THE
AMERICAN HERITAGE
ILLUSTRATED
ENCYCLOPEDIC
DICTIONARY

Adapted and developed from the lexical databases of
Houghton Mifflin Company of Boston, Massachusetts.
Lexical Databases, Copyright © 1987
Houghton Mifflin Company

Special features and captions from the
READER'S DIGEST ILLUSTRATED ENCYCLOPEDIC DICTIONARY
First Edition, Copyright © 1987
The Reader's Digest Association, Inc. of
Pleasantville, New York
Used by permission

Language Families of the World map on
pages 938–939 is reprinted from *Geography* by
Arthur Getis and Judith M. Getis, pages 84–85.
© 1982 Houghton Mifflin Company.

Library of Congress Cataloging-in-Publication Data

The American heritage illustrated encyclopedic
    dictionary.

    "Adapted and developed from the lexical databases
of Houghton Mifflin Company . . . special features and
captions from the Reader's Digest illustrated
encyclopedic dictionary, first edition, c1987, the
Reader's Digest Association"—Verso t.p.
    1. English language—Dictionaries. 2. Americanisms.
I. Houghton Mifflin Company. II. Reader's Digest
Association.
PE1628.A624 1987   423   87-4039
ISBN 0-395-44295-8

Manufactured in the United States of America

THE
AMERICAN HERITAGE
ILLUSTRATED
ENCYCLOPEDIC
DICTIONARY

Houghton Mifflin Company • Boston

THE AMERICAN HERITAGE
ILLUSTRATED ENCYCLOPEDIC DICTIONARY

Houghton Mifflin

COORDINATING EDITOR
Pamela B. DeVinne

EDITORS
Kaethe Ellis, Susan M. Innes, David A. Jost,
James P. Marciano

CONTRIBUTING EDITORS
Walter M. Havighurst, Ramona Michaelis,
Trudy Nelson, Anne D. Steinhardt

PRODUCTION MANAGER
Christopher Leonesio

PRODUCTION COORDINATOR
Donna L. Muise

EDITORIAL PRODUCTION ASSISTANTS
Patricia McTiernan, Margaret Anne Miles

ART ASSISTANT
Tom Flynn

EDITORIAL DEPARTMENT SECRETARY
Cara Murray

COMPOSITION KEYBOARDING
Brenda Bregoli-Sturtevant, Celester Jackson,
Ron Perkins, Tracy Weiner

Reader's Digest

EDITOR
David Rattray

ART EDITOR
Richard J. Berenson

ART ASSOCIATE
Morris Karol

EDITORIAL ASSISTANT
Vita Gardner

PICTURE EDITOR
Robert J. Woodward

CONTRIBUTING EDITOR
Madeleine Walker

CONTRIBUTING PICTURE RESEARCHER
Mary Leverty

CONTRIBUTING COPY EDITOR
Marsha Lutch Lloyd

READER'S DIGEST GENERAL BOOKS
Editorial Director: John A. Pope, Jr.
Managing Editor: Jane Polley
Art Director: David Trooper
Group Editors: Norman B. Mack
Susan J. Wernert

PREFACE

The English language was born fifteen hundred years ago when the Saxon invaders of the Roman province of Britain started raising children in their new homeland. Children are the inventors of language. In the earliest centuries of its existence, English remained almost identical with the Saxon dialects spoken by the settlers' forebears in what is now Germany and Denmark, across the North Sea. From A.D. 793 to 1066, England was invaded again and again by Norsemen, and for two centuries much of northern Britain was under Danish rule. Our language has retained a slightly Scandinavian flavor ever since. Following the Conquest of 1066, by French-speaking Normans, English as we know it came into being, a peculiar Germanic tongue whose vocabulary is more than two-thirds French in origin. With the Age of Exploration came the British Empire (a term coined by Queen Elizabeth's astrologer John Dee) and the language expanded in many different directions at once. Thousands of new words for new concepts and things flowed in from Latin and Greek. The vocabularies of politics, commerce, and the arts soaked up words from French, Italian, Spanish, Dutch, and other languages. At the same time, English-speaking settlers put down roots in new countries all over the globe, and within a few generations there were as many new dialects of English as there were British colonies. By the end of the 20th century, World English has already become the most important language on the planet, and North American its leading dialect. The day is at hand when everyone on earth will know at least some North American, regardless of his or her home language.

A language serving so many different communities and fields represents a body of information too vast for any one person to master. Hence the need for dictionaries. Everybody needs one nowadays. It was established some years ago that there are more dictionaries than television sets in North America. The basic purpose served by a dictionary is to furnish a word's correct spelling and syllabication, meaning, and pronunciation. In a language as vast as World English, spellings, meanings, and pronunciations fluctuate almost as rapidly as the ebb and flow of the events they mirror. As North American English becomes Number One in science, industry, and politics worldwide, people are coming to expect the dictionary to provide authoritative information about not only words but the objects and ideas they denote. This has led to a need for a new type of dictionary, one that provides all that traditional dictionaries give, and then some. In the present work we have accounted for more than 200,000 meanings coming from all of the many varieties of English, with special emphasis on North American but extensive coverage of all the rest. We continued to add important new words to the text up until the last days before the book went to press. In addition to such traditional features as word origins, usage notes, illustrative quotations, and synonyms, we have added the most extensive biographical and geographic coverage ever provided in a dictionary, together with several hundred illustrated feature articles, and 2,300 four-color pictures. Each of the pictures was chosen for its information value, the better to identify, visualize, or understand the item in question.

There is another feature that, although intangible, looms larger than all of the foregoing put together, and that is the element of due proportion and measure that we have brought to the writing of this book. Dictionary writing, like medicine, is partly a science, mostly an art. Estimates vary as to the actual number of words present in the language at any given time. Some authorities fix this at around 340,000 live items. Yet many of these are so trivial or so ephemeral that they do not really belong in a reference book. The dictionary writer, in attempting to meet the need for all-round usefulness, must rely heavily on intuition, judgment, guesswork. In a dictionary with additional encyclopedic material, the editor has to make strong-minded choices, to include or to exclude, every step of the way. At the same time, by our choice of quotations as well as our own use of English in the articles, definitions, and captions you will read in the following pages, we have tried to keep the focus on the book's highest object, which is the thing of rare beauty that is our language. According to the Book of Proverbs, ''A word fitly spoken is like apples of gold in a setting of silver.'' It is to help our readers find many such words that we offer the present book.

—The Editor

HOW TO USE THIS DICTIONARY

FINDING THE WORD YOU WANT

All the entries in this Dictionary are listed in strict alphabetical order, letter by letter. This applies equally to hyphenated entries and entries that consist of two or more words:

> **run·ny** (rŭn′ē) *adj.*
> **Run·ny·mede** (rŭn′ē-mēd′).
> **run off** *intr.v.*
> **run-off** (rŭn′ôf′, -ŏf′) *n.*
> **run-of-the-mill** (rŭn′əv-*th*ə-mĭl′) *adj.*

Single letters, word parts, and abbreviations are also listed in alphabetical order:

> **i, I** (ī) *n., pl.* **i's** or **I's.**
> **I** (ī) *pron.*
> **i–¹.** Variant of **y-.**
> **i–².** Variant of **in-** (not).
> **IA** Iowa (used with a Zip Code).
> **i.a.** in absentia.

When an entry word contains a number, it is listed (in numerical order, where necessary) before a word that has a letter in the same position:

> **u·ra·ni·um** (yŏŏ-rā′nē-əm) *n.*
> **uranium 235** *n.*
> **uranium 238** *n.*
> **uranium dioxide** *n.*

However, when an entry begins with a number, it is listed as though it were spelled out in full:

> **two-fold** (tōō′fōld′, -fōld′) *adj.* **1.** Having two components . . . .
> **2, 4, 5-T** (tōō′fôr′fīv′tē′) *n.* **Trichlorophenoxyacetic acid** *(see).*
> **two-hand·ed** (tōō′hăn′dĭd) *adj.* **1.** Requiring the use of two hands at once: *a two-handed sledgehammer* . . . .

Words that have the same spelling but different etymologies are listed separately and distinguished by raised numbers:

> **bay¹** (bā) *n.* **1.** *Abbr.* **b., B.** A body of water partly enclosed by land, but having a wide outlet to the sea. . . . [Middle English *baye,* from Old French *baie,* from Old Spanish *bahia,* perhaps from Iberian.]
> **bay²** *n.* **1.** *Architecture.* A part of a building or other structure . . . [Middle English, from Old French *baee,* an opening, from *baer,* to gape, from Medieval Latin *batāre,* to yawn, gape.]

Proper names
Mac- and **Mc-** entries are also listed in strict alphabetical order— that is, **Mc** is not listed as if it were spelled **Mac:**

> **Ma·cau·lay** (mə-kô′lē), Thomas Babington, 1st Baron
> **Mba·bane** (əm-bä-bän′).
> **Mc·Cau·ley** (mə-kô′lē), Mary Ludwig Hays

Towns and cities named after saints appear at **Saint** or **St.,** following conventional spelling. Biographies of saints appear at the name of the saint: for example, Saint Paul is entered at **Paul.**

Names of people and places are alphabetized up to the first period, by surname or distinguishing proper name:

> **Wash·ing·ton¹** (wŏsh′ĭng-tən, wôsh′-).
> **Washington².**
> **Washington, Booker Taliaferro** (1856–1915).
> **Washington, George** (1732–1799).
> **Washington, Martha Dandridge Custis** (1731–1802).
> **Washington, Mount.**

Fictional and legendary characters are entered with the forename or title first, if this is how they are best known:

> **Don Qui·xo·te**
> **Rob·in Hood**

Fixed phrases
Fixed phrases of two or more words whose meaning cannot be worked out from the literal sense of the individual words are entered under the key word (usually the first noun). For example, **throw the book at** will be listed under **book; hand over fist** is listed under **hand.** The only exceptions to this rule are phrases that function as nouns, such as **green thumb** or **cold feet.** These are listed in their alphabetical place.

Fixed verb phrases with a special meaning, such as **come across** (to meet) or **put down** (to rebuke), will either be listed under the verb or, if they can be used in several ways—as adjectives or nouns, for example—will be entered separately.

Inflections
Inflections are grammatically different forms of a word, such as the plural of a noun, the past tense of a verb, or the comparative degree of an adjective. Inflections are shown in shortened form, unless the entry has only one syllable or the first syllable is a vowel standing alone:

> **ear·ly** (ûr′lē) *adj.* **-lier, -liest.**
> **o·bey** (ō-bā′) *v.* **obeyed, obeying, obeys.**

Plurals
Plural forms of nouns are shown when these are irregular (that is, when the plural is not formed simply by adding *-s* or *-es*) and when more than one plural is possible:

> **ra·di·us** (rā′dē-əs) *n., pl.* **-dii** (-dē-ī′) or **-uses.**
> **car·go** (kär′gō) *n., pl.* **-goes** or **-gos.**

In cases where it is difficult to tell whether a word takes a singular or a plural verb, the Dictionary indicates what construction to use:

> **ge·net·ics** (jə-nĕt′ĭks) *n.* **1.** *Used with a singular verb.* The biology of heredity; . . . **2.** *Used with a singular or plural verb.* The genetic constitution of an individual, group, or class.

Verbs
The principal parts of all verbs, whether regular or irregular, are shown following the base form, in the order past tense, past participle (if different), present participle, 3rd person singular present tense:

> **al·ter** (ôl′tər) *v.* **-tered, -tering, -ters.**

Adjectives and adverbs
The comparative and superlative forms of all adjectives and adverbs are shown following the base form, in the order comparative, superlative:

> **air·y** (âr′ē) *adj.* **-ier, -iest.**

Alternate forms of entry words

The first form given is always the preferred one. When a word has an alternate but still acceptable written form, this is shown after the entry word in one of two positions.

When an alternate form of a word is so close to the preferred spelling that it shares the same pronunciation, it is shown immediately after the entry word and before the pronunciation:

me·di·e·val, me·di·ae·val (mĕ'dē-ē'vəl, mĕ-dē'vəl) *adj.*

Alternate British or chiefly British spellings of common words are shown like this:

col·or (kŭl'ər) *n.* Also *chiefly British* **col·our.**

When an alternate form of a word is different enough in spelling to require a pronunciation of its own, this is shown after the part of speech:

bi·o·log·i·cal (bī'ə-lŏj'ĭ-kəl) *adj.* Also **bi·o·log·ic** (-lŏj'ĭk).

Alternate forms that need qualifying, for example because they are found in a particular variety of English or apply only to specific senses of a word, are also shown in this way:

where·so·ev·er (hwâr'sō-ĕv'ər, wâr'-) *conj.* Also *poetic* **where·so·e'er** (-âr').
di·van . . . *n.* Also **di·wan** (dĭ-wän') (for senses 2, 5).

Alternate forms that fall more than ten places away from their preferred form in the alphabetical list are entered as follows:

foetus. Variant of **fetus.**

Definitions

When an entry word has several meanings, these are listed with the central meaning shown first:

fell¹ (fĕl) *tr.v.* **felled, felling, fells.** **1.** To cause to fall; cut or knock down: *fell a tree; fell an opponent.* **2.** To sew or finish (a seam) with the raw edges flattened, turned under, and stitched down.

The different meanings of a word are indicated by numbers, or, in the case of closely related meanings, by lower-case letters. Any italic label, such as *Informal, Chemistry,* or *Southwestern U.S.,* that comes before the first definition number of a word applies to all the numbered meanings of that word. However, if it follows a letter or number, it applies to the definition(s) covered by that letter or number:

ear·ful (îr'fŏŏl') *n. Informal.* **1.** A quantity of information or gossip. **2.** A severe reprimand.
ef·flo·resce (ĕf'lə-rĕs') *intr.v.* **-resced, -rescing, -resces.** **1.** To blossom; flower; bloom. **2.** *Chemistry.* **a.** To become a powder by losing water of crystallization. **b.** To become covered with a powdery deposit, as by evaporation.

In the example at **earful,** the label *Informal* applies to senses **1** and **2.** In the example at **effloresce,** the label *Chemistry* applies to senses **2a** and **2b.**

Cross-references

Cross-references, usually shown in **boldface** print, direct you to another entry word in the dictionary where further information will be found.

GUIDANCE ON THE USE OF WORDS

Some words or uses of a word are associated with a particular context—for example, a geographic area or a special style of speech or writing. Such specialized uses are marked by a range of italic labels.

Historical labels

Archaic indicates that a word is no longer in common use and will be found only in certain contexts, such as poetry or legal texts. Occasionally a modern author might use such words to give an old-fashioned "feel" to a piece of writing. *Obsolete* indicates that there is no evidence of a word or meaning being used since 1714, other than for literary effect.

Geographic labels

Words, spellings, or meanings that occur in specific areas of the English-speaking world are labeled accordingly:

bushed (bŏŏsht) *adj.* . . . **2.** *Chiefly Australian & Canadian.* Lost or confused.

Regional indicates that an expression is commonly used in one area and little used—even if known—in other areas. Such expressions bear area labels, such as *Southwestern U.S.* and *New England.* Often an expression may be common to several areas and yet not be used in American speech in general. These expressions are labeled *Regional:* for example, the use of **fair¹** as a verb in *The weather will fair today.*

Field labels

Many definitions are labeled according to the field of knowledge with which they are concerned. These labels are merely an aid to orientation; they are not to be interpreted as stating that the sense is not used outside the special field, only that the sense being defined is of primary concern within that field. Such labels are especially useful when a word has many senses; for example, senses 5, 7, 8, 9, 10, 11, and 13 of **base¹** are labeled *Sports, Military, Architecture, Heraldry, Linguistics, Mathematics,* and *Chemistry,* respectively.

Stylistic labels

Informal indicates that a word or meaning is typically used by speakers addressing one another directly on familiar terms, as in a casual conversation. Informal terms are often mildly humorous or euphemistic in tone, for example, *creepy* or *funny bone.*

Slang indicates a closer degree of familiarity between speakers, or between reader and author, than *Informal.* Slang words are often associated with "in-groups" within the community, such as servicemen. The distinguishing feature of slang is the striving for rhetorical effect through the use of extravagant and often facetious figures of speech. Slang is usually transitory and either dies out or is incorporated into the standard vocabulary as its rhetorical aspect is lost.

Nonstandard indicates that a word or meaning is in widespread use but is regarded as incorrect by most educated speakers of English. For example, the use of *disinterested* to mean "uninterested" is labeled *Nonstandard.* Controversial uses and those on which guidance may be helpful are dealt with more fully in usage notes.

Short notes describing a particular attitude on the part of the user will be found after some words or meanings. "Used derogatorily," for example, indicates that the speaker wishes to show contempt or disapproval. "Considered offensive" indicates that a word or meaning might cause offense, even when the speaker intends none.

Foreign-language labels are used at some expressions from other languages which, though fairly common, are still felt by the native speaker as not belonging to English. Such words are represented in italic type by many publications. The language from which they come is indicated in the Dictionary by a label:

ad in·ter·im (ăd ĭn′tər-əm) *adv. Abbr.* **ad int.** *Latin.* In the meantime; meanwhile. —**ad in·ter·im** *adj.*

Many terms that appear to be foreign have been incorporated into the vocabulary of a special field such as law or medicine. These are given the label of the field rather than a language label. Thus the entry:

no·lo con·ten·de·re (nō′lō kən-tĕn′də-rē′) *n. Law.* A plea made by the defendant . . . . [Latin, "I do not wish to contend."]

Usage notes

Occasionally the use of a word or phrase may require extended discussion. The paragraphs labeled *Usage* following many of the entries in this Dictionary supply information on the conventions observed by most users of the language. They identify areas of controversy over the meaning or grammatical use of a word so that the reader can see what the linguistic "state of play" is in contemporary English and make confident decisions in speaking and writing. The usage notes never tell a reader what to do or how to react; they simply present the alternatives. It is enough to know in what circumstances a usage is preferred, or avoided—for example, in formal writing, or in very informal speech. What was frowned upon a generation ago may be widely accepted today; but the reader who understands what the norms are will at least know when they are being disregarded.

GUIDE TO PRONUNCIATION

All pronunciations are shown in parentheses following the entry word or any alternate form of it. If part of an entry has already appeared separately elsewhere in the Dictionary, its pronunciation is not repeated. Similarly, entry words followed by raised numbers, indicating that they have the same spelling but a different origin, are assumed to have the same pronunciation, unless otherwise indicated.

Pronunciation Symbols

The set of symbols used in this Dictionary is designed to enable the reader to reproduce a satisfactory pronunciation with no more than a quick reference to the key.

A shorter form of the key below appears in the margins at intervals throughout the Dictionary.

Spellings	Symbols	Spellings	Symbols
pat	ă	noise	oi
pay	ā	out	ou
care	âr	book	o͝o
father, are	ä	boot	o͞o
bib	b	pop	p
church	ch	roar	r
deed, milled	d	sauce	s
pet	ĕ	ship, dish	sh
be	ē	tight, stopped	t
fife, phase, rough	f	thin, path	th
gag	g	this, bathe	*th*
hat	h	cut	ŭ
which	hw	fur, term, firm,	ûr
pit	ĭ	word, heard	
pie, by	ī	valve	v
pier	îr	with, which	w
judge	j	yes	y
kick, cat, pique	k	zebra, xylem,	z
lid, needle	l (nēd′l)	size	
mum	m	vision, pleasure,	zh
no, sudden	n (sŭd′n)	garage	
thing	ng	about, item,	ə
pot, horrid	ŏ	edible, gallop,	
toe, hoarse	ō	circus, peaceful	
caught, paw, for	ô	butter	ər

Foreign		Stress Marks	
French ami	à	Primary stress: ′	
French feu,	œ	**in·cite′** (ĭn-sīt′)	
German schön			
French tu,	ü	Secondary stress: ′	
German über		**in′sight′** (ĭn′sīt′)	
German ich,	KH		
Scottish loch			
French bon	N		
French Compiègne	y′ (kôN-pyĕn′y′)		

Alternate pronunciations

All pronunciations given are acceptable in all circumstances. When more than one is given, the first is assumed to be the most common, but the difference in frequency may be insignificant.

Americans do not all speak alike; nevertheless, they can understand one another, at least on the level of speech sounds. For most words a single set of symbols can represent the pronunciation found in each regional variety of American English, provided the symbols are planned to enable the reader to reproduce a satisfactory pronunciation. When a single pronunciation is given in this Dictionary, the reader will supply those features of his own regional speech that are suggested by his reading of the key. The policy of this Dictionary is to record pronunciations used in educated speech. In every community, educated speech is accepted and understood by everyone, including those who do not themselves use it.

To save space, where alternate pronunciations are given, only that part of the word that varies from the standard form is repeated:

glo·ri·fi·ca·tion (glôr′ə-fĭ-kā′shən, glōr′-) *n.*

Explanatory Notes

ə: this nonalphabetical symbol is called a *schwa*. The symbol is used in the Dictionary to represent a reduced vowel, that is, a vowel that receives the weakest level of stress (which can be thought of as no stress) within a word and that therefore nearly always has a different quality than it would have if it were stressed, as in **telegraph** (tĕl′ə-grăf′) and **telegraphy** (tə-lĕg′rə-fē). Vowels are never reduced to a single vowel sound; the schwa sound varies, sometimes according to the vowel it is representing and often according to the sounds surrounding it.

âr, îr, ûr: these symbols represent vowels that have been altered by the *r* that follows. This situation can be understood by considering the words **Mary, merry,** and **marry.** In some regional varieties of American English, all three words are pronounced alike (mĕr′ē). However, in many individual American speech patterns, the three words are distinguished. It is this pattern that the Dictionary represents, thus: **Mary** (mâr′ē), **merry** (mĕr′ē), **marry** (măr′ē). However, in some words all three pronunciations are heard, grading indistinctly one into another. For these words the Dictionary represents only (â), for example, **care** (kâr), **dairy** (dâr′ē).

In words such as **hear, beer,** and **dear,** the vowel could be represented by (ē) were it not for the effect of the following *r*, which makes it approach (ĭ) in sound. In this Dictionary a special symbol (îr) is used for this combination, as in **beer** (bîr).

The symbol (ûr), used in **her** (hûr), **fur** (fûr), etc., has a regular regional variant that is not separately recorded. In one pattern the effect of the *r* is heard simultaneously with the vowel; in the other, some, but not all, such syllables are heard with a vowel like (ŭ) before the onset of the *r*.

ôr, ŏr, ŏr: there are regional differences in the distinctions among various pronunciations of the syllable -*or*-. In pairs such as **horse, hoarse,** the vowel varies between (ô) and (ō). In this Dictionary these vowels are represented as follows: **horse** (hôrs), **hoarse** (hôrs, hōrs). Other words for which both forms are shown include **more** (môr, mōr), **glory** (glôr'ē, glōr'-). Another group of words with variation in the pronunciation of -*or*- syllables includes words such as **forest** and **horrid,** in which the pronunciation of *o* before *r* varies between (ô) and (ŏ). In these words the (ôr) pronunciation is given first: **forest** (fôr'ĭst, fŏr'-), **horrid** (hôr'ĭd, hŏr'-).

Syllabic Consonants

Two consonants are often represented as complete syllables. These are *l* and *n* (called *syllabics*) when they occur after stressed syllables ending in or followed by *d* or *t* in such words as **cradle** (krād'l), **rattle** (răt'l), **redden** (rĕd'n), **cotton** (kŏt'n), and **midden** (mĭd'n). Syllabic *n* is not shown following -*nd*- or -*nt*-, as in **abandon** (ə-băn'dən) and **mountain** (moun'tən); but syllabic *l* is shown in that position: **spindle** (spĭnd'l).

Stress

In this Dictionary, *stress,* the relative degree of loudness with which the syllables of a word (or phrase) are spoken, is indicated in three different ways. An unmarked syllable has the weakest stress in the word. The strongest, or *primary,* stress is marked with a bold mark ('). An intermediate level of stress, here called *secondary,* is marked with a similar but lighter mark (').

Words of one syllable show no stress mark, since there is no other stress level to which the syllable is compared.

Syllabication

All entry words of more than one syllable, as well as their alternate and derived forms, are divided into syllables by centered dots that show where the word can be hyphenated. No syllable dots are shown for words that have already appeared as separate entries.

Pronunciations are also syllabicated for the sake of clarity, although the syllabication of the phonetic form does not necessarily match the syllabication of the graphic form of the entry word. The former follows phonological rules; the latter represents the established practice of printers and editors in breaking words at the end of a line.

THE ORIGINS OF WORDS

The text in square brackets at the end of the entry gives the etymology, or historical derivation, of the entry word, except in the instances mentioned below. If a word is native to the language, the etymology normally traces its history back to the earlier stages of English—Old English (A.D. 450–1100) and Middle English (1100–1500). If the word is derived from a foreign language, the etymology usually traces it back to its earliest written form in the language of its origin:

ef·fi·gy (ĕf'ə-jē) . . . [Middle English *effigie,* from Latin *effigiēs,* likeness, image, from *effingere,* to form, portray : *ex-,* out of + *fingere,* to fashion, shape.]

The etymologies are intended to be easily readable and therefore no special abbreviations have been used. The languages mentioned in the derivations (Old French, Old High German, Old Norse, for example), which are frequently earlier forms of modern languages, are all defined in the body of the Dictionary. So too are technical terms such as "back-formation," "unattested," "akin," and "folk etymology."

Source words are usually printed in *italics*. They are omitted altogether, however, if identical to the entry word or to the source word listed just before. Where the source word is itself an entry in the Dictionary, it is usually printed in SMALL CAPITALS; this alerts the reader to the fact that there is further information at that entry (either in its definition or in its etymology):

frank·in·cense . . . [Middle English *frank encens,* from Old French *franc encens* : *franc,* free, superior, FRANK + *encens,* INCENSE.]

A cross-reference in **bold** type indicates that the reader should consult the etymology of this word, where more information will be found:

dis·crete . . . [Middle English, from Latin *discrētus,* separate. See **discreet.**]

Many words are combinations of other words or word parts. This is shown in a number of ways, as in the example of **frankincense** above, or in simpler cases:

pul·sar . . . [From *puls*ating st*ar.*]
mel·a·nous . . . [MELAN(O)- + -OUS.]

In the cases of some words, the combination is so obvious that the etymology can be omitted entirely—for example, at **evergreen** (ever + green) or **eventuality** (eventual + ity). (The only other class of words usually not given an etymology is that of proper nouns, including trademarks.)

Some words, by contrast, have uncertain origins. If evidence is lacking or highly unreliable, the etymology will be limited to the simple explanation "origin obscure," often preceded by a century date to indicate when the word first appeared in written form in English:

flunk . . . [19th century : origin obscure.]

In the case of a source word which is in turn of unknown origin, the obelisk or dagger symbol † is printed after it:

Men·sa[1] . . . [Latin *mēnsa*†, table.]

A special effort has been made to include in the etymologies information that explains the origin and changes in meaning of certain words and phrases. Such etymologies may trace a word or phrase back to a Biblical allusion, a name of a person or place, or a historical incident, for example:

mav·er·ick . . . [After Samuel A. *Maverick* (1803–70), Texas cattleman who did not brand his calves.]
quark . . . [From a line in James Joyce's *Finnegans Wake,* "Three quarks for Muster Mark!"]

READING THE ENTRIES

The examples numbered below are a guide to the symbols and terms used in creating the entries in this Dictionary. They summarize and illustrate the information given on the preceding pages and act as a quick source of reference for the reader. Each example is printed in blue to make it stand out from the surrounding text and given a number that is keyed to the explanatory notes alongside.

KEY

1 Entry word.

2 Parentheses enclose **pronunciation**.

3 Words made up of **two or more elements** are entered separately.

4 Main **inflected forms** of verb.

5 **Cross-reference** to entry word with **Synonym list**.

6 **Usage note** comments on problems of spelling, grammar, style, or meaning.

7 **Cross-reference** to entry word with **Usage note**.

8 **Note** in entry indicates limitations of **usage**.

9 Italic label indicates **part of speech**.

10 **Alternate spelling** with same pronunciation as entry word.

11 **Boldface dots** divide entry word into **syllables**.

12 **Irregular plural** of entry word.

13 Parentheses enclose **object of verb**.

14 **Alternate spelling** entered separately.

15 **Cross-reference** to related entry word.

16 Brackets enclose **etymology**.

17 **Example phrase** shows word used in context.

18 **Numbers** distinguish entry words with the **same spelling but different origins**.

19 Italic label indicates **usage level** of word or sense.

20 **Alternate spelling** of entry word with different pronunciation.

21 **Cross-reference** to etymology of another entry word.

22 **Derived forms** made up of the entry word and a word part that is entered elsewhere.

23 Italic label indicates **geographic area** of use.

---

1 **cli·ma·tol·o·gy** (klī′mə-tŏl′ə-jē) *n.* The meteorological study of climate. [CLIMAT(E) + -LOGY.] —**cli·ma·to·log·ic** (klī′mə-tə-lŏj′ĭk), **cli·ma·to·log·i·cal** *adj.* —**cli·ma·tol·o·gist** (klī′mə-tŏl′ə-jĭst) *n.*

2 **cli·max** (klī′măks′) *n.* **1. a.** The point of greatest intensity, excitement, or interest in any series or progression of events; the culmination. **b.** Such a point in a literary or dramatic work. **2.** An orgasm. **3.** *Rhetoric.* **a.** A series of statements or ideas in an ascending order of force or intensity. **b.** The final statement in such a series. **4.** The stage in ecological development or evolution in which the community of organisms becomes stable. —See Synonyms at **summit**. ~*v.* **climaxed, -maxing, -maxes.** —*intr.* To reach a climax. —*tr.* To bring to a climax. [Latin, rhetorical climax, from Greek *klimax*, ladder.]

3 **climax community** *n. Ecology.* The mature or stabilized stage in a successional series of communities, usually associated with maximum complexity, when dominant species are completely adapted to environmental conditions, as in tropical rain forests.

4 **climb** (klīm) *v.* climbed or *archaic* clomb (klōm), climbing, climbs. —*tr.* To move up or mount, especially by using the hands and feet; ascend. —*intr.* **1.** To rise to a higher position; move upward: *The sun climbed in the sky.* **2.** To rise slowly or with effort in rank, status, or fortune. **3.** To slant or slope upward. **4.** To grow in an upward direction, as some plants do, by twining about or clinging to another object for support. **5.** To move in a specified direction **5** by or as if by clambering: *climbed out of the window.* —See Synonyms at **rise**. ~*n.* **1.** An act of climbing; an ascent. **2.** A place to be climbed. [Climb, clomb; Middle English *climben*, *clomb*, Old English *climban*, *clamb* (or *clomb*).] —**climb·a·ble** *adj.*

6 *Usage:* Both *up* and *down* are used with this verb in standard English. *Climb up* has been said to contain an unnecessary element, in that climbing implies ascent. By the same token, *climb down* is said to be self-contradictory, but both uses are well established. **climb down** *intr.v.* **1.** To move downward by using the limbs. **2.** To retreat in an argument or dispute; back down.

7 ~*tr.v.* To descend by using the limbs. —See Usage note at **climb**. **climb·er** (klī′mər) *n.* **1.** Something or someone that climbs; especially, a person who climbs mountains. **2.** *Informal.* A person seek- **8** ing to gain a higher social or professional position. Used derogatorily. **3.** A plant that grows upward by clinging to or twining about something.

9 **climbing irons** *pl.n.* Iron bars with spikes or spurs attached, which are strapped to a shoe or boot and used in climbing telegraph poles, trees, or ice slopes.

clime (klīm) *n. Poetic.* Climate or region. [Middle English, region of the earth, zone, from Late Latin *clīma*, CLIMATE.]

-clinal *suffix.* Indicates a slope or inclination; for example, **anticlinal, synclinal.** [-CLINE + -AL.]

10 **cli·mo·graph**, **cli·ma·graph** (klī′mə-grăf′, -gräf′) *n. Meteorology.* A graph in which one climatic feature at a location is plotted against another, for example temperature against humidity. Also called "climagram," "climogram." [CLIMATE + -GRAPH.]

clin-. Variant of clino-.

11 **cli·nan·dri·um** (klī-năn′drē-əm) *n., pl.* **-dria** (-drē-ə). *Botany.* A hollow containing the anther in the upper part of the column of an orchid. [New Latin, "stamen bed" : CLIN(O)- + -andrium, "stamen," from Greek *anēr* (stem *andr-*), man.]

clinch (klĭnch) *v.* clinched, clinching, clinches. —*tr.* **1.** To fix or **13** secure (a nail or bolt, for example) by bending down or flattening the end that has been driven through something. **2.** To fasten together in this way. **3.** To settle definitely and conclusively; make final. **4.** *Nautical.* To fasten with a clinch. —*intr.* **1.** In boxing and wrestling, to hold the opponent's body with one or both arms to prevent or hinder his movements. **2.** *Informal.* To embrace. ~*n.* **1.** The act of clinching. **2.** Something that clinches, such as a clinched nail or clamp. **3.** The clinched part of a nail, bolt, rivet, or the like. **4.** In boxing and wrestling, the act or an instance of clinching. **5.** *Nautical.* A knot in a rope made by a half hitch with the end of the rope fastened back by seizing. Also called "clench." **6.** *Informal.* An amorous or romantic embrace. [Variant of CLENCH.]

clinch·er (klĭn′chər) *n.* **1.** One that clinches; specifically, a tool for clinching nails or bolts. **2.** *Informal.* A decisive point, fact, or remark, as in an argument.

14 **clincher-built.** Variant of clinker-built.

cline (klīn) *n. Ecology.* A continuous variation in form within **23** members of a species or population, resulting from gradual changes or transitions in the environment over a wide range. **2.** Loosely, a

continuum. [Greek *klinein*, to slope, lean.]

-cline *suffix.* Indicates slope; for example, **anticline, syncline.** [Greek *klinein*, to slope.]

cling (klĭng) *intr.v.* **clung** (klŭng), **clinging, clings. 1.** To hold fast or adhere to something, as by grasping, sticking, or entwining. **2. a.** To stay near; remain close. **b.** To resist separation. **3.** To hold on, often stubbornly; remain attached: *cling to old-fashioned ideas.* [Cling, clung (past tense), clung (past participle); Middle English *clingen, clong* (past singular), *clungen* (past plural), *clungen*, Old English *clingan, clang, clungon, clungen*.] —**cling·er** *n.*

15 **cling·stone** (klĭng′stōn′) *n.* A fruit, especially a peach, having pulp that adheres partially to the stone. Compare **freestone**. —**clingstone** *adj.*

cling·y (klĭng′ē) *adj.* **-gier, -giest.** Tending to cling: *a clingy dress.*

clin·ic (klĭn′ĭk) *n.* **1.** An establishment, often a department of a hospital specializing in a particular branch of medicine, devoted to the treatment and care of outpatients. **2.** A medical establishment run by several specialists working cooperatively. **3.** A private hospital or nursing home. **4.** A group meeting or seminar devoted to the **16** study of problems in a particular field, or offering to teach certain skills to those who attend: *a tennis clinic.* [French *clinique*, originally "a bedridden person," from Greek *klinikē*, medical treatment at sickbed, from *klinikos*, "of a bed," doctor who visits bedridden persons, from *klinē*, bed.]

-clinic *suffix.* Indicates: **1.** Inclination or slope; for example, **isoclinic. 2.** A specified number of oblique axial intersections; for example, **triclinic.** [-CLINE + -IC.]

clin·i·cal (klĭn′ĭ-kəl) *adj.* **1.** Pertaining to or connected with a clinic. **2.** Of or pertaining to direct observation and treatment of patients: *a clinical lecture.* **3.** Analytical; highly objective; rigorously scientific: *clinical details.* **4.** Suggestive of a hospital or clinic; austere; **17** antiseptic: *a clinical style of decor.* ~*n.* A class in which medical students are instructed in the examination and treatment of patients at the bedside. —**clin·i·cal·ly** *adv.*

cli·ni·cian (klĭ-nĭsh′ən) *n.* A doctor, psychologist, or psychiatrist specializing in clinical studies or practice. [French *clinicien*, from *clinique*, CLINIC.]

18 **clink¹** (klĭngk) *n.* A soft, sharp, ringing sound. ~*v.* clinked, clinking, clinks. —*intr.* To make a clink. —*tr.* To cause to clink. [Middle English, from Middle Dutch *klinken*.]

clink² *n. Slang.* Prison. [16th century (as *the Clink*, name of former prison near London) : origin obscure.]

clink·er (klĭng′kər) *n.* **1.** The incombustible residue, fused into irregular lumps, that remains after the combustion of coal. **2.** A partially vitrified brick or a mass of bricks fused together. **3.** An extremely hard burned brick. **4.** Vitrified matter expelled by a vol- **19** cano. **5.** *Slang.* A conspicuous mistake or failure. ~*intr.v.* clinkered, -ering, -ers. To form clinker while burning. [Earlier clincart, klincard, from obsolete Dutch *klinckaerd*, "one that clinks" (from its clinking sound when struck), from Middle Dutch *klinken, clinken*, CLINK.]

20 **clink·er-built** (klĭng′kər-bĭlt′) *adj.* Also clinch·er-built (klĭn′chər-). Built with overlapping planks or boards. Said of ships or boats. Compare **carvel-built**. [From *clinker*, a fastening or clinching with nails, from Middle English *clinken*, probably variant of *clenchen*, **21** CLENCH.]

clino-, clin- *prefix.* Indicates slope or slant; for example, **clinometer, clinandrium.** [New Latin, from Greek *klinein*, to slope, and *klinē*, bed.]

cli·nom·e·ter (klī-nŏm′ə-tər, klĭ-) *n.* An instrument for measuring the angle of an incline, as of an embankment. Also called "incli- **22** nometer." [CLINO- + -METER.] —**cli·no·met·ric** (klī′nə-mĕt′rĭk), **cli·no·met·ri·cal** *adj.* —**cli·nom·e·try** (klī-nŏm′ə-trē) *n.*

clin·quant (klĭng′kənt; *French* klăn-kän′) *adj. Archaic.* Adorned with gold or silver. ~*n. Archaic.* Imitation gold leaf; tinsel. [French, "glistening," from *clinquer*, to glitter, clink, from Middle Dutch *clinken*, CLINK.]

cli·o·met·rics (klī′ə-mĕt′rĭks) *n. Used with a singular verb.* The use of statistics in the study of history. —**cli·o·met·ric** *adj.*

clip¹ (klĭp) *tr.v.* clipped, clipping, clips. **1.** To cut off or cut out with or as if with scissors or shears: *clip an article from a newspaper; clipped three seconds off the record.* **2.** To make shorter by cutting; trim. **3.** To cut off the edge of: *clip a coin.* **4. a.** To cut short (a word or words) by leaving out letters or syllables. **b.** To enunciate with clarity and precision: *clip one's speech.* **5.** *British.* To punch a hole in (a ticket). **6.** *Informal.* To hit with a sharp blow. **7.** *Slang.* To cheat or overcharge.

LIST OF ABBREVIATIONS USED IN ENTRIES

Abbr.		A.T.C.; F.O.	n.	noun	marble; lawn mower.
adj.	adjective	**lovable; red.**	*pl.n.*	plural noun	**environs; cattle.**
adv.	adverb	**merrily; moreover.**	*prep.*	preposition	**with; despite.**
comb. form	combining form	**all-; -in.**	*pron.*	pronoun	**she; myself.**
conj.	conjunction	**and; inasmuch as.**	*tr.v.*	transitive verb	**hire; repatriate.**
interj.	interjection	**hi; ouch.**	*v.*	verb (transitive and	**grow; advertise.**
intr.v.	intransitive verb	**emigrate; subside.**		intransitive)	

---

gha·ri·al (gä′rē-əl) *n.* A reptile, the gavial *(see).*

ghar·ry, ghar·ri (găr′ē, gär′ē) *n., pl.* **-ries.** A small horse-drawn carriage in India. [Hindi *gāṛī.*]

ghast·ly (găst′lē, gäst′-) *adj.* **-lier, -liest. 1.** Terrifying; dreadful: *a ghastly accident.* **2.** Having a deathlike pallor: *"amid the dim and ghastly glare of a snowy night"* (Washington Irving). **3.** Extremely unpleasant or bad: *a ghastly little book.* ~*adv.* Dreadfully; horribly. [Middle English *gastlich,* Old English *gāstlīc,* spiritual, ghostly, ghastly, from *gāst,* soul, ghost.] —**ghast·li·ness** *n.*

Synonyms: grim, grisly, gruesome, lurid, macabre.

ghat, ghaut (gôt, gät) *n.* In India: **1.** A mountain pass. **2.** A mountain chain. **3.** A flight of steps down to the bank of a river. **4.** An area beside a river, used for bathing. [Hindi *ghāt,* from Sanskrit *ghaṭṭa,* perhaps from *ghṛṣṭa,* rubbed.]

Ghats (gôts, gäts). Two coastal mountain ranges in India, forming the edges of the Deccan plateau. The Western Ghats extend approximately 1,500 kilometers (932 miles) along the west coast and rise to 2,698 meters (8,852 feet) at Anai Mudi. The Eastern Ghats extend approximately 1,400 kilometers (880 miles) along the east coast, rising to 2,637 meters (8,651 feet) at Doda Betta.

gha·zi (gä′zē) *n., pl.* **-zies. 1.** A Muslim warrior who has fought successfully against infidels. Often used as a title of honor. **2.** A high-ranking Turkish warrior. [Arabic *ghāzī,* participle of *ghazā,* he made war.]

Ghazzah. See Gaza.

ghee (gē) *n.* Clarified butter from the butterfat of buffalo or other milk. It is used in cooking, especially in India and neighboring countries. [Hindi *ghī,* from Sanskrit *ghṛta,* present participle of *ghṛ†,* to sprinkle.]

Ghent (gĕnt). *Flemish* **Gent** (gĕnt); *French* **Gand** (gäɴ). A city and port in northwest-central Belgium, the capital of East Flanders.

ghe·rao (gə-rou′) *n.* In India, a coercive tactic adopted during industrial disputes whereby workers surround an employer and detain him on his own premises until he agrees to their demands. ~*tr.v.* **gheraoed, -raoing, -raoes.** To coerce (an employer) by using this technique. [Bengali *gherāo,* to surround, from Indic *gher-* (unattested), causative of *ghir-* (unattested), "to go around," from Dravidian.]

gher·kin (gûr′kĭn) *n.* **1.** A small cucumber, especially one used for pickling. **2.** A tropical American vine, *Cucumis anguria,* bearing prickly, edible fruit. **3.** The fruit of this vine. [Dutch *agurk(je),* from Low German *agurke,* from Lithuanian *agurkas,* from Polish *ogorek, ogurek,* from Medieval Greek *angourion,* probably from Greek *agouros,* youth, "unripe," from *aōros* : *a-,* not + *ōros,* time.]

ghet·to (gĕt′ō) *n., pl.* **-tos** or **-toes. 1.** A slum section of a city occupied predominantly by members of a minority group who live there because of social or economic pressure. **2.** A section or quarter in a European city to which Jews were formerly restricted. **3.** An area occupied by a group, institution, or the like, with a distinctive, and often exclusive, specified common trait: *a cultural ghetto.* [Italian *ghetto†.*]

Ghib·el·line (gĭb′ə-lēn′, -lĭn′, -lĭn) *n.* Any of the members of the aristocratic political faction who fought during the Middle Ages for German imperial control of Italy, in opposition to the Guelphs, who favored papal control. Compare **Guelph.** [Italian *Ghibellino,* from Middle High German *Waiblingen,* name of a Hohenstaufen estate.]

Ghi·ber·ti (gē-bĕr′tē), **Lorenzo** (c.1378–1455). Italian goldsmith and sculptor. He is best known for his series of bronze panels for the doors of the baptistry of Florence Cathedral, depicting scenes from the Old and New Testaments.

ghilgai. Variant of **gilgai.**

ghil·lie (gĭl′ē) *n., pl.* **-lies. 1.** A low-cut sports shoe with fringed laces, originally worn by the Scots. **2.** Variant of **gillie.** [Scottish Gaelic *gille,* boy, servant, GILLIE.]

ghost (gōst) *n.* **1.** The spirit of a dead person, supposed to haunt living persons or former habitats; a specter; a phantom; a wraith. **2.** *Archaic.* The animus or soul as opposed to the body. **3.** A returning or haunting memory or image. **4.** A slight trace or vestige of something; a hint; a semblance: *a ghost of a smile; a ghost of a chance.* **5.** A faint, false secondary image, such as: **a.** A displaced image in a mirror caused by reflection from the front of the glass. **b.** A displaced image in a photograph caused by the optical system of the camera. **c.** A secondary image on a television or radar screen caused by reflected waves. **d.** A false spectral line caused by imperfections in the diffraction grating. **6.** *Printing.* A variation or unevenness of color intensity on a surface intended to be solidly tinted, as the result of irregular distribution of ink. **7.** *Obsolete.* The Holy Ghost. **8.** *Informal.* A ghostwriter. **9.** A nonexistent publication listed in bibliographies. In this sense, also called "ghost edition." **10.** A ghost word. —**give up the ghost.** To die. ~*v.* **ghosted, ghosting, ghosts.** —*intr. Informal.* To work as a ghostwriter. —*tr.* **1.** To haunt. **2.** *Informal.* To write (a work) as a ghostwriter. [Middle English *gost, gast,* Old English *gāst,* from Germanic.]

ghost crab *n.* Any of several light-colored burrowing crabs of the genus *Ocypoda,* frequenting the tide line along sandy shores.

ghost dance *n.* Either of two religious dances practiced chiefly by certain North American Indians of the southwestern United States and California during the latter half of the 19th century to invoke a return of their former condition.

ghost gum *n.* Any of various Australian eucalyptus trees with a smooth, whitish trunk and branches.

ghost·ly (gōst′lē) *adj.* **-lier, -liest. 1.** Pertaining to or resembling a ghost or apparition; spectral; eerie. **2.** Pertaining to the spirit or to religion; spiritual. —**ghost·li·ness** *n.*

ghost town *n.* A town, especially a boom town of the West, that has now been completely abandoned.

ghost word *n.* A word that has come into a language through the perpetuation of a misreading of a manuscript, a typographical error, or a misunderstanding. For example, in *Ye Olde Sweete Shoppe, Ye* is a ghost word, the *y* having been a misreading of the runic letter thorn.

ghost·write (gōst′rīt′) *v.* **-wrote** (-rōt′), **-written** (-rĭt′n), **-writing, -writes.** —*intr.* To work as a ghostwriter. —*tr.* To write (something) as a ghostwriter.

ghost·writ·er (gōst′rī′tər) *n.* A person who is hired to write for another person who then takes credit of authorship. Also informally called "ghost."

ghoul (gōōl) *n.* **1.** One who delights in what is revolting, macabre, or loathsome. **2.** A grave robber. **3. a.** A malevolent ghost. **b.** An evil spirit or demon in Muslim folklore supposed to plunder graves and feed on corpses. [Arabic *ghūl,* from *ghāla,* he took suddenly.] —**ghoul·ish** *adj.* —**ghoul·ish·ly** *adv.* —**ghoul·ish·ness** *n.*

GHQ, G.H.Q. general headquarters.

ghyll. Variant of **gill** (stream or ravine).

gi gill (liquid measure).

Gi gilbert (unit of magnetomotive force).

GI (jē′ī′) *n., pl.* **GIs** or **GI's.** A serviceman in or ex-serviceman of any of the U.S. armed forces. ~*adj.* **1.** Pertaining to or characteristic of a GI. **2.** In conformity to or accordance with U.S. military regulations or procedures. **3.** Issued by an official U.S. military supply department. [Abbreviation of *general issue* or *government issue.*]

GI 1. general issue. **2.** Government Issue.

G.I. Government Issue.

Gia·co·met·ti (jä′kō-mĕt′ə), **Alberto** (1901–66). Swiss painter and sculptor. From 1922 to 1935 he experimented with cubism but later evolved a distinctive, elongated style of representing the human figure.

gi·ant (jī′ənt) *n.* **1. a.** A person or thing of extraordinary size or strength. **b.** A person of outstanding importance or achievement: *He is a giant in his field.* **2. a.** *Greek Mythology.* Any of a race of manlike beings of enormous strength and stature who warred with the Olympians, by whom they were finally destroyed. **b.** Any similar being in folklore or myth. ~*adj.* Of immense size; gigantic; huge. [Middle English *geant,* from Old French, from Vulgar Latin *gangante* (unattested), from Latin *gigās* (stem *gigant-*), from Greek *gigas†.*]

giant anteater *n.* See **anteater.**

giant axon *n.* A giant fiber *(see).*

giant chromosome *n.* A chromosome consisting of many parallel strands of chromatids that have failed to separate after duplication. Giant chromosomes, which occur in the salivary glands of *Drosophila* and other insects, are used to study gene activity.

gi·ant·ess (jī′ən-tĭs) *n.* A female giant.

giant fiber *n. Zoology.* A nerve fiber with a very large diameter found in many invertebrate animals that is capable of rapid conduction of impulses. Also called "giant axon."

giant hogweed *n.* **giant hogweeds** or collectively **giant hogweed.** A very tall plant, *Heracleum mantegazzianum,* with clusters of small white flowers, found especially on waste ground.

gi·ant·ism (jī′ən-tĭz′əm) *n.* **1.** The condition of being a giant. **2.** *Pathology.* Gigantism *(see).*

KEY

24 **Cross-reference** to more common word with same meaning.

25 **Quotation** from well-known author shows entry word used in context.

26 **Synonym list** gives words with closely related meanings.

27 **Geographic** entry.

28 Italic label indicates **foreign language.**

29 **Dagger** in etymology indicates obscure origin.

30 **Biographical** entry.

31 Italic label indicates sense of entry word is **no longer current.**

32 **Subject labels** precede specialized meanings.

33 **Fixed phrases** shown at key entry word.

34 **Comparative** form of modifier.

35 **Superlative** form of modifier.

36 Dashes introduce **intransitive** and **transitive** uses of **verb.**

37 **Abbreviations** included in dictionary word list.

38 Wavy dash introduces **new part of speech.**

39 **Alternate term** for entry word.

40 **Scientific names** of plants and animals given.

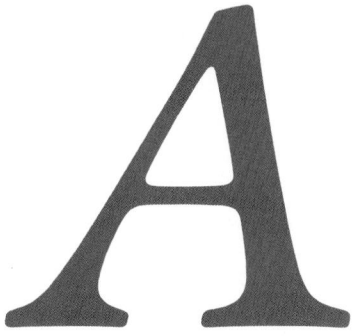

a, A (ā) *n., pl.* **a's** or **A's. 1.** The first letter of the modern English alphabet. See feature at **alphabet. 2.** Any of the speech sounds represented by this letter. **3.** Anything shaped like the letter **A. 4. A** The best or highest in quality, class, or rank: *grade A milk.* **5. A** The highest mark awarded for academic work. **6. A a.** The sixth tone in the scale of C major. **b.** The key or a scale in which A is the tonic. **c.** A written or printed note representing A. **d.** A string, key, or pipe tuned to the pitch of A. **7. A** A human blood type of the ABO group. See **ABO.**

a, A, a., A. *Note:* As an abbreviation or symbol, *a* may be a small or a capital letter, with or without a period. Established forms or those generally preferred precede the definition. When no form is given, all four forms are in general use in that sense. **1. a.** about. **2. a.** academician; academy. **3. a** acceleration. **4. A, a., A.** acre. **5. a.** acreage. **6. a.** acting. **7. a.** adjective. **8. a.** afternoon. **9. A.** alto. **10. a., A.** amateur. **11. A.** America; American. **12. A** ammeter. **13. A** ampere. **14. a.** anonymous. **15. a., A.** answer. **16. a.** anterior. **17. a, a.** are (measurement). **18. A** area. **19. a** *Physics.* atto-. **20. a.** before. [Latin *ante*] **21. a.** in the year. [Latin *annō*] **22.** *Physics.* **A** Helmholtz function. **23. a.** year. [Latin *annus*] **24.** The first in a series.

a¹ (ə; *emphatic* ā). Indefinite article functioning as an adjective. **1.** Used before nouns and noun phrases that denote a single, but unspecified, person or thing: *a region; a man.* **2.** Used before plural nouns modified by *few, good many,* or *great many: a few donations.* **3.** One kind of: *birds of a feather.* **4.** Any: *a broken leg soon mends; not a drop to drink.* **5.** Used before mass nouns to indicate: **a.** A particular type of: *a good education.* **b.** A unit of: *a beer.* **6.** Used before nouns that indicate a state or action, to denote a single instance: *had a long wait; cut prices at a stroke.* **7.** One like: *a Casanova.* **8.** A certain: *A Mrs. Brown just called.* **9.** A type of: *Chianti is a wine.* **10.** A work of art by: *It's a Picasso.* See **an.** [Middle English *a(n),* from Old English *an, ān,* one.]

Usage: The general rule of thumb is that *a* is used before words beginning with a consonant, and *an* before those beginning with a vowel, but difficulties may arise over abbreviations and words beginning with *u* and *h.* In all such cases it is the *sound* of the letters that determines which form is used, so it is *an M.B.A., a union, an umbrella, a hair, an heir.*

In a few cases, *a* or *an* are used almost interchangeably. When *h* is in an unstressed syllable at the beginning of a word, *an* is sometimes used (*an hotel*) but it sounds old-fashioned. In rapid speech, however, the *h* may be so reduced in strength that the use of *an* sounds quite natural, so that variation occurs between *a habitual worry* and *an habitual worry.*

a² (ə). Indefinite article functioning as a preposition. In every; to each; per: *once a month; 50 cents a pound.* [Middle English *a, o,* reduced form of *an, on,* in, at, ON.]

a³ (ə, ā) *v. Regional.* Have: *He'd a come if he could.* [Middle English *a, ha,* reduced forms of *haven, habben,* to HAVE.]

a–¹ *prefix.* Indicates without, not, or opposite to; for example, **amoral, acotyledon.** [Greek *a-, an-,* not.]

a–² *prefix.* Indicates: **1.** On or in; for example, **aboard, abed. 2.** In the act of; for example, **a-fishing, a-going. 3.** In a specified state or manner; for example, **aloud, asleep.**

a–³ Indicates: **1.** Up, out, or away; for example, **arise, awake. 2.** Intensified action; for example, **abide, amaze.** [Middle English *a-,* up, out, away, Old English *ā-,* reduced form of *ar-, or-,* from Germanic.]

a–⁴ Indicates of or from; for example, **anew, afresh.** [Middle English *a-, o-,* reduced form of OF.]

Å angstrom.

A–1, A–one (ā'wŭn') *adj.* **1.** *Informal.* Excellent; splendid. **2.** Having a hull and equipment in top condition. Said of a ship. [The symbol used by Lloyd's Register of Shipping to designate ships in first-class condition.]

A1C airman first class.

aa *Pharmacology.* ana (in prescriptions).

AA 1. Alcoholics Anonymous. **2.** antiaircraft.

AAA American Automobile Association.

Aa·chen (ä'кнən). *French* **Aix-la-Cha·pelle** (ĕks'lä-shä-pĕl'). City in North Rhine-Westphalia, Germany, near the Dutch and Belgian borders. Charlemagne made it the northern capital of his empire, and from 936 to 1531 many Holy Roman Emperors were crowned in its cathedral. It is now an important industrial and manufacturing center.

Aalborg. See **Ålborg.**

Aalesund. See **Ålesund.**

Aal·to (äl'tō), **Alvar** (1898–1976). Finnish architect whose work is noted for the use of contrasting materials, such as pine boarding with rough concrete. One of his finest buildings is the Paimio Tuberculosis Sanatorium, Finland (1929–33).

A & M 1. agricultural and mechanical. **2.** ancient and modern.

A. & R. artists and repertory (or repertoire).

aard·vark (ärd'värk') *n.* A burrowing mammal, *Orycteropus afer,* of southern Africa, having a stocky, hairy body, large ears, a long, tubular snout, and powerful digging claws for excavating ant and termite nests. Also called "ant bear." [Obsolete Afrikaans, "earth-pig" : *aarde,* earth, from Dutch, from Middle Dutch *aerde* + *vark,* pig, from Middle Dutch *varken,* little pig; akin to FARROW (litter of pigs).]

aard·wolf (ärd'wŏolf') *n., pl.* **-wolves** (-wŏolvz'). A hyenalike mammal, *Proteles cristatus,* of southern and eastern Africa, having gray fur with black stripes, and feeding mainly on termites and insect larvae. [Afrikaans, "earth-wolf" : *aarde,* earth (see **aardvark**) + *wolf,* WOLF.]

Aarhus. See **Århus.**

Aar·on (âr'ən, ăr'-). The original high priest of the Hebrew nation, the elder brother of Moses. Exodus 28:1–4; 40:12–13.

Aaron's rod *n.* **1.** Any of several flowering plants having tall, erect stems; especially, *Thermopsis caroliniana,* of the southeastern United States, having compound leaves and erect clusters of yellow flowers. **2.** A common Eurasian plant, *Verbascum thapsus,* with whitish downy leaves and erect clusters of yellow flowers. See **mullein. 3.** *Architecture.* A rod-shaped molding decorated with a design of leaves, scrolls, or a twined serpent. [After the rod of the high priest Aaron, which blossomed and produced almonds (Numbers 17:8).]

Ab. Variant of **Av.**

ab–¹ *prefix.* Indicates a position or quality off, outside of, opposite to, or removed from another specified position or quality; for example, **abomasum, aboral, abnormal.** [Latin, from *ab,* away from. In Latin compounds, *ab-* becomes *a-* before *m, p,* and *v; au-* before *f;* and *abs-* before *t.*]

ab–² *prefix.* Indicates a centimeter-gram-second electromagnetic unit of measurement; for example, **abcoulomb.** [Short for ABSOLUTE.]

AB A human blood type of the ABO group. See **ABO.**

a.b. able-bodied seaman.

A.B. 1. able-bodied seaman. **2.** Bachelor of Arts. [Latin *Artium Baccalaureus*]

a·ba, ab·ba (ə-bä') *n.* **1.** A light fabric woven from the hair of camels or goats. **2.** A loose-fitting sleeveless garment of this fabric worn by Arabs. [Arabic *'abā'.*]

ABA 1. American Bankers Association. **2.** Also **A.B.A.** American Bar association. **3.** American Booksellers Association.

ab·a·ca (ăb'ə-kä') *n.* A Philippine plant, *Musa textilis,* related to the banana. Its leafstalks are the source of **Manila hemp** *(see).* [Spanish *abacá,* from Tagalog *abaká.*]

a·back (ə-băk') *adv.* **1.** *Nautical.* Facing into a headwind in such a way that the sails are pressed against the mast. **2.** *Archaic.* Back; backward. [Middle English *abak,* Old English *on bæc* : ON + *bæc,* BACK.]

ab·a·cus (ăb'ə-kəs) *n., pl.* **-cuses** or **-ci** (-sī'). **1.** A manual calculating device consisting of a frame holding parallel rods strung with movable counters. **2.** A slab on the top of the capital of a column. [Latin *abacus,* from Greek *abax* (stem *abak-*), slab, mathematical

aardvark *The aardvark of southern Africa (whose name comes from the Afrikaans for "earth pig") feeds on insects, breaking up termite nests with its powerful front claws and gathering up the insects with its 45-centimeter-long (18-inch) tongue. It is the sole member of the scientific order Tubilidentata—so called because the aardvark's teeth are a mass of small tubes, quite unlike those of any other mammal.*

aardwolf *A small member of the hyena family, the aardwolf lives in the dry plains of southern and eastern Africa. It has a weak jaw with small teeth and lives chiefly on termites and insect larvae.*

table, originally a drawing board covered with dust, from Hebrew *'ābhāq,* dust.]

Ab·a·dan (ä'bə-dän', ăb'ə-dăn'). City in southwest Iran, on Abadan Island in the Shatt al Arab. A major oil-refining and oil-exporting center, it was severely damaged in the 1980 war with Iraq.

a·baft (ə-băft', ə-bäft') *adv. Nautical.* Toward the stern.
~*prep. Nautical.* Behind: *abaft the mainmast.* [Middle English *o(n) baft* : ON + *baft,* from Old English *beæftan,* behind : *be,* at, BY + *æftan,* behind.]

abalone *Found in warm seas, the abalone is a marine snail prized both for its tasty flesh and for its shell that provides mother-of-pearl. This is a small tropical abalone.*

ab·a·lo·ne (ăb'ə-lō'nē) *n.* Any of the various large, edible marine gastropod mollusks of the genus *Haliotis,* having an ear-shaped shell with a row of holes and a colorful, pearly interior often used for making ornaments. [American Spanish *abulón*†.]

ab·amp (ăb'ămp') *n.* An abampere.

ab·am·pere (ăb-ăm'pîr') *n.* A centimeter-gram-second electromagnetic unit of current, equal to the current that produces a force of two dynes per centimeter of length on each of two infinitely long straight parallel wires one centimeter apart. It is equal to ten amperes. [AB- (absolute) + AMPERE.]

a·ban·don (ə-băn'dən) *tr.v.* **-doned, -doning, -dons. 1.** To forsake; desert: *abandon one's child.* **2.** To leave or leave behind; withdraw from: *abandon ship.* **3.** To surrender one's claim or right to. **4.** To give up completely and irrevocably; relinquish: *abandon hope.* **5.** To end prematurely: *abandon play because of rain.* **6.** To yield (oneself) completely and without restraint, as to emotion. **7.** To relinquish (property) to an insurer in order to make a full claim in case of damage or partial loss.
~*n.* A complete surrender of inhibitions. [Middle English *abandounen,* from Old French *abandoner,* from *(metre) a bandon,* "(to put) in one's power" : *a,* to, at, from Latin *ad,* to + *bandon,* power, from *ban,* jurisdiction, power, from Frankish *ban* (unattested); akin to Old English *gebann,* proclamation, BANNS.] **—a·ban·don·ment** *n.*

a·ban·doned (ə-băn'dənd) *adj.* **1.** Forsaken; deserted. **2.** Completely uninhibited. **3.** Shameless; immoral.

a·base (ə-bās') *tr.v.* **abased, abasing, abases.** To lower in rank, prestige, or esteem; humble; humiliate. —See Synonyms at **degrade.** [Middle English *abassen,* from Old French *abaissier,* from Vulgar Latin *abbassiāre* (unattested) : *ad-,* to + *bassiāre* (unattested), to lower, from Late Latin *bassus,* low.] **—a·base·ment** *n.*

a·bash (ə-băsh') *tr.v.* **abashed, abashing, abashes.** To make ashamed or uneasy; disconcert. [Middle English *abaisen, abashen,* to gape with surprise, be dumbfounded, from Norman French *abaiss-,* variant of Old French *e(s)bass-,* present stem of *e(s)bahir* : *es-,* from Latin *ex-,* out of + *baer,* to gape, from Latin *batāre* (unattested), to yawn, gape.] **—a·bash·ment** *n.*

Aberdeen Angus *A stocky Scottish breed of cattle that grows quickly and produces high-quality beef.*

a·bate (ə-bāt') *v.* **abated, abating, abates.** *—tr.* **1.** To reduce in amount, degree, or intensity; lessen. **2.** To deduct from an amount; subtract. **3.** *Law.* **a.** To put an end to: *abate a nuisance.* **b.** To make void: *abate a writ.* *—intr.* **1.** To subside: *The storm abated.* **2.** *Law.* To become void. —See Synonyms at **decrease.** [Middle English *abaten,* from Old French *abatre,* to beat down, from Vulgar Latin *abbattuere* (unattested) : *ad-,* at, to (used here to express completed action) + *battuere*†, to beat.]

a·bate·ment (ə-bāt'mənt) *n.* **1.** Diminution in degree or intensity; moderation. **2.** The amount abated; reduction. **3.** *Law.* The act of abating; elimination or annulment.

ab·at·toir (ăb'ə-twär') *n.* A slaughterhouse. [19th century : French, from *abattre,* to fell. See **abate.**]

ab·ax·i·al (ăb-ăk'sē-əl) *adj.* Facing away from the axis. Said of the lower surface of leaves. Compare **adaxial.**

abba. Variant of **aba.**

Ab·ba (ăb'ə) *n.* **1.** In the New Testament, God. Mark 14:36. **2. abba.** Father. Used as a title of honor in several Eastern churches. [Middle English, from Late Latin, from Greek, from Aramaic *abbā,* father.]

ab·ba·cy (ăb'ə-sē) *n., pl.* **-cies.** The office, term, or jurisdiction of an abbot. [Middle English *abbatie,* from Late Latin *abbātia,* from *abbās* (stem *abbāt-*), ABBOT.]

Ab·bas·sid (ə-băs'ĭd, ăb'ə-sĭd). Also **Ab·bas·side** (-īd). Arabic dynasty (750–1258) that expanded the Moslem Empire to cover much of Asia Minor, North Africa, and parts of Spain. It took its name from al-Abbas (*c.* 566–652), uncle of the prophet Mohammed, and its authority was based chiefly on the religious prestige enjoyed by the prophet's descendants. **—Ab·bas·sid, Ab·bas·side** *adj. & n.*

ab·ba·tial (ə-bā'shəl) *adj.* Of or pertaining to an abbey, abbot, or abbess. [Middle English *abbacyal,* from Late Latin *abbātiālis,* from *abbās* (stem *abbāt-*), ABBOT.]

ab·bé (ăb'ā, ă-bā') *n., pl.* **abbés.** In France, originally the superior of an abbey, now any priest. Used especially as a title. [French, from Old French, from Late Latin *abbās,* ABBOT.]

ab·bess (ăb'ĭs) *n., pl.* **-besses.** The female superior of a convent of nuns. [Middle English *abbesse,* from Old French, from Late Latin *abbātissa,* from *abbās* (stem *abbāt-*), ABBOT.]

Ab·be·vil·li·an (ăb'ə-vĭl'ē-ən) *adj.* Of or designating the earliest Paleolithic archaeological sites in Europe, characterized by bifacial stone hand axes. Formerly called "Chellian." [After *Abbeville,* France, site of the archaeological finds.]

ab·bey (ăb'ē) *n., pl.* **-beys. 1.** A monastery or convent. **2.** A church that is or once was part of an abbey. [Middle English, from Old French *abaie,* from Late Latin *abbātia,* from *abbās,* ABBOT.]

ab·bot (ăb'ət) *n.* The superior of a monastery. [Middle English *abbod,* Old English *abbod, abbad,* from Late Latin *abbās* (stem *abbāt-*), from Late Greek *abbās,* from Aramaic *abbā,* father, ABBA.]

abbr., abbrev. abbreviation.

ab·bre·vi·ate (ə-brē'vē-āt') *tr.v.* **-ated, -ating, -ates. 1.** To make shorter by removing or leaving out parts. **2.** To reduce (a word or phrase) to a shorter form intended to represent the full form. [Middle English *abbreviaten,* from Late Latin *abbreviāre,* to shorten : *ab-,* off, or *ad-,* toward + *brevis,* short.] **—ab·brev·i·at·or** *n.*

ab·bre·vi·a·tion (ə-brē'vē-ā'shən) *n. Abbr.* **abbr., abbrev. 1.** The act or product of abbreviating. **2.** A shortened form of a word or phrase used chiefly in writing to represent the complete form; for example, *Mass.* for Massachusetts. Compare **contraction.**

ABC[1] (ā'bē'sē') *n., pl.* **ABC's. 1.** *Usually* **ABC's.** The alphabet. **2. ABC's.** The rudiments of reading and writing. **3.** An alphabetical guidebook or instruction manual.

ABC[2] **1.** American Broadcasting Company. **2.** atomic, biological, and chemical. **3.** Australian Broadcasting Commission.

ab·cou·lomb (ăb-ko͞o'lŏm', -lōm') *n.* A centimeter-gram-second electromagnetic unit of charge, equal to the charge passing in one second through any cross section of a conductor carrying a steady current of one abampere. It is equal to ten coulombs. [AB- (absolute) + COULOMB.]

ab·di·cate (ăb'dĭ-kāt') *v.* **-cated, -cating, -cates.** *—tr.* To relinquish (power or responsibility) formally. *—intr.* To relinquish formally high office or responsibility. Used especially of a monarch. [Latin *abdicāre,* to disclaim : *ab-,* away from + *dicāre,* to proclaim.] **—ab·di·ca·ble** (ăb'dĭ-kə-bəl) *adj.* **—ab·di·ca·tion** (ăb'dĭ-kā'shən) *n.* **—ab·di·ca·tor** (ăb'dĭ-kā'tər) *n.*

ab·do·men (ăb'də-mən, ăb-dō'mən) *n.* **1.** The part of the body in vertebrates that lies between the thorax and the pelvis, and that encloses the viscera; the belly. **2.** In arthropods, the major posterior part of the body. [16th century : Latin *abdōmen*†, belly.] **—ab·dom·i·nal** (ăb-dŏm'ə-nəl) *adj.* **—ab·dom·i·nal·ly** *adv.*

ab·du·cens nerve (ăb-do͞o'sənz, -dyo͞o'-) *n.* Either of the 6th pair of cranial nerves, which supply one of the eye muscles. [Latin *abdūcens,* "leading away," present participle of *abdūcere,* to ABDUCT.]

ab·duct (ăb-dŭkt') *tr.v.* **-ducted, -ducting, -ducts. 1.** To carry off (a person) by force; kidnap. **2.** *Physiology.* To draw away from the median line of a bone or muscle or from an adjacent part or limb. [Latin *abdūcere* (past participle *abductus*) : *ab-,* away + *dūcere,* to lead.] **—ab·duc·tion** *n.* **—ab·duc·tor** *n.*

Ab·dul Rah·man (ăb'do͝ol räKH'mən), **Tunku** (1903–73). Malaysian statesman who negotiated the independence of Malaya from Britain in 1957 and helped establish the Federation of Malaysia in 1963. He was the first prime minister of Malaya (1957–63) and of Malaysia (1963–70).

a·beam (ə-bēm') *adv.* At right angles to the keel of a ship or length of an aircraft or directly opposite the middle of its side. [A- (in the direction of) + BEAM (keel).]

a·be·ce·dar·i·an (ā'bē-sē-dâr'ē-ən) *n.* Also **a·be·ce·da·ry** (ā'bē-sē'-də-rē). **1.** One who teaches or studies the alphabet. **2.** One who is just learning; a novice.
~*adj.* Arranged alphabetically. [Middle English, from Medieval Latin *abecedārium,* alphabet, from Late Latin *abecedārius,* pertaining to the alphabet, from the first four letters.]

a·bed (ə-bĕd') *adv.* In bed.

A·bed·ne·go (ə-bĕd'nĭ-gō'). One of the three young men, the others being Meshach and Shadrach, who came unharmed out of the fiery furnace in Babylon. Daniel 3:12–30.

A·bel (ā'bəl). The second son of Adam and Eve, slain by his elder brother, Cain. Genesis 4:2. [Middle English, from Late Latin, from Greek, from Hebrew *Hebhel,* akin to Assyrian *ablu,* son.]

Ab·e·lard (ăb'ə-lärd'), **Peter** (1079–1142). *French* **Pierre A·bé·lard** (à-bā-lár'). French philosopher and theologian whose application of the principles of ancient Greek logic to the doctrines of the medieval Catholic Church led him into great controversy and charges of heresy. In Paris he secretly married one of his pupils, Héloise, after she bore him a child. Héloise's family had Abelard castrated; she became a nun and he became a monk.

a·bele (ə-bēl') *n.* A tree, the **white poplar** *(see).* [16th century : Dutch *abeel,* from Old French *abel, aubel,* from Medieval Latin *albellus,* diminutive of Latin *albus,* white.]

a·be·li·a (ə-bē'lē-ə) *n.* Any of various shrubs of the genus *Abelia,* having tubular red, pink, or white flowers and widely grown as garden ornamentals.

A·be·li·an group (ə-bē'lē-ən, ə-bēl'yən) *n. Algebra.* A **commutative group** *(see).* [After Niels Henrik *Abel* (1802–29), Norwegian mathematician.]

a·bel·mosk (ā'bəl-mŏsk') *n.* A hairy plant, *Hibiscus abelmoschus,* of tropical Asia, having large yellow flowers and musk-scented seeds that are used in perfumery. Also called "musk mallow." [New Latin *Abelmoschus,* from Arabic *ḥabb-al-musk* (vulgar pronunciation *ḥabb-el-mosk*), "grain of musk" : *ḥabb,* grain + *mosk,* MUSK.]

Ab·er·deen (ab'ər-dēn'). City, port, and administrative center of Grampian Region, northeast Scotland, on the North Sea coast at the mouth of the Dee River. Granted a royal charter in 1176, it has a 14th-century cathedral and a university formed by the amalgamation in 1860 of its two ancient colleges, King's College (founded 1494) and Marischal College (founded 1593). It is known as the "Granite City" because the local stone is used in many of its buildings. Aberdeen is the third-largest fishing port in Britain and the main town servicing the North Sea oil industry.

Aberdeen An·gus (ăng'gəs) *n.* Any of a breed of black, hornless beef cattle that originated in Scotland.

PRONUNCIATION KEY

ă, pat; ā, pay; âr, care;
ä, father, are; b, bib;
ch, church; d, deed; ĕ, pet;
ē, be; f, fife; g, gag; h, hat;
hw, which; ĭ, pit; ī, pie;
îr, pier; j, judge; k, kick;
l, lid, needle; m, mum;
n, no, sudden; ng, thing;
ŏ, pot; ō, toe; ô, paw, for;
oi, noise; ou, out; o͝o, book;
o͞o, boot; p, pop; r, roar;
s, sauce; sh, ship, dish;
t, tight; th, thin, path;
th, this, bathe; ŭ, cut; ûr, fur;
v, valve; w, with; y, yes;
z, zebra, size; zh, vision;
ə, about, item, edible,
gallop, circus, peaceful

IN FOREIGN WORDS:

à, *Fr.* ami; œ, *Fr.* feu, *Ger.* schön; ü, *Fr.* tu, *Ger.* über; KH, *Ger.* ich, *Scot.* loch; N, *Fr.* bon; y', *Fr.* Compiègne

STRESS MARKS:

Primary stress: '
in·cite' (ĭn-sīt')
Secondary stress: '
in'sight' (ĭn'sīt')

ISLANDS OF CIVILIZATION

Abbeys preserved Europe's intellectual and artistic traditions in the Middle Ages

Abbeys have their roots in the early religious communities of the Middle East and Greece. The first European abbey, however, was built in 529 on the rugged peak of Monte Cassino, Italy, by St. Benedict, founder of Western monasticism. The abbot—from Aramaic *abba* ("father")—was seen both as the representative of Christ and as the monastery's temporal authority. The name abbey was given to a monastic community under an abbot or abbess, but it was used loosely for other religious foundations—and often as another word for monastery.

The monastic life was attractively secure when, outside, governments were weak and life unruly. In Christian Western Europe 100 abbeys were founded in the 7th century and 100 more by 750. For six centuries, abbeys were islands of civilization all over Europe. A large abbey could serve a considerable area as an administrative, intellectual, and spiritual center. Some could house 1,000 people—several hundred monks, servants, and guests. Many became extremely wealthy and were famed for their splendid buildings.

In Britain, as a consequence of his break with the papacy and his need for additional income, Henry VIII dissolved the monasteries (1536–40). Most abbeys were destroyed, leaving only some abbey churches such as Westminster Abbey. Several have been restored, but few new ones have been built.

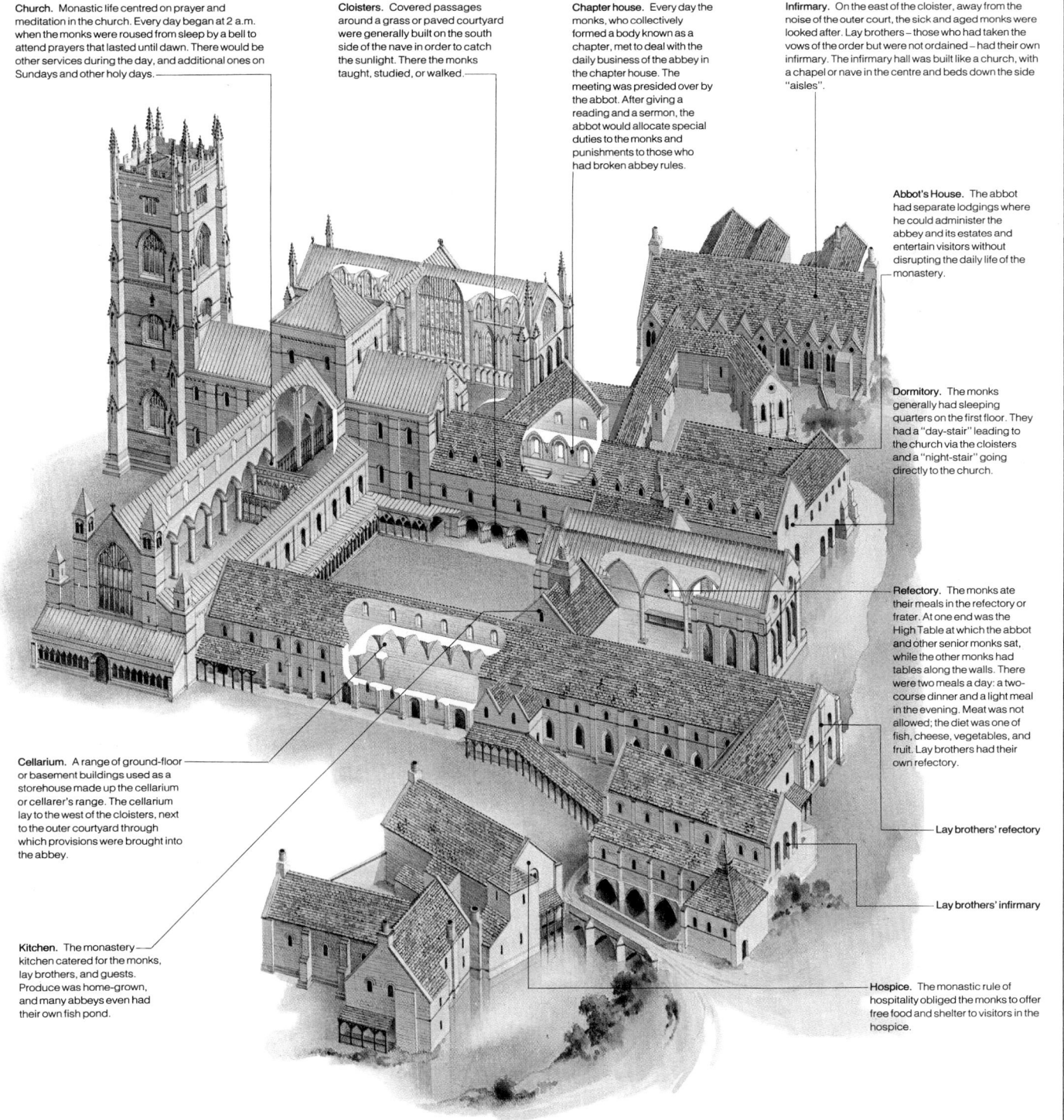

Church. Monastic life centred on prayer and meditation in the church. Every day began at 2 a.m. when the monks were roused from sleep by a bell to attend prayers that lasted until dawn. There would be other services during the day, and additional ones on Sundays and other holy days.

Cloisters. Covered passages around a grass or paved courtyard were generally built on the south side of the nave in order to catch the sunlight. There the monks taught, studied, or walked.

Chapter house. Every day the monks, who collectively formed a body known as a chapter, met to deal with the daily business of the abbey in the chapter house. The meeting was presided over by the abbot. After giving a reading and a sermon, the abbot would allocate special duties to the monks and punishments to those who had broken abbey rules.

Infirmary. On the east of the cloister, away from the noise of the outer court, the sick and aged monks were looked after. Lay brothers – those who had taken the vows of the order but were not ordained – had their own infirmary. The infirmary hall was built like a church, with a chapel or nave in the centre and beds down the side "aisles".

Abbot's House. The abbot had separate lodgings where he could administer the abbey and its estates and entertain visitors without disrupting the daily life of the monastery.

Dormitory. The monks generally had sleeping quarters on the first floor. They had a "day-stair" leading to the church via the cloisters and a "night-stair" going directly to the church.

Refectory. The monks ate their meals in the refectory or frater. At one end was the High Table at which the abbot and other senior monks sat, while the other monks had tables along the walls. There were two meals a day: a two-course dinner and a light meal in the evening. Meat was not allowed; the diet was one of fish, cheese, vegetables, and fruit. Lay brothers had their own refectory.

Cellarium. A range of ground-floor or basement buildings used as a storehouse made up the cellarium or cellarer's range. The cellarium lay to the west of the cloisters, next to the outer courtyard through which provisions were brought into the abbey.

Kitchen. The monastery kitchen catered for the monks, lay brothers, and guests. Produce was home-grown, and many abbeys even had their own fish pond.

Lay brothers' refectory

Lay brothers' infirmary

Hospice. The monastic rule of hospitality obliged the monks to offer free food and shelter to visitors in the hospice.

Ab·er·deen·shire (ăb′ər-dēn′shǐr′). Former county of northeast Scotland. Since 1975 it has been part of Grampian Region.

Aberdeen terrier *n.* The **Scottish terrier** *(see).*

ab·er·rant (ă-bĕr′ənt) *adj.* **1.** Deviating from the proper or expected course. **2.** Deviating from what is normal; untrue to type. —**ab·er·rance, ab·er·ran·cy** *n.*

ab·er·ra·tion (ăb′ə-rā′shən) *n.* **1.** A deviation from the proper or expected course. **2.** A departure from the normal or typical. **3.** An abnormal alteration in one's mental state; a lapse in mental capacities. **4.** *Optics.* **a.** A defect of focus, such as blurring or distortion, in an image. **b.** A physical defect in an optical element, as in a mirror or lens, that causes such an imperfection. See **chromatic aberration, spherical aberration, astigmatism, coma. 5.** The apparent displacement of the position of a celestial body in the direction of motion of an observer on Earth, caused by the motion of the Earth. [Latin *aberrātiō,* diversion, from *aberrāre,* to go astray : *ab-,* from + *errāre,* to stray.]

a·bet (ə-bĕt′) *tr.v.* **abetted, abetting, abets.** To encourage and assist; especially, to incite to a criminal act. [Middle English *abetten,* from Old French *abeter,* to entice : *a-,* from Latin *ad-,* to + *beter,* to bait, from Germanic.] —**a·bet·ment** *n.* —**a·bet·ter, a·bet·tor** *n.*

ab ex·tra (ăb ĕk′strə) *adv. Latin.* From without.

a·bey·ance (ə-bā′əns) *n.* **1.** The condition of being temporarily set aside or suspended. **2.** *Law.* A condition of undetermined ownership, as of an estate that has not yet been assigned. [Norman French *abeiance,* variant of Old French *abeance,* desire, from *abaer,* "to gape at," yearn for : *a-,* from Latin *ad-,* to + *baer,* to gape (see **abash**).] —**a·bey·ant** *adj.*

ab·far·ad (ăb-făr′ăd′, -əd) *n.* A centimeter-gram-second electromagnetic unit of capacitance, equal to the capacitance of a capacitor having a charge of one abcoulomb and a potential difference of one abvolt. It is equal to 10⁹ farads. [AB- (absolute) + FARAD.]

ab·hen·ry (ăb-hĕn′rē) *n., pl.* **-ries.** A centimeter-gram-second electromagnetic unit of inductance, equal to the inductance resulting from a current variation of one abampere per second that produces an induced electromotive force of one abvolt. It is equal to 10⁻⁹ henry. [AB- (absolute) + HENRY.]

ab·hor (ăb-hôr′) *tr.v.* **-horred, -horring, -hors. 1.** To regard with horror or loathing; abominate. **2.** To reject vehemently; shun. [Middle English *abhorren,* from Latin *abhorrēre,* to shrink from : *ab-,* from + *horrēre,* to shudder, bristle.] —**ab·hor·rence** *n.* —**ab·hor·rer** *n.*

ab·hor·rent (ăb-hôr′ənt, -hŏr′-) *adj.* **1.** Disgusting; loathsome; repellent. **2.** In opposition; completely contrary: *Carelessness was abhorrent to his nature.* —**ab·hor·rent·ly** *adv.*

A·bib (ä-vēv′) *n.* In the ancient Hebrew calendar, an earlier name for the month of **Nisan** *(see).* [Hebrew *'ābhībh,* "(month of) fresh barley," "spring."]

a·bide (ə-bīd′) *v.* **abode** (ə-bōd′) or **abided, abiding, abides.** —*tr.* **1.** To put up with; tolerate: *can't abide hypocrisy.* **2.** To withstand; persevere under: *abide the horrors of war.* **3.** *Archaic.* To wait patiently for: *"I will abide the coming of my Lord"* (Tennyson). —*intr.* **1.** To remain in one place or state. **2.** To continue; endure: *"Who can abide in the fierceness of his anger?"* (Cotton Mather). **3.** *Archaic.* To dwell or sojourn. —See Synonyms at **bear.** —**abide by. 1.** To conform to; comply with. **2.** To accept the consequences of; rest satisfied with. [Middle English *abiden,* Old English *ābīdan : a-* (intensive) + *bīdan,* to remain, await.] —**a·bid·ance** *n.*

a·bid·ing (ə-bī′dǐng) *adj.* Lasting; enduring: *an abiding devotion.* —**a·bid·ing·ly** *adv.*

Ab·i·djan (ăb′ī-jän′). The capital of the Ivory Coast, on the Gulf of Guinea. It lies on an enclosed lagoon and is the country's leading port and industrial center.

ab·i·et·ic acid (ăb′ē-ĕt′ǐk) *n.* A yellowish resinous powder, C₁₉H₂₉COOH, occurring naturally in rosin and used in lacquers, varnishes, and soaps. [19th century : from Latin *abiēs†* (stem *abiēt-*), fir (the acid occurs in its resin).]

ab·i·gail (ăb′ə-gāl′) *n. Archaic.* A lady's maid. [From the name of a serving maid in *The Scornful Lady* (c. 1613), play by Beaumont and Fletcher.]

Ab·i·gail (ăb′ə-gāl′). The wife of David. I Samuel 25:14-44. [Hebrew *Abhīgayil,* "my father is joy."]

Ab·i·lene¹ (ăb′ə-lēn′). A city in central Kansas, west of Topeka. It was originally a boisterous cow town and terminus of the Abilene trail, a cattle-driving route from Texas to Kansas. Dwight D. Eisenhower lived in Abilene during his youth; the Eisenhower Center includes his family homestead, a museum, a library, and his grave.

Abilene². A city in west-central Texas. Originally a shipping center for cattle, Abilene is now the financial, commercial, and educational center of a large part of western Texas.

a·bil·i·ty (ə-bǐl′ə-tē) *n., pl.* **-ties. 1.** The quality of being able to do something; the fact of having the requisite means, skill, strength, mental capacity, or legal power. **2.** A natural or acquired skill or talent. [Middle English *abilite,* from Old French *habilite,* from Latin *habilitās,* from *habilis,* ABLE.]

Synonyms: aptitude, capacity, competence, skill, talent.

–ability, –ibility *suffix.* Indicates: **1.** Ability to undergo the specified action or process; for example, **wearability. 2.** Possession of a specified quality; for example, **variability.** [-ABLE + -ITY or -IBLE + -ITY.]

ab in·i·ti·o (ăb′ ǐ-nǐsh′ē-ō) *adv. Latin.* From the beginning.

ab in·tra (ăb′ ǐn′trə) *adv. Latin.* From within.

a·bi·o·gen·e·sis (ā′bī-ō-jĕn′ə-sǐs, ăb′ē-ō-) *n.* The hypothetical development of living organisms from nonliving matter as is assumed to have occurred in the origin of life on earth. Also called "autogenesis." See **primordial soup, spontaneous generation.** [A- (without) + BIO- + -GENESIS.] —**a·bi·o·ge·net·ic** (ā′bī-ō-jə-nĕt′ǐk) *adj.*

a·bi·ot·ic (ā′bī-ŏt′ǐk) *adj.* Devoid of life; inanimate. Said especially of environments or environmental factors.

ab·ject (ăb′jĕkt′, ăb-jĕkt′) *adj.* **1.** Of the most contemptible kind: *an abject liar.* **2.** Of the most miserable kind; wretched: *abject poverty.* **3.** Humble and often ingratiating in manner; servile. —See Synonyms at **mean** (ignoble). [Middle English, "rejected," from Latin *abjectus,* cast away, from the past participle of *abjicere,* to cast away : *ab-,* away from + *jacere,* to throw.] —**ab·jec·tion** *n.* —**ab·ject·ly** *adv.*

ab·jure (ăb-jōōr′) *tr.v.* **-jured, -juring, -jures. 1. a.** To repudiate or recant solemnly. **b.** To renounce under oath; forswear. **2.** To abstain from; give up. [Middle English *abjuren,* from Old French *abjurer,* from Latin *abjūrāre : ab-,* away + *jūrāre,* to swear.] —**ab·ju·ra·tion** *n.* —**ab·jur·er** *n.*

abl. ablative.

ab·late (ă-blāt′) *tr.v.* **-lated, -lating, -lates.** To remove by ablation. [Back-formation from ABLATION.]

ab·la·tion (ă-blā′shən) *n.* **1.** Surgical excision or amputation of any part of the body. **2.** The totality of erosive processes by which a glacier or ice sheet is reduced. **3.** *Aerospace.* The dissipation of heat generated by atmospheric friction, especially in the atmospheric reentry of a spacecraft or missile, by means of a melting **heat shield** *(see).* [Late Latin *ablātiō,* from *ablātus,* removed (past participle of *auferre,* to carry away) : *ab-,* away from + *-lātus,* carried.]

ab·la·tive (ăb′lə-tĭv) *n. Abbr.* **abl. 1.** The grammatical case in certain Indo-European languages, such as Latin, that denotes separation, direction away from, and sometimes manner or agency. **2.** A form or construction in this case. [Middle English, from Old French *ablatif,* from Latin *ablātīvus,* "expressing removal," from *ablātus,* removed. See **ablation.**] —**ab·la·tive** *adj.*

ablative absolute *n.* In Latin grammar, an adverbial phrase syntactically independent from the rest of the sentence and containing two main constituents, both in the ablative case. It is usually used to express cause, circumstance, or time; for example, in the sentence *Regibus expulsis, leges respublica condit (The kings having been expelled, the republic sets up laws),* the phrase *Regibus expulsis* is the ablative absolute.

ab·la·tor (ă-blā′tər) *n.* A **heat shield** *(see).* [ABLAT(ION) + -OR.]

ab·laut (ăb′lout′, äp′-) *n. Linguistics.* A patterned change in root vowels of verb forms, characteristic of Indo-European languages, indicating alteration of tense, aspect, or function; for example, *ring, rang, rung.* Also called "gradation," "vowel gradation." Compare **umlaut.** [German *Ablaut,* "off sound" : *ab,* off, away from, from Old High German *aba* + *Laut,* sound, from Middle High German *lūt,* from Old High German *hlūt.*]

a·blaze (ə-blāz′) *adj.* **1.** On fire. **2.** Radiant; aglow.

a·ble (ā′bəl) *adj.* **abler, ablest. 1.** Having sufficient ability or resources. **2. a.** Capable; competent: *an able administrator.* **b.** Talented; gifted. **3.** Legally qualified: *able to inherit.* [Middle English, from Old French, from Latin *habilis,* manageable, apt, expert, from *habēre,* to hold, handle.]

–able, –ible *suffix.* Indicates: **1.** Able to undergo the specified action; for example, **debatable, drinkable, collapsible. 2.** Having or sharing a specified quality; for example, **knowledgeable, comfortable, fashionable. 3.** Causing or deserving; for example, **honorable, objectionable.** [Middle English, from Old French, from Latin *-ābilis, -ibilis,* forms (with different vowel stems) of the passive adjectival suffix *-bilis.*]

a·ble-bod·ied (ā′bəl-bŏd′ēd) *adj.* Physically strong and healthy.

able-bodied seaman *n. Abbr.* **a.b., A.B.** A merchant seaman certified for all seaman's duties. Also called "able seaman."

a·bloom (ə-blōōm′) *adj.* In bloom; flowering. —**a·bloom** *adv.*

ab·lu·tion (ə-blōō′shən) *n.* **1.** A washing or cleansing of the body, especially as part of a religious ceremony. **2.** The liquid used in such cleansing. **3. ablutions.** The act of washing oneself. Usually used humorously. [Middle English, from Latin *ablūtiō,* from *abluere,* to wash away : *ab-,* away from + *luere,* to wash, from *lavere,* variant of *lavāre,* to wash.] —**ab·lu·tion·ar·y** *adj.*

a·bly (ā′blē) *adv.* In an able manner; capably.

ABM antiballistic missile.

abn airborne.

Ab·na·ki (ăb-nä′kē) *n., pl.* **-kis** or collectively **Abnaki** (for senses 1, 2). **1.** A tribe of North American Indians of Maine, New Brunswick, and southern Quebec. **2.** A member of the Abnaki. **3.** The Algonquian language of the Abnaki.

ab·ne·gate (ăb′nǐ-gāt′) *tr.v.* **-gated, -gating, -gates.** To deny to oneself; give up; renounce. [Latin *abnegāre,* to refuse, reject : *ab-,* away from + *negāre,* to deny.]

ab·ne·ga·tion (ăb′nǐ-gā′shən) *n.* **1.** Renunciation. **2.** Self-denial or self-sacrifice; self-abnegation.

ab·nor·mal (ăb-nôr′məl) *adj.* **1.** Not normal; untypical; irregular. **2.** Peculiar; deviant. [Latin *abnormis,* departing from normal : *ab-,* away from + *norma,* rule, norm.] —**ab·nor·mal·ly** *adv.*

ab·nor·mal·i·ty (ăb′nôr-măl′ə-tē) *n., pl.* **-ties. 1.** The condition of not being normal. **2.** An abnormal phenomenon; an irregularity. **3.** A physical defect or deformity.

abnormal psychology *n.* The study of behavioral abnormalities and mental disorders in human beings.

ABO (ā-bē′ō′) *n.* A classification of human blood types according to their compatibility in transfusion, which depends on the presence or

Abraham, Plains of. A plateau near Quebec, where the British under Gen. James Wolfe defeated the French under Gen. Louis Montcalm in 1759 and effectively won Canada for Britain.

a·bran·chi·ate (ā-brăng′kē-ĭt, -āt′) *adj. Zoology.* Having no gills. [A- (without) + Greek *brankhia,* gills. See **branchia.**]

ab·ra·sion (ə-brā′zhən) *n.* **1.** The process of wearing down or rubbing away by means of friction. **2.** A scraped or worn area; a graze. [Medieval Latin *abrāsiō,* from Latin *abrādere,* to ABRADE.]

ab·ra·sive (ə-brā′sĭv, -zĭv) *adj.* **1.** Causing abrasion; harsh; rough. **2.** Harsh in manner; rude.
~*n.* A substance that abrades, especially emery, pumice, or similar material, used to clean or smooth surfaces.

ab·re·act (ăb′rē-ăkt′) *tr.v.* **-acted, -acting, -acts.** *Psychology.* To release repressed emotions by abreaction. [Translation of German *abreagieren* : AB- (away from) + *reagieren,* to react.]

ab·re·ac·tion (ăb′rē-ăk′shən) *n. Psychology.* The release of the tension resulting from conflict or from repressed emotion, achieved either unconsciously or through conscious examination and the acting out, in imagination, words, or action, of the situation causing the conflict.

a·breast (ə-brĕst′) *adv.* **1.** Side by side. **2.** Up to date; aware: *abreast of the news.* [Middle English *abrest* : A- + BREAST.]

a·bridge (ə-brĭj′) *tr.v.* **abridged, abridging, abridges.** **1.** To reduce the length of (a written text); condense. **2.** To cut short. **3.** To limit or curtail (freedom or rights). [Middle English *abregen,* from Old French *abregier,* from Late Latin *abbreviāre,* to ABBREVIATE.] —**a·bridg·er** *n.*

a·bridg·ment (ə-brĭj′mənt) *n.* Also chiefly British **a·bridge·ment.** *Abbr.* **abr.** **1. a.** The action of abridging. **b.** The state of being abridged. **2.** A condensation of a book, play, or the like; an abridged version.

a·broad (ə-brôd′) *adv.* **1.** Out of one's own country. **2.** In a foreign country or countries. **3.** Away from one's place of residence; outdoors. **4.** On the move; at large; circulating. **5.** Broadly; widely. **6.** *Archaic.* Not on target; astray; in error.
~*n.* A foreign country; foreign countries collectively: *a student from abroad.* [Middle English *abro(o)d,* "broadly, widely scattered" : A- (on, in) + *brood,* BROAD.]

ab·ro·gate (ăb′rō-gāt′, -rə-) *tr.v.* **-gated, -gating, -gates.** To abolish or annul by authority. —See Synonyms at **nullify.** [Latin *abrogāre* : *ab-,* away + *rogāre,* to ask, propose.] —**ab·ro·ga·tion** *n.* —**ab·ro·ga·tor** *n.*

a·brupt (ə-brŭpt′) *adj.* **1.** Unexpectedly sudden. **2.** Curt; brusque. **3.** Touching on one subject after another with sudden transitions: *abrupt, nervous prose.* **4.** Steeply inclined. **5.** *Biology.* Appearing to be cut or broken off short; truncate. [Latin *abruptus,* past participle of *abrumpere,* to break off : *ab-,* off + *rumpere,* to break.] —**a·brupt·ly** *adv.* —**a·brupt·ness** *n.*

A·bruz·zi (ä-brōōt′tsē) Also **A·bruz·zo** (-tsō). Region of central Italy, bordering on the Adriatic in the east. It is mountainous, containing the highest peak in the Apennines, Monte Corno (2,914 meters; 9,560 feet), and is fairly poor, with small-scale agriculture and industry. Its capital is L'Aquila.

abs absolute temperature.

abs. **1.** absence; absent. **2.** absolute; absolutely. **3.** abstract.

Ab·sa·lom (ăb′sə-ləm) In the Old Testament, David's favorite son, killed when rebelling against his father. II Samuel 13–39.

ab·scess (ăb′sĕs′) *n.* A localized collection of pus in any part of the body, surrounded by an inflamed area and often caused by bacterial infection.
~*intr.v.* **abscessed, -scessing, -scesses.** To form an abscess. [Latin *abscēssus,* "a going away (of bad humors)," hence, collection of pus, from *abscēdere,* to go away : *abs-, ab-,* away from + *cēdere,* to go.]

ab·scise (ăb-sīz′) *v.* **-scised, -scising, -scises.** —*tr.* To remove; cut off. —*intr.* To be shed by abscission. [Latin *abscindere* (past participle *abscissus*) : *abs-, ab-,* away + *scindere,* to cut.]

ab·scis·sa (ăb-sĭs′ə) *n., pl.* **-sas** or **-scissae** (-sĭs′ē′). *Mathematics.* The coordinate representing the distance of a point from the *y*-axis in a plane Cartesian coordinate system, measured along a line parallel to the *x*-axis. Compare **ordinate.** [New Latin *(linea) abscissa,* "cut-off (line)," from Latin *abscissus,* past participle of *abscindere,* to cut off, ABSCISE.]

ab·scis·sion (ăb-sĭzh′ən) *n.* **1.** The act of cutting off. **2.** The process by which plant parts, such as leaves and flowers, are shed. A layer of cells forms at the base of the plant part and then disintegrates, causing the part to become separated.

ab·scond (ăb-skŏnd′) *intr.v.* **-sconded, -sconding, -sconds.** To leave quickly and secretly and hide oneself, especially in order to escape imprisonment, arrest, or prosecution. [Latin *abscondere* : *abs-, ab-,* away + *condere,* to hide.] —**ab·scond·er** *n.*

ab·seil (äp′zīl′) *intr.v.* **-seiled, -seiling, -seils.** **1.** In mountaineering and caving, to descend a steep or vertical rock face using a rope attached above and secured around the body. **2.** To descend from a helicopter by means of a rope.
~*n.* An instance of abseiling. [German *abseilen,* to descend by means of a rope : *ab-,* down + *Seil,* rope.]

ab·sence (ăb′səns) *n. Abbr.* **abs.** **1.** The state of being away. **2.** The time during which one is away. **3.** Lack: *an absence of corroborating evidence.* **4.** Inattention; abstraction: *absence of mind.*

ab·sent (ăb′sənt) *adj. Abbr.* **abs.** **1.** Missing or not present. **2.** Not existent; lacking. **3.** Inattentive.
~*tr.v.* (ăb-sĕnt′) **absented, -senting, -sents.** **1.** To keep (oneself)

away. **2.** To withdraw (oneself). [Middle English, from Old French, from Latin *absēns,* present participle of *abesse,* to be away : *abs-, ab-,* away from + *esse,* to be.] —**ab·sent·ly** *adv.*

ab·sen·tee (ăb′sən-tē′) *n.* One who is absent.
~*adj.* **1.** Habitually absent or not in residence: *absentee landlords.* **2.** Of or pertaining to one that is absent: *an absentee vote.*

ab·sen·tee·ism (ăb′sən-tē′ĭz′əm) *n.* Habitual failure to appear, especially for work.

ab·sent-mind·ed (ăb′sənt-mīn′dĭd) *adj.* Heedless of one's immediate surroundings or activity, especially because of preoccupation with unrelated matters; inattentive and forgetful. —See Synonyms at **abstracted, forgetful.** —**ab·sent-mind·ed·ly** *adv.* —**ab·sent-mind·ed·ness** *n.*

ab·sinthe, ab·sinth (ăb′sĭnth) *n.* **1.** A pale-green liqueur that has a high alcoholic content and is flavored with aniseed and wormwood or a wormwood substitute. **2.** A plant, **wormwood** (see). [French, from Latin *absinthium,* wormwood, from Greek *apsinthion,* of Mediterranean origin.]

ab·so·lute (ăb′sə-lōōt′) *adj. Abbr.* **abs.** **1.** Perfect in quality or nature; complete: *an absolute vacuum.* **2.** Not mixed; pure; unadulterated: *absolute alcohol.* **3. a.** Not limited by restrictions or exceptions; unconditional: *absolute freedom.* **b.** Unqualified in extent or degree; total: *an absolute pardon.* **4.** Not limited by constitutional provisions or other restraints: *an absolute monarch.* **5.** Unrelated to and independent of anything else: *an absolute value.* **6.** Not to be doubted or questioned; positive; certain: *absolute truth.* **7.** *Grammar.* **a.** Designating a construction in a sentence that is syntactically independent of the main clause. For example, in *Their ship having sailed, we went home,* the construction *Their ship having sailed* is an absolute phrase. **b.** Pertaining to or characterizing a transitive verb when its object is implied but not stated; for example, *inspires* in *We have a teacher who inspires.* **c.** Pertaining to or characterizing an adjective or pronoun that stands alone, the noun it modifies being implied but not stated; for example, *Theirs* and *best* in *Theirs were the best.* **8.** *Physics.* **a.** Pertaining to measurements or units of measurement derived from fundamental relationships of space, mass, and time. **b.** Pertaining to absolute temperature. **c.** Indicating a pressure measurement that is not relative to atmospheric pressure. Compare **gauge.** **9.** *Law.* Complete and unconditional; having no encumbrances; final.
~*n.* Something that is absolute. —**the Absolute.** *Philosophy.* **1.** Something regarded as the ultimate basis of all thought and being. **2.** Something regarded as independent of and unrelated to anything else. **3.** In the philosophy of Hegel, the ultimate condition toward which everything is moving. [Middle English *absolut,* from Latin *absolūtus,* completed, unfettered, unconditional, from the past participle of *absolvere,* to free from, complete : *ab-,* away from + *solvere,* to loose.] —**ab·so·lute·ness** *n.*

absolute alcohol *n.* Ethyl alcohol containing no more than one percent of water by weight.

absolute ceiling *n.* The maximum altitude above sea level at which an aircraft or missile can maintain horizontal flight under standard atmospheric conditions.

absolute humidity *n.* The humidity of a gas, especially air, expressed as the mass of water vapor in grams per cubic meter of gas. Compare **relative humidity.**

ab·so·lute·ly (ăb′sə-lōōt′lē, ăb′sə-lōōt′ lē) *adv. Abbr.* **abs.** **1.** Definitely and completely; positively; unquestionably. **2.** *Grammar.* In an absolute manner: *The verbs in "Man proposes, God disposes" are used absolutely.*
~*interj.* Used to express complete agreement.

absolute magnitude *n. Astronomy.* A measure of the brightness of a star or other astronomical body equal to the apparent magnitude it would have if it were 10 parsecs or 32.6 light-years from the Earth.

absolute majority *n.* A majority of over 50 percent of a total, as of votes cast or seats obtained. Compare **relative majority.**

absolute music *n.* Instrumental music designed not to represent images or actions but to have an intellectual and emotional content that depends solely on its rhythmic, melodic, and contrapuntal structures. Compare **program music.**

absolute permeability *n.* The **magnetic constant** (see).

absolute permittivity *n.* See **permittivity.**

absolute pitch *n.* **1.** The precise pitch of an isolated tone, as established by its rate of vibration measured on a standard scale. **2.** The ability to identify the pitch of any tone heard, or to reproduce a tone without reference to another previously sounded. Also called "perfect pitch." Compare **relative pitch.**

absolute scale *n.* A scale of temperature with absolute zero as the minimum and scale units equal in magnitude to centigrade degrees. It is equivalent to the **thermodynamic scale** (see).

absolute temperature *n. Abbr.* **abs** Temperature measured or calculated on the absolute scale.

absolute value *n. Mathematics.* **1.** The numerical value or magnitude of a quantity, as of a vector or of a negative integer, without regard to its sign. **2.** The modulus of a complex number, equal to the square root of the sum of the squares of the real and imaginary parts of the number.

absolute zero *n. Physics.* The temperature at which substances possess minimal energy, equal to $-273.15°C$ or $-459.67°F$.

ab·so·lu·tion (ăb′sə-lōō′shən) *n.* **1.** Forgiveness; release from obligation or punishment. **2.** *Roman Catholic Church.* **a.** The formal remission of sin imparted by a priest as part of the sacrament of

absence of either of two antigens, A and B. Blood types are classified as A, B, AB, or O.

a·board (ə-bôrd′, ə-bōrd′) *adv.* On or onto a ship, train, airplane, or other passenger vehicle.
∼*prep.* On, in, onto, or into (a ship, train, or the like). [Middle English : A- (on) + BOARD.]

a·bode (ə-bōd′). Past tense and past participle of **abide.**
∼*n.* A dwelling place or home. [Middle English *abod,* from *abiden,* ABIDE.]

ab·ohm (ăb-ōm′) *n.* A centimeter-gram-second electromagnetic unit of resistance equal to 10^{-9} ohm. [AB- (absolute) + OHM.]

a·bol·ish (ə-bŏl′ĭsh) *tr.v.* **-ished, -ishing, -ishes.** To do away with (an institution or practice, for example); put an end to. [Middle English *abolysshen,* from Old French *abolire* (present stem *aboliss-*), from Latin *abolēre,* to destroy.] **—a·bol·ish·a·ble** *adj.* **—a·bol·ish·er** *n.* **—a·bol·ish·ment** *n.*
Synonyms: *eradicate, extirpate.*

ab·o·li·tion (ăb′ə-lĭsh′ən) *n.* **1.** An act of abolishing or state of being abolished; annulment; extinction. **2.** *Sometimes* **Abolition.** The ending of slavery and the slave trade, especially in the United States. [Latin *abolitiō,* from *abolitus,* past participle of *abolēre,* ABOLISH.] **—ab·o·li·tion·ar·y** *adj.*

ab·o·li·tion·ist (ăb′ə-lĭsh′ə-nĭst) *n.* **1.** One who wishes to abolish a law, institution, or the like. **2.** *Sometimes* **Abolitionist.** A supporter of the abolition of slavery, especially in the United States during the period before the Civil War. **—ab·o·li·tion·ism** *n.*

ab·o·ma·sum (ăb′ō-mā′səm) *n., pl.* **-sa** (-sə). The fourth division of the stomach in ruminant animals, in which true digestion takes place. [New Latin : AB- (away from) + OMASUM.] **—ab·o·ma·sal** *adj.*

A-bomb (ā′bŏm′) *n.* An **atomic bomb** *(see).*

a·bom·i·na·ble (ə-bŏm′ə-nə-bəl) *adj.* **1.** Detestable; loathsome. **2. a.** Thoroughly unpleasant. **b.** Of extremely poor quality. [Middle English, from Old French, from Latin *abōminābilis,* from *abōminārī,* to ABOMINATE.] **—a·bom·i·na·bly** *adv.*

abominable snowman *n.* A legendary humanlike animal reportedly inhabiting the high Himalayas. Also called "yeti." [Translation of Tibetan *metohkangmi* : *metoh,* abominable + *kangmi,* snowman.]

a·bom·i·nate (ə-bŏm′ə-nāt′) *tr.v.* **-nated, -nating, -nates.** To detest; abhor. [Latin *abōminārī,* "to shun as a bad omen" : *ab-,* away from + *ōmen* (stem *ōmin-*), omen.] **—a·bom·i·na·tor** *n.*

a·bom·i·na·tion (ə-bŏm′ə-nā′shən) *n.* **1.** Something or someone that causes great revulsion or abhorrence. **2.** An intense dislike or loathing for someone or something.

ab·o·ral (ă-bôr′əl, -bōr′-) *adj. Biology.* Opposite to or away from the mouth. [AB- (away from) + ORAL.] **—ab·o·ral·ly** *adv.*

ab·o·rig·i·nal (ăb′ə-rĭj′ə-nəl) *adj.* **1.** Native; indigenous: *The Indians are among the aboriginal inhabitants of South America.* **2.** Of or pertaining to aborigines.
∼*n.* **1.** An aborigine. **2. Aboriginal.** An Australian Aborigine. **—ab·o·rig·i·nal·ly** *adv.*

ab·o·rig·i·ne (ăb′ə-rĭj′ə-nē′) *n.* **1.** An indigenous inhabitant of a region. **2. Aborigine.** A member of the indigenous dark-skinned people of Australia. **3. Aborigine.** Any of the languages of this people. **4. aborigines.** The plants and animals native to a geographical area. [Latin *Aborīginēs,* pre-Roman tribes inhabiting Latium, probably an alteration of some tribal name, reshaped by folk etymology as if derived from *ab orīgine,* "from the beginning."]

a·born·ing (ə-bôr′nĭng, ə-bōr′-) *adv.* While coming into being or getting under way: *The project almost died aborning.* [A- (in the act of) + BORN + -ING.]

a·bort (ə-bôrt′) *v.* **aborted, aborting, aborts.** —*intr.* **1. a.** To miscarry. Used of a pregnant mammal. **b.** To be expelled prematurely from the womb. Used of a fetus. **2.** To cease organic growth before full development or maturation. **3.** To end prematurely; especially, to terminate an operation involving a missile or a space vehicle before completion. —*tr.* **1. a.** To cause the abortion of (a fetus). **b.** To terminate prematurely the pregnancy of. **2.** To interfere with or terminate the normal development of. **3.** To bring to an end prematurely or before scheduled completion: *Equipment failure forced us to abort the space mission.* [Latin *abortāre,* frequentative of *aborīrī* (past participle *abortus*), to die, disappear, miscarry : *ab,* off, away, hence, badly + *orīrī,* to arise, appear, be born.]

a·bor·ti·cide (ə-bôr′tə-sīd′) *n.* **1.** The destruction of a fetus within the womb. **2.** The drug used in this process. [ABORT + -CIDE.]

a·bor·ti·fa·cient (ə-bôr′tə-fā′shənt) *adj.* Causing abortion.
∼*n.* Anything used to induce abortion. [ABORT(ION) + -FACIENT.]

a·bor·tion (ə-bôr′shən) *n.* **1.** The premature expulsion of a fetus from the womb, which may be either spontaneous (a miscarriage) or induced. Compare **stillbirth. 2.** An operation to remove a fetus from the womb. **3.** Cessation of normal growth, especially of an organ, prior to full development or maturation. **4.** An aborted organism. **5.** Anything malformed or incompletely developed. **6.** An action or plan that has not been carried to a successful conclusion.

a·bor·tion·ist (ə-bôr′shən-ĭst) *n.* One who performs abortions.

a·bor·tive (ə-bôr′tĭv) *adj.* **1.** Failing to accomplish an intended objective; fruitless. **2.** Partially or imperfectly developed. **3.** Causing abortion; abortifacient. **—a·bor·tive·ly** *adv.*

aboulia. Variant of **abulia.**

a·bound (ə-bound′) *intr.v.* **abounded, abounding, abounds. 1.** To be present in great numbers or large amount. **2.** To have a large number or amount; teem: *The rivers here abound in game fish. Her letters abound with playful humor.* [Middle English *abounden,* from Old French *abonder,* from Latin *abundāre,* to overflow : *ab-,* away from + *undāre,* to flow, from *unda,* wave.]

a·bout (ə-bout′) *adv. Abbr.* **a. 1.** Approximately; roughly. **2.** Nearly; almost. **3.** To a reversed position or direction: *She turned about and retraced her steps.* **4.** In no particular direction; with no particular destination: *wandering about.* **5. a.** All around; on every side. **b.** In various places; here and there: *scattered about; lying about.* **6.** In the area or vicinity. **7.** In succession; one after another: *Turn about is fair play.* **8.** Prevailing; current: *There's a lot of flu about.* **9.** *Informal.* In an extreme degree. Used ironically as an understatement: *About time.* **10.** Into existence; so as to occur: *How did it come about? Bring it about.*
∼*prep.* **1.** On all sides of; surrounding. **2.** In the vicinity of; around: *somewhere about 110°.* **3.** In and around; here and there in; through. **4.** Almost the same as; close to; near. **5.** In reference to; relating to. **6.** On, attached to, or in the possession or character of: *He has his wits about him; an air of caution about her.* **7.** On the verge of doing something. Used with an infinitive: *The chorus is about to sing.* **8.** Willing or prepared. Used in the negative and with an infinitive to indicate determination: *I'm not about to give up now.* **9.** Involved with or engaged in: *going about his work cheerfully; make me a cup while you're about it.*
∼*adj.* Out of bed, after sleep or illness: *up and about.* [Middle English *about,* Old English *abūtan, onbūtan* : ON + *būtan,* outside of.]
Usage: *about, around, round.* These terms are sometimes interchangeable, as adverbs and prepositions. However, *around* either specifies or suggests complete encirclement of something, whereas *about* and *round* are less exact and indicate, more or less, semiencirclement: *The children gathered about* (or *round*) *the fire place; then they danced around the table.* • The construction *not about to,* or a variant with *about* and a negative, is used to emphasize intention or express determination. The construction is principally appropriate to informal speech or writing.

a·bout-face (ə-bout′fās′) *n.* **1.** A reversal of orientation, accomplished by a pivotal movement from a stationary position; a movement resulting in the body facing the opposite direction. **2.** A change to an opposite opinion or point of view.
∼*intr.v.* **about-faced, -facing, -faces. 1.** To make an about-face. **2.** To reverse direction.

a·bout-turn (ə-bout′tûrn′) *n. Chiefly British.* An about-face.

a·bove (ə-bŭv′) *adv.* **1.** Overhead; on high: *the clouds above.* **2.** In heaven; heavenward. **3.** Upstairs: *a table in the dining room above.* **4.** In a higher place. **5.** On the top or upper side. **6.** Beyond a given amount or figure: *designed for children of 12 and above.* **7.** Upstream: *the rapids above.* **8.** In an earlier part of the text: *figures quoted above.* Also used in combination: *the above-mentioned figures.* **9.** In or to a higher rank or position: *promoted to the grade above.*
∼*prep.* **1.** Over; higher than: *situated above the treeline.* **2. a.** Superior to; of more importance than: *placed his country above his family ties.* **b.** Of higher rank or status than. **3. a.** Beyond the level or reach of: *above suspicion.* **b.** Beyond the grasp or understanding of: *The political discussion was above me.* **4.** In preference to. **5.** Too honorable to engage in: *above petty intrigue.* **6.** Greater than, as in weight, price, age, temperature, or pitch: *above the age of 65; a shot heard above the music.* **7.** North of: *Canada is directly above the United States.* **8.** Upstream from. **—above all.** Most of all. **—above and beyond.** In addition to.
∼*n.* Something that is above: *as the above should make clear.*
∼*adj.* Appearing earlier in the same text: *flaws in the above interpretation.* [Middle English *aboven, abuven,* Old English *abufan* : A- (on) + *bufan,* above.]
Usage: *The above, cf. above,* and other such uses, are common in business and legal writing, but they are often considered awkward or stilted and are usually avoided in popular writing.

a·bove·board (ə-bŭv′ bôrd′, -bōrd′) *adv.* Without deceit or trickery.
∼*adj.* Honest; not concealed: *an open and aboveboard agreement.* [Originally a gambling term, "above the gambling table, not changing cards under the table."]

a·bove·ground (ə-bŭv′ground′) *adj.* **1.** Located on or above the surface of the ground: *an aboveground nuclear explosion.* **2.** Not hidden or secret; open. **3.** Using conventional standards, means, or procedures: *the aboveground press.*

ab o·vo (ăb ō′vō) *adv. Latin.* From the start. [Literally, "from the egg."]

abp., Abp. archbishop.

abr. abridged; abridgment.

ab·ra·ca·dab·ra (ăb′rə-kə-dăb′rə) *n.* **1.** A word held to possess supernatural powers to ward off disease or disaster. **2.** A formula spoken by conjurors when performing a trick. **3.** Jargon; mumbo jumbo; gibberish. [Late Latin, from Late Greek *abrasadabra,* a magic word used by a Gnostic sect, probably derived from *Abraxas,* name of a Gnostic deity.]

a·brade (ə-brād′) *tr.v.* **abraded, abrading, abrades. 1.** To rub off or wear away by or as if by friction. **2.** *Geology.* To wear away as a result of corrosion. [Latin *abrādere,* to scrape off : *ab-,* off + *rādere,* to scrape.] **—a·bra·dant** *adj. & n.* **—a·brad·er** *n.*

A·bra·ham (ā′brə-hăm′). The first patriarch and progenitor of the Hebrew people; father of Isaac. Genesis 11–25. [Middle English, from Late Latin, from Late Greek, from Hebrew *Abhrāhām,* "father of a multitude," altered from *Abram,* "high father."]

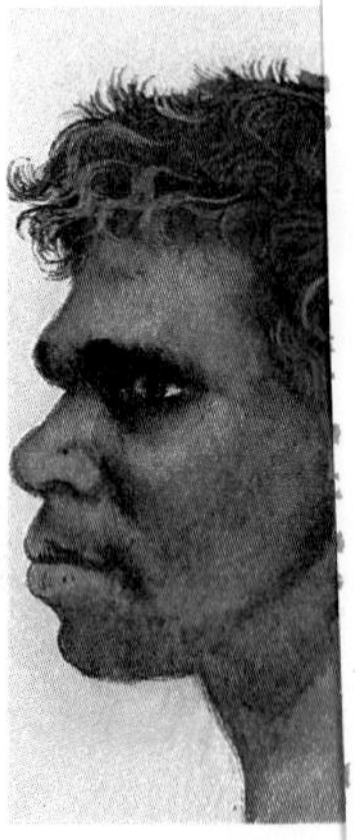

Aborigine *The only s… members of the Austra… Aborigines are thought… reached Australia from… 40,000 years ago. By t… are nomadic hunters, b… arrival of Europeans in… century, their numbers… —from about 300,000 … of about 200,000—and… settled in towns.*

penance. **b.** The specific words spoken by a priest in granting this remission.

ab·so·lut·ism (ăb′sə-lo͞o′tĭz′əm) *n.* **1.** A system of government in which all power is vested in a monarch or dictator. **2.** The political theory reflecting this system. —**ab·so·lut·ist** *n. & adj.*

ab·solve (ăb-zŏlv′, -sŏlv′) *tr.v.* **-solved, -solving, -solves. 1.** To pronounce free of blame or guilt. **2.** To relieve of a requirement or obligation. **3. a.** To grant a remission of sin to. **b.** To pardon or remit (a sin). [Middle English *absolven,* from Latin *absolvere,* to free from : *ab-,* away from + *solvere,* to loose, free.] —**ab·solv·a·ble** *adj.* —**ab·solv·er** *n.*

ab·sorb (ăb-sôrb′, -zôrb′) *v.* **-sorbed, -sorbing, -sorbs.** —*tr.* **1.** To take in through or as if through pores or interstices; soak in or up. **2.** To occupy the full attention, interest, or time of; engross. **3. a.** To take in so as to make part of an existing whole; incorporate. **b.** To take into the mind; assimilate. **4.** To receive (the impact of a projectile) without recoil. **5.** To defray (costs). **6.** To take in and use up (marketable goods): *The market could not absorb the increased sugar production.* **7.** *Physiology.* **a.** To assimilate (the products of digestion). **b.** To take up (gases and fluids) through surface tissues. **8.** *Chemistry.* To take in (a gas or liquid) and hold by means of physical forces. Compare **adsorb. 9.** *Physics.* To receive (electromagnetic radiation, for example) and retain fully, without reflection or transmission. —*intr.* To cause or undergo absorption: *The sponge was too dry to absorb well.* [Old French *absorber,* from Latin *absorbēre* : *ab-,* away from + *sorbēre,* to suck.] —**ab·sorb·a·bil·i·ty** *n.* —**ab·sorb·a·ble** *adj.* —**ab·sorb·er** *n.*

ab·sorbed (ăb-sôrbd′, -zôrbd′) *adj.* Engrossed. —See Synonyms at **abstracted.** —**ab·sorb·ed·ly** (ăb-sôr′bĭd-lē, -zôr′-) *adv.*

absorbed dose *n. Physics.* A **dose** *(see).*

ab·sor·be·fa·cient (ăb-sôr′bə-fā′shənt, -zôr′-) *adj.* Inducing or causing absorption.
∼*n.* A medicine that induces absorption. [ABSORB + -FACIENT.]

ab·sorb·ent (ăb-sôr′bənt, -zôr′-) *adj.* Capable of absorbing something: *absorbent cloth.*
∼*n.* A substance having this capability. —**ab·sorb·en·cy** *n.*

absorbent cotton *n.* Loose cotton that is sterilized, pressed into wads, and used as an absorbent or protective material, as in dressing wounds. Also called "cotton wool."

ab·sorb·ing (ăb-sôr′bĭng, -zôr′-) *adj.* Fully occupying one's time or attention; engrossing. —**ab·sorb·ing·ly** *adv.*

ab·sorp·tance (ăb-sôrp′təns, -zôrp′-) *n.* The ratio of the absorbed flux of incident radiation to the incident flux for a given body or surface. Compare **reflectance, transmittance.** [ABSORPT(ION) + -ANCE.]

ab·sorp·tion (ăb-sôrp′shən, -zôrp′-) *n.* **1.** The act or process of absorbing or the state of being absorbed. **2.** A state of mental concentration. [Latin *absorptiō,* from *absorbēre,* to ABSORB.] —**ab·sorp·tive** *adj.*

absorption nebula *n. Astronomy.* A dark **nebula** *(see).*

absorption spectrum *n. Physics.* The spectrum of dark lines or bands observed when radiation traverses an absorbing medium. Compare **emission spectrum.**

ab·sorp·tiv·i·ty (ăb′sôrp-tĭv′ĭ-tē, -zôrp-) *n.* The absorptance of a body per unit of radiation path length, measured under conditions in which the surfaces of the sample do not influence the amount of absorption.

ab·stain (ăb-stān′) *intr.v.* **-stained, -staining, -stains. 1.** To do without or refrain by one's own choice: *abstain from alcohol.* **2.** To withhold one's vote. [Middle English *absteinen, abstenen,* from Old French *abstenir,* from Latin *abstinēre,* to hold (oneself) back : *abs-, ab-,* away from + *tenēre,* to hold.] —**ab·stain·er** *n.*

ab·ste·mi·ous (ăb-stē′mē-əs) *adj.* **1.** Sparing or restrained, especially in one's consumption of food and alcohol. **2.** Restricted to bare necessities; marked by moderation; sparing: *an abstemious household.* [Latin *abstēmius* : *abs-, ab-,* away from + *-tēmus,* from *tēmētum*†, alcoholic drink, mead, wine.] —**ab·ste·mi·ous·ly** *adv.* —**ab·ste·mi·ous·ness** *n.*

ab·sten·tion (ăb-stĕn′shən) *n.* **1.** The act or habit of abstaining. **2. a.** A deliberate act of refraining from voting. **b.** One who abstains from voting. [Late Latin *abstentiō* (stem *abstentiōn-*), from Latin *abstinēre,* to ABSTAIN.]

ab·ster·gent (ăb-stûr′jənt) *adj.* Scouring or cleansing.
∼*n.* A scouring agent.

ab·sti·nence (ăb′stə-nəns) *n.* **1. a.** Denial of the appetites; abstention. **b.** Abstention from alcoholic drinks. **2.** *Roman Catholic Church.* Abstention from certain foods, especially meat, on days of penitential observance. [Middle English, from Old French, from Latin *abstinentia,* from *abstinēns,* present participle of *abstinēre,* to ABSTAIN.] —**ab·sti·nent** *adj.* —**ab·sti·nent·ly** *adv.*
Synonyms: *continence, self-denial, temperance.*

ab·stract (ăb-străkt′, ăb′străkt′) *adj. Abbr.* **abs., abstr. 1.** Considered apart from concrete existence or specific objects and actions. **2.** Theoretical; not applied or practical. **3.** Not easily understood; abstruse. **4.** Thought of or stated without reference to a specific instance. **5.** Designating a genre of art that does not represent scenes or objects naturalistically, but in which the intellectual and emotional content depends solely on intrinsic form.
∼*n.* (ăb′străkt′) *Abbr.* **abs., abstr. 1.** A statement summarizing the important points of a given text. **2.** The concentrated essence of a larger whole. **3.** Something abstract, such as a term. **4.** An abstract work of art. —**in the abstract.** Apart from actual substance or experience; in theory rather than in reality.
∼*tr.v.* (ăb-străkt′, ăb′străkt′) **abstracted, -stracting, -stracts. 1.** To take away; remove. **2.** To remove without permission; steal. **3.** To consider theoretically; think of (a quality or attribute) without reference to a particular example or object. **4.** To detach or disengage (thoughts or the attention). **5.** To summarize. [Middle English, from Latin *abstractus,* "removed from (concrete reality)," past participle of *abstrahere,* to pull away, remove : *abs-, ab-,* away from + *trahere,* to pull.] *n.* —**ab·stract·ly** *adv.* —**ab·stract·ness** *n.* —**ab·strac·tor, ab·stract·er** *n.*

ab·stract·ed (ăb-străk′tĭd) *adj.* **1.** Removed or separated from something; apart. **2.** Lost or deep in thought; preoccupied; meditative. —See Synonyms at **forgetful.** —**ab·stract·ed·ly** *adv.* —**ab·stract·ed·ness** *n.*
Synonyms: *absent-minded, absorbed.*

abstract expressionism *n.* A school of painting that flourished after World War II until the early 1960's, characterized by the active and free application of the paint to the canvas, as by splattering, and its nonrepresentational design.

ab·strac·tion (ăb-străk′shən) *n.* **1.** The act or process of abstracting: *the abstraction of metal from ore.* **2. a.** The act or process of separating the inherent qualities or properties from the actual physical object or concept to which they belong. **b.** A product of this process; a general idea or word expressing a quality: *Beautiful things are concrete, but beauty is an abstraction.* **3.** Preoccupation. **4.** An abstract work of art.

ab·strac·tion·ism (ăb-străk′shə-nĭz′əm) *n.* The theory and practice of abstract art. —**ab·strac·tion·ist** *n. & adj.*

abstract noun *n.* A noun that refers to a quality rather than a thing or to an abstract idea as opposed to a material object. Compare **concrete noun.**

abstract of title *n. Law.* A statement of the history of an unregistered piece of land, for the purpose of establishing ownership.

ab·struse (ăb-stro͞os′) *adj.* Difficult to understand because intellectually complicated or somewhat obscure. [Latin *abstrūsus,* past participle of *abstrūdere,* to hide : *abs-, ab-,* away + *trūdere,* to push.] —**ab·struse·ly** *adv.* —**ab·struse·ness** *n.*

ab·surd (ăb-sûrd′, ăb-zûrd′) *adj.* **1.** Foolishly incongruous or unreasonable; ridiculous. **2.** Reflecting or dealing with the absurd. —See Synonyms at **foolish.**
∼*n. Sometimes* **Absurd.** A 20th-century philosophical concept, embodied in many modern novels and plays, emphasizing the cruelty, ludicrousness, and ultimate futility of human life. Preceded by *the.* [French *absurde,* from Latin *absurdus.*] —**ab·surd·ism** *n.* —**ab·surd·ist** *n. & adj.* —**ab·surd·i·ty, ab·surd·ness** *n.* —**ab·surd·ly** *adv.*

A·bu-Bekr (ä′bo͞o-bĕk′ər) (573–634). First caliph of the Muslim Empire, who ruled from 632. He made Islam a political and military force throughout Arabia after the death of his son-in-law, the prophet Muhammad.

A·bu Dha·bi (ä′bo͞o dä′bē). Sheikdom and town in eastern Arabia on the Persian Gulf. The town is the capital of the United Arab Emirates. With enormous oil revenues, the sheikdom is one of the richest states in the world in terms of per capita income.

A·bu·ja (ä-bo͞o′jə). New city inaugurated as the capital of Nigeria in 1982. It lies some 480 kilometers (300 miles) northeast of Lagos (the former capital), in a more central position.

a·bu·li·a, a·bou·li·a (ə-bo͞o′ lē-ə) *n. Psychology.* Loss or impairment of the ability to decide or act independently. [New Latin, from Greek *aboulia,* irresolution : *a-,* without + *boulē,* will.] —**a·bu·lic** *adj.*

a·bun·dance (ə-bŭn′dəns) *n.* Also **a·bun·dan·cy** (-dən-sē). **1.** A great quantity; a plentiful amount. **2.** Fullness to overflowing: *"My thoughts . . . are from the abundance of my heart"* (Thomas De Quincey). **3.** Affluence; wealth. **4.** *Chemistry.* The relative amount of a substance in a particular environment, especially the proportion of a particular element or mineral in the earth's crust, usually expressed in parts per million or as a percentage. **5.** *Physics.* The ratio of the number of atoms of a given isotope to the total number of atoms of the element in a given sample, especially the proportion in a naturally occurring sample.

a·bun·dant (ə-bŭn′dənt) *adj.* **1.** In plentiful supply; more than sufficient; ample. **2.** Amply supplied; abounding. Used with *in.* [Middle English *abundaunt,* from Old French *abundant,* from Latin *abundāns* (stem *abundant-*), present participle of *abundāre,* to ABOUND.] —**a·bun·dant·ly** *adv.*

ab ur·be con·di·ta (ăb ûr′bē kŏn′dĭ-tə) *Abbr.* **A.U.C.** *Latin.* From the founding of the city. Used to indicate the date in ancient Rome, the base year being 753 B.C.

a·buse (ə-byo͞oz′) *tr.v.* **abused, abusing, abuses. 1.** To use wrongly or improperly; misuse. **2.** To hurt or injure by maltreatment. **3.** To speak to in a contemptuous, coarse, or insulting way; revile.
∼*n.* (ə-byo͞os′). **1.** Misuse. **2.** A corrupt practice or custom. **3.** Maltreatment: *child abuse.* **4.** Insulting or coarse language. [Middle English *abusen,* from Old French *abuser,* from *abus,* improper use, from Latin *abūsus,* a using up, past participle of *abūtī,* to use up, make (improper) use of : *ab-,* away + *ūtī,* to USE.] —**a·bus·er** *n.*
Synonyms: *ill-treat, maltreat, mistreat, misuse.*

A·bu Sim·bel (ä′bo͞o sĭm′bəl). Village in southern Egypt on the Nile River and the site of the massive temples constructed by Ramses II *c.* 1250 B.C. The temples were raised over 60 meters (200 feet) in order to escape the rising waters of Lake Nasser, caused by the completion of the Aswan High Dam in 1966.

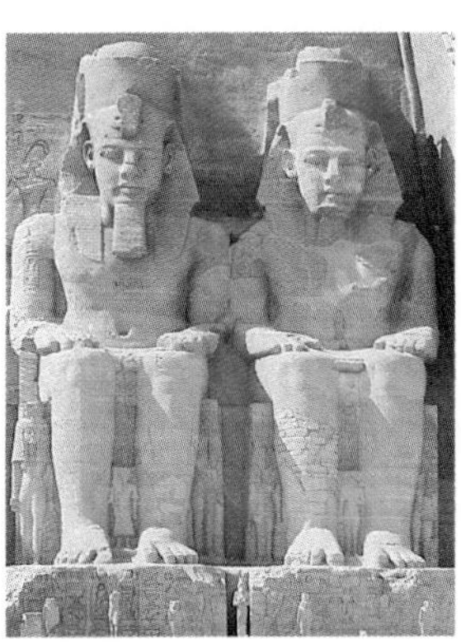

Abu Simbel *Giant statues of the Egyptian pharaoh Ramses II guard the temple complex he built in the Nile Valley near the village of Abu Simbel. Statues and temples were raised 61 meters (200 feet) above their original site in the 1960's to rescue them from the lake formed by the Aswan High Dam.*

a·bu·sive (ə-byōō′sĭv, -zĭv) *adj.* **1.** Of, pertaining to, or characterized by abuse. **2.** Marked by or using insulting or contemptuous language. —**a·bu·sive·ly** *adv.* —**a·bu·sive·ness** *n.*

a·but (ə-bŭt′) *v.* **abutted, abutting, abuts.** —*intr.* To touch at one end or side; lie adjacent. Used with *on, upon,* or *against.* —*tr.* To border upon; be next to. [Middle English *abutten,* from Old French *abouter,* to border on : *a,* to + *bout,* end.]

a·bu·ti·lon (ə-byōō′tə-lŏn′) *n.* Any of various shrubs or plants of the genus *Abutilon;* especially, the **flowering maple** (*see*). [New Latin, from Arabic *aubūṭīlūn.*]

a·but·ment (ə-bŭt′mənt) *n.* **1.** The act or process of abutting. **2. a.** That on which something abuts. **b.** The point of contact of two abutting objects or parts. **3.** *Architecture.* That element which shares a common boundary or surface with its neighbor. **4.** *Engineering.* **a.** A structure that supports an arch or the end of a bridge. **b.** A structure that anchors the cables of a suspension bridge.

a·but·tal (ə-bŭt′l) *n.* **1.** An abutment. **2. abuttals.** *Law.* The parts, especially of a piece of land, that abut against other property; boundaries.

ab·volt (ăb′vōlt′, ăb-vōlt′) *n. Abbr.* **abv.** A centimeter-gram-second electromagnetic unit of potential difference or electromotive force, equal to the potential difference between two points such that one erg of work must be performed to move a one-abcoulomb charge from one of the points to the other. It is equal to 10^{-8} of a volt. [AB-(absolute) + VOLT.]

ab·watt (ăb′wŏt′, ăb-wŏt′) *n. Abbr.* **abw.** A centimeter-gram-second electromagnetic unit of power, equal to the power dissipated by a current of one abampere flowing between two points with a potential difference of one abvolt. It is equal to 10^{-7} watt. [AB (absolute) + WATT.]

a·bysm (ə-bĭz′əm) *n.* An abyss. [Middle English *abi(s)me,* from Old French, from Late Latin *abyssus,* ABYSS.]

a·bys·mal (ə-bĭz′məl) *adj.* **1.** Unfathomable; very great: *abysmal ignorance.* **2.** Of or resembling an abyss. **3.** *Informal.* Extremely poor in quality. —**a·bys·mal·ly** *adv.*

a·byss (ə-bĭs′) *n.* **1. a.** A very steep gorge or deep crack in a mountain or on the earth. **b.** An unfathomable chasm; a yawning gulf. **2.** Any immeasurably great depth or void. **3. a.** Primeval chaos. **b.** The bottomless pit; hell. [Late Latin *abyssus,* from Greek *abussos* (*limnē*), "bottomless (lake)" : *a-,* not + *bussos,* bottom.]

a·bys·al (ə-bĭs′əl) *adj.* **1.** Abysmal. **2.** Of or pertaining to the depths of the oceans, usually below 1,000 fathoms: *abyssal plain.*

Ab·ys·sin·i·a (ăb′ə-sĭn′ē-ə). See **Ethiopia.**

Ab·ys·sin·i·an (ăb′ə-sĭn′ē-ən) *adj.* Of or pertaining to Ethiopia or its inhabitants.
~*n.* An inhabitant of Ethiopia.

Abyssinian cat *n.* A short-haired cat of a breed developed from Near Eastern stocks, having a reddish-brown coat tipped with small black markings.

ac alternating current.

Ac The symbol for the element actinium.

a.c. *Medicine.* before meals. [New Latin *ante cibum*]

A.C. **1.** Air Corps. **2.** aircraftman. **3.** alternating current. **4.** appellation controlée. **5.** athletic club. **6.** before Christ. [New Latin *ante Christum*] **7.** Companion of the Order of Australia.

a/c, A/C **1.** account; account current. **2.** air conditioning.

a·ca·cia (ə-kā′shə) *n.* **1.** Any of various chiefly tropical trees of the genus *Acacia,* having compound leaves and small yellow or white flowers. Some species yield gums having a wide variety of uses. **2.** A related tree, the **locust** (*see*). **3.** A substance, **gum arabic** (*see*). [Latin, from Greek *akakia,* probably from Egyptian.]

acad. academic; academy.

ac·a·deme (ăk′ə-dēm′) *n.* **1.** *Sometimes* **Academe.** The world of scholarship and higher education; scholarly or academic life or its associated environment. **2.** *Archaic.* A place of learning; a university. **3.** *Archaic.* A scholar, teacher, or pedant. [Pseudo-Greek form of Greek *Akadēmia,* ACADEMY.]

ac·a·de·mi·a (ăk′ə-dē′mē-ə) *n.* The academic world; academe. [New Latin, from Latin *Academīa,* ACADEMY.]

ac·a·dem·ic (ăk′ə-dĕm′ĭk) *adj. Abbr.* **acad.** **1.** Of, pertaining to, or characteristic of a university, college, or other institution of learning. **2.** Scholarly to the point of being impractical or unaware of the outside world. **3.** Pertaining to or based on formal education, as in the humanities or sciences, rather than on practical or vocational training: *an education geared to children with academic ability.* **4.** Formalistic; conventional: *academic painters.* **5.** Merely theoretical; speculative: *"I took an academic interest in the thought of stealing the car"* (John Knowles). **6.** **Academic.** Of or pertaining to the Academy and philosophy of Plato.
~*n.* A member of a university or college; especially, a university teacher. —**ac·a·dem·i·cal·ly** *adv.*

academic freedom *n.* Liberty to pursue, discuss, and teach knowledge without hindrance or censorship.

ac·a·de·mi·cian (ăk′ə-də-mĭsh′ən) *n. Abbr.* **A.** A member of an academy or society of the arts or sciences.

ac·a·dem·i·cism (ăk′ə-dĕm′ə-sĭz′əm) *n.* Also **a·cad·e·mism** (ə-kăd′ə-mĭz′əm). Traditional formalism; conventionalism, especially in art.

A·ca·dé·mie Fran·çaise (à-kà-dā-mē′ frȧN-sĕz′) *n. French.* An association of 40 French intellectuals, scholars, and writers founded by Cardinal Richelieu in 1635, whose role is to pronounce on the correct usage of the French language.

a·cad·e·my (ə-kăd′ə-mē) *n., pl.* **-mies.** *Abbr.* **A., acad.** **1.** An association of artists or scholars. **2.** A school for special instruction: *a naval academy.* **3. a.** A secondary school, especially a private one. **b.** In Scotland, a grammar school. **4. Academy. a.** The grove near Athens where Plato taught. **b.** The philosophy of Plato. **c.** The disciples of Plato. [Latin *Academīa,* from Greek *Akadēmia,* the Platonic school of philosophy, from *Akadēmia, Akadēmeia,* name of the place in Athens where Plato taught, after *Akadēmos,* legendary Attic hero.]

Academy Award *n.* Any of the golden statuettes awarded annually by the Academy of Motion Picture Arts and Sciences for achievement in motion pictures. Also called "Oscar."

A·ca·di·a (ə-kā′dē-ə). *French* **A·ca·die** (ȧ-kȧ-dē′). Region and former French colony in eastern Canada, encompassing Nova Scotia, Cape Breton Island, Prince Edward Island, New Brunswick, and part of Maine. Nova Scotia was ceded to Britain in 1713, and many of its inhabitants migrated or were deported (1755) to the southern colonies, including Louisiana, where their descendants came to be called Cajuns (from "Acadians"). The rest of Acadia, excluding Maine, came under British rule in 1763.

A·ca·di·an (ə-kā′dē-ən) *adj.* Of or pertaining to Acadia or its inhabitants.
~*n.* Any of the early French settlers of Acadia or their descendants. See **Cajun.**

Acadia National Park. A scenic recreation area on Mount Desert Island off the coast of southern Maine. The rugged terrain includes glacier-scoured areas and a wave-eroded coastline.

a·ca·jou (ă-kə-zhōō′) *n.* Mahogany. [French, cashew, from Portuguese *(a)caju,* from Tupi, mahogany, probably by confusion with Tupi *agapú.*]

acantho–, acanth– *prefix.* Indicates thorns; for example, **acanthocephalan.** [New Latin, from Greek *akanthos,* thorn plant, from *akantha,* thorn : *ak-,* sharp + *antha,* of Mediterranean origin.]

a·can·tho·ceph·a·lan (ə-kăn′thō-sĕf′ə-lən) *n.* Any of various parasitic worms of the phylum Acanthocephala, having a proboscis armed with hooked spines. [New Latin *Acanthocephala,* "thornheads" (from the spiky proboscis) : ACANTHO- + -*cephala,* neuter plural of -*cephalus,* -CEPHALOUS.]

a·can·thoid (ə-kăn′thoid′) *adj.* Resembling a thorn or spine. [ACANTH(O)- + -OID.]

ac·an·thop·ter·yg·i·an (ăk′ən-thŏp′tə-rĭj′ē-ən) *n.* Any fish of the superorder Acanthopterygii, which includes fishes having spiny fins, such as bass, perch, and mackerel. Compare **malacopterygian.** [New Latin *Acanthopterygii* : ACANTHO- + Greek *pterugion,* diminutive of *pterux,* wing, fin, from *pteron,* feather, wing.] —**ac·an·thop·ter·yg·i·an** *adj.*

a·can·thus (ə-kăn′thəs) *n., pl.* **-thuses** or **-thi** (-thī′). **1.** Any of various plants of the genus *Acanthus,* native to the Mediterranean region, having large, segmented, thistlelike leaves. **2.** An architectural ornament patterned after the leaves of the acanthus, used especially on capitals of Corinthian columns. [New Latin, from Greek *akanthos,* thorn plant, from *akantha,* thorn. See **acantho-.**] —**a·can·thine** (ə-kăn′thĕn′) *adj.*

a cap·pel·la (ä kə-pĕl′ə) *adv. Music.* Without instrumental accompaniment. [Italian, "in the manner of the chapel (or choir)."] —**a cap·pel·la** *adj.*

a ca·pric·cio (ä kə-prēt′chō) *adv. Music.* At whatever tempo and with whatever expression the performer or conductor desires. Used as a direction. [Italian, "capriciously."]

A·ca·pul·co (de Juá·rez) (ä′kə-pōōl′kō də hwär′əs). A city of southern Mexico on the Pacific Ocean. Acapulco is a fashionable resort and has a fine natural harbor surrounded by cliffs and promontories.

ac·a·ri·a·sis (ăk′ə-rī′ə-sĭs) *n.* Infestation with mites or ticks. [New Latin : ACAR(ID) + -IASIS.]

a·car·i·cide (ə-kăr′ə-sīd′) *n.* A substance lethal to ticks and mites; a miticide. [ACARI(D) + -CIDE.] —**a·car·i·ci·dal** *adj.*

ac·a·rid (ăk′ə-rĭd) *n.* Any arachnid of the order Acarina, which includes the mites and ticks. [New Latin *Acaridae* (family), from *Acarus* (genus), from Greek *akari†,* a kind of mite.] —**ac·a·rid** *adj.*

ac·a·roid resin (ăk′ə-roid′) *n.* A gum obtained from various Australian grass trees, and used in varnishes, lacquers, and paper. Also called "acaroid gum," "gum accroides." [New Latin *acaroides,* from Greek *akari,* a kind of mite that bred in wax or resin. See **acarid.**]

a·car·pous (ā-kär′pəs) *adj. Botany.* Producing no fruit; sterile. [A-(not) + -CARPOUS.]

ac·a·rus (ăk′ə-rəs) *n., pl.* **-ri** (-rī′). A mite, especially one of the genus *Acarus.* [New Latin *Acarus.* See **acarid.**]

ac·a·ta·lec·tic (ā′kăt′ə-lĕk′tĭk) *adj.* Designating a line of verse having the required number of syllables in the last foot.
~*n.* An acatalectic line. [Late Latin *acatalēcticus,* from Greek *akatalēktikos* : *a-,* not + *katalēktikos,* CATALECTIC.]

a·cau·date (ā-kô′dāt′) *adj. Zoology.* Having no tail. [A- (not) + CAUDATE.]

a·cau·les·cent (ā′kô-lĕs′ənt) *adj. Botany.* Stemless, or nearly so. [A-(not) + CAULESCENT.]

acc. **1.** acceptance. **2.** accompanied. **3.** account; accountant. **4.** accusative. **5.** according to.

Accad. See **Akkad.**

Accadian. Variant of **Akkadian.**

ac·cede (ăk-sēd′) *intr.v.* **-ceded, -ceding, -cedes.** **1.** To give one's assent; agree. Often used with *to.* **2.** To take up or come into an office or high-ranking position. Used with *to: accede to the throne.*

Abyssinian cat *A short-haired breed, the Abyssinian is a domestic cat thought to be closely related to the sacred species of ancient Egypt.*

3. To become a party, as to an agreement. Used with *to*: *accede to a treaty.* —See Synonyms at **assent.** [Middle English *acceden,* from Latin *accēdere,* to go near, agree : *ad-*, to + *cēdere,* to go.] —**ac·ced·ence** (ăk-sē′dəns) *n.* —**ac·ced·er** *n.*

ac·cel·er·an·do (ä-chĕl′ə-rän′dō) *adj. Music.* Gradually accelerating or quickening in time. Used as a direction. [Italian, from Latin *accelerandum,* gerund of *accelerāre,* to ACCELERATE.] —**ac·cel·er·an·do** *n. & adv.*

ac·cel·er·ate (ăk-sĕl′ə-rāt′) *v.* **-ated, -ating, -ates.** —*tr.* **1.** To increase the speed of. **2.** To cause to occur sooner than expected or usual: *Hard work accelerated her promotion.* **3.** *Physics.* To cause a change of velocity in. —*intr.* **1.** To move or act faster. **2.** *Physics.* To change in velocity. —See Synonyms at **speed.** [Latin *accelerāre* : *ad-* (intensive) + *celerāre,* to hasten, from *celer,* swift.] —**ac·cel·er·a·tive** (ăk-sĕl′ə-rā′tĭv) *adj.*

ac·cel·er·a·tion (ăk-sĕl′ə-rā′shən) *n.* **1. a.** The act of accelerating. **b.** The state of being accelerated. **2. a.** *Physics. Symbol* **a** The rate of change of velocity with respect to time. **b.** Broadly, the ability to increase speed: *a car with good acceleration.*

acceleration of free fall *n. Symbol* **g** The acceleration of freely falling bodies under the influence of terrestrial gravity in a vacuum. The standard value is 9.80665 meters per second per second (approximately 32 feet per second per second) at sea level. Also called "acceleration due to gravity" or "acceleration of gravity."

ac·cel·er·a·tor (ăk-sĕl′ə-rā′tər) *n.* **1.** A device that controls the speed of a motor vehicle, especially by means of a pedal regulating the fuel intake to the engine. **2.** A substance that increases the speed of a chemical reaction. **3.** *Physics.* Any device, such as a cyclotron or linear accelerator, that accelerates charged subatomic particles or nuclei to energies useful for research. In this sense, also called "particle accelerator," "atom smasher."

ac·cel·er·om·e·ter (ăk-sĕl′ə-rŏm′ə-tər) *n.* Any of various devices used to measure acceleration. [ACCELER(ATION) + -METER.]

ac·cent (ăk′sĕnt′) *n.* **1.** *Linguistics.* The relative prominence given to a particular syllable of a word by greater intensity *(stress accent),* or by variation or modulation of pitch or tone *(pitch accent).* **2.** Vocal prominence or emphasis given to a particular syllable, word, or phrase. **3.** A characteristic pronunciation, especially: **a.** One that is typical of a particular regional or social group. **b.** One determined by the phonetic habits of the speaker's native language carried over to his use of another language. **4.** A mark or symbol used in printing and writing for any of various purposes, as: **a.** A mark used in certain languages to indicate the vocal quality to be given to a particular letter: *an acute accent.* **b.** A mark used to indicate the stressed syllables of a spoken word. **c.** A mark used to indicate an unusual or unexpected stress pattern, especially in poetry; for example, *venturèd, Déliláh.* **5.** Rhythmically significant stress in a line of verse. **6.** *Music.* **a.** Special stress given to a musical note within a phrase. **b.** A mark representing this stress. **c.** The rhythmical pattern of a piece of music based on the primary beat in each bar. **7.** *Mathematics.* **a.** A mark, or one of several marks, used as a superscript to distinguish variables represented by the same symbol; for example, x', x''. **b.** A mark used as a superscript to indicate the first derivative of a variable. **c.** Any of various marks used as a superscript to indicate a unit. See **prime. 8.** A distinctive character or quality: *a modern building but with a classical accent.* **9.** A strongly contrasting detail. **10.** Particular emphasis: *a mechanics course with the accent on practical experience.*
∼*tr.v.* (ăk′sĕnt′, ăk-sĕnt′) **accented, -centing, -cents. 1.** To stress or emphasize the pronunciation of. **2.** To mark with a written or printed accent. **3.** To draw attention to; accentuate: *"the effect of appropriate drapery in accenting feminine graces"* (Edward Bellamy). [Middle English, from Old French, from Latin *accentus,* accentuation, originally "song added to (speech)" (translation of Greek *prosōidia,* PROSODY) : *ad-*, to + *cantus,* song, from the past participle of *canere,* to sing.]

ac·cen·tor (ăk-sĕn′tər) *n.* Any of various sparrowlike songbirds of the family Prunellidae, most of which frequent mountainous regions. [Late Latin, "one who sings with another" : Latin *ad-*, to + *cantor,* singer, from *cantus,* song (see **accent**).]

ac·cen·tu·al (ăk-sĕn′cho͞o-əl) *adj.* **1.** Of or pertaining to accent. **2.** Designating verse rhythm based on stress accents rather than on the number of syllables. —**ac·cen·tu·al·ly** *adv.*

ac·cen·tu·ate (ăk-sĕn′cho͞o-āt′) *tr.v.* **-ated, -ating, -ates. 1.** To give greater prominence or emphasis to; heighten or emphasize. **2.** To mark or pronounce with a stress or accent. [Medieval Latin *accentuāre,* from Latin *accentus,* ACCENT.] —**ac·cen·tu·a·tion** *n.*

ac·cept (ăk-sĕpt′) *v.* **-cepted, -cepting, -cepts.** —*tr.* **1.** To take or receive (something offered) willingly. **2.** To receive as adequate, satisfactory, or admissible: *accepted his excuse.* **3.** To admit, as to a group or place: *accepted in the best circles.* **4.** To regard with favor or approval. **5. a.** To regard as usual, proper, or right. **b.** To regard as true; believe in: *accept a witness's version of what happened.* **6. a.** To bear up under resignedly or patiently: *accept one's fate.* **b.** To submit to without argument. **7. a.** To respond to affirmatively: *accept an invitation.* **b.** To take upon oneself (a duty or responsibility, for example); undertake. **8.** To be able to hold (something applied or inserted): *This wood will not accept oil paints.* **9.** *Commerce.* To consent to pay (a bill, for example), as by a signed agreement. —*intr.* To receive or agree to something willingly. —See Synonyms at **assent.** [Middle English *accepten,* from Old French *accepter,* from Latin *acceptāre,* frequentative of *accipere* (past participle *acceptus*), to receive, "take to oneself" : *ad-*, to + *capere,* to take.]

ac·cept·a·ble (ăk-sĕp′tə-bəl) *adj.* **1.** Satisfactory; adequate. **2.** Welcome; gratifying: *a most acceptable gift.* **3.** Tolerable. —**ac·cept·a·bil·i·ty, ac·cept·a·ble·ness** *n.* —**ac·cept·a·bly** *adv.*

ac·cep·tance (ăk-sĕp′təns) *n. Abbr.* **acc. 1.** The act or process of accepting. **2.** The state or condition of being accepted or acceptable. **3.** Favorable reception; approval. **4.** Belief in something; agreement; assent. **5.** *Commerce.* **a.** A formal indication by a party of willingness to pay a bill of exchange when it falls due, as by writing the word *accepted* and affixing his signature across the face of the document. **b.** The bill itself when so endorsed. **6.** *Law.* Assent by one party, through conduct or the spoken word, to the terms and conditions of offer of another so that a contract becomes legally binding between them.

ac·cep·tant (ăk-sĕp′tənt) *adj.* Accepting willingly.

ac·cep·ta·tion (ăk′sĕp-tā′shən) *n.* **1.** The usual or accepted meaning, as of a word or expression. **2.** *Archaic.* **a.** Favorable reception. **b.** Belief or assent.

ac·cept·ed (ăk-sĕp′tĭd) *adj.* Generally approved, believed, or recognized.

ac·cep·tor, ac·cept·er (ăk-sĕp′tər) *n.* **1.** *Commerce.* One who formally accepts a bill of exchange. **2.** *Physics.* An impurity that accepts electrons in a semiconductor, thus increasing the p-type semiconductivity. Compare **donor. 3.** *Chemistry.* An atom, molecule, or group that can accept a pair of electrons in forming a coordinate bond. Compare **donor. 4.** *Electronics.* A resonant circuit with the inductance and capacitance in series, which produces a large current at a particular frequency. Compare **rejector.**

ac·cess (ăk′sĕs′) *n.* **1.** A means of approaching or entering; a passage or entrance. **2.** The right or ability to enter, approach, or make use of. **3.** The state or quality of being approachable or reachable: *easy of access.* **4.** A sudden onset or outburst: *an access of rage.*
∼*tr.v.* **accessed, -cessing, -cesses. 1.** To retrieve from a computor's storage files: *to access data.* **2.** To obtain access to; reach. [Middle English, from Old French *acces,* arrival, from Latin *accessus,* from the past participle of *accēdere,* to arrive : *ad-*, to + *cēdere,* to come.]

ac·ces·si·ble (ăk-sĕs′ə-bəl) *adj.* **1.** Easily reached or entered. **2.** Easily obtained. **3.** Easily understood or appreciated: *a very accessible writer.* **4.** Susceptible; open: *accessible to flattery.* —**ac·ces·si·bil·i·ty, ac·ces·si·ble·ness** *n.* —**ac·ces·si·bly** *adv.*

ac·ces·sion (ăk-sĕsh′ən) *n.* **1.** The attainment of rank or high office. **2. a.** Increase by means of something added. **b.** An addition or acquisition; especially, a library book added to an existing collection. **3.** *Law.* **a.** The addition to or increase in value of property by means of improvements or natural growth. **b.** The right of a proprietor to ownership of such addition or increase. **4.** Agreement; assent. **5.** The act of formally accepting or becoming a party to a treaty or agreement: *Britain's accession to the Treaty of Rome.* **6.** Access; admittance. **7.** A sudden outburst; an access.
∼*tr.v.* **accessioned, -sioning, -sions.** To record as acquired. —**ac·ces·sion·al** *adj.*

ac·ces·so·rize (ăk-sĕs′ə-rīz′) *tr.v.* **-rized, -rizing, -rizes.** To provide with accessories.

ac·ces·so·ry (ăk-sĕs′ər-ē) *n., pl.* **-ries.** Also **ac·ces·sa·ry** (for sense 2). **1.** Something supplementary; an adjunct, as: **a.** A small, minor, or decorative item of clothing, such as a belt or scarf. **b.** A minor or additional part, device, or attachment, as for a motor vehicle. **2. a.** One who incites or aids another in the commission of a crime, but is not present at the time of the crime. Used in the phrase *accessory before the fact.* **b.** One who aids a criminal after the commission of a crime, but was not present at the time of the crime. Used in the phrase *accessory after the fact.* —See Synonyms at **appendage.**
∼*adj.* Also **ac·ces·sa·ry** (for sense 2). **1.** Having a secondary, supplementary, or subordinate function. **2.** Serving to aid or abet a criminal either before or after the commission of the crime, without being present at the time the crime was committed. [Middle English *accessorie,* from Medieval Latin *accessōrius,* from *accessor,* helper, accessory, subordinate, from Latin *accessus,* ACCESS.] —**ac·ces·so·ri·al** (ăk′sə-sôr′ē-əl, -sōr′-) *adj.* —**ac·ces·so·ri·ly** *adv.* —**ac·ces·so·ri·ness** *n.*

accessory fruit *n.* A **pseudocarp** *(see).*

accessory nerve *n.* Either of the 11th pair of cranial nerves, which supply certain muscles in the neck and, with the vagus nerve, supply the internal laryngeal muscles.

ac·ciac·ca·tu·ra (ä-chä′kə-to͝or′ə) *n., pl.* **-ture** (-to͝or′ā) or **-turas** (-to͝or′əz). *Music.* A short grace note, usually immediately below a principal note, sounded immediately before or at the same time in order to add sustained dissonance. Compare **appoggiatura.** [Italian *acciaccatura,* "crushing sound," from *acciaccare*†, to crush.]

ac·ci·dence (ăk′sə-dəns, -dĕns′) *n.* The part of grammar that deals with the inflections of words. [Latin *accidentia,* accidental or supplementary things, hence, inflections, from *accidere,* to happen (see **accident**).]

ac·ci·dent (ăk′sə-dənt, -dĕnt′) *n.* **1.** An unexpected and undesirable event, especially one resulting in damage, injury, or death; a mishap. **2.** Anything that occurs unexpectedly or unintentionally: *By a happy accident, I met him at the bus stop.* **3.** A property or attribute that is not essential to our conception of the nature of something. **4.** Any incidental or nonessential feature; an adjunct or accessory. **5.** Fortune; chance: *rich by accident of birth.* **6.** *Geology.* An irregu-

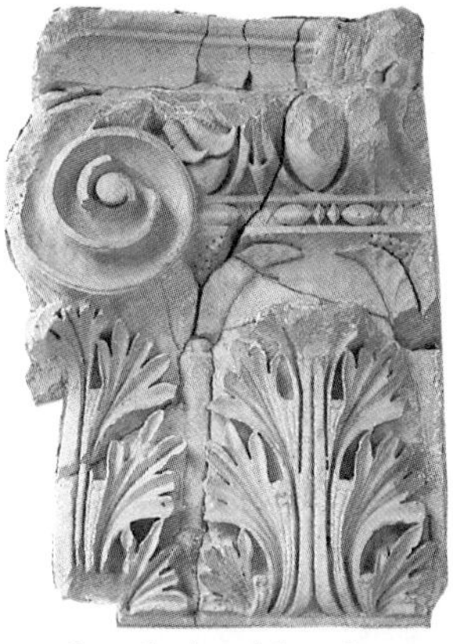

acanthus *Greek and, later, Roman architects used acanthus-leaf designs to decorate Corinthian columns.*

PRONUNCIATION KEY

ă, pat; ā, pay; âr, care;
ä, father, are; b, bib;
ch, church; d, deed; ĕ, pet;
ē, be; f, fife; g, gag; h, hat;
hw, which; ĭ, pit; ī, pie;
îr, pier; j, judge; k, kick;
l, lid, needle; m, mum;
n, no, sudden; ng, thing;
ŏ, pot; ō, toe; ô, paw, for;
oi, noise; ou, out; o͝o, book;
o͞o, boot; p, pop; r, roar;
s, sauce; sh, ship, dish;
t, tight; th, thin, path;
th, this, bathe; ŭ, cut; ûr, fur;
v, valve; w, with; y, yes;
z, zebra, size; zh, vision;
ə, about, item, edible, gallop, circus, peaceful

IN FOREIGN WORDS:

à, *Fr.* ami; œ, *Fr.* feu, *Ger.* schön; ü, *Fr.* tu, *Ger.* über;
KH, *Ger.* ich, *Scot.* loch;
N, *Fr.* bon; y′, *Fr.* Compiègne

STRESS MARKS:

Primary stress: ′
in·cite′ (ĭn-sīt′)
Secondary stress: ′
in′sight′ (ĭn′sīt′)

lar or unusual natural formation. [Middle English, from Old French, from Latin *(rēs) accidēns* (stem *accident-*), "(a thing) happening," from *accidere,* to fall upon, happen : *ad-,* to + *cadere,* to fall.]

ac·ci·den·tal (ăk′sə-dĕn′tl) *adj.* **1.** Occurring unexpectedly and unintentionally: *a verdict of accidental death.* **2.** Of or characterizing a nonessential property or attribute; supplementary; incidental. **3.** *Music.* Of or designating a sharp, flat, or natural not indicated in the key signature.
∼*n.* **1.** A factor or attribute that is not essential. **2.** *Music.* An accidental note or the symbol indicating this. **—ac·ci·den·tal·ly** *adv.*

accident insurance *n.* Insurance against injury or death because of accident.

ac·ci·dent-prone (ăk′sə-dənt-prōn′) *adj.* Especially liable to suffer an accident or injury.

ac·ci·die (ăk′sə-dē) *n.* Also **a·ce·di·a** (ə-sē′dē-ə). Spiritual torpor; apathy. [Late Latin, from Greek *akēdia, akēdeia,* indifference, apathy : *a-,* not + *kēdos,* care.]

ac·cip·i·ter (ăk-sĭp′ə-tər) *n.* Any hawk of the genus *Accipiter,* characterized by short wings and a long tail. [Latin, hawk.] **—ac·cip·i·trine** (ăk-sĭp′ə-trīn′, -trĭn) *adj.*

ac·claim (ə-klām′) *v.* **-claimed, -claiming, -claims.** *—tr.* **1.** To greet, especially publicly, with enthusiastic praise or approval. **2.** To acknowledge or declare with enthusiastic and unanimous approval: *acclaimed as the best play in town.* *—intr.* To shout approval. —See Synonyms at **praise.**
∼*n.* Enthusiastic applause or approval. [Latin *acclāmāre,* to shout at : *ad-,* to + *clāmāre,* to shout.] **—ac·claim·er** *n.*

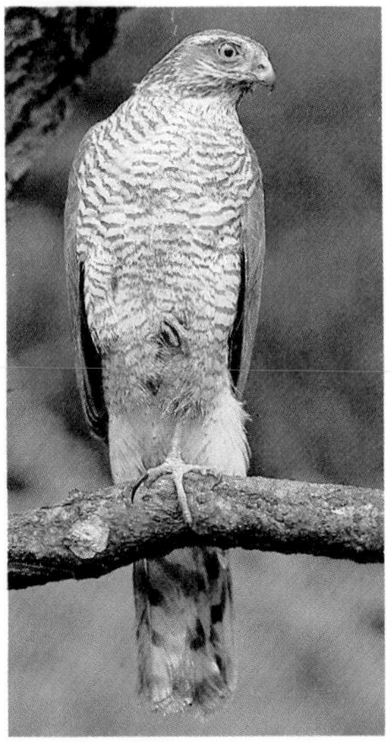

accipiter *The sparrow hawk (above) and its larger relative, the goshawk, are both accipiters, a worldwide genus containing more than 40 species of hawk.*

ac·cla·ma·tion (ăk′lə-mā′shən) *n.* **1.** The act of acclaiming or being acclaimed. **2.** A public expression of enthusiastic approval or praise. **3.** An expression of overwhelming or unanimous assent, as by cheers or shouts, taken as a vote of approval without a formal ballot: *The president was renominated by acclamation.* **—ac·clam·a·to·ry** (ə-klăm′ə-tôr′ē, -tōr′ē) *adj.*

ac·cli·mate (ə-klī′mĭt, ăk′lə-māt′) *v.* **-mated, -mating, -mates.** *—tr.* To accustom (something or someone) to a new environment or situation; adapt; acclimatize. *—intr.* To become accustomed to a new environment. [French *acclimater* : *ac-,* from Latin *ad,* to + *climate,* CLIMATE.]

ac·cli·ma·tion (ăk′lə-mā′shən) *n.* **1.** Acclimatization. **2.** The adaptation of an organism to its immediate natural climatic environment. Compare **acclimatization.**

ac·cli·ma·ti·za·tion (ə-klī′mə-tə-zā′shən) *n.* **1.** The process of acclimatizing or the state of being acclimatized. **2.** The climatic adaptation, often over several generations, of an organism that has been moved to a new environment. Compare **acclimation.**

ac·cli·ma·tize (ə-klī′mə-tīz′) *v.* **-tized, -tizing, -tizes.** *—tr.* To acclimate (someone or something). *—intr.* To acclimate. **—ac·cli·ma·tiz·a·ble** *adj.* **—ac·cli·ma·tiz·er** *n.*

ac·cliv·i·ty (ə-klĭv′ə-tē) *n., pl.* **-ties.** An upward slope. Compare **declivity.** [Latin *acclīvitās,* from *acclīvis,* uphill : *ad-,* to + *clīvus,* slope.]

ac·co·lade (ăk′ə-lād′, ăk′ə-läd′) *n.* **1.** An expression of praise or approval: *critics' accolades.* **2.** An award or honor: *the highest accolade of the literary world.* **3.** The ceremonial bestowal of knighthood, as by a tap on the shoulder with the flat of a sword or, formerly, by an embrace. [French, from Provençal *acolada,* an embrace, from *acolar,* to embrace, from Vulgar Latin *accollāre* (unattested), to hug around the neck : *ad-,* to + *collum,* neck.]

ac·com·mo·date (ə-kŏm′ə-dāt′) *v.* **-dated, -dating, -dates.** *—tr.* **1.** To do a favor or service for; oblige. **2.** To furnish or supply with something needed; especially, to provide with lodging or housing. **3. a.** To contain comfortably or have space for. **b.** To admit the inclusion of: *The party accommodates a wide range of moderate views.* **4.** To adapt, adjust, or make fit. Often used with *to.* **5.** To bring into harmony or agreement; settle; reconcile. *—intr.* To become adjusted, as the eye to focusing on objects at a distance. —See Synonyms at **contain.** [Latin *accommodāre,* to make fit : *ad-,* to + *commodus,* fit, "conforming with the (right) measure" : *con-,* with + *modus,* measure.] **—ac·com·mo·da·tive** *adj.*

ac·com·mo·dat·ing (ə-kŏm′ə-dā′tĭng) *adj.* Helpful and obliging. **—ac·com·mo·dat·ing·ly** *adv.*

ac·com·mo·da·tion (ə-kŏm′ə-dā′shən) *n.* **1.** The act of accommodating or the state of being accommodated; adaptation, adjustment, or reconciliation. **2.** Anything that meets a need; a convenience. **3. accommodations. a.** Space for living or staying; lodgings. **b.** A seat or compartment on a public vehicle. **4.** An arrangement by which opposing views are settled; a compromise. **5.** *Physiology.* Adaptation or adjustment in an organism, organ, or part, as takes place in the lens of the eye to permit retinal focus of images of objects at different distances. **6.** *Commerce.* A loan or other financial favor.

accommodation bill *n.* A bill of exchange endorsed by a guarantor to ensure the credit of the drawer.

accommodation ladder *n. Nautical.* A portable ladder or stairway hung from the side of a ship.

ac·com·pa·ni·ment (ə-kŭm′pə-nē-mənt, ə-kŭmp′nē-) *n.* **1.** Something that accompanies; a concomitant. **2.** Something added for embellishment, completeness, or symmetry; a complement. **3.** *Music.* A vocal or instrumental part that supports a solo part.

ac·com·pa·nist (ə-kŭm′pə-nĭst, ə-kŭmp′nĭst) *n. Music.* A performer, such as a pianist, who plays an accompaniment.

ac·com·pa·ny (ə-kŭm′pə-nē, ə-kŭmp′nē) *v.* **-nied, -nying, -nies.** *—tr.* **1.** To go along with; join in company. **2.** To supplement; add to: *the caption accompanying an illustration.* **3.** To coexist or occur with. **4.** To perform a musical accompaniment to or for. *—intr.* To play a musical accompaniment. [Middle English *accompanien,* from Old French *accompagner* : *ac-,* from Latin *ad-,* to + *compain(g),* companion, from Late Latin *compāniō,* COMPANION.]
Synonyms: *chaperone, conduct, escort.*

ac·com·plice (ə-kŏm′plĭs) *n.* One who aids or abets another in wrongdoing, especially in a criminal act. —See Synonyms at **partner.** [Middle English, from *a complice,* a COMPLICE (influenced by ACCOMPLISH).]

ac·com·plish (ə-kŏm′plĭsh) *tr.v.* **-plished, -plishing, -plishes. 1.** To succeed in doing; achieve. **2.** To reach the end of; complete; finish. —See Synonyms at **perform, reach.** [Middle English *accomplissen,* from Old French *accomplir* (present stem *accompliss-*), to complete : *ac-,* from Latin *ad-,* to + *complir,* to complete, from Latin *complēre,* "to fill up," to finish : *com-* (intensive) + *plēre,* to fill.] **—ac·com·plish·a·ble** *adj.* **—ac·com·plish·er** *n.*

ac·com·plished (ə-kŏm′plĭsht) *adj.* **1.** Skilled; proficient, especially through training and practice. **2.** Sophisticated; having many social accomplishments.

ac·com·plish·ment (ə-kŏm′plĭsh-mənt) *n.* **1.** The act of accomplishing or the state of being accomplished; completion. **2.** Something completed successfully; an achievement. **3.** A quality or faculty that contributes to a person's social poise; a social skill. **4.** Any talent or skill.

ac·cord (ə-kôrd′) *v.* **-corded, -cording, -cords.** *—tr.* **1.** To cause to conform or agree; bring into harmony. **2.** To grant or bestow: *I accord you my blessing.* *—intr.* To be consistent, in agreement, or in harmony. —See Synonyms at **agree.**
∼*n.* **1.** Agreement, harmony, or conformity. Used especially in the phrase *in accord with.* **2.** A settlement or compromise between conflicting opinions; especially, a settlement of points at issue between nations; a treaty. **—of one's own accord.** Voluntarily. **—with one accord.** Unanimously. [Middle English *acorden,* from Old French *acorder,* from Vulgar Latin *accordāre* (unattested), "to be heart-to-heart with" : Latin *ad-,* to + *cor* (stem *cord-*), heart.]

ac·cord·ance (ə-kôr′dəns) *n.* **1.** Agreement; conformity. Used especially in the phrase *in accordance with.* **2.** The act of granting.

ac·cord·ant (ə-kôr′dənt) *adj.* In agreement or harmony; corresponding; consonant. Usually used with *with.* **—ac·cord·ant·ly** *adv.*

ac·cord·ing as (ə-kôr′dĭng) *conj.* **1.** Consistently with the way in which; to the extent. **2.** Depending on whether.

ac·cord·ing·ly (ə-kôr′dĭng-lē) *adv.* **1.** In a way that corresponds or accords with what the circumstances imply or demand; appropriately. **2.** Consequently.

according to *prep. Abbr.* **acc. 1.** In accordance with. **2.** In proportion to. **3.** In the report of; as stated or shown by.

ac·cor·di·on (ə-kôr′dē-ən) *n.* A portable musical instrument with a small keyboard and free metal reeds that sound when air is forced past them by pleated bellows operated by the player. See **piano accordion.** [German *Akkordion,* from *Akkord,* agreement, "harmony," from French *accord,* from Old French *acorder,* to ACCORD.] **—ac·cor·di·on·ist** *n.*

ac·cost (ə-kôst′, ə-kŏst′) *tr.v.* **-costed, -costing, -costs. 1.** To approach and speak to, especially boldly or accusingly. **2.** To solicit sexually. [Old French *accoster,* from Vulgar Latin *accostāre* (unattested), to come alongside someone : Latin *ad-,* near + *costa,* side, rib.]

ac·couche·ment (ȧ-ko͞osh-mäN′) *n.* A confinement; childbirth.

ac·cou·cheur (ȧ-ko͞o-shœr′) *n. Feminine* **ac·cou·cheuse** (ȧ-ko͞o-shœz′). A midwife or obstetrician. [French, "one attending at the bedside" : *ac-,* at + *coucheur,* from *couche,* bed.]

ac·count (ə-kount′) *n.* **1.** A written or oral narration or description: *an eyewitness account of the accident.* **2.** An explanatory statement or report; especially, a statement explaining and justifying one's conduct: *called to give an account of his behavior.* **3.** A demonstration or exposition, as of one's qualities or abilities: *gave a good account of herself at the interview.* **4.** A particular version, report, or stated opinion: *by all accounts a formidable character.* **5.** Worth, standing, or importance: *a man of some account.* **6.** Consideration; notice: *taking into account the level of inflation.* **7.** Profit; advantage: *turned her talents to good account.* **8.** A precise list or enumeration of monetary transactions. **9.** *Abbr.* **a/c, A/C, acct., acc.** *Finance.* **a.** A business relationship involving the exchange of money or credit: *a bank account.* **b.** The client or customer involved in such a relationship. **c.** The amount of money held by a depositor in a bank. **d.** A statement recording all transactions relating to an account during a particular period and showing the current balance. **—call to account. 1.** To hold answerable. **2.** To reprimand. **—on account. 1.** On credit. **2.** In part payment. **—on account of. 1.** Because of. **2.** For the sake of: *Don't wait on account of me.* **3.** *Regional.* Because. **—on no account.** Under no circumstances. **—on one's own account. 1.** On one's own behalf. **2.** At one's own risk.
∼*tr.v.* **accounted, -counting, -counts.** To consider or esteem: *"Your honor is accounted a merciful man"* (Shakespeare). **—account for. 1.** To provide a reckoning of (people or funds, for example): *Six survivors have been accounted for.* **2.** To provide an explanation or justification for: *They couldn't account for the thumping noise in the cellar.* **3.** To be the explanation or cause of. **4.** To kill, capture, or disable. [Middle English, from Old French *acont,*

acompt, from *acunter, acompter,* "to count up to," reckon : *ac-,* from Latin *ad-,* to + *cunter, compter,* to COUNT (compute).]

ac·count·a·ble (ə-koun'tə-bəl) *adj.* **1.** Liable to be called to account for one's conduct; answerable. Used with *to* or *for.* **2.** Capable of being explained. —**ac·count·a·bil·i·ty, ac·count·a·ble·ness** *n.* —**ac·count·a·bly** *adv.*

ac·count·an·cy (ə-koun'tən-sē) *n.* The practice, profession, or business of an accountant.

ac·count·ant (ə-koun'tənt) *n. Abbr.* **acc.** One who keeps, audits, and inspects the financial records of individuals or business concerns and prepares financial reports and tax returns.

account executive *n.* An employee of an advertising firm who manages the account of one or more clients.

ac·count·ing (ə-koun'tĭng) *n.* The principles and methods involved in keeping a financial record of business transactions and in preparing statements concerning the assets, liabilities, and operating results of a business.

ac·cou·ter (ə-kōō'tər) *tr.v.* **-tered, -tering, -ters.** Also *chiefly British* **ac·cou·tre** (-tər) **-tred, -tring, -tres.** To equip or attire, especially with a particular type of outfit or uniform. Usually used in the passive. [French *accoutrer,* from Old French *acoustrer,* from Vulgar Latin *acconsūtūrāre* (unattested), to equip (with clothes) : Latin *ad-,* to + *consūtūra* (unattested), sewing, clothes, from Latin *consuere,* to sew together : *con-,* together + *suere,* to sew.]

ac·cou·ter·ment (ə-kōō'tər-mənt) Also *chiefly British* **ac·cou·tre·ment** (-tər-mənt, -trə-mənt) *n.* **1.** The act of accoutering. **2.** **accouterments.** Equipment, adornments, or accessories; especially, the equipment other than arms and uniform issued to a soldier. **3.** **accouterments.** The outward forms whereby a thing may be recognized; trappings.

Ac·cra (ə-krä', ăk'rə). The capital of Ghana, located on the Gulf of Guinea. It was originally the capital of an ancient Ga kingdom and became the capital of the Gold Coast, a British colony, in 1876. It developed into the country's economic center after the completion in 1923 of a railway to the mining and agricultural regions inland.

ac·cred·it (ə-krĕd'ĭt) *tr.v.* **-ited, -iting, -its. 1. a.** To ascribe or attribute to someone. **b.** To credit (someone) with something. **2. a.** To supply with credentials or authority; authorize. **b.** To appoint as an ambassador or envoy. **3.** To recognize or certify as meeting a prescribed standard. [French *accréditer,* from *(mettre) à crédit,* "(to put) to CREDIT."] —**ac·cred·it·ed** *adj.*

ac·cred·i·ta·tion (ə-krĕd'ə-tā'shən) *n.* The act of accrediting or the condition of being accredited; especially, the granting of approval to an institution of learning by an official reviewing body after the school has met specific requirements.

ac·crete (ə-krēt') *v.* **-creted, -creting, -cretes.** —*tr.* To attract or attach (additional elements) so as to cause increased growth. —*intr.* **1.** To grow together; fuse. **2.** To become attached, so as to cause increased growth. Used with *to.* [Back-formation from ACCRETION.]

ac·cre·tion (ə-krē'shən) *n.* **1.** Growth or increase in size by the gradual addition, fusion, or inclusion of external elements; specifically, the process by which an astronomical body increases in size or mass as a result of gravitationally attracting less dense material surrounding or adjoining it. **2.** Something added externally to promote such growth or increase. **3.** *Biology.* **a.** Any growing together of plant or animal tissues that are normally separate. **b.** A build-up of foreign matter in a cavity. **4.** *Geology.* A slow build-up of material, such as deposition of a water-borne sediment. **5.** *Law.* **a.** An increase of land through a process of natural growth, as by alluvial deposit. **b.** An increase in the share of a property when a joint owner or beneficiary dies or fails to take up his share. [Latin *accrēscere* (past participle *accrētus*), to ACCRUE.] —**ac·cre·tion·ar·y, ac·cre·tive** *adj.*

accretion theory *n.* The theory that the continents have increased in size during geological time as continental drift has moved the landmasses about the globe, building up new mountain ranges.

ac·crue (ə-krōō') *intr.v.* **-crued, -cruing, -crues. 1.** To come to someone or something as a gain or addition. **2.** To increase or accumulate, as by natural growth or as interest on capital. **3.** *Law.* To become enforceable or permanent. Used of a right. [Middle English *acrewen,* probably from Old French *accreue,* growth, from the past participle of *accreistre,* to increase, from Latin *accrēscere* : *ad-,* in addition + *crēscere,* to grow.] —**ac·cru·al, ac·crue·ment** *n.*

acct. account.

ac·cul·tur·ate (ə-kŭl'chə-rāt') *v.* **-ated, -ating, -ates.** —*tr.* To cause to change by the process of acculturation. —*intr.* To change or be modified by acculturation.

ac·cul·tur·a·tion (ə-kŭl'chə-rā'shən) *n.* The modification of the culture of an individual or group through prolonged contact with a different culture; especially, the modification of a primitive culture through contact with an advanced culture. [AD- (toward) + CULTUR(E) + -ATION.]

ac·cum·bent (ə-kŭm'bənt) *adj. Botany.* Resting against another part. Said especially of cotyledons. [Latin *accumbēns* (stem *accumbent-*), present participle of *accumbere,* to recline : *ad-,* near to + *-cumbere,* to recline.] —**ac·cum·ben·cy** *n.*

ac·cu·mu·late (ə-kyōōm'yə-lāt') *v.* **-lated, -lating, -lates.** —*tr.* To amass or gather; pile up; collect. —*intr.* To grow or increase; mount up. —See Synonyms at **gather.** [Latin *accumulāre* : *ad-,* in addition + *cumulāre,* to pile up, from *cumulus,* a heap.] —**ac·cu·mu·la·ble** *adj.*

ac·cu·mu·la·tion (ə-kyōōm'yə-lā'shən) *n.* **1.** The act or process of accumulating; amassing or growing, as into a heap or large amount.

2. A mass or quantity that has accumulated or been accumulated. **3.** The growth of capital by retention of interest or profit.

ac·cu·mu·la·tive (ə-kyōōm'yə-lā'tĭv, -lə-tĭv) *adj.* **1.** Characterized by or showing the effects of accumulation; cumulative. **2.** Having a tendency to amass material or wealth; acquisitive. —**ac·cu·mu·la·tive·ly** *adv.* —**ac·cu·mu·la·tive·ness** *n.*

ac·cu·mu·la·tor (ə-kyōōm'yə-lā'tər) *n.* **1.** Someone or something that accumulates. **2.** A register or electrical circuit in a calculator or computer that stores figures for computation. **3.** *Chiefly British.* A **storage battery** *(see),* especially one used in a motor vehicle. **4.** *British.* A kind of bet, a **parlay** *(see).*

ac·cu·ra·cy (ăk'yər-ə-sē) *n.* Exactness; correctness.

ac·cu·rate (ăk'yər-ĭt) *adj.* **1. a.** Having no errors; correct. **b.** Marked by or showing careful attention to what is true or correct. **2.** Deviating only slightly or within acceptable limits from a standard. [Latin *accūrātus,* done with care, past participle of *accūrāre,* to attend to carefully : *ad-,* to + *cūrāre,* to care for, attend to, from *cūra,* care.] —**ac·cu·rate·ly** *adv.* —**ac·cu·rate·ness** *n.*

ac·curs·ed (ə-kûr'sĭd, ə-kûrst') *adj.* Also **ac·curst** (ə-kûrst'). **1.** Under a curse; doomed. **2.** Abominable; hateful. [Middle English *acursed,* from *acursen,* to curse, from Old English *ācursian* : *ā-* (intensive) + *cursian,* to curse, from *curs,* CURSE.] —**ac·curs·ed·ly** *adv.* —**ac·curs·ed·ness** *n.*

ac·cu·sal (ə-kyōō'zəl) *n.* An accusation.

ac·cu·sa·tion (ăk'yōō-zā'shən) *n.* **1.** The act of accusing or the fact of being accused. **2.** An allegation. **3.** *Law.* A formal charge brought before a court against a person, stating that he is guilty of some punishable offense.

ac·cu·sa·tive (ə-kyōō'zə-tĭv) *adj. Abbr.* **acc.** Of, pertaining to, or designating the case of a noun, pronoun, adjective, or participle that is the direct object of a verb or the object of certain prepositions.
~*n.* The accusative case. [Middle English, from Latin *(casus) accūsātīvus,* "(case) indicating accusation" (mistranslation of Greek *aitiatikos ptōsis,* "case of causation"), from *accūsāre,* to ACCUSE.] —**ac·cu·sa·tive·ly** *adv.*

ac·cu·sa·to·ri·al (ə-kyōō'zə-tôr'ē-əl, -tōr'ē-əl) *adj.* Of or designating a procedure of criminal justice in which the judge assesses the validity of an accusation as argued by a prosecutor. Compare **inquisitorial.**

ac·cu·sa·to·ry (ə-kyōō'zə-tôr'ē, -tōr'ē) *adj.* Containing or implying an accusation.

ac·cuse (ə-kyōōz') *tr.v.* **-cused, -cusing, -cuses.** —*tr.* **1.** To charge with a shortcoming or error; blame. **2.** To bring charges against (someone) for a crime or offense. Used with *of.*
~*intr.* To make an accusation. [Middle English *acusen,* from Old French *acuser,* from Latin *accūsāre,* to accuse, "call to account" : *ad-,* to + *causa,* CAUSE.] —**ac·cus·er** *n.* —**ac·cus·ing·ly** *adv.*

ac·cused (ə-kyōōzd') *n., pl.* **accused.** *Law.* The defendant in a criminal case. Preceded by *the.*

ac·cus·tom (ə-kŭs'təm) *tr.v.* **-tomed, -toming, -toms.** To familiarize, as by constant practice, use, or habit. Often used reflexively. [Middle English *accustomen,* from Old French *aco(u)stumer* : *a-,* from Latin *ad-,* to + *costume,* CUSTOM.]

ac·cus·tomed (ə-kŭs'təmd) *adj.* **1.** Usual, characteristic, or normal: *sitting in her accustomed place.* **2.** In the habit of; used. Used with *to: accustomed to sleeping late.* —See Synonyms at **usual.**

ace (ās) *n.* **1. a.** A single pip or spot on a playing card, die, or domino. **b.** A playing card, die, or domino having one spot or pip. **2.** In racket games: **a.** A serve which one's opponent is unable to reach. **b.** Any serve which one's opponent fails to return. **3.** In golf, a hole in one stroke. **4.** A military aircraft pilot who has destroyed five or more enemy aircraft. **5.** *Informal.* A person with great skill in a particular activity. —**within an ace of.** Very close to: *within an ace of victory.*
~*adj. Informal.* **1.** Highly skilled; expert. **2.** *Informal.* Of the highest quality; really good.
~*tr.v.* **aced, acing, aces. 1.** In racket games, to serve an ace against. **2.** *Slang.* To receive a grade of A on: *She aced the exam.* [Middle English *aas,* from Old French *as,* from Latin *ās,* unit. See **as** (Roman coin).]

-acean *suffix.* Indicates an animal belonging to a taxonomic class or order; for example, cetacean. [New Latin *-acea* and *-aceae,* neuter and feminine plural of *-aceus,* -ACEOUS.]

acedia. Variant of **accidie.**

A·cel·da·ma¹ (ə-sĕl'də-mə). The potter's field near Jerusalem purchased by the priests as a burying ground for strangers with the reward that Judas had received for betraying Jesus and later had returned to them. Matthew 27:7. [Greek *Akeldama,* from Aramaic *ḥăqēl dĕmā,* "field of blood."]

Aceldama² *n.* Any place with dreadful associations.

a·cel·lu·lar (ā-sĕl'yə-lər) *adj. Biology.* Containing no cells; not made up of cells.

a·cen·tric (ā-sĕn'trĭk) *adj.* **1.** Having no center. **2.** Not centered; placed off-center. [A- (not) + CENTRIC.]

-aceous *suffix.* Indicates: **1.** Of or pertaining to; for example, sebaceous. **2.** Resembling or of the nature of; for example, farinaceous. **3.** Belonging to a taxonomic category, especially a botanical family; for example, orchidaceous. [New Latin *-aceus,* from Latin *-āceus,* "of a specific kind or group," originally an extension of an adjectival suffix *-āx,* (stem *-āc-*).]

a·ceph·a·lous (ā-sĕf'ə-ləs) *adj.* **1.** *Zoology.* Headless or lacking a clearly defined head. **2.** Having no leader: *an acephalous tribe.*

[Medieval Latin *acephalus*, headless, from Greek *akephalos* : *a-* (not) + -CEPHALOUS.]

ac·e·rate (ăs′ə-rāt′) *adj.* Also **ac·e·rat·ed** (-rā′tĭd). *Biology.* Pointed at one end; needle-shaped. [Latin *ācer*, sharp.]

ac·er·bate (ăs′ər-bāt) *tr.v.* **-bated, -bating, -bates.** To vex; annoy. [Latin *acerbāre*, to make sour, from *acerbus*, ACERBIC.]

a·cerb·ic (ə-sûr′bĭk) *adj.* Also **a·cerb** (ə-sûrb′). 1. Sour; bitter; astringent. 2. Harsh in manner or speech; cutting. [Latin *acerbus*, sharp, bitter.]

a·cer·bi·ty (ə-sûr′bə-tē) *n., pl.* **-ties.** 1. Sourness of taste. 2. Acrimony; sharpness of speech or manner. 3. An instance of this.

ac·e·rose (ăs′ə-rōs′) *adj. Botany.* Slender and sharp-pointed, as a pine needle is. [Incorrect use (by Linnaeus as if from Latin *ācer*, sharp, ACERATE) of Latin *acerōsus*, from *acus* (stem *acer-*), chaff.]

acet. acetone.

acet. a. acetic acid.

ac·e·tab·u·lum (ăs′ə-tăb′yə-ləm) *n., pl.* **-la** (-lə). 1. *Anatomy.* The cup-shaped cavity in the hipbone into which the head of the thighbone fits. 2. *Zoology.* A sucker, such as that of an octopus or cuttlefish. [Latin *acētābulum*, vinegar cup, from *acētum*, vinegar; akin to *ācer*, sharp.] **—ac·e·tab·u·lar** *adj.*

ac·e·tal (ăs′ə-tăl) *n.* 1. A colorless, flammable, volatile liquid, $CH_3CH(OC_2H_5)_2$, used in cosmetics and as a solvent. 2. Any of the class of compounds formed from aldehydes combined with alcohols. [German *Azetal* : ACET(O)- + AL(COHOL).]

ac·et·al·de·hyde (ăs′ĭt-ăl′də-hīd′) *n.* A colorless, flammable liquid, CH_3CHO, used to manufacture acetic acid, perfumes, and drugs. Also called "aldehyde." [ACET(O)- + ALDEHYDE.]

a·cet·a·mide (ə-sĕt′ə-mīd′, ăs′ĭt-ăm′īd′) *n.* Also **a·cet·a·mid** (ə-sĕt′-ə-mĭd, ăs′ĭt-ăm′ĭd). The crystalline amide of acetic acid, CH_3CONH_2, used as a wetting agent and in lacquers and explosives. Also called "ethanamide." [German *Azetamid* : ACET(O)- + AMIDE.]

ac·et·an·i·lide (ăs′ĭt-ăn′ə-līd′) *n.* Also **ac·et·an·i·lid** (-lĭd). A white crystalline compound, $C_6H_5NH(COCH_3)$, used medicinally to relieve pain and reduce fever. [ACET(O)- + ANIL(INE) + -IDE.]

ac·e·tate (ăs′ə-tāt) *n.* 1. A salt or ester of acetic acid. 2. Cellulose acetate or any of various products, especially fibers and fabrics, derived from it. [ACET(O)- + -ATE.] **—ac·e·tat·ed** *adj.*

a·ce·tic (ə-sē′tĭk) *adj.* Of, pertaining to, or containing acetic acid or vinegar. [Latin *acētum*, vinegar, akin to *ācer*, sharp.]

acetic acid *n. Abbr.* **acet. a.** A clear, colorless organic acid, CH_3COOH, with a distinctive pungent odor, widely used as a solvent and in industry. It is the characteristic ingredient of vinegar. Also called "ethanoic acid" and, when at least 99.8 percent pure, "glacial acetic acid."

acetic anhydride *n.* An organic liquid, $(CH_3CO)_2O$, with a pungent odor, combining with water to produce acetic acid and used as an acetylating agent.

a·cet·i·fy (ə-sĕt′ə-fī′) *v.* **-fied, -fying, -fies.** *—tr.* To convert (a neutral liquid) to acetic acid or vinegar. *—intr.* To become acetic; turn into acetic acid or vinegar. [ACET(O)- + -FY.] **—a·cet·i·fi·ca·tion** *n.* **—a·cet·i·fi·er** *n.*

aceto-, acet– *prefix.* Indicates the presence of acetic acid or the acetyl radical; for example, **acetophenetidin, acetify.** [Latin *acētum*, vinegar.]

ac·e·to·a·ce·tic acid (ăs′ə-tō-ə-sē′tĭk, ə-sē′tō-) *n.* A syrupy, colorless acid, CH_3COCH_2COOH, excreted in the urine and found in abnormal quantities in the urine of diabetics.

ac·e·tone (ăs′ə-tōn′) *n. Abbr.* **acet.** A colorless, volatile, extremely flammable liquid, CH_3COCH_3, widely used as an organic solvent and, in especially pure grades, to clean and dry electronic component materials. Also called "propanone." [German *Azeton* : ACET(O)- + -ONE.] **—ac·e·ton·ic** (ăs′ə-tŏn′ĭk) *adj.*

acetone body *n. Biochemistry.* A **ketone body** (see).

ac·e·to·phe·net·i·din (ăs′ə-tō-fə-nĕt′ə-dĭn) *n.* A white powder or crystalline solid, $CH_3CONHC_6H_4OC_2H_5$, used in medicine to reduce fever and relieve pain. Also called "phenacetin." [ACETO- + PHEN(O)- + ET(HYL) + -ID(E) + -IN.]

ac·e·tous (ăs′ə-təs, ə-sē′təs) *adj.* Also **a·ce·tose** (ăs′ə-tōs′). 1. Of, pertaining to, or producing acetic acid or vinegar. 2. Having an acetic taste; sour-tasting. [Late Latin *acētōsus*, vinegary, from *acētum*, vinegar.]

a·ce·tum (ə-sē′təm) *n.* An acetic acid solution of a drug. [Latin *acētum*, akin to *ācer*, sharp.]

ac·e·tyl (ăs′ə-tĭl, ə-sĕt′l) *n.* The acetic acid radical CH_3CO. [ACET(O)- + -YL.] **—ac·e·tyl·ic** (ăs′ə-tĭl′ĭk) *adj.*

a·cet·y·late (ə-sĕt′l-āt′) *v.* **-lated, -lating, -lates.** *—tr.* To introduce an acetyl group into (an organic molecule), using a reagent such as acetic anhydride. *—intr.* To undergo introduction of an acetyl group. **—a·cet·y·la·tion** *n.*

ac·e·tyl·cho·line (ăs′ə-tĭl-kō′lēn′, ə-sĕt′l-) *n.* A white crystalline compound, $C_7H_{17}NO_3$, released at some nerve endings when a nerve impulse is transmitted from one nerve fiber to another. [ACETYL + CHOLINE.]

ac·e·tyl·cho·lin·es·ter·ase (ăs′ə-tĭl-kō′lə-nĕs′tə-rās′) *n.* An enzyme, **cholinesterase** (see).

a·cet·y·lene (ə-sĕt′l-ēn′, -ən) *n.* A colorless, highly flammable or explosive gas, C_2H_2, used for metal welding and cutting and as an illuminant. Also called "ethyne." [ACETYL + -ENE.] **—a·cet·y·len·ic** *adj.*

acetylene series *n.* A series of unsaturated aliphatic hydrocarbons, each containing a triple carbon bond, having chemical properties resembling acetylene and having the general formula C_nH_{2n-2}, with acetylene being the simplest member. Also called "alkyne series."

a·ce·tyl·sal·i·cyl·ic acid (ə-sĕt′l-săl′ə-sĭl′ĭk) *n.* A common drug, **aspirin** (see).

ace·y·deuc·y (ā′sē-dōō′sē, -dyōō′sē) *n.* A variation of backgammon. [ACE + DEUCE.]

A·chae·a (ə-kē′ə). Also **A·cha·ia** (ə-kī′ə, ə-kā′ə). Greek **A·khaï·a** (ə-kī′ə, ə-kā′ə). A region of ancient Greece occupying the north part of the Peloponnese on the Gulf of Corinth. The cities of the region banded together in the early 3rd century B.C. to form the Achaean League, which defeated Sparta but was eventually beaten by the Romans. Rome annexed Achaea in 146 B.C. and later gave the name to a Roman province comprising all of Greece south of Thessaly. The name Achaea is now used for a modern prefecture in the northern Peloponnese, whose capital is Patras.

A·chae·an (ə-kē′ən) *n.* Also **A·cha·ian** (ə-kī′ən). 1. A native or inhabitant of Achaea. 2. A Greek, especially of the Mycenaean era. **—A·chae·an** *adj.*

A·chae·me·nid (ə-kē′mə-nĭd, ə-kĕm′ə-) *n.* A member of the ruling dynasty of Persia from the time of Cyrus the Great to the death of Darius III (559–330 B.C.). [Greek *Akhaimenidēs*, from *Akhaimenēs*, founder of the dynasty.] **—A·chae·me·nid** *adj.*

A·cha·tes (ə-kā′tēz) *n.* A loyal friend. [After *Achates*, the faithful companion of Aeneas, in Virgil's epic poem the *Aeneid.*]

ache (āk) *intr.v.* **ached, aching, aches.** 1. To suffer, or cause one to suffer, a dull, sustained pain. 2. *Informal.* To yearn painfully. *~n.* A dull, steady pain. [Middle English *aken*, Old English *acan.*]

A·che·be (ə-chē′bā), Chinua (1930–). Nigerian Ibo novelist and poet, whose writings deal with the conflict arising when traditional African society faces Western culture. His works include the novels *Things Fall Apart* (1958) and *A Man of the People* (1966).

a·chene (ə-kēn′) *n. Botany.* A dry, thin-walled, one-seeded fruit, such as that of the buttercup and dandelion, that does not split open when ripe. [New Latin *achēnium*, "one that does not yawn or split open" : A- (not) + Greek *khainein*, to yawn.] **—a·che·ni·al** (ə-kē′nē-əl) *adj.*

A·cher·nar (ā′kər-när′) *n.* A star in the constellation Eridanus that is one of the brightest stars in the sky and is 114 light-years from Earth. [Arabic *ākhir al-nahr*, "the end of the river" (referring to the star's position in Eridanus).]

Ach·e·ron (ăk′ə-rŏn′) *n. Greek Mythology.* 1. The river of woe over which Charon ferried the souls of the dead to Hades. 2. The underworld; Hades.

Ach·e·son (ăch′ə-sən), **Dean Gooderham** (1893–1971). U.S. lawyer and statesman. He was secretary of state under President Harry S Truman and later became a presidential adviser. He promoted the Marshall Plan and helped establish NATO.

A·cheu·li·an, A·cheu·le·an (ə-shōō′lē-ən) *adj. Archaeology.* Of or designating a stage of culture of the European Lower Paleolithic Age, about 250,000 years ago, characterized by symmetrical stone hand axes. [French *acheuléen*, after *St. Acheul*, village in northern France and site of the archaeological finds from which the culture was classified.]

à che·val (ä shə-väl′) *adv.* Positioned so as to straddle a line on a gambling table between two numbers or cards. Used especially in roulette. [French, "on horseback."]

a·chieve (ə-chēv′) *v.* **achieved, achieving, achieves.** *—tr.* 1. To accomplish; succeed in doing. 2. To attain or get as a result of one's efforts, skill, or perseverance: *We inched up the rock face until we achieved the ledge. —intr.* To attain a satisfactory standard: *schoolchildren who fail to achieve.* **—See Synonyms at** *perform, reach.* [Middle English *acheven*, from Old French *achever*, "to bring to a head," from *a chef*, "to a head" : *a*, to, from Latin *ad-* + *chef*, head, from Latin *caput.*] **—a·chiev·a·ble** *adj.* **—a·chiev·er** *n.*

a·chieve·ment (ə-chēv′mənt) *n.* 1. The act of accomplishing, attaining, or finishing something. 2. Something that has been accomplished successfully, especially by means of skill, practice, or perseverance. 3. *Heraldry.* A coat of arms.

A·chil·les (ə-kĭl′ēz). *Greek Legend.* The greatest of the Greek warriors at the siege of Troy, who killed the Trojan Hector and was himself later killed by Paris. He was the son of Peleus and Thetis.

Achilles' heel *n.* A small but significant weakness; a vulnerable point. [From Achilles' being vulnerable only in the heel.]

Achilles' tendon *n.* The large tendon running from the heel bone to the calf muscle of the leg.

Ach·ill Island (ăk′ĭl). A rugged and mountainous island in the Republic of Ireland off the west coast of County Mayo. With an area of 148 square kilometers (57 square miles), it is the largest offshore Irish island.

a·chi·o·te (ä′chē-ō′tē) *n.* The seeds of the **annatto** (see) or a preparation made from them, used to flavor and impart a yellow or reddish color to various foods. [Spanish, from Nahuatl (Aztec) *achi(y)otl.*]

Achitophel. See **Ahithophel.**

ach·la·myd·e·ous (ăk′lə-mĭd′ē-əs) *adj. Botany.* Having no floral envelope; without calyx or corolla. [A- (not) + CHLAMYDEOUS.]

a·chon·drite (ā-kŏn′drīt′) *n.* A stony meteorite that contains no **chondrules** (see). **—a·chon·drit·ic** (ā′kŏn-drĭt′ĭk) *adj.*

a·chon·dro·pla·si·a (ā-kŏn′drō-plā′zhē-ə) *n.* Abnormal development of cartilage at the ends of the long bones, resulting in congenital dwarfism. [A- (not) + CHONDRO- + -PLASIA.] **—a·chon·dro·plas·tic** (ā-kŏn′drō-plăs′tĭk) *adj.*

acorn *The fruit of the oak was once an important food used for raising pigs. In England's New Forest, farmers still exercise the ancient right of pannage, when pigs are let loose to feed on the acorns that fall in the autumn.*

ach·ro·mat·ic (ăk'rə-măt'ĭk) *adj.* **1.** Free from color; having no hue. Said of neutral colors like gray, black, and white. **2.** *Optics.* Refracting light without spectral color separation. **3.** *Biology.* Not readily absorbing color from standard dyes. **4.** *Music.* Having only the diatonic tones of the scale. [Greek *akhrōmatos,* colorless : *a-,* not, without + *khrōma,* color.] —**ach·ro·mat·i·cal·ly** *adv.* —**a·chro·ma·tism** (ā-krō'mə-tĭz'əm), **a·chro·ma·tic·i·ty** (ā-kro'mə-tĭs'ə-tē) *n.*

achromatic lens *n.* A combination of lenses to produce images free of chromatic aberrations.

a·chro·ma·tize (ā-krō'mə-tīz') *tr.v.* **-tized, -tizing, -tizes.** To make achromatic; rid of color.

a·chro·ma·tous (ā-krō'mə-təs) *adj.* **1.** Without color. **2.** With less color than is usual or needed. [Greek *akhrōmatos,* ACHROMATIC.]

a·chro·mic (ā-krō'mĭk) *adj.* Also **a·chro·mous** (ā-krō'məs). Colorless. [A- (not) + CHROMIC.]

a·cic·u·la (ə-sĭk'yə-lə) *n., pl.* **-lae** (-lē'). A needlelike object or part, such as a bristle, spine, or crystal. [New Latin, from Latin *acicula,* hairpin, diminutive of *acus,* needle.] —**a·cic·u·lar, a·cic·u·late** (ə-sĭk'yə-lĭt, -lāt'), **a·cic·u·lat·ed** *adj.*

ac·id (ăs'ĭd) *n.* **1.** *Chemistry.* **a.** Any of a large class of substances, the aqueous solutions of which can turn litmus indicators red, can react with and dissolve certain metals to form salts, can react with bases or alkalis to form salts, or have a sour taste. **b.** A substance that ionizes in solution to give the positive ion of the solvent. **c.** A substance capable of giving up a proton. **d.** Any molecule or ion that can combine with another by forming a covalent bond with two electrons of the other. In this sense, also called "Lewis acid." **2.** A substance with a sour taste. **3.** *Slang.* A hallucinogen, **LSD** *(see).* **4.** A sarcastic, bitter, or scornful quality: *a letter oozing with acid.*

~*adj.* **1.** *Chemistry.* **a.** Of or pertaining to an acid. **b.** Having a high concentration of acid. **2.** Having a sour taste. **3.** Having or indicative of a biting, sharp, or unkind nature; caustic: *an acid wit.* **4.** *Geology.* Designating an igneous rock containing more than 66 percent silica. **5.** Designating soil having a pH value below 7.2. [Latin *acidus,* sharp, sour, from *acēre,* to be sour, akin to *ācer,* sharp.] —**ac·id·ly** *adv.* —**ac·id·ness** *n.*

ac·id-fast (ăs'ĭd-făst', -fäst') *adj.* Not readily decolorized by acid. Said of stained tissues and microorganisms. —**ac·id-fast·ness** *n.*

a·cid-head (ăs'ĭd-hĕd) *n. Slang.* A person who habitually uses the drug LSD.

a·cid·ic (ə-sĭd'ĭk) *adj.* **1.** Acid. **2.** Tending to form an acid.

a·cid·i·fy (ə-sĭd'ə-fī') *v.* **-fied, -fying, -fies.** —*tr.* To make acid. —*intr.* To become acid. —**a·cid·i·fi·a·ble** *adj.* —**a·cid·i·fi·ca·tion** (ə-sĭd'ə-fĭ-kā'shən) *n.* —**a·cid·i·fi·er** *n.*

ac·i·dim·e·ter (ăs'ĭ-dĭm'ə-tər) *n.* A hydrometer used to determine the relative density of acid solutions. Also called "acidometer." —**ac·i·di·met·ric** (ăs'ĭ-dĭ-mĕt'rĭk) *adj.* —**ac·i·dim·e·try** *n.*

a·cid·i·ty (ə-sĭd'ə-tē) *n.* **1.** The state, quality, or degree of being acid. **2.** *Medicine.* Excessive acidity, **hyperacidity** *(see).*

ac·i·do·phil·ic (ăs'ĭ-dō-fĭl'ĭk) *adj. Microbiology.* **1.** Growing well in an acid medium. **2.** Easily stained with acid dyes. [ACID + -PHILIC.] —**a·cid·o·phil** (ə-sĭd'ə-fĭl'), **a·cid·o·phile** (ə-sĭd'ə-fīl') *n.*

ac·i·doph·i·lus milk (ăs'ĭ-dŏf'ə-ləs) *n.* Milk containing bacterial cultures that thrive in dilute acid, often used in treating gastrointestinal disorders. [New Latin *acidophilus,* "acid-loving" : Latin *acidus,* ACID + -PHILOUS.]

ac·i·do·sis (ăs'ĭ-dō'sĭs) *n.* A condition of pathologically high acidity of the blood and body tissues. —**ac·i·dot·ic** (ăs'ĭ-dŏt'ĭk) *adj.*

acid precipitation *n.* Precipitation having an abnormally high sulfuric and nitric acid content caused by industrial pollution.

acid rain *n.* Acid precipitation falling as rain.

acid rock *n.* A type of rock music supposedly inspired by the drug LSD, characterized by freely improvised instrumental passages.

acid salt *n.* A salt of a polybasic acid in which one or more acid hydrogen atoms have not been replaced by positive ions, as in sodium bicarbonate ($NaHCO_3$).

acid test *n.* A rigorous or decisive test of worth or quality. [From the test of gold in nitric acid.]

a·cid·u·late (ə-sĭj'ə-lāt') *tr.v.* **-lated, -lating, -lates.** To make slightly acid. [ACIDUL(OUS) + -ATE.] —**a·cid·u·la·tion** *n.*

a·cid·u·lous (ə-sĭj'ə-ləs) *adj.* **1.** Rather sour in taste. **2.** Sour in feeling or manner; biting; caustic. [Latin *acidulus,* sourish, diminutive of *acidus,* sour, ACID.]

acid value *n.* The amount of free acid in a fat, oil, or the like, expressed as the number of milligrams of potassium hydroxide necessary to neutralize the free acid in one gram of the substance.

ac·i·er·ate (ăs'ē-ə-rāt') *tr.v.* **-ated, -ating, -ates.** To convert (iron) into steel. [French *acier,* steel, from Latin *aciēs,* sharpness, from *ācer,* sharp + -ATE.] —**ac·i·er·a·tion** (ăs'ē-ə-rā'shən) *n.*

ac·i·nac·i·form (ăs'ĭ-năs'ə-fôrm') *adj. Botany.* Resembling a scimitar in shape: *acinaciform leaves.* [Latin *acinācēs,* short saber, from Greek *akinakēs,* from Iranian + -FORM.]

ac·i·nar (ăs'ĭ-nər) *adj. Anatomy.* Of or pertaining to an acinus.

a·cin·i·form (ə-sĭn'ə-fôrm') *adj.* Having the shape of a cluster of grapes or of a berry such as the raspberry. [ACIN(US) + -FORM.]

ac·i·nous (ăs'ĭ-nəs) *adj.* Consisting of small lobules or acini.

ac·i·nus (ăs'ĭ-nəs) *n., pl.* **-ni** (-nī'). **1.** *Botany.* Any of the small divisions or drupelets of an aggregate fruit such as the raspberry. **2.** The stone or seed of a grape or berry. **3.** *Anatomy.* Any of the small saclike dilations composing a compound gland. [New Latin, from Latin *acinus,* berry (especially a grape), probably of Mediterranean origin.]

-acious *suffix.* Indicates a tendency toward or abundance of something; for example, **fallacious.** [French *-acieux,* from Latin *-ācius* and *-āx* (stem *-āc-*), adjectival suffixes.]

-acity *suffix.* Indicates a quality or state of being; for example, **tenacity.** [French *acité,* from Latin *-ācitās,* from *-āx* (stem *-āc-*), -ACIOUS.]

ack-ack (ăk'ăk') *n. Military Slang.* **1.** An antiaircraft gun. **2.** Antiaircraft fire. Also used adjectivally: *an ack-ack gun.* [British telephonic code for *AA,* abbreviation for ANTIAIRCRAFT.]

ackee. Variant of **akee.**

ac·knowl·edge (ăk-nŏl'ĭj) *tr.v.* **-edged, -edging, -edges. 1.** To admit or accept the existence, reality, or fact of: *acknowledge one's mistakes.* **2.** To accept as valid or as having authority. **3. a.** To express recognition of. **b.** To express thanks or gratitude for. **4.** To report the receipt of. **5.** *Law.* To accept or certify as legally binding: *acknowledge a deed.* [Middle English, blend of *acknowen,* to recognize, acknowledge, Old English *oncnāwan* : *on,* ON + *cnāwan,* to KNOW and KNOWLEDGE.] —**ac·knowl·edge·a·ble** *adj.*

Synonyms: *admit, avow, concede, confess, own.*

ac·knowl·edg·ment, ac·knowl·edge·ment (ăk-nŏl'ĭj-mənt) *n.* **1.** The act of admitting, or accepting responsibility for, something. **2.** Recognition of someone's or something's existence, validity, authority, or right. **3.** An answer or response in return for something done. **4. a.** An expression or token of appreciation or thanks. **b. acknowledgments.** An author's expression of thanks, at the beginning or end of a book, to those who have helped him. **5.** A formal declaration made to authoritative witnesses to ensure legal validity.

a·clin·ic (ā-klĭn'ĭk) *adj. Geology.* Having no inclination or dip. [Greek *aklinēs,* not inclining to either side : *a-,* not + *klinein,* to lean.]

aclinic line *n.* The **magnetic equator** *(see).*

ACLU American Civil Liberties Union.

ac·me (ăk'mē) *n.* The highest point of attainment; the peak. —See Synonyms at **summit.** [Greek *akmē,* point, summit.]

ac·ne (ăk'nē) *n.* An inflammatory disease of the sebaceous glands, characterized by pimples on the face, neck, and upper torso, that is common in adolescents. [New Latin, misreading of Greek *akmē,* eruption on the face, point, ACME.]

ac·node (ăk'nōd') *n. Mathematics.* A point with coordinates that satisfy the equation of a curve, but that does not lie on the curve. Also called "isolated point." [Latin *acus,* needle + NODE (comparing the isolated point to a needle prick).]

a·cock (ə-kŏk') *adj.* In a cocked position. —**a·cock** *adv.*

ac·o·lyte (ăk'ə-līt') *n.* **1.** One who assists a priest in the performance of a religious service or ceremony; especially, in the Roman Catholic Church, an altar server who carries a candle. **2.** An attendant or follower. [Middle English *acolite,* from Old French, from Medieval Latin *acolytus,* variant of *acoluthus,* from Greek *akolouthos,* follower, following. See **anacoluthon.**]

A·con·ca·gua, Mount (ä'kōn-kä'gwä). A mountain in the Andes in western Argentina, near the Chilean border. It rises to 6,960 meters (22,835 feet), and until recent surveys revealed Ojos del Salado to be higher, it was regarded as the highest peak in the Western Hemisphere.

ac·o·nite (ăk'ə-nīt') *n.* **1.** Any plant of the genus *Aconitum,* such as **monkshood. 2.** The dried, poisonous root of monkshood, *A. napellus,* sometimes used in medicine to relieve pain or to reduce fever. [Latin *aconītum,* from Greek *akoniton,* possibly from *akonitos,* "dustless," unconquerable (with reference to the deadly properties of the plant) : *a-,* without + *-konitos,* "dusty," from *koniein,* to raise dust, struggle, from *konis,* dust.]

Açôres. See **Azores.**

a·corn (ā'kôrn', ā'kərn) *n.* The fruit of the oak tree, consisting of a thick-walled nut usually set in a woody, cuplike base. [Middle English, variant of *akern,* from Old English *æcern.*]

acorn barnacle *n.* A barnacle, such as *Balanus balanoides,* that lives attached to rocks and has a conical shell.

acorn tube *n.* A small, acorn-shaped vacuum tube used in very high frequency devices. Also *chiefly British* "acorn valve."

acorn worm *n.* Any of the wormlike marine animals with an acorn-shaped proboscis that belong to the genus *Balanoglossus* or related genera.

a·cot·y·le·don (ā'kŏt-ə-lēd'n) *n. Botany.* A plant having no cotyledons, or seed leaves, such as a moss or fern. —**a·cot·y·le·don·ous** (ā'kŏt-ə-lēd'ə-nəs) *adj.*

a·cous·tic (ə-ko͞o'stĭk) *adj.* Also **a·cous·ti·cal** (-stĭ-kəl). **1.** Of or pertaining to sound, the sense of hearing, or the science of sound. **2. a.** Designed to carry, absorb, or control sound: *an acoustic delay line.* **b.** Designating a device that is operated by sound waves: *an acoustic mine.* **c.** Designating a device that is designed to assist hearing: *an acoustic aid.* **3.** Not using electronic amplification. Said of a musical instrument, especially a guitar. [Greek *akoustikos,* pertaining to hearing, from *akouein,* to hear.] —**a·cous·ti·cal·ly** *adv.*

ac·ous·ti·cian (ăk'o͞o-stĭsh'ən) *n.* A specialist in acoustics.

acoustic nerve *n.* Either of the eighth pair of cranial nerves, each consisting of a *cochlear nerve,* which conducts acoustic stimuli to the brain, and a *vestibular nerve,* which conducts stimuli related to bodily equilibrium to the brain. Also called "auditory nerve," "vestibulocochlear nerve."

a·cous·tics (ə-ko͞o'stĭks) *n.* Also **a·cous·tic** (-tĭk) (for sense 2).

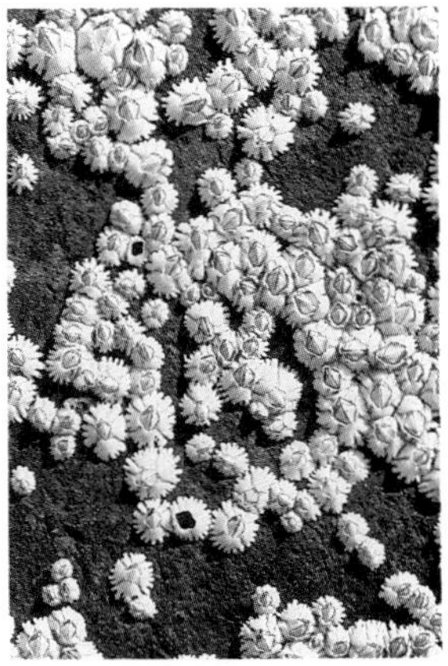

acorn barnacle *As a larva, the acorn barnacle has no bony shell. It floats freely in the sea until it lands on a suitable rock; then it uses a cement gland in its head to fix itself permanently to the spot. Once settled, it grows a shell with a hinged lid, which it opens at high tide to feed.*

PRONUNCIATION KEY

ă, pat; ā, pay; âr, care;
ä, father, are; b, bib;
ch, church; d, deed; ĕ, pet;
ē, be; f, fife; g, gag; h, hat;
hw, which; ĭ, pit; ī, pie;
îr, pier; j, judge; k, kick;
l, lid, needle; m, mum;
n, no, sudden; ng, thing;
ŏ, pot; ō, toe; ô, paw, for;
oi, noise; ou, out; o͝o, book;
o͞o, boot; p, pop; r, roar;
s, sauce; sh, ship, dish;
t, tight; th, thin, path;
th, this, bathe; ŭ, cut; ûr, fur;
v, valve; w, with; y, yes;
z, zebra, size; zh, vision;
ə, about, item, edible, gallop, circus, peaceful

IN FOREIGN WORDS:

à, *Fr.* ami; œ, *Fr.* feu, *Ger.* schön; ü, *Fr.* tu, *Ger.* über;
KH, *Ger.* ich, *Scot.* loch;
N, *Fr.* bon; y', *Fr.* Compiègne

STRESS MARKS:

Primary stress: '
in·cite' (ĭn-sīt')
Secondary stress: '
in'sight' (ĭn'sīt')

1. *Used with a singular verb.* The scientific study of sound, especially of its production, perception, and interaction with materials and other forms of radiation. **2.** *Used with a plural verb.* The quality and fidelity of the sound experienced in a particular room, auditorium, or other enclosed space: *a hall with poor acoustics.*

ac·quaint (ə-kwānt') *tr.v.* **-quainted, -quainting, -quaints. 1.** To make familiar. Used reflexively and with *with: acquaint oneself with the rules of the game.* **2.** To inform. Used with *with: acquaint someone with one's plans.* **3.** To cause to know personally. Used in the passive and with *with: I see you're already acquainted with each other.* [Middle English *aqueynten, acointen,* from Old French *acointer,* from Medieval Latin *accognitāre,* from Latin *accognitus,* past participle of *accognōscere,* to know perfectly : *ad-* (intensive) + *cognōscere,* to know : *co-, com-,* completely + *gnōscere,* to know.]

ac·quain·tance (ə-kwān'təns) *n.* **1.** Knowledge of or information about someone or something, especially when based on direct experience. **2.** Knowledge of a person acquired by a relationship less intimate than friendship. **3.** A person whom one knows, but who is not a close friend. **—ac·quain·tance·ship** *n.*

ac·qui·esce (ăk'wē-ĕs') *intr.v.* **-esced, -escing, -esces.** To accept, consent, or comply passively or without protest. Often used with *in: acquiesce in a ruling.* **—See Synonyms at assent.** [Latin *acquiēscere,* to remain at rest, agree tacitly : *ad-,* at, to + *quiēscere,* to rest, from *quiēs,* rest, QUIET.]

ac·qui·es·cence (ăk'wē-ĕs'əns) *n.* **1.** Passive assent or agreement without protest. **2.** The state of acquiescing or a tendency to acquiesce. **3.** *Law.* Failure to object to something such as an infringement of a right, taken as signifying acceptance or consent. **—ac·qui·es·cent** *adj.* **—ac·qui·es·cent·ly** *adv.*

ac·quire (ə-kwīr') *tr.v.* **-quired, -quiring, -quires. 1.** To gain possession of. **2.** To get, especially by one's own efforts or qualities: *acquire a reputation for honesty.* **3.** To locate (an object in the atmosphere or in space) for the purpose of tracking: *acquire a target.* [Middle English *acqueren,* from Old French *acquerre,* from Latin *acquīrere,* to add to, get : *ad-,* in addition to + *quaerere,* to seek, obtain.]

acquired characteristic (ə-kwīrd') *n.* A nonhereditary change in an organ caused by use or disuse or by environmental factors.

acquired immune deficiency syndrome *n.* AIDS (see).

acquired taste *n.* Something that initially seems unpleasant, but for which one develops a liking.

ac·quire·ment (ə-kwīr'mənt) *n.* **1.** The act of acquiring. **2.** An attainment, such as a skill or social accomplishment.

ac·qui·si·tion (ăk'wə-zĭsh'ən) *n.* **1.** The act of acquiring. **2.** Something or someone acquired, especially as an addition to an established category or group. **3.** *Aerospace.* The process of locating a satellite, guided missile, or moving target so that its track or orbit can be determined. [Middle English *acquisicioun,* from Latin *acquīsītiō* (stem *acquīsītiōn-*), from *acquīrere,* to ACQUIRE.]

ac·quis·i·tive (ə-kwĭz'ə-tĭv) *adj.* **1.** Eager to acquire material possessions. **2.** Tending to acquire and retain ideas or information: *an acquisitive mind.* **—ac·quis·i·tive·ly** *adv.* **—ac·quis·i·tive·ness** *n.*

ac·quit (ə-kwĭt') *tr.v.* **-quitted, -quitting, -quits. 1.** To clear of a criminal charge; declare to be not guilty. **2.** To release or discharge from duty or obligation. **3.** To conduct (oneself) in a specified way: *In her first formal speech she acquitted herself well.* [Middle English *acquiten,* from Old French *aquiter,* from Vulgar Latin *acquītāre* (unattested), "to bring to rest," set free : *ad-,* to + *quitāre, quiētāre* (unattested), to put to rest, set free, from *quiēs,* QUIET.] **—ac·quit·ter** *n.*

ac·quit·tal (ə-kwĭt'l) *n.* The judgment of a jury or judge that a person is not guilty of a crime as charged.

ac·quit·tance (ə-kwĭt'əns) *n.* A written release from an obligation or debt.

a·cre (ā'kər) *n.* **1.** *Abbr.* **A, a., A.** A unit of area used in land measurement and equal to 4840 square yards or 4046.86 square meters or 0.4047 hectares. **2. acres.** Property in the form of land. **3.** *Usually* **acres.** *Informal.* A wide expanse of space: *acres of room.* [Middle English *acre,* Old English *æcer,* field, acre; akin to Latin *ager,* field.]

A·cre (ä'kər, ā'kər, ä'krə). *Hebrew* **Ak·ko** (äk'ō). *Arabic* **Ak·ka** (äk'ə). Town and port in northern Israel on the Bay of Haifa. During the Crusades it changed hands many times between Christians and Arabs. It finally fell to the Saracens in 1291 and became part of the Ottoman Empire in the 16th century. During World War I it was won by the British and became part of the Palestinian protectorate. Acre was ceded to the Arabs in the UN partition of Palestine (1948), but was captured by Israel shortly afterward.

a·cre·age (ā'kər-ĭj, ā'krĭj) *n.* Area of land in acres.

a·cred (ā'kərd) *adj.* Comprising or possessing many acres of land. Used chiefly in combination: *a many-acred estate.*

ac·rid (ăk'rĭd) *adj.* **1.** Harsh and irritating to the taste or smell. **2.** Bitterly caustic in language or tone. [From Latin *ācer* (stem *ācr-*), sharp, bitter (probably influenced by ACID).] **—a·crid·i·ty** (ə-krĭd'ə-tē), **ac·rid·ness** *n.* **—ac·rid·ly** *adv.*

ac·ri·dine (ăk'rĭ-dēn', -dĭn) *n.* A coal tar derivative, $C_{13}H_9N$, that has a strongly irritating odor and is used in the manufacture of dyes and synthetics.

ac·ri·fla·vine (ăk'rĭ-flā'vēn') *n.* A brown or orange powder, $C_{14}H_{14}N_3Cl$, derived from acridine and used as an antiseptic. [ACRI(DINE) + FLAVIN.]

ac·ri·mo·ni·ous (ăk'rĭ-mō'nē-əs) *adj.* Bitter and caustic in speech,

tone, or manner; rancorous. **—ac·ri·mo·ni·ous·ly** *adv.* **—ac·ri·mo·ni·ous·ness** *n.*

ac·ri·mo·ny (ăk'rĭ-mō'nē) *n.* Bitterness or ill-natured animosity, especially in speech or manner. [Latin *ācrimōnia,* sharpness, from *ācer,* sharp.]

acro– *prefix.* Indicates: **1.** A height or summit; for example, **acrophobia. 2.** An outer end, tip, or point; for example, **acrogen. 3.** An extremity of the body; for example, **acromegaly.** [Greek *akros,* topmost, extreme.]

ac·ro·bat (ăk'rə-băt') *n.* **1.** A performer, as in a circus, who is skilled in feats of agility and balance. **2.** One adept at quick changes of position, political stance, or the like. [French *acrobate,* from Greek *akrobatēs,* "one who walks on tiptoe," from *akrobatein,* to walk on tiptoe : ACRO- + *bat-,* stem of *bainein,* to walk.] **—ac·ro·bat·ic** (ăk'rə-băt'ĭk) *adj.* **—ac·ro·bat·i·cal·ly** *adv.*

ac·ro·bat·ics (ăk'rə-băt'ĭks) *n.* **1.** *Used with a singular verb.* The art of an acrobat. **2.** *Used with a plural verb.* The feats performed by an acrobat. **3.** *Used with a plural verb.* Any manifestation of spectacular mental or physical agility.

ac·ro·car·pous (ăk'rō-kär'pəs) *adj. Botany.* Having the spore-bearing capsule at the end or top of a leafy stem or stalk, as in many mosses. [New Latin *acrocarpus,* from Greek *akrokarpos,* bearing fruit at the top : ACRO- + -CARPOUS.]

ac·ro·cy·a·no·sis (ăk'rō-sī'ə-nō'sĭs) *n.* Slow circulation of the blood through the small vessels in the skin, resulting in bluish-purple discoloration of the hands and feet.

ac·ro·dont (ăk'rə-dŏnt') *adj. Zoology.* Having or designating teeth that lack roots and are fused to the bony ridge of the jaw, as in certain reptiles. [ACR(O)- + -ODONT.]

ac·ro·drome (ăk'rə-drōm') *adj.* Also **a·crod·ro·mous** (ə-krŏd'rə-məs). Designating a pattern of leaf venation in which there are two or more main veins, each terminating at the leaf tip. [ACRO- + -DROMOUS.]

ac·ro·gen (ăk'rə-jən) *n.* A flowerless plant, such as a fern or moss, in which all growth proceeds from the tip. [ACRO- + -GEN.] **—ac·ro·gen·ic** (ăk'rə-jĕn'ĭk), **a·crog·e·nous** (ə-krŏj'ə-nəs) *adj.* **—a·crog·e·nous·ly** *adv.*

a·cro·le·in (ə-krō'lē-ĭn) *n.* A colorless, flammable, poisonous liquid, $CH_2:CHCHO$, having an acrid odor and vapors dangerous to the eyes. Also called "propenal." [ACR(ID) + OLEIN.]

ac·ro·meg·a·ly (ăk'rō-mĕg'ə-lē) *n.* Pathological enlargement of the bones of the hands, feet, and face, resulting from excess production of growth hormone by the pituitary gland. [French *acromégalie,* "enlargement of extremities" : ACRO- + Greek *megal-,* stem of *megas,* big.] **—ac·ro·me·gal·ic** (ăk'rō-mĭ-găl'ĭk) *n. & adj.*

ac·ro·nym (ăk'rə-nĭm') *n.* A word formed from the initial letters of a name, such as *NATO,* from *North Atlantic Treaty Organization,* or by combining initial letters or parts of a series of words, such as *radar,* from *radio detecting and ranging.* [ACR(O)- + -ONYM.] **—ac·ro·nym·ic** (ăk'rə-nĭm'ĭk), **a·cron·y·mous** (ə-krŏn'ə-məs) *adj.*

a·crop·e·tal (ə-krŏp'ə-təl) *adj. Botany.* Developing upward toward the apex from the base, as certain forms of inflorescence do. [ACRO- + -PETAL.] **—a·crop·e·tal·ly** *adv.*

ac·ro·pho·bi·a (ăk'rə-fō'bē-ə) *n.* Abnormally intense fear of being in high places. [ACRO- + -PHOBIA.] **—ac·ro·pho·bic** *adj.*

a·crop·o·lis (ə-krŏp'ə-lĭs) *n.* **1.** The fortified citadel of an ancient Greek city. **2. the Acropolis.** The citadel of Athens, which is the site of the Parthenon. [Greek *akropolis,* "upper city" citadel : ACRO- + *polis,* city.]

ac·ro·some (ăk'rə-sōm') *n.* A structure in the head of a sperm that contains enzymes to break down the egg wall and allow fertilization. [ACRO- + -SOME (body).]

ac·ro·spire (ăk'rə-spīr') *n. Botany.* The first sprout from a germinating grain seed. [Variant (influenced by ACRO-) of dialectal *akerspire,* "ear-sprout" : *aker,* ear of grain, ultimately from Old English *æhher, ēar* + Middle English *spire,* Old English *spīr.*]

a·cross (ə-krôs', ə-krŏs') *prep.* **1.** On or at the other side of: *across the road.* **2.** So as to cross; over; through: *draw lines across the paper.* **3.** From one side of to the other: *a bridge across a river.* **4.** Extending throughout: *across all social classes.* *—adv.* **1.** From one side to the other: *The bridge swayed when he ran across.* **2.** On or to the opposite side: *We came across by ferry.* [Middle English *acros,* on *croice,* from Old French *a croix, en croix,* "in the form of a CROSS," hence "transversely."]

a·cross-the-board (ə-krôs'thə-bôrd', -bōrd', ə-krŏs'-) *adj.* **1.** Affecting all categories or members, especially in an occupation or industry: *an across-the-board wage increase.* **2.** Wagering equal amounts on the same contestant to win, place, or show: *an across-the-board bet in horse racing.*

a·cros·tic (ə-krôs'tĭk, ə-krŏs'-) *n.* A poem or series of lines in which certain letters, usually the first in each line, form a name, motto, or message when read in sequence. [French *acrostiche,* from Old French, from Greek *akrostikhis,* "end-line" : ACRO- + *stikhos,* line of verse.] **—a·cros·tic** *adj.* **—a·cros·ti·cal·ly** *adv.*

ac·ry·late resin (ăk'rĭ-lāt') *n.* Any of a class of acrylic resins used in emulsion paints, adhesives, plastics, and textile and paper finishes. Also called "acrylate."

a·cryl·ic (ə-krĭl'ĭk) *adj.* Based on or relating to acrylic acid. *—n.* **1.** Acrylic fiber. **2.** Acrylic resin. **3.** Acrylic paint. [ACR(O)-LEIN) + -YL + -IC.]

acrylic acid *n.* An easily polymerized, colorless, corrosive liquid, $H_2C:CHCOOH$, used as a monomer for acrylate resins. Also called "propenoic acid."

acrylic fiber *n.* Any of numerous synthetic fibers polymerized from acrylonitrile. Also called "acrylic."

acrylic paint *n.* A paint based on acrylic resin, which dries quickly to give a semigloss finish. Also called "acrylic."

acrylic resin *n.* Any of numerous thermoplastic or thermosetting polymers or copolymers of acrylic acid, methacrylic acid, esters of these acids, or acrylonitrile. They are used to produce synthetic rubbers, exceptionally clear, lightweight plastics resistant to weather and corrosion, and other resin forms for many manufactured products including aircraft canopies and windows, contact lenses, refrigerator parts, protective coatings, and lubricant additives. Also called "acrylic."

ac·ry·lo·ni·trile (ăk'rĭ-lō-nī'trəl) *n.* A colorless, liquid organic compound, H_2C:CHCN, used in the manufacture of acrylic rubber and fibers. [ACRYL(IC RESIN) + NITRILE.]

act (ăkt) *n.* **1.** The process of doing or performing something: *caught in the act of stealing.* **2. a.** Something that is done or performed; a deed: *a charitable act.* **b.** A deed indicative or symptomatic of a particular condition: *an act of faith; an act of lunacy.* **3.** An enactment, edict, or decree, as of a judicial or legislative body. **4.** *Usually* **acts.** A formal written record of proceedings or transactions. **5.** One of the major divisions or sections of a play, drama, or opera. **6.** A performance that forms part of a longer presentation, as in a variety show or circus: *a juggling act.* **7.** *Informal.* A display of insincere behavior; a pose: *put on an act.*
~*v.* **acted, acting, acts.** —*tr.* **1.** To play the part of; assume the dramatic role of. **2.** To perform on the stage: *act a drama.* **3.** To behave like or pose as; impersonate: *act the fool.* **4.** To behave in a manner appropriate to: *Act your age.* **5.** *Obsolete.* To activate; animate. —*intr.* **1.** To behave or conduct oneself: *He acts as if he owns the place.* **2. a.** To perform in a dramatic role or roles; be an actor. **b.** To be suitable for theatrical performance: *This scene acts well.* **3.** To behave affectedly or unnaturally; pretend; pose. **4.** To take action; do something: *promised to act on my suggestion.* **5.** To operate or function in a specified way: *His mind acts quickly.* **6.** To function in a particular capacity; serve: *This valve acts as an additional safeguard.* **7.** To perform actions or duties as a substitute for someone or something else: *A coin can act as a screwdriver.* **8.** To produce a desired or characteristic effect: *The drug will act in an hour.* —**act out. 1.** To express by acting or mime. **2.** To enact. —**act up.** *Informal.* To misbehave, malfunction, or give trouble. [Middle English *acte,* from Latin *āctus,* the process of action, and *āctum,* a thing done, both from *āctus,* past participle of *agere,* to drive, to do.] —**ac·ta·bil·i·ty** (ăk'tə-bĭl'ə-tē) *n.* —**act·a·ble** *adj.*

Usage: The nouns *act* and *action* are distinct in meaning. An *act* is the deed accomplished by means of an *action*; when Brutus killed Caesar, he committed the *act* of murder by means of the *action* of stabbing. We speak of a *stop-action movie camera* (i.e., one that can arrest physical motion), but a criminal is *caught in the act* (i.e., of committing a crime). A baseball pitcher may throw with an *unnatural action* (i.e., a physical movement difficult for the human arm); a parent who abandons a child performs an *unnatural act* (the deed is contrary to nature, not the series of activities with which it is performed).

A.C.T. Australian Capital Territory.

Ac·tae·on (ăk-tē'ən). *Greek Mythology.* A young hunter who, having inadvertently observed Artemis while she was bathing, was turned by her into a stag and killed by his own dogs.

ACTH *n.* A pituitary hormone synthesized or extracted from mammalian pituitaries for use in stimulating secretion of cortisone and other adrenal cortex hormones. Also called "corticotropin." [*A*drenocortico*t*ropic *h*ormone.]

ac·tin (ăk'tĭn) *n.* A muscle protein, active with myosin in muscular contraction. [Latin *āctus,* an ACT + -IN.]

ac·ti·nal (ăk'tĭ-nəl, ăk-tī'-) *adj. Zoology.* Of or designating the part of a sea anemone or similar animal from which the tentacles or rays radiate. [ACTIN(O)- + -AL.] —**ac·ti·nal·ly** *adv.*

act·ing (ăk'tĭng) *adj.* **1.** *Abbr.* **a.** Temporarily assuming the duties or authority of another: *acting chairman.* **2.** Containing directions for use in a dramatic performance: *an acting text.*
~*n.* The art or occupation of an actor.

ac·tin·i·a (ăk-tĭn'ē-ə) *n., pl.* **-iae** (-ē-ē'). Also **ac·tin·i·an** (-ən). A sea anemone, or a related animal. [New Latin *actinia,* "the radially structured ones," from Greek *aktis* (stem *aktin-*), ray.]

ac·tin·ic (ăk-tĭn'ĭk) *adj.* Of, pertaining to, or designating electromagnetic radiation, such as ultraviolet radiation, that can produce chemical change. [ACTIN(O)- + -IC.] —**ac·tin·i·cal·ly** *adv.*

ac·ti·nide (ăk'tĭ-nīd') *n.* Any of a series of chemically similar, mostly synthetic, radioactive elements with atomic numbers ranging from 89 (actinium) to 103 (lawrencium). Also called "actinoid." [ACTIN(O)- + -IDE.]

ac·ti·nism (ăk'tĭn-ĭz'əm) *n.* The intrinsic property in radiation that produces photochemical activity. [ACTIN(O)- + -ISM.]

ac·tin·i·um (ăk-tĭn'ē-əm) *n. Symbol* **Ac** A radioactive element found in uranium ores and used, in equilibrium with its decay products, as a source of alpha rays. Its longest lived isotope is Ac 227 with a half-life of 21.7 years. Atomic number 89, melting point 1,050°C, boiling point (estimated) 3,200°C, specific gravity (calculated) 10.07, valence 3. [New Latin : ACTIN(O)- + -IUM.]

actino-, actin- *prefix.* Indicates: **1.** Radial or tentacled structure; for example, **actinoid. 2.** Radiation or radioactivity; for example, **actinometer.** [New Latin, from Greek *aktis,* ray.]

ac·ti·noid (ăk'tĭ-noid') *adj.* Having a radial form, as a starfish.
~*n. Chemistry.* An actinide. [ACTIN(O)- + -OID.]

ac·tin·o·lite (ăk-tĭn'ə-līt') *n. Mineralogy.* A greenish variety of **amphibole** *(see).* [ACTINO- (from its radiated forms) + -LITE.]

ac·ti·nom·e·ter (ăk'tĭ-nŏm'ə-tər) *n.* Any of several instruments for measuring the intensity of radiation. [ACTINO- + -METER.] —**ac·ti·no·met·ric** (ăk'tĭ-nō-mĕt'rĭk) *adj.* —**ac·ti·nom·e·try** *n.*

ac·ti·no·mor·phic (ăk'tĭ-nō-môr'fĭk) *adj.* Also **ac·ti·no·mor·phous** (-fəs). *Biology.* Having radial symmetry; divisible vertically through two or more planes into similar halves. Compare **zygomorphic.** [ACTINO- + -MORPHIC.]

ac·ti·no·my·cete (ăk'tĭ-nō-mī'sēt') *n.* Any of numerous generally filamentous and often pathogenic microorganisms of the order Actinomycetales, resembling both bacteria and fungi. [ACTINO- + -MYCETE.]

ac·ti·no·my·cin (ăk'tĭ-nō-mī'sĭn) *n.* Any of various often toxic antibiotic substances found in soil bacteria and used to treat some forms of cancer. [New Latin *Actinomyces,* a genus of soil bacteria : ACTINO- + Greek *mukēs,* fungus (see **-mycin**).]

ac·ti·no·my·co·sis (ăk'tĭ-nō-mī-kō'sĭs) *n.* An inflammatory infection of cattle, pigs, and sometimes man, caused by microorganisms of the genus *Actinomyces,* and characterized by lumpy tumors of the neck, chest, and abdomen. Also called "lumpy jaw." [ACTINO- + MYCOSIS.] —**ac·ti·no·my·cot·ic** (ăk'tĭ-nō-mī-kŏt'ĭk) *adj.*

ac·ti·non (ăk'tĭ-nŏn') *n. Symbol* **An** A radioactive inert gaseous isotope of radon, with a half-life of 3.92 seconds. [ACTIN(O)- + -ON.]

ac·ti·no·u·ra·ni·um (ăk'tĭ-nō-yŏŏ-rā'nē-əm) *n.* The isotope of uranium with mass number 235, fissionable with slow neutrons.

ac·ti·no·zo·an (ăk'tĭ-nō-zō'ən) *n. Zoology.* An **anthozoan** *(see).* [New Latin *actinozoa,* "the radiated life-forms" : ACTINO- + -ZOA.]

ac·tion (ăk'shən) *n.* **1.** The state or process of acting, functioning, or doing; the condition of exerting energy or being in operation: *sprang into action; temporarily out of action.* **2.** Something done; an act or deed: *Actions speak louder than words.* **3.** Movement, posture, or gesture. **4.** Style or manner of movement: *a horse with good action.* **5.** Activity; initiative; especially, organized activity in support of a cause or group: *The authorities decided to take action.* **6.** The exertion or transmission of energy, force, or influence: *the action of water on a stone.* **7. a.** The operating parts of a mechanism: *the action of a gun.* **b.** The way in which a mechanism works. **8.** The series of events and episodes that form the plot of a story or play. **9.** A judicial process; a lawsuit, especially one undertaken to obtain redress or enforce a claim. **10. a.** Armed combat: *troops sent into action.* **b.** A military engagement. **11.** *Slang.* The most important or exciting activity in a field: *For a banker, New York is where the action is.* **12.** *Slang.* The activity of betting or gambling.

ac·tion·a·ble (ăk'shən-ə-bəl) *adj.* Giving just cause for legal action. —**ac·tion·a·bly** *adv.*

action painting *n.* A school of abstract painting that exploits the random effects of spontaneous techniques such as dribbling and splattering paint onto the canvas. See **tachisme.** —**action painter** *n.*

action potential *n.* The voltage change occurring across the membrane of a nerve or muscle cell during transmission of a nerve impulse.

action replay *n. British.* An **instant replay** *(see).*

action stations *pl.n.* The positions taken up by members of a military force prior to going into action.
~*interj.* Used as a signal to order troops to take up positions ready to go into action.

Ac·ti·um (ăk'tə-əm, ăk'shē-əm). A promontory in ancient Greece, at the mouth of the Ambracian Gulf. In 31 B.C. it was the scene of a sea and land battle in which the forces of Octavian (later the emperor Augustus) led by Agrippa decisively defeated Mark Antony and Cleopatra.

ac·ti·vate (ăk'tə-vāt') *tr.v.* **-vated, -vating, -vates. 1.** To set in motion or action; make active. **2.** To set up or organize (a military unit or post, for example). **3.** To purify (sewage) by aeration. **4.** *Chemistry.* To accelerate a reaction in, as by heat. **5.** *Physics.* To make radioactive. —**ac·ti·va·tion** (ăk'tə-vā'shən) *n.* —**ac·ti·va·tor** *n.*

ac·ti·vat·ed alumina (ăk'tə-vā'tĭd) *n.* Highly adsorbent aluminum oxide in granular form, used to filter oil, dry gases, or catalyze a reaction.

activated carbon *n.* Highly adsorbent carbon obtained by heating granulated charcoal to exhaust contained gases, used in gas absorption, solvent recovery, or deodorization, and as an antidote to certain poisons. Also called "activated charcoal."

activated sludge *n.* A mass of sewage through which compressed air has been blown or which has been aerated by mechanical agitation. It is added to untreated sewage to increase the rate of bacterial decomposition.

ac·tive (ăk'tĭv) *adj.* **1.** In a state of action, motion, or operation. **2.** Given to or characterized by action or activity; lively; vigorous: *an active mind; over eighty, but still active.* **3.** Producing action or change; especially, producing a particular or characteristic effect: *an active ingredient.* **4.** Marked by or engaging in effective or productive activity; contributing; participating: *an active member of a club; gave active encouragement to the conspirators.* **5.** Capable of action or effective operation; not passive or dormant: *an active volcano.* **6.** Characterized by energetic action or activity; busy. **7. a.** Designating a verb inflection or voice indicating that the subject of the sentence is performing or causing the action expressed by the verb. In the sentence *John bought a book, bought* is in the active voice. Compare **passive. b.** Expressing action rather than a state of

PRONUNCIATION KEY

ă, pat; ā, pay; âr, care;
ä, father, are; b, bib;
ch, church; d, deed; ĕ, pet;
ē, be; f, fife; g, gag; h, hat;
hw, which; ĭ, pit; ī, pie;
îr, pier; j, judge; k, kick;
l, lid, needle; m, mum;
n, no, sudden; ng, thing;
ŏ, pot; ō, toe; ô, paw, for;
oi, noise; ou, out; ŏŏ, book;
ōō, boot; p, pop; r, roar;
s, sauce; sh, ship, dish;
t, tight; th, thin, path;
th, this, bathe; ŭ, cut; ûr, fur;
v, valve; w, with; y, yes;
z, zebra, size; zh, vision;
ə, about, item, edible,
gallop, circus, peaceful

IN FOREIGN WORDS:

à, *Fr.* ami; œ, *Fr.* feu, *Ger.* schön; ü, *Fr.* tu, *Ger.* über; KH, *Ger.* ich, *Scot.* loch; N, *Fr.* bon; y', *Fr.* Compiègne

STRESS MARKS:

Primary stress: '
in·cite' (ĭn-sīt')
Secondary stress: '
in'sight' (ĭn'sīt')

being. Said of verbs such as *run, speak, move.* **8.** Producing profit, interest, or dividends: *active accounts.* **9.** Marked by or engaging in full military duties: *on active service; active troops.*
~*n.* **1.** The active voice. **2.** A construction or form in the active voice. [Middle English, from Old French *actif,* from Latin *āctīvus,* from *āctus,* ACT.] —**ac·tive·ly** *adv.* —**ac·tive·ness** *n.*

    Synonyms: *dynamic, energetic, lively, vigorous.*

ac·tiv·ist (ăk′tĭv-ĭst) *n.* One who favors vigorous and direct action, especially in support of a political cause. —**ac·tiv·ism** *n.*

ac·tiv·i·ty (ăk-tĭv′ə-tē) *n., pl.* **-ties. 1.** The state or condition of being active. **2.** Energetic action or movement. **3.** A pursuit or occupation, especially when recreational. **4.** The intensity of a radioactive source.

act of God *n. Law.* An unforeseeable or inevitable occurrence, such as a tornado, caused by nature and not by man.

ac·to·my·o·sin (ăk′tō-mī′ə-sĭn) *n.* A system of actin and myosin

BRITAIN'S GREATEST CLASSICAL ARCHITECT
Robert Adam designed houses down to the last detail

Robert Adam (1728–82) led the neoclassical movement in British domestic architecture and was the outstanding exponent of this revived classical style. The most gifted of four Scots architect brothers, he lived for four years in Italy, where his intensive study of classical antiquities, particularly the Palace of Diocletian at Spalato (now Split, Yugoslavia), inspired him to develop his own style. In 1763 he went into partnership in London with his brother James and together, by a series of romantically elegant variations on classical originals, they transformed the prevailing Palladian fashion.

But Robert Adam was more than a distinguished architect. He was equally outstanding as an interior designer and planned and executed his houses down to the last detail of fireplaces, plasterwork, furniture, carpets, and door fittings. His interior designs, characterized by the use of the oval, lines of decorative motifs in plaster, and painted panels in low relief, were also based on ancient Greek and Roman designs. Adam created complete harmony of exterior and interior. Commissions poured in, and in the last year of his life he designed 25 private houses and eight public buildings.

Among his works in and around London are Kenwood House, Syon House, Osterley Park, and 20 Portman Square, his finest town house. His other works include Charlotte Square in Edinburgh; Harefield House, Yorkshire; and Kedleston Hall, Derbyshire.

OSTERLEY PARK DRAWING ROOM *Horace Walpole described it as "worthy of Eve before the Fall." The rich effects of the ornamented ceiling and complementary pattern in the carpet are enhanced by the silk-brocaded walls.*

OSTERLEY PARK HOUSE *Adam's modernization of a Tudor house is a perfect example of his style of complete harmony of exterior and interior. His work on the house took almost 20 years to complete.*

that with other substances constitutes muscle fiber and is responsible for muscular contraction. [ACT(IN) + MYOSIN.]

ac·tor (ăk′tər) *n.* **1.** A performer in a play, film, or broadcast. **2.** One who takes part; a participant.

ac·tress (ăk′trĭs) *n.* A female actor.

Acts of the Apostles *n. Used with a singular verb.* The fifth book of the New Testament. Also called "Acts."

ac·tu·al (ăk′chōō-əl) *adj.* **1.** Existing in fact, rather than in theory or imagination; real: *The actual cost far exceeded the original estimate.* **2.** Being, existing, or acting at the present moment. —*See Synonyms at* **real.** [Middle English *actuel,* from Old French, from Late Latin *āctuālis,* "pertaining to acts," from Latin *āctus,* an ACT.]

ac·tu·al·i·ty (ăk′chōō-ăl′ə-tē) *n., pl.* **-ties. 1.** The state or fact of being actual; reality. **2.** actualities. Actual conditions or facts.

ac·tu·al·ize (ăk′chōō-ə-līz′) *tr.v.* **-ized, -izing, -izes. 1.** To make actual; realize in action. **2.** To describe or portray realistically. —**ac·tu·al·i·za·tion** (ăk′chōō-ə-lə-zā′shən) *n.*

ac·tu·al·ly (ăk′chōō-ə-lē, ăk′chə-lē) *adv.* **1.** In fact; in reality. **2.** Believe it or not: *I not only gambled, I actually won.*

ac·tu·ar·y (ăk′chōō-ĕr′ē) *n., pl.* **-ies.** A statistician who calculates insurance risks and premiums. [Latin *āctuārius,* secretary of accounts, from *āctus,* public employment, state business, the process of action, ACT.] —**ac·tu·ar·i·al** (ăk′chōō-ĕr′ē-əl) *adj.*

ac·tu·ate (ăk′chōō-āt′) *tr.v.* **-ated, -ating, -ates. 1.** To put into action or motion: *actuate a mechanism.* **2.** To move to action; impel: *actuated by greed.* [Medieval Latin *āctuāre,* from Latin *āctus,* an ACT.] —**ac·tu·a·tion** (ăk′chōō-ā′shən) *n.* —**ac·tu·a·tor** *n.*

a·cu·i·ty (ə-kyōō′ə-tē) *n.* Keenness, sharpness, or acuteness, especially of the senses or the mind: *visual acuity.* [Middle English *acuitie,* from Medieval Latin *acuitās,* from Latin *acuere,* to sharpen, from *acus,* needle.]

a·cu·le·ate (ə-kyōō′lē-ĭt, -āt′) *adj.* **1.** Having a sting, as a bee does. **2.** Having prickles or thorns. [Latin *aculeātus,* from *aculeus,* diminutive of *acus,* needle, sting. See **acuity.**]

a·cu·men (ə-kyōō′mən) *n.* The ability to make quick, shrewd, and accurate judgments; keenness of insight. [Latin *acūmen,* (mental) sharpness, from *acuere,* to sharpen, from *acus,* needle.]

a·cu·mi·nate (ə-kyōō′mə-nĭt, -nāt′) *adj. Biology.* Tapering to a sharp point: *acuminate leaves.* [Latin *acūminātus,* past participle of *acūmināre,* to sharpen, from *acūmen,* sharpness, ACUMEN.] —**a·cu·mi·na·tion** *n.*

ac·u·punc·ture (ăk′yŏŏ-pŭngk′chər) *n.* A traditional Chinese therapeutic technique whereby fine needles are inserted into the skin at particular points. This may stimulate nerves, causing the pituitary gland to release painkilling endorphins. Also called "stylostixis." [Latin *acū,* with a needle, from *acus,* needle + PUNCTURE.]

a·cut·ance (ə-kyōō′təns) *n.* The sharpness of outline in a photograph.

a·cute (ə-kyōōt′) *adj.* **1.** Having a sharp point or tip; not blunt. **2.** Keenly perceptive or discerning; shrewd; penetrating. **3.** Reacting readily to impressions; sensitive: *an acute sense of smell.* **4.** Serious enough to cause concern; critical; severe: *acute shortages.* **5.** Having a powerful, usually unpleasant, effect; keen; intense: *acute pain.* **6.** *Medicine.* Reaching a crisis rapidly. Said of a disease. Compare **chronic. 7.** *Music.* High in pitch; shrill. **8.** *Geometry.* **a.** Designating an angle less than 90°. **b.** Designating a triangle with all three interior angles less than 90°. —*See Synonyms at* **critical, sharp.** [Latin *acūtus,* sharp, from *acuere,* to sharpen, from *acus,* needle.] —**a·cute·ly** *adv.* —**a·cute·ness** *n.*

acute accent *n.* A mark (′) indicating: **1.** A raised pitch or rising tone, in certain languages such as Chinese and Ancient Greek. **2.** Primary stress of a spoken sound or syllable. **3.** Metrical stress in poetry. **4.** A particular sound quality or vowel length in certain languages such as French.

a·cy·clic (ā-sī′klĭk, ā-sĭk′lĭk) *adj.* **1.** *Botany.* Not having or forming whorls; not cyclic. **2.** *Chemistry.* Having an open-chain molecular structure rather than a ring-shaped structure.

ac·yl (ăs′əl) *n. Chemistry.* Any radical having the general formula RCO-, derived from an organic acid. [AC(ID) + -YL.]

ad¹ (ăd) *n. Informal.* An advertisement.

ad² *n.* In racket games, an **advantage** *(see).*

ad– *prefix.* Indicates motion toward; for example, **adhere.** [Latin, from *ad,* to, toward, at. In borrowed Latin compounds *ad-* indicates: **1.** Motion toward, as in **advent. 2.** Proximity, as in **adjacent. 3.** Addition, increase, as in **accrue. 4.** Relationship, dependence, as in **adjunct. 5.** Intensified action, as in **accelerate.** Before *c, f, g, l, n, q, r, s,* and *t, ad-* is assimilated to *ac-, af-, ag-, al-, an-, acq-, ar-, as-,* and *at-;* before *sc, sp, st,* and *gn,* it is reduced to *a-*.]

–ad *suffix. Biology.* Indicates direction toward a specified anatomical part; for example, **dorsad.** [Coined from Latin *ad,* toward.]

A.D. anno Domini (usually small capitals A.D.).

    Usage: In formal usage, A.D. precedes the date, which is always a specific year rather than a century: *He died A.D. 961* (not *in the tenth century A.D.*). Informally it is often used like B.C., which always follows the date and may be applied to any specified period (year, century, or era). When neither abbreviation appears, the time is assumed to be after Christ.

A.D.A. 1. American Dental Association. **2.** Americans for Democratic Action.

a·dac·ty·lous (ā-dăk′tə-ləs) *adj.* Having no fingers or toes.

ad·age (ăd′ĭj) *n.* A short maxim or proverb. [French, from Old French, from Latin *adagium,* proverb.]

a·da·gi·o (ə-dä′jō, -jē-ō′) *adv. Music.* Slowly. Used as a direction.

~*n., pl.* **adagios.** **1.** *Music.* A composition or movement played in this tempo. **2.** In ballet, a section of a pas de deux, in which the ballerina and her partner perform steps requiring lyricism and great skill in lifting, balancing, and turning. [Italian *adagio,* "at ease" : *ad-,* at, from Latin, at, toward + *agio,* ease, from Old Provençal *aize,* from Vulgar Latin *adjacēs* (unattested), variant of Latin *adjacēns,* convenient, ADJACENT.] **—a·da·gi·o** *adj.*

Ad·am[1] (ăd'əm). **1.** The first man and progenitor of mankind, according to the Bible. Genesis 2:7. **2.** The unregenerate side of human nature: *the old Adam.* **—not know someone from Adam.** To be completely ignorant of the identity of. [Late Latin, from Hebrew *ādām,* "man," from *adāmāh,* earth.] **—A·dam·ic** (ə-dăm'ĭk) *adj.*

Adam[2] *adj.* In, pertaining to, or characteristic of the neoclassical style of furniture and architecture originated by Robert and James Adam: *an Adam fireplace.*

Adam (ăd'əm), **Robert** (1728–92). British architect. Adam built in a delicate classical style, a development of the Palladian tradition, and was equally outstanding as an interior designer. In 1763 he went into partnership in London with his brother **James** (1730–94).

ad·a·mant (ăd'ə-mənt, -mănt') *n.* **1.** A stone of uncertain identity formerly believed to be unbreakable. **2.** Any substance of exceptional hardness and resilience.

~*adj.* **1.** Unshakably firm in purpose or opinion; unyielding. **2.** Adamantine. —See Synonyms at **inflexible.** [Middle English *adama(u)nt,* diamond, magnet, from Old French *adamaunt,* from Latin *adamās* (stem *adamant-*), from Greek *adamas,* hard metal, steel, diamond, possibly, "unbreakable" : *a-* not + *daman,* to tame, break down.] **—ad·a·mant·ly** *adv.*

ad·a·man·tine (ăd'ə-măn'tēn', -tĭn, -tīn') *adj.* **1.** Made of or resembling adamant. **2.** Having the hardness or luster of a diamond. **3.** Unyielding; inflexible.

Ad·am·ite (ăd'ə-mīt') *n.* A descendant of Adam; a human being.

Ad·ams (ăd'əmz), **Abigail** (1744–1818). U.S. letter writer and first lady (1797–1801) as the wife of President John Adams. During frequent separations caused by the Revolutionary War, she wrote constantly to her husband, providing a vivid picture of her life and times in Massachusetts.

Adams, Ansel (1902–84). U.S. photographer. The American wilderness, from Death Valley to the Sierra Nevada, was the raw material for his magnificent photographs. Adams also worked tirelessly for the preservation of wilderness areas in the United States.

Adams, John (1735–1826). First vice president (1789–97) and second president (1797–1801) of the United States. Adams played a leading part in the American Revolution, shaping the Constitution and helping draft the Declaration of Independence.

Adams, John Couch (1819–92). British astronomer who was the first to predict the position of Neptune. Adams calculated the position of the new planet, purely mathematically, in 1845. However the planet was not discovered until Urbain Leverrier's independent prediction had been made and confirmed in 1846.

Adams, John Quincy (1767–1848). Sixth president of the United States (1825–29) and son of John Adams. As secretary of state (1817–25) he helped formulate the Monroe Doctrine. He later became an active campaigner against slavery.

Adam's apple *n.* The projection of the largest laryngeal cartilage at the front of the throat, especially in men. [Translation of Hebrew *tappūah hāādām.*]

ad·ams·ite (ăd'əmz-īt') *n. Symbol* **DM** A yellow crystalline compound, $(C_6H_4)_2(NH)AsCl$, used dispersed in air as a poison gas. [After Roger *Adams* (1889–1971), U.S. chemist.]

Adam's needle *n.* A plant, the **Spanish bayonet** *(see).* [From the spines on its leaves and with allusion to Genesis 3:7: ". . . they sewed fig leaves together, and made themselves aprons."]

a·dapt (ə-dăpt') *v.* **adapted, adapting, adapts.** —*tr.* **1.** To adjust to a new environment or situation. **2.** To modify for a different use or purpose: *adapt a stage play for the radio.* —*intr.* To become adapted. [Latin *adaptāre,* to fit to : *ad-* to + *aptāre,* to fit, from *aptus,* APT.]

a·dapt·a·ble (ə-dăp'tə-bəl) *adj.* Capable of adapting or of being adapted. —See Synonyms at **flexible.** **—a·dapt·a·bil·i·ty** (ə-dăp'tə-bĭl'ə-tē), **a·dapt·a·ble·ness** *n.*

ad·ap·ta·tion (ăd'ăp-tā'shən) *n.* **1. a.** The act or process of adapting. **b.** The state of being adapted. **2.** Something that has adapted or been adapted so as to suit a new or special use or situation: *a new adaptation for radio.* **3.** An adjustment or process of adjustment, often hereditary, by which a species or individual improves its condition in relationship to its environment. **4.** The responsive alteration of a sense organ to repeated stimuli of a particular type. **—ad·ap·ta·tion·al** *adj.* **—ad·ap·ta·tion·al·ly** *adv.*

a·dapt·er, a·dap·tor (ə-dăp'tər) *n.* **1.** One that adapts. **2.** A device used to connect an electrical plug of one type into a supply point having a different fitting. **3.** A device that enables several electrical plugs to be fitted into one supply point. **4.** Any device that enables one part of an apparatus or machine to be fitted into another part having a different size or fitting.

a·dap·tive (ə-dăp'tĭv) *adj.* Tending toward, fit for, or having a capacity for adaptation. **—a·dap·tive·ly** *adv.* **—a·dap·tive·ness** *n.*

adaptive radiation *n.* The evolution of one relatively unspecialized species into several related species characterized by different specializations that fit them for life in various environments. See feature, next page.

A·dar (ä-där') *n.* The sixth month of the year in the Hebrew calendar. See feature at **calendar.** [Hebrew *Adhār,* from Akkadian *ad(d)aru,* "the dark or cloudy month," from *adāru,* to be dark.]

Adar She·ni (shā-nē') *n.* An intercalary Hebrew month, **Veadar** *(see).* [Hebrew *Adhār shēnī,* "second Adar."]

ad·ax·i·al (ăd-ăk'sē-əl) *adj.* Facing toward the axis. Said of the upper surface of leaves. Compare **abaxial.**

ADC, a.d.c., A.D.C. aide-de-camp.

add (ăd) *v.* **added, adding, adds.** —*tr.* **1.** To join or unite so as to increase in size, quantity, or scope. **2.** To combine (a column of figures, for example) to form a total. Often used with *up.* **3.** To say or write further. **4.** To provide as an additional feature or quality; impart: *Wine can add zest to a meal.* —*intr.* **1.** To create or constitute an addition. Used with *to.* **2.** To find a sum in arithmetic. **—add up.** *Informal.* **1.** To come to a correct or desired total: *His figures don't add up.* **2.** To be reasonable, plausible, or consistent; make sense. **—add up to.** *Informal.* To mean; amount to. [Middle English *adden,* from Latin *addere,* to add, "to put to" : *ad-,* to + *-dere,* to put, from *dare,* to give.] **—add·a·ble, add·i·ble** *adj.*

Ad·dams (ăd'əmz), **Charles** (1912–). U.S. cartoonist. Addams is known for the macabre humor and gothic settings of his cartoons, many of which have appeared in *The New Yorker.*

Addams, Jane (1860–1935). U.S. social reformer. In 1889 she opened Hull House, a settlement house in a slum neighborhood of Chicago offering adult-education courses and activities for the poor and foreign-born of the area. Addams became a leader of the pacifist movement in the early 1900's and was awarded a Nobel Peace Prize in 1931.

ad·dax (ăd'ăks') *n.* An antelope, *Addax nasomaculatus,* of northern Africa having long, spirally twisted horns. [Latin *addāx,* of African origin.]

add·ed value (ăd'ĭd) *n. Economics.* The increase in the value of goods occurring in the process of production. It is measured as the difference between the producer's total revenue and the cost to him of raw materials.

ad·dend (ăd'ĕnd', ə-dĕnd') *n.* Any of a set of numbers to be added. [Shortened from ADDENDUM.]

ad·den·dum (ə-dĕn'dəm) *n., pl.* **-da** (-də). Something added or to be added; especially, a supplement, appendix, or list of matter wrongly omitted from a publication. [Latin, neuter of *addendus,* gerundive of *addere,* to ADD.]

ad·der (ăd'ər) *n.* **1.** Any of various venomous snakes of the family Viperidae, especially the common viper, *Vipera berus,* of Eurasia. **2.** Any of several similar snakes, such as the **hognose snake** *(see),* or puff adder, of North America. [Middle English *addre,* from *an addre,* mistaken from *a naddre,* Old English *nǣdre,* snake.]

ad·der's-tongue (ăd'ərz-tŭng') *n.* **1.** Any of several ferns of the genus *Ophioglossum*; especially, *O. vulgatum,* of the Northern Hemisphere, having a single sterile, leaflike frond, and a spore-bearing stalk. **2.** Any of various plants of the genus *Erythronium,* such as the **dogtooth violet** *(see).* [From the spike sticking out from the base of the frond of the fern, suggesting a snake's tongue.]

ad·dict (ə-dĭkt') *tr.v.* **-dicted, -dicting, -dicts.** **1.** To cause to become physiologically or psychologically dependent, especially on a drug. Usually used in the passive and with *to.* **2.** To devote (oneself) excessively or compulsively.

~*n.* (ăd'ĭkt). **1.** One who is addicted, especially to a drug. **2.** *Informal.* A devotee: *a TV addict.* [Latin *addīctus,* "given over," one awarded to another as a slave, past participle of *addīcere,* to award to : *ad-,* to + *dīcere,* to say, pronounce, adjudge.] **—ad·dic·tion** *n.* **—ad·dic·tive** *adj.*

Ad·dis Ab·a·ba (ăd'ĭs ăb'ə-bə). Capital and largest city of Ethiopia, located in the center of the country on a plateau more than 2,440 meters (8,000 feet) above sea level. It became the capital in 1889. Captured by the Italians in 1936 and made the capital of Italian East Africa, it was liberated by the Allies in 1941 and returned to Ethiopia.

Ad·di·son (ăd'ə-sən), **Joseph** (1672–1719). British essayist, poet, and Whig politician. He is best known for his witty, elegant essays, which were mainly contributed to two periodicals: Richard Steele's *Tatler,* and the *Spectator,* founded by Steele and Addison.

Addison's disease *n.* A disease caused by failure of the adrenal cortex to function and marked by a bronzelike skin pigmentation, anemia, and prostration. [After Thomas *Addison* (1793–1860), British physician who discovered it.]

ad·di·tion (ə-dĭsh'ən) *n.* **1.** The act or process of adding. **2. a.** The result of adding. **b.** Something or someone added. **3.** The process of combining numbers so as to find their sum. **4.** A part added to a building; an extension. —See Synonyms at **appendage.** **—in addition.** Besides; also. **—in addition to.** Over and above; as well as. —See Usage note at **together.**

ad·di·tion·al (ə-dĭsh'ə-nəl) *adj.* In addition; added; extra.

ad·di·tion·al·ly (ə-dĭsh'ə-nə-lē) *adv.* Furthermore; in addition. —See Synonyms at **also.**

ad·di·tive (ăd'ə-tĭv) *adj.* **1.** Marked by, produced by, or involving addition. **2.** Designating any of certain colors of wavelengths that may be mixed with one another to produce other colors. Compare **subtractive.** See **primary color.**

~*n.* A substance added in small amounts to something else, especially a food or drink, to improve, strengthen, or otherwise alter it.

ad·dle (ăd'l) *v.* **-dled, -dling, -dles.** —*tr.* To muddle; confuse: *His brain is addled by too much drink.* —*intr.* **1.** To become rotten. Used of an egg. **2.** To become confused.

~*adj.* Mixed-up; confused. Usually used in combination: *addle-*

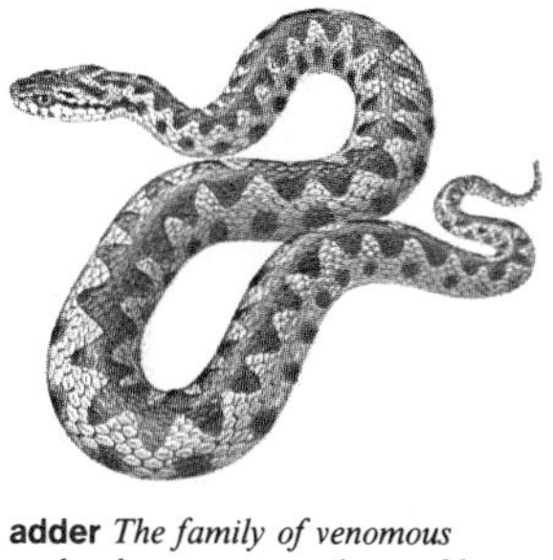

adder *The family of venomous snakes known commonly as adders, or vipers, includes some that are extremely dangerous to man—among them the puff adders of Africa. The common adder of Europe and Asia,* Vipera berus *(above), will not, however, attack man unless provoked; and its bite is very rarely fatal. The death adder of Australia is a member of the cobra family and is not related to adders; it is so named only because it superficially resembles them.*

PRONUNCIATION KEY

ă, pat; ā, pay; âr, care;
ä, father, are; b, bib;
ch, church; d, deed; ĕ, pet;
ē, be; f, fife; g, gag; h, hat;
hw, which; ĭ, pit; ī, pie;
îr, pier; j, judge; k, kick;
l, lid, needle; m, mum;
n, no, sudden; ng, thing;
ŏ, pot; ō, toe; ô, paw, for;
oi, noise; ou, out; ŏŏ, book;
ōō, boot; p, pop; r, roar;
s, sauce; sh, ship, dish;
t, tight; th, thin, path;
th, this, bathe; ŭ, cut; ûr, fur;
v, valve; w, with; y, yes;
z, zebra, size; zh, vision;
ə, about, item, edible, gallop, circus, peaceful

IN FOREIGN WORDS:

à, *Fr.* ami; œ, *Fr.* feu, *Ger.* schön; ü, *Fr.* tu, *Ger.* über;
KH, *Ger.* ich, *Scot.* loch;
N, *Fr.* bon; y', *Fr.* Compiègne

STRESS MARKS:

Primary stress: '
in·cite' (ĭn-sīt')
Secondary stress: '
in'sight' (ĭn'sīt')

adaptive radiation

EVOLUTION OF NEW SPECIES BY ADAPTATION
How various animal and plant species evolve

Living beings are always more or less like their parents, but never exactly like them. Because of this, according to the Darwinian theory of evolution, species change over thousands of generations. In any species, those members best adapted to their environment survive and breed, and their progeny tend to inherit the characteristics that best fit them to survive. The species becomes even better adapted through the generations and in time may change so much that it is a new species.

Sometimes the changes involve a single line of evolving plants or animals—as in man's line of descent from apelike ancestors to modern human beings. More often, however, one species in the past has become the ancestor of various related kinds, all alike in some ways but each adapted to survive in slightly different ways.

This fanning-out process is called adaptive radiation.

All the cat family come from the same ancestors and hunt in broadly the same way, but large cats such as lions can hunt large prey, and smaller cats hunt smaller prey. Large cats, such as lions, tigers, and leopards, have evolved different camouflage so they can hunt in different places.

Some of the most striking examples occur when one kind of animal becomes cut off in one part of the world. Charles Darwin observed an example on the Galápagos Islands in the Pacific Ocean, where 13 species of finch had adapted to the different local environments on the various islands. The marsupials, or pouched mammals, of Australia, which nowadays lead very varied lives, are another example.

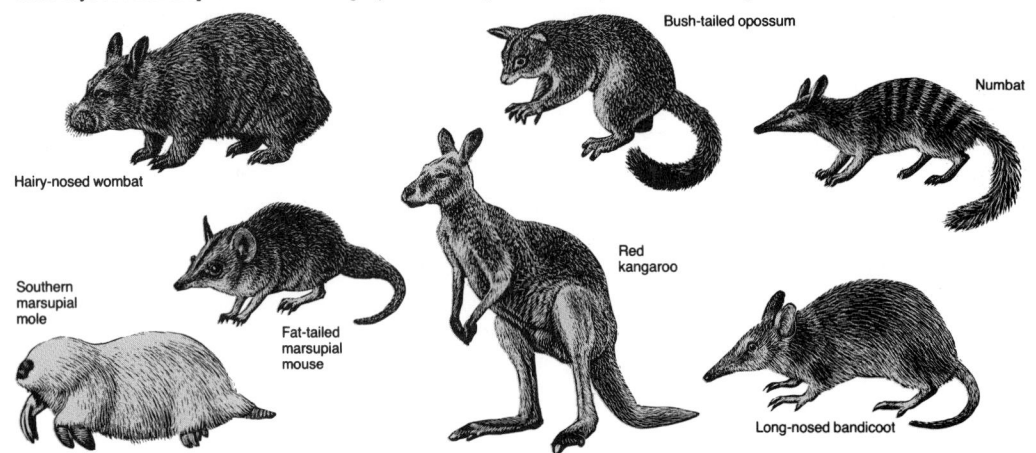

Bush-tailed opossum

Numbat

Hairy-nosed wombat

Southern marsupial mole

Fat-tailed marsupial mouse

Red kangaroo

Long-nosed bandicoot

AUSTRALIAN MARSUPIALS *Cut off in Australia, the common ancestor of the marsupials produced generations of young that adapted to various environments and eventually diversified into different species. The hairy-nosed wombat has strong legs for burrowing and the fat-tailed mouse anticipates shortages by storing fat in its tail. Long hind legs give the red kangaroo speed in its search for sparse food,* *and the bush-tailed opossum can hang from branches with its clawless hind digit. The pointed muzzle of the long-nosed bandicoot helps it to root for worms. The numbat has powerful claws to dig up ants' nests and a long, sticky tongue to mop up the ants. The marsupial mole has a horny shield to protect its nose as it burrows in the harsh desert.*

brained. [Middle English *adel,* rotten, putrid, Old English *adela,* filth, urine; akin to Middle Low German *adele†.*]

ad·dress (ə-drĕs′) *tr.v.* **-dressed, -dressing, -dresses. 1.** To speak to; especially, to use a certain form in speaking to: *I addressed her by her first name.* **2.** To make a formal speech to. **3.** To direct (a spoken or written comment) to the attention of. Used with *to: Please address your remarks to the chairman.* **4.** To mark (a letter, parcel, or the like) with the name of the person and place to which it is to be delivered. **5. a.** To direct (oneself) in speech. Used with *to.* **b.** To direct the efforts or attention of (oneself): *address oneself to a task.* **c.** To direct one's efforts or attention to (a problem, for example). **6.** To consign (a ship or its cargo) to an agent or factor. **7.** To adjust and aim a golf club or billiard cue when preparing to strike (a ball).
~*n.* (ə-drĕs′; *also* ăd′rĕs *for senses 3,4,7*). **1.** A formal spoken or written communication: *polite forms of address.* **2.** A formal speech. **3.** The location at which a particular organization or person may be found or reached. **4.** Information giving details of this, written on a letter, parcel, or the like. **5.** Skillfulness, adroitness, or tact in handling a situation. **6.** The act of consigning a ship or its cargo, as to an agent or factor. **7.** *Computer Science.* A number used in information storage or retrieval that is assigned to a specific memory location. **8.** *Usually* **addresses.** Courteous attention; wooing. Used chiefly in the phrase *pay one's addresses.* **9.** Manner or bearing of a person, especially in conversation. [Middle English *addressen,* from Old French *addresser,* from Vulgar Latin *addrictiāre* (unattested), to straighten, direct oneself toward : *ad-,* + *directiāre* (unattested), to straighten, from Latin *dīrectus,* DIRECT.] **—ad·dress·er, ad·dres·sor** *n.*

ad·dress·a·ble (ə-drĕs′ə-bəl) *adj.* Accessible through an address, as in a computer memory.

ad·dress·ee (ăd′rĕs-ē′, ə-drĕs′ē′) *n.* One to whom something, such as a letter, is addressed.

Ad·dress·o·graph (ə-drĕs′ə-grăf′) *n.* A trademark for a machine that prints addresses on letters.

ad·duce (ə-dōōs′, ə-dyōōs′, ă-) *tr.v.* **-duced, -ducing, -duces.** To cite as an example, explanation, or means of proof; bring forward for consideration. [Latin *addūcere,* to bring to (someone) : *ad-,* toward + *dūcere,* to lead.] **—ad·duce·a·ble, ad·duc·i·ble** *adj.*

ad·du·cent (ə-dōō′sənt, ə-dyōō′-, ă-) *adj. Physiology.* Drawing toward or together; adducting. Said of a muscle.

ad·duct (ə-dŭkt′, ă-) *tr.v.* **-ducted, -ducting, -ducts.** To pull or draw (a limb) toward the main axis. Used of a muscle. [Back-formation from ADDUCTOR.] **—ad·duc·tion** *n.* **—ad·duc·tive** *adj.*

ad·duc·tor (ə-dŭk′tər, ă-) *n.* A muscle that adducts. [Latin *adductor,* "a bringer toward," from *addūcere,* to ADDUCE.]

–ade *suffix.* Indicates a sweetened drink of; for example, **lemonade.** [French *-ade,* from Provençal, Portuguese, and Spanish *-ada* and Italian *-ata,* all from Latin *-āta,* feminine of *-ātus,* "furnished with," past participial ending of verbs in *-āre.*]

Ad·e·laide (ăd′ə-lād′). Capital of South Australia, on the Torrens River in the southeast of the state. The products of its manufacturing industries include textiles, cars, and electronics, and it exports agricultural goods.

A·dé·lie Land (ə-dā′lē). Also **Adélie Coast.** Region of Antarctica on the coast of Wilkes Land, claimed by the French.

Adélie penguin *n.* A common Antarctic penguin, *Pygoscelis adeliae,* of medium size, with white underparts and black back and head. It lives and breeds in large exposed rookeries.

–adelphous *suffix. Botany.* Indicates stamens united by their filaments to form a specified number of groups; for example, **diadelphous.** [New Latin *-adelphus,* "having the stamens grouped together (in a 'brotherhood')," from Greek *adelphos,* brother.]

a·demp·tion (ə-dĕmp′shən) *n. Law.* The invalidation of a bequest, especially as a result of some action by the testator during his lifetime, such as the disposal of the property in question. [Latin *ademptiō,* a taking away, from *adimere* (past participle *ademptus*), to take to (oneself), take away : *ad-,* toward + *emere,* to buy, "take."]

A·den (ăd′n, ād′n). Capital and chief port of South Yemen on the Gulf of Aden, the western arm of the Arabian Sea. It has always been one of the chief ports of southern Arabia. It was annexed by Britain in 1839, and became a major trading and refueling station after the opening of the Suez Canal in 1869. Aden is the country's industrial and commercial center.

A·den·au·er (ăd′n-ou′ər, ād′n-), **Konrad** (1876–1967). German statesman and first chancellor of the Federal Republic of Germany. In 1946 Adenauer, a former Rhineland politician who had been twice imprisoned by the Nazis, became leader of the Christian

Democratic Union (CDU), which won the first West German elections in 1949. Under Adenauer West Germany embarked on a program of economic reconstruction and gained membership in NATO and the European Economic Community.

ad·en·ec·to·my (ăd′n-ĕk′tə-mē) *n., pl.* **-mies.** Surgical excision of a gland. [ADEN(O)- + -ECTOMY.]

ad·e·nine (ăd′n-ēn′, -ĭn) *n. Biochemistry.* A purine derivative, $C_5H_5N_5$, that is a constituent of nucleic acid in the pancreas, spleen, and other organs. [ADEN(O)- + -INE.]

ad·e·ni·tis (ăd′n-ī′tĭs) *n.* Inflammation of a lymph node or gland. [ADEN(O)- + -ITIS.]

adeno-, aden- *prefix.* Indicates a gland or glands; for example, **adenocarcinoma.** [New Latin, from Greek *adēn,* gland.]

ad·e·no·car·ci·no·ma (ăd′n-ō-kär′sə-nō′mə) *n., pl.* **-mata** (-mə-tə) or **-mas.** A malignant tumor originating in glandular tissue. **—ad·e·no·car·ci·nom·a·tous** (ăd′n-ō-kär′sə-nŏm′ə-təs, -nō′mə-təs) *adj.*

ad·e·no·hy·poph·y·sis (ăd′n-ō-hī-pŏf′ĭ-sĭs) *n.* The front section of the pituitary gland. Compare **neurohypophysis.**

ad·e·noid (ăd′n-oid′) *adj.* Also **ad·e·noi·dal** (ăd′n-oid′l). **1.** Glandlike; glandular. **2.** Of or pertaining to the adenoids.

ad·e·noi·dal (ăd′n-oid′l) *adj.* **1.** Variant of **adenoid. 2. a.** Having a nasal or constricted tone: *an adenoidal singer.* **b.** Breathing through the mouth; open-mouthed.

ad·e·noids (ăd′n-oidz′) *pl.n.* Lymphoid tissue growths in the nose above the throat that when swollen may obstruct nasal breathing, induce postnasal discharge, and make speech difficult. [Greek *adenoeidēs* : ADEN(O)- + -OID.]

ad·e·no·ma (ăd′n-ō′mə) *n., pl.* **-mata** (-mə-tə) or **-mas.** An epithelial tumor of glandular origin and structure that is usually benign or of low-grade malignancy. [ADEN(O)- + -OMA.] **—ad·e·nom·a·tous** (ăd′n-ŏm′ə-təs) *adj.*

a·den·o·sine (ə-dĕn′ə-sēn′) *n.* An organic compound, $C_{10}H_{13}N_5O_4$, that is a structural component of nucleic acids. [Blend of ADENINE and RIBOSE.]

adenosine diphosphate *n.* **ADP** *(see).*

adenosine monophosphate *n.* **AMP** *(see).*

adenosine triphosphate *n.* **ATP** *(see).*

ad·e·no·vir·us (ăd′n-ō-vī′rəs) *n.* Any of a group of viruses that cause respiratory infections producing symptoms like those of the common cold.

a·dept (ə-dĕpt′) *adj.* Highly skilled; expert. —See Synonyms at **proficient.**
~*n.* (ăd′ĕpt′). One who is thoroughly proficient or highly skilled; an expert. [Latin *adeptus,* "having attained (knowledge or skill)," past participle of *adipīscī,* to attain : *ad-,* toward + *apīscī,* to reach for.] **—a·dept·ly** *adv.* **—a·dept·ness** *n.*

ad·e·quate (ăd′ĭ-kwĭt) *adj.* **1. a.** Sufficient for a particular purpose or need. **b.** Able to satisfy a requirement or standard; suitable. **c.** Having the necessary qualities to meet the demands of a situation: *proved adequate to the task.* **2.** Barely satisfactory or sufficient. [Latin *adaequatus,* past participle of *adaequāre,* to make equal to : *ad-,* toward + *aequāre,* to make equal, from *aequus,* EQUAL.] **—ad·e·qua·cy** (ăd′ĭ-kwə-sē), **ad·e·quate·ness** *n.* **—ad·e·quate·ly** *adv.*
Usage: The prepositions *to* and *for* following this word are becoming interchangeable. *To* is generally recommended in contexts such as *adequate to his needs, adequate to the task*; but *for* is increasingly common: *There was adequate food for our purposes.*

ad·here (ăd-hîr′) *intr.v.* **-hered, -hering, -heres. 1.** To stick fast or together by or as if by grasping, suction, or being glued. Often used with *to.* **2.** To be devoted as a follower or supporter. Used with *to.* **3.** To follow closely or strictly. Used with *to*: *adhere to a plan.* [Latin *adhaerēre,* to stick to : *ad,* toward + *haerēre,* to stick.]

ad·her·ence (ăd-hîr′əns) *n.* **1.** The act or state of adhering; adhesion. **2.** Fidelity or attachment, as to a party, cause, or set of rules.

ad·her·ent (ăd-hîr′ənt) *adj.* **1.** Sticking or holding fast; attached. **2.** *Botany.* Growing or fused together; adnate.
~*n.* A supporter, as of a cause, idea, or individual. **—ad·her·ent·ly** *adv.*

ad·he·sion (ăd-hē′zhən) *n.* **1. a.** The act or state of sticking together. **b.** Firm physical contact between surfaces: *the wallpaper's adhesion to the wall.* **2.** Loyalty or attachment; adherence. **3.** Assent or agreement, especially to join or associate oneself. **4.** The physical attraction or joining together of two substances; especially, the molecular attraction of dissimilar substances. Compare **cohesion. 2.** *Biology & Medicine.* An abnormal joining together of two organic parts. [Latin *adhaesiō,* from *adhaerēre,* to ADHERE.]

ad·he·sive (ăd-hē′sĭv) *adj.* **1.** Tending to adhere; sticky. **2.** Gummed so as to adhere.
~*n.* An adhesive substance, such as paste or glue. **—ad·he·sive·ly** *adv.* **—ad·he·sive·ness** *n.*

ad hoc (ăd hŏk′) *adj. Latin.* For a specific purpose, case, or situation: *an ad hoc committee.* [Latin, "toward this."] **—ad hoc** *adv.*

ad ho·mi·nem (ăd hŏm′ĭ-nĕm) *adj. Latin.* **1.** Appealing to personal interests, prejudices, or emotions rather than to reason: *an argument ad hominem.* **2.** Attacking an opponent personally, rather than answering the opponent's arguments. [Latin, "to the man."] **—ad ho·mi·nem** *adv.*

ad·i·a·bat·ic (ăd′ē-ə-băt′ĭk, ā′dī-ə-) *adj. Physics.* Of, pertaining to, or designating a reversible thermodynamic process executed at constant entropy; loosely, occurring without gain or loss of heat. [Greek *adiabatos,* "impassable (to heat)" : *a-,* not + *diabatos,* passable, from *diabainein,* to go through : *dia,* through + *bainein,* to go.] **—ad·i·a·bat·i·cal·ly** *adv.*

a·dieu (ə-dyōō′, ə-dōō′) *interj.* Good-by; farewell.
~*n., pl.* **adieus** or **adieux** (ə-dyōōz′, ə-dōōz′). A farewell. [Middle English, from Old French, from *a dieu,* "(I commend you) to God" : *a,* to, from Latin *ad* + *dieu,* God, from Latin *deus,* god.]

ad in·fi·ni·tum (ăd ĭn′fə-nī′təm) *adv. Abbr.* **ad inf.** *Latin.* To infinity; endlessly.

ad in·ter·im (ăd ĭn′tər-əm) *adv. Abbr.* **ad int.** *Latin.* In the meantime; meanwhile. **—ad in·ter·im** *adj.*

a·di·os (ä′dē-ōs′, ăd′ē-ōs′) *interj.* Good-by; farewell. [Spanish, translation of French *adieu,* ADIEU.]

ad·i·pose (ăd′ə-pōs′) *adj.* Of or related to animal fat; fatty.
~*n.* The fat found in adipose tissue. [New Latin *adiposus,* from Latin *adeps*† (stem *adip-*), fat.] **—ad·i·pose·ness, ad·i·pos·i·ty** (ăd′ə-pŏs′ə-tē) *n.*

adipose fin *n.* An additional dorsal fin in certain fishes, such as the salmon, consisting mostly of fatty tissue and usually without supporting rays.

adipose tissue *n.* Connective tissue in the body that contains stored cellular fat.

Ad·i·ron·dack Mountains (ăd′ə-rŏn′dăk′). Also **Ad·i·ron·dacks** (-dăks). Group of mountains in eastern New York State. The highest peak is Mt. Marcy (1,628 meters; 5,344 feet). The region's lakes and forests attract many tourists, and there are also numerous winter sports resorts, including Lake Placid, site of the Winter Olympic Games of 1932 and 1980.

ad·it (ăd′ĭt) *n.* A horizontal, or near horizontal, passage cut in a hill slope for mining or drainage purposes. [Latin *aditus,* access, from the past participle of *adīre,* to approach : *ad-,* toward + *īre,* to go.]

A·di·va·si (ä′dĭ-vä′sē) *n., pl.* **-sis** or collectively **Adivasi.** A member of any of the aboriginal peoples of India.

adj. 1. adjective. **2.** adjourned. **3.** adjutant.

ad·ja·cent (ə-jā′sənt) *adj.* **1.** Lying or being close in space or time. **2.** Having a common border; contiguous or adjoining. [Middle English, from Latin *adjacēns* (stem *adjacent-*), present participle of *adjacēre,* to lie near : *ad-,* near to + *jacēre,* to lie, "be thrown down," intransitive of *jacere,* to lay, throw.] **—ad·ja·cen·cy** *n.* **—ad·ja·cent·ly** *adv.*

adjacent angle *n.* Either of two angles having a common side and a common vertex and lying on opposite sides of the common side.

ad·jec·tive (ăj′ĭk-tĭv) *n. Abbr.* **adj., a. 1.** A part of speech comprising a class of words that modify a noun or other substantive by limiting, qualifying, or specifying. **2.** A word belonging to this class, such as *nice* in *a nice house.* **3.** A word used as an adjective, such as *brick* in *a brick house.*
~*adj.* **1.** Pertaining to or functioning as an adjective. **2.** Dependent; subordinate. **3.** *Law.* Concerned with court procedure as opposed to legal principles. Compare **substantive. 4.** Requiring the use of a mordant to make permanent: *adjective dyes.* [Middle English, from Old French *adjectif,* from Latin *adjectīvus,* "attributive," from *adjectus,* "attributed," added, from *adjicere,* to throw to, add : *ad-,* to + *jacere,* to throw.] **—ad·jec·ti·val** (ăj′ĭk-tī′vəl) *adj.* **—ad·jec·ti·val·ly** *adv.*

ad·join (ə-join′) *v.* **-joined, -joining, -joins.** —*tr.* **1.** To be next to; be contiguous to. **2.** To attach; append. Used with *to.* —*intr.* To be nearby or contiguous: *in the adjoining room.* [Middle English *adjoinen,* from Old French *ajoindre,* from Latin *adjungere,* to join to : *ad-,* to + *jungere,* to join.]

ad·journ (ə-jûrn′) *v.* **-journed, -journing, -journs.** —*tr.* To break off (especially a meeting or court session) until a later time. —*intr.* **1.** To suspend transfer or proceedings to another time or place. **2.** To move from one place to another. Often used humorously: *We adjourned to the living room.* [Middle English *ajournen,* from Old French *ajourner,* "to put off to an appointed day" : *a-,* to, from Latin *ad-* + *jour,* day, from Late Latin *diurnum,* day, from *diurnus,* daily, from *diēs,* day.] **—ad·journ·ment** *n.*

adjt. adjutant.

ad·judge (ə-jŭj′) *tr.v.* **-judged, -judging, -judges. 1.** To determine or settle by judicial procedure; adjudicate. **2.** To order or pronounce judicially; rule. **3.** To award (costs or damages, for example) by law. **4.** To consider or pronounce to be; deem. [Middle English *ajugen,* from Old French *ajuger,* from Latin *adjūdicāre,* to ADJUDICATE.]

ad·ju·di·cate (ə-jōō′dĭ-kāt′) *v.* **-cated, -cating, -cates.** —*tr.* **1.** To hear and settle (a case) by judicial procedure. **2.** To pronounce judicially; adjudge: *was adjudicated a bankrupt.* —*intr.* To act as a judge. Usually used with *on* or *upon.* [Latin *adjūdicāre,* to award to (judicially) : *ad-,* to + *jūdicāre,* to be a judge, from *jūdex,* a judge.] **—ad·ju·di·ca·tion** (ə-jōō′dĭ-kā′shən) *n.* **—ad·ju·di·ca·tive** (ə-jōō′dĭ-kā′tĭv, -kə-tĭv) *adj.* **—ad·ju·di·ca·tor** *n.*

ad·junct (ăj′ŭngkt′) *n.* **1.** Something attached to another thing but in a subordinate or incidental relation. **2.** A person associated with another in a subordinate or auxiliary capacity; a helper; an assistant. **3.** A word or words added to clarify or modify other words in a sentence, but not grammatically essential to the sentence. **4.** *Logic.* A nonessential attribute of a thing. —See Synonyms at **appendage.**
~*adj.* Added or connected in a subordinate or auxiliary capacity: *an adjunct clause.* [Latin *adjunctum,* from *adjunctus,* past participle of *adjungere,* to ADJOIN.] **—ad·junc·tion** (ə-jŭngk′shən) *n.* **—ad·junc·tive** (ə-jŭngk′tĭv) *adj.*

PRONUNCIATION KEY

ă, pat; ā, pay; âr, care; ä, father, are; b, bib; ch, church; d, deed; ĕ, pet; ē, be; f, fife; g, gag; h, hat; hw, which; ĭ, pit; ī, pie; îr, pier; j, judge; k, kick; l, lid, needle; m, mum; n, no, sudden; ng, thing; ŏ, pot; ō, toe; ô, paw, for; oi, noise; ou, out; ŏŏ, book; ōō, boot; p, pop; r, roar; s, sauce; sh, ship, dish; t, tight; th, thin, path; *th,* this, bathe; ŭ, cut; ûr, fur; v, valve; w, with; y, yes; z, zebra, size; zh, vision; ə, about, item, edible, gallop, circus, peaceful

IN FOREIGN WORDS:

à, *Fr.* ami; œ, *Fr.* feu, *Ger.* schön; ü, *Fr.* tu, *Ger.* über; KH, *Ger.* ich, *Scot.* loch; N, *Fr.* bon; y′, *Fr.* Compiègne

STRESS MARKS:

Primary stress: ′ **in·cite′** (ĭn-sīt′)
Secondary stress: ′ **in′sight′** (ĭn′sīt′)

ad·ju·ra·tion (ăj′ŏŏ-rā′shən) *n.* An earnest or solemn appeal. —**ad·jur·a·to·ry** (ə-jŏŏr′ə-tôr′ē, -tōr′ē) *adj.*

ad·jure (ə-jŏŏr′) *tr.v.* **-jured, -juring, -jures. 1.** To command or enjoin solemnly, as under oath or penalty. **2.** To appeal to or entreat earnestly. [Middle English *adjuren,* from Latin *adjūrāre,* to swear to : *ad-,* to + *jūrāre,* to swear.] —**ad·jur·er, ad·ju·ror** *n.*

ad·just (ə-jŭst′) *v.* **-justed, -justing, -justs.** —*tr.* **1.** To change so as to match or fit; cause to correspond. **2.** To adapt; change so as to harmonize with new conditions. **3.** To regulate so as to make accurate or efficient. **4.** To decide how much is to be paid on (an insurance claim). —*intr.* To adapt oneself, as to changed conditions; become suited or fit. [Obsolete French *adjuster,* from Old French *ajoster,* from Vulgar Latin *adjuxtāre* (unattested), to put close to : Latin *ad-,* near to + *juxtā,* close by, near.] —**ad·just·a·ble** *adj.* —**ad·just·a·bly** *adv.* —**ad·just·er, ad·jus·tor** *n.*

ad·just·ment (ə-jŭst′mənt) *n.* **1.** The act of adjusting or state of being adjusted. **2.** A slight alteration or modification. **3.** A means for adjusting. **4.** The settlement of a debt or claim.

ad·ju·tant (ăj′ŏŏ-tənt) *n.* **1.** *Abbr.* **adj., adjt.** *Military.* A staff officer who helps a commanding officer with and is responsible for administrative work. **2.** An assistant. **3.** A stork, the **marabou** (*see).* [Latin *adjūtāns* (stem *adjūtant-*), present participle of *adjūtāre,* to assist, AID.] —**ad·ju·tan·cy, ad·ju·tant·ship** *n.*

adjutant general *n., pl.* **adjutants general.** *Abbr.* **A.G., AG** *Military.* **1.** An adjutant of a military unit having a general staff. **2.** An officer in charge of the National Guard of one of the states of the United States. **3. Adjutant General.** The chief administrative officer, a major general, of the U.S. Army.

adjutant stork *n.* The marabou (*see).* [Alluding to the military stiffness of its posture and gait.]

ad·ju·vant (ăj′ə-vənt) *adj.* Helping or contributing.
~*n.* One that aids; specifically, an ingredient that increases the effectiveness of a medicine.

Ad·ler (ăd′lər), **Alfred** (1870–1937). Austrian physician and psychiatrist. Originally a follower of Sigmund Freud, Adler broke away in 1911. He rejected Freud's emphasis on sexuality and held that much behavior arises from subconscious efforts to compensate for feelings of inferiority and that neurosis results from overcompensation. —**Ad·le·ri·an** (ăd-lîr′ē-ən) *adj. & n.*

ad lib (ăd lĭb′) *adv.* **1.** Without preparation; spontaneously. **2.** Without limit; freely. —See Synonyms at **extemporaneous.**

ad-lib (ăd-lĭb′) *v.* **-libbed, -libbing, -libs.** *Informal.* —*tr.* To improvise and deliver without rehearsal (words, music, or the like). —*intr.* To improvise a speech, lines, or the like; extemporize.
~*n.* Words, music, or actions ad-libbed.
~*adj.* Spoken or performed spontaneously; impromptu. [Shortened from AD LIBITUM.] —**ad-lib·ber** *n.*

ad lib·i·tum (ăd lĭb′ə-təm) *adv. Abbr.* **ad lib., ad libit.** *Music.* Without limit or restriction; performed as desired. Used as a direction. Compare **obbligato.** [Latin, "to the desire."]

ad li·tem (ăd lī′təm) *adv. Law.* For a lawsuit or action. Said of a guardian appointed for such a purpose.

ad loc (ăd lŏk′) *adv.* To (or at) the place already mentioned. [Latin *ad locum.*]

Adm. admiral; admiralty.

ad·man (ăd′măn′) *n., pl.* **-men** (-měn′). *Informal.* A man employed in the advertising business.

ad·meas·ure (ăd-mězh′ər) *tr.v.* **-ured, -uring, -ures.** To divide and distribute proportionally; apportion. [Middle English *amesuren,* from Old French *amesurer,* to measure out to.] —**ad·meas·ure·ment** *n.* —**ad·meas·ur·er** *n.*

Ad·me·tus (ăd-mē′təs) *Greek Mythology.* A king of Thessaly and the husband of Alcestis.

admin. administration; administrator.

ad·min·is·ter (ăd-mĭn′ĭs-tər) *v.* **-tered, -tering, -ters.** —*tr.* **1.** To have charge of; direct; manage (the affairs of a person, business, government, or the like). **2. a.** To give or perform in a formal or ritualistic way: *administer the last rites.* **b.** To apply or give as a remedy: *administer a sedative.* **3.** To dispense; put into operation: *administer justice.* **4.** To manage or dispose of (trusts and estates) under a will or an official appointment. **5.** To impose, offer, or tender (an oath, for example). —*intr.* **1.** To act as an administrator. **2.** To attend to the needs of others; minister. Used with *to: administering to their pleasure.* [Middle English *administren,* from Old French *administrer,* from Latin *administrāre,* to be an aid to : *ad-,* to + *ministrāre,* to serve, from *minister,* servant.] —**ad·min·is·tra·ble** (ăd-mĭn′ĭs-trə-bəl) *adj.* —**ad·min·is·trant** (ăd-mĭn′ĭs-trənt) *adj. & n.*

ad·min·is·trate (ăd-mĭn′ĭs-trāt′) *tr.v.* **-trated, -trating, -trates.** To administer; be in charge of the affairs of.

ad·min·is·tra·tion (ăd-mĭn′ĭs-trā′shən) *n. Abbr.* **admin. 1.** The management of affairs, especially in government or business. **2.** The people who make up the managing body of any institution, public or private. **3.** *Often* **Administration.** The executive branch of government or its term of office: *a member of the Reagan administration.* **4.** *Law.* The management and disposal of a trust or estate. **5.** The dispensing, applying, or tendering of something, such as an oath, sacrament, or medicine. —**ad·min·is·tra·tive** (ăd-mĭn′ĭ-strā′tĭv, -strə-tĭv) *adj.* —**ad·min·is·tra·tive·ly** *adv.*

ad·min·is·tra·tor (ăd-mĭn′ĭs-trā′tər) *n. Abbr.* **admin. 1.** One who administers, especially public or business affairs. **2.** *Law.* A person appointed to administer an estate.

ad·mi·ra·ble (ăd′mər-ə-bəl) *adj.* Deserving admiration; excellent. —**ad·mi·ra·ble·ness** *n.* —**ad·mi·ra·bly** *adv.*

ad·mi·ral (ăd′mər-əl) *n.* **1.** The commander in chief of a navy or fleet. **2.** *Abbr.* **Adm.** In the U.S., British, or Canadian Navy: **a.** An officer holding the next-to-highest rank, who commands a whole fleet. **b.** An **Admiral of the Fleet,** a rear admiral, or a vice admiral *(all of which see).* **3.** The ship carrying an admiral; a flagship. **4.** Any of various brightly colored butterflies of the genera *Limenitis* and *Vanessa.* [Middle English *a(d)miral,* from Medieval Latin *a(d)mīrālis* (reshaped as if from *admīrārī,* to admire), from Old French *amiral,* from Arabic *'amīr-al-,* "commander of" : *'amīr,* commander, EMIR + *al,* the.]

Admiral of the Fleet *n.* In the U.S., British, or Canadian navy, the officer holding the highest rank, equivalent to field marshal or general of the army. Also called "Admiral," "Fleet Admiral."

ad·mi·ral·ty (ăd′mər-əl-tē) *n., pl.* **-ties.** *Abbr.* **Adm. 1. a.** A court exercising jurisdiction over all maritime causes. **b.** Maritime law. **2. Admiralty.** The British government department that controls naval affairs.

Ad·mi·ral·ty Islands (ăd′mər-əl-tē). Group of 40 volcanic islands in the southwest Pacific Ocean. The islands lie in the Bismarck Archipelago, and are part of Papua New Guinea. Lorengau, the administrative center and chief port, is on Manus, the largest island.

ad·mi·ra·tion (ăd′mə-rā′shən) *n.* **1. a.** A feeling of pleasure and approval. **b.** A feeling of disinterested and pleased respect. **2.** An object of wonder; a marvel: *His success made him the admiration of all his friends.* **3.** *Archaic.* Wonder. —See Synonyms at **regard.**

ad·mire (ăd-mīr′) *tr.v.* **-mired, -miring, -mires. 1.** To look at with pleasure and approval: *stood in front of the mirror admiring himself.* **2.** To have a high opinion of; regard with respect. **3.** *Archaic.* To marvel or wonder at. [Latin *admīrārī,* to wonder at : *ad-,* to, at + *mīrārī,* to wonder, from *mīrus,* wonderful.] —**ad·mir·ing** *adj.* —**ad·mir·ing·ly** *adv.*

ad·mir·er (ăd-mīr′ər) *n.* One who admires; especially, a man who is attracted to a particular woman.

ad·mis·si·ble (ăd-mĭs′ə-bəl) *adj.* **1.** Capable of being accepted; allowable. Said especially of evidence in a court case. **2.** Qualified or permitted to enter. —**ad·mis·si·bil·i·ty** (ăd-mĭs′ə-bĭl′ə-tē), **ad·mis·si·ble·ness** *n.* —**ad·mis·si·bly** *adv.*

ad·mis·sion (ăd-mĭsh′ən) *n.* **1. a.** The act of admitting or allowing to enter. **b.** The state of being allowed to enter. **2.** The right to enter; access. **3.** The cost of entering; entrance fee. **4.** The act or process of acceptance and entry into a position or situation; appointment. **5.** A confession of crime or wrongdoing. **6.** A voluntary acknowledgment that something is true. —See Usage note at **admittance.** [Middle English *admissioun,* from Latin *admissiō* (stem *admissiōn-*), from *admittere* (past participle *admissus*), to ADMIT.] —**ad·mis·sive** (ăd-mĭs′ĭv) *adj.*

ad·mit (ăd-mĭt′) *v.* **-mitted, -mitting, -mits.** —*tr.* **1.** To permit to enter. **2.** To serve as an authorization of entrance: *This ticket admits the whole group.* **3.** To permit to join or exercise certain rights, functions, or privileges. **4.** To have room for; be able to accommodate. **5.** To allow the possibility of; permit. **6.** To acknowledge; confess: *admit the truth.* **7.** To grant as true or valid, as for the sake of argument; concede. **8.** To acknowledge as being lawful or valid. —*intr.* **1.** To allow the possibility; permit. Used with *of.* **2.** To allow entrance; afford access. Used with *to: This door admits to the main hall.* —See Synonyms at **acknowledge.** [Middle English *admitten,* from Latin *admittere,* to send in to : *ad-,* to + *mittere,* to send.]

ad·mit·tance (ăd-mĭt′əns) *n.* **1.** The act of admitting or entering. **2.** Permission to enter; the power or right of entrance. **3.** *Electricity.* The reciprocal of impedance. It is the ratio of a voltage to a current, is measured in siemens, and may be expressed as a complex quantity, the real part of which is conductance and the imaginary part susceptance.

Usage: **Admittance** applies largely to physical entry to a specific place (*admittance to the jury room*). In the corresponding sense of entry, *admission* is used figuratively (*admission of evidence to the court record*) or, when physical entry is involved, in the additional sense of right or privilege of participation (*admission to a club; price of admission to a theater*).

ad·mit·ted·ly (ăd-mĭt′ĭd-lē) *adv.* By general admission; granted that: *admittedly the quality is poor.*

ad·mix·ture (ăd-mĭks′chər) *n.* **1. a.** The act of mingling or mixing. **b.** The state of being mingled or mixed. **2.** That which is mingled or mixed; a mixture. **3.** Anything added in mixing; an ingredient. [From Latin *admixtus,* past participle of *admiscēre,* to mix into : *ad,* to + *miscēre,* to mix.]

ad·mon·ish (ăd-mŏn′ĭsh) *tr.v.* **-ished, -ishing, -ishes. 1.** To reprove mildly or kindly, but firmly. **2.** To counsel against something; caution; warn. **3.** To remind or advise about something forgotten or disregarded, by means of a warning, reproof, or exhortation. —See Synonyms at **warn.** [Middle English *admonissen,* back-formation from *admonesten* (the stem *admonest-* was mistaken for a past participle), from Old French *admonester,* from Vulgar Latin *admonestāre* (unattested), variant of Latin *admonēre,* to bring to (someone's) mind : *ad-,* to + *monēre,* to remind, advise.] —**ad·mon·ish·er** *n.* —**ad·mon·ish·ing·ly** *adv.* —**ad·mon·ish·ment** *n.*

Synonyms: rebuke, reprimand, reproach, reprove.

ad·mo·ni·tion (ăd′mə-nĭsh′ən) *n.* **1.** A mild rebuke or warning. **2.** Cautionary advice. [Middle English *admonicioun,* from Old

French *amonition,* from Latin *admonitiō* (stem *admonitiōn-*), from *admonēre,* to ADMONISH.]

ad·mon·i·to·ry (ăd-mŏn′ə-tôr′ē, -tōr′ē) *adj.* Cautionary.

ad·nate (ăd′nāt′) *adj. Biology.* Joined to or fused with another part or organ. Said of parts not usually united. [Latin *adnātus,* past participle of *adnāscī, agnāscī,* to be born in addition to. See **agnate.**] —**ad·na·tion** (ăd-nā′shən) *n.*

ad nau·se·am (ăd nô′zē-əm) *adv. Latin.* To a sickening or tedious degree.

ad·noun (ăd′noun′) *n. Grammar.* An adjective used as a noun, as in *the bold* and *the brave.* [AD- (additional) + NOUN (by analogy with ADVERB).] —**ad·nom·i·nal** (ăd-nŏm′ə-nəl) *adj.*

a·do (ə-dōō′) *n.* Bustle; fuss; trouble; bother. [Middle English, from the phrase *at do,* "to do" : *at,* from Old Norse *at* (used with infinitive), to + *don,* to DO.]

a·do·be (ə-dō′bē) *n.* 1. a. Clay or loess, probably wind-blown in origin, found in the deserts of the southwestern United States and Mexico. b. A sun-dried brick made from this or a similar material. 2. A structure built with such bricks. [Spanish *adobe,* from Arabic *aṭṭoba, al-ṭōba,* "the brick."] —**a·do·be** *adj.*

ad·o·les·cence (ăd′l-ĕs′əns) *n.* 1. The period of physical and psychological development from the onset of puberty to maturity. 2. The condition of a person during that period.

ad·o·les·cent (ăd′l-ĕs′ənt) *adj.* 1. Of, pertaining to, or undergoing adolescence. 2. Immature in attitude or behavior; puerile: *adolescent dreams.* —*n.* An adolescent person. —See Synonyms at **young.** [Middle English, from Old French, from Latin *adolēscēns* (stem *adolēscent-*), present participle of *adolēscere,* to grow up : *ad-,* toward + *alēscere,* to grow, "be nourished," inceptive of *alere,* to nourish.]

Ad·o·nai (ăd′ō-nī′). *Hebrew.* Lord. Used in Judaism as a spoken substitute for the name of God. See **Tetragrammaton.** [Hebrew *adōnāi,* "my lord(s)," from Phoenician *adōn,* lord.]

A·don·ic (ə-dŏn′ĭk, ə-dō′nĭk) *adj.* 1. Of or designating a verse measure consisting of a dactyl followed by a spondee or trochee. 2. Of or pertaining to Adonis. —*n.* An Adonic verse. [This meter was said to have been first used in verses lamenting Adonis's death.]

A·don·is¹ (ə-dŏn′ĭs, ə-dō′nĭs). *Greek Mythology.* A youth loved by Aphrodite for his striking beauty. [Greek *Adōnis,* from Phoenician *adōn,* lord. See also **Adonai.**]

Adonis² *n.* A young man of great physical beauty.

a·dopt (ə-dŏpt′) *tr.v.* **adopted, adopting, adopts.** 1. To take into one's family through legal means and bring up as one's own child. 2. To select and bring into a new relationship, as a friend, heir, or citizen, for example. 3. To take and follow (a course of action, for example) by choice or assent: *adopt a new technique.* 4. To take up and use (an idea or word, for example) as one's own. 5. To take on or assume: *"He adopted the important air of a herald in red and gold"* (Stephen Crane). 6. To vote to accept: *adopt a resolution.* 7. To choose as a standard or required textbook or reference book in a school course. [Latin *adoptāre,* to choose for oneself : *ad-,* to + *optāre,* to choose, desire.] —**a·dopt·a·ble** *adj.* —**a·dopt·er** *n.* —**a·dop·tion** *n.*

a·dopt·ed (ə-dŏp′tĭd) *adj.* Related by adoption: *an adopted child.*

a·dop·tive (ə-dŏp′tĭv) *adj.* 1. Related by adoption: *an adoptive parent.* 2. Tending to adopt. —**a·dop·tive·ly** *adv.*

a·dor·a·ble (ə-dôr′ə-bəl, ə-dōr′-) *adj.* 1. Delightful; lovable; charming. 2. *Archaic.* Worthy of or eliciting worship. —**a·dor·a·bil·i·ty** (ə-dôr′ə-bĭl′ə-tē), **a·dor·a·ble·ness** *n.* —**a·dor·a·bly** *adv.*

ad·o·ra·tion (ăd′ə-rā′shən) *n.* 1. The act of worship. 2. Profound love or regard.

a·dore (ə-dôr′, ə-dōr′) *tr.v.* **adored, adoring, adores.** 1. To worship with divine honors. 2. *Informal.* To love deeply. 3. *Informal.* To like very much: *He adores being tickled.* —See Synonyms at **revere.** [Middle English *adoren,* from Old French *adorer,* from Latin *adōrāre,* to pray to : *ad-,* to + *ōrāre,* to speak, pray.] —**a·dor·er** *n.* —**a·dor·ing·ly** *adv.*

a·dorn (ə-dôrn′) *tr.v.* **adorned, adorning, adorns.** 1. To be a decoration to; lend beauty to: *"the pale mimosas that adorned the favourite promenade"* (Ronald Firbank). 2. To decorate; furnish with ornaments. 3. To add luster or distinction to. [Middle English *adornen,* from Old French *adorner,* from Latin *adornāre,* to put ornaments on : *ad-,* to + *ornāre,* to furnish, deck.] —**a·dorn·er** *n.* —**a·dorn·ment** *n.*

ADP *n.* An organic compound, $C_{10}H_{15}N_5O_{10}P_2$, that is formed when ATP undergoes hydrolysis of the terminal phosphate bond and releases its energy. [Adenosine *d*iphosphate.]

A.D.P. automatic data processing.

ad rem (ăd rĕm′) *adj. Latin.* To the point; pertinent. —**ad rem** *adv.*

ad·re·nal (ə-drē′nəl) *adj.* 1. At, near, or on the kidneys. 2. Of or pertaining to the adrenal glands or their secretions. —*n.* An adrenal gland. [AD- (toward, near) + RENAL.]

adrenal cortex *n.* The three-zoned center of the adrenal glands.

adrenal gland *n.* Either of two small dissimilarly shaped endocrine glands, one located above each kidney, consisting of the cortex, which secretes corticosteroid hormones, and the medulla, which secretes epinephrine. Also called "suprarenal gland."

a·dren·a·lin (ə-drĕn′əl-ĭn) *n.* Also **ad·ren·a·line.** 1. A secretion of the adrenal glands, **epinephrine** *(see).* 2. Broadly, a substance that is supposed to cause heightened emotion and a sudden increase in physical strength, as during fear or anger. [ADRENAL + -INE.]

ad·re·ner·gic (ăd′rə-nûr′jĭk) *adj.* Of, relating to, or having chemi-

cal activity like that of epinephrine. Said of certain nerve fibers. [ADREN(ALINE) + Greek *ergon,* work, action.]

ad·re·no·cor·ti·co·trop·ic (ə-drē′nō-kôr′tĭ-kō-trŏp′ĭk, -trō′pĭk) *adj.* Also **ad·re·no·cor·ti·co·troph·ic** (-trŏf′ĭk, -trō′fĭk). Stimulating or otherwise acting upon the cortex of the adrenal gland. [ADREN(AL) + CORTICO- + -TROPIC.]

adrenocorticotropic hormone *n.* A hormone, **ACTH** *(see).*

A·dri·an (ā′drē-ən), Edgar Douglas, 1st Baron (1889-1977). British physiologist. His research on nerve cells led to major advances in the understanding of the nervous and muscular systems. He won the 1932 Nobel Prize for physiology and medicine.

Adrian IV, born Nicholas Breakspear (c. 1100-1159). Also **Ha·dri·an IV** (hā′drē-ən). Pope (1154-59); the only English pope.

Adrianople. See **Edirne.**

A·dri·at·ic (ā′drē-ăt′ĭk) *adj.* Of or pertaining to the Adriatic Sea or to the peoples inhabiting its islands and coasts.

Adriatic Sea. A northern arm of the Mediterranean, between Italy and the Balkan Peninsula. It is c. 800 kilometers (500 miles) long, from the Gulf of Venice in the north to the Strait of Otranto.

a·drift (ə-drĭft′) *adv.* 1. Without anchor or steering; drifting. 2. Purposelessly; aimlessly. 3. Wrong; not according to plan: *His schemes went badly adrift.* 4. *Chiefly British Informal.* Unfastened or unattached: *Your shoelace has come adrift.* —**a·drift** *adj.*

a·droit (ə-droit′) *adj.* 1. Dexterous; deft. 2. Resourceful and quick-thinking under pressure. —See Synonyms at **dexterous.** [French, from *à droit,* "rightly" : *à,* to, at, from Latin *ad-* + *droit,* right, from Latin *dīrectus,* DIRECT.] —**a·droit·ly** *adv.* —**a·droit·ness** *n.*

ad·sci·ti·tious (ăd′sĭ-tĭsh′əs) *adj.* Not inherent or essential; added as a supplementary part. [From Latin *adscītus,* derived, assumed, past participle of *adscīscere,* to approve, arrogate to oneself : *ad-,* to + *scīscere,* to seek to know, assume, inceptive of *scīre,* to know.]

ad·sorb (ăd-sôrb′, -zôrb′) *tr.v.* **-sorbed, -sorbing, -sorbs.** To take up by adsorption. Compare **absorb.** [AD- + Latin *sorbēre,* to drink in, suck.]

ad·sor·bate (ăd-sôr′bĭt, -zôr′-) *n.* An adsorbed substance.

ad·sor·bent (ăd-sôr′bənt, -zôr′-) *adj.* Capable of adsorption. —*n.* An adsorbent material, such as activated carbon.

ad·sorp·tion (ăd-sôrp′shən, -zôrp′-) *n.* The assimilation of gas, vapor, or dissolved matter by the surface of a solid. [ADSORB + -TION.] —**ad·sorp·tive** *adj.*

adsuki bean. Variant of **adzuki bean.**

ad·u·lar·i·a (ăj′ōō-lâr′ē-ə) *n. Mineralogy.* A variety of **orthoclase** *(see).* [Italian, from French *adulaire,* after Adula, mountain group in Switzerland.]

ad·u·late (ăj′ōō-lāt′) *tr.v.* **-lated, -lating, -lates.** To praise excessively or fawningly. [Back-formation from ADULATION.] —**ad·u·la·tor** *n.* —**ad·u·la·to·ry** (ăj′ōō-lə-tôr′ē, -tōr′ē) *adj.*

ad·u·la·tion (ăj′ōō-lā′shən) *n.* Excessive praise or flattery. [Middle English *adulacioun,* from Old French *adulation,* from Latin *adulātiō,* from *adulārī†,* to flatter.]

a·dult (ə-dŭlt′, ăd′ŭlt) *n.* 1. One who has attained maturity or legal age. 2. A fully grown, mature organism, such as an insect that has completed its final stage of metamorphosis. —*adj.* 1. Fully developed and mature. 2. Pertaining to, befitting, or intended for mature persons: *adult education.* 3. Sexually explicit; pornographic. Used euphemistically: *adult films.* [Latin *adultus,* past participle of *adolēscere,* to grow up. See **adolescent.**] —**a·dult·hood** *n.*

a·dul·ter·ant (ə-dŭl′tər-ənt) *n.* A substance that adulterates. —*adj.* Adulterating.

a·dul·ter·ate (ə-dŭl′tə-rāt′) *tr.v.* **-ated, -ating, -ates.** To make impure, spurious, or inferior by adding extraneous or improper ingredients. —*adj.* 1. Spurious; adulterated; corrupt: *"prefer the adulterate enjoyments of the town to the genuine pleasures of a country"* (Smollett). 2. Adulterous. [Latin *adulterāre,* to pollute, commit adultery.] —**a·dul·ter·a·tion** (ə-dŭl′tə-rā′shən) *n.* —**a·dul·ter·a·tor** *n.*

a·dul·ter·er (ə-dŭl′tər-ər) *n.* A person, especially a man, who commits adultery.

a·dul·ter·ess (ə-dŭl′trĭs, ə-dŭl′tər-ĭs) *n.* A woman who commits adultery.

a·dul·ter·ine (ə-dŭl′tə-rīn′, -rĭn) *adj.* 1. Characterized by adulteration; spurious; fake. 2. Unauthorized by law; illegal. 3. Born of adultery: *adulterine children.* [Latin *adulterīnus* from *adulterāre,* to commit adultery, ADULTERATE.]

a·dul·ter·ous (ə-dŭl′tər-əs, -trəs) *adj.* Characterized by, inclined to, or having committed adultery. —**a·dul·ter·ous·ly** *adv.*

a·dul·ter·y (ə-dŭl′tər-ē, -trē) *n., pl.* **-ries.** Voluntary sexual intercourse between a married person and a partner other than the lawful husband or wife. [Middle English *adulterie, a(d)vouterie,* from Old French *avoutrie, avoutire,* from Latin *adulterium,* from *adulter,* adulterer, from *adulterāre,* to ADULTERATE.]

ad·um·bral (ăd-ŭm′brəl) *adj.* In shadow. [AD- (in) + Latin *umbra,* shadow.]

ad·um·brate (ăd′əm-brāt′, ə-dŭm′-) *tr.v.* **-brated, -brating, -brates.** 1. To give a sketchy outline of. 2. To prefigure indistinctly; foreshadow. 3. To disclose partially or guardedly. 4. To overshadow; obscure. [Latin *adumbrāre,* to overshadow : *ad-,* to + *umbra,* shadow.] —**ad·um·bra·tion** (ăd′əm-brā′shən) *n.* —**ad·um·bra·tive** (ə-dŭm′brə-tĭv) *adj.* —**ad·um·bra·tive·ly** *adv.*

a·dust (ə-dŭst′) *adj.* 1. Burnt; scorched. 2. Melancholy; gloomy. [Middle English, from Latin *adūstus,* from the past participle of *adūrere,* to set fire to : *ad-* + *ūrere,* to burn.]

adobe *An adobe mission building in New Mexico built of sun-dried bricks that are made from a mixture of clay and straw.*

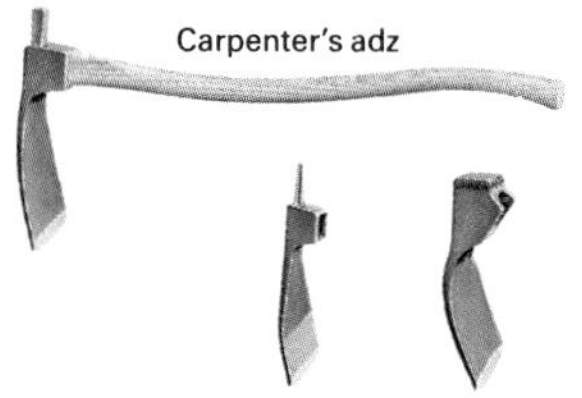
Carpenter's adz
Shipwright's adz
Fencer's adz

adz *A carpenter's cutting tool on a handle. The adz is a forerunner of the plane, and has been in common use for more than 5,000 years.*

adv. adverb; adverbial.

ad va·lo·rem (ăd və-lôr′əm, -lōr′-) *adj. Latin. Abbr.* **a.v., ad val.** In proportion to the value: *ad valorem duties on imported goods.* **—ad va·lo·rem** *adv.*

ad·vance (ăd-văns′, -väns′) *v.* **-vanced, -vancing, -vances.** *—tr.* **1.** To move or bring forward in position. **2.** To put forward; propose; suggest. **3.** To aid the growth or progress of; further. **4.** To raise in rank; promote. **5.** To cause to occur sooner; hasten. **6.** To raise in amount or rate; increase. **7.** To pay (money or interest) before legally due. **8.** To supply or lend, especially on credit. *—intr.* **1.** To go or move forward or onward. **2.** To make progress; improve; grow. **3.** To rise in rank, position, or value.
~n. **1.** The act or process of moving or going forward. **2.** Improvement; progress. **3.** A rise or increase of price or value. **4. advances.** Personal approaches made to secure acquaintance, favor, or an agreement; overtures. **5. a.** The furnishing of funds or goods on credit. **b.** The funds or goods so furnished; a loan. **6.** A payment of money before legally or normally due. **—in advance. 1.** In front. **2.** Ahead of time; beforehand; early. Often used with *of.*
~adj. **1.** Made or given ahead of time; prior. **2.** Going before; in front; forward. [Middle English *advancen,* from Old French *avancier,* from Vulgar Latin *abantiāre* (unattested), from Latin *abante,* "from before" : *ab-,* away from + *ante,* before.] **—ad·vance·ment** *n.* **—ad·vanc·er** *n.*
Synonyms: *forward, further, promote.*

ad·vanced (ăd-vănst′, -vänst′) *adj.* **1. a.** Far on in development or progress: *The child is very advanced for her age.* **b.** Far on in life: *advanced in years.* **2.** Ahead of contemporary thought or practice: *advanced ideas.* **3.** At a high level of difficulty: *advanced mathematics.*

advanced gas-cooled reactor *n. Abbr.* **A.G.R.** A type of nuclear reactor in which the coolant is gaseous carbon dioxide, the moderator is graphite, and the fuel is ceramic uranium dioxide in a stainless-steel casing.

advance guard *n. Military.* A detachment of troops sent ahead of the main force to reconnoiter and provide protection.

ad·van·tage (ăd-văn′tĭj, ăd-vän′-) *n.* **1.** A factor favorable or conducive to success. **2.** Benefit or profit; gain. **3.** A position of relative superiority: *has the advantage.* **4.** In racket games, the first point scored after deuce, or the resulting score. In this sense, also called "ad," "vantage." **—take advantage of. 1.** To put to good use; avail oneself of. **2.** To profit selfishly by; exploit. **3.** To seduce. Used euphemistically. **—to advantage.** So as to produce a good or favorable effect: *She uses her husky voice to advantage.*
~tr.v. **advantaged, -taging, -tages.** To afford profit or gain to; benefit. [Middle English *avantage,* from Old French, "the condition of being ahead," from *avant,* before, from Latin *abante,* (from) before. See **advance.**]

ad·van·ta·geous (ăd′văn-tā′jəs, ăd′vən-) *adj.* Affording benefit or gain; profitable; useful. **—ad·van·ta·geous·ly** *adv.* **—ad·van·ta·geous·ness** *n.*

ad·vec·tion (ăd-vĕk′shən) *n. Meteorology.* The transfer of heat or water vapor by horizontally moving air. [Latin *advectiō* (stem *advectiōn-*), conveyance, from *advehere* (past participle *advectus*), to carry to : *ad-,* to + *vehere,* to carry.]

ad·vent (ăd′vĕnt′) *n.* The coming or arrival, especially of something expected or momentous: *"a melodious tinkle of strings announced the advent of the minstrels"* (Ronald Firbank). [Middle English, from Latin *adventus,* from the past participle of *advenīre,* to come to.]

Advent *n.* **1.** The birth of Christ. **2.** See **Second Coming. 3.** The period including four Sundays before Christmas, the first of which is called Advent Sunday.

Ad·vent·ist (ăd′vĕn-tĭst) *n.* A member of any of several Christian denominations that believe Christ's second coming and the end of the world are near at hand. See **Seventh-Day Adventist. —Ad·vent·ism** *n.*

ad·ven·ti·ti·a (ăd′vĕn-tĭsh′ē-ə) *n.* The outermost covering of an organ, especially of a blood vessel. [New Latin, from Latin *adventīcius,* ADVENTITIOUS.]

ad·ven·ti·tious (ăd′vĕn-tĭsh′əs) *adj.* **1.** Acquired by accident; added by chance; not inherent: *adventitious scribblings in the margins of a manuscript.* **2.** *Biology.* Appearing in an unusual place or in an irregular or sporadic manner: *adventitious shoots.* [Latin *adventīcius,* "arriving (from outside)," from *adventus,* arrival, ADVENT.] **—ad·ven·ti·tious·ly** *adv.* **—ad·ven·ti·tious·ness** *n.*

ad·ven·tive (ăd-vĕn′tĭv) *adj. Biology.* Not native to, and not fully established in, a new habitat or environment; locally or temporarily naturalized: *an adventive weed.*
~n. Biology. An adventive organism. [Latin *adventus,* arrival, ADVENT.] **—ad·ven·tive·ly** *adv.*

Advent Sunday *n.* The first of the four Sundays of Advent; the Sunday nearest to the last day of November.

ad·ven·ture (ăd-vĕn′chər) *n.* **1.** An undertaking of a hazardous nature; a risky enterprise: *Fording the stream was an adventure.* **2.** An unusual experience or course of events marked by excitement and suspense. **3.** Participation in hazardous or exciting experiences: *a wandering life, full of adventure.* **4.** A financial speculation or business venture.
~v. **adventured, -turing, -tures.** *—tr.* To venture upon; risk; dare. *—intr.* **1.** To take risks; engage in hazardous activities. **2.** To dare to enter or embark. Used with *on* or *upon.* [Middle English *aventure,* from Old French, from Vulgar Latin *(rēs) adventūra* (unattested), "(a thing) that will happen," from Latin *adventūrus,* future participle of *advenīre,* to arrive. See **advent.**]

ad·ven·tur·er (ăd-vĕn′chər-ər) *n.* **1.** One who adventures. **2.** A mercenary soldier. **3.** A heavy speculator. **4.** One who seeks wealth and social position by unscrupulous means.

ad·ven·ture·some (ăd-vĕn′chər-səm) *adj.* Daring; venturesome. **—ad·ven·ture·some·ly** *adv.* **—ad·ven·ture·some·ness** *n.*

ad·ven·tur·ess (ăd-vĕn′chər-ĭs) *n.* A woman who seeks social and financial advancement by dubious means.

ad·ven·tur·ism (ăd-vĕn′chə-rĭz′əm) *n.* Recklessness in political or financial activities. **—ad·ven·tur·ist** *n.* & *adj.*

ad·ven·tur·ous (ăd-vĕn′chər-əs) *adj.* **1.** Inclined to undertake new and daring enterprises or activities; bold; daring: *trails for adventurous hikers.* **2.** Hazardous; risky. —See Synonyms at **reckless. —ad·ven·tur·ous·ly** *adv.* **—ad·ven·tur·ous·ness** *n.*

ad·verb (ăd′vûrb′) *n. Abbr.* **adv. 1.** A part of speech comprising a class of words that modify a verb, adjective, whole sentence, or other adverb. **2.** A word belonging to this class, such as *rapidly* in *He runs rapidly.* [Middle English, from Old French *adverbe,* from Latin *adverbium* (translation of Greek *epirrhēma,* "added word") : *ad-,* additional + *verbum,* word.]

ad·ver·bi·al (ăd-vûr′bē-əl) *adj.* Of, pertaining to, or used as an adverb: *an adverbial phrase.*
~n. **1.** An adverb. **2.** A word, phrase, or clause functioning as an adverb. *Nicely* and *in a nice way* can both be adverbials. **—ad·ver·bi·al·ly** *adv.*

ad ver·bum (ăd vûr′bəm) *adv. Latin.* Word for word; verbatim.

ad·ver·sar·i·al (ăd′vər-sâr′ē-əl) *adj.* Involving, or considered to involve, adversaries or strongly opposed interests: *an adversarial relationship.*

ad·ver·sar·y (ăd′vər-sĕr′ē) *n., pl.* **-ies.** An opponent; an enemy. **—the Adversary.** The Devil. [Middle English *adversarie,* from Latin *adversārius,* opponent, from *adversus,* ADVERSE.]

ad·ver·sa·tive (ăd-vûr′sə-tĭv) *adj. Grammar.* Expressing antithesis or opposition. Said of words and clauses.
~n. An adversative word, such as *however* or *but.* [Latin *adversātivus,* from *adversāri,* to be opposed to, from *adversus,* ADVERSE.] **—ad·ver·sa·tive·ly** *adv.*

ad·verse (ăd-vûrs′, ăd′vûrs′) *adj.* **1.** Antagonistic in design or effect; hostile; opposed: *adverse criticism.* **2.** Contrary to one's interests or welfare; unfavorable; unpropitious: *adverse circumstances.* **3.** In an opposite or opposing direction or position: *adverse winds.* **4.** *Botany.* Facing the axis or main stem. —See Synonyms at **contrary.** [Middle English, from Old French *advers,* from Latin *adversus,* past participle of *advertere,* to turn toward (with hostility).] **—ad·verse·ly** *adv.* **—ad·verse·ness** *n.*

adverse possession *n. Law.* Occupation of a property in a way that threatens the rights of the owner.

ad·ver·si·ty (ăd-vûr′sə-tē) *n., pl.* **-ties. 1.** A state of hardship, suffering, or affliction; misfortune. **2.** A calamitous event. —See Synonyms at **misfortune.**

ad·vert[1] (ăd-vûrt′) *intr.v.* **-verted, -verting, -verts.** To call attention; refer: *advert to a problem.* [Middle English *a(d)verten,* from Old French *a(d)vertir,* from Vulgar Latin *advertīre* (unattested), from Latin *advertere,* to turn toward. See **adverse.**] **—ad·vert·ence, ad·vert·en·cy** *n.* **—ad·vert·ent** *adj.* **—ad·vert·ent·ly** *adv.*

ad·vert[2] (ăd′vûrt′) *n. Chiefly British Informal.* An advertisement.

ad·ver·tise (ăd′vər-tīz′) *v.* **-tised, -tising, -tises.** *—tr.* **1. a.** To make public announcement of: *advertise a vacancy.* **b.** To cause to be generally or publicly known: *Roosevelt did not conceal his disability, but he did not advertise it.* **2.** To proclaim publicly the qualities or advantages of (a product or service, for example) so as to increase sales. **3.** *Archaic.* To warn or notify. *—intr.* **1.** To call the attention of the public to a product, service, or the like: *The store advertises on television.* **2.** To ask in a public notice, as in a newspaper; make a public request. Often used with *for: I'm advertising for a new roommate.* [Middle English *a(d)vertisen,* from Old French *a(d)vertir* (present participle *advertissant*), TO ADVERT.] **—ad·ver·tis·er** *n.*

ad·ver·tise·ment (ăd′vər-tīz′mənt, ăd-vûr′tĭs-, -tĭz-) *n. Abbr.* **advt.** Any public notice, such as a poster, newspaper display, television, film, or radio announcement, designed to sell a product, publicize a vacancy or service, influence opinion, or the like.

ad·ver·tis·ing (ăd′vər-tī′zĭng) *n.* **1.** The action of attracting public attention, as to a product or business. **2.** The business of preparing and distributing advertisements for publication or broadcast. **3.** Printed or broadcast advertisements collectively.

ad·vice (ăd-vīs′) *n.* **1.** Opinion from one not immediately concerned as to what could or should be done in a given situation; counsel. **2.** *Often* **advices.** Information or a report, especially when communicated from a distance: *advices from an ambassador.* **3.** A formal notice regarding a financial transaction: *a stock-purchase advice.* [Middle English *a(d)vise,* from Old French *a(d)vis,* opinion, from Vulgar Latin *advīsum* (unattested), opinion, probably from some such phrase as *ad (meum) vīsum,* "according to (my) view" : *ad,* to + *vīsum,* view, from the neuter past participle of *vidēre,* to see.]

ad·vis·a·ble (ăd-vī′zə-bəl) *adj.* Worthy of being recommended or suggested; prudent; expedient. **—ad·vis·a·bil·i·ty** (ăd-vī′zə-bĭl′ə-tē), **ad·vis·a·ble·ness** *n.* **—ad·vis·a·bly** *adv.*

ad·vise (ăd-vīz′) *v.* **-vised, -vising, -vises.** *—tr.* **1.** To offer advice to; counsel: *aides who advise the president.* **2.** To recommend by way of advice; suggest: *My broker advised caution.* **3.** To inform; notify: *advise a person of a decision.* *—intr.* **1.** To offer or be able to give advice. **2.** To consult; take counsel. Used with *with: You should*

PRONUNCIATION KEY

ă, pat; ā, pay; âr, care;
ä, father, are; b, bib;
ch, church; d, deed; ĕ, pet;
ē, be; f, fife; g, gag; h, hat;
hw, which; ĭ, pit; ī, pie;
îr, pier; j, judge; k, kick;
l, lid, needle; m, mum;
n, no, sudden; ng, thing;
ŏ, pot; ō, toe; ô, paw, for;
oi, noise; ou, out; o͝o, book;
o͞o, boot; p, pop; r, roar;
s, sauce; sh, ship, dish;
t, tight; th, thin, path;
th, this, bathe; ŭ, cut; ûr, fur;
v, valve; w, with; y, yes;
z, zebra, size; zh, vision;
ə, about, item, edible,
gallop, circus, peaceful

IN FOREIGN WORDS:

à, *Fr.* ami; œ, *Fr.* feu, *Ger.* schön; ü, *Fr.* tu, *Ger.* über;
KH, *Ger.* ich, *Scot.* loch;
N, *Fr.* bon; y′, *Fr.* Compiègne

STRESS MARKS:

Primary stress: ′
in·cite′ (ĭn-sīt′)
Secondary stress: ′
in′sight′ (ĭn′sīt′)

advise with your associates before making a decision. [Middle English *a(d)visen,* from Old French *a(d)viser,* from Vulgar Latin *advīsāre* (unattested), to observe (influenced by Latin *advīsum,* ADVICE) : Latin *ad-,* to, at + *vīsere,* desiderative of *vidēre* (past participle *vīsus*), to see.] **—ad·vi·so·ry** *adj.*

Usage: In the sense of "inform" or "notify," the use of *advise* is usually restricted to business correspondence.

ad·vised (ăd-vīzd′) *adj.* Considered; thought out. Used chiefly in the combinations *well-advised* and *ill-advised.* **—ad·vis·ed·ly** (ăd-vī′zĭd-lē) *adv.*

ad·vise·ment (ăd-vīz′mənt) *n.* **1.** Careful consideration. **2.** Consultation.

ad·vis·er, ad·vi·sor (ăd-vī′zər) *n.* A person who offers advice, especially in an official or professional capacity.

ad·vo·caat, ad·vo·kaat (ăd′vō-kät′) *n.* A sweet, thick, yellow Dutch liqueur made of raw egg yolks and brandy. [Dutch, shortened from *advocaatenborrel,* from *advocaat,* ADVOCATE (noun) + *borrel,* drink.]

ad·vo·ca·cy (ăd′və-kə-sē) *n.* Active support, as of a cause.

ad·vo·cate (ăd′və-kāt′) *tr.v.* **-cated, -cating, -cates.** To speak in favor of; recommend. —See Synonyms at **support.**

~n. (ăd′və-kĭt, -kāt′). **1.** A person who argues for a cause or idea; a supporter or defender. **2.** A person who pleads on another's behalf; an intercessor. **3.** *Law.* In Scotland and South Africa, a **barrister** *(see).* —See Usage note at **lawyer.** [Middle English *a(d)vocat,* a lawyer, from Old French, from Latin *advocātus,* "one summoned (to give evidence)," from *advocāre,* to call or summon to : *ad,* to + *vocāre,* to call.] **—ad·vo·ca·to·ry** (ăd-vŏk′ə-tôr′ē, -tōr′ē) *adj.*

ad·vow·son (ăd-vou′zən) *n.* In English ecclesiastical law, the right to nominate the successor to a vacant benefice. [Middle English *avoweson, advounson,* from Norman French *a(d)voeson,* variant of Old French *avoueson,* from Medieval Latin *advocātiō,* presentation, summoning, from Latin *advocāre,* to summon, ADVOCATE.]

advt. advertisement.

ad·y·na·mi·a (ăd′ə-nā′mē-ə, ā′dī-năm′ē-ə) *n.* Loss of energy or strength, especially after illness; feebleness or debility. [A- (not) + Greek *dunamis,* power, from *dunasthai,* to be able.] **—ad·y·nam·ic** (ăd′ə-năm′ĭk, ā′dī-năm′ĭk) *adj.*

ad·y·tum (ăd′ə-təm) *n., pl.* **-ta** (-tə). The sanctum in an ancient temple. [Latin, from Greek *aduton,* neuter of *adutos,* not to be entered : *a-,* not + *duein*†, to enter, sink.]

adz, adze (ădz) *n.* An axlike tool with an arched blade at right angles to the handle, used for dressing wood. [Middle English *adse,* Old English *adesa*†.]

ad·zu·ki bean (ăd-zo͞o′kē) *n.* Also **ad·su·ki bean** (ăd-so͞o′kē, -zo͞o′-). A plant, *Phaseolus angularis,* with yellow flowers and pods bearing edible seeds, widely cultivated as a food crop in the Orient. [Japanese *azuki,* "red bean."]

A.E.A. Actor's Equity Association.

A.E. and P. Ambassador Extraordinary and Plenipotentiary.

AEC, A.E.C. Atomic Energy Commission.

ae·ci·o·spore (ē′sē-ō-spôr′, -spōr′). Also **ae·cid·i·o·spore** (ē-sĭd′-ē-ō-spôr′, -spōr) *n. Botany.* A rust spore, formed in a chainlike series in an aecium. [*Aecium* + *spore.*]

ae·ci·um (ē′sē-əm, ē′shē-əm) *n., pl.* **-cia** (-sē-ə, -shē-ə). Also **ae·cid·i·um** (ē-sĭd′ē-əm), *pl.* **-ia** (-ē-ə). *Botany.* A cuplike structure in rust fungi, containing chains of aeciospores. [New Latin, from Greek *aikia,* injury (rust fungi are destructive), from *aikēs,* unseemly.] **—ae·ci·al** (ē′sē-əl, -shē-əl) *adj.*

a·e·des (ā-ē′dēz) *n., pl.* **aedes.** Any mosquito of the genus *Aedes,* such as *A. aegypti,* which transmits yellow fever and dengue. [New Latin *Aedes,* from Greek *aēdēs,* unpleasant : *a-,* not + *ēdos,* pleasant.]

ae·dile (ē′dīl′) *n.* In ancient Rome, an elected official who was responsible for public works and games and for the supervision of markets, the grain supply, and the water supply. [Latin *aedīlis,* "(one) concerned with buildings," from *aedēs,* house.]

Ae·ge·an (ĭ-jē′ən) *adj.* **1.** Of or pertaining to the Aegean Sea. **2.** Of, pertaining to, or designating the prehistoric civilization that flourished in the Aegean area in the Bronze Age.

Aegean Sea. A northeastern arm of the Mediterranean between Greece and Turkey. It is roughly 630 kilometers (380 miles) long and 300 kilometers (186 miles) wide and contains numerous, mainly Greek islands. The **Aegean Islands** include the Cyclades, the Dodecanese, and the Sporades.

Ae·gi·na (ē-jī′nə). *Greek* **Ai·gi·na** (ā′gĭn-ə). Greek town and island in the Aegean, near Athens. It was a prosperous and important city-state in the 5th century B.C., but declined in importance after defeat by the Athenians, who expelled its inhabitants.

Ae·gir (ăg′ər). *Norse Mythology.* The god of the sea.

ae·gis (ē′jĭs) *n.* Also **e·gis. 1.** *Greek Mythology.* The shield of Zeus, lent by him to Athena. **2.** Protection or sponsorship: *a conference held under the aegis of the World Health Organization.* Compare **auspices.** [Latin, from Greek *aigis* (often depicted as a goatskin, and associated by folk etymology with *aix,* stem *aig-,* goat).]

Ae·gis·thus (ē-jĭs′thəs). In Greek legend, the son of Thyestes and lover of Clytemnestra.

Ael·fric (ăl′frĭk), also called "Grammaticus" (*c.* 955–*c.* 1020). English abbot and writer. He is considered to be the greatest prose writer of Anglo-Saxon times. His prolific output included *Homilies* (the first Christian texts written in English), *Lives of the Saints,* a Latin grammar, and translations of Latin religious literature.

-aemia. Variant of **-emia.**

Ae·ne·as (ĭ-nē′əs). In classical legend, a Trojan prince, the son of Anchises and Aphrodite, who, as recounted in the Aeneid, escaped the sack of Troy and after an arduous sea voyage settled in Italy, where his descendants eventually founded Rome.

Ae·ne·id (ĭ-nē′ĭd) *n.* An epic poem in Latin by Virgil, telling of the adventures of Aeneas after the destruction of Troy.

a·e·ne·ous (ā-ē′nē-əs) *adj.* Having a brassy or golden-green color. [Latin *aeneus, aenus,* of bronze or copper, from *aes,* bronze, copper.]

Ae·o·li·an (ē-ō′lē-ən) *adj.* **1.** Of or pertaining to Aeolus, god of the winds. **2.** *Music.* Of or designating a mode represented by the white notes of the scale of A on the piano keyboard. **3. aeolian.** Of or caused by the action of the wind. Said of erosion.

~n. **1.** A member of one of the major Greek tribes that settled in central Greece and on the west coast of Asia Minor. **2.** Aeolic.

Aeolian harp *n.* A musical instrument consisting of an open box with strings stretched across it that sound when wind passes over them. Also called "wind harp."

Aeolian Islands. See **Lipari Islands.**

Ae·ol·ic (ē-ŏl′ĭk) *n.* One of the four main dialects of ancient Greek, spoken in Thessaly, Boeotia, and in the coastal region of Asia Minor north of Ionia. Compare **Arcado-Cyprian, Attic-Ionic, Doric.**

ae·ol·i·pile (ē-ŏl′ə-pīl′) *n.* A prototype steam turbine invented *c.* 100 B.C., consisting of a hollow sphere fitted with projecting angled exhaust jets and mounted to permit free rotation about the steam inlet axis. [Latin *aeolipila,* from Greek *aiolipulē,* "wind-vent" : *Aiolos,* AEOLUS + *pulē,* gate.]

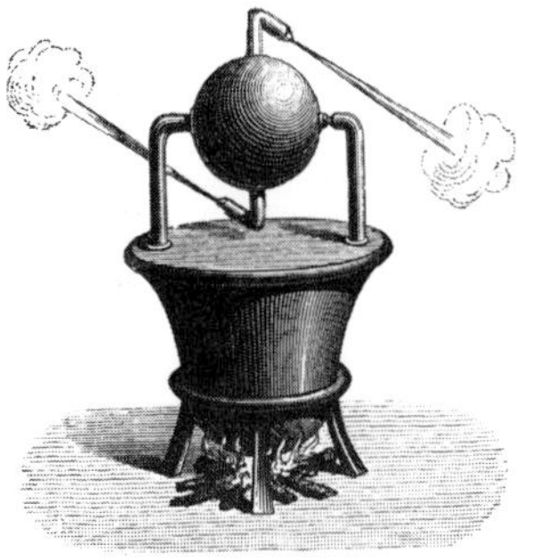

aeolipile *The Greek engineer Hero of Alexandria invented this simple form of steam turbine in 100 B.C. A closed caldron produced steam that passed into a hollow ball and then escaped through narrow, bent pipes, causing the ball to rotate. It was not until the 1600's, however, that the idea of using steam for power was really exploited.*

Ae·o·lus (ē′ə-ləs). *Greek Mythology.* The god of the winds. [Latin, from Greek *Aiolos,* from *aiolos*†, quick-moving.]

aeon. Variant of **eon.**

aer·ate (âr′āt′) *tr.v.* **-ated, -ating, -ates. 1.** To charge (liquid) with a gas, especially carbon dioxide. **2.** To expose to the circulation of air for purification. **3.** To supply (blood) with oxygen. [AER(O)- + -ATE.] **—aer·a·tion** (âr-ā′shən) *n.*

aer·a·tor (âr′ā′tər) *n.* A device for aerating liquids.

aer·i·al (âr′ē-əl, ā-ĭr′ē-əl) *adj.* **1.** Existing or functioning in the air: *an aerial telephone cable.* **2.** Reaching high into the air; lofty. **3.** Light and airy; insubstantial; imaginary. **4.** Of, by, or from aircraft: *an aerial photograph.* **5.** *Botany.* Borne in the air rather than underground or under water: *aerial roots.*

~n. (âr′ē-əl). *Electronics.* An **antenna** *(see).* [Latin *āerius,* from Greek *aērios,* from *aēr,* air.]

aer·i·al·ist (âr′ē-əl-ĭst) *n.* An acrobat who performs on a tightrope, trapeze, or similar apparatus.

aerial ladder *n.* A ladder that can be extended to reach high places, especially one mounted on a fire engine.

aer·ie (âr′ē, ăr′ē, ĭr′ē) *n.* Also **aer·y, eyr·ie. 1.** The nest of an eagle or other predatory bird, built on a crag or other high place. **2.** A room, house, or fortification built on a height. [Medieval Latin *aeria, aerea,* from Old French *aire, aere,* from Latin *ārea,* open field, threshing floor, bird's nest (possibly influenced by Latin *ager,* native place, acre).]

aero-, aer- *prefix.* Indicates: **1.** Air, gas, or the atmosphere; for example, **aerate, aerosphere. 2.** Aircraft; for example, **aeromedicine.** [Middle English, from Old French, from Latin, from Greek, from *aēr,* air.]

aer·o·bal·lis·tics (âr′ō-bə-lĭs′tĭks) *n. Used with a singular verb.* The ballistics of missiles and other projectiles in the atmosphere.

aer·o·bat·ics (âr′ō-băt′ĭks) *n. Used with a singular or plural verb.* The performance of stunts, such as rolls and loops, in an airplane or glider. [AERO- + (ACRO)BATICS.]

aer·obe (âr′ōb′) *n.* An organism, such as a bacterium, requiring molecular oxygen or air to live. [French *aérobie,* "air-life" : AERO- + Greek *bios,* life.]

aer·o·bic (â-rō′bĭk) *adj.* **1.** Of or indicating a process, such as respiration, dependent on molecular oxygen or air. **2.** Of or pertaining to aerobes. **3.** Of or pertaining to aerobics. **—aer·o·bic·al·ly** *adv.*

aer·o·bics (â-rō′bĭks) *n. Used with a singular verb.* A system of vigorous physical exercises, sometimes combined with dance routines, designed to speed up the breathing and stimulate blood circulation. [AERO- + Greek *bios,* life + -ICS.]

aer·o·bi·ol·o·gy (âr′ō-bī-ŏl′ə-jē) *n.* The study of airborne microorganisms, pollen, spores, and the like, especially those causing disease.

aer·o·bi·o·sis (âr′ō-bī-ō′sĭs) *n.* Life in the presence of molecular oxygen or air. [AERO- + -BIOSIS.]

aerodrome. *Chiefly British.* Variant of **airdrome.**

aer·o·dy·nam·ic (âr′ō-dī-năm′ĭk) *adj.* **1.** Of or pertaining to aerodynamics. **2.** Embodying aerodynamic principles; streamlined: *the car's sleek aerodynamic lines.*

aer·o·dy·nam·ics (âr′ō-dī-năm′ĭks) *n. Used with a singular verb.* The dynamics of gases, especially of atmospheric interactions with moving objects. See feature, next page.

aer·o·dyne (âr′ə-dīn′) *n.* Any heavier-than-air aircraft that derives its lift chiefly from motion. [AERO- + *-dyne,* from Greek *dunamis,* power, from *dunasthai,* to be able.]

aer·o·em·bo·lism (âr′ō-ĕm′bə-lĭz′əm) *n.* The presence of nitrogen bubbles in the blood and tissues caused by a sudden reduction in atmospheric pressure, as occurs in decompression sickness.

aer·o engine (âr′ō) *n.* An engine used to power an aircraft.

aerofoil. *Chiefly British.* Variant of **airfoil.**

aer·o·gram, aer·o·gramme (âr′ə-grăm′) *n.* An airmail letter written on a standard, lightweight form that folds into the shape of an envelope and can be sent at a low postage rate. Also called "air letter." [AERO- + -GRAM.]

BASICS OF FLIGHT
How control, thrust, and lift keep an airplane in the air

When, on December 17, 1903, the Wright brothers in Kitty Hawk, North Carolina, made the first powered flight in an airplane, Wilbur Wright acknowledged his debt to a British engineer of 100 years before.

The work done by Sir George Cayley between 1799 and 1809 laid the foundations of modern aerodynamics. Models and gliders designed by him proved that heavier-than-air flight was possible. Cayley also established the principles that govern the flight of airplanes: that an aircraft needs a lifting force to raise it into the air, a system of control, and a means of propulsion.

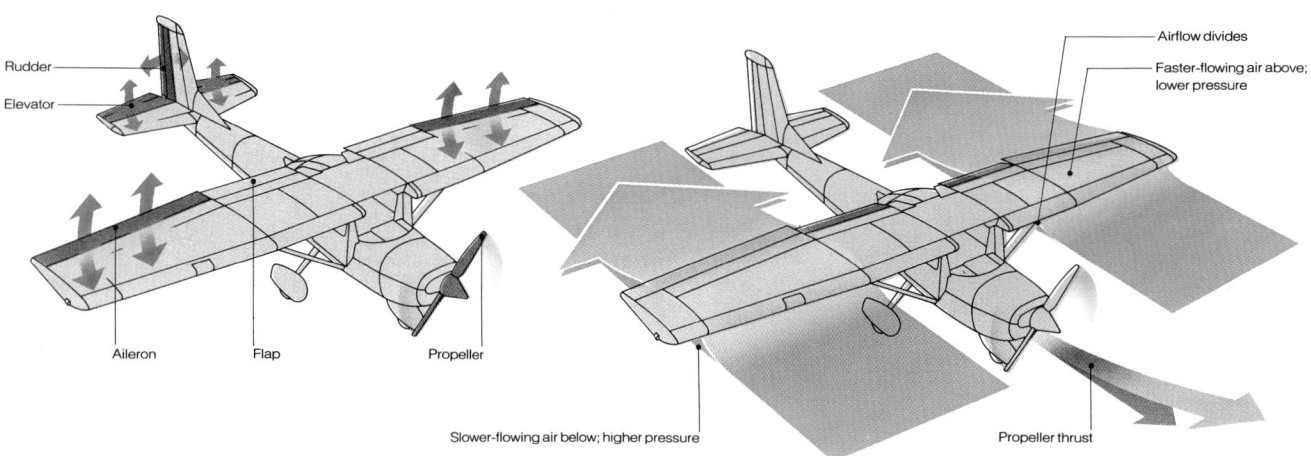

CONTROL AND THRUST *On a simple, light aircraft, a propeller powered by an internal-combustion engine provides thrust through the air. The moving control surfaces consist of ailerons and flaps on the wings and a rudder and elevators on the tail.*

LIFT *Air passing over the curved top surface of the wing has farther to go, and therefore travels faster, than the air passing under the flatter, bottom surface. The pressure of the slower-moving air under the wing is greater, and the wings lift.*

aer·o·lite (âr′ə-līt′) *n.* A chiefly silicious meteorite. [AERO- + -LITE.] —**aer·o·lit·ic** (âr′ə-lĭt′ĭk) *adj.*

aer·ol·o·gy (âr-ŏl′ə-jē) *n.* Total atmospheric meteorology as opposed to surface-based study; climatology. [AERO- + -LOGY.] —**aer·o·log·ic** (âr′ə-lŏj′ĭk), **aer·o·log·i·cal** *adj.* —**aer·ol·o·gist** (âr-ŏl′ə-jĭst) *n.*

aer·o·me·chan·ics (âr′ō-mĭ-kăn′ĭks) *n. Used with a singular verb.* The science of the motion and equilibrium of air and other gases, comprising aerodynamics and aerostatics. —**aer·o·me·chan·i·cal** *adj.* —**aer·o·me·chan·i·cal·ly** *adv.*

aer·o·med·i·cine (âr′ō-mĕd′ə-sĭn) *n.* The medical study and treatment of disturbances, disorders, and diseases resulting from or associated with atmospheric flight. Compare **aviation medicine.** —**aer·o·med·i·cal** *adj.*

aer·o·me·te·or·o·graph (âr′ō-mē′tē-ôr′ə-grăf′, -gräf′) *n.* An aircraft instrument for simultaneously recording temperature, atmospheric pressure, and humidity.

aer·om·e·ter (âr-ŏm′ə-tər) *n.* A device for determining the weight and density of air or other gas.

aer·o·naut (âr′ə-nôt′) *n.* A pilot or navigator of a balloon or lighter-than-air craft. [French *aéronaute* : AERO- (air) + Greek *nautēs,* sailor. See **nautical.**]

aer·o·nau·tics (âr′ə-nô′tĭks) *n. Used with a singular verb.* **1.** The science of aircraft design and construction. **2.** The theory and practice of aircraft navigation. —**aer·o·nau·tic, aer·o·nau·ti·cal** *adj.*

aer·on·o·my (âr-ŏn′ə-mē) *n.* The study of the upper atmosphere, especially of regions of ionized gas. [AERO- + -NOMY.]

aer·o·pause (âr′ə-pôz′) *n.* The region of the atmosphere above which aircraft cannot fly. [AERO- + -PAUSE.]

aer·o·pha·gia (âr′ə-fā′jə) *n.* The abnormal, spasmodic swallowing of air, especially as a symptom of hysteria.

aer·o·pho·bi·a (âr′ə-fō′bē-ə) *n.* The abnormal fear of air or of drafts.

aer·o·phyte (âr′ə-fīt′) *n. Botany.* An **epiphyte** (*see*).

aeroplane. *Chiefly British.* Variant of **airplane.**

aer·o·sol (âr′ə-sôl′, -sŏl′, -sōl′) *n.* **1.** A gaseous suspension of fine solid or liquid particles. **2. a.** A substance, such as a detergent, insecticide, or paint, packaged under pressure with a gaseous propellant for release as an aerosol. **b.** A container from which an aerosol is released; an aerosol bomb. [AERO- + SOL(UTION).]

aerosol bomb *n.* A usually hand-held container or dispenser from which an aerosol is released.

aer·o·space (âr′ō-spās′) *adj.* **1.** Of or designating Earth's atmosphere and the space beyond. **2.** Of or pertaining to the science or technology of flight. —**aer·o·space** *n.*

aerospace vehicle *n.* A vehicle capable of flight both within and outside Earth's atmosphere.

aer·o·sphere (âr′ō-sfîr′) *n.* The lower portion of the atmosphere in which both unmanned and manned flight is possible; the troposphere and stratosphere.

aer·o·stat (âr′ō-stăt′) *n.* An aircraft, especially a balloon or dirigible, deriving its lift from the buoyancy of surrounding air rather than from aerodynamic motion. [French *aérostat* : AERO- + -STAT.] —**aer·o·stat·ic** (âr′ō-stăt′ĭk), **aer·o·stat·i·cal** *adj.*

aer·o·stat·ics (âr′ō-stăt′ĭks) *n. Used with a singular verb.* The science of gases in equilibrium and of the equilibrium of balloons or aircraft under changing atmospheric flight conditions.

aer·o·ther·mo·dy·nam·ics (âr′ō-thûr′mō-dī-năm′ĭks) *n. Used with a singular verb.* The study of the thermodynamics of gases, especially at high relative velocities.

ae·ru·go (ĭ-rōō′gō) *n.* **Verdigris** (*see*). [Latin *aerūgō,* from *aes* (stem *aer-*), copper, bronze.]

aer·y¹ (âr′ē, ā′ə-rē) *adj. Poetic.* Ethereal; insubstantial.

aery². Variant of **aerie.**

Aes·chy·lus (ĕs′kə-ləs, ēs′-) (c. 525–456 B.C.). Greek dramatist. He wrote some 90 plays, of which 7 complete tragedies survive. His best-known work is the trilogy of the *Oresteia* (458 B.C.): *Agamemnon, Choephori,* and *Eumenides.* His plays are concerned with the justice of the gods and are based on tales from mythology and history.

Aes·cu·la·pi·an (ĕs′kyōō-lā′pē-ən) *adj.* Of or pertaining to the healing art; medical: *the Aesculapian art.*

Aes·cu·la·pi·us (ĕs′kyōō-lā′pē-əs). The Roman god of medicine and healing; identified with the Greek god Asclepius.

Ae·sir (ā′sîr, ē′sîr) *pl.n.* The gods of Norse mythology. [Old Norse, plural of *āss,* a god.]

Ae·sop (ē′sŏp′, ē′səp) (6th century B.C.). Supposed author of *Aesop's Fables.* Nothing is known for certain about his life, but he is said to have been Greek and born a slave and to have been deformed. The fables are moral tales, originating in folklore, with animal protagonists. Among the best-known are "The Tortoise and the Hare" and "The Fox and the Grapes."

Ae·so·pi·an (ē-sō′pē-ən) *adj.* Also **Ae·sop·ic** (ē-sŏp′ĭk). **1.** In the manner of Aesop's animal fables. **2.** Expressed allegorically or obliquely so as to elude political censorship.

aes·thete, es·thete (ĕs′thēt′) *n.* A person who has, or affects to have, a sensitive appreciation of the beautiful, especially in art. [Back-formation from AESTHETIC.]

aes·thet·ic, es·thet·ic (ĕs-thĕt′ĭk) *adj.* **1.** Of or pertaining to aesthetics. **2.** Of or concerning the criticism of taste or the appreciation of the beautiful. **3.** Having or showing a well-developed sense of beauty. [French *esthétique,* from German *ästhetisch,* from New Latin *aestheticus,* from Greek *aisthētikos,* pertaining to sense perception, from *aisthēta,* perceptible things, from *aisthenasthai,* to perceive.] —**aes·thet·i·cal·ly** *adv.*

aes·the·ti·cian, es·the·ti·cian (ĕs′thə-tĭsh′ən) *n.* A specialist in aesthetics or the theory of beauty.

aes·thet·i·cism, es·thet·i·cism (ĕs-thĕt′ə-sĭz′əm) *n.* **1.** The pursuit of the sensuously beautiful; devotion to beauty and refined taste. Sometimes used derogatorily to characterize an excessive or affected appreciation of beauty. **2. a.** The belief that beauty is the basic principle from which all other principles, especially moral principles, are derived. **b.** The belief that art and artists should be judged according to aesthetic considerations alone.

aes·thet·ics, es·thet·ics (ĕs-thĕt′ĭks) *n. Used with a singular verb.* The branch of philosophy dealing with the nature and perception of the beautiful.

aes·ti·val, es·ti·val (ĕs′tə-vəl, ĕs-tī′-) *adj.* Of or appearing in summer. [Middle English *estival*, from Old French, from Latin *aestivālis*, from *aestīvus*, from *aestās*, summer.]

aes·ti·vate, es·ti·vate (ĕs′tə-vāt′) *intr.v.* **-vated, -vating, -vates.** To pass the summer, especially in a state of dormancy, as lungfish and some other animals do. Compare **hibernate.** [Latin *aestīvāre*, from *aestīvus*, AESTIVAL.]

aes·ti·va·tion, es·ti·va·tion (ĕs′tə-vā′shən) *n.* **1.** *Zoology.* A state of dormancy or torpor during the summer or periods of drought. Compare **hibernation. 2.** *Botany.* The arrangement of petals, sepals, and other floral organs in the unopened bud.

ae·ta·tis su·ae (ē-tā′tĭs sōō′ē). *Abbr.* **aetat., aet.** *Latin.* Of his (or her) age.

Aethelred. See **Ethelred.**

Aethelstan. See **Athelstan.**

ae·ther (ē′thər) *n.* **1. Aether.** *Greek Mythology.* The poetic personification of the clear upper air breathed by the Olympians. **2.** Variant of **ether** (sense 3).

aethereal. Variant of **ethereal.**

aetiology. Variant of **etiology.**

AF, A.F. 1. air force. **2.** Anglo-French. **3.** audio frequency.

Af. Africa; African.

a.f. audio frequency.

a·far (ə-fär′) *adv.* At or to a distance; far away. [Middle English *afer*, from *on fer*, at a distance, and *of fer*, from a distance, from *fer*, FAR.]

Afars and Issas, French Territory of the. See **Djibouti.**

AFB air force base.

a·feard, a·feared (ə-fîrd′) *adj. Regional & Archaic.* Afraid; frightened: *"Be not afeared; the isle is full of noises"* (Shakespeare). [Middle English *afered*, Old English *āfǣred*, past participle of *āfǣran*, to frighten : *ā-*, intensive prefix + *fǣran*, to frighten, from *fǣr*, fear.]

af·fa·ble (ăf′ə-bəl) *adj.* Easy to speak to; approachable; amiable. [Old French, from Latin *affābilis*, from *affāri*, to speak to : *ad-*, to + *fārī*, to speak.] **—af·fa·bil·i·ty** *n.* **—af·fa·bly** *adv.*

af·fair (ə-fâr′) *n.* **1.** Anything that has been done or is to be done or dealt with. **2. affairs. a.** Personal or business concerns in general: *a man of affairs.* **b.** Matters or events of public interest: *affairs of state.* **3.** Any object or contrivance: *Our first car was a ramshackle affair.* **4.** A private matter; a personal concern. **5.** A matter causing scandal and controversy: *the Dreyfus affair.* **6.** A sexual relationship, usually of limited duration, between two people who are not married to one another. [Middle English *afere*, from Old French *afaire*, from the phrase *a faire*, "to do" : *a*, to, from Latin *ad-* + *faire*, to do, from Latin *facere*.]

af·faire d'hon·neur (á-fâr′ dô-nœr′) *n. French.* A matter in which honor is at stake; a duel.

af·fect[1] (ə-fĕkt′) *tr.v.* **-fected, -fecting, -fects. 1.** To have an effect on; bring about a change in. **2.** To touch or move the emotions of. **3.** To have an adverse effect on; especially, to attack or infect. Used of disease, pain, or the like. **4.** To allot or assign. Used only in the passive.
—n. (ăf′ĕkt). *Psychology.* **1.** A feeling or emotion as distinguished from cognition, thought, or action. **2.** A strong feeling having active consequences. [Latin *afficere* (past participle *affectus*), to do something to, exert influence on : *ad-*, to + *facere*, to do.]
Synonyms: *impress, influence, move, strike, touch.*
Usage: *Affect* and *effect* have no senses in common; therefore the tendency to confuse the words must be guarded against closely. As verbs, *affect* (the more common) is used principally in the senses of influence (*how smoking affects health*) and pretense or imitation (*affecting nonchalance to hide fear*), whereas *effect* applies only to accomplishment or execution (*reductions designed to effect economy; means adopted to effect an end*). As nouns, the terms can be kept straight by remembering that *affect* is now confined to psychology.

af·fect[2] (ə-fĕkt′) *tr.v.* **-fected, -fecting, -fects. 1.** To simulate in order to make some desired impression; pretend to feel: *affect indifference.* **2.** To imitate; assume: *affect an American accent.* **3. a.** To display a preference for. **b.** *Archaic.* To fancy; love. **c.** To tend to by nature; tend to frequent: *affect crystalline form.* [Middle English *affecter*, from Latin *affectāre*, to strive after, frequentative of *afficere* (past participle *affectus*), to AFFECT.] **—af·fect·er** *n.*

af·fec·ta·tion (ăf′ĕk-tā′shən) *n.* **1.** A pretense or false display. **2.** An artificial behavior adopted to impress others. [Latin *affectātiō* (stem *affectātiōn-*), from *affectāre*, to strive after, AFFECT.]

af·fect·ed[1] (ə-fĕk′tĭd) *adj.* Emotionally stirred or moved.

affected[2] *adj.* **1.** Assumed or simulated to impress others. **2.** Speaking or behaving in an artificial or insincere way to make a particular impression. **3.** Disposed or inclined. Used with *to* or *toward*: *was well affected to their cause.* **4.** Fancied; taken up: *a book much affected by experts in the subject.* **—af·fect·ed·ly** *adv.* **—af·fect·ed·ness** *n.*

af·fect·ing (ə-fĕk′tĭng) *adj.* Full of pathos; touching; moving: *an affecting sight.* —See Synonyms at **moving. —af·fect·ing·ly** *adv.*

af·fec·tion (ə-fĕk′shən) *n.* **1.** A fond or tender feeling toward another. **2.** *Often* **affections.** Feeling or emotion. **3.** Any pathological condition of the mind or body. **4.** The act of affecting or state of being affected. **5.** Mental disposition or tendency. —See Syn-

onyms at **love.** [Middle English *affecioun*, from Old French *affection*, from Latin *affectiō* (stem *affectiōn-*), (friendly) disposition, from *afficere*, to AFFECT.] **—af·fec·tion·al** *adj.* **—af·fec·tion·al·ly** *adv.*

af·fec·tion·ate (ə-fĕk′shə-nĭt) *adj.* **1.** Having or showing fond feelings or affection; loving; tender. **2.** *Archaic.* Strongly or favorably disposed. Used with *to.* **—af·fec·tion·ate·ly** *adv.* **—af·fec·tion·ate·ness** *n.*

af·fec·tive (ə-fĕk′tĭv) *adj.* **1.** *Psychology.* Pertaining to or resulting from emotions or feelings rather than from thought. **2.** Pertaining to or arousing affection or emotion; emotional. **—af·fec·tiv·i·ty** (ăf′ĕk-tĭv′ə-tē) *n.*

af·fen·pin·scher (ăf′ən-pĭn′chər, ä′fən-) *n.* Any of a breed of small dogs of European origin, having dark, wiry, shaggy hair and a tufted muzzle. [German *Affenpinscher*, "monkey-terrier" (so called because its face resembles a monkey's) : *Affe*, monkey, APE + *Pinscher*, terrier (see **Doberman pinscher**).]

af·fer·ent (ăf′ər-ənt) *adj.* Directed toward a central organ or section, as are nerves that conduct impulses from the periphery of the body inward to the brain or spinal cord. Compare **efferent.** [Latin *afferēns* (stem *afferent-*), present participle of *afferre*, to bring toward : *ad-*, toward + *ferre*, to bring.]

af·fet·tu·o·so (ăf′fĕt-tōō-ō′zō) *adv. Music.* With tender or passionate feeling. Used as a direction. [Italian.] **—af·fet·tu·o·so** *adj.*

af·fi·ance (ə-fī′əns) *tr.v.* **-anced, -ancing, -ances.** To promise (oneself or another) in marriage; betroth. [Middle English *affiaunce*, from Old French *affiance*, "trust," from *affier*, to trust to, from Medieval Latin *affīdāre* : Latin *ad-*, to + *fīdāre*, variant of Latin *fīdere*, to trust.]

af·fi·ant (ə-fī′ənt) *n. Law.* One who makes an affidavit. [Old French, present participle of *affier*, to trust to. See **affiance**.]

af·fi·da·vit (ăf′ə-dā′vĭt) *n. Law.* A written declaration made under oath before a notary public or other authorized officer. [Medieval Latin *affīdāvit*, "he has pledged," from *affīdāre*, to trust to. See **affiance**.]

af·fil·i·ate (ə-fĭl′ē-āt′) *v.* **-ated, -ating, -ates.** *—tr.* **1.** To adopt as an associate or subsidiary member or branch of a group or larger organization: *an affiliated member; a union affiliated with the AFL-CIO.* **2.** To associate (oneself) as a subordinate or subsidiary. Used with *with.* **3.** *Law.* To impute the paternity of (an illegitimate child). Used with *upon* or *to.* *—intr.* To associate or connect oneself: *We decided to affiliate.*
~n. (ə-fĭl′ē-ĭt). A person or organization associated with another in a subordinate relationship. [Medieval Latin *affīliāre*, "to take to oneself as a son" : *ad-*, to + *fīlius*, son.] **—af·fil·i·a·tion** (ə-fĭl′ē-ā′shən) *n.*

af·fine (ə-fīn′) *adj.* **1.** Of or pertaining to a mathematical transformation of coordinates that is equivalent to a translation, contraction, or expansion with respect to a fixed origin and fixed coordinate system. **2.** Of or pertaining to the geometry of affine transformations. [Old French *affin*, AFFINED.]

af·fined (ə-fīnd′) *adj.* Joined by kinship or affinity. [French *affiné*, from Old French *affin*, closely related, from Latin *affīnis*, neighboring, allied by marriage : *ad-*, near to + *fīnis*, border.]

af·fin·i·ty (ə-fĭn′ə-tē) *n., pl.* **-ties. 1.** A natural personal attraction or liking: *A good swimmer, she always seemed to have an affinity to water.* **2.** Relationship by marriage or adoption rather than by blood. **3.** An inherent similarity between organisms or things: *The language has some affinities with Russian.* **4.** A chemical or physical attraction or attractive force. —See Synonyms at **likeness.** [Middle English *affinite*, from Old French *afinite*, from Latin *affīnitās*, from *affīnis*, AFFINED.]

af·firm (ə-fûrm′) *v.* **-firmed, -firming, -firms.** *—tr.* **1.** To declare positively or firmly; maintain the truth or existence of, especially in response to a question or doubt: *affirmed his innocence of the accusations.* **2.** To ratify or confirm. *—intr. Law.* To declare solemnly and formally to tell the truth, but without taking an oath: *Witnesses may swear or affirm.* —See Synonyms at **assert.** [Middle English *affermen*, from Old French *afermer*, from Latin *affirmāre*, "to give firmness to," strengthen, assert : *ad-*, to + *firmāre*, to make firm, from *firmus*, firm.] **—af·firm·a·ble** *adj.* **—af·firm·a·bly** *adv.* **—af·firm·ant** *adj. & n.* **—af·firm·er** *n.*

af·fir·ma·tion (ăf′ər-mā′shən) *n.* **1.** The act of affirming or state of being affirmed. **2.** *Law.* A solemn and formal declaration to tell the truth, as made by a person who conscientiously objects to taking an oath. **3.** Any formal or solemn declaration.

af·firm·a·tive (ə-fûr′mə-tĭv) *adj.* **1.** Responding with the word *yes* or any other expression of agreement or consent: *an affirmative reply.* **2.** Asserting that something is true as represented; confirming. **3.** *Logic.* Designating a proposition in which the predicate states something about the subject to be true; for example, *Apples have seeds* is an affirmative proposition.
~n. **1.** A word or phrase showing agreement or assent: *My request was answered in the affirmative.* **2.** The side in a debate that upholds a proposition.
~interj. Used, especially in a military context, in place of *yes* to express confirmation or consent. Compare **negative. —af·firm·a·tive·ly** *adv.*
Usage: The expressions *in the affirmative* and *in the negative*, as in *she answered in the affirmative*, are generally regarded as pompous. *She answered yes* would be more acceptable even at the most formal levels of style.

affirmative action *n.* Action taken to provide opportunities, as in admissions or employment, for members of groups suffering from the effects of past or present discrimination. Also used adjectivally: *an affirmative-action employer.*

af·fix (ə-fĭks′) *tr.v.* **-fixed, -fixing, -fixes. 1.** To secure (an object) to another; attach: *affix a label to a parcel.* **2.** To impute; attribute: *affix blame for the error to him.* **3.** To place at the end; append: *affix a postscript.* ～*n.* (ăf′ĭks). **1.** Something that is attached, joined, or added. **2.** *Grammar.* A word element, such as a prefix or suffix, that can only occur attached to a base, stem, or root. [Medieval Latin *affixāre* : Latin *ad-*, to + *fixāre*, to fix, frequentative of *fīgere* (past participle *fīxus*), to fasten.] —**af·fix·er** *n.*

af·fla·tus (ə-flā′təs) *n.* A creative impulse; an inspiration. Used chiefly in the phrase *divine afflatus.* [Latin *afflātus*, inspiration, past participle of *afflāre*, to breathe on : *ad-*, toward + *flāre*, to blow.]

af·flict (ə-flĭkt′) *tr.v.* **-flicted, -flicting, -flicts.** To inflict physical or mental suffering upon; cause great distress to. [Middle English *afflicten*, from Latin *afflīgere* (past participle *afflīctus*), to dash against : *ad-*, to + *flīgere*, to strike.] —**af·flict·er** *n.* —**af·flic·tive** *adj.* —**af·flic·tive·ly** *adv.*

af·flic·tion (ə-flĭk′shən) *n.* A condition or cause of pain, suffering, or distress, such as disease or grief.

af·flu·ence (ăf′lōō-əns) *n.* **1.** A plentiful supply of material goods; the state of being affluent; wealth. **2.** An abundance.

af·flu·ent (ăf′lōō-ənt) *adj.* **1.** Amply supplied with material goods and comforts; wealthy: *the affluent society.* **2.** Copious; abundant. **3.** Flowing freely. ～*n.* A stream or river that flows into another or other body of water; a tributary. [Middle English, from Old French, from Latin *affluēns* (stem *affluent-*), present participle of *affluere*, to flow to : *ad-*, toward + *fluere*, to flow.] —**af·flu·ent·ly** *adv.*

af·flux (ăf′lŭks′) *n.* A flowing toward a particular area: *an afflux of blood to the head.* [Medieval Latin *affluxus*, from Latin, past participle of *affluere*, to flow to. See **affluent.**]

af·ford (ə-fôrd′, ə-fōrd′) *tr.v.* **-forded, -fording, -fords. 1.** To have the financial means for; be able to meet the expense of. Preceded by *can* or *be able.* **2.** To be able to spare or give up. Preceded by *can* or *be able.* **3.** To be able to do or bear (something) without incurring serious loss, difficulty, or criticism. Preceded by *can* or *be able: He can afford to take a tolerant attitude.* **4.** To provide or give: *The balcony affords a marvelous view.* [Middle English *aforthen*, Old English *geforthian*, to further, achieve, carry out, from *forthian*, to promote, from *forth*, forward.] —**af·ford·a·ble** *adj.*

af·for·est (ə-fôr′ĭst, ə-fŏr′-) *tr.v.* **-ested, -esting, -ests.** To convert (open land) into forest. [Medieval Latin *afforestāre* : *ad-*, to + *forestāre*, from Late Latin *forestis*, FOREST.] —**af·for·es·ta·tion** (ə-fôr′ĭs-tā′shən, ə-fŏr′-) *n.*

af·fran·chise (ə-frăn′chīz′) *tr.v.* **-chised, -chising, -chises.** To free from servitude; liberate from obligation or liabilities. [15th century : alteration of Old French *affranchis* (stem *affranchiss-*), to free, from *franchis*, to free.] —**af·fran·chise·ment** *n.*

af·fray (ə-frā′) *n. Law.* A public quarrel or brawl noisy enough to disturb those not involved. —See Synonyms at **conflict.** ～*tr.v.* **affrayed, -fraying, -frays.** *Archaic.* To frighten. [Middle English, from Old French *effray, esfrei*, from *affreer, esfreer*, to fight in public, from Vulgar Latin *exfridāre* (unattested), "to break the peace" : Latin *ex*, out of + Frankish *frithuz* (unattested), peace.]

af·fri·cate (ăf′rĭ-kĭt) *n. Phonetics.* A speech sound produced when the breath stream is completely stopped and then released at articulation; for example, the *t* plus *sh* sound in *churn* or *clutch* or the *j* sound in *judge.* Also called "affricative." [Latin (*vox*) *affricāta*, "rubbed" (sound), feminine past participle of *affricāre*, to rub against : *ad-*, to + *fricāre*, to rub.] —**af·fri·cate** (ăf′rĭ-kāt′) *v.* —**af·fri·ca·tion** (ăf′rĭ-kā′shən) *n.* —**af·fri·ca·tive** *adj. & n.*

af·fric·a·tive (ə-frĭk′ə-tĭv) *adj.* Of, pertaining to, or forming an affricate. ～*n.* An **affricate** (see).

af·fright (ə-frīt′) *tr.v.* **-frighted, -frighting, -frights.** *Archaic.* To frighten; terrify. ～*n. Archaic.* **1.** Terror. **2.** A cause of terror. —**af·fright·ment** *n.*

af·front (ə-frŭnt′) *tr.v.* **-fronted, -fronting, -fronts. 1.** To slight or insult openly; cause offense to. **2.** *Archaic.* To meet face to face defiantly; confront. —See Synonyms at **offend.** ～*n.* **1.** An open or intentional slight or insult. **2.** Anything that causes offense. [Middle English *affronten*, from Old French *afronter*, from Vulgar Latin *affrontāre* (unattested) : Latin *ad-*, to + *frōns* (stem *front-*), forehead, FRONT.]

af·fu·sion (ə-fyōō′zhən) *n.* A pouring on of water, especially as in baptism. [Latin *affūsiō* (stem *affūsiōn-*), from *affūsus*, past participle of *affundere*, to pour on : *ad-*, to + *fundere*, to pour.]

Af·ghan (ăf′găn′, -gən) *n.* **1.** A native or inhabitant of Afghanistan or a person of Afghan descent. **2.** A major language of Afghanistan, Pashto (see). **3. afghan.** A coverlet of wool, knitted or crocheted in colorful geometric designs. **4. afghan.** A type of sheepskin or goatskin coat, usually decorated with embroidery. —**Af·ghan** *adj.*

Afghan hound *n.* A large, slender dog of an ancient breed, having long, thick hair, a pointed muzzle, and drooping ears.

af·ghan·i (ăf-găn′ē) *n.* The basic monetary unit of Afghanistan, equal to 100 puls. See feature at **currency.**

Af·ghan·i·stan (ăf-găn′ĭ-stăn′). Arid, landlocked state of west-central Asia, dominated by mountains radiating from the Hindu Kush. Only 10 percent is cultivable, yet normally 85 percent of workers are in farming, mostly at subsistence level. The country is rich in minerals, but only gas and goal are exploited to any extent. Dried fruit, gas, skins, cotton, and wool are the main exports, and the country is famed for its carpets. Afghanistan lies astride ancient invasion routes and is ethnically diverse as a result. Most people are Muslim, and less than 8 percent are literate. The area was part of the Persian Empire and was later conquered by Alexander the Great. It fell to the Arabs, who introduced Islam (8th century), and later to Genghis Khan (1220) and Tamerlane (14th century). The country was part of the Mogul Empire (16th century), until an Afghan chief revolted and founded the present state (1747). This buffer state between Russia and British India survived to win complete independence (1919) and was proclaimed a republic (1973). A military coup (1978) led to an unpopular regime dependent on the U.S.S.R. and to Soviet occupation of the country (1979). Area, 647,497 square kilometers (249,934 square miles). Population, 15,500,000. Capital, Kabul.

a·fi·ci·o·na·do (ə-fĕ′sē-ə-nä′dō, ə-fĭs′ē-ə-) *n., pl.* **-dos. 1.** An enthusiastic admirer or follower; a devotee. **2.** A devotee of bullfighting. [Spanish, from the past participle of *aficionar*, to incite affection, from *aficion*, from Latin *affectiō*, AFFECTION.]

a·field (ə-fēld′) *adv.* Off the usual or desired track; away from one's home or usual environment. Used chiefly in the phrase *far afield.*

a·fire (ə-fīr′) *adj.* **1.** On fire. **2.** Intensely interested and involved: *He was afire with enthusiasm about the new project.* —**a·fire** *adv.*

a·flame (ə-flām′) *adj.* **1.** On fire; flaming. **2.** Keenly excited and interested: *aflame with a desire to learn.* —**a·flame** *adv.*

af·la·tox·in (ăf′lə-tŏk′sĭn) *n.* A poison, produced by the fungus *Aspergillus flavus*, growing on peanuts and cereals, that is thought to cause certain cancers. [*A(spergillus) fla(vus)* + TOXIN.]

AFL-CIO, A.F.L.-C.I.O. The American Federation of Labor and Congress of Industrial Organizations.

a·float (ə-flōt′) *adj.* **1.** Floating. **2.** On a boat or ship away from the shore; at sea. **3.** In circulation; being spread about: *All sorts of rumors were afloat.* **4.** Awash; flooded. **5.** Drifting about; moving without guidance. **6.** Out of debt. —**a·float** *adv.*

a·flut·ter (ə-flŭt′ər) *adj.* In a flutter; nervous and excited.

a·foot (ə-fŏŏt′) *adj.* **1.** Being prepared or carried out; astir: *some nasty business afoot.* **2.** Walking; on foot. —**a·foot** *adv.*

a·fore (ə-fôr′, ə-fōr′) *adv.* **1.** *Archaic & Regional.* Before. **2.** *Nautical.* In front. ～*prep.* **1.** *Archaic.* Before. **2.** *Nautical.* In front of. ～*conj. Archaic.* Before. [Middle English *afor(e)n*, Old English *onforan* : ON + *foran*, dative of *for*, FORE.]

a·fore·men·tioned (ə-fôr′mĕn′shənd, ə-fōr′-) *adj.* Mentioned previously or before. Used especially in legal documents. ～*n., pl.* **aforementioned.** The person mentioned already. Preceded by *the.*

a·fore·said (ə-fôr′sĕd′, ə-fōr′-) *adj.* Spoken of or referred to earlier. ～*n., pl.* **aforesaid.** The person, thing, or fact already stated or referred to. Preceded by *the.*

a·fore·thought (ə-fôr′thôt′, ə-fōr′-) *adj.* Planned or intended beforehand; premeditated. Used chiefly in the legal phrase *malice aforethought.*

a·fore·time (ə-fôr′tīm′, ə-fōr′-) *adv. Archaic.* At a former or past time; previously. —**a·fore·time** *adv.*

a for·ti·o·ri (ä fôr′shē-ôr′ē, ā fôr′shē-ō′rī) *adv.* With greater reason; all the more: *If there are to be cuts in the education budget, then a fortiori there should be cuts in the defense budget.*

a·foul (ə-foul′) *adj.* In or into a condition of entanglement, conflict, or collision. —**run** (or **fall**) **afoul of.** To become entangled with; come into collision with. —**a·foul** *adj.*

afp alpha-fetoprotein.

Afr. Africa; African.

a·fraid (ə-frād′) *adj.* **1.** Filled with fear; frightened or apprehensive: *afraid of snakes.* **2.** Disinclined; averse: *not afraid of work.* **3.** Filled with regret. Used especially as a polite way of lessening the force of

AFGHANISTAN

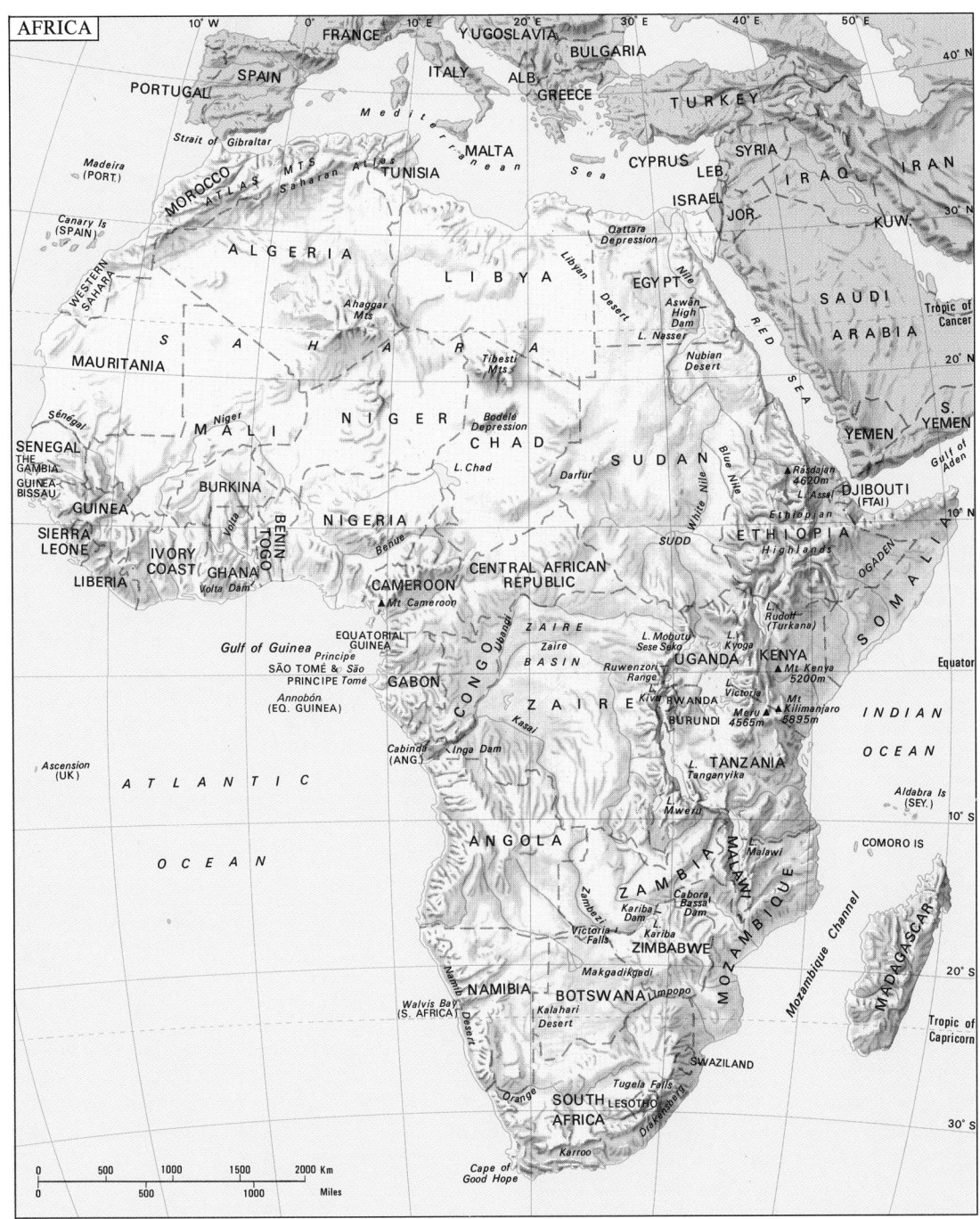

AFRICA

an unpleasant statement: *I'm afraid that I disagree with you.* [Middle English *af(f)raied,* past participle of *affraien,* to frighten, from Old French *affreer,* to AFFRAY.]

af·reet, af·rit (ăf′rēt′, ə-frēt′) *n. Arabic Mythology.* A powerful evil spirit or gigantic and monstrous demon. [Arabic *'ifrīt,* probably from Persian *āfrīda,* "a created being," from *āfrīdan,* to create.]

a·fresh (ə-frĕsh′) *adv.* Anew; again; from the beginning: *start afresh.*

Af·ri·ca (ăf′rĭ-kə). *Abbr.* **Af., Afr.** The second-largest continent after Asia, consisting mostly of high, monotonous plateaus, which drop dramatically to narrow coastal plains. It has a very short coastline for its area and has few inlets with deep harbors. Africa has few fold mountains: only the Atlas ranges in the northeast, part of the great Alpine-Himalayan system, and the older, smoother Cape ranges in the far south. Some ranges, such as the rugged Drakensberg and Ruwenzori, are the edges of tilted plateaus, while the others are generally of volcanic origin. The Great Rift Valley slashes through the continent from the mouth of the Zambezi to Djibouti and continues in the Red Sea. The valley encloses Lakes Malawi and Turkana, while Lakes Tanganyika and Mobutu Sese Seko lie in an arm to the west. Africa's largest lake, Victoria, lies in a shallow depression between the two arms of the valley. Africa's longest rivers, the Nile, Zaire (Congo), and Niger, are among the 10 longest in the world. Many rivers leave the plateaus by spectacular falls, such as

those on the Tugela River in South Africa, and these provide great potential for hydroelectric schemes. There are also vast areas of inland drainage, with no outlet to the sea, the Chad and Makgadikgadi depressions being two of them. Two thirds of the continent lies within the Tropics, and though temperatures are much modified by altitude, Africa is the hottest continent. It is also one of the driest: one third of it has less than 250 millimeters (10 inches) of rain a year. The Sahara, covering 25 percent of the total area, and the Namib and Kalahari deserts are among the world's harshest. Savannas, increasingly dry as they near the deserts, cover another 40 percent of the land. Soils in Africa are often poor, but rich chernozems (black earths) cover much of the East African highlands, and the alluvium of the great river valleys provides good soils. Soil erosion, frequently the result of overgrazing by livestock, is a problem in many countries. Arable land covers less than 7.5 percent of the continent, yet farming provides a living for some 75 percent of its people, the highest proportion of any continent. Africa's great strength lies in its vast and varied mineral reserves. It has 30 percent of the Western world's known mineral resources apart from oil, and already produces more than 10 percent of the world's oil. Many African countries, especially those with fewer natural resources, are finding tourism an increasingly valuable source of foreign exchange. The continent's sunny climate, warm seas, sandy

African marigold *An annual plant native to Mexico.*

African violets Saintpaulias, *or African violets, are native to tropical Africa, but they are now grown as popular houseplants around the world. Varieties exist in a range of colors from white to dark blue.*

agama *The red-headed agama (above) is one member of this desert-dwelling family of lizards.*

beaches, and scenery are a good base for development, while another asset is its remarkably varied wildlife, in many places preserved in national park and game reserves. Area, 30,334,562 square kilometers (11,712,252 square miles).

Af·ri·can (ăf'rĭ-kən) *adj. Abbr.* **Afr., Af.** Of or pertaining to Africa, or any of its peoples, languages, fauna, or the like.
~n. **1.** A native or inhabitant of Africa. **2.** A member of any of the indigenous peoples of Africa.

Af·ri·can·der, Af·ri·kan·der (ăf'rĭ-kăn'dər) *n.* **1.** Any of a breed of cattle with a humped back and large, spreading horns, originally developed in South Africa. **2.** *Obsolete.* An Afrikaner. [Afrikaans *Afrikaander,* alteration (influenced by *Hollander*) of Dutch *Afrikaner.*] **—Af·ri·can·der, Af·ri·kan·der** *adj.*

Af·ri·can·ism (ăf'rĭ-kə-nĭz'əm) *n.* A characteristically African feature; especially, a word or expression from an African language when used in a non-African language.

Af·ri·can·ist (ăf'rĭ-kən-ĭst) *n.* A specialist in African affairs, culture, or languages.

Af·ri·can·ize (ăf'rĭ-kən-īz') *tr.v.* **-ized, -izing, -izes.** To make African; especially, to transfer to African control or give a specifically African character to. **—Af·ri·can·i·za·tion** (ăf'rĭ-kən-ĭ-zā'shən) *n.*

African lily *n.* A plant, *Agapanthus africanus,* native to southern Africa, having rounded clusters of blue, violet, or white flowers.

African mahogany *n.* **1.** Any of several African trees of the genus *Khaya;* especially, *K. ivorensis,* having wood similar to that of true mahogany. **2.** The wood of this tree, used for furniture, musical instruments, and boat interiors. **3.** Any of various other African woods resembling true mahogany.

African marigold *n.* A widely cultivated plant, *Tagetes erecta,* native to Mexico, having finely divided foliage and showy, rounded, orange or yellow flowers.

African National Congress *n. Abbr.* **A.N.C.** A South African resistance movement favoring majority rule. It is banned in South Africa.

African trypanosomiasis *n.* **Sleeping sickness** *(see).*

African violet *n.* Any of several plants of the genus *Saintpaulia,* native to tropical East Africa and widely cultivated as house plants; especially, *S. ionantha,* having violet, white, or pink flowers. Also called "saintpaulia."

Af·ri·kaans (ăf'rĭ-käns', -känz') *n.* A language developed from 17th-century Dutch among the Afrikaners. It shares with English official-language status in the Republic of South Africa. Also called "Taal," formerly "Cape Dutch." **—Af·ri·kaans** *adj.*

Afrikander. Variant of **Africander.**

Af·ri·kan·er (ăf'rĭ-kä'nər) *n.* An Afrikaans-speaking descendant of the Dutch settlers of South Africa. **—Af·ri·kan·er** *adj.*

Af·ri·kan·er·dom (ăf'rĭ-kä'nər-dəm) *n.* The sense of solidarity among Afrikaners; loyalty to and pride in the cultural and political values of the Afrikaner people and their pioneer origins.

Af·ro (ăf'rō) *n., pl.* **-ros.** A hairstyle in which the hair is shaped into a round frizzy mass.
~adj. **1.** Of or for an Afro. **2.** Directly or indirectly African in style. [Perhaps short for AFRO-AMERICAN.]

Afro- *prefix.* Indicates Africa or African or African and; for example, **Afro-American.** [Latin *Āfr-,* stem of *Āfer,* an African.]

Af·ro-A·mer·i·can (ăf'rō-ə-mĕr'ĭ-kən) *adj.* Of or pertaining to American blacks of African ancestry, their history, or their culture.
~n. An American black of African ancestry.

Af·ro-A·si·at·ic (ăf'rō-ā'zhē-ăt'ĭk) *n.* A family of languages of southwestern Asia and northern Africa. Also called "Hamito-Semitic," "Semito-Hamitic." **—Af·ro-A·si·at·ic** *adj.*

af·ror·mo·si·a (ăf'rôr-mō'zē-ə, -mō'zhə) *n.* **1.** Any of several North and West African trees of the genus *Pericopsis.* **2.** The hard teaklike wood of this tree. [AFRO- + *Ormosia* (genus name), from Greek *hormos,* necklace, alluding to the use of its berries in making necklaces.]

aft (ăft, äft) *adv.* At, in, toward, or close to the stern of a vessel or the back of an aircraft. [Probably shortening of ABAFT.] **—aft** *adj.*

aft. afternoon.

af·ter (ăf'tər, äf'-) *prep.* **1.** Following in place or order: *D comes after C.* **2.** Following in time; subsequent to: *Come after dinner.* **3.** Following continually: *week after week of cold weather.* **4.** In quest or pursuit of: *The police are after them.* **5. a.** Considering; bearing in mind: *After the way he treated her, I'm not surprised she left.* **b.** In spite of: *After all my work, the job still wasn't finished on time.* **6.** Concerning: *He asked after you.* **7.** Next to or lower than in order or importance: *Football is his favorite sport after bicycling.* **8.** In the style of; in imitation of: *a painting after the style of Picasso.* **9.** With the same name as; in honor or memory of: *named after her mother.* **10.** Past the hour of; past: *It's ten after three.* **11.** According to the nature or desires of; in accordance with: *a person after my own heart.* **—after all. 1.** When everything is considered. **2.** Eventually; ultimately.
~adv. **1.** Behind; in the rear. **2.** At a later time; afterward.
~adj. **1.** Subsequent in time or place; later; following: *in after years.* Often used in combination: *afterglow.* **2.** *Nautical.* Nearer the stern of a vessel; further aft.
~conj. Following or subsequent to the time that: *I saw her after I arrived.* [Middle English *after,* Old English *æfter.*]

af·ter·birth (ăf'tər-bûrth', äf-) *n.* The placenta and fetal membranes expelled from the uterus after birth of the offspring. Also called "secundines."

af·ter·burn·er (ăf'tər-bûr'nər, äf'-) *n.* **1.** A device for increasing the thrust of a jet engine by burning additional fuel with the uncombined oxygen in the exhaust gases. **2.** A device for removing or neutralizing harmful gases in the exhaust of an internal-combustion engine, especially as fitted to a car.

af·ter·care (ăf'tər-kâr', äf'-) *n.* Treatment or special care given to someone after discharge from an institution, such as a hospital.

af·ter·damp (ăf'tər-dămp', äf'-) *n.* An asphyxiating mixture of gases, primarily nitrogen and carbon dioxide, left in a mine after a fire or explosion.

af·ter·deck (ăf'tər-dĕk', äf'-) *n. Nautical.* The part of a deck lying between the middle and stern of a ship.

af·ter·ef·fect (ăf'tər-ə-fĕkt', äf'-) *n. Often* **aftereffects.** An effect that follows some time after its cause or after an initial effect.

af·ter·glow (ăf'tər-glō', äf'-) *n.* **1.** The light emitted or remaining after removal of a source of illumination, as: **a.** The atmospheric glow after sunset. **b.** The glow of an incandescent metal as it cools. **c.** Emission from a phosphor after removal of excitation. **2.** The comfortable feeling following a pleasant experience. **3.** A lingering pleasant impression, as of past happiness or success.

af·ter·heat (ăf'tər-hēt', äf'-) *n.* The heat produced in a nuclear reactor after it has been shut down, as a result of residual radioactivity in the fuel elements.

af·ter-hours (ăf'tər-ourz', äf'-) *adj.* **1.** Occurring or done after closing time or after the normal working period. **2.** Open after a legal or established closing time: *an after-hours club.*

af·ter·im·age (ăf'tər-ĭm'ĭj, äf'-) *n.* A visual image that persists after a visual stimulus ceases. Also called "photogene."

af·ter·life (ăf'tər-līf', äf'-) *n.* **1.** A life believed to follow death. **2.** The part of one's life that follows a particular event.

af·ter·math (ăf'tər-măth', äf'-) *n.* **1.** A resulting state or period, especially following a disaster or misfortune: *in the aftermath of the explosion.* **2.** A second growth or crop of grass in one season. [AFTER + obsolete *math,* mowing, Middle English *math* (unattested), Old English *mǣth.*]

af·ter·noon (ăf'tər-no͞on', äf'-) *n.* **1.** *Abbr.* **a., aft.** The part of the day from noon until evening. **2.** The closing part: *in the afternoon of one's life.*
~adj. Of or occurring in the afternoon.

af·ter·noons (ăf'tər-no͞onz', äf'-) *adv. Informal.* Regularly in the afternoon; on any afternoon.

af·ter·pains (ăf'tər-pānz', äf'-) *pl.n.* The cramps or pains following childbirth, resulting from the contraction of the uterus.

af·ters (ăf'tərz, äf'-) *n. British Informal.* Dessert.

af·ter·sen·sa·tion (ăf'tər-sĕn-sā'shən, äf'-) *n.* A sensory impression, such as an afterimage or aftertaste, that persists or recurs after removal of a stimulus.

af·ter·shave lotion (ăf'tər-shāv', äf'-) *n.* An astringent lotion, usually scented, applied to the face after shaving. Also called "aftershave."

af·ter·shock (ăf'tər-shŏk', äf'-) *n.* A relatively small earthquake following a large-magnitude earthquake, occurring fairly close to the focus, and probably caused by mechanical readjustment in the earth's mantle following the release of energy by the main shock.

af·ter·taste (ăf'tər-tāst', äf'-) *n.* **1.** A taste that remains in the mouth after the substance causing it is no longer present. **2.** A usually unpleasant feeling that remains after an event or experience.

af·ter·thought (ăf'tər-thôt', äf'-) *n.* **1.** An idea, response, or explanation that occurs to one after an event or decision. **2.** A later addition to something completed: *The last paragraph was a bit of an afterthought.*

af·ter·time (ăf'tər-tīm', äf'-) *n.* The time to come; the future.

af·ter·ward (ăf'tər-wərd, äf'-) *adv.* Also **af·ter·wards** (-wərdz). At a later time; subsequently.

af·ter·word (ăf'tər-wûrd', äf'-) *n.* Something added to the end of a literary work, such as an epilogue.

Ag The symbol for the element silver. [Latin *argentum.*]

A.G., AG 1. adjutant general. **2.** attorney general.

a·ga, a·gha (ä'gə) *n.* A high-ranking official of the Ottoman Empire. [Turkish *ağa,* "lord."]

A·ga·dir (ä'gə-dîr', ăg'ə-). Port in southwest Morocco. In 1911 it was the scene of an international crisis known as the Agadir Incident, when Britain forcibly protested at the sending by Germany of a gunboat to Agadir. War was averted owing to French arbitration. In 1960 earthquakes virtually destroyed the town, killing over 10,000 of its inhabitants.

a·gain (ə-gĕn') *adv.* **1.** Once more; another time; anew. **2.** Back to a previous place, position, or state: *He left home, but went back again.* **3.** Furthermore; moreover. **4.** On the other hand: *He might go, and again he might not.* **—again and again.** Repeatedly; frequently. **—as much again. 1.** The same amount again. **2.** Twice as much. [Middle English *again, ayen,* Old English *ongēan,* in return, toward, against, from Germanic : ON + *gagin* (unattested), straight.]

a·gainst (ə-gĕnst') *prep.* **1.** In a direction or course opposite to: *row against the current.* **2.** So as to come into forcible contact with: *waves dashing against the shore.* **3.** In contact with so as to rest or press on: *He leaned against the tree.* **4.** In opposition or resistance to: *the war against crime; 10 votes for and 12 against.* **5.** Contrary to: *against my better judgment; against all the odds.* **6.** In contrast or comparison with the setting or background of: *dark colors against a fair skin.* **7.** In preparation for; in anticipation of: *food stored against winter.* **8.** As a defense or safeguard from, or from the effects of: *protection against the cold; insurance against fire and theft.* **9.** Unfavorable or disadvantageous to: *Her age is against her.* [Middle English *against, ayenst,* alteration of *ayenes, againes,* from *again, ayen,* against. See **again.**]

A·ga Khan (ä′gə kän′) *n.* A hereditary title of the religious and spiritual leader of the sect of Ismaili Muslims.

Aga Khan III (1877–1957). The title of Aga Sultan Sir Mahomed Shah, leader (imam) of the Ismaili Muslim sect. He represented India at the League of Nations in the 1930's, becoming president of the League in 1937. He appointed his grandson, **Aga Khan IV** (formerly Prince Karim; 1936–) to be his successor as imam, in preference to his son (the prince's father), Prince Aly Khan.

a·gal (ə-gäl′) *n.* A cord worn wound around the head by many desert Arabs that keeps the kaffiyeh (headdress) in place. [Arabic *'īgal,* cord, rope.]

ag·a·ma (ăg′ə-mə) *n.* Any of various small, long-tailed, insect-eating lizards of the family Agamidae, found in Old World tropics. [Carib.]

Ag·a·mem·non (ăg′ə-mĕm′nŏn′). *Greek Mythology.* The king of Mycenae, leader of the Greeks against Troy, husband of Clytemnestra, and father of Orestes, Electra, and Iphigenia.

a·ga·mete (ā′gə-mēt′, ā-găm′ēt′) *n. Biology.* A single-celled organism that reproduces asexually.

a·gam·ic (ā-găm′ĭk) *adj.* Also **ag·a·mous** (ăg′ə-məs). *Biology.* Occurring or reproducing without the union of male and female cells; asexual or parthenogenetic. [Late Latin *agamus,* unmarried, from Greek *agamos* : *a-,* not + -GAMOUS.] **—a·gam·i·cal·ly** *adv.*

ag·a·mo·gen·e·sis (ăg′ə-mō-jĕn′ə-sĭs, ā′găm-ō-) *n. Biology.* Asexual reproduction, as by budding, cell division, or parthenogenesis. [AGAM(IC) + GENESIS.] **—ag·a·mo·ge·net·ic** (ăg′ə-mō-jə-nĕt′ĭk) *adj.*

A·ga·na (ə-gä′nyə). Capital of Guam, on the west coast of the island. It was almost completely destroyed in World War II. U.S. military bases on the island are important to Agana's economy.

ag·a·pan·thus (ăg′ə-păn′thəs) *n.* Any plant of the genus *Agapanthus,* which includes the **African lily** *(see).* [New Latin : Greek *agapē,* love, AGAPE + *anthos,* flower.]

a·gape[1] (ə-gāp′, ə-găp′) *adv.* In a state of wonder or amazement, often with the mouth wide open. **—a·gape** *adj.*

a·ga·pe[2] (ä′gə-pā′) *n., pl.* **-pae** (-pē′). **1.** Christian love. **2.** In the early Christian Church, the **love feast** *(see)* accompanied by a celebration of the Eucharist. [Greek *agapē*†, love.]

a·gar (ä′gär, ä′gär) *n.* Also **a·gar-a·gar** (ä′gär′ä′gär, ä′gär′ä′gär). A mucilaginous material prepared from certain marine algae and used as a base for bacterial culture media, as a laxative, and for thickening certain foods. [Malay, "jelly, gelatin."]

ag·a·ric (ăg′ə-rĭk, ə-găr′ĭk) *n.* **1.** Any fungus of the family Agaricaceae, including the common cultivated mushroom, *Agaricus campestris,* and the **fly agaric** *(see).* **2.** The dried fruiting body of the fungus *Fomes laricis,* formerly used in medicine. [Latin *agaricum,* from Greek *agarikon,* perhaps after *Agaria,* city in Sarmatia.]

Ag·as·siz (ăg′ə-sē), **(Jean) Louis Rodolphe** (1807–73). Swiss-born U.S. naturalist and geologist. He won fame for his pioneering studies of fossil fishes, and was the first man to recognize from geological evidence that ice ages had once occurred in the Northern Hemisphere.

ag·ate (ăg′ĭt) *n.* **1.** A fine-grained quartz, a variety of chalcedony, with color banding or irregular clouding. **2.** A child's marble made of this material or a glass imitation of it. **3.** A tool with agate parts, such as a bookbinder's burnisher. **4.** A printer's type size, approximately 5½ points. [Old French, from Latin *achātēs,* from Greek *akhātēs*†.]

a·ga·ve (ə-gä′vē, ə-gä′-) *n.* Any of numerous fleshy-leaved tropical American plants of the genus *Agave,* which includes the **century plant** *(see).* Some species yield valuable fibers. [New Latin, "noble (plant)" (probably so named because of its height), from Greek *agauē,* feminine of *agauos*†, noble.]

age (āj) *n.* **1.** The period or amount of time during which someone or something has existed. **2.** An advanced stage of life or existence; the state of being old. **3.** That time in life when a person becomes eligible or entitled to do something, such as being qualified to assume certain civil and personal rights and responsibilities. Used chiefly in the phrases *of age* and *under age.* **4.** Any of the various stages of life: *at an awkward age.* **5.** *Sometimes* **Age.** Any period in history or geology designated by a specified characteristic: *the atomic age; the Stone Age.* **6.** A generation: *future ages.* **7.** *Often* **ages.** *Informal.* A very long time: *We waited an age. They left ages ago.* **8.** *Psychology.* See **mental age.** **—come of age. 1.** To reach the age at which one is considered legally an adult. **2.** To reach a state of maturity.

~v. **aged, aging, ages** or *chiefly British* **aged, ageing, ages.** *—tr.* To cause to grow or seem older or more mature. *—intr.* **1.** To become old. **2.** To show signs of old age. **3.** To mature with age. Used especially of alcoholic drinks. [Middle English, from Old French *age, aage,* from Vulgar Latin *aetāticum* (unattested), from Latin *aetās* (stem *aetāt-*), age.] **—ag·er** *n.*

-age *suffix.* Indicates: **1.** Collectively; for example, **acreage, baggage. 2.** Relation to or connection with; for example, **parentage. 3.** Result, action, or process; for example, **passage, spillage. 4.** Condition or position; for example, **vagabondage, marriage. 5.** Charge or fee; for example, **postage, cartage. 6.** Residence or place; for example, **vicarage, orphanage. 7.** Rate; for example, **mileage.** [Middle English, from Old French, from Late Latin *-āticum,* from the neuter of *-āticus* : Latin *-ātus,* -ATE + -IC.]

a·ged (ā′jĭd *for senses 1,4;* ājd *for senses 2,3, and occasionally for other senses*) *adj.* **1.** Old; advanced in years. **2.** Of the age of: *aged three.* **3.** Having undergone the process of aging; matured. **4.** *Geology.* Near the base level of erosion. —See Synonyms at **old. —a·ged·ness** *n.*

A·gee (ā′jē), **James** (1909–55). U.S. writer. His most influential work, done in collaboration with the photographer Walker Evans, was *Let Us Now Praise Famous Men* (1941), a harrowing documentary account of the lives of Alabama sharecroppers during the Depression.

age group *n.* All the people of a particular age or between two particular ages, considered as a group.

age·ing. *Chiefly British.* Variant of **aging.**

age·ism (ā′jĭz′əm) *n.* Unfair discrimination based on age, especially against middle-aged and elderly people. **—age·ist** *adj. & n.*

age·less (āj′lĭs) *adj.* **1.** Never seeming to grow old. **2.** Existing forever; eternal. **—age·less·ly** *adv.* **—age·less·ness** *n.*

a·gen·cy (ā′jən-sē) *n., pl.* **-cies. 1.** Action; operation; power: *Rust occurs through the agency of moisture in the air.* **2. a.** A business or service authorized to act for others: *an employment agency.* **b.** The office or premises from which such a business operates. **3.** An organization set up by a government department or international body. [Latin *agentia,* from *agēns,* acting, AGENT.]

a·gen·da (ə-jĕn′də) *n.* A list of things to be done, especially the program for a meeting. [Latin, plural of *agendum,* neuter gerundive of *agere,* to do.]

a·gen·e·sis (ā-jĕn′ə-sĭs) *n.* Also **ag·e·ne·sia** (ăj′ə-nē′zhə). *Biology.* Failure of an organism, organ, or part to develop.

a·gent (ā′jənt) *n.* **1.** One that acts or has the power or authority to act. **2. a.** One who acts for or as the representative of another: *an actor's agent.* **b.** A sales representative: *an insurance agent.* **3.** A means by which something is done or caused; an instrument. **4.** A force or substance that causes changes: *a chemical agent.* [Middle English, from Latin *agēns* (stem *agent-*), present participle of *agere,* to act, drive, do.] **—a·gen·tial** (ā-jĕn′shəl) *adj.*

Agent Orange *n.* A powerful toxic herbicide containing the chemical 2,4,5-T, used as a defoliant. [After the color of the identifying stripe on the barrels containing the herbicide.]

a·gent pro·vo·ca·teur (ȧ-zhäN′ prô-vô-kȧ-tœr′) *n., pl.* **agents provocateurs** (*pronounced as singular*). A person employed to associate with individuals or groups suspected of seditious or other criminal activities and to incite them to commit illegal acts so as to incur punishment. [French, "provocative agent."]

age of consent *n. Law.* The age at which a person may choose to have sexual intercourse.

Age of Reason *n.* The period of the **Enlightenment** *(see),* especially in Britain, France, and the United States. Preceded by *the.*

age-old (āj′ōld′) *adj.* Very old or of long standing.

ag·e·ra·tum (ăj′ə-rā′təm) *n.* **1.** Any of various plants of the genus *Ageratum*; especially, *A. houstonianum,* a commonly cultivated species having clusters of usually violet-blue flowers. **2.** Loosely, any of several other plants having similar flower clusters. [New Latin *Ageratum,* from Latin *agēraton,* from Greek, neuter of *agēratos,* ageless : *a-,* not + *-gēratos,* from *gēras,* old age.]

ag·gie (ăg′ē) *n.* A playing marble. [AG(ATE) + -IE.]

ag·gior·na·men·to (äd-jôr′nä-mĕn′tō) *n., pl.* **-ti** (-tē). *Italian.* The process or an instance of modernizing an institution or organization.

ag·glom·er·ate (ə-glŏm′ə-rāt′) *v.* **-ated, -ating, -ates.** *—tr.* To form or collect into a rounded mass. *—intr.* To take the shape of a rounded mass.

~adj. (ə-glŏm′ər-ĭt). Gathered into a rounded mass.

~n. (ə-glŏm′ər-ĭt). **1.** A confused or jumbled mass of things clustered together; a heap. **2.** A volcanic rock consisting of angular and rounded fragments fused together. [Latin *agglomerāre* : *ad-,* to + *glomerāre,* to wind into a ball, from *glomus* (stem *glomer-*), ball.] **—ag·glom·er·a·tive** (ə-glŏm′ər-ə-tĭv, -ə-rā′tĭv) *adj.* **—ag·glom·er·a·tor** (ə-glŏm′ə-rā′tər) *n.*

ag·glom·er·a·tion (ə-glŏm′ə-rā′shən) *n.* **1.** The action of agglomerating or the state of being agglomerated. **2.** A confused or jumbled mass; an agglomerate.

ag·glu·ti·nate (ə-glo͞ot′n-āt′) *v.* **-nated, -nating, -nates.** *—tr.* **1.** To join together by causing adhesion, as with glue. **2.** *Linguistics.* To form (words) by combining words, or words and word elements. **3.** *Physiology.* To cause (red blood cells or microorganisms) to clump together. *—intr.* **1.** To join together into a group or mass. **2.** *Linguistics.* To form words by agglutination. **3.** To undergo agglutination. [Latin *agglūtināre* : *ad-,* to + *glūtināre,* to glue, from *glūten,* glue.] **—ag·glu·ti·nant** *adj. & n.*

ag·glu·ti·na·tion (ə-glo͞ot′n-ā′shən) *n.* **1.** The process of agglutinating; adhesion of distinct parts. **2.** A mass formed in this manner. **3.** *Linguistics.* The process of forming words by combining component units that retain their original forms and meanings with little change, as in the formation of *houseboat* from *house* and *boat.*

ag·glu·ti·na·tive (ə-glo͞ot′n-ā′tĭv) *adj.* **1.** Tending toward, concerning, or characteristic of agglutination. **2.** *Linguistics.* Designating a language, such as Turkish, in which words are formed primarily by means of agglutination.

ag·glu·ti·nin (ə-glo͞ot′n-ĭn) *n.* An antibody that induces agglutination in blood cells or microorganisms. [AGGLUTIN(ATION) + -IN.]

ag·grade (ə-grād′) *tr.v.* **-graded, -grading, -grades.** To fill and raise the level of (the bed of a stream or a beach, for example) by depositing sediment. [AD- (toward) + GRADE.] **—ag·gra·da·tion** (ăg′rə-dā′shən) *n.* **—ag·gra·da·tion·al** *adj.*

ag·gran·dize (ə-grăn′dīz′, ăg′rən-dīz′) *tr.v.* **-dized, -dizing, -dizes.**

Agamemnon *A golden death mask, known as the Agamemnon mask after the legendary king who led the Greeks in the siege of Troy. The mask, dating from about the 16th century B.C., is now in the National Museum, Athens.*

agave *Members of this genus of tropical plant are used in the manufacture of the Mexican drink tequila.*

ageratum *An American tropical plant now widely cultivated.*

1. To increase the scope of; enlarge; extend. 2. To make greater in power, influence, stature, or reputation. 3. To make (something) seem greater; exaggerate. [French *aggrandir* (present stem *aggrandiss-*) : *a,* to, from Latin *ad-* + *grandir,* to grow larger, from Latin *grandīre,* from *grandis,* great, GRAND.] **—ag·gran·dize·ment** *n.* **—ag·gran·diz·er** *n.*

ag·gra·vate (ăg′rə-vāt′) *tr.v.* **-vated, -vating, -vates.** 1. To make worse or more serious: *Sunlight can aggravate certain skin conditions.* 2. *Informal.* To annoy or exasperate; provoke; irritate. [Latin *aggravāre,* to make heavier : *ad-,* in addition to + *gravāre,* to burden, from *gravis,* heavy.] **—ag·gra·vat·ing** *adj.* **—ag·gra·va·tor** *n.*

Usage: The word *aggravate* is widely used to mean "to irritate," as in *The mechanic's surliness aggravated me no end.* But many still insist that the word should be used only to mean "to make worse," in referring to a situation or condition, as in: *The plight of the small farmer has been aggravated by the drought. Kim's bad luck was aggravated by his refusal to get sufficient rest.*

ag·gra·va·tion (ăg′rə-vā′shən) *n.* 1. The action of aggravating. 2. The state of being aggravated. 3. A thing that irritates or makes worse or more troublesome. 4. *Informal.* Exasperation; bother.

ag·gre·gate (ăg′rə-gĭt′) *adj.* 1. Gathered together so as to make a whole; total. 2. *Botany.* Crowded or massed into a dense cluster. 3. *Geology.* Consisting of a mixture of mineral or rock fragments separable by mechanical means. Said of rock.
~*n.* 1. Any total or whole considered with reference to its constituent parts; a group of distinct particulars massed together; a gross amount: *"an empire is the aggregate of many states under one common head"* (Edmund Burke). 2. The mineral materials, such as sand or stone, used in making concrete. **—in the aggregate.** Considered collectively or as a whole.
~*tr.v.* (ăg′rə-gāt′) **aggregated, -gating, -gates.** 1. To gather into a mass, sum, or whole. 2. To total; add up to. [Middle English *aggregat,* from Latin *aggregātus,* past participle of *aggregāre,* to add to (the flock), attach to : *ad-,* to + *gregāre,* to herd, from *grex* (stem *greg-*), flock.] **—ag·gre·gate·ly** *adv.* **—ag·gre·ga·tion** (ăg′rə-gā′shən) *n.* **—ag·gre·ga·tive** (ăg′rə-gā′tĭv, ăg′rə-gə-tĭv) *adj.* **—ag·gre·ga·tor** *n.*

aggregate fruit *n.* A fruit, such as a raspberry or blackberry, consisting of a cluster of drupelets formed from the ovaries of a single flower.

ag·gress (ə-grĕs′) *v.* **-gressed, -gressing, -gresses.** —*intr.* To start an attack or a quarrel. —*tr.* To commit an act of aggression against. [Latin *aggredī* (past participle *aggressus*), to approach (with hostility), attack : *ad-,* toward + *gradī,* to step, go.]

ag·gres·sion (ə-grĕsh′ən) *n.* 1. The act or an instance of commencing an attack, invasion, or quarrel; an assault. 2. The habit or practice of launching attacks. 3. *Psychology.* Hostile action or behavior.

ag·gres·sive (ə-grĕs′ĭv) *adj.* 1. Inclined to provoke argument or hostility; belligerent. 2. Assertive; bold; forceful: *an aggressive salesman.* **—ag·gres·sive·ly** *adv.* **—ag·gres·sive·ness** *n.*

ag·grieve (ə-grēv′) *tr.v.* **-grieved, -grieving, -grieves.** 1. To distress or afflict. 2. To injure unjustly; give reason for just complaint. [Middle English *agreven,* from Old French *agrever,* from Latin *aggravāre,* to make heavier, AGGRAVATE.]

ag·grieved (ə-grēvd′) *adj.* 1. Hurt or offended, especially because of wrongful or unfair treatment. 2. *Law.* Treated unjustly by a decision of the court or other legal authority. **—ag·griev·ed·ly** (ə-grē′vĭd-lē) *adv.* **—ag·griev·ed·ness** *n.*

agha. Variant of **aga.**

a·ghast (ə-găst′, ə-gäst′) *adj.* Shocked, as by something horrible; appalled: *stood aghast at the sight.* [Middle English *agast,* past participle of *agasten,* to frighten : *a-* (intensive) + *gasten,* to frighten, Old English *gæstan,* from *gāst,* ghost.]

ag·ile (ăj′əl, ăj′īl) *adj.* 1. Able to move in a quick and easy fashion; active. 2. Mentally alert. —See Synonyms at **nimble.** [Middle English, from Old French, from Latin *agilis,* easily moved, light, nimble, from *agere,* to drive.] **—ag·ile·ly** *adv.* **—ag·ile·ness, a·gil·i·ty** (ə-jĭl′ə-tē) *n.*

a·gin (ə-gĭn′) *prep. Regional.* Against.

A·gin·court (ăj′ĭn-kôrt′). *French* **A·zin·court** (ȧ-zăN-ko͝or′). Village in northern France, scene of a decisive battle that took place in 1415 when an English army led by Henry V defeated a much larger French force. The victory, largely due to the superiority of the English archers, left nearly 6,000 French dead while the English losses were few.

ag·ing (ā′jĭng) *n.* Also *chiefly British* **age·ing.** 1. The process of becoming old or mature. 2. Any artificial process for imparting the characteristics and properties of age.

ag·i·o (ăj′ē-ō) *n., pl.* **-os.** *Finance.* 1. A premium paid for changing one kind of money into another. 2. An allowance or premium for the difference in value between two currencies being exchanged. 3. Agiotage. [Italian *ag(g)io,* alteration of dialectal *lajjē,* from Medieval Greek *allagion,* exchange, from *allagē,* change, from *allos,* other.]

ag·i·o·tage (ăj′ē-ə-tĭj, ăzh′ə-täzh′) *n. Finance.* 1. The business of brokerage; speculation in stocks and shares. 2. Exchange transactions, especially of currencies. [French, from *agioter,* to practice stockjobbing, from *agio,* stockbroking, from Italian *aggio,* AGIO.]

a·gist (ə-jĭst′) *tr.v.* **agisted, agisting, agists.** *Law.* To feed and take care of (cattle or horses belonging to others) in return for payment. [Middle English *agisten,* to pasture, from Old French *agister,* "to provide lodging for" : *a-,* from Latin *ad-,* to + *gister,* to lodge, from Vulgar Latin *jacitāre* (unattested), to make lie down, frequentative of Latin *jacēre,* to lie, intransitive of *jacere,* to throw.] **—a·gist·ment** *n.*

ag·i·tate (ăj′ə-tāt′) *v.* **-tated, -tating, -tates.** —*tr.* 1. To move with violence or sudden forcefulness: *a storm agitating the ocean.* 2. To excite or trouble; disturb: *Signs of the approaching storm agitated the birds.* 3. To arouse interest in (a cause, for example) by the written or spoken word; discuss; debate. 4. *Archaic.* To ponder over; consider. —*intr.* To stir up public interest in a cause: *agitate for better working conditions.* [Latin *agitāre,* frequentative of *agere,* to do, drive.] **—ag·i·tat·ed·ly** *adv.*

ag·i·ta·tion (ăj′ə-tā′shən) *n.* 1. The act of agitating. 2. The state of being agitated; disturbance; commotion. 3. Extreme emotional disturbance. 4. The stirring up of public interest, especially in favor of political or social change. **—ag·i·ta·tion·al** *adj.*

a·gi·ta·to (ä′jē-tä′tō) *adv. Music.* Agitated; fast and stirring. Used as a direction. [Italian, from Latin *agitātus,* past participle of *agitāre,* to AGITATE.] **—a·gi·ta·to** *adj.*

ag·i·ta·tor (ăj′ə-tā′tər) *n.* 1. A person who agitates, especially one who engages in political agitation. 2. A machine for stirring or shaking. **—ag·i·ta·to·ri·al** (ăj′ə-tə-tôr′ē-əl, -tōr′ē-əl) *adj.*

a·git·prop (ăj′ĭt-prŏp′) *n.* Political agitation and propaganda, especially in aid of left-wing or radical causes. [Shortened from Russian *Agitpropbyuro,* a Communist Party propaganda department, from *agitatsya-propaganda,* agitation-propaganda.] **—a·git·prop** *adj.*

A·gla·ia (ə-glā′ə, ə-glī′ə). *Greek Mythology.* One of the three **Graces** *(see).* [Greek, personification of *aglaia,* splendor, from *aglaos,* bright, splendid.]

a·gleam (ə-glēm′) *adj.* Brightly shining. **—a·gleam** *adv.*

ag·let (ăg′lĭt) *n.* Also **ai·glet** (ā′glĭt) 1. A tag or metal sheath on the end of a lace, cord, or ribbon to facilitate its passing through eyelet holes. 2. A similar device used as an ornament. [Middle English, from Old French *aguillette,* diminutive of *aguille,* needle, from Late Latin *acūcula,* pin, pine needle, diminutive of Latin *acus,* needle.]

a·gley (ə-glā′, ə-glī′) *adv.* Also **a·glee** (ə-glē′). *Scottish.* Off to the wrong direction; awry: *"The best laid schemes o' mice an' men / Gang aft agley"* (Robert Burns). [Scottish, "squintingly" : *a-,* on + *gley,* to squint, from Middle English (Scottish dialect) *gleyen*†.]

a·glim·mer (ə-glĭm′ər) *adj.* Lighting up faintly; glimmering. **—a·glim·mer** *adv.*

a·glit·ter (ə-glĭt′ər) *adj.* Glittering; sparkling. **—a·glit·ter** *adv.*

a·glow (ə-glō′) *adj.* Glowing; in a glow. **—a·glow** *adv.*

ag·ma (ăg′mə) *n.* A phonetic symbol, **eng** *(see).*

ag·mi·nate (ăg′mə-nĭt, -nāt′) *adj.* Also **ag·mi·nat·ed** (-nā′tĭd). Gathered in clusters. [Latin *agmen* (stem *agmin-*), moving multitude, troop.]

ag·nail (ăg′nāl′) *n.* 1. A hangnail. 2. A painful sore or swelling around a fingernail or toenail; a whitlow. [Middle English *agnail,* Old English *angnægl,* "painful prick in the flesh" : *ang-,* painful + *nægl,* (iron) nail.]

ag·nate (ăg′nāt′) *adj.* 1. Related on or descended from the father's or male side. 2. From a common source; akin.
~*n.* A relative on the male or father's side only. [Middle English, from Latin *agnātus,* "born in addition," past participle of *agnāsci,* to be born in addition to : *ad-,* in addition + *nāscī, gnāscī,* to be born.] **—ag·nat·ic** (ăg-năt′ĭk) *adj.* **—ag·nat·i·cal·ly** *adv.* **—ag·na·tion** *n.*

Ag·ni (ŭg′nē). *Hinduism.* The Vedic god of fire and guardian of man. [Sanskrit *agniḥ,* fire.]

ag·no·men (ăg-nō′mən) *n., pl.* **-nomina** (-nŏm′ə-nə). 1. An additional cognomen given to an ancient Roman, often in honor of military victories, as Publius Cornelius Scipio *Africanus.* 2. A nickname. [Latin *agnōmen* : *ad-,* additional + *(g)nōmen,* name.]

Ag·non (ăg′nôn′), **Shmuel Yosef,** born Samuel Czaczkes (1888–1970). Israeli novelist. Born in Galicia (now in the U.S.S.R.), he moved to Palestine in 1907. His dramatic and influential novels, written in Hebrew, include *A Guest for the Night* (1938) and *The Day Before Yesterday* (1945). He was awarded the Nobel Prize for literature in 1966.

ag·nos·tic (ăg-nŏs′tĭk) *n.* Someone who doubts the existence or knowability of God but does not deny the possibility that God exists.
~*adj.* 1. Pertaining to agnostics. 2. Uncertain or uncommitted on any particular question at issue. [19th century : A- (not) + GNOSTIC (coined by T.H. Huxley as a description of his own views, as opposed to those of Victorian "gnostics," who believed that there were immaterial or spiritual phenomena).] **—ag·nos·ti·cal·ly** *adv.*

ag·nos·ti·cism (ăg-nŏs′tə-sĭz′əm) *n.* The philosophical view that it is impossible to know whether or not God exists; doubt as to the existence or knowability of God.

Ag·nus De·i (ăg′nəs dē′ī, äg′no͞os dā′ē) *n.* 1. The Lamb of God, an emblem of Christ, derived from John 1:29 and Isaiah 53:7. 2. A representation of this. 3. A wax disk stamped with this emblem and blessed by the pope. 4. a. A threefold prayer said or sung shortly after the Eucharistic Prayer in the Mass. b. A musical setting of the Latin text of this prayer. [Latin.]

a·go (ə-gō′) *adj.* Gone by; past: *two years ago.*
~*adv.* In the past: *It happened long ago.* [Middle English *ago(n),* past participle of *agon,* to go away, be past, Old English *āgān* : *ā-* (intensive) + *gān,* to go.]

a·gog (ə-gŏg′) *adv.* In a state of keen anticipation; highly excited: *The court was all agog to hear the verdict.* [Middle English, from Old French *en gogues,* "in merriments," from *gogue,* merriment, probably imitative of hubbub.] **—a·gog** *adj.*

agouti *A burrowing rodent native to South and Central America, the agouti is a fast runner about the size of a rabbit.*

PRONUNCIATION KEY

ă, pat; ā, pay; âr, care; ä, father, are; b, bib; ch, church; d, deed; ĕ, pet; ē, be; f, fife; g, gag; h, hat; hw, which; ĭ, pit; ī, pie; îr, pier; j, judge; k, kick; l, lid, needle; m, mum; n, no, sudden; ng, thing; ŏ, pot; ō, toe; ô, paw, for; oi, noise; ou, out; o͝o, book; o͞o, boot; p, pop; r, roar; s, sauce; sh, ship, dish; t, tight; th, thin, path; *th,* this, bathe; ŭ, cut; ûr, fur; v, valve; w, with; y, yes; z, zebra, size; zh, vision; ə, about, item, edible, gallop, circus, peaceful

IN FOREIGN WORDS:

ȧ, *Fr.* ami; œ, *Fr.* feu, *Ger.* schön; ü, *Fr.* tu, *Ger.* über; KH, *Ger.* ich, *Scot.* loch; N, *Fr.* bon; y′, *Fr.* Compiègne

STRESS MARKS:

Primary stress: ′ in·cite′ (ĭn-sīt′)
Secondary stress: ′ in′sight′ (ĭn′sīt′)

á go·go, á go-go (ä gō-gō′) *adj. Informal.* Unlimited; galore: *champagne á gogo.* [French, "in a joyful manner," from *gogo,* probably reduplication of the first syllable of *gogue,* merriment, from Old French. See **agog.**] **—á go·go** *adv.*

-agogue, -agog *suffix.* Indicates: **1.** A leader or inciter of; for example, **demagogue. 2.** *Medicine.* Something that stimulates the flow of; for example, **emmenagogue.** [Late Latin *-agōgus,* from Greek *-agōgos,* from *agōgos,* leading, drawing forth, from *agein,* to lead.]

a·gone (ə-gôn′, ə-gŏn′) *adj. Archaic.* Gone; gone by; past. [Middle English *agon,* AGO.] **—a·gone** *adv.*

a·gon·ic (ā-gŏn′ĭk, ə-gŏn′-) *adj.* Having no angle. [Greek *agōnos* : *a-,* not + *gōnia,* angle.]

agonic line *n.* An imaginary line on the earth's surface connecting points where the magnetic declination is zero.

ag·o·nist (ăg′ə-nĭst) *n. Physiology.* A muscle whose contraction effects movement of a part of the body. It is opposed by contraction in another muscle, the **antagonist** *(see).* [Back-formation from ANTAGONIST.]

ag·o·nis·tic (ăg′ə-nĭs′tĭk) *adj.* **1.** Striving to overcome in argument; competitive; combative. **2.** Straining to achieve effect. **3.** Of or pertaining to contests, originally those of the ancient Greeks. [Late Latin *agōnisticus,* from Greek *agōnistikos,* from *agōnistēs,* contestant, from *agōn,* contest.] **—ag·o·nis·ti·cal·ly** *adv.*

ag·o·nize (ăg′ə-nīz′) *v.* **-nized, -niz·ing, -niz·es.** *—intr.* **1.** To be in extreme pain or suffer great anguish. **2.** To make a prolonged or intense mental effort: *We agonized over the decision all night.* *—tr.* To cause great pain or anguish to. [Old French *agoniser,* from Late Latin *agōnizāre,* from Greek *agōnizesthai,* to contend for a prize, to struggle, from *agōnia,* contest, AGONY.] **—ag·o·niz·ing·ly** *adv.*

ag·o·ny (ăg′ə-nē) *n., pl.* **-nies. 1.** The suffering of intense physical or mental pain. **2.** A sudden or intense emotion of a particular sort: *an agony of doubt.* **3.** A violent or intense struggle. **—last agony** or **agonies.** The struggle that precedes death. [Middle English *agonie,* from Old French, from Late Latin *agōnia,* from Greek, contest, anguish, from *agōn,* contest, from *agein,* to drive.]

agony column *n. Informal.* **1.** A newspaper column containing advertisements chiefly about missing relatives or friends. **2.** *British.* A newspaper or magazine feature that prints letters from troubled readers together with a columnist's replies and advice.

ag·o·ra[1] (ăg′ə-rə) *n., pl.* **-rae** (-rē′, -rī′) or **-ras. 1.** A marketplace in ancient Greece, customarily used for holding meetings of the people's assembly. **2.** The assembly itself. [Greek *agora,* from *ageirein,* to assemble.]

a·go·ra[2] (ä′gə-rä′) *n., pl.* **-rot** or **-roth** (-rōt′). An Israeli monetary unit equal to 1/100 of the shekel of Israel. See feature at **currency.** [Hebrew *'agōrāh,* from *āgōr,* to collect.]

ag·o·ra·pho·bi·a (ăg′ə-rə-fō′bē-ə) *n.* Abnormal fear of open spaces or of going out in public. [New Latin : Greek *agora,* open space, AGORA + -PHOBIA.] **—ag·o·ra·pho·bic** (ăg′ə-rə-fō′bĭk, -fŏb′ĭk) *adj.*

a·gou·ti (ə-go͞o′tē) *n., pl.* **-tis** or **-ties.** Any of several burrowing rodents of the genus *Dasyprocta,* of tropical America, having grizzled brownish or dark-gray fur. [French, from Spanish *agutí,* from Guarani *acutí.*]

agr. agricultural; agriculture.

A.G.R. advanced gas-cooled reactor.

A·gra (ä′grə). City in north-central India in Uttar Pradesh on the Jumna River. It was a capital of the Mogul Empire in the 16th and 17th centuries. The Taj Mahal was built here by Shah Jahan. Modern Agra is an important commercial city whose products include carpets and glassware.

a·graffe (ə-grăf′) *n.* **1.** A hook-and-loop clasp on armor and clothing. **2.** In stonemasonry, a cramp iron for holding stones together. [French *agrafe,* from Old French *agrafer,* to hook on to : *a-,* to, from Latin *ad-* + *grafer,* to hook, from *grafe,* hook, from Old High German *krāpfo.*]

a·gran·u·lo·cy·to·sis (ā-grăn′yə-lō-sī-tō′sĭs) *n.* A drug-induced disease marked by high fever, lesions of the mucous membranes, and a marked decrease in granular white blood corpuscles. [New Latin : A- (not) + GRANULE + -CYT(E) + -OSIS.]

a·gra·pha (ăg′rə-fə) *pl.n. Often* **Agrapha.** The sayings of Jesus not recorded in the Gospels. [Greek, "things unwritten," neuter plural of *agraphos,* unwritten : *a-,* not + *graphein,* to write.]

a·graph·i·a (ā-grăf′ē-ə) *n. Pathology.* Acquired inability to write, caused by disease of the parietal lobe of the brain. [New Latin : A- (not) + Greek *graphein,* to write.] **—a·graph·ic** *adj.*

a·grar·i·an (ə-grâr′ē-ən) *adj.* **1.** Relating to or concerning the land and its ownership, cultivation, and tenure. **2.** Pertaining to agricultural or rural matters.
∼*n.* A person who favors equitable distribution of land. [From Latin *agrārius,* from *ager* (stem *agri-*), land, field.]

a·grar·i·an·ism (ə-grâr′ē-ə-nĭz′əm) *n.* A movement for equitable distribution of land and for agrarian reform.

a·gree (ə-grē′) *v.* **a·greed, a·gree·ing, a·grees.** *—intr.* **1.** To grant consent; be willing. Used with the infinitive: *He agreed to accompany us.* **2.** To correspond; be in accord: *The copy agrees with the original.* **3.** To be of one opinion. Often used with *with.* **4.** To come to an understanding or to terms. Used with *about, upon,* or *on*: *Is it possible to agree on such great problems?* **5.** To be beneficial to the constitution or health. Used with *with*: *Spicy food does not agree with him.* **6.** *Grammar.* To correspond in gender, number, case, or person. *—tr.* **1.** To grant or concede: *He agreed that we should go.* **2.** *Chiefly British.* To come to an understanding or settlement regarding: *agree terms.* —See Synonyms at **assent.** [Middle English *agreen,* from Old French *agreer,* from Vulgar Latin *aggrātāre* (unattested), to be pleasing to : *ad-,* to + *grātus,* pleasing, beloved, agreeable.]
Synonyms: *accord, coincide, conform, correspond, harmonize.*

a·gree·a·ble (ə-grē′ə-bəl) *adj.* **1.** Pleasing; pleasant; to one's liking: *an agreeable painting.* **2.** Ready to consent or submit: *They needed a lift, and I was agreeable.* **—a·gree·a·bil·i·ty, a·gree·a·ble·ness** *n.* **—a·gree·a·bly** *adv.*

a·greed (ə-grēd′) *adj.* **1.** Determined by common consent: *the agreed meeting place.* **2.** Of one opinion: *Both parties were agreed.* **3.** Allowed; granted. Used as an interjection.

a·greed-val·ue policy (ə-grēd′văl′yo͞o) *n.* An insurance policy requiring the insurer to pay the insured the full face value of the policy in the event of total loss, regardless of the actual value of the property lost. Also called "valued policy."

a·gree·ment (ə-grē′mənt) *n.* **1.** The act of agreeing. **2.** The state of being agreed; concord; harmony. **3.** An arrangement between parties regarding a course of action; a covenant; a treaty. **4.** *Law.* **a.** A properly executed and legally binding contract. **b.** The writing or document embodying this. **5.** *Grammar.* Correspondence in gender, number, case, or person between words.

a·gres·tal (ə-grĕs′təl) *adj. Botany.* Growing wild, especially in cultivated areas. [From Latin *agrestis,* rural, from *ager* (stem *agr-*), field, land.]

a·gres·tic (ə-grĕs′tĭk) *adj.* Also **a·gres·ti·cal** (-tĭ-kəl). **1.** Rural; rustic. **2.** Unpolished; crude.

ag·ri·busi·ness (ăg′rə-bĭz′nĭs) *n.* Farming engaged in as a large-scale business, including the production, processing, and distribution of farm products and the manufacture of farm machinery, equipment, and supplies. [AGRI(CULTURE) + BUSINESS.]

agric. agriculture; agriculturist.

A·gric·o·la (ə-grĭk′ə-lə), **Georgius,** born Georg Bauer (1494–1555). German mineralogist. In his book *De Re Metallica,* published in 1556, he dealt with mineralogy, geology, and mining, and produced the first systematic and scientific description of minerals and ores.

Agricola, Gnaeus Julius (*c.*A.D. 40–93). Roman general and conqueror of Britain. A consul in *c.* 71, he was governor of Britain (*c.* 78–85). An enlightened ruler, he circumnavigated the mainland and pacified most of the island, subduing northern Wales and advancing far into Scotland.

ag·ri·cul·ture (ăg′rĭ-kŭl′chər) *n. Abbr.* **agr., agric.** The science or occupation of cultivating the soil, producing crops, and raising livestock; farming. [Latin *agricultūra,* originally *agrī cultūra,* "cultivation of land" : *agrī,* genitive of *ager,* land + *cultūra,* cultivation, CULTURE.] **—ag·ri·cul·tur·al** (ăg′rĭ-kŭl′chə-rəl) *adj.* **—ag·ri·cul·tur·al·ly** *adv.* **—ag·ri·cul·tur·ist** (ăg′rĭ-kŭl′chə-rĭst), **ag·ri·cul·tur·al·ist** *n.*

Agri Dagi. See **Ararat, Mount.**

ag·ri·mo·ny (ăg′rə-mō′nē) *n., pl.* **-nies. 1.** Any of various plants of the genus *Agrimonia,* having compound leaves, long clusters of small yellow flowers, and bristly fruits. **2.** Any of several other plants, such as the **hemp agrimony** *(see).* [Middle English *agrimonie,* from Old French *aigremoine,* from Latin *agrimōnia,* alteration of *argemōnia,* from Greek *argemōnē, argemōnia,* poppy, perhaps from Hebrew *'argāmān,* red-purple.]

ag·ri·ol·o·gy (ăg′rē-ŏl′ə-jē) *n.* The study of primitive cultures. [Greek *agrios,* wild, from *agros,* open field + -LOGY.] **—ag·ri·o·log·i·cal** (ăg′rē-ə-lŏj′ĭ-kəl) *adj.*

A·grip·pa (ə-grĭp′ə), **Marcus Vipsanius** (63–12 B.C.). Roman general and statesman, the adviser of the emperor Augustus, whose daughter Julia he married. He was in command of the fleet that defeated the forces of Mark Antony and Cleopatra at Actium.

Ag·rip·pi·na (ăg′rə-pī′nə, -pē′-), known as "the Elder" (*c.* 13 B.C.–A.D. 33). Roman matron, daughter of Agrippa, granddaughter of Augustus, and mother of the emperor Caligula. She accompanied her husband, Germanicus Caesar, on all his campaigns and was famous for her courage. After Germanicus's death Tiberius banished her to the island of Pandataria, where she died of starvation.

Agrippina, known as "the Younger" (*c.* A.D. 15–59). Roman empress, daughter of Agrippina the Elder and mother of the emperor Nero. She was known for her ambition and ruthlessness, and it is thought that she murdered her third husband, her uncle the emperor Claudius. She managed to place Nero on the throne and exerted considerable power through her son. Eventually they quarreled, and Nero had her murdered.

agro- *prefix.* Indicates field, earth, or soil; for example, **agronomy.** [Greek *agros,* open field.]

ag·ro·bi·ol·o·gy (ăg′rō-bī-ŏl′ə-jē) *n.* The science of plant and animal growth and nutrition as related to soil variation and crop yield. **—ag·ro·bi·o·log·ic** (ăg′rō-bī′ə-lŏj′ĭk), **ag·ro·bi·o·log·i·cal** *adj.* **—ag·ro·bi·o·log·i·cal·ly** *adv.* **—ag·ro·bi·ol·o·gist** (ăg′rō-bī-ŏl′ə-jĭst) *n.*

a·grol·o·gy (ə-grŏl′ə-jē) *n.* The applied science of soils in relation to crops. Compare **pedology.** [AGRO- + -LOGY.] **—ag·ro·log·ic** (ăg′rə-lŏj′ĭk), **ag·ro·log·i·cal** *adj.* **—ag·ro·log·i·cal·ly** *adv.* **—a·grol·o·gist** (ə-grŏl′ə-jĭst) *n.*

ag·ro·nom·ics (ăg′rə-nŏm′ĭks) *n. Used with a singular verb.* Agronomy.

a·gron·o·my (ə-grŏn′ə-mē) *n.* The application of the various soil and plant sciences to soil management and the raising of crops; scientific agriculture. [French *agronomie* : AGRO- + -NOMY.] **—ag·ro·nom·ic** (ăg′rə-nŏm′ĭk), **ag·ro·nom·i·cal** *adj.* **—a·gron·o·mist** (ə-grŏn′ə-mĭst) *n.*

ag·ros·tol·o·gy (ăg′rə-stŏl′ə-jē) *n.* The botanical study of grasses.

agrimony *This common European wildflower,* Agrimonia eupatoria, *has had many uses in the past—from curing snakebites to producing a dye for wool. An infusion from its leaves is still used as a tonic.*

ailanthus *This tree,* Ailanthus altissima, *was introduced to the Western world in the 1750's. It was given the name "tree of heaven" because its branches are said to reach toward Paradise, but the name rightly belongs to the related species* Ailanthus moluccana.

[Greek *agrōstis,* a kind of wild grass, from *agros,* field + -LOGY.]
a·ground (ə-ground′) *adv.* On the ground or bottom; stranded, as in shallow water: *The ship ran aground.* **—a·ground** *adj.*
a·gue (ā′gyōō) *n.* **1.** An attack of malarial fever, with alternate fever and chills. **2.** A recurrent chill or fit of shivering. [Middle English, from Old French *ague,* from Medieval Latin *(fēbris) acūta,* "sharp (fever)," feminine of *acūtus,* sharp, past participle of *acuere,* to sharpen, from *acus,* needle.] **—a·gu·ish** (ā′gyōō-ĭsh) *adj.* **—a·gu·ish·ly** *adv.* **—a·gu·ish·ness** *n.*
a·gue·weed (ā′gyōō-wēd′) *n.* **1.** A plant, *Gentiana quinquefolia,* of eastern North America, having clusters of pale blue-violet or white flowers. **2.** A plant, **boneset** *(see).*
A·gul·has, Cape (ə-gŭl′əs). Headland in South Africa, the most southerly point of Africa. Its meridian (longitude 20° E) marks the division between the Atlantic and Indian oceans.
ah (ä) *interj.* Used to express various emotions, such as surprise, delight, pain, satisfaction, or regret. See **ooh.** [Middle English *a(h),* from Old French.]
A.H. in the year of the Hegira. Used to indicate the date in the Muslim world, the base year being A.D. 622. [Latin *anno Hegirae*]
a·ha (ä-hä′) *interj.* Used to express surprise, triumph, or pleasure. [Middle English : AH + HA.]
A·hab (ā′hăb′). A king of Israel in the 9th century B.C., husband of Jezebel. I Kings 16:29.
A·has·u·e·rus (ə-hăz′yōō-ē′rəs). A king of ancient Persia, often identified with Xerxes; the husband of Esther. Esther 1:1.
a·head (ə-hĕd′) *adv.* **1.** At or to the front or leading position. **2.** Before in space or in time; in advance. **3.** Onward; forward. **—ahead of.** In front of. **—get ahead.** To attain success. **—a·head** *adj.*
a·hem (ə-hĕm′) *interj.* Used to attract attention or to express doubt or warning. [Imitative. See **hem².**]
a·him·sa (ə-hĭm′sä′) *n.* An Indian doctrine of nonviolence, expressing belief in the sacredness of all living creatures and the possibility of reincarnation. It is strictly practiced by the Jains and subscribed to by Buddhists and Hindus. [Sanskrit *ahiṁsā,* noninjury : *a-,* without + *hiṁsā,* injury, from *hiṁsati,* he injures.]
a·his·tor·i·cal (ā′hĭ-stôr′ĭ-kəl, ā′hĭ-stŏr′-) *adj.* Also **a·his·tor·ic** (ā′-hĭ-stôr′ĭk, -stŏr′ĭk). Not historical; unrelated to history.
A·hith·o·phel (ə-hĭth′ə-fĕl). Also in Douay Bible **A·chit·o·phel** (ə-kĭt′-). A counselor of David, who became an adviser to Absalom in his rebellion and hanged himself when his advice was disregarded.
Ah·ma·da·bad, Ah·me·da·bad (ä′məd-ə-bäd′). Capital of Gujarat state, India. Founded in 1412 as the capital of the former Gujarat kingdom, it is the largest town of Gujarat as well as being the state's cultural and commercial center. Ahmadabad's textile industry is one of the largest in India.
-aholic. Variant of **-holic.**
a·hoy (ə-hoi′) *interj. Nautical.* Used to hail a ship or person, or to attract attention. [AH + HOY (interjection).]
A.H.Q. army headquarters.
Ah·ri·man (ä′rĭ-mən) *n.* In Zoroastrianism, the spirit of evil, understood by some as the arch rival of **Ormazd** *(see).* [Persian *Ahrīman,* probably from Avestan *aṅra mainyu,* "the evil spirit" : *aṅra,* evil, hostile, probably from Iranian root *ans-*†, to hate + *mainyu,* spirit.]
A·hu·ra Maz·da (ä-hōōr′ə măz′də). **Ormazd** *(see).*
Ah·ve·nan·maa (äKH′vĕ-nän-mä′). Also **Å·land Islands** (ō′län). Province of Finland, comprising about 80 inhabited islands and 6,000 uninhabited islets in the Baltic Sea between Finland and Sweden at the entrance to the Gulf of Bothnia. Ahvenanmaa, the largest island, is the site of the capital, Maarianhamina.
ai (ī) *n., pl.* **ais.** See **sloth** (sense 2a). [Portuguese, from Tupi *ai, hai.*]
A.I. **1.** artificial insemination. **2.** artificial intelligence.
ai·a (ī′ə) *n. South African.* **1.** A child's nursemaid or nanny, especially a native woman. **2.** *Informal.* An old native woman. [Portuguese, nurse. Compare **ayah.**]
aid (ād) *v.* **aided, aiding, aids.** *—intr.* To help; assist. *—tr.* To give help or assistance to. **—**See Synonyms at **help.**
∼n. **1.** The act or result of helping; assistance; cooperation. **2. a.** One that helps; an assistant or helper. **b.** A device that helps: *a hearing aid; a teaching aid.* **3. Foreign aid** *(see).* **4.** An aide-de-camp or aide. **5.** In medieval England: **a.** Any of several revenues or subsidies paid to the king. **b.** A money payment to a feudal lord by a vassal. [Middle English *eyden, aiden,* from Old French *aider,* from Latin *adjūtāre,* frequentative of *adjuvāre,* to give aid to, help : *ad,* to + *juvāre*†, to help.] **—aid·er** *n.*
A.I.D. **1.** acute infectious disease. **2.** Agency for International Development. **3.** artificial insemination by donor.
Ai·dan (ā′dən), **Saint** (*c.* A.D. 600–51). Irish monk. From the monastery at Iona he was sent as a missionary to Northumbria in 635. He founded a famous monastery at (Holy Island) Lindisfarne and became its first bishop.
aide (ād) *n.* **1.** An aide-de-camp. **2.** An assistant; a helper: *a president's aide.* [French, from *aider,* to help, AID.]
aide-de-camp (ād′də-kămp′) *n., pl.* **aides-de-camp** (ādz′-). *Abbr.* **ADC, a.d.c., A.D.C.** A naval or military officer acting as secretary and confidential assistant to a superior officer of general or flag rank. [French, "camp assistant."]
aide-mé·moire (ād′mĕm-wär′) *n., pl.* **aides-mé·moire** (ādz′-). A statement in summary form, usually of the terms of an agreement, to be used in drafting a formal document. [French, "help memory."]
AIDS (ādz) *n.* An abnormal, ultimately fatal condition of the body's immune system, in which the body's defenses against disease are permanently weakened. [*A*cquired *I*mmune *D*eficiency *S*yndrome.]
Aigina. See **Aegina.**
aiglet. Variant of **aglet.**
ai·grette, ai·gret (ā-grĕt′, ā′grĕt) *n.* **1.** An ornamental tuft of upright plumes, especially the tail feathers of an egret. **2.** An ornament or item of jewelry, such as a spray of gems, resembling such a tuft. [French. See **egret.**]
ai·guille (ā-gwēl′) *n.* **1.** A sharp, pointed mountain peak. **2.** A needle-shaped drill for boring holes in rock or masonry. [French, "needle," from Old French, AGLET.]
ai·guil·lette (ā′gwĭ-lĕt′) *n.* An ornamental cord or braid worn on the shoulder of a military uniform. [French, AGLET.]
A.I.H. artificial insemination by husband.
Ai·ken (ā′kən), **Charles Avery** (1872–1965). U.S. painter and graphic artist. He is noted for his watercolors of flowers and landscapes. Aiken also originated the technique of making prints from plaster blocks.
Aiken, Conrad Potter (1889–1973). U.S. poet, novelist, and critic. He won a Pulitzer Prize for his *Selected Poems* in 1929. Among his most famous works is *Collected Poems* (1953), which earned him the recognition he had long been denied.
ai·ki·do (ī′kē-dō′, ī-kē′dō) *n.* A 20th-century Japanese martial art similar to judo.
ail (āl) *v.* **ailed, ailing, ails.** *—intr.* **1.** To feel ill or have pain; be unwell. **2.** To be in a weak or unsound condition: *The economy is ailing.* *—tr.* To cause pain; make ill or uneasy; trouble: *What ails you?* [Middle English *eilen,* Old English *eglan,* to trouble, from *egle,* troublesome.]
ai·lan·thus (ā-lăn′thəs) *n.* A deciduous tree, *Ailanthus altissima,* native to China and widely grown for ornament, especially in urban areas. It has compound leaves and clusters of small greenish flowers with a strong odor. Also called "tree of heaven." [New Latin, from Amboinese (an Indonesian language) *ai lanto,* "tree (of) heaven"; Latin form influenced by Greek *anthos,* flower.]
ai·le·ron (ā′lə-rŏn′) *n.* A movable control surface on the trailing edge of an airplane wing. [French, diminutive of *aile,* wing, from Old French, from Latin *āla.*]
ail·ment (āl′mənt) *n.* A physical or mental disorder; especially, a mild illness.
ai·lu·ro·phile (ā-lōōr′ə-fīl′) *n.* A person who loves cats. [Greek *ailouros,* cat + -PHILE.]
ai·lu·ro·phobe (ā-lōōr′ə-fōb′) *n.* A person with an intense fear or dislike of cats. [Greek *ailouros,* cat + -PHOBE.]
aim (ām) *v.* **aimed, aiming, aims.** *—tr.* To direct (a weapon, remark, or blow, for example) at someone or something. *—intr.* **1.** To direct a weapon. **2. a.** To direct one's efforts toward something; strive: *aim at perfection.* **b.** To intend; propose; plan. Used with *for* or with an infinitive: *We are aiming for an early start. We aim to get to the bottom of this.*
∼n. **1.** The act of aiming or pointing. **2.** The sighting or line of fire of something aimed: *take aim.* **3.** A purpose; an intention; a plan. **—**See Synonyms at **intention.** [Middle English *aimen,* to guess, aim, from Old French *aesmer,* to guess at : *a-,* at, to, from Latin *ad-* + *esmer,* to guess, from Latin *aestimāre,* to ESTIMATE.]
aim·less (ām′lĭs) *adj.* Without direction or purpose. **—aim·less·ly** *adv.* **—aim·less·ness** *n.*
ain¹ (ān) *adj. Scottish.* Own.
ain². Variant of **ayin.**
ain't (ānt). *Nonstandard.* Contraction of *am not.* Also extended in use to mean *are not, is not, has not,* and *have not.*
Usage: Although widely used in colloquial speech, *ain't* is considered nonstandard by educated speakers. It should always be avoided in writing or formal speech, unless you are deliberately trying to create a humorous effect or using a fixed phrase like *Things ain't what they used to be. Aren't I* (as in *aren't I coming too?*) has sometimes also been attacked on the grounds that it misleadingly suggests a corresponding form *I are.* But the full form, *am I not,* is so formal that in many contexts it may be considered ridiculously stilted, and *aren't I* is therefore a quite acceptable usage in educated English. The form *amn't I* has some currency in regional English, but is considered nonstandard.
Ai·nu (ī′nōō) *n., pl.* **-nus** or collectively **Ainu.** **1.** A member of an aboriginal Caucasian people inhabiting the northernmost islands of Japan. **2.** The language of this people. [Ainu, "man."]
aï·o·li (ī-ō′lē) *n.* Garlic-flavored mayonnaise. [French, from *ail,* garlic.]
air (âr) *n.* **1. a.** A colorless, odorless, tasteless, gaseous mixture, mainly nitrogen (approximately 78 percent) and oxygen (approximately 21 percent) with lesser amounts of argon, carbon dioxide, neon, helium, and other gases. **b.** This mixture with varying amounts of moisture, low-altitude pollutants, and particulate matter, enveloping Earth; the atmosphere. **c.** The air or atmosphere in an enclosed space: *The air in the conference room is invariably half cigar smoke.* **d.** In ancient thought, one of the four elements. **2. a.** The sky; the firmament. **b.** The space above the ground: *leaped into the air.* **3.** An atmospheric movement; a breeze; a wind. **4.** The sky as a medium of transport or conveyance: *sent it by air.* **5.** Utterance; public expression: *give air to one's grievances.* **6.** A peculiar or characteristic impression; an appearance or aura: *an air of excitement.* **7.** Personal bearing, appearance, or manner; mien: *He has an air of gentility.* **—**See Synonyms at **bearing.** **8. airs.** Affectations; haughty manner: *She gives herself airs.* **9.** *Music.* A

melody or tune, especially: **a.** The soprano or treble part in a harmonized composition. **b.** A solo for voice or instrument, with or without accompaniment. **10.** *Archaic.* Breath. —**clear the air.** To dispel emotional differences and tensions. —**in the air. 1.** In circulation; prevalent. **2.** Uncertain; not settled; being thought out or formulated. —**on the air.** Broadcast, or being broadcast, on radio or television. —**take the air.** To go outdoors for fresh air; take a short walk or ride. —**up in the air.** Not decided; uncertain. —**walk on air.** To feel elated or extremely happy.
~*tr.v.* **aired, airing, airs. 1.** To expose (a room or laundry, for example) to air or warmth, in order to dry, cool, or freshen; ventilate. **2.** To give public utterance to; circulate: *air one's grievances.* —See Synonyms at **vent.** [Blend of senses of several origins: 1. Atmosphere: Middle English *eir, ayr,* from Old French *air,* from Latin *āēr,* from Greek *āēr,* breath, atmospheric air; 2. Manner, appearance: French *air,* from Old French *aire,* nature, quality, originally "place of origin," from Latin *ager,* place, field, and Latin *ārea,* open space, threshing floor, AREA; 3. Melody: Italian *aria,* ARIA. In English these senses have interacted inextricably, with the first prevailing.]
AIR 1. artist in residence. **2.** All India Radio.
air bag *n.* A safety device designed for use in cars, consisting of a large bag that inflates upon collision and prevents passengers from pitching forward.
air base *n.* A base of operations for military aircraft.
air battery *n.* A rechargeable battery in which the current is produced as a result of oxidation of a metal.
air bearing *n.* A device that uses compressed air to separate working parts, for example of a dental drill, to reduce noise level.
air bed *n.* An inflatable mattress, especially one used for supporting patients with extensive burns.
air bladder *n. Biology.* **1.** An air-filled structure near the spinal column in many fishes, which functions to maintain buoyancy or, in some species, as an aid in respiration or hearing. Also called "swim bladder." **2.** Any air-filled saclike structure, such as one of the dilated parts of the thallus in certain seaweeds.
air·boat (âr′bōt′) *n.* A swamp boat *(see).*
air·borne (âr′bôrn′, -bōrn′) *adj. Abbr.* **abn 1.** Carried by or through the air: *airborne pollen.* **2.** Transported in aircraft: *airborne troops.* **3.** Flying; in flight.
air brake *n.* A brake operated by compressed air.
air brick *n.* A brick with holes running through it, built into a wall as a means of ventilation.
air bridge *n.* A transport link by aircraft between two distant points.
air·brush (âr′brŭsh′) *n.* An atomizer using compressed air to spray paint or other liquids on a surface.
~*tr.v* **airbrushed, -brushing, -brushes.** To paint or coat (a surface) using an airbrush.
air·burst (âr′bûrst′) *n.* An explosion of a bomb or shell in the atmosphere.
air·bus (âr′bŭs′) *n.* A usually wide-bodied jet airplane carrying a large number of passengers over relatively short distances.
air chamber *n.* **1.** Any enclosure filled with air for a special purpose. **2.** Such a compartment, especially in a hydraulic system, in which air elastically compresses and expands to regulate the flow of a fluid.
air command *n.* A unit of the U.S. Air Force that is larger than an air force.
air-con·di·tion (âr′kən-dĭsh′ən) *tr.v.* **-tioned, -tioning, -tions.** To provide with or ventilate by air conditioning. —**air-con·di·tioned** *adj.*
air conditioning *n.* **1.** *Abbr.* **a/c, A/C** A system or apparatus for controlling, especially lowering, the temperature and humidity of a building or vehicle. **2.** The condition so produced. —**air conditioner** *n.*
air-cool (âr′kōōl′) *tr.v.* **-cooled, -cooling, -cools.** To cool (an engine, for example) by a flow of air.
air corridor *n.* An air route established by international agreement, along which aircraft are allowed to fly.
air cover *n.* **1.** Protection for ground operations provided by military aircraft. **2.** The aircraft so employed.
air·craft (âr′krăft′, -kräft′) *n., pl.* **aircraft.** Any machine or device, such as an airplane, helicopter, glider, or balloon, capable of flight in the air by means of buoyancy or aerodynamic forces.
aircraft carrier *n.* A large naval ship designed as a mobile air base at sea, having a long flat deck to serve as a landing strip.
air·craft·man (âr′krăft′mən, -kräft′mən) *n., pl.* **-men** (-mĭn). *Abbr.* **A.C.** A serviceman of the lowest rank in the British Royal Air Force.
air·craft·wom·an (âr′krăft′wŏŏm′ən, -kräft′wŏŏm′ən) *n., pl.* **-women** (-wĭm′ĭn) *Abbr.* **A.C.W.** A servicewoman of the lowest rank in the British Women's Royal Air Force.
air cushion *n.* **1.** An inflatable cushion. **2.** The downward flow of air that lifts and supports a Hovercraft. **3.** An air spring *(see).*
air-cush·ion vehicle (âr′kŏŏsh′ən) *n.* A vehicle supported by a cushion of air, a Hovercraft *(see).*
air division *n.* A unit of the U.S. Air Force larger than a wing and smaller than an air command.
air door *n.* A strong current of warm air directed upward and used instead of a conventional door to prevent heat loss from a building. Also called "air curtain."
air·drome (âr′drōm′) *n.* Also *chiefly British* **aer·o·drome** (âr′ə-drōm′). **1.** An airport. **2.** A landing field. **3.** An airplane hangar.

[Earlier *aerodrome* : AERO- + -DROME.]
air-drop (âr′drŏp′) *n.* A delivery, as of supplies or troops, by parachute from aircraft in flight.
~*tr.v.* **airdropped, -dropping, -drops.** To drop (supplies or troops, for example) from an aircraft.
air-dry (âr′drī′) *tr.v.* **-dried, -drying, -dries.** To dry by exposure to the air.
~*adj.* Sufficiently dry so that further exposure to air will not evaporate moisture.
Aire·dale (âr′dāl′) *n.* A large terrier of a breed developed in England, having a wiry tan coat marked with black. Also called "Airedale terrier." [After *Airedale,* a valley in Yorkshire, England.]
air embolism *n. Pathology.* Obstruction of blood flow from the heart by the presence of air in the circulation, resulting from surgery, injury, or the like.
air·field (âr′fēld′) *n.* An area with hard-surfaced runways where aircraft can take off and land, but usually smaller than an airport and without its facilities for travelers.
air·flow (âr′flō′) *n.* The air currents caused by the motion of an object such as an airplane or motor vehicle.
air·foil (âr′foil′) *n.* Also *chiefly British* **aer·o·foil** (âr′ə-foil′). An aircraft part or surface, such as a wing, propeller blade, or rudder, the shape and orientation of which control stability, direction, lift, thrust, or propulsion.
air force *n. Abbr.* **AF, A.F. 1.** The aviation branch of a country's armed forces. **2.** A unit of the U.S. Air Force larger than an air division and smaller than an air command.
air·frame (âr′frām′) *n.* An aircraft body excluding its engine.
air freight *n.* **1.** A system of transporting freight by air. **2.** The amount charged for this service. —**air-freight** *v.*
air gas *n.* A manufactured fuel gas, **producer gas** *(see).*
air·glow (âr′glō′) *n.* A faint photochemical light in the upper atmosphere, observable in regions of low and middle latitude. Compare **aurora.**
air gun *n.* A gun discharged by compressed air.
air·head (âr′hĕd′) *n.* An area of hostile or enemy-controlled territory secured by paratroops.
air hole *n.* **1.** A hole or opening through which gas or air may pass. **2.** An opening in the frozen surface of a body of water. **3.** *Aviation.* An **air pocket** *(see).*
air hostess *n.* A stewardess on an aircraft.
air·i·ly (âr′ə-lē) *adv.* **1.** In a light spirit; gaily; jauntily. **2.** In a light manner; delicately; gently.
air·i·ness (âr′ē-nĭs) *n.* **1.** The quality or state of being light or airy. **2.** Delicacy. **3.** Gaiety; jauntiness.
air·ing (âr′ĭng) *n.* **1.** Exposure to fresh or warm air for ventilation or drying. **2.** Public disclosure or discussion: *giving the whole subject an airing.*
air lane *n.* A regular route of travel for aircraft; an airway.
air layering *n.* A method of plant propagation in which a twig or shoot attached to the parent plant is wrapped in moist sphagnum moss or polyethylene plastic so that it will form roots and can later be removed and replanted.
air·less (âr′lĭs) *adj.* **1.** Without air. **2.** Lacking fresh air; stuffy. **3.** Without a breeze or wind; still. —**air·less·ness** *n.*
air letter *n.* **1.** An airmail letter. **2.** An aerogram *(see).*
air·lift (âr′lĭft′) *n.* An operation by which passengers, troops, or supplies are transported by air when surface routes are blocked.
~*tr.v.* **airlifted, -lifting, -lifts.** To transport by air, as when ground routes are blocked.
air·line (âr′līn′) *n.* **1.** A system for the scheduled transport of passengers and freight by air. **2.** A business organization providing such a system of air transport. **3.** An air route. **4.** The shortest distance between two geographical points; a direct line.
air·lin·er (âr′lī′nər) *n.* A large airplane designed for carrying passengers.
air lock *n.* **1.** An airtight chamber, usually located between two regions of unequal pressure, in which air pressure can be regulated so as to allow access or communication between the regions while maintaining their pressure difference. **2.** A bubble or pocket of air or vapor, as in a pipe, that stops the normal flow of fluid through the conducting part.
air mail, air·mail (âr′māl′) *n.* **1.** The system of conveying mail by aircraft. **2.** Mail conveyed by aircraft. —**air·mail** *adj.*
air·mail (âr′māl′) *tr.v.* **-mailed, -mailing, -mails.** To send (a letter, for example) by air mail.
air·man (âr′mən) *n., pl.* **-men** (-mĭn). A pilot, navigator, or member of any technical profession dealing primarily with aircraft, especially one serving in an air force.
air mass *n. Meteorology.* A large body of air with only small horizontal variations of temperature, pressure, and moisture content.
air mile *n.* A unit of distance in air navigation. See **nautical mile.**
air piracy *n.* The hijacking of an airplane in flight. —**air pirate** *n.*
air·plane (âr′plān′) *n.* Also *chiefly British* **ae·ro·plane** (âr′ə-plān′). A winged flying vehicle that is heavier than air and is powered by jet engines or propellers. [French *aéroplane,* from Late Greek *aeroplanos,* wandering in the air : AERO- + -*planos,* wandering, from *planasthai,* to wander.]
air plant *n. Botany.* An **epiphyte** *(see).*
air pocket *n.* A downward air current that causes an aircraft to lose altitude abruptly. Also called "air hole."
air·port (âr′pôrt′, -pōrt′) *n.* A tract of leveled land where aircraft can take off and land, especially one equipped with hard-surfaced land-

ing strips, a control tower, hangars, facilities for passengers and cargo, and usually a customhouse.

air pump *n.* A piece of equipment for compressing, removing, or forcing a flow of air.

air raid *n.* An attack by hostile military aircraft, especially when armed with bombs. —**air-raid** (âr′rād′) *adj.*

air rifle *n.* A low-powered rifle using manually compressed air to fire small pellets.

air sac *n. Biology.* An air-filled space, such as one of the spaces in a bird's body that forms a connection between the lungs and the bone cavities, or a dilation in the trachea of many insects.

air scoop *n.* An air inlet on an aircraft, designed to take in air for ventilation or pressure.

air·screw (âr′skrōō′) *n. British.* The propeller of an airplane.

air-sea rescue (âr′sē′) *n.* A rescue at sea, carried out by aircraft.

air·ship (âr′shĭp′) *n.* A self-propelled lighter-than-air craft with directional control surfaces; a dirigible.

air·sick·ness (âr′sĭk′nĭs) *n.* Nausea resulting from nervous tension or changes in pressure or motion in an aircraft. —**air·sick** *adj.*

air sock *n.* A **windsock** (see).

air·space (âr′spās′) *n.* The portion of the atmosphere above a particular land area; especially, the air above a nation or other political subdivision, considered to be under its jurisdiction.

air speed *n.* Speed, especially of an aircraft, relative to the air.

air spray *n.* **1.** A device for spraying liquids using compressed air; an aerosol. **2.** The liquid sprayed by such a device.

air spring *n.* An enclosed volume of air which, by its resilience, acts as a spring or shock absorber. Also called "air cushion."

air·stream (âr′strēm′) *n.* **1.** The current of air passing over a surface. **2.** A wind, especially at high altitude.

air·strip (âr′strĭp′) *n.* A cleared area serving as an airfield; a landing strip.

airt (ârt) *n. Scottish.* Any of the points on the compass; a direction, especially of the wind. [Middle English *art*, from Scottish Gaelic *aird*, probably from Old Irish *aird†*.]

air terminal *n.* See **terminal** (sense 4b).

air·tight (âr′tīt′) *adj.* **1.** Impermeable to air or other gas. **2.** Having no weak points; sound: *an airtight excuse.*

air time *n.* **1.** The period of time during which a radio or television station broadcasts. **2.** An amount of broadcasting time allocated or available for a particular purpose.

air-to-air missile (âr′tə-âr′) *n.* A missile, usually guided, designed to be fired from aircraft at aircraft.

air-to-surface missile (âr′tə-sûr′fĭs) *n.* A missile, usually guided, designed to be fired from aircraft at targets on the ground. Also called "air-to-ground missile."

air-traf·fic control (âr′trăf′ĭk) *n. Abbr.* **A.T.C.** **1.** A system of directing aircraft movements in which the required speed, direction, and altitude of each aircraft in a given area is communicated by radio to its pilot. **2.** The people operating this system. —**air-traf·fic control·ler** *n.*

air·waves (âr′wāvz′) *pl.n.* The medium used for the transmission of radio and television signals: *a new program coming to you over the airwaves.*

air·way (âr′wā′) *n.* **1.** A passageway for a current of air, as to the lungs or to a mine. **2.** A designated route of passage for an aircraft; an air lane.

air·wom·an (âr′wŏom′ən) *n., pl.* **-women** (-wĭm′ĭn) A female airman.

air·wor·thy (âr′wûr′thē) *adj.* Prepared and in fit condition to fly. Said of aircraft. —**air·wor·thi·ness** *n.*

air·y (âr′ē) *adj.* **-ier, -iest. 1.** Having the constitution or nature of air. **2.** High in the air; lofty; towering. **3. a.** Open to the air; breezy; full of fresh air. **b.** Spacious; uncluttered. **4.** Resembling air; immaterial: *an airy apparition.* **5.** Insubstantial; irrational; unrealistic: *airy political views.* **6.** Light as air; graceful or delicate: *an airy veil.* **7.** Nonchalant or breezy in manner.

air·y-fair·y (âr′ē-fâr′ē) *adj.* **1.** Extremely light and delicate; insubstantial. **2.** *Informal.* Unrealistic; fanciful: *airy-fairy notions.*

Aisha. See **Ayesha.**

aisle (īl) *n.* **1.** A part of a church divided laterally from the nave by a row of pillars or columns. **2.** A passageway between rows of seats, such as in a church or auditorium. —**rolling in the aisles.** *Informal.* Overwhelmed by laughter. [Middle English *eile* (influenced by *ile, isle,* ISLE), from Old French *ele, aile,* wing of a building, from Latin *āla,* wing.]

ait. Variant of **eyot.**

aitch (āch) *n.* The letter *h.* [Obsolete *ache,* from French *hache,* probably from Vulgar Latin *haccat†* (unattested), of obscure origin.]

aitch·bone (āch′bōn′) *n.* **1.** The rump bone in cattle. **2.** The cut of meat containing this bone. [Middle English *hachbone,* from phrase *an hach boon,* originally *a nachebon : nache, nage,* buttock, from Old French *nache,* from Late Latin *natica,* from Latin *natis,* buttock + *bon,* BONE.]

Aix-en-Pro·vence (ĕks′äN-prô-väNs′). City and spa in Bouches-du-Rhône department, southeast France. It has been the capital of Provence since the 12th century and is an important cultural center.

Aix-la-Chapelle. See **Aachen.**

a·jar¹ (ə-jär′) *adv.* Partially opened. Said of doors and windows: *Please leave the door ajar.* [Middle English *on char,* "in the act of turning" : ON + *char,* a turn, Old English *cierr* (see **char**).] —**a·jar** *adj.*

ajar² *adv.* Not harmonious; jarring: *ajar with the times.* [A- (on, in

Ajax *During the sack of Troy, according to Greek legend, the Greek hero Ajax, son of Ileus of Lochis, raped the priestess Cassandra on the altar of the goddess Athena. On this vase, dating from about 450 B.C., the naked priestess clasps the goddess's statue for protection as Ajax grabs her hair.*

the act of) + JAR (discord).] —**a·jar** *adj.*

A·jax¹ (ā′jăks). *Greek Mythology.* A Greek warrior of great stature and prowess who fought against Troy; son of Telamon of Salamis.

Ajax². *Greek Mythology.* A Greek warrior of small stature and arrogant character who fought against Troy; son of Ileus of Locris.

AK Alaska (used with a Zip Code).

AK 47 *n.* A type of rifle, a **Kalashnikov** *(see).*

a.k.a. also known as.

Ak·bar (ăk′bär′), known as "the Great" (1542–1605). The greatest of India's Mogul emperors, who reigned from 1556. His conquests added most of northern India to the Mogul Empire.

ak·ee, ack·ee (ăk′ē, ä-kē′) *n.* **1.** A tropical tree, *Blighia sapida,* native to Africa and cultivated in the West Indies, having fragrant flowers and capsules containing black seeds. **2.** The edible aril surrounding these seeds, used in tropical cooking. [Native name in Liberia.]

Akhaïa. See **Achaea.**

A·khe·na·ton (ä′kə-nä′tən) (died *c.* 1360 B.C.). Also **Ikh·na·ton** (ĭk-), **A·men·ho·tep IV** (ä′mən-hō′tĕp). King of Egypt, who reigned from *c.* 1379–*c.* 1360 B.C. Originally named Amenhotep IV, he changed his name on rejecting the old gods and initiating the worship of the sun god Aten (Aton). He built a new capital at Tell-el-Amarna.

Akh·ma·to·va (äKH-mät′ə-və, äKH′-, -mä′tə-), **Anna,** pen name of Anna Andreevna Gorenko (1889–1966). Russian poet. Her intense and lyrical poems, often dealing with tragic love, have established her as one of the foremost 20th-century Russian poets.

a·kim·bo (ə-kĭm′bō) *adj.* With the hands on the hips and the elbows bowed outward. Used chiefly in the phrase *with arms akimbo.* [Middle English *in kenebowe,* "in keen bow," "in a sharp curve," probably from Old Norse *i keng boginn* (unattested), "bent like a bow" : *keng,* accusative of *kengr†,* a curve, hook + *boginn,* accusative of *bogi,* a bow.] —**a·kim·bo** *adv.*

a·kin (ə-kĭn′) *adj.* **1.** Of the same kin; related. **2.** Having a similar quality or character; analogous. Often used with *to.* **3.** *Linguistics.* Related in origin; cognate. Said of languages or of words in different languages derived from the same source. [A- (of) + KIN.]

Akka. See **Acre.**

Ak·kad or **Ac·cad** (ăk′ăd′, ä′käd′). Ancient region of central Mesopotamia, now in Iraq. The Akkadian empire flourished from *c.* 2340 B.C. to *c.* 2240 B.C., especially under Sargon, who ruled from his capital at Agade (or Akkad).

Ak·ka·di·an, Ac·ca·di·an (ə-kā′dē-ən) *n.* **1.** A native or inhabitant of Akkad. **2.** The Semitic language spoken in ancient Akkad. ~*adj.* Of, pertaining to, or relating to the Akkadians or their Semitic language.

Akko. See **Acre.**

Ak·ron (ăk′rən). City in northeastern Ohio. It became known as the rubber capital of the world in the early 20th century.

Ak·sum or **Ax·um** (ăk′sŏŏm). Town in northern Ethiopia that was the center of the northern Ethiopian empire from the 1st to the 8th centuries A.D. Its kings were converted to Christianity in the 4th century. According to tradition, the Ark of the Covenant was brought here from Jerusalem and placed in the Church of St. Mary of Zion, where the emperors of Ethiopia were crowned.

–al¹ *suffix.* Indicates a relation to or connection with; for example, **adjectival.** [Middle English *-al, -el,* from Old French, from Latin *-ālis.*]

–al² *suffix.* Indicates the act or process of doing or experiencing the action specified; for example, **denial, arrival.** [Middle English *-aille,* from Old French, from Latin *-ālia,* substantive neuter plural of *-ālis,* adjectival suffix.]

–al³ *suffix. Chemistry.* Indicates an aldehyde, an organic compound; for example, **ethanal, butanal.** [*Al*dehyde.]

Al The symbol for the element aluminum.

AL 1. Alabama (used with a Zip Code). **2.** American League. **3.** American Legion.

al. alcohol; alcoholic.

à la (ä′lä, ä′lə, ăl′ə) *prep.* Also **a la.** In the style or manner of; in accordance with: *mushrooms à la grecque; a poem à la Ogden Nash.* [French, short for *à la mode de,* "in the manner of."]

a·la (ā′lə) *n., pl.* **alae** (ā′lē). *Biology.* A winglike structure or part, such as the flattened part of certain bones, the membranous border of some seeds, or one of the side petals of certain flowers, such as the sweet pea. [Latin *āla,* wing]

Ala. Alabama.

a.l.a. all letters answered.

Al·a·bam·a (ăl′ə-băm′ə). State in the southeastern United States. It was admitted as the 22nd state in 1819. Montgomery is the capital and Birmingham the largest city. Alabama is still a major cotton-growing state, but since World War II mining and manufacturing have accounted for the largest share of the state's income. Products include coal, oil, steel, chemicals, and textiles. —**Al·a·ba·mi·an** (ăl′ə-bā′mē-ən), **Al·a·bam·an** *adj. & n.*

al·a·bas·ter (ăl′ə-băs′tər, -bäs′tər) *n.* **1.** A dense, translucent, white or tinted, fine-grained gypsum, often used in sculpture. **2.** A variety of hard calcite, translucent and sometimes banded. **3.** Pale yellowish pink to yellowish gray. ~*adj.* Also **al·a·bas·trine** (ăl′ə-băs′trĭn, -băs′trīn). Of or similar to alabaster; smooth and white. [Middle English *alabastre,* from Old French, from Latin *alabaster,* from Greek *alabast(r)os,* perhaps of Egyptian origin.]

à la carte (ä′lä kärt′, ăl′ə) *adj.* Having a separate price for each item. Said of a menu or part of a menu. Compare **prix fixe, table d'hôte.**

[French, "by the menu."] —**à la carte** *adv*.

a·lack (ə-lăk') *interj*. Also **a·lack·a·day** (ə-lăk'ə-dā'). *Archaic*. Used to express sorrow, regret, or alarm. [Middle English *alacke*, "ah, (what) loss!" : probably *a, ah*, AH + LACK, by analogy with *alas*.]

a·lac·ri·ty (ə-lăk'rə-tē) *n*. **1**. Cheerful willingness; eagerness. **2**. Lively action; sprightliness. [Latin *alacritās*, from *alacer* (stem *alacr-*), lively, eager.] —**a·lac·ri·tous** *adj*.

A·lad·din (ə-lăd'n). In the *Arabian Nights*, a boy who acquires a magic lamp and a magic ring with which he can summon two genies to fulfill any desire.

A·lain-Four·nier (ä'lăɴ-fōōr-nyä'), pen name of Henri Alban Fournier (1886–1914). French novelist. He is principally remembered for his novel *Le Grand Meaulnes* (1913), translated into English as *The Lost Domain*. He was killed in battle in World War I.

à la king (ä' lä kĭng', äl'ə) *adj*. Prepared in a cream sauce with green pepper and mushrooms: *chicken à la king*.

Alamannian, Alamannic. Variants of **Alemannic**.

Alamein. See El Alamein.

Al·a·mo (ăl'ə-mō'). A chapel built in 1744 as part of the Mission of San Antonio de Valero at San Antonio, Texas. During the Texas Revolution against Mexican rule some 182 revolutionaries were besieged here from February 24 to March 6, 1836, by Gen. Santa Anna and an army of thousands. All the insurgents, including Davy Crockett, William B. Travis, and Jim Bowie, were killed.

à la mode (ä' lä mōd', äl'ə) *adj*. **1**. According to or in style or fashion; fashionable. **2. a**. Served with ice cream. **b**. Braised with vegetables and served in a rich, brown sauce. [French, "in the fashion."]

a·la·mode (ä'lə-mōd', äl'ə-mōd') *n*. A lustrous plain-weave silk fabric, used especially for head coverings and scarfs. [From À LA MODE.]

Al·a·mo·gor·do (ăl'ə-mə-gôr'dō). A town in southern New Mexico. The first atomic bomb was exploded at the White Sands Missile Range, 97 kilometers (60 miles) northwest of the city, in a test on July 16, 1945.

Al·an·brooke (ăl'ən-brŏŏk'), **Alan Francis Brooke, 1st Viscount** (1883–1963). British field marshal. During World War II he was commander in chief of the home forces from 1940 to 1941 and chief of the Imperial General Staff from 1941 to 1946.

Åland Islands. See Ahvenanmaa.

al·a·nine (ăl'ə-nēn') *n*. An amino acid, $CH_3CH(NH_2)COOH$, a constituent of most proteins. [German *Alanin* : AL(DEHYDE) + *-an* (euphonic infix) + -IN(E).]

a·lar (ā'lər) *adj*. **1**. Of, pertaining to, or having wings or alae. **2**. Shaped like or resembling a wing. **3**. *Anatomy*. Pertaining to the armpit; axillary. [Latin *alāris*, from *āla*, wing.]

Al·a·ric (ăl'ə-rĭk) (c. A.D. 370–410). King of the Visigoths. In 395 he invaded and plundered Greece, and from 400 onward he attacked Italy, capturing Rome in 410.

a·larm (ə-lärm') *n*. **1**. A sudden fear caused by an awareness of danger; fright. **2**. A warning of approaching or existing danger. **3**. An electrical or mechanical device that serves to warn of danger, fire, or the like by means of a sound or signal. **4. a**. The sounding mechanism of an alarm clock. **b**. An alarm clock. **5**. *Archaic*. A call to arms. **6**. *Fencing*. A stamp on the ground with the advancing foot. —See Synonyms at **fear**.
~*tr.v*. **alarmed, alarming, alarms**. **1**. To fill with alarm or apprehension. **2**. To warn of approaching or existing danger. —See Synonyms at **frighten**. [Middle English *alarme*, from Old French, from Old Italian *allarme*, from *all'arme*, "to arms!" : *alla*, to, from Latin *ad illam*, to that, from *ille*, that + *arme*, arms, from Latin *arma*.] —**a·larm·a·ble** *adj*. —**a·larm·ing·ly** *adv*.

alarm bird *n*. Any of various Australian birds, such as the kookaburra, having a characteristic loud cry.

alarm clock *n*. A clock that can be set to sound a bell or buzzer at any desired hour, especially to wake a person up. Also called "alarm."

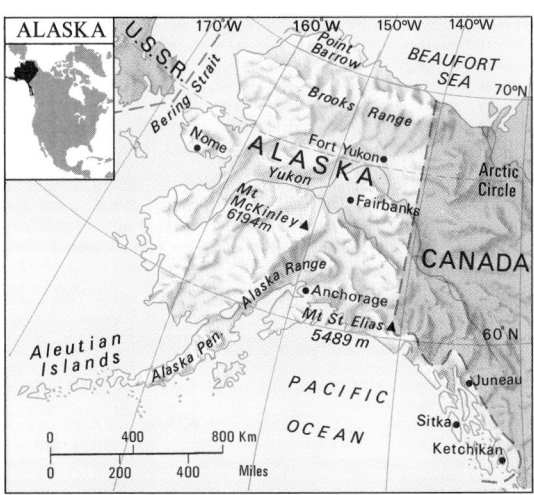

a·larm·ist (ə-lär'mĭst) *n*. A person who needlessly alarms or attempts to alarm himself or others, as by inventing or spreading frightening rumors and prophesying political or social calamities. —**a·larm·ism** *n*. —**a·larm·ist** *adj*.

a·lar·um (ə-lär'əm, ə-lăr'-) *n*. *Archaic*. **1**. An alarm, especially a call to arms. **2**. A clamorous confusion onstage, especially in Elizabethan drama. Used chiefly in the phrase *alarums and excursions*. [Middle English *alarom, alarme*, ALARM.]

a·lar·y (ā'lər-ē) *adj*. **1**. Of or pertaining to wings. **2**. Resembling a wing; wing-shaped. [Latin *alārius*, from *āla*, wing.]

a·las (ə-lăs', ə-läs') *interj*. An exclamation expressing regret, grief, compassion, or alarm. [Middle English, from Old French : *a*, AH + *las*, wretched, from Latin *lassus*, weary.]

Alas. Alaska.

a·las·ka (ə-lăs'kə) *n*. **1**. A kind of heavy-duty rubberized overshoe. **2. a**. A heavy dress and coat fabric of cotton and wool. **b**. A yarn made of cotton and wool. [After ALASKA.]

A·las·ka (ə-lăs'kə). Largest state in the United States, situated in the extreme northwest of North America, and separated from the rest of the country by Canada. It has a total area of 1,530,694 square kilometers (591,004 square miles) but fewer people than any other mainland territory, and was admitted as the 49th state in 1959. Alaska is mostly mountainous, and much of it is frozen all year. Gold was once mined extensively, but platinum and coal mining are now more important. Mining, oil, and natural gas are the most valuable industries. Fishing and timber are also important. Its capital is now Juneau but may be moved to Willow, near the largest city, Anchorage. —**A·las·kan** *adj. & n*.

Alaskan malamute *n*. A dog, the **malamute** (see).

a·las·tor (ə-lăs'tôr) *n*. Often **Alastor**. An avenging deity or spirit, frequently evoked in Greek tragedy; a masculine personification of Nemesis. [Greek *alastōr*, "unforgetting one," from *alastos*, unforgettable : *a-*, not + *lathein, lanthanesthai* (stem *las-*), to forget.]

a·late (ā'lāt') *adj*. Also **a·lat·ed** (ā'lā'tĭd). *Biology*. Having thin, winglike extensions or parts; winged. [Latin *ālātus*, from *āla*, wing.]

Al-'Ayzariyah. See Bethany.

alb (ălb) *n*. A long white linen robe with tapered sleeves worn by a priest, especially during Mass. [Middle English *albe, aube*, Old English *albe*, from Medieval Latin *(vestis) alba*, "white (garment)," from Latin *albus*, white.]

Alb. Albania; Albanian.

Al·ba·ce·te (äl'bä-sā'tĕ). Province of southeast-central Spain. The provincial capital, Albacete, was the site of battles between Moors and Christians in 1145 and 1146.

al·ba·core (ăl'bə-kôr', -kōr') *n., pl*. **-cores** or collectively **albacore**. A large marine fish, *Thunnus alalunga*, of warm seas, having edible flesh that is a major source for canned tuna. [Portuguese *albacor*, from Arabic *al-bakrah* : *al*, the + *bakr*, young camel.]

Al·ban (ôl'bən), **Saint** (died c. A.D. 304). First Christian martyr in Britain. A soldier in the Roman army in Britain, he was executed for having given shelter to a Christian priest, who converted him to Christianity. In 793 an abbey was founded on the site of his martyrdom, and the town of St. Albans grew around it.

Al·ba·ni·a (ăl-bā'nē-ə, -băn'yə, ôl-). *Abbr*. **Alb**. *Albanian* **Shqip·e·ri** (shkyĭp-ə-rē'). Country lying on the Adriatic Sea. Most of the country is either mountainous or swampy. It is fast developing its rich mineral resources, hydroelectric potential, and manufacturing, but farming remains the major occupation. After more than four centuries of Turkish rule, Albania proclaimed its independence in 1912, and that independence was guaranteed by the Allied powers after World War I. The country became a republic in 1925. In 1944 the Communist Party gained control, and Albania became a satellite of the U.S.S.R. It declared itself the first atheist state, abolishing all public worship in 1967. In 1961 it broke with the Soviets and in 1968 withdrew from the Warsaw Pact after the Soviet intervention in Czechoslovakia. After 1961 it was closely tied, diplomatically and commercially, with China, but relations between the two countries deteriorated after the death of Mao Ze-dong in 1976.

alabaster Tree of Jesse, *a medieval carving in alabaster at the Victoria and Albert Museum, London. Alabaster is a type of gypsum—the mineral from which plaster of Paris is made.*

Area, 28,748 square kilometers (11,097 square miles). Population, 2,600,000. Capital, Tirana.

Al·ba·ni·an (ăl-bā′nē-ən, -bān′yən, ôl-) *adj. Abbr.* **Alb.** Of or pertaining to Albania, its inhabitants, or its language.
~*n.* **1.** A native or inhabitant of Albania. **2.** The Indo-European language of Albania.

Al·ba·ny (ôl′bə-nē). Capital city, since 1797, of the state of New York, on the west bank of the Hudson River at the head of deep-water navigation. A major urban-renewal project in the downtown area was initiated in the 1960's.

al·ba·ta (ăl-bā′tə) *n.* A metallic alloy, **nickel silver** *(see).* [Latin *albata,* "clothed in white," from *albus,* white.]

al·ba·tross (ăl′bə-trôs′, -trŏs′) *n., pl.* **-trosses** or collectively **albatross.** **1.** Any of various large, web-footed birds of the family Diomedeidae, chiefly of the oceans of the Southern Hemisphere, having a hooked beak and long, narrow wings. The wandering albatross, *Diomedea irrorata,* has the largest wingspan of any bird. **2.** An obvious handicap, constant burden, or heavy cross to bear. [Alteration (influenced by Latin *albus,* white) of Portuguese *alcatraz,* pelican, from Arabic *al-ghaṭṭās* : *al,* the + *ghaṭṭās,* white-tailed sea eagle. Sense 2 is a reference to S.T. Coleridge's Ancient Mariner, who sinned by killing an albatross and who had to wear it around his neck in penance.]

Al Bayda. See **Zawiyat al Bayda.**

al·be·do (ăl-bē′dō) *n., pl.* **-dos.** The fraction of incident electromagnetic radiation reflected by a surface. [Late Latin *albēdō,* whiteness, from Latin *albus,* white.]

Al·bee (ăl′bē), **Edward (Franklin)** (1928–). U.S. playwright. His most successful play has been *Who's Afraid of Virginia Woolf?* (1962), a savage and comic play about a power struggle between an academic couple. He won Pulitzer Prizes for two later plays, *A Delicate Balance* (1967) and *Seascape* (1975).

al·be·it (ôl-bē′ĭt, ăl-) *conj.* Although; even though; notwithstanding. [Middle English *al be it,* "let it be entirely (that)" : *al,* ALL + *be,* subjunctive of *been,* to BE + IT.]

Al·bé·niz (ăl-bā′nēth, -nēs), **Isaac Manuel Francisco** (1860–1909). Spanish composer and concert pianist. He used traditional folk songs and is known for his piano music, especially *Iberia.*

Al·bert I (ăl′bərt) (1875–1934). King of the Belgians (1909–34). During World War I he was commander in chief of the Belgian army and led the Belgian and French forces that reconquered Belgium in 1918.

Albert, Lake. See **Mobutu (Sese Seko) Lake.**

Albert, Prince (1819–1861). Prince Consort and husband of Queen Victoria. He was a strong influence on the queen and an active patron of the arts, sciences, and industry.

Al·ber·ta (ăl-bûr′tə). Province in western Canada. The capital and largest city is Edmonton. Wheat and cattle farming were the basis of the province's economy until the discovery of petroleum and natural gas in the early 1960's.

Al·ber·ti (ăl-bâr′tē), **Leon Battista** (1404–72). Italian Renaissance architect. Among the buildings that he designed are the churches of Santa Maria Novella in Florence (built 1446–51) and Sant' Andrea in Mantua (1472–94). Alberti was also an accomplished painter, musician, and writer.

Al·ber·tus Mag·nus (ăl-bûr′təs măg′nəs), **Saint,** born Albert, Count von Bollstadt (*c.* 1206–80). German theologian, scholastic philosopher, and scientist. He taught at various German schools, then at Paris (1245) and Cologne (1248–54), where Thomas Aquinas was one of his students. His reputation as an alchemist stemmed from his extensive knowledge of chemistry and physical sciences. He was beatified in 1622 and canonized in 1932.

al·bes·cent (ăl-bĕs′ənt) *adj.* Becoming white or moderately white; whitish. [Latin *albēscēns* (stem *albescent-*), from *albescere,* to become white, from *albus,* white.]

Al·bi (ăl-bē′). Capital of Tarn department in the Languedoc region of southern France, on the Tarn River. It was the center of the heresy of the Albigenses in the 12th and 13th centuries.

Al·bi·gen·ses (ăl′bə-jĕn′sēz′) *pl.n.* The members of a Catharist religious sect that flourished in southern France in the 12th and 13th centuries, and was eradicated by the Inquisition under Pope Innocent III, following the Albigensian Crusade. See **Catharism.** [Medieval Latin, inhabitants of *Albiga,* ALBI (where the sect was dominant).] —**Al·bi·gen·si·an** (ăl′bə-jĕn′sē-ən, -jĕn′shən) *adj.* —**Al·bi·gen·si·an·ism** *n.*

al·bin·ism (ăl′bə-nĭz′əm) *n.* **1.** Absence of normal pigmentation in a person, animal, or plant. **2.** The condition of being an albino. [French *albinisme,* from German *Albinismus,* from ALBINO.] —**al·bin·ic** (ăl-bĭn′ĭk), **al·bin·is·tic** (ăl′bə-nĭs′tĭk) *adj.*

al·bi·no (ăl-bī′nō) *n., pl.* **-nos.** An organism lacking normal pigmentation; especially, a person having abnormally pale skin, very light hair, and lacking normal eye coloring, or an animal, such as a rabbit, having white hair or fur and red eyes. [Portuguese, from *albo,* white, from Latin *albus* (originally applied to black Africans having albinism).]

Al·bi·no·ni (ăl′bə-nō′nē), **Tomaso** (1671–1750). Italian violinist and composer, court musician to the Duke of Mantua. He wrote about 50 operas and was the first composer to write concertos for solo violin.

Al·bi·on (ăl′bē-ən) *Archaic & Literary.* England or Great Britain. [Latin *Albiōn,* from Celtic *alb-* (unattested), high. See also **Alps.**]

al·bite (ăl′bīt′) *n.* A widely distributed white feldspar, NaAlSi₃O₈, one of the common rock-forming plagioclase group. [Swedish *albit,*

alder *The alder tree likes damp soil and, like clover, can fix nitrogen from the air.*

from Latin *albus,* white.] —**al·bit·ic** (ăl-bĭt′ĭk), **al·bit·i·cal** *adj.*

Ål·borg, Aal·borg (ôl′bôrg′). City and port in northern Jutland, Denmark, on the Lim Fjord.

al·bum (ăl′bəm) *n.* **1.** A book or binder with blank pages for the insertion and preservation of stamps, photographs, keepsakes, autographs, or the like. **2. a.** A long-playing phonograph record, usually of popular music. **b.** A set of phonograph records stored together in sleeves in one booklike holder. **3.** A printed collection of miscellaneous musical compositions. **4.** A tall, handsomely printed book, especially popular in the 19th century, often having a profusion of illustrations and short, sentimental texts. [Latin, blank tablet, neuter of *albus,* white.]

al·bu·men (ăl-byōō′mĭn) *n.* **1.** The white of an egg, consisting of a mixture of proteins (albumins). **2.** The material stored in a plant seed; the endosperm. **3.** Variant of **albumin.** [Latin *albūmen,* from *albus,* white.]

al·bu·min, al·bu·men (ăl-byōō′mən) *n.* Any of several simple, water-soluble proteins that are coagulated by heat and are found in egg white, blood serum, milk, various animal tissues, and many plant juices and tissues. [ALBUM(EN) + -IN.]

al·bu·mi·noid (ăl-byōō′mə-noid′) *adj.* Also **al·bu·mi·noi·dal** (-byōō′mə-noi′dəl). Resembling albumin.
~*n. Biochemistry.* **Scleroprotein** *(see).*

al·bu·mi·nous (ăl-byōō′mə-nəs) *adj.* Of, like, or containing albumin.

al·bu·mi·nu·ri·a (ăl-byōō′mə-nŏor′ē-ə, -nyŏor′ē-ə) *n.* The presence of albumin and other serum proteins in the urine, sometimes indicative of kidney disease. Also called "proteinuria." [ALBUMIN + -URIA.] —**al·bu·mi·nu·ric** (ăl-byōō′mə-nŏor′ĭk, -nyŏor′ĭk) *adj.*

al·bu·mose (ăl′byə-mōs′, -mōz′) *n.* Any of a class of albuminous substances formed by enzymatic action on proteins during digestion. [French : *album(ine),* ALBUM(IN) + -OSE.]

Al·bu·quer·que (ăl′bə-kûr′kē). A town in the United States, on the upper Rio Grande. It is the largest city in New Mexico.

al·bur·num (ăl-bûr′nəm) *n. Botany.* **Sapwood** *(see).* [Latin, from *albus,* white.]

alc. alcohol; alcoholic.

Al·ca·ic (ăl-kā′ĭk) *adj.* Of or designating a verse form used in Greek and Latin poetry, consisting of strophes having four lines each containing four feet.
~*n. Often* **Alcaics.** Verse composed in Alcaic strophes. [Late Latin *Alcaicus,* from Greek *Alkaïkos,* "of Alcaeus" (*fl.* 600 B.C.), Greek lyric poet.]

al·cai·de, al·cay·de (ăl-kī′dē) *n.* In former times, the commander or governor of a fortress in Spain, Portugal, or Latin America. [Spanish, from Arabic *al-qā'id,* the commander, from *qād,* to command.]

al·cal·de (ăl-käl′dē) *n.* The mayor or chief judicial official of a Spanish or Latin-American town. [Spanish, from Arabic *al-qāḍī* : *al,* the + *qāḍī,* judge, from *qaḍā,* to judge.]

Al·ca·traz (ăl′kə-trăz′). A rocky island in San Francisco Bay, California. The island served as a federal prison until 1963.

al·ca·zar (ăl-kăz′ər, ăl′kə-zär′) *n.* A Spanish palace or fortress, originally one built by the Moors. [Spanish *alcázar,* from Arabic *al-qaṣr* : *al,* the + *qaṣr,* castle, from Latin *castra,* fort, plural of *castrum,* camp.]

Al·cá·zar de San Juan (ăl′kə-zär′ də săn wän′). Town of Roman origin in the Ciudad Real province of central Spain. It was the center of the order of San Juan from the 14th to the 16th century.

Al·ces·tis (ăl-sĕs′tĭs). *Greek Mythology.* The wife of King Admetus of Thessaly. She agreed to die in place of her husband and was later rescued from Hades by Hercules.

al·che·mist (ăl′kə-mĭst) *n.* A practitioner of alchemy. —**al·che·mis·tic, al·che·mis·ti·cal** (ăl′kə-mĭs′tĭ-kəl) *adj.*

al·che·mize (ăl′kə-mīz′) *tr.v.* **-mized, -mizing, -mizes.** To transform by or as if by alchemy; transmute.

al·che·my (ăl′kə-mē) *n.* **1.** In medieval Europe, a philosophy and branch of science that sought to find a way of turning base metals into gold, a universal cure, and the elixir of life. **2.** Any seemingly magical power or process of transmuting. —See Synonyms at **magic.** [Middle English, from Old French *alquemie,* from Medieval Latin *alchymia,* from Arabic *al-kīmiyā',* "the art of transmutation" : *al,* the + *kīmiyā',* from Greek *khēm(e)ia,* "art of transmutation (of metals)."] —**al·chem·i·cal** (ăl-kĕm′ĭ-kəl), **al·chem·ic** *adj.* —**al·chem·i·cal·ly** *adv.*

al·che·rin·ga (ăl′chə-rĭng′gə) *n.* Also **al·che·ra** (ăl′chə-rə). In Australian Aboriginal mythology, the **Dreamtime** *(see).* [Native Australian.]

Al·ci·bi·a·des (ăl′sĭ-bī′ə-dēz′) (*c.* 450–404 B.C.). Athenian general and politician. He was brought up by his uncle, Pericles, and became a protégé of Socrates. His brilliant political career foundered during the Peloponnesian War against Sparta (431–404 B.C.), when he commanded a disastrous military attack on Syracuse in 415.

Alc·me·ne (ălk-mē′nē). *Greek Mythology.* Amphitryon's wife, who gave birth to Hercules after being seduced by Zeus.

Al·cock (ôl′kŏk), **Sir John William** (1892–1919). British aviator. On June 14, 1919, together with Sir Arthur Whitten Brown, he made the first nonstop flight across the Atlantic Ocean. They flew from Newfoundland to Ireland in a Vickers-Vimy bomber, taking 16 hours 27 minutes.

al·co·hol (ăl′kə-hôl′) *n.* **1.** *Abbr.* **al., alc.** A colorless volatile flammable liquid, C₂H₅OH, synthesized or obtained by fermentation of sugars and starches, and widely used, either pure or denatured, as a solvent or in drugs, cleaning solutions, explosives, and intoxicating beverages. Also called "ethanol," "ethyl alcohol," "grain alcohol." **2.** Intoxicating drink containing alcohol. **3.** Any of a series of compounds that contain a hydroxyl group bound to a hydrocarbon group. Simple examples are methanol (CH_3OH) and butanol (C_4H_9OH). [New Latin *alcohol (vini),* spirit (of wine), from Medieval Latin *alcohol,* fine powder of antimony used to tint the eyelids, any powder obtained by sublimation, quintessence, from Arabic *al-koḥl, al-kuḥl :* *al,* the + *koḥl, kuḥl,* KOHL.]

al·co·hol·ic (ăl′kə-hôl′ĭk, -hŏl′ĭk) *adj. Abbr.* **al., alc.** **1.** Of, pertaining to, or resulting from alcohol. **2.** Containing or preserved in alcohol. **3.** Suffering from alcoholism.
—*n.* A person who drinks habitually and to excess, and is unable to stop doing so; a sufferer from alcoholism.

al·co·hol·ic·i·ty (ăl′kə-hôl-ĭs′ə-tē) *n.* Alcoholic content.

Alcoholics Anonymous *n. Abbr.* **A.A.** A fellowship of alcoholics who wish to stop drinking and stay sober.

al·co·hol·ism (ăl′kə-hôl-ĭz′əm) *n.* **1.** Habitual excessive consumption of alcohol. **2.** A chronic pathological condition resulting from this, chiefly affecting the nervous and gastroenteric systems and characterized by mental disturbance, muscular incoordination, and eventually cirrhosis of the liver.

al·co·hol·ize (ăl′kə-hôl-īz′) *tr.v.* **-ized, -izing, -izes.** To make alcoholic; saturate, mix, or treat with alcohol. —**al·co·hol·i·za·tion** *n.*

al·co·hol·om·e·ter (ăl′kə-hôl-ŏm′ə-tər) *n.* A hydrometer for determining the percentage of alcohol in liquids.

alcohol thermometer *n.* A simple glass thermometer containing alcohol colored with a red dye, used instead of a mercury thermometer for measuring lower temperatures.

Al·co·ran, Al·ko·ran (ăl′kô-răn′, -rän′) *n.* The sacred book of the Muslims, the **Koran** (*see*).

Al·cott (ôl′kət, -kŏt), **Louisa May** (1832–88). U.S. novelist. Her most famous work, *Little Women* (1868–69), was a largely autobiographical account of herself and her family.

al·cove (ăl′kōv′) *n.* **1. a.** A recessed or partly enclosed area connected to or forming part of a room. **b.** Any arched niche or recess, as in a wall. **2.** A secluded bower or similar enclosed structure in a garden. [French *alcôve,* from Spanish *alcoba,* from Arabic *al-qubbah,* "the vault."]

Al·cuin (ăl′kwĭn) (735–804). English scholar and theologian. In 781 he became an adviser to Charlemagne, whose court became the center of the revival of learning and the arts that came to be known as the Carolingian Renaissance.

Al·cy·o·ne (ăl-sī′ə-nē) *n.* **1.** *Astronomy.* The brightest star in the Pleiades, in the constellation Taurus. **2.** *Greek Mythology.* One of the **Pleiades** (*see*).

Ald. alderman.

Al·dab·ra (ăl-dăb′rə). Group of four coral islands in the Indian Ocean north of Madagascar, famous for its giant tortoises and other wildlife. Formerly British, it joined the Seychelles in 1976.

Al·deb·a·ran (ăl-dĕb′ə-rən) *n.* A double star in the constellation Taurus, one of the brightest stars in the sky, 68 light-years from Earth. [Middle English, from Medieval Latin *Aldebaran,* from Arabic *al-dabarān,* "the follower (of the Pleiades)" : *al,* the + *dabarān,* following, from *dabar,* to follow.]

al·de·hyde (ăl′də-hīd′) *n.* **1.** Any of a class of highly reactive organic chemical compounds obtained by oxidation of primary alcohols, characterized by the common group CHO (the **aldehyde group**), and used in the manufacture of resins, dyes, and organic acids. Examples are formaldehyde (HCHO) and butanal (C_3H_7CHO). **2.** Such a compound, **acetaldehyde** (*see*). [German *Aldehyd,* from New Latin, abbreviation of *al(cohol) dehyd(rogenatum),* "dehydrogenized alcohol."]

al den·te (äl dĕn′tē) *adj.* Cooked so as to be still slightly firm. Said of pasta. [Italian, "to the tooth."] —**al den·te** *adv.*

al·der (ôl′dər) *n.* **1.** Any of various deciduous shrubs or trees of the genus *Alnus,* growing in cool, moist places, and having toothed rounded leaves, woody cones, and reddish wood used in underwater construction and cabinet work. **2.** Any of several similar shrubs or trees. [Middle English *alder,* Old English *aler, alor;* akin to Old Norse *ölr,* Latin *alnus.*]

alder fly *n.* Any insect of the group Sialoidea, related to the lacewings, found near water and having large wings.

al·der·man (ôl′dər-mən) *n., pl.* **-men** (-mĭn). **1.** *Abbr.* **Ald., Aldm.** In many town and city governments, a member of the municipal legislative body. **2.** *Abbr.* **Ald., Aldm.** In England and Wales before 1974, a member of the higher branch of a municipal or borough council, elected by the councilors themselves. **3.** In Anglo-Saxon England: **a.** A high-ranking noble. **b.** The chief officer of a shire. [Middle English *alderman,* partly guild official, Old English *(e)aldormann,* viceroy : *(e)aldor,* chief, "elder," from *(e)ald,* old + MAN.] —**al·der·man·cy** *n.* —**al·der·man·ic** (ôl′dər-măn′ĭk) *adj.*

Al·der·ney¹ (ôl′dər-nē). Northernmost island of the larger Channel Islands. It was part of the domain of Normandy from the 11th century, but is today included in the bailiwick of Guernsey, although it is self-governing.

Alderney² *n., pl.* **-neys.** One of a breed of small dairy cattle originally bred in the Channel Islands.

Al·dine (ôl′dīn′, -dēn′) *adj.* Of, pertaining to, or published by the press of Aldus **Manutius** (*see*) and his family.

Aldm. alderman.

aldo– *prefix.* Indicates the presence of an aldehyde group; for example, **aldohexose, aldopentose.** [From ALDEHYDE.]

al·do·hex·ose (ăl′dō-hĕk′sōs, -sōz) *n.* An aldose sugar that has six carbon atoms in its molecules.

al·dol (ăl′dôl′, -dŏl′) *n.* **1.** A thick colorless to pale-yellow liquid, $CH_3CH(OH)CH_2CHO$, obtained from acetaldehyde and used to make perfumes and in ore flotation. **2.** Any of a class of organic chemical compounds that have a hydroxyl group and an aldehyde group in their molecules on adjacent carbon atoms.

al·do·pent·ose (ăl′dō-pĕn′tōs, -tōz) *n.* An aldose sugar that has five carbon atoms in its molecules.

al·dose (ăl′dōs′, -dōz′) *n. Chemistry.* Any of a class of monosaccharide sugars containing an aldehyde group. Compare **ketose.** Also called "aldose sugar."

al·dos·te·rone (ăl-dŏs′tə-rōn′) *n.* A steroid hormone, secreted by the adrenal cortex, that regulates salt and water balance by its action on the kidneys.

al·dox·ime (ăl-dŏk′sēm′) *n.* A chemical compound formed by reaction of an aldehyde with hydroxylamine and having the characteristic group ·CHNON or :CNOH in its molecules.

al·drin (ôl′drĭn) *n.* A brownish-white crystalline pesticide. [After Kurt *Alder* (1902–58), German chemist.]

Aldus Manutius. See **Manutius.**

ale (āl) *n.* A fermented alcoholic drink containing malt and formerly made without hops, similar to but often heavier than beer. [Middle English *ale,* Old English *alu, ealu.*]

a·le·a·to·ry (ā′lē-ə-tôr′ē, -tōr′ē) *adj.* **1.** Dependent upon chance or luck. **2.** Using or consisting of elements chosen at random or arrived at by chance. Said of musical or other artistic compositions. [Latin *āleātōrius,* from *āleātor,* gambler, from *ālea†,* dice.]

A·lec·to (ə-lĕk′tō). *Greek Mythology.* One of the **Furies** (*see*).

a·lee (ə-lē′) *adv. Nautical.* At, on, or to the leeward side. Compare **aweather.**

al·e·gar (ăl′ə-gər, ā′lə-). *n.* Vinegar produced by the fermentation of ale; malt vinegar. [Middle English : ALE + (VINE)GAR.]

ale·house (āl′hous′) *n.* **1.** In former times, a place where ale was sold and drunk. **2.** *British Informal.* A pub.

Aleichem, Sholem. See **Sholem Aleichem.**

Al·e·man·ni (ăl′ə-măn′ī) *pl.n.* A group of Germanic tribes that settled in Alsace and nearby areas during the 4th century A.D. [Latin, from Germanic *Alamanniz* (unattested); akin to Gothic *alamannam* (dative plural), mankind : probably ALL + MAN.]

Al·e·man·nic, Al·a·man·nic (ăl′ə-măn′ĭk) *n.* The High German dialect of the Alemanni, forms of which are now spoken in Alsace and parts of southern Germany and Switzerland.
—*adj.* Also **Al·e·man·ni·an, Al·a·man·ni·an** (ăl′ə-măn′ē-ən). Of or pertaining to the Alemanni or their language.

a·lem·bic (ə-lĕm′bĭk) *n.* **1.** An apparatus formerly used for distilling. **2.** Something that purifies or transforms by a process comparable to distillation. [Middle English, from Old French *alambic,* from Medieval Latin *alambicus,* from Arabic *al-anbīg :* *al,* the + *anbīg,* still, from Greek *ambix†* (stem *ambik–*), cup.]

Al·en·con (ăl-äN-sôN′). Capital of Orne department, in Normandy, northwestern France. It is famous for "point d'Alençon" lace.

a·leph, a·lef (ä′lĭf) *n.* The first letter of the Hebrew alphabet. See feature at **alphabet.** [Hebrew *āleph,* "ox"; akin to ALPHA.]

a·leph-null (ä′lĭf-nŭl′) *n. Mathematics.* The first **transfinite number** (*see*). Also called "aleph-zero." [ALEPH (symbol for transfinite number) + NULL (smallest possible entity).]

A·lep·po (ə-lĕp′ō). Arabic **Ha·leb** (hä-lĕb′). City in northwest Syria, which was probably first settled as long ago as 6000 B.C. It was once a major station on the caravan route across Syria to Baghdad, and was a center of Christianity in the Middle East.

a·lert (ə-lûrt′) *adj.* **1.** Vigilantly attentive; watchful: *alert to danger.* **2.** Mentally responsive and perceptive; quick. **3.** Brisk; lively.
—*n.* **1.** A warning signal of attack or danger; especially, a siren warning of an air raid. **2.** The period of time during which such a warning is in effect. —**on the alert.** Watchful and prepared for danger or emergency.
—*tr.v.* **alerted, alerting, alerts.** To notify or cause to be aware of approaching or potential danger; warn: *a campaign alerting people to the dangers of smoking.* [French *alerte,* from Italian *all'erta,* "on the watch" : *alla,* at the, from Latin *ad illam,* from *ille,* that + *erta,* watch, from *(torre)erta,* watchtower, "high (tower)," from Latin *ērectus,* raised, ERECT.]

Å·le·sund, Aa·le·sund (ô′lə-sŏon′). Fishing port and town in Norway, dating from the 9th century. It is the headquarters for cod and halibut trawling and of the Arctic sealing fleet.

Al·etsch Glacier (ăl′ĭch). Glacier in the Bernese Alps. It occupies 171 square kilometers (66 square miles) and is the largest glacier in Europe.

a·leu·rone (ə-lŏor′ōn′, ăl′yə-rōn′) *n.* A protein consisting of minute granules, forming the outermost layer of the endosperm in cereal grains. [German *Aleuron,* from Greek *aleuron,* flour.] —**al·eu·ron·ic** (ăl′yə-rŏn′ĭk) *adj.*

A·leut (ə-lōot′, ăl′yōot′) *n., pl.* **Aleuts** or collectively **Aleut.** Also **A·leu·tian** (for sense 1). **1.** A member of the Eskimo people inhabiting the Aleutian Islands. **2.** A subfamily of the Eskimo-Aleut family of languages, spoken in the Aleutian Islands. [Russian *aleút,* probably from Chukchi *aliut,* "beyond the shore."]

A·leu·tian (ə-lōo′shən) *adj.* Of or pertaining to the Aleuts, their language, or their culture.
—*n.* **1.** Variant of **Aleut** (sense 1). **2. Aleutians.** The Aleutian Islands.

Aleutian Islands. Also **Aleutians.** Archipelago of volcanic islands

alder fly *An insect often found in spring near ponds and muddy streams. It is related to the lacewing fly. Alder flies, which are poor fliers, get their name because they breed on waterside plants, including alder trees.*

alexanders *This member of the parsley family is a native of Macedonia but is now common on roadsides and wasteland throughout Europe and much of North America. Its name is a reference to its country of origin—the home of the Greek conqueror Alexander the Great.*

Alexander the Great *A silver coin showing the head of the fourth-century* B.C. *Macedonian conqueror. The coin was minted either on the Greek island of Rhodes or in Alexandria, Egypt—both parts of Alexander's vast empire.*

PRONUNCIATION KEY

ă, pat; ā, pay; âr, care; ä, father, are; b, bib; ch, church; d, deed; ĕ, pet; ē, be; f, fife; g, gag; h, hat; hw, which; ĭ, pit; ī, pie; îr, pier; j, judge; k, kick; l, lid, needle; m, mum; n, no, sudden; ng, thing; ŏ, pot; ō, toe; ô, paw, for; oi, noise; ou, out; o͝o, book; o͞o, boot; p, pop; r, roar; s, sauce; sh, ship, dish; t, tight; th, thin, path; *th*, this, bathe; ŭ, cut; ûr, fur; v, valve; w, with; y, yes; z, zebra, size; zh, vision; ə, about, item, edible, gallop, circus, peaceful

IN FOREIGN WORDS:

à, *Fr.* ami; œ, *Fr.* feu, *Ger.* schön; ü, *Fr.* tu, *Ger.* über; KH, *Ger.* ich, *Scot.* loch; N, *Fr.* bon; y', *Fr.* Compiègne

STRESS MARKS:

Primary stress: ′ **in·cite′** (ĭn-sīt′)
Secondary stress: ′ **in′sight′** (ĭn′sīt′)

extending westward for nearly 2,000 kilometers (1,250 miles) from the tip of the Alaska Peninsula. There are radar stations (part of the Distant Early Warning Line) and military bases on the islands, which are of vital strategic importance because of their proximity to the U.S.S.R.

ale·wife¹ (āl′wīf′) *n., pl.* **-wives** (-wīvz′). A fish, *Alosa* (or *Pomolobus*) *pseudoharengus,* closely related to the herrings, of North American Atlantic waters and some inland lakes. Also called "oldwife." [Alteration (by association with ALEWIFE, alehouse keeper, "pot-bellied woman") of obsolete *allowes* (plural), probably from French *alose,* shad, from Gaulish Latin *alōsa*†.]

alewife² *n., pl.* **-wives.** Formerly, a woman who kept an alehouse.

Al·ex·an·der I (ăl′ĭg-zăn′dər, -zän′-) (1777–1825). Czar of Russia. He came to the throne in 1801 when his father, Paul I, was murdered. His plans to liberalize his country's government were delayed by prolonged wars with Napoleon, until eventually he was converted to rigid conservatism.

Alexander II (1818–81). Czar of Russia. Considered the ablest and most liberal of the Romanov dynasty, he came to the throne in 1855 and immediately began a program of political, educational, and military reforms. In 1861 he emancipated Russia's 10 million male serfs and their families, an act that won him the title "Czar liberator." He was assassinated by a member of a revolutionary party.

Alexander III (1845–94). Czar of Russia. He came to the throne after the assassination of his father, the liberal Alexander II, and immediately abandoned all reforms, reaffirming his "faith in the principle of autocracy." He pursued extreme reactionary policies, persecuted Jews and reformers, increased repressive police powers, and let the education system decline.

Alexander VI, born Rodrigo Borgia (*c.*1431–1503). Pope (1492–1503). On achieving the papacy (through bribery), he is said to have commented, "God has given us the papacy. Let us enjoy it." He used papal wealth and power for the advancement of his illegitimate children, and together with his son, Cesare Borgia, he embarked on the conquest of central Italy for the benefit of his family and himself. He was also a great patron of the arts.

Alexander Nev·sky (nĕv′skē, nĕf′-) (1220–63). Russian hero and saint, Prince of Novgorod (1236) and Grand Duke of Kiev and Novgorod (1246) and Vladimir (1252). He is famous for defeating the Swedes in 1240 in a battle near the Neva River (thus acquiring the name Nevsky). In 1242 he won a victory against the Teutonic Knights on the frozen waters of Lake Peipus.

Alexander of Tu·nis (to͞o′nĭs, tyo͞o′-), **Harold Alexander, 1st Earl** (1891–1969). British field marshal. In World War II he oversaw the evacuation of the British forces from Dunkirk and Burma. He directed the campaign that brought about the Allied victory in North Africa (1943), and then led the successful invasions of Sicily and Italy (1944–45), ending the war as Allied supreme commander in the Mediterranean. He was governor general of Canada (1946–52) and British minister of defense (1952–54).

al·ex·an·ders (ăl′ĭg-zăn′dərz, -zän′dərz) *pl.n.* An umbelliferous plant, *Smyrnium olusatrum,* native to southern Europe, whose stems were formerly eaten like celery. [Middle English, from Old French from Medieval Latin *alexandrum,* perhaps alteration (through association with *Alexander* the Great) of Latin *holus atrum,* "black vegetable" : *holus,* vegetable + *atrum,* neuter of *ater,* black.]

Alexander the Great (356–323 B.C.). King of Macedonia and conqueror of an empire that covered much of Asia. He was the son of the founder of the Macedonian Empire, Philip II, and the pupil of Aristotle. Alexander ascended the throne after the murder of his father in 336 B.C. He forcibly united the warring Greek states and in 334 invaded the Persian Empire with some 35,000 men, defeating its king, Darius III, at Issus. Within four years Alexander had conquered Asia Minor, Syria, Egypt (where he founded Alexandria), Babylonia, and Persia itself. He then invaded northern India and defeated the Indian king, Porus, in 327. A mutiny in his army prevented his advancing to the Ganges, and he returned reluctantly to Babylon, where he died of a fever.

Al·ex·an·dra¹ (ăl′ĭg-zăn′drə, -zän′-) (1844–1925). Queen consort of Edward VII. The eldest daughter of King Christian IX of Denmark, she married Edward in 1863, when he was the prince of Wales.

Alexandra² (1872–1918). Last czarina of Russia. A German princess and the granddaughter of Queen Victoria, she married Nicholas II in 1894. During World War I she was in charge of the government and, under the influence of the monk Rasputin, ruled disastrously. After the Revolution in 1917 she and her family were imprisoned and later shot.

Al·ex·an·dri·a (ăl′ĭg-zăn′drē-ə, -zän′-). Egypt's leading port, standing at the western tip of the Nile Delta on the Mediterranean Sea. It was founded by Alexander the Great in 332 B.C. and became a repository of Jewish, Arab, and Hellenistic culture, famous for its two royal libraries. Its pharos (lighthouse) was one of the Seven Wonders of the Ancient World. Early Christianity flourished there, and Alexandria remains the seat of the patriarch of the Eastern Orthodox Church. It was captured by the Arabs in A.D. 642 and soon after was replaced by Cairo as the capital of Egypt.

Al·ex·an·dri·an (ăl′ĭg-zăn′drē-ən, -zän′drē-ən) *adj.* **1.** Of or pertaining to Alexander the Great. **2.** Of or pertaining to Alexandria in Egypt. **3.** Of, characteristic of, or designating the learned school of Hellenistic literature, science, and philosophy that flourished in Alexandria in the last three centuries B.C. **4.** Characterized by the careful study or imitation of earlier forms and masterpieces, rather than by originality. Said of writers and literary works. **5.** Of or designating the school of early Christian philosophy and theology of Alexandria.

~*n.* **1.** A native or inhabitant of Alexandria, Egypt, especially of Hellenistic times. **2.** A scholar, writer, or theologian of the Alexandrian school.

al·ex·an·drine (ăl′ĭg-zăn′drĭn, -zän′-) *n. Often* **Alexandrine. 1.** The commonest French verse form, consisting of a line of twelve syllables with a caesura usually falling after the sixth syllable. **2.** A line of English verse composed in iambic hexameter, usually with a caesura after the third foot. [French *alexandrin,* from Old French, from *Alexandre,* title of a romance about Alexander the Great, written in this meter.] **—al·ex·an·drine, Al·ex·an·drine** *adj.*

al·ex·an·drite (ăl′ĭg-zăn′drīt′, -zän′drīt′) *n.* A greenish mineral that appears red in artificial light, used as a gemstone. It is a form of chrysoberyl. [German *Alexandrit,* named in honor of Czar ALEXANDER I.]

a·lex·i·a (ə-lĕk′sē-ə) *n.* A disorder in which cerebral lesions cause loss of the ability to read. Also called "word blindness." Compare **dyslexia.** [New Latin : A- (without) + Greek *lexis,* speech, from *legein,* to speak.]

a·lex·in (ə-lĕk′sĭn) *n.* Also **a·lex·ine** (ə-lĕk′sēn). A blood component, **complement** *(see).* [German *Alexin,* "protection (from bacteria)," from Greek *alexein,* to protect, ward off.]

a·lex·i·phar·mic (ə-lĕk′sĭ-fär′mĭk) *adj.* Preventing or resisting effects of poison or infection; antidotal; prophylactic.

~*n.* An antidote. [Obsolete *alexipharmac,* from French *alexipharmaque,* from Greek *alexipharmakos* : *alexein,* to ward off + *pharmakon,* poison (see **pharmaco-**).]

al·fal·fa (ăl-făl′fə) *n.* A plant, *Medicago sativa,* native to Eurasia, having compound leaves with three leaflets, and clusters of small purple flowers. It is widely cultivated for forage and is used as a commercial source of chlorophyll. Also called "lucerne." [Spanish, from Arabic *al-faṣfaṣah,* best fodder.]

Al Fatah *n.* See **Fatah.**

al·fil·a·ri·a, al·fil·e·ri·a (ăl-fĭl′ə-rē′ə) *n.* A plant, *Erodium cicutarium,* native to Europe but widely naturalized in North America, having finely divided leaves and small pink or purplish flowers. Also called "filaree," "pin clover." [American Spanish *alfilerillo,* from Spanish, diminutive of *alfiler,* a pin, from Arabic *al-khilāl,* thorn, pin.]

Al·fred the Great (ăl′frĭd) (849–99). King of Wessex. He became ruler of Wessex in 871 and conducted several wars against the Danes, driving them from Wessex. Alfred built Britain's first navy, reorganized Wessex's army, and set up a complex of fortified earthworks. He was also an able administrator and drew up a legal code and encouraged scholarship.

al·fres·co (ăl-frĕs′kō) *adv.* In the fresh air; outdoors: *Let's eat alfresco.*

~*adj.* Taking place outdoors; outdoor: *an alfresco meal.* [Italian, "in the fresh (air)" : *a il,* in the + *fresco,* fresh, FRESCO.]

Al Furāt. See **Euphrates.**

Al Fustat. See **Cairo.**

Alf·vén wave (ălf-văn′) *n. Physics.* A transverse wave propagated through a plasma, such as the matter in a star, under the influence of magnetohydrodynamic forces. [After Hannes Olof Gösta *Alfvén* (1908–), Swedish astrophysicist.]

Alg. Algeria.

al·gae (ăl′jē) *pl.n. Singular* **al·ga** (ăl′gə). Primitive, chiefly aquatic, one-celled or multicellular plants that lack true stems, roots, and leaves but contain chlorophyll. Included among the algae are kelps and other seaweeds, and the diatoms. [Latin *algae,* plural of *alga*†, seaweed.] **—al·gal** (ăl′gəl) *adj.*

al·gar·ro·ba (ăl′gə-rō′bə) *n.* **1.** A tree, the **mesquite** *(see).* **2.** A tree, the **carob** *(see).* **3.** The edible pod of either of these trees. [Spanish, from Arabic *al-kharrūbah* : *al,* the + *kharrūbah,* CAROB.]

Al·gar·ve (ăl-gär′və, ăl-). Former kingdom and province of southernmost Portugal, now the district of Faro. Farming and fishing are the main occupations, and it is also noted for cork.

al·ge·bra (ăl′jə-brə) *n.* **1.** A generalization of arithmetic in which symbols, usually letters of the alphabet, represent numbers and are related by operations that hold for all numbers in the set. **2.** A set of entities (such as matrices, propositions, or vectors) together with operations for combining these entities to give other members of the set. See **algebraic structure.** [Medieval Latin, from Arabic *al-jebr, al-jabr,* "the (science of) reuniting" (referring to the solving of algebraic equations) : *al,* the + *jabr,* reunification, bone-setting.] **—al·ge·bra·ist** (ăl′jə-brā′ĭst) *n.*

al·ge·bra·ic (ăl′jə-brā′ĭk) *adj.* **1.** Of, pertaining to, or involving algebra. **2.** Designating an expression, equation, or function in which only numbers, letters, and arithmetical operations are contained or used. **3.** Indicating or restricted to a finite number of algebraic operations. **—al·ge·bra·i·cal·ly** *adv.*

algebraic logic *n.* A method of presenting a problem for a calculator or computer with the operations entered in the order in which they would be written out.

algebraic number *n.* **1.** Any positive or negative number. **2.** A number that is a root of a polynomial equation with rational coefficients.

algebraic operation *n.* Addition, subtraction, multiplication, division, exponentiation, root extraction, or any finite combination of these operations.

algebraic structure *n.* The general set of operations and relationships in an algebra, considered independently of the particular mathematical entities used.

al·ge·bra·ic sum *n.* The sum of algebraic quantities produced by arithmetic addition, in which negative quantities are added by the subtraction of corresponding positive quantities. For example, the algebraic sum of 6 and −2 is 4.

Al·ge·ci·ras (ăl′jə-sîr′əs). Port and tourist center in southern Spain, situated on the Mediterranean Sea across the bay from Gibraltar.

Al·ger (ăl-zhā′). *English* **Al·giers** (ăl-jîrz′). Capital of Algeria and an ancient Mediterranean port. It was taken by the French (1830), and during World War II was the seat of the French government in exile and headquarters of the Allied forces in North Africa.

Al·ger (ăl′jər), **Horatio** (1832–99). U.S. author. His first successful novel was *Ragged Dick* (1867). He wrote more than a hundred books based on the formula that a poor boy—with hard work, honesty, gumption, and a little (or a lot) of luck—could become rich and famous.

Al·ge·ri·a (ăl-jîr′ē-ə). *Abbr.* **Alg.** *French* **Al·gé·rie** (ăl′zhə-rē′). Country in northwest Africa bordering on the Mediterranean Sea, the second-largest country in Africa, after Sudan. Arab armies conquered Algeria in the 7th century, and the north fell to the Ottoman Turks in 1519. The French invaded the country in 1830, and in 1871 the north became three departments of France. Algeria gained its independence, after a long terrorist and guerrilla campaign, in 1962. The country has two distinct regions: the northern cultivated region of the Mediterranean littoral and the Atlas Mts. (about 15 percent of the country), and the arid wastes of the Sahara in the south. Algeria has extensive deposits of oil and natural gas, which account for 90 percent of its exports. Area, 2,381,741 square kilometers (919,352 square miles). Population, 17,400,000. Capital, Alger (Algiers). —**Al·ge·ri·an** *adj. & n.*

–algia *n. suffix.* Indicates pain or a painful condition; for example, **neuralgia**. [Greek, from *algos*†, pain.]

al·gi·cide (ăl′jə-sīd′) *n.* A chemical used to kill algae in water.

al·gid (ăl′jĭd) *adj.* Chilly; clammy. Said especially of the skin. [Latin *algidus*, from *algēre*†, to be cold.] —**al·gid·i·ty** *n.*

Algiers. See **Alger.**

al·gin (ăl′jĭn) *n.* A gelatinous substance consisting of alginic acid or its salts or esters, obtained from certain algae, especially the giant kelp, and used as an emulsifier, a thickener for foods, and a fabric dressing. [ALG(AE) + -IN.]

al·gi·nate (ăl′jə-nāt′) *n.* A salt or ester of alginic acid.

al·gin·ic acid (ăl-jĭn′ĭk) *n.* A gelatinous substance obtained from certain seaweeds. See **algin.**

algo– *prefix.* Indicates pain; for example, **algolagnia**. [Greek, from *algos*†, pain.]

al·goid (ăl′goid′) *adj.* Of or resembling algae.

Al·gol (ăl′gŏl′, ăl′gôl′) *n.* A double, eclipsing, variable star in the constellation Perseus, almost as bright as Polaris. [Arabic *al ghūl*, "the ghoul" : *al,* the + *ghūl,* GHOUL.]

AL·GOL (ăl′gŏl′, ăl′gôl′) *n.* An arithmetical language by which numerical procedures may be precisely presented to a computer in a standard form. [*Al*gorithmic *O*riented *L*anguage.]

al·go·lag·ni·a (ăl′gō-lăg′nē-ə) *n.* Sexual gratification derived from inflicting or experiencing pain. See **masochism, sadism.** [New Latin : ALGO- + Greek *lagneia,* lust, from *lagnos,* lustful.] —**al·go·lag·ni·ac** *n. & adj.*

al·gol·o·gy (ăl-gŏl′ə-jē) *n.* The study of algae. [ALG(AE) + -LOGY.] —**al·go·log·i·cal** (ăl′gə-lŏj′ĭ-kəl) *adj.* —**al·gol·o·gist** (ăl-gŏl′ə-jĭst) *n.*

al·gom·e·ter (ăl-gŏm′ə-tər) *n.* An apparatus for determining sensitivity to pain caused by pressure. [ALGO- + -METER.] —**al·go·met·ric** (ăl′gə-mĕt′rĭk), **al·go·met·ri·cal** *adj.* —**al·gom·e·try** (ăl-gŏm′ə-trē) *n.*

Al·gon·ki·an (ăl-gŏng′kē-ən) *n., pl.* **–ans** or collectively **Algonkian** (for sense 2). **1.** *Geology.* In Canada, the late **Proterozoic** (*see*). **2.** Variant of **Algonquian.** [After the rock formations in the Great Lakes district, homeland of the Algonquin Indians.]

Al·gon·qui·an (ăl-gŏng′kwē-ən, -kē-ən) *n., pl.* **–ans** or collectively **Algonquian** (for sense 2). Also **Al·gon·ki·an** (-kē-ən). **1.** A principal family of about 50 North American Indian languages spoken in an area stretching from the Atlantic to the Rocky Mountains, and from Labrador in the north to North Carolina and Tennessee in the south, and used by such tribes as the Ojibwa, Delaware, Cree, Fox, Blackfoot, Illinois, and Shawnee. **2.** A member of a tribe using a language of this family. [From ALGONQUIN.] —**Al·gon·qui·an, Al·gon·ki·an** *adj.*

Al·gon·quin (ăl-gŏng′kwĭn, -kĭn) *n., pl.* **–quins** or collectively **Algonquin** (for sense 1). Also **Al·gon·kin** (-kĭn) **1.** A member of any of several Algonquian-speaking North American Indian tribes formerly inhabiting the region along the Ottawa River and near the northern tributaries of the St. Lawrence River. See **Ottawa.** **2.** The Algonquian language of these tribes. [Canadian French, from earlier *Algoumequins*† (plural).]

al·go·pho·bi·a (ăl′gō-fō′bē-ə) *n.* Abnormal fear of pain. [New Latin : ALGO- + -PHOBIA.]

al·go·rism (ăl′gə-rĭz′əm) *n.* **1.** The Arabic system of numbers; the decimal system. **2.** Variant of **algorithm.** [Middle English *algorisme,* from Old French, from Medieval Latin *algorismus,* after Muhammad ibn-Musa AL-KHWARIZMI.]

al·go·rithm (ăl′gə-rĭth′əm) *n.* Also **al·go·rism** (-rĭz′əm). *Mathematics.* Any mechanical or recursive computational procedure. [Variant (influenced by ARITHMETIC) of ALGORISM.] —**al·go·rith·mic** (ăl′gə-rĭth′mĭk) *adj.*

algorithmic language *n.* An arithmetical language presenting numerical procedures to a computer in a standard form.

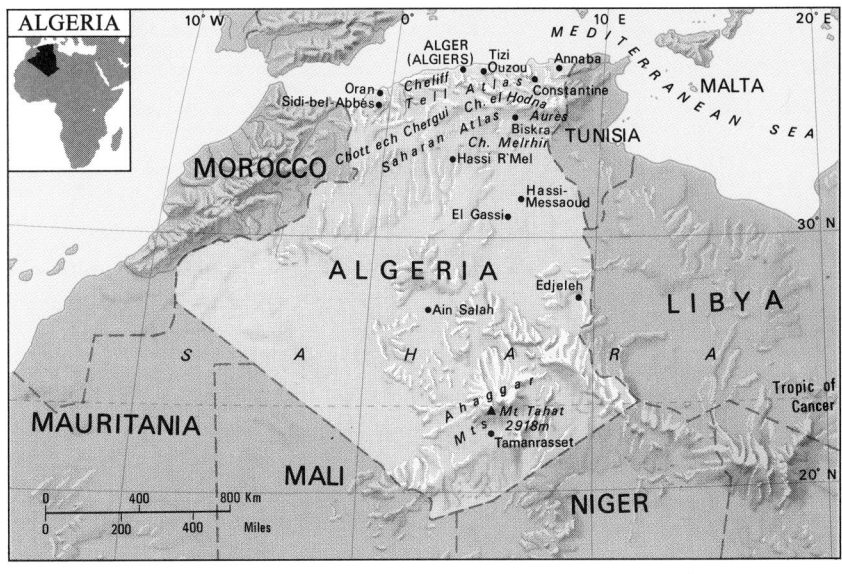

Al·ham·bra, the (ăl-hăm′brə). Citadel and palace, overlooking Granada in southern Spain. It was built by the Moorish kings in the 13th and 14th centuries and is the best example of Moorish architecture in Spain.

A·li (ä′lē) (*c.* 600–61). Fourth caliph of Islam (656–61). He was the cousin and son-in-law (by his marriage to Fatima) of the prophet Muhammad and one of the first converts to Islam. His reign was marred by conflict between his supporters and rivals, and after his assassination, Islam came to be divided into Sunnites and Shiites, the Shiites holding that Ali and his descendants had the only valid claim to the caliphate.

A·li (ä-lē′), **Muhammad,** originally Cassius Marcellus Clay (1942–). U.S. boxer. He won the world heavyweight championship in 1964. He became a Black Muslim, changed his name, and refused military service in 1967. For this last action he was stripped of his title. He regained the championship by defeating George Foreman in 1974, losing it briefly in 1978 and regaining it again that year.

a·li·as (ā′lē-əs, āl′yəs) *n., pl.* **–ases.** An assumed name. ~*adv.* Otherwise named or known as: *Johnson, alias Rogers.* [Latin *aliās,* otherwise, from *alius,* other.]

A·li Ba·ba (ä′lē bä′bə). In the *Arabian Nights,* a poor woodcutter who gains entrance to the treasure cave of the forty thieves by saying the magic words "Open, Sesame!"

al·i·bi (ăl′ə-bī′) *n., pl.* **–bis. 1.** *Law.* **a.** A form of defense whereby a defendant attempts to prove that he was elsewhere when the crime in question was committed. **b.** The evidence supporting this. **2.** *Informal.* An excuse. ~*tr.v.* **alibied, -bling, -bis.** *Informal.* To provide an excuse or alibi for. [Latin *alibī,* elsewhere : *alius,* other + *ubī,* where.]

al·i·ble (ăl′ə-bəl) *adj.* Having nutrients; nourishing. [Latin, *alibilis,* from *alere,* to nourish.]

A·li·can·te (ä′lē-kän′tē). Mediterranean port and tourist resort in the Valencia region of southeastern Spain. It is the capital of Alicante province.

Al·ice-band (ăl′ĭs-bănd′) *n.* A firm, U-shaped headband worn over the crown and tucked behind the ears. [After the headband worn by Alice in Sir John Tenniel's (1820–1914) illustrations of *Through the Looking-Glass.*]

Al·ice-in-Won·der·land (ăl′ĭs-ĭn-wŭn′dər-lănd′) *adj.* Absurd; fantastic. [After the fantastic logic and events of Wonderland in Lewis Carroll's book.]

Al·ice Springs (ăl′ĭs). Town in Northern Territory, Australia, lying almost at the midpoint of the continent. It is a center for tourism and transport.

al·i·cy·clic (ăl′ĭ-sī′klĭk, -sĭk′lĭk) *adj.* Of, pertaining to, or designating chemical compounds having both aliphatic and cyclic characteristics or structures. Examples of alicyclic compounds include cyclohexane and sucrose. [German *alicyclisch* : ALI(PHATIC) + CYCLIC.]

al·i·dade (ăl′ə-dād′) *n.* Also **al·i·dad** (-dăd). **1.** A surveying instrument consisting of a rule with sights at each end, used on a plane table to draw lines of sight onto distant objects. Also called "sight rule." **2.** A similar rule with a telescope mounted parallel to it. **3.** The index of a graduated surveying instrument such as an astrolabe. [French, from Medieval Latin *alidada,* from Arabic *al-'iḍāda,* "the revolving radius of a circle," from *'aḍud,* humerus.]

a·li·en (ā′lē-ən, āl′yən) *adj.* **1.** Owing political allegiance to a country other than the one in which one is resident; foreign: *a large alien population.* **2. a.** Belonging to, characteristic of, or derived from another place, society, or person; not one's own; unfamiliar; strange: *the problems of adjusting to an alien culture.* **b.** Belonging or pertaining to another planet or world: *an alien spaceship.* **3.** Inconsistent or incompatible; repugnant. Used with *to: Lying is alien to his nature.* —See Synonyms at **extrinsic.**

Ali Baba *In the* Arabian Nights *story, the 40 thieves conceal themselves in large oil jars at Ali Baba's house, planning to kill him because he knows the secret of their magic cave. But, as this 19th-century illustration shows, Ali and his servant Morgiana discover their hiding place, and Morgiana kills the thieves by pouring boiling oil over them.*

~*n.* **1.** A foreign resident of a country who has not been naturalized. **2.** A member of another family, people, region, or the like; especially, a being from another planet or world. **3.** A person who is excluded from some group; an outsider. **4.** *Ecology.* A plant native to one region but naturalized in another.
~*tr.v.* **aliened, -ening, -ens.** *Law.* To alienate (property). [Middle English, from Old French, from Latin *aliēnus,* belonging to another, from *alius,* other.]

a·li·en·a·ble (āl′yə-nə-bəl, ā′lē-ə-) *adj. Law.* Capable of being transferred to the ownership of another. Said typically of property. —**a·li·en·a·bil·i·ty** *n.*

a·li·en·age (āl′yə-nĭj, ā′lē-ə-) *n.* The state or condition of being alien or an alien.

a·li·en·ate (āl′yə-nāt′, ā′lē-ə-) *tr.v.* **-ated, -ating, -ates.** **1.** To cause (someone previously friendly or affectionate) to become unfriendly or indifferent; estrange. **2.** To dissociate or isolate (oneself). **3.** To cause to be transferred; turn away: *"he succeeded . . . in alienating the affections of my only ward"* (Oscar Wilde). **4.** *Law.* To transfer (property) to the ownership of another. [Latin *aliēnāre,* from *aliēnus,* ALIEN.] —**a·li·en·a·tor** *n.*

a·li·en·at·ed (āl′yə-nā′tĭd, ā′lē-ə-) *adj. Psychology.* **1.** Suffering from alienation. **2.** Loosely, out of sympathy with one's immediate social environment.

a·li·en·a·tion (āl′yə-nā′shən, ā′lē-ə-) *n.* **1.** The condition of being an outsider; a state of isolation. **2.** *Psychology.* A state of estrangement between the self and the objective world, or between different parts of the personality. **3.** The act of alienating, as: **a.** Estrangement; disaffection: *"In the decades after 1795 there was a profound alienation between classes in Britain"* (E.P. Thompson). **b.** *Law.* The transference of property, or the title to it, to another. **4.** In Marxist theory, the sense of loss of personal identity and worth caused in workers by the fragmentation of labor, mechanization, and lack of control over the means of production. **5.** In the theater, the distancing of the audience from the action of the play by dramatic devices: *Brecht's alienation effects.* [Sense 4: translation of German *Entäusserung.* Sense 5: short for *alienation effect,* translation of German *Verfremdungseffekt.*]

a·li·en·ee (āl′yə-nē′, ā′lē-ə-nē′) *n. Law.* A person to whom ownership of property is transferred.

a·li·en·ist (āl′yə-nĭst, ā′lē-ə-nĭst) *n.* **1.** *Archaic.* A doctor specializing in mental illness. **2.** *Law.* A psychiatrist who has been accepted by a court as an expert on the mental competence of principals or witnesses appearing before it. [French *aliéniste,* from *aliéné,* insane, from Latin *aliēnātus,* "estranged," past participle of *aliēnāre,* to ALIENATE.]

a·li·en·or (āl′yə-nôr′, ā′lē-ə-) *n. Law.* A person who transfers ownership of property to another.

a·lif (ä′lĭf) *n.* The first letter of the Arabic alphabet. See feature at **alphabet.** [Arabic.]

a·li·form (ā′lə-fôrm′, ăl′ə-) *adj.* Shaped like a wing; alar. [Latin *āla,* wing + -FORM.]

a·light¹ (ə-līt′) *intr.v.* **alighted** or **alit** (ə-lĭt′), **alighting, alights.** **1.** To come down and settle, as after flight. Used with *on* or *upon: a bird alighting on a branch.* **2. a.** To get out of (a vehicle, for example). **b.** To dismount. Used with *from.* **3.** To come upon by chance. Used with *on* or *upon: His gaze alighted on an old vase.* [Middle English *ali(g)hten,* Old English *ālīhtan : ā-* (intensive) + *līhtan,* to dismount, lighten, from *līht,* LIGHT (adjective).]

alight² *adj.* **1.** Burning. **2.** Lighted; lit up. Used after the noun: *Her face was alight with intelligence.* [Middle English *alight,* Old English *ālīht,* past participle of *ālīhtan,* to light up : *ā-* + *līhtan,* to light, from *līht,* LIGHT.] —**a·light** *adv.*

a·lign (ə-līn′) *v.* **aligned, aligning, aligns.** —*tr.* **1.** To arrange in a line. **2.** To ally (oneself, for example) with one side of an argument, cause, policy, or the like. **3.** To bring (two or more parts of a machine, for example) into correct relation with one another. —*intr.* To fall into line or position. [French *aligner,* from Old French : *a-,* from Latin *ad-,* to + *ligne,* LINE.] —**a·lign·er** *n.*

a·lign·ment (ə-līn′mənt) *n.* **1.** Arrangement or position in a straight line. **2.** A ground plan, as of a railway. **3.** The act of aligning or the condition of being aligned: *In the new political alignment; all parties opposed the government.* **4.** The correct or proper adjustment or positioning of related parts, as of a machine.

alignment chart *n. Mathematics.* A **nomogram** (see).

a·like (ə-līk′) *adj.* Having a close resemblance; similar. Usually used after the noun: *His sons are alike.*
~*adv.* In the same way or manner, or to the same degree: *They dress and walk alike.* [Middle English *ilik,* Old English *gelīc : ge-* (collective prefix) + *līc,* form.] —**a·like·ness** *n.*

al·i·ment (ăl′ə-mənt) *n. Formal.* **1.** Food; nourishment. **2.** Something that supports or sustains. **3.** In Scots law, alimony or maintenance.
~*tr.v.* (ăl′ə-mĕnt′) **alimented, -menting, -ments.** *Formal.* To supply with food or other sustenance. [Middle English, from Latin *alimentum,* from *alere,* to nourish.] —**al·i·men·tal** (ăl′ə-mĕn′təl) *adj.* —**al·i·men·tal·ly** *adv.*

al·i·men·ta·ry (ăl′ə-mĕn′trē, -tə-rē) *adj.* **1.** Of or pertaining to food or nutrition. **2.** Providing nourishment.

alimentary canal *n.* The mucous-membrane-lined tube of the digestive system, extending from the mouth to the anus and including the esophagus, stomach, and intestines.

al·i·men·ta·tion (ăl′ə-mĕn-tā′shən) *n.* **1.** The act or process of giving or receiving nourishment. **2.** Support; sustenance.

al·i·mo·ny (ăl′ə-mō′nē) *n., pl.* **-nies. 1.** *Law.* An allowance for support made under court order and usually given by one spouse to the other after divorce or legal separation. **2.** Sustenance; support. [Latin *alimōnia,* nutriment, support, from *alere,* to nourish.]

al·i·phat·ic (ăl′ə-făt′ĭk) *adj.* Of, pertaining to, or designating organic chemical compounds with reactions characteristic of compounds with open chains of carbon atoms rather than the closed chains of **aromatic** (see) compounds. See **alicyclic.** [From Greek *aleiphar* (stem *aleiphat-*), oil, from *aleiphein,* to anoint.]

al·i·quant (ăl′ə-kwŏnt) *adj.* Of, pertaining to, or designating a number or quantity that is not an exact factor or divisor of some other number or quantity. [New Latin *aliquantus,* from Latin, "a certain quantity" : *alius,* some + *quantus,* how much.]

al·i·quot (ăl′ə-kwŏt′, -kwət) *adj.* **1.** *Mathematics.* Of, pertaining to,

---

alien message

MESSAGES AIMED AT THE STARS

Man's attempts to communicate with alien civilizations

The first deliberate messages from Earth to alien civilizations have already been sent. Two identical "letters," in the form of engraved metal plaques, were fixed to the Pioneer 10 and 11 spacecraft that were launched by the United States in the early 1970's. Neither probe was aimed at any particular star. So both could drift through the emptiness of interstellar space, unnoticed but untarnished, for millions of years—until long after every 20th-century artifact on Earth has crumbled to dust.

Even if the letters are found by beings from another planet, a reply will take some time. Although scientists calculate that our own galaxy alone may contain as many as a million Earth-type planets—or about one for every 100,000 of its stars—the distances they are from Earth are so vast that even a reply sent at the speed of light could take many thousands of years to reach us.

A second message, which took only three minutes to transmit but which will take 24,000 years to arrive, was sent in 1974. It was a powerful radio signal beamed from the 305-meter-wide (1,000-foot) radio telescope at Arecibo, Puerto Rico. The message was aimed at a cluster of 300,000 stars known as M13 in the constellation of Hercules, 24,000 light-years away. The signal consists of 1,679 on-off pulses that make up a strip of pictograms carefully designed to show the basic details of terrestrial life. Even the total number of pulses was chosen to avoid ambiguity; 1,679 can be arranged into a rectangular pattern in only one way—as 73 rows of 23 pulses each.

Because humans have only recently learned to send messages to the stars, and because interstellar communications are so slow, any message that reaches Earth *from* outer space in the near future will almost certainly have come from a civilization far in advance of our own. Despite years of listening, however, astronomers have yet to hear any intelligible signal.

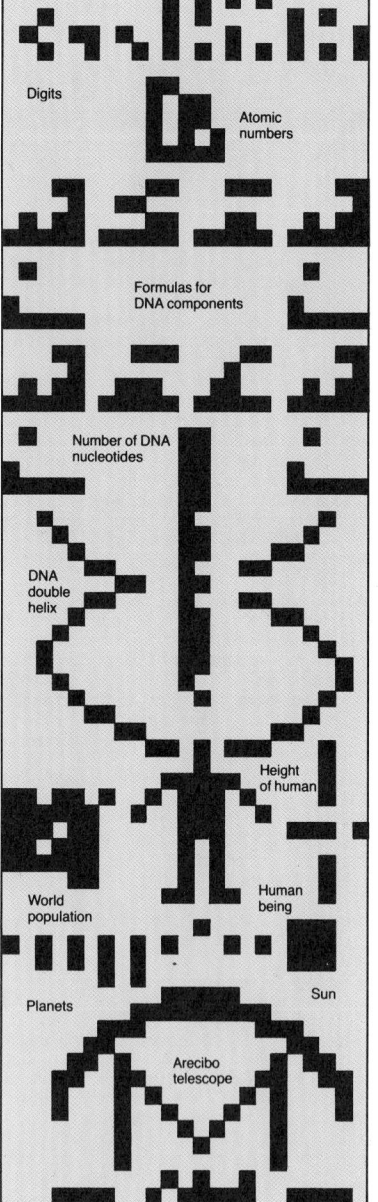

Digits
Atomic numbers
Formulas for DNA components
Number of DNA nucleotides
DNA double helix
Height of human
World population
Human being
Planets
Sun
Arecibo telescope

PEACE FROM EARTH *Plaques on the Pioneer space probes show two human figures drawn to scale against an outline of the craft—with the man holding up his hand in greeting. On the right are representations of the universe's basic building block, the hydrogen atom, the sun's position in relation to various radio sources, and the probe's journey from Earth.*

OVER AND OUT *The pictogram message that was flashed to the stars from Puerto Rico. It includes details about terrestrial arithmetic and atomic numbers, and the chemicals on which all life on earth is based. The message also contains simple pictures of a human figure, with an indication of its size, and of the giant Arecibo radio telescope itself.*

or designating an exact divisor or factor of a quantity, especially of an integer. **2.** Contained exactly or an exact number of times. [French *(partie) aliquote,* aliquot (part), from Medieval Latin *(pars) aliquotae,* from Latin *aliquot,* some, several : *alius,* some, other + *quot,* how many.]

a·lit. Alternate past tense of **alight.**

a·li·un·de (ă'lē-ŭn'dē, ăl'ē-) *adv. Law.* From another source; from elsewhere: *evidence aliunde.* [Latin, from elsewhere : *alius,* other + *unde,* whence.]

a·live (ə-līv') *adj.* **1.** Having life; in a living state. **2.** In existence or operation; not extinct or inactive: *keep love alive.* **3.** In a state of animation; full of life; lively: *Her performance was splendidly alive.* **4.** Now living. Used as an intensive, usually with a superlative: *the strongest man alive.* **5.** Aware; sensitive: *alive to the moods of others.* **6.** Swarming: *The square was alive with happy people.* —See Synonyms at **living.** —**alive and kicking.** Lively; active. —**look alive.** To be alert. Used in the imperative. [Middle English *alive, on live,* Old English *on līfe* : ON + *līfe,* dative of *līf,* LIFE.] —**a·live·ness** *n.*

a·liz·a·rin (ə-lĭz'ə-rĭn) *n.* Also **a·liz·a·rine** (-rĭn, -rēn'). An orange-red compound, $C_{14}H_8O_4$, used as a dyestuff. [French *alizarine,* from *alizari,* madder, from Spanish, from Arabic *al-'aṣārah,* the juice pressed out : *al,* the + *'aṣara,* he pressed.]

al·ka·hest (ăl'kə-hĕst') *n.* The hypothetical universal solvent once sought by alchemists. [Medieval Latin *alchahest,* probably coined as a pseudo-Arabic word by Paracelsus.]

al·ka·les·cent (ăl'kə-lĕs'ənt) *adj.* Becoming alkaline; slightly alkaline. [ALKAL(I) + -ESCENT.] —**al·ka·les·cence, al·ka·les·cen·cy** *n.*

al·ka·li (ăl'kə-lī') *n., pl.* **-lis** or **-lies. 1.** *Chemistry.* A soluble base such as ammonia or a hydroxide or carbonate of an alkali metal, the aqueous solution of which is bitter, slippery, and caustic. **2.** Any of various soluble mineral salts found in natural water and arid soils. [Middle English *alcaly,* from Medieval Latin *alcali,* from Arabic *al-qalīy,* the ashes (of saltwort), from *qalay,* to fry.]

al·ka·li·fy (ăl'kə-lə-fī', ăl-kăl'ə-fī') *v.* **-fied, -fying, -fies.** —*tr.* To make alkaline; alkalize. —*intr.* To become alkaline.

alkali metal *n.* Any of a group of soft, white, low-density, low-melting, highly reactive metallic elements, including lithium, sodium, potassium, rubidium, cesium, and francium. The alkali metals constitute Group I of the periodic table of the elements.

al·ka·lim·e·ter (ăl'kə-lĭm'ə-tər) *n.* **1.** An apparatus for measuring alkalinity. **2.** An apparatus for measuring the amount of carbon dioxide evolved from a solid. —**al·ka·lim·e·try** (ăl'kə-lĭm'ə-trē) *n.*

al·ka·line (ăl'kə-lĭn, -līn') *adj.* **1.** Of, relating to, containing, or having the nature of an alkali. **2.** Designating a soil having a pH greater than 7.

alkaline earth *n.* **1.** An oxide of an alkaline-earth metal. **2.** Loosely, an alkaline-earth metal. —**al·ka·line-earth** *adj.*

alkaline-earth metal *n.* Any of a group of silvery, fairly reactive metallic elements, especially calcium, strontium, and barium, but generally including beryllium, magnesium, and radium. The alkaline-earth metals constitute Group II of the periodic table of the elements.

al·ka·lin·i·ty (ăl'kə-lĭn'ĭ-tē) *n.* The alkali concentration or alkaline quality of an alkali-containing substance or solution.

al·ka·lize (ăl'kə-līz') *v.* **-lized, -lizing, -lizes.** Also **al·ka·lin·ize** (-lĭn-īz'), **-ized, -izing, -izes.** —*tr.* To make alkaline. —*intr.* To become an alkali. —**al·ka·li·za·tion** *n.*

al·ka·loid (ăl'kə-loid') *n.* Any of various physiologically active nitrogen-containing organic bases derived from plants, including nicotine, quinine, cocaine, atropine, and morphine. [German : AL-KAL(I) + -OID.] —**al·ka·loi·dal** (ăl'kə-loid'l) *adj.*

al·ka·lo·sis (ăl'kə-lō'sĭs) *n.* Pathologically high alkali content in the blood and tissues. [New Latin : ALKAL(I) + -OSIS.]

al·kane series (ăl'kān') *n. Chemistry.* The **paraffin** series *(see).* [AL-K(YL) + -ANE.]

al·ka·net (ăl'kə-nĕt') *n.* **1. a.** A European plant, *Alkanna tinctoria,* the roots of which yield a red dye. **b.** The root of this plant, or a dye prepared from it. **2.** Any of several hairy plants of the genus *Anchusa,* native to the Old World, having clusters of blue flowers. Also called "bugloss." [Middle English, from Spanish *alcaneta,* diminutive of *alcana,* henna, from Medieval Latin *alchanna,* from Arabic *al-ḥinnā',* the HENNA.]

al-Kartum, Al Khartum. See **Khartoum.**

al·kene (ăl'kēn') *n.* Any of a class of unsaturated aliphatic hydrocarbons that contain at least one double carbon-carbon bond in their molecules. The simplest alkenes have only one double bond and form a series (the *alkene series*) with the general formula C_nH_{2n}. The first members of the series are ethene ($CH_2{:}CH_2$), propene ($CH_3CH_2{:}CH_2$), and butene ($C_2H_5CH_2{:}CH_2$). Also called "olefine." [ALK(YL) + -ENE.]

Al Khalil. See **Hebron.**

al-Khwa·riz·mi (ăl'KHwä-rēz'mē), **Muhammad ibn-Musa** (*c.* 780–*c.* 850). Arab mathematician. His work introduced the Hindu system of notation into Arabic mathematics, and a 10th-century Latin translation of it introduced this system, now known as "Arabic numerals," to Western mathematics. The word "algebra" comes from the title of al-Khwarizmi's treatise on it, and the word for the calculating procedure he discussed, "algorism" (algorithm), is derived from his name.

al·kie, al·ky (ăl'kē) *n., pl.* **-kies.** *Slang.* An alcoholic.

Alkoran. Variant of **Alcoran,** the **Koran** *(see).*

al·kox·ide (ăl-kŏk'sīd') *n. Chemistry.* Any of a class of chemical compounds that are salts formed by removing a hydrogen atom from the hydroxyl group of an alcohol. Sodium methoxide, $NaOCH_3$, is a simple example. [ALK(YL) + OX(Y)- + -IDE.]

al·kyd resin (ăl'kĭd) *n.* A widely used durable synthetic resin derived from glycerol and phthalic anhydride. Also called "alkyd." [Blend of ALKYL and ACID.]

al·kyl (ăl'kəl) *n. Chemistry.* A monovalent radical, such as ethyl or propyl, having the general formula C_nH_{2n+1}. [German : ALC(OHOL) + -YL.]

al·kyl·a·tion (ăl'kə-lā'shən) *n. Chemistry.* Any process in which an alkyl group is added to or substituted in a molecule, as in the reaction of alkenes with alkanes to make high-octane fuels.

al·kyl·ben·zene (ăl'kəl-bĕn'zēn') *n. Chemistry.* Any of a class of hydrocarbons with molecules that have an alkyl group joined to a benzene ring. Toluene ($C_6H_5{\cdot}CH_3$) is the simplest example.

al·kyne series (ăl'kīn') *n.* A series of hydrocarbons, the **acetylene series** *(see).* [ALKY(L) + -(I)NE.]

all (ôl) *adj.* **1.** The total entity or extent of: *All Europe was threatened.* **2.** The entire or total number, amount, or quantity of: *All animals are alike in some respects.* Often used after a pronoun: *I like them all.* **3.** Every one of a group or class: *All the staff were present.* **4.** The greatest possible: *in all honesty.* **5. a.** Many: *all sorts of books.* **b.** Every. Used in the phrase *all manner of.* **6.** Any whatsoever: *beyond all doubt.* **7.** Nothing but; only: *He was all skin and bones.*

~pron. **1.** Each and every one: *Education for all.* **2. a.** Each and every thing: *Ten ships sailed and all have now docked.* **b.** Everything collectively: *He remembered all he saw.*

~n. **1.** Everything one has: *She gave her all.* **2.** The whole number; totality. —**all and sundry.** Everyone without restriction. —**all in all. 1.** With everything being taken into account. **2.** Of the highest importance. —**at all. 1. a.** To some or any extent: *He can't walk at all.* **b.** Whatever: *He did no work at all.* Used as an intensive in negative sentences. **2. a.** Ever: *Do you see him at all now?* **b.** To any extent; in any way: *Does he feel better at all?* Used in questions to suggest some doubt in the speaker's mind. —**for all.** To the limited extent that: *for all I care.* —**in all.** Including everyone or everything: *That makes twelve packages in all.*

~adv. **1.** Wholly; entirely; completely: *This is all wrong.* **2.** *Informal.* Very; thoroughly: *The coat was all dirty.* **3.** Each; apiece: *a score of five all.* **4.** Exclusively: *The cake is all for you.* **5. a.** To a great extent or degree: *happens all too often.* **b.** To such an extent: *all the more reason not to trust him.* —**all about.** Mainly or exclusively concerned with: *This book is all about trout fishing.* —**all along.** Over a period of time; consistently: *I hoped all along that he'd come.* —**all but.** Nearly; almost: *He all but fainted.* —**all in.** *Informal.* Tired; exhausted. —**all of.** Not less than: *It's all of ten miles.* —**all that.** Particularly. Used in the negative: *It wasn't all that difficult.* —**all there.** *Informal.* Mentally competent or alert. —**all the same. 1.** Nevertheless. **2.** Of little importance: *It's all the same to me.* [Middle English *al(le),* Old English *all, eall.*]

Usage: *All* can occur with either a singular or plural verb, according to whether an uncountable or a countable noun respectively is present or understood. *All is not lost, all human life is there, all (members) were present,* are equally correct. The use of *of* before the definite article in such phrases is optional: *all (of) the members*; it is often preferred in American English and omitted in British English, especially in writing.

all-[1] *comb. form.* Indicates: **1.** Wholly or entirely; for example, **all-night, all-wool. 2.** Extremely; very; for example, **all-important. 3.** Representing the whole of; for example, **all-American. 4.** Every kind of; for example, **all-weather.**

all-[2]. Variant of **allo-.**

al·la bre·ve (ä'lə brĕv'ā). *adv. Music.* In duple or quadruple time with the half note being the unit of time. [Italian, "according to the breve."] —**al·la bre·ve** *adj.*

Al·lah (ăl'ə, ä'lə) *n.* The supreme being in the Muslim religion. [Arabic *Allāh* : *al,* the + *Ilāh,* god.]

Al·la·ha·bad (ăl'ə-hə-băd', -bäd'). City in Uttar Pradesh, northern India, at the confluence of the Ganges and Jumna rivers. It was an important center of the movement for Indian national independence.

al·la·man·da, al·la·man·de (ăl'ə-măn'də) *n.* Any of several woody vines of the genus *Allamanda,* native to tropical America, having showy, funnel-shaped yellow flowers. [After Jean N.S. *Allamand* (1713–87), Swiss scientist.]

all-A·mer·i·can (ôl'ə-mĕr'ĭ-kən) *adj.* **1.** Representative of the best of its kind in the United States. **2.** *Sports.* Chosen as the best amateur in the United States at a particular position or event: *an all-American halfback.* **3.** Composed of Americans or American materials exclusively. **4.** Entirely within the territorial limits of the United States. **5.** Of all the Americas.

~n. Often **All-American.** An all-American athlete.

al·lan·ite (ăl'ə-nīt') *n.* A rare brown mineral found in certain igneous rocks, consisting of an aluminosilicate of calcium, iron, and several lanthanoid elements. [After T. *Allan* (1777–1833), British mineralogist.]

al·lan·toid (ə-lăn'toid) *adj.* Also **al·lan·toi·dal** (ăl'ən-toid'l). **1.** Of or having an allantois. **2.** *Botany.* Shaped like a sausage.

~n. The allantois. [French *allantoïde,* from Old French, from Greek *allantoeidēs (humēn),* "the sausage-shaped (membrane)" : *allantos*†, sausage + -OID.]

al·lan·to·is (ə-lăn'tō-ĭs) *n., pl.* **allantoides** (ăl'ən-tō'ə-dēz). A membranous sac that develops from the hindgut in the embryos of mam-

alkanet *An upright, hairy plant with tiny blue flowers that look like birds' eyes. It has spread all over southern Europe and eastern North America. Egyptian women made henna, a red dye for hair and nails, from it.*

PRONUNCIATION KEY

ă, pat; ā, pay; âr, care; ä, father, are; b, bib; ch, church; d, deed; ĕ, pet; ē, be; f, fife; g, gag; h, hat; hw, which; ĭ, pit; ī, pie; îr, pier; j, judge; k, kick; l, lid, needle; m, mum; n, no, sudden; ng, thing; ŏ, pot; ō, toe; ô, paw, for; oi, noise; ou, out; o͝o, book; o͞o, boot; p, pop; r, roar; s, sauce; sh, ship, dish; t, tight; th, thin, path; *th,* this, bathe; ŭ, cut; ûr, fur; v, valve; w, with; y, yes; z, zebra, size; zh, vision; ə, about, item, edible, gallop, circus, peaceful

IN FOREIGN WORDS:

à, *Fr.* ami; œ, *Fr.* feu, *Ger.* schön; ü, *Fr.* tu, *Ger.* über; KH, *Ger.* ich, *Scot.* loch; N, *Fr.* bon; y', *Fr.* Compiègne

STRESS MARKS:

Primary stress: '
in·cite' (ĭn-sīt')
Secondary stress: '
in'sight' (ĭn'sīt')

mals, birds, and reptiles. In mammals it takes part in the formation of the umbilical cord and the placenta. [New Latin, from Greek *allantoeidēs*, ALLANTOID.] —**al·lan·to·ic** (ăl′ən-tō′ĭk) *adj.*

al·lar·gan·do (ä′lär-gän′dō) *adv. Music.* To be performed more slowly. Used as a direction. [Italian, from *allargare*, to make slow, widen, ultimately from Latin *largus*, abundant, LARGE.]

all-a·round (ôl′ə-round′) *adj.* Also **all-round** (ôl′round′). 1. Comprehensive in extent or depth: *a program of all-around vocational training.* 2. Able to do many or all things well; versatile: *an all-around athlete.*

al·lay (ə-lā′) *tr.v.* **-layed, -laying, -lays.** 1. To lessen or relieve (pain or grief, for example); reduce the intensity of. 2. To calm or pacify (fear, for example); set at rest. —See Synonyms at **relieve.** [Middle English *alaien*, Old English *ālecgan* : *ā-*, away, aside + *lecgan*, to lay.] —**al·lay·er** *n.*

all clear *n.* 1. A signal, usually by siren, that an air raid is over. 2. An indication of the absence of immediate obstacles or impending danger. 3. Official approval to proceed: *We need the all clear from the boss.*

al·le·ga·tion (ăl′ə-gā′shən) *n.* 1. The act of alleging. 2. A statement offered without proof, especially regarding the wrongdoings of another; a mere assertion. 3. *Law.* A statement, charge, or claim put forward by a party to be proved or supported with evidence. [Middle English, from Latin *allēgātiō* (stem *allēgātiōn-*), from *allēgāre*, to dispatch, adduce: *ad-*, toward + *lēgāre*, to charge.]

al·lege (ə-lĕj′) *tr.v.* **-leged, -leging, -leges.** 1. To assert to be true; affirm; declare. 2. To assert without proof. 3. To bring forward (a plea or excuse, for example) in support or denial of a claim or accusation. 4. *Archaic.* To cite or quote, as in confirmation. —See Synonyms at **assert.** [Middle English *alleg(g)en*, from Norman French *alegier*, Old French *esligier*, from Vulgar Latin *exlītigāre* (unattested), to clear of charges in lawsuit: *ex-*, out of + *lītigāre*, to LITIGATE.] —**al·leg·er** *n.*

al·leged (ə-lĕjd′, ə-lĕj′ĭd) *adj.* Claimed to exist or to be as described but without proof; merely supposed: *the alleged theft.* —**al·leg·ed·ly** (ə-lĕj′ĭd-lē) *adv.*

Al·le·ghe·ny Mountains (ăl′ə-gā′nē). Also **Al·le·ghe·nies** (-nēz). Mountain range forming the western part of the Appalachian Mts. in the eastern United States. The range stretches some 800 kilometers (500 miles) through Pennsylvania, Maryland, Virginia, and West Virginia and rises to 1,480 meters (4,860 feet) at Spruce Knob in West Virginia.

al·le·giance (ə-lē′jəns) *n.* 1. Loyalty, or the obligation of loyalty, as to a nation, sovereign, or cause. 2. The obligations of a vassal to his overlord. —See Synonyms at **fidelity.** [Middle English *allegeaunce*, from Old French *ligeance*, from *li(e)ge*, LIEGE.] —**al·le·giant** *adj.*

al·le·gor·i·cal (ăl′ə-gôr′ĭ-kəl, -gŏr′ĭ-kəl) *adj.* Also **al·le·gor·ic** (ăl′-ə-gôr′ĭk, -gŏr′ĭk). Pertaining to, characteristic of, or having the nature of allegory. —**al·le·gor·i·cal·ly** *adv.*

al·le·go·rize (ăl′ə-gô-rīz′, -gə-rīz′) *v.* **-rized, -rizing, -rizes.** —*tr.* 1. To express as, or in the form of, an allegory. 2. To interpret allegorically. —*intr.* To use or make allegory. —**al·le·go·ri·za·tion** (ăl′ə-gə-rə-zā′shən) *n.* —**al·le·go·riz·er** *n.*

al·le·go·ry (ăl′ə-gôr′ē, -gōr′ē) *n., pl.* **-ries.** 1. The representation of a subject in a story, play, or picture, using the people or events portrayed to illustrate deeper or more general truths: *The story of the Holy Grail is an allegory of man's spiritual quest.* 2. An instance of such representation. 3. Any symbolic representation. [Middle English *allegorie*, from Old French, from Latin *allēgoria*, from Greek, from *allēgorein*, to speak figuratively, "speak in other terms" : *allos*, other + *agoreuein*, to speak (in public), from *agora*, an assembly.] —**al·le·go·rist** *n.*

al·le·gret·to (ăl′ə-grĕt′ō, ä′lə-) *adv. Music.* In quick tempo; slower than allegro but faster than andante. Used as a direction.
~*n., pl.* **allegrettos.** *Music.* A movement or passage in this tempo. [Italian, diminutive of ALLEGRO.] —**al·le·gret·to** *adj.*

al·le·gro (ə-lĕg′rō, ə-lā′grō) *adv. Music.* In rapid tempo; faster than allegretto but slower than presto. Used as a direction.
~*n., pl.* **allegros.** *Music.* A movement or passage in this tempo. [Italian, "lively," from Latin *alacer*, brisk.] —**al·le·gro** *adj.*

al·lele (ə-lēl′) *n.* Any of the alternative forms of a gene, which occupy the same relative position on homologous chromosomes. Also called "allelomorph." [German *Allel*, short for ALLELOMORPH.] —**al·le·lic** (ə-lē′lĭk, ə-lĕl′ĭk) *adj.*

al·le·lo·morph (ə-lē′lə-môrf′, ə-lĕl′ə-) *n.* An allele. [Greek *allēlōn*, reciprocally, from *allos*, another + -MORPH.] —**al·le·lo·mor·phic** (ə-lē′lə-môr′fĭk) *adj.* —**al·le·lo·mor·phism** (ə-lē′lə-môr′fĭz′əm) *n.*

al·le·lu·ia (ăl′ə-lōō′yə) *interj.* Used as a Christian expression of praise to God or of thanksgiving.
~*n., pl.* **alleluias.** 1. A part of the Catholic Mass beginning and ending with this word. 2. A musical setting of this. [Middle English, from Medieval Latin *allēlūja*, from Late Greek *allēlouia*, from Hebrew *hallelūyāh*, HALLELUJAH.]

al·le·mande (ăl′ə-mănd′, äl′ə-mănd′) *n.* 1. **a.** A lively, late 18th-century dance in ³/₄ time. **b.** A movement in square dancing and country dancing. 2. *Music.* The first movement of a 17th- or 18th-century classical suite. [French, feminine of *allemand*, German, from Latin *Alemannus*, singular of ALEMANNI.]

Al·len (ăl′ən), **Ethan** (1738–89). U.S. Revolutionary soldier. He commanded the Green Mountain Boys, who helped capture Fort Ticonderoga from the British (1775).

Allen, Fred, born John Florence Sullivan (1894–1956). U.S. humorist. Allen was noted for his work in vaudeville, radio, and early television and for his dry humor and deadpan delivery.

Allen, Woody, born Allen Stewart Konigsberg (1935–). U.S. film director, comic actor, and writer. His films include *Play It Again Sam* (1972), *Sleeper* (1973), *Annie Hall* (1977, two Academy Awards), and *Manhattan* (1979).

---

allegory

UNIVERSAL THEMES IN WORDS AND PICTURES
Great art that shimmers with layers of meaning

Since ancient times, artists have used allegory to express abstract themes vividly. In Greek and Roman frescoes, for instance, bulls are often more than just animals; they symbolize fertility or virility as well. In medieval religious paintings, a dove may be a mark of divine favor or a symbol of peace.

Many allegories have been literary rather than pictorial. John Bunyan's *The Pilgrim's Progress* (published in 1678) traces the hero's journey through places such as Vanity Fair and the Slough of Despond in order to illustrate the Christian's search for salvation. Jonathan Swift's book, *Gulliver's Travels* (1726) is both an adventure story and a bitter satire on the follies of mankind. And George Orwell's *Animal Farm* (1945) hides an attack on the leadership of the international Communist movement and the U.S.S.R. beneath a simple tale about a revolt by farm animals. So close is the parallel that figures such as Marx, Lenin, Trotsky, and Stalin can be identified among the animals.

LOVE CONQUERS ALL *In this allegorical painting,* Mars and Venus, *by the 15th-century Italian painter Sandro Botticelli, Mars, symbolizing war, is soothed into a peaceful sleep by the Roman goddess of love—illustrating the Christian belief that violence should be overcome by gentleness. The painting was designed to commemorate a marriage.*

Al·len·de (ä-yĕn′dā), **Salvador** (1908–73). Chilean statesman, president of Chile (1970–1973) and the first democratically elected Marxist head of government. He attempted to achieve socialism by gradual peaceful change, including land reform and nationalization, but many measures, especially the nationalization of foreign investments, were controversial, and financial credit was withdrawn from the Chilean economy. Right-wing opposition to Allende in Chile was encouraged by U.S. intervention, and his government was overthrown by a military coup in 1973, in which he was killed.

al·ler·gen (ăl′ər-jən) *n.* A substance that causes an allergy. [German *Allergen* : *Allergie,* ALLER(GY) + -GEN.] —**al·ler·gen·ic** (ăl′ər-jĕn′ĭk) *adj.*

al·ler·gic (ə-lûr′jĭk) *adj.* **1.** Characteristic of or concerning allergy. **2.** Having an allergy. **3.** *Informal.* Having a dislike; averse. Used with *to*: *allergic to work.*

al·ler·gist (ăl′ər-jĭst) *n.* A doctor specializing in allergies.

al·ler·gy (ăl′ər-jē) *n., pl.* **-gies. 1.** Excessive sensitivity to some environmental factor or substance, such as pollens, particular foods, dust, or microorganisms, causing an adverse physical reaction. **2.** *Informal.* A dislike; an aversion. [German *Allergie,* "altered reaction" : ALL(O)- + Greek *ergon,* work, effect.]

al·le·thrin (ăl′ə-thrĭn′) *n.* A synthetic amber liquid insecticide, similar to pyrethrin. [ALL(YL) + (PYR)ETHRIN.]

al·le·vi·ate (ə-lē′vē-āt′) *tr.v.* **-ated, -ating, -ates.** To make more bearable; reduce (pain or grief, for example). —See Synonyms at **relieve.** [Late Latin *alleviāre,* to lighten : Latin *ad-,* toward + *levis,* light.] —**al·le·vi·a·tion** (ə-lē′vē-ā′shən) *n.* —**al·le·vi·a·tor** *n.*

al·le·vi·a·tive (ə-lē′vē-ā′tĭv) *adj.* Also **al·le·vi·a·to·ry** (ə-lē′vē-ə-tôr′ē, -tōr′ē). Promoting alleviation.

al·ley¹ (ăl′ē) *n., pl.* **-leys. 1.** A narrow street or passageway between or behind buildings. **2.** A path between flowerbeds or trees in a garden or park. **3.** A **bowling alley** *(see).* **4.** Either of the parallel lanes at the sides of a tennis court, reserved for use in doubles play. —**up one's alley.** *Slang.* Compatible with one's interests or qualifications. [Middle English *aley,* from Old French *alee,* from the feminine past participle of *aler,* to go, from Latin *ambulāre,* to walk.]

alley² *n., pl.* **-leys.** A large playing marble; often used as the shooter. [Short for ALABASTER.]

Al·leyn (ăl′ən, -ĕn′, -ān′), **Edward** (1566–1626). English actor, one of the finest of the Elizabethan stage. Alleyn created the leading roles in Marlowe's *Tamburlaine* and *Doctor Faustus.*

al·ley·way (ăl′ē-wā′) *n.* A narrow passage between buildings.

All Fools' Day *n.* April 1, **April Fools' Day** *(see).*

all fours *pl.n.* **1.** All four limbs of an animal or person: *A baby crawls on all fours.* **2.** *Used with a singular verb.* A card game, **seven-up** *(see).*

all hail *interj. Archaic.* All health. Used as a greeting.

All·hal·low·mas (ôl′hăl′ō-məs) *n.* Also **All·hal·lows** (ôl′hăl′ōz). *Archaic.* **All Saints' Day** *(see).*

all-heal (ôl′hēl′) *n.* Any of several plants reputed to have healing powers, such as **valerian** and **self-heal** *(both of which see).*

al·li·a·ceous (ăl′ē-ā′shəs) *adj. Botany.* **1.** Belonging to the same genus (*Allium*) as onions and garlic. **2.** Tasting or smelling of onions or garlic. [Latin *allium*†, garlic + -ACEOUS.]

al·li·ance (ə-lī′əns) *n.* **1. a.** A formal pact of union joining nations or parties in a common cause. **b.** The nations or parties so conjoined. **2.** The act of allying or the state of being allied. **3.** Any union or relationship based on kinship, marriage, or common interest. **4.** A sharing or affinity of qualities or characteristics. **5.** *Botany.* A subclass of related plant families. [Middle English *alliaunce,* from Old French *aliance,* from *alier,* to ALLY.]

al·lied (ə-līd′, ăl′īd′) *adj.* **1.** Joined, especially in a pact; united. **2.** Of a similar nature; related: *allied studies.* **3. Allied.** Of or pertaining to the Allies.

Al·lies (ăl′īz′, ə-līz′) *pl.n.* **1.** In World War I, the nations allied against the Central Powers of Europe. They were France, Great Britain, and initially Russia, and later many others, including the United States. **2.** In World War II, the nations, primarily the United Kingdom, the U.S.S.R., and the United States, allied against the Axis powers.

al·li·ga·tor (ăl′ə-gā′tər) *n.* **1.** Either of two large, amphibious reptiles, *Alligator mississipiensis,* of the southeastern United States, or *A. sinensis,* of China, having sharp teeth and powerful jaws, and differing from crocodiles in having a broader, shorter snout. **2.** Loosely, any crocodilian reptile. **3.** Leather made from the hide of an alligator. **4.** A tool or machine having strong, adjustable toothed jaws for gripping or crushing. [Obsolete *alagarto,* from Spanish *el lagarto* : *el,* the, from Latin *ille,* that + *lagarto,* lizard, from Latin *lacertus,* LIZARD.]

alligator pear *n.* A tree, the **avocado** *(see),* or its fruit. [Folk etymology, variant of AVOCADO (the trees are said to grow in places infested by alligators).]

all-im·por·tant (ôl′ĭm-pôr′tənt) *adj.* Of vital importance.

all-in·clu·sive (ôl′ĭn-klōō′sĭv) *adj.* Including everything; comprehensive.

Al·ling·ham (ăl′ĭng-əm), **Margery Louise** (1904–66). British detective-story writer. She created a popular fictional detective in the deceptively mild Albert Campion and wrote a number of ingenious and later serious thrillers including *The Crime at Black Dudley* (1928), *Flowers for The Judge* (1936), *Tiger in The Smoke* (1952), and *The China Governess* (1963).

all-in wrestling (ôl′ĭn′) *n.* Professional wrestling with few restrictions on holds. —**all-in wrestler** *n.*

al·lit·er·ate (ə-lĭt′ə-rāt′) *v.* **-ated, -ating, -ates.** —*intr.* **1.** To use alliteration in speech or writing. **2.** To have or contain alliteration. —*tr.* To form or arrange with alliteration. [Back-formation from ALLITERATION.] —**al·lit·er·a·tor** *n.*

al·lit·er·a·tion (ə-lĭt′ə-rā′shən) *n.* The occurrence in a phrase or line of speech or writing of two or more words having the same initial sound; for example, *wailing in the winter wind.* [New Latin *alliterātiō* (stem *alliterātiōn-*) : Latin *ad-,* to + *littera,* LETTER.]

al·lit·er·a·tive (ə-lĭt′ə-rā′tĭv, -ər-ə-tĭv) *adj.* Of or characterized by alliteration. —**al·lit·er·a·tive·ly** *adv.* —**al·lit·er·a·tive·ness** *n.*

al·li·um (ăl′ē-əm) *n.* Any of various plants of the genus *Allium,* characterized by their pungent odor, and including the onion, leek, chive, garlic, and shallot. [New Latin *Allium,* from Latin *allium, ālium*†, garlic.]

all-night (ôl′nīt′) *adj.* **1.** Continuing throughout the night. **2.** Open all night: *an all-night diner.*

allo-, all- *prefix.* Indicates divergence, opposition, or difference; for example, **allopathy.** [Greek, other, altered, from *allos,* other.]

al·lo·bar (ăl′ə-bär′) *n. Physics.* A mixture of isotopes differing in composition from the natural isotopic composition of the element. [ALLO- + Greek *baros,* weight]

al·lo·cate (ăl′ə-kāt′) *tr.v.* **-cated, -cating, -cates. 1.** To designate for a special purpose; set apart: *allocate funds to clean up toxic chemical dumps.* **2.** To distribute as a share; apportion; allot. **3.** To determine the location of; locate. —See Synonyms at **assign.** [Medieval Latin *allocāre,* to place to : Latin *ad-,* toward + *locāre,* to place, from *locus,* place, LOCUS.] —**al·lo·ca·ble** (ăl′ə-kə-bəl) *adj.*

al·lo·ca·tion (ăl′ə-kā′shən) *n.* **1.** The act of allocating or the state of being allocated. **2.** A portion or share that has been allocated.

al·lo·chem (ăl′ə-kĕm′) *n. Geology.* A discrete particle, such as a fossil, oolite, or intraclast, found in a limestone. [ALLO- + CHEM(ICAL), referring to rocks, such as limestones, deposited from solution].

al·lo·cu·tion (ăl′ə-kyōō′shən) *n.* A formal and authoritative speech or address. [Latin *allocūtiō,* from *alloqui* (past participle *allocūtus*), to speak to : *ad-,* to + *loquī,* to speak.]

al·lo·di·um, a·lo·di·um (ə-lō′dē-əm) *n., pl.* **-dia** (-dē-ə). Land held in absolute ownership, and without obligation or service to any feudal overlord. [Medieval Latin *allodium,* from Frankish *al-ōd-* (unattested), "complete property" : *al-,* ALL + *ōd-* (unattested), property.] —**al·lo·di·al** *adj.* —**al·lo·di·al·ly** *adv.*

al·log·a·my (ə-lŏg′ə-mē) *n. Botany.* **Cross-fertilization** *(see).* [ALLO- + -GAMY.] —**al·log·a·mous** *adj.*

al·lo·graph (ăl′ə-grăf′, -gräf′) *n.* **1.** Writing, especially a signature, made by one person on behalf of another. **2.** Any of several ways of representing a sound in writing, or of writing a letter of the alphabet. [ALLO- + -GRAPH.]

al·lom·er·ism (ə-lŏm′ə-rĭz′əm) *n.* Similarity in crystalline form in substances that have different chemical compositions. [ALLO- + Greek *meros,* part.] —**al·lom·er·ous** *adj.*

al·lom·e·try (ə-lŏm′ə-trē) *n. Biology.* The study of the change in proportion of various parts of an organism as a consequence of growth. [ALLO- + -METRY.] —**al·lo·met·ric** (ăl′ə-mĕt′rĭk) *adj.*

al·lo·morph (ăl′ə-môrf′) *n.* **1.** *Mineralogy.* A **paramorph** *(see).* **2.** *Linguistics.* Any of the variant forms of a morpheme; for example, the phonetic *s* of *cats, z* of *dogs,* and *iz* of *horses* are allomorphs of the English morpheme *s.* [ALLO- + -MORPH.] —**al·lo·mor·phic** (ăl′ə-môr′fĭk) *adj.* —**al·lo·mor·phism** *n.*

al·lo·path (ăl′ə-păth′) *n.* Also **al·lop·a·thist** (ə-lŏp′ə-thĭst). A person who practices allopathy.

al·lop·a·thy (ə-lŏp′ə-thē) *n.* Medical treatment by orthodox means, using drugs that alleviate the symptoms of the disease. Compare **homeopathy.** [German *Allopathie* : ALLO- + -PATHY.] —**al·lo·path·ic** (ăl′ə-păth′ĭk) *adj.* —**al·lo·path·i·cal·ly** *adv.*

al·lo·pat·ric (ăl′ə-păt′rĭk) *adj. Ecology.* Occurring in separate, widely differing areas. Compare **sympatric.** [From ALLO- + Greek *patra,* fatherland, from *patēr,* father.] —**al·lo·pat·ri·cal·ly** *adv.*

al·lo·phane (ăl′ə-fān′) *n.* An amorphous clay mineral, essentially hydrous aluminum silicate. [Greek *allophanēs,* "appearing otherwise" : ALLO- + -PHANE.]

al·lo·phone (ăl′ə-fōn′) *n. Linguistics.* Any of the variant forms of a phoneme; for example, the aspirated *p* of *pit* and the unaspirated *p* of *spit* are allophones of the English phoneme *p.* [ALLO- + -PHONE.] —**al·lo·phon·ic** (ăl′ə-fŏn′ĭk) *adj.*

al·lo·pu·ri·nol (ăl′ō-pyŏŏr′ə-nôl′) *n.* A drug, $C_5H_4N_4O$, used in the treatment of gout, that acts by reducing the amount of uric acid in the blood and tissues. [ALLO- + PURIN(E) + -OL.]

all-or-none (ôl′ər-nŭn′) *adj.* Designating a physiological response, especially a nerve impulse, that will only occur if the stimulus that elicits it is above a certain threshold value. Above this threshold the response is maximal.

all-or-noth·ing (ôl′ər-nŭth′ĭng) *adj.* Depending upon or prepared to accept only complete success: *He had an all-or-nothing approach to the venture.*

al·lot (ə-lŏt′) *tr.v.* **-lotted, -lotting, -lots. 1.** To distribute; apportion. **2.** To give or assign; allocate: *allot three weeks to a project.* —See Synonyms at **assign.** [Middle English *allotten,* from Old French *aloter* : *a-,* from Latin *ad-,* to + *lot,* a portion, lot, from Frankish *lot* (unattested).] —**al·lot·tee** *n.* —**al·lot·ter** *n.*

al·lot·ment (ə-lŏt′mənt) *n.* **1.** The act of allotting. **2.** That which is allotted. **3.** A portion of a serviceman's pay set aside for a member of his family or for insurance.

al·lo·trope (ăl′ə-trōp′) *n.* Any of the different crystalline or molecu-

allium *This species of wild garlic,* Allium ursinum, *known as ramson, or bear's garlic, flavors the milk of any cow that eats it. The* Allium *genus contains about 280 species, including numerous garden flowers and all the onion family.*

PRONUNCIATION KEY

ă, pat; ā, pay; âr, care;
ä, father, are; b, bib;
ch, church; d, deed; ĕ, pet;
ē, be; f, fife; g, gag; h, hat;
hw, which; ĭ, pit; ī, pie;
îr, pier; j, judge; k, kick;
l, lid, needle; m, mum;
n, no, sudden; ng, thing;
ŏ, pot; ō, toe; ô, paw, for;
oi, noise; ou, out; ŏŏ, book;
ōō, boot; p, pop; r, roar;
s, sauce; sh, ship, dish;
t, tight; th, thin, path;
th, this, bathe; ŭ, cut; ûr, fur;
v, valve; w, with; y, yes;
z, zebra, size; zh, vision;
ə, about, item, edible, gallop, circus, peaceful

IN FOREIGN WORDS:

à, *Fr.* ami; œ, *Fr.* feu, *Ger.* schön; ü, *Fr.* tu, *Ger.* über; KH, *Ger.* ich, *Scot.* loch; N, *Fr.* bon; y′, *Fr.* Compiègne

STRESS MARKS:

Primary stress: ′
in·cite′ (ĭn-sīt′)
Secondary stress: ′
in′sight′ (ĭn′sīt′)

lar forms of an element that displays allotropy. [Back-formation from ALLOTROPY.]

al·lot·ro·py (ə-lŏt′rə-pē) *n.* The existence, especially in the solid state, of two or more crystalline or molecular structural forms of an element. Diamond and graphite, for example, are allotropic forms of carbon. [ALLO- + -TROPY.] —**al·lo·trop·ic** (ăl′ə-trŏp′ĭk), **al·lo·trop·i·cal** *adj.* —**al·lo·trop·i·cal·ly** *adv.*

all′ ot·ta·va (äl ō-tä′və). *adv. Music.* Symbol **va** To be played an octave higher or lower than written. [Italian, "at the octave."] —**all′ ot·ta·va** *adj.*

all out *adv.* With maximum effort, determination, or strength: *She went all out to win the contest.*

all-out (ôl′out′) *adj.* Using all one's resources; holding nothing in reserve: *an all-out effort.*

all over *adv.* **1.** In every possible place; everywhere. **2.** *Informal.* Typically; in every respect: *He refused to back down—that's him all over.*

all-o·ver (ôl′ō′vər) *adj.* Covering an entire surface.

al·low (ə-lou′) *v.* **-lowed, -low·ing, -lows.** —*tr.* **1.** To raise or constitute no objection, restraint, or bar to; let happen or be done; permit: *Do the rules allow a recount?* **2.** To acknowledge or admit; concede: *allow the legality of a claim.* **3.** To permit to have. **4.** To make provision for: *allow time for a coffee break.* **5.** To permit the presence of: *No pets allowed.* **6.** To provide (the needed amount): *allow funds in case of emergency.* **7.** To grant as a discount or in exchange: *They allowed me twenty dollars on my old typewriter.* —*intr.* **1.** To make an allowance or provision. Used with *for: allow for bad weather.* **2.** To permit or accommodate; be susceptible. Used with *of: a clause allowing of several interpretations.* [Middle English *allowen,* from Old French *al(l)ouer,* to permit, approve, a blend of: (a) Medieval Latin *allocāre,* to assign, ALLOCATE, and (b) Latin *allaudāre,* to give praise to : *ad-,* to + *laudāre,* to praise, LAUD.]

al·low·a·ble (ə-lou′ə-bəl) *adj.* That may be allowed; permissible.

al·low·ance (ə-lou′əns) *n.* **1.** The act of allowing. **2.** A regular provision of money, food, or the like, as to a dependent. **3.** Money provided for a particular purpose: *a clothing allowance.* **4.** A price reduction granted as in exchange for used merchandise; a discount. **5.** A consideration for something that might happen: *an allowance for breakage.* **6. allowances.** A taking into account of modifying factors or extenuating circumstances: *make allowances for his age.* **7.** An allowed difference in dimension of closely mating machine parts.
~*tr.v.* **allowanced, -ancing, -ances. 1.** To restrict to an allowance. **2.** To put on an allowance.

al·low·ed·ly (ə-lou′ĭd-lē) *adv.* By general admission; admittedly.

al·loy (ăl′oi′, ə-loi′) *n.* **1.** A macroscopically homogeneous mixture or solid solution of two or more metals or of a metal with an element such as carbon, with the atoms of one replacing or occupying interstitial positions between atoms of the other. **2.** Anything added that lowers value or purity.
~*tr.v.* (ə-loi′, ăl′oi′) **alloyed, -loying, -loys. 1.** To combine (metals) to form an alloy. **2.** To lower the purity or value of (a metal) by mixing with an inferior metal. **3.** To debase or reduce in purity by the addition of an inferior element. [Old French *aloi,* from *aloier, aleier,* to alloy, to bind, from Latin *alligāre,* to bind to, ALLY.]

al·loyed junction (ə-loid′, ăl′oid′) *n. Electronics.* A semiconductor junction formed by alloying a metal contact with a wafer of semiconducting material.

alloy steel *n.* Any of various types of steel that contain large amounts of other metals, such as chromium, vanadium, or tungsten, used for special purposes. Compare **carbon steel.**

all-pur·pose (ôl′pûr′pəs) *adj.* Fulfilling many different functions; capable of being used in various ways: *an all-purpose vehicle.*

all right *adj.* **1.** Satisfactory; as desired; average. **2.** Correct. **3.** Not injured or sick. **4.** Permissible: *Is it all right to leave now?*
~*adv.* **1.** To one's satisfaction. **2.** Safely. **3.** Very well; yes. Used to express agreement or concession. **4.** Without a doubt: *He's a fool, all right!*
Usage: It is still not acceptable to write *all right* as a single word, *alright,* despite the parallel to words like *already* and *altogether* and despite the fact that in casual speech the expression is often pronounced as if it were one word.

all-right (ôl′rīt′) *adj. Slang.* **1.** Dependable; honorable: *He's an all-right guy.* **2.** Good; excellent: *an all-right movie.*

all-round. Variant of **all-around.**

all-round·er (ôl′roun′dər) *n. Chiefly British.* A person who has many talents or abilities, especially in sport.

All Saints' Day *n.* November 1, a church festival in honor of all saints.

all-seed (ôl′sēd′) *n. Botany.* Any of several plants having many seeds, such as **knotgrass** (see).

All Souls' Day *n.* November 2, observed by the Roman Catholic Church as a day of prayer for souls in purgatory.

all·spice (ôl′spīs′) *n.* **1.** A tropical American tree, *Pimenta officinalis,* having small white flowers and aromatic berries. **2.** The dried berries of this tree, used whole or ground as a spice. Also called "pimento." [ALL + SPICE, after its supposed flavor of nutmeg, cloves, and cinnamon.]

all-star (ôl′stär′) *adj.* Made up wholly of star performers: *a play with an all-star cast.*
~*n. Sports.* A player chosen for an all-star team.

all-time (ôl′tīm′) *adj. Informal.* Of all time: *one of the all-time greats of football.*

all told *adv.* In all; altogether; with everything or everyone considered: *over 50 deaths all told.*

al·lude (ə-lōōd′) *intr.v.* **-luded, -luding, -ludes.** To make an indirect reference; refer, without identifying specifically. Used with *to: When he said he had received expert help, the speaker was alluding to his wife.* [Latin *allūdere,* to play with, jest at : *ad-,* to + *lūdere,* to play, from *lūdus,* game.]

al·lure (ə-lōōr′) *tr. v.* **-lured, -luring, -lures.** To entice with something desirable; tempt.
~*n.* The power to entice or tempt; fascination; strong attraction. [Middle English *aluren,* from Old French *aleurrer : a-,* to + *leurrer,* to lure, from *loirre, leurre,* LURE.] —**al·lure·ment** *n.* —**al·lur·er** *n.*

al·lur·ing (ə-lōōr′ĭng) *adj.* Tempting, enticing, or fascinating. —**al·lur·ing·ly** *adv.*

al·lu·sion (ə-lōō′zhən) *n.* **1.** The act of alluding **2.** An indirect, but pointed or meaningful, reference. [Late Latin *allūsiō* (stem *allūsiōn-*), a playing with, from Latin *allūdere* (past participle *allūsus*), to play with, ALLUDE.]

al·lu·sive (ə-lōō′sĭv) *adj.* Containing or making allusions; suggestive. —**al·lu·sive·ly** *adv.* —**al·lu·sive·ness** *n.*

al·lu·vi·al (ə-lōō′vē-əl) *adj.* **1.** Of, pertaining to, or composed of alluvium. **2.** Found in alluvium: *alluvial gold.*

alluvial fan *n.* A fan-shaped accumulation of alluvium deposited at the mouth of a ravine. Also called "alluvial cone."

alluvial plain *n.* A plain resulting from the deposit of alluvium.

al·lu·vi·on (ə-lōō′vē-ən) *n.* **1.** Alluvium. **2.** The flow of water against a shore or bank. **3.** Inundation by water; flooding. **4.** *Law.* The formation of new land, especially along a river bed, by deposited alluvium. Compare **avulsion.** [Latin *alluviō* (stem *alluviōn-*), from *alluere,* to wash against : *ad-,* to + *lavere,* to wash.]

al·lu·vi·um (ə-lōō′vē-əm) *n., pl.* **-viums** or **-via** (-vē-ə). Any sediment deposited by flowing water, as in a river bed, flood plain, or delta. Also called "alluvion." [Latin, from the neuter of *alluvius,* alluvial, from *alluere,* to wash against. See **alluvion.**]

all-weath·er (ôl′wĕth′ər) *adj.* Suitable for or usable in any kind of weather: *all-weather garments.*

al·ly¹ (ə-lī′, ăl′ī′) *v.* **-lied, -lying, -lies.** —*tr.* **1.** To unite or connect in a formal relationship or bond, as by treaty, marriage, or other arrangement. Used with *to* or *with: The United States allies itself with Great Britain.* **2.** To connect or associate. Used chiefly in the passive. —*intr.* To enter into an alliance.
~*n.* (ăl′ī, ə-lī′) *pl.* **allies. 1.** One that is united with another in some formal or personal relationship. See **Allies. 2.** A close associate or supporter. **3.** *Biology.* A plant or animal species or other group that is related to another such group. —See Synonyms at **partner.** [Middle English *al(l)ien,* from Old French *alier,* from Latin *alligāre,* to bind to : *ad-,* to + *ligāre,* to bind.]

ally². Variant of **alley** (a marble).

al·lyl (ăl′ĭl) *n.* The univalent organic radical CH_2:$CHCH_2$. [Latin *allium†,* garlic + -YL (so called because it was first obtained from garlic).] —**al·lyl·ic** (ə-lĭl′ĭk) *adj.*

allyl alcohol *n.* A colorless, poisonous, flammable liquid, CH_2:$CHCH_2OH$, used in poison gas, resins, plastics, and herbicides.

allyl resin *n.* Any of a class of synthetic resins derived from allyl alcohol esters and dibasic acids, and used as laminating adhesives and in varnishes and molding compounds.

almacantar. Variant of **almucantar.**

Al Madinah. See **Medina.**

Al·ma·gest (ăl′mə-jĕst′) *n.* **1.** A comprehensive work on astronomy and geometry compiled by Ptolemy about A.D. 150. **2.** *Sometimes* **almagest.** In medieval science, any similar work concerned with astronomy or alchemy. [Middle English *almageste,* from Old French, from Arabic *al-majisti : al,* the + Greek *megistē (suntaxis),* greatest (collection), feminine of *megistos,* superlative of *megas,* great.]

al·ma ma·ter, Al·ma Ma·ter (ăl′mə mä′tər, ăl′mə) *n.* **1.** The school, college, or university that one has attended. **2.** The anthem or school song of an institution of higher learning. [Latin, "cherishing or fostering mother."]

al·ma·nac (ôl′mə-năk, ăl′-) *n.* **1.** An annual publication including calendars with weather forecasts, astronomical information, tide tables, and other related tabular information. **2.** An annual publication composed of various lists, charts, and tables of useful information in many unrelated fields. [Middle English *almenak,* from Medieval Latin (Roger Bacon) *almanac(h)†.*]

Al Manamah. See **Manama.**

al·man·dine (ăl′mən-dēn′) *n.* Also **al·man·dite** (-dīt′). A deep violet-red garnet, essentially $Fe_3Al_2(SiO_4)_3$, found in metamorphic rocks and used as a gemstone. [Variant of earlier *alabandine,* from Middle English *alabandina,* from Late Latin *(gemma) alabandīna,* "(gem) of *Alabanda,*" town in Caria, ancient district of Asia Minor, famous for jewelry.]

Al·ma-Tad·e·ma (ăl′mə-tăd′ə-mə), **Sir Lawrence** (1836–1912). Dutch-born British painter. He is famous for his grand romantic paintings set in classical Greece and Rome and ancient Egypt.

al·me·mar (ăl-mē′mär) *n. Judaism.* A kind of pulpit, a **bema** (see). [Hebrew *almēmār,* from Arabic *al-minbar,* the pulpit.]

Al·me·rí·a (ăl′mä-rē′ä). Seaport on the Gulf of Almería in the Mediterranean and the capital of Almería province in the Andalusia region of Spain.

---

al·might·y (ôl-mī′tē) *adj.* **1.** All-powerful; omnipotent: *almighty God.* **2.** *Informal.* Great. Used as an intensive: *an almighty din.* —*n.* **the Almighty.** God. —*adv. Slang.* Extremely: *almighty scared.* [Middle English *almighty,* Old English *ealmihtig : eall,* ALL + *mihtig,* from *miht,* MIGHT.] —**al·might·i·ly** *adv.*

al·mond (ä′mənd, ăm′ənd, äl′mənd, ăl′-) *n.* **1.** A small tree, *Prunus amygdalus,* native to the Mediterranean region, having pink flowers and fruit containing an edible nut. **2.** The nut itself, ellipsoid in shape, and having a soft yellowish-brown shell. **3.** Something having the oval, pointed shape of an almond. **4.** Pale tan. [Middle English *almande,* from Old French, from Late Latin *amandula,* corruption of Latin *amygdala,* from Greek *amugdalē.*] —**al·mond** *adj.*

al·mon·er (ăl′mə-nər, ä′mə-) *n.* **1.** One who distributes alms, as for a church or royal family. **2.** *British.* Formerly, a social worker in a hospital. [Middle English *a(u)moner,* from Norman French, from Old French *aumosnier,* from *amosne,* alms, from Vulgar Latin *alemosina* (unattested), from Late Latin *eleēmosyna,* ALMS.]

al·mon·ry (ăl′mən-rē, ä′mən-) *n., pl.* **-ries.** The house of an almoner; a place at which alms are distributed.

Al·mo·ra·vides (ăl-môr′ə-vīdz′, -môr′-). Also **Al·mo·ra·vids** (-vĭdz′). A Berber dynasty and Muslim sect, based in the western Sahara, that conquered northwestern Africa and much of Spain in the 11th and 12th centuries. [Arabic *al-murābitūn,* "holy ones," from *murābit,* holy-man.]

al·most (ôl′mōst′, ôl-mōst′) *adv.* Slightly short of; not quite; all but; very nearly. [Middle English *almost,* Old English *(e)almǣst,* completely, for the most part : *eall,* ALL + *mǣst,* MOST.]

alms (ämz) *pl.n.* Money or goods given to the poor as charity. [Middle English *almes, almesse,* from Old English *ælmesse,* from Common Germanic *alemosina* (unattested), alteration (through influence of Latin *alimōnia;* see **alimony**) of Late Latin *eleēmosyna,* from Greek *eleēmosunē,* pity, from *eleēmōn,* pitiful, from *eleos†,* pity.]

alms·house (ämz′hous′) *n.* **1.** A poorhouse. **2.** *British.* A house founded and supported by a charity to provide accommodation for the poor and elderly.

alms·man (ämz′mən) *n., pl.* **-men** (-mĭn). One dependent on alms for support.

al·mu·can·tar (ăl′myōō-kăn′tər) *n.* Also **al·ma·can·tar** (ăl′mə-kăn′tər). *Astronomy.* **1.** A circle on the celestial sphere that is parallel to the horizontal plane. **2.** An instrument for measuring azimuth and altitude. [Middle English, from Medieval Latin *almucantarath,* from Arabic *almukantarāt,* the sundial.]

al·ni·co (ăl′nĭ-kō′) *n.* Any of a class of hard, strong alloys of aluminum, cobalt, copper, iron, nickel, and sometimes niobium or tantalum, used to make strong permanent magnets. [*Al*uminium *ni*ckel *co*balt.]

alodium. Variant of **allodium.**

al·oe (ăl′ō) *n.* Any of various plants of the genus *Aloe,* mostly native to southern Africa, having fleshy, spiny-toothed leaves and red or yellow flowers. [Middle English *aloe,* Old English *aluwe,* from Latin *aloē,* from Greek, probably of Oriental origin.] —**al·o·et·ic** (ăl′ō-ĕt′ĭk) *adj.*

al·oes (ăl′ōz) *n. Used with a singular verb.* **1.** A cathartic drug derived from the aloe, **bitter aloes** (see). **2.** The fragrant wood of a tree, *Aquilaria agallocha,* of tropical Asia. In this sense, also called "aloes wood," "eaglewood."

a·loft (ə-lôft′, ə-lŏft′) *adv.* **1.** In or into a high place; high or higher up. **2.** *Nautical.* In or toward the upper rigging. —*prep.* On top of: *A strange flag was flying aloft the main mast.* [Middle English, from Old Norse *ā lopt : ā,* on, in + *lopt,* air, sky.]

a·lo·ha (ä-lō′hä′) *interj.* Used in Hawaii to express greeting or farewell. [Hawaiian, "love."]

al·o·in (ăl′ō-ĭn) *n.* A bitter crystalline compound obtained from the aloe and used as a laxative. [ALO(E) + -IN.]

a·lone (ə-lōn′) *adj.* **1.** Apart from others; single; solitary. **2. a.** Excluding anything or anyone else; with nothing further; only: *Man cannot live by bread alone.* **b.** Taking no one or nothing else into account: *The price alone should have made you suspicious.* **3.** Unique or by oneself in a particular position, belief, or ability: *I wasn't alone in opposing his plan.* **4.** To take action independently of others. —**leave alone.** *Informal.* To refrain from tampering or interfering with. —**let alone.** Not to speak of or think of; even less: *I haven't a minute to spare, let alone an hour.* [Middle English, from *al one :* ALL + ONE.] —**a·lone** *adv.* —**a·lone·ness** *n.*

a·long (ə-lông′, ə-lŏng′) *adv.* **1.** With a progressive onward motion; forward: *walking along at a brisk pace.* **2.** In association; together. Usually used with *with.* **3.** As company; as a companion: *Bring your son along.* **4.** In a line; from one to another: *Read the note, and pass it along.* —**be along.** *Informal.* To come; arrive at a place: *Our guests should be along very soon.* —**get along. 1.** To manage successfully; survive. **2.** To be compatible; agree: *Do the cat and dog get along?* —*prep.* **1.** Over or through the length of: *running along the road.* **2.** In a line with; following the length or path of: *trees growing along the river.* [Middle English *along,* Old English *andlang,* "extending opposite" : *and-,* against, facing + *lang,* extending, LONG.]

a·long·shore (ə-lông′shôr′, -shōr′, ə-lŏng′-) *adv.* Along, near, or by the shore, either on land or in the water.

a·long·side (ə-lông′sīd′, ə-lŏng′sīd′) *adv.* Along, near, at, or to the side of something, especially a ship. —*prep.* By the side of; side by side with.

a·loof (ə-lōōf′) *adj.* Distant, especially in one's relations with other people; reserved. —*adv.* At a distance, but within view; apart; withdrawn. [From obsolete *aloufe!* (nautical use), "(steer the ship) up into the wind!" : A- (to) + *loufe,* LUFF.] —**a·loof·ly** *adv.* —**a·loof·ness** *n.*

al·o·pe·ci·a (ăl′ə-pē′shē-ə, -pē′shə) *n.* Loss of hair; baldness. [Latin *alopēcia,* mange of fox, baldness, from Greek *alōpekia,* from *alōpēx,* fox.] —**al·o·pe·cic** (ăl′ə-pē′sĭk) *adj.*

a·loud (ə-loud′) *adv.* **1.** Louder than a whisper; audibly: *afraid to say it aloud.* **2.** With the voice; not silently: *Read aloud.*

Al·o·y·si·us (ăl′ō-ĭsh′ē-əs, -ĭsh′əs), **Saint,** born Luigi Gonzaga (1568-91). Italian Jesuit, patron saint of youth; canonized in 1726.

alp (ălp) *n.* **1.** A shoulder high on a mountain side; especially, a gentle, grassy slope above a valley, often used as summer pasture. **2.** A high mountain peak, especially one of the **Alps** (see).

al·pac·a (ăl-păk′ə) *n.* **1.** A domesticated South American mammal, *Lama pacos,* related to the llama, and having fine, long wool. **2. a.** The silky wool of this animal. **b.** Cloth made from this wool. **3.** A glossy cotton or rayon and wool fabric, usually black. [Spanish, from Aymara *alpaco,* from *packo,* reddish brown.]

al·pen·glow (ăl′pən-glō′) *n.* A rosy glow appearing around snow-covered mountain peaks at sunrise or dusk on a clear day. [Partial translation of German *Alpenglühen : Alpen,* ALPS + *glühen,* to glow.]

al·pen·horn (ăl′pən-hôrn′) *n.* Also **alp·horn** (ălp′hôrn′). A curved wooden horn, sometimes as long as 20 feet, used especially formerly by herdsmen in the Alps to call cows to pasture. [German *Alpenhorn : Alpen,* ALPS + *Horn,* HORN]

al·pen·stock (ăl′pən-stŏk′) *n.* A long staff with an iron point, used by mountain climbers. [German *Alpenstock : Alpen,* ALPS + *Stock,* a staff, from Old High German *stoc.*]

al·pes·trine (ăl-pĕs′trĭn) *adj. Botany.* Growing at high altitudes; alpine or subalpine. [Medieval Latin *alpestris,* mountainous, from *Alpes,* the ALPS.]

al·pha (ăl′fə) *n.* **1.** The first letter in the Greek alphabet, written A, α. Transliterated in English as *A, a.* See feature at **alphabet. 2.** The first of anything; beginning. **3.** *Astronomy.* The brightest or main star in a constellation. **4.** *Physics* **a.** An alpha particle. **b.** An alpha ray. —*adj. Chemistry.* Closest to the functional group of atoms in a molecule. [Middle English, from Latin, from Greek, from a Phoenician word akin to Hebrew *āleph,* ALEPH.]

alpha and omega *n.* **1.** The first and the last: *"I am Alpha and Omega, the beginning and the ending, saith the Lord"* (Revelation 1:8). **2.** The most important part of something.

Alpha A·quil·ae (ə-kwĭl′ē) *n.* A star, **Altair** (see).

al·pha·bet (ăl′fə-bĕt′, -bət) *n.* **1.** The set of letters in which a language or group of languages is written, arranged in the order fixed by custom. **2.** Any system of characters or symbols representing sounds, words, or things: *the semaphore alphabet.* **3.** The basic or elementary principles of anything; rudiments. [Latin *alphabētum,* from Greek *alphabētos :* ALPHA + BETA.] See feature, next page.

al·pha·bet·i·cal (ăl′fə-bĕt′ĭ-kəl) *adj.* Also **al·pha·bet·ic** (-bĕt′ĭk). **1.** Arranged in the customary order of the letters of an alphabet. **2.** Of, pertaining to, or expressed by an alphabet. —**al·pha·bet·i·cal·ly** *adv.*

al·pha·bet·ize (ăl′fə-bə-tīz′) *tr.v.* **-ized, -izing, -izes. 1.** To arrange in or put into alphabetical order. **2.** To express by or supply with an alphabet. —**al·pha·bet·i·za·tion** (ăl′fə-bĕt′ə-zā′shən) *n.* —**al·pha·bet·iz·er** *n.*

Alpha Cen·tau·ri (sĕn-tôr′ē) *n.* A double star in Centaurus, the brightest in the constellation, 4.4 light-years from Earth.

Alpha Cru·cis (krōō′sĭs) *n.* A double star in the constellation Crux, approximately 230 light-years from Earth.

alpha decay *n. Physics.* A form of radioactive decay in which an unstable nucleus emits an alpha particle, transforming into a lighter nucleus.

al·pha·fe·to·pro·tein (ăl′fə-fē′tō-prō′tēn) *n. Abbr.* **afp** A protein formed in the fetus and present in the amniotic fluid surrounding it in the womb. Its presence in high levels is used as a prenatal diagnostic test for such abnormal conditions as spina bifida. See **amniocentesis.**

Alpha Le·o·nis (lē-ō′nĭs) *n.* A star, **Regulus** (see).

al·pha·nu·mer·ic (ăl′fə-nōō-mĕr′ĭk, -nyōō-mĕr′ĭk) *adj.* Also **al·pha·mer·ic** (ăl′fə-mĕr′ĭk). **1. a.** Consisting of alphabetical and numerical symbols. **b.** Consisting of such symbols and also of punctuation marks, mathematical symbols, and other conventional symbols used in computer work. **2.** Of, pertaining to, or employing an alphanumeric code or system.

alpha particle *n. Symbol* α A positively charged composite particle consisting of two protons and two neutrons; a helium-atom nucleus.

alpha privative *n.* The Greek negative prefix *a-* (*an-* before vowels). See **a-** (negative prefix).

alpha ray *n.* A narrow stream of alpha particles.

alpha rhythm *n.* One of the electroencephalographic waveforms found in recordings of the electrical activity of the adult brain, characteristically 8 to 12 smooth, regular oscillations per second in subjects at rest. Also called "alpha wave." Compare **beta rhythm.**

al·pho·sis (ăl-fō′sĭs) *n. Pathology.* Lack of skin pigment, as in albinism. [New Latin : Greek *alphos,* kind of leprosy + -OSIS.]

al·pine (ăl′pīn′) *adj.* **1.** Of or pertaining to high mountains.

aloe *A colorful plant native to Africa. There are at least 275 species of aloe, but new types are still being discovered. This one grows wild in the Namib Desert of Namibia.*

ABC's OF WRITTEN COMMUNICATION
Letters of the alphabet replaced symbolic pictures

The alphabet developed from ancient writing systems in which each word was represented by a picture (pictography), as in Egyptian hieroglyphics, or later by a symbol (ideography), as in Chinese. In these systems many thousands of symbols had to be learned.

Around 2000 B.C., systems developed in the Middle East in which each symbol stood for a syllable of the spoken language. A syllabary, as it was called, was much simpler to learn than a pictographic system because it contained far fewer symbols. The Japanese began using a syllable script known as *kana* as late as A.D. 800, and it is still in use.

The alphabet made written language even easier to learn, especially as successive developments reduced the number of letters needed in most languages to between 20 and 40. The number of letters used depends upon the number of sounds the alphabet was devised to represent.

The first alphabet was the North Semitic, which emerged about 1700 B.C. at the eastern end of the Mediterranean. From this alphabet stemmed the Hebrew, the Arabic, and the Phoenician, which was introduced into Europe by the Greeks about 1000 B.C. The Greeks modified the Phoenician, standardizing the direction of the written lines to read from left to right, rather than in various different directions. They also added symbols for vowel sounds.

All Western alphabets evolved from the Greek. First came the Etruscan in central Italy about 800 B.C. This led to the Latin or Roman, and the subsequent variations of it that suited the language of different countries, including English. In eastern Europe, the Cyrillic alphabet, from which developed the Bulgarian, and then the Russian, Ukrainian, and Serbian, was devised from the Greek in the 9th century A.D. by St. Cyril, a Greek missionary.

In the chart below, the transliteration column shows the Roman (English) equivalent of the Hebrew, Arabic, Greek, and Cyrillic letters.

ROMAN	GREEK			CYRILLIC (Russian)		HEBREW			ARABIC		
form	form	name	transliteration	form	transliteration	form	name	transliteration	form	name	transliteration
A a	Αα	alpha	a	А а	a	א	'aleph, 'alef	'	ا	'alif	'
B b	Ββ	beta	b	Б б	b	ב	bēth	b(bh)	ب	bā	b
C c	Γγ	gamma	g	В в	v	ג	gimel	g(gh)	ت	tā	t
D d	Δδ	delta	d	Г г	g	ד	dāleth	d(dh)	ث	thā	th
E e	Εε	epsilon	e	Д д	d	ה	hē	h	ج	jīm	j
F f	Ζζ	zēta	z	Е е	e	ו	vav waw	w	ح	ḥā	ḥ
G g	Ηη	ēta	ē	Ё ё	yo	ז	zayin	z	خ	khā	kh
H h	Θθ	thēta	th	Ж ж	zh	ח	ḥeth	ḥ	د	dāl	d
I i	Ιι	iota	i	З з	z	ט	ṭeth	ṭ	ذ	dhāl	dh
J j	Κκ	kappa	k	И и, Й й	i, ī	י	yod, yodh	y	ر	rā	r
K k	Λλ	lambda	l	К к	k	ך כ	kāph	k(kh)	ز	zāy	z
L l	Μμ	mu	m	Л л	l	ל	lāmedh	l	س	sīn	s
M m	Νν	nu	n	М м	m	ם מ	mēm	m	ش	shīn	sh
N n	Ξξ	xi	x	Н н	n	ן נ	nūn	n	ص	ṣād	ṣ
O o	Οο	omicron	o	О о	o	ס	samekh	s	ض	ḍād	ḍ
P p	Ππ	pi	p	П п	p	ע	'ayin	'	ط	ṭā	ṭ
Q q	Ρρ	rhō	r, rh	Р р	r	ף פ	pē	p(ph)	ظ	ẓā	ẓ
R r	Σσς	sigma	s	С с	s	ץ צ	sade, ṣadhe	ṣ	ع	'ayn	'
S s	Ττ	tau	t	Т т	t	ק	qōph	q	غ	ghayn	gh
T t	Υυ	upsilon	u	У у	u	ר	rēsh	r	ف	fā	f
U u	Φφ	phi	ph	Ф ф	f	שׂ	sin	s	ق	qāf	q
V v	Χχ	chi khi	kh	Х х	kh	שׁ	shin	sh	ك	kāf	k
W w	Ψψ	psi	ps	Ц ц	ts	ת	tāv, tāw	t(th)	ل	lām	l
X x	Ωω	ōmega	ō	Ч ч	ch				م	mīm	m
Y y				Ш ш	sh				ن	nūn	n
Z z				Щ щ	shch				ه	hā	h
				Ъ ъ	'				و	wāw	w
				Ь ь	'				ى	yā	y
				Ы ы	y						
				Э э	e						
				Ю ю	yu						
				Я я	ya						

2. a. *Biology.* Living or growing on mountains above the treeline. **b.** *Botany.* Small enough to be suitable for growing in a rock garden. **3.** Intended for or concerned with mountaineering. **4. Alpine. a.** Of, pertaining to, or characteristic of the Alps or their inhabitants. **b.** Of or pertaining to a subdivision of the Caucasian race predominant around the Alps. **5.** *Geology.* Of, pertaining to, or designating the last great mountain-building period. It began in mid-Tertiary times and resulted in the main fold-mountain ranges of Europe and Asia, including the Alps. **6. Alpine.** Of or designating downhill and slalom skiing events. Compare **Nordic.**
~*n.* *Botany.* An alpine plant. [Latin *Alpīnus,* of the ALPS.]

al·pine azalea *n.* A low-growing, shrubby plant, *Loiseleuria procumbens,* of northern regions, having small evergreen leaves and clusters of small pink or white flowers.

al·pin·ist (ăl'pĭ-nĭst) *n. Sometimes* **Alpinist.** A mountain climber. —**al·pin·ism** *n.*

Alps (ălps). A major mountain system consisting of a great arc of fold mountains, which runs for *c.* 800 kilometers (500 miles) from the north shore of the Ligurian Sea through southeast France, northern Italy, Switzerland, Germany, and Austria into northwest Yugoslavia. The highest peak, Mont Blanc, in Haute-Savoie, France, rises to 4,807 meters (15,771 feet).

Al Qahira. See **Cairo.**

Al Quds. See **Jerusalem.**

al·read·y (ôl-rĕd'ē) *adv.* **1.** By a specified or implied time: *already dead when they found him.* **2.** As early or soon as this: *Is he back already?* **3.** Before; previously: *I've already asked her and don't feel like asking again.* **4.** *Slang.* For goodness' sake! Used as an intensive to show irritation: *That's enough already!* [Middle English *al redy :* ALL + READY.]

Usage: The use of *already* with the simple past tense is common in informal speech: *I already got it, he already went.* In formal English, however, only the *have* form of the verb is acceptable: *He has already gone.*

al·right (ôl'rīt') *adv.* Nonstandard. All right. —See Usage note at **all right.**

Al·sace (ăl-săs', -săs'). Region of eastern France, lying on the border with West Germany. Annexed by Germany, along with Lorraine, after the Franco-Prussian War of 1870, it was returned to France by the Treaty of Versailles (1919).

Al·sa·tian (ăl-sā'shən) *adj.* Of or pertaining to Alsace, its inhabitants, or their culture.
~*n.* **1.** A native or inhabitant of Alsace. **2.** *Chiefly British.* A dog, a German shepherd *(see).*

al·sike clover (ăl'sĭk', -sīk') *n.* A plant, *Trifolium hybridum,* native to Eurasia and widely cultivated for forage, having compound leaves and pink or whitish flowers. [After *Alsike,* town in Sweden, where it was first found.]

al·so (ôl'sō) *adv.* Besides; in addition; too. [Middle English *also,* from Old English *(e)alswā,* even so, altogether thus : *(e)al-,* all + *swā,* so.]

Synonyms: additionally, besides, furthermore, moreover, too.

Usage: The use of *also* as a connective word, in the sense of "and," should be avoided in formal written English. *He studied French and German, also Russian and Greek* is a poorly constructed sentence, which would be better in the form *He studied French and German and also Russian and Greek.*

Al·sop (ôl'səp, ŏl'-), **Joseph Wright, Jr.** (1910–) and **Stewart Johonnot Oliver** (1914–74). U.S. journalists. Known for their astute reporting of politics and the Washington scene, the Alsop brothers wrote many articles, columns, and books. From 1946 to 1958 they collaborated on the column "Matter of Fact."

al·so-ran (ôl'sō-răn') *n.* **1.** A horse or dog that fails to finish in the first three, or sometimes four, places in a race. **2.** *Informal.* One that is defeated in a race, election, or other competition; a loser or failure.

alt (ălt) *n. Music.* The first octave above the treble staff. Used chiefly in the phrase *in alt.* [Latin *altus,* high, deep.]

alt. altitude.

Al·tai Mountains (ăl'tī). Central Asian mountain range. It lies mostly in the U.S.S.R., but spreads into western China and Mongolia. Belukha, the highest peak in the U.S.S.R., rises to 4,506 meters (14,783 feet).

Al·ta·ic (ăl-tā'ĭk) *n.* A language family of Europe and Asia, including Turkic, Tungus, Mongolian, and possibly Korean. [After the ALTAI MOUNTAINS, where the languages originated.] —**Al·ta·ic** *adj.*

Al·tair (ăl-târ', -tīr') *n.* A very bright, double, variable star in the constellation Aquila, approximately 15.7 light-years from Earth. Also called "Alpha Aquilae." [Arabic *al-tā'ir,* "the star."]

Al·ta·mi·ra (ăl'tə-mîr'ə). Caves lying 21 kilometers (13 miles) southwest of Santander in northern Spain, containing magnificent Stone Age wall paintings discovered in 1879.

al·tar (ôl'tər) *n.* **1.** An elevated place or structure upon which sacrifices are offered or incense burned, or before which religious ceremonies are enacted. **2.** In Christian churches, a table or similar structure upon which the Eucharist is celebrated. —**lead to the altar.** To marry. [Middle English *alter,* Old English *altar,* from Late Latin *altāre,* "high place," from Latin *altus,* high.]

altar boy *n.* An attendant who assists a priest in the performance of a religious service, especially in the Roman Catholic Church; an acolyte.

al·tar·piece (ôl'tər-pēs') *n.* A painting, carving, or the like placed above and behind an altar.

alt·az·i·muth (ălt-ăz'ə-məth) *n.* A mounting for astronomical telescopes that permits both horizontal (azimuth) rotation and vertical (altitude) rotation. [ALT(ITUDE) + AZIMUTH.]

Alt·dorf (ält'dôrf', ält'-). Town in central Switzerland, the capital of Uri canton, home of the legendary hero William Tell. A bronze statue erected in 1895 marks the spot where Tell is supposed to have shot an apple, with his crossbow, off the head of his son.

Alt·dor·fer (ält'dôr'fər, ält'-) **Albrecht** (*c.* 1480–1538). German painter. He is often regarded as the first true landscape painter as many of his scenes contain no figures or only insignificant ones.

al·ter (ôl'tər) *v.* **-tered, -tering, -ters.** —*tr.* **1.** To modify or make different, usually without changing the fundamental nature of. **2.** To adjust or remake (a garment) for a better fit. **3.** To castrate or spay. —*intr.* To change or become different. —See Synonyms at **change.** [Middle English *alteren,* from Old French *alterer,* from Medieval Latin *alterāre,* from Latin *alter,* other.] —**al·ter·a·bil·i·ty** (ôl'tər-ə-bĭl'ə-tē), **al·ter·a·ble·ness** *n.* —**al·ter·a·ble** *adj.* —**al·ter·a·bly** *adv.*

al·ter·a·tion (ôl'tə-rā'shən) *n.* **1.** The act or procedure of altering. **2.** The condition resulting from altering; a modification; a change.

al·ter·a·tive (ôl'tə-rā'tĭv) *adj.* **1.** Tending to alter or produce alteration. **2.** *Medicine.* Tending to restore normal health.
~*n.* Also **al·ter·ant** (ôl'tər-ənt). An alterative treatment or medicine.

al·ter·cate (ôl'tər-kāt') *intr.v.* **-cated, -cating, -cates.** To argue or dispute vehemently. [Latin *altercārī,* to have differences with another, from *alter,* another.]

al·ter·ca·tion (ôl'tər-kā'shən) *n.* A heated and noisy quarrel.

al·ter e·go (ôl'tər ē'gō) *n.* **1.** Another side of oneself; a second self. **2.** An intimate or inseparable friend; a constant companion. [Latin, "other I."]

al·ter·nate (ôl'tər-nāt', ăl'-) *v.* **-nated, -nating, -nates.** —*intr.* **1.** To occur in successive turns. Usually used *with: The rainy season alternates with the dry season.* **2.** To pass from one state, action, or place to a second, back to the first, and so on repeatedly. Usually used with *between: alternate between optimism and pessimism.* **3.** To change direction regularly. Used of an electric current or voltage. —*tr.* **1.** To do or perform by turns. **2.** To cause to follow in turns; interchange regularly.
~*adj.* (ôl'tər-nĭt, ăl'-). **1.** Happening or following in turns; succeeding each other continuously: *alternate rain and sunshine.* **2.** Every other one of a series: *on alternate days.* **3.** In place of another; substitute: *an alternate plan.* **4.** *Botany.* **a.** Growing at alternating intervals on either side of a stem. Said especially of leaves. Compare **opposite. b.** Arranged alternately between other parts, as stamens are between petals.
~*n.* (ôl'tər-nĭt, ăl'-). A person acting in the place of another; a substitute. [Latin *alternāre,* from *alternus,* by turns, interchangeable, from *alter,* other.] —**al·ter·nate·ness** *n.*

alternate angle *n. Geometry.* An angle on one side of a **transversal** *(see)* that cuts two lines, having one of the intersected lines as a side.

al·ter·nate·ly (ôl'tər-nĭt-lē, ăl'-) *adv.* In alternate order or place; by turns.

al·ter·nat·ing current (ôl'tər-nā'tĭng, ăl'-) *n. Abbr.* **ac, A.C.** An electric current that reverses direction in a circuit at regular intervals, especially one that varies sinusoidally.

al·ter·na·tion (ôl'tər-nā'shən, ăl'-) *n.* Successive changes from one state to another and back again.

alternation of generations *n.* The occurrence within the life cycle of many plants and certain animals of alternating sexual and asexual reproduction. Also called "digenesis," "heterogenesis," "metagenesis," "xenogenesis."

al·ter·na·tive (ôl-tûr'nə-tĭv, ăl-) *n.* **1.** The possibility or necessity of choosing only one of two or more things, courses of action, or the like: *You have the alternative of paying a fine or going to prison.* **2.** Either or any of the things from which one is to be chosen: *Is there any alternative to taking the train?* —See Synonyms at **choice.**
~*adj.* **1.** Offering or necessitating a choice between two or more things or courses; constituting an alternative. **2.** *Grammar.* Indicating that the words or phrases connected are alternatives: *an alternative conjunction.* **3.** Different from or opposed to conventional and established types: *alternative medicine; the alternative press.* —**al·ter·na·tive·ly** *adv.*

Usage: Alternative is widely used to denote simply "one of a set of possible courses of action," but many traditionalists continue to insist that its use be restricted to situations in which only two possible choices present themselves. In this stricter sense, *alternative* is incompatible with all numerals *(there are three alternatives),* and the use of *two,* in particular, is held to be redundant *(the two alternatives are life and death)* would be unacceptable to traditionalists). Similarly, traditionalists reject as unacceptable sentences like *there is no other alternative* on the grounds that it is equivalent to the simpler *there is no alternative.*

al·ter·na·tor (ôl'tər-nā'tər, ăl'-) *n.* An electric generator that produces alternating current.

al·the·a, al·thae·a (ăl-thē'ə) *n.* **1.** Any plant of the genus *Althaea,* which includes the hollyhock. **2.** A shrub, the **rose of Sharon** *(see).* [Latin, marsh mallows, from Greek *althaia,* "healer," from *althein,* to heal.]

Al·thing (äl'thĭng, ôl'-) *n.* The Icelandic parliament. [Icelandic, from Old Norse *althingi,* assembly of all. See **all, thing.**]

alt·horn (ălt'hôrn') *n.* A brass instrument that sometimes replaces the French horn. Also called "alto horn." [German *Althorn : alt,*

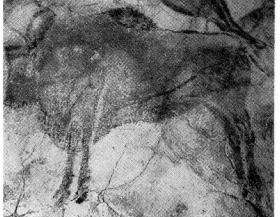

Altamira *Detail of one of the Stone Age wall paintings found in 1879 by a 12-year-old boy in a cave in northern Spain. The paintings, which date from about 12,000 B.C., are now known by the name of the nearby village.*

alyssum *A plant once believed to be a cure for rabies. The species shown here is* Alyssum saxatile, *an evergreen that flowers in the Northern Hemisphere from April to June.*

amaranth *A genus of plants grown for their tassellike flowers. This species is love-lies-bleeding,* Amaranthus caudatus.

alto, from Italian *alto,* ALTO + *Horn,* HORN.]

al·though (ôl-*thō*′) *conj.* Regardless of the fact that; even though. [Middle English : *al,* ALL + THOUGH.]

Usage: *Although* and *though* are often interchangeable: *I came to work, (al)though I was ill; (Al)though I was ill, I came to work. Though* is more colloquial and tends to occur when the clause it introduces is in second position in the sentence. *Although* is preferred with clauses in first position. Note that *though* has a certain mobility in some constructions *(Angry though I was. . .),* which does not extend to *although.*

al·tim·e·ter (ăl-tĭm′ə-tər) *n.* An instrument for determining altitude, used especially in aircraft and commonly based on sensing of pressure changes with altitude or on determination of the frequency delay in a radio signal reflected from the ground. [Latin *altus,* high + -METER.] **—al·tim·e·try** (ăl-tĭm′ə-trē) *n.*

al·ti·plan·a·tion (ăl′tĭ-plə-nā′shən) *n. Geology.* The process in which terraces are formed in rock on a hillside by weathering. [Latin *altus,* high + PLANATION.]

al·ti·pla·no (äl′tē-plä′nō) *n.* A high plateau, as in the Andes of Bolivia, Peru, and Argentina. [American Spanish, from Latin *altus,* high + Latin *planum,* plain.]

al·tis·si·mo (ăl-tĭs′ə-mō′) *adj. Music.* **1.** Of the highest pitch. **2.** Of or in the octave G to F, two octaves above the treble staff. [Italian, "highest," superlative of *alto,* high, from Latin *altus,* high.] **—al·tis·si·mo** *n. & adv.*

al·ti·tude (ăl′tə-to͞od′, -tyo͞od′) *n. Abbr.* **alt. 1.** The height of a thing above a particular level, especially above sea level or above the earth's surface. Also called "elevation." **2.** *Often* **altitudes.** A high location or area: *the difficulty of breathing at high altitudes.* **3.** *Astronomy.* The angular distance of a celestial object above the horizon. **4.** *Geometry.* The perpendicular distance from the base of a geometric figure or solid to the opposite vertex, parallel side, or parallel surface. **5.** A high position or rank. [Middle English, from Latin *altitūdō,* from *altus,* high.] **—al·ti·tud·i·nal** (ăl′tə-to͞od′n-əl, -tyo͞od′n-əl) *adj.*

altitude sickness *n.* Illness with symptoms such as nausea, breathlessness, and exhaustion, caused by oxygen deficiency, as encountered at high altitudes. Also called "mountain sickness."

al·to (ăl′tō) *n., pl.* **-tos.** *Abbr.* **A.** *Music.* **1.** A low, female singing voice; a contralto. **2.** A high male singing voice; a countertenor. **3.** The range between soprano and tenor. **4.** A singer whose voice lies within this range. **5.** An instrument that plays notes within this range, such as an alto saxophone. **6.** A vocal or instrumental part written for such a voice or instrument.

~adj. Pertaining to or playing notes within this range. [Italian, "high," from Latin *altus,* high.]

alto clef *n.* The C clef that places middle C on the third line of the staff.

al·to·cu·mu·lus (ăl′tō-kyo͞o′myə-ləs) *n.* A cloud formation of rounded, fleecy, white or gray masses arranged in bands or waves, occurring at 6,000 to 20,000 feet. [Latin *altus,* high + CUMULUS.]

al·to·geth·er (ôl′tə-gĕth′ər, ôl′tə-gĕth′ər) *adv.* **1.** Entirely; completely; utterly. **2.** With all included or counted; in all; all told: *Altogether 100 people were there.* **3.** On the whole; with everything considered: *Altogether, I'm sorry it happened.* **—in the altogether.** *Informal.* Naked; nude. [Middle English *al togeder* : *al,* ALL + TOGETHER.]

Usage: *Altogether* should be distinguished from *all together. All together* is used of a group to indicate that its members performed or underwent an action collectively: *The nations stood all together. The prisoners were herded all together. All together* can be used only if it is possible to rephrase the sentence so that *all* and *together* may be separated by other words: *The books lay all together in a heap. All the books lay together in a heap.*

al·to-re·lie·vo (ăl′tō-rĭ-lē′vo) *n., pl.* **-vos.** Also *Italian* **al·to-ri·lie·vo** (äl′tō-rē-lyā′vō), *pl.* **-vi** (-vē). **High relief** *(see).* [Italian *alto rilievo,* "high relief."]

al·to·stra·tus (ăl′tō-strā′təs, -străt′əs) *n.* An extended cloud formation of bluish or gray sheets or layers occurring at 6,000 to 20,000 feet. [Latin *altus,* high + STRATUS.]

al·tri·cial (ăl-trĭsh′əl) *adj.* Of or characterizing birds that are helpless and naked when hatched, such as young pigeons. Compare **precocial.** [Latin *altrīcēs,* plural of *altrix,* feminine of *altōr,* nourisher, from *alere,* to nourish.]

al·tru·ism (ăl′tro͞o-ĭz′əm) *n.* **1.** Concern for the welfare of others, as opposed to egoism; selflessness. **2.** *Zoology.* Instinctive cooperative behavior by an animal that apparently protects or benefits other members of its species, and its species in general, rather than itself. [Italian *attrui,* others, from Latin *alteri,* plural of *alter,* other.] **—al·tru·ist** *n.* **—al·tru·is·tic** (ăl′tro͞o-ĭs′tĭk) *adj.* **—al·tru·is·ti·cal·ly** *adv.*

al·u·del (ăl′yə-dĕl′) *n. Chemistry.* A pear-shaped glass apparatus, open at both ends, formerly used to collect condensed mercury and other liquids. [Middle English *alutel,* from Old French *aludel,* from Spanish, from Arabic *al-'uthāl,* the vessel.]

al·u·la (ăl′yə-lə) *n., pl.* **-lae** (-lē′). **1.** The feathers attached to the part of a bird's wing corresponding to the thumb. Also called "bastard wing." **2.** A small lobe near the base of the wing in certain insects. [New Latin, diminutive of Latin *āla,* wing.] **—al·u·lar** (ăl′yə-lər) *adj.*

al·um (ăl′əm) *n.* Any of various double sulfates of a trivalent metal such as aluminum, chromium, or iron, and a univalent metal or radical such as potassium, sodium, or ammonium; especially, potassium aluminum sulfate (*potash alum,* $K_2SO_4 \cdot Al_2(SO_4)_3 \cdot 12H_2O$), which is widely used as a mordant and size for paper and, medicinally, as an astringent and styptic. See **chrome alum.** [Middle English, from Old French, from Latin *alūmen*†.]

a·lu·mi·na (ə-lo͞o′mə-nə) *n.* Any of several forms of aluminum oxide, Al_2O_3, occurring naturally as corundum, in a hydrated form in bauxite, and with various impurities as ruby, sapphire, and emery. It is used in aluminum production, in abrasives, refractories, ceramics, and electrical insulation, and as an absorbent material. [New Latin, from Latin *alūmen* (stem *alūmin-*), ALUM.]

a·lu·min·ate (ə-lo͞o′mə-nāt′, -nĭt) *n.* A chemical compound containing the negative ion AlO_2^-.

a·lu·mi·nif·er·ous (ə-lo͞o′mə-nĭf′ər-əs) *adj.* Containing or yielding aluminum, alumina, or alum. [Latin *alūmen* (stem *alūmin-*), ALUM + -FEROUS.]

a·lu·min·ize (ə-lo͞o′mə-nīz′) *tr.v.* **-ized, -izing, -izes.** To coat or cover with aluminum or aluminum paint.

a·lu·min·o·sil·i·cate (ə-lo͞o′mə-nō-sĭl′ə-kāt′) *n.* Any of a large number of complex inorganic crystalline substances or glasses, consisting of silicate compounds in which some of the silicon atoms have been replaced by aluminum atoms. Many are found naturally in rocks and minerals. [ALUMIN(UM) + SILICATE.]

a·lu·mi·no·ther·my (ə-lo͞o′mə-nō-thûr′mē) *n. Chemistry.* The reduction of metal oxides to metals using aluminum powder, a process that produces great heat and that is used in welding and in incendiary devices.

a·lu·mi·nous (ə-lo͞o′mə-nəs) *adj.* Of, pertaining to, or containing aluminum or alum.

a·lu·mi·num (ə-lo͞o′mə-nəm) *n.* Also *chiefly British* **al·u·min·i·um** (ăl′yə-mĭn′ē-əm). *Symbol* **Al** A silvery-white, ductile metallic element, the most abundant in the earth's crust, but found only in combination, chiefly in bauxite. It is used to form many hard, light, corrosion-resistant alloys. Atomic number 13, atomic weight 26.98, melting point 660.2°C, boiling point 2,467°C, specific gravity 2.69, valence 3. [New Latin, earlier *alumium* : ALUMINA + -IUM.]

aluminum foil *n.* Aluminum in the form of a very thin sheet, used chiefly as a protective wrapping for foodstuffs. Also called "foil."

aluminum oxide *n.* A white crystalline compound, Al_2O_3, occurring naturally as **alumina** *(see).*

aluminum sulfate *n.* A white crystalline compound, $Al_2(SO_4)_3$, used chiefly in papermaking, water purification, sanitation, and tanning.

a·lum·na (ə-lŭm′nə) *n., pl.* **-nae** (-nē′). A female graduate or former student of a school, college, or university. [Latin, feminine of *alumnus.*]

a·lum·nus (ə-lŭm′nəs) *n., pl.* **-ni** (-nī′). A male graduate or former student of a school, college, or university. [Latin *alumnus,* a pupil, foster son, from *alere,* to nourish.]

al·um·root (ăl′əm-ro͞ot′, -ro͝ot′) *n.* Any of various North American plants of the genus *Heuchera,* having clusters of small white, reddish, or green flowers and astringent roots.

A·lun·dum (ə-lŭn′dəm) *n.* A trademark for a hard, artificial abrasive of fused alumina, used in making oilstones and grinding wheels.

al·u·nite (ăl′yə-nīt′) *n.* A gray mineral, chiefly $KAl_3(SO_4)_2(OH)_6$, used in making alum and fertilizer. Also called "alumstone." [French, from *alun,* ALUM.]

al·ve·o·lar (ăl-vē′ə-lər) *adj.* **1.** Of or pertaining to an alveolus. **2.** *Anatomy.* **a.** Pertaining to the section of the jaw containing the tooth sockets. **b.** Pertaining to the alveoli of the lungs. **3.** *Phonetics.* Formed with the tip of the tongue touching or near the hard ridge behind the upper teeth, as the English *t, d,* and *s.*

~n. Phonetics. An alveolar consonant or sound. [French *avéolaire,* from *alvéole,* ALVEOLUS.]

al·ve·o·late (ăl-vē′ə-lĭt) *adj.* Having alveoli; deeply pitted; honeycombed. [Latin *alveolātus,* hollowed, from ALVEOLUS.] **—al·ve·o·la·tion** (ăl-vē′ə-lā′shən) *n.*

al·ve·o·lus (ăl-vē′ə-ləs) *n., pl.* **-li** (-lī′). **1.** A small cavity or pit, such as a honeycomb cell. **2.** A tooth socket in the jawbone. **3.** An air sac of the lungs, at the end of a bronchiole, through which exchange of respiratory gases takes place. [Latin, small cavity, diminutive of *alveus,* a cavity, hollow, from *alvus,* a hollow, belly.]

al·ways (ôl′wāz, -wĭz) *adv.* **1.** On every occasion; every time: *always leaves at six.* **2.** Ceaselessly; forever: *friends always.* **3.** Continually; repeatedly: *He's always fiddling with his car.* **4.** In every instance: *Cats always have whiskers.* **5.** As a possibility; as a last resort: *You could always just refuse.* [Middle English *alwayes,* adverbial genitive of *alwei,* Old English *ealne weg,* "along all the way" : *ealne,* accusative of *eall,* ALL + *weg,* WAY.]

al·ys·sum (ə-lĭs′əm) *n.* **1.** Any of various plants of the genus *Alyssum,* having dense clusters of yellow or white flowers. Also called "madwort." **2.** See **sweet alyssum.** [New Latin, from Greek *alusson,* madwort (believed to cure rabies), from neuter of *alussos,* curing rabies : *a-,* not + *lussa,* rabies, madness.]

Alz·heim·er's disease (älts′hī′mərz, älts′-) *n.* A degenerative disease of the brain, often occurring in middle age, causing progressive loss of mental faculties. Also called "presenile dementia." [After Alois *Alzheimer* (1864–1915), German doctor.]

am (ăm; *unstressed* əm). The first person singular, present indicative of **be.**

am, AM amplitude modulation.

Am The symbol for the element americium.

Am. America; American.

a.m. ante meridiem

A.M. 1. ante meridiem. **2.** in the year of the world. [Latin *anno mundi*] **3.** Master of Arts. [Latin *Artium Magister*]

a·mah, a·ma (ä′mə, ä′mä) *n.* In the Orient, a maidservant who looks after children; especially, a wet nurse. [Portuguese *ama,* wet nurse, from Medieval Latin *amma,* from Latin *amma* (unattested), mother.]

a·main (ə-mān′) *adv. Archaic & Poetic.* **1.** With strength and intensity. **2.** With speed or haste. **3.** Greatly; exceedingly. [A- (on, by) + MAIN (strength).]

Am·a·lek·ite (ăm′ə-lĕk-īt′, ə-măl′ə-kīt′) *n.* A member of an ancient nomadic tribe reputedly descended from Esau's grandson Amalek and hostile to the Israelites. Genesis 36:12–16. Exodus 17:13. I Samuel 15:7. [Hebrew *'Amālēqī,* after *'Amālēq,* Amalek.]

a·mal·gam (ə-măl′gəm) *n.* **1.** Any of various alloys of mercury with other metals, such as tin or silver: *dental amalgam.* **2.** Any combination or mixture of diverse elements. [Middle English *amalgame,* from Old French, from Medieval Latin *amalgama*†.]

a·mal·ga·mate (ə-măl′gə-māt′) *v.* **-mated, -mating, -mates.** —*tr.* **1.** To mix so as to make a unified whole; blend; unite; combine. **2.** To mix or alloy (a metal) with mercury. —*intr.* **1.** To combine, unite, or consolidate. **2.** To form an amalgam with mercury. Used of metals. —See Synonyms at **mix.** —**a·mal·ga·ma·tive** (ə-măl′gə-mā′tĭv, -mə-tĭv) *adj.* —**a·mal·ga·ma·tor** *n.*

a·mal·ga·ma·tion (ə-măl′gə-mā′shən) *n.* **1.** The act of or condition resulting from amalgamating. **2.** A merger, as of several companies. **3.** *Chemistry.* The dissolving of a metal in mercury to form an alloy.

a·mand·la (ə-mänd′lə) *interj. South African.* Power. Used as a slogan by supporters of Black Power. [Zulu.]

am·a·ni·ta (ăm′ə-nī′tə, -nē′tə) *n.* Any of various mushrooms of the genus *Amanita,* most of which are extremely poisonous. See **death cup, fly agaric.** [From Greek *amanitai*† (plural), a type of fungus.]

a·man·ta·dine (ə-măn′tə-dēn′) *n.* An antiviral drug, $C_{10}H_{17}NHCl$, used in the treatment of influenza and Parkinson's disease. [Alteration (through influence of *amine*) of *adamantane,* an organic compound, from ADAMANT.]

a·man·u·en·sis (ə-măn′yo͞o-ĕn′sĭs) *n., pl.* **-ses** (-sēz). **1.** One employed to take dictation or to copy manuscript. **2.** A personal assistant to a writer. [Latin *āmanuensis,* from *(servus) ā manū,* "(slave) at hand(writing)" : *ab-,* by + *manus,* hand.]

am·a·ranth (ăm′ə-rănth) *n.* **1.** Any of various plants of the genus *Amaranthus,* having clusters of small greenish, red, or purplish flowers. See **pigweed, tumbleweed, love-lies-bleeding. 2.** *Poetic.* An imaginary flower that never fades. **3.** Deep reddish purple. [New Latin *amaranthus,* variant (influenced by *-anthus,* flower) of Latin *amarantus,* from Greek *amarantos,* unfading : *a-,* not + *marainein,* to waste, wither.]

am·a·ran·thine (ăm′ə-răn′thĭn, -thīn′) *adj.* **1.** Of, pertaining to, or resembling the amaranth. **2.** Eternally beautiful; unfading; everlasting. **3.** Deep purple in color.

am·a·relle (ăm′ə-rĕl′) *n.* A variety of sour cherry having pale-red fruit. [German *Amarelle,* from Medieval Latin *amarellum,* from Latin *amārus,* bitter.]

am·a·ret·to (ăm′ə-rĕt′ō) *n.* An almond-flavored Italian liqueur. [Italian, "bitter," from *amaro,* bitter; referring to bitter almonds, on which the liqueur is based.]

Am·a·ril·lo (ăm′ə-rĭl′ō). A city of northern Texas. It is a commercial, banking, and industrial center of the Texas Panhandle. The discovery of gas (1918) and oil (1921) spurred the city's growth.

am·a·ryl·lis (ăm′ə-rĭl′ĭs) *n.* **1.** A bulbous plant, *Amaryllis belladonna,* native to southern Africa, having large, lilylike reddish or white flowers. Also called "belladonna lily." **2.** Any of several related or similar plants. [After AMARYLLIS.]

Amaryllis. A shepherdess who appears in the pastoral poetry of Virgil and other classical writers. [Latin girl's name, from Greek *Amarullis.*]

a·mass (ə-măs′) *tr.v.* **amassed, amassing, amasses. 1.** To pile or gather up in a mass. **2.** To collect for oneself; accumulate, especially for one's own pleasure or profit. —See Synonyms at **gather.** [Old French *amasser* : *a-,* to, from Latin *ad-* + *masser,* to gather together, from *masse,* a MASS.] —**a·mass·a·ble** *adj.* —**a·mass·er** *n.* —**a·mass·ment** *n.*

am·a·teur (ăm′ə-tûr′, -tər, -ə-cho͝or′, -chər, -tyo͝or′) *n.* **1.** A person who engages in any art, science, study, or sporting activity as a pastime rather than as a profession. **2.** *Abbr.* **a., A.** A sportsman or sportswoman who has never participated in competition for money or a livelihood. **3.** One lacking professional skill or judgment in a certain area, as in art.
~*adj.* **1.** *Abbr.* **a., A.** Pertaining to or performed by an amateur or amateurs. **2.** *Abbr.* **a., A.** Made up of amateurs: *an amateur orchestra.* **3.** Not professional; unskillful. [French, from Latin *amātōr,* a lover, from *amāre,* to love.] —**am·a·teur·ism** *n.*

am·a·teur·ish (ăm′ə-tûr′ĭsh, -cho͝or′ĭsh, -tyo͝or′ĭsh) *adj.* Characteristic of an amateur; not professional; unskillful. —**am·a·teur·ish·ly** *adv.* —**am·a·teur·ish·ness** *n.*

A·ma·ti[1] (ä-mä′tē). A family of violin makers in Cremona, Italy, in the 16th and 17th centuries. They include **Andrea Amati** (*c.* 1505–75) who established the early design for the modern violin. His grandson **Nicolò Amati** (1596–1684) was the most famous craftsman and was also the teacher of Stradivari and Guarneri.

Amati[2] *n.* A violin, cello, or similar instrument made by Nicolò Amati or any of the members of his family.

am·a·tive (ăm′ə-tĭv) *adj.* Amorous. [Medieval Latin *amātīvus,* from Latin *amāre,* to love.] —**am·a·tive·ness** *n.*

am·a·tol (ăm′ə-tôl′, -tōl′) *n.* A highly explosive mixture of ammonium nitrate and trinitrotoluene. [*Am*monium + trinitro*tol*uene.]

am·a·to·ry (ăm′ə-tôr′ē, -tōr′ē) *adj.* Also **am·a·to·ri·al** (ăm′ə-tôr′ē-əl, -tōr′ē-əl). Of, pertaining to, or expressive of love, especially sexual love: *amatory verse.* [Latin *amātōrius,* from *amātōr,* a lover, from *amāre,* to love.]

am·au·ro·sis (ăm′ô-rō′sĭs) *n.* Partial or complete blindness, especially when not associated with disease of the eye. [Greek *amaurōsis,* from *amauroun,* to darken, from *(a)mauros*†, dark.] —**am·au·rot·ic** (ăm′ô-rŏt′ĭk) *adj.*

a·maze (ə-māz′) *tr.v.* **amazed, amazing, amazes. 1.** To affect with surprise or great wonder; astonish. **2.** *Obsolete.* To bewilder. —See Synonyms at **surprise.**
~*n. Archaic & Poetic.* Amazement; wonder. [Middle English *amasen,* Old English *āmasian*†, to bewilder. See **maze.**] —**a·maz·ed·ly** (ə-mā′zĭd-lē) *adv.*

a·maze·ment (ə-māz′mənt) *n.* **1.** A state of extreme surprise or wonder; astonishment. **2.** *Obsolete.* Bewilderment; perplexity.

a·maz·ing (ə-mā′zĭng) *adj.* Causing amazement; greatly surprising; wonderful. —**a·maz·ing·ly** *adv.*

Am·a·zon[1] (ăm′ə-zŏn′, -zən) *n.* **1.** *Greek Mythology.* A member of a nation of female warriors reputed to have lived in Scythia, near the Black Sea. **2.** *Often* **amazon.** Any tall, vigorous, athletic woman. [Middle English, from Latin *Amāzon,* from Greek. Probably of non-Indo-European origin but interpreted by the Greeks as *a-,* without + *mazos,* breast (from the belief that the Amazons removed their right breasts in order to make it easier to use their bows.] —**Am·a·zo·ni·an** (ăm′ə-zō′nē-ən) *adj.*

Amazon[2]. *Portuguese* **Ri·o Am·a·zo·nas** (rē′o͞o ăm′ə-zō′nəs). River formed by the confluence of the Ucayali and Marañón rivers, it flows 6,570 kilometers (4,082 miles) from northern Peru across northern Brazil into the Atlantic Ocean. It carries so great a volume of water (more than any other river) that fresh water is to be found in the ocean some 320 kilometers (200 miles) from its mouth. Its vast basin covers an area of more than 6,475,000 square kilometers (2,500,000 square miles). It is the second-longest river in the world, after the Nile. —**Am·a·zo·ni·an** (ăm′ə-zō′nē-ən) *adj.*

Amazon ant *n.* Any of several small red ants of the genus *Polyergus,* that take over and enslave the young ants of other species. [After the legend that the Amazons raised captured children.]

am·a·zon·ite (ăm′ə-zən-īt′) *n.* A blue-green variety of microcline, often used as a semiprecious stone. Also called "amazon stone." [After the AMAZON River, near which it is found.]

amb., Amb. ambassador.

am·bas·sa·dor (ăm-băs′ə-dər, -dôr′) *n. Abbr.* **amb., Amb. 1.** A diplomatic official of the highest rank appointed and accredited as representative in residence by one government to another. Called in full "ambassador extraordinary and plenipotentiary." **2.** Any of various diplomatic officials of the highest rank. **3.** A diplomatic official heading his or her country's permanent mission to certain international organizations, such as the United Nations. **4.** Any authorized messenger or representative. **5.** One who stands for or represents a particular belief, set of values, or culture: *an ambassador for change.* [Middle English *ambassadour,* from Old French *ambassadeur,* from Old Italian *ambasciator,* from Vulgar Latin *ambactiātor* (unattested), from Medieval Latin *ambactia,* mission, from Germanic *ambakhtaz* (unattested), from Latin *ambactus,* vassal, probably from Celtic.] —**am·bas·sa·do·ri·al** (ăm-băs′ə-dôr′ē-əl, -dōr′ē-əl) *adj.* —**am·bas·sa·dor·ship** *n.*

am·bas·sa·dress (ăm-băs′ə-drĭs) *n.* **1.** The wife of an ambassador. **2.** A female ambassador or representative.

am·ber (ăm′bər) *n.* **1.** A hard, translucent, brownish-yellow fossil resin, found chiefly along the shores of the Baltic Sea, and used for making jewelry and other ornamental objects. **2.** Medium to dark or deep orange yellow. **3.** An amber-toned stage light used to simulate sunlight. [Middle English *ambre,* from Old French, from Medieval Latin *ambra, ambar,* from Arabic *'anbar,* ambergris, amber.] —**am·ber** *adj.*

am·ber·gris (ăm′bər-grĭs′, -grēs′) *n.* A waxy, grayish substance, mainly cholesterol, formed in the intestines of sperm whales and found floating at sea or washed ashore. It is used as a fixative in perfumes. [Middle English *ambregris,* from Old French *ambre gris* : AMBER + *gris,* gray, from Frankish *gris* (unattested).]

am·ber·oid (ăm′bə-roid′) *n.* Also **am·broid** (ăm′broid′). A synthetic form of amber made by melting together small pieces of amber and other resins under pressure.

ambi– *prefix.* Indicates both; for example, **ambiversion.** [Latin, round, on both sides.]

am·bi·ance, am·bi·ence (ăm′bē-əns, äɴ-byäɴs′) *n.* **1.** The atmosphere or character of a place: *a strange ambiance.* **2.** A pleasant or congenial atmosphere or environment: *a restaurant lacking in ambiance.* [French, from *ambiant,* surrounding, from Latin *ambiēns,* AMBIENT.]

am·bi·dex·trous (ăm′bĭ-dĕk′strəs) *adj.* **1.** Able to use both hands with equal facility. **2.** Unusually dexterous or adroit, especially in more than one activity; versatile. **3.** Deceptive; hypocritical. [Late Latin *ambidexter* : Latin *ambi-,* AMBI- + *dexter,* right-handed.] —**am·bi·dex·ter** (ăm′bĭ-dĕk′stər) *n. & adj.* —**am·bi·dex·ter·i·ty** (ăm′bĭ-dĕk-stĕr′ə-tē) *n.* —**am·bi·dex·trous·ly** *adv.*

am·bi·ent (ăm′bē-ənt) *adj.* Surrounding; designating or pertaining to the immediate environment: *the ambient temperature.* [Latin *ambiēns* (stem *ambient-*), present participle of *ambīre,* to go round : *ambi-,* round + *īre,* to go.]

am·bi·gu·i·ty (ăm′bĭ-gyo͞o′ə-tē) *n., pl.* **-ties. 1.** The state of being ambiguous. **2.** Something ambiguous.

amaryllis *A plant named after a shepherdess in classical pastoral poetry. It is a native of southern Africa.*

Amazons *A portrayal of these legendary women warriors in battle. The relief is part of the decoration of a chariot made in Ionia—a Greek colony in present-day Turkey—in the sixth century* B.C.

PRONUNCIATION KEY

ă, pat; ā, pay; âr, care;
ä, father, are; b, bib;
ch, church; d, deed; ĕ, pet;
ē, be; f, fife; g, gag; h, hat;
hw, which; ĭ, pit; ī, pie;
îr, pier; j, judge; k, kick;
l, lid, needle; m, mum;
n, no, sudden; ng, thing;
ŏ, pot; ō, toe; ô, paw, for;
oi, noise; ou, out; o͝o, book;
o͞o, boot; p, pop; r, roar;
s, sauce; sh, ship, dish;
t, tight; th, thin, path;
th, this, bathe; ŭ, cut; ûr, fur;
v, valve; w, with; y, yes;
z, zebra, size; zh, vision;
ə, about, item, edible, gallop, circus, peaceful

IN FOREIGN WORDS:

à, *Fr.* ami; œ, *Fr.* feu, *Ger.* schön; ü, *Fr.* tu, *Ger.* über; KH, *Ger.* ich, *Scot.* loch; N, *Fr.* bon; y′, *Fr.* Compiègne

STRESS MARKS:

Primary stress: ′
in·cite′ (ĭn-sīt′)
Secondary stress: ′
in′sight′ (ĭn′sīt′)

am·big·u·ous (ăm-bĭg′yo͞o-əs) *adj.* **1.** Open to more than one interpretation. **2.** Doubtful or uncertain. [Latin *ambiguus,* uncertain, "going about," from *ambigere,* to wander about : *ambi-,* around + *agere,* to drive, lead.] **—am·big·u·ous·ly** *adv.* **—am·big·u·ous·ness** *n.*

am·bit (ăm′bĭt) *n.* **1.** The external boundary of something; a circuit. **2.** The sphere or scope of something. [Middle English, from Latin *ambitus,* a going round, from *ambīre* (past participle *ambitus*), to go round. See **ambient.**]

am·bi·tion (ăm-bĭsh′ən) *n.* **1.** An eager or strong desire to achieve success, distinction, fortune, or the like; will to succeed. **2.** A strong desire to achieve a particular end. **3.** The object or goal desired. [Middle English *ambicioun,* from Old French *ambition,* from Latin *ambitiō* (stem *ambitiōn-*), a going round (for votes), from *ambīre,* to go round. See **ambient.**]

am·bi·tious (ăm-bĭsh′əs) *adj.* **1.** Full of, characterized by, or motivated by ambition. **2.** Greatly desirous; eager. Used with *of* or an infinitive: *"I am not ambitious of ridicule"* (Edmund Burke). **3.** Showing or requiring much skill, ambition, or effort; challenging: *an ambitious plan.* **—am·bi·tious·ly** *adv.* **—am·bi·tious·ness** *n.*

ambulacrum ***The underside of a starfish's arms—the part of the body known as the ambulacrum—is covered with the trunklike appendages shown here. The appendages are the animal's feet.***

am·biv·a·lence (ăm-bĭv′ə-ləns) *n.* Also **am·biv·a·len·cy** (-lən-sē). The simultaneous existence in a person's mind of mutually conflicting feelings or thoughts toward or about something or someone. [German *Ambivalenz* (coined by Freud) : AMBI- + VALENCE]. **—am·biv·a·lent** (ăm-bĭv′ə-lənt) *adj.* **—am·biv·a·lent·ly** *adv.*

am·bi·ver·sion (ăm′bĭ-vûr′zhən, -shən) *n. Psychology.* The condition of showing both introversion and extroversion. [AMBI- + (IN-TRO)VERSION or (EXTRO)VERSION.] **—am·bi·vert** (ăm′bĭ-vərt) *n.*

am·ble (ăm′bəl) *intr.v.* **-bled, -bling, -bles. 1.** To move along smoothly by lifting first both legs on one side and then both on the other. Used of horses and other animals. **2.** To walk slowly; move with a leisurely gait. **3.** To ride an ambling horse.
∼n. **1.** An ambling gait, especially that of a horse. **2.** An unhurried pace. **3.** A leisurely walk. [Middle English *amblen,* from Old French *ambler,* from Latin *ambulāre,* to AMBULATE.] **—am·bler** *n.*

Am·bler (ăm′blər), **Eric** (1909–). British novelist. He has written many successful thrillers, including *The Mask of Dimitrios* (1939), *A Passage of Arms* (1959), and *Send No More Roses* (1977).

am·blyg·o·nite (ăm-blĭg′ə-nīt′) *n.* A white or creamy white mineral with composition $(Li,Na)Al(PO_4)(F,OH)$. It is an important source of lithium. [German *Amblygonit,* "the stone with obtuse angles (in its crystals)" : Greek *amblugōnios,* having obtuse angles : *amblus,* blunt + *gōnia,* angle + -ITE.]

am·bly·o·pi·a (ăm′blē-ō′pē-ə) *n.* Dimness of vision without apparent physical defect or disease of the eye. [New Latin, from Greek *ambluōpia* : *amblus,* blunt, dim + -OPIA.] **—am·bly·op·ic** (ăm′blē-ō′pĭk, -ŏp′ĭk) *adj.*

am·bo (ăm′bō) *n., pl.* **-bos** or **ambones** (ăm-bō′nēz). Either of the two pulpits or raised stands in early Christian churches from which parts of the service were chanted or read. [Medieval Latin, from Greek *ambōn*†, pulpit, a raised edge or rim.]

am·boy·na, am·boi·na (ăm-boi′nə) *n.* The reddish-brown, curly-grained wood of a tree, *Pterocarpus indicus,* of southeastern Asia, used for decorative cabinetwork. [After *Amboina* in the Moluccas, Indonesia.]

ambroid. Variant of **amberoid.**

Am·brose (ăm′brōz′), **Saint** (*c.* A.D. 340–397). Bishop of Milan and leader of the early Christian Church. He was influential in imposing orthodoxy on the early Church and strengthening the power of the Church against the state.

am·bro·si·a (ăm-brō′zhə, -zhē-ə) *n.* **1.** *Greek & Roman Mythology.* The food of the gods, thought to impart immortality. Compare **nectar. 2.** Anything with an especially delicious flavor or fragrance. **3. Beebread** *(see).* [Latin, from Greek, "immortality," from *ambrotos,* immortal : *a-,* not + *mbrotos,* archaic form of *brotos,* mortal.] **—am·bro·si·al, am·bro·si·an** *adj.*

ambrosia beetle *n.* Any of various small bark beetles that tunnel into solid wood and feed on fungi. [After *ambrosia fungus,* on which the beetles feed.]

Am·bro·si·an chant (ăm-brō′zē-ən) *n.* A type of liturgical chant, supposedly introduced by St. Ambrose and used to the present day in the Cathedral of Milan.

am·bro·type (ăm′brō-tīp′) *n.* In early photography, a positive picture produced by backing a glass negative with black paper or paint. [Greek *ambro(tos),* immortal (see **ambrosia**) + -TYPE.]

am·bry (ăm′brē) *n., pl.* **-bries.** Also **aum·bry** (ôm′brē). **1.** In churches, a niche near the altar for keeping sacred vessels and vestments. **2.** *Archaic.* A small storeroom or cupboard. [Middle English *aumry,* from Old French *almarie, aumaire,* from Medieval Latin *almārium,* store, from Latin *armārium,* from *arma,* tools, ARMS.]

ambs·ace (āmz′ās′) *n.* **1.** Double aces, the lowest throw at dice. **2.** Misfortune; bad luck. **3.** The smallest amount or most worthless thing possible. [Middle English *ambes as,* from Old French, from Latin *ambās ās,* "both aces" : *ambās,* feminine accusative of *ambō,* both + *ās,* a unit (see **ace**).]

am·bu·la·crum (ăm′byə-lā′krəm) *n., pl.* **-cra** (-krə). *Zoology.* One of the five radial areas on the undersurface of the starfish and similar echinoderms, on which the tube feet are borne. [New Latin, from Latin *ambulācrum,* avenue (hence the row of pores for protrusion of the tube feet), from *ambulāre,* to AMBULATE.]

am·bu·lance (ăm′byə-ləns) *n.* A vehicle specially equipped to transport the sick or injured. [French, from *(hôpital) ambulant,* itinerant (hospital), from Latin *ambulāns* (stem *ambulant-*), present participle of *ambulāre,* to AMBULATE.]

ambulance chaser *n. Slang.* **1.** A lawyer or a lawyer's agent who obtains clients by persuading accident victims to sue for damages. **2.** A lawyer avid for clients.

am·bu·lant (ăm′byə-lənt) *adj.* Moving or walking about; shifting from place to place. [French. See **ambulance.**]

am·bu·late (ăm′byə-lāt′) *intr.v.* **-lated, -lating, -lates.** To walk from place to place; move about. [Latin *ambulāre,* to go about, walk : *ambi-,* around, about + *-ul-, -el-* (unattested), to go.] **—am·bu·la·tion** *n.*

am·bu·la·to·ry (ăm′byə-lə-tôr′ē, -tōr′ē) *adj.* **1.** Of, pertaining to, or adapted for walking. **2.** Capable of walking; not bedridden. **3.** Moving about; not stationary. **4.** *Law.* Capable of being changed or revoked, as a will during the life of the testator.
∼n., pl. **ambulatories. 1.** An aisle around the east end of a church. **2.** A covered place for walking, as in a cloister.

am·bus·cade (ăm′bə-skād′) *n.* An ambush.
∼tr.v. **ambuscaded, -cading, -cades.** To ambush. [Old French *embuscade,* from Old Italian *imboscata,* feminine past participle of *imboscare,* to ambush, from Vulgar Latin *imboscāre* (unattested), to AMBUSH.] **—am·bus·cad·er** *n.*

am·bush (ăm′bo͝osh′) *n.* **1.** A lying in wait to attack by surprise. **2.** A surprise attack made from a concealed position. **3. a.** Those in hiding to make such an attack. **b.** Their hiding place. **4.** Any hidden peril or trap.
∼tr.v. **ambushed, -bushing, -bushes.** To attack from a concealed position. [Middle English *embushen,* to ambush, from Old French *embuschier,* from Vulgar Latin *imboscāre* (unattested), "to hide in the bushes" : *in,* in + *boscus* (unattested), bush, from Germanic.] **—am·bush·er** *n.*

A.M.D.G. To the greater glory of God. Used as the motto of the Jesuits. [Latin *ad majorem Dei gloriam.*]

ameba. Variant of **amoeba.**

ameer. Variant of **emir.**

a·me·li·o·rate (ə-mēl′yə-rāt′) *v.* **-rated, -rating, -rates.** *—tr.* To make better; improve. *—intr.* To become better. [French *améliorer,* to improve, from Old French *ameillorer* : *a-,* to, from Latin *ad-* + *meillor,* better, from Latin *melior,* better.] **—a·me·li·o·ra·ble** (ə-mēl′yə-rə-bəl) *adj.* **—a·me·li·o·ra·tive** (ə-mēl′yə-rā′tĭv, -rə-tĭv) *adj.* **—a·me·li·o·ra·tor** *n.*

a·me·li·o·ra·tion (ə-mēl′yə-rā′shən) *n.* **1.** The act of ameliorating or the state of being ameliorated. **2.** Something resulting from amelioration; an improvement. **3.** *Linguistics.* A change in the meaning of a word to a more favorable sense. For example, the word *shrewd* has undergone amelioration from its earlier senses of "mischievous" and "dangerous." Also called "melioration."

a·men (ā-mĕn′, ä-) *interj.* Used at the end of a prayer or a statement to express concurrence, ratification, or approval.
∼n. **1.** An utterance of this interjection. **2.** Any expression of conviction or assent. [Middle English *amen,* Old English *amen,* from Late Latin, from Greek, from Hebrew *āmēn,* certainly, verily.]

A·men, A·mon (ä′mən, ăm′ən). *Egyptian Mythology.* The god of life and reproduction, represented as a man with a ram's head. Sometimes identified with **Amen-Ra** *(see).*

a·me·na·ble (ə-mē′nə-bəl, ə-mĕn′ə-) *adj.* **1.** Willing to follow advice or suggestion; tractable; responsive. **2.** Responsible to authority; accountable. **3.** Open or liable to testing, criticism, or judgment. —See Synonyms at **obedient.** [Norman French (legal use), from French *amener,* to lead, bring, from Old French : *a-,* to, from Latin *ad-* + *mener,* to lead, from Latin *mināre,* to drive (cattle), from *minārī,* "to shout at," threaten, from *minae,* threats.] **—a·me·na·bil·i·ty** (ə-mē′nə-bĭl′ə-tē, ə-mĕn′ə-), **a·me·na·ble·ness** *n.* **—a·me·na·bly** *adv.*

a·mend (ə-mĕnd′) *v.* **amended, amending, amends.** *—tr.* **1.** To remove the faults or errors of; correct; rectify. **2.** To improve; better. **3.** To alter formally (a legislative measure, for example) by adding, deleting, or rephrasing. *—intr.* To improve one's conduct; reform. —See Synonyms at **correct.** [Middle English *amenden,* from Old French *amender,* alteration of Latin *ēmendāre,* to free from faults : *ex-,* removal, out of + *menda, mendum,* defect, fault.] **—a·mend·a·ble** *adj.* **—a·mend·er** *n.*

a·mend·a·to·ry (ə-mĕn′də-tôr′ē, -tōr′ē) *adj.* Serving or tending to amend; constituting an amendment.

a·mend·ment (ə-mĕnd′mənt) *n.* **1.** The act or process of amending. **2.** A correction, alteration, or improvement. **3.** An alteration formally proposed for or made in a legislative measure.

a·mends (ə-mĕndz′) *pl.n.* Reparation or compensation made as satisfaction for insult or injury. Used chiefly in the phrase *make amends.* —See Synonyms at **reparation.** [Middle English *amendes,* from Old French, plural of *amende,* reparation, from *amender,* to AMEND.]

Amenhotep IV. See **Akhenaton.**

a·men·i·ty (ə-mĕn′ə-tē, ə-mē′nə-) *n., pl.* **-ties. 1.** Pleasantness; agreeableness. **2.** A feature or facility that increases physical or material comfort: *recreational amenities.* **3. amenities.** Social courtesies; pleasantries; civilities. [Middle English *amenite,* from Old French, from Latin *amoenitās,* from *amoenus*†, pleasant, delightful.]

a·men·or·rhe·a, a·men·or·rhoe·a (ā-mĕn′ə-rē′ə) *n.* Abnormal suppression or absence of menstruation. [New Latin : A- (not) + Greek *mēn,* month + -RRHEA.]

Amen-Ra (ä′mən-rä′) The chief national god of ancient Egypt during the period of Theban domination, regarded as the sun god.

am·ent¹ (ăm′ənt, ā′mənt) *n. Botany.* A **catkin** (*see*). [New Latin *amentum,* from Latin *ammentum,* a thong, strap.] **—am·en·ta·ceous** (ăm′ən-tā′shəs, ā′mən-) *adj.* **—am·en·tif·er·ous** (ăm′ən-tĭf′ər-əs, ā′mən-) *adj.*

a·ment² (ā′mənt, ā′mĕnt′) *n. Psychology.* A mentally deficient or feeble-minded person. [Latin *āmēns* (stem *āment-*) : *ā-,* out of, away from + *mēns,* mind.]

a·men·tia (ā-mĕn′shə) *n. Psychology.* Subnormal mental development; feeble-mindedness. [Latin *āmentia,* from *āmēns,* AMENT.]

Amer. America; American.

A·mer·a·sian (ăm′ə-rā′zhən, -shən) *n.* A person of mixed American and Asian descent. **—A·mer·a·sian** *adj.*

a·merce (ə-mûrs′) *tr.v.* **amerced, amercing, amerces. 1.** To punish by a fine imposed arbitrarily at the discretion of the court. **2.** To punish by imposing any arbitrary penalty. [Middle English *amercien,* from Norman French *amercier,* from *a merci,* at the mercy of : *a-,* to, from Latin *ad-* + *merci,* mercy, from Latin *mercēs,* wages.] **—a·merce·ment** *n.* **—a·merc·er** *n.*

A·mer·i·ca (ə-mĕr′ə-kə). *Abbr.* **A., Am., Amer. 1.** The United States of America. **2.** North America, Central America, and South America together. In this sense, also called "the Americas." [After *Americus* Vespucius (Latinized form of Amerigo VESPUCCI).]

A·mer·i·can (ə-mĕr′ə-kən) *adj. Abbr.* **A., Am., Amer. 1.** Of, relating to, belonging to, or characteristic of the United States of America, its language, people, culture, government, or history. **2.** Of or pertaining to the Americas. **3.** Of or pertaining to the American Indians. **4.** Indigenous to the Americas. Often used with plant and animal names: *American elm; American elk.* *~n. Abbr.* **A., Am., Amer. 1.** A native or inhabitant of America. **2.** A citizen of the United States. **3.** American English.

A·mer·i·ca·na (ə-mĕr′ə-kä′nə, -kăn′ə, -kā′nə) *pl.n.* **1.** Objects relating to American history, folklore, or geography. **2.** A collection of such objects. [AMERIC(A) + -ANA.]

American Beauty *n.* A type of rose bearing large, long-stemmed, purplish-red flowers.

American dream *n.* **1.** The democratic and egalitarian ideals espoused by Americans. **2.** The material affluence that the United States traditionally offers its inhabitants.

American eagle *n.* The **bald eagle** (*see*), especially as it appears on the Great Seal of the United States.

American elk *n.* The **wapiti** (*see*).

American English *n.* The English language as used in the United States. Also called "American."

American Federation of Labor *n. Abbr.* **AFL, A.F.L., A.F.** of **L.** A federation of U.S. labor unions organized in 1886, and merged with the Congress of Industrial Organizations in 1955.

American Indian *n.* A member of any of the aboriginal peoples of North America (except the Innuit, or Eskimos), South America, and Central America, considered to belong to the Mongoloid ethnic division of the human species.

A·mer·i·can·ism (ə-mĕr′ə-kə-nĭz′əm) *n.* **1.** A custom, trait, or tradition originating in or peculiar to the United States. **2.** A usage of language characteristic of American English. **3.** Allegiance to the United States and its values and institutions.

A·mer·i·can·ist (ə-mĕr′ə-kə-nĭst) *n.* **1.** A specialist in some facet of America, such as its history or geology. **2.** An anthropologist specializing in the study of American aboriginal culture.

A·mer·i·can·ize (ə-mĕr′ə-kə-nīz′) *v.* **-ized, -izing, -izes.** *—tr.* To cause to become American in character, spirit, or form. *—intr.* To become American in character, spirit, or form. **—A·mer·i·can·i·za·tion** (ə-mĕr′ə-kə-nə-zā′shən, -nī-zā′shən) *n.*

American plan *n.* A system of hotel tariffs in which a guest pays a fixed daily rate for room, meals, and service. Compare **European plan.**

American Revolution *n.* The war fought between Great Britain and her colonies in North America (1775–83) by which the colonies won independence. Also called "Revolutionary War" and, in Great Britain, "War of American Independence." See feature, next page.

American robin *n.* See **robin** (sense 1).

American sable *n.* See **sable** (sense 1).

American Sa·mo·a (sə-mō′ə). Also **Eastern Samoa.** An unincorporated territory of the United States comprising the seven easternmost islands of the Samoan archipelago, lying in the South Pacific Ocean *c.* 1,000 kilometers (620 miles) northeast of Fiji. The islands are administered by the U.S. Department of the Interior. The capital is Pago Pago on Tutuila, the main island.

American Spanish *n.* The variety of Spanish spoken in the Americas.

American Standard Version *n. Abbr.* **ASV, ARV** A revised version of the Authorized Version of the Bible published in the United States in 1901. Also called "American Revised Version."

Americas, the. The landmasses and islands between the main bodies of the Atlantic and Pacific oceans, also known as the New World or Western Hemisphere. With some 28 percent of the world's land, the Americas approach Asia in size, but have only just over a quarter of Asia's population. They stretch for more than 15,300 kilometers (*c.* 9,500 miles), through more degrees of latitude than any other continent. Two areas with roughly the same north-south extent result from a division at the Isthmus of Panama: North America (Panama and all lands and islands to the north) and South America. These in turn can be divided into North America (Mexico and lands to the north); South America (as above); and Central America. A cultural division can be made into North America (or

Anglo-America) and Latin America (all lands south of the United States); virtually all of Latin America was for 300 years part of either the Spanish or Portuguese empires. The region of Pre-Columbian civilization of Central America (southern Mexico, Belize, Guatemala, western Honduras, and El Salvador) is sometimes called Middle America.

America's Cup *n.* An international yachting trophy awarded to the winner of a yacht race between a selected challenger and a selected American yacht. It was first won by the yacht *America* in 1851.

am·er·i·ci·um (ăm′ə-rĭsh′ē-əm) *n. Symbol* **Am** A white metallic transuranic element of the actinide series, having isotopes with mass numbers from 237 to 246 and half-lives from 25 minutes to 7,950 years. Its longest-lived isotopes, Am-241 and Am-243, are alpha-ray emitters used as radiation sources in research. Atomic number 95, specific gravity 13.67, valences 3, 4, 5, 6. [New Latin, from AMERICA (where it was first produced).]

Amerigo Vespucci. See **Vespucci.**

Am·er·in·di·an (ăm′ə-rĭn′dē-ən) *n.* Also **Am·er·ind** (ăm′ə-rĭnd′). An American Indian or an Eskimo. [AMER(ICAN) + INDIAN.] **—Am·er·in·di·an, Am·er·ind·ic** *adj.*

am·e·thyst (ăm′ə-thĭst) *n.* **1.** A purple or violet form of transparent quartz used as a gemstone. **2.** A purple variety of corundum, used as a gemstone. Also called "oriental amethyst." **3.** Moderate to reddish purple. [Middle English *ametist,* from Old French *ametiste,* from Latin *amethystus,* from Greek *amethustos,* amethyst, "anti-intoxicant" (amethyst was thought to be a remedy for intoxication) : *a-,* not + *methuskein,* to intoxicate, from *methuein,* to be drunk, from *methu,* wine.] **—am·e·thys·tine** (ăm′ə-thĭs′tĭn, -tīn′) *adj.*

amethystine python *n.* The largest Australian python, *Liasis amethystinus.* Also called "rock python."

am·e·tro·pi·a (ăm-ə-trō′pē-ə) *n.* Any eye abnormality, such as near sightedness, farsightedness, or astigmatism, resulting from faulty refraction. [New Latin : Greek *ametros,* beyond measure, disproportionate : *a-,* without + *metron,* measure + -OPIA.]

Am·har·ic (ăm-hăr′ĭk, ăm-hä′rĭk) *n.* A southern Semitic language, the official language in Ethiopia. **—Am·har·ic** *adj.*

a·mi·a·ble (ā′mē-ə-bəl) *adj.* **1.** Friendly and likable; good-natured; agreeable. **2.** Cordial; congenial. [Middle English, from Old French, from Late Latin *amīcābilis,* AMICABLE.] **—a·mi·a·bil·i·ty** (ā′mē-ə-bĭl′ə-tē), **ami·a·ble·ness** *n.* **—a·mi·a·bly** *adv.*

am·i·an·thus (ăm′ē-ăn′thəs) *n.* Also **am·i·an·tus** (-təs). An asbestos with fine, silky fibers. [Latin *amiantus,* from Greek *amiantos* (*lithos*), "unpolluted (stone)" : *a-,* not + *miainein,* to pollute, defile.]

am·i·ca·ble (ăm′ĭ-kə-bəl) *adj.* Characterized by or showing friendliness; especially, made in a spirit of good will and without rancor: *an amicable settlement of their dispute.* [Middle English, from Late Latin *amīcābilis,* from Latin *amīcus,* friend.] **—am·i·ca·bil·i·ty** (ăm′ĭ-kə-bĭl′ə-tē), **am·i·ca·ble·ness** *n.* **—am·i·ca·bly** *adv.*

am·ice (ăm′ĭs) *n.* In Christian churches, a liturgical vestment consisting of an oblong piece of white linen worn round the neck and shoulders and partly under the alb. [Middle English *amyse,* perhaps from Old French *amis,* plural of *amit,* amice, from Latin *amictus,* mantle, "(a garment) thrown around one," from *amicīre,* to throw round : *ambi-,* round + *jacere,* to throw.]

A·mi·ci (ä-mē′chē), **Giovanni Battista** (1786–1863). Italian astronomer. He is noted for his improvements in designing scientific instruments, especially telescopes and microscopes, and particularly for his development of the achromatic lens.

a·mi·cus cu·ri·ae (ə-mē′kəs kyŏŏr′ē-ī′) *n.,pl.* **amici curiae** (ə-mē′kē kyŏŏr′ē-ī′). *Law.* A person invited to advise a court on a matter of law in a case to which he is not a party. [Latin, "friend of the court."]

a·mid (ə-mĭd′) *prep.* Also **a·midst** (ə-mĭdst′). Surrounded by, in the middle of, or in the course of. —See Synonyms at **among.** [Middle English *amidde,* Old English *onmiddan* : ON + *middan,* dative singular of *midd(e),* middle.]

am·ide (ăm′īd′, -ĭd) *n.* **1.** An organic compound, such as acetamide, containing the CONH₂ group. **2.** A compound with a metal replacing hydrogen in ammonia, such as *sodium amide,* NaNH₂. [AM(MONIA) + -IDE.] **—a·mid·ic** (ə-mĭd′ĭk) *adj.*

am·i·dol (ăm′ĭ-dôl′, -dōl′) *n.* A colorless crystalline compound (NH₂)₂C₆H₃OH·2HCl, used as a photographic developer. [German *Amidol* (trademark) : *amide* + *phenol.*]

a·mid·ships (ə-mĭd′shĭps′) *adv.* Also **a·mid·ship** (-shĭp′). *Nautical.* To, near to, or in the middle of a ship

A·mi·ens (ăm′ē-ənz, ä-myăN′). City in northern France dating from pre-Roman times. Situated in the Somme valley north of Paris, it is the principal city and capital of the Somme department. It has been a center of textile manufacturing since the Middle Ages, and its fine Gothic cathedral is the largest church in France.

a·mi·go (ə-mē′gō) *n., pl.* **-gos.** A friend. [Spanish, from Latin *amīcus,* friend.]

A·min Da·da (ä-mēn′ dä-dä′), **Idi** (*c.* 1925–). President of Uganda from 1971 to 1979. He became commander in chief of the Ugandan army in 1966, and in 1971 led the military coup that overthrew President Milton Obote. In 1972 he ordered the expulsion of Uganda's 80,000-strong Asian community. Thereafter his rule became increasingly brutal and repressive, and in 1979 he fled the country after being deposed in a Tanzanian-backed coup.

Amindivi Islands. See **Lakshadweep.**

a·mine (ə-mēn′, ăm′ĭn) *n.* Any of a group of organic compounds of nitrogen, such as ethylamine, C₂H₅NH₂, that may be considered ammonia derivatives in which one or more hydrogen atoms has

amethyst *The ancient Greeks wore amulets made of this semiprecious stone, believing that it could prevent drunkenness, dispel sleep, sharpen the intellect, and act as an antidote to poison.*

THE BIRTH OF A GREAT NATION

How Puritan ideals from the Old World inspired revolution in the New

When Britain drove the French from Canada (1763) the writ of empire ran from Labrador to the Gulf of Mexico. Troops and administrators were needed to control the land, and King George III imposed a succession of new taxes on the 13 American colonies to help pay the costs.

The colonists resisted. They were independent people, struggling to open virgin lands and steeped in the Puritan principles of self-help. From England's own traditions they inherited a belief that governments derived their power from the consent of the governed, that liberty was a natural right. The colonists demanded "No taxation without representation" and refused to buy British imports that were taxed, a move that halved British trade to America by 1769. Parlia-

ment at length dropped the duties, but kept a tax on tea as a token of English supremacy. It was a provocative gesture: in 1773 colonists dressed as Indians held what history would call the Boston Tea Party, boarding a newly arrived ship and hurling 342 chests of tea into the harbor.

An angry Parliament reacted by closing Boston harbor and sending more troops. As tensions mounted, citizens formed militias and began drilling and stockpiling weapons. On the morning of April 19, 1775, British soldiers sent to seize arms were faced by local militiamen across the green at Lexington, Massachusetts. Shots were fired, and the conflict began. Early in 1776 Parliament blockaded the colonies and hired German mercenaries to help quell the uprising.

Outcry followed in America. A committee appointed by the Continental Congress issued a declaration, written chiefly by Thomas Jefferson. "We hold these truths to be self-evident," it stated, "that all men are created equal, that they are endowed by their Creator with certain inalienable rights, that among these are life, liberty, and the pursuit of happiness." Congress unanimously approved the Declaration of Independence at Philadelphia on July 4, 1776.

The war itself dragged on until, in 1781, 7,000 British soldiers surrendered to General Washington at Yorktown, Virginia. The rebels had won, and in 1783 Parliament accepted the inevitable—eight years after the skirmish at Lexington, Britain formally recognized the United States of America.

MEN OF IDEAS *Pictured on a snuffbox lid are Benjamin Franklin (1706–90), right, with the philosophers Voltaire (1694–1778), left, and Rousseau (1712–78). Franklin persuaded the French to back the American colonists.*

LEADERS OF THE EMPIRE *An 18th-century print shows George III (1760–1820) with the elder Pitt (left) and James Wolfe, the minister and general who won Canada from the French (1763). A major part of their American empire was soon to be in revolt against the English king.*

THE VOICE OF INDEPENDENCE *Thomas Jefferson (1743–1826) insisted that Parliament should have no authority in America. His pen wrote the echoing words that among man's rights were: "Life, liberty, and the pursuit of happiness."*

FIRST PRESIDENT *George Washington (1732–99) commanded the colonial troops throughout the Revolutionary War. In 1789 he answered his country's call once more—and became the first President of the United States.*

BUNKER HILL (1775) *British troops fought all day to move the Patriot farmers from a promontory overlooking Boston. The fierce resistance of the colonists set the pattern for the long war.*

BIRTH OF A NATION *Thomas Jefferson and his committee laid the Declaration of Independence before Congress in the State House, Philadelphia, on July 4, 1776. A young brigade major, John Trumbull, painted the historic moment from sketches made at the scene. To the right of Jefferson is Benjamin Franklin, to the left are John Adams, Roger Sherman, and Robert Livingston. Their words, unanimously accepted by Congress, summed up the new ideas of liberty and equality, and set the 13 colonies on a course of freedom from the British empire.*

been replaced by a hydrocarbon radical. [AM(MONIUM) + -INE.]

–amine *suffix.* Indicates an amine; for example, **methylamine.**

a·mi·no (ə-mē′nō, ăm′ə-nō′) *adj.* Pertaining to or consisting of an amine or other chemical compound containing NH₂ combined with a nonacid organic radical. [Independent use of AMINO-.]

amino– *prefix.* Indicates replacement of one of the hydrogen atoms in ammonia by a nonacid organic radical; for example, **aminophenol.** [From AMINE.]

amino acid *n.* Any organic compound containing both an amino group (NH₂) and a carboxyl group (COOH). Amino acids are essential components of proteins.

a·mi·no·ac·i·de·mi·a (ə-mē′nō-ăs′ĭ-dē′mē-ə, ăm′ə-nō-) *n.* A condition marked by excess amino acids in the blood.

a·mi·no·ac·i·du·ri·a (ə-mē′nō-ăs′ĭ-dŏŏr′ē-ə, -dyŏŏr′-, ăm′ə-nō-) *n.* A condition marked by excess amino acids in the urine.

a·mi·no·ben·zo·ic acid (ə-mē′nō-běn-zō′ĭk, ăm′ə-nō-) *n.* Any of three benzoic acid derivatives, NH₂C₆H₄COOH, especially the yellowish para form, which is part of the vitamin B complex.

a·mi·no·phe·nol (ə-mē′nō-fē′nôl′, -nŏl′, ăm′ə-nō-) *n.* One of three organic compounds with composition C₆H₄NH₂OH, used as photographic developers and dye intermediates.

a·mi·no·py·rine (ə-mē′nō-pī′rēn′, ăm′ə-nō-) *n.* A colorless crystalline compound, C₁₃H₁₇N₃O, used to reduce fever and relieve pain. [AMINO- + (ANTI)PYRINE.]

amir. Variant of **emir.**

A·mis (ā′mĭs), **Kingsley** (1922–). British novelist, poet, and critic. His first novel, *Lucky Jim* (1954), a satire on provincial university life, became an immediate popular success. His other works include *Jake's Thing* (1978), *The Green Man* (1969), *The Riverside Villas Murder* (1973), and *Russian Hide-and-Seek* (1980).

A·mish (ä′mĭsh, ăm′ĭsh, ā′mĭsh) *pl.n.* An orthodox U.S. Anabaptist sect that separated from the Mennonites in the late 17th century. [German *amisch,* after Jacob *Amman,* 17th-century Swiss Mennonite bishop.] —*adj.* Of or pertaining to this sect or its members.

a·miss (ə-mĭs′) *adj.* Out of proper order, wrong, or out of place in the circumstances: *What is amiss?* —*adv.* In an improper, erroneous, or defective way. —**take amiss.** To misunderstand; feel offended by. [Middle English *a mis* : A- (on, at) + *mis,* a mistake, from *missen,* to MISS.]

a·mi·to·sis (ā′mī-tō′sĭs) *n. Biology.* Cell division characterized by simple nuclear cleavage without the formation of chromosomes. [New Latin : A- (not) + MITOSIS.] —**a·mi·tot·ic** (ā′mī-tŏt′ĭk) *adj.* —**a·mi·tot·i·cal·ly** *adv.*

am·i·ty (ăm′ə-tē) *n., pl.* **-ties.** Peaceful and cordial relations, especially between nations; friendship. [Middle English *amite,* from Old French *amitie,* from Medieval Latin *amīcitās,* from Latin *amīcus,* friend.]

Am·man (ə-măn′, ə-män′). The capital and by far the largest and most modern city of Jordan, on the Jabbok (Zarqa) River in the north of the country. Since 1948 remains from the Chalcolithic period (*c.* 4000 B.C.–*c.* 3000 B.C.) have been unearthed on the site.

am·me·ter (ăm′mē′tər) *n. Abbr.* **A** An instrument that measures electric current. [AM(PERE) + -METER.]

am·mine (ăm′mēn′, ə-mēn′) *n.* Any of a class of chemical compounds, such as aniline, derived from replacement of hydrogen atoms in ammonia by univalent hydrocarbon radicals. [AMM(ONIA) + -INE.] —**am·mi·no** (ăm′ə-nō′, ə-mē′nō) *adj.*

am·mo (ăm′ō) *n. Informal.* Ammunition.

am·mo·cete (ăm′ə-sēt′) *n.* The blind, wormlike larva of the lamprey. [New Latin *Ammocoetes* (former genus name), "ones that lie in sand" : Greek *ammos,* sand + *koitē,* bed, from *keisthai,* to lie.]

am·mo·nia (ə-mōn′yə) *n.* **1.** A colorless, pungent gas, NH₃, extensively used to manufacture fertilizers and a wide variety of nitrogen-containing organic and inorganic chemicals. **2.** A solution of ammonia in water, **ammonium hydroxide** *(see).* [New Latin, from Latin *(sal) ammōniācus,* "(salt) of Amen," from Greek *ammōniakos,* from *Ammōn,* AMEN (it was originally obtained from a region near the temple of Amen, in Libya).]

am·mo·ni·ac¹ (ə-mō′nē-ăk′) *adj.* Also **am·mo·ni·a·cal** (ăm′ə-nī′ə-kəl). Of, containing, or similar to ammonia.

ammoniac² *n.* A strong-smelling gum resin from the stems of a plant, *Dorema ammoniacum,* of northern Asia, formerly used in medicine as an expectorant and stimulant. Also called "gum ammoniac." [Middle English *ammonyak,* from Latin *ammōniacum,* from Greek *ammōniakon,* neuter of *ammōniakos,* of Amen. See **ammonia.**]

am·mo·ni·ate (ə-mō′nē-āt′) *tr.v.* **-ated, -ating, -ates.** To treat or combine with ammonia. —*n.* A compound that contains ammonia. —**am·mo·ni·a·tion** *n.*

ammonia water *n. Chemistry.* Ammonium hydroxide.

am·mon·i·fi·ca·tion (ə-mŏn′ə-fĭ-kā′shən, ə-mō′nə-) *n.* **1.** Impregnation with ammonia or an ammonium compound. **2.** The generation of ammonia or ammonium compounds by the action of bacteria on nitrogenous organic matter in soil.

am·mon·i·fy (ə-mŏn′ə-fī′, ə-mō′nə-) *v.* **-fied, -fying, -fies.** —*tr.* To subject to ammonification. —*intr.* To undergo ammonification. [AMMONI(A) + -FY.]

am·mon·ite¹ (ăm′ə-nīt′) *n.* **1.** The coiled, flat, chambered shell of any of various extinct cephalopod mollusks of the subclass Ammonoidea, found as fossils in Mesozoic formations. **2.** Any mollusk of the subclass Ammonoidea. [New Latin *Ammonītēs,* from Latin *(cornus) Ammōnis,* "(horn) of Amen" (because it resembles the

horns of Amen), from *Ammōnis,* genitive of *Ammōn,* AMEN.]

ammonite² *n.* **1.** An explosive mixture of ammonium nitrate and a small quantity of TNT or a similar substance. **2.** A nitrogenous fertilizer made from animal wastes. [*Ammonium* + *nitrate.*]

Am·mo·nite (ăm′ə-nīt′) *n.* A member of a Semitic people living east of the river Jordan, mentioned frequently in the Old Testament. [Late Latin *Ammonītēs,* the Ammonites, from Hebrew *'Ammōn,* city or people of Amman, from Canaanite *'am-,* "folk."]

am·mo·ni·um (ə-mō′nē-əm) *n.* The chemical ion NH₄⁺. [New Latin : AMMON(IA) + -IUM.]

ammonium carbonate *n.* A white powder with composition (NH₄)HCO₃·(NH₄)CO₂NH₂, used in baking powders, smelling salts, and fire-extinguishing compounds. Also called "sal volatile."

ammonium chloride *n.* A slightly hygroscopic white crystalline compound, NH₄Cl, used in dry cells, as a soldering flux, as an expectorant, and in various industrial applications. Also called "sal ammoniac."

ammonium hydroxide *n.* A colorless basic aqueous solution of ammonia, NH₄OH, used as a household cleanser and to manufacture a wide variety of products including textiles, rayon, rubber, fertilizers, and plastics. Also called "ammonia water."

ammonium nitrate *n.* A colorless crystalline salt, NH₄NO₃, used in fertilizers, explosives, and solid rocket propellants.

ammonium sulfate *n.* A brownish-gray to white crystalline salt, (NH₄)₂SO₄, used in fertilizers and water purification.

am·mu·ni·tion (ăm′yə-nĭsh′ən) *n.* **1. a.** Bullets, shells, or the like, along with their fuses and primers, that can be fired from guns or otherwise propelled. **b.** Any nuclear, biological, chemical, or explosive material used in warfare. **2.** Any means of attack or defense, such as facts that can be used in an argument. [Obsolete French *amunition,* from phrase *l'amunition,* misinterpretation of *la munition,* the MUNITION.]

am·ne·si·a (ăm-nē′zhə) *n.* Partial or total loss of memory, especially through shock, psychological disturbance, brain damage, or illness. [New Latin, from Greek *amnēsia* : *a-,* not + *mnasthai,* to remember.] —**am·ne·si·ac** (ăm-nē′zē-ăk′, -zhē-ăk′) *n. & adj.* —**am·nes·tic** (ăm-nĕs′tĭk) *adj.*

am·nes·ty (ăm′nəs-tē) *n., pl.* **-ties. 1.** A general pardon granted by a government, especially to people guilty of political offenses. **2.** A period during which this is in force. **3.** A period of immunity during which penalties for past infringements are waived. —*tr.v.* **amnestied, -tying, -ties.** To grant an amnesty to. [Greek *amnēstia,* "forgetfulness," from *amnēstos,* forgotten : *a-,* not + *mnasthai,* to remember.]

Amnesty International *n.* An organization that investigates violations of human rights and campaigns for the release of prisoners of conscience and the humane treatment of political prisoners.

am·ni·o·cen·te·sis (ăm′nē-ō-sĕn-tē′sĭs) *n., pl.* **-ses** (-sēz′). The withdrawal of a sample of amniotic fluid from a pregnant woman, usually for the diagnosis of genetic or developmental disorders in the fetus. [AMNION + Greek *kentesis,* a puncturing, from *kentein,* to prick.]

am·ni·og·ra·phy (ăm′nē-ŏg′rə-fē) *n.* Radiography of the amnion in order to examine the placenta and umbilical cord. [AMNIO(N) + -GRAPHY.]

am·ni·on (ăm′nē-ən, -ŏn′) *n., pl.* **-ons** or **-ni·a** (-nē-ə). A thin, tough, membranous sac that contains a watery fluid in which the embryo of a mammal, bird, or reptile is suspended. It is the inner of two embryonic membranes. Compare **chorion.** [New Latin, from Greek *amnion,* caul, diminutive of *amnos,* lamb.] —**am·ni·ot·ic** (ăm′nē-ŏt′-ĭk), **am·ni·on·ic** (ăm′nē-ŏn′ĭk) *adj.*

am·ni·os·co·py (ăm′nē-ŏs′kə-pē) *n., pl.* **-pies.** Examination of the interior of the amniotic sac by means of an instrument passed through the wall of the abdomen. [AMNIO(N) + -SCOPY.] —**am·ni·o·scope** (ăm′nē-ə-skōp′) *n.*

am·n't (ăm′ənt) *Chiefly Regional.* Contraction of *am not.* —See Usage note at **ain't.**

a·moe·ba, a·me·ba (ə-mē′bə) *n., pl.* **-bas** or **-bae** (-bē). Any of various protozoans of the genus *Amoeba* and related genera, occurring in water, soil, and as internal animal parasites, characteristically having an indefinite, changeable form and moving by means of pseudopodia. [New Latin, from Greek *amoibē,* change, from *ameibein,* to change.] —**a·moe·bic** (ə-mē′bĭk) *adj.*

am·oe·bae·an, am·oe·be·an (ăm′ē-bē′ən) *adj.* Alternately answering, as dialogue. [Late Latin *amoebaeus,* from Greek *amoibaios,* from *amoibē,* change. See **amoeba.**]

am·oe·bi·a·sis, am·e·bi·a·sis (ăm′ə-bī′ə-sĭs) *n., pl.* **-ses** (-sēz′). An infection caused by amoebas, especially by *Entamoeba histolytica.* [New Latin : AMOEB(A) + -IASIS.]

amoebic dysentery *n.* An infectious, inflammatory disease of the colon, caused by *Entamoeba histolytica* and resulting in severe pain and diarrhea.

a·moe·bo·cyte (ə-mē′bə-sīt′) *n.* Any cell, such as a leucocyte, having amoebic form. [AMOEB(A) + -CYTE.]

a·moe·boid (ə-mē′boid′) *adj.* Of or resembling an amoeba, especially in changeable form and means of locomotion.

amok. Variant of **amuck.**

a·mo·le (ə-mō′lē) *n.* **1.** Any of several plants, chiefly of southwestern North America, with parts, as roots or bulbs, used as soap. **2.** The parts of an amole used as soap. [Spanish, from Nahuatl *amol(li).*]

Amon. Variant of **Amen.**

a·mong (ə-mŭng′) *prep.* Also **a·mongst** (ə-mŭngst′). **1.** In the midst

ammonite *The fossil remains of a number of types of extinct shellfish are known as ammonites. This ammonite, dating from perhaps 200 million years ago, was found in West Germany.*

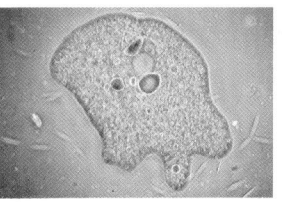

amoeba *The microscopic amoeba is the simplest form of animal life. It reproduces by splitting in two.*

of; surrounded by. **2.** In the group, number, or class of: *among the fastest runners in the country; among other things.* **3.** In the company of; in association with: *traveling among a group of tourists.* **4.** With or by many or most of: *a custom popular among the Greeks.* **5.** By the joint action of: *Among us, we will get the job done.* **6.** With portions to each of: *Distribute this among them.* **7.** Each with the other of; between one another in a group of: *Don't fight among yourselves.* [Middle English *among,* Old English *on gemang* : *on,* in, ON + *gemang,* a crowd.]

a·mon·til·la·do (ə-mŏn′tə-lä′dō) *n., pl.* **-dos.** A fairly pale medium-dry sherry. [Spanish *(vino) amontillado,* "(wine) made in Montilla" : *a-,* to, from Latin *ad-* + *Montilla,* Spanish town.]

a·mor·al (ā-môr′əl, ā-mŏr′-) *adj.* **1.** Not admitting of moral distinctions or judgments; outside the sphere of morality; nonmoral. **2.** Lacking moral judgment or sensibility; unable to distinguish between right and wrong. [A- (not) + MORAL.] —**a·mo·ral·i·ty** (ā′mô-răl′ə-tē, -mə-), **a·mor·al·ism** *n.* —**a·mor·al·ly** *adv.*

a·mo·ret·to (ăm′ə-rĕt′ō, ä′mə-) *n., pl.* **-retti** (-rĕt′ē) or **-tos.** A cupid. [Italian, diminutive of *Amore,* Cupid, from Latin *Amor,* from *amor,* love, from *amāre,* to love.]

am·o·rist (ăm′ə-rĭst) *n.* One who is dedicated to or writes about love. [From Latin *amor,* love.]

Am·o·rite (ăm′ə-rīt′) *n.* A member of a people inhabiting Canaan before the Israelites, mentioned frequently in the Old Testament. [Hebrew *Emōrī.*]

a·mo·ro·so (ä′mə-rō′sō, ăm′ə-) *adv. Music.* In a loving manner; tenderly. Used as a direction. [Italian, "amorous."] —**a·mo·ro·so** *adj.*

am·o·rous (ăm′ər-əs) *adj.* **1.** Strongly attracted to love, especially sexual love. **2.** Indicative of love: *an amorous glance.* **3.** Of or concerned with love: *an amorous poem.* **4.** In love; enamored. Sometimes used with *of.* [Middle English, from Old French, from Medieval Latin *amōrōsus,* from Latin *amor,* love.] —**am·or·ous·ly** *adv.* —**am·or·ous·ness** *n.*

a·mor·phism (ə-môr′fĭz′əm) *n.* The state or quality of being amorphous, especially with respect to lack of crystalline structure.

a·mor·phous (ə-môr′fəs) *adj.* **1.** Without definite form; lacking a specific shape. **2.** Of no particular type or character; formless; indeterminate. **3.** Lacking distinct crystalline structure. [Greek *amorphos* : A- (without) + -MORPHOUS.] —**a·mor·phous·ly** *adv.* —**a·mor·phous·ness** *n.*

am·or·ti·za·tion (ăm′ər-tə-zā′shən, ə-môr′tə-) *n.* **1. a.** The act or process of amortizing or the condition of being amortized. **b.** The money set aside for this purpose. **2.** In reckoning the yield of a bond bought at a premium, the periodic subtraction from its current yield of a proportionate share of the premium between the purchase date and the maturity date.

am·or·tize (ăm′ər-tīz′, ə-môr′tīz′) *tr.v.* **-tized, -tizing, -tizes. 1.** *Finance.* To liquidate (a debt) by installment payments or payment into a sinking fund. **2.** *Accounting.* **a.** To reduce gradually the book value of (an asset) over a period equal to its projected useful life. **b.** To provide for the cost of replacing (an asset) by periodic payments into a sinking fund. **3.** *Law.* To transfer (property) in mortmain. [Middle English *amortisen,* from Old French *amortir* (present stem *amortiss-*), from Vulgar Latin *admortīre* (unattested), to deaden : *ad-,* to + *mortus* (unattested), dead, from Latin *mors* (stem *mort-*), death.] —**am·or·tiz·a·ble** *adj.*

a·mor·tize·ment (ə-môr′tĭz-mənt) *n.* Amortization.

A·mos[1] (ā′məs). A Hebrew prophet of the 8th century B.C.

Amos[2] *n.* A book of the Old Testament containing the prophecies of Amos.

a·mount (ə-mount′) *n. Abbr.* **amt. 1.** The total figure or quantity; a sum or aggregate: *could only raise half the amount needed.* **2.** A quantity or supply: *attracted a tremendous amount of interest.* **3.** A principal plus its interest, as in a loan. **4.** The overall effect or meaning; import. ~*intr.v.* **amounted, amounting, amounts. 1.** To add up in number or quantity: *The total purchase amounts to ten dollars.* **2.** To be equivalent or tantamount: *accusations amounting to an indictment.* [Middle English *amounten,* to rise, from Old French *amonter,* from *amont,* upward, "to the mountain" : *a-,* to, from Latin *ad-* + *mont,* mountain, from Latin *mōns* (stem *mont-*).]

a·mour (ə-moor′) *n.* A love affair, especially an illicit one: *His latest amours were in all the gossip columns.* [Middle English, from Old French, from Old Provençal *amor,* from Latin *amor,* love, from *amāre,* to love.]

a·mour-pro·pre (ə-moor′prôp′rə) *n.* Self-esteem. [French, "self-love."]

Amoy. See Xiamen.

amp (ămp) *n.* **1.** An ampere. **2.** *Informal.* An amplifier.

AMP[2] (ā′ĕm-pē′) *n.* A mononucleotide, $C_{10}H_{14}N_5O_7P$, found in animal cells, that is reversibly convertible to ADP and ATP. [*A*denosine *m*ono*p*hosphate.]

am·pe·lop·sis (ăm′pə-lŏp′sĭs) *n.* Any of several woody vines of the genus *Ampelopsis,* having small greenish or yellowish flowers and occurring in warm regions of Asia and America. [New Latin *Ampelopsis* : Greek *ampelos,* grapevine, + -OPSIS.]

am·per·age (ăm′pər-ĭj, ăm′pîr′-) *n.* The strength of an electric current expressed in amperes.

am·pere (ăm′pîr′) *n. Abbr.* **A 1.** A unit of electric current in the meter-kilogram-second system. It is the steady current that when flowing in straight parallel wires of infinite length and negligible cross section, separated by a distance of one meter in free space, produces a force between the wires of 2×10^{-7} newtons per meter

of length. One ampere is equal to one coulomb per second. **2.** A former unit of electric current, the international ampere, equal to 0.999835 ampere. Also shortened to "amp." [After André-Marie AMPÈRE.]

Am·père (ăm′pîr′), **André-Marie** (1775–1836). French physicist and mathematician. He formulated Ampère's law, a mathematical description of the magnetic field produced by a current-carrying conductor. The SI unit of electric current is named after him.

am·pere-hour (ăm′pîr-our′) *n.* The electric charge transferred past a specific circuit point by a current of one ampere in one hour.

am·pere-turn (ăm′pîr-tûrn′) *n.* A unit of magnetomotive force equal to the magnetomotive force around a path linking one turn of a conducting loop carrying a current of one ampere.

am·per·sand (ăm′pər-sănd′) *n.* The character or sign (&) representing *and.* [From *and per se and,* "& by itself (equals) *and,*" phrase formerly used to explain the character.]

am·phet·a·mine (ăm-fĕt′ə-mēn′, -mĭn) *n.* **1.** A colorless volatile liquid, $C_9H_{13}N$, used primarily as a central nervous system stimulant. **2.** A phosphate or sulfate of amphetamine used as a central nervous system stimulant. [*Alpha methyl phenyl ethyl amine.*]

amphi- *prefix.* Indicates: **1.** On both sides; on both ends; of both kinds; both; for example, **amphibious. 2.** Around; on all sides; for example, **amphithecium.** [Latin, from Greek, from *amphi,* around, on both sides, on all sides.]

am·phi·ar·thro·sis (ăm′fē-är-thrō′sĭs) *n., pl.* **-ses** (-sēz′). A relatively immobile joint between bony surfaces connected by ligaments or elastic cartilage.

am·phib·i·an (ăm-fĭb′ē-ən) *n.* **1.** Any of various cold-blooded, smooth-skinned, vertebrate organisms of the class Amphibia, such as a frog, toad, or salamander, characteristically hatching as aquatic larvae that breathe by means of gills and metamorphosing to an adult form having air-breathing lungs. **2.** Any amphibious organism. **3.** An aircraft that can take off and land either on land or on water. **4.** A vehicle that can move over land and on water. ~*adj.* Of or pertaining to an amphibian, especially one of the Amphibia. [New Latin *Amphibia,* plural of *amphibium,* an amphibian, from Greek *amphibion,* neuter of *amphibios,* AMPHIBIOUS.]

am·phi·bi·ot·ic (ăm′fĭ-bī-ŏt′ĭk) *adj.* Living in water during an early stage of development and on land during the adult stage.

am·phib·i·ous (ăm-fĭb′ē-əs) *adj.* **1.** Living or able to live both on land and in water. **2. a.** Able or trained to operate on both land and water: *amphibious troops.* **b.** Involving operations on both land and water: *an amphibious invasion.* **3.** Of a mixed or twofold nature. [Greek *amphibios,* "living a double life" : AMPHI- + *bios,* life.] —**am·phib·i·ous·ly** *adv.* —**am·phib·i·ous·ness** *n.*

am·phi·bole (ăm′fĭ-bōl′) *n.* Any of a large group of structurally similar hydrated double silicate minerals including hornblende and several types of asbestos, containing various combinations of sodium, calcium, magnesium, iron, and aluminum. [French, from Late Latin *amphibolus,* ambiguous (from its many varieties), from Greek *amphibolos,* doubtful, from *amphiballein,* to throw around, doubt : AMPHI- + *ballein,* to throw.] —**am·phi·bol·ic** (ăm′fĭ-bŏl′ĭk) *adj.*

am·phib·o·lite (ăm-fĭb′ə-līt′) *n.* A metamorphic rock composed chiefly of amphibole with some plagioclase and quartz. [AMPHIBOL(E) + -ITE.]

am·phi·bol·o·gy (ăm′fĭ-bŏl′ə-jē) *n., pl.* **-gies.** Also **am·phib·o·ly** (ăm-fĭb′ə-lē) *pl.* **-lies. 1.** Ambiguity arising from a grammatical construction that can be understood in more than one way. **2.** A statement, as *flying planes can be dangerous,* containing amphibology. [Middle English *amphibologie,* from Late Latin *amphibologia,* from *amphibolia,* from Greek *amphibolos,* ambiguous. See **amphibole.**] —**am·phib·o·log·i·cal** (ăm-fĭb′ə-lŏj′ĭ-kəl) *adj.* —**am·phib·o·log·i·cal·ly** *adv.*

am·phib·o·lous (ăm-fĭb′ə-ləs) *adj.* Having two meanings; ambiguous; equivocal. [Greek *amphibolos.* See **amphibole.**]

am·phi·brach (ăm′fə-brăk′) *n.* A trisyllabic metrical foot having one accented or long syllable between two unaccented or short syllables, as in the word *remember.* [Latin *amphibrachys,* from Greek *amphibrakhus* : *amphi-,* on both sides + *brakhus,* short.]

am·phi·coe·lous, am·phi·ce·lous (ăm′fĭ-sē′ləs) *adj.* Concave on both ends or sides, as the vertebrae of most fishes are. [Late Greek *amphikoilos* : AMPHI- + *koilos,* hollow.]

am·phic·ty·o·ny (ăm-fĭk′tē-ə-nē) *n., pl.* **-nies.** In ancient Greece, a group of neighboring states associated for a common religious or political purpose, especially the protection and maintenance of a common religious center or shrine, such as the one at Delphi. [Greek *amphiktuonia,* from *amphiktuones,* neighbors : AMPHI- + *ktizein,* to found.] —**am·phic·ty·on·ic** (ăm-fĭk′tē-ŏn′ĭk) *adj.*

am·phi·mix·is (ăm′fĭ-mĭk′sĭs) *n.* True sexual reproduction, with fusion of sperm and egg nuclei. Compare **apomixis.** [New Latin : AMPHI- + Greek *mixis,* a mingling, from *mignunai,* to mingle.] —**am·phi·mic·tic** (ăm′fĭ-mĭk′tĭk) *adj.*

am·phi·ox·us (ăm′fē-ŏk′səs) *n.* A primitive chordate organism, the **lancelet** *(see).* [New Latin, "sharp at both ends" : AMPHI- + Greek *oxus,* sharp.]

am·phi·pod (ăm′fĭ-pŏd′) *n.* Any of numerous small crustaceans of the order Amphipoda, which includes the beach fleas. [New Latin *Amphipoda,* "having feet on both sides" : AMPHI- + -POD.]

am·phi·pro·style (ăm-fĭp′rə-stīl′, ăm′fĭ-prō′-) *adj.* Having a prostyle or set of columns at each end, but none along the sides. Said especially of an ancient temple. [Latin *amphiprostylos,* from Greek *am-*

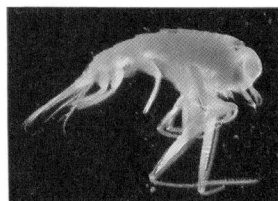

phiprostulos, "with pillars in front and behind" : AMPHI- + *prostulos,* with pillars in front (see **prostyle**).] —**am·phi·pro·style** *n.*

am·phis·bae·na (ăm′fĭs-bē′nə) *n.* **1.** A mythological serpent having a head at each end of its body. **2.** A wormlike burrowing lizard of the genus *Amphisbaena.* [Latin, from Greek *amphisbaina,* "one that goes in both directions" : *amphis,* both ways, + *bainein,* to go.] —**am·phis·bae·nic** *adj.*

am·phi·sty·lar (ăm′fĭ-stī′lər) *adj. Architecture.* Having columns at both front and back or on each side. [AMPHI- + Greek *stulos,* a pillar.]

am·phi·the·a·ter (ăm′fə-thē′ə-tər) *n.* Also *chiefly British* **am·phi·the·a·tre.** **1.** An oval or round structure having tiers of seats rising gradually outward from an open space or arena at the center. **2.** A public place where contests are held; an arena. **3.** A level area surrounded by upward sloping ground. **4.** An upper, sloping gallery in a theater. [Latin *amphitheatrum,* from Greek *amphitheatron* : AMPHI- + THEATER.] —**am·phi·the·at·ric** (ăm′fə-thē-ăt′rĭk), **am·phi·the·at·ri·cal** *adj.* —**am·phi·the·at·ri·cal·ly** *adv.*

am·phi·the·ci·um (ăm′fĭ-thē′shē-əm, -sē-əm) *n., pl.* **-ci·a** (-shē-ə, -sē-ə). *Botany.* The outer layer of cells of the spore-containing capsule of a moss. [New Latin : AMPHI- + Greek *thēkion,* diminutive of *thēkē,* a case.]

am·phit·ri·chous (ăm-fĭt′rĭ-kəs) *adj.* Having a flagellum or flagella at both ends, as certain microorganisms do. [AMPHI- + -TRICHOUS.]

Am·phi·tri·te (ăm′fĭ-trī′tē). *Greek Mythology.* The goddess of the sea, wife of Poseidon, and one of the Nereids.

am·phit·ro·pous (ăm-fĭt′rə-pəs) *adj. Botany.* Partly inverted, so that the point of attachment is near the middle. Said of an ovule. [AM-PHI- + -TROPOUS.]

am·pho·ra (ăm′fər-ə) *n., pl.* **-rae** (-rē) or **-ras.** A large two-handled jar with a narrow neck, used by the ancient Greeks and Romans to carry wine or oil. [Latin *amphora,* from Greek *amphoreus, amphiphoreus* : AMPHI- + *phoreus,* a bearer, from *pherein,* to bear.] —**am·pho·ral** (ăm′fər-əl) *adj.*

am·pho·ter·ic (ăm′fə-tĕr′ĭk) *adj. Chemistry.* Capable of reacting either as an acid or a base. [Greek *amphoteros,* either of two, from *amphō,* both.]

am·pi·cil·lin (ăm′pə-sĭl′ĭn) *n.* An antibiotic given orally or by injection primarily to treat a variety of infections of the urinary, respiratory, and intestinal tracts. [AM(INO-) + P(EN)ICILLIN.]

am·ple (ăm′pəl) *adj.* **-pler, -plest.** **1.** Large in extent or capacity; spacious: *an ample living room.* **2.** Large in degree, scope, or amount: *a family of ample means.* **3.** Rather stout; portly: *an ample figure.* **4.** Enough or more than enough for a particular need or purpose. [Middle English, from Old French, from Latin *amplus†,* wide, ample.] —**am·ple·ness** *n.*

am·plex·i·caul (ăm-plĕk′sĭ-kôl′) *adj. Botany.* Having a base that clasps or encircles the stem, as some leaves do. [New Latin *amplexicaulis,* embracing stem : Latin *amplexus,* past participle of *amplectī,* to wind around : AM(BI)- + *plectere,* to plait + *caulis,* stem.]

am·pli·fi·ca·tion (ăm′plə-fĭ-kā′shən) *n.* **1.** The act or result of amplifying; especially, the process of expanding a statement, narrative, or the like, as for clarification or rhetorical effect. **2. a.** Material used to amplify a statement. **b.** A statement so amplified. **3.** *Physics.* **a.** The process of increasing the magnitude of a variable quantity, especially of a voltage or current, without altering any other quality. **b.** The result of such a process.

am·pli·fi·er (ăm′plə-fī′ər) *n.* **1.** One that amplifies, enlarges, or extends. **2.** Any of various electronic devices or circuits that increase the current or voltage of a signal fed into them; for example, an audio-frequency amplifier that feeds the loudspeakers in a radio, record-player, or the like.

am·pli·fy (ăm′plə-fī′) *v.* **-fied, -fying, -fies.** —*tr.* **1.** To enlarge (a statement or idea, for example) by adding material that clarifies, illustrates, or otherwise expands. **2.** To extend, enhance, or increase, as in scope or importance. **3.** *Physics.* To produce amplification of. —*intr.* To write or discourse at greater length on what has been written or said. [Middle English *amplifien,* from Old French *amplifier,* from Latin *amplificāre* : *amplus,* AMPLE + *facere,* to make.]

am·pli·tude (ăm′plə-tōōd′, -tyōōd′) *n.* **1.** Greatness of size or extent; magnitude. **2.** Fullness of scope; breadth or range, as of mind. **3.** *Astronomy.* The angular distance along the horizon from true east or west to the intersection of the vertical circle of a celestial body with the horizon. **4.** *Physics.* The maximum value of a periodically varying quantity. **5.** *Mathematics.* **a.** The maximum ordinate value of a periodic curve. **b.** The angle made with the positive horizontal axis by the vector representation of a complex number. In this sense, also called "argument." [Latin *amplitūdō,* from *amplus,* AM-PLE.]

amplitude modulation *n. Abbr.* **AM, am** The encoding of a carrier wave by variation of its amplitude in accordance with an input signal. Compare **frequency modulation**.

am·ply (ăm′plē) *adv.* In an ample manner; largely; liberally; sufficiently.

am·poule, am·pule (ăm′pōōl, -pyōōl) *n.* A small glass tube, sealed after filling and used chiefly as a container for a hypodermic injection solution. [French, from Old French, from Latin *ampulla,* AM-PULLA.]

am·pul·la (ăm-pōōl′ə, -pŭl′ə) *n., pl.* **-pullae** (-pōōl′ē, -pŭl′ē). **1.** A nearly round bottle with two handles used by the ancient Romans for wine, oil, or perfume. **2. a.** A container used for wine or water at the Eucharist. **b.** A vessel for consecrated wine or holy oil.

3. *Anatomy.* A small dilation in a canal or duct, especially in the semicircular canal of the ear. [Latin, diminutive of *amp(h)ora,* AM-PHORA.] —**am·pul·lar** (ăm-pōōl′ər, -pŭl′ər) *adj.*

am·pul·la·ceous (ăm′pōō-lā′shəs) *adj.* Resembling an ampulla; bladder-shaped. [Latin *ampullāceus* : AMPULL(A) + -ACEOUS.]

am·pu·tate (ăm′pyōō-tāt′) *tr.v.* **-tated, -tating, -tates.** To cut off (a bodily part, usually a limb), especially by surgery. [Latin *amputāre,* to cut around : AM(BI)- + *putāre,* to cut.] —**am·pu·ta·tion** *n.*

am·pu·tee (ăm′pyōō-tē′) *n.* A person who has had one or more limbs removed by amputation.

am·ri·ta, am·ree·ta (ŭm-rē′tə) *n. Hindu Mythology.* **1.** The ambrosia, prepared by the gods, that bestows immortality. **2.** The immortality achieved by drinking this ambrosia. [Sanskrit *amṛta,* "deathless" : *a-,* without + *mṛta,* death.]

Am·rit·sar (ŭm-rĭt′sər). The administrative center and largest city in the Punjab, northwestern India, on the border with Pakistan. Founded in 1577 by the fourth guru of the Sikhs, Ram Das, it has remained the center of the Sikh faith. In 1919 it was the scene of a massacre in which hundreds of Indian nationalists were killed by British-led troops.

Am·ster·dam (ăm′stər-dăm′). The capital and largest city of the Netherlands, in North Holland province. It lies on the Ij, an arm of the Ijsselmeer, and is linked to the North Sea by a ship canal. The city has one of the world's most important stock exchanges and is a major center of the diamond-cutting industry. Among its many museums, the Rijksmuseum, which houses a large collection of Dutch paintings, is outstanding.

amt. amount.

amu *Physics.* atomic mass unit.

a·muck (ə-mŭk′) *adv.* Also **a·mok** (ə-mŭk′, ə-mŏk′). **1.** In a frenzy to do violence or kill. **2.** In a wild, frantic, or uncontrollable manner. Used in the phrase *run amok.* [Malay *amok,* furious attack.]

A·mu Dar·ya (ä′mōō där′yə). Ancient name **Ox·us** (ŏk′səs). A river that rises in the Pamir Mts. of central Asia and flows *c.* 2,580 kilometers (1,600 miles) northwest to the Aral Sea.

am·u·let (ăm′yə-lĭt) *n.* An object worn, especially around the neck, as a charm against evil or injury. [Latin *amulētum†.*]

A·mund·sen (ä′mən-sən), **Roald** (1872–1928). Norwegian explorer. He was the first to navigate the Northwest Passage (1903–06), and he fixed the position of the North Magnetic Pole. He became the first person to reach the South Pole in 1911, 34 days ahead of Robert Falcon Scott. With the Italian explorer Umberto Nobile he was the first to make a flight over the North Pole. Amundsen died on a flight to the Arctic to search for Nobile, whose airship had crashed.

A·mur (ä-mōōr′). *Chinese* **Hei·long Ji·ang** (hā′lōōng′ jē-äng′). One of the principal waterways of Asia. It is formed by the confluence of the Shilka and Argun on the northern border of Manchuria and flows some 2,900 kilometers (1,800 miles) to the Sea of Japan. For more than 1,600 kilometers (1,000 miles) it serves as the border between China and the U.S.S.R.

a·muse (ə-myōōz′) *tr.v.* **amused, amusing, amuses.** **1.** To occupy in an agreeable, pleasing, or entertaining fashion. **2.** To cause to laugh or smile by giving pleasure. [Old French *amuser,* "to cause to idle away time" : *a,* to, from Latin *ad-* + *muser,* to idle, MUSE.] —**a·mus·er** *n.*

a·muse·ment (ə-myōōz′mənt) *n.* **1.** The pleasurable occupation of time or the attention; diversion; entertainment: *sang for the amusement of her guests.* **2.** The state of being amused, entertained, or pleased. **3.** Something that amuses.

amusement park *n.* A commercially operated enterprise that offers various forms of entertainment, as rides on a merry-go-round, and often has stands where refreshments are sold.

a·mus·ing (ə-myōō′zĭng) *adj.* **1.** Entertaining or pleasing. **2.** Arousing laughter. —**a·mus·ing·ly** *adv.* —**a·mus·ing·ness** *n.*

a·myg·dale (ə-mĭg′dāl) *n.* An amygdule. [Greek *amugdalē,* AL-MOND.]

a·myg·da·loid (ə-mĭg′də-loid) *n.* A volcanic rock containing many amygdules.
~*adj.* Also **a·myg·da·loi·dal** (ə-mĭg′də-loid′l) (for sense 2). **1.** Almond-shaped. **2.** *Geology.* Resembling amygdaloid. [Latin *amygdala,* ALMOND + -OID.]

a·myg·dule (ə-mĭg′dōōl, -dyōōl) *n.* A small gas bubble in lavar or other igneous rock that has filled with secondary minerals such as zeolite, calcite, or quartz. [Latin *amygdala,* ALMOND (from its shape) + (NOD)ULE.]

am·yl (ăm′əl) *n.* Any univalent organic radical with the formula C_5H_{11}. See **pentyl**. [Latin *amylum,* starch, AMYLUM.]

am·y·la·ceous (ăm′ə-lā′shəs) *adj.* Of, pertaining to, or resembling starch; starchy. [AMYL(O)- + -ACEOUS.]

amyl acetate *n.* An organic compound, $CH_3COOC_5H_{11}$, used commercially in isomeric mixtures as a flavoring agent, as a paint and lacquer solvent, and in the preparation of penicillin. Also called "banana oil," "pear oil."

amyl alcohol *n.* Any of eight isomers of the composition $C_5H_{11}OH$, one of which, $CH_3CH_2CH(CH_3)CH_2OH$, is the principal constituent of fusel oil.

am·y·lase (ăm′ə-lās′, -lāz′) *n.* Any of various enzymes that convert starch or glycogen to sugar. [AMYL(O)- + -ASE.]

am·yl·ene (ăm′ə-lēn) *n. Chemistry.* Pentene (see).

amyl nitrite *n.* The nitrous acid ester of isoamyl alcohol, $(CH_3)_2CHCH_2CH_2NO_2$, used in medicine as a vasodilator, mainly in the treatment of angina pectoris.

amphitheater *This amphitheater in Athens, built in the second century A.D., can seat 5,000 spectators. It is still used for music festivals and for performances of ancient Greek plays.*

amylo-, amyl- *prefix*. Indicates starch; for example, **amylolysis**, **amylase**. [Latin *amylum*, starch, AMYLUM.]

am·y·loid (ăm′ə-loid′) *n.* **1.** A starchlike substance. **2.** *Pathology.* A hard starchlike protein deposited in tissues in certain degenerative diseases. [AMYL(O)- + -OID.] —**am·y·loid** *adj.*

am·y·lol·y·sis (ăm′ə-lŏl′ə-sĭs) *n.* The enzymatic conversion of starch to sugars. [AMYLO- + -LYSIS.] —**am·y·lo·lyt·ic** (ăm′ə-lō-lĭt′ĭk) *adj.*

am·y·lo·pec·tin (ăm′ə-lō-pĕk′tĭn) *n.* The major and insoluble portion of starch. Compare **amylose.**

am·y·lop·sin (ăm′ə-lŏp′sĭn) *n.* The starch-digesting amylase produced by the pancreas. [AMYLO- + (TRY)PSIN.]

am·y·lose (ăm′ə-lōs′, -lōz′) *n.* The relatively soluble portion of starch. Compare **amylopectin.** [AMYL(O)- + -OSE.]

am·y·lum (ăm′ə-ləm) *n.* Starch. [Latin, from Greek *amulon*, starch, the finest flour, from neuter of *amulos,* "not ground in a mill": A- (not) + *mulē,* mill.]

a·my·o·to·ni·a (ā-mī′ə-tō′nē-ə) *n.* Lack of muscle tone. [New Latin : A- (without) + MYO- + -TONIA.]

an[1] (ăn, ən). The indefinite article, a form of *a* used before words beginning with a vowel or with an unpronounced *h: They saw an elephant. The work took an hour.* —See Usage note at **a.** [Middle English *an,* Old English *ān,* one.]

an[2], **an'** (ăn, ən) *conj. Archaic.* And if; if. [Middle English *an,* Old English *an,* short for AND.]

An *Physics.* actinon.

an– *prefix.* Indicates not or without; for example, **anaerobe, anosmia.** [Greek *an-,* not, without, lacking.]

–an[1] *suffix.* Indicates: **1.** Pertaining to, belonging to, or resembling; for example, **American, Mexican. 2.** Believing in or adhering to; for example, **Anglican, Darwinian.** [Latin *-ānus,* adjectival suffix.]

–an[2] *suffix. Chemistry.* Indicates: **1.** A heterocyclic compound; for example, **furan. 2.** An anhydride of a carbohydrate; for example, **dextran.** [Latin *-ānus,* adjectival suffix.]

an. 1. before. [Latin *ante*] **2.** in the year. [Latin *annō*]

an·a[1] (ăn′ə, ä′nə) *n., pl.* **ana** or **anas. 1.** A collection of a person's memorable sayings. **2.** A collection of anecdotes and other information relating to or illustrating the character of a person or place. [Independent use of -ANA.]

an·a[2] (ăn′ə) *adv. Abbr.* **aa** *Pharmacology.* Both in the same quantity; of each. Used to refer to ingredients in prescriptions. [Middle English, from Medieval Latin, from Greek, to the amount of, literally "up."]

ana– *prefix.* Indicates: **1.** Upward progression; for example, **anabolism, anaphase. 2.** Reversion; for example, **anaplasia. 3.** Renewal or intensification; for example, **anaphylaxis.** In borrowed Greek compounds, *ana-* indicates: **1.** Upward, as in **anabasis. 2.** According to, as in **analogy. 3.** Back, as in **anabiosis. 4.** Backward, reversed, as in **anachronism. 5.** Again, anew, as in **anaphora.** Greek, from *ana,* up, throughout, according to.]

–ana, –iana *suffix.* Indicates a collection of assorted material, as facts, anecdotes, objects, and pictures, relating to or illustrating the character of a specified place, person, topic, or period; for example, **Victoriana.** [New Latin, from Latin *-āna,* "the things pertaining to," neuter plural of *-ānus,* -AN.]

an·a·bae·na (ăn′ə-bē′nə) *n.* Any of various freshwater algae of the genus *Anabaena,* sometimes occurring in drinking water and causing a bad taste and odor. [New Latin *Anabaena,* from Greek *anabainein,* to go up (from their periodic rise to the surface) : *ana-,* up + *bainein,* to go.]

an·a·ban·tid (ăn′ə-băn′tĭd) *n.* Any of various tropical freshwater fishes of the family Anabantidae, which includes the **Siamese fighting fish** (see). [New Latin *Anabantidae* : *Anabas* (stem *Anabant-*), type genus, from Greek *anabas,* aorist participle of *anabainein,* to go up + -IDAE.]

An·a·bap·tist (ăn′ə-băp′tĭst) *n.* A member of one of the radical movements of the Reformation that insisted that only adult baptism was valid and held that true Christians should not bear arms, use force, or hold government office. [New Latin *anabaptista,* "one who is rebaptized," from Late Greek *anabaptizein,* to baptize again : Greek *ana-,* again + *baptizein,* to baptize, from *baptein,* to dip.] —**An·a·bap·tism** *n.* —**An·a·bap·tist** *adj.*

an·a·bas (ăn′ə-băs′) *n.* Any member of the genus *Anabas,* which includes freshwater fishes of Africa and Asia, resembling perch. [New Latin *Anabas.* See **anabantid.**]

a·nab·a·sis (ə-năb′ə-sĭs) *n., pl.* **-ses** (-sēz′). A large-scale military advance; specifically, the expedition across Asia Minor (401 B.C.) made by Greek mercenaries led by Cyrus the Younger of Persia, as described by Xenophon. [Greek, a going up or forward, from *anabainein,* to go up. See **anabaena.**]

an·a·bat·ic (ăn′ə-băt′ĭk) *adj.* Of, pertaining to, or designating rising wind currents. [Late Greek *anabatikos,* from Greek, rising, from *anabainein,* to go up. See **anabaena.**]

an·a·bi·o·sis (ăn′ə-bī-ō′sĭs) *n.* A restoring to life from a deathlike condition; resuscitation. [New Latin, from Greek *anabiōsis,* from *anabioun,* to come back to life : *ana-,* back + *bioun,* to live, from *bios,* life.]

an·a·bi·ot·ic (ăn′ə-bī-ŏt′ĭk) *adj.* In a state resembling death, but capable of resuscitation.

an·a·bol·ic (ăn′ə-bŏl′ĭk) *adj.* Of, pertaining to, or characterized by anabolism.

anabolic steroid *n.* Any of a group of synthetic sex hormones used to increase muscle size and strength, as in debilitated underweight patients and in athletes.

a·nab·o·lism (ə-năb′ə-lĭz′əm) *n.* The metabolic process by which simple substances are synthesized into the complex materials of living tissue; constructive metabolism. Compare **catabolism.** [ANA- + (META)BOLISM.]

a·nab·o·lite (ə-năb′ə-līt′) *n.* A product of anabolism. —**a·nab·o·lit·ic** (ə-năb′ə-lĭt′ĭk) *adj.*

a·nach·ro·nism (ə-năk′rə-nĭz′əm) *n.* **1.** The representation of something as existing or happening at other than its proper or historical time. **2. a.** Anything out of its proper time. **b.** Someone or something no longer appropriate to or in harmony with the time. [French *anachronisme,* from Greek *anakhronismos,* from *anakhronizein,* to be an anachronism : *ana-,* backward, reversed + *khronizein,* to belong to a particular time, from *khronos,* time (see **chronic**).] —**a·nach·ro·nis·tic** (ə-năk′rə-nĭs′tĭk), **a·nach·ro·nous** (ə-năk′rə-nəs) *adj.* —**a·nach·ro·nis·ti·cal·ly, a·nach·ro·nous·ly** *adv.*

an·a·cli·nal (ăn′ə-klī′nəl) *adj.* Designating valleys and similar formations that progress in an opposite direction to the dip of surrounding rock strata. [ANA- + -CLINAL.]

an·a·cli·sis (ăn′ə-klī′sĭs) *n.* Psychological dependence on others. [New Latin, from Greek *anaklisis,* a leaning back, from *anaklinein,* to lean on.] —**an·a·clit·ic** (ăn′ə-klĭt′ĭk) *adj.*

an·a·co·lu·thon (ăn′ə-kə-lōō′thŏn′) *n., pl.* **-thons** or **-tha** (-thə). A statement characterized by an abrupt change to a second grammatical construction inconsistent with the first, sometimes used for rhetorical effect; for example, *I warned him that if he continues to drink, what will become of him?* [Late Latin, from Greek *anakolouthon,* inconsistent, from *anakolouthos,* inconsistent : *an-,* not + *akolouthos,* following : *a-,* together + *keleuthos†,* path.] —**an·a·co·lu·thic** *adj.*

an·a·con·da (ăn′ə-kŏn′də) *n.* **1.** A large, nonvenomous, arboreal snake, *Eunectes murinus,* of South America, that constricts its prey. **2.** Any of several similar or related snakes. [Unexplained alteration of Sinhalese *henakandayā,* whip snake (originally applied to a snake of Sri Lanka) : *hena,* lightning + *kanda,* stem.]

A·nac·re·on (ə-năk′rē-ən, -ŏn′) (*c.* 572–*c.* 488 B.C.). Greek poet, noted for his songs praising love and wine.

A·nac·re·on·tic (ə-năk′rē-ŏn′tĭk) *adj.* Characteristic of or in the style of the poems of Anacreon; specifically, convivial or amatory.

an·a·cru·sis (ăn′ə-krōō′sĭs) *n.* **1.** One or more unstressed syllables at the beginning of a line of verse, before the reckoning of the normal meter begins. **2.** *Music.* An upbeat. [New Latin, from Greek *anakrousis,* a pushing back of a tune, from *anakrouein,* to strike up: ANA- + *krouein,* to strike.]

an·a·dem (ăn′ə-dĕm′) *n. Poetic.* A wreath or garland for the head. [Latin *anadēma,* from Greek, from *anadein,* to bind up : ANA- + *dein,* to bind.]

an·a·di·plo·sis (ăn′ə-dĭ-plō′sĭs) *n., pl.* **-ses** (-sēz′). Rhetorical repetition at the beginning of a phrase of the word or words with which the previous phrase ended; for example, *ruined his reputation—his reputation that had taken so long to establish.* [Latin *anadiplōsis,* from Greek, from *anadiploun,* to reduplicate.]

a·nad·ro·mous (ə-năd′rə-məs) *adj.* Migrating up rivers from the sea to breed in fresh water, as salmon do. Compare **catadromous.** [Greek *anadromos,* a running up : ANA- + *dromos,* a running.]

anaemia. Variant of **anemia.**

an·aer·obe (ăn′ə-rōb′, ăn-âr′ōb′) *n.* A microorganism, such as a bacterium, able to live in the absence of free oxygen.

an·aer·o·bic (ăn′ə-rō′bĭk, ăn-âr′ō′-) *adj.* **1.** Of or designating a process, such as respiration, that does not require free oxygen. **2.** Of or pertaining to anaerobes. —**an·aer·o·bi·cal·ly** *adv.*

anaesthesia. Variant of **anesthesia.**

an·a·glyph (ăn′ə-glĭf) *n.* **1.** An ornament carved in low relief. **2.** A photographic process whereby two superimposed images of an object, usually in red and green, produce a three-dimensional effect when viewed through red and green lenses. [Greek *anagluphos,* wrought in low relief, from *anagluphein,* to carve in relief : *ana-,* up + *gluphein,* to carve.] —**an·a·glyph·ic** (ăn′ə-glĭf′ĭk) *adj.*

an·a·go·ge, an·a·go·gy (ăn′ə-gō′jē) *n.* A mystical interpretation of a word, passage, or text; specifically, scriptural exegesis that detects hidden spiritual allusions or meanings. [Late Latin *anagōgē,* from Late Greek, spiritual uplift, from *anagein,* to uplift, lead up : ANA- + *agein,* to lead.] —**an·a·gog·ic** (ăn′ə-gŏj′ĭk), **an·a·gog·i·cal** *adj.* —**an·a·gog·i·cal·ly** *adv.*

an·a·gram (ăn′ə-grăm′) *n.* A word or phrase formed by reordering the letters of another word or phrase: *"Pear" is an anagram of "reap."* [French *anagramme,* from New Latin *anagramma* : ANA- + -GRAM.] —**an·a·gram·mat·ic** (ăn′ə-grə-măt′ĭk) *adj.* —**an·a·gram·mat·i·cal·ly** *adv.*

an·a·gram·ma·tize (ăn′ə-grăm′ə-tīz′) *tr.v.* **-tized, -tiz·ing, -tizes.** To make an anagram of.

a·nal (ā′nəl) *adj.* **1.** Of, pertaining to, or near the anus. **2.** *Psychoanalysis.* Of, pertaining to, or designating: **a.** The stage of psychosexual development of the infant in which gratification is derived from sensations associated with the anus. **b.** Personality traits originating during toilet training and distinguished as **anal-expulsive** or **anal-retentive** (both of which see). Compare **genital, oral.** [New Latin *analis,* from Latin *ānus,* ANUS.]

anal. 1. analogous; analogy. **2.** analysis; analytic.

a·nal·cime (ə-năl′sēm′) *n. Mineralogy.* A white or colorless zeolite, found in some dolerites and basalts. [French, from Greek *analkimos,* weak (from its weak electric power) : AN- (not) + *alkimos,* strong, from *alkē,* strength.]

a·nal·cite (ə-năl′sīt′) *n.* Analcime.

an·a·lects (ăn′ə-lĕkts′) *pl.n.* Also **an·a·lec·ta** (ăn′ə-lĕk′tə). Selections or parts of a literary work or group of works. [Latin *analecta,* from Greek *analekta,* neuter plural of *analektos,* select, from *analegein,* to gather : *ana-,* up + *legein,* to gather.] —**an·a·lec·tic** (ăn′ə-lĕk′tĭk) *adj.*

an·a·lem·ma (ăn′ə-lĕm′ə) *n.* A graduated scale, in the shape of a figure eight, indicating the sun's declination and the equation of time for every day of the year, usually found on sundials and globes. [Latin, a sundial, from Greek *analēmma,* a support, from *analambanein,* to take up, restore. See **analeptic.**] —**an·a·lem·mat·ic** (ăn′ə-lĕ-măt′ĭk) *adj.*

an·a·lep·tic (ăn′ə-lĕp′tĭk) *adj.* Restorative or stimulating. ~*n.* An analeptic medication. [Greek *analēptikos,* from *analambanein,* to take up, restore : *ana-,* up + *lambanein,* to take.]

a·nal-ex·pul·sive (ā′nəl-ĭk-spŭl′sĭv) *adj. Psychoanalysis.* Of, designating, or exhibiting personality traits such as conceit, suspicion, ambition, and generosity, originating in habits, attitudes, or values associated with infantile pleasure in the expulsion of feces.

anal fin *n.* An unpaired fin in fishes, located on the ventral median line between the tail and the anus.

an·al·ge·si·a (ăn′əl-jē′zē-ə, -zhə) *n. Medicine.* Insensibility to pain without loss of consciousness. [New Latin, from Greek *analgēsia,* want of feeling : AN- (not) + *algēsia,* sense of pain, from *algein,* to feel pain, from *algos,* pain.]

an·al·ge·sic (ăn′əl-jē′zĭk, -sĭk) *n.* A drug or other substance that reduces or eliminates pain. ~*adj.* Of or causing analgesia.

a·nal·i·ty (ā-năl′ə-tē) *n., pl.* **-ties.** *Psychoanalysis.* The quality or state of being anal.

an·a·log (ăn′ə-lôg′, -lŏg′) *adj.* **1.** Of, pertaining to, or constituting an analogue. **2.** Designating a watch or clock in which the time is indicated by means of hands moving around a dial in the traditional manner. **3.** Designating a means of recording sound in which the changes to the recording medium are continuous and analogous to the changes in the wave form of the sound. ~*n.* Variant of **analogue.** Compare **digital.**

analog computer *n.* A computer in which numerical data are represented by analogous physical magnitudes or electrical signals. Compare **digital computer.**

analog data *pl.n. Used with a singular or plural verb.* Data presented or collected in continuous form, as temperature variation or voltage measurement.

an·a·log·i·cal (ăn′ə-lŏj′ĭ-kəl) *adj.* Also **an·a·log·ic** (-lŏj′ĭk) Of, pertaining to, consisting of, or based upon an analogy. —**an·a·log·i·cal·ly** *adv.*

a·nal·o·gist (ə-năl′ə-jĭst) *n.* One who looks for or reasons from analogies.

a·nal·o·gize (ə-năl′ə-jīz′) *v.* **-gized, -gizing, -gizes.** —*tr.* To make an analogy to. —*intr.* To think or reason by analogy.

a·nal·o·gous (ə-năl′ə-gəs′) *adj. Abbr.* **anal. 1.** Similar or alike in a way that permits the drawing of an analogy; comparable in certain respects. **2.** *Biology.* Similar in function but not in evolutionary origin, as the gills of a fish and the lungs of a mammal. Compare **homologous.** [Latin *analogus,* from Greek *analogos,* proportionate, resembling : *ana-,* according to + *logos,* proportion, word, from *legein,* to speak.] —**a·nal·o·gous·ly** *adv.* —**a·nal·o·gous·ness** *n.*

an·a·logue, an·a·log (ăn′ə-lôg′, -lŏg′) *n.* **1.** Something that bears an analogy to something else. **2.** *Biology.* An organ or structure that is similar in function to one in another kind of organism, but is of dissimilar evolutionary origin. **3.** *Chemistry.* A structural derivative of a parent compound. [French, from Greek *analogos,* ANALOGOUS.]

a·nal·o·gy (ə-năl′ə-jē) *n., pl.* **-gies.** *Abbr.* **anal. 1. a.** Correspondence in some respects between things otherwise dissimilar: *to draw an analogy.* **b.** A statement illustrating such correspondence. **2.** A form of logical inference, or an instance of it, based on the assumption that if two things are known to be alike in some respects, then they will be alike in other respects. **3.** *Biology.* Correspondence in function or position but not in evolutionary origin. **4.** *Linguistics.* The creation of new forms on the model of known ones: *A child might say "teached" instead of "taught" by analogy with "reached."* —See Synonyms at **likeness.** [Latin *analogia,* from Greek, from *analogos,* ANALOGOUS.]

an·al·pha·bet·ic (ăn′ăl′fə-bĕt′ĭk) *adj.* **1.** Not alphabetical. **2.** Unable to read; illiterate. ~*n.* A person who cannot read; an illiterate.

a·nal·re·ten·tive (ā′nəl-rĭ-tĕn′tĭv) *adj. Psychoanalysis.* Of, designating, or exhibiting personality traits such as meticulousness, avarice, and obstinacy, originating in habits, attitudes, or values associated with infantile pleasure in the retention of feces.

a·nal·y·sand (ə-năl′ə-sănd′) *n.* A person who is being psychoanalyzed. [From ANALYZE (by analogy with MULTIPLICAND).]

analyse. *Chiefly British.* Variant of **analyze.**

a·nal·y·sis (ə-năl′ə-sĭs) *n., pl.* **-ses** (-sēz′). *Abbr.* **anal. 1.** The breaking down of a complex intellectual or substantial whole, for example, an argument or a set of statistics, into its constituent elements in order to examine its nature, significance, and interrelationships. Compare **synthesis. 2.** A statement of the results of such a study. **3.** *Chemistry.* **a.** Separation of a substance into constituents or the determination of its composition. **b.** The stated findings of such separation or determination. **4.** *Mathematics.* **a.** Methodology principally involving algebra and calculus as opposed to synthetic geometry, group theory, and number theory. **b.** The method

of proof in which a known truth is sought as a consequence of reasoning from the thing to be proved. **5.** Psychoanalysis. —**in the last** (or **final**) **analysis.** When everything has been taken into account; in the end. [Medieval Latin, from Greek *analusis,* a loosening, from *analuein,* to undo : *ana-,* back + *luein,* to loosen, free.]

analysis si·tus (sī′təs) *n.* Formerly, **topology** (*see*). [New Latin, "analysis of region."]

an·a·lyst (ăn′ə-lĭst) *n.* **1.** One who analyzes. **2.** A psychoanalyst. **3.** A systems analyst.

an·a·lyt·ic (ăn′ə-lĭt′ĭk) *adj.* Also **an·a·lyt·i·cal** (-ĭ-kəl). *Abbr.* **anal. 1.** Of, pertaining to, or based on analysis: *adopted an analytic approach to the problem.* **2.** Showing an ability to analyze and reason from a perception of the parts and interrelations of a subject; skilled in analysis: *an analytic mind.* **3.** *Linguistics.* Characteristically expressing grammatical distinctions by using two or more words instead of an inflected form: *English is analytic in its use of the comparative "more beautiful" instead of "beautifuler."* **4.** *Philosophy.* Designating a statement or proposition whose truth depends entirely on the meaning of the words of which it is composed rather than any fact about the world. In this sense, compare **synthetic.** —**an·a·lyt·i·cal·ly** *adv.*

analytical balance *n.* A balance for chemical analysis.

analytical reagent *n.* A chemical of high purity containing known amounts of contaminants and therefore suitable for use in a quantitative analysis.

analytic geometry *n.* The analysis of geometric structures and properties principally by algebraic operations on variables defined in terms of position coordinates. Also called "coordinate geometry."

an·a·lyt·ics (ăn′ə-lĭt′ĭks) *n. Used with a singular verb.* The branch of logic dealing with analysis.

an·a·lyze (ăn′ə-līz′) *tr.v.* **-lyzed, -lyzing, -lyzes. 1.** To separate into constituent elements or basic principles so as to elucidate the interrelation of the parts and the nature or significance of the whole; examine methodically. **2.** To make a chemical or mathematical analysis of. **3.** To psychoanalyze. [French *analyser,* from *analyse,* ANALYSIS.] —**an·a·lyz·a·ble** *adj.* —**an·a·lyz·er** *n.*

Anam. See **Annam.**

an·am·ne·sis (ăn′ăm-nē′sĭs) *n., pl.* **-ses** (-sēz′). **1.** *Psychology.* A recalling to memory; recollection. **2.** *Medicine.* The complete case history of a patient. **3.** *Often* **Anamnesis.** That part of the Eucharist which recalls Christ's passion. [New Latin, from Greek *anamnēsis,* from *anamimnēskein,* to recall to memory : *ana-,* back + *mimnēskein,* to call to mind.] —**an·am·nes·tic** (ăn′ăm-nĕs′tĭk) *adj.* —**an·am·nes·ti·cal·ly** *adv.*

an·a·mor·phic (ăn′ə-môr′fĭk) *adj.* Having, producing, or designating different optical magnification along mutually perpendicular radii: *an anamorphic lens.* [ANA- + -MORPHIC.]

an·a·mor·pho·sis (ăn′ə-môr′fə-sĭs, -môr-fō′sĭs) *n., pl.* **-ses** (-sēz′). *Optics.* An image distorted so that it can be viewed without distortion only from a special angle or with a special instrument. [Medieval Greek *anamorphōsis,* "a forming anew," from Late Greek *anamorphoun,* to transform : *ana-,* again + *morphoun,* to form, from *morphē,* form.]

A·nan·da (ə-năn′də, ä′nən-də) (5th–4th century B.C.). Favorite disciple of Buddha. He was the Buddha's first cousin and is known as the "beloved disciple."

an·an·drous (ăn-ăn′drəs) *adj. Botany.* Having no stamens. [Greek *anandros,* "without a man" : AN- + *anēr* (stem *andr-*), man.]

an·an·thous (ăn-ăn′thəs) *adj. Botany.* Lacking flowers. Said of some angiosperms. [AN- + -ANTHOUS.]

an·a·pest, an·a·paest (ăn′ə-pĕst′) *n.* **1.** A metrical foot composed of two short syllables followed by one long one, written (˘ ˘ ´). **2.** A line of verse in this meter: " *'Twas the night before Christmas and all through the house*" (Clement Moore). [Latin *anapaestus,* from Greek *anapaistos,* "struck back" (an anapest being a dactyl reversed) : *ana-,* back + *paiein,* to strike.] —**an·a·pest·ic** *adj.*

an·a·phase (ăn′ə-fāz′) *n. Biology.* The stage of mitosis in which the daughter chromosomes move toward the poles of the nuclear spindle. [ANA- + PHASE.]

a·naph·o·ra (ə-năf′ər-ə) *n.* **1.** The deliberate repetition in rhetoric of a word or phrase at the beginning of several successive verses, clauses, or paragraphs. **2.** Reference to an antecedent by the use of a grammatical substitute, as a pronoun. [Late Latin, from Greek *anaphora,* repetition, from *anapherein,* to repeat : *ana-,* again + *pherein,* to carry.]

an·a·phor·ic (ăn′ə-fôr′ĭk, -fŏr′ĭk) *adj. Grammar.* Referring to an antecedent: *the anaphoric pronoun "one" in "May I have another one?"*

an·aph·ro·dis·i·a (ăn-ăf′rə-dĭz′ē-ə, -dĭzh′ə) *n.* Absence or decline of sexual desire. [AN- + Greek *aphrodisia,* sexual desire (see **aphrodisiac**).] —**an·aph·ro·dis·i·ac** (ăn-ăf′rə-dĭz′ē-ăk′) *adj.* & *n.*

an·a·phy·lac·toid (ăn′ə-fə-lăk′toid′) *adj. Pathology.* **1.** Of or pertaining to an anaphylactic reaction that occurs without causing antibodies. **2.** Of or pertaining to a toxic reaction caused in an unsensitized person by an excessive dose of a substance that causes anaphylaxis in a sensitized person.

an·a·phy·lax·is (ăn′ə-fə-lăk′sĭs) *n.* Hypersensitivity to a foreign substance induced by a small preliminary or sensitizing injection of the substance. [New Latin : ANA- + (PRO)PHYLAXIS.] —**an·a·phy·lac·tic** (ăn′ə-fə-lăk′tĭk) *adj.* —**an·a·phy·lac·ti·cal·ly** *adv.*

an·a·pla·si·a (ăn′ə-plā′zhə) *n. Biology.* Reversion of cells or tissues to a more primitive or less differentiated form. [ANA- + -PLASIA.]

an·a·plas·tic (ăn′ə-plăs′tĭk) *adj.* **1.** Pertaining to or involving the restoration of a lost or absent part, as by plastic surgery. **2.** Of or pertaining to anaplasia of cells.

an·a·plas·ty (ăn′ə-plăs′tē) *n.* Plastic surgery. [French *anaplastie*, from Greek *anaplasis*, remodeling, from *anaplassein*, to form anew : ANA- + *plassein*, to mold.]

an·arch (ăn′ärk′) *n.* A leader or advocate of anarchy.

an·ar·chic (ăn-är′kĭk) *adj.* Also **an·ar·chi·cal** (-kĭ-kəl). **1.** Of, like, or promoting anarchy. **2.** Lacking order or control; chaotic. —**an·ar·chi·cal·ly** *adv.*

an·ar·chism (ăn′ər-kĭz′əm) *n.* **1.** The theory that all forms of government are oppressive and undesirable, and should be abolished and replaced by voluntary cooperation. **2.** Active resistance and terrorism against the state, as used by some anarchists. **3.** Rejection of all forms of coercive control and authority.

an·ar·chist (ăn′ər-kĭst) *n.* **1.** An advocate of anarchism. **2.** One who actively promotes anarchism or anarchy, as by the use of terrorism, to destabilize the existing order.

an·ar·chis·tic (ăn′ər-kĭs′tĭk) *adj.* Of, pertaining to, or tending toward anarchism.

anarcho– *prefix.* Indicates anarchistic tendencies or anarchism; for example, **anarcho-syndicalism.** [Medieval Latin, from Greek *anarkhos*, without a ruler. See **anarchy.**]

an·ar·cho-syn·di·cal·ism (ăn-är′kō-sĭn′dĭ-kə-lĭz′əm) *n.* A revolutionary doctrine, **syndicalism** *(see).* [ANARCHO- + SYNDICALISM.]

an·ar·chy (ăn′ər-kē) *n., pl.* **-chies. 1.** Absence of any form of political authority. **2.** Political disorder and confusion. **3.** Any state of disorder or confusion, especially when caused by absence of a recognized authority or cohesive principle: *classroom anarchy.* [Greek *anarkhia*, from *anarkhos*, without a ruler : AN- + *arkhos*, ruler, -ARCH.]

an·ar·thri·a (ăn-är′thrē-ə) *n.* Loss of the ability to speak. [New Latin, from Greek *anarthros*, not articulated. See **anarthrous.**] —**an·arth·ric** (ăn-är′thrĭk) *adj.*

an·ar·throus (ăn-är′thrəs) *adj. Zoology.* Lacking joints; unjointed. [Greek *anarthros*, not articulated : AN- (without) + *arthron*, joint, article.]

an·a·sar·ca (ăn′ə-sär′kə) *n.* A general accumulation of serum in the subcutaneous connective tissue, resulting in swelling of the trunk and legs. [New Latin, from Greek *ana sarka*, "throughout the body" : *ana*, throughout + *sarka*, accusative of *sarx*, flesh.] —**an·a·sar·cous** (ăn′ə-sär′kəs) *adj.*

An·as·ta·si·a (ăn′ə-stā′zhə), **Grand Duchess** (1901-*c.* 1918). Youngest daughter of the last czar of Russia, Nicholas II. She is thought to have been killed with the rest of her family after the Russian Revolution, but several women have since claimed to be her without conclusive proof, most notably (from 1920) a woman known as Anna Anderson.

an·as·tig·mat (ăn-ăs′tĭg-măt′) *n.* A compound lens corrected for astigmatism and for at least one off-axis zone in the image plane. [AN- (not) + ASTIGMAT(IC).]

an·as·tig·mat·ic (ăn-ăs′tĭg-măt′ĭk) *adj.* **1.** Not astigmatic. Said of a lens that forms an accurate point image of a point object. **2.** Of or designating a compound lens in which the separate components compensate for the astigmatism of each. [AN- + ASTIGMATIC.]

a·nas·to·mose (ə-năs′tə-mōz′, -mōs′) *v.* **-mosed, -mosing, -moses.** —*tr.* To join by anastomosis. —*intr.* To become connected by anastomosis. [Back-formation from ANASTOMOSIS.]

a·nas·to·mo·sis (ə-năs′tə-mō′sĭs) *n., pl.* **-ses** (-sēz′). **1.** The union or connection of branches, as of rivers, veins of leaves, or blood vessels. **2.** A surgical connection of separate or severed hollow organs to form a continuous channel. [New Latin, from Greek *anastomōsis*, an outlet, opening, from *anastomoun*, to furnish with a mouth : *ana-*, up + *stoma*, a mouth, opening.] —**a·nas·to·mot·ic** (ə-năs′tə-mŏt′ĭk) *adj.*

a·nas·tro·phe (ə-năs′trə-fē) *n.* Inversion, as for rhetorical effect, of the normal syntactic order of words; for example, *to market went she.* [Greek *anastrophē*, a turning upside down, from *anastrephein*, to turn upside down : *ana-*, back + *strephein*, to turn.]

anat. anatomical; anatomy.

an·a·tase (ăn′ə-tās′, -tāz′) *n.* A rare blue or light-yellow to black mineral consisting of titanium dioxide in tetragonal form. Formerly called "octahedrite." [French, from Greek *anatasis*, extension (from its long crystals), from *anateinein*, to extend, stretch up : *ana-*, up + *teinein*, to stretch.]

a·nath·e·ma (ə-năth′ə-mə) *n., pl.* **-mas. 1.** Someone or something cursed, reviled, shunned, or detested: *Fascism was anathema to her.* **2.** A formal ecclesiastical pronouncement of damnation; a denunciation or excommunication. **3.** Any vehement denunciation; an imprecation; a curse. [Late Latin, a curse, a person cursed, an offering, from Greek *anathēma*, votive offering, from *anatithenai*, to dedicate : *ana-*, up + *tithenai*, to put.]

a·nath·e·ma·tize (ə-năth′ə-mə-tīz′) *tr.v.* **-tized, -tizing, -tizes.** To proclaim an anathema on; denounce or curse. —**a·nath·e·ma·ti·za·tion** (ə-năth′ə-mə-tĭ-zā′shən) *n.*

An·a·to·li·a (ăn′ə-tō′lē-ə). Also **A·sia Mi·nor** (ā′zhə mī′nər, ā′shə). The Asian part of Turkey. In ancient times it was the great meeting place of Oriental and Occidental commerce. The region was slowly conquered by the Ottoman Turks in the 14th and 15th centuries and remained part of the Ottoman Empire until the republic of Turkey was established.

An·a·to·li·an (ăn′ə-tō′lē-ən, -tōl′yən) *n.* **1.** A native or inhabitant of Anatolia. **2.** Any of a family of extinct Indo-European languages of ancient Anatolia. —**An·a·to·li·an** *adj.*

an·a·tom·i·cal (ăn′ə-tŏm′ĭ-kəl) *adj.* Also **an·a·tom·ic** (-tŏm′ĭk). *Abbr.* **anat. 1.** Of or pertaining to anatomy. **2.** Of or pertaining to dissection. **3.** Structural as opposed to functional. —**an·a·tom·i·cal·ly** *adv.*

a·nat·o·mist (ə-năt′ə-mĭst) *n.* An expert in or student of anatomy.

a·nat·o·mize (ə-năt′ə-mīz′) *tr.v.* **-mized, -mizing, -mizes. 1.** To dissect. **2.** To analyze in minute detail. —**a·nat·o·mi·za·tion** (ə-năt′ə-mĭ-zā′shən) *n.*

a·nat·o·my (ə-năt′ə-mē) *n., pl.* **-mies.** *Abbr.* **anat. 1.** The structure of a plant or animal, or of any of its parts. **2.** The science of the shape and structure of organisms and their parts. **3.** A treatise on this science. **4.** The dissection of a plant or animal to disclose the various parts, their positions, structure, and interrelation. **5.** Any detailed examination or analysis: *The psychologist wrote a book entitled "The Anatomy of Depression."* **6.** The human body. [Middle English *anatomie*, from Old French, from Late Latin *anatomia*, from Greek *anatomē*, dissection, from *anatemnein*, to dissect : *ana-*, up + *temnein*, to cut.]

a·nat·ro·pous (ə-năt′rə-pəs) *adj. Botany.* Inverted so that the micropyle is next to the hilum, and the embryonic root is at the other end. Said of an ovule. [ANA- + -TROPOUS.]

anatto. Variant of **annatto.**

An·ax·ag·o·ras (ăn′ăk-săg′ə-rəs) (*c.* 500-428 B.C.). Greek philosopher. Born in Clazomenae, Asia Minor (now in Turkey), he moved to Athens, where he gained the friendship of Pericles. He taught that the universe was composed of an infinite number of elements and gave the true explanation of solar eclipses.

A·nax·i·man·der (ə-năk′sə-măn′dər) (*c.*611-*c.*547 B.C.). Greek philosopher and astronomer from Miletus, Asia Minor (now in Turkey). One of the earliest thinkers to speculate on the origin of the universe, he held that it arose out of the separation of opposite qualities from one primordial substance and that animal life had evolved from the sea.

An·ax·im·e·nes (ăn′ăk-sĭm′ə-nēz′) (*c.* 570-*c.* 500 B.C.). Greek philosopher from Miletus, Asia Minor (now in Turkey). He held that the fundamental matter of the universe was air or vapor and that all other substances were derived from it by condensation, compression, or rarefaction.

an·bur·y (ăn′bĕr′ē) *n.* **1.** A soft tumor afflicting horses and oxen. **2.** A disease of root crops, such as turnips, in which the roots are swollen or distorted. [16th century : perhaps from *ang-*, "painful" (as in Old English *angnægl*, AGNAIL) + *-bury*, BERRY (referring to the reddish tumor).]

anc. ancient.

–ance, –ancy *suffix.* Indicates an action, quality, or condition; for example, **riddance, compliancy.** [Middle English *-ance, -aunce,* from Old French *-ance,* from Latin *-antia,* abstract noun suffix of *-ant-,* stem of *-āns,* present participle ending, -ANT.]

an·ces·tor (ăn′sĕs′tər) *n.* **1.** Any person from whom one is descended, especially if more remote than a grandparent; a forebear. **2.** An early or original type of a later person or thing; a precursor: *The clavichord is one of the ancestors of the modern piano.* **3.** *Biology.* The actual or hypothetical organism or stock from which later kinds have evolved. [Middle English *ancestre, ancessour,* from Old French *ancestre, ancessor,* from Latin *antecessor,* "one that goes before," from *antecessus,* past participle of *antecēdere,* to go before : ANTE- + *cēdere,* to go.]

an·ces·tral (ăn-sĕs′trəl) *adj.* Of, pertaining to, evolved from, or inherited from an ancestor or ancestors: *The family lived on the ancestral farm.* —**an·ces·tral·ly** *adv.*

an·ces·tress (ăn′sĕs′trĭs) *n.* A female ancestor.

an·ces·try (ăn′sĕs′trē) *n., pl.* **-tries. 1.** Ancestral descent or lineage. **2.** Ancestors collectively. [Middle English *ancestrie,* from Old French *ancesserie,* from *ancessour,* ANCESTOR.]

An·chi·ses (ăng-kī′sēz′, ăn-). *Greek and Roman Mythology.* The father of Aeneas, rescued by his son from the ruins of Troy.

an·chor (ăng′kər) *n.* **1.** A heavy, usually metal, object attached to a vessel by a cable and cast overboard to keep the vessel in place, usually by flukes that grip the bottom. **2.** Something used to keep an object firmly in position. **3.** Someone or something providing security or stability. **4.** *Radio & Television.* An anchorperson. —**at anchor.** Anchored. ~*v.* **anchored, -choring, -chors.** —*tr.* **1.** To hold fast by or as if by an anchor. **2.** To act as the anchorperson of (a news broadcast, for example). —*intr.* To drop anchor or lie at anchor. Used of a ship. [Middle English *anker,* Old English *ancer, ancor,* from Latin *anc(h)ora,* from Greek *ankura.*]

an·chor·age (ăng′kər-ĭj) *n.* **1.** A place for anchoring. **2.** A fee charged for the privilege of anchoring. **3. a.** The act of anchoring. **b.** The condition of being at anchor. **4.** Something that provides stability or support.

An·chor·age (ăng′kər-ĭj). Chief port and largest city of Alaska. It is situated on Cook Inlet in the southern part of the state, and was founded in 1915 as the headquarters for the building of the Alaska Railway.

an·cho·ress (ăng′kər-ĭs) *n.* A female anchorite.

an·cho·rite (ăng′kə-rīt′) *n.* Also **an·cho·ret** (-rĕt). A person who has retired into seclusion, usually for religious reasons; a hermit; a recluse. [Middle English, from Medieval Latin *anchorīta,* variant of Late Latin *anchorēta,* from Late Greek *anakhōrētēs,* "one who withdraws (from the world)," from *anakhōrein,* to withdraw : Greek *ana-*, back + *khōrein*, to make room.] —**an·cho·rit·ic** (ăng′kə-rĭt′-ĭk) *adj.*

an·chor·man (ăng′kər-măn′) *n., pl.* -**men** (-měn′). **1.** One who plays a crucial part in providing strength, stability, or cohesion. **2.** The runner, usually the strongest in a team, who performs the last stage of a relay race. **3.** The presenter or coordinator of a broadcast involving several different contributors or correspondents.

an·chor·per·son (ăng′kər-pûr′sən) *n.* An anchorman or anchorwoman.

anchor ring *n. Mathematics.* A torus *(see).*

an·chor·wom·an (ăng′kər-wŏŏm′ən) *n., pl.* -**women** (-wĭm′ĭn). A woman who presents or coordinates a broadcast involving several different contributors or correspondents.

an·cho·vy (ăn′chō′vē, ăn-chō′vē) *n., pl.* -**vies** or collectively **anchovy.** Any of various small, herringlike marine fishes of the family Engraulidae. Several species, especially *Engraulis encrasicholus,* are widely used as food fish. [Spanish *anchova, anchoa,* perhaps from Basque *anchu.*]

anchovy pear *n.* **1.** A tropical American tree, *Grias cauliflora,* that bears edible fruit similar in taste to the mango. **2.** The fruit of the anchovy pear. [The fruit is so called after its use, like anchovies, as a first course or hors d'oeuvre.]

an·chu·sa (ăng-kyōō′sə-, -zə) *n.* Any plant of the genus *Anchusa.* See **bugloss.** [New Latin *Anchusa,* from Latin *anchūsa,* a plant used as a cosmetic, from Greek *ankhousa†,* alkanet.]

anchylose. Variant of **ankylose.**

an·cien ré·gime (äN-syăN′ rā-zhĕm′) *n.* **1.** The political and social system existing in France before the Revolution of 1789. **2.** Any system or regime that has been superseded. [French, "old regime."]

an·cient¹ (ān′shənt) *adj. Abbr.* **anc. 1.** Having lived or existed for a long time; very old. **2.** Of, existing in, or occurring in times long past; especially, belonging to the historical period prior to the fall of the Western Roman Empire (A.D. 476). —See Synonyms at **old.** ~*n.* **1.** A person who lived in ancient times, especially one belonging to any of the classical civilizations of antiquity. **2. ancients.** The ancient Greek and Roman authors. **3.** A very old person. [Middle English *ancien,* from Old French, from Vulgar Latin *anteānus* (unattested), "going before," from Latin *ante,* before.] —**an·cient·ness** *n.*

an·cient² *n. Obsolete.* **1.** An ensign; a flag. **2.** A flag-bearer or lieutenant. [Variant of ENSIGN.]

Ancient Greek *n.* The Greek language of historical antiquity, from its first documentation in the 14th century B.C. until the time of the late Roman Empire, divided into two principal dialect areas, **East Greek** and **West Greek** (*both of which see*).

ancient history *n.* **1.** The history of ancient times. **2.** *Informal.* Common knowledge, especially of a recent event that has lost its original impact or importance.

ancient light *n.* A window whose light has long been enjoyed and according to common law may not be obstructed by an adjacent owner.

an·cient·ly (ān′shənt-lē) *adv.* In ancient times.

an·cil·lar·y (ăn′sə-lĕr′ē) *adj.* **1.** Of secondary importance; subordinate: *"For Degas, sculpture was never more than ancillary to his painting"* (Herbert Read). **2.** Helping; auxiliary: *She was a member of the ancillary staff in the hospital.* ~*n., pl.* **ancillaries.** One who works in a subordinate or auxiliary capacity. [Latin *ancillāris,* servile, from *ancilla,* maidservant, feminine diminutive of *anculus,* servant.]

an·cip·i·tal (ăn-sĭp′ə-təl) *adj.* Flattened and two-edged, as certain plant stems are. [From Latin *anceps* (stem *ancipit-*), two-headed : AMBI- + *caput,* head.]

an·con (ăng′kŏn′) *n., pl.* **ancones** (ăng-kō′nēz). A projecting bracket used in classical architecture to carry the upper elements of a cornice; a console. [Latin *ancōn,* from Greek *ankōn,* elbow, bend of the arm.] —**an·co·nal** (ăng-kō′nəl) *adj.*

An·co·na (ăng-kō′nə). Adriatic port and capital of the province of the same name in central Italy.

-ancy. Variant of **-ance.**

an·cy·lo·sto·mi·a·sis (ăn′sə-lō-stō-mī′ə-sĭs, ăng′kə-lō-) *n.* A disease caused by hookworm infestation of the intestine and marked by progressive anemia. Also called "hookworm disease." [New Latin : *Ancylostoma,* hookworm (genus), "hook-mouth" : Greek *ankulos,* crooked + *stoma,* mouth + -IASIS.]

Ancyra. See **Ankara.**

and (ənd, an; *stressed* ănd) *conj.* **1.** Together with or along with; also; in addition; as well as. Used to connect words, phrases, or clauses, especially those having the same grammatical function: *trials and tribulations; a long and happy life.* **2. a.** Added to; plus: *Two and two makes four.* **b.** Prepared, served, eaten, or drunk with as a unit: *bread and butter; gin and tonic.* **3.** As a result. Used to express an actual or likely consequence: *She felt tired and went to bed. One more remark like that and I'll knock your block off.* **4.** Next in time; then: *paid the bill and left.* **5.** *Informal.* Used instead of *to* after verbs such as *go, come,* or *try: try and find it; come and see.* **6.** Used, especially in news broadcasting, to initiate discussion of an announced topic: *The Middle East—and Egypt has announced . . .* **7.** Used as a connection between identical words to express repetition, continuation, or progression: *rolled over and over; waited and waited; getting hotter and hotter.* **8.** Used to express a contrast in quality between things of the same basic type: *There are cameras and cameras.* **9.** Used, especially after *good* and *nice,* to give adverbial force to the words preceding it: *nice and warm.* **10.** Used to introduce a comment or parenthetic remark: *Here's our meal—and not a minute too early! After that—and this is the funny part— he fell into the pool.* **11.** *Archaic.* If: *and it please you.* [Middle English *and,* Old English *and, ond.*]

Usage: Although frowned upon by some, the use of *and* to begin a sentence has a long and respectable history: *"And it came to pass in those days"* (Luke 2:1).

AND (ănd) *n. Computer Science.* A logic operator equivalent to the sentential connective "and." [From AND.]

An·da·lu·sia (ăn′də-lōō′zhə). Spanish **An·da·lu·cí·a** (än′dä-lōō-thē′ə). The largest region in Spain, covering much of the south of the country. It was the last part of Spain to be reconquered from the Moors in the 15th century and contains some magnificent Moorish architecture, including the historic towns of Seville, Granada, and Córdoba. —**An·da·lu·sian** *n. & adj.*

an·da·lu·site (ăn′də-lōō′sīt′) *n.* A mineral consisting of aluminum silicate, Al₂SiO₅, usually found in prisms of various colors. [French *andalousite,* discovered in ANDALUSIA.]

An·da·man and Nic·o·bar Islands (ăn′də-mən; nĭk′ə-bär′). Indian possessions in the Bay of Bengal. The Andamans comprise more than 200 small islands, the Nicobars 19. Port Blair on South Andaman Island is the capital.

An·da·man·ese (ăn′də-mə-nēz′, -nēs′) *n., pl.* **Andamanese. 1.** A member of a Negrito people native to the Andaman Islands. **2.** The agglutinative language of this people, not known to be connected with any other language family. —**An·da·man·ese** *adj.*

an·dan·te (än-dän′tā, ăn-dăn′tē) *adv. Music.* In a moderate tempo; faster than adagio, but slower than allegretto. Used as a direction: *performed andante.* ~*n. Music.* A movement or passage in a moderate tempo. [Italian, "walking," present participle of *andare,* to walk, from Vulgar Latin *ambitāre* (unattested), from Latin *ambulāre,* to AMBULATE.] —**an·dan·te** *adj.*

an·dan·ti·no (än′dän-tē′nō, ăn′dăn-) *adv. Music.* In a tempo slightly faster than andante. Used as a direction. ~*n., pl.* **andantinos.** *Music.* A movement or passage in this tempo. [Italian, diminutive of ANDANTE.] —**an·dan·ti·no** *adj.*

An·de·an (ăn′dē-ən, ăn-dē′ən) *adj.* Of, pertaining to, or resembling the Andes or their inhabitants.

An·der·sen (ăn′dər-sən), Hans Christian (1805–75). Danish writer, famous chiefly for his fairy tales. The son of a poor shoemaker, he made his reputation with the publication in 1835 of his first collection of fairy tales, *Eventyr* ("Tales Told for Children").

An·der·son (ăn′dər-sən), Carl David (1905–). U.S. physicist. In 1936 he was awarded the Nobel Prize for his discovery of the positively charged particle, the positron.

Anderson, Marian (1902–). U.S. contralto singer. She was most famous for her interpretation of Negro spirituals and was the first black singer to perform at the Metropolitan Opera in New York, making her debut in 1955.

Anderson, Maxwell (1888–1959). U.S. playwright. Many of his dramas, including *Winterset* (1935), were written in verse. He also cowrote *What Price Glory?* (1924) and *Knickerbocker Holiday* (1938).

Anderson, Sherwood (1876–1941). U.S. author of novels and short stories. Most of his often autobiographical works detail the frustrations of life in small Midwestern towns. Anderson's best-known work is *Winesburg, Ohio* (1919), a collection of interrelated short stories and sketches.

An·des (ăn′dēz). Mountain system running along the Pacific coast of South America for 8,000 kilometers (5,000 miles). It is higher than any other mountain range in the world except the Himalayas. Its maximum width is 480 kilometers (300 miles), and its highest peak, Ojos del Salado on the Chile-Argentina border (7,084 meters; 23,241 feet), is the highest mountain in the Western Hemisphere.

an·de·site (ăn′dī-zīt′) *n.* A fine-grained volcanic rock containing plagioclase and feldspar. [German *Andesit,* from the ANDES.]

AND gate *n. Computer Science.* A logic circuit with two or more input wires that emits a signal only if all input wires receive coincident signals. See **OR gate.** [So called because the emission of the signal is comparable to the use of the conjunction *and* in logic.]

An·dhra Pra·desh (ăn′drə prə-dāsh′). State in southeastern India, bordering on the Bay of Bengal. It was created in 1956 from the Telegu-speaking regions of Madras and Hyderabad. The capital is Hyderabad.

and·i·ron (ănd′ī′ərn) *n.* Either of a pair of metal supports for holding up logs in a fireplace. Also called "firedog." [Middle English *aundiren,* variant of Old French *andier,* firedog, from Gaulish *andero-* (unattested), young bull (andirons were often decorated with heads of animals at the top).]

and/or (ănd′ôr′) *conj.* Used to indicate that either *and* or *or* may be used to connect words, phrases, or clauses, depending upon what meaning is intended.

Usage: And/or is mainly used in legal, commercial, and technical contexts, where it is a succinct way of setting forth three distinct and exclusive possibilities: either of two things considered separately, or the two in combination (that is, one or the other or both). Thus, *an offense punishable by a fine and/or imprisonment* means "either by a fine, or by imprisonment, or both."

An·dor·ra (ăn-dôr′ə, -dŏr′ə). Tiny, independent state high in the eastern Pyrenees on the Franco-Spanish border. It is an ancient coprincipality and still pays nominal dues to the president of France and the Spanish bishop of Urgel. Area, 453 square kilome-

Andes *Aerial view of the northernmost section of the mountains that stretch the length of South America. Here, in Colombia, the Andes are a cordillera—a series of parallel ranges—more than 320 kilometers (200 miles) wide and rising to more than 2,700 meters (9,000 feet).*

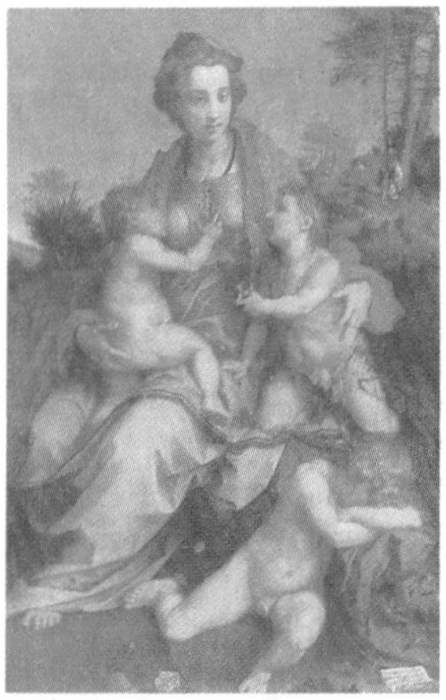

Andrea del Sarto painting *A symbolic portrait of Charity by the Florentine painter. The canvas is now in the Louvre, Paris.*

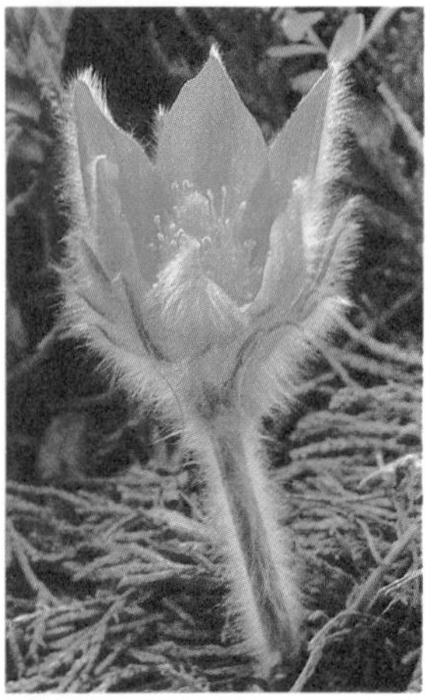

anemone *There are 150 species in the* Anemone *genus varying in color between white, yellow, purple, and red. This is* Anemone patens.

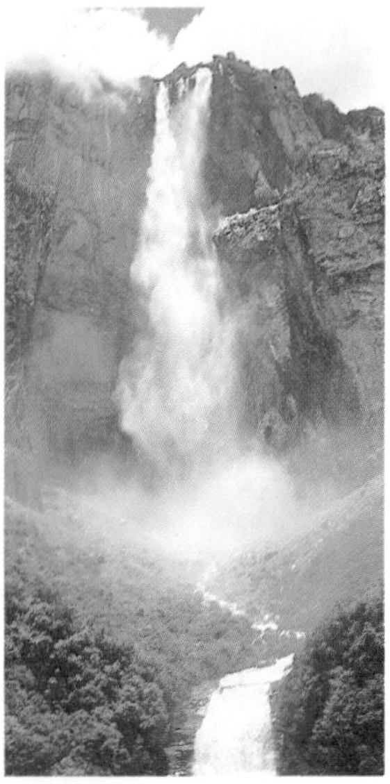

Angel Fall *The highest uninterrupted waterfall in the world lies in the Guiana Highlands of southeast Venezuela, where a river cascades over the edge of the Auyán-Tapuí plateau.*

ters (175 square miles). Population, 31,000. Capital, Andorra la Vella. See map at **France.**

an·dra·dite (ăn-drä'dīt', ăn'drə-dīt') *n.* A green to brown or black calcium-iron garnet, $Ca_3Fe_2(SiO_4)_3$, used as a gem. [After José B. de *Andrada* e Silva (1763–1838), Brazilian geologist.]

An·dre·a del Sar·to (än-drā'ä dĕl sär'tō), born Andrea d'Agnolo (1486–1530). Florentine painter. He painted chiefly religious subjects in the classical manner of Raphael and is best known for the fresco cycle of the life of John the Baptist in the Chiostro dello Scalzo, Florence.

An·drew (ăn'dro͞o'). One of the Apostles, the brother of Simon called Peter. [Middle English, from Latin *Andreas,* from Greek, probably from *andreios,* manly, from *anēr* (stem *andr-*), man.]

andro–, andr– *prefix.* Indicates: **1.** The male sex or masculine; for example, **androgen. 2.** *Botany.* Stamen or anther; for example, **androecium.** [Greek, from *anēr* (stem *andr-*), man.]

an·droe·ci·um (ăn-drē'shē-əm, -shəm) *n., pl.* **-cia** (-shē-ə, -shə). The stamens of a flower considered collectively. [New Latin : ANDR(O)- + Greek *oikion,* residence, diminutive of *oikos,* house.] **—an·droe·cial** (ăn-drē'shəl) *adj.*

an·dro·gen (ăn'drə-jən) *n.* Any of the steroid hormones that develop and maintain masculine characteristics, such as the growth of facial hair. Compare **estrogen.** [ANDRO- + -GEN.] **—an·dro·gen·ic** (ăn'drə-jĕn'ĭk) *adj.*

an·drog·y·nous (ăn-drŏj'ə-nəs) *adj.* **1.** Having both female and male characteristics. **2.** *Botany.* Composed of staminate and pistillate flowers. Said of the flower spikes of certain sedges. [Latin *androgynus,* from Greek *androgunos* : ANDRO- + -GYNOUS.] **—an·drog·y·ny** (ăn-drŏj'ə-nē) *n.*

an·droid (ăn'droid') *adj.* Possessing human features.
~*n.* In science fiction, a synthetic person created from biological materials, as distinguished from a robot. Also called "humanoid." [Late Greek *androeidēs,* manlike : ANDR(O)- + -OID.]

An·drom·a·che (ăn-drŏm'ə-kē). *Greek Mythology.* The faithful wife of Hector, captured by the Greeks at the fall of Troy.

An·drom·e·da[1] (ăn-drŏm'ə-də). *Greek Mythology.* The daughter of Cepheus and Cassiopeia, who married Perseus after he had rescued her from a sea monster.

Andromeda[2] *n.* A constellation in the Northern Hemisphere near Lacerta and Perseus.

An·dro·pov (ăn-drŏp'ôf, -ŏv), **Yuri Vladimirovich** (1914–84). General secretary of the Communist Party of the U.S.S.R (1982) after the death of Leonid Brezhnev; president (1983). Andropov was Soviet ambassador to Hungary in 1956 when that country was invaded by the U.S.S.R. From 1967 until May of 1982 he was chairman of the K.G.B., the Soviet security police, leaving that post just six months before achieving the country's most important political appointment.

An·dros[1] (ăn'drəs). Largest of the Bahama Islands. Andros is in the western group of islands and is the only island in the Bahamas that is traversed by streams.

An·dros[2] (ăn'drəs, -drŏs). Greek island in the Aegean Sea. It is the northernmost of the Cyclades. Andros was colonized by Athens in the 5th century B.C. and later came under the control of Macedonia, Rome, Venice, and Turkey. In 1829 it became part of Greece.

An·dros (ăn'drəs, -drŏs), **Sir Edmund** (1637–1714). British colonial administrator. As governor of the Dominion of New England his autocratic manner and vigorous enforcement of unpopular laws angered the colonists, and in 1689 the people of Boston revolted and threw Andros into jail. He soon after returned to England.

an·dros·ter·one (ăn-drŏs'tə-rōn') *n.* A male sex hormone excreted in urine and synthetically produced from cholesterol. [ANDRO- + STER(OL) + -ONE.]

-androus *suffix. Botany.* Indicates a specified number or type of stamens; for example, **monandrous.** [New Latin *-andrus,* from Greek *-andros,* "having men," from *anēr* (stem *andr-*), man.]

-andry *suffix.* Indicates the state or custom of having a specified number of husbands; for example, **monandry.** [Greek *anēr* (stem *andr-*), man.]

-ane *suffix. Chemistry.* Indicates a saturated hydrocarbon; for example, **hexane, propane.** [Variant of -ENE, -INE, or -ONE.]

a·near (ə-nîr) *adv. Archaic.* **1.** Near. **2.** Nearly; almost.
~*tr.v.* **aneared, anearing, anears.** *Archaic.* To approach: *"The castle tonight . . . anears its fall"* (Elizabeth Barrett Browning). **—a·near** *prep.*

an·ec·dot·age (ăn'ĭk-dō'tĭj) *n.* **1.** Anecdotes collectively. **2.** Garrulous old age or senility. Used humorously. [Sense 2 is a blend of ANECDOTE and DOTAGE.]

an·ec·dot·al (ăn'ĭk-dōt'l) *adj.* Characterized by, containing, or given to telling anecdotes.

an·ec·dote (ăn'ĭk-dōt') *n.* A short account of some interesting, biographical, or humorous incident. [French, from Greek *anekdota,* "things unpublished," from *anekdotos,* unpublished : AN- (not) + *ekdotos,* given out, from *ekdidonai,* to give out : *ek-,* out + *didonai,* to give.] **—an·ec·dot·ist** (ăn'ĭk-dō'tĭst), **an·ec·dot·al·ist** (ăn'ĭk-dōt'l-ĭst) *n.*

an·ec·dot·ic (ăn'ĭk-dŏt'ĭk) *adj.* Also **an·ec·dot·i·cal** (-ĭ-kəl). **1.** Anecdotal. **2.** Full of or given to telling anecdotes.

an·e·cho·ic (ăn'ĕ-kō'ĭk) *adj.* Neither having nor producing echoes: *an anechoic chamber.* [AN- (not) + ECHOIC.]

a·ne·mi·a, a·nae·mi·a (ə-nē'mē-ə) *n.* A pathological deficiency in the oxygen-carrying material of the blood, measured in unit volume concentrations of hemoglobin, red blood cell volume, and red blood cell number.

a·ne·mic, a·nae·mic (ə-nē'mĭk) *adj.* **1.** Of, relating to, or suffering from anemia. **2.** Listless and weak; pallid. **3.** Lacking in vigor.

anemo– *prefix.* Indicates wind; for example, **anemology.** [Greek *anemos,* wind.]

a·nem·o·chore (ə-nĕm'ə-kôr', -kōr') *n.* A plant, such as the dandelion, having seeds, spores, or similar reproductive parts that are dispersed by the wind. [ANEMO- + -CHORE.]

a·nem·o·graph (ə-nĕm'ə-grăf', -gräf') *n.* A recording anemometer. [ANEMO- + -GRAPH.] **—a·nem·o·graph·ic** *adj.*

an·e·mog·ra·phy (ăn'ə-mŏg'rə-fē) *n.* The science of recording wind direction and force. [ANEMO- + -GRAPHY.]

an·e·mol·o·gy (ăn'ə-mŏl'ə-jē) *n.* The scientific study of winds. [ANEMO- + -LOGY.]

an·e·mom·e·ter (ăn'ə-mŏm'ə-tər) *n.* An instrument for measuring and indicating wind force and speed. [ANEMO- + -METER.] **—an·e·mo·met·ric** (ăn'ə-mə-mĕt'rik), **an·e·mo·met·ri·cal** *adj.*

an·e·mom·e·try (ăn'ə-mŏm'ə-trē) *n.* The determination of wind force and velocity. [ANEMO- + -METRY.]

a·nem·o·ne (ə-nĕm'ə-nē) *n.* **1.** Any of various plants of the genus *Anemone,* of the North Temperate Zone, having white, yellow, purple, or red cup-shaped flowers. Some species are also called "windflower." See **pasqueflower, wood anemone. 2.** A marine invertebrate, the **sea anemone** *(see).* [Latin *anemōnē,* from Greek, perhaps from Semitic.]

anemone fish *n.* Any of various small, brightly colored marine fishes of the genus *Amphiprion,* found near sea anemones.

an·e·moph·i·lous (ăn'ə-mŏf'ə-ləs) *adj.* Pollinated by wind-dispersed pollen. [ANEMO- + -PHILOUS.] **—an·e·moph·i·ly** *n.*

an·en·ceph·al·y (ăn'ĕn-sĕf'ə-lē) *n.* Congenital absence of part or all of the brain. [AN- + *-encephaly* : ENCEPHAL(O)- + -Y (state or condition).] **—an·en·ce·phal·ic** (ăn-ĕn'sə-făl'ĭk) *adj.*

a·nent (ə-nĕnt') *prep. Archaic & Scottish.* Regarding; concerning. [Middle English *anent, onevent,* Old English *onemn, on efen,* alongside, together : ON + *efen,* EVEN.]

an·er·oid (ăn'ə-roid') *adj.* Not using fluid. [French *anéroïde* : A- (not) + Greek *nēron,* water.]

aneroid barometer *n.* A barometer in which variations of atmospheric pressure are measured by the relative bulges of a thin elastic metal disc covering a partially evacuated chamber, the movements being magnified by a train of levers to move a needle over a calibrated scale.

an·es·the·sia, an·aes·the·sia (ăn'ĭs-thē'zhə) *n.* **1.** Total or partial loss of sensation, especially tactile sensibility induced by disease or an anesthetic. **2.** Artificially induced unconsciousness or local or general insensibility to pain. [New Latin from Greek *anaisthēsia,* lack of sensation : AN- + *aisthēsis,* feeling.]

an·es·the·si·ol·o·gy, an·aes·the·si·ol·o·gy (ăn'ĭs-thē'zē-ŏl'ə-jē) *n.* The medical study and application of anesthetics.

an·es·thet·ic, an·aes·thet·ic (ăn'ĭs-thĕt'ĭk) *adj.* **1.** Relating to or resembling anesthesia. **2.** Causing anesthesia. **3.** Insensitive.
~*n.* An agent that causes unconsciousness or insensitivity to pain.

a·nes·the·tist, a·naes·the·tist (ə-nĕs'thĭ-tĭst) *n.* A person, usually a physician, trained to administer anesthetics.

a·nes·the·tize, a·naes·the·tize (ə-nĕs'thĭ-tīz') *tr.v.* **-tized, -tizing, tizes.** To induce anesthesia in.

an·es·trus (ăn-ĕs'trəs) *n.* An interval of sexual dormancy between two periods of estrus.

Aneto, Pico de. See **Pico de Aneto.**

an·eu·rysm, an·eu·rism (ăn'yə-rĭz'əm) *n.* A pathological blood-filled dilatation of a blood vessel. [Greek *aneurusma,* from *aneurunein,* to dilate : *ana-,* "throughout" + *eurunein,* to dilate, widen, from *eurus,* wide.] **—an·eu·rys·mal** (ăn'yə-rĭz'məl) *adj.*

a·new (ə-no͞o', ə-nyo͞o') *adv.* **1.** Again. **2.** In a new and different way, form, or manner. [Middle English *anewe, of newe,* Old English *of nīwe* : OF + *nīwe,* NEW.]

an·frac·tu·os·i·ty (ăn-frăk'cho͞o-ŏs'ə-tē) *n., pl.* **-ties. 1.** The state or quality of being anfractuous. **2.** Something anfractuous, such as a winding passage or a complicated process.

an·frac·tu·ous (ăn-frăk'cho͞o-əs) *adj.* Full of twists and turns; winding; tortuous. [French *anfractueux,* from Late Latin *anfractuōsus,* from Latin *anfractus,* a winding : *an-,* from AMBI- + *fractus,* past participle of *frangere,* to break.]

an·ga·ry (ăng'gə-rē) *n. International Law.* The right of a belligerent state to seize, use, or destroy the property of a neutral, provided that full compensation is made. [Late Latin *angaria,* enforced service to a lord, from Greek *angareia,* impressment for public service, from *angaros,* mounted courier, perhaps of Persian origin.]

an·gel (ān'jəl) *n.* **1.** *Theology.* **a.** An immortal, spiritual being attendant upon God, conventionally represented as a winged being of human form. **b.** In medieval angelology, one of nine orders of spiritual beings (listed from the highest to lowest in rank): seraphim, cherubim, thrones, dominations or dominions, virtues, powers, principalities, archangels, and angels. **2.** A guardian spirit or guiding influence. **3.** A sweet-tempered or kind person, especially a child or a woman. **4.** *Christian Science.* God's thoughts passing to man. **5.** *Informal.* A financial backer of an enterprise, especially a dramatic production. [Middle English, from Old French *angele,* from Late Latin *angelus,* from Greek *angelos* (translation of Hebrew *mal'ākh*), messenger, perhaps of Persian origin.]

An·gel Fall (ān'jəl). The highest waterfall in the world, with a drop of 980 meters (3,215 feet). Set among the dense forests of southeastern Venezuela, it was discovered in 1935 and named after James Angel, a U.S. pilot who crashed nearby in 1937.

an·gel·fish (ān′jəl-fĭsh′) *n., pl.* **-fishes** or collectively **angelfish.** **1.** Any of several brightly colored fishes of the family Chaetodontidae, of warm seas, having laterally compressed bodies. **2.** A fresh-water fish, *Pterophyllum scalare,* native to rivers of South America, having a laterally compressed, usually striped body. Also called "scalare." [After its fancied resemblance to the brilliance of an angel and, in some species, alluding to its fins as an angel's wings.]

angel food cake *n.* Also **angel cake.** A white, almond-flavored sponge cake.

an·gel·ic (ăn-jĕl′ĭk) *adj.* Also **an·gel·i·cal** (-ĭ-kəl). **1.** Of or consisting of angels: *angelic hosts.* **2.** Suggestive of or resembling an angel, as in innocence, kindness, or beauty. **—an·gel·i·cal·ly** *adv.*

an·gel·i·ca (ăn-jĕl′ĭ-kə) *n.* **1.** Any of various plants of the genus *Angelica,* having compound leaves and clusters of small white or greenish flowers; especially, *A. archangelica,* whose aromatic seeds, leaves, stems, and roots are used in medicine and as flavoring. **2.** The candied stem of this plant, used especially for decorating cakes and sweet dishes. [New Latin, from Medieval Latin *(herba) angelica,* "angelic (herb)," from Late Latin, feminine of *angelicus,* from Greek *angelikos,* from *angelos,* messenger. See **angel.**]

An·gel·i·co (ăn-jĕl′ĭ-kō), **Fra** (1387–1455). Florentine painter, famous for his frescos of religious subjects. His real name was Guido di Pietro, which he changed when he became a Dominican monk. His best-known work is the cycle of 35 paintings that decorates the sanctuary of the Church of SS. Annunziata.

an·gel·ol·o·gy (ān′jə-lŏl′ə-jē) *n.* The branch of theology having to do with angels. [ANGEL + -LOGY.]

angel shark *n.* Any of several raylike sharks of the genus *Squatina,* having a broad, flat head and body.

An·ge·lus, an·ge·lus (ăn′jə-ləs) *n. Roman Catholic Church.* **1.** A devotional prayer at morning, noon, and night to commemorate the Annunciation. **2.** A bell rung as a summons to recite this prayer. [Medieval Latin, *"Angelus (Domini . . .),"* "The Angel (of the Lord)" (the beginning of the liturgy commemorating the Incarnation), from *angelus,* ANGEL.]

an·ger (ăng′gər) *n.* A feeling of extreme displeasure, hostility, indignation, or exasperation toward someone or something.
~v. **angered, -gering, -gers.** *—tr.* To make angry; enrage. *—intr.* To become angry. [Middle English, from Old Norse *angr,* grief.]
Synonyms: *fury, indignation, ire, rage, resentment, wrath.*

an·ger·ly (ăng′gər-lē) *adv. Archaic.* In an angry manner; angrily.

An·gers (än-zhā′). Town of pre-Roman origin, the capital of Maine-et-Loire department in western France. Formerly the capital of Anjou, it boasts a rich heritage of medieval architecture.

An·ge·vin (ăn′jə-vĭn) *adj.* **1.** Of or pertaining to Anjou. **2.** Of or pertaining to the ruling house of Anjou, especially as represented by the Plantagenet kings of England, from Henry II, the son of Geoffrey, Count of Anjou, to Richard II (1154–1399). [French, from Old French, from Medieval Latin *Andegavīnus,* from *Andegavia,* ANJOU.] **—An·ge·vin** *n.*

an·gi·na (ăn-jī′nə) *n.* **1.** Any disease, such as croup or diphtheria, in which spasmodic and painful suffocation or spasms occur. **2.** Angina pectoris. [Latin, quinsy, from Greek *ankhonē,* a strangling.] **—an·gi·nal** *adj.*

angina pec·to·ris (pĕk′tər-ĭs) *n.* Severe paroxysmal pain in the chest characterized by feelings of suffocation and apprehension and caused by a momentary lack of adequate blood supply to the heart. [New Latin, "angina of the chest."]

angio-, angi- *prefix.* Indicates: **1.** Blood or lymph vessel; for example, **angiography. 2.** Seed vessel; for example, **angiosperm.** [Greek *angeion,* vessel, diminutive of *angos*†, vessel.]

an·gi·og·ra·phy (ăn′jē-ŏg′rə-fē) *n.* The x-ray examination of blood vessels after the injection of a radiopaque dye. **—an·gi·o·gra·phic** (ăn′jē-ə-grăf′ĭk) *adj.*

an·gi·ol·o·gy (ăn′jē-ŏl′ə-jē) *n.* The study of blood and lymph vessels.

an·gi·o·ma (ăn′jē-ō′mə) *n., pl.* **-mas** or **-mata** (-mə-tə). A tumor composed of lymph and blood vessels. [ANGIO- + -OMA.] **—an·gi·om·a·tous** (ăn′jē-ŏm′ə-təs) *adj.*

an·gi·o·sperm (ăn′jē-ə-spûrm′) *n. Botany.* Any plant of the class Angiospermae, characterized by having seeds enclosed in an ovary; a flowering plant. **—an·gi·o·sper·mous** (ăn′jē-ə-spûr′məs) *adj.*

an·gi·o·ten·sin (ăn′jē-ō-tĕn′sĭn) *n.* A protein in the blood that causes constriction of blood vessels and stimulates secretion of the hormone aldosterone from the adrenal cortex. [ANGIO- + TENS(ION) + -IN.]

Ang·kor (ăng′kôr′). Major archaeological site in northwestern Kampuchea (Cambodia), the capital of the Khmer empire from the 9th to the 15th century. The ruins include two major Hindu temple complexes, Angkor Wat (12th century) and Angkor Thom (13th century).

Angl. Anglican.

an·gle¹ (ăng′gəl) *intr.v.* **-gled, -gling, -gles. 1.** To fish with a hook and line. **2.** To try to get something by deceitful or indirect means. Used with *for: angle for an invitation.*
~n. Obsolete. A fishhook or fishing tackle. [Middle English *anglen,* from *angel,* a fishhook, Old English *angul, ongul.*]

angle² *n.* **1.** *Geometry.* **a.** The figure formed by two lines diverging from a common point. **b.** The figure formed by two planes diverging from a common line. **c.** The rotation required to superimpose either of two such lines or planes on the other. **d.** The space between such lines or surfaces. **e.** A **solid angle** *(see).* **2.** An angular or projecting corner, as of a building. **3. a.** The place, position, or direction from which an object is presented to view. **b.** *Informal.* A particular aspect of a complex whole, viewed separately: *He deals with the advertising angle.* **c.** *Informal.* A particular viewpoint: *From his angle, it's a disaster.* **4.** *Slang.* A scheme; a devious method.
~v. **angled, -gling, -gles.** *—tr.* **1.** To move or turn at an angle. **2.** To aim or hit (a ball, for example) at an angle. **3.** *Informal.* To impart a particular bias or point of view to (a story or report, for example). *—intr.* To move or proceed by angles: *The path angled through the woods.* [Middle English, from Old French, from Latin *angulus,* angle, corner.]

An·gle (ăng′gəl) *n.* A member of a Germanic people that migrated to England from southern Denmark in the 5th century A.D., founded the kingdoms of Northumbria, East Anglia, and Mercia, and together with the Jutes and Saxons formed the Anglo-Saxon peoples. [Latin *Anglī, Anglii* (plural), from Germanic; related to Old English *angul,* fishhook; perhaps alluding to the shape of the original homeland, the Angul district of Schleswig.]

angle bracket *n.* Either of the punctuation marks, < >, used to enclose written or printed material, or to indicate an integral in quantum mechanics.

angle iron *n.* A length of steel or iron having an L-shaped cross-section, used as part of a structural framework.

angle of attack *n.* **1.** The acute angle between the chord of an airfoil and a line representing the undisturbed relative airflow. **2.** Any other acute angle between two reference lines designating the cant of an airfoil relative to the oncoming air.

angle of incidence *n.* **1.** *Physics.* The angle formed by the path of a body or of radiation incident on a surface and a perpendicular to the surface at the point of impact. **2.** *Aviation.* The angle of attack.

angle of reflection *n.* The acute angle formed by the path of a reflected body or reflected radiation with a perpendicular to the surface at the point of reflection.

angle of refraction *n.* The acute angle formed by the path of refracted radiation with a perpendicular to the refracting surface at the point of refraction.

angle of repose *n.* The maximum angle to the horizontal that a pile of rocks, soil, or the like can sustain without sliding.

angle of view *n.* The angle included by two lines drawn from opposite extreme corners of an image to the center of a lens.

angle of yaw *n.* The angle between an aircraft's longitudinal axis and its line of travel, as seen from above.

angle plate *n.* **1.** A right-angled metal bracket, used on the face plate of a lathe to hold pieces being worked. **2.** A flat steel plate in the shape of a right-angled triangle, used to strengthen frameworks, connect structural members, and the like.

an·gler (ăng′glər) *n.* **1.** A fisherman who uses a hook. **2.** An anglerfish.

an·gler·fish (ăng′glər-fĭsh′) *n., pl.* **-fishes** or collectively **anglerfish.** Any of various marine fishes of the order Lophiiformes (or Pediculati), having a long dorsal fin ray that is suspended over the mouth and serves as a lure to attract prey.

An·gle·sey (ăng′gəl-sē). Island separated from the northwestern mainland of Wales by the Menai Strait. Formerly a separate county, it has been part of the new county of Gwynedd since 1974.

angle shades *n. Used with a singular verb.* A common European moth, *Phlogophora meticulosa,* that resembles a withered leaf when the wings are folded. [From the angular markings of the wings.]

an·gle·site (ăng′glə-sīt′) *n.* A lead sulphate mineral, occurring in white or tinted crystals. [After ANGLESEY, where it was first found.]

an·gle·worm (ăng′gəl-wûrm′) *n.* A worm, such as an earthworm, used as bait in fishing.

An·gli·a (ăng′glē-ə). The medieval Latin name for England. [Latin, from *Anglī,* the ANGLE(S).]

An·gli·an (ăng′glē-ən) *n.* **1.** An Angle. **2.** The Old English dialects of Northumbrian and Mercian.
~adj. Of or pertaining to the Angles.

An·gli·can (ăng′glĭ-kən) *adj. Abbr.* **Angl.** Of, pertaining to, or characteristic of the Church of England or any of the churches related to it in origin and communion, such as the Protestant Episcopal Church.
~n. A member of the Church of England or of any of the churches related to it. [Medieval Latin *Anglicānus,* from *Anglicus,* English, from Latin *Anglī,* ANGLE(S.)]

Anglican Communion *n.* The Church of England and those Episcopal churches, chiefly in English-speaking countries, that share with it substantially the same doctrine and are in communion with the Archbishop of Canterbury. Also called "Anglican Church."

An·gli·can·ism (ăng′glĭ-kə-nĭz′əm) *n.* The doctrine, system, and practice of the Anglicans.

An·gli·ce (ăng′glə-sē) *adv.* In the English form: *Firenze, Anglice Florence.* [Medieval Latin *Anglicē,* adverb of *Anglicus,* English, from Latin *Anglī,* the ANGLE(S).]

An·gli·cism (ăng′glə-sĭz′əm) *n. Often* **anglicism. 1.** A word, phrase, or idiom peculiar to the English language, especially as it is spoken in England. **2.** Attachment to or admiration of English customs or values.

An·gli·cize, an·gli·cize (ăng′glə-sīz′) *v.* **-cized, -cizing, -cizes.** *—tr.* To make English in form, idiom, style, or character. *—intr.* To become Anglicized. **—An·gli·ci·za·tion** (ăng′glə-sĭ-zā′shən) *n.*

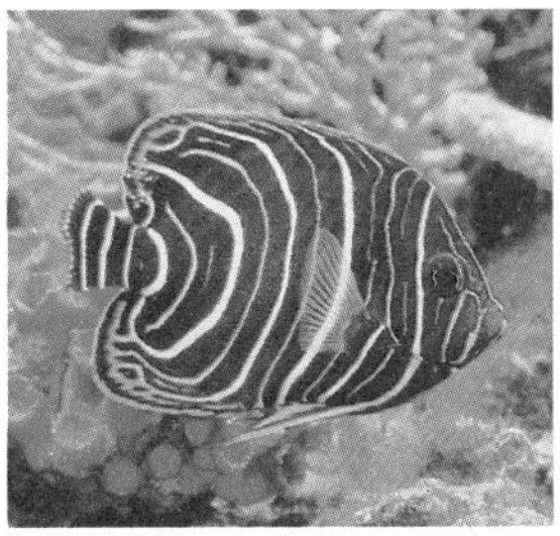
angelfish *These small, brilliantly colored fish are found mainly on coral reefs in the Indian Ocean and the Pacific.*

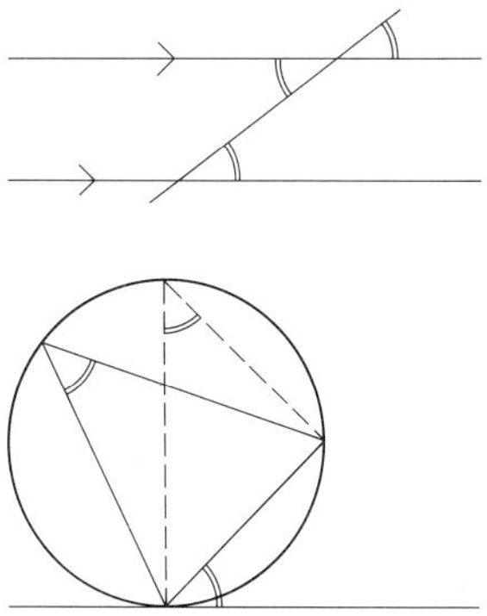
angle *Angles are formed whenever lines or planes cross each other or diverge from a common point. In each of these drawings, all the marked angles are equal.*

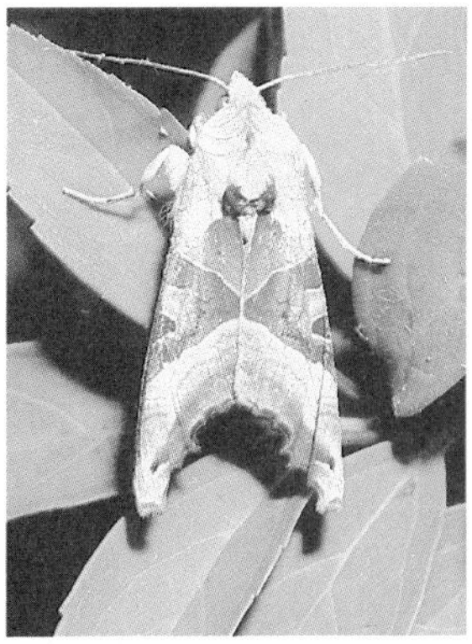
angle shades moth *When this common moth folds its wings, it resembles a withered leaf.*

an·gling (ăng'glĭng) n. The act, process, or art of fishing with a hook and line and usually a rod.

An·glo (ăng'glō) n., pl. **-glos.** Informal. An Anglo-American, especially a white resident of the United States who is not of Latin descent. [Short for ANGLO-AMERICAN.] —**An·glo** adj.

Anglo– prefix. Indicates: **1.** English or England; for example, **Anglophile. 2.** Involving the English or British and; for example, Anglo-Israeli relations. [New Latin, from Medieval Latin Anglī, the English people, from Latin, the ANGLE(s).]

An·glo-A·mer·i·can (ăng'glō-ə-mĕr'ə-kən) n. An American, especially a resident of the United States, whose language, ancestry, and culture are English. —**An·glo-A·mer·i·can** adj.

An·glo-Cath·o·lic (ăng'glō-kăth'lĭk, -kăth'ə-lĭk) n. A member of the Anglican Communion who inclines toward the Roman Catholic Church in matters of ritual and worship. —**An·glo-Cath·o·lic** adj. —**An·glo-Ca·thol·i·cism** (ăn'glō-kə-thŏl'ə-sĭz'əm) n.

An·glo-French (ăng'glō-frĕnch') n. Abbr. **AF, A.F.** Norman French (see). Also called "Anglo-Norman." —**An·glo-French** adj.

An·glo-In·di·an (ăng'glō-ĭn'dē-ən) n. **1.** A person of British and Indian descent. **2.** A person of British origin living in India during British rule. **3.** The dialect of English used in India. —**An·glo-In·di·an** adj.

An·glo-I·rish (ăng'glō-ī'rĭsh) pl.n. Inhabitants of Ireland of English origin. Preceded by the. —**An·glo-Ir·ish** adj.

An·glo-Nor·man (ăng'glō-nôr'mən) n. **1.** Any of the Norman people who settled in England after 1066, or a descendant of these settlers. **2.** Abbr. **AN, A.N.** The Norman-French language spoken by these people. —**An·glo-Nor·man** adj.

An·glo·phile (ăng'glə-fīl') n. An admirer of England and English customs or manners. —**An·glo·phile** adj. —**An·glo·phil·i·a** (ăng'glə-fĭl'ē-ə).

An·glo·phobe (ăng'glə-fōb') n. One who has an aversion to England and English customs or manners. —**An·glo·phobe** adj. —**An·glo·pho·bi·a** (ăng'glə-fō'bē-ə) n.

An·glo·phone (ăng'glə-fōn') adj. **1.** Of, pertaining to, or being an English-speaking individual, especially in a country where two or more languages are spoken. Compare **Francophone.** —**An·glo·phone** n.

An·glo-Sax·on (ăng'glō-săk'sən) n. Abbr. **AS, A.S., AS. 1.** A member of one of the Germanic peoples (Angles, Saxons, and Jutes) who settled in Britain in the 5th and 6th centuries A.D. **2.** Any of the descendants of these peoples who were dominant in England until the Norman Conquest of 1066. **3. a. Old English** (see). **b.** Plain, unadorned English. **4.** Any person of English ancestry. —**An·glo-Sax·on** adj.

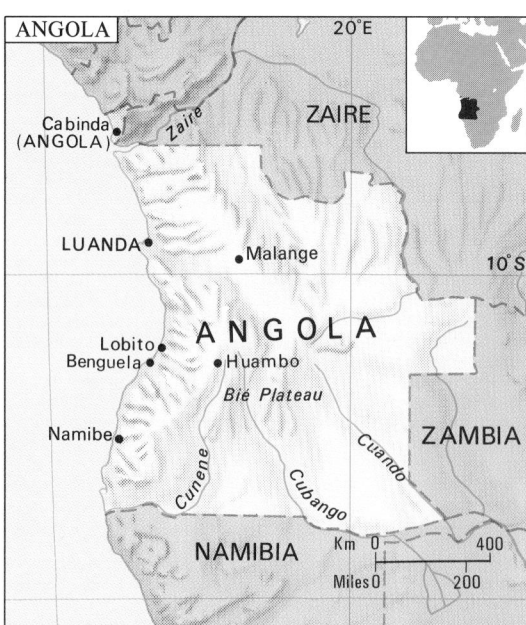

An·go·la (ăng-gō'lə). Country in southwest Africa. Formerly Portuguese West Africa, it gained its independence in 1975 after a long guerrilla war. A civil war then ensued between the three former independence groups: the National Front for the Liberation of Angola (FNLA), the National Union for the Total Independence of Angola (UNITA), and the People's Movement for the Liberation of Angola (MPLA). The Cuban-backed MPLA eventually gained control over most of the country. The country has great hydroelectric potential and considerable mineral resources. Coffee, oil, diamonds, and iron ore are the chief exports. Area, 1,246,700 square kilometers (481,226 square miles). Population, 7,100,000. Capital, Luanda. —**An·go·lan** n. & adj.

An·go·ra¹ (ăng-gôr'ə, -gōr'ə) n. **1.** Often **angora. a.** The hair of the Angora goat. **b.** The fine, light hair of the Angora rabbit, some-

times blended with wool in fabrics. **c.** A yarn or fabric made from either of these fibers. **2.** An Angora cat. **3.** An Angora goat. **4.** An Angora rabbit. [From ANGORA (Ankara), name given first to the goat and its wool.]

Angora². See **Ankara.**

Angora cat n. A long-haired domestic cat similar to the Persian cat.

Angora goat n. Any of a breed of domestic goats having long, silky hair.

Angora rabbit n. Any of a breed of domestic rabbits having long, soft, usually white hair.

an·gos·tu·ra bark (ăng'gə-stŏor'ə, -styŏor'ə) n. The bitter, aromatic bark of either of two Brazilian trees, Galipea officinalis or Cusparia trifoliata, used as a tonic. [From Angostura, former name of Ciudad Bolívar.]

Angostura bitters pl.n. A trademark for a tonic used to flavor alcoholic drinks. [After ANGOSTURA BARK.]

an·gry (ăng'grē) adj. **-gri·er, -gri·est. 1.** Feeling or showing anger; incensed or enraged. **2.** Indicative of or resulting from anger: an angry silence. **3.** Having a menacing aspect; seeming to threaten: angry clouds. **4.** Inflamed: an angry sore. [Middle English, from ANGER.] —**an·gri·ly** (ăng'grə-lē) adv. —**an·gri·ness** n.

angry young man n. **1.** Any of a group of British writers of the 1950's whose works are characterized by vigorous social protest. **2.** Any young man with strongly felt radical or anti-Establishment views. [Perhaps from Angry Young Man (1951), an autobiography by L. A. Paul (1901–), British journalist.]

angst (ängkst) n. A feeling of anxiety. [German Angst, from Middle High German angest, from Old High German angust.]

ang·strom, Ång·ström (ăng'strəm) n. Symbol **Å** A unit of length that is equal to one hundred-millionth (10^{-8}) of a centimeter, used especially to specify radiation wavelengths. Also called "angstrom unit." [After Anders Jonas ÅNGSTRÖM.]

Ång·ström (ăng'strəm, ông'-), **Anders Jonas** (1814–74). Swedish physicist. He was a founder of the science of spectroscopy, and the angstrom unit of measurement is named after him. He laid the foundations of modern spectral analysis and discovered by investigating the solar spectrum that there is hydrogen in the sun's atmosphere.

An·guil·la (ăng-gwĭl'ə, ăn-). One of the Leeward Islands in the Caribbean Sea, discovered by Columbus in 1493. A British colony ruled from St. Kitts since the 17th century, it was linked with St. Kitts-Nevis as a British associated state in 1962. The Anguillans sought independence from Britain and St. Kitts in 1967 and again in 1969, when British troops and London police quelled their revolt. The island finally became a separate self-governing dependency in 1980. —**An·guil·lan** adj. & n.

an·guil·li·form (ăng-gwĭl'ə-fôrm') adj. Having the elongated shape of an eel. [New Latin anguilla, from Latin, eel, diminutive of anguis, snake + -FORM.]

an·guine (ăng'gwĭn) adj. Of, pertaining to, or resembling a snake; snakelike. [Latin anguīnus, from anguis, snake.]

an·guish (ăng'gwĭsh) n. Extreme pain, especially mental pain; torment; torture.
~v. **anguished, -guishing, -guishes.** —tr. To cause to suffer or feel anguish. —intr. To suffer or feel anguish. [Middle English anguisshe, from Old French anguisse, from Latin angustia, straightness, narrowness, from angustus, narrow.]

an·guished (ăng'gwĭsht) adj. Filled with or expressing anguish: an anguished cry.

an·gu·lar (ăng'gyə-lər) adj. **1.** Having, forming, or consisting of an angle or angles. **2.** Measured by an angle or degrees of an arc. **3.** Bony and lean; gaunt. **4.** Lacking grace or smoothness in movement or manner; awkward: an angular gait. [Latin angulāris : angulus, ANGLE + -āris, -AR.] —**an·gu·lar·ly** adv. —**an·gu·lar·ness** n.

angular acceleration n. Physics. The rate of change of angular velocity with respect to time.

an·gu·lar·i·ty (ăng'gyə-lăr'ə-tē) n., pl. **-ties. 1.** The state or quality of being angular. **2. angularities.** Angular forms, outlines, or corners.

angular momentum n. Physics. **1.** The vector product of the position vector and linear momentum of a particle in motion relative to an axis. **2.** The sum of such products, one for each component particle of an extended body, expressible as the product of the angular velocity and the moment of inertia of the body. Also called "moment of momentum."

angular velocity n. Physics. A vector quantity describing rotational motion, the magnitude of which is the time rate of change of angle, and the direction of which is along the axis of rotation.

an·gu·late (ăng'gyə-lĭt, -lāt') adj. Also **an·gu·lat·ed** (-lā'tĭd). Having angles or an angular shape.
~v. (-lāt') **angulated, -lating, -lates.** —tr. To cause to become angular. —intr. To become angular. [Latin angulātus, past participle of angulāre, to make angular, from angulus, ANGLE.] —**an·gu·late·ly** adv.

an·gu·la·tion (ăng'gyə-lā'shən) n. **1.** The formation of angles. **2.** An angular part, position, or formation. **3.** The measurement of angles.

an·hin·ga (ăn-hĭng'gə) n. A bird, the **water turkey** (see). [Portuguese, from Tupi.]

an·hy·dride (ăn-hī'drīd') n. **1.** A chemical compound formed from another by the removal of water. **2.** A compound that forms an acid or a base when water is added to it. **3.** An organic compound containing two carboxyl groups from which a single water molecule has been removed, leaving the group -CO·O·CO-. [ANHYDR(OUS) + -IDE.]

an·hy·drite (ăn-hī'drīt') *n.* A white to grayish or reddish mineral of anhydrous calcium sulfate, CaSO₄, occurring as layers in gypsum deposits. [ANHYDR(OUS) + -ITE.]

an·hy·drous (ăn-hī'drəs) *adj.* Without water, especially water of crystallization. [Greek *anudros,* waterless : *an-,* without + *hudōr,* water.]

an·i·con·ic (ăn'ī-kŏn'ĭk) *adj.* Not in human or animal form. Said of mythical symbols, portrayals of gods, or the like. [AN- (not) + ICONIC.]

an·il (ăn'ĭl) *n.* 1. The indigo plant. 2. The blue dye obtained from the indigo plant. [French, from Portuguese, from Arabic *an-nīl,* the indigo plant, from Persian *nīl,* indigo.]

an·ile (ăn'ĭl, ā'nīl') *adj.* Feeble and frail like an old woman. [Latin *anīlis,* from *anus,* old woman.] —**a·nil·i·ty** (ā-nĭl'ə-tē) *n.*

an·i·line, an·i·lin (ăn'ə-lĭn) *n.* A colorless, oily, poisonous benzene derivative, C₆H₅NH₂, used in the manufacture of rubber, dyes, resins, pharmaceuticals, and varnishes.
~*adj.* Derived from aniline. [German *Anilin* : ANIL + -INE.]

aniline dye *n.* Any of numerous synthetic dyes, originally those derived from aniline.

an·i·ma (ăn'ə-mə) *n.* 1. The soul. 2. In the psychology of Carl Jung: **a.** The soul, or true inner self. Compare **persona. b.** The feminine inner personality, as present in the unconscious of the male. Compare **animus.** [Latin, feminine of *animus,* mind, ANIMUS.]

an·i·mad·ver·sion (ăn'ə-măd-vûr'zhən, -shən) *n.* 1. Hostile criticism. 2. A considered and usually censorious or critical remark. Used with *on* or *upon.* [Latin *animadversiō,* from *animadvertere,* to ANIMADVERT.]

an·i·mad·vert (ăn'ə-măd-vûrt') *intr.v.* -**verted, -verting, -verts.** To remark or comment critically, usually with strong disapproval or censure. Used with *on* or *upon.* [Latin *animadvertere,* to direct the mind to, censure : *animus,* mind + *advertere,* to turn toward : *ad-,* to + *vertere,* to turn.]

an·i·mal (ăn'ə-məl) *n.* 1. Any organism of the kingdom Animalia, distinguished from plants by certain typical characteristics, such as the power of locomotion, fixed structure and limited growth, nonrigid cell walls, specialized sense organs and rapid response to stimuli, and nonphotosynthetic metabolism. 2. Any such organism other than a human being; especially, a mammal. 3. A person of inhuman character or behavior; someone who is bestial or brutish. 4. A person considered in terms of a characteristic quality or interest: *Her husband is the complete domestic animal.* 5. Animality: *Drinking releases the animal in him.*
~*adj.* 1. Of, pertaining to, or characteristic of animals. 2. Produced by or derived from animals: *animal fat.* 3. Pertaining to the sensual or physical as distinct from the spiritual nature of human beings. [Latin, an animal, from *animālis,* living, from *anima,* feminine of *animus,* breath, soul.]

animal cracker *n.* A small cookie baked in the shape of an animal.

an·i·mal·cule (ăn'ə-măl'kyōōl) *n.* Also **an·i·mal·cu·lum** (-kyə-ləm) *pl.* -**cula** (-kyə-lə). 1. A microscopic or minute organism usually regarded as an animal, as an amoeba or paramecium. 2. *Archaic.* A tiny animal, such as a mosquito. [New Latin *animalculum,* diminutive of ANIMAL.] —**an·i·mal·cu·lar** (ăn'ə-măl'kyə-lər) *adj.*

animal heat *n.* The heat generated in an animal's body.

animal husbandry *n.* The care and breeding of domestic animals such as cattle, pigs, sheep, and horses.

an·i·mal·ism (ăn'ə-mə-lĭz'əm) *n.* 1. A state of sound health resulting from the full satisfaction of physical drives. 2. A state of brutish indifference to all but the physical appetites. 3. The doctrine that human beings are purely animal with no spiritual nature. —**an·i·mal·ist** *n.* —**an·i·mal·is·tic** (ăn'ə-mə-lĭs'tĭk) *adj.*

an·i·mal·i·ty (ăn'ə-măl'ə-tē) *n.* 1. The characteristics or nature of an animal. 2. Animals collectively; the animal kingdom. 3. The animal as distinct from the spiritual nature of mankind.

an·i·mal·ize (ăn'ə-mə-līz') *tr.v.* -**ized, -izing, -izes.** 1. To make coarse and brutal. 2. To endow (a deity) with the attributes, especially the form, of an animal. —**an·i·mal·i·za·tion** *n.*

animal kingdom *n.* The category of living organisms that includes all animals. Compare **mineral kingdom, plant kingdom.**

animal magnetism *n.* 1. Magnetic personal presence. 2. Sensuality. 3. Hypnotism or mesmerism.

animal spirits *pl.n.* Buoyancy that results from good physical health and vitality.

animal starch *n.* Glycogen (see).

an·i·mate (ăn'ə-māt') *tr.v.* -**mated, -mating, -mates.** 1. To give life to; fill with life. 2. To impart interest or zest to; enliven. 3. To fill with spirit, courage, or resolution; encourage. 4. To impart motion or activity to. 5. To make, design, or produce (a film, for example) by means of animation.
~*adj.* (-mĭt). 1. Possessing life; living. 2. Lively; vivacious. [Latin *animāre,* to fill with breath, from *anima,* breath, soul. See **animal.**]

an·i·mat·ed (ăn'ə-mā'tĭd) *adj.* 1. Filled with life, activity, vigor, or spirit; enlivened: *an animated discussion.* 2. Made or designed so as to seem alive and moving: *an animated doll.* 3. Involving or using animation: *an animated film.* —**an·i·mat·ed·ly** *adv.*

animated cartoon *n.* A motion picture involving the animation of cartoon figures. Also called "cartoon."

animated oat *n.* A grass, *Avena sterilis,* of the Mediterranean region, having seeds that move or twist in response to changes in moisture.

an·i·ma·tion (ăn'ə-mā'shən) *n.* 1. The act, process, or result of animating. 2. The condition or quality of being animate; liveliness; spirit; vitality. 3. **a.** An optical illusion of continuous movement achieved by the rapid succession of separate, still, but gradually varying images, utilized for entertainment in animated cartoons, for example. **b.** The art or process of achieving this illusion.

a·ni·ma·to (ä'nə-mä'tō, ăn'ə-) *adv. Music.* In an animated or lively manner. Used as a direction. [Italian, from Latin *animātus,* past participle of *animāre,* to ANIMATE.] —**a·ni·ma·to** *adj.*

an·i·ma·tor, an·i·mat·er (ăn'ə-mā'tər) *n.* 1. One that animates. 2. An artist or technician who produces an animated cartoon.

an·i·mism (ăn'ə-mĭz'əm) *n.* 1. Any of various cultural beliefs whereby natural phenomena and things animate and inanimate are held to possess individual innate souls. 2. Any belief in spiritual beings or spiritual forces. 3. The hypothesis, first advanced by Pythagoras and Plato, of an immaterial force animating the universe. 4. An 18th-century doctrine that viewed the soul as the vital principle and source of both the normal and the abnormal phenomena of life. [German *Animismus,* from Latin *anima,* breath, soul. See **animal.**] —**an·i·mist** (ăn'ə-mĭst) *n.* —**an·i·mis·tic** (ăn'ə-mĭs'tĭk) *adj.*

an·i·mos·i·ty (ăn'ə-mŏs'ə-tē) *n., pl.* -**ties.** Active hostility or open enmity. [Middle English *animosite,* from Old French, from Late Latin *animōsitās,* vehemence, spirit, from Latin *animōsus,* bold, spirited, from *animus,* soul, mind.]

an·i·mus (ăn'ə-məs) *n.* 1. An animating motive; an intention or purpose. 2. A feeling of animosity; bitter hostility or hatred. 3. In the psychology of Carl Jung, the masculine inner personality, as present in the unconscious of the female. Compare **anima.** [Latin, mind, soul.]

an·i·on (ăn'ī'ən) *n.* A negatively charged ion that migrates to an anode, as in electrolysis. Compare **cation.** [Greek, "that which goes up" (i.e., toward the anode), neuter present participle of *anienai,* to go up : *an(a)-,* up + *ienai,* to go.] —**an·i·on·ic** (ăn'ī-ŏn'ĭk) *adj.*

an·ise (ăn'ĭs) *n.* 1. A plant, *Pimpinella anisum,* native to the Mediterranean region, having clusters of small yellowish-white flowers and licorice-flavored seeds. 2. Aniseed. [Middle English *anis,* from Old French, from Latin *anīsum,* from Greek *anison†.*]

an·i·seed (ăn'ĭ-sēd') *n.* The licorice-flavored seed of the anise plant, used in medicine and as flavoring. [Middle English *anis seed* : ANISE + SEED.]

an·i·sei·ko·ni·a (ăn-ī'sī-kō'nē-ə) *n.* An ocular defect in which the perception of image, shape, and size differ in each eye. [New Latin : ANIS(O)- + Greek *eikōn,* image.] —**an·i·sei·kon·ic** (ăn-ī'sī-kŏn'ĭk) *adj.*

an·i·sette (ăn'ə-sĕt', -zĕt') *n.* An anise-flavored liqueur. [French, diminutive of *anis,* ANISE.]

aniso– *prefix.* Indicates not equal or alike; for example, **anisomerous.** [New Latin, from Greek *anisos,* unequal : AN-, not + *isos,* equal (see **iso-**).]

an·i·sog·a·my (ăn'ī-sŏg'ə-mē) *n. Biology.* A union between markedly different gametes. [ANISO- + -GAMY.] —**an·i·sog·a·mous** (ăn'ī-sŏg'ə-məs) *adj.*

an·i·sole (ăn'ə-sōl') *n.* A colorless liquid, C₆H₅OCH₃, used as a solvent, vermicide, and flavoring. [ANIS(E) + -OLE.]

an·i·som·er·ous (ăn'ī-sŏm'ər-əs) *adj. Botany.* Having or designating floral whorls that have unequal numbers of parts. [ANISO- + -MEROUS.]

an·i·so·met·ric (ăn-ī'sə-mĕt'rĭk) *adj.* 1. Not isometric. 2. Denoting a crystal that has unequal axes. [French *anisométrique* : AN- (not) + ISOMETRIC.]

an·i·so·me·tro·pi·a (ăn-ī'sə-mə-trō'pē-ə) *n. Pathology.* Difference in the refractive power of the eyes. [New Latin : Greek *anisometros* : AN- (not) + *isometros,* ISOMETR(IC) + -OPIA.]

an·i·so·trop·ic (ăn-ī'sə-trŏp'ĭk) *adj.* 1. Not isotropic. 2. *Physics.* Having properties that differ according to the direction of measurement. [AN- (not) + ISOTROPIC.] —**an·i·sot·ro·pi·cal·ly** *adv.* —**an·i·sot·ro·pism** (ăn'ī-sŏt'rə-pĭz'əm), **an·i·sot·ro·py** (ăn'ī-sŏt'rə-pē) *n.*

An·jou (ăn'jōō). Ancient region of western France, ruled by the powerful counts of Anjou in the early Middle Ages. From their line came Geoffrey Plantagenet (1131–51), Count of Anjou and the father of the English king Henry II. See **Angevin.**

An·ka·ra (ăng'kə-rə, äng'-) In ancient times known as **An·cy·ra** (ăn-sī'rə), later **An·go·ra** (ăng-gôr'ə, -gōr'ə). The capital and second-largest city of Turkey, lying 900 meters (3,000 feet) above sea level in the west-central part of the country.

an·ker·ite (ăng'kə-rīt') *n.* A dolomitelike mineral in which iron partially replaces magnesium. [German *Ankerit,* after M.J. *Anker* (died 1843), Austrian mineralogist.]

ankh (ăngk) *n.* An **ansate cross** *(see).* [Egyptian *'nh,* soul, life.]

an·kle (ăng'kəl) *n.* 1. The joint, consisting of the talus bone and related structures, that connects the foot with the leg. 2. The slender section of the leg immediately above the foot. [Middle English *ankel* and *anclowe,* probably from Old Norse *ankula* (unattested) and Old English *anclēow.*]

an·kle·bone (ăng'kəl-bōn') *n.* The **talus** *(see).*

an·klet (ăng'klĭt) *n.* 1. An ornament worn around the ankle. 2. A sock that reaches just above the ankle. [ANKL(E) + -LET.]

an·ky·lose, an·chy·lose (ăng'kə-lōs', -lōz') *v.* -**losed, -losing, -loses.** —*tr.* To join or consolidate by ankylosis. —*intr.* To become joined or consolidated by ankylosis. [Back-formation from ANKYLOSIS.]

an·ky·lo·sis, an·chy·lo·sis (ăng'kə-lō'sĭs) *n.* 1. *Anatomy.* The consolidation of bones or their parts forming a single unit. 2. *Pathology.* The stiffening of a joint as the result of abnormal bone fusion, surgery, or growth of fibrous tissue within the joint. [New Latin, from Greek *ankulōsis,* stiffening of the joints, from *ankuloun,* to bend, from *ankulos,* bent, curved, crooked.] —**an·ky·lot·ic** (ăng′kə-lŏt′ĭk) *adj.*

an·lace (ăn′lĭs, -lās′) *n.* A two-edged medieval dagger. [Middle English *anlas, anelas*†.]

an·la·ge (än′lä′gə) *n., pl.* **-gen** (-gən) or **-ges. 1.** *Embryology.* The initial cell structure from which an embryonic part or organ develops; a primordium. **2.** A fundamental principle; a foundation. [German *Anlage,* from Middle High German *anlāge,* a request, a laying on : *ane-,* on, from Old High German *ana* + *lāge,* act of laying, from Old High German *āga.*]

ann. 1. annals. **2.** annual. **3.** annuity.

an·na (ä′nə) *n.* **1.** A former monetary unit of India, Burma, and Pakistan, equal to 1/16 of a rupee. **2.** A copper coin worth one anna. [Hindi *ānā,* from Sanskrit *áṇu-*†, small.]

an·na·berg·ite (ăn′nə-bûr′gīt′) *n.* A rare mineral consisting of hydrated nickel arsenate, $Ni_3(AsO_4)_2 \cdot 8H_2O$. Also called "nickel bloom." [After *Annaberg,* Saxony, where it was discovered.]

An·na Com·ne·na (ăn′ə kŏm-nē′nə) (1083–*c.* 1148). Byzantine princess and historian, daughter of the emperor Alexis I Comnenus. She wrote the *Alexiad,* a history of her father's reign, one of the great works of medieval historical literature.

an·nal·ist (ăn′ə-lĭst) *n.* One who writes annals; a historian. [French *annaliste,* from Old French, from *annales,* annals, from Latin *annālēs,* ANNALS.] —**an·nal·is·tic** *adj.*

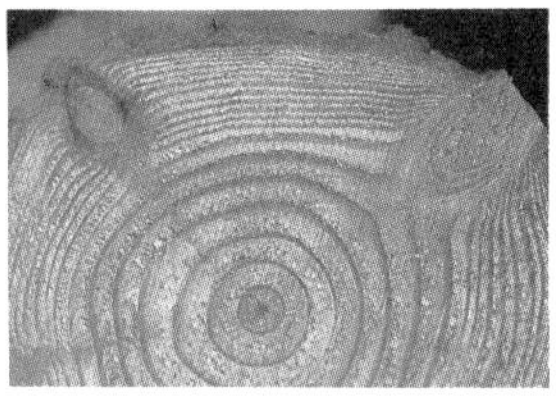

annual ring *A section through a larch tree showing a ring for each year's growth. The rings' markings are created by fast growth in spring, followed by slow growth in summer and no growth in winter.*

an·nals (ăn′əlz) *pl.n. Abbr.* **ann. 1.** A chronological record of the events of successive years. **2.** Any descriptive account or record; a history. **3.** A periodical journal compiling the records and reports of a particular learned field, society, or the like. [Latin *(lĭbrī) annālēs,* "yearly (books)," from *annālis,* yearly, from *annus,* year.]

An·nam or **A·nam** (ă-năm′, ăn′ăm′). Former kingdom, lying in central Vietnam. Originally centered on the Red River valley, it was ruled by China from 111 B.C. until A.D. 939 and came under French influence in the 19th century. Its capital was Hué.

An·na·mese (ăn′ə-mēz′, -mēs′) *n., pl.* **Annamese** (for sense 1). Also **An·na·mite** (ăn′ə-mīt′). **1.** A native or inhabitant of Annam. **2.** Formerly, the Vietnamese language. —**An·na·mese** *adj.*

An·nap·o·lis (ə-năp′ə-lĭs). Capital of the state of Maryland, on the Atlantic seaboard. It was the site of the Annapolis Convention of 1786, which led to the drafting of the Constitution in 1787. It is the seat of the U.S. Naval Academy.

An·na·pur·na (ăn′ə-po͝or′nə, -pûr′-). Himalayan mountain in north-central Nepal. Annapurna I, one of the world's highest peaks, rises to 8,078 meters (26,503 feet) and was scaled by French mountaineers in 1950.

an·nates (ăn′āts′) *pl.n. Roman Catholic Church.* A full year's revenue formerly paid to the pope by a bishop or other ecclesiastic on first being appointed. [French, plural of *annate,* from Medieval Latin *annāta,* a year's revenue, from Latin *annus,* year, + *-āta,* "product of" (past participial ending forming nouns).]

an·nat·to, a·nat·to (ə-nä′tō) *n., pl.* **-tos.** Also **ar·nat·to** (är-nä′tō). **1.** A small tropical American tree, *Bixa orellana,* having red or pinkish flowers and seeds used in cooking. See **achiote. 2.** A yellowish-red dye obtained from the pulp of annatto seeds. [Cariban (the name of the tree).]

Anne (ăn), **(Elizabeth Alice Louise)** (1950–). British princess, second child and only daughter of Elizabeth II. She has represented Great Britain in equestrian events at the Olympic Games.

Anne, Queen (1665–1714). Queen of England, Scotland, and Ireland from 1702, the last monarch of the Stuart line. She was the second daughter of James II and came to the throne on the death of William III. She was the last English monarch to exercise the royal veto over legislation, in 1707.

an·neal (ə-nēl′) *tr.v.* **-nealed, -nealing, -neals. 1.** To subject (glass or metal) to a process of heating and slow cooling in order to toughen and reduce brittleness. **2.** To temper. **3.** To strengthen (the will or determination, for example).
~*n.* An act of or treatment by annealing. [Middle English *anelen,* Old English *onǣlan* : ON + *ǣlan,* to set fire to, from *āl,* fire.]

an·ne·lid (ăn′ə-lĭd) *adj.* Also **an·nel·i·dan** (ə-nĕl′ə-dən). Of or belonging to the phylum Annelida, which includes the earthworms, leeches, and other worms having cylindrical segmented bodies.
~*n.* Also **an·nel·i·dan.** An annelid worm. [New Latin *Annelida,* from French *annélide* : *annelés,* ringed, from *anneler,* to encircle, from Old French *annel,* ring, from Latin *annellus,* diminutive of *ānulus,* small ring + -IDE.]

Anne of Cleves (klēvz) (1515–57). Fourth wife of Henry VIII of England, sister of the German Protestant prince William, Duke of Cleves. She married Henry in January 1540, but the marriage was never consummated and they were divorced in July 1540.

an·nex (ə-nĕks′, ăn′ĕks′) *tr.v.* **-nexed, -nexing, -nexes. 1.** To add or join; append or attach, especially to something larger or more significant. **2.** To incorporate (territory) into an existing state, country, or empire. **3.** To add or attach, as an attribute, condition, or consequence. **4.** To take possession of without permission.
~*n.* (ăn′ĕks′, -ĭks). **1.** An auxiliary building added on to, or situated near, a larger one. **2.** An addition to a record or document; an appendix or addendum. [Middle English *annexen,* from Old French *annexer,* from Latin *annectere* (past participle *annexus*), to bind to : *ad-,* to + *nectere,* to tie.] —**an·nex·a·ble** *adj.*

an·nex·a·tion (ăn′ĕk-sā′shən) *n.* **1.** The act or process of annexing. **2.** The condition of being annexed. **3.** Something that has been annexed. —**an·nex·a·tion·al** *adj.* —**an·nex·a·tion·ism** *n.* —**an·nex·a·tion·ist** *n. & adj.*

annexe. *Chiefly British.* Variant of **annex.**

An·nie Oak·ley (ăn′ē ōk′lē) *n. Slang.* A complimentary ticket of admittance; a free ticket or pass. [After *Annie Oakley* (1860–1926), American sharpshooter, from the association of the punched ticket with one of her bullet-riddled targets.]

an·ni·hi·late (ə-nī′ə-lāt′) *v.* **-lated, -lating, -lates.** —*tr.* **1.** To destroy completely; wipe out; reduce to nonexistence. **2.** To nullify or render void; abolish. **3.** *Informal.* To overwhelm completely; render helpless or ineffective. —*intr. Physics.* To participate in annihilation, as an electron and a positron do. [Late Latin *annihilāre,* to reduce to nothing : Latin *ad-,* to + *nihil,* nothing.] —**an·ni·hi·la·ble** (ə-nī′ə-lə-bəl) *adj.* —**an·ni·hi·la·tive** (ə-nī′ə-lā′tĭv, -lə-tĭv), **an·ni·hi·la·to·ry** (ə-nī′ə-lə-tôr′ē, -tōr′ē) *adj.* —**an·ni·hi·la·tor** *n.*

an·ni·hi·la·tion (ə-nī′ə-lā′shən) *n.* **1.** The act or process of annihilating. **2.** The condition or result of having been annihilated; utter destruction. **3.** *Theology.* The destruction of the soul at the death of the body. **4.** *Physics.* The phenomenon in which a particle and an antiparticle, such as an electron and a positron, disappear with a resultant release of energy approximately equivalent to the sum of their masses.

an·ni·hi·la·tion·ism (ə-nī′ə-lā′shə-nĭz′əm) *n. Theology.* The doctrine that the souls of the wicked are destroyed at death.

an·ni·ver·sa·ry (ăn′ə-vûr′sə-rē) *n., pl.* **-ries. 1.** The annual recurrence of the date on which a notable event took place in some preceding year: *a wedding anniversary.* **2.** A commemorative celebration on this date. [Middle English *anniversarie,* from Medieval Latin *(diēs) anniversāria,* "anniversary (day)," from Latin *anniversārius,* "returning yearly" : *annus,* year + *versus,* past participle of *vertere,* to turn.] —**an·ni·ver·sa·ry** *adj.*

an·no Dom·i·ni (ăn′ō dŏm′ə-nī′, dŏm′ə-nē) *adv. Abbr.* **A.D.** In a specified year of the Christian era: *He died A.D. 961.* —See Usage note at **A.D.** [Latin, "in the year of the Lord."]

an·no·tate (ăn′ə-tāt′) *v.* **-tated, -tating, -tates.** —*tr.* To provide (a literary work) with critical commentary or explanatory notes; gloss. —*intr.* To gloss a text. [Latin *annotāre,* to note down : *ad-,* to + *notāre,* to mark, from *nota,* a mark, note.] —**an·no·ta·tive** *adj.* —**an·no·ta·tor** *n.*

an·no·ta·tion (ăn′ə-tā′shən) *n.* **1.** The act or process of annotating. **2.** A critical or explanatory note; a commentary.

an·nounce (ə-nouns′) *v.* **-nounced, -nouncing, -nounces.** —*tr.* **1.** To bring to public notice; declare or proclaim officially or formally. **2.** To proclaim the presence, readiness, or arrival of: *announce a visitor.* **3.** To make known in advance; serve to indicate: *The footsteps announced the presence of an unexpected visitor.* —*intr.* To serve as a broadcasting announcer. [Middle English *announcen,* from Old French *annoncer,* from Latin *annuntiāre* : *ad-,* to + *nuntiāre,* to announce, from *nuntius,* messenger.]

an·nounce·ment (ə-nouns′mənt) *n.* **1.** The act of announcing. **2.** Something that has been announced. **3.** A printed or published statement or notice, as in a newspaper.

an·nounc·er (ə-noun′sər) *n.* **1.** Someone who announces. **2.** One who provides program continuity and delivers news bulletins on television or radio.

an·noy (ə-noi′) *v.* **-noyed, -noying, -noys.** —*tr.* **1.** To bother or irritate; anger slightly. **2.** To injure or harm; molest. —*intr.* To behave in an annoying manner.
~*n. Archaic.* Something that annoys. [Middle English *anoien,* from Old French *anoier, enuier,* from Late Latin *inodiāre,* to make odious, from Latin *in odiō,* "in hatred," odious : *in,* in + *odiō,* ablative of *odium,* hatred.] —**an·noy·er** *n.* —**an·noy·ing·ly** *adv.*

Synonyms: *bother, irk, irritate, provoke, vex.*

an·noy·ance (ə-noi′əns) *n.* **1.** Something that annoys; a nuisance. **2.** The act of annoying. **3.** Vexation; irritation.

an·nu·al (ăn′yo͞o-əl) *adj. Abbr.* **ann. 1.** Recurring, done, or performed every year; yearly. **2.** Of or pertaining to the year; determined by a year's time: *an annual income.* **3.** *Botany.* Living and growing for only one year or season. Compare **perennial, biennial.**
~*n.* **1. a.** A periodical published yearly; a yearbook. **b.** A special issue, as of a children's comic book, published yearly. **2.** A plant that lives and grows for only one year or season. [Middle English *annuel,* from Old French, from Late Latin *annuālis,* from Latin *annus,* year.] —**an·nu·al·ly** *adv.*

annual parallax *n. Astronomy.* **Parallax** *(see)* in a celestial body caused by motion of the earth around the sun, defined by the angle subtended at the celestial body by the earth's radius. Also called "heliocentric parallax."

annual ring *n.* Any of the concentric layers of wood, especially in a tree trunk, indicating a year's growth in temperate climates and seasonal growth in regions of wet and dry seasons. Also called "growth ring."

an·nu·i·tant (ə-no͞o′ə-tənt, ə-nyo͞o′-) *n.* A person who receives or is qualified to receive an annuity.

an·nu·i·ty (ə-no͞o′ə-tē, ə-nyo͞o′-) *n., pl.* **-ties.** *Abbr.* **ann. 1. a.** The annual payment of an allowance or income. **b.** The sum of money involved in such a payment. **2.** The right to receive or the obligation to make an annuity. **3. a.** The interest or dividends paid annually on an investment of money. **b.** The investment made. [Middle English *annuite,* from Old French, from Medieval Latin *annuitās,* yearly payment, from Latin *annus,* yearly, from *annus,* year.]

an·nul (ə-nŭl′) *tr.v.* **-nulled, -nulling, -nuls. 1.** To make or declare void or invalid; nullify or cancel (a marriage or a law, for example).

PRONUNCIATION KEY

ă, pat; ā, pay; âr, care;
ä, father, are; b, bib;
ch, church; d, deed; ĕ, pet;
ē, be; f, fife; g, gag; h, hat;
hw, which; ĭ, pit; ī, pie;
îr, pier; j, judge; k, kick;
l, lid, needle; m, mum;
n, no, sudden; ng, thing;
ŏ, pot; ō, toe; ô, paw, for;
oi, noise; ou, out; o͝o, book;
o͞o, boot; p, pop; r, roar;
s, sauce; sh, ship, dish;
t, tight; th, thin, path;
th, this, bathe; ŭ, cut; ûr, fur;
v, valve; w, with; y, yes;
z, zebra, size; zh, vision;
ə, about, item, edible,
gallop, circus, peaceful

IN FOREIGN WORDS:

à, *Fr.* ami; œ, *Fr.* feu, *Ger.* schön; ü, *Fr.* tu, *Ger.* über; KH, *Ger.* ich, *Scot.* loch; N, *Fr.* bon; y′, *Fr.* Compiègne

STRESS MARKS:

Primary stress: ′
in·cite′ (ĭn-sīt′)
Secondary stress: ′
in′sight′ (ĭn′sīt′)

2. To obliterate the existence or effect of; annihilate. —See Synonyms at **nullify.** [Middle English *annullen,* from Old French *annuller,* from Late Latin *annullāre,* to make into nothing : Latin *ad-,* to + *nullus,* none, null.] **—an·nul·la·ble** *adj.*

an·nu·lar (ăn′yə-lər) *adj.* Forming or shaped like a ring. [Old French *annulaire,* from Latin *annulāris, ānulāris,* from *annulus, ānulus,* ring.] **—an·nu·lar·i·ty** (ăn′yə-lăr′ə-tē) *n.* **—an·nu·lar·ly** *adv.*

annular eclipse *n.* A solar eclipse in which the moon covers all but a bright ring around the circumference of the sun.

annular ligament *n.* A ligament or fibrous band that encircles a part of the body, such as the ankle or wrist.

an·nu·late (ăn′yə-lĭt, -lāt) *adj.* Also **an·nu·lat·ed** (-lā′tĭd). Having or consisting of rings or ringlike segments. [Latin *annulātus, ānulātus,* from *annulus, ānulus,* ring. See **annulet.**] **—an·nu·late·ly** *adv.*

an·nu·la·tion (ăn′yə-lā′shən) *n.* **1.** The act or process of forming rings. **2.** A ringlike structure or segment.

an·nu·let (ăn′yə-lĭt) *n.* **1.** *Architecture.* A ringlike molding around the capital of a pillar. **2.** *Heraldry.* A ring shape. **3.** A small ring. [Diminutive formation from Latin *annulus, ānulus,* ring.]

an·nul·ment (ə-nŭl′mənt) *n.* **1.** The act of annulling. **2.** A retrospective as well as prospective invalidation, especially of an unconsummated marriage.

an·nu·lus (ăn′yə-ləs) *n., pl.* **-luses** or **-li** (-lī′). **1.** A ringlike figure, part, structure, or marking. **2.** *Geometry.* The figure bounded by and containing the area between two concentric circles. [Latin *annulus, ānulus,* ring.]

an·nun·ci·ate (ə-nŭn′sē-āt′) *tr.v.* **-ated, -ating, -ates.** To announce; proclaim. [Latin *annuntiāre,* to ANNOUNCE.] **—an·nun·ci·a·to·ry** (ə-nŭn′sē-ə-tôr′ē, -tōr′ē) *adj.*

an·nun·ci·a·tion *n.* **1.** The act of announcing. **2.** The angel Gabriel's announcement of the Incarnation to the Virgin Mary. Luke 1:26–38. **3. Annunciation.** The festival, on March 25, in celebration of this event.

Annunciation lily *n.* The **Madonna lily** *(see).* [From its frequent depiction in paintings of the Annunciation.]

an·nun·ci·a·tor (ə-nŭn′sē-ā′tər) *n.* **1.** An electrical signaling device used in hotels or offices to indicate the source of calls on a switchboard. **2.** A signaling device indicating the position of a train.

an·nus mi·rab·i·lis (ăn′əs mĭ-răb′ə-lĭs) *n.* **1.** A remarkable or fateful year. **2.** The year 1666, memorable for the Great Fire of London and the English victory over the Dutch. [New Latin, "wondrous year," originally designating the year 1588 in a forecast of its disasters.]

a·no·a (ə-nō′ə) *n.* A small buffalo, *Anoa depressicornis,* of Celebes and the Philippines, having short, pointed horns. [Native name in Celebes.]

an·ode (ăn′ōd′) *n.* **1.** Any positively charged electrode, as of an electrolytic cell or electron tube. **2.** The negatively charged terminal of a primary cell or of a storage battery that is supplying current. [Greek *anodos,* a way up (i.e., from the positive pole into the electrolyte) : *ana-,* up + *hodos,* road, way.] **—an·od·al** (ăn-ō′dəl), **an·od·ic** (ăn-ŏd′ĭk) *adj.*

an·o·dize (ăn′ə-dīz′) *tr.v.* **-dized, -dizing, -dizes.** To coat (a metallic surface) electrolytically with a protective oxide. [ANOD(E) + -IZE.] **—an·o·di·za·tion** *n.*

an·o·dyne (ăn′ə-dīn′) *adj.* **1.** Able to soothe or relieve pain. **2.** Relaxing; soothing. **3.** Watered-down; insipid; innocuous: *anodyne references to progress and freedom.*
~n. **1.** A medicine that relieves pain. **2.** Anything that soothes or comforts. [Latin *anōdynus,* from Greek *anōdunos,* free from pain : AN- (without) + *odunē,* pain.] **—an·o·dyn·ic** (ăn′ə-dĭn′ĭk) *adj.*

an·o·e·sis (ăn′ō-ē′sĭs) *n. Psychology.* A state of consciousness involving sensation but not thought. [A- (without) + Greek *noēsis,* thought, understanding.] **—an·o·et·ic** (ăn′ō-ĕt′ĭk) *adj.*

a·noint (ə-noint′) *tr.v.* **anointed, anointing, anoints. 1.** To apply oil, ointment, or a similar substance to. **2.** To put oil on as a sign of sanctification or consecration in a religious ceremony. [Middle English *anointen,* from Old French *enoindre* (past participle *enoint*), from Latin *inunguere* : *in-,* upon + *unguere,* to smear, anoint.] **—a·noint·er** *n.* **—a·noint·ment** *n.*

a·no·le (ə-nō′lē) *n.* Any of various chiefly tropical New World lizards of the genus *Anolis,* characterized by a distensible throat flap and the ability to change color. Also called "chameleon." [New Latin *Anolis,* from French *anolis,* anole, from Cariban *anoli.*]

a·nom·a·lis·tic (ə-nŏm′ə-lĭs′tĭk) *adj.* Also **a·nom·a·lis·ti·cal** (-tĭ-kəl). Of or pertaining to the astronomical anomaly.

anomalistic month *n.* A month measured as the interval between two successive passages of the moon through perigee and equal to 27.55455 mean solar days.

anomalistic year *n.* A year measured as the interval between two successive passages of the earth through perihelion and equal to 365.25964 mean solar days.

a·nom·a·lous (ə-nŏm′ə-ləs) *adj.* Deviating from the normal or common order, form, or rule; abnormal, deviant, or irregular. [Late Latin *anōmalos,* from Greek, uneven, irregular : AN- (not) + *homalos,* even, from *homos,* same.] **—a·nom·a·lous·ly** *adv.* **—a·nom·a·lous·ness** *n.*

a·nom·a·ly (ə-nŏm′ə-lē) *n., pl.* **-lies. 1.** Deviation from the normal or common order, form, or rule; abnormality. **2.** Anything anomalous, irregular, or abnormal. **3.** *Astronomy.* **a.** The angular deviation, as observed from the sun, of a planet from its perihelion. **b.** The angular deviation of a satellite from its perigee. [Latin *anōmalia,* from Greek *anōmalia.* See **anomalous.**]

an·o·mie, an·o·my (ăn′ə-mē) *n.* **1.** The absence of the social consensus necessary for governing a society. **2.** The state of alienation experienced by an individual or class in such a situation. **3.** Disorientation of the personality resulting in unsocial behavior. [Greek *anomia,* lawlessness, from *anomos,* without law : A- (without) + *nomos,* law.] **—a·nom·ic** (ə-nŏm′ĭk, -nō′mĭk) *adj.*

a·non (ə-nŏn′) *adv.* **1.** In a short time; soon. **2.** At another time; again. **3.** *Archaic.* At once; immediately: *"The same is he that heareth the word, and anon with joy receiveth it"* (Matthew 13:20). [Middle English *anon, onon,* from Old English *on ān,* "in one," at once : *on,* in, ON + *ān,* one.]

anon. anonymous.

an·o·nym (ăn′ə-nĭm′) *n.* **1.** An anonymous publication or person. **2.** A pseudonym. [French *anonyme,* noun use of adjective, ANONYMOUS.]

an·o·nym·i·ty (ăn′ə-nĭm′ə-tē) *n., pl.* **-ties. 1.** The state or quality of being anonymous. **2.** One that is anonymous.

a·non·y·mous (ə-nŏn′ə-məs) *adj. Abbr.* **a., anon. 1.** Having an unknown name. **2.** Of unknown or undeclared authorship, origin, or agency: *an anonymous donation.* **3.** Inconspicuous; lacking in individuality. [Late Latin *anōnymus,* from Greek *anōnumos,* nameless : AN- (without) + *onoma,* name.] **—a·non·y·mous·ly** *adv.* **—a·non·y·mous·ness** *n.*

a·noph·e·les (ə-nŏf′ə-lēz′) *n.* Any of various mosquitoes of the genus *Anopheles,* many of which carry the malaria parasite and transmit the disease to humans by their bite. [New Latin *Anopheles,* "the hurtful ones," from Greek *anōphelēs,* useless, hurtful : AN- (without) + *ophelos,* advantage.] **—a·noph·e·line** (ə-nŏf′ə-līn′) *adj.* & *n.*

an·o·rak (ăn′ə-răk′) *n.* A padded waterproof and windproof jacket with a hood. [Eskimo (Greenland) *ánorâq.*]

an·o·rec·tic (ăn′ə-rĕk′tĭk) *adj.* Also **an·o·rex·ic** (-rĕk′sĭk). **1.** Marked by anorexia. **2.** Suppressing or causing loss of appetite.
~n. **1.** One that is anorectic. **2.** An anorectic drug. [Greek *anorektos* : AN- (without) + *oregein,* to reach out for.]

an·o·rex·i·a (ăn′ə-rĕk′sē-ə) *n.* **1.** Loss of appetite. **2.** Anorexia nervosa. [Late Latin *anorexia,* from Greek : AN- (without) + *orexis,* a longing, from *oregein,* to reach out for.]

anorexia ner·vo·sa (nûr-vō′sə, -zə) *n.* An illness thought to be psychological in origin in which the patient, usually a young woman, refuses to eat over a long period. Compare **bulimia nervosa.** [New Latin, " nervous anorexia."]

anorexic. Variant of **anorectic.**

an·or·thite (ăn-ôr′thīt′) *n.* A plagioclase feldspar with high calcium oxide content, occurring in igneous rocks. [French : AN- (not) + Greek *orthos,* straight (from its oblique crystals) + -ITE.] **—an·or·thit·ic** (ăn′ôr-thĭt′ĭk) *adj.*

an·or·tho·site (ăn-ôr′thə-sīt′) *n.* A plutonic rock, chiefly plagioclase. [French *anorthose* (see **anorthite**) + -ITE.]

an·os·mi·a (ăn-ŏz′mē-ə) *n.* Loss of the sense of smell. [New Latin : AN- (without) + Greek *osmē,* smell + -IA.] **—an·os·mic** *adj.*

an·oth·er (ə-nŭth′ər) *adj.* **1.** Distinctly different from the first: *That's another matter.* **2.** Some other; any other: *in another country; Come again another day.* **3. a.** Additional; one more: *Take another cake.* **b.** Reminiscent of the specified phenomenon: *another Hitler; another Babylon.*
~pron. **1.** A different one. **2.** One of the same kind. **3.** An additional one. [Middle English *an other.*]

A·nou·ilh (ä-no͞o-ē′), **Jean** (1910–). French dramatist. Many of his plays written during the Nazi occupation of France were derived from classical tradition, for example, *Eurydice* (1942) and *Antigone* (1944). Two of the best-received of his postwar plays were *Ring Around the Moon* (1948) and *Becket* (1959).

an·ov·u·lant (ăn-ŏv′yə-lənt) *n.* A drug that prevents ovulation. [AN- (not) + OVUL(ATION) + -ANT.] **—an·ov·u·lant** *adj.*

an·ov·u·la·to·ry (ăn-ŏv′yə-lə-tôr′ē, -tōr′ē) Of, pertaining to, or characterized by the failure or suppression of ovulation. [AN- (without) + OVUL(ATION) + -ORY.]

an·ox·e·mi·a (ăn′ŏk-sē′mē-ə) *n.* An abnormally low concentration of oxygen in the blood. [New Latin : AN- (without) + OX(Y)- + -EMIA.] **—an·ox·e·mic** *adj.*

an·ox·i·a (ă-nŏk′sē-ə) *n.* **1.** Absence or lack of oxygen. **2.** The condition resulting from a deficiency in the supply of oxygen to the tissues; especially, **hypoxia** *(see).* [AN- (without) + OX(Y)- + -IA.] **—an·ox·ic** *adj.*

ans. answer.

an·sate (ăn′sāt′) *adj.* Also **an·sat·ed** (-sā′tĭd). Having a handle or a part resembling a handle. [Latin *ānsātus,* from *ānsa,* handle.]

ansate cross *n.* A cross shaped like a T with a loop at the top used, especially in Egyptian art, as a symbol of life. Also called "ankh," "crux ansata."

An·schluss (ăn′shlo͝os′) *n. Often* **anschluss.** A union; specifically, the political union of Nazi Germany and Austria in 1938. [German, from *anschliessen,* to join: *an-* to, up + *schliessen,* to close.]

An·selm (ăn′sĕlm′), **Saint** (*c.*1033–1109). Italian theologian and philosopher and archbishop of Canterbury from 1093 until his death. In his *Proslogion* the argument for the existence of God marks him as one of the founders of Scholasticism.

an·ser·ine (ăn′sə-rīn′) *adj.* Also **an·ser·ous** (-sər-əs) (for sense 3). **1.** Of, belonging to, or pertaining to the subfamily Anserinae, which includes geese, swans, and certain ducks. **2.** Resembling a goose; gooselike. **3.** Stupid; silly; foolish. [New Latin *Anserinae,* from Latin *ānserīnus,* gooselike: *ānser,* goose + *-īnus,* -INE.]

an·swer (ăn′sər) *n. Abbr.* **ans., a., A. 1.** A spoken or written reply, as

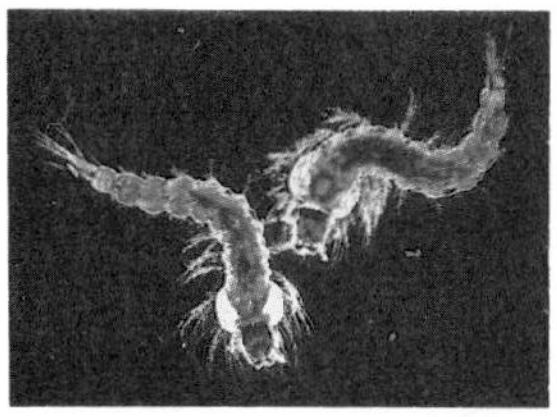

anopheles *Larvae of an anopheles mosquito. Adult females carry and transmit malaria to humans.*

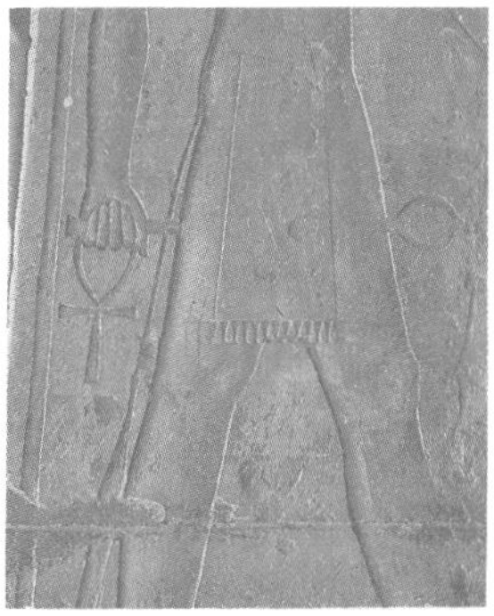

ansate cross *Detail of a 15th-century* B.C. *Egyptian relief, showing an ankh, or ansate cross, the symbol of life, being carried by the pharaoh Tuthmosis III.*

to a question, request, statement, accusation, or letter. **2. a.** A solution or result, as to a problem. **b.** The correct response or solution. **3.** An act in response or retaliation. **4.** *Law.* A defendant's defense against charges filed against him. **5.** *Music.* A phrase in a fugue similar to the subject but in a different voice. **6.** A counterpart; an equivalent: *America's answer to the royal family.*
~*v.* **answered, -swering, -swers.** —*intr.* **1.** To respond in words or action. Used with *to.* **2. a.** To be liable or accountable. Used with *for.* **b.** To atone; make amends. Used with *for.* **3.** To serve the purpose; suffice; do: *use three words where one would answer.* **4.** To correspond; match. Used with *to: answering to the description.* —*tr.* **1. a.** To reply to. **b.** To say in reply. **2.** To respond correctly to; solve. **3.** To fulfill the demands of; serve: *"my fortune has answered my desires"* (Izaak Walton). **4.** To conform or correspond to. **5.** To be responsible for; meet; discharge (a claim or debt, for example). **6.** To offer an explanation or justification for (an accusation, charge, or the like). **7.** To attend to a signal or summons from: *answer the phone.* —**answer back.** To give a rude or defiant reply instead of showing politeness or deference. [Middle English *answer(e),* Old English *andswaru.*] —**an·swer·er** *n.*
Synonyms: *reply, respond, retort.*
an·swer·a·ble (ăn′sər-ə-bəl) *adj.* **1.** Responsible; accountable; liable. Used with *for* or *to: Members of Congress are answerable to their constituents.* **2.** Able to be answered. **3.** *Archaic.* Corresponding; suitable. Used with *to.* —See Synonyms at **responsible.** —**an·swer·a·bil·i·ty, an·swer·a·ble·ness** *n.* —**an·swer·a·bly** *adv.*
answering machine *n.* A machine that can be plugged into a telephone line to record any message a caller may wish to leave.
answering service *n.* A commercial service that deals with telephone calls and telephone messages for its clients.
ant (ănt) *n.* Any of various social insects of the family Formicidae, characteristically having wings in the males and fertile females, and living in colonies that have a complex social organization. [Middle English *ante, amete,* Old English *æmette.*]
ant–. Variant of **anti-.**

ant *There are some 10,000 species of this insect worldwide, all living in colonies consisting of a queen ant and up to 500,000 worker ants. Shown here are the winged queen and a worker of the species,* Lasius flavus.

ant

HALF A MILLION SOCIAL INSECTS WORKING IN HARMONY
Specialist roles for ants in an efficiently run society

Man is not the only animal to herd livestock, grow crops—or enslave others of his own kind. Ants do all these things as well. Many ant species breed sap-sucking aphids in their nests. The ants drive the aphids out to pasture on nearby plants, then "milk" them by licking off the sweet honeydew they exude. South American leaf-cutter ants spread a compost of chewed leaves inside their nest as a bed on which they grow fungus for food.

A species of ant native to Europe and North America, and known to scientists as *Formica sanguinea,* raids the nests of other ants to capture slaves. The hunters carry off pupae—ants in the dormant stage between larva and adult. When the captives emerge as adults, they are put to work extending the nest, caring for the young, and collecting food for their captors.

Most ants live in nests in highly organized colonies of up to half a million insects. Each colony has a single queen to lay all the eggs, and a few winged males whose only function is to fertilize the queen on its one marriage flight; then they die. The rest of the colony consists of wingless and sterile female ants, which act as workers and soldiers.

A few species, such as the army ants of South America and the driver ants of Africa, have no permanent homes. They remain endlessly on the march in columns of up to 1,500,000 ants, eating anything in their path. Once, a tethered horse was reduced to a skeleton in three hours.

READY FOR SEWING *Weaver ants of Southeast Asia and Australia make their nests by sewing together leaves with silk. It is produced by ant larvae that they carry in their mouths. Here workers, each able to carry three times its own weight, maneuver two leaves into position.*

–ant *suffix.* Indicates performing, promoting, or causing a specified state or action; for example, **deodorant.** [Middle English, from Old French, from Latin *-āns* (stem *-ant-*), present participial ending of first conjugation verbs.]
ant. 1. antenna. **2.** antonym.
an·ta (ăn′tə) *n., pl.* **-tae** (-tē). *Architecture.* **1.** A thickening of the projecting end of the lateral wall of a Greek temple. **2.** A pier that constitutes one boundary of the porch. [Latin *antae* (plural), door jamb.]
ant·ac·id (ănt-ăs′ĭd) *adj.* Correcting acidity; neutralizing acids.
~*n.* A substance, as medicinal remedy, that neutralizes acid, especially in the stomach. [ANT(I)- + ACID.]
An·tae·us (ăn-tē′əs) *n. Greek Mythology.* A giant, invincible while touching the ground, who was lifted into the air by Hercules and crushed to death.
an·tag·o·nism (ăn-tăg′ə-nĭz′əm) *n.* **1.** Active, and often mutual, resistance, opposition, or hostility. **2.** The condition of being an opposing principle, force, or factor. **3.** The opposing action of two muscles such that the contraction of one is accompanied by the relaxation of the other. **4.** The interaction of two substances, such as drugs or hormones, such that one partly or wholly inhibits the action of the other. [French *antagonisme.* See ANTAGONIST, -ISM.]
an·tag·o·nist (ăn-tăg′ə-nĭst) *n.* **1.** One who opposes and actively competes with another; an adversary. **2.** *Anatomy.* A muscle whose action opposes that of another muscle. Compare **agonist. 3.** *Pharmacology.* A drug that counteracts or neutralizes another drug. [French *antagoniste,* from Late Latin *antagonista,* from Greek *antagōnistēs : antagōnizesthai,* to struggle against (see **antagonize**) + *-istes,* -IST.] —See Synonyms at **opponent.**
an·tag·o·nis·tic (ăn-tăg′ə-nĭs′tĭk) *adj.* Arising from or characterized by antagonism. —**an·tag·o·nis·ti·cal·ly** *adv.*
an·tag·o·nize (ăn-tăg′ə-nīz′) *tr.v.* **-nized, -nizing, -nizes. 1.** To incur or provoke the dislike or hostility of. **2.** To counteract. [Greek *antagōnizesthai,* to struggle against : *anti-,* against + *agōnizesthai,* to struggle, from *agōn,* contest (see **agony**).]
Antakya. See **Antioch.**
An·ta·nan·a·ri·vo (ăn′tə-năn′ə-rē′vō). Formerly **Ta·nan·a·rive** (tə-năn′ə-rēv′). The capital of Madagascar. It is the largest city in the country and was founded in the early 17th century as a walled citadel.
Ant·arc·tic (ănt-ärk′tĭk, -är′tĭk) *adj.* Of or pertaining to the regions surrounding the South Pole.
~*n.* **the Antarctic.** Antarctica and its surrounding waters. [Middle English *Antartik,* from Medieval Latin *Antarcticus,* from Latin *antarcticus,* southern, from Greek *antarktikos : anti-,* opposite + ARCTIC.]
Ant·arc·ti·ca (ănt-ärk′tĭ-kə, -är′tĭ-kə). The coldest, stormiest, and driest continent, lying over the South Pole. It has 9 percent of the world's land, *c.* 13,338,500 square kilometers (11,500,000 square miles), 95 percent of it covered by an ice sheet more than 3 kilometers (1.9 miles) thick in places, making up 90 percent of the world's permanent ice and snow. Temperatures average –50°C (–58°F) at the pole, and the world's lowest recorded temperature, –88.2°C (–126.9°F), occurred near a Soviet base, Vostok. Antarctica's rocks are believed to contain coal, gas, metal ore, and oil deposits, but their extraction through the constantly moving ice sheet would be extremely difficult. The surrounding seas are a potentially rich source of food. There is no permanent population in Antarctica, but many countries have made territorial claims in the continent; these have been held in abeyance in the interests of international cooperation for exploration and scientific research. The Antarctic Treaty of 1959 forbids any military use of the area.
Antarctic Circle *n.* A parallel of latitude 66°32′ south, along which the sun does not set on one day of the year, around December 22.
An·tar·es (ăn-târ′ēz, -tär′ēz) *n.* A double and variable star, the brightest in the southern sky, about 424 light-years from Earth in the constellation Scorpius. [Greek *antarēs,* "opposing Mars" (that is, rivaling Mars in color) : ANTI- + ARES.]
ant bear *n.* **1.** An anteater. **2.** An aardvark *(see).*
ant cow *n.* An aphid that yields a honeylike substance on which ants feed.
an·te (ăn′tē) *n.* **1.** In poker, the stake that each player must put into the pool before receiving his hand, or before receiving new cards. **2.** An amount paid or to be paid in advance, especially as one's share in a financial venture.
~*tr.v.* **anted** or **-teed, -teing, -tes.** In poker, to put (one's stake) into the pool. Often used with *up.* [Latin *ante,* before.]
ante– *prefix.* Indicates: **1.** In front of; for example, **anteroom. 2.** Previous to; for example, **antenatal.** [Latin, from *ante,* before, in front of, previous to.]
ant·eat·er (ănt′ē′tər) *n.* **1.** Any of several tropical American mammals of the family Myrmecophagidae, that lack teeth and feed on ants and termites; especially, *Myrmecophaga tridactyla,* having a long, narrow snout, a long, sticky tongue, and a long, shaggy-haired tail. This species is also called "giant anteater" and sometimes "ant bear." **2.** Any of several other animals that feed on ants, such as the echidna, the pangolin, and the aardvark.
an·te·bel·lum (ăn′tē-bĕl′əm) *adj.* Belonging to the period prior to a war, especially the American Civil War. [Latin *ante bellum,* before the war.]
an·te·cede (ăn′tə-sēd′) *tr.v.* **-ceded, -ceding, -cedes.** To go before in rank, place, or time; precede. [Latin *antecēdere :* ANTE- + *cēdere,* to go.]

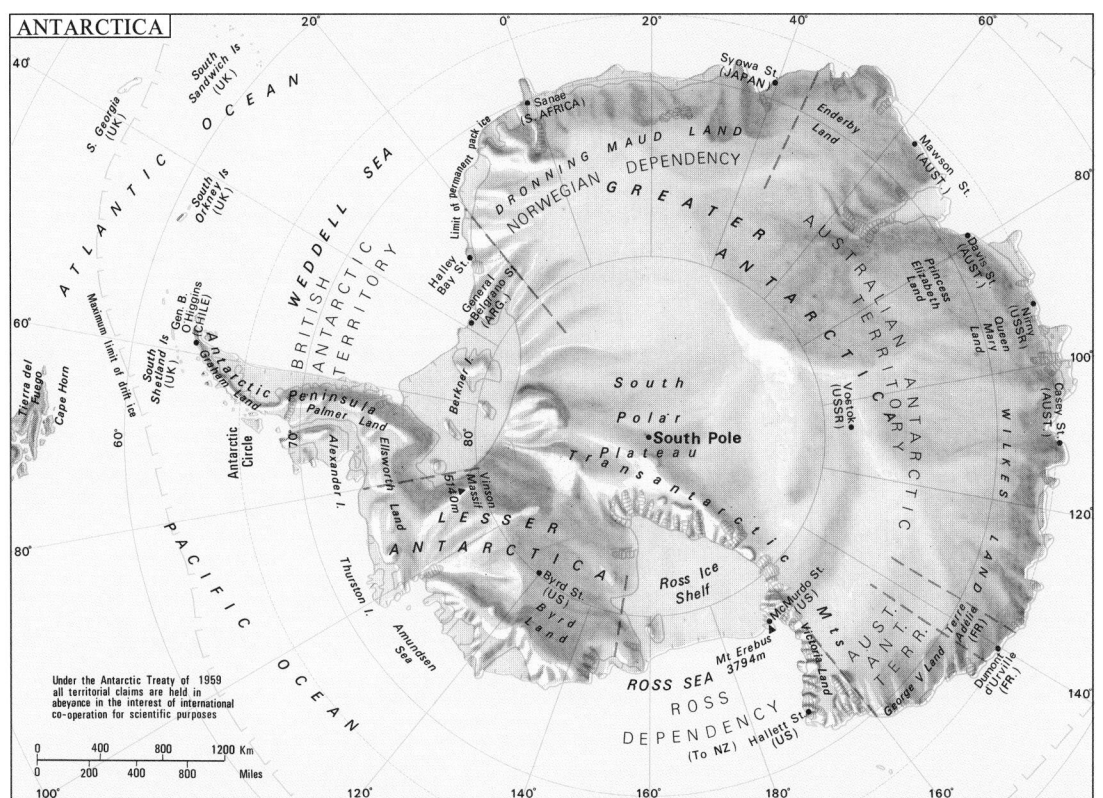

ANTARCTICA

Under the Antarctic Treaty of 1959 all territorial claims are held in abeyance in the interest of international co-operation for scientific purposes

Antarctica *The continent around the South Pole is largely covered by a vast ice sheet that in places extends over the sea, ending in spectacular ice cliffs like these.*

an·te·ce·dence (ăn′tə-sēd′ns) *n.* Precedence.

an·te·ce·dent (ăn′tə-sēd′nt) *adj.* Going before; preceding; prior.
~*n.* **1.** An occurrence or circumstance that precedes another, often having a causal relationship with what follows. **2. antecedents.** One's ancestors, ancestry, or past life. **3.** *Grammar.* The word, phrase, or clause to which a relative pronoun refers. **4.** *Mathematics.* The first term of a ratio. **5.** *Logic.* The first proposition or premise within a conditional proposition. —**an·te·ce·dent·ly** *adv.*

an·te·cham·ber (ăn′tē-chām′bər) *n.* A smaller room serving as an entrance into a larger room; an anteroom. [French *antichambre* : *anti-*, before + *chambre*, room, CHAMBER.]

an·te·cha·pel (ăn′tē-chăp′əl) *n.* An inner porch or vestibule at the western end of a chapel.

an·te·choir (ăn′tē-kwīr′) *n.* A place in front of the choir reserved for the clergy and choir members.

an·te·date (ăn′tĭ-dāt′) *tr.v.* **-dated, -dating, -dates. 1.** To be of an earlier date than; precede in time. **2.** To give a date earlier than the actual date to (a document, manuscript, or the like), especially in order to deceive: *antedate a check.* **3.** To assign a date to (a historical period or event) that is earlier than previously thought. **4.** *Archaic.* To bring about sooner than expected.
~*n.* A date given to an event or a document that is earlier than the actual date.

an·te·di·lu·vi·an (ăn′tĭ-də-lōō′vē-ən) *adj.* **1.** Occurring or belonging to the era before the Flood. Genesis 7, 8. **2. a.** Very old; antiquated. **b.** Old-fashioned; extremely conservative.
~*n.* **1.** A person or thing existing before the Flood. **2.** A very old person. [From ANTE- + Latin *dīluvium*, flood (see diluvial).]

an·te·fix (ăn′tĭ-fĭks′) *n., pl.* **-fixes** or **antefixa** (ăn′tĭ-fĭk′sə). *Architecture.* An upright ornament along the eaves of a tiled roof to conceal the joints between the rows of tiles. [Latin *antefīxus*, "fastened before" (the joints) : *ante-*, before + *fīxus*, past participle of *fīgere*, to fasten.] —**an·te·fix·al** *adj.*

an·te·lope (ăn′tə-lōp) *n., pl.* **-lopes** or collectively **antelope. 1.** Any of various slender, swift-running, long-horned ruminants of the family Bovidae, of Africa and Asia. **2.** An animal that resembles a true antelope, such as the **pronghorn** *(see).* **3.** Leather made from the hide of an antelope. [Middle English, from Old French *antelop*, a fabulous oriental beast, from Medieval Latin *anthalopus*, from Late Greek *antholops†*.]

an·te·me·rid·i·an (ăn′tē-mə-rĭd′ē-ən) *adj.* Of, pertaining to, or taking place in the morning. [Latin *antemerīdiānus* : *ante-*, before + *merīdiānus*, MERIDIAN.]

an·te me·rid·i·em (ăn′tē mə-rĭd′ē-əm) *adv. Abbr.* **a.m., A.M.** Before noon. Used chiefly in the abbreviated form to specify the hour: *10:30* A.M. [Latin : *ante-*, before + *merīdiēs*, midday, noon (see **meridian**).]

an·te mor·tem (ăn′tē môr′təm) *adj. Latin.* Before death.

an·te·na·tal (ăn′tē-nāt′l) *adj.* Of, pertaining to, or occurring before birth; prenatal.

an·ten·na (ăn-tĕn′ə) *n., pl.* **-tennae** (-tĕn′ē) (for sense 1) or **-nas** (for sense 2). **1.** One of the paired, flexible, jointed sensory appendages on the head of an insect, myriapod, or crustacean. **2.** *Abbr.* **ant.** A metallic apparatus for sending and receiving electromagnetic waves. In this sense, also called "aerial." [Medieval Latin, from Latin *antemna, antenna†*, sail yard.] —**an·ten·nal** *adj.*

an·ten·nule (ăn-tĕn′yōol) *n. Zoology.* A small antenna, especially either of the first pair in crustaceans. [French, diminutive of *antenne*, ANTENNA.]

an·te·pen·di·um (ăn′tē-pĕn′dē-əm) *n., pl.* **-dia** (-dē-ə). **1.** A hanging for the front of an altar. **2.** A pulpit cloth. [Medieval Latin : Latin *ante-*, in front of + *pendēre*, to hang.]

an·te·pe·nult (ăn′tē-pē′nŭlt′, -pĭ-nŭlt′) *n.* The third syllable from the end in a word; for example, *te* is the antepenult of the word *antepenult.* [Late Latin *antepaenultima*, feminine of *antepaenultimus*, ANTEPENULTIMATE.]

an·te·pe·nul·ti·mate (ăn′tē-pĭ-nŭl′tə-mĭt) *adj.* Third from the end in a series.
~*n.* An antepenult. [Late Latin *antepaenultimus* : Latin ANTE- + *paenultimus*, PENULT.]

an·te·post (ăn′tē-pōst′) *adj. Chiefly British.* **1.** Made before the runners' numbers are posted on the board. Said of a racing bet. **2.** Occurring in or pertaining to the period before a horse race.

an·te·ri·or (ăn-tîr′ē-ər) *adj.* **1.** Placed in front; located forward. **2.** Prior in time; earlier. **3.** *Zoology.* **a.** Of, pertaining to, or located near the head in lower animals. **b.** Of or pertaining to the front of the body in higher animals and man; ventral. **c.** Located on or near the front of the body or of an organ. **4.** *Botany.* In front of and facing away from the axis or stem. Said of part of a flower or leaf. Compare **posterior.** [Latin, comparative of *ante*, before.] —**an·te·ri·or·i·ty** (ăn-tîr′ē-ôr′ə-tē) *n.* —**an·te·ri·or·ly** *adv.*

an·te·room (ăn′tē-rōōm′, -rōōm′) *n.* A room that leads into a larger room and that is often used as a waiting room.

ant·he·li·on (ănt-hē′lē-ən, ăn-thē′-) *n., pl.* **-lia** (-lē-ə) or **-ons.** A luminous, white, halolike area occasionally seen in the sky opposite the Sun on the **parhelic circle** *(see).* [Greek *anthēlion*, from *anthēlios*, opposite the sun : *anti*-, opposite + *hēlios*, sun.]

ant·hel·min·tic (ănt′hĕl-mĭn′tĭk, ăn′thĕl-) *adj.* Also **ant·hel·min·thic** (-thĭk). Acting to expel or destroy intestinal worms.
~*n.* An anthelmintic remedy; a vermifuge. [ANT(I)- + Greek *helmins* (stem *helminth-*), worm.]

an·them (ăn′thəm) *n.* **1.** A song of praise or loyalty, as to a nation. **2.** A choral composition, often set to words from the Bible. **3.** A religious chant sung in alternation as part of a church service. [Middle English *antem, antefn*, Old English *antefn*, antiphonal song, from Medieval Latin *antiphōna*, from Late Greek, "sung responses," neuter plural of *antiphōnos*, singing in response : *anti-*, opposite + *phōnē*, voice.]

an·the·mi·on (ăn-thē′mē-ən) *n., pl.* **-mia** (-mē-ə). A pattern of honeysuckle, lotus, or palm leaves in a radiating cluster, used especially as a motif in ancient Greek art and architecture. [Greek, diminutive of *anthemon*, name of a plant, from *anthos*, flower.]

an·ther (ăn′thər) *n. Botany.* The organ that forms the upper end of a stamen, and that produces and discharges pollen. [New Latin

anteater *Using its tubular snout, the giant anteater (above) probes inside an ant colony or termite mound before capturing the insects on its long, sticky tongue. It has powerful front claws that can rip open a rock-hard anthill, and its stomach contains special grit to crush the insects' shells.*

anthera, from Medieval Latin *anthēra,* pollen, from Latin, medicine composed of flowers, from Greek *anthēros,* flowery, from *anthos,* flower.] **—an·ther·al** *adj.*

an·ther·id·i·um (ăn'thə-rĭd'ē-əm) *n., pl.* **-ia** (-ē-ə). *Botany.* An organ that produces male gametes in the algae, fungi, mosses, and ferns. Compare **archegonium.** [New Latin : *anthera,* ANTHER + -IDIUM.] **—an·ther·id·i·al** *adj.*

an·ther·o·zo·id (ăn'thər-ə-zō'ĭd) *n. Botany.* A male sex cell produced by an antheridium. [ANTHER + ZO(O)ID.]

an·the·sis (ăn-thē'sĭs) *n. Botany.* The blooming or time of full bloom of a plant. [New Latin, from Greek *anthēsis,* from *anthein,* to bloom, from *anthos,* flower.]

ant·hill (ănt'hĭl') *n.* **1.** A mound formed by ants or termites in digging or building a nest. **2.** Anything suggestive of this, such as a teeming city or an overcrowded building.

antho- *prefix. Botany.* Indicates a plant or flower; for example, **anthocyanin.** [Greek *anthos,* blossom, flower.]

an·tho·cy·a·nin (ăn'thō-sī'ə-nĭn) *n.* Any of a class of water-soluble pigments, found in the sap of certain plants, that impart red, purple, or blue coloring to flowers, fruits, and autumn leaves. [ANTHO- + CYANIN(E).]

an·tho·di·um (ăn-thō'dē-əm) *n., pl.* **-dia** (-dē-ə). *Botany.* The flower head of composite plants, such as the aster, thistle, and golden rod. [New Latin, from Greek *anthōdēs,* flowerlike : ANTHO- + -OID.]

an·thol·o·gize (ăn-thŏl'ə-jīz') *tr.v.* **-gized, -gizing, -gizes.** To compile or include in an anthology.

an·thol·o·gy (ăn-thŏl'ə-jē) *n., pl.* **-gies. 1.** A collection of literary pieces, such as poems, short stories, or plays, usually suggesting a common theme. **2.** Any collection of works of art, such as paintings, based on a specific period, theme, or subject. [New Latin *anthologia,* from Medieval Greek, from Greek, "flower gathering," a collection : ANTHO- + -LOGY.] **—an·tho·log·i·cal** (ăn'thə-lŏj'ĭ-kəl) *adj.* **—an·thol·o·gist** *n.*

An·tho·ny (ăn'thə-nē, -tə-), **Saint** (*c.* A.D. 250-350). Egyptian hermit and monk, known as St. Anthony of Egypt and St. Anthony the Abbot. He forsook a wealthy inheritance and went into the desert to become a hermit. Although he established no order, he is considered to be the founder of Christian monasticism.

Anthony, Susan Brownell (1820-1906). U.S. feminist leader and suffragette. She played a major part in getting the first legislation passed giving married women legal rights over their children, property, and wages. In 1869, with Elizabeth Stanton, she founded the National American Woman Suffrage Association.

Anthony of Pad·u·a (păj'ōō-ə), **Saint** (1195-1231). Portuguese friar, the most celebrated follower of St. Francis of Assisi. He gained a reputation as a miracle worker before his death in Padua.

-anthous *suffix.* Indicates a flower; for example, **ananthous.** [New Latin *-anthus,* from Greek *anthos,* flower.]

an·tho·zo·an (ăn'thə-zō'ən) *n.* Any of various marine organisms of the class Anthozoa, growing singly or in colonies, and including the corals and sea anemones. Also called "actinozoan." [New Latin *Anthozoa,* "flowerlike organisms" : ANTHO- + -ZOA.] **—an·tho·zo·an, an·tho·zo·ic** *adj.*

an·thra·cene (ăn'thrə-sēn') *n.* A crystalline hydrocarbon, $C_6H_4(CH)_2C_6H_4$, extracted from coal tar and used in the manufacture of dyes and organic chemicals. [Greek *anthrax* (stem *anthrak-*), ANTHRAX + -ENE.]

an·thra·cite (ăn'thrə-sīt') *n.* A hard coal containing more than 85 percent carbon and little volatile matter, that burns with a clean flame. Also called "hard coal." [Greek *anthrakitēs,* a kind of coal, from ANTHRAX.] **—an·thra·cit·ic** (ăn'thrə-sĭt'ĭk) *adj.*

an·thrac·nose (ăn-thrăk'nōs') *n.* Any of several diseases of plants caused by fungi and characterized by black spots on the leaves, twigs, or fruit. [French : Greek *anthrax,* charcoal, carbuncle, ANTHRAX + Greek *nosos,* disease.]

an·thrax (ăn'thrăks') *n.* **1.** *Pathology.* An infectious, often fatal disease of warm-blooded animals, especially of cattle and sheep, caused by the bacterium *Bacillus anthracis.* It is transmissible to man, capable of affecting various organs, and especially characterized by malignant ulcers. **2.** A lesion caused by this disease. [Latin, virulent ulcer, from Greek *anthrax†,* charcoal, carbuncle, pustule.]

anthrop. anthropological; anthropology.

an·throp·ic (ăn-thrŏp'ĭk) *adj.* Also **an·throp·i·cal** (-ĭ-kəl). Of or pertaining to humans or the era of human life. [Greek *anthrōpikos,* from *anthrōpos,* human being.]

anthropo-, anthrop- *prefix.* Indicates man or human; for example, **anthropoid, anthroposophy.** [From Greek *anthrōpos,* human being.]

an·thro·po·cen·tric (ăn'thrə-pə-sĕn'trĭk) *adj.* **1.** Regarding the human race as the central fact of the universe. **2.** Interpreting reality exclusively in terms of human values and experience. **—an·thro·po·cen·tric·i·ty** (ăn'thrə-pō-sĕn-trĭs'ə-tē), **an·thro·po·cen·trism** (-sĕn'trĭz'əm) *n.*

an·thro·po·gen·e·sis (ăn'thrə-pə-jĕn'ə-sĭs) *n.* The scientific study of the origin of man. [New Latin : ANTHROPO- + -GENESIS.] **—an·thro·po·ge·net·ic** (ăn'thrə-pō-jə-nĕt'ĭk) *adj.*

an·thro·po·gen·ic (ăn'thrə-pə-jĕn'ĭk) *adj.* Of, pertaining to, or originating as a result of human activity. [ANTHROPO- + -GENIC.]

an·thro·po·ge·og·ra·phy (ăn'thrə-pō-jē-ŏg'rə-fē) *n.* The science of the geographical distribution of human communities.

an·thro·poid (ăn'thrə-poid') *adj.* **1.** Resembling man, as the tailless semi-erect apes of the family Pongidae, which includes gorillas, chimpanzees, orangutans, and gibbons. **2.** Resembling or charac-

anthurium *The bright waxy flowers of this tropical American plant have made it a popular potted plant around the world. This species,* Anthurium scherzerianum, *comes from Guatemala.*

teristic of an ape; apelike. **3.** Shaped like a human being: *an anthropoid sarcophagus.*
~*n.* **1.** Any member of the family Pongidae. **2.** A person resembling an ape in appearance, behavior, or intelligence. [Greek *anthrōpoeidēs* : ANTHROP(O)- + -OID.] **—an·thro·poid·al** (ăn'thrə-poid'l) *adj.*

an·thro·pol·o·gy (ăn'thrə-pŏl'ə-jē) *n. Abbr.* **anthrop., anthropol.** The scientific study of the origin and of the physical, social, and cultural development and behavior of mankind. [New Latin *anthropologia* : ANTHROPO- + -LOGY.] **—an·thro·po·log·ic** (ăn'thrə-pə-lŏj'ĭk), **an·thro·po·log·i·cal** *adj.* **—an·thro·po·log·i·cal·ly** *adv.* **—an·thro·pol·o·gist** *n.*

an·thro·pom·e·try (ăn'thrə-pŏm'ə-trē) *n.* The study of or technique for measuring the various sizes and proportions of the human body, for use in anthropological classification and comparison. [ANTHROPO- + -METRY.] **—an·thro·po·met·ric** (ăn'thrə-pə-mĕt'rĭk), **an·thro·po·met·ri·cal** *adj.* **—an·thro·pom·e·trist** *n.*

an·thro·po·mor·phism (ăn'thrə-pə-môr'fĭz'əm) *n.* The attribution of human form, motivation, characteristics, or behavior to inanimate objects, animals, gods, or natural phenomena. **—an·thro·po·mor·phic** *adj.*

an·thro·po·mor·phize (ăn'thrə-pə-môr'fīz') *tr.v.* **-phized, -phizing, -phizes.** To ascribe human characteristics to.

an·thro·po·mor·phous (ăn'thrə-pə-môr'fəs) *adj.* **1.** Having or suggesting human form and appearance. **2.** Of or pertaining to anthropomorphism. [Greek *anthrōpomorphos* : ANTHROPO- + -MORPHOUS.] **—an·thro·po·mor·phous·ly** *adv.*

an·thro·pop·a·thism (ăn'thrə-pŏp'ə-thĭz'əm) *n.* The attribution of human feelings to nonhuman beings, such as gods, animals, inanimate objects, or natural phenomena. [From Greek *anthrōpopathēs,* with human feelings : ANTHROPO- + *pathos,* feeling (see **-pathy**).]

an·thro·poph·a·gus (ăn'thrə-pŏf'ə-gəs) *n., pl.* **-gi** (-jī'). An eater of human flesh; cannibal. [Latin *anthrōpophagus,* from Greek *anthrōpophagos,* man-eating : ANTHROPO- + -PHAGOUS.] **—an·thro·po·phag·ic** (ăn'thrə-pə-făj'ĭk), **an·thro·poph·a·gous** (-pŏf'ə-gəs) *adj.* **—an·thro·poph·a·gy** (ăn'thrə-pŏf'ə-jē) *n.*

an·thro·pos·o·phy (ăn'thrə-pŏs'ə-fē) *n.* A 20th-century religious system of thought derived from theosophy by Rudolph Steiner, that centers on human beings rather than God and concentrates on the development of all the human faculties. [ANTHROPO- + -SOPHY.] **—an·thro·po·soph·ic** (ăn'thrə-pə-sŏf'ĭk) *adj.* **—an·thro·pos·o·phist** (-pŏs'ə-fĭst) *n.*

-anthropus *suffix.* Indicates man; for example, **pithecanthropus.** [New Latin, from Greek *anthrōpos,* human being.]

an·thu·ri·um (ăn-thŏor'ē-əm) *n.* Any of various tropical American plants of the genus *Anthurium,* many of which are cultivated as potted plants for their showy foliage. [New Latin *Anthurium,* "flower-tail" : ANTH(O)- + Greek *oura,* tail.]

an·ti (ăn'tī', ăn'tē) *n., pl.* **-tis.** *Informal.* A person who is opposed, as to a policy or proposal. [Noun use of ANTI-.] **—an·ti** *adj.*

anti-, ant- *prefix.* Indicates: **1. a.** Opposition to; for example, **antismoking, antiabortion. b.** Hostility toward; for example, **antiSemitic, antiwoman. 2.** Opposite to, especially in character; for example, **anticlimax, antihero. 3.** Reciprocal correspondence to; for example, **antilogarithm. 4.** Converse operation to; for example, **anticyclone, anticlockwise. 5.** Action against or prevention of; for example, **antifreeze, antidepressant.** *Note:* Many compounds other than those entered here may be formed with *anti-.* In forming compounds, *anti-* is normally joined to the following element without a space or hyphen: *antibody.* However, if the second element begins with a capital letter, it is separated with a hyphen: *anti-British.* It is also preferable to use the hyphen if the second element begins with *i: anti-intellectual.* The hyphen may always be used to aid clarity, as in nonce coinages: *anti-antivivisection,* or when the compound brings together three or more vowels: *anti-aesthetic.* [In borrowed Greek compounds *anti-* indicates : **1.** Over against, opposite, as in **antichrist. 2.** Against, opposite, as in **antipathy. 3.** Responding to, as in **antiphon. 4.** Instead of, as in **antonomasia. 5.** Mirroring, counterfeiting, as in **antirrhinum.** Greek, from *anti,* opposite, against.]

an·ti·a·bor·tion (ăn'tē-ə-bôr'shən, ăn'tī-) *adj.* Opposed to abortion. **—an·ti·a·bor·tion·ist** *n.*

an·ti·air·craft (ăn'tē-âr'krăft', -kräft', ăn'tī-) *adj. Abbr.* **AA** Defensive, especially from a surface position, against aircraft or missile attack.
~*n.* An antiaircraft weapon.

an·ti·al·ler·gic (ăn'tē-ə-lûr'jĭk, ăn'tī-) *adj.* Also **an·ti·al·ler·gen·ic** (-ăl'ər-jĕn'ĭk). Preventing or relieving allergies.

an·ti·bal·lis·tic missile (ăn'tē-bə-lĭs'tĭk, ăn'tī-) *n. Abbr.* **ABM** A defensive missile designed to intercept and destroy a ballistic missile in flight.

an·ti·bar·y·on (ăn'tē-băr'ē-ŏn', ăn'tī-) *n.* The antiparticle of the **baryon** (*see*).

An·tibes (äN-tēb'). Fashionable resort on the French Riviera, lying across the Bay of Angels from Nice. It is the center of one of Europe's largest flower-producing regions and is noted for the collection of Picasso's paintings in the Grimaldi Museum.

an·ti·bi·o·sis (ăn'tē-bī-ō'sĭs, ăn'tī-) *n.* An association between two or more organisms, particularly microorganisms, that is injurious to one of them. [New Latin : ANTI- + -BIOSIS.]

an·ti·bi·ot·ic (ăn'tē-bī-ŏt'ĭk, ăn'tī-) *n.* Any of various substances, such as penicillin and streptomycin, produced by certain fungi, bacteria, and similar organisms, that are effective in inhibiting the growth of or destroying microorganisms and are widely used in the prevention and treatment of diseases. ~*adj.* **1.** Of or pertaining to antibiotics. **2.** Of or pertaining to antibiosis. [New Latin *antibioticus* : ANTI- + BIOTIC.] —**an·ti·bi·ot·i·cal·ly** *adv.*

an·ti·bod·y (ăn′tĭ-bŏd′ē) *n., pl.* **-ies. 1.** Any of various proteins in the blood that are generated in reaction to the invasion of foreign substances, which they neutralize, thus producing immunity against infections. **2.** An object composed of antimatter. [20th century : translation of German *Antikörper* : ANTI- + *Körper*, body.]

an·tic (ăn′tĭk) *n.* **1.** *Often* **antics.** A ludicrous or extravagant act or gesture; a caper; a prank. **2.** *Archaic.* A clown; a jester. ~*adj. Archaic.* Ludicrous; odd; fantastic. [Italian *antico*, "grotesque," "ancient" (originally with reference to fantastic sculptures found in ancient Roman ruins, hence, anything fantastic or grotesque), from Latin *antiquus*, ANTIQUE.]

an·tic·i·pant (ăn-tĭs′ə-pənt) *adj.* **1.** Coming or acting in advance. **2.** Expectant. ~*n.* One who anticipates.

an·tic·i·pate (ăn-tĭs′ə-pāt′) *tr.v.* **-pated, -pating, -pates. 1.** To sense or realize beforehand; foresee. **2.** To look forward to as likely or certain; expect. **3.** To act in advance so as to prevent or counter; forestall. **4.** To foresee and fulfill or satisfy in advance. **5.** To cause to happen in advance; accelerate; precipitate. **6.** To consider prematurely; bring up before the proper time. **7.** To use in advance, as income not yet available. **8.** To pay (a debt) before it is due. —See Synonyms at **expect.** [Latin *anticipāre*, to take before : *ante-*, before + *capere*, to take.] —**an·tic·i·pa·tor** *n.* —**an·tic·i·pa·to·ry** (ăn-tĭs′ə-pə-tôr′ē, -tōr′ē) *adj.*

Usage: Some traditionalists hold that *anticipate* should not be used simply as a synonym for *expect.* They would restrict its use to senses in which it suggests some advance action, either to fulfill *(anticipate my desires)* or to forestall *(anticipate her opponent's next move).* Others accept its use in the senses of "to feel or realize beforehand" and "to look forward to" (often with the implication of foretasting pleasure): *He is anticipating a visit with his son.*

an·tic·i·pa·tion (ăn-tĭs′ə-pā′shən) *n.* **1.** The act of anticipating. **2.** The act or state of looking forward to something. **3.** Foreknowledge; intuition; premonition. **4.** *Law.* The use or assignment of funds from a trust fund before legitimately available for use. **5.** *Music.* The introduction of a note or notes of a new chord before the previous chord is resolved.

an·ti·cler·i·cal (ăn′tē-klĕr′ĭ-kəl, ăn′tī-) *adj.* Opposed to the influence and power of the clergy, especially in political affairs. —**an·ti·cler·i·cal** *n.* —**an·ti·cler·i·cal·ism** *n.*

an·ti·cli·max (ăn′tē-klī′măks′) *n.* **1.** A decline viewed in disappointing contrast with a previous rise: *the anticlimax of a brilliant career.* **2.** Something trivial or commonplace coming to conclude a series of significant events. **3.** *Rhetoric.* **a.** A sudden descent from the impressive or significant to the ludicrous or inconsequential. **b.** An instance of this; for example, *For God, for country, and for my dog.* —**an·ti·cli·mac·tic** (ăn′tē-klī-măk′tĭk) *adj.*

an·ti·cli·nal (ăn′tī-klī′nəl) *adj.* Sloping downward in opposite directions, as an anticline. [ANTI- + -CLINAL.]

an·ti·cline (ăn′tī-klīn′) *n. Geology.* A fold with strata sloping downward on both sides from a common crest. [ANTI- + -CLINE.]

an·ti·clock·wise (ăn′tē-klŏk′wīz′) *adv. Chiefly British.* Counterclockwise. —**an·ti·clock·wise** *adj.*

an·ti·co·ag·u·lant (ăn′tē-kō-ăg′yə-lənt, ăn′tī-) *n.* A substance that suppresses or counteracts coagulation, especially of the blood. ~*adj.* Acting as an anticoagulant.

an·ti·co·in·ci·dence circuit (ăn′tē-kō-ĭn′sə-dəns) *n.* A specific binary logic element designed to provide input signals to a device according to fixed rules.

an·ti·con·vul·sant (ăn′tē-kən-vŭl′sənt, ăn′tī-) *n.* A drug that reduces or prevents convulsions. —**an·ti·con·vul·sant, an·ti·con·vul·sive** (ăn′tē-kən-vŭl′sĭv, ăn′tī-) *adj.*

an·ti·cy·clone (ăn′tē-sī′klōn′) *n.* An extensive system of winds spiraling outward from a high-pressure center, circling clockwise in the Northern Hemisphere and counterclockwise in the Southern Hemisphere. —**an·ti·cy·clon·ic** (ăn′tē-sī-klŏn′ĭk) *adj.*

an·ti·de·pres·sant (ăn′tē-dĭ-prĕs′ənt) *n.* Any drug that relieves the symptoms of depression. —**an·ti·de·pres·sant, an·ti·de·pres·sive** (ăn′tē-dĭ-prĕs′ĭv, ăn′tī-) *adj.*

an·ti·di·u·ret·ic hormone (ăn′tē-dī′ə-rĕt′ĭk, ăn′tī-) *n.* A hormone, vasopressin *(see).*

an·ti·dote (ăn′tĭ-dōt′) *n.* **1.** A remedy or other agent to counteract or neutralize the effects of a poison. **2.** Anything that relieves or counteracts an unwanted condition. [Latin *antidotum*, from Greek *antidoton*, from *antididonai*, to give as a remedy against : ANTI- + *didonai*, to give.] —**an·ti·dot·al** (ăn′tĭ-dōt′l) *adj.*

an·ti·e·lec·tron (ăn′tē-ĭ-lĕk′trŏn′, ăn′tī-) *n.* A positron *(see).*

an·ti·en·zyme (ăn′tē-ĕn′zīm′, ăn′tī-) *n.* A substance that neutralizes or counteracts an enzyme. —**an·ti·en·zy·mat·ic** (ăn′tē-ĕn′zī-măt′ĭk, ăn′tī-), **an·ti·en·zy·mic** (-ĕn′zī′mĭk) *adj.*

An·tie·tam (ăn-tē′təm). Creek in northern Maryland, emptying into the Potomac River. The bloody and inconclusive Battle of Antietam (or Sharpsburg, as it was called by the Confederates) was fought on its banks on September 17, 1862.

an·ti·feb·rile (ăn′tē-fĕb′rəl, -fē′brəl, -brĭl′, ăn′tī-) *adj.* Able to reduce fever; antipyretic. ~*n.* An antifebrile drug or agent.

an·ti·fer·ro·mag·ne·tism (ăn′tē-fĕr′ō-măg′nə-tĭz′əm, ăn′tī-) *n. Physics.* The property of certain substances that have relative permeabilities resembling paramagnetic substances but behave as ferromagnetic substances when their temperature is changed.

an·ti·foul·ing (ăn′tē-fou′lĭng, ăn′tī-) *adj.* Designed to prevent build-up on surfaces, clogging of valves, and the like.

antifouling paint *n.* A paint applied to ships' bottoms to prevent the growth of barnacles and other marine organisms.

an·ti·freeze (ăn′tī-frēz′) *n.* A substance, often a liquid such as ethylene glycol or alcohol, mixed with another liquid to lower the freezing point of the latter; especially, the liquid added to the cooling water of an internal-combustion engine to prevent freezing.

an·ti·gen (ăn′tĭ-jən) *n.* Any substance that, when introduced into the body, stimulates the production of an antibody. [ANTI- + -GEN.] —**an·ti·gen·ic** (ăn′tĭ-jĕn′ĭk) *adj.* —**an·ti·gen·i·cal·ly** *adv.* —**an·ti·ge·nic·i·ty** (ăn′tĭ-jə-nĭs′ə-tē) *n.*

An·tig·o·ne (ăn-tĭg′ə-nē). *Greek Mythology.* The daughter of Oedipus and Jocasta, who performed funeral rites over the body of her brother Polynices in defiance of her uncle Creon.

An·tig·o·nus I (ăn-tĭg′ə-nəs) (382-301 B.C.). King of Macedonia (after 306 B.C.). He was one of Alexander the Great's generals, and after Alexander's death he warred against other eastern governors in an attempt to gain sole control of Asia. He was killed in battle during his unsuccessful invasion of Egypt.

an·ti·grav·i·ty (ăn′tē-grăv′ə-tē, ăn′tī-) *n.* The effect of reducing or canceling a gravitational field. ~*adj.* Canceling or reducing gravity or protecting against its effect.

An·ti·gua and Bar·bu·da (ăn-tē′gə, -gwə; bär-bōō′də). Island state in the Leeward Islands of the Caribbean. Discovered by Columbus (1493), it became a British colony (1667) and was a British associated state from 1967 until independence in 1981. The islands of Redonda (uninhabited) and Barbuda are included in its territory, but the Barbudans are seeking independence. Antigua is a communications and business center for the Caribbean area. Formerly dependent on sugar, it now relies on tourism and cotton. Area, 442 square kilometers (171 square miles). Population, 72,000. Capital, St. John's. —See map at **Latin America.** —**An·ti·guan** *adj.* & *n.*

an·ti·ha·la·tion backing (ăn′tē-hā-lā′shən, ăn′tī-) *n.* A backing applied to a photographic film, consisting of a dye or pigment that absorbs light, to prevent halation that would otherwise occur as a result of light being reflected back into the emulsion.

an·ti·he·ro (ăn′tē-hîr′ō, ăn′tī-) *n.* A main character in a dramatic or literary work who is characterized by a lack of traditional heroic qualities.

an·ti·his·ta·mine (ăn′tē-hĭs′tə-mēn′, -mĭn, ăn′tī-) *n.* Any of various drugs used to reduce physiological effects associated with histamine production in allergies and colds. —**an·ti·his·ta·min·ic** (ăn′tē-hĭs′tə-mĭn′ĭk, ăn′tī-) *adj.*

an·ti·knock (ăn′tī-nŏk′, ăn′tī-) *n.* A substance, such as tetraethyl lead, added to gasoline to reduce engine knock.

An·ti-Leb·a·non Mountains (ăn′tī-lĕb′ə-nən). Range of mountains on the Lebanon-Syria border. The highest peak, Mt. Hermon, rises to 2,814 meters (9,232 feet).

an·ti·lep·ton (ăn′tē-lĕp′tŏn′, ăn′tī-) *n. Physics.* The antiparticle of any **lepton** *(see).*

An·til·les (ăn-tĭl′ēz). Two groups of islands in the West Indies. The Greater Antilles include Cuba, Hispaniola (Haiti and the Dominican Republic), Jamaica, and Puerto Rico; the Lesser Antilles include the Leeward Islands, the Windward Islands, the Netherlands Antilles, Trinidad and Tobago, and Barbados.

an·ti·log·a·rithm (ăn′tē-lô′gə-rĭth′əm, ăn′tī-lŏg′ə-, ăn′tī-) *n.* The number for which a given logarithm stands; for example, where log *x* equals *y*, the *x* is the antilogarithm of *y.* Also called "antilog." See **logarithm.** —**an·ti·log·a·rith·mic** *adj.*

an·ti·ma·cas·sar (ăn′tē-mə-kăs′ər, ăn′tī-) *n.* A protective or decorative covering for the backs of chairs and sofas. [ANTI- + MACASSAR (OIL).]

an·ti·mag·net·ic (ăn′tē-măg-nĕt′ĭk, ăn′tī-) *adj.* Impervious to the effect of a magnetic field; magnetization-resistant. Said especially of watch movements.

an·ti·ma·lar·i·al (ăn′tē-mə-lâr′ē-əl, ăn′tī-) *adj.* Effective against malaria. ~*n.* An antimalarial drug.

an·ti·mat·ter (ăn′tĭ-măt′ər) n. A hypothetical form of matter consisting of antiparticles and having positron-surrounded nuclei composed of antiprotons and antineutrons. See **antiparticle**.

an·ti·mere (ăn′tĭ-mîr′) n. Biology. A part or division corresponding to an opposite or similar part in an organism characterized by bilateral or radial symmetry. [ANTI- + -MERE.]

an·ti·mi·cro·bi·al (ăn′tĕ-mī-krō′bē-əl) adj. Capable of destroying or suppressing the growth of microorganisms.
~n. An antimicrobial agent.

an·ti·mis·sile (ăn′tĕ-mĭs′əl, ăn′tī-) n. A missile designed to intercept and destroy another missile in flight.

an·ti·mo·ni·al (ăn′tə-mō′nē-əl) adj. Of or containing antimony.
~n. A medicine with antimony as an ingredient.

an·ti·mo·ny (ăn′tə-mō′nē) n. Symbol **Sb** A metallic element having four allotropic forms the most common of which is a hard, extremely brittle, lustrous, silver-white, crystalline material. It is used in a wide variety of alloys, especially with lead in battery plates, and in the manufacture of flame-proofing compounds, paints, semiconductor devices, and ceramic products. Atomic number 51, atomic weight 121.75, melting point 630.5°C, boiling point 1,380°C, specific gravity 6.684, valences 3, 5. [Middle English, from Medieval Latin *antimonium*†.]

antimony glance n. An antimony ore, **stibnite** (see).

an·ti·ne·o·plas·tic (ăn′tĕ-nē′ō-plăs′tĭk, ăn′tī-) adj. Inhibiting the growth or spread of malignant tumors.

an·ti·neu·tri·no (ăn′tĕ-nōō-trē′nō, -nyōō-trē′nō, ăn′tī-) n., pl. **-nos**. Physics. The **antiparticle** (see) of the neutrino.

an·ti·neu·tron (ăn′tĕ-nōō′trŏn′, -nyōō′trŏn′, ăn′tī-) n. Physics. The **antiparticle** (see) of the neutron.

ant·ing (ăn′tĭng) n. The placing or rubbing by some birds of ants in their plumage, possibly to repel parasites.

an·ti·node (ăn′tĭ-nōd′) n. Physics. The region or point of maximum amplitude between adjacent **nodes** (see).

an·ti·no·mi·an (ăn′tĭ-nō′mē-ən) n. Theology. A member of a Christian sect holding that faith alone is sufficient for salvation and that it is not necessary to obey any moral law.
~adj. 1. Of or pertaining to such a sect or doctrine. 2. Opposed to universal applicability of moral laws. [From Medieval Latin *antinomus*, from Greek : ANTI- + *nomos*, law.] **—an·ti·no·mi·an·ism** n.

an·tin·o·my (ăn-tĭn′ə-mē) n., pl. **-mies**. 1. Opposition or contradiction, especially between two laws or rules. 2. Contradiction between propositions that seem equally necessary and reasonable; a paradox. [Latin *antinomia*, from Greek : ANTI- + *nomos*, law.]

an·ti·nu·cle·on (ăn′tĕ-nōō′klē-ŏn′, -nyōō′klē-ŏn′, ăn′tī-) n. Physics. The **antiparticle** (see) of a nucleon.

An·ti·och (ăn′tē-ŏk′). Turkish **An·ta·kya** (än-täk′yə). Ancient city in southeastern Turkey, lying on the Orontes River near its mouth on the Mediterranean. St. Paul preached here and followers of Christ first adopted the name "Christian" here.

An·ti·o·chus (ăn-tī′ō-kəs). A Seleucid dynasty ruling in Syria (280-64 B.C.). Its most important member was **Antiochus III**, known as "the Great" (242-187; ruled 223-187). He conquered much of Asia Minor, but was forced to yield his territories after he was defeated by the Romans (190).

an·ti·ox·i·dant (ăn′tĕ-ŏk′sə-dənt, ăn′tī-) n. A chemical compound or substance that inhibits oxidation. **—an·ti·ox·i·dant** adj.

an·ti·par·al·lel (ăn′tĕ-păr′ə-lĕl′, ăn′tī-) adj. 1. Physics. Parallel but rotating or pointing in opposite directions: *antiparallel spin*. 2. Mathematics. **a.** Designating two parallel lines that cut another pair of parallel lines in such a way that the interior opposite angles of the quadrilateral so formed are supplementary. **b.** Having the same magnitude but opposite senses. Said of vectors. Compare **parallel**.

an·ti·par·ti·cle (ăn′tĕ-pär′tĭ-kəl, ăn′tī-) n. A subatomic particle, such as a positron, antiproton, or antineutron, having the same mass, average lifetime, spin, magnitude of magnetic moment, and magnitude of electric charge as the particle to which it corresponds, but having the opposite sign of electric charge, opposite intrinsic parity, and opposite direction of magnetic moment. See **annihilation**.

an·ti·pas·to (ăn′tĕ-pä′stō, ăn′tē-päs′tō) n., pl. **-tos** or **-ti** (-tē). An appetizer; an hors d'oeuvre. [Italian : ANTI- (before) + *pasto*, food, from Latin *pastus*, past participle of *pascere*, to feed.]

An·tip·a·ter (ăn-tĭp′ə-tər) (c. 398-319 B.C.). Macedonian general and ruler. He acted as regent of Macedonia from 334 to 323 during Alexander the Great's Asian campaign and again from 321 to 319 for the mentally deficient Philip III and the infant Alexander IV. After his death the centralized unity of the Macedonian empire quickly disintegrated.

an·tip·a·thet·ic (ăn-tĭp′ə-thĕt′ĭk) adj. Also **an·tip·a·thet·i·cal** (-ĭ-kəl). 1. Having an inherent feeling of aversion, repugnance, or opposition. Often used with *to*: *antipathetic to new ideas*. 2. Causing a feeling of antipathy. **—an·tip·a·thet·i·cal·ly** adv.

an·tip·a·thy (ăn-tĭp′ə-thē) n., pl. **-thies**. 1. A strong feeling of aversion or opposition. 2. The object of this feeling. [Latin *antipathia*, from Greek *antipatheia*, from *antipathēs*, of opposite feelings : ANTI- (opposite) + *pathos*, feeling (see **-pathy**).]

an·ti·pe·ri·od·ic (ăn′tĕ-pîr′ē-ŏd′ĭk, ăn′tī-) adj. Preventing regular recurrence of disease or fever.
~n. An antiperiodic drug.

an·ti·per·i·stal·sis (ăn′tĕ-pĕr′ə-stŏl′sĭs, -stăl′sĭs, ăn′tī-) n. Physiology. Contractions of the alimentary canal that push food back toward the mouth. Compare **peristalsis**.

an·ti·per·son·nel (ăn′tĕ-pûr′sə-nĕl′, ăn′tī-) adj. Military. Designed to inflict casualties on the military personnel or civilian population of an enemy country rather than on equipment or arms.

an·ti·per·spi·rant (ăn′tĕ-pûr′spər-ənt, ăn′tī-) n. A preparation applied to the skin to reduce or prevent perspiration.

an·ti·phlo·gis·tic (ăn′tĕ-flə-jĭs′tĭk, ăn′tī-) adj. Reducing inflammation. **—an·ti·phlo·gis·tic** n.

an·ti·phon (ăn′tə-fŏn′, -fən) n. 1. A plainsong setting of words, usually from the Bible, sung as a response as part of a liturgy. 2. A plainsong setting of a short liturgical text chanted or sung as a response before or after a psalm, psalm verse, or canticle. 3. A response; an answer: *a resounding antiphon of dissent*. [Late Latin *antiphona*, from Greek *antiphōna*, sung responses, ANTHEM.]

an·tiph·o·nal (ăn-tĭf′ə-nəl) adj. 1. Pertaining to or resembling an antiphon. 2. Sung or played as a response or in alternation (as in antiphony).
~n. Variant of **antiphonary**. **—an·tiph·o·nal·ly** adv.

an·tiph·o·nar·y (ăn-tĭf′ə-nĕr′ē) n., pl. **-ies**. Also **an·tiph·o·nal** (-nəl). A bound collection of antiphons, especially of the responsive choral parts of the divine office.

an·tiph·o·ny (ăn-tĭf′ə-nē) n., pl. **-nies**. 1. Responsive or antiphonal singing or chanting. 2. A composition that is sung in alternation or responsively; an antiphon. 3. A musical or other sound effect that answers or echoes another.

an·tiph·ra·sis (ăn-tĭf′rə-sĭs) n., pl. **-ses** (-sēz′). The use of a word in a sense contrary to its normal or accepted meaning for ironic or humorous effect; for example, *He is just a mere baby of thirty years*. [Late Latin, from Greek, from *antiphrazein*, "to speak by using the opposite sense": *anti-*, opposite + *phrazein*, to speak.]

an·ti·pod·al (ăn-tĭp′ə-dəl) adj. 1. Of, pertaining to, or situated on the opposite side or opposite sides of the earth. 2. Diametrically opposed; exactly opposite.

an·ti·pode (ăn′tĭ-pōd′) n. A direct or exact opposite or contrary. [Back-formation from ANTIPODES.]

an·tip·o·des (ăn-tĭp′ə-dēz′) pl.n. 1. Any two places or regions that are on opposite sides of the Earth. 2. Often **Antipodes**. Australia and New Zealand. [Middle English, from Latin, from Greek, plural of *antipous* (stem *antipod-*), with the feet opposite : ANTI- + *pous*, foot.] **—an·tip·o·de·an** (ăn-tĭp′ə-dē′ən) n. & adj.

an·ti·pope (ăn′tĭ-pōp′) n. A person claiming to be or elected pope in opposition to the one considered to have been chosen by church law. [Middle English, from Old French *antipape*, from Medieval Latin *antipāpa* : ANTI- + *pāpa*, POPE.]

an·ti·pro·ton (ăn′tĕ-prō′tŏn′, ăn′tī-) n. Physics. The **antiparticle** (see) of the proton.

an·ti·py·ret·ic (ăn′tĕ-pī-rĕt′ĭk) adj. Reducing or tending to reduce fever.
~n. Medication that reduces fever. **—an·ti·py·re·sis** (ăn′tĕ-pī-rē′sĭs) n.

an·ti·py·rine (ăn′tĕ-pī′rēn′) n. A white powder, $C_{11}H_{12}N_2O$, used to reduce fever and relieve pain. [German *Antipyrin* (trademark) : ANTI- + PYR(O)- + -INE.]

antiq. 1. antiquarian; antiquary. 2. antiquity.

an·ti·quar·i·an (ăn′tĭ-kwâr′ē-ən) adj. Abbr. **antiq.** 1. Of or pertaining to antiquaries or the study of antiquities. 2. Dealing in or having to do with old or rare books.
~n. An antiquary. **—an·ti·quar·i·an·ism** n.

an·ti·quar·y (ăn′tə-kwĕr′ē) n., pl. **-ies**. Abbr. **antiq.** A student of, collector of, or dealer in antiquities or antiques. [Latin *antīquārius*, from adjective, of antiquity, from *antīquus*, ANTIQUE.]

an·ti·quate (ăn′tə-kwāt′) tr.v. **-quated, -quating, -quates**. 1. To make obsolete or old-fashioned. 2. To give an antique appearance to. [Latin *antīquāre*, to leave in its ancient state, from *antīquus*, ANTIQUE.] **—an·ti·qua·tion** n.

an·ti·quat·ed (ăn′tə-kwā′tĭd) adj. 1. So old as to be no longer useful or applicable; outmoded; obsolete: *antiquated laws*. 2. Very old; aged. **—an·ti·quat·ed·ness** n.

an·tique (ăn-tēk′) adj. 1. Belonging to, made in, or typical of an earlier period. 2. Of or belonging to ancient times; especially, of, from, or characteristic of ancient Greece or Rome. 3. Of or dealing in antiques. 4. Old-fashioned. —See Synonyms at **old**.
~n. 1. An object having special value because of its age; especially, a piece of furniture or other work of art valued for its workmanship, beauty, and age. 2. The style or manner of ancient times, especially that of ancient Greek or Roman art. Preceded by *the*: *an admirer of the antique*.
~tr.v. **antiqued, -tiquing, -tiques**. To give the appearance of an antique to. [French, from Latin *antīquus*, ancient, former.] **—an·tique·ly** adv. **—an·tique·ness** n. **—an·tiqu·er** n.

an·tiq·ui·ty (ăn-tĭk′wə-tē) n., pl. **-ties**. Abbr. **antiq.** 1. Often **Antiquity**. Ancient times, especially the times preceding the Middle Ages. 2. The people of ancient times. 3. The quality of being old or ancient; considerable age: *a carving of great antiquity*. 4. Often **antiquities**. Something belonging to or dating from a time long past.

an·ti·ra·chit·ic (ăn′tĕ-rə-kĭt′ĭk, ăn′tī-) adj. Curing or preventing rickets.
~n. An antirachitic drug or food.

an·tir·rhi·num (ăn′tə-rī′nəm) n. Any plant of the genus *Antirrhinum*, such as a **snapdragon** (see). [New Latin, from Greek *antirrhinon*, "plant having snoutlike flowers" : *anti-*, counterfeiting + *rhis*† (stem *rhin-*), nose (see **rhino-**).]

an·ti·scor·bu·tic (ăn′tĕ-skôr-byōō′tĭk, ăn′tī-) adj. Curing or preventing scurvy.
~n. A food or drug that cures or prevents scurvy.

antler *Found on the heads of most species of deer, antlers are normally confined to the male and are used during the breeding season in contests between rivals. Made of bone, they are shed at the end of each mating season and regrow with more spikes every year. The antlers of the barren ground caribou (above) can have a spread of up to 1.2 meters (4 feet).*

an·ti·Sem·ite (ăn′tē-sĕm′īt′, ăn′tī-) *n.* A person who is hostile toward or prejudiced against Jews. —**an·ti·Se·mit·ic** (ăn′tē-sə-mĭt′-ĭk, ăn′tī-) *adj.* —**an·ti·Sem·i·tism** *n.*

an·ti·sep·sis (ăn′tə-sĕp′sĭs) *n.* The destruction of microorganisms that cause disease, fermentation, or putrefaction. Compare **asepsis.**

an·ti·sep·tic (ăn′tə-sĕp′tĭk) *adj.* **1.** Of, pertaining to, or designating antisepsis. **2.** Capable of producing antisepsis. **3.** Thoroughly clean. **4.** *Informal.* Devoid of enlivening or enriching qualities; austere; clinical.
~*n.* An antiseptic drug or agent. —**an·ti·sep·ti·cal·ly** *adv.*

an·ti·se·rum (ăn′tē-sîr′əm, ăn′tī-) *n., pl.* **-rums** or **-ra** (-rə). Human or animal serum containing antibodies against at least one antigen, used to treat or provide immunity to an infection.

an·ti·slav·er·y (ăn′tē-slā′və-rē, -slāv′rē, ăn′tī-) *adj.* Opposed to or against slavery.

an·ti·so·cial (ăn′tē-sō′shəl, ăn′tī-) *adj.* **1.** Shunning the society of others; unsociable. **2.** Upsetting or offensive to other people: *antisocial behavior.* **3.** Opposed to or interfering with the social order or the general welfare of society. —**an·ti·so·cial·ly** *adv.*

an·ti·spas·mod·ic (ăn′tē-spăz-mŏd′ĭk, ăn′tī-) *adj.* Easing or preventing spasms.
~*n.* An antispasmodic drug.

an·ti·stat·ic (ăn′tē-stăt′ĭk, ăn′tī-) *adj.* Preventing or inhibiting the build-up of static electricity.

an·tis·tro·phe (ăn-tĭs′trə-fē) *n.* **1.** In ancient Greek choral poetry or drama, the movement following and in the same meter as the strophe, sung while the chorus moves in the opposite direction from that of the strophe. **2.** The second stanza, and those like it, in a poem consisting of alternating stanzas in contrasting metric form. [Late Latin, from Greek *antistrophē* : ANTI- + STROPHE.] —**an·ti·stroph·ic** (ăn′tī-strŏf′ĭk) *adj.* —**an·ti·stroph·i·cal·ly** *adv.*

an·ti·sub·ma·rine (ăn′tē-sŭb′mə-rēn′, -sŭb′mə-rēn′, ăn′tī-) *adj. Abbr.* **AS** Directed against enemy submarines.

an·ti·tank (ăn′tē-tăngk′, ăn′tī-) *adj. Abbr.* **AT** Designed or used for combat against tanks or other armored vehicles.

an·tith·e·sis (ăn-tĭth′ə-sĭs) *n., pl.* **-ses** (-sēz′). **1.** Direct contrast; opposition. **2.** The direct or exact opposite: *Despair is the antithesis of hope.* **3. a.** The juxtaposition of sharply contrasting ideas in balanced or parallel words, phrases, or grammatical structures; for example, *They died that we might live.* **b.** The second and contrasting part of such a juxtaposition. **4.** In Hegelian philosophy, the second stage of the dialectic process. [Late Latin, from Greek, opposition, from *antitithenai,* to oppose : ANTI- + *tithenai,* to set, place.]

an·ti·thet·i·cal (ăn′tə-thĕt′ĭ-kəl) *adj.* Also **an·ti·thet·ic** (-ĭk). **1.** Pertaining to, of the nature of, or including antithesis. **2.** Directly opposed in every respect. —See Synonyms at **opposite.** [Late Latin *antitheticus,* from Greek *antithetikos,* from *antitithenai,* to oppose. See **antithesis.**] —**an·ti·thet·i·cal·ly** *adv.*

an·ti·tox·ic (ăn′tĭ-tŏk′sĭk) *adj.* **1.** Counteracting a toxin or poison. **2.** Of, pertaining to, or constituting an antitoxin.

an·ti·tox·in (ăn′tĭ-tŏk′sĭn) *n.* **1.** An antibody formed in response to and capable of neutralizing a poison of biological origin. **2.** An animal serum containing such antibodies.

an·ti·trades (ăn′tĭ-trādz′, ăn′tī-) *pl.n.* The westerly winds above the trade winds of the tropics, which become the westerly winds of the middle latitudes.

an·ti·trust (ăn′tē-trŭst′, ăn′tī-) *adj.* Opposing or concerned with the regulation of trusts, cartels, or similar business monopolies.

an·ti·tus·sive (ăn′tē-tŭs′ĭv, ăn′tī-) *adj.* Capable of relieving coughing.
~*n.* An antitussive drug.

an·ti·type (ăn′tĭ-tīp′) *n.* One that is foreshadowed or represented by a symbol or earlier type, such as a figure in the New Testament who has a counterpart in the Old Testament. [Medieval Latin *antitypus,* from Greek *antitupos,* "opposite to the die" (hence, anything resembling the impression made by a die or stamp) : *anti-,* opposite + *tupos,* die (see **type**).] —**an·ti·typ·i·cal** (ăn′tī-tĭp′ĭ-kəl) *adj.*

an·ti·ven·in (ăn′tē-vĕn′ĭn, ăn′tī-) *n.* **1.** An antitoxin active against a particular venom. **2.** An antiserum containing such an antitoxin. [ANTI- + VEN(OM) + -IN.]

ant·ler (ănt′lər) *n.* Either of a pair of hard, bony, deciduous growths, usually elongated and branched, that characteristically grow on the heads of male deer and related animals. [Middle English *aunteler,* from Old French *antoillier,* from Vulgar Latin *anteoculāris* (unattested), "before the eyes" : ANTE- + Latin *oculus,* eye.] —**ant·lered** (ănt′lərd) *adj.*

Ant·li·a (ănt′lē-ə) *n.* A constellation in the Southern Hemisphere near Hydra and Vela. [Latin *antlia,* pump, from Greek *antlia, antlos,* bucket.]

ant lion *n.* Any insect of the family Myrmeleontidae, of which the adults resemble dragonflies; especially, the larva of such an insect, which digs holes to trap ants and other insects for food. Also called "doodlebug."

An·to·ne·scu (ăn′tə-nĕs′kŏo), **Ion** (1882–1946). Romanian marshal and prime minister. He was chief of staff of the Romanian army and was appointed prime minister with unlimited powers on September 5, 1940, by King Carol II. For the rest of World War II Antonescu acted as Hitler's puppet and connived at violent pogroms against the Jews. He was executed for his war crimes in 1946.

An·to·nine Wall (ăn′tə-nīn′) A defensive Roman frontier in Scotland that stretched for *c.* 58 kilometers (36 miles) between the Clyde and the Firth of Forth. It was built in A.D. 142 on the orders of the emperor Antoninus Pius. Small traces of the wall remain.

An·to·ni·o·ni (ăn-tō′nē-ō′nē), **Michelangelo** (1912–). Italian film director. He developed a highly visual style in which realism was subordinated to a metaphorical treatment of subject. Among his most famous films are *L'Avventura* (1959), *The Red Desert* (1964), *Blow-up* (1966), and *Zabriskie Point* (1969).

Antonius, Marcus. See Mark Antony.

an·to·no·ma·sia (ăn-tə-nō-mā′zhə) *n.* **1.** The substitution of a title or epithet for a proper name, as in calling a king "His Majesty." **2.** The substitution of a personal name for a common noun to designate a member of a group or class, as in calling a libertine "a Don Juan." [Latin, from Greek, from *antonomazein,* to name instead : *ant(i)-,* instead of + *onomazein,* to name, from *onoma,* name.] —**an·ton·o·mas·tic** (ăn-tŏn′ə-măs′tĭk) *adj.*

an·to·nym (ăn′tə-nĭm′) *n. Abbr.* **ant.** A word having a meaning opposite to that of another word; for example, *light* is an antonym of *dark.* Compare **synonym.** [ANT(I)- + -ONYM.] —**an·ton·y·mous** (ăn-tŏn′ə-məs) *adj.* —**an·ton·y·my** (ăn-tŏn′ə-mē) *n.*

an·tre (ăn′tər) *n. Chiefly Poetic.* A cavern or cave. [French, from Latin *antrum,* cave. See **antrum.**]

An·trim (ăn′trĭm). A predominantly agricultural county in northeastern Northern Ireland. Its county town is Belfast.

an·trorse (ăn′trôs′) *adj. Biology.* Directed forward and upward. [New Latin *antrorsus* : perhaps blend of ANTERIOR and DEXTRORSE.] —**an·trorse·ly** *adv.*

an·trum (ăn′trəm) *n., pl.* **-tra** (-trə). A cavity, usually in bone; especially, either of the sinuses in the upper jaw opening into the nose. [Late Latin, cavity in the body, from Latin, cave, from Greek *antron.*]

Ant·wer·pen (ănt′vĕr′pən). *French* **An·vers** (än′vâr′); *English* **Ant·werp** (ănt′wûrp′). One of Europe's busiest ports, lying on the Scheldt River in northern Belgium. It was a trading center as early as the 8th century, and the world's first stock exchange was founded here in 1460. It has been one of the leading centers of the diamond industry since the 15th century.

A·nu·bis (ə-nōo′bĭs, ə-nyōo′-). *Egyptian Mythology.* A jackal-headed god, son of Osiris, who conducted the dead to judgment.

A·nu·ra·dha·pu·ra (ə-nə-rä′də-pŏor′ə). Market town in northern Sri Lanka and capital of North Central province. It was founded in the 5th century B.C. and became the capital of the Sinhalese kingdom and a major center of Buddhism.

a·nu·ran (ə-nŏor′ən, ə-nyōor′-) *adj.* Of or belonging to the Anura, an order of amphibians containing the frogs and toads; salientian.
~*n.* A frog or toad. Also called "salientian." [New Latin *Anura* : AN- (without) + Greek *oura,* tail.]

an·u·re·sis (ăn′yə-rē′sĭs) *n.* Inability to urinate. [AN- (without) + Greek *ouresis,* urination, from *ourein,* to urinate, from *ouran,* urine.] —**an·u·ret·ic** (ăn′yə-rĕt′ĭk) *adj.*

a·nu·ri·a (ə-nŏor′ē-ə, ə-nyŏor′-) *n.* The pathological condition characterized by failure of the kidneys to produce urine. [New Latin : AN- (not) + -URIA.] —**a·nu·ric** *adj.*

a·nu·rous (ə-nŏor′əs, ə-nyŏor′-) *adj.* Having no tail; tailless. [AN- + -UROUS.]

a·nus (ā′nəs) *n., pl.* **anuses.** The excretory opening at the end of the alimentary canal. [Latin *ānus,* ring.]

Anvers. See Antwerpen.

an·vil (ăn′vĭl) *n.* **1.** A heavy block of iron or steel with a smooth, flat top on which metals are shaped by hammering. **2.** A part of a tool or device that resembles an anvil in shape or function, such as: **a.** The lower part of a telegraph key. **b.** The fixed jaw in a set of calipers, against which the object to be measured is placed. **3.** *Anatomy.* A bone, the **incus** (see). [Middle English *anvil(t),* anvelt, Old English *anfealg,* anfilt : *an,* ON + *-fealt,* "beaten."]

anx·i·e·ty (ăng-zī′ə-tē) *n., pl.* **-ties.** **1.** A state of uneasiness and distress about future uncertainties; apprehension; worry. **2.** A cause of such uneasiness; a worry. **3.** *Psychiatry.* Intense fear or dread lacking an unambiguous cause or a specific threat. **4.** Eagerness: *his anxiety to go home.* [Latin *anxietās* (stem *anxietāt-*), from *anxius,* ANXIOUS.]

Synonyms: concern, solicitude, worry.

anx·ious (ăngk′shəs, ăng′shəs) *adj.* **1.** Worried and strained about some uncertain event or matter; uneasy. **2.** Attended with, showing, or causing much anxieties: *This is an anxious time for her.* **3.** Eagerly or earnestly desirous. Used with *to: The child was anxious to please the teacher.* —See Synonyms at **eager.** [Latin *anxius,* from *angere,* to torment, choke.] —**anx·ious·ly** *adv.* —**anx·ious·ness** *n.*

an·y (ĕn′ē) *adj.* **1. a.** One or some, taken at random from three or more; a, an, or some: *Any book will do. Pick any four numbers.* **b.** Each and every one: *Any child knows that.* **c.** The whole amount; all: *We will turn over any profit to charity.* **2. a.** Some, regardless of quantity, number, or extent: *Did you buy any butter?* **b.** Even the smallest amount or quantity: *Don't make any noise!* **c.** Unlimited in extent, quantity, or number: *any amount of luck; any number of books.* **3.** Of an ordinary or indeterminate kind. Used in negative statements, often with *just: Edwin can't wear just any tie.* **4.** No matter how large or small: *not at any price.*
~*pron.* **1.** Any one or ones among three or more. **2.** Any quantity or part; some. **3.** Anybody; any person.
~*adv.* **1.** To any degree or extent. Used with comparative forms: *Is he any better now?* **2.** *Informal.* At all: *The medicine didn't help any.* [Middle English *any,* eny, Old English *ænig.*]

Usage: Any may be used with either a singular or a plural verb:

Anubis *A bronze statuette of the jackal-headed Egyptian god, probably made during the Ptolemaic period (323–30 B.C.).*

Any of these books would be suitable implies "any *one* of . . ."; *Are any available?* implies "some." In negative constructions, *any* is the accepted usage. *I haven't any money* does not have a corresponding form *I haven't some money.* There is, however, a more formal alternative, *I have no money.*

An·yang (än′yäng′). Agricultural trading center in Henan province, northeast China. It was the capital of the Shang dynasty *c.* 1711–1066 B.C.

an·y·bod·y (ĕn′ē-bŏd′ē, -bŭd′ē, bə-dē) *pron.* Any person, no matter who.
~*n., pl.* **anybodies.** A person of some consequence: *everybody who is anybody.*

an·y·how (ĕn′ē-hou′) *adv.* **1.** In any case; at any rate. **2.** Carelessly; neglectfully.

an·y·more (ĕn′ē-môr′, -mōr′) *adv.* Any longer; from now on. Used in negative and interrogative constructions: *The store doesn't accept credit cards anymore.*

an·y·one (ĕn′ē-wŭn′, -wən) *pron.* Any person, no matter who; any body: *Anyone who disagrees with this editorial can write a letter to the editor.*
Usage: A controversy arises over the appropriate pronoun to use in certain types of sentence where *anyone* is the subject: *Anyone can do what — wants.* The use of the traditionally neutral pronoun *he* in this context may be misleading if females are involved, and in recent years has attracted criticism as being sexist. On the other hand, the use of *she* sounds odd and possibly insulting, and to use *he or she* is extremely awkward. For such reasons, the use of *they, their,* or the like, long-attested but widely condemned, has taken on a new respectability as an idiomatic solution to the problem. The traditional grammarian, however, would wish the singular sense of *anyone* to be matched by a singular pronoun and verb, and this principle is still the safest one to follow in formal speech or writing.

an·y·place (ĕn′ē-plās′) *adv.* Anywhere.

an·y·road (ĕn′ē-rōd′) *adv. British Regional.* Anyway.

an·y·thing (ĕn′ē-thĭng′) *pron.* Any object, act, occurrence, or matter whatever.
~*adv.* To any degree or extent; at all: *The movie wasn't anything like we'd expected.* —**anything but.** By no means; not at all. —**like anything.** *Informal.* Used as an intensive: *She screamed like anything.* —**or anything.** *Informal.* Something similar: *Did he argue or anything?*

an·y·time (ĕn′ē-tīm′) *adv.* At any time.

an·y·way (ĕn′ē-wā′) *adv.* **1.** Nevertheless; at any rate; in any case. **2.** In any manner or by any means whatever. **3.** Carelessly; neglectfully.

an·y·ways (ĕn′ē-wāz′) *adv. Nonstandard.* Anyway.

an·y·where (ĕn′ē-hwâr′) *adv.* **1.** To, in, or at any place. **2.** To any extent or degree; at all: *We aren't anywhere near being finished.* —**anywhere from** (or **between**). Any quantity, degree, time, or the like between given bounds: *It could last anywhere from 20 minutes to an hour.* —**get anywhere.** To succeed to any degree: *I don't see how he can get anywhere with his attitude.* —**get nowhere.** To fail to succeed: *I got nowhere with my proposal.*

an·y·wise (ĕn′ē-wīz′) *adv.* In any way or manner. [Old English *on ǣnige wīsan,* in any wise.]

An·zac (ăn′zăk′) *n.* **1.** A soldier in the Australian and New Zealand Army Corps formed in World War I. **2.** Any soldier from New Zealand or Australia. —**An·zac** *adj.*

A-OK, A-O·kay (ā′ō-kā′) *adj.* Functioning perfectly; excellent; fine. [From the phrase *all systems o.k.*]

Aorangi. See Mount Cook.

a·o·rist (ā′ər-ĭst) *n.* A verb tense originally used in classical Greek. It usually denotes past action without indicating completion, continuation, or repetition of this action. [Greek *(khronos) aoristos,* "the indefinite (tense)" : A- (not) + *horistos,* definable, from *horizein,* to delimit, from *horos†,* boundary, limit.] —**a·o·rist, a·o·ris·tic** *adj.* —**a·o·ris·ti·cal·ly** *adv.*

a·or·ta (ā-ôr′tə) *n., pl.* **-tas** or **-tae** (-tē) *Anatomy.* The main trunk of the systemic arteries, carrying oxygenated blood from the left side of the heart to the arteries of all limbs and organs except the lungs. [New Latin, from Greek *aortē,* aorta, "appendices (of the heart)," from *aeirein,* to raise up.] —**a·or·tic** (ā-ôr′tĭk), **a·or·tal** (ā-ôr′tl) *adj.*

aortic arch *n.* The section of the aorta that passes over the top of the heart and back down to the fourth thoracic vertebra.

Aotearoa. See New Zealand.

a·ou·dad (ä′ōō-dăd′, ou′dăd′) *n.* A wild sheep, *Ammotragus lervia,* of northern Africa, having long, curved horns and a beardlike growth of hair on the neck and chest. Also called "Barbary sheep." [French, from Berber *audad.*]

ap. apothecary.

a.p. 1. additional premium. **2.** author's proof.

A.P. Associated Press.

a·pace (ə-pās′) *adv.* At a rapid pace; rapidly; swiftly. [Middle English *apas, apace,* step by step, from Old French *a pas* : *a,* to, from Latin *ad* + *pas,* step, PACE.]

a·pache (ə-päsh′) *n., pl.* **apaches** (ə-päsh′). A member of the Parisian underworld. [French, from (English) APACHE (alluding to the tribe's warlike or violent character).]

A·pach·e (ə-păch′ē) *n., pl.* **-es** or collectively **Apache** (for sense 1). **1.** A member of a formerly nomadic tribe of North American Indians inhabiting the southwestern United States and northern Mexico. **2.** Any of the Athapascan languages of the Apache. [Spanish, probably from Zuñi *Apachu,* enemy.]

aphid *Greenfly (top) and blackfly are both aphids—soft-bodied insects that feed on the sap of plants and often act as carriers of plant diseases. Many species are milked by ants for their honeydew, a sugary secretion exuded by the aphids' bodies.*

Aphrodite *The Venus de Milo, as it is known, is a statue of the Greek goddess Aphrodite, dating from about 100 B.C. It was found on the Greek island of Milos and is in the Louvre, Paris.*

apanage. Variant of **appanage.**

ap·a·re·jo (ŏp′ə-rā′hō, -rā′ō) *n., pl.* **-jos.** *Southwestern U.S.* A packsaddle made of a stuffed leather pad. [Mexican Spanish, from Spanish, equipment, from *aparejar,* to prepare.]

a·part (ə-pärt′) *adv.* **1. a.** In pieces. **b.** To pieces. **2. a.** Separately or at a distance in time, place, or position: *Over the years, they grew apart.* **b.** To one side; aside. **3.** One from another: *It's easy to confuse the two pictures if you see them apart.* **4.** Independently or separately in consideration or thought. **5.** Out of consideration or set aside; aside: *These few problems apart, it's all going well.* —**apart from. 1.** With the exception of. **2.** Besides: *Apart from me, there are four others.*
~*adj.* Having individualizing features or characteristics. Used after the noun: *a race apart.* [Middle English, from Old French *a part,* to the side : *a,* to + PART.]

a·part·heid (ə-pärt′hīt′, -hāt′) *n.* **1.** An official policy of racial segregation practiced in the Republic of South Africa with a view to promoting and maintaining white ascendancy. **2.** A condition of separateness; separation or segregation. [Afrikaans, "apartness" : *apart,* separate, from French *à part,* APART + *-heid,* -HOOD.]

a·part·ment (ə-pärt′mənt) *n. Abbr.* **apt. 1.** A room or suite of rooms designed for housekeeping and generally located in a building occupied by more than one household. **2.** A building that comprises a number of apartments. **3.** A room. [French *appartement,* from Italian *appartamento,* from *apparare,* to separate, from *a parte,* APART.]

apartment house *n.* A building divided into apartments. Also called "apartment building."

ap·as·tron (ă-păs′trŏn, -trŏn′) *n., pl.* **-tra** (-trə). *Astronomy.* The point in an orbit around a star that is farthest from the star; especially, this point in the orbit of one star around another in a binary system. [New Latin, from Greek : *ap(o)-,* away from + *astron,* star.]

ap·a·tet·ic (ăp′ə-tĕt′ĭk) *adj. Zoology.* Pertaining to or designating coloration serving as natural camouflage to an animal. [Greek *apatētikos,* deceptive, from *apateuein,* to cheat, from *apatē†,* deceit, fraud.]

ap·a·thet·ic (ăp′ə-thĕt′ĭk) *adj.* **1.** Feeling or showing little or no emotion. **2.** Uninterested; indifferent; listless. —See Synonyms at **indifferent.** [Blend of APATHY and PATHETIC.] —**ap·a·thet·i·cal·ly** *adv.*

ap·a·thy (ăp′ə-thē) *n.* **1.** Lack of emotion or feeling. **2.** Lack of interest or absence of response, especially to what is generally found exciting, interesting, or moving; indifference. [Greek *apatheia,* from *apathēs,* without feeling : A- (without) + *pathos,* feeling.]

ap·a·tite (ăp′ə-tīt′) *n.* A natural, variously colored form of calcium fluoride phosphate, Ca₅F(PO₄)₃, with chlorine, hydroxyl, or carbonate sometimes replacing the fluoride. It is a source of phosphorus compounds and is used in the manufacture of fertilizers. [German *Apatit,* "the deceptive stone" (often mistaken for other minerals), from Greek *apatē,* deceit. See **apatetic.**]

ape (āp) *n.* **1.** Any of various large, tailless Old World primates of the family Pongidae, including the chimpanzee, gorilla, gibbon, and orang-utan. **2.** Broadly, any monkey. **3.** A mimic or imitator. **4.** *Informal.* A large, clumsy, coarse person.
~*tr.v.* **aped, aping, apes.** To mimic. —See Synonyms at **imitate.** [Middle English *ape,* Old English *apa,* from Germanic *apan-* (unattested).]

a·peak (ə-pēk′) *adv. Nautical.* In a vertical or almost vertical position or direction. [Earlier *apike* : A- + PIKE (peak).]

A·pel·les (ə-pĕl′ēz) (*fl.* 4th century B.C.). Greek painter. He was court painter to Philip II of Macedon and Alexander the Great and was considered the greatest painter of his time. No copies of his paintings exist.

ape-man (āp′măn′) *n., pl.* **-men** (-mĕn′). Loosely, any of several extinct primates considered intermediate between apes and modern man.

Ap·en·nines (ăp′ə-nīnz′). Mountain system running about 1,350 kilometers (840 miles) along the length of peninsular Italy. It has two active volcanoes, Vesuvius and Etna. The highest peak, at 2,914 meters (9,560 feet), is Monte Corno.

a·per·çu (ä′pĕr-sü′) *n., pl.* **-çus** (-sü′). A brief outline; summary. [Past participle of *apercevoir,* to PERCEIVE.]

a·pe·ri·ent (ə-pîr′ē-ənt) *adj.* Gently purgative; laxative.
~*n.* A mild laxative. [Latin *aperiēns* (stem *aperient-*), present participle of *aperīre,* to uncover, open.]

a·pe·ri·od·ic (ā′pîr′ē-ŏd′ĭk) *adj.* **1.** Not occurring at regular intervals; irregular. **2.** *Electronics.* Of or designating a circuit that is not capable of resonance at the frequency used. —**a·pe·ri·od·i·cal·ly** *adv.* —**a·pe·ri·o·dic·i·ty** (ā′pîr′ē-ə-dĭs′ə-tē) *n.*

a·pé·ri·tif (ä-pĕr′ə-tēf′) *n.* An alcoholic drink taken to stimulate the appetite before a meal. [French, from Old French *aperitif,* from Medieval Latin *aperitīvus,* from Latin *aperīre,* open.]

ap·er·ture (ăp′ər-chōōr′, -chər) *n.* **1.** A hole, gap, slit, or other opening; an orifice. **2.** *Optics.* **a.** A usually adjustable opening in an optical instrument that limits the amount of light passing through a lens or onto a mirror. **b.** The effective diameter of a lens or mirror divided by its focal length. See **f-number. 3.** The diameter of a radio telescope. [Latin *apertūra,* from *apertus,* open, from the past participle of *aperīre,* to open.] —**ap·er·tur·al** *adj.*

aperture card *n.* A punched card upon which some portion of a microfilmed document is mounted.

a·pet·al·ous (ā-pĕt′l-əs) *adj. Botany.* Having no petals. —**a·pet·al·y** (ā-pĕt′l-ē) *n.*

a·pex (ā′pĕks′) *n., pl.* **apexes** or **apices** (ā′pə-sēz′, ăp′ə-) **1.** The highest point of something; the vertex. **2.** The culmination, as of an activity or effort. **3.** The pointed end of something; the tip. **3.** *Astronomy.* A point on the celestial sphere toward which the solar system moves relative to neighboring stars. —See Synonyms at **summit.** [Latin *apex*, point, summit, top.]

A·PEX, A·pex (ā′pĕks′) *n.* A system of discount air fares available on bookings paid for in advance of a minimum stipulated period. [*A*dvance *P*urchase *Ex*cursion.]

a·phaer·e·sis, a·pher·e·sis (ə-fĕr′ə-sĭs) *n.*, *pl.* **-ses** (-sēz′). The loss of one or more letters or sounds from the beginning of a word, as in *round* for *around* or *most* for *almost*. [Late Latin, from Greek *aphairesis*, a taking away, from *aphairein*, to take away from : *ap(o)-*, away from + *hairein†*, to take.] —**aph·ae·ret·ic** (ăf′ə-rĕt′ĭk) *adj.*

a·pha·gi·a (ə-fā′jē-ə, -jə) *n.* Inability to swallow. [New Latin : A- (not) + -PHAGIA.]

aph·a·nite (ăf′ə-nīt′) *n.* Any igneous rock with constituents so fine that they cannot be seen by the naked eye. [French : Greek *aphanēs*, unseen : A- (not) + *phainesthai*, to be seen, from *phainein*, to see + -ITE.] —**aph·a·nit·ic** (ăf′ə-nĭt′ĭk) *adj.* —**aph·a·nit·ism** *n.*

a·pha·sia (ə-fā′zhə) *n.* Partial or total loss of the ability to use or articulate words, usually resulting from brain damage. [New Latin, from Greek : A- (without) + -PHASIA.] —**a·pha·si·ac** (ə-fā′zē-ăk′) *n.* —**a·pha·sic** (ə-fā′zĭk) *adj.* & *n.*

a·phe·li·on (ə-fē′lē-ən, ə-fēl′yən, ə-fēl′yən) *n.*, *pl.* **-lia** (-lē-ə). The point on the orbit of a planet or comet that is farthest from the sun. Compare **perihelion.** [New Latin, variant of *aphelium* : Greek *ap(o)-*, away from + *hēlios*, Sun.]

a·phe·li·o·trop·ic (ə-fē′lē-ə-trŏp′ĭk) *adj. Biology.* Turning away from the sun, as roots do. [AP(O)- (away from) + HELIOTROPIC.] —**a·phe·li·o·trop·i·cal·ly** *adv.* —**a·phe·li·ot·ro·pism** (ə-fē′lē-ŏt′rə-pĭz′əm) *n.*

aph·e·sis (ăf′ə-sĭs) *n*, *pl.* **-ses** (-sēz′). The loss of a short unstressed vowel from the beginning of a word, for example, *squire* for *esquire*. [New Latin, from Greek *aphesis*, a letting go, from *aphienai*, to let go : *ap(o)-*, away + *hienai†*, to send.] —**a·phet·ic** (ə-fĕt′ĭk) *adj.* —**a·phet·i·cal·ly** *adv.*

a·phid (ā′fĭd, ăf′ĭd) *n.* Any of various small, soft-bodied insects of the family Aphididae, such as greenflies, that feed by sucking sap from plants. Also called "plant louse." [From New Latin *aphis* (stem *aphid-*), APHIS.] —**a·phid·i·an** (ə-fĭd′ē-ən) *adj.* & *n.*

aphid lion. The larva of any of several insects of the family Chrysopidae, such as the lacewing, that feed on aphids.

a·phis (ā′fĭs, ăf′ĭs) *n.*, *pl.* **aphides** (ā′fĭ-dēz′, ăf′ə-). An aphid, especially one of the genus *Aphis*. [New Latin *Aphis* (coined by Linnaeus), of obscure origin but perhaps due to a misreading of Greek *koris*, bug.]

a·pho·ni·a (ā-fō′nē-ə) *n.* Voicelessness or loss of speech as a result of disease or injury to the organs of speech. [New Latin, from Greek *aphōnia*, voicelessness, from *cphōnos*, voiceless : A- (without) + *phōnē*, voice.]

a·phon·ic (ā-fŏn′ĭk, ā-fō′nĭk) *adj.* **1.** *Pathology.* Affected with or having aphonia. **2.** *Phonetics.* Voiceless.

aph·o·rism (ăf′ə-rĭz′əm) *n.* A pithy statement of a truth or opinion; a maxim; an adage. —See Synonyms at **saying.** [Old French *aphorisme*, from Greek *aphorismos*, a delimitation, from *aphorizein*, to mark off by boundaries : *ap(o)-*, off, away from + *horizein*, to limit, from *horos†*, boundary, limit.] —**aph·o·ris·tic** (ăf′ə-rĭs′tĭk) *adj.* —**aph·o·ris·ti·cal·ly** *adv.*

aph·o·rize (ăf′ə-rīz′) *intr.v.* **-rized, -rizing, -rizes.** To express oneself, as in speaking, in or as if in aphorisms.

a·pho·tic (ā-fō′tĭk) *adj.* **1.** Without light. **2.** Of or designating the ocean zone below the level at which photosynthesis can occur (about 200 meters or 656 feet). [A- (not) + PHOTIC.]

aph·ro·dis·i·ac (ăf′rə-dĭz′ē-ăk′) *adj.* Stimulating or intensifying sexual desire.
~*n.* Anything having aphrodisiac properties, such as a drug or food. [Greek *aphrodisiakos*, from *aphrodisia*, aphrodisiac pleasures, from *aphrodisios*, of Aphrodite.]

Aph·ro·di·te (ăf′rə-dī′tē) *Greek Mythology.* The goddess of love and beauty, identified with the Roman goddess Venus. Also called "Cytherea."

a·phyl·lous (ā-fĭl′əs) *adj. Botany.* Having or bearing no leaves. [Greek *aphullos* : A- (not) + -PHYLLOUS.] —**a·phyl·ly** (ā′fĭl′ē) *n.*

A·pi·a (ä-pē′ä). Capital and only port of Western Samoa, on the northern coast of Upolu Island. Vailima, the former home of Robert Louis Stevenson, is the residence of the head of state.

a·pi·an (ā′pē-ən) *adj.* Of or pertaining to bees. [Latin *apiānus*, from *apis†*, bee.]

a·pi·ar·i·an (ā′pē-âr′ē-ən) *adj.* Of or pertaining to bees or to the breeding and care of bees.
~*n.* An apiarist.

a·pi·a·rist (ā′pē-ər-ĭst, ā′pē-är′ĭst) *n.* A beekeeper.

a·pi·ar·y (ā′pē-ĕr′ē) *n.*, *pl.* **-ies.** A place containing a number of beehives, in which bees are kept and raised, usually for their honey. [Latin *apiārium*, beehive, from *apis†*, bee.]

ap·i·cal (ăp′ĭ-kəl, ā′pĭ-) *adj.* **1.** Of, pertaining to, located at, or constituting the apex. **2.** *Phonetics.* Of or designating consonants articulated with the tip of the tongue, as *t*, *d*, and *s*. [New Latin *apicalis*, from Latin *apex* (stem *apic-*), APEX.]

apices. Alternate plural of **apex.**

a·pic·u·late (ə-pĭk′yə-lĭt) *adj. Botany.* Ending with a sharp, abrupt tip: *an apiculate leaf*. [From New Latin *apiculus*, a sharp point, diminutive of *apex* (stem *apic-*), APEX.]

a·pi·cul·ture (ā′pĭ-kŭl′chər) *n.* The breeding and care of bees. [Latin *apis†*, bee + CULTURE.] —**a·pi·cul·tur·al** *adj.* —**a·pi·cul·tur·ist** *n.*

a·piece (ə-pēs′) *adv.* To or for each one; each: *Give them an apple apiece.* [Middle English *a pece* : A + PIECE.]

A·pis (ā′pĭs) *n.* A sacred bull of the ancient Egyptians.

ap·ish (ā′pĭsh) *adj.* **1.** Slavishly or foolishly imitative. **2.** Silly; foolish. [AP(E) + -ISH.] —**ap·ish·ly** *adv.* —**ap·ish·ness** *n.*

a·piv·o·rous (ā-pĭv′ər-əs) *adj.* Feeding on bees. [Latin *apis†*, bee + -VOROUS.]

APL (ā′pē-ĕl′) *n.* A computer programming language designed for use at remote terminals. [*A Programming Language.*]

a·pla·cen·tal (ā′plə-sĕn′təl) *adj.* Having no placenta. Said of marsupials and monotremes. [A- (not) + PLACENT(A) + -AL.]

ap·la·nat·ic (ăp′lə-năt′ĭk) *adj.* Of, pertaining to, or designating optical systems that correct for spherical aberration and coma. [Greek *aplanētos*, unable to go astray : A- (not) + *planētos*, *planēs*, wandering, from *planasthai*, to wander.]

a·plan·o·spore (ā-plăn′ə-spôr′, -spōr′) *n.* A nonmotile, asexual spore characteristic of the green algae. [A- (not) + Greek *planos*, wandering + SPORE.]

a·pla·sia (ə-plā′zhə) *n.* Defective development or congenital absence of tissue, of an organ, or of an organ part. [New Latin : A- (not) + -PLASIA.]

a·plas·tic (ā-plăs′tĭk) *adj.* **1.** Lacking form. **2.** *Pathology.* Of, relating to, or characterized by aplasia: *aplastic anemia.* [A- (not) + -PLASTIC.]

a·plen·ty (ə-plĕn′tē) *adj.* Being in abundance. Used after the noun: *goods aplenty.*
~*adv.* **1.** In abundance. **2.** To an extreme degree.

ap·lite (ăp′līt′) *n.* Also **hap·lite** (hăp′-). A fine-grained, light-colored granitic rock consisting primarily of orthoclase and quartz. [German *Aplit* : Greek *haplous*, single, simple (see **haploid**) + -ITE.] —**ap·lit·ic** (ā-plĭt′ĭk) *adj.*

a·plomb (ə-plŏm′, ə-plŭm′) *n.* Self-confidence; poise; assurance. [French, uprightness, from Old French *a plomb*, perpendicularly, according to the plummet : *a*, to + *plomb*, plummet, lead weight, from Latin *plumbum*, lead.]

ap·ne·a, ap·noe·a (ăp′nē-ə) *n.* Temporary suspension of respiration. [New Latin, from Greek *apnoia*, absence of respiration : A- (without) + *pnoē*, breathing, from *pnein*, to breathe.] —**ap·ne·ic, ap·noe·ic** (ăp-nē′ĭk) *adj.*

apo-, ap- *prefix.* Indicates: **1.** Being away from; for example, **aphelion. 2.** Lack of; for example, **apogamy. 3.** Separation of; for example, **apocarpous. 4.** *Geology.* Derived from; for example, **apophysis. 5.** *Chemistry.* Derived from; for example **apomorphine.** [In borrowed Greek compounds, *apo-* indicates: **1.** Away from, as in **apogee. 2.** Away, off, as in **apothecary. 3.** Return, as in **apodosis. 4.** Intensive action, as in **aposiopesis. 5.** Keeping off, defense, as in **apology. 6.** Change from an existing state, as in **apotheosis. 7.** Reversal, as in **Apocalypse.** Greek *apo-*, from *apo*, away from, off.]

Apoc. 1. Apocalypse. **2.** Apocrypha; Apocryphal.

A·poc·a·lypse (ə-pŏk′ə-lĭps′) *n.* **1.** *Abbr.* **Apoc.** The last book of the New Testament, **Revelation** *(see)*. **2.** *apocalypse.* A prophetic disclosure or revelation; especially, a vision of the end of the world. **3.** *apocalypse.* An event marked by violent destruction and upheaval. [Middle English *Apocalipse*, from Late Latin *Apocalypsis*, from Greek *apokalupsis*, revelation, from *apokaluptein*, to uncover : *apo-*, reversal + *kaluptein*, to cover.]

a·poc·a·lyp·tic (ə-pŏk′ə-lĭp′tĭk) *adj.* Also **a·poc·a·lyp·ti·cal** (-tĭ-kəl). **1.** Of or pertaining to a prophetic disclosure or revelation. **2.** Portending violent disaster or ultimate doom. **3.** Suggesting the end of the world: *an apocalyptic spectacle.* —**a·poc·a·lyp·ti·cal·ly** *adv.*

ap·o·carp (ăp′ə-kärp′) *n. Botany.* An apocarpous fruit. [Back-formation from APOCARPOUS.]

ap·o·car·pous (ăp′ə-kär′pəs) *adj. Botany.* Having distinctly separated carpels. [APO- + -CARPOUS.] —**ap·o·car·py** (ăp′ə-kär′pē) *n.*

ap·o·ca·tas·ta·sis (ăp′ō-kə-tăs′tə-sĭs) *n. Theology.* The doctrine of Universalism *(see)*. [Latin, from Greek, restoration, from *apokathistanai*, to re-establish, "set back down" : *apo-*, back + *kata-*, down + *histanai*, (cause) to stand.]

ap·o·chro·mat·ic (ăp′ō-krō-măt′ĭk) *adj. Optics.* Corrected for both chromatic and spherical aberration. —**ap·o·chro·ma·tism** (ăp′-ə-krō′mə-tĭz′əm) *n.*

a·poc·o·pe (ə-pŏk′ə-pē) *n.* A cutting off or omitting of the last sound or syllable of a word; for example, *goin'* for *going*. [Latin *apocopē*, from Greek *apokopē*, from *apokoptein*, to cut off : *apo-*, off + *koptein*, to cut.]

ap·o·crine (ăp′ə-krĭn′, -krīn′, -krēn′) *adj.* Of, pertaining to, or designating a gland that loses part of its cytoplasm in secretion. Compare **holocrine, merocrine.** [APO- + Greek *krinein*, to separate.]

A·poc·ry·pha (ə-pŏk′rə-fə) *n.* Used with a singular or plural verb. *Abbr.* **Apoc. 1.** The 14 books of the Septuagint included in the Vulgate but considered uncanonical by Protestants. Eleven of these books are accepted in the Roman Catholic canon, and appear in the Douay Bible. **2.** Various early Christian writings proposed as additions to the New Testament, but rejected by the major canons. **3.** *apocrypha.* Any writings of questionable authorship or authenticity. [Middle English *Apocripha*, from Medieval Latin *scripta apocrypha*, hidden writings (that is, hidden and excluded from the canon because spurious); from Late Latin *apocryphus*, hidden, from

Apis *A bronze statuette of this sacred bull that was worshiped by ancient Egyptians. The statuette, found at Memphis, Egypt, dates from the fourth century* B.C.

Greek *apokruphos*, from *apokruptein*, to hide away : *apo-*, away + *kruptein*, to hide.]

a·poc·ry·phal (ə-pŏk'rə-fəl) *adj.* **1.** Of questionable authorship or authenticity. **2.** False; counterfeit. **3. Apocryphal. Apoc.** Of or pertaining to the Apocrypha. —**a·poc·ry·phal·ly** *adv.*

ap·o·cyn·thi·on (ăp'ə-sĭn'thē-ən) *n.* The point at which a spacecraft launched from earth into orbit around the moon is most distant from the moon. Compare **pericynthion, apolune.** [APO- (away) + *cynthion*, from CYNTHIA (goddess of the moon).]

ap·o·dal (ăp'ə-dəl) *adj. Zoology.* Having no limbs, feet, or footlike appendages. [From Greek *apous* (stem *apod-*) : A- (without) + *pous*, foot.]

ap·o·dic·tic (ăp'ə-dĭk'tĭk) *adj.* Clearly proven or demonstrated; incontestable. [Latin *apodicticus*, from Greek *apodeiktikos*, from *apodeiknunai*, to point out or away from : *apo-*, away from + *deiknunai*, to show.]

a·pod·o·sis (ə-pŏd'ə-sĭs) *n., pl.* **-ses** (-sēz'). *Grammar.* The clause stating the conclusion or consequence of a conditional sentence. Compare **protasis.** [New Latin, from Greek, response (to the protasis), "a giving back," from *apodidonai*, give up or back : *apo-*, back + *didonai*, to give.]

ap·o·dous (ăp'ə-dəs) *adj.* Apodal.

ap·o·en·zyme (ăp'ō-ĕn'zīm') *n.* An inactive enzyme that needs to be combined with a **coenzyme** (*see*) to become functional.

a·pog·a·my (ə-pŏg'ə-mē) *n. Botany.* In ferns, the production of the sporophyte directly from a cell of the gametophyte, without the formation of gametes. Compare **apospory.** [APO- (away from) + -GAMY.] —**ap·o·gam·ic** (ăp'ə-găm'ĭk), **a·pog·a·mous** (ə-pŏg'ə-məs) *adj.*

ap·o·gee (ăp'ə-jē) *n.* **1.** The point in the orbit of the moon or of an artificial satellite most distant from the earth. Compare **perigee.** **2.** The farthest or highest point; the apex. [French *apogée*, from New Latin *apogaeum*, from Greek *apogaion*, neuter of *apogaios*, "away from the earth" : *apo-*, away from + *gaia, gē*, earth.] —**ap·o·ge·an** (ăp'ə-jē'ən) *adj.*

a·po·lit·i·cal (ā'pə-lĭt'ĭ-kəl) *adj.* Having no association with or interest in politics. —**a·po·lit·i·cal·ly** *adv.*

A·pol·li·naire (ä'pô-lē-nâr'), **Guillaume,** born Wilhelm Apollinaris de Kostrowitzky (1880–1918). French poet and leading figure in avant-garde literary and painting circles.

a·pol·lo (ə-pŏl'ō) *n., pl.* **-los.** A young man of great physical beauty. [After APOLLO (the god).]

A·pol·lo[1] (ə-pŏl'lo). *Greek & Roman Mythology.* The god of the sun, prophecy, music, medicine, and poetry.

Apollo[2] *n.* Any of a series of 17 U.S. spacecraft designed to land people on the moon. The first 10 Apollo craft were used to test various aspects of the program, the first moon landing (July, 1969) being achieved by Apollo 11. The remaining members of the series also made manned moon landings, except Apollo 13, which was safely aborted. [After APOLLO (the god).]

Ap·ol·lo·ni·an (ăp'ə-lō'nē-ən) *adj.* **1.** Of or pertaining to Apollo or his cult. **2.** *Often* **apollonian.** In the philosophy of Nietzsche, characteristic of or embodying the theoretical, rational, calm, harmonious qualities of human nature. Compare **dionysian. 3. apollonian.** Noble; dignified; serene. —**Ap·ol·lo·ni·an** *n.*

Ap·ol·lo·ni·us of Per·ga (ăp'ə-lō'nē-əs, pûr'gə) (c. 262 B.C.–c. 190 B.C.). Greek mathematician. He was the first to define, in his work on conic sections, the curves called the parabola, hyperbola, and ellipse.

Apollonius of Rhodes (rōdz). Greek poet of the late 3rd and early 2nd centuries B.C. His epic *Argonautica* recounts the adventures of the Argonauts. Apollonius was also librarian at Alexandria.

a·pol·o·get·ic (ə-pŏl'ə-jĕt'ĭk) *adj.* **1.** Making an apology or excuse. **2.** Conveying self-recrimination and regret: *an apologetic smile.* **3.** Explaining or defending in speech or writing.

~*n.* A formal defense or apology. —**a·pol·o·get·i·cal·ly** *adv.*

a·pol·o·get·ics (ə-pŏl'ə-jĕt'ĭks) *n.* Used with a singular verb. The branch of theology that deals with the defense and proof of Christianity.

ap·o·lo·gi·a (ăp'ə-lō'jē-ə, -jə) *n.* A formal defense or justification. [Latin, APOLOGY.]

a·pol·o·gist (ə-pŏl'ə-jĭst) *n.* A person who argues in defense or justification of another person or cause.

a·pol·o·gize (ə-pŏl'ə-jīz') *intr.v.* **-gized, -gizing, -gizes. 1.** To make excuse for or regretful acknowledgment of a fault or offense. **2.** To make a formal defense or justification in speech or writing. —**a·pol·o·giz·er** *n.*

ap·o·logue (ăp'ə-lôg', -lŏg') *n.* A moral fable. [French *apologue*, from Latin *apologus*, from Greek *apologos*, fable : *apo-*, away, off + *logos*, discourse.]

a·pol·o·gy (ə-pŏl'ə-jē) *n., pl.* **-gies. 1.** A statement, either written or verbal, expressing regret or asking pardon for a fault or offense. **2.** A formal justification or defense. **3.** An inferior substitute: *a poor apology for a dinner.* [French *apologie*, from Late Latin *apologia*, from Greek *apologiā*, speech in defense : *apo-*, defense + *logos*, discourse, speech.]

ap·o·lune (ăp'ə-lōōn') *n.* The point at which a spacecraft launched from the moon into lunar orbit is farthest from the moon. Also called "aposelene." Compare **perilune, apocynthion.** [APO- (away from) + *lune*, from Latin *lūna*, moon.]

ap·o·mict (ăp'ə-mĭkt') *n. Biology.* An organism, especially a plant, that is the result of apomixis. [APO- + Greek *miktos*, mixed, from *mignunai*, to mix.]

ap·o·mix·is (ăp'ə-mĭk'sĭs) *n.* An asexual reproductive process in which a new individual is produced from a female cell or cells other than the egg cell, often in a manner that mimics sexual reproduction. [New Latin : APO- + Greek *mixis*, a mingling, from *mignunai*, to mix.]

ap·o·mor·phine (ăp'ə-môr'fēn') *n.* A poisonous white crystalline alkaloid, $C_{17}H_{17}NO_2$, derived from morphine and used medicinally as an emetic, expectorant, and hypnotic.

ap·o·neu·ro·sis (ăp'ə-nōō-rō'sĭs, ăp'ə-nyōō-) *n., pl.* **-ses** (-sēz'). A sheetlike membrane, resembling a flattened tendon, that forms the end of certain muscles and connects them to bones. [New Latin, from Greek *aponeurōsis*, from *aponeurousthai*, to become a nerve : *apo-* (change) + *neuron*, nerve.] —**ap·o·neu·rot·ic** (ăp'ə-nōō-rŏt'ĭk, ăp'ə-nyōō-) *adj.*

apophthegm. Variant of **apothegm.**

a·poph·y·ge (ə-pŏf'ə-jē) *n. Architecture.* The curvature at the top and bottom of the shaft of a column. [Greek *apophugē*, "escape" : *apo-*, away + *phugē*, flight.]

a·poph·yl·lite (ə-pŏf'ə-līt', ăp'ə-fĭl'īt') *n.* A white, pale-pink, or pale-green crystalline mineral, essentially $KCa_4FSi_4O_{10} \cdot 8H_2O$. [APO- + PHYLLITE.]

a·poph·y·sis (ə-pŏf'ə-sĭs) *n., pl.* **-ses** (-sēz') **1.** *Biology.* A swelling, projection, or outgrowth of an organ or part. **2.** *Geology.* A branch from a dike or vein. [New Latin, from Greek *apophusis*, side-shoot : *apo-*, off, away + *phusis*, growth, from *phuein*, to grow.] —**a·poph·y·sate** (ə-pŏf'ə-sāt'), **a·poph·y·se·al** (ə-pŏf'ə-sē'əl) *adj.*

ap·o·plec·tic (ăp'ə-plĕk'tĭk) *adj.* **1.** Of, resembling, or causing apoplexy. **2.** Having or exhibiting symptoms of apoplexy. **3.** *Informal.* **a.** Of a sort to cause apoplexy: *We found him in an apoplectic fury.* **b.** Extremely annoyed. —**ap·o·plec·ti·cal·ly** *adv.*

ap·o·plex·y (ăp'ə-plĕk'sē) *n.* Sudden loss of muscular control, with diminution or loss of sensation and consciousness, resulting from rupture or blocking of a blood vessel in the brain; a stroke. [Middle English *apoplexie*, from Old French, from Late Latin *apoplēxia*, from Greek, from *apoplēssein*, to cripple by a stroke : *apo-* (intensive) + *plēssein*, to strike.]

a·port (ə-pôrt', ə-pōrt') *adv. Nautical.* On or toward the port, or left, side.

ap·o·se·le·ne (ăp'ō-sə-lē'nē) *n.* An **apolune** (*see*). [APO- (away from) + Greek *selēnē*, moon.]

ap·o·se·mat·ic coloration (ăp'ə-sə-măt'ĭk) *n.* **Warning coloration** (*see*). [APO- (away from) + SEMATIC.]

ap·o·si·o·pe·sis (ăp'ə-sī'ə-pē'sĭs) *n., pl.* **-ses** (-sēz'). A sudden and dramatic breaking off in the middle of a sentence, as though the speaker were unwilling or unable to continue, often done for rhetorical effect. [Late Latin *aposiōpēsis*, from Greek, a becoming silent, from *aposiōpān*, to maintain silence : *apo-* (intensifier) + *siōpān*, to be silent, from *siōpē*, silence.] —**ap·o·si·o·pet·ic** (ăp'ə-sī'ə-pĕt'ĭk) *adj.*

ap·o·spor·y (ăp'ə-spôr'ē, -spōr'ē, ə-pŏs'pə-rē) *n. Botany.* In mosses and ferns, the development of the gametophyte directly from a cell of the sporophyte, without spore formation. Compare **apogamy.** [APO- (away from) + SPOR(E) + -Y (state).]

a·pos·ta·sy (ə-pŏs'tə-sē) *n., pl.* **-sies.** An abandonment of one's religious faith or of any cause or principle to which one was attached. [Middle English *apostasie*, from Late Latin *apostasia*, from Greek, desertion, revolt, from *apostanai*, "to stand away from," rebel : *apo-*, away from + *stanai*, to stand.]

a·pos·tate (ə-pŏs'tāt', -tĭt) *n.* One who is guilty of apostasy. [Middle English, from Late Latin *apostata*, from Greek *apostatēs*, deserter, rebel, from *apostanai*, to rebel. See **apostasy.**] —**a·pos·tate** *adj.*

a·pos·ta·tize (ə-pŏs'tə-tīz') *intr.v.* **-tized, -tizing, -tizes.** To give up or abandon one's faith, political party, or cause.

a pos·te·ri·o·ri (ä' pō-stîr'ē-ôr'ē, -ōr'ē, -ôr'ī', -ōr'ī', ā' pō-stîr'-) *adj. Logic.* Of, pertaining to, or designating arguments, propositions, or knowledge derived from reasoning from facts or particulars to general principles, or from effects to causes; inductive; empirical. Compare **a priori.** [Latin, "from the subsequent."] —**a pos·te·ri·o·ri** *adv.*

a·pos·tle (ə-pŏs'əl) *n.* **1.** *Usually* **Apostle.** Any of the twelve disciples chosen by Christ to preach His gospel. Luke 6:13–16. **2.** A missionary of the early Christian Church. **3.** A leader of the first Christian mission to a country or region. **4.** Any of the twelve members of the Mormon administrative council. **5.** One who leads or advocates a new cause. [Middle English *apostel, apostle*, Old English *apostol*, from Late Latin *apostolus*, from Greek *apostolos*, messenger, envoy, from *apostellein*, to send away from : *apo-*, away from + *stellein*, to place.]

Apostles' Creed *n.* A Christian creed traditionally ascribed to the twelve Apostles.

Apostle spoon, apostle spoon *n.* A spoon, usually of silver, with a handle ending in the figure of an Apostle.

ap·os·tol·ic (ăp'ə-stŏl'ĭk) *adj.* **1.** Of, pertaining to, or contemporary with the Apostles. **2.** Of, pertaining to, or conforming to the faith, teaching, or practice of the Apostles. **3.** Of or pertaining to the pope as successor to Saint Peter.

Apostolic Father *n.* A church father who received personal instruction from the twelve Apostles or from their disciples.

apostolic see *n.* **1.** A bishopric founded, according to tradition, by one of the Apostles. **2. Apostolic See.** The See of Rome founded, according to tradition, by the Apostle Peter.

apostolic succession *n.* The doctrine that authority in the Christian Church is derived from the Apostles through an unbroken succession of bishops.

a·pos·tro·phe¹ (ə-pŏs′trə-fē) n. The superscript sign (′) used in punctuation to indicate the omission of a letter or letters from a word, the omission of a number or numbers, as from a date, the possessive case, and certain plurals, especially those of numbers and letters. [French, from Old French, from Late Latin apostrophus, from Greek (prosōidia) apostrophos, "(accent of) turning away," sign of elision, from apostrephein, to turn away : apo-, away + strephein, to turn.] —**ap·os·troph·ic** (ăp′ə-strŏf′ĭk) adj.

apostrophe² n. A digression in discourse; especially, a rhetorical device by which a speaker or writer breaks off to address an absent or imaginary person. [Latin apostrophē, from Greek, from apostrephein, to turn away. See **apostrophe** (sign).] —**ap·os·troph·ic** (ăp′ə-strŏf′ĭk) adj.

a·pos·tro·phize (ə-pŏs′trə-fīz′) v. -phized, -phizing, -phizes. —tr. To address by apostrophe. —intr. To speak or write in apostrophe.

apothecaries' measure n. A system of liquid volume measure used in pharmacy.

apothecaries' weight n. A system of weights used in pharmacy and based on an ounce equal to 480 grains and a pound equal to 12 ounces.

a·poth·e·car·y (ə-pŏth′ə-kĕr′ē) n., pl. -ries. Abbr. ap. One who prepares and sells drugs and medicines; a pharmacist. [Middle English, from Medieval Latin apothecārius, from Late Latin, from Latin apothēca, storehouse, from Greek apothēkē, from apotithenai, to put away : apo-, away + tithenai, to put.]

ap·o·the·ci·um (ăp′ə-thē′shē-əm, -sē-əm) n., pl. -cia (-shē-ə, -sē-ə). An open disk-shaped or cup-shaped fruiting body in certain fungi that is lined with a layer bearing spores. [New Latin, from Latin apothēca, storehouse (see **apothecary**.)] —**ap·o·the·cial** (ăp′ə-thē′shəl) adj.

ap·o·thegm (ăp′ə-thĕm′) n. A terse and witty instructive saying; maxim. [Greek apophthegma, a pointed saying, from apophthenges-thai, to speak out plainly : apo-, away from + phthengesthai, to speak; akin to phthongos, sound (see **diphthong**.)] —**ap·o·theg·mat·ic** (ăp′ə-thĕg-măt′ĭk) adj. —**ap·o·theg·mat·i·cal·ly** adv.

ap·o·them (ăp′ə-thĕm′) n. Geometry. In a regular polygon, the perpendicular distance from the center to any of the sides. [APO-, away from + Greek thema, position, THEME.]

a·poth·e·o·sis (ə-pŏth′ē-ō′sĭs, ăp′ə-thē′ə-sĭs) n., pl. -ses (-sēz′). 1. Exaltation to divine rank or stature; deification. 2. An exalted or glorified ideal. 3. The culmination or highest development; the quintessence. [Late Latin apotheōsis, from Greek apotheōsis, from apotheoun, to deify : apo- (change) + theos, god.]

ap·o·the·o·size (ăp′ə-thē′ə-sīz′, ə-pŏth′ē-ə-sīz′) tr.v. -sized, -sizing, -sizes. To glorify, exalt, or deify.

ap·o·tro·pa·ic (ăp′ə-trō-pā′ĭk) adj. Having the power to avert or purpose of averting evil: an apotropaic ritual. [Greek apotropaios, from apotrepein, to turn away : apo- away + trepein, to turn.] —**ap·o·tro·pa·i·cal·ly** adv.

app. 1. apparatus. 2. appendix. 3. applied. 4. appoint; appointed.

Ap·pa·la·chi·a (ăp′ə-lā′chē-ə, -chə, -lăch′ē-ə, -lăch′ə). The region including the Appalachian Mountains. In popular usage, Appalachia is often thought to include only the isolated mountain regions of western Virginia and West Virginia. The people living in these areas have long been among the poorest in the United States.

Ap·pa·la·chi·an (ăp′ə-lā′chən, -lā′chē-ən, -lăch′ən) adj. Of, from, or pertaining to the Appalachian Mountains, the Appalachian mountain region, or the inhabitants of the region and their culture.

Appalachian Mountains. Also **Ap·pa·la·chi·ans** (-ənz). Mountain range in eastern North America, stretching from Newfoundland to Alabama. It includes the Alleghenies, Blue Ridge, and Cumberland mountains. The highest peak, Mt. Mitchell (2,037 meters; 6,684 feet), is in North Carolina.

Appalachian Trail. A network of mountain trails covering 3,300 kilometers (2,050 miles). It extends from Mt. Katahdin in central Maine to Springer Mt. in northern Georgia and is the longest continuous hiking path in the world.

ap·pall (ə-pôl′) tr.v. -palled, -palling, -palls. To fill with consternation, dismay, or horror. [Middle English ap(p)allen, from Old French apalir, to grow pale : a-, to, from Latin ad-, to + palir, from Latin pallescere, from pallēre, to be pale.]

ap·pall·ing (ə-pô′lĭng) adj. 1. Causing dismay; frightful; horrifying. 2. Informal. Very bad; terrible: The child had really appalling manners. —**ap·pall·ing·ly** adv.

ap·pa·loo·sa (ăp′ə-loō′sə) n. A horse of a breed developed in northwestern North America, characteristically having a spotted rump. [Probably after the Palouse Indians, who bred the horse.]

ap·pa·nage, ap·a·nage (ăp′ə-nĭj) n. 1. Land or some other source of revenue given by a king for the maintenance of a member of the ruling family. 2. A perquisite. 3. A natural or rightful attribute or adjunct. [French apanage, from Old French, from apaner, to make provisions for, from Medieval Latin appānāre : Latin ad-, to + pānis, bread.]

ap·pa·rat (ăp′ə-rät, ä′pə-rät′) n. The organization and administrative apparatus of a political party, especially that of the Communist party in the U.S.S.R. and other Communist countries. [Russian, from German, APPARATUS.]

ap·pa·rat·chik (ä′pə-rä′chĭk) n., pl. -chiks or -chiki (-chĭ-kē). 1. One who belongs to a Communist apparat. 2. An official, as a bureaucrat, who is slavishly devoted to the organization for which he

works or to his superiors. [Russian : APPARAT + -chik, suffix indicating agent, adherent, member.]

ap·pa·ra·tus (ăp′ə-rā′təs, -răt′əs) n., pl. apparatus or -tuses. Abbr. app. 1. The totality of things provided or necessary for the accomplishment of a particular task or purpose. 2. A machine, instrument, or other piece of equipment with a specific function. 3. Physiology. A group of organs having a collective function: the respiratory apparatus. 4. A political, bureaucratic, or other organizational system. 5. A set of principles or standards, as for judging or testing. [Latin apparātus, from the past participle of apparāre, to prepare : ad-, to + parāre, to make ready.]

apparatus crit·i·cus (krĭt′ĭ-kəs) n. 1. Reference materials used in literary research. 2. Special appendixes, notes, or glossaries in an edition of a text. Also called "critical apparatus." [New Latin, "critical apparatus."]

ap·par·el (ə-păr′əl) n. 1. Clothing, especially outer garments; attire. 2. Something that covers or adorns. 3. The equipment of a vessel, especially a sailing ship. ~tr.v. appareled, -eling, -els. Also Chiefly British -elled, -elling, -els. 1. To clothe; dress. 2. To adorn; embellish. [Middle English appareil, from Old French apareil, preparation, furnishings, from apareillier, to prepare, from Vulgar Latin appariculāre (unattested), from Latin apparāre : ad-, to + parāre, to make ready.]

ap·par·ent (ə-păr′ənt, ə-pâr′-) adj. 1. Readily seen; open to view; visible. 2. Readily understood or perceived; plain or obvious: His pleasure was apparent to everyone. 3. Appearing as such but not necessarily so; seeming: an apparent advantage. —See Synonyms at **evident**. [Middle English, from Old French aparent, present participle of aparoir, to APPEAR.] —**ap·par·ent·ness** n.

apparent horizon n. See **horizon** (sense 1).

ap·par·ent·ly (ə-păr′ənt-lē, ə-pâr′-) adv. 1. So far as one can tell; evidently. 2. According to the information one has: Apparently they're going to cut the interest rate. 3. Seemingly but perhaps not actually.

apparent magnitude n. Astronomy. **Magnitude** (see).

apparent time n. **Local time** (see).

ap·pa·ri·tion (ăp′ə-rĭsh′ən) n. 1. A ghostly figure; a specter. 2. A sudden or unusual sight. 3. The act of appearing; appearance. [Middle English apparicioun, from Old French apparition, from Late Latin apparitiō (stem apparitiōn-), appearance, epiphany (translation of Greek epiphaneia), from Latin appārēre, to APPEAR.] —**ap·pa·ri·tion·al** adj.

ap·par·i·tor (ə-păr′ə-tər) n. An official who was fomerly sent to carry out the orders of an ecclesiastical or civil court. [Latin, from appārēre, to serve, APPEAR (as a servant).]

ap·pas·sio·na·to (ə-päsh′ə-nä′tō) adv. Music. In an impassioned manner. Used as a direction. [Italian, "impassioned," past participle of appassionare, to inspire with passion : ap- (intensive) + passionare, from passione, from Late Latin passiō, PASSION.] —**ap·pas·sio·na·to** adj.

ap·peal (ə-pēl′) n. 1. An earnest or urgent request, entreaty, or supplication. 2. A resort or application to some higher authority, as for sanction, corroboration, or a decision: an appeal to reason. 3. The power of attracting interest or of arousing sympathy: For her the great appeal of crossword puzzles was the intellectual challenge. 4. Law. a. The transfer of a case from a lower to a higher court for a new hearing. b. A request for a new hearing. c. A case so transferred. 5. A campaign to raise funds or resources, usually for a charitable cause: launched an appeal on behalf of the refugees. ~v. appealed, -pealing, -peals. —intr. 1. To make an earnest or urgent request, as for help or sympathy. 2. To resort or have recourse to some higher authority, as for sanction, corroboration, or a decision. 3. To be attractive or interesting. 4. Law. To make or apply for an appeal. —tr. Law. To transfer or apply to transfer (a case) to a higher court for rehearing. [Middle English appelen, apelen, from Old French apeler, from Latin appellāre, to apply to, entreat, address.] —**ap·peal·a·ble** adj. —**ap·peal·er** n. —**ap·peal·ing·ly** adv.

ap·pear (ə-pîr′) intr.v. -peared, -pearing, -pears. 1. To come into view; become visible: A plane appeared in the sky. 2. To come into existence: New strains of viruses appear periodically. 3. To seem or look to be: They appeared unhappy. 4. To seem likely: It appears they will be late. 5. To come before the public; be presented or published. 6. To present oneself formally; especially, in law, to present oneself before a court as defendant, plaintiff, or counsel. [Middle English apperen, aperen, from Old French aparoir, from Latin appārēre : ad-, toward + pārēre†, to show.]

ap·pear·ance (ə-pîr′əns) n. 1. The act or an instance of appearing. 2. An act or instance of being present: put in an appearance. 3. The outward aspect of someone or something. 4. Something that appears; a phenomenon. 5. An apparition. 6. A pretense or semblance; a false show. 7. appearances. Outward indications: Appearances can be deceptive.

ap·pease (ə-pēz′) tr.v. -peased, -peasing, -peases. 1. To bring peace to; soothe. 2. To placate or conciliate by yielding to the demands of. 3. To satisfy or relieve: appease thirst. —See Synonyms at **pacify**. [Middle English appesen, apesen, from Old French apaisier : ap-, to + pais, peace, from Latin pāx.] —**ap·peas·a·ble** adj. —**ap·peas·a·bly** adv. —**ap·peas·er** n.

ap·pease·ment (ə-pēz′mənt) n. 1. a. The act of appeasing. b. The condition of being appeased. 2. The policy of granting concessions to potential enemies with the aim of maintaining peace.

ap·pel (ə-pĕl′) n. Fencing. 1. A quick stamp of the foot used as a feint to produce an opening. **2.** A blow with a weapon to produce an opening. [French, a call, challenge, from *appeler*, to call, from Old French *apeler*, to APPEAL.]

ap·pel·lant (ə-pĕl′ənt) *adj.* Of or pertaining to an appeal; appellate. —*n.* One who appeals a court decision.

ap·pel·late (ə-pĕl′ĭt) *adj.* Having the power to hear appeals and to reverse court decisions: *an appellate court.* [Latin *appellātus*, past participle of *appellāre*, to APPEAL.]

ap·pel·la·tion (ăp′ə-lā′shən) **1.** A name, title, or epithet. **2.** The act of naming. [Middle English *appellacioun*, from Latin *appellātiō* (stem *appellātiōn-*), from *appellāre*, to APPEAL.]

ap·pel·la·tion con·trô·lée (ȧ′pĕ-lȧ′syôN kôN′trō-lā′) *n. French.* A designation awarded to wines of high quality that are produced in limited amounts from specific regions. ["Certified name."]

ap·pel·la·tive (ə-pĕl′ə-tĭv) *adj.* **1.** Of or relating to the assignment of names. **2.** *Grammar.* Used to designate a class; common: *appellative nouns.*
—*n.* A name or descriptive epithet. [Middle English, from Late Latin *appellātīvus*, from *appellāre*, to call by name, APPEAL.] —**ap·pel·la·tive·ly** *adv.*

ap·pel·lee (ăp′ə-lē′) *n. Law.* One against whom an appeal has been taken. [Old French *apele*, from *apeler*, to APPEAL.]

ap·pend (ə-pĕnd′) *tr.v.* **-pended, -pending, -pends. 1.** To add as a supplement. **2.** To attach; fix. Used with *to.* [Latin *appendere* : *ad-*, to + *pendere*, to hang.]

ap·pend·age (ə-pĕn′dĭj) *n.* **1.** Something appended, especially something of lesser importance. **2.** *Biology.* Any part or organ that is joined to an axis or trunk, such as an arthropod limb.
Synonyms: accessory, addition, adjunct, attachment.

ap·pen·dant (ə-pĕn′dənt) *adj.* **1.** Hanging attached; suspended. **2.** Accompanying; attendant: *faith and its appendant hope.* **3.** *Law.* Belonging as a subsidiary right.
—*n.* **1.** Something attached or added. **2.** *Law.* A subsidiary right.

ap·pen·dec·to·my (ăp′ən-dĕk′tə-mē) *n., pl.* **-mies.** The surgical removal of the vermiform appendix. [Latin *appendix* (stem *appendic-*) + -ECTOMY.]

ap·pen·di·ci·tis (ə-pĕn′də-sī′tĭs) *n.* Inflammation of the vermiform appendix. [APPENDIX + -ITIS.]

ap·pen·dic·u·lar (ăp′ən-dĭk′yə-lər) *adj.* **1.** Of, pertaining to, or consisting of an appendage or appendages. **2.** Of or pertaining to the vermiform appendix. **3.** *Biology.* Of or pertaining to limbs: *appen-*

dicular skeleton. [Latin *appendicula*, diminutive of *appendix* (stem *appendic-*), APPENDIX.]

ap·pen·dix (ə-pĕn′dĭks) *n., pl.* **-dixes** or **-dices** (-də-sēz′) *Abbr.* **app. 1. a.** An appendage. **b.** A collection of supplementary material at the end of a book. **2.** The **vermiform appendix** (see). [Latin *appendix*, appendage, from *appendere*, to APPEND.]
Usage: In its medical sense, the plural is *appendixes.* In the sense of "supplementary material at the end of a book," formal usage still prefers *appendices.*

ap·per·ceive (ăp′ər-sēv′) *tr.v.* **-ceived, -ceiving, -ceives. 1.** To be conscious of perceiving. **2.** *Psychology.* To perceive in terms of past perceptions. [Middle English *apperceiven*, *aperceiven*, from Old French *aperceivre* : *a-*, toward + *perceivre*, to PERCEIVE.]

ap·per·cep·tion (ăp′ər-sĕp′shən) *n.* **1.** Conscious perception with full awareness. **2.** *Psychology.* The process of understanding by which newly observed qualities of something are related to past experience. —**ap·per·cep·tive** (ăp′ər-sĕp′tĭv) *adj.*

Ap·pert (ȧ-pâr′), **Nicolas** (*c.* 1749–1841). French inventor of preserving food by enclosing it in sealed jars.

ap·per·tain (ăp′ər-tān′) *intr.v.* **-tained, -taining, -tains.** To belong as a function or part; pertain properly. Used with *to.* [Middle English *apperteinen*, from Old French *apartenir*, from Vulgar Latin *appartenere* (unattested), variant of Late Latin *appertinēre*, to PERTAIN.]

ap·pe·stat (ăp′ə-stăt′) *n.* The mechanism in the hypothalamus of the brain that controls appetite. [APPE(TITE) + -STAT.]

ap·pe·tence (ăp′ə-təns) *n.* Also **ap·pe·ten·cy** (-tən-sē) *pl.* **-cies. 1.** A strong craving or desire. **2.** A tendency or proclivity; a propensity. [Latin *appetentia*, from *appetēns* (stem *appetent-*), present participle of *appetere*, to strive after, desire eagerly. See **appetite.**]

ap·pe·tite (ăp′ə-tīt′) *n.* **1.** A desire for food or drink. **2.** Any physical craving or desire. **3.** A strong wish or urge: *Some students have a great appetite for learning.* [Middle English *appetit, apetit*, from Old French *apetit*, from Latin *appetītus*, from *appetere*, to strive after, desire eagerly : *ad-*, toward + *petere*, to seek.] —**ap·pe·ti·tive** (ăp′ə-tī′tĭv, ə-pĕt′ə-tĭv) *adj.*

ap·pe·tiz·er (ăp′ə-tī′zər) *n.* **1.** A food or drink served before a meal, or before the main course of a meal, to stimulate the appetite. **2.** Something that stimulates the senses or arouses expectations.

ap·pe·tiz·ing (ăp′ə-tī′zĭng) *adj.* Stimulating or appealing to the appetite.

Ap·pi·an Way (ăp′ē-ən) *n.* Roman road connecting Rome and Capua, and later extended to Brundisium (Brindisi), some 589 kilo-

---

apple

THE STONE-AGE FRUIT THAT BECAME PART OF POPULAR LEGEND

A symbol of fruitfulness and a charm for lovers—but not in the Garden of Eden

The apple has been eaten by man since at least the New Stone Age—nearly 6,000 years ago—when it grew wild in Europe and western Asia. So great was its appeal that it entered into mythology as a symbol of fruitfulness and has been thought of as a love charm, a means to perpetual youth, and a medicine. But despite popular belief it is not mentioned in the Bible as the fruit Eve ate in the Garden of Eden. The Book of Genesis refers only to "the fruit of the tree which is in the midst of the garden."

Today's apple, of which there are several thousand varieties, has been developed, frequently by grafting, from the wild apple to produce strains that are resistant to disease and have particular flavors and colors.

Apples may be divided into two main groups, the sweetest for eating, and sharper varieties for cooking and for making alcoholic drinks such as cider and apple brandy (calvados or applejack).

Rhode Island Greening, a cooking apple, dates from colonial days.

Winesap is an old favorite cider apple.

Chenango Strawberry apple ripens early.

Rome Beauty is a large apple used for cooking.

Grimes Golden is a richly flavored winter apple.

Jonathan apple is good for eating and cooking.

Roxbury Russet ripens late and gains sweetness in storage.

Spitzenburg was the favorite apple of Thomas Jefferson.

York Imperial, an excellent keeper, comes from eastern Pennsylvania.

meters (366 miles). It was inaugurated in 312 B.C. by the censor Appius Claudius Caecus.

appl. applied.

ap·plaud (ə-plôd′) v. **-plauded, -plauding, -plauds.** —*intr.* To express approval, especially by clapping the hands. —*tr.* **1.** To express approval of, especially by clapping the hands. **2.** To praise; approve. [Latin *applaudere,* to clap at : *ad-,* to + *plaudere†,* to clap.] —**ap·plaud·er** n.

ap·plause (ə-plôz′) n. Publicly expressed approval, especially when shown by the clapping of hands. [Medieval Latin *applausus,* from Latin, past participle of *applaudere,* to APPLAUD.]

ap·ple (ăp′əl) n. **1. a.** A tree, *Pyrus malus,* of temperate regions, having fragrant pink or white flowers and edible fruit. **b.** The firm, rounded fruit of this tree, having skin that is red, yellow, or green. **2. a.** Any of several trees or plants having fruit resembling the apple, such as the **custard apple** *(see).* **b.** The fruit of any of these trees or plants. **3.** The hard wood of an apple tree. —**apple of one's eye.** A precious or much-loved person or thing: *My granddaughter is the apple of my eye.* [Middle English *appel,* Old English *æppel.*]

ap·ple·cart (ăp′əl-kärt′) n. A cart loaded with apples. —**upset the applecart.** To spoil a plan or scheme.

apple green n. Moderate to vivid yellowish green. —**ap·ple-green** (ăp′əl-grēn′) adj.

ap·ple·jack (ăp′əl-jăk′) n. Brandy distilled from cider. [APPLE + JACK (fellow, chap).]

ap·ple-pie bed (ăp′əl-pī′) n. A bed which has been made with one of the sheets folded double as a joke, so that one cannot lie down. [Perhaps alteration of French *nappe pliée,* folded sheet.]

apple-pie order n. *Informal.* Excellent order: *The guests left their room in apple-pie order.*

ap·ple-pol·ish (ăp′əl-pŏl′ĭsh) intr.v. **-ished, -ishing, -ishes.** *Informal.* To seek favor by toadying. —**ap·ple-pol·ish·er** n.

ap·ple sauce (ăp′əl-sôs′) n. **1.** Apples stewed to a pulp, sweetened, and sometimes spiced. **2.** *Slang.* Foolishness; nonsense.

Appleseed, Johnny. See John **Chapman.**

Ap·ple·ton layer (ăp′əl-tən) n. The **F layer** *(see)* of the ionosphere. [After Sir Edward *Appleton* (1892–1965), British physicist.]

ap·pli·ance (ə-plī′əns) n. **1.** A device or instrument; especially, one operated by electricity and designed for household use, such as a refrigerator or vacuum cleaner. **2.** An attachment or accessory; especially, one that adapts a tool for a different use. —See Synonyms at **tool.** [From APPLY.]

ap·pli·ca·ble (ăp′lĭ-kə-bəl, ə-plĭk′ə-) adj. **1.** Capable of being applied; appropriate. **2.** In force; effective: *New rates are applicable from Monday.* —**ap·pli·ca·bil·i·ty** n. —**ap·pli·ca·bly** adv.

ap·pli·cant (ăp′lĭ-kənt) n. One who applies, as for a job. [Latin *applicāns* (stem *applicant-*), present participle of *applicāre,* to APPLY.]

ap·pli·ca·tion (ăp′lĭ-kā′shən) n. **1.** The act of applying or putting something on. **2.** Anything that is applied, such as a cosmetic or curative agent. **3.** The act of putting something to a special use or purpose. **4. a.** A method of applying or using; a specific use: *industrial applications.* **b.** The capacity of being usable; relevance: *The theory has no application in this case.* **5.** Attention, diligence, or effort. **6. a.** A formal request, as for employment or admission. **b.** A written statement making such a request. **c.** The printed form upon which such a statement is often made: *fill out an application.* [Middle English *applicacioun,* from Latin *applicātiō* (stem *applicātiōn-*), from *applicāre,* to APPLY.]

ap·pli·ca·tive (ăp′lĭ-kā′tĭv, ə-plĭk′ə-) adj. **1.** Characterized by actual application to something. **2.** Of practical use; applicatory. —**ap·pli·ca·tive·ly** adv.

ap·pli·ca·tor (ăp′lĭ-kā′tər) n. An instrument for applying something, such as a medicament or glue.

ap·pli·ca·to·ry (ăp′lĭ-kə-tôr′ē, -tōr′ē, ə-plĭk′ə-) adj. Of practical value; useful.

ap·plied (ə-plīd′) adj. Abbr. **app., appl.** Intended to have practical consequences; capable of being put to practical use: *applied physics.* Compare **theoretical.**

ap·pli·qué (ăp′lĭ-kā′) n. A decoration or ornament, as in needlework, made by cutting pieces of one material and applying them to the surface of another.

~adj. Of or like appliqué.

~tr.v. **appliquéd, -quéing, -qués.** To decorate with appliqué work. [French, past participle of *appliquer,* to put on, apply, from Latin *applicāre,* to APPLY.]

ap·ply (ə-plī′) v. **-plied, -plying, -plies.** —*tr.* **1.** To bring near to or into contact with something; put on or onto: *apply the glue to both surfaces.* **2.** To put to or adapt for a special use: *This principle is applied in glass manufacture.* **3.** To use (an epithet, for example) with reference to a particular person or thing. Used with *to.* **4.** To devote (oneself or one's efforts) to something. **5.** To bring into operation: *applied the brakes.* —*intr.* **1.** To be pertinent or relevant. **2.** To request or seek employment, acceptance, or admission. Used with *for* or *to.* [Middle English *applien, aplien,* from Old French *aplier,* from Latin *applicāre,* to join to, apply to : *ad-,* to + *plicāre,* to fold together.]

ap·pog·gia·tu·ra (ə-pŏj′ə-tŏŏr′ə) n. *Music.* A grace note of varying length, usually one step above or below the note it precedes. Compare **acciaccatura.** [Italian, "a supporting," from *appoggiare,* to lean on, from Vulgar Latin *appodiāre* (unattested) : Latin *ad-,* to +

podium, balcony, from Greek *podion,* small foot, base, diminutive of *pous* (stem *pod-*), foot.]

ap·point (ə-point′) tr.v. **-pointed, -pointing, -points.** Abbr. **app., appt. 1.** To select or designate to fill an office or position. **2.** To fix or set by authority or by mutual agreement. **3.** To order, require, or enjoin with authority; prescribe. **4.** To furnish; equip. Used chiefly in the passive and in combination: *a well-appointed apartment.* **5.** *Law.* To direct the disposition of (property) to a person or persons in exercise of a power granted for this purpose by a preceding deed. [Middle English *appointen, apointen,* from Old French *apointier,* to arrange, from *(rendre) à point,* "(to bring) to a point" : *a-,* to + POINT.] —**ap·point·ee** (ə-poin′tē′, ăp′oin-tē′) n.

ap·point·ive (ə-poin′tĭv) adj. Pertaining to or filled by appointment: *an appointive office.*

ap·point·ment (ə-point′mənt) n. **1.** The act of appointing or state of being appointed, as to an office or position. **2.** The office or position to which a person has been appointed. **3.** An arrangement to do something or meet someone at a particular time and place. **4.** *Usually* **appointments.** Fittings or equipment. **5.** *Law.* The act of directing the disposition of property by virtue of a power granted under a preceding deed.

ap·point·or (ə-poin′tər, ə-poin′tôr′) n. *Law.* One who executes a power of appointment of property.

Ap·po·mat·tox (ăp′ə-măt′əks). Town in central Virginia where the Civil War came to a close. The Confederate general Robert E. Lee surrendered to the Union general Ulysses S. Grant here on April 9, 1865.

ap·port (ə-pôrt′, ə-pōrt′) n. **1.** In spiritualism, the act of conjuring up or transporting a material object. **2.** The object so transported. [Middle English *a bringing,* from Old French *aport,* from Medieval Latin *apportum,* offering, contribution, from Latin *apportāre* : *ad-,* near to + *portāre,* to carry.]

ap·por·tion (ə-pôr′shən, ə-pōr′-) tr.v. **-tioned, -tioning, -tions.** To divide and assign according to some plan or proportion; allot; partition. —See Synonyms at **assign.** [French *apportionner* : *a-,* to + *portionner,* to divide into portions, from PORTION.]

ap·por·tion·ment (ə-pôr′shən-mənt, ə-pōr′-) n. **1. a.** The act of apportioning or the condition of being apportioned. **b.** An amount apportioned. **2.** The proportional distribution of the number of members of the U.S. House of Representatives on the basis of the population of each state.

ap·pose (ă-pōz′) tr.v. **-posed, -posing, -poses. 1.** To put or apply (one thing) to another. **2.** To arrange (things) near to each other or side by side. [Back-formation from APPOSITION (by analogy with COMPOSE, COMPOSITION).]

ap·po·site (ăp′ə-zĭt) adj. Fitting; suitable; appropriate. —See Synonyms at **relevant.** [Latin *appositus,* "situated near," past participle of *appōnere,* to place near to, apply to. See **apposition.**] —**ap·po·site·ly** adv. —**ap·po·site·ness** n.

ap·po·si·tion (ăp′ə-zĭsh′ən) n. **1.** *Grammar.* **a.** A construction in which one noun or noun phrase is placed after another to explain it, both having the same function in the sentence. In the sentence *Copley, the famous painter, was born in Boston, Copley* and *the famous painter* are in apposition. **b.** The relationship between such nouns or noun phrases. **2.** A placing side by side or next to each other. **3.** *Biology.* The growth in thickness of a cell wall by deposition of successive layers of material. [Middle English *apposicioun,* from Medieval Latin *appositiō* (stem *appositiōn-*), from Latin *appōnere* (past participle *appositus*), to place near to, apply to : *ad-,* near to + *pōnere,* to put.] —**ap·po·si·tion·al** adj. —**ap·po·si·tion·al·ly** adv.

ap·pos·i·tive (ə-pŏz′ə-tĭv) adj. Of, pertaining to, or being in apposition.

~n. A word or phrase that is in apposition. [From APPOSITION.] —**ap·pos·i·tive·ly** adv.

ap·prais·al (ə-prā′zəl) n. **1.** The act of appraising. **2.** An account or evaluation of the merits and defects of someone or something. **3.** An expert or official valuation of something, as for taxation.

ap·praise (ə-prāz′) tr.v. **-praised, -praising, -praises. 1.** To evaluate the importance or worth of, especially in an official capacity. **2.** To estimate the quality, amount, size, and other features of; judge. —See Synonyms at **estimate.** [Middle English *appreisen,* partly from *preise,* value, PRAISE, partly from Old French *aprisier,* from Late Latin *appretiāre,* to set a value on : *ad-,* to + *pretiāre,* to value, from Latin *pretium,* price.] —**ap·prais·a·ble** adj. —**ap·praise·ment** n. —**ap·prais·er** n.

ap·pre·cia·ble (ə-prē′shə-bəl) adj. Capable of being noticed, estimated, or measured; noticeable. —See Synonyms at **perceptible.** —**ap·pre·cia·bly** adv.

ap·pre·ci·ate (ə-prē′shē-āt′) v. **-ated, -ating, -ates.** —*tr.* **1.** To be fully aware of or sensitive to; realize: *He doesn't appreciate the difficulties involved.* **2.** To recognize the quality, significance, or magnitude of; value: *appreciated their freedom.* **3.** To be thankful or show gratitude for. **4.** To enjoy and understand critically or emotionally: *appreciates fine wines.* **5.** To raise in value or price. —*intr.* To go up in value or price: *Their art collection appreciates every year.* [Late Latin *appretiāre,* to set a value on : *ad-,* to + *pretiāre,* to value, from *pretium,* price.] —**ap·pre·ci·a·tor** n.

Synonyms: *cherish, esteem, prize, treasure, value.*

ap·pre·ci·a·tion (ə-prē′shē-ā′shən) n. **1.** Gratefulness; gratitude. **2.** Awareness or delicate perception, especially of aesthetic qualities or values: *an appreciation of Manet's brushwork.* **3.** An assessment of the true nature of someone or something: *a fair appreciation of*

apricot *Although the apricot is native to central Asia and China, it is widely cultivated in other parts of the world for canning and jam making.*

the economic situation. **4.** A usually favorable expression of criticism. **5.** A rise in value or price.

ap·pre·cia·tive (ə-prē′shə-tĭv, -shē-ā′tĭv) *adj.* Capable of or showing appreciation. **—ap·pre·cia·tive·ly** *adv.*

ap·pre·hend (ăp′rĭ-hĕnd′) *v.* **-hended, -hending, -hends.** *—tr.* **1.** To take into custody; arrest. **2.** To grasp mentally; understand. **3.** To look forward to fearfully; anticipate with anxiety. *—intr.* To understand. [Middle English *apprehenden,* from Latin *apprehendere,* to lay hold of, seize : *ad-,* to + *prehendere,* to seize.]

Synonyms: *comprehend, grasp, understand.*

ap·pre·hen·si·ble (ăp′rĭ-hĕn′sə-bəl) *adj.* Capable of being apprehended or understood. **—ap·pre·hen·si·bly** *adv.*

ap·pre·hen·sion (ăp′rĭ-hĕn′shən) *n.* **1.** A fearful or uneasy anticipation of the future. **2.** A seizing or capturing; an arrest. **3.** The ability to apprehend or understand; understanding. **4.** An opinion or estimate. [Middle English *apprehensioun,* from Late Latin *apprehensiō* (stem *apprehensiōn-*), from *apprehendere* (past participle *apprehensus*), APPREHEND.]

Synonyms: *foreboding, misgiving, presentiment.*

ap·pre·hen·sive (ăp′rĭ-hĕn′sĭv) *adj.* **1.** Anxious or fearful about the future; uneasy. **2.** Capable of understanding; quick to apprehend. **3.** Aware; cognizant. **—ap·pre·hen·sive·ly** *adv.* **—ap·pre·hen·sive·ness** *n.*

ap·pren·tice (ə-prĕn′tĭs) *n.* **1.** One bound by legal agreement to work for another for a given length of time in return for instruction in a trade, art, or business. **2.** A person who is learning a trade or occupation, especially as a member of a labor union. **3.** A beginner; a learner.

~tr.v. **apprenticed, -ticing, -tices.** To place or take on as an apprentice; bind by indenture. [Middle English *aprentis,* from Old French, from *aprendre,* to learn, from Latin *appre(he)ndere,* to APPREHEND.] **—ap·pren·tice·ship** *n.*

ap·pressed (ə-prĕst′) *adj.* Lying flat or pressed closely against something, as leaves on a stem. [Latin *appressus,* past participle of *apprimere,* to press to : *ad-,* to + *premere,* to press.]

ap·prise (ə-prīz′) *tr.v.* **-prised, -prising, -prises.** To cause to know; make aware; inform. Used with *of.* [French *apprendre* (past participle *appris*), to cause to learn, inform, from Old French *aprendre,* to learn, from Latin *appre(he)ndere,* to APPREHEND.]

ap·proach (ə-prōch′) *v.* **-proached, -proaching, -proaches.** *—intr.* To come near or nearer in space, time, or magnitude. *—tr.* **1.** To come near or nearer to. **2.** To come close to in appearance, quality, condition, or other characteristics; approximate: *Her talent approaches genius.* **3.** To make a proposal to; make overtures to. **4.** To begin to deal with or work on. **5.** To bring or draw closer: *The scientist approached the microscope to the slide.*

~n. **1.** The act of coming or drawing near. **2.** A fairly close resemblance; an approximation. **3.** A way or means of reaching someone or a destination; an access: *All approaches to the town are blocked.* **4.** The method used in dealing with or accomplishing something: *We took a logical approach to the problem.* **5.** *Often* **approaches.** An advance or overture made by one person to another. **6.** In golf, the stroke following the drive from the tee with which the player tries to get the ball onto the putting green. **7.** The last stage in an aircraft's flight before it lands: *We are now commencing the approach to the airport.* **8. approaches.** *Military.* Works such as trenches or bulwarks for the protection of troops besieging a fortified position. [Middle English *aprochen,* from Old French *aprochier,* from Late Latin *appropiāre,* to go nearer to : *ad-,* to + *propius,* nearer, from *prope,* near.]

ap·proach·a·ble (ə-prō′chə-bəl) *adj.* **1.** Capable of being approached or reached; accessible. **2.** Easily approached; receptive to overtures; friendly. **—ap·proach·a·bil·i·ty** *n.*

ap·pro·bate (ăp′rə-bāt′) *tr.v.* **-bated, -bating, -bates.** To give permission or approval for; sanction or authorize. [Middle English *approbaten,* from Latin *approbāre,* to APPROVE.] **—ap·pro·ba·tive** (ăp′rə-bā′tĭv, ə-prō′bə-tĭv), **ap·pro·ba·to·ry** (ə-prō′bə-tôr′ē, -tōr′ē) *adj.*

ap·pro·ba·tion (ăp′rə-bā′shən) *n.* **1.** Praise; commendation. **2.** Official approval. —See Synonyms at **regard.**

ap·pro·pri·a·ble (ə-prō′prē-ə-bəl) *adj.* Capable of being appropriated.

ap·pro·pri·ate (ə-prō′prē-ĭt) *adj.* Suitable for a particular person, condition, occasion, or place; proper or fitting: *A book would be an appropriate gift.* —See Synonyms at **fit.**

~tr.v. (ə-prō′prē-āt′) **appropriated, -ating, -ates. 1.** To set apart for a specific use. **2.** To take possession of or make use of exclusively for oneself, often without permission. [Middle English *appropriaten,* from Late Latin *appropriāre* (past participle *appropriātus*), to make one's own : Latin *ad-,* to + *proprius,* own.] **—ap·pro·pri·ate·ly** *adv.* **—ap·pro·pri·ate·ness** *n.* **—ap·pro·pri·a·tive** (ə-prō′prē-ā′tĭv, -ə-tĭv) *adj.* **—ap·pro·pri·a·tor** *n.*

ap·pro·pri·a·tion (ə-prō′prē-ā′shən) *n.* **1.** The act of appropriating for a specific use or purpose. **2.** The act of appropriating to oneself. **3.** Public funds set aside for a specific purpose.

ap·prov·al (ə-pro͞o′vəl) *n.* **1.** The act or an instance of approving. **2.** Commendation; favorable regard; good opinion. **—on approval.** For examination or trial by a potential customer without the obligation to buy.

ap·prove (ə-pro͞ov′) *v.* **-proved, -proving, -proves.** *—tr.* **1.** To confirm or consent to officially; sanction; ratify: *approve the proposals.* **2.** To view with approval; commend. **3.** *Obs.* To prove or demonstrate: *"the letter he spoke of which approves him an intelligent party"* (Shakespeare). *—intr.* To feel, voice, or demonstrate approval. Usually used with *of*: *approve of capital punishment.* [Middle English *approven,* from Old French *aprover,* from Latin *approbāre,* to make good, admit as good : *ad-,* to + *probus,* good.] **—ap·prov·a·ble** *adj.* **—ap·prov·ing·ly** *adv.*

Synonyms: *certify, endorse, ratify, sanction.*

approved school *n. Chiefly British.* Formerly, a school for young offenders. Compare **community home.**

approx. approximate; approximately.

ap·prox·i·mate (ə-prŏk′sə-mĭt) *adj. Abbr.* **approx. 1.** Almost exact, correct, complete, or perfect. **2.** Very similar; closely resembling. **3.** Close together; near.

~v. (ə-prŏk′sə-māt′) **approximated, -mating, -mates.** *—tr.* **1.** To come close to; be nearly the same as. **2.** To cause to approach; bring near. *—intr.* To come near or close in degree, nature, quality, or other characteristics. [Late Latin *approximātus,* past participle of *approximāre,* to come near to : Latin *ad-,* to + *proximāre,* to come near, from *proximus,* nearest.]

ap·prox·i·mate·ly (ə-prŏk′sə-mĭt-lē) *adv.* Almost but not exactly; about: *It's approximately two o'clock.*

ap·prox·i·ma·tion (ə-prŏk′sə-mā′shən) *n.* **1.** The act, process, or result of approximating. **2.** A nearly accurate account, calculation, or estimate: *an approximation of the facts.* **3.** *Mathematics.* An inexact result or relationship, adequate for a given purpose. **—ap·prox·i·ma·tive** (ə-prŏk′sə-mā′tĭv, -mə-tĭv) *adj.* **—ap·prox·i·ma·tive·ly** *adv.*

appt. appoint; appointed.

ap·pulse (ə-pŭls′, ă-pŭls′) *n.* An apparent close approach of two celestial bodies in which no occultation or eclipse occurs. [Latin *appulsus,* approach, from past participle of *appellere,* to drive toward : *ad-,* toward + *pellere,* to drive.]

ap·pur·te·nance (ə-pûrt′n-əns) *n.* **1.** Something added to another more important thing; an appendage; an accessory. **2. appurtenances.** Equipment, such as clothing or tools, used for a specific purpose or task; gear. **3.** *Law.* A right, privilege, or minor property that is considered as accompanying the principal property for purposes such as passage of title, conveyance, or inheritance. [Middle English *appurtenaunce,* from Norman-French *apurtenance,* variant of Old French *apertenance,* from Vulgar Latin *appertinentia* (unattested), from Late Latin *appertinēre,* to APPERTAIN.]

ap·pur·te·nant (ə-pûrt′n-ənt) *adj.* **1.** *Law.* Constituting an appurtenance. **2.** Belonging, accessory, or relating.

Apr. April.

a·prax·i·a (ā-prăk′sē-ə) *n.* The inability to perform coordinated movements as a result of lesions in the cerebral cortex. [New Latin, from Greek, inaction : *a-,* without + Greek *praxis,* action, from *prassein,* to do.] **—a·prac·tic** (ā-prăk′tĭk) *adj.*

a·près- *comb. form.* Indicates a time following a specified period or activity; for example, **après-ski.** [French, "after."]

a·près-ski (ä′prā-skē′, ăp′rā-) *n.* Social activities in the afternoon or evening at a ski resort. **—a·près-ski** *adj.*

a·pri·cot (ăp′rĭ-kŏt′, ā′prĭ-) *n.* **1.** A tree, *Prunus armeniaca,* native to western Asia and Africa, widely cultivated for its edible fruit. **2.** The juicy, yellow-orange peachlike fruit of this tree. **3.** Moderate, light, or strong orange to orange yellow. [Earlier *abrecock,* perhaps from obsolete Catalan *abercoc,* from Arabic *al-birqūq,* "the apricot," from Late Greek *praikokion,* from Latin *(prūnum) praecoquum,* "early-ripening (plum)," from *praecoquere,* to ripen early : *prae-,* before + *coquere,* to ripen, cook.] **—a·pri·cot** *adj.*

A·pril (ā′prəl) *n. Abbr.* **Apr.** The fourth month of the year according to the Gregorian calendar. April has 30 days. See feature at **calendar.** [Middle English, from Latin *aprīlis,* perhaps "month of Venus," from Etruscan *apru,* from Greek *Aphrō,* short form of *Aphroditē,* APHRODITE.]

April fool *n.* The victim of a trick played on April Fools' Day.

April Fools' Day *n.* April 1, marked as a day for playing practical jokes. Also called "All Fools' Day."

a pri·o·ri (ä′ prē-ôr′ē, -ōr′ē, ā′ prī-ôr′ī′, -ōr′ī′) *adj.* **1.** *Logic.* Pertaining to or proceeding from a known or assumed cause or general principle to a necessarily related effect or conclusion; deductive. **2. a.** Based on reason alone; not provable empirically. **b.** Based on a hypothesis or convention rather than on experiment or experience. **3.** Claimed as true without examination; not supported by factual study. Compare **a posteriori.** [Latin, "from the previous (causes or hypotheses)."] **—a·pri·or·i·ty** (ä′prē-ôr′ə-tē, ā′prī-) *n.*

a·pron (ā′prən) *n.* **1.** A garment worn over all or part of the front of the body to protect one's clothes or as a decorative part of a costume. **2.** Anything resembling an apron in appearance or function. **3.** The hard-surfaced area in front of and around airport hangars and terminal buildings. **4.** The part of a stage in a theater extending in front of the curtain. **5. a.** A platform of planking or other material at the entrance to a dock. **b.** A covering or structure along the shoreline of a body of water for protection against erosion. **c.** A platform serving a similar purpose below a dam or in a sluiceway. **6.** A continuous conveyor belt. **7.** *Geology.* An area covered by sand and gravel deposited at the front of a glacial moraine. **8.** A panel, board, or the like between a windowsill and a board. **9.** A metal plate that protects a machine operator, gunner, or the like from pieces of flying debris. **—tied to someone's apron strings.** Dominated by, controlled by, or dependent on another person, usually a wife or mother.

~tr.v. **aproned, aproning, aprons.** To cover, protect, or provide with an apron; put an apron or aprons on. [Middle English *(an) apron,* originally *(a) napron,* from Old French *naperon,* diminutive

PRONUNCIATION KEY

ă, pat; ā, pay; âr, care; ä, father, are; b, bib; ch, church; d, deed; ĕ, pet; ē, be; f, fife; g, gag; h, hat; hw, which; ĭ, pit; ī, pie; îr, pier; j, judge; k, kick; l, lid, needle; m, mum; n, no, sudden; ng, thing; ŏ, pot; ō, toe; ô, paw, for; oi, noise; ou, out; o͝o, book; o͞o, boot; p, pop; r, roar; s, sauce; sh, ship, dish; t, tight; th, thin, path; *th,* this, bathe; ŭ, cut; ûr, fur; v, valve; w, with; y, yes; z, zebra, size; zh, vision; ə, about, item, edible, gallop, circus, peaceful

IN FOREIGN WORDS:

à, *Fr.* ami; œ, *Fr.* feu, *Ger.* schön; ü, *Fr.* tu, *Ger.* über; KH, *Ger.* ich, *Scot.* loch; N, *Fr.* bon; y′, *Fr.* Compiègne

STRESS MARKS:

Primary stress: ′ **in·cite′** (ĭn-sīt′)
Secondary stress: ′ **in′sight′** (ĭn′sīt′)

of *nape,* tablecloth, from Latin *mappa,* napkin.]

apron stage *n.* A part of the Elizabethan stage that extends into the area occupied by the audience.

ap·ro·pos (ăp′rə-pō′) *adj.* Appropriate; pertinent; opportune.
~*adv.* **1.** Pertinently; relevantly; opportunely. **2.** By the way; incidentally. Used to introduce a remark.
~*prep.* Also **apropos of.** Speaking of; with reference to. [French *à propos,* "to the purpose."]

a·pro·tic (ā-prō′tĭk) *adj. Chemistry.* Having no protons; not producing or accepting hydrogen ions. Used of substances or solutions that are not hydrogen acids or hydroxide bases. [A- (without) + PROT(ON) + -IC.]

apse (ăps) *n.* **1.** *Architecture.* A semicircular or polygonal, usually domed, projection of a building, especially at the altar or east end of a church. Also called "apsis." **2.** *Astronomy.* An orbital position, **apsis** *(see).* [Medieval Latin *apsis, absis.* See **apsis.**] —**ap·si·dal** (ăp′sə-dəl) *adj.*

ap·sis (ăp′sĭs) *n., pl.* **-sides** (-sə-dēz′) **1.** *Astronomy.* The point of greatest or least distance of a celestial body from a center of attraction. Also called "apse." **2.** *Architecture.* An apse. [Medieval Latin *apsis,* architectural apse, from Latin, arch, vault, orbit, from Greek *apsis, hapsis,* "a fastening together," from *haptein*†, to fasten.]

apt (ăpt) *adj.* **1.** Exactly suitable; appropriate: *That was an apt reply.* **2.** Likely: *The handle is apt to break off.* **3.** Having a tendency; inclined: *He is apt to stammer when he is excited.* **4.** Quick to learn or understand. —See Synonyms at **fit, relevant.** [Middle English, from Latin *aptus,* fit, suited, from the past participle of *apere,* to fasten.] —**apt·ly** *adv.* —**apt·ness** *n.*

APT (ā′pē-tē′) *n.* A computer programming language designed for use with computer-controlled machine tools. [*A*utomatically *Pro*grammed *T*ool.]

apt. apartment.

ap·ter·al (ăp′tər-əl) *adj. Architecture.* Having no columns along the sides. [Greek *apteros,* wingless, APTEROUS.]

ap·ter·ous (ăp′tər-əs) *adj.* **1.** *Zoology.* Having no wings: *an apterous insect.* **2.** *Botany.* Having no winglike parts or extensions. [Greek *apteros,* wingless : *a-,* without + -PTEROUS.]

ap·ter·yg·i·al (ăp′tə-rĭj′ē-əl) *adj. Zoology.* Without wings or fins. [A- (without) + Greek *pterux* (stem *pterug-*), wing, fin.]

ap·ter·yx (ăp′tə-rĭks) *n.* A bird, the **kiwi** *(see).* [New Latin : A- (without) + Greek *pterux,* wing, from *pteron,* feather, wing.]

ap·ti·tude (ăp′tə-to͞od′, -tyo͞od′) *n.* **1.** A natural or acquired talent, skill, or ability: *an aptitude for sculpture.* **2.** Quickness in learning and understanding; intelligence. **3.** The state or quality of being fitting; aptness. —See Synonyms at **ability.** [Middle English, from Late Latin *aptitūdō,* fitness, from *aptus,* APT.]

aptitude test *n.* A standardized test designed to measure the ability of an individual to develop skills or acquire knowledge.

A·pu·lei·us (ăp′yə-lē′əs), **Lucius,** also known as "Apuleius of Madaura" (A.D. *c.* 125–*c.* 180). Roman philosopher and satirist, born in Numidia. His most famous work, *The Golden Ass,* or *Metamorphoses,* is the story of a man who is changed into an ass.

A·pu·lia (ə-po͞ol′yə). *Italian* **Pu·glia** (po͞o′lyä). A farming region, chiefly low-lying, in southeast Italy. Its southern portion forms the heel of the Italian "boot." Bari is the chief city.

A·pus (ā′pəs) *n.* A constellation in the Southern Hemisphere near Musca and Pavo. [New Latin, from Latin *apus,* the swallow, from Greek *apous,* the swift, "footless" (probably because the swift is seldom seen perching) : *a-,* without + *pous,* foot.]

a·py·ret·ic (ā′pī-rĕt′ĭk) *adj.* Without fever. [A- (without) + Greek *puretos,* fever.]

aq. aqueous.

A·qa·ba (ä′kə-bə, ăk′ə-). Jordan's only seaport, located at the head of the Gulf of Aqaba, an arm of the Red Sea between the Sinai Peninsula and Saudi Arabia.

aq·ua (ăk′wə, ä′kwə) *n., pl.* **aquae** (ăk′wē, ä′kwī′) or **-uas. 1.** *Pharmacology.* Liquid; solution, especially in water. **2.** The color aquamarine. [Latin, water.] —**aq·ua** *adj.*

aqua- *prefix.* Indicates water; for example, **aquarium, aquanaut.** [Latin.]

aq·ua·cade (ăk′wə-kād′, ä′kwə-) *n.* A water show with swimmers and divers. [AQUA + (CAVAL)CADE.]

aq·ua·cul·ture (ăk′wə-kŭl′chər, ä′kwə-) *n.* The farming of sea organisms, as shellfish, for human use.

Aq·ua·dag (ăk′wə-dăg′, ä′kwə-) *n.* A trademark for a colloidal suspension of graphite in water, used as a lubricant and conducting coating.

aqua fortis *n.* Also **aq·ua·for·tis** (ăk′wə-fôr′tĭs, ä′kwə-). *Chemistry.* **Nitric acid** *(see).* [New Latin, "strong water."]

Aqua Lung *n.* A trademark for an underwater breathing apparatus.

aq·ua·ma·rine (ăk′wə-mə-rēn′, ä′kwə-) *n.* **1.** A transparent blue-green variety of beryl, used as a gemstone. **2.** Pale blue to light greenish blue. [New Latin *aqua marīna,* from Latin, sea water : *aqua,* AQUA- + *marīnus,* of the sea, MARINE.] —**aq·ua·ma·rine** *adj.*

aq·ua·naut (ăk′wə-nôt′, ä′kwə-) *n.* A person trained to live in underwater installations and conduct or assist in scientific research. [AQUA- + Greek *nautēs,* sailor.]

aq·ua·plane (ăk′wə-plān′, ä′kwə-) *n.* A board on which a person rides in a standing position while it is pulled over the water by a motorboat.
~*intr.v.* **aquaplaned, -planing, -planes.** To ride on an aquaplane. [AQUA- + PLANE (surface).]

aqua re·gi·a (rē′jē-ə, -jə) *n.* A corrosive, fuming mixture of concentrated hydrochloric and nitric acids, used for testing metals and dissolving platinum and gold. Also called "nitrohydrochloric acid." [New Latin, "royal water" (because it dissolves gold and platinum, which were known as the "noble metals").]

aq·ua·relle (ăk′wə-rĕl′, ä′kwə-) *n.* A drawing in transparent water colors. [French, from obsolete Italian *acquarella,* water color, from *acqua,* water, from Latin *aqua.*] —**aq·ua·rel·list** *n.*

a·quar·ist (ə-kwâr′ĭst) *n.* One who keeps an aquarium.

a·quar·i·um (ə-kwâr′ē-əm) *n., pl.* **-ums** or **-ia** (-ē-ə). **1.** A tank, bowl, or other water-filled enclosure in which living aquatic animals and plants are kept. **2.** A place for the public exhibition of such animals and plants. [19th century : noun use of Latin *aquārius,* of water, from *aqua,* water, formed by analogy with *vivarium.*]

A·quar·i·us (ə-kwâr′ē-əs) *n.* **1.** A constellation in the equatorial region of the Southern Hemisphere near Pisces and Aquila. **2. a.** The 11th sign of the **zodiac** *(see).* Also called the "Water Bearer." **b.** One born under this sign. [Latin *aquārius,* from *aqua,* water.] —**A·quar·i·an** (ə-kwâr′ē-ən) *n. & adj.*

a·quat·ic (ə-kwŏt′ĭk, ə-kwăt′-) *adj.* **1.** Living or growing in or on the water. **2.** Taking place in or on the water.
~*n.* **1.** An aquatic organism. **2. aquatics.** Aquatic sports. [Old French *aquatique,* from Latin *aquāticus,* from *aqua,* water.]

aq·ua·tint (ăk′wə-tĭnt′, ä′kwə-) *n.* **1.** A process of etching capable of producing several tones by varying the etching time of different areas of a copper plate so that the resulting print resembles the flat tints of an ink or wash drawing. **2.** An etching made in this way.
~*tr.v.* **aquatinted, -tinting, -tints.** To etch in aquatint. [French *aquatinte,* from Italian *acqua tinta,* "tinted water," water color, hence aquatint (which imitates water color) : *acqua,* water + *tinta,* tinted, from Latin *tincta,* feminine of *tinctus,* dyed (see **tint**).]

a·qua·vit (ä′kwə-vēt′) *n.* A strong, clear Scandinavian liquor distilled from potato or grain mash and flavored with caraway seed. [Swedish, Danish, and Norwegian *akvavit,* from Medieval Latin *aqua vītae,* "water of life."]

aqua vi·tae (vī′tē) *n.* **1.** Whiskey, brandy, or other strong liquor. **2.** Alcohol. [Middle English *aquavite,* from Medieval Latin *aqua vītae,* "water of life," originally an alchemist's term for alcohol or spirits.]

aq·ue·duct (ăk′wə-dŭkt′) *n.* **1.** A manmade channel designed to transport water over long distances, usually by gravity. **2.** An elevated structure supporting a channel or canal passing over a river or low ground. **3.** *Anatomy.* A channel or passage carrying fluid in the body. [Latin *aquae ductus* : *aquae,* genitive of *aqua,* water + DUCT.] See feature, next page.

aqueduct *The Pont du Gard was built by the Romans in the first century* A.D. *to carry water across a valley in Provence, France.*

a·que·ous (ā′kwē-əs, ăk′wē-) *adj. Abbr.* **aq. 1.** Pertaining to, similar to, containing, or dissolved in water; watery. **2.** *Geology.* Formed from matter deposited by water, as are certain sedimentary rocks. [Medieval Latin *aqueus,* from Latin *aqua,* water.]

aqueous humor *n.* A clear, lymphlike fluid in the chamber of the eye between the cornea and the lens. Compare **vitreous humor.**

aqui– *prefix.* Indicates water; for example, **aquiculture.** [Latin, from *aqua,* water.]

aq·ui·cul·ture (ăk′wĭ-kŭl′chər, ä′kwĭ-) *n.* A method of cultivation, **hydroponics** *(see).* —**aq·ui·cul·tur·al** *adj.*

aq·ui·fer (ăk′wə-fər, ä′kwə-) *n.* A water-bearing rock, rock formation, or group of formations. [AQUI- + -FER.] —**a·quif·er·ous** (ə-kwĭf′ər-əs) *adj.*

Aq·ui·la (ăk′wə-lə) *n.* A constellation in the Northern Hemisphere and the Milky Way near Aquarius and Serpens Cauda. [Latin *aquila,* EAGLE.]

aq·ui·le·gi·a (ăk′wə-lē′jē-ə, -jə) *n.* A plant, the **columbine** *(see).* [New Latin, from Medieval Latin *aquilēgia, aquilēja*†, columbine.]

aq·ui·line (ăk′wə-līn′, -lĭn) *adj.* **1.** Of or similar to an eagle. **2.** Curved or hooked like an eagle's beak: *an aquiline nose.* [Latin *aquilīnus,* from *aquila,* eagle. See **eagle.**]

A·qui·nas (ə-kwī′nəs), **Saint Thomas** (*c.* 1225–74). Italian Doctor of the Church, theologian, and philosopher, the outstanding representative of the medieval system of thought known as Scholasticism. By far the most influential example of Aquinas's application of Aristotelian methods to Christian theology is *Summa Theologica* (1267–73).

Arab *A light-framed horse with a deep chest and great stamina. All thoroughbred racehorses are descended from Arab stallions.*

Aq·ui·taine (ăk′wə-tān′). Region of southwest France, stretching north from the Pyrenees to the Garonne River. It formed the Roman province of Aquitania and was subsequently part of the Visigothic and Frankish kingdoms.

a·quiv·er (ə-kwĭv′ər) *adj.* Marked by quivering: *all aquiver with anticipation.*

Ar 1. The symbol for the element argon. **2.** The symbol for an aromatic group in an organic compound.

AR Arkansas (used with a Zip Code).

-ar[1] *suffix.* Indicates like, pertaining to, or of the nature of; for example, **titular, polar, spectacular.** [Middle English *-ar, -er,* from Old French *-er,* from Latin *-āris,* dissimulated alteration (after bases ending in *l*) of *-ālis,* -AL.]

-ar[2] *suffix.* Indicates someone performing or involved with a specified occupation; for example, **bursar, burglar.** [Middle English variant of **-er**[1].]

Ar. 1. Arabia; Arabian. **2.** Arabic. **3.** Aramaic.

A·ra (âr′ə) *n.* A constellation in the Southern Hemisphere near the constellations Norma and Telescopium. [Latin *āra,* altar.]

Ar·ab (ăr′əb) *n.* **1.** A native or inhabitant of Arabia. **2.** A member of a Semitic people originally from Arabia, but later widely scattered throughout the Middle East, North Africa, and the Arabian Penin-

aqueduct

MOVING WATER BY AQUEDUCT

Bridges and channels transporting water to cities

The first aqueducts were built in the Middle East before 700 B.C., but it was the Romans who took water supply most seriously, making it a deliberate part of their public health policy. Several Roman aqueducts can still be seen: for example at Nîmes in France, at Segovia in Spain, and in Rome. It is a tribute to the engineering skills of the Romans that many of the aqueducts of today are based on the principles they pioneered. California has the most advanced system of aqueducts in the world, because the bulk of the water supply comes from the north while most of the demand is in the south.

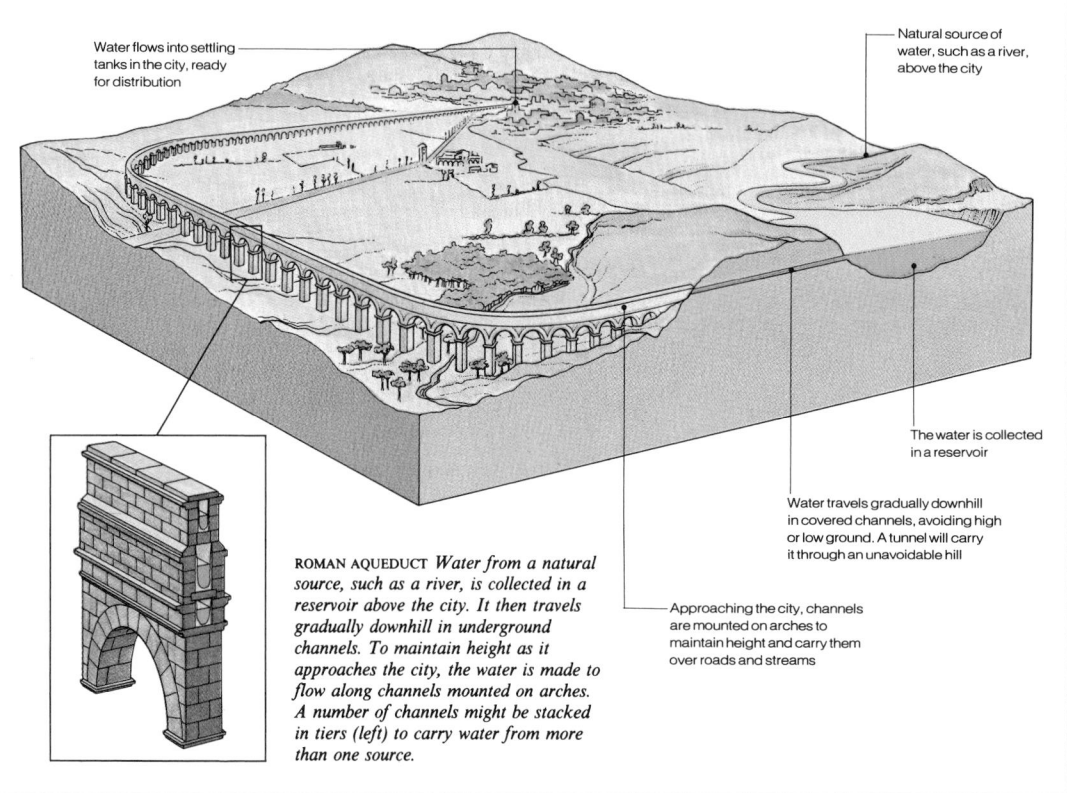

Water flows into settling tanks in the city, ready for distribution

Natural source of water, such as a river, above the city

The water is collected in a reservoir

Water travels gradually downhill in covered channels, avoiding high or low ground. A tunnel will carry it through an unavoidable hill

Approaching the city, channels are mounted on arches to maintain height and carry them over roads and streams

ROMAN AQUEDUCT *Water from a natural source, such as a river, is collected in a reservoir above the city. It then travels gradually downhill in underground channels. To maintain height as it approaches the city, the water is made to flow along channels mounted on arches. A number of channels might be stacked in tiers (left) to carry water from more than one source.*

sula. **3.** A horse of a swift, graceful breed native to Arabia, used mainly for riding. **4.** A street Arab; waif.
—*adj.* Of or pertaining to the Arabs or Arabia. [Middle English, from Latin *Arabs,* from Greek *Arabs, Araps,* from Arabic *'arab.*]
Arab. 1. Arabia; Arabian. **2.** Arabic.
ar·a·besque (ăr'ə-bĕsk') *n.* **1.** A complex and ornate design with intertwined flowers, leaves, and geometrical figures. **2.** A ballet position in which the dancer stands on one leg, with the other leg extended backward and the arms stretched out.
—*adj.* Pertaining to, resembling, or formed as an arabesque. [French, from Italian *arabesco,* "made or done in Arabic fashion."]
A·ra·bi·a (ə-rā'bē-ə). *Abbr.* **Ar., Arab.** Peninsula in southwest Asia, including Saudi Arabia and its adjoining states to the south and east. It is estimated to have about a third of the world's petroleum reserves.
A·ra·bi·an (ə-rā'bē-ən) *adj. Abbr.* **Ar., Arab.** Of or pertaining to Arabia or the Arabs; Arab.
—*n.* **1.** A native or inhabitant of Arabia. **2.** A horse of a breed native to Arabia; an Arab.
Arabian camel *n.* The **dromedary** *(see).*
Arabian Nights A collection of oriental stories of love and adventure dating from the 10th century A.D. and including the stories of Aladdin and Sinbad. Also called the "Thousand and One Nights."
—*adj.* Sumptuous and exotic: *an Arabian Nights costume.*
Arabian Sea. The northwestern part of the Indian Ocean, bounded by eastern Africa, Arabia, and western India.
Ar·a·bic (ăr'ə-bĭk) *adj.* Of or pertaining to Arabia, the Arabs, their language, or their culture.
—*n. Abbr.* **Ar., Arab. 1.** The Southwest Semitic language of the Arabs, which is now (in a variety of dialects) the prevailing language of the Arabian peninsula and most of the Middle East and North Africa. **2.** The literary language of the Koran, as employed in formal usage in Arabic-speaking countries; classical Arabic.
Arabic numeral *n.* One of the numerical symbols 1, 2, 3, 4, 5, 6, 7, 8, 9, and 0. Compare **Roman numeral.**
a·rab·i·nose (ə-răb'ə-nōs', -nōz') *n.* A pentose sugar, $C_5H_{10}O_5$, found in plant gums, pectins, and mucilages, especially of certain conifers. It is used in bacteriology as a constituent of culture media.

[*Arabin,* from (GUM) ARAB(IC) + -IN + -OSE.]
Ar·ab·ist (ăr'ə-bĭst) *n.* **1.** A specialist in the Arabic language or culture, or in the politics of the Arab world. **2.** A supporter of Arab interests.
ar·a·ble (ăr'ə-bəl) *adj.* Fit for the cultivation of crops.
—*n.* Arable land. [Middle English, from Old French, from Latin *arābilis,* from *arāre,* to plough.]
Arab League *n.* An association of independent Arab nations formed in 1945 by Iraq, Jordan, Lebanon, Saudi Arabia, Egypt, Syria, and Yemen. There are now 22 members, including the Palestine Liberation Organization.
Ar·a·by (ăr'ə-bē). *Poetic.* Arabia.
a·ra·ceous (ə-rā'shəs) *adj. Botany.* Aroid. [New Latin *Araceae* (family), from Latin *arum,* ARUM.]
A·rach·ne (ə-răk'nē). *Greek Mythology.* A maiden who was transformed into a spider by Athena for beating her in a weaving contest. [Latin *Arachnē,* from Greek *Arakhnē,* from *arakhnē†,* spider.]
a·rach·nid (ə-răk'nĭd) *n.* Any of various arthropods of the class Arachnida, such as a spider, scorpion, tick, or mite, characteristically having four pairs of legs, simple eyes, and no antennae. Also called "arachnoid." [New Latin *Arachnida,* from Greek *arakhnē,* spider, ARACHNE.] —**a·rach·ni·dan** (ə-răk'nə-dən) *adj. & n.*
a·rach·noid (ə-răk'noid') *n.* **1.** The middle of the three delicate membranes covering the spinal cord and brain, lying between the pia mater and the dura mater. **2.** An arachnid.
—*adj.* **1.** Of or pertaining to the arachnoid membrane. **2.** Of, pertaining to, or resembling the arachnids. **3.** Covered with or consisting of thin, soft, entangled hairs like the threads of a cobweb. [New Latin *arachnoides,* from Greek *arakhnoeidēs,* cobweblike : *arakhnē,* spider, ARACHNE + -OID.]
Ar·a·fat (ăr'ə-făt'), **Yasir** (1929–). Leader of Al Fatah and of the Palestine Liberation Organization (PLO). In 1974 Arab leaders endorsed him as the spokesman for all Palestinians, but in recent years his influence has diminished as more militant terrorist groups have sought to gain control.
Ar·a·gon (ăr'ə-gŏn'). *Spanish* **Ar·a·gón** (ä'rä-gōn'). Region of northeast Spain. It became an independent kingdom (1035) and united with Castile (1479) to form the nucleus of modern Spain.
A·ra·gon (ăr-ə-gôN'), **Louis** (1897–1982). French poet and novelist,

one of the founders of literary surrealism. In 1919 he helped found the surrealist journal *Littérature*.

Ar·a·go·nese (ăr'ə-gə-nēz', -nēs) *adj.* Of or pertaining to Aragon, its inhabitants, their language, or their culture.
~*n., pl.* **Aragonese.** A native or inhabitant of Aragon.

a·rag·o·nite (ə-răg'ə-nīt', ăr'ə-gə-) *n.* An orthorhombic mineral form of calcium carbonate, dimorphous with calcite. [After ARAGON, where it was first found.]

A·ral Sea (ăr'əl). The fourth-largest inland body of water in the world, covering some 68,682 square kilometers (26,518 square miles) in the southern U.S.S.R.

Ar·am (ăr'əm). A Biblical name for ancient Syria.

Aram, Eugene (1704–59). English philologist. Largely self-taught, Aram was the first man to demonstrate that the Celtic languages belong to the Indo-European group. In 1759 he was executed for the murder, 14 years earlier, of his friend Daniel Clark.

Ar·a·ma·ic (ăr'ə-mā'ĭk) *n.* A Northwest Semitic language used as the commercial lingua franca for nearly all of southwestern Asia after about 300 B.C. and still spoken in parts of Syria and Lebanon. Compare **Biblical Aramaic.** —**Ar·a·ma·ic** *adj.*

Ar·a·me·an, Ar·a·mae·an (ăr'ə-mē'ən) *adj.* Of or pertaining to Aram, its inhabitants, language, or culture.
~*n.* **1.** A native or inhabitant of Aram. **2.** The Aramaic language.

Ar·an (ăr'ən) *adj.* Knitted from undyed wool in an elaborate cable-stitch pattern that originated in the Aran Islands off the west coast of Ireland: *an Aran sweater.*

ar·a·pai·ma (ăr'ə-pī'mə) *n.* A large South American freshwater food fish, *Arapaima gigas,* sometimes attaining a length of 15 feet. Also called "pirarucu." [Spanish and Portuguese, from Tupi.]

Ar·a·rat, Mount (ăr'ə-răt'). *Turkish* **A·gri Da·gi** (ä'rē dä-ē'). Massif in eastern Turkey. Great Ararat (5,165 meters; 16,945 feet) is its highest peak and is traditionally regarded as the resting place of Noah's Ark.

ar·a·ro·ba (ăr'ə-rō'bə) *n.* **1.** A Brazilian tree, *Andira araroba,* having yellowish wood from which a medicinal powder is obtained. **2.** The powder itself, found in cavities in the wood. In this sense, also called "Goa powder." See **chrysarobin.** [Portuguese, probably from Tupi : *arara,* parrot + *yba,* tree.]

Ar·au·ca·ni·an (ăr'ô-kā'nē-ən) *n.* Also **A·rau·can** (ə-rô'kən). **1.** A South American Indian language family spoken in Chile and the western pampas of Argentina. **2.** A member of any of the Araucanian-speaking peoples. —**Ar·au·ca·ni·an** *adj.*

ar·au·car·i·a (ăr'ô-kăr'ē-ə) *n.* Any of several evergreen trees of the coniferous genus *Araucaria.* See **bunya, monkey puzzle.** [New Latin *Araucaria,* from Spanish *Araucano,* (tree) of *Araucania,* region of Chile.]

Ar·a·wak (ăr'ə-wäk') *n., pl.* **-waks** or collectively **Arawak. 1.** An Indian people now living chiefly in certain regions of the Guianas. **2.** A member of the Arawak. **3.** The Arawakan language of the Arawak.

Ar·a·wa·kan (ăr'ə-wä'kən) *n., pl.* **-kans** or collectively **Arawakan. 1.** A member of a group of Indian people living in a wide area of South America including Venezuela, Colombia, the Guianas, Peru, Bolivia, Paraguay, and the Amazon basin of Brazil. **2.** A language family that consists of the languages spoken by the Arawakan peoples.

ar·ba·lest (är'bə-lĭst) *n.* Also **ar·be·list.** A medieval weapon designed on the crossbow principle and used for firing arrows, stones, balls, and other missiles. [Middle English *arbelast, arblast,* Old English *arblast,* from Old French *arbaleste,* from Late Latin *arcuballista* : Latin *arcus,* bow + BALLISTA.] —**ar·ba·lest·er** *n.*

ar·bi·ter (är'bĭ-tər) *n.* **1.** One chosen or appointed to judge or decide a disputed issue; an arbitrator. **2.** One who has the power to judge or ordain at will. **3.** One who has the authority to make influential judgments: *an arbiter of taste.* —See Synonyms at **judge.** [Middle English *arbitre,* from Old French, from Latin *arbiter†,* judge.]

ar·bi·tra·ble (är'bĭ-trə-bəl) *adj.* Subject to arbitration; capable of being referred to an arbitrator.

ar·bi·trage (är'bĭ-träzh') *n.* The purchase of securities, commodities, or the like, on one market for immediate resale on another in order to profit from a price discrepancy. [French, arbitration, from *arbitrer,* to ARBITRATE.]

ar·bit·ra·ment (är-bĭt'rə-mənt) *n.* **1.** The act of arbitrating. **2.** The judgment or award made by an arbitrator. [Middle English, from Old French *arbitrement,* from *arbitrer,* to ARBITRATE.]

ar·bi·trar·y (är'bĭ-trĕr'ē) *adj.* **1.** Determined by chance, whim, or impulse, not by reason or law. **2.** Based on or subject to individual judgment or discretion. **3.** Established by a court or judge rather than by a specific law or statute. **4.** Not limited by law; absolute; despotic: *the arbitrary power of a dictator.* —See Synonyms at **dictatorial.** [Middle English, from Latin *arbitrārius,* from *arbiter,* ARBITER.] —**ar·bi·trar·i·ly** (är'bĭ-trâr'ə-lē) *adv.* —**ar·bi·trar·i·ness** *n.*

ar·bi·trate (är'bĭ-trāt') *v.* **-trated, -trating, -trates.** —*tr.* **1.** To judge or decide as or in the manner of an arbitrator. **2.** To submit to settlement or judgment by arbitration. —*intr.* **1.** To serve as an arbitrator or arbiter. **2.** To refer a dispute to arbitration. [Latin *arbitrārī* (past participial stem *arbitrāt-*), from *arbiter,* ARBITER.]

ar·bi·tra·tion (är'bĭ-trā'shən) *n.* The process by which the parties to a dispute submit their differences to the judgment of an impartial party appointed by mutual consent or statutory provision. —See Synonyms at **mediation.**

ar·bi·tra·tor (är'bĭ-trā'tər) *n.* **1.** A person chosen to settle the issue between parties engaged in a dispute or controversy. **2.** One having the ability or power to make authoritative decisions; an arbiter. —See Synonyms at **judge.**

ar·bor¹ (är'bər) *n.* **1.** A shady garden shelter or bower, often made of rustic work or latticework, on which climbing plants, as vines or roses, are grown. **2.** *Obsolete.* An orchard or garden.

arbor² *n.* **1.** An axis or shaft supporting a rotating part on a lathe. **2.** A rotating shaft fitted with a device for holding work while it is being machined. **3.** An axle or spindle of a wheel, as in a watch or a clock. **4.** *Archaic.* A tree. [French *arbre* (in a Latinized respelling), axle, axis, tree, from Latin *arbor†,* tree.]

Arbor Day *n.* In the United States, Canada, Australia, and New Zealand, a day set apart annually for the community planting of trees.

ar·bo·re·al (är-bôr'ē-əl, är-bōr'-) *adj.* **1.** Of, pertaining to, or resembling a tree. **2.** Living in trees: *Some monkeys are arboreal animals.* —**ar·bo·re·al·ly** *adv.*

ar·bo·re·ous (är-bôr'ē-əs, är-bōr'-) *adj.* **1.** Having many trees; wooded. **2.** Resembling or characteristic of a tree; treelike.

ar·bo·res·cent (är'bə-rĕs'ənt) *adj.* Having the form or characteristics of a tree; treelike. [Latin *arborēscēns* (stem *arborēscent-*), present participle of *arborēscere,* to grow to be a tree, from *arbor†,* tree.] —**ar·bo·res·cence** *n.*

ar·bo·re·tum (är'bə-rē'təm) *n., pl.* **-tums** or **-ta** (-tə). A place where many different species and varieties of trees and shrubs are grown for scientific study and public exhibition. [New Latin, from Latin *arborētum,* a place where trees are grown, from *arbor†,* tree. See **arbor** (shaft).]

ar·bo·ri·cul·ture (är'bər-ĭ-kŭl'chər, är-bôr'ĭ-, är-bōr'ĭ-) *n.* The cultivation of trees for ornament or for the production of timber. [Latin *arbor†,* tree + *-culture,* by analogy with *agriculture.*] —**ar·bo·ri·cul·tur·al** *adj.* —**ar·bo·ri·cul·tur·ist** *n.*

ar·bor·ist (är'bər-ĭst) *n.* One who specializes in the cultivation and care of trees.

ar·bor·i·za·tion (är'bər-ə-zā'shən) *n.* **1.** A treelike shape or arrangement, as in certain minerals or fossils. See **dendrite. 2.** The formation of such a shape or arrangement.

ar·bo·rize (är'bə-rīz') *intr.v.* **-rized, -rizing, -rizes.** To have or form many branches.

ar·bor·vi·tae, arbor vi·tae (är'bər-vī'tē) *n.* **1. a.** Any of several evergreen shrubs and trees of the genus *Thuja,* having tiny, scalelike leaves and egg-shaped cones. **b.** A similar tree of the genus *Thujopsis.* **2.** *Anatomy.* The white matter of the cerebellum seen in cross section, having the appearance of a tree. [New Latin *arbor vitae,* "tree of life," referring to the tree's remaining green all year.]

arbour. *Chiefly British.* Variant of **arbor.**

ar·bo·vi·rus (är'bə-vī'rəs) *n.* Any of various viruses that are transmitted by arthropods, especially insects, and cause such diseases as encephalitis and yellow fever. [*Ar*thropod-*bo*rne *virus.*]

Ar·buth·not (är-bŭth'nət, är'bəth-nŏt'), **John** (1667–1735). Scottish physician and essayist. His five anti-Whig pamphlets, published as *The History of John Bull* (1712), were satirical pieces that introduced the character of John Bull to English tradition.

ar·bu·tus (är-byōō'təs) *n.* **1.** Any of several broad-leaved evergreen trees of the genus *Arbutus,* having clusters of white or pinkish flowers, especially the **strawberry tree** *(see).* **2.** A plant, **trailing arbutus** *(see).* [New Latin *Arbutus,* from Latin *arbūtus†,* strawberry tree, referring to the appearance of its berries.]

arc (ärk) *n.* **1.** Anything shaped like a bow, curve, or arch. **2.** In geometry, a segment of a curve. **3.** *Electricity.* A luminous discharge of electric current crossing a gap between two electrodes.
~*adj. Mathematics.* Designating an inverse trigonometric function: *the arc sine of a quantity.*
~*intr.v.* **arced** (ärkt) or **arcked, arcing** (är'kĭng) or **arcking, arcs.** To form an arc. [Middle English *ark,* Old English *arc,* from Latin *arcus,* bow, arc.]

ar·cade (är-kād') *n.* **1.** *Architecture.* **a.** A series of arches supported by columns, piers, or pillars. **b.** An arched, roofed building or part of a building. **2.** A roofed passageway or lane, especially one with shops on either side. [French, from Italian *arcata,* from *arco,* arch, from Vulgar Latin *arca* (unattested). See **arch.**]

Ar·ca·di·a (är-kā'dē-ə) *n.* **1.** A mountainous region of ancient Greece whose inhabitants, isolated from the rest of the world, lived a simple, pastoral life. **2.** A place or region thought to epitomize rustic contentment and simplicity.

Ar·ca·di·an (är-kā'dē-ən) *adj.* **1.** Of, pertaining to, or characteristic of Arcadia. **2.** *Often* **arcadian.** Rustic, peaceful, and simple; pastoral. —See Synonyms at **rural.**
~*n.* **1.** A native of Arcadia. **2.** *Often* **arcadian.** A person who leads or prefers a simple, rural life. **3.** The Ancient Greek dialect of Arcadia, belonging to Arcado-Cyprian.

Ar·ca·do·-Cyp·ri·an (är-kā'dō-sĭp'rē-ən) *n.* One of the four main dialects of ancient Greek, comprising Arcadian, Pamphylian, and Cypriot. Compare **Aeolic, Attic-Ionic, Doric.** —**Ar·ca·do·-Cyp·ri·an** *adj.*

Ar·ca·dy (är'kə-dē) *n. Poetic.* Arcadia.

ar·cane (är-kān') *adj.* Known or understood only by those having special, secret knowledge; esoteric. [Latin *arcānus,* closed, secret, from *arcēre,* to shut, from *arca,* chest.]

ar·ca·num (är-kā'nəm) *n., pl.* **-na** (-nə). **1.** A profound secret; a mystery. **2.** The reputed great secret of nature that alchemists sought to find. **3.** An elixir. [Latin *arcānum,* a mystery, secret, from the neuter of *arcānus,* closed, secret, ARCANE.]

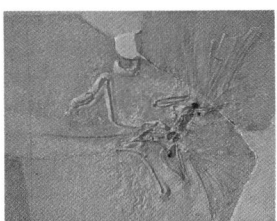

archaeopteryx *The long-extinct archaeopteryx, one of the earliest flying animals, lived about 150 million years ago. This is the fossilized imprint of its body, with the shape of the wings visible as feathery lines radiating from the skeleton.*

arc·bou·tant (är′bōō-tän′) *n.*, *pl.* **arcs-boutants** (är′bōō-tän′). *French.* A **flying buttress** (see).

arch[1] (ärch) *n.* **1.** A curved structure, especially of masonry, forming the upper edge of an opening or a support, as in a bridge or doorway. **2.** Any similar structure, such as a monument. **3.** Anything curved like an arch. **4.** *Anatomy.* Any of various arch-shaped structures, especially the structure in the foot formed by the tarsal and metatarsal bones. **5.** One of the three basic patterns by which fingerprints are classified, consisting of numerous curved ridges one above the other. Compare **loop, whorl.**
~*v.* **arched, arching, arches.** —*tr.* **1.** To supply with an arch. **2.** To cause to form an arch or similar curve: *arch one's eyebrows.* **3.** To span: *"the rude bridge that arched the flood"* (Emerson). —*intr.* **1.** To form an arch or archlike curve: *Elm trees arched over the road.* **2.** To move in a course shaped like an arch: *The football arched over the goal post.* [Middle English *arche,* from Old French, from Vulgar Latin *arca* (unattested), plural noun from Latin *arcus,* bow, ARC.]

arch[2] *adj.* **1.** Chief; principal. Used before the noun: *an arch-thief.* **2.** Mischievous; roguish: *an arch glance.* [From ARCH-.] —**arch′ly** *adv.* —**arch′ness** *n.*

arch– *prefix.* Indicates: **1.** Highest rank or chief status; for example, **archduke, archbishop. 2.** Ultimate of a kind; for example, **archfiend.** [Middle English *arche-, arch-,* from Old English *ærce-, arce-, erce-,* and Old French *arch(e)-,* both from Latin *arch(i)-,* from Greek *arkh(i)-,* from *arkhos,* chief, ruler, from *arkhein†,* to begin, rule.]

–arch *suffix.* Indicates a ruler or leader; for example, **monarch, matriarch.** [Middle English *-arche,* from Old French, from Late Latin *-archa,* from Latin *-archēs,* from Greek *-arkhēs,* from *arkhos,* ruler, from *arkhein†,* to rule.]

arch. 1. archaic; archaism. **2.** archery. **3.** archipelago. **4.** architect; architectural; architecture.

Arch. archbishop.

Archaean. Variant of **Archean.**

archaeo–, archeo– *prefix.* Indicates ancient times or an early condition; for example, **archaeology, archaeopteryx.** [New Latin, from Greek *arkhaio-,* from *arkhaios,* ancient, from *arkhē,* beginning, from *arkhein†,* to begin.]

ar·chae·o·as·tron·o·my (är′kē-ō-ə-strŏn′ə-mē) *n.* The study of megalithic sites and other ancient structures with a view to showing that they were built to align with or predict astronomical observations. —**ar·chae·o·as·tron·o·mer** *n.*

ar·chae·ol·o·gy, ar·che·ol·o·gy (är′kē-ŏl′ə-jē) *n.* The systematic recovery by scientific methods and study of material evidence, such as graves, buildings, tools, and pottery, of man's life, culture, and history in former times. [French *archéologie,* from Late Latin *archaeologia,* "the study of antiquity," from Greek *arkhaiologia* : ARCHAEO- + -LOGY.] —**ar·chae·o·log·i·cal** (är′kē-ə-lŏj′ĭ-kəl), **ar·chae·o·log·ic** *adj.* —**ar·chae·olo·gist** *n.*

ar·chae·o·mag·net·ism (är′kē-ō-măg′nə-tĭz′əm) *n.* A technique used in archaeology for dating clay objects by measuring the extent to which they have been magnetized by the earth's magnetic field. —**ar·chae·o·mag·net·ic** (är′kē-ō-măg-nĕt′ĭk) *adj.*

ar·chae·op·ter·yx (är′kē-ŏp′tər-ĭks) *n.* An extinct primitive bird of the genus *Archaeopteryx,* of the Jurassic period, having wings, feathers, teeth, and a long tail, and representing a transitional form between reptiles and birds. [New Latin, "ancient bird" : ARCHAEO- + Greek *pterux,* bird, wing, from *pteron,* feather, wing.]

ar·chae·o·zo·ol·o·gy (är′kē-ō-zō-ŏl′ə-jē) *n.* The scientific study of ancient animal remains, especially fossilized bones, as evidence of early domestication, the hunting habits of a given culture, climatic changes, and the like.

ar·cha·ic (är-kā′ĭk) *adj.* *Abbr.* **arch. 1.** Belonging to a much earlier time; ancient: *archaic sculpture.* **2.** No longer current or applicable; antiquated: *archaic laws.* **3.** Of, pertaining to, or characteristic of words and language that were once common but are now used chiefly to suggest an earlier style or period. —See Synonyms at **old.** [French *archaïque,* from Greek *arkhaikos,* from *arkhaios,* from *arkhē,* beginning, from *arkhein†,* to begin.] —**ar·cha·i·cal·ly** *adv.*

archaic smile *n.* A representation of the human mouth with slightly upturned corners, characteristic of early Greek sculpture.

ar·cha·ism (är′kē-ĭz′əm, är′kā-) *n.* *Abbr.* **arch. 1.** An archaic word or expression. **2.** An archaic style or quality. **3.** The imitation of archaic styles, as in literature or art. [New Latin *archaeismus,* from Greek *arkhaïsmos,* from *archaios,* ancient, ARCHAIC.] —**ar·cha·ist** *n.* —**ar·cha·is·tic** (är′kē-ĭs′tĭk, är′kā-) *adj.*

ar·cha·ize (är′kē-īz′, är′kā-) *v.* **-ized, -izing, -izes.** —*tr.* To impart an archaic quality or character to. —*intr.* To use archaisms. [Greek *arkhaïzein,* from *arkhaios,* ancient, ARCHAIC.] —**ar·cha·iz·er** *n.*

arch·an·gel (ärk′ān′jəl) *n.* *Theology.* **1.** A celestial being next in rank above an angel. **2. archangels.** The eighth of the nine orders of angels. See **angel.** [Middle English, from Norman-French *archangele,* from Late Latin *archangelus,* from Greek *arkhangelos* : ARCH- + ANGEL.] —**arch·an·gel·ic** (ärk′ān-jĕl′ĭk) *adj.*

Archangel. See **Arkhangelsk.**

arch·bish·op (ärch-bĭsh′əp) *n.* *Abbr.* **abp., Abp., Arch., Archbp.** A bishop of the highest rank, heading an archdiocese or province. [Middle English *erchebishop, archebishop,* Old English *ærcebiscop, arcebiscop,* from Late Latin *archiepiscopus,* from Late Greek *arkhiepiskopos* : ARCH- + *episkopos,* BISHOP.]

THE GROWTH OF THE ARCH

How a simple skill transformed construction

The arch is a curved or pointed span joining the walls on either side of an opening. The Egyptians made small ones from 4000 B.C., but it was the Roman development of the arch that revolutionized architecture. They built their arches over wooden frames, extending the span to more than 30 meters (90 feet) high and wide. With buttressed walls, buildings became huge, airy, and spectacular.

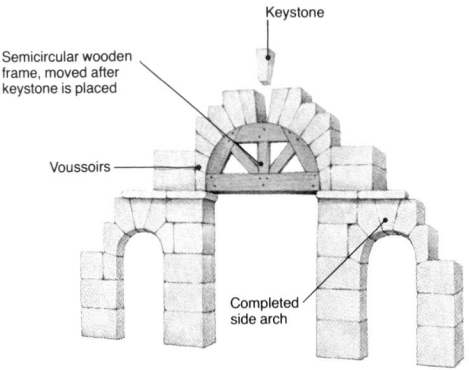

THE SEMICIRCULAR ARCH *Made from wedge-shaped masonry blocks called voussoirs, and built over a frame. A keystone, dropped into place, locks the voussoirs in place.*

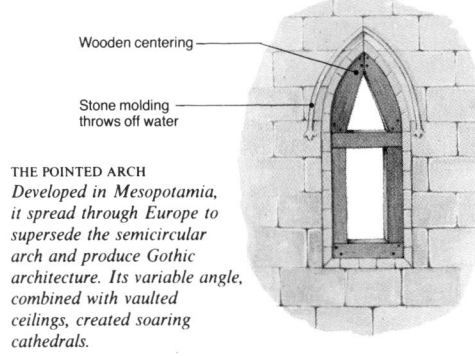

THE POINTED ARCH
Developed in Mesopotamia, it spread through Europe to supersede the semicircular arch and produce Gothic architecture. Its variable angle, combined with vaulted ceilings, created soaring cathedrals.

THE SEGMENTAL ARCH *A shallow, less than semicircular curve gives a wide base. It was common in Europe from the 16th century for bridge building.*

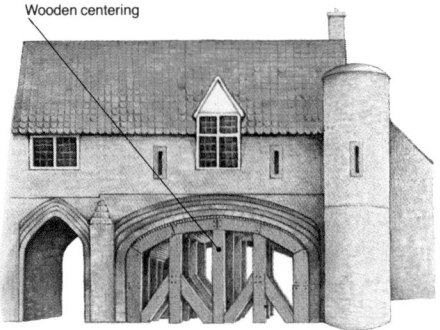

THE ELLIPTICAL ARCH *A half-oval curve gave a low rise-to-span ratio. It used less stone and its very shallow curve was ideal for bridges.*

arch·bish·op·ric (ärch-bĭsh′ə-prĭk) *n.* **1.** The rank, office, or term of an archbishop. **2.** The jurisdiction of an archbishop.
arch·dea·con (ärch-dē′kən) *n.* A clergyman, chiefly in the Anglican Church, in charge of temporal and other affairs in a diocese, with powers delegated from the bishop. [Middle English *archedeken,* Old English *ærcediakon,* from Late Latin *archidiāconus,* from Late Greek *arkhidiakonos* : ARCH- + DEACON.]
arch·dea·con·ry (ärch-dē′kən-rē) *n., pl.* **-ries.** The office, jurisdiction, residence, or district of an archdeacon.
arch·di·o·cese (ärch-dī′ə-sĭs, -sēs′, -sēz′) *n.* A diocese under an archbishop's jurisdiction. **—arch·di·oc·e·san** (ärch′dī-ŏs′ə-sən) *adj.*
arch·du·cal (ärch-do͞o′kəl, -dyo͞o′kəl) *adj.* Of or pertaining to an archduke or an archduchy.
arch·duch·ess (ärch-dŭch′ĭs) *n.* **1.** The wife or widow of an archduke. **2.** A woman having a rank equivalent to that of an archduke; especially, an Austrian princess.
arch·duch·y (ärch-dŭch′ē) *n., pl.* **-ies.** The territory over which an archduke or an archduchess has authority.
arch·duke (ärch-do͝ok′, -dyo͝ok′) *n.* In certain royal families, especially that of imperial Austria, a nobleman having a rank equivalent to that of a sovereign prince.
Ar·che·an (är-kē′ən) *adj. Geology.* Of, pertaining to, or designating the oldest rocks of the Precambrian era, predominantly igneous in composition.
arched (ärcht) *adj.* **1.** Forming an arch or a curve like that of an arch. **2.** Provided, made, or covered with an arch or arches.
ar·che·go·ni·um (är′kə-gō′nē-əm) *n., pl.* **-nia** (-nē-ə). *Botany.* A multicellular female sex organ of mosses, ferns, and conifers, which produces a single gamete. Compare **antheridium.** [New Latin, diminutive of Greek *arkhegonos,* primal parent : ARCH- (chief) + *-gonos,* race.] **—ar·che·go·ni·al** *adj.* **—ar·che·go·ni·ate** (är′kə-gō′nē-ĭt) *adj.*
arch·en·e·my (ärch-ĕn′ə-mē) *n., pl.* **-mies.** **1.** A chief or principal enemy. **2.** *Often* **Archenemy.** The devil; Satan.
arch·en·ter·on (är-kĕn′tə-rŏn′, -rən) *n.* The embryonic digestive tract, essentially a cavity in the gastrula. [New Latin : ARCH- + ENTERON.] **—arch·en·ter·ic** (är′kĕn-tĕr′ĭk) *adj.*
archeo-. Variant of **archaeo-.**
archeology. Variant of **archaeology.**
arch·er (är′chər) *n.* **1.** One who engages in archery. **2. Archer.** The constellation and sign of the zodiac **Sagittarius** *(see).* [Middle English, from Old French *archier,* from Late Latin *arcārius,* alteration of *arcuārius,* "of a bow," from Latin *arcus,* bow, ARC.]
Ar·cher (är′chər), **Frederick Scott** (1813–57). British photographer. He invented the wet collodion process, by which more than one photograph could be printed from a glass negative.
Archer, Thomas (*c.* 1668–1743). English baroque architect. Among the churches he designed are St. John's, Smith Square, London, and St. Paul's, Deptford.
arch·er·fish (är′chər-fĭsh′) *n., pl.* **-fishes** or collectively **archerfish.** Any of several small freshwater Indo-Australian fishes of the family Toxotidae, capable of capturing insects by squirting water at them.
arch·er·y (är′chə-rē) *n. Abbr.* **arch.** **1.** The art, sport, or skill of shooting with a bow and arrows. **2.** The equipment of an archer. **3.** A troop or body of archers.
ar·che·spore (är′kə-spôr′, -spōr′) *n.* Also **ar·che·spo·ri·um** (är′kə-spôr′ē-əm, -spōr′ē-əm) *pl.* **-sporia** (-spôr′ē-ə, -spōr′ē-ə). *Botany.* A cell or mass of cells producing spores in a sporangium. [New Latin *archesporium* : ARCH- + *spora,* SPORE.] **—ar·che·spo·ri·al** *adj.*
ar·che·type (är′kə-tīp′) *n.* **1.** An original model or type after which other similar things are patterned; a prototype. **2.** A perfect or typical example. **3.** In the psychology of C. G. Jung, an inherited idea in the individual unconscious that is thought to derive from the collective experience of mankind as a whole. —See Synonyms at **ideal.** [Latin *archetypum,* from Greek *arkhetupon,* neuter of *arkhetupos,* "first-molded" : ARCH- + *tupos,* mold, stamp, TYPE.] **—ar·che·typ·al** (är′kə-tī′pəl), **ar·che·typ·i·cal** (-tĭp′ĭ-kəl) *adj.* **—ar·che·typ·i·cal·ly** *adv.*
arch·fiend (ärch-fēnd′) *n.* **1.** A chief or foremost fiend. **2.** *Often* **Archfiend.** The devil; Satan.
ar·chi·di·ac·o·nal (är′kĭ-dī-ăk′ə-nəl) *adj.* Of or pertaining to an archdeacon, his duties, or his office. [From Late Latin *archidiāconus,* ARCHDEACON.]
ar·chi·di·ac·o·nate (är′kĭ-dī-ăk′ə-nĭt) *n.* The office or status of an archdeacon. [Medieval Latin *archidiāconātus,* from Late Latin *archidiāconus,* ARCHDEACON.]
ar·chi·e·pis·co·pal (är′kē-ĭ-pĭs′kə-pəl) *adj.* Of or pertaining to an archbishop or an archbishopric. [Medieval Latin *archiepiscopālis,* from Late Latin *archiepiscopus,* ARCHBISHOP.]
ar·chi·e·pis·co·pate (är′kē-ĭ-pĭs′kə-pĭt, -pāt′) *n.* The rank, office, or term of an archbishop. [Medieval Latin *archiepiscopātus,* from Late Latin *archiepiscopus,* ARCHBISHOP.]
archil. Variant of **orchil.**
Ar·chi·lo·chi·an (är′kĭ-lō′kē-ən) *adj.* Of, pertaining to, or characteristic of Archilochus, Greek satiric poet of the 7th century B.C., or of the verse form invented by him.
ar·chi·mage (är′kə-māj′) *n.* A great magician or chief wizard. [Late Greek *arkhimagos* : ARCH- + *magos,* magician. See **magi.**]
ar·chi·man·drite (är′kə-măn′drīt′) *n.* In the Eastern Orthodox Church: **1.** A cleric ranking below a bishop. **2.** The head of a monastery or group of monasteries. [Late Latin *archimandrītēs, archimandrīta,* from Late Greek *arkhimandritēs* : ARCH- + *mandra†,* monastery, from Greek, enclosure, cattle pen.]
Ar·chi·me·de·an (är′kə-mē′dē-ən, -mĭ-dē′ən) *adj.* Of or pertaining to Archimedes or his inventions.
Archimedean screw *n.* An ancient apparatus for raising water, consisting of either a spiral tube around an inclined axis or an inclined tube containing a tight-fitting, broad-threaded screw. Also called "Archimedes' screw."
Ar·chi·me·des (är′kə-mē′dēz) (*c.* 287–212 B.C.). Greek mathematician and inventor from Syracuse. He is considered, with Karl F. Gauss and Isaac Newton, one of the three greatest mathematicians of all time. He discovered and analyzed the principle of the lever and invented the Archimedean screw for raising water. His most famous discovery, the principle of buoyancy, is said to have come to him when he observed the amount of water his body displaced in his bath. In his excitement he ran naked through the streets shouting "Eureka!" ("I have found it"). When Syracuse fell to the Romans, he was killed, it is said, while drawing geometric figures in the sand.
Archimedes' principle *n.* The principle that the apparent loss in the weight of a body immersed in a fluid is equal to the weight of the fluid displaced.
ar·chine, ar·shin (är-shēn′) *n.* A Russian unit of linear measure equivalent to 28 inches. [Russian *arshin,* of Turkic origin; akin to Turkish and Kazan Tatar *aršyn,* an ell.]
ar·chi·pel·a·go (är′kə-pĕl′ə-gō′) *n., pl.* **-goes** or **-gos.** *Abbr.* **arch.** **1.** A large group of islands. **2.** A sea containing many groups of islands, such as the Aegean. [From *Archipelago,* the Aegean Sea, from Italian *Arcipelago,* "the Chief Sea" (a misinterpretation of Greek *Aigaion pelagos,* the Aegean Sea) : ARCH- + Greek *pelagos,* sea.] **—ar·chi·pe·lag·ic** (är′kə-pə-lăj′ĭk) *adj.*
archit. architecture.
ar·chi·tect (är′kə-tĕkt′) *n. Abbr.* **arch.** **1.** One who designs and supervises the construction of buildings or other large structures, such as ships. **2.** Any planner or deviser: *the architect of European unity.* [French *architecte,* from Latin *architectus,* from Greek *arkhitektōn,* master builder : ARCH- + *tektōn,* builder, craftsman.]
ar·chi·tec·ton·ic (är′kə-tĕk-tŏn′ĭk) *adj.* **1.** Of or pertaining to architecture or design. **2.** Having qualities characteristic of architecture; designed and structured. **3.** *Philosophy.* Of or pertaining to the scientific systematization of knowledge. [Latin *architectonicus,* architectural, from Greek *arkhitektonikos,* from *arkhitektōn,* ARCHITECT.] **—ar·chi·tec·ton·i·cal·ly** *adv.*
ar·chi·tec·ton·ics (är′kə-tĕk-tŏn′ĭks) *n. Used with a singular verb.* **1.** The science of architecture. **2.** Structural design, as in a musical work. **3.** *Philosophy.* The scientific systematization of knowledge.
ar·chi·tec·ture (är′kə-tĕk′chər) *n. Abbr.* **arch., archit.** **1.** The art and science of designing and erecting buildings. **2.** A structure or structures collectively. **3.** A particular style and method of design and construction: *Byzantine architecture.* **4.** The planning or design evidenced in any structure or arrangement: *the architecture of nature.* [French, from Latin *architectūra,* from *architectus,* ARCHITECT.] **—ar·chi·tec·tur·al** *adj.* **—ar·chi·tec·tur·al·ly** *adv.*
ar·chi·trave (är′kə-trāv′) *n. Architecture.* **1.** The lowermost part of an entablature, resting directly on top of a column as in classical architecture. Also called "epistyle." **2.** The molding around a door or window. [Old French, from Old Italian, "chief beam" : ARCH- + *trave,* beam, from Latin *trabs.*]
ar·chi·val (är-kī′vəl) *adj.* Of, pertaining to, or kept in archives.
archival standards *pl.n.* Standards set by the U.S. Bureau of Standards to assure permanence of microfilm images.
ar·chive (är′kīv′) *n. Often* **archives.** **1.** An organized body of records pertaining to an organization, institution, or the like. **2.** A place in which such records are preserved. **3.** Any repository of evidence or information: *the archives of the mind.* [French *archive,* from Late Latin *archī(v)um,* from Greek *arkheion,* public office (plural *arkheia,* public records, archives), from *arkhē,* beginning, hence first place, government, from *arkhein†,* to begin.]
ar·chi·vist (är′kə-vĭst, är′kī′-) *n.* One who is in charge of archives.
ar·chi·volt (är′kə-vōlt′) *n.* Also **ar·chi·vault** (-vôlt′). *Architecture.* A decorative molding carried around an arched wall opening. [Italian *archivolto* : *arco,* arch, from Latin *arcus,* ARC + *volta,* VAULT.]
ar·chon (är′kŏn′, -kən) *n.* **1.** Any of the nine principal governing officials of ancient Athens. **2.** Any of various officials of the Byzantine Empire. **3.** *Often* **Archon.** In certain Gnostic systems, any of several powers believed to be superior to the angels. [Latin *archōn,* from Greek *arkhōn,* "ruler," from the present participle of *arkhein†,* to rule.] **—ar·chon·ship** *n.*
arch·priest (ärch-prēst′) *n.* Formerly, a priest holding first rank among the members of a cathedral chapter, acting as chief assistant to a bishop. Now used only as a title of honor. [Middle English *archeprest,* from Old French *archeprestre,* from Late Latin *archipresbyter* : ARCHI- + *presbyter,* PRIEST.] **—arch·priest·hood, arch·priest·ship** *n.*
arch·way (ärch′wā′) *n.* **1.** A passageway under an arch. **2.** An arch covering or enclosing an entrance or passageway.
-archy *suffix.* Indicates rule or government; for example, **oligarchy.** [Middle English *-archie,* from Old French, from Latin *-archia,* from Greek *-arkhia,* from *-arkhēs,* -ARCH.]
ar·ci·form (är′sə-fôrm′) *adj.* Formed like an arc. [Latin *arci-,* from *arcus,* bow, ARC + -FORM.]
arc jet *n.* An arc-jet engine.
arc-jet engine (ärk′jĕt′) *n.* A rocket engine that operates by heating the propellant gas with an electric arc.
arcked. Alternate past tense and past participle of **arc.**

archaic smile *This enigmatic expression, typical of early Greek sculpture, appears here on a statue of the goddess Persephone carved in about 510 B.C.*

archerfish *A freshwater fish of Southeast Asia that catches insects by shooting them down from overhanging foliage with a jet of water. An adult archerfish can hit its prey with remarkable accuracy over a distance of up to about 90 centimeters (3 feet).*

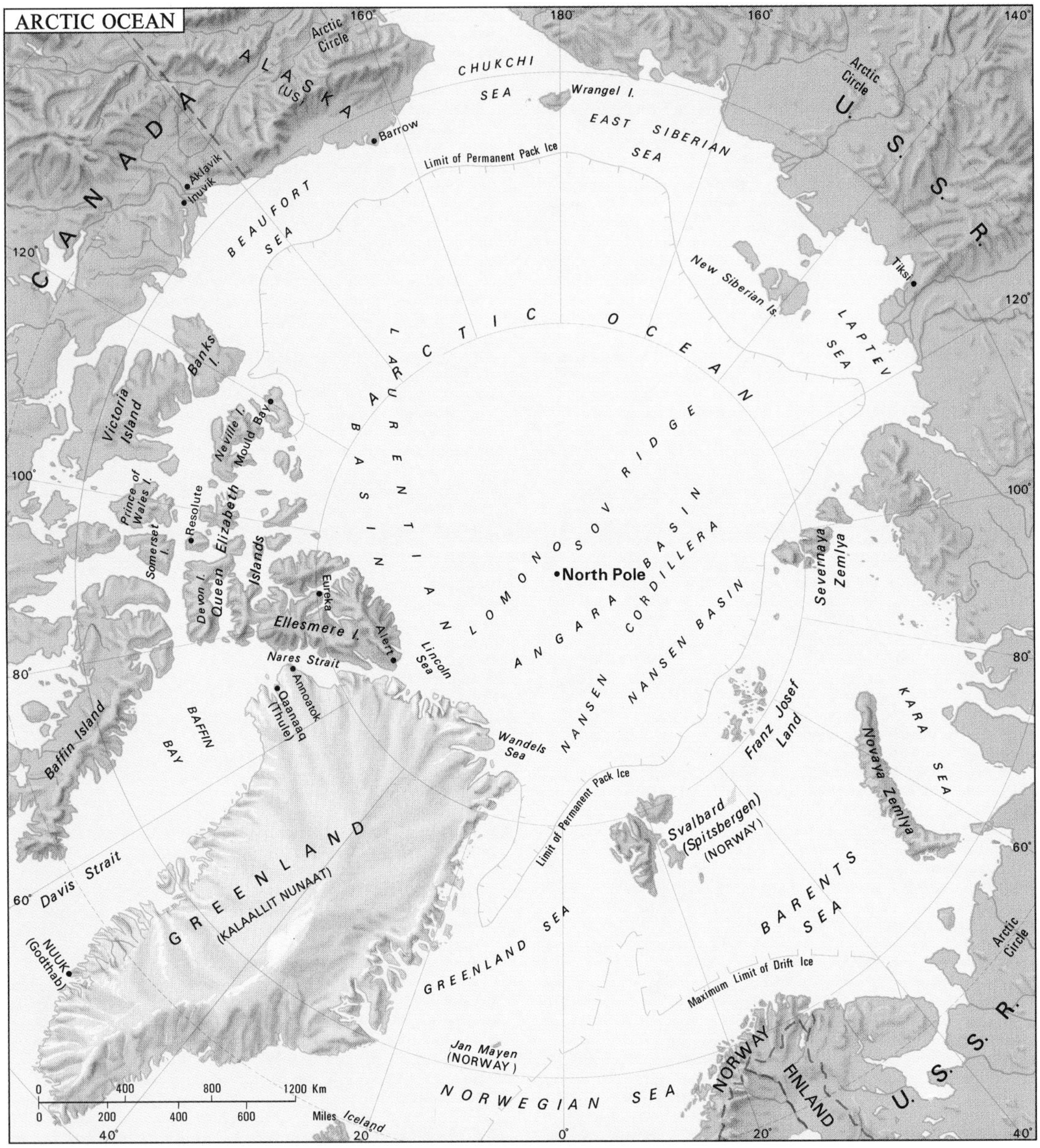

ARCTIC OCEAN

[Map of the Arctic Ocean region, showing Canada, Alaska, Greenland, the U.S.S.R., the North Pole, and surrounding seas including the Beaufort Sea, Chukchi Sea, East Siberian Sea, Laptev Sea, Kara Sea, Barents Sea, Greenland Sea, Norwegian Sea, and Baffin Bay. Features labeled include the Lomonosov Ridge, Nansen Basin, Angara Basin, Nansen Cordillera, Laurentian Basin, and various islands such as Wrangel I., New Siberian Is., Franz Josef Land, Novaya Zemlya, Severnaya Zemlya, Svalbard (Spitsbergen) (Norway), Jan Mayen (Norway), Banks I., Victoria Island, Ellesmere I., Baffin Island, Iceland. The Arctic Circle is marked.]

arctic fox *Found throughout the tundra regions of the Northern Hemisphere, the arctic fox has a very thick coat, rounded ears, and furred feet. It feeds on small birds, rodents, and carrion left by polar bears.*

arcking. Alternate present participle of **arc.**

arc lamp *n.* A lamp in which the light is produced by an electric arc between two closely spaced electrodes. Often carbon electrodes are used to produce an intense white light.

arc·tic (ärk′tĭk, är′tĭk) *adj.* **1.** *Usually* **Arctic.** Of, pertaining to, or characteristic of a geographical area extending from the North Pole to the northern timberline. **2. a.** Characteristic of the North Pole or polar regions; extremely cold. **b.** Suitable for very cold conditions: *arctic clothing.*
~*n.* A warm, waterproof overshoe. [Middle English *artik,* from Latin *ar(c)ticus,* from Greek *arktikos,* from *arktos,* bear, hence the northern constellation Ursa Major, the Great Bear, hence "north."] **—arc·ti·cal·ly** *adv.*

Arc·tic, the (ärk′tĭk, är′tĭk). Northernmost area of the earth, centered on the North Pole.

Arctic Archipelago. A group of more than 50 large islands in the Arctic Ocean between North America and Greenland. The islands are part of the Northwest Territories, Canada.

Arctic Circle *n.* A parallel of latitude 66°33′ north, along which the sun does not set on one day in the year, around June 21.

Arctic Current. See **Labrador Current.**

arctic fox *n.* A fox, *Alopex lagopus,* inhabiting arctic regions, having fur that is white or light-gray in winter and brown or blue-gray in summer. Also called "blue fox."

Arctic Ocean. The world's smallest ocean, covering some 14,000,-000 square kilometers (5,500,000 square miles) over the North Pole. It is covered by pack ice throughout the year, and its main outlet is the East Greenland Current, which takes icebergs far into the Atlantic Ocean.

arctic tern *n.* A tern, *Sterna paradisaea,* that breeds in the Arctic and migrates to the Antarctic, southern Africa, and South America.

Arc·to·gae·a (ärk′tə-jē′ə) *n.* The zoogeographical region that includes the Palaearctic, Nearctic, Ethiopian, and Oriental regions. Compare **Notogaea.** [New Latin, "north earth," from Greek *arktos,* bear, Ursa Major, north + *gaia,* earth.] **—Arc·to·gae·an** *adj.*

Arc·tu·rus (ärk-tŏŏr′əs, -tyŏŏr′əs) *n.* The brightest star in the constellation Boötes, approximately 36 light-years from earth. [Middle English *Artur, Arcturus,* from Latin *Arcturus,* from Greek *Arktouros,* "guardian of the Bear" (from its position behind the tail of Ursa Major) : *arktos,* bear + *ouros,* a guard.] **—Arc·tu·ri·an** *adj.*

ar·cu·ate (är′kyŏŏ-ĭt, -āt′) *adj.* Also **ar·cu·at·ed** (-ā′tĭd). Having the form of a bow; curved; arched: *arcuate veins in a leaf; arcuate horns.* [Latin *arcuātus,* past participle of *arcuāre,* to bend like a bow, from *arcus,* bow.] **—ar·cu·ate·ly** *adv.*

ar·cu·a·tion (är′kyŏŏ-ā′shən) *n.* **1.** The process of curving or the state of being curved. **2.** *Architecture.* The use of arches or vaults in building.

ar·cus se·ni·lis (är′kəs sə-nī′lĭs) *n.* A narrow, opaque circle around the cornea of the eye, often seen in old people. [Latin, "senile bow."]

arc-weld (ärk′wĕld′) *tr.v.* **-welded, -welding, -welds.** To weld by means of heat produced by an electric arc between an electrode and the part being welded. **—arc-weld·ing** *n.*

ard (ärd) *n.* A primitive plow, used in prehistoric times and now in some less developed countries. [Middle English, from Old Norse *arthr,* plow, from Latin *arātrum.*]

–ard, –art *suffix.* Indicates: **1.** One who does something to excess; for example, **drunkard, braggart.** **2.** One who is characterized by a particular, especially an undesirable, quality; for example, **sluggard.** [Middle English, from Old French from Germanic *-hart, -hard,* "bold, hardy," often in proper names such as *Raynard, Gerhart.*]

ar·deb (är'dĕb') *n.* A unit of dry measure in several countries of the Near East, usually equal to 5.6 U.S. bushels but with variations in different localities. [Colloquial Arabic *ardabb,* from Greek *artabē,* probably from Egyptian.]

ar·den·cy (är'dən-sē) *n.* The state or quality of being ardent.

Ar·dennes (är-dĕnz'). Wooded plateau in southeastern Belgium, extending into France and Luxembourg.

ar·dent (är'dənt) *adj.* **1. a.** Expressing or characterized by warmth of passion, emotion, or desire. **b.** Displaying or characterized by strong enthusiasm or devotion; fervent; zealous: *"an impassioned age, so ardent and serious in its pursuit of art"* (Walter Pater). **2.** Glowing; flashing; fierce: *ardent eyes.* **3.** Hot as fire; burning: *an ardent sun.* [Middle English *ardaunt,* from Old French *ardant,* from Latin *ardēns* (stem *ardent-*), present participle of *ardēre,* to burn.] —**ar·dent·ly** *adv.*

ardent spirits *pl.n.* Strong alcoholic drinks, such as whiskey.

ar·dor (är'dər) *n.* Also *chiefly British* **ar·dour.** **1. a.** Great warmth or intensity, as of emotion, passion, or desire. **b.** Fervent enthusiasm or devotion; zeal: *"the dazzling conquest of Mexico gave a new impulse to the ardor of discovery"* (William H. Prescott). **2.** Intense heat, as of fire. [Middle English *ardour,* from Old French, from Latin *ardor,* from *ardēre,* to burn.]

ar·du·ous (är'jŏŏ-əs) *adj.* **1.** Demanding great care, effort, or exertion; strenuous. **2.** Testing severely the powers of endurance; full of hardships: *a long, arduous journey.* **3.** Hard to climb or surmount; steep: *an arduous path.* —See Synonyms at **burdensome, hard.** [Latin *arduus,* high, steep, difficult.] —**ar·du·ous·ly** *adv.* —**ar·du·ous·ness** *n.*

are¹ (är). Present tense, indicative plural, and second person singular of **be.**

are² (âr, är) *n. Abbr.* **a, a.** A metric unit of area equal to 100 square meters. [French, from Latin *ārea,* AREA.]

ar·e·a (âr'ē-ə) *n.* **1.** A flat, open, or unoccupied piece of ground. **2.** A part of the earth's surface; a region. **3.** A distinct spatial extent; a part, section, or locality having a particular function or characteristic quality: *a residential area; a room with a living area and a dining area.* **4.** A field of study or activity: *the whole area of finance.* **5.** *Abbr.* **A** The measure of a planar region or of the surface of a solid. **6.** A section of computer storage set aside for a particular purpose. [Latin *ārea†,* open field.] —**ar·e·al** *adj.*
   Synonyms: district, locality, region, zone.

Area Code, area code *n.* A number, often with three digits, assigned to a telephone area, as in the United States and Canada, used when placing a call to another area.

a·re·ca (ə-rē'kə, ăr'ĭ-kə) *n.* Any of various tall palms of the genus *Areca,* of southeast Asia, having white flowers and red or orange egg-shaped nuts. See **betel palm.** [New Latin *Areca,* from Portuguese *areca,* from Malayalam *aṭekka, aṭakka.*]

a·re·na (ə-rē'nə) *n.* **1.** The area in the center of an ancient Roman amphitheater where contests and other spectacles were held. **2.** Any similar place: *a boxing arena.* **3.** A sphere or field of conflict, interest, or activity: *the political arena.* [Latin *(h)arēna,* sand, arena covered with sand, perhaps from Etruscan.]

ar·e·na·ceous (ăr'ə-nā'shəs) *adj.* **1.** Sandlike in appearance or qualities: *arenaceous limestone.* **2.** Growing in sandy areas. [Latin *(h)arēnaceus :* *(h)arēna,* sand, ARENA + -ACEOUS.]

arena stage *n.* The stage of a theater-in-the-round.

arena theater *n.* A **theater-in-the-round** (see).

ar·ene (ăr'ēn') *n. Chemistry.* An aromatic hydrocarbon or a derivative of an aromatic hydrocarbon. [AR(OMATIC) + -ENE.]

ar·e·nic·o·lous (ăr'ə-nĭk'ə-ləs) *adj.* Growing or living in sand. [Latin *(h)arēna,* sand, ARENA + -COLOUS.]

aren't (ärnt, är'ənt). Contraction of *are not.*

a·re·o·la (ə-rē'ə-lə) *n., pl.* **-lae** (-lē') or **-las.** Also **ar·e·ole** (âr'ē-ōl'). **1.** *Biology.* A small space or interstice, such as an area bounded by small veins in a leaf or an insect's wing. **2.** *Anatomy.* A small, dark-colored area around a center portion, as about a nipple or part of the iris of the eye. [New Latin, from Latin *āreola,* diminutive of *ārea,* open place, AREA.] —**a·re·o·lar, a·re·o·late** *adj.*

Ar·e·op·a·gus (ăr'ē-ŏp'ə-gəs) *n.* The highest council of ancient Athens. [Greek *Areios pagos,* Ares' hill.] —**Ar·e·op·a·gite** (ăr'ē-ŏp'ə-jīt', -gīt') *n.* —**Ar·e·op·a·git·ic** (ăr'ē-ŏp'ə-jĭt'ĭk) *adj.*

Ar·es (âr'ēz'). *Greek Mythology.* The god of war, identified with the Roman god Mars. [Greek *Ares†,* god of war, the planet Mars.]

a·rête (ə-rāt') *n.* A sharp, narrow mountain ridge or spur. [French *arête,* fishbone, spiny ridge, from Old French *areste,* from Latin *arista†,* fishbone, spine, beard of grain.]

ar·e·thu·sa (ăr'ə-thŏŏ'zə, -sə) *n.* Any of several orchids of the genus *Arethusa,* especially *A. bulbosa,* of eastern North America, having a solitary rose-purple flower fringed with yellow. [After the nymph ARETHUSA.]

Ar·e·thu·sa (ăr'ə-thŏŏ'zə, -sə). *Greek Mythology.* A nymph who was turned into a spring so as to avoid the attentions of the river god Alpheus. [Latin, from Greek *Arethousa.*]

A·re·ti·no (ä'rä-tē'nō), **Pietro** (1492-1556). Italian writer and satirist. He wrote five comedies, but was best known for his satirical attacks on the wealthy and powerful, which, together with a collection of lewd poems, *Sonnetti Lussuriosi* (1524), compelled him to flee Rome in 1527. For the rest of his life he lived in Venice, amassing wealth by writing satires or by being paid not to write them.

arg. argent.

Arg. Argentina.

argal. Variant of *argol.*

ar·ga·li (är'gə-lē) *n., pl.* **-lis** or collectively **argali.** A large wild sheep, *Ovis ammon,* of mountainous regions of central and northern Asia, the male of which has massive, spirally curved horns. [Mongolian *argali,* mountain goat.]

Ar·gand diagram (är'gänd', -gänd') *n. Mathematics.* A diagram in which complex numbers are represented in a coordinate system with two perpendicular axes determining the real and imaginary parts of the number. The number $x + iy$ is the point (x, y) or the directed line segment from the origin to the point (x,y). [After Jean-Robert *Argand* (1768-1822), French mathematician.]

ar·gent (är'jənt) *n.* **1.** *Poetic.* Silver or anything resembling it. **2.** *Abbr.* **arg.** *Heraldry.* The metal silver, represented by the color white. [Middle English, from Old French, from Latin *argentum.*] —**ar·gent** *adj.*

ar·gen·tic (är-jĕn'tĭk) *adj.* Of or containing silver. Said especially of chemical compounds containing silver having a valence of 2 or 3. [Latin *argentum,* silver + -IC.]

ar·gen·tif·er·ous (är'jən-tĭf'ər-əs) *adj.* Bearing or producing silver. [ARGENT + -FEROUS.]

Ar·gen·ti·na (är'jən-tē'nə) *Abbr.* **Arg.** Country of South America. It was a Spanish colony from 1620 until independence was proclaimed in 1816. Since 1929 the military have intervened in the government several times, most notably in 1943, a move that paved the way for the rise of Col. Juan Perón (president 1945-55, 1973-74). He was succeeded by his third wife, Isabel, who was deposed by the military (1976). In 1982 Argentinian forces occupied South Georgia and the Falkland Islands, which the country claims, but were expelled by a British task force. Argentina is among the most developed Latin-American countries and was the most prosperous until the recent political instability. The fertile pampas and sheep ranches of Patagonia provide most of its exports: meat, cere-

ard *A farmer using an ard in Morocco. The ard is a primitive type of plowshare, having no moldboard or other device for turning the soil.*

als, hides and skins, wool, and linseed oil. It has few mineral resources, but does produce most of its own oil. Area, 2,776,889 square kilometers (1,072,157 square miles). Population, 27,900,000. Capital, Buenos Aires. [Spanish *(Tierra) Argentina,* "silvery (land)," (with reference to the rivers and lakes), from Latin, feminine of *argentīnus,* silvery, ARGENTINE.] **—Ar·gen·tine** (är′jən-tēn′, -tīn′), **Ar·gen·tin·i·an** (är′jən-tĭn′ē-ən) *n. & adj.*

ar·gen·tine (är′jən-tīn′, -tēn′) *adj.* Silvery.
∼n. **1.** Any of various silvery metals. **2.** Any of several small, silvery marine fishes of the family Argentinidae. [French *argentin,* from Latin *argentīnus,* from *argentum,* silver, ARGENT.]

ar·gen·tite (är′jən-tīt′) *n.* A valuable silver ore, Ag_2S, with a lustrous, lead-gray color. [Latin *argentum,* silver, ARGENT + -ITE.]

ar·gen·tous (är-jĕn′təs) *adj.* Of or containing silver. Said especially of chemical compounds containing silver with a valence of 1. [Latin *argentum,* silver + -OUS.]

ar·gil (är′jĭl) *n.* Clay, especially that used by potters. [Middle English *argil, argilla,* from Latin *argilla,* from Greek *argillos.*]

ar·gil·la·ceous (är′jə-lā′shəs) *adj.* Containing, made of, or resembling clay; clayey. [Latin *argillāceus* : *argilla,* ARGIL + -ACEOUS.]

ar·gil·lite (är′jə-līt′) *n.* A metamorphic rock, intermediate between shale and slate, that does not possess true slaty cleavage. [Latin *argilla,* ARGIL + -ITE.] **—ar·gil·lit·ic** (är′jə-lĭt′ĭk) *adj.*

ar·gi·nine (är′jə-nēn′) *n.* An essential amino acid, $C_6H_{14}N_4O_2$, obtained from plant and animal protein or the digestive action of bacteria. [German *Arginin* : perhaps Greek *arginoeis,* bright, white + -INE.]

Ar·give (är′jīv′, -gīv′) *adj.* **1.** Of or pertaining to Argos. **2.** Of or pertaining to the Greeks or Greece.
∼n. A Greek, especially an inhabitant of Argos.

argle-bargle. Variant of **argy-bargy.**

Ar·go (är′gō) *n.* **1.** *Greek Mythology.* The ship in which Jason sailed in search of the Golden Fleece. **2.** A constellation in the Southern Hemisphere, now known by the names of its four smaller parts, **Carina, Puppis, Pyxis,** and **Vela** *(all of which see).*

ar·gol, ar·gal (är′gəl) *n.* Crude tartar deposited on casks as a by-product of winemaking. [Middle English *argoile,* from Norman-French *argoil*†.]

ar·gon (är′gŏn′) *n. Symbol* **Ar** A colorless, odorless, inert gaseous element constituting approximately one percent of the earth's atmosphere, from which it is commercially obtained by fractionation of liquid air for use in electric lamps, fluorescent tubes, electronic valves, and as an inert gas shield in arc-welding. Atomic number 18, atomic weight 39.94, melting point −189.4°C, boiling point −185.9°C. [Greek, neuter of *argos,* inert, idle, "not working" : *a-,* without + *ergon,* work.]

ar·go·naut (är′gə-nôt′) *n.* A mollusk, the **paper nautilus** *(see).* [New Latin *Argonauta* (genus name), from Latin, ARGONAUT.]

Ar·go·naut (är′gə-nôt′) *n. Greek Mythology.* One who sailed with Jason on the *Argo* in search of the Golden Fleece. [Latin *Argonauta,* from Greek *Argonautēs* : *Argō,* name of Jason's ship + *nautēs,* sailor, from *naus,* ship.] **—Ar·go·nau·tic** (är′gə-nô′tĭk) *adj.*

Ar·gonne (är-gŏn′, är′gŏn′). Wooded, hilly region of eastern France, forming a natural barrier between the districts of Champagne and Lorraine. It was a major battleground throughout World War I.

Ar·gos (är′gŏs′, -gəs). A city of ancient Greece, in the northeastern Peloponnese. Occupied from the early Bronze Age, it is possibly Greece's oldest city. Argos was one of the strongest cities of ancient Greece until the rise of Sparta and later flourished as a trade center under Roman control.

ar·go·sy (är′gə-sē) *n., pl.* **-sies.** **1.** A large merchant ship. **2.** A fleet of such ships. [Earlier *argose, ragusye,* from Italian *ragusea,* vessel of *Ragusa,* former name of the port of Dubrovnik, Yugoslavia.]

ar·got (är′gō, -gət) *n.* A specialized vocabulary or set of idioms used by a particular class or group; especially, the jargon of the underworld. [French *argot*†.] **—ar·got·ic** (är-gŏt′ĭk) *adj.*

ar·gu·a·ble (är′gyo͞o-ə-bəl) *adj.* **1.** Open to argument; questionable. **2.** That can be supported by argument. —See Synonyms at **doubtful.** **—ar·gu·a·bly** *adv.*

ar·gue (är′gyo͞o) *v.* **-gued, -guing, -gues.** *—tr.* **1.** To put forward reasons for or against; debate. **2.** To prove or attempt to prove by reasoning; maintain in argument; contend. **3.** To give evidence of; indicate: *"similarities can always be used to argue descent"* (Isaac Asimov). **4.** To persuade or influence, as by presenting reasons: *He argued me into going.* *—intr.* **1.** To put forward reasons for or against an opinion, procedure, proposal, or the like. **2.** To quarrel; engage in a dispute. —See Synonyms at **discuss.** [Middle English *arguen,* from Old French *arguer,* to blame, argue against, from Latin *arguere,* to make clear, assert, prove.] **—ar·gu·er** *n.*
Synonyms: *bicker, haggle, quarrel, squabble, wrangle.*

ar·gu·fy (är′gyə-fī′) *v.* **-fied, -fying, -fies.** *Regional.* *—tr.* To argue over. *—intr.* To argue stubbornly; wrangle. **—ar·gu·fi·er** *n.*

ar·gu·ment (är′gyə-mənt) *n.* **1. a.** A discussion in which reasons are put forward in support of or against an opinion, procedure, proposal, or the like; a debate. **b.** A quarrel; a contention. **2. a.** A course of reasoning aimed at demonstrating the truth or falsehood of something. **b.** A fact or statement advanced in support of or against a plan of action, suggestion, proposal, or the like. **3.** A summary or short statement of the plot or subject of a literary work. **4.** *Logic.* The minor premise in a syllogism. **5.** *Mathematics.* **a.** The independent variable of a function. **b.** The **amplitude** *(see)* of a complex number. [Middle English, from Old French, from Latin *argūmentum,* from *arguere,* to ARGUE.]
Synonyms: *controversy, dispute, wrangling.*

ar·gu·men·ta·tion (är′gyə-mĕn-tā′shən) *n.* **1.** The act or process of presenting and elaborating an argument. **2.** Deductive reasoning in debate. **3.** A debate.

ar·gu·men·ta·tive (är′gyə-mĕn′tə-tĭv) *adj.* **1.** Given to excessive arguing; disputatious. **2.** Of or characterized by argument; controversial: *an argumentative discourse.* **—ar·gu·men·ta·tive·ly** *adv.* **—ar·gu·men·ta·tive·ness** *n.*

ar·gu·men·tum (är′gyə-mĕn′təm) *n., pl.* **-ta** (-tə). *Logic.* An argument, proof, or appeal to reason in support or refutation of a proposition. [Latin, "argument."]

argumentum ad hom·i·nem (ăd hŏm′ə-nĕm′) *n.* An argument appealing to personal prejudices and emotions rather than to logic or reason. [Latin, "argument to the man."]

Ar·gus (är′gəs). *Greek Mythology.* A giant with a hundred eyes who was made guardian of Io and later slain by Hermes.

Ar·gus-eyed (är′gəs-īd′) *adj.* Extremely observant; vigilant.

argus pheasant *n.* A large bird, *Argusianus argus,* having long tail feathers marked with brilliantly colored eyelike spots. [After the eyelike markings, imagined to resemble the numerous eyes of Argus.]

ar·gy-bar·gy (är′jē-bär′jē) *n.* Also **ar·gle-bar·gle** (är′gəl-bär′gəl). *Chiefly British Informal.* Quarreling; bickering. [19th century : Scottish, variant of *argle-bargle,* reduplication of *argue,* altered through confusion with or perhaps through influence of *haggle.*] **—ar·gy-bar·gy** *v.*

ar·gyle, ar·gyll (är′gīl′) *n.* **1.** A geometric knitting pattern of varicolored, diamond-shaped areas on a solid color background. **2.** A sock knit in an argyle pattern. [After Campbell of *Argyle* (Argyll), the clan whose tartan was adapted for this pattern.]

Ar·gyll (är-gīl′, är′gīl′). Also **Ar·gyll·shire** (-shĭr). Former county in west-central Scotland, since 1975 divided between Highland and Strathclyde regions.

ar·hat (är′hət) *n.* A Buddhist monk who has reached the state of nirvana. [Sanskrit, "(one) deserving respect," from *arhati,* "he deserves."]

År·hus (ôr′ho͞os′). Commercial and industrial city, on Århus Bay in Jutland, Denmark. It is Denmark's second-largest city and one of its oldest. Until 1948 its name was spelled "Aarhus."

a·ri·a (är′ē-ə) *n. Music.* **1.** An air; a melody. **2.** A solo vocal piece with instrumental accompaniment, as in an opera or oratorio. [Italian *aria,* melody, "(atmospheric) air," from Latin *āēra,* accusative of *āēr,* air, from Greek *aēr.*]

Ar·i·ad·ne (ăr′ē-ăd′nē). *Greek Mythology.* The daughter of Minos and Pasiphae who gave Theseus the thread with which to find his way out of the Minotaur's labyrinth.

Ar·i·an[1] (ăr′ē-ən, âr′-) *adj.* Of or pertaining to Arius or Arianism.
∼n. A believer in Arianism.

Arian[2]. Variant of **Aryan.**

-arian *suffix.* Indicates: **1.** Sect; for example, **Unitarian.** **2.** Belief, advocacy; for example, **authoritarian, vegetarian.** [Latin *-ārius,* -ARY + -AN.]

Ar·i·an·ism (ăr′ē-ə-nĭz′əm, âr′-) *n. Theology.* The doctrines of Arius, denying that Jesus was of the same substance as God and holding instead that he was only the highest of created beings.

ar·id (ăr′ĭd) *adj.* **1.** Very dry; lacking sufficient rainfall to support agriculture; parched. **2.** Lacking interest or feeling; lifeless; dull. [French *aride,* from Latin *āridus,* from *ārēre,* to be dry or parched.] **—a·rid·i·ty** (ə-rĭd′ə-tē), **ar·id·ness** *n.* **—ar·id·ly** *adv.*

ar·i·el (ăr′ē-əl, âr′-) *n.* A gazelle, *Gazella arabica* (or *dama*), native to Arabia. [Arabic *'aryal,* stag.]

Ar·ies (âr′ēz′, âr′ē-ēz′, ăr′-) *n.* **1.** A constellation in the Northern Hemisphere near Taurus and Pisces. **2. a.** The first sign of the **zodiac** *(see).* Also called the "Ram." **b.** One born under this sign. [Latin *ariēs,* ram.]

a·ri·et·ta (ăr′ē-ĕt′ə) *n.* Also **a·ri·ette** (-ĕt′). A short aria. [Italian, diminutive of ARIA.]

a·right (ə-rīt′) *adv.* Properly; correctly. [Middle English *aright,* Old English *ariht, on riht* : A- (on) + *riht,* RIGHT (noun).]

ar·il (ăr′əl) *n. Botany.* An outer covering or appendage of some seeds, arising at or near the hilum. It is often fleshy or brightly colored, as in the yew. [New Latin *arillus,* from Medieval Latin *arillus*†, raisin, grape seed.] **—ar·il·late** (ăr′ə-lāt′) *adj.*

aril *The waxy red aril, or coating, of nutmeg seeds is used to make mace, an aromatic spice. The seeds grow inside a fleshy fruit that splits open when ripe.*

ar·il·lode (ăr′ə-lōd′) *n. Botany.* An appendage or covering that resembles an aril but arises from the micropyle rather than the hilum. [New Latin *arillus,* ARIL + -ODE (like).]

a·rio·so (ä-ryō′sō) *adv. Music.* In the style of an aria. Used as a direction.
∼n., pl. **ariosos.** A piece of recitative sung in this style, rather than the usual declamatory style. [Italian, from ARIA.] **—a·rio·so** *adj.*

A·ri·os·to (ä′rē-ô′stō), **Ludovico** (1474–1533). Italian poet and dramatist. He is chiefly remembered for his epic comic masterpiece, *Orlando Furioso,* published in its final form in 1532.

a·rise (ə-rīz′) *intr.v.* **arose** (ə-rōz′), **arisen** (ə-rĭz′ən), **arising, arises.** **1.** To get up, as from a sitting or prone position. **2.** To move upward; ascend. **3.** To come into being; originate. **4.** To result, issue, or proceed. Used with *from.* **5.** To become apparent. [Middle English *arisen,* Old English *ārīsan* : A- (up) + *rīsan,* RISE.]

a·ris·ta (ə-rĭs′tə) *n., pl.* **-tae** (-tē). A bristlelike part, such as the awns of grasses or the antennae of certain insects. [New Latin, from Latin *arista*†, beard of grain, spine.] **—a·ris·tate** *adj.*

Ar·is·tar·chus of Sa·mos (ăr′ĭs-tär′kəs; sā′mŏs) *(fl.* 270 B.C.). Greek

PRONUNCIATION KEY

ă, pat; ā, pay; âr, care;
ä, father, are; b, bib;
ch, church; d, deed; ĕ, pet;
ē, be; f, fife; g, gag; h, hat;
hw, which; ĭ, pit; ī, pie;
îr, pier; j, judge; k, kick;
l, lid, needle; m, mum;
n, no, sudden; ng, thing;
ŏ, pot; ō, toe; ô, paw, for;
oi, noise; ou, out; o͝o, book;
o͞o, boot; p, pop; r, roar;
s, sauce; sh, ship, dish;
t, tight; th, thin, path;
th, this, bathe; ŭ, cut; ûr, fur;
v, valve; w, with; y, yes;
z, zebra, size; zh, vision;
ə, about, item, edible,
gallop, circus, peaceful

IN FOREIGN WORDS:

à, *Fr.* ami; œ, *Fr.* feu, *Ger.* schön; ü, *Fr.* tu, *Ger.* über; KH, *Ger.* ich, *Scot.* loch; N, *Fr.* bon; y′, *Fr.* Compiègne

STRESS MARKS:

Primary stress: ′
in·cite′ (ĭn-sīt′)
Secondary stress: ′
in′sight′ (ĭn′sīt′)

astronomer of the Alexandrian school. He was one of the first men to propose that the sun was the center of the universe and that the earth moves around it.

ar·is·toc·ra·cy (ăr′ĭs-tŏk′rə-sē) *n., pl.* **-cies.** **1.** A hereditary privileged ruling class or nobility. **2.** Government by the nobility or by a privileged minority or upper class. **3.** A state or country having this form of government. **4.** *Rare.* **a.** Government by the best citizens. **b.** A state having such government. **5.** Any group or class considered to be superior. [Old French *aristocratie,* from Late Latin *aristocratia,* from Greek *aristokratia,* "rule by the best (citizens)" : *aristos,* best + -CRACY.]

a·ris·to·crat (ə-rĭs′tə-krăt′, ăr′ĭs-tə-) *n.* **1.** A member of the nobility or aristocracy. **2.** A person having the tastes, opinions, manners, and other characteristics of an upper class. **3.** A person who advocates government by an aristocracy. **4.** One that is superior in a specified field: *The aristocrat of pianos.* [French *aristocrate,* from *aristocratie,* ARISTOCRACY.] **—a·ris·to·crat·ic, a·ris·to·crat·i·cal** *adj.* **—a·ris·to·crat·i·cal·ly** *adv.*

Ar·is·toph·a·nes (ăr′ĭs-tŏf′ə-nēz′) (*c.* 448–*c.* 387 B.C.). Greek comic poet and dramatist, considered the greatest of ancient writers of satirical comedy. Among his surviving plays are *The Clouds* (423), *Lysistrata* (411), and *The Frogs* (405).

Ar·is·to·te·li·an (ăr′ĭs-tə-tē′lē-ən, -tēl′yən) *adj.* Of or pertaining to Aristotle or his philosophy.
~n. A follower of Aristotle or his teachings.

Aristotelian logic *n.* Aristotle's deductive method of logic and the logical system based on this, especially the theory of the syllogism.

Ar·is·tot·le (ăr′ĭs-tŏt′l) (384–322 B.C.). Greek ethical, metaphysical, and political philosopher, who wrote on most branches of learning, including physics and biology, and whose influence extended for more than a thousand years. From 367 to 347 he studied under Plato; from 342 to *c.* 339 he was tutor to Alexander the Great. He returned to Athens and opened a school, the Lyceum, in 335. The most important of his surviving works are the six-volume treatise on logic, *Organon,* the *Physics,* the *Nicomachean Ethics,* and the *Politics.* The fundamental propositions of Aristotle's system of thought were that theory should follow upon the empirical observation of nature and things and that logic, based upon the syllogism, was the essential method of all rational inquiry.

a·rith·me·tic (ə-rĭth′mə-tĭk) *n.* **1.** The mathematics of integers under simple operations such as addition, subtraction, multiplication, division, involution, and evolution. **2.** Counting or problem-solving involving arithmetic operations.
~adj. **ar·ith·met·ic** (ăr′ĭth-mĕt′ĭk). Also **ar·ith·met·i·cal** (-ĭ-kəl). Of or pertaining to arithmetic. [Middle English *ar(i)smet(r)yk, arithmet(r)ik,* from Old French *ar(i)smetique,* from Latin *arithmētica,* from Greek *arithmētikē (tekhnē),* "(the art) of counting," from the feminine of *arithmētikos,* of counting, from *arithmein,* to count, from *arithmos,* number.] **—ar·ith·met·i·cal·ly** *adv.*

a·rith·me·ti·cian (ə-rĭth′mə-tĭsh′ən) *n.* An arithmetic expert.

ar·ith·met·ic mean (ăr′ĭth-mĕt′ĭk) *n.* The number obtained by dividing the sum of a set of quantities by the number of quantities in the set. Also called "average," "mean."

ar·ith·met·ic progression (ăr′ĭth-mĕt′ĭk) *n.* A sequence, such as the odd integers 1, 3, 5, 7, . . . , in which each term after the first is formed by adding a constant to each preceding term.

ar·ith·met·ic series (ăr′ĭth-mĕt′ĭk) *n.* A series in which the terms form an arithmetic progression, as in 1 + 3 + 5 + ...

-arium *suffix.* Indicates a place or housing for; for example, **planetarium, terrarium.** [Latin, from the neuter of *-ārius,* -ARY.]

A·ri·us (ə-rī′əs, âr′ē-əs) (*c.* 250–336). Christian priest of Alexandria, whose teaching gave rise to the Arianism heresy.

A·ri·zo·na (ăr′ə-zō′nə). A state in the southwestern United States. The capital and largest city is Phoenix. The state includes the Grand Canyon, the Painted Desert, and the Petrified Forest National Park. It joined the Union in 1912.

Ar·ju·na (är′jo͞o-nə). *Hinduism.* The prince in the **Bhagavad-Gita** *(see)* to whom Krishna, disguised as a charioteer, expounds the whole nature of being, including the nature of God and the means by which human beings can come to know him.

ark (ärk) *n.* **1. Ark.** The chest containing the Ten Commandments written on stone tablets which represented to the Hebrews a sacred symbol of God's presence and was carried by them during their desert wanderings. Numbers 10:35. Also called "Ark of the Covenant." **2.** The **Holy Ark** *(see).* **3.** The boat built by Noah in readiness for the Flood. Genesis 6–9. **4.** Any large, commodious boat. **5.** A place of shelter or refuge. [Middle English *ark,* Old English *arc, aerc, earc,* from Common Germanic *ark-* (unattested), from Latin *arca,* chest, box, coffer.]

Ar·kan·sas (är′kən-sô′). A state in the central-southwestern United States. The capital and largest city is Little Rock. Most of its eastern border is formed by the Mississippi River. It joined the Union in 1836.

Ar·khan·gelsk (är-kăn′gĕlsk, -KHän′-). *English* **Arch·an·gel** (ärk′ān′-jəl). City and major timber port of the U.S.S.R., in the northwest on the Northern Dvina River.

ar·kose (är-kōz′) *n.* Coarse-grained sandstone containing at least 25 percent feldspar as well as quartz. [French.]

Ark·wright, (ärk′rīt′) **Sir Richard** (1732–92). British inventor. He patented his invention, a machine for spinning called a water frame, in 1769. He also established cotton mills that were among the earliest examples of the new factory system.

Arles (ärlz). City and port on the Rhône delta in Provence in southern France. It was one of the leading cities in the Western Roman Empire (a Roman arena is still used for bullfights and plays) and the capital of a medieval kingdom.

arm[1] (ärm) *n.* **1.** Either of the upper limbs of the human body connecting the hand and wrist to the shoulder. **2.** A part similar to an arm, such as the forelimb of an animal, a branch of a tree, or a long part projecting from a central support in a machine. **3.** Anything designed to cover or support the human arm, such as a sleeve on an article of clothing or a projecting support on a chair or sofa. **4.** Anything branching out from a large mass: *an arm of the sea.* **5.** An administrative or functional branch, as of an organization. **6.** Power; authority: *the long arm of the law.* **7.** *Mathematics.* Either of the two straight lines that form an angle. **8.** *Physics.* Any of the resistors forming a Wheatstone bridge or similar circuit. **—arm in arm.** With arms linked one through the other. **—at arm's length.** At a distance; not on friendly or intimate terms. **—twist someone's arm.** To coerce or put pressure on someone. **—with open arms.** Cordially; hospitably. [Middle English *arm,* Old English *arm, earm.*]

arm[2] *n.* **1.** A weapon, especially a firearm. **2.** A branch of a military force, such as the infantry, cavalry, or air force.
~v. **armed, arming, arms.** *—intr.* **1.** To supply or equip oneself with weapons. **2.** To prepare oneself for or as if for warfare. *—tr.* **1.** To equip with weapons. **2.** To prepare for war; fortify. **3.** To provide with anything that strengthens, increases efficiency, or prepares. **4.** *Military.* To prepare (a bomb, for example) for detonation, as by releasing a safety device. [Back-formation from ARMS (plural).] **—arm·er** *n.*

ar·ma·da (är-mä′də, -mā′də) *n.* **1.** A fleet of warships. **2.** Any large mobile force. **3. Armada.** The **Spanish Armada** *(see).* [Spanish, from Medieval Latin *armāta,* army, fleet, from Latin *armātus,* past participle of *armāre,* to arm, from *arma,* arms.]

ar·ma·dil·lo (är′mə-dĭl′ō) *n., pl.* **-los.** Any of several omnivorous, burrowing mammals of the family Dasypodidae, of southern North America and Central and South America, having a covering of armorlike, jointed, bony plates. [Spanish, diminutive of *armado,* armor-plated, past participle of *armar,* to arm, from Latin *armāre,* from *arma,* arms.]

Ar·ma·ged·don (är′mə-gĕd′n) *n.* **1.** The scene of a final battle between the forces of good and evil, prophesied in the Bible to occur at the end of the world. Revelation 16:16. **2.** Any great conflict causing widespread destruction. [Late Latin *Armagedōn,* from Greek, from Hebrew *har megiddōn,* the mountain region of *Megiddo,* site of several great battles in the Old Testament.]

Ar·magh (är-mä′). A market town in the county of Armagh, in the south of Northern Ireland. It is the seat of both the Roman Catholic and Protestant primates of Ireland.

Ar·ma·gnac (är′mən-yăk′) *n.* A dry brandy of superior quality made in the department of Gers in southwestern France. [After *Armagnac,* former name of the region.]

ar·ma·ment (är′mə-mənt) *n.* **1.** The weapons and supplies of war with which a military unit is equipped. **2.** *Often* **armaments.** All the military forces and war equipment of a country. **3.** A military force equipped for war. **4.** The process of arming for war. [Late Latin *armāmentum* (singular), from Latin *armāmenta* (plural), implements, equipment, from *arma,* tools, ARMS.]

ar·ma·men·tar·i·um (är′mə-mĕn-târ′ē-əm) *n., pl.* **-taria** (-târ′ē-ə). **1.** The complete equipment of a physician or medical institution, including medicines, supplies, and instruments. **2.** All the articles used in a field of activity; paraphernalia. [Latin, store of weapons. See **armament, -arium.**]

ar·ma·ture (är′mə-cho͝or′) *n.* **1.** *Electricity.* **a.** The rotating part of a dynamo consisting essentially of copper wire wound around an iron core. **b.** The moving part of an electromagnetic device such as a relay, buzzer, or loud-speaker. **c.** A piece of soft iron connecting the poles of a magnet. **2.** *Biology.* The protective covering or structure of an animal or plant. **3.** A framework serving as a supporting core for clay sculpture. **4.** *Archaic.* Armor. [Latin *armātūra,* equipment, from *armāre,* to arm, from *arma,* weapons, tools.]

arm·band (ärm′bănd′) *n.* A strip of material worn around the upper arm for identification or as a sign of mourning.

arm·chair (ärm′châr′) *n.* A chair, usually upholstered, with supports at the sides for the arms or elbows.
~adj. Remote from active involvement; purely theoretical: *an armchair warrior.*

armed (ärmd) *adj.* **1.** Equipped with weapons. **2.** Having or characterized by an arm or arms of a specified kind or number. Usually used in combination: *strong-armed.* **3.** Ready to face adversity.

armed forces *pl.n.* The military forces of a country or countries. Also called "armed services."

Ar·me·ni·a (är-mē′nē-ə, -mēn′yə). Ancient Asian kingdom centered on Mt. Ararat and now divided between Turkey, Iran, and the Armenian Soviet Socialist Republic. Established in the 8th century B.C., it became the world's first country to make Christianity the state religion (A.D. 303). It was partitioned between Persia and the Eastern Roman Empire (A.D. 387), and thereafter endured many conquerors. Between 1894 and 1915 the Turks massacred most of the Armenians because they were Christians.

Ar·me·ni·an (är-mē′nē-ən, -mēn′yən) *n.* **1.** A native or inhabitant of Armenia. **2.** The Indo-European language of the Armenians. **—Ar·me·ni·an** *adj.*

Armenian Church *n.* The independent church of the Armenians, founded in about A.D. 300 and similar to the Eastern Orthodox

Arjuna *The legendary Indian hero, with a red quiver slung across him, fires an arrow in battle. His charioteer is the blue-skinned Hindu god Krishna.*

armadillo *All species of armadillo are protected by small plates of bone covered with horny skin. They are found in southern North America and Central and South America. This is a Brazilian armadillo that grows to about 45 centimeters (18 inches) long; some species can reach a length of 90 centimeters (3 feet).*

armor

PROTECTIVE COVERING FOR COMBAT
The continuing struggle to provide a defense against new arms technology

Armor made of rigid plates was originally worn by the Greeks in about 700 B.C. Several other types, including scale armor (overlapping metal plates attached to fabric) and mail (interlocking metal rings) were widely used by soldiers of the Roman Empire. In 11th-century Europe, mail was the predominant armor; whalebone, wax-hardened leather (cuir bouilli), or metal plates came into use as additional protection from the end of the 13th century.

Mail was the most used form of armor in early medieval Europe because it was readily available. From the 14th century, plate armor was used increasingly, perhaps to give greater protection against the longbow and the halberd. In turn, weapon design changed in response to the new plate armor—swords, for example, were more pointed to penetrate the gaps between plates, and stronger to smash through the plates.

The great period of the suit (or harness) of armor was the 15th century. By the early 16th century, magnificent custom-made suits, often elaborately etched and gilded, proclaimed the wealth and status of the wearer, and horse armor was sometimes made to match the rider's suit. Apart from the chamfron to cover a horse's head, armor for horses was never widely used.

The average weight of full armor was about 22.7 kilograms (50 pounds)—no more than the weight of the equipment carried by a modern soldier. The popular belief that a knight had to be hoisted into his saddle with a crane is a myth; the main source of discomfort was heat.

During the 14th and 15th centuries jousts and tournaments became popular as a sport, rather than a military exercise, and specially reinforced armor was designed for combatants.

With the growing ascendancy of the infantry and firearms, full armor became obsolete. Light armor consisting of a cuirass (back and breast plate) and a helmet continued to be worn by certain cavalry units until the 20th century. During World War I there was a renewed need for head protection, this time from gas as well as bullets. In World War II gas masks and helmets were issued in vast numbers and bullet-resistant vests were made from a form of scale armor.

Today the term "armored" usually refers to vehicles and aircraft, but the armed forces, the police, and bomb-disposal units all depend on equipment such as flame-resistant headgear and body suits, gas masks, and riot shields. Bullet-proof vests have fiber-glass inserts over which impact-absorbing ceramic plates fit.

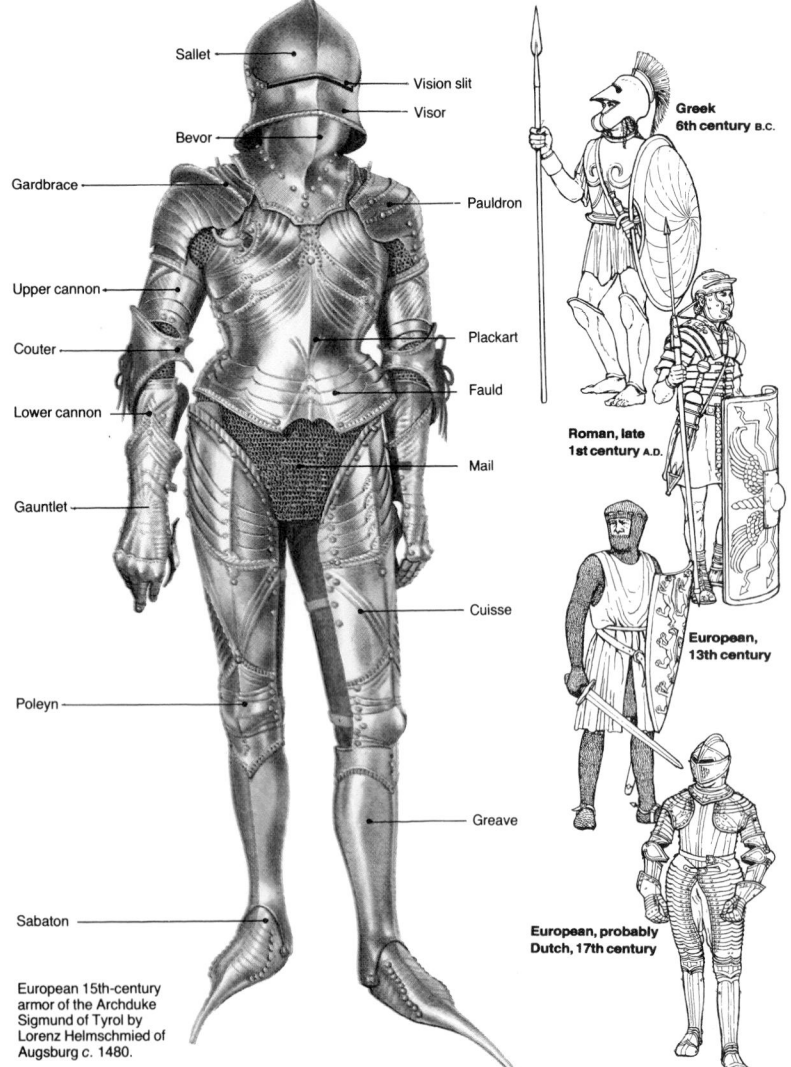

Sallet
Vision slit
Visor
Bevor
Gardbrace
Pauldron
Upper cannon
Plackart
Couter
Fauld
Lower cannon
Mail
Gauntlet
Cuisse
Poleyn
European,
13th century
Greave
Sabaton
European, probably
Dutch, 17th century
Greek
6th century B.C.
Roman, late
1st century A.D.

European 15th-century armor of the Archduke Sigmund of Tyrol by Lorenz Helmschmied of Augsburg c. 1480.

Church in its practices and doctrines.

Armenian Soviet Socialist Republic. The smallest of the 15 constituent republics of the U.S.S.R., lying in the southwest of the country on the southern flanks of the Caucasus Mts. The capital is Yerevan.

ar·met (är′mĕt) *n.* A medieval light helmet with a neck guard and movable visor. [Old French *armet,* partly from *arme,* singular of *armes,* ARMS, and partly from Old Spanish *almete,* from Old French *helmet,* HELMET.]

arm·ful (ärm′fŏŏl′) *n., pl.* **-fuls.** As much as one or both arms can hold.

arm·hole (ärm′hōl′) *n.* An opening for the arm in a garment.

ar·mi·ger (är′mĭ-jər) *n.* **1.** An armorbearer for a knight; a squire. **2.** A person entitled to heraldic arms. [Latin *armiger : arma,* ARMS + *gerere,* to carry.]

ar·mil·lar·y sphere (är′mə-lĕr′ē, är-mĭl′ə-rē) *n.* An astronomical model with solid rings, all circles of a single sphere, used to display relationships among the principal circles on the celestial sphere. [Old French *armillaire,* from Medieval Latin *armilla,* ring, from Latin *arm ring,* from *armus,* arm.]

Ar·min·i·an·ism (är-mĭn′ē-ən-ĭz′əm) *n.* The doctrine of Jacobus Arminius and his followers, opposing the Calvinist doctrine of absolute predestination and holding that salvation is possible for all. It was the basis of the Methodist position of John and Charles Wesley. —**Ar·min·i·an** *adj. & n.*

Ar·min·i·us (är-mĭn′ē-əs), **Jacobus** (1560–1609). Theologian of the Dutch Reformed Church. His opposition to the strict predestinarianism of John Calvin became known as Arminianism and had a wide influence throughout Europe.

ar·mip·o·tent (är-mĭp′ə-tənt) *adj. Archaic.* Mighty in arms or battle. [Middle English, from Latin *armipotēns : arma,* ARMS + *potēns* (stem *potent-*), POTENT.] —**ar·mip·o·tence** *n.*

ar·mi·stice (är′mə-stĭs) *n.* A temporary cessation or suspension of hostilities by mutual consent; a truce. [French, from New Latin *armistitium : Latin arma,* ARMS + *-stitium,* "stoppage."]

Armistice Day *n.* November 11, celebrated as the anniversary of the armistice of World War I in 1918. It has been called **Veterans Day** *(see)* since 1954.

arm·let (ärm′lĭt) *n.* **1.** A band or bracelet worn on the arm for ornament or identification. **2.** A small arm, as of the sea.

ar·moire (ärm-wär′, ärm′ər) *n.* A large, ornate cabinet or wardrobe. [Old French, variant of *armaire,* from Latin *armārium,* closet, from *arma,* weapons, tools.]

ar·mor (är′mər) *n.* Also British **ar·mour.** **1.** A defensive covering, such as chain mail, leather, or metal plates, worn as protection against weapons. **2.** Any tough protective covering, such as the bony scales or plates covering certain animals, or metal plates on tanks or warships. **3.** Anything serving as a safeguard or protection. **4.** The armored vehicles of an army collectively.
~*tr.v.* **armored, -moring, -mors.** To cover with armor. [Middle English *armure,* from Old French, from Latin *armātūra,* equipment, from *armāre,* to arm, from *arma,* ARMS.]

ar·mor·bear·er (är′mər-bâr′ər) *n.* One who carries the arms or armor of a warrior.

ar·mor·clad (är′mər-klăd′) *adj.* Wearing or covered with armor.

ar·mored (är′mərd) *adj.* **1.** Clad with armor or a protective covering, such as scales. **2.** Equipped with armored vehicles, as a military unit.

armored car *n.* **1.** A light, armored, military vehicle usually having a mounted machine gun and used especially for reconnaissance. **2.** A light armored van used for transporting money or valuables.

ar·mor·er (är′mər-ər) *n.* **1.** One who makes or repairs armor. **2.** A manufacturer of weapons. **3.** *Military.* A serviceman in charge of maintenance and repair of the small arms of a unit.

ar·mo·ri·al (är-môr′ē-əl, är-mōr′-) *adj.* Of or pertaining to heraldry or heraldic arms.
~*n.* A book containing coats of arms. [From *armory,* a rare word for heraldry + -AL.]

Ar·mor·i·ca (är-môr′ə-kə, -mōr′-). A literary name for Brittany.

Ar·mor·i·can (är-môr′ĭ-kən) *adj.* Also **Ar·mor·ic** (är-môr′ĭk). **1.** Of or pertaining to Armorica or the people or language of Amorica. **2.** *Geology.* Hercynian.
~*n.* Also **Ar·mor·ic. 1.** A native or inhabitant of Armorica. **2.** The language of Armorica; Breton.

armor plate *n.* Hard steel plate used to cover warships, vehicles, and fortifications. —**ar·mor-plat·ed** *adj.*

ar·mor·y (är′mər-ē) *n., pl.* **-ies. 1.** A storehouse for arms; an arsenal. **2.** A building for storing arms and military equipment, especially one serving as a headquarters for military reserve personnel. **3.** An arms factory. [Middle English *armourie,* from *armure,* ARMOUR.]

ar·mour. *British.* Variant of **armor.**

arm·pit (ärm′pĭt′) *n.* The hollow under the arm at the shoulder.

arm·rest (ärm′rĕst′) *n.* A support for the arm, as on a piece of furniture or the inner surface of the door of a vehicle.

arms (ärmz) *pl.n.* **1.** Weapons. **2.** Warfare. **3.** Heraldic bearings. **4.** Insignia, as of a state, official, family, or organization. —**bear arms against.** To attack with arms; wage war on. —**in** (or **under) arms.** Armed. —**lay down one's arms.** To surrender. —**order arms.** *Military.* To bring a rifle vertically against the right side of the body with the butt touching the ground. —**shoulder arms.** *Military.* To hold a rifle in a sloping position with the barrel over the shoulder and the butt in the hand. —**up in arms.** Aroused to anger and ready to protest. [Middle English *armes,* from Old

French, from Latin *arma,* weapons, tools.]
arms race *n.* A continuous build-up of weapons and forces by two or more competing nations in order to maintain equality or superiority of military power.
Arm·strong (ärm′strông′), **Louis** (1900–71). U.S. jazz musician, popularly known as "Satchmo." He was born in New Orleans. In 1922 he joined King Oliver's band in Chicago and quickly rose to national fame as both a trumpeter and a singer.
Armstrong, Neil Alden (1930–). U.S. astronaut and first man to walk on the moon. In July, 1969, he commanded Apollo XI on its mission to the moon, and on July 20 he set the lunar module *Eagle* down on the surface. Millions of people watched a live television transmission of his first steps on the moon.
ar·my (är′mē) *n., pl.* **-mies.** **1.** A large body of men organized and trained for warfare on land. **2.** The entire military land forces of a country. **3.** A tactical and administrative military unit consisting of a headquarters, two or more army corps, and auxiliary forces. **4.** Any large group of people organized for a specific cause. **5.** A large multitude, as of people or animals. —See Synonyms at **multitude.** [Middle English *armee,* from Old French, from Medieval Latin *armāta,* army, fleet, from Latin *armātus,* past participle of *armāre,* to arm, from *arma,* arms.]
army ant *n.* Any of various chiefly tropical New World ants of the subfamily Dorylinae, forming large colonies that move from place to place. Also called "legionary ant."
ar·my·worm (är′mē-wûrm′) *n.* Any of various insect larvae that travel in large groups, destroying crops; especially, the caterpillar of a New World moth, *Leucania* (or *Pseudaletia*) *unipuncta.*
arnatto. Variant of **annatto.**
Arne (ärn), **Thomas Augustine** (1710–78). British composer. Largely self-taught, he wrote songs, oratorios, and operas. The song "Rule, Britannia" comes from his opera *Alfred* (1740).
Arn·hem (ärn′hĕm′, är′nəm). Industrial town and port on the Lower Rhine River in the eastern Netherlands. It was the site of a major defeat inflicted upon British airborne troops in September 1944.
Arnhem Land. Northernmost part of Northern Territory in Australia, site of the largest of the country's 17 aboriginal reservations.
ar·ni·ca (är′nĭ-kə) *n.* **1.** Any of various alpine or arctic plants of the genus *Arnica,* having bright-yellow, rayed flowers. **2.** A tincture of the dried flower heads of *A. montana,* used for sprains and bruises. [18th century : New Latin *Arnica*†.]
Ar·no (är′nō). River of central Italy. It rises in the Apennines and flows some 240 kilometers (150 miles) to the Ligurian Sea. In 1966 it flooded, causing severe damage to art treasures in Florence.
Ar·no (är′nō), **Peter,** born Curtis Arnoux Peters (1904–68). U.S. cartoonist. His drawings, with their urbane, satirical observations on the foibles of café and high society, were a noted feature of *The New Yorker* from 1925 on.
Ar·nold (är′nəld), **Benedict** (1741–1801). Revolutionary soldier and traitor. Arnold was appointed commander of West Point in 1780. Troubled by debts and embittered by what he considered unfair treatment by the Continental Congress, he offered to surrender the fort to the British for 20,000 pounds. The British go-between, Maj. John André, was captured while carrying papers implicating Arnold, and the plot was foiled. Arnold fled, first to New York and later to England (1781).
Arnold, Matthew (1822–88). British poet, critic, and essayist. His famous poem "Dover Beach" (1867) expressed his personal moral and religious doubts. He is most widely known for his classic study *Culture and Anarchy* (1869), a trenchant polemic against the materialism of Victorian society.
ar·oid (ăr′oid′, âr′-) *adj.* Also **a·ra·ceous** (ə-rā′shəs). Of or belonging to the Araceae, a family of plants that includes the arums and callas.
~*n.* Any of various plants of the family Araceae.
a·roint (ə-roint′) *tr.v.* **arointed, arointing, aroints.** *Archaic.* Begone: *"Aroint thee, witch!"* (Shakespeare). [Origin unknown.]
a·ro·ma (ə-rō′mə) *n.* **1.** A pleasant, characteristic odor, as of a plant, spice, or food. **2.** A distinctive, intangible quality; an aura. —See Synonyms at **smell.** [Latin *arōma,* from Greek *arōma*†, aromatic herb or spice.]
ar·o·mat·ic (ăr′ə-măt′ĭk) *adj.* **1.** Having an aroma; fragrant, sweet-smelling, or spicy. **2.** *Chemistry.* Of, pertaining to, or containing the 6-carbon ring characteristic of the benzene series and related organic groups. Compare **aliphatic.**
~*n.* An aromatic plant or substance. [Middle English, from Old French *aromatique,* from Late Latin *arōmaticus,* from Greek *arōmatikos* : AROMA (stem *arōmat-*) + -IC.] —**ar·o·mat·i·cal·ly** *adv.*
ar·o·ma·tic·i·ty (ăr′ə-mə-tĭs′ə-tē, ə-rō′mə-) *n.* **1.** Aromatic quality or character. **2.** The characteristic structure or properties of the aromatic chemical compounds.
a·ro·ma·tize (ə-rō′mə-tīz′) *v.* **-tized, -tizing, -tizes.** —*tr.* **1.** To make aromatic or fragrant. **2.** *Chemistry.* To change (a compound) into an aromatic compound. —*intr.* To become aromatic. Used of chemical compounds. —**a·ro·ma·ti·za·tion** *n.*
arose. Past tense of **arise.**
a·round (ə-round′) *adv.* **1.** In all directions from a specific point: *famous for miles around.* **2.** On or to all sides or in all directions; about: *looked around in vain.* **3.** Along a circuit: *passed the plate around.* **4.** In or toward the opposite direction, position, or attitude; round: *swung around at the noise.* **5.** From one place to another; here and there; about: *wander around.* **6.** *Informal.* Close at hand; nearby: *He waited around all day.* **7.** In circumference: *a pole three feet around.* **8.** In existence; about: *There is at least one around somewhere.* **9.** *Informal.* To a specific place: *when you come around again.* —**get around.** *Informal.* **1.** To avoid and so overcome (a problem, for example). **2.** To have wide knowledge of worldly matters. —**get around to.** *Informal.* To find time or occasion to give one's attention to.
~*prep.* **1.** On all sides of: *the world around us.* **2.** So as to enclose, surround, or envelop. **3.** About the circumference or periphery of: *a path around the lake.* **4.** About the central point of: *the earth's motion around the sun.* **5.** In or to a place or places within or near: *driving around the countryside.* **6.** On or to the other side of: *the house around the corner.* **7.** Approximately; about: *around 20 guests.* **8.** So as to get past or avoid: *a way around the problem.* —See Usage note at **about.** [Middle English : A- (on) + ROUND (noun).]
a·rous·al (ə-rou′zəl) *n.* The act of arousing or state of being aroused.
a·rouse (ə-rouz′) *tr.v.* **aroused, arousing, arouses.** **1.** To awaken from or as if from sleep. **2.** To excite or stimulate. —See Synonyms at **provoke.** [16th century : A- (intensive) + ROUSE, by analogy with *rise, arise, wake, awake,* and the like.] —**a·rous·er** *n.*
Arp (ärp), **Jean** or **Hans** (1887–1966). French sculptor and painter. Arp was an experimental artist who produced abstract works in a variety of forms, including collages, full rounded sculptures, painted wood reliefs, and painted cutouts.
ar·peg·gi·o (är-pĕj′ē-ō, -pĕj′ō) *n., pl.* **-os.** *Music.* **1.** The playing of the notes of a chord in rapid succession rather than simultaneously. **2.** A chord played or sung in this manner. [Italian *arpeggio,* "chord played as on a harp," from *arpeggiare,* to play the harp, from *arpa,* harp, from Germanic *harpon-* (unattested), HARP.] —**ar·peg·gi·oed** *adj.*
ar·pent (är-päɴ′) *n.* An old French unit of land measurement approximately equivalent to an acre. [French, from Old French, from Vulgar Latin *arependis* (unattested), variant of Latin *arepennis,* half acre, of Gaulish origin; related to Old Irish *airchenn* (a land measure).]
arquebus. Variant of **harquebus.**
arr. **1.** arrival; arrive; arrived. **2.** arranged (by).
ar·rack (ăr′ək, ə-răk′) *n.* A strong, alcoholic drink of the Middle and Far East, usually distilled from rice or molasses. [Arabic *'araq,* sweet juice, liquor, as in *'araq at-tamr,* fermented juice of the date.]
ar·raign (ə-rān′) *tr.v.* **-raigned, -raigning, -raigns.** **1.** *Law.* To call before a court to answer to an indictment. **2.** To call to account; charge; accuse. [Middle English *arreinen,* from Old French *araisnier,* from Vulgar Latin *adrationāre* (unattested), "to call to account" : *ad-,* to + Latin *ratiō,* reason, from *rērī* (past participle *ratus*), to think, reckon.] —**ar·raign·er** *n.*
ar·raign·ment (ə-rān′mənt) *n.* The act or procedure of arraigning or being arraigned; especially, the formal summoning of a prisoner in a law court to answer to an indictment.
Ar·ran (ăr′ən). A granite island at the mouth of the Firth of Clyde in western Scotland.
ar·range (ə-rānj′) *v.* **-ranged, -ranging, -ranges.** —*tr.* **1.** To put into a deliberate order or relation; dispose: *arrange flowers in a vase.* **2.** To plan or prepare for: *arrange a picnic.* **3.** To agree about; settle: *arrange the date of the marriage.* **4.** *Music.* To rescore (music) for other instruments or voices, or for another style of performance. —*intr.* **1.** To come to an agreement: *arranged to meet on Sunday.* **2.** To make preparations; plan: *arranged for a trip south.* [Middle English *arangen, arengen,* from Old French *arangier, arengier* : *a-,* from *ad,* to + *rengier,* to put in a line, from *renc, reng,* line, row, from Frankish *hring* (unattested), circle, ring.] —**ar·rang·er** *n.*
ar·range·ment (ə-rānj′mənt) *n.* **1.** The act or process of arranging. **2.** The condition, manner, or result of being arranged; disposal; order. **3.** Something that has been arranged. **4.** A collection or set of things that have been arranged: *a floral arrangement.* **5.** *Often* **arrangements.** A provision or plan made in preparation for some undertaking. **6.** An agreement; settlement; disposition: *an arrangement to share the rent.* **7.** *Music.* **a.** An adaptation of a composition for other voices or instruments, or to another style or level of difficulty. **b.** A composition so adapted.
ar·rant (ăr′ənt) *adj.* Notorious; unmitigated; thoroughgoing: *an arrant knave.* [14th century : variant of ERRANT, wandering; pejorative sense developed through frequent use in phrases such as *arrant* (i.e., vagabond) *thief.*] —**ar·rant·ly** *adv.*
ar·ras (ăr′əs) *n.* **1.** A tapestry. **2.** A wall hanging, especially of tapestry. [Middle English, from Norman-French *(drap de) Arras,* (cloth of) ARRAS.]
Ar·ras (ăr′əs). Administrative center of Pas-de-Calais department on the Scarpe River of northern France. It was a famous woolen and tapestry center in the Middle Ages.
ar·ray (ə-rā′) *tr.v.* **-rayed, -raying, -rays.** **1.** To arrange or draw up (troops, for example) in battle order. **2.** To deck in finery; adorn.
~*n.* **1.** An orderly arrangement, especially of troops. **2.** An impressive display of numerous persons or objects. **3.** Splendid attire; finery. **4.** *Mathematics.* **a.** A rectangular arrangement of quantities in rows and columns, as in a matrix or determinant. **b.** Numerical data linearly ordered by magnitude. **5.** *Law.* A list of the jurors impaneled to try a case. **6.** *Electronics.* A regular arrangement of antennas used for radar or radio astronomy. —See Synonyms at **multitude.** [Middle English *arayen, arrayen,* from Old French *areer, arayer,* from Vulgar Latin *arrēdāre* (unattested), to arrange : *ad,* towards + *rēdāre* (unattested), to provide, from Germanic.]

armillary sphere *This piece of astronomical equipment was made in Florence in 1554 and is now in the Science Museum, London. The movable rings of the sphere were used to display the supposed relationships between the principal celestial bodies.*

armorial bearing *This coat of arms is in the form known as quartering of six. The top left section is inherited from the father; the others are the coats of arms of families to which the first is related by marriage.*

ar·ray·al (ə-rā′əl) *n.* **1.** The act or process of arraying. **2.** Something arrayed; an array.
ar·rear (ə-rîr′) *n.* **1.** *Usually* **arrears.** An unpaid and overdue debt, or an unfulfilled obligation. **2.** *Usually* **arrears.** The state of being behind in fulfilling contractual obligations or payments. Used with *in*: *in arrears on his rent.* [Middle English *ar(r)ere,* behind, from Old French *arriere, arrere,* from Late Latin *ad retrō,* backward : *ad-,* toward + *retrō,* backward, behind.]
ar·rear·age (ə-rîr′ĭj) *n.* **1.** The state of being in arrears. **2.** An amount owed in payment. **3.** *Rare.* Something held in reserve.
ar·rest (ə-rĕst′) *tr.v.* **-rested, -resting, -rests. 1.** To prevent the motion, progress, growth, or spread of; stop or check. **2.** To seize and hold under authority of the law. **3.** To capture and hold briefly (the attention, for example); engage.
~*n.* **1. a.** The act of arresting. **b.** The state of being arrested. **2.** A device for arresting motion, especially of a moving part. **—under arrest.** Detained in legal custody. [Middle English *aresten,* from Old French *arester,* from Vulgar Latin *arrestāre* (unattested), to cause to stop : Latin *ad-,* to + *restāre,* to stop, stay behind : *re-,* back + *stāre,* to stand.] **—ar·rest·er** *n.* **—ar·rest·ment** *n.*
ar·rest·a·ble (ə-rĕs′tə-bəl) *adj.* Liable to incur or lead to arrest if committed: *an arrestable offense.*
ar·rest·ing (ə-rĕs′tĭng) *adj.* Attracting and holding the attention; striking. **—ar·rest·ing·ly** *adv.*
arrest of judgment *n. Law.* **1.** A request by the accused before being sentenced that judgment be postponed owing to some irregularity. **2.** The suspension of judgment by a court if an indictment does not disclose an offense known to law.
Ar·rhe·ni·us (ə-rē′nē-əs, ə-rā′-), **Svante August** (1859–1927). Swedish chemist, a pioneer of modern physical chemistry. His research into the aqueous solutions of bases and acids led to the discovery, called the Arrhenius theory, of electrolytes, for which he was awarded the Nobel Prize in chemistry in 1903.
ar·rhyth·mi·a (ə-rĭth′mē-ə) *n.* Any irregularity in the force or rhythm of the heartbeat. [New Latin, from Greek, from *arrhuthmos,* unrhythmical : *a-,* not + *rhuthmos,* RHYTHM.]
ar·rhyth·mic (ə-rĭth′mĭk) *adj.* Also **ar·rhyth·mi·cal** (-mĭ-kəl). **1.** Lacking rhythm or regularity of rhythm. **2.** *Pathology.* Characterized by arrhythmia. **—ar·rhyth·mi·cal·ly** *adv.*
ar·ri·ère-ban (ăr′ē-âr-băn′, -băn′) *n.* **1.** In medieval France, a royal proclamation by which vassals were summoned to military service. **2.** The vassals so summoned. [French, from Old French *arriereban,* alteration of *arban, herban,* from Old High German *heriban* : *heri,* army + *ban,* proclamation.]
ar·ri·ère-pen·sée (ăr′ē-âr-päɴ-sā′) *n.* An intention or a thought which is not disclosed, often because of an ulterior motive. [French, "behind thought."]
ar·ris (ăr′ĭs) *n., pl.* **arris** or **-rises.** *Architecture.* The sharp edge or ridge formed by two surfaces meeting at an angle, as in a molding. [Old French *areste* (modified), ridge, ARÊTE.]
ar·ri·val (ə-rī′vəl) *n. Abbr.* **arr. 1.** The act of arriving. **2.** One that arrives or has arrived. Also used adjectivally: *the arrival lounge at the airport.* **3.** The reaching of a goal or objective as a result of some process or effort.
ar·rive (ə-rīv′) *intr.v.* **-rived, -riving, -rives. 1.** To reach a destination; come to a particular place. **2.** To reach a goal or object through some process or effort. Usually used with *at*: *arrive at a decision.* **3.** To come at length; take place: *The day of crisis has arrived.* **4.** *Informal.* To achieve success or recognition. **5.** *Informal.* To be born. [Middle English *ariven,* from Old French *ariver,* from Vulgar Latin, *arripāre* (unattested), to land, come to shore : Latin *ad-,* to + *rīpa,* shore.] **—ar·riv·er** *n.*
ar·ri·ve·der·ci (ə-rē′və-dâr′chē) *interj. Italian.* Goodbye.
ar·ri·viste (ă-rē-vēst′) *n., pl.* **-vistes** (-vēst′). A social climber or opportunist; an upstart. [French, from *arriver,* to ARRIVE.]
ar·ro·ba (ə-rō′bə) *n.* **1.** An old unit of weight in Spanish-speaking countries equal to about 25 pounds. **2.** An old unit of weight in Portuguese-speaking countries equal to about 32 pounds. **3.** A liquid measure used in Spanish-speaking countries, having varying value, but approximately equal to 16 liters (17 quarts) when used to measure wine. [Spanish and Portuguese, from Arabic *ar-rub'*, the quarter (of a quintal).]
ar·ro·gance (ăr′ə-gəns) *n.* The state or quality of being arrogant; insolent pride; haughtiness.
ar·ro·gant (ăr′ə-gənt) *adj.* **1.** Excessively convinced of one's own importance; haughty. **2.** Characterized by or arising from haughty self-importance. —See Synonyms at **proud.** [Middle English, from Latin *arrogāns* (stem *arrogant-*), present participle of *arrogāre,* ARROGATE.] **—ar·ro·gant·ly** *adv.*
ar·ro·gate (ăr′ə-gāt′) *tr.v.* **-gated, -gating, -gates. 1.** To appropriate presumptuously; claim or assume without right. **2.** To attribute to another without justification. [Latin *arrogāre,* to claim for oneself : *ad-,* to + *rogāre,* to ask.] **—ar·ro·ga·tion** *n.* **—ar·ro·ga·tive** (ăr′ə-gā′tĭv) *adj.* **—ar·ro·ga·tor** (ăr′ə-gā′tər) *n.*
ar·ron·disse·ment (â-rôɴ-dēs-mäɴ′) *n. French.* **1.** The chief administrative subdivision of a department in France. **2.** A municipal subdivision of some large French cities. [French, from *arrondir,* to make round, round out, from *rond,* ROUND.]
ar·row (ăr′ō) *n.* **1.** A straight, thin shaft, shot from a bow and usually made of light wood with a pointed head at one end and flight-stabilizing feathers at the other. **2.** Anything similar in form, function, or speed, such as a sign or symbol used to indicate direction. [Middle English *arewe, arwe,* Old English *arwe, earh.*]
ar·row·head (ăr′ō-hĕd′) *n.* **1.** The pointed, removable striking tip of an arrow. **2.** Something shaped like an arrowhead, such as a mark indicating a limit on a drawing. **3.** Any aquatic or marsh plant of the genus *Sagittaria,* especially *S. sagittifolia,* having arrowhead-shaped leaves and purple-spotted white flowers.
ar·row·root (ăr′ō-ro͞ot′, -ro͝ot′) *n.* **1.** A tropical American plant, *Maranta arundinacea,* having roots that yield an edible starch. **2.** The edible starch from this plant and from certain plants of the genera *Manihot, Curcuma,* and *Tacca.* [After the use of the root by the American Indians to absorb poison from arrow wounds.]
ar·row·wood (ăr′ō-wo͝od′) *n.* Any of several small shrubs of the genus *Viburnum,* having straight tough stems formerly used by American Indians to make arrows.
arrow worm *n.* Any of various small, transparent marine worms of the phylum Chaetognatha, having prehensile bristles on each side of the mouth.
ar·roy·o (ə-roi′ō) *n., pl.* **-os.** *Southwestern U.S.* **1.** A deep gully cut by a stream; a dry ravine. **2.** A brook or creek. [Spanish, from Vulgar Latin *arrugium* (unattested), variant of Latin *arrugia*†, mine-shaft.]
ar·se·nal (är′sə-nəl) *n.* **1.** An establishment for the storing, manufacturing, or repairing of arms, ammunition, and other war materiel. **2.** A stock of weapons. **3.** A collection or storehouse: *an arsenal of debating points.* [Italian *arsenale, arzanale,* originally, naval dockyard, from Arabic *dār-aṣ-ṣinā'ah* : *dār,* house + *aṣ-,* variant of *al-,* the + *ṣinā'ah,* manufacture, from *ṣana'a,* he made.]
ar·se·nate (är′sə-nĭt, -nāt′) *n.* A salt or ester of arsenic acid.
ar·se·nic (är′sə-nĭk) *n.* **1.** *Symbol* **As** A highly poisonous metallic element having three allotropic forms, yellow, black, or gray, of which the brittle, crystalline gray form is the most common. Arsenic and its compounds are used in insecticides, weed killers, solid-state doping agents, and various alloys. Atomic number 33, atomic weight 74.922, valence 3 or 5. Gray arsenic melts at 817°C (at 28 atm pressure), sublimes at 613°C, and has a specific gravity of 5.73. **2.** Arsenic trioxide.
~*adj.* **ar·sen·ic** (är-sĕn′ĭk). Of or containing arsenic. Used especially of chemical compounds containing arsenic with a valence of 5. [Middle English, from Old French, from Latin *arsenicum, arrenicum,* from Greek *arsenikon, arrhenikon,* yellow orpiment, alteration (influenced by *arsenikos, arrhenikos,* male, virile) of Syriac *zarnīkā,* from Iranian; akin to Avestan *zarniya,* gold.]
ar·sen·ic acid (är-sĕn′ĭk) *n.* A poisonous, white, translucent crystalline compound, H_3AsO_4, used to manufacture arsenates.
ar·sen·i·cal (är-sĕn′ĭ-kəl) *adj.* Of or containing arsenic.
~*n.* A drug or preparation containing arsenic.
arsenical nickel *n.* A nickel ore, **niccolite** *(see).*
ar·se·nic trioxide (är′sə-nĭk) *n.* A poisonous, white powder, As_2O_3, used in insecticides, rat poison, and weed killers. Also loosely called "arsenic."
ar·se·nide (är′sə-nīd′) *n.* A compound of arsenic with a more electropositive element. [ARSEN(IC) + -IDE.]
ar·se·ni·ous (är-sē′nē-əs) *adj.* Of or containing arsenic. Used especially of chemical compounds containing arsenic with a valence of 3.
ar·se·no·py·rite (är′sə-nō-pī′rīt′) *n.* A silver-white to gray arsenic ore, essentially FeAsS. Also called "mispickel." [ARSEN(IC) + PYRITE.]
arshin. Variant of **archine.**
ar·sine (är-sēn′, är′sēn′) *n.* A colorless, flammable, very poisonous gas, AsH_3, used as a military poison gas, as a solid-state doping agent, and in organic synthesis. [ARS(ENIC) + -INE.]
ar·sis (är′sĭs) *n., pl.* **-ses** (-sēz′). **1.** Originally, the unaccented or shorter part of a foot of verse. **2.** In modern usage, the accented or longer part of a foot of verse. **3.** *Music.* The upbeat, or unaccented part, of a measure. Compare **thesis.** [Late Latin, accented syllable, "raising of the voice," from Greek, unaccented syllable, "raising of the foot in beating time," from *aeirein,* to lift.]
ar·son (är′sən) *n.* The crime of maliciously burning property belonging to someone else, or of burning one's own property for some improper or illegal purpose, as to collect insurance. [Norman French (legal use), from Old French, from Medieval Latin *arsiō* (stem *arsion-*), act of burning, from Latin *ardēre* (past participle *arsus*), to burn.] **—ar·son·ist** *n.*
ars·phen·a·mine (ärs-fĕn′ə-mēn′) *n.* A yellow hygroscopic arsenical powder, $C_{12}H_{12}N_2O_2As{\cdot}2HCl{\cdot}2H_2O$, formerly used to treat syphilis. A trademark is "Salvarsan." [ARS(ENIC) + PHEN(YL) + AMINE.]
art[1] (ärt) *n.* **1.** Human effort to imitate, supplement, alter, or counteract the work of nature. **2.** The conscious production or arrangement of sounds, colors, forms, words, movements, or other elements in a manner that affects the sense of beauty; especially, the production of the beautiful in a graphic or plastic medium, for example, painting and sculpture. **3.** The product of these activities; human works of beauty, collectively. Also used adjectivally: *an art exhibition.* **4.** High quality of conception or execution, as found in works of beauty; aesthetic value. **5.** Any field or category of art, such as music, ballet, or literature. **6. arts.** Nonscientific branches of learning, for example, languages or philosophy. **7. a.** A system of principles and methods employed in the performance of a set of activities: *the art of building.* **b.** A trade or craft that applies such a system of principles and methods: *pursuing the baker's art.* **8.** Any skill or faculty, whether acquired by study and practice or based on intuition: *the art of conversation.* **9. a.** *Usually* **arts.** Artful devices; stratagems; tricks. **b.** Artfulness; contrivance; cunning. **10.** *Print-*

arrowhead *A freshwater plant of wide distribution with arrowhead-shaped leaves. Some species have edible tubers.*

PRONUNCIATION KEY

ă, pat; ā, pay; âr, care;
ä, father, are; b, bib;
ch, church; d, deed; ĕ, pet;
ē, be; f, fife; g, gag; h, hat;
hw, which; ĭ, pit; ī, pie;
îr, pier; j, judge; k, kick;
l, lid, needle; m, mum;
n, no, sudden; ng, thing;
ŏ, pot; ō, toe; ô, paw, for;
oi, noise; ou, out; o͝o, book;
o͞o, boot; p, pop; r, roar;
s, sauce; sh, ship, dish;
t, tight; th, thin, path;
th, this, bathe; ŭ, cut; ûr, fur;
v, valve; w, with; y, yes;
z, zebra, size; zh, vision;
ə, about, item, edible,
gallop, circus, peaceful

IN FOREIGN WORDS:

à, *Fr.* ami; œ, *Fr.* feu, *Ger.* schön; ü, *Fr.* tu, *Ger.* über;
KH, *Ger.* ich, *Scot.* loch;
N, *Fr.* bon; y', *Fr.* Compiègne

STRESS MARKS:

Primary stress: ′
in·cite′ (ĭn-sīt′)
Secondary stress: ′
in′sight′ (ĭn′sīt′)

ing. Illustrative material as distinguished from text. **—get something down to a fine art.** To become skilled at doing something through constant repetition or practice. [Middle English, from Old French, from Latin *ars* (stem *art-*).]

art². *Archaic.* Second person singular, present indicative of **be.** Used with *thou.*

-art. Variant of **-ard.**

art. 1. article. **2.** artificial. **3.** artillery.

Ar·taud (är-tō′), **Antonin** (1896–1948). French poet and dramatist. His view that the theater ought to harrow and disquiet the audience was put forward in two treatises, *Manifesto of the Theater of Cruelty* (1932) and *The Theater and its Double* (1938). His own plays were unsuccessful, but his theories had a great influence on the generation of dramatists of the absurd.

art de·co (dĕk′ō) *n. Sometimes* **Art Deco.** A style of decoration and architecture popular in the 1920's and 1930's, characterized by bold geometrical and rectilinear shapes and the use of man-made materials, such as plastic and steel. [Shortened from French *arts décoratifs,* decorative arts.]

artefact. Variant of **artifact.**

ar·tel (är-tĕl′) *n.* A cooperative enterprise of industrial or agricultural workers in the U.S.S.R. [Russian *artel'*, from Italian *artieri,* plural of *artiere,* artisan, from *arte,* art, work, from Latin *ars* (stem *art-*).]

Ar·te·mis (är′tə-mĭs). *Greek Mythology.* The virgin goddess of the hunt and the moon, and twin sister of Apollo. Identified with the Roman goddess Diana.

ar·te·mis·i·a (är′tə-mĭzh′ē-ə, -mĭz′ē-ə) *n.* Any of various plants of the genus *Artemisia,* which includes sagebrush and wormwood. [Middle English, from Latin, from Greek, "plant sacred to Artemis," from ARTEMIS.]

ar·te·ri·al (är-tîr′ē-əl) *adj.* **1.** Of, like, or in an artery or arteries. **2.** Of or designating the blood in the arteries that has absorbed oxygen in the lungs and is bright red. **3.** Of or designating a route in a transport or communications system carrying a main flow and having many branches. **—ar·te·ri·al·ly** *adv.*

ar·te·ri·al·ize (är-tîr′ē-əl-īz′) *tr.v.* **-ized, -izing, -izes.** To convert (venous blood) into arterial blood by absorption of oxygen in the lungs. **—ar·te·ri·al·i·za·tion** *n.*

arterio-, arter- *prefix.* Indicates an artery or the arteries; for example, **arteriosclerosis.** [Greek *artērio-,* from *artēria,* ARTERY.]

ar·te·ri·og·ra·phy (är-tîr′ē-ŏg′rə-fē) *n.* The x-ray examination of an artery that has been injected with a radiopaque substance. **—ar·te·ri·o·gram** (är-tîr′ē-ə-grăm′) *n.* **—ar·te·ri·o·graph·ic** *adj.*

ar·te·ri·ole (är-tîr′ē-ōl′) *n. Anatomy.* One of the small terminal branches of an artery that subdivides into capillaries. [New Latin *arteriola,* diminutive of Latin *artēria,* ARTERY.] **—ar·te·ri·o·lar** (är-tîr′ē-ō′lär′, -lər) *adj.*

ar·te·ri·o·scle·ro·sis (är-tîr′ē-ō-sklə-rō′sĭs) *n.* A chronic disease in which thickening and hardening of arterial walls interferes with blood circulation. Also called "hardening of the arteries." [ARTERIO- + SCLEROSIS.] **—ar·te·ri·o·scle·rot·ic** (är-tîr′ē-ō-sklə-rŏt′ĭk) *adj.*

ar·te·ri·o·ve·nous (är-tîr′ē-ō-vē′nəs) *adj.* Of, pertaining to, or connecting the arteries and veins.

ar·te·ri·tis (är′tə-rī′tĭs) *n.* Inflammation of an artery. [ARTER(IO)- + -ITIS.]

ar·ter·y (är′tər-ē) *n., pl.* **-ies. 1.** *Anatomy.* Any of a branching system of muscular tubes that carry blood away from the heart. **2.** A major route in a transportation or communications system, which local routes join. [Middle English *arterie,* from Latin *artēria,* from Greek; probably related to *airein,* to raise.]

ar·te·sian well (är-tē′zhən) *n.* A well drilled through impermeable strata to reach water capable of rising to the surface by internal hydrostatic pressure. [French *(puit) artésien,* (well) of *Artois* (former French province), where such wells were first drilled.]

art form *n.* Any activity that can be considered as a medium of artistic expression.

art·ful (ärt′fəl) *adj.* **1.** Deceitful or tricky; cunning; crafty. **2.** Having or showing skill, especially in finding the means to an end; clever; ingenious. **3.** Exhibiting art or technical skill. **4.** *Archaic.* Artificial. —See Synonyms at **sly.** **—art·ful·ly** *adv.* **—art·ful·ness** *n.*

Artful Dodger *n.* A person who manages to escape from difficulties, usually in an ingenious and engaging way. [After the young pickpocket in Dickens's novel *Oliver Twist* (1838).]

ar·thral·gia (är-thrăl′jə, -jē-ə) *n.* Pain in a joint. [ARTHR(O)- + -ALGIA.] **—ar·thral·gic** *adj.*

ar·thri·tis (är-thrī′tĭs) *n.* Inflammation of a joint or joints, producing pain and stiffness. See **osteoarthritis, rheumatoid arthritis.** [Latin, from Greek : ARTHR(O)- + -ITIS.] **—ar·thrit·ic** (är-thrĭt′ĭk) *adj. & n.*

arthro-, arthr- *prefix.* Indicates joint; for example, **arthropod, arthritis.** [Greek *arthron.*]

ar·thro·mere (är′thrə-mîr′) *n.* One of the body segments of an arthropod. [ARTHRO- + -MERE.] **—ar·thro·mer·ic** (är′thrə-mĕr′ĭk, -mîr′ĭk) *adj.*

ar·throp·a·thy (är-thrŏp′ə-thē) *n.* Any disease of a joint. [ARTHRO- + -PATHY.]

ar·thro·pod (är′thrə-pŏd′) *n.* Any of numerous invertebrate organisms of the phylum Arthropoda, which includes the insects, crustaceans, arachnids, millipedes, and centipedes, having a horny, segmented external covering and jointed limbs. [New Latin *Ar-*

thropoda : ARTHRO- + -POD.] **—ar·throp·o·dous** (är-thrŏp′ə-dəs), **ar·throp·o·dal** *adj.*

ar·thro·sis (är-thrō′sĭs) *n., pl.* **-ses** (-sēz′). **1.** A connection or joint between bones. **2.** A degenerative process in a joint. [New Latin, from Greek *anthrosis:* ARTHR(O)- + -OSIS.]

ar·thro·spore (är′thrə-spôr′, -spōr′) *n. Botany.* A sporelike cell characteristic of segmented filamentous fungi or certain algae. [ARTHRO- + SPORE.] **—ar·thro·spor·ic, ar·thro·spor·ous** *adj.*

---

art deco

MASS-MARKET MODERNISM

Bright colors, bold designs, and manmade material

Art deco sprang, like jazz, from the mood of its age. It was confident and brash and a powerful reaction against the ornateness and tradition in art that existed before World War I. The name came from a Paris exhibition of decorative arts in 1925. The influences were cubism and the Fauvists—the bold colorists led by Matisse. The style was simple and geometric, inspired by tribal art and Egyptian motifs uncovered in 1922 in Tutankhamen's tomb. The materials, popularized by the avant-garde designers at the Bauhaus in Dessau, Germany, were manmade—glass, plastic, metal—and the products were unashamedly for a mass market.

FUNCTIONAL *A sun-ray pattern is etched in bold color on this art deco decanter and glasses. The lines are typical of the style, simple and angular, matching the geometric design.*

A FIGURINE REVOLUTION *Bold geometric designs gave a new look to 1920's figurines, as in Gerdago's ivory dancer (1925).*

CREATION *A 1920's art deco version of William Blake's 1794 painting of the Creation is at Rockefeller Center in New York City.*

MASS PRODUCTION *A major influence was the need for items that could be mass-produced. This lady's cigarette case, in enamel on silver, is an example.*

AMBITIOUS SWIRLS *Gunta Stolzl, one of the trend-setting Bauhaus group, whose original ideas gave such impetus to the art deco movement, wove this tapestry (1927–29). Its geometric shapes form complex swirls of striking colors.*

Arthurian legend

THE KING FROM CAMELOT

How the legend of Arthur and the Round Table grew through the centuries

Most modern historians agree that the British hero Arthur did exist, but he may not have been a king. He was probably a cavalry chieftain who defeated invading Saxons in the 6th century. The tales of his prowess spread. He was first written about in the 10th-century Welsh chronicles, *Annales Cambriae*. Stories of Arthur were embroidered by Geoffrey of Monmouth in his 12th-century *History of the Kings of Britain*.

Geoffrey makes Arthur a great king who won many famous victories and held court at Camelot. The site of Camelot is uncertain but may have been Cadbury Castle, near Yeovil, Somerset. Called to fight in Rome, Arthur left his nephew Modred to guard the kingdom, but

Modred betrayed his trust and abducted Arthur's queen, Guinevere. When Arthur returned he defeated Modred in battle but was mortally wounded. He was taken to the sacred Isle of Avalon to be healed.

Breton minstrels brought the story of Arthur to Europe. Local legends were added to it and French writers worked in new themes, including the Round Table, a means of avoiding disputes over precedence among the knights. Also added were the stories of Sir Lancelot and Guinevere and of the Holy Grail, the chalice from the Last Supper in which Christ's blood was preserved. The legend of Arthur ends with the prediction that he will one day return and rule England.

EXCALIBUR *Magic played a great part in the legends of King Arthur. This 13th-century French illumination shows Arthur proving his right to the kingdom by pulling the sword Excalibur from an anvil when others had failed.*

HOLY GRAIL *The legend combined with religious themes in the 12th century. A woman bears the Grail, which Galahad set out to find.*

MAGIC ARM *As Arthur dies, Bedivere throws Excalibur into a lake, to be caught by a mysterious arm.*

Ar·thur (är′thər). Legendary British king of the 6th century A.D., whose court was at Camelot.

Arthur, Chester Alan (1830–86). 21st U.S. president (1881–85). Known as a staunch defender of the spoils system, Arthur became vice president in 1881. He became president on September 19, 1881, after James A. Garfield's assassination, and to everyone's surprise supported the 1883 Pendleton Act that created the Civil Service Commission to regulate federal appointments.

Ar·thu·ri·an (är-thōor′ē-ən) *adj.* Of or pertaining to King Arthur and his Knights of the Round Table: *Arthurian legends.*

ar·ti·choke (är′tə-chōk′) *n.* **1.** A thistlelike plant, *Cynara scolymus,* having a large flower head with numerous fleshy, scalelike bracts. **2.** The unopened flower head of this plant, cooked and eaten as a vegetable. Also called "globe artichoke." **3.** The **Jerusalem artichoke** *(see).* [Italian (northern dialect) *articiocco, arciciocco,* alteration of *arcicioffo,* from Old Spanish *alcarchofa,* from Arabic *al-kharshūf,* the artichoke.]

ar·ti·cle (är′tĭ-kəl) *n. Abbr.* **art. 1.** An individual thing belonging to a class; an item: *an article of clothing.* **2.** A piece of material goods or property. **3.** A particular section or item of a series in a document, such as a contract, constitution, or creed: *the Articles of Confederation.* **4.** A nonfictional literary composition that forms an independent part of a publication, as of a newspaper, magazine, or reference work. **5.** *Grammar.* Any of a class of words used to signal nouns and to specify their application. In English, the articles are *a* and *an* (indefinite articles) and *the* (definite article). **6.** A specific part or detail; a particular.
~*tr.v.* **articled, -cling, -cles. 1.** To bind, as for a period of training or apprenticeship, by articles set forth in a contract: *an articled clerk.* **2.** *Archaic.* To make specific or formal charges against; accuse. [Middle English, from Old French, from Latin *articulus,* small joint, division, part, diminutive of *artus,* joint.]

article of faith *n.* **1.** A belief that is an essential part of a church's creed. **2.** Any deeply held conviction.

articles of association *pl.n.* **1.** The set of rules by which a registered company is administered. **2.** The document in which these rules are set down, which must by law be open to public inspection.

Articles of Confederation *pl.n.* The first constitution of the United States, adopted by the original 13 states in 1781 and lasting until 1788 when the present Constitution was ratified.

ar·tic·u·lar (är-tĭk′yə-lər) *adj.* Of or pertaining to a joint or joints. [Middle English *articuler,* from Latin *articulāris,* from *articulus,* small joint, ARTICLE.] —**ar·tic·u·lar·ly** *adv.*

ar·tic·u·late (är-tĭk′yə-lĭt) *adj.* **1.** Capable of, speaking in, or characterized by clear, expressive language. **2.** Spoken in or divided into clear and distinct words or syllables. **3.** Endowed with the power of speech. **4.** *Biology.* Having joints or segments.
~*v.* (är-tĭk′yə-lāt′) **articulated, -lating, -lates.** —*tr.* **1.** To utter (a speech sound or sounds) by moving the necessary organs of speech. **2.** To pronounce distinctly and carefully; enunciate. **3.** To express in coherent verbal form; give words to (an emotion, for example). **4.** To unite by means of a joint or joints. —*intr.* **1.** To utter a speech sound or sounds. **2.** To speak clearly and distinctly. **3.** To form a joint; be jointed. [Latin *articulātus,* jointed, distinct, past participle of *articulāre,* to divide into joints, utter distinctly, from *articulus,* small joint, ARTICLE.] —**ar·tic·u·late·ly** *adv.* —**ar·tic·u·late·ness** *n.*

ar·tic·u·la·tion (är-tĭk′yə-lā′shən) *n.* **1.** The act or process of speaking. **2.** *Phonetics.* **a.** The movements of speech organs employed in producing a particular speech sound. **b.** Any speech sound, especially a consonant. **3. a.** A jointing together or an instance of being jointed together. **b.** The method or manner of jointing. **4.** *Zoology.* **a.** A joint between bones, or between movable parts of an outside shell. **b.** The manner in which jointed parts are connected. **5.** *Botany.* **a.** A joint between two separable parts, such as a leaf and a stem. **b.** A node, or a space on a stem between two nodes. —See Synonyms at **diction.** —**ar·tic·u·la·tive** (är-tĭk′yə-lə-tĭv, -lā′tĭv), **ar·tic·u·la·to·ry** (är-tĭk′yə-lə-tôr′ē, -tōr′ē) *adj.*

ar·tic·u·la·tor (är-tĭk′yə-lā′tər) *n.* **1.** A person or thing that articulates. **2.** *Phonetics.* An organ used in producing speech sounds, such as the tongue, lips, hard palate, or glottis.

ar·ti·fact (är′tə-făkt′) *n.* Also **ar·te·fact. 1.** An object produced or shaped by human workmanship; especially, a simple tool, weapon, or ornament of archaeological or historical interest. **2.** *Biology.* A structure or substance not normally present, but produced by some external agency or action; especially, a structure seen in a microscopic specimen after fixation that is not present in the living tissue. [Latin *arte,* by skill, ablative or *ars,* ART + *factum,* something made, from past participle of *facere,* to make.]

ar·ti·fice (är′tə-fĭs) *n.* **1.** A crafty expedient; an artful device or stratagem. **2.** Subtle but base deception; trickery. **3.** Ingenuity; cleverness; skill. [French, from Old French, craftsmanship, from Latin *artificium,* from *artifex,* craftsman : *ars* (stem *art-*), ART + *-fex,* -maker, from *facere,* to make.]
Synonyms: *dodge, feint, finesse, guile, maneuver, ruse, stratagem, subterfuge, trick, wile.*

ar·tif·i·cer (är-tĭf′ə-sər) *n.* **1.** A skilled worker; a craftsman. **2.** One that contrives, devises, or constructs something: *"The labyrinth . . . was built by Daedalus, a most skilled artificer"* (Thomas Bulfinch).

ar·ti·fi·cial (är′tə-fĭsh′əl) *adj. Abbr.* **art. 1.** Made by man, rather than occurring in nature. **2.** Made in imitation of something natural. **3.** Feigned; pretended. **4.** Affected; forced. [Middle English, from Old French, from Latin *artificiālis,* from *artificium,* ARTIFICE.]

—ar·ti·fi·ci·al·i·ty (är′tə-fĭsh′ē-ăl′ə-tē) n. —ar·ti·fi·cial·ly adv.
Synonyms: counterfeit, ersatz, simulated, synthetic.

artificial cinnabar n. Chemistry. **Mercuric sulfide** (see).

artificial horizon n. **1.** A gyroscopic instrument displaying a line on a flight indicator that lies within the horizontal plane, and about which the pitching and banking movements of an airplane are shown. **2.** A level reflecting surface, such as a dish of mercury, used with a sextant on land to establish a horizontal reference in a navigational or astronomical instrument.

artificial insemination n. Abbr. **A.I.** The introduction of semen into the female reproductive organs by means other than sexual contact.

artificial intelligence n. Abbr. **A.I.** The branch of computer science concerned with ways of programming and designing computers to mimic human mechanisms of reasoning.

artificial kidney n. A **kidney machine** (see).

artificial respiration n. Any of various methods for restoring normal breathing in an asphyxiated but living person, usually through rhythmic forcing of air into and out of the lungs by means of mouth-to-mouth breathing or manual pressure on the chest.

artificial satellite n. Aerospace. A man-made **satellite** (see).

artificial silk n. **Rayon** (see).

ar·til·ler·ist (är-tĭl′ər-ĭst) n. An artilleryman; a gunner.

ar·til·ler·y (är-tĭl′ər-ē) n. Abbr. **art.**, **arty**. **1.** Large-caliber firing weapons, such as howitzers, cannons, and missile launchers on suitable mounts, which are served by crews. **2.** Troops armed with such guns. **3.** The branch of an armed force that specializes in the use of large, mounted guns. **4.** The science of the use of guns; gunnery. **5.** Catapults, crossbows, slings, and similar devices for discharging missiles. [Middle English artil(le)rie, from Old French artillerie, from artillier, alteration (influenced by art, ART) of atillier, to fortify, arm, from Latin apticulāre (unattested), from aptāre, to fit, adapt, from aptus, fitting, APT.]

ar·til·ler·y·man (är-tĭl′ər-ē-mən) n., pl. **-men** (-mĭn). A soldier in the artillery.

ar·ti·o·dac·tyl (är′tē-ō-dăk′təl) n. Any of various hoofed mammals of the order Artiodactyla, which includes cattle, deer, camels, and hippopotamuses, having an even number of toes, either two or four, on each foot. [New Latin Artiodactyla, "the even-toed ones" : Greek artios, even, matching + DACTYL.] —ar·ti·o·dac·tyl, ar·ti·o·dac·ty·lous adj.

ar·ti·san (är′tə-zən, -sən) n. A skilled manual worker; a craftsman. [Old French, from Italian artigiano, from Vulgar Latin artitiānus (unattested), a skilled laborer, from Latin artītus, skilled in arts, from artīre, to instruct in the arts, from ars (stem art-), ART.]

art·ist (är′tĭst) n. **1.** One who creates works of art; especially, a painter or sculptor. **2.** Anyone whose work shows skill, imagination, or other artistic qualities. **3.** An artiste. **4.** Slang. One who is adept at, or keen on, a particular activity: a con artist. [Old French artiste, from Italian artista, one skilled in the arts, from arte, ART.]

ar·tiste (är-tēst′) n. A public performer or entertainer, especially a singer or dancer. [French, from Old French, ARTIST.]

ar·tis·tic (är-tĭs′tĭk) adj. **1.** Of, relating to, or befitting art or artists. **2.** Appreciative of or sensitive to art or beauty. —ar·tis·ti·cal·ly adv.

art·ist·ry (är′tĭs-trē) n. Artistic ability, quality, or workmanship.

art·less (ärt′lĭs) adj. **1.** Without guile, cunning, or deceit; ingenuous; naive. **2.** Free of artificiality; natural; simple. **3.** Lacking art or skill; crude. **4.** Uncultured; ignorant. —art·less·ly adv. —art·less·ness n.

art nou·veau (ärt nōō-vō′) n. Sometimes **Art Nouveau.** A style of decoration and architecture first current in the 1890's, characterized particularly by depiction of leaves and flowers in sinuous, flowing lines. [French, "new art."]

art·sy-craft·sy (ärt′sē-krăft′sē, -krăft′-) adj. Also **art·y-craft·y** (är′tē-krăf′tē, -kräf′-). Informal. **1.** Decorative rather than useful or comfortable: artsy-craftsy furniture. **2.** Pretentiously or self-consciously artistic.

art·work (ärt′wûrk′) n. **1.** Work in the graphic or plastic arts; especially, small handmade decorative or artistic objects. **2.** Printing. The illustrative and decorative matter in a publication, as opposed to the text.

art·y (är′tē) adj. **-ier**, **-iest**. Also **art·sy** (ärt′sē). Informal. Showy or affected in trying to appear artistic. —art·i·ly adv. —art·i·ness n.

A·ru·ba (ə-rōō′bə). Island of the Netherlands Antilles, in the Leeward Islands off the coast of Venezuela. Tourism and the refining of Venezuelan oil are the major industries.

ar·um (âr′əm) n. **1.** Any of various plants of the genus Arum, such as the cuckoopint, having arrow-shaped leaves and small flowers on a spadix surrounded by or enclosed within a spathe. **2.** Any of several similar or related plants, such as the **calla** (see). In this sense, also called "arum lily." [New Latin Arum, from Latin arum, cuckoopint, from Greek aron†.]

a·run·di·na·ceous (ə-rŭn′də-nā′shəs) adj. Of, pertaining to, or resembling a reed; reedlike. [Latin arundināceus, from (h)arundō†, reed.]

aruspex. Variant of **haruspex.**

-ary suffix. Indicates of, engaged in, or connected with; for example, **functionary, parliamentary, reactionary.** [Middle English -arie, from Old French -arie, -aire, from Latin -ārius, -āria, -ārium, noun suffixes, from -ārius, adjective suffix.]

Ar·y·an (âr′ē-ən) n. Also **Ar·i·an.** **1.** A member of the prehistoric people that spoke Proto-Indo-European. **2.** A member of any of the peoples descended from this people; especially, any speaker of an Indic or Iranian language. **3.** Proto-Indo-European, or a language

THE "NEW ART" OF 1900

A style of flowing lines and ornamental motifs

Art nouveau, and its successor art deco, were both modernist trends that reacted against the emphasis in 19th-century art on history and tradition.

The new style aimed to produce designs of high esthetic quality suitable for machine production. It was characterized by organic forms based on flowers and the human body.

The leading exponents included the English illustrator Aubrey Beardsley (1872–98); the Scottish architect and designer Charles Rennie Mackintosh (1868–1928); the Belgian architect and designer Victor Horta (1861–1947); the Spanish architect Antonio Gaudí (1852–1926); the Austrian artist Gustav Klimt (1868–1910); and the French glassmakers René Lalique (1860–1945) and Emile Gallé (1846–1904).

FRENCH *The wrought-iron railings at the entrance to the Louvre metro station in Paris were designed by Hector Guimard (1867–1942).*

ENGLISH *A silver box made for the English store Liberty & Co. about 1900. It is an art nouveau version of a traditional Celtic design.*

SCOTTISH *A tall-backed chair, designed in 1902. Its white-painted woodwork and flower pattern is typical of Charles Rennie Mackintosh's work.*

SPANISH *Casa Battló in Barcelona (1905) was designed by the architect Antonio Gaudí. Although Gaudí developed his own style, the curving lines are characteristically art nouveau.*

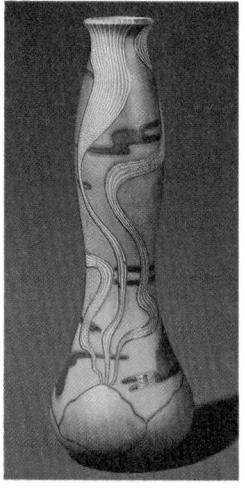

HUNGARIAN *An elongated, curved, glazed stoneware vase designed by the Hungarian artist Jozsef Rippl-Rónai (1861–1927) about 1890.*

ENGLISH *The flowing pattern of leaves and flowers is typical of the textile and wallpaper designs of William Morris (1834–96).*

AUSTRIAN *Gustav Klimt was a leading art nouveau painter. In Salome (1909) elaborate patterns and gold leaf enhance the sensuality of the skin.*

or language group descended from it, especially Indo-Aryan. **4.** In Nazi ideology, a Caucasian gentile, especially of Nordic type. *~adj.* Of or pertaining to Aryans or their culture or language. [Sanskrit *ārya* (adjective and noun), noble, Aryan.]

ar·yl (ăr'əl) *n. Chemistry.* **1.** A radical or group derived from an aromatic hydrocarbon by removal of a hydrogen atom, for example, the phenyl group C_6H_5. **2.** An organometallic compound in which a metal atom is directly bound to an aryl group. [AR(OMATIC) + -YL.]

ar·y·te·noid (ăr'ə-tē'noid', ə-rĭt'n-oid') *adj. Anatomy.* **1.** Of, pertaining to, or designating either of two small cartilages attached to the back of the larynx and to the vocal cords. **2.** Of, pertaining to, or designating any of three small muscles of the larynx. *~n.* An arytenoid cartilage or muscle. [New Latin *arytaenoides,* from Greek *(khondros) arutainoeidēs,* "the ladle-shaped (cartilage)" : *arutaina,* ladle, from *aruein†,* to draw water + -OID.] **—ar·y·te·noi·dal** *adj.*

as¹ (ăz; weak form əz) *adv.* **1.** To the same extent or degree: *just as smart; twice as wide.* **2.** For instance: *large carnivores, as the bear or lion.* **3.** Considered in the specified way: *workers as distinct from management.* *~conj.* **1.** To the same degree or quantity that. Often used as the consequent in correlative constructions: *as sweet as sugar; not so bad as you suggest.* **2.** In the same manner or way that: *Think as I think; treat him as you would a friend.* **3.** At the same time that; while: *As we were leaving, it began to snow.* **4.** For the reason that; since; because: *could not call as we had no phone.* **5.** Though: *Unaccustomed as I am to public speaking.* **6.** With the result that: *so changed as to be unrecognizable.* **7.** *Informal.* That: *I don't know as I can.* **—as far as.** To the extent that: *She is right, as far as I know.* **—as from** (or **of**). Starting from a specified time. **—as if** (or **though**). In the same way that it would be if. **—as is.** *Informal.* Just the way it is; without making changes. *~pron.* **1.** A fact that: *He is a fool, as everyone knows.* **2.** Which also; so too: *Jean comes from California, as does her husband.* **3.** *Regional.* Who or which: *Those as want to can come with me.* *~prep.* In the role, capacity, or function of: *acting as a mediator.* **—as for.** With regard to; concerning: *As for me, I prefer walking.* [Middle English *as* (adverb and conjunction), reduced form of Old English *alswā, ealswā, aelswā,* just as, likewise, ALSO.]

Usage: In positive comparisons, the double use of *as* is required: *He's as tall as I am.* In negative comparisons, traditional grammar prescribes *so . . . as* (*He's not so tall as I am*), but *as . . . as* is still widely used. Several *as* constructions are potentially ambiguous. A sentence such as *He came as I was leaving* could be interpreted to mean either "He came at the same time as I left" or "He came because I was leaving." In consequence, many speakers prefer *because* to *as* in such contexts. A similar ambiguous case is *He likes her as much as Jim,* which could mean "as much as he likes Jim" or "as much as Jim likes her." This prompts some speakers to use *I* in place of *me* in such sentences as: *He likes her as much as I (do), He likes her as much as (he likes) me.* See also **like, than.**

as² (ăs) *n., pl.* **asses** (ăs'ēz', ăs'ĭz). **1.** An ancient Roman copper coin of low value, a quarter of a **sesterce** *(see).* **2.** A unit of weight in ancient Rome equal to about one troy pound. [Latin *ās,* a whole, unit, copper coin, perhaps from Etruscan.]

As The symbol for the element arsenic.

AS 1. Anglo-Saxon. **2.** antisubmarine.

As. Asia; Asian.

AS., A.S. Anglo-Saxon.

ASA, A.S.A. American Standards Association (used in photography, preceded by a number, as a measurement of film speed).

as·a·fet·i·da, as·a·foet·i·da (ăs'ə-fĕt'ə-də) *n.* A yellow-brown, bitter, unpleasantly pungent resinous material obtained from the roots of several plants of the genus *Ferula,* used as a spice in oriental cuisine, and formerly used in medicine. [Middle English *asa-fetida,* from Medieval Latin *asafoetida* : *asa,* gum, from Persian *azā†,* mastic + Latin *foetida,* feminine of *foetidus,* FETID.]

a.s.a.p., asap As soon as possible.

as·a·ra·bac·ca (ăs'ə-rə-băk'ə) *n.* A creeping, perennial plant, *Asarum europaeum,* with shiny, kidney-shaped leaves and dull, purple flowers. [Alteration of obsolete *asarabacara,* from Spanish *asarabácara,* from Latin *bácara,* clary, from Latin *baccaris,* plant with aromatic roots, from Greek *bakkaris.*]

as·a·rum (ăs'ə-rəm) *n.* The dried, strong-scented roots of the wild ginger, formerly used in medicine and as a flavoring agent. [New Latin, from Latin, wild spikenard, from Greek *asaron†.*]

as·bes·tos (ăs-bĕs'təs, ăz-) *n. Abbr.* **asb.** Any of the fibrous variety of four distinct incombustible, chemical-resistant silicate minerals, used for fireproofing, electrical insulation, building materials, brake linings, and chemical filters. See **chrysotile, crocidolite.** *~adj.* Of, made of, or containing asbestos. [17th century : Middle English *asbeston,* a mythical stone with unquenchable heat, from Old French, from Latin, from Greek, from *asbestos,* inextinguishable : A- (not) + *sbennunai,* to extinguish.] **—as·bes·tine** (ăs-bĕs'tĭn, -tēn), **as·bes·tic** *adj.*

as·bes·to·sis (ăs'bĕs-tō'sĭs, ăz'-) *n.* A lung disease caused by prolonged inhalation of asbestos particles, characterized by breathlessness. [New Latin : ASBEST(OS) + -OSIS.]

as·ca·ri·a·sis (ăs'kə-rī'ə-sĭs) *n.* Infestation with nematode worms of the species *Ascaris lumbricoides,* usually in the intestines, but also in the liver, lungs, or stomach. [New Latin : Late Latin *ascaris,* ASCA-RID + -IASIS.]

as·ca·rid (ăs'kə-rĭd) *n.* Any of various nematode worms of the fam-

ily Ascaridae, such as the common intestinal parasite *Ascaris lumbricoides.* [Late Latin *ascaris* (stem *ascarid-*), intestinal worm, from Greek *askaris†.*]

as·cend (ə-sĕnd') *v.* **-cended, -cending, -cends.** *—intr.* **1.** To go or move upward; rise. **2.** To rise gradually. **3.** To slope upward. *—tr.* **1.** To move upward upon or along; climb. **2.** To succeed to. Used in the phrase *ascend the throne.* **—See Synonyms at rise.** [Middle English *ascenden,* from Latin *ascendere* : *ad-,* towards + *scandere,* to climb.] **—as·cend·a·ble, as·cend·i·ble** *adj.*

as·cen·dan·cy (ə-sĕn'dən-sē) *n.* Also **as·cen·den·cy, as·cen·dance** (-dəns), **as·cen·dence.** The state of being in the ascendant; superiority or decisive advantage.

as·cen·dant (ə-sĕn'dənt) *adj.* Also **as·cen·dent. 1.** Inclining or moving upward; ascending; rising. **2.** Dominant in position or influence; superior. *~n.* **1.** The position or state of being dominant or in a position of decisive advantage: *in the ascendant.* **2.** *Astrology.* The section of the zodiac that rises in the east at the time of a particular event, such as a person's birth. **3.** *Rare.* An ancestor.

as·cend·er (ə-sĕn'dər) *n.* **1.** One that ascends. **2.** *Printing.* **a.** The part of certain lower-case letters that extends above most other lower-case letters. **b.** Any letter containing such a part, as *d, f,* or *k.*

as·cend·ing (ə-sĕn'dĭng) *adj.* Moving, going, or growing upward: *a tree with ascending branches.* **—as·cend·ing·ly** *adv.*

as·cen·sion (ə-sĕn'shən) *n.* **1.** The act or process of ascending; ascent. **2.** *Astronomy.* The rising of a star above the horizon. **—the Ascension.** The ascent of Christ into heaven, celebrated on Ascension Day, the 40th day after Easter. Acts 1:9. [Middle English *ascencion,* from Latin *ascensiō* (stem *ascension-*), from *ascendere,* ASCEND.] **—as·cen·sion·al** *adj.*

As·cen·sion (ə-sĕn'shən). Island in the South Atlantic Ocean, 1,130 kilometers (700 miles) northwest of St. Helena. Britain made it a dependency of St. Helena in 1922. Rocky and barren, it has an airstrip and a U.S. tracking station.

as·cent (ə-sĕnt') *n.* **1.** The act or process of ascending. **2.** An advancement, especially in social status. **3.** An upward slope or incline. [17th century (Shakespeare and the King James Bible); from ASCEND (by analogy with DESCEND, DESCENT).]

as·cer·tain (ăs'ər-tān') *tr.v.* **-tained, -taining, -tains. 1.** To discover through examination or experimentation; find out for certain. **2.** *Archaic.* To make definite. [Middle English *ascertainen,* from Old French *acertainer, acertener* : *a-,* from Latin *ad-,* to + *certain,* CERTAIN.] **—as·cer·tain·a·ble** *adj.* **—as·cer·tain·a·ble·ness** *n.* **—as·cer·tain·a·bly** *adv.* **—as·cer·tain·ment** *n.*

as·cet·ic (ə-sĕt'ĭk) *n.* A person who renounces material comforts and leads a life of austere self-discipline, especially as an act of religious devotion. *~adj.* Also **as·cet·i·cal** (ə-sĕt'ĭ-kəl). Pertaining to or characteristic of an ascetic; self-denying; austere. **—See Synonyms at severe.** [Greek *askētikos,* from *askētēs,* hermit, "one who exercises (self-discipline)", from *askein†,* to exercise.] **—as·cet·i·cal·ly** *adv.*

as·cet·i·cism (ə-sĕt'ə-sĭz'əm) *n.* **1.** Ascetic practice or discipline. **2.** A doctrine or theory supporting this practice, such as the belief that the ascetic life releases the soul from bondage to the body and permits union with the divine.

Asch (ăsh), **Sholem** or **Shalom** (1880-1957). Polish writer who wrote in modern Yiddish. A prolific novelist, his most controversial works were those in which he sought to reconcile Judaism and Christianity: *The Nazarene* (1939), *The Apostle* (1943), *Mary* (1949), and *The Prophet* (1955). He lived in the United States from 1909 until 1956, then in Israel until his death.

As·cham (ăs'kəm), **Roger** (1515-68). English humanist scholar. Latin secretary to Edward VI, Mary I, and Elizabeth I, his historical importance rests largely on his advocacy of the use of the vernacular in literature.

as·cid·i·an (ə-sĭd'ē-ən) *n.* Any of various saclike marine animals of the class Ascidiacea, which includes the sea squirts. *~adj.* Of or belonging to the Ascidiacea. [New Latin *Ascidia* (genus name), from Greek *askidion,* little wineskin, from *askos†,* wineskin. See **ascus.**]

as·cid·i·um (ə-sĭd'ē-əm) *n., pl.* **-ia** (-ē-ə). *Botany.* A sac-shaped or bottle-shaped part or organ, such as a leaf of a pitcher plant. [New Latin, from Greek *askidion,* little wineskin, from *askos†,* wineskin. See **ascus.**]

as·ci·tes (ə-sī'tēz) *n.* An abnormal accumulation of serous fluid in the abdominal cavity. [Middle English *aschytes,* from Late Latin *ascītēs,* from Greek *askītēs,* from *askos†,* bag, belly. See **ascus.**] **—as·cit·ic** (ə-sīt'ĭk), **as·cit·i·cal** *adj.*

As·cle·pi·us (ə-sklē'pē-əs). *Greek Mythology.* Apollo's son, the god of medicine, identified with the Roman god Aesculapius.

asco– *prefix.* Indicates a saclike or bladderlike part; for example, ascospore. [New Latin, from Greek *askos†,* bag, bladder. See **ascus.**]

as·co·carp (ăs'kə-kärp') *n. Botany.* A globular structure containing the spore sacs of ascomycetous fungi. [ASCO- + -CARP.] **—as·co·car·pous** *adj.*

as·co·go·ni·um (ăs'kə-gō'nē-əm) *n., pl.* **-nia** (-nē-ə). *Botany.* A female reproductive structure of certain fungi. [New Latin : ASCO- + -GONIUM.] **—as·co·go·ni·al** *adj.*

as·co·my·cete (ăs'kō-mī'sēt', -mī'sēt') *n. Botany.* Any of numerous fungi that produce spores in a saclike structure, or ascus. [New

Latin *Ascomycetes* : ASCO- + -MYCETE.] —**as·co·my·ce·tous** (ăs′-kō-mĭ-sē′təs) *adj.*

a·scor·bic acid (ə-skôr′bĭk) *n.* A white, crystalline vitamin, $C_6H_8O_6$, found in citrus fruits, tomatoes, potatoes, and leafy green vegetables. It is used to prevent scurvy. Also called "vitamin C." [A- (not) + SCORB(UT)IC.]

as·co·spore (ăs′kə-spôr′, -spōr′) *n. Botany.* A sexual spore formed in an ascus. —**as·co·spo·rous** (ăs′kə-spôr′əs, -spōr′-), **as·co·spo·ric** (ăs′kə-spôr′ĭk, -spōr′-) *adj.*

as·cot (ăs′kət, -kŏt′) *n.* A kind of scarf or necktie, knotted so that its broad ends are laid flat upon each other. [After *Ascot*, Berkshire, where it was probably first worn.]

As·cot (ăs′kət) A village in Berkshire, in southern England. The Royal Ascot meeting, a week of horse races on Ascot Heath, was begun by Queen Anne in 1711.

as·cribe (ə-skrīb′) *tr.v.* **-cribed, -cribing, -cribes.** **1.** To attribute to a specified cause, source, author: *The Iliad is ascribed to Homer.* **2.** To assign as a quality or characteristic. —See Synonyms at **attribute.** [Middle English *ascriben*, from Latin *ascrībere*, to add to in writing : *ad-*, in addition + *scrībere*, to write.] —**as·crib·a·ble** *adj.*

as·crip·tion (ə-skrĭp′shən) *n.* **1.** The act of ascribing. **2.** A statement that ascribes. [Latin *ascrīptiō*, from *ascrībere*, ASCRIBE.]

as·cus (ăs′kəs) *n., pl.* **asci** (ăs′ī, -kī). *Botany.* A saclike structure in certain fungi, containing ascospores. [New Latin, from Greek *askos†*, wineskin, bag, bladder, belly.]

as·dic (ăz′dĭk) *n.* A sonar device used in antisubmarine warfare. [*Anti-Submarine Detection Investigation Committee.*]

-ase *suffix. Chemistry.* Indicates an enzyme; for example, amyl**ase.** [*Diastase.*]

a·sea (ə-sē′) *adv.* Toward or on the sea; at sea.

ASEAN Association of Southeast Asian Nations.

a·seis·mic (ā-sīz′mĭk) *adj.* Having no earthquakes: *an aseismic region.*

a·sep·sis (ə-sĕp′sĭs) *n.* The state of being free of pathogenic organisms. Compare **antisepsis.** [A- (without) + SEPSIS.]

a·sep·tic (ə-sĕp′tĭk) *adj.* **1.** Of or pertaining to asepsis. **2.** Lacking animation or emotion: *an aseptic smile.* [A- (not) + SEPTIC.]

a·sex·u·al (ā-sĕk′shōō-əl) *adj.* **1.** Having no evident sex or sex organs; sexless. **2.** Pertaining to or characterizing reproduction involving a single individual, and without male or female gametes, as in binary fission or budding. **3.** Having no apparent interest in or desire for sex. [A- (not) + SEXUAL.] —**a·sex·u·al·i·ty** (ā-sĕk′shōō-ăl′ə-tē) *n.* —**a·sex·u·al·ly** *adv.*

As·gard (ăs′gärd′, äz′-). Also **As·garth** (-gärth), **As·gar·dhr** (-gär′thr′). *Norse Mythology.* The heavenly residence of the gods and slain heroes of war.

asgmt. assignment.

ash¹ (ăsh) *n.* **1.** The soft, powdery, grayish-white to black residue left over when something is burnt. **2.** *Geology.* Pulverized particulate matter ejected by volcanic eruption. **3. ashes.** Ruins: *Bombs reduced the town to ashes.* **4. ashes.** Human remains, especially after cremation. [Middle English *asshe*, Old English *asce, æsce.*]

ash² *n.* **1.** Any of various trees of the genus *Fraxinus*; especially, *F. excelsior*, having compound leaves, clusters of small greenish flowers, and winged seeds. **2.** The durable, close-grained, elastic wood of any of these trees. Compare **mountain ash.** [Middle English *asshe*, Old English *æsc.*]

ash³ *n.* The alphabetical digraph (æ) used especially in Old English. [Old English *æsc*, the name of the letter in the runic alphabet.]

a·shamed (ə-shāmd′) *adj.* **1.** Feeling shame or guilt. **2.** Reluctant through fear of resulting humiliation or shame: *Don't be ashamed to ask for help.* **3.** Feeling inferior, inadequate, or embarrassed: *ashamed of her torn coat.* [Middle English, Old English *āscamod*, past participle of *āscamian*, to feel shame : *ā-*, intensive + *scamian*, to be ashamed.] —**a·sham·ed·ly** (ə-shā′mĭd-lē) *adv.* —**a·sham·ed·ness** (ə-shā′mĭd-nĭs) *n.*

A·shan·ti¹ (ə-shän′tē, -shän′-) An ancient powerful kingdom of the Ashanti people of Africa. It was annexed to the British Gold Coast colony in 1901, and is now an administrative region of Ghana, with Kumasi as the capital.

Ashanti² *n., pl.* **-tis** or collectively **Ashanti.** **1.** An inhabitant of Ashanti. **2.** A dialect of **Twi** *(see)*, spoken by the Ashantis.

ash blonde *adj.* Very fair or pale blonde.

ash can *n.* A large metal receptacle for trash.

Ashe (ăsh), **Arthur Robert** (1943-). American tennis player. He was the first black to win the United States championship (1968) and the Wimbledon championship (1975). He also won the Australian championship (1970).

ash·en¹ (ăsh′ən) *adj.* **1.** Consisting of ashes. **2.** Resembling ashes in color; very pale: *Her face was ashen with grief.*

ashen² *adj.* Of, pertaining to, or made from the wood of the ash tree.

Ash·er¹ (ăsh′ər). A son of Jacob. Genesis 49:20.

Asher² *n.* The tribe of Israel descended from Asher.

ash·et (ăsh′ĭt) *n. Scottish.* A large plate or serving dish. [French *assiette*, a seating of guests at dinner, hence, course, dish, from Old French *assiette*, from Vulgar Latin *assedita* (unattested), a sitting, seating, from Latin *assiduus*, past participle of *assidēre*, to sit by, from *ad-* at, by + *sedēre*, to sit.]

Ash·ke·lon or **Ash·qe·lon** (ăsh′kə-lŏn′). Site of an ancient city in southwestern Israel. Herod greatly enlarged the city and built fine public buildings, many of which have been excavated in the 20th century. It was destroyed by Saladin in 1270.

Ash·ke·na·zi (äsh′kə-nä′zē) *n., pl.* **-nazim** (-nä′zĭm). A central or eastern European Jew, generally Yiddish-speaking. Compare **Sephardi.** —**Ash·ke·na·zic** *adj.*

Ash·ke·na·zy (äsh′kə-nä′zē), **Vladimir Davidovich** (1937-). Russian-born pianist and conductor. He is noted especially for his interpretations of the 19th-century masters. He took Icelandic nationality in 1972.

ash-key (ăsh′kē′) *n.* The winged seed of the ash tree. [After its keylike shape.]

Ash·kha·bad (äsh′kə-băd′, -bäd′). The capital of the Turkmen Soviet Socialist Republic, situated in a fertile oasis. After an earthquake in 1948 the city had to be almost entirely rebuilt.

ash·lar, ash·ler (ăsh′lər) *n.* **1.** A squared block of building stone. **2.** Masonry of such stones. **3.** A thin, dressed rectangle of stone for facing walls. In this sense, also called "ashlar veneer." [Middle English *asheler*, from Old French *aisselier*, beam, from Latin *axilla*, diminutive of *axis*, board, plank, probably variant of *assis*, akin to *asser†*, beam.]

ash-leaved maple (ăsh′lēvd′). A tree, the **box-elder** *(see).*

Ash·ley (ăsh′lē), **Laura** (1925-85). British designer. Ashley's designs for clothing, fabrics, linens, and household appurtenances evoked the English countryside and the Welsh retreat where she established a studio and school.

a·shore (ə-shôr′, ə-shōr′) *adv.* **1.** Toward or on the shore. **2.** On land; aground.

ash·plant (ăsh′plănt′) *n.* A staff or walking stick made from an ash sapling.

Ashqelon. See **Ashkelon.**

ash·ram (äsh′rəm, -räm′) *n.* **1.** A Hindu religious retreat or hermitage. **2.** Loosely, the meeting place of any eastern religious community. [Sanskrit *āśrama*, from *ā*, toward + *śrama*, religious training.]

Ash Sham. See **Damascus.**

Ash·ton (ăsh′tən), **Sir Frederick William Mallandaine** (1904-). British dancer and choreographer, born in Ecuador. He joined the Vic-Wells (later Royal) Ballet in 1933 and made his name as a mime and character dancer. His ballets include *The Dream* (1964) and *A Month in the Country* (1976). He was director of the Royal Ballet from 1963 to 1970.

Ash·to·reth (ăsh′tə-rĕth′). The ancient Syrian and Phoenician goddess of sexual love and fertility. Identified with Astarte.

ash·tray (ăsh′trā′) *n.* A receptacle for tobacco ashes.

A·shur¹ (ä′shōōr′). Town on the banks of the Tigris River, in northern Iraq. It was the religious capital of Assyria in ancient times, when it was known as Qal'at Shargat. The town was destroyed by the Babylonians in 614 B.C.

A·shur² (ä′shōōr′). Also **As·shur, As·sur, A·sur.** *Assyrian Mythology.* The principal deity and god of war and empire.

Ash Wednesday *n.* The seventh Wednesday before Easter and the first day of Lent, on which Roman Catholics customarily have ashes placed on the forehead as a sign of penitence.

ash·y (ăsh′ē) *adj.* **-ier, -iest.** **1.** Pertaining to, resembling, or covered with ashes. **2.** Ashen; pale.

A·sia (ā′zhə, ā′shə). *Abbr.* **As.** The largest of the continents, making up about 33 percent of the earth's land area. It has an even greater proportion of the world's people: roughly three out of every five humans live in Asia. This great landmass both physically and culturally falls into five broad subcontinents. North Asia comprises the part of the U.S.S.R. east of the Ural Mts. The Far East is made up of the temperate and subtropical parts in the east, where most people are of Mongoloid origin. The hot, dry lands of the west, whose inhabitants are largely of Semitic stock, many of whom are Moslems, make up the Middle East. The generally humid tropical lands of the south can be divided into two: Middle South Asia is the subcontinent of India (including Pakistan, Bangladesh, and Sri Lanka), with largely Dravidian and Indo-Aryan people; Southeast Asia, the remainder of the continent, has great ethnic and cultural diversity, many of its people being derived from other parts of Asia in historic times. See map, next page.

Asia Minor. See **Anatolia.**

A·sian (ā′zhən, ā′shən) *adj. Abbr.* **As.** Of or pertaining to Asia or its people.
—*n.* **1.** A native or inhabitant of Asia. **2.** *British.* A person of Indian, Pakistani, or Bangladeshi extraction.

A·si·at·ic (ā′zhē-ăt′ĭk) *adj.* Asian. —**A·si·at·ic** *n.*

a·side (ə-sīd′) *adv.* **1.** On or to one side: *stand aside.* **2.** Out of one's thoughts or mind; away from consideration: *Put doubts aside.* **3.** In reserve: *put a little money aside.* **4.** Apart; dispensed with: *all joking aside.* —**aside from.** Excluding; excepting.
—*n.* **1.** A piece of dialogue that other actors on stage are supposed by dramatic convention not to hear. **2.** A remark made in an undertone, not intended to be heard by anyone present. **3.** A parenthetical departure; a digression.

as·i·nine (ăs′ə-nīn′) *adj.* **1.** Of or resembling an ass. **2.** Utterly stupid: *an asinine remark.* [Latin *asinīnus*, from *asinus*, ass.] —**as·i·nine·ly** *adv.* —**as·i·nin·i·ty** (ăs′ə-nĭn′ə-tē) *n.*

Asiut. See **Asyut.**

ask (ăsk, äsk) *v.* **asked, asking, asks.** —*tr.* **1.** To put a question to. **2.** To seek information about; inquire about. **3.** To make a request of or for: *asked her forgiveness.* **4. a.** To require or call for. **b.** To expect or demand: *ask too much of a child; How much are they asking for their home?* **5.** To invite. —*intr.* **1.** To inquire. Used with *about.* **2.** To make a request. Often used with *for.* —**ask after.** To inquire about the health or well-being of. —**ask for.** *Informal.* To

ash *In pre-Christian times the ash tree was worshiped by northern peoples as a symbol of the life-force. Its strong, straight-grained wood is commonly used for oars, ax shafts, and tool handles.*

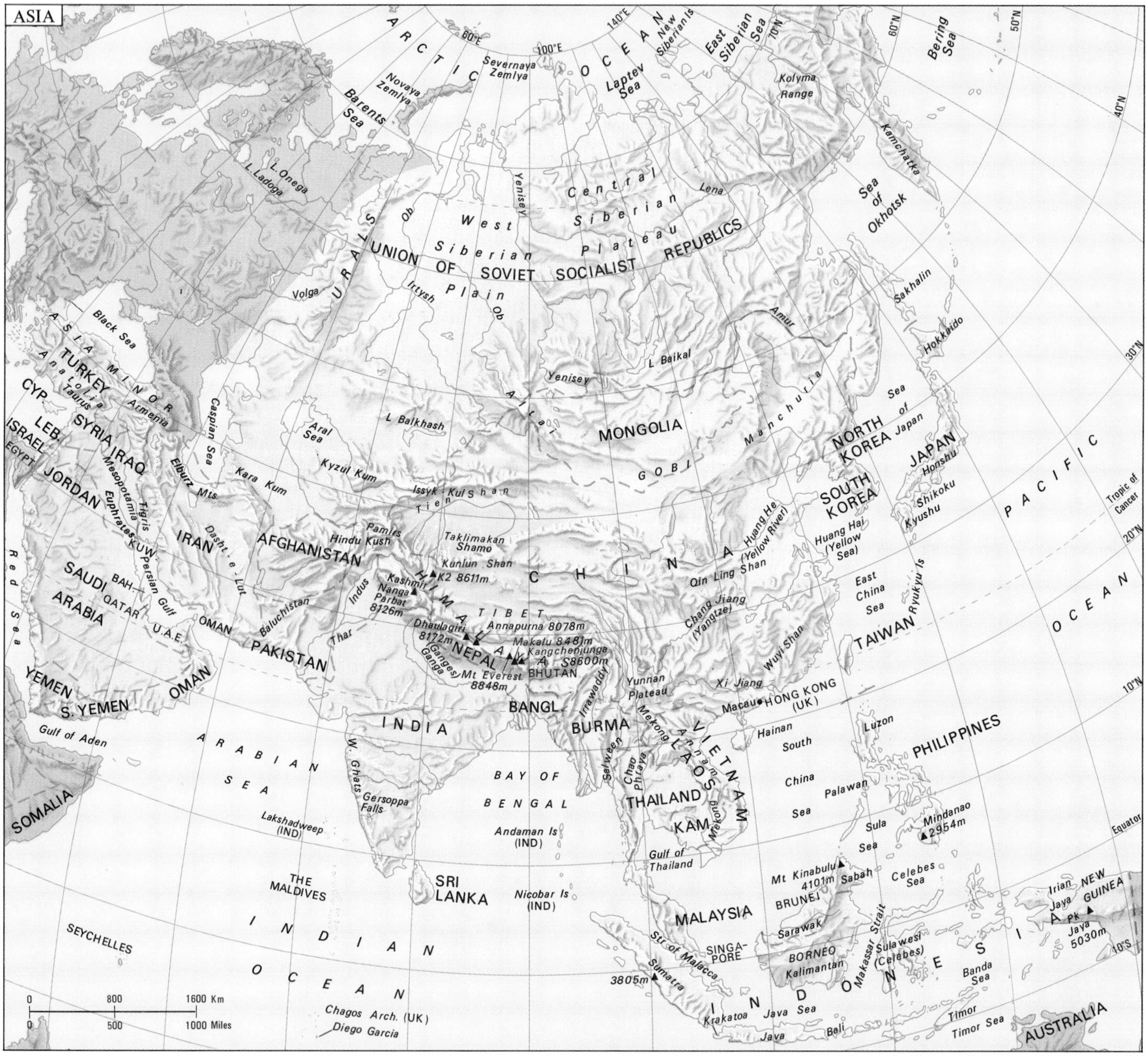

asparagus *The young shoots of Asparagus officinalis, a member of the lily family, have been a delicacy for at least 2,000 years.*

act in a manner that provokes (trouble, punishment, or the like): *He's really asking for it.* [Middle English *asken, axen,* Old English *āscian, ācsian.*] —**ask·er** *n.*
　Synonyms: *examine, inquire, interrogate, query, question.*
a·skance (ə-skăns′) *adv.* Also **a·skant** (ə-skănt′). **1.** With a sideways or oblique glance. **2.** With disapproval, suspicion, or distrust. [Earlier *a scanche, a sca(u)nce, a sconce,* obliquely, of unknown origin.]
a·ska·ri (ə-skä′rē) *n.* In parts of Africa, a native soldier or watchman, formerly one in the service of colonial authorities. [Arabic *'askarī,* soldier.]
a·skew (ə-skyōō′) *adj.* Crooked; oblique.
　~*adv.* To one side; obliquely; awry. [16th century : A- (on) + SKEW.]
a·slant (ə-slănt′, ə-slänt′) *adj.* Oblique; slanting.
　~*adv.* At a slant; obliquely.
　~*prep.* Obliquely over or across; athwart. [A- (on) + SLANT.]
a·sleep (ə-slēp′) *adj.* **1.** Sleeping. **2.** Inactive; dormant. **3.** Numb: *My leg is asleep.* **4.** Dead. Used euphemistically.
　~*adv.* Into a state of sleep. [A- (on) + SLEEP, replacing Middle English *o slepe,* from Old English *on slǣpe.*]
a·slope (ə-slōp′) *adv.* At a slope or slant.
　~*adj.* Sloping.
As·ma·ra (ăz-mä′rə). The capital of the province of Eritrea in northern Ethiopia.
As·mo·de·us (ăz′mə-dē′əs). In Jewish demonology, king of the demons. [Latin *Asmodaeus,* from Greek *Asmodaios,* from Middle He-

brew *Ashmǝday,* from Avestan *Aēsma-daēva,* "spirit of anger" : *aēsma-,* anger + *daēva-,* demon.]
A·so, Mount (ä′sō). Also **A·so·san** (ä′sō-sän′). A volcanic mountain in central Kyushu in Japan. It has one of the largest craters in the world, containing five volcanic cones. The highest peak is Takadake (1,593 meters; 5,225 feet). One peak, Naka-dake, is active.
a·so·cial (ā-sō′shəl) *adj.* **1.** Avoiding the society of others; not gregarious. **2.** Inconsiderate of others; self-centered.
asp¹ (ăsp) *n.* **1.** A viper, *Vipera aspis,* of southern Europe, with a brown skin marked with black stripes. **2.** The venomous snake that killed Cleopatra, probably the Egyptian cobra, *Naja haje.* **3.** The **horned viper** (see). [Middle English *aspis,* from Latin, from Greek *aspis†.*]
asp² *n. Rare.* A tree, the aspen. [See **aspen.**]
Aspadana. See **Isfahan.**
as·par·a·gine (ə-spăr′ə-jēn′) *n.* A nonessential amino acid, $C_4H_8N_2O_3$, found mainly in asparagus, potatoes, and beetroot. [ASPARAG(US) + -INE.]
as·par·a·gus (ə-spăr′ə-gəs) *n.* Any of several plants of the genus *Asparagus,* native to Eurasia, having small scales or needlelike branchlets rather than true leaves; especially, the widely cultivated species *A. officinalis,* the young shoots of which are cooked and eaten as a vegetable. [Latin, from Greek *asparagos, aspharagos†.*]
asparagus beetle *n.* A small, spotted beetle, *Crioceris asparagi,* that infests and damages asparagus plants.
asparagus fern *n.* An ornamental asparagus plant, *Asparagus plumosus,* native to southern Africa, having fernlike foliage.

as·par·tic acid (ə-spär′tĭk) *n.* Also **as·pa·rag·ic acid** (ăs′pə-răj′ĭk). A nonessential amino acid, $C_4H_7NO_4$, found especially in young sugar cane and sugar beet. [*Aspartic,* irregularly from ASPARAGUS (because it is obtained by hydrolysis of a crystalline amino acid found in asparagus) + ACID.]

A.S.P.C.A. American Society for the Prevention of Cruelty to Animals.

as·pect (ăs′pĕkt′) *n.* **1.** Appearance to the eye, especially when seen from a specific view. **2. a.** An angle or viewpoint of an idea or problem: *study the case from every possible aspect.* **b.** A particular feature or element of a problem or idea: *a different aspect of the same problem.* **3.** A particular facial expression, mien, or air: *a matron of grim aspect.* **4.** A position facing or commanding a given direction; an exposure. **5.** A side or surface facing in a particular direction: *the ventral aspect of the body.* **6.** *Astronomy.* The relative positions of two celestial bodies. **7.** *Astrology.* The configuration of the stars or planets in relation to one another or to the subject. **8.** *Grammar.* A category of the verb denoting primarily the relation of the action to the passage of time, especially in reference to completion, duration, or repetition. Compare **mood. 9.** *Archaic.* A gaze; a look. [Middle English, from Latin *aspectus,* a view, past participle of *aspicere,* look at : *ad-,* at + *specere,* to look.]

aspect ratio *n.* **1.** The width-to-height ratio of a television image. It is 4:3 in most countries. **2.** The width-to-length ratio of the conductivity channel in an integrated circuit.

a·spec·tu·al (ă-spĕk′cho͞o-əl) *adj. Grammar.* Of or pertaining to the aspect of a verb.

as·pen (ăs′pən) *n.* Any of several trees of the genus *Populus,* having leaves that flutter readily on the breeze because of their flattened leafstalks. *P. Tremuloides,* of North America, is often called "quaking aspen."
~adj. **1.** Of or relating to an aspen. **2.** Shivering or trembling like the leaves of an aspen. [Middle English *aspen,* "of an aspen" (adjective misinterpreted as a noun), replacing *aspe,* an aspen, Old English *æspe,* of Germanic origin.]

As·pen (ăs′pən). A city of west-central Colorado, in the Sawatch range of the Rocky Mts. It was founded *c.* 1879 by silver prospectors and is now a popular ski resort.

as·per·ate (ăs′pə-rāt′) *tr.v.* **-ated, -ating, -ates.** To make uneven; roughen. [Latin *asperāre,* from *asper*†, rough.]

as·per·ges (ə-spûr′jēz) *n. Roman Catholic Church.* A short rite, preceding the High Mass on Sundays, that consists of sprinkling the congregation with holy water. [Latin *asperges me, Domine,* "thou wilt sprinkle me, Lord", first words of the rite, from *aspergere,* to sprinkle, ASPERSE.]

as·per·gil·lo·sis (ăs-pûr′jĭ-lō′sĭs) *n.* An infectious disease of the mucous membranes, lungs, and other parts of the body, caused by certain fungi of the genus *Aspergillus.* [New Latin : ASPERGILL(US) + -OSIS.]

as·per·gil·lum (ăs′pər-jĭl′əm) *n., pl.* **-la** (-lə) or **-lums.** Also **as·per·gill** (-jĭl). *Roman Catholic Church.* A brush, perforated container, or other instrument used for sprinkling holy water. [New Latin *aspergillum,* sprinkler, from Latin *aspergere,* to sprinkle on, ASPERSE.]

as·per·gil·lus (ăs′pər-jĭl′əs) *n., pl.* **-gilli** (-jĭl′ī′). Any of various fungi of the genus *Aspergillus,* which includes many common molds. [New Latin, from *aspergillum,* ASPERGILLUM, from its resemblance to an aspergillum brush.]

as·per·i·ty (ă-spĕr′ə-tē) *n. pl.* **-ties. 1.** Roughness or harshness, as of surface, weather, or sound: *the asperity of the climate.* **2.** Ill temper; irritability. [Latin *asperitās,* from *asper*†, rough.]

as·perse (ə-spûrs′) *tr.v.* **-persed, -persing, -perses. 1.** To spread false charges against; defame; slander. **2.** *Rare.* To sprinkle with water or dust. [Latin *aspergere* (past participle *aspersus*), to sprinkle on, spatter : *ad-,* to + *spargere,* to strew, scatter.] **—as·pers·er, as·per·sor** *n.* **—as·per·sive** *adj.* **—as·per·sive·ly** *adv.*

as·per·sion (ə-spûr′zhən, -shən) *n.* **1.** A calumnious report or remark; slander. Often used in the phrase *cast aspersions on.* **2.** The act of defaming or slandering. **3.** *Rare.* A sprinkling; especially, a baptism by sprinkling.

as·phalt (ăs′fôlt′) *n.* Also **as·phal·tum** (ăs-fôl′təm), **as·phal·tus** (-təs). **1.** A brownish-black solid or semisolid mixture of bitumens obtained from native deposits or as a petroleum by-product, used in paving, roofing, and waterproofing. Also called "mineral pitch." **2.** Mixed asphalt and crushed stone gravel or sand, used for paving or roofing.
~tr.v. **asphalted, -phalting, -phalts.** To pave or coat with asphalt. [Middle English, *asp(h)alt, aspaltoun,* from Late Latin *asphaltus,* from Greek *asphaltos, asphalton,* bitumen, pitch, origin obscure.] **—as·phal·tic** (ăs-fôl′tĭk) *adj.*

as·phal·tite (ăs′fôl-tīt′) *n.* A solid, dark-colored complex of hydrocarbons, found in natural veins and deposits.

a·spher·ic (ā-sfîr′ĭk, ā-sfĕr′-) *adj.* Also **a·spher·i·cal** (-ĭ-kəl). Not spherical. Said of lenses and mirrors designed with parabaloidal or other surfaces in order to reduce aberrations.

as·pho·del (ăs′fə-dĕl′) *n.* **1.** An unidentified flower of classical legend, said to resemble the narcissus and to cover the Elysian Fields. **2.** Any of several plants of the genus *Asphodeline* or the genus *Asphodelus,* of the Mediterranean region, having clusters of white or yellow flowers. See **bog asphodel.** [Latin *asphodelus,* from Greek *asphodelos*†.]

as·phyx·i·a (ăs-fĭk′sē-ə) *n.* Unconsciousness or death ocurring when oxygen is prevented from reaching the tissues; suffocation. [New Latin, from Greek *asphuxia,* stopping of the pulse : *a-,* not + *sphuxis,* heartbeat, pulsation, from *sphuzein*†, to throb.] **—as·phyx·i·al** *adj.*

as·phyx·i·ant (ăs-fĭk′sē-ənt) *adj.* Inducing or tending to induce asphyxia.
~n. A substance or condition that causes asphyxia.

as·phyx·i·ate (ăs-fĭk′sē-āt′) *v.* **-ated, -ating, -ates.** *—tr.* To cause asphyxia in; smother. *—intr.* To undergo asphyxia; suffocate. **—as·phyx·i·a·tion** *n.* **—as·phyx·i·a·tor** *n.*

as·pic[1] (ăs′pĭk) *n.* A clear jelly made of stock and gelatin and used to make a meat, fish, or vegetable mold or as a garnish in cookery. [French *(sauce)* or *(ragoût) à l'aspic,* from *aspic,* ASPIC (snake), from the fancied resemblance of the different colors of the jelly to those of the snake.]

aspic[2] *n. Poetic & Archaic.* The asp, a poisonous snake. [Old French, from *aspe,* from Latin *aspis,* ASP (snake).]

aspic[3] *n.* A species of lavender, *Lavandula spica,* that yields a fragrant oil used in perfumery. [French, from Old French, from Old Provençal *espic,* spike (of a grain such as barley), from Latin *spīca,* spike.]

as·pi·dis·tra (ăs′pə-dĭs′trə) *n.* Any of several Asian plants of the genus *Aspidistra*; especially, *A. lurida,* having long, tough, evergreen leaves and small brownish flowers. This species is widely cultivated as a house plant. [New Latin *Aspidistra* : Greek *aspis*† (stem *aspid-*), shield (referring to the shape of the leaves) + *-istra,* after *Tupistra* (a genus of the lily family).]

as·pi·rant (ăs′pər-ənt, ə-spīr′ənt) *n.* One who aspires, especially after advancement, honors, or a high position.
~adj. **1.** Aspiring after recognition or distinction: *aspirant poets.* **2.** *Poetic.* Rising; ascending.

as·pi·rate (ăs′pə-rāt′) *tr.v.* **-rated, -rating, -rates. 1.** *Phonetics.* **a.** To pronounce (a vowel or word) with the initial release of breath associated with English *h,* as in *hurry.* **b.** To follow (a consonant, especially a stop consonant) with a puff of breath that is clearly audible before the next sound begins, as in English *p, t,* and *k* before vowels. **2.** *Medicine.* To remove (fluids or gases) from the body by means of an aspirator.
~n. (ăs′pər-ĭt). *Phonetics.* **1.** The speech sound represented by the English *h.* **2.** Any speech sound followed by a puff of breath.
~adj. (ăs′pər-ĭt). *Phonetics.* Aspirated. Said of a speech sound. [Latin *aspīrāre,* to breathe upon, aspirate : *ad-,* to + *spīrāre,* to breathe.]

as·pi·ra·tion (ăs′pə-rā′shən) *n.* **1.** Expulsion of breath in speech. **2.** *Phonetics.* **a.** The pronunciation of an aspirate. **b.** The puff of air accompanying the release of a stop consonant. **3.** *Medicine.* Removal of fluids or gases from the body with an aspirator. **4. a.** A strong desire for high achievement. **b.** An object of such desire; an ambition.

as·pi·ra·tor (ăs′pə-rā′tər) *n.* **1.** Any device that removes liquids or gases from a space by suction, especially one used medically to evacuate a bodily cavity. **2.** A suction pump used to create a partial vacuum.

as·pir·a·to·ry (ə-spīr′ə-tôr′ē, -tōr′ē) *adj.* Of, concerning, or suited for breathing or suction.

as·pire (ə-spīr′) *intr.v.* **-pired, -piring, -pires. 1.** To have a great ambition or ultimate goal: *aspired to stardom.* **2.** To strive toward an end; aim. **3.** *Archaic.* To rise upward; soar. [Middle English *aspiren,* from Old French *aspirer,* from Latin *aspīrāre,* to breathe upon, desire, ASPIRATE.] **—as·pir·er** *n.* **—as·pir·ing·ly** *adv.*

as·pi·rin (ăs′pər-ĭn, -prĭn) *n.* **1.** A white crystalline compound, $CH_3COOC_6H_4COOH$, commonly used in tablet form to relieve pain, fever, and inflammation. Also called "acetylsalicylic acid." **2.** A tablet of aspirin. [German, from AC(ETYL) + *spir(aeic acid),* old name for salicylic acid, from SPIRAEA + -IN.]

as·pir·ing (ə-spīr′ĭng) *adj.* Aiming for recognition or distinction: *an aspiring young lawyer.*

a·squint (ə-skwĭnt′) *adv.* With a sidelong glance. [Middle English : perhaps A- (on) + Dutch *schuinte*†, a slope, slant, from *schuin,* sideways, slanting.] **—a·squint** *adj.*

As·quith (ăs′kwĭth), **Herbert Henry, 1st Earl of Oxford and Asquith** (1852–1928). British Liberal politician, prime minister (1908–16). His government passed the Parliament Act of 1911 and took away the power of veto from the House of Lords. It also introduced unemployment insurance and old-age pensions. In 1915 he formed a coalition government with the Conservatives and a year later was forced to resign in favor of Lloyd George. He remained leader of the Liberal Party until 1926.

ass (ăs) *n., pl.* **asses** (ăs′ĭz). **1.** Any of several hoofed mammals of the genus *Equus*; especially, *E. asinus* of Africa and *E. hemionus* of Asia, resembling and closely related to the horses and zebras but having longer ears. See **donkey, onager. 2.** A stupid person, especially one who is vain and self-important. [Middle English *asse,* Old English *assa,* from Old Celtic *as(s)in* (unattested), from Latin *asinus.*]

assagai. Variant of **assegai.**

as·sai[1] (ä-sī′) *n.* **1.** Any of several palm trees of the genus *Euterpe,* of tropical South America, having edible, fleshy purple fruit. **2.** A beverage made from this fruit. [Brazilian Portuguese *assaí,* from Tupi *assahi.*]

assai[2] *adv. Music.* Very. Used in directions: *allegro assai.* [Italian, "enough," from Vulgar Latin *ad satis* (unattested), "to the point of sufficiency." See **assets.**]

as·sail (ə-sāl′) *tr.v.* **-sailed, -sailing, -sails. 1.** To attack with or as if with violent blows; assault. **2.** To attack verbally, as with ridicule

aspen *The constant rustling of the aspen's leaves—caused by the slenderness of the stalks that hold them to the tree—was formerly thought to indicate someone's secret grief or guilt. Another theory was that the tree trembled because it had provided the wood for Christ's cross.*

aspidistra *An east Asian plant popular as an indoor evergreen in Victorian Britain. It was able to thrive in the extremes of temperature and dim light often found in Victorian homes.*

or censure. **3.** To trouble: *She was assailed by doubts.* —See Synonyms at **attack.** [Middle English *asailen,* from Old French *asaillir,* from Medieval Latin *assalīre* from Latin *assilīre,* to jump on : *ad-,* to + *salīre,* to leap.] **—as·sail·a·ble** *adj.* **—as·sail·a·ble·ness** *n.* **—as·sail·er** *n.* **—as·sail·ment** *n.*

as·sail·ant (ə-sā′lənt) *n.* A person who assails another.

As·sam (ə-săm′, ăs′əm). A state in the far northeast of India, almost isolated from the rest of the country by Bangladesh. The capital is Shillong. It is a tea-growing region, but also has important oil reserves and refineries.

As·sa·mese (ăs′ə-mēz′, -mēs′) *adj.* Of or pertaining to Assam, its people, or their language.
∼*n., pl.* **Assamese. 1.** A native or inhabitant of Assam. **2.** The Indo-European Indic language of the Assamese.

as·sas·sin (ə-săs′ĭn) *n.* **1.** A murderer, especially one who carries out a plot to kill a prominent public figure. **2. Assassin.** A member of a secret order of Muslim fanatics who terrorized and killed Christian Crusaders. [French, from Medieval Latin *assassīnus,* from Arabic *ḥashshāshīn,* plural of *ḥashshāsh,* "hashish eater," (originally referring to members of an Ismaili sect who took the drug before attacking their enemies), from *ḥashīsh,* HASHISH.]

as·sas·si·nate (ə-săs′ə-nāt′) *tr.v.* **-nated, -nating, -nates. 1.** To murder (a prominent person). **2.** To injure or destroy treacherously: *assassinated her good name.* **—as·sas·si·na·tive** *adj.* **—as·sas·si·na·tor** (ə-săs′ə-nā′tər) *n.*

as·sas·si·na·tion (ə-săs′ə-nā′shən) *n.* **1.** Murder, especially of a prominent person. **2.** Malicious injury, especially of a person's good reputation: *character assassination.*

assassin bug *n.* Any of various predatory insects of the large family Reduviidae, having short, curved, powerful beaks adapted for sucking blood and capable of inflicting a painful bite on humans. Some species transmit disease. See **kissing bug.**

as·sault (ə-sôlt′) *n.* **1.** A violent attack, either physical or verbal. **2.** *Military.* **a.** An attack upon a fortified area or place. **b.** The concluding stage of an attack in which there is close combat with the enemy. **3.** *Law.* An unlawful attempt or threat to injure another physically. **4.** Rape.
∼*tr.v.* **assaulted, -saulting, -saults.** To make an assault on. —See Synonyms at **attack.** [Middle English *assaut,* from Old French *asaut, assaut,* from Vulgar Latin *assaltus* (unattested), variant of Latin *assultus,* past participle of *assilīre,* ASSAIL.] **—as·sault·er** *n.*

assault and battery *n. Law.* The threat to make a physical attack on someone and the carrying out of the threat.

assault course *n.* **1.** A military exercise in which troops are made to go over a course of physical obstacles. **2.** Any procedure presenting a series of difficulties.

as·say (ăs′ā′, ă-sā′) *n.* **1. a.** The qualitative or quantitative analysis of a substance, especially of an ore or drug. **b.** A substance to be so analyzed. **c.** The result of such an analysis. **2.** Any analysis or examination. **3.** *Obsolete.* An attempt; an essay.
∼*v.* (ă-sā′, ăs′ā′) **assayed, -saying, -says.** —*tr.* **1.** To subject to chemical analysis; make an assay of. **2.** To examine by trial or experiment; put to a test: *assay one's ability.* **3.** To evaluate; assess. **4.** To attempt; try. —*intr.* To be shown by analysis as having a certain proportion, usually of a precious metal. —See Synonyms at **estimate.** [Middle English, from Old French *assai, essai,* trial, ESSAY.] **—as·say·a·ble** *adj.* **—as·say·er** *n.*

assay office *n.* An office or laboratory in which ore is analyzed to determine the proportion of precious metal it contains.

as·se·gai, as·sa·gai (ăs′ə-gī′) *n.* **1.** A light spear or javelin used by southern African tribesmen. **2.** A tree, *Curtisia faginea,* of southern Africa, the wood of which is used for making spears.

as·sem·blage (ə-sĕm′blĭj) *n.* **1. a.** The act of assembling. **b.** The state of being assembled. **2.** A collection of people or things. **3.** A fitting together of parts, as of a machine. **4.** A sculpture consisting of an arrangement of miscellaneous objects, such as scraps of metal, cloth, or string.

as·sem·ble (ə-sĕm′bəl) *v.* **-bled, -bling, -bles.** —*tr.* **1.** To bring or gather together into a group or whole. **2.** To fit or join together the parts of. **3.** *Computer Science.* To run an assembler program on (data). —*intr.* **1.** To gather together; congregate. **2.** To be capable of undergoing assembly: *The kit assembles into a bookcase.* —See Synonyms at **gather.** [Middle English *assemblen,* from Old French *assembler,* from Vulgar Latin *assimulāre* (unattested), to bring together : Latin *ad-,* to + *simul,* together, at the same time.] **—as·sem·bler** *n.*

as·sem·bler (ə-sĕm′blər) *n.* **1.** A person or device that assembles something. **2.** *Computer Science.* A program that converts input data into machine code. Compare **compiler.**

as·sem·bly (ə-sĕm′blē) *n., pl.* **-blies.** *Abbr.* **assy. 1. a.** The act of assembling. **b.** The state of being assembled. **2.** A group of persons gathered together for a common purpose, usually legislative, religious, educational, or social. **3. Assembly.** In certain U.S. states, the lower house of the legislature. **4. a.** The putting together of manufactured parts to make a completed product, such as a machine or electronic circuit. **b.** A set of parts so assembled. **5.** *Military.* The signal calling troops to form ranks.

assembly language *n. Computer Science.* A programming language that is a close approximation of machine code.

assembly line *n.* A line of factory workers and equipment on which the product being assembled passes consecutively from operation to operation until completed. Also called "production line." **—as·sem·bly-line** *adj.*

as·sem·bly·man (ə-sĕm′blē-mən) *n., pl.* **-men** (-mĭn). A member of a legislative assembly.

Assembly of God *n.* A Pentecostal congregation founded in the United States in 1914.

assembly time *n. Computer Science.* The time required for an assembler to translate symbolic language into machine code.

as·sent (ə-sĕnt′) *intr.v.* **-sented, -senting, -sents.** To express agreement; concur. Used with *to*: *assent to his plan.*
∼*n.* **1.** Agreement, as to a proposal; compliance. **2.** Acquiescence; consent. [Middle English *assenten,* from Old French *assenter,* from Latin *assentārī,* frequentative of *assentīre,* "to join in feeling," agree with : *ad-,* toward + *sentīre,* to feel, think.] **—as·sent·er, as·sen·tor** (ə-sĕn′tər) *n.* **—as·sent·ing·ly** *adv.* **—as·sent·ive** *adj.* **—as·sent·ive·ness** *n.*
Synonyms: *accede, accept, acquiesce, agree, concur, consent, subscribe.*

as·sen·ta·tion (ăs′ĕn-tā′shən) *n.* Ill-considered or servile agreement with another's opinions.

as·sert (ə-sûrt′) *tr.v.* **-serted, -serting, -serts. 1.** To state or express positively or forcefully; affirm. **2.** To defend or maintain (one's rights, for example). **3.** To put (oneself) forward, forcefully or boldly. [Latin *asserere,* "to join to oneself," maintain, claim : *ad-,* to + *serere,* to join.] **—as·sert·a·ble, as·sert·i·ble** *adj.* **—as·sert·er, as·ser·tor** (ə-sûr′tər) *n.*
Synonyms: *affirm, allege, asseverate, aver, avow, declare.*

as·ser·tion (ə-sûr′shən) *n.* **1.** The act of asserting or declaring. **2.** A declaration stated positively but with no support or attempt at proof. **—as·ser·tion·al** *adj.*

as·ser·tive (ə-sûr′tĭv) *adj.* Inclined to bold or confident assertion; aggressive. **—as·ser·tive·ly** *adv.* **—as·ser·tive·ness** *n.*

assertiveness training *n.* A method of training individuals to behave in a boldly self-confident manner.

as·ser·to·ry (ə-sûr′tər-ē) *adj.* Asserting or affirming.

as·ses[1]**.** Plural of **as** (Roman coin).

ass·es[2]**.** Plural of **ass.**

as·sess (ə-sĕs′) *tr.v.* **-sessed, -sessing, -sesses. 1.** To estimate the value of (property) for taxation. **2.** To set or determine the amount of (a tax, fine, or other payment). **3.** To charge (a person or property) with a tax, fine, or other special payment. **4.** To evaluate; appraise. —See Synonyms at **estimate.** [Middle English *assessen,* from Old French *assesser,* from Latin *assidere* (past participle *assessus*), "to sit beside," be an assistant judge (hence, Medieval Latin, to tax) : *ad-,* near to + *sedēre,* to sit.] **—as·sess·a·ble** *adj.*

as·sess·ment (ə-sĕs′mənt) *n.* **1.** The act of assessing. **2.** An account of an act of assessing. **3.** An amount assessed, as for taxation or costing purposes. **4.** An evaluation; an appraisal.

as·ses·sor (ə-sĕs′ər) *n.* **1.** An official who makes assessments, as for taxation. **2.** An assistant to a judge, selected for his special knowledge of a particular area. **3.** Any adviser or assistant. **—as·ses·so·ri·al** (ăs′ə-sôr′ē-əl, -sōr′-) *adj.*

as·set (ăs′ĕt′) *n.* **1.** A useful or valuable quality, person, or thing. **2.** A valuable item that is owned. [Back-formation from ASSETS.]

as·sets (ăs′ĕts′) *pl.n.* **1.** *Accounting.* The entries on a balance sheet showing all of a person's or enterprise's properties and claims against others that may be applied, directly or indirectly, to cover liabilities. Assets include the value of tangible things, such as cash and stock, and that of intangibles, such as a trademark or goodwill. **2.** The entire property owned by a person, especially a dead person or a bankrupt, which can be used to settle debts. [Norman French *asetz* (legal use), from Old French *asez,* "enough (to satisfy creditors)," from Vulgar Latin *ad satis* (unattested), "to the point of sufficiency," enough : Latin *ad-,* to + *satis,* sufficient.]
Synonyms: *belongings, effects, property, possessions.*

as·sev·er·ate (ə-sĕv′ə-rāt′) *tr.v.* **-ated, -ating, -ates.** To declare seriously or positively; affirm. —See Synonyms at **assert.** [Latin *asseverāre,* to assert earnestly : *ad-,* to + *sevērus,* earnest, serious.] **—as·sev·er·a·tion** *n.*

as·sib·i·late (ə-sĭb′ə-lāt′) *tr.v.* **-lated, -lating, -lates.** *Phonetics.* To make sibilant; pronounce with a hissing sound. [AD- (in addition to) + SIBILATE.] **—as·sib·i·la·tion** *n.*

as·si·du·i·ty (ăs′ə-do͞o′ə-tē, -dyo͞o′ə-tē) *n., pl.* **-ties. 1.** Close and constant application; unflagging effort; diligence. **2. assiduities.** Constant personal attentions; solicitude.

as·sid·u·ous (ə-sĭj′o͞o-əs) *adj.* **1.** Constant in application or attention; diligent; devoted: *an assiduous churchgoer.* **2.** Unceasing; persistent. —See Synonyms at **busy.** [Latin *assiduus,* from *assidēre,* to sit beside, attend to : *ad-,* near to + *sedēre,* to sit.] **—as·sid·u·ous·ly** *adv.* **—as·sid·u·ous·ness** *n.*

as·sign (ə-sīn′) *tr.v.* **-signed, -signing, -signs. 1.** To set apart or fix for a particular purpose; designate. **2.** To select for a duty or office; appoint. **3.** To give out as a task; allot. **4.** To ascribe; attribute. **5.** *Law.* To transfer (property, rights, or interests). **6.** *Military.* To place (a unit or personnel) integrally into a particular organization. Compare **attach.** —See Synonyms at **attribute, commit.**
∼*n. Law.* An assignee. [Middle English *assignen,* from Old French *assigner,* from Latin *assignāre,* to mark out : *ad-,* to + *signāre,* to mark, from *signum,* sign.] **—as·sign·a·bil·i·ty** *n.* **—as·sign·a·ble** *adj.* **—as·sign·a·bly** *adv.* **—as·sign·er** *n.*
Synonyms: *allocate, allot, apportion.*

as·sig·nat (ăs′ĭg-năt′; *French* à-sē-nyà′) *n.* Any of the notes of the paper currency issued in France (1789–96) by the revolutionary government on the security of confiscated lands. [French, from

Latin *assignātum*, "something assigned," past participle of *assignāre*, ASSIGN.]

as·sig·na·tion (ăs′ĭg-nā′shən) *n*. 1. The act of assigning. 2. Something assigned; an assignment. 3. An appointment for a meeting between lovers; a tryst.

as·sign·ee (ə-sī′nē′, ăs′ĭ-nē′) *n. Law*. 1. A person to whom a transfer of property, rights, or interest is made. 2. One appointed to act for another; a deputy; an agent.

as·sign·ment (ə-sīn′mənt) *n. Abbr.* **asgmt.** 1. The act of assigning. 2. Something assigned, such as a task. 3. A position or post of duty to which one is assigned. 4. *Law*. **a.** The transfer of a claim, right, interest, or property. **b.** The document or deed by which this transfer is made. **c.** That which is transferred. —See Synonyms at **task.**

as·sign·or (ə-sī′nôr′, ə-sī′nər, ăs′ə-nôr′) *n. Law*. A person who makes an assignment.

as·sim·i·la·ble (ə-sĭm′ə-lə-bəl) *adj*. Capable of being assimilated. —**as·sim·i·la·bil·i·ty** *n*.

as·sim·i·late (ə-sĭm′ə-lāt′) *v*. **-lated, -lating, -lates.** —*tr*. 1. *Biology*. **a.** To consume and incorporate into the body; digest. **b.** To transform (digested food) into living tissue; metabolize constructively. 2. To absorb and incorporate (knowledge, for example). 3. To cause to belong or become integrated: *Can the community assimilate these newcomers?* 4. To make similar; cause to assume a resemblance. 5. *Linguistics*. To alter (a sound) by assimilation. —*intr*. To become assimilated. [Middle English *assimilaten*, from Latin *assimilāre, assimulāre*, to make similar to : *ad-*, to + *simulāre, similāre*, to simulate, from *similis*, similar.] —**as·sim·i·la·tor** *n*.

as·sim·i·la·tion (ə-sĭm′ə-lā′shən) *n*. 1. **a.** The act or process of assimilating. **b.** The condition or process of being assimilated. 2. *Biology*. The process by which the molecules of digested food are incorporated into living tissue; constructive metabolism. 3. *Linguistics*. The process by which a sound is modified to make it resemble an adjacent sound. For example, the prefix *in-*, as in *intolerable*, becomes *im-* in *impossible* by assimilation. 4. The process whereby a group, especially a minority or immigrant group, gradually adopts the characteristics of another culture.

as·sim·i·la·tive (ə-sĭm′ə-lā′tĭv, -lə-tĭv) *adj*. Also **as·sim·i·la·to·ry** (-lə-tôr′ē, -tōr′ē). Marked by or causing assimilation.

As·si·si (ə-sē′zē, -sē). Town in the Umbrian region of central Italy, lying on the slopes of the Apennines. St. Francis of Assisi was born here in 1182 and the convent built immediately after his canonization in 1228 still stands.

as·sist (ə-sĭst′) *v*. **-sisted, -sisting, -sists.** —*tr*. 1. To aid; help. 2. To aid in a professional capacity: *assist a surgeon in an operation.* —*intr*. 1. To give aid or support. 2. To be present; attend. Usually used with *at*. —See Synonyms at **help.**
~*n*. 1. An act of giving aid; help. 2. **a.** In baseball, a handling of the ball that enables a runner to be put out. **b.** In ice hockey, a pass of the puck to the teammate scoring a goal. [Middle English *assisten*, from Old French *assister*, from Latin *assistere*, to stand beside, help : *ad-*, near to + *sistere*, to stand.] —**as·sist·er** *n*.

as·sis·tance (ə-sĭs′təns) *n*. 1. The act of assisting. 2. Aid.

as·sis·tant (ə-sĭs′tənt) *n. Abbr.* **asst.** 1. One that assists; a helper; especially, a professional aide. 2. A person serving customers in a shop.
~*adj. Abbr.* **asst.** 1. Holding an auxiliary position; subordinate. 2. Giving aid; auxiliary.

assistant professor *n*. A college teacher who ranks above an instructor and below an associate professor.

as·sis·tant·ship (ə-sĭs′tənt-shĭp′) *n*. An academic position that carries a stipend and usually involves part-time teaching or research, given to a qualified graduate student.

Assiut. See **Asyut.**

as·size (ə-sīz′) *n*. 1. *English History*. **a.** A session of a legislative or judicial body or court. **b.** A decree, verdict, or edict rendered at such a session. 2. **assizes. a.** Any of the periodic court sessions formerly held in each of the counties of England and Wales for the trial of civil or criminal cases. Its functions are now carried out by the High Court and Crown Court. **b.** The time or place of such sessions. [Middle English *assise*, from Old French, feminine of *assis*, past participle of *as(s)eeir*, to seat, from Vulgar Latin *assedēre* (unattested), from Latin *assidēre*, to sit beside, be an assistant judge. See **assiduous.**]

assn. association.

assoc. associate; association.

as·so·ci·a·ble (ə-sō′shē-ə-bəl, -shə-bəl) *adj*. Capable of being associated. —**as·so·ci·a·bil·i·ty, as·so·ci·a·ble·ness** *n*.

as·so·ci·ate (ə-sō′shē-āt′, -sē-āt′) *v*. **-ated, -ating, -ates.** —*tr*. 1. To bring into company with another; join in a relationship. 2. To connect or join together; combine; link. 3. To connect in the mind or imagination: *I always associate the Lake District with Wordsworth.* —*intr*. 1. To join in or form a league, union, or association. 2. To keep company. —See Synonyms at **join.**
~*n*. (ə-sō′shē-ĭt, -sē-ĭt, -shē-āt′, -sē-āt′). *Abbr.* **assoc.** 1. A person united with another or others in some action, enterprise, or business; a partner; a colleague. 2. A companion; a comrade. 3. Anything that habitually accompanies or is associated with another; an attendant circumstance. 4. A member of an institution or society who is granted only partial status or privileges. —See Synonyms at **partner.**
~*adj*. (ə-sō′shē-ĭt, -sē-ĭt, -shē-āt′, -sē-āt′). *Abbr.* **assoc.** 1. Joined with another or others and having equal or nearly equal status: *an associate editor.* 2. Having partial status or privileges: *an associate*

member of the club. 3. Following or accompanying; concomitant. [Middle English *associaten*, from Latin *associāre*, to join to : *ad-*, to + *sociāre*, to join, from *socius*, companion.]

associate professor *n*. A college or university teacher who ranks below a full professor and above an assistant professor.

as·so·ci·a·tion (ə-sō′sē-ā′shən, -shē-) *n*. 1. The act of associating. 2. The state of being associated. 3. *Abbr.* **assn., assoc.** An organized body of people who have some interest, activity, or purpose in common; a society. 4. A mental connection or relation between thoughts, feelings, ideas, or sensations. 5. *Chemistry*. Any of various processes of chemical combination, such as hydration, solvation, or complex-ion formation, depending on relatively weak chemical bonding. 6. *Ecology*. A large community of organisms in a specific area with one or two dominant species. —**as·so·ci·a·tion·al** *adj*.

association football *n. Chiefly British*. The official name for **soccer** *(see).*

as·so·ci·a·tion·ism (ə-sō′sē-ā′shən-ĭz′əm, -shē-) *n*. The psychological theory that association is the basic principle of all mental activity. —**as·so·ci·a·tion·ist** *n. & adj.*

Association of Southeast Asian Nations. *Abbr.* **ASEAN** An alliance formed in 1967 to stimulate economic growth in Southeast Asia. Its members are Indonesia, Malaysia, the Philippines, Singapore, and Thailand.

as·so·ci·a·tive (ə-sō′shē-ā′tĭv, -sē-ā′tĭv, -shə-tĭv) *adj*. 1. Of, characterized by, resulting from, or causing association. 2. *Mathematics*. Independent of the grouping of elements. Said of mathematical operations: *If* $a + (b + c) = (a + b) + c$, *the operation indicated by* $+$ *is associative.* —**as·so·ci·a·tive·ly** *adv*.

as·soil (ə-soil′) *tr.v.* **-soiled, -soiling, -soils.** *Rare*. 1. To absolve or pardon. 2. To atone for. [Middle English *assoilen*, from Norman French *as(s)oilier*, from Old French *assoldre* (stem *assoil-*), from Latin *absolvere*, to set free from : *ab-*, away from + *solvere*, to loosen, set free.]

as·so·nance (ăs′ə-nəns) *n*. 1. Resemblance in sound, especially in the vowel sounds of words. 2. A partial rhyme in which the accented vowel sounds correspond but the consonants differ, as in *brave* and *vain*. 3. Rough similarity; approximate agreement. [French, from Latin *assonāns*, present participle of *assonāre*, to sound in response to : *ad-*, to + *sonāre*, to sound.] —**as·so·nant** *adj. & n.*

as·sort (ə-sôrt′) *v*. **-sorted, -sorting, -sorts.** —*tr*. 1. To separate into groups according to kinds; classify. 2. To supply with a variety of goods. —*intr*. 1. To fall into a class; match. Often used with *with.* 2. To associate; consort. Used with *with.* [Old French *assorter* : *a-*, from Latin *ad-*, to + *sorte*, kind, from Vulgar Latin *sorta* (unattested), kind, from Latin *sors* (stem *sort-*), chance, fortune, lot.] —**as·sort·a·tive** (ə-sôr′tə-tĭv) *adj*. —**as·sort·er** *n*.

as·sort·ed (ə-sôr′tĭd) *adj*. 1. Consisting of a number of different kinds; various. 2. Placed in classes; classified. 3. Suited or matched. Often used in combination: *well-assorted; ill-assorted.* —See Synonyms at **miscellaneous.**

as·sort·ment (ə-sôrt′mənt) *n*. 1. The act of assorting; separation into classes. 2. A collection of various things; a variety.

Assouan, Assuan. See **Aswan.**

A.S.S.R. Autonomous Soviet Socialist Republic.

asst. assistant.

as·suage (ə-swāj′) *tr.v.* **-suaged, -suaging, -suages.** 1. To make less severe or burdensome; ease: *assuage her grief.* 2. To satisfy; appease, as thirst. 3. To pacify or calm. —See Synonyms at **relieve.** [Middle English *aswagen*, from Old French *assouagier*, from Vulgar Latin *assuāviāre* (unattested), to sweeten : *ad-*, to + *suāvis*, sweet.] —**as·suage·ment** *n*. —**as·suag·er** *n*.

as·sua·sive (ə-swā′sĭv, -zĭv) *adj*. Soothing. [AD- + *-suasive*, as in PERSUASIVE but influenced by ASSUAGE.]

as·sume (ə-soom′) *tr.v.* **-sumed, -suming, -sumes.** 1. To put on; don (a garment, for example). 2. To take upon oneself; undertake: *assume responsibility.* 3. To appropriate or usurp. **b.** To invest oneself formally with: *assume the presidency.* 4. To take on; adopt: *"the god assumes a human form"* (John Ruskin). 5. To feign; affect. 6. To take for granted; suppose. 7. *Theology*. To receive, as into heaven. —See Synonyms at **presume.** [Middle English *assumen*, from Latin *assūmere*, to take to oneself, adopt : *ad-*, to + *sūmere*, to take.] —**as·sum·a·ble** *adj*. —**as·sum·a·bly** *adv*. —**as·sum·er** *n*.

as·sumed (ə-soomd′) *adj*. 1. Pretended; adopted; fictitious: *an assumed name.* 2. Taken for granted. —**as·sum·ed·ly** (ə-soo′mĭd-lē) *adv*.

as·sum·ing (ə-soo′mĭng) *adj*. Presumptuous or arrogant.
~*conj*. Accepting as provisionally true, for the sake of argument; supposing: *Assuming you miss the train, how will you get there?* —**as·sum·ing·ly** *adv*.

as·sump·sit (ə-sŭmp′sĭt) *n. Law*. 1. An agreement or promise not under seal; a contract. 2. A legal action to enforce or recover damages for a breach of such an agreement. [New Latin, "he undertook," from *assūmere*, to undertake, ASSUME.]

as·sump·tion (ə-sŭmp′shən) *n*. 1. The act of assuming. 2. A statement accepted or supposed to be true without proof or demonstration. 3. Presumption or arrogance. 4. *Logic*. A minor premise. 5. **Assumption. a.** *Theology*. The bodily taking up of the Virgin Mary into heaven. **b.** A church feast on August 15 celebrating this event. [Middle English, from Latin *assumptiō* (stem *assumptiōn-*); a taking up, adoption, from *assūmere*, ASSUME.]

as·sump·tive (ə-sŭmp′tĭv) *adj*. 1. Of or characterized by assumption: *assumptive facts.* **2.** Taken for granted. **3.** Presumptuous; assuming. —**as·sump·tive·ly** *adv.*

as·sur·ance (ə-shoor′əns) *n.* **1. a.** The act of assuring. **b.** The state of being assured. **2.** A statement or indication that inspires confidence. **3. a.** Freedom from doubt; certainty. **b.** Self-confidence. **4.** Boldness; audacity. **5.** *Chiefly British.* Insurance making provision for events that are certain rather than probable, especially for death. —See Synonyms at **certainty.**

as·sure (ə-shoor′) *tr.v.* **-sured, -suring, -sures.** **1.** To inform confidently, with a view to removing doubt. **2.** To cause to feel sure; convince. **3.** To give confidence to; reassure. **4.** To make certain; ensure: *This will assure the success of our enterprise.* **5.** To make safe or secure. **6.** To insure, especially against death. [Middle English *assuren,* from Old French *assurer,* from Medieval Latin *assēcūrāre,* to make sure : Latin *ad-,* to + *sēcūrus,* SECURE.] —**as·sur·a·ble** *adj.* —**as·sur·er** *n.*

as·sured (ə-shoord′) *adj.* **1.** Undoubted; guaranteed; made certain. **2.** Confident; bold. **3.** Insured, especially against death. —See Synonyms at **sure.**

~*n., pl.* **assured.** **1.** A person whose life is insured. **2.** A person who stands to benefit from a life insurance policy. —**as·sur·ed·ly** (ə-shoor′id-lē) *adv.* —**as·sur·ed·ness** *n.*

as·sur·gent (ə-sûr′jənt) *adj.* **1.** Rising or tending to rise. **2.** *Botany.* Slanting or curving upward; ascending. [Latin *assurgēns* (stem, *assurgent-*), present participle of *assurgere,* to rise up to : *ad-,* to + *surgere,* to SURGE.] —**as·sur·gen·cy** *n.*

assy. assembly.

Assyr. Assyrian.

As·syr·i·a (ə-sîr′ē-ə). An ancient civilization of western Asia, which began to develop at the beginning of the 3rd millennium B.C. around the city of Ashur on the upper Tigris River. The zenith of the Assyrian Empire was reached between the 9th and 7th centuries B.C. when it was extended from the Mediterranean across Arabia and Armenia. Its capital, Nineveh, fell in 612 B.C. to the Medes and Babylonians.

As·syr·i·an (ə-sîr′ē-ən) *adj.* Of or pertaining to Assyria, its people, their language or culture.

~*n.* **1.** A native or inhabitant of Assyria. **2.** *Abbr.* **Assyr.** The Semitic language of Assyria.

As·syr·i·ol·o·gy (ə-sîr′ē-ŏl′ə-jē) *n.* The study of the ancient civilization of Assyria. —**As·syr·i·ol·o·gist** *n.*

a·sta·ble (ā-stā′bəl) *adj.* **1.** Not stable. **2.** *Electronics.* Designating or pertaining to a component or circuit that can exist in two distinct states.

As·taire (ə-stâr′), **Fred,** born Frederick Austerlitz (1899–). U.S. dancer and actor. His first film with Ginger Rogers, *Flying Down to Rio* (1933), marked the start of one of Hollywood's most famous partnerships. Among his other films are *Top Hat* (1935), *Easter Parade* (1948), and *Daddy Long Legs* (1955). In 1949 he was awarded a special Academy Award.

As·tar·te (ə-stär′tē). *Phoenician Mythology.* The goddess of love and fertility. [Latin *Astartē,* from Greek, from Phoenician *'strt,* akin to Hebrew *'Ashtoreth.*]

a·sta·sia (ə-stā′zhə) *n.* Inability to stand because of poor muscular coordination. [New Latin, from Greek instability, from *astatos,* unstable : *a-,* not + *statos,* standing.]

a·stat·ic (ā-stăt′ĭk) *adj.* **1.** Unsteady; unstable. **2.** *Physics.* Pertaining to or designating a device having two magnetic coils to compensate for the earth's magnetic field: *an astatic galvanometer.* —**a·stat·i·cal·ly** *adv.* —**a·stat·i·cism** (ā-stăt′ə-sĭz′əm) *n.*

as·ta·tine (ăs′tə-tēn′) *n. Symbol* **At** A highly unstable radioactive element that resembles iodine in solution and accumulates in the thyroid gland. Its longest lived isotope is At 210, having a half-life of 8.3 hours, used in medicine as a radioactive tracer. Atomic number 85, valences probably 1, 3, 5, and 7. [Greek *astatos,* unstable : *a-,* not + *statos,* standing + -INE.]

as·ter (ăs′tər) *n.* **1.** Any of various tall, perennial plants of the genus *Aster,* having rayed, daisylike flowers ranging in color from white to bluish purple or pink. See **Michaelmas daisy. 2.** The **China aster** *(see).* **3.** *Biology.* A star-shaped structure appearing in the cytoplasm of the cell and associated with the centrosome during mitosis. [New Latin, from Latin *astēr,* star, from Greek.]

-aster *suffix.* Indicates inferiority or fraudulence; for example, **poetaster.** [Middle English, from Latin, suffix denoting either smallness or partial resemblance (often pejorative).]

as·te·ri·at·ed (ă-stîr′ē-ā′tĭd) *adj. Mineralogy.* Exhibiting asterism. [Greek *asterios,* starry, from *astēr,* star.]

as·ter·isk (ăs′tə-rĭsk′) *n.* **1.** A star-shaped figure (*) used in printing to indicate an omission or a reference to a footnote. **2.** *Linguistics.* This sign used to indicate an unattested form or entity.

~*tr.v.* **asterisked, -isking, -isks.** To indicate by means of an asterisk; mark with an asterisk. [Late Latin *asteriscus,* from Greek *asteriskos,* little star, asterisk, diminutive of *astēr,* star.]

as·ter·ism (ăs′tə-rĭz′əm) *n.* **1.** Three asterisks in triangular form used to call attention to a following passage. **2.** *Astronomy.* **a.** A cluster of stars. **b.** A constellation. **3.** In mineralogy, a six-rayed starlike figure observed in some crystal structures using reflected or transmitted light. [Greek *asterismos,* from *asterizein,* to arrange in constellations, from *astēr,* star.] —**as·ter·is·mal** *adj.*

a·stern (ə-stûrn′) *adv. Nautical.* **1.** Behind a vessel. **2.** Toward the rear of a vessel. **3.** To the rear; backward. [17th century : A- (toward) + STERN, formed by analogy with *ahead.*] —**a·stern** *adj.*

a·ster·nal (ā-stûr′nəl) *adj. Anatomy.* **1.** Not connected to the sternum. **2.** Lacking a sternum.

as·ter·oid (ăs′tə-roid′) *n.* **1.** *Astronomy.* Any of numerous celestial bodies with characteristic diameters between one and several hundred miles and orbits lying in a zone, the *asteroid belt,* chiefly between Mars and Jupiter. Also called "minor planet," "planetoid." **2.** *Zoology.* A starfish.

~*adj.* Also **as·ter·oi·dal** (ăs′tə-roid′l). Star-shaped. [Greek *asteroeidēs,* like a star : *astēr,* star + -OID.]

Asterope. Variant of **Sterope.**

as·the·ni·a (ăs-thē′nē-ə) *n.* Also **as·the·ny** (ăs′thə-nē). *Pathology.* Loss or lack of strength; weakness. [New Latin, from Greek *astheneia,* from *asthenēs,* weak : *a-,* without + *sthenos†,* strength.]

as·then·ic (ăs-thĕn′ĭk) *adj.* **1.** Of or having a slender, long-limbed physique. **2.** Of or having asthenia.

~*n.* A slender, long-limbed person. —**as·then·i·cal** *adj.*

as·the·no·pi·a (ăs′thə-nō′pē-ə) *n.* Eyestrain, especially with headache and dimming of the vision. [New Latin, from ASTHEN(IA) + -OPIA.] —**as·the·nop·ic** (ăs′thə-nŏp′ĭk) *adj.*

as·then·o·sphere (ăs-thĕn′ə-sfîr′) *n.* A deformable zone in the earth's mantle lying between the lithosphere and the mesosphere (a depth of between 30 and 150 miles). [Greek *asthenēs,* weak (see **asthenia**) + SPHERE.]

asth·ma (ăz′mə) *n.* A chronic respiratory disease, often allergic in origin and marked by labored breathing, a sense of chest constriction, and coughing or gasping. [Middle English *asma,* from Medieval Latin, from Greek *asthma†.*] —**asth·mat·ic** (ăz-măt′ĭk) *adj. & n.* —**asth·mat·i·cal·ly** *adv.*

As·ti (ä′stē). Town in the Piedmont region of northwest Italy, famous for its sparkling white wine, Asti Spumante.

as·tig·mat·ic (ăs′tĭg-măt′ĭk) *adj.* **1.** Of or having astigmatism. **2.** Correcting astigmatism. —**as·tig·mat·i·cal·ly** *adv.*

a·stig·ma·tism (ə-stĭg′mə-tĭz′əm) *n.* **1.** A refractive defect of a lens that prevents focusing of sharp, distinct images. It occurs when the lens has different curvatures in two different directions. **2.** Faulty vision caused by such defects in the lens of the eye. [A- (without) + Greek *stigma* (stem *stigmat-*), spot, (tattoo) mark, "focus," from *stizein,* to tattoo.]

a·stil·be (ə-stĭl′bē) *n.* Any plant of the genus *Astilbe,* cultivated as garden plants for their ornamental pink or white plumelike flower clusters. [New Latin : A- (not) + Greek *stilbē,* from *stilbos,* glittering, with reference to the small, inconspicuous individual flowers.]

a·stir (ə-stûr′) *adj.* **1.** Moving about. **2.** Out of bed; awake. [Scottish *asteer* : A- (on) + *steer,* variant of STIR (noun).]

a·stom·a·tous (ā-stŏm′ə-təs, ā-stō′mə-) *adj.* Also **as·tom·ous** (ăs′tə-məs), **a·stom·a·tal** (ā-stŏm′ə-təl, ā-stō′mə-). *Biology.* Having no mouth or stomata.

As·ton (ăs′tən), **Francis William** (1877–1945). British physicist and chemist. In 1922 he was awarded the Nobel Prize in chemistry for the development of the mass spectograph, which led to the discovery of a number of isotopes of nonradioactive elements and the accurate atomic weights of elements.

a·ston·ied (ə-stŏn′ēd) *adj. Archaic.* Bewildered; dazed. [Middle English *aston(y)ed,* past participle of *astonen,* ASTONISH.]

a·ston·ish (ə-stŏn′ĭsh) *tr.v.* **-ished, -ishing, -ishes.** To fill with sudden wonder or amazement; surprise greatly. —See Synonyms at **surprise.** [Extension (with verbal suffix *-ish,* as in ABOLISH, FINISH) of obsolete *astony,* Middle English *astonen, astonien,* from Old French *estoner,* from Vulgar Latin *extonāre* (unattested), to strike with thunder, stun : Latin *ex-,* out of + *tonāre,* to thunder.] —**a·ston·ish·ing** *adj.* —**a·ston·ish·ing·ly** *adv.*

a·ston·ish·ment (ə-stŏn′ĭsh-mənt) *n.* **1.** Great surprise or amazement. **2.** A cause of amazement; a marvel.

As·tor (ăs′tər), **John Jacob** (1763–1848). U.S. fur trader and land investor. He founded the fortune of the Astors, one of the United States' wealthiest families.

Astor, Nancy Witcher Langhorne, Viscountess (1879–1964). British Conservative politician, born in the United States. Her second husband was **Waldorf Astor, 2nd Viscount Astor** (1879–1952), the great-great-grandson of John Jacob Astor. When she succeeded to the peerage in 1919, she was elected to his old seat of Plymouth and thus became the first woman to sit in the House of Commons. She held the seat until 1945.

a·stound (ə-stound′) *tr.v.* **astounded, astounding, astounds.** To strike with sudden wonder. —See Synonyms at **surprise.** [Originally the past participle of obsolete *astone,* to amaze, from Middle English *astonen,* ASTONISH.] —**a·stound·ing·ly** *adv.*

a·strad·dle (ə-străd′l) *adv.* In a straddling position; astride.

~*prep.* So as to straddle; astride.

As·trae·a (ă-strē′ə). *Greek Mythology.* The goddess of justice. [New Latin, from Greek *astraios,* starry, from *astēr,* star.]

as·tra·gal (ăs′trə-gəl) *n. Architecture.* A narrow, convex molding, often having the form of beading. [Latin *astragalus,* from Greek *astragalos,* ankle bone (from the shape of the molding).]

as·trag·a·lus (ə-străg′ə-ləs) *n., pl.* **-li** (-lī′). A bone, the **talus** *(see).* [New Latin, from Greek *astragalos.*] —**as·trag·a·lar** *adj.*

as·tra·khan, as·tra·chan (ăs′trə-kăn′, -kən) *n.* **1.** The curly or wavy fur made from the wool of young lambs from the region of Astrakhan. **2.** A fabric with a curly, looped pile, made to resemble this fur.

As·tra·khan (ăs′trə-kăn′, -kən). City on the delta islands of the Volga, in the southwest U.S.S.R. The city was taken from the Tatars by Ivan the Terrible in 1556.

as·tral (ăs′trəl) *adj.* **1.** Of, pertaining to, consisting of, emanating from, or resembling the stars. **2.** *Biology.* Pertaining to or shaped like an aster; star-shaped. **3.** In theosophy, consisting of or pertaining to a substance from which a higher, nonphysical body is made; mystical. [Late Latin *astrālis,* from Latin *astrum,* star, from Greek *astron.*] —**as·tral·ly** *adv.*

as·tra·pho·bi·a (ăs′trə-fō′bē-ə) *n.* Fear of lightning and thunder. [New Latin : Greek *astrapē,* lightning + -PHOBIA.]

a·stray (ə-strā′) *adv.* **1.** Away from the correct path or direction. **2.** Away from the right or good; toward evil or wrong ways. **3.** In the manner of one that strays: *My glasses have gone astray.* [Middle English *astray, astraie,* from Old French *estraie,* past participle of *estraier,* to STRAY.] —**a·stray** *adj.*

as·trict (ə-strĭkt′) *tr.v.* **-tricted, -tricting, -tricts.** To bind, especially by moral or legal obligations. [Latin *astrictus,* past participle of *astringere,* to bind fast, ASTRINGE.] —**as·tric·tion** *n.*

as·tric·tive (ə-strĭk′tĭv) *adj.* Astringent. —*n.* An astringent. —**as·tric·tive·ly** *adv.* —**as·tric·tive·ness** *n.*

a·stride (ə-strīd′) *adv.* **1.** With the legs separated so that one is on each side: *rode the horse astride.* **2.** With the legs wide apart. —*prep.* **1.** Upon or over and with a leg on each side of. **2.** With a part on each side of; spanning or bridging.

as·tringe (ə-strĭnj′) *tr.v.* **-tringed, -tringing, -tringes.** To draw together; constrict. [Latin *astringere,* to bind together : *ad-,* to + *stringere,* to bind.]

as·trin·gent (ə-strĭn′jənt) *adj.* **1.** Tending to draw together or constrict tissue; contracting; styptic. **2.** Harsh; severe: *an astringent wit.* **3.** Sharp-tasting; acidic. —*n.* **1.** An astringent substance or drug, such as alum, used to constrict soft tissue and reduce superficial bleeding. **2.** An astringent cosmetic preparation; especially, a lotion for toning up the complexion. —**as·trin·gen·cy** *n.* —**as·trin·gent·ly** *adv.*

as·tri·on·ics (ăs′trē-ŏn′ĭks) *n. Used with a singular verb.* Electronics used in astronautics. [Irregularly from ASTRO(NAUTICS) + (ELEC-TR)ONICS.]

astro-, astr- *prefix.* Indicates: **1.** Star or star-shaped; for example, **astrocyte. 2.** Outer space; for example, **astronautics. 3.** Astronomical; for example, **astrophysics.** [Middle English, from Old French, from Latin, from Greek *astron,* star.]

as·tro·bi·ol·o·gy (ăs′trō-bī-ŏl′ə-jē) *n.* **Exobiology** *(see).*

as·tro·bleme (ăs′trō-blēm′) *n.* An ancient crater on the earth's surface formed by the impact of a meteorite. [ASTRO- + Greek *blēma,* a shot, wound.]

as·tro·chem·is·try (ăs′trō-kĕm′ĭs-trē) *n.* The study of the composition and reactions of substances present in celestial objects and interstellar matter.

as·tro·com·pass (ăs′trō-kŭm′pəs, -kŏm′-) *n.* A navigational instrument for determining direction relative to a fixed star.

as·tro·cyte (ăs′trə-sīt′) *n.* A star-shaped cell, especially a neuroglial cell. [ASTRO- + -CYTE.]

as·tro·cy·to·ma (ăs′trō-sī-tō′mə) *n., pl.* **-mas** or **-mata** (-mə-tə). A malignant brain tumor composed of astrocytes. [ASTROCYT(E) + -OMA.]

as·tro·dome (ăs′trə-dōm′) *n.* **1.** A transparent dome on the top of an aircraft, through which celestial observations are made for navigation. **2. Astrodome.** An enclosed stadium, used mainly for sports events, with a translucent dome.

as·tro·dy·nam·ics (ăs′trō-dī-năm′ĭks) *n. Used with a singular verb.* The dynamics of celestial bodies.

as·tro·ge·ol·o·gy (ăs′trō-jē-ŏl′ə-jē) *n.* The study of the structure, composition, and formation of rocks and minerals on other planets.

as·troid (ăs′troid′) *n. Geometry.* A type of plane curve; a hypocycloid that has four cusps. [ASTRO- + -OID (referring to its starlike shape).]

astrol. astrologer; astrological; astrology.

as·tro·labe (ăs′trə-lāb′) *n.* A medieval instrument consisting of a graduated vertical circle with a movable arm, used to determine the altitude of the sun or other celestial bodies for astronomical or navigational purposes. [Middle English, from Old French, from Medieval Latin *astrolabium,* from Greek *(organon) astrolabon,* "(instrument) for taking the stars" : ASTRO- + *lambanein,* to take.]

as·trol·o·gy (ə-strŏl′ə-jē) *n. Abbr.* **astrol.** The study of the positions and aspects of heavenly bodies with a view to assessing or predicting their supposed influence on human characteristics and the course of human affairs. [Middle English *astrologie,* from Old French, from Latin *astrologia,* from Greek, from *astrologos,* astronomer, (later) astrologer : ASTRO- + -LOGY.] —**as·trol·o·ger, as·trol·o·gist** *n.* —**as·tro·log·ic** (ăs′trə-lŏj′ĭk), **as·tro·log·i·cal** *adj.* —**as·tro·log·i·cal·ly** *adv.*

as·trom·e·try (ə-strŏm′ə-trē) *n.* The scientific measurement of the positions and movements of celestial bodies. [ASTRO- + -METRY.] —**as·tro·met·ric** (ăs′trə-mĕt′rĭk), **as·tro·met·ri·cal** *adj.*

astron. astronomer; astronomical; astronomy.

as·tro·naut (ăs′trə-nôt′) *n.* A person trained to pilot, navigate, or otherwise participate in the flight of a spacecraft. [ASTRO- + Greek *nautēs,* sailor, from *naus,* ship.]

as·tro·nau·tics (ăs′trə-nô′tĭks) *n. Used with a singular verb.* The science and technology of space flight. [ASTRO- + Latin *nautica,* neuter plural of *nauticus,* NAUTICAL.] —**as·tro·nau·tic, as·tro·nau·ti·cal** *adj.* —**as·tro·nau·ti·cal·ly** *adv.*

as·tro·nav·i·ga·tion (ăs′trō-năv′ə-gā′shən) *n.* **1.** Navigation of outer space, as in spacecraft. **2. Celestial navigation** *(see).* —**as·tro·nav·i·ga·tor** *n.*

as·tron·o·mer (ə-strŏn′ə-mər) *n. Abbr.* **astron.** A scientist specializing in astronomy. [Middle English, from Late Latin *astronomus,* from Greek *astronomos,* "star-arranger" : ASTRO- + -*nomos,* from *nemein,* to arrange (see -nomy).]

as·tro·nom·i·cal (ăs′trə-nŏm′ĭ-kəl) *adj.* Also **as·tro·nom·ic** (-nŏm′ĭk). **1.** *Abbr.* **astron.** Of or pertaining to astronomy. **2.** Inconceivably large; immense. —**as·tro·nom·i·cal·ly** *adv.*

astronomical telescope *n.* A reflecting or refracting telescope designed for astronomical observation. Compare **terrestrial telescope.**

astronomical unit *n. Abbr.* **A.U.** A unit of length used in measuring astronomical distances, equal to the distance of the earth from the sun, approximately 93 million miles.

astronomical year *n.* A **tropical year** *(see).*

as·tron·o·my (ə-strŏn′ə-mē) *n. Abbr.* **astron.** The scientific study of the universe beyond the earth, especially the observation, calculation, and theoretical interpretation of the positions, dimensions, distribution, motion, composition, and evolution of celestial bodies and phenomena. [Middle English *astronomie,* from Old French, from Latin *astronomia,* from Greek, from *astronomos,* ASTRONOMER.]

as·tro·pho·tog·ra·phy (ăs′trō-fə-tŏg′rə-fē) *n.* Astronomical photography. —**as·tro·pho·to·graph·ic** (ăs′trō-fō′tə-grăf′ĭk) *adj.*

as·tro·phys·ics (ăs′trō-fĭz′ĭks) *n. Used with a singular verb.* The branch of astronomy concerned with the theoretical physics of celestial bodies and phenomena. —**as·tro·phys·i·cal** *adj.* —**as·tro·phys·i·cist** *n.*

as·tro·sphere (ăs′trō-sfîr′) *n. Biology.* **1.** The central portion of a cell aster; the centrosphere. **2.** The entire cell aster with the exception of the centrosome. [ASTRO- + -SPHERE.]

As·tro·Turf (ăs′trō-tûrf′) *n.* A trademark for an artificial grasslike surfacing material made of nylon and vinyl, used especially on sports fields.

As·tu·ri·as (ə-stōŏr′ē-əs, ə-styōŏr′-). Region and old kingdom (established in 718) in northern Spain, coinciding with the present-day province of Oviedo. The 9th-century shrine at Santiago de Compostela remains a spiritual center of Christian Spain. —**As·tu·ri·an** *n. & adj.*

Asturias, Miguel Angel (1899-1974). Guatemalan novelist, poet, and diplomat. In 1923 he settled in Paris and came under the influence of André Breton. *Men of Corn* (1949) is usually considered to be his best novel. He received the Nobel Prize for literature (1967).

as·tute (ə-stōōt′, ə-styōōt′) *adj.* Keen in judgment. —See Synonyms at **shrewd.** [Latin *astūtus,* from *astus,* craft.] —**as·tute·ly** *adv.* —**as·tute·ness** *n.*

As·ty·a·nax (ə-stī′ə-năks′). *Greek Mythology.* The young son of Hector and Andromache, flung from the walls of Troy by the conquering Greeks.

a·sty·lar (ā-stī′lər) *adj.* Not having columns or pilasters. [A- (without) + Greek *stulos,* pillar.]

A·sun·ción (ə-sōōn-syŏn′). Chief port, industrial center, and capital of Paraguay, on the Paraguay River.

a·sun·der (ə-sŭn′dər) *adv.* **1.** Into separate parts or pieces. **2.** Apart from each other, either in position or direction. [Middle English *asonder,* Old English *onsundran, onsundrum : on,* on + *sundran, sundrum,* singly, separately, from *sunder,* apart, separate.] —**a·sun·der** *adj.*

Asur. Variant of **Ashur.**

A·swan (ăs′wän, äs-wän′). Also **As·souan** or **As·suan.** City in southern Egypt, on the Nile River. It was an important station in the trade between ancient Egypt and the Sudan.

Aswan High Dam. Dam built on the Nile River c. 11 kilometers (7 miles) south of Aswan, opened in 1971. The building costs were largely supplied by the U.S.S.R. The dam is 114 meters (375 feet) high and 3,600 meters (11,800 feet) long. Its reservoir, Lake Nasser, is one of the largest artificial lakes in the world.

a·syl·lab·ic (ā′sĭ-lăb′ĭk) *adj.* Not syllabic.

a·sy·lum (ə-sī′ləm) *n.* **1.** A place offering protection or safety. **2.** Formerly, a temple or church affording sanctuary for criminals or debtors. **3.** Protection and immunity from extradition granted by a government to a political refugee from another country. **4.** Formerly, an institution for the care of the severely handicapped and especially the mentally ill. —See Synonyms at **shelter.** [Middle English *asilum,* from Latin *asylum,* from Greek *asulon,* sanctuary, from *asulos,* inviolable : *a-,* without + *sulon†,* right of seizure.]

a·sym·met·ric (ā′sĭ-mĕt′rĭk) *adj.* Also **a·sym·met·ri·cal** (-mĕt′rĭ-kəl). *Abbr.* **asym.** Not symmetrical. —**a·sym·met·ri·cal·ly** *adv.*

asymmetric atom *n. Chemistry.* An atom that is attached to four different groups in a molecule, such that the compound exhibits optical isomerism.

a·sym·me·try (ā-sĭm′ə-trē) *n.* Lack of symmetry or balance. [Greek *asummetria : a-,* without + *summetria,* SYMMETRY.]

a·symp·to·mat·ic (ā′sĭmp-tə-măt′ĭk) *adj.* Neither causing nor exhibiting symptoms. —**a·symp·to·mat·i·cal·ly** *adv.*

as·ymp·tote (ăs′ĭm-tōt′, -ĭmp-) *n. Mathematics.* **1.** A straight line that approaches a curve so that the perpendicular distance from a moving point on the curve to the line approaches zero as the point moves an infinite distance from the origin. **2.** A plane that approaches a curved surface at infinite distance from the origin. [New Latin *asymptota,* from Greek *(grammē) asumptōtos,* "(a line) not falling together" : *a-,* not + *sumptōtos,* from *sumpiptein,* to fall together : *sun-,* together + *piptein,* to fall.] —**as·ymp·tot·ic** (ăs′ĭm-tŏt′ĭk, -ĭmp-), **as·ymp·tot·i·cal** *adj.* —**as·ymp·tot·i·cal·ly** *adv.*

a·syn·chro·nism (ā-sĭng′krə-nĭz′əm) *n.* Also **a·syn·chro·ny** (-krə-nē). Lack of synchronism.

a·syn·chro·nous (ā-sĭng′krə-nəs) *adj.* Not synchronous. —**a·syn·chro·nous·ly** *adv.*

a·syn·de·ton (ə-sĭn′də-tŏn′) *n., pl.* **-tons** or **-ta** (-tə). The omission of conjunctions from constructions in which they would normally be used; for example: *He wrote, he drew, he painted.* Compare **parataxis.** [Late Latin, from Greek *asundeton,* from *asundetos,* "without conjunctions," unconnected : *a-,* not + *sundetos,* bound together, from *sundein,* to bind together : *sun-,* together + *dein,* to bind.] —**as·yn·det·ic** (ăs′ĭn-dĕt′ĭk) *adj.* —**as·yn·det·i·cal·ly** *adv.*

a·syn·tac·tic (ā′sĭn-tăk′tĭk) *adj.* Not syntactic.

As·yut or **As·iut** or **As·siut** (ăs-yo͞ot′). An industrial city in central Egypt, on the Nile River.

at[1] (ăt, *weak form* ət) *prep.* **1. a.** In the location of: *at the market.* **b.** In the position of: *at the center of the page.* **2.** To or toward the direction of: *Look at him.* **3.** Present in; attending: *at the dance.* **4.** In the duration of; during: *at night.* **5.** In the state or condition of: *at peace with one's conscience; at liberty.* **6.** In the manner of: *at a run.* **7.** To the extent or amount of: *at thirty cents a pound.* **8.** On the exact or approximate moment of: *at three o'clock.* **9.** Because of: *rejoice at a victory.* **10.** Engaged in: *at war.* **11.** According to: *at one's discretion.* **12.** Dependent upon: *at the mercy of the court.* **13.** Maintaining or in accordance with a given rate, speed, or degree: *driving at 55 miles per hour.* [Middle English *at, atte,* Old English *æt.*]

at[2] (ăt) *n., pl.* **at.** A monetary unit equal to 1/100 of the kip of Laos. [Thai.]

aT *Physics.* attotesla.

At The symbol for the element astatine.

AT antitank.

At·a·brine (ăt′ə-brĭn, -brēn′). A trademark for a yellow, bitter, crystalline compound, quinacrine hydrochloride, used primarily as an antimalarial drug.

A·ta·ca·ma Desert (ăt′ə-kăm′ə). Arid region of northwestern Chile. It is one of the world's driest areas, much of it having no recorded rainfall. It has some nitrate and copper reserves.

a·tac·tic (ā-tăk′tĭk) *adj. Chemistry.* Of or pertaining to a polymer with a nonregular arrangement of groups along its chain. Compare **stereospecific.** [A- (not) + -TACTIC.]

ataghan. Variant of **yataghan.**

Atahualpa *When taken prisoner by Francisco Pizarro, the Inca Atahualpa offered as ransom to fill a room of 169 cubic meters (5,984 cubic feet) halfway up with gold, and to fill the entire room twice over with silver. Despite the vast amount of Inca treasure collected—some 6,080 kilograms (13,420 pounds) of gold and 11,790 kilograms (26,000 pounds) of silver—Atahualpa was garroted by the Spaniards.*

A·ta·hual·pa or **A·ta·huall·pa** (ăt′ə-wäl′pə). Also **A·ta·ba·li·pa** (-bä′lə-pə). (*c.* 1502–33). The last Inca to rule Peru, captured and executed by the Spaniards.

At·a·lan·ta (ăt′ə-lăn′tə). *Greek Mythology.* A maiden who agreed to marry any man who could outrun her, and who was defeated by Hippomenes when he dropped three golden apples that she paused to pick up.

at·a·man (ăt′ə-măn′) *n., pl.* **-mans.** A Cossack chief. [Russian, from Polish *hetman,* from German *Hauptmann,* captain, from Middle High German *houbetman,* from Old High German *houbitman* : *houbit,* head + *man,* man.]

at·a·rac·tic (ăt′ə-răk′tĭk) *adj.* Also **at·a·rax·ic** (-răk′sĭk). Pertaining to or producing calmness and peace of mind.
∼*n.* Also **at·a·rax·ic.** A drug that reduces nervous tension; a tranquilizer. [Greek *ataraktos,* undisturbed : *a-,* not + *taraktos,* disturbed, from *tarattein,* to disturb.]

at·a·rax·i·a (ăt′ə-răk′sē-ə) *n.* Peace of mind; emotional tranquillity. [Greek *ataraxia,* from *ataraktos,* ATARACTIC.]

A·ta·türk (ăt′ə-tûrk′), **Kemal,** born Mustafa Kemal (1881–1938). Turkish national leader, the founder of modern Turkey. In 1919 he organized the Turkish Nationalist Party and set up a rival government to the Ottoman sultan at Ankara. In 1923, after a civil war, he was elected the first president of the Turkish republic, a position that he held until his death. His rule was marked by westernization and internal reform. The name "Atatürk" means "Father of the Turks."

a·tav·ic (ə-tăv′ĭk) *adj.* Of or concerning a remote ancestor.

at·a·vism (ăt′ə-vĭz′əm) *n.* **1.** The reappearance of a characteristic in an organism after several generations of absence, caused by a recessive gene or complementary genes. **2.** An individual or part displaying atavism. Also loosely called "reversion," "throwback." **3.** Reversion to a primitive or earlier state of behavior. [French *atavisme,* from Latin *atavus,* ancestor, great-great-great-grandfather : *atta,* father + *avus,* grandfather.] —**at·a·vist** *n.* —**at·a·vis·tic** (ăt′ə-vĭs′tĭk) *adj.* —**at·a·vis·ti·cal·ly** *adv.*

a·tax·i·a (ə-tăk′sē-ə, ā-) *n.* Also **a·tax·y** (ə-tăk′sē, ā-). Loss or lack of muscular coordination. [Greek *ataxia,* from *ataktos,* disorderly : *a-,* not + *taktos,* ordered, from *tattein,* to arrange.]

a·tax·ic (ə-tăk′sĭk, ā-) *adj.* Of or pertaining to ataxia.
∼*n.* An individual exhibiting symptoms of ataxia.

A.T.C. Air Traffic Control.

ate. Past tense of **eat.**

-ate[1] *suffix.* Indicates: **1.** Possessing; for example, **nervate, affectionate. 2.** Shaped like; for example, **lyrate. 3.** Having the general characteristics of; for example, **Latinate.** [Middle English *-at,* from Old French, from Latin *-ātus,* ending of the past participle of verbs in *-āre* (first conjugation). It thus appears in: **1.** Participial adjectives; for example, **ornate. 2.** Nouns converted from adjectives, either in Latin or in English; for example, **associate. 3.** Verbs originally formed from the corresponding nouns and adjectives in *-ate;* for example, **aggregate, conjugate;** and subsequently, by analogy with these, adopted directly from Latin, taking participial form but infinitive sense; for example, **desiccate, eradicate.**]

-ate[2] *suffix.* Indicates: **1.** The product of a specified process; for example, **distillate. 2.** *Chemistry.* **a.** The salt of an oxygen acid; for example, **nitrate, sulfate. b.** The ester of an oxygen acid or carboxylic acid; for example, **acetate, stearate.** [Special use of -ATE[1].]

-ate[3] *suffix.* Indicates: **1.** Rank or status; for example, **magistrate. 2.** A group of people performing a specified function or holding a specified office; for example, **electorate.** [Latin *-ātus,* an abstract suffix made up of the *-āt-* of *-ātus,* participial ending (-ATE[1]) and the feminine *-us* of fourth declension nouns. It originally designated the collective status of a group, as in **senate,** later the power of a specific type of ruler, as in **triumvirate.**]

-ate[4] *suffix.* Indicates: **1.** To cause to become; for example, **activate. 2.** To supply or impregnate with; for example, **oxygenate.** [Abstracted from verbs of Latin origin ending in *-ate.* See **-ate**[1].]

at·el·ier (ăt′l-yā′) *n.* A workshop or artist's studio. [French, from Old French *astelier,* woodpile, hence carpenter's shop, from *astele,* splinter, shaving, chip, from Late Latin *astella,* variant of Latin *astula, assula,* diminutive of *assis,* board, plank, probably variant of *axis.* See **ashlar.**]

a tem·po (ä tĕm′pō) *adv. Music.* In normal time; resuming the original tempo. Used as a direction. [Italian, "in time."]

a·tem·po·ral (ā-tĕm′pər-əl) *adj.* Independent of time; timeless.

A·ten, A·ton (ä′tən). *Egyptian Mythology.* A sun god, regarded during the reign of Akhenaton as the only god.

Ath·a·bas·ka or **Ath·a·bas·ca** (ăth′ə-băs′kə). River in northern Alberta in Canada, rising in the Rockies and flowing 1,230 kilometers (765 miles) northeast into Lake Athabaska.

Ath·a·na·sian (ăth′ə-nā′zhən) *adj.* Of or pertaining to Athanasius.
∼*n.* A follower of Athanasius and his teachings.

Athanasian creed *n.* A Christian creed or profession of faith dating from about A.D. 425, expounding the doctrine of the Trinity. [After St. ATHANASIUS.]

Ath·a·na·si·us (ăth′ə-nā′shəs), **Saint** (A.D. *c.* 297–373). Doctor of the Christian Church and patriarch of Alexandria (328–373). He played an important part at the First Council of Nicaea in the debate against Arianism. He was formerly thought to be the author of the Athanasian creed.

Ath·a·pas·can (ăth′ə-păs′kən) *n.* Also **Ath·a·bas·can** (-băs′kən). **1.** A North American Indian language stock, including languages of Alaska and northwest Canada, of the coast of Oregon and California, and the Navaho and Apache languages of the southwestern United States. **2.** A member of an Athapascan-speaking people.
∼*adj.* Of or designating this language stock. [From the name of Lake *Athabaska* in western Canada, Northern Cree *athapaskaaw,* "there is scattered grass."]

a·the·ism (ā′thē-ĭz′əm) *n.* **1.** Disbelief in or denial of the existence of God. Compare **agnosticism. 2.** Godlessness; wickedness. **3.** The doctrine that there is no deity. [Old French *atheisme,* from *athee,* atheist, from Greek *atheos,* godless : *a-,* without + *theos,* god.]

A·the·ist (ā′thē-ĭst) *n.* One who denies the existence of God.

a·the·is·tic (ā′thē-ĭs′tĭk) *adj.* Also **a·the·is·ti·cal** (-tĭ-kəl). **1.** Pertaining to or characteristic of atheism or atheists. **2.** Inclined to atheism. —**a·the·is·ti·cal·ly** *adv.*

ath·e·ling, aeth·e·ling (ăth′ə-lĭng, ăth′-) *n.* An Anglo-Saxon nobleman or prince. [Middle English *atheling,* Old English *ætheling,* prince : *æthel,* noble + *-ing,* descendant of.]

Ath·el·stan, Aeth·el·stan (ăth′əl-stən′) (895–940). King of Mercia and Wessex, the first Saxon ruler to establish his authority over all of England. He was elected king of Mercia in *c.* 924 and a year later was crowned king of the whole country.

a·the·mat·ic (ā′thē-măt′ĭk) *adj.* **1.** *Music.* Not based on themes. **2.** *Linguistics.* Designating a verb that has no vowel between the stem and the ending.

A·the·na (ə-thē′nə). Also **A·the·ne** (-nē). *Greek Mythology.* The goddess of wisdom and the arts. Identified with the Roman goddess Minerva. Also called "Pallas Athena."

ath·e·ne·um, ath·e·nae·um (ăth′ə-nē′əm) *n.* **1.** An institution, such as a literary club or scientific academy, for the promotion of learning. **2.** A library, reading room, or similar place. [Late Latin *Athēnaeum,* a Roman school of art, after Greek *Athēnaion,* the temple of Athena at Athens, where philosophy was taught, from *Athēnē,* ATHENA.]

Ath·ens (ăth′ənz). *Greek* **A·thi·ne, A·thi·nai** (ə-thē′nĭ′). Capital and industrial center of Greece, in the east of the country near the Saronic Gulf. At the time of the Persian Wars (500–499 B.C.) it was the most powerful Greek city state and the cradle of democracy. The zenith of its cultural achievements and imperial power was reached during the time of Pericles (443–429 B.C.), when Socrates, Sophocles, Aeschylus, and Euripides all flourished. It became the capital of modern Greece when the country won its independence from Turkey in 1834.

a·ther·man·cy (ə-thûr′mən-sē, ā-) *n. Physics.* The inability of substances to transmit infrared radiation. [Greek *athermantos,* not heated : A-(not) + *thermantos,* from *thermē,* heat.] —**a·ther·man·ous** *adj.*

ath·er·o·ma (ăth′ə-rō′mə) *n., pl.* **-mas** or **-mata** (-mə-tə). *Pathology.* **1.** A deposit or degenerative accumulation of pulpy, acellular, lipid-containing materials, especially in arterial walls. **2.** A form of arteriosclerosis characterized by such deposits. [New Latin, from Latin, from Greek *athērōma,* a cyst full of gruellike pus, from *athēra,* gruel, from *athērƚ,* beard of grain.] —**ath·er·o·ma·to·sis** (ăth′ə-rō-mə-tō′sĭs) *n.* —**ath·er·o·ma·tous** (ăth′ə-rŏ′mə-təs) *adj.*

ath·er·o·scle·ro·sis (ăth′ə-rō-sklə-rō′sĭs) *n. Pathology.* A disease in which fatty deposits form in the arteries and obstruct the blood flow; atheromatous arteriosclerosis; atheroma. [*atheroma + sclerosis.*] —**ath·er·o·scle·rot·ic** (ăth′ə-rō-sklə-rŏt′ĭk) *adj.*

a·thirst (ə-thûrst′) *adj.* **1.** Strongly desirous; eager. Usually used with *for: athirst for freedom* **2.** *Archaic.* Thirsty.

ath·lete (ăth′lēt′) *n.* **1.** One who takes part in competitive sports, especially track and field events. **2.** A person possessing the natural prerequisites for sports competition, such as strength, speed, agility, and endurance. [Middle English, from Latin *athlēta,* from Greek *athlētēs,* contestant, from *athlein,* to contend for an award, from *athlon*†, award, prize.]

athlete's foot *n.* A chronic fungal infection of the skin of the foot, usually causing itching, blisters, and cracking.

ath·let·ic (ăth-lĕt′ĭk) *adj.* **1.** Of, pertaining to, or befitting athletics or athletes. **2.** Physically strong; muscular. **3.** Physically active and agile. —**ath·let·i·cal·ly** *adv.* —**ath·let·i·cism** (ăth-lĕt′ə-sĭz′əm) *n.*

ath·let·ics (ăth-lĕt′ĭks) *n.* **1.** *Used with a plural verb.* **a.** Physical activities, such as competitive sports or games. **b.** Track and field sporting events. **2.** *Used with a singular verb.* The principles or practice of athletic exercises and training.

athletic supporter *n.* A **jockstrap** (*see*).

ath·o·dyd (ăth′ə-dĭd) *n.* A simple jet engine. See **ramjet, pulsejet.** [*Aerothermodynamic duct.*]

at-home (ət-hōm′) *n.* An informal reception at one's home.

-athon, -thon *suffix.* Indicates a prolonged or strenuous event or activity, often involving financial sponsorship; for example, **telethon, talkathon.** [Abstracted from MARATHON.]

Ath·os, Mount (ăth′ŏs, ā′thŏs). A mountain peak, rising to 2,030 meters (6,660 feet) at the southern tip of the Athos Peninsula in northeast Greece. It is the site of the virtually independent group of 20 monasteries of the Order of St. Basil of the Eastern Orthodox Church. In 1927 Mount Athos was granted the status of a theocratic republic under the suzerainty of Greece.

a·thwart (ə-thwôrt′) *adv.* **1.** From side to side; crosswise; transversely. **2.** So as to thwart or obstruct; perversely.
~*prep.* **1.** From one side to the other of; across. **2.** Contrary to; against. **3.** *Nautical.* Across the course, line, or length of. [Middle English : A- (on) + THWART (side).]

a·tilt (ə-tĭlt′) *adv.* **1.** In a tilted position; inclined upward. **2.** As if tilting with a lance: *"Break a lance, and run atilt at death"* (Shakespeare). —**a·tilt** *adj.*

-ation *suffix.* Indicates: **1.** Action or process of; for example, **strangulation, negotiation.** **2.** State, condition, or quality of; for example, **isolation, moderation.** **3.** Result or product of; for example, **dramatization, civilization.** [Middle English *-acioun,* from Old French *-ation,* from Latin *-ātiō* (stem *-ātiōn-*), abstract noun suffix, from *-ātus.* See **-ate¹, -ion.**]

-ative *suffix.* Indicates relation, nature, or tendency; for example, **authoritative, illustrative, formative.** [Middle English, from Old French *-atif,* from Latin *-ātīvus,* from *-ātus.* See **-ate¹, -ive.**]

Atkins, Tommy. See **Tommy Atkins.**

Atl. Atlantic.

At·lan·ta (ăt-lăn′tə). The capital of Georgia, in the northwest part of the state. It was founded in 1837, but had to be almost entirely rebuilt after being burned during the Civil War on November 15, 1864, just before Gen. William Tecumseh Sherman began his "march to the sea" from the town. Today it is the largest city in Georgia and the cultural and business center of the state.

At·lan·te·an (ăt′lăn-tē′ən, ăt-lăn′tē-ən) *adj.* **1.** Of, pertaining to, or resembling Atlas. **2.** Of or pertaining to Atlantis. [Latin *Atlanteus* : *Atlas* (stem *Atlant-*), ATLAS + -AN.]

at·lan·tes. *Architecture.* Plural of **atlas** (sense 4).

At·lan·tic (ăt-lăn′tĭk) *adj.* **1.** *Abbr.* **Atl.** Of, in, near, upon, or pertaining to the Atlantic Ocean. **2.** Of or pertaining to Atlas or to the Atlas Mountains.
~*n.* The Atlantic Ocean. [Latin *(mare) Atlanticum,* from Greek *(pelagos) Atlantikos,* "(the sea) of Atlas" (the sea lying beyond the Atlas Mountains), from *Atlas* (stem *Atlant-*), ATLAS.]

Atlantic Charter *n.* A declaration of the aims of the Allied Nations concerning a postwar settlement in World War II, made jointly by Churchill and Roosevelt after a meeting at sea in August 1941.

Atlantic City. A resort and convention city on the Atlantic coast of New Jersey. The city thrives almost exclusively on tourism and legalized gambling, introduced in 1978.

Atlantic Ocean. The world's second-largest ocean, with an area of 82,217,000 square kilometers (31,744,000 square miles). Its average depth is 3,660 meters (12,000 feet). It is divided into two great basins, the North Atlantic and the South Atlantic, the former with clockwise-flowing currents, the latter with counterclockwise currents. Down the center of the ocean, running for 16,000 kilometers (10,000 miles) is the Mid-Atlantic Ridge. See map, next page.

Atlantic salmon *n.* A food fish, *Salmo salar,* of northern Atlantic waters. See **salmon.**

At·lan·tis (ăt-lăn′tĭs). Legendary island in the Atlantic west of Gibraltar, said by Plato to have sunk beneath the sea.

at·las (ăt′ləs) *n., pl.* **atlases** or **atlantes** (ăt-lăn′tēz) (for sense 4).) **1.** A bound collection of maps. **2.** Any volume of tables, charts, or plates that systematically illustrate a subject: *anatomical atlas.* **3.** A large size of drawing paper, measuring 26 by 33 or 34 inches. **4.** *Plural* **atlantes.** *Architecture.* A figure of a man used as a masonry column on a building to support an entablature. **5.** *Anatomy.* The top or first cervical vertebra of the neck, which supports the skull.

[From representations of the Titan ATLAS upholding the heavens, common in 16th-century books of maps.]

At·las (ăt′ləs). *Greek Mythology.* A giant, one of the Titans, who was condemned to support the heavens upon his shoulders for rebelling against the gods. [Latin, from Greek *Atlas* (stem *Atlant-*); the name was subsequently applied to the Atlas Mts. in northwest Africa and then to the sea nearby (Atlantis, Atlantic).]

Atlas Mountains. Series of fold mountain ranges extending from Morocco through Algeria into Tunisia. They form a climatic barrier between the Mediterranean lowlands and the Sahara. The highest peak is Jebel Toubkal (4,165 meters; 13,665 feet).

atm. atmosphere; atmospheric.

at·man (ăt′mən) *n. Hinduism.* **1.** The individual soul; the principle of life. **2. Atman.** The universal soul, from which all individual souls arise; Brahma. [Sanskrit *ātman,* breath, spirit, soul.]

atmo– *prefix.* Indicates the presence of or relation to vapor; for example, **atmosphere.** [New Latin, from Greek *atmos,* vapor, breath.]

at·mol·y·sis (ăt-mŏl′ə-sĭs) *n., pl.* **-ses** (-sēz). The separation of a mixture of gases, each with different diffusibility, by diffusion through a porous material. [ATMO- + -LYSIS.]

at·mom·e·ter (ăt-mŏm′ə-tər) *n.* An instrument that measures the rate of water evaporation. [ATMO- + -METER.] —**at·mo·met·ric** (ăt′mō-mĕt′rĭk) *adj.* —**at·mom·e·try** *n.*

atmos. atmosphere; atmospheric.

at·mos·phere (ăt′mə-sfîr′) *n.* **1.** *Abbr.* **atm., atmos.** The gaseous mass or envelope surrounding a celestial body, especially that surrounding the earth, and retained by the body's gravitational field. **2.** The quality of the air or climate in a specific place: *a very smoky atmosphere.* **3.** *Abbr.* **atm** *Physics.* A unit of pressure equal to 1.01325 × 10⁵ newtons per square meter at sea level. **4.** A psychological environment: *He grew up in an atmosphere of austerity.* **5.** The predominant tone or mood of a work of art. **6. a.** A pervading quality, effect, or mood, especially as associated with a particular place: *a dark old house with a depressing atmosphere.* **b.** A distinctively exotic or romantic quality or effect: *a Greek restaurant with lots of atmosphere.* [New Latin *atmosphaera,* "sphere of vapor" : ATMO- + -SPHERE.] See feature, page 117.

at·mos·pher·ic (ăt′mə-sfîr′ĭk, -sfĕr′ĭk) *adj.* Also **at·mos·pher·i·cal.** *Abbr.* **atm., atmos.** **1.** Of, pertaining to, or existing in the atmosphere. **2.** Produced by, dependent on, or coming from the atmosphere. —**at·mos·pher·i·cal·ly** *adv.*

atmospheric pressure *n.* The pressure exerted by the atmosphere. At sea level it has a mean value of 1.01325 × 10⁵ newtons per square meter (760 mmHg) but reduces with increasing altitude.

at·mos·pher·ics (ăt′mə-sfîr′ĭks) *n. Used with a singular verb.* **1.** Electromagnetic radiation produced by natural phenomena such as lightning. **2.** Radio interference produced by such radiation. Also called "spherics."

a·toll (ă′tôl′, ā′tôl′, ā′-) *n.* A ringlike coral reef that nearly or entirely encloses a lagoon. [Malayalam *atoḷu,* "reef," native name for the Maldive Islands.]

at·om (ăt′əm) *n.* **1.** Anything considered an irreducible constituent of a specified system. **2.** The irreducible, indestructible material unit of ancient **atomism** (*see*). **3.** *Physics & Chemistry.* A unit of matter, the smallest unit of an element, consisting of a dense, central, positively charged **nucleus** (*see*) surrounded by a system of electrons, equal in number to the number of nuclear protons, the entire structure having an approximate diameter of 10⁻⁸ centimeter and characteristically remaining undivided in chemical reactions except for limited removal, transfer, or exchange of outer electrons. **4.** This unit regarded as a source of nuclear energy. [Middle English *attome, attomus,* from Latin *atomus,* from Greek *atomos,* indivisible : *a-,* not + *temnein,* to cut. See **-tome, -tomy.**]

a·tom·ic (ə-tŏm′ĭk) *adj.* **1.** Of or relating to an atom or atoms. **2.** Of or employing atomic energy: *an atomic submarine.* **3.** Very small; infinitesimal. —**a·tom·i·cal·ly** *adv.*

atomic age *n.* Also **Atomic Age.** The current era as characterized by the discovery, technological applications, and sociopolitical consequences of atomic energy.

atomic bomb *n.* Nuclear **bomb** (*see*).

atomic clock *n.* An extremely precise timekeeping device regulated in correspondence with a characteristic invariant frequency of an atomic or molecular system.

atomic energy *n.* Nuclear **energy** (*see*).

atomic heat *n.* The product of an element's atomic weight and its specific heat capacity.

at·o·mic·i·ty (ăt′ə-mĭs′ə-tē) *n.* **1.** The state of being composed of atoms. **2.** *Chemistry.* **a.** The number of atoms in a molecule. **b.** Valence.

atomic mass *n.* The mass of an atomic system or constituent, usually expressed in atomic mass units.

atomic mass unit *n. Abbr.* **amu** A unit of mass equal to ¹/₁₂ the mass of the carbon isotope with mass number 12, approximately 1.6604 × 10⁻²⁴ gram.

atomic number *n. Symbol* **Z** The number of protons in an atomic nucleus. Also called "proton number."

atomic pile *n.* A nuclear **reactor** (*see*).

atomic power *n.* Nuclear **power** (*see*).

atomic reactor *n.* A nuclear **reactor** (*see*).

atomic theory *n.* **1.** The physical theory of the structure, properties, and behavior of the atom. **2.** Atomism.

Athena *The Greek goddess of wisdom. This Roman statuette dates from 130 A.D. and is in the Athens National Museum.*

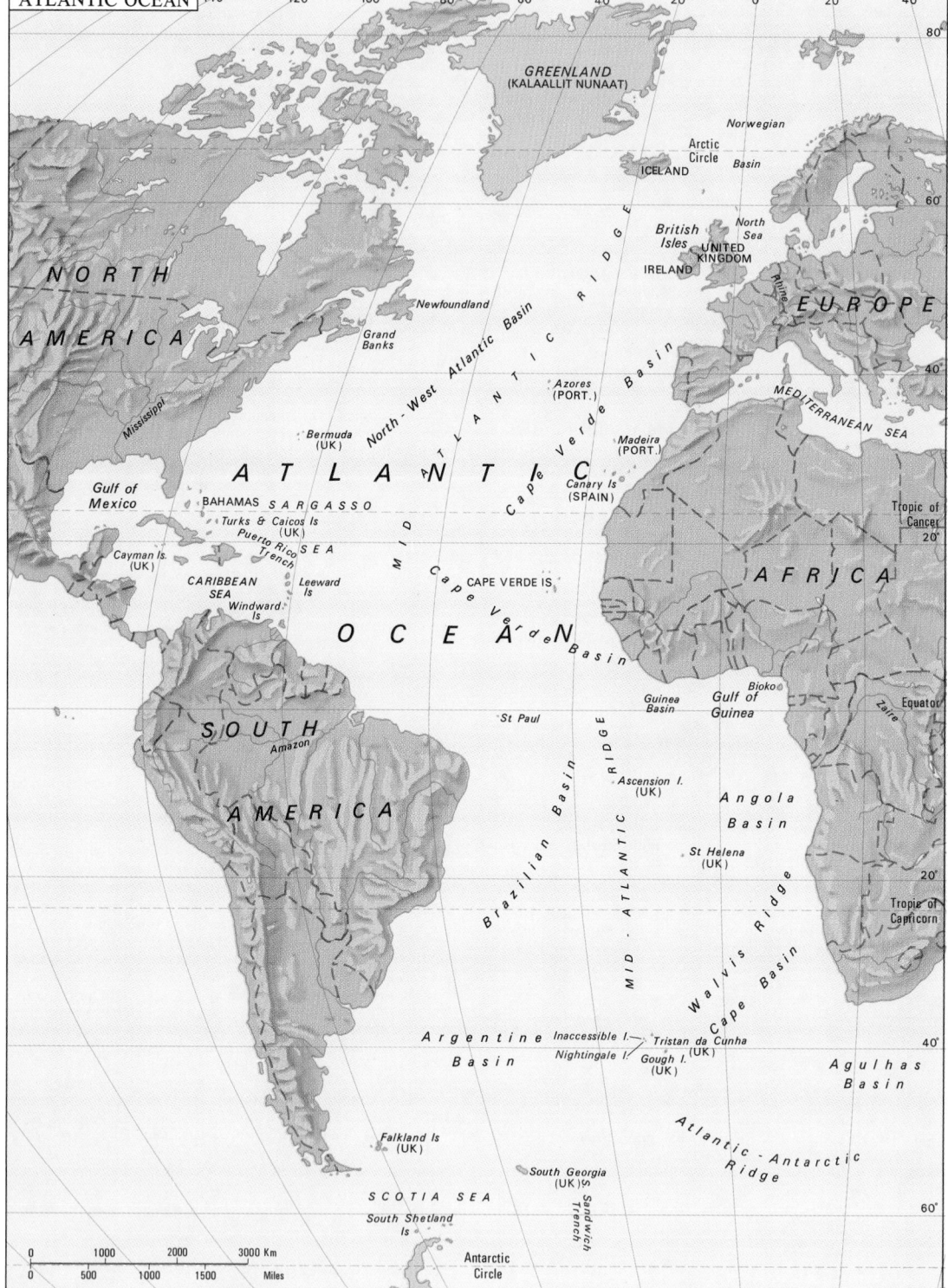

ATLANTIC OCEAN

atomic volume *n.* The ratio of an element's atomic weight to its density.

atomic weight *n. Abbr.* **at wt** The average weight of an atom of an element, usually expressed relative to one atom of the carbon isotope taken to have a standard weight of 12. Also called "relative atomic mass."

at·om·ism (ăt´əm-ĭz´əm) *n.* **1.** The ancient theory of Democritus, Epicurus, and Lucretius, according to which simple, indivisible, and indestructible atoms are the basic components of the entire universe. **2.** In sociology, any theory according to which social institutions and processes arise solely from the acts of individual men. **3.** In political theory: **a.** The division or tendency to divide into subclasses, groups, or units of a given society. **b.** Such a tendency accompanied by or arising from a strong subjective individualism. **—at·om·ist** *n.* **—at·om·is·tic, at·om·is·ti·cal** *adj.* **—at·om·is·ti·cal·ly** *adv.*

at·om·ize (ăt´əm-īz´) *tr.v.* **-ized, izing, -izes. 1.** To reduce or separate into atoms. **2. a.** To reduce (a liquid) to a spray. **b.** To spray (a liquid) in this form. **3.** To subject to bombardment with atomic weapons. **4.** To reduce to individual parts or units; fragment. **—at·om·i·za·tion** *n.*

at·om·iz·er (ăt´əm-ī´zər) *n.* A device for producing a fine spray, especially of perfume or medicine.

atom smasher *n.* An atomic particle **accelerator** (see).

at·o·my¹ (ăt´ə-mē) *n., pl.* **-mies.** *Archaic.* **1.** A tiny particle. **2.** A tiny being: *"Drawn with a team of little atomies"* (Shakespeare). [Latin *atomī*, plural of *atomus,* ATOM.]

atomy² *n., pl.* **-mies.** *Archaic.* A skeleton or a gaunt person. [From ANATOMY, misinterpreted as *an atomy.*]

Aton. Variant of **Aten.**

a·to·nal (ā-tō´nəl) *adj. Music.* Lacking a tonal center or established

key. Compare **serial, twelve-tone.** —**a·to·nal·ism** *n.* —**a·to·nal·ly**
adv.

a·to·nal·i·ty (ā′tō-năl′ə-tē) *n. Music.* **1.** The lack of a tonal center or
key in musical composition, or the deliberate disregarding of it,
especially as an alternative to the diatonic system. **2.** The theory of
atonal composition.

a·tone (ə-tōn′) *v.* **atoned, atoning, atones.** —*intr.* **1.** To make
amends, as for a sin or fault. Used with *for.* **2.** *Archaic.* To agree.
—*tr. Archaic.* **1.** To expiate. **2.** To reconcile or harmonize. **3.** To
conciliate; appease. [Middle English *atonen,* to be reconciled, from
at one, of one mind, in accord : AT + ONE.] —**a·ton·a·ble, a·tone·a·**
ble *adj.* —**a·ton·er** *n.*

a·tone·ment (ə-tōn′mənt) *n.* **1.** Amends or reparation made for an
injury or wrong; expiation; recompense. **2.** In the Hebrew scriptures, man's reconciliation with God after having transgressed the
covenant. **3.** Atonement. *Theology.* **a.** The redemptive life, suffering, and death of Christ. **b.** The reconciliation of God and man
thus brought about by Christ. **4.** *Christian Science.* The radical obedience and purification, exemplified in the life of Jesus, by which
humanity finds man's oneness with God. **5.** *Archaic.* Reconciliation; concord.

a·ton·ic (ā-tŏn′ĭk) *adj.* **1.** Not accented: *atonic words and syllables.*
2. *Pathology.* Pertaining to, caused by, or characterized by atony.
—*n.* A word, syllable, or sound that is unaccented. [French *ato-*
nique, from Greek *atonos.* See **atony.**] —**at·o·nic·i·ty** (ăt′ə-nĭs′ə-tē,
ā′tō-) *n.*

at·o·ny (ăt′ə-nē) *n.* **1.** *Pathology.* **1.** Insufficient muscular tone.
2. *Phonetics.* Lack of accent or stress. [Late Latin *atonia,* from
Greek, from *atonos,* not stretched : *a-,* without + *tonos,* a stretching, TONE.]

a·top (ə-tŏp′) *adv. Archaic.* On or at the top.
—*prep.* On top of. —**a·top** *adj.*

-ator *suffix.* Indicates one that acts or does; for example, **aviator,**
radiator. [Middle English *-atour,* from Old French, from Latin *-ātor*
: *-ātus,* -ATE + -OR.]

-atory *suffix.* Indicates pertinence to, characteristic of, result of, or
effect of; for example, **placatory, perspiratory, amendatory.** [Mid-
dle English, from Latin *-ātōrius : -ātus,* -ATE + *-ōrius,* -ORY.]

ATP *n. Biochemistry.* A nucleotide, $C_{10}H_{16}N_5O_{13}P_3$, occurring in
plant and animal cells, that is a major energy source for vital processes. The energy is released when ATP is converted to ADP.
[*adenosine triphosphate.*]

at·ra·bil·ious (ăt′rə-bĭl′yəs) *adj.* Also **at·ra·bil·i·ar** (-bĭl′ē-ər). **1.** Inclined to melancholy; gloomy. **2.** Having a peevish disposition;
surly. [Latin *ātra bīlis,* black bile (translation of Greek *melankhōlia,*
MELANCHOLY) : *ātra,* feminine of *āter,* black + *bīlis,* BILE.] —**at·ra·**
bil·ious·ness *n.*

A·treus (ā′trōōs′, ā′trē-əs). *Greek Mythology.* A king of Mycenae,
father of Agamemnon and Menelaus.

a·tri·o·ven·tric·u·lar (ā′trē-ō-věn-trĭk′yə-lər) *adj. Anatomy.* Pertaining to the atria and the ventricles of the heart. [New Latin *atrio-,*
heart chamber, ATRIUM + VENTRICULAR.]

a·trip (ə-trĭp′) *adj. Nautical.* Just clear of the bottom; aweigh. Said
of an anchor. [A- (on) + TRIP (to raise an anchor).] —**a·trip** *adv.*

a·tri·um (ā′trē-əm) *n., pl.* **atria** (ā′trē-ə) or **-ums. 1.** An open central
court, especially in an ancient Roman house. **2.** A body cavity or
chamber; especially, either of the two upper chambers of the heart,
from which the blood passes to the ventricles. Also called "auricle."
3. A court in front of a church, often surrounded by colonnades.
[Latin *ātrium;* akin to *āter,* black, blackened (by fire), perhaps with
reference to the part of a Roman house blackened by smoke from
the hearth.] —**a·tri·al** (ā′trē-əl) *adj.*

a·tro·cious (ə-trō′shəs) *adj.* **1.** Extremely evil or cruel; monstrous:
an atrocious crime. **2.** Exceptionally bad; terrible: *atrocious decor;*
atrocious behavior. [Latin *ātrōx* (stem *ātrōc-*), "dark-looking," horrible, cruel; akin to *āter,* black.] —**a·tro·cious·ly** *adv.* —**a·tro·cious·**
ness *n.*

a·troc·i·ty (ə-trŏs′ə-tē) *n., pl.* **-ties. 1.** Atrocious condition, quality,
or behavior; monstrousness; vileness. **2. a.** An atrocious action,
situation, or object; an outrage. **b. atrocities.** Savage or brutal acts
committed in wartime.

at·ro·phy (ăt′rə-fē) *n., pl.* **-phies. 1.** *Pathology.* The emaciation or
wasting of tissues, organs, or the entire body. **2.** Any wasting away
or diminution: *moral atrophy.*
—*v.* **atrophied, -phying, -phies.** —*tr.* To cause to waste away.
—*intr.* To waste away; wither. [Late Latin *atrophia,* from Greek,
from *atrophos,* ill-nourished : *a-,* without + *trophē,* nourishment,
from *trephein,* to feed.] —**a·tro·phic** (ā-trō′fĭk) *adj.*

at·ro·pine (ăt′rə-pēn′) *n.* An extremely poisonous, bitter, crystalline
alkaloid, $C_{17}H_{23}NO_3$, obtained from belladonna and related plants.
It is used in medicine to dilate the pupil of the eye and as an
antispasmodic. [New Latin *Atropa,* genus of belladonna, deadly
nightshade, from Greek *atropos,* unchangeable, inflexible. See **Atro·**
pos.]

At·ro·pos (ăt′rə-pŏs′, -pəs). *Greek Mythology.* One of the three
Fates *(see).* She cuts the thread of life. [Greek, from *atropos,* inexorable, inflexible : *a-,* not + *trop-,* stem of *trepein,* to turn.]

A.T.S. 1. American Temperance Society. **2.** Army Transport Serv·
ice.

at·ta·boy (ăt′ə-boi′) *interj.* Used to express encouragement or approval.

at·tach (ə-tăch′) *v.* **-tached, -taching, -taches.** —*tr.* **1.** To fasten on
or affix to; connect or join. **2.** To connect as an adjunct or associ-

OUR MULTILAYERED ATMOSPHERE
A barrier of gases protecting Earth from space

The atmosphere is a mixture of gases encircling
Earth and held by Earth's gravity. This invisible
mixture of nitrogen, oxygen, argon, carbon dioxide, and water vapor protects the planet from
harmful radiation and makes life on Earth possible. The atmosphere's density decreases with
height, but not at a uniform rate. Above about
90 kilometers (55 miles) the air is extremely rarefied but it extends thousands of miles above
Earth.

Different layers of atmosphere are distinguished by their temperatures. The troposphere
extends 18 kilometers (11 miles) above Earth. It
is warmed by solar rays reradiated from Earth's
surface. This causes convection currents that
bring changes in the weather. Temperature in
the troposphere decreases with height to -60°C
(-76°F), but in the stratosphere it rises to near
freezing point. The stratosphere extends to 50

kilometers (30 miles). It contains ozone, which
absorbs ultraviolet rays from the sun. In the
mesosphere, which extends to 80 kilometers (50
miles) above Earth, temperature drops to
-113°C (-173°F). These three layers form the
lower atmosphere. In the rarefied upper atmosphere, temperature rises, reaching 227°C
(441°F) even at night where thermosphere and
exosphere meet 450 kilometers (280 miles) above
Earth.

The upper atmosphere absorbs much harmful
radiation and in doing so produces electrically
charged particles—ions. In this region, called
the ionosphere, layers of greater ion concentration—the D, E, and F layers—exist, although
they vary daily or seasonally. Man uses them to
bounce radio waves around the earth. Farther
out in the ionosphere are two Van Allen belts,
zones of radiation concentration.

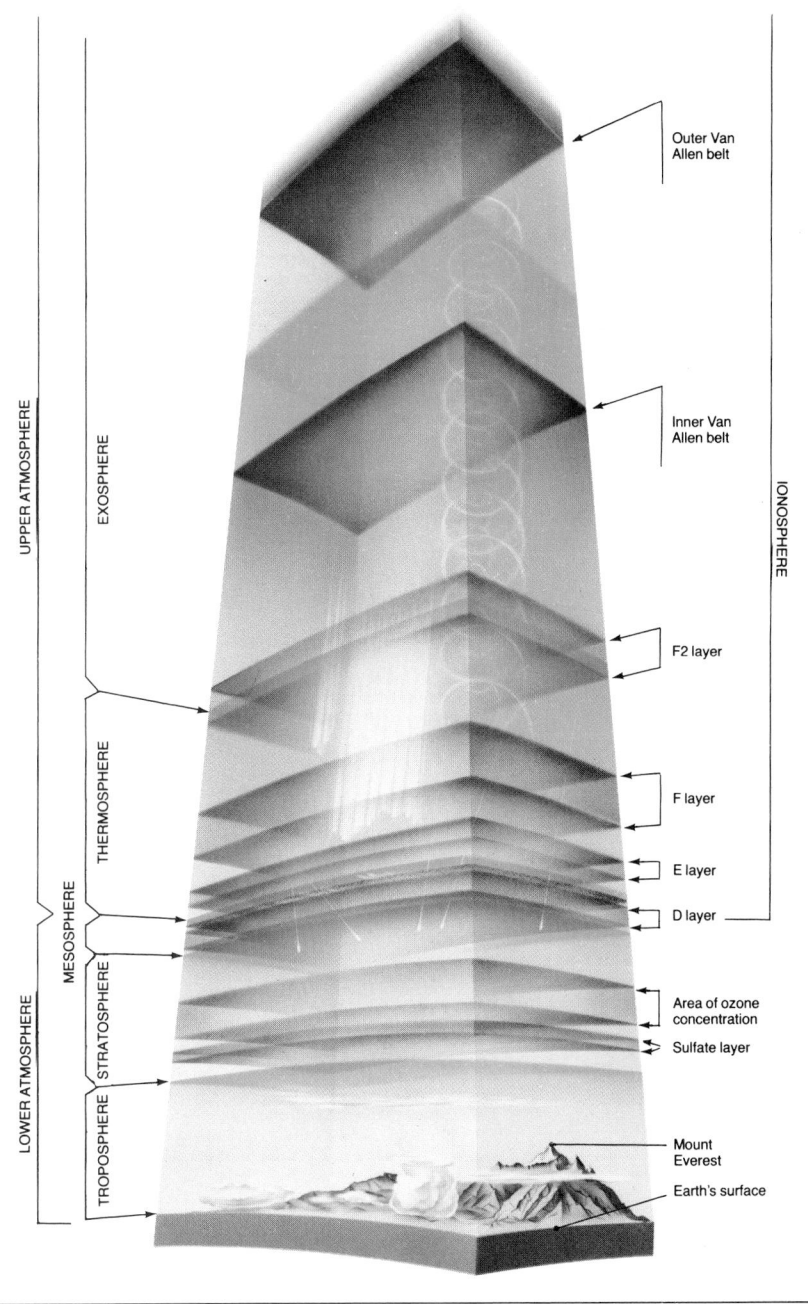

ated part. **3.** To affix or append; add, as a signature. **4.** To ascribe or assign: *I attach no significance to the threat.* **5.** To bind by personal ties, as of affection or loyalty. Usually used in the passive with *to*: *He's very attached to his mother.* **6.** To appoint officially. **7.** *Military.* To assign (personnel) to a unit on a temporary basis. Compare **assign. 8.** *Law.* To seize (persons or property) by legal writ. **9.** *Law.* To order the withholding of payment of (a debt) because a third party holds judgment for money against the creditor. **10.** To cause (oneself) to be part of or associated with a particular group. *—intr.* **1.** To become attached; adhere. **2.** To be an integral part of something: *Misery attaches to such a way of life.* [Middle English *attachen,* from Old French *attacher, estachier,* to fasten (with a stake), from *estache,* STAKE.] **—at·tach·a·ble** *adj.* **—at·tach·er** *n.*

at·ta·ché (ăt′ə-shā′, ə-tă′shā′) *n.* A person officially assigned to the staff of a diplomatic mission to serve in some particular capacity: *a cultural attaché.* [French, "one attached (to a diplomatic mission)," past participle of *attacher,* ATTACH.]

attaché case *n.* A briefcase resembling a small suitcase, with hinges and flat sides, used for carrying papers.

at·tached (ə-tăcht′) *adj.* Married, engaged, or committed to a serious romantic relationship.

at·tach·ment (ə-tăch′mənt) *n.* **1.** The act of attaching or the condition of being attached. **2.** Something that serves to attach one thing to another; a tie, band, or fastening. **3.** Fond regard; affection. **4.** A supplementary part; an accessory: *an attachment for a blender.* **5.** *Law.* **a.** The legal seizure of a person or property. **b.** The writ ordering such a seizure. **6.** *Law.* The procedure by which debts are attached. —See Synonyms at **appendage.**

at·tack (ə-tăk′) *v.* **-tacked, -tacking, -tacks.** *—tr.* **1.** To set upon with violent force; begin hostilities against or conflict with. **2.** To bombard with hostile criticism. **3.** To start work on with purpose and vigor: *attack a problem.* **4.** To begin to affect harmfully: *a disease that attacks crops.* *—intr.* **1.** To make an attack; launch an assault. **2.** To play offensively or take the initiative in a sport or game.

∼n. **1.** The act of attacking; an assault. **2.** A hostile criticism. **3.** An occurrence of or seizure by a disease or medical condition, especially one whose main symptoms recur at intervals: *an attack of asthma.* **4.** The act of setting to work on any task or undertaking: *made an attack on the problem.* **5.** *Music.* **a.** The manner in which a passage or phrase is begun. **b.** Force and incisiveness in performing. **6.** *Sports.* The offensive players, or the positions taken up by them, in a game between two teams. [French *attaquer,* from Old French, from Old Italian *attaccare,* variant of *estaccare* (unattested), to attach, join (battle), from *stacca* (unattested), STAKE.] **—at·tack·er** *n.*

Synonyms: *assail, assault, beset, bombard, storm.*

at·tain (ə-tān′) *v.* **-tained, -taining, -tains.** *—tr.* **1.** To gain, reach, or accomplish by mental or physical effort. **2.** To arrive at, as in time: *attain a ripe old age.* *—intr.* To succeed in gaining or reaching something; arrive at. Usually used with *to*: *He attained to the highest office in the land.* —See Synonyms at **reach.** [Middle English *atteignen,* from Norman-French, from Old French *ataindre* (stem *ataign-*), to reach to, from Vulgar Latin *attangere* (unattested), from Latin *attingere* : *ad-,* to + *tangere,* to touch.] **—at·tain·a·ble** *adj.* **—at·tain·a·bil·i·ty, at·tain·a·ble·ness** *n.*

at·tain·der (ə-tān′dər) *n.* **1.** The loss of all civil rights following a sentence of death or outlawry for a capital offense. See **bill of attainder. 2.** *Obsolete.* Dishonor. [Middle English *attendre,* conviction, from Norman French, noun use of *ateindre,* from Old French *ataindre,* to ATTAIN.]

at·tain·ment (ə-tān′mənt) *n.* **1.** The act of attaining. **2.** Something that is attained; an accomplishment or acquisition.

at·taint (ə-tānt′) *tr.v.* **-tainted, -tainting, -taints. 1.** *Law.* To condemn by a sentence of attainder. **2.** *Archaic.* To impart stigma to; disgrace. **3.** *Obsolete.* To accuse or prove guilty. Used with *of.*

∼n. **1.** Attainder. **2.** *Archaic.* A disgrace; a stigma. [Middle English *attaynten,* from Old French *ataint,* past participle of *ataindre,* to convict, originally, to ATTAIN (sense development influenced by TAINT).]

at·tar (ăt′ər) *n.* Also **ot·tar** (ŏt′ər), **ot·to** (ŏt′ō). A fragrant essential oil or perfume obtained from the petals of flowers, especially certain species of roses *(attar of roses).* [Persian *'aṭṭār,* perfumed, from *'iṭr,* perfume, from Arabic.]

at·tempt (ə-tĕmpt′) *tr.v.* **-tempted, -tempting, -tempts. 1.** To endeavor to do or achieve; try. **2.** To try to climb (a mountain). **3.** *Archaic.* To tempt. **4.** *Archaic.* To attack.

∼n. **1. a.** An effort or try. **b.** A try at conquering or winning something: *an attempt on the world record.* **2.** An attack; an assault: *an attempt on one's life.* **3.** The result of an attempt, especially when unsuccessful. [Middle English *attempten,* from Old French *attempter,* from Latin *attemptāre* : *ad-,* to + *temptāre,* to try, TEMPT.] **—at·tempt·a·ble** *adj.* **—at·tempt·er** *n.*

At·ten·bor·ough (ăt′n-bûr′ə, -bər-ə), **Sir Richard** (1923–). British film actor, director, and producer. He produced two films, including *The L-Shaped Room* (1962). Films he has directed include *Oh What a Lovely War!* (1968) and *Ghandi* (1982). He was knighted in 1976.

at·tend (ə-tĕnd′) *v.* **-tended, -tending, -tends.** *—tr.* **1.** To be present at; go to: *attend medical school; attend lectures.* **2.** To accompany as a circumstance or follow as a result: *The speech was attended by wild applause.* **3.** To accompany as an attendant or servant; wait upon. **4.** To take care or charge of (a sick person, for example). **5.** To listen to; heed: *Attend my warning.* **6.** *Archaic.* To wait for; expect. *—intr.* **1.** To be present. **2.** To pay attention; heed. Used with *to.* **3.** To remain ready to serve; wait. Used with *on* or *upon*: *We attend upon your wishes.* **4.** To apply or direct oneself. Used with *to*: *Please attend to the matter at once.* **5.** To deal with the needs of; take care of. Used with *to*: *attend to a patient.* [Middle English *attenden,* from Old French *atendre,* from Latin *attendere,* to stretch toward, direct attention to : *ad-,* toward + *tendere,* to stretch.] **—at·tend·er** *n.*

at·ten·dance (ə-tĕn′dəns) *n.* **1.** The act of attending. **2.** The persons or number of persons who are present, as at a class.

at·ten·dant (ə-tĕn′dənt) *n.* **1.** One who attends; especially, one who waits on another. **2.** One who is present, as at a class. **3.** An accompanying thing or circumstance; a consequence or concomitant. **4.** One who is employed to provide a service, as to a customer: *flight attendant.*

∼adj. Accompanying or consequent: *attendant circumstances.* **—at·ten·dant·ly** *adv.*

at·ten·tion (ə-tĕn′shən) *n. Abbr.* **attn. 1.** Concentration of the mental powers upon an object; a close or careful observing or listening. **2.** The ability or power to concentrate mentally. **3. a.** Observation; notice: *Your suggestion has come to our attention.* **b.** Consideration with a view to deciding on a course of action: *an injury requiring prompt attention.* **4.** Respectful consideration: *attention to the feelings of others.* **5.** *Usually* **attentions.** An act of courtesy, consideration, or gallantry indicating romantic interest. **6.** *Military.* **a.** A posture assumed by a soldier, with the body erect, eyes to the front, arms at the sides, and heels together. **b.** A command to assume this position. [Middle English *attencioun,* from Latin *attentiō* (stem *attentiōn-*), from *attendere,* ATTEND.] **—at·ten·tion·al** *adj.*

at·ten·tive (ə-tĕn′tĭv) *adj.* **1.** Paying attention; observant; listening. **2.** Courteous or devoted; considerate; thoughtful. **—at·ten·tive·ly** *adv.* **—at·ten·tive·ness** *n.*

at·ten·u·ate (ə-tĕn′yo͞o-āt′) *v.* **-ated, -ating, -ates.** *—tr.* **1.** To make slender, fine, or small. **2.** To reduce in strength, force, value, or amount; weaken. **3.** To lessen in density; dilute or rarefy (a liquid or gas). **4.** *Bacteriology.* To make (a pathogenic microorganism) less virulent, as by treating with heat or chemicals. *—intr.* To become thin, weak, fine, or reduced in power.

∼adj. (ə-tĕn′yo͞o-ĭt) **1.** Thinned; diluted; weakened. **2.** *Botany.* Gradually tapering to a point; slender and pointed. [Latin *attenuāre,* to make thin : *ad-,* to + *tenuāre,* to make thin, from *tenuis,* thin.] **—at·ten·u·a·ble** *adj.*

at·ten·u·a·tion (ə-tĕn′yo͞o-ā′shən) *n.* **1.** An act or instance of attenuating or the state of being attenuated. **2.** *Physics.* **a.** The loss in energy of radiation, sound, or the like, as it passes through matter, primarily as a result of absorption or scattering. **b.** The power loss suffered by an electric current passing through a circuit.

at·ten·u·a·tor (ə-tĕn′yo͞o-ā′tər) *n.* Any device or object that causes attenuation; especially, a device that reduces the power of a wave, signal, or the like, without causing distortion.

at·test (ə-tĕst′) *v.* **-tested, -testing, -tests.** *—tr.* **1.** To affirm to be correct, true, or genuine; corroborate. **2.** To certify by signature or oath; affirm officially. **3.** To supply evidence or proof of: *His vast holdings attest his wealth.* **4.** To constitute documentary or other material proof of the former existence of. Used especially in archaeology and historical linguistics. **5.** To put under oath. *—intr.* To bear witness; give testimony. Used with *to*: *I attest to his good faith.*

∼n. Archaic. An act of attesting. [French *attester,* from Old French, from Latin *attestārī* : *ad-,* to + *testārī,* to be a witness, from *testis,* witness.] **—at·test·ant** (ə-tĕs′tənt) *n.* **—at·tes·ta·tion** (ăt′ĕs-tā′shən, ăt′ə-stā′-) *n.* **—at·test·er, at·tes·tor** (ə-tĕs′tər) *n.*

at·tic (ăt′ĭk) *n.* **1.** A story or room directly below the roof of a house. **2.** *Architecture.* A low wall or story above the cornice of a classical façade. [French *attique,* "attic story," a top story above or enclosed by columns in an Attic style.]

At·tic (ăt′ĭk) *adj.* **1.** Of, pertaining to, or characteristic of ancient Attica, Athens, or the Athenians. **2.** *Sometimes* **attic.** Characterized by classical purity and simplicity.

∼n. The ancient Greek dialect of Athens, in which the bulk of classical Greek literature is written, belonging to Attic-Ionic.

At·ti·ca (ăt′ĭ-kə). Region of ancient Greece, occupying the area around Athens. According to Greek legend, there were four Attic tribes, unified into a single community by Theseus.

At·tic-I·on·ic (ăt′ĭk-ī-ŏn′ĭk) *n.* One of the four main dialects of ancient Greek, spoken in Attica and Ionia. Compare **Aeolic, Arcado-Cyprian, Doric.**

At·ti·cism (ăt′ə-sĭz′əm) *n.* **1.** Something characteristic of the Attic Greek language. **2.** An expression or style of expression characterized by simplicity, conciseness, and elegance.

Attic salt *n.* Dry, delicate, pointed wit. Also called "Attic wit."

At·ti·la (ăt′ə-lə, ə-tĭl′ə), also known as "Attila the Hun," "the Scourge of God" (died A.D. 453). Leader of the Huns and the most notorious of the barbarian invaders of the Roman Empire. After 441 he attacked the empire repeatedly from the east, gaining much territory, but was checked at Constantinople (443), in Gaul (451), and in Italy (452).

at·tire (ə-tīr′) *tr.v.* **-tired, -tiring, -tires.** To dress, especially in elaborate or splendid garments; clothe.

∼n. **1.** Clothing, especially of an elaborate or special kind: *formal attire.* **2.** *Heraldry.* The antlers of a deer. [Middle English *attiren,* from Old French *atirier,* to arrange into ranks, put in order : *a-,* from Latin *ad-,* to + *tire,* order, rank (see **tier**).]

PRONUNCIATION KEY

ă, pat; ā, pay; âr, care; ä, father, are; b, **bib**; ch, **church**; d, **deed**; ĕ, pet; ē, be; f, **fife**; g, **gag**; h, **hat**; hw, **which**; ĭ, pit; ī, pie; îr, pier; j, **judge**; k, **kick**; l, lid, needle; m, **mum**; n, no, sudden; ng, **thing**; ŏ, pot; ō, toe; ô, **paw**, for; oi, noise; ou, **out**; o͝o, **book**; o͞o, **boot**; p, **pop**; r, **roar**; s, sauce; sh, **ship**, **dish**; t, tight; th, **thin**, **path**; *th*, **this**, bathe; ŭ, **cut**; ûr, **fur**; v, valve; w, **with**; y, **yes**; z, zebra, size; zh, vision; ə, about, item, edible, gallop, circus, peaceful

IN FOREIGN WORDS:

à, *Fr.* ami; œ, *Fr.* **feu**, *Ger.* schön; ü, *Fr.* **tu**, *Ger.* **über**; KH, *Ger.* **ich**, *Scot.* **loch**; N, *Fr.* bon; y′, *Fr.* Compiègne

STRESS MARKS:

Primary stress: ′ **in·cite′** (ĭn-sīt′)
Secondary stress: ′ **in′sight′** (ĭn′sīt′)

at·ti·tude (ăt′ə-to͞od′, -tyo͞od′) *n.* **1.** A position of the body or manner of carrying oneself, indicative of a mood or condition: *"men . . . sprawled alone or in heaps, in the careless attitudes of death"* (John Reed). **2.** A state of mind or feeling with regard to some matter. **3.** A way of behaving; disposition. **4.** *Aeronautics.* The orientation of an aircraft's axes relative to some reference line or plane, such as the horizon. **5.** *Aerospace.* The orientation of a spacecraft relative to its direction of motion. **6.** A ballet position in which a dancer stands on one leg with the other leg raised and bent backward. [French, from Italian *attitudine,* disposition, from Late Latin *aptitūdō,* faculty, fitness, from Latin *aptus,* fit, APT.] **—at·ti·tu·di·nal** (ăt′ə-to͞od′n-əl, -tyo͞od′-) *adj.*

at·ti·tu·di·nize (ăt′ə-to͞od′n-īz′, -tyo͞od′-) *intr.v.* **-nized, -nizing, -nizes.** To assume an affected attitude.

Att·lee (ăt′lē), **Clement Richard Attlee, 1st Earl** (1883–1967). British politician. In 1935 he became leader of the Labour Party. He was deputy prime minister in Churchill's wartime coalition government (1940–45). As prime minister from 1945 to 1951 he presided over the establishment of the National Health Service, the expansion of public ownership of industry, and the granting of independence to India. He received his peerage in 1955.

attn. attention.

atto– *prefix. Symbol* **a** Indicates one quintillionth (10^{-18}); for example, **attotesla.** [Danish or Norwegian *atten,* eighteen, from Old Norse *āttjān.*]

at·torn (ə-tûrn′) *intr.v.* **-torned, -torning, -torns.** *Law.* To acknowledge a new owner as landlord. [Middle English *attournen,* from Old French *atorner,* to turn to, assign to : *a-,* from Latin *ad-,* to + *torner,* to turn, from Latin *tornāre,* to TURN.] **—at·torn·ment** *n.*

at·tor·ney (ə-tûr′nē) *n., pl.* **-neys.** *Abbr.* **atty.** A person legally appointed or empowered to act for another; especially an attorney at law. —See Usage note at **lawyer.** [Middle English *attourney,* from Old French *atorne,* "one appointed," past participle of *atorner,* to appoint, ATTORN.] **—at·tor·ney·ship** *n.*

attorney at law *n.* One who is qualified to represent clients in a court of law and to advise them on legal matters; a lawyer.

attorney general *n., pl.* **attorneys general. 1.** The chief law officer and legal counsel of the government of a state or nation. **2.** In some states, a public prosecutor.

Attorney General *n., pl.* **Attorneys General.** *Abbr.* **A.G., Atty. Gen.** The chief law officer and legal counsel of the government of the United States, who is also a Cabinet member and head of the Department of Justice.

at·to·tes·la (ăt′ō-tĕs′lə) *n. Abbr.* **aT** *Physics.* One quintillionth (10^{-18}) of a tesla.

at·tract (ə-trăkt′) *v.* **-tracted, -tracting, -tracts.** *—tr.* **1.** To cause to draw near or adhere. **2.** To draw or direct to oneself by some quality or action: *attract attention.* **3.** To evoke interest or admiration in; allure. *—intr.* To possess or use the power of attraction; be magnetic or alluring. [Middle English *attracten,* from Latin *attrahere* (past participle *attractus*) : *ad-,* toward + *trahere,* to draw.] **—at·tract·a·ble** *adj.* **—at·trac·tor, at·tract·er** (ə-trăk′tər) *n.*

at·tract·ant (ə-trăk′tənt) *n.* A substance that attracts, especially a chemical produced by insects and other animals to attract opposite-sexed members of the same species. See **pheromone.**

at·trac·tion (ə-trăk′shən) *n.* **1.** The act of attracting. **2.** The quality or power of attracting; allure; charm. **3.** A feature, characteristic, or factor that attracts: *Money was not the least of her attractions.* **4.** A public spectacle or entertainment. **5.** A force that causes one body to attract another body with which it is not in contact: *gravitational attraction; magnetic attraction.*

at·trac·tive (ə-trăk′tĭv) *adj.* **1.** Having the power to attract. **2.** Pleasing to the eye or mind; appealing. **3.** Personally engaging; charming. **—at·trac·tive·ly** *adv.* **—at·trac·tive·ness** *n.*

at·trib·ute (ə-trĭb′yət, -yo͞ot′) *—tr.v.* **-uted, -uting, -utes.** To regard or assign as belonging to or resulting from someone or something; ascribe: *attribute a painting to Rembrandt; attributed his downfall to greed.*

∼n. (ăt′rə-byo͞ot′). **1.** A quality or characteristic belonging to a person or thing; a distinctive feature: *Travel has lost the attributes of privilege and fashion"* (John Cheever). **2.** An object associated with and serving to identify a character, person, or office: *Lightning bolts are the attribute of Zeus.* **3.** *Grammar.* An adjective or a phrase used as an adjective. —See Synonyms at **quality.** [Latin *attribūtum,* "quality belonging to something," noun use of past participle of *attribuēre* : *ad-,* to + *tribuēre,* to allot, grant (see **tribute**).] **—at·trib·ut·a·ble** *adj.* **—at·trib·ut·er, at·trib·u·tor** (ə-trĭb′yə-tər) *n.*

Synonyms: *ascribe, assign, credit, impute.*

at·tri·bu·tion (ăt′rə-byo͞o′shən) *n.* **1.** The act of attributing. **2.** Something that is ascribed; an attribute.

at·trib·u·tive (ə-trĭb′yə-tĭv) *adj.* **1.** *Grammar.* Pertaining to or designating an adjective or a word or phrase used adjectivally that is joined directly to the noun it modifies without a linking verb. For example, in the sentence *The young girl is ill, young* is an attributive adjective. Compare **predicative. 2.** Of or having the nature of an attribution or attribute. **3.** Of an attributed origin: *an attributive Rubens.*

∼n. Grammar. An attributive adjective or adjectival phrase. **—at·trib·u·tive·ly** *adv.* **—at·trib·u·tive·ness** *n.*

at·trit·ed (ə-trī′tĭd) *adj.* Worn down by attrition. [Latin *attrītus,* from past participle of *atterere,* to rub away. See **attrition.**]

at·tri·tion (ə-trĭsh′ən) *n.* **1.** A rubbing away or wearing down by friction, especially of rock particles during transport by wind or water. **2.** The act or result of gradually wearing down and exhausting an opponent by constant stress and harassment: *a war of attrition.* **3.** A gradual reduction in membership or personnel through retirement, resignation, or death. **4.** *Theology.* Repentance for sin motivated by fear of punishment rather than by love of God. In this sense, compare **contrition.** [Middle English *attricioun,* from Medieval Latin *attrītiō* (stem *attrītiōn-*), "chastisement," from Latin, a rubbing against, from *atterere,* to rub against : *ad-,* against + *terere,* to rub.]

at·tune (ə-to͞on′, -tyo͞on′) *tr.v.* **-tuned, -tuning, -tunes. 1.** To bring into harmony. **2.** To accustom to a special perception; make aware: *an ear attuned to dissonance.* **3.** To tune (an instrument). [16th century : AD- (to) + TUNE.]

atty. attorney.

Atty. Gen. attorney general.

a·twit·ter (ə-twĭt′ər) *adj.* In a state of nervous excitement.

At·wood (ăt′wo͝od′), **Margaret** (1939–). Canadian writer. Her works include a collection of poems, *The Circle Game* (1966), and the novels *The Edible Woman* (1969) and *Lady Oracle* (1976).

at wt atomic weight.

a·typ·i·cal (ā-tĭp′ĭ-kəl) *adj.* Also **a·typ·ic** (ā-tĭp′ĭk). Not typical; varying from the type. **—a·typ·i·cal·ly** *adv.*

Au The symbol for the element gold. [Latin *aurum.*]

A.U. astronomical unit.

au·bade (ō-bäd′) *n.* **1.** A musical composition intended to be played or sung at dawn or early in the morning. **2.** A poem appropriate to this time of day. [French, from Old French, from Old Provençal *auba, alba,* dawn, from Vulgar Latin *alba* (unattested), feminine of Latin *albus,* white.]

au·ber·gine (ō′bər-zhēn′) *n.* **1.** A vegetable, the **eggplant** *(see).* **2.** Blackish purple. [French, from Catalan *albergínia,* from Arabic *al-bādindjān,* from Persian *bādin-gān,* from Sanskrit *vātimgana.*]

Au·brey (ô′brē), **John** (1626–97). English antiquarian and writer. His work, *Brief Lives* (published in the 19th century), contains brilliant sketches of his contemporaries.

Aubrey hole *n.* Any of the 56 holes that form the outer ring of the circle at **Stonehenge.** [After John AUBREY.]

au·brie·tia, au·bre·tia (ô-brē′shə) *n.* Any trailing plant of the genus *Aubrietia,* having purple or red flowers and widely cultivated in gardens. [New Latin, after Claude *Aubriet,* 18th-century French painter of animals and flowers, in whose honor it was named.]

aubrietia *A perennial plant that thrives in limy soil and is commonly grown in rock gardens and borders.* Aubrietia deltoidea, *shown here, is a native of southern Europe and Asia Minor.*

au·burn (ô′bərn) *n.* Moderate reddish brown to brown. [Middle English *aborne,* blond, from Old French *auborne, alborne,* from Medieval Latin *alburnus,* whitish, from Latin *albus,* white.] **—au·burn** *adj.*

Au·bus·son (ō-bo͞o-sôɴ′). Town in Creuse department in central France. It has been famous for its manufacture of carpets and tapestries since the 16th century.

A.U.C. ab urbe condita.

Auck·land (ôk′lənd). The largest city and chief port of New Zealand, on an isthmus in the northern part of North Island. It was the capital until 1865.

au cou·rant (ō ko͞o-räɴ′) *adj.* Informed on current affairs; up-to-date. [French, "in the current."]

auc·tion (ôk′shən) *n.* **1.** A public sale in which property or items of merchandise are sold to the highest bidder. **2.** The bidding in the game of bridge.

∼tr.v. **auctioned, -tioning, -tions.** To sell at or by an auction. Often used with *off.* [Latin *auctiō* (stem *auctiōn-*), (a sale by) increase (of bids), from *augēre,* to increase.]

auction bridge *n.* A variety of the game of bridge in which tricks made in excess of the contract are scored toward game. Compare **contract bridge.**

auc·tion·eer (ôk′shə-nîr′) *n.* A person who conducts an auction and controls the bidding.

∼tr.v. **auctioneered, -eering, -eers.** To act as an auctioneer.

auctioneer bird *n.* A small Australian black-headed bird, *Orthonyx spaldingi,* that lives in mountain scrub and has a loud call. Also called "chowchilla."

auc·to·ri·al (ôk-tôr′ē-əl, -tōr′-) *adj.* Of or pertaining to an author. [Latin *auctor,* AUTHOR + -IAL.]

au·da·cious (ô-dā′shəs) *adj.* **1.** Fearlessly daring; bold. **2.** Lacking restraint or tact; arrogantly insolent. —See Synonyms at **brave, reckless.** [Latin *audāx* (stem *audāc-*), bold, from *audēre,* to dare, "be eager," from *avidus,* AVID.] **—au·da·cious·ly** *adv.* **—au·da·cious·ness** *n.*

au·dac·i·ty (ô-dăs′ə-tē) *n., pl.* **-ties. 1.** Boldness; daring. **2.** Unrestrained impudence; presumption. **3.** An instance of boldness or presumption. —See Synonyms at **temerity.**

Au·den (ôd′n), **Wystan Hugh** (1907–73). British poet. In the 1930's he was a member of the literary circle that included Christopher Isherwood, with whom he wrote several verse dramas. He immigrated to the United States in 1939 and became a citizen (1946).

au·di·bil·i·ty (ô′də-bĭl′ə-tē) *n.* The capacity to be heard.

au·di·ble (ô′də-bəl) *adj.* Capable of being heard. [Late Latin *audībilis,* from Latin *audīre,* to hear.] **—au·di·ble·ness** *n.* **—au·di·bly** *adv.*

au·di·ence (ô′dē-əns) *n.* **1.** A gathering of spectators or listeners, as at a concert, play, or film. **2.** The readers, hearers, or viewers reached by a book, radio broadcast, or television program. **3.** A formal meeting or conference, as with a king or pope. **4.** An opportunity to be heard or to express one's views. **5.** The act of hearing or attending. [Middle English, from Old French, from Latin *audi-*

Audubon painting *The pictures of the 19th-century American naturalist John James Audubon form a detailed record of birds such as this red-billed blue magpie.*

auger *A tool used to make holes in wood. The screw at the end pulls the tool into the wood when the auger is turned.*

entia, from *audiēns* (stem *audient-*), present participle of *audīre,* to hear.]

au·di·ent (ô′dē-ənt) *adj.* Hearing; listening. [Latin *audiēns* (stem *audient-*), present participle of *audīre,* to hear.]

au·dile (ô′dīl′) *adj. Psychology.* Capable of learning chiefly from auditory, rather than tactile or visual, stimuli.
~*n.* An audile person. [Latin *audīre,* to hear, by analogy with *tactile*]

au·di·o (ô′dē-ō′) *adj.* **1.** Of or pertaining to audible sound. **2. a.** Of or pertaining to the broadcasting of sound. **b.** Of or pertaining to the high-fidelity reproduction of sound.
~*n.* **1.** The audio part of television equipment. **2.** Audio broadcasting or reception. **3.** Audible sound. Compare **video.** [Independent use of AUDIO-.]

audio– *prefix.* Indicates sound or hearing; for example, **audiometer.** [Latin *audīre,* to hear.]

audio frequency *n. Abbr.* **a.f., A.F., AF** A frequency in a range, usually between 15 hertz and 20,000 hertz, characteristic of signals audible to the normal human ear.

au·di·o·lin·gual (ô′dē-ō-lĭng′gwəl) *adj.* Designating an approach to language learning that involves speaking and listening rather than reading and writing.

au·di·ol·o·gy (ô′dē-ŏl′ə-jē) *n.* The scientific study of hearing; especially, the study and treatment of hearing defects. —**au·di·o·log·i·cal** (ô′dē-ō-lŏj′ĭ-kəl) *adj.* —**au·di·ol·o·gist** *n.*

au·di·om·e·ter (ô′dē-ŏm′ə-tər) *n. Medicine.* An instrument for measuring hearing thresholds for pure tones of normally audible frequencies. —**au·di·o·met·ric** (ô′dē-ō-mĕt′rĭk) *adj.* —**au·di·om·e·try** *n.*

au·di·o·phile (ô′dē-ō-fīl′) *n.* One who has a great interest in high-fidelity sound reproduction.

au·di·o·tape (ô′dē-ō-tāp′) *n.* A sound tape recording, as opposed to a videotape.

au·di·o·typ·ist (ô′dē-ō-tī′pĭst) *n.* One who types directly from tape recordings as opposed to written material. Compare **copy typist.** —**au·di·o·typ·ing** *n.*

au·di·o·vis·u·al (ô′dē-ō-vĭzh′ŏŏ-əl) *adj. Abbr.* **A.V. 1.** Both audible and visible. **2.** Of or pertaining to educational materials, such as sound filmstrips, that present information in audible and visible form.

audio-visual aids *pl.n.* Also **audio-visuals.** Educational materials that present information in audible and visible form.

au·dit (ô′dĭt) *n.* **1.** An examination of records or accounts to check their accuracy. **2.** An adjustment or correction of accounts. **3.** An examined and verified account. **4.** *Rare.* An audience or hearing.
~*v.* **audited, -diting, -dits.** —*tr.* **1.** To examine, verify, or correct (accounts, records, or claims). **2.** To register for and attend a (college course) without receiving academic credit. —*intr.* To examine accounts. [Middle English, from Latin *audītus,* a hearing, from the past participle of *audīre,* to hear.]

au·di·tion (ô-dĭsh′ən) *n.* **1.** The act or sense of hearing. **2.** A presentation of something heard; a hearing. **3.** A trial performance, as by an actor or musician, to demonstrate ability or skill.
~*v.* **auditioned, -tioning, -tions.** —*tr.* To test in an audition. —*intr.* To perform or be tested in an audition. [Latin *audītiō* (stem *audītiōn-*), from *audīre,* to hear. See **audit.**]

au·di·tive (ô′də-tĭv) *adj.* Auditory.

au·di·tor (ô′də-tər) *n.* **1.** One who hears; a listener. **2.** One who audits accounts. **3.** One who audits a course of study. [Middle English *auditour,* from Old French *auditeur,* from Latin *audītor,* hearer (in Medieval Latin, also one who audits accounts), from *audīre,* to hear.]

au·di·to·ri·um (ô′də-tôr′ē-əm, -tōr′-) *n., pl.* **-toriums** or **-toria** (-tôr′ē-ə, -tōr′-). **1.** The part of a theater, school, or other public building where an audience sits. **2.** A large building for public meetings or artistic performances. [Latin *audītōrium,* from *audīre,* to hear.]

au·di·to·ry (ô′də-tôr′ē, -tōr′ē) *adj.* Of or pertaining to the sense, the organs, or the experience of hearing. [Late Latin *audītōrius,* from Latin *audīre,* to hear.]

auditory nerve *n. Anatomy.* The **acoustic nerve** *(see).*

Au·du·bon (ô′də-bŏn′, -bən), **John James** (1785–1851). American naturalist and painter, born in Haiti. He was the first ornithologist to ring birds so as to discover their migratory habits. His *Birds of America* (1827–38) is a classic of both naturalism and art.

au fait (o fĕ′) *adj. French.* **1.** Skilled or knowledgeable; expert. **2.** Conversant or familiar. Often used with *with.* [Literally, "to the point."]

Auf·klä·rung (ouf′klā′rŏŏng) *n. German.* The Enlightenment.

au fond (o fôN′) *adv. French.* Basically; essentially. [Literally, "at the bottom."]

auf Wie·der·seh·en (ouf vē′dər-zā′ən) *interj. German.* Until we see one another again; farewell.

Aug. August.

Au·ge·an Stables (ô-jē′ən) *pl.n.* **1.** *Greek Mythology.* The stables of King Augeas that had not been cleaned for thirty years and which Hercules had to clean as one of his twelve labors. **2.** A place or state of extreme filth or corruption. [After *Augeas,* king of Elis in Greek mythology.]

au·gend (ô′jĕnd′) *n. Mathematics.* A quantity to which another quantity, the addend, is added. [Latin *augendum,* "the thing to be increased," gerundive of *augēre,* to increase.]

au·ger (ô′gər) *n.* **1.** A tool with a corkscrew-shaped bit, for boring holes in wood. **2.** A large tool for boring into the earth. [Middle

English *an auger,* originally *a nauger,* Old English *nafogār,* "tool for piercing wheel hubs."]

Auger effect (ō-zhā′) *n. Physics.* The emission of an electron instead of a photon by an excited ion when a vacancy in an inner electron shell is filled. [After Pierre *Auger* (born 1899), French physicist.]

aught¹ (ôt) *pron.* Also *regional* **ought. 1.** All: *For aught we know he may have changed his name.* **2.** *Archaic.* Anything whatever; any least part.
~*adv.* Also *regional* **ought.** At all; in any respect. [Middle English *aught, ought,* Old English *āuht, āwiht,* "ever a thing," anything.]

aught² (ôt) *n.* Also **ought. 1.** A cipher; the symbol 0; zero. **2.** *Archaic.* Nothing. [From *an aught,* originally *a* NAUGHT.]

au·gite (ô′jīt′) *n.* A dark-green to black pyroxene mineral that contains aluminum, iron, and magnesium. [Latin *augītēs,* a precious stone, from Greek *augitēs,* from *augē,* ray, brightness.]

aug·ment (ôg-mĕnt′). *v.* **-mented, -menting, -ments.** —*tr.* **1.** To make greater, as in size, extent, or quantity; enlarge; increase: *He augmented his salary by writing.* **2.** *Music.* To increase (a perfect or major interval) by a semitone. Compare **diminish.** —*intr.* To become greater; enlarge. —See Synonyms at **increase.**
~*n.* (ôg′mĕnt′). A morphological indication of past tense in Greek and Sanskrit verbs, consisting of the prefixing of a vowel or the lengthening of the initial vowel. [Middle English *augmenten,* from Old French *augmenter,* from Late Latin *augmentāre,* from *augmentum,* increase, from Latin *augēre,* to increase.] —**aug·ment·a·ble** *adj.*

aug·men·ta·tion (ôg′mĕn-tā′shən) *n.* **1. a.** The act or process of augmenting. **b.** The condition of being augmented. **2.** Something that enlarges or increases; an addition. **3.** *Music.* The repetition of a theme in notes of usually double the value of those originally assigned to it. Compare **diminution.**

aug·men·ta·tive (ôg-mĕn′tə-tĭv) *adj.* Also **aug·men·tive** (ôg-mĕn′tĭv). **1.** Having the tendency or ability to augment. **2.** Designating a word or affix that produces an increase in size or intensity when added to another word, such as *super-* in *superstar.* Compare **diminutive.**
~*n.* Also **aug·men·tive.** An augmentative word or affix.

aug·ment·ed (ôg-mĕn′tĭd) *adj. Music.* Increased from the corresponding major or perfect interval by a semitone. Said of an interval.

au gra·tin (ō grät′n, grăt′n; *French* ō grà-tăN′) *adj.* Covered with breadcrumbs and sometimes grated cheese and browned in an oven or under a broiler: *cauliflower au gratin.* [French, "with the crust (of bread crumbs)."] —**au gratin** *adv.*

Augs·burg (ougz′bûrg′, ôgz′-). Industrial city in Bavaria in West Germany, on the Lech River. It was the home of the great banking families of Fugger and Welser.

au·gur (ô′gər) *n.* **1.** One of a group of religious officials of ancient Rome who foretold events by observing and interpreting signs and omens. **2.** A seer or prophet; a soothsayer.
~*v.* **augured, -guring, -gurs.** —*tr.* **1.** To predict or prognosticate, as from signs or omens. **2.** To serve as an omen of; betoken. —*intr.* **1.** To conjecture or foretell from signs or omens. **2.** To be a sign or omen. Used in the phrase *augur ill* or *well.* —See Synonyms at **foretell.** [Latin *augur, auger : au-,* perhaps from *avis,* bird + *gerere,* to do, perform (with reference to observing birds' flight or examining their viscera as a means of divination). See **auspice.**] —**au·gu·ral** (ô′gyə-rəl) *adj.*

au·gu·ry (ô′gyə-rē) *n., pl.* **-ries. 1.** The art, ability, or practice of auguring; divination. **2.** The rite performed by an augur. **3.** A sign or omen; an indication. [Middle English *augurie,* from Old French, from Latin *augurium,* from *augur,* AUGUR.]

au·gust (ô-gŭst′) *adj.* **1.** Inspiring awe or admiration; majestic. **2.** Venerable for reasons of age or high rank. —See Synonyms at **grand.** [Latin *augustus,* venerable, magnificent.] —**au·gust·ly** *adv.* —**au·gust·ness** *n.*

Au·gust (ô′gəst) *n. Abbr.* **Aug.** The eighth month of the year according to the Gregorian calendar. August has 31 days. See feature at **calendar.** [Middle English *August,* Old English *August,* from Latin *(mensis) Augustus,* (month) of Augustus, after the emperor AUGUSTUS.]

Au·gus·ta (ô-gŭs′tə). The capital of Maine, in the southwestern part of the state on the Kennebec River. A trading post was established here in the early 17th century.

Au·gus·tan (ô-gŭs′tən) *adj.* **1.** Pertaining to or characteristic of the emperor Augustus or his reign or times. **2.** Pertaining to or characteristic of any era resembling the reign of Augustus, as in classicism and refinement.
~*n.* A writer in an Augustan age.

Augustan age *n.* **1.** The golden age of Latin literature during the reign of Augustus (27 B.C.–A.D. 14), to which Horace, Livy, and Ovid belonged. **2.** A similar period of great literary achievement, as during the 18th century in England.

Au·gus·tine of Can·ter·bur·y (ô′gə-stēn′, ô-gŭs′tĭn; kăn′tər-bĕr′ē), **Saint** (died c. 605). Founder of the Christian Church in southern Britain and first archbishop of Canterbury. A Benedictine prior, he was appointed by Pope Gregory I to lead an evangelizing mission to Britain in 597. He was received by King Ethelbert of Kent, who gave him land at Canterbury. Ethelbert adopted the Christian faith, and in 598 Augustine was ordained as bishop of the English at Arles.

Augustine of Hip·po (hĭp′ō), **Saint** (A.D. 354–430). Latin Father and Doctor of the Church. Raised as a Christian, he abandoned the faith for Manichaeism after studying in Carthage. He later came under the influence of St. Ambrose, Bishop of Milan, and in 387 was baptized as a Christian. In 391 he was chosen by the Christians of Hippo (in present-day Algeria) to be their priest. He remained in Hippo for the rest of his life, becoming bishop *c.* 395. His *Confessions* (*c.* 400) and *The City of God* (after 412) are eloquent and moving testaments of Christian piety and belief.

Au·gus·tin·i·an (ô′gə-stĭn′ē-ən) *adj.* **1.** Pertaining to St. Augustine of Hippo or his doctrines. **2.** Designating or belonging to any of several orders following or influenced by the rule of St. Augustine. ~*n.* **1.** A follower of the principles and doctrines of St. Augustine of Hippo. **2.** A monk or friar belonging to an Augustinian orders. —**Au·gus·tin·i·an·ism.**

Au·gus·tus (ô-gŭs′təs) *n.* **1.** A title of the Roman emperors. **2.** After Hadrian, the title of the senior emperor as distinct from his junior colleague, the **Caesar** *(see).* [Latin *Augustus,* AUGUST, "Imperial Majesty," adopted by Octavian as a personal title when he acquired supreme power.]

Augustus, born Gaius Octavius, later "Gaius Julius Caesar Octavianus." Known as Octavian (63 B.C.–A.D. 14). First Roman emperor, the grand-nephew of Julius Caesar. Named by Caesar as his heir, Octavian became leader of the faction against Mark Antony. In 43 B.C. he, Mark Antony, and Lepidus formed the Second Triumvirate, whose armies defeated Brutus and Cassius at Philippi in 42. Antony's intrigues with Cleopatra led to the appointment of Octavian as general in 31. Following the defeat of Antony and Cleopatra at Actium in the same year, Octavian controlled all the lands of the empire. In 29 the senate named him *imperator,* or emperor, and in 27 gave him the honorary title Augustus. He subsequently devoted himself to consolidating Caesar's conquests, restoring civilian rule in Rome, building roads, and reforming the taxation system.

au jus (ō zho͞o′) *adj.* Served with the natural juices or gravy: *roast beef au jus.* [French, "with juice."]

auk (ôk) *n., pl.* **auks** or collectively **auk.** Any of several sea birds of the family Alcidae, of northern regions, having a squat body, short wings, and black and white plumage, such as the **razorbill** *(see).* See **great auk, little auk.** [Norwegian *alk, alka,* from Old Norse *ālka.*]

auk·let (ôk′lĭt) *n.* Any of various small auks of the genus *Aethia* and related genera, of northern Pacific coasts and waters.

au lait (ō lā′) *adj.* Cooked or served with milk. [French, "with milk."]

auld (ôld) *adj. Scottish.* Old.

auld lang syne (ôld lăng zīn′) *n.* The good old days long past. [Scottish, "old long since" : AULD + LANGSYNE.]

au·lic (ô′lĭk) *adj. Archaic.* Pertaining to a royal court; courtly. [French *aulique,* from Latin *aulicus,* from Greek *aulikos,* from *aulē,* court.]

Aulic Council *n.* The emperor's privy council in the Holy Roman Empire from 1498, when it was established by Maximilian I, until the dissolution of the Empire in 1806.

aumbry. Variant of **ambry.**

au na·tu·rel (ō nä-tü-rel′) *adj.* **1.** In a natural state; nude. **2.** Cooked simply. Said of food. [French, "in the natural."]

aunt (ănt, änt) *n.* **1.** The sister of one's father or mother. **2.** The wife of one's uncle. [Middle English *aunte,* from Norman French, from Old French *ante,* from Latin *amita,* paternal aunt.]

aunt·ie, aunt·y (ăn′tē, än′-) *n.* Variant of **aunt.** Used as a familiar form of address.

Aunt Sally *n., pl.* **Aunt Sallies.** *British.* **1.** A fairground game in which sticks or balls are thrown at a wooden dummy. **2. a.** Someone or something that is the object of insults or derision. **b.** Any easy target of criticism; a scapegoat. [After the fairground dummy, usually the head of an old woman smoking a clay pipe.]

au pair (ō pâr′) *n.* Also **au pair girl.** A foreign girl who lives with a family, doing housework and looking after the children in exchange for room and board.
~*intr.v.* **au paired, au pairing, au pairs.** To work as an au pair. [French, "on equal basis," by exchange of services rather than money.]

au·ra (ôr′ə) *n., pl.* **-ras** or **aurae** (ôr′ē). **1.** An invisible breath or emanation. **2.** A distinctive air or quality that characterizes a person or thing: *an aura of nobility.* **3.** An emanation of light said to surround a person and to be visible to those claiming psychic powers. **4.** A subjective sensation, as of a cold breeze or flashes of light, preceding the onset of an attack in certain nervous disorders, especially epilepsy. [Middle English, from Latin, from Greek, : "breath, breeze," akin to *aēr,* AIR.]

au·ral¹ (ôr′əl) *adj.* Of, pertaining to, or perceived by the ear.
~*n.* An aural examination in music. [Latin *auris,* ear + -AL.]

aural² (ôr′əl) *adj.* Characterized by or pertaining to an aura.

au·rar. Plural of **eyrir.**

au·re·ate (ôr′ē-ĭt) *adj.* **1.** Of a golden color; gilded. **2.** Speaking in or characterized by a florid and pompous style. [Middle English *aureat,* from Medieval Latin *aureātus,* from Latin *aureus,* golden, from *aurum,* gold.] —**au·re·ate·ly** *adv.* —**au·re·ate·ness** *n.*

Au·re·li·an (ô-rēl′yən). Latin name, "Lucius Domitius Aurelianus." (A.D. *c.* 215–75). Roman emperor (270–75). In a series of victories he held the barbarians in check beyond the Rhine and regained Britain, Gaul, Spain, Syria, and Egypt for the empire.

au·re·ole (ôr′ē-ōl′) *n.* Also **au·re·o·la** (ô-rē′ə-lə). **1.** A circle of light or radiance surrounding the head or body of a representation of a deity or holy person; a halo. **2.** A bright, circumferential region around a luminous celestial body, such as the sun or moon, especially when observed through a haze or fog. **3.** *Geology.* A zone around an intrusion which has been altered by the heat and chemicals generated during the intrusion of the magma. [Middle English *aureole, auriole,* from Old French *auriole,* from Medieval Latin *(corōna) aureola,* golden (crown), from Latin *aureolus,* golden; from *aurum,* gold.]

Au·re·o·my·cin (ôr′ē-ō-mī′sĭn) *n.* A trademark for **chlortetracycline** *(see).*

au·re·us (ôr′ē-əs) *n., pl.* **aurei** (ôr′ē-ī′). A gold coin of the late Roman Republic and of the Roman Empire.

au re·voir (ō rə-vwär′) *interj. French.* Until we meet again; good-by.

au·ric (ôr′ĭk) *adj.* Of, pertaining to, derived from, or containing gold, especially with valence 3. [Latin *aurum,* gold.]

au·ri·cle (ôr′ĭ-kəl) *n.* Also **au·ric·u·la** (ô-rĭk′yə-lə) *pl.* **-lae** (-lē′) or **-las.** **1.** *Anatomy.* **a.** The external part of the ear; the pinna. **b.** An **atrium** *(see)* of the heart. **2.** *Biology.* Any earlike part, process, or appendage, especially at the base of an organ. [Latin *auricula,* diminutive of *auris,* ear.] —**au·ri·cled** (ôr′ĭ-kəld) *adj.*

au·ric·u·la (ô-rĭk′yə-lə) *n., pl.* **-las** or **-lae** (-lē′). **1.** A species of primrose, *Primula auricula,* native to the Alps but widely cultivated, having clusters of variously colored flowers. Also called "bear's-ear." **2.** Variant of **auricle.** [New Latin, "little ear" (from the shape of the leaves), from Latin, AURICLE.]

au·ric·u·lar (ô-rĭk′yə-lər) *adj.* **1.** Of or pertaining to the sense or organs of hearing. **2.** Perceived by or spoken into the ear: *an auricular confession.* **3.** Having the shape of an ear. **4.** Of or pertaining to an auricle of the heart.
~*n.* **auriculars.** The feathers covering the opening of the ear in some birds, such as owls. [Late Latin *auriculāris,* from *auricula,* AURICLE.] —**au·ric·u·lar·ly** *adv.*

au·ric·u·late (ô-rĭk′yə-lĭt, -lāt′) *adj.* Also **au·ric·u·lat·ed** (-lā′tĭd). **1.** Having ears or earlike parts or extensions: *an auriculate leaf.* **2.** Having the shape of an ear. [Latin *auricula,* AURICLE.] —**au·ric·u·late·ly** *adv.*

au·rif·er·ous (ô-rĭf′ər-əs) *adj.* Containing gold; gold-bearing. Said of rocks or gravels. [Latin *aurifer* : *aurum,* gold + -FER.]

au·ri·form (ôr′ə-fôrm′) *adj.* Ear-shaped. [Latin *auris,* ear + -FORM.]

Au·ri·ga (ô-rī′gə) *n.* A constellation in the Northern Hemisphere near Lynx and Perseus. Also called the "Charioteer." [Latin *aurīga,* charioteer.]

Au·rig·na·cian (ôr′ĭg-nā′shən, ôr′ēn-yā′shən) *adj. Sometimes* **aurignacian.** *Archaeology.* Of or relating to the Old World Upper Paleolithic culture between Mousterian and Solutrean, associated with Cro-Magnon man, and characterized by artifacts such as figures of stone and bone, paintings on the walls of caves, and the use of dress and adornment. [After *Aurignac,* commune in the French Pyrenees, near which such artifacts were found.]

au·rochs (ou′rŏks′, ô′-) *n.* **1.** An extinct bovine mammal, *Bos taurus primigenius,* of northern Africa, Europe, and western Asia, believed to be the forerunner of domestic cattle. Also called "urus." **2.** Loosely, the European bison, or wisent. [German, from Old High German *ūrohso* : *ūro,* bison, from Germanic *ūrus* (unattested) + *ohso,* ox.]

au·ro·ra (ô-rôr′ə, ô-rōr′ə) *n., pl.* **-ras** or **aurorae** (ô-rôr′ē, ô-rōr′ē). **1.** High-altitude, many-colored, flashing luminosity, visible in night skies of polar and sometimes temperate zones, and thought to be caused by the capture of charged particles, especially ones of solar origin, by the earth's magnetic field. Compare **airglow.** **2.** *Poetic.* The dawn. **3.** *Rare.* An early part or stage; a beginning. [Latin *aurōra,* dawn.]

Au·ro·ra (ô-rôr′ə, ô-rōr′ə). *Roman Mythology.* The goddess of the dawn, identified with the Greek goddess Eos.

aurora aus·tra·lis (ô-strā′lĭs) *n.* Aurora occurring in southern regions. Also called "southern lights." [New Latin : AURORA + AUSTRAL.]

aurora bo·re·al·is (bôr′ē-ăl′ĭs, bōr′-) *n.* Aurora occurring in northern regions. Also called "northern lights." [New Latin : AURORA + BOREAL.]

au·ro·ral (ô-rôr′əl, ô-rōr′-) *adj.* Also *poetic* **au·ro·re·an** (ô-rôr′ē-ən, ô-rōr′-) (for sense 1). **1.** Pertaining to or resembling the dawn. **2.** *Meteorology.* Pertaining to, caused by, or like an aurora. —**au·ro·ral·ly** *adv.*

au·rous (ôr′əs) *adj.* Of or pertaining to gold, especially with valence 1. [Late Latin *aurōsus,* from Latin *aurum,* gold.]

au·rum (ôr′əm) *n. Symbol* **Au** The element gold. [Latin, gold.]

Aus. **1.** Australia; Australian. **2.** Austria; Austrian.

Auschwitz. See **Oświęcim.**

aus·cul·tate (ô′skəl-tāt′) *tr.v.* **-tated, -tating, -tates.** *Medicine.* To examine by auscultation. [Back-formation from AUSCULTATION.] —**aus·cul·ta·tive** *adj.* —**aus·cul·ta·to·ry** (ô-skŭl′tə-tôr′ē, -tōr′ē) *adj.*

aus·cul·ta·tion (ô′skəl-tā′shən) *n.* **1.** *Medicine.* Diagnostic monitoring with a stethoscope or other instrument of sounds within the body. **2.** The act of listening. [Latin *auscultātiō* (stem *auscultātiōn-*), from *auscultāre,* to listen to.]

aus·form (ôs′fôrm′) *tr.v.* **-formed, -forming, -forms.** To subject (a metal, especially steel) to deformation, quenching, and tempering while it is in the austenite temperature range, in order to improve its wear properties. [*Aus*tenitic de*form.*]

Aus·gleich (ous′glīKH′) *n., pl.* **-gleiche** (-glī′KHə). *German.* Compromise; agreement; specifically, the treaty between Hungary and Austria in 1867 organizing their dual monarchy.

Augustus *Bronze head portraying Rome's first emperor. The head is part of a 2,000-year-old Roman statue found at Merowe in the Sudan.*

aurochs *The earliest cattle in Europe to be domesticated, aurochs were large, brown or black, and had horns measuring as much as 1 meter (3 feet) from tip to tip. They are thought to have become extinct in 1627.*

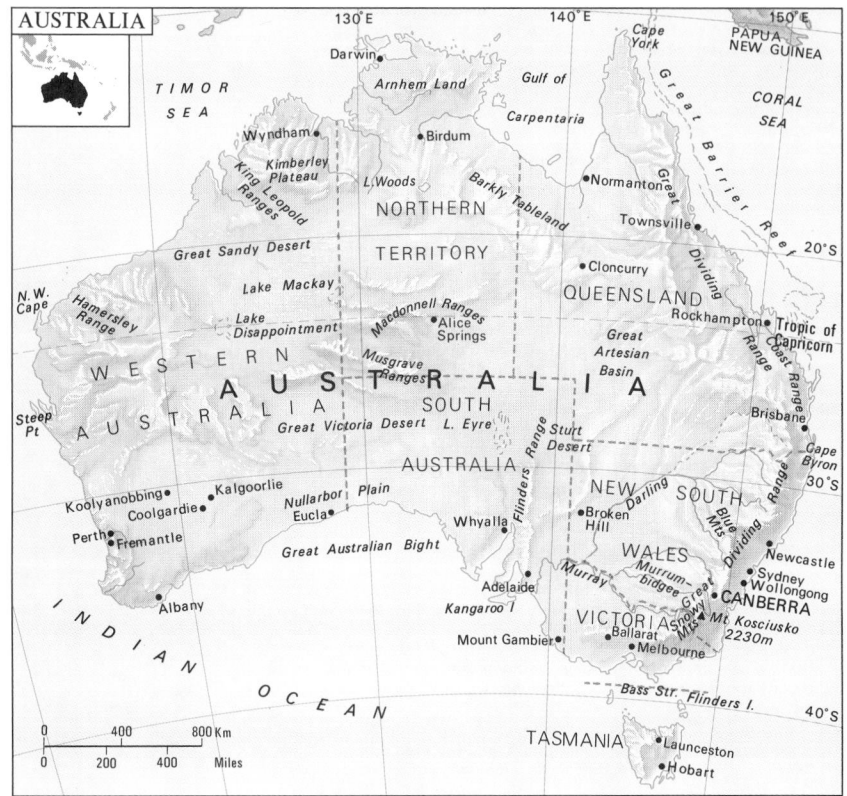

AUSTRALIA

aus·pex (ô'spĕks') *n., pl.* **auspices** (ô'spə-sēz'). An augur of ancient Rome, especially one who interpreted omens taken from the actions of birds. [Latin. See **auspice.**]

aus·pi·cate (ô'spĭ-kāt') *tr.v.* **-cated, -cating, -cates.** *Rare.* To begin or inaugurate with a ceremony designed to bring good luck. [Latin *auspicāri,* from *auspex,* bird augur. See **auspice.**]

aus·pice (ô'spĭs) *n., pl.* **auspices** (ô'spə-sēz'). **1.** *Usually* **auspices.** Protection or support; patronage. Used in the phrase *under the auspices of.* Compare **aegis. 2.** A portent, omen, or augury, especially when observed in the actions of birds. **3.** Observation of and divination from the actions of birds. [Latin *auspicium,* bird divination, from *auspex* (stem *auspic-*), a bird augur : *au-,* from *avis,* bird + *-spex,* from *specere,* to look.]

aus·pi·cious (ô-spĭsh'əs) *adj.* **1.** Attended by favorable circumstances; promising. **2.** Marked by success; fortunate; prosperous. —See Synonyms at **favorable.** —**aus·pi·cious·ly** *adv.* —**aus·pi·cious·ness** *n.*

Aus·sie (ô'sē) *n. Slang.* An Australian. —**Aus·sie** *adj.*

Aust. 1. Australia; Australian. **2.** Austria; Austrian.

Aus·ten (ôs'tən), **Jane** (1775–1817). English novelist. Although her subject matter and personal experience may have been limited, her novels, which include *Sense and Sensibility* (1811), *Pride and Prejudice* (1813), *Mansfield Park* (1814), and *Emma* (1816), are notable for their incisive social satire, irony, and wit and for their fine observation of manners and morality.

aus·ten·ite (ôs'tə-nīt') *n.* **1.** A nonmagnetic solid solution of ferric carbide or carbon in iron, used in making corrosive-resistant steel. **2.** Any solid solution based on the gamma phase of iron, especially when stabilized by the addition of nickel. [After Sir William Roberts-Austen (1843–1902), British metallurgist.]

aus·ten·it·ic (ôs'tə-nĭt'ĭk) *adj.* Designating a form of steel that con-

tains sufficient nickel, nickel and chromium, or manganese to maintain the structure of austenite: *austenitic stainless steel.*

Aus·ter (ôs'tər) *n. Poetic.* The south wind. [Latin *auster†,* south wind, the south.]

aus·tere (ô-stîr') *adj.* **1.** Severe or stern in disposition or appearance; somber; grave: *"an austere man that never laughed or smiled"* (Alan Paton). **2.** Strict or severe in moral discipline; ascetic. **3.** Without adornment or ornamentation; simple; bare. **4.** *Archaic.* Bitter or sour to the taste. —See Synonyms at **severe.** [Middle English, from Old French, from Latin *austērus,* from Greek *austēros,* harsh, rough, severe.] —**aus·tere·ly** *adv.* —**aus·tere·ness** *n.*

aus·ter·i·ty (ô-stĕr'ə-tē) *n., pl.* **-ties. 1.** The quality of being austere. **2.** Severely simple living conditions, especially as an economic policy: *wartime austerity.* **3.** *Usually* **austerities.** An ascetic habit or practice: *Hermits were renowned for their austerities.*

Aus·ter·litz (ô'stər-lĭts'). A town in Moravia, in southern Czechoslovakia. Nearby, Napoleon won a brilliant victory (December 2, 1805) over the Russian and Austrian armies under Czar Alexander I and Emperor Francis II. Tolstoy described the battle in his *War and Peace.*

Aus·tin (ôs'tən) *adj.* Augustinian. Now used only in the phrase *Austin Friars.* [Shortening of *Augustine.*]

Austin. The capital of Texas, in the south-central part of the state, on the Colorado River. It is the commercial center of a large ranching, poultry, dairy, cotton, and grain area, with diversified manufactures. The main campus of the University of Texas is in Austin.

Austin, Stephen Fuller (1793–1836). Colonizer and political leader in Texas. He founded a colony in the area in 1822. Although he originally worked to make Texas a state of Mexico, he helped the Texas settlers gain their independence in 1836.

aus·tral (ôs'trəl) *adj.* **1.** Of, pertaining to, or coming from the south: *austral winds.* **2. Austral.** Australian; Australasian. [Middle English, from Latin *austrālis,* from *auster†,* south, AUSTER.]

Aus·tral·a·sia (ôs'trəl-ā'zhə, -shə). An imprecise term referring to lands in the Pacific Ocean. The name is used in a broad sense to include the Malay Archipelago, Micronesia, Polynesia, and Melanesia in addition to New Zealand, the island of New Guinea, and Australia. It is used more commonly to refer simply to Australia and New Zealand and their dependencies (or former dependencies), such as Papua New Guinea. —**Aus·tral·a·sian** *n. & adj.*

Aus·tra·lia (ô-strāl'yə). *Abbr.* **Aus., Aust.** Island commonwealth lying between the Indian and Pacific oceans. Nearly half of it is desert or dry scrub. About 85 percent of its people live in towns, and nearly 20 percent of its workers are in manufacturing, the chief products being steel, aluminum, vehicles, textiles, and machinery. However, minerals, wool, beef, and sugar are still the main exports. The population, about 75 percent of British or Irish descent, includes some 140,000 aborigines. Dutch navigators were the first Europeans to sight Australia (1606), and Capt. James Cook claimed the east coast for Britain (1770). The first colony, a penal settlement, was established at Sydney Cove (1788), and by 1850 there were colonies at what are now the other six state capitals. Discovery of gold in New South Wales and Victoria (1851) stimulated their growth, and in 1901 the Commonwealth of Australia, a federation of six former colonies (Tasmania, Victoria, South Australia, Western Australia, Queensland, and New South Wales), was born. Northern Territory came under federal control, and the Capital Territory was created in 1911. Australia became a dominion within the Commonwealth in 1931. Since 1945 traditional ties with Europe have weakened. Australia signed the ANZUS Pact (1952) and was a member of SEATO (1954–77); some Australians now favor a republican government. Area, 7,686,848 square kilometers (2,967,123 square miles). Population, 13,500,000. Capital, Canberra.

Australia Day *n.* In Australia, the national holiday held on January 26 or the first Monday following it to commemorate the landing of the British in 1788.

Aus·tra·lian (ô-strāl'yən) *n.* **1.** A native or citizen of the Commonwealth of Australia. **2.** An aborigine of Australia. **3.** Any of the languages of the Australian aborigines. **4.** English as it is spoken by Australians.

~adj. **1.** Of or pertaining to Australia or its inhabitants and their languages or cultures. **2.** *Ecology.* Of or designating the zoogeographic region that includes Australia, the islands adjacent to it, and New Guinea.

Australian Alps (ălps). A chain of mountain ranges forming a segment of the Great Dividing Range, occupying the southeastern corner of Australia.

Australian Antarctic Territory. A territory claimed by Australia, including all the islands and lands south of latitude 60° and between longitudes 160° and 45° east, except for Adélie Land.

Australian ballot *n.* A printed ballot that bears the names of all candidates and the texts of propositions and is distributed to the voter at the polls to be marked in secret.

Australian Capital Territory. *Abbr.* **A.C.T.** Formerly **Federal Capital Territory.** The name for the separate administrative unit enclosed by New South Wales in Australia, comprising the national capital, Canberra, and land around it. The territory has an area of 2,430 square kilometers (940 square miles).

Australian crawl *n.* A swimming stroke, a variation of the **crawl** (*see*) executed with an eight-beat flutter kick to each stroke.

Australian Rules *n. Used with a singular verb.* In Australia, a variety of football played on an oval field between teams of 18 players.

Australian terrier *n.* A small dog of a breed developed in Australia, having a coarse blackish coat with tan markings.

Aus·tra·loid (ôs′trə-loid′) *adj.* Of or pertaining to an ethnic group including the Australian aborigines. [AUSTRAL(IAN) + -OID.] —**Aus·tra·loid** *n.*

aus·tra·lo·pith·e·cine (ô-strā′lō-pĭth′ə-sīn′) *n.* Any of several extinct humanlike primates of the genera *Australopithecus* and *Paranthropus* or *Zinjanthropus,* known chiefly from late Pliocene and Pleistocene fossil remains found in southern and eastern Africa. ~*adj.* Of, pertaining to, or characteristic of the australopithecines. [New Latin *Australopithecus,* "southern ape" : AUSTRAL + New Latin *pithēcus,* ape, from Greek *pithēkos* (see **pithecanthropus**).]

Aus·tra·sia (ô-strā′zhə, -shə). The eastern portion of the Frankish kingdom from the 6th to the 8th century, consisting of parts of eastern France, western Germany, and the Netherlands. It was eventually absorbed by the empire of the Carolingian kings. —**Aus·tra·sian** *adj.*

Aus·tri·a (ô′strē-ə). *Abbr.* **Aus., Aust.** German **Ös·ter·reich** (œs′tə-rīKH). Landlocked Alpine republic in Central Europe. A former territory of Rome and of Charlemagne's empire, it came under the Habsburgs (1246), who were also Holy Roman Emperors (1438–1806). Under the statesman Prince Metternich, the arbiter of Europe, the Habsburgs built a vast multinational empire, which was a bulwark against the Turks. However, discontent grew within the empire. The Hungarians forced the dual monarchy of Austria-Hungary on Francis Joseph I (1867), and the assassination of the empire's heir, Archduke Francis Ferdinand, in Sarajevo (1914) unleashed World War I. In 1919 Austria was defeated, reduced to its German-speaking area, and became a republic. After suffering economic collapse, it was annexed by Hitler (1938). After World War II the Allies occupied the country until 1955, when a federal republic, obligated to remain neutral, was set up. Austria has reserves of oil, gas, lignite, and iron ore. It exports iron and steel, machinery, wooden goods, timber from its vast forests, and livestock products. Tourism is a major industry. Area, 83,849 square kilometers (32,366 square miles). Population, 7,500,000. Capital, Vienna. —**Aus·tri·an** *n. & adj.*

Aus·tri·a·Hun·ga·ry (ôs′trē-ə-hŭng′gə-rē). Two states ruled (1867–1918) by the Hapsburgs, one as emperors of Austria (Austria, Bohemia, Moravia, Austrian Poland, Austrian Silesia, and Slovenia), the other as kings of Hungary (Hungary, Transylvania, Croatia, and lands along the Dalmatian coast).

Austro–¹ *prefix.* Indicates southern; for example, **Austro-Asiatic.** [Latin *auster†,* the south, AUSTER.]

Austro–² *prefix.* Indicates Austrian; for example, **Austro-Hungarian.**

Aus·tro-A·si·at·ic, Aus·tro·a·si·at·ic (ôs′trō-ā′zhē-ăt′ĭk) *n.* A family of languages of southeastern Asia, believed to have once been dominant in northeastern India and Indochina. —**Austro-Asiatic** *adj.*

Aus·tro·Hun·gar·i·an (ôs′trō-hŭng-gâr′ē-ən) *adj.* Of or pertaining to Austria-Hungary.

Aus·tro·ne·sia (ôs′trō-nē′zhə, -shə). The islands in the Pacific Ocean, including Indonesia, Melanesia, Micronesia, and Polynesia.

Aus·tro·ne·sian (ôs′trō-nē′zhən, -shən) *adj.* Of or pertaining to Austronesia, its peoples, or their languages. ~*n.* A family of languages spoken in Austronesia, including the Indonesian, Melanesian, Micronesian, and Polynesian subfamilies. Also called "Malayo-Polynesian."

aut–. Variant of **auto–.**

au·ta·coid, au·to·coid (ô′tə-koid′) *n.* An organic substance, such as a hormone, formed by the cells of an organ and secreted into the blood or lymph to act on the cells of other parts of the organism. [AUT(O)- + Greek *akos,* cure.]

au·tar·chy (ô′tär′kē) *n., pl.* **-chies.** 1. Absolute rule or power; autocracy. 2. A country under such rule. 3. Variant of **autarky.** [Greek *autarkhia,* from *autarkhos,* self-governing : AUT(O)- + -ARCH.] —**au·tar·chic** (ô-tär′kĭk), **au·tar·chi·cal** *adj.*

au·tar·ky (ô′tär′kē) *n., pl.* **-kies.** 1. A policy of national self-sufficiency and nonreliance on imports or economic aid. 2. A self-sufficient region or country. [Greek *autarkeia,* self-sufficiency, from *autarkēs,* self-sufficient : AUT(O)- + *arkein,* to suffice.] —**au·tar·kic** (ô-tär′kĭk), **au·tar·ki·cal** *adj.*

au·te·col·o·gy (ô′tĭ-kŏl′ə-jē) *n.* The ecology of a species or an individual organism. Compare **synecology.** [AUT(O)- + ECOLOGY.]

auth. 1. authentic. 2. author. 3. authorized. 4. authority.

au·then·tic (ô-thĕn′tĭk) *adj. Abbr.* **auth.** 1. a. Conforming to fact and therefore worthy of trust, reliance, or belief: *authentic records.* b. Having an undisputed origin; genuine: *an authentic Chippendale chair.* 2. *Law.* Executed with due process of law: *an authentic deed.* 3. *Music.* a. Designating a medieval mode having a range from its final note to the octave above it. b. Designating a cadence with the dominant chord immediately preceding the tonic chord. Compare **plagal.** —See Synonyms at **real.** [Middle English *autentik,* from Old French *autentique,* from Late Latin *authenticus,* from Greek *authentikos,* genuine, authoritative, from *authentēs†,* perpetrator, author.] —**au·then·ti·cal·ly** *adj.*

au·then·ti·cate (ô-thĕn′tĭ-kāt′) *tr.v.* **-cated, -cating, -cates.** 1. To establish as worthy of belief: *authenticate a story.* 2. To confirm as genuine; prove or verify the origin of: *authenticate a painting.* 3. To invest (a deed, for example) with legal validity. —See Synonyms at **confirm.** —**au·then·ti·ca·tion** *n.* —**au·then·ti·ca·tor** (ô-thĕn′tĭ-kā′tər) *n.*

au·then·tic·i·ty (ô′thĕn-tĭs′ə-tē) *n.* The condition or quality of being authentic, trustworthy, or genuine. —See Synonyms at **truth.**

au·thor (ô′thər) *n.* 1. *Abbr.* **auth.** a. The original writer of a literary work, as a book, essay, or article. b. One who practices writing as a profession. c. An author's works collectively: *reading my favorite author.* 2. The beginner, originator, or creator of anything: *the author of the universe; the author of a theory.* ~*tr.v.* **authored, -thoring, -thors.** 1. To be the author of; write. 2. To originate; create: *author a new fashion.* [Middle English *autour,* from Old French *autor,* from Latin *auctor,* creator, from *augēre* (past participle *auctus*), to create, increase.] —**au·thor·i·al** (ô-thôr′ē-əl, ô-thōr′-) *adj.*

au·thor·ess (ô′thər-ĭs) *n.* A female author. Sometimes considered disparaging.

au·thor·i·tar·i·an (ə-thôr′ə-târ′ē-ən, ə-thōr′-, ô-) *adj.* 1. Characterized by or favoring absolute obedience to authority, as against individual freedom. 2. Favoring strong government powers. ~*n.* One who believes in or practices authoritarian policies or methods. —**au·thor·i·tar·i·an·ism** *n.*

au·thor·i·ta·tive (ə-thôr′ə-tā′tĭv, ə-thōr′-, ô-) *adj.* 1. Having or arising from proper authority; official: *authoritative sources.* 2. Having a commanding air; wielding authority: *an authoritative voice.* —**au·thor·i·ta·tive·ly** *adv.* —**au·thor·i·ta·tive·ness** *n.*

au·thor·i·ty (ə-thôr′ə-tē, ə-thōr′-, ô-) *n., pl.* **-ties.** *Abbr.* **auth.** 1. The right or power to act, command, enforce laws, exact obedience, determine, or judge. 2. a. A person or group invested with this right or power. b. **authorities.** Government officials having this right or power. Preceded by *the.* 3. Power delegated to others; authorization: *You have my authority to decide.* 4. *Often* **Authority.** A public agency or corporation with administrative powers limited to a specified field: *the Transit Authority.* 5. a. An accepted source of expert information or advice: *This book is an authority on civil law.* b. A quotation or citation from such a source used in defense or support of one's actions, opinions, or the like. 6. An expert in a given field: *an authority on plants.* 7. Power to influence or persuade resulting from knowledge or experience: *write with authority.* 8. A claim to be accepted or believed: *on the authority of the press.* 9. An authoritative statement or decision that provides adequate grounds for a course of action or that may be taken as a precedent. [Middle English *autorite, auctorite,* from Old French *auctorite,* from Latin *auctōritās* (stem *auctōritāt-*), from *auctor,* AUTHOR.]

au·thor·i·za·tion (ô′thər-ə-zā′shən) *n.* 1. The act of conferring authority; permission. 2. Written permission. 3. Legal power, right, or sanction.

au·thor·ize (ô′thə-rīz′) *tr.v.* **-ized, -izing, -izes.** 1. To grant authority or power to. 2. To approve or give permission for; sanction: *authorize a highway project.* 3. To be sufficient grounds for; justify. [Middle English *autorisen,* from Old French *autoriser,* from Medieval Latin *auctorizāre,* from Latin *auctor,* AUTHOR.] —**au·thor·iz·er** *n.*

au·thor·ized (ô′thə-rīzd′) *adj. Abbr.* **auth.** 1. Invested with authority; authoritative. 2. Having official permission. 3. Sanctioned by law or command.

Authorized Version *n. Abbr.* **A.V.** The **King James Bible** (see).

au·thor·ship (ô′thər-shĭp′) *n.* 1. The profession or occupation of writing. 2. A source or origin, as of a book or idea.

au·tism (ô′tĭz′əm) *n.* A condition of abnormal subjectivity marked by absorption in self-centered thought and behavior and an inability to communicate or to relate to other people. Also called "infantile autism." [New Latin *autismus* : AUT(O)- + -ISM.] —**au·tis·tic** (ô-tĭs′tĭk) *adj.*

au·to (ô′tō) *n., pl.* **-tos.** *Informal.* An automobile.

auto–, aut– *prefix.* Indicates: 1. Acting or directed from within; for example, **autogenesis, autism.** 2. Self; same; for example, **autobiography.** 3. Indicates self-propelled; automotive; for example, **autogiro.** [Greek, from *autos†,* self.]

auto. 1. automatic. 2. automotive.

au·to·an·ti·bod·y (ô′tō-ăn′tĭ-bŏd′ē) *n., pl.* **-ies.** An antibody that acts against cells of the organism in which it is formed. See **autoimmune.**

au·to·bahn (ou′tō-bän′) *n., pl.* **-bahns** or **-bahnen** (-bä′nən). A German expressway. [German *Autobahn* : AUTO- (automobile) + *Bahn,* road, from Middle High German *ban, bane.*]

au·to·bi·og·ra·phy (ô′tō-bī-ŏg′rə-fē, -bē-) *n., pl.* **-phies.** 1. The written story of one's own life; memoirs. 2. Such writings as a literary form. —**au·to·bi·og·ra·pher** *n.* —**au·to·bi·o·graph·ic** (ô′tō-bī′ə-grăf′ĭk), **au·to·bi·o·graph·i·cal** *adj.* —**au·to·bi·o·graph·i·cal·ly** *adv.*

au·to·ca·tal·y·sis (ô′tō-kə-tăl′ə-sĭs) *n., pl.* **-ses** (-sēz′). Catalysis of a chemical reaction by one of the products of the reaction.

au·to·ceph·a·lous (ô′tō-sĕf′ə-ləs) *adj.* Independent of outside authority; having its own head. Said especially of Eastern Christian churches. [Late Greek *autokephalos* : *auto-,* self + *kephalē,* head.]

au·to·chrome (ô′tə-krōm′) *n.* A photographic plate once used in three-color photography. [French : AUTO- + -CHROME.]

au·toch·thon (ô-tŏk′thən) *n., pl.* **-thons** or **-thones** (-thə-nēz′). 1. **autochthons** or **autochthones.** The earliest known or aboriginal inhabitants of a particular place. 2. *Ecology.* Any indigenous plant or animal. [Greek *autokhthōn,* "one sprung from the land itself," indigenous : AUTO- + *khthōn,* earth.]

au·toch·tho·nous (ô-tŏk′thə-nəs) *adj.* Also **au·toch·tho·nal** (ô-tŏk′thə-nəl), **au·toch·thon·ic** (ô′tŏk-thŏn′ĭk). Native to a particular place; aboriginal; indigenous. —**au·toch·thon·ism** (ô-tŏk′thə-nĭz′əm), **au·toch·tho·ny** *n.* —**au·toch·tho·nous·ly** *adv.*

au·to·clave (ô′tō-klāv′) *n.* A strong, pressurized, steam-heated vessel, used to establish special conditions for chemical reactions, for sterilization, and for cooking.

~*tr.v.* **autoclaved, -claving, -claves.** To process in an autoclave. [French, "self-locking" : AUTO- + Latin *clāvis*, key.]

autocoid. Variant of **autacoid.**

au·toc·ra·cy (ô-tŏk′rə-sē) *n., pl.* **-cies. 1.** Government by a single person having unlimited power; despotism. **2.** A country or state having this form of government. [From AUTOCRAT.]

au·to·crat (ô′tə-krăt′) *n.* **1.** A ruler having absolute or unrestricted power; a despot. **2.** Any arrogant and domineering person. [French *autocrate,* from Greek *autokratēs,* ruling by oneself : AUTO- + -CRAT.] —**au·to·crat·ic, au·to·crat·i·cal** *adj.* —**au·to·crat·i·cal·ly** *adv.*

au·to·cross (ô′tō-krôs′) *n. Chiefly British.* A form of automobile racing, with races held on a rough grass track.

au·to·da·fé (ou′tō-də-fā′, ô′tō-) *n., pl.* **au·tos-da-fé** (ou′tōz-, ô′tōz-). **1.** The public announcement of the sentences imposed on persons tried by the Inquisition. **2.** The public execution of these sentences by the secular authorities, especially the burning of condemned heretics at the stake. [Portuguese *auto da fé,* "act of the faith" : *auto,* act, from Latin *āctus,* ACT + *da,* of the + *fé,* faith, from Latin *fidēs.*]

au·to·di·dact (ô′tō-dī′dăkt′) *n.* A person who is self-taught. [Greek *autodidaktos,* self-taught : AUTO- + *didaktos,* taught (see didactic).] —**au·to·di·dac·tic** (ô′tō-dī-dăk′tĭk) *adj.*

au·to·dyne (ô′tə-dīn′) *n.* A heterodyne radio device in which one valve serves as both oscillator and detector. [AUTO- + (HETERO)-DYNE.] —**au·to·dyne** *adj.*

au·toe·cious (ô-tē′shəs) *adj. Biology.* Completing all stages of a life cycle on the same host. Said especially of certain rust fungi. Compare **heteroecious.** [AUT(O)- + -*oecious,* from Greek *oikos,* house.] —**au·toe·cism** (ô-tē′sĭz′əm) *n.*

au·to·er·o·tism (ô′tō-ĕr′ə-tĭz′əm) *n.* Also **au·to·e·rot·i·cism** (ô′-tō-ĭ-rŏt′ə-sĭz′əm). Self-arousal and self-satisfaction of sexual desire, as by masturbation. —**au·to·e·rot·ic** (ô′tō-ĭ-rŏt′ĭk) *adj.*

au·tog·a·my (ô-tŏg′ə-mē) *n.* **1.** *Botany.* Fertilization of a flower by its own pollen; self-fertilization. **2.** *Biology.* The union of nuclei within and arising from a single cell, as in certain protozoans. [AUTO- + -GAMY.] —**au·tog·a·mous** (ô-tŏg′ə-məs) *adj.*

au·to·gen·e·sis (ô′tō-jĕn′ə-sĭs) *n.* Also **au·tog·e·ny** (ô-tŏj′ə-nē). *Biology.* Abiogenesis *(see).* —**au·to·ge·net·ic** (ô′tō-jə-nĕt′ĭk) *adj.* —**au·to·ge·net·i·cal·ly** *adv.*

au·tog·e·nous (ô-tŏj′ə-nəs) *adj.* Also **au·to·gen·ic** (ô′tə-jĕn′ĭk). Self-generated; self-produced. [Greek *autogenēs,* self-producing : AUTO- + -GENOUS.] —**au·tog·e·nous·ly** *adv.*

au·to·gi·ro, au·to·gy·ro (ô′tō-jī′rō) *n., pl.* **-ros.** An aircraft powered by a conventional propeller and supported in flight by a freewheeling horizontal rotor mounted above the fuselage that provides lift. [AUTO- + Greek *guros,* circle.]

au·to·graft (ô′tō-grăft′, -grăft′) *n. Medicine.* A tissue graft obtained from the body of the recipient.

au·to·graph (ô′tə-grăf′, -gräf′) *n.* **1.** A person's own signature or handwriting. **2.** A manuscript in the author's handwriting. ~*tr.v.* **autographed, -graphing, -graphs. 1.** To write one's name or signature on or in; sign. **2.** To write in one's own handwriting. ~*adj.* **1.** Written in a person's own handwriting. **2.** Containing signatures or autographs. [Latin *autographum,* from Greek *autographon,* autograph manuscript, from *autographos,* written by oneself : AUTO- + -GRAPH.] —**au·to·graph·ic, au·to·graph·i·cal** *adj.* —**au·to·graph·i·cal·ly** *adv.*

au·tog·ra·phy (ô-tŏg′rə-fē) *n.* **1.** The writing of something in one's own handwriting. **2.** Autographs collectively.

au·to·harp (ô′tō-härp′) *n.* A musical instrument, similar to a zither, on which a desired chord can be selected by depressing a particular damper. [Originally a trademark : AUTO- (self) + HARP.]

au·to·hyp·no·sis (ô′tō-hĭp-nō′sĭs) *n.* **1.** The act or process of hypnotizing oneself. **2.** A self-induced hypnotic state. —**au·to·hyp·not·ic** (ô′tō-hĭp-nŏt′ĭk) *adj.*

au·to·im·mune (ô′tō-ĭ-myōon′) *adj.* Of, relating to, or caused by the action of antibodies against the body's own tissues: *an autoimmune disease.* —**au·to·im·mu·ni·ty** *n.* —**au·to·im·mu·ni·za·tion** (ô′tō-ĭm′yə-nə-zā′shən) *n.*

au·to·in·fec·tion (ô′tō-ĭn-fĕk′shən) *n.* Infection, as with recurrent boils, caused by germs or viruses persisting on or in the body.

au·to·in·oc·u·la·tion (ô′tō-ĭn-ŏk′yə-lā′shən) *n.* **1.** Inoculation with a vaccine made from microorganisms derived from the recipient. **2.** A secondary infection caused by a disease already in the body.

au·to·in·tox·i·ca·tion (ô′tō-ĭn-tŏk′sə-kā′shən) *n.* Self-poisoning caused by endogenous microorganisms, metabolic wastes, or other toxins in the body. Also called "autotoxemia."

au·to·i·on·i·za·tion (ô′tō-ī′ə-nə-zā′shən) *n. Physics.* A process in which an excited atom or molecule emits an electron rather than a photon when it decays. See **Auger effect.**

au·to·load·ing (ô′tō-lō′dĭng) *adj.* **Semiautomatic** *(see).*

au·tol·y·sate (ô-tŏl′ə-sāt′, -zāt′) *n. Biochemistry.* An end product of autolysis.

au·tol·y·sin (ô-tŏl′ə-sĭn, ô′tə-lī′sĭn) *n. Biochemistry.* A substance that causes autolysis. [AUTOLYS(IS) + -IN.]

au·tol·y·sis (ô-tŏl′ə-sĭs) *n. Biochemistry.* The destruction of tissues or cells of an organism by self-produced enzymes. [AUTO- + -LYSIS.] —**au·to·lyt·ic** (ô′tə-lĭt′ĭk) *adj.*

au·to·mak·er (ô′tō-mā′kər) *n.* A manufacturer of automobiles.

au·to·mat (ô′tə-măt′) *n.* A restaurant in which the customers obtain food from closed compartments by inserting coins in a slot. [From trademark *Automat,* from AUTOMATIC.]

au·to·mate (ô′tə-māt′) *v.* **-mated, -mating, -mates.** —*tr.* **1.** To convert (a process, factory, or machine) to automation. **2.** To control or operate by automation. —*intr.* To convert to or make use of automation. [Back-formation from AUTOMATIC.]

au·to·mat·ic (ô′tə-măt′ĭk) *adj. Abbr.* **auto. 1. a.** Acting or operating in a manner essentially independent of external influence or control; self-moving. **b.** Self-regulating. **2.** Lacking volition, intention, or conscious planning; involuntary; reflex. **3.** Occurring as a matter of course or routine: *automatic weekly inspections.* **4.** Having an automatic transmission. Said of a motor vehicle. **5.** Capable of firing continuously until ammunition is exhausted. Said of firearms. Compare **semiautomatic.** —See Synonyms at **spontaneous.** ~*n.* **1.** An automatic firearm, especially an automatic pistol. **2.** An automatic machine, vehicle, or device. [Greek *automatos,* acting by itself, spontaneous, acting of one's own will : AUTO- + -*matos,* willing.] —**au·to·mat·i·cal·ly** *adv.*

au·tom·a·tic·i·ty (ô-tŏm′ə-tĭs′ə-tē) *n.* **1.** The state of being automatic. **2.** Automatic action.

automatic pilot *n.* An aircraft control mechanism that automatically maintains altitude, preset course, and steadiness. Also called "autopilot," "robot pilot."

automatic pistol *n.* A pistol that can be fired automatically or semiautomatically.

automatic rifle *n.* A light machine gun that can be fired automatically or semiautomatically, normally the latter.

automatic transmission *n.* A device in a motor vehicle that enables gear changes to be operated mechanically rather than manually according to car or engine speed.

au·to·ma·tion (ô′tə-mā′shən) *n.* **1.** Automatically controlled operation of a process, equipment, or a system. **2.** The act or process of conversion to such operation. **3.** The totality of mechanical and electronic techniques and equipment used to achieve such operation. **4.** The condition of being automatically controlled or operated. [AUTOM(ATIC) + -ATION.] —**au·to·ma·tive** *adj.*

au·tom·a·tism (ô-tŏm′ə-tĭz′əm) *n.* **1. a.** The state or quality of being automatic. **b.** Automatic mechanical action. **2.** *Philosophy.* The theory that all living organisms are automatons. **3.** *Physiology.* **a.** The automatic operation of organs and cells, such as the beating of the heart. **b.** Performance of an act without conscious control, as in the operation of the reflexes. **4.** The effort at suspension of consciousness made by certain surrealist writers and artists in order to express subconscious ideas and feelings. [French *automatisme* : *automate,* AUTOMATON + -*isme,* -ISM.] —**au·tom·a·tist** *n.*

au·tom·a·tize (ô-tŏm′ə-tīz′) *tr.v.* **-tized, -tizing, -tizes.** To make automatic.

au·tom·a·ton (ô-tŏm′ə-tən, -tŏn′) *n., pl.* **-tons** or **-ta** (-tə). **1.** See **robot** (sense 2). **2.** One that behaves in an automatic or mechanical fashion. [Latin, self-operating machine, from Greek *automaton,* neuter of *automatos,* AUTOMATIC.] —**au·tom·a·tous** *adj.*

au·to·mo·bile (ô′tō-mō-bēl′, -mō′bēl′, ô′tə-mō-bēl′) *n.* A self-propelled passenger vehicle that usually has four wheels and an internal-combustion engine, used for land transport. [French : AUTO- + MOBILE.] —**au·to·mo·bil·ist** *n.*

au·to·mo·tive (ô′tə-mō′tĭv) *adj. Abbr.* **auto. 1.** Self-moving; self-propelling. **2.** Of or pertaining to self-propelled vehicles.

au·to·net·ics (ô′tə-nĕt′ĭks) *n. Used with a singular verb.* The study of automatic guidance and control systems. [AUTO- + -*netics,* as in CYBERNETICS.]

au·to·nom·ic (ô′tə-nŏm′ĭk) *adj.* **1.** Of, relating to, or controlled by the autonomic nervous system. **2.** Resulting from internal causes; self-generated; spontaneous. —**au·to·nom·i·cal·ly** *adv.*

autonomic nervous system *n.* The division of the vertebrate nervous system that regulates involuntary action, as of the intestines, heart, and glands, and consists of the **sympathetic nervous system** and the **parasympathetic nervous system** *(both of which see).*

au·ton·o·mous (ô-tŏn′ə-məs) *adj.* **1. a.** Independent. **b.** Self-contained. **2. a.** Independent of the laws of another state or government; self-governing. **b.** Of or pertaining to an autonomy. **3.** Autonomic. [Greek *autonomos,* self-ruling : AUTO- + *nomos,* law.] —**au·ton·o·mous·ly** *adv.*

au·ton·o·my (ô-tŏn′ə-mē) *n., pl.* **-mies. 1.** The condition or quality of being self-governing. **2.** Self-government or the right of self-government; self-determination; independence. **3.** A self-governing state, community, or group. **4.** A condition or personal independence. [Greek *autonomia,* from *autonomos,* AUTONOMOUS.] —**au·ton·o·mist** *n.*

au·to·phyte (ô′tə-fīt′) *n. Botany.* An autotrophic plant. [AUTO- + -PHYTE.] —**au·to·phyt·ic** (ô′tə-fĭt′ĭk) *adj.*

au·to·pi·lot (ô′tō-pī′lət) *n.* An **automatic pilot** *(see).*

au·to·plas·ty (ô′tō-plăs′tē) *n.* Surgical repair or replacement with tissue taken from another part of the patient's body. [AUTO- + -PLASTY.] —**au·to·plas·tic** *adj.* —**au·to·plas·ti·cal·ly** *adv.*

au·top·sy (ô′tŏp′sē, ô′təp-) *n., pl.* **-sies.** The examination and dissection of a dead body to determine the cause of death. Also called "necropsy," "post-mortem." [New Latin *autopsia,* from Greek, a seeing for oneself : AUT(O)- + Greek *opsis,* sight.] —**au·top·sy** *v.*

au·to·ra·di·og·ra·phy (ô′tō-rā′dē-ŏg′rə-fē) *n.* A process for producing an image of the amount and distribution of radioactive material in an object by means of direct exposure to a photographic plate to radiation emitted by the object. Also called "radioautography." —**au·to·ra·di·o·graph** (ô′tō-rā′dē-ə-grăf′, -gräf′) *n.* —**au·to·ra·di·o·graph·ic** *adj.*

au·to·ro·ta·tion (ô'tō-rō-tā'shən) n. Rotation of the blades of a helicopter in free unpowered descent.

au·to·some (ô'tə-sōm') n. Any chromosome that is not a sex chromosome. [AUTO- + (CHROMO)SOME.] —**au·to·so·mal** adj.

au·to·sug·ges·tion (ô'tō-səg-jĕs'chən) n. Psychology. The process by which a person induces self-acceptance of an opinion, belief, or plan of action. —**au·to·sug·gest** v. —**au·to·sug·gest·i·bil·i·ty** n. —**au·to·sug·gest·i·ble** adj. —**au·to·sug·ges·tive** adj.

au·tot·o·mize (ô-tŏt'ə-mīz') v. -mized, -mizing, -mizes. —tr. To cause the autotomy of (a body part). —intr. To undergo autotomy.

au·tot·o·my (ô-tŏt'ə-mē) n. Zoology. The spontaneous casting off of a body part, such as the tail of certain lizards, for self-protection. —**au·to·tom·ic** (ô'tə-tŏm'ĭk) adj.

au·to·tox·e·mi·a (ô'tō-tŏk-sē'mē-ə) n. Also **au·to·tox·i·co·sis** (ô'-tō-tŏk'sĭ-kō'sĭs). Autointoxication (see).

au·to·tox·in (ô'tō-tŏk'sĭn) n. A poison that acts on the organism in which it is generated. —**au·to·tox·ic** adj.

au·to·trans·form·er (ô'tō-trăns-fôr'mər) n. An electrical transformer in which the primary and secondary coils have some or all windings in common.

au·to·troph (ô'tə-trŏf', -trōf') n. Biology. An autotrophic organism, such as a green plant. [Back-formation from AUTOTROPHIC.]

au·to·tro·phic (ô'tə-trō'fĭk, -trŏf'ĭk) adj. Biology. Designating or characterizing plants or certain microorganisms capable of manufacturing their own food from inorganic materials, as in photosynthesis. —**au·to·tro·phi·cal·ly** adv. —**au·tot·ro·phy** (ô-tŏt'rə-fē) n.

aut·ox·i·da·tion (ôt-ŏk'sə-dā'shən) n. Chemistry. 1. An oxidation reaction that involves atmospheric oxygen as the oxidizing agent. 2. An oxidation reaction that is induced by a second reaction taking place in the system.

au·tumn (ô'təm) n. 1. The season of the year between summer and winter, strictly lasting from the autumnal equinox to the winter solstice and considered to be from September to November in the Northern Hemisphere and from March to May in the Southern Hemisphere. Also called "fall." 2. A time or period of maturity verging on decline: in the autumn of one's life. [Middle English autumpne, from Old French autompne, from Latin autumnus, perhaps of Etruscan origin.] —**au·tum·nal** (ô-tŭm'nəl) adj. —**au·tum·nal·ly** adv.

autumnal equinox n. 1. The **equinox** (see) of September 22 or 23 in the Northern Hemisphere, or March 21 or 22 in the Southern Hemisphere, when the sun crosses the celestial equator going toward the equator, marking the start of autumn. 2. Astronomy. The point in Virgo on the celestial sphere at which the celestial equator and the ecliptic intersect. Compare **vernal equinox**.

autumn crocus n. A plant, Colchicum autumnale, native to Europe and northern Africa, having pink or purplish flowers that bloom in the autumn. Also called "meadow saffron."

au·tun·ite (ô-tŭn'īt', ô'tən-īt') n. A yellowish fluorescent, minor ore of uranium with composition $Ca(UO_2)_2(PO_4)_2 \cdot 10\text{-}12H_2O$. [After Autun, France, where it was discovered.]

Au·vergne (ō-vârn') n. A mainly agricultural region and former province of central France.

aux. auxiliary.

aux·e·sis (ôg-zē'sĭs, ôk-sē'-) n. Biology. An increase in the size of a cell or tissue without cell division. [Greek auxēsis, growth, from auxanein, to grow, increase.]

aux·il·ia·ry (ôg-zĭl'yər-ē, -zĭl'ər-ē) adj. Abbr. aux. 1. Giving assistance or support; aiding; helping. 2. Subsidiary; supplementary; additional. 3. Held in or used as a reserve: auxiliary troops. 4. Nautical. Equipped with a motor to supplement the sails.

~n., pl. auxiliaries. 1. One that assists or helps; an assistant. 2. A group or organization that assists or is supplementary to a larger one. 3. auxiliaries. Foreign troops serving a country in wartime. 4. An auxiliary verb. 5. Nautical. A sailing vessel equipped with a motor. 6. Naval. A vessel for use in other than combat services, such as a supply ship. [Latin auxiliārius, from auxilium, help.]

auxiliary verb n. Grammar. A verb that accompanies particular forms of the main verb of a clause to form a phrasal unit expressing the tense, mood, voice, or aspect of the main verb. Have, may, can, must, and will are some auxiliary verbs, as in He will come.

aux·in (ôk'sĭn) n. Any of several plant hormones, or similar synthetic substances, that affect growth by increasing cell elongation. [Greek auxein, to grow + -IN] —**aux·in·ic** adj.

aux·o·chrome (ôk'sə-krōm) n. A group of atoms that produces or intensifies the color of a dye. [auxo- (increasing), from Greek auxein, to grow + -CHROME.]

Av (ŏv, äb) n. Also **Ab** (äb, ôv). The 11th month of the year on the Hebrew calendar, usually coinciding with August. See feature at **calendar**. [Hebrew ābh, from Akkadian abu.]

av. 1. avenue. 2. average. 3. avoirdupois.

Av. avenue.

a.v. ad valorem.

A.V. 1. audio-visual. 2. Authorized Version.

a·vail (ə-vāl') v. availed, availing, avails. —tr. To be of use or advantage to; assist; help. —intr. To be of use value, or advantage; serve. —**avail oneself of.** To make use of.

~n. Use, benefit, or advantage. Now used chiefly in the phrase to or of no avail. [Middle English availen : A- (intensive) + vailen, to avail, from Old French valoir (stem vail-), to be worth, from Latin valēre, to be strong, be worth.] —**a·vail·ing·ly** adv.

a·vail·a·ble (ə-vā'lə-bəl) adj. 1. Accessible for use; obtainable. 2. At the disposal of an employer, visitor, or the like. —**a·vail·a·bil·i·ty,**

a·vail·a·ble·ness n. —**a·vail·a·bly** adv.

av·a·lanche (ăv'ə-lănch', -länch') n. 1. A fall or slide of a large mass of snow, rock, or other material down a mountainside. 2. Something resembling such an overwhelming fall or slide.

~v. avalanched, -lanching, -lanches. —intr. To fall, as an avalanche. —tr. To overwhelm. [French, from Swiss French avalantse, altered (through influence of avaler, to descend) from Savoyard lavantse, from Vulgar Latin (unattested) labanca†.]

avalanche lily n. A plant, Erythronium montanum, of western North America, having nodding white flowers. [So called because it grows near the snow line and blooms when the snow begins to melt.]

Av·a·lon (ăv'ə-lŏn'). Celtic Mythology. An island paradise in the western seas where King Arthur and other heroes went at death.

a·vant-garde (ä'vänt-gärd'; French ä-väN-gàrd') n. A group, as of writers and artists, regarded as pre-eminent in the invention and application of new styles and techniques in a given field.

~adj. 1. Of or belonging to the avant-garde, as in the arts. 2. Ahead of the times. [French, VANGUARD.]

av·a·rice (ăv'ə-rĭs) n. An extreme desire to amass wealth; greed; cupidity. [Middle English, from Old French, from Latin avāritia, from avārus, greedy, from avēret, to desire.]

av·a·ri·cious (ăv'ə-rĭsh'əs) adj. Immoderately fond of accumulating wealth. —**av·a·ri·cious·ly** adv. —**av·a·ri·cious·ness** n.

a·vast (ə-văst', ə-väst') interj. Used as a nautical command to stop: Avast heaving there. [Shortened from Dutch houd vast, "hold fast" : houd, imperative of houden, to hold, + vast, fast.]

av·a·tar (ăv'ə-tär') n. 1. a. One regarded as the incarnation or embodiment of some known model or category. b. An entity regarded as an extreme or notably complete manifestation of its kind; exemplar; archetype. 2. In Hindu mythology, the descent to earth of a deity in human or animal form. Used as a generic term for the incarnations of Vishnu. [Sanskrit avatāra, descent, from avatarati, he descends : ava, down + tarati, he crosses.]

a·vaunt (ə-vônt', ə-vänt') interj. Archaic. Used as a command to be gone. [Middle English, from Old French avant, "forward," "go away!" See **vanguard**.]

avdp. avoirdupois.

A·ve (ä'vā) n., pl. Aves. The Ave Maria.

ave., Ave. avenue.

Ave·bur·y (ăv'bə-rē, -brē). A village on the Marlborough Downs, Wiltshire, in southern England. It is situated on one of the most important prehistoric sites in Europe, lying within a Neolithic ring of upright stones older and larger than those at Stonehenge.

A·ve Ma·ri·a (ä'vā mə-rē'ə). n. 1. A Roman Catholic prayer, based on the greetings of Gabriel and Elizabeth to the Virgin Mary. Luke 1:28, 42. Also called "Ave," "Hail Mary." 2. a. A recitation of this prayer. b. The hour when it is customarily said. 3. One of the small beads on a rosary used to count recitations of this prayer. [Middle English, from Medieval Latin, "Hail Mary!"]

a·venge (ə-vĕnj') v. avenged, avenging, avenges. —tr. 1. To take revenge or exact satisfaction for (a wrong or injury). 2. To take vengeance on behalf of. —intr. To take vengeance. [Middle English avengen : a-, from Latin ad-, to + vengen, to revenge, from Old French vengier, from Latin vindicāre, from vindex (stem vindic-), protector, avenger.] —**a·veng·er** n. —**a·veng·ing·ly** adv.

a·vens (ăv'ĭnz) n., pl. -enses or collectively avens. 1. Any of various plants of the genus Geum, having irregularly shaped leaves, white, yellow, or reddish flowers, and plumed seed clusters. 2. Any of several related plants of the genus Dryas, of mountainous and arctic regions. [Middle English avence, from Old French, from Medieval Latin avencia†.]

Av·en·tine (ăv'ən-tīn', -tēn'). One of the seven hills of Rome.

a·ven·tu·rine (ə-vĕn'chə-rēn', -rĭn) n. Also **a·ven·tu·rin** (ə-vĕn'-chə-rĭn). 1. An opaque or semitranslucent brown glass flecked with small metallic particles, often of copper or chromic oxide. 2. Any of several varieties of quartz or feldspar flecked with particles of mica, hematite, or other materials. Also called "sunstone." [French, from aventure, accident, ADVENTURE; so called because of its accidental discovery.] —**a·ven·tu·rine** adj.

av·e·nue (ăv'ə-nōō', -nyōō') n. Abbr. av., Av., ave., Ave. 1. a. A wide street or thoroughfare. b. Any path resembling such a thoroughfare. 2. a. A road, normally lined with trees. b. Chiefly British. A drive or road, usually tree-lined, leading to a country house. 3. An opening or means of approach to a given place, activity, or goal: new avenues of trade. [French, from Old French, approach, avenue, feminine past participle of avenir, to approach, arrive, from Latin advenīre, to come to : ad-, to + venīre, to come.]

a·ver (ə-vûr') tr.v. averred, averring, avers. 1. To declare in a positive manner; affirm. 2. Law. To assert formally as a fact; justify or prove (a plea). —See Synonyms at **assert**. [Middle English averren, from Old French averer, from Medieval Latin advērāre, to assert as true : ad-, to + vērus, true.] —**a·ver·ment** n. —**a·ver·ra·ble** adj.

av·er·age (ăv'rĭj, ăv'ər-ĭj) n. Abbr. av., avg. 1. Something such as an amount, degree, or standard that is considered typical, normal, or representative. 2. Mathematics. a. A number that typifies a set of numbers of which it is a function. b. The arithmetic mean (see). 3. A ratio, relative proportion, or degree indicating position or achievement: a goal average; batting averages. 4. Law. a. The incurrence of and loss due to damage at sea to a ship or cargo. b. The equitable distribution of such a loss among concerned parties. c. Any charges incurred through such a loss. —**on the average.** As a mean rate, amount, or the like.

~adj. 1. Of, pertaining to, or constituting a mathematical average.

avatar A representation of one of the incarnations, or avatars, of the Hindu god Vishnu. The carving is in the Horniman Museum, London.

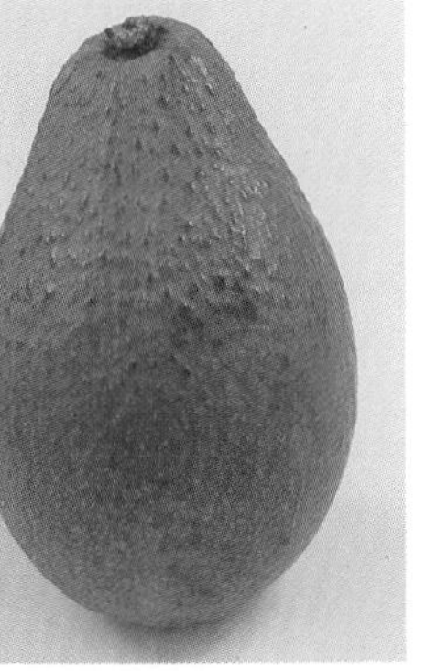

avocado *Avocado trees, which are native to the Americas, are now grown in other parts of the world for their pear-shaped fruit that are rich in protein, fats, and vitamins.*

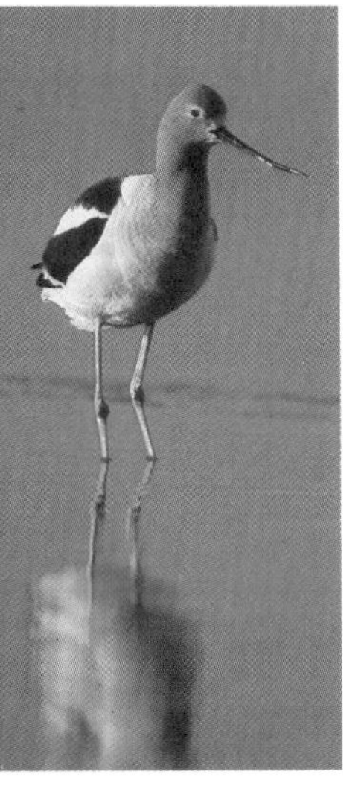

avocet *The upturned bills of this worldwide group of wading birds act as scoops. By sweeping them through the water, avocets collect the small crustaceans that form the major part of their diet.*

2. Typical; usual. **3.** *Law.* Assessed in compliance with the laws of average.
~*v.* **averaged, -aging, -ages.** —*tr.* **1.** To calculate the average of; especially, to calculate the arithmetic mean of (a set of numbers, quantities, or the like). **2.** To accomplish or obtain an average of: *average three hours work a day.* **3.** To distribute proportionately. —*intr.* **1.** To be or amount to an average. **2.** To buy or sell more goods or shares to obtain more than an average price. —**average out. 1.** *Informal.* To attain an average eventually. **2.** To work out so as to attain an average. [Alteration (by *-age,* as in *damage*) of obsolete *averie,* financial loss on damaged shipping, hence such loss shared equitably among investors, hence numerical average, from Old French *avarie,* damage to shipping, from Old Italian *avaria,* from Arabic *'awārīyah,* damaged goods, from *'awar,* fault, blemish.]
Synonyms: *fair, indifferent, mediocre, medium, middling, run-of-the-mill, so-so, tolerable.*

A·ver·ro·ës (ə-vĕr′ō-ēz′, ăv′ə-rō′ēz), (1126–98). *Arabic* **ibn-Rushd** (ĭb′ən-rŏŏsht′). Spanish-Arabian philosopher. He attempted to bring together the Islamic and Greek traditions of thought.

a·verse (ə-vûrs′) *adj.* **1.** Opposed; reluctant; disinclined. Usually used with *to.* **2.** *Botany.* Turned away from the central stem or axis: *averse leaves.* [Latin *āversus,* past participle of *āvertere,* AVERT.] —**a·verse·ly** *adv.* —**a·verse·ness** *n.*

a·ver·sion (ə-vûr′zhən, -shən) *n.* **1.** Intense dislike. Used with *to.* **2.** A feeling of extreme repugnance. **3.** A greatly disliked person or thing: *a pet aversion.*

aversion therapy *n.* A form of therapy designed to overcome an addiction or a harmful habit by associating it, in the mind of the patient, with something unpleasant, such as vomiting.

a·vert (ə-vûrt′) *tr.v.* **averted, averting, averts. 1.** To turn away: *avert one's eyes.* **2.** To ward off or prevent: *avert disaster.* [Middle English *averten,* from Old French *avertir,* from Vulgar Latin *āvertīre* (unattested), variant of Latin *āvertere* : *ab-,* away from + *vertere,* to turn.] —**a·vert·ed·ly** *adv.* —**a·vert·i·ble, a·vert·a·ble** *adj.*

Av·e·ry (ā′və-rē), **Oswald Theodore** (1877–1955). Canadian-born bacteriologist. In 1944 he isolated and identified DNA.

A·ves·ta (ə-vĕs′tə) *n.* The sacred writings of the Zoroastrian religion, the **Zend-Avesta** *(see).* [Middle Persian *apastāk†,* text.]

A·ves·tan (ə-vĕs′tən) *n.* The dialect of Old Iranian, in which the Avesta was written. Also called "Zend."
~*adj.* Of or pertaining to the Avesta or to the language in which it was written.

avg. average.

av·go·lem·o·no (ăv′gō-lĕm′ə-nō) *n.* A Greek chicken soup or sauce made with eggs and lemons. [Modern Greek *avgolemono* : *avgon,* egg + *lemonion,* lemon.]

a·vi·an (ā′vē-ən) *adj. Zoology.* Of, pertaining to, or characteristic of birds. [Latin *avis,* bird.]

a·vi·ar·y (ā′vē-ĕr′ē) *n., pl.* **-ies.** A large enclosure built to house live birds. [Latin *aviārium,* from *avis,* bird.] —**av·i·a·rist** *n.*

a·vi·a·tion (ā′vē-ā′shən, ăv′ē-) *n. Abbr.* **avn. 1.** The operation of aircraft. **2.** The production of aircraft. **3.** Military aircraft. [French, from Latin *avis,* bird.] —**a·vi·ate** *v.*

aviation medicine *n.* The branch of medicine comprising **aeromedicine** and **space medicine** *(both of which see).*

a·vi·a·tor (ā′vē-ā′tər, ăv′ē-) *n.* One who operates an aircraft; pilot. [French *aviateur,* from *aviation,* AVIATION.]

a·vi·a·trix (ā′vē-ā′trĭks, ăv′ē-) *n., pl.* **-trixes.** A woman who operates an aircraft.

Av·i·cen·na (ăv′ə-sĕn′ə), (980–1037). *Arabic* **ibn-Si·na** (ĭb′ən-sē′nə). Persian philosopher and physician. His most famous work was the *Canon of Medicine.*

a·vi·cul·ture (ā′vĭ-kŭl′chər, ăv′ĭ-) *n.* The raising or keeping of birds. [Latin *avis,* bird + CULTURE.] —**a·vi·cul·tur·ist** *n.*

av·id (ăv′ĭd) *adj.* **1. a.** Eager. Often used with *of* or *for*: *avid for adventure.* **b.** Greedy. **2.** Enthusiastic; ardent: *an avid sportsman.* —See Synonyms at **eager.** [French *avide,* from Latin *avidus,* from *avēre,* to long for. See **avarice.**] —**av·id·ly** *adv.*

av·i·din (ăv′ə-dĭn) *n.* A protein in egg albumin, capable of inactivating biotin, consequently causing a deficiency of this vitamin in the consumer. [AVID + -IN, from its affinity for biotin.]

a·vid·i·ty (ə-vĭd′ə-tē) *n.* **1. a.** Eagerness. **b.** Greed. **2.** *Chemistry.* **a.** The dissociation-dependent strength of an acid or base. **b.** Degree of **affinity** *(see).*

a·vi·fau·na (ā′və-fô′nə, ăv′ə-) *n.* All the birds of a specific region. [New Latin : Latin *avis,* bird + FAUNA.] —**a·vi·fau·nal** *adj.*

A·vi·gnon (à-vē-nyôN′). Industrial city in Vaucluse department in southeastern France, on the Rhône River. It was the seat of several antipopes from 1378 to 1408 and still contains the papal palace, one of the greatest of medieval fortress-castles.

A·vi·la (ä′və-lə). Capital of the province of the same name, in central Spain, on the upper Adaja River.

a·vi·on·ics (ā′vē-ŏn′ĭks, ăv′ē-) *n. Used with a singular verb.* The science and technology of electronics applied to aeronautics and astronautics. [AVI(ATION) + (ELECTR)ONICS.] —**a·vi·on·ic** *adj.*

a·vir·u·lent (ā-vĭr′yə-lənt, ā-vĭr′ə-lənt) *adj. Medicine.* Not infectious or virulent.

a·vi·ta·min·o·sis (ā-vī′tə-mĭn-ō′sĭs) *n.* Any disease caused by deficiency of vitamins. [A- (without) + VITAMIN + -OSIS.]

av·i·zan·dum (ăv′ə-zăn′dəm) *n. British.* **1.** In Scots law, a judge's decision to delay giving judgment for a certain time. **2.** The period of this delay. [Medieval Latin, "a being considered," gerund of *avisare,* to consider. See **advise.**]

avn. aviation.

av·o·ca·do (ăv′ə-kä′dō) *n., pl.* **-dos. 1.** A tropical American tree, *Persea americana,* cultivated for its edible fruit. **2.** The oval or pear-shaped fruit of this tree, having leathery green or blackish skin, a large seed, and bland, greenish-yellow pulp. Also called "alligator pear." **3.** A dull green. [Spanish *aguacate,* from Nahuatl *ahuacatl,* "testicle" (from the shape of the fruit).]

av·o·ca·tion (ăv′ō-kā′shən) *n.* **1.** An activity engaged in, usually for enjoyment, in addition to one's regular work or profession; hobby. **2.** *Archaic.* One's regular work or profession. [Latin *āvocātiō* (stem *āvocātiōn-*), a calling away, diversion, from *āvocāre,* to call away : *ab-,* away + *vocāre,* to call.]

av·o·cet (ăv′ə-sĕt′) *n.* Any of several long-legged shore birds of the genus *Recurvirostra,* having a long, slender, upturned beak. [French *avocette,* from Italian *avosetta†.*]

a·vo·di·re (ăv′ə-də-rā′, -dĭ-rā′) *n.* **1.** A tree, *Turreanthus africana,* of western Africa, having light-colored wood with a clearly marked grain. **2.** The wood of this tree, used in cabinetwork. [French *avodiré†.*]

A·vo·ga·dro number (ä′və-gä′drō, ăv′ə-) *n.* Also **Avogadro's number.** *Abbr.* **N** The number of molecules in one mole of a substance, approximately 6.0225 × 10^{23}. Also called "Avogadro constant." [After Amedeo *Avogadro* (1776–1856), Italian physicist.]

Avogadro's law *n.* The principle that equal volumes of different gases under identical conditions of pressure and temperature contain the same number of molecules. Also called "Avogadro's hypothesis." [After Amedeo *Avogadro.*]

a·void (ə-void′) *tr.v.* **avoided, avoiding, avoids. 1.** To keep away from; stay clear of; shun. **2.** To prevent from happening. **3.** *Law.* To annul or make void (a contract or deed). —See Synonyms at **escape.** [Middle English *avoiden,* from Norman-French *avoider,* from Old French *esvuidier,* "to empty out," hence, to leave : *es-,* from Latin *ex-,* out + *vuidier,* to empty, from *vuide,* VOID.] —**a·void·a·ble** *adj.* —**a·void·a·bly** *adv.* —**a·void·er** *n.*

a·void·ance (ə-void′ns) *n.* **1.** The act of avoiding or shunning something. **2.** *Law.* A making void; an annulment. **3.** *Anthropology.* The custom, common among many primitive tribes, by which a member of a family may not meet or speak to another member.

av·oir·du·pois (ăv′ər-də-poiz′) *n. Abbr.* **av., avdp., avoir. 1.** Avoirdupois weight. **2.** *Informal.* Weight; heaviness. Said of a person. [Middle English *avoir de pois,* "commodities sold by weight," from Old French *aver de peis* : *aver,* property, from *aver, aveir,* to possess, have, from Latin *habēre,* to have + *de,* of, from Latin *dē* + *pois, peis,* weight, from *peser,* to weigh, POISE.]

avoirdupois weight *n.* A system of weights and measures, formerly used in most English-speaking countries, based on a pound containing 16 ounces or 7,000 grains and equal to 453.59 grams.

A·von[1] (ā′vŏn, ā′vən). Also **Upper Avon.** English river that rises near Naseby, Northamptonshire, and flows 155 kilometers (96 miles) through Stratford-upon-Avon to the Severn River near Tewkesbury, Gloucestershire.

Avon[2]. Also **Lower Avon.** English river that rises near Tetbury, Gloucestershire, and flows some 121 kilometers (75 miles) through Bath and Bristol to the Severn estuary at Avonmouth.

Avon[3]. A county in southwest England, created in 1974 and comprising Bath, Bristol, and areas formerly in Somerset and Gloucestershire. Its administrative center is Bristol.

a·vouch (ə-vouch′) *tr.v.* **avouched, avouching, avouches. 1.** To take responsibility for; guarantee. **2.** To assert positively; affirm. **3.** To acknowledge one's responsibility for; confess; avow. [Middle English *avouchen,* from Old French *avochier,* from Latin *advocāre,* to call on (as adviser) : *ad-,* to + *vocāre,* to call.]

a·vow (ə-vou′) *tr.v.* **avowed, avowing, avows.** To acknowledge openly; confess: *avow guilt.* —See Synonyms at **acknowledge, assert.** [Middle English *avowen,* from Old French *avouer,* from Latin *advocāre,* to call on (as adviser), appeal to. See **avouch.**] —**a·vow·a·ble** *adj.* —**a·vow·a·bly** *adv.* —**a·vow·er** *n.*

a·vow·al (ə-vou′əl) *n.* An admission or acknowledgment.

a·vowed (ə-voud′) *adj.* Frankly acknowledged; confessed: *an avowed rebel.* —**a·vow·ed·ly** (ə-vou′ĭd-lē) *adv.*

a·vul·sion (ə-vŭl′shən) *n.* **1.** A ripping off or forcible separation, as of a part of the body by injury. **2.** A part removed in this way. **3.** *Law.* The removal of soil from one property to another by the movement of floodwater, a shift in the course of a boundary stream, or encroachment by the sea. In this sense, compare **alluvion.**

a·vun·cu·lar (ə-vŭng′kyə-lər) *adj.* **1.** Of, pertaining to, or resembling an uncle, especially a benevolent uncle. **2.** Benevolent; kindly and friendly. [Latin *avunculus,* maternal uncle.]

a·vun·cu·late (ə-vŭng′kyə-lĭt) *n.* Customs regulating relations between a maternal uncle and his nephew in certain societies and concerning various duties and rights, especially of inheritance. [Latin *avunculus,* maternal uncle + -ATE (group, rank).]

A·WACS, A·wacs (ā′wăks′) *n.* A defense system of aircraft equipped with radar used by the U.S. Air Force to detect enemy bombers. [*A*irborne *W*arning *A*nd *C*ontrol *S*ystem.]

a·wait (ə-wāt′) *v.* **awaited, awaiting, awaits.** —*tr.* **1.** To wait for. **2.** To be in store for. —*intr* To wait. —See Synonyms at **expect.** [Middle English *awaiten,* from Old North French *awaitier,* watch for, wait for: *a-,* to + *waitier,* to watch, WAIT.]

a·wake (ə-wāk′) *v.* **awoke** (ə-wōk′) or *rare* **awaked, awaked** or **awoken** (ə-wō′kən) or *rare* **awoke, awaking, awakes.** —*tr.* **1.** To rouse from sleep; waken. **2.** To stir up or excite (memories or fears, for example). —*intr.* **1.** To wake up. **2.** To become alert. **3.** To be-

come aware or cognizant. Often used with *to*: *They awoke to reality.* —See Usage note at **wake**.
~*adj.* **1.** Not asleep. **2.** Alert; vigilant; watchful. [Middle English *awaken, awakien,* Old English *awacan, awacian* : A- (intensive) + *wacan, wacian,* to be awake, WAKE.]
a·wak·en (ə-wā′kən) *v.* **-ened, -ening, -ens.** —*tr.* To cause to wake up. —*intr.* To wake up; awake. —See Usage note at **wake.** [Middle English *awak(e)nen,* Old English *āwæcnan, āwæcnian* : A- (on) + *wæcnan, wæcnian,* to WAKE.]
a·wak·en·ing (ə-wā′kən-ĭng) *adj.* **1.** Waking up. **2.** Rousing; exciting.
~*n.* **1.** The act of waking; an emergence from sleep. **2.** A stirring up; a rousing of attention, awareness, or interest.
a·ward (ə-wôrd′) *tr.v.* **awarded, awarding, awards. 1.** To grant as merited or due. **2.** To declare as legally due: *awarded damages.* **3.** To bestow for performance or quality: *award a prize.*
~*n.* **1.** A decision, especially one made by a judge or arbitrator. **2.** Something awarded, such as a medal or a sum of money. [Middle English *awarden,* from Norman French *awarder,* variant of Old North French *eswarder,* to judge after careful observation : *es-,* from Latin *ex-,* out + *warder,* to observe, keep, judge, from Germanic.] **—a·ward·ee** (ə-wôr-dē′) *n.* **—a·ward·a·ble** *adj.* **—a·ward·er** *n.*
a·ware (ə-wâr′) *adj.* **1.** Conscious; cognizant. Often used with *of*: *aware of their limitations.* **2.** Well-informed; knowledgeable: *politically aware.* **3.** *Informal.* Sensitive and perceptive: *an aware person.* [Middle English *awar, iwar,* Old English *gewær.*] **—a·ware·ness** *n.*
a·wash (ə-wŏsh′, ə-wôsh′) *adj.* **1.** Level with or washed by waves. **2.** Flooded. **3.** Floating on waves. **—a·wash** *adv.*
a·way (ə-wā′) *adv.* **1. a.** From a particular place or position; off. **b.** To or at another place or position. **2.** At a distance. **3.** In a different direction; aside: *He glanced away.* **4.** Out of existence: *The music faded away.* **5.** From one's possession or notice: *He gave the money away.* **6.** Continuously; persistently: *He worked away at his job.* **7.** Immediately: *Fire away!* **8.** *Informal.* In a penal or mental institution: *put away for robbery.* **9.** So as to pass a period of time in a specified activity: *danced the night away.* **10.** At or on an opponent's playing field or location: *playing away on Saturday.* **—away with. 1.** Take away. **2.** Go away: *Away with you!* **—do away with. 1.** To get rid of. **2.** To murder.
~*adj.* **1.** Absent. **2.** At a distance: *He is miles away.* **3. a.** Played on an opponent's playing field or location. **b.** Of, pertaining to, or occurring at an away match or game: *six away goals.*
~*interj.* Used as an order of dismissal. [Middle English *away, on way,* from Old English *aweg, oweg, onweg,* "on the way (from)" : *a-, on,* ON + *weg,* WAY.]
awe (ô) *n.* **1. a.** An emotion of mingled reverence, dread, and wonder inspired by something majestic or sublime. **b.** Respect, tinged with fear, for authority. **2.** *Archaic.* The power to inspire reverence or fear. —*tr.v.* **awed, awing** or **aweing, awes.** To inspire with awe. [Middle English *awe, age, aghe,* from Old Norse *agi.*]
a·wea·ry (ə-wîr′ē) *adj. Poetic.* Tired; weary.
a·weath·er (ə-wĕth′ər) *adv. Nautical.* To windward. Compare **alee.**
a·weigh (ə-wā′) *adj. Nautical.* Hanging just clear of the bottom. Said of an anchor. [A- (on) + WEIGH.]
awe-in·spir·ing (ô′ĭn-spīr′ĭng) *adj.* Causing great admiration or wonder; spellbinding.
awe·some (ô′səm) *adj.* **1.** Inspiring awe. **2.** Expressing or characterized by awe. **—awe·some·ly** *adv.* **—awe·some·ness** *n.*
awe-strick·en (ô′strĭk′ən) *adj.* Also **awe-struck** (-strŭk′). Full of awe.
aw·ful (ô′fəl) *adj.* **1.** Extremely bad or unpleasant; terrible; horrible. **2.** Dreadful; appalling; fearsome. **3.** Used as an intensive: *an awful fool; an awful lot of people.* [Middle English *awful, aweful* : AWE + -FUL.] **—aw·ful·ness** *n.*
aw·ful·ly (ô′fə-lē, ô′flē) *adv.* **1.** In an extremely unpleasant manner; horribly. **2.** Used as an intensive: *He's awfully late.*
a·while (ə-hwīl′) *adv.* For a short time.
Usage: *Awhile,* an adverb, is never preceded by a preposition such as *for,* but the two-word form *a while* may be preceded by a preposition. In writing, each of the following is acceptable: *stay awhile; stay for a while; stay a while* (but not *stay for awhile*).
awk·ward (ôk′wərd) *adj.* **1.** Not graceful; ungainly. **2.** Not dexterous; clumsy; unskillful. **3.** Hard to handle; unwieldy: *an awkward bundle.* **4.** Difficult or dangerous: *an awkward climb.* **5.** Inconvenient; uncomfortable: *an awkward pose.* **6.** Causing embarrassment; trying: *an awkward predicament.* **7.** Embarrased; ill-at-ease: *I felt awkward.* **8.** Difficult to cope with; contrary; perverse. [Middle English *awkeward,* "in the wrong direction," awry : *awke,* backhanded, perverse, wrong, from Old Norse *afugr,* turned backwards + -WARD.] **—awk·ward·ly** *adv.* **—awk·ward·ness** *n.*
Synonyms: *awkward, bungling, clumsy, gauche, inept, maladroit, ungainly.*
awkward age *n.* The period between childhood and adulthood; adolescence.
awl (ôl) *n.* A pointed tool for making holes, as in wood or leather. [Middle English *aule, al,* Old English *æl.*]
awl·wort (ôl′wûrt′, -wôrt′) *n.* A small aquatic plant, *Subularia aquatica,* of the Northern Hemisphere, having narrow, pointed leaves and minute white flowers. [From the shape of its leaves.]
awn (ôn) *n. Botany.* A slender, bristlelike terminal part, such as those found on the spikelets of many grasses. [Middle English *awne, agene,* from Old Norse *ögn*; akin to Gothic *ahana,* chaff.]
awn·ing (ô′nĭng) *n.* A rooflike structure, as of canvas, stretched over a frame as a shelter from the weather. [17th century (nautical use) : origin obscure.]
a·woke. A past tense of **awake.**
a·wok·en. A past participle of **awake.**
A·WOL, a·wol (ā′wôl′) *adj.* Absent without leave, especially from the military service.
~*n.* One that is AWOL. **—A·WOL** *adv.*
a·wry (ə-rī′) *adv.* **1.** Turned or twisted to one side; askew. **2.** Away from the correct course; amiss; wrong. [Middle English *awrie, on wry* : ON + *wry,* twisted, WRY.] **—a·wry** *adj.*
ax, axe (ăks) *n., pl.* **axes. 1.** A tool having a head with a sharp cutting edge mounted on a handle, used for felling, chopping, or splitting trees and wood. **2.** Any similar tool or weapon, such as a battle-ax. **3.** Anything that acts drastically to remove or reduce something: *The ax fell on the research program.* **—get the ax.** To be fired from one's job. **—have an ax to grind.** To pursue a private, selfish, or subjective aim.
~*tr.v.* **axed, axing, axes. 1.** To work on with an ax. **2. a.** To cancel (a project, for example). **b.** To reduce substantially (manpower or expenditure, for example). **c.** To dismiss from employment. [Middle English *ax, axe,* Old English *æx, aces.*]
ax. axiom.
ax·el (ăk′səl) *n.* A jump in figure skating involving one and a half turns in the air. [After *Axel* Paulsen (died 1938), Norwegian skater.]
a·xen·ic (ā-zĕn′ĭk, ā-zē′nĭk) *adj. Biology.* Free of symbionts or parasites; uncontaminated. Said of cultures or culture media. [A- (without) + XEN(O)- + -IC.]
ax·es. 1. Plural of **axis. 2.** Plural of **ax.**
ax·i·al (ăk′sē-əl) *adj.* **1.** Pertaining to or forming an axis. **2.** Located on, around, or in the direction of an axis. [AXI(S) + -AL.] **—ax·i·al·ly** *adv.*
ax·il (ăk′sĭl) *n.* The angle between the upper surface of a leafstalk, flower stalk, branch, or similar part, and the stem or axis from which it arises. [Latin *axilla,* armpit, AXILLA.]
ax·il·la (ăk-sĭl′ə) *n., pl.* **axillae** (ăk-sĭl′ē). The armpit, or an analogous part such as the underside of a bird's wing. [Latin *axilla,* armpit.]
ax·il·lar (ăk-sĭl′ər, ăk′sə-lər) *adj.* Axillary.
~*n.* One of the feathers in the axilla of a bird's wing.
ax·il·lar·y (ăk′sə-lĕr′ē) *adj.* **1.** *Anatomy.* Of, relating to, or near the armpit. **2.** *Botany.* Of, pertaining to, or located in an axil: *axillary buds.*
~*n., pl.* **axillaries.** An axillar.
ax·i·ol·o·gist (ăk′sē-ŏl′ə-jĭst) *n.* An expert in or student of axiology.
ax·i·ol·o·gy (ăk′sē-ŏl′ə-jē) *n. Philosophy.* The study of the nature of values and value judgments. [Greek *axios,* worth + -LOGY.] **—ax·i·o·log·i·cal** (ăk′sē-ə-lŏj′ĭ-kəl) *adj.* **—ax·i·o·log·i·cal·ly** *adv.*
ax·i·om (ăk′sē-əm) *n.* **1.** A self-evident or universally recognized truth; a maxim. **2.** An established rule, principle, or law. **3.** *Abbr.* **ax.** *Mathematics & Logic.* A statement or proposition requiring no proof, as: **a.** An undemonstrated proposition concerning an undefined set of elements, properties, functions, and relationships; a postulate. **b.** A self-evident, self-consistent, or accepted principle. [Latin *axiōma,* from Greek, "that which is thought fitting or worthy," from *axioun,* to think worthy, from *axios,* worthy.]
ax·i·o·mat·ic (ăk′sē-ə-măt′ĭk) *adj.* Also **ax·i·o·mat·i·cal** (-ĭ-kəl). **1.** Of, pertaining to, or resembling an axiom; self-evident. **2.** Based on logical axioms: *axiomatic method; axiomatic set theory.* **3.** Containing axioms; aphoristic. **—ax·i·o·mat·i·cal·ly** *adv.*
ax·is (ăk′sĭs) *n., pl.* **axes** (ăk′sēz′). **1.** A straight line about which a body or geometrical object rotates or may be conceived to rotate. **2.** *Mathematics.* **a.** A line, half-line, or line segment serving to orient a space or object, especially a line about which the object is symmetrical. **b.** A reference line from which distances or angles are measured in a coordinate system. **3.** A center line to which parts of a structure or body may be referred. **4.** *Fine Arts.* An imaginary line to which elements of the work are referred for measurement or symmetry. **5.** *Anatomy.* **a.** The second cervical vertebra, on which the head turns. **b.** Any of various central structures, such as the spinal column. **c.** An imaginary line through the center of the body or one of its parts, used as a positional referent. **6.** *Botany.* The main stem or central part about which organs or plant parts such as branches are arranged. **—the Axis** or **the Axis powers.** The alliance of Germany and Italy (1936), later including Japan and other nations, that opposed the Allies in World War II. [Latin *axis,* hub, axis, axle.]
axis deer *n.* A deer, *Axis axis,* of central Asia, having a brown coat with white spots. Also called "chital." [Latin *axis*†, given by Pliny as the Indian name of an unidentified animal.]
ax·le (ăk′səl) *n.* **1.** A supporting shaft or bar upon which a wheel or wheels revolve. **2.** The spindle of an axletree. **3.** Either end of an axletree. [Middle English *axil, axel,* from Old Norse *öxull.*]
ax·le·tree (ăk′səl-trē′) *n.* A crossbar or rod supporting a vehicle, as a drawn cart, and having terminal spindles on which the wheels revolve.
ax·man (ăks′mən) *n., pl.* **-men** (-mĭn). A man who wields an ax; especially a worker who fells trees or chops logs.
Ax·min·ster (ăks′mĭn′stər) *n.* A kind of carpet with a long, soft cut-wool pile, formerly handmade in Axminster, England.
ax·o·lotl (ăk′sə-lŏt′l) *n.* Any of several western North American and Mexican salamanders of the genus *Ambystoma,* especially *A. mexicanum.* [Nahuatl : *atl,* water + *xolotl,* servant, spirit.]

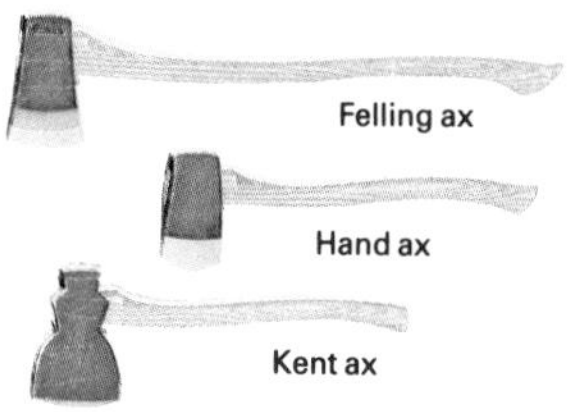

ax *One of mankind's oldest tools and weapons. The first axes, chipped from stone or flint and with no handles, were in use more than 600,000 years ago. The three modern types shown here are a felling ax (top), a hand ax (center), and a Kent ax.*

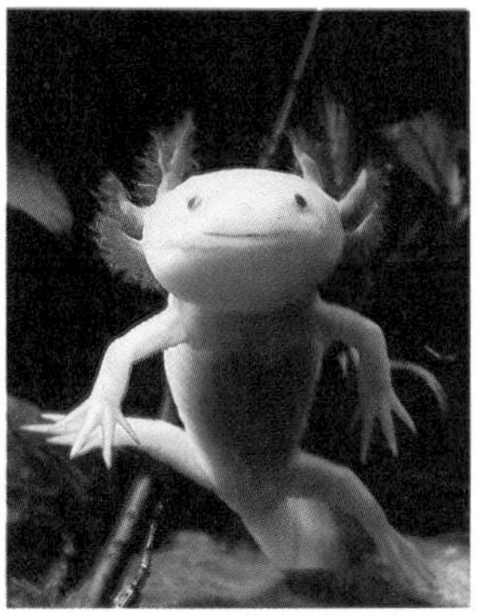

axolotl *Most animals become capable of breeding only when they are adult. This rare Mexican amphibian, however—usually mates and gives birth to a new generation while it is still in its larval form (above).*

PRONUNCIATION KEY

ă, **pat**; ā, **pay**; âr, **care**;
ä, **father**, **are**; b, **bib**;
ch, **church**; d, **deed**; ĕ, **pet**;
ē, **be**; f, **fife**; g, **gag**; h, **hat**;
hw, **which**; ĭ, **pit**; ī, **pie**;
îr, **pier**; j, **judge**; k, **kick**;
l, **lid**, **needle**; m, **mum**;
n, **no**, **sudden**; ng, **thing**;
ŏ, **pot**; ō, **toe**; ô, **paw**, **for**;
oi, **noise**; ou, **out**; ŏŏ, **book**;
ōō, **boot**; p, **pop**; r, **roar**;
s, **sauce**; sh, **ship**, **dish**;
t, **tight**; th, **thin**, **path**;
th, **this**, **bathe**; ŭ, **cut**; ûr, **fur**;
v, **valve**; w, **with**; y, **yes**;
z, **zebra**, **size**; zh, **vision**;
ə, **about**, **item**, **edible**,
gallop, **circus**, **peaceful**

IN FOREIGN WORDS:

à, *Fr.* **ami**; œ, *Fr.* **feu**, *Ger.* **schön**; ü, *Fr.* **tu**, *Ger.* **über**; KH, *Ger.* **ich**, *Scot.* **loch**; N, *Fr.* **bon**; y′, *Fr.* **Compiègne**

STRESS MARKS:

Primary stress: ′
in·cite′ (ĭn-sīt′)
Secondary stress: ′
in′sight′ (ĭn′sīt′)

Ayers Rock *The biggest single rock in the world lies in the Ayers Rock-Mount Olga National Park in the south of Australia's Northern Territory. Made largely of sandstone, it is some 6 kilometers (4 miles) long by 2.4 kilometers (1.5 miles) wide and rises to 348 meters (1,143 feet) above the surrounding desert. The feature is named after Henry Ayers, a former governor of South Australia.*

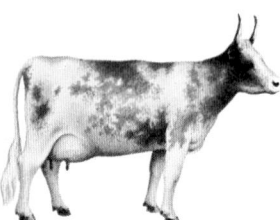

Ayrshire *A sturdy breed of dairy cow from Scotland. It produces milk with a high butterfat content and makes good beef when crossed with the beef shorthorn.*

ax·on (ăk′sŏn′) *n.* Also **ax·one** (ăk′sōn′). The long unbranched process extending from the cell body of a nerve cell that generally conducts impulses away from the nerve cell. Also called "neuraxon." [New Latin, from Greek *axōn*, axis.]

Axum. See **Aksum.**

a·yah (ä′yə, ä′ə, ī′ə) *n.* A native maid or nurse in India. [Hindi *āyā*, from Portuguese *aia*, nursemaid, from Latin *avia*, grandmother.]

a·ya·tol·lah (ī′ə-tō′lə, -tôl′ə) *n.* In the Shiite branch of Islam, a religious leader of the highest rank. [Arabic *āyatollāh*, sign of God.]

aye¹, ay (ī) *n.* A vote or voter voting in favor of a proposal.
~*adv.* Yes; yea. [16th century : probably the same word as the pronoun *I*, used as an affirmative answer.]

aye², ay (ā) *adv. Regional & Poetic.* Always; ever. [Middle English *ay, ei*, from Old Norse *ei*.]

aye-aye (ī′ī′) *n.* A small, nocturnal, arboreal mammal, *Daubentonia madagascariensis*, of Madagascar, related to the lemurs. [French, from Malagasay *aiay*, probably imitative of its cry.]

Ayer (âr), **Sir Alfred Jules** (1910–). British philosopher. His book *Language, Truth and Logic* (1936) was the first and most influential exposition of logical positivism in English.

A·yers Rock (ā′ərz). The largest monolith in the world, situated in the southwestern part of Northern Territory in Australia.

Ay·e·sha or **A·i·sha** (ä-ē′shə) (611–78). The third and favorite wife of Muhammad, the founder of Islam. She led an unsuccessful revolt against Muhammad's successor, Ali.

a·yin, a·in (ä′yĭn) *n.* The 16th letter of the Hebrew alphabet. See feature at **alphabet.** [Hebrew *'ayin*.]

Ay·ma·ra (ī′mä-rä′) *n., pl.* **-ras** or collectively **Aymara** (for sense 1). **1.** A member of an Indian people inhabiting Bolivia and Peru. **2.** A language family including that spoken by the Aymara people. —**Ay·ma·ran** *adj. & n.*

Ayr·shire¹ (âr′shîr, -shər). Formerly, a county in southwest Scotland, since 1975 part of Strathclyde Region.

Ayrshire² *n.* Any of a breed of brown and white dairy cattle originating in Ayrshire in the late 18th century.

A·yub Khan (ä′yōōb kän′), **Mohammad** (1907–74). Pakistani army commander and politician. He seized the presidency by a military coup in 1958. In 1965 he was confirmed in the presidency by a national election. He resigned in 1969.

A·yur·ve·da (ä′yŏŏr-vā′də, -vĕ′də) *n.* The ancient Hindu science of health and medicine, consisting of the following branches: removal of foreign substances and bodies from the body; cure of diseases by sharp instruments; cure of diseases affecting the whole body; treatment of mental illnesses supposed to be caused by demoniacal influence; treatment of children's diseases; and the doctrines of antidotes, elixirs, and aphrodisiacs. [Sanskrit : *āyur*, life + *veda*, knowledge.]

AZ Arizona (used with a Zip Code).

az. azimuth.

a·zal·e·a (ə-zāl′yə) *n.* Any of a group of deciduous or evergreen shrubs, part of the genus *Rhododendron*, of the North Temperate Zone, many of which are cultivated for their showy, variously colored flowers. [New Latin, "the dry plant" (growing in dry soil), from Greek, feminine of *azaleos*, dry.]

a·zan (ä-zän′) *n.* The Muslim summons to prayer, called by the muezzin from a minaret of a mosque five times a day. [Arabic *adhān*, from *adhina*, to proclaim. See **muezzin.**]

A·za·ña y Dí·az (ə-zän′yə ē dē′əz), **Manuel** (1880–1940). Spanish writer and politician. He was prime minister from 1931 to 1933 and again in 1936. In May 1936 he was elected president. He fled to France in 1939 after the Nationalist victory in the civil war.

A·za·ni·a (ə-zään-yə, -ē-ə). South Africa. Used by black African nationalists. [Latin *Azania*, Africa, probably from Arabic *Zanj*, a dark-skinned African.]

az·a·thi·o·prine (ăz′ə-thī′ə-prēn′) *n.* A drug that suppresses the body's immune response, used mainly to assist the survival of organ transplants. [*Aza-*, variant of AZO- + THIO- + P(U)RINE.]

A·za·zel (ə-zā′zəl, ăz′ə-zĕl′). In ancient Hebrew tradition, the rebel leader of the angels who seduced mankind. [Hebrew *'azāzēl*, "removal," hence scapegoat (ritually "sent" into the wilderness) : *'ez*, goat + *'azl*, to go.]

a·zed·a·rach (ə-zĕd′ə-răk′) *n.* **1.** A tree, the **chinaberry** (*see*). **2.** The astringent bark of this tree, formerly used as an emetic. [French *azedarac*, from Persian *āzād-dirakht* : *āzād*, free + *dirakht*, tree.]

a·ze·o·trope (ə-zē′ə-trōp′) *n.* A mixture of two or more liquids that, at a given pressure and temperature, boils without change of composition (the composition of the vapor is the same as that of the boiling liquid). [A- (not, without) + Greek *zeō*, (infinitive *zein*, boil) + -TROPE.] —**a·ze·o·trop·ic** *adj.*

A·zer·bai·jan or **A·zer·bai·dzhan Soviet Socialist Republic** (ăz′ər-bī-jän′, ä′zər-). Constituent republic of the U.S.S.R., in southeastern Transcaucasia. It was formed from territory ceded by Persia to Russia in 1813 and 1828. The capital is Baku, a center of rich oilfields. More than half the people are Turkic-speaking Azerbaijanis, who are Shiite Muslims.

A·zer·bai·ja·ni (ăz′ər-bī-jä′nē, ä′zər-) *n., pl.* **-nis** or collectively **Azerbaijani.** **1.** A native or inhabitant of Azerbaijan S.S.R. **2.** The Turkic language of Azerbaijanis.

a·zide (ā′zīd′) *n. Chemistry.* **1.** An inorganic compound containing the negative ion N_3^-. **2.** An organic compound containing the group $-N_3$. **3.** The group or radical N_3. [AZO- + -IDE.]

A·zil·ian (ə-zĭl′yən) *adj. Archaeology.* Of or denoting a western Eu-

ropean culture, especially of France and Spain, following the Magdalenian era and preceding the Neolithic. [After Le Mas d'*Azil*, village in the French Pyrenees, where such artifacts were found.]

az·i·muth (ăz′ə-məth) *n. Abbr.* **az. 1.** The horizontal angular distance from a fixed reference direction to a position, object, or object referent, as to a great circle intersecting a celestial body, usually measured clockwise in degrees along the horizon from a point due south. **2.** *Military.* The lateral deviation of a projectile or bomb. [Middle English, from Old French *azimut*, from Arabic *as-sumūt*, plural of *as-samt*, "the way," compass bearing, from Latin *semita†*, path.] —**az·i·muth·al** (ăz′ə-mŭth′əl) *adj.* —**az·i·muth·al·ly** *adv.*

azimuthal equidistant projection *n.* A map projection of the earth designed so that a straight line from a given point on the map to any other point gives the shortest distance between the two points.

Azincourt. See **Agincourt.**

az·ine (ăz′ēn′, ā′zēn′) *n.* A six-membered heterocyclic compound, such as pyridine, containing one or more atoms of nitrogen in the ring. [AZ(O)- + -INE.]

azine dye *n.* Any of various dyes derived from **phenazine** (*see*).

az·o (ăz′ō) *adj. Chemistry.* Containing a nitrogen group. [From AZO-.]

azo-, az- *prefix. Chemistry.* Indicates the presence of a nitrogen group, especially one attached at both ends in a covalent bond to other groups; for example, **azobenzene, azole.** [French *azote*, nitrogen, "lifeless" (unlike the life-sustaining oxygen) : A- (not) + Greek *zōē*, life.]

az·o·ben·zene (ăz′ō-bĕn′zēn, -bĕn-zēn′) *n.* A yellow or orange crystalline compound, $C_6H_5N_2C_6H_5$, used in the manufacture of dyes and as a fumigant.

Aztec

MYSTIC WARRIORS OF ANCIENT MEXICO
Aztecs practiced mass human sacrifice

The Aztecs were warrior nomads who settled on a lake island in Central America in the 14th century. The island grew into Tenochtitlán, a great, waterbound city of about 200,000 people supported by intensive agriculture, markets, and tribute from subject peoples in the countryside. The Aztecs believed that their world was protected by a god, Huitzilopochtli, who fought darkness each night so the sun would rise next day. To give the god strength, they sacrificed human beings, cutting the hearts from living victims, usually criminals or prisoners of war. In 1519 the Spanish conquistador, Hernando Cortés, landed in Mexico with 600 soldiers, overthrew the Aztec king, Montezuma, and claimed the country as a Spanish colony.

GIFTS TO A GOD *In a 16th-century Indian painting of an Aztec human sacrifice, one priest holds a victim's legs while another cuts out the still-beating heart. An earlier victim is being dragged away.*

AZTEC IMAGE *The stone carving of an Aztec god is probably of Huitzilopochtli himself. His image was usually decorated with skulls, stylized earrings, and open hands, apparently receiving a skull as an offering. At the dedication of his temple in Tenochtitlán (1487), it took four days to sacrifice the 20,000 victims.*

azo dye *n.* Any of various red, brown, or yellow acidic or basic dyes containing the azo groups.

a·zo·ic (ā-zō′ĭk, ə-) *adj.* Of or pertaining to geological periods that precede the appearance of life. [A- (not) + -ZOIC.]

az·ole (ăz′ōl′, ā′zōl′) *n.* **1.** Any organic compound having a five-membered heterocyclic ring. **2. Pyrrole** *(see).* [AZ(O)- (because it contains atoms of nitrogen) + -OLE.]

a·zon·ic (ā-zŏn′ĭk) *adj.* Not restricted to any particular zone or region; not local. [A- (not) + ZONE + -IC.]

A·zores (ā′zôrz, ə-zôrz′). *Portuguese* **A·çô·res** (ä-sō′rĭs). Group of nine volcanic islands in the Atlantic Ocean, forming three administrative districts of Portugal. Lying some 1,190 kilometers (740 miles) west of mainland Portugal, they were settled by the Portuguese in the mid-15th century. The islanders live by fishing, farming, and tourism. Ponta Delgada on São Miguel Island is the capital.

az·o·te·mi·a (ăz′ə-tē′mē-ə) *n.* **Uremia** *(see).* [New Latin : French *azote*, nitrogen (see **azo-**) + NAEMIA.] —**az·o·te·mic** *adj.*

az·oth (ăz′ŏth′, -ôth′) *n. Alchemy.* **1.** Mercury. **2.** Paracelsus's universal remedy. [Arabic *az-zā'ūq*, the mercury.]

a·zo·to·bac·ter (ā-zō′tō-băk′tər, ə-) *n.* Any of various nitrogen-fixing bacteria of the family Azotobacteraceae. [New Latin : French *azote*, nitrogen (see **azo-**) + BACTER(IA).]

az·o·tu·ri·a (ăz′ə-tŏŏr′ē-ə, -tyŏŏr′-) *n.* Increase of nitrogenous substances, especially urea, in the urine. [New Latin : French *azote*, nitrogen (see **azo-**) + -URIA.]

Az·ov, Sea of (ăz′ôf′). The northern arm of the Black Sea, in the Ukraine, southern European U.S.S.R. The shallow sea, maximum depth *c.* 15 meters (50 feet), has important fisheries. It is connected with the Black Sea by Kerch Strait.

Az·ra·el (ăz′rā-ĕl′). The angel who separates the soul from the body at death in Moslem and Jewish legend. [Arabic *Azrā'īl*, from Hebrew *'Azar'ēl*, "God has helped."]

Az·tec (ăz′tĕk′) *n.* **1.** A member of an Indian people of Central Mexico who established a great empire that was overthrown by Cortés in the 16th century. **2.** The language of this people, Nahuatl. ～*adj.* Also **Az·tec·an** (ăz′tĕk′ən). Of the Aztecs, their language, culture, or empire. [Spanish *Azteca*, from Nahuatl *Aztecatl* (plural *Azteca*) : *Azt(a)lan*, the supposed place of origin of the people, "near the crane"; *aztatl* (plural *azta*), crane + *tlan*, near + *-tecatl*, suffix denoting origin.]

az·ure (ăzh′ər) *n.* **1. a.** Light purplish blue, like a summer sky. **b.** *Heraldry.* The color blue. **2.** An azure pigment. **3.** *Poetic.* The blue sky. [Middle English, from Old French *azur* from Old Spanish *azul*, *azur*, from Arabic *allāzaward*, lapis lazuli, from Persian *lāzhuward*, LAPIS LAZULI.] —**az·ure** *adj.*

az·u·rite (ăzh′ə-rīt′) *n.* An azure-blue vitreous mineral of basic copper carbonate, $2CuCO_3 \cdot Cu(OH)_2$, used as a copper ore and as a gemstone. [French : Old French *azur*, AZURE + -ITE.]

az·y·gous (ăz′ĭ-gəs) *adj. Biology.* Occurring singly; unpaired. [New Latin *azygos*, from Greek *azugos*, unwedded, unpaired : *a-*, without + *zugon*, yoke.]

azalea *Gardeners all over the world cultivate this hardy shrub, which is related to the rhododendron and belongs to the heath family.*

B

Ba *The symbol of the soul or life after death in ancient Egyptian religion. It was portrayed by a bird with a human head.*

baboon *Members of the monkey family, baboons are native to the drier areas of Arabia and Africa and live mainly on the ground, in troops of up to 150 animals. They feed on vegetation, insects, and small animals.*

b, B (bē) *n., pl.* **b's** or **B's. 1.** The second letter of the modern English alphabet. See feature at **alphabet. 2.** Any of the speech sounds represented by this letter. **3. B** A human blood type of the ABO group. See **ABO. 4.** The second in a series. **5.** The second best or highest in quality or rank: *grade B meat; a mark of B on an English theme.* **6. B** *Music.* **a.** The seventh tone in the scale of C major, or the second tone in the relative minor scale. **b.** The key or a scale in which B is the tonic. **c.** A written or printed note representing this tone. **d.** A string, key, or pipe tuned to the pitch of this tone. **7. B** Something second-rate; especially, something that is the inferior or secondary item of a pair. Often used adjectivally: *a B film; the B side of a record.* **8. B** A fairly soft pencil or pencil-lead. Often used adjectivally: *a B pencil.*
b, B, b., B. *Note:* As an abbreviation or symbol, *b* may be a small or a capital letter, with or without a period. Established forms or those generally preferred precede the definition. When no form is given, all four forms are in general use in that sense. **1. B.** bachelor. **2. B.** bacillus. **3. b** *Physics.* barn. **4. B** baryon number. **5. b., B.** base. **6. b., B.** *Music.* basso. **7. B.** Baumé scale. **8. b., B.** bay. **9. B.** Bible. **10. B** *Chess.* bishop. **11. b., B.** bolivar. **12. b., B.** book. **13. b., B.** born. **14. B** The symbol for the element boron. **15. b** *Cricket.* bowled. **16. b., B.** breadth. **17. B.** British. **18. b., B.** brother. **19. B.** brotherhood.
B- *Military.* bomber: *a B-52.*
Ba¹ The symbol for the element barium.
Ba² (bä) *n.* In ancient Egyptian religion, the soul or life after death represented as a bird with a human head. [Egyptian.]
B.A. 1. Bachelor of Arts. **2.** British Academy. **3.** British Association (for the Advancement of Science).
baa (bă, bä) *intr.v.* **baaed, baaing, baas.** To make a bleating sound, as a sheep does.
—n. The bleat of a sheep. [Imitative.]
Baa·der-Mein·hof Gang (bä'dər-mīn'hôf') *n.* A West German revolutionary group, also known as the Red Army Faction, committed to the destruction of capitalism through acts of terrorism and violence. The group's original leading members, Andreas Baader (1943–77) and Ulrike Meinhof (1934–76), both died in prison.
Ba·al (bā'əl) *n., pl.* **-alim** (-ə-lĭm) **1. a.** Any of various local fertility and nature gods of the ancient Semitic peoples, considered to be false idols by the Hebrews. **b.** The chief god of the Phoenicians and Canaanites. **2.** *Sometimes* **baal.** Any false god or idol. [Hebrew *bá'al,* owner, master, lord.] **—Ba·al·ism** *n.*
Ba·al·bek, Baal·bek (bäl'bĕk', bā'əl-). Village in east Lebanon, site of an ancient Phoenician city, probably devoted to Baal. It is now a tourist center famous for its extensive Roman ruins.
Baal Shem Tov (bäl' shĕm' tōv'), original name Israel ben Eliezer (c. 1700–60). Polish-born Jewish religious leader and mystic and founder of Chassidism. His name means "Master of the Holy Name."
baas (bäs) *n., pl.* **baas.** *South African.* **1.** A master or boss. **2.** Sir; master. Used as a term of address, chiefly by black South Africans to whites. [Afrikaans, from Dutch *baas,* master or captain.]
baas·skap (bäs'kăp) *n. South African.* The condition of mastery or overlordship; especially, the political supremacy of South African whites over blacks. [Afrikaans, from Dutch : *baas,* master + *-skap,* -SHIP.]
Bab (bäb), **the,** title of Ali Muhammad of Shiraz (c. 1819–50). Persian founder of Babism and one of the three central figures of the Bahai faith, who proclaimed himself as the Bab (or "Gateway") to the truth.
Bab. Babylonia; Babylonian.
ba·ba (bä'bə) *n.* A sponge cake leavened with yeast, sometimes made with raisins and usually flavored with rum. Also called "rum baba." [French, from Polish, "old woman."]
Babar. See **Baber.**
ba·bas·su (bä'bə-soo') *n.* A Brazilian palm tree, *Orbignya martiana* (or *O. speciosa*), bearing hard nuts that yield an oil similar to coconut oil. [Brazilian Portuguese *babaçú,* probably a native name.]
Bab·bage (băb'ĭj), **Charles** (1792–1871). British mathematician and inventor. He designed a computer that was based on principles like those used in modern computers. Input data was stored on punched cards.
bab·bitt (băb'ĭt) *tr.v.* **-bitted, -bitting, -bitts.** To line or face with Babbitt (metal).
Bab·bitt¹ (băb'ĭt) *n.* A member of the American middle class whose attachment to its ideals is such as to make him a model of narrow-mindedness and self-satisfaction. Used disparagingly. [After George F. *Babbitt,* main character in Sinclair Lewis's novel *Babbitt* (1922).] **—Bab·bitt·ry** *n.*
Babbitt² *n.* A trademark for a soft, silvery antifriction alloy composed of tin with small amounts of copper and antimony. [After Isaac *Babbitt* (1799–1862), U.S. inventor.]
bab·ble (băb'əl) *v.* **-bled, -bling, -bles.** *—intr.* **1.** To utter an incoherent or meaningless confusion of words or sounds: *"the telescreen was still babbling away about pig iron and the overfulfillment of the Ninth Three-Year Plan"* (George Orwell). **2.** To talk foolishly or idly; chatter. **3.** To make a continuous low, murmuring sound, as flowing water does. *—tr.* **1.** To utter in a rapid, indistinct voice. **2.** To blurt out impulsively; disclose without careful consideration. *~n.* **1.** Inarticulate or meaningless talk or sounds. **2.** Idle or foolish talk; chatter; prattle. **3.** A continuous murmuring sound. **4.** Jargon, especially that characteristic of a particular field of interest or activity. Used in combination: *psychobabble; Eurobabble.* [Middle English *babelen,* of imitative origin.]
bab·bler¹ (băb'lər) *n.* **1.** One who babbles. **2.** A small songbird of the Old World family Timaliidae, occurring especially in Southeast Asia and having a loud babbling cry.
babbler² *n. Australian Slang.* A cook at a camp or sheep ranch. [From *babbling brook,* rhyming slang for *cook.*]
babe (bāb) *n.* **1.** *Archaic.* A baby; an infant. **2.** *Slang.* An innocent or naive person. **3.** *Slang.* A term of familiar address, usually used to a girl or young woman. [Middle English *babe,* imitative of a baby's sounds.]
ba·bel (bā'bəl, băb'əl) *n. Often* **Babel. 1.** A confusion of sounds, voices, or languages: *"in the babel of two hundred voices he would forget himself"* (Joseph Conrad). **2.** A scene of noise and confusion. —See Synonyms at **noise.** [After BABEL.]
Ba·bel (bā'bəl, băb'əl). A city (now thought to be Babylon) in Shinar where, according to Genesis 11:1–9, an attempt to construct a tower to reach heaven incurred the wrath of God, who interrupted the work by making the builders unable to understand one another's language. [Hebrew *Bābhél,* from Akkadian *Bāb-ilu,* "gate of God."]
Ba·ber or **Ba·bar** or **Ba·bur** (bä'bər), original name Zahir ud-Din Muhammad (1483–1530). Mongol conqueror of India. A descendant of Genghis Khan and Tamerlane, he made periodic raids into India from 1519 to 1524. After he occupied Delhi and Agra (1526), he established the Mogul dynasty, which ruled India until 1857.
Ba·bi (bä'bē) *n.* **1.** Babism. **2.** A follower of the Bab.
bab·i·ru·sa, bab·i·rus·sa, bab·i·rous·sa (băb'ə-roo'sə, bä'bə-) *n.* A hairless wild pig, *Babyrousa babyrussa,* of the East Indies, having four long, upward-curving tusks in the male. [Malay *bābīrūsa : bābī,* hog + *rūsa,* deer.]
Bab·ism (bä'bĭz'əm) *n.* The beliefs and practices of a 19th-century Persian religious sect, founded about 1844 by the **Bab** *(see),* in which polygamy, concubinage, begging, trading in slaves, and the use of alcohol or drugs were forbidden. Also called "Babi."
bab·ka (băb'kə) *n.* A coffee cake flavored with orange rind, rum, almonds, and raisins. [Polish, "little old woman," diminutive of *baba,* old woman.]
ba·boon (bă-boon') *n.* **1.** Any of several chiefly African omnivorous monkeys of the genus *Papio* (or *Chaeropithecus*) and related genera, having an elongated, doglike muzzle and large teeth. See **gelada, hamadryas. 2.** *Slang.* A large, clumsy, often coarse person. [Middle English *baboyne,* from Old French *babuin,* gaping figure, baboon, perhaps a blend of *babine,* pendulous lip, and *baboue,* grimace.]
ba·bu, ba·boo (bä'boo) *n.* **1.** A form of address in Hindi equivalent

or similar to *Mister,* placed before a man's full name or after his first name. **2. a.** A Hindu clerk possessing a prerequisite degree of literacy in English. Considered offensive. **b.** A native of India who has acquired some superficial education in English. Used derogatorily. [Hindi *bābū,* "father."]

Babur. See **Baber.**

ba·bush·ka (bə-bo͝osh′kə) *n.* A woman's headscarf, folded triangularly and tied under the chin. [Russian, "grandmother," diminutive of *baba,* old woman.]

ba·by (bā′bē) *n., pl.* **-bies. 1.** A newborn or very young boy or girl; an infant. **2.** The youngest member of a family or group. **3.** A newborn or very young animal. **4.** An adult or young person who acts like an infant. **5.** *Slang.* **a.** A girlfriend or boyfriend. **b.** A term of familiar address, usually used to a woman or girl. **6.** *Slang.* An object of personal concern or interest: *The project was his baby.*
∼*adj.* **1.** Of or pertaining to a baby or babies. **2.** Infantile; childish. **3.** Small in comparison with others of the same kind.
∼*tr.v.* **babied, -bying, -bies.** To treat oversolicitously; coddle. —See Synonyms at **pamper.** [Middle English *babie,* imitative.] **—ba·by·hood** *n.*

baby blue *n.* Very light to very pale greenish or purplish blue. **—ba·by-blue** *adj.*

ba·by-blue-eyes (bā′bē-blo͞o′īz′) *n.* *Used with a singular or plural verb.* A low-growing plant, *Nemophila menziesii,* of California, having bell-shaped blue flowers.

baby carriage *n.* A small four-wheeled carriage for an infant. Also called "baby buggy," "buggy."

baby face *n. Slang.* **1.** A plump, smooth face like a baby's. **2.** An adult having a baby face. **—ba·by-faced** *adj.*

baby grand *n.* A small grand piano.

ba·by·ish (bā′bē-ĭsh) *adj.* **1.** Like a baby; childlike. **2.** Childish; immature. **—ba·by·ish·ly** *adj.* **—ba·by·ish·ness** *n.*

Bab·y·lon[1] (băb′ə-lən, -lŏn′). City in ancient Mesopotamia, some 88 kilometers (55 miles) south of modern Baghdad. Founded in the 2nd millennium B.C., it flourished as Hammurabi's capital. It was virtually destroyed by the Assyrians under Sennacherib (*c.* 689 B.C.), but rose again, achieving vast wealth as the capital of a neo-Babylonian empire. Nebuchadnezzar II rebuilt the city, and his Hanging Gardens were one of the Seven Wonders of the World. Babylon fell to Cyrus the Great (538 B.C.) and became a minor center of the Persian Empire.

Babylon[2] *n.* **1.** A place of great luxury and corruption. **2.** A place of captivity or exile. **3.** In Rastafarian ideology, the corrupt and materialistic values of the West. See **Zion.** [After BABYLON.]

Bab·y·lo·ni·a (băb′ə-lō′nē-ə). *Abbr.* **Bab.** Empire of ancient Mesopotamia. Created in the 2nd millennium B.C., it rose to greatness under Hammurabi. It then fell to successive invaders and eventually to the Assyrians (*c.* 722 B.C.). A native king established a neo-Babylonian empire (*c.* 625 B.C.), and under Nebuchadnezzar II this was expanded to include Mesopotamia and Palestine. The empire declined after his death and fell to the Persians (538 B.C.).

Bab·y·lo·ni·an (băb′ə-lō′nē-ən) *adj. Abbr.* **Bab. 1.** Of or pertaining to ancient Babylonia or Babylon, their people, culture, or language. **2.** Characterized by a luxurious, pleasure-seeking, and immoral way of life.
∼*n. Abbr.* **Bab. 1.** A native or inhabitant of ancient Babylon or Babylonia. **2.** The Semitic language of the Babylonians, a form of Akkadian.

Babylonian captivity *n.* **1.** The deportation of the Jews to Babylonia and their period of exile there, initiated by Nebuchadnezzar II in 597 B.C. and formally terminated by Cyrus in 538 B.C. Also called "Babylonian exile." **2.** The period (1309–78) when the French popes resided at Avignon rather than Rome.

ba·by's-breath, ba·bies'-breath (bā′bēz-brĕth′) *n.* **1.** Any plant of the genus *Gypsophila;* especially, *G. paniculatum,* having numerous small white flowers in branching clusters. **2.** Any of several other plants with small, pleasantly scented flowers.

baby sitter *n.* A person who looks after one or more children while the parents are out, especially in the evening. **—ba·by-sit** *v.*

baby talk *n.* **1.** The early speech of a very young child. **2.** The infantile speech of an adult imitating a very young child.

ba·by-tears (bā′bē-tîrz′) *n.* Also **ba·by's-tears** (bā′bēz-tîrz′). *Used with a singular or plural verb.* A creeping plant, *Helxine soleirolii,* native to Corsica, having numerous very small leaves and minute green flowers.

baby tooth *n.* A **milk tooth** *(see).*

Ba·car·di (bə-kär′dē) *n.* **1.** A trademark for a brand of rum originally distilled in Cuba. **2.** A cocktail made with this rum, containing lime or lemon juice and sugar or grenadine.

bac·ca·lau·re·ate (băk′ə-lôr′ē-ĭt) *n.* **1.** The university degree of **Bachelor** *(see).* **2.** A farewell address in the form of a sermon delivered to a graduating class. [Medieval Latin *baccalaureātus,* from *baccalaureus,* variant (influenced by *bacca lauri,* "laurel berry") of *baccalārius,* BACHELOR.]

bac·ca·rat (bä′kə-rä′, băk′ə-) *n.* A card game in which two or more players bet against a dealer and the winner is the player holding two or three cards totaling closest to nine. [French *baccara*†.]

bac·cate (băk′āt′) *adj.* **1.** Bearing berries. **2.** Resembling a berry in texture or form. [Latin *baccatus,* "having berries," from *bāca, bacca,* berry, perhaps akin to BACCHUS.]

Bac·chae (băk′ē) *pl.n.* The priestesses and female followers of Bacchus. [Latin, from Greek *Bakkhai,* plural of *Bakkhē,* priest of BACCHUS.]

bac·cha·nal (băk′ə-năl′, -näl′, băk′ə-nəl) *n.* **1.** A participant in the Bacchanalia. **2.** *Sometimes* **bacchanals.** The Bacchanalia. **3.** Any drunken or riotous celebration. **4.** A reveler.
∼*adj.* Bacchanalian. [Latin *bacchānālis,* of BACCHUS.]

Bac·cha·na·li·a (băk′ə-nāl′yə, -nā′lē-ə) *n., pl.* **Bacchanalia. 1.** The ancient Roman festival in honor of Bacchus. **2. bacchanalia.** A riotous or drunken festivity; a revel. [Latin *bacchānālia,* neuter plural of *bacchānālis,* BACCHANAL.]

bac·cha·na·lian (băk′ə-nāl′yən, -nā′lē-ən) *adj.* **1.** Of or pertaining to the Bacchanalia. **2.** Characterized by riotous, drunken revelry; orgiastic.
∼*n.* A drunken reveler; a bacchanal.

bac·chant (bə-kănt′, -känt′, băk′ənt) *n., pl.* **-chants** or **-chantes** (-kăn′tēz, -kän′tēz, -kănts′, -känts′). **1.** A priest or votary of Bacchus. **2.** A boisterous reveler.
∼*adj.* **1.** Wine-loving. **2.** Riotous; carousing. [Latin *bacchāns* (stem *bacchant-*), present participle of *bacchārī,* to celebrate the festival of Bacchus, from Greek *bakkhān,* from *Bakkhos,* BACCHUS.]

bac·chante (bə-kăn′tē, -kän′tē, -kănt′, -känt′) *n.* **1.** A priestess or female votary of Bacchus. **2.** A female participant in a drunken or orgiastic revel. [French, from Latin *bacchāns,* BACCHANT.]

Bac·chic (băk′ĭk) *adj.* **1.** Of or pertaining to Bacchus. **2. bacchic.** Drunken and carousing; bacchanalian.

Bac·chus (băk′əs). The god of grape-growing, wine, and pleasure, often identified with Dionysus. [Latin, from Greek *Bakkhos.*]

bac·cif·er·ous (băk-sĭf′ər-əs) *adj. Botany.* Bearing berries. [Latin *baccifer* : *bacca,* berry + -FEROUS.]

bac·ci·form (băk′sə-fôrm′) *adj.* Having the shape of a berry. [Latin *bacca,* berry + -FORM.]

bac·cy (băk′ē) *n. Chiefly British Informal.* Tobacco.

bach[1] (băch) *intr.v.* **bached, baching, baches.** Also **batch.** *Slang.* To live alone and keep house for oneself, especially in a makeshift fashion. Used especially in the expression *bach it.* [Short for BACHELOR.]

bach[2] (băch) *n. New Zealand.* A small cottage or beach house. [Short for BACHELOR.]

Bach (bäKH), **Johann Sebastian** (1685–1750). German composer and musician. Among his religious works are over 200 cantatas, the *St. Matthew Passion* (1729), and the Mass in B minor (1733–38). His many orchestral pieces include the six *Brandenburg Concertos* (1721), and he wrote numerous compositions for the keyboard, including *The Well-Tempered Clavier* (1722, 1744) and the *Goldberg Variations* (1742). Of those of his 20 children who became musicians, two are especially renowned. **Carl Philipp Emanuel Bach** (1714–88) played an important part in the development of the symphony; **Johann Christian Bach** (1735–82) became music master to the British royal family and is sometimes known as the English or London Bach. See feature, next page.

Bachan. See **Batjan.**

bach·e·lor (băch′ə-lər, băch′lər) *n.* **1.** An unmarried man. **2.** In feudal times, a young knight in the service of another knight. Also called "bachelor-at-arms." See **knight bachelor. 3. Bachelor.** *Abbr.* **B. a.** A college or university degree signifying completion of the undergraduate curriculum and graduation. **b.** A person who holds such a degree. **4.** A young male fur seal who is kept from the breeding territory by older males. In this sense, also called "bachelor seal." [Middle English *bacheler,* from Old French, squire, from Vulgar Latin *baccalārius*†.] **—bach·e·lor·dom** *n.* **—bach·e·lor·hood** *n.* **—bach·e·lor·ship** *n.*

Bachelor of Arts *n. Abbr.* **B.A., A.B. 1.** An academic degree conferred by a college or university upon a person who has completed his or her undergraduate studies, usually in the arts or humanities. Compare **Master of Arts, Doctor of Philosophy. 2.** A person who has received this degree.

Bachelor of Science *n. Abbr.* **B.S., B.Sc., S.B. 1.** An academic degree conferred by a college or university upon a person who has completed his or her undergraduate studies in the sciences or some social sciences. Compare **Master of Science, Doctor of Philosophy. 2.** A person who has received this degree.

bach·e·lor's-but·ton (băch′ə-lərz-bŭt′n, băch′lərz-) *n.* **1.** A plant, the **cornflower** *(see).* **2.** The common European daisy. See **daisy. 3.** Any of various plants of the daisy family having buttonlike flower heads.

Bach trumpet (bäKH) *n.* A small modern trumpet designed to simplify the playing of the high trumpet parts found in the works of J.S. Bach and similar composers.

ba·cil·lar·y (băs′ə-lĕr′ē, bə-sĭl′ə-rē) *adj.* Also **ba·cil·lar** (bə-sĭl′ər, băs′ə-lər). **1.** Of, pertaining to, or caused by bacilli. **2.** Rod-shaped. From BACILLUS.]

ba·cil·li·form (bə-sĭl′ə-fôrm) *adj.* Rod-shaped.

ba·cil·lus (bə-sĭl′əs) *n., pl.* **-li** (-ī′). **1.** *Abbr.* **B.** Any rod-shaped bacterium. Compare **coccus, spirillum. 2.** Any of various rod-shaped, aerobic bacteria of the genus *Bacillus,* often occurring in chainlike formations. —See Usage note at **germ.** [New Latin, from Late Latin, diminutive of Latin *baculum,* rod, stick.]

bac·i·tra·cin (băs′ə-trā′sĭn) *n.* An antibiotic obtained from the bacterium *Bacillus subtilis* and usually used externally to treat skin infections. [BACI(LLUS) + Margaret *Tracy,* an American child in whose blood it was first isolated in 1945 + -IN.]

back[1] (băk) *n.* **1. a.** The region of the vertebrate body located nearest the spine, in man consisting of the rear area from the neck to the pelvis. **b.** The analogous dorsal region in other animals, such as insects. **2. a.** The backbone or spine. **b.** The surface of the human

Babylon *A replica of a tower that once stood in the ancient Mesopotamian capital. The tower is dedicated to Ishtar, the Babylonian goddess of love and fertility.*

Bacchae *A follower of the wine god Bacchus beats a hand drum in a marble frieze from a first-century Roman villa.*

THE GREATEST OF A MUSICAL FAMILY

Heredity, faith, and craft were elements in Bach's musical genius

For Johann Sebastian Bach (1685–1750), the composing and playing of music was an art whose "aim and final reason ... should be none else but the Glory of God and the recreation of the mind." That principle infuses not only Bach's religious works such as the Passions, the many Cantatas, and the B-minor Mass, but also his secular music, including the Well-tempered Clavier, the Art of Fugue, and other works created to teach keyboard students.

Bach occupied about midpoint in a family line that produced successful musicians for over 200 years. Of his 20 children from two marriages (his first wife having died in 1720), Wilhelm Friedemann (1710–84), Carl Philipp Emanuel (1714–88), Johann Christoph Friedrich (1732–95), and Johann Christian (1735–82) became admired composers. In a distinguished if unspectacular career that took him never farther than 200 miles from his birthplace at Eisenach, Bach held a number of musical posts culminating in the position of musical director at St. Thomas Church, Leipzig.

BACH IN HIS SIXTIES *The authenticity of Bach portraits has been much debated among scholars, but this painting by Elias Gottlob Haussmann almost certainly shows Bach as he looked in 1746. He is holding a copy of his six-part canon BWV 1076.*

body, or any part of it, or any part of the body of an animal, that is located on the side facing away from the front: *the back of the leg.* **3. a.** The part, area, or surface farthest from the front. **b.** The upper or convex side of something: *the back of one's hand.* **4.** The part opposite to or behind that adapted for use or view. **5.** The reverse or underside, as of a coin or sheet of paper. **6. a.** A part that supports or strengthens from the rear: *the back of a chair.* **b.** Something that covers the back; for example, that part of a garment that covers the back. **7. a.** The part of a book where the pages are stitched together into the binding. **b.** The binding itself. **8. a.** In certain games, such as football or hockey, a player taking a position behind the front line of players. **b.** The position of such a player. **—at the back of one's mind.** In one's memory or subconscious. **—back to front.** The wrong way round; reversed. **—behind someone's back.** Without someone's knowledge or approval. **—get off someone's back.** *Informal.* To cease pestering or scolding someone. **—get (or put) someone's back up.** *Informal.* To annoy or antagonize. **—in back of.** At the rear of; behind. **—on one's back.** Incapacitated or helpless; bedridden. **—put one's back into.** To put great effort into. **—stab in the back.** To attack or betray (a friend or colleague). **—the back of beyond.** A very remote, insignificant, and inaccessible place. **—turn one's back on. 1.** To ignore the plight of; forsake. **2.** To turn away from; renounce. **—with one's back to the wall.** In a desperate position from which one cannot retreat. ~*v.* **backed, backing, backs.** —*tr.* **1.** To cause to move backward or in a reverse direction. **2.** To furnish or strengthen with a back, backing, or lining. **3. a.** To provide with support, assistance, or encouragement. **b.** To provide a musical backing for. **4.** To bring forward evidence in support of; substantiate. Often used with *up*: *backing up an argument with facts.* **5.** To bet on. **6.** To form the back or background of. **7.** To endorse by signing on the back of. —*intr.* **1.** To move backward. **2.** To shift counterclockwise in direction, as from south to southeast. Used of the wind. Compare **veer.** **3.** To have the back facing in a particular direction: *the house backs onto the park.* **—back and fill. 1.** To maneuver a sailing vessel in a narrow channel by alternately filling and spilling the sails. **2.** To vacillate in one's actions or decisions. **—back down.** To withdraw from a position, opinion, or commitment; abandon a former stand. **—back off.** To retreat or draw away. **—back out.** To withdraw from an enterprise, commitment, or plan, especially before completion: *He announced he was backing out of the project.* ~*adj.* **1.** Located at the rear. **2.** Distant from a center of activity; remote. **3.** Of a past date; not current. **4.** Owing or due from an earlier time; in arrears. **5.** Moving in a backward direction. **6.** *Phonetics.* Articulated with the tongue pulled to the rear of the mouth. ~*adv.* **1.** At, to, or toward the rear or back; backward. **2.** In, to, or toward a former location. **3.** In, to, or toward a former time. **4.** In, to, or toward a past time. **5.** Away; at a distance: *Stand back!* **6.** In reserve or concealment. **7.** In check. **8.** In return. **9.** In retort.

—back and forth. From one place to another and back again; to and fro. **—go back on. 1.** To fail to keep (a promise or commitment). **2.** To betray or desert (a person). [Middle English *bak,* Old English *bæc,* from Germanic *bakam* (unattested).]

back² *n.* A shallow vat or tub used chiefly by brewers. [Dutch *bak,* from French *bac,* from Old French, from Vulgar Latin *bacca* (unattested), a water vessel, perhaps from Celtic.]

back·ache (băk′āk′) *n.* A usually persistent ache or pain in the lower back.

back·bench·er (băk′běn′chər) *n. Chiefly British.* **1.** Any of the Members of Parliament, who sit on the rear benches of the House of Commons and are not ministers or shadow ministers. Also called "bencher." See **front bench, crossbench.** **2.** One occupying an equivalent position in a similar legislative body.

back·bite (băk′bīt′) *v.* **-bit** (-bĭt′), **-bitten** (-bĭt′n) or *informal* **-bit, -biting, -bites.** —*tr.* To slander the character or reputation of (an absent person). —*intr.* To speak spitefully or slanderously of a person in his absence. **—back·bit·er** *n.*

back·blocks (băk′blŏks′) *pl.n. Australian.* A remote and sparsely populated area, especially in the interior of Australia. **—back·block·er** *n.*

back·board (băk′bôrd′, -bōrd′) *n.* **1.** A board that can be worn, or one that can be placed under the mattress of a bed, to support the back. **2.** *Basketball.* The elevated, vertical board from which the basket projects.

back·bone (băk′bōn′) *n.* **1.** The vertebrate spine or spinal column. **2.** Anything that resembles a backbone in appearance or position, such as the keel of a ship. **3.** A main support or major sustaining factor: *"Doubt and the Land League were the backbone of the conflict with England"* (Sean O'Faolain). **4.** Strength of character; fortitude; determination. **5.** The main ridge of a mountain range or the main range of mountains in a region. **—See Synonyms at courage. —back·boned** *adj.*

back·break·ing (băk′brā′kĭng) *adj.* Demanding great physical exertion; exhausting; arduous. **—back·break·er** *n.*

back·chat (băk′chăt′) *n. Chiefly British.* Back talk.

back·cloth (băk′klôth′, -klŏth′) *n. Chiefly British.* **1.** A large, usually painted, cloth forming the background to a stage set. **2.** A setting or background.

back·comb (băk′kōm′) *v.* **-combed, -combing, -combs.** —*tr.* To comb (the hair) from the ends toward the roots to give fullness. —*intr.* To backcomb the hair.

back country *n.* A remote, sparsely populated area.

back·court (băk′kôrt′, -kōrt′) *n.* **1.** In tennis and other racket games, the part of a court between the service line and the base line. **2.** In other games, such as handball or basketball, the part of the playing area farthest from the goal or target wall.

back·cross (băk′krôs′, -krŏs′) *v.* **-crossed, -crossing, -crosses.** *Genetics.* —*tr.* To mate (a first-generation hybrid) with a parent or member of the parental stock. —*intr.* To breed or cross in this way. ~*n. Genetics.* The act or result of backcrossing.

back·date (băk′dāt′) *tr.v.* **-dated, -dating, -dates.** To make retroactive by assigning an earlier date to: *The June pay raise was backdated to January.*

back door *n.* **1.** A door to a building other than the front or main door. **2.** An unfair, covert, or underhand method used to obtain a promotion, job, or the like: *He got into the company through the back door.*

back·door (băk′dôr′, -dōr′) *adj.* Done or formed secretly or surreptitiously; clandestine.

back·drop (băk′drŏp′) *n.* **1.** A painted curtain or screen forming the background to a stage set. **2.** The setting, as of a historical event.

backed (băkt) *adj.* Having or furnished with a back or backing. Usually used in combination: *a low-backed chair.*

back end *n. British Informal.* Autumn.

back·er (băk′ər) *n.* **1.** One who supports, gives aid to, or invests in a person, group, or enterprise. **2.** One who bets on a contestant.

back·field (băk′fēld′) *n.* **1.** *Football.* The players stationed behind the line of scrimmage. **2.** The area occupied by these players.

back·fill (băk′fĭl′) *tr.v.* **-filled, -filling, -fills.** To refill (an excavated ditch).

back·fire (băk′fīr′) *n.* **1.** An explosion of prematurely ignited fuel or of unburned exhaust gases in an internal-combustion engine. **2.** A fire started purposely in the path of an oncoming fire so that the latter will be extinguished on reaching an area that has already been burned out. **3.** An explosion of ammunition in the breech of a gun. ~*intr.v.* **backfired, -firing, -fires. 1.** To explode in or make the sound of a backfire. **2.** To start or employ a backfire. **3.** To produce an unexpected and undesired result: *His plot backfired on him.*

back·for·ma·tion (băk′fôr-mā′shən) *n. Linguistics.* **1.** A new word created by removing from an existing word what is mistakenly thought to be an affix, as *laze* from *lazy* or *edit* from *editor.* **2.** The process of forming words in this way.

back·gam·mon (băk′găm′ən) *n.* A game for two persons, played on a specially marked board with pieces whose moves are determined by throws of dice. [BACK (referring to the movement of the pieces) + GAMMON (a type of victory in the game).]

back·ground (băk′ground′) *n.* **1.** The ground located behind closer areas. **2. a.** The space in pictorial representation, usually appearing as if in the distance, arranged to provide relief for the principal objects. **b.** The general scene or surface against or upon which designs, patterns, figures, or the like are seen or represented. **3.** An area or position of relative obscurity or unimportance. **4.** The underlying or supporting causes of or the contributory circumstances connected with an occurrence or development; the context in which something occurs. **5. a.** A person's experience, training, and education, often in a specified area. **b.** A person's social class, personal history, or family circumstances. **6. a.** Music or sounds heard as accompaniment to dialogue or action in a dramatic performance, film, or broadcast. **b.** Subdued music played in a public place, such as a restaurant or airport, to create atmosphere. **7.** Radiation at a constant low level at any specific location, usually due to traces of naturally occurring radioactive elements and cosmic rays. Also called "background radiation." **8.** Noise or interference, usually at a constant level, that is picked up by electronic devices. —**back·ground** *adj.*

back·ground·er (băk′groun′dər) *n. Slang.* An informal meeting at which an official provides background information, as to news reporters, about a governmental issue.

back·hand (băk′hănd′) *n.* **1.** In sports such as tennis and table tennis, a stroke or motion, as of a racket, made with the back of the hand facing outward and the arm typically held across the body. Compare **forehand**. **2.** Handwriting characterized by letters that slant to the left.
~*adj.* Backhanded.
~*adv.* With a backhanded stroke or motion.
~*tr.v.* **backhanded, -handing, -hands.** To perform, hit, or catch backhand.

back·hand·ed (băk′hăn′dĭd) *adj.* **1.** Made with the back of the hand or with the back of the hand facing outward and moving away from the body. **2.** Slanting toward the left. **3.** Containing a disguised insult or rebuke: *a backhanded compliment.* **4.** Twisted or formed in a direction opposite to the normal one: *backhanded rope.* —**back·hand·ed·ly** *adv.* —**back·hand·ed·ness** *n.*

back·hand·er (băk′hăn′dər) *n.* **1.** A backhanded stroke or hit. **2.** *British Informal.* A bribe. **3.** An indirect verbal attack.

back·hoe (băk′hō′) *n.* A machine used in excavating, having a digging device attached to a hinged extension that draws it toward the operator with a motion like that used in hoeing.

back·ing (băk′ĭng) *n.* **1.** Material that provides support or strength from the back. **2.** Support or aid; endorsement. **3.** Those who provide aid or support. **4.** A musical accompaniment for a performer.

back·lash (băk′lăsh′) *n.* **1.** A strongly adverse, usually delayed, reaction to some prior development that has been construed as a threat, as in the context of morality or social or race relations. **2.** A sudden or violent backward whipping motion. **3.** A snarl in the part of a fishing line wound round the reel. **4.** The play resulting from loose connections between gears or other mechanical elements, which is most evident on reversal of movement.

back·less (băk′lĭs) *adj.* Having no back; especially, of a dress, cut to the waist or very low at the back.

back·list (băk′lĭst′) *n.* A publisher's list of older titles kept in print.

back·log (băk′lôg′, -lŏg′) *n.* **1.** An accumulation, especially of unfinished work or unfilled orders. **2.** A reserve supply or source. **3.** A large log placed at the back of a fire to support other logs and maintain heat.

back matter *n. Printing.* End matter (see).

back number *n.* **1.** An out-of-date periodical or newspaper. **2.** *Informal.* An out-of-date or old-fashioned person or thing.

back·pack (băk′păk′) *n.* **1.** A knapsack, often mounted on a lightweight frame, that is worn on the back to carry camping supplies. **2.** A piece of equipment made for use while being carried on the back.
~*v.* **backpacked, -packing, -packs.** —*intr.* To hike while carrying supplies in a backpack. —*tr.* To carry in a backpack. —**back·pack·er** *n.*

back·ped·al (băk′pĕd′l) *intr.v.* **-aled, -aling, -als** or *chiefly British* **-alled, -alling.** **1.** To turn the pedals backward, as on a bicycle. **2.** To withdraw from or qualify a previous commitment, stance, opinion, or the like. **3.** In boxing, to go backward.

back projection *n.* The projection of a film onto a screen from behind the screen, often used as a background for a scene being filmed from the front.

back·rest (băk′rĕst′) *n.* A support or rest for the back.

back·room (băk′rōōm′, -rŏŏm′) *adj.* Of or pertaining to a planning department or scientific laboratory in which confidential work, often governmental and military, is carried out and from which indirect influence is often exercised. —**back room** *n.*

backroom boy *n. Chiefly British Informal.* A person engaged in backroom work.

back·rush (băk′rŭsh′) *n.* The seaward return of water after the landward motion of a wave.

back·saw (băk′sô′) *n.* A saw that is reinforced by a metal band along its back edge.

back·scat·ter (băk′skăt′ər) *n.* The deflection of waves or particles through angles greater than 90° by electromagnetic or nuclear forces. Also called "backscattering."

back·scratch·er (băk′skrăch′ər) *n.* **1.** A long-handled implement made of wood or plastic, used to scratch one's own back. **2.** *Informal.* One involved in the giving and receiving of favors for personal gain, often in an underhand way, as in politics or business. —**back·scratch·ing** *n.*

back seat *n.* **1.** A seat in the back, especially of a vehicle or an auditorium. **2.** *Informal.* A subordinate position. Used chiefly in the phrase *take a back seat.*

back-seat driver (băk′sēt′) *n. Informal.* **1.** A passenger in a car who constantly advises, corrects, or nags the driver. **2.** Any person who persists in giving unsolicited advice.

back·set (băk′sĕt′) *n.* **1.** A setback; reversal. **2.** An eddy or countercurrent in water.

backsheesh, backshish. Variants of **baksheesh.**

back·side (băk′sīd′) *n.* **1.** The back or rear part of something. **2.** *Informal.* The buttocks; rump.

back·sight (băk′sīt′) *n.* **1.** In surveying, a reading taken facing backward to a previous position. **2.** *Chiefly British.* The sight on a rifle nearer the stock.

back·slap·ping (băk′slăp′ĭng) *adj.* Excessively hearty. —**back·slap·ping** *n.*

back·slide (băk′slīd′) *intr.v.* **-slid** (-slĭd′), **-slid** or **-slidden** (-slĭd′n), **-sliding, -slides.** To revert to a bad habit, sin, wrongdoing, or the like. —**back·slid·er** *n.*

back·space (băk′spās′) *intr.v.* **-spaced, -spacing, -spaces.** To move the carriage of a typewriter back one or more spaces by striking the key used for this purpose.
~*n.* The key on a typewriter used for backspacing. Also called "backspacer," "backspace key."

back·spin (băk′spĭn′) *n.* A spin that tends to retard, arrest, or reverse the linear motion of an object, especially of a ball.

back·stage (băk′stāj′) *adv.* **1.** In or toward the dressing rooms, wings, or other areas behind the performing area in a theater. **2.** In or toward a place closed to public view; privately.
~*adj.* (băk′stāj′). **1.** Occurring or situated behind the performing area of a theater. **2.** Not open or known to the public; private or concealed.

back·stairs (băk′stârz′) *n.* A secondary staircase at the back of a house especially one formerly used by servants.
~*adj.* Also **back·stair** (-stâr′). **1.** Furtive; clandestine. **2.** Scandalous.

back·stay (băk′stā′) *n.* **1.** A rope or shroud extending from the top of the mast aft to the ship's side or stern to help support the mast. **2.** A support at or for the back of something.

back·stitch (băk′stĭch′) *n.* A stitch made by inserting the needle at the midpoint of the preceding stitch, so that each stitch overlaps another by half its length. —**back·stitch** *v.*

back·stop (băk′stŏp′) *n.* **1.** A screen or fence used to prevent a ball from being thrown or hit far out of a playing area, as in baseball or tennis. **2.** *Baseball.* A catcher. **3.** A device that prevents excessive backward movement, as of a machine part.
~*tr.v.* **backstopped, -stopping, -stops.** **1.** To serve as a backstop for. **2. a.** To support. **b.** To substitute for (another) in an emergency.

back straight *n. Chiefly British.* The backstretch.

back·street (băk′strēt′) *n.* A minor or side street, especially one away from a main thoroughfare.
~*adj.* **1.** Situated on or pertaining to a backstreet. **2.** Operating or performed illegally or secretly: *a backstreet abortion.*

back·stretch (băk′strĕch′) *n.* The part of an oval racecourse farthest from the spectators and opposite the homestretch, usually a straightaway.

back·stroke (băk′strōk′) *n.* **1.** A swimming stroke that resembles an inverted crawl. It is executed with the swimmer on his back, using a flutter kick, and moving his arms in backward circular strokes. **2.** A backhanded stroke. **3.** A stroke or motion made in return or as a recoil.

back·swim·mer (băk′swĭm′ər) *n.* Any of various insects of the family Notonectidae that swim or float on their backs.

back·sword (băk′sôrd′, -sōrd′) *n.* **1.** A sword with only one cutting edge. **2.** A stick used in fencing practice, a **singlestick** *(see).* **3.** One who fights with a backsword.

back talk *n.* Impudent contradiction; an insolent retort.

back-to-back (băk′tə-băk′) *adj.* **1.** Facing away from each other. **2.** *British.* Having the backs facing or adjoining. Said of rows of houses. **3.** *Informal.* In succession: *two films back-to-back.*
~*n. British.* A back-to-back house. —**back-to-back** *adv.*

back·track (băk′trăk′) *intr.v.* **-tracked, -tracking, -tracks.** **1.** To go back over the course by which one has come. **2.** To reverse one's position or policy; retreat.

back up *tr.v.* **1.** To support or help, especially through reinforcement, confirmation, or safeguards. **2.** *Printing.* To print the reverse side of (a sheet). **3.** *Computer Science.* To provide a duplicate copy of (a data file). —*intr.v.* To accumulate.

back·up (băk′ŭp′) *n.* **1. a.** A reserve supply, as of provisions. **b.** One kept in reserve, as a safeguard or substitute, for example. **2. a.** Support or backing. **b.** A background accompaniment, as for a musical performer. **3.** *Computer Science.* A copy of a data file made and kept in case of computer failure. **4.** An overflow caused by clogged plumbing.
~*adj.* **1.** Kept in reserve; standby: *a back-up pilot.* **2.** Supporting; auxiliary.

back·veld (băk′fĕlt′, -vĕlt′) *n. South African.* A remote, rural, thinly populated area. [Afrikaans *backvelt,* "back field."] —**back·veld** *adj.* —**back·veld·er** *n.*

back·ward (băk′wərd) *adj.* **1. a.** Directed or facing toward the back or rear. **b.** Directed toward the beginning or start. **c.** Directed toward the past; regressive. **2. a.** Done with the back leading or first: *a backward somersault.* **b.** Done or arranged in reverse or in a manner contrary to the usual. **3.** Unwilling to act; reluctant; shy. **4.** Behind others in progress or development.

THE EARLIEST FORMS OF LIFE ON EARTH
Without microscopic bacteria, plants and animals could not survive

Bacteria are some of the simplest of all organisms. Traces have been found in rocks as much as 3,100 million years old; they probably represent the earliest stages of the development of life on earth.

Bacteria originated in the ocean, and today are found in greatest abundance in seas, lakes, and other moist environments.

Although many bacteria cause disease, others perform functions that are essential to life. Some bacteria break down the vast range of organic matter in the soil; without them the soil would become sterile and grow nothing. Others turn nitrogen from the air into a form that can be used as plant food. There are also bacteria that break down waste products in the gut of the host animal.

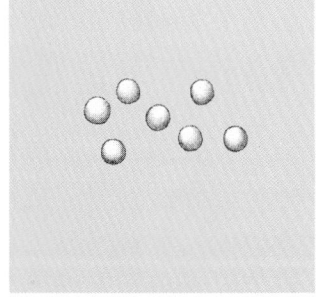 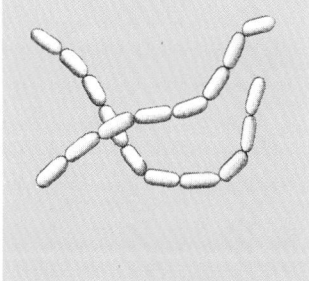 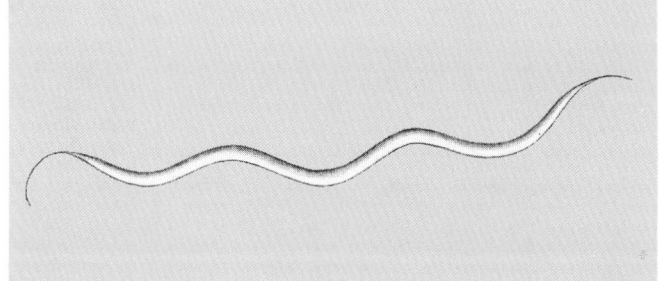

BACTERIA SHAPES *Bacteria occur in enormous numbers. Most of them reproduce by cell division—one cell dividing into two new ones. In this way a single bacterial cell can produce 16 million progeny in 24 hours. There are three main shapes, illustrated from left to right: spherical (coccus), rodlike (bacillus), and spiral (spirillum).*

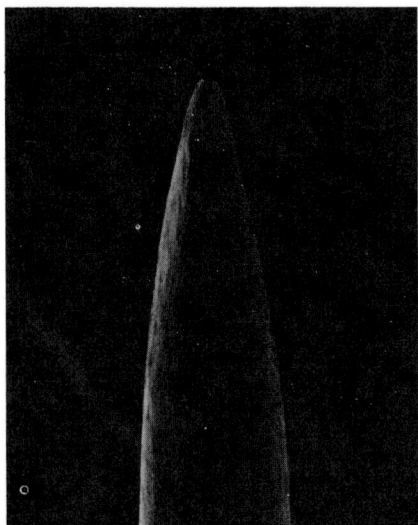 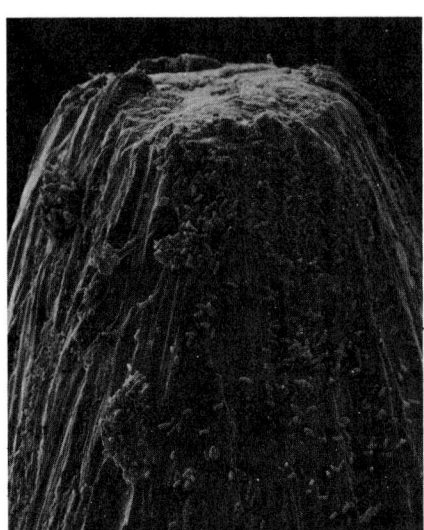 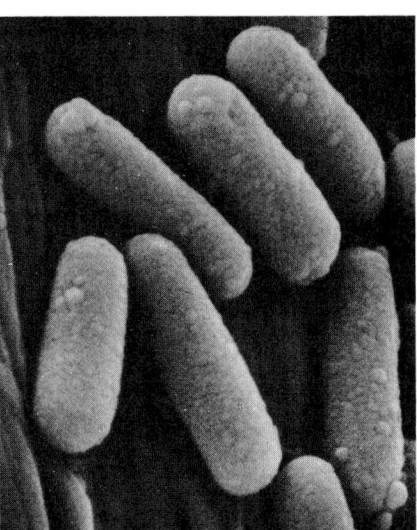

BACTERIA SIZES *Bacteria are tiny, ranging from about 0.0001 to 0.0005 millimeter in length. They are so profuse that a single drop of saliva may contain millions of them, and a gram of garden soil billions. These bacteria on the point of a pin have been magnified (left to right) 50, 1,250, and 31,250 times.*

Bactrian camel *This largely domesticated two-humped camel is used throughout central Asia for riding and to supply meat, hides, wool, and some milk. Unlike the single-humped dromedary, Bactrian camels can survive in cold desert regions as well as hot ones.*

~*adv.* Also **back·wards. 1.** To or toward the back or rear. **2.** With the back leading. **3.** In a manner or order contrary to the usual or expected; in reverse. **4.** To, toward, or into the past. —**back·ward·ly** *adv.* —**back·ward·ness** *n.*

back·wash (băk′wŏsh′, -wôsh′) *n.* **1.** Water moved backward, as by the action of oars or a motor. **2.** A backward flow of air, as from the propeller of an aircraft. **3.** A flow of water back down a beach after a wave has broken. **4.** A condition resulting from some disturbing or irregular event; an aftermath.

back·wa·ter (băk′wô′tər, -wŏt′ər) *n.* **1.** Water held or pushed back by or as if by a dam or current; especially, a body of stagnant or still water thus formed. **2.** A place or situation regarded as stagnant or backward: *a cultural backwater.*

back·woods (băk′wŏŏdz′, -wŏŏdz′) *pl.n.* **1.** Heavily wooded, uncultivated areas. **2.** Any remote, thinly populated, and backward area. —**back·woods** *adj.*

back·woods·man (băk′wŏŏdz′mən, -wŏŏdz′mən) *n., pl.* **-men** (-mĭn). **1.** One who lives or was brought up in a backwoods area, especially one who is unfamiliar with the customs of urban life; a rustic. **2.** *British.* A peer who rarely or never attends the House of Lords.

back yard, back·yard (băk′yärd′) *n.* **1.** A yard at the rear of a house. **2.** A region or sphere of special concern, especially one that is geographically close: *a war in America's back yard.*

ba·con (bā′kən) *n.* The salted and often smoked meat from the back and sides of a pig. —**bring home the bacon.** *Informal.* **1.** To provide food and other necessities. **2.** To make good; succeed. —**save one's bacon.** To escape harm or loss. [Middle English *bacon, ba-koun,* from Old French *bacon, bacun,* from Frankish *bako* (unattested), ham, from Germanic *bakkon* (unattested), perhaps akin to *bakam* (unattested), BACK.]

Ba·con (bā′kən), **Francis** (1910–). British painter. He is best known for his disturbing portraits in which subjects are distorted and invested with feelings of terror.

Bacon, Francis, 1st Baron Verulam, Viscount St. Albans (1561-1626). English philosopher, politician, and Lord Chancellor. His many influential writings include *The Advancement of Learning* (1605) and the *Novum Organum* (1620), in which he put forward a new theory of scientific knowledge based on observation and experiment that came to be known as the inductive method.

Bacon, Roger (*c.* 1214-94). English scientist, encyclopedist, philosopher, alchemist, and Franciscan monk; for these diverse skills he was called *Doctor Mirabilis* ("Admirable Doctor").

Ba·co·ni·an (bā-kō′nē-ən) *adj.* Of, pertaining to, or characteristic of the works or thought of the philosopher Francis Bacon.

~*n.* **1.** A follower of the doctrines of Francis Bacon. **2.** One who believes that Francis Bacon wrote Shakespeare's plays.

bact. bacteria; bacterial.

bac·te·re·mi·a (băk′tə-rē′mē-ə) *n.* The presence of viable bacteria in the blood. [New Latin : BACTER(IO)- + -EMIA.] —**bac·te·re·mic** *adj.* —**bac·te·re·mi·cal·ly** *adv.*

bac·te·ri·a (băk-tîr′ē-ə) *pl.n. Singular* **-rium** (-əm). *Abbr.* **bact.** Microorganisms, usually single-celled, constituting the class Schizomycetes, occurring in a wide variety of forms. Most bacteria are either free-living saprophytes, bringing about decomposition, or parasites, many of which cause disease. —See Usage note at **germ.** [New

Latin, plural of *bacterium*, from Greek *baktērion*, diminutive of *baktron*, rod.] —**bac·te·ri·al** *adj.* —**bac·te·ri·al·ly** *adv.*

bac·te·ri·cide (băk-tîr′ə-sīd′) *n.* A substance that destroys bacteria. [BACTERI(O)- + -CIDE.] —**bac·te·ri·ci·dal** *adj.*

bac·te·rin (băk′tə-rĭn) *n.* A vaccine prepared from dead bacteria. [BACTER(IO)- + -IN.]

bacterio-, bacteri-, bacter- *prefix.* Indicates bacteria, bacterial activity, or relationship to bacteria; for example, **bacteriophage, bactericide, bacteroid.** [From BACTERIA.]

bac·te·ri·ol·o·gy (băk-tîr′ē-ŏl′ə-jē) *n. Abbr.* **bacteriol.** The study of bacteria, especially in relation to medicine and agriculture. [BACTERIO- + -LOGY.] —**bac·te·ri·o·log·i·cal** (băk-tîr′ē-ə-lŏj′ĭ-kəl), **bac·te·ri·o·log·ic** *adj.* —**bac·te·ri·o·log·i·cal·ly** *adv.* —**bac·te·ri·ol·o·gist** *n.*

bac·te·ri·ol·y·sis (băk-tîr′ē-ŏl′ə-sĭs) *n.* The dissolution of bacteria, especially by the action of specific antibodies. [New Latin : BACTERIO- + -LYSIS.] —**bac·te·ri·o·lyt·ic** (băk-tîr′ē-ə-lĭt′ĭk) *adj.*

bac·te·ri·o·phage (băk-tîr′ē-ə-fāj′) *n.* A virus that is parasitic on and destroys bacteria. Also called "phage." [BACTERIO- + -PHAGE.] —**bac·te·ri·o·phag·ic, bac·te·ri·oph·a·gous** (băk-tîr′ē-ŏf′ə-gəs) *adj.* —**bac·te·ri·o·phag·i·cal·ly** *adv.*

bac·te·ri·o·sta·sis (băk-tîr′ē-ō-stā′sĭs) *n.* The arresting or inhibition of bacterial growth and reproduction, usually by the action of drugs. [New Latin : BACTERIO- + -STASIS.] —**bac·te·ri·o·stat·ic** (băk-tîr′ē-ō-stăt′ĭk) *adj.* —**bac·te·ri·o·stat·i·cal·ly** *adv.*

bac·te·ri·um (băk-tîr′ē-əm) *n.* Singular of **bacteria.**

bac·te·roid (băk′tə-roid′) *adj.* Also **bac·te·roi·dal** (băk′tə-roid′l). Resembling bacteria in appearance or action.
~*n.* Any of various irregularly shaped bacteria, such as those occurring on the roots of leguminous plants. [BACTER(IO)- + -OID.]

Bac·tri·an camel (băk′trē-ən) *n.* A two-humped camel, *Camelus bactrianus,* native to central and southwestern Asia and used as a beast of burden. Compare **dromedary.**

bac·u·li·form (băk′yə-lə-fôrm′, bə-kyōō′lə-) *adj.* Rod-shaped. [Latin *baculum,* stick, staff + -FORM.]

bad¹ (băd) *adj.* **worse** (wûrs), **worst** (wûrst). **1.** Inferior; poor in quality. **2.** Evil; wicked; sinful. **3.** Misbehaving; disobedient; naughty. **4.** Disagreeable; unpleasant; disturbing: *bad news.* **5.** Unfavorable: *bad reviews.* **6.** Rotten; spoiled; decomposed. **7.** Harmful in effect; detrimental: *bad habits.* **8.** Not able to be recovered or discharged: *a bad debt.* **9. a.** Faulty or incorrect: *bad grammar.* **b.** Incompetent: *bad at sums.* **10.** Not valid or genuine: *a bad check.* **11.** Severe; violent; intense: *a bad cold.* **12.** In poor health; in pain; ill. **13.** Sorry; regretful; unhappy: *Don't feel bad about it.* **14.** *Slang.* Very good; excellent. —**in bad.** *Informal.* In trouble or disfavor. —**not half** (or **so**) **bad.** *Informal.* Rather good; acceptable.
~*n.* Wickedness: *go to the bad.*
~*adv. Informal.* Badly. [Middle English *badde,* perhaps from Old English *bæddel,* effeminate man, hermaphrodite.] —**bad·ness** *n.*

bad². *Archaic.* A past tense of **bid.**

bad blood *n.* Bitterness; animosity.

bad·der·locks (băd′ər-lŏks′) *n. Used with a singular or plural verb.* An edible seaweed, *Alaria esculenta,* having long, yellowish-green fronds. [18th century : origin obscure.]

bad·dy, bad·die (băd′ē) *n., pl.* **-dies.** *Informal.* A criminal or villain, especially as portrayed in a film, play, or book.

bade. A past tense of **bid.**

Ba·den¹ (bäd′n). Also **Ba·den bei Wien** (bī vēn′). Spa town in Lower Austria, near Vienna, at the foot of the Wienerwald.

Baden². Health resort in Aargau canton, northern Switzerland, famous for its hot springs.

Baden³. Former state in southwestern West Germany. Bounded by the Main and Rhine rivers, it is now part of Baden-Württemberg.

Ba·den-Ba·den (bäd′n-bäd′n). Fashionable spa town in Baden-Württemberg, West Germany. Its hot springs have been known since Roman times.

Ba·den-Pow·ell (bäd′n-pō′əl), **Robert Stephenson Smyth, 1st Baron** (1857–1941). British general, founder of the Boy Scout movement. As a soldier he is famous for his heroic defense of Mafeking during the Boer War.

Ba·den-Würt·tem·berg (bäd′n-vûrt′əm-bĕrg′). State of West Germany. It was formed (1952) by the amalgamation of Baden and Württemberg. Stuttgart is its capital.

bad faith *n.* A dishonest and deceiving attitude.

badge (băj) *n.* **1.** A small metal disk worn on clothing, bearing a design, slogan, or the like. **2.** A device or emblem worn as an insignia of rank, office, or membership in an organization or as an award or honor. **3.** Any characteristic mark or symbol. —See Synonyms at **sign.** [Middle English *bag(g)e*†.]

badg·er (băj′ər) *n.* **1.** Any of several large carnivorous, burrowing animals of the family Mustelidae, such as *Meles meles,* of Eurasia, or *Taxidea taxus,* of North America, typically having black and white stripes on the head, short legs, long claws on the front feet, and a heavy, silvery grizzled coat. **2.** The fur or hair of a badger. **3.** Any of several mammals related to or resembling the badger, uch as the **honey badger** (*see*), or, in Australia, the wombat or the bandicoot.
~*tr.v.* **badgered, -ering, -ers.** To harass persistently; pester. —See Synonyms at **harass.** [16th century : perhaps BADGE (from the white mark on its forehead).]

bad·i·nage (băd′ə-näzh′) *n.* Light, playful banter; flippant repartee. [French, from *badin,* fool, joker, from Provençal, from *badar,* to gape, from Vulgar Latin *batāre* (unattested).]

bad·lands (băd′lăndz′) *pl.n.* An area of barren land characterized by roughly eroded ridges, peaks, and plateaus.

Bad·lands (băd′lăndz′). A heavily eroded arid region of southwestern South Dakota, characterized by gullies and sharply indented ridges. It is now a national monument.

Badlands *This arid, heavily eroded plateau in South Dakota, also known as the Big Badlands, got its name because explorers found it difficult to cross. The area has given its name to similar regions around the world.*

---

badger

THE UNDERGROUND LIFE OF THE BADGER

The fastidious housekeeper that hunts by night

During the day most badgers in Europe live in groups in a set—a labyrinth of underground tunnels and chambers that penetrates up to 18 meters (20 yards) into woodland hillside and that they keep scrupulously clean. It is only at night that they emerge to search for bedding and food, which includes earthworms, insects, small mammals, snails, and berries. Sometimes they leave a trail of scent behind them so that they can find their way back home.

There are eight species of badger, six of which are found only in south and southeast Asia. The Eurasian badger, which is found from western Europe to China, has a silver-gray body with bold black-and-white stripes on its head. The American badger, which is widespread in North America, is a smaller animal with a gray body, a single white stripe from its muzzle to its shoulders, and black patches on its cheeks. It is found in the western part of North America, usually in open, dry country. For most of the time it lives alone. It burrows rapidly with its powerful claws and can defend itself fiercely from an attacker if cornered.

EURASIAN BADGER *This species of badger is some 900 millimeters (35 inches) long, with strong claws for burrowing.*

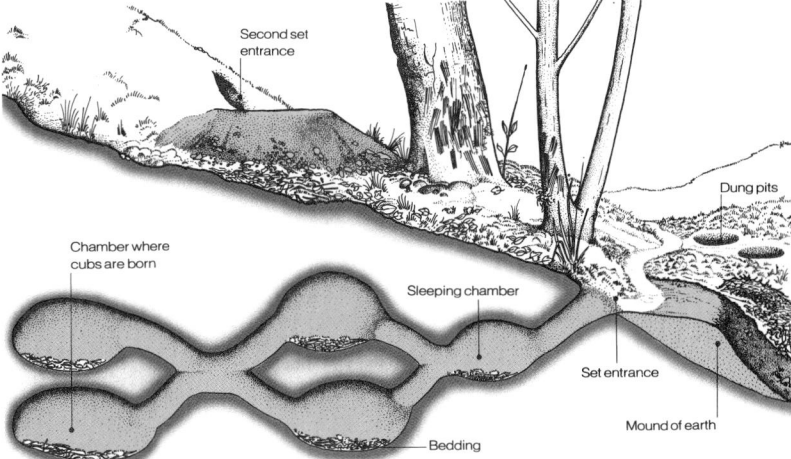

BADGER'S SET *The badger digs a deep set at the base of a tree, building up a mound of earth at the entrance. It sharpens its claws against the tree.*

Second set entrance

Dung pits

Chamber where cubs are born

Sleeping chamber

Set entrance

Mound of earth

Bedding

bad·ly (băd′lē) *adv.* **worse, worst. 1.** In a bad manner. **2.** Very much; greatly.

bad·min·ton (băd′mĭn′tən) *n.* **1.** A game played by volleying a shuttlecock back and forth over a high, narrow net by means of a light, long-handled racket. **2.** *Chiefly British.* A drink usually made with claret, soda water, and sugar and served cold. [After BADMINTON.]

Bad·min·ton (băd′mĭn′tən). A village in Avon, England, in the Cotswolds. Annual horse trials are held on the grounds of Badminton House (built 1682), the country seat of the dukes of Beaufort. The game of badminton is reputed to have originated here.

bad-mouth (băd′mouth′, -mouth′) *tr.v.* **-mouthed, -mouthing, -mouths.** *Slang.* To criticize or disparage, often spitefully or unfairly; run down.

bad news *n. Used with a singular verb. Slang.* A troublesome or undesirable person, thing, or situation.

Baeda. See **Bede.**

Bae·de·ker (bā′dĭ-kər) *n.* **1.** Any of a series of guidebooks to Europe and the Middle East produced by the German publisher Karl Baedeker (1801–59) or his company. **2.** Any guidebook.

Baeke·land (bāk′lănd′), **Leo Hendrick** (1863–1944). Belgian-born U.S. chemist and inventor. He invented the first plastic that hardens permanently on heating and does not soften when reheated, which he called **Bakelite** *(see).* He also invented the first commercially successful photographic printing paper.

Baer (bâr), **Karl Ernst von** (1792–1876). Estonian-born German zoologist. He made pioneering researches in the mammalian reproductive system, discovering the mammalian egg, and is considered to be one of the founders of the science of embryology.

Ba·ez (bī′ĕz′, bī-ĕz′), **Joan** (1941–   ). U.S. folk singer and political activist.

Baf·fin (băf′ĭn), **William** (1584–1622). English navigator. While searching for the Northwest Passage (1615–16), he discovered Baffin Bay and explored the northern part of Baffin Island.

Baffin Island. Formerly **Baffin Land.** The largest island in the Canadian Arctic Archipelago, and at 476,068 square kilometers (183,810 square miles) the fifth-largest island in the world.

baf·fle (băf′əl) *tr.v.* **-fled, -fling, -fles. 1.** To foil; thwart; frustrate: *The police were baffled by the lack of clues.* **2.** To perplex to the point of helplessness; bewilder. **3.** To impede the force or movement of; interfere with. —See Synonyms at **puzzle.** ~*n.* Any structure used to impede, regulate, or alter the flow of a fluid or to control the emission or distribution of sound. Also called "baffle plate." [Perhaps obscurely related to French *bafouer,* to hoodwink, deceive, from Old French *beffert†,* ridicule.] —**baf·fle·ment** *n.* —**baf·fler** *n.*

baf·fling (băf′lĭng) *adj.* **1.** Of a nature that defies solution or understanding; bewildering. **2.** *Nautical.* Shifting in direction and tending to impede or interfere with progress. Said of winds.

bag (băg) *n.* **1.** A container in the form of a sack or pouch, made from a flexible material, such as paper, cloth, plastic, or leather. **2.** A woman's handbag. **3.** A suitcase, satchel, or other piece of hand luggage. **4.** An organic sac or pouch, such as the udder of a cow. **5.** Something resembling a bag or pouch. **6.** *Nautical.* The bulging part of a sail. **7. a.** The amount held in a bag; bagful. **b.** *British.* Any of various units of dry measure. **8.** The amount of game killed or permitted to be killed in a single day during one shooting expedition, or by one member of a shoot. **9.** *Informal.* A collection of persons or things: *His friends were a mixed bag.* **10.** *Baseball.* A base. **11.** *Slang.* An area of interest, activity or skill: *Cooking is not my bag.* **12.** *Slang.* An unpleasant or unattractive woman: *a disagreeable old bag.* **13.** A small amount of heroin, marijuana, or some other drug wrapped in paper. —**bag and baggage.** With all one's belongings; completely: *He moved out bag and baggage.* —**holding the bag.** *Informal.* Having full responsibility or blame thrust upon one. —**in the bag.** *Slang.* Assured of successful outcome; virtually accomplished or won. ~*v.* **bagged, bagging, bags.** —*tr.* **1.** To put into a bag. **2.** To cause to bulge like a bag. **3.** To capture or kill (game). **4.** *Informal.* **a.** To gain possession of; capture or steal. **b.** *British Informal.* To reserve the right to do or have. Used especially by children: *Bags I. Bags that piece of cake.* **5.** *Australian Slang.* To disparage; belittle. —*intr.* **1.** To hang or bulge loosely. **2.** To swell out. [Middle English *bagge,* from Old Norse *baggi†.*]

ba·gasse (bə-găs′) *n.* The dry pulp remaining from sugar cane or sugar beet after the juice has been extracted, used for making paper and as a fuel. [French, from Spanish *bagazo,* dregs, from *baga,* pod, husk, from Latin *bāca, bacca,* berry.]

bag·a·telle (băg′ə-tĕl′) *n.* **1.** An unimportant or insignificant thing; a trifle. **2.** A short piece of light verse or music. **3.** A game played on an oblong table with a cue and balls. [French, from Italian *bagatella,* diminutive formation perhaps from Latin *bāca, bacca,* berry.]

Bagdad. See **Baghdad.**

Bage·hot (băj′ət), **Walter** (1826–77). British economist, journalist, political theorist, and literary critic. He wrote *The English Constitution* (1867), an analysis of the comparative powers of the British organs of government.

ba·gel, bei·gel (bā′gəl) *n.* A ring-shaped roll with a tough, chewy texture, made from plain yeast dough that is dropped briefly into nearly boiling water and then baked. [Yiddish *beygel,* ultimately from Middle High German *bouc,* ring, bracelet, from Old High German *boug.*]

bagworm *The caterpillar of the bagworm builds a case, or bag (above), of twigs, leaves, or fiber in which it lies while it changes from caterpillar to adult. The female remains in the bag until she has been fertilized by the winged male, then lays her eggs in it before dying.*

bag·ful (băg′fŏŏl′) *n., pl.* **-fuls** or **bagsful.** The amount held by or contained in a bag.

bag·gage (băg′ĭj) *n.* **1.** The trunks, bags, and suitcases in which one carries one's belongings while traveling; luggage. **2.** The movable equipment and supplies of an army; impedimenta. **3.** *Informal.* A badly behaved, impudent, or saucy girl or woman. **4.** A set of ideas, beliefs, theories, or the like, especially when out-of-date or redundant. [Middle English *bagage,* from Old French, from *bague†,* bundle, pack.]

bag·ging (băg′ĭng) *n.* Coarse material used for making bags.

bag·gy (băg′ē) *adj.* **-gier, -giest.** Bulging or hanging loosely: *baggy trousers.* —**bag·gi·ly** *adv.* —**bag·gi·ness** *n.*

Bagh·dad or **Bag·dad** (băg′dăd′). The capital of Iraq since 1920, reputed to be the fabled city of the *Arabian Nights.* Situated on the Tigris River near the center of the country, it was built by the Abbassid caliph al-Mansur (8th century) on the site of an old Babylonian town. Modern Baghdad is an important industrial, commercial, and cultural center in the Arab world.

bag lady *n.* A homeless woman, especially one in a big city, who carries all her possessions in a shopping bag.

bag·man (băg′mən) *n., pl.* **-men** (-mĭn). **1.** *Slang.* A person who collects money for racketeers. **2.** *British.* A traveling salesman. **3.** *Australian.* A tramp; a swagman.

bagn·io (băn′yō) *n., pl.* **-ios. 1.** A brothel. **2.** *Obsolete.* A prison for slaves in the Orient. **3.** *Obsolete.* A public bathhouse in Italy or Turkey. [Italian *bagno,* "bath," from Latin *balneum,* from Greek *balaneion†.*]

bag of bones *n. Informal.* A very thin person or animal.

bag·pipe (băg′pīp′) *n.* Often **bagpipes.** A musical instrument having a flexible bag inflated either by being blown into through a tube with valves or by bellows, a double-reed melody pipe, and from one to four drone pipes. —**bag·pip·er** *n.*

ba·guette (bă-gĕt′) *n.* Also **ba·guet** (for senses 1, 2, 3). **1.** A gem cut into the form of a narrow rectangle. **2.** The form of such a gem. **3.** *Architecture.* A narrow, convex molding. **4.** A long, stick-shaped loaf of French bread. [French, "small rod," from Italian *bacchetta,* diminutive of *bacchio,* rod, from Latin *baculum,* stick, staff.]

bag·worm (băg′wûrm′) *n.* The larva of any of several moths of the family Psychidae, that encloses itself in a characteristic fibrous case, and that feeds upon and destroys tree foliage.

bah (bä, bă) *interj.* Used to express impatient rejection or contempt. [Probably from French (imitative).]

ba·ha·dur (bə-hŏ′dŏŏr, -hä′dŏŏr) *n.* A Hindu title of respect. Often used with the names of army officers. [Hindi *bahādur,* hero, from Persian *bahādur†,* brave.]

Ba·ha·i (bä-hä′ē, -hī′) *adj.* Of, pertaining to, or designating a religion founded in 1863 by the Iranian religious leader Bahaullah (1817–92), developed from **Babism** *(see),* and emphasizing the spiritual unity of all mankind. ~*n.* A teacher of or believer in the Bahai faith. [Persian *bahā′ī,* "of glory," from *Bahā′ u′llāh,* Bahaullah, "Glory of God."] —**Ba·ha·ism** (bə-hä′ĭz′əm, -hī′ĭz′əm) *n.* —**Ba·ha·ist** *adj. & n.*

Ba·ha·mas (bə-hä′məz). Also **Ba·ha·ma Islands** (-mə). Island state in the Atlantic Ocean, comprising some 700 islands and islets and numerous cays. Columbus made his first landfall here in 1492. The islands became a British colony (1717), internally self-governing (1964), and independent within the Commonwealth (1973). Tourism, including gambling, provides more than 60 percent of state revenues. Agriculture, fishing, and small industries are developing, but 80 percent of food requirements are still imported. Some 80 percent of the people are black descendants of slaves. Area, 13,935 square kilometers (5,379 square miles). Population, 200,000. Capital, Nassau on New Providence Island. See map at **Cuba.** —**Ba·ha·mi·an** (bə-hä′mē-ən) *adj. & n.*

Ba·ha·sa Indonesia (bä-hä′sə) *n.* The Malay language that is the official language of Indonesia.

Bahasa Malaysia *n.* Also **Bahasa Malay.** The Malay language that is the official language of Malaysia.

Ba·hi·a (bä-ē′ə, bə-hē′ə). State of northeast Brazil. Its capital is Salvador (also called Bahia).

Bahía de Cochinos. See **Bay of Pigs.**

Bah·rain or **Bah·rein** (bä-rān′). Arab country comprising a group of low, sandy islands off eastern Arabia. It was the first Arabian state to strike oil (1932), but this is now running out. However, oil revenues have created a welfare state and new industries, including oil refining (of imported and home-produced oil) and ship repairing. Bahrain is also a banking, communications, and tax-free entrepôt center for the Persian Gulf region. Area, 622 square kilometers (240 square miles). Population, 400,000. Capital, Manama, on Bahrain Island. See map at **Gulf States.**

Bahr el Azraq. See **Blue Nile.**

Bahret Lut. See **Dead Sea.**

baht (bät) *n., pl.* **bahts** or **baht. 1.** The basic monetary unit of Thailand, equal to 100 satangs. See feature at **currency. 2.** A note worth one baht. [Thai *bāt.*]

ba·hu·vri·hi (bä′hŏŏ-vrē′hē) *adj.* Designating a word made up of two elements, the first of which describes a feature of the second; for example, *graybeard.* Compare **dvandva.** [Sanskrit "having much rice," a compound made in this way.] —**ba·hu·vri·hi** *n.*

Bai·kal or **Bay·kal, Lake** (bī-kôl′, -käl′). The world's deepest lake, located in Siberia in the U.S.S.R. Its maximum depth is 1,742 meters (5,714 feet), and it covers 31,492 square kilometers (12,159 square miles).

bail¹ (bāl) *n.* **1.** Security, usually a sum of money, exchanged for the release of an arrested person, as a guarantee of his appearance for trial. **2.** Release from imprisonment provided by the payment of such security. **3.** The person who provides such security. —**jump bail.** To fail to appear in court when required after having been allowed bail. —**stand** (or **go**) **bail for.** To supply bail for; act as security for. ~*tr.v.* **bailed, bailing, bails. 1.** To secure the release of (a person) by providing bail. Often used with *out.* **2.** To release (a person) for whom bail has been paid. **3.** To deliver or transfer (property) to another for a special purpose, but without permanent transference of ownership. [Middle English *baile,* "custody," from Old French *bail,* from *baillier,* to take charge of, carry, from Latin *bājulāre,* from *bājulus†,* carrier.] —**bail·er** *n.*

bail² *v.* **bailed, bailing, bails.** Also *chiefly British* **bale.** —*tr.* **1.** To remove (water) from a boat by repeatedly filling a container and emptying it over the side. **2.** To empty (a boat) of water by this means. Usually used with *out.* —*intr.* To empty a boat of water by scooping or dipping. ~*n.* Also *chiefly British* **bale.** A container used for bailing. [Middle English *baille,* bucket, from Old French, probably from Vulgar Latin *bājula* (unattested), "carrier (of water)," from Latin *bājulus,* carrier. See **bail** (security).] —**bail·er** *n.*

bail³, bale (bāl) *n.* **1.** The arched, hooplike handle of a pail, kettle, or similar container. **2.** An arch or hoop, such as those used to support the top of a covered wagon. **3.** *Australian & New Zealand.* A frame used to secure the head of a cow while it is being milked. —**bail up.** *Australian & New Zealand.* To secure (a cow) in a bail. [Middle English *baile,* handle, probably from Old Norse *beygla,* bow, from *beygja* to bend.]

bail⁴ *n.* **1.** *Cricket.* One of the two small bars of wood placed across the top of the stumps to form the wicket. **2.** A pole or bar used to separate horses in an open stable. **3.** The hinged bar on a typewriter holding the paper against the platen. —**bail up.** *Australian.* **1.** To hold up in order to rob. **2.** To accost in order to speak to. [Middle English, from Old French *bail(e),* enclosed court, from *bailler†* to enclose.]

bail·a·ble (bā′lə-bəl) *adj.* **1.** Eligible for bail. **2.** Allowing or admitting of bail: *a bailable offense.*

Baile Átha Cliath. See **Dublin.**

bail·ee (bā-lē′) *n.* A person to whom property is bailed.

bai·ley (bā′lē) *n., pl.* **-leys.** The outer wall of a castle or the space enclosed by it. [Middle English *bailly, baile,* variant of BAIL (in cricket).]

Bailey bridge *n.* A temporary steel bridge that can be assembled rapidly from prefabricated parts. [Designed by Sir Donald *Bailey* (born 1901), British engineer.]

bail·ie (bā′lē) *n.* A Scottish municipal magistrate, elected by town councilors. [Middle English *bailli,* from Old French, variant of *baillif,* BAILIFF.]

bail·iff (bā′lĭf) *n.* **1.** A court attendant entrusted with a variety of duties, such as the custody of prisoners under arraignment, the protection of jurors, and the maintenance of order in a courtroom during a trial. **2.** An official who assists a British sheriff and who has the power to execute writs, processes, and arrests. **3.** *Chiefly British.* An agent who administers an estate on behalf of a landowner; a steward. [Middle English *baillif,* from Old French, from Medieval Latin *bājulīvus,* from Latin *bājulus,* carrier, "person in charge." See **bail** (security).]

bail·i·wick (bā′lĭ-wĭk′) *n.* **1.** The office or district of a bailiff. **2.** A person's specific area of interest, skill, or authority. [Middle English *bailliwik* : BAILIE + WICK.]

bail·ment (bāl′mənt) *n. Law.* **1.** The process of providing bail for an accused person. **2.** The act of delivering goods or personal property to another in trust.

bail·or (bā′lər, bā-lôr′) *n. Law.* A person who bails property to another.

bail out *intr.v.* **1.** To parachute from an aircraft. **2.** *Slang.* To abandon a project or enterprise. —*tr.v. Informal.* To extricate (another) from a difficult situation.

bail·out (bāl′out′) *n.* A rescue from financial difficulties.

bails·man (bālz′mən) *n., pl.* **-men** (-mĭn). *Law.* One who provides bail or security for another.

Bai·ly's beads (bā′lēz) *pl. n.* Bright spots of sunlight that appear briefly around the edge of the moon's disk immediately before and after the central phase in a solar eclipse, caused by the sun's shining through lunar valleys. [After Francis *Baily* (1774-1844), British astronomer.]

bain-ma·rie (băn′mə-rē′) *n., pl.* **bains-ma·rie** (băn′mə-rē′). A device consisting of a large pan containing hot water in which smaller pans may be set to cook the contents slowly or keep them warm. [French, from Medieval Latin *balneum Mariae,* "bath of Mary" (mistranslation of Medieval Greek *kaminos Marias,* "furnace of Mary"), after *Mary,* sister of Moses and an alleged alchemist.]

Bai·ram (bī-räm′, bī′räm) *n.* Either of two Muslim festivals occurring after Ramadan: *Lesser Bairam* occurs at the end of Ramadan and lasts for 3 days; *Greater Bairam* occurs 70 days later and lasts for 4 days. [Turkish *bayrām.*]

Baird (bârd), **John Logie** (1888-1946). British electrical engineer noted for his pioneering work in the field of television and in the use of radar and fiber optics.

bairn (bârn) *n. Scottish.* A child. [Middle English *barn,* Old English *bearn.*]

Bairns·fa·ther (bârnz′fä′thər), **Charles Bruce** (1888-1959). British cartoonist and author, famous for his World War I cartoon character "Old Bill."

bait¹ (bāt) *n.* **1.** Food or other lure placed on a hook or in a trap and used in the catching of fish, birds, or other animals. **2.** Any enticement; a temptation. **3.** *Chiefly British.* **a.** A stop for food or rest during a journey or a break from work. **b.** The food or drink consumed during such a break. ~*v.* **baited, baiting, baits.** —*tr.* **1.** To place food or other lure in or on (a trap or fishing hook). **2.** To lure or entice, especially by trickery or strategy. **3.** To set dogs upon (a chained animal, for example) for sport. **4.** To attack or torment, especially with persistent insult, criticism, or ridicule. **5.** To tease. **6.** *Archaic.* To feed (an animal) on a journey. —*intr. Archaic.* To stop for food or rest during a journey. —See Synonyms at **harass.** [Middle English, partly from Old Norse *beita,* to hunt with dogs, harass, and partly from Old Norse *beita* (a separate word), pasture, food, fish bait.] —**bait·er** *n.*

bait² *Falconry.* Variant of **bate.**

bai·za (bī′zä) *n.* A monetary unit of Oman equal to ¹/₁,₀₀₀ of the rial-omani. See feature at **currency.** [Arabic, from Hindi *paisā.*]

baize (bāz) *n.* A cotton or woolen material resembling felt, often bright green in color, and used chiefly as a cover for gaming and billiard tables. [French *baie* (plural *baies*), from *bai,* BAY (probably its original color).]

Baja California. See **Lower California.**

bake (bāk) *v.* **baked, baking, bakes.** —*tr.* **1. a.** To cook with continuous, even, dry heat, especially in an oven. **b.** To make by baking: *bake a cake; bake bread.* **2.** To harden, dry, or otherwise affect by subjecting to heat in or as if in an oven. —*intr.* **1.** To cook food, primarily bread, cakes, or pastry, by baking. **2.** To become cooked by baking. **3.** To become hard, dry, or otherwise affected by exposure to steady, dry heat. **4.** *Informal.* To feel very hot. ~*n.* **1. a.** The act or process of baking. **b.** The amount baked. **2.** A social gathering at which food is baked and served. Sometimes used in combination: *a clambake.* [Middle English *baken,* Old English *bacan.*]

baked Alaska *n.* A dessert consisting of ice cream covered with meringue, which is baked for a short time at a high temperature.

Ba·ke·lite (bā′kə-līt′) *n.* A trademark for any of a group of thermosetting plastics having high chemical and electrical resistance and used in a variety of manufactured articles. [After Leo BAEKELAND.]

bak·er (bā′kər) *n.* **1.** One who bakes and sells bread, cakes, or the like. **2.** A portable oven.

Bak·er, Mount (bā′kər). Peak, 3,287 meters (10,778 feet) high, in northwestern Washington, in the Cascade Range just south of the Canadian border.

baker's dozen *n.* A group of 13; one dozen plus one. [After the former custom among bakers of adding an extra roll to every dozen purchased as a safeguard against the possibility that 12 rolls might weigh light.]

Bak·ers·field (bā′kərz-fēld′). A city in south-central California, at the southern end of the fertile San Joaquin Valley. It is an oil, mining, and agricultural center. Gold was discovered in the region in 1855 and petroleum in 1899.

bak·er·y (bā′kə-rē) *n., pl.* **-ies. 1.** A place where products such as bread, cake, and pastries are baked. Also called "bakehouse." **2.** A shop where baked goods are sold. In this sense, also called "bakeshop."

bak·ing (bā′kĭng) *n.* **1.** The act or process of baking. **2.** The amount baked. ~*adj. Informal.* Extremely hot. ~*adv.* Used as an intensive: *baking hot.*

baking powder *n.* Any of various powdered mixtures of sodium bicarbonate, starch, and at least one slightly acidic compound such as cream of tartar, used as a raising agent in baking.

baking soda *n.* A chemical compound, **sodium bicarbonate** *(see).*

ba·kla·va (bä′klə-vä′) *n.* A dessert made of paper-thin layers of pastry, chopped nuts, and honey. [Turkish.]

bak·sheesh (băk′shēsh′) *n.* Also **bak·shish, back·sheesh, back·shish.** In Turkey, Egypt, India, and other Eastern countries, a tip, gratuity, or charitable gift. [Persian *bakhshīsh,* from *bakhshīdan,* to give.]

Bakst (bäkst), **Léon** (c. 1866-1924). Russian artist noted for his work in modernizing theater design. His best-known works were for ballets produced by Sergei Diaghilev in Paris.

Ba·ku (bä-kōō′). Port in the southern U.S.S.R., on the Caspian Sea. Since the 1870's it has been a center of Russian oil production.

Ba·ku·nin (bə-kōō′nĭn, bä-), **Mikhail Aleksandrovich** (1814-76). Russian anarchist and political theorist. Imprisoned in Russia for his revolutionary activities and exiled to Siberia, he escaped to London (1861). After many arguments with Marx, his brand of anarchism took final shape as the antithesis of Marx's communism.

BAL¹ (băl) *n.* A colorless, oily, viscous liquid, $C_3H_5(SH)_2(OH)$, used as an antidote for poisoning caused by lewisite, organic arsenic compounds, and heavy metals including mercury and gold. [B(RITISH) + A(NTI-) + L(EWISITE).]

BAL² *n. Computer Science.* A low-level assembly language. [B(ASIC) A(SSEMBLY) L(ANGUAGE).]

bal. balance.

bal·a·cla·va (băl′ə-klä′və) *n. Sometimes* **Balaclava. 1.** A woolen hood almost completely covering the head and neck. **2.** A similar hood often covering the shoulders as well, worn by soldiers and sailors, and originally worn by soldiers fighting in the Crimean

War. Also called "balaclava helmet." [After BALAKLAVA.]

Ba·la·kla·va (băl′ə-klä′və). A small port in southern Crimea in the U.S.S.R., now part of Sevastopol. It is famous for the battle between Russian troops and Turkish and British troops (1854) in the Crimean War, during which the British Light Brigade made a hopeless charge against heavy Russian guns.

bal·a·lai·ka (băl′ə-lī′kə) *n.* A Russian musical instrument with a triangular body and three strings. [Russian.]

bal·ance (băl′əns) *n. Abbr.* **bal.** **1. a.** A weighing device typically consisting of a rigid beam, horizontally suspended by a low-friction support at its center, with identical weighing pans hung at either end, one of which holds an unknown weight while the effective weight in the other is changed by known amounts until the beam is level and motionless. Also called "beam balance." **b.** Any of various other weighing devices, such as a **spring balance** *(see).* **2.** A critical state in which the outcome is still to be determined: *lives hanging in the balance.* **3.** A stable state characterized by cancellation of all forces, weights, or the like by equal opposing ones. **4.** A state of bodily equilibrium. **5.** A stable mental or psychological state; emotional equilibrium. **6.** A harmonious or satisfying arrangement or proportion of parts or elements, as in a design or composition. **7. a.** An influence or force tending to produce equilibrium; a counterpoise. **b.** A control or mechanism for achieving balance; specifically, a control balancing the average sound level from a high-fidelity system. **8.** The difference in magnitude between opposing forces, weights, or influences, representing the excess held by one side over another: *The balance of control lies with the parents.* **9. a.** Equality of totals in the debit and credit sides of an account. **b.** The difference between such totals, either on the credit or the debit side of an account. **10.** *Informal.* Anything that remains or is left over. **11.** *Chemistry.* Equality of the number, kinds, and net electric charge of reacting species on each side of a chemical equation. **12.** *Mathematics.* Equality with respect to the net number of reduced symbolic quantities on each side of an equation. **13.** A **balance wheel** *(see).* **14.** A dance movement first toward and then away from one's partner. **15. Balance.** *Astronomy.* A constellation and sign of the zodiac, **Libra** *(see).* —See Synonyms at **proportion, remainder.** —**on balance.** All things considered. —**strike a balance.** To achieve a state or position between extremes.

~*v.* **balanced, -ancing, -ances.** —*tr.* **1.** To weigh or poise in or as if in a balance. **2.** To compare as if weighing in the mind. **3.** To bring into or maintain in a state of equilibrium. **4.** To act as an equalizing weight or force to; offset; counterbalance. **5. a.** To calculate the difference between the debits and credits of (an account). **b.** To reconcile or equalize the sums of the debits and credits of (an account). **c.** To settle by paying what is owed. **6.** To bring into or keep in equal or satisfying proportion or harmony. **7.** *Mathematics.* To bring (an equation) into mathematical balance. **8.** *Chemistry.* To bring (a chemical equation) into chemical balance. **9.** To move toward and then away from (one's dance partner). —*intr.* **1.** To be in or come into equilibrium. **2.** To be equal or equivalent. **3.** To sway or waver as if losing or regaining equilibrium. **4.** To be in or come into a state of balance. Used of a chemical or mathematical equation. **5.** To move toward and then away from one's dance partner. [Middle English, from Old French, from Vulgar Latin *bilancia* (unattested), scales, from Late Latin *(lībra) bilanx* (stem *bilanc-*), (a balance) having two scales : Latin *bi-*, double + *lanx*†, scale, plate, pan.]

balance of nature *n.* The state of stability achieved by plant and animal communities in their natural environment by means of such interactions as adaptation and competition.

balance of payments *n.* A systematic recording of a nation's total payments to foreign countries and international institutions, including the price of imports and the outflow of capital and gold, and its total receipts from abroad, including the price of exports and the inflow of capital and gold.

balance of power *n.* **1.** A distribution of power between nations, often by means of alliance and counteralliance, whereby no one nation is able to dominate or conquer the others. **2.** Any similar distribution of power.

balance of terror *n.* A balance of power between nations, especially the Eastern and Western blocs, maintained by an equivalent distribution of nuclear weapons.

balance of trade *n.* The difference in value between the total exports and imports of a nation.

bal·anc·er (băl′ən-sər) *n.* **1.** One that balances. **2.** A rudimentary insect wing, a **halter** *(see).*

balance sheet *n. Abbr.* **B.S.** A statement of the assets and liabilities of a business, association, or individual at a given date.

balance wheel *n.* A wheel that regulates rate of movement in machine parts; especially, a wheel that swings back and forth against a hair spring in a watch or small clock. Also called "balance."

Bal·an·chine (băl′ən-chēn′), **George,** born Georgy Melitonovich Balanchivadze (1904–83). Russian-born U.S. ballet dancer, choreographer, and director. In 1948 he was appointed artistic director of the New York City Ballet. He choreographed over 100 ballets, including *Firebird* (1950) and *Don Quixote* (1965).

Ba·la·ra·ma (bŭl′ə-rä′mə). *Hinduism.* See **Rama.**

bal·as (băl′əs) *n.* A rose-red to orange spinel, used as a semiprecious gem. [Middle English, from Old French *balais,* from Medieval Latin *balascus,* from Arabic *bálakhsh,* from Persian *Badhakhshān,* a region in northeastern Iran, where the gem is found.]

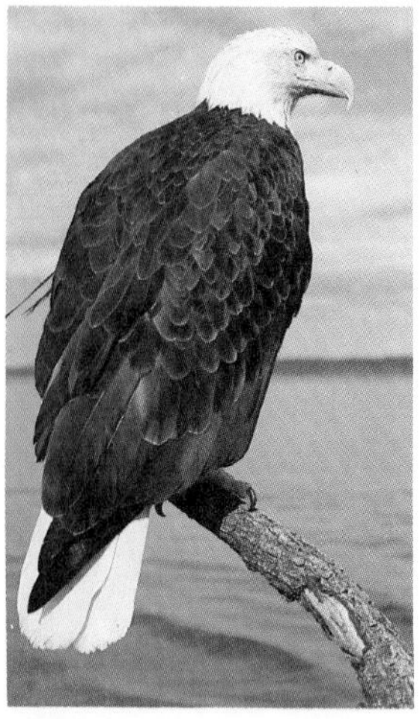

bald eagle *In their spectacular courtship display, a pair of bald eagles may plummet through the air with their claws locked together, breaking apart just before they reach the ground. The bald eagle, which nests near water, is native to North America and is the national emblem of the United States. It is classified as an endangered species.*

PRONUNCIATION KEY

ă, pat; ā, pay; âr, care;
ä, father, are; b, bib;
ch, church; d, deed; ĕ, pet;
ē, be; f, fife; g, gag; h, hat;
hw, which; ĭ, pit; ī, pie;
îr, pier; j, judge; k, kick;
l, lid, needle; m, mum;
n, no, sudden; ng, thing;
ŏ, pot; ō, toe; ô, paw, for;
oi, noise; ou, out; o͝o, book;
o͞o, boot; p, pop; r, roar;
s, sauce; sh, ship, dish;
t, tight; th, thin, path;
th, this, bathe; ŭ, cut; ûr, fur;
v, valve; w, with; y, yes;
z, zebra, size; zh, vision;
ə, about, item, edible, gallop, circus, peaceful

IN FOREIGN WORDS:

à, *Fr.* ami; œ, *Fr.* feu, *Ger.* schön; ü, *Fr.* tu, *Ger.* über;
KH, *Ger.* ich, *Scot.* loch;
N, *Fr.* bon; y′, *Fr.* Compiègne

STRESS MARKS:

Primary stress: ′
in·cite′ (ĭn-sīt′)
Secondary stress: ′
in′sight′ (ĭn′sīt′)

ba·la·ta (bə-lä′tə) *n.* **1.** A tropical American tree, *Manilkara bidentata,* that yields a latexlike sap. **2.** A tough, nonelastic gum obtained from this sap and used for golf-ball covers, industrial belting, and gaskets. [American Spanish, from Cariban.]

Ba·la·ton, Lake (băl′ə-tŏn′). The largest lake in Central Europe, situated in western Hungary. It has an area of 600 square kilometers (230 square miles) and many lakeside resorts.

bal·bo·a (băl-bō′ə) *n.* **1.** The basic monetary unit of Panama, equal to 100 centesimos. See feature at **currency.** **2.** A coin worth one balboa. [After Vasco Núñez de BALBOA.]

Bal·bo·a (băl-bō′ə), **Vasco Núñez de** (1475–1519). Spanish explorer. While serving as governor of Darién on the Isthmus of Panama, he heard stories of a great body of water to the south. He set out with an exploring party on September 1, 1513, and on September 25 first sighted the Pacific Ocean, which he called El Mar del Sur (the South Sea).

bal·brig·gan (băl-brĭg′ən) *n.* **1.** A knitted unbleached cotton fabric, often used in the manufacture of underwear. **2.** *Usually* **balbriggans.** Underwear made of this fabric. [After *Balbriggan,* Irish seaport where it was first manufactured.]

bal·co·ny (băl′kə-nē) *n., pl.* **-nies.** **1.** A platform that projects from the wall of a building and is surrounded by a railing, balustrade, or parapet. **2.** A gallery that projects over the main floor in a theater or auditorium. [Italian *balcone,* from Germanic *balkon* (unattested).]

bald (bôld) *adj.* **balder, baldest.** **1.** Having little or no hair on the top of the head. **2.** Lacking natural or usual covering: *a bald spot on the lawn.* **3.** Having the tread worn away through use. Said of a tire. **4.** Having white feathers or markings on the head: *a bald eagle.* **5.** Lacking ornament; bare; unadorned. **6.** Undisguised; blunt: *a bald statement.* [Middle English *ballede,* perhaps Old English *bællede* (unattested), from *ball-* (unattested), "white patch."] —**bald·ly** *adv.* —**bald·ness** *n.*

bal·da·chin, bal·da·quin (bôl′də-kĭn, băl′-) *n.* Also **bal·da·chi·no** (băl′də-kē′nō). **1.** A rich fabric of silk and gold brocade. **2.** A canopy of fabric carried in church processions or placed over an altar, throne, or dais. **3.** *Architecture.* A stone or marble structure built in the form of a canopy, especially over the altar of a church. [Italian *baldacchino,* from Old Italian, from *Baldacco,* BAGHDAD, famous in the Middle Ages for its brocades.]

bald cypress *n.* A cone-bearing but deciduous tree, *Taxodium distichum,* of the southeastern United States, growing in swamps and damp ground.

bald eagle *n.* A North American eagle, *Haliaeetus leucocephalus,* having a dark body and a white head and tail. It appears on the national emblem of the United States. Also called "American eagle."

Bal·der (bôl′dər). *Norse Mythology.* The god of peace and light, son of Odin and Frigg, renowned for his goodness and beauty.

bal·der·dash (bôl′dər-dăsh′) *n.* Nonsense. [16th century ("froth," "mixture of drinks") : origin obscure.]

bald-faced (bôld′fāst′) *adj.* **1.** Having a white face or face markings. **2.** Brash; undisguised.

bald·head (bôld′hĕd′) *n.* **1.** A person whose head is bald. **2.** Any of several birds having white markings on the head.

bald·head·ed (bôld′hĕd′ĭd) *adj.* Having a bald head.

balding (bôl′dĭng) *adj.* Becoming bald.

bald·pate (bôld′pāt′) *n.* **1.** A baldheaded person. **2.** An American duck, the **widgeon** *(see).*

bal·dric (bôl′drĭk) *n.* A belt, usually of ornamented leather, worn over one shoulder and across the chest to support a sword or bugle. [Middle English *baud(e)rik,* from Old French *baldrei, baudrei*†.]

Bald·win (bôld′wĭn), **James Arthur** (1924–). U.S. author and dramatist whose first novel, *Go Tell It on the Mountain* (1953), was based on his early experiences of religion and deprivation in Harlem, New York City.

Baldwin, Stanley, 1st Earl Baldwin of Bewdley (1867–1947). British Conservative prime minister (1923–29; 1935–37). As prime minister, he responded to the General Strike of 1926 with an anti-union bill, the Trade Disputes Act of 1927, and was at the political center of the events leading to Edward VIII's abdication.

bale[1] (bāl) *n. Abbr.* **bl.** A large bound package or bundle of raw or processed material.

~*tr.v.* **baled, baling, bales.** To wrap or form into bales. [Middle English, probably from Old French, from Germanic.] —**bal·er** *n.*

bale[2] *n. Poetic.* **1.** Evil influence. **2.** Mental suffering; anguish. [Middle English *bale,* Old English *bealu,* from Germanic.]

bale[3]. Variant of **bail** (to empty a boat).

bale[4]. Variant of **bail** (hoop or hooplike device).

Bâle. See **Basel.**

Bal·e·ar·ic Islands (băl′ē-ăr′ĭk). *Spanish* **Is·las Ba·le·a·res** (ēz′läz bä′lā-ä′rās). Archipelago in the Mediterranean, off the east coast of Spain. A Spanish province, it includes the islands of Mallorca (Majorca), Menorca (Minorca), Ibiza, and Formentera. Because of the islands' mild climate, the principal local industry is tourism.

ba·leen (bə-lēn′) *n.* **Whalebone** *(see).* [Middle English *balene,* whale, baleen, from Old French *baleine,* from Latin *balaena,* whale.]

bale·ful (bāl′fəl) *adj.* **1.** Harmful or malignant in intent or effect. **2.** Portending evil; dire. —**bale·ful·ly** *adv.* —**bale·ful·ness** *n.*

Usage: *Baleful* and *baneful* overlap in meaning, but *baleful* usually applies to that which menaces or foreshadows evil: *a baleful look. Baneful* is used most often of that which is actually harmful or destructive: *the baneful effects of pollution.*

Ba·len·ci·a·ga (bə-lĕn′sē-ä′gə), **Cristóbal** (1895–1972). Spanish fashion designer. He settled in Paris in 1937 and became noted for his stark, elegant designs.

Bal·four (băl′fo͝or′), **Arthur James, 1st Earl** (1848–1930). British Conservative prime minister (1902–05). He served as foreign secretary in Lloyd George's cabinet from 1916 to 1919.

Balfour Declaration *n.* A statement by A.J. Balfour on November 2, 1917, that Britain would support the establishment of a national home for Jews in Palestine, on condition that the rights of existing non-Jewish communities there would be safeguarded.

Ba·li (bä′lē). Indonesian island east of Java. Mountainous and volcanic with a tropical climate and fertile soil, it is sometimes called the "Jewel of the East." The Balinese are renowned for the delicacy of their arts and crafts. Bali resisted the spread of Islam through Indonesia in the 16th and 17th centuries and has been Hindu since the 7th century A.D.

Ba·li·nese (bä′lə-nēz′, -nēs′) *adj.* Of or pertaining to Bali, its people, culture, or language.
~*n.* **1.** A native or inhabitant of Bali. **2.** The Indonesian language spoken in Bali.

Baliol, John de. See **Balliol.**

balk (bôk) *v.* **balked, balking, balks.** Also **baulk.** —*intr.* **1.** To stop short and refuse to go on. **2.** To refuse obstinately or show great reluctance; shrink. Used with *at: He balked at the very idea of compromise.* **3.** *Sports.* To make an incomplete or misleading move, especially an illegal one. —*tr.* **1.** To put obstacles in the way of; check or thwart. **2.** *Archaic.* To allow to go by; miss: *balk an opportunity.* —See Synonyms at **frustrate, hinder.**
~*n.* Also **baulk. 1.** A hindrance, check, or defeat. **2.** A blunder or failure. **3. a.** In baseball, an illegal move; especially, a false move made by the pitcher to throw the ball when there are runners on base. **b.** In various other sports, an incomplete or misleading move. **4. a.** An unplowed strip of land. **b.** A ridge between furrows. **5.** A wooden beam or rafter. **6.** On a billiard table, the space between the cushion and the balk line. [Old English *balc,* ridge, hindrance, from Old Norse *bálkr,* partition, from Germanic *balkuz* (unattested).] —**balk·er** *n.*

Bal·kan (bôl′kən) *adj.* Of or pertaining to the Balkans or their inhabitants.

Bal·kan·ize (bôl′kə-nīz′) *tr.v.* **-ized, -izing, -izes.** *Sometimes* **balkanize.** To divide (a region or territory) into small, often mutually hostile, units. [From the division of the Balkan countries by the Great Powers in the early 20th century.] —**Bal·kan·i·za·tion** *n.*

Bal·kans (bôl′kənz). Also **Balkan Peninsula.** Region of southeast Europe. Formerly part of the Roman and Byzantine empires, it broke into rival states, which, with the exception of Montenegro, fell to the Ottoman Turks by 1500. Nationalist movements arose, and by 1908 Greece, Romania, Bulgaria, Serbia, and Montenegro were independent, but Bosnia, Croatia, Dalmatia, and Hercegovina were part of Austria-Hungary, and Macedonia, Albania, and Thrace were still Turkish. The First Balkan War (1912–13) resulted in independence for Albania, and the division of Macedonia between Bulgaria, Greece, Montenegro, and Serbia. The Second Balkan War (1913) and World War I, largely the result of Austrian pressure on Serbia, led to the emergence of Yugoslavia, comprising Serbia, Montenegro, Bosnia, Dalmatia, Slovenia, Hercegovina, and part of Macedonia. Most of Thrace remained Turkish.

Bal·kis (băl′kĭs). The name given in the Koran to the Queen of Sheba.

balk line *n.* On a billiard table, a line drawn parallel to one end, from behind which a player makes the opening shot.

balk·y (bô′kē) *adj.* **-ier, -iest.** Given to stopping at obstacles, real or imagined. Said especially of horses.

ball¹ (bôl) *n.* **1. a.** A spherical or almost spherical body. **b.** Anything approximately spherical: *a ball of flame.* **2. a.** Any of various rounded movable objects used in sports and games. **b.** A game, especially baseball, played with such an object. **3. a.** *Sports.* A ball moving, thrown, hit, or kicked in a particular manner: *a low ball.* **b.** *Cricket.* One delivery of the ball by the bowler. **4. a.** A solid projectile of spherical or pointed shape, such as that shot from a cannon. **b.** Projectiles of this kind collectively. **5.** A rounded part or protuberance, especially of the body: *the ball of the foot.* **6.** *Mathematics.* A three-dimensional region formed by the set of points that are less than a fixed distance from a given point; the interior of a sphere. —**keep the ball rolling.** To make sure that a project, event, or the like continues. —**on the ball.** *Slang.* Alert, competent, or efficient. —**play ball. 1.** To begin or resume a ball game or other activity. **2.** *Informal.* To cooperate. —**set** (or **start**) **the ball rolling.** *Informal.* To get something under way.
~*v.* **balled, balling, balls.** —*tr.* To form into a ball. —*intr.* To become formed into a ball. [Middle English *bal,* from Old Norse *böllr,* from Germanic *balluz* (unattested).]

ball² *n.* A formal gathering for social dancing. —**have a ball.** *Informal.* To have a very enjoyable time. [French *bal,* from Old French, from *baller,* to dance, from Late Latin *ballāre,* from Greek *ballizein.*]

Ball (bôl), **John** (died 1381). English priest and rebel who became one of the leaders of the Peasants' Revolt (1381) and was executed after the failure of the revolt.

Ball, Lucille (1911–). U.S. comedienne. After a moderately successful career as a model and film actress, she premiered in the television series "I Love Lucy" in 1951. It was a hit show for six seasons and still appears around the world in syndication. A fine comedienne who ranges from slapstick to pathos, Ball has since appeared in other television series, musical comedies, and motion pictures.

bal·lad (băl′əd) *n.* **1.** A narrative poem, often of folk origin and intended to be sung, consisting of simple stanzas and usually having a recurrent refrain. **2.** The music for such a poem. **3.** A popular song of a romantic or sentimental nature, in which the same melody is used for each stanza. [Middle English *balade,* from Old French *ballade,* from Provençal *balada,* piece to be accompanied by dancing, from *balar,* to dance, from Late Latin *ballāre.* See **ball** (dance).]

bal·lade (bə-läd′, bă-) *n.* **1.** *Prosody.* A verse form usually consisting of three stanzas of eight or ten lines each, with the same concluding line in each stanza, and an envoy, or brief final stanza, ending with the same last line as that of the preceding stanzas. **2.** A musical composition, usually for the piano, having the romantic or dramatic quality of a ballad. [Earlier form of BALLAD.]

bal·lad·eer (băl′ə-dîr′) *n.* One who sings ballads.

bal·lad·ist (băl′ə-dĭst′) *n.* A singer or writer of ballads.

bal·lad·ry (băl′ə-drē) *n.* Ballads collectively.

ballad stanza *n.* A four-line stanza often used in ballads, rhyming in the second and fourth lines, and having four metrical feet in the first and third lines, and three in the second and fourth.

ball-and-sock·et joint (bôl′ən-sŏk′ĭt) *n.* **1.** A joint consisting of a spherical knob or knoblike part fitted into a socket so that some degree of motion is possible in nearly any direction. **2.** *Anatomy.* A freely movable joint, such as the hip or shoulder joint, in which the rounded head of a long bone fits into a rounded cavity.

bal·last (băl′əst) *n.* **1.** Any heavy material placed in the hold of a ship or the gondola of a balloon to enhance stability. **2.** Coarse gravel or crushed rock laid to form a bed for roads or railroads. **3.** That which gives stability, especially to character. **4.** *Electronics.* A circuit element, such as a resistor, used to stabilize or maintain the current in a circuit.
~*tr.v.* **ballasted, -lasting, -lasts. 1.** To stabilize or provide with ballast. **2.** To fill (a road or railroad bed) with ballast. [Perhaps from Old Swedish or Old Danish *barlast,* "bare load" (cargo carried only for its weight) : *bar,* bare + *last,* load.]

ball bearing *n.* **1.** A friction-reducing bearing, consisting essentially of a ring-shaped track containing freely revolving hard metal balls against which a rotating shaft or other part turns, either in direct contact with the balls or with a second matched ring. **2.** A hard ball used in such a bearing.

ball boy *n.* In tennis, a court attendant who collects the ball when it is out of play.

ball cock *n.* A self-regulating device controlling the supply of water in a tank, cistern, or toilet by means of a floating hollow ball connected to a valve that opens or closes with a change in water level.

bal·le·ri·na (băl′ə-rē′nə) *n.* **1.** A principal female dancer in a corps de ballet. **2.** Any female ballet dancer. Compare **prima ballerina.** [Italian, from *ballare,* to dance. See **ball** (dance).]

bal·let (bă-lā′, băl′ā′) *n.* **1.** An artistic dance form characterized by grace and precision of movement and an elaborate formal technique. Sometimes preceded by *the.* **2.** A theatrical presentation of group or solo dancing to a musical accompaniment, usually in costume and with scenic effects, and conveying a story, theme, or atmosphere. **3.** A musical composition written or used for ballet. **4.** A company or group that performs ballet. [French, from Italian *balletto,* diminutive of *ballo,* a dance. See **ball** (dance).] —**bal·let·ic** (bă-lĕt′ĭk) *adj.*

bal·let·o·mane (bă-lĕt′ə-măn′) *n.* An ardent admirer of the ballet. [Blend of BALLET and MANIA.] —**bal·let·o·ma·ni·a** (bă-lĕt′ə-mā′nē-ə, -măn′yə) *n.*

ball·flow·er (bôl′flou′ər) *n. Architecture.* An ornament in the form of a ball cupped in the petals of a circular flower.

ball game *n.* **1.** A game played with a ball. **2.** *Informal.* A state of affairs; business: *This makes the election a whole new ball game.*

ball girl *n.* In tennis, a court attendant who collects the ball when it is out of play.

Bal·liol or **Bal·iol** (băl′yəl, bā′lē-əl), **John de** (1249–1315). Scottish king, given the Scottish crown (1292) by Edward I of England, who acted as arbitrator in the contest for the throne. Balliol rose against English domination (1295), but was defeated by the English (1296) and fled to France.

bal·lis·ta (bə-lĭs′tə) *n., pl.* **-tae** (-tē′). A military engine used in ancient and medieval warfare to hurl heavy projectiles. [Latin, from Greek *ballein,* to throw.]

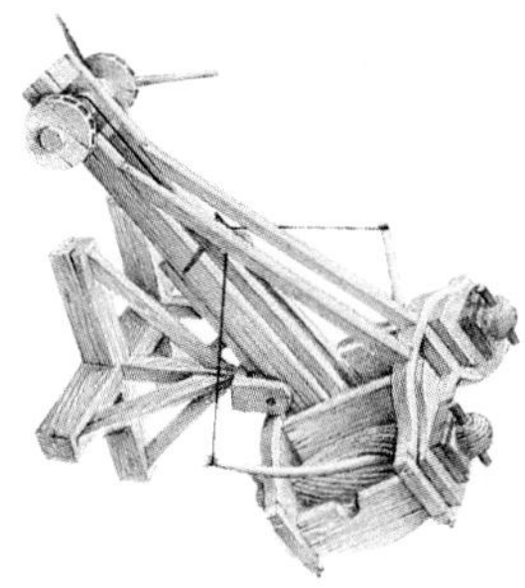

ballista *An ancient missile launcher that operated like a crossbow: the two arms were pulled back, then released to fire the missile.*

bal·lis·tic (bə-lĭs′tĭk) *adj.* **1.** Of or pertaining to ballistics. **2.** Of or pertaining to projectiles, their motion, or their effects. **3.** Of, pertaining to, or designating a measuring instrument that relies on a short impulse or current pulse to cause a movement, the magnitude of which is related to the quantity to be measured: *a ballistic galvanometer.* [From BALLISTA.] —**bal·lis·ti·cal·ly** *adv.*

ballistic missile *n.* A projectile that assumes a free-falling trajectory after an internally guided, self-powered ascent. Compare **guided missile.**

bal·lis·tics (bə-lĭs′tĭks) *n. Used with a singular verb.* **1. a.** The study of the dynamics of projectiles. **b.** The study of the flight characteristics of projectiles. **2. a.** The study of the functioning of firearms. **b.** The study of the firing, flight, and effect of ammunition. —**bal·lis·ti·cian** (băl′ĭ-stĭsh′ən) *n.*

ball lightning *n.* A rare form of atmospheric lightning in which the electrical discharge occurs as a slow-moving, luminous sphere of ionized gas. Also called "fireball."

ball of fire *n. Informal.* A lively, dynamic person.

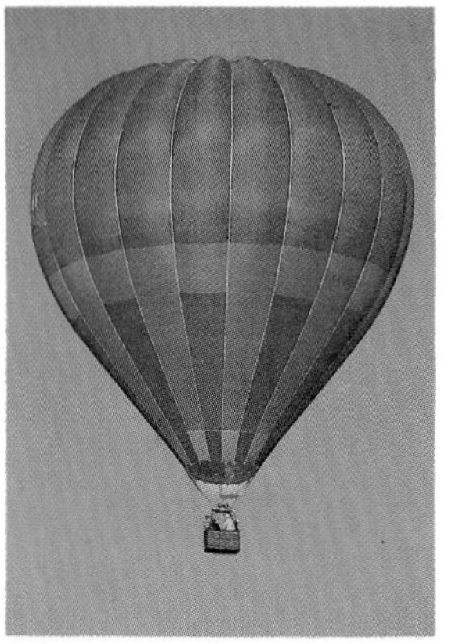

balloon *The earliest 18th-century balloons were filled with air, heated by burning wood or straw. In this modern hot-air balloon, however, the air is heated by a gas burner. Other balloons are inflated with gases that are lighter than air: hydrogen or, more usually, helium.*

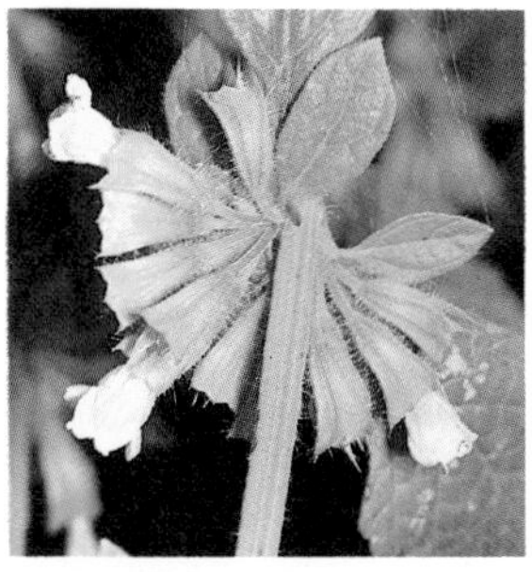

balm Melissa officinalis, *or balm, is a fragrant perennial herb native to Europe. The stems and lemon-scented leaves have long been used for medicinal purposes, and today the plant is sometimes used as a mild stimulant or tonic.*

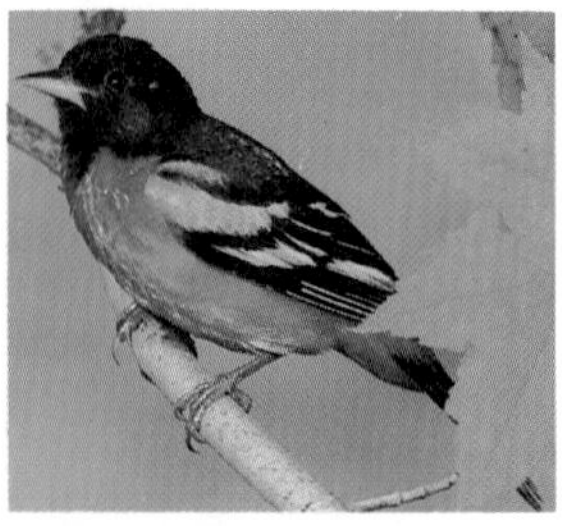

Baltimore oriole *The most common oriole species in North America east of the Rockies. Migrating flocks of Baltimore orioles sometimes raid orchards, causing considerable damage to fruit crops.*

bal·lo·net (băl′ə-nā′) *n.* One of several small auxiliary gasbags placed inside a balloon or a nonrigid airship that can be inflated or deflated during flight to control and maintain shape and buoyancy. [French *ballonnet,* diminutive of *ballon,* BALLOON.]

bal·loon (bə-lo͞on′) *n.* **1.** A spherical or pear-shaped, flexible, nonporous bag inflated with a gas lighter than air, such as helium, that causes it to rise and float in the atmosphere; especially, such a bag with sufficient capacity to lift a suspended gondola. See **barrage balloon, hot-air balloon. 2.** A small brightly colored, inflatable rubber bag used as a toy or decoration. **3.** A rounded or irregularly shaped outline containing the words a character in a cartoon is represented as saying.
~*v.* **ballooned, -looning, -loons.** —*intr.* **1.** To ascend or ride in a balloon. **2.** To expand or swell out like a balloon. —*tr.* To cause to expand by or as if by inflating. [French *ballon,* from Italian *ballone,* augmentative of *balla,* BALL.] **—bal·loon·ist** *n.*

balloon flower *n.* A plant, *Platycodon grandiflorum,* native to Asia, cultivated for its showy, blue, bell-shaped flowers.

balloon sail *n.* A comparatively large foresail, used when going before the wind in races to supplement or replace a jib.

balloon tire *n.* A pneumatic tire with a wide tread, inflated to low pressure, and now used chiefly on trucks.

balloon vine *n.* An ornamental tropical climbing plant, *Cardiospermum halicacabum,* with balloonlike seed capsules.

bal·lot (băl′ət) *n.* **1.** A written or printed paper or ticket used to cast or register a vote, especially a secret vote. **2.** The act, process, or system of voting, especially by the use of secret ballots or voting machines. **3.** A list of candidates running for office; ticket. **4.** The total of all votes cast in an election. **5.** The right to vote; the franchise. **6.** Formerly, a small ball used to register a vote.
~*v.* **balloted, -loting, -lots.** —*intr.* **1.** To cast a ballot; vote. **2.** To draw lots. —*tr.* To obtain a vote from: *The union balloted its membership.* [Italian *ballotta,* small ball or pebble used for voting, diminutive of *balla,* BALL.] **—bal·lot·er** *n.*

ballot box *n.* **1.** A box in which a voter places his or her completed ballot. **2.** The process or system of secret voting; the ballot: *The government's popularity will be tested at the ballot box.*

bal·lotte·ment (bə-lŏt′mənt) *n.* A technique for detecting or examining a floating object in the body, as: **1.** The use of a finger to push sharply against the uterus and detect the presence or position of a fetus by its return impact. **2.** A test for a floating kidney in which the kidney is moved by alternating external digital pressures. [French, a tossing, from *ballotter,* to toss, from *ballotte,* diminutive of *balle,* BALL.]

ball·park (bôl′pärk′) *n.* A park or stadium in which ball games are played. **—in the ballpark.** *Informal.* Within the proper range; approximately right.
~*adj. Informal.* Approximate: *a ballpark figure.*

ball-peen hammer (bôl′pēn′) *n.* A hammer having one end of the head hemispherical.

ball·play·er (bôl′plā′ər) *n.* One who plays baseball.

ball-point pen (bôl′point′) *n.* A pen having as its writing point a small ball bearing that transfers ink stored in a cartridge onto a writing surface. Also called "ball point."

ball·room (bôl′ro͞om′, -ro͝om′) *n.* A large room for dancing.

ballroom dancing *n.* Formal, social dancing with conventional rhythms and steps, such as the waltz and foxtrot.

ball valve *n.* A valve regulated by the position of a free-floating ball that moves in response to fluid or mechanical pressure. It is often used as a one-way valve.

bal·ly·hoo (băl′ē-ho͞o′) *n., pl.* **-hoos.** *Informal.* **1.** Sensational or clamorous advertising. **2.** Noisy shouting or uproar.
~*tr.v.* **ballyhooed, -hooing, -hoos.** *Informal.* To advertise by sensational methods; publicize exaggeratedly. [20th century (U.S.) : origin obscure.]

ballyrag. Variant of **bullyrag.**

balm (bäm) *n.* **1.** An aromatic, oily resin exuded by various chiefly tropical trees and shrubs and used in medicine. **2.** Any tree or shrub yielding such a substance, such as the balm of Gilead. **3.** Any aromatic ointment, oil, unguent, or similar substance. **4.** An aromatic herb, *Melissa officinalis,* native to Europe, having clusters of small, fragrant white flowers. Also called "lemon balm." **5.** Any of several similar aromatic plants. **6.** A pleasing, aromatic fragrance. **7.** Something that soothes, heals, or comforts. [Middle English *baume, basme,* from Old French *basme,* from Latin *balsamum,* BALSAM.]

bal·ma·caan (băl′mə-kăn′) *n.* A loose, full overcoat with raglan sleeves, originally made of rough, woolen cloth. [After *Balmacaan,* an estate near Inverness, Scotland.]

balm of Gil·e·ad (gĭl′ē-əd, -ăd′) *n.* **1.** An aromatic evergreen tree of the genus *Commiphora;* especially, *C. opobalsamum,* of Africa and Asia Minor. **2.** A fragrant resin obtained from this tree. **3.** A North American deciduous tree, *Populus candicans,* having broad, heart-shaped leaves. **4.** A fragrant resin obtained from the **balsam fir** *(see).*

Bal·mor·al¹ (băl-môr′əl, -mŏr′əl) *n.* **1.** A brimless Scottish cap with a flat, round top. **2.** *Sometimes* **balmoral.** A heavy, laced walking shoe. [After BALMORAL Castle.]

Balmoral². A castle in Grampian Region, close to the Dee River. It is the private residence of the British monarch in Scotland.

balm·y (bä′mē) *adj.* **-ier, -iest. 1.** Having the quality or fragrance of balm. **2.** Mild and pleasant: *a balmy breeze.* **3.** *Slang.* Eccentric in behavior. [Sense 3, variant of BARMY.] **—balm·i·ly** *adv.* **—balm·i·ness** *n.*

bal·ne·al (băl′nē-əl) *adj.* Of or pertaining to baths or bathing. [From Latin *balneum,* bath, from Greek *balaneion*†, bath.]

bal·ne·ol·o·gy (băl′nē-ŏl′ə-jē) *n.* The therapeutic use of mineral baths. [Latin *balneum,* bath (see **balneal**) + -LOGY.]

ba·lo·ney, bo·lo·ney (bə-lō′nē) *n.* **1.** Variant of **bologna. 2.** *Slang.* Nonsense. [Perhaps from BOLOGNA (sausage).]

bal·sa (bôl′sə) *n.* **1.** A tree, *Ochroma lagopus,* of tropical America, having wood that is unusually light in weight. **2.** The wood of this tree. **3.** A raft consisting of a frame fastened to buoyant cylinders of wood or metal. [Spanish *balsa*†, raft.]

bal·sam (bôl′səm) *n.* **1.** An oily or gummy oleoresin, usually containing benzoic or cinnamic acids, obtained from the exudations of various trees and shrubs, and used as a base for cough syrups, other medications, and perfumes. See **balsam of Peru, balsam of Tolu, Canada balsam. 2.** Any similar substance, especially a fragrant ointment used as medication. **3.** Any of various trees yielding an aromatic, resinous substance; especially, the **balsam fir** *(see).* **4.** Any of several plants of the genus *Impatiens;* especially, *I. balsamina,* cultivated for its double flowers of various colors. [Latin *balsamum,* from Greek *balsamon,* from Hebrew *bāśām,* "spice."]

balsam apple *n.* A tropical vine, *Momordica balsamina,* native to the Old World, having yellow flowers and warty, orange fruit.

balsam fir *n.* A small, evergreen tree, *Abies balsamea,* of northeastern North America. It yields Canada balsam. Also called "balsam," "Canada balsam."

bal·sam·ic (bôl-săm′ĭk) *adj.* **1.** Of, pertaining to, or resembling balsam. **2.** Containing or yielding balsam.

bal·sam·if·er·ous (bôl′sə-mĭf′ər-əs) *adj.* Yielding balsam.

balsam of Peru *n.* The aromatic resin of a tropical American tree, *Myroxylon pereirae,* used to make perfume and other products.

balsam of To·lu (tə-lo͞o′) *n.* The aromatic resin of a tropical American tree, *Myroxylon toluiferum,* used in cough remedies and in the manufacture of perfumes. Also called "tolu."

balsam pear *n.* A tropical vine, *Momordica charantia,* native to the Old World, having yellow-orange fruit.

balsam poplar *n.* A North American tree, *Populus balsamifera,* having large buds coated with a gummy, fragrant resin. Also called "tacamahac."

Balt (bôlt) *n.* A member of the Baltic-speaking people inhabiting the southeastern shores of the Baltic Sea and formerly occupying a wide area bounded by Gdańsk, Riga, Moscow, and Kiev.

Bal·tha·zar¹ (băl-thā′zər, -thăz′ər, bôl′thə-zär′, băl′-). Also **Bal·tha·sar.** One of the three Magi who traveled to see the infant Jesus.

Balthazar² *n.* A wine bottle that holds as much as 16 standard bottles. [Probably after BALTHAZAR (the Magus).]

Bal·ti (bŭl′tē) *n.* A Tibeto-Burman language of the people of northern Kashmir.

Bal·tic (bôl′tĭk) *adj.* **1.** Of or pertaining to the Baltic Sea, or to the Baltic States and their inhabitants or cultures. **2.** Of or designating a group of languages of the Indo-European family, consisting of Lithuanian, Lettish, and Old Prussian. See **Balto-Slavic.**
~*n.* The Baltic language group.

Baltic Sea. Arm of the Atlantic Ocean bounded by Denmark, Sweden, Finland, the U.S.S.R., Poland, and Germany. It opens to the North Sea by channels between Denmark and Sweden and via the Kiel and Göta canals. It is relatively shallow, with very low salinity, and can freeze for between three to five months of the year.

Baltic States. Territories on the southeast coast of the Baltic Sea, comprising the Latvian, Lithuanian, and Estonian republics of the U.S.S.R. They have been subject to Russian rule since the 18th century, except for a brief period of independence between World War I and World War II.

Bal·ti·more (bôl′tə-môr′, -mōr′). Industrial city, seaport, and cultural center in northern Maryland. Situated at the mouth of the Patapsco River, it has been a busy port and shipbuilding center since the 18th century. In 1827 it was the starting point of the first public railway.

Baltimore oriole *n.* An American songbird, *Icterus galbula,* of which the male has bright-orange, black, and white plumage. [After George Calvert, 1st Baron *Baltimore* (1605–75); (the colors of the male are the same as those in Lord Baltimore's coat of arms).]

Bal·to-Sla·vic (bôl′tō-slä′vĭk, -slăv′ĭk) *n.* A subfamily of the Indo-European language family, composed of the Baltic group and the Slavic group.

Ba·lu·chi (bə-lo͞o′chē) *n., pl.* **-chis** or collectively **Baluchi. 1.** A native or inhabitant of Baluchistan. **2.** The Iranian language of the Baluchi people. **—Ba·lu·chi** *adj.*

Ba·lu·chi·stan (bə-lo͞o′chĭ-stăn′, -stän′). Province in Pakistan, bordering on Iran and Afghanistan. An arid and mountainous region, its inhabitants are mostly Muslim Baluchi and Pathan nomads. Quetta is the capital.

ba·lu·chi·ther·i·um (bə-lo͞o′chĭ-thîr′ē-əm) *n., pl.* **-ther·i·a** (-thîr′ē-ə). An extinct, rhinoceroslike mammal of the genus *Baluchitherium,* of the Oligocene and Miocene epochs, which was one of the largest land mammals ever to have lived. [New Latin.]

bal·un (băl′ən) *n.* An electrical device for coupling an aerial to a transmission line. [*bal*anced + *un*balanced (impedance).]

bal·us·ter (băl′ə-stər) *n.* One of the posts or supports of a handrail, as on a bannister. [French *balustre,* from Italian *balaustro,* from *balaustra,* flower of the pomegranate (from the shape of the post), from Latin *balaustium,* from Greek *balaustion*†.]

bal·us·trade (băl′ə-strād′) *n.* A rail and the row of posts that support it, as along the edge of a staircase. [French, from Italian *balaustrata,* from *balaustro,* BALUSTER.]

Bal·zac (bôl′zăk′, băl′-), **Honoré de** (1799–1850). French author. Often considered the greatest French novelist and the founder of the realist school of fiction, Balzac portrayed French society in a series of works known collectively as *La Comédie Humaine.*

Bam·a·ko (băm′ə-kō). Port on the Niger River and the capital of Mali in West Africa.

Bam·ba·ra (băm-bä′rä) *n., pl.* **-ras** or collectively **Bambara.** **1.** A member of a Negroid people of the upper Niger River valley. **2.** The Mande language of this people.

bam·bi·no (băm-bē′nō, bäm-) *n., pl.* **-nos** or **-ni** (-nē). **1.** Used as an affectionate term for a child or baby. **2.** A representation of the infant Jesus. [Italian, diminutive of *bambo,* child.]

bam·boo (băm-bo͞o′) *n., pl.* **-boos. 1.** Any of various mostly tropical grasses of the subfamily Bambusoideae, having hard-walled stems with ringed joints. **2.** The hollow woody stems of these plants, used in building, making furniture and utensils, and in certain crafts. **3.** Any of various tall, bamboolike grasses such as those of the genera *Arundinaria* and *Dendrocalamus.* [Earlier *bamboos* (misunderstood as plural), from Dutch *bamboes,* unexplained variant of Portuguese *mambu,* from Malay.] **—bam·boo** *adj.*

Bamboo Curtain *n.* A political and especially an ideological barrier existing between the People's Republic of China and other major powers, such as the United States and the U.S.S.R., especially during the leadership of Mao Ze-dong. [Formed by analogy with IRON CURTAIN.]

bam·boo·zle (băm-bo͞o′zəl) *tr.v.* **-zled, -zling, -zles.** *Informal.* **1.** To trick or deceive by elaborate misinformation; hoax. **2.** To mystify or confuse. —See Synonyms at **deceive.** [Probably a cant variant of *bumbazzle,* from *bombace,* padding, BOMBAST.] **—bam·boo·zle·ment** *n.*

ban¹ (băn) *tr.v.* **banned, banning, bans. 1.** To prohibit, especially by official decree. **2.** *Archaic.* To heap curses upon; execrate. **3.** *South African.* To deprive (a person suspected of illegal political activity) of the right of free movement and association with others.
∼*n.* **1.** A prohibition, especially one imposed by law or official decree. **2.** *Archaic.* An excommunication or condemnation by church officials. **3.** In feudal times, a summons to arms. **4.** *Archaic.* Censure through public opinion. **5.** *Archaic.* A curse or imprecation. [Middle English *bannen,* to summon, banish, curse, partly from Old English *bannan,* to summon, proclaim, and partly from Old Norse *banna,* to prohibit, curse, both ultimately from Germanic *bannan* (unattested).]

ban² (bän) *n., pl.* **bani** (bä′nē). A monetary unit equal to 1/100 of the leu of Romania. See feature at **currency.** [Romanian, from Serbo-Croatian *bān,* lord, from Turkish; akin to *bayan,* rich.]

ba·nal (bə-näl′, -năl′, bā′nəl) *adj.* Lacking originality, depth, and inspiration; trite and drearily predictable: *a banal love story.* See Synonyms at **trite.** [French, commonplace, from Old French, common to everyone, shared (as by tenants in a feudal jurisdiction), from *ban,* summons to military service, from Frankish *ban* (unattested).] **—ba·nal·i·ty** (bə-năl′ə-tē, bā-) *n.* **—ba·nal·ly** *adv.*

ba·nan·a (bə-năn′ə) *n.* **1.** Any of several treelike tropical or subtropical plants of the genus *Musa;* especially, *M. sapientum,* having long, broad leaves and hanging clusters of edible fruit. **2.** The crescent-shaped fruit of any of these plants, having white, pulpy flesh and thick, easily removed yellow, green, or reddish skin. [Portuguese and Spanish, from a native name in Guinea.]

banana oil *n.* **1.** A liquid mixture of nitrocellulose and amyl acetate, or a similar solvent, having a bananalike odor. **2.** An organic compound, **amyl acetate** *(see).* **3.** *Slang.* Insincere flattery.

banana republic *n. Informal.* A small country, especially in Central America, often economically dependent on a single crop, such as bananas, and regarded as politically unstable.

ba·na·nas (bə-năn′əz) *adj. Slang.* Crazy; wild. Often used in the phrase *go bananas.* [20th century : origin obscure.]

banana split *n.* A dessert consisting of a banana cut lengthwise and served with ice cream, syrup, fruit, nuts, and whipped cream.

ba·nau·sic (bə-nô′sĭk) *adj.* Materialistic and practical, especially to the point of being dull or pedestrian. [Greek *banausikos,* suitable for artisans, from *baunos,* forge.]

ban·co (băng′kō, bäng′-) *n., pl.* **-cos.** A bet in certain gambling games for the entire amount the banker offers to accept.
∼*interj.* Used to announce a banco. [Italian *banco, banca,* BANK (financial establishment).]

band¹ (bănd) *n.* **1.** A thin strip of flexible material used to encircle and bind one object or to hold a number of objects together: *a rubber band.* **2.** A narrow strip of fabric used to trim, finish, or reinforce articles of clothing. Often used in combination: *a waistband.* **3.** Any strip or stripe that contrasts with its surroundings in color, texture, or material. **4. a.** A neckband or collar. **b. bands.** The two strips hanging from the front of a collar as part of the dress of certain clergymen, scholars, and lawyers. **c.** A high collar popular in the 16th and 17th centuries. **5.** *Architecture.* A flat strip along a wall. **6.** *Biology.* Any chromatically or functionally differentiated strip or stripe in or on an organism. **7.** *Physics.* **a.** A range of some physical variable, as of radiation wavelength or frequency, between well-defined limits; especially, a range of emitted or absorbed wavelengths in a spectrum. **b.** A restricted range of very closely spaced electron energy levels in solids, the distribution and nature of which determine the electrical properties of a material. **8.** The cords across the back of a book, to which the quires or sheets are attached. **9.** A track on a phonograph record. **10.** *Computer Science.* The recording area on a magnetic disk or drum.
∼*tr.v.* **banded, banding, bands. 1.** To tie, bind, or encircle with a band. **2.** To mark with a band or bands. [Middle English, from Old French *bande,* bond, tie, link, from Germanic.]

band² *n.* **1. a.** A group of people, especially when joined together for a common purpose: *a band of robbers.* **b.** A group of animals, as a flock or herd. **2.** A group of musicians who play together, especially: **a.** One not including stringed instruments. **b.** One playing popular music, such as jazz or rock. **3.** *Anthropology.* A self-sufficient subdivision of a tribe.
∼*v.* **banded, banding, bands.** —*tr.* To assemble or unite in a group. —*intr.* To form a group; unite. Often used with *together*: *to band together to oppose legislation.* [Middle English, from Old French *bande,* a troop, from Medieval Latin *banda,* from Germanic.]

band³ *n. Archaic.* **1.** *Usually* **bands.** A physical restraint; a manacle or fetter. **2.** A moral or legal restraint; a bond. [Middle English, from Old Norse.]

Ban·da (băn′də), **Hastings Kamuzu** (*c.* 1906–). African statesman. He practiced medicine in the United Kingdom during World War II and then in the United States. In 1958 he returned to Malawi (then called Nyasaland) to lead the fight for independence from the British, which was achieved in 1964. He became president in the same year and life president in 1966, when Malawi was declared a republic.

band·age (băn′dĭj) *n.* A strip of fabric or other material used as a protective covering for a wound or other injury.
∼*tr.v.* **bandaged, -aging, -ages.** To apply a bandage to. [French, from *bande,* BAND (strip).] **—band·ag·er** *n.*

Band-Aid (bănd′ād′) *n.* A trademark for a small adhesive plaster with a gauze pad in the center, used on minor wounds.

ban·dan·na, ban·dan·a (băn-dăn′ə) *n.* A large handkerchief or scarf, usually brightly colored. [Probably from Portuguese *bandana,* from Hindi *bāndhnū,* a dyeing process in which the cloth is tied at various points, from *bāndhnā,* to tie, from Sanskrit *bandhnāti.*]

Ban·da·ra·na·i·ke (băn′də-rə-nī′ə-kə), **Sirimavo Ratwatte Dias** (1916–). The world's first woman prime minister. She succeeded her husband, S.W.R.D. Bandaranaike, to the presidency of the Sri Lanka Freedom Party after his assassination. She served as prime minister from 1960 until 1965 and from 1970 to 1977.

Bandaranaike, Solomon West Ridgeway Dias (1899–1959). Sri Lankan statesman who was prime minister of what was then Ceylon (1956–59). He was assassinated by a Buddhist monk.

Ban·dar Se·ri Be·ga·wan (bün′där sĕr′ē bə-gä′wən). Formerly **Brunei Town** (bro͞o-nī′). Capital of Brunei. Situated near the mouth of the Brunei River, it is partly built on piles.

b. & b. bed and breakfast.

band·box (bănd′bŏks′) *n.* A lightweight, rounded box originally designed to hold collars but now used for any small articles of dress. **—as if one came out of a bandbox.** Extremely smart and neat.

ban·deau (băn-dō′) *n., pl.* **-deaux** (-dōz′) or **-deaus.** A narrow band for the hair; a fillet. [French, from Old French *bandel,* diminutive of *bande,* BAND (strip).]

ban·de·ril·la (băn′də-rē′ə, -rēl′yə) *n.* In bullfighting, a decorated barbed dart that is thrust into the bull's neck or shoulder muscles by a banderillero. [Spanish, diminutive of *bandera,* banner, from Vulgar Latin *bandāria* (unattested), BANNER.]

ban·de·ril·le·ro (băn′də-rē-âr′ō, -rēl-yâr′ō) *n., pl.* **-ros.** In bullfighting, one who implants the banderillas. [Spanish, from BANDERILLA.]

ban·de·role, ban·de·rol (băn′də-rōl′) *n.* Also **ban·ne·rol** (băn′ə-rōl′). **1.** A narrow forked flag or streamer attached to a staff or lance or flown from a masthead. **2.** *Art & Architecture.* A representation of a ribbon or scroll bearing an inscription. **3.** A square flag, sometimes carried at a funeral and placed over a tomb. [French, from Italian *banderuola,* diminutive of *bandiera,* banner, from Vulgar Latin *bandāria* (unattested), BANNER.]

ban·di·coot (băn′dĭ-ko͞ot′) *n.* **1.** Any of several ratlike marsupials of the family Peramelidae, of Australia and adjacent islands, having a long, tapering snout and long hind legs. **2.** Any of several large rats of the genera *Bandicota* and *Nesokia,* of southeastern Asia. In this sense, now usually called "bandicoot rat" and sometimes "mole-rat." [Telegu *pandikokku* : *pandi,* pig + *kokku,* rat.]

ban·dit (băn′dĭt) *n., pl.* **-dits** or **banditti** (băn-dĭt′ē). A robber; especially, an outlaw who belongs to a gang. [Italian *bandito,* from the past participle of *bandire,* to BAN.] **—ban·dit·ry** *n.*

band leader *n.* One who conducts a band, especially a large band that plays popular dance music.

band·mas·ter (bănd′măs′tər, -mäs′-) *n.* One who conducts a band, especially a military or brass band.

ban·dog (băn′dôg′, -dŏg′) *n.* A dog formerly kept chained up as a watchdog or because of its ferocious nature. [Middle English *banddogge* : BAND (fetter) + DOG.]

ban·do·leer, ban·do·lier (băn′də-lîr′) *n.* A belt fitted with small pockets or loops for carrying cartridges and worn across the chest by soldiers. [French *bandoulière,* from Spanish *bandolera,* from *banda,* sash, probably from Germanic.]

ban·dore (băn′dôr′, -dōr′) *n.* A 16th-century stringed, bass musical instrument resembling the lute. Also called "pandore." [Portuguese *bandurra,* from Late Latin *pandūra,* a three-stringed lute, from Greek *pandoura.*]

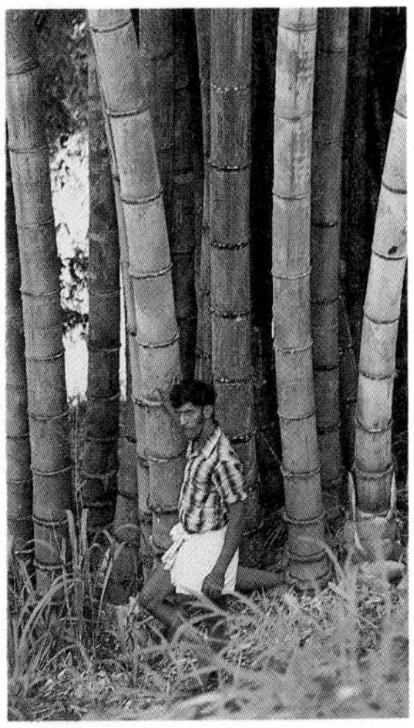

bamboo *A group of perennial grasses found in tropical and subtropical regions of the Eastern and Western hemispheres. Bamboo grows rapidly and there are approximately 200 different species. Giant varieties, like the one shown here, are used to build houses and even road bridges. Split bamboo is woven into mats, baskets, and hats.*

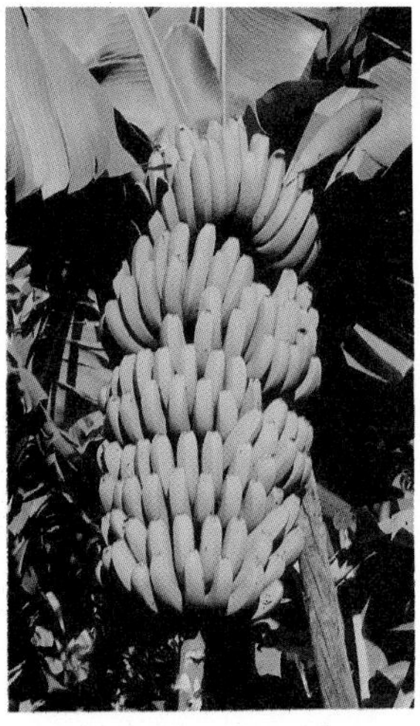

banana *Originating in southwest Asia, bananas are now an important commercial crop grown in tropical and subtropical climates around the world.*

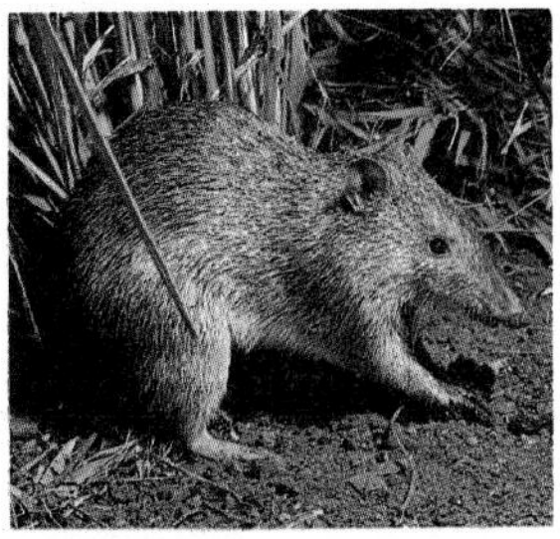

bandicoot *These marsupials are found in Australia and New Guinea. The female carries her young in a pouch on her belly. Largely nocturnal, bandicoots feed mostly on insects and mice, although some species are vegetarian, and others prey on a number of small mammals and lizards.*

band-pass filter (bănd′păs′) *n. Electronics.* A filter that blocks all signals but those within a selected frequency range.

band saw *n.* A power saw consisting essentially of a toothed metal band coupled to and continuously driven round the circumferences of two wheels.

band shell *n.* A bandstand equipped at the rear with a concave, almost hemispheric wall that serves as a sounding board.

bands·man (băndz′mən) *n., pl.* **-men** (-mĭn). A musician who plays an instrument in a band, especially a military or brass band.

band spectrum *n.* A molecular spectrum in which a number of bands of closely spaced lines occur as a result of emission or absorption of radiation.

band·stand (bănd′stănd′) *n.* A platform for a band or orchestra, usually outdoors and having a roof.

Ban·dung (bän′dŏŏng′). City in Indonesia, in western Java. The Bandung Conference (1955) was attended by representatives of 29 African and Asian countries opposed to colonialism.

band·wag·on (bănd′wăg′ən) *n.* **1.** An elaborately decorated wagon used to transport musicians in a parade. **2.** *Informal.* A cause or party that attracts increasing numbers of adherents. **—climb** (or **jump**) **on the bandwagon.** *Informal.* To support or shift one's support to a party, cause, or enterprise that appears likely to win or succeed.

band·width (bănd′wĭdth′) *n. Electronics.* **1.** The frequency range used by a transmitted signal on either side of the carrier frequency. **2.** The range of frequencies over which an amplifier gives a power amplification that falls within a stipulated fraction of the maximum value.

ban·dy¹ (băn′dē) *tr.v.* **bandied, bandying, bandies.** **1.** To toss, throw, or strike back and forth: *"A sunrise breeze bandied the curtains"* (Truman Capote). **2.** To exchange (words or blows). **3.** To discuss in a casual or frivolous manner. **4.** To pass round or along indiscriminately. [Perhaps from French *bander,* to form sides (as for a game), oppose oneself against, from BAND (group).]

bandy² *adj.* Bowed or bent in an outward curve: *bandy legs.* ~*n., pl.* **bandies.** *Chiefly British.* **1.** An early form of hockey. **2.** A stick, bent at one end, used in playing this game. [Adjective sense from noun (hockey stick), obscurely related to BANDY (toss, throw).]

ban·dy-leg·ged (băn′dē-lĕg′ĭd) *adj.* Having **bowlegs** *(see)*; bowlegged. [From BANDY (curved stick).]

bane (bān) *n.* **1.** Someone or something that is a nuisance or cause of distress: *the bane of one's life.* **2.** *Poetic.* Fatal injury or ruin. **3.** A cause of death, destruction, or ruin. **4.** A deadly poison. Used in combination: *henbane; wolf's-bane.* [Middle English *bane,* Old English *bana,* slayer, cause of death or destruction, ruin.]

bane·ber·ry (bān′bĕr′ē) *n., pl.* **-ries.** **1.** Any plant of the genus *Actaea,* especially *A. spicata,* having clusters of white flowers and red or white poisonous berries. **2.** A berry of any of these plants.

bane·ful (bān′fəl) *adj.* **1.** Full of venom or harm. **2.** Destructive; pernicious: *"Criticism is really, in itself, a baneful and injurious employment"* (Matthew Arnold). **—See Usage note at baleful.**

Banff (bămf). A town in southwestern Alberta, Canada, in the Rocky Mts. near Lake Louise. It is a famous winter resort and tourist center.

bang¹ (băng) *n.* **1.** The sudden loud noise of an explosion. **2.** A sudden loud impact or thump. **3.** *Informal.* A sudden burst of action. **4.** *Slang.* A sense of excitement; a thrill. **—with a bang.** With notable success.

~*v.* **banged, banging, bangs.** —*tr.* **1.** To hit noisily; strike heavily and repeatedly: *banging the table with his fist.* **2.** To close suddenly and loudly; slam. **3.** To handle noisily or violently: *bang the dishes in the sink.* **4.** To hit sharply: *I've banged my elbow.* —*intr.* **1.** To make a sudden loud noise. **2.** To crash noisily against something. **3.** To strike with a sudden loud noise.

~*adv.* **1.** With a bang. **2.** Exactly; precisely: *bang on time.* **3.** Suddenly; completely: *If we make one mistake, bang go our hopes of winning.* **—bang on.** *Informal.* Exactly right: *That answer was bang on.* [16th century: perhaps from Scandinavian, akin to Old Norse *bang,* a hammering.]

bang² *n. Often* **bangs.** Hair cut in a fringe straight across the forehead.

~*tr.v.* **banged, banging, bangs.** To cut (hair) straight across the forehead. [Perhaps ultimately from Old Norse *banga,* to cut off.]

bang³. Variant of **bhang.**

Ban·ga·lore (băng′gə-lôr′, -lōr′). Capital city of Karnataka state in south India, 290 kilometers (180 miles) west of Madras.

bangalore torpedo *n.* A piece of metal pipe filled with an explosive, used primarily to clear a path through barbed wire or to detonate land mines. [After BANGALORE, where it was first used.]

bang·er (băng′ər) *n. Chiefly British.* **1.** A firework that explodes with a sudden loud noise. **2.** *Informal.* A sausage. [Sense 2: probably from the sputtering sound made in cooking.]

Bangkok. See Krung Thep.

Ban·gla·desh (băng′lə-dĕsh′, băng′-). Formerly **East Pak·i·stan** (păk′ĭ-stăn′). Muslim country of south Asia, lying mostly in the fertile Ganges-Brahmaputra delta. Formerly part of Bengal, it became East Pakistan on Indian independence (1947), but Calcutta, Bengal's chief port and industrial center for its jute, became part of India. Disastrously weakened economically, East Pakistan was neglected by the government in West Pakistan. Unrest erupted into a savage civil war (1971), and independent Bangladesh was born. Sheik Mujibur Rahman, the East Bengali leader, was released from prison in West Pakistan to form the country's first government

(1972) but was killed in a military coup (1975). A countercoup installed another military regime, and Gen. Ziaur Rahman took over the government the same year. He was elected president (1978) but was assassinated (1981). A bloodless military coup (1982) was led by Gen. Hussein Ershad, who became president (1983). Despite some industrialization and advances that have made more than 75 percent of the land cultivable, political instability, droughts, floods, and cyclones have kept Bangladesh a poor country dependent on foreign aid. Area, 143,998 square kilometers (55,583 square miles). Population, 87,000,000. Capital, Dacca. **—Bang·la·desh·i** *adj. & n.*

ban·gle (băng′gəl) *n.* **1.** A rigid bracelet or anklet, especially one with no clasp. **2.** An ornament hung from a bracelet, necklace, or the like. [Hindi *bangrī†,* glass bracelet.]

Ban·gor (băng′gôr, -gər). A river port of southern Maine, on the Penobscot River. It is the gateway to an extensive resort and lumbering region.

bang·tail (băng′tāl′) *n.* **1.** An animal's tail that has been cut straight across and short. **2.** An animal, especially a horse, with such a tail. [Probably BANG (cut) + TAIL.]

Ban·gui (bäng-gē′). Capital of the Central African Republic. Situated on the Ubangi River, it is the chief port of the country and also handles goods for Chad.

bang up *tr.v.* **1.** To cause damage or injury to. **2.** *Chiefly British.* To raise; increase: *bang up a price.*

bang-up (băng′ŭp′) *adj. Slang.* Excellent: *a bang-up job.*

Bang·we·u·lu, Lake (băng′wə-ŏŏ′lŏŏ). A shallow lake bordered by swamps, on a plateau in northeast Zambia. It was discovered by David Livingstone in 1868.

ba·ni. Plural of **ban** (currency).

ban·i·an (băn′yən) *n.* **1.** A member of a Hindu merchant or trader caste, whose members eat no meat. **2.** A loose shirt, jacket, or gown worn in India. **3.** Variant of **banyan.** [Portuguese, from Gujarati *vāṇiyo,* from Sanskrit *vāṇija,* merchant.]

ban·ish (băn′ĭsh) *tr.v.* **-ished, -ishing, -ishes.** **1.** To force to leave a country or place by official decree; exile. **2.** To drive away; expel: *He banished all doubts from his mind.* [Middle English *banishen,* from Old French *banir* (present stem *baniss-*), from Vulgar Latin *bannīre* (unattested), from Germanic *bannjan* (unattested), to BAN.] **—ban·ish·er** *n.* **—ban·ish·ment** *n.*

Synonyms: *deport, exile, expatriate, extradite, transport.*

ban·is·ter, ban·nis·ter (băn′ĭ-stər) *n.* **1.** *Usually* **banisters.** The handrail or balustrade of a staircase. **2.** A baluster. [From earlier *barrister,* variant BALUSTER.]

ban·jo (băn′jō) *n., pl.* **-jos** or **-joes.** A fretted stringed musical instrument, having a long narrow neck and a hollow circular body with a stretched diaphragm of vellum upon which the bridge rests. [Probably of African origin.] **—ban·jo·ist** *n.*

banjo clock *n.* A wall clock of a type made in the United States in the 19th century, resembling a banjo in shape.

Ban·jul (băn-jŏŏl′). Formerly **Bath·urst** (băth′ərst). Capital of Gambia, in West Africa. Situated at the mouth of the Gambia River, it is a port and the country's only sizable town.

bank¹ (băngk) *n.* **1.** Any piled-up mass, as of snow or clouds; a mound; a ridge. **2.** A steep natural incline. **3.** An artificial embankment, especially one built on a bend in a road to help vehicles to

---

baneberry *The poisonous fruit of* Actaea spicata, *a European bush found in limestone woodlands, gets its common name from the old English word* bane, *meaning "poison."*

---

corner safely. **4. a.** *Often* **banks.** The slope of land adjoining a body of water, especially adjoining a lake, river, or sea. **b.** A part of a town situated on one side of a river flowing through it: *the Left Bank.* **5.** *Often* **banks.** A large elevated area of a sea floor. **6.** The cushion of a billiard or pool table. **7.** *Aviation.* The lateral tilt of an aircraft when turning. —See Usage note at **shoal.**
~*v.* **banked, banking, banks.** —*tr.* **1.** To border or protect with a ridge or embankment. Often used with *up.* **2.** To pile up; amass. Often used with *up: bank up earth along a wall.* **3.** To cover (a fire) with ashes or fresh fuel to ensure continued low burning. Often used with *up.* **4.** To construct with a slope rising to the outside edge. Often used with *up.* **5.** *Aviation.* To tilt (an aircraft) laterally in flight. **6.** In billiard games, to strike (a ball) so that it rebounds from the table's cushion. —*intr.* **1.** To take the form of or rise in a bank or banks. **2.** *Aviation.* To tilt an aircraft laterally when turning. **3.** To round a sloping embankment, especially at speed. [Middle English *banke,* probably from Old Danish *banke,* sandbank, from Germanic *bankon* (unattested).]
bank² *n. Abbr.* **bk. 1.** A business establishment or organization authorized to perform one or more of the following services: receive and safeguard money and other valuables; lend money at interest; negotiate bills of exchange, such as checks and drafts; purchase and exchange foreign currency; issue currency. **2.** The offices or building in which such an establishment, or a branch of such an organization, is located. **3. a.** The funds owned by a gambling establishment. **b.** The funds held by a dealer or banker in some gambling games. **4. a.** The reserve pieces, cards, chips, or play money, from which the players may draw, in games such as poker or dominoes. **b.** The player holding this stock. **5.** A supply or stock held in reserve: *a blood bank.* **6.** Any place of safekeeping or storage. **7.** *Obsolete.* A moneychanger's table or place of business.
~*v.* **banked, banking, banks.** —*tr.* To deposit (money) in a bank. —*intr.* **1.** To transact business with a bank; especially, to maintain a bank account. **2.** To operate a bank. **3.** To hold the bank in some gambling games. **4.** *Informal.* To depend or rely. Used with *on* or *upon.* —See Synonyms at **rely.** [French *banque,* from Italian *banca,* bench, moneychanger's table, from Germanic *bank* (unattested), BENCH.]
bank³ *n.* **1.** A set of similar or matched things arranged in a row: *a bank of desks.* **2.** A row of keys on a keyboard. **3.** *Nautical.* A bench for rowers in a galley. **4.** A row of oars in a galley. **4.** The lines of type under a newspaper headline. **5.** *Printing.* A slanting table on which type matter in galleys or sheets is stored or corrected before being made up in pages. **6.** A row of fixed electrical contacts forming part of an automatic switching unit in a telephone circuit. ~*tr.v.* **banked, banking, banks.** To arrange or set up in a row: *"Every street was banked with purple-blooming trees"* (Doris Lessing). [Middle English *bank,* from Old French *banc,* from Germanic *bank* (unattested), BENCH.]
bank·a·ble (băng′kə-bəl) *adj.* **1.** Acceptable to or at a bank. **2.** *Informal.* Guaranteed to bring profit: *a bankable movie star.*
bank acceptance *n.* A draft or bill of exchange drawn upon and accepted by a bank. Also called "banker's acceptance."
bank account *n.* **1.** An agreement between a bank and a customer whereby money is deposited with the bank and can be added to or withdrawn. **2.** The amount the customer deposits with the bank.
bank annuities *pl.n. Chiefly British.* **Consols** (see).
bank barn *n.* A barn built into a hillside as protection against cold, with a back entrance at the second-floor level.
bank·book (băngk′bŏŏk′) *n.* A book held by a person having a deposit account at a bank, in which deposits and withdrawals are recorded by the bank. Also called "passbook."
bank·card (băngk′kärd′) *n.* A credit card issued by a bank.
bank discount *n.* The interest on a loan, computed in advance, and deducted at the time the loan is made.
bank·er¹ (băng′kər) *n.* **1.** A person who owns or manages a bank. **2.** The player in charge of the bank in games such as poker or dominoes.
banker² *n.* A person or boat engaged in cod fishing on the Newfoundland banks.
banker³ *n.* A workbench used by masons and sculptors.
Bank·head (băngk′hĕd′), **Tallulah** (1903–68). U.S. actress. Noted as much for her extravagant lifestyle as for her performances on stage and screen, she did, however, win acclaim for her appearances in plays such as *The Little Foxes* by Lillian Hellman (1939).
bank holiday *n.* **1.** A weekday on which banks are legally closed. **2.** *British.* One of five days regarded as legal holidays, when banks are ordered to remain closed.
bank·ing (băng′kĭng) *n. Abbr.* **bkg.** The business of a bank or the occupation of a banker.
bank manager *n.* The person in charge of a local branch of a bank.
bank·note (băngk′nōt′) *n.* A note issued by an authorized bank representing its promise to pay a specific sum to the bearer on demand and acceptable as money. Also called "bank bill."
bank paper *n.* **1.** Banknotes. **2.** Securities, drafts, bills of exchange, and other commercial paper acceptable to a bank.
bank rate *n.* The rate of discount established by a country's central bank or banks.
bank·roll (băngk′rōl′) *n.* **1.** A roll of paper money. **2.** *Informal.* A person's ready cash.
~*tr.v.* **bankrolled, -rolling, -rolls.** *Slang.* To provide financial backing for (a business enterprise, for example).
bank·rupt (băngk′rŭpt′, -rəpt) *n. Abbr.* **bkpt. 1.** *Law.* An individual

or corporate debtor, who, after a voluntary petition to the court or one invoked by creditors, is judged legally insolvent. His remaining property is then administered for his creditors or distributed among them in accordance with the law. **2.** Any person unable to pay his creditors in full. **3.** One who is or has become devoid of some resource or quality: *an intellectual bankrupt.*
~*adj.* **1.** Subject to legal procedure because of insolvency; legally declared a bankrupt. **2.** Financially ruined; impoverished. **3.** Completely lacking in some quality; destitute: *morally bankrupt.*
~*tr.v.* **bankrupted, -rupting, -rupts.** To cause to become bankrupt. [16th century : from Italian *banca rotta,* "broken bench," symbol of an insolvent moneychanger : *banca,* moneychanger's bench + *rotta,* past participle of *rompere,* to break (assimilated to Latin *rupta*).] —**bank·rupt·cy** *n.*
bankrupt worm *n.* A roundworm of the genus *Trichostrongylus* that causes gastroenteritis in sheep and cattle. [So called because it can bring bankruptcy to cattle raisers.]
Banks (băngks), **Sir Joseph** (1743–1820). British botanist and explorer. His most famous expedition was the circumnavigation of the world with Captain James Cook on the *Endeavour* (1768–71). He discovered and catalogued many species of animal and plant life, especially from Australia, and promoted the introduction of crop plants from their native regions to other parts of the world.
bank·si·a (băngk′sē-ə) *n.* Any shrub or tree of the Australian genus *Banksia,* whose flowers are borne on densely packed spikes that form cylindrical heads.
bank statement *n.* A statement showing the transactions and current balance of a bank account, especially one that is sent on a regular basis to the holder of the account.
ban·ner (băn′ər) *n.* **1.** A strip of cloth, either hung overhead or carried between poles, bearing a message or slogan. **2.** A piece of cloth attached to a staff and used as a standard by a monarch, knight, or military commander. **3. a.** The flag of a nation, state, army, or sovereign. **b.** An ensign bearing a motto, emblem, or legend, as of a society or trade union. **4.** A headline spanning the width of a newspaper page. Also called "banner headline." **5.** A principle, ideal, or slogan: *The Party is campaigning under the banner of democracy.*
~*adj.* Outstanding; superior. [Middle English *banere,* from Norman-French, from Old French *baniere,* from Vulgar Latin *bandāria* (unattested), from Late Latin *bandum,* standard, from Germanic.]
banner cloud *n.* A type of cloud that forms in clear skies on the side of a mountain peak sheltered from the wind, as air rising to pass over the peak cools.
ban·ner·et¹, ban·ner·ette (băn′ər-ĭt, -ə-rĕt′) *n.* A small banner. [Middle English *baneret,* from Old French *banerete,* diminutive of *baniere,* BANNER.]
ban·ner·et² *n.* **1.** A feudal knight entitled to lead men into battle under his own standard. **2.** This knight's rank between knight bachelor and baron. Also called "knight banneret." [Middle English *baneret,* from Old French, "bannered," from *baniere,* BANNER.]
bannerol. Variant of **banderole.**
bannister. Variant of **banister.**
Ban·nis·ter (băn′ə-stər), **Sir Roger Gilbert** (1929–). British middle-distance runner, the first man to break the four-minute mile barrier (May 6, 1954) with a time of 3 minutes 59.4 seconds. He was British mile champion (1951, 1953, and 1954) and European 1,500-meters champion and record holder.
ban·nock (băn′ək) *n.* Also **bon·nock** (bŏn′ək). *Scottish & British Regional.* A griddlecake, usually unleavened, made of oatmeal, barley, or wheat flour and sometimes containing dried fruit. [Middle English *bannok,* Old English *bannuc,* perhaps from Celtic.]
Ban·nock·burn (băn′ək-bûrn′, băn′ăk-bûrn′). Small town now in Central Region, Scotland, on the Bannock River, a tributary of the Forth River. It is the site of the battle (1314) where the Scots, under Robert the Bruce, won a famous victory over the English, under Edward II.
banns, bans (bănz) *pl.n.* A spoken or published announcement in a church of an intended marriage, usually read out on three successive Sundays. [Middle English *banes,* plural of *bane, ban,* proclamation, BAN.]
ban·quet (băng′kwĭt) *n.* **1.** An elaborate and sumptuous meal. **2.** A ceremonial dinner honoring a particular guest or occasion.
~*v.* **banqueted, -queting, -quets.** —*tr.* To entertain at a banquet. —*intr.* To partake of a banquet; feast. [Old French, diminutive of *banc,* bench, from Germanic.] —**ban·quet·er** *n.*
ban·quette (băng-kĕt′) *n.* **1.** *Military.* A platform lining a trench or parapet wall where soldiers may stand when firing. **2.** *Southern U.S.* A sidewalk. **3.** A long upholstered bench, either placed against or built into a wall. **4.** Any ledge or shelf, as on a buffet. [French, from Italian *banchetta,* diminutive of *banca,* bench, from Germanic.]
ban·shee, ban·shie (băn′shē) *n.* A female spirit in Gaelic folklore believed to presage a death in the family by wailing outside the house. [Irish Gaelic *bean sídhe,* "woman of the fairies," from Old Irish *ben síde : ben,* woman + *síde†,* fairy folk.]
ban·tam (băn′təm) *n.* **1.** Any of various breeds of small domestic fowl. **2.** A small but aggressive person.
~*adj.* **1.** Diminutive; miniature. **2.** Spirited or aggressive. [From the belief that the fowl were native to *Bantam,* village in Java.]
ban·tam·weight (băn′təm-wāt′) *n.* A boxer weighing between 112 and 118 pounds.

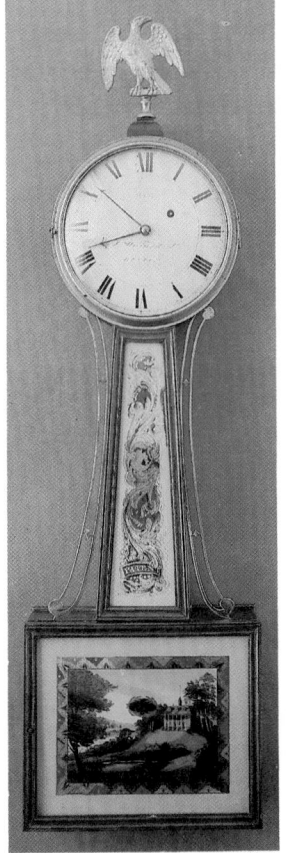

banjo clock *A 19th-century American clock design named for its resemblance to the musical instrument. The case accommodates a small falling weight. The example illustrated was made in 1841.*

baobab *An African member,* Adansonia digitata, *of a family of tropical flowering trees. The thick, barrel-shaped trunk acts as a water reservoir, enabling the tree to survive long droughts.*

ban·ter (băn′tər) *n.* Good-humored teasing or playful repartee.
~*v.* **bantered, -tering, -ters.** —*tr.* To tease or mock gently. —*intr.* To exchange mildly teasing remarks. [17th century : origin obscure.] —**ban·ter·er** *n.* —**ban·ter·ing·ly** *adv.*

Ban·ting (băn′tĭng), **Sir Frederick Grant** (1891–1941). Canadian physiologist. In 1921, in collaboration with Charles H. Best, he discovered a technique for isolating the hormone insulin from pancreatic tissue and thus discovered a treatment for diabetics. He was awarded the Nobel Prize (1923) jointly with his professor at Toronto University, John J.R. Macleod, but gave half of his share of the prize to Best.

bant·ling (bănt′lĭng) *n. Archaic.* A young child; a brat. [16th century : perhaps a variant of German *Bänkling,* bastard, from *Bank,* bench (i.e., "a child begotten on a bench"), from Old High German *banc.*]

Ban·try Bay (băn′trē). Atlantic inlet on the southwest coast of County Cork, Republic of Ireland.

Ban·tu (băn′to͞o) *n., pl.* **Bantus** or collectively **Bantu. 1.** A member of any of several Negroid tribes of central and southern Africa. **2.** A family of languages spoken by the Bantu, including Kongo, Luba, Kikuyu, Luganda, Nyanja, Swahili, and Zulu.
~*adj.* Of or pertaining to any of the Bantu peoples or their languages.

Ban·tu·stan (băn′to͞o-stän′) *n. South African.* A **homeland** *(see).*

banx·ring (băngks′rĭng′) *n.* A small squirrellike animal from Java. Also called "tree-shrew." [Javanese.]

ban·yan, ban·ian (băn′yən) *n.* A tree, *Ficus benghalensis,* of tropical India and the East Indies, having large, oval leaves, reddish fruit, and many aerial roots that develop into additional trunks. Compare **peepul.** [Originally name applied to one such tree near Bandar Abbas, Iran, beneath which Hindu banians had built a pagoda.]

ban·zai (bän-zī′) *n.* A Japanese battle cry, patriotic cheer, or greeting. [Japanese, "(may you live) ten thousand years," from Chinese *wàn sùi* : *wàn,* ten thousand + *sùi,* year.]

banzai attack *n.* A desperate, suicidal attack, as practiced by Japanese troops in World War II. Also called "banzai charge."

ba·o·bab (bā′ō-băb′, bä′-) *n.* A tree, *Adansonia digitata,* of tropical Africa, having an extremely thick trunk, large, pendulous white flowers, and hard-shelled, fleshy fruit called "monkey bread." [New Latin (16th century) : probably a native Central African name.]

bap., bapt. 1. baptism. **2.** baptized.

Bap., Bapt. Baptist.

bap·tism (băp′tĭz′əm) *n. Abbr.* **bap., bapt. 1.** A Christian sacrament, symbolic of spiritual regeneration, in which, as a result of immersion or sprinkling with water, accompanied by the recital of a form of words, the recipient is considered cleansed of original sin, given a name, and admitted into Christianity or a specific Christian church. **2.** Any ceremony, trial, or experience by which one is initiated, purified, or given a name. **3.** *Christian Science.* A submergence in Spirit or purification by Spirit. [Middle English *bapteme,* from Old French *bapteme, baptesme,* from Late Latin *baptisma,* from Greek, from *baptizein,* to BAPTIZE.] —**bap·tis·mal** (băp-tĭz′məl) *adj.* —**bap·tis·mal·ly** *adv.*

baptism of fire *n.* **1.** A soldier's first experience of actual combat conditions. **2.** Any severe ordeal experienced for the first time.

Bap·tist (băp′tĭst) *n. Abbr.* **Bap., Bapt. 1.** A member of any of various Protestant denominations believing that the sacrament of baptism should be given only to adult members upon a profession of faith and usually by immersion. **2. baptist.** One who baptizes. —**the Baptist.** John the Baptist. —**Bap·tist** *adj.*

bap·tis·ter·y, bap·tis·try (băp′tĭs-trē) *n., pl.* **-ies. 1.** A part of a church, or a separate building, where baptisms take place. **2.** A font used for baptism. **3.** A tank for baptizing by total immersion used in Baptist churches.

bap·tize (băp-tīz′, băp′tīz′) *v.* **-tized, tizing, -tizes.** —*tr.* **1.** To dip or immerse (a person) in water or to sprinkle water on (a person) during a baptismal ceremony. **2. a.** To cleanse or purify. **b.** To initiate. **3.** To give a first or Christian name to; christen. —*intr.* To administer baptism. [Middle English *baptizen,* from Old French *baptiser,* from Late Latin *baptizāre,* from Greek *baptizein,* from *baptein,* to dip.] —**bap·tiz·er** *n.*

bar[1] (bär) *n.* **1.** A relatively long, straight, rigid piece of any solid material used, for example, as a support, barrier, or structural or mechanical member, or to fasten something. **2. a.** A solid oblong block of a substance, such as soap or candy. **b.** A rectangular block of a precious metal. **c.** A unit of quantity based on such a block. **3.** Anything that impedes or prevents; an obstacle. **4.** A sandbar. **5.** A stripe or band, such as one formed by light or color. **6.** *British.* The heating element in an electric fire. **7.** *Heraldry.* A pair of horizontal parallel lines drawn across a shield. **8.** *Law.* **a.** The nullifying, defeating, or preventing of a claim or action. **b.** The process by which this is done. **9.** The railing in a courtroom enclosing the part of the room where the judges and lawyers sit, witnesses are heard, and prisoners are tried. **10. a.** Lawyers collectively. Preceded by *the.* **b.** The legal profession collectively. Preceded by *the.* **11. a.** A particular system of law courts. **b.** Any tribunal or place of judgment. **12.** *Music.* **a.** A vertical line dividing a staff into equal measures. Also *British* "bar line." **b.** A measure. **c.** A **double bar** *(see).* **13. a.** A counter at which alcoholic drinks and sometimes meals or snacks are served. **b.** An establishment or room containing such a counter. **14. a.** A counter where goods or services of a specified kind are sold or provided: *a hat bar.* **b.** An establishment or room containing such a counter: *a snack bar.* **15.** *British.* An insignia added to a military decoration indicating that it has been awarded a second time. **16.** Variant of **barre.** —**behind bars.** In prison. —See Synonyms at **obstacle.** —See Usage note at **shoal.**
~*tr.v.* **barred, barring, bars. 1.** To fasten securely with a bar. **2.** To keep in or out with or as if with bars. **3.** To obstruct or impede; block. **4.** To exclude. **5.** To mark with bars or stripes. **6.** *Music.* To indicate measures in (a piece of music) by using bars. **7.** *Law.* To stop (an action or claim) by legal objection. —See Synonyms at **hinder.**
~*prep.* Excluding; except for; barring: *That was his best performance, bar none.* [Middle English *barre,* from Old French, from Vulgar Latin (unattested) *barra*†.]

bar[2] *n.* A unit of pressure equal to 10^5 newtons per square meter or 0.98697 standard atmosphere. [German, from Greek *baros,* weight.]

BAR Browning automatic rifle.

bar. 1. barometer; barometric. **2.** barrel.

Ba·rab·bas (bə-răb′əs). A condemned thief whose release was demanded of Pilate by the multitude instead of that of Jesus. Matthew 27:15–26.

Ba·ra·ka (bə-rä′kə), **Imamu Amiri,** born (Everett) LeRoi Jones (1934–). U.S. playwright and poet. He is a leading black nationalist politician and founder of the Black Community Development and Defense Organization (1968).

bar·a·the·a (băr′ə-thē′ə) *n.* A soft fabric of silk and cotton or silk and wool. [19th century : origin obscure.]

barb[1] (bärb) *n.* **1.** A sharp point projecting in reverse direction to the main point of a weapon or tool, as on an arrow, fishhook, or spear. **2.** A cutting or biting remark. **3.** *Botany.* A hooked bristle or hairlike projection. **4.** *Ornithology.* Any of the many parallel filaments projecting from the main shaft of a feather. **5.** Any of various Old World freshwater fishes of the genus *Barbus* (or *Puntius*) and related genera, many of which are popular in home aquariums. **6.** Any of the small folds of mucous membrane below the tongue of horses and cattle. **7.** A white linen covering for a woman's head, throat, and chin, worn in medieval times; nowadays worn by certain orders of nuns. **8.** *Obsolete.* A beard.
~*tr.v.* **barbed, barbing, barbs.** To provide or furnish with a barb or barbs. [Middle English *barbe,* beard, beardlike appendage, from Old French, from Latin *barba,* beard.]

barb[2] *n.* **1.** A hardy racehorse of a breed that originated in northern Africa. **2.** Any of a breed of domestic pigeons having dark plumage. **3.** *Australian.* A type of sheepdog, a black **kelpie** *(see).* [French *barbe,* Barbary horse, from Italian *barbero,* BARBARY.]

barb[3] *n. Slang.* A barbiturate.

Bar·ba·dos (bär-bā′dōs, -dəs). Prosperous West Indian island, the most easterly of the Antilles. It was probably first visited by the Portuguese, who named it Los Barbados ("bearded") because of its numerous bearded fig trees. The British first landed in 1605 and began colonizing it in 1627. The island was a British colony until 1966 when it became independent within the Commonwealth. The economy is based on sugar and tourism. It is densely populated, and over 80 percent of the people are black descendants of African slaves. Area, 431 square kilometers (166 square miles). Population, 250,000. Capital, Bridgetown. See map at **Trinidad and Tobago.**

Barbados gooseberry *n.* A cactus, the **blade-apple** *(see).*

bar·bar·i·an (bär-bâr′ē-ən) *n.* **1.** Originally, a foreigner; especially, one not Greek or Roman and therefore regarded as uncivilized. **2.** One belonging to a people or tribe considered to have a primitive civilization. **3.** A fierce, brutal, or cruel person. **4.** An insensitive, uncultured person; a boor.
~*adj.* Characteristic of or resembling a barbarian; rough and uncivilized. [French *barbarien,* from Latin *barbaria,* foreign country, from *barbarus,* BARBAROUS.] —**bar·bar·i·an·ism** *n.*

bar·bar·ic (bär-băr′ĭk) *adj.* **1.** Of, pertaining to, or characteristic of a barbarian or barbarians. **2.** Marked by crudeness or wildness of taste, style, or manner. **3.** Extremely cruel and inhuman.

bar·ba·rism (bär′bə-rĭz′əm) *n.* **1.** An instance, act, trait, or custom characterized by brutality or coarseness. **2. a.** The use of words or forms considered incorrect or nonstandard in a language. **b.** A specific word or form so used. **3.** Anything that offends against accepted standards of taste or manners. [Old French *barbarisme,* from Latin *barbarismus,* from Greek *barbarismos,* foreign or incorrect speech, from *barbaros,* foreign, BARBAROUS.]
Usage: *Barbarism* applies to an uncivilized condition generally, with emphasis on crudity of taste, and to crudity of expression in particular. *Barbarity* primarily denotes grossly cruel behavior.

bar·bar·i·ty (bär-băr′ə-tē) *n., pl.* **-ties. 1.** Harsh or cruel conduct. **2.** An inhuman, brutal act. **3.** Crudity; coarseness. —See Usage note at **barbarism.**

bar·ba·rize (bär′bər-īz′) *v.* **-ized, -izing, -izes.** —*tr.* To make crude or barbarous; corrupt. —*intr.* To become barbarous.

Barbarossa. See **Frederick I.**

bar·ba·rous (bär′bər-əs) *adj.* **1.** Primitive in culture and customs; uncivilized. **2.** Characterized by savagery; cruel; brutal. **3.** Lacking refinement or culture; coarse; boorish. **4.** Of, pertaining to, or designating language that violates classical or accepted usage standards. —See Synonyms at **cruel.** [Latin *barbarus,* from Greek *barbaros,* non-Greek, foreign, rude.] —**bar·ba·rous·ly** *adv.* —**bar·ba·rous·ness** *n.*

Bar·ba·ry (bär′bə-rē). A region of the North African coast from Egypt to the Atlantic Ocean. It takes its name from the Berbers, inhabitants of the area since the 2nd millennium B.C. It fell to the

Arabs (7th century A.D.), who introduced Islam. Between the 16th and 19th centuries, it was notorious for its pirates.

Barbary ape *n.* A tailless monkey, *Macaca sylvanus*, of Gibraltar and northern Africa. A species of macaque, it is the only monkey found wild in Europe. Also called "magot."

Barbary sheep *n.* The aoudad *(see).*

bar·bas·co (bär-băs′kō) *n., pl.* -cos. Any of several tropical American trees of the genus *Lonchocarpus*, used locally as the source of a poison for killing fish. [American Spanish, from Spanish, perhaps from Latin *verbascum†*, a plant, mullein.]

bar·bate (bär′bāt) *adj. Biology.* Having a beard, or tufted hairs resembling a beard. [Latin *barbātus*, from *barba*, beard.]

bar·be·cue (bär′bĭ-kyoō′) *n.* 1. a. A pit or outdoor fireplace for cooking meat or other food. b. A grill or similar apparatus used for cooking food outdoors. 2. Meat or other food cooked over an open fire or on a spit. 3. A social gathering, usually held outdoors, at which food is prepared on a barbecue.
~*tr.v.* barbecued, -cuing, -cues. To roast or grill over hot charcoal or an open fire. [American Spanish *barbacoa*, from Haitian Creole, framework of sticks set on posts, from Taino.]

barbed (bärbd) *adj.* 1. Having a barb or barbs. 2. Piercing or stinging: *a barbed statement.*

barbed wire *n.* Twisted strands of fencing wire with barbs at regular intervals. Also called "barbwire."

bar·bel (bär′bəl) *n.* 1. Any of the slender, whiskerlike sensory organs on the head of certain fishes, such as catfish. 2. Any of several Old World freshwater fish of the genus *Barbus*, resembling the carp but with a longer snout. [Middle English, from Old French, from Late Latin *barbellus*, diminutive of *barbus*, barbel (the fish), from Latin *barba*, beard (from its beardlike fleshy filaments).]

bar·bell (bär′bĕl′) *n.* A bar with adjustable weights at each end, used in weightlifting.

bar·bel·late (bär′bə-lāt′) *adj.* Having minute, hooked bristles or hairs. [From New Latin *barbella*, short stiff hair, diminutive of Latin *barbula*, little beard, diminutive of *barba*, beard.]

bar·ber (bär′bər) *n.* One whose business is to cut hair and to shave or trim beards.
~*tr.v.* barbered, -bering, -bers. 1. To cut the hair of. 2. To shave or trim the beard of. [Middle English *barbour*, from Old French *barbeor*, from Medieval Latin *barbātor*, from *barba*, beard, from Latin.]

Bar·ber (bär′bər), **Samuel** (1910–81). U.S. composer. A musical prodigy, he wrote his first opera at the age of six. Barber's 1956 opera *Vanessa*, with a libretto by Gian-Carlo Menotti, won a Pulitzer Prize.

bar·ber·ry (bär′bĕr′ē) *n., pl.* -ries. A shrub of the genus *Berberis*, having small leaves, clusters of yellow flowers, and small orange or red berries. [Variant (influenced by BERRY) of Middle English *barbere*, from Old French *berberis†*.]

bar·ber·shop (bär′bər-shŏp′) *n.* The place of business of a barber.
~*adj. Informal.* Of or designating male voices singing sentimental songs in close, usually four-part, harmony: *a barbershop quartet.*

barber's itch *n.* Any of various infections of the skin beneath a beard, especially ringworm. Not in technical usage.

bar·bet (bär′bĭt) *n.* Any of various tropical birds of the family Capitonidae, having a broad bill bristled at the base and brightly colored plumage, and related to the toucans. [French, from Latin *barbātus*, BARBATE.]

bar·bette (bär-bĕt′) *n.* 1. A platform or mound within a fort high enough to permit firing of guns over the parapet. 2. An armored protective cylinder around a revolving turret on a warship. [French, diminutive of *barbe*, beard.]

bar·bi·can (bär′bĭ-kən) *n.* A tower or other fortification on the approach to a castle or town, especially one at a gate or drawbridge. [Middle English, from Old French *barbacane†*.]

bar·bi·cel (bär′bə-sĕl′) *n. Ornithology.* Any of the minute projections that fringe the edges of the barbules of feathers and interlock with those on adjacent barbules. [New Latin *barbicella*, diminutive of Latin *barba*, beard.]

bar·bi·tal (bär′bə-tôl′) *n.* A barbiturate drug, $C_8H_{12}N_2O_3$, used as a sedative or to induce sleep. [BARBIT(URIC ACID) + (VERON)AL.]

bar·bi·tu·rate (bär-bĭch′ər-ĭt, -ə-rāt′) *n.* 1. A salt or ester of barbituric acid. 2. Any of a group of barbituric acid derivatives used as sedatives or to induce sleep. Prolonged use may lead to dependence. [BARBITUR(IC ACID) + -ATE.]

bar·bi·tu·ric acid (bär′bə-toōr′ĭk, -tyoōr′ĭk) *n.* An organic acid, $C_4H_4N_2O_3$, used in the manufacture of barbiturates and some plastics. [Partial translation of German *Barbitursäure* : *Barbitur*, perhaps from the name *Barbara* + UR(IC) + *Säure*, ACID.]

Bar·bi·zon school (bär′bə-zŏn′) *n.* A 19th-century group of landscape painters in France, including Corot, Daubigny, Millet, and Rousseau. [After *Barbizon*, a small village near Paris, where they worked.]

Barbuda. See **Antigua and Barbuda.**

bar·bule (bär′byoōl′) *n. Biology.* A small barb or pointed projection; especially, any of the small projections fringing the edges of the barbs of feathers. [Latin *barbula*, diminutive of *barba*, beard.]

Bar·busse (bär-büs′), **Henri** (1873–1935). French novelist and journalist who came to fame with the publication of his novel *Under Fire* (1916), based on his experiences in World War I. His disillusionment led him first to pacifism and later to communism.

barb·wire (bärb′wīr′) *n.* Barbed wire *(see).*

Bar·ca (bär′kə). The name of a prominent family of ancient Carthage, whose members included Hannibal and other Carthaginian generals.

bar·ca·role, bar·ca·rolle (bär′kə-rōl′) *n.* 1. A Venetian gondolier's song, with a rhythm suggestive of rowing. 2. A musical composition imitating this. [French, from Italian *barcaruola*, from *barcaruolo*, gondolier, from *barca*, barge, from Late Latin *barca*, BARK (ship).]

Bar·ce·lo·na (bär′sə-lō′nə). Capital of Barcelona province, in Catalonia, northeast Spain, on the Mediterranean coast. Founded by the Carthaginians, it prospered under the Romans and the Visigoths. It was captured by the Moors (713) and by Charlemagne (801). With the incorporation of Catalonia into Spain, the city grew as the center of Catalan separatist, anarcho-syndicalist, and socialist movements. In the Civil War (1936–39) it was the seat of the Republican government. Barcelona is a major cultural center and an enclave of Catalan art and literature. It is the largest port in Spain and a leading commercial and industrial center.

B.Arch. Bachelor of Architecture.

bar·chan, bar·chane, bar·khan (bär-kän′) *n.* A type of crescent-shaped sand dune, concave on the side sheltered from the prevailing wind. [Russian *barkhan*, from Kirghiz.]

bar chart *n.* A bar graph *(see).*

bar code *n.* A code in the form of vertical lines and numbers printed on a book or item of merchandise, for example, so that it can be identified by an optical scanner.

bar·code (bär′kōd′) *tr. v.* -coded, -coding, -codes. To provide with a bar code.

bard¹ (bärd) *n.* 1. Any of an ancient Celtic order of singing poets who composed and recited verses on the legends and history of their people. 2. Any poet, especially an exalted national poet. —See Synonyms at **poet.** [Middle English, from Gaelic and Irish *bárd* and Welsh *bardd*.] —**bard·ic** *adj.*

bard², barde (bärd) *n.* Any piece of armor used to protect or ornament a horse.
~*tr.v.* barded, barding, bards. To equip (a horse) with bards. [Old French *barde*, probably from Old Italian *barda*, from Arabic *barda'ah*, stuffed packsaddle.]

Bard of Avon. William Shakespeare, so called because he was born and buried at Stratford-on-Avon.

bar·dol·a·try (bär-dôl′ə-trē) *n.* Inordinate admiration of Shakespeare and his works. Usually used facetiously. [BARD (Shakespeare) + -LATRY.] —**bar·dol·a·ter** *n.*

Bar·dot (bär-dō′), **Brigitte** (1934–). French actress and model. Among her best-known films are *And God Created Woman* (1956) and *Shaloko* (1968).

bare¹ (bâr) *adj.* barer, barest. 1. Without the usual or appropriate covering or clothing; naked: *a bare chest.* 2. Exposed to view; unconcealed: *laid bare the secret agreements.* 3. Lacking the usual furnishings, equipment, or decoration: *walls bare of pictures.* 4. Without addition, adornment, or qualification; simple; plain: *the bare facts.* 5. Just sufficient; mere: *the bare necessities of life.* 6. Empty: *a bare cupboard.* 7. *Obsolete.* Bareheaded. —See Synonyms at **empty.**
~*tr.v.* bared, baring, bares. 1. To make bare; strip of covering. 2. To expose; reveal: *The dog bared its teeth.* —See Synonyms at **strip.** [Middle English *bare*, Old English *bær*, from Germanic *bazaz* (unattested).] —**bare·ness** *n.*

bare². *Archaic.* Past tense of **bear** (to carry).

bare·back (bâr′băk′) *adj. Also* bare·backed (-băkt′). On a horse or pony, with no saddle: *a bareback rider.* —**bare·back** *adv.*

bare·faced (bâr′fāst′) *adj.* 1. a. Having no covering over the face. b. Having no beard. 2. Unconcealed; without disguise. 3. Presumptuous and shameless; brazen: *a barefaced lie.* —See Synonyms at **shameless.** —**bare·fac·ed·ly** (bâr′fā′sĭd-lē, -fāst′lē) *adv.* —**bare·fac·ed·ness** *n.*

bare·foot (bâr′foōt′) *adj. Also* bare·foot·ed (-foōt′ĭd). Wearing nothing on the feet. —**bare·foot** *adv.*

barefoot doctor *n.* A medical worker, especially in rural areas of developing countries, who carries out such tasks as treating simple injuries and ailments, or assisting at childbirth.

ba·rege, ba·rège (bə-rĕzh′) *n.* A sheer fabric woven of silk or cotton and wool, used for women's apparel. [French *barège*, first made in *Barèges*, southwestern France.]

bare·hand·ed (bâr′hăn′dĭd) *adj.* 1. Having no covering on the hands. 2. With the hands alone; unaided by tools or weapons. —**bare·hand·ed** *adv.*

bare·head·ed (bâr′hĕd′ĭd) *adj.* Having no head covering. —**bare·head·ed** *adv.*

bare·legged (bâr′lĕg′ĭd, -lĕgd′) *adj.* Having the legs uncovered. —**bare·leg·ged** *adv.*

bare·ly (bâr′lē) *adv.* 1. By a very little; hardly; only just. 2. Meagerly; scantily. 3. *Archaic.* Without disguise; openly.

Bar·en·boim (bär′ən-boim′), **Daniel** (1942–). Israeli pianist and conductor. He married (1967) the cellist Jacqueline du Pré and has been musical director of the Orchestre de Paris since 1975.

Bar·ents (bär′ənts), **Willem** (c. 1550–97). Dutch navigator. Barents commanded expeditions (1594, 1595, 1596–97) to find the Northwest Passage. He discovered Spitsbergen on his third voyage and died after being trapped in the ice off Novaya Zemlya. The accuracy of his charts and meteorological data guaranteed his reputation as one of the most important Arctic explorers.

Barents Sea. Shallow section of the Arctic Ocean lying between Svalbard and Novaya Zemlya. The North Atlantic Current keeps

Barbary ape *The Moors—who occupied Gibraltar for most of the period between A.D. 711 and 1462— are thought to have introduced these small apes to the Rock from their native North Africa. The apes are now the only wild monkeys in Europe. Legend has it that when they leave the Rock, the British will follow.*

barge *A large flat-bottomed boat for carrying freight. This one is on a canal in Holland.*

bargeboard *Bargeboards are built against the edge of a gable roof and usually decorated with ornate carving. This Tudor example is at Rottingdean in Sussex, England.*

bark *The Portuguese naval training ship* Sagres II *(above) is a modern barque. It has three masts: the forward two are square-rigged; the stern, or mizzenmast, has a fore-and-aft rig.*

its southern ports ice-free all the year. The sea floor is potentially rich in oil and gas; this and the desire of the U.S.S.R. to command the shipping lanes to the strategic ice-free port of Murmansk have led to disputes over the Norwegian-Soviet border across the sea.

bar·fly (bär′flī′) *n., pl.* **-flies.** *Slang.* One who frequents bars.

bar·gain (bär′gĭn) *n.* **1.** An agreement or deal made between parties, especially one involving the sale and purchase of goods or services. **2.** The terms or conditions of such an agreement: *He met his part of the bargain by handing over the goods.* **3.** The property acquired or services rendered as a result of such an agreement. **4.** Something offered or acquired at a price advantageous to the buyer. **—into the bargain.** Over and above what is expected. **—strike a bargain.** To agree on the terms of a transaction.
~*v.* **bargained, -gaining, -gains.** —*intr.* **1.** To negotiate the terms of a sale, exchange, or other agreement. **2.** To arrive at an agreement. —*tr.* To exchange or trade: *He bargained his watch for a meal.* **—bargain away.** To give up or lose (something of value, such as rights or freedom) without getting anything substantial in return. **—bargain for.** To expect; count on: *got more than she'd bargained for.* **—bargain on.** To rely on. [Middle English *bargaynen,* from Old French *bargaignier,* haggle in the market, probably from Germanic.] **—bar·gain·er** *n.*

bargaining chip *n.* Also *chiefly British* **bargaining counter.** Something offered by one side in negotiations to try to get concessions from the other side.

barge (bärj) *n.* **1.** A long, large boat, usually flat-bottomed, used chiefly on inland waterways for transporting freight. It may have its own power or be towed by other craft. **2.** A large pleasure boat used for parties, pageants, or formal ceremonies. **3.** *Slang.* Any old or unwieldy boat or ship. **4.** *Naval.* A power boat reserved for the use of a flag officer.
~*v.* **barged, barging, barges.** —*tr.* To carry by barge. —*intr. Informal.* **1.** To move about clumsily. **2.** To collide. Used with *into.* **3.** To enter or interrupt rudely and abruptly; intrude. Used with *in* or *into.* [Middle English, from Old French *barge,* perhaps from Medieval Latin *barica* (unattested), from Greek *baris,* BARK (ship).]

barge·board (bärj′bôrd′, -bōrd′) *n. Architecture.* A board, often ornately carved, attached along the projecting edge of a gable roof. [*Barge,* perhaps akin to Medieval Latin *bargus,* gallows.]

bar·gee (bär-jē′) *n. British.* A bargeman.

barge·man (bärj′mən) *n., pl.* **-men** (-mĭn). The master or a crew member of a barge.

barge·pole (bärj′pōl′) *n.* A stout pole used for guiding and pushing a barge.

bar graph *n.* A graph consisting of parallel, usually vertical, bars or rectangles with lengths proportional to specific quantities in a set of data. Also called "bar chart."

Ba·ri (bä′rē). Seaport in Italy, on the Adriatic Sea. Once the Roman colony of Barium, it was held successively by Goths, Lombards, Byzantines, Normans, and Venetians and became part of the kingdom of Naples (1557).

ba·ril·la (bə-rēl′yə, -rē′yə) *n.* **1.** Either of two Old World plants, *Salsola kali* or *S. soda,* or a similar plant, *Halogeton soda,* that were formerly burned to obtain a form of sodium carbonate. **2.** The sodium carbonate thus obtained. [Spanish *barrilla*†.]

bar·ite (bâr′īt′) *n.* A colorless crystalline mineral of barium sulfate that is the chief source of barium chemicals. Also called "barytes," "heavy spar." [Greek *barutēs,* weight, from *barus,* heavy.]

bar·i·tone (bâr′ə-tōn′) *n.* Also **bar·y·tone. 1.** A male singer or voice having a range higher than a bass and lower than a tenor. **2.** A part written for a baritone. **3.** A brass wind instrument with a similar range.
~*adj.* **1.** Of, pertaining to, or having the range of a baritone. **2.** Having the second-lowest range in a family of instruments: *the baritone saxophone.* [Italian *baritono,* from Greek *barutonos,* deep sounding : *barus,* heavy, + *tonos,* pitch, TONE.]

bar·i·um (bâr′ē-əm, băr′-) *n. Symbol* **Ba** A soft, silvery-white, alkaline-earth metal, used to deoxidize copper, in various alloys, and in rat poison. Atomic number 56, atomic weight 137.34, melting point 725°C, boiling point 1,140°C, specific gravity 3.50, valence 2. [BAR(YTA) + -IUM.] **—bar·ic** *adj.*

barium enema *n.* A preparation of barium sulfate infused into the rectum in order to reveal the large intestine by x-ray.

barium hydroxide *n.* A white, poisonous, crystalline compound, $Ba(OH)_2$, used in the extraction of beet sugar. Also called "baryta."

barium meal *n.* A preparation of barium sulfate swallowed before x-ray examination of the stomach and small intestine.

barium oxide *n.* A white soluble powder, BaO, used as a dehydrating agent and in the manufacture of certain types of glass. Also called "baryta."

barium sulfate *n.* A fine white powder, $BaSO_4$, used as a pigment, as a filler for textiles, rubbers, and plastics, and as an indicator in x-ray photography of the digestive tract. Also called "baryta."

barium yellow *n.* **1.** A pigment made of barium chromate, $BaCrO_4$. **2.** Light or moderate greenish yellow to brilliant yellow.

bark[1] (bärk) *n.* **1.** The characteristic harsh, abrupt, usually gruff sound of a dog and certain other animals. **2.** Any similar sound, such as a gunshot or cough.
~*v.* **barked, barking, barks.** —*intr.* **1.** To utter a bark. **2.** *Informal.* To cough. **3.** To speak sharply; snap: *He barked at his assistant.* **4.** *Informal.* To work as a barker. —*tr.* To utter sharply in a loud, harsh voice. [Middle English *berken,* to bark, Old English *beorcan.*]

bark[2] *n.* **1.** The protective outer covering of the woody stems, branches, and main trunks of trees and other woody plants, consisting of dead cells. **2.** A specific kind of bark used for a special purpose, as in tanning or medicine.
~*tr.v.* **barked, barking, barks. 1.** To remove bark from (a tree or log). **2.** To rub off the skin of; bruise. **3.** To tan, dye, or treat medically using bark. [Middle English *barke,* from Old Norse *börkr,* from North Germanic *barkuz* (unattested).]

bark[3] *n.* Also **barque** (bärk). **1.** A sailing ship with from three to five masts, all of them square-rigged except the after mast, which is fore-and-aft rigged. Compare **barkentine. 2.** *Poetic.* Any boat, especially a small sailing vessel. [Middle English *barke,* boat, from Old French *barque,* probably from Italian *barca,* from Late Latin, small boat, bark, barge, from Greek *baris,* Egyptian barge, akin to Coptic *bari,* barge.]

bark beetle *n.* Any of various small beetles of the family Scolytidae that damage trees by boring along the surface of the wood beneath the bark.

bar·ken·tine (bär′kən-tēn′) *n.* Also **bar·quen·tine.** A sailing ship with from three to five masts of which only the foremast is square-rigged, the other masts being fore-and-aft rigged. Compare **bark.** [Probably blend of BARK (boat) and BRIGANTINE.]

bark·er[1] (bär′kər) *n.* **1.** An animal or person making a barking sound. **2.** *Informal.* An employee who stands before the entrance to a show and attracts customers with loud, colorful sales talk.

barker[2] *n.* A person or machine that removes bark from trees or prepares it for tanning.

barkhan. Variant of **barchan.**

Bark·hau·sen effect (bärk′hou′zən) *n.* A phenomenon exhibited by ferromagnetic materials, in which the process of magnetization and demagnetization proceeds in discrete jumps. [First described by Heinrich *Barkhausen* (1881–1956), German physicist.]

barking deer *n.* The **muntjac** *(see).*

bark·y (bär′kē) *adj.* **-ier, -iest.** Covered with, containing, or resembling bark.

bar·ley (bär′lē) *n.* **1.** A widely cultivated cereal grass of the genus *Hordeum*; especially, *H. vulgare,* bearing bearded flower spikes with edible seeds. **2.** The grain of this plant, used as food and in making beer, ale, and whiskey. See **pearl barley.** [Middle English *barrlig,* originally "of barley," Old English *bærlic,* from *bære, bere,* barley.]

bar·ley·corn (bär′lē-kôrn′) *n.* **1.** The seed or grain of barley. **2.** Formerly, a unit of measure equal to the width of a grain of barley, or approximately $1/3$ inch.

Barleycorn, John. See **John Barleycorn.**

barley sugar *n.* A clear, hard candy made by boiling down sugar, formerly with an extract of barley added.

barley water *n.* A drink prepared by boiling pearl barley in water, to which lemon juice is often added.

barley wine *n.* A very strong beer.

bar line *n. British.* A vertical line dividing a musical staff into equal measures; a bar.

barm (bärm) *n.* The yeasty foam that rises to the surface of fermenting malt liquors. [Middle English *berme,* Old English *beorma.*]

bar·maid (bär′mād′) *n.* A woman who serves drinks in a bar.

bar·man (bär′mən) *n., pl.* **-men** (-mĭn). *Chiefly British.* A bartender.

Bar·me·ci·dal (bär′mə-sīd′l) *adj.* Also **Bar·me·cide** (bär′mə-sīd′). Plentiful or abundant in appearance only; illusory: *a Barmecide feast.* [From *Barmecide,* name of an 8th-century noble Persian family, one of whom served a beggar an imaginary feast in the *Arabian Nights.*]

bar mitz·vah, bar miz·vah (bär mĭts′və) *n. Judaism.* **1.** A thirteen-year-old Jewish male, considered an adult and thenceforth responsible for his moral and religious duties. **2.** The ceremony conferring and celebrating this status.
~*tr.v.* **bar mitzvahed, -vahing, -vahs.** To admit to the status of bar mitzvah. [Hebrew, "son of commandment."]

barm·y (bär′mē) *adj.* **-ier, -iest. 1.** Full of barm; frothy; foamy. **2.** *British Informal.* Slightly mad; foolish.

barn (bärn) *n.* **1.** A large farm building used for storing grain, hay, and other farm products, and for sheltering livestock. **2.** Any building that resembles a barn in being uncomfortably large and bare. **3.** A large shed for the housing of railroad cars, trucks, or other vehicles. **4.** *Physics. Symbol* **b** A unit of area equal to 10^{-24} square centimeter, used to express nuclear cross sections. [Middle English *bern,* from Old English *bern, berern* : *bere,* BARLEY + *ern, ærn,* house, from Germanic *razn-* (unattested) (see **ransack**).]

bar·na·cle (bär′nə-kəl) *n.* **1.** Any of various marine crustaceans of the order Cirripedia that, in the adult stage, form a hard shell from which feathery food-catching appendages protrude and which remain attached to a submerged surface, thus fouling ship bottoms. See **acorn barnacle, goose barnacle. 2.** Formerly, the barnacle goose. [Middle English *bernak, bernacle,* barnacle goose, from Medieval Latin *bernaca, bernecat*†, barnacle, barnacle goose (from the belief that the geese were produced from the shellfish that supposedly clung to trees).] **—bar·na·cled** *adj.*

barnacle goose *n.* A waterfowl, *Branta leucopsis,* of northern Europe and Greenland, having black, white, and gray plumage.

Bar·nard (bär′nərd, bär-närd′), **Christiaan Neethling** (1923–). South African surgeon noted for pioneering heart transplant operations. He performed the world's first heart transplant (December 3, 1967) at the Groote Schuur Hospital, Cape Town. The recipient was Louis Washkansky, who died of pneumonia 18 days after the operation.

Bar·nard (bär′nərd), **Edward Emerson** (1857–1923). U.S. astronomer. He is noted for his discovery of Jupiter's fifth satellite (1892) and for his discovery of Barnard's star (1916).

Barnard's star *n.* A star in the constellation Ophiuchus, 6 light-years from the sun and the second-nearest star system to the sun. It has an extremely large proper motion, which indicates the presence of an orbiting system of planets.

barn dance *n.* **1.** A social gathering, usually held in a barn, with music and square dancing. **2.** *Chiefly British.* A kind of country dance.

barn door *n.* **1.** The door of a barn. **2.** A target so large that it is hard to miss.

bar·ney (bär'nē) *n. British.* A noisy quarrel.
~*intr.v.* **barneyed, -neying, -neys.** To quarrel noisily. [19th century : origin obscure.]

barn owl *n.* A long-legged owl, *Tyto alba,* having light-brown and white plumage and a heart-shaped face, and often frequenting barns and other buildings.

barn·storm (bärn'stôrm') *v.* **-stormed, -storming, -storms.** —*intr.* **1.** To travel about the country making political speeches, especially in an election campaign. **2.** To tour rural areas presenting theatrical performances, often in makeshift theaters. **3.** To tour rural areas giving exhibitions of stunt flying, especially in the early days of aviation. —*tr.* To travel through in order to go barnstorming. **—barn·storm·er** *n.*

barn swallow *n.* A widely distributed bird, *Hirundo rustica,* having a deeply forked tail, a dark-blue back, and tan underparts. [The bird often builds its nest in the eaves of barns.]

Bar·num (bär'nəm), **P(hineas) T(aylor)** (1810–91). U.S. showman who first popularized "freak shows" in 1842. Among his exhibits were Chang and Eng, the original Siamese twins. His circus was established in 1871 and in 1881 merged with that of his great rival, James A. Bailey.

barn·yard (bärn'yärd') *n.* The area of ground surrounding a barn, often enclosed by a fence; a farmyard.
~*adj.* **1.** Of or pertaining to a barnyard: *a barnyard fence.* **2.** Rustic; earthy: *barnyard humor.*

baro- *prefix.* Indicates weight or pressure; for example, **barometer.** [From Greek *baros,* weight.]

Ba·ro·da (bə-rō'də). City in southeast Gujarat state, India. Once the capital of the princely state of Baroda, it is distinguished by many fine public buildings, palaces, and Hindu temples.

bar·o·gram (băr'ə-grăm') *n.* A graphic record produced by a barograph. [BARO- + -GRAM.]

bar·o·graph (băr'ə-grăf', -gräf') *n.* A self-recording barometer. [BARO- + -GRAPH.] **—bar·o·graph·ic** *adj.*

ba·rom·e·ter (bə-rŏm'ə-tər) *n.* **1.** *Abbr.* **bar.** An instrument for measuring atmospheric pressure, used in weather forecasting and in determining altitude. The main types are the **aneroid barometer** and the **mercury barometer** *(both of which see).* **2.** Anything that gives notice of fluctuations; an indicator: *This election will be a barometer of the government's popularity.* [BARO- + -METER.] **—bar·o·met·ric** (băr'ə-mĕt'rĭk), **bar·o·met·ri·cal** *adj.* **—bar·o·met·ri·cal·ly** *adv.* **—ba·rom·e·try** *n.*

barometric gradient *n.* A **pressure gradient** *(see).*

bar·on (băr'ən) *n.* **1.** Formerly: **a.** A feudal tenant holding his rights and title directly from the king or another feudal superior. **b.** A lord or nobleman; a peer. **2.** A member of the lowest rank of nobility in Great Britain, certain European countries, and Japan. **3.** *Abbr.* **Bn., bn.** The rank or title of such a nobleman. **4.** A man with great and coercive power in a specified sphere of commercial activity; a magnate. **5.** A cut of beef consisting of a double sirloin. Also called "baron of beef." [Middle English, from Norman French, from Old French, accusative of *ber,* from Medieval Latin *barō*† (stem *barōn-*), man, warrior.]

bar·on·age (băr'ə-nĭj) *n.* **1.** The rank, title, or dignity of a baron. **2.** A list of barons. **3.** All of the peers of a kingdom.

bar·on·ess (băr'ə-nĭs) *n.* **1.** The wife or widow of a baron. **2.** A woman holding a barony in her own right.

bar·on·et (băr'ə-nĭt, băr'ə-nĕt') *n.* **1.** A British hereditary title of honor, ranking next below a baron, held by commoners. **2.** *Abbr.* **Bart., Bt.** The bearer of such a title. [Middle English, diminutive of BARON.]

bar·on·et·age (băr'ə-nĭt-ĭj, -nĕt'ĭj) *n.* **1.** The rank or dignity of a baronet. **2.** A list of baronets. **3.** Baronets collectively.

bar·on·et·cy (băr'ə-nĭt-sē, -nĕt'sē) *n., pl.* **-cies.** The dignity or rank of a baronet.

ba·rong (bă-rông', -rŏng') *n.* A large, broad-bladed knife used by the Moros of the Philippines. [Native Philippine name, probably akin to Malay PARANG.]

ba·ro·ni·al (bə-rō'nē-əl) *adj.* **1.** Of or pertaining to a baron or barony. **2.** Suited for or befitting a baron; stately; grand.

bar·o·ny (băr'ə-nē) *n., pl.* **-nies.** **1.** The domain of a baron. **2.** The rank or dignity of a baron. **3.** In Ireland, a division of a county. **4.** In Scotland, a large estate.

ba·roque (bə-rōk') *adj.* **1.** *Often* **Baroque. a.** Of, pertaining to, or designating a style in art and architecture developed in Europe from the late 16th to the early 18th centuries, typified by elaborate and ornate scrolls, curves, and other symmetrical ornamentation. **b.** Of, pertaining to, or designating music of this period, characterized especially by chromaticism and elaborate ornamentation. **2.** Ornate or flamboyant in style; richly ornamented. **3.** Irregular in shape: *baroque pearls.*
~*n.* **1.** *Often* **Baroque.** The baroque style in art, architecture, and music. **2.** The period during which baroque styles flourished, from the late 16th to the early 18th centuries. **3.** Any elaborate or ornate style. [French (originally used of pearls), from Portuguese *barroco*†, and Spanish *barrueco*†; (in architecture), from Italian *barroco*†.] See feature, next page.

bar·o·re·cep·tor (băr'ə-rĭ-sĕp'tər) *n. Physiology.* A group of nerve endings, found in the walls of various blood vessels and the heart, that is sensitive to changes in blood pressure.

bar·o·scope (băr'ə-skōp') *n.* Any instrument or device for estimating atmospheric pressure; especially, a manometer with one leg open to the atmosphere. [BARO- + -SCOPE.]

bar·o·stat (băr'ə-stăt) *n.* **1.** Any device for maintaining a constant pressure, as in the cabin of an airplane. **2.** A device used on gas turbines that regulates the input and output pressures of the fuel--metering equipment, in order to compensate for variations of atmospheric pressure. [BARO- + -STAT.]

Ba·rot·se·land (bə-rŏt'sē-lănd'). A former kingdom in central Africa, now Western province, Zambia, inhabited by the Lozi people. Under their chief, Lewanika (died 1916), the kingdom became part of the protectorate of Northern Rhodesia; and when Zambia became independent (1964), Barotseland tried unsuccessfully to become a separate kingdom.

ba·rouche (bə-ro͞osh') *n.* A four-wheeled carriage with a collapsible top, two double seats inside opposite each other, and a box seat outside in front for the driver. [German *Barutsche,* from Italian *baroccio,* earlier *biroccio* (unattested), from Late Latin *birotium,* two-wheeled, from Latin *birotus* : BI- + *rota,* wheel.]

barque. Variant of **bark** (ship).

barquentine. Variant of **barkentine.**

bar·rack[1] (băr'ĭk) *tr.v.* **-racked, -racking, -racks.** To house in barracks.

barrack[2] *v.* **-racked, -racking, -racks.** —*intr.* **1.** *British.* To jeer or shout at a player, speaker, or team. **2.** *Australian.* To shout support for a team. Used with *for.* —*tr. British.* To shout against; jeer at. [From native Australian *borak,* banter, chaff.] **—bar·rack·er** *n.*

bar·racks (băr'ĭks) *n., pl.* **barracks.** *Used with a singular or plural verb.* **1. a.** *Abbr.* **bks.** A building or group of buildings used to house soldiers. **b.** A post or station of the state police. **2.** Any large building used for temporary accommodation. **3.** Any unadorned or unattractive building. [From French *baraque,* from Italian *baracca,* soldier's tent, from Spanish *barraca,* mud hut, perhaps from Catalan *barraca*†.]

barracks bag *n.* A soldier's cloth bag, usually with a drawstring, for the storage of clothing or laundry in the barracks.

bar·ra·coon (băr'ə-ko͞on') *n.* Formerly, a barracks in which slaves and convicts were temporarily confined. [Spanish *barracón,* augmentative of *barraca,* hut. See **barracks.**]

bar·ra·cu·da (băr'ə-ko͞o'də) *n., pl.* **-das** or collectively **barracuda.** Any of various voracious, mostly tropical, marine fishes of the genus *Sphyraena;* especially, *S. barracuda,* having a long, narrow body and projecting jaws with fanglike teeth. [American Spanish *barracuda*†.]

bar·rage[1] (băr'ĭj) *n.* An artificial obstruction in a watercourse, used especially to promote irrigation or prevent flooding. [French, from *barrer,* BAR.]

bar·rage[2] (bə-räzh') *n.* **1.** A heavy curtain of artillery fire often placed in front of friendly troops to screen and protect them. **2.** Any rapid, concentrated discharge of missiles, or heavy, blanket bombardment. **3.** An overwhelming, concentrated outpouring, as of words or blows: *a barrage of questions.* **4.** A deciding bout in fencing.
~*tr.v.* **barraged, -raging, -rages.** To direct a barrage at. [French, from *(tir de) barrage,* barrier (fire), from BARRAGE (barrier).]

barrage balloon *n.* A balloon anchored singly or as one of a series, supporting cables or nets in order to hinder the passage of low-flying enemy aircraft.

bar·ra·mun·da (băr'ə-mŭn'də) *n., pl.* **-das** or collectively **barramunda.** Also **bar·ra·mun·di** (-mŭn'dē) *pl.* **-dis** or collectively **barramundi.** Any of several Australian food fishes, such as the river fish *Scleropages leichhardtdii,* or the lungfish *Neoceratodus forsteri.* [From a native Australian name.]

bar·ran·ca (bə-răng'kə) *n. Southwestern U.S.* A deep ravine or gorge. [Spanish, probably from Iberian.]

Bar·ran·quil·la (băr'ən-kē'ə, -yə). A large seaport in northern Colombia, on the Magdalena River near its mouth on the Caribbean Sea.

bar·ra·tor, bar·ra·ter (băr'ə-tər) *n. Law.* One who commits barratry. [Middle English, from Norman-French *baratour,* from Old French *barateor,* swindler, from *barater,* to cheat, BARTER.]

bar·ra·try (băr'ə-trē) *n., pl.* **-tries.** **1.** *Law.* Formerly, the offense of exciting or stirring up quarrels or groundless lawsuits. **2.** *Maritime Law.* An unlawful breach of duty on the part of a ship's master or crew that is to the prejudice or disadvantage of the ship's owner. **3.** The sale or purchase of positions in the church or state. [Middle English *barratrie,* the purchase of church offices, from Old French *baraterie,* deception, from *barater,* to cheat, BARTER.] **—bar·ra·trous** *adj.* **—bar·ra·trous·ly** *adv.*

Bar·rault (bá-rō'), **Jean Louis** (1910–). French actor, director, and producer. He was producer-director with the Comédie Française (1940–46) and director of the Theâtre de France (1959–68). His film credits include *La Symphonie Fantastique* (1942) and *Les Enfants du Paradis* (1944).

barn owl *The barn owl, which often nests in old barns, has extremely sensitive hearing and, with its silent flight, can hunt rodents by sound alone, even in complete darkness.*

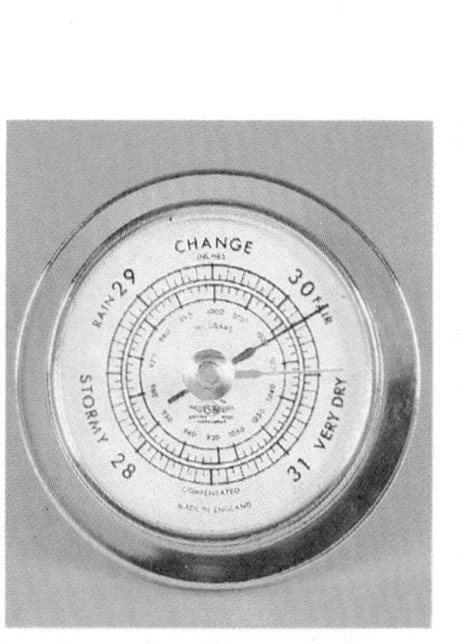

barometer *A modern aneroid barometer. Barometers are used to measure changes in air pressure as an aid to weather forecasting.*

barracuda *A fierce predator of tropical and sometimes temperate waters. It can grow to nearly 2.5 meters (8 feet) long and weigh about 18 kilograms (40 pounds).*

baroque

THE ART OF 17TH-CENTURY ROMAN CATHOLIC EUROPE
An extravagant style of painting, sculpture, and architecture

The baroque was predominantly a style of Roman Catholic Europe, reaching its finest expression in mid-17th-century Rome.

The style is characterized by the subordination of the various parts of a building, sculpture, or painting to an overall dramatic, three-dimensional, even theatrical effect. Lines are curved and bold, decoration is elaborate, and composition makes a direct appeal to the emotions.

The outstanding exponents of the baroque in Rome were the sculptor and architect Gianlorenzo Bernini (1598–1680), the architect Francesco Borromini (1599–1667), and the painter Michelangelo da Caravaggio (c. 1565–1610). Under the auspices of the Jesuits, the baroque style spread to the German-speaking countries and to the Spanish Netherlands, where the Flemish painter Peter Paul Rubens (1577–1640) reigned supreme.

RELIGIOUS REALISM *In religious paintings such as* The Supper at Emmaus, *Caravaggio pioneered a new style of intense realism and dramatic use of light and shade.*

RELIGIOUS RAPTURE The Ecstasy of St. Teresa, *a group by Bernini, stands in a side chapel of Santa Maria della Vittoria in Rome. The swirling drapery and the ecstatic central figure portray an intense religious experience.*

RELIGIOUS DRAMA *The vault of a chapel completed about 1700 in San Carlo ai Catinari in Rome is an exuberant example of how Antonio Gherardi (1644–1702) combined sculpture and architecture into one overwhelming and dramatic whole.*

barre, bar (bär) *n.* A bar fixed to a wall in a studio to aid ballet dancers when practicing. [French.]

bar·ré (bä-rā′) *n. Music.* A technique, used by guitar and lute players, of laying the forefinger over some or all of the strings and so changing the pitch. [French, "barred."]

barred owl *n.* A North American owl, *Strix varia,* having barred, brownish plumage, a streaked belly, and a strident, hooting cry.

bar·rel (băr′əl) *n.* **1.** A large, nearly cylindrical container, traditionally made of wooden staves bound together with hoops, and having a flat top and bottom of equal diameter and, usually, sides that bulge outward in the middle. **2.** The quantity that a barrel with a given or standard capacity will hold. **3.** *Abbr.* **bar., bbl, bbl., bl.** Any of various units of volume or capacity. In the U.S. Customary System it varies, as a liquid measure, from 31 to 42 gallons as established by law or usage. **4.** The metal, cylindrical part of a firearm through which the bullet travels. **5.** A cylinder that contains a movable piston. **6.** The drum of a capstan. **7.** The cylinder within the mechanism of a timepiece that contains the mainspring. **8.** The cylindrical part or hollow shaft of any of various other instruments and mechanisms. **9.** The ink container of a fountain pen. **10.** *Informal.* A large quantity: *a barrel of fun.* **—over a barrel.** Helpless; defenseless. **—scrape the (bottom of the) barrel.** To use one's last and poorest resources.

~v. **barreled** or **barrelled, -reling** or **-relling, -rels.** *—tr.* To put or pack in a barrel or barrels. *—intr. Informal.* To move at high speed. Usually used with *along.* [Middle English *barel,* from Old French *baril,* probably from *barre,* BAR (rod).]

barrel chair *n.* A large, upholstered chair having a high, rounded back resembling a half-barrel.

bar·rel-chest·ed (băr′əl-chĕs′tĭd) *adj.* Having a very large outward-curving chest.

bar·rel·house (băr′əl-hous′) *n.* **1.** A disreputable, old-time saloon or bawdyhouse. **2.** An early style of jazz characterized by free group improvization and an accented two-beat rhythm.

barrel organ *n.* A portable musical instrument operated by the action of a revolving barrel with pegs or pins that open air valves leading from a bellows to a series of pipes.

barrel roll *n.* A flight maneuver in which an aircraft makes a complete rotation on its longitudinal axis while approximately maintaining its original direction.

barrel vault *n. Architecture.* A simple vault with a continuous semicircular section.

bar·ren (băr′ən) *adj.* **1. a.** Not producing offspring; childless or fruitless. **b.** Incapable of producing offspring; infertile; sterile. **2.** Lacking vegetation, especially useful vegetation; unproductive. **3.** Unproductive of results or gains; unprofitable. **4.** Devoid; lacking: *writing barren of insight.* **5.** Lacking in liveliness or interest. —See Synonyms at **empty, sterile.**
~*n. Usually* **barrens.** A tract of unproductive land, often with a scrubby growth of trees: *the pine barrens of New Jersey.* [Middle English *barein(e),* from Norman French, from Old French *baraigne, barhaine†.*] —**bar·ren·ly** *adv.* —**bar·ren·ness** *n.*

bar·ren·wort (băr′ən-wərt) *n.* A European perennial herbaceous plant, *Epimedium alpinum,* with clusters of red and yellow flowers. [From the belief that it caused sterility.]

bar·ret (băr′ĭt) *n.* A flat cap; especially, a **biretta** *(see).* [French, *barrette,* from Italian *barretta, berretta,* BIRETTA.]

bar·rette (bə-rĕt′, bä-) *n.* A small clasp used by women for holding the hair in place. Also *British* "hair-slide." [French, diminutive of *barre,* BAR.]

bar·ri·cade (băr′ə-kād′, băr′ə-kād′) *n.* **1.** A structure set up across a road, as a means of defense or to obstruct passage. **2.** Anything acting to obstruct passage; a barrier. —See Synonyms at **bulwark.**
~*tr.v.* **barricaded, -cading, -cades. 1.** To close off or block with a barricade. **2.** To keep in or out by means of a barricade. [French, from *barrique,* barrel (the earliest barricades were made of earth-filled barrels), from Spanish *barrica,* from *barril,* akin to Old French *baril,* BARREL.] —**bar·ri·cad·er** *n.*

Bar·rie (băr′ē), **Sir James Matthew** (1860–1937). Scottish novelist and dramatist. His first novel, *The Little Minister* (1891), was an immediate success. With *The Little White Bird* (1902), he began the Peter Pan cycle, which was continued with the play *Peter Pan* (1904), *Peter Pan in Kensington Gardens* (1906), and *Peter Pan and Wendy* (1908). His later plays include *What Every Woman Knows* (1908) and *Dear Brutus* (1917). He was made a baronet (1913).

bar·ri·er (băr′ē-ər) *n.* **1.** A fence, wall, or other structure built to prevent or control access or passage. **2.** Anything, material or immaterial, that acts to obstruct or prevent passage. **3.** A boundary or limit. **4.** Anything that separates or holds apart: *social barriers.* **5.** A movable gate that keeps racehorses in line before the start of a race. **6. barriers.** The palisades or fences enclosing the lists of a medieval tournament. **7.** *Geology.* An **ice barrier** *(see).* —See Synonyms at **obstacle.** [Middle English; from Norman French *barrere,* from Old French *barriere,* probably from *barre,* BAR.]

barrier beach *n.* A long, narrow bar of sand built up parallel to a coastline by wave action, and exposed at high tide. Also called "barrier island."

barrier reef *n.* A long, narrow ridge of coral or rock parallel to and relatively near a coastline, separated from the coastline by a lagoon too deep for coral growth.

bar·ring (bär′ĭng) *prep.* Unless (something) occurs; excepting: *Barring strong headwinds, the plane will arrive on time.*

bar·ri·o (bä′ryō) *n., pl.* **-os. 1.** An enclave, ward, or urban district in a Latin-American country or in the Philippines. **2.** A chiefly Spanish-speaking community or neighborhood, especially in a U.S. city. [Spanish, from Arabic *barrī,* of an open area, from *barr,* open area, open country, outside.]

bar·ris·ter (băr′ĭ-stər) *n. Chiefly British.* A lawyer admitted to plead at the bar in the superior courts. Compare **advocate, solicitor.** —See Usage note at **lawyer.** [16th century : from BAR (railing) + *-rister,* perhaps by analogy with *minister.*]

bar·room (bär′ro͞om′, -ro͝om′) *n.* A room or building in which alcoholic beverages are sold at a counter or bar.

bar·row¹ (băr′ō) *n.* **1. a.** A flat, rectangular tray or cart, having handles at each end. **b.** The load carried on such a tray. **2.** A **wheelbarrow** *(see).* [Middle English *bar(o)we,* Old English *bearwe,* basket, wheelbarrow.]

barrow² *n. Archaeology.* A large mound of earth or stones placed over a burial site. Also called "mound." [Middle English *borewe, burgh,* Old English *beorg,* from Germanic *bergaz* (unattested).]

barrow³ *n.* A pig that has been castrated before reaching sexual maturity. [Middle English *barow,* Old English *bearg, barg.*]

Bar·ry (băr′ē). Port in South Glamorgan, on the Bristol Channel in southern Wales. Barry Island, a popular holiday resort, is joined to the mainland south of Barry.

Bar·ry·more (băr′ĭ-môr′, -mōr′). Family of U.S. actors. **Lionel** (1878–1954) first appeared on stage at age six. Among his films were *Free Soul* (1931), for which he won an Oscar, and the Dr. Kildare series. His sister, **Ethel** (1879–1959), appeared mainly in the theater but also made motion pictures, including the Oscar-winning *None but the Lonely Heart* (1944). Their younger brother, **John** (1882–1942), was known as "the Great Profile." He appeared on stage as Hamlet and Richard III and in many popular motion pictures, including *Dinner at Eight* (1933).

bar sinister *n.* **1.** A heraldic bend or baton sinister held to signify bastardy. Not in technical usage. **2.** A hint or proof of illegitimate birth.

Bart. baronet.

bar·tend·er (bär′tĕn′dər) *n.* One who mixes and serves alcoholic drinks at a bar. Also *especially British* "barman."

bar·ter (bär′tər) *v.* **-tered, -tering, -ters.** —*intr.* **1.** To trade goods or services without the exchange of money. **2.** To haggle or bargain. —*tr.* To exchange (goods or services) without using money: *He bartered his watch for food.*
~*n.* **1.** The act or practice of bartering. **2.** Any exchange, as of agreements or concessions by two or more sides; a bargaining. **3.** Something that is bartered. [Middle English *barteren,* probably from Old French *barater,* to barter, cheat, perhaps from Vulgar Latin *prattāre* (unattested), cheat, do, from Greek *prattein,* to do, manage.] —**bar·ter·er** *n.*

Barth (bärt), **Karl** (1886–1968). Swiss Protestant theologian, who advocated a return to the principles of the Reformation and the teachings of the Bible. In his books *Epistle to the Romans* (1918) and *Church Dogmatics,* which he started in 1932 and completed in 1962, he emphasized the sovereignty of God and the inherent sinfulness of mankind.

Barthes (bärt), **Roland** (1915–80). French philosopher and social critic. He wrote on structuralism, modern linguistics, and semiology—the science of signs or sign language, which he extended to clothing, sports, and fashions in general.

Bar·thol·di (bär-thŏl′dē, -tôl′dē), **Frédéric Auguste** (1834–1904). French sculptor. He is best known for his monumental figure of *Liberty Enlightening the World,* the Statue of Liberty in New York Harbor, presented to the United States by France and dedicated in 1886. The statue was extensively restored in preparation for a gala July 4, 1986, centennial celebration.

Bar·thol·o·mew (bär-thŏl′ə-myo͞o′), **Saint,** sometimes called "Nathanael." One of the Twelve Apostles. Mark 3:18.

bar·ti·zan, bar·ti·san (bär′tə-zən, bär′tə-zăn′) *n. Architecture.* A small, overhanging turret on a wall or tower. [Spurious architectural term (coined by Sir Walter Scott), from Scottish *bartisane,* corruption of *bratticing,* from BRATTICE.] —**bar·ti·zaned** *adj.*

Bart·lett (bärt′lĭt) *n.* A widely grown English variety of pear having large, juicy, yellow fruit. [Named after Enoch *Bartlett* (1779–1860), U.S. merchant who cultivated and popularized it.]

Bar·tók (bär′tôk), **Béla** (1881–1945). Hungarian pianist and composer. In 1940 he took up residence in the United States. His compositions blend elements of Eastern European folk music with dissonant harmonies. In addition to three piano concertos, he composed the music for the opera *Duke Bluebeard's Castle* (1911) and for the ballet *The Miraculous Mandarin* (1919). His most popular work is the *Concerto for Orchestra* (1943).

Bar·ton (bärt′n), **Clara,** in full Clarissa Harlowe Barton (1821–1912). U.S. founder of the American Red Cross. She first did battlefield relief work during the Civil War. The U.S. branch of the Red Cross was organized in 1881.

Bar·uch (bâr′ək, bə-ro͞ok′) *n.* A book of the Old Testament Apocrypha.

Ba·ruch (bə-ro͞ok′), **Bernard Mannes** (1870–1965). U.S. financier and statesman. He accumulated a large fortune on Wall Street and after 1916 devoted much of his time to governmental advisory commissions. Baruch was widely known as a confidant and adviser of every president from Woodrow Wilson to John F. Kennedy.

bar·y·cen·ter (băr′ə-sĕn′tər) *n. Physics.* **Center of mass** *(see).* [Greek *barus,* heavy + CENTER.]

bar·y·on (băr′ē-ŏn′) *n.* Any of a family of subatomic particles, including the nucleon and hyperon multiplets, that participate in strong interactions, have half-integral spins, and are generally more massive than mesons. [Greek *barus,* heavy + -ON.] —**bar·y·on·ic** *adj.*

baryon number *n. Symbol* **B** A conserved quantum number equal to the difference between the number of baryons and the number of antibaryons in a system of subatomic particles.

Ba·rysh·ni·kov (bə-rĭsh′nĭ-kôf′), **Mikhail** (1948–). Russian-born U.S. dancer and choreographer. Until his defection in 1974 Baryshnikov danced with the Kirov Ballet in Leningrad. In the United States he has danced with the American Ballet Theater, appeared on television and in motion pictures, and choreographed numerous works, including the classic *Nutcracker.*

ba·ry·ta (bə-rī′tə) *n.* **1. Barium hydroxide** *(see).* **2. Barium oxide** *(see).* **3. Barium sulfate** *(see).* [From BARYTES + *-a,* as in *soda,* etc.]

ba·ry·tes (bə-rī′tēz) *n.* A mineral, **barite** *(see).*

barytone. Variant of **baritone.**

bas·al (bā′səl, -zəl) *adj.* **1.** Pertaining to, located at, or forming a base. **2.** Of primary importance; basic. —**bas·al·ly** *adv.*

basal complex *n.* The part of the earth's crust that lies below any sedimentary rock or sediment and extends down to the Moho; it is usually Precambrian in age. Also called "basement complex."

basal ganglia *pl.n.* Several masses of gray matter situated deep within the brain that are concerned with the unconscious control of voluntary movements.

basal metabolic rate *n. Abbr.* **BMR** The rate at which energy is used by an organism at complete rest, expressed in terms of heat production per unit of body surface area per day.

basal metabolism *n.* The least amount of energy required to maintain vital functions, such as respiration and digestion, in an organism at complete rest.

ba·salt (bə-sôlt′, bā′sôlt′) *n.* **1.** A hard, fine-grained, dense, dark

barrier reef *The Great Barrier Reef—the largest barrier reef in the world and the largest structure built by any living creature—runs for more than 1,900 kilometers (1,180 miles) off the coast of Queensland, northeast Australia, and is up to 160 kilometers (100 miles) wide. Formed by coral polyps, the ridge is made up of more than 2,500 separate reefs, some of which, as here, are topped by coral islands.*

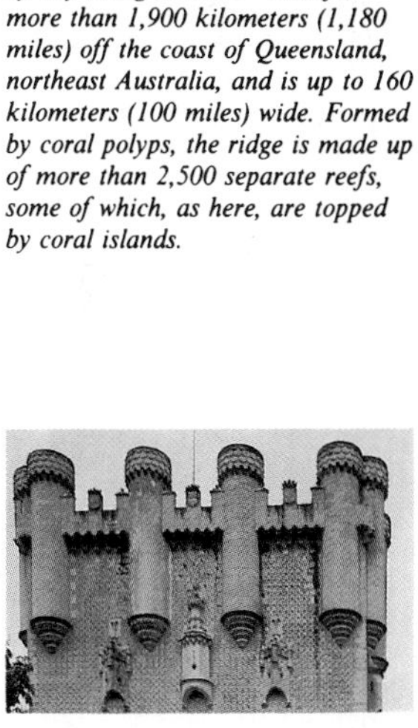

bartizan *Overhanging turrets, or bartizans, jut from the walls of the Alcazar castle at Segovia in southern Spain.*

PRONUNCIATION KEY

ă, pat; ā, pay; âr, care;
ä, father, are; b, bib;
ch, church; d, deed; ĕ, pet;
ē, be; f, fife; g, gag; h, hat;
hw, which; ĭ, pit; ī, pie;
îr, pier; j, judge; k, kick;
l, lid, needle; m, mum;
n, no, sudden; ng, thing;
ŏ, pot; ō, toe; ô, paw, for;
oi, noise; ou, out; o͝o, book;
o͞o, boot; p, pop; r, roar;
s, sauce; sh, ship, dish;
t, tight; th, thin, path;
th, this, bathe; ŭ, cut; ûr, fur;
v, valve; w, with; y, yes;
z, zebra, size; zh, vision;
ə, about, item, edible, gallop, circus, peaceful

IN FOREIGN WORDS:

ä, *Fr.* ami; œ, *Fr.* feu, *Ger.* schön; ü, *Fr.* tu, *Ger.* über; KH, *Ger.* ich, *Scot.* loch; N, *Fr.* bon; y′, *Fr.* Compiègne

STRESS MARKS:

Primary stress: ′
in·cite′ (ĭn-sīt′)
Secondary stress: ′
in′sight′ (ĭn′sīt′)

basalt *A common volcanic rock formed from the molten magma of the earth's interior. As it cools, it cracks along natural planes of cleavage, often forming hexagonal columns like these at the Giant's Causeway in Northern Ireland.*

bascule *The roadway of Tower Bridge in London is an example of this kind of counterbalanced apparatus.*

basilisk *A lizard found near Central American rivers and streams. It can run for short distances along the surface of the water on its hind legs, balancing itself upright with its long tail. Its prominent crest, which can be raised like a cockscomb, has caused it to be named after a mythical creature that was reared by a serpent from a rooster's egg.*

volcanic rock composed chiefly of plagioclase, augite, and magnetite and often having a glassy appearance. **2.** A kind of black, unglazed pottery. In this sense, also called "basaltware." [Earlier *basaltes,* from Latin *basaltēs,* manuscript error for *basanītēs (lapis),* touchstone, from Greek *basanitēs,* from *basanos,* from Egyptian *bakhan.*] **—ba·sal·tic** *adj.*

B.A.Sc. 1. Bachelor of Agricultural Science. **2.** Bachelor of Applied Science.

bas·cule (băs′kyo͞ol) *n.* **1.** A device counterbalanced so that when one end is lowered, the other is raised. **2.** A bridge that incorporates such a device. **3.** A road, forming part of a bridge, that can be raised and lowered. [French, seesaw, from earlier *basse cule,* variant (influenced by *basse,* low) of earlier *bacule* : *bat(t)re,* to beat, BATTER + *cul,* buttocks, from Latin *cūlus.*]

base[1] (bās) *n. Abbr.* **b., B. 1. a.** The lowest or supporting part or layer; a foundation. **b.** An infrastructure: *the nation's industrial base.* **2.** The fundamental principle or underlying concept of a system or theory. **3.** The fundamental ingredient from which a mixture is prepared; a chief constituent: *a paint with an oil base.* **4.** The fact, observation, or premise from which a measurement, study, or reasoning process is begun. **5.** *Sports.* **a.** A goal, starting point, or safety area. **b.** In baseball, any of the four corners of the infield, marked by a bag or plate, which players must pass in order to score. **6.** A center of organization, supply, or activity; a headquarters. **7.** *Military.* **a.** A fortified center of operations. **b.** A supply center for a large force. **8.** *Architecture.* The lowest part of a structure, considered as a separate architectural unit: *the base of a column.* **9.** *Heraldry.* The lower part of a shield. **10.** *Linguistics.* **a.** A morpheme or morphemes regarded as a form to which affixes or other bases may be added; a root or stem. For example, in the words *filled* and *refill, fill* is the base. **b. Base component** *(see).* **11.** *Mathematics.* **a.** The side or face of a geometric figure or solid to which an altitude is drawn or is considered to be drawn. **b.** The number that is raised to various powers to generate the principal counting units of a number system. **c.** The number raised to the logarithm of a designated number in order to produce that designated number. **12.** A line used as a reference for measurement or calculations. **13.** *Chemistry.* **a.** Any of a large class of compounds, including the hydroxides and oxides of metals, that have a bitter taste and are slippery in solution, and have the ability to turn litmus blue and to react with acids to form salts. **b.** A molecular or ionic substance capable of combining with a proton to form a new substance. **c.** A substance that provides a pair of electrons for a coordinate bond with an acid. Also called "Lewis base." **14.** *Biology.* **a.** The region of a part or organ, such as a leaf, that is closest to its point of attachment. **b.** The point of attachment of such an organ. **15.** *Electronics.* **a.** The region in a transistor between the emitter and the collector. **b.** The electrode attached to this region.
~adj. **1.** Forming or serving as a base. **2.** Situated at or near the base or bottom.
~tr.v. **based, basing, bases. 1.** To provide with a base: *a mixture based on alcohol; a firm based in San Francisco.* **2.** To provide an intellectual basis for; establish. Used with *on* or *upon.* **3.** To provide the imaginative basis or central idea for: *The play was based on a novel by Dickens.* [Middle English, from Old French, from Latin *basis,* pedestal, base, from Greek.]

Synonyms: *basis, foundation, grounds.*

Usage: *Base* and *basis* both have the written plural *bases,* but the pronunciation differs. The plural form of *base* is (bā′sĭz); the plural of *basis,* (bā′sēz′). *Base* is mainly used literally and refers to the lowest or supporting part or layer of something. It is occasionally used figuratively, as in *the industrial base of the economy. Basis* is nearly always used figuratively to mean foundation, as in the *basis of an argument.*

base[2] *adj.* **baser, basest. 1.** Having or proceeding from low moral standards; treacherous; contemptible. **2.** Inferior in quality or value; shabby. **3.** Not precious; common: *a base metal.* **4.** Valueless, or greatly depreciated in value; debased: *base currency.* **5.** Corrupted by extraneous elements: *base Latin.* **6. a.** *Archaic.* Of low birth, rank, or position. **b.** Characteristic of a person of low station; servile; menial. **7.** *Obsolete.* Short in stature. —See Synonyms at **mean** (ignoble). [Middle English *bas,* low, inferior, from Old French, from Late Latin *bassus,* fat, low.] **—base·ly** *adv.* **—base·ness** *n.*

base·ball (bās′bôl′) *n.* **1.** A game played with a wooden bat and hard ball by two opposing teams of nine players, each team batting and fielding alternately, the players batting having to run a course of four bases laid out in a diamond pattern in order to score. **2.** The ball used in this game.

base·board (bās′bôrd′, -bōrd′) *n.* **1.** A molding that conceals the joint between an interior wall and a floor. Also *chiefly British* "skirting board." **2.** Any board or plate that serves as a base of something.

base·born (bās′bôrn′) *adj. Archaic.* **1.** Of humble birth. **2.** Born of unmarried parents; illegitimate. **3.** Ignoble; contemptible.

base·burn·er (bās′bûr′nər) *n.* A stove or furnace that automatically replenishes consumed coal or other fuel from above.

base component *n.* In transformational grammar, a set of rules specifying the deep structure of the language. Also called "base."

base hit *n. Baseball.* A hit by which the batter reaches base safely, without an error or force play being made.

Ba·sel (bä′zəl) or **Basle** (bäl). *French* **Bâle** (bäl). City in Switzerland, the capital of Basel canton. It lies on the Rhine River, at the meeting point of the French, German, and Swiss borders. It is a major business and industrial center.

basela. Variant of **bonsella.**

base·less (bās′lĭs) *adj.* Having no basis or foundation.

base level *n.* The lowest level to which a land surface can be reduced by the action of running water.

base·line (bās′līn′) *n.* **1.** A line or imaginary level used as a base for measurement or comparison, as in surveying. **2.** In tennis and badminton, a line bounding each end of a court, marking the limits of play. **3.** In baseball, a path between successive bases.

base·ment (bās′mənt) *n.* **1.** The substructure or foundation of a building. **2.** The lowest habitable story of a building, usually below ground level. Often used adjectivally: *a basement flat.* [Probably from Dutch (obsolete), perhaps from Italian *basamento,* foundation (of a column), from *basare,* to BASE.]

basement complex *n.* A **basal complex** *(see).*

base metal *n.* Any relatively common, inexpensive metal, such as iron or copper, as distinguished from a precious metal, such as gold or silver.

ba·sen·ji (bə-sĕn′jē) *n., pl.* **-jis.** A small dog of a breed originally from Africa, having a short, smooth coat, and not uttering the barking sound characteristic of most dogs. [Bantu.]

base point *n. Heraldry.* The lowest point on a shield.

base rate *n. British.* The rate of interest offered by clearing banks, used as a basis for lending rates.

ba·ses[1]. Plural of **basis.** —See Usage note at **base.**

bas·es[2]. Plural of **base.** —See Usage note at **base.**

bash (băsh) *tr.v.* **bashed, bashing, bashes.** *Informal.* To strike or smash with a heavy and crushing blow. Often used with *in.* **—bash into.** *Informal.* To crash into; collide with.
~n. **1.** *Informal.* A heavy, crushing blow. **2.** *British Informal.* An attempt; a try. **3.** *Slang.* A celebration; a party. [17th century : imitative, perhaps a blend of BANG + *-sh,* as in SMASH or CRASH.]

ba·shaw (bə-shô′) *n. Obsolete.* A **pasha** *(see).*

bash·ful (băsh′fəl) *adj.* **1.** Inclined to shrink from notice through shyness; diffident; self-conscious. **2.** Characterized by, showing, or resulting from social shyness or self-consciousness. —See Synonyms at **shy.** [Middle English *baschen,* short for *abashen,* to ABASH + -FUL.] **—bash·ful·ly** *adv.* **—bash·ful·ness** *n.*

bash·i-ba·zouk (băsh′ē-bə-zo͞ok′) *n.* A member of the Turkish irregulars, a 19th-century cavalry troop noted for its brutality. [Turkish *başıbozuk,* irregular soldier : *baş,* head + *bozuk,* depraved, out of order.]

Bash·kir (băsh′kîr) *n., pl.* **-kirs** or collectively **Bashkir. 1.** A member of a Mongoloid people living in the Bashkir A.S.S.R. **2.** The Turkic language of this people.

Bashkir Autonomous Soviet Socialist Republic. Also **Bash·kir·i·a** (băsh-kîr′ē-ə). An administrative division in eastern European U.S.S.R. in the southwest Urals. It has large mineral deposits and its main agricultural crop is grain. The capital and main administrative and industrial center is Ufa.

basi–, baso– *prefix.* Indicates: **1.** The base or lower part; for example, **basipetal. 2.** A chemical base; for example, **basophil.** [Latin *basis,* BASIS.]

ba·sic (bā′sĭk) *adj.* **1. a.** Of, pertaining to, or constituting a basis; underlying; fundamental. **b.** Simple; unadorned; without extras: *a basic salary.* **2.** *Chemistry.* **a.** Producing, resulting from, or pertaining to a base. **b.** Containing a base, especially in excess of acid. **3.** *Geology.* Containing little silica. Said of igneous rocks. **4.** *Metallurgy.* Of, designating, or produced by a steel-making process in which the furnace is lined with a basic material, such as magnesium oxide. The lining combines with acidic impurities in the ore to form basic slag.

BASIC *n. Computer Science.* A simple high-level computer-programming language. [*B*eginner's *A*ll-purpose *S*ymbolic *I*nstruction *C*ode.]

ba·si·cal·ly (bā′sĭk-lē) *adv.* Fundamentally; essentially.

Basic English *n.* A simplified, copyrighted form of English with a vocabulary of 850 English words and a short list of words in international use, intended to provide a basis for an auxiliary language and for the introductory teaching of English. [Coined by C.K. OGDEN to represent *B*ritish *A*merican *S*cientific *I*nternational *C*ommercial.]

ba·sic·i·ty (bā-sĭs′ə-tē) *n. Chemistry.* The quality or degree of being a base.

basic oxide *n.* A metallic oxide that is a base or that forms a hydroxide if combined with water.

basic process *n.* A method of steel production that uses a furnace lined with a basic refractory material.

basic rock *n.* A dark-colored igneous rock containing less than 52 percent silica bound up in its feldspar and rich in iron and magnesium.

ba·sics (bā′sĭks) *pl.n.* Fundamental or rudimentary principles or practices: *back to basics.*

basic salt *n.* A salt formed from a base by replacement of only part of the hydroxide or oxide content, as in basic lead carbonate, $2PbCO_3 \cdot Pb(OH)_2$.

basic slag *n.* Furnace slag containing a sufficiently high proportion of calcium phosphate to make it useful as a fertilizer. It is produced during the course of basic-process steel making.

basic training *n.* The initial period of training of a recruit in the armed forces.

ba·sid·i·o·my·cete (bə-sĭd′ē-ō-mī′sēt′, -mī-sēt′) *n.* Any fungus of the class Basidiomycetes, which includes the mushrooms, puffballs, and other fungi that produce spores on a basidium. [New Latin *Basidiomycetes* : BASIDI(UM) + -MYCETE.] **—ba·sid·i·o·my·ce·tous** (bə-sĭd′ē-ō-mī-sē′təs) *adj.*

ba·sid·i·o·spore (bə-sĭd′ē-ō-spôr′, -spōr′) *n.* A spore formed on a basidium. [BASIDI(UM) + SPORE.]

ba·sid·i·um (bə-sĭd′ē-əm) *n., pl.* **-ia** (-ē-ə) A club-shaped structure characteristic of basidiomycetous fungi, which produces sexual spores, usually four, at the tips. [New Latin, from Greek *basidion,* diminutive of BASIS.] **—ba·sid·i·al** *adj.*

Ba·sie (bā′sē) **Count,** born William Basie (1904–84). U.S. jazz musician noted for his "big band" sound. One of the great jazz pianists, he was influenced by Harlem ragtime music.

ba·si·fy (bā′sə-fī′) *tr.v.* **-fied, -fying, -fies.** *Chemistry.* To make basic. [BAS(E) + -FY.] **—ba·si·fi·ca·tion** *n.* **—ba·si·fi·er** *n.*

bas·il (băz′əl, bā′zəl) *n.* **1.** An herb, *Ocimum basilicum,* native to the Old World, having spikes of small white flowers and aromatic leaves used as seasoning. Also called "sweet basil." **2.** A related plant, *Calamintha vulgaris,* native to Europe, having dense clusters of small pink or purplish flowers. This species is also called "wild basil." [Middle English *basile,* from Old French, from Medieval Latin *basilicum,* from Greek *basilikon,* "royal," from *basileus*†, king.]

Bas·il (băz′əl, bā′zəl), **Saint,** called "the Great" (*c.* A.D. 330–*c.* 379). Bishop of Caesarea in Cappadocia (from 370) who is credited with the authorship of the liturgy of St. Basil, which is still used on certain days in the Eastern Orthodox Church. He was one of the chief opponents of the heresy of Arianism.

bas·i·lar (băs′ə-lər) *adj.* Also **bas·i·lar·y** (-lĕr′ē). Pertaining to or located at or near the base, especially the base of the skull. [New Latin *basilaris,* from Latin *basis,* BASE (bottom).]

ba·sil·ic (bə-sĭl′ĭk) *adj.* Also **ba·sil·i·cal** (-ĭ-kəl,) **ba·sil·i·can** (-kən). Of or pertaining to a basilica.

ba·sil·i·ca (bə-sĭl′ĭ-kə) *n.* **1.** Any of various oblong buildings of ancient Rome having two rows of columns dividing the interior into a nave and two side aisles, used as a court or place of assembly. **2.** A building of this kind or design used as a Christian church. **3.** *Roman Catholic Church.* **a.** Any of several ancient churches in Rome. **b.** A church or cathedral accorded certain special ceremonial rights. [Latin, from Greek *basilikē (stoa),* "royal (portico, court)," from *basileus*†, king.]

bas·i·lisk (băs′ə-lĭsk′, băz′-) *n.* **1.** A legendary serpent or dragon with lethal breath and glance. Compare **cockatrice. 2.** Any of various tropical American lizards of the genus *Basiliscus,* having an erectile crest at the back of the head. [Middle English, from Latin *basiliscus,* from Greek *basiliskos,* "princelet," diminutive of *basileus*† king; the serpent was believed to have a mark resembling a crown on its head.]

ba·sin (bā′sən) *n.* **1.** An open, rounded vessel with sides that narrow toward the base, used especially for holding or mixing liquids. **2.** The amount such a vessel will hold. **3.** A washbasin; a sink. **4. a.** An artificially enclosed area of a river or harbor, so designed that the water level remains unaffected by tidal changes. **b.** A small enclosed or partly enclosed body of water. **5.** A region drained by a single river system. Also called "river basin." **6.** A vast depression on the earth's surface, filled by an ocean. Also called "ocean basin." **7.** *Geology.* **a.** A tract of land in which the rock strata are tilted toward a common center. **b.** Any bowl-shaped depression in the surface of the land. [Middle English *ba(s)cin,* from Old French *bacin,* from Late Latin *bacchinus* (unattested), from Vulgar Latin *bacca* (unattested), water vessel, BACK (vat).]

bas·i·net (băs′ə-nĕt′, băs′ə-nĭt) *n.* A light, round, close-fitting medieval helmet, often with a visor. [Middle English *bacinet,* from Old French, diminutive of *bacin,* BASIN.]

ba·sip·e·tal (bā-sĭp′ə-təl) *adj. Botany.* Developing or growing in order from the top toward the base. Said of certain leaves and flowers. Compare **acropetal.** [BASI- + -PETAL.] **—ba·sip·e·tal·ly** *adv.*

ba·sis (bā′sĭs) *n., pl.* **-ses** (-sēz′). **1.** A foundation upon which something rests. **2.** The chief or most stable component of anything; a fundamental ingredient. **3.** A principle; a criterion. —See Synonyms and Usage note at **base.** [Latin, pedestal, foot, base, from Greek.]

bask (băsk, bäsk) *intr.v.* **basked, basking, basks. 1.** To expose oneself pleasantly to warmth. **2.** To thrive in the presence of a pleasant or advantageous influence. [Middle English *basken,* probably from Scandinavian; akin to Norwegian dialectal *baska,* to splash in the water, and Old Norse *batha,* to BATHE.]

bas·ket (băs′kĭt) *n.* **1. a.** A container made of interwoven material, such as rushes, twigs, or strips of wood, often having a handle. **b.** The amount a basket will hold. **2.** Something resembling a basket in shape or function, such as the container suspended from a hot-air balloon. **3.** *Basketball.* **a.** Either of the two goals, each consisting of a metal hoop from which an open-bottomed circular net is suspended. **b.** The score, normally worth two points, made by throwing the ball through the basket. [Middle English, from Norman French and Old French *basket*†.]

bas·ket·ball (băs′kĭt-bôl′) *n.* **1.** A game played between two teams of five players each, the object being to throw the ball through an elevated basket on the opponent's side of the rectangular court. **2.** The round, inflated ball used in this game.

basket chair *n.* A chair made of wickerwork or cane.

basket hilt *n.* A sword hilt with a basket-shaped guard serving to cover and protect the hand.

bas·ket·ry (băs′kĭt-rē) *n.* **1.** The craft or process of making baskets. **2.** Baskets collectively.

basket star *n.* Any of various marine organisms of the class Ophiuroidea, related to the starfishes, and having slender, many-branched arms. Also called "basket fish."

basket weave *n.* A textile weave consisting of double threads interlaced to produce a checkered pattern similar to that of a woven basket.

basking shark *n.* A very large shark, *Cetorhinus maximus,* that feeds on plankton and often floats near the surface of the water.

Basle. See **Basel.**

bas mitzvah, bas mizvah. Variants of **bat mitzvah.**

baso-. Variant of **basi-.**

ba·so·phil (bā′so-fĭl) *n.* A cell, especially a white blood cell, having granules that exhibit an affinity for basic dyes. [BASO- + -PHIL(E).] **—ba·so·phil·ic, ba·soph·i·lous** (bə-sŏf′ə-ləs) *adj.*

Ba·so·tho (bə-so͞o′to͞o, -sō′tō) *n, pl.* **-thos** or collectively **Basotho.** A member of an African people, a **Mosotho** *(see).*

basque (băsk) *n.* A woman's close-fitting bodice. [French, variant (influenced by *basquine,* petticoat) of earlier *baste,* from Provençal *basta,* perhaps from Germanic.]

Basque (băsk) *n.* **1.** A member of a people of unknown origin inhabiting the western Pyrenees in France and Spain. **2.** The language of the Basques, of no known relationship to any other language. [French, from Latin *Vascō* † (stem *Vascōn-*), whence also GASCON.] **—Basque** *adj.*

Bas·ra (băs′rə, bŭs′-). Iraq's only port, on the Shatt al Arab in the southeast of the country.

bas-re·lief (bä′rĭ-lēf′) *n. Sculpture.* Relief that projects very little from the background. Also called "basso-relievo," "low relief." [French, from Italian *bassorilievo,* low relief : *basso,* low, BASE + *rilievo,* RELIEF.]

bass¹ (băs) *n., pl.* **basses** or collectively **bass. 1.** Any of several North American freshwater fishes of the family Centrarchidae, related to but larger than the sunfishes. See **largemouth bass** and **smallmouth bass. 2.** Any of various marine fishes of the family Serranidae, such as the **sea bass** and the **striped bass** *(both of which see).* [Middle English, from dialect *barse,* from Old English *bærs.*]

bass² (bās) *n.* **1.** A low-pitched tone. **2.** The notes in the lowest register of a musical instrument. **3.** The lowest part in vocal or instrumental part music. **4.** A male singing voice of the lowest range. **5.** A man who has such a singing voice. **6.** A musical instrument that produces notes in a low register; especially, a **double bass** *(see)* or a **bass guitar** *(see).* **7.** The response to the low-frequency notes of an audio-frequency amplifier, especially in a record player or tape recorder.
~*adj.* **1.** Having a deep tone; low in pitch. **2.** Being the largest and having lowest range of a family of instruments: *a bass recorder.*

bass³ (băs) *n.* A fibrous plant product, **bast** *(see).* [Variant of BAST.]

Bas·sa·no (bə-sä′nō), **Jacopo,** also known as Giacomo da Ponte (1510–92). Italian painter of the Venetian school. He is one of the earliest known artists to depict rustic life in both secular and religious scenes.

bass clef (bās) *n.* A musical clef that designates F below middle C as being on the fourth line above the bottom of the staff. Also called "F clef."

bass drum (bās) *n.* A large drum having a cylindrical body and two drumheads, both of which can be struck to produce a low, resonant sound.

bas·set (băs′ĭt) *n.* A dog, the **basset hound** *(see).* [French, Old French, from *basset,* short and low, from *bas,* BASE.]

basset horn *n.* An alto clarinet in F, having a range of three and a half octaves and sounding notes a fifth lower than they are written. [German *Bassetthorn,* part translation of French *cor de bassette,* from Italian *corno di bassetto* : *corno,* horn + *di,* of + *bassetto,* diminutive of BASSO.]

basset hound *n.* A short-haired dog of a breed originating in France, having a long body, short, crooked forelegs, and long, drooping ears.

bass fiddle (bās) *n. Informal.* A **double bass** *(see).*

bass guitar (bās) *n.* An electric guitar that has the same pitch as a double bass. Also called "bass."

bass horn (bās) *n.* A **tuba** *(see).*

bas·si·net (băs′ə-nĕt′) *n.* An oblong basket, often resting on legs, used as a crib for an infant. [French, small basin, from Old French *bacinet,* diminutive of *bacin,* BASIN.]

bass·ist (bā′sĭst) *n.* **1.** A person who plays a double bass. **2.** A person who plays a bass guitar.

bas·so (băs′ō, bä′sō) *n., pl.* **-sos** or **-si** (-sē). *Abbr.* **b., B.** A bass singer, especially an operatic bass. [Italian, from Late Latin *bassus,* fat, short, low.]

basso continuo *n.* A **continuo** *(see).* [Italian, "continuous bass."]

bas·soon (bə-so͞on′, bă-) *n.* A low-pitched woodwind instrument with a double reed, having a long wooden body attached to a lateral tube that leads to the mouthpiece. [French *basson,* from Italian *bassone,* augmentative of *basso,* BASS.] **—bas·soon·ist** *n.*

basso os·ti·na·to (ŏs′tĭ-nä′tō) *n.* A **ground bass** *(see).* [Italian, "persistent bass."]

basso pro·fun·do (prə-fŭn′dō, prō-fo͞on′dō) *n., pl.* **basso profundos** or **bassi profundi** (-dē) *Music.* **1.** A bass voice of the lowest range. **2.** A singer having such a voice. [Italian, "deep bass."]

bas·so-re·lie·vo (băs′ō-rĭ-lē′vō) *n., pl.* **-vos.** Also *Italian* **bas·so-ri·**

bas-relief *A detail of a bas-relief carving on a wall in Persepolis, Iran.*

basset hound *Descended from bloodhound stock, the basset has an excellent sense of smell and is used for hunting hares, rabbits, and pheasants.*

PRONUNCIATION KEY

ă, pat; ā, pay; âr, care;
ä, father, are; b, bib;
ch, church; d, deed; ĕ, pet;
ē, be; f, fife; g, gag; h, hat;
hw, which; ĭ, pit; ī, pie;
îr, pier; j, judge; k, kick;
l, lid, needle; m, mum;
n, no, sudden; ng, thing;
ŏ, pot; ō, toe; ô, paw, for;
oi, noise; ou, out; o͝o, book;
o͞o, boot; p, pop; r, roar;
s, sauce; sh, ship, dish;
t, tight; th, thin, path;
th, this, bathe; ŭ, cut; ûr, fur;
v, valve; w, with; y, yes;
z, zebra, size; zh, vision;
ə, about, item, edible,
gallop, circus, peaceful

IN FOREIGN WORDS:

à, *Fr.* ami; œ, *Fr.* feu, *Ger.* schön; ü, *Fr.* tu, *Ger.* über; KH, *Ger.* ich, *Scot.* loch; N, *Fr.* bon; y′, *Fr.* Compiègne

STRESS MARKS:

Primary stress: ′
in·cite′ (ĭn-sīt′)
Secondary stress: ′
in′sight′ (ĭn′sīt′)

lie·vo (bä′sō-rĕ-lyä′vō) *pl.* **-vi** (-vē). *Sculpture.* **Bas-relief** *(see).* [Italian, BAS-RELIEF.]

bass saxophone (băs) *n.* A large saxophone with a low range, usually supported on a stand while being played.

Bass Strait (băs). A channel separating mainland Australia from Tasmania. It is 240 kilometers (150 miles) at its widest point and 290 kilometers (180 miles) long.

bass viol (băs) *n. Music.* **1.** A **double bass** *(see).* **2.** A **viola da gamba** *(see).*

bass·wood (băs′wŏŏd′) *n.* **1.** Any of several linden trees of eastern North America; especially, *Tilia americana,* having clusters of fragrant yellowish flowers. **2.** The soft, light-colored wood of any of these trees.

bast (băst) *n. Botany.* **1.** The fibrous or somewhat woody outer layer of the stems of certain plants, such as flax, hemp, and ramie, used to make cordage and textiles. Also called "bass." **2.** A plant tissue, **phloem** *(see).* [Middle English *baste,* Old English *bæst,* from Common Germanic *bastaz* (unattested).]

bas·tard (băs′tərd) *n.* **1.** An illegitimate child. **2.** *Slang.* **a.** A mean, disagreeable, or obnoxious person. Used derogatorily. **b.** A person, especially a man. Used familiarly or humorously: *lucky bastard.* **c.** A tedious or difficult task or problem. **3.** Any product of irregular, inferior, or dubious origin. —*adj.* **1.** Born of unwed parents; illegitimate. **2.** Not genuine; spurious. **3.** Of inferior breed or kind. **4.** Resembling a known kind or species, but not truly such: *bastard toadflax.* [Middle English, from Old French, perhaps *(fils de) bast,* "packsaddle (son)," from Medieval Latin *bastum,* packsaddle, perhaps from Vulgar Latin *bastāre* (unattested), to carry, from Greek *bastazein†,* to lift, bear.] —**bas·tard·ly** *adj.*

bas·tard·ize (băs′tər-dīz′) *tr.v.* **-ized, -izing, -izes.** To debase; corrupt. —**bas·tard·i·za·tion** *n.*

bastard toadflax *n.* Any plant of the genus *Comandra;* especially, *C. umbellata,* of eastern North America, having rounded clusters of small greenish flowers.

bastard wing *n. Ornithology.* An **alula** *(see).*

bat

THE MAMMAL THAT CAN FLY

How some bat species "see" in the dark

Bats are the only mammals that fly. There are nearly 950 species, which can be grouped according to what they eat. Fruit bats, which often have wingspans of up to 1.5 meters (5 feet), feed on fruit and nectar; some species of insect-eating bats feed on flowers, birds, lizards, or fish, as well as insects; and vampire bats live on blood that they obtain by making a small incision in a sleeping animal.

Most bats are nocturnal and navigate by echolocation, sending out sounds and sensing the shape and location of an object from the echoes. However, fruit bats—a large number among the bat species—do not use echolocation.

BAT ANATOMY *The wing is a double layer of skin supported by the forelimb and hind limb, and in some species by the tail.*

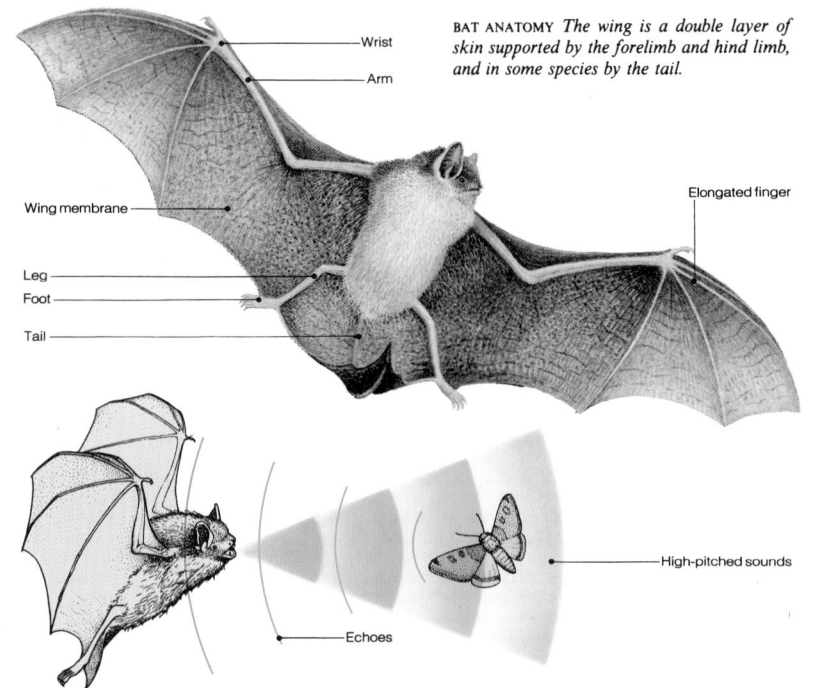

Wrist
Arm
Wing membrane
Leg
Foot
Tail
Elongated finger
High-pitched sounds
Echoes

ECHOLOCATION *To find food and navigate at night, a bat emits high-pitched sounds. Echoes are reflected from prey such as moths, or from obstacles, and are picked up by the bat.*

bas·tard·y (băs′tər-dē) *n.* The condition of being of illegitimate birth; illegitimacy.

baste¹ (bāst) *tr.v.* **basted, basting, bastes.** To sew loosely with large running stitches so as to hold together temporarily; tack. [Middle English *basten,* from Old French *bastir,* from Common Germanic *bastjan* (unattested), to sew with bast, from *bastaz* (unattested), BAST.]

baste² *tr.v.* **basted, basting, bastes.** To pour pan drippings or sauce over (meat) while cooking. [16th century : origin obscure.]

baste³ *tr.v.* **basted, basting, bastes.** **1.** To beat vigorously; thrash. **2.** To berate. [Perhaps ultimately from Old Norse *beysta,* to thrash, strike.]

Bas·ti·a (băs′tē-ə, bäs′-). Port on the northeast coast of Corsica, France, and the largest city on the island.

bas·tille, bas·tile (băs-tēl′) *n.* **1.** A prison. **2.** A fortress. [Middle English, from Old French, variant of *bastide,* from Provençal *bastida,* from the past participle of *bastir,* to build.]

Bas·tille (băs-tēl′). A fortress in Paris used as a prison until captured on July 14, 1789, at the outset of the French Revolution.

bas·ti·na·do (băs′tə-nā′dō, -năd′ō) *n., pl.* **-does.** Also **bas·ti·nade** (-tə-nād′, -năd′). **1.** A beating with a stick or cudgel, especially on the soles of the feet. **2.** A stick or cudgel. —*tr.v.* **bastinadoed, -doing, -does.** Also **bas·ti·nade, -naded, -nading, -nades.** To subject to a beating, especially on the soles of the feet. [Spanish *bastonada,* from *baston,* stick, BATON.]

bast·ing (bā′stĭng) *n.* **1.** The act of sewing together loosely. **2.** The thread used to baste. **3. bastings.** The loose stitches used to baste material; tacking.

bas·ti·on (băs′chən, băs′tē-ən) *n.* **1.** A projecting part of a rampart or other fortification. **2.** Any well-fortified or defended position. **3.** A person, place, or institution regarded as a defender or stronghold of a belief, cause, or the like. —See Synonyms at **bulwark.** [French, from earlier *bastillon,* from Old French *bastille,* BASTILLE.]

bast·naes·ite, bast·nas·ite (băst′nə-sīt′) *n.* A yellowish to reddish-brown mineral, a fluorocarbonate of several lanthanide elements, used as a rare-earth ore. [Swedish *bastnäsit,* after *Bastnäs,* Sweden, where it was discovered.]

Ba·su·to (bə-sōō′tō) *n., pl* **-tos** or collectively **Basuto.** **1.** A **Mosotho** *(see).* **2.** The dialect of **Sotho** *(see)* spoken in Lesotho. In both senses, not in current usage.

Basutoland. See **Lesotho.**

bat¹ (băt) *n.* **1.** A stout wooden stick or club; a cudgel. **2.** A blow, as with a stick. **3. a.** *Baseball.* A rounded wooden club, wider and heavier at the hitting end and tapering at the handle, used to strike the ball. **b.** *Cricket.* A wooden club having a broad, flat-surfaced hitting end and a narrow handle. **c.** The club or racket used in other games, such as table tennis. **4.** *Cricket.* A batsman. **5.** *Slang.* A binge; a spree. —**at bat.** *Baseball & Cricket.* Taking one's turn batting. —**go to bat for.** *Informal.* To support or defend. —**(right) off the bat.** *Informal.* Without hesitation; immediately. —*v.* **batted, batting, bats.** —*tr.* **1.** To hit with, or as if with, a club or bat. **2.** *Baseball.* To have (some specified score) as a batting average. **3.** *Informal.* To discuss or consider at length. Usually used with *around.* —*intr.* **1.** *Baseball.* **a.** To use a bat. **b.** To have a turn at bat. **2.** *Slang.* To go from place to place; wander. [Middle English *bat,* late Old English *batt,* cudgel, probably from Old French *batte,* club, from *battre,* to beat.]

bat² *n.* **1.** Any of various nocturnal flying mammals of the order Chiroptera, having membranous wings that extend from the forelimbs to the hind limbs or tail. The order is subdivided into the **fruit bats** and the **insectivorous bats** *(both of which see).* **2.** *Slang.* A small-minded, nagging person, usually a woman. Used chiefly in the phrase *old bat.* —**have bats in the belfry.** *Slang.* To be eccentric; have foolish or crazy ideas. [16th-century variant of Middle English *bakke,* from Scandinavian; akin to Middle Swedish *-bakka,* from Old Norse *-blaka* in *ledhrblaka,* "leather-flapper," bat.]

bat³ *tr.v.* **batted, batting, bats.** To wink or flutter: *to bat one's eyelashes.* —**not bat an eye.** To evince no sign of surprise or emotion. [Probably a variant of BATE (flap).]

bat. battalion.

Ba·taan (bə-tăn′, -tän′). A mountainous, jungle-covered peninsula of western Luzon, the Philippines. In World War II it was the scene of defensive action by U.S. and Filipino troops who resisted the Japanese advance for three months (1942).

Batavia. See **Jakarta.**

batch¹ (băch) *n.* **1.** The amount of loaves, cakes, or the like produced at one baking. **2.** The quantity of something produced as the result of one operation: *a batch of cement.* **3.** The quantity of material needed for one operation: *a batch of dough.* **4.** Any group of persons or things treated or regarded as a set: *He was working on a second batch of inquiries.* [Middle English *bacche,* Old English *bæcce* (unattested), from *bacan,* to BAKE.]

batch². Variant of **bach** (to live alone).

batch processing *n. Computer Science.* A system in which data is accumulated and processed together as a single unit. Compare **time-sharing.**

bate¹ (bāt) *tr.v.* **bated, bating, bates.** **1.** To lessen the force of; hold back: *with bated breath.* **2.** To take away; subtract. [Middle English *baten,* variant of *abaten,* to ABATE.]

bate² *intr.v.* **bated, bating, bates.** Also **bait.** *Falconry.* To flap the wings wildly, as if in impatience. [Middle English *baten,* from Old French *bat(t)re,* to beat, BATTER.]

ba·teau (bă-tō′) *n., pl.* **-teaux** (-tōz′). A light, flat-bottomed boat, used especially in Louisiana and Canada. [Canadian French, from French, from Old French *batel,* from Old English *bāt,* BOAT.]

Bates (bāts), **Henry Walter** (1825–92). British naturalist and explorer who gave his name to Batesian mimicry, a phenomenon he discovered in the Amazon valley.

Bates, Herbert Ernest (1905–74). British novelist and short-story writer. During World War II he served with the Royal Air Force and, as "Flying Officer X," wrote many short stories based on his experiences. He also wrote war novels under his own name, the best known of which is *Fair Stood the Wind for France* (1944). His other novels include *The Darling Buds of May* (1958) and *A Moment in Time* (1964).

Bates·i·an mimicry (bāt′sē-ən) *n.* A defense mechanism that confers a degree of protection against predators on an otherwise defenseless species of animal, in which the harmless species bears a strong resemblance to another species that is dangerous or unpalatable to its predators. Also called "protective coloring."

Bate·son (bāt′sən), **William** (1861–1926). British biologist, one of the founders of the science of genetics.

bat·fish (băt′fĭsh′) *n., pl.* **-fishes** or collectively **batfish.** Any of various marine fishes of the family Ogcocephalidae, having a flattened body and fleshy pectoral and pelvic fins, and living on the sea floor.

bat·fowl (băt′foul′) *intr.v.* **-fowled, -fowling, -fowls.** To catch roosting birds at night by blinding them with a light. [BAT (club) + FOWL, later associated with BAT (animal) and the use of a blinding light.]

bath[1] (băth, bäth) *n., pl.* **baths** (băthz, băths, bäthz, bäths). **1.** The act of washing, dipping, or immersing the body in water. **2.** The water used for bathing. **3.** *Chiefly British.* A bathtub. **4.** A liquid, or a liquid and its container, used to regulate the temperature of, soak, or otherwise act upon an immersed object. **5.** A bathroom. **6.** *Usually* **baths.** A public building with facilities for swimming and, sometimes, for washing. **7.** *Often* **baths.** A resort providing therapeutic baths; a spa. [Middle English *bath,* Old English *bæth.*]

bath[2] (băth) *n.* An ancient Hebrew unit of liquid measure, equal to approximately 10 U.S. gallons. [Hebrew.]

Bath (băth, bäth). City in Avon, on the Lower Avon River in southwest England. Its Roman baths are considered to be among the best of the Roman remains in Britain. It was a fashionable spa town in the 18th century and has many elegant Georgian buildings.

Bath brick *n.* Fine calcareous and siliceous silt pressed into blocks and used for scouring and polishing metal. [After BATH.]

Bath chair *n. Sometimes* **bath chair.** A hooded wheelchair used especially by invalids, as at a spa. [After BATH, where it was first used.]

bathe (bāth) *v.* **bathed, bathing, bathes.** —*intr.* **1.** To take a bath; wash oneself. **2.** To go swimming. **3.** To become immersed in or as if in liquid. —*tr.* **1.** To immerse in liquid. **2.** To wash or wet. **3.** To apply a liquid to for soothing or healing purposes. **4.** To suffuse: *The garden was bathed in sunlight.* [Middle English *bathen,* Old English *bathian.*] —**bath·er** *n.*

ba·thet·ic (bə-thĕt′ĭk) *adj.* Characterized by bathos. [Probably a blend of BATHOS and PATHETIC.] —**ba·thet·i·cal·ly** *adv.*

bath·house (băth′hous′, bäth′-) *n.* **1.** A building equipped for bathing. **2.** A building with dressing rooms for swimmers.

bathing beauty *n.* An attractive young woman in a bathing suit, especially one who is a contestant in a beauty contest.

bathing machine *n.* In former times, a small hut on wheels that could be moved to the edge of the sea, and in which bathers changed their clothes.

bathing suit *n.* A garment worn for swimming; a swimsuit. Also *chiefly British* "bathing costume."

bath·mat (băth′măt′, bäth′-) *n.* A washable mat used in front of a bathtub.

batho–. Variant of **bathy-.**

bath·o·lith (băth′ə-lĭth′) *n.* Also **bath·o·lite** (-līt′). A large irregularly shaped body of igneous rock that has melted and intruded surrounding strata at great depths, and usually covering more than 100 square kilometers (40 square miles). [German : BATHO- + -LITH.] —**bath·o·lith·ic** *adj.*

ba·thom·e·ter (bə-thŏm′ə-tər) *n.* An instrument used to measure the depth of water. [BATHO- + -METER.]

bath·o·pho·bi·a (băth′ə-fō′bē-ə) *n.* An abnormal fear of depths.

ba·thos (bā′thŏs′) *n.* **1. a.** A ludicrously abrupt transition from an elevated or inspired to a commonplace style. **b.** An anticlimax. **c.** The lowest point; a nadir. **2. a.** Insincere or grossly sentimental pathos. **b.** Extreme triteness or dullness. —See Usage note at **pathos.** [Greek, depth, from *bathus,* deep.]

bath·robe (băth′rōb′, bäth′-) *n.* A loose-fitting robe worn before and after bathing and for lounging; a dressing gown.

bath·room (băth′ro͞om′, -ro͝om′, bäth′-) *n.* A room equipped for taking a bath or shower and usually also containing a washbasin and toilet.

bath salts *pl.n.* Crystals for scenting or softening bath water.

Bath·she·ba (băth-shē′bə, băth′shĭ-bə). The wife of Uriah and later of David and, by David, the mother of Solomon. II Samuel 11–12.

bath·tub (băth′tŭb′, bäth′-) *n.* An oblong tub for bathing. Also *chiefly British* "bath."

Bath·urst[1] (băth′ərst). City in New South Wales, Australia, on the Macquarie River. It was the scene of a gold rush in 1851.

Bathurst[2]. See **Banjul.**

bathy–, batho– *prefix.* Indicates deepness or some relationship to depth; for example, **bathyscaph, bathometer.** [From Greek *bathus,* deep, and *bathos,* depth, from *bathus.*]

bath·y·al (băth′ē-əl) *adj.* Of, pertaining to, or designating a zone on the continental slope between 200 and 2,000 meters (650 and 6,550 feet) below sea level. [BATHY- + -AL.]

ba·thym·e·try (bə-thĭm′ə-trē) *n.* The measurement of the depth of large bodies of water. [French *bathymétrie* : BATHY- + -METRY.] —**bath·y·met·ric** (băth′ə-mĕt′rĭk) **bath·y·met·ri·cal** *adj.* —**bath·y·met·ri·cal·ly** *adv.*

bath·y·pe·lag·ic (băth′ə-pə-lăj′ĭk) *adj.* Of, relating to, or living in the depths of the ocean, especially below 2,000 feet.

bath·y·scaph (băth′ĭ-skăf′) *n.* Also **bath·y·scaphe** (-skăf, -skāf′). A free-diving, self-contained, deep-sea research vessel, consisting essentially of a large flotation hull with a manned observation capsule fixed to its underside. [BATHY- + Greek *skaphē,* basin, light boat.]

bath·y·sphere (băth′ĭ-sfîr′) *n.* A reinforced, spherical deep-diving chamber, manned, and lowered by cable.

bath·y·ther·mo·graph (băth′ə-thûr′mə-grăf′, -gräf′) *n.* An instrument that records water temperature as a function of depth.

ba·tik, bat·tik (bə-tēk′, băt′ĭk) *n.* **1.** A method of dyeing print into a fabric in which the parts of the cloth not intended to be dyed are covered with removable wax. **2.** The print that is dyed into cloth by this method. **3.** The cloth so dyed. [Malay, from Javanese, "painted."] —**ba·tik** *adj.*

Ba·tis·ta y Zal·dí·var (bə-tēs′tə ē zäl-dē′vär), **Fulgencio** (1901–73). Cuban president (1940–44; 1954–58). His repressive and authoritarian style of government proved unpopular, and, on New Year's Day, 1959, he was ousted by a revolutionary movement led by Fidel Castro.

ba·tiste (bə-tēst′, bă-) *n.* A fine, plain-woven fabric made from various fibers and used especially for clothing. [Earlier *baptist cloth* (translation of French *toile de Batiste*), first made by *Baptiste* of Cambrai (13th century).]

Ba·tjan, Ba·chan (bä′chän). A large island, 2,367 square kilometers (914 square miles) in area, in the Moluccas, Indonesia, lying southwest of Halmahera Island.

bat·man (băt′mən) *n., pl.* **-men** (-mĭn). In the British armed forces, a soldier who is an officer's personal servant. [Obsolete *bat,* packsaddle, from Middle English *batt,* from Old French *ba(s)t,* from (unattested), a carrying, perhaps from Vulgar Latin *bastum* (unattested), a carrying, perhaps from *bastāre* (unattested), to carry (see **bastard**) + MAN.]

bat mitz·vah, bat miz·vah (bät mĭts′və) *n.* Also **bas mitz·vah** (bäs), **bas miz·vah.** *Judaism.* **1.** A Jewish girl, usually between twelve and fourteen years, considered an adult and thenceforth responsible for her moral and religious duties. **2.** In some congregations, the ceremony marking the arrival of a girl's religious commitment. See **bar mitzvah.** [Hebrew *baṯ mitzvāh,* "daughter of commandment."]

ba·ton (bə-tŏn′, băt′n) *n.* **1.** A short staff carried by some public and military officials as a symbol of office. **2.** A slender wooden stick or rod used by a conductor to direct an orchestra or band. **3.** The hollow metal rod with heavy rubber tips twirled by a drum major or majorette. **4.** *British.* A short thick stick used by the police as a weapon. **5.** *Heraldry.* A shortened narrow **bend** *(see)* on a coat of arms, often signifying bastardy. [French *bâton,* from Old French *baston,* from Vulgar Latin *baston-* (unattested), from Late Latin *bastum,* stick.]

Bat·on Rouge (băt′n ro͞ozh′). Capital of Louisiana. Situated on the Mississippi River at the head of oceangoing navigation, it is also a major industrial and commercial center.

bat·o·pho·bi·a (băt′ə-fō′bē-ə) *n.* An abnormal fear of being near an object of great height, such as a skyscraper or mountain. [Gk. *batos,* passable + -PHOBIA.]

ba·tra·chi·an (bə-trā′kē-ən) *adj.* Of or pertaining to frogs and toads. ∼*n.* A frog or toad. [New Latin *Batrachia* (former order name, now Salienta), from Greek *batrakhos*†, frog.]

bats (băts) *adj. Slang.* Eccentric; insane.

bats·man (băts′mən) *n., pl.* **-men** (-mĭn). **1.** *Baseball & Cricket.* A batter. **2.** *Aeronautics.* A ground official who signals to landing aircraft with a pair of bats.

batt (băt) *n.* A mass of cotton fibers, **batting** *(see).*

batt. battalion.

bat·tal·i·on (bə-tăl′yən) *n. Abbr.* **bat., batt., bn., Bn. 1.** A tactical military unit, typically consisting of a headquarters company and four infantry companies, or a headquarters battery and four artillery batteries. **2.** An indefinite number of military troops. **3.** *Often* **battalions.** A large group or number. [French *battaillon,* from Italian *battaglione,* augmentative of *battaglia,* troop, BATTLE.]

bat·ten[1] (băt′n) *intr.v.* **-tened, -tening, -tens. 1. a.** To become fat. **b.** To feed gluttonously; gorge oneself. **2.** To thrive and prosper, especially at another's expense: *slum landlords who batten on the poor.* [Ultimately from Old Norse *batna,* to improve.]

batten[2] *n.* **1.** A strip of wood used in building to support tiles, slates, laths, or the like. **2.** A narrow strip of wood, used for flooring. **3.** Any of several flexible strips of wood placed in pockets at the outer edge of a sail to keep it flat. ∼*tr.v.* **battened, -tening, -tens. 1.** To furnish with battens: *batten a sail.* **2.** To fasten or make secure with battens. Usually used with *up* or *down*: *batten down the hatches.* [French *bâton,* BATON.]

Bat·ten (băt′n), **Jean** (1909–). New Zealand aviator and the first

bat *The only flying mammals, most bats—such as the long-eared bat shown here—find their way by listening to the echoes of their high-pitched squeaks bouncing off objects in their path. They feed on insects, which they catch on the wing at night. Fruit bats, however, feed largely on fruit and have large eyes to help them see at night. During the day, bats roost in caves and dark buildings, usually hanging upside down to sleep.*

PRONUNCIATION KEY

ă, pat; ā, pay; âr, care; ä, father, are; b, bib; ch, church; d, deed; ĕ, pet; ē, be; f, fife; g, gag; h, hat; hw, which; ĭ, pit; ī, pie; îr, pier; j, judge; k, kick; l, lid, needle; m, mum; n, no, sudden; ng, thing; ŏ, pot; ō, toe; ô, paw, for; oi, noise; ou, out; o͝o, book; o͞o, boot; p, pop; r, roar; s, sauce; sh, ship, dish; t, tight; th, thin, path; *th*, this, bathe; ŭ, cut; ûr, fur; v, valve; w, with; y, yes; z, zebra, size; zh, vision; ə, about, item, edible, gallop, circus, peaceful

IN FOREIGN WORDS:

à, *Fr.* ami; œ, *Fr.* feu, *Ger.* schön; ü, *Fr.* tu, *Ger.* über; KH, *Ger.* ich, *Scot.* loch; N, *Fr.* bon; y′, *Fr.* Compiègne

STRESS MARKS:

Primary stress: ′ **in·cite′** (ĭn-sīt′)
Secondary stress: ′ **in′sight′** (ĭn′sīt′)

woman to make a solo flight from England across the South Atlantic Ocean to South America (1935).

bat·ter¹ (băt′ər) v. **-tered, -tering, -ters.** —tr. **1. a.** To hit heavily and repeatedly with violent blows. **b.** To subject a child or woman to persistent violence or psychological cruelty. Used chiefly in the phrases *battered baby* and *battered wife.* **2.** To damage by heavy wear. —intr. To pound repeatedly with heavy blows. —n. *Printing.* **1.** A damaged area on the face of type or on a plate. **2.** The defect in print resulting from such damaged type. [Middle English *bateren,* from Norman-French, from Old French *bat(t)re,* to beat, from Latin *battuere.*]

bat·ter² n. A thick, beaten liquid mixture, as of flour, milk, and eggs, used in cooking. [Middle English *bater,* from Norman-French *batour,* from Old French *bateüre,* akin to BATTER (beat).]

batter

PORTABLE STOREHOUSE OF POWER
How electricity can be made by chemical reaction

A battery cell contains two plates of dissimilar metals (called electrodes) immersed in acid, alkaline, or salt solution (the electrolyte). When a wire is connected to the two electrodes, a chemical reaction between electrolyte and electrode causes free electrons to move along the wire. The movement is electric current. This was discovered by the Italian physicist Alessandro Volta in 1800. It is the basis of all batteries, which are portable sources of electricity. The wet battery, as used in motor cars, consists of lead plates immersed in sulfuric acid. The dry battery, as used in a flashlight, has electrodes of zinc and carbon in a damp paste of chemicals.

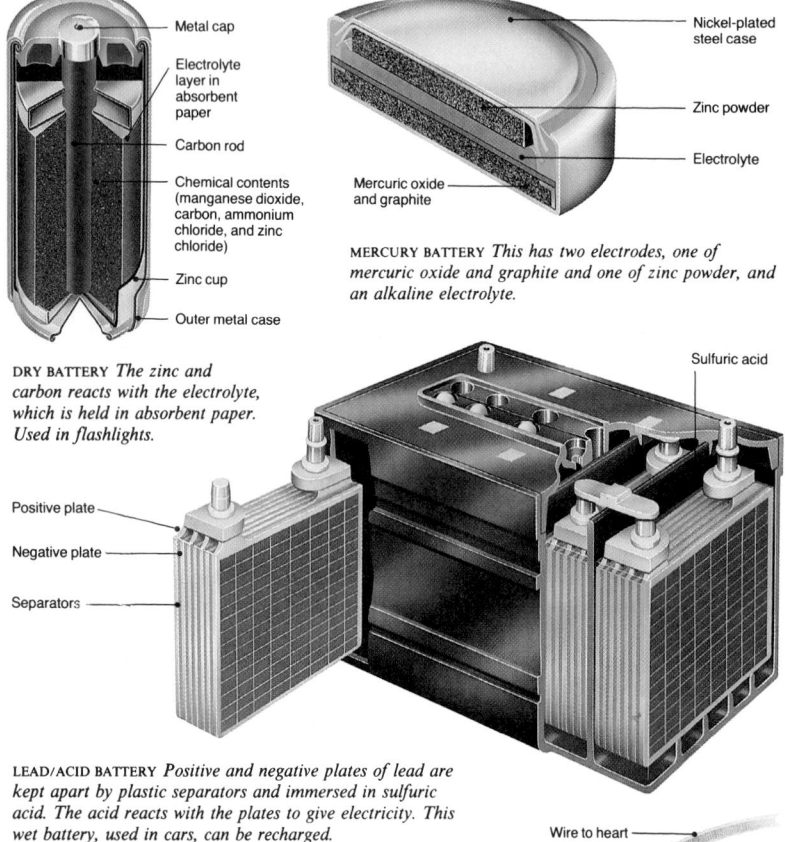

Metal cap

Electrolyte layer in absorbent paper

Carbon rod

Chemical contents (manganese dioxide, carbon, ammonium chloride, and zinc chloride)

Zinc cup

Outer metal case

DRY BATTERY *The zinc and carbon reacts with the electrolyte, which is held in absorbent paper. Used in flashlights.*

Nickel-plated steel case

Zinc powder

Electrolyte

Mercuric oxide and graphite

MERCURY BATTERY *This has two electrodes, one of mercuric oxide and graphite and one of zinc powder, and an alkaline electrolyte.*

Sulfuric acid

Positive plate

Negative plate

Separators

LEAD/ACID BATTERY *Positive and negative plates of lead are kept apart by plastic separators and immersed in sulfuric acid. The acid reacts with the plates to give electricity. This wet battery, used in cars, can be recharged.*

LITHIUM BATTERY *Power is created by a reaction between an iodine complex, the lithium, and an electrolyte of a thin layer of lithium iodide. This type of battery is quite small and light. It is used to provide the electricity in some heart pacemakers.*

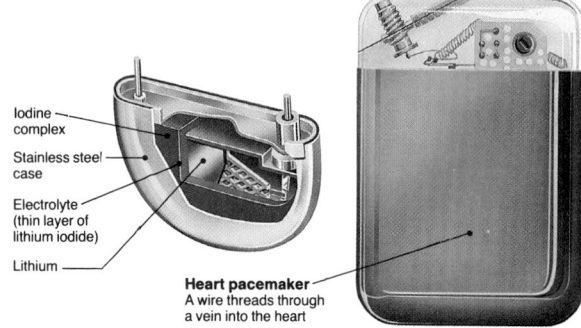

Iodine complex

Stainless steel case

Electrolyte (thin layer of lithium iodide)

Lithium

Wire to heart

Heart pacemaker A wire threads through a vein into the heart

batter³ n. A slope, as of the outer side of a wall, that recedes from bottom to top.
~tr.v. **battered, -tering, -ters.** To construct so as to slope thus. [Middle English *batter†.*]

batter⁴ n. *Baseball & Cricket.* The player whose turn it is to bat.

bat·ter·ing-ram (băt′ər-ĭng-răm′) n. Also **battering ram. 1.** A heavy beam used in ancient warfare to batter down walls and gates. **2.** Any device resembling this or used for similar purposes.

Bat·ter·sea (băt′ər-sē). Part of the Greater London borough of Wandsworth, on the south bank of the Thames River. The river at Battersea is crossed by three of London's most famous bridges, the Albert (built 1873), the Battersea (1890), and the Chelsea (1937).

bat·ter·y (băt′ə-rē) n., pl. **-ies. 1.** A number of **primary cells** (see) connected together to provide a source of electric current. **2.** One or more primary cells connected together in which the electrolyte is in the form of a paste. Also *chiefly British* "dry battery." **3.** One or more **secondary cells** (see) connected together as a source of electric current; especially, the device used for this purpose in a motor vehicle. Also *chiefly British* "accumulator." **4. a.** A beating or pounding. **b.** *Law.* The unlawful beating of another person. Compare **assault and battery. 5. a.** An emplacement for one or more pieces of artillery. **b.** A set of guns or other heavy artillery, as on a warship. **c.** *Abbr.* **btry.** The basic tactical artillery unit, corresponding to the company in the infantry. **6.** An array or grouping of like things to be used together. **7.** The pitcher and catcher on a baseball team. **8.** The percussion section of an orchestra. **9.** A system of keeping poultry confined in cages in order to produce high yields of eggs. Often used adjectivally: *battery hens.* [French *batterie,* from *battre,* from Old French *bat(t)re,* to BATTER.]

Bat·ter·y, the (băt′ə-rē). Also **Battery Park.** A park at the southern tip of Manhattan Island on the upper end of New York Bay in New York City. Coastal artillery was mounted here during Colonial and Revolutionary times.

battik. Variant of **batik.**

bat·ting (băt′ĭng) n. **1.** The action of one who bats. **2.** Cotton or wool fiber wadded together and used for stuffing furniture and mattresses. Also called "batt," "cotton batting." [Sense 2, from the beating of raw cotton or wool to clean it.]

bat·tle (băt′l) n. **1.** A large-scale combat between armed forces. **2.** Armed fighting; combat. **3.** Any intense competition; a struggle. ~v. **battled, -tling, -tles.** —intr. To engage in or as if in battle. —tr. To fight against; force: *He battled his way through the crowd.* —**give battle.** To begin fighting. [Middle English *bataille,* from Old French, from Vulgar Latin *battālia* (unattested), from Late Latin *battuālia,* fighting and fencing exercises, from Latin *battuere,* to BATTER.]

Bat·tle (băt′l). Town in East Sussex, England. The Battle of Hastings was fought (1066) on a ridge, called Senlac, to the southeast. William the Conqueror built an abbey to commemorate his victory over the Saxon king, Harold II.

bat·tle-ax, bat·tle-axe (băt′l-ăks′) n., pl. **-axes. 1.** A heavy broadheaded ax, formerly used as a weapon. **2.** *Slang.* An overbearing woman; a virago.

battle cruiser n. A warship with less heavy armor than a battleship, and with the speed of a cruiser.

battle cry n. **1.** A shout uttered by troops in battle. **2.** A slogan used by the proponents of a cause.

bat·tle·dore (băt′l-dôr′, -dōr′) n. **1.** An early form of badminton played with a flat wooden racket and a shuttlecock. Also called "battledore and shuttlecock." **2.** The racket used in this game. [Middle English *batildore,* perhaps from Old Provençal *batedor,* a beater, from *bat(t)re,* to beat, BATTER.]

battle fatigue n. **Combat fatigue** (see).

bat·tle·field (băt′l-fēld′) n. A field or area where an actual or figurative battle is fought. Also called "battleground."

bat·tle·front (băt′l-frŭnt′) n. The area where opponents meet or clash in battle: *a contest that was fought on political and military battlefronts.*

bat·tle·ment (băt′l-mənt) n. Usually **battlements.** A parapet built on top of a wall, with indentations for defense or decoration. [Middle English *batelment,* from Old French *bataillier,* to provide with battlements, from *batailles,* battlements, plural of *bataille,* BATTLE.] —**bat·tle·ment·ed** adj.

battle royal n., pl. **battles royal. 1.** A battle in which numerous combatants participate. **2.** A fight to the finish. **3.** An intense altercation.

bat·tle·ship (băt′l-shĭp′) n. Any of a class of warships of the largest size, carrying the greatest number of guns and batteries and clad with the heaviest armor.

battleship gray n. Medium gray.

bat·tle·wag·on (băt′l-wăg′ən) n. *Slang.* A battleship.

bat·tue (bă-tōō′, -tyōō′; *French* bà-tü′) n. **1.** The driving of wild game from cover by beaters toward waiting hunters. **2.** A hunt employing this procedure. **3.** Wholesale massacre, as of a defenseless crowd. [French, from the feminine past participle of *bat(t)re,* to beat, BATTER.]

bat·ty (băt′ē) adj. **-tier, -tiest.** *Slang.* Eccentric; crazy.

bau·ble (bô′bəl) n. **1.** A small, showy ornament or trinket, such as a Christmas tree decoration. **2.** A baton surmounted by a grotesquely carved head, carried by a court jester as a mock scepter of his office. [Middle English *babel, babulle,* from Old French *babel, baubel†,* plaything.]

baud (bôd) n. **1.** A unit for the speed of telegraphic or telephonic transmission equal to a transmission speed of one unit element per second. **2.** *Computer Science.* A unit of speed in data transmission, as one bit per second for binary signals. [After J. M. E. *Baudot* (1845–1903), French engineer and inventor of a telegraph system.]

Baude·laire (bōd-lâr′), **Charles** (1821–67). French poet and literary, art, and music critic. He discovered Edgar Allan Poe and translated many of his works. Baudelaire published an autobiographical novel, *La Fanfarlo* (1847), and his only volume of poetry, *Les Fleurs du Mal* (1857, revised 1861).

Bau·douin I (bō-dwăɴ′) (1930–). King of Belgium. He ascended to the throne in 1951, succeeding his father, Leopold III. He married Fabiola de Mora y Aragon in 1960.

Bau·haus (bou′hous′). An institute founded in 1919 by Walter Gropius in Weimar, Germany, for the study of art, design, and architecture and noted for its development of a style of functional architecture and its experimental use of building materials. It was closed by the Nazis in 1933. [German, "architecture house."]

bau·hin·i·a (bô-hĭn′ē-ə) *n.* Any plant of the leguminous genus *Bauhinia,* consisting of woody climbers with flattened stems and showy flowers, widely cultivated for ornament. [After Jean (1541–1613) and Gaspard (1560–1624) *Bauhin,* Swiss physicians and botanists.]

baulk. Variant of **balk.**

Baum (băm, bôm), **L(yman) Frank** (1856–1919). U.S. novelist famous for writing *The Wonderful Wizard of Oz* (1900).

Bau·mé scale (bō-mā′) *n. Abbr.* **Bé, B.** A hydrometer scale in which 1 degree Baumé is equivalent to 145 $(1-v)$ for liquids heavier than water and $140v-130$ for liquids lighter than water, where v is the reciprocal of the relative density of the liquid at 60°F. [After Antoine *Baumé* (1728–1804), French pharmacist, inventor of a hydrometer.]

baum marten (boum) *n.* The fur of any of several Eurasian martens. [Partial translation of German *Baummarder*: *Baum,* tree, from Old High German *boum* + MARTEN.]

baux·ite (bôk′sīt′) *n.* The principal ore of aluminum. It is composed mainly of aluminum hydroxide, with some iron hydroxide, and forms as a result of leaching of the soil in tropical conditions. It is used as an abrasive and catalyst. Compare **laterite.** [French, first found at Les *Baux,* southern France.]

Bav. Bavaria; Bavarian.

Ba·va·ri·a (bə-vâr′ē-ə). *German* **Bay·ern** (bī′ərn). Largest state in West Germany, lying in the extreme south. The Bavarian Alps contain West Germany's highest peak, the Zugspitze (2,963 meters; 9,721 feet). Beer, grain, salt, graphite, lignite, and iron ore are the region's chief products. The capital is Munich.

Ba·var·i·an (bə-vâr′ē-ən) *n. Abbr.* **Bav. 1.** A native or inhabitant of Bavaria. **2.** The High German dialect spoken in Bavaria and Austria. **—Ba·var·i·an** *adj.*

baw·bee, bau·bee (bô′bē′) *n. Scottish Informal.* A halfpenny. [After Alexander Orok of *Sillebawby,* 16th-century Scottish master of the mint.]

bawd (bôd) *n.* **1.** A woman who keeps a brothel; a madam. **2.** A prostitute. [Middle English *bawde,* probably from Old French *baude, baud,* lively, bold, from Old High German *bald,* bold.]

bawd·ry (bô′drē) *n.* Obscene or coarse language on the subject of sex. [Middle English *bawdery,* from BAWD.]

bawd·y (bô′dē) *adj.* **-ier, -iest.** Humorously coarse; vulgar; lewd. **—bawd·i·ly** *adv.* **—bawd·i·ness** *n.*

bawd·y·house (bô′dē-hous′) *n.* A house of prostitution.

bawl (bôl) *v.* **bawled, bawling, bawls.** *—intr.* **1.** To cry loudly, as from pain or annoyance; howl. **2.** To cry out loudly and vehemently; shout. *—tr.* To utter in a loud, vehement voice. **—bawl out.** *Informal.* To reprimand or scold in a loud voice.
~n. A loud, extended outcry; a wail. [Middle English *baulen,* probably from Scandinavian, of imitative origin, akin to Icelandic *baula,* to low.] **—bawl·er** *n.*

bay[1] (bā) *n.* **1.** *Abbr.* **b., B.** A body of water partly enclosed by land, but having a wide outlet to the sea. **2.** A broad stretch of low land between hills. **3.** An arm of prairie partly enclosed by woodland. [Middle English *baye,* from Old French *baie,* from Old Spanish *bahia,* perhaps from Iberian.]

bay[2] *n.* **1.** *Architecture.* A part of a building or other structure marked off by vertical elements. **2. a.** A **bay window** *(see).* **b.** Any opening or recess in a wall. **3.** An extension of a building; a wing. **4.** A compartment in a barn, used for storing hay or grain. **5.** A ship's sickbay. **6.** A compartment in an aircraft: *the bomb bay.* **7.** *British.* A dead end in a railway station marking the termination of a line, with a platform surrounding it on three sides. [Middle English, from Old French *baee,* an opening, from *baer,* to gape, from Medieval Latin *batāre,* to yawn, gape.]

bay[3] *adj.* Reddish-brown: *a bay colt.*
~n. **1.** A reddish-brown color. **2.** An animal, especially a horse, of this color. [Middle English, from Old French *bai,* from Latin *badius.*]

bay[4] *n.* **1.** A deep, prolonged barking, especially of hounds closing in on prey. **2.** The position of one cornered by pursuers and forced to turn and fight at close quarters. **3.** The position of someone or something checked or kept at a safe distance.
~v. **bayed, baying, bays.** *—intr.* To utter a deep, prolonged bark or howl. *—tr.* **1.** To pursue or challenge with barking: *"I had rather be a dog, and bay the moon"* (Shakespeare). **2.** To express by barking. **3.** To bring to bay: *"too big for the dogs which tried to bay it"* (William Faulkner). [Middle English *baien,* short for *abaien,* from Old French *abaiier, abayer,* from Vulgar Latin *abbaiāre* (unattested).]

bay[5] *n.* **1.** The true laurel, *Laurus nobilis,* native to the Mediterranean area, having stiff, glossy, aromatic leaves. See **bay leaf.** Also called "bay laurel," "bay tree," "laurel." **2.** Any of several similar trees or shrubs, such as the **sweet bay** *(see).* **3.** *Usually* **bays.** A crown or wreath made of the leaves and branches of the bay or similar plants, conferred or awarded in classical times as a sign of honor. **4. bays.** Renown; honor. [Middle English *baye,* laurel berry, from Old French *baie,* from Latin *bāca,* berry.]

ba·ya·dere (bī′ə-dîr′, -dâr′) *n.* A fabric with vividly contrasting horizontal stripes. [French *bayadère,* Hindu dancing girl, from Portuguese *bailadeira,* from *bailar,* to dance.]

Ba·yard (bā′ərd, bī′-, bä-yär′), **Pierre de Terrail, Seigneur de** (*c.* 1473–1524). French soldier known for his fearlessness and chivalry.

bay·ber·ry (bā′bĕr′ē) *n., pl.* **-ries. 1.** Any of several aromatic shrubs or small trees of the genus *Myrica;* especially, *M. pensylvanica,* of eastern North America, bearing gray, waxy berries. **2.** A tropical American tree, *Pimenta acris,* yielding an oil used in making bay rum. Also called "bay rum tree." **3.** The fruit of any of these trees or shrubs.

Bayern. See **Bavaria.**

Bayes·i·an (bā′zē-ən) *adj.* Of or designating a method or theory for reassessing the probability of a proposition in the light of new relevant information. [After Thomas *Bayes* (1701–61), British mathematician.]

Ba·yeux (bä-yo͞o′, bā-). Small town in northwestern France, in the Calvados department of Normandy. It was the first French town (June 8, 1944) to be liberated from Nazi occupation by the Allies in World War II.

Bayeux tapestry *n.* An 11th- or 12th-century tapestry, 50 centimeters (20 inches) wide by 70.5 meters (231 feet) long, embroidered with scenes depicting the Norman Conquest of England, and preserved in the town of Bayeux.

Baykal. See **Baikal, Lake.**

Bayle (bāl), **Pierre** (1647–1706). French philosopher, a forerunner of the 18th-century philosophes. Although he was brought up as a Calvinist, he devoted his writings to the cause of religious tolerance and skeptical subversion of Christian belief. His most famous work was the *Dictionnaire Historique et Critique* (1697).

bay leaf *n.* The dried, aromatic leaf of the bay, *Laurus nobilis,* or of the bayberry, *Pimenta acris,* used as seasoning in cooking.

Bay·lis (bā′lĭs), **Lilian Mary** (1874–1937). English theater manager. She became manager of the Old Vic, London (1912), and created a theater for the production of Shakespeare's plays. In 1931 she assumed the management of the Sadler's Wells theater and transformed it into a center for opera and ballet.

bay lynx *n.* The **bobcat** *(see).*

Bay of Pigs (pĭgz). *Spanish* **Ba·hí·a de Co·chin·os** (bä-ē′ə dā kə-chē′nōs). Bay on the southern coast of Cuba, the site of the unsuccessful Bay of Pigs invasion of April 17, 1961, when a force of about 1,500 U.S.-trained troops, rebels against the regime of Fidel Castro, landed here from Guatemala.

bay·o·net (bā′ə-nĭt, -nĕt′, bā′ə-nĕt′) *n.* A knife or spike adapted to fit the muzzle end of a rifle and used in close combat.
~tr.v. **bayoneted** or **bayonetted, -neting** or **-netting, -nets.** To stab or prod with a bayonet. [French *baïonnette,* first manufactured at BAYONNE, France.]

bayonet fitting *n. Chiefly British.* A method of fastening two cylindrical parts together, similar to the original method of attaching a bayonet to a rifle. It is used in fitting light bulbs into holders, two pins on the bulb cap engaging with two L-shaped slots on the holder.

Ba·yonne (bā-ōn′, bä-yôn). Port in the Pyrénées-Atlantique department of France, now joined with the resort of Biarritz. The town gave its name to the bayonet, which was first used by local Basques in the 17th century.

bay·ou (bī′o͞o, bī′ō) *n., pl.* **-ous.** *Southern U.S.* A marshy, sluggish body of water tributary to a lake or river. [Louisiana French, from Choctaw *bayuk.*]

Bay·reuth (bī-roit′). Industrial city of Bavaria, southeast West Germany. Richard Wagner lived here from 1872 to 1883, and the Festival Theater, devoted to the performance of his operas, was opened in 1876.

bay rum *n.* An aromatic liquid obtained by distilling the leaves of the bayberry tree, *Pimenta acris,* with rum, and now also synthesized from alcohol, water, and various oils.

bay rum tree *n.* See **bayberry** (sense 1).

Bay Street *n.* The controlling financial interests of Canada. [After the main street of the financial district of Toronto.]

bay tree *n.* **1.** A tree, the **bay** *(see).* **2.** The **California laurel** *(see).*

bay window *n.* **1.** A large window or series of windows projecting from the wall of a building and forming a recess within. Also called "bay." **2.** *Slang.* A protruding belly; paunch.

bay·wood (bā′wo͝od′) *n.* The wood of a tropical American mahogany, *Swietenia macrophylla.* [After the *Bay* of Campeche, Mexico.]

ba·zaar, ba·zar (bə-zär′) *n.* **1.** An Oriental market, usually consisting of an area of streets lined with shops and stalls. **2.** A shop or part of a store for the sale of miscellaneous articles. **3.** A fair at which miscellaneous articles are sold, usually for charitable purposes. [Earlier *bazarro, bazar,* probably from Italian *bazarro,* from Turkish, from Persian *bāzār,* from Middle Persian *bāchār,* from Old Persian *abēcharish*†.]

battlement *Archers shot arrows through the open sections in castle walls, known as embrasures, and hid behind the solid sections (merlons). Slits in the merlons enabled the archers to see out.*

bay *The sacred tree of the god Apollo. In ancient Rome, a garland of its leaves was the highest honor bestowed on a warrior.*

ba·zoo·ka (bə-zōō′kə) *n.* A portable military weapon consisting of a long, metal, smoothbore tube for firing small, armor-piercing, explosive rockets at short range. [After the *bazooka,* a crude wind instrument made of pipes, invented by Bob Burns (1896–1956), U.S. comedian.]

bb, b.b. ball bearing.

BB (bē′bē) *n.* A standard size of lead shot that measures about .46 cm (or 0.18 in.) in diameter. [Perhaps from the letter *b.*]

B.B.A. Bachelor of Business Administration.

BBB, B.B.B. Better Business Bureau.

BBC, B.B.C. British Broadcasting Corporation.

BB gun *n.* A small air rifle firing BB shot.

bbl, bbl. barrel (of oil).

B.C. **1.** Bachelor of Chemistry. **2.** Bachelor of Commerce. **3.** before Christ (usually small capitals, B.C.). —See Usage note at **A.D.** **4.** British Columbia.

B.C.E. **1.** Bachelor of Chemical Engineering. **2.** Bachelor of Civil Engineering.

B cell *n.* A lymphocyte derived from bone marrow that takes part in the immune response. [*B*one-marrow-derived + CELL.]

BCG Bacillus Calmette-Guérin (a strain of tuberculosis bacillus used in a vaccine against the disease).

B.Ch.E. Bachelor of Chemical Engineering.

B.C.L. **1.** Bachelor of Common Law. **2.** Bachelor of Civil Law.

B.C.S. **1.** Bachelor of Chemical Science. **2.** Bachelor of Commercial Science.

bd. **1.** board. **2.** bond. **3.** *Bookbinding.* bound.

B.D. **1.** Bachelor of Divinity. **2.** bank draft. **3.** bills discounted.

bdel·li·um (dĕl′ē-əm) *n.* **1.** An aromatic gum resin similar to myrrh, produced by various trees of the genus *Commiphora,* of western Asia and Africa. **2.** A substance mentioned in the Bible, variously interpreted to be carbuncle, rock crystal, pearl, or gum resin. Numbers 11:7. [Latin, from Greek *bdellion,* probably from Hebrew *bədōlaḥ.*]

bd. ft. board foot.

bds. bound in boards.

B.D.S. Bachelor of Dental Surgery.

be (bē) *v.*

	1st person	2nd person	3rd person
Present Tense			
singular	**am** (ăm)	**are** (är)†	**is** (ĭz)
plural	**are**	**are**	**are**

†*Archaic 2nd person singular* **art** (ärt)

	1st person	2nd person	3rd person
Past Tense			
singular	**was** (wŭz; wŏz)	**were** (wûr)‡	**was**
plural	**were**	**were**	**were**

‡*Archaic 2nd person singular* **wast** (wŏst) *or* **wert** (wûrt)

Present Participle: **being** (bē′ĭng)   Present Subjunctive: **be**
Past Participle: **been** (bĭn)   Past Subjunctive: **were**

Used as an auxiliary verb in certain constructions, as: **a.** With the past participle of a transitive verb to form the passive voice: *The competition is held annually. Our club may be disbanded for lack of funds.* **b.** With the present participle of a verb to express a continuing action: *We are working to improve housing conditions.* **c.** With the present participle or the infinitive of a verb, to express intention, obligation, or future action: *All visitors are to leave by 10:00 p.m. The finals are to be held in London.* **d.** *Archaic.* With the past participle of certain intransitive verbs to form the perfect tense: *Christ is risen from the dead.* —*intr.* **1.** To exist in actuality; have reality or life: *I think, therefore I am.* **2.** To exist in a specified place; stay; reside: *"Oh, to be in England,/ Now that April's there"* (Robert Browning). **3.** To occupy a specified position: *The food is on the table.* **4.** To take place; occur: *Her party was last week.* **5.** To go. Used chiefly in the past and perfect tenses: *Have you ever been to Italy?* **6.** *Archaic.* To belong; befall. Used in the subjunctive: *Peace be unto you.* **7.** Used as a copula linking a subject and a predicate nominative, adjective, or pronoun, in such senses as: **a.** To equal in meaning or identity: *"To be a Christian was to be a Roman"* (James Bryce). **b.** To signify; indicate: *A is excellent, C is passable, F is failing.* **c.** To belong to a specified class or group: *A human is a primate.* **d.** To have or show a specified essential quality or characteristic: *She is courageous. All men are mortal.* **e.** To have or show a specified quality or characteristic at a particular time: *I'm busy just now.* **f.** To represent or embody the essential character of; symbolize: *She is the liberal party.* [1. Be; been: Middle English *be(e)n; be(o)n,* Old English *bēon; bēon,* to come to be. 2. Am; art; is; are (singular and plural): Middle English *am; art, eart; is; are* (singular), *aren* (plural); Old English *eam, eom; eart; is; (e)aron* (plural only), from Germanic *es-* (unattested) and *ar-* (unattested). 3. Was; were: Middle English *wes, was; ware, were* (singular), *weren, were* (plural); Old English *wæs; wære* (singular), *wæron* (plural), from Germanic *wes-* (unattested).]

Usage: When pronouns follow a form of the verb *to be,* the nominative is traditionally required, on the grounds that the pronoun denotes the same entity as the subject. Thus, the rules require *it is I, that must be she,* and so forth. The rules create problems, however, when the pronoun after *to be* denotes an entity that is also understood to be the object of some other verb or preposition. Shall

beagle *The stamina of this breed— along with its acute sense of smell— has made it popular as a hunting dog. It is often used in packs to hunt hares.*

we say *it is I she loves* or *it is me she loves?* There is no strict rule, but given the natural tendency to use objective forms like *me* rather than nominatives like *I* in undecided cases, the use of *me* is entirely defensible here. It should also be noted that the use of the nominative following *to be* sounds stilted when the verb has been contracted. Nevertheless, a purist would say *it's I* rather than *it's me,* or *that's they* rather than *that's them.*

be– *prefix.* Indicates: **1.** A complete or profuse covering or affecting; for example, **becloud, besmear. 2.** A thorough or excessive degree; for example, **bewilder. 3.** An action that causes a condition to exist; for example, **besot, befriend.** [Middle English, Old English, weak form of *bī-,* BY. In Middle English *be-* indicates: 1. Thoroughly, as in **beloved, betray.** 2. On all sides, as in **besiege.** 3. About, over, in relation to, as in **betroth, bequest.** Old English *be-, bi-* indicates: 1. About, over, as in **bethink.** 2. On all sides, as in **beset.** 3. Away, away from, as in **benumb.**]

Be The symbol for the element beryllium.

Bé Baumé scale.

B.E. **1.** Bachelor of Education. **2.** Bachelor of Engineering. **3.** Bank of England. **4.** Board of Education.

B/E **1.** bill of entry. **2.** bill of exchange.

beach (bēch) *n.* **1.** The shore of a body of water. **2.** The sand or pebbles on a shore. **3.** The accumulation of shingle, sand, and rocks on the coast between the lowest level reached by spring tides and the highest point attained by storm waves. ~*tr.v.* **beached, beaching, beaches.** To haul or drive (a boat for example) ashore. [16th century : origin obscure.]

beach buggy *n.* A car usually open and fitted with balloon tires, used for driving on beaches and sand.

beach·comb·er (bēch′kō′mər) *n.* **1.** One who collects flotsam and jetsam from beaches and port areas; especially, a vagrant who makes a living in this way. **2.** A long wave rolling in toward a beach. [Sense 2, from COMB, in the sense "to break with foam."]

beach flea *n.* Any of various small, jumping crustaceans of the family Talitridae, living on sandy beaches at or near the tide line. Also called "sand hopper."

beach·head (bēch′hĕd′) *n.* **1.** A position on an enemy shoreline captured by advance troops of an invading force. **2.** A first achievement that opens the way for further development.

beach·la·mar (bēch′lə-mär′) *n.* A dialect, **bêche-de-mer** (*see*). [Alteration of Portuguese *bicho do mar.*]

beach pea *n.* Either of two similar North American plants, *Lathyrus maritimus,* of the Atlantic coast, or *L. littoralis,* of the Pacific coast, having purplish flowers and sprawling stems.

beach plum *n.* A seacoast shrub, *Prunus maritima,* of northeastern North America, having white flowers and edible plumlike fruit.

beach wormwood *n.* A seacoast plant, *Artemisia stelleriana,* originally native to Asia but now widespread, covered with dense, white down and having small yellow flowers. Also called "dusty miller."

bea·con (bē′kən) *n.* **1. a.** A signal fire lit on a hill or other high place; especially, one used to warn of an enemy's approach. **b.** *Chiefly British.* A hill suitable for such a fire. **2.** A lighthouse or other signaling or guiding device on a coast. **3.** A radio transmitter that emits a characteristic signal as a warning or guide. **4.** Anything that warns or guides. ~*v.* **beaconed, -coning, -cons.** —*tr.* To provide a beacon for. —*intr.* To serve as a beacon. [Middle English *beken,* sign, standard, Old English *bēacen.*]

bead (bēd) *n.* **1.** A small, ball-shaped piece of glass, metal, wood, or other material pierced for stringing or threading. **2. beads. a.** A necklace made of such pieces. **b.** A rosary. **3.** Any small, round object, especially: **a.** A small drop of moisture. **b.** A bubble of gas in a liquid. **c.** A small knob of metal on the muzzle of a rifle or gun, used for sighting. **4.** *Architecture.* A strip of stone or wood, with one molded edge placed flush against a wall, door, or window frame. Also called "bead butt." **5.** *Chemistry.* A **borax bead** (*see*). **6.** *Metallurgy.* A small blob of metal from a welding rod applied to the material to be welded in order to test the nature of the weld. **—count** (or **say** or **tell**) **one's beads.** To pray with a rosary. ~*v.* **beaded, beading, beads.** —*tr.* To ornament or cover with beads. —*intr.* To collect into beads. [Middle English *bede, bead,* prayer, prayer bead, bead, Old English *gebed,* prayer, from Germanic *bedh-* (unattested).]

bead·ing (bē′dĭng) *n.* **1.** Beads or material used for beads. **2.** Ornamentation with beads. **3.** *Architecture.* A narrow, half-rounded molding. **4.** Any narrow strip of trimming. **5.** A narrow piece of openwork lace through which ribbon may be run. **6.** Bubbles or froth, as on the rim of a glass.

bea·dle (bēd′l) *n.* **1.** Formerly, a minor parish official in an English church, whose duties included keeping order and ushering during services. **2.** An official at certain English universities who supervises and walks before processions. **3.** *Judaism.* A **shammes** (*see*). [Middle English *bedele, bidel,* herald, messenger, beadle, from Old French *bedel* (of Germanic origin), replacing Old English *bydel.*]

bea·dle·dom (bēd′l-dəm) *n.* Petty bureaucratic officiousness.

bead test *n.* *Chemistry.* A test to identify the component elements of a substance. See **borax bead.**

bead·work (bēd′wûrk′) *n.* **1.** Decorative work in beads. **2.** *Architecture.* Beaded molding.

bead·y (bē′dē) *adj.* **-ier, -iest. 1.** Small, round, and shiny: *beady eyes.* **2.** Decorated or covered with beads.

bea·gle (bē′gəl) *n.* Any of a breed of small hounds having short legs, drooping ears, and a smooth coat with white, black, and tan markings. [Middle English *begle*, perhaps from Old French *bee-gueule*, noisy person : probably *beer*, to gape, from (unattested) Vulgar Latin *batāre* (see **bay**, opening) + *gueule*, throat, from Latin *gula*.]

beak (bēk) *n.* **1.** The horny, projecting structure forming the mandibles of a bird; a bill. **2.** A part or organ resembling this, as in some turtles, insects, or fish. **3.** Any hard, cone-shaped, or pointed structure or part. **4.** *Informal.* A person's nose. **5.** *British Slang.* **a.** A schoolmaster. **b.** A judge. [Middle English *bec, bek,* from Old French *bec,* from Latin *beccus,* from Gaulish.]

beak·er (bē′kər) *n.* **1. a.** A large drinking cup with a wide mouth. **b.** The contents of such a cup. **2.** An open glass cylinder with a pouring lip, used as a standard laboratory container or vessel for mixing and heating. [Middle English *biker, beker,* from Old Norse *bikarr,* probably from Vulgar Latin *bicārium* (unattested), perhaps from Greek *bikos,* drinking-jar.]

Beaker Folk *pl.n.* An ancient people inhabiting Europe in the Bronze Age, whose artifacts, especially metal beakers, have been found in their round burial barrows. Also called "Beaker People."

be-all and end-all (bē′ôl′ ənd ĕnd′ôl′) *n.* The chief aim or consideration, to the exclusion of all others. [From Shakespeare's *Macbeth* (1605), Act I, scene 7, in which Macbeth considers the murder of Duncan: ". . . this blow/Might be the be-all and the end-all. . . ."]

beam (bēm) *n.* **1.** A squared-off log or large, oblong piece of timber, metal, or stone, used especially in construction. **2.** *Nautical.* **a.** The breadth of a ship at the widest point. **b.** A transverse structural member of the framing of a vessel, used to support a deck and to brace the sides against stress. **c.** The shank of an anchor. **3.** A steel tube or wooden roller with flanged ends on which the warp is wound in a loom. **4.** An oscillating lever connected to an engine piston rod and used to transmit power to the crankshaft. **5.** The bar of a balance, from which weighing pans are suspended. **6.** Either of the main stems of a deer's antlers. **7.** The main horizontal bar on a plow to which the share, colter, and handles, if any, are attached. **8. a.** A ray of light or other electromagnetic radiation. **b.** A group of particles traveling together in close parallel trajectories. **9.** A **radio beam** (see). **—broad in the beam.** *Informal.* Wide-hipped; fat. **—off the beam. 1.** Not following the radio beam. Said of an aircraft. **2.** *Informal.* Not on the right track; mistaken. ∼*v.* **beamed, beaming, beams. —***tr.* **1.** To emit or transmit: *beaming the message.* **2.** To express by means of a broad or radiant smile. **—***intr.* **1.** To radiate light; shine. **2.** To smile expansively. [Middle English *beme, beem,* Old English *bēam,* tree, beam.]

beam compass *n.* A form of compass used for drawing large circles. It consists of a horizontal beam along which two vertical legs slide, one fitted with a pin to act as a center and the other with a pen or pencil. Not in technical usage. Also called "trammel."

beam-ends (bēm′ĕndz′) *pl.n.* The ends of a ship's beams. **—on the beam-ends.** Listing so far over that the beams are nearly vertical and there is danger of capsizing. **—on one's beam-ends.** *Informal.* Having no money at all.

beam hole *n.* A hole through a nuclear-reactor shield enabling a beam of radiation to be used for experimental purposes.

beam rider *n.* A guided missile that steers itself along the axis of a scanned beam of microwave radiation. **—beam riding** *n.*

beam·y (bē′mē) *adj.* **-ier, -iest. 1.** Broad at the beam. Said of a ship. **2.** Emitting beams, as of light; radiant.

bean (bēn) *n.* **1.** Any of several plants of the genus *Phaseolus,* having compound leaves, white or yellow flowers, and seed-bearing pods. See **lima bean, string bean. 2.** The edible seed or pod of any of these plants. **3.** Any of several related plants bearing similar pods and seeds. See **broad bean. 4.** Any of various other seeds or pods resembling beans, such as the coffee bean or the vanilla bean. **5. beans.** *Slang.* A small amount: *I don't know beans about the stock market.* **6.** *Slang.* The head. **7.** *British Slang.* A fellow; a chap: *old bean.* **—full of beans.** *Informal.* Very lively; energetic. **—spill the beans.** *Informal.* To disclose what was not meant to be disclosed. [Middle English *ben(e),* Old English *bēan.*]

bean·bag (bēn′băg′) *n.* A small bag filled with dried beans and used for throwing in games.

bean ball *n.* A baseball pitch aimed at the batter's head.

bean caper *n.* A plant of the genus *Zygophyllum;* especially, *Z. fabago,* a shrub of the Middle East, bearing edible buds used as capers.

bean curd *n.* A soft soybean cheese of the Orient. Also called "tofu." [Translation of Chinese (Mandarin) *dou⁴ fu³: dou⁴,* bean + *fu³,* curdled.]

bean·feast (bēn′fēst′) *n. British Informal.* **1.** An annual dinner given by a firm for its employees. **2.** A party or celebration. [19th century : beans and bacon were always served at such annual dinners.]

bean·ie (bē′nē) *n.* A small brimless cap.

bean·o (bē′nō) *n.* A form of bingo, especially one using beans as markers. [Perhaps blend of BINGO and BEAN.]

bean·pole (bēn′pōl′) *n.* **1.** A thin pole used to support bean plants. **2.** *Slang.* A very tall, thin person.

bean sprout *n.* A young, tender shoot of certain beans, such as the soybean or the mung bean, used in Chinese cooking.

bean·stalk (bēn′stôk′) *n.* The stem of a bean plant.

bean tree *n.* Any of various trees, such as the catalpa, that bear beanlike fruit.

bear[1] (bâr) *v.* **bore** (bôr, bōr) or *archaic* **bare** (bâr), **borne** (bôrn, bōrn) (for all senses) or **born** (for sense 11 only), **bearing, bears.** **—***tr.* **1.** To support; hold up: *bore him on her shoulders.* **2.** To carry

---

beak

THE MANY SHAPES OF BEAKS
How birds have adapted to the demands of their diets

The shape of a bird's beak depends on its feeding habits. Scavengers, such as gulls and crows, have all-purpose beaks so that they can feed on a wide range of animals and plants. The diets of some birds, however, have become very specialized in order to avoid competition for food, and their beaks have adapted to the demands of these specialized diets.

WIGEON *Wide beak shears grass and plants.*

OYSTERCATCHER *Beak can pry open the shell of prey.*

WOODPECKER *Tapering beak chisels into bark for insects.*

WOODCOCK *Long, thin beak probes for worms in soft earth.*

SWIFT *Wide beak for catching insects on the wing.*

HUMMINGBIRD *Long, narrow beak for collecting nectar.*

MERGANSER *Serrated beak for gripping slippery fish.*

HERON *Long, daggerlike beak for seizing fish.*

PUFFIN *Large, triangular beak can hold several fish.*

AVOCET *Long, upcurved beak skims food from water surface.*

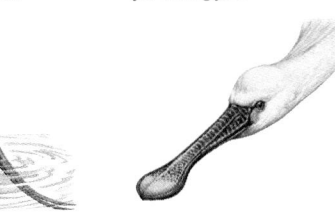
SPOONBILL *Spatulate beak sifts food from the shallows.*

PELICAN *Pouch beneath long, pointed beak holds fish.*

COCKATOO *Hooked beak for cracking nuts.*

TOUCAN *Huge, brightly colored beak reaches for fruit.*

MACAW *Hooked beak for cracking nuts.*

GOLDEN EAGLE *Strong, hooked beak for tearing flesh.*

OWL *Short, hooked beak for catching prey.*

PETREL *Narrow, hooked beak for catching fish.*

bearberry Arctostaphylos uva-ursi, *the bearberry, is an evergreen shrub that bears small white or pink flowers and red berries. It grows on wetlands and bogs in the cooler regions of the Northern Hemisphere.*

bearded reedling *A native of Europe and Asia, the bearded reedling is a member of the babbler family and lives in reedbeds on lakes and marshes. It is also called the bearded tit. The bird gets its name because the male (above) has a "beard" of black feathers beneath its beak.*

Beardsley lithograph *This study of Isolde (Iseult)—the Irish princess in the tragic Arthurian love story* Tristan and Isolde—*was first published in* The Studio, *an art magazine, in October 1895.*

on one's person; convey. **3.** To carry as if in the mind; maintain: *bearing love for others.* **4.** To transmit at large; bring: *bearing glad tidings.* **5.** To have as a visible characteristic; show: *bearing a scar on his right arm.* **6.** To have as a visible quality or form; exhibit: *"A thousand different shapes it bears"* (Abraham Cowley). **7.** To conduct or carry (oneself) in a particular way. **8.** To be accountable for; assume. **9.** To tolerate; endure: *couldn't bear her husband.* **10.** To be capable of undergoing; admit of: *doesn't bear thinking about.* **11.** To give birth to. —See Usage note below. **12.** To produce; yield. **13.** To offer; render: *bearing witness.* **14.** To move by steady pressure; push: *"boats against the current, borne back ceaselessly into the past"* (F. Scott Fitzgerald). —*intr.* **1.** To yield a product; produce. **2.** To withstand stress, difficulty, or attrition. Often used with *up.* **3.** To have relevance; apply. Used with *on.* **4.** To turn or proceed in a specified direction: *"I bore right, to avoid the Beduin"* (T.E. Lawrence). —See Synonyms at **convey.** —**bear down on** (or **upon**). **1.** To come toward in an aggressive or threatening way. **2.** To exert pressure or weight on. —**bear out.** To prove right or justified; confirm: *The results bear out her claims.* —**bear up.** To withstand stress or difficulty. —**bear with.** To be patient or tolerant with. [Bear, bore, borne; Middle English *beren, bare, boren,* Old English *beran, bær, boren.*]

Synonyms: *abide, endure, stand, suffer, tolerate.*

Usage: In its literal sense the past participle *born* is used only of mammals and only with *to be: The baby was born.* It may also be used figuratively: *A star is born. Borne,* said of the act of birth, refers only to the mother's role, but it can be used actively or passively: *She has borne three children. Three children were borne by her* (but *born to her*). In all other senses of *bear* the past participle is *borne*: *The soil has borne abundant crops. Such a burden cannot be borne by anyone.*

bear² *n.* **1.** Any of various usually omnivorous mammals of the family Ursidae, having a shaggy coat, strong claws, and a short tail, and walking with the entire lower surface of the foot touching the ground. See **black bear, brown bear, grizzly bear, polar bear.** **2.** Any of various animals resembling a bear in some respect, such as the **koala** *(see).* **3.** A person who is awkward, clumsy, or ill-mannered. **4. Bear.** *Astronomy.* Either of two constellations, **Ursa Major** or **Ursa Minor** *(both of which see).* **5.** *Stock Market.* An investor or concern that sells securities or commodities in the expectation that prices will fall. Compare **bull.**
∼*v.* **beared, bearing, bears.** —*tr.* To engage in speculative selling so as to lower the price of (stocks and shares) or prices in (a market). —*intr.* To fall in price. Compare **bull.**
∼*adj.* Characterized by falling prices: *a bear market.* Compare **bull.** [Middle English *bere,* Old English *bera.* Stock market senses, 18th century : originally probably *bearskin jobber,* alluding to the proverb, *To sell the bear's skin before one has caught the bear.*]

bear·a·ble (bâr'ə-bəl) *adj.* Capable of being borne; endurable; tolerable. —**bear·a·bly** *adv.*

bear-bait·ing (bâr'bā'tĭng) *n.* The former sport of setting dogs to attack or torment a chained bear.

bear·ber·ry (bâr'bĕr'ē) *n., pl.* **-ries.** A trailing shrub, *Arctostaphylos uva-ursi,* of the Northern Hemisphere, having small evergreen leaves, white or pink flowers, and red berries. Also called "kinnikinnick" and sometimes "crowberry."

beard (bîrd) *n.* **1. a.** The hair on the chin, cheeks, and throat of a man: *three days' growth of beard.* **b.** This hair allowed to grow and cover the skin: *a foot-long beard.* **2.** Any similar hairy or hairlike growth such as that on or near the face of certain mammals. **3.** A tuft or group of bristles on certain plants, especially cereals; an awn. **4.** The barb or hook of a fishhook, arrow, or the like. **5.** The gills of an oyster. **6.** *Printing.* The part of a piece of type between the face and the shoulder; the neck.
∼*tr.v.* **bearded, bearding, beards.** **1.** To furnish with a beard. **2.** To grasp by the beard. **3.** To confront boldly: *beard the lion in his den.* [Middle English *berd,* Old English *beard.*]

bearded iris *n.* Any of many varieties of iris having beardlike growths at the bases of the three lower, recurved petals.

bearded reedling *n.* A small Eurasian marsh bird, *Panurus biarmicus,* having black, mustachelike markings in the male. Also called "bearded tit," "reedling."

bearded vulture *n.* A bird, the **lammergeier** *(see).*

beard·less (bîrd'lĭs) *adj.* **1. a.** Having no beard. **b.** Having the beard shaved off; clean-shaven. **2. a.** Not old enough to have a beard. **b.** Immature; inexperienced. —**beard·less·ness** *n.*

Beards·ley (bîrdz'lē), **Aubrey Vincent** (1872–98). British illustrator. His flowing designs, characteristic of the art nouveau style, are usually figurative ink drawings done in black and white, contrasting areas of elaborate intricacy with stark white spaces and dense black shadows. Works that he illustrated include Wilde's *Salome,* Pope's *Rape of the Lock,* and Ben Jonson's *Volpone.*

bear·er (bâr'ər) *n.* **1.** One that carries or supports. **2. a.** A porter. **b.** *British.* A domestic or personal servant, especially in India. **3.** A person who presents for payment a check or other redeemable note. **4.** A **pallbearer** *(see).* **5.** Any fruit-bearing plant.

bear garden *n.* **1.** Formerly, a place where bears were confined and exhibited, as for bearbaiting. **2.** A place or scene of tumult.

bear grass *n.* **1.** A tall plant, *Xerophyllum tenax,* of northwestern North America, having narrow, grasslike leaves and white flowers in a large terminal cluster. **2.** Any of several similar or related plants, especially any of several species of yucca.

bear hug *n.* A very tight, enveloping hug or embrace.

bear·ing (bâr'ĭng) *n.* **1.** The manner in which a person carries or conducts himself; deportment. **2.** *Engineering.* **a.** Any part that supports another part or structure. **b.** A device that supports, guides, and reduces the friction of motion between fixed and moving machine parts. **3.** Anything that bears weight or acts as a support. **4.** The part of an architectural arch or beam that rests on a support. **5. a.** The act or period of producing fruit or offspring. **b.** The quantity produced; the yield. **6.** Direction, especially angular direction measured from one position to another using geographical or celestial reference lines. **7.** *Usually* **bearings.** The position or situation of a person or object relative to the surroundings. **8.** Relevance; relationship; connection: *This has no bearing on the subject.* **9.** *Heraldry.* A charge or device on a field.

Synonyms: *air, carriage, demeanor, manner, mien, presence.*

bearing rein *n.* A rein for a horse, a **checkrein** *(see).*

bear·ish (bâr'ĭsh) *adj.* **1.** Like a bear; clumsy, boorish, or surly. **2.** Causing, expecting, or characterized by falling stock-market prices. Compare **bullish.** —**bear·ish·ly** *adv.* —**bear·ish·ness** *n.*

bé·ar·naise sauce (bā-är-nāz') *n.* A sauce made from butter, egg yolks, lemon juice or vinegar, and flavored with tarragon, shallots, and chervil. Also called "sauce béarnaise." [French *béarnaise,* feminine of *béarnais,* of Béarn, region in southwestern France.]

bear's-ear (bârz'îr') *n.* A plant, the **auricula** *(see).*

bear·skin (bâr'skĭn') *n.* **1.** Something, such as a rug, made from the skin of a bear. **2.** A tall military headdress made of black fur. —**bear·skin** *adj.*

beast (bēst) *n.* **1.** Any animal except a human; especially, any large, four-footed animal. **2.** The qualities of an animal; animal nature. **3.** A brutal or vile person. [Middle English *beste,* from Old French, from Latin *bēstia*†.]

beast·ly (bēst'lē) *adj.* **-lier, -liest.** **1.** Of or like a beast; bestial. **2.** *Informal.* Disagreeable; nasty; abominable.
∼*adv. Chiefly British Informal.* Used as an intensive: *It's beastly cold outside.* —**beast·li·ness** *n.*

beast of burden *n.* An animal used for transporting loads.

beast of prey *n.* An animal that kills and eats other animals.

beat (bēt) *v.* **beat, beaten** (bēt'n) or **beat, beating, beats.** —*tr.* **1. a.** To strike or hit repeatedly. **b.** To strike (a drum, for example) in order to produce a noise. **2.** To punish by hitting or whipping; flog. **3.** To pound or strike against repeatedly: *waves beating the shore.* **4.** To shape or break by repeated blows; forge. **5.** To make flat by pounding or trampling. **6.** To mix rapidly with an instrument to a frothy consistency: *beat two eggs in a bowl.* **7.** To flap (wings, for example). **8.** To sound (a signal), as on a drum. **9.** To mark or count (time or rhythm) with the hands or with a baton. **10.** To disturb (bushes, for example) in order to drive out game for shooting. **11.** To defeat or subdue. **12.** *Informal.* To excel or surpass. **13.** *Informal.* To avoid or counter the effects of; circumvent: *beat the traffic.* **14.** To precede or arrive in advance of; forestall: *They beat us to it.* **15.** *Slang.* To perplex or baffle. —*intr.* **1.** To inflict repeated blows. **2.** To throb or pulsate rhythmically. **3.** *Physics.* **a.** To cause beating by superposing waves of different frequencies. **b.** To undergo beating. Said of waves of alternating electrical signals. **4.** To emit sound when struck: *The gong beat thunderously.* **5.** To sound a signal, as on a drum. **6.** To admit of rapid whipping to a froth. **7.** To hunt through woods or undergrowth to drive out game. **8.** *Nautical.* To progress against the wind by tacking. —See Synonyms at **defeat, pulsate.** —**beat about** (or **around**) **the bush.** To approach a subject in a roundabout manner. —**beat a retreat.** To flee or withdraw. —**beat back.** To force to retreat or withdraw. —**beat down.** To force or persuade (a seller) to accept a lower price. —**beat it.** *Slang.* To get going; go away. Usually used in the imperative. —**beat off.** To drive away. —**beat up.** *Informal.* To give a thorough beating to; thrash.
∼*n.* **1.** A stroke or blow, especially one that produces a sound or acts as a signal. **2.** A periodic pulsation or throb. **3.** *Physics.* An amplitude pulse produced by beating. **4.** *Music.* **a.** A regular and rhythmical unit of time. **b.** The pulse given to a piece of music by the recurrence of this unit. **c.** The gesture given by a conductor or the symbol representing this unit of time. **5.** The measured and rhythmical sound of verse; meter. **6.** The area regularly covered by a policeman, sentry, or newspaper reporter. **7.** A process of disturbing the undergrowth to drive out game when shooting. **8.** A member of the **beat generation** *(see).* **9.** *Slang.* The reporting of a news item obtained ahead of one's competitors. —See Synonyms at **rhythm.**
∼*adj. Informal.* Worn-out; exhausted. [Beat, beat, beaten; Middle English *beten, bette, beten,* Old English *bēatan, bēot, bēaten.*]

beat·en (bēt'n) *adj.* **1.** Defeated; completely baffled. **2.** Made thin or formed by hammering. **3.** Worn by many footsteps; much traveled: *a beaten path.* **4.** Exhausted; worn-out. —**off the beaten track** (or **path**). **1.** In a remote, out-of-the-way place. **2.** Not well-known; unusual.

beat·er (bē'tər) *n.* **1.** One that beats, especially an instrument for beating: *a carpet beater.* **2.** A person who drives wild game from under cover for a hunter.

beat generation *n.* In the 1950's, a group of young Americans, including Jack Kerouac, Allen Ginsberg, and William Burroughs, who expressed disillusionment with Western values and turned for inspiration to Eastern religion, trying experimental literary forms and adopting a bohemian lifestyle. [Perhaps from BEATEN (exhausted).]

be·a·tif·ic (bē'ə-tĭf'ĭk) *adj.* Showing or producing exalted joy or

bearing

HOW MACHINERY IS KEPT MOVING SAFELY AND SMOOTHLY

The modern use of an old device to minimize friction between moving parts

When, in ancient Egypt and Mesopotamia, building blocks were hauled over logs, the logs were acting as bearings as they rolled. Today's bearings fulfill a similar function: they cut down the friction between two parts of a mechanism, at least one of which is moving. By minimizing friction, they ease movement and reduce wear.

Bearings are now essential components of all kinds of modern machinery. They can be classified according to their shape. The three most common types are journal bearings, roller bearings, and ball bearings. The journal bearing is the simplest, the oldest, and still the most commonly used of the three. It originated in about 1000 B.C. among the Celts of France and Germany who fitted a wooden insert between the wheel hub and axle of a cart.

The idea of the roller bearing was also put to use by the Celts—as wooden rollers fitted inside a sleeve on a hub. Ball bearings first came into general use in the bicycle in 1868.

bearskin *Tall fur hat that is part of the ceremonial dress of the British Guards regiments. First used by the Grenadier Guards in the 18th century, it is seen here worn by a soldier of the Scots Guards.*

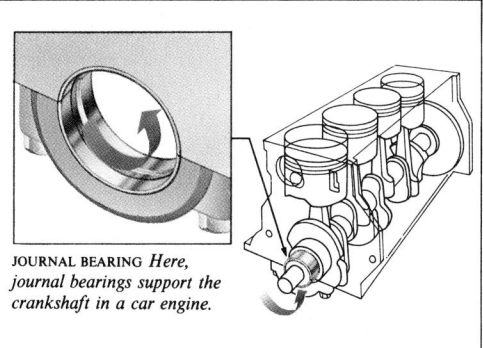

JOURNAL BEARING *Here, journal bearings support the crankshaft in a car engine.*

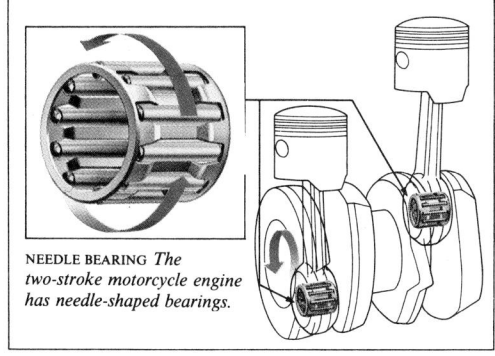

NEEDLE BEARING *The two-stroke motorcycle engine has needle-shaped bearings.*

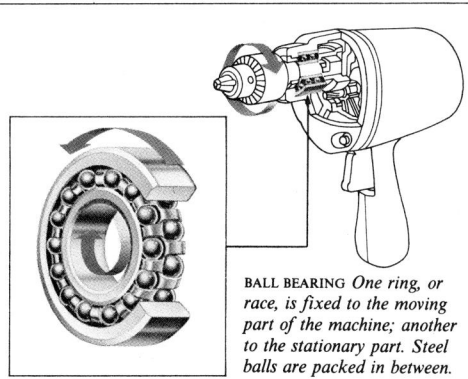

BALL BEARING *One ring, or race, is fixed to the moving part of the machine; another to the stationary part. Steel balls are packed in between.*

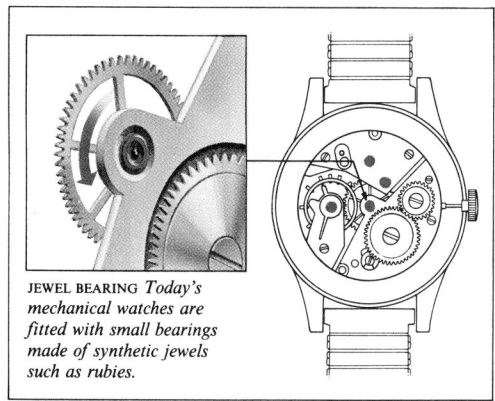

JEWEL BEARING *Today's mechanical watches are fitted with small bearings made of synthetic jewels such as rubies.*

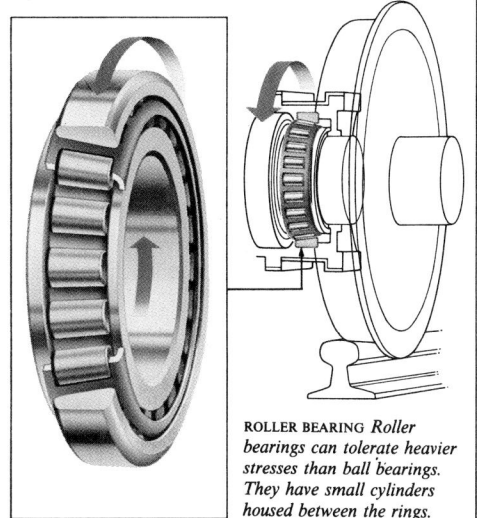

ROLLER BEARING *Roller bearings can tolerate heavier stresses than ball bearings. They have small cylinders housed between the rings.*

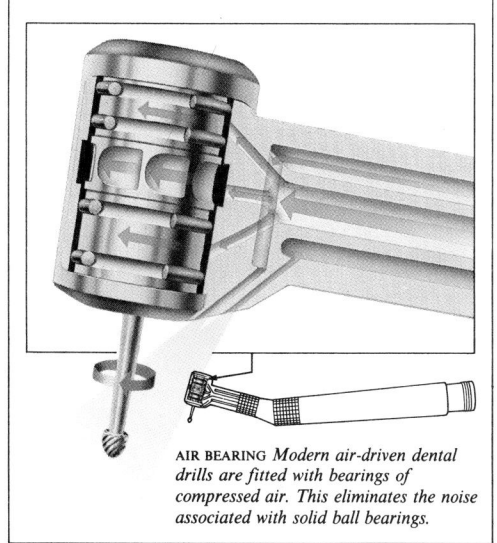

AIR BEARING *Modern air-driven dental drills are fitted with bearings of compressed air. This eliminates the noise associated with solid ball bearings.*

blessedness: *a beatific smile.* [Late Latin *beātificus* : Latin *beātus*, blessed, from the past participle of *beāre*, to make happy + *facere*, to do.] —**be·a·tif·i·cal·ly** *adv.*

be·at·i·fy (bē-ăt′ə-fī) *tr.v.* **-fied, -fying, -fies. 1.** To make blessedly happy. **2.** *Roman Catholic Church.* To proclaim (a deceased person)

to be one of the blessed and thus worthy of public religious honor, usually prior to canonization. **3.** To exalt above all others. [Late Latin *beātificāre*, from *beātificus*, BEATIFIC.] —**be·at·i·fi·ca·tion** *n.*

beat·ing (bē′tĭng) *n.* **1.** Punishment by whipping, flogging, or thrashing. **2.** A defeat. **3.** A throbbing or pulsation, as of the heart.

4. *Physics.* The periodic alternation of amplitude maxima and minima produced by interference between two waves of different frequency.

be·at·i·tude (bē-ăt′ə-tōōd′, -tyōōd′) *n.* **1.** Supreme blessedness or happiness. **2. Beatitude.** Any of the nine declarations of blessedness made by Jesus in the Sermon on the Mount. Matthew 5:3–11. [Latin *beātitūdo,* from *beātus,* blessed. See **beatific.**]

Beat·les (bēt′əlz), **the.** English pop group, comprising John Lennon, Ringo Starr, Paul McCartney, and George Harrison. They were all born in Liverpool and began performing together in Liverpool clubs in 1960. They first gained international fame in 1962, with records such as "Love Me Do" and "Please Please Me." For the next eight years they were the most famous pop group in the world. The group disbanded in 1970.

beat·nik (bēt′nĭk) *n.* **1.** A member of the **beat generation** *(see).* **2.** Especially in the 1950's, a person whose dress and behavior showed pointed, often exaggerated, disregard for conventional norms. [BEAT + -NIK.]

Bea·ton (bēt′n), **Sir Cecil Walter Hardy** (1904–80). English photographer, internationally famous for his portraits of celebrities. He also designed many theatrical productions, including *My Fair Lady* (stage, 1956; film, 1964).

Be·a·trix (bē′ə-trĭks′), in full Beatrix Wilhelmina Armgard (1938–). Queen of the Netherlands. She became queen in April 1980 after the abdication of her mother, Juliana.

beau (bō) *n., pl.* **beaus** (bōz) or **beaux. 1.** The sweetheart of a woman or girl. **2.** A man excessively interested in fine clothes and social etiquette; a dandy. [French, fine, handsome, from Latin *bellus,* pretty, handsome, fine.]

Beau Brum·mell (bō brŭm′əl) *n.* A dandy; fop. [After George Bryan ("*Beau*") BRUMMELL.]

Beau·fort scale (bō′fərt) *n.* A scale on which successive ranges of wind velocities are assigned code numbers from 0 to 12 or from 0 to 17, corresponding to names from *calm* to *hurricane.* [After Sir Francis *Beaufort* (1774–1857), British admiral.]

Beaufort Sea. Sea in the Arctic Ocean, lying between Point Barrow, Alaska, and the Canadian Arctic Archipelago. It is never free of pack ice.

beau geste (bō zhĕst′) *n., pl.* **beaux gestes** (bō zhĕst′) or **beau gestes** (bō zhĕst′). **1.** A gracious gesture. **2.** A gesture noble in form but meaningless in substance. [French, "beautiful gesture."]

Beau·har·nais (bō-är-nā′), **Alexandre, Vicomte de** (1760–94). French general, who fought on the side of the Colonists in the American Revolution and then in France in the Revolutionary army. He was guillotined during the Reign of Terror.

Beauharnais, Joséphine de. See **Joséphine.**

beau i·de·al (bō ī-dē′əl) *n., pl.* **beau ideals. 1.** The concept of perfect beauty. **2.** An idealized type or model. [French *beau idéal,* "ideal beauty."]

Beau·jo·lais[1] (bō′zhə-lā′). Hilly region of east-central France, lying west of the Saône River between Mâcon and Lyon. It is one of the most famous wine districts in France.

Beau·jo·lais[2] (bō′zhə-lā′) *n. Often* **beaujolais.** A light red or white wine from central France.

Beau·mar·chais (bō-mär-shā′), **Pierre Augustin Caron de** (1732–99). French dramatist. His two most famous plays, both rich in subversive innuendo against feudal privileges, served as the basis for Rossini's *The Barber of Seville* and Mozart's *The Marriage of Figaro.*

beau monde (bō mŏnd′; *French* bō môN′d) *n., pl.* **beaux mondes** (bō mŏnd′) or **beau mondes** (bō mŏndz′). Fashionable society. [French, "beautiful world."]

Beau·mont (bō′mŏnt), **Francis** (1584–1616). English dramatist who collaborated with John Fletcher from *c.* 1606 until *c.* 1616. Their most famous joint work was *The Maid's Tragedy* (1611). Beaumont is credited with the sole authorship of *The Woman Hater* (1607) and *The Knight of the Burning Pestle* (*c.* 1607).

Beaune (bōn). Small town in Côte-d'Or department in southeastern France. The center of the Burgundy wine industry, its vineyards date from the period of Roman occupation.

Beau·re·gard (bō′rə-gärd′), **Pierre Gustave Toutant de** (1818–93). Confederate army officer in the Civil War. He gave the order to fire on Fort Sumter and fought at the first Battle of Bull Run (1861) and the Battle of Shiloh (1862).

beaut (byōōt) *n. Slang.* Something outstanding of its kind. [Short for BEAUTY.]

beau·te·ous (byōō′tē-əs, -tyəs) *adj.* Beautiful, especially to the sight. —**beau·te·ous·ly** *adv.* —**beau·te·ous·ness** *n.*

beau·ti·cian (byōō-tĭsh′ən) *n.* One skilled in cosmetic treatment, especially one working in a beauty salon. [BEAUT(Y) + -ICIAN.]

beau·ti·ful (byōō′tə-fəl) *adj.* **1.** Pleasing to the senses. **2.** Pleasing to the mind: *a beautiful irony.* **3.** Excellent. **4.** Desirable; of great worth: *Small is beautiful.* —*n.* Beauty, as an aesthetic or philosophical principle. Preceded by *the.* —**beau·ti·ful·ly** *adv.* —**beau·ti·ful·ness** *n.*
Synonyms: comely, fair, handsome, lovely, pretty.

beautiful people *pl.n.* People who are prominent and fashionable, especially in international society.

beau·ti·fy (byōō′tə-fī) *v.* **-fied, -fying, -fies.** —*tr.* To make beautiful; adorn. —*intr.* To become beautiful. [BEAUT(Y) + -FY.] —**beau·ti·fi·ca·tion** *n.* —**beau·ti·fi·er** *n.*

beau·ty (byōō′tē) *n., pl.* **-ties. 1.** A quality that appeals to the senses or the mind through harmony of form or color, excellence of art-

istry or craftsmanship, truthfulness, originality, or some other, often unspecifiable, property. **2.** Appearance or sound that arouses a strong, contemplative delight; loveliness: *a woman who has preserved her youthful beauty.* **3.** A person or thing that arouses such delight; especially, a woman widely regarded as beautiful. **4.** A part, characteristic, or attribute that arouses such delight; a specific excellence or grace. **5.** The feature that is most effective, gratifying, or telling: *The beauty of the venture is that we stand to lose nothing.* **6.** *Informal.* An outstanding or conspicuous example. [Middle English *beau(l)te,* from Old French *bealte, beaute,* from Vulgar Latin *bellitās* (unattested), from Latin *bellus,* pretty, handsome, fine.]

beau·ty·ber·ry (byōō′tē-bĕr′ē) *n., pl.* **-ries.** Any shrub of the genus *Callicarpa,* having glistening, purplish, berrylike fruit. *C. americana,* of southeastern North America, is also called "Bermuda mulberry," "French mulberry."

beauty contest *n.* A competition in which a number of girls or women are judged on the basis of appearance.

beauty queen *n.* A girl or woman who has won a beauty contest or who enters such contests.

beauty salon *n.* An establishment providing services that include hair treatment, manicures, facials, and the like. Also called "beauty parlor," "beauty shop."

beauty sleep *n.* Sleep, especially in the hours before midnight, supposed to preserve a youthful appearance.

beauty spot *n.* **1.** Formerly, a small black mark glued on a woman's face or shoulders to accentuate the fairness of her skin. Also called "patch." **2.** A mole or freckle. **3.** A place of outstanding natural beauty.

Beau·vais (bō-vā′). Town in the Oise department in northern France. Its world-famous tapestry works, established as a royal factory in the 17th century, was destroyed in World War II. The Cathedral of St. Pierre, intended to be the largest in Christendom, was never completed, but its Gothic choir remains the loftiest (48 meters; 157 feet) in the world.

Beau·voir (bō-vwär′), **Simone de** (1908–86). French writer and feminist thinker. For many years the lover of Jean Paul Sartre, she devoted much of her writing to the exploration of existentialist themes. Her best-known works are the feminist treatise *The Second Sex* (1949–50), her autobiography, and a study of different cultures' treatment of old age, *The Coming of Age* (1970).

beaux. Alternative plural of **beau.**

beaux-arts (bō-zàr′) *pl.n. French.* The fine arts.

bea·ver[1] (bē′vər) *n.* **1.** A large, amphibious rodent of the genus *Castor,* of Eurasia and North America, having thick brown fur, webbed hind feet, a paddlelike, hairless tail, and chisellike front teeth adapted for gnawing bark and felling trees used to build dams. **2.** The fur of a beaver. **3. a.** A full beard. **b.** A bearded man. **4.** A top hat, originally made of the beaver's underfur. **5.** A napped wool fabric, similar to felt, used for outer garments. **6.** Grayish brown to light or dark grayish yellowish brown.
—*intr.v.* **beavered, -vering, -vers.** *Chiefly British.* To work with determination. Used with *away.* [Middle English *bever,* Old English *be(o)for.*]

beaver[2] *n.* **1.** A movable piece of medieval armor attached to a helmet or breastplate to protect the mouth and chin. **2.** The visor on a helmet. [Middle English *baviere,* from Old French, *bib,* from *baver,* to slaver, from *beve,* saliva, from (unattested) Vulgar Latin *baba* (imitative).]

bea·ver·board (bē′vər-bôrd′, -bōrd′) *n.* A light, semirigid building material of compressed wood pulp, used for walls and partitions. [From the former trademark *Beaverboard.*]

Bea·ver·brook (bē′vər-brŏŏk′), **William Maxwell Aitken, 1st Baron** (1879–1964). British press baron, financier, and politician, born in Canada. He came to England in 1910, was elected to Parliament, and remained in the House of Commons until 1917, when he was given a peerage. He gained control of the *Daily Express* in 1916 and the *Evening Standard* in 1923. He was minister of aircraft production (1940–41), of war production (1942), and lord privy seal (1943–45). His writings include *Politicians and the War, 1914–1916* (1928, 1932), and *Men and Power: 1917–1918* (1956).

be·bop (bē′bŏp′) *n.* A type of music, **bop** *(see).* [Imitative of a two-beat phrase in this music.]

be·calm (bĭ-käm′) *tr.v.* **-calmed, -calming, -calms. 1.** To render (a ship) motionless for lack of wind. **2.** To make calm or still; soothe.

be·came. Past tense of **become.**

be·cause (bĭ-kôz′, -kŭz′) *conj.* **1.** For the reason that; since. **2.** *Nonstandard.* The fact that: *Because you're here doesn't mean that I'm ready.* —**because of.** By reason of; on account of. [Middle English *bi cause* : *bi,* BY + CAUSE.]
Usage: In clauses introduced by *The reason that . . .* or *The reason is . . . ,* the use of *because* is common but superfluous. In a sentence like *The reason why you're tired is because you went to bed late* the notion of "cause" is expressed twice; it is sufficient to say *The reason you're tired is that you went to bed late,* or, more simply, *You're tired because you went to bed late.*

bec·ca·fi·co (bĕk′ə-fē′kō) *n., pl.* **-cos.** Any small songbird or warbler of various genera, eaten as a delicacy in Italy. [Italian, "figpecker" : *beccare,* to peck, from *becco,* beak, from Latin *beccus,* BEAK + *fico,* fig, from Latin *ficus,* FIG.]

bé·cha·mel sauce (bā′shə-mĕl′) *n.* A white sauce, made from butter, flour, milk or cream, and seasonings. Also called "sauce béchamel." [French *sauce béchamelle,* after Louis de *Béchamel,* steward of Louis XIV, who invented it.]

beaver

THE DAM BUILDERS
How the work of beavers helps to improve the environment

At one time beavers were valued only for their fur. Today, they are legally protected in most countries. North American beavers are recognized as natural conservationists; for the dams they build help to control the flow of mountain streams, preventing soil erosion and creating new homes for plants and animals.

Beavers, which are found mainly in North America and in the forests of northern Europe and Asia, are rodents—gnawing animals. They have powerful jaws and chisellike front teeth that enable them to gnaw on bark and vegetation for food and to fell trees for their dams.

The ponds that form above the dams become natural moats, keeping predators away from the wooden lodges that the beavers build. Dozens of animals may work together to construct a dam from wood, stones, mud, and weeds. The result can be huge: frequently 200 meters (about 650 feet) long and 4 meters (13 feet) high, and even up to 550 meters (1,800 feet) long.

Food store   Ventilated roof   Living area   Dam

BEAVERS' LODGE *Protected by the lake that forms behind their dam, beavers build dens called lodges, just above the water. Each lodge may be occupied by a family of up to ten animals—the parents and two litters of young—and several families may share the same lake, all helping to maintain or enlarge a single dam. The animals, who can stay submerged for up to 15 minutes, enter and leave the lodges through underwater passages.*

PADDLE AND RUDDER *The beaver's webbed feet serve as paddles, and its broad tail as a rudder. An adult can be 1 meter (3 feet 3 inches) long and weigh up to 15 kilograms (about 33 pounds).*

---

be·chance (bĭ-chăns′, -chäns′) *v.* **-chanced, -chancing, -chances.** *Rare.* —*intr.* To happen; chance. —*tr.* To befall; happen to.

bêche-de-mer (bĕsh′də-mâr′) *n., pl.* **bêches-de-mer** (bĕsh′də-mâr′). **1.** A marine animal, the **trepang** *(see),* or a food prepared from it. **2.** A lingua franca that combines Malay and English, spoken in the southwest Pacific. In this sense, also called "beach-la-mar." [French, from earlier *biche de mer,* from Portuguese *bicho do mar,* "sea worm" : *bicho,* worm, from Late Latin *bēstulus,* diminutive of Latin *bēstia,* BEAST + *mar,* sea, from Latin *mare.* The designation of the language is probably from the use of trepang as an important trade item in this area.]

Bech·u·a·na (bĕch′oō-ä′nə) *n., pl.* **-nas** or collectively **Bechuana.** **1.** A former name for a member of a Bantu people inhabiting Botswana in south-central Africa. **2.** A language, **Tswana** *(see).*

Bechuanaland. See **Botswana.**

beck¹ (bĕk) *n.* A gesture of beckoning or summons. —**at someone's beck and call.** Having to carry out someone's every wish. [Middle English, from *beknen,* from BECKON.]

beck² *n. British.* A small brook. [Middle English, from Old Norse *bekkr.*]

beck·et (bĕk′ĭt) *n. Nautical.* A device, such as a looped rope, hook and eye, strap, or grommet, for holding or fastening loose ropes, spars, or oars in position. [18th century : origin obscure.]

Beck·et (bĕk′ĭt), **Saint Thomas,** also known as "Thomas à Becket" (c. 1118-70). English cleric. He entered the household of Theobald, archbishop of Canterbury, in c. 1142 and was appointed archdeacon of Canterbury in 1154. In the same year Henry II made him his chancellor. Appointed archbishop of Canterbury in 1162, he fell into disfavor with Henry by becoming the spokesman for the Church. Charged in 1164 with misappropriating crown funds as chancellor, Becket fled the country and remained in exile for six years. He returned in 1170 and immediately became embroiled in the controversy surrounding Henry's illegal appointment of his eldest son as archbishop of York. At Henry's behest, four knights of the royal household murdered Becket in Canterbury Cathedral on December 29. He was canonized in 1173.

Beck·ett (bĕk′ĭt), **Samuel** (1906-   ). Irish playwright, novelist and critic. He settled in Paris in 1937, and many of his works are written in both French and English. His first novel, *Murphy* (1938), was followed by *Watt* (1942-44), *Malone Dies* (1951), and *Molloy* (1951). He is known to a wider audience for his plays in the style of the theater of the absurd, especially *Waiting for Godot* (1952), *Endgame* (1957), *Krapp's Last Tape* (1959), and *Happy Days* (1961). In 1969 he won the Nobel Prize for literature.

Beck·mann (bĕk′män), **Max** (1884-1950). German painter and printmaker. Beckmann developed an expressionist manner under the influence of Edvard Munch, and in the 1920's he came to his most lasting style, the painting of brutal, often grotesque, large figurative canvases. Persecuted by the Nazis, he fled to Amsterdam in 1937 and in 1947 settled in the United States, where he died.

Beck·mann thermometer (bĕk′mən, -män) *n.* A mercury thermometer with a small adjustable range, used in scientific experiments for the accurate measurement of small temperature changes. [After Ernst *Beckmann* (1853-1923), German chemist.]

beck·on (bĕk′ən) *v.* **-oned, -oning, -ons.** —*tr.* **1.** To signal or summon (another), as by nodding or waving. **2.** To attract as if with gestures; invite: *"a lovely, sunny country that seemed to beckon them on to the Emerald City"* (L. Frank Baum). —*intr.* **1.** To make a summoning or signaling gesture. **2.** To be attractive or enticing. ~*n.* A gesture or motion of summons. [Middle English *beknen,* Old English *bēcnan, bīecnan.*] —**beck·on·er** *n.* —**beck·on·ing·ly** *adv.*

be·cloud (bĭ-kloud′) *tr.v.* **-clouded, -clouding, -clouds.** **1.** To darken with clouds. **2.** To confuse; obscure.

be·come (bĭ-kŭm′) *v.* **-came** (-kām′), **-come, -coming, -comes.** —*intr.* To grow or come to be: *After two months together, the relationship was becoming predictable.* —*tr.* **1.** To be appropriate or suitable to: *"it would not become me . . . to interfere with parties"* (Jonathan Swift). **2.** To show to advantage; look good with or on. —**become of.** To be the fate or subsequent condition of; happen to. [Middle English *becomen,* Old English *becuman* : BE- + COME.]

be·com·ing (bĭ-kŭm′ĭng) *adj.* **1.** Appropriate; suitable; proper. **2.** Pleasing or attractive to the eye. —**be·com·ing·ly** *adv.* —**be·com·ing·ness** *n.*

Bec·que·rel (bĕ-krĕl′, bĕk′ə-rĕl′), **Antoine Henri** (1852-1908). French physicist, grandson of **Antoine César Becquerel** (1788-1878), one of the first investigators of electrochemistry, and son of **Alexandre Edmond Becquerel** (1820-91), the inventor of the phosphoroscope. Principally devoted to the study of the effect of the earth's magnetism on the atmosphere, he discovered radioactivity in uranium (1896) and shared the Nobel Prize for physics (1903) with Marie and Pierre Curie.

bed (bĕd) *n.* **1. a.** A piece of furniture for reclining and sleeping, typically consisting of a flat, rectangular frame, a mattress resting on springs, and bedclothes. **b.** A bedstead. **c.** A mattress or a mattress with bedclothes. **2. a.** Rest or sleep. **b.** Any place or surface upon which one may rest or sleep. **c.** A place where one may sleep for the night; a lodging. **3. a.** Sexual intercourse. **b.** A situation of

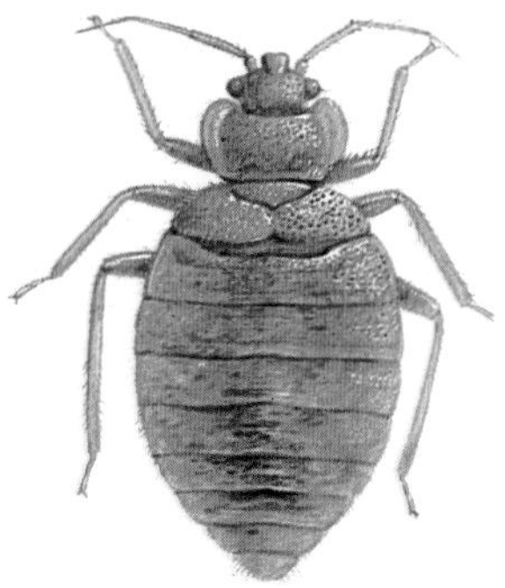

bedbug *This blood-sucking insect—which is 4–6 millimeters (1/4 inch) long—is so named because it feeds at night, sometimes on sleeping humans. It is not common nowadays in most developed countries.*

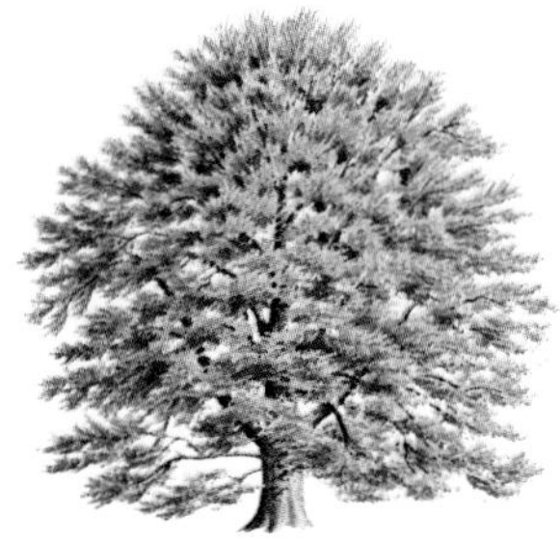

beech *The knot-free and supple, fine-grained wood of this tree is ideal for making chairs. The prickly fruit are known as mast.*

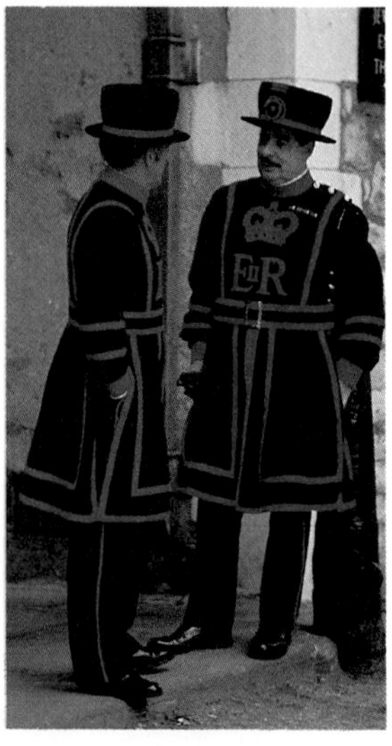

beefeater *Yeomen warders of the Tower of London in their day uniform. First formed as a royal bodyguard for the coronation of Henry VII in 1485, the yeomen are thought to have acquired their nickname from an envious reference to their generous rations.*

sexual intimacy. **4. a.** A small plot of cultivated or planted land: *a flower bed.* **b.** Part of a river or sea bed used for cultivation, especially of oysters. **5.** The bottom of a watercourse or other body of water. **6.** A supporting, underlying, or securing part, especially: **a.** A layer of food on which another kind of food rests: *lobster on a bed of rice.* **b.** A foundation of crushed rock or a similar substance for a road or railway; roadbed. **c.** A layer of mortar upon which stones or bricks are laid. **d.** The flat underside of something, as of a brick. **e.** The heavy table of a printing press in which the type form is placed. **7.** *Geology.* **a.** A rock mass of large horizontal extent bounded, especially above, by physically different material. **b.** A deposit, as of ore or lava, parallel to the local stratification. Compare **mass, vein.** **—put** (or **go**) **to bed.** In journalism, to send or go to press; have or be printed.
~*v.* **bedded, bedding, beds.** —*tr.* **1.** To provide with a bed or sleeping place. **2.** To put to bed. **3.** To embed. **4.** To make a bed for; spread litter for. Usually used with *down: She bedded down the sheep under a lean-to.* **5.** To plant in a prepared bed of soil. **6.** To lay flat or arrange in layers. **7.** To have sexual intercourse with. —*intr.* **1.** To go to bed. Usually used with *down.* **2.** To form layers or strata. [Middle English *bed(e),* Old English *bed(d).*]

B.Ed. Bachelor of Education.

bed and board *n.* Sleeping accommodation and meals.

bed and breakfast *n. Abbr.* **b. & b. 1.** Overnight accommodation and breakfast. **2.** A guest house or private house providing this. **—bed-and-breakfast** *adj.*

be·daub (bĭ-dôb′) *tr.v.* **-daubed, -daubing, -daubs. 1.** To smear; soil. **2.** To ornament in a vulgar and showy fashion.

be·daz·zle (bĭ-dăz′əl) *tr.v.* **-zled, -zling, -zles.** To dazzle so completely as to confuse or blind. **—be·daz·zle·ment** *n.*

bed·bug, bed bug (bĕd′bŭg′) *n.* A wingless, bloodsucking insect of the genus *Cimex*; especially, *C. lectularius,* that has a flat, reddish body and a disagreeable odor and that often infests dirty human dwellings.

bed·cham·ber (bĕd′chām′bər) *n.* A bedroom.

bed·clothes (bĕd′klōz′, -klōthz′) *pl.n.* Coverings, such as sheets and blankets, used on a bed.

bed·ding (bĕd′ĭng) *n.* **1.** Bedclothes. **2.** Straw or similar material for animals to sleep on. **3.** Something that forms a foundation or bottom layer. **4.** *Geology.* Stratification or layering of rocks.

Bede (bēd), **Saint.** Also **Bae·da** (bē′də). (*c.* 673–735). Anglo-Saxon Benedictine monk and scholar known as the "the Venerable Bede." His theological works gained him the title of Doctor of the Church, the only Englishman so honored. He is best known for his *Historia Ecclesiastica Gentis Anglorum (Ecclesiastical History of the English Nation),* a record of the spread of Christianity and Anglo-Saxon culture in Britain. He was canonized in 1899.

be·deck (bĭ-dĕk′) *tr.v.* **-decked, -decking, -decks.** To deck out or adorn in a showy fashion; cover with decorations.

bedes·man (bēdz′mən) *n., pl.* **-men** (-mĭn). Formerly, an almsman. [Variant of *beadsman,* an almsman who had promised to pray (or say the rosary) for his benefactor.]

be·dev·il (bĭ-dĕv′əl) *tr.v.* **-iled, -iling, -ils** or *chiefly British* **-illed, -illing. 1.** To torment devilishly; plague; harass. **2.** To worry, annoy, or frustrate. **3.** To possess as with a devil; bewitch. **4.** To spoil; ruin. **—be·dev·il·ment** *n.*

be·dew (bĭ-do͞o′, -dyo͞o′) *tr.v.* **-dewed, -dewing, -dews.** To wet with or as if with dew.

bed·fel·low (bĕd′fĕl′ō) *n.* **1.** A person with whom one shares a bed; a bedmate. **2.** A temporary associate, collaborator, or ally.

Bed·ford (bĕd′fərd). Town in central England, on the Great Ouse River. The county town of Bedfordshire, it was the site of a British victory over the Saxons in 571.

Bedford cord *n.* A heavy cotton or woolen fabric in a ribbed weave with wide or narrow raised cords, similar to corduroy. [After BEDFORD, where it was made.]

Bed·ford·shire (bĕd′fərd-shîr, -shər). County in central England, most of it lying in the fertile valley of the Great Ouse River. Its county town is Bedford.

be·dight (bĭ-dīt′) *tr.v.* **-dight, -dight** or **-dighted, -dighting, -dights.** *Archaic.* To dress or adorn. [Middle English *bedighten* : *be-,* thoroughly + DIGHT.]

be·dim (bĭ-dĭm′) *tr.v.* **-dimmed, -dimming, -dims.** To make dim.

be·di·zen (bĭ-dī′zən, -dĭz′ən) *tr.v.* **-zened, -zening, -zens.** To dress or ornament vulgarly or tastelessly. [BE- + DIZEN.] **—be·di·zen·ment** *n.*

bed jacket *n.* A jacket worn when sitting up in bed.

bed·lam (bĕd′ləm) *n.* **1.** Any place or scene of noisy uproar and confusion. **2.** *Archaic.* A lunatic asylum; madhouse. [Middle English *Bedlem, Bethlem,* Hospital of St. Mary of *Bethlehem,* in south-eastern London, which was an asylum at one time.]

bed linen *n.* The sheets and pillowcases used on a bed.

Bed·ling·ton terrier (bĕd′lĭng-tən) *n.* A dog of a breed developed in England, having long legs and a woolly grayish or brownish coat. [After *Bedlington,* northeastern England.]

bed·mate (bĕd′māt′) *n.* One with whom a bed is shared.

bed molding *n. Architecture.* **1.** The molding between the corona and frieze of an entablature. **2.** Any molding below a projection.

bed of roses *n.* A state of idyllic comfort or luxury.

Bed·ou·in, Bed·u·in (bĕd′o͞o-ĭn) *n., pl.* **-ins** or collectively **Bedouin** or **Beduin.** An Arab of any of the nomadic tribes of the deserts of North Africa, Arabia, Jordan, and Syria. [Middle English *Bedoin,* from Old French *beduin,* from Arabic *badāwīn,* desert dwellers, plural of *badāwī,* from *badw,* desert.] **—Bed·ou·in** *adj.*

bed·pan (bĕd′păn′) *n.* **1.** A metal, glass, or plastic receptacle for the excreta of people who are bedridden. **2.** A **warming pan** *(see).*

bed·plate (bĕd′plāt′) *n.* A metal plate, frame, or platform serving as a base or support for a machine.

bed·post (bĕd′pōst′) *n.* Any of the four vertical posts at the corners of some beds.

be·drag·gled (bĭ-drăg′əld) *adj.* Wet, limp, and untidy. Said of the hair, clothes, or appearance.

bed·rid·den (bĕd′rĭd′n) *adj.* Confined to one's bed because of illness or infirmity. [Middle English *bedreden, bedrede,* Old English *bedrida,* from noun, "one who is bedridden" : BED + *rīda,* a rider, from *rīdan,* to RIDE.]

bed·rock (bĕd′rŏk′) *n.* **1.** The solid rock that underlies all soil, sand, clay, gravel, and loose material on the earth's surface. **2.** The lowest or bottom level. **3.** Fundamental principles.

bed·roll (bĕd′rōl′) *n.* A portable roll of bedding used especially by campers and others who sleep outdoors. Compare **sleeping bag.**

bed·room (bĕd′ro͝om′, -ro͞om′) *n.* A room for sleeping in.

bed·side (bĕd′sīd′) *n.* The space alongside a bed, especially the bed of a sick person.
~*adj.* Near a bed: *a bedside table.*

bedside manner *n.* The attitude and conduct of a doctor in the presence of a patient, intended to inspire confidence and allay fears.

bed·sit·ter (bĕd′sĭt′ər) *n. Chiefly British.* An **efficiency apartment** *(see).* Also called "bedsit," "bed-sitting room."

bed·sore (bĕd′sôr′, -sōr′) *n.* A pressure-induced ulceration of the skin with necrosis and sometimes deep muscular infection, occurring during long confinement in bed. Also called "decubitus ulcer," "pressure sore."

bed·spread (bĕd′sprĕd′) *n.* A usually decorative bed covering.

bed·spring (bĕd′sprĭng′) *n.* **1.** The network of springs supporting the mattress of a bed. **2.** Any of these springs.

bed·stead (bĕd′stĕd′) *n.* The frame of a bed, which supports the mattress.

bed·straw (bĕd′strô′) *n.* Any of various plants of the genus *Galium,* such as *G. verum* (lady's bedstraw), having whorled leaves, small white or yellow flowers, and prickly burrs. [After its former use as a mattress stuffing.]

bed·time (bĕd′tīm′) *n.* The time when one goes or should go to bed.

Beduin. Variant of **Bedouin.**

bed-wet·ting (bĕd′-wĕt′ĭng) *n.* Urinating in bed, especially when considered as a condition that may require medical or psychiatric treatment; nocturnal **enuresis** *(see).* **—bed-wet·ter** *n.*

bee[1] (bē) *n.* **1.** Any of various winged, hairy-bodied, usually stinging insects of the order Hymenoptera, including many solitary species, such as the **mason bee** and **leaf-cutter bee** *(both of which see),* as well as the social members of the family Apidae. They are characterized by structures for sucking nectar and gathering pollen from flowers. See **bumblebee, honeybee. 2.** A social gathering where people combine work, competition, and amusement: *a spelling bee.* [Middle English *bee,* Old English *bēo.*]

bee[2] *n.* A **bee block** *(see).* [Middle English *bege,* a ring of metal, Old English *bēag.*]

Bee·be (bē′bē), **(Charles) William** (1879–1962). U.S. naturalist and author. From 1919 on he was director of the New York Zoological Society's department of tropical research. In 1934 he made a record descent into the ocean in a bathysphere he had helped design.

bee block *n. Nautical.* A piece of hardwood on either side of a bowsprit through which forestays are reeved. Also called "bee."

bee·bread (bē′brĕd′) *n.* A brownish substance consisting of a mixture of pollen and nectar, fed by bees to their larvae. Also called "ambrosia."

beech (bēch) *n.* **1.** Any tree of the genus *Fagus,* characterized by smooth, light-colored bark and edible nuts partly enclosed in a prickly husk, especially, *F. grandifolia,* of eastern North America, and *F. sylvatica,* of Europe. **2.** Any tree of the genus *Nothofagus,* of the Southern Hemisphere, similar to the northern beeches but with evergreen leaves. **3.** The wood of any of these trees. [Middle English *beche,* Old English *bēce.*] **—beech** *adj.*

Bee·cham (bē′chəm), **Sir Thomas** (1879–1961). British symphony conductor. He founded the London Philharmonic (1932) and the Royal Philharmonic (1946) orchestras and did much to popularize the works of Frederick Delius.

beech·drops (bēch′drŏps′) *n., pl.* **beechdrops.** A leafless plant, *Epifagus virginiana,* of eastern North America, that has brownish or purplish flowers and is parasitic on the roots of the beech tree.

Bee·cher (bē′chər), **Henry Ward** (1813–87). U.S. clergyman and reformer. He was well known for his opposition to slavery, his passionate sermons, and his unorthodox private life.

Beecher, Lyman (1775–1863). U.S. clergyman and reformer. He was a fiery preacher, a strong abolitionist, and patriarch of a remarkable family that included Henry Ward Beecher and Harriet Beecher Stowe.

beech marten *n.* A **stone marten** *(see).*

beech mast *n.* The nuts of the beech tree; beechnuts.

beech·nut (bēch′nŭt′) *n.* The small, triangular nut of the beech tree, which provides food for livestock.

bee-eat·er (bē′ē′tər) *n.* Any of various chiefly tropical Old World birds of the family Meropidae, having brightly colored plumage and a downward-curving bill, and feeding chiefly on bees.

beef (bēf) *n., pl.* **beeves** (bēvz) or **beefs** (only form for sense 4).

1. The flesh of a slaughtered full-grown bull, ox, or cow. **2.** A full-grown bull, ox, or cow, especially one intended for use as meat. **3.** *Informal.* Human muscle; brawn. **4.** *Slang.* A complaint. ~*intr.v.* **beefed, beefing, beefs.** *Slang.* To complain. —**beef up.** *Slang.* To reinforce; build up; fill out. [Middle English *boef, beef,* beef, ox, from Old French *boef,* from Latin *bōs* (stem *bov-*), ox.] —**beef** *adj.*

beef bour·gui·gnon (bŏōr'gē-nyôn') *n.* Also *French* **boeuf bour·gui·gnon** (bœf'bŏōr-gē-nyôn'). Braised cubes of beef simmered in a seasoned sauce with red wine, mushrooms, carrots, and onions. [Partial translation of French *boeuf bourguignon,* beef Burgundy style, from *Bourgogne,* BURGUNDY.]

beef·burg·er (bēf'bûr'gər) *n.* A hamburger.

beef·cake (bēf'kāk') *n. Slang.* **1.** A photograph, as in an advertisement, of a scantily clothed man showing off his muscular physique. **2.** Such photographs collectively. **3.** Men who appear, or look as though they might appear, in such photographs. Compare **cheesecake.** [BEEF + (CHEESE)CAKE.]

beef cattle *pl.n.* Cows, bulls, or oxen bred and raised for meat.

beef·eat·er (bēf'ē'tər) *n.* A yeoman of the royal guard in England or a yeoman warder of the Tower of London, wearing a characteristic red and gold or red and black uniform. [17th century : popular term for a well-fed servant.]

bee fly *n.* Any of various flies of the family Bombyliidae, resembling bees and having larvae that are parasitic on the young of bees, wasps, and other insects.

beef·steak (bēf'stāk') *n.* A thick slice of beef, as from the loin or the hindquarters, suitable for grilling or frying.

beefsteak fungus *n.* An edible fungus, *Fistularia hepatica,* growing on decaying wood and having a large, irregularly shaped reddish cap.

beef stro·ga·noff (strô'gə-nôf', -nŏf', strō-gän'ôf) *n.* Thinly sliced beef fillet sautéed and served with mushrooms and sour cream. [After Count Paul *Stroganoff,* 19th-century Russian diplomat.]

beef tea *n.* Broth made from beef extract or by boiling pieces of lean beef, often used as a restorative and for invalids.

beef Wellington *n.* Roast fillet of beef, covered with paté de foie gras and pastry, and baked. [After the 1st Duke of WELLINGTON.]

beef·wood (bēf'wŏod') *n.* Any of various trees of the genus *Casuarina,* mostly native to Australia, having small, scalelike leaves and flowers and very hard wood. Also called "she-oak." [Perhaps from its reddish color.]

beef·y (bē'fē) *adj.* **-ier, -iest. 1.** Resembling beef. **2.** Muscular in build; heavy; brawny. —**beef·i·ness** *n.*

bee·hive (bē'hīv') *n.* **1.** A hive, either natural or manmade, for bees. **2.** Any place teeming with activity. **3.** A hairstyle in which the hair is backcombed and piled on top of the head.

bee·keep·er (bē'kē'pər) *n.* One who keeps bees; apiarist.

bee·line (bē'līn') *n.* A fast, direct course. Used chiefly in the phrase *make a beeline for.* [From the belief that a pollen-laden bee flies straight back to its hive.]

Be·el·ze·bub (bē-ĕl'zĭ-bŭb'). **1.** The Devil. **2.** In Milton's *Paradise Lost,* the chief of the fallen angels, next to Satan in power. [Late Latin, from Greek *Beelzeboub,* from Hebrew *bá'al zəbūb,* "lord of flies," god of the Ekronites (II Kings 1:2) : *bá'al,* lord + *zəbūb,* fly.]

bee moth *n.* A pyralid moth, such as *Galleria mellonella,* that lays its eggs in beehives, where the larvae feed on the honeycombs and the young bees. Also called "wax moth."

been. Past participle of **be.**

been·to, bin·tu (bĭn'tōo) *n. British Informal.* An African or Asian who has lived in Britain for part of his life, especially one who has received his education there, and has since returned to his country of origin. Used in various African and Asian countries. [From *been to* (Britain).] —**been·to** *adj.*

bee orchid *n.* A European orchid, *Ophrys apifera,* having a flower that resembles a bumblebee.

beep (bēp) *n.* A high-pitched sound such as that emitted by a car horn or some types of electrical apparatus. ~*v.* **beeped, beeping, beeps.** —*intr.* To make a beep. —*tr.* To cause to make a beep. [Imitative.]

beep·er (bē'pər) *n.* **1.** One that beeps. **2.** A small portable electronic device that emits a beeping signal when the person carrying it is being paged.

beer (bîr) *n.* **1.** A fermented alcoholic beverage brewed from malt and flavored with hops. **2.** Any of various drinks made from extracts of roots and plants. **3.** A glass or mug of such a drink. [Middle English *ber(e),* Old English *bēor,* from a West Germanic word, from Late Latin *biber,* a drink, from Latin *bibere,* to drink.]

beer and skittles *n. Slang.* Easygoing existence.

beer belly *n.* A person's stomach that is excessively large from the regular consumption of beer or some other alcoholic beverage.

Beer·bohm (bîr'bŏm'), **Sir (Henry) Max(imilian)** (1872–1956). English caricaturist and writer, called by George Bernard Shaw "the incomparable Max." He was the half-brother of the actor-producer Sir Herbert Beerbohm Tree. His first satirical essays, *The Works of Max Beerbohm,* and his first caricatures, *Caricatures of Twenty-five Gentlemen,* both appeared in 1896. His only novel, *Zuleika Dobson,* an Oxford fantasy, was published in 1911. After 1910 he lived, apart from the World War II years, in Rapallo, Italy. He was knighted in 1939.

Beer·she·ba (bîr-shē'bə). *Hebrew* **Be·'er She·va'** (bîr shĕ'və). Town in southern Israel. It was famous in Biblical times as the abode of Isaac and Jacob and as the place where Abraham made his cov-

---

bee

INSIDE A BEEHIVE

A rigid caste system separates queen, drone, and worker

Most of the 12,000 species of bees in the world are solitary insects, coming together only to mate. Honeybees, on the other hand, live in highly organized colonies—sometimes in hives provided for them by beekeepers. Each colony contains, on average, a single queen—a fertile female who lives for between four and five years—a few dozen drones, or male bees, and about 60,000 worker bees—sterile females.

The workers, who rarely live more than a few months, collect nectar for the hive's winter food store of honey, build honeycombs from wax produced by their bodies, and bring pollen to the hive to feed the young larvae. In a good summer, a single colony can produce 30 kilograms (66 pounds) of honey.

The drones have to be fed by the workers because they are unable to feed themselves. The drones' only function is to fertilize a young queen before she takes over a colony from a dead or aging queen, or flies off with half the workers (known as swarming) to found a new one. Fertilization takes place in midair during a mating flight by the queen. The five or six drones who succeed in mating with the queen die soon afterward. The remainder survive till the end of summer; then they are driven out of the colony by the workers to die.

From this single flight, the queen derives all the sperm she needs for a lifetime of egg laying. Thereafter, between early spring and late autumn each year, she lays eggs at the rate of about one a minute—up to 1,500 a day. Depending on the population balance of the colony, these eggs are either fertilized with the sperm she has stored in her body—and develop into females as workers or queens—or laid unfertilized—and hatch into male drones. Eggs that will grow into queens are identical at first to the eggs of the workers. But the queen eggs are laid in larger cells in the honeycomb and are given extra amounts of royal jelly—a milky substance that the workers secrete in their saliva and feed to the larvae.

As long as the existing queen remains healthy, she produces from glands on her head a pheromone known as queen substance that has the effect of calming the workers and preventing them from raising new queens. But when she sickens or dies, the pheromone supply is cut off, and the workers immediately start to rear new queens to replace her.

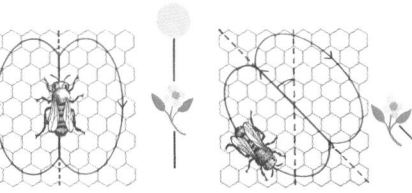

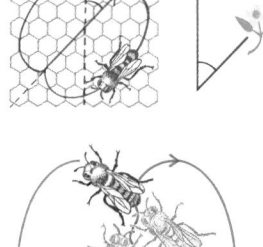

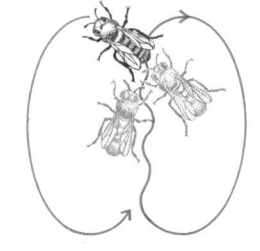

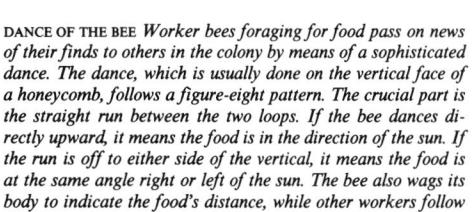

DANCE OF THE BEE *Worker bees foraging for food pass on news of their finds to others in the colony by means of a sophisticated dance. The dance, which is usually done on the vertical face of a honeycomb, follows a figure-eight pattern. The crucial part is the straight run between the two loops. If the bee dances directly upward, it means the food is in the direction of the sun. If the run is off to either side of the vertical, it means the food is at the same angle right or left of the sun. The bee also wags its body to indicate the food's distance, while other workers follow the dancer, apparently to help them memorize the information.*

---

enant with the Philistines. The city is still, as it has been for centuries, a watering place and market center for the nomadic Bedouins of the Negev.

beer·y (bîr'ē) *adj.* **-ier, -iest. 1.** Smelling or tasting of beer. **2.** Affected or produced by beer.

bee's knees *n.* Used with a singular verb. *Chiefly British Informal.* A person or thing considered to be marvelous. Preceded by *the.*

beest·ings (bē'stĭngz) *n.* Used with a singular or plural verb. The first milk given by a cow or other mammal after parturition; colostrum. [Middle English *bestynge* (singular), Old English *bēsting* (untested), from *bēost,* beestings, akin to Middle Dutch *biest,* Old High German *biost†.*]

bees·wax (bēz'wăks') *n.* **1.** The yellowish to dark-brown wax secreted by the honeybee for making honeycombs. **2.** Commercial wax obtained by processing and purifying the crude wax of the honeybee, used in making candles, crayons, and polishes. ~*tr.v.* **beeswaxed, -waxing, -waxes.** To polish with this wax. [From *bee's wax.*]

bees·wing (bēz'wĭng') *n.* **1.** A thin crust of tartar scales that sometimes forms on old port or other old wines. **2.** Wine affected by this crust. [From *bee's wing.*]

beet (bēt) *n.* **1.** Any of several widely cultivated plants of the genus *Beta;* especially, *B. vulgaris,* having leaves sometimes eaten as greens and a thickened, fleshy root. See **sugar beet. 2.** The bulbous root of this plant, characteristically dark red in color, eaten as a vegetable. Also *chiefly British* "beetroot." [Middle English *bete,* Old English *bēte,* from Latin *bēta†.*]

Bee·tho·ven (bā'tō-vən), **Ludwig van** (1770–1827). German composer. He was an outstanding representative of the transition from the classical to the romantic era of musical composition. He was born in Bonn, but settled in Vienna (1792). In 1801 his hearing began to fail and by 1819 he was deaf. He wrote music of all genres,

bee orchid *The flower of this plant appears to have a female bumblebee resting on it. The ruse attracts male bumblebees, which try to mate with the female and in doing so pollinate the flower.*

including 9 symphonies, 5 piano concertos, 1 violin concerto, 32 piano sonatas, 10 violin sonatas, 5 cello sonatas, 2 Masses, and 1 opera, *Fidelio.*

bee·tle¹ (bēt′l) *n.* **1.** Any of numerous insects of the order Coleoptera, having biting mouth parts and front wings modified to form horny wing covers that overlie the membranous rear wings when at rest. **2.** Loosely, any insect resembling a beetle.
~*intr.v.* **beetled, -tling, -tles.** To hurry off; scuttle. Usually used with *off.* [Middle English *bityl,* Old English *bitula, biter,* from *bītan,* to BITE.]

beetle² *adj.* Jutting; overhanging: *beetle brows.*
~*intr.v.* **beetled, -tling, -tles.** To overhang. [Middle English *bitel-(brouwe),* origin obscure.]

beetle³ *n.* **1.** A heavy mallet with a large wooden head. **2.** A small wooden household mallet. **3.** A heavy wooden club used in stamping and finishing handmade linen. **4.** A cloth-finishing machine that stamps cloth with revolving wooden hammers.
~*tr.v.* **beetled, -tling, -tles. 1.** To pound with a beetle. **2.** To stamp and finish (cloth) with a beetle. [Middle English *betel,* Old English *bētel,* from Germanic *bautilaz* (unattested), from *bautan* (unattested), to BEAT.]

bee·tle-browed (bēt′l-broud′) *adj.* Having projecting and shaggy eyebrows.

beet·root (bēt′rōōt′, -rōōt′) *n. British.* The beet.

beet sugar *n.* The sugar that is obtained from sugar beets.

beeves. A plural of **beef.**

be·fall (bĭ-fôl′) *v.* **-fell** (-fĕl′), **-fallen** (-fôl′ən), **-falling, -falls.** —*intr.* To come to pass; happen. —*tr.* To happen to: *"There shall no evil befall thee"* (Psalms 91:10). —See Synonyms at **happen.**

be·fit (bĭ-fĭt′) *tr.v.* **-fitted, -fitting, -fits.** To be suitable to or appropriate for.

be·fit·ting (bĭ-fĭt′ĭng) *adj.* Appropriate; suitable; proper. —**be·fit·ting·ly** *adv.*

be·fog (bĭ-fôg′, -fŏg′) *tr.v.* **-fogged, -fogging, -fogs. 1.** To cover or obscure with or as if with fog; make foggy. **2.** To cause confusion in; muddle.

be·fool (bĭ-fōōl′) *tr.v.* **-fooled, -fooling, -fools. 1.** To make a fool of; hoodwink; trick; deceive. **2.** To treat as a fool.

be·fore (bĭ-fôr′, -fōr′) *adv.* **1.** In front; ahead; in advance. **2.** In the past; previously.
~*prep.* **1.** In front of; ahead of. **2.** Prior to. **3.** Awaiting: *Your happiness lies before you.* **4.** In or into the presence of: *She ordered the man to be brought before her.* **5.** Under the consideration or jurisdiction of: *the case before the court.* **6.** In preference to; sooner than. **7.** In advance of, or in precedence to, as in rank, condition, or development: *The princess is before him in the line of succession.*
~*conj.* **1.** In advance of the time when: *before he went.* **2.** Rather than; sooner than: *She would die before she would betray her cause.* [Middle English *before(n),* Old English *beforan,* from Germanic : *bi-* (unattested), BY + *forana* (unattested), from the front.]

be·fore·hand (bĭ-fôr′hănd′, bĭ-fōr′-) *adv.* In anticipation; in advance; early: *We arrived beforehand.* —**be·fore·hand** *adj.*

be·fore·time (bĭ-fôr′tīm′, bĭ-fōr′-) *adv. Rare.* Formerly.

be·foul (bĭ-foul′) *tr.v.* **-fouled, -fouling, -fouls. 1.** To make dirty; soil. **2.** To speak badly of; cast aspersions upon.

be·friend (bĭ-frĕnd′) *tr.v.* **-friended, -friending, -friends. 1.** To make friends with; initiate friendship with. **2.** To act as a friend to; aid; assist.

be·fud·dle (bĭ-fŭd′l) *tr.v.* **-dled, -dling, -dles. 1.** To confuse; perplex. **2.** To stupefy with or as if with alcoholic drink.

beg¹ (bĕg) *v.* **begged, begging, begs.** —*tr.* **1.** To ask for as charity. **2.** To ask earnestly for, or of; entreat. **3.** To leave (a point) unresolved. —*intr.* **1.** To solicit alms. **2.** To make a humble or urgent plea. —**beg off.** To seek release from (a penalty or obligation). —**go begging.** To be unclaimed or unwanted. [Middle English *beggen†.*]
Synonyms: beseech, crave, entreat, implore, importune.

beg² (bĕg, bāg) *n.* A governor or other official of the Ottoman Empire or Mogul Empire; bey. [Ottoman Turkish, BEY.]

be·gan. Past tense of **begin.**

be·get (bĭ-gĕt′) *tr.v.* **-got** (-gŏt′) or *rare* **-gat** (-găt′) **-gotten** (-gŏt′n) or **-got, -getting, -gets. 1.** To father; sire. **2.** To cause to exist. [Middle English *begeten,* to acquire, procreate, Old English *begietan.*] —**be·get·ter** *n.*

beg·gar (bĕg′ər) *n.* **1.** One who solicits alms. **2.** One who has no money; an impoverished person; a pauper. **3.** A rascal; rogue: *lucky beggar.* —**beggars can't be choosers.** People who have nothing must accept what is offered.
~*tr.v.* **beggared, -garing, -gars. 1.** To impoverish; make a beggar of. **2.** To exhaust the resources of: *His beauty beggars all description.* [Middle English *begger(e), beggar(e),* from *beggen,* to BEG.]

beg·gar·ly (bĕg′ər-lē) *adj.* Of or pertaining to a beggar; very poor or meager: *a beggarly pension.* —**beg·gar·li·ness** *n.*

beg·gar-my-neigh·bor (bĕg′ər-mī-nā′bər) *n.* A simple card game of chance in which, by means of face cards, one must capture all one's opponents' cards.
~*adj.* Helping oneself at the expense of others: *a beggar-my-neighbor policy.*

beg·gar's-lice (bĕg′ərz-līs′) *pl.n.* **1.** Used with a singular or plural verb. Any of several plants bearing small, prickly fruit that cling readily to clothing or the fur of animals, such as the **stickseed** (*see*). **2.** The seeds of such a plant.

beg·gar-ticks (bĕg′ər-tĭks′) *pl.n.* **1.** Used with a singular or plural

verb. Any of several plants having seeds that cling to clothing, often by means of barbed bristles; especially, the **bur marigold** and the **tick trefoil** (*both of which see*). **2.** The seeds of any of these plants.

beg·gar·y (bĕg′ə-rē) *n.* **1.** Extreme poverty; penury. **2.** The state or condition of being a beggar. **3.** Beggars collectively.

be·gin (bĭ-gĭn′) *v.* **-gan** (-găn′), **-gun** (-gŭn′), **-ginning, -gins.** —*intr.* **1.** To start; commence. **2.** To come into being: *when life began.* —*tr.* **1.** To start to do; commence. **2.** To be the cause or origin of: *It was her obstinacy that began the quarrel.* **3.** To show some likelihood of or capacity for: *doesn't begin to tackle the problem.* —**to begin with.** As a start; in the first place. [Begin, began, begun; Middle English *beginnen, bigan, begun,* Old English *beginnan, began, begunnen,* from West Germanic *bi-ginnan* (unattested) : *bi-,* BE + *-ginnan* (unattested), origin obscure.]
Synonyms: commence, inaugurate, initiate, start.

Be·gin (bā′gĭn), **Menachem** (1913-). Israeli politician, born in Brest in the U.S.S.R. He was sent to a labor camp in Siberia in 1941 for Zionist activities. Released in 1942, he went to Palestine, where he joined the Zionist underground movement, Irgun, which was campaigning for an independent Jewish state, and became its leader (1943-48). He helped found the Herut (Freedom) Party (1948), became its leader, and was elected to the Knesset. He became joint-chairman of the newly founded Likud Party (1973), led it to electoral victory, and became prime minister (1977-83). He shared the Nobel Peace Prize with Anwar el-Sadat (1978).

be·gin·ner (bĭ-gĭn′ər) *n.* **1.** One who begins something. **2.** One who is just starting to learn or do something; novice.

be·gin·ning (bĭ-gĭn′ĭng) *n.* **1.** The act or process of bringing, or being brought, into being; start; commencement. **2.** The time when something begins or is begun: *"In the beginning God created the heaven and the earth"* (Genesis 1:1). **3.** The place where something begins or is begun: *at the beginning of the road.* **4.** The source or origin of something: *"The fear of the Lord is the beginning of wisdom"* (Psalms 111:10). **5.** The first part: *the beginning of the play.* **6.** *Often* **beginnings.** The early or rudimentary phase: *the beginnings of history; the beginnings of an agreement.*

be·gird (bĭ-gûrd′) *tr.v.* **-girt** (-gûrt′) or **-girded, -girt, -girding, -girds.** To gird or encircle; surround.

be·gone (bĭ-gôn′, -gŏn′) *interj.* Used as an order of dismissal. [Middle English : BE (imperative) + GONE.]

be·go·nia (bĭ-gōn′yə) *n.* Any of various plants of the genus *Begonia,* mostly native to the tropics but widely cultivated, having leaves that are often brightly colored or veined and irregular, waxy flowers of various colors. [New Latin, after Michel *Bégon* (1638-1710), French governor in the West Indies and patron of science.]

be·gor·ra (bĭ-gôr′ə) *interj.* Used to express surprise, alarm, or the like. It is used only humorously, as a supposed characteristic of Irish speakers. [Euphemistic for *by God!*]

be·got. Past tense and alternative past participle of **beget.**

be·got·ten. Past participle of **beget.**

be·grime (bĭ-grīm′) *tr.v.* **-grimed, -griming, -grimes.** To smear or soil with dirt or grime.

be·grudge (bĭ-grŭj′) *tr.v.* **-grudged, -grudging, -grudges. 1. a.** To envy the possession or enjoyment of: *She begrudged his youth.* **b.** To envy for a possession: *She begrudged him his youth.* **2.** To give with reluctance.

be·guile (bĭ-gīl′) *tr.v.* **-guiled, -guiling, -guiles. 1.** To deceive by guile; delude: *"The serpent beguiled me and I did eat"* (Genesis 3:13). **2. a.** To take away from by guile; cheat. Used with *of* or *out of.* **b.** To divert; distract the attention of: *"to beguile you from the grief of a loss so overwhelming"* (Lincoln). **3.** To attract strongly; fascinate. **4.** To cause to vanish unnoticed or without pain: *"The history of a soldier's wound beguiles the pain of it"* (Lawrence Sterne). —See Synonyms at **deceive, lure.** [BE- + GUILE (verb).] —**be·guile·ment** *n.* —**be·guil·er** *n.*

be·guine (bĭ-gēn′) *n.* **1.** A ballroom dance in the rhythm of a bolero based on a dance originating in Martinique and St. Lucia. **2.** The music for this dance. [American French *béguine,* from French *béguin,* hood, flirtation (as in *avoir un béguin pour quelqu'un,* "to be sweet on someone"), probably from Old French *Beguine,* BEGUINE.]

Be·guine (bĕg′ēn′) *n.* A member of any of several Roman Catholic lay sisterhoods existing in the Netherlands since the 12th century. [Old French *Beguine,* perhaps after Lambert le *Bègue* (Lambert the Stammerer), priest of Liège who founded the community.]

be·gum (bē′gəm) *n.* A Muslim lady of high rank. [Urdu *begam,* from Ottoman Turkish *begim,* possessive of *beg,* BEY.]

be·gun. Past participle of **begin.**

be·half (bĭ-hăf′, -häf′) *n.* Interest, support, or benefit. Used chiefly in the phrases *in behalf of* and *on behalf of.* —See Usage note below. [Middle English *(on min) behalfe,* "on my side" : *be,* BY + *half,* side, HALF.]
Usage: *In behalf of* and *on behalf of* have distinct senses. *In behalf of* means "in the interest of" or "for the benefit of": *We raised money in behalf of the orphans. We acted in their behalf.* *On behalf of* means "as the agent of" or "on the part of": *The guardian sued on behalf of the minor child. On whose behalf did he act?*

Be·han (bē′ən), **Brendan** (1923-64). Irish writer. He joined the I.R.A. in 1937, was arrested in England in 1940, and was sentenced to three years in a reform school. The years were described in *The Borstal Boy* (1958). In 1942 he was convicted in Dublin of attempted murder and sentenced to 14 years' imprisonment. He was released in 1946. His prison years provided the experience for his most famous play, *The Quare Fellow* (1954). His later works include *Brendan Behan's Island* (1962) and *Confessions of an Irish Rebel* (1965).

be·have (bĭ-hāv′) *v.* **-haved, -having, -haves.** —*intr.* **1.** To act, react, function, or perform in a particular way. **2. a.** To conduct oneself in a specified way. **b.** To conduct oneself in a proper way. —*tr.* **1.** To conduct (oneself) properly. **2.** To conduct (oneself) in a specified way. [Middle English *behaven,* to hold oneself in a certain way : *be-,* thoroughly + *haven,* to HAVE.]

be·hav·ior (bĭ-hāv′yər) *n.* Also *chiefly British* **be·hav·iour. 1.** The manner in which one behaves; deportment; demeanor. **2.** The actions or reactions of persons or things under specified circumstances. —**be·hav·ior·al** *adj.* —**be·hav·ior·al·ly** *adv.*

behavioral science *n.* A science, such as sociology, psychology, or anthropology, that seeks to discover general truths about human social behavior. —**behavioral scientist** *n.*

be·hav·ior·ism (bĭ-hāv′yə-rĭz′əm) *n.* The psychological school holding that objectively observable organismic behavior constitutes the only valid scientific basis for psychological data and investigation and stressing the role of environment as a determinant of human and animal behavior. —**be·hav·ior·ist** *n.* —**be·hav·ior·is·tic** *adj.*

behavior therapy *n. Psychology.* Any method of treating psychological disorders that involves the patient's learning new patterns of behavior. It includes **aversion therapy** *(see).*

be·head (bĭ-hĕd′) *tr.v.* **-headed, -heading, -heads.** To separate the head from; decapitate. [Middle English *beheveden,* Old English *behēafdian : be-,* away from + *hēafdian,* to behead, from *hēafod,* HEAD.]

be·he·moth (bĭ-hē′məth, bē′ə-môth′) *n.* **1.** A huge animal, possibly the hippopotamus. Job 40:15-24. **2.** An enormous, or enormously powerful, person or thing. [Hebrew *bəhēmôth,* intensive plural ("great beasts") of *bəhēmāh,* beast.]

be·hest (bĭ-hĕst′) *n.* An order or authoritative command; a request or bidding. Used chiefly in the phrase *at the behest of.* [Middle English *behest,* promise, command, Old English *behǣs.*]

be·hind (bĭ-hīnd′) *adv.* **1.** In, to, or toward the rear: *He walked behind.* **2.** In a place or condition that has been passed or left: *He left his gloves behind.* **3.** In arrears; late: *fell behind in her payments.* **4.** Below the standard level; in an inferior position: *fall behind in class.* **5.** Slow: *His watch is running behind.* **6.** *Rare.* In reserve; yet to come: *There is no more behind.* ~*prep.* **1.** At the back of or in the rear of: *She sat behind him.* **2.** On the farther side of; beyond: *behind the door.* **3.** In a place or time that has been passed or left by: *Their worries are behind them.* **4.** After (a set time); later than: *The project was behind schedule.* **5.** Inferior to; less advanced than: *behind us in technology.* **6.** Hidden or concealed by: *behind the scenes.* **7.** Serving to support: *He had the army behind him.* ~*n. Informal.* The buttocks. [Middle English *bihinden,* Old English *behindan, bihindan : bi-,* BY + *hindan,* from behind.]

be·hind·hand (bĭ-hīnd′hănd′) *adv.* **1.** In arrears. **2.** Behind time; slow. **3.** In a backward state. —**be·hind·hand** *adj.*

Behn (bĕn), **Aphra** (1640-89). English writer, the first Englishwoman to make a professional career in letters. Her poetry is largely forgotten, but *Oroonoko* (1688) retains its place in English literary history as one of the earliest English novels.

be·hold (bĭ-hōld′) *tr.v.* **-held** (-hĕld′), **-holding, -holds.** To gaze at; look upon. —See Synonyms at **see.** ~*interj.* Used to express amazement or draw attention. [Middle English *beholden,* Old English *behealdan,* to possess, hold, observe.]

be·hold·en (bĭ-hōl′dən) *adj.* Obliged; indebted. [Middle English *beholden,* bound by obligation, Old English *behealden,* past participle of *behealdan,* to hold, BEHOLD.]

be·hoof (bĭ-hŏŏf′) *n. Rare.* Benefit; advantage; use. [Middle English *behove,* Old English *behōf.*]

be·hoove (bĭ-hŏŏv′) *tr. v.* **-hooved, -hooving, -hooves.** To be necessary or proper for. Used impersonally: *It behooves us to consider the question carefully.* [Middle English *behoven,* Old English *behōfian,* to require, be needful or fitting.]

Beh·ring (bâr′ĭng), **Emil (Adolph) von** (1854-1917). German bacteriologist. He is most famous for his work in serum therapy. For his demonstrations of serum immunization against diphtheria and tetanus he received the Nobel Prize in physiology and medicine in 1901. Behring coined the word "antitoxin."

Behring, Vitus. See **Bering.**

Bei·der·becke (bī′dər-bĕk′), **Bix,** born Leon Bismark Beiderbecke (1903-31). U.S. jazz musician. He was a self-taught pianist and cornet player and was the first white jazz musician to be recognized as a luminary of the jazz world by black musicians.

beige (bāzh) *n.* **1.** Light grayish brown, or yellowish brown to grayish yellow. **2.** A soft fabric of unbleached and originally undyed wool. [French, from Old French *bege†.*] —**beige** *adj.*

beigel. Variant of **bagel.**

Bei·jing (bā′jĭng′). Also **Pe·king** (pē′kĭng′, pä′-). Formerly (1928-49) **Pei·ping** (pā′pĭng′). Capital and second-largest city of China. It is a major cultural, communications, and industrial center. Founded by the Zhou as a frontier town on the North China Plain (c. 700 B.C.), the city was Kublai Khan's capital of Khanbalik (1264-67). The Ming made it their capital (1421), and it remained China's capital until 1912. Foreign troops occupied the city in 1860 and during the Boxer Rebellion (1900-01), and thereafter foreign garrisons were stationed in it. The city changed hands many times in the civil war following the formation of the Chinese Republic (1911-12). The Communists took Beijing (1949) and made it China's capital once

more. In it is preserved the Inner or Tatar City containing the Imperial or Forbidden City.

be·ing (bē′ĭng) *n.* **1. a.** Existence or a state of existence. **b.** A condition of particular existence. **2.** An object, idea, or symbol that exists, is thought to exist, or is represented as existing. **3.** A person: *"The artist after all is a solitary being"* (Virginia Woolf). **4.** One's basic or essential nature. **5.** *Philosophy.* **a.** That which can be conceived as existing. **b.** Absolute existence in its perfect and unqualified state; the essence of existence.

Bei·ra (bā′rə). Port in Mozambique, at the mouth of the Pungoe River. It is a beach resort and railway terminal, handling trade for Zimbabwe and Malawi.

Bei·rut or **Bey·routh** (bā-rŏŏt′). Capital and chief port of Lebanon. Founded by the Phoenicians, it was an important Greek and Roman trade center. It fell to the Arabs (635) and was much fought over during the Crusades. The Ottoman Turks took the city and later allowed the Druses to control it. The French captured Beirut (1918), and it became Lebanon's capital (1920). The city prospered as the chief financial and trade center of the Middle East, but from 1958 was severely damaged in the country's factional strife, in which the Syrians intervened (1976). It became a stronghold of the PLO and suffered at the hands of the Israelis until most of the PLO was evacuated (1982). Serious factional fighting resumed in 1983.

Be·ja (bā′jə) *n., pl.* **Beja. 1.** A member of a pastoral people living as nomads in the area between the Nile and the Red Sea. **2.** The Cushitic language of this people.

be·ja·bers (bē-jā′bərz) *interj.* Used to express surprise, alarm, or the like. [Euphemistic for *By Jesus!*]

Bé·jart (bā-zhär′), **Maurice,** born Maurice Jean de Berger (1927-). French dancer and choreographer. In 1954 he formed *Les Ballets de l'Etoile,* later renamed the *Ballet Théâtre de Paris.*

be·jew·el (bĭ-jŏŏ′əl) *v.* **-eled, eling, els** or *chiefly British* **-elled, -elling.** To adorn with or as if with jewels.

bel (bĕl) *n.* A unit used for comparing two levels of power, voltage, current, or sound intensity equal to the logarithm to the base 10 of the ratio of the two levels. See **decibel.** [After Alexander Graham BELL.]

Bel (bĕl). *Babylonian Mythology.* The god of heaven and earth.

be·la·bor (bĭ-lā′bər) *tr.v.* **-bored, -boring, -bors. 1.** To beat, hit, or whip; attack with blows. **2.** To attack verbally. **3.** To go over repeatedly or for an absurd amount of time; harp on: *to belabor a point.*

be·lah (bē′lə) *n.* Any of various types of Australian tree, especially the casuarina. [From a native Australian name.]

Be·las·co (bə-lăs′kō), **David,** known as "the bishop of Broadway" (1853-1931). U.S. playwright, producer, and director, famous for his realistic stage settings and innovative lighting effects. Among his productions were *Madame Butterfly* (1900), *The Girl of the Golden West* (1905), and *Laugh, Clown, Laugh* (1923).

be·lat·ed (bĭ-lā′tĭd) *adj.* Tardy; after the appropriate time: *a belated birthday card.* [Past participle of obsolete *belate,* to delay : BE- + LATE.] —**be·lat·ed·ly** *adv.* —**be·lat·ed·ness** *n.*

Be·lau (bə-lou′). Formerly **Pa·lau** (pə-) or **Be·lew** (bə-lŏŏ′). Four volcanic islands and numerous islets in the Caroline Islands, in the west Pacific Ocean. When the group opted to become part of the Federated States of Micronesia (1978), Belau broke away. The republic is in "free association" with the United States, which will be responsible for its defense until 1996. The people, largely Micronesian, live by fishing and farming. Area, 465 square kilometers (179 square miles). Population, 10,000 (1977). Capital, Koror. See map at **Pacific Ocean.**

be·lay (bĭ-lā′) *v.* **-layed, -laying, -lays.** —*tr.* **1.** *Nautical.* To secure or make fast (a rope) by winding on a cleat or pin. **2.** To secure (a mountain climber) at the end of a length of rope. —*intr.* **1.** To be made secure. **2.** *Nautical.* To stop. Used in the imperative. ~*n.* In mountain climbing, the securing of a rope on a rock or other projection. [Middle English *beleggen,* to beset, surround, Old English *belecgan,* to cover, surround. Current senses (from 16th century), from Dutch *beleggen.*]

be·lay·ing pin (bĭ-lā′ĭng) *n. Nautical.* A short, removable wooden or metal pin, fitted in a hole in the rail of a boat, and used for securing running gear.

bel can·to (bĕl kän′tō) *n.* A style of operatic singing characterized by rich tonal lyricism and brilliant display of vocal technique. [Italian, "beautiful singing."]

belch (bĕlch) *v.* **belched, belching, belches.** —*intr.* **1.** To expel gas noisily from the stomach through the mouth; eruct. **2.** To expel the contents violently; erupt: *The volcano belched with a roar.* **3.** To issue spasmodically; gush forth. —*tr.* **1.** To expel (gas) noisily from the stomach through the mouth; eruct. **2.** To eject violently from within: *The volcano belched hot lava.* ~*n.* A belching; an eructation. [Middle English *belchen,* perhaps Old English *bealcan* or *b(i)elcan* (unattested).] —**belch·er** *n.*

bel·dam, bel·dame (bĕl′dəm) *n.* An old woman, especially one who is loathsome or ugly. [Middle English, grandmother : Old French *bel-,* prefix indicating respect, from BELLE + DAME.]

be·lea·guer (bĭ-lē′gər) *tr.v.* **-guered, -guering, -guers. 1.** To besiege by surrounding with troops. **2.** To harass; plague; beset. [Dutch *belegeren : be-,* around + *leger,* camp, from Middle Dutch.] —**be·lea·guer** *n.* —**be·lea·guer·ment** *n.*

Be·lém (bə-lĕm′). Formerly **Pa·rá** (pə-rä′). Seaport on the Pará River in northern Brazil. It is a communications and market center for much of the Amazon basin.

bel·em·nite (bĕl′əm-nīt′) *n.* A pointed, cigar-shaped fossil, the internal shell of any of various extinct cephalopods related to the cuttlefish. Also called "thunderstone." [New Latin *belemnites,* from Greek *belemnon,* dart; from the superstitious belief that such fossils were thunderbolts.]

bel esprit (bĕl′es-prĕ′) *n., pl.* **beaux esprits** (bōz′ ĕs-prĕ′). *French.* A witty and intelligent person. ["Fine mind."]

Be·lew. See **Belau.**

Bel·fast (bĕl′făst′, bĕl-făst′). Capital and largest city of Northern Ireland. Because of its large natural harbor on Belfast Lough, it has enjoyed a substantial trade and was a flourishing shipbuilding center. In the 19th century it was also one of the great linen centers of the world.

bel·fry (bĕl′frē) *n., pl.* **-fries.** **1.** A tower or steeple in which one or more bells are hung. **2.** The part of a tower or steeple in which the bells are hung. [Middle English *berfrey* (altered through influence of *bell*), portable siege tower, bell tower, from Old French *berfrei,* from Germanic, probably from *bergan* (unattested), protect + *frithuz* (unattested), shelter.] —**bel·fried** *adj.*

Belg. Belgian; Belgium.

Bel·gae (bĕl′gī′, -jē′) *pl.n.* An ancient Gallic people who formerly inhabited what is now Belgium and northern France.

Bel·gian (bĕl′jən) *n. Abbr.* **Belg.** A native or inhabitant of Belgium. See **Fleming, Walloon.** —**Bel·gian** *adj.*

Belgian Congo. See **Zaire.**

Belgian hare *n.* A large, reddish-brown rabbit of a domestic breed developed in England from Belgian stock.

Bel·gic (bĕl′jĭk) *adj.* Of or pertaining to Belgium or the Belgians, to the Netherlands, or to the Belgae.

Bel·gium (bĕl′jəm) *Abbr.* **Belg.** Kingdom of northwest Europe, whose strategic position made it the "cockpit of Europe." It was a Roman province and later part of Charlemagne's empire. United under the dukes of Burgundy (14th century), it fell to the Habsburgs (1477) and passed to Spain. Napoleon occupied the country (1797), and after the Battle of Waterloo (1815), it became part of the United Netherlands. Belgium won its independence (1830), and its neutrality was guaranteed by the Great Powers (1839), but this was violated by Germany in both world wars. Belgium joined the Benelux Union (1948) and was a founding member of the EEC. The country is culturally divided into Dutch-speaking Flanders to the north of Brussels and French-speaking Wallonia to the south. Apart from coal, Belgium has few raw materials, yet it is one of the world's most industrialized countries, with over half its workers in manufacturing. Following land improvements, more than half its area is farmed intensively. Engineering goods, textiles, chemicals, glass, and foodstuffs are the main products and exports. Area, 30,513 square kilometers (11,781 square miles). Population, 9,900,-000. Capital, Brussels.

Bel·grade (bĕl′grăd′, -gräd′, bĕl′grăd′). *Serbo-Croatian* **Be·o·grad** (bā′ə-gräd′). The capital and largest city of Yugoslavia, lying at the confluence of the Danube and Sava rivers. Founded as a Celtic fortress (3rd century B.C.), it became (12th century) the capital of Serbia, which fell to the Ottoman Turks (1521). A major Turkish stronghold, garrisoned until 1867, Belgrade was made the capital of independent Serbia (1882) and (1918) of the Kingdom of the Serbs, Croats, and Slovenes (which became Yugoslavia in 1929).

Bel·gra·vi·a (bĕl-grä′vē-ə). Fashionable residential district in southwestern London, England. It is named after Belgrave Square, which is included in the district.

Be·li·al (bē′lē-əl, bĕl′yəl). A satanic personification of wickedness and ungodliness alluded to in the New Testament. II Corinthians 6:15. [Hebrew *bəlīyya'al,* "uselessness" : *bəlīy,* without + *ya'al,* use.]

be·lie (bĭ-lī′) *tr.v.* **-lied, -lying, -lies.** **1.** To misrepresent or picture falsely; disguise: *"He spoke roughly in order to belie his air of gentility"* (James Joyce). **2.** To show to be false: *Their laughter belied their grief.* **3.** To disappoint or leave unfulfilled. **4.** *Archaic.* To tell lies about; slander; defame. [Middle English *belien,* Old English *belēogan.*] —**be·li·er** *n.*

be·lief (bĭ-lēf′) *n.* **1.** The mental act, condition, or habit of placing trust or confidence in a person or thing. **2.** Mental acceptance or conviction in the truth or existence of something. **3.** Something believed or accepted as true; especially, a particular tenet, or a body of tenets, accepted by a group of people. —See Synonyms at **opinion.** [Middle English *beleve,* Old English *bileafe, gelēafa.*]

be·lieve (bĭ-lēv′) *v.* **-lieved, -lieving, -lieves.** —*tr.* **1.** To accept as true or real. **2.** To credit with truthfulness; trust. **3.** To expect or suppose; think: *I believe that he will come shortly.* —*intr.* **1.** To have faith, especially religious faith. **2.** To have faith or confidence; trust. Used with *in: I believe in his ability.* **3.** To have confidence in the truth, value, or existence of something. Used with *in: Her gardener did not believe in artificial fertilizers.* [Middle English *bileven, beleven,* Old English *belēfan, gelēfan,* from Germanic *galaubjan* (unattested), hold dear; akin to **lief.**] —**be·liev·a·ble** *adj.* —**be·liev·er** *n.*

be·like (bĭ-līk′) *adv. Archaic.* Perhaps; probably.

be·lit·tle (bĭ-lĭt′l) *tr.v.* **-tled, -tling, -tles.** **1.** To represent or speak of as small or unimportant; disparage. **2.** To cause to seem less or little. —See Synonyms at **decry.** —**be·lit·tle·ment** *n.* —**be·lit·tler** *n.*

Be·lize¹ (bə-lēz′). Formerly **British Hon·du·ras** (hŏn-dŏor′əs, -dyŏor′-). Low-lying country of the Central American mainland. Nearly half of it is forested, and British loggers in search of hardwoods were the first outsiders to settle here (17th century). The territory was made a British colony (1884), became internally self-governing (1964), and changed its name to Belize (1973). Belize gained independence within the Commonwealth (1981). Fish, forest products, sugar, and citrus fruits are the main products and exports. Agriculture is being expanded, but this has been hampered by devastating hurricanes and floods. Area, 22,965 square kilometers (8,867 square miles). Population, 145,000. Capital, Belmopan. See map at **Central American States.**

Belize² Port and the largest city of Belize. It was the capital until 1970, when it was replaced by Belmopan.

bell¹ (bĕl) *n.* **1.** A hollow, metal instrument, usually cup-shaped with a flared opening and having a clapper suspended inside. It emits a metallic tone when struck. **2.** A device consisting of an electromagnetically operated hammer that repeatedly strikes a hemispherical metal disk to make a ringing sound as a signal. **3.** Something shaped like a bell, as: **a.** The round, flared mouth of some musical wind instruments. **b.** The corolla of a flower. **c.** A hollow, usually inverted vessel, such as a diving bell. **4.** *Nautical.* **a.** A stroke on a bell to mark the half-hour intervals. **b.** The time indicated by the striking of a bell, divided into half hours. —**ring a bell.** To remind one of something previously known or experienced.
~*v.* **belled, belling, bells.** —*tr.* **1.** To put a bell on. **2.** To shape or cause to flare like a bell. —*intr.* To flare like a bell. [Middle English *belle,* Old English *belle,* perhaps akin to **BELL².**]

bell² *n.* The bellowing or baying cry of certain animals, such as a deer in rut or a beagle on the hunt.
~*intr.v.* **belled, belling, bells.** To bellow; bay. [Middle English *bellen,* to bay, Old English *bellan.*]

Bell (bĕl), **Alexander Graham** (1847–1922). U.S. inventor, born in Edinburgh. He went to Canada in 1870 and settled in New England shortly afterward. He was the inventor of the telephone, the first electrical transmission of speech by his apparatus taking place in 1876. The Bell Telephone Company was founded in 1877. He also invented the audiometer, an early hearing aid, and flat and cylindrical wax recorders for phonographs.

bel·la·don·na (bĕl′ə-dŏn′ə) *n.* **1.** A poisonous Eurasian plant, *Atropa belladonna,* having purplish-red, bell-shaped flowers and small black poisonous berries. Also called "deadly nightshade." **2.** An atropine powder or tincture derived from the leaves and roots of the belladonna and used to treat asthma, colic, and hyperacidity. [Italian, "fair lady" (supposedly from its use in cosmetics).]

belladonna lily *n.* A plant, the **amaryllis** (see).

Bel·la·trix (bĕ-lā′trĭks) *n.* A giant star, the third brightest in the constellation Orion.

Bel·lay (bə-lā′), **Joachim du** (1524–60). French poet. One of the founders of a group of poets known as the Pléiade, du Bellay wrote sonnets, satires on literary conventions and pretensions, and a manifesto of the Pléiade's poetic principles.

bell-bird (bĕl′bûrd′) *n.* **1.** Any of various tropical American birds of the genus *Procnias,* family Cotingidae, having a characteristic bell-like call. **2.** A New Zealand honeyeater, *Anthornis melanura.*

bell-bot·toms (bĕl′bŏt′əmz) *pl.n.* Trousers with legs that flare out at the bottom. —**bell-bot·tom, bell-bot·tomed** *adj.*

bell·boy (bĕl′boi′) *n.* A boy or man employed by a hotel to carry luggage, run errands, and the like. Also called "bellhop."

bell buoy *n.* A buoy fitted with a warning bell that is activated by the movement of the waves.

Bellerophon *A Greek terra cotta, made in Melos about 450 B.C., shows the legendary Greek hero on the winged horse Pegasus battling with the Chimera. The Chimera was part lion, part goat, and part dragon and is usually portrayed as a lion with a goat's head on its back.*

BELGIUM

NORTH SEA

NETHERLANDS

ANTWERP

GERMAN FEDERAL REPUBLIC

WEST FLANDERS

EAST FLANDERS

Oostende (Ostend)

Brugge (Bruges)

Zelzate

Antwerpen (Antwerp)

Herentals

LIMBURG

Gent (Ghent)

Mechelen (Malines)

Genk

Ieper (Ypres)

Passchendaele

BRUSSEL (BRUSSELS)

Leuven (Louvain)

Menen (Menin)

Kortrijk (Courtrai)

Oudenaarde (Audenarde)

Waterloo

BRABANT

Liège

Verviers

Spa

Botrange 692 m

Tournai (Doornik)

BELGIUM

Namur

NAMUR

Mons (Bergen)

Charleroi

Dinant

LIÈGE

FRANCE

Bastogne (Bastenaken)

Oesling

Sûre

LUXEMBOURG

LUXEMBOURG

LUXEMBOURG

Differdange

Esch

Gutland

0   50   100 Km
0   25   100   Miles

belle (bĕl) *n.* **1.** An attractive and much-admired girl or woman. **2.** The most attractive girl or woman at a specified place: *the belle of the ball.* [French, "beautiful," from Latin *bella,* feminine of *bellus,* handsome, pretty.]
belle é·poque (bĕl ā-pŏk′) *n.* The period preceding World War I. [French, "fine period."]
Bel·ler·o·phon (bĕ-lĕr′ə-fŏn′). *Greek Mythology.* The Corinthian hero who, with the aid of the winged horse Pegasus, slew the Chimera.
belles-let·tres (bĕl-lĕt′rə) *pl.n. Used with a singular verb.* Literature regarded for its aesthetic value rather than for its didactic or informative content. [French, "fine letters" (literature).] **—bel·let·rism** *n.* **—bel·let·rist** *n.* **—bel·le·tris·tic** (bĕl′ə-trĭs′tĭk) *adj.*
bell·flow·er (bĕl′flou′ər) *n.* Any of various plants of the genus *Campanula,* characteristically having blue, bell-shaped flowers. See **harebell, bluebell.**
bell·hop (bĕl′hŏp′) *n.* A **bellboy** *(see).*
bel·li·cose (bĕl′ĭ-kōs′) *adj.* Warlike in manner or temperament; pugnacious. [Middle English, from Latin *bellicōsus,* from *bellicus,* of war, from *bellum,* earlier *duellum,* war.] **—bel·li·cose·ly** *adv.* **—bel·li·cos·i·ty** (bĕl′ĭ-kŏs′ə-tē), **bel·li·cose·ness** *n.*
bel·lig·er·en·cy (bə-lĭj′ər-ən-sē) *n.* The state of being at war or engaged in a warlike conflict.
bel·lig·er·ent (bə-lĭj′ər-ənt) *adj.* **1.** Given to or marked by hostile or aggressive behavior. **2.** Of, pertaining to, or engaged in warfare: *the belligerent powers.*
~*n.* A person or state engaging in warfare. [Latin *belligerāns* (stem *belligerant-*), present participle of *belligerāre,* to wage war, from *belliger,* waging war : *bellum,* war + *gerere,* to bear, carry.] **—bel·lig·er·ence** *n.* **—bel·lig·er·ent·ly** *adv.*
Synonyms: *contentious, pugnacious, quarrelsome.*
Bel·li·ni (bə-lē′nē), **Gentile** (*c.* 1429–1507). Venetian painter of the Renaissance, son of Jacopo and brother of Giovanni.
Bellini, Giovanni (*c.* 1430–1516). Venetian painter of the Renaissance, son of Jacopo and brother of Gentile, the most illustrious of the family. His *Madonna with Saints,* an altarpiece for the church of Frari, Venice, was praised by John Ruskin as one of the three most beautiful paintings in the world. His coloring and atmospheric landscapes had a great influence, especially through his pupil Titian, on the development of the Venetian school.
Bellini, Jacopo (*c.* 1400–1470). Venetian painter of the Renaissance, father of the painters Gentile and Giovanni. Most of his famous paintings have been lost, including the *Crucifixion* for the cathedral at Verona.
bell jar *n.* A cylindrical glass vessel with a rounded top and an open base used to protect and display fragile objects or to establish a controlled atmosphere or environment in scientific experiments.
bell magpie *n.* A bird, the **currawong** *(see).*
bell·man (bĕl′mən) *n., pl.* **-men** (-mĭn). A **town crier** *(see).*
bell metal *n.* An alloy of tin and copper with small amounts of zinc and lead, used to make bells.
bell-mouthed (bĕl′mou*th*d′, -moutht′) *adj.* Having a flaring, bell-shaped mouth, as a flask might.
Bel·loc (bĕl′ŏk′, -ək), **Hilaire,** born Joseph Hilary Pierre Belloc (1870–1953). British writer and politician, born in France. He became a British citizen in 1902 and was a Liberal M.P. (1906–10). He is famous chiefly for his droll verse, especially *The Bad Child's Book of Beasts* (1896).
bel·low (bĕl′ō) *v.* **-lowed, -lowing, -lows.** *—intr.* **1.** To roar, as a bull does. **2.** To shout in a deep voice. *—tr.* To utter in a loud and powerful voice.
~*n.* **1.** The roar of a bull, elephant, or other large animal. **2.** A very loud utterance; a shout. **3.** The sound of artillery, thunder, or the like. [Middle English *belwen,* Old English *belgan* (unattested).]
Bel·low (bĕl′ō), **Saul** (1915–). U.S. novelist, born in Quebec, Canada. His novels include *Dangling Man* (1944), *The Adventures of Augie March* (1953), and his most famous one, *Herzog* (1964). He won the Nobel Prize in 1976.
bel·lows (bĕl′ōz, -əz) *n. Used with a singular or plural verb.* **1.** An apparatus for producing a strong current of air, as for sounding a pipe organ or increasing the draft to a fire. It consists of a flexible, valved air chamber that is contracted and expanded by pumping to force the air through a nozzle. **2.** Something resembling a bellows, such as the pleated windbag of an accordion. [Middle English *belwes, belows,* plural of *belu, below,* probably from Old English *belga,* plural of *bel(i)g, bœlig,* bag, bellows. See **belly.**]
bell pepper *n.* **1.** A pepper plant, *Capsicum frutescens grossum,* cultivated for its edible fruit. **2.** The mild-flavored, bell-shaped fruit of this plant, usually red when ripe but often eaten when green. Also called "sweet pepper."
bell pull *n.* A sash, cord, or handle that is pulled to ring a bell.
bell-ring·er (bĕl′rĭng′ər) *n.* **1.** One who rings church bells, especially on ceremonial occasions. **2.** One who plays musical handbells.
bells of Ireland *n. Used with a singular or plural verb.* A plant, the **shellflower** *(see).*
bell·weth·er (bĕl′wĕ*th*′ər) *n.* **1.** A male sheep, usually castrated, with a bell hung from its neck, that leads a flock of sheep. **2.** One that is followed, such as a leader. **3.** One that acts as a standard or representative.
bel·ly (bĕl′ē) *n., pl.* **-lies.** **1.** The part of the body of mammals between the rib cage and the pelvis that contains the intestines; the abdomen. **2.** The underside of the body of certain other vertebrates, such as snakes, amphibians, and fish. **3. a.** The stomach. **b.** Appetite for food; gluttony. **4.** Any part that bulges or protrudes: *the belly of a sail.* **5.** The deep, hollow interior of something: *a ship's belly.* **6.** The bulging part of a muscle. **7.** The front part of the body of a stringed musical instrument. In this sense, also called "table." **8.** The womb; the uterus. *—v.* **bellied, -lying, -lies.** *—intr.* To swell out; bulge: *"mud-colored clouds bellied downwards from the sky"* (Thomas Hardy).
~*tr.* To cause to bulge. [Middle English *bely, baly,* Old English *bel(i)g, bœl(i)g,* bag, purse, bellows.]
bel·ly·ache (bĕl′ē-āk′) *n. Informal.* An ache or pain in the stomach or abdomen.
~*intr.v.* **bellyached, -aching, -aches.** *Slang.* To grumble or complain, especially in a whining manner. **—bel·ly·ach·er** *n.*
bel·ly·band (bĕl′ē-bănd′) *n.* **1.** A band passed around the belly of an animal to secure something, such as a saddle. **2.** An encircling cloth band for holding in the protruding navel of a baby.
bel·ly·but·ton (bĕl′ē-bŭt′n) *n. Informal.* The **navel** *(see).*
belly dance *n.* A dance performed by women, originally in the Middle East, in which the hips and naked abdomen jerk and undulate. **—bel·ly-dance** *v.* **—belly dancer** *n.*
belly flop *n.* A dive in which the front of the body hits against the surface of the water. **—belly-flop** *v.*
bel·ly·ful (bĕl′ē-fo͝ol′) *n. Informal.* An amount that satisfies or exceeds what one desires or can endure.
belly landing *n.* A landing of an aircraft onto the underside of its fuselage, without the use of its undercarriage.
belly laugh *n.* A deep, unrestrained laugh.
Bel·mo·pan (bĕl′mə-păn′). Capital of Belize since 1970. After the former capital, Belize City, was devastated by Hurricane Hattie and its storm wave (1961), it was decided to build a new capital on higher ground 80 kilometers (50 miles) inland.
Be·lo Ho·ri·zon·te (bā′lō hôr′ĭ-zŏn′tē). City in eastern Brazil. An important manufacturing and marketing center, it was the first of Brazil's planned cities, built 1895–97.
be·long (bĭ-lông′, -lŏng′) *intr.v.* **-longed, -longing, -longs.** **1.** To be the property or concern of. Used with *to*: *"the earth belongs to the living"* (Thomas Jefferson). **2.** To be part of or in natural association with something. **3.** To be a member of an organization. Used with *to*: *belong to a club.* **4.** To have a proper or suitable place: *Those clothes belong in the drawer.* **5.** *Informal.* To be socially acceptable: *made her feel she belonged.* [Middle English *belongen* : *be-,* thoroughly + *longen,* to suit (see **long,** to yearn).]
be·long·ing (bĭ-lông′ĭng, bĭ-lŏng′-) *n.* **1. belongings.** Personal possessions; effects. **2.** Close and secure relationship: *a sense of belonging.* —See Synonyms at **assets.**
Be·lo·rus·sian (bĕl′ō-rŭsh′ən) *adj.* Also **Bye·lo·rus·sian** (byĕl′-). Of or pertaining to the Belorussian S.S.R., its people, or their language.
~*n.* Also **Bye·lo·rus·sian.** **1.** A native or inhabitant of the Belorussian S.S.R. **2.** The Slavonic language of the Belorussians. Also called "White Russian."
Belorussian Soviet Socialist Republic. Also **Be·lo·rus·sia** (bĕl′-ō-rŭsh′ə), **Bye·lo·rus·sia** (byĕl′-). Constituent republic of the U.S.S.R., bordering on Poland. The capital is Minsk. Peat is the region's most important mineral resource. Western Belorussia, awarded to Poland by the Treaty of Riga (1921), was overrun by Soviet troops (1939) and annexed to the U.S.S.R. The republic is popularly known as "White Russia."
be·lov·ed (bĭ-lŭv′ĭd, -lŭvd′) *adj.* Held in great affection.
~*n.* One that is loved. [Middle English, past participle of *beloven,* to love thoroughly : *be-,* thoroughly + *loven,* to LOVE.]
be·low (bĭ-lō′) *adv.* **1.** In or to a lower place; beneath. **2. a.** On or to a lower floor; downstairs. **b.** *Nautical.* On or to a lower deck. **3.** Farther down or on, as on a page. **4.** In or to hell or Hades. **5.** On earth. **6.** In a lower rank or class.
~*prep.* **1.** Lower than; beneath. **2.** Unworthy of or unsuitable to the rank or dignity of. **3.** Downstream of. **4.** South of. [Middle English *biloogh*e : *bi,* BY + *loogh, lowe,* LOW.]
Usage: *below, under, beneath, underneath. Below,* in its principal physical sense, denotes only position lower than a given point of reference. *Under* specifies position directly below, lower than the point of reference and in approximately vertical line with it. *Below* is also used to indicate direction and distance in a horizontal plane: *a town on the Hudson below Albany. Beneath* may have the basic sense of *below* or, more often, of *under. Underneath* combines the basic sense of *under* with that of at least partial concealment. Figuratively, *below* indicates deficiency or lesser status in a general way: *below normal; below one's rank. Under* indicates specific deficiency or explicitly subordinate relationship: *under legal age; serve under a captain. Beneath* applies to deficiency in moral or social senses: *beneath ordinary decency; beneath one's level.*
Beloye More. See **White Sea.**
Bel·shaz·zar (bĕl-shăz′ər). The son of Nebuchadnezzar II and the last king of Babylon, who was warned of his downfall and death by the handwriting on the wall. Daniel 5.
belt (bĕlt) *n.* **1.** A band of leather, cloth, or other flexible material, worn round the waist to support clothing, secure tools or weapons, or serve as decoration. **2.** *Sports.* A belt worn as a mark of distinction: *won a black belt in judo.* **3.** A **seat belt** *(see).* **4.** A strip of armor surrounding a warship at the water line. **5.** A continuous band of a flexible material for transferring motion or power or conveying materials from one wheel or shaft to another. See **conveyor belt, fan belt.** **6. a.** An encircling route or highway. **b.** A **belt line** *(see).* **7.** A geographical, sociological, or meteorological region,

bellflower *There are about 300 varieties of bellflower, including the harebell shown here, which is the "bluebell of Scotland."*

bell jar *An open-ended glass cover used as a display case for fragile objects and in scientific experiments. Antoine Lavoisier (1743–94) used the bell jar shown here to investigate combustion, by which he discovered the presence of oxygen in the air.*

especially an elongated one, that is distinctive in some specific way. **8.** A narrow channel. **9.** *Slang.* A powerful blow; a punch. **—below the belt. 1.** *Boxing.* In the area below the waistline, where a blow is foul. **2.** *Informal.* Not according to the rules; unfair. **—tighten one's belt.** To become more thrifty and frugal.
~v. **belted, belting, belts.** *—tr.* **1.** To encircle; gird. **2.** To attach with or as if with a belt. **3.** To mark with or as if with a belt. **4.** To strike with a belt. **5.** *Slang.* To strike forcefully; punch. **6.** *Slang.* To sing in a loud and forceful manner. Often used with *out*: *belt out a note.* *—intr. Slang.* To run, ride, or drive very quickly. [Middle English *belt,* Old English *belt,* from Common Germanic *baltjaz* (unattested), from Latin *balteus,* probably from Etruscan.]

Bel·tane (bĕl′tān′, -tĭn) *n.* **1.** May Day in the old Scottish calendar. **2.** The ancient Celtic May Day celebration. [Middle English *beltane,* from Scottish Gaelic *bealltainn,* probably from Old Celtic *belote(p)nia* (unattested).]

belt drive *n.* A mechanism for transmitting power between drive shafts by means of a belt connecting pulleys on a shaft. Compare **direct drive.**

belt highway *n.* A highway that skirts an urban area.

belt·ing (bĕl′tĭng) *n.* **1.** Belts collectively. **2.** The material used to make belts. **3.** *Informal.* A physical beating.

belt line *n.* A transportation line, as of trains, trolleys, or buses, that makes a complete circuit of an urban area.

be·lu·ga (bə-lo͞o′gə) *n.* **1.** The **white whale** *(see).* **2.** A sturgeon, *Huso huso,* of the Black and Caspian seas, whose roe is used for caviar. Also called "beluga sturgeon." [Russian *byeluga,* sturgeon, and *byelukha,* white whale : *byelii,* white + *-uga, -ukha,* augmentative suffix.]

bel·ve·dere (bĕl′və-dîr′) *n.* A structure, such as a summerhouse or an open roofed gallery, situated so as to command a fine view. [Italian, "beautiful view."]

be·ma (bē′mə) *n., pl.* **-mata** (-mə-tə). Also **bi·mah** (bē′mə), *pl.* **-mahs. 1.** *Judaism.* The platform from which services are conducted in a synagogue. Also called "almemar." **2.** *Eastern Orthodox Church.* The enclosed area about the altar; the sanctuary. [Late Latin *bēma,* from Greek, platform.]

beluga *The beluga, or white whale, is found along coasts in the Arctic and the far north. Adults are about 4 meters (13 feet) long.*

Bem·ba (bĕm′bə) *n. pl.* **-bas** or collectively **Bemba. 1.** A member of a south-central African people, living mainly in Zambia. **2.** The language of this people.

Be·mel·mans (bē′məl-mənz, bĕm′əl-), **Ludwig** (1898–1962). U.S. artist and author. Born in Austria, he immigrated to New York in 1914. His experiences in the restaurant and hotel business form the basis for many of his whimsical short stories and novels, often illustrated with his own drawings and water colors.

be·mire (bĭ-mīr′) *tr.v.* **-mired, -miring, -mires. 1.** To soil with mud. **2.** To bog down in mud. Usually used in the passive.

be·moan (bĭ-mōn′) *v.* **-moaned, -moaning, -moans.** *—tr.* **1.** To lament; mourn over. **2.** To express pity or grief for. *—intr.* To mourn; lament.

be·muse (bĭ-myo͞oz′) *tr.v.* **-mused, -musing, -muses.** To confuse or stupefy.

be·mused (bĭ-myo͞ozd′) *adj.* **1.** Confused; bewildered. **2.** Deep in thought; engrossed.

ben¹ (bĕn) *n. Scottish.* The inner room or parlor of a house.
~adv. Scottish. Inside; within.
~adj. Scottish. Inner.
~prep. Scottish. Within. [Middle English *ben, binne(n),* within, Old English *binnan* : *be,* BY + *innan,* within.]

ben² *n. Scottish.* A mountain peak. Used in names of mountains: *Ben Nevis.* [Scottish Gaelic *beann,* peak, height.]

ben³ *n.* Any of several Asiatic trees of the genus *Moringa,* bearing winged seeds that yield an oil used in perfumes and cosmetics. [Dialectal Arabic *bēn,* from Arabic *bān.*]

Ben·a·dryl (bĕn′ə-drĭl) *n.* A trademark for diphenhydramine, an antihistamine drug used mainly to treat allergy symptoms and, in combination with a hypnotic, to induce sleep.

Benares. See **Varanasi.**

Ben Bel·la (bĕn bĕl′ə), **Ahmed** (1919–). Algerian revolutionary leader and politician. He was the leader of the terrorist wing of the Algerian nationalist movement against France after World War II, and he helped found the National Liberation Front (1954). When Algeria gained its independence (1962), he became its first prime minister, after serving six years in prison. He was elected Algeria's first president (1963) but was ousted by a coup (1965).

bench (bĕnch) *n.* **1.** A long seat, usually made of wood or stone and without a back, for two or more persons. **2.** A thwart in a boat. **3. a.** The seat for judges in a courtroom. **b.** The office or position of a judge. **4.** The judge or judges composing a court. **5. a.** A seat occupied by persons in some official capacity. **b.** The office of the persons occupying such a seat. **6.** A strong worktable, such as one used in carpentry. **7.** A platform on which animals, especially dogs, are exhibited. **8.** *Sports.* **a.** The place where the players on a team sit while they are not participating in the game. **b.** The reserve players on a team. **9.** *Geology.* **a.** A level, narrow stretch of land interrupting a slope. **b.** A level elevation of land along a shore or coast, especially one marking a former shoreline. **10.** The working platform in a quarry or a mine.
~adj. Used in work done at a bench: *a bench plane.*
~tr.v. **benched, benching, benches. 1.** To furnish with a bench or benches. **2.** To seat on a bench, especially in a judicial capacity. **3.** To show (dogs) in a bench show. **4.** To keep out of or remove from a game. [Middle English *bench,* Old English *benc.*]

bench·er (bĕn′chər) *n. British.* **1.** A member of the inner or higher bar who acts as a governor of one of the Inns of Court. **2.** A **backbencher** *(see).*

Bench·ley (bĕnch′lē), **Robert Charles** (1889–1945). U.S. actor, film director, drama critic, and comic essayist. He is best remembered for his essays, represented in *The Benchley Roundup* (1954).

bench mark *n.* **1.** *Abbr.* **B.M.** A surveyor's mark made on some stationary object of previously determined position and elevation, and used as a reference point in tidal observations and surveys. **2.** A standard or reference point against which something is measured; a touchstone.

bench warrant *n. Law.* A warrant issued by a judge or court, ordering the arrest of an offender.

bend¹ (bĕnd) *v.* **bent** (bĕnt) or *rare* **bended, bending, bends.** *—tr.* **1.** To bring (a bow, for example) into tension by pulling or exerting pressure. **2. a.** To cause to assume a curved or angular shape. **b.** To force to assume a different shape or direction. **3.** To cause to swerve from a straight line; turn; deflect. **4.** To turn or direct (one's eyes or attention, for example): *"And to my cries . . . Thine ear with favor bend"* (Milton). **5.** To influence coercively; subdue. **6.** To decide; resolve. Used in the passive, with *on*: *He was bent on leaving.* **7.** To apply (the mind) closely; concentrate. **8.** *Nautical.* To fasten: *bend a mainsail onto the boom.* *—intr.* **1. a.** To turn or be altered from straightness or from an initial shape or position: *Wire bends easily.* **b.** To assume a curved, crooked, or angular form or direction: *The saplings bent in the wind.* **2.** To take a new direction; swerve. **3.** To incline the body; stoop. **4.** To bow in submission; yield. **5.** To apply oneself closely; concentrate. Used with *to.* **—bend over backward.** *Informal.* To make a considerable effort.
~n. **1.** The act or fact of bending. **2.** The state of being bent. **3.** Something bent; a curve; crook. **4.** *Nautical.* **a. bends.** The thick planks in a ship's side; the wales. **b.** A knot that joins a rope to a rope or another object. **—round the bend.** *Chiefly British Informal.* Mad or eccentric; dotty. **—the bends. Caisson disease** *(see).* [Bend, bent, bent; Middle English *benden, bente* and *bende, bente* and *bende,* Old English *bendan, bende, bended.*]

bend² *n. Heraldry.* A band passing from the upper dexter corner of the escutcheon to the lower sinister corner. [Middle English *bend,* Old English *bend,* ribbon, band.]

Ben Day *n.* Also **ben·day** (bĕn-dā′), **Ben·day, ben·day. 1.** A method of adding a tone to a printed image by imposing a transparent sheet of dots or other patterns on the image at some stage of a photographic reproduction process. **2.** A screen or pattern used in this process. [After Benjamin *Day* (1838–1916), New York printer.]

bend·er (bĕn′dər) *n.* **1.** One that bends. **2.** *Slang.* A drinking spree.

bend sinister *n. Heraldry.* A band passing from the upper sinister corner of the escutcheon to the lower dexter corner.

be·neath (bĭ-nēth′) *adv.* **1.** In a lower place; below. **2.** Underneath.
~prep. **1.** Below; under. **2.** Covered by: *The earth lay beneath a blanket of snow.* **3.** Under the power or influence of. **4.** Lower than in rank or station; inferior to: *An earl is beneath a duke.* **5.** Unworthy of; unbefitting: *It is beneath him to beg.* —See Usage note at **below.** [Middle English *benethe(n),* Old English *binithan* : *bi,* BY + *nithan, neothan,* from below, BELOW.]

Ben·e·dic·i·te (bĕn′ə-dĭs′ə-tē) *n.* **1.** A canticle, used in various Christian churches, beginning *"Benedicite, omnia opera Domini Domino"* ("All ye works of the Lord, bless the Lord"). **2. benedicite.** An invocation of a blessing, especially before meals. [Middle English, from Latin, imperative of *benedīcere,* to bless.]

ben·e·dict (bĕn′ə-dĭkt′) *n.* Also **ben·e·dick** (-dĭk′). A confirmed bachelor who has recently married. [After *Benedick,* a character in Shakespeare's *Much Ado About Nothing* (1598–99).]

Ben·e·dict (bĕn′ə-dĭkt′), **Saint** (*c.*480–*c.*543). Italian monk, founder of the Benedictine order, known from his birthplace as "Benedict of Nursia." After studying in Rome, he lived as a hermit in Subiaco, then moved to Monte Cassino, where he founded the first Benedictine monastery and established the principles of the order and of western monasticism in general in the book *The Rule of St. Benedict.*

Ben·e·dic·tine (bĕn′ə-dĭk′tĭn, -tēn′) *adj.* Of or pertaining to St. Benedict of Nursia or his monastic order.
~n. (bĕn′ə-dĭk′tĭn, -tēn′ *for sense 1*; bĕn′ə-dĭk′tēn′ *for sense 2).* **1.** A monk or nun belonging to the order founded by St. Benedict. **2.** A trademark for a liqueur made originally by Benedictine monks.

ben·e·dic·tion (bĕn′ə-dĭk′shən) *n.* **1.** A blessing or the act of blessing. **2.** An invocation of divine blessing, usually at the end of a service. **3. Benediction.** *Roman Catholic Church.* A short service consisting of prayers, the singing of a Eucharistic hymn, and the blessing of the congregation with the Host. Also called "Benediction of the Blessed Sacrament." **4.** The state of blessedness. [Middle English *benediccioun,* from Old French *benediction,* from Latin *benedictiō* (stem *benedictiōn-*), from *benedictus,* blessed, from *benedīcere,* to bless : *bene,* well + *dīcere,* to say.] **—ben·e·dic·tive, ben·e·dic·to·ry** *adj.*

Benedict's solution *n.* A solution of potassium, sodium tartrates, copper sulfate, and sodium carbonate, used to detect the presence of reducing sugars, especially in urine. [After S.R. *Benedict* (1884–1936), U.S. chemist.]

Ben·e·dic·tus (bĕn′ə-dĭk′təs) *n.* **1.** A short canticle that begins, *"Benedictus qui venit in nomine Domini"* ("Blessed is he that cometh in the name of the Lord"). Matthew 21:9. **2.** A canticle starting *"Benedictus Dominus Deus Israel"* ("Blessed be the Lord God of Israel"). Luke 1:68. **3.** A musical setting of either of these canticles.

[Latin, "blessed." See **benediction.**]
ben·e·fac·tion (bĕn'ə-făk'shən) *n.* **1.** The act of conferring help or a benefit. **2.** A charitable gift or deed. [Late Latin *benefactiō* (stem *benefactiōn-*), from *benefactus*, past participle of *beneficere*, to do well : Latin *bene*, well + *facere*, to do.]
ben·e·fac·tor (bĕn'ə-făk'tər) *n.* One who gives financial or other aid. [Late Latin, from *benefactiō*, BENEFACTION.]
ben·e·fac·tress (bĕn'ə-făk'trĭs) *n.* A female benefactor.
be·nef·ic (bə-nĕf'ĭk) *adj.* Exerting a beneficent influence; beneficent. [Latin *beneficus.* See **beneficence.**]
ben·e·fice (bĕn'ə-fĭs) *n.* **1. a.** A church office, such as a rectory, endowed with fixed capital assets. **b.** The revenue from such assets. **2.** A piece of land granted in feudal tenure to a vassal.
~*tr.v.* **beneficed, -ficing, -fices.** To endow or provide with a benefice. [Middle English, from Old French, from Medieval Latin *beneficium*, from Latin, favor, benefit, from *beneficus*, beneficent. See **beneficence.**]
be·nef·i·cence (bə-nĕf'ə-səns) *n.* **1.** The quality of charity or kindness: *nature's beneficence.* **2.** A charitable act or gift. [French, from Latin *beneficentia*, from *beneficus*, beneficent, generous : *bene*, well + *facere*, to do.]
be·nef·i·cent (bə-nĕf'ə-sənt) *adj.* **1.** Characterized by or performing acts of kindness or charity: *"even cruel savage brutes . . . have at times . . . beneficent impulses"* (W.H. Hudson). **2.** Conferring benefit; beneficial. —**be·nef·i·cent·ly** *adv.*
ben·e·fi·cial (bĕn'ə-fĭsh'əl) *adj.* **1.** Promoting a favorable result; enhancing well-being; advantageous. **2.** *Law.* Receiving or having the right to receive proceeds or other advantages: *a beneficial interest in sales.* [From BENEFICE, in the obsolete sense "benefit."] —**ben·e·fi·cial·ly** *adv.* —**ben·e·fi·cial·ness** *n.*
ben·e·fi·ci·ar·y (bĕn'ə-fĭsh'ē-ĕr-ē, -fĭsh'ə-rē) *n., pl.* **-ies. 1.** One who receives a benefit. **2.** *Law.* The recipient of funds, property, or other benefits from an insurance policy, will, or similar settlement. **3.** The holder of an ecclesiastical benefice.
~*adj.* Pertaining to or holding a feudal benefice. [Latin *beneficiārius*, of a favor, from *beneficium*, favor, BENEFICE.]
ben·e·fit (bĕn'ə-fĭt) *n.* **1.** Anything that promotes or enhances well-being; an advantage. **2.** A payment or series of payments made, for example by the government or by an insurance company, to one in need: *unemployment benefits.* **3.** A public entertainment, performance, or social event held to raise funds for a person or cause. **4.** *Archaic.* An act of charity; a kindly deed.
~*v.* **benefited, -fiting, -fits.** —*tr.* To be helpful or advantageous to. —*intr.* To gain advantage; profit. Used with *from.* [Middle English *benfet*, from Norman French, from Latin *benefactum*, benefit, good deed, from *bene facere*, to do well : *bene*, well + *facere*, to do.]
benefit of clergy *n.* **1.** The exemption from trial or punishment except by church court given to the clergy in the Middle Ages. **2.** The church's official approval. Used euphemistically: *cohabiting without benefit of clergy.*
benefit of the doubt *n.* A favorable judgment granted in the absence of full evidence.
benefit society *n.* An association that guarantees its members financial aid in times of need, as by hospitalization insurance, by the collection of dues. Also called "benefit association."
Be·ne·lux (bĕn'ə-lŭks). Economic union established (1948) by Belgium, the Netherlands, and Luxembourg. It came into effect (1960) as the world's first completely free international market for goods and labor.
Be·neš (bĕn'ĕsh'), **Eduard** (1884-1948). Czechoslovakian politician. He served under Tomáš Masaryk as foreign minister (1918–35) and succeeded him as president. He resigned from the presidency after the Munich Agreement (1938). He was again elected president (1946), but after the imposition of a Soviet-style constitution, he once more resigned. He died soon afterward.
Be·nét (bĭ-nā'), **Stephen Vincent** (1898-1943). U.S. poet and short-story writer. He is remembered chiefly for his long narrative poem of the Civil War, *John Brown's Body* (1928).
be·nev·o·lence (bə-nĕv'ə-ləns) *n.* **1.** An inclination or tendency to perform charitable acts; goodwill. **2.** A kindly act. **3.** In medieval England, a compulsory tax or payment exacted by some sovereigns without the consent of Parliament.
be·nev·o·lent (bə-nĕv'ə-lənt) *adj.* **1.** Characterized by benevolence; kindly. **2.** Of or concerned with charity: *a benevolent fund.* —See Synonyms at **kind.** [Middle English, from Latin *benevolēns* (stem *benevolent-*), "wishing well" : *bene*, well + *volēns*, present participle of *velle*, to wish.] —**be·nev·o·lent·ly** *adv.*
B. Eng. Bachelor of Engineering.
Ben·gal (bĕn-gôl', bĕng-). Region of eastern India and Bangladesh, a state of India before the partition into India and Pakistan (1947). The western part became the Indian state of West Bengal, whose capital is Calcutta. The eastern part became East Pakistan (1947) and Bangladesh (1971).
Bengal, Bay of. Large bay in the Indian Ocean, bordered by Sri Lanka and India on the west, Bangladesh on the north, and Burma and Thailand on the east.
Ben·ga·li (bĕn-gô'lē, bĕng-gô'-) *n.* **1.** An inhabitant of Bengal. **2.** The modern Indic language spoken in Bengal. It is the official language of Bangladesh and the main language of the Indian state of West Bengal.
~*adj.* Of or characteristic of Bengal, its inhabitants, or its language.
ben·ga·line (bĕng'gə-lēn', bĕng'gə-lēn') *n.* A fabric having a cross-

wise ribbed effect, made of silk, wool, or synthetic fibers. [French, after its similarity to a fabric made in BENGAL.]
Bengal light *n.* A type of firework that burns with a brilliant, sustained blue light, formerly used for signaling. [First made in and exported from BENGAL.]
Ben·gha·zi or **Ben·ga·si** (bĕn-gä'zē). Town in northeastern Libya, on the Mediterranean coast. It is the second-largest town in the country and the most important port. From 1951 to 1972 the city shared the status of being the nation's capital with Tripoli.
Ben·guel·a (bĕn-gĕl'ə, -gwĕl'ə, bĕng-). Seaport of Angola. It gives its name to the Benguela Current, a cold current flowing northward along the west coast of southern Africa.
Ben-Gur·i·on (bĕn-gōōr'ē-ən), **David**, born David Grün (1886–1973). Israeli politician, born in Poland. He settled in Palestine (1906) and became an active member of the Zionist campaign for an independent Jewish nation. He founded the Mapai Party in 1930. After World War II he led the resistance movement against the British, and when Israel was created (1948), he became prime minister. He held the office until 1953 and was again prime minister (1955–63).
be·night·ed (bĭ-nī'tĭd) *adj.* **1.** In moral or intellectual darkness; unenlightened; ignorant. **2.** Overtaken by darkness or night. —**be·night·ed·ly** *adv.* —**be·night·ed·ness** *n.*
be·nign (bĭ-nīn') *adj.* **1.** Of a kind disposition. **2.** Manifesting gentleness and mildness. Often said of weather. **3.** Tending to promote well-being; beneficial. **4.** *Pathology.* Not malignant: *a benign tumor.* Compare **malignant.** —See Synonyms at **favorable, kind.** [Middle English *benigne*, from Old French, from Latin *benīgnus*, "well-born" : *bene*, well + -GENOUS.] —**be·nign·ly** *adv.*
be·nig·nant (bĭ-nĭg'nənt) *adj.* **1.** Favorable; beneficial. **2.** Kind and gracious. —**be·nig·nant·ly** *adv.*
be·nig·ni·ty (bĭ-nĭg'nə-tē) *n., pl.* **-ties.** Also **be·nig·nan·cy** (-nən-sē). **1.** The quality or condition of being benign. **2.** A kindly or gracious act.
Be·nin¹ (bə-nĭn', -nēn'). Formerly (until 1975) **Da·ho·mey** (də-hō'mē). Republic of West Africa. Formerly several ancient African kingdoms colonized by France, it gained its independence (1960). It is one of the smallest countries in Africa, and, despite rich reserves of offshore petroleum, chromite, and iron ore, is one of the poorest and least industrially developed, largely because of political instability. The mainstays of the economy are palm products, cotton, and coffee. Area, 112,522 square kilometers (43,484 square miles). Population, 3,350,000. Capital, Porto Novo. See map at **West African States.**
Benin² or **Benin City.** Port in southeastern Nigeria, on the Benin River. It is the center of Nigeria's rubber industry. From the 14th to the 17th century it was the capital of the African kingdom of Benin, noted for its bronze works of art.
ben·i·son (bĕn'ə-zən, -sən) *n.* A blessing or benediction. [Middle English *benes(u)n*, from Old French *beneisson*, from Latin *benedictiō*, BENEDICTION.]
ben·ja·min (bĕn'jə-mən) *n.* A resin, **benzoin** *(see).* Also called "gum benjamin." [Variant (influenced by the name) of earlier *benjoin*, BENZOIN.]
Ben·ja·min¹ (bĕn'jə-mən). The youngest son of Jacob and Rachel, favorite son of Jacob. Genesis 35:18. [Hebrew, "son of the right hand" : *bēn*, son + *yāmīn*, right hand.]
Benjamin² *n.* The tribe of Israel descended from Benjamin. —**Benja·mite** (bĕn'jə-mīt) *adj.* & *n.*
benjamin bush *n.* The **spicebush** *(see).*
ben·ne, ben·ni (bĕn'ē) *n.* A plant, the **sesame** *(see),* or its seeds or oil. [Of African origin, akin to Mandingo *bēne.*]
ben·net (bĕn'ĭt) *n.* See **herb bennet.**
Ben·nett (bĕn'ĭt), **(Enoch) Arnold** (1867-1931). English novelist and dramatist. Most of his novels are set in the "Five Towns" of the Midlands pottery district. Influenced by the French realist writers, Bennett specialized in a sympathetic depiction of everyday life among the lower middle classes. His novels include *The Old Wives' Tale* (1908) and the *Clayhanger* trilogy (1910-16).
Ben Ne·vis (bĕn nĕ'vĭs, nĕv'ĭs). Highest mountain in Great Britain, rising to 1,343 meters (4,406 feet), in the Lochaber district of the Scottish Highlands.
ben·ny (bĕn'ē) *n., pl.* **-nies.** *Slang.* An amphetamine tablet. [From BENZEDRINE.]
Ben·ny (bĕn'ē), **Jack**, born Benjamin Kubelsky (1894-1974). He enjoyed a long career in vaudeville, motion pictures, radio, and television. Known for his famous delayed delivery, complete with arched eyebrow and bemused stare, he built many routines on his so-called reputation as a miser, his never-changing age of thirty-nine, and his supposed lack of skill as a violinist.
bent¹ (bĕnt). Past tense and past participle of **bend.**
~*adj.* **1.** Deviating from a straight line; crooked. **2.** On a fixed course of action; determined. Used with on: *"I perceived he was bent on refusing my mediation"* (Emily Brontë). **3.** *Chiefly British Slang.* **a.** Corrupt; dishonest. **b.** Homosexual. **4.** *Archaic.* Heading toward; on the way to.
~*n.* **1.** The state of being crooked. **2.** An individual tendency, disposition, or inclination: *"The natural bent of my mind was to science"* (Thomas Paine). **3.** The limit of endurance. Used chiefly in the phrase *to the top of one's bent.* **4.** A structural member or framework used for strengthening a bridge or trestle transversely.
bent² *n.* **1.** Any of several grasses of the genus *Agrostis,* some species of which are used in lawn mixtures and for hay. Also called "bent

Benin *A sculpted head, depicting a queen of the Benin, a West African people. Cast in bronze, it dates probably from the 16th century.*

grass." **2.** The stiff stalk of various grasses. **3.** *Rare.* A moor; a heath. [Middle English *bent,* grassy plain, Old English *beonet-* (attested in place names), from West Germanic *binut-* (unattested).]

Ben·tham (bĕn′thəm), **Jeremy** (1748-1832). English political theorist and philosopher. He was one of the first Englishmen to systematically analyze law and legislation, and he laid the foundations of the ethical system known as utilitarianism.

Ben·tham·ism (bĕn′thə-mĭz′əm) *n.* The utilitarian philosophy of Jeremy Bentham. See **utilitarianism.** —**Ben·tham·ite** *n. & adj.*

ben·tho·graph (bĕn′thə-grăf′, -gräf′) *n.* A steel sphere containing cameras and lights, designed to be lowered to great depths for underwater exploration.

ben·thos (bĕn′thŏs) *n.* **1.** The bottom of the sea or of a lake, especially at considerable depths. **2.** The organisms living on sea or lake bottoms. [Greek, depth of the sea.] —**ben·thic** (bĕn′thĭk), **ben·thal** (bĕn′thəl), **ben·thon·ic** (bĕn·thŏn′ĭk) *adj.*

Ben·tinck¹ (bĕn′tĭngk), **Lord William Henry Cavendish** (1774-1839). English colonial statesman. As the first governor general of British India (1828-35) he suppressed suttee, the burning of widows on their husbands' graves.

Bentinck², **Lord William Henry Cavendish.** See **Portland, 3rd Duke of.**

Bent·ley (bĕnt′lē), **Edmund Clerihew** (1875-1956). British man of letters. His detective story *Trent's Last Case* (1913) is a classic, but he is famous chiefly for inventing the short verse biography called a "clerihew."

Ben·ton (bĕn′tn), **Thomas Hart** (1889-1975). U.S. painter. His paintings and murals, executed in a flat, realistic style known as regionalism, portrayed everyday life in the Midwest and South. He won wide acclaim for his paintings of American farm life and his mural *The History of Missouri* in the state capitol at Jefferson City.

ben·ton·ite (bĕn′tə-nīt′) *n.* Either of two principally aluminum silicate clays, containing some magnesium and iron, distinguished by sodium or calcium content with corresponding high or low swelling capacity, and used in cements, adhesives, fillers, and as a drilling mud in oil wells. [After Fort *Benton,* north-central Montana.] —**ben·ton·it·ic** (bĕn′tə-nĭt′ĭk) *adj.*

bent·wood (bĕnt′wŏod′) *n.* Wood that has been steamed until pliable and then bent into shape.

~adj. Of or designating a style of furniture made of wood so treated.

be·numb (bĭ-nŭm′) *tr.v.* **-numbed, -numbing, -numbs. 1.** To make numb, especially by cold. **2.** To make inactive; stupefy. [Middle English *benomen,* past participle of *benimen,* to take away, Old English *beniman* : *be-,* away + *niman,* to take.] —**be·numb·ment** *n.*

Benz (bĕnz, bĕnts), **Karl Friedrich** (1844-1929). German engineer. He is credited with manufacturing the first car to be driven by an internal-combustion engine, patented in 1886. His company merged with the Daimler Motor Company (1926) to become Daimler-Benz AG, the makers of the famous Mercedes Benz, named after his wife.

benz–. Variant of **benzo–.**

benz·al·de·hyde (bĕn-zăl′də-hīd′) *n.* A colorless or yellowish, strongly reactive, volatile oil, C₆H₅CHO, used as a solvent, flavoring, and in perfumery. [German *Benzaldehyd* : *benzoin* + *aldehyde.*]

Ben·ze·drine (bĕn′zə-drēn′) *n.* A trademark for a brand of **amphetamine** *(see).*

ben·zene (bĕn′zēn′, bĕn-zēn′) *n.* A clear, colorless, highly refractive, flammable liquid, C₆H₆, derived from petroleum and used to manufacture a wide variety of chemical products including detergents, insecticides, and motor fuels. In nontechnical usage, also called "benzol." [BENZ(OIN) + -ENE.]

benzene hexachloride *n.* **Hexachlorocyclohexane** *(see).*

benzene ring *n.* The hexagonal ring structure in the benzene molecule and its substitutional derivatives, each vertex of which is occupied and distinguished by a carbon atom. Also called "benzene nucleus."

benzene series *n.* A series of chemically related aromatic hydrocarbons containing the benzene ring, the simplest member of which is benzene.

ben·zi·dine (bĕn′zə-dēn′) *n.* A yellowish, white, or reddish-gray aromatic amine, NH₂C₆H₄NH₂, crystalline powder, C₁₂H₁₂N₂, used in the manufacture of dyes and to detect bloodstains.

benzine (bĕn′zēn′, bĕn-zēn′) *n.* A mixture of hydrocarbons, **ligroin** *(see).* [German *Benzin* : BENZ(OIN) + -INE.]

benzo– or **benz–** *prefix.* Indicates benzene or benzoic acid: for example, *benzophenone.* [From BENZOIN.]

ben·zo·ate (bĕn′zō-at′) *n.* A salt or ester of benzoic acid.

benzoate of soda *n. Chemistry.* **Sodium benzoate** *(see).*

ben·zo·caine (bĕn′zə-kān′) *n.* A white, odorless, tasteless crystalline ester, C₉H₁₁NO₂, used as a local anesthetic.

ben·zo·di·az·e·pine (bĕn′zō-dī-ăz′ə-pēn′) *n.* Any of several chemical compounds used as sedatives and muscle relaxants. [BENZO- + DIAZEP(AM) + -INE.]

ben·zo·ic acid (bĕn-zō′ĭk) *n.* A white crystalline acid, C₆H₅COOH, used to season tobacco and in perfumes, dentifrices, and germicides.

ben·zo·in (bĕn′zō-ĭn, -zoin′) *n.* **1.** Any of several resins containing benzoic acid, obtained as a gum from various trees of the genus *Styrax* and used in ointments, perfumes, and medicine. Also called "benjamin," "gum benzoin." **2.** Any of various aromatic shrubs and trees of the genus *Lindera,* which includes the **spicebush** *(see).* **3.** A white or yellowish crystalline compound, C₁₄H₁₂O₂, derived from benzaldehyde and used as an antiseptic. [Earlier *benjoin,*

from French, from New Latin *benzoe,* from Arabic *lubān jāwī,* "frankincense of Java."]

ben·zol (bĕn′zôl, -zōl) *n.* **Benzene** *(see).* Not in technical usage.

ben·zo·phe·none (bĕn′zō-fī-nōn′, -fē′nōn′) *n.* A white crystalline compound, (C₆H₅)₂CO, used in perfumery and in medicine. Also called "diphenylketone."

ben·zo·py·rene (bĕn′zō-pī′rēn′) *n.* A yellow, crystalline, aromatic hydrocarbon, C₂₀H₁₂, that is a carcinogen found in coal tar and cigarette smoke.

ben·zo·yl (bĕn′zō-īl′) *n.* The univalent radical C₆H₅CO derived from benzoic acid.

benzoyl peroxide *n.* A flammable, white, granular solid, (C₆H₅CO)₂O₂, used as a bleaching agent for flour, fats, waxes, and oils, as a polymerization catalyst, and in pharmaceuticals.

ben·zyl (bĕn′zĭl, -zēl′) *n.* The univalent radical C₆H₅CH₂ derived from toluene.

Beograd. See **Belgrade.**

Be·o·wulf (bā′ə-wŏolf′). The hero of an anonymous Old English epic poem believed to have been composed in northern England in the early 8th century.

be·queath (bĭ-kwēth′, -kwēth′) *tr.v.* **-queathed, -queathing, -queaths. 1.** *Law.* To give or leave (property) by will. **2.** To pass on or hand down: *His mother bequeathed to him a love of paintings.* [Middle English *bequethen,* Old English *becwethan,* to say, bequeath : *be-,* about, over + *cwethan,* to say, speak.] —**be·queath·al** *n.* —**be·queath·er** *n.* —**be·queath·ment** *n.*

be·quest (bĭ-kwĕst′) *n.* **1.** The act of bequeathing. **2.** That which is bequeathed; a legacy. [Middle English : *be-,* about + *-quiste,* a decree, Old English *-cwiss.*]

be·rate (bĭ-rāt′) *tr.v.* **-rated, -rating, -rates.** To rebuke or scold harshly. —See Synonyms at **scold.** [BE- + RATE (verb).]

Ber·ber (bûr′bər) *n.* **1.** A member of one of several Muslim tribes of North Africa. **2.** The branch of the Afro-Asiatic languages spoken by these tribes. —**Ber·ber** *adj.*

Ber·be·ra (bûr′bĕr-ə). Port on the Gulf of Aden in northern Somalia. The town was captured from the Egyptians by Britain (1884); from then until 1941 it was the capital of British Somaliland.

ber·ber·ine (bûr′bə-rēn′) *n.* A bitter-tasting yellow alkaloid, C₂₀H₁₉NO₅, obtained from the root of a North American plant, *Hydrastis canadensis,* from the barberry, and from other plants, and used in medicine as a tonic. [German *Berberin* : New Latin *Berberis* (genus), from Old French *berberis,* BARBERRY + -in, -INE.]

ber·ber·is (bûr′bə-rəs) *n.* Any shrub of the genus *Berberis,* many species of which are grown in gardens for their ornamental foliage, flowers, or berries. See **barberry.** [19th century : Medieval Latin *barbaris,* barberry.]

ber·ceuse (bĕr-sœz′) *n., pl.* **-ceuses** *(pronounced as singular).* **1.** A cradlesong or lullaby. **2.** A musical composition with a soothing accompaniment, usually in moderate ⁶/₈ time. [French, from *bercer,* to rock.]

Berch·tes·ga·den (bĕrKH′təs-gäd′n). Town in the Bavarian Alps of West Germany. It lies in a deep valley, surrounded on three sides by Austrian territory. The chalets and air-raid shelters of Hitler, Goering, and other Nazi leaders are on the Obersalzberg peak overlooking the town.

be·reave (bĭ-rēv′) *tr.v* **-reaved** or **-reft** (-rĕft′), **-reaving, -reaves. 1.** To deprive, as of life or hope: *"To a man bereft of the sense of purpose"* (G. Wilson Knight). **2.** To leave desolate, especially by the death of a loved one: *"cry aloud for the man who is dead, for the woman and children bereaved"* (Alan Paton). [Middle English *bireven,* Old English *berēafian.*] —**be·reave·ment** *n.* —**be·reav·er** *n.*

be·reft (bĭ-rĕft′). Past participle of **bereave.**

~adj. **1. a.** Deprived of something: *bereft of his dignity.* **b.** Lacking something needed or expected: *a dictionary bereft of pictures.* **2.** Suffering the death of a loved one; bereaved.

Ber·e·ni·ce's Hair (bĕr′ə-nī′sēz) *n.* **Coma Berenices** *(see).*

Ber·en·son (bĕr′ən-sən), **Bernard** (1865-1959). U.S. art critic and historian, born in Lithuania. He is most famous for his writings on the Italian Renaissance, especially the comprehensive *Italian Painters of the Renaissance* (1894-1907).

be·ret (bə-rā′) *n.* A round, visorless cloth cap, worn originally by men in the Basque country. [French *béret,* from Old Gascon *barret,* cap, from Late Latin *birrus*†, hooded cape.]

beretta. Variant of **biretta.**

berg (bûrg) *n.* **1.** An **iceberg** *(see).* **2.** *South African.* A mountain.

Berg (bĕrKH), **Alban** (1885-1935). Austrian composer. A pupil of Arnold Schoenberg, he adopted his atonal manner and, with Anton von Webern and Schoenberg, formed the "Second Viennese School" of composers. He is best known for his two operas, *Wozzeck* (1925) and *Lulu* (1937), for the chamber *Lyric Suite* (1926), and his last completed work, the *Violin Concerto* (1936).

Ber·ga·mo (bĕr-gä′mō). Industrial city in the Lombardy region of northern Italy, lying in the foothills of the Alps between the Brembo and Serio rivers.

ber·ga·mot (bûr′gə-mŏt′) *n.* **1.** A small, spiny tree, *Citrus aurantium bergamia,* bearing sour, pear-shaped fruit, the rind of which yields an aromatic oil. Also called "bergamot orange." **2.** The oil itself, used in perfumery. Also called "bergamot oil." **3.** Any of several plants of the genus *Monarda;* especially the **wild bergamot** *(see).* [French *bergamote,* from Italian *bergamotta,* probably from Turkish *beg-armûdī,* "bey's pear."]

Ber·gen¹ (bûr′gən, bĕr′-). Norway's second-largest city, built on Bergen Fiord in the southwest of the country. Founded (c. 1070) by

King Olaf III, it was the capital of Norway in the 12th and 13th centuries and is now the center of the country's oil industry.

Bergen². See **Mons.**

Bergerac, Cyrano de. See **Cyrano de Bergerac.**

Ber·gi·us process (bûr′gē-əs) *n.* A process for the manufacture of diesel oil and gasoline from coal by hydrogenation of finely powdered coal with a catalyst at high temperatures. [After Friedrich *Bergius* (1884-1949), German chemist.]

Berg·man (bûrg′mən), **(Ernst) Ingmar** (1918-). Swedish film director. *Smiles of a Summer Night* (1955) announced the main elements of his highly distinctive style: a slow pace, laconic dialogue, and the heavy use of symbolism to explore the psychological states of his characters. Most critics consider his finest achievement to be his studies of psychosis, such as *The Silence* (1963) and *Persona* (1966).

Bergman, Ingrid (1915-82). Swedish film and stage actress, who gained international fame in the Hollywood version of *Intermezzo* (1939). Thereafter she retained her place as one of the great international film stars. She won an Academy Award for best actress in *Gaslight* (1944), *Anastasia* (1956), and *Murder on the Orient Express* (1974). She was awarded an Emmy for her portrayal of Golda Meir in *A Woman Called Golda* (1982).

berg·schrund (bĕrk′shro͞ont′) *n. Geology.* A crevasse at the head of a glacier that separates the moving ice from stationary ice adhering to the valley walls. [German *Bergschrund* : *Berg*, mountain from Old High German *bĕrg* + *Schrunde*, crack, from Old High German *scrunta*.]

Berg·son (bĕrg′sən), **Henri** (1859-1941). French philosopher. The central item in Bergson's philosophy is the opposition between the life force and the material world. He also assigned an important role to intuition, as opposed to the rational intelligence, in man's perception of reality. Among his best-known works are *Time and Free Will* (1889), *Creative Evolution* (1907), and *The Creative Mind* (1934).

Berg·so·ni·an (bĕrg-sō′nē-ən) *adj.* Of or pertaining to Henri Bergson or to his philosophy. **—Berg·so·ni·an** *n.*

Berg·son·ism (bĕrg′sə-nĭz′əm) *n.* Bergson's philosophy, which asserts that the flow of time as personally experienced is free and unrestricted rather than measured as on a clock and contends that all living forms arise from a persisting natural force, the **élan vital** *(see).*

berg wind *n.* A hot wind that blows from the plateau in South Africa down to the coast. [Afrikaans, "hill wind."]

be·rhyme (bĭ-rīm′) *tr.v.* **-rhymed, -rhyming, -rhymes.** **1.** To celebrate in verse. **2.** To lampoon in verse.

Be·ri·a (bĕr′ē-ə), **Lavrenti Pavlovich** (1899-1953). Soviet politician, born in Georgia. In 1946 he became a member of the Politburo and, on Stalin's death (1953), was appointed first deputy premier under Malenkov. In July 1953 he was arrested with six others, convicted of conspiracy, and executed.

ber·i·ber·i (bĕr′ē-bĕr′ē) *n.* A thiamine (vitamin B₁) deficiency disease of the peripheral nervous system, endemic in eastern and southern Asia, and characterized by partial paralysis of the extremities, emaciation, and anemia. [Singhalese, reduplication of *beri*, weakness.]

Ber·ing (bâr′ĭng), **Vitus.** Also **Beh·ring.** (1680-1741). Danish navigator in the employ of Russia. On the first voyage (1725) he explored the northern coast of Siberia. In 1728 he set out from Kamchatka Peninsula and traversed the Bering Strait, proving (though he did not realize it at the time) that Asia and North America are separate continents.

Bering Sea. Part of the North Pacific Ocean, lying north of the Aleutian Islands and connected to the Arctic Ocean by the Bering Strait.

Bering Strait. A narrow stretch of water (90 kilometers; 56 miles wide), separating Alaska from Siberia and connecting the Arctic Ocean and the Bering Sea. It is believed that in prehistoric times the strait formed a land bridge by which the original inhabitants of North America arrived from Asia.

Bering time *n.* The time in western Alaska and the Aleutian Islands, which lie in the 11th time zone west of Greenwich, England. [After the BERING SEA.]

Berke·le·ian (bär′klē-ən, bûr′-) *adj.* Of or pertaining to George Berkeley or his philosophy. **—Berke·le·ian** *n.*

Berke·le·ian·ism (bär′klē-ə-nĭz′əm, bûr′-) *n.* The philosophy of George Berkeley, holding that material objects have no existence independent of a mind perceiving them and that the uniform and continuous nature of the universe must be maintained by a divine mind always perceiving everything.

Berke·ley¹ (bûrk′lē). A city of western California, located on San Francisco Bay. Americans purchased the site from a Spanish family in 1853. The settlement, first called Oceanview, was renamed Berkeley in 1866. A large campus of the University of California is in Berkeley.

Berkeley². A suburb of St. Louis in eastern Missouri. The first International Air Meet in the United States was held here in 1910.

Berke·ley (bûrk′lē), **Busby,** born William Berkeley Enos (1895-1976). U.S. dance director. His trademark, lavish dance routines with precisely synchronized chorus lines, first appeared in *The Gold Diggers* series (1933-37) and *Footlight Parade* (1933).

Berke·ley (bärk′lē), **George** (1685-1753). Irish philosopher and clergyman. His important treatises are the *Essay Towards a New Theory of Vision* (1709) and the *Treatise Concerning the Principles of*

Human Knowledge (1710). The basic tenet of his philosophy, directed against the materialism of Thomas Hobbes, was that to be is to perceive or to be perceived.

ber·ke·li·um (bər-kē′lē-əm, bûrk′lē-əm) *n. Symbol* **Bk** A synthetic transuranic element having 9 isotopes with mass numbers from 243 to 250 and half-lives from 3 hours to 1,380 years. Atomic number 97, valences 3, 4. [New Latin, after BERKELEY, California.]

Berk·shire¹ (bärk′shîr, -shər). Also **Berks** (bärks). A chiefly agricultural county in south-central England, lying in the Thames basin. The county town is Reading.

Berk·shire² (bûrk′shîr, -shər) *n.* A pig of a domestic breed that originated in Berkshire, England, having a black body with white feet and face.

Berk·shire Hills (bûrk′shîr, -shər). Also **Berk·shires.** A range of wooded hills in western Massachusetts. The highest elevation is Mt. Greylock (1,065 meters; 3,491 feet). There are many resorts, state parks, and forests in the area.

ber·ley, bur·ley (bûr′lē) *n. Australian.* **1.** Ground bait for angling. **2.** *Slang.* Nonsense.

ber·lin (bər-lĭn′) *n.* **1.** A light wool used in tapestry or for making clothing, especially gloves. Also called "Berlin wool." **2.** Also **ber·line.** A four-wheeled covered carriage with a seat behind. **3.** Also **ber·line.** A limousine with a glass window between the front and rear seats. [After BERLIN.]

Ber·lin (bûr-lĭn′). City divided since 1949 into East Berlin (belonging to East Germany) and West Berlin (belonging to West Germany). It is situated in the center of East Germany on the Spree and Havel rivers. It was the center of the Prussian state and from 1871 was the capital of the German empire. East Berlin is now the capital of East Germany. The two parts of the city are divided by the Berlin Wall, a wire and concrete barrier erected by the East German government in August 1961.

Berlin, Irving, born Israel Baline (1888-). U.S. composer, born in Russia. Although he never learned to read music or play the piano, except in the key of F sharp, he became the most versatile and successful of 20th-century popular songwriters. He has written more than 1,500 songs. His first major success was Alexander's Ragtime Band (1911). Among his most famous musical comedies are *Top Hat* (1935), and *Annie Get Your Gun* (1946).

berline. Variant of **berlin** (senses 2, 3).

Ber·li·oz (bĕr′lē-ōz′; *French* bĕr-lyôz′), **(Louis) Hector** (1803-69). French composer, the leading representative of the romantic movement in French music. An early work, the *Symphonie Fantastique* (1830), is notable for its freedom from classical form and expansive scoring for a very large orchestra. His other most famous works are the symphonies *Harold in Italy* (first performed 1834) and *Romeo and Juliet* (1839), the operas *Benvenuto Cellini* (1838) and *The Trojans* (1855, 1858), the "concert opera" *The Damnation of Faust* (1846), and the oratorio *The Childhood of Christ* (1854).

berm, berme (bûrm) *n.* **1. a.** A narrow ledge or shelf, as along a slope. **b.** A shoulder of a road. **2.** A ledge between the parapet and the moat in a fortification. [French *berme*, from Dutch *berm*, slope, edge of a dike or dam, from Middle Dutch *berme*, perhaps akin to Old Norse *barmr*, brim.]

Ber·mu·da (bər-myo͞o′də). A self-governing British colony in the North Atlantic Ocean, comprising about 300 coral islands, some 20 of which are inhabited. The capital, Hamilton, is on the largest of the islands, called Bermuda or Great Bermuda. Bermuda has been a British colony since 1609 and relies on tourism.

Bermuda grass *n.* A grass, *Cynodon dactylon,* that has wiry, creeping rootstocks and is used for lawns and pasturage in warm regions. Also called "scutch grass," "wiregrass."

Bermuda lily *n.* A plant, the **Easter lily** *(see).*

Bermuda mulberry *n.* The **beautyberry** *(see).*

Bermuda rig *n.* A fore-and-aft rig, distinguished by a tall triangular mainsail, widely used on cruising and racing vessels. Also called "Marconi rig." **—Ber·mu·da-rigged** *adj.*

Bermuda shorts *pl.n.* Shorts that end slightly above the knees. Also called "Bermudas."

Bermuda Triangle. Area of the North Atlantic Ocean remarkable for the number of ships and airplanes that have disappeared without explanation in its waters. The triangle lies approximately in the area between latitude 25° to 40°N and longitude 55° to 85°W, between Bermuda, Puerto Rico, and Florida.

Bern (bûrn, bĕrn). Also **Berne.** The capital of Switzerland, situated on the Aar River in the west-central part of the country. The city joined the Swiss Confederation (1353) and became its capital (1848). Bern is also the name of the canton that surrounds the city.

Ber·na·dette (bûr′nə-dĕt′), **Saint,** born Marie Bernarde Soubirous (1844-79). French girl whose visions of the Virgin Mary at a grotto near her birthplace, Lourdes, led to the establishment of a shrine there. She had her first visions when she was 14 (1858). She was canonized in 1933.

Bernadotte, Jean Baptiste Jules. See **Charles XIV.**

Ber·nard·ine (bûr′nər-dīn, -dēn′) *adj.* **1.** Of or pertaining to St. Bernard of Clairvaux. **2.** Of or pertaining to the Cistercians, the order of monks reformed by St. Bernard in 1115.
~*n.* A member of a Cistercian order.

Ber·nard of Clair·vaux (bər-närd′ əv klâr-vō′), **Saint.** (c. 1090-1153). French mystic and Doctor of the Church. He entered the Cistercian order (1112) and was sent to establish a monastery (1115) at Clairvaux, where he remained abbot for the rest of his life. He is sometimes called the second founder of the Cistercian broth-

Berkshire *Developed in the Thames Valley of England in the 19th century, the traditional Berkshire pig is now becoming rare. It is a small pork-producing pig that has been crossed with other breeds as bacon has become more important commercially.*

Bernini

MASTERPIECES IN MARBLE

A sculptor and architect who left his imprint on Rome

Gianlorenzo Bernini (1598-1680) was the son of a sculptor who worked in Rome for Pope Paul V. Gianlorenzo began sculpting as a boy and attracted a patron in the pope's nephew, Cardinal Scipione Borghese, for whom he made *Aeneas and Anchises* (1618-19), *The Rape of Proserpina* (1621-22), and *David* (1623). These established him as an unmatched master, and his reputation became international. His greatest achievements are to be seen in Rome, in tombs, busts, statues, buildings, and fountains.

Bernini was a splendid sculptor in white marble, but his use of polychrome marble, on its own or combined with gilded bronze, is outstanding. He used the combination in the tomb of Pope Urban VIII (1628-47) and of Pope Alexander VII (1671-78). Characteristic of his style are swirling movement in draperies and ecstatic gestures and facial expressions.

His architecture includes St. Peter's Piazza, much work in St. Peter's Basilica, and several churches, including St. Andrea al Quirinale (1658-70). His busts, among them one of Louis XIV (at Versailles), are the finest pieces of baroque portrait sculpture. The most notable of his fountains are the Triton, the Moro, and the Four Rivers.

Perhaps Bernini's most characteristic masterpiece is the chapel he created (1645-52) for the Cornaro family in the church of Santa Maria della Vittoria. Saint Theresa and the angel are flanked by members of the Cornaro family. The group combines white and colored marble, gilded bronze, and natural light filtering from a window behind the figures.

A MOMENT CAUGHT FOREVER Apollo and Daphne *(1622-24), in the Borghese Museum, Rome, shows Bernini's unrivaled skill in portraying movement in pose, drapery, and gesture.*

erhood. His simple devotion to the Virgin Mary and the infant Christ make him a precursor of the movement known as the *devotio moderna*. His most influential writings, apart from his sermons (more than 300 of which survive), were *On the Steps of Humility and Pride* (c. 1125) and *On the Love of God* (c. 1127).

Bern·hardt (bûrn′härt′, bĕrn′-), **Sarah,** born Henriette Rosine Bernard, known as "the Divine Sarah" (1844-1923). French actress, one of the most renowned in the history of the theater. She made her debut at the Comédie Française (1862), but her great reputation did not begin until her appearance there as *Phèdre* (1874). In 1912 she appeared in two films, *La Dame aux Camélias* and *Queen Elizabeth*. She continued acting all over the world even after her leg was amputated (1915).

Ber·ni·ni (bĕr-nē′nē), **Giovanni Lorenzo** or **Gianlorenzo** (1598-1680). Italian sculptor, painter, and architect, the outstanding representative of the Italian baroque. He was appointed architect to St. Peter's in Rome (1629) and made the great ornate baldachin over the high altar and the *Cathedra Petri* monument enshrining St. Peter's throne. He later decorated the apse of St. Peter's with a group of the Fathers of the Church, designed the colonnade around the piazza at the front of the church, and created the royal staircase in the Vatican.

Ber·noul·li (bər-nōō′lē), **Daniel** (1700-82). Swiss physician, mathematician, and physicist, son of Jean. He was one of the first natural philosophers who could properly be called a mathematical physicist. He anticipated the law of the conservation of energy and did important pioneering work in the molecular theory of gases; he also contributed to probability theory and the theory of differential equations. He is best known for his formulation of **Bernoulli's law,** which appears in *Hydrodynamica* (1738).

Bernoulli, Jacques or **Jakob** (1654-1705). Swiss mathematician, brother of Jean. He was professor of natural philosophy at Basel (1687-1705). He is one of the most important founders of the theory of ordinary calculus and the calculus of variations. He was the first user of the word "integral," in his solution to the problem of the isochronal curve.

Bernoulli, Jean or **Johann** (1667-1748). Swiss mathematician, brother of Jacques and father of Daniel. He succeeded his brother as professor of natural philosophy at the University at Basel. He is important for his development of integral and exponential calculus.

Bernoulli distribution *n. Statistics.* The **binomial distribution** *(see).* [After Jacques BERNOULLI.]

Bernoulli effect *n.* The phenomenon of internal pressure reduction with increased stream velocity in a fluid. [After Daniel BERNOULLI.]

Bernoulli's law *n.* **1.** *Statistics.* The probability theorem stating that for a very large number of independent repeated Bernoulli trials the observed relative frequency of successes will approximate the probability of success on each trial. Also called "law of large numbers." **2.** *Physics.* The relationship between internal fluid pressure and fluid velocity, essentially a statement of the conservation of energy, that has as a consequence the Bernoulli effect. Also called "Bernoulli's theorem." [Statistics law, after Jacques BERNOULLI; physics law, after Daniel BERNOULLI.]

Bernoulli trial *n. Statistics.* An experiment having just two possible results, usually denoted *success* and *failure,* with the property that the occurrence of one excludes the occurrence of the other in any given trial. [After Jacques BERNOULLI.]

Bern·stein (bûrn′stīn′), **Leonard** (1918-). U.S. symphony conductor and composer. He was the permanent conductor of the New York Philharmonic (1958-70). He has written a number of serious choral and symphonic works, but is best known for his musical comedies, including *On The Town* (1944) and *West Side Story* (1957).

Ber·ra (bĕr′ə), **Yogi,** born Lawrence Peter Berra (1925-). U.S. baseball player and manager. Considered one of the best catchers in the history of baseball, Berra played for the New York Yankees from 1946 to 1963. In 1972 he was elected to the Baseball Hall of Fame.

berretta. Variant of **biretta.**

ber·ry (bĕr′ē) *n., pl.* **-ries. 1.** Any of various usually fleshy, edible fruits, such as the strawberry, blackberry, or raspberry. **2.** *Botany.* A fleshy fruit, such as the grape, date, or tomato, that usually has two or more seeds and does not split open when ripe. **3.** Any of various seeds or dried kernels, such as that of the coffee plant. **4.** The small, dark egg of certain crustaceans or fishes.
~*intr.v.* **berried, -rying, -ries. 1.** To hunt for or gather berries. **2.** To produce or bear berries. [Middle English *berye,* Old English *beri(g)e.*]

Ber·ry (bĕr′ē), **Chuck,** born Charles Edward Anderson Berry (1926-). U.S. popular songwriter and singer. He was one of the first singers in the 1950's to evolve the rock 'n' roll style.

ber·seem (bər-sēm′) *n.* A clover, *Trifolium alexandrinum,* native to northern Africa and southwestern Asia, and grown for soil improvement in dry regions of southwestern North America. Also called "Egyptian clover." [Arabic *barsīm, birsīm,* from Coptic *bersīm.*]

ber·serk (bər-sûrk′, -zûrk′) *adj.* **1.** Destructively or frenetically violent. **2.** Deranged.
~*n.* A berserker. **—ber·serk** *adv.*

ber·serk·er (bər-sûr′kər, -zûr′-) *n.* A fierce ancient Norse warrior who fought in battle with frenzied violence and fury. [Icelandic *berserkr,* "bear's skin" : *björn* (stem *ber-*), a bear + *serkr,* shirt, SARK.]

berth (bûrth) *n.* **1.** A usually built-in bed or bunk in a ship or railroad sleeping car. **2.** *Nautical.* A space at a wharf for a ship to dock or anchor. **3.** *Nautical.* Enough space for a ship to maneuver; sea room. **4.** A position of employment, especially on a ship. **—give a wide berth to.** To stay at a substantial distance from; avoid.
~*v.* **berthed, berthing, berths.** *—tr.* **1.** To bring (a ship) to a berth. **2.** To provide (a ship) with a berth. **3.** To provide a bunk for, as on a ship or train. *—intr.* To come to a berth; dock. [Probably BEAR (verb, in nautical sense, "to sail in a certain direction") + -TH (noun suffix expressing result).]

ber·tha (bûr'thə) *n.* A wide, deep collar, often of lace, that covers the shoulders of a low-necked dress. [French *berthe,* after Queen *Bertha,* mother of Charlemagne.]

Ber·til·lon system (bûr'tə-lŏn'; *French* bĕr-tē-yôN') *n.* A former system for identifying persons, especially criminal, by means of a record of various body measurements, coloring, markings, and the like. [After Alphonse *Bertillon* (1853–1914), French criminologist.]

Ber·wick·shire (bĕr'wĭk-shîr', -shər). A former county of Scotland, since 1975 included in Borders Region.

ber·yl (bĕr'əl) *n.* A mineral, essentially aluminum beryllium silicate, $Be_3Al_2Si_6O_{18}$, occurring in hexagonal prisms. It is the chief source of beryllium and is used as a gem. [Middle English, from Old French, from Latin *bēryllus,* from Greek *bērullos,* perhaps of Dravidian origin.] **—beryl·line** (bĕr'ə-lĭn, -lĭn') *adj.*

be·ryl·li·um (bə-rĭl'ē-əm) *n. Symbol* **Be** A lightweight, corrosion-resistant, rigid, steel-gray metallic element used as an aerospace structural material, as a moderator and reflector in nuclear reactors, and in a copper alloy used for springs, electrical contacts, and nonsparking tools. Atomic number 4, atomic weight 9.0122, melting point 1,287°C, boiling point 2,970°C, specific gravity 1.848, valence 2. [New Latin, from BERYL.]

Ber·ze·li·us (bər-zā'lē-əs, -zē'-), **Jöns Jakob, Baron** (1779–1848). Swedish chemist, one of the most important founders of modern chemistry. He made enormous contributions to the development of the science in atomic weights (he published a table of these in 1828), electrochemical theory (by his experiments in electrolysis of various solutions), and the discovery of the elements selenium and thorium and the isolation of silicon. He coined the words "isomerism," "allotropy," and "protein." His most important publication was the *Theory of Chemical Proportions and the Chemical Action of Electricity* (1814).

Bes (bĕs). *Egyptian Mythology.* A god of music and revelry.

Be·san·çon (bə-zäN-sôN'). Industrial city in eastern France, on the Doubs River. It is famous for watches and clocks.

Bes·ant (bĕz'ənt), **Annie,** born Annie Wood (1847–1933). English freethinker and theosophist. In 1889 she became a disciple of Helena Blavatsky and for the rest of her life devoted herself to theosophy. She later became the founder-president of the India Home Rule League (1916) and president of the Indian National Congress (1917).

be·seech (bĭ-sēch') *tr.v.* **-sought** (-sôt') or **-seeched, -seeching, -seeches.** **1.** To address an earnest or urgent request to; implore. **2.** To request earnestly; beg for. **—See Synonyms at beg.** [Middle English *besechen,* to seek : *be-,* thoroughly + *sechen, seken,* to SEEK.] **—be·seech·er** *n.* **—be·seech·ing·ly** *adv.*

be·seem (bĭ-sēm') *tr.v.* **-seemed, -seeming, -seems.** *Archaic.* To be appropriate for; befit. [Middle English *besemen,* to seem, appear to do well : *be-,* thoroughly + *semen,* to SEEM.]

be·set (bĭ-sĕt') *tr.v.* **-set, -setting, -sets.** **1.** To attack from all sides. **2.** To trouble persistently; harass: *beset by doubts.* **3.** To surround; hem in. **4.** To stud, as with jewels. **—See Synonyms at attack.** [Middle English *besetten,* Old English *besettan* : *be-,* on all sides + SET (place).] **—be·set·ment** *n.*

be·set·ting (bĭ-sĕt'ĭng) *adj.* Constantly troubling or attacking.

be·shrew (bĭ-shrōō') *tr.v.* **-shrewed, -shrewing, -shrews.** *Archaic.* To invoke evil upon; curse. [Middle English *beshrewen,* to corrupt, curse : *be-,* thoroughly + *shrewen,* to curse, from *shrewe,* SHREW.]

be·side (bĭ-sīd') *prep.* **1.** Next to; at or by the side of. **2.** In comparison with. **3.** Except for. **—See Usage note at besides.** **4.** Wide of; unrelated to: *beside the point.* **—beside oneself.** Out of one's senses with excitement, grief, rage, or the like; extremely agitated. ~*adv.* In addition to. [Middle English *biside,* Old English *be sīdan* : *be,* BY + *sīdan,* dative of *sīde,* SIDE.]

be·sides (bĭ-sīdz') *adv.* **1.** In addition; also; over and above. **2.** Moreover; furthermore. **3.** Otherwise; else. **—See Synonyms at also.** ~*prep.* **1.** In addition to. **2.** Except for. [Middle English *bisides,* adverbial genitive of *biside,* BESIDE.]

Usage: In modern usage, the senses *in addition to* and *except for* are conveyed more often by *besides* than *beside.* Thus: *He had few friends besides us.*

be·siege (bĭ-sēj') *tr.v.* **-sieged, -sieging, -sieges.** **1.** To surround with aggressive intent in order to compel surrender; lay siege to. **2.** To crowd round; hem in. **3.** To harass or importune, as with requests. [Middle English *besegen* : *be-,* on all sides + *sege,* SIEGE.] **—be·siege·ment** *n.* **—be·sieg·er** *n.*

be·smear (bĭ-smîr') *tr.v.* **-smeared, -smearing, -smears.** **1.** To smear over. **2.** To tarnish; defile.

be·smirch (bĭ-smûrch') *tr.v.* **-smirched, -smirching, -smirches.** **1.** To make dirty; soil. **2.** To dim the purity or luster of (someone's reputation, for example); tarnish; dishonor. **—be·smirch·er** *n.* **—be·smirch·ment** *n.*

be·som (bē'zəm) *n.* **1.** A bundle of twigs attached to a handle and

used as a broom. **2.** In curling, the broom used to sweep the ice from the path of a curling stone. **3.** *Rare.* The broom plant. ~*tr. v.* **besomed, -soming, -soms.** To sweep using a besom. [Middle English *besem,* Old English *bes(e)ma,* from West Germanic *besmo-* (unattested).]

be·sot·ted (bĭ-sŏt'ĭd) *adj.* **1.** Muddled or stupefied, especially with liquor. **2.** Infatuated.

be·sought. Past tense and past participle of **beseech.**

be·span·gle (bĭ-spăng'gəl) *tr.v.* **-spangled, -spangling, -spangles.** To ornament or cover with spangles.

be·spat·ter (bĭ-spăt'ər) *tr.v.* **-tered, -tering, -ters.** **1.** To spatter or soil thoroughly, as with mud. **2.** To cast aspersions on; defame.

be·speak (bĭ-spēk') *tr.v.* **-spoke** (-spōk') or *archaic* **-spake** (-spāk'), **-spoken** (-spō'kən) or **-spoke, -speaking, -speaks.** **1.** To be or give a sign of; indicate; signify. **2.** *Archaic.* To speak to; address. **3.** To engage or claim in advance; reserve. **4.** To foretell; portend.

be·spec·ta·cled (bĭ-spĕk'tə-kəld) *adj.* Wearing eyeglasses.

be·spoke (bĭ-spōk') *adj.* Also **be·spo·ken** (bĭ-spō'kən). *Chiefly British.* **1.** Made-to-order. Usually said of clothing. **2.** Dealing in custom-made articles: *a bespoke tailor.*

be·spread (bĭ-sprĕd') *tr.v.* **-spread, -spreading, -spreads.** To cover or spread over, usually thickly.

be·sprent (bĭ-sprĕnt') *adj. Poetic.* Besprinkled. [Middle English *bespreynt,* past participle of *besprengen,* to besprinkle, Old English *besprengan* : *be-,* around, over + *sprengan,* to scatter, burst.]

be·sprin·kle (bĭ-sprĭng'kəl) *tr.v.* **-kled, -kling, -kles.** To sprinkle over, as with water. [Middle English *besprengelen,* frequentative of *besprengen,* to besprinkle. See **besprent.**]

Bes·sa·ra·bi·a (bĕs'ə-rā'bē-ə). Historic region in southwest European U.S.S.R., now forming parts of the Ukraine and Moldavia. Russia gained the area (1812), but it declared itself the independent republic of Moldavia (1918) and voted for union with Romania. Romania was forced formally to cede it to the U.S.S.R. (1940).

Bes·sel equation (bĕs'əl) *n.* The differential equation, $x^2f''(x) + xf'(x) + (x^2-n^2)f(x) = 0$. [After Friedrich Wilhelm *Bessel* (1784–1846), German astronomer and mathematician.]

Bessel function *n.* Any of the solutions of the Bessel equation, having many applications in mathematical physics, including the representation of current density and magnetic field strength, and in problems of heat conduction.

Bes·se·mer (bĕs'ə-mər), **Sir Henry** (1813–98). British engineer and inventor. Over his lifetime he patented more than 100 inventions. He is most famous for inventing the **Bessemer process.** He was knighted in 1879.

Bessemer converter *n.* A large pear-shaped container in which molten pig iron is converted to steel by the Bessemer process. [After Sir Henry BESSEMER.]

Bessemer process *n.* A method for making steel by blasting compressed air through molten iron, burning out excess carbon and other impurities. [After Sir Henry BESSEMER.]

best (bĕst) **1.** Superlative of **good.** **2.** Superlative of **well.** ~*adj.* **1.** Surpassing all others in quality; most excellent. **2.** Most satisfactory, suitable, or useful; most desirable or attractive: *the best solution.* **3.** Greatest; largest: *It took the best part of a week.* ~*adv.* **1.** In the best way; most creditably, attractively, or advantageously. **2.** To the greatest degree or extent; most: *"He was certainly the best hated man in the ship"* (Somerset Maugham). **—had best.** Should; ought to; would be wisest to. ~*n.* **1.** That which is best among several. Preceded by *the.* **2.** The best person or persons. Preceded by *the.* **3.** The best condition or quality: *look your best.* **4.** One's best clothing. **5.** The best effort one can make: *doing his best.* **6.** One's warmest wishes or regards: *Give them my best.* **—at best.** **1.** When interpreted most favorably. **2.** Under the most favorable conditions. **—for the best.** For the ultimate good. **—get** (or **have**) **the best of.** To defeat, surpass, or outwit. **—make the best of.** To do as well as possible under unfavorable conditions. ~*tr.v.* **bested, besting, bests.** To prevail over; surpass; defeat: *"I'm a rough customer, I expect, but I know when I'm bested"* (Nathanael West). [Middle English *best,* Old English *bet(e)st.*]

Best (bĕst), **Charles Herbert** (1899–1978). Canadian physician and physiologist, famous for collaborating with John J.R. MacLeod and Sir Frederick Banting in the extraction of the hormone insulin from a dog's pancreas (1921) and the subsequent demonstration that it could be used to arrest the progress of diabetes mellitus, then a fatal disease.

be·stead (bĭ-stĕd') *tr.v.* **-steaded** or **-stead, -steading, -steads.** *Archaic.* To be of service to; avail; aid. ~*adj. Archaic.* Placed; located. [BE- + STEAD (to help).]

bes·tial (bĕs'chəl, bĕst'yəl) *adj.* **1.** Of or pertaining to an animal. **2.** Having the qualities of or behaving in the manner of a brute; savage; depraved. **3.** Subhuman in intelligence. [Middle English, from Old French, from Late Latin *bēstiālis,* from Latin *bēstia,* BEAST.] **—bes·tial·ly** *adv.*

bes·ti·al·i·ty (bĕs'chē-ăl'ĭ-tē, bĕs'tē-ăl'-) *n., pl.* **-ties. 1.** The quality of being bestial; animal nature. **2.** An action or conduct marked by repugnant carnality or brutality. **3.** Sexual relations between a human being and an animal; sodomy.

bes·tial·ize (bĕs'chə-līz', bĕst'yə-) *tr.v.* **-ized, -izing, -izes.** To make bestial; brutalize.

bes·ti·ar·y (bĕs'chē-ĕr'ē, bĕs'tē-) *n., pl.* **-ies. 1.** A medieval collection of allegorical fables about the habits and traits of animals, each fable followed by an interpretation of its moral significance. **2.** A modern version of such a collection. [Medieval Latin *bēstiārium,* from Latin *bēstia,* BEAST.]

be·stir (bǐ-stûr′) *tr.v.* **-stirred, -stirring, -stirs.** To cause to become active; rouse. Usually used reflexively: *She bestirred herself and went for a walk.*

best man *n.* The bridegroom's chief attendant at a wedding.

be·stow (bǐ-stō′) *tr.v.* **-stowed, -stowing, -stows. 1.** To present as a gift or honor; confer. Used with *on* or *upon.* **2.** To give in marriage. **3.** To apply; use: *"On Hester Prynne's story . . . I bestowed much thought"* (Nathaniel Hawthorne). **4.** *Archaic.* To store; house. [Middle English *bestowen :* be- (intensive) + STOW.] **—be·stow·able** *adj.* **—be·stow·al, be·stow·ment** *n.*

be·strew (bǐ-strōō′) *tr.v.* **-strewed, -strewed** or **-strewn** (-strōōn′), **-strewing, -strews. 1.** To strew (a surface) with things so as to cover it. **2.** To scatter or cast things profusely on a surface. **3.** To lie scattered over or about.

be·stride (bǐ-strīd′) *tr.v* **-strode** (-strōd′), **-stridden** (-strĭd′n), **-striding, -strides. 1.** To sit or stand on with the legs widely spread; straddle. **2.** To step over. [Middle English *bestriden,* Old English *bestrīdan : be-,* over + *strīdan,* to STRIDE.]

best seller *n.* A book or other product that is among those sold in the largest numbers. **—best-sell·ing** (bĕst′sĕl′ĭng) *adj.*

bet (bĕt) *n.* **1.** An agreement between two parties such that the one proved wrong about an uncertain outcome will forfeit a stipulated thing or sum to the other; a wager. **2.** The fact, event, or outcome on which a wager is made. **3.** The object or amount risked in a wager; the stake. **4. a.** A plan or course of action: *Your best bet is to leave now.* **b.** *Informal.* A view; opinion: *My bet is that she won't come.* **—hedge one's bets. 1.** To protect oneself from possible loss by betting on more than one outcome. **2.** To guard against risk; cover oneself.

~*v.* **bet** or rare **betted, betting, bets.** *—tr.* **1.** To stake (an object or amount, for example) in a bet. **2.** To make a bet with. **3.** To make a bet on (a contestant or an outcome). **4.** To predict confidently. *—intr.* To make or place a bet. **—you bet.** *Informal.* Surely. [16th century : perhaps short for ABET in the sense of "instigation."]

be·ta (bā′tə, bē′-) *n.* **1.** The second letter in the Greek alphabet, written B, β. Transliterated in English as *B, b,* and sometimes, for Modern Greek words, as *V, v.* See feature at **alphabet. 2.** The second item in a series or system of classification. **3.** *Chiefly British.* A second-class mark for an examination, essay, or the like. **4.** *Physics.* **a.** A **beta particle** *(see).* **b.** A **beta ray** *(see).* [Greek *bēta,* from Hebrew *bēth,* BETH.]

beta blocker *n.* Any of a group of drugs that slow down the action of the heart by blocking the action of nerve endings called *beta-receptors.* They are used to treat abnormal heart conditions and high blood pressure.

be·ta·ine (bē′tə-ēn′) *n.* A sweet, crystalline alkaloid, $C_5H_{11}NO_2$, occurring in sugar beets and other plants and formerly used in treatment of muscular degeneration. [Latin *bēta,* BEET + -INE.]

be·take (bǐ-tāk′) *tr.v.* **-took** (-tōōk′), **-taken, -taking, -takes. 1.** To cause (oneself) to go or move. **2.** *Archaic.* To commit or apply (oneself) to something: *He betook himself to fasting.*

Be·tan·court (bĕ-tän-kōōr′), **Romulo** (1908–81). Venezuelan politician. He founded the National Democratic Party (1935), later renamed Democratic Action. He spent several years in exile, but served twice as president.

beta particle *n.* A high-speed electron or positron, especially one emitted in radioactive decay.

beta ray *n.* A stream of beta particles, especially of electrons.

beta rhythm *n.* The waveform occurring in electroencephalograms of the adult brain, characteristically having a frequency from 18 to 30 cycles per second and associated with an alert waking state. Also called "beta wave." Compare **alpha rhythm.**

be·ta·tron (bā′tə-trŏn′, bē′-) *n.* A fixed-radius magnetic induction electron **accelerator** *(see)* capable of accelerating electrons to energies of a few million to a few hundred million electron volts. [BETA + -TRON.]

be·tel (bēt′l) *n.* A climbing Asiatic plant, *Piper betle,* the leaves of which are chewed with the betel nut, especially in southeastern Asia, to induce both stimulating and narcotic effects. [Portuguese *betel, betle,* from Malayalam *veṭṭila.*]

Be·tel·geuse, Be·tel·geux (bĕt′l-jōōz′, bĕt′l-joez′) *n.* A bright-red intrinsic-variable star, about 600 light years from Earth, in the constellation Orion. [French *Bételgeuse,* from Arabic *bīt al-jauzā',* "shoulder of the Giant (Orion)."]

betel nut *n.* Also **be·tel·nut** (bēt′l-nŭt′). The seed of the fruit of the betel palm, chewed, together with betel leaves and lime, by many people of southeastern Asia.

betel palm *n.* A palm tree, *Areca catechu,* of tropical Asia, having featherlike leaves and orange or scarlet fruit. See note at **betel nut.**

bête noire (bĕt nwär′) *n., pl.* **bêtes noires** *(pronounced as singular).* Someone or something that one especially dislikes or avoids. [French, "black beast."]

beth (bĕt) *n.* The second letter of the Hebrew alphabet. See feature at **alphabet.** [Hebrew *bēth,* "house."]

Beth·a·ny (bĕth′ə-nē). *Arabic* **Al-'Ay·zar·i·yah** (ăl-ī′zə-rē′ə, -yə). Small village at the southeastern foot of the Mount of Olives, in the Israeli-occupied West Bank. The miracle of Lazarus's resurrection took place here (the Arabic name means "Lazarus").

Be·the (bā′tə), **Hans Albrecht** (1906–). American physicist, born in Germany. His chief work has been the study of nuclear reactions in stars, especially that by which hydrogen is converted to helium.

He was awarded the Nobel Prize in physics (1967).

beth·el (bĕth′əl, bē′thĕl′) *n.* **1.** A hallowed or holy place. **2.** A chapel for seamen. **3.** *Chiefly British.* A Nonconformist chapel. [Hebrew *bēth 'Ēl,* "house of God."]

Beth·el (bĕth′əl). A town of Biblical Palestine, about 18 kilometers (11 miles) north of Jerusalem. Genesis 28:19.

Be·thes·da (bə-thĕz′də). An urban center in west-central Maryland, forming a residential suburb of Washington, D.C. The National Institutes of Health, the National Cancer Institute, and the Naval Medical Center are located in Bethesda.

be·think (bǐ-thĭngk′) *v.* **-thought** (-thôt′), **-thinking, -thinks.** *—tr.* **1.** To reflect upon; think about; consider. **2.** To remind (oneself); remember. *—intr. Archaic.* To meditate; ponder. [Middle English *bethinken,* Old English *bethencan : be-,* about + *thencan,* to THINK.]

Beth·le·hem (bĕth′lĭ-hĕm, -lē-əm). Small market town in the Judaean Hills, south of Jerusalem, in the Israeli-occupied West Bank. Traditionally held to be the birthplace of Christ, it was the home and probably the birthplace of David, who was annointed King of Israel by Samuel here.

Be·thune (bǐ-thōōn′), **Mary McLeod** (1875–1955). U.S. educator. Noted for her work on behalf of education for blacks and improved racial relations, she served as an adviser on minority affairs for President Franklin D. Roosevelt. In 1945 she was an observer with the U.S. delegation to the first United Nations meeting in San Francisco.

be·tide (bǐ-tīd′) *v.* **-tided, -tiding, -tides.** *—tr.* To happen to: *Woe betide you if you harm his son.* *—intr.* To take place; befall. **—See** Synonyms at **happen.** [Middle English *betiden : be-,* thoroughly + *tiden,* to happen, Old English *tīdan.*]

be·times (bǐ-tīmz′) *adv.* **1.** Early; in good time: *He awoke betimes.* **2.** *Archaic.* Quickly; soon. [Middle English, adverbial genitive of *betime : be,* BY + TIME.]

bê·tise (bā-tēz′) *n., pl.* **bêtises** *(pronounced as singular).* **1.** A foolish or gauche remark or action. **2.** Folly; ignorance. [French.]

Bet·je·man (bĕch′ə-mən), **Sir John** (1906–84). British poet laureate (1972–84). He produced many collections of poems, including a verse autobiography, *Summoned by Bells* (1960), and wrote extensively on Victorian architecture.

be·to·ken (bǐ-tō′kən) *tr.v.* **-kened, -kening, -kens.** To give a sign or portent of: *Those clouds betoken snow.* **—See** Synonyms at **foretell.** [Middle English *betokenen,* Old English *bitācnian* (unattested).] **—be·to·ken·er** *n.*

bet·o·ny (bĕt′ə-nē) *n., pl.* **-nies. 1.** Any of several plants of the genus *Stachys;* especially, *S. officinalis,* native to Eurasia, having a spike of reddish-purple flowers. **2.** A plant, the **lousewort** *(see).* [Middle English *betone,* from Old French *betoine,* from Latin *bētonica, vettonica,* probably after the *Vettones,* an ancient Iberian tribe.]

be·took. Past tense of **betake.**

be·tray (bǐ-trā′) *tr.v.* **-trayed, -traying, -trays. 1.** To give aid or information to an enemy of; commit treason against or be a traitor to: *betray one's nation.* **2.** To be disloyal or faithless to. **3.** To divulge in a breach of confidence: *"A servant . . . betrayed their presence . . . to the Germans"* (William Styron). **4.** To make known unintentionally: *"Only the young have the right to betray their ignorance"* (Henry Adams). **5.** To show unintentionally; reveal; indicate: *His shaking hands betrayed his nervousness.* **6.** To deceive; lead astray. **7.** *Archaic.* To seduce and forsake (a woman). **—See** Synonyms at **reveal, deceive.** [Middle English *betrayen : be-,* thoroughly + *trayen,* to betray, from Old French *trair,* from Latin *trādere : trāns-,* over + *dare,* to give.] **—be·tray·al, be·tray·ment** *n.* **—be·tray·er** *n.*

be·troth (bǐ-trōth′, -trôth′) *tr.v.* **-trothed, -trothing, -troths. 1.** To promise to give in marriage. **2.** To promise to marry.

be·troth·al (bǐ-trō′thəl) *n.* Also **be·troth·ment** (bǐ-trōth′mənt, -trôth′-). **1.** The act of becoming betrothed or of betrothing. **2.** A mutual promise to marry; an engagement.

be·trothed (bǐ-trōthd′, -trôtht′) *adj.* Engaged to be married.
~*n., pl.* **betrothed.** A person who is engaged to be married.

bet·ter¹ (bĕt′ər). **1.** Comparative of **good. 2.** Comparative of **well.**
~*adj.* **1.** Greater in excellence or higher in quality. **2.** More useful, suitable, or desirable. **3.** Larger; greater: *the better part of a summer.* **4.** Healthier than before. **—better off.** In a better or wealthier condition.
~*adv.* **1.** In a more useful, suitable, or desirable way. **2.** To a greater or higher extent or degree. **3.** More: *better than a year.* **—go one better.** To outdo or improve upon someone or something. **—had better.** Ought to; would be wise to. **—think better of.** To change one's mind about (a course of action) after reconsideration.
~*n.* **1.** Something more useful, excellent, desirable, or suitable. Usually used with *the.* **2.** *Usually* **betters.** One's superiors, especially in social standing, competence, or intelligence. **—for the better.** Resulting in an improvement. **—for better or for worse.** Whatever happens subsequently; despite any future setbacks. **—get** (or **have**) **the better of. 1.** To overcome; defeat. **2.** To gain an advantage over.
~*v.* **bettered, -tering, -ters.** *—tr.* **1.** To improve. Often used reflexively. **2.** To surpass or exceed. *—intr.* To become better. **—See** Synonyms at **improve.** [Middle English *bettre,* Old English *betera.*]

bet·ter², bet·tor (bĕt′ər) *n.* One who bets.

better half *n.* A spouse. Used humorously.

bet·ter·ment (bĕt′ər-mənt) *n.* **1.** An improvement. **2.** *Usually* **betterments.** *Law.* Any improvement, excluding mere repairs, that adds to the value of real property.

betting shop *n. Chiefly British.* Licensed premises where bets may be placed; a bookmaker's shop.

be·tween (bĭ-twēn′) *prep.* **1.** Intermediate in the space separating two places or things. **2.** Intermediate to two times, quantities, or degrees: *between 11:00 and 12:00.* **3.** At a point in relation to two specified points, such that a perpendicular from the first point can be dropped to the line joining the two other points. **4.** Connecting spatially: *a path between the house and the road.* **5.** Connecting in reciprocal action or effort: *an agreement between workers and management.* **6.** By the combined efforts of: *Between them, they succeeded.* **7.** In the combined possession of: *They had three dollars between them.* **8.** Either one or the other of: *choose between riding and walking.* **—between you and me.** In strictest confidence. *~adv.* In an intermediate space, position, or time; in the interim. **—in between.** In an intermediate position or situation. [Middle English *betwene*, Old English *betwēonum*.]

be·tween·times (bĭ-twēn′tīmz′) *adv.* In the interval; between other acts.

be·twixt (bĭ-twĭkst′) *adv. Archaic & Poetic.* Between. *~prep. Archaic & Poetic.* Between. **—betwixt and between.** In an intermediate or indecisive state; in a middle position; neither wholly one nor the other. [Middle English *betwix(te)*, Old English *betwēohs, betwihs.*]

Beu·lah (byōō′lə). **1.** In the Old Testament, the land of Israel. Isaiah 62:4. **2.** The land of peace described in Bunyan's *Pilgrim's Progress.*

BeV *Physics.* Billion electron volts. The abbreviation **GeV** (gigaelectron volts) is preferred in standard international usage.

Bev·an (bĕv′ən), **Aneurin,** known as "Nye" (1897–1960). British politician. A coal miner and trade unionist, he was a Labour member of Parliament (1929–60). As minister of health (1945–51) he was the chief architect of the National Health Service.

bev·el (bĕv′əl) *n.* **1.** The angle or inclination of a line or surface that meets another at any angle other than 90 degrees. **2.** A rule with an adjustable arm, used to measure or draw angles or to fix a surface at an angle. In this sense, also called "bevel square." *~adj.* Inclined at an angle; slanted. *~v.* **beveled, -eling, -els.** Also *chiefly British* **-elled, -elling.** *—tr.* To cut at an inclination that forms an angle other than a right angle. *—intr.* To be inclined; slope. [Old French *bevel* (unattested), from *baif*, open-mouthed, from *bayer*, to gape. See **bay** (space).]

bevel gear *n.* Either of a pair of gears with teeth surfaces cut so that the gear shafts are not parallel.

bev·er·age (bĕv′rĭj, bĕv′ə-rĭj) *n.* Any of various liquid refreshments, usually excluding water. [Middle English *beverege*, from Old French *bevrage*, from Vulgar Latin *biberāticum* (unattested), from Latin *bibere*, to drink.]

Bev·er·ly Hills (bĕv′ər-lē). City in California, completely surrounded by greater Los Angeles. It adjoins Hollywood and is famous as the residential area of wealthy stars of show business.

Bev·in (bĕv′ĭn), **Ernest** (1881–1951). British trade unionist and politician. Bevin became secretary of the dock workers' union (1911) which became the Transport and General Workers' Union (1921). He entered Parliament (1940) and joined Churchill's war cabinet as minister of labor and national service. As foreign secretary (1945–51) he played an important part in the establishment of NATO.

bev·y (bĕv′ē) *n., pl.* **-ies. 1.** A group of animals or birds, especially larks or quail. **2.** A group, especially of girls. [15th century : origin obscure.]

be·wail (bĭ-wāl′) *v.* **-wailed, -wailing, -wails.** *—tr.* To express sorrow or regret over; cry or complain about. *—intr.* To wail or lament. **—be·wail·er** *n.* **—be·wail·ment** *n.*

be·ware (bĭ-wâr′) *v.* **-wared, -waring, -wares.** *—tr.* To be on guard against; be cautious of. Used chiefly in the imperative or infinitive. *—intr.* To be wary or careful. Used chiefly in the imperative or infinitive, sometimes with *of.* [Middle English *be war* : BE (imperative) + *war(e),* WARY.]

Bew·ick (byōō′ĭk), **Thomas** (1753–1828). English illustrator and wood engraver whose best-known work is his *History of British Birds* (1797–1804).

be·wil·der (bĭ-wĭl′dər) *tr.v.* **-dered, -dering, -ders. 1.** To confuse or befuddle, especially with numerous conflicting situations, objects, or statements. **2.** *Rare.* To cause to become lost. **—See Synonyms** at **puzzle.** [BE- + archaic *wilder,* to stray, probably from WILDERNESS.] **—be·wil·der·ing·ly** *adv.*

be·wil·der·ment (bĭ-wĭl′dər-mənt) *n.* **1.** The condition of being bewildered. **2.** A situation of perplexity or confusion.

be·witch (bĭ-wĭch′) *tr.v.* **-witched, -witching, -witches. 1.** To place under one's power by magic; cast a spell over. **2.** To captivate completely; fascinate. [Middle English *bewicchen* : *be-,* thoroughly + *wicchen,* to bewitch, Old English *wiccian.*] **—be·witch·er** *n.* **—be·witch·ing·ly** *adv.* **—be·witch·ment** *n.*

be·wray (bĭ-rā′) *tr.v.* **-wrayed, -wraying, -wrays.** *Archaic.* To disclose, especially inadvertently; betray. [Middle English *bewreien* : *be-,* thoroughly + *wreien,* to accuse, Old English *wrēgan,* from Germanic *wrōgian* (unattested).]

bey (bā) *n.* **1.** A provincial governor in the Ottoman Empire. **2.** A native ruler of the former kingdom of Tunis. **3. a.** A Turkish title of honor and respect. **b.** A Turkish form of address equivalent to *Mr.* [Turkish, prince, lord, gentleman, from Ottoman Turkish *beg.*]

be·yond (bē-ŏnd′) *prep.* **1.** Farther away than; on the far side of.

2. After a specified time; later than. **3. a.** Past or outside the limits, reach, or scope of. **b.** Not comprehensible to: *It's beyond me.* **4.** In addition to; besides. *~adv.* Farther along; to the farther side. *~n. Sometimes* **Beyond.** That which is outside the scope of human experience; especially, life after death: *the Great Beyond.* [Middle English *beyonde,* Old English *begeondan* : *be,* BY + *geondan,* farther, from *geond,* YONDER.]

Beyrouth. See **Beirut.**

bez·ant, bez·zant (bĕz′ənt, bə-zănt′) *n.* Also **byz·ant** (bĭz′ənt, bĭ-zănt′). **1.** A gold coin issued in Byzantium; a solidus. **2.** *Architecture.* A flat disk, used as an ornament. **3.** *Heraldry.* A round gold mark. [Middle English *besant,* from Old French, from Latin *Bȳzantius,* of BYZANTIUM.]

bez·el, bez·il (bĕz′əl) *n.* **1.** A slanting surface or bevel on the edge of various cutting tools. **2.** The upper, faceted portion of a cut gem, above the girdle. **3.** A groove or flange designed to hold the beveled edge of a watch crystal or a gem. [Probably from Old French *besel*† (unattested).]

be·zique (bə-zēk′) *n.* **1.** A card game similar to whist for two players, played with two packs of cards with all of the cards from two to six removed. **2.** The highest-scoring combination in this game, that of queen of spades and knave of diamonds. [French *bésigue*†.]

be·zoar (bē′zôr′, -zōr′) *n.* A hard gastric or intestinal mass, found chiefly in ruminants and once considered an antidote to poison. [Middle English *bezear,* from Old French *bezar,* from Arabic *bā-zahr,* from Persian *pād-zahr* : *pād,* protecting against, + *zahr,* poison, from (unattested) Old Persian *jathra.*]

bf, bf. boldface.

b.f. 1. boldface. **2.** *Accounting.* brought forward.

B/F *Accounting.* brought forward.

B.F.A. Bachelor of Fine Arts.

Bha·ga·vad-Gi·ta (bä′gə-väd-gē′tə) *n.* A sacred Hindu text that is incorporated into the *Mahabharata,* an ancient Sanskrit epic. It takes the form of a philosophical dialogue in which Krishna, disguised as a charioteer, explains to the prince Arjuna the whole nature of being. [Sanskrit *Bhagavad-gītā,* "Song of the Blessed One" : *Bhágaḥ,* god of wealth, "the allotter," from *bhájati,* apportion, enjoy + *gītā,* a song.]

bha·ji·a (bä′jē-ə) *n.* Also **bha·gi** (bä′jē). An Indian savory consisting of a vegetable deep-fried in gram flour batter. [Hindi.]

bhak·ti (bŭk′tē) *n. Hinduism.* The devotional way of achieving salvation, open to all irrespective of sex or caste. [Sanskrit, "portion," from *bhajati,* he allocates.]

bhang (băng) *n.* **1.** A plant, **hemp** *(see).* **2.** Any of several narcotics made from hemp. [Hindi *bhāng,* from Sanskrit *bhaṅgā*†, hemp.]

bha·ra·ta na·tyam (bŭr′ə-tə nät′yəm) *n.* Also **bha·ra·ta na·tya** (-yə). A traditional Hindu dance, formerly performed as a religious ceremony, involving pantomime and song. [Sanskrit, "Bharata's dancing" : *Bharata,* supposed author of a classical treatise on dance and drama + *nātyam,* dancing, dramatic art.]

bhin·di (bĭn′dē) *n.* Okra, as used in Indian dishes. [Hindi.]

Bho·pal (bō-päl′). The capital city of Madhya Pradesh state in central India. A major railway junction and trade center, it is the site of the 19th-century Táj-ul-Masjid, the largest mosque in India.

bhp, b.hp. brake horsepower.

Bhu·tan (bōō-tän′, -tän′). Isolated kingdom in the eastern Himalayas. Although independent, its foreign affairs have been directed by Great Britain (1910–49) and since then by India. The country's eight fertile valleys opening onto the plains of India support more than 95 percent of its people. The main sources of foreign exchange are tourism and exports of timber, postage stamps, fruit, and handicrafts. Less than 5 percent of the people are literate. Area, 47,000 square kilometers (18,142 square miles). Population, 1,300,000. Capital, Thimphu. See map at **India.**

Bhu·tan·ese (bōō′tə-nēz′, -nēs′) *n., pl.* **Bhutanese.** Also **Bhu·ta·ni** (bōō-tä′nē), *pl.* **-nis** or collectively **Bhutani. 1.** A native or inhabitant of Bhutan. **2.** The Sino-Tibetan language spoken in Bhutan. *~adj.* Of or characteristic of Bhutan, its people, or their language or culture.

Bhut·to (bōō′tō), **Zulfikar Ali** (1928–79). Pakistani politician. In 1963 he was appointed foreign minister, quarreled with the government over the peace terms with India (1965), and formed his own opposition party, the Pakistan People's Party (1967). In 1971 he became president of Pakistan and subsequently prime minister (1973). In 1977 he won a massive victory at the polls; but his opponents claimed that he had rigged the elections, and in July he was deposed by an army coup. Two years later he was executed for alleged crimes against the state.

Bi The symbol for the element bismuth.

bi–¹. Variant of **bio-.**

bi–², **bin–** *prefix.* Indicates: **1.** Two; for example, **binocular.** **2. a.** Appearance or occurrence in intervals of two; for example, **bicentennial.** **b.** Appearance or occurrence twice during; for example, **biannual.** **3.** Occurrence on both sides or directions; for example, **biconcave, bilateral. 4.** *Chemistry.* **a.** An acid salt, in which only part of the hydrogen of the acid has been replaced; for example, **sodium bicarbonate. b.** An organic compound containing a double radical; for example, **biphenyl.** [Latin *bi-, bin-,* from *bis,* twice.]

Usage: **Bimonthly** and **biweekly** mean "once every two months" and "once every two weeks." For "twice a month" and "twice a week," the words **semimonthly** and **semiweekly** should be used. But

bezant *An example of this Byzantine gold coin, with a portrait of Justinian I, who ruled in Constantinople A.D. 527–65.*

there is a great deal of confusion over the distinction, and a writer is well advised to substitute expressions like "every two months" or "twice a month" where possible. However, used as nouns to denote "a publication that appears every two months," the words with *bi-* are unavoidable.

Bi·a·fra (bē-ä′frə, -äf′rə). Former region of eastern Nigeria, chiefly peopled by the Ibo. It seceded as Biafra (1967-70), reverting only after a savage civil war. It now forms the federal states of Anambra, Imo, and Cross River. —**Bi·af·ran** *adj. & n.*

Biafra, Bight of. The eastern arm of the Gulf of Guinea on the west coast of Africa, stretching from the Niger delta to northern Gabon.

Bia·ly·stok (bē-ä′lĭ-stôk′). Industrial and railway city in northeast Poland. Nearly half of the city's population was killed during the Nazi occupation (1941-44).

bi·an·nu·al (bī-ăn′yōō-əl) *adj.* Happening twice each year; semiannual. —**bi·an·nu·al·ly** *adv.*

    Usage: There is confusion between this word and *biennial. Biannual* means "twice a year"; *biennial* means "once in two years" or "lasting for two years."

Bi·ar·ritz (bē′ə-rĭts′). Seaside resort and spa in southwestern France, on the Bay of Biscay. It is a fashionable gambling resort.

bi·as (bī′əs) *n.* **1.** A line cutting diagonally across the grain of fabric: *cut cloth on the bias.* **2. a.** Preference or inclination that inhibits impartial judgment; prejudice. **b.** A particular instance of this. **3. a.** A weight or irregularity in a ball that causes it to swerve, as in lawn bowling. **b.** The tendency of such a ball to swerve. **4.** The fixed voltage applied to an electrode, in a valve, transistor, or electronic circuit. **5.** *Statistics.* **a.** An influence that distorts the true expected value of a statistic. **b.** A distortion in findings from an oversight in investigation.

  ~adj. Slanting or diagonal; oblique: *a bias fold.*

  ~adv. Obliquely; aslant.

  ~tr.v. **biased** or **biassed, biasing** or **biassing, biases** or **biasses. 1.** To cause to have a prejudiced view; prejudice or influence. **2.** To apply a small voltage to (an electrode). [French, from Old French *biais,* oblique, from Old Provençal, perhaps from Greek *epikarsios†,* oblique.]

  Usage: Bias has generally been defined as "uninformed or unintentional inclination"; as such it may operate either for or against someone or something. Recently *bias* has been used in the sense of "adverse action or discrimination": *Congress included a provision in the Civil Rights Act of 1964 banning racial bias in employment.*

bias binding *n.* A strip of material cut across the grain of a fabric used to strengthen hems, finish edges, or the like.

bi·ath·lete (bī-ăth′lēt′) *n.* One who takes part in a biathlon.

bi·ath·lon (bī-ăth′lən, -lŏn′) *n.* An athletic competition that combines events in cross-country skiing and rifle-shooting. [BI- + Greek *athlon,* contest.]

bi·au·ric·u·lar (bī′ô-rĭk′yə-lər) *adj.* Also **bi·au·ric·u·late** (-lĭt, -lāt′). Possessing two auricles.

bi·ax·i·al (bī-ăk′sē-əl) *adj.* Having two axes. Used especially of crystals that have two optic axes. —**bi·ax·i·al·i·ty** (bī-ăk′sē-ăl′ə-tē) *n.* —**bi·ax·i·al·ly** *adv.*

bib (bĭb) *n.* **1.** A piece of cloth or plastic worn under the chin by small children, to protect the clothing during meals. **2.** The part of an apron, smock, or pair of overalls worn over the chest. **3.** A European food fish, *Gadus luscus,* related to the cod, with a barbel on its lower jaw. Also called "pout," "whiting pout."

  ~v. **bibbed, bibbing, bibs.** *—tr.* To drink; imbibe. *—intr.* To indulge in drinking; tipple. [Middle English *bibben,* to tipple, drink, perhaps from Latin *bibere.*]

Bib. Bible; Biblical.

bib and tucker *n. Informal.* Clothing; an outfit. Usually used in the phrase *one's best bib and tucker.*

bibb (bĭb) *n.* **1.** A bracket on the mast of a ship to support the trestletrees. **2.** A bibcock *(see).* [Variant of BIB (napkin).]

bib·ber (bĭb′ər) *n.* A tippler; a drinker: *a wine-bibber.* [From BIB (to drink).]

bib·cock (bĭb′kŏk′) *n.* A tap with a nozzle that is bent downward. Also called "bibb." [BIB (napkin) + COCK.]

bi·be·lot (bĭb′lō; *French* bē-blō′) *n.* A trinket or small decorative curio. [French, from Old French *beubelet,* from a reduplication of *bel,* beautiful, from Latin *bellus,* handsome, fine.]

bibl., Bibl. Biblical.

Bi·ble (bī′bəl) *n. Abbr.* **B., Bib. 1.** The sacred book of Christianity, a collection of ancient writings including the books of both the Old Testament and the New Testament, and, in the Roman Catholic Bible, the deuterocanonical books. See **Old Testament, New Testament, Apocrypha, King James Bible, Revised Version, Revised Standard Version, Douay Bible, Vulgate, New English Bible, Jerusalem Bible. 2.** The Old Testament, the sacred book of Judaism. See **Hebrew Scriptures. 3. bible.** Any book or collection of writings constituting the guiding text of a religion, political movement, or individual lifestyle. **4. bible.** Any book considered authoritative in its field. [Middle English, from Old French, from Medieval Latin *biblia,* from Greek *(ta) biblia,* "(the) books," plural of *biblion,* book, originally a diminutive of *biblos, bublos,* papyrus, scroll, book, after *Bublos,* Phoenician port from which the Egyptian papyrus was exported to Greece.]

Bible Belt *n.* Those sections of the United States, especially in the South and Middle West, where Protestant fundamentalism prevails. [Coined by H.L. MENCKEN, *c.* 1925.]

Bible paper *n.* A thin, strong, opaque printing paper used for Bi-

bib *An embroidered chestpiece, or bib, on a Palestinian dress from Bethlehem.*

bles and reference books. Also called "India paper."

Bible thumper *n. Informal.* A person who enthusiastically, dogmatically, and often aggressively expounds and refers to the Bible or religion. —**Bible-thumping** *n. & adj.*

Bib·li·cal (bĭb′lĭ-kəl) *adj. Sometimes* **biblical.** *Abbr.* **Bib., Bibl., bibl. 1.** Of, pertaining to, or contained in the Bible. **2.** In keeping with the nature of the Bible, especially: **a.** Suggestive of the personages or times depicted in the Bible. **b.** Suggestive of the prose or narrative style of the King James Bible. [Obsolete *biblic,* probably from Medieval Latin *biblicus,* from *biblia,* BIBLE.] —**Bib·li·cal·ly** *adv.*

Biblical Aramaic *n.* A form of Aramaic that was the original language of the non-Hebrew portions of the Old Testament, such as certain passages in Ezra, Daniel, and Jeremiah. Also called "Chaldee." Compare **Aramaic.**

Bib·li·cist (bĭb′lə-sĭst) *n.* Also **Bib·list** (bĭb′lĭst). **1.** An expert on the Bible. **2.** A person who interprets the Bible literally. **3.** One who emphasizes the authority of the Bible rather than tradition. [From obsolete *biblic,* BIBLICAL.] —**Bib·li·cism** *n.*

biblio- *prefix.* Indicates books; for example, **bibliomania.** [Greek *biblion,* book. See **Bible.**]

bib·li·o·film (bĭb′lē-ō-fĭlm′) *n.* A type of microfilm used especially to photograph the pages of books.

bibliog. bibliographer; bibliography.

bib·li·og·ra·pher (bĭb′lē-ŏg′rə-fər) *n.* Also **bib·li·o·graph** (bĭb′lē-ə-grăf′, -gräf′). *Abbr.* **bibliog. 1.** An expert in the description and cataloguing of printed matter. **2.** One who compiles a bibliography.

bib·li·og·ra·phy (bĭb′lē-ŏg′rə-fē) *n., pl.* **-phies.** *Abbr.* **bibliog. 1. a.** A list of the works of a particular author or publisher, or of sources of information in print on a particular subject. **b.** A list of sources used as reference for the writing of a book, thesis, or the like. **2. a.** The description and identification of the editions, dates of issue, authorship, and typography of books or other written material. **b.** A compilation of such information. [French *bibliographie,* from New Latin *bibliographia* : BIBLIO- + -GRAPHY.] —**bib·li·o·graph·ic** (bĭb′lē-ə-grăf′ĭk), **bib·li·o·graph·i·cal** *adj.* —**bib·li·o·graph·i·cal·ly** *adv.*

bib·li·ol·a·try (bĭb′lē-ŏl′ə-trē) *n.* **1.** Excessive adherence to a literal interpretation of the Bible. **2.** Extreme devotion to or concern with books. [BIBLIO- + -LATRY.] —**bib·li·ol·a·ter** *n.* —**bib·li·ol·a·trous** *adj.*

bib·li·o·man·cy (bĭb′lē-ō-măn′sē) *n., pl.* **-cies.** Divination by interpretation of a passage chosen at random from a book, especially the Bible. [BIBLIO- + -MANCY.]

bib·li·o·ma·ni·a (bĭb′lē-ō-mā′nē-ə, -mān′yə) *n.* An exaggerated liking for acquiring and owning books. [BIBLIO- + -MANIA.] —**bib·li·o·ma·ni·ac** *n. & adj.* —**bib·li·o·ma·ni·a·cal** (bĭb′lē-ō-mə-nī′ə-kəl) *adj.*

bib·li·o·phile (bĭb′lē-ə-fīl′) *n.* Also **bib·li·o·phil** (-fĭl′), **bib·li·oph·i·list** (bĭb′lē-ŏf′ə-lĭst). **1.** One who loves books. **2.** A book collector. [French : BIBLIO- + -PHILE.] —**bib·li·o·phil·ic** (bĭb′lē-ə-fĭl′ĭk) *adj.,* **bib·li·oph·i·lism** (bĭb′lē-ŏf′ə-lĭz′əm), **bib·li·oph·i·ly** *n.* —**bib·li·oph·i·lis·tic** (bĭb′lē-ŏf′ə-lĭs′tĭk) *adj.*

bib·li·o·pole (bĭb′lē-ə-pōl′) *n.* Also **bib·li·op·o·list** (bĭb′lē-ŏp′ə-lĭst). A person who deals in rare books. [Latin *bibliopōla,* from Greek *bibliopōlēs* : BIBLIO- + *pōlēs,* seller, from *pōlein,* to sell.] —**bib·li·o·pol·ic** (bĭb′lē-ə-pŏl′ĭk) *adj.,* —**bib·li·op·o·ly** (bĭb′lē-ŏp′ə-lē) *n.*

bib·li·o·the·ca (bĭb′lē-ə-thē′kə) *n.* **1.** A book collection; a library. **2.** A catalogue of books. [Latin *bibliothēca,* from Greek *bibliothēkē,* "case for books" : BIBLIO- + *thēkē,* receptacle, case.] —**bib·li·o·the·cal** *adj.*

Biblist. Variant of **Biblicist.**

bib·u·lous (bĭb′yə-ləs) *adj.* Given to or marked by convivial drinking. [Latin *bibulus,* from *bibere,* to drink.] —**bib·u·lous·ly** *adv.* —**bib·u·lous·ness** *n.*

bi·cam·er·al (bī-kăm′ər-əl) *adj.* Composed of two houses, chambers, or branches: *a bicameral legislature.* [BI- + Late Latin *camera,* room, CHAMBER.] —**bi·cam·er·al·ism** *n.*

bi·cap·su·lar (bī-kăp′sə-lər, -syōō-lər) *adj. Botany.* **1.** Having two capsules. **2.** Having a capsule with two locules.

bi·carb (bī-kärb′) *n. Informal.* **Sodium bicarbonate** *(see).*

bi·car·bon·ate (bī-kär′bə-nāt′, -nĭt) *n.* The radical group HCO₃ or a compound, such as sodium bicarbonate, containing it. Also called "hydrogen carbonate."

bicarbonate of soda *n.* **Sodium bicarbonate** *(see).*

bice blue (bīs) *n.* Moderate blue, the color of azurite. [Partial translation of French *azur bis,* "dark blue" : AZURE + *bis,* brown, tawny, from Old French *bis†.*]

bice green *n.* Moderate yellow green, the color of malachite. [See **bice blue.**]

bi·cen·ten·a·ry (bī′sĕn-tĕn′ər-ē, -ə-rē) *n., pl.* **-ries.** *Chiefly British.* A bicentennial. —**bi·cen·ten·a·ry** *adj.*

bi·cen·ten·ni·al (bī′sĕn-tĕn′ē-əl) *adj.* **1.** Happening once every 200 years. **2.** Lasting for 200 years. **3.** Pertaining to a 200th anniversary.

  ~n. A 200th anniversary or its celebration.

bi·cen·tric (bī-sĕn′trĭk) *adj.* Having two centers. —**bi·cen·tric·i·ty** (bī-sĕn-trĭs′ə-tē) *n.*

bi·ceph·a·lous (bī-sĕf′ə-ləs) *adj.* Two-headed.

bi·ceps (bī′sĕps′) *n., pl.* **biceps** or **-cepses** (-sĕp′sĭz). Any muscle having two heads or points of origin, especially: **a.** The large muscle at the front of the upper arm that flexes the elbow joint. **b.** The large muscle at the back of the thigh that flexes the knee joint.

[New Latin, from Latin, "two-headed" : BI- + *-ceps,* from *caput,* head.]
bi·chlo·ride (bī-klôr′īd′, -klōr′-) *n. Chemistry.* **Dichloride** *(see).*
bi·chro·mate (bī-krō′māt′, -mĭt). *Chemistry.* A **dichromate** *(see).*
bi·cip·i·tal (bī-sĭp′ə-təl) *adj.* Of or pertaining to the biceps. [New Latin *biceps* (stem *bicipit-*), BICEPS.]
bick·er (bĭk′ər) *intr.v.* **-ered, -ering, -ers. 1.** To engage in a petty quarrel; squabble. **2.** *Poetic.* To flicker; glisten; quiver. —See Synonyms at **argue.**
~*n.* A petty quarrel; a tiff. [Middle English *bikeren*†, to attack.] **—bick·er·er** *n.*
bi·col·or (bī′kŭl′ər) *adj.* Also **bi·col·ored** (bī′kŭl′ərd). Having two colors.
bi·con·cave (bī′kŏn-kāv′, bī-kŏn′kāv′) *adj.* Concave on both sides or surfaces. **—bi·con·cav·i·ty** (bī′kŏn-kăv′ə-tē) *n.*
bi·con·di·tion·al (bī′kən-dĭsh′ən-əl) *n. Logic.* **1.** A statement containing two propositions related in such a way that one can be true only if the other is true, and false only if the other is false. **2.** The relation that exists between two such propositions. Compare **equivalence. —bi·con·di·tion·al** *adj.*
bi·con·vex (bī′kŏn-vĕks′, bī-kŏn′vĕks′) *adj.* Convex on both sides or surfaces. **—bi·con·vex·i·ty** *n.*
bi·corn (bī′kôrn′) *adj.* Also **bi·cor·nu·ate** (bī-kôr′nyo͞o-ĭt, -āt′). **1.** Having two horns or two horn-shaped parts. **2.** Shaped like a crescent. [Latin *bicornis* : BI- + *cornū,* HORN.]
bi·cor·po·ral (bī-kôr′pər-əl) *adj.* Also **bi·cor·po·re·al** (bī′kôr-pôr′ē-əl, -pōr′ē-əl). Having two distinct bodies or main parts.
bi·cul·tur·al (bī-kŭl′chər-əl) *adj.* Of or relating to two separate cultures in one community. **—bi·cul·tur·al·ism** *n.*
bi·cus·pid (bī-kŭs′pĭd) *adj.* Also **bi·cus·pi·date** (-pə-dāt′). Having two points or cusps, as the crescent moon or the **mitral valve** *(see)* of the heart do.
~*n.* A bicuspid tooth, especially a **premolar** *(see).* [New Latin *bicuspis* (stem *bicuspid-*) : BI- + Latin *cuspis,* point, CUSP.]
bi·cy·cle (bī′sĭk′əl, -sĭ-kəl) *n.* A vehicle, usually designed for one person, consisting of a metal frame mounted upon two wire-spoked wheels with narrow rubber tires, one behind the other. It has a seat, handlebars for steering, brakes, and two pedals or a small motor by which it is driven.
~*intr.v.* **bicycled, -cling, -cles.** To ride or travel on a bicycle. [French : BI- + Greek *kuklos,* circle, wheel.] **—bi·cy·clist** *n.*
bicycle pump *n.* A portable hand pump for inflating bicycle tires.
bi·cy·clic (bī-sī′klĭk, -sĭk′lĭk) *adj.* Also **bi·cy·cli·cal** (bī-sī′klĭ-kəl, -sĭk′lĭ-kəl). **1.** Consisting of or having two cycles. **2.** *Botany.* Composed of or arranged in two distinct whorls, as are the petals or stamens of a flower. **3.** *Chemistry.* Consisting of or having molecules containing two fused rings.
bid (bĭd) *v.* For transitive senses 1, 2, 3: **bade** (băd, bād) or *archaic* **bad** (băd), **bidden** (bĭd′n) or **bid, bidding, bids.** For remaining senses: **bid, bid, bidding, bids.** —*tr.* **1. a.** To direct; command. **b.** To enjoin politely. **2.** To utter (a greeting or salutation). **3.** To invite to attend; summon. **4.** *Card Games.* To state one's intention to take (tricks of a certain number or suit): *bid four hearts.* **5.** To offer or propose (an amount) as a price. —*intr.* **1.** To make an offer to pay or accept a specified price. **2.** To seek to win or attain something; strive: *bid for the contract.* —See Synonyms at **command. —bid defiance.** To refuse to submit; offer resistance. **—bid fair.** To appear likely; seem. ***Note:*** In these phrases the past tense and past participle is **bid.**
~*n.* **1. a.** An offer or proposal of a price, as for an item at an auction or for a contract. **b.** The amount offered or proposed. **2.** An invitation, especially one offering membership in a group or club. **3.** *Card Games.* **a.** The act of bidding. **b.** The number of tricks or points declared. **c.** The trump or no-trump declared. **d.** The turn of a player to bid. **4.** A serious attempt to gain something; a striving: *a bid for the party leadership.* [Bid, bade, bidden; from two verbs: 1. Middle English *bidden,* ask, beseech, demand, command, *bad, beden,* Old English *biddan, bæd* (plural *bǣdon*), *(ge)beden.* 2. Middle English *beden,* to offer, present, proclaim, command (last sense adopted from *bidden*), *bead, boden,* Old English *bēodan, bēad* (plural *budon*), *(ge)boden.*] **—bid·der** *n.*
b.i.d. *Medicine.* twice a day. [Latin *bis in die*]
bi·dar·ka (bī-där′kə) *n.* A hide-covered canoe used by Eskimos of Alaska. [Russian *baidarka,* diminutive of *baidara*†.]
bid·da·ble (bĭd′ə-bəl) *adj.* **1.** Worth bidding on. Said of a hand or suit in cards. **2.** Docile; tractable. **—bid·da·bil·i·ty** *n.*
bid·den. A past participle of **bid.**
bid·ding (bĭd′ĭng) *n.* **1.** A demand that something be done; a command. **2.** A request to appear; a summons. **3. a.** The act of making bids, as at an auction or in playing cards. **b.** The bids collectively. **—at the bidding of.** At the service of; on the command of. **—do the bidding of.** To follow the orders of.
bid·dy[1] (bĭd′ē) *n., pl.* **-dies.** A hen; a fowl. [Perhaps imitative of a call used for hens.]
biddy[2] *n., pl.* **-dies.** *Slang.* A garrulous or interfering old woman. [Pet form of *Bridget,* a feminine name.]
bide (bīd) *v.* **bided** or **bode** (bōd), **bided, biding, bides.** —*intr.* **1.** To stay in some condition or state; remain the same: *"England shall bide till Judgement Tide"* (Rudyard Kipling). **2. a.** To wait or tarry: *bide for a while.* **b.** To stay: *bide at home.* **c.** To be left; remain: *"Waters stink soon, if in one place they bide"* (John Donne). —*tr.* To await. Used only in the phrase *bide one's time.* [Bide, bode; Middle English *biden, bod* (past singular), Old English *bīdan, bād.*]
bi·den·tate (bī-dĕn′tāt′) *adj.* **1.** *Biology.* Having two teeth or two toothlike projecting parts. **2.** *Chemistry.* Designating a ligand that can coordinate at two separate positions to the same atom or ion.
bi·det (bē-dā′) *n.* A basinlike fixture designed to be straddled for washing the genitals and the posterior parts. [French, "small horse," possibly from Old French *bider*†, to trot.]
Bie·der·mei·er (bē′dər-mī′ər) *adj.* **1.** Of, pertaining to, or designating a type of German furniture of the first half of the 19th century, modeled after Empire styles. **2.** Staid and conventional; philistine. [After Gottlieb *Biedermeier,* the imaginary humdrum author of poems written by L. Eichroth (1827–92), German poet.]
Biel (bēl). *French* **Bienne** (byĕn). Town in Bern canton in northwest Switzerland, renowned for its clocks.
Bie·le·feld (bē′lə-fĕlt′). Major industrial city in North Rhine-Westphalia in West Germany, long famous as a linen center.
bi·en·ni·al (bī-ĕn′ē-əl) *adj.* **1.** Lasting or living for two years. **2.** Happening every second year. **3.** *Botany.* Having a normal life cycle of two years. Compare **annual, perennial.**
~*n.* **1.** An event that occurs once every two years. **2.** A plant that normally requires two years to reach maturity, producing leaves in the first year, blooming and producing fruit in its second year, and then dying. —See Usage note at **biannual.** [From BIENNIUM.] **—bi·en·ni·al·ly** *adv.*
bi·en·ni·um (bī-ĕn′ē-əm) *n., pl.* **-ums** or **-ennia** (-ĕn′ē-ə). A two-year period. [Latin : BI- + *annus,* year.]
bier (bîr) *n.* A stand on which a corpse, or a coffin containing a corpse, is placed to lie in state or to be carried to the grave. [Middle English *bere,* Old English *bēr, bǣr.*]
Bierce (bîrs), **Ambrose Gwinnett** (1842–*c.* 1914). U.S. writer. His scathing wit and fascination with the supernatural influenced many of his works, including *The Fiend's Delight* (1872), *Can Such Things Be?* (1893), and *The Devil's Dictionary* (1906). He disappeared in Mexico and is thought to have died there in a battle.
bi·fa·cial (bī-fā′shəl) *adj.* **1.** Having two faces, fronts, or façades. **2.** *Botany.* Having upper and lower surfaces that are distinct and dissimilar. Said of leaves. **3.** Having two opposing surfaces that are alike.
biff (bĭf) *tr.v.* **biffed, biffing, biffs.** *Slang.* To strike or punch.
~*n. Slang.* A blow or cuff. [Imitative.]
bi·fid (bī′fĭd) *adj. Biology.* Divided or cleft into two parts or lobes. [Latin *bifidus* : BI- + -FID.] **—bi·fid·i·ty** *n.* **—bi·fid·ly** *adv.*
bi·fi·lar (bī-fī′lər) *adj. Physics.* Fitted with or involving the use of two threads or wires, as in certain types of electrical measuring instruments or resistors. [BI- + FILAR.] **—bi·fi·lar·ly** *adv.*
bi·flag·el·late (bī-flăj′ə-lĭt, -lāt′) *adj. Biology.* Having two flagella: *a biflagellate protozoan.*
bi·fo·cal (bī-fō′kəl) *adj.* **1.** Having two different focal lengths. **2.** Correcting for both near and distant vision.
bi·fo·cals (bī-fō′kəlz) *pl.n.* Spectacles with bifocal lenses, used for both near and distant vision.
bi·fo·li·ate (bī-fō′lē-ĭt, -āt′) *adj.* Having two leaves.
bi·fo·li·o·late (bī-fō′lē-ə-lāt′, -lĭt) *adj.* Having two leaflets.
bi·fo·rate (bī-fôr′āt′, -fōr′āt′, bī′fə-rāt′) *adj. Biology.* Having two openings or perforations. [BI- + Latin *forātus,* past participle of *forāre,* to pierce, bore.]
bi·forked (bī′fôrkt′) *adj.* Divided into two branches; bifurcate.
bi·form (bī′fôrm′) *adj.* Also **bi·formed** (-fôrmd′). Having a combination of features or qualities of two distinct forms, as a sphinx does.
bi·fur·cate (bī′fər-kāt′, bī-fûr′kāt′) *v.* **-cated, -cating, -cates.** —*tr.* To divide or separate into two parts or branches. —*intr.* To separate into two parts; fork.
~*adj.* (bī′fər-kāt′, -kĭt, bī-fûr-kāt′, -kĭt). Also **bi·fur·cat·ed** (-kā′tĭd). Forked or divided into two parts. [Medieval Latin *bifurcātus* (adjective), from Latin *bifurcus,* two-forked : BI- + *furca,* forked stake (see **fork**).] **—bi·fur·cate·ly** *adv.* **—bi·fur·ca·tion** *n.*
big (bĭg) *adj.* **bigger, biggest. 1.** Of considerable size, number, quantity, magnitude, or extent; large. **2. a.** *Obsolete.* Of great force or violence: *"Farewell the plumed troop and the big wars"* (Shakespeare). **b.** Having great intensity; great; strong. **3.** Grown-up. **4.** Elder. **5.** Pregnant. Used with *with: big with child.* **6.** Filled up; brimming over. **7.** Having or exercising considerable authority, control, or influence. **8.** Conspicuous in position, wealth, or importance; prominent; influential. **9.** Of great significance; important; momentous. **10.** Loud and firm; resounding. **11.** Bountiful; generous; kindly. **12.** *Informal.* **a.** Self-important; boastful; pompous. **b.** Ambitious: *big ideas.* **—big on.** *Informal.* Enthusiastic about: *big on women's rights.*
~*adv. Slang.* **1. a.** Pompously; pretentiously; boastfully: *"Toad talked big about all he was going to do in the days to come"* (Kenneth Grahame). **b.** Ambitiously: *think big.* **2.** With considerable success; in an outstanding manner: *His speech went down big at the conference.* [Middle English *big, byg,* strong, stout, full-grown, probably of Scandinavian origin.] **—big·gish** *adj.* **—big·ness** *n.*
big·a·mous (bĭg′ə-məs) *adj.* **1.** Involving bigamy. **2.** Guilty of bigamy. **—big·a·mous·ly** *adv.*
big·a·my (bĭg′ə-mē) *n., pl.* **-mies.** *Law.* The criminal offense of marrying one person while still legally married to another. [Middle English *bigamie,* from Old French, from *bigame,* bigamous, from Late Latin *bigamus* : BI- + -GAMOUS.] **—big·a·mist** *n.*
Big Apple *n.* New York. Used as a nickname, preceded by *the.*
big·ar·reau (bĭg′ə-rō′) *n.* Any of several varieties of sweet cherry

PRONUNCIATION KEY

ă, pat; ā, pay; âr, care;
ä, father, are; b, bib;
ch, church; d, deed; ĕ, pet;
ē, be; f, fife; g, gag; h, hat;
hw, which; ĭ, pit; ī, pie;
îr, pier; j, judge; k, kick;
l, lid, needle; m, mum;
n, no, sudden; ng, thing;
ŏ, pot; ō, toe; ô, paw, for;
oi, noise; ou, out; o͝o, book;
o͞o, boot; p, pop; r, roar;
s, sauce; sh, ship, dish;
t, tight; th, thin, path;
th, this, bathe; ŭ, cut; ûr, fur;
v, valve; w, with; y, yes;
z, zebra, size; zh, vision;
ə, about, item, edible, gallop, circus, peaceful

IN FOREIGN WORDS:

à, *Fr.* ami; œ, *Fr.* feu, *Ger.* schön; ü, *Fr.* tu, *Ger.* über; KH, *Ger.* ich, *Scot.* loch; N, *Fr.* bon; y′, *Fr.* Compiègne

STRESS MARKS:

Primary stress: ′
in·cite′ (ĭn-sīt′)
Secondary stress: ′
in′sight′ (ĭn′sīt′)

with firm, often light-colored flesh. [French, from *bigarrer*, to variegate : BI- + Old French *garre*†, variegated.]

big band *n.* A large dance or jazz band.

big-bang theory (bǐg'bǎng') *n.* A theory that the universe originated as a small, very dense mass that exploded, throwing out matter in all directions, from which galaxies and stars formed. The theory accounts for the **expanding universe** and the **microwave background** (*both of which see*). Compare **steady-state theory.**

Big Ben *n.* **1.** The bell in the clock tower of the Houses of Parliament in London. **2. a.** The clock itself. **b.** Loosely, the clock tower.

Big Bend. A section of the Columbia River in east-central Washington where the river is forced by lava beds to make a big bend westward before resuming its southerly course.

Big Bend National Park. A park in western Texas on the Mexican border, located in a triangle formed by the Rio Grande. The river and its deep canyons, the desert plain, and the Chisos Mts. offer sharp contrasts in wilderness scenery.

Big Bertha *n.* A large cannon used by the Germans in World War I. [Translation of German *dicke Bertha*, "fat Bertha," after *Bertha Krupp von Bohlen und Halbach* (1886–1957), proprietress of the Krupp Works, where the cannon was made.]

big brother *n.* **1.** An older brother or someone with whom one has a similar protective relationship. **2. Big Brother.** A vague, threatening figure representing the all-seeing, omnipresent power of an authoritarian government. [Sense 2, after *Big Brother*, a character in George Orwell's novel *1984* (1949).]

big business *n.* **1.** Commercial operations on a large scale, especially when regarded as powerful or manipulative. **2.** Any activity or undertaking regarded as commercially successful.

big deal *n. Informal.* An impressive achievement or proposition. ~*interj. Informal.* Used ironically to express contempt.

Big Dipper *n.* A cluster of seven stars in the constellation Ursa Major, four forming the bowl and three the handle of a dipper-shaped configuration. Also called the "Plow," the "Wain," the "Wagon."

bi·gem·i·nal (bī-jĕm'ə-nəl) *adj.* Occurring in pairs; twinned. [Late Latin *bigeminus*, doubled : BI- + Latin *geminus*, paired, double, twin.]

big·eye (bǐg'ī') *n.* Any of several tropical or subtropical marine fishes of the family Priacanthidae, having large eyes and reddish scales.

big game *n.* **1.** Large animals or fish hunted or caught for sport. **2.** *Slang.* An important objective. —**big-game** (bǐg'gām') *adj.*

big·gie (bǐg'ē) *n. Informal.* **1.** A bigwig; big wheel. **2.** Something, as a corporation, that is considered big or important.

big gun *n. Slang.* An important person; a bigwig.

big·head (bǐg'hĕd') *n.* **1.** *Informal.* Conceit; egotism. **2.** Any of various diseases of animals characterized by swelling of the head. —**big·head·ed** (bǐg'hĕd'ĭd) *adj.* —**big·head·ed·ness** *n.*

big·heart·ed (bǐg'här'tĭd) *adj.* Generous; charitable. —**big·heart·ed·ly** *adv.* —**big·heart·ed·ness** *n.*

big·horn (bǐg'hôrn') *n.* A wild sheep, *Ovis canadensis,* of the mountains of western North America, having massive, curved horns in the male. Also called "mountain sheep," "Rocky Mountain sheep."

Big·horn (bǐg'hôrn'). A river rising in west-central Wyoming and flowing *c.* 742 kilometers (461 miles) northward to join the Yellowstone River in southern Montana.

bight (bīt) *n.* **1. a.** A loop in a rope. **b.** The middle or slack part of an extended rope. **2.** A bend or curve, especially in a shoreline. **3.** A wide bay formed by such a bend or curve. ~*tr.v.* **bighted, bighting, bights.** To tie in or secure with a bight of a rope. [Middle English *byght*, bend, bay, armpit, Old English *byht*, bend, angle.]

big league *n.* **1.** A major league. **2.** Big time. —**big leaguer** *n.*

big-league (bǐg'lēg') *adj.* **Major-league** (*see*).

big·mouth (bǐg'mouth') *n. Slang.* A loud-mouthed or gossipy person. —**big-mouthed** (bǐg'mouthd', -moutht') *adj.*

big·no·ni·a (bǐg-nō'nē-ə) *n.* A tropical American plant of the genus *Bignonia*; especially, the **cross-vine** (*see*). [New Latin, after the Abbé Jean-Paul Bignon (1662–1743), librarian to Louis XV.]

big·ot (bǐg'ət) *n.* A person of strong conviction or prejudice, especially in matters of religion, race, or politics, who is intolerant of those who feel differently. [French, from Old French *bigot*†, a pejorative term for the Normans.] —**big·ot·ed** *adj.* —**big·ot·ed·ly** *adv.* —**big·ot·ed·ness** *n.*

big·ot·ry (bǐg'ə-trē) *n.* The attitude, state of mind, or behavior characteristic of a bigot; intolerance.

big shot *n. Slang.* An important, powerful, or influential person.

big stick *n. Informal.* A display or threat of force.

big-tick·et (bǐg'tǐk'ĭt) *adj. Informal.* Having a high price.

big time *n. Slang.* The most prestigious level of attainment in a competitive field. —**big-time** (bǐg'tīm') *adj.* —**big-tim·er** *n.*

big top *n. Informal.* **1.** The main tent of a circus. **2.** The circus.

big tree *n.* The **giant sequoia** (*see*).

big wheel *n. Slang.* A person of importance.

big·wig (bǐg'wǐg') *n. Informal.* An important person; a dignitary.

Bi·har (bǐ-här'). State in east-central India, crossed by the Ganges. Patna is the capital. Buddha passed his early years in Bihar, and the town of Buddh Gaya is a leading Buddhist center.

Bi·ha·ri (bē-hä'rē) *n.* **1.** A native or inhabitant of Bihar. **2.** The Indic language spoken in northeastern India. —**Bi·ha·ri** *adj.*

bi·jou (bē'zhōō') *n., pl.* **-joux** (-zhōōz'). **1.** A small, exquisitely wrought trinket. **2.** Any charming, delicately made thing. [French,

from Breton *bizou*, ring with a stone, from *biz*†, finger.]

bi·jou·te·rie (bē-zhōō'tə-rē) *n.* **1.** Jewelry and trinkets. **2.** A collection of jewelry or trinkets. [French, from BIJOU.]

bike (bīk) *n.* **1.** A bicycle. **2.** A motorcycle. **3.** A motorbike. ~*intr.v.* **biked, biking, bikes.** To ride a bike. [Short for BICYCLE.]

bi·ker (bī'kər) *n.* A motorcyclist, especially one who belongs to a motorcycle gang.

bi·ki·ni (bǐ-kē'nē) *n.* A brief two-piece bathing suit worn by women. [French, after BIKINI Atoll (referring to the "atomic" impact of the first bikinis).]

Bi·ki·ni (bǐ-kē'nē). Atoll in the west-central Pacific Ocean, part of the Ralik, or western, chain of the Marshall Islands, now a commonwealth of the United States. The area was used by the U.S. government to test nuclear bombs (1946–58).

Bi·ko (bē'kō), **Steve,** born Bantu Stephen Biko (1947–77). Black South African political leader, honorary president of the Black People's Convention. In 1969 he cofounded the radical "Black Consciousness" movement, the South African Students' Organization. He was expelled from the University of Natal (1973) and joined the Black Community Program to rally black opposition to the Nationalist regime. He spent several periods in police detention and died in September 1977, six days after being arrested.

bi·la·bi·al (bī-lā'bē-əl) *adj.* **1.** *Phonetics.* Pronounced or articulated with both lips. Said of certain consonants, such as *b, p,* and *m.* **2.** Pertaining to or having a pair of lips. ~*n. Phonetics.* A bilabial sound or consonant. —**bi·la·bi·al·ly** *adv.*

bi·la·bi·ate (bī-lā'bē-ĭt, -āt') *adj. Botany.* Having two lips. Said of a flower or corolla.

bil·an·der (bǐl'ən-dər, bī'lən-) *n.* A small two-masted sailing vessel, used especially on canals in the Low Countries. [Dutch *bijlander,* "ship that sails by the land" : *bij,* by + *land,* land.]

bi·lat·er·al (bī-lǎt'ər-əl) *adj.* **1.** Of, pertaining to, or having two sides; two-sided. **2.** Having two symmetrical sides. **3.** Affecting or undertaken by two sides equally; binding on both parties. **4.** Occurring on one of two sides after affecting the other: *bilateral recurrence of breast cancer.* **5.** Pertaining to descent through both the paternal and maternal lines. Compare **unilateral.** —**bi·lat·er·al·ism, bi·lat·er·al·ness** *n.* —**bi·lat·er·al·ly** *adv.*

bilateral symmetry *n.* The arrangement of the parts of an organism or organ in such a way that it can be divided into two halves that are mirror images of each other along only one plane. Compare **radial symmetry.**

Bil·ba·o (bǐl-bä'ō). Major port of Spain, on the Nervión River near the Bay of Biscay. It is the largest city of the three Basque provinces and the center of a heavily industrialized, iron-producing region.

bil·ber·ry (bǐl'bĕr'ē) *n., pl.* **-ries.** **1.** Any of several shrubby or woody plants of the genus *Vaccinium,* having edible blue or blackish berries. The European species, *V. myrtillus,* is also called "whortleberry." **2.** The fruit of any of these plants. [Probably from Scandinavian, akin to Danish *bøllebaer* : *bolle,* ball, round roll + *baer,* berry.]

bil·bo (bǐl'bō) *n., pl.* **-boes** or **-bos.** A kind of well-tempered sword, used in former times. [After BILBAO, famous for its ironworks.]

bil·boes (bǐl'bōz) *pl.n.* An iron bar with sliding fetters, formerly used to shackle the feet of prisoners. [16th century : origin obscure.]

Bil·dungs·ro·man (bǐl'dǔngs-rō-män', -dǔngz-) *n.* A novel concerning the hero's early life and development. [German, "education novel."]

bile (bīl) *n.* **1.** *Physiology.* A bitter, alkaline, brownish-yellow or greenish-yellow liquid that is secreted by the liver, stored in the gall bladder, and discharged into the duodenum, where it aids in digestion, chiefly by emulsifying fats so that they can be more easily absorbed. Bile contains the pigments bilirubin and biliverdin. **2.** Bitterness of temper; irascibility; ill humor; spleen. **3.** In medieval physiology, either of two humors: *black bile,* thought to cause melancholy or *yellow bile,* thought to cause anger. [French, from Latin *bīlis,* from Old Latin *bis(t)lis* (unattested), perhaps from Celtic.]

bile acid *n.* Any of the liver-generated steroid acids that appear in the bile as sodium salts.

bile duct *n.* Any of the ducts that drain bile from the liver. They join to form the *common bile duct,* which opens into the duodenum.

bile salt *n.* **1.** Any of the sodium salts found in the bile. **2.** A mixture of ox-gall salts used medicinally as a hepatic stimulant or laxative.

bilge (bǐlj) *n.* **1.** The lowest inner part of a ship's hull. **2.** Water that collects in this part. Also called "bilge water." **3.** The bulge of a barrel or cask. **4.** *Slang.* Stupid talk; nonsense. ~*v.* **bilged, bilging, bilges.** —*intr.* **1.** To spring a leak in the bilge. **2.** To bulge or swell. —*tr.* To break open the bilge of. [Probably variant of BULGE.] —**bilg·y** *adj.*

bilge keel *n.* Either of two beams or fins fastened lengthwise along the outside of a ship's bilge to inhibit heavy rolling.

bil·har·zi·a·sis (bǐl'här-zī'ə-sĭs) *n.* A disease, **schistosomiasis** (*see*). [New Latin : *Bilharzia,* schistosomes discovered by T. *Bilharz* (1825–62), German parasitologist + -IASIS.]

bil·i·ar·y (bǐl'ē-ĕr'ē) *adj.* Of or pertaining to bile or to bile ducts: *biliary colic.*

biliary cirrhosis *n.* Progressive inflammatory disease of the liver caused by bile-duct obstruction.

bi·lin·e·ar (bī-lǐn'ē-ər) *adj. Mathematics.* Linear with respect to each of two variables or positions.

bi·lin·gual (bī-lǐng'gwəl) *adj.* **1.** Able to speak two languages with

bilberry *The bilberry's berrylike flowers appear in early summer, and the blue-gray edible berries in autumn. The bilberry grows on poor soil in northern temperate mountainous areas.*

equal skill. **2.** Written or expressed in two languages. **3.** In which two languages are used equally: *a bilingual city.*
~*n.* A bilingual person. [Latin *bilinguis* : BI- + *lingua*, tongue.] —**bi·lin·gual·ly** *adv.*

bi·lin·gual·ism (bī-lǐng′gwǝ-lǐz′ǝm) *n.* Habitual use of two languages, especially in speaking.

bil·ious (bǐl′yǝs) *adj.* **1.** Of, pertaining to, or containing bile; biliary. **2.** Pertaining to, characterized by, or experiencing gastric distress, especially nausea and vomiting, caused by sluggishness of the liver or gallbladder. **3.** Reminiscent of bile, especially in color; sickly. **4.** Of a peevish disposition; sour-tempered; irascible. —**bil·ious·ly** *adv.* —**bil·ious·ness** *n.*

bil·i·ru·bin (bǐl′ǝ-rōō′bǐn, bǐl′ǝ-) *n.* A reddish-yellow organic compound, $C_{33}H_{36}O_6N_4$, occurring in bile and derived from hemoglobin during normal and pathological destruction of erythrocytes. [Latin *bīlis*, BILE + *ruber*, red.]

-bility *suffix.* Indicates quality or state of being; for example, **capability, visibility.** [Middle English *-bilite*, from Old French, from Latin *-bilitās*, from *-bilis*, adjective suffix. See **-able.**]

bil·i·ver·din (bǐl′ǝ-vûr′dǐn) *n.* A green compound, $C_{33}H_{34}O_4N_4$, occurring in bile, sometimes formed by oxidation of bilirubin. [Swedish : *bili-*, from Latin *bīlis*, BILE + obsolete French *verd*, green, from Latin *viridis*, from *virēre*, to be green.]

bilk (bǐlk) *tr.v.* **bilked, bilking, bilks.** **1.** To defraud, cheat, or swindle. Often used with *out of.* **2.** To evade payment of. **3.** To balk or frustrate. **4.** To elude.
~*n.* **1.** One who cheats. **2.** A hoax or swindle. [Perhaps an alteration of BALK (to refuse to go farther), originally used in cribbage, "to deprive an opponent of his score."] —**bilk·er** *n.*

bill¹ (bǐl) *n.* **1.** An itemized statement of money owed for goods or services supplied. **2.** A statement or list of particulars, such as a playbill or menu. **3.** The entertainment offered by a theater. **4.** An advertising poster or similar public notice. **5.** A piece of legal paper money; a banknote. **6.** A **bill of exchange** *(see)* or a similar commercial note. **7.** A draft of a proposed law presented for approval to a legislative body. **8.** *Law.* A **bill of indictment** *(see).* —**fill** (or **fit**) **the bill.** *Informal.* To be quite satisfactory; meet all necessary requirements. —**foot the bill.** *Informal.* To pay the complete cost of.
~*tr.v.* **billed, billing, bills.** **1.** To present a statement of costs or charges to. **2.** To enter on a statement of costs or a particularized list. **3.** To advertise, announce, or schedule, either by public notice or as part of a program. [Middle English *bille*, from Norman French, from Medieval Latin *billa*, variant of *bulla*, seal affixed to a document, document, from Latin, bubble, ball, amulet.]

bill² *n.* **1.** The beak of a bird. **2.** A beaklike mouth-part, such as that of a turtle. **3.** The visor of a cap. **4.** The tip of the fluke of an anchor.
~*intr.v.* **billed, billing, bills.** To touch beaks together. —**bill and coo.** To kiss and murmur amorously. [Middle English *bile.*]

bill³ *n.* **1.** A pruning implement, a **billhook** *(see).* **2.** A halberd or similar weapon with a hooked blade and a long handle. [Middle English *bil*, Old English *bil.*]

bil·la·bong (bǐl′ǝ-bông′, -bǒng) *n. Australian.* **1.** A dead-end channel extending from the main stream of a river. **2.** A stream bed filled with water only in the rainy season. **3.** A stagnant pool or backwater. [Native Australian name : *billa*, river, water + *bong*, dead.]

bill·board (bǐl′bôrd′, -bōrd′) *n.* **1.** A structure for the display of advertisements in public places or alongside highways. Also *chiefly British* "hoarding." **2.** *Broadcasting.* The opening listing of title, sponsors, products, talent, and the like, designed to stimulate audience interest in the program to follow.

bill·er (bǐl′ǝr) *n.* **1.** A clerk who makes out bills. **2.** A machine for making out bills.

bil·let¹ (bǐl′ǐt) *n.* **1.** A lodging for troops in a nonmilitary building. **2.** A written order directing that such quarters be provided. **3.** Any assigned quarters. **4.** *Informal.* A position of employment; a job.
~*v.* **billeted, -leting, -lets.** —*tr.* **1.** To quarter (soldiers), especially in nonmilitary buildings. **2.** To serve (a person) with an order to provide such quarters. **3.** To assign lodging to. —*intr.* To be quartered; lodge. [Middle English *bylet*, from Old French *billette, bullette*, diminutives of *bulle*, document, from Medieval Latin *bulla*, document, BILL.]

billet² *n.* **1.** A short, thick piece of firewood. **2.** *Architecture.* One of a series of square or log-shaped decorations forming part of a molding. **3.** A bar of iron or steel in an intermediate stage of manufacture. **4. a.** The part of a harness strap that passes through a buckle. **b.** A loop or pocket for securing the tongue of a harness strap. [Middle English, from Old French *billette, billot*, diminutive of *bille*, log, block, tree trunk, from Medieval Latin *billus, billa*, branch, trunk, probably from Celtic; akin to Irish *bile†*, sacred tree, large tree.]

bil·let-doux (bǐl′ā-dōō′, bǐl′ē-) *n., pl.* **billets-doux** (-dōōz′). A love letter. [French : *billet*, short note, from Old French *billette, bullette*, short note, BILLET¹ + *doux*, sweet.]

bill·fish (bǐl′fǐsh′) *n., pl.* **-fishes** or collectively **billfish. 1.** Any of various fishes of the family Istiophoridae, such as a marlin or sailfish, having an elongated, swordlike or spearlike snout and upper jaw. **2.** Any of various other fishes having long, pointed jaws.

bill·fold (bǐl′fōld′) *n.* A folding pocket-sized case for carrying money and personal documents; a wallet.

bill·head (bǐl′hěd′) *n.* A sheet of paper with a business name and address printed at the top, used for making out bills.

bill·hook (bǐl′hŏŏk′) *n.* An implement with a curved blade attached to a handle, used especially for clearing brush and for rough pruning. Also called "bill."

bil·liard (bǐl′yǝrd) *adj.* Of, pertaining to, or used in billiards.
~*n.* A shot in billiards; a carom.

bil·liards (bǐl′yǝrdz) *n. Used with a singular verb.* **1.** A game played on a rectangular, cloth-covered table with raised, cushioned edges, in which a long, tapering cue is used to hit three small, hard balls against one another or the side cushions of the table. **2.** Any of several similar games, such as one played on a table with pockets. Compare **pool, snooker.** [French *billard*, bent stick, billiard cue, from Old French, from *bille*, log. See **billet** (stick).]

bill·ing (bǐl′ǐng) *n.* **1.** The relative importance of performers as indicated by the position and type size in which their names are listed on programs, theater billboards, or advertisements. **2. a.** Advertising. **b.** Often **billings.** The total amount of business done in a specific period, as by a company.

Bil·lings (bǐl′ǐngz). A city in southern Montana, on the Yellowstone River. Founded in 1882 by the Northern Pacific Railroad, Billings today is a trade and manufacturing center for the surrounding area. Yellowstone National Park is nearby.

Billings, Josh. See Henry Wheeler **Shaw.**

bil·lings·gate (bǐl′ǐngz-gāt′; *British* bǐl′ǐngz-gǐt) *n.* Foul-mouthed abuse. [With allusion to scurrilous fishmongers at BILLINGSGATE.]

Billingsgate. Formerly, the oldest market in London, situated at the north end of London Bridge until it moved to West India Dock (1982). It had been principally a fish market since the 16th century.

bil·lion (bǐl′yǝn) *n., pl.* **billion** (for senses 1 and 2), or **-lions** (for sense 3). **1.** The cardinal number represented by 1 followed by 9 zeros, usually written 10^9. Also *British* "milliard." **2.** *Chiefly British.* The cardinal number represented by 1 followed by 12 zeros, usually written 10^{12}. **3.** An indefinitely large number. [French : BI- + (M)ILLION.] —**bil·lion** *adj.*

bil·lion·aire (bǐl′yǝ-nâr′) *n.* A person whose wealth amounts to at least a billion dollars, pounds, or comparable monetary units. [*billion* + millio*naire.*]

bil·lionth (bǐl′yǝnth) *n.* **1.** The ordinal number one billion in a series. **2.** One of a billion equal parts. —**bil·lionth** *adj. & adv.*

bill of attainder *n.* A former legislative act, last used in the 18th century, pronouncing a person guilty of a crime, usually treason, without trial and subjecting that person to **attainder** *(see).*

bill of exchange *n. Abbr.* **B/E** A written order directing that a specified sum of money be paid to a specified person on a specified date. Also called "bill."

bill of fare *n.* A menu.

bill of health *n.* A certificate stating whether or not there is infectious disease aboard a ship or in its port of departure, and given to the ship's master for presentation at the next port of arrival. —**clean bill of health.** *Informal.* A statement that someone or something is in a satisfactory condition.

bill of indictment *n. Law.* A written statement charging someone with a crime, formerly presented to a grand jury to be ratified. Also called "bill."

bill of lading *n. Abbr.* **B/L** A document listing and acknowledging receipt of goods for shipment.

bill of rights *n.* **1.** A formal summary of those rights and liberties considered essential to a people or group of people. **2. Bill of Rights.** The first ten amendments to the Constitution of the United States. **3. Bill of Rights.** A declaration of rights restricting the power of the Crown, enacted by the English Parliament in 1689.

bill of sale *n. Abbr.* **b.s.** A document that attests a transference of the ownership of personal property.

bil·lon (bǐl′ǝn) *n.* **1.** An alloy of gold or silver with a greater proportion of another metal such as tin or copper, used in making coins. **2.** An alloy of silver with a high percentage of copper, used in making medals and tokens. [French, from Old French, ingot, from *bille*, log. See **billet** (stick).]

bil·low (bǐl′ō) *n.* **1.** A large wave or ocean swell. **2.** A great swell or surge, as of smoke or sound.
~*v.* **billowed, -lowing, -lows.** —*intr.* **1.** To surge or roll in or as if in billows. **2.** To swell out: *The sails billowed in the wind.* —*tr.* To cause to swell or rise in billows. [Old Norse *bylgja*.] —**bil·low·i·ness** *n.* —**bil·low·y** *adj.*

bill·post·er (bǐl′pō′stǝr) *n.* One who posts notices, posters, or advertisements. Also called "billsticker." —**bill·post·ing** *n.*

bil·ly¹ (bǐl′ē) *n., pl.* **-lies.** *Informal.* A billy club *(see).* [Probably from the name *Billy*, pet form of William.]

billy² *n., pl.* **-lies.** *Australian.* A metal pot or kettle used in camp cooking. [Short for *billycan* : *billa*, a native Australian word for water + CAN (container).]

billy club *n.* A short wooden club, especially a policeman's club.

bil·ly·cock (bǐl′ē-kŏk′) *n. British.* A man's felt hat with a low crown, similar to a derby. [Possibly after *Billy* or William *Coke*, nephew of Thomas William Coke, Earl of Leicester (1752-1842), for whom the first billycock was made.]

billy goat *n. Informal.* A male goat. Compare **nanny goat.**

Bil·ly the Kid (bǐl′ē). See William H. **Bonney.**

bi·lo·bate (bī-lō′bāt) *adj.* Also **bi·lo·bat·ed** (-bā′tǐd), **bi·lobed** (bī′lōbd′). Divided into or having two lobes.

bi·loc·u·lar (bī-lŏk′yǝ-lǝr) *adj.* Also **bi·loc·u·late** (-lǐt, -lāt′). *Biology.* Divided into or containing two chambers, cavities, or cells. [BI- + LOCULUS.]

Bi·lox·i¹ (bǝ-lŭk′sē, -lŏk′sē) *n., pl.* **-is** or collectively **Biloxi.** One of a tribe of Siouan-speaking North American Indians originally inhabiting the area of the lower Mississippi River.

Bi·lox·i². A city in southeastern Mississippi, on a peninsula between Biloxi Bay and Mississippi Sound, on the Gulf of Mexico. It is a popular resort, and its industries include fishing, boatbuilding, shrimp and oyster packing, and the manufacture of small appliances. Old Biloxi was first settled by the French in 1699.

bil·sted (bĭl′stĕd′) *n.* A tree, the **sweet gum** (see). [Origin obscure.]

bil·tong (bĭl′tông′, -tŏng′) *n. South African.* Narrow strips of meat, salted and dried in the sun. [Afrikaans : *bil,* buttock + *tong,* tongue.]

bimah. Variant of **bema.**

bi·man·u·al (bī-măn′yōō-əl) *adj.* Using or requiring the use of both hands. —**bi·man·u·al·ly** *adv.*

bi·max·il·lar·y (bī-măk′sə-lĕr′ē) *adj.* Pertaining to the two halves of the maxilla.

bi·mes·tri·al (bī-mĕs′trē-əl) *adj.* Bimonthly. [Latin *bimē(n)stris* : BI- + *mēnsis,* month.]

bi·me·tal·lic (bī′mə-tăl′ĭk) *adj.* 1. Consisting of two metals. 2. Of, based on, or employing the principles of bimetallism.

bimetallic strip *n.* A strip consisting of two metals welded together, each metal having a different coefficient of expansion, so that a change of temperature causes the strip to buckle. Bimetallic strips are used in switches, thermostats, and the like.

bi·met·al·lism (bī-mĕt′l-ĭz′əm) *n.* 1. The use of gold and silver as the monetary standard of currency and value. 2. The doctrine advocating such a standard. —**bi·met·al·list** *n.*

Bi·mi·nis (bĭm′ə-nēz). A group of small islands in the Straits of Florida, the northwestern section of the Bahamas. According to legend, the Biminis are the site of the Fountain of Youth sought by Juan Ponce de León.

bi·mod·al (bī-mōd′l) *adj.* Having two distinct statistical modes. —**bi·mo·dal·i·ty** (bī′mō-dăl′ə-tē) *n.*

bi·mo·lec·u·lar (bī′mə-lĕk′yə-lər) *adj.* Pertaining to, consisting of, or affecting two molecules.

bi·month·ly (bī-mŭnth′lē) *adj.* 1. Happening every two months. 2. Happening twice a month; semimonthly.
—*adv.* 1. Once every two months. 2. Twice a month; semimonthly.
—*n., pl.* **bimonthlies.** A publication issued bimonthly. —See Usage note at **bi-.**

bi·morph (bī′môrf′) *n.* Also **bimorph cell.** *Electronics.* A cell consisting of two piezoelectric crystals cemented together so that a voltage applied to the cell causes one crystal to expand and the other to contract or so that a mechanical deformation of the cell causes a voltage to be generated. Bimorphs are used in microphones, vibration detectors, record player pickups, and the like.

bi·mor·phe·mic (bī′môr-fē′mĭk) *adj.* Consisting of two morphemes.

bi·mo·tored (bī-mō′tərd) *adj.* Possessing, especially powered by, two motors.

bin (bĭn) *n.* 1. A storage receptacle or container. 2. *Slang.* A loony bin (see). 3. A storage rack containing one kind of wine.
—*tr.v.* **binned, binning, bins.** To place or store in a bin. [Middle English *binne,* Old English *binn, binne,* basket, crib.]

bin-. Variant of **bi-.**

bi·nal (bī′nəl) *adj.* Twofold; double. [New Latin *binalis,* twin, from Latin *bini,* two by two.]

bi·na·ry (bī′nə-rē) *adj.* 1. Characterized by or composed of two different parts; twofold; double. 2. *Chemistry.* Consisting of or containing only molecules consisting of just two kinds of atoms. 3. Of, designating, or belonging to a number system that has 2 as its base. 4. Of or pertaining to an alloy consisting of two components. 5. *Music.* Having two subjects or themes.
—*n., pl.* **binaries.** An entity consisting of two distinct parts, especially a **binary star** (see). [Late Latin *bīnārius,* from *bīnī,* two by two.]

binary code *n. Computer Science.* A code consisting of a unique group of bits, each having two possible values, used to represent each of a set of numbers or letters.

binary coded decimal *n. Abbr.* **BCD** A number in binary code expressed in groups of four bits, each group representing one digit of the decimal number.

binary digit *n.* Either of the digits 0 or 1 used to express a number in the binary notation.

binary fission *n.* **Fission** (see), especially of a cell or of an atomic nucleus, that results in just two approximately equal products.

binary measure *n. Music.* A measure of two beats to the bar.

binary notation *n. British.* The **binary numeration system** (see).

binary numeration system *n.* A system of numeration, based on 2, in which the numerals are represented as sums of powers of 2 and in which all numerals can be written using the symbols 0 and 1. The system is used in computers, as the digits 0 and 1 can be represented by an electrical system in the "off" and "on" states.

binary operation *n.* An operation, such as addition, that is applied to two elements of a set to produce a single element of the set.

binary star *n.* A stellar system consisting of two stars orbiting about a common center of mass and often appearing as a single visual or telescopic object. Also called "binary," "double star."

bi·nate (bī′nāt′) *adj. Botany.* Consisting of two parts or divisions; growing in pairs: *a binate leaf.* [Latin *bīnī,* two by two.] —**bi·nate·ly** *adv.*

bi·na·tion·al (bī-năsh′ə-nəl) *adj.* Of, relating to, or involving two nations.

bin·au·ral (bī-nôr′əl, bĭn-ôr′əl) *adj.* 1. Having or related to two ears;

hearing with both ears. 2. Of or pertaining to sound transmission from two sources, which may vary acoustically, as in tone or pitch, relative to a listener. Compare **stereophonic.**
—*n.* Binaural sound recording or transmission. [BIN- + AURAL.]

bind (bīnd) *v.* **bound** (bound), **binding, binds.** —*tr.* 1. To tie or secure, as with a rope or cord. 2. To fasten or wrap by encircling with a belt, girdle, or the like. 3. To bandage. Often used with *up: bind up a wound.* 4. To hold or restrain with or as if with bonds. 5. To compel, obligate, or unite, as with a sense of moral duty. 6. *Law.* To place under legal obligation by contract or oath. 7. To make certain or irrevocable: *bind a bargain.* 8. To hold or employ as an apprentice; indenture. Often used with *out* or *over.* 9. To cause to cohere or stick together in a mass. 10. To enclose and fasten (a book) between covers. 11. To furnish with an edge or border for reinforcement or ornamentation. 12. To constipate. 13. *Chemistry.* To cause to form a chemical bond. —*intr.* 1. To tie up or fasten anything. 2. To be tight and uncomfortable. 3. To become stiff, compact, or solid; cohere; jam. 4. To be obligatory or compulsory. 5. *Chemistry.* To form a chemical bond. —**bind off.** In knitting, to cast off (stitches). —**bind over.** *Law.* To hold on bail or place under bond.
—*n.* 1. Something that binds. b. The act of binding. c. The state of being bound. 2. *Informal.* A difficult situation or dilemma. 3. *Music.* A tie (see). 4. A twining plant, bine (see). [Bind, bound, bound; Middle English *binden, bond, b(o)unden,* Old English *bindan, band* (plural *bundon*), *bunden.*]

bind·er (bīn′dər) *n.* 1. One who binds books by trade; a bookbinder. 2. Something used to tie or fasten, such as a cord, rope, or band. 3. A notebook cover with rings or clamps for holding sheets of paper. 4. A material used to ensure uniform consistency, solidification, or adhesion to a surface, as the eggs in batter or the gum in paint. 5. a. An attachment on a reaping machine that ties grain in bundles. b. A machine for reaping and tying grain. 6. *Law.* A payment or written statement making an agreement legally binding until the completion of a formal contract, especially an insurance contract. 7. A beam or steel girder supporting floor joists.

bind·er·y (bīn′də-rē) *n., pl.* **-ies.** A place where books are bound.

bin·di-eye (bĭn′dē-ī′) *n.* Any small Australian perennial herb of the genus *Calotis,* having burrlike fruit. [20th century : origin obscure.]

bind·ing (bīn′dĭng) *n.* 1. The action or process of one that binds. 2. Something that binds or is used as a binder. 3. The cover that holds together the pages of a book. 4. A strip sewn or attached over or along the edge of something for protection, reinforcement, or ornamentation.
—*adj.* 1. Serving to bind. 2. Uncomfortably tight and confining. 3. Having the power to hold to an agreement or commitment; obligatory. —**bind·ing·ly** *adv.* —**bind·ing·ness** *n.*

binding energy *n. Symbol* E_B 1. The net energy required to decompose a system, especially an atomic nucleus, into its constituent particles. Also called "mass defect." 2. The net energy required to remove a particle from a system, especially to remove an electron from its orbit in an atom or molecule. See **ionization potential.**

bin·dle·stiff (bĭnd′l-stĭf′) *n. Slang.* A migrant worker or hobo who carries his own bedroll. [*Bindle,* alteration of BUNDLE + STIFF.]

bind·weed (bīnd′wēd′) *n.* 1. Any of several trailing or twining plants of the genera *Convolvulus* and *Calystegia,* having pink or white trumpet-shaped flowers. 2. Any of various similar trailing or twining plants.

bine (bīn) *n.* 1. The flexible stem of any of various climbing and twining plants, such as the hop, woodbine, or bindweed. 2. Any of these plants. [Variant of dialectal *bind,* clinging vine, Middle English *bynde,* from BIND.]

Bi·net-Si·mon scale (bī-nā′sī′mən) *n.* A scale evaluating mental ability through a series of early psychological tests of childhood intelligence. Also called "Binet scale," "Binet-Simon test." See **Stanford-Binet scale.** [After Alfred *Binet* (1857-1911) and Théodore *Simon* (1873-1961), French psychologists.]

Bing (bĭng), **Sir Rudolph** (1902–). Opera impresario, born in Austria, but a naturalized British citizen after 1946. He was the general manager of the Glyndebourne opera festival (1934-49) and gained international recognition for his work at the Metropolitan Opera in New York, where he was the general manager (1950-72).

binge (bĭnj) *n. Slang.* 1. A drunken spree or revel. 2. A burst of self-indulgence in something, especially after a period of restraint.
—*intr.v.* **binged, binging, binges.** *Informal.* To be uncontrolled and self-indulgent, especially by overeating. [British dialectal *binge†,* to fill a boat with water, to drink heavily.]

bin·go (bĭng′gō) *n.* A game of chance in which players place markers on a pattern of numbered squares according to numbers drawn and announced by a caller. Compare **lotto, keno.**
—*interj.* 1. Used by a player to announce a win. 2. Used to express pleasurable surprise or unexpected satisfaction. [Originally the winner's exclamation, from *bing,* ringing sound, sound expressing surprise (imitative).]

bin·man (bĭn′mən) *n., pl.* **-men** (-mĭn). *British.* A trash or garbage collector.

bin·na·cle (bĭn′ə-kəl) *n.* The nonmagnetic stand on which a ship's compass case is supported. [Earlier *bittacle,* from Middle English *bitakle,* from Spanish *bitácula* or Portuguese *bitácola,* from Latin *habitāculum,* little house, from *habitāre,* to dwell, abide, from *habēre,* to have.]

bin·oc·u·lar (bə-nŏk′yə-lər, bī-) *adj.* 1. Pertaining to, used by, or

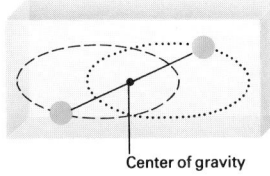
Center of gravity

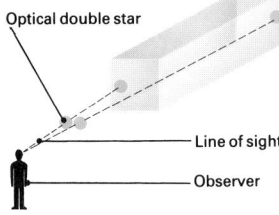
Optical double star
Line of sight
Observer

binary star *Many stars are in pairs, revolving around a common center of gravity, and appearing from earth to be a single star (upper illustration). An optical double star is a pair that are actually very far from each other, but lie in almost the same line of sight (lower illustration).*

binary numeration system

COUNTING IN "DOUBLING UP"

A mathematical "language" for the computer

Human beings count in tens (the decimal system) because we have ten fingers and thumbs. A computer, however, "thinks" in terms of just two possibilities and so counts in twos. Either a signal is passing a point in the computer's circuitry or it is not. The binary system, or counting in twos, is just as convenient for computer design as the decimal system is for humans.

In the familiar decimal system, with hundreds, tens, units, and so on, moving a number one place to the left has the effect of multiplying its value by 10. Thus, 357 in the decimal system means 3 hundreds + 5 tens + 7 units. The binary system uses only two symbols, 0 and 1, and moving a number one place to the left has the effect of doubling its value.

In the binary system all numbers are composed of successive doublings of the numbers 1 and 0. The value of 0 can, of course, be doubled an infinite number of times and it will still be 0. The value of 1, as it is doubled, becomes: 2, 4, 8, 16, 32, 64, 128, 256, and so on. So the three-figure number 357 is written in the binary system as 101100101. This is because it is made up of 256 + 0 + 64 + 32 + 0 + 0 + 4 + 0 + 1. The chart below explains why this is so:

Binary scale	256	128	64	32	16	8	4	2	1	
Binary numbers:	1	0	1	1	0	0	1	0	1	
Decimal equivalent:	256	0	+ 64	+ 32	0	0	+ 4	0	+ 1	= 357

The first ten binary numbers are:

Binary numbers	1	10	11	100	101	110	111	1000	1001	1010
Decimal equivalent	1	2	3	4	5	6	7	8	9	10
Explanation	1	2 + 0	2 + 1	4 + 0 + 0	4 + 0 + 1	4 + 2 + 0	4 + 2 + 1	8 + 0 + 0 + 0	8 + 0 + 0 + 1	8 + 0 + 2 + 0

Fractions are represented by figures to the right of the "binary point," which is similar to the decimal point, except that it halves the value of each number to the right, instead of dividing it by 10 as happens in the decimal system.

Clearly the number of digits employed in the binary codes makes the system too cumbersome for anything but the simplest calculations in mental arithmetic. But, when the system is applied to computers, the difficulties raised by the length of the sequences are far outweighed by the ease of handling just two signals, which can be represented in electromagnetic terms by the presence or absence of a pulse. For this reason, digital computers—those built to process purely numerical information—all work with the binary system.

Modern computers can store and integrate millions of "bits" (*binary digits*), and since the pulses travel at the speed of light, they can perform millions of calculations per second.

---

involving both eyes at the same time. **2.** Having two eyes arranged to produce stereoscopic vision.
~*n.* Often **binoculars.** An optical device, especially a pair of field glasses, designed for use by both eyes at once. [BIN- + OCULAR.] —**bin·oc·u·lar·i·ty** *n.* —**bin·oc·u·lar·ly** *adv.*
binocular vision *n.* The ability of both eyes to focus on the same object at the same time, possessed by primates (including man) and predators (such as owls).
bi·no·mi·al (bī-nō'mē-əl) *adj.* Consisting of or pertaining to two names or terms.
~*n.* **1.** *Mathematics.* An expression consisting of two terms connected by a plus or minus sign; a polynomial in two terms. **2.** A taxonomic name in **binomial nomenclature** (*see*). [New Latin *binōmium* : BI- + Greek *nomos*, portion, part.] —**bi·no·mi·al·ly** *adv.*
binomial distribution *n.* *Statistics.* The frequency distribution of the probability of a specified number of successes in an arbitrary number of repeated independent Bernoulli trials. Also called "Bernoulli distribution."
binomial nomenclature *n.* A system of naming plants and animals by a double name, the first of which is the name of the genus and the second that of the species within the genus; for example, *Odobenus rosmarus,* the walrus.
binomial theorem *n.* A mathematical theorem that specifies the expansion of a binomial to any power without requiring the explicit multiplication of the binomial terms. If *n* is a positive integer, $(x + a)^n = x^n + (n/1!) ax^{n-1} + [n(n-1)/2!]a^2x^{n-2} + \ldots a^n.$
binto. Variant of **beento.**
bin·tu·rong (bĭn'tyə-rŏng) *n.* An arboreal mammal, *Arctictis binturong,* of Southeast Asia, closely related to the palm civets. It has shaggy hair and a prehensile tail. [Malay.]
bi·nu·cle·ate (bī-nōō'klē-ĭt, -āt', bī-nyōō'-) *adj.* Also **bi·nu·cle·ar** (-ər), **bi·nu·cle·at·ed** (-ā'tĭd). Having two nuclei.
Bin·yon (bĭn'yən), **Laurence** (1869–1943). English poet and art critic. His most valuable pieces of art criticism and history were on Oriental subjects. He is best known for his poem "For the Fallen," from which the quatrain beginning "They shall grow not old" is traditionally recited at services honoring the war dead.
bio–, bi– *prefix.* Indicates: **1.** Life or living organisms; for example, **biocide, bionics. 2.** Biology; for example, **biophysics.** [Greek, from *bios,* life, mode of life.]
bi·o·as·say, bi·o·as·say (bī'ō-ăs'ā', -ă-sā') *n.* Evaluation of the activity of a drug, hormone, or other substance by comparison of its effect with that of a standard on a test organism. —**bi·o·as·say** *v.*
bi·o·as·tro·nau·tics (bī'ō-ăs'trə-nô'tĭks) *n. Used with a singular verb.* The study of the biological and medical effects of space flight.
bi·o·cat·a·lyst (bī'ō-kăt'l-ĭst) *n.* A substance, especially an enzyme, that initiates or modifies the rate of a biological process. —**bi·o·cat·a·lyt·ic** (bī'ō-kăt'l-ĭt'ĭk) *adj.*
biochemical oxygen demand *n. Abbr.* **BOD** The amount of oxygen required to meet the metabolic needs of microorganisms in a sample of water in a given period of time, used as a measure of the organic pollution of water. Also called "biological oxygen demand."
bi·o·chem·is·try (bī'ō-kĕm'ĭ-strē) *n.* The chemistry of biological substances and processes. —**bi·o·chem·i·cal** *adj.* —**bi·o·chem·i·cal·ly** *adv.* —**bi·o·chem·ist** *n.*
bi·o·cide (bī'ə-sīd') *n.* A substance, such as a pesticide or an antibiotic, that is capable of destroying living organisms. [BIO- + -CIDE.] —**bi·o·ci·dal** *adj.*
bi·o·cli·ma·tol·o·gy (bī'ō-klī'mə-tŏl'ə-jē) *n.* The study of the effects of climatic conditions on organic life.
bi·o·de·grad·a·ble (bī'ō-dĭ-grā'də-bəl) *adj.* Capable of being decomposed by natural biological processes: *a biodegradable detergent.*
bi·o·en·er·get·ics (bī'ō-ĕn-ər-jĕt'ĭks) *n. Used with a singular verb.* The study of energy relationships between organisms, particularly the cycle of energy in a natural community. —**bi·o·en·er·get·ic** *adj.*
bi·o·en·gi·neer·ing (bī'ō-ĕn'jə-nîr'ĭng) *n.* **1.** The design and manufacture of aids or replacements for defective or missing organs, such as artificial limbs, heart pacemakers, and hearing aids. **2.** The design, manufacture, and use of equipment for industrial biosynthetic processes, such as fermentation.
bi·o·feed·back (bī'ō-fēd'băk') *n.* A technique whereby one seeks consciously to regulate a bodily function thought to be involuntary, such as heartbeat or blood pressure, by using an instrument to monitor the function and to signal changes in it.
bi·o·fla·vo·noid (bī'ō-flā'və-noid') *n.* Any of a group of biologically active substances found widely in plants and functioning in the maintenance of the walls of small blood vessels. Also called "vitamin P." [BIO- + FLAVON(E) + -OID.]
biog. biographer; biographical; biography.
bi·o·gas (bī'ō-găs') *n.* A mixture of methane and carbon dioxide produced through bacterial action.
bi·o·gen·e·sis (bī'ō-jĕn'ə-sĭs) *n.* Also **bi·og·e·ny** (bī-ŏj'ə-nē). **1.** The doctrine that living organisms develop only from other living organisms and not from nonliving matter. Compare **abiogenesis. 2.** The generation of living organisms from other living organisms. —**bi·o·ge·net·ic, bi·o·ge·net·i·cal, bi·og·e·nous** *adj.* —**bi·o·ge·net·i·cal·ly** *adv.*
bi·o·gen·ic (bī'ō-jĕn'ĭk) *adj.* Developing or produced by living organisms. —**bi·o·gen·i·cal·ly** *adv.*
bi·o·ge·og·ra·phy (bī'ō-jē-ŏg'rə-fē) *n.* The biological study of the

geographical distribution of plants and animals. —**bi·o·ge·o·graph·ic, bi·o·ge·o·graph·i·cal** *adj.*

bi·og·ra·pher (bī-ŏg′rə-fər, bē-) *n. Abbr.* **biog.** One who writes a biography.

bi·o·graph·i·cal (bī′ə-grăf′ĭ-kəl) *adj.* Also **bi·o·graph·ic** (-grăf′ĭk). *Abbr.* **biog. 1.** Containing, consisting of, or pertaining to the facts or events in a person's life. **2.** Of or pertaining to biography as a literary form. —**bi·o·graph·i·cal·ly** *adv.*

bi·og·ra·phy (bī-ŏg′rə-fē, bē-) *n., pl.* **-phies.** *Abbr.* **biog. 1.** An account of a person's life written by another; a life history. **2.** Such writings as a literary form. [New Latin *biographia,* from Medieval Greek : BIO- + -GRAPHY.]

biol. biological; biology.

bi·o·log·i·cal (bī′ə-lŏj′ĭ-kəl) *adj.* Also **bi·o·log·ic** (-lŏj′ĭk). *Abbr.* **biol. 1.** Of or pertaining to biology. **2.** Of, pertaining to, caused by, or affecting life or living organisms.

~*n. Pharmacology.* A drug derived from a biological source. —**bi·o·log·i·cal·ly** *adv.*

biological clock *n.* An intrinsic biological mechanism responsible for the periodicity or other time-dependent aspects of certain classes of behavior in living organisms.

biological control *n.* The control of pests using other organisms, usually their natural predators, parasites, or diseases.

biological oxygen demand *n.* **Biochemical oxygen demand** *(see).*

biological warfare *n.* Warfare in which disease-producing microorganisms or organic biocides are used to destroy livestock, crops, or human life.

bi·ol·o·gy (bī-ŏl′ə-jē) *n. Abbr.* **biol. 1.** The science of life and life processes, including the study of structure, functioning, growth, origin, evolution, ecology, and distribution of living organisms. **2.** The life processes or characteristic phenomena of any group or category of living organisms. **3.** The plant and animal life of a specific region or place. [German *Biologie* : BIO- + -LOGY.] —**bi·ol·o·gist** *n.*

bi·o·lu·mi·nes·cence (bī′ō-lōō′mə-něs′əns) *n.* The emission of visible light by living organisms such as the firefly, various fish, fungi, bacteria, and other organisms. It is the result of the biochemical oxidation of the compound luciferin. Compare **fluorescence, phosphorescence.** —**bi·o·lu·mi·nes·cent** *adj.*

bi·ol·y·sis (bī-ŏl′ə-sĭs) *n.* Death caused or accompanied by lysis. [New Latin : BIO- + -LYSIS.] —**bi·o·lyt·ic** (bī′ə-lĭt′ĭk) *adj.*

bi·o·mass (bī′ō-măs′) *n.* The total mass of living matter within a given volume of environment.

bi·ome (bī′ōm′) *n. Ecology.* A community of living organisms of a single major ecological region, such as a desert or tropical forest. [BI(O-) + -OME.]

bi·om·e·try (bī-ŏm′ĭ-trē) *n.* Also **bi·o·met·rics** (bī′ō-mĕt′rĭks). *Used with a singular verb.* The statistical study of biological data. —**bi·o·met·ric, bi·o·met·ri·cal** *adj.* —**bi·o·met·ri·cal·ly** *adv.*

bi·o·morph (bī′ō-môrf′) *n.* In art and sculpture, a form representing a living object. [BIO- + -MORPH.] —**bi·o·morph·ic, bi·o·morph·ic·al** *adj.*

bi·on·ic (bī-ŏn′ĭk) *adj.* **1.** Of or pertaining to bionics. **2.** In science fiction, having certain functions carried out by electronic equipment instead of by the normal physiological processes.

bi·on·ics (bī-ŏn′ĭks) *n. Used with a singular verb.* The application of biological principles to the study and design of engineering systems, especially electronic systems. [BI(O)- + (ELECTR)ONICS.]

bi·o·nom·ics (bī′ə-nŏm′ĭks) *n. Used with a singular verb.* **Ecology** *(see).* [French *bionomique,* pertaining to ecology, from *bionomie,* ecology : BIO- + -NOMY.] —**bi·o·nom·ic, bi·o·nom·i·cal** *adj.* —**bi·o·nom·i·cal·ly** *adv.*

bi·ont (bī′ŏnt′) *n.* A living organism. —**bi·on·tic** (bī-ŏn′tĭk) *adj.*

bi·o·phys·ics (bī′ō-fĭz′ĭks) *n. Used with a singular verb.* The physics of biological processes. —**bi·o·phys·i·cal** *adj.* —**bi·o·phys·i·cal·ly** *adv.* —**bi·o·phys·i·cist** *n.*

bi·o·plasm (bī′ō-plăz′əm) *n.* Living protoplasm, especially as distinguished from its nonliving content. [BIO- + -PLASM.]

bi·op·sy (bī′ŏp′sē) *n., pl.* **-sies.** The examination of tissues removed from the body as an aid to medical diagnosis. [French *biopsie* : BI(O)- + -OPSY.] —**bi·op·sic** *adj.*

bi·o·rhythm (bī′ō-rĭth′əm) *n.* A phenomenon found to a greater or lesser extent in most organisms whereby patterns of growth, behavior, or the like exhibit a natural periodic cycle in response to environmental changes or to various internal control mechanisms. —**bi·o·rhyth·mic** *adj.*

bi·o·scope (bī′ō-skōp′) *n.* **1.** An early film projector, used about 1900. **2.** *South African.* A cinema. [BIO- + -SCOPE.]

-biosis *suffix.* Indicates a specific way of living; for example, **symbiosis.** [New Latin, from Greek *biōsis,* way of life, from *bioun,* to live, from *bios,* mode of life.]

bi·o·sphere (bī′ə-sfîr′) *n.* The totality of regions of the earth that support self-sustaining and self-regulating ecological systems. [BIO- + -SPHERE.]

bi·o·sta·tis·tics (bī′ō-stə-tĭs′tĭks) *n. Used with a singular verb.* Statistical techniques used in studies of health and social welfare.

bi·o·syn·the·sis (bī′ō-sĭn′thə-sĭs) *n., pl.* **-ses** (-sēz′). The production of complex substances from simple ones by or with living organisms. —**bi·o·syn·thet·ic** *adj.* —**bi·o·syn·thet·i·cal·ly** *adv.*

bi·o·ta (bī-ō′tə) *n.* The animal and plant life of a particular region considered as a total ecological entity. [New Latin, from Greek *biotē,* way of life, from *bios,* life.]

bi·o·tech·nol·o·gy (bī′ō-těk-nŏl′ə-jē) *n.* **1.** The manipulation of the physiology of microorganisms, especially bacteria, usually by genetic techniques, to produce useful chemicals on an industrial scale. See **genetic engineering. 2.** Ergonomics *(see).*

bi·ot·ic (bī-ŏt′ĭk) *adj.* Pertaining to life or specific life conditions. [Greek *biōtikos,* from *bios,* mode of life.]

biotic potential *n.* **1.** The likelihood of survival of a specific organism in a specific environment, especially in an unfavorable environment. **2.** The growth rate of a population that maintains a stable age distribution.

bi·o·tin (bī′ə-tĭn) *n.* A colorless crystalline vitamin, $C_{10}H_{16}N_2O_3S$, part of the vitamin B complex found in large quantities in liver, egg

birch *Druids believed the birch had powers of purification, so its twigs were used to drive out spirits. Echoes of this belief still survive in one of the wood's traditional uses: as the source of the twiggy house-cleaning brooms known as besoms.*

---

biological clock

RHYTHMS OF LIFE

Internal clocks keep us in step with the sun

Nearly all plants and animals have built-in biorhythms: regular cycles of activity, such as the annual blooming of some plants, the daily dawn chorus of birds, or the 28-day cycle of menstruation in women. Many of these changes follow a circadian, or 24-hour pattern. In humans, the most obvious examples are sleeping and eating; but there are also less noticeable daily variations in body temperature, pulse rate, blood pressure, and speed of cell growth.

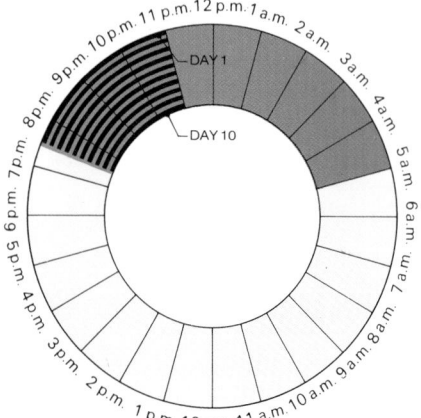

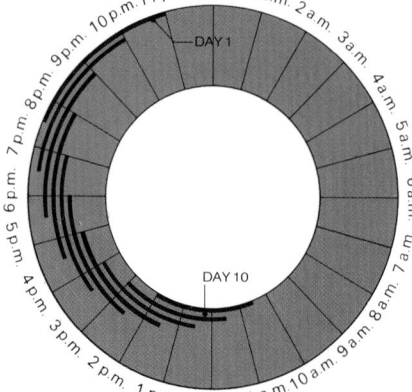

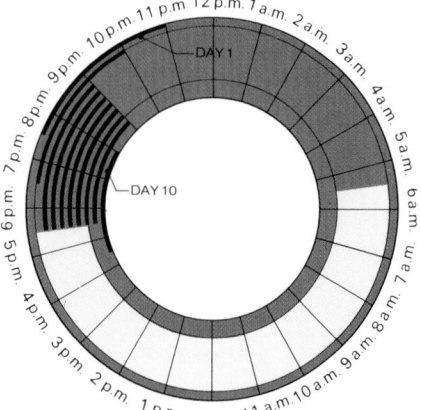

THE EFFECT OF DARKNESS *Diagram A shows the normal evening activity period of a nocturnal animal. If the animal is confined in total darkness (B), that 3-hour period drifts forward by about an hour each day as the animal slips into a 23-hour routine. If, on the other hand, the same animal is put into an environment where day and night are both 12 hours long (C), the activity period drifts at first, then synchronizes with the new cycle. If the cycle is changed a second time, the activity period will drift again.*

yolk, milk, and yeast. [Greek *biotos,* life, from *bios,* life, mode of life + -IN.]

bi·o·tite (bī′ə-tīt′) *n.* A dark-brown to black mica, $K(Mg, Fe)_3AlSi_3O_{10}(OHF)_2$, found in igneous and metamorphic rocks. [German *Biotit,* after Jean Baptiste *Biot* (1774–1862), French physicist.] **—bi·o·tit·ic** (bī′ə-tĭt′ĭk) *adj.*

bi·o·tope (bī′ə-tōp′) *n.* A limited ecological region or niche, such as a dung heap, in which the environment is suitable for certain forms of life. [BIO- + Greek *topos,* place (see **topic**).]

bi·o·type (bī′ə-tīp′) *n.* A group of organisms having identical genetic but varying physical characteristics. **—bi·o·typ·ic** *adj.*

bip·a·rous (bĭp′ər-əs) *adj.* **1.** *Biology.* Producing two offspring in a single birth. **2.** *Botany.* Having two axes or branches. Said of certain flower clusters. [BI- + -PAROUS.]

bi·par·ti·san (bī-pär′tə-zən) *adj.* Consisting of or supported by members of two parties, especially two major political parties. **—bi·par·ti·san·ism** *n.* **—bi·par·ti·san·ship** *n.*

bi·par·tite (bī-pär′tīt′) *adj.* Also **bi·part·ed** (-pär′tĭd). **1.** Having or consisting of two parts. **2.** Having two corresponding parts, one for each party: *a bipartite treaty.* **3.** *Botany.* Divided into two, almost to the base. Said of certain leaves. [Latin *bipartītus,* past participle of *bipartīre,* to divide into two parts : BI- + *partīre,* to part, from *pars* (stem *part-*), a share, part.] **—bi·par·tite·ly** *adv.* **—bi·par·ti·tion** (bī′pär-tĭsh′ən) *n.*

bi·ped (bī′pĕd′) *n.* An animal with two feet.
~*adj.* Also **bi·ped·al** (bī-pĕd′l). Having two feet; two-footed. [Latin *bipēs,* "two-footed" : BI- + -PED.]

bi·pet·al·ous (bī-pĕt′l-əs) *adj. Botany.* Having two petals; dipetalous.

bi·phen·yl (bī-fĕn′əl, -fē′nəl) *n.* A colorless crystalline compound, $C_6H_5C_6H_5$, used as a heat-transfer agent, in fungicides, and in organic synthesis. Also called "diphenyl."

bi·pin·nate (bī-pĭn′āt′) *adj. Botany.* Having opposite leaflets that are subdivided into opposite leaflets. Said of compound leaves. **—bi·pin·nate·ly** *adv.*

bi·plane (bī′plān′) *n.* An early aircraft distinguished by single or paired wings fixed at two different levels, especially one above and one below the fuselage. Compare **monoplane.**

bi·pod (bī′pŏd′) *n.* A stand having two legs, as for the support of an instrument or a weapon. [BI- + -POD.]

bi·po·lar (bī-pō′lər) *adj.* **1.** Pertaining to or having two poles. **2.** Relating to or involving both of Earth's poles. **3.** Having or expressing two opposite or contradictory ideas or qualities. **—bi·po·lar·i·ty** (bī′pō-lăr′ə-tē) *n.*

bi·pro·pel·lant (bī′prə-pĕl′ənt) *n.* A two-component rocket propellant, such as liquid hydrogen and liquid oxygen, combined as fuel and oxidizer. Also called "dipropellant."

bi·quad·rat·ic (bī′kwŏ-drăt′ĭk) *adj. Mathematics.* Of or pertaining to the fourth degree.
~*n. Mathematics.* An algebraic equation of the fourth degree.

bi·quar·ter·ly (bī-kwôr′tər-lē) *adj.* Happening or appearing twice during each three-month period of a year.

bi·ra·cial (bī-rā′shəl) *adj.* Of, for, or consisting of members of two races. **—bi·ra·cial·ism** *n.*

bi·ra·di·al (bī-rā′dē-əl) *adj. Biology.* Both bilaterally and radially symmetrical.

bi·ra·mous (bī-rā′məs) *adj. Biology.* Having two branches, as in an arthropod appendage.

birch (bûrch) *n.* **1.** Any of several deciduous trees of the genus *Betula,* common in the Northern Hemisphere, and having white, yellowish, or gray bark that can be separated from the wood in sheets. **2.** The hard, close-grained wood of any of these trees. **3.** A rod or bundle of twigs from a birch tree, used to administer a whipping.
~*tr.v.* **birched, birching, birches.** To whip (someone) with or as if with birch twigs or a birch rod. [Middle English *birche,* Old English *birce, beorc(e).*] **—birch** *adj.*

Birch·er (bûr′chər) *n.* Also **Birch·ite** (bûr′chīt′), **Birch·ist** (bûr′chĭst). **1.** A member of the **John Birch Society** *(see).* **2.** A supporter of its doctrines and activities. **—Birch·ism** *n.*

bird (bûrd) *n.* **1.** Any member of the class Aves, which includes warm-blooded, egg-laying feathered vertebrates with forelimbs modified to form wings. **2.** A bird hunted as game. **3.** *Slang.* A rocket or guided missile. **4.** A target, a **clay pigeon** *(see).* **5.** The feather-tipped object used in playing badminton, a **shuttlecock** *(see).* **6.** *Slang.* One who is odd or remarkable. **7.** *British Slang.* A young woman. **8.** *Slang.* A sound of disapproval or derision. Used chiefly in the expressions *give someone the bird; get the bird.* **9.** *British Slang.* A prison sentence; imprisonment. Used chiefly in the phrase *do bird.* **—a bird in the hand.** A certainty; something achieved. **—for the birds.** *Slang.* Objectionable or worthless. **—the birds and the bees.** Human reproduction and sexuality, as explained to children. Often used humorously. [Middle English *byrd, bryd,* young bird, Old English *bridd*†. Sense 8, short for *bird-time,* rhyming slang for *time.*] See feature, next page.

bird·bath (bûrd′băth′) *n.* A garden trough or basin filled with water in which birds may bathe.

bird·brain (bûrd′brān′) *n. Slang.* A silly, frivolous person. **—bird-brained** *adj.*

bird·cage (bûrd′kāj′) *n.* A cage for birds.

bird·call (bûrd′kôl′) *n.* **1.** The song of a bird. **2. a.** An imitation of the song of a bird. **b.** A small device for producing this.

bird cherry *n.* A cherry tree, *Prunus padus,* native to Eurasia, having clusters of white flowers and small black fruit.

bird colonel *n. Slang.* A full colonel. [From the eagle insignia worn by a full colonel.]

bird dog *n.* **1.** A dog used to hunt game birds; gun dog. **2.** *Slang.* One who seeks out something for another.

bird-dog (bûrd′dôg′, -dŏg′) *v.* **-dogged, -dog·ging, -dogs.** *—intr.* To watch closely. *—tr.* To seek out; follow.

bird·farm (bûrd′färm′) *n. Slang.* An aircraft carrier.

bird-foot violet (bûrd′fo͝ot′) *n.* Also **bird's-foot violet** (bûrdz′-). A North American violet, *Viola pedata,* having blue flowers and leaves divided into narrow lobes.

bird·house (bûrd′hous′) *n.* **1.** An aviary. **2.** A small box made as a nesting place for birds.

bird·ie (bûr′dē) *n.* **1.** *Informal.* A small bird. **2.** *Golf.* One stroke under par for any hole. **3.** A **shuttlecock** *(see).*

bird·lime (bûrd′līm′) *n.* **1.** A sticky substance smeared on branches to capture small birds. **2.** Something that captures and ensnares.
~*tr.v.* **birdlimed, -liming, -limes. 1.** To smear with birdlime. **2.** To catch with birdlime.

bird louse *n.* A **louse** *(see).*

bird·man (bûrd′mən) *n., pl.* **-men** (-mĭn). **1.** A person who is interested in birds; ornithologist. **2.** *Slang.* An aviator.

bird of paradise *n.* Any of various birds of the family Paradisaeidae, native to New Guinea and adjacent areas, usually having brilliant plumage and long tail feathers in the male.

bird-of-par·a·dise flower *n.* (bûrd′əv-păr′ə-dīs′) *n.* A perennial plant, *Strelitzia reginae,* having purple bracts and large orange or yellow flowers with blue tongues. [After its stalks of colorful flowers resembling birds of paradise.]

bird of passage *n.* A migratory bird or a transient person.

bird of prey *n.* Any of various predatory carnivorous birds, such as the eagle or hawk, having powerful claws and a strong bill.

bird pepper *n.* **1.** A tropical plant, *Capsicum frutescens,* that is the probable ancestor of the mild peppers and many of the hot peppers. **2.** The narrow, extremely pungent fruit of this plant.

bird·seed (bûrd′sēd′) *n.* A mixture of various kinds of seeds used for feeding birds, especially caged birds.

bird's-eye (bûrdz′ī′) *adj.* **1.** Dappled or patterned with spots thought to resemble birds' eyes: *bird's-eye maple.* **2.** Seen from high above or from a remote distance: *a bird's-eye view.*
~*n.* **1.** Any of various plants having small, brightly colored flowers, such as the bird's-eye primrose or the bird's-eye speedwell. **2. a.** A fabric woven with a pattern of small diamonds, each having a dot in the center. **b.** The pattern of such a fabric.

bird's-eye primrose *n.* A plant, *Primula farinosa,* native to Eurasia, having clusters of small, purplish, yellow-throated flowers.

bird's-eye speedwell *n.* A weak-stemmed plant, *Veronica chamaedrys,* native to Eurasia, having small, bright-blue flowers.

bird's-foot (bûrdz′fo͝ot′) *n., pl.* **bird's-foots. 1.** A European plant, *Ornithopus perpusillus,* with small whitish flowers and curved pods. **2.** Any of various other plants that have flowers, leaves, or pods resembling a bird's foot or claw.

bird's-foot fern *n.* A fern, *Pellaea mucronata,* native to California, having fronds with wiry leaves grouped to resemble a bird's foot.

bird's-foot trefoil *n.* A sprawling plant, *Lotus corniculatus,* having yellow flowers and seed pods resembling the claws of a bird.

bird's-nest fungus (bûrdz′nĕst′) *n.* Any of various fungi of the family Nidulariaceae, having a cuplike fruiting body containing several round, egglike structures that enclose the spores.

bird's-nest orchid *n.* A brown parasitic orchid, *Neottia nidus-avis,* that grows in woods in Europe and Asia and has thick intertwining roots.

bird's-nest soup *n.* A Chinese soup made from a gelatinous coating on the nests of certain swifts native to the Orient. [Translation of Chinese (Mandarin) *yen^{4} wo^{1} t'ang^{1}* : *yen^{4},* the swallow or swift + *wo^{1},* nest + *t'ang^{1},* soup.]

birds of a feather *pl.n.* People who are alike in some way. Used chiefly in the saying *Birds of a feather flock together.*

bird·song (bûrd′sông′, -sŏng′) *n.* **1.** The singing of birds. **2.** A bird's cry or call.

bird spider *n.* Any spider of the tropical American family Aviculariidae, which is large and hairy and preys on birds.

bird watcher *n.* A person who observes and identifies birds in their natural surroundings. **—bird watch·ing** *n.*

bird·y·back (bûr′dē-băk′) *n.* The transporting of loaded truck trailers by airplane. [BIRD + -Y + (PIGGY)BACK.]

bi·re·frin·gence (bī′rĭ-frĭn′jəns) *n.* The resolution or splitting of a light wave into two waves with mutually perpendicular vibration directions by an optically anisotropic medium such as a crystal of calcite, topaz, or quartz. Also called "double refraction." **—bi·re·frin·gent** *adj.*

bi·reme (bī′rēm′) *n.* An ancient galley equipped with two tiers of oars on each side. [Latin *birēmis* : BI- + *rēmus,* oar.]

bi·ret·ta, be·ret·ta (bə-rĕt′ə) *n.* Also **ber·ret·ta, bir·ret·ta.** A stiff square cap that is worn by Roman Catholic clergy and is black for a priest, purple for a bishop, and red for a cardinal. Also called "barret." [Italian *berretta* or Spanish *birreta,* from Medieval Latin *birretum,* cap, from Late Latin *birrus,* hooded cloak. See **beret.**]

Birk·beck (bûr′bĕk, bûrk′-), **George** (1776–1841). British educational reformer. His lectures to workingmen in Glasgow (1800–04) led to the establishment of the first Mechanics' Institute in Britain (1823). He was one of the founders of London University (1827).

Bir·ken·head (bûr′kən-hĕd′). Industrial port in Merseyside in northwest England, on the Mersey River, opposite Liverpool.

bird of paradise *Count Raggi's bird of paradise,* Paradisaea raggiana *(above), was discovered in New Guinea in 1873. It was named after the Marquis Francis Raggi, a French amateur ornithologist.*

bird of paradise flower *A native of southern Africa, this exotic plant resembles the plumed head of a bird of paradise, found in the forests of New Guinea and northern Australia. The species shown here is* Strelitzia reginae.

bird's-nest orchid *In European woodlands this orchid feeds on decaying leaves. Its tangled roots, looking like an untidy bird's nest, give the plant its name.*

bird

BUILT FOR FLIGHT

How adaptations of anatomy have made birds masters of the air

Birds had feathers before they could fly, but it was feathers that made flight possible. The earliest known ancestor of the birds, called archaeopteryx, lived 150 million years ago and was a halfway stage between reptile and bird. Its feathers were modified scales use-ful in temperature control. The nearest it came to flight may have been weak flapping that helped it to glide between trees. Birds may have come to fly by chance, perhaps by flapping their forelimbs while run-ning on their hind legs or leaping from tree to tree.

Birds have evolved into some 8,600 species, most of which have thrived by mastery of the air. A bird has become perfectly adapted for flight. As well as feath-ers, which maintain lift, it has light bones, big breast muscles, and a fast-beating heart.

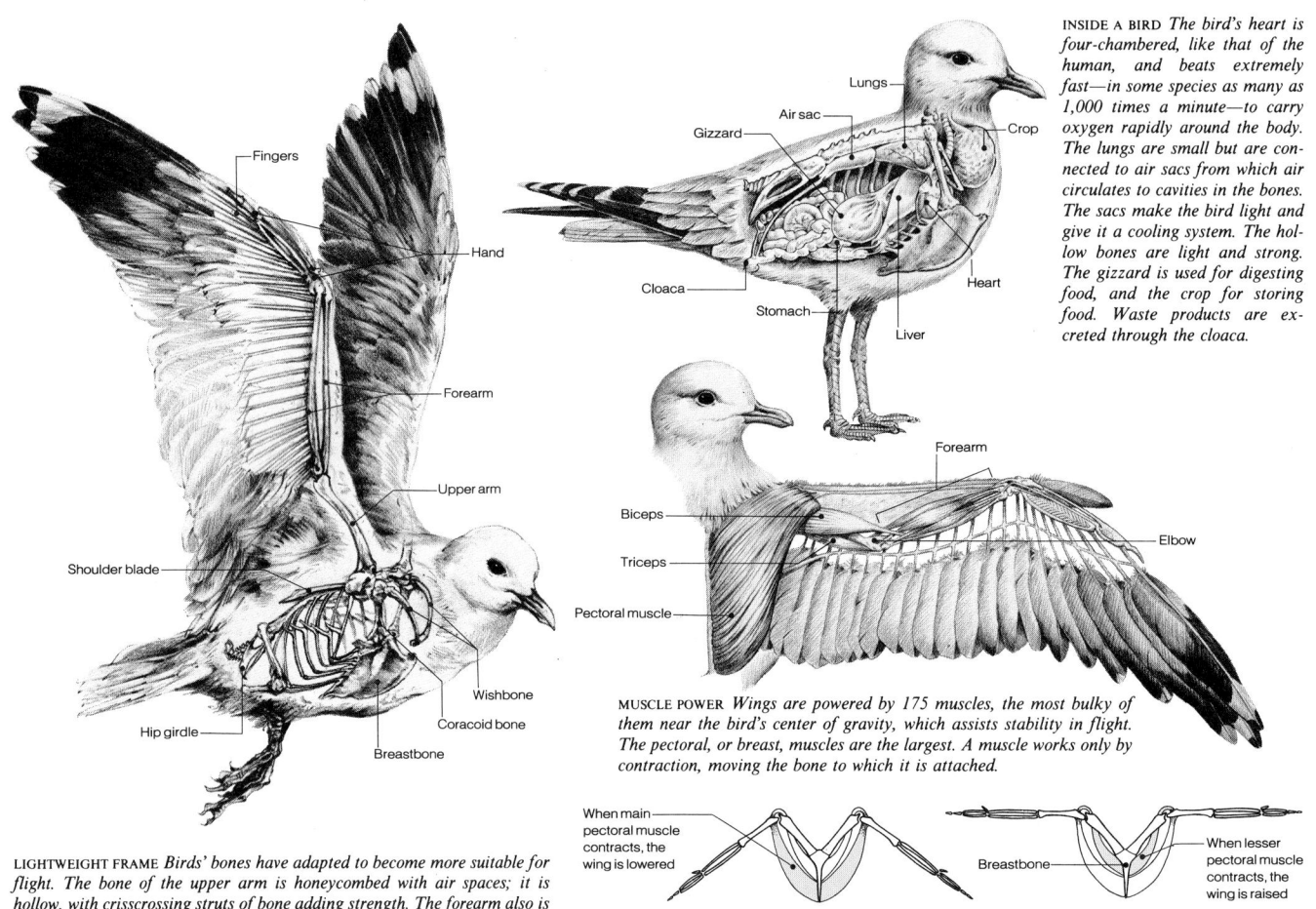

INSIDE A BIRD *The bird's heart is four-chambered, like that of the human, and beats extremely fast—in some species as many as 1,000 times a minute—to carry oxygen rapidly around the body. The lungs are small but are con-nected to air sacs from which air circulates to cavities in the bones. The sacs make the bird light and give it a cooling system. The hol-low bones are light and strong. The gizzard is used for digesting food, and the crop for storing food. Waste products are ex-creted through the cloaca.*

MUSCLE POWER *Wings are powered by 175 muscles, the most bulky of them near the bird's center of gravity, which assists stability in flight. The pectoral, or breast, muscles are the largest. A muscle works only by contraction, moving the bone to which it is attached.*

LIGHTWEIGHT FRAME *Birds' bones have adapted to become more suitable for flight. The bone of the upper arm is honeycombed with air spaces; it is hollow, with crisscrossing struts of bone adding strength. The forearm also is hollow with cross struts, and in large birds many other bones have a simi-larly light but strong structure. The wishbone and coracoid bones act as bracing struts when the wings are spread in flight. The powered muscles for flight are attached to the breastbone and to the wings.*

USING THE MUSCLES IN FLIGHT *Contraction of the main pectoral muscle produces the downward wing beat, the chief power stroke. The wing is raised by contraction of the lesser pectoral mus-*

cle. This is below the arm bone it has to raise; the lifting is managed by a "rope and pulley" attachment connected to the upper surface of the bone.

Birkenhead, Frederick Edwin Smith, 1st Earl of (1872–1930). British lawyer and politician. He was solicitor general (1915), attor-ney general (1915–19), Lord Chancellor (1919–22), and secretary of state for India (1924–28).

bir·kie (bûr′kē) *adj. Scottish.* Cheeky and lively; cocky. [Perhaps from Scandinavian; compare Old Norse *berkja,* to bark, boast.]

birl¹ (bûrl) *v.* **birled, birling, birls.** —*tr.* To cause (a floating log) to spin rapidly by rotating with the feet. —*intr.* To whirl; hum. ~*n.* A whirring noise; hum. [Blend of BIRR and WHIRL.]

birl², **birle** (bûrl) *tr.v.* **birled, birling, birls** or **birles.** *Scottish.* To pour out (drink). [Old English *byrelian;* akin to *byrele,* cup-bearer.]

birl·ing (bûr′lĭng) *n.* A game of skill, originating among lumber-jacks, in which two competitors try to balance on a floating log while spinning it with their feet. Also called "logrolling." [From BIRL (spin around).]

Bir·ming·ham¹ (bûr′mĭng-əm). City in the West Midlands in Eng-land, the second-largest city in the United Kingdom and center of the automobile industry. It owes its leading industrial position partly to the fact that it lies equidistant from London, Bristol, Man-chester, and Liverpool and partly to its proximity to large deposits of iron and coal.

Bir·ming·ham² (bûr′mĭng-hăm′). The largest city in Alabama. It is the center of a mining and industrial region.

Birobidzhan. See **Jewish Autonomous Region.**

birr¹ (bûr) *n.* A whirring sound. ~*intr.v.* **birred, birring, birrs.** To make this sound. [Middle English

bir(re), byrr, strong wind, onrush, from Old Norse *byrr,* favorable wind.]

birr² *n.* The basic monetary unit of Ethiopia, equal to 100 cents. See feature at **currency.** [Amharic.]

birretta. Variant of **biretta.**

birth (bûrth) *n.* **1.** The beginning of existence; the fact of being born. **2.** Any beginning or origin. **3. a.** The act of bearing young; parturition. **b.** The passage of a child or other young mammal from the uterus. **4.** Ancestry; parentage: *a man of noble birth.* **5.** Origin; lineage: *a Southerner by birth.* —**give birth to.** To bring forth. ~*tr.v.* **birthed, birthing, births.** *Chiefly Regional.* **1.** To deliver (a baby). **2.** To bear (a child). [Middle English *birth,* from Old Norse *byrth.*]

birth canal *n.* The cavity of the uterus and the vagina traversed by the fetus during birth.

birth certificate *n.* An official record of a person's parentage and the date, time, and place of birth.

birth control *n.* **1.** Voluntary limitation or control of conception, especially by planned use of contraceptive techniques. **2.** Contra-ceptive materials.

birth·day (bûrth′dā′) *n.* **1.** The day of one's birth. **2.** The anniver-sary of one's birth.

Birthday honors *pl.n. British.* Decorations or titles conferred on the sovereign's official birthday.

birthday suit *n. Informal.* A state of complete nakedness. Used humorously.

birth•ing (bûr′thĭng) *adj.* Pertaining to or used during the act of giving birth: *a bad birthing position.* **—birth•ing** *n.*
birth•mark (bûrth′märk′) *n.* A mole, mark, or blemish present on the body from birth; nevus.
birth•place (bûrth′plās′) *n. Abbr.* **b.pl.** The place where someone is born or where something originates.
birth•rate (bûrth′rāt′) *n.* The number of live births in a specified population per unit time, especially per thousand of the population per year. Also called "natality."
birth•right (bûrth′rīt) *n.* **1.** Any privilege granted a person by virtue of birth. **2.** Any special privilege accorded the first-born. —See Synonyms at **right.**
birth•stone (bûrth′stōn′) *n.* A jewel associated with a specific month and thought to bring good luck to a person born in that month.
birth trauma *n.* **1.** An injury sustained by an infant during birth. **2.** An emotional shock sustained by an infant during birth.
birth•wort (bûrth′wûrt′, -wôrt′) *n.* Any of several climbing plants of the genus *Aristolochia,* such as the European species *A. clematitis,* having reddish or brownish, usually unpleasantly scented flowers. [Formerly given to women in childbirth.]
bis (bĭs) *adv.* Twice; again; encore. Used chiefly as a direction in music. [French, from Latin, twice.]
BIS, B.I.S. **1.** Bank for International Settlements. **2.** British Information Service.
Bis•cay, Bay of (bĭs′kā). The section of the Atlantic Ocean east of a line running roughly from Ushant Island, off Brittany, to Cape Ortegal in northwestern Spain.
biscay green *n.* A moderate yellow green color.
bis•cuit (bĭs′kĭt) *n., pl.* **-cuits** or **biscuit.** **1.** A small cake of shortened bread leavened with baking powder or soda. **2.** *British.* A thin, crisp cracker of unleavened bread. **3.** Pale brown; beige. **4.** *Ceramics.* Pottery that has been fired once but not glazed. Also called "bisque." **—take the biscuit.** *British Informal.* To be the most surprising or outstanding instance of something ever encountered. [Middle English *besquite,* from Old French *bescoit, bescuit,* from (unattested) Medieval Latin *biscoctus (panis),* "twice-cooked (bread)" : Latin *bis-,* BI- + *coctus,* past participle of *coquere,* to cook.]
bise (bēz) *n.* A cold, dry, northerly wind that blows in Switzerland and the adjacent areas of France and Italy. [Middle English, from Old French, from Germanic; akin to Old Swedish *bisa,* whirlwind.]
bi•sect (bī′sĕkt′, bī-sĕkt′) *v.* **-sected, -secting, -sects.** *—tr.* To cut or divide into two equal parts. *—intr.* To split; fork: *The road bisects at the junction.* [BI- + -SECT.] **—bi•sec•tion** *n.* **—bi•sec•tion•al** *adj.* **—bi•sec•tion•al•ly** *adv.*
bi•sec•tor (bī′sĕk′tər, bī-sĕk′-) *n.* Anything that bisects, especially a straight line or plane that bisects an angle.
bi•ser•rate (bī-sĕr′āt′) *adj. Biology.* **1.** Having serrations that are themselves serrated; doubly serrate: *biserrate leaves.* **2.** Serrated on both sides: *biserrate antennae.*
bi•sex•u•al (bī-sĕk′sho͞o-əl) *adj.* **1.** Of or pertaining to both sexes. **2.** Having both male and female organs; hermaphroditic. Said of some plants and animals. **3.** Sexually attracted to members of both sexes.
~n. **1.** A bisexual organism; a hermaphrodite. **2.** A person who is sexually attracted to members of both sexes. **—bi•sex•u•al•ism, bi•sex•u•al•i•ty** *n.* **—bi•sex•u•al•ly** *adv.*
bish•op (bĭsh′əp) *n.* **1.** *Abbr.* **bp.** A high-ranking Christian clergyman, in modern churches usually in charge of a diocese and having the power to confirm and ordain, and in some churches regarded as having received the highest ordination in unbroken succession from the apostles. **2.** *Abbr.* **B** A miter-shaped chessman that can move diagonally across any number of unoccupied spaces of the same color linked in a straight line. **3.** Mulled port spiced with oranges, sugar, and cloves. [Middle English *bisshop,* Old English *biscop, bisceop,* from Vulgar Latin *biscopus* (unattested), variant of Late Latin *episcopus,* from Greek *episkopos,* guardian, overseer : *epi-,* on, over + *skopos,* one who watches.]
bish•op•ric (bĭsh′əp-rĭk) *n.* **1.** The office or rank of a bishop. **2.** The diocese of a bishop. [Middle English *bisshopriche, bisshoprike,* Old English *bisceoprīce* : BISHOP + *rīce,* realm.]
bishop's weed *n.* A plant, the **ground elder** *(see).*
Bis•marck (bĭz′märk′). The capital of North Dakota, on the Missouri River in the south-central part of the state. Bismarck was originally a camp for the men who were building the Northern Pacific Railroad. [It was named after Prince Otto von BISMARCK in the hope of attracting German investment in the railroad.]
Bismarck, Prince Otto Eduard Leopold von (1815–98). German politician, known as the "Iron Chancellor." In 1862 he became prime minister of Prussia and was largely responsible for the successful war against Austria (1866) and the creation of the North German Confederation, excluding Austria (1867). After the Franco-Prussian War (1870–71) he became chancellor of the new German empire. His chancellorship (1871–90) was notable for a complex series of foreign alliances and for his sweeping social reforms, introduced in the mid-1880's, by which he sought to stem the advance of German socialism.
Bismarck Archipelago. Group of volcanic islands in the southwest Pacific Ocean, now part of Papua New Guinea. The largest island is New Britain.
bis•muth (bĭz′məth) *n. Symbol* **Bi** A white, crystalline, brittle, highly diamagnetic metallic element used in alloys to form sharp castings for objects sensitive to high temperatures and in various low-melting alloys for fire-safety devices. Atomic number 83, atomic weight 208.980, melting point 271.3°C, boiling point 1,560°C, specific gravity 9.747, valences 3, 5. [New Latin *bisemutum,* Latinization of German *Wismut*†.] **—bis•muth•al, bis•muth•ic** *adj.*
bis•muth•in•ite (bĭz-mŭth′ə-nīt) *n.* A gray, natural form of bismuth sulfide that occurs in veins associated with tin, copper, lead, and other ores, and is used as a source of bismuth. Also called "bismuth glance."
bis•na•ga (bĭs-nä′gə) *n.* Any of several spiny, globe-shaped or barrel-shaped cacti of the southwestern United States and Mexico. [Spanish *biznaga,* alteration of *vitznauac,* from Nahuatl *huitznahuac* : *huitztli,* spine + *nahuac,* around.]
bi•son (bī′sən, -zən) *n., pl.* **bison.** **1.** A hoofed mammal, *Bison bison,* of western North America, having a dark-brown coat, a shaggy mane, and short, curved horns. Also called "buffalo." **2.** A similar, somewhat smaller animal, *B. bonasus,* of Europe. In this sense, also called "wisent." [Latin *bisōn,* from Germanic.]
bisque[1] (bĭsk) *n.* **1. a.** A thick, rich soup made from meat, fish, or shellfish. **b.** A thick cream soup made of vegetables that have been purėed. **2.** Ice cream mixed with crushed macaroons or nuts. [French *bisque*†.]
bisque[2] *n.* **1.** *Ceramics.* **Biscuit** *(see).* **2.** Pale orange yellow to yellowish gray. [From BISCUIT.]
bisque[3] *n.* An advantage allowed an inferior player in certain games; especially, a free point taken when desired in a tennis set. [French *bisque*†.]
Bis•sau (bĭ-sou′). Capital, largest city, and chief port of Guinea-Bissau in West Africa.
bis•sex•tile (bī-sĕks′tĭl, -tīl′, bĭ-) *adj.* **1.** Of or pertaining to a leap year. **2.** Of or pertaining to the extra day falling in a leap year.
~n. A leap year. [Late Latin *bissextilis,* from Latin *bissextus,* intercalary day in the Julian calendar, which followed February 24, the sixth day before the calends of March : *bis,* twice, BI- + *sextus,* sixth.]
bi•sta•ble (bī-stā′bəl) *adj.* Having two stable states: *a bistable circuit.*
bis•ter, bis•tre (bĭs′tər) *n.* **1.** A water-soluble, yellowish-brown pigment made from soot obtained from beech or other wood. **2.** Grayish to yellowish brown. [French *bistre*†.] **—bis•ter, bis•tered** *adj.*
bis•tort (bĭs′tôrt′) *n.* Any of several plants of the genus *Polygonum,* especially: **1.** A Eurasian plant, *P. bistorta,* having pointed clusters of small, pinkish flowers. **2.** A similar plant, *P. bistortoides,* of the mountains of western North America, having oval clusters of pink or white flowers. [Old French *bistorte,* "twice-twisted" : Latin *bis,* twice, BI- + *tortus,* past participle of Latin *torquēre,* to twist.]
bis•tou•ry (bĭs′tə-rē) *n., pl.* **-ries.** A long, narrow surgical knife for minor incisions. [French *bistouri,* from Old French *bistorie, bistorit,* dagger, from Italian (northern dialect) *bistorino* (unattested), variant of *pistorino,* "of Pistoia," from *Pistoja,* Pistoia, Italy (where sharp knives were made).]
bis•tro (bē′strō, bĭs′trō) *n., pl.* **-tros.** A small bar, restaurant, or nightclub. [French *bistro*†.]
bi•sul•cate (bī-sŭl′kāt′) *adj.* Cleft or cloven, as a hoof. [BI- + SULCATE.]
bi•sul•fate (bī-sŭl′fāt′) *n. Chemistry.* The inorganic acid group HSO_4 or any compound containing it.
bi•sul•fide (bī-sŭl′fīd′) *n. Chemistry.* A **disulfide** *(see).*
bi•sul•fite (bī-sŭl′fīt′) *n. Chemistry.* The inorganic acid group HSO_3 or any compound containing it.
bit[1] (bĭt) *n.* **1.** A small piece, portion, or amount. **2.** A brief amount of time; moment. **3. a.** An entertainment routine given regularly by a performer; act. **b.** A short scene or episode in a play, movie, or the like. **4.** A **bit part** *(see).* **5.** *Informal.* **a.** A particular kind of action, situation, or behavior: *She did the whole bit.* **b.** A matter being considered: *What's this bit about inflation?* **6.** *Informal.* An amount equal to one eighth of a dollar. Used only in multiples of two. **7.** *British.* Formerly, a small coin: *a threepenny bit.* **—a bit.** Somewhat; to some extent. **—a bit of.** **1.** Some. **2.** In some way; to some degree: *a bit of a bore.* **—a bit of all right.** *British Informal.* An attractive thing or person, especially a woman. **—bit by bit.** Little by little; gradually. **—do one's bit.** To make one's contribution; do one's share. **—every bit as.** Quite as; to the same degree as. **—to bits.** **1.** Into small pieces or fragments. **2.** To distraction: *thrilled to bits.* [Middle English *bit,* Old English *bita,* piece bitten off, morsel.]
bit[2] *n.* **1.** The sharp part of a tool, such as the blade of a knife, plane, or the like. **2.** A pointed and threaded tool for drilling and boring that is secured in a brace, bitstock, or drill press. **3.** The part of a key that enters the lock and engages the bolt or tumblers. **4.** The metal mouthpiece of a bridle, serving to control, curb, and direct an animal. See **bridle.** **5.** Anything that controls, guides, or curbs. **6.** The gripping end of a pair of pincers. **7.** The copper end of a soldering iron. **—take the bit in one's teeth.** To start up and proceed uncontrollably.
~tr.v. **bitted, bitting, bits.** **1.** To place a bit in the mouth of (a horse). **2.** To check or control, as if with a bit. **3.** To make or grind a bit on (a key). [Middle English *bitt,* cutting edge, mouthpiece of a bridle, Old English *bite,* a sting, bite.]
bit[3] *n. Computer Science.* **1.** A single character of a language having just two characters, such as either of the binary digits 0 or 1. **2.** A unit of information equivalent to the choice of either of two equally likely states of an information-containing system. **3.** A unit of in-

bison *The bison—known as the buffalo in its native North America—was hunted almost to extinction with the coming of frontiersmen to the prairies. "Buffalo Bill" Cody alone shot 3,000 in one year. Their population dropped from about 40 million in 1830 to less than 1,000 in 1894, when they became a protected species in the United States.*

PRONUNCIATION KEY

ă, pat; ā, pay; âr, care;
ä, father, are; b, bib;
ch, church; d, deed; ĕ, pet;
ē, be; f, fife; g, gag; h, hat;
hw, which; ĭ, pit; ī, pie;
îr, pier; j, judge; k, kick;
l, lid, needle; m, mum;
n, no, sudden; ng, thing;
ŏ, pot; ō, toe; ô, paw, for;
oi, noise; ou, out; o͝o, book;
o͞o, boot; p, pop; r, roar;
s, sauce; sh, ship, dish;
t, tight; th, thin, path;
th, this, bathe; ŭ, cut; ûr, fur;
v, valve; w, with; y, yes;
z, zebra, size; zh, vision;
ə, about, item, edible,
gallop, circus, peaceful

IN FOREIGN WORDS:

à, *Fr.* ami; œ, *Fr.* feu, *Ger.* schön; ü, *Fr.* tu, *Ger.* über; KH, *Ger.* ich, *Scot.* loch; N, *Fr.* bon; y', *Fr.* Compiègne

STRESS MARKS:

Primary stress: ′
in•cite′ (ĭn-sīt′)
Secondary stress: ′
in′sight′ (ĭn′sīt′)

bittern *The courting male bittern makes a loud booming call—and the bird's name is thought to derive from the Latin term* butitaurus, *meaning "bird that bellows like an ox." Bitterns, which are native to Europe and Asia, breed in reedbeds.*

bittersweet *The common name for woody nightshade—*Solanum dulcamara. *Bittersweet grows in woods, hedges, and on sand dunes. Its poisonous, glossy red berries (above) taste first bitter, then sweet.*

blackbird *Evolution originally fitted blackbirds to live in woodland clearings, but many have adapted to living in gardens as well, so that they are now one of the commonest songbirds. This is a male bird; females have light brown plumage.*

formation storage capacity, as of a computer memory. [BI(NARY) (DIGI)T.]

bit[4]. Past tense and alternate past participle of **bite**.

bi·tar·trate (bī-tär′trāt′) *n. Chemistry.* The tartrate of an acid.

bitch (bĭch) *n.* **1.** A female dog or other canine animal. **2.** *Slang.* A spiteful woman. Used derogatorily. **3.** *Slang.* A complaint. **4.** *Slang.* A difficult or confounding problem.
∼*intr.v.* **bitched, bitching, bitches.** *Slang.* **1.** To talk spitefully. **2.** To complain; grumble. **3.** To botch; bungle. Used with *up.* [Middle English *bicche,* Old English *bicce,* female dog, from Germanic *bekjōn-* (unattested).]

bitch·y (bĭch′ē) *adj.* **-ier, -iest.** *Slang.* Malicious, spiteful, or ill-tempered. **—bitch·i·ly** *adv.* **—bitch·i·ness** *n.*

bite (bīt) *v.* **bit** (bĭt), **bitten** (bĭt′n), **biting, bites.** —*tr.* **1.** To cut, grip, or tear with or as if with the teeth. **2.** To pierce the skin of with the teeth, fangs, or stinger. **3.** To cut into with a sharp instrument, such as a knife or drilling bit. **4.** To grip, grab, or seize. **5.** To eat into; corrode. **6.** To cause to sting or smart. **7.** *Informal.* To irritate. —*intr.* **1.** To grip, cut into, or injure something with or as if with the teeth. **2.** To have a stinging effect or a sharp taste. **3.** To have the desired, usually unpleasant, effect: *The new tax is really beginning to bite.* **4.** To take or swallow bait. **5.** To be taken in by a ploy or deception. **—bite the dust. 1.** To fall dead, especially in combat. **2.** To be badly defeated. **3.** To become useless.
∼*n.* **1.** The act of biting. **2.** A wound or injury resulting from biting. **3.** A stinging or smarting sensation. **4.** An incisive, penetrating quality. **5.** An amount of food taken into the mouth at one time; mouthful. **6.** *Informal.* A light meal or snack. **7.** An attempt by a fish to take the bait on an angler's line. **8. a.** A secure grip or hold applied by a tool or machine upon a working surface. **b.** A surface, as on a file, applying such a grip. **9.** *Dentistry.* The angle at which the upper and lower teeth meet when they come into contact. **10.** The corrosive action of acid upon an etcher's metal plate. **—put the bite on.** *Slang.* To borrow money from. [Bite, bit, bitten; Middle English *biten, bot* (past plural *biten*), *biten,* Old English *bītan, bāt* (past plural *biton*), *biten.*] **—bit·er** *n.*

Bi·thy·ni·a (bĭ-thĭn′ē-ə). An ancient country in Asia Minor, in northwestern present-day Turkey. Originally inhabited by Thracians, by the end of the 1st century B.C. it had been absorbed into the Roman Empire.

bit·ing (bī′tĭng) *adj.* **1.** Causing a stinging sensation. **2.** Incisive; caustic. —See Synonyms at **incisive.** **—bit·ing·ly** *adv.*

bit part *n.* A small role in a play or film, having only a few spoken lines.

bit·stock (bĭt′stŏk′) *n.* A brace or handle in which a drilling or boring bit is secured.

bitt (bĭt) *n.* Either of a pair of vertical posts set on the deck of a ship and used to secure cables.
∼*tr.v.* **bitted, bitting, bitts.** To wind (a cable) around a bitt. [Middle English, probably of Low German origin, akin to Low German and Dutch *beting.*]

bit·ten. Past participle of **bite.**

bit·ter (bĭt′ər) *adj.* **-terer, -terest. 1.** Having or being a taste that is sharp, acrid, and unpleasant. **2.** Causing sharp pain to the body or discomfort to the mind; harsh. **3.** Difficult or distasteful to accept or admit: *the bitter truth.* **4.** Exhibiting or proceeding from strong animosity: *bitter foes.* **5.** Marked by resentfulness or rancor: *a bitter old man.*
∼*n. British.* A sharp-tasting beer made with hops.
∼*v.* **bittered, -tering, -ters.** —*tr.* To make bitter. —*intr.* To become bitter. [Middle English *bitter,* Old English *biter.*] **—bit·ter·ly** *adv.* **—bit·ter·ness** *n.*

bitter almond *n.* A variety of the common almond, *Prunus amygdalus amara,* having bitter kernels that yield a highly poisonous oil, which is used for flavoring when the prussic acid in it has been removed.

bitter aloes *pl.n. Used with a singular verb.* A cathartic drug derived from the juice of the fleshy leaves of a tropical plant, *Aloe barbadensis.* See **aloe.**

bitter apple *n.* A plant, the **colocynth** *(see),* or its fruit.

bitter end *n.* **1.** *Nautical.* The end of a rope or cable that is wound around a bitt. **2.** A final, painful, or difficult conclusion; the absolute end.

bit·ter·ling (bĭt′ər-lĭng) *n.* A small colorful freshwater fish, *Rhodeus sericeus,* related to the carp and often kept in aquariums. [German: BITTER + -LING.]

bit·tern[1] (bĭt′ərn) *n.* Any of several wading birds of the genera *Botaurus* and *Ixobrychus,* having mottled, brownish plumage, and notable for its deep, resonant cry. [Middle English *botor, bitter,* from Old French *butor,* from Vulgar Latin *būtitaurus* (unattested), perhaps "bird (that bellows like) an ox" (after its booming call) : Latin *būtiō,* bittern + *taurus,* ox, bull.]

bittern[2] *n.* The solution of bromides, magnesium, and calcium salts remaining after sodium chloride has been crystallized out of sea water. [From BITTER.]

bit·ter·nut (bĭt′ər-nŭt′) *n.* A hickory tree, *Carya cordiformis,* of eastern North America, having nuts with bitter kernels.

bitter orange *n.* The **Seville orange** *(see).*

bitter principle *n. Pharmacology.* Any of a large number of bitter substances, frequently of vegetable origin.

bit·ter·root (bĭt′ər-ro͞ot′, -ro͝ot′) *n.* A plant, *Lewisia rediviva,* of western North America, having showy pink or white flowers and a starchy, edible root.

bit·ters (bĭt′ərz) *pl.n.* A bitter, usually alcoholic liquid made with herbs or roots and used in cocktails or as a tonic.

bit·ter·sweet (bĭt′ər-swēt′) *n.* **1.** A North American woody vine, *Celastrus scandens,* having orange or yellowish fruits that split open to expose seeds enclosed in fleshy scarlet arils. **2.** A sprawling vine, *Solanum dulcamara,* native to Eurasia, having purple flowers and poisonous scarlet berries. Also called "woody nightshade."
∼*adj.* **1.** Bitter and sweet at the same time. **2.** Producing a mixture of pain and pleasure.

bit·ter·weed (bĭt′ər-wēd′) *n.* Any of various plants that yield or contain a bitter principle, such as the **ragweed** *(see),* or plants of the genus *Picris.*

bit·ter·wood (bĭt′ər-wo͝od′) *n.* **1.** The wood of the tree *Quassia amara.* See **quassia. 2.** Any of various other trees from whose bitter wood a substitute for quassia is obtained.

bi·tu·men (bĭ-to͞o′mən, bī-tyo͞o′-) *n.* Any of various mixtures of hydrocarbons, occurring naturally or obtained by distillation from coal or petroleum, found in asphalt and tar, and used for surfacing roads and for waterproofing. [Middle English *bithumen,* from Latin *bitūmen,* probably from Gaulish *bet* (unattested).] **—bi·tu·mi·noid** *adj.*

bi·tu·mi·nize (bĭ-to͞o′mə-nīz′, bī-tyo͞o′-) *tr.v.* **-nized, -nizing, -nizes.** To treat with bitumen. **—bi·tu·mi·ni·za·tion** *n.*

bi·tu·mi·nous (bĭ-to͞o′mə-nəs, bĭ-tyo͞o′-, bī-) *adj.* **1.** Like or containing bitumen. **2.** Of or pertaining to bituminous coal.

bituminous coal *n.* A mineral coal that burns with a smoky, yellow flame, yielding volatile bituminous constituents. Also called "soft coal."

bi·va·lent (bī-vā′lənt) *adj.* **1.** *Chemistry.* Having a valence of 2; divalent. **2.** *Genetics.* Composed of two homologous chromosomes or two sets of such chromosomes.
∼*n. Genetics.* A pair of homologous chromosomes associated together during meiosis. **—bi·va·lence, bi·va·len·cy** *n.*

bi·valve (bī′vălv′) *n.* Any mollusk of the class Bivalvia (or Pelecypoda), having a shell consisting of two dorsally hinged valves. Bivalves include oysters, cockles, clams, scallops, and mussels. Also called "lamellibranch," "pelecypod."
∼*adj.* Also **bi·val·vate** (-văl′vāt′), **bi·val·vu·lar** (-văl′vyə-lər) (for sense 2). **1.** Having a two-valved shell. **2.** Consisting of two similar separable parts.

biv·ou·ac (bĭv′o͞o-ăk, bĭv′wăk) *n.* A temporary encampment made by soldiers in the field.
∼*intr.v.* **bivouacked, -acking, -acks** or **-acs.** To encamp in a bivouac. [French, earlier *biwacht,* probably from Swiss German *beiwacht,* "supplementary night watch," from German *Beiwache, Beiwacht* : *bei,* by, at + *Wache,* watch.]

bi·week·ly (bī-wēk′lē) *adj.* **1.** Happening every two weeks. **2.** Happening twice a week; semiweekly.
∼*n., pl.* **biweeklies.** A publication issued every two weeks.
∼*adv.* **1.** Every two weeks. **2.** Twice a week; semiweekly.

bi·year·ly (bī-yîr′lē) *adj.* **1.** Biennial. **2.** Biannual. **—bi·year·ly** *adv.*

bi·zarre (bĭ-zär′) *adj.* Strikingly unconventional and far-fetched in style or appearance; odd; grotesque. —See Synonyms at **fantastic.** [French, originally "handsome," "brave," from Spanish *bizarro,* from Basque *bizar,* beard ("bearded," hence "spirited").] **—bi·zarre·ly** *adv.* **—bi·zarre·ness** *n.*

Bi·zet (bē-zā′), **Georges,** born Alexandre César Léopold Bizet (1838–75). French composer. His reputation rests chiefly on the opera *Carmen* (1873–74) and the *Arlésienne* suite.

Bk The symbol for the element berkelium.

bk. 1. bank. **2.** book.

bkg. banking.

bkpg. bookkeeping.

bkpt. bankrupt.

bks. 1. barracks. **2.** books.

bl. 1. bale. **2.** barrel. **3.** black. **4.** blue.

B.L. 1. Bachelor of Laws. **2.** Bachelor of Letters; Bachelor of Literature.

B/L bill of lading.

B.L.A. Bachelor of Liberal Arts.

blab (blăb) *v.* **blabbed, blabbing, blabs.** —*tr.* To reveal (a secret), especially through indiscretion. —*intr.* **1.** To talk of secret matters. **2.** To chatter indiscreetly.
∼*n.* **1.** A person who blabs. **2.** Lengthy chatter. [Middle English *blabben,* akin to *blabberen,* to BLABBER.] **—blab·by** *adj.*

blab·ber (blăb′ər) *intr.v.* **-bered, -bering, -bers.** To chatter.
∼*n.* **1.** Idle chatter. **2.** One who blabs. [Middle English *blabberen,* from an imitative Germanic root *blab-* (unattested).]

blab·ber·mouth (blăb′ər-mouth′) *n., pl.* **-mouths** (-mouthz). *Slang.* One who chatters indiscreetly and at length.

black (blăk) *n. Abbr.* **bl., blk. 1.** An achromatic color value of minimum lightness or maximum darkness; one extreme of the neutral gray series, the opposite being white. Although strictly a response to zero stimulation of the retina, the perception of black appears to depend on contrast with surrounding color stimuli. **2.** Clothing of this color, especially for mourning. **3.** *Often* **Black. a.** Any member of a Negroid people. **b.** Loosely, any member of a dark-skinned ethnic group. **4.** The black-colored chess or checker pieces, or the player using them. **—in the black.** On the credit side of a ledger; prosperous.
∼*adj.* **blacker, blackest.** *Abbr.* **bl., blk. 1.** Being of the darkest achromatic visual value; producing or reflecting comparatively little light and having no predominant hue. **2.** Having no light whatso-

ever: *a black cave.* **3.** *Often* **Black. a.** Belonging to a Negroid group. **b.** Loosely, belonging to an ethnic group having dark skin. **4.** Dark in color or having parts that are dark in color. Used with animal and plant names: *black bass; black birch.* **5.** Soiled, as from soot. **6.** Evil; sinister: *black deeds.* **7.** Cheerless and depressing; gloomy. **8.** Angered; sullen; threatening: *a black look.* **9.** Attended with disaster; calamitous. **10.** Of or designating a form of humor dealing with the abnormal and grotesque aspects of life and society and evoking a sense of the comedy of human despair and failure. **11.** Indicating or incurring censure or dishonor: *a black record of environmental pollution.* **12.** Wearing black clothing: *the black knight.* **13.** Served without milk or cream. Said of coffee. **14.** Evading the attention of the tax authorities; illegal: *the black market.* **15.** Purporting to originate from one's own side, when in fact being enemy propaganda: *black radio.* **16.** *British.* Boycotted or not approved by a trade union: *black labor.*

~*tr.v.* **blacked, blacking, blacks. 1.** To make black or dirty; soil. **2.** To put black dye, paint, or polish on. **3.** To bruise (an eye) with a blow. **4.** *British.* To refuse to have anything to do with (a cargo, for example) because of trade union objections. [Middle English *blak,* Old English *blæc.*] **—black·ly** *adv.* **—black·ness** *n.*

Usage: The preferred term for a person today is *black* rather than *Negro.* Another acceptable term is *Afro-American.* The noun and the adjective *black* are usually but not invariably lower-cased: *"Together, blacks and whites can move our country beyond racism"* (Whitney Young, Jr.).

Black (blăk), **Joseph** (1728–99). Scottish chemist and physicist. He rediscovered what was then called "fixed air" (carbon dioxide) and formulated the concepts of latent heat and specific heat.

black alder *n.* **1.** A deciduous holly, *Ilex verticillata,* of eastern North America, bearing bright-scarlet berries. **2.** A tree, *Alnus glutinosa,* native to Eurasia, having dark bark.

black·a·moor (blăk'ə-mo͝or') *n.* Any dark-skinned person; especially, a North African. [Earlier *black More* : BLACK + MOOR.]

black-and-blue (blăk'ən-blo͞o') *adj.* Discolored from coagulation of blood below the surface of the skin.

Black and Tan *n.* An auxiliary member of the Royal Irish Constabulary, mostly British ex-servicemen, specially recruited to suppress the Sinn Fein rebellion of 1920–21. [After the color of the uniform.]

black-and-tan terrier (blăk'ən-tăn') *n.* A **Manchester terrier** *(see).*

black and white *n.* **1.** Print or writing: *Be sure to get the agreement in black and white.* **2.** Tones of black and white. **3.** A picture or photograph in tones of black and white.

black-and-white (blăk'ən-hwīt', -wīt') *adj.* **1.** Pertaining or restricted to film or photography in tones of black and white: *a black-and-white television set.* **2.** Presenting exaggeratedly simplistic ideas, usually polarized in moral terms.

black art *n.* **Black magic** *(see).*

black·ball (blăk'bôl') *n.* **1.** A small, black ball used as a negative ballot. **2.** A negative vote that blocks the admission of an applicant to an organization.

~*tr.v.* **blackballed, -balling, -balls. 1.** To vote against; especially, to veto the admission of. **2.** To exclude from a social group; ostracize. [From the small black ball dropped into a ballot box to represent an adverse vote.] **—black·ball·er** *n.*

black bass *n.* Any of several North American freshwater game fishes of the genus *Micropterus.*

black bear *n.* Either of two black or dark-brown bears, *Ursus* (or *Euarctos*) *americanus,* of North America, or *Selenarctos thibetanus,* of Asia. The Asian species has a pale V-shaped chest marking.

Blackbeard. See Edward **Teach.**

black belt *n.* **1. a.** The rank of expert in a system of self-defense such as judo or karate. **b.** The black-colored sash that symbolizes this rank. **c.** A person who holds this rank. **2.** A region of rich, black soil. **3.** An area with a predominantly black population.

black·ber·ry (blăk'bĕr'ē, -bər-ē) *n., pl.* **-ries. 1.** Any of several woody plants of the genus *Rubus,* having canelike, usually thorny stems and black, glossy, edible berries. Also called "bramble." See **black raspberry, dewberry, loganberry. 2.** The fruit of any of these plants.

blackberry lily *n.* A plant, *Belamcanda chinensis,* having spotted orange flowers and a seed cluster that resembles a blackberry.

black bile *n.* One of the four **humors** *(see)* of medieval physiology, supposed to cause melancholia.

black bindweed *n.* A vine, *Polygonum convolvulus,* native to Europe and naturalized as a weed in North America.

black birch *n.* A North American tree, *Betula lenta,* having dark, brownish bark and twigs and leaves that yield an aromatic oil.

black·bird (blăk'bûrd') *n.* **1.** Any of various New World birds of the family Icteridae, having black or predominantly black plumage in the male. **2.** A common Eurasian bird, *Turdus merula,* of the thrush family, of which the male is black with a yellow bill and the female is brown. See **cowbird, grackle, redwing.**

black·board (blăk'bôrd', -bōrd') *n.* A panel with a black or sometimes colored surface for writing on with chalk, used especially in schools; chalkboard.

blackboard jungle *n.* **1.** A school with a reputation for violence by pupils. **2.** The phenomenon of aggression and violence in schools. [From the title of a book (1954) by Evan Hunter, popularized as a film.]

black·bod·y (blăk'bŏd'ē) *n., pl.* **-ies.** *Physics.* A theoretically perfect absorber of all incident radiation.

blackbody radiation *n.* The thermal radiation emitted by a blackbody at a given temperature. The total amount of radiation emitted is given by the **Stefan-Boltzmann law** and the spectral energy distribution by **Planck's formula** *(both of which see).*

black book *n.* A record of people liable to punishment. **—in someone's black book.** In disfavor with someone.

black box *n.* **1.** A device or theoretical construct, especially an electric circuit, with known or specified performance characteristics but unknown or unspecified constituents and means of operation. **2.** A **flight recorder** *(see).* **3.** Any device used for automatically recording the details of a journey. See **tachograph.**

black bread *n.* Coarse rye bread.

black bryony *n.* A climbing European plant, *Tamus communis,* having small, greenish flowers and poisonous red berries.

black·buck (blăk'bŭk') *n.* An antelope, *Antilope cervicapra,* of India, of which the male has a dark back and spiral horns. Also called "sasin."

Black·burn (blăk'bərn). Industrial town in northwest England, in the central Lancashire coal field. It is located on the Leeds-Liverpool canal.

black·cap (blăk'kăp') *n.* **1.** The **black raspberry** *(see).* **2.** A small European bird, *Sylvia atricapilla,* of which the male is gray with a black crown. **3.** Any of various other black-crowned birds.

black·cock (blăk'kŏk') *n.* The male of the **black grouse** *(see).*

black cohosh *n.* A tall plant, *Cimicifuga racemosa,* of eastern North America, having long clusters of small, whitish flowers.

black crappie *n.* An edible North American fish, *Pomoxis nigromaculatus,* having dark, mottled coloring.

black currant *n.* **1.** A widely cultivated Eurasian shrub, *Ribes nigrum,* producing clusters of small edible black berries. **2.** The fruit of this shrub.

black·damp (blăk'dămp') *n.* A gas composed of a mixture of carbon dioxide and nitrogen, found in mines after fires and explosions of combustible gases. Also called "chokedamp."

Black Death *n.* A form of plague that was pandemic throughout Europe and much of Asia during periods in the 14th century. [From the dark splotches it causes on the skin.]

black diamond *n.* **1.** A variety of diamond, **carbonado** *(see).* **2. black diamonds.** Coal.

black dog *n.* A melancholy state or mood; depression. Usually preceded by *the.*

black earth *n.* A type of soil, **chernozem** *(see).* **—black-earth** *adj.*

black·en (blăk'ən) *v.* **-ened, -ening, -ens.** —*tr.* **1.** To make black. **2.** To stain (someone's reputation, for example); defame. —*intr.* To become black or dark. **—black·en·er** *n.*

Black·ett (blăk'ĭt), **Patrick Maynard Stuart, Baron** (1897–1974). British physicist. For his contributions to the study of cosmic radiation, he was awarded the Nobel Prize for physics (1948).

black eye *n.* **1.** A bruised discoloration of the flesh surrounding the eye, resulting from a blow. **2.** A heavy defeat; bad setback.

black-eyed pea (blăk'īd') *n.* The edible seed of the **cowpea** *(see).*

black-eyed Susan *n.* **1.** Any of several North American plants of the genus *Rudbeckia*; especially, *R. hirta,* having hairy stems and leaves, and flowers with orange-yellow rays and dark-brown centers. **2.** A vine, *Thunbergia alata,* native to tropical Africa, having white or orange-yellow flowers with purple throats.

black·face (blăk'fās') *n.* **1.** Make-up for a conventionalized comic travesty of blacks, as in a minstrel show. **2.** An actor in a minstrel show. **3.** *Printing.* Boldface type. **4.** *British.* A black-faced sheep.

black·fish (blăk'fĭsh') *n., pl.* **-fishes** or collectively **blackfish. 1.** Any of various dark-colored fishes, such as: **a.** A freshwater fish, *Dallia pectoralis,* of far northern regions. **b.** The **tautog** *(see).* **2.** The **pilot whale** *(see).* **3.** A female salmon that has recently spawned. Compare **redfish.**

black flag *n.* The flag used by pirates, the **Jolly Roger** *(see).*

black fly *n.* Any of various small, dark-colored, bloodsucking flies of the family Simuliidae. Also called "buffalo gnat."

black·fly (blăk'flī') *n., pl.* **-flies** or collectively **blackfly.** A black aphid, *Aphis fabae,* that feeds in large masses on bean plants, spinach, dock, and the like.

Black·foot (blăk'fo͝ot') *n., pl.* **-feet** or collectively **Blackfoot. 1.** Any of three tribes of Algonquian-speaking Indians formerly inhabiting the regions of Montana, Alberta, and Saskatchewan. **2.** A member of one of these tribes. **3.** The Algonquian language spoken by these peoples. [Translation of Blackfoot *Siksika*; said to be so named because the soles of their moccasins were black from walking across burned prairie.] **—Black·foot** *adj.*

black-foot·ed ferret (blăk'fo͝ot'ĭd) *n.* A weasellike mammal, *Mustela nigripes,* of central North America, related to the polecat and having yellowish fur and dark feet. Also called "ferret."

Black Forest. See **Schwarzwald.**

Black Friar *n.* A Dominican friar. [After the black mantles worn by the Dominican friars.]

black frost *n.* A condition in which the air temperature falls below the freezing point without frost forming, causing blackening and internal damage in vegetation.

black gold *n.* Crude oil.

black grouse *n.* A Eurasian game bird, *Lyrurus tetrix.* of which the black male is called "blackcock," the mottled female is called "greyhen," and for which the collective plural is "black game."

black·guard (blăg'ərd, -ärd) *n.* **1.** A scoundrel. **2.** A scurrilous person.

~*adj.* Of or like a blackguard; foulmouthed.

black currant *The cultivated fruit of this shrub is rich in vitamin C and is used mainly in soft drinks and for making jam.*

blackface *Once a Scottish breed, the blackface is now widespread. Kept mainly for meat, the sheep does not yield a heavy fleece, but the wool is long and flowing.*

black grouse *A male black grouse, or blackcock, fans its tail as part of its courtship display. In the mating season, these northern European game birds gather at communal mating grounds known as leks, often returning to the same site year after year. Females have brown plumage.*

~v. **blackguarded, -guarding, -guards.** —*tr.* To abuse or revile. —*intr.* To behave like a blackguard. [Originally, the kitchen workers and menials of a noble household or of an army.] —**black·guard·ism** *n.* —**black·guard·ly** *adj. & adv.*

Black Hand *n.* A secret society organized for acts of terrorism and blackmail, composed mainly of Sicilians active in the United States in the early 20th century. Compare **Mafia.**

Black Hawk (blăk′hôk′), original name Makataimeshekiakiak (1767–1838). U.S. Indian leader. Resenting an 1804 treaty that ceded all of his tribe's lands east of the Mississippi River to the United States, he led 1,000 Fox and Sauk Indians in the Black Hawk War. His autobiography is a classic statement of Indian indignation toward white intrusion.

black·head (blăk′hĕd′) *n.* **1.** A plug of dried fatty matter capped with blackened dust and epithelial debris that clogs a pore of the skin. Also called "comedo." **2.** *Veterinary Medicine.* An infectious, often fatal, liver and intestinal disease of turkeys and some wildfowl. Also called "infectious enterohepatitis." **3.** Any of various birds with dark head markings.

black·heart (blăk′härt′) *n.* **1.** A disease of potatoes and other plants, in which the inner tissues darken. **2.** Abnormal blackening of the stems in woody plants, probably caused by extreme cold. **3.** A variety of dark-skinned purple-fleshed cherry.

black·heart·ed (blăk′här′tĭd) *adj.* Evil by nature; wicked.

Black·heath (blăk′hēth′). District and former village in southeast Greater London in England, in the boroughs of Greenwich and Lewisham. Its common was used as a rallying-point by Wat Tyler and Jack Cade for attacks on London in the rebellions of 1381 and 1450.

Black Hills. Rugged mountains of southwest South Dakota and

northeast Wyoming. Harney Peak (2,209 meters; 7,242 feet) is the highest peak. The region is rich in mineral resources.

black hole *n.* A region in space caused by a star collapsing under its own gravitational force to such an extent that its gravitational field prevents any matter, light, or other electromagnetic radiation leaving the region. See **singularity, white hole.**

Black Hole of Calcutta *n.* **1.** A small dungeon at Calcutta, India, in which 123 of the 146 British prisoners confined there on June 20, 1756, died of suffocation. **2. black hole of Calcutta.** An uncomfortable, confined space.

black horehound *n.* A strong-smelling plant, *Ballota nigra,* native to Europe, having clusters of purple flowers.

black humor *n.* The humor of the morbid and the absurd, especially as a literary genre.

black·ing (blăk′ĭng) *n.* **1. Lamp black** *(see).* **2.** A black paste or liquid used as shoe polish.

black·ish (blăk′ĭsh) *adj.* Somewhat black. —**black·ish·ly** *adv.*

black·jack¹ (blăk′jăk′) *n.* A small leather-covered bludgeon with a short, flexible shaft or strap, used as a hand weapon. ~*tr.v.* **blackjacked, -jacking, -jacks. 1.** To hit with a blackjack. **2.** To coerce by threats. [BLACK + JACK (tool).]

black·jack² *n.* An oak tree, *Quercus marilandica,* of the southeastern United States, having blackish bark. Also called "blackjack oak." [BLACK + JACK (tool).]

blackjack³ *n.* A card game in which the object is to accumulate cards with a total count nearer to 21 than that of the dealer. Also called "twenty-one." [BLACK + JACK (knave in cards).]

blackjack⁴ *n.* A tankard made of tarred or waxed leather. [BLACK + Middle English *jakke,* leather coat, container, from Old French *jacque* (see **jacket**).]

blackjack⁵ *n.* Sphalerite or zinc sulfide ore. [BLACK + JACK (impertinent, worthless person); miners' term for this worthless mixture in lead ore.]

black lead *n.* **Graphite** *(see).*

black·leg (blăk′lĕg′) *n.* **1.** *Veterinary Medicine.* An infectious, usually fatal, gas gangrene affecting the heavily muscled upper parts of the legs of sheep and cattle. **2.** A bacterial or fungous plant disease that causes the stems of plants to turn black. **3.** One who cheats in gambling, especially a professional gambler; cardsharp. **4.** *British.* A strikebreaker; scab.

black letter *n.* *Printing.* **1.** A heavy typeface having very broad counters and thick, ornamental serifs. Also called "gothic," "church text," "Old English." **2.** Loosely, any heavy, black typeface. —**black-let·ter** *adj.*

black light *n.* Invisible ultraviolet or infrared radiation.

black·list (blăk′lĭst′) *n.* A list of persons or organizations to be disapproved of, boycotted, or suspected of disloyalty. ~*tr.v.* **blacklisted, -listing, -lists.** To place (a name) on a blacklist.

black lung *n.* A disease suffered by coal miners involving chronic inflammation of the lungs as a result of inhaling coal dust.

black magic *n.* Magic as practiced in league with the Devil; witchcraft. Also called "black art." —See Synonyms at **magic.**

black·mail (blăk′māl′) *n.* **1.** Extortion by the threat of exposure or criminal prosecution. **2.** Money extorted in this manner. **3.** Tribute formerly paid to freebooters along the Scottish border for protection against pillage. ~*tr.v.* **blackmailed, -mailing, -mails. 1.** To extort money or something of value from (a person) by means of blackmail. **2.** To coerce or influence the behavior of by means of blackmail. [BLACK + *mail,* tribute, Middle English *maill, male,* Old English *māl,* agreement, from Old Norse *māl,* speech, agreement.] —**black·mail·er** *n.*

Black Ma·ri·a (mə-rī′ə) *n.* A police van, used especially for transporting offenders.

black mark *n.* A sign of disapprobation, discredit, or the like.

black market *n.* **1.** The illicit trade in goods or currencies in violation of price controls, rationing, or other restrictions. **2.** A place where such trade takes place.

black-mar·ket (blăk′mär′kĭt) *tr.v.* **-keted, -keting, -kets.** To trade (goods) on a black market. —**black marketer, black marketeer** *n.*

black mass *n.* A travesty of the Roman Catholic Mass practiced by Satanists.

black measles *n.* A severe form of measles, characterized by a dark rash due to subcutaneous bleeding.

black medic, black medick *n.* A cloverlike plant, *Medicago lupulina,* native to Europe, having compound leaves, small yellow flower heads, and black pods. Also called "nonesuch."

Black·more (blăk′mōr′, -môr′), **Richard Doddridge** (1825–1900). British novelist and poet. He wrote several volumes of verse and published 15 novels, but he is remembered now only for his historical romance *Lorna Doone* (1869).

Black Muslim *n.* A member of the **Nation of Islam** *(see).*

black mustard *n.* A plant, *Brassica nigra,* native to Eurasia, having clusters of yellow flowers. Its pungent seeds, ground to a powder, are a source of the condiment mustard.

black-necked stork *n.* The **jabiru** *(see).*

black nightshade *n.* A plant, the **deadly nightshade** *(see).*

black oak *n.* A deciduous tree, *Quercus velutina,* of eastern North America, having hard, durable wood. Also called "quercitron."

black out *tr.v.* **1.** To cause or produce the blacking out of (a city, theater, or radio station, for example). **2.** To suppress or delete for political reasons or by censorship. —*intr.v.* To undergo a blackout; especially, to suffer a temporary loss of consciousness, memory, or vision.

---

black hole

THE INVISIBLE GIANTS

Stars so dense that not even light can escape their pull

When a star dies, its nuclear fuel exhausted, it cools and contracts dramatically. In a star the size of our sun, this contraction eventually produces a dense dwarf star, a thimbleful of whose matter would weigh about 10 tons. But in a very large star—several times as massive as the sun —many physicists believe that there is no limit to the contraction. The star collapses under the pull of its gravity until nothing, not even light, can escape. It becomes a black hole.

By their very nature, black holes cannot be seen directly. But their presence can be deduced from their effect on nearby material. What may be the first known black hole was found in the 1970's about 6,000 light-years away in the constellation of Cygnus the Swan. The area around the hole is known as Cyg X-1; it gives off strong x-rays—the result, astronomers believe, of material being compressed and heated just before it is sucked in.

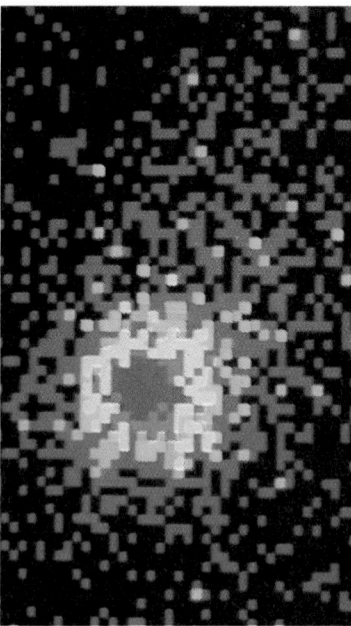

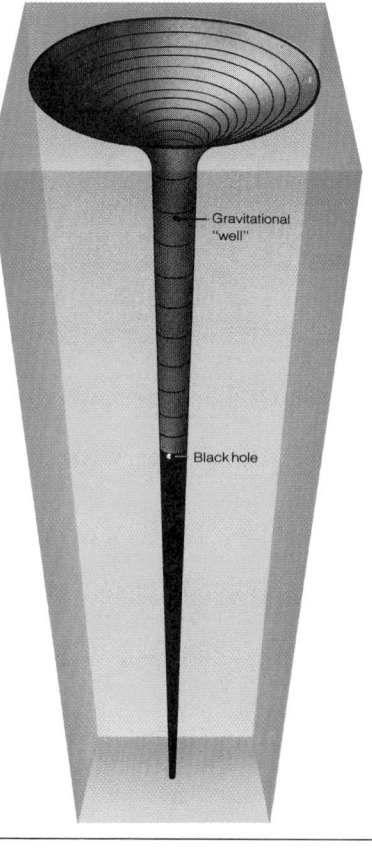

— Gravitational "well"

— Black hole

CYG X-1 *A color-coded impression (above) of the x-rays given off by Cyg X-1. They suggest that a giant star has an invisible companion, possibly a black hole, about 15 times as massive as the sun. A black hole cannot yet be described, but some theorists envisage one as a gravitational "well" or funnel (right) pouring matter from our universe into another as yet unknown.*

black·out (blăk'out') *n.* **1.** The extinguishing or concealing of lights that might be visible to enemy aircraft during an air raid at night. Compare **dim-out. 2.** A temporary loss of electric power. **3.** In the theater, the sudden extinguishing of all stage lights to indicate passage of time, or to mark the end of an act or a scene. **4.** A temporary loss of consciousness or vision. **5.** A suppression or stoppage, as of news for political reasons. **6.** A temporary loss or stoppage of radio or television communication or broadcasting caused by a technical fault, a strike, or the like.

Black Panther *n.* A member of a militant organization of black Americans.

black pepper *n.* See **pepper.**

black·poll (blăk'pōl') *n.* A North American warbler, *Dendroica striata,* of which the male has a black cap.

black poplar *n.* An ornamental poplar tree, *Populus nigra,* native to Eurasia, having spreading branches and pointed, triangular leaves. See **Lombardy poplar.**

Black Power *n.* A movement among black Americans emphasizing racial pride and social equality through the creation of black political and cultural institutions.

Black Prince. See **Edward, Prince of Wales.**

black pudding *n. Chiefly British.* **Blood pudding** *(see).*

black raspberry *n.* **1.** A prickly shrub, *Rubus occidentalis,* of eastern North America, bearing black fruit. **2.** The fruit of this plant. Also called "blackcap."

black rat *n.* A type of **rat** *(see).*

Black Rod *n.* A British official, the chief usher of various institutions, including the House of Lords.

black rot *n.* Any of various plant diseases, particularly affecting fruits and vegetables, caused by fungi or bacteria and resulting in darkening of the leaves and decay.

Black Sash *n.* A movement in South Africa of women against apartheid.

Black Sea. A sea lying between Europe and Asia. It is connected to the Mediterranean Sea by the Bosporus, the Sea of Marmara, and Dardanelles. The main Soviet Black Sea port of Odessa, frozen for three months, is kept open all year by icebreakers.

black sheep *n.* **1.** A sheep with black fleece. **2.** A person considered undesirable or disgraceful by his family or peer group.

Black Shirt *n.* A member of a fascist party organization, especially Mussolini's Italian Fascist party. [After the black shirts of Italian Fascist uniforms.]

black·smith (blăk'smĭth') *n.* **1.** One who forges and shapes iron with an anvil and hammer. **2.** One who makes, repairs, and fits horseshoes. [Middle English *blaksmith,* "a worker in black metal" (iron).] **—black·smith·ing** *n.*

black·snake (blăk'snāk') *n.* **1.** Any of various dark-colored, nonvenomous snakes, such as the black racer, *Coluber constrictor,* or the black rat snake, *Elaphe obsoleta,* of North America. **2.** *Western U.S.* A long, tapering, braided rawhide or leather whip with a snapper on the end. **3.** Any of various venomous black snakes, such as the Australian species *Pseudechis porphyriacus.*

black spot *n.* Any of various plant diseases caused by fungi or bacteria and resulting in small black spots on the leaves.

black spruce *n.* An evergreen tree, *Picea mariana,* of northern North America, growing mostly in bogs. Sometimes called "spruce pine."

Black·stone (blăk'stən, -stōn'), **Sir William** (1723–80). British jurist. His enduring fame rests on his monumental four-volume *Commentaries on the Laws of England* (1765–69), the most comprehensive single treatment of the body of English law.

black·strap (blăk'străp') *n.* A dark, very thick molasses used in the manufacture of industrial alcohol, and as an ingredient in cattle feed. Also called "blackstrap molasses."

black-tailed deer (blăk'tāld') *n.* Also **black·tail deer** (blăk'tāl'). The **mule deer** *(see).*

black tea *n.* A dark tea, the leaf of which is fully fermented or oxidized before drying. Compare **green tea, oolong.**

black·thorn (blăk'thôrn') *n.* A thorny Eurasian shrub, *Prunus spinosa,* having clusters of white flowers and bluish-black, plumlike fruit. Also called "sloe."

black tie *n.* **1.** A black bow tie worn with a dinner jacket. **2.** Semiformal evening wear for men, typically requiring a black dinner jacket. Compare **white tie. —black-tie** *adj.*

black·top (blăk'tŏp') *n.* A bituminous material, such as asphalt, used to pave roads.
~*tr.v.* **blacktopped, -topping, -tops.** To pave with blacktop.

black velvet *n.* A drink consisting of stout and champagne.

black vomit *n.* **1.** A vomit consisting of bloody matter. **2.** Severe yellow fever with symptomatic regurgitation of such vomit.

black vulture *n.* A carrion-eating bird, *Coragyps atratus,* of central North America and South America, having black plumage and a bald, black head.

black walnut *n.* **1.** A deciduous walnut tree, *Juglans nigra,* of eastern North America, having dark, hard wood and edible nuts. **2.** The grained wood of this tree, used for cabinetwork.

Black Watch *n.* **1.** A Highland regiment of the British Army, the men of which wear uniforms of a dark-blue and dark-green tartan. **2.** *Often* **black watch.** The tartan of the Black Watch.

black·wa·ter fever (blăk'wô'tər, -wŏt'ər) *n.* A severe, frequently fatal malaria with symptomatic excretion of blood in the urine caused by destruction of red blood cells.

black widow *n.* A New World spider, *Latrodectus mactans,* of which the extremely venomous female is black with red markings. [From the fact that the female eats its mate.]

blad·der (blăd'ər) *n.* **1.** *Anatomy.* Any of various distensible membranous sacs found in most animals, especially the **urinary bladder** *(see).* **2.** Anything resembling such a sac: *the bladder of a football.* **3.** *Botany.* An inflated, hollow structure, such as the air sac in certain seaweeds. **4.** *Pathology.* A blister, pustule, or cyst filled with fluid or air. [Middle English *bladdre,* Old English *blǣdre.*]

bladder campion *n.* A plant, *Silene cucubalus,* native to Europe, having white flowers and an inflated calyx.

blad·der·nose (blăd'ər-nōz') *n.* An aquatic mammal, the **hooded seal** *(see).*

blad·der·nut (blăd'ər-nŭt') *n.* Any of several shrubs or small trees of the genus *Staphylea,* of the North Temperate Zone, having small, whitish flowers and inflated seed pods.

bladder worm *n.* The bladderlike, encysted larva of the tapeworm.

blad·der·wort (blăd'ər-wûrt', -wôrt') *n.* Any of various aquatic plants of the genus *Utricularia,* having violet or yellow flowers, and, in most species, small bladders that trap minute aquatic animals.

bladder wrack *n.* A rockweed, *Fucus vesiculosus,* having forked, brownish-green fronds with air-filled bladders.

blade (blād) *n.* **1.** The flat-edged cutting part of a sharpened tool or weapon. **2. a.** A sword. **b.** A swordsman. **3.** A dashing young man. **4.** Any flat, thin structural member or section, such as the flat part of an oar or propeller. **5.** *Anatomy.* The **scapula** *(see).* **6.** *Botany.* **a.** The leaf of a grass or similar plant. **b.** The expanded, usually green part of a leaf, as distinguished from the leafstalk. **7.** The upper surface of the tongue, just behind the tip. [Middle English *blade,* Old English *blæd,* leaf, blade.] **—blad·ed** *adj.*

blade-ap·ple (blăd'ăp'əl) *n.* A spiny, vinelike, tropical American cactus, *Pereskia aculeata,* having true leaves, white flowers, and pulpy yellow fruit. Also called "Barbados gooseberry."

blah (blä) *n. Slang.* **1.** Worthless nonsense; drivel. **2. blahs.** A general feeling of physical or psychological discomfort or dissatisfaction.
~*adj.* Dull and uninteresting. [Imitative.]

blain (blān) *n.* A skin sore; blister; blotch. [Middle English *blein, blain,* an inflammatory swelling, Old English *blegen.*]

Blake (blāk), **Robert** (1599–1657). English admiral who was on the Parliamentarian side in the English Civil War. He pursued Prince Rupert to the Mediterranean (1650) and virtually destroyed the Royalist fleet there.

Blake, William (1757–1827). British poet and painter. He trained as an engraver and illustrated his own poems. Both his poems and his paintings have a mystical, visionary quality. His first important volumes of poetry were the childlike *Songs of Innocence* (1789) and *Songs of Experience* (1794). In these and his later, prophetic volumes, such as *The Marriage of Heaven and Hell* (c. 1790), Blake railed against both cruelty and injustice and made a plea for the freedom of the human spirit.

blame (blām) *tr.v.* **blamed, blaming, blames. 1.** To hold responsible; accuse. **2.** To find fault with; censure. **3.** To place responsibility for (something) on a person or thing: *blamed the accident on the cyclist.* —See Synonyms at **criticize.**
~*n.* **1.** The responsibility for a fault or error. **2.** Censure; condemnation. **—be to blame.** To be guilty or responsible. Used with *for.* [Middle English *blamen,* from Old French *blamer,* earlier *blasmer,* from Vulgar Latin *blastēmāre* (unattested), alteration of Late Latin *blasphēmāre,* to reproach, BLASPHEME.] **—blam·a·ble, blame·a·ble** *adj.* **—blam·er** *n.*

blame·ful (blām'fəl) *adj.* Deserving of blame; blameworthy. **—blame·ful·ly** *adv.* **—blame·ful·ness** *n.*

blame·less (blām'lĭs) *adj.* Free from blame or guilt; innocent. **—blame·less·ly** *adv.* **—blame·less·ness** *n.*

blame·wor·thy (blām'wûr'thē) *adj.* Deserving of blame; reprehensible. **—blame·wor·thi·ness** *n.*

Blanc (bläN), **Louis** (1811–82). Spanish-born French politician and political theorist. His lasting importance rests on his writings, especially the *Organization of Work* (1839), one of the most influential of early socialist treatises.

Blanc, Mont. See **Mont Blanc.**

blanc fixe (blăngk'fĭks') *n.* Powdered barium sulfate used as a white base for water-color pigments. [French, "fixed white."]

blanch (blănch, blänch) *v.* **blanched, blanching, blanches.** Also **blench** (blĕnch). *—tr.* **1.** To take color from; bleach. **2.** To whiten (a growing food plant, such as celery) by covering to cut off direct light. **3.** To whiten (a metal) by soaking in acid or by coating with tin. **4. a.** To loosen the skin of (almonds, for example) by scalding. **b.** To boil (food) briefly to remove strong or bitter flavors or to kill enzymes prior to freezing. **5.** To cause to turn pale. *—intr.* To turn white or become pale as through shock or illness. [Middle English *blaunchen,* from Old French *blanchir,* from *blanche,* feminine of *blanc,* white, from Vulgar Latin *blancus* (unattested), from Germanic.] **—blanch·er** *n.*

blanc·mange (blə-mänj'; *French* bläN-mäNzh') *n.* A flavored and sweetened milk pudding, thickened with cornstarch and set with gelatin in a mold. [Middle English *blancmanger,* dish of chopped chicken or fish with rice, from Old French, "white food" : *blanc,* white (see **blanch**) + *manger,* food, from *mangier,* to eat (see **mange**).]

bland (blănd) *adj.* **blander, blandest. 1.** Characterized by a moderate, undisturbing, or tranquil quality: **a.** Pleasant in manner; ingratiating. **b.** Free of irritation; soothing: *a bland diet.* **c.** Mild; balmy.

black widow *The black widow spider is so called because the female sometimes devours the male after mating. She is recognizable by her red mottling and is seen here with an egg sac. Black widow spiders are highly venomous, but their bite is seldom fatal to humans.*

bladder campion *This plant grows from 22 centimeters (9 inches) to 60 centimeters (2 feet) high and has white—and very occasionally pink—flowers. A native of Europe, it is widely naturalized in the United States and blooms from June to August.*

2. Lacking a distinctive character; mediocre. [Latin *blandus,* caressing, flattering, "soft-spoken."] —**bland·ly** *adv.* —**bland·ness** *n.*

blan·dish (blăn′dĭsh) *tr.v.* **-dished, -dishing, -dishes.** To coax by flattery or wheedling; cajole. [Middle English *blandishen,* from Old French *blandir* (present stem *blandiss-*), from Latin *blandīrī,* from *blandus,* flattering, BLAND.] —**blan·dish·er** *n.* —**blan·dish·ment** *n.*

blank (blăngk) *adj.* **blanker, blankest. 1.** Bearing no writing, print, or marking of any kind. **2.** Not finished or filled in: *a blank questionnaire.* **3.** Having no finishing grooves or cuts: *a blank key.* **4. a.** Expressing nothing; vacant. **b.** Vacuous; having no inspiration: *my mind was blank.* **c.** Confused, uncomprehending: *a blank look.* **5.** Devoid of activity or character; empty. **6.** Barren; fruitless: *blank efforts.* **7.** Utter; complete: *a blank refusal.* **8.** Having no openings or ornamentation: *a blank wall.* —See Synonyms at **empty.**

~*n.* **1.** An empty space; void: *His memory was a complete blank.* **2. a.** An empty space on a document to be filled in. **b.** A document having one or more such spaces. **3.** An unfinished material, part, or article, such as a key form, that is prepared ready for eventual finishing. **4.** A gun cartridge with a charge of powder but no bullet. Also called "blank cartridge." **5.** A lottery ticket that wins no prize. **6.** A mark, usually a dash (—), indicating the omission of a word or letter. **7.** The center white circle of a target; the bull's eye. **8.** Something used to seal an opening. **9.** Any goal or target. —**draw a blank.** *Informal.* To fail utterly; achieve nothing.

~*tr.v.* **blanked, blanking, blanks. 1.** To remove from view; obliterate: *The strong glare of the sun blanked it from view.* **2.** To omit; delete; invalidate. Often used with *out.* **3.** To prevent (an opponent in a game or sport) from scoring. **4.** To punch or stamp from flat stock, especially with a die. Often used with *out.* **5.** To seal or block (an opening or means of access). Often used with *off.* [Middle English *bla(u)nk,* white, not written on, from Old French *blanc.* See **blanch.**] —**blank·ly** *adv.* —**blank·ness** *n.*

blank check *n.* **1.** A check that has been signed, but which has not had the amount filled in. **2.** Unrestrained freedom of action or choice.

blank endorsement *n.* An endorsement on a check or negotiable note that names no payee, making it payable to the bearer. Also called "endorsement in blank."

blan·ket (blăng′kĭt) *n.* **1.** A large piece of wool or other thick cloth used as a covering for warmth, especially on a bed. **2.** A thick layer that covers or encloses: *a blanket of snow.*

~*adj.* Covering a wide range of conditions or requirements: *a blanket insurance policy.*

~*tr.v.* **blanketed, -keting, -kets. 1.** To cover with or as if with a blanket. **2.** To conceal or suppress as if with a blanket. **3.** *Nautical.* To cut off (a sail boat) from the wind by passing close on the windward side. [Middle English, originally, a white woolen material, from Old French *blanquet, blanchet,* diminutive of *blanc,* white. See **blanch.**]

blanket stitch *n.* The buttonhole stitch, as used for edging around a blanket.

blank verse *n.* Verse consisting of unrhymed lines, usually of iambic pentameter.

blan·quette de veau (blän-kĕt′də-vō′) A stew or fricassee of veal in a white sauce. [French, white dish of veal. See **blanket.**]

Blan·qui (blän-kē′), **Louis Auguste** (1805–81). French revolutionary leader and political theorist. He fought for the deposition of Napoleon III and proclamation of the Paris Commune. His ideas, close to those of Karl Marx, were expressed in his treatise, *Critique Sociale,* published four years after his death.

Blan·tyre (blăn-tîr′). Also **Blan·tyre-Lim·be** (-lĭm′bā). The oldest and largest town in Malawi, in the Shire Highlands. It was founded as a mission of the Church of Scotland by David Livingstone (1876) and named after the village where he was born.

blare (blâr) *v.* **blared, blaring, blares.** —*intr.* To sound loudly and insistently. —*tr.* To utter or proclaim loudly.

~*n.* A loud, strident noise. [Middle English *bleren,* to bellow, from Middle Dutch.]

blar·ney (blär′nē) *n.* Smooth, flattering talk.

~*v.* **blarneyed, -neying, -neys.** —*tr.* To beguile with blarney. —*intr.* To flatter. [After the *Blarney Stone.*]

Blar·ney (blär′nē). A village in County Cork, Republic of Ireland. Blarney Castle (*c.* 1446) has on its southern wall the famous Blarney Stone, said to impart gifts of eloquence and flattery to those who kiss it.

Blas·co I·bá·ñez (blä′skō ē-bän′yäs), **Vicente** (1867–1928). Spanish politician and novelist. He founded the republican paper *El Pueblo* (1891), was elected to the Spanish parliament (1901), and spent more than 30 periods in prison for his antimonarchist views before settling in France (1923). His most famous novel is *The Four Horsemen of the Apocalypse* (1916).

bla·sé (blä-zā′, blä′zā) *adj.* **1.** Indifferent, unexcited, or lacking enthusiasm, especially as a result of habitual and excessive indulgence. **2.** Filled with ennui; weary. [French, past participle of *blaser,* to blunt, cloy, "to cause to be bloated with strong liquor," from Middle Dutch *blasen,* to blow up, cause to swell.]

blas·pheme (blăs-fēm′) *v.* **-phemed, -pheming, -phemes.** —*tr.* **1.** To speak of (God or something sacred) in an irreverent or impious manner. **2.** To revile; execrate: *"and every tongue/ Cursed and blasphemed me as he passed"* (P.B. Shelley). —*intr.* To utter blasphemy. [Middle English *blasfemen, blasphemen,* from Old French *blasfemer,* from Late Latin *blasphēmāre,* to reproach, blaspheme,

from Greek *blasphēmein,* from *blasphēmos,* evil-speaking, BLASPHE-MOUS.] —**blas·phem·er** *n.*

blas·phe·mous (blăs′fə-məs) *adj.* Impiously irreverent. —See Synonyms at **profane.** [Late Latin *blasphēmus,* from Greek *blasphēmos,* evil-speaking, impious.] —**blas·phe·mous·ly** *adv.* —**blas·phe·mous·ness** *n.*

blas·phe·my (blăs′fə-mē) *n., pl.* **-mies. 1. a.** Any contemptuous or profane act, utterance, or writing concerning God or something considered sacred. **b.** The act of claiming for oneself the attributes and rights of God. **2.** An irreverent or impious act, attitude, or utterance in regard to something considered inviolable or sacrosanct.

blast (blăst, bläst) *n.* **1. a.** A strong gust of wind. **b.** The battering effect of such a gust. **2.** A forcible stream of air or other gas from an opening, especially one in a blast furnace to aid combustion. **3. a.** The blowing of a whistle or wind instrument. **b.** The sound or noise produced by this. **4. a.** An explosion. **b.** A charge of explosive. **c.** The powerful, destructive rush of air resulting from an explosion. **5.** Any disease of plants that results in failure of flowers to open, or failure of fruit or seeds to mature. **6.** A violent verbal assault or outburst. **7.** A big or wild party. —See Synonyms at **wind.** —**(at) full blast.** At full speed, volume, or capacity.

~*v.* **blasted, blasting, blasts.** —*tr.* **1.** To tear to pieces by or as if by explosion; blow up. **2.** To cause to deteriorate; ruin; frustrate: *His dreams were all blasted by the news of his rejection.* **3.** To cause to shrivel, wither, or mature imperfectly by or as if by blast or blight. **4.** To make, dislodge, or open (something) by or as if by explosion: *blast a channel through the reefs.* **5.** *Slang.* To attack or criticize vigorously. **6.** *Slang.* To damn. Used euphemistically. —*intr.* **1.** To detonate explosives. **2.** To emit a sudden loud noise. **3.** To wither, shrivel, or mature imperfectly. **4.** *Slang.* To attack or criticize with vigor. **5.** *Slang.* To shoot. Sometimes used with *away.* **6.** *Electronics.* To distort sound recording or transmission by overloading a microphone or loud-speaker.

~*interj. Informal.* Used to express annoyance or frustration. [Middle English *blast,* Old English *blæst.*] —**blast·er** *n.*

-blast *suffix* Indicates a germ, sprout, or growth; for example, **erythroblast.** [Greek *blastos,* shoot, bud.]

blast·ed (blăs′tĭd, bläs′-) *adj.* **1.** Blighted; withered; shriveled. **2.** *Slang.* Damned.

blas·te·ma (blă-stē′mə) *n., pl.* **-mas** or **-mata** (-mə-tə). **1.** A segregated region of embryonic cells from which a specific organ develops. **2.** A mass of undifferentiated animal cells that develops into a new tissue or organ during regeneration of lost parts. [New Latin, from Greek *blastēma,* offspring, offshoot, from *blastos,* sprout, bud.] —**blas·te·mal** (blă-stē′məl), **blas·te·mat·ic** (blăs′tə-măt′ĭk), **blas·te·mic** (blă-stē′mĭk) *adj.*

blast furnace *n.* Any furnace in which combustion is intensified by a blast of air, especially a furnace for smelting iron by blowing air through a hot mixture of ore, coke, and flux.

-blastic *suffix.* Indicates buds, sprouts, or growth; for example, **diploblastic.**

blasting gelatin *n.* A **dynamite** *(see)* containing nitrocellulose in addition to nitroglycerin.

blasto– *prefix.* Indicates growth, budding, or germination; for example, **blastoderm.** [Greek *blastos.* See **-blast.**]

blas·to·coel, blas·to·coele (blăs′tə-sēl′) *n. Embryology.* The cavity of a **blastula** *(see).* Also called "segmentation cavity." [BLASTO- + *-coel,* variant of -CELE.] —**blas·to·coel·ic** *adj.*

blas·to·cyst (blăs′tə-sĭst) *n. Embryology.* **1.** The **blastula** *(see)* of mammals. **2.** The **germinal vesicle** *(see).* —**blas·to·cys·tic** *adj.*

blas·to·derm (blăs′tə-dûrm′) *n.* **1.** The layer of cells surrounding the blastocoel. It gives rise to the **germinal disc** *(see)* from which the embryo develops in most placental vertebrates. **2.** The embryonic structure resulting from cleavage in heavily yolked eggs, such as those of birds. [BLASTO- + -DERM.] —**blas·to·der·mat·ic, blas·to·derm·ic** *adj.*

blas·to·disc, blas·to·disk (blăs′tə-dĭsk′) *n. Embryology.* The **germinal disc** *(see).*

blast off *intr.v.* To commence flight; take off. Used of rockets or space vehicles.

blast-off, blast·off (blăst′ôf′, bläst′-) *n.* The launching of a rocket or space vehicle.

blas·to·gen·e·sis (blăs′tə-jĕn′ĭ-sĭs) *n. Biology.* **1.** The theory that inherited characteristics are transmitted from parent to offspring by germ plasm. **2.** Reproduction by budding or other asexual means. —**blas·to·ge·net·ic** (blăs′tə-jə-nĕt′ĭk), **blas·to·gen·ic** *adj.*

blas·to·mere (blăs′tə-mîr′) *n.* A cell formed during the cleavage of a fertilized ovum. [BLASTO- + -MERE.] —**blas·to·mer·ic** (blăs′tə-mĕr′ĭk) *adj.*

blas·to·pore (blăs′tə-pôr′, -pōr′) *n.* The mouthlike opening into the primitive intestinal cavity of the gastrula. [BLASTO- + PORE (orifice).] —**blas·to·po·ral** *adj.*

blas·tu·la (blăs′chōō-lə) *n., pl.* **-las** or **-lae** (-lē′). An early embryonic form, resulting from cleavage and consisting essentially of a hollow cellular sphere. Also called "blastosphere." [New Latin, from Greek *blastos,* bud, germ.] —**blas·tu·lar** (blăs′chōō-lər) *adj.* —**blas·tu·la·tion** (blăs′chōō-lā′shən) *n.*

bla·tant (blā′tənt) *adj.* **1.** Offensively conspicuous; obtrusive; obvious: *a blatant lie.* **2.** Unpleasantly loud and noisy. [First used by Spenser ("the blattant beast," a symbol of calumny), probably from Latin *blatīre,* to blab, gossip.] —**bla·tan·cy** *n.* —**bla·tant·ly** *adv.*

Usage: *Blatant* and *flagrant* are often confused. In the sense that causes the confusion, *blatant* has the meaning of "outrageous" or "egregious." *Flagrant* emphasizes wrong or evil that is glaring or notorious. Therefore, one who blunders may be guilty of a *blatant* (but not *flagrant*) error; one who intentionally violates a pledge commits a *flagrant* act.

blath·er (blăth′ər) *v.* **-ered, -ering, -ers.** Also **bleth·er** (blĕth′ər). —*intr.* To talk nonsense; babble. —*tr.* To speak foolishly or nonsensically.
~*n.* Also **bleth·er.** Absurd or foolish talk; nonsense. [Middle English *blether,* from Old Norse *bladhra,* to prattle, akin to *bladhra,* bladder.] **—blath·er·er** *n.*

blath·er·skite (blăth′ər-skīt′) *n.* **1.** A babbling, foolish person. **2.** Absurd and foolish talk. [Earlier *bletherskate* : BLATHER + SKATE (fish).]

Bla·vat·sky (blə-văt′skē), **Helena Petrovna,** born Helena Petrovna Hahn (1831–91). Russian theosophist. She began the theosophist movement in Russia in the late 1850's and founded the Theosophical Society in New York. Her demonstrations of supernatural phenomena were declared fraudulent by the London Society for Psychical Research (1885).

blaze[1] (blāz) *n.* **1.** A brilliant burst of fire; a flame. **2. a.** Any bright, hot, steady light or glare. **b.** Any bright, conspicuous display: *a blaze of color; a blaze of publicity.* **3.** A destructive fire, especially one that spreads rapidly. **4.** A sudden outburst, as of emotion or activity. **5. blazes.** *Slang.* Hell. Used euphemistically especially in the phrase *go to blazes* and as an intensive: *gallop like blazes; What he blazes is going on here?*
~*v.* **blazed, blazing, blazes.** —*intr.* **1.** To burn with a bright flame. **2.** To shine brightly. **3.** To be deeply excited, as by emotion. **4.** To shoot rapidly and continuously. Used with *away.* —*tr.* To shine or be resplendent with: *Her eyes blazed fire.* [Middle English *blase,* Old English *blæse,* torch, bright fire.] **—blaz·ing·ly** *adv.*
Synonyms: *flame, flare, flash, glare, glow, incandescence.*

blaze[2] *n.* **1.** A white or light-colored spot or stripe on the face of a horse or other animal. **2.** A mark cut on a tree to indicate a trail.
~*tr.v.* **blazed, blazing, blazes. 1.** To mark (a tree) by cutting the bark. **2.** To indicate (a trail) by marking trees in this manner. **3.** To make (a trail) into new, unexplained areas of knowledge or research. Used in the phrase *blaze the trail.* [Probably from Middle Low German *bles.*]

blaz·er (blā′zər) *n.* **1.** One that blazes. **2.** A lightweight, informal sports jacket, often striped or brightly colored.

blaz·ing (blā′zĭng) *adj.* Very hot.
~*adv.* Used as an intensive: *blazing hot.*

blazing star *n.* **1.** A North American plant, *Chamaelirium luteum,* having a long cluster of small white flowers. Also called "devil's bit." **2.** Any of various North American plants of the genus *Liatris,* having clusters of tuftlike purple or pinkish flowers. Also called "button snakeroot." **3.** A plant, *Mentzelia laevicaulis,* of western North America, having large, pale-yellow flowers.

bla·zon (blā′zən) *tr.v.* **-zoned, -zoning, -zons. 1.** To describe (a coat of arms) in proper heraldic terms. **2.** To paint or depict (a coat of arms) with accurate heraldic detail. **3.** To adorn or embellish with or as if with blazons. **4.** To announce publicly; proclaim loudly and widely. Often used with *abroad.*
~*n.* **1.** A heraldic charge or coat of arms. **2. a.** The heraldic description or representation of a heraldic charge or coat of arms. **b.** The heraldic terms used to describe coats of arms. **3.** An ostentatious or showy display. [Middle English *blasoun,* shield, coat of arms, from Old French *blason*†.] **—bla·zon·er** *n.* **—bla·zon·ment** *n.*

bla·zon·ry (blā′zən-rē) *n., pl.* **-ries. 1.** The art of properly and accurately describing or representing heraldic bearings. **2.** Coats of arms and heraldic bearings collectively. **3.** Any showy or brilliant display.

bld. boldface.

bldg. building.

bleach (blēch) *v.* **bleached, bleaching, bleaches.** —*tr.* **1.** To remove the color from, as by means of sunlight or chemical agents. **2.** To make white or colorless. —*intr.* To become white or colorless.
~*n.* **1.** Any chemical agent used for bleaching, by either oxidation or reduction. **2.** The degree of bleaching obtained. **3.** The act of bleaching. [Middle English *blechen,* Old English *blǣcan.*]

bleach·er (blē′chər) *n.* **1.** One that bleaches. **2.** *Usually* **bleachers.** An unroofed outdoor grandstand for seating spectators. [Sense 2, from the bleaching effect of exposure to sun.]

bleaching powder *n.* Any powder, such as chlorinated lime or calcium hypochlorite, used in solution as a bleach.

bleak[1] (blēk) *adj.* **bleaker, bleakest. 1.** Exposed to the elements; unsheltered; barren. **2.** Cold and cutting; harsh. **3.** Offering no hope or encouragement: *bleak prospects.* **4.** Gloomy and somber; depressing; dreary. [Middle English *bleike,* pale, from Old Norse *bleikr,* shining, white.] **—bleak·ly** *adv.* **—bleak·ness** *n.*

bleak[2] *n.* A European freshwater fish of the genus *Alburnus,* related to the carp, having silvery scales used in the manufacture of artificial pearls. [Middle English *bleke,* probably from Old Norse *bleikja,* "white color."]

blear (blîr) *tr.v.* **bleared, blearing, blears. 1.** To blur (the eyes) with or as if with tears. **2.** To blur; dim.
~*adj.* Bleary. [Middle English *bleren,* probably of Low German origin, akin to Low German *blerr-*† (in *blerr-oged,* bleary-eyed).]

blear·y (blîr′ē) *adj.* **-ier, -iest. 1.** Blurred or dimmed as by tears or lack of sleep. Said of the eyes. **2.** Vague or indistinct; blurred. **3.** Exhausted; worn-out. **—blear·i·ly** *adv.* **—blear·i·ness** *n.*

blear·y-eyed (blîr′ē-īd′) *adj.* Also **blear-eyed** (blîr′īd′). **1.** With eyes blurred by or as if by tears or lack of sleep. **2.** Dull of mind or perception.

bleat (blēt) *v.* **bleated, bleating, bleats.** —*intr.* **1.** To utter the cry of a goat, sheep, or calf. **2.** To utter any similar sound, especially a whine. —*tr.* To utter in a whining voice.
~*n.* **1.** The characteristic cry of a goat, sheep, or calf. **2.** Any similar sound, such as a whining cry. [Middle English *bleten,* Old English *blǣtan.*] **—bleat·er** *n.*

bleb (blĕb) *n.* **1.** A small blister or pustule. Compare **bulla. 2.** An air bubble. [Variant of BLOB.] **—bleb·by** *adj.*

bleed (blēd) *v.* **bled** (blĕd), **bleeding, bleeds.** —*intr.* **1.** To lose or emit blood. **2.** To suffer injury or death, as in battle. **3.** To feel sympathetic grief or anguish: *My heart bleeds for you.* **4.** To exude sap or a similar fluid, as a bruised plant does. **5.** *Slang.* To pay out money, especially an exorbitant amount. **6.** To become mixed or run, as dyes in wet cloth or paper. **7.** To show through a layer of paint, as a stain or resin in wood. **8.** *Printing.* To be printed so as to go over the edge or edges of a page, either purposely or by trimming the margins too closely. Often used with *off.* —*tr.* **1. a.** To take blood from, either surgically or with leeches. **b.** To extract sap or juice from. **2.** To exude (blood or sap, for example). **3. a.** To draw liquid or gaseous contents from; especially, to remove air from a hydraulic brake system or from a radiator in a central-heating system. **b.** To draw off (liquid or gaseous matter) from a container. **4.** *Slang.* To obtain large amounts of money from, especially by improper means. **5.** *Printing.* **a.** To print (an illustration, for example) so that it will go over the edge or edges of a page. **b.** To trim (a page or sheet, for example) too closely so as to mutilate the printed or illustrative matter. **6.** To feed (continuous small amounts of fluid) into a system.
~*n.* *Printing.* **1.** Illustrative matter that purposely bleeds. **2.** A page trimmed so as to bleed. Also called "bleed page." **3.** The part thus trimmed off. [Bleed, bled, bled; Middle English *bleden, bledde, bledde,* Old English *blēdan, blēdde, blēdd,* from Common Germanic *blōthjan* (unattested), from *blōtham* (unattested), BLOOD.]

bleed·er (blē′dər) *n.* **1.** A **hemophiliac** *(see).* **2.** A bloodletter.

bleed·ing-heart (blē′dĭng-härt′) *n.* **1.** Any of several plants of the genus *Dicentra,* having nodding, pink flowers; especially, the widely cultivated species *D. spectabilis,* native to Japan. **2.** A person who is considered excessively sympathetic toward those who claim to be underprivileged or exploited.

bleeding-heart *A pink flower similar in appearance to the fuchsia; it is native to Japan and Siberia.*

bleep (blēp) *n.* A high-pitched noise of short duration produced electronically.
~*intr.v.* **bleeped, bleeping, bleeps.** To blip. [Imitative.]

blem·ish (blĕm′ĭsh) *tr.v.* **-ished, -ishing, -ishes.** To impair or spoil by a flaw; mar.
~*n.* A flaw or defect; a stain; a disfigurement. [Middle English *blemisshen,* from Old French *blemir, blesmir* (present stem *blemiss-*), to make pale, from Germanic.] **—blem·ish·er** *n.*
Synonyms: *defect, fault, flaw, imperfection.*

blench[1] (blĕnch) *intr.v.* **blenched, blenching, blenches.** To draw back or shy away, as in fear; quail; flinch. —See Synonyms at **recoil.** [Middle English *blenchen,* to deceive, start aside, evade, Old English *blencan,* to deceive.] **—blench·er** *n.*

blench[2]**.** Variant of **blanch.**

blend (blĕnd) *v.* **blended** or **blent** (blĕnt), **blending, blends.** —*tr.* **1.** To combine or mix so as to render the constituent parts indistinguishable from one another. **2.** To mix (different varieties or grades of coffee or tea, for example) so as to obtain a new mixture of some particular quality or consistency. —*intr.* **1.** To form a uniform mixture; intermingle. **2.** To become merged into one; unite. **3.** To pass imperceptibly into one another: *"standing motionless beside that door, as though trying to make myself blend with the dark wood"* (William Faulkner). —See Synonyms at **mix.**
~*n.* **1.** That which is blended; a mixture. **2.** The act of blending. **3.** *Linguistics.* A word produced by combining parts of other words, such as *smog,* from *smoke* and *fog;* a portmanteau word. **4.** To go together; harmonize: *The new carpet blends well with the curtains.* [Middle English *blenden,* from Old Norse *blanda* (stem *blend-*).]

blende (blĕnd) *n.* **1.** Any of various shiny minerals composed chiefly of metallic sulfides. **2.** A mineral, **sphalerite** *(see).* [German *Blende,* short for *blendendes Erz,* "deceptive ore" (often mistaken, on account of its metallic gleam, for a lead ore), from *blenden,* to blind, deceive, from Old High German *blenten.*]

blended whiskey *n.* Whiskey that is a blend of two or more straight whiskeys, or a blend of whiskey and neutral spirits.

blend·er (blĕn′dər) *n.* **1.** One that combines or blends. **2.** A mechanical device with rotating blades used for chopping, mixing, or liquefying foods.

Blen·heim Palace (blĕn′əm). The country seat of the dukes of Marlborough, outside Woodstock in Oxfordshire. The palace, designed by Sir John Vanbrugh, is considered to be one of the finest examples of the baroque in English architecture.

blen·ny (blĕn′ē) *n., pl.* **-nies.** Any of numerous small, elongated marine fishes of the families Blenniidae and Clinidae, especially a fish of the genus *Blennius,* which has a long dorsal fin and long, rayed pelvic fins. [Latin *blennius, blendius,* from Greek *blennos,* "slime" (from the slimy coating on its scales).]

blent. Alternate past tense and past participle of **blend.**

bleph·a·ri·tis (blĕf′ə-rī′tĭs) *n.* Inflammation of the eyelid. [New Latin : Greek *blepharon*†, eyelid + -ITIS.]
bleph·a·ro·spasm (blĕf′ə-rō-spăz′əm) *n.* Uncontrollable winking, caused by involuntary contraction of an eyelid muscle. [New Latin *blepharospasmus* : BLEPHAR(ITIS) + SPASM.]
Blé·riot (blā-ryō′, blĕr′ē-ō), **Louis** (1872–1936). French inventor and aviator. On July 25, 1909, he flew his 25-horsepower airplane over the English Channel from Calais to Dover, the first time that an airplane had flown across open sea.
bles·bok (blĕs′bŏk′) *n., pl.* **-boks** or collectively **blesbok.** Also **bles·buck** (-bŭk′), *pl.* **-bucks** or collectively **blesbuck.** An African antelope, *Damaliscus albifrons,* having a reddish-brown coat and a face marked with white. [Afrikaans : *bles,* white mark on animal's face + *bok,* buck.]

blesbok *Great herds of blesbok used to roam the grasslands of southern Africa. Hunting has now made the antelope rare in the wild, but it is preserved on private farms and in game reserves.*

bless (blĕs) *tr.v.* **blessed** (blĕst) or **blest, blessing, blesses. 1.** To make holy by religious rite; sanctify. **2.** To make the sign of the cross over, so as to sanctify. **3.** To invoke divine favor upon. **4.** To preserve from evil. Used as an exclamation: *Bless my soul!* **5.** To honor as holy; glorify: *Bless the Lord.* **6.** To confer well-being or prosperity upon. **7.** To endow or favor. Usually used in the passive: *blessed with good health.* **—bless you.** Used conventionally as an interjection after a person has sneezed. [Middle English *blessen,* Old English *blētsian, blœdsian,* from Common Germanic *blōthisōjan* (unattested), "to hallow with blood," from *blōtham* (unattested), BLOOD.] **—bless·er** *n.*
bless·ed (blĕs′ĭd) *adj.* Also **blest** (blĕst). **1.** Made sacred by a religious rite; consecrated. **2.** Worthy of profound respect or worship. **3.** *Roman Catholic Church.* Enjoying the eternal happiness of heaven. Used as a title for those who have been beatified. **4.** Enjoying happiness; fortunate. **5.** Bringing happiness or bliss. **6.** Damned. Used euphemistically or as an intensive. **—bless·ed·ly** *adv.* **—bless·ed·ness** *n.*
Bles·sed Sacrament (blĕs′ĭd) *n. Roman Catholic Church.* The consecrated Host.
Bles·sed Virgin (blĕs′ĭd) *n. Abbr.* **B.V.** The Virgin Mary.
bless·ing (blĕs′ĭng) *n.* **1. a.** The act of one who blesses. **b.** The prescribed words or ceremony for such an act. **2.** An expression or utterance of good wishes. **3.** A special favor granted by God. **4.** Anything promoting or contributing to happiness, well-being, or prosperity; a boon: *a blessing in disguise.* **5.** Approval: *This plan has my blessing.* **6.** A short prayer before or after a meal.
blest. 1. Alternate past tense and past participle of **bless. 2.** Variant of **blessed.**
blet (blĕt) *n.* Internal softening or incipient decay of certain fruits. The medlar is edible only when it has reached this state. [French *blettir,* become overripe, from *blet(te),* overripe, from Old French, from Germanic.]
blether. Variant of **blather.**
bleu cheese (blœ) *n.* Blue cheese.
blew. Past tense of **blow.**
blew·its (blo͞o′əts) *n. Used with a singular verb.* An edible mushroom, *Tricholoma saevum,* having a bluish stalk and a pale brown cap. [Probably from BLUE.]
Bligh (blī), **William** (1754–1817). British admiral, known chiefly from the mutiny of his ship the *Bounty* (1789). He accompanied James Cook on the explorer's last expedition (1776–79) as sailing master and served as governor of New South Wales (1805–08).
blight (blīt) *n.* **1.** Any of several plant diseases that result in sudden dying of leaves, growing tips, or an entire plant. **2.** An environmental condition, such as air pollution, that injures or kills plants or animals. **3.** Something that withers hopes or ambitions, impairs growth, or halts prosperity. **4.** The state or result of being blighted; dilapidation; decay: *urban blight.*
~v. **blighted, blighting, blights.** *—tr.* **1.** To cause to decline or decay. **2.** To ruin; destroy. **3.** To frustrate: *a mishap that blighted his hopes.* *—intr.* To suffer blight. [17th century : origin obscure.]
blight·er (blī′tər) *n. Chiefly British Slang.* **1.** An annoying or contemptible person. **2.** A person. Used affectionately: *You lucky blighter!*
blight·y (blī′tē) *n. Often* **Blighty.** *British Slang.* England; home. Used especially by soldiers serving abroad. [Hindi *bilāyatī, wilāyatī,* "foreign," "English," from Arabic *wilāyat,* district, realm, from *waliya,* he rules.]
bli·mey (blī′mē) *interj. British Slang.* Used to express surprise, irritation, or the like. [From *(God) blind me!*]
blimp¹ (blĭmp) *n.* A nonrigid, buoyant aircraft, such as a barrage balloon. [Probably (type) B + LIMP.]
blimp² *n. Chiefly British.* One whose views exhibit a blend of ultraconservative jingoism and misinformation. [After Colonel *Blimp,* a cartoon character invented by David Low.] **—blimp·ish** *adj.*
blind (blīnd) *adj.* **blinder, blindest. 1.** Without the sense of sight. **2.** Of or for sightless persons. **3.** Performed without the use of sight, relying wholly on instruments: *blind flying.* **4.** Performed without preparation, forethought, or knowledge: *a blind attempt.* **5.** Unable or unwilling to perceive or understand: *blind to all her faults.* **6.** Not based on reason or evidence: *blind faith.* **7.** *Informal.* Drunk. **8.** Acting without human control: *blind fate.* **9. a.** Difficult to comprehend or see; illegible: *blind writings.* **b.** Illegibly or incompletely addressed: *blind mail.* **10.** Hidden from sight: *a blind seam.* **11.** Affording poor visibility to an oncoming driver: *a blind corner.* **12.** Closed at one end: *a blind alley.* **13.** Having no opening: *a blind wall.* **14.** *Botany.* Failing to flower. Said of cultivated plants. **15.** *Informal.* Used as an intensive: *didn't take a blind bit of notice.*
~n. **1. a.** Something that hinders vision or shuts out light: *a Venetian blind.* **b.** A piece of fabric, usually mounted on rollers, used to cover a window. Also "window shade." **2.** A shelter for concealing hunters, especially duck hunters. **3.** Any subterfuge or front; a decoy. **4.** *British Slang.* A drinking bout. **5.** In poker, a bet made before seeing one's cards.
~adv. **1.** Without being able to see; blindly: *fly blind.* **2.** *Informal.* Into a stupor: *They drank themselves blind.* Also used as an intensive, chiefly in the phrase *blind drunk.* **3.** Without a filling, or with a temporary filling of dried peas, beans, or the like inserted merely to retain shape during cooking: *bake a pastry shell blind.*
~tr.v. **blinded, blinding, blinds. 1.** To deprive of sight. **2.** To dazzle. **3.** To deprive (a person) of the powers of perception or judgment. **4.** To eclipse. **5.** To deprive of light; darken. [Middle English *blind,* Old English *blind,* blind, obscure.] **—blind·ly** *adv.* **—blind·ness** *n.*
blind alley *n.* **1.** A passageway open only at one end; a dead end. **2.** *Informal.* Any project or situation that offers no prospect of progress or development.
blind date *n. Informal.* **1.** A social engagement between two people, usually a man and a woman, who have not previously met. **2.** Either of the persons keeping such an engagement.
blind·er (blīn′dər) *n.* **1.** One that causes blinding. **2. blinders.** A pair of leather flaps attached to a horse's bridle to curtail side vision. Also called "blinkers." **3.** *Western U.S.* A cloth used to cover a horse's eyes during saddling or shoeing. **4.** *British Slang.* A bout of drinking. Used chiefly in the phrase *go on a blinder.*
blind·fish (blīnd′fĭsh′) *n., pl.* **-fishes** or collectively **blindfish.** Any of various fishes having rudimentary, nonfunctioning eyes; especially, the **cavefish** *(see).*
blind·fold (blīnd′fōld′) *tr.v.* **-folded, -folding, -folds. 1.** To cover the eyes with or as if with a bandage. **2.** To hamper the sight or comprehension of; mislead; delude.
~n. A bandage over the eyes.
~adj. **1.** With eyes covered. **2.** Reckless. [Middle English *blindfolde, blindfelde,* past participle of *blindfellen,* to strike blind, from Old English *geblindfellian,* "to strike blind" : *ge-,* Y- + BLIND + *fellan,* to strike down, FELL.]
blind gut *n.* **1.** A digestive cavity having only one opening. **2.** *Anatomy.* The **cecum** *(see).*
blind hinge *n.* A hinge so constructed that it allows the hinged piece to swing shut by its own weight unless held open.
blind·ing (blīn′dĭng) *adj.* **1.** Tending to make sightless. **2.** Dazzling; overpowering. **—blind·ing·ly** *adv.*
blind·man's buff (blīnd′mănz′) *n.* A game in which one person, blindfolded, tries to catch and identify one of the other players. [*Buff,* short for BUFFET (a blow).]
blind side *n.* The side away from which one is directing one's attention.
blind spot *n.* **1.** *Anatomy.* The small, optically insensitive region where the optic nerve enters the retina of the eye. **2.** Any part of an area that cannot be directly observed, especially that part of a motor-vehicle driver's surroundings that is not reflected in the vehicle's mirrors and cannot be seen without sharply turning the head. **3.** An area where radio reception is weak. **4.** A subject about which one is markedly ignorant or prejudiced.
blind staggers *n. Used with a singular verb.* A disease of horses, **staggers** *(see).*
blind·sto·ry (blīnd′stôr′ē, -stōr′ē) *n., pl.* **-ries.** *Architecture.* A story having no windows.
blind·worm (blīnd′wûrm′) *n.* A lizard, the **slowworm** *(see).* [Perhaps so called because its eyes close after death.]
bli·ni (blē′nē, blĭn′ē) *pl.n.* Small buckwheat pancakes served with caviar or sour cream. [Russian, plural of *blin,* pancake, from Old Russian *blinŭ, mlinŭ.*]
blink (blĭngk) *v.* **blinked, blinking, blinks.** *—intr.* **1.** To close and open one or both eyes rapidly. **2.** To look through half-closed eyes, as in a bright glare; squint. **3.** To shine with intermittent gleams; flash on and off. **4.** To pretend not to be aware of something, especially something unpleasant. Used with *at.* **5.** To become startled or dismayed. Usually used with *at.* *—tr.* **1.** To close and open (the eyes or an eye) rapidly. **2.** To ignore or refuse to acknowledge. —See Usage note below.
~n. **1.** The act or an instance of blinking; a brief closing of the eyes. **2.** A quick look or glimpse; a glance. **3.** The time it takes to blink. **4.** A flash of light; a gleam; a twinkle; a glimmer. **5.** An **iceblink** *(see).* **—on the blink.** *Slang.* Not in proper working condition; out of order. [Middle English *blinken,* partly a variant of *blenchen,* BLENCH (flinch), and perhaps partly from Middle Dutch *blinken,* to glitter.]
Usage: The verb *blink* used transitively and without a preposition expresses evasion in the sense of deliberate refusal to face or recognize: *blink* (not *blink at*) *ugly facts.* In an intransitive sense, *blink at* (or more frequently, *wink at*) expresses evasion by condoning or tolerating: *blink at dishonest practices.* The first construction pertains basically to shirking and the second to complicity.
blink·er (blĭng′kər) *n.* **1.** A light that blinks in order to convey a message or warning, as, for example, on a control panel. **2.** *Slang.* An eye. **3. blinkers.** Goggles. **4. blinkers. Blinders** *(see).*
blink·ered (blĭng′kərd) *adj.* **1.** Wearing blinders. Said of a horse. **2.** Showing unwillingness or inability to understand; obtuse.
blintz (blĭnts) *n.* Also **blin·tze** (blĭn′tsə). A thin, folded pancake filled with cream cheese or cottage cheese, fruit, or seasoned

mashed potatoes, and often served with sour cream. [Yiddish *blintse,* from Russian *blinyets,* diminutive of *blin,* BLINI.]

blip (blĭp) *n.* **1.** A spot of light on a radar screen. **2.** A regularly repeated sound. **3.** A brief interruption of the sound received in a television program as a result of blipping.
~*intr. v.* **blipped, blipping, blips. 1.** To produce a blip. **2.** To interrupt recorded sounds, as on a videotape: *blipped the expletive from the TV show.* [Imitative.]

bliss (blĭs) *n.* **1.** Serene happiness. **2.** The ecstasy of salvation; spiritual joy. —See Synonyms at **ecstasy.** [Middle English *blis(se),* Old English *bliss, blīths,* from Common Germanic *blīthsjo* (unattested), from *blīthiz* (unattested), BLITHE.] —**bliss•ful** *adj.* —**bliss•ful•ly** *adv.* —**bliss•ful•ness** *n.*

blis•ter (blĭs′tər) *n.* **1.** A thin, rounded swelling of the skin, containing watery serum, caused by burning or friction. **2.** A similar swelling on a plant. **3.** An air bubble on a painted surface or in a casting. **4.** A rounded, often transparent protuberance on certain aircraft, used for observation or as a gun position.
~*v.* **blistered, -tering, -ters.** —*tr.* **1.** To cause a blister or blisters to form upon. **2.** To reprove harshly. —*intr.* To break out in blisters. [Middle English *blester, blister,* possibly from Old French *blestre,* from Middle Dutch *bluyster,* "swelling."] —**blis•ter•y** *adj.*

blister beetle *n.* Any of various beetles of the family Meloidae that secrete a substance capable of blistering the skin. Some species cause damage to crops. See **Spanish fly.**

blister copper *n.* An almost pure form of copper produced in an intermediate stage of copper refining. [From its blistered surface caused by release of gas in the refining process.]

blis•ter•ing (blĭs′tər-ĭng) *adj.* **1.** Intensely hot. **2.** Harshly condemnatory; scathing: *a blistering attack on government policy.* **3.** Very rapid: *a blistering pace.*

blister pack *n.* A type of package for pills or tablets with plastic bubbles that are pushed in to eject the pill or tablet through the backing foil.

blister rust *n.* Any of several diseases of pine trees, caused by various fungi of the genus *Cronartium,* and resulting in cankers and blisters on the bark.

B.Lit. or **B.Litt.** Bachelor of Letters. [Latin *Baccalaureus Litterarum.*]

blithe (blīth, blīth) *adj.* **1.** Filled with gaiety; cheerful. **2.** Frivolous; casual; carefree: *blithe optimism.* —See Synonyms at **jolly.** [Middle English *blithe,* Old English *blīthe,* from Common Germanic *blīthiz*† (unattested), gentle, mild.] —**blithe•ly** *adv.* —**blithe•ness** *n.*

blith•er (blĭth′ər) *intr.v.* **-ered, -ering, -ers.** To blather. [Alteration of BLATHER.]

blith•er•ing (blĭth′ər-ĭng) *adj.* **1.** Talking senselessly; jabbering. **2.** *British Informal.* Stupid; silly.

blithe•some (blīth′səm, blīth′-) *adj.* Cheerful; merry. —**blithe•some•ly** *adv.* —**blithe•some•ness** *n.*

blitz (blĭts) *n.* **1.** A blitzkrieg. **2.** An intensive air raid or series of air raids. **3.** Any intense campaign or effort: *I'm ready for a blitz on the spare room.* —**the Blitz.** The period in 1940–41 during which British cities and towns were subjected to continual nighttime bombing by the German Luftwaffe.
~*tr.v.* **blitzed, blitzing, blitzes.** To subject to a blitz. [Short for BLITZKRIEG.]

blitz•krieg (blĭts′krēg′) *n.* **1.** A swift, sudden military offensive, usually by combined air and land forces. **2.** Any swift, concerted effort. [German *Blitzkrieg,* "lightning war."]

bliz•zard (blĭz′ərd) *n.* **1.** A violent windstorm accompanied by intense cold and driving, powdery snow or ice crystals. **2.** A very heavy snowstorm with high winds. [19th century : originally American, perhaps imitative.]

blk. 1. black. **2.** block. **3.** bulk.

bloat (blōt) *v.* **bloated, bloating, bloats.** —*tr.* **1.** To cause to swell up or inflate, as with liquid or gas. **2. a.** To puff up, as with vanity. **b.** To puff up (the face or body), as from overeating. **3.** To cure (herring or other fish) by soaking in brine and half-drying in smoke. —*intr.* To become swollen or inflated.
~*n. Veterinary Medicine.* A swelling of the rumen or intestinal tract of a domestic animal, caused by the gases of fermentation of green forage. [From *bloat,* swollen, earlier *blowt,* soft, flabby, from Middle English *blout,* probably from Old Norse *blautr,* soft, wet, soaked.]

bloat•er (blō′tər) *n.* A herring lightly smoked and salted.

blob (blŏb) *n.* **1.** A soft, amorphous mass. **2.** A shapeless splotch or daub of color.
~*tr.v.* **blobbed, blobbing, blobs.** To splash or mark with blobs; splotch. [Middle English, bubble (imitative).]

bloc (blŏk) *n.* A group of persons, parties, or nations united for common action or by a common interest. [French, BLOCK.]

Bloch (blŏk), **Ernest** (1880–1959). Swiss-born U.S. composer. He is famous for his chamber music, such as the Piano Quintet (1923) and his five string quartets, and also for works with Jewish themes, including the *Israel Symphony* (1916).

block (blŏk) *n. Abbr.* **blk. 1.** A large, solid piece of wood, stone, or other hard substance having one or more flat sides. **2. a.** Such a piece used in construction work. **b.** A child's toy model of such a piece: *a set of building blocks.* **3.** A large solid piece of wood, especially: **a.** One on which chopping or cutting is done: *a butcher's block.* **b.** One on which people were formerly beheaded. Usually preceded by *the.* **c.** One from which a horse may be mounted. **4.** A piece of wood, stone, or metal engraved for use in printing. **5. a.** A pulley or a system of pulleys set in a casing. **b.** The casing holding the pulleys. See **block and tackle. 6.** The casting containing the cylinders of an internal-combustion engine. **7.** A group acting or regarded as a unit; a bloc. **8.** A set or quantity of like items sold, handled, or regarded as a unit, such as theater tickets, shares, or postage stamps. **9.** A large building divided into separate units, such as apartments or offices. **10. a.** A rectangular section of a city or town bounded on each side by consecutive streets. **b.** A segment of a street bounded by successive cross streets, including its buildings and inhabitants. **c.** The distance between these streets: *The theater is three blocks away.* **11.** A length of railway track controlled by signals. See **block system. 12.** Something that hinders; an obstacle. **13.** An act of obstructing or hindering. **14.** *Sports.* An act of bodily obstruction; specifically, in football, legal interference with an opposing player to clear the path of the ballcarrier. **15.** In athletics, a **starting block** *(see).* **16.** *Medicine.* Interruption, especially obstruction, of a neural, digestive, or other physiological process. See **heart block, nerve block. 17.** *Psychology.* Sudden cessation of a thought or creative process without an immediate observable cause, sometimes considered to be a consequence of repression. **18.** *Slang.* A person's head. Used chiefly in the phrase *knock someone's block off.* **19.** *Computer Science.* A group of words or numbers treated as a unit in a storage device. —**off one's block.** Mad; crazy. —**on the block.** Up for auction. —See Synonyms at **obstacle.**
~*v.* **blocked, blocking, blocks.** —*tr.* **1.** To shape into a block or blocks. **2.** To support, strengthen, or retain in place by means of a block or blocks. **3.** To shape, mold, or form with or on a block: *block a hat.* **4.** To stop or impede the passage of or movement through; hinder or obstruct: *block traffic; block a piece of legislation.* **5.** *Sports.* To impede the movement of (one's opponent or the ball) by means of physical interference. **6.** *Medicine.* To interrupt the proper functioning of (a physiological process). **7.** To stamp or emboss a design or lettering on (the cover of a book), especially using gold or other foil. **8.** *Finance.* To restrict or prevent the use or conversion of (currency or assets). **9.** *Psychology.* To repress or fail to recognize (an area or subject that causes pain or anxiety). Often used with *out.* —*intr. Sports.* To obstruct the movement of an opponent. —See Synonyms at **hinder.** —**block out. 1.** To plan or project broadly without details; sketch out. **2.** To obscure from view. —**block up. 1.** To raise on a block or blocks, as a house or boat. **2.** To fill with solid material: *block up the windows of an old house.* [Middle English *blok(ke),* from Old French *bloc,* from Middle Dutch *blok,* trunk of a tree, from Germanic.] —**block** *adj.* —**block•er** *n.*

Block (blŏk), **Herbert Lawrence,** known as "Herblock" (1909–). U.S. editorial cartoonist. His works have appeared in *The Washington Post* and 200 other newspapers nationwide. In 1942 and 1954 he was awarded a Pulitzer Prize.

block•ade (blŏ-kād′) *n.* **1.** The closing off of a country, city, harbor, or other area to traffic and communication by hostile ships or forces. **2.** The forces employed to close such an area. —**run a blockade.** To succeed in getting through a blockade.
~*tr.v.* **blockaded, -ading, -ades.** To set up a blockade against. [From BLOCK (after AMBUSCADE).] —**block•ad•er** *n.*

block•ade-run•ner (blŏ-kād′rŭn′ər) *n.* A ship or person that goes through or past a blockade. —**block•ade-ru•ning** *n.*

block•age (blŏk′ĭj) *n.* **1.** The act of blocking or obstructing. **2.** An obstruction.

block and tackle *n.* An apparatus of pulley blocks and ropes or cables used for hauling and hoisting heavy objects.

block•bust•er (blŏk′bŭs′tər) *n. Informal.* **1.** A powerful bomb capable of destroying large areas. **2.** Anything of devastating effect. **3.** A film or play that attracts large audiences and earns large amounts of money.

block diagram *n.* **1.** A diagram of a system, such as a computer program or electrical circuit, in which the essential units are represented by rectangles or blocks that are connected by lines showing the relationship between the units. **2.** A diagram that gives a three-dimensional representation of a landform or section of country.

block-graze (blŏk′grāz′) *tr.v.* **-grazed, -grazing, -grazes.** *Chiefly Australian.* To graze (livestock) on an area of land until it is bare before moving them to the next area.

block•head (blŏk′hĕd′) *n.* A stupid person; a dolt.

block•house (blŏk′hous′) *n.* **1.** A military fortification constructed of concrete or other sturdy material, with loopholes for defensive firing or for observation. **2.** *Aerospace.* A heavily reinforced building used for protecting personnel and equipment during launch operations of missiles, rockets, or the like. **3.** A house made of squared timbers.

block•ish (blŏk′ĭsh) *adj.* **1.** Like or resembling a block. **2.** Dull; stupid. —**block•ish•ly** *adv.* —**block•ish•ness** *n.*

block lava *n.* Lava formed into sharp, angular blocks.

block letter *n.* **1.** A plain capital letter printed or written sans serif, often used when filling in forms. Also called "block capital." **2.** *Printing.* A sans-serif style of type. —**block-let•ter** *adj.*

block plane *n.* A small plane used by carpenters for cutting across the grain of wood.

block printing *n.* Printing from engraved or carved wooden or linoleum blocks.

block release *n. British.* A system whereby trainees and apprentices may leave work for a set period in order to study at a college. Compare **day release.**

block system *n.* A system for controlling and safeguarding the flow

blister beetle *One of the 2,000 species of the family* Meloidae *that secrete a substance containing cantharidin, an irritant chemical.*

PRONUNCIATION KEY

ă, pat; ā, pay; âr, care;
ä, father, are; b, bib;
ch, church; d, deed; ĕ, pet;
ē, be; f, fife; g, gag; h, hat;
hw, which; ĭ, pit; ī, pie;
îr, pier; j, judge; k, kick;
l, lid, needle; m, mum;
n, no, sudden; ng, thing;
ŏ, pot; ō, toe; ô, paw, for;
oi, noise; ou, out; ŏŏ, book;
ōō, boot; p, pop; r, roar;
s, sauce; sh, ship, dish;
t, tight; th, thin, path;
th, this, bathe; ŭ, cut; ûr, fur;
v, valve; w, with; y, yes;
z, zebra, size; zh, vision;
ə, about, item, edible,
gallop, circus, peaceful

IN FOREIGN WORDS:

à, *Fr.* ami; œ, *Fr.* feu, *Ger.* schön; ü, *Fr.* tu, *Ger.* über; KH, *Ger.* ich, *Scot.* loch; N, *Fr.* bon; y′, *Fr.* Compiègne

STRESS MARKS:

Primary stress: ′
in•cite′ (ĭn-sīt′)
Secondary stress: ′
in′sight′ (ĭn′sīt′)

of railway trains, in which the track is divided into sections or blocks, each controlled by automatic signals.

block tin *n.* An impure commercial form of tin cast in blocks.

block vote *n.* A single vote cast by the representative of a large group, as at a union conference, for example, that is held to represent the votes of all the members of that group.

block·y (blŏk′ē) *adj.* **-ier, -iest.** Resembling a block; stocky.

Bloem·fon·tein (blōōm′fŏn-tān′). City in South Africa, capital of the Orange Free State. Founded as a Boer fort (1846), it is unofficially called the judicial capital of South Africa because the appellate division of the Supreme Court sits here.

Blois (blwä). City in north-central France, lying on the Loire River. Its historical importance dates from the 6th century when it became the seat of the powerful counts of Blois, the ancestors of the royal Capetian line.

bloke (blōk) *n. Chiefly British Slang.* A fellow; a man.

blond (blŏnd) *adj.* **-er, -est. 1.** Having fair hair and skin and usually light eyes. **2.** Of a flaxen or golden color or of any light shade of auburn or pale yellowish brown: *blond hair.* **3.** Light-colored: *blond furniture.*
~*n.* A blond person. [Old French, probably from Germanic.] —**blond·ish** *adj.* —**blond·ness** *n.*
Usage: Blond as an adjective may be used of both sexes. *Blonde* and *brunette* as nouns are used only of females.

blonde (blŏnd) *adj.* **blonder, blondest.** Blond.
~*n.* A blonde woman or girl. [Old French, feminine of *blond.*]

Blon·din (blôn-dăn′), **Charles,** born Jean François Gravelet (1824–97). French acrobat and stunt performer whose speciality was tightrope walking. He walked across Niagara Falls several times, the first time in 1859, in a variety of ways—with a man on his back, on stilts, and blindfolded.

blood (blŭd) *n.* **1.** The fluid circulated by the heart through the vertebrate vascular system, carrying oxygen and nutrients throughout the body and waste materials to excretory channels. It consists of **blood plasma** *(see)* in which are suspended red blood cells (erythrocytes), white cells (leucocytes), and platelets. **2.** A functionally similar fluid in an invertebrate. **3.** A fluid resembling blood, such as the juice of certain plants. **4.** Loosely, life; lifeblood. **5.** Bloodshed; murder. **6.** Temperament; temper; disposition. **7.** Descent from a common ancestor; parental lineage. **8.** Family relationship; kinship. **9.** Descent from noble or royal lineage. Preceded by *the: a princess of the blood.* **10.** Recorded descent from purebred stock. Said of animals. **11.** Racial or national ancestry. **12.** Members or personnel, especially ones providing fresh or new impetus: *new blood in the organization.* **13.** A dashing young man; a rake; a dandy. —**blood is thicker than water.** Family ties and loyalties are stronger than any others. —**in cold blood.** Dispassionately; deliberately; coldly. —**in one's blood.** Fundamental or inherent in one's character. —**make one's blood boil.** To make extremely angry. —**make one's blood run cold.** To terrify.
~*tr.v.* **blooded, blooding, bloods. 1. a.** To give (a hound or hunting dog) its first taste of blood. **b.** To initiate a novice who has successfully followed hounds from find to death by marking the face with the blood of the fox. **2.** To initiate (a new member or recruit) into an organization. **3.** To subject (recruits) to the baptism of fire.
~*adj.* Purebred: *a blood mare.* [Middle English *blood,* Old English *blōd,* from Common Germanic *blōtham* (unattested).]

blood-and-thunder (blŭd′ən-thŭn′dər) *adj.* Designating or pertaining to a melodramatic, action-packed book or film.

blood bath *n.* A savage and indiscriminate killing; a massacre.

blood brother *n.* **1.** One's brother by birth. **2.** A boy or man who swears to treat another as his brother, often at a ceremony where the blood of the two is mingled.

blood count *n.* **1.** The number of red and white blood cells in a specific volume of blood. **2.** The determination of this number.

blood·cur·dling (blŭd′kûrd′lĭng) *adj.* Causing great horror; terrifying. —**blood·cur·dling·ly** *adv.*

blood donor *n.* A person who gives blood for transfusion.

blood·ed (blŭd′ĭd) *adj.* **1.** Having blood or a temperament of a specified kind. Used in combination: *a cold-blooded reptile; a hot-blooded person.* **2.** Thoroughbred.

blood feud *n.* A long-lasting dispute, usually between families or tribes, involving killing on both sides.

blood fluke *n.* A trematode worm, such as a **schistosome** *(see),* that lives in the blood vessels of its host.

blood group *n.* Any of several immunologically distinct, genetically determined classes of human blood, clinically identified by characteristic agglutination reactions based on the presence or absence of certain antigens. Also called "blood type."

blood-guilt (blŭd′gĭlt′) *n.* Guilt owing to murder or bloodshed.

blood heat *n.* The usual temperature (37°C; 98.6°F) of human blood.

blood·hound (blŭd′hound′) *n.* **1.** One of a breed of hounds with a smooth coat, drooping ears, sagging jowls, and a keen sense of smell. **2.** *Informal.* Any relentless pursuer.

blood·less (blŭd′lĭs) *adj.* **1.** Having no blood. **2.** Pale and anemic in color. **3.** Achieved without bloodshed. **4.** Lacking spirit or emotion. —**blood·less·ly** *adv.* —**blood·less·ness** *n.*

Bloodless Revolution *n.* The **Glorious Revolution** *(see).*

blood·let·ting (blŭd′lĕt′ĭng) *n.* **1.** The bleeding of a vein as a supposedly therapeutic measure; bleeding; venesection. **2.** A draining away, as of lifeblood. **3. Bloodshed** *(see).* —**blood·let·ter** *n.*

blood·line (blŭd′līn′) *n.* Direct line of descent; strain; pedigree.

blood money *n.* **1.** Money paid as compensation to the next of kin of a murder victim. **2.** Money paid to a hired killer. **3.** Money gained at the cost of another's life or livelihood.

blood plasma *n.* The pale-yellow or gray-yellow, protein-containing fluid portion of the blood in which the blood cells are normally suspended. Also called "plasma."

blood platelet *n.* A constituent of blood, a **platelet** *(see).*

blood poisoning *n.* Any condition in which the blood contains poisons or the bacteria that produce them; **septicemia** or **toxemia** *(both of which see).*

blood pressure *n.* Pressure of the blood against the walls of the arteries, primarily maintained by contraction of the left ventricle.

blood pudding *n.* A sausage prepared from cooked swine's blood and suet. Also *chiefly British* "black pudding."

---

blood

THE BODY'S INTERNAL TRANSPORT SYSTEM

The liquid that supports life in every cell of the body

Every cell of living tissue in the body is linked by the flow of blood. As it circulates, it acts as a transport system—carrying oxygen, vitamins, and nutrients to the body's tissues and waste products away from them. The blood has a defense mechanism that fights infection and a self-sealing power to repair wounds. It also carries hormones to the organs that need them, and it distributes body heat.

Human blood contains red cells, white cells, and platelets in a clear fluid called plasma. The red blood cells absorb oxygen in the lungs to provide energy for the body. The heart pumps oxygenated blood around the body and returns it, with waste products such as carbon dioxide, to the lungs. White blood cells defend the body against attacks by bacteria. Platelets enable the blood to clot after a cut.

Lungs
Carbon dioxide from venous blood is breathed out and oxygen is supplied to form arterial blood

Head
Carotid arteries carry blood to the head; jugular veins lead it away

Artery

Heart

Aorta

Vein

Liver
Products of digestion are absorbed from blood that comes to the liver from the intestines

Arm
The brachial artery takes blood into the arms; the basilic and cephalic veins carry it away

Kidneys
On each circuit of the body, some of the blood passes through the kidneys to be filtered

Intestines
Blood flows to the intestines from branches of the aorta; returning blood flows through the liver before passing into the main bloodstream

Leg
Blood flows in along the femoral artery and returns to the circulation through the femoral vein

CIRCULATION *The heart pumps blood through the lungs to absorb oxygen, then through the aorta, a large blood vessel, to the main arteries. These divide and subdivide before reaching the minute blood vessels called capillaries, which permeate the tissue and pass oxygen to it. Blood from the capillaries returns to the heart through the veins.*

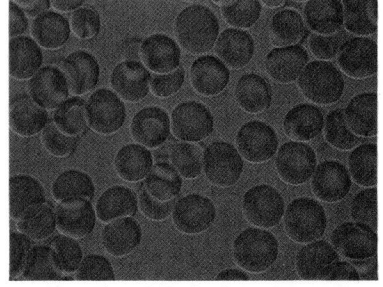

RED CELLS *The red blood cells, erythrocytes, contain hemoglobin, an iron-carrying protein that makes the blood red and transports oxygen around the body.*

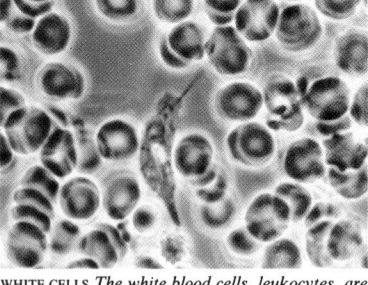

WHITE CELLS *The white blood cells, leukocytes, are part of the body's defense mechanism. They surround and "digest" any foreign bodies, such as bacteria in the blood.*

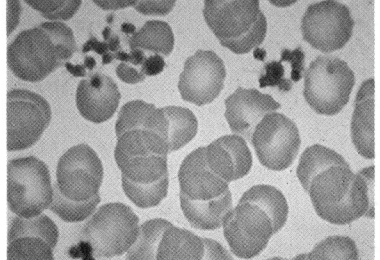

PLATELETS *Minute cells, called platelets (seen above as small, dark spots among red blood cells), cluster together and enable the blood to clot when a blood vessel is injured.*

blood rain *n.* Rain in which the raindrops are colored by fine, reddish dust particles brought from desert regions by the wind.
blood red *n.* Moderate to vivid red. **—blood-red** (blŭd′rĕd′) *adj.*
blood relation *n.* A person who is related by birth rather than by marriage. Also called "blood relative." **—blood relationship** *n.*
blood·root (blŭd′ro͞ot′, -ro͝ot′) *n.* See **sanguinaria.**
blood sausage *n.* **Blood pudding** *(see).*
blood serum *n.* Blood plasma with the fibrin removed.
blood·shed (blŭd′shĕd′) *n.* **1.** The shedding of blood. **2.** Carnage. Also called "bloodletting." **—blood·shed·der** *n.*
blood·shot (blŭd′shŏt′) *adj.* Red and inflamed: *bloodshot eyes.*
blood·stain (blŭd′stān′) *n.* A stain caused by blood. **—blood·stained** *adj.*
blood·stock (blŭd′stŏk′) *n.* Thoroughbred horses, especially racehorses.
blood·stone (blŭd′stōn′) *n.* A variety of deep-green chalcedony flecked with red jasper. Also called "heliotrope."
blood·stream (blŭd′strēm′) *n.* The stream of blood flowing through the circulatory system of a living body.
blood·suck·er (blŭd′sŭk′ər) *n.* **1.** Any animal that sucks blood, as a leech. **2.** One who clings to or preys upon another; a parasite. **—blood·suck·ing** *adj.* & *n.*
blood test *n.* Examination of a blood sample in order to determine the level of alcohol or drugs, the presence of bacteria, the blood group, or the like.
blood·thirst·y (blŭd′thûr′stē) *adj.* **1. a.** Thirsting for bloodshed; murderous; cruel. **b.** Thirsting for violence. **2.** Displaying or pandering to such feelings: *a bloodthirsty film.* **—blood·thirst·i·ly** *adv.* **—blood·thirst·i·ness** *n.*
blood type *n.* **Blood group** *(see).*
blood vessel *n.* Any elastic, tubular canal, such as an artery, vein, or capillary, through which blood circulates.
blood·worm (blŭd′wûrm′) *n.* Any of various segmented worms of the genera *Polycirrus* and *Enoplobranchus,* having bright-red bodies and often used for bait.
blood·wort (blŭd′wûrt′, -wôrt′) *n.* Any of various chiefly South American plants of the family Haemodoraceae, having roots that contain a red juice.
blood·y (blŭd′ē) *adj.* **-ier, -iest. 1.** Stained with blood. **2.** Of, characteristic of, or containing blood. **3.** Accompanied by or giving rise to bloodshed: *a bloody fight.* **4.** Bloodthirsty; cruel. **5.** Suggesting the color of blood; blood-red. **6.** *British Slang.* Used as an intensive: *bloody fool.*
~*adv. British Slang.* Used as an intensive: *a bloody good film.*
~*tr.v.* **bloodied, -ying, -ies.** To stain, spot, or color with or as if with blood. **—blood·i·ly** *adv.* **—blood·i·ness** *n.*
bloody mary, Bloody Mary *n.* A drink made with vodka, tomato juice, and seasonings.
Bloody Mary. See **Mary I.**
bloom¹ (blo͞om) *n.* **1.** The flower or blossoms of a plant. **2. a.** The condition or time of being in flower: *a rose in bloom.* **b.** A condition or time of vigor, freshness, and beauty; prime: *the bloom of girlhood.* **3.** A fresh, rosy complexion. **4.** *Botany.* A delicate, powdery coating, such as that found on some fruits, such as the plum, or on some leaves and stems. **5.** A similar coating, as on newly minted coins. **6.** A cloudy appearance on old paint or varnish.
~*v.* **bloomed, blooming, blooms.** *—intr.* **1.** To bear flowers. **2.** To shine with health and vigor; glow. **3.** To grow or flourish. *—tr.* **1.** To cause to flower. **2.** To cause to flourish. **3.** *British.* To coat the outer surface of (a lens) with a thin transparent layer so as to minimize reflection. [Middle English *blom, blome,* from Old Norse *blōm, blōmi.*] **—bloom·y** *adj.*
bloom² *n.* **1.** A large bar of steel prepared for rolling. **2.** A mass of wrought iron ready for further working. [Middle English *blome,* lump of metal, Old English *blōma.*]
bloom·er (blo͞o′mər) *n.* **1. a.** A plant that blooms. **b.** One who attains full development of his or her abilities. **2.** *Slang.* A blunder.
bloom·ers (blo͞o′mərz) *pl.n.* **1.** A costume formerly worn by women and girls that was composed of loose trousers gathered about the ankles and sometimes worn under a short skirt. **2.** Women's long and usually loose underpants. [After Amelia *Bloomer* (1818–94), U.S. reformer who advocated this type of undergarment.]
bloom·ing (blo͞o′mĭng) *adj.* **1.** Flowering; blossoming. **2.** Flourishing; growing. **3.** *Slang.* Utter; thorough. Used as an intensive: *a blooming idiot.* [Sense 3, probably a euphemism for BLOODY.] **—bloom·ing·ly** *adv.* **—bloom·ing·ness** *n.*
bloop·er (blo͞o′pər) *n.* **1.** *Baseball.* A short, weakly hit fly ball that carries just beyond the infield. **2.** *Informal.* A clumsy mistake, especially one made in public; a faux pas. [From *bloop,* sound of such a hit (imitative).]
blos·som (blŏs′əm) *n.* **1.** A flower or mass of flowers, especially on a plant that yields edible fruit. **2.** The condition or time of flowering: *peach trees in blossom.*
~*intr.v.* **blossomed, -soming, -soms. 1.** To come into flower; bloom. **2.** To develop; flourish: *She blossomed into a beauty.* [Middle English *blosme,* Old English *blōstm, blōstma.*] **—blos·som·y** *adj.*
blot¹ (blŏt) *n.* **1.** A spot; a stain: *a blot of ink.* **2.** A stain on one's reputation or character; a disgrace. **3.** Something that detracts from beauty or excellence: *That factory is a blot on the landscape.*
~*v.* **blotted, blotting, blots.** *—tr.* **1.** To spot or stain. **2.** To bring moral disgrace to. **3.** To obliterate; cancel. Used with *out: "Whosoever hath sinned against me, him will I blot out of my book"* (Exodus 32:33). **4.** To make obscure; darken; hide. Usually used with *out: clouds blotting out the moon.* **5.** To destroy utterly; annihilate. Used with *out.* **6.** To dry or soak up with absorbent material. *—intr.* **1.** To spill or spread in a blot or blots. **2.** To become blotted; absorb or soak up: *a paper that blots easily.* —See Synonyms at **erase.** [Middle English *blot, blotte,* perhaps from Old French *blotte, blostre,* clod of earth, probably from Germanic.]
blot² *n.* **1.** An exposed piece in backgammon. **2.** *Archaic.* A weak point. [Probably from Dutch *bloot,* "naked," from Middle Dutch, naked, poor.]
blotch (blŏch) *n.* **1.** A spot or blot; a splotch. **2.** A discoloration on the skin; a blemish. [Probably a blend of BLOT and BOTCH.] **—blotched** *adj.* **—blotch·i·ness** *n.* **—blotch·y** *adj.*
blot·ter (blŏt′ər) *n.* **1.** A piece or pad of blotting paper, especially one with a firm backing. **2.** A book containing daily records of occurrences or transactions: *a police blotter.*
blotting paper *n.* Absorbent paper used to soak up excess ink.
blot·to (blŏt′ō) *adj. Informal.* Very drunk. [Perhaps from BLOT.]
blouse (blouz, blous) *n.* **1.** A woman's or child's loosely fitting shirtlike garment extending from the neck to the waist or slightly below the waist. **2.** A loosely fitting garment resembling a long shirt, sometimes belted at the waist, often worn by European workmen. **3.** A jacket or tunic worn as part of a uniform.
~*v.* **bloused, blousing, blouses.** *—intr.* To hang loosely. *—tr.* To make full and loose. [French *blouse*†.]
blou·son (blou′sŏn′, blo͞o′zŏn′) *n.* A short, loose jacket similar in style to a blouse and fitting tightly at the waist and often at the wrists. [French *blouson*†.]
blow¹ (blō) *v.* **blew** (blo͞o), **blown** (blōn), **blowing, blows.** *—intr.* **1.** To be in a state of motion, as the wind. **2. a.** To move along or be carried by or as if by the wind: *Her hat blew away.* **b.** To be brought into a specified state by the action of the wind: *The door blew open. The chimney blew down.* **3.** To expel a current of air, as from the mouth or from a bellows. **4.** To produce a sound by expelling a current of air, as in sounding a wind instrument. **5.** To breathe hard; pant. **6.** To storm: *It blew all night.* **7.** To spout water and air. Used of a whale. **8.** *Slang.* To boast. Used with *off.* **9.** *Slang.* To go away; depart. **10.** To break down as a result of excess current. Used of fuses or electronic components. *—tr.* **1.** To cause to move by means of a current of air. **2.** To bring into a specified state by means of a current of air: *The wind blew the door shut.* **3.** To clear out or make free of obstruction by forcing air through: *to blow one's nose.* **4. a.** To shape or form (glass, for example) by forcing air or gas through the material when molten. **b.** To shape or form by forcing air through the mouth: *blow a smoke ring.* **5. a.** To cause (a wind instrument) to sound. **b.** To sound: *The bugle blew reveille.* **6.** To cause (a horse) to be out of breath. **7.** To cause to explode or bring into a specified state by means of an explosion. Used with *up, down, apart,* or other adverbs: *The bomb blew the windows out.* **8.** To lay or deposit eggs in. Used of a fly. **9.** To burn out or destroy (a fuse or other component) by excess current. **10.** *Slang.* To spend (money) freely. **11.** *Slang.* To handle ineptly; bungle: *blew his only chance.* **12.** *Informal.* To curse; damn. Used euphemistically: *I'm blowed if I'll do it!* **—blow hot and cold.** To vacillate between favor and opposition. **—blow over. 1.** To subside; wane: *The storm blew over quickly.* **2.** To be forgotten: *The scandal will soon blow over.* **—blow through.** *Australian & New Zealand Informal.* To leave.
~*n.* **1. a.** A blast of air or wind. **b.** A storm. **2.** The act of blowing. **3.** A sound produced by blowing. [Blow, blew, blown; Middle English *blowen, blew, blowen,* Old English *blāwan, blēow, blāwen.*]
blow² *n.* **1.** A sudden hard stroke or hit, as with the fist or an instrument. **2.** A setback or unexpected shock. **—come to blows.** To begin to fight. [Middle English (northern dialect) *blaw,* perhaps from Germanic *bleuwan* (unattested), to strike.]
blow³ *n.* A mass of blossoms. Used chiefly in the phrase *in full blow.*
~*v.* **blew** (blo͞o), **blown** (blōn), **blowing, blows.** *—intr.* To bloom. *—tr.* **1.** To cause to bloom. **2.** To produce (blossoms). [Middle English *blowen,* to blossom, Old English *blōwan.*]
blow-by-blow (blō′bī-blō′) *adj.* Described exactly and in a detailed way: *a blow-by-blow account of the accident.*
blow-dry (blō′drī′) *n.* A method of styling the hair by drying it with a hand-held hair drier and shaping it with a brush at the same time. **—blow-dri·er** *n.* **—blow-dry** *v.*
blow·er (blō′ər) *n.* **1.** One that blows, especially a mechanical device, such as a fan. **2.** *Slang.* A braggart. **3.** *British Informal.* A telephone.
blow·fish (blō′fĭsh′) *n., pl.* **-fishes** or collectively **blowfish.** The **puffer** *(see).*
blow·fly (blō′flī′) *n., pl.* **-flies.** Any of several flies of the family Calliphoridae that deposit their eggs in carcasses or carrion or in open sores and wounds. See **bluebottle.**
blow·hard (blō′härd′) *n. Slang.* A boaster; a braggart.
blow·hole (blō′hōl′) *n.* **1.** A nostril at the highest point on the head of whales and other cetaceans. **2.** A hole in ice through which whales, dolphins, seals, and other aquatic mammals come up for air. **3.** A vent to permit the escape of air or other gas. **4.** A virtually vertical vent that reaches from the roof of a sea cave to the cliff top.
blow in *intr.v. Informal.* To arrive casually or without warning.
blow-in (blō′ĭn′) *n. Australian Informal.* A stranger or newcomer, especially one who is unwelcome.
blow·lamp (blō′lămp) *n.* A **blowtorch** *(see).*
blown (blōn) *adj.* Completely expanded or opened. Often used in combination: *a full-blown flower.*
blow off *tr.v.* To release or let off (steam from a boiler, for example).

PRONUNCIATION KEY

ă, pat; ā, pay; âr, care;
ä, father, are; b, bib;
ch, church; d, deed; ĕ, pet;
ē, be; f, fife; g, gag; h, hat;
hw, which; ĭ, pit; ī, pie;
îr, pier; j, judge; k, kick;
l, lid, needle; m, mum;
n, no, sudden; ng, thing;
ŏ, pot; ō, toe; ô, paw, for;
oi, noise; ou, out; o͝o, book;
o͞o, boot; p, pop; r, roar;
s, sauce; sh, ship, dish;
t, tight; th, thin, path;
th, this, bathe; ŭ, cut; ûr, fur;
v, valve; w, with; y, yes;
z, zebra, size; zh, vision;
ə, about, item, edible, gallop, circus, peaceful

IN FOREIGN WORDS:

à, *Fr.* ami; œ, *Fr.* feu, *Ger.* schön; ü, *Fr.* tu, *Ger.* über; KH, *Ger.* ich, *Scot.* loch; N, *Fr.* bon; y′, *Fr.* Compiègne

STRESS MARKS:

Primary stress: ′
in·cite′ (ĭn-sīt′)
Secondary stress: ′
in′sight′ (ĭn′sīt′)

bluebell *Common name for the wood hyacinth, a perennial plant with dark-blue or violet bell-shaped flowers. Bluebells flower in early summer in woodlands.*

blueberry *Grape-colored edible berries that grow well only in very acidic, well-drained, but moist soils.*

bluebottle *The large shiny-bodied relative of the common housefly makes a distinctive buzzing noise when it flies. The eggs it lays hatch into maggots that feed on carrion. Bluebottles may also lay eggs on household meat that has been left uncovered.*

—*intr.v.* **1.** To be released or let off. Used of gas or liquid under pressure. **2.** *Informal.* To give vent to pent-up emotions.

blow·off (blō′ôf′, -ŏf′) *n.* **1.** Something blown off, such as a gas. **2.** A device or channel for blowing off something.

blow out *intr.v.* **1.** To be extinguished by a current of air. Used of a candle or other flame. **2.** To burst suddenly. Used of a tire. **3.** To burn out or melt. Used of a fuse or other electrical device. **4.** To eject gas or oil in an uncontrolled flow. Used of a gas or oil well. —*tr. v.* To extinguish (a candle, for example) by blowing.

blow·out (blō′out′) *n.* **1. a.** A sudden rupture or bursting, as of a car tire. **b.** The hole made in this way. **2.** A sudden escape of a confined gas. **3.** The burning out of a fuse. **4.** An uncontrolled flow from a gas or oil well. **5.** A basin-shaped or trough-shaped depression formed by wind eddying in a sand dune or sand deposit. **6.** *Slang.* A very large party or social affair.

blow·pipe (blō′pīp′) *n.* **1.** A metal tube through which a flow of gas is mixed with a controlled flow of air to concentrate the heat of a flame. **2.** A long narrow pipe through which darts or pellets may be blown. **3.** A long narrow iron pipe used to gather, work, and blow molten glass.

blow·torch (blō′tôrch′) *n.* **1.** A portable burner for mixing gas and oxygen to produce a very hot flame for welding, flame cutting, glass blowing, or the like. **2.** A portable hand burner fueled by paraffin or bottled gas and used by plumbers for soldering and by painters for removing old paint. Also called "blowlamp."

blow up *intr.v.* **1.** To come into being: *A storm blew up off the coast.* **2.** To explode. **3.** To lose one's temper. —*tr. v.* **1.** To cause to explode. **2.** To enlarge the size of (a photographic print). **3.** To increase the importance of. **4.** To fill with air.

blow·up (blō′ŭp′) *n.* **1.** An explosion. **2.** A violent outburst of temper. **3.** A photographic enlargement.

blow·y (blō′ē) *adj.* **-ier, -iest.** Windy; breezy.

blow·zy, blow·sy (blou′zē) *adj.* **-zier, -ziest** or **-sier, -siest. 1.** Having a coarsely ruddy and bloated appearance. **2.** Disheveled; frowzy; unkempt: *blowzy hair.* —See Synonyms at **sloppy.** [From obsolete *blowse,* beggar wench, slattern, perhaps from *blowzy,* windy, from BLOW.]

blub (blŭb) *intr.v.* **blubbed, blubbing, blubs.** *British.* To blubber.

blub·ber[1] (blŭb′ər) *v.* **-bered, -bering, -bers.** —*intr.* To weep and sob in a noisy manner. —*tr.* To utter while crying and sobbing: *The child blubbered his name.* —See Synonyms at **cry.**

~*n.* A loud weeping and sobbing. [Middle English *bloberen, blubren,* to bubble, foam, from *blober, bluber,* foam, bubble (imitative).] —**blub·ber·er** *n.* —**blub·ber·ing·ly** *adv.*

blubber[2] *n.* **1.** The thick layer of fat between the skin and the muscle layers of whales and other marine mammals. **2.** Excessive body fat.

~*adj.* Swollen and protruding. [Middle English *blober, bluber,* foam, bubble, entrails, fish, or whale oil. See **blubber** (verb).] —**blub·ber·y** *adj.*

Blü·cher (blo͞o′kər), **Gebhard Leberecht von, Prince of Wahlstatt** (1742–1819). Prussian field marshal. His astute leadership of the Prussian army played a crucial part in the campaigns against Napoleon, culminating in 1815 when he arrived at Waterloo in time to secure Wellington's famous victory.

bludg·eon (blŭj′ən) *n.* A short, heavy club, usually of wood, that has one end loaded or thicker than the other.

~*tr.v.* **bludgeoned, -eoning, -eons. 1.** To hit with or as if with a bludgeon. **2.** To threaten or bully. [18th century : origin obscure.] —**bludg·eon·er, bludg·eon·eer** (blŭj′ə-nîr′) *n.*

blue (blo͞o) *n.* **1.** *Abbr.* **bl.** Any of a group of colors that may vary in lightness and saturation, whose hue is that of a clear sky; the hue of that portion of the spectrum lying between green and violet; one of the additive or light primaries; one of the psychological primary hues, evoked in the normal observer by radiant energy of wavelength approximately 475 nanometers. **2. a.** Any pigment or dye imparting this color. **b. Bluing** *(see).* **3. a.** Any object of this color. **b.** Blue dress or clothing: *the girls in blue.* **4.** A person who wears a blue uniform. **5.** *Sometimes* **Blue. a.** A member of the Union Army in the Civil War. **b.** The Union Army itself. Compare **gray. 6. blues.** The blue uniform of the U.S. Navy. **7.** A small blue butterfly of the family Lycaenidae. **8.** A **bluestocking** *(see).* **9.** *British Informal.* A member of the Conservative Party or loosely, a politically conservative person. Used chiefly in the phrase *a true blue.* —**into the blue.** At a far distance or into the unknown. —**out of the blue. 1.** From an unexpected, unforeseen, or unknown source. **2.** At a completely unexpected time. —**the blue. 1.** The sea. **2.** The sky.

~*adj.* **bluer, bluest. 1.** *Abbr.* **bl.** Of the color blue. **2.** Bluish, or having parts that are blue or bluish. Used with plant and animal names: *blue spruce, blue whale.* **3.** Having a gray or purplish color, as from cold or contusion. **4.** Wearing blue. **5. a.** Gloomy; depressed. **b.** Dismal; dreary: *a blue day.* **c.** *Music.* Of or pertaining to the blues. **6.** *Physics.* Designating one of the three quark colors, the others being green and red. **7.** Puritanical; strict. **8.** Fiercely intellectual. Usually said of a woman. **9.** Aristocratic; patrician. **10. a.** Indecent; risqué: *a blue joke.* **b.** Pornographic: *blue films.* —**true blue.** *Informal.* **1.** Loyal and sincere. **2.** Genuine or real.

~*v.* **blued, bluing, blues.** —*tr.* **1.** To make blue. **2.** To use bluing on. **3.** *Slang.* To squander; waste. —*intr.* To become blue. [Middle English *bleu, blewe,* from Old French *bleu,* from Common Romance *blāvus* (unattested), from Germanic.] —**blue·ly** *adv.* —**blue·ness** *n.*

blue asbestos *n.* A variety of commercial asbestos, **crocidolite** *(see).*

blue baby *n.* An infant born with bluish skin caused by inadequate oxygenation of the blood, a symptom of a congenital malformation of the heart.

blue-back salmon (blo͞o′băk′) *n.* The sockeye salmon *(see).*

blue·beard (blo͞o′bîrd′) *n.* *Often* **Bluebeard.** Any man thought to be a wife-slayer or a killer of women. [French *Barbe-bleue,* character in fairy tale (by Charles PERRAULT) who murdered a number of wives in succession.]

blue·beat (blo͞o′bēt′) *n.* A type of rhythmic West Indian popular music in 12/8 time with the accent on the third beat in every group of three beats.

blue·bell (blo͞o′bĕl′) *n.* **1.** A European plant, *Endymion nonscriptus,* having a one-sided cluster of fragrant, blue-violet flowers. **2.** The **harebell** *(see),* which is the bluebell of Scotland. **3.** Any of various other plants with blue, bell-shaped flowers.

blue·ber·ry (blo͞o′bĕr′ē, -bər-ē) *n., pl.* **-ries. 1.** Any of several North American shrubs of the genus *Vaccinium,* having small, urn-shaped flowers and edible berries. **2.** The juicy, blue, purplish, or blackish berry of any of these shrubs.

blue·bird (blo͞o′bûrd′) *n.* Any of several North American birds of the genus *Sialia,* having blue plumage and, in the male of most species, a rust-colored breast.

blue blood *n.* **1.** Noble or aristocratic descent. **2.** A member of the aristocracy or other high social group. [Translation of Spanish *sangre azul*; probably from the blue color of the veins of fair-complexioned aristocrats.] —**blue-blood·ed** *adj.*

blue·blos·som (blo͞o′blŏs′əm) *n.* A shrub, *Ceanothus thyrsiflorus,* of the west coast of the United States, having profuse clusters of small blue flowers.

blue·bon·net (blo͞o′bŏn′ĭt) *n.* **1.** A plant, *Lupinus subcarnosus,* of Texas and adjacent regions, having compound leaves and clusters of blue flowers. **2.** Any of several other plants having blue flowers. **3.** A broad, blue woolen cap worn in Scotland. **4.** A Scotsman wearing such a cap.

blue·book (blo͞o′bo͝ok′) *n.* **1.** An official publication of the British government, so named from its blue covers. **2.** An official list of persons in the employ of the U.S. government. **3.** *Informal.* A book listing socially prominent people. **4.** A blank notebook with blue covers in which to write college examinations.

blue·bot·tle (blo͞o′bŏt′l) *n.* **1.** Any of several flies of the genus *Calliphora,* having a bright metallic-blue body and breeding in decaying organic matter. **2.** A plant, the **cornflower** *(see).*

blue cheese *n.* Any of various cheeses having a greenish-blue mold and a sharp flavor. Also called "bleu cheese."

blue chip *n.* **1.** *Finance.* A stock that sells at a high price because of public confidence in its long record of steady earnings. Also called "blue-chip stock." **2.** A valuable asset held in reserve. **3.** A blue-colored gambling chip of high value. —**blue-chip** *adj.*

blue cohosh *n.* A plant, *Caulophyllum thalictroides,* of eastern North America, having compound leaves and a cluster of greenish or purplish flowers.

blue-col·lar (blo͞o′kŏl′ər) *adj.* Of or pertaining to wage earners in jobs performed in clothing such as overalls and often involving manual labor, especially when such workers are regarded as a social class. Compare **white-collar.**

blue devils *pl.n.* **1.** *Slang.* Delirium tremens. **2.** *Informal.* A feeling of depression or despondency.

blue-eyed Mary (blo͞o′īd′) *n.* A plant, *Collinsia verna,* of eastern North America, having two-lipped blue and white flowers.

Blue·fields (blo͞o′fēldz′). A port in southeast Nicaragua, the most important of the country's Caribbean ports. British and Dutch pirate ships used it as a harbor in the 16th and 17th centuries.

blue·fish (blo͞o′fĭsh′) *n., pl.* **-fishes** or collectively **bluefish. 1.** A voracious bluish-colored food and game fish, *Pomatomus saltatrix,* of temperate and tropical waters of the Atlantic and Indian oceans. **2.** Broadly, any of various other fishes that are predominantly blue in color.

blue fox *n.* **1.** The **arctic fox** *(see)* during its summer color phase, when its pelt is bluish gray. **2.** The fur of such a fox.

blue·gill (blo͞o′gĭl′) *n.* A common, edible sunfish, *Lepomis macrochirus,* of North American lakes and streams.

blue·grass (blo͞o′grăs′, -gräs′) *n.* **1.** Any of several grasses of the genus *Poa*; especially, *P. pratensis,* native to Eurasia but naturalized throughout North America. This species is also called "Kentucky bluegrass." **2.** A type of folk music that originated in the southern United States, characterized by rapid tempos, jazzlike improvisation, and emphasis on nonelectrified stringed instruments, such as banjos and guitars.

Blue·grass Country (blo͞o′grăs′). Also **Bluegrass Region** or **the Bluegrass.** Area in central Kentucky noted for its abundant bluegrass and also for the breeding of racehorses.

blue-green algae (blo͞o′grēn′) *n.* Algae of the division Cyanophyta (or Myxophyceae), considered to be among the simplest forms of plants.

blue grouse *n.* A wildfowl, *Dendragapus obscurus,* of Western North America, having predominantly gray plumage.

blue·gum (blo͞o′gŭm′) *n.* Also **blue gum.** A tall timber tree, *Eucalyptus globulus,* native to Australia, having aromatic leaves that yield a medicinal oil and outer bark that peels off in shreds.

blue·head (blo͞o′hĕd′) *n.* A marine fish, *Thalassoma bifasciatum,* of tropical Atlantic waters, of which the male has a blue head and a green body.

blueing. Variant of **bluing.**

blueish. Variant of **bluish.**

blue·jack·et (blo͞o′jăk′ĭt) *n.* A sailor in the U.S. or British navy. [From the blue jacket of the Navy.]

blue jay *n.* A common North American bird, *Cyanocitta cristata,* having a crested head and predominantly blue plumage.

blue jeans *pl.n.* Heavy blue denim trousers. See **jean** (sense 2).

blue law *n.* **1.** One of a body of laws in colonial New England designed to enforce certain moral standards. **2.** A law designed to regulate Sunday activities.

blue mold *n.* Any of several fungi of the genus *Penicillium,* forming a bluish growth on food and other surfaces.

Blue Mountains. Uplifted, eroded part of the Columbia Plateau in northeastern Oregon and southeastern Washington. Lava flows cover much of the surface. The slopes are used for lumbering, and the surrounding lowlands for irrigated farming and dairying.

Blue Nile. *Arabic* **Bahr el Az·raq** (bä′hər ăl äz′rŏk). A river rising in northwestern Ethiopia and flowing *c.* 1,610 kilometers (1,000 miles) southeast and then northwest to Sudan. At Khartoum it joins the White Nile to form the Nile.

blue·nose (blo͞o′nōz′) *n.* **1.** A puritanical person. **2.** Usually **Bluenose.** A person or ship from Nova Scotia.

blue note *n. Music.* A flatted note, especially the third or seventh note of a chord, in place of an expected major interval.

blue-pen·cil (blo͞o′pĕn′səl) *tr.v.* **-ciled, -ciling, -cils.** To edit, revise, or correct with or as if with a blue pencil; especially, to censor.

blue peter *n. Nautical.* A blue flag with a white square in the center, flown to signal that a ship is ready to sail. [Probably from the Christian name *Peter.*]

blue·print (blo͞o′prĭnt′) *n.* **1.** A photographic reproduction, as of architectural plans or technical drawings, rendered as white lines on a blue background. Also called "cyanotype." **2.** Any carefully designed plan or model.
~*tr.v.* **blueprinted, -printing, -prints.** **1.** To make a blueprint of. **2.** To lay a plan for.

blue ribbon *n.* **1.** The first prize; highest award or honor. **2.** The badge of various temperance societies. **—blue-rib·bon** *adj.*

Blue Ridge. Also **Blue Ridge Mountains.** A range of the Appalachian Mts. extending from southern Pennsylvania to northern Georgia. It is a major recreation area noted for its resorts and scenery.

blues (blo͞oz) *n. Sometimes used with a singular verb.* **1.** A state of depression or melancholy. **2.** A style of jazz evolved from black southern American secular songs and usually distinguished by slow tempo and flatted thirds and sevenths.

blue shift *n.* A shift of spectral lines toward shorter wavelengths, observed in the spectra of stars that are approaching the solar system. Compare **red shift.**

blue-sky law (blo͞o′skī′) *n.* A law designed to protect the public from buying fraudulent securities.

blue spruce *n.* An evergreen tree, *Picea pungens,* of the Rocky Mountain region, having bluish-green needles.

blue·stock·ing (blo͞o′stŏk′ĭng) *n.* A serious, intellectual, or scholarly woman. [After the *Blue Stocking Society,* name given derisively to a group of 18th-century intellectuals who met in the London houses of several prominent women. Some of the male members wore ordinary blue stockings instead of formal black silk.] **—blue·stock·ing** *adj.*

blue·stone (blo͞o′stōn′) *n.* **1.** A bluish-gray sandstone used for paving and building. **2.** Any similar stone.

blue tit *n.* A common European songbird, *Parus caeruleus,* with a blue crown and wings, a yellow breast, and a white face.

blu·ets (blo͞o′ĭts) *n. Used with a singular or plural verb.* A slender, low-growing plant, *Houstonia caerulea,* of eastern North America, having small, light-blue flowers with yellow centers. Also called "innocence," "Quaker-ladies." [French *bleuet, bluet,* diminutives of *bleu,* BLUE.]

blue vitriol *n. Chemistry.* The blue hydrated crystalline form of **copper sulfate** *(see).*

blue·weed (blo͞o′wēd′) *n.* A plant, **viper's bugloss** *(see).*

blue whale *n.* A very large whale, *Sibbaldus musculus,* having a bluish-gray back and longitudinal grooves along the throat and belly. Also called "sulphur-bottom," "Sibbald's rorqual."

bluff[1] (blŭf) *v.* **bluffed, bluffing, bluffs.** *—tr.* **1.** To mislead, deceive, or hoodwink. **2.** To impress, deter, or intimidate by a display of confidence greater than the facts support. **3.** To try to mislead (opponents) in poker by heavy betting on a poor hand or by little or no betting on a good one. *—intr.* To feign strength when in a state of weakness, or, to feign weakness when strong.
~*n.* **1.** The act or practice of bluffing. **2.** One who bluffs. **—call someone's bluff.** To challenge or expose someone's bluff. [19th century (as poker term) : Dutch *bluffen,* to boast, from Middle Dutch, to swell up.] **—bluff·a·ble** *adj.* **—bluff·er** *n.*

bluff[2] *n.* A steep headland, promontory, river bank, or cliff.
~*adj.* **bluffer, bluffest.** **1.** Presenting a broad, steep front. **2.** Having a rough, blunt, but not unkind manner. —See Synonyms at **gruff.** [17th century (nautical use) : origin obscure.] **—bluff·ly** *adv.* **—bluff·ness** *n.*

blu·ing, blue·ing (blo͞o′ĭng) *n.* **1.** Any of various coloring agents used to counteract the yellowing of laundered fabrics. Also called "blue." **2.** A rinsing agent used to give a silver tint to graying hair.

blu·ish, blue·ish (blo͞o′ĭsh) *adj.* Somewhat or slightly blue. **—blu·ish·ness** *n.*

Blum (blo͞om), **Léon** (1872–1950). French statesman, cofounder of the Socialist Party (1905), becoming its leader in 1920. He was premier in 1936–37 and again in 1938 and 1946–47.

Blun·den (blŭn′dən), **Edmund Charles** (1896–1974). British writer. He is best known for *Undertones of War* (1928), a collection of prose and poetry derived from his experiences in World War I.

blun·der (blŭn′dər) *n.* A stupid and serious mistake usually caused by ignorance, stupidity, or confusion. —See Synonyms at **error.**
~*v.* **blundered, -dering, -ders.** *—intr.* **1.** To move awkwardly or clumsily, as if blind; stumble. **2.** To make a stupid mistake because of ignorance or confusion. *—tr.* **1.** To botch or bungle. **2.** To say stupidly or thoughtlessly. [Middle English *blund(e)ren, blond(e)ren,* to proceed blindly, bungle, probably from Old Norse *blunda,* to shut the eyes.] **—blun·der·er** *n.* **—blun·der·ing·ly** *adv.*

blun·der·buss (blŭn′dər-bŭs′) *n.* **1.** A short musket with a wide bore and flaring muzzle, formerly used to scatter shot at close range. **2.** A stupid, clumsy person. [Alteration (influenced by BLUNDER) of Dutch *donderbus* : *donder,* thunder, + *bus,* gun, from Middle Dutch *busse,* box, tube, from Late Latin *buxis,* BOX.]

blunge (blŭnj) *tr.v.* **blunged, blunging, blunges.** To mix (clay, for example) with water for use in making ceramics, usually by means of a machine. [Blend of BLEND + PLUNGE.]

blung·er (blŭn′jər) *n.* A large vat in which water and clay or a similar substance are mixed. [From *blunge.*]

blunt (blŭnt) *adj.* **blunter, bluntest.** **1.** Having a thick, dull edge or end; not sharp or pointed. **2. a.** Having an abrupt and frank manner; brusque. **b.** Direct; straightforward: *a blunt refusal.* **3.** Slow to understand or perceive; dull. —See Synonyms at **gruff.**
~*v.* **blunted, blunting, blunts.** *—tr.* **1.** To make blunt. **2.** To make less sensitive or alert: *senses blunted by too much drinking.* **3.** To lessen the force or destructiveness of: *blunt the enemy's attack.* *—intr.* To become blunt. [Middle English *blont, blunt*†, dull, blunt, stupid.] **—blunt·ly** *adv.* **—blunt·ness** *n.*

blur (blûr) *v.* **blurred, blurring, blurs.** *—tr.* **1.** To make indistinct and hazy in outline or appearance; obscure. **2.** To smear or stain; smudge. **3.** To lessen the perception of; dim. *—intr.* To become indistinct or smudged.
~*n.* **1.** A blot or smudge. **2.** A hazy and indistinct visual or mental image. [16th century : perhaps akin to BLEAR.] **—blur·ry** *adj.*

blurb (blûrb) *n.* A brief commendatory publicity notice, as on a book jacket. [Coined in the early 1900's by Gelett *Burgess* (1866–1951), American humorist and illustrator.]

blurt (blûrt) *tr.v.* **blurted, blurting, blurts.** To utter suddenly and impulsively. Often used with *out.* [Probably imitative.]

blush (blŭsh) *v.* **blushed, blushing, blushes.** *—intr.* **1.** To become suddenly red in the face from modesty, embarrassment, or shame; flush: *"There's a blush for won't, and a blush for shan't / And a blush for having done it"* (Keats). **2.** To become red or rosy. **3.** To feel ashamed or regretful about something. Usually used with *at* or *for.* *—tr.* **1.** To give a reddish hue to. **2.** To reveal by blushing.
~*n.* **1.** A sudden reddening of the face from modesty, embarrassment, or shame. **2.** A red or rosy color. **—at** (or **on**) **first blush.** At first sight or glance.
~*adj.* Having the rosy color of a blush. [Middle English *blusshen, blisshen,* Old English *blyscan.*] **—blush·ful** *adj.* **—blush·ing·ly** *adv.*

blush·er (blŭsh′ər) *n.* **1.** One that blushes. **2.** A cosmetic used to give color to the cheeks.

blus·ter (blŭs′tər) *v.* **-tered, -tering, -ters.** *—intr.* **1.** To blow in loud, violent gusts, as wind in a storm. **2.** To speak noisily and boastfully. **3.** To threaten ineffectually. *—tr.* To force or bully (one's way) with swaggering threats.
~*n.* **1.** A violent, gusty wind. **2.** Turbulence or noisy confusion. **3.** Swaggering talk. [Middle English *blusteren,* probably akin to Low German *blüstern.*] **—blus·ter·er** *n.* **—blus·ter·y, blus·ter·ous** *adj.*

blvd. boulevard.

b.m. board measure.

B.M. **1.** Bachelor of Medicine. **2.** Bachelor of Music. **3.** bench mark. **4.** British Museum.

B.M.E. **1.** Bachelor of Mechanical Engineering. **2.** Bachelor of Mining Engineering.

BMR basal metabolic rate.

B.M.S. Bachelor of Marine Science.

B.Mus. Bachelor of Music.

bn., Bn. **1.** baron. **2.** battalion.

B.N.A. British North America.

B'nai B'rith (bnā′ brĭth′) *n.* A Jewish international fraternal society. [Hebrew *bənē bərīth,* "sons of the covenant."]

bo (bō) *n., pl.* **bos.** *Slang.* A fellow; a pal. Often used as a form of address. [Probably short for HOBO or BOZO.]

b.o. **1.** box office. **2.** branch office. **3.** buyer's option.

B.O. *n. Informal.* Body odor; an unpleasant bodily smell.

bo·a (bō′ə) *n.* **1.** Any of various large, nonvenomous, chiefly tropical snakes of the family Boidae, which includes the python, anaconda, boa constrictor, and other snakes that coil around and crush their prey. **2.** A long, fluffy scarf made of fur, feathers, or other soft material. [New Latin *Boa* (genus), from Latin *boa*†, a large water snake.]

boa constrictor *n.* A large, nonvenomous snake, *Constrictor constrictor,* of tropical America, having brown markings, which kills its prey by constriction.

blue jay *North America's blue jay (above) is distinguished from the European jay by its coloring and by its mobile crest, shown here in the lowered position. But the birds have many similar habits. Both, for instance, bury acorns as a winter food reserve.*

blue tit *Insects and insect larvae are the chief food of the European blue tit, which often hunts upside down on the branches of trees.*

PRONUNCIATION KEY

ă, pat; ā, pay; âr, care;
ä, father, are; b, bib;
ch, church; d, deed; ĕ, pet;
ē, be; f, fife; g, gag; h, hat;
hw, which; ĭ, pit; ī, pie;
îr, pier; j, judge; k, kick;
l, lid, needle; m, mum;
n, no, sudden; ng, thing;
ŏ, pot; ō, toe; ô, paw, for;
oi, noise; ou, out; o͝o, book;
o͞o, boot; p, pop; r, roar;
s, sauce; sh, ship, dish;
t, tight; th, thin, path;
th, this, bathe; ŭ, cut; ûr, fur;
v, valve; w, with; y, yes;
z, zebra, size; zh, vision;
ə, about, item, edible, gallop, circus, peaceful

IN FOREIGN WORDS:

à, *Fr.* ami; œ, *Fr.* feu, *Ger.* schön; ü, *Fr.* tu, *Ger.* über; KH, *Ger.* ich, *Scot.* loch; N, *Fr.* bon; y', *Fr.* Compiègne

STRESS MARKS:

Primary stress: ′
in·cite′ (ĭn-sīt′)
Secondary stress: ′
in′sight′ (ĭn′sīt′)

Boadicea. See **Boudicca.**

Bo·a·ner·ges¹ (bō'ə-nûr'jēz). The name given by Jesus to the Apostles John and James. Mark 3:17.

Boanerges² n. *Used with a singular verb.* A vociferous, loud-voiced preacher or orator. [Hebrew *bənē reghesh,* "sons of thunder."]

boar (bôr, bōr) n. **1.** An uncastrated male pig. **2.** A wild boar *(see).* [Middle English *bor,* Old English *bār,* from West Germanic *bairoz* (unattested).]

board (bôrd, bōrd) n. *Abbr.* **bd. 1.** A long, flat slab of sawed lumber; plank. **2.** A flat piece of wood or similarly rigid material, adapted for a special use: *a diving board; a notice board.* **3.** A flat, usually specially marked surface on which a game is played. **4.** The hard pasteboard cover of a book. **5. boards. a.** The stage of a theater. **b.** The acting profession. In both senses, preceded by *the.* **6. a.** A table, especially one set for serving food. **b.** Food or meals collectively: *board and lodging.* **7.** A table at which official meetings are held; a conference table. **8.** *Used with a singular or plural verb.* **a.** The directors of a company. Also used adjectively: *a board meeting.* **b.** Any committee, body of administrators, or the like: *a board of trustees.* **9.** A panel, usually plastic, on which an electrical circuit is mounted, especially one serving as a base for a printed circuit: *printed circuit board.* **10.** *Nautical.* **a.** The side of a ship. **b.** A leeboard. **c.** A centerboard. **—across the board.** *Informal.* **1.** Designating a bet that a horse or dog will win, place, or show. **2.** Affecting all members or divisions equally. **—by the board.** Overboard. **—go by the board.** To be ruined, unnoticed, or ignored. **—on board.** Aboard. **—sweep the board.** To win every possible prize, event, or the like. **—tread the boards.** To perform on or as if on a theater stage.
~v. **boarded, boarding, boards.** —*tr.* **1.** To cover or close with boards. Used with *up: board up a door.* **2.** To furnish with meals in return for payment. **3.** To house where board is furnished. **4.** To enter or go aboard (a ship or public vehicle). **5.** To come alongside (a ship), especially in order to force one's way aboard. **6.** In ice hockey, to block (an opposing player) into the boards surrounding the rink. —*intr.* To receive meals, or meals and lodging, in return for payment. [Middle English *bord,* Old English *bord,* plank, table, border, ship's side.]

board·er (bôr'dər, bōr'-) n. **1.** One who pays a stipulated sum to stay in someone else's house and receive regular meals; lodger. **2.** A person who is detailed to go aboard an enemy ship.

board foot n., *pl.* **board feet.** *Abbr.* **bd. ft.** A unit of lumber measurement equal to the volume of a piece of wood one foot square by one inch thick.

boarding house, board·ing·house (bôr'dĭng-hous', bōr'-) n. A private home that takes in paying guests and provides meals and lodging.

boarding school n. A school where pupils are provided with meals and lodging. Compare **day school.**

board measure n. *Abbr.* **b.m.** Measurement of lumber in board feet.

board of trade n. **1.** An association of bankers and businessmen formed to promote common commercial interests; a **chamber of commerce** *(see).* **2. Board of Trade.** A British government committee dealing with problems of trade and commerce.

board rule n. A measuring stick for determining a volume of lumber in board feet.

board·walk (bôrd'wôk', bōrd'-) n. **1.** A path made of wooden planks. **2.** A promenade, especially of planks, along a beach or waterfront.

boar·fish (bôr'fĭsh', bōr'-) n., *pl.* **-fishes** or collectively **boarfish.** Any of several marine fishes of the genus *Antigonia,* having a deep, flattened body, bright red coloring, and spiny fins.

boar·hound (bôr'hound', bōr'-) n. A large dog, such as the Great Dane, used for hunting wild boars.

boar·ish (bôr'ĭsh, bōr'-) adj. Like a boar; coarse; lecherous; brutish. **—boar·ish·ly** adv. **—boar·ish·ness** n.

boart. Variant of **bort.**

Bo·as (bō'ăz'), **Franz** (1858-1942). German-born U.S. anthropologist. Boas laid special emphasis on the systematic analysis of language structures and culture and is considered one of the founders of American anthropology.

boast¹ (bōst) v. **boasted, boasting, boasts.** —*intr.* To speak with excessive pride about one's own accomplishments, talents, or possessions. Often used with *of* or *about.* —*tr.* **1.** To brag about with excessive pride. **2.** To take pride in, or be enhanced by the possession of: *The school boasts excellent sporting facilities.*
~n. **1.** An instance of excessive self-praise. **2.** Something that one is proud of. [Middle English *bosten,* from *bost,* bragging, threat, perhaps from Germanic, akin to German dialectal *bauste(r)n,* to swell.] **—boast·er** n. **—boast·ing·ly** adv.
Synonyms: **brag, crow, vaunt.**

boast² *tr.v.* **boasted, boasting, boasts.** To shape or form (stone) roughly with a broad chisel. [Origin obscure.]

boast·ful (bōst'fəl) adj. Tending to boast or brag. **—boast·ful·ly** adv. **—boast·ful·ness** n.

boat (bōt) n. **1.** A relatively small, usually open craft of a size that might be carried on a ship. **2.** A ship. Not in nautical usage. **3.** A dish shaped somewhat like a boat: *a gravy boat.* **—burn one's boats.** *Chiefly British.* To commit oneself irrevocably to a course of action; burn one's bridges. **—in the same boat.** In the same predicament. **—miss the boat.** *Informal.* To lose an opportunity by failing to act at the right moment. **—rock the boat.** To upset the

bobcat *A North American wild cat that grows to about 75 centimeters (30 inches) long. It lives in forests, swamps, and deserts and is sometimes found even on the outskirts of towns. The bobcat's main prey are rabbits and hares.*

existing state of affairs; behave disruptively.
~v. **boated, boating, boats.** —*intr.* To travel by boat. —*tr.* To transport by boat. [Middle English *bo(o)t,* from Old English *bāt* and Old Norse *bātr.*]

boat·bill (bōt'bĭl') n. A nocturnal tropical American wading bird, *Cochlearius cochlearius,* having a large bill shaped like an inverted boat. Also called "boat-billed heron."

boat·er (bō'tər) n. **1.** One who boats. **2.** A stiff straw hat with a flat crown.

boat hook n. A pole with a metal point and hook at one end, used to maneuver boats and other floating objects.

boat·house (bōt'hous') n. A shed built at the water's edge or over the water, in which boats are kept.

boat·load (bōt'lōd') n. The number of passengers or quantity of cargo that a boat carries or can safely carry.

boat·man (bōt'mən) n., *pl.* **-men** (-mĭn). One who works on, deals with, or operates boats. **—boat·man·ship** n.

boat people *pl.n.* Refugees, especially those from Vietnam or other parts of Southeast Asia, who have made their escape in small boats.

boat·swain, bo's'n, bo·sun (bō'sən) n. A warrant officer or petty officer in charge of a ship's deck crew, rigging, anchors, and cables, who has a whistle as his badge of office. [Middle English *botswein,* Old English *bātswān* : BOAT + SWAIN.]

boatswain's chair n. A short board secured by ropes and used as a seat by sailors when working aloft or over a ship's side.

boat train n. A train scheduled to take passengers to catch or meet a particular ship.

Bo·az (bō'ăz). The husband of Ruth. Ruth 2:4.

bob¹ (bŏb) n. **1. a.** A quick jerking movement of the head or body. **b.** A quick bow or curtsy. **2.** A short line at the end of a stanza of verse. **3. a.** Any small knoblike dangling object: *a plumb bob.* **b. bobs.** Small, unimportant objects: *bits and bobs.* **4.** A fishing float or cork. **5.** A small lock or curl of hair. **6.** A short haircut on a woman or child, in which the hair is cut to the same length all round the back and sides of the head. **7.** The docked tail of a horse. **8.** A polishing disk rotated by a spindle and impregnated with an abrasive. **9.** In bell-ringing, one of several types of change. **10.** A tap or a light blow.
~v. **bobbed, bobbing, bobs.** —*intr.* **1.** To move up and down: *The cork bobbed on the water.* **2.** To curtsy or bow. **3.** To grab at floating or hanging objects with the teeth. Usually used with *for: He bobbed for apples.* **4.** To fish with a bob. —*tr.* **1.** To move (especially the head) up and down. **2.** To cut short: *She bobbed her hair.* **3.** To hit lightly and quickly; tap. **—bob up.** To appear suddenly, as a cork emerging from under water. [As "a pendent object," Middle English *bobbe†,* cluster of flowers or fruit. As verb "to move up and down," Middle English *bobben* (probably imitative).] **—bob·ber** n.

bob² n., *pl.* **bob.** *British Slang.* A shilling (five pence). [19th century : origin obscure.]

bob·bin (bŏb'ĭn) n. **1.** A spool or reel that holds thread or yarn for spinning, weaving, knitting, sewing, or making lace. **2.** Narrow braid used as trimming. **3.** A spool wound with insulated wire that forms part of an electromagnetic device, such as an electric bell. [French *bobine* (expressive).]

bob·bi·net (bŏb'ə-nĕt') n. A machine-woven net fabric with hexagonal meshes. [*bobbin* + *net.*]

bobbin lace n. An intricate handmade lace made by interlacing thread around small notched pins or bobbins stuck into a pillow according to a certain pattern. Also called "pillow lace."

bob·ble (bŏb'əl) v. **-bled, -bling, -bles.** —*intr.* To bob up and down. —*tr.* To fumble (a ball, for example).
~n. **1.** A fumble or a miss; a blunder. **2.** *Chiefly British.* An ornamental woolly ball, as on a knitted hat. [Frequentative of BOB (verb).]

bob·by (bŏb'ē) n., *pl.* **-bies.** *British Informal.* A policeman. [After Sir Robert PEEL, who was Home Secretary of England when the Metropolitan Police Force was created (1828).]

bob·by·daz·zler (bŏb'ē-dăz'lər) n. *British Informal.* A striking or exceptional person or thing.

bobby pin n. A small metal hair clip with the ends pressed tightly together. Also *British* "hairgrip." [From BOB (lock of hair).]

bobby socks, bobby sox *pl.n. Informal.* Ankle socks worn by girls or women. [From the name *Bobby,* pet form for the name *Robert* (influenced by BOBBY PIN).]

bob·by·sox·er (bŏb'ē-sŏk'sər) n. *Informal.* A teenage girl of the 1940's who followed current fads. [From the BOBBY SOCKS worn by the teenage girls.]

bob·cat (bŏb'kăt') n. A wild cat, *Lynx rufus,* of North America, having reddish-brown fur with dark markings, tufted ears, and a short tail. Also called "bay lynx." [From its bobbed tail.]

bob·o·link (bŏb'ə-lĭngk') n. An American migratory songbird, *Dolichonyx oryzivorus,* of which the male has black, white, and yellowish plumage in the breeding season. Also called "reedbird." [Originally *bobolincon;* imitative of its call.]

bob skate n. A skate having two parallel bearing edges. [BOB(SLED) + SKATE.]

bob·sled (bŏb'slĕd') n. **1.** A long racing sled with a steering mechanism controlling the front runners. **2. a.** A long sled made of two shorter sleds joined in tandem. **b.** Either of these two smaller sleds.
~*intr.v.* **bobsledded, -sledding, -sleds.** To ride or race in a bobsled. [From BOB (to cut short).]

bob·stay (bŏb'stā') n. *Nautical.* A rope or chain used to steady the bowsprit. [From BOB (up-and-down motion).]

bob·tail (bŏb′tāl′) *n.* **1.** A short or shortened tail. **2.** A horse or other animal having such a tail.
~*adj.* **1.** Having the tail short or cut short: *a bobtail nag.* **2.** Cut short; abbreviated; curtailed.
~*tr.v.* **bobtailed, -tailing, -tails. 1.** To cut the tail of (a horse or other animal); dock. **2.** To cut short; abbreviate.

bob·white (bŏb-hwīt′) *n.* A small North American quail, *Colinus virginianus,* having brown plumage with white markings. Sometimes called "partridge." [Imitative of its call.]

bo·cac·cio (bə-kä′chō, -chē-ō′) *n., pl.* **-cios.** A rockfish, *Sebastodes paucispinus,* of American Pacific waters. [Mexican Spanish, probably from Spanish *bocacha,* big mouth.]

bo·cage (bō′kàzh′) *n.* The representation of woodland scenes in ceramics. [French, from Old French, BOSCAGE.]

Boc·cac·cio (bō-kä′chē-ō, -chō), **Giovanni** (1313-75). French-born Italian poet and writer. His reputation rests chiefly on *Il Decameron* (1348-53), a collection of 100 tales exposing the nature of man, set against the melancholy background of the Black Death.

Boc·cher·i·ni (bō′kə-rē′nē), **(Ridolfo) Luigi** (1743-1805). Italian cellist and composer. He made his name as a composer, especially as a developer and prolific composer of chamber music.

boc·cie or **boc·ci** or **boc·ce** (bŏch′ē) *n.* A game of Italian origin similar to bowling that is played with wooden balls on a long narrow dirt or clay court. [Ital. *bocce,* pl. of *boccia,* ball.]

bock beer (bŏk) *n.* A strong dark beer, the first that is drawn from the vats in springtime. Also called "bock." [German *Bockbier,* short for *Eimbockbier* : *Eimbock, Einbeck* (town in Lower Saxony) + *Bier,* BEER.]

bod (bŏd) *n. Slang.* Body. [Shortened from BODY.]

BOD 1. biochemical oxygen demand. **2.** biological oxygen demand.

bode[1] (bōd) *tr.v.* **boded, boding, bodes. 1.** To be an omen of: *His ill will bodes no good.* **2.** *Obsolete.* To predict; foretell. —*intr.* To be a sign or omen: *The fine weather bodes well for the game.* —See Synonyms at **foretell.** [Middle English *boden,* Old English *bodian,* to announce, proclaim, from *boda,* messenger.]

bode[2]. Alternate past tense of **bide.**

bo·de·ga (bō-dā′gə) *n.* **1.** A wineshop, sometimes combined with a grocery, especially in a Spanish-speaking country. **2.** A warehouse for wine storage. [Spanish, from Latin *apothēca,* from Greek *apothēkē,* storehouse, from *apotithenai,* to put away : *apo-,* away + *tithenai,* to put, place.]

Bodensee. See **Constance, Lake.**

bodge (bŏj) *tr.v.* **bodged, bodging, bodges.** To spoil through clumsiness; make a mess of; botch.
~*n.* A carelessly done piece of work. [Variant of BOTCH.]

bod·ger (bŏj′ər) *adj.* Also **bod·gie** (bŏj′ē). *Australian Informal.* **1.** Worthless; inferior. **2.** False or assumed. Said especially of names.
~*n. British.* One who makes chairs out of beech wood. [From BODGE.]

bod·gie (bŏj′ē) *n. Australian.* **1.** An unruly and unconventionally dressed young man, especially in the 1950's. **2.** A worthless or uncouth person.
~*adj.* Variant of **bodger.**
~*tr.v.* **bodgied, -giing, -gies.** *Australian Informal.* To patch (something) up, especially temporarily. Used with *up.*

Bodh Gaya. See **Buddh Gaya.**

bo·dhi·satt·va (bō′dĭ-sŭt′və) *n. Buddhism.* One who, out of compassion, forgoes nirvana in order to save others. [Sanskrit, "one whose essence is enlightenment" : *bodhi,* enlightenment, from *bodhati,* he awakes + *sattva,* essence, from *sat, sant,* existing.]

bod·ice (bŏd′ĭs) *n.* **1.** The fitted part of a dress that extends from the waist to the shoulder. **2.** A woman's laced outer garment, worn like a vest over a blouse. **3.** *Obsolete.* A corset. [Originally *bodies,* plural of BODY (originally referring to the two sides of a whalebone corset).]

bod·ied (bŏd′ēd) *adj.* **1.** Having a body. **2.** Having a specified kind of body: *strong-bodied; full-bodied wine.*

bod·i·less (bŏd′ē-lĭs, bŏd′ə-) *adj.* Having no body, form, or substance; incorporeal. **—bod·i·less·ness** *n.*

bod·i·ly (bŏd′ə-lē) *adj.* **1.** Of, pertaining to, within, or exhibited by the body. **2.** Physical as opposed to mental or spiritual.
~*adv.* **1.** In the flesh; in person: *He was bodily but not mentally present.* **2.** As a complete physical entity: *He carried her bodily from the room.*

bod·ing (bō′dĭng) *n.* An omen or foreboding, especially of evil.

bod·kin (bŏd′kĭn) *n.* **1.** A small, sharply pointed instrument for making holes in fabric or leather. **2.** A blunt needle for pulling tape or ribbon through a series of loops or a hem. **3.** A long hairpin, usually with an ornamental head. **4.** *Printing.* A pointed tool for extracting letters from set type when correcting. [Middle English *boidekyn†.*]

Bod·lei·an (bŏd′lē-ən, bŏd-lē′ən) *n.* The library of Oxford University. It is one of the five libraries that automatically receive a free copy of every book published in the United Kingdom, in accordance with the copyright laws. [After Sir Thomas *Bodley* (1545-1613), English diplomat who refounded it (1603).]

Bo·do·ni (bō-dō′nē) *n. Printing.* A style of typeface. [Designed by Giambattista *Bodoni* (1740-1813), Italian printer.]

bod·y (bŏd′ē) *n., pl.* **-ies. 1. a.** The entire material structure and substance of an organism, especially of a human being or an animal. **b.** A corpse or carcass. **2. a.** The trunk or torso of a human

being or animal. **b.** The part of a garment covering the torso. **3.** *Informal.* A person. **4. a.** *Law.* A group of individuals regarded as an entity; a corporation. **b.** A number of persons, concepts, or things regarded collectively; a group: *We walked out in a body; a legislative body.* **5.** The main or central part of something, as: **a.** The nave of a church or the auditorium of a theater. **b.** The central content of a book or document as opposed to the prefatory matter, codicils, indexes, and the like. **c.** The passenger- and cargo-carrying part of an aircraft, ship, or vehicle. **d.** The sound box of a musical instrument. **e.** The majority: *The body of party opinion favored the reform.* **6. a.** Any bounded mass of matter: *a body of water.* **b.** Any perceptible three-dimensional piece of matter: *a foreign body in one's ear; heavenly bodies.* **7.** Consistency of substance, as in paint, textiles, wine, and the like: *a sauce with body.* **8.** *Printing.* The part of a block of type underlying the impression surface.
~*tr.v.* **bodied, -ying, -ies.** To give form or shape to. Usually followed by *forth:* "*Imagination bodies forth the form of things unknown*" (Shakespeare). [Middle English *body,* Old English *bodig,* from Germanic *bot-* (unattested), container.]

body blow *n.* **1.** In boxing, a blow delivered to the front of the body above the waist. **2.** A serious setback; a major disappointment.

body building *n.* The strengthening of the body by means of physical exercises, especially in a way that makes the muscles prominent. **—body builder** *n.*

body cavity *n.* The internal cavity of all multicellular animals except sponges, which contains the heart, digestive tract, and many other organs.

body-centered (bŏd′ē-sĕn′tərd) *adj.* Having a lattice point at the center of the body as well as at the corners. Said of a crystal. Compare **face-centered.**

body corporate *n. Law.* A corporation *(see).*

body count *n.* The total number of persons killed in a battle or war.

bod·y·guard (bŏd′ē-gärd′) *n.* **1.** A person or group of persons, usually armed, responsible for the physical safety of one or more specific persons. **2.** An escort or retinue.

body image *n.* A person's concept of the identity, shape, and relative positions of the different parts of his body.

body language *n.* Unspoken communication through conscious and unconscious gestures and positioning of the body.

body louse *n.* A parasitic louse, *Pediculus humanus,* afflicting humans.

body paint *n.* Paint that is applied directly to the body for decoration.

body politic *n.* The people collectively of a politically organized nation or state.

body pop·ping *n.* A type of dancing characterized by convulsive body movements and mimed robotic gestures, popular in the 1980's. It is often combined with **breakdancing** *(see).* [20th century : origin obscure.]

bod·y·shoot (bŏd′ē-shōōt′) *tr.v.* **-shot, -shooting, -shoots.** *Australian.* To surf (a wave) without a board.

body shop *n.* A shop or garage where the bodies of automotive vehicles are repaired.

body snatcher *n.* In former times, a person who stole corpses from graves for dissection.

body stocking *n.* A tight one-piece undergarment for the torso, sometimes also with sleeves and legs.

body suit *n.* A tight-fitting one-piece garment for the torso.

body surfing *n.* A form of surfing without a board in which one swims with a wave and allows it to carry one toward the shore. **—bod·y·surf** *v.*

body wall *n.* The part of an animal's body that encloses the body cavity, made up of ectoderm and mesoderm.

body work *n.* The act or process of repairing the bodies of automotive vehicles.

bod·y·work (bŏd′ē-wûrk′) *n.* The usually metal external structure of a motor vehicle.

Boehme, Jakob. See **Böhme.**

boehm·ite (bā′mīt′, bō′-) *n.* A natural, white, hydrated aluminum hydroxide, AlO(OH), that occurs as orthorhombic crystals in some bauxites. [German *Böhmit,* after J. *Böhm,* 20th-century German scientist.]

Boe·o·tia (bē-ō′shə). Region of ancient Greece, lying north of Attica and the Gulf of Corinth. In the 7th century B.C. the cities of the region formed the Boeotian League, although they never succeeded in escaping from the dominance of Thebes.

Boe·o·tian (bē-ō′shən) *adj.* **1.** Of or pertaining to Boeotia or its inhabitants. **2.** Stupid; boorish.
~*n.* **1.** An inhabitant of Boeotia. **2.** A stupid, boorish person.

Boer (bōr, bôr, bōōr) *n.* A Dutch colonist or a descendant of a Dutch colonist in South Africa. [Dutch, "peasant," "farmer," from Middle Dutch *gheboer.*] **—Boer** *adj.*

Boer War *n.* A war (1899-1902) in which Great Britain defeated the Boers of the Orange Free State and the Transvaal Republic in South Africa. Also called "Anglo-Boer War."

Bo·e·thi·us (bō-ē′thē-əs), **Anicius Manlius Severinus** (*c.* 480-*c.* 524). Roman philosopher. His famous work, *De Consolatione Philosophiae (On the Consolation of Philosophy),* written in prison in the weeks before his execution without trial by Theodoric the Ostrogoth, became one of the most influential accounts of classical thought.

boeuf bourguignon *n. French.* Beef bourguignon *(see).*

bof·fin (bŏf′ən) *n. British Informal.* A scientist or technical expert, originally one carrying out work for the Royal Air Force. [20th century : origin obscure.]

bof·fo (bŏf′ō) *adj.* Extremely successful; excellent; great. [Short for slang *boffola,* hit, success.]

Bo·fors gun (bō′fôrz′) *n.* A double-barreled, automatic antiaircraft gun. [First made at the munitions works in *Bofors,* Sweden.]

bog (bŏg, bôg) *n.* **1.** Permanently water-logged ground, with a surface layer of decaying vegetation, particularly *Sphagnum* mosses, which forms highly acid peat. **2.** An area of such ground; a marsh; a swamp.

~*v.* **bogged, bogging, bogs.** —*tr.* To hinder; slow; impede. Usually used with *down.* —*intr.* To be hindered and slowed. Usually used with *down: bogged down in work.* [Scottish and Irish Gaelic *bogach,* from *bog,* soft.] —**bog·gish** *adj.* —**bog·gish·ness** *n.*

Bo·garde (bō′gärd′), **Dirk,** born Derek Niven van den Bogaerde (1921–). British actor and writer. Among his most famous films are *The Servant* (1963) and *Death in Venice* (1971).

Bo·gart (bō′gärt′), **Humphrey DeForest** (1899–1957). U.S. actor. In the 1930's, 1940's, and 1950's he appeared in numerous roles as a reticent, tough hero with a soft heart, in films such as *Casablanca* (1942), *The African Queen* (1951), and, with the actress Lauren Bacall (whom he married in 1945), *To Have and Have Not* (1944) and *The Big Sleep* (1946).

bog asphodel *n.* Either of two related bog plants, *Narthecium ossifragum,* of Europe, or *N. americanum,* of the southeastern United States, having a spike of yellow flowers and irislike leaves.

bog·bean (bŏg′bēn′, bôg′-) *n.* An aquatic or creeping plant, *Menyanthes trifoliata,* with pink or white flowers in spikes, and three-lobed leaves held conspicuously above the surface. Also called "buckbean."

bo·gey (bō′gē) *n., pl.* **-geys. 1.** In golf: **a.** An estimated score. **b.** One stroke over par on a hole. **2.** *Military Slang.* Any unidentified flying aircraft. **3.** *Slang.* A bit of mucus from the nose. **4.** Variant of **bogy.**

bo·gey·man (bŏog′ē-măn′, bō′gē-, bōo′gē-) *n.* Variant of **boogieman.**

bog·gle (bŏg′əl) *v.* **-gled, -gling, -gles.** —*intr.* **1.** To hesitate or evade as if in fear or doubt. Usually used with *at.* **2.** To shy away with fright or astonishment; be overcome. **3.** To botch; bungle. —*tr.* To cause to be overcome, as with fright or astonishment. ~*n.* The act of boggling. [Probably from *boggle,* Northern dialectal variant of BOGLE.] —**bog·gler** *n.*

bog·gy (bŏg′ē, bôg′ē) *adj.* **-gier, -giest. 1.** Like a bog; swampy. **2.** Full of bogs. —**bog·gi·ness** *n.*

bog hole *n.* A hole containing soft mud or quicksand.

bo·gie¹, bo·gy (bō′gē) *n., pl.* **bogies. 1.** A railway coach or locomotive undercarriage with two, four, or six wheels that swivel so that curves may be negotiated. Also called "bogie truck." **2.** One of several wheels or supporting and aligning rollers inside the tread of a tractor or tank. In this sense, also called "bogie wheel." **3.** A small railway truck used for transporting coal, ores, or the like. [19th century : Northern England dialect, origin obscure.]

bogie². Variant of **bogy** (hobgoblin).

bo·gle (bō′gəl) *n.* A hobgoblin, a **bogy** *(see).* [Scottish *bogill;* akin to Welsh *bwg,* ghost, *bwgwl,* menace, akin to Cornish *buccaboo,* the devil, BUGABOO.]

bog moss *n.* Peat moss *(see).*

bog myrtle *n.* The sweet myrtle *(see).*

Bog·nor Re·gis (bŏg′nər rē′jĭs). Resort town on the coast of West Sussex, in southern England. It gained the title "Regis" after George V convalesced here in 1929.

bo·gong (bō′gŏng) *n.* An edible nocturnal Australian moth. [From a native Australian language.]

bog orchid *n.* An orchid, *Malaxis* (or *Hammarkya) paludosa,* growing in bogs, with yellow-green flowers and oval leaves that usually have small bulbils on their edges.

Bo·go·tá (bō′gə-tä′). Largest city and capital of Colombia, on a high plateau in the Andes Mts. where several rivers meet to form the Bogotá River.

bog rosemary *n.* A low-growing evergreen shrub, *Andromeda polifolia,* growing in wet ground, and having small pink bell-like flowers. Also called "marsh andromeda," "moorwort."

bog rush *n.* A densely tufted plant, *Schoenus nigricans,* with narrow, wiry leaves and stems carrying black, pointed spikes.

bog·trot·ter (bŏg′trŏt′ər, bôg′-) *n. Slang.* An Irishman. Used derogatorily.

bo·gus (bō′gəs) *adj.* Counterfeit; fake. [19th century (U.S.) : perhaps of African origin; compare Hausa *boko,* deceit, fraud.]

bog·wood (bŏg′wŏod′, bôg′-) *n.* Wood that has been preserved in a peat bog. Also called "bog oak."

bo·gy¹, bo·gie, bo·gey (bō′gē) *n., pl.* **-gies. 1.** An evil or mischievous spirit; a hobgoblin. Also called "bogle." **2.** Something that causes annoyance or harassment. [Originally used as proper name; compare BOGLE, BUGBEAR.] —**bo·gy·ism** *n.*

bogy². Variant of **bogie** (railroad car undercarriage).

bogyman. Variant of **boogieman.**

Bo Hai or **Po Hai** (bō′hī′). Formerly **Gulf of Chih·li** (jē′lē′). Inlet of the Yellow Sea between Shandong and Liaoning provinces in northeast China, with important oil and natural-gas resources.

bo·hea (bō-hē′) *n.* A black Chinese tea. The name originally referred to the choicest grade but later was applied to an inferior variety. [Chinese (Fujian dialect) *bu-i,* corresponding to Mandarin *wŭ-yí,* after *Wu-yi Shan,* a range of hills in northern Fujian Prov-

ince, where the black tea is grown.]

bo·he·mi·a, Bo·he·mi·a (bō-hē′mē-ə) *n.* **1.** A community of persons with artistic or literary tastes whose manners and moral standards are unconventional. **2.** The district in which bohemians live.

Bo·he·mi·a (bō-hē′mē-ə). *Czech* **Če·chy** (chĕKH′ē). A historic region of present-day western Czechoslovakia and a former kingdom. The Czechs, a west Slav people, settled in the area between the 1st and 5th centuries A.D. They maintained the independence of Bohemia until the 15th century, when the crown passed to Hungary and then to the Habsburgs. Nationalist efforts by the Czechs in the 19th century failed to re-establish an independent Bohemia, and it became a province of the new republic of Czechoslovakia (1918), losing its provincial status in an administrative reorganization (1948).

Bo·he·mi·an (bō-hē′mē-ən) *n.* **1.** A native or inhabitant of Bohemia. **2.** A Gypsy. **3.** *Archaic.* The language of the Czechs. **4. bohemian.** A person with artistic or literary interests who disregards conventional standards of behavior. —**Bo·he·mi·an** *adj.* —**Bo·he·mi·an·ism** *n.*

Bohemian Brethren *pl.n.* A Protestant religious society organized in the 15th century by the Hussites.

Böhm (bœm), **Karl** (1894–1981). Austrian conductor. He was conductor of the Vienna State Opera (1943–45 and 1954–56) and throughout his career was closely associated with the Vienna Philharmonic.

Böh·me or **Boeh·me** (bĕ′mə), **Jakob** (1575–1624). German theosophist and mystic. His several books describe evil as a necessary antithesis to good.

Bohr (bôr), **Niels Henrik David** (1885–1962). Danish physicist. His pioneering theoretical work used quantum theory to explain and develop the nuclear model of the atom put forward by Ernest Rutherford. He was awarded the Nobel Prize in physics (1922). His son **Aage Niels Bohr** (1922–) also won a Nobel Prize for physics (1975).

Bohr-Som·mer·feld theory (bôr′zŏm′ər-fĕlt′) *n.* A modification of the Bohr theory, allowing for elliptical as well as circular orbits. [After Arnold *Sommerfeld* (1868–1951), German physicist who produced the modification.]

Bohr theory *n.* A model of atomic structure, in which electrons travel around the nucleus in certain orbits representing specific energy states determined by quantum theory, a jump from one orbit to another being accompanied by the emission or absorption of a quantum of energy. The model explains the spectrum of the hydrogen atom. [After Niels BOHR.]

boil¹ (boil) *v.* **boiled, boiling, boils.** —*intr.* **1.** To vaporize a liquid by the application of heat. **2.** To reach the **boiling point** *(see).* **3.** To undergo the action of boiling; especially, to cook by boiling. **4.** To be in a state of agitation; boiling water; seethe. **5.** To be greatly excited, as with rage or passion. —*tr.* **1.** To heat to the boiling point. **2.** To cook or clean by boiling. **3.** To separate by evaporation as a result of boiling. —**boil away.** To evaporate by boiling. —**boil down. 1.** To reduce in bulk or size by boiling. **2.** To condense or summarize. —**boil down to.** To be in essence; amount to. —**boil over. 1.** To overflow while boiling. **2.** To explode in rage or passion. —**boil up.** *Australian & New Zealand.* To make tea. ~*n.* The state, condition, or act of boiling. [Middle English *boillen,* from Old French *bo(u)illir,* from Latin *bullīre,* to bubble, boil.]

boil² *n.* A painful swelling of the skin and subcutaneous tissue with a hard pus-filled center, caused by bacterial infection, usually occurring at a hair follicle. Also called "furuncle." Compare **carbuncle.** [Middle English *bile, bule, boyl,* Old English *bȳl, bȳle.*]

Boi·leau-Des·pré·aux (bwä-lō′dā-prā-ō′), **Nicolas** (1636–1711). French poet and critic. His most celebrated work, *The Art of Poetry* (1674), a treatise in verse, was a comprehensive summation of classical rules and conventions in French literature.

boil·er (boi′lər) *n.* **1.** An enclosed vessel in which water is heated and circulated, either as hot water or as steam, for heating or power. **2.** A container for boiling liquids, such as a double boiler. **3.** A storage tank for hot water. **4.** A hen, usually old and tough, to be cooked by boiling. Also called "boiling fowl." **5.** *Australian Informal.* A nagging old woman; an old bag.

boil·er·mak·er (boi′lər-mā′kər) *n.* **1.** One who makes or repairs boilers. **2.** *Slang.* A drink of whiskey with beer as a chaser.

boil·er·plate (boi′lər-plāt′) *n.* **1.** A steel plate used in making the shells of steam boilers. **2.** Journalistic material, such as syndicated features, available in plate or mat form.

boil·er·room (boi′lər-rōom′, -rōom′) *adj. Informal.* Of, relating to, or involving usually illegal, high-pressure telephone sales tactics, as used in selling stock, commodities, or land.

boiler suit *n. British.* Coveralls or overalls.

boil·ing (boi′lĭng) *adj. Informal.* Very hot. ~*adv.* Used as an intensive: *boiling hot.*

boiling point *n.* **1.** *Abbr.* **bp, b.p.** The temperature at which a liquid boils, especially under standard atmospheric conditions. **2.** *Informal.* The point at which a person loses his temper.

boil·ing-wa·ter reactor (boi′lĭng-wô′tər) *n. Abbr.* **BWR** A type of nuclear reactor in which boiling water is used as both moderator and coolant.

boil off *tr.v.* To remove (impurities) from a liquid mixture by boiling. —*intr.v.* To be removed by boiling. Used of impurities, fractions, and the like in liquid mixtures.

boil-off (boil′ôf′, -ŏf′) *n.* The vaporization of a liquid, such as a rocket fuel.

Bois de Bou·logne (bwä′də bōo-lōn′). A large park in west Paris, situated between the suburbs of Neuilly and Boulogne-Billancourt. It includes within its boundaries the two famous racecourses of Auteuil and Longchamps.

bois de rose (bwä′də rōz′) *n.* Dusty deep pink. [French, "rose-wood."]

Boi·se (boi′zē, -sē). Capital and largest city of Idaho in the south-western part of the state on the Boise River. It is an important trade, transportation, and food-processing center for a largely agricultural region.

bois·ter·ous (boi′stər-əs, -strəs) *adj.* **1.** Rough and stormy; violent and turbulent. **2.** Loud, noisy, and unrestrained. [Middle English *boistres,* variant of *boist(e)ous*†, rude, fierce, stout.] —**bois·ter·ous·ly** *adv.* —**bois·ter·ous·ness** *n.*

bok choy (bŏk choi′) *n.* Variant of **pak choi.**

Bokhara. See **Bukhara.**

Bok·mål (bŏŏk′môl′, bōk′-) *n.* One of the two officially recognized and mutually intelligible forms of Norwegian. It is the language in which newspapers and most literature are written. Also called "Dano-Norwegian," formerly "Riksmål." Compare **Nynorsk.** [Norwegian, "book language."]

bo·la (bō′lə) *n.* Also **bo·las** (-ləs). A rope with weights attached, used in South America to catch cattle or game by entangling the legs. [American Spanish *bolas,* plural of Spanish *bola,* ball, from Latin *bulla,* bubble, round object.]

bola tie. Variant of **bolo tie.**

bold (bōld) *adj.* **bolder, boldest. 1.** Fearless and daring; courageous. **2.** Requiring or exhibiting courage and bravery. **3.** Unduly forward and brazen in manner. **4.** Clear and distinct to the eye; standing out prominently: *bold handwriting.* **5.** Steep, as a cliff. **6.** *Printing.* Designating thick, heavy type; boldface. —See Synonyms at **brave, shameless.** —**make bold.** To take the liberty; dare. [Middle English *bold,* Old English *bald, beald.*] —**bold·ly** *adv.* —**bold·ness** *n.*

boldface (bōld′fās′) *n. Abbr.* **bf, bf., b.f., bld.** *Printing.* Type that has thick, heavy lines so as to give a conspicuous black impression. Compare **lightface.**
~*adj. Abbr.* **bf, bf., b.f., bld.** Printed in boldface.
~*tr.v.* **boldfaced, -facing, -faces. 1.** To mark (copy) for printing in boldface. **2.** To print or set in boldface. See **bola.**

bold-faced (bōld′fāst′) *adj.* **1.** Impudent; brazen. **2. a.** Printed or set in boldface. **b.** Marked for printing in boldface.

bole¹ (bōl) *n.* The trunk of a tree. [Middle English, from Old Norse *bolr.*]

bole² *n.* **1.** Any of various fine soft clays; especially, a reddish-brown variety used as a pigment. **2.** Moderate reddish brown. [Middle English, a red clay, from Medieval Latin *bōlus,* clod of earth, BOLUS.] —**bole** *adj.*

bo·lec·tion (bō-lĕk′shən) *n. Architecture.* A molding that projects from the surface of a panel. [18th century : origin obscure.]

bo·le·ro (bō-lâr′ō) *n., pl.* **-ros. 1.** A short jacket, usually with no front fastening, worn by both men and women. **2.** A Spanish dance in triple time. **3.** The music for this dance. [Spanish, apparently from *bola,* ball. See **bola.**]

bo·le·tus (bō-lē′təs) *n., pl.* **-tuses** or **-ti** (-tī′). Also **bo·lete** (bō′lēt′). Any fungus of the genus *Boletus,* having an umbrella-shaped cap with spore-bearing tubules on the underside. Some species are poisonous and others edible. [New Latin *Boletus,* from Latin *bōlētus*†, fungus.]

Bo·leyn (bŏŏl′ĭn, bō-lĭn′), **Anne** (*c.* 1507–36). Second wife of Henry VIII and mother of Elizabeth I. In order to marry her, Henry VIII divorced his first wife, Catherine of Aragon, thus breaking with the Roman Catholic Church and providing the occasion for the official Reformation in England. Henry and Anne were secretly married (January 1533). She produced no male heir and was convicted of adultery and beheaded (1536).

bo·lide (bō′līd) *n.* A meteoric fireball. [French, from Latin *bolis,* from Greek *bolis†,* missile.]

bol·i·var (bŏl′ə-vər; bō-lē′vär) *n., pl.* **-vars** or **bolivares** (bō-lē-vä′rĕs). *Abbr.* **b., B. 1.** The basic monetary unit of Venezuela, equal to 100 centimos. **2.** A coin worth one bolivar. See feature at **currency.** [After Simón BOLÍVAR.]

Bo·lí·var (bō-lē′vär), **Simón** (1783–1830). Venezuelan revolutionary hero, known as "the Liberator." He defeated the Spanish forces at Boyacá (1819) and was made president of Greater Colombia (now Colombia, Venezuela, and Ecuador). He helped liberate (1823–34) Peru and present-day Bolivia (named after him) and became the most powerful man on the continent.

Bo·liv·i·a (bə-lĭv′ē-ə). A landlocked republic in west-central South America. The country was named after Simón Bolívar who helped win its independence from Spain (1825). The western half of the country is dominated by the Andes Mts. and includes the populated plateau of the altiplano, 3,900 meters (13,000 feet) high, containing Lake Titicaca; the east is a lowland region of forests and plains. Most of the population is concentrated in the southern Andes plateau. Area, 1,098,581 square kilometers (424,165 square miles). Population, 5,600,000. Judicial capital, Sucre; administrative capital, La Paz. —**Bo·liv·i·an** *adj. & n.*

boll (bōl) *n.* The rounded seed pod of certain plants, such as flax or cotton. [Middle English *bolle,* from Middle Dutch.]

Böll (bœl), **Heinrich** (1917–). German writer. His short stories include the collection, *Traveller, If you Come to Spa* (1950); his novels include *Tomorrow and Yesterday* (1957), *The Clown* (1963), and *The Lost Honor of Katharina Blum* (1975). He was awarded the Nobel Prize for literature in 1972.

BOLIVIA

bol·lard (bŏl′ərd) *n.* **1.** A thick post on a ship or wharf, used for securing ropes and hawsers. **2.** *British.* **a.** A small marker post on a traffic island. **b.** A post placed on a pavement, path, or street to prevent traffic from driving or parking there. [Middle English : probably BOLE (tree trunk) + -ARD.]

bol·lix (bŏl′ĭks) *tr.v.* **-lixed, -lixing, -lixes.** Also **bol·lox** (-əks), **-loxed, -loxing, -loxes.** *Slang.* To throw into confusion; botch or bungle. Usually used with *up.* [From earlier *bollocks, ballocks,* testicles, Middle English *ballocks,* Old English *beallucas.*]

boll weevil *n.* A small, grayish, long-snouted beetle, *Anthonomus grandis,* of Mexico and the southern United States, having destructive larvae that hatch in and damage cotton bolls.

boll·worm (bōl′wûrm′) *n.* **1.** The larval stage of various moths, such as *Pectinophora gossypiella,* that feeds on and destroys cotton bolls. **2.** The corn earworm (*see*).

bo·log·na (bə-lō′nə, -nē, -nyə) *n.* Also *informal* **ba·lo·ney** (-nē), **bo·lo·ney.** A seasoned smoked sausage of mixed meats. [After BOLOGNA, where it was originally made.]

Bo·lo·gna (bə-lō′nyə). An industrial town in the Emilia-Romagna region of north-central Italy. It has one of the world's oldest universities, founded as a law school (A.D. 425) and established as a university in the 11th century.

bo·lom·e·ter (bō-lŏm′ə-tər) *n.* An instrument that measures radiant heat by detecting the change in electrical resistance produced in prepared metal foil strips by the heating effect of the incident radiation. [Greek *bolē,* beam, ray + -METER.] —**bo·lo·met·ric** (bō′-lō-mĕt′rĭk) *adj.*

bolo tie, bola tie *n.* A necktie consisting of a piece of cord with an ornamental bar or clasp. [Alteration of BOLA + TIE.]

Bol·she·vik (bōl′shə-vĭk′, bŏl′-) *n., pl.* **-viks** or **-viki** (-vē′kē). **1. a.** A member of the Communist Party of the Soviet Union. **b.** A member of the left-wing majority group of the Russian Social Democratic Party adopting Lenin's theses on party organization (1903). Compare **Menshevik. 2.** *Often* **bolshevik.** Any extreme radical: *a literary bolshevik.* [Russian *Bol'shevik,* "one of the majority" : *bol'shii,* greater, from *bol'shoi,* large + noun suffix *-vik.*] —**Bol·she·vik** *adj.*

Bol·she·vism (bōl′shə-vĭz′əm, bŏl′-) *n.* Also **bolshevism. 1.** The strategy developed by the Bolsheviks between 1903 and 1917 with a view to seizing state power and establishing the dictatorship of the proletariat. **2.** Soviet Communism.

Bol·she·vist (bōl′shə-vĭst, bŏl′-) *n.* Also **bolshevist.** A Bolshevik. —**Bol·she·vist, Bol·she·vis·tic** *adj.*

bol·son (bōl′sən) *n. Southwestern U.S.* A flat arid valley surrounded by mountains and draining into a shallow central lake. [Spanish, "big pouch," augmentative of *bolsa-,* purse, from Late Latin *bursa.*]

bol·ster (bōl′stər) *n.* **1.** A long, narrow pillow or cushion, typically hard and stiff. **2.** A structural support, such as a horizontal bar across the top of a post or column.
~*tr.v.* **bolstered, -tering, -sters. 1.** To support or prop up, as with a pillow. **2.** To support or strengthen: *bolster one's confidence.* **3.** To apply padding to. [Middle English *bolster,* Old English *bolster,* cushion.] —**bol·ster·er** *n.*

bolt¹ (bōlt) *n.* **1.** A bar made of wood or metal that slides into a socket and is used to fasten doors and gates. **2.** A metal bar or rod in the mechanism of a lock, thrown or withdrawn by turning the key. **3.** A fastener consisting of an externally threaded cylindrical piece, formed from a pin, rod, or wire and having a head at one end. It is designed to be inserted through holes in assembled parts and secured by a mating nut that is tightened by application of torque.

boll *The boll of the cotton plant, shown here, produces the white strands that are spun into yarn.*

4. a. A sliding metal bar that positions the cartridge in breech-loading rifles, closes the breech, and ejects the spent cartridge. **b.** A similar device in any breech mechanism. **5.** A short, heavy arrow with a thick head, used especially with a crossbow. **6.** A flash of lightning or a thunderbolt. **7.** A sudden movement toward or away from something. **8.** A large roll of cloth of a definite length, especially as it comes from the loom. **—bolt from the blue.** A sudden, usually shocking, surprise. **—shoot one's bolt.** To do all that one can; exhaust one's resources.
~v. **bolted, bolting, bolts.** —tr. **1.** To secure or lock with or as if with a bolt or bolts. **2.** To arrange or roll (lengths of cloth, for example) on a bolt. **3.** To eat hurriedly and with little chewing; gulp. **4.** Archaic. To shoot or discharge (an arrow or other missile). **5.** To desert or withdraw support from (a political party). **6.** To utter impulsively; blurt out. —intr. **1.** To move or spring suddenly toward or from something. **2.** To break from the rider's control and run away. Used of a horse. **3.** To make off suddenly; run away. **4.** To break away from a political party or its policies. **5.** Horticulture. To flower or produce seeds prematurely.
~adv. Rigidly straight. Used in the phrase bolt upright. [Middle English bolt, Old English bolt, heavy arrow.]
bolt² tr.v. **bolted, bolting, bolts.** To pass through a sieve; sift. [Middle English bulten, bolten, from Old French buleter, from Middle Dutch biutelen.]
Bolt (bōlt), **Robert Oxton** (1924–). British playwright. His most popular successes have been A Man for All Seasons (1960) and Vivat! Vivat Regina! (1970). He has also written numerous screenplays and won Academy Awards for Dr. Zhivago (1965) and A Man for All Seasons (1966).
bolt·er¹ (bōl′tər) n. **1.** A horse given to bolting. **2.** One who gives up membership in or withdraws support from his political party.
bolt·er² n. **1.** A machine for bolting flour. **2.** One who operates a bolter.
Bol·ton (bōl′tən). Industrial town in the metropolitan county of Greater Manchester, in northwest England. It was the center of the woolen trade from the 14th to the 18th century, when its economy shifted to cotton spinning.
bol·to·ni·a (bōl-tō′nē-ə) n. Any of several North American plants of the genus Boltonia, having daisylike flowers with white, violet, or pinkish rays. [New Latin, after James Bolton, 18th-century botanist.]
bolt·rope (bōlt′rōp′) n. A rope sewn into the outer edge of a sail to prevent the sail from tearing.
Boltz·mann (bōlts′män), **Ludwig** (1844–1906). Austrian physicist, one of the founders of modern physics, whose chief contribution was the kinetic theory of gases. He developed the Stefan-Boltzmann law.
Boltzmann constant n. Physics. Symbol **k** The ratio of the universal gas constant to the Avogadro constant. It has the value $1.380\ 622 \times 10^{-23}$ joule per kelvin. [After Ludwig BOLTZMANN.]
bo·lus (bō′ləs) n., pl. **-luses. 1.** A small round mass, particularly of chewed food. **2.** Pharmacology. A large pill or tablet. [Medieval Latin bōlus, from Greek bōlos†, lump, clod.]
bo·ma (bŏm′ə, bō′mə) n. In Central and East Africa: **1.** A protective enclosure for domestic animals; a camp; a stockade. **2.** A military or police post. **3.** A magistrate's office. [Swahili.]
Bo·ma (bō′mə). A port and railway terminus on the Zaire River in southwest Zaire. It was an important slave market up to the 19th century and was the capital of the Congo Free State (the Belgian Congo after 1908) from 1886 to 1926.
bomb (bŏm) n. **1.** An explosive weapon detonated by impact, proximity to an object, a timing mechanism, or other predetermined means. **2.** Any of various weapons detonated to release smoke, gas, pellets, poisons, or other destructive materials. **3.** Football. A very long forward pass designed to achieve great yardage in a single play. **4.** A container for a radioactive substance used in radiotherapy: a cobalt bomb. **5. a.** A vessel for storing compressed gas. **b.** A portable, manually operated container that ejects a spray, foam, or gas under pressure. **6.** A spherical mass of molten rock ejected into the air during a volcanic eruption. **7.** Chiefly British Slang. A lot of money: It cost a bomb. **8.** Chiefly British Slang. An old car. **9.** Slang. A dismal failure or complete fiasco. **—the bomb.** Often **Bomb. 1.** The atom or hydrogen bomb. **2.** Nuclear weapons collectively.
~v. **bombed, bombing, bombs.** —tr. To attack, damage, or destroy with a bomb or bombs. —intr. **1.** To drop a bomb or bombs. **2.** Slang. To go, especially to drive, quickly. Often used with along. **3.** Slang. To fail miserably. Usually used with out. [French bombe, from Italian bomba, probably from Latin bombus, booming, humming, from Greek bombos.]
bom·bard (bŏm′bärd′) n. An early form of cannon that fired stone balls.
~tr.v. (bŏm-bärd′) **bombarded, -barding, -bards. 1.** To attack with bombs, explosive shells, or missiles. **2.** To attack persistently with arguments, criticism, or the like. **3.** Physics. To subject (an atom, nucleus, or the like) to a stream of high energy particles. **4.** Archaic. To attack with a bombard. —See Synonyms at attack. [Middle English bombarde, cannon, from Old French, from Medieval Latin bombarda, probably from Latin bombus, booming. See bomb.] **—bom·bard·er** n. **—bom·bard·ment** n.
bom·bar·dier (bŏm′bər-dîr′) n. **1.** Military. The member of an aircraft crew who operates the bombing equipment. **2.** British. A corporal in the artillery. **3.** Formerly, a soldier who operated a

bombard. [French, from Old French bombarde, BOMBARD.]
bombardier beetle n. Any of various beetles of the genus Brachinus and related genera, that expel an acrid secretion from the posterior end of the abdomen.
bom·bar·don (bŏm-bärd′n, bŏm′bər-dən) n. **1.** A brass musical instrument resembling a tuba but with a lower pitch; a bass or contrabass tuba. **2.** A 16-foot reed stop on the organ. [French, from Italian bombardone, augmentative of bombardo, from bombarda, bombard, from Medieval Latin. See bombard.]
bom·bast (bŏm′băst′) n. **1.** Grandiloquent and pompous speech or writing. **2.** Formerly, a soft material used for padding. [Earlier bombace, cotton padding, from Old French, from Late Latin bombax, cotton, silk, alteration of Latin bombyx, silkworm, silk, from Greek bombux, of Oriental origin, akin to Turkish pambuk, cotton.] **—bom·bast·er** n.
bom·bas·tic (bŏm-băs′tĭk) adj. Characterized by bombast; pompous; grandiloquent. **—bom·bas·ti·cal·ly** adv.
bom·bax (bŏm′băks′) n. Any of various trees of the genus Bombax, especially the cotton tree. [New Latin, from Late Latin. See bombast.]
bombax cotton n. The silky, cottonlike fiber produced by various trees of the genus Bombax.
Bom·bay (bŏm-bā′). An industrial city and port on the northwest coast of India, built on the islands of Bombay and Salsette and connected to the mainland by a causeway. It is the capital of Maharashtra state and India's main seaport and commercial center.
Bombay duck n. **1.** A food fish, Harpodon nehereus, of India. **2.** The dried flesh of this fish or a dish prepared from it.
bom·ba·zine (bŏm′bə-zēn′) n. A fine twilled fabric of silk and worsted or cotton, often dyed black and used for mourning clothes. [French bombasin, from Late Latin bombacīnum, variant of bombȳcīnum, from Latin, neuter of bombȳcīnus, silken, from bombyx, silk. See bombast.]
bomb bay n. The compartment in the fuselage of a military aircraft from which bombs are dropped.
bomb calorimeter n. A device used to measure the calorific value of fuels, foods, and the like by burning them in oxygen at high pressure and noting the rise in temperature of the calorimeter and its contents.
bombe (bŏm; French bôⁿb) n. A dessert consisting of two or more layers of ice cream of different flavors or textures frozen in a round or melon-shaped mold. [French, "bomb" (from its shape).]
bombed (bŏmd) adj. Slang. Drunk or under the influence of drugs.
bomb·er (bŏm′ər) n. **1.** A military aircraft designed to carry and drop bombs. **2.** One who plants or drops bombs.
bom·bo·ra, bom·boo·ra (bŏm-bō′rə) n. Australian. A dangerous stretch of water above a submerged reef. [From a native Australian language.]
bomb·proof (bŏm′prōōf′) adj. Designed and constructed to resist destruction by bombs.
bomb rack n. A framework or mechanical holder for bombs on a military aircraft.
bomb·shell (bŏm′shĕl′) n. **1.** A bomb. **2.** A shocking surprise.
bomb shelter n. A shelter, often below ground, built to withstand attacks by bombing.
bomb·sight (bŏm′sīt′) n. A device in aircraft for aiming bombs.
bomb·site (bŏm′sīt′) n. Also **bomb site.** A derelict area, often an open space, where the buildings have been destroyed by bombing.
bom·by·cid (bŏm′bĭ-sĭd) n. A moth of the family Bombycidae, which includes the silkworm. [New Latin Bombycidae, from Latin bombyx, silkworm. See bombast.]
Bon (bŏn) n. A Japanese Buddhist festival held in July to honor ancestral spirits. Also called "Feast of Lanterns." [Japanese bon, basin, sacrificial vessel (later used as a festive lantern), from Chinese (Mandarin) pén.]
bo·na fi·de (bō′nə fīd′, fī′dē, bŏn′ə) adj. **1.** Done or made in good faith; sincere: a bona fide offer. **2.** Authentic; genuine: a bona fide Rembrandt. [Latin, "in good faith."]
bona fi·des (fī′dēz) n. Law. Honest intention; good faith. [Latin, "good faith."]
Usage: Bona fides is a singular Latin noun that takes a singular verb: His bona fides is not in question. Use of a plural verb is incorrect, and arises from confusion with the adjectival form bona fide, as in a bona fide traveler.
bo·nan·za (bə-năn′zə) n. **1.** A rich mine, vein, or pocket of ore. **2.** Any source of great wealth or prosperity. [Spanish, fair weather, prosperity, from Vulgar Latin bonacia (unattested), from Latin bonus, good (after Latin malacia, calm at sea, taken as if from malus, bad).]
Bo·na·parte (bō′nə-pärt′), **Jérôme** (1784–1860). Napoleon's youngest brother, king of Westphalia (1807–13). He lost the Westphalian crown when Germany was liberated from Napoleon (1813). He then took part in the French army's campaigns and fought at Waterloo. He became marshal of France (1850) and president of the senate under Napoleon III.
Bonaparte, Joseph (1768–1844). Napoleon's eldest brother, king of Naples (1806–08) and of Spain (1808–13).
Bonaparte, Louis (1778–1846). Brother of Napoleon, king of Holland (1806–10). He served with Napoleon in the Italian campaign (1796–97) and was his aide-de-camp in Egypt (1798–99). He was the father of Napoleon III.
Bonaparte, Lucien (1775–1840). Brother of Napoleon. He played an important part in Napoleon's coup of 18 Brumaire (1799), but,

disillusioned with his brother's policies, he went to Italy. He was reconciled with Napoleon at Elba.

Bonaparte, Napoleon. See **Napoleon I.**

Bo·na·part·ist (bō′nə-pär′tĭst) *n.* A follower or supporter of Napoleon Bonaparte, his policies and dynastic claims, or of the Bonaparte family. —**Bo·na·part·ism** *n.*

bon ap·pe·tit (bŏn′ ä-pā-tē′) *interj.* Used to wish someone a good appetite and a pleasant meal. [French.]

bo·na va·can·ti·a (bō′nə və-kăn′tē-yə) *pl.n. Law.* Unclaimed goods. [Latin, goods without an owner.]

bon·bon (bŏn′bŏn′) *n.* A candy having a center of fondant, fruit, or nuts, and coated with chocolate or fondant. [French, baby-talk reduplication of *bon,* good, from Latin *bonus.*]

bon·bon·niere (bŏn′bŏn-yâr′) *n.* **1.** A small ornate box or dish for candy. **2.** A confectioner's store.

bond (bŏnd) *n.* **1.** Anything that binds, ties, or fastens together, as: **a.** A shackle; a fetter. **b.** A cord, rope, or band. **2.** Often **bonds.** *Archaic.* Captivity; confinement. **3.** Often **bonds.** A uniting force or tie; a link. **4.** A binding agreement; a covenant. **5.** The duty, promise, or obligation by which one is bound: *"To trust a man on his oath or bond"* (Shakespeare). **6. a.** A substance or an agent that causes two or more objects or parts to cohere. **b.** Such a union or cohesion. **7.** *Chemistry.* A **chemical bond** *(see).* **8.** *Law.* **a.** Any written and sealed obligation, especially one requiring payment of a stipulated amount of money on or before a given day. **b.** A sum of money paid as bail or surety. **c.** One who acts as bail; bondsman. **9.** *Finance.* **a.** A certificate of debt issued by a government or corporation, guaranteeing payment of the original investment plus interest by a specified future date. **b.** *South African.* A company loan or mortgage on a house or property. **10.** *Commerce.* The state or condition of storing taxable goods in a warehouse until the taxes or duties due on them are paid. Used chiefly in the phrase *in bond.* **11.** An insurance contract in which an agency guarantees payment to an employer in the event of unforeseen financial loss through the actions of an employee. **12.** Any overlapping arrangement of bricks or other masonry components in a wall. **13. Bond paper** *(see).*
—*v.* **bonded, bonding, bonds.** —*tr.* **1.** To mortgage or place a guaranteed bond on. **2.** To furnish a bond or surety for. **3.** To place (an employee, for example) under bond or guarantee. **4.** To join securely, as with glue or cement. **5.** To lay (bricks or other building materials) in an overlapping pattern for solidity. —*intr.* To secure or hold something together with or as if with a bond. [Middle English *bond, band,* from Old Norse *band.*] —**bond·a·ble** *adj.* —**bond·er** *n.*

Bond (bŏnd), **Edward** (1934–). British playwright. His plays include *Saved* (1965), *Lear* (1972), and *The Women* (1978). He also wrote the libretto for the German composer Hans Werner Henze's opera *We Come to the River* (1976).

bond·age (bŏn′dĭj) *n.* **1.** The condition of a slave or serf; serfdom; servitude. **2.** A state of subjection to any force, power, or influence. **3.** In early English law, villeinage *(see).* **4.** The condition or practice of deriving sexual pleasure from being tied or chained up or tying or chaining up another. —See Synonyms at **servitude.** [Middle English, from Anglo-Latin *bondāgium,* from Middle English *bonde,* serf, peasant, from Old English *bōnda,* householder, from Old Norse *bōndi, būandi,* "tiller of the soil," husbandman, from the present participle of *būa,* to live, dwell.]

bonded warehouse *n.* A warehouse certified by the U.S. Department of Internal Revenue in which dutiable goods are stored pending payment of duties or taxes.

bond·hold·er (bŏnd′hōl′dər) *n.* The owner of a bond or bonds.

bond·ing (bŏn′dĭng) *n. Anthropology.* The forming of close, specialized human relationships, such as those that link parent and child, husband and wife, or friend and friend.

bond·maid (bŏnd′mād′) *n.* A female bondservant.

bond paper *n.* A superior grade of strong white paper made wholly or in part from rag pulp. Also called "bond."

bond·ser·vant (bŏnd′sûr′vənt) *n.* **1.** A person obligated to service without wages. **2.** A slave or serf. Also called "bondslave." [*Bond-,* from Middle English *bonde,* serf. See **bondage.**]

bonds·man (bŏndz′mən) *n., pl.* **-men** (-mĭn). **1.** A male bondservant. **2.** A person who provides bond or surety for another.

bond·wom·an (bŏnd′wŏom′ən) *n.* A female bondservant.

bone (bōn) *n.* **1. a.** The dense, semirigid, porous, calcified connective tissue of the skeleton of most vertebrates. **b.** Any of numerous anatomically distinct skeletal structures made of this material. **c.** A piece of this material. **2. bones. a.** The skeleton. **b.** The body. **3.** An animal structure or material, such as ivory, resembling bone. **4.** Something made of bone or of material resembling bone, especially: **a.** A piece of whalebone or similar material used as a corset stay. **b. bones.** *Informal.* Dice. **5. bones.** Essentials; basic principles. Used chiefly in the phrase *the bare bones.* **6. a. bones.** Flat clappers made of bone or wood used by the end man in a minstrel show. **b. Bones.** *Used with a singular verb.* The end man in a minstrel show. —**bone of contention.** The subject of a dispute. —**feel in one's bones.** To have an intuition of. —**have a bone to pick with.** To have grounds for a dispute with. —**make no bones about.** To be frank and candid about.
—*adv.* Used as an intensive: *bone dry; bone idle.*
—*tr.v.* **boned, boning, bones. 1.** To remove the bones from. **2.** To stiffen (a corset or piece of clothing) with whalebone or similar material. **3.** To fertilize with bone meal. —**bone up.** *Informal.* To study intensively, usually at the last minute. Often used with *on.*

[Middle English *bon, ban,* from Old English *bān,* from Germanic *bainam* (unattested).] See feature, next page.

bone ash *n.* The white, powdery calcium phosphate ash of burned bones, used as a fertilizer, in making ceramics, and in cleaning and polishing compounds.

bone·black (bōn′blăk′) *n.* Also **bone black.** A black pigment containing about 10 percent charcoal, made by roasting bones in an airtight container, and used in polishes, as a filtering medium, and in decolorizing sugar.

bone china *n.* Porcelain made of clay mixed with bone ash.

bone conduction *n.* The transmission of sound by bone, especially to the inner ear by the bones of the skull.

bone·fish (bōn′fĭsh′) *n., pl.* **-fishes** or collectively **bonefish.** A marine game fish, *Albula vulpes,* of warm, shallow waters, having silvery scales. [From its many small bones.]

bone·head (bōn′hĕd′) *n. Slang.* A stupid person; dunce. —**bone·head·ed** *adj.* —**bone·head·ed·ness** *n.*

bone marrow *n.* The tissue contained in the bone cavities that in early life forms the blood cells and platelets.

bone meal *n.* Bones crushed and ground to a coarse powder, used as plant fertilizer and animal feed.

bon·er (bō′nər) *n. Slang.* A blunder. [BON(E) + -ER.]

bone·set (bōn′sĕt′) *n.* Any of various plants of the genus *Eupatorium;* especially, *E. perfoliatum,* of eastern North America, having broad clusters of small white flowers. Also called "thoroughwort" and sometimes "agueweed" or "feverwort." [From its use as a folk medicine.]

bone·set·ter (bōn′sĕt′ər) *n.* A person with no medical qualifications who tends to broken bones or dislocated limbs.

bone·yard (bōn′yärd′) *n. Informal.* A cemetery.

bon·fire (bŏn′fīr′) *n.* A large outdoor fire. [Middle English *banefyre,* a fire in which bones were burned : BON(E) + FIRE.]

bong (bŏng, bông) *n.* A deep ringing sound, as of a bell. —*v.* **bonged, bonging, bongs.** —*tr.* To announce or proclaim with or as if with a deep ringing sound: *bong the hour.* —*intr.* To ring. [Imitative.]

bon·go (bŏng′gō) *n., pl.* **-gos.** An antelope, *Boocercus eurycerus,* of central Africa, having a reddish-brown coat with narrow, vertical white stripes and spirally twisted horns. [Native African name.]

bongo drums *pl.n.* A pair of connected drums having parchment heads that can be tuned, played by beating with the hands. Also called "bongos," "bongoes." [American Spanish *bongó* (probably imitative).]

Bon·hoef·fer (bŏn′hŏf-ər), **Dietrich** (1906–45). German Protestant theologian and philosopher. In 1933 he denounced Hitler in a radio broadcast, and two years later he was forbidden to teach and banned from Berlin. He then worked for the anti-Nazi underground movement. In 1945 after spending two years in prison, during which time he wrote *Letters and Papers from Prison,* he was executed for alleged participation in a plot to assassinate Hitler. His most important philosophical work was his *Ethics,* compiled from his notes and published posthumously (1949).

bon·ho·mie (bŏn′ə-mē′) *n.* An outgoing affable disposition; good nature; geniality. [French, from *bonhomme,* good-natured man.]

bon·i·face (bŏn′ə-fĭs, -făs′) *n.* An innkeeper. [After *Boniface,* an innkeeper in *The Beaux' Stratagem* by George Farquhar (1678–1707), British dramatist.]

Bon·i·face (bŏn′ə-fās′), **Saint** (A.D. 675–754). English monk, known as "the Apostle of Germany." He was born in Devonshire, and his English name was Winfrid or Wynfrith. Pope Gregory II gave him the name of Boniface (718) and encouraged his missionary work in Germany, where he made many converts to Christianity and founded monasteries. He was killed by a mob in Friesland.

bo·ni·to (bə-nē′tō) *n., pl.* **-tos** or collectively **bonito. 1.** Any of several marine food and game fishes of the genus *Sarda,* related to and resembling the tuna. **2.** Any of several similar fishes. [Spanish, "beautiful" (from its appearance), from Latin *bonus,* good.]

bon·kers (bŏng′kərz) *adj. Slang.* Mad; eccentric; crazy. [20th century : origin obscure.]

bon mot (bôn mō′) *n., pl.* **bons mots** (bôn′mōz′). A clever saying, usually a terse and apt witticism. [French, "good word."]

Bonn (bŏn). Capital since 1949 of West Germany, on the Rhine River in the western part of the country. It was founded as a Roman garrison (1st century A.D.). Its baroque architectural character is due to its having been rebuilt in 1685 after being destroyed by Elector Frederick III of Brandenburg.

Bon·nard (bô-när′), **Pierre** (1867–1947). French painter and lithographer noted for his use of dazzling light and color.

bonne (bôn) *n.* A female servant; maid. [French, feminine of *bon,* good, from Latin *bonus.*]

bonne bouche (bôn′ bōōsh′) *n., pl.* **bonnes bouches** (*pronounced as singular*). **1.** Something small and tasty, often eaten at the end of a meal. **2.** A short pleasing item, such as a musical encore. [French, "good mouth."]

bonne femme (bôn′ fĕm′) *adj.* Designating simple, home-style cooking. [French (*à la*) *bonne femme,* "(in the manner of) a good housewife."]

bon·net (bŏn′ĭt) *n.* **1.** A hat that is held in place by ribbons tied under the chin, worn by women and girls. **2.** *Scottish.* A brimless cap worn by men. **3.** A feather headdress worn by some American Indians. **4.** A removable metal plate over a valve or other machinery part. **5.** *Chiefly British.* The hood of an automobile. **6.** A wind screen for a chimney. **7.** *Nautical.* A strip of canvas laced to a

bone

THE SCAFFOLDING OF THE HUMAN BODY

Bone is light, flexible, yet stronger than steel

The human body, like those of other animals, is built around a skeleton of bone. This internal scaffolding not only supports the flesh and decides the shape of the body, but is jointed to make movement possible. Bone is made of two-thirds calcium, phosphorus, and magnesium and one-third collagen, a protein giving elasticity. This combination gives strength greater than that of mild steel, with only one-third the weight.

Bone consists of alternate horizontal and vertical layers of minerals containing collagen fibers, compacted on the outside to form hard ivory bone, and spongy in the center, where cavities hold bone marrow, which makes red blood cells and contains much of the body's stored fat cells.

Bones are classified as long (a thigh bone), short (a finger bone), flat (a shoulder bone), or irregular (a heel bone). In the embryo they are modeled in soft cartilage (gristle) and membrane. Bone-forming (ossification) centers develop later, and at birth all major bones have ossification centers near the middle. In childhood, secondary ossification centers develop near the ends (epiphyses) of long bones, which is where growth mainly occurs.

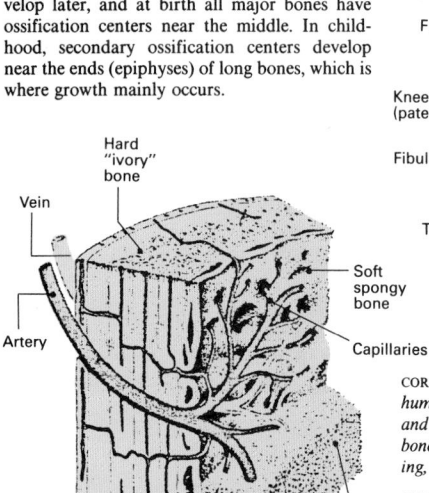

Skull · Collarbone (clavicle) · Pectoral girdle · Shoulder blade (scapula) · Breastbone (sternum) · Humerus · Ribs · Vertebral column · Radius · Ulna · Pelvic girdle · Carpals · Metacarpals · Phalanges · Femur · Kneecap (patella) · Fibula · Tibia · Tarsals · Metatarsals · Phalanges

Tough, dense, elastic, the cartilage surface of most adult joints has no blood supply of its own; it gets nutrients from tissue fluids. The body's cartilage distribution is shown in gray.

Hard "ivory" bone · Vein · Artery · Soft spongy bone · Capillaries · Bone marrow

CORE OF MAN *More than 200 bones make up the human frame. All but the brain box are flexible and jointed. In reaction with contracted muscles, bones make possible all movement, such as breathing, walking, bending, and grasping.*

BONE STRUCTURE *Inside the hard ivory bone are layers (lamellae) containing Haversian canals, which carry blood and osteoblasts. These cells continually dissolve bone, replacing it with new minerals—the process that renews broken bones.*

---

fore-and-aft sail to increase sail area.
~*tr.v.* **bonneted, -neting, nets.** To put a bonnet on. [Middle English *bonet,* from Old French, from Medieval Latin *abonnis†,* cap.] —**bon·net·ed** *adj.*
bonnet monkey *n.* A macaque, *Macaca radiata,* having a thatch of hair on the head resembling a bonnet.
Bon·ne·ville Salt Flats (bŏn′ə-vĭl′). A very flat region of the Great Salt Lake Desert in northwest Utah. It forms part of the bed of the now-vanished ancient Lake Bonneville, named after a 19th-century French fur trader and explorer. The flats are regularly used in attempts to set land speed records.
Bon·ney (bŏn′ē), **William H.,** known as "Billy the Kid" (1859–81). U.S. outlaw. By the age of 21 he had murdered 21 men, two of them during an escape from jail after he had been sentenced to death. Sheriff Pat Garrett fulfilled a campaign promise by fatally shooting him, bringing to an end Bonney's murderous career.
Bonnie Prince Charlie. See **Stuart, Charles Edward.**
bonnock. Variant of **bannock.**
bon·ny (bŏn′ē) *adj.* **-nier, -niest.** Also **bon·nie.** *Chiefly Scottish.* **1.** Pleasing or attractive to the eye; pretty; fair. **2.** Healthy; robust. **3.** Cheerful; pleasant. [Perhaps from Old French *bon,* good, from Latin *bonus.*] —**bon·ni·ly** *adv.* —**bon·ni·ness** *n.*
bon·ny·clab·ber (bŏn′ē-klăb′ər) *n. British Regional.* Sour clotted milk. [Probably from Irish *bainne clabair,* "milk of the churn-dasher" : *bainne,* milk, from Middle Irish *banne,* milk, drop + *clabair,* genitive of *clabaire†,* dasher (part of a churn).]
bon·sai (bŏn-sī′) *n., pl.* **bonsai. 1.** The art of producing dwarfed trees or shrubs by growing them from normal seed in small, shallow pots and restricting root and shoot growth by pruning. **2.** A tree or

bonnet monkey *This southern Indian monkey's name comes from its distinctive cap of long hair. It lives in troops of about two dozen.*

---

shrub grown by this method. [Japanese, "potted plant" : *bon,* basin, pot + *sai,* to plant.]
bon·spiel (bŏn′spēl′) *n.* Also **bon·spell** (-spəl). *Scottish.* A curling match. [Probably from Dutch *bon(d)spel* (unattested), "league game" : *bond,* league, from Middle Dutch *bont* + *spel,* game, from Middle Dutch, from Germanic *spillōn* (unattested), to play (see **spiel**).]
bon·te·bok (bŏn′tə-bŏk′) *n.* A rare South African antelope, *Damaliscus dorcas dorcas* (or *pygargus*), having a dark reddish coat, white underparts and rump, and a white mark on the face. [Afrikaans : *bont,* spotted, from Middle Dutch, probably from Latin *punctus,* spotted, pierced (see **point**) + *bok,* buck, from Middle Dutch *boc.*]
bon ton (bŏn′tŏn′) *n.* **1.** Sophisticated manners; style. **2.** Stylish or fashionable society. [French, "good tone."]
bo·nus (bō′nəs) *n., pl.* **-nuses. 1.** Something given or paid in addition to the usual or expected, especially an extra payment to employees at Christmas or for higher productivity. **2.** An extra dividend paid to shareholders from profits. **3.** Money paid to a state by a company in return for a corporate charter. **4.** A grant from the government to veterans of the armed forces. **5.** An incidental, extra, or unexpected benefit. **6.** A premium paid for a loan. [Latin *bonus,* good.]
   Synonyms: *bounty, dividend, grant, gratuity, premium, reward, subsidy.*
bonus issue *n.* A **scrip issue** (see).
bon vi·vant (bôn vē-vän′) *n., pl.* **bons vivants** (*pronounced as singular*). *French.* A person who enjoys good food and drink and lives luxuriously.
bon voy·age (bôn vwä-yàzh′) *interj.* Used to wish a departing traveler a pleasant journey. [French, "good journey."]
bon·y (bō′nē) *adj.* **-ier, -iest. 1.** Of, pertaining to, resembling, or made of bone. **2.** Having an internal skeleton of bones rather than cartilage. Said of fish. **3.** Having many bones. **4.** Having protruding or prominent bones; lean; gaunt. —**bon·i·ness** *n.*
bonze (bŏnz) *n.* A Mahayana Buddhist monk, especially of China, Japan, and adjacent countries. [French *bonze* or Portuguese *bonzo,* from Japanese *bonsō,* from Chinese *fàn sēng* : *fàn,* Buddhist, from Sanskrit *brahmanas* + *sēng* monk.]
bon·zer (bŏn′zər) *adj. Australian Slang.* Excellent; very good. Not in current usage. [Perhaps from BONANZA.]
boo¹ (bōō) *n., pl.* **boos.** A vocal sound uttered to show contempt, scorn, or disapproval.
   ~*interj.* Used to frighten or surprise, or to express disapproval or derision.
   ~*v.* **booed, booing, boos.** —*intr.* To utter "boo." —*tr.* To say "boo" to; jeer at. [Imitative.]
boo² *n. Slang.* Marijuana. [Origin unknown.]
boob (bōōb) *n. Slang.* A stupid or foolish person; a simpleton. [Short for BOOBY.]
boob·oi·sie (bōōb′wä-zē′) *n.* The class of the population composed of the stupid and gullible. [BOOB + (BOURGE)OISIE (coined by H.L. MENCKEN).]
boo-boo (bōō′bōō′) *n., pl.* **-boos.** *Slang.* **1.** A stupid or thoughtless mistake; a blunder. **2.** A slight physical injury, especially on a child.
boob tube *n. Slang.* Television.
boo·by (bōō′bē) *n., pl.* **-bies. 1.** A stupid or childish person. **2.** *Slang.* A woman's breast. **3.** Any of several tropical sea birds of the genus *Sula,* typically with brightly colored bills and feet, resembling and related to the gannets. [Spanish *bobo,* from Latin *balbus,* stammering.]
booby hatch *n.* **1.** *Nautical.* A raised covering over a small hatchway. **2.** *Slang.* A mental hospital. [Sense 1, from BOOBY (bird), since these birds commonly light there at sea. Sense 2, from BOOBY (stupid person).]
booby prize *n.* An insignificant or comical prize given to the person who receives the lowest score in a game or contest.
booby trap *n.* **1.** A concealed or camouflaged device designed to be triggered by some unsuspecting action of the intended victim. **2.** Any device or situation that catches a person off guard.
boo·by-trap (bōō′bē-trăp′) *tr.v.* **-trapped, -trapping, -traps.** To fit with a booby trap.
boo·dle (bōō′dl) *n. Slang.* **1. a.** Money, especially counterfeit money. **b.** Money accepted as a bribe. **2.** Stolen goods; swag. **3.** A crowd or mob; caboodle.
   ~*v.* **boodled, -dling, -dles.** *Slang.* —*intr.* To accept a bribe. —*tr.* To bribe or swindle. [Dutch *boedel,* estate, effects, from Middle Dutch *bōdel,* riches, property.] —**boo·dler** *n.*
boo·gie (bōō′gē) *n.* Strongly rhythmic rock music.
   ~*intr.v.* **boogied, -gieing, -gies.** To dance to rock music. [Shortened from BOOGIE-WOOGIE.]
boog·ie-man (bōōg′ē-măn′, bōō′gē-) *n., pl.* **-men** (-mĕn′). Also **boog·y·man, boog·ey·man, bo·gy·man** (bō′gē-), **bo·gey·man.** A hobgoblin; a terrifying specter. [*Boogie,* alteration of *booger,* from dialectal *boggart,* specter, hobgoblin, akin to BOGLE.]
boog·ie-woog·ie (bōōg′ē-wōōg′ē) *n.* A style of jazz piano-playing characterized by a repeated rhythmic and melodic pattern in the bass. [20th century : probably of African origin; compare Hausa *buga,* to beat (drums), West African English (Sierra Leone) *bogi* (bogi), to dance.] —**boog·ie-woog·ie** *adj.*
boo-hoo (bōō′hōō′) *intr.v.* **-hooed, -hooing, -hoos.** To weep or pretend to weep noisily.
   ~*n., pl.* **boohoos.** Noisy or pretended weeping. [Imitative.]

book (bŏŏk) *n. Abbr.* **b., B., bk.** **1.** A volume made up of written or printed pages fastened along one side, and having cardboard, leather, or paper protective covers. **2.** Any written or printed literary work. **3.** A bound volume of blank or ruled pages. **4. a.** Any of the volumes in which financial transactions are recorded. **b. books.** Such records collectively. **5.** A main division of a larger written or printed work: *a book of the Old Testament.* **6.** A **libretto** (*see*). **7.** The script of a play. **8. Book.** The Bible. Often preceded by *the.* **9. books.** *Informal.* Studies; lessons: *She's at her books.* **10.** Something regarded as a source of knowledge: *the book of life.* **11.** A number of similar items bound together between covers or in a small packet: *a book of matches.* **12.** A record of bets placed on a race. **13.** In card games, the number of tricks needed before any tricks can have scoring value, as the first six tricks taken by the declaring side in bridge. **14.** A bundle of tobacco leaves sliced lengthwise. **—bring to book. 1.** To compel to explain or account for. **2.** To reprimand. **—by the book.** Strictly according to established rules. **—close the books. 1.** In bookkeeping, to make no further entries in and to draw up statements from the records as they stand. **2.** To bring to an end. **—in one's book.** In one's opinion. **—in someone's good** (or **bad**) **books.** In favor (or disfavor) with someone. **—keep books.** To keep financial records. **—like a book.** Thoroughly; completely: *She knows him like a book.* **—make book.** *Slang.* To accept bets as a bookmaker, especially on a sporting event. **—one for the books.** *Informal.* Something noteworthy. **—on the books. 1.** Recorded or registered. **2.** Enlisted or enrolled. **—throw the book at.** *Slang.* **1.** To make all possible charges against (an offender or lawbreaker, for example). **2.** To reprimand or punish severely. ~*tr.v.* **booked, booking, books. 1.** To list or register in or as if in a book. **2.** To record charges against (a person) on a police blotter. **3.** To arrange for in advance; reserve (tickets, for example). **4.** To hire (entertainers, for example). [Middle English *bok,* Old English *bōc,* written document, composition.]

book·bind·er·y (bŏŏk′bīn′də-rē) *n., pl.* **-ies.** A business establishment where books are bound.

book·bind·ing (bŏŏk′bīn′dĭng) *n.* The art, trade, or profession of binding books. **—book·bind·er** *n.*

book·case (bŏŏk′kās′) *n.* A piece of furniture with shelves for holding books.

book club *n.* **1.** An organization that sells books, usually at a discount, to members who have agreed to buy a minimum number. **2.** A club for the reading and discussion of books.

book end *n.* A prop placed at the end of a row of books to keep them upright.

book·ie (bŏŏk′ē) *n. Slang.* A **bookmaker** (*see*).

book·ing (bŏŏk′ĭng) *n.* **1.** An engagement, as for a performance by an entertainer. **2.** A reservation, as of tickets or a hotel room. **3.** The recording of a person's name on a police blotter.

book·ish (bŏŏk′ĭsh) *adj.* **1.** Of, relating to, or resembling a book. **2.** Fond of books; studious. **3.** Relying on book learning rather than practical experience. **—book·ish·ly** *adv.* **—book·ish·ness** *n.*

book jacket *n.* A **dust jacket** (*see*).

book·keep·ing (bŏŏk′kē′pĭng) *n. Abbr.* **bkpg.** The art or practice of recording the accounts and transactions of a business. **—book·keep·er** *n.*

book learning *n.* Knowledge gained from books rather than from practical experience. Also called "booklore." **—book-learn·ed** *adj.*

book·let (bŏŏk′lĭt) *n.* A small bound book or pamphlet, usually with paper covers.

book·louse (bŏŏk′lous′) *n., pl.* **-lice** (-līs′). Any of various small, often wingless insects of the order Psocoptera (or Corrodentia), some species of which damage books.

book·mak·er (bŏŏk′mā′kər) *n.* **1.** One who edits, prints, publishes, or binds books. **2.** Someone who accepts bets, as on a horse race, and pays out winning bets. Also called "bookie."

book·man (bŏŏk′mən) *n., pl.* **-men** (-mĭn). **1.** One who is fond of books and reading. **2.** One who belongs to the literary world, such as a writer, critic, publisher, or bookseller.

book·mark (bŏŏk′märk′) *n.* A marker, such as a ribbon or a strip of leather, placed between the pages of a book.

book·mo·bile (bŏŏk′mō-bēl′) *n.* A small truck or trailer equipped to serve as a mobile lending library.

Book of Common Prayer *n.* The book of services and prayers used in the Church of England and, with certain modifications, in the other churches of the Anglican Communion.

Book of Kells. See **Kells.**

Book of Mormon *n.* The sacred text of the Mormon Church. See **Mormon.**

book·plate (bŏŏk′plāt′) *n.* A label usually pasted on the inside cover of a book that bears the owner's name or other identification.

book·rack (bŏŏk′răk′) *n.* **1.** A small rack or shelf for books. **2.** A frame or rack for supporting an open book. Also called "bookstand," "bookrest."

book review *n.* A critical analysis of a book.

book·sel·ler (bŏŏk′sĕl′ər) *n.* A person who sells books.

book·stall (bŏŏk′stôl′) *n.* A stall or stand where newspapers, magazines, or books are sold.

book·stand (bŏŏk′stănd′) *n.* **1.** A small counter where newspapers, magazines, or books are sold. **2.** A **bookrack** (*see*).

book·store (bŏŏk′stôr′, -stōr′) *n.* A store where books are sold. Also called "bookshop."

book value *n.* The value of a company's assets as set down in its financial records.

book·worm (bŏŏk′wûrm′) *n.* **1.** Any of various insects, especially booklice and silverfish, that infest books and feed on the paste in the bindings. **2.** One who spends much time reading or studying.

Boole (bŏŏl), **George** (1815–64). British mathematician and logician. He developed a calculus of symbolic logic, which was one of the first systems to show the use of symbolic mathematics as a tool in logical inference. It became one of the foundations of computer technology.

Bool·e·an algebra (bŏŏ′lē-ən) *n.* Any of various algebraic systems based on mathematical forms and relationships borrowed from the symbolic logic of George Boole.

boom¹ (bŏŏm) *v.* **boomed, booming, booms.** *—intr.* **1.** To make a deep, resonant, usually sustained sound: *His voice boomed down the corridor.* **2.** To flourish or progress usually with sudden rapid growth: *Business boomed.* *—tr.* To give forth or utter with a deep, resonant sound. Often used with *out.* ~*n.* **1.** A booming sound, as of an explosion. **2.** A time of general prosperity and economic growth. **3.** A sudden increase, as in growth, wealth, or popularity: *an investment boom; a baby boom.* ~*adj.* Of or resulting from a boom: *boom prices.* [Middle English *bomben, bummen* (imitative).]

boom² *n.* **1.** *Nautical.* A long spar extending from a mast to hold or extend the foot of a sail. **2.** A long pole extending upward at an angle from the mast of a derrick to support or guide objects lifted or suspended. **3. a.** A barrier composed of a chain of floating logs enclosing other free-floating logs. **b.** The area enclosed by such a barrier. **4.** A floating barrier serving to obstruct navigation or protect the entrance to a waterway. **5.** A long, movable arm used to maneuver an overhead microphone. ~*tr.v.* **boomed, booming, booms. 1.** *Nautical.* To extend (a sail) on a boom. Used with *out.* **2.** To obstruct (a river or the mouth of a harbor, for example) wih a floating barrier. [Dutch, tree, pole, from Middle Dutch.]

boom·er (bŏŏ′mər) *n.* **1.** A large male kangaroo. **2.** *Australian & New Zealand Informal.* Anything large, successful, or exciting.

boo·mer·ang (bŏŏ′mə-răng′) *n.* **1.** A flat, curved wooden missile, some types of which can be hurled so that they return to the thrower. It is used as a weapon by Australian aborigines. **2.** A statement or course of action that rebounds to the disadvantage of its originator. ~*intr.v.* **boomeranged, -anging, -angs.** To result in adverse effect upon the originator; backfire. [Native Australian word, variously recorded as *wo-mur-rāng, būmarin.*]

boom town *n.* A town which expands rapidly due to sudden prosperity, often through the discovery of local mineral resources.

boon¹ (bŏŏn) *n.* **1.** Something granted to benefit or please; a blessing: *Those phrase books are a boon to travellers.* **2.** A favor or request. [Middle English *bone,* prayer, thing prayed for, hence favor, from Old Norse *bōn,* prayer, request.]

boon² *adj.* Jolly; convivial. Used chiefly in the phrase *boon companion.* [Middle English *bone,* "good," from Old French *bon,* from Latin *bonus.*]

boon·docks (bŏŏn′dŏks′) *pl.n. Slang.* **1.** Wild and dense brush; jungle. Preceded by *the.* **2.** Back country; hinterland. Preceded by *the.* [Tagalog *bundok,* mountain.]

boon·dog·gle (bŏŏn′dô′gəl, -dŏg′əl) *intr.v.* **-gled, -gling, -gles.** *Informal.* To waste time on pointless and unnecessary work. ~*n.* Pointless, unnecessary, and time-wasting work. [20th century : origin obscure.] **—boon·dog·gler** *n.*

Boone (bŏŏn), **Daniel** (1734–1820). U.S. frontiersman and folk hero. He undertook the colonization of Kentucky, founding Boonesboro (or Boonesborough) on the Kentucky River (1775) after leading settlers across the Appalachian Mts.

boon·ies (bŏŏ′nēz) *pl.n. Slang.* See **Boondocks** (sense 2). [Shortening and alteration of BOONDOCKS.]

boor (bŏŏr) *n.* **1.** A peasant. **2.** A person with rude, clumsy manners and little respect for the feelings of others. [Dutch *boer,* farmer, peasant, from Middle Dutch *gheboer.*]

boor·ish (bŏŏr′ĭsh) *adj.* Like a boor; rude; ill-mannered. **—boor·ish·ly** *adv.* **—boor·ish·ness** *n.*

boost (bŏŏst) *v.* **boosted, boosting, boosts.** *—tr.* **1.** To raise or lift by or as if by pushing up from behind or below. **2.** To increase; raise: *boost production.* **3.** To encourage; help to improve: *boost someone's reputation; boost morale.* **4.** To promote or publicize; advocate actively. **5.** *Slang.* To steal, especially to shoplift. *—intr. Slang.* To steal. **—See Synonyms at lift.** ~*n.* **1.** A lift or help. **2.** An increase: *a boost in salary.* **3.** Anything that encourages or improves.

boost·er (bŏŏ′stər) *n.* **1.** Any device for increasing power or effectiveness. **2.** A person, thing, or event that is a source of encouragement or progress. **3.** *Electronics.* A radio-frequency amplifier. **4. a.** A rocket that assists the main propulsive system of an aircraft or spacecraft. **b.** A rocket used to launch a missile or space vehicle. In this sense, also called "booster rocket," "launch vehicle." **5.** A supplementary dose of a vaccine injected to maintain immunity. In this sense, also called "booster shot." **6.** A **supercharger** (*see*). **7.** *Slang.* One who shoplifts.

booster cable *n.* An electric cable used to connect a discharged automobile battery to a power source for charging. Also called "jumper cable," *chiefly British* "jump lead."

boot¹ (bŏŏt) *n.* **1.** A piece of footwear, usually of leather or rubber,

booby *There are six species of booby, a tropical relative of the gannet. Boobies catch fish by diving from high in the air. The conspicuously colored feet are used in displays to attract mates and warn off rivals.*

that covers the foot and part or all of the legs. **2.** A protective sheath for a horse's leg. **3.** An instrument of torture formerly used to crush the foot and leg. **4.** Any protective covering or sheath, especially a rubber sheath fitted over a coupling between two shafts. **5.** *British.* An automobile trunk. **6. a.** *Informal.* A kick. **b.** *Slang.* A swift, pleasurable feeling; thrill. **7.** A marine or navy recruit in basic training. **8.** *Slang.* A rude dismissal, as from work. Used with *the.*
~*tr.v.* **booted, booting, boots. 1.** To put boots on. **2.** *Informal.* To kick. **3.** *Informal.* To discharge; dismiss. Usually used with *out.* [Middle English *bote,* from Old French *bote†.*]

boot² *intr.v.* **booted, booting, boots.** *Archaic.* To be of help or advantage; avail.
~*n.* **1.** *Regional.* Something given in addition. **2.** *Archaic.* Advantage; avail. **—to boot.** In addition; besides. [Middle English *bote,* Old English *bōt,* advantage, addition, recompense.]

boot·black (boot'blăk') *n.* A person who cleans and polishes shoes for a living.

boot camp *n.* A training camp for marine or navy recruits.

boot·ed (boo'tĭd) *adj.* **1.** Wearing boots. **2.** *Zoology.* In birds, having a horny sheath (in poultry, feathers) covering the lower part of the legs.

boo·tee (boo'tē) *n.* Also **boo·tie.** A soft, usually knitted, shoe for a baby. [Diminutive of BOOT (shoe).]

Bo·ö·tes (bō-ō'tēz) *n.* A constellation in the Northern Hemisphere near Virgo and Canes Venatici which contains the star Arcturus. [Latin *Boötēs,* from Greek, "plowman," from *boötein,* to plow, from *bous,* ox.]

booth (booth) *n., pl.* **booths** (boothz, booths). **1.** A small enclosed compartment, usually accommodating only one person and providing privacy: *a telephone booth.* **2.** A seating area in a restaurant that has a table and seats whose backs serve as partitions. **3.** A small stall or stand for the display and sale of goods, as at a fairground. [Middle English *both, b(o)uth,* from Old Danish *bōth,* dwelling, stall.]

Booth (booth). Family of actors, including **Junius Brutus** (1796–1852), a British-born Shakespearean actor who immigrated to the United States in 1821 and continued his highly acclaimed career. His two sons were born in America. **Edwin Thomas** (1833–93) began with supporting roles in his father's productions and later achieved accolades for a career highlighted by a 100-night appearance as Hamlet. The younger son, **John Wilkes** (1838–65), though also a talented actor, is infamous for the assassination of President Abraham Lincoln.

Booth, Charles (1840–1916). British social scientist. His 17-volume work, *Life and Labour of the People in London* (1891–1903), was one of the great early contributions to the modern study of social science.

Booth, William (1829–1912). British religious leader, the founder of the Salvation Army. He became a minister in the Methodist New Connection Church (1852). In 1861 he left the church to devote himself to independent evangelical work, establishing the East London Revival Society, later known as the Christian Mission (1865). In 1878 this organization became the Salvation Army, with Booth as its first general.

boot·jack (boot'jăk') *n.* A forked device for holding a boot secure while the foot is being withdrawn.

boot·lace (boot'lās') *n.* A strong lace for tying boots or shoes.

bootlace fungus *n.* The **honey fungus** (see).

bootlace worm *n.* A dark brown ribbon worm, *Lineus longissimus,* found in shallow waters. They grow up to 6 meters (20 feet) in length, and are the longest worms in existence.

boot·leg (boot'lĕg') *v.* **-legged, -legging, -legs.** —*tr.* To make, sell, or transport (alcoholic liquor, for example) for sale illegally. —*intr.* To engage in bootlegging.
~*n.* Goods smuggled or illicitly produced or sold.
~*adj.* Produced, sold, or transported for sale illegally: *bootleg gin.* [From smugglers' practice of carrying liquor in the legs of tall boots.] **—boot·leg·ger** *n.*

boot·less (boot'lĭs) *adj.* Having no advantage or benefit; useless; unavailing; fruitless: *a bootless effort.* **—boot·less·ly** *adv.* **—boot·less·ness** *n.*

boot·lick (boot'lĭk') *v.* **-licked, -licking, -licks.** —*tr.* To be servile toward. —*intr.* To behave in a servile manner. **—boot·lick·er** *n.*

boots (boots) *n., pl.* **boots.** *British.* A servant in a hotel who cleans and shines shoes.

boot·strap (boot'străp') *n.* **1.** A leather or cloth loop sewn at each side or the top rear of a boot to help in pulling it on. **2.** *Computer Science.* A subroutine used to establish the full routine or another routine.
~*tr.v.* **-strapped, -strapping, -straps.** To establish (a program) with a bootstrap.
~*adj.* **1.** Undertaken or accomplished with minimal resources or help. **2.** Designating a technique or device for loading the first few programs into a computer so that the remaining programs can be introduced by way of an input device: *a bootstrap loader.* **3.** Denoting an electronic device, such as an amplifier, that uses the output voltage to bias the input. **4.** Denoting a self-consistent theory of nuclear interactions. **—by one's (own) bootstraps.** By one's own efforts.

boot tree *n.* A **shoetree** (see).

boo·ty (boo'tē) *n., pl.* **-ties. 1.** Plunder taken from an enemy in time of war. **2.** Any seized or stolen goods. **3.** Any valuable prize, award, or gain. [Middle English *bottyne,* from Old French *butin,* from Middle Low German *būte,* exchange, from Common Germanic *būti-ōn* (unattested).]

booze (booz) *Slang. n.* **1.** Alcoholic drink; especially, hard liquor. **2.** A drinking spree.
~*intr.v.* **boozed, boozing, boozes.** To drink alcoholic beverages excessively or chronically. [Middle English *bousen,* to carouse, from Middle Dutch *būsen†.*] **—booz·er** *n.* **—booz·y** *adj.*

bop¹ (bŏp) *tr.v.* **bopped, bopping, bops.** *Informal.* To hit or strike.
~*n.* A blow; a punch. [Imitative.]

bop² *n.* **1.** A style of jazz with a fast driving rhythm, very complex harmonies, and demanding virtuoso skills and techniques. Also called "bebop." **2.** *Informal.* A dance or a session of dancing to disco or pop music.
~*intr. v* **bopped, bopping, bops.** *Informal.* To dance to disco or pop music. [Short for BEBOP.]

Bo·phu·tha·tswa·na (bō'poo-tä-tswä'nə). One of the segregated areas known as Bantu homelands in South Africa. It consists of a number of widely separated districts located in Cape Province, the Orange Free State, and the Transvaal. It officially became a republic in 1977, but its independence has been recognized only by South Africa. Area, 40,430 square kilometers (15,610 square miles). Population, 1,200,000. Capital, Mmabatho.

bop·per (bŏp'ər) *n.* **1.** *Informal.* One who bops or plays bop. **2.** A **teenybopper** (see).

bor. borough.

bo·ra¹ (bôr'ə, bōr'ə) *n.* A violent cold wind from the northeast blowing on the Dalmatian coast of Yugoslavia in winter. [Italian (Venetian dialect), from Latin *Boreās,* BOREAS.]

bora² *n.* *Australian.* An Aboriginal initiation ceremony for boys going into manhood. [From a native Australian language.]

bo·rac·ic (bə-răs'ĭk, bô-) *adj.* Variant of **boric.** [Medieval Latin *borax* (stem *borac-*), BORAX + -IC.]

bo·rac·ite (bôr'ə-sīt', bōr'-) *n.* A white mineral consisting of borate and magnesium chloride, $Mg_6Cl_2B_{14}O_{26}$, found in some gypsum beds.

bor·age (bôr'ĭj, bŏr'-) *n.* A plant, *Borago officinalis,* native to southern Europe and northern Africa, having hairy leaves and star-shaped blue flowers. The young, cucumber-flavored leaves are sometimes used as seasoning. [Middle English, from Old French *bourrache,* from Medieval Latin *borrāgō,* probably from Arabic *abū 'āraq,* "father of sweat" (from its use medicinally as a sudorific).]

bo·rane (bôr'ān', bōr'-) *n.* Any of a series of boron-hydrogen compounds. [BOR(ON) + -ANE.]

bora ring *n.* *Australian.* A circle inside which an Aboriginal bora takes place.

bo·rate (bôr'āt', bōr'-) *n.* A salt or ester of boric acid.

bo·rax (bôr'ăks', -əks, bōr'-) *n.* **1.** A hydrated **sodium borate** (see). **2.** An anhydrous sodium borate used in the manufacture of glass and various ceramics. [Middle English *boras, borax,* from Old French *boras,* from Medieval Latin *borax,* from Arabic *būraq,* from Persian *būrah†.*]

borax bead *n.* A bead made of fused borax supported on a platinum wire, used in qualitative chemical analysis. When a substance of unknown composition is fused with the bead in a flame, the bead may change color depending on the presence of certain elements in the substance.

Bo·ra·zon (bôr'ə-zŏn', bōr'-) *n.* A trademark for an extremely hard boron nitride formed at very high pressures and temperatures. [BOR(ON) + AZ(O)- + -ON.]

bor·bo·ryg·mus (bôr'bə-rĭg'məs) *n.* Rumbling in the abdomen due to movement of fluid and gases in the intestines. [New Latin, from Greek (imitative).]

Bor·deaux¹ (bôr-dō'). A port in southwestern France, at the mouth of the Garonne River. Although it is an industrial town, its economy rests chiefly on the trade in Bordeaux wines.

Bor·deaux² (bôr-dō') *n., pl.* **Bordeaux** (bôr-dōz'). Any of the red or white wines produced in the regions around Bordeaux.

Bordeaux mixture *n.* A mixture of copper sulfate, lime, and water, used as a fungicide. [Translation of French *bouillie bordelaise.*]

bor·de·laise sauce (bôr-də-lĕz') *n.* A brown sauce made with Bordeaux wine and often with mushrooms. Also called "sauce bordelaise."

bor·del·lo (bôr-dĕl'ō) *n., pl* **-los.** A house of prostitution; a brothel. [Middle English, from Old French *bordel,* smallholding, small farm, diminutive of *borde,* from Frankish; akin to BOARD.]

Bor·den (bôrd'n), **Gail** (1801–74). U.S. surveyor and inventor. Concerned with the difficulty of transporting wholesome foods for long distances on the Western frontier, Borden developed a dried-beef biscuit (1851) and a method of condensing milk (patented 1856). His products were widely used during the Civil War.

Borden, Lizzie Andrew (1860–1927). Fall River, Massachusetts, woman who was accused of the ax murders of her father and stepmother on August 4, 1892. After a sensational trial, she was acquitted in June, 1893. The crime, still unsolved, has inspired many works of fiction, nonfiction, theater, and dance.

bor·der (bôr'dər) *n.* **1.** A margin, rim, or edge around or along something. **2.** A design or a decorative strip on the edge or rim of something, such as a plate. **3.** A strip of ground, around a lawn or along the side of a path for example, in which flowers or shrubs are planted. **4.** The line or frontier area separating political divisions or geographical regions; a boundary. **—the Borders.** The boundary

and adjacent areas between England and Scotland. —See Synonyms at **boundary.**
~*adj.* Of, pertaining to, forming, or located on a border.
~*tr.v.* **bordered, -dering, -ders. 1.** To put a border, rim, or edging on. **2.** To lie along or adjacent to the border of. —**border on** (or **upon**). **1.** To adjoin. **2.** To be almost like; approach in character: *an act that borders on heroism.* [Middle English *bordure,* from Old French, from *border,* to border, from *bord,* side of a vessel, border, from Frankish *bord* (unattested), board, plank.]
    Synonyms: brim, brink, brow, edge, margin, rim, verge.
bor·der·er (bôr′dər-ər) *n.* A person who lives on or near a border, especially the border between Scotland and England.
bor·der·land (bôr′dər-lănd′) *n.* **1.** Land located on or near a border or frontier. **2.** An uncertain or indeterminate area, situation, or condition.
bor·der·line (bôr′dər-līn′) *n.* Also **border line. 1.** A line that establishes or marks a border; a demarcation. **2.** An indefinite or indeterminate division beween two qualities or conditions: *the borderline between genius and madness.*
~*adj.* **1.** Verging on any quality or condition; indeterminate; dubious: *a borderline case of paranoia.* **2.** Not quite or only just measuring up to an accepted standard, especially of behavior: *a borderline gesture.*
Borders Region. Since 1975 an administrative region of Scotland, in the southeast on the border with England. It includes the former counties of Roxburgh, Verwick, Peebles, and Selkirk. The administrative center is Newtown St. Boswells.
Border States. The former slave states of Delaware, Maryland, Kentucky, and Missouri, adjacent to the free states of the North and caught between opposing forces in the Civil War. None of the Border States seceded.
border terrier *n.* A small, hardy, rough-coated breed of terrier, bred to hunt foxes in the border country of Scotland and England.
Bor·det (bôr-dā′), **Jules** (1870–1961). Belgian serologist and immunologist. He helped develop the technique that led to the Wassermann test for syphilis. In 1906 he discovered the bacillus of whooping cough. He was awarded the Nobel Prize for medicine (1919).
bor·de·tel·la per·tus·sis (bôr′də-tĕl′ə pər-tŭs′ĭs) *n.* The coccobacillus that causes whooping cough. [NLat. : *Bordetella,* genus name (after Jules *Bordet,* 1870–1961) + *pertussis,* whooping cough.]
bor·dure (bôr′jər) *n. Heraldry.* A border around a shield. [Middle English, BORDER.]
bore¹ (bôr, bōr) *v.* **bored, boring, bores.** —*tr.* **1.** To make a hole in or through, as with a drill or lathe. **2.** To make (a tunnel or well, for example) by drilling, digging, or burrowing. **3.** To make (one's way) with difficulty. —*intr.* **1.** To make a hole in or through something by or as if by drilling. **2.** To advance steadily or laboriously.
~*n.* **1.** A hole made by or as if by drilling, especially in order to find water or minerals; specifically, in Australia, an artesian well. Also called "borehole." **2. a.** The hollow part of a hole, tube, or cylinder. **b.** The interior diameter of this. **3.** The caliber of a firearm. Often used in combination: *12-bore.* **4.** A drilling tool. [Middle English *boren,* Old English *borian.*]
bore² *tr.v.* **bored, boring, bores.** To tire or weary with dullness, repetition, or tediousness.
~*n.* **1.** A tiresome or tedious person or activity. **2.** A nuisance; a bother. [18th century : origin obscure.]
bore³ *n.* A high wave traveling upstream in the tidal reaches of certain rivers, caused by the surge of a flood tide upstream in a narrowing estuary or by colliding tidal currents. Also called "eagre." [Middle English *bare,* from Old Norse *bāra,* wave, billow.]
bore⁴. Past tense of **bear.**
bo·re·al (bôr′ē-əl, bōr′-) *adj.* **1.** Pertaining to the north; northern. **2.** Of or concerning the north wind. **3.** **Boreal.** Of or pertaining to the coniferous forest areas of the North Temperate Zone and Arctic region. **4.** **Boreal.** Of or designating a climatic zone with short summers and hard winters. **5.** **Boreal.** Of or designating a climatic period of cold winters and warm summers (7500 B.C. to 5500 B.C.). [Middle English *boriall,* from Late Latin *boreālis,* from BOREAS.]
Bo·re·as (bôr′ē-əs, bōr′-). **1.** The north wind. **2.** The god personifying the north wind in Greek mythology. [Middle English, from Latin *Boreās,* from Greek *Boreas.*]
bore·cole (bôr′kōl′, bōr′-) *n.* A vegetable, kale *(see).* [Dutch *boerenkool,* "peasants' cabbage" : *boer,* BOOR (peasant) + *kool,* cabbage, from Latin *caulis,* stalk (see **cole**).]
bore·dom (bôr′dəm, bōr′-) *n.* The condition of being bored.
bore·hole (bôr′hōl′, bōr′-) *n.* A bore, as for water or minerals; specifically, in South Africa, a narrow well drilled through to an underground source of water, which is usually pumped to the surface by means of a windmill.
bor·er (bôr′ər, bōr′-) *n.* **1.** A tool used for boring or drilling. **2.** One who works with such a tool. **3.** An insect or insect larva, such as the **corn borer** *(see),* that bores into plant material. **4.** Any of various mollusks that bore into soft rock or plant material.
Borg (bôrg), **Björn** (1956–). Swedish tennis player. He won his first major title at the Italian championships (1974) and from 1976 until 1980 won the Wimbledon men's singles championships five consecutive times, a record for the 20th century.
Bor·ges (bôr′hās), **Jorge Luis** (1899–1986). Argentinian writer. He was a poet, essayist, and literary critic, but he is best known for the metaphysical fantasy of his short stories, such as the collection *Ficciones* (1945).

Bor·gia (bôr′jä, -zhə), **Cesare** (c. 1475–1507). Italian soldier and politician, illegitimate son of Pope Alexander VI. The pope used his son to consolidate a papal empire, making him archbishop of Valenzia and then a cardinal. He was supposedly the model of the ruler in Machiavelli's *The Prince* (1532).
Borgia, Lucrezia (1480–1519). Italian noblewoman, daughter of Pope Alexander VI and sister of Cesare. Her three marriages helped increase the political power of the Borgia family. Later, her court at Ferrara became a cultural center of the Italian Renaissance.
Borgia, Rodrigo. See **Alexander VI.**
bo·ric (bôr′ĭk, bōr′-) *adj.* Also **bo·rac·ic** (bə-răs′ĭk). Of, pertaining to, derived from, or containing boron or boric acid.
boric acid *n.* A white or colorless crystalline compound, H_3BO_3, used as an antiseptic, preservative, and fireproofing agent. Also called "orthoboric acid."
boric oxide *n.* A hard, colorless, transparent glass, B_2O_3, used in heat-resistant glassware, as a fire-resistant paint additive, and in the production of boron.
bo·ride (bôr′īd, bōr′-) *n.* A binary compound of boron with a more electropositive element or radical. [BOR(ON) + -IDE.]
bor·ing¹ (bôr′ĭng, bōr′-) *n.* **1.** The making of a hole by or as if by drilling. **2.** A hole made in this way. **3. borings.** The material, chips, or dust produced by such drilling.
boring² *adj.* Uninteresting and tiresome; dull.
    Synonyms: dreary, humdrum, irksome, monotonous, tedious, tiresome.
Bor·laug (bôr′lôg′), **Norman Ernest** (1914–). U.S. agronomist. For his contribution to progress in agriculture and attempts to overcome world hunger, he was awarded the Nobel Peace Prize (1970).
Bor·mann (bôr′män′), **Martin Ludwig.** (1900– c. 1945). German Nazi leader. He met Hitler in 1924 and became an important figure in the Nazi hierarchy. In 1942 he became Hitler's private secretary. He disappeared after Hitler's suicide in 1945 and was sentenced to death in his absence at the Nuremberg trials (1946). It is now thought that he committed suicide in May 1945.
born (bôrn). A past participle of **bear** (to give birth to). —See Usage note at **bear** (to carry).
~*adj.* **1.** *Abbr.* **b., B.** Brought into life or being. **2.** Having or appearing to have a specified innate quality or talent: *a born artist.*
Born (bôrn), **Max** (1882–1970). British theoretical physicist, born in Germany. He played an important part in the development of the new quantum and wave mechanics and was awarded the Nobel Prize for physics (1954).
born-a·gain (bôrn′ə-gĕn′) *adj.* **1.** Characteristic of or being a person who has undergone a personal, and usually very emotional conversion or reconversion, to Christianity, often through revelation or a similar experience; evangelical. **2.** Characterized by renewal, resurgence, or return: *born-again enthusiasm.*
borne¹ (bôrn, bōrn). A past participle of **bear** (to carry). —**borne in on** (or **upon**). Brought to the notice of; realized by: *The extent of our dilemma was gradually borne in on us.* —See Usage note at **bear** (to carry).
borne² *adj.* Carried or supported in a specified way. Often used in combination: *windborne; seaborne.*
Bor·ne·o (bôr′nē-ō). The largest island of the Malay Archipelago, lying north of Java and southwest of the Philippines. It is the third-largest island in the world. Kalimantan state, which occupies 70 percent of the island, belongs to Indonesia; the states of Sarawak in the west and Sabah in the north belong to Malaysia; and Brunei, in the northwest, is a British protectorate. The interior of the island consists of dense jungle and mountains, the coastal regions of mangrove swamp. The island is one of the most thinly populated parts of the nonpolar world.
bor·ne·ol (bôr′nē-ôl′, -ōl′) *n.* A solid terpene alchohol, $C_{10}H_{17}OH$, obtained from the tree *Dryobalanops camphora* and used in perfumery, the manufacture of celluloid, and as an antiseptic. [BORNEO + -OL.]
born·ite (bôr′nīt′) *n.* A brownish-bronze copper ore with composition Cu_5FeS_4. [After Ignaz von *Born* (1742–91), Austrian mineralogist.]
Bo·ro·bu·dur (bôr′ə-bə-dōōr′, bōr′-). One of the greatest of Buddhist shrines, in central Java in Indonesia. The monument was built in *c.* A.D. 800 and, although badly weathered, still stands.
Bo·ro·din (bôr′ə-dēn′), **Alexander Porfirevich.** (1834–87). Russian composer. His output was small, since he was primarily a chemist, but he is remembered for his opera, *Prince Igor* (unfinished at his death), and his two string quartets.
Bo·ro·di·no (bôr′ə-dē′nō). A village in central European U.S.S.R., west of Moscow. Nearby, Napoleon defeated the Russian forces defending Moscow on September 7, 1812. The battle, with heavy casualties on both sides, is described in Tolstoy's *War and Peace.*
bo·ron (bôr′ŏn′, bōr′-) *n. Symbol* **B** A nonmetallic element, extracted chiefly from kernite and borax, and used in flares, propellant mixtures, nuclear-reactor control elements, abrasives, and hard metallic alloys. It exists in two allotropic forms: a soft, brown, amorphous variety and a hard crystalline form. Atomic number 5, atomic weight 10.811, melting point 2,300°C, sublimation 2,550°C, specific gravity (crystal) 2.34, valence 3. [BOR(AX) + (CARB)ON.]
boron carbide *n.* An extremely hard, black, crystalline compound, B_4C, used as an abrasive, in control rods for nuclear reactors, and as a reinforcing filament in composite structural materials.
boron chamber *n. Physics.* A type of particle detector that detects and counts slow neutrons by their effect on boron atoms.

boron nitride *n.* An inert white solid, BN, used as a lubricant, heat shield, and insulator at high temperatures. It has two crystalline forms: one similar to graphite and the other, **borazon** *(see),* similar to diamond.

bo·ro·sil·i·cate glass (bôr′ō-sĭl′ĭ-kĭt, bŏr′ō-, -kāt′) *n.* A strong heat-resistant glass that contains a proportion of boron atoms in place of silicon atoms (up to five percent boric oxide).

bor·ough (bûr′ō, bûr′ə) *n.* Abbr. **bor.** **1.** A self-governing incorporated town in certain U.S. states. **2.** Any of the five administrative units of New York City. **3.** *British.* **a.** A town that was originally incorporated by royal charter and had a municipal corporation and certain rights, such as self-government. Compare **burgh.** **b.** A town that makes up the constituency of a member of Parliament. **c.** Any of the 32 divisions that make up Greater London. [Middle English *burgh, borugh,* Old English *burg, burh,* fortress, fortified town.]

bor·ough-Eng·lish (bûr′ō-ĭng′glĭsh) *n.* An old custom in certain boroughs of England whereby the right to inherit an estate went to the youngest son or, in default of issue, to the youngest brother. [Middle English, from Norman French *(tenure en) Burgh Engloys,* (tenure in) English borough.]

Bor·rel·i·a (bə-rĕl′ē-ə, -rē′lē-ə) *n.* A genus of locomotive helical bacteria of the family Spirochaetaceae, some of which cause relapsing fever in humans. [New Latin, after Amédée *Borrel* (1867–1936).]

Bor·ro·mi·ni (bôr′ō-mē′nē), **Francesco,** born Francesco Castelli (1599–1667). Baroque architect. He revolutionized architecture by conceiving a building as a collection of geometric shapes and by treating light and space as elements of the design.

bor·row (bŏr′ō, bôr′ō) *v.* **-rowed, -rowing, -rows.** —*tr.* **1.** To obtain or receive (something) on loan with the promise or understanding of returning it or its equivalent. **2.** To adopt or use as one's own: *They borrowed his ideas.* **3.** In subtraction, to increase a figure in the minuend by ten and make up for it by decreasing the next, larger denomination by one. **4.** *Nonstandard.* To lend. —*intr.* **1.** To take or receive a loan; obtain or receive something. **2.** *Golf.* To play a ball, especially when putting, so as to allow for the slope or wind. [Middle English *borwen,* Old English *borgian.*] —**bor·row·er** *n.*

bor·row·ing (bŏr′ō-ĭng, bôr′-) *n.* Something that is borrowed, especially a word borrowed from one language for use in another.

borscht, borsht (bôrsht) *n.* Also **borsch** (bôrsh). A Russian soup made from beets and sometimes cabbage, served hot or cold, often with sour cream. [Russian *borshch,* "cow parsnip" (the original base of the soup).]

borscht circuit *n. Slang.* The predominantly Jewish resort hotels of the Catskill Mountains that employ entertainers. [From the popularity of BORSCHT in their cuisine.]

bor·stal (bôr′stəl) *n. British.* A disciplinary institution for young offenders, aged 15 to 21. [After *Borstal* near Rochester, England, where the Borstal Institution for young offenders was established in 1901.]

bort, boart (bôrt) *n.* **1.** Poor-quality diamonds used for industrial cutting and abrasion. **2.** An impure diamond, a **carbonado** *(see).* [Perhaps from Dutch *boort,* perhaps from Old French *bourt,* bastard, from Latin *burdus,* hinny.] —**bort·y** *adj.*

bor·zoi (bôr′zoi) *n.* A rather large, slenderly built dog of a breed originating in Russia, having a narrow, pointed head and a silky, predominantly white coat. Also called "Russian wolfhound." [Russian *borzoi†,* "swift."]

bos·cage, bos·kage (bŏs′kĭj) *n.* A mass of trees or shrubs; a thicket. [Middle English *boskage,* from Old French *boscage,* from *bosc,* forest, from Germanic.]

Bosch (bŏs, bôs, bŏsh, bôsh), **Hieronymus** (c. 1450–1516). Flemish painter. He was strikingly original, producing surrealistically grotesque and allegorical canvases that have nothing in common with the prevailing Flemish style of the period.

Bosch (bŏsh, bôsh), **Karl** (1874–1940). German industrialist and chemist. He developed the Bosch process, but was more famous for his contribution to developing methods for the high-pressure synthesis of gases, especially ammonia. For this latter work he shared the Nobel Prize in chemistry with Friedrich Bergius (1884–1949).

Bosch process (bŏsh) *n.* A method of making hydrogen by the action of carbon monoxide on steam over a hot catalyst. [After K. BOSCH.]

Bose (bōs), **Sir Jagadis Chandra** (1858–1937). Indian physicist, plant physiologist, and founder of the Bose Research Institute in Calcutta. His most important work was in plant physiology. He was the inventor of an instrument used to measure the growth of plants.

Bose (bōs), **Satyenda Nath** (1894–1974). Indian physicist. In 1924 he was able to derive a radiation law for black bodies without using classical electrodynamics, as Max Planck had done. His work led to the **Bose-Einstein statistics.**

Bose-Ein·stein statistics (bōs′īn′shtīn, -stīn) *pl.n.* Quantum statistics concerning a system of identical bosons for which there can be any number of particles in the same quantum state simultaneously. [After S.N. BOSE and A. EINSTEIN.]

bosh (bŏsh) *n. Informal.* Meaningless talk or opinions; nonsense. [Turkish *boş,* empty, useless.]

bosk (bŏsk) *n.* A small wooded area or thicket. [Back-formation from BOSKY.]

bos·ky (bŏs′kē) *adj.* **1.** Covered with bushes, shrubs, or trees. **2.** Shaded by trees or bushes. [Middle English *bosk,* wooded, from *bosk, bush,* bush, from Old Norse *buskr.*] —**bos·ki·ness** *n.*

bo's'n. Variant of **boatswain.**

Bos·ni·a and Her·ce·go·vi·na (bŏz′nē-ə; hĕrt′sə-gō-vē′nə). Historic

Balkan provinces, joined in 1946 to form one of the constituent republics of Yugoslavia. They are situated in the Dinaric Alps in the west-central part of the country. Sarajevo, in Bosnia, is the capital.

Bos·ni·an (bŏz′nē-ən) *adj.* Also **Bos·ni·ac** (-nē-ăk′). Of or pertaining to Bosnia.

~*n.* Also **Bos·ni·ac.** **1.** A native of Bosnia. **2.** The Serbo-Croatian language of this people.

bos·om (bŏŏz′əm, bŏŏ′zəm) *n.* **1.** The chest of a human being; especially, the female breasts. **2.** The part of a garment covering the chest. **3.** The midst or heart: *"Deep in the bosom of the hills"* (George Eliot). **4.** A close enveloping relationship: *in the bosom of her family.* **5.** The chest considered as the source of feelings, hopes, and desires.

~*adj.* Beloved; intimate: *a bosom friend.* [Middle English *bosom,* Old English *bosom.*]

bos·om·y (bŏŏz′ə-mē, bŏŏ′zə-mē) *adj.* Having large breasts; busty.

bos·on (bō′sŏn) *n.* A particle, such as a photon, pion, or alpha particle, having zero or integral spin and obeying Bose-Einstein statistics. Compare **fermion.** [J.C. BOSE + -ON.]

Bos·po·rus (bŏs′pər-əs). The strait joining the Black Sea and the Sea of Marmara. Istanbul lies on its northern shore. Currents moving in opposite directions make the waters extremely turbulent.

boss¹ (bôs, bŏs) *n.* **1. a.** An employer or supervisor of workers; manager; foreman. **b.** A person who makes decisions or exercises authority. **2.** A professional politician who controls a party or political machine often by underhand or shady means.

~*v.* **bossed, bossing, bosses.** —*tr.* **1.** To supervise or control. **2.** To command in an arrogant or domineering manner. Often used with *around.* —*intr.* To be or act as a boss.

~*adj. Slang.* First-rate; topnotch. [Dutch *baas,* master, from Middle Dutch *baes,* from Germanic *basa-* (unattested).]

boss² *n.* **1.** A circular or knoblike protuberance, as on a shield. **2.** A raised area used as ornamentation. **3.** *Architecture.* A raised ornament, as at the intersection of the ribs in vaulted roofs. **4.** *Machinery.* **a.** An enlarged part of a shaft to which another shaft is coupled or to which a wheel or gear is keyed. **b.** A hub, especially of a propeller. **5.** A metal ornament used for protecting the corners or centers of books. **6.** *Geology.* An intrusive mound of igneous rock.

~*tr.v.* **bossed, bossing, bosses.** **1.** To decorate with bosses. **2.** To emboss. [Middle English *boce,* from Old French, from Vulgar Latin *bottia†* (unattested).]

boss³ (bôs, bŏs) *n.* A cow or calf. [Origin unknown.]

bossa nova (bŏs′ə nō′və) *n.* **1.** A rhythmic dance similar to the samba, originating in Brazil. **2. a.** A complex dance rhythm extending over two bars. **b.** A musical composition using this rhythm, as one written for the dance. [Portuguese, "new voice."]

bos·sism (bô′sĭz′əm, bŏs′ĭz′əm) *n.* The domination of a political organization by a political boss.

boss·y¹ (bô′sē, bŏs′ē) *adj.* **-ier, -iest.** Commanding, domineering, or overbearing. —**boss·i·ly** *adv.* —**boss·i·ness** *n.*

bossy² *adj.* Decorated with studs or similar raised ornaments.

bossy³ *n., pl.* **-sies.** *Informal.* A cow or calf. [From BOSS (cow).]

boss·y-boots (bô′sē-bŏŏts′, bŏs′ē-) *n. British Informal.* A bossy person.

Bos·ton¹ (bô′stən, bŏs′tən). Capital of Massachusetts, in the eastern part of the state on Boston Bay, an arm of the Atlantic Ocean. It played a prominent role in the developing opposition to colonial rule that led to the American Revolution. In the 19th century it was one of the centers of the movement to abolish slavery in the South. Today it is a major financial center and a leading port. Its industries include publishing, food processing, and the manufacture of machinery and electronic equipment. Tourism is also important to its economy.

Boston². Port in Lincolnshire in east-central England. Puritans sailed from Boston to Massachusetts Bay (1630) and gave the American settlement its name.

Boston bag *n.* A handbag or satchel for books and papers, with handles on both sides of the top opening.

Boston bull *n.* A dog, the **Boston terrier** *(see).*

Boston cream pie *n.* A cake with a custard filling.

Boston fern *n.* A fern, *Nephrolepis exaltata bostoniensis,* having arching or drooping fronds with opposite leaflets.

Boston ivy *n.* A widely cultivated climbing woody vine, *Parthenocissus tricuspidata,* native to Asia, that has three-lobed leaves and that frequently covers the outer walls of buildings. Also called "Japanese ivy."

Boston lettuce *n.* A type of cultivated lettuce forming a rounded head and having soft-textured, yellow-green leaves.

Boston rocker *n.* A 19th-century American wooden rocking chair with a curved seat, a high spindled back, and usually a headpiece with stenciled decorations.

Boston Tea Party *n.* A protest staged by American colonists in Boston (December 16, 1773) against the British tax on imported tea. The colonists, disguised as Indians, boarded British ships in Boston Harbor and threw chests of tea overboard.

Boston terrier *n.* A small dog of a breed that originated in New England as a cross between a bull terrier and a bulldog. Also called "Boston bull."

bosun. Variant of **boatswain.**

Bos·well (bŏz′wĕl′, -wəl) *n.* An assiduous and devoted admirer, student, and recorder of another's words and deeds. [After James Boswell.] —**Bos·wel·li·an** *adj.*

Boswell, James (1740–95). Scottish lawyer and author. He practiced law all his life, but his greatest interest was literature. His most famous work is the biography *The Life of Samuel Johnson* (1791).

Bos•worth Field (bŏz′wûrth′). Site of the final battle in the Wars of the Roses, near Leicester in central England, where Richard III, the last Plantagenet king, was defeated on August 22, 1485, by Henry Tudor.

bot, bott (bŏt) *n.* The parasitic larva of a botfly. [Middle English, probably of Low German origin; akin to Dutch *bot*†.]

bot. 1. botanical; botanist; botany. **2.** bottle.

bo•tan•i•cal (bə-tăn′ĭ-kəl) *adj.* Also **bo•tan•ic** (bə-tăn′ĭk). *Abbr.* **bot.** Of or pertaining to plants, plant life, or the science of botany.
~*n.* A drug, medicinal preparation, or similar substance obtained from a plant or plants. [French *botanique,* from Late Latin *botanicus,* from Greek *botanikos,* from *botanē*†, pasture, herb, plant.] **—bo•tan•i•cal•ly** *adv.*

botanical garden *n.* A place where plants are grown for scientific study and public exhibition, and at which herbaria and libraries are maintained.

botanical Latin *n.* An international language used by botanists to name and describe all new plant species.

bot•a•nist (bŏt′n-ĭst) *n. Abbr.* **bot.** One who specializes in the study of plants.

bot•a•nize (bŏt′n-īz′) *v.* **-nized, -nizing, -nizes.** —*intr.* **1.** To secure plants for botanical study. **2.** To examine plants scientifically. —*tr.* To investigate (an area) for botanical study. **—bot•a•niz•er** *n.*

bot•a•ny (bŏt′n-ē) *n., pl.* **-nies.** *Abbr.* **bot. 1.** The study of plants, covering their classification, form, function, ecology, and economic importance. **2.** The plant life of a particular area or period. **3.** The characteristics of a plant group: *the botany of grasses.* **4.** A particular system of botany: *the botany of Linnaeus.* [From BOTANICAL.]

Bot•a•ny Bay (bŏt′n-ē). Inlet of the Tasman Sea, just south of Sydney in Australia. It was visited by Capt. James Cook (1770) and given its name by Sir Joseph Banks, the botanist in Cook's crew, for the variety of new flora he found on its shores.

Botany wool *n.* The wool of the merino sheep. [After BOTANY BAY.]

bo•tar•go (bə-târ′gō) *n.* A relish made from the roe of tuna or mullet. [From Italian *bottarga* (obsolete), from Egyptian Arabic *batārikh,* roe, from Coptic.]

botch (bŏch) *tr.v.* **botched, botching, botches. 1.** To ruin through clumsiness. Often used with *up.* **2.** To make or perform clumsily; bungle. **3.** To repair or mend clumsily.
~*n.* A ruined or defective piece of work: *"I have made a miserable botch of this description"* (Nathaniel Hawthorne). [Middle English *bocchen*†, to patch up, mend.] **—botch•er** *n.*

botch•y (bŏch′ē) *adj.* **-ier, -iest.** Carelessly or clumsily done or made; imperfect. **—botch•i•ly** *adv.*

bot•fly (bŏt′flī′) *n., pl.* **-flies.** Also **bot fly.** Any of various winged insects, chiefly of the families Gasterophilidae, Oestridae, and Cuterebridae, having larvae that are parasitic on man, livestock, rodents, and other animals. See **bots.**

both (bōth) *adj.* One and the other; two in conjunction: *Both boys arrived.*
~*pron.* The one and the other: *Both are patriots.*
~*conj.* Used with *and* to show that each of two coordinated words or things in coordinated phrases or clauses is included: *both Keats and Shelley.* [Middle English *bothe, bathe,* from Old Norse *bāthir.*]

Bo•tha (bō′tə), **Louis** (1862–1919). South African general in the Second Anglo-Boer War and first prime minister of the Union of South Africa after its establishment in 1910.

Botha, Pieter Willem (1916–). Prime minister of the Republic of South Africa since September 1978.

both•er (bŏ*th*′ər) *v.* **-ered, -ering, -ers.** —*tr.* **1.** To irritate, particularly by small annoyances; pester; harass. **2. a.** To make agitated or nervous; fluster. **b.** To make confused or perplexed; bewilder; puzzle. **3.** To disturb, as by asking questions or by intrusion. **4.** To give trouble to: *a back condition that bothers him constantly.* —*intr.* To trouble or concern oneself. —See Synonyms at **annoy.**
~*n.* **1.** A cause or state of disturbance or confusion. **2.** A person or thing that causes annoyance or disturbance. **3.** *British Slang.* Aggressive behavior or disturbance.
~*interj. Chiefly British.* Used to express mild irritation. [18th century : Anglo-Irish, perhaps akin to POTHER.]

both•er•a•tion (bŏ*th*′ə-rā′shən) *n.* Irritation; vexation; bother.
~*interj.* Used to express irritation.

both•er•some (bŏ*th*′ər-səm) *adj.* Causing vexation or irritation; troublesome.

Both•ni•a, Gulf of (bŏth′nē-ə). The northernmost arm of the Baltic Sea, lying between Sweden and Finland and separated from the Baltic by the Ahvenanmaa. The gulf is 725 kilometers (450 miles) long and is ice-covered for five months of the year.

Both•well (bŏth′wəl), **James Hepburn, 4th Earl of** (*c.* 1536–78). Scottish courtier, the third husband of Mary, Queen of Scots. He helped suppress the rebellion led by the Earl of Moray (1565) and became the adviser and confidant of the queen. In 1567 he was acquitted of the murder of her husband, Lord Darnley. He was forced to flee to Denmark soon after his own marriage to Mary.

both•y (bŏ*th*′ē, bŏth′-) *n., pl.* **bothies.** *Scottish.* A hut or other shelter, used by people, especially shepherds, working outdoors. [18th century : perhaps akin to BOOTH.]

bo tree (bō) *n.* An Asiatic tree, the **peepul** *(see).* According to Buddhist tradition, this is the tree under which the Buddha attained enlightenment. [Singhalese *bo,* from Pali *bodhi(taru),* "(tree of) wisdom," from Sanskrit *bodhi,* wisdom, enlightenment, from *bodhati,* he awakes.]

bot•ry•oi•dal (bŏt′rē-oid′l) *adj.* Also **bot•ry•oid** (bŏt′rē-oid′). Formed like a bunch of grapes. Said especially of minerals. [Greek *botruoeidēs* : *botrus*†, bunch of grapes + -OID.] **—bot•ry•oi•dal•ly** *adv.*

bots (bŏts) *n. Used with a singular or plural verb.* A disease of horses and cattle caused by infestation of the intestines with botfly larvae.

Bot•swa•na (bŏt-swä′nə). Formerly **Bech•u•a•na•land** (bĕch′wän′-ə-lănd′, bĕch′ə-). Republic in southern Africa between Namibia in the west and Zimbabwe in the east, north of South Africa. It was named Botswana when it gained independence (1966). The country is a high tableland, mostly covered by arid desert sands. Cattle breeding is the chief economic activity, but important reserves of nickel, copper, diamonds, and coal were discovered in the 1960's. Area, 600,372 square kilometers (231,805 square miles). Population, 800,000. Capital, Gaborone. See map, next page.

bott. Variant of **bot.**

botte (bŏt) *n.* In fencing, a hit with the sword. [French, "hit."]

Bot•ti•cel•li (bŏt′ĭ-chĕl′ē), **Alessandro di Mariano di Vanni Filipepi,** known as "Sandro" (*c.* 1444–1510). Italian painter of the Florentine Renaissance. His flowing draftmanship is seen to advantage in his two best-known paintings, *Primavera* and the *Birth of Venus.*

bot•tle (bŏt′l) *n. Abbr.* **bot., btl. 1.** A receptacle, usually glass, having a narrow neck and mouth that can be plugged, corked, or capped. **2.** The quantity a bottle contains. In the case of wine bottles, this is usually between 70 and 75 centiliters. **3. a.** A bottle filled with milk or other liquid and used to feed a baby. **b.** Intoxicating drink: *took to the bottle.* **4.** *Physics.* A configuration of magnetic fields used to confine a plasma in a fusion reactor.
~*tr.v.* **bottled, -tling, -tles.** To place in a bottle. **—bottle up. 1.** To hold in; restrain: *bottled up her emotions.* **2.** To seal up; block. **—hit the bottle.** *Slang.* To drink alcoholic liquor to excess. [Middle English *botel,* from Old French *botele, botaille,* from Medieval Latin *butticula,* diminutive of Late Latin *buttis,* cask, BUTT.] **—bot•tler** *n.*

bot•tle•brush (bŏt′l-brŭsh′) *n.* **1.** Any of various shrubs or trees of the genera *Callistemon* and *Melaleuca,* native to Australia. They have dense spikes of red flowers with protruding stamens that suggest a brush used to clean bottles. **2.** Any of various similar plants of the genus *Greyia,* native to southern Africa.

bottle club *n.* A private establishment where patrons may purchase bottles of liquor and keep them for consumption after legal closing hours.

bottled gas *n.* Gas, such as butane or propane, stored under pressure in portable tanks.

bottle-feed (bŏt′l-fēd′) *tr.v.* **-fed** (-fĕd), **-feeding, -feeds.** To feed (a baby) from a bottle rather than from the breast.

bottle gentian *n.* A plant, *Gentiana andrewsii,* of eastern and central North America, having deep-blue flowers that remain closed. Also called "closed gentian."

bottle gourd *n.* A vine, the **calabash** *(see),* or its fruit.

bottle green *n.* Dark bluish green. **—bot•tle-green** *adj.*

bot•tle•neck (bŏt′l-nĕk) *n.* **1.** The narrow part of a bottle near the top. **2. a.** A point on a road where traffic is held up because of an obstruction or narrow section. **b.** The hold-up so caused. **3. a.** Part of a process which is slower than other parts and delays the entire process. **b.** The delay caused. **4.** *Music.* A style of playing the guitar, especially in blues and country-and-western music, with a hollow metal cylinder which is held around the finger and slid along the strings.
~*tr.v.* **bottlenecked, -necking, -necks.** To impede or slow down by creating a bottleneck.

bot•tle-nosed dolphin (bŏt′l-nōzd′) *n.* Any of several marine mammals of the genus *Tursiops,* having a short, protruding beak. Also called "bottlenose."

bottle tree *n.* Any of several trees of the genus *Brachychiton,* native to Australia, characterized by a bottlelike swelling of the trunk.

bot•tom (bŏt′əm) *n.* **1. a.** The lowest or deepest part of anything. **b.** The far end of something. **c.** The last place, as on a list. **d.** The worst or least favorable point: *started life at the bottom.* **2.** The underside. **3.** The supporting part of something; a foundation; base. **4.** The basic underlying cause or origin: *to find out what's at the bottom of the dispute.* **5.** The land below a body of water: *a river bottom.* **6.** *Often* **bottoms.** Low-lying alluvial land adjacent to a river; bottom land. **7. a.** *Nautical.* The part of a ship's hull below the water line. **b.** A ship: *"English merchants did much of their overseas trade in foreign bottoms"* (G.M. Trevelyan). **8. bottoms.** The trousers of pajamas. **9.** *Informal.* The buttocks. **10.** The seat of a chair. **11.** Staying power, as of a horse; stamina.
~*adj.* Lowest; undermost; fundamental.
~*v.* **bottomed, -toming, -toms.** —*tr.* **1.** To provide with an underside or foundation. **2.** To provide (a chair) with a bottom. **3.** To establish on a foundation or basis; ground; found. Used with *on* or *upon*: *The theory is bottomed on questionable assumptions.* **4.** To grasp the meaning of; fathom: *bottom a mystery.* —*intr.* To rest on or touch the bottom: *The submarine bottomed on the ocean floor.* **—at bottom.** Basically; actually. **—bottom out.** To descend to the lowest point possible, after which only a rise may occur: *Coffee bottomed out in the market.* **—bottoms up.** *Informal.* Drain your glass. [Middle English *botme,* Old English *botm,* from Germanic.] **—bot•tom•er** *n.*

botfly *A type of fly that bears some resemblance to a bee. The botfly often lays its eggs on horses' legs. When the horse licks the spot, the eggs are swallowed and later hatch into parasitic larvae inside the horse's stomach. The full-grown larvae, or maggots, eventually pass out in the animal's manure and undergo the transformation to adults in the soil.*

bottle-nosed dolphin *Dolphins—members of the air-breathing whale family—were once land mammals but readapted to life in the sea. Among the world's most intelligent animals, they communicate by using a vocabulary of grunts, squeaks, and whistles produced by forcing air past valves and flaps in their breathing holes.*

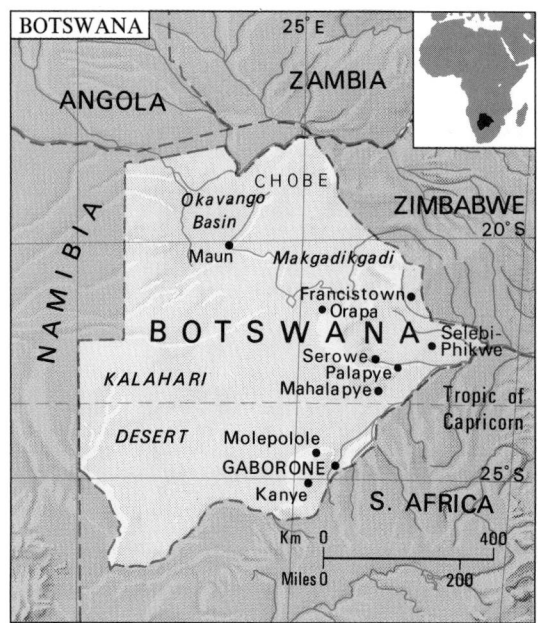

BOTSWANA   25° E

ANGOLA   ZAMBIA

NAMIBIA

CHOBE
Okavango
Basin   ZIMBABWE
20° S
Maun   Makgadikgadi
Francistown
Orapa
BOTSWANA   Selebi-
Phikwe
KALAHARI   Serowe
Palapye
Mahalapye   Tropic of
Capricorn
DESERT   Molepolole
GABORONE   25° S
Kanye   S. AFRICA

Km 0   400
Miles 0   200

bottom break *n.* A branch arising from the stem base of a plant.
bottom drawer *n. British.* A hope chest (*see*).
bottom fauna *n.* Marine vegetation growing in the benthic region of the ocean depths.
bottom land *n.* Low land along a river.
bot·tom·less (bŏt′əm-lĭs) *adj.* 1. Having no bottom. 2. Too deep to be measured. 3. Difficult or impossible to understand; unfathomable. 4. Having no limit; limitless. —**bot·tom·less·ly** *adv.*
bottom line *n.* 1. The lowest line in a financial statement, showing net income or loss. 2. The results or basic implications of anything. 3. The main or essential point.
bot·tom-line (bŏt′əm-līn′) *adj.* Concerned exclusively with costs and profits.
bot·tom·most (bŏt′əm-mōst′) *adj.* Deepest; most profound.
bottom round *n.* A cut of meat, as a steak or roast, taken from the outer section of a round of beef.
bot·tom·ry (bŏt′əm-rē) *n.* A contract by which a shipowner borrows money to finance a voyage, pledging the vessel as security. [BOTTOM (a ship) + -RY, by analogy with Dutch *bodemerij.*]
bot·u·lin (bŏch′ōō-lĭn) *n.* Any of several nerve toxins produced by the bacterium *Clostridium botulinum* and found in improperly canned or improperly smoked foods. [New Latin *botulinus,* from Latin *botulus,* sausage.]
bot·u·li·num (bŏch′ə-lī′nəm) *n.* A bacterium, *Clostridium botulinum,* that secretes botulin. [New Latin, from Latin *botulus,* sausage.]
bot·u·lism (bŏch′ō-lĭz′əm) *n.* An often fatal food poisoning caused by botulin and characterized by vomiting, abdominal pain, coughing, muscular weakness, and visual disturbance. [German *Botulismus,* "sausage-poisoning," from Latin *botulus,* sausage.]
bou·chée (bōō-shā′) *n.* A puff pastry case usually with a creamed filling. [French, "mouthful."]
Bou·cher (bōō-shā′), **François** (1703-70). French painter. He was an outstanding representative of the rococo style of the 18th century, noted for his tapestries and *fêtes galantes.*
bou·clé (bōō-klā′) *n.* 1. A type of yarn, usually three-ply and having one thread looser than the others, which produces a rough-textured cloth. 2. Fabric woven or knitted from this yarn. [French, "curled."]
Bou·dic·ca (bōō-dĭk′ə). Also **Bo·a·di·ce·a** (bō-ăd′ə-sē′ə) (died A.D. 60). Queen of the Iceni people of eastern Britain. When her husband, King Prasutagus, died in 59 or 60, she led the **Iceni** of what is now Norfolk and Suffolk in a fierce and temporarily successful onslaught against the Romans who had seized her late husband's kingdom.
bou·doir (bōō′dwär′, -dwôr′) *n.* A woman's private sitting room, dressing room, or bedroom. [French, "place for pouting," from Old French *bouder,* to pout, sulk (imitative).]
bouf·fant (bōō-fänt′) *adj.* Puffed-out; full: *a bouffant hair style.* [French, present participle of *bouffer,* to swell, puff up (the cheeks), from Old French (imitative).]
bouffe (bōōf) *n.* Comic opera. See opera buffa.
Bou·gain·ville (bōō′gən-vĭl′). Volcanic island in the South Pacific Ocean, the largest of the Solomon Islands. It forms part of Papua New Guinea.
Bougainville, Louis Antoine de (1729-1811). French navigator and explorer. In c. 1764 he established a short-lived French colony on the Falkland Islands and in 1766-69 made a voyage around the world with a crew that included astronomers and naturalists.
bou·gain·vil·le·a, bou·gain·vil·lae·a (bōō′gən-vĭl′ē-ə, -vĭl′yə) *n.* Any of several woody tropical American vines of the genus *Bougainvillea,* having inconspicuous flowers surrounded by showy red,

purple, or orange bracts. [After Louis Antoine de BOUGAINVILLE.]
bough (bou) *n.* A large branch of a tree. [Middle English *bow, bough,* Old English *bōg, bōh,* from Germanic.]
bought. Past tense and past participle of **buy.**
bought·en. *Regional.* A past participle of **buy.**
bou·gie (bōō′zhē, -jē) *n.* 1. A wax candle. 2. *Medicine.* **a.** A slender, pliable implement inserted into a bodily canal, such as the urethra or rectum, to dilate the passageway. **b.** A suppository. [French, from Old French, a fine wax imported from *Bougie* (Arabic *Bujiya*), town in Algeria.]
bouil·la·baisse (bōō′yə-bās′) *n.* A highly seasoned fish stew made with several kinds of fish and shellfish. [French, earlier *bouilleabaisse,* from Provençal *bouiabaisso,* "boil (and) settle" (jocular command to the pot, because the fish is rapidly cooked).]
bouil·lon (bōō′yŏn′, bōōl′yŏn′, -yən) *n.* The stock, often served as a broth, made from the liquid in which beef or chicken is simmered. [French, from Old French, from *boulir,* to boil, from Latin *bullīre.*]
bouillon cube *n.* A small cube of evaporated seasoned meat, poultry, or vegetable stock.
boul. boulevard.
Bou·lan·ger (bōō-län-zhā′), **Georges Ernest Jean Marie** (1837-91). French general and politician. After the Franco-Prussian War he rallied the extreme right wing in France against Germany for the loss of Alsace-Lorraine. For a time he was the most popular French politician, but was dismissed from the government and the army (1887) by republicans who viewed him as a potential military dictator.
Boulanger, Nadia (1887-1979). French teacher of musical composition. She taught and influenced several generations of modern composers, including Milhaud, Copland, and Elliott Carter.
boul·der, bowl·der (bōl′dər) *n.* A large rounded mass of rock lying on the surface of the ground, or sometimes embedded in the soil, and generally different in composition from other rocks in the immediate vicinity. [Middle English *bulder (ston),* from Scandinavian, akin to dialectal Swedish *bullersten,* stone in a stream : *buller-,* "rounded object."]
boulder clay *n.* An unstratified clay deposited by glaciers and ice sheets. Also called "till."
Boulder Dam. See Hoover Dam.
bou·le[1] (bōō′lē, bōō-lā′) *n.* 1. **a.** Boule. The senate of 400 members founded in ancient Athens by Solon. **b.** A legislative assembly in any of the states of ancient Greece. 2. Boule. The lower house of the modern Greek legislature. [Greek *boulē,* "will," "council."]
bou·le[2] (bōōl) *n.* A pear-shaped synthetic sapphire, ruby, or other alumina-based gem, produced by fusing and tinting alumina. [French, "ball," from Latin *bulla,* bubble, ball.]
boule[3]. Variant of **buhl.**
boules (bōōl) *n. Used with a singular verb.* A version of bowling played in France with metal balls on a hard surface. [French, "bowls."]
boul·e·vard (bōōl′ə-värd′, bōō′lə-) *n. Abbr.* **blvd., boul.** A broad city street, often tree-lined and landscaped. [French, from Old French *boloart, belouart,* rampart, promenade converted from an old rampart, from Middle Dutch *bolwerc,* from Middle High German, BULWARK.]
bou·le·var·dier (bōō′lə-vär-dyā′, bōōl′ə-vär-dîr′) *n.* A man-about-town. [French, a man who frequents boulevards, from BOULEVARD.]
bou·le·ver·se·ment (bōō′lə-vĕr′sə-mäN′) *n.* 1. A reversal. 2. A violent uproar; tumult. [French, from Old French *bouleverser,* to overturn : *boule,* ball + *verser,* to overturn, from Latin *versare,* to turn.]
Bou·lez (bōō-lĕz′), **Pierre** (1925-). French composer and conductor. He is a leading composer of the French avant garde, in particular as an adherent of 12-tone atonality. His best-known works are *Le Marteau sans Maître* (1955) and *Pli selon Pli* (1960).
boulle. Variant of **buhl.**
Bou·logne(-sur-Mer) (bōō-lōn′sür-mâr′, -loin′-). Port and resort in Pas-de-Calais department in northwest France, on the English Channel. It has grown from its Celtic origins to be the leading fishing port in France.
Boult (bōlt), **Sir Adrian Cedric** (1889-1983). British orchestral conductor. In 1930 he became conductor of the new BBC Symphony Orchestra, with whom he stayed until 1950, when he became musical director of the London Philharmonic.
Bou·mé·di·enne (bōō-mā-dē-ĕn′), **Houari** (1928-78). Algerian independence leader and politician. He studied in Cairo in the early 1950's, then returned secretly to Algeria in 1955 to take part in guerrilla action against the French. He was head of the National Liberation Army operating from Tunisia (1960-67), and when Algeria gained its independence he served under Ahmed Ben Bella as minister of defense. He directed an army coup that overthrew Ben Bella (1965) and assumed the presidency of Algeria.
bounce (bouns) *v.* **bounced, bouncing, bounces.** —*intr.* 1. **a.** To rebound elastically from an impact, as a rubber ball. **b.** To collide and rebound elastically several times in succession. 2. To walk or move in a springy or excited way: *The child bounced into the room.* 3. *Informal.* To be sent back by a bank as valueless: *The check bounced.* 4. *Informal.* To recover after a setback. Used with *back.* —*tr.* 1. To cause (a body, such as a ball) to collide and rebound. 2. To cause to rebound repeatedly. 3. *Slang.* To expel by force. 4. *Slang.* To dismiss from employment.
~*n.* 1. A bound or rebound. 2. A sudden spring or leap. 3. **a.** A loud or heavy blow or thump. **b.** *Archaic.* The sound of an explo-

sion: *"He speaks plain cannon fire, and smoke and bounce"* (Shakespeare). **4.** Capacity to bounce; spring: *A ball with bounce.* **5.** Spirit; liveliness. **6.** *Slang.* Expulsion; dismissal. **7.** *British.* An instance of impudent bluff: *"The whole story is a bounce of his own"* (Thomas De Quincey). [Middle English *bunsen, bonchen,* to beat, thrust, stamp (probably imitative).]

bounc·er (boun'sər) *n.* **1.** One that bounces. **2.** A person employed to expel disorderly people from a public place.

bounc·ing (boun'sĭng) *adj.* **1.** Vigorous; healthy: *a bouncing baby.* **2.** Spirited; lively.

bouncing Bet *n.* A plant, the **soapwort** *(see).* [*Bet,* pet form of *Elizabeth* (from its flower clusters, suggesting bouncing girls).]

bounc·y (boun'sē) *adj.* **-ier, -iest. 1. a.** Characterized by a capacity to bound or spring. **b.** Elastic; springy. **2.** Having vigor and buoyancy; lively. **—bounc·i·ly** *adv.*

bound¹ (bound) *intr.v.* **bounded, bounding, bounds. 1.** To leap forward or upward; spring. **2.** To progress quickly by bounds. ~*n.* **1.** A leap; jump. **2.** A bounce. [French *bondir,* to bounce, originally "to rebound," from Old French, to resound, from Vulgar Latin *bombitīre* (unattested), to hum, buzz, from Latin *bombīre,* to buzz, from *bombus,* a deep hollow sound, buzz, from Greek *bombos.*]

bound² *n.* **1.** *Usually* **bounds.** Boundary; limit: *His joy knew no bounds.* **2. bounds.** The territory on, within, or near limiting lines: *the bounds of the kingdom.* **—See Synonyms at boundary. —out of bounds. 1.** In an area outside official boundaries. **2.** Transgressing moral or conventional limits. ~*v.* **bounded, bounding, bounds.** *—tr.* **1.** To set a limit to. **2.** To constitute the boundary or limit of. **3.** To identify and set the boundaries of; demarcate. *—intr.* To border on another country, state, or place; adjoin. **—See Synonyms at limit.** [Middle English *bounde,* from Old French *bunde,* from Medieval Latin *bodina,* from Gaulish *bodina†* (unattested).]

bound³. Past tense and past participle of **bind.** ~*adj.* **1. a.** Confined by bonds; tied. **b.** Restricted; obstructed. Often used in combination: *snowbound.* **2.** Under legal or moral obligation; under contract: *bound by his promise.* **3.** Indentured: *a bound apprentice.* **4.** *Abbr.* **bd.** Encased in a cover or binding: *bound volumes.* **5.** Predetermined; certain: *We are bound to be late.* **6.** Constipated. **—bound up in.** Wholly dedicated to: *She is bound up in her career.*

bound⁴ *adj.* **1.** Heading for; going toward: *bound for Sydney.* Often used after an expression of direction: *outward bound; homeward bound.* **2.** Intended for; on one's way to: *bound for a career in medicine.* [Middle English *boun,* prepared, ready to go, from Old Norse *būinn,* past participle of *būa,* to dwell, prepare.]

bound·a·ry (boun'drē, -də-rē) *n., pl.* **-ries. 1.** Something that indicates a border or limit. **2.** The border or limit so indicated. [From dialect *bounder,* from BOUND (limit).]

Synonyms: *border, bound, confine, end, frontier, limit.*

boundary layer *n. Physics.* The nearly motionless fluid layer found immediately adjacent to the surface of a solid, past which the fluid flows.

boundary rider *n. Australian.* A person employed to ride around the boundary of a sheep or cattle ranch and maintain the fences.

bound·en (boun'dən) *adj.* **1.** Obligatory: *his bounden duty.* **2.** *Archaic.* Under obligation; obliged. [From *bounden,* obsolete past participle of BIND.]

bound·er (boun'dər) *n.* **1.** One that bounds. **2.** *Chiefly British Informal.* A man who fails to behave like a gentleman.

bound form *n.* A linguistic element that always occurs as part of another word, as *-ly* in *lovely.* Compare **free form.**

bound·less (bound'lĭs) *adj.* Without limit; infinite. **—See Synonyms at infinite. —bound·less·ly** *adv.* **—bound·less·ness** *n.*

boun·te·ous (boun'tē-əs) *adj.* **1.** Giving generously and kindly. **2.** Copious; plentiful. [Middle English *bountevous, bounteuous,* from Old French *bontif, bontive,* benevolent, from *bonte,* BOUNTY.] **—boun·te·ous·ly** *adv.* **—boun·te·ous·ness** *n.*

boun·ti·ful (boun'tĭ-fəl) *adj.* **1.** Generous. **2.** Abundant; plentiful. **—boun·ti·ful·ly** *adv.* **—boun·ti·ful·ness** *n.*

boun·ty (boun'tē) *n., pl.* **-ties. 1.** Liberality in giving. **2.** Something that is given liberally. **3.** A reward, inducement, or payment, especially one given by a government for acts beneficial to the state, such as killing predatory animals or enlisting for military service. **—See Synonyms at bonus.** [Middle English *bounte,* from Old French *bonté,* from Latin *bonitās* (stem *bonitāt-*), goodness, from *bonus,* good.]

bounty hunter *n.* One who hunts predatory animals or criminals and outlaws for a bounty.

bou·quet (bō-kā', boō-for sense 1; boō-kā' for sense 2) *n.* **1.** A cluster of flowers; a nosegay. **2.** The fragrance typical of a wine or a liqueur. **3.** A compliment; praise. **—See Synonyms at smell.** [French, from Old North French *bosquet,* clump, diminutive of Old French *bosc,* forest, from Germanic.]

bou·quet gar·ni (bō-kā' gär-nē', boō-) *n., pl.* **bouquets garnis** (bō-kāz'gär-nē', boō-). A bunch of herbs tied together or wrapped in cheesecloth, immersed in a soup, stew, or the like as seasoning. [French, "garnished bouquet."]

bour·bon (bûr'bən) *n.* A whiskey distilled from a fermented mash containing not less than 51 percent corn. [After *Bourbon* County, Kentucky.]

Bour·bons (boor'bənz). Members of the French royal line descending from Louis I, Duke of Bourbon (c. 1270-1342). They make up one of the most powerful ruling houses in modern European history. The first Bourbon king of France was Henry IV, and the line occupied the French throne until 1793 (when the French monarchy was abolished); it was briefly restored in 1814 and ruled again until the overthrow of Charles X in the July Revolution of 1830. The Bourbons have been kings of Spain since 1700, and another branch of the family ruled in Naples and Sicily from 1734 until 1860.

bour·don (boor'dən) *n.* **1.** The monotonic drone bass of a bagpipe. **2.** An organ stop, commonly of the 16-foot pipes. [Middle English *burdoun,* from Old French *bourdon,* drone, from Vulgar Latin *burdō* (stem *burdon-*) (unattested), of imitative origin.]

Bourdon gauge *n.* A type of pressure gauge having a narrow spiral tube attached to a pointer and closed at one end, which tends to uncoil as the pressure in the tube increases. [After Eugène *Bourdon* (1808-84), French inventor.]

bourg (boorg; *French* boor) *n.* **1.** A French medieval village, especially one situated near a castle. **2.** A French market town. [Middle English, fortified town, from Old French, from Late Latin *burgus.*]

bour·geois¹ (boor-zhwä', boor'zhwä') *n., pl.* **bourgeois. 1.** One belonging to the bourgeoisie. **2.** The middle classes; the bourgeoisie. **3.** One whose attitudes and behavior are marked by conformity to the standards and conventions of the middle class. **4.** In Marxist theory, a member of the property-owning class; a capitalist, as opposed to a member of the proletariat. ~*adj.* **1.** Of or typical of the middle class. Often used derogatorily to suggest such qualities as mediocrity or a preoccupation with respectability and material values. **2.** In Marxist theory, of, pertaining to, or dominated by the property-owning class. [French, from Old French *burgeis,* from *bourg,* fortified town, BOURG.]

bour·geois² (bər-jois') *n. Printing.* A size of type, approximately 9-point. [French, middle class, perhaps from its middling size between long primer and brevier.]

bour·geoise (boor-zhwäz', boor'zhwäz') *n., pl.* **-geoises** (-zhwä'zĭz). A female member of the bourgeoisie. **—bour·geoise** *adj.*

bour·geoi·sie (boor'zhwä-zē') *n.* **1.** The middle classes. **2.** In Marxist theory, the social group opposed to the proletariat in the class struggle; the capitalist class. [French.]

bour·geoi·si·fy (boor-zhwä'sə-fī) *tr. v.* **-fied, -fying, fies.** To turn (a member of the working class) into a member of the bourgeoisie; impart bourgeois values to. **—bour·geoi·si·fi·ca·tion** *n.*

bourgeon. Variant of **burgeon.**

Bourgogne. See **Burgundy** (region).

Bour·gui·ba (boor-gē'bə), **Habib ben Ali** (1903-). Tunisian politician. His political career began in the 1930's, when he formed a nationalist party opposed to French rule and was several times imprisoned. He was finally released (1954) to take part in the pre-independence negotiations and was elected prime minister of independent Tunisia (1956). He became president (1957) and was re-elected several times before being voted president for life (1975).

Bourke-White (bûrk'hwīt'), **Margaret** (1906-71). U.S. photographer and author. Her many photographic books and essays explored such diverse subjects as the rural South, Soviet life, and the emancipation of concentration camp victims. She was an editor of *Life* magazine for 33 years.

bourn¹, bourne (bôrn, bōrn, boōrn) *n.* A stream or small brook. [Middle English *burne,* variant of *burn,* BURN (brook).]

bourn², bourne *n. Archaic.* **1.** The terminal point of a journey or course of action; a goal. **2.** A boundary, as between properties. [French *borne,* from Old French, BOUND (limit).]

Bourne·mouth (bôrn'məth, bōrn'-, boōrn'-). Resort town on England's southern coast, at the eastern border of Dorset. Until 1974 it was in Hampshire.

bour·rée (boo-rā', boō-) *n.* **1.** An old French dance resembling the gavotte, and usually in quick duple time beginning with an upbeat. **2.** The music for this dance. [French, "faggot" (probably from its rude movements), from *bourrer,* to stuff, from Old French *bourre,* stuffing, fluff, from Late Latin *burra,* shaggy garment.]

Bourse (boors) *n.* The stock exchange of a city of continental Europe, especially Paris. [French, "purse," from Late Latin *bursa,* from Greek.]

bour·sin (boor-săn', boōr'săn) *n.* A soft, creamy French cheese, flavored with herbs and garlic or peppercorns.

bouse (bouz) *v.* **boused, bousing, bouses.** Also **bowse.** *Nautical.* *—tr.* To hoist or pull up with a tackle. *—intr.* To hoist. [16th century : origin obscure.]

bou·stro·phe·don (boō'strə-fēd'n, -fē'dŏn) *n.* An ancient method of writing in which the lines are inscribed alternately from right to left and from left to right. [Greek *boustrophēdon,* turning like an ox (while ploughing) : *bous,* ox + *strephein,* to turn.] **—bou·stroph·e·don·ic** (boō-strŏf'ə-dŏn'ĭk) *adj.*

bout (bout) *n.* **1.** A contest between antagonists; a match: *a wrestling bout.* **2.** A period of time spent in a particular way or state; a spell: *bouts of depression and drinking.* [Earlier *bought,* a turn (as in ploughing), Middle English *bought,* bend, turn, from Middle Low German *bucht.*]

bou·tique (boō-tēk') *n.* A small retail shop that specializes in gifts, fashionable clothes, or accessories. [French, from Old Provençal *botica,* from Greek *apothēkē,* storeroom, from *apotithenai,* to put away : *apo-,* away + *tithenai,* to place, put.]

bou·ton (boō-tôn') *n.* A club-shaped enlargement at the end of a nerve fiber. [Fr., button.]

bou·ton·niere, bou·ton·nière (boō'tə-nîr', -tən-yâr') *n.* A flower or

bowerbird *The bowerbird gets its name from the unusual courtship behavior of the male. It attracts a mate by building a bower and adorning it with brightly colored shells, flowers, and feathers.*

bowline knot *A bowline forms a loop that cannot close.*

small bunch of flowers worn in a buttonhole, usually on a lapel. [French.]

bou·var·di·a (bōō-vär′dē-ə) *n.* Any of several tropical American shrubs of the genus *Bouvardia,* having clusters of white or red, often fragrant flowers. [New Latin *Bouvardia;* after Charles *Bouvard* (died 1658), French physician.]

Bou·vier des Flan·dres (bōō-vyā′ də flän′dərz; *French* bōō-vyā′ dä flän′dr′) *pl.* **Bouviers des Flandres** (*pronounced as singular*). A rough-coated dog of a breed originally used in Belgium for herding and guarding cattle. [French, "cowherd of Flanders."]

bou·zou·ki (bōō-zōō′kē, bə-) *n.* A Greek fretted string instrument resembling the mandolin. [Modern Greek *mpouzouki,* perhaps from Turkish *büyük,* large.]

Bo·vet (bō-vā′), **Daniel** (1907–). Italian pharmacologist, born in Switzerland. For his discovery of gallamine and development of antihistamines, sulfa drugs, and other muscle relaxants used in surgery, he was awarded the Nobel Prize for medicine (1957).

bo·vid (bō′vĭd) *adj.* Of or belonging to the family Bovidae, which includes hoofed, hollow-horned ruminants such as cattle, sheep, goats, and buffaloes.
~*n.* A member of the Bovidae. [New Latin *Bovidae,* from Latin *bōs* (stem *bov-*), ox, cow.]

bo·vine (bō′vīn′, -vēn′) *adj.* **1.** Of, pertaining to, or resembling an ox, cow, or other ruminant animal of the genus *Bos.* **2.** Sluggish; dull; stolid.
~*n.* A bovine animal. [Late Latin *bovīnus,* from Latin *bōs* (stem *bov-*), ox, cow.]

bow¹ (bou) *n.* **1.** The front section of a ship or boat. **2.** The oar or oarsman closest to the bow of a boat.
~*adj.* Of or close to the bow. [Middle English, from Middle Low German *boog.*]

bow² (bou) *v.* **bowed, bowing, bows.** —*intr.* **1.** To bend or curve downward; stoop. **2.** To incline the body or head or bend the knee in greeting, consent, courtesy, acknowledgment, submission, or veneration. **3.** To yield or comply; defer: *I bow to your superior knowledge.* —*tr.* **1.** To bend (the head, knee, or body) in order to express greeting, consent, courtesy, submission, or veneration. **2.** To convey (greeting or consent, for example) by bowing. **3.** To escort deferentially and with bows: *He bowed us into the restaurant.* **4.** To cause to acquiesce or submit. **5.** To oppress; overburden. Often used with *down: Grief bowed him down.* —See Synonyms at **yield.** —**bow and scrape.** To behave in an obsequious manner. —**bow out.** To remove oneself from a situation or agreement.
~*n.* An inclination of the head or body, as in greeting, consent, courtesy, acknowledgment, submission, or veneration. —**make one's bow.** To enter or retire formally. —**take a bow.** To recognize and accept applause or an introduction. [Middle English *bowen,* Old English *būgan.*]

bow³ (bō) *n.* **1.** Something that is bent, curved, or arched: *a bow in a road.* **2.** A weapon consisting of a curved rod of a resilient material, especially wood, held tightly in an arch by a taut bowstring strung from end to end and used to propel arrows. **3.** An archer, or archers collectively. **4.** A rod having horsehair drawn tightly between its two raised ends, used in playing instruments such as the violin, cello, or viola. **5. a.** A knot usually having two loops and two ends; a bowknot. **b.** This knot made with ribbon or braid and used to decorate the hair, clothing, or the like. **6.** The loop forming the handle of a pair of scissors or large key. **7. a.** A frame for the lenses of a pair of eye glasses. **b.** The part of such a frame passing over the ear. **8.** A rainbow. **9.** An ox-bow.
~*v.* **bowed, bowing, bows.** —*tr.* **1.** To bend (something) into the shape of a bow. **2.** To play (a stringed instrument) with a bow. —*intr.* **1.** To bend into a curve or bow. **2.** To play a stringed instrument with a bow. [Middle English *bowe,* Old English *boga,* bow, arch.]

bow compass (bō) *n.* A drawing compass with legs that are connected by an adjustable metal spring band. Also called "bow-spring compass."

Bowd·ler (boud′lər), **Thomas** (1754–1825). British editor, famous for his expurgated editions of classic literary works, especially his *Family Shakespeare* (1818).

bowd·ler·ize (bōd′lə-rīz′, boud′-) *tr.v.* **-ized, -izing, -izes.** To expurgate prudishly. [After Thomas BOWDLER.] —**bowd·ler·ism** *n.* —**bowd·ler·i·za·tion** *n.*

bow·el (bou′əl, boul) *n.* **1.** An intestine, especially in humans. **2.** *Often* **bowels.** The digestive tract below the stomach. **3. bowels.** The inner depths of anything: *in the bowels of the ship.* **4. bowels.** *Archaic.* The seat of pity or the gentler emotions.
~*tr.v.* **boweled, -eling, -els.** *Also Chiefly British* **-elled, -elling.** To remove the bowels or entrails from; disembowel. [Middle English *b(o)uel,* from Old French *bo(u)el, boiel,* from Latin *botellus,* diminutive of *botulus,* sausage.]

bowel movement *n.* **1.** The discharge of waste matter from the body; defecation. **2.** The matter discharged; feces.

Bow·en (bō′ən), **Elizabeth Dorothea Cole** (1899–1973). British novelist and short-story writer, born in Ireland. Her first collection of short stories, *Encounters,* appeared in 1923; her first novel, *The Hotel,* in 1927. Her most popular novels were *The House in Paris* (1935) and *The Heat of the Day* (1949).

bow·er¹ (bou′ər) *n.* **1.** A shaded, leafy recess; an arbor. **2.** *Poetic.* A private chamber; a boudoir. **3.** *Poetic.* A rustic cottage; a country retreat.
~*tr.v.* **bowered, -ering, -ers.** *Poetic.* To enclose in or as if in a bower; embower. [Middle English *bour,* dwelling, inner apartment, Old English *būr.*] —**bow·er·y** *adj.*

bower² *n.* In the game of euchre, either of the two highest cards, the jack of trumps (*right bower*) or the jack of the same color as the trump (*left bower*). [German *Bauer,* "farmer," "peasant," jack (in cards), from Middle High German *būre, gebūre,* from Old High German *gibūro.*]

bower³ *n.* The heaviest of a ship's anchors, carried at the bow. Also called "bower anchor."

bow·er·bird (bou′ər-bûrd′) *n.* **1.** Any of various songbirds of the family Ptilonorhynchidae, of Australia and New Guinea. The males of many species build bowers of grasses, twigs, and colored materials to attract females. **2.** *Australian Informal.* A person who collects trivia.

bow·er·y (bou′ər-ē, bou′rē) *n.* A farm or plantation owned by one of the early Dutch settlers of New York. [Dutch *bouwerij,* farm, estate, from *bouwen,* to cultivate, from Middle Dutch.]

Bow·er·y, the (bou′ər-ē, bou′rē). A street and section of lower Manhattan in New York City. The street was once a road to the farm, or *bouwerie,* owned by Peter Stuyvesant.

bow·fin (bō′fĭn′) *n.* A primitive, bony, freshwater fish, *Amia calva,* of central and eastern North America. Also called "dogfish," "mudfish."

bow·front (bō′frŭnt′) *adj.* Having an outward-curving front: *a bowfront bureau.*

bow·head (bō′hĕd′) *n.* A whale, *Balaena mysticetus,* of Arctic seas, having a large head. [From the curved top of its head.]

Bow·ie (bō′ē, bōō′ē), **James** (1796–1836). Texas soldier. He was a colonel of the Texan forces during their struggle for independence from Mexico. He popularized the bowie knife, which was probably designed by his brother, Rezin P. Bowie. He died during the heroic defense of the Alamo.

bow·ie knife (bō′ē, bōō′ē) *n.* A single-edged, steel hunting knife, about 38 centimeters (15 inches) in length, having a hilt and a crosspiece. [After Col. James BOWIE.]

bow·knot (bō′nŏt′) *n.* A knot with large, decorative loops.

bowl¹ (bōl) *n.* **1. a.** A hemispherical container, wider than deep, for food or fluids. **b.** The contents of such a vessel. **2.** A bowl-shaped part of something, such as a spoon or pipe. **3. a.** A bowl-shaped building such as an amphitheater or a football stadium. **b.** Any of various football games played after the usual season between selected teams. **4.** A bowl-shaped topographical depression. **5.** *Archaic.* A drinking goblet. [Middle English *bolle,* Old English *bolla.*]

bowl² *n.* **1.** A large, wooden ball weighted or slightly flattened so as to roll with a bias. **2.** A roll or throw of the ball, as in bowling. **3.** *Machinery.* A revolving cylinder or drum.
~*v.* **bowled, bowling, bowls.** —*intr.* **1.** To participate in a game of bowling. **2.** To throw or roll a ball in bowls or tenpin bowling. **3.** To move smoothly and rapidly. Usually used with *along.* **4.** *Cricket. Abbr.* **b** To deliver the ball from one end of the pitch toward the batsman at the other, keeping the arm straight throughout. —*tr.* **1.** To throw or roll (a ball) in bowling. **2.** To make or achieve by bowling. **3.** *Cricket. Abbr.* **b** To retire (a batsman) with a bowled ball that knocks the bails off the wicket. Used with *out.* —**bowl over. 1.** To knock over (a person or thing); cause to fall. **2.** *Informal.* To take by surprise; astound. [Middle English *boule, bowle,* originally "ball," from Old French *boule,* from Latin *bulla.*]

bowlder. Variant of **boulder.**

bow·leg (bō′lĕg′) *n.* A leg having an outward curvature in the region of the knee.

bow·leg·ged (bō′lĕg′ĭd, -lĕgd′) *adj.* Having bowlegs.

bowl·er¹ (bō′lər) *n.* One that bowls.

bowler² *n. Chiefly British.* A man's hat, a **derby** (*see*). [After John *Bowler,* 19th-century London hatmaker.]

bow·line (bō′lĭn, -līn′) *n.* **1.** *Nautical.* A rope leading from the weather edge of a square sail to the bow to hold it forward when sailing close-hauled. **2.** A knot forming a loop that does not slip. In this sense, also called "bowline knot." —**on a bowline.** *Nautical.* Close-hauled. [Middle English *bouline,* probably from Middle Low German *bōline : boog,* BOW (of a ship) + *līne,* line.]

bowl·ing (bō′lĭng) *n.* **1.** A game played by rolling a ball down a wooden alley to knock down a triangular group of ten pins. Also called "tenpins." **2.** Any of various similar games, such as skittles or ninepins. **3. Lawn bowling** (*see*).

bowling alley *n.* **1.** A smooth, level, wooden alley used in bowling. **2.** A building or room containing such alleys.

bowling green *n.* A level grassy area for lawn bowling.

bow·man¹ (bō′mən) *n., pl.* **-men** (-mĭn). *Archaic.* An archer.

bow·man² (bou′mən) *n., pl.* **-men** (-mĭn). An oarsman stationed at the bow of a boat.

Bow·man's capsule (bō′mənz) *n. Anatomy.* In vertebrates, the cup-shaped end of a kidney tubule that surrounds a knot of blood capillaries and with them forms the Malpighian body. [After Sir William *Bowman* (1816–92), English surgeon.]

Bowman's glands *n.* The olfactory glands, which keep the olfactory surface moist.

bow·man's root (bō′mənz) *n.* A plant, *Gillenia trifoliata,* of eastern North America, having compound leaves and small white or pinkish flowers. Also called "Indian physic."

bow pen (bō) *n.* A bow compass with a pen at the end of one leg.

bow saw (bō) *n.* A type of saw with a narrow blade held in a large frame, used for cutting curves.

bowse. *Nautical.* Variant of **bouse.**

bow·shot (bō'shŏt') n. The distance an arrow can be shot.
bow-spring compass (bō'sprĭng) n. A **bow compass** (see).
bow·sprit (bou'sprĭt', bō'-) n. A spar extending forward from the stem of a ship. [Middle English *bouspret*, from Middle Low German *bōchsprēt, bugsprēt*.]
Bow Street runner n. A member of the first organized police force in London, set up in 1748 by Bow Street magistrate's court.
bow·string (bō'strĭng') n. The string of a bow.
bowstring hemp n. **1.** Any of various plants of the genus *Sansevieria*, having thick, erect leaves. **2.** The fiber from the leaves of these plants, used for cordage and in packing.
bow tie (bō) n. A man's small tie tied in the shape of a bow.
bow window (bō) n. A bay window built in a curve.
bow-wow (bou'wou'; bou'wou' *for sense 2) n.* **1.** An imitation or representation of the bark of a dog. **2.** A dog. Used by or to children. [Imitative.]
bow·yer (bō'yər) n. **1.** An archer. **2.** One who makes bows.
box¹ (bŏks) n. **1.** A rigid, usually rectangular container, typically having a lid or cover. **2.** The amount or quantity such a container can hold. **3.** A separate compartment in a public place, such as a theater, for the accommodation of a small group. **4. a.** A small structure serving as a shelter: *a sentry box.* **b.** Any of various containers used for a particular purpose: *a money box.* **5.** *British.* A small country house: *a shooting box.* **6.** A **box stall** (see). **7.** The raised seat for a driver of a coach or carriage. **8.** *Baseball.* **a.** An area marked out by chalk lines where the batter stands. **b.** Any of various designated areas for other team members, such as the pitcher, catcher, and coaches. **9.** Featured printed matter, enclosed by lines, a border, or white space and placed within or between text columns. **10.** A cut in the side of a tree through which sap is collected. **11.** An insulating, enclosing, or protective casing or part in a machine. **12.** An awkward or perplexing situation; predicament. —*tr.v.* **boxed, boxing, boxes. 1.** To pack or put in a box. **2.** To confine in or as if in a box. Often used with *in* or *up.* **3.** *Nautical.* To boxhaul. —**box the compass. 1.** To name the points of the compass in proper order. **2.** To make a complete revolution or reversal. —**the box.** *Chiefly British Informal.* Television. [Middle English *box*, Old English *box*, from Late Latin *buxis*, variant of Latin *pyxis*, box (made of boxwood), from Greek *puxis*, from *puxos*, box tree.]
box² n. A blow or slap with the hand: *a box on the ear.* —*v.* **boxed, boxing, boxes. 1.** To hit with the hand or fist. **2.** To take part in a boxing match with. —*intr.* To fight with the fists; spar. [Middle English *box†.*]
box³ n., *pl.* **box** or **boxes. 1.** Any evergreen tree or shrub of the genus *Buxus*; especially, *B. sempervirens*, used for hedges, borders, and garden mazes. Also called "boxwood." **2.** The wood of this tree, **boxwood** (see). **3.** Any of several trees whose timber or foliage resembles that of box. [Middle English *box*, Old English *box*, from Latin *buxus*, from Greek *puxos*.]
Box and Cox n. *Sometimes* **box and cox. 1.** Two people who live in the same house but never see each other. **2.** Two people who take turns to perform the same role, function, or position. [After a stage farce by J. Maddison Morton (1811–91) in which two characters share a room in this way.] —**Box and Cox** v.
box calf n. Calfskin treated with chromium salts and having square markings on the grain. [After Joseph *Box*, 19th-century London bootmaker.]
box camera n. A camera shaped like a box with a simple lens and viewfinder.
box·car (bŏks'kär') n. An enclosed and covered railway car for the transportation of freight.
box coat n. **1.** A heavy overcoat formerly worn by coachmen. **2.** A coat designed to hang loose from the shoulders. [From BOX (seat for coach driver).]
box·el·der (bŏks'ĕl'dər) n. A widely cultivated maple tree, *Acer negundo*, of North America, having compound leaves with lobed leaflets. Also called "ash-leaved maple."
box·er¹ (bŏk'sər) n. One who boxes; specifically, a pugilist.
boxer² n. A short-haired dog of a breed developed in Germany, having a brownish coat and a short, square-jawed muzzle. [German *Boxer*, from English BOXER.]
Box·er (bŏk'sər) n. A member of a secret society in China that attempted in 1900 to drive foreigners from the country by violence and to force Chinese Christians to renounce their religion. [Rough translation of Mandarin Chinese *yì hé quán*, "righteous harmonious fists," altered from *yì hé tuán*, "Righteous Harmonious Brigade" (name of the society) : *yì*, righteousness + *hé*, harmony + *tuán*, brigade.]
boxer shorts *pl.n.* Men's full-cut undershorts.
box·fish (bŏks'fĭsh') n., *pl.* **-fishes** or collectively **boxfish.** A fish, the **trunkfish** (see).
box girder n. A hollow girder with a square or rectangular section.
box·haul (bŏks'hôl') *tr.v.* **-hauled, -hauling, -hauls.** To turn (a square-rigged ship) about on its heel by bracing the foresails against the wind and steering round.
box·ing¹ (bŏk'sĭng) n. Material used for boxes.
boxing² n. The sport or profession of fighting with the fists; especially, the modern sport of fighting with gloved hands, inside a raised ring.
Boxing Day n. *British.* The first weekday after Christmas, observed as a holiday in Britain and other Commonwealth countries, when Christmas boxes were traditionally given to household employees and other service workers.

boxing glove n. A heavily padded leather glove worn in boxing.
box jellyfish n. A highly venomous jellyfish, *Chironex fleckeri*, common in Australian waters.
box kite n. A tailless kite consisting of a rectangular, box-shaped frame, encircled with cloth or paper bands.
box lacrosse n. *Chiefly Canadian.* A form of lacrosse played in an enclosure by teams of seven players. Also informally called "boxla."
box lunch n. A lunch packed in a container, as a box, especially for traveling.
box office n. **1.** A ticket office, as of a theater or stadium. **2.** The drawing power of a theatrical entertainment or of a performer; popular appeal. —**box-of·fice** *adj.*
box pleat n. A double pleat formed by two facing folds.
box score n. A printed summary of a baseball or basketball game, in the form of a table listing each player and the statistics for his performance.
box seat n. A seat in a box at a theater, concert hall, or stadium.
box set n. A stage set with a ceiling and three walls.
box spanner n. A type of spanner with a socket that fits over the nut.
box spring n. A bedspring consisting of a frame enclosed with cloth and containing rows of coiled springs.
box stall n. An enclosed stall for a single animal.
box·thorn (bŏks'thôrn') n. A shrub, the **matrimony vine** (see).
box turtle n. Any of several North American turtles of the genus *Terrapene*, having a high-domed shell.
box·wood (bŏks'wood') n. **1.** The hard, light-yellow wood of the box tree, used to make musical instruments, rulers, inlays, and engraving blocks. **2.** A shrub or tree, **box** (see).
box·y (bŏk'sē) *adj.* **-ier, -iest.** Like a box.
boy (boi) n. **1.** A male child or youth. **2.** *Informal.* A grown man; fellow. Often used in the plural to imply a spirit of camaraderie among a group of men: *a night out with the boys.* **3.** A manservant. —*interj.* Used as a mild exclamation. [Middle English *boye, bay, bye*, originally "male servant," "knave," possibly from Norman French *abuié, embuié* (unattested), "fettered," from Old French *embuier*, to fetter, from Vulgar Latin *imboiāre* (unattested) : *in-*, in + *boiae*, collar for the neck, fetters, from Greek *boeiai (dorai)*, ox(hides), hence thongs made from oxhide, from *bous*, ox.] —**boy·hood** n.
bo·yar (bō-yär') n. Also **bo·yard. 1.** A member of a former Russian aristocratic order abolished by Peter I. **2.** A member of a former aristocratic class of Romania. [Earlier *boiaren*, from Russian *boyarin*, from Old Russian, "of the highest rank," from Old Slavic *boljarinŭ*, from Old Turkic *boila*, a title.]
boy·cott (boi'kŏt') *tr.v.* **-cotted, -cotting, -cotts.** To abstain from using, buying, or dealing with, as a protest or means of coercion. —*n.* The act or an instance of boycotting. [After Charles C. *Boycott* (1832–97), land agent for the Earl of Erne, in County Mayo, Ireland, who was ostracized by the tenants for refusing to lower the rents.] —**boy·cott·er** n.
boy·friend (boi'frĕnd') n. Also **boy friend. 1.** A male friend. **2.** A favored male sexual or romantic partner; a sweetheart or lover.
boy·ish (boi'ĭsh') *adj.* Characteristic of or befitting a boy: *a boyish prank.* —**boy·ish·ly** *adv.* —**boy·ish·ness** n.
Boyle (boil), **Robert** (1627–91). Irish physicist and chemist, sometimes called "the father of chemistry" since his precision in defining chemical elements and chemical reactions was a major step in separating the science of chemistry from alchemy.
Boyle's law n. The principle that at a fixed temperature the pressure of a gas varies inversely with its volume. The law is obeyed only by a hypothetical ideal gas. Real gases approximately obey Boyle's law at high temperatures and low pressures. [After R. BOYLE.]
Boy Scout n. A member of a worldwide organization of young men and boys, founded in England in 1908, for character development and citizenship training.
boy·sen·ber·ry (boi'zən-bĕr'ē) n., *pl.* **-ries. 1.** A prickly bramble hybridized from the loganberry and various blackberries and raspberries. **2.** The large, wine-red, edible berry borne by this plant. [After Rudolph *Boysen*, 20th-century U.S. horticulturist.]
Boz (bŏz). Pen name of Charles *Dickens* (see).
bo·zo (bō'zō) n., *pl.* **-zos.** *Slang.* **1.** A fellow; guy. **2.** A dunce; fool. [Possibly from Spanish *bozot*, "down growing on the cheeks of youths."]
bp, b.pt. boiling point.
bp. bishop.
B.P. 1. Bachelor of Pharmacy. **2.** Bachelor of Philosophy. **3.** bills payable. **4.** British Pharmacopoeia.
B/P bills payable.
bpd, b.p.d. barrels per day.
B.Pd., B.Pe. Bachelor of Pedagogy.
B.P.E. Bachelor of Physical Education.
B.Ph., B.Phil. Bachelor of Philosophy.
bpi, b.p.i. bits per inch.
b.pl. birthplace.
B.P.O.E. Benevolent and Protective Order of Elks.
Br The symbol for the element bromine.
br. 1. branch. **2.** bridge. **3.** *Law.* brief. **4.** bronze. **5.** brother. **6.** brown.
Br. 1. Breton. **2.** Britain; British. **3.** Brother (religious).
B/R bills receivable.
bra (brä) n. A brassiere. —**bra·less** *adj.*

Bow Street Runner *One of the group of paid full-time "thief takers," who were the ancestors of modern policemen. The group was formed by the English novelist and playwright Henry Fielding after he became a magistrate at London's Bow Street Court in 1748. A runner's job was to detect and arrest criminals and to protect travelers from highwaymen and footpads.*

boxer *Often used as police and guide dogs, boxers are a hybrid breed descended from bulldogs and mastiffs.*

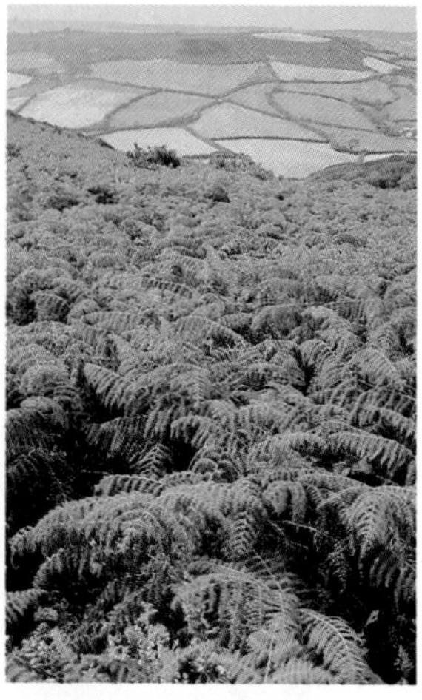

bracken *The largest and most common of British ferns, seen here on a hillside in Dorset, England.*

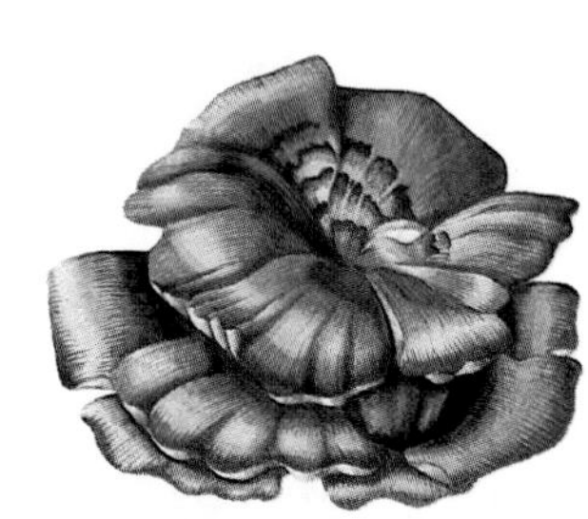

bracket fungus *A large, sometimes platelike, inedible fungus that grows on oak or beech trees in midwinter.*

PRONUNCIATION KEY

ă, pat; ā, pay; âr, care; ä, father, are; b, bib; ch, church; d, deed; ĕ, pet; ē, be; f, fife; g, gag; h, hat; hw, which; ĭ, pit; ī, pie; îr, pier; j, judge; k, kick; l, lid, needle; m, mum; n, no, sudden; ng, thing; ŏ, pot; ō, toe; ô, paw, for; oi, noise; ou, out; o͝o, book; o͞o, boot; p, pop; r, roar; s, sauce; sh, ship, dish; t, tight; th, thin, path; *th*, this, bathe; ŭ, cut; ûr, fur; v, valve; w, with; y, yes; z, zebra, size; zh, vision; ə, about, item, edible, gallop, circus, peaceful

IN FOREIGN WORDS:

à, *Fr.* ami; œ, *Fr.* feu, *Ger.* schön; ü, *Fr.* tu, *Ger.* über; KH, *Ger.* ich, *Scot.* loch; N, *Fr.* bon; y', *Fr.* Compiègne

STRESS MARKS:

Primary stress: ′ **in·cite′** (ĭn-sīt′)
Secondary stress: ′ **in′sight′** (ĭn′sīt′)

Bra·bant (brə-bănt′, -bänt′). A densely populated industrial and agricultural province of central Belgium, whose center is Brussels. It is the southern part of the old duchy of Brabant, which is now divided between Belgium and the Netherlands.

brab·ble (brăb′əl) *intr.v.* **-bled, -bling, -bles.** To quarrel noisily; to wrangle.
∼*n.* A petty dispute; a squabble. [Possibly from Middle Dutch *brabelen,* to jabber (imitative).] **—brab·bler** *n.*

brace (brās) *n., pl.* **braces** or **brace** (for sense 13 only). **1.** A device that holds or fastens two or more parts together or in place; a clamp. **2.** Any device that steadies or holds something erect, such as a supporting beam in a building. **3. braces.** *Chiefly British.* A pair of suspenders. **4.** *Medicine.* An appliance used to support a bodily part. **5.** *Often* **braces.** *Dentistry.* An arrangement of adjustable bands and wires fixed to the teeth to correct irregular alignment. **6.** *Nautical.* A rope by which a yard is controlled and secured on a square-rigged ship. **7.** *Archery.* A protective pad strapped to the bow arm. **8.** *Music.* A leather loop that slides to change the tension on the cords of a drum. **9.** *Music.* **a.** A symbol connecting two or more staves. **b.** A set of connected staves. **10.** A cranklike handle with an adjustable aperture at one end for securing and turning a bit. See **brace and bit. 11.** *Printing.* One of two symbols, { }, used to connect written or printed lines that should be considered together or are related in some way. **12.** *Mathematics.* Either of a pair of symbols, { }, used to indicate aggregation or to clarify the grouping of quantities when parentheses and square brackets have already been used. Also informally called "bracket." **13.** *pl.* **brace.** A pair of like things: *a brace of partridges.* —See Synonyms at **couple.**
∼*v.* **braced, bracing, braces.** —*tr.* **1.** To provide or strengthen with a brace or braces. **2.** To support or hold steady with or as if with a brace or braces. **3.** To prepare or position so as to be ready for an impact or danger. **4.** To invigorate; stimulate. **5.** *Nautical.* To turn (the yards of a ship) by the braces. —*intr.* **1.** To get ready; make preparations. **2.** *Military.* To assume a position of rigid attention. **—brace up.** To summon one's strength or endurance. [Middle English, arm guard, support, from Old French *brace,* the two arms, from Latin *bracchia,* plural of *bracchium,* arm, from Greek *brakhiōn.*]

brace and bit *n.* A hand tool for boring holes, consisting of a drilling bit rotated by a handle.

brace·let (brās′lĭt) *n.* **1.** An ornamental band or chain encircling the wrist. **2. bracelets.** *Slang.* Handcuffs. [Middle English, from Old French *bracelet,* diminutive of *bracel,* "little arm," armlet, from Latin *bracchiāle,* from *bracchium,* arm.]

brac·er[1] (brā′sər) *n.* **1.** Something or someone that braces. **2.** *Informal.* A stimulating drink, especially an alcoholic one; a tonic.

bracer[2] *n.* An arm or wrist guard worn by archers and fencers. [Middle English, arm guard, from Old French *brasseure,* from *bras,* arm, from Latin *bracchium.*]

bra·ce·ro (brə-sâr′ō) *n., pl.* **-ros.** A Mexican agricultural or industrial laborer permitted to enter the United States and work for a limited period of time. Compare **wetback.** [Spanish, manual laborer, from *brazo,* arm, from Latin *bracchium,* from Greek *brakhiōn.*]

bra·chi·a (brā′kē-ə, brăk′ē-ə) *n.* Plural of **brachium.**

bra·chi·al (brā′kē-əl, brăk′ē-) *adj.* Of, pertaining to, or resembling the arm or a similar or homologous part. [Latin *bracchialis,* from *bracchium,* arm, BRACHIUM.]

bra·chi·ate (brā′kē-ĭt, brăk′ē-, -āt′) *adj. Botany.* Having widely spreading branches arranged in pairs.
∼*intr.v.* (brā′kē-āt′, brăk′ē-) **brachiated, -ating, -ates.** To swing by the arms from branch to branch, as certain apes do. [Latin *bracchiātus,* from *bracchium,* arm, BRACHIUM.] **—bra·chi·a·tion** *n.*

brach·i·o·pod (brăk′ē-ə-pŏd′, brā′kē-) *n.* Any of various marine invertebrates of the phylum Brachiopoda, having bivalve dorsal and ventral shells and tentacled structures on either side of the mouth, used for feeding. Also called "lamp shell." [BRACHI(UM) + -POD.] **—brach·i·o·pod** *adj.*

bra·chi·o·saur·us (brăk′ē-ō-sôr′əs, brā′kē-) *n.* A dinosaur belonging to the genus *Brachiosaurus,* which grew up to 50 tons in weight and was the heaviest known dinosaur. [BRACHI(UM) + -SAURUS.]

bra·chis·to·chrone (brə-kĭs′tə-krōn′) *n. Mathematics.* A curve that is the path of an object falling freely between two points in the shortest possible time. [Greek *brakhistos,* shortest, superlative of *brakhus,* short + *khronos,* time.]

bra·chi·um (brā′kē-əm, brăk′ē-) *n., pl.* **brachia** (brā′kē-ə, brăk′ē-ə). An arm or a homologous anatomical structure, such as a flipper or wing. [Latin *bracchium,* arm, forearm, from Greek *brakhiōn.*]

brachy- *comb. form.* Indicates shortness; for example, **brachyuran.** [Greek *brakhus,* short.]

brach·y·ce·phal·ic (brăk′ē-sə-făl′ĭk) *adj.* Also **brach·y·ceph·a·lous** (-sĕf′ə-ləs). Having a short, almost round head, the width of which is at least 80 percent as great as the length. Compare **dolichocephalic, mesocephalic.** See **cephalic index.** [BRACHY- + -CEPHALIC.] **—brach·y·ceph·a·ly** (brăk′ē-sĕf′ə-lē), **brach·y·ceph·a·lism** (brăk′ē-sĕf-ə-lĭz′əm) *n.*

brach·y·dac·tyl·ic (brăk′ē-dăk-tĭl′ĭk) *adj.* Also **brach·y·dac·ty·lous** (-dăk′tə-ləs). Having abnormally short fingers or toes. [BRACHY- + -DACTYLIC.] **—brach·y·dac·tyl·i·a** (brăk′ē-dăk-tĭl′ē-ə), **brach·y·dac·ty·ly** (brăk′ē-dăk′tə-lē) *n.*

bra·chyl·o·gy (bră-kĭl′ə-jē) *n., pl.* **-gies. 1.** Brief, concise speech. **2.** A shortened or condensed phrase or expression. [Late Latin *brachylogia,* from Greek *brakhulogia* : BRACHY- + -LOGY.]

bra·chyp·ter·ous (bră-kĭp′tər-əs) *adj.* Having short wings. Said of certain insects. [Greek *brakhupteros* : BRACHY- + -PTEROUS.] **—bra·chyp·ter·ism** (bră-kĭp′tə-rĭz′əm) *n.*

brach·y·u·ran (brăk′ē-yo͝or′ən) *adj.* Also **brach·y·u·ral** (-əl), **brach·y·u·rous** (-əs). Of or belonging to the Brachyura, a group of crustaceans characterized by a short abdomen concealed under the cephalothorax, and including the true crabs.
∼*n.* A member of the Brachyura. [New Latin *Brachyura,* "short-tailed ones" : BRACHY- + *-ura,* plural of *-urus,* -UROUS.]

brac·ing (brā′sĭng) *adj.* Invigorating; strengthening.
∼*n.* **1.** A brace. **2.** Braces collectively; a system of braces. **—brac·ing·ly** *adv.* **—brac·ing·ness** *n.*

brack·en (brăk′ən) *n.* **1.** A fern, *Pteridium aquilinum,* having tough stems and branching, finely divided fronds. Also called "brake." **2.** An area overgrown with this fern. **3.** Any large, coarse fern. [Middle English (northern dialect) *braken,* from Old Norse *brakni* (unattested).]

brack·et (brăk′ĭt) *n.* **1.** A simple rigid structure in the shape of an L, one arm of which is fixed to a vertical surface, with the other projecting horizontally to support a shelf or other weight. **2.** Any of various functionally similar fixtures adapted to support loads. **3.** A small shelf or shelves supported by brackets. **4. a.** Either of a pair of symbols, [ ], used to enclose written or printed material or to indicate a mathematical expression considered in some sense a single quantity. Also called "square bracket." **b.** An **angle bracket** *(see).* **c.** *Informal.* A **brace** *(see).* **5.** A section or group within a classification, especially one of taxpayers according to income. **6.** *Military.* The space between two rounds of artillery, the first aimed beyond a target and the second aimed short of it, used to determine range.
∼*tr.v.* **bracketed, -eting, -ets. 1.** To support or hold with a bracket or brackets. **2. a.** To place (qualifying, explanatory, or unrelated material) within brackets. Often used with *off.* **b.** *Mathematics.* To put within brackets, especially angle brackets, to indicate a specified relationship. **c.** To enclose in a brace. Often used with *together.* **3.** To classify or group together. **4.** *Military.* To fire beyond and short of (a target) in order to determine range. [Earlier *bragget,* from Old French *braguette,* codpiece, diminutive of *brague,* mortise, breeches (in plural), from Old Provençal *braga,* from Latin *brāca.*]

bracket fungus *n.* Any of various fungi that form shelflike growths on tree trunks and wood structures.

brack·ish (brăk′ĭsh) *adj.* **1.** Containing some salt; briny. Usually said of water. **2.** Distasteful; unpalatable. [From obsolete *brack,* briny, brine, from Dutch *brak,* salty, from Middle Dutch *brac*†.] **—brack·ish·ness** *n.*

bract (brăkt) *n.* A leaflike plant part, usually small but sometimes showy and brightly colored, located below a flower or an inflorescence. [New Latin *bractea,* from Latin *bractea,* properly *brattea*†, metal plate or leaf.] **—brac·te·al** (brăk′tē-əl) *adj.*

brac·te·ate (brăk′tē-ĭt, -āt′) *adj. Botany.* Bearing bracts. [New Latin *bracteatus,* from *bractea,* BRACT.]

brac·te·o·late (brăk′tē-ə-lĭt, -lāt′) *adj. Botany.* Bearing small bracts, or bracteoles.

brac·te·ole (brăk′tē-ōl) *n.* Also **bract·let** (brăkt′lĭt). *Botany.* A small or secondary bract. [New Latin *bracteola,* from Latin, diminutive of *bractea,* metal plate or leaf. See **bract.**]

brad (brăd) *n.* A tapered nail with a small head or a slight side projection instead of a head. [Middle English *brad, brod,* from Old Norse *broddr,* spike.]

brad·awl (brăd′ôl′) *n.* A small awl with a chisel edge, used to make holes in wood for brads or screws.

Brad·bur·y (brăd′bĕr′ē), **Ray Douglas** (1920–). U.S. science fiction writer. Most of his works are a combination of social criticism and technological fantasy. His most successful novels have been *Fahrenheit 451* (1953), *Something Wicked This Way Comes* (1962), and *The Halloween Tree* (1972).

Brad·ford (brăd′fərd). Textile manufacturing town in the county of West Yorkshire in northern England, on the eastern slopes of the Pennines. It has been an important wool center since the 14th century and since the 18th century the most important worsted center in the country, both for its spinning mills and for its wool exchange.

Bradford, William (1590–1657). English Puritan colonist in America. A signer of the *Mayflower Compact* and an original settler of Plymouth Plantation, he was elected governor for 30 1-year terms and led the colony through its difficult early times.

Brad·laugh (brăd′lô), **Charles** (1833–91). British secularist and politician. In the 1860's and 1870's he campaigned for a number of unpopular causes, such as birth control, national education, and votes for women. In 1880 he was elected to the House of Commons for Northampton, but was refused permission to take his seat when he insisted on the right to affirm, rather than swear on the Bible. Eventually, after being re-elected by Northampton twice, he won the right for an atheist to sit in Parliament (1886).

Brad·ley (brăd′lē), **Omar Nelson** (1893–1981). U.S. general. He played a major part in the Allied victory in World War II. He was appointed chief of staff of the U.S. Army (1948) and was promoted to general (1950). He retired from the army in 1953.

brady- *prefix.* Indicates slowness; for example, **bradycardia.** [New Latin, from Greek *bradus*†, slow.]

Bra·dy (brā′dē), **Mathew B.** (*c.* 1823–96). U.S. photographer. He learned the daguerrotype process from Samuel Morse and opened his own studio in New York in 1844. He was famous for his por-

brachiation

HOW A GIBBON SWINGS THROUGH THE TREES
Acrobatic traveling by long-armed primates

The ability to brachiate (from the Latin *bracchiatus:* having arms) is a characteristic of all apes, although not all of them make frequent use of it. The undisputed masters of the art are the gibbons and siamangs, whose slight bodies, long arms, and hooked fingers are ideal for moving through trees. A gibbon traveling by this means (below) normally moves at human walking pace. But when excited, it can plunge through the tree-tops, or canopy, at astonishing speeds, covering 9 meters (30 feet) with each jump. Although gibbons have thumbs, they move so fast they do not have time to hook the thumbs around the branches.

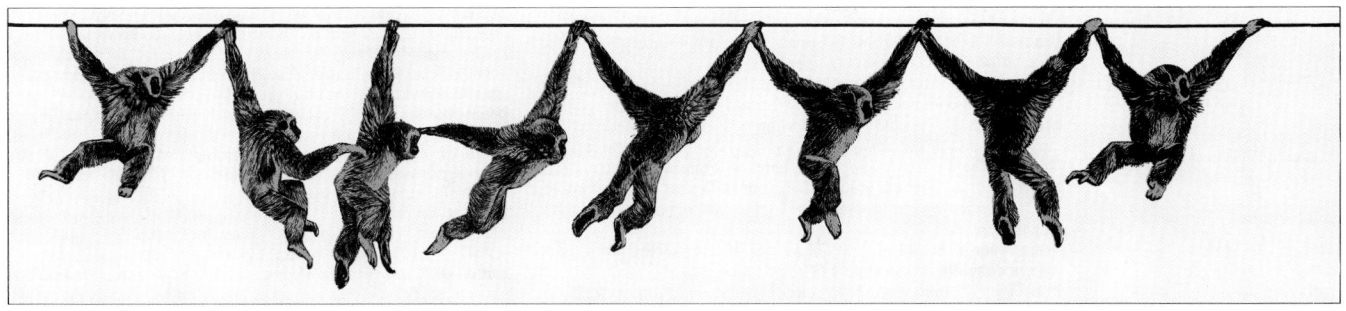

traits and was appointed official Union photographer of the Civil War (1861).

brad·y·car·di·a (brăd´ĭ-kär´dē-ə) *n.* Abnormally slow heartbeat, as less than 50 beats per minute. [New Latin : BRADY- + Greek *kardia,* heart (see cardia).] —**brad·y·car·dic** *adj.*

brad·y·kin·in (brăd´ĭ-kī´nən, brā´də-) *n.* A protein, $C_{50}H_{73}N_{15}O_{11}$, found in blood plasma that causes contraction of smooth muscle and dilates blood vessels. [BRADY- + Greek *kin(ēsis),* motion + -IN.]

brad·y·lex·i·a (brăd´ĭ-lĕk´sē-ə) *n.* A slowness of reading not attributable to lack of intelligence. [BRADY- + Greek *lexis,* speech, *legein,* to speak.]

brad·y·lo·gia (brăd´ə-lō´jə, -jē-ə) *n.* Abnormally slow speech. [New Latin : BRADY- + Greek *-logia,* -logy.]

brae (brā) *n. Scottish.* A hillside; slope. [Middle English (Scottish and northern dialects) *bra,* from Old Norse *brā,* eyelash.]

brag (brăg) *v.* **bragged, bragging, brags.** —*intr.* To talk boastfully about oneself, one's possessions, or the like. Often used with *about.* —*tr.* To assert boastfully: *He used to brag he'd become president.* —See Synonyms at **boast.** ~*n.* **1.** Arrogant or boastful speech or behavior. **2.** A braggart; boaster. **3.** A card game similar to poker. ~*adj.* **bragger, braggest.** Exceptionally fine; first-rate. [Middle English *braggen,* probably from *bragt,* "spirited," "mettlesome," hence boastful.] —**brag·ger** *n.*

Bra·ga (brä´gə). A city in northwestern Portugal, the capital of Braga district. It is said to have been founded by the Carthaginians and was an important settlement during Roman times. The city is now an agricultural trade center.

Bra·gan·ça (brə-gän´sə). Also **Bra·gan·za** (-zə). Town in northeast Portugal, capital of the province of the same name. It lies in the Sierra de la Culebra, almost on the border with Spain. Its 12th-century castle was the seat of the Bragança family who ruled Portugal from 1640 to 1910 and Brazil from 1822 to 1889.

Bragg (brăg), **Sir William Henry** (1862–1942). British physicist. He shared the Nobel Prize in physics (1915) with his son, **Sir William Lawrence Bragg** (1890–1971), for their analysis of x-ray spectra and the structure of crystals.

brag·ga·do·ci·o (brăg´ə-dō´shē-ō) *n., pl.* **-os. 1.** A braggart. **2. a.** Empty or pretentious bragging. **b.** Swaggering manner; cockiness. [After *Braggadocchio,* name coined by Spenser for his personification of boasting : *braggad-,* alteration of BRAGGART + *-occio,* Italian augmentative suffix.]

Bragg angle *n.* The angle between an incident x-ray beam and a set of crystal planes for which the reflected or transmitted radiation displays maximum intensity as a result of constructive interference. [After Sir William Lawrence BRAGG.]

brag·gart (brăg´ərt) *n.* One given to loud, empty boasting; a bragger. [French *bragard,* from *braguer,* to brag, obscurely related to Middle English *braggen,* BRAG.] —**brag·gart** *adj.*

Bragg's law *n.* The fundamental law of x-ray crystallography, $n\lambda = 2d\sin\theta$, where n is an integer, λ is the wavelength of a beam of x-rays incident on a crystal with lattice planes separated by distance d, and θ is the Bragg angle.

Bra·gi (brä´gē). Also **Bra·ge** (brä´gə). *Norse Mythology.* The son of Odin, husband of Ithunn, and god of poetry.

Bra·he (brä´ə), **Tycho** (1546–1601). Danish astronomer. His precise fixing of the planets and the stars, by far the most accurate positioning achieved until then, formed the foundation for **Johannes Kepler's** laws of planetary motion. He also made a detailed study of the supernova (first observed 1572) known as Tycho's star.

Brah·ma¹ (brä´mə) *n. Hinduism.* **1.** The personification of divine reality in its creative aspect as a member of the Hindu triad. See **Vishnu, Shiva. 2.** Variant of **Brahman.** [Sanskrit *bráhman,* prayer,

the universal soul, the Absolute, akin to *brahmán-,* priest. See **Brahman.**]

Brah·ma² (brä´mə, brä´-) *n. Sometimes* **brama.** A large domestic fowl of a breed originating in Asia, and having feathered legs. [Short for *Brahmaputra;* first brought from Lakhimpur, India, on the BRAHMAPUTRA river.]

Brah·man (brä´mən) *n., pl.* **-mans** (for senses 2, 3). Also **Brah·ma** (-mə), **Brah·min** (-mĭn). **1.** Also **Brah·ma.** *Hinduism.* The essential divine reality of the universe; the eternal spirit from which all being originates and to which all returns. **2.** Also **Brah·min.** *Hinduism.* A member of the highest caste, originally composed only of priests. **3.** Also **Brah·ma, Brah·min.** One of a breed of domestic cattle developed in the southern United States from stock originating in India, and having a hump between the shoulders and a pendulous dewlap. [Sanskrit *brāhmaṇas,* member of the Brahman caste, from *brahmán-,* priest.] —**Brah·man·ic** (brä-măn´ĭk), **Brah·man·i·cal** *adj.*

Brah·man·ism (brä´mən-ĭz´əm) *n.* Also **Brah·min·ism** (brä´mĭn-). **1.** The religious practices and beliefs of ancient India as reflected in the Vedas, the earliest religious texts. **2.** The social and religious system of the Brahmans and orthodox Hindus of India, characterized by a caste system and various forms of pantheism. —**Brah·man·ist** *n.*

Brah·ma·pu·tra (brä´mə-pōō´trə). A river rising in the Himalayas in southwestern Tibet and flowing 2,895 kilometers (1,800 miles) through northeastern India to join the Ganges River in Bangladesh. The river's lower course is sacred to Hindus.

Brah·min (brä´mĭn) *n.* **1.** Variant of **Brahman** (except for sense 1). **2.** A highly cultured and socially exclusive person, especially a member of one of the old New England families. —**Brah·min·ic** (brä-mĭn´ĭk), **Brah·min·i·cal** *adj.*

Brah·min·ism (brä´mĭn-ĭz´əm) *n.* **1.** Variant of **Brahmanism. 2.** The attitude or conduct typical of a social or cultural elite.

Brahms (brämz), **Johannes** (1833–97). German composer. His work was a blend of classical tradition with the new Romantic impulse. He wrote a relatively small number of large-scale works, including four symphonies (1876–85), the *German Requiem* (1868), two piano concertos (1881), a violin concerto (1878), and numerous chamber works.

braid (brād) *tr.v.* **braided, braiding, braids. 1.** To interweave three or more strands of; plait. **2.** To decorate or edge with an ornamental trim. **3.** To produce by interweaving: *braid a rug.* **4.** To fasten or entwine (hair) with a band or ribbon. ~*n.* **1.** A narrow length of fabric, hair, or other material that has been braided or plaited. **2.** A thin, flat, woven strip of cloth with a regular diagonal pattern, used for binding or decorating fabrics; an ornamental trim. **3.** A ribbon or band entwined in or used to fasten the hair. [Middle English *breyden,* to move quickly, pull, twist, braid, Old English *bregdan.*] —**braid·er** *n.*

braid·ing (brä´dĭng) *n.* **1.** A length of braid. **2.** Braided work.

brail (brāl) *n.* A line used to bring in a sail before furling it. ~*tr.v.* **brailed, brailing, brails.** To gather in (a sail) with brails. Usually used with *up.* [Middle English *brayle,* from Old French *brail, braiel,* belt, girdle, from Medieval Latin *brācāle,* from Latin *brāca,* breeches.]

Braille (brāl) *n.* Also **braille.** A system of writing and printing for the blind, in which varied arrangements of raised dots representing letters and numerals can be identified by touch. [After Louis BRAILLE.]

Braille (brāl), **Louis** (1809–52). French inventor of the Braille system. He was blinded himself at the age of three.

brain (brān) *n.* **1.** The portion of the central nervous system in the vertebrate cranium that is responsible for the interpretation of sensory impulses, the coordination and control of bodily activities, and the exercise of emotion, memory, and thought. **2.** A functionally similar portion of the invertebrate nervous system. **3. a.** Intellectual capacity or potential; mind: *She has a good brain.* **b.** *Often* **brains.** Intelligence; intellectual ability. **4.** *Informal.* A highly intelligent or intellectual person. **5.** *Often* **brains.** The planner or organizer of an enterprise or undertaking. **6. brains.** The brain of a calf, pig, or sheep used as food. **7.** An automatic device, as a computer, that is central to a computation or control process. —See Synonyms at **mind.** —**on the brain.** Obsessively in the mind or thoughts. —**pick someone's brains.** To elicit and use the ideas, knowledge, or thoughts of. —**rack one's brains.** To make a great mental effort. ~*tr.v.* **brained, braining, brains. 1.** To smash in the skull of. **2.** *Slang.* To hit on the head. [Middle English *brain,* Old English *brægen.*] See feature, previous page.

brain·child (brān'chīld') *n. Informal.* An original idea, plan, or the like, attributed to a specific person or group.

brain coral *n.* Any of several corals of the genus *Meandrina,* forming rounded colonies that resemble the surface of the human brain.

brain death *n.* Cessation of respiration and other vital reflexes due to irreversible brain damage, although the heart may continue beating with the aid of life-support systems. —**brain dead** *adj.*

brain drain *n.* The emigration of highly skilled or trained people, such as scientists or doctors, to another country, especially for higher salaries.

brain fever *n. Pathology.* Any of several diseases of the brain, such as **encephalitis** or **meningitis** *(both of which see).*

brain·less (brān'lĭs) *adj.* **1.** Devoid of intelligence; stupid. **2.** Lacking a brain. —**brain·less·ly** *adv.* —**brain·less·ness** *n.*

brain·pan (brān'păn') *n.* The part of the skull that contains the brain; the cranium.

brain·pick·ing (brān'pĭk'ĭng) *n.* The act of probing another's mind for information. —**brain·pick·er** *n.*

brain·pow·er (brān'pou'ər) *n.* **1.** Intellectual power or ability. **2.** People with well-developed mental ability.

brain scanner *n.* A **CAT scanner** *(see)* used to x-ray the brain.

brain·sick (brān'sĭk') *adj.* Of, pertaining to, or induced by insanity; mad. —**brain·sick·ly** *adv.* —**brain·sick·ness** *n.*

brain·stem (brān'stĕm') *n.* The part of the brain consisting of the medulla oblongata, pons, midbrain, and part of the forebrain, connecting the spinal cord to the forebrain and cerebrum.

brain·storm (brān'stôrm') *n.* **1.** A sudden and violent disturbance in the brain. **2. a.** A sudden clever idea. **b.** A foolish idea.

brain·storm·ing (brān'stôr'mĭng) *n.* A method of attacking problems or creating original ideas by intense discussion and spontaneous idea swapping within a group.

brain·teas·er (brān'tē-zər) *n. Informal.* A difficult or puzzling problem. Also called "brain-twister."

brain trust *n. Also Chiefly British.* **brains trust.** A group of experts who serve as unofficial advisers and policy planners, especially in a government. —**brain truster** *n.*

brain·wash (brān'wŏsh', -wôsh') *tr.v.* **-washed, -washing, -washes.** To subject to brainwashing. [Back-formation from BRAINWASH-ING.]

brain·wash·ing (brān'wŏsh'ĭng, -wôsh'ĭng) *n.* Intensive indoctrination, usually political, aimed at changing a person's basic convictions and attitudes and replacing them with a fixed and

brain

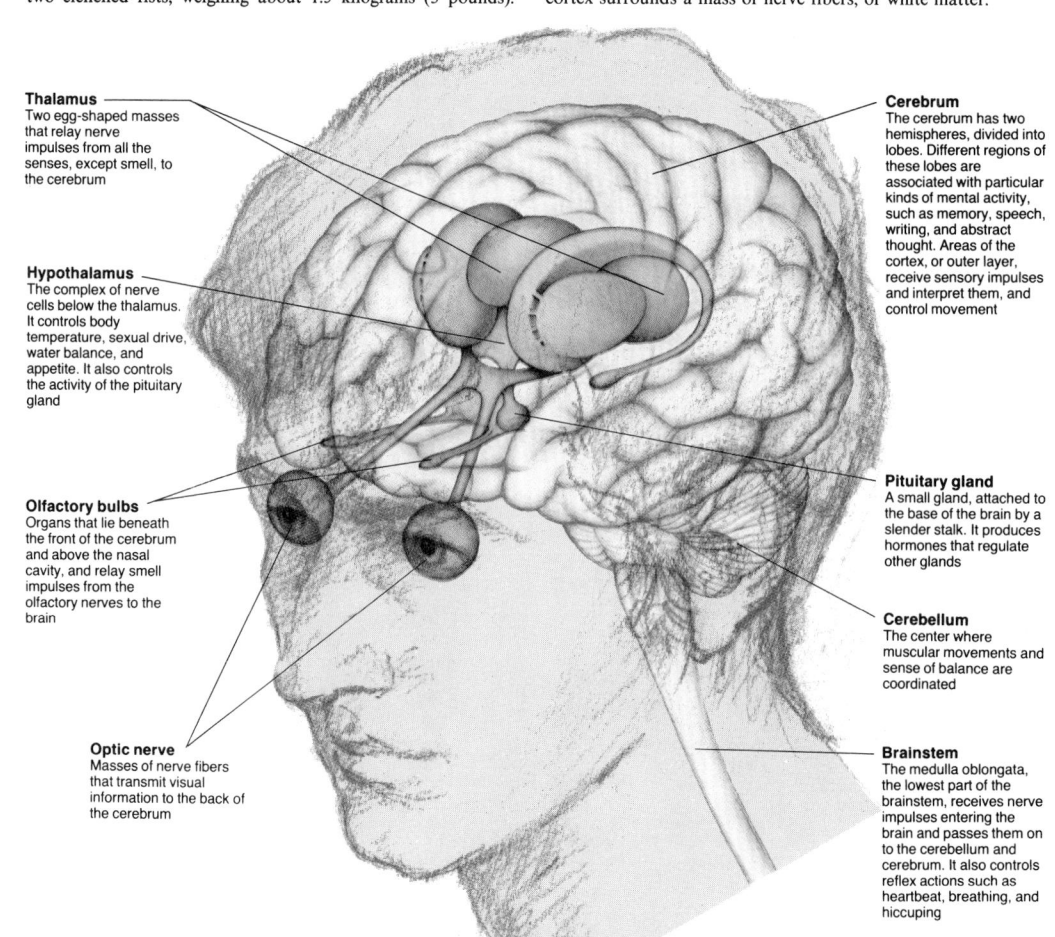

THE MASTER CONTROLLER OF THE HUMAN BODY

A communications system that processes information from the senses

Wrinkled and grooved like an oversized walnut, the human brain consists of some 100 billion nerve cells and a complex system of interlinked pathways between them. This soft, gray mass of nerve tissue controls all the activities of the body, both conscious and unconscious, as well as being the seat of sensations, skills, emotions, intelligence, and memory.

All this potential is contained in a volume about the size of two clenched fists, weighing about 1.5 kilograms (3 pounds).

There are three main parts: the cerebrum, the largest and most developed part of the brain; the cerebellum; and the brainstem, which is an extension of the spinal cord.

The surface of the cerebrum has a layer of gray matter, known as the cortex, which is convoluted into folds to give it the maximum possible area for receiving and interpreting the stream of unsifted information that is relayed to it from the senses. The cortex surrounds a mass of nerve fibers, or white matter.

Thalamus
Two egg-shaped masses that relay nerve impulses from all the senses, except smell, to the cerebrum

Hypothalamus
The complex of nerve cells below the thalamus. It controls body temperature, sexual drive, water balance, and appetite. It also controls the activity of the pituitary gland

Olfactory bulbs
Organs that lie beneath the front of the cerebrum and above the nasal cavity, and relay smell impulses from the olfactory nerves to the brain

Optic nerve
Masses of nerve fibers that transmit visual information to the back of the cerebrum

Cerebrum
The cerebrum has two hemispheres, divided into lobes. Different regions of these lobes are associated with particular kinds of mental activity, such as memory, speech, writing, and abstract thought. Areas of the cortex, or outer layer, receive sensory impulses and interpret them, and control movement

Pituitary gland
A small gland, attached to the base of the brain by a slender stalk. It produces hormones that regulate other glands

Cerebellum
The center where muscular movements and sense of balance are coordinated

Brainstem
The medulla oblongata, the lowest part of the brainstem, receives nerve impulses entering the brain and passes them on to the cerebellum and cerebrum. It also controls reflex actions such as heartbeat, breathing, and hiccuping

unquestioned set of beliefs. [Translation of Mandarin Chinese *hsi³ nao³* : *hsi³*, to wash + *nao³*, brain.]

brain wave *n.* **1.** A fluctuation of electric potential between parts of the brain, as seen on an electroencephalogram. **2.** *Informal.* A sudden inspiration or brilliant idea.

brain·y (brā′nē) *adj.* **-ier, -iest.** *Informal.* Intelligent; learned; smart. **—brain·i·ly** *adv.* **—brain·i·ness** *n.*

braise (brāz) *tr.v.* **braised, braising, braises.** To cook (meat or vegetables) by browning in fat, then simmering in a small quantity of liquid in a covered container. [French *braiser*, from *braise*, hot charcoal, from Old French *brese*, from Germanic.]

brake¹ (brāk) *n.* **1.** A device for slowing or stopping motion, as of a vehicle or machine, especially by contact friction. **2.** *Often* **brakes.** Anything serving to slow or stop action or movement. **3.** A device for separating the fibers of flax or hemp by crushing or beating. **4.** A heavy harrow for breaking clods of earth. **5.** A handle on a pump or other machine. **~v.** **braked, braking, brakes.** **—tr.** **1.** To reduce the speed of with or as if with a brake. **2.** To crush (flax or hemp) in a brake. **3.** To break up (clods of earth) with a harrow. **—intr.** To operate or apply a brake or brakes. [Middle English *brake*, crushing instrument, pestle, flax brake, from Middle Dutch *braeke*.]

brake² *n.* Any of several ferns, especially **bracken** (see). [Middle English, variant of BRACKEN.]

brake³ *n.* An area overgrown with dense brushwood, briars, and undergrowth; a thicket. [Middle English *(ferne) brake*, Old English *(fearn)braca*, bed of fern : FERN + *bracu* (unattested), dense growth, thicket.]

brake⁴. Variant of **break** (carriage).

brake⁵. *Archaic.* Past tense of **break.**

brake·age (brā′kĭj) *n.* The action or capacity of a brake.

brake band *n.* A flexible belt that is tightened around a brake drum to arrest the motion of a wheel or shaft.

brake drum *n.* A metal cylinder to which pressure is applied in order to arrest rotation of a wheel or shaft attached to the cylinder.

brake fluid *n.* The liquid used in a hydraulic brake cylinder.

brake horsepower *n.* *Abbr.* **bhp., b.hp.** The useful horsepower of an engine, usually determined from the force exerted on a dynamometer connected to the engine's drive shaft.

brake light *n.* A red light on the back of a vehicle which lights up when the brakes are applied.

brake lining *n.* A renewable thin strip on the outside of a brake shoe to minimize wear.

brake·man (brāk′mən) *n., pl.* **-men** (-mĭn). A railroad employee who assists the conductor and checks on the operation of the train's brakes.

brake shoe *n.* A curved metal block that presses against and thereby arrests the rotation of a wheel or brake drum.

brak·ing rocket *n.* *Aerospace.* A **retrorocket** (see).

bram·ble (brăm′bəl) *n.* **1.** Any prickly plant or shrub of the genus *Rubus*, especially the blackberry. **2.** Any similar prickly shrub or bush such as the dog rose. [Middle English *brembel*, Old English *brǣmbel, brēmel*.] **—bram·bly** *adj.*

bram·bling (brăm′blĭng) *n.* A finch, *Fringilla montifringilla*, of northern Eurasia, having black, white, and rust-brown plumage. Also called "cock of the north." [BRAMB(LE) + -LING.]

Bram·ley (brăm′lē) *n.* A variety of cooking apple with firm juicy flesh. Also called "Bramley's seedling." [After Matthew *Bramley*, 19th-century English butcher, who may first have grown it.]

bran (brăn) *n.* **1.** The seed husk or outer coating of cereals such as wheat, rye, and oats, separated from the flour by sifting. **2.** Cereal by-products used as a food. [Middle English *bran, bren*, from Old French *bran*, perhaps from Gaulish *brenno-†* (unattested).]

branch (brănch, bränch) *n.* *Abbr.* **br.** **1.** A secondary woody stem or limb growing from the trunk or main stem of a tree, bush, or shrub, or from another secondary limb. **2.** Any part resembling or suggestive of a branch. **3.** A limited part of a larger or more complex body, such as: **a.** An academic or vocational field of specialization. **b.** A local unit of a business, enterprise, bank, or the like. **c.** A division of a family, tribe, or other group believed to stem from a common ancestor. **4.** *Linguistics.* A subdivision of a family of languages. **5. a.** A tributary of a river. **b.** Any small stream, creek, or brook. **6.** *Geometry.* A part of a curve that is separated, as by discontinuities or extreme points. **7.** *Computer Science.* A change from a main program sequence into a subroutine. **~v.** **branched, branching, branches.** **—intr.** **1.** To put forth or spread out in branches. **2.** To separate into subdivisions; diverge. **3.** *Computer Science.* To depart from a sequence of instructions as a result of a branch. **—tr.** **1.** To separate (something) into or as if into branches. **2.** To embroider with a design of flowers or foliage. **—branch off.** **1.** To divide into branches; fork. **2.** To separate from the main part or course; diverge. **—branch out.** To enlarge the scope of one's interest, business, or activities. [Middle English *braunche*, from Old French *branche*, from Late Latin *branca*, foot, paw.] **—branched** *adj.* **—branch·less** *adj.* **—branch·y** *adj.*

-branch *suffix.* *Zoology.* Indicates gills; for example, **elasmobranch.** [New Latin *-branchia*, from Latin *branchia*, BRANCHIA.]

branched chain *n.* *Chemistry.* A chain of atoms in a molecule with one or more side chains attached.

bran·chi·a (brăng′kē-ə) *n., pl.* **-chiae** (-kē-ē). *Zoology.* A gill or similar breathing organ. [Latin, from Greek *brankhia†*, gills.] **—bran·chi·al** *adj.*

bran·chi·ate (brăng′kē-ĭt, -āt′) *adj.* Having branchiae or gills.

bran·chi·o·pod (brăng′kē-ə-pŏd′) *n.* Any of various crustaceans of the subclass Branchiopoda, characteristically having a segmented body and flattened, limblike appendages. The group includes the water fleas. [New Latin *Branchiopoda* : BRANCHIA + -POD.]

branch line *n.* A minor railway line that branches off from a main line.

branch water *n.* Plain water, especially when mixed with liquor. [From *branch water*, water from a stream.]

Bran·cu·si (brän-kōō′zē, -sē), **Constantin** (1876–1957). Romanian sculptor, who settled in Paris in 1904. He broke sharply with the realist tradition in sculpture, making abstract sculptures of great geometric simplicity, chiefly in metal and stone.

brand (brănd) *n.* **1. a.** A trademark or distinctive name identifying a product or a manufacturer. **b.** The make of a product thus marked: *a popular brand of soap.* **2.** A particular type: *a strange brand of humor.* **3.** A mark indicating identity or ownership, burned on the hide of an animal with a hot iron. **4.** A mark formerly burned into the flesh of criminals or slaves. **5.** Any mark of disgrace or notoriety; a stigma. **6.** An iron that is heated and used for branding. **7.** A piece of burning or charred wood. **8.** *Archaic.* A sword: *"So flash'd and fell the brand Excalibur"* (Tennyson). **9.** A disease of plants caused by the rust fungus *Puccinia arenariae* in which brown spots appear on the leaves. **~tr.v.** **branded, branding, brands.** **1.** To mark with or as if with a brand. **2.** To mark with disgrace or infamy; stigmatize. [Middle English *brand*, fire, torch, sword.]

Bran·deis (brăn′dīs), **Louis Dembitz** (1856–1941). Associate Justice U.S. Supreme Court (1916–39). As a young lawyer sensitive to the many social and economic problems of the day, he felt that law should be used to help the average citizen. Later, his liberalism and ardent defense of individual rights were the basis for many of his Supreme Court decisions.

Bran·den·burg¹ (brăn′dən-bûrg′). A former principality in Prussia, now lying in central East Germany, stretching at its greatest extent in the 18th century from west of the Elbe River beyond the Oder north to the Baltic Sea. Its center was Berlin. In 1701 Elector Frederick III took the title King of Prussia, and thereafter the history of Brandenburg is the history of Prussia.

Brandenburg². An industrial town in East Germany, on the Havel River. It was the headquarters of the ruling Hohenzollern family of Brandenburg (15th–early 18th century).

brand·ing iron *n.* A metal rod heated and used for branding.

bran·dish (brăn′dĭsh) *tr.v.* **-dished, -dishing, -dishes.** **1.** To wave or flourish (a weapon, for example) menacingly. **2.** To display ostentatiously. **~n.** A menacing or defiant wave or flourish. [Middle English *braundisshen*, from Old French *brandir* (present stem *brandiss-*), from *brand*, sword, blade, from Germanic.] **—bran·dish·er** *n.*

brand·ling (brănd′lĭng) *n.* A common reddish-brown earthworm, *Eisenia foetida*, often used as bait by fishermen. [BRAND (because of its red markings) + -LING.]

brand name *n.* See **trade name** (sense 1).

brand-new (brănd′nōō′, -nyōō′) *adj.* In fresh and unused condition; completely new.

Bran·do (brăn′dō), **Marlon** (1924–). U.S. actor, chiefly famous for his appearance in films, most notably in *A Streetcar Named Desire* (1951). One of the outstanding representatives of method acting, he also won critical acclaim for *On the Waterfront* (1954).

Brandt (brănt, bränt), **Willy,** born Herbert Ernst Karl Frahm (1913–). West German politician. He was elected to the Bundestag (1949) and became mayor of West Berlin (1957). He was chancellor (1969–74) until the revelation that one of his close aides was an East German spy. He was awarded the Nobel Peace Prize (1971) for his efforts to reduce tension between East and West.

bran·dy (brăn′dē) *n., pl.* **-dies.** A strong alcoholic drink distilled from wine or from fermented fruit juice. **~tr.v.** **brandied, -dying, -dies.** To mix, flavor, or preserve with brandy. [Earlier *brandy wine*, from Dutch *brandewijn, brantwijn* : *brant*, past participle of *branden*, to burn, distil + WINE.]

brandy bottle *n.* A plant, the **yellow water lily** (see).

Bran·dy·wine (brăn′dē-wīn′). A creek in southern Pennsylvania and northern Delaware. It was here on September 11, 1777, that Gen. William Howe's British and Hessian troops defeated George Washington's army, largely made up of militiamen. Later that month Howe's forces entered Philadelphia.

branks (brăngks) *n. Used with a singular or plural verb.* A metal bridle with a bit to restrain the tongue, formerly used to punish scolds. [Perhaps an alteration of earlier *bernaks*, plural of Middle English *bernak*, bridle, from Norman French *bernact†*.]

bran·ni·gan (brăn′ĭ-gən) *n. Slang.* **1.** A noisy or confused quarrel. **2.** A spree; binge. [Probably from the proper name *Brannigan*.]

brant (brănt) *n., pl.* **brant** or **brants.** Also *British* **brent** (brĕnt). Any of several wild geese of the genus *Branta*, that breed in Arctic regions; especially, *B. bernicla*, having a black neck and head. [Probably from Scandinavian, akin to Swedish *brandgas*, "burnt goose" (from its black color) : *brand*, firebrand, from Old Norse *brandr* + *gas*, goose.]

Brant (brănt), **Joseph,** original name Thayendanegea (1742–1807). Indian leader. He supported Britain in the French and Indian War and remained loyal during the American Revolution, in which he led Mohawk warriors on devastating attacks on frontier settlements. After the war he settled in what is now Ontario, Canada.

Braque (bräk), **Georges** (1882–1963). French painter, a leading member of the School of Paris and cofounder of the cubist movement. His landscapes of 1908, painted after he had seen Picasso's *Demoiselles d'Avignon,* and described by Matisse as composed of little cubes, gave rise to the term "cubism." He later abandoned the cubist manner, painting still lifes with a flat perspective, large interior scenes, and in the 1950's the large black birds against a blue sky that dominate his last period.

brash¹ (brăsh) *adj.* **brasher, brashest. 1.** Hasty and unthinking; rash. **2.** Impudent; cocky. **3.** Brittle. Said of wood or timber. —See Synonyms at **shameless.** [Perhaps imitative, influenced by BREAK and RASH.] —**brash·ly** *adv.* —**brash·ness** *n.*

brash² *n.* A mass or pile of rubble or fragments. [Perhaps from French *brèche,* breach, from Old French, from Old High German

brehha, fracture, from *brehhan,* to break.]

Brasil. See **Brazil.**

Bra·sí·lia (brə-zĭl'yə). Capital of Brazil, a new town built in the central highlands of the country, 970 kilometers (603 miles) northwest of Rio de Janeiro. The city was laid out by the architect Lúcio Costa in the shape of an airplane; the civic buildings were almost all designed by Oscar Niemeyer.

brasilin. Variant of **brazilin.**

brass (brăs, bräs) *n.* **1.** An alloy of copper (more than 50 percent) and zinc with other metals in varying lesser amounts. **2.** Ornaments, objects, or utensils made of brass. **3.** *Often* **brasses.** *Music.* **a.** The family of wind instruments, such as the French horn and trombone, made of brass. **b.** *Sometimes used with a plural verb.* The section of an orchestra made up of these instruments. **4.** A memorial plaque made of brass, often inscribed with a representation of a dead person. See **brass rubbing. 5.** *Engineering.* A bushing sleeve or similar lining for a bearing, made from a copper alloy. **6.** *Informal.* Blatant self-assurance; effrontery; nerve. **7.** *Slang. Used with a plural verb.* High-ranking military officers or other high officials: *the top brass.* **8.** *Northern English Informal.* Money. [Middle English *bras,* Old English *bræs.†*] —**brass** *adj.*

bras·sard (brə-särd', brăs'ärd') *n.* Also **bras·sart** (brə-särt', brăs'-ärt'). **1.** A cloth badge worn around the upper arm. **2.** A piece of armor for the arm. [French, from *bras,* arm, from Latin *brachium,* from Greek *brakhiōn.*]

brass·bound (brăs'bound', bräs'-) *adj.* **1.** Strengthened or ornamented with brass: *a brassbound wooden box.* **2.** Firmly and inflexibly established; rigid: *a brassbound tradition.*

brass·col·lar (brăs'kŏl'ər) *adj.* Voting the straight party ticket with no variation.

bras·se·rie (brăs'ə-rē', brăs-rē') *n.* **1.** A bar in which food may be served. **2.** A French-style restaurant. [French, "brewery."]

brass hat *n. Slang.* **1.** A high-ranking military officer. **2.** Any high-ranking official. [Because of the gold braid on his cap.]

bras·si·ca (brăs'ĭ-kə) *n.* Any plant of the genus *Brassica,* indigenous to the Mediterranean region but widely cultivated as vegetables, such as cabbages, Brussels sprouts, and rutabagas. [Latin, "cabbage."]

brass·ie, brass·y (brăs'ē, brä'sē) *n., pl.* **-ies.** A wooden golf club with a brass-plated sole, used for long low shots.

bras·siere, bras·sière (brə-zîr') *n.* A woman's undergarment worn to support and give contour to the breasts. Also called "bra." [French *brassière,* from Old French *braciere,* armor for the arm, arm guard, from *bras,* arm, from Latin *bracchium,* from Greek *brakhiōn.*]

brass knuckles *pl.n.* A weapon consisting of a metal strip or chain with holes or links into which the fingers fit.

brass rubbing *n.* **1.** The process of reproducing on paper the design on a memorial brass by rubbing with graphite or the like. **2.** The impression produced in this way.

brass tacks *pl.n. Informal.* Essential facts or details: *getting down to brass tacks.*

brass·y (brăs'ē, brä'sē) *adj.* **-ier, -iest. 1.** Of or decorated with brass. **2.** Resembling brass in color. **3.** Resembling or characterized by the sound of brass instruments; strident. **4.** Cheap and showy. **5.** *Informal.* Brazen; insolent; impudent. —**brass·i·ly** *adv.* —**brass·i·ness** *n.*

brat (brăt) *n.* A child, especially an ill-mannered one. [Perhaps from dialectal *brat,* coarse garment, Middle English *brat,* Old English *bratt,* cloak, from Old Irish *bratt†.*] —**brat·tish, brat·ty** *adj.*

Bra·ti·sla·va (brăt'ĭ-slä'və). Industrial city in southern Czechoslovakia, on the Danube River near the Austrian and Hungarian borders, the third-largest city in the country. From 1541 to 1784 it was the capital of Hungary.

brat·tice (brăt'ĭs) *n.* A partition, especially one erected in a mine for ventilation. ~*tr.v.* **bratticed, -ticing, -tices.** To equip with a brattice. [Middle English *bretais,* defensive structure, from Norman French *breteske,* variants of Old French *bretesque,* from Medieval Latin *(turris) brittisca,* perhaps "British (tower)," parapet (this type of fortification originated in Britain), probably from Latin *Britto,* BRITON.]

brat·tle (brăt'l) *n. Chiefly Scottish.* A rattling or clattering sound. ~*intr.v.* To make a brattle. [Imitative.]

brat·wurst (brăt'wûrst'; *German* brät'vŏŏrsht') *n.* A sausage made with finely chopped, seasoned fresh pork. [German *Bratwurst,* from Old High German *brātwurst* : *brāt(o),* meat + *wurst,* sausage, WURST.]

Braun (broun), **Eva** (1912–45). German salesgirl, mistress and wife of Adolf Hitler. She went to live with him in 1936, but the liaison was kept secret and she was never seen in public with him. They married hours before committing suicide on April 30, 1945.

Braun, Wernher von (1912–77). U.S. aeronautical physicist, born in Germany. He worked on weapons and rocket research in Germany (1932–45), including the V-2 rockets that were used to bombard London (1944–45). After surrendering to Allied troops, he went to New Mexico to join the U.S. Army Ordnance Corps research and testing station at White Sands. He was the director of the army team that put the first American satellite, Explorer I, into space (January 1958). He retired in 1972.

Braunschweig. See **Brunswick.**

Braun·schwei·ger (broun'shwī'gər) *n.* A smoked liver sausage. [German *Braunschweig,* Brunswick, West Germany.]

bra·va (brä'vä, brä-vä') *interj.* Used to express approval in applauding a woman.

---

brass instruments

THE POWERHOUSE OF MUSIC
Instruments that provide the strength of band and orchestra

Brass is the collective term for metal instruments that are blown directly through a cup-shaped or funnel-shaped mouthpiece. They include the trumpet, trombone, French horn, tuba, saxhorn, flugelhorn, cornet, and bugle. The saxophone is metal, but counts as woodwind because it has a reed mouthpiece.

Sound from a brass instrument is originated by air vibrated by the player's lips against the mouthpiece, which, together with the bell and

bore of the tube, also controls the quality of tone. A cupped mouthpiece, cylindrical bore, and narrow bell give a hard, bright tone as in the trumpet. A funnel-shaped mouthpiece, conical bore, and wide bell give the soft sound of the horn. Most brass instruments have valves that change the sounding length of the tube to give a wider range of notes. A trombone's tube length is varied by a telescopic slide operated by the player.

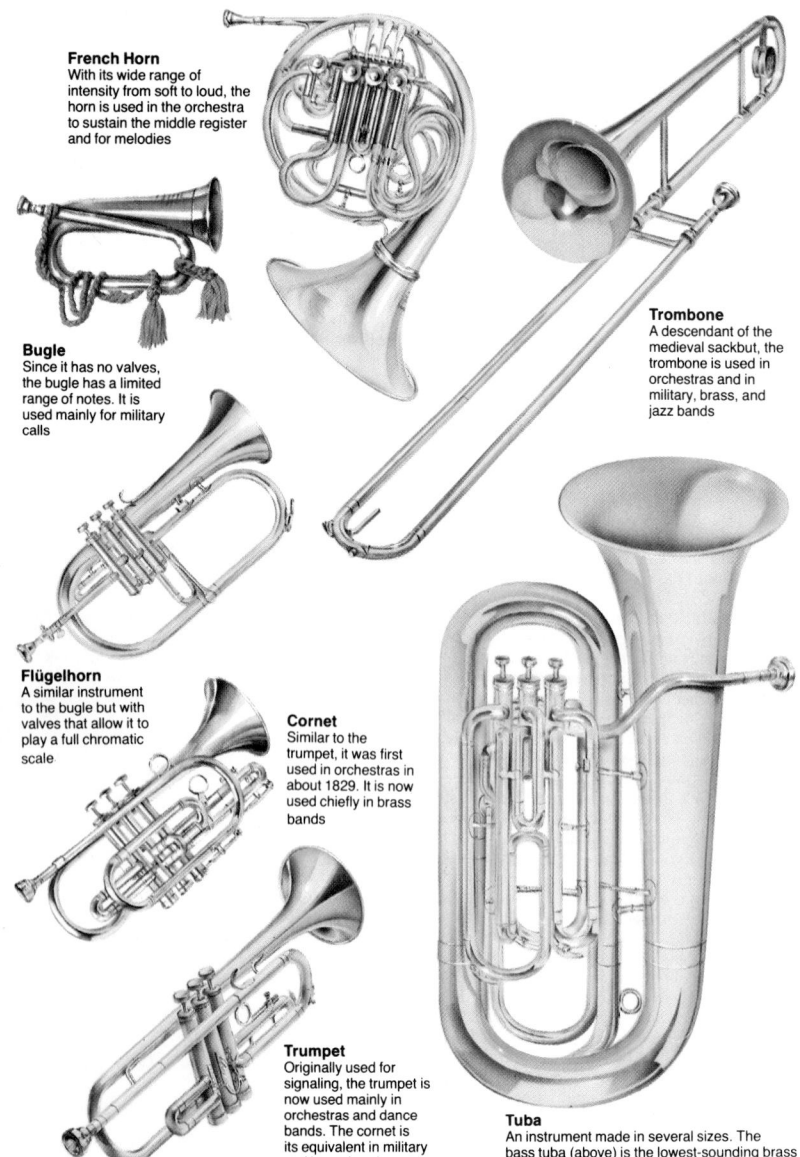

French Horn
With its wide range of intensity from soft to loud, the horn is used in the orchestra to sustain the middle register and for melodies

Bugle
Since it has no valves, the bugle has a limited range of notes. It is used mainly for military calls

Flügelhorn
A similar instrument to the bugle but with valves that allow it to play a full chromatic scale

Cornet
Similar to the trumpet, it was first used in orchestras in about 1829. It is now used chiefly in brass bands

Trumpet
Originally used for signaling, the trumpet is now used mainly in orchestras and dance bands. The cornet is its equivalent in military and brass bands

Trombone
A descendant of the medieval sackbut, the trombone is used in orchestras and in military, brass, and jazz bands

Tuba
An instrument made in several sizes. The bass tuba (above) is the lowest-sounding brass instrument of the orchestra

~*n.* A shout or cry of "brava." [Ital., fem. of *bravo,* bravo.]

bra·va·do (brə-vä′dō) *n., pl.* **-does** or **-dos.** **1.** Defiant or swaggering show of courage; false bravery. **2.** *Rare.* An instance of such behavior. [Spanish *bravada, bravata,* from *bravo,* BRAVE.]

Bra·vais lattice (brä′vā, brä-vā′) *n. Physics.* A **space lattice** *(see).* [After Auguste *Bravais* (died 1863), French physicist.]

brave (brāv) *adj.* **braver, bravest.** **1.** Possessing or displaying courage; valiant. **2.** Making a fine display; splendid. **3.** *Archaic.* Excellent.

~*n.* **1.** A North American Indian warrior. **2.** *Obsolete.* A boast or challenge. **3.** *Obsolete.* A bully.

~*tr. v.* **braved, braving, braves.** **1.** To undergo or face courageously. **2.** To defy; challenge. [Old French *brave,* courageous, noble, from Italian and Spanish *bravo,* from Vulgar Latin *brabus* (unattested), wild, savage, altered from Latin *barbarus,* foreign, barbarous, from Greek *barbaros.*] **—brave·ly** *adv.* **—brave·ness** *n.*

Synonyms: *audacious, bold, courageous, daring, dauntless, doughty, fearless, gallant, game, gritty, intrepid, mettlesome, plucky, undaunted, valiant, valorous.*

brave new world *n.* A future that holds out a promise of social progress and human contentment. Often used ironically. [After the title of a novel (1932) by Aldous Huxley, which was itself taken from Shakespeare's *The Tempest* (*c.* 1611).]

brav·er·y (brā′və-rē, brāv′rē) *n., pl.* **-ies.** **1.** The state or quality of being brave; courage. **2.** Splendor, as of attire; show. —See Synonyms at **courage.**

bra·vo[1] (brä′vō, brä-vō′) *interj.* Used to express approval.

~*n., pl.* **bravos.** A shout or cry of "bravo." [Italian, fine, BRAVE.]

bra·vo[2] (brä′vō) *n., pl.* **-voes** or **-vos.** A hired assassin; killer. [Italian, "brave."]

bra·vu·ra (brə-vyo͝or′ə) *n.* **1.** *Music.* **a.** Brilliant technique or style in performance. **b.** A piece of music requiring this. **2.** A bold or showy manner. [Italian, "bravery," spirit, from *bravo,* BRAVE.] **—bra·vu·ra** *adj.*

braw (brô) *adj.* **brawer, brawest.** *Scottish.* Fine or splendid. [Earlier *brawf,* Scottish variant of BRAVE.]

brawl (brôl) *n.* A noisy quarrel or fight.

~*intr.v.* **brawled, brawling, brawls.** **1.** To fight or quarrel noisily. **2.** To flow noisily: *a brawling stream.* [Middle English *brawlen, brallen,* probably related to Dutch and Low German *brallen* (imitative).] **—brawl·er** *n.* **—brawl·ing·ly** *adv.*

brawn (brôn) *n.* **1.** Solid and well-developed muscles. **2.** Muscular strength and power. **3.** *British.* A pickled or preserved preparation, made from meat of the head or feet of a pig. [Middle English, from Norman French *braun,* variant of Old French *braon,* flesh, muscle.]

brawn·y (brô′nē) *adj.* **-ier, -iest.** Strong and muscular. **—brawn·i·ly** *adv.* **—brawn·i·ness** *n.*

bray[1] (brā) *v.* **brayed, braying, brays.** —*intr.* **1.** To utter the loud, harsh cry of a donkey. **2.** To sound loudly and harshly. —*tr.* To utter loudly and harshly.

~*n.* **1.** A loud, harsh cry, as of a donkey. **2.** Any sound resembling this. [Middle English *brayen,* to make noise, roar, from Old French *braire,* probably from Celtic.] **—bray·er** *n.*

bray[2] *tr.v.* **brayed, braying, brays.** **1.** To crush and pound in or as if in a mortar. **2.** To spread (printing ink) thinly over type. [Middle English *brayen,* from Old French *breier,* to break, from Germanic.]

bray·er (brā′ər) *n. Printing.* A small hand roller used to spread ink thinly and evenly over type.

Braz. Brazil; Brazilian.

braze[1] (brāz) *tr.v.* **brazed, brazing, brazes.** *Archaic.* To make hard like brass. [Middle English *brasen,* Old English *brasian,* from *bræs,* BRASS.]

braze[2] *tr.v.* **brazed, brazing, brazes.** To solder (two pieces of metal) together using a hard solder with a high melting point. [Probably from French *braser,* from Old French, to burn, from *brese,* burning coals, from Germanic.] **—braz·er** *n.*

bra·zen (brā′zən) *adj.* **1.** Made of brass. **2.** Resembling brass in color, quality, or hardness. **3.** Having a loud, resonant sound like that of a brass trumpet. **4.** Impudent; bold. —See Synonyms at **shameless.**

~*tr.v.* **brazened, -zening, -zens.** To face or undergo with bold or brash self-assurance. Usually used with *out.* [Middle English *brasen,* Old English *bræsen,* from *bræs,* BRASS.] **—bra·zen·ly** *adv.* **—bra·zen·ness** *n.*

bra·zen·faced (brā′zən-fāst′) *adj.* Impudent and shameless.

bra·zier[1] (brā′zhər) *n.* One who works in brass. [Middle English *brasier,* from *bras,* BRASS.]

brazier[2] *n.* A metal stand for holding burning coals or charcoal, usually used outdoors. [French *brasier,* from *braise,* burning coals, from Old French *brese,* from Germanic.]

Bra·zil (brə-zĭl′). *Abbr.* **Braz.** *Portuguese* **Bra·sil** (brä-). Republic in eastern South America and the largest Latin American country, occupying nearly half of the South American continent. The capital is Brasília. Northern and western Brazil consists of the densely forested lowlands of the Amazon basin and is sparsely inhabited by South American Indian tribes. The more temperate southern part of the country produces three quarters of the national agricultural and industrial output. Brazil contains huge deposits of iron ore, perhaps a quarter of the world's total. It produces a quarter of the world's coffee. The country was ruled by Portugal from 1500 until 1822. It became a republic (1889) when Emperor Pedro II was forced to abdicate. Area, 8,511,965 square kilometers (3,286,488 square miles). Population, 119,000,000. See map, next page. **—Bra·zil·i·an** *adj. & n.*

braz·i·lin, bras·i·lin (brăz′ə-lĭn, brə-zĭl′ən) *n.* A crystalline compound, $C_{16}H_{14}O_5$, obtained from brazilwood and used as a dye. [French *brésiline,* from *brésil,* brazilwood.]

Brazil nut *n.* **1.** A tree, *Bertholletia excelsa,* of tropical South America, bearing hard, round, woody pods that contain the nuts. **2.** The edible nut of this tree. Also called "brazil." [After BRAZIL.]

bra·zil·wood (brə-zĭl′wo͝od′) *n.* The red wood of any of several tropical trees of the genus *Caesalpinia,* used especially for cabinetwork and as the source of a red or purple dye, brazilin. [Middle English *brasil,* from Old French *bresil,* "red-dye wood," probably from *brese,* burning coals, from Germanic.]

Braz·os (brăz′əs). A river of eastern New Mexico and central Texas. It flows 1,400 kilometers (870 miles) to the Gulf of Mexico at Freeport, southwest of Galveston.

Braz·za·ville (brăz′ə-vĭl′). Capital and largest city of the Congo. It is on the Zaire River and is an important port, receiving rubber, wood, and agricultural products and sending them on to the coast for export. The city was founded (1880) by the French explorer Savorgnan de Brazza (1852–1905) and was the capital of French Equatorial Africa (1910–58).

breach (brēch) *n.* **1.** A violation or infraction, as of a law, obligation, contract, or promise. **2.** A gap or rift, especially in a solid structure such as a dike or fortification. **3.** A breaking up or disruption of friendly relations; an estrangement. **4.** The leaping of a whale from the water. **5.** The breaking of waves or surf.

~*v.* **breached, breaching, breaches.** —*tr.* To make a hole or gap in; break through. —*intr.* To leap from the water. Used of a whale. [Middle English *breche, brek,* partly from Old French *breche,* from Old High German *brehha,* from *brehhan,* to break, and partly from Old English *brǣc, brēc,* from *brecan,* to break.]

Synonyms: *encroachment, infraction, infringement, transgression, trespass, violation.*

breach of promise *n. Law.* Formerly, the failure to fulfill a promise, especially a promise to marry someone.

breach of the peace *n. Law.* A disturbance of public order caused, for example, by fighting or rioting.

bread (brĕd) *n.* **1.** A staple food made from flour or meal mixed with a liquid, usually combined with a leavening agent, and kneaded, shaped into loaves, and baked. **2.** Food in general, regarded as necessary for sustaining life. **3. a.** The necessities of life; livelihood: *earn one's bread.* **b.** *Slang.* Money.

~*tr.v.* **breaded, breading, breads.** To coat with breadcrumbs, as before cooking. [Middle English *bread, bred,* Old English *brēad.*]

bread and butter *n. Informal.* **1.** A means of support; a livelihood. **2.** A staple, but not exclusive, source of income.

bread-and-but·ter (brĕd′n-bŭt′ər) *adj.* **1.** Providing a basic income: *a bread-and-butter job.* **2.** Of fundamental concern; basic: *an election campaign fought on bread-and-butter issues.* **3.** Expressing gratitude for hospitality: *a bread-and-butter note.*

bread·bas·ket (brĕd′băs′kĭt, -bäs′kĭt) *n.* **1.** An important cereal-producing region. **2.** *Slang.* The stomach.

bread·board (brĕd′bôrd′, -bōrd′) *n.* **1.** A board on which bread is sliced. **2.** An experimental model, especially of an electronic circuit; prototype.

bread·fruit (brĕd′fro͞ot′) *n., pl.* **-fruits** or collectively **breadfruit.** **1.** A tree, *Artocarpus communis,* of Polynesia, having deeply lobed leaves and round, usually seedless fruit. **2.** The edible fruit of this tree, having a texture like that of bread when baked or roasted.

bread·line (brĕd′līn′) *n.* A line of persons waiting to be given free food, either from a relief agency or as charity. **—on the breadline.** Living at subsistence level; destitute.

bread mold *n.* A fungus, *Rhizopus nigricans,* that forms a dense, cottony growth on bread and other foods.

bread·nut (brĕd′nŭt′) *n.* **1.** A tree, *Brosimum alicastrum,* of Central America and the West Indies, bearing round, nutlike fruit. **2.** The fruit of this tree, ground to produce a substitute for wheat flour.

breadth (brĕdth) *n.* **1.** *Abbr.* **b., B.** The measure or dimension from side to side of something, as distinguished from length or thickness; width. **2.** An extent or piece of something, usually conforming to a standard width: *a breadth of canvas.* **3.** Wide extent or scope. **4.** Freedom from narrowness, as of views or interests. [Middle English *brede,* Old English *brǣdu,* from Germanic *braidjōn* (unattested), from *braithaz* (unattested), BROAD.]

breadth·wise (brĕdth′wīz′) *adv.* Also **breadth·ways** (-wāz′). In the direction of the breadth. **—breadth·wise** *adj.*

bread·win·ner (brĕd′wĭn′ər) *n.* One who supports a family or household by his or her earnings.

break (brāk) *v.* **broke** (brōk) or *archaic* **brake** (brāk), **broken** (brō′kən), **breaking, breaks.** —*tr.* **1.** To separate or reduce to pieces with sudden or violent force; smash. **2.** To crack without actually separating into pieces. **3.** To render unusable or inoperative. **4.** To part or pierce the surface of. **5.** To cause to burst. **6.** To fracture a bone of. **7.** To force or make a way through; penetrate: *break the sound barrier.* **8.** To force one's way out of; escape from. **9.** To put an end to by force or strong opposition: *break a strike.* **10.** To fail to conform to; act contrary to; violate. **11. a.** To bring abruptly to an end: *A scream broke the silence.* **b.** To discontinue temporarily; interrupt; suspend: *break a journey.* **12.** To cause to give up a habit. Used with *of.* **13.** To train to obey; tame; especially, to accustom (a horse) to the saddle. **14.** To disrupt or destroy the order or regularity of: *break ranks.* **15.** To destroy the completeness of: *break a set*

Brazil nuts *These edible nuts are harvested from a South American tree,* Bertholletia excelsa. *The nuts are contained in segmented shells that fit inside large spherical seedpods.*

breadfruit *In the 17th century this Pacific island fruit was introduced from Tahiti to the West Indies. It was during an expedition to collect the plant that the mutiny on H.M.S* Bounty *took place.*

PRONUNCIATION KEY

ă, pat; ā, pay; âr, care;
ä, father, are; b, bib;
ch, church; d, deed; ĕ, pet;
ē, be; f, fife; g, gag; h, hat;
hw, which; ĭ, pit; ī, pie;
îr, pier; j, judge; k, kick;
l, lid, needle; m, mum;
n, no, sudden; ng, thing;
ŏ, pot; ō, toe; ô, paw, for;
oi, noise; ou, out; o͝o, book;
o͞o, boot; p, pop; r, roar;
s, sauce; sh, ship, dish;
t, tight; th, thin, path;
th, this, bathe; ŭ, cut; ûr, fur;
v, valve; w, with; y, yes;
z, zebra, size; zh, vision;
ə, about, item, edible,
gallop, circus, peaceful

IN FOREIGN WORDS:

à, *Fr.* ami; œ, *Fr.* feu, *Ger.* schön; ü, *Fr.* tu, *Ger.* über; KH, *Ger.* ich, *Scot.* loch; N, *Fr.* bon; y′, *Fr.* Compiègne

STRESS MARKS:

Primary stress: ′
in·cite′ (ĭn-sīt′)
Secondary stress: ′
in′sight′ (ĭn′sīt′)

BRAZIL

VENEZUELA · GUYANA · Mt Roraima 2810m · SURINAM · FR. GUIANA · ATLANTIC OCEAN · COLOMBIA · Guiana Highlands · Negro · AMAPÁ · Mouths of the Amazon · Marajó I. · Belém · São Luís · Fortaleza · Manaus · Amazon · P A R Á · Teresina · Natal · Juruá · Purus · Madeira · B R A Z I L · PERNAMBUCO · Recife · São Francisco · ALAGOAS · SERGIPE · Maceió · Tocantins · Xingu · Tapajós · Brazilian Highlands · GOIÁS · B A H I A · Salvador · Mato Grosso · Cuiabá · Goiânia · BRASÍLIA · MINAS GERAIS · ESPÍRITO SANTO · Sabará · Belo Horizonte · OuroPrêto · Congonhas · SÃO PAULO · Campinas · Rio de Janeiro · São Paulo · Santos · GUANABARA · Curitiba · PARANÁ · Itaipú Dam · SANTA CATARINA · RIO GRANDE DO SUL · Pôrto Alegre · Rio Grande · URUGUAY · PACIFIC OCEAN · PERU · ANDES · BOLIVIA · CHILE · PARAGUAY · ARGENTINA · Paraguay · Paraná · Uruguay · Equator · Tropic of Capricorn · Km 0 400 800 1200 1600 · Miles 0 200 400 600 800

breaker *There are three ways in which a wave breaks into foam against a reef or shoreline: plunging breakers (shown here) surge up from a steeply rising bottom and curl over to break with a sudden crash; spilling breakers break slowly over a long stretch of the seabed; surging breakers neither spill nor plunge— they break as they flow over the beach face.*

of books. **16.** To lessen in force or effect: *break a fall.* **17.** To weaken or destroy, as in spirit or health: *"For a hero loves the world till it breaks him"* (W.B. Yeats). **18.** To overwhelm with grief or sorrow: *break one's heart.* **19.** To cause to be without money or to go into bankruptcy. **20.** *Military.* To reduce in rank; demote. **21.** To reduce to or exchange for smaller monetary units: *break a ten-dollar bill.* **22.** To surpass or outdo: *break a record.* **23.** To make known (news, for example). **24.** To find the solution or key to; decipher. **25.** *Law.* To invalidate (a will) by judicial action. **26.** *Tennis.* To win a game against (the service of an opponent). **27.** *Electricity.* To open: *break a circuit.* —*intr.* **1.** To become separated into pieces or fragments; come apart. **2.** To become unusable or inoperative. **3.** To give way; collapse. **4.** To diminish or discontinue abruptly: *His fever broke.* **5.** To rise to or emerge from the surface of the water. Used of fish. **6.** To move away or escape suddenly. **7.** To weaken in spirit, resolve, or self-control: *He broke under torture.* **8. a.** To come into being or public notice, especially suddenly: *The story broke at 12:00.* **b.** To dawn. **9.** To come to an end after a long time: *The cold spell finally broke.* **10.** To be overwhelmed with sorrow. Used of the heart. **11.** To begin abruptly to utter, express, or do something: *Her face broke into a smile. The horse broke into a gallop.* **12.** To interrupt or discontinue an activity. Often used with *up: The meeting broke up after noon.* **13.** *Linguistics.* To undergo breaking. Used of a vowel. **14.** To collapse or crash into surf or spray. Used of waves. **15. a.** To change from one tone quality to another, as from emotion. Used of the voice. **b.** To change from one musical register to another. **16.** In boxing and wrestling, to disengage from one's opponent after a clinch. —**break bread.** To eat or share a meal. —**break camp.** To pack up and leave a campsite. —**break even.** To operate economically, making neither a profit nor a loss. —**break (new) ground.** To discover or pioneer: *broke ground in cancer research.* —**break in on** (or **upon**). To interrupt or intrude on. —**break into. 1.** To enter forcibly, suddenly, or illegally. **2.** To interrupt. **3.** To begin to draw on (a reserve): *break into one's savings.* **4.** To become employed or established in a profession or sphere of activity: *trying to break into publishing.* —**break off. 1.** To stop suddenly, as in speaking. **2.** To discontinue (a relationship). —**break the ice.** To get started, as in an enterprise or conversation. —**break with. 1.** To discontinue a relationship with. **2.** To depart from (a tradition or precedent, for example).
~*n.* Also **brake** (for sense 19). **1.** The act of breaking; a separating into parts. **2.** The result of breaking; a fracture or crack. **3. a.** A beginning; a coming into being: *the break of day.* **b.** An opening; a clearing. **4.** A dash, especially to escape: *made a break for it.* **5.** An interruption or disruption of continuity or regularity. **6.** A brief rest or holiday, as from work. **7.** A sudden or marked change. **8.** *Informal.* A chance occurrence; especially, an unexpected opportunity. **9.** A severing of ties. **10.** A sudden decline in prices, especially in the stock market. **11.** *Prosody.* A pause in a line; a caesura. **12.** *Tennis.* An instance of winning a game against an opponent's

serve. **13.** *Electricity.* Interruption of a flow of current. **14.** *Music.* **a.** The point at which a register or a tonal quality changes to another register or a tonal quality. **b.** The change itself. **c.** In jazz, an improvised solo cadenza played during the pause between the regular phrases or choruses of a melody. **15.** *Baseball & Cricket.* The swerving of a ball from a straight path of flight when thrown. **16.** *Billiards.* The opening shot. **17.** *Billiards & Croquet.* A run or unbroken series of successful shots. **18.** *Bowling.* Failure to score a strike or a spare in a given frame. **19.** A high, open, horse-drawn carriage with four wheels. [Break, broke, broken; Middle English *breken, brok* (or *brak*), *broken*, Old English *brecan, bræc* (plural *bræcon*), *brocen*, from Germanic *brekan* (unattested).]
  Synonyms: *burst, crack, crush, fracture, rupture, shatter, shiver, smash, splinter, split.*

break·a·ble (brā′kə-bəl) *adj.* Capable of being broken. —See Synonyms at **fragile.**
~*n.* **breakables.** Articles capable of being broken easily. —**break·a·ble·ness** *n.*

break·age (brā′kĭj) *n.* **1.** The act or result of breaking. **2.** A quantity or article broken. **3. a.** Loss or damage as a result of breaking. **b.** An allowance in compensation for such a loss or damage.

break away *intr.v.* **1.** To withdraw, especially from a main group. **2.** To depart from former ways or tradition.

break·a·way (brāk′ə-wā′) *adj.* **1.** Withdrawing, or favoring withdrawal, from a main group: *a breakaway political faction.* **2.** Designed to break or fall apart easily: *breakaway stage scenery.*
~*n.* **1.** One that breaks away. **2.** *Australian.* A sudden mad rush, as of cattle, for example; a stampede.

break·bone fever (brāk′bōn′) *n.* A viral disease, **dengue** (see).

break·danc·ing (brāk′dăn′sĭng) *n.* A type of dance incorporating gymnastics such as handsprings, popular in the 1980's. It may accompany **body popping** (see). [20th century : origin obscure.]

break down *intr.v.* **1.** To fail to function; cease to be useful or operable. **2.** To have a physical or mental collapse. **3.** To become seriously distressed or upset. **4.** To end prematurely or inconclusively: *Peace talks have broken down.* **5.** To undergo chemical decomposition. —*tr.v.* **1.** To distress; upset. **2.** To overcome (opposition, for example). **3.** To consider in parts; analyze. **4.** To effect chemical decomposition in. **5.** To demolish; destroy.

break·down (brāk′doun′) *n.* **1. a.** The act or an instance of failing to function or ceasing to be effective. **b.** The condition resulting from this. **2.** *Electricity.* The failure of an insulator or insulating medium to prevent discharge or current flow. **3.** A collapse in physical or mental health. **4.** An analysis, outline, or summary consisting of itemized data or essentials. **5.** Disintegration or decomposition into parts or elements. **6.** An electrical discharge between electrodes that occurs at a certain voltage in a gas discharge tube.

break·er¹ (brā′kər) *n.* **1.** One that breaks. **2.** A machine or plant for breaking up some hard substance, such as rock or coal. **3.** *Electricity.* A **circuit breaker** (see). **4.** A wave that crests or breaks into foam, especially against a shoreline.

breaker² *n.* A small water cask for use on a ship's lifeboat. [Spanish *bareca, barrica,* BARREL.]

break-e·ven point (brāk′ē′vən) *n.* The stage at which a business, project, or speculator can operate economically without making a loss, but not yet making a profit.

break·fast (brĕk′fəst) *n.* The first meal of the day. [Middle English *brekfast, brekefast,* from *breken faste,* to break (one's) fasting.] —**break·fast** *v.* —**break·fast·er** *n.*

break·front (brāk′frŭnt′) *n.* A high, wide cabinet or bookcase having a central section projecting beyond the end sections.

break in *tr.v.* **1.** To train (a horse, for example) to obey; tame. **2.** To accustom to duties. **3.** To wear or use until comfortable or suited to one's requirements. —*intr.v.* **1.** To break into premises, usually to steal. **2.** To interrupt a speaker.

break-in (brāk′ĭn′) *n.* **1.** An act of forcible entry, as into a building, dwelling, or office, for an illegal purpose such as theft. **2.** A training or testing period of someone or something that is new.

break·ing (brā′kĭng) *n.* *Linguistics.* The change of a simple vowel to a diphthong, often caused by the influence of neighboring consonants. Also called "vowel fracture."

breaking and entering *n.* *Law.* The gaining of unauthorized access, as by forcing a lock, to another's premises for the purpose of committing a crime.

breaking point *n.* **1.** The point at which the stress on a material is sufficient to cause it to break. **2.** The stage at which a person is no longer able to bear psychological stress.

break·neck (brāk′nĕk′) *adj.* Dangerous: *breakneck speed.*

break out *intr.v.* **1.** To begin or arise suddenly. **2.** To escape, as from prison. **3.** To become affected with eruptions or with a rash. Used of the skin, or of a skin-disease sufferer.

break-out (brāk′out′) *n.* An escape, as from prison.

Breakspear, Nicholas. See **Adrian IV.**

break through *intr.v.* **1.** To penetrate an obstacle or defense. **2.** To overcome a difficulty and be able to make progress.

break·through (brāk′thrōō′) *n.* **1.** An act of breaking through an obstacle or restriction. **2.** A military offensive that penetrates an enemy's lines of defense. **3.** A major achievement or success that permits further progress, as in scientific research.

break up *tr.v.* **1.** To disband or disrupt. **2. a.** To take apart; separate. **b.** To fragment, as by cutting or digging. **3.** To put a stop to; discontinue. **4.** *Informal.* To convulse with laughter. —*intr.v.* **1. a.** To end. Used of a relationship. **b.** To part. Used of partners, especially in or as in a marriage. **2.** *British.* To begin the holiday period at the end of a school term. **3.** To melt in the spring thaw. Used of ice on a frozen river or lake. **4.** *Informal.* To be overcome by laughter or emotion.

break·up (brāk′ŭp′) *n.* **1.** The act of breaking up; a separation or dispersal. **2.** A collapse; dissolution.

break·wa·ter (brāk′wô′tər, -wŏt′ər) *n.* A structure that protects a harbor or shore from the full impact of waves.

bream (brēm) *n., pl.* **bream. 1.** Any of several European freshwater fishes of the genus *Abramis,* having a deep, flattened body and silvery scales. **2.** Any of several similar or related fishes. [Middle English *breme,* from Old French *breme, bresme,* from Germanic.]

breast (brĕst) *n.* **1. a.** Either of two fleshy milk-secreting organs on a woman's chest; the human mammary gland. **b.** A homologous organ in other mammals. **2.** A source of nourishment. **3. a.** The front of the body, extending from the neck to the abdomen. **b.** A homologous part in other animals. **4.** This part of the human body regarded as the seat of affection or emotion. **5.** The section of a garment that covers this part of the body. **6.** Anything likened to this part of the body: *the breast of a hill.* **7.** A coal face. **—make a clean breast of.** To make a full confession of.

∼*tr.v.* **breasted, breasting, breasts. 1.** To meet with the breast: *The runner breasted the tape just ahead of the others.* **2.** To encounter or face bravely. **3.** To come to the breast of: *The figure breasted the hill.* [Middle English *brest,* Old English *brēost.*]

breast·bone (brĕst′bōn′) *n. Anatomy.* The **sternum** *(see).*

breast·feed (brĕst′fēd′) *v.* **-fed** (-fĕd′), **-feeding, -feeds.** *—tr.* To feed (a baby) mother's milk from the breast; suckle. *—intr.* To feed a baby in this way.

breast·plate (brĕst′plāt′) *n.* **1.** A piece of armor that covers the breast. **2.** A square cloth set with 12 precious stones representing the 12 tribes of Israel, worn by a Jewish high priest. **3.** The plastron of a turtle's or tortoise's shell.

breast stroke *n.* A swimming stroke in which one lies face down in the water and extends the arms in front of the head, then sweeps them both back laterally under the surface of the water while performing a frog kick.

breast·work (brĕst′wûrk′) *n.* A temporary, quickly constructed fortification, usually breast-high. —See Synonyms at **bulwark.**

breath (brĕth) *n.* **1.** The air inhaled and exhaled in respiration. **2.** The act or process of breathing; respiration. **3.** The capacity to breathe, especially as evidence of life. **4.** A single respiration. **5.** Exhaled air, as evidenced by vapor, odor, or heat. **6.** A momentary pause or rest. **7. a.** A momentary stirring of air. **b.** A slight gust of fragrant air. **8.** A trace or suggestion: *a breath of scandal.* **9.** A soft-spoken sound; a whisper. **10.** *Phonetics.* Exhalation of air without vibrating the vocal cords, as in the articulation of *p* and *s.* Compare **voice. —catch one's breath. 1.** To pause until one's normal breathing is regained. **2.** To be left breathless for a moment, as in admiration. **—in the same breath.** At the same time. **—out of breath.** Breathless, as from exertion. **—save one's breath.** Not to waste time in pointless excuses, pleading, or the like. **—take someone's breath away.** To leave one as if breathless from awe or surprise. **—under** (or **below**) **one's breath.** In a whisper or muted voice. [Middle English *breth,* vapor, air from the lungs, Old English *brǣth,* odor, exhalation.]

breath·a·lyze (brĕth′ə-līz′) *tr.v.* **-lyzed, -lyzing, -lyzes.** To test (a driver) for excessive consumption of alcohol, using a Breathalyzer.

Breath·a·lyz·er (brĕth′ə-lī′zər) *n.* A trademark for a device used to test whether a driver has consumed an excessive amount of alcohol, consisting of crystals which react to the presence of alcohol in the driver's breath by changing color. [BREATH + (AN)ALYZE + -ER.]

breathe (brēth) *v.* **breathed, breathing, breathes.** *—intr.* **1.** To inhale and exhale. **2.** To be alive; live. **3.** To move or stir gently, as air does. **4.** To take in oxygen for combustion. Used of machinery. **5.** To come into contact with, or allow the passage of, air: *open the wine and let it breathe.* *—tr.* **1.** To inhale and exhale during respiration. **2.** To impart (a quality) as if by breathing; instill: *breathe life into a portrait.* **3.** To exhale; emit. **4.** To utter, especially quietly; whisper: *Don't breathe a word of this.* **5.** To express; evince; manifest. **6.** To allow (a person or animal) to rest or regain breath. **7.** *Phonetics.* To utter with a voiceless exhalation of air. [Middle English *brethen,* from *breth,* BREATH.] **—breath·a·ble** *adj.*

breath·er (brē′*th*ər) *n.* **1.** One who breathes in a specified manner. **2.** *Informal.* A short rest period. **3.** An opening for ventilation.

breath·ing (brē′*th*ĭng) *n.* **1.** The act or process of respiration. **2.** Either of two marks used in writing Greek, indicating aspiration of an initial sound (‘), called *rough breathing,* or the absence of such aspiration (’), called *smooth breathing.*

breathing room *n.* Breathing space.

breathing space *n.* **1.** Sufficient space to permit ease of breathing or movement. **2.** Time allowing an opportunity to rest or solve a problem. In this sense, also called "breathing spell."

breathing spell *n.* See **breathing space** (sense 2).

breath·less (brĕth′lĭs) *adj.* **1.** Out-of-breath. **2.** Holding the breath from excitement or suspense. **3.** Inspiring or marked by sudden excitement that takes the breath away: *a breathless flight.* **4.** Having no air or breeze; still. **5.** Without breath; not breathing; dead. **—breath·less·ly** *adv.* **—breath·less·ness** *n.*

breath·tak·ing (brĕth′tā′kĭng) *adj.* Inspiring awe; deeply impressive or exciting. **—breath·tak·ing·ly** *adv.*

breath test *n. British.* A test for intoxication, usually using a Breathalyzer.

breath·y (brĕth′ē) *adj.* **-ier, -iest.** Marked by audible or noisy breathing: *a breathy voice.*

brec·ci·a (brĕch′ē-ə, brĕsh′-) *n.* Rock composed of angular fragments cemented in a fine matrix. [Italian, from Old High German *brehha,* breaking, fragment, from *brehhan,* to break.] **—brec·ci·at·ed** (brĕch′ē-ā′tĭd, brĕsh′-) *adj.*

Brecht (brĕkt, brĕKHt), **Bertolt** (1898–1956). German playwright. His most popular work, *The Threepenny Opera,* with music by Kurt Weill, was produced in 1928. In 1933 he fled to Denmark to escape the Nazis, and in 1941 came to the United States, where he wrote *The Caucasian Chalk Circle.* He settled in East Berlin (1949) and was awarded the Stalin Peace Prize (1954). **—Brecht·i·an** *adj. & n.*

bred. Past tense and past participle of **breed.**

Bre·da (brā-dä′). Industrial town in the southern Netherlands, at the confluence of the Merk and Aa rivers. Charles II of England lived here during much of his exile and issued the Declaration of Breda (1660) announcing the conditions for his return to the English throne.

brede (brēd) *n. Archaic.* An ornamental embroidered edging. [Alteration of BRAID.]

breech (brēch) *n.* **1.** The lower rear portion of the human trunk; the buttocks. **2.** The lower part of a pulley. **3.** The part of a firearm to the rear of the barrel or, in a cannon, to the rear of the bore. [Middle English *breech,* Old English *brēc,* breeches, plural of *brōc,* leg covering.]

breech·block (brēch′blŏk′) *n.* The metal part that closes the breech end of the barrel of a breechloading gun and that is removed to insert a cartridge and replaced before firing.

breech·cloth (brēch′klŏth′) *n.* Also **breech·clout** (-klout′). A loincloth.

breech delivery *n.* Delivery of a baby with the buttocks or feet appearing first. Also called "breech birth."

breech·es (brĭch′ĭz) *pl.n.* **1.** Trousers extending to or just below the knee. **2.** *Informal & Regional.* Any trousers. [Plural of BREECH.]

breeches buoy *n.* An apparatus used for rescues at sea, consisting of sturdy canvas breeches for the rescued person's legs, attached at the waist to a ring buoy that is suspended from a pulley running along a rope from ship to shore or from ship to ship.

breech·ing (brĭch′ĭng, brē′chĭng) *n.* **1.** The strap of a harness that passes behind a draft animal's haunches. **2.** The parts of a gun that make up the breech. **3.** Formerly, a rope securing the breech of a cannon to the side of a ship to control the recoil.

breech·load·er (brēch′lō′dər) *n.* Any gun or firearm loaded at the breech. **—breech·load·ing** *adj.*

breech presentation *n.* The position of a fetus during labor in which the buttocks or feet appear first in the cervix.

breed (brēd) *v.* **bred** (brĕd), **breeding, breeds.** *—tr.* **1.** To produce (offspring); give birth to or hatch. **2.** To bring about; engender. **3. a.** To cause to reproduce; raise. **b.** To develop new or improved strains in (animals or plants) by selection, hybridization, and similar methods. *—intr.* **1.** To produce offspring. **2.** To be engendered; arise: *Panic bred in this atmosphere.*

∼*n.* **1.** A genetic strain or type of organism, usually a domestic animal, having consistent and recognizable inherited characteristics; especially, such a strain developed and maintained by man. **2.** A kind or type: *a new breed of university student.* [Middle English *breden, bred,* Old English *brēdan, bredd* (unattested).]

breed·er (brē′dər) *n.* **1.** A person who breeds animals or plants. **2.** An animal kept to produce offspring. **3.** One that breeds; a cause; source. **4.** A breeder reactor.

breeder reactor *n.* A nuclear reactor that produces, as well as consumes, fissionable material; especially, one that produces more fissionable material than it consumes.

breed·ing (brē′dĭng) *n.* **1.** One's line of descent: *a woman of noble breeding.* **2.** Training in the proper forms of social and personal conduct. —See Usage note at **culture.**

breeding ground *n.* **1.** A place to which animals go to breed. **2.** A place or set of circumstances that encourages certain ideas or conditions.

breeks (brēks) *pl.n. Chiefly Scottish.* Breeches; trousers. [Middle English (northern dialect) *breke,* variant of *brech,* BREECH.]

breeze¹ (brēz) *n.* **1.** A light air current; a gentle wind. **2.** *Meteorology.* A wind of from 6.5 to 50 kilometers (4 to 31 miles) per hour. **3.** *Chiefly British Informal.* A commotion or disturbance; an argument. **4.** *Informal.* An easily accomplished task. —See Synonyms at **wind.**

∼*intr.v.* **breezed, breezing, breezes. 1.** To blow lightly. **2.** *Informal.* To move in a quick and usually nonchalant manner: *She breezed in an hour late* **3.** To progress swiftly and effortlessly: *breezed through the test.* **—breeze up.** *Nautical.* To blow more strongly. Used of wind. [Perhaps from Old Spanish *briza*†, northeast wind.]

breeze² *n. British.* The refuse left when coal, coke, or charcoal is burned, used in brickmaking and as a concrete filler. [French *braise,* burning coals, from Old French *brese,* from Germanic.]

breeze·way (brēz′wā′) *n.* A roofed, open-sided passageway connecting two structures, such as a house and a garage.

breez·y (brē′zē) *adj.* **-ier, -iest. 1.** Exposed to breezes; windy. **2.** Fresh and animated; lively; sprightly. **3.** Casual; nonchalant. **—breez·i·ly** *adv.* **—breez·i·ness** *n.*

breg·ma (brĕg′mə) *n., pl.* **-mata** (-mə-tə). *Anatomy.* The junction of the sagittal and coronal sutures at the top of the skull. **—breg·mat·ic** (brĕg′măt′ĭk) *adj.*

bream *A European freshwater fish that lives in lakes and slow-flowing rivers. Adult bream grow to between 300 and 500 millimeters (12–20 inches) long.*

PRONUNCIATION KEY

ă, pat; ā, pay; âr, care;
ä, father, are; b, bib;
ch, church; d, deed; ĕ, pet;
ē, be; f, fife; g, gag; h, hat;
hw, which; ĭ, pit; ī, pie;
îr, pier; j, judge; k, kick;
l, lid, needle; m, mum;
n, no, sudden; ng, thing;
ŏ, pot; ō, toe; ô, paw, for;
oi, noise; ou, out; ŏŏ, book;
ōō, boot; p, pop; r, roar;
s, sauce; sh, ship, dish;
t, tight; th, thin, path;
th, this, bathe; ŭ, cut; ûr, fur;
v, valve; w, with; y, yes;
z, zebra, size; zh, vision;
ə, about, item, edible, gallop, circus, peaceful

IN FOREIGN WORDS:

à, *Fr.* ami; œ, *Fr.* feu, *Ger.* schön; ü, *Fr.* tu, *Ger.* über;
KH, *Ger.* ich, *Scot.* loch;
N, *Fr.* bon; y′, *Fr.* Compiègne

STRESS MARKS:

Primary stress: ′
in·cite′ (ĭn-sīt′)
Secondary stress: ′
in′sight′ (ĭn′sīt′)

Bre·men (brĕm'ən, brā'mən). City in northern West Germany, capital of the state of the same name, on the Weser River. It is West Germany's second most important port after Hamburg and in the Middle Ages was a leading member of the Hanseatic League.

Bre·mer·ha·ven (brĕm'ər-hä'vən, -hā'-). Port in northern West Germany, on the estuary of the Weser River. It has a deep natural harbor and is the largest fishing port in continental Europe.

brems·strah·lung (brĕms'shträ'lŏng) n. The electromagnetic radiation produced by an electrically charged subatomic particle, such as an electron, subjected to a change in velocity, as by deceleration in the electric field of an atomic nucleus. [German, "braking radiation" : *Bremse*, brake + *Strahlung*, radiation.]

Bren·dan (brĕn'dən), **Saint** (c. 484–c. 577). Irish abbot, also known variously as "Brenainn" (in Modern Irish), "Brandanus" (in Latin), and "Brandon." He is the legendary hero of a number of sea voyages, including one to America, and almost certainly visited the Scottish isles.

Bren·del (brĕn'dəl), **Alfred** (1931–). Austrian pianist. Although admired for his interpretation of the 19th-century masters generally, he has made his name as a performer of Schubert and Beethoven.

Bren gun (brĕn) n. A .303 caliber gas-operated, air-cooled light machine gun, adopted by the British Army in World War II. [BR(NO), Czechoslovakia, where it was first made + *En(field)*, England, where it was later manufactured.]

Bren·ner Pass (brĕn'ər). One of the lowest Alpine passes, connecting Innsbruck, Austria, with Bolzano, Italy. It has been the major northern entrance to Italy since Roman times, but a road was not constructed through it until 1772. A railway through the pass, requiring 30 tunnels and 60 large bridges, was completed in 1867.

brent *British*. Variant of **brant**.

br'er (brûr, brĕr) n. *Southern U.S. Informal*. Brother.

Bre·scia (brĕsh'ə, brā'shə). Industrial city in northern Italy, at the junction of the Garza River and the Po plain. It is the capital of the province of the same name.

Brest¹ (brĕst). Port and naval station in northwest France, on the Brittany coast. Its large landlocked harbor was built by Cardinal Richelieu (1631) as a military base and arsenal, with a roadstead (24 kilometers; 14 miles long) leading to open water.

Brest². Formerly **Brest-Li·tovsk** (brĕst'lĭ-tôfsk'). Industrial city in the Belorussian S.S.R. in the U.S.S.R., near the Polish border. It belonged to Lithuania, then Poland, before being ceded to Russia (1795). Germany and the U.S.S.R. signed the treaty of Brest-Litovsk ending World War I on the eastern front (March 1918).

Bretagne. See **Brittany**.

breth·ren (brĕth'rən). Plural of **brother**. Used chiefly in archaic, ceremonial, or ironic contexts.

Bret·on (brĕt'n) n. 1. A native or inhabitant of Brittany. 2. The Celtic language of Brittany. [French, from Old French, BRITON.] —**Bret·on** *adj*.

Bre·ton (brə-tôN'), **André** (1896–1966). French poet and literary theorist, founder of surrealism. He began to write after World War I, at first linking himself with dadaism, but breaking with that movement to write the first manifesto of surrealism (1924).

Breu·er (broi'ər) **Josef** (1842–1925). Austrian physician and psychologist. He collaborated with Freud in writing *Studies in Hysteria* (1895). He was the first man to relieve hysteria by cathartic methods, and it was his therapy that provided the basis of Freud's development of the theory of psychoanalysis.

Breughel. See **Bruegel**.

breve (brĕv, brēv) n. 1. A symbol (˘) placed over a vowel to show that it has a short sound. Compare **macron**. 2. *Prosody*. A similar symbol used to indicate that a syllable is short or unstressed. 3. *Music*. A single note equivalent to two whole notes. 4. *Archaic*. A letter of authority, especially one from a pope. [Middle English, variant of *bref*, BRIEF.]

bre·vet (brə-vĕt', brĕv'ĭt) n. *Abbr*. **brev.**, **bvt.** A commission, often granted as an honor, promoting a military officer in rank without an increase in pay or authority.
—*tr.v.* **brevetted** or **-veted, -vetting** or **-veting, -vets**. To promote by brevet.
—*adj.* Held or awarded by brevet. [Middle English, from Old French *brevet*, diminutive of *bref*, letter, BRIEF.] —**bre·vet·cy** (brə-vĕt'sē) n.

bre·vi·ar·y (brē'vē-ĕr-ē, brĕv'ē-) n., pl. **-ies**. A book containing the hymns, offices, and prayers said or sung by Roman Catholic clergy at the canonical hours. [Latin *breviārium*, summary, abridgment, from *breviāre*, to abridge, from *brevis*, short, BRIEF.]

bre·vier (brə-vîr') n. *Printing*. Formerly, a size of type, 8-point. [Dutch, "type size for breviaries," from Latin *breviārium*, BREVIARY.]

brev·i·ty (brĕv'ə-tē) n. 1. Briefness of duration. 2. Concise expression; terseness. [Latin *brevitās*, from *brevis*, BRIEF.]

brew (broo) v. **brewed, brewing, brews**. —*tr.* 1. To make (ale or beer, for example) from malt and other ingredients by infusion, boiling, and fermentation. 2. To make (a beverage) by boiling, steeping, or mixing various ingredients. 3. To concoct; devise. —*intr.* 1. To brew ale or beer. 2. To be in the process of infusion. 3. To be imminent; impend. Used of storms. 4. To be in preparation. Used of plots, quarrels, or the like.
—*n.* 1. A beverage made by brewing. 2. The quality or quantity of beverage brewed at one time. 3. A concoction. [Middle English *brewen*, Old English *brēowan*, from Germanic.] —**brew·er** n.

brew·age (broo'ĭj) n. 1. Something prepared by brewing. 2. The process of brewing.

brewer's yeast n. 1. A yeast, *Saccharomyces cerevisiae*, used in brewing and as a source of B complex vitamins. 2. The yeast obtained as a by-product of brewing.

brew·er·y (broo'ər-ē) n., pl. **-ies**. An establishment for the manufacture of malt liquors.

brew·is (broo'ĭs, brooz) n. *Regional*. 1. A broth. 2. Bread soaked in broth, gravy, milk, or the like. [Middle English *browis, brewes,* from Old French *broez, bro(u)ez,* from *breu,* broth.]

Brey·ten·bach (brā'tən-bŭKH), **Breyten** (1939–). South African poet, a member of the so-called *Sestigers* (people of the sixties). After living in Paris for some years, he returned to South Africa in the 1970's and was imprisoned under the country's Terrorism Act.

Brezh·nev (brĕzh'nĕf), **Leonid Ilyich** (1906–82). Soviet politician and president. He joined the Komsomol (Communist Youth) in 1923 and the party in 1931. For the next 20 years he advanced his career as a protégé of Khrushchev in the Ukraine. In 1957 he was promoted to membership of the Presidium (now the Politburo) and became its chairman (1960). In 1964, when Khrushchev was dismissed, he replaced him as first secretary of the party. He became president in 1977. In 1968 when Soviet troops entered Czechoslovakia, he enunciated the "Brezhnev doctrine," which asserts that the U.S.S.R. has the right to enter any Warsaw Pact country in which the authority of the Communist government is threatened.

Bri·an Bo·ru (brī'ən bə-roo') (c. 926–1014). King of Ireland. Most of his life was spent fighting the Danes and their allies, the Norse of Ireland, Iceland, the Hebrides, and the Orkneys. In 1014 his forces routed the Danish coalition at Clontarf, ending Norse power in Ireland. He was killed at the end of the battle.

Bri·and (brē-äN'), **Aristide** (1862–1932). French politician and lawyer who became prime minister for the first of 11 times in 1909. His greatest achievements were as foreign minister (1925–32), when he was the chief architect of the Locarno Pact, guaranteeing the borders of Belgium, France, and Germany, and the Kellogg-Briand Pact (a declaration against war signed by 62 countries). He shared the Nobel Peace Prize (1926) with Gustav Stresemann.

bri·ar¹, **bri·er** (brī'ər) n. 1. A shrub or small tree, *Erica arborea*, of southern Europe, having a hard, woody root used to make tobacco pipes. Also called "tree heath." 2. A pipe made from briar-root or from a similar wood. [French *bruyère*, heath, from Gallo-Roman *brūcaria* (unattested), from Gaulish *brūko* (unattested).]

briar². Variant of **brier** (bush).

Bri·ar·e·us (brī-âr'ē-əs). *Greek Mythology*. A giant who aided Zeus and the Olympians against the Titans.

bri·ar·root (brī'ər-root', -root') n. The hard, woody root of the briar, *Erica arborea*.

bribe (brīb) n. 1. Anything, such as money, property, or a favor, offered or given to someone in a position of trust to induce him to act dishonestly. 2. Something offered or serving to influence or persuade.
—*v.* **bribed, bribing, bribes**. —*tr.* 1. To give, offer, or promise a bribe to. 2. To gain influence over or corrupt by bribery. —*intr.* To give, offer, or promise bribes. [Middle English *briben,* to purloin, steal, from Old French *briber, brimbert,* to beg.] —**brib·a·ble** *adj.* —**brib·er** n.

brib·er·y (brī'bə-rē) n., pl. **-ies**. The act of giving, offering, or taking a bribe.

bric-a-brac (brĭk'ə-brăk') n. Miscellaneous, usually small, objects displayed in a room as ornaments and valued for their antiquity, rarity, or curiosity value. [French, from obsolete *à bric et à brac*, at random, perhaps based on *bric*, piece.]

brick (brĭk) n. 1. A molded, rectangular block of clay, baked by the sun or in a kiln until hard, and used as a building and paving material. 2. These blocks collectively. 3. Any object shaped like a brick. 4. *Informal*. A trustworthy or obliging person. 5. *Informal*. A tactless blunder. Used in the phrase *drop a brick*.
—*tr.v.* **bricked, bricking, bricks**. 1. To construct, line, or pave with brick. 2. To close or wall with brick. Usually used with *up* or *in*: *He bricked up the windows of the old house.* [Middle English *brike, breke,* probably from Middle Dutch *bricke,* akin to Middle Low German *brike†*.] —**brick** *adj.* —**brick·y** *adj.*

brick·bat (brĭk'băt') n. 1. A piece of brick, especially one used as a weapon or missile. 2. A critical remark.

brick·lay·er (brĭk'lā'ər) n. A person who lays brick. —**brick·lay·ing** n.

brick red n. 1. Moderate reddish brown. 2. Moderate to strong brown. —**brick-red** *adj.*

brick·work (brĭk'wûrk') n. 1. A structure made of bricks. 2. Construction with bricks.

brick·yard (brĭk'yärd') n. A place where bricks are made.

bri·dal (brīd'l) n. A marriage ceremony; wedding.
—*adj.* Of or pertaining to a bride or a marriage ceremony; nuptial. [Middle English *bridale,* wedding feast, Old English *brȳdealu,* "bride ale" : BRIDE + ALE.]

bridal wreath n. Any of various shrubs of the genus *Spiraea*, cultivated for their profuse white flowers.

bride¹ (brīd) n. A woman who has recently been married or is about to be married. [Middle English *bride,* Old English *brȳd,* from Germanic *brūdhiz* (unattested).]

bride² n. A loop, bar, or tie connecting pattern segments in lacework or needlework. [French, "bridle," from Middle High German *brīdel,* rein.]

Bride (brīd), **Saint** (c. 453–c. 523). Also **Bridg·et** (brĭj′ĭt) or **Brig·id** (brĭj′ĭd, brē′ĭd). Irish holy woman, buried at Downpatrick with St. Patrick and St. Columba and, like them, a patron saint of Ireland. Her feast day is February 1.

bride·groom (brīd′grōōm′, -grōōm′) n. A man who has recently been married or is about to be married. [Alteration (influenced by GROOM) of Middle English *bridegome*, Old English *brȳdguma : brȳd*, BRIDE + *guma*, man.]

bride price n. In certain societies, money or goods given by a bridegroom's family to the bride's family. Also called "bride wealth."

brides·maid (brīdz′mād′) n. A woman, usually young and unmarried, who attends the bride at a wedding. Compare **maid of honor**, **matron of honor**.

bride·well (brīd′wĕl′, -wəl) n. A prison for petty offenders. [After *St. Bride's Well*, London, site of such a prison (16th century).]

bridge¹ (brĭj) n. *Abb.* **br. 1.** A structure spanning and providing passage over a road, waterway, railway, or other obstacle. **2. a.** Anything resembling such a structure in form. **b.** Anything which forms a connection: *a bridge between peoples.* **3.** The upper bony ridge of the human nose. **4.** The part of a pair of eyeglasses that rests against this ridge. **5.** *Music.* **a.** A thin, upright piece of wood in some stringed instruments that supports the strings above the soundboard. **b.** A transitional passage connecting two subjects or movements. **6.** *Dentistry.* A fixed replacement for one or several, but not all, of the natural teeth, anchored at each end to a natural tooth. Also called "bridgework." **7.** *Nautical.* A crosswise platform or area above the main deck of a ship from which the ship is controlled. **8.** In games such as billiards, a notched piece of wood or a rest made with the hand on which to steady the cue. Also called "rest." **9.** *Electricity.* Any of various circuits containing a branch that connects two points of equal potential and consequently carries no current when the circuit is suitably adjusted. **10.** A platform above a theater stage. **—burn one's bridges.** To eliminate the possibility of retreat. **—**v. **bridged, bridging, bridges. 1.** To build a bridge over. **2.** To cross by or as if by a bridge. **3.** To form a link across (a period of time, for example). [Middle English *brigge*, Old English *brycg*, from Germanic.] **—bridge·a·ble** adj.

bridge² n. Any of several card games derived from whist, played with one pack of cards divided equally among four people. [19th century : origin obscure.]

bridge·board (brĭj′bôrd′, -bōrd′) n. A notched board at either side of a staircase, that supports the treads and risers.

bridge·build·er (brĭj′bĭl′dər) n. One who works for better relations between opposing groups; a conciliator. **—bridge·build·ing** n.

bridge·head (brĭj′hĕd′) n. **1.** A military position established by advance troops on the enemy's side of a river or pass to afford protection for the main attacking force. **2.** Any foothold established in hostile territory. [Translation of French *tête de pont*.]

Bridge of Sighs n. A stone bridge of the 16th century, in Venice, connecting the Doge's palace to the state prison, so named because prisoners were taken over the bridge from the hall in which they had been sentenced to the prison. The bridge over the Cam River, behind St. John's College, Cambridge, England, resembles the Venetian original and is often called by the same name.

Bridg·es (brĭj′ĭz), **Robert Seymour** (1844–1930). British poet, who became poet laureate in 1913. His poems are admired for their metrical invention and lyrical simplicity. His long poetic disquisition on the growth of the human soul, *The Testament of Beauty* (1929), is considered his finest achievement.

Bridget, Saint. See **St. Bride.**

Bridg·et of Sweden (brĭj′ĭt), **Saint** (1302–73). Swedish nun and patron saint of Sweden, who founded the Order of the Most Holy Savior (Bridgettines) for nuns and monks. She settled in Rome (1350), founded a house where she sheltered the poor, campaigned for Church reform, and worked, unsuccessfully, to bring the papacy back to Rome from Avignon. Her feast day is October 8.

Bridge·town (brĭj′toun′). Capital and largest city of Barbados, in the West Indies. It is the country's only seaport.

Bridge·wa·ter Canal (brĭj′wô′tər, -wŏt′ər). An inland canal in northwestern England, connecting Worsley to Liverpool. It was one of the great engineering feats of the early Industrial Revolution, completed in 1761 for the Duke of Bridgewater by James Brindley (1716–72). Brindley avoided the use of locks by designing the canal as an aqueduct on arches, allowing the water to flow by the natural force of gravity.

bridge·work (brĭj′wûrk′) n. *Dentistry.* **1.** A bridge. **2.** Prosthetics involving a bridge or bridges.

bridg·ing (brĭj′ĭng) n. Wooden braces between beams, as of a floor or roof, that provide reinforcement and distribution of stress.

bridging loan n. A short-term loan made by a bank to enable a house purchaser to buy a new house before the purchaser's previous house has been sold.

Bridg·man (brĭj′mən), **Percy Williams** (1882–1961). U.S. physicist who investigated the conduction of electricity in metals, the properties of crystals, and the behavior of matter when subjected to high pressure. For his contributions to the last of those fields he was awarded the Nobel Prize in physics (1946).

Bridg·wa·ter (brĭj′wô′tər, -wŏt′ər). Port and market town in Somerset, southwestern England, on an estuary of the Parrett River on the Bristol Channel. It was the site of medieval wool and wine fairs and now produces bricks and plastics.

bri·dle (brīd′l) n. **1.** The harness fitted around a horse's head, nor-mally consisting of a headstall, bit, and reins, used to restrain or guide the animal. **2.** Any device or condition that controls or restrains free movement; a curb or check. **3.** *Nautical.* A span of chain, wire, or rope that can be secured at both ends to an object and slung from its center point. **4.** A bridling gesture. **—**v. **bridled, -dling, -dles.** **—**tr. **1.** To put a bridle on. **2.** To control or restrain with or as if with a bridle. **—**intr. **1.** To lift the head and draw in the chin as an expression of scorn or resentment. **2.** To become scornful or angry; take offense. [Middle English *bridel*, Old English *brīdel*, from Germanic.] **—bri·dler** n.

bridle hand n. The left hand, in which the reins are usually held, as by a cavalry soldier.

bridle path n. A pathway suitable for horses.

bri·doon (brĭ-dōōn′) n. A part of certain military bridles that consists of a rein and a bit resembling a snaffle, which may be reined independently of the curb bit. [French *bridon*, from *bride*, a bridle. See **bride** (loop).]

Brie¹ (brē). Agricultural region of northern France, lying east of Paris between the Seine and Marne valleys. It is a region of wheat and sugar-beet cultivation, but is famous more for its rose nurseries and, above all, for Brie cheese.

Brie² n. A soft, white, mold-ripened, whole-milk cheese. [French, first made in BRIE.]

brief (brēf) adj. **briefer, briefest.** **1.** Short in time or duration. **2.** Short in length or extent. **3.** Condensed in expression; succinct. **4.** Curt; abrupt. **—**n. **1.** A short or condensed statement. **2.** A condensation or abstract of a large document or series of documents. **3.** *Abbr.* **br.** *Law.* A document containing all facts and points of law pertinent to a specific case, filed by an attorney before arguing the case in court. **4.** *Roman Catholic Church.* A papal letter pertaining to matters of discipline. **5.** A set of instructions; a briefing. **6. briefs.** Short, tight-fitting underpants. **7.** *British Slang.* A lawyer. **—in brief.** In short; in a few words. **—**tr.v. **briefed, briefing, briefs. 1.** To give concise preparatory instructions or advice to. **2.** To summarize. **3.** *British.* To send a legal brief to (an attorney). **4.** *British.* To authorize and retain (an attorney) as counsel. [As an adjective, Middle English *bref*, from Old French *bref*, from Latin *brevis;* as a noun, Middle English *bref*, letter of authority, from Old French *brief*, from Late Latin *breve*, summary, from Latin, neuter of *brevis*, short.] **—brief·ly** adv. **—brief·ness** n.

brief·case (brēf′kās′) n. A portable rectangular case of leather or similar material, used for holding books and papers. [From BRIEF (document).]

brief·ing (brē′fĭng) n. **1.** The act or procedure of giving or receiving concise preparatory instructions, information, or advice. **2.** The information conveyed during this procedure.

brief·less (brēf′lĭs) adj. Having no brief, thus no clients. Said of a lawyer.

bri·er¹ (brī′ər) n. Also **bri·ar.** Any of various thorny plants or bushes, especially a prickly-stemmed rosebush.

brier². Variant of **briar** (shrub).

brig¹ (brĭg) n. A two-masted sailing ship, developed from the brigantine and differing from it mainly by being square-rigged on both masts. [Short for BRIGANTINE.]

brig² n. **1.** A ship's prison. **2.** *Military Slang.* A guardhouse. [Probably from BRIG (ship).]

bri·gade (brĭ-gād′) n. **1. a.** A military unit consisting of a variable number of combat battalions. **b.** A former unit of the U.S. Army composed of two or more regiments commanded by a brigadier general. **2.** A group of persons organized for a specific purpose: *a fire brigade.* **—**tr.v. **brigaded, -gading, -gades.** To form into a brigade. [French, from Old French, from Old Italian *brigata*, troop, company, from *brigare*, to form a troop, fight, from *briga*, strife, perhaps from Celtic.]

brig·a·dier (brĭg′ə-dîr′) n. A brigadier general. [French, from BRIGADE.]

brigadier general n., pl. **brigadier generals.** An officer ranking above a colonel and below a major general in the U.S. Army, Air Force, and Marine Corps. Also called "brigadier."

brig·and (brĭg′ənd) n. A robber, especially one of a gang of bandits. [Middle English *brigaunt*, foot soldier, bandit, from Old French *brigand*, from Italian *brigante*, from the past participle of *brigare*, to fight. See **brigade.**] **—brig·and·age** (brĭg′ənd-ĭj), **brig·and·ism** n.

brig·an·dine (brĭg′ən-dēn′) n. A protective jacket made of canvas or leather lined with overlapping scales or plates, worn in medieval times.

brig·an·tine (brĭg′ən-tēn′) n. A two-masted sailing ship, square-rigged on the foremast and differing from a brig mainly by being fore-and-aft rigged with square topsails on the mainmast. [French, from Old French *brigandin*, from Italian *brigantino*, "pirate ship."]

bright (brīt) adj. **brighter, brightest. 1.** Emitting or reflecting light; shining. **2. a.** Vivid or brilliant in color. **b.** Characterizing a dye that produces a highly saturated color. **3.** Glorious; splendid. **4.** Full of promise and hope; auspicious. **5.** Happy; cheerful. **6.** Clever; intelligent. **—See Synonyms at intelligent. —**n. **1.** A thin, flat paintbrush used for highlighting. **2. brights.** High-beam headlights. **—**adv. In a bright manner. [Middle English *bright*, Old English *beorht*, from Germanic.] **—bright·ly** adv.

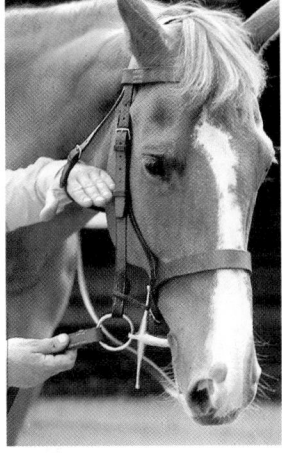

bridle *The bit and reins by which a horse is controlled by its rider.*

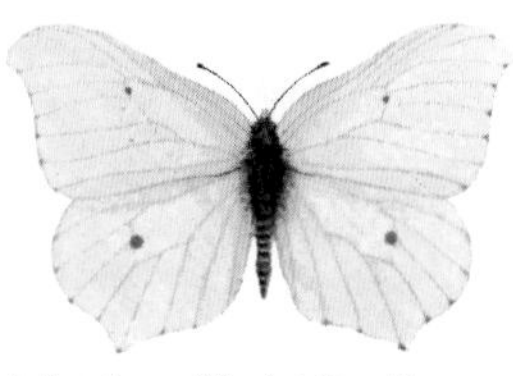

brimstone *The bright yellow brimstone butterfly of Europe and Asia takes its common English name from the color of brimstone, an early word for sulfur.*

Synonyms: *brilliant, incandescent, lambent, luminous, lustrous, radiant.*

Bright (brīt), **John** (1811–89). British politician and one of the founders of the Anti-Corn Law League (1839). He was a leading campaigner in the movement that led to both the Second Reform Act (1867) and the Third (1884). From 1858 he represented Birmingham in Parliament, serving in Gladstone's administrations as president of the Board of Trade (1868–70) and Chancellor of the Duchy of Lancaster (1873–74 and 1880–82). He resigned from the cabinet in 1882 in protest against the bombardment of Alexandria, Egypt.

bright•en (brīt'n) *v.* **-ened, -ening, -ens.** —*tr.* To make bright or brighter. —*intr.* To become bright or brighter.

bright•ness (brīt'nĭs) *n.* **1.** The state or quality of being bright. **2. a.** The effect or sensation by means of which an observer is able to distinguish differences in luminance. **b.** *Physics.* **Luminance** *(see).* No longer in technical usage. **3.** The dimension of a color that represents its similarity to one of a series of achromatic colors ranging from very dim (dark) to very bright (dazzling).

Brigh•ton (brīt'n). Resort town on an old Saxon site on the East Sussex coast. Formerly known as Brighthelmstone, it became a fashionable resort after 1783, when the Prince of Wales, later George IV, began to frequent it. The famous pavilion, designed by John Nash in a combination of Chinese and Indian styles, was built for George IV.

Bright's disease *n.* Any of a group of kidney diseases marked by albumin in the urine and edema. [After Richard *Bright* (1789–1858), British physician who first described it.]

bright•work (brīt'wûrk') *n.* Metal parts or fixtures, especially on a ship, made bright by polishing.

Brigid, Saint. See **St. Bride.**

brill (brĭl) *n., pl.* **brills** or collectively **brill.** An edible flatfish, *Scophthalmus rhombus,* of European waters. [15th century : origin obscure.]

Bril•lat-Sa•va•rin (brē-yä'säv-ə-răɴ'), **Anthelme** (1755–1826). French politician and writer. He is best known for his *Physiologie de Goût* (1825), a witty dissertation on the art of dining.

bril•li•ance (brĭl'yəns) *n.* Also **bril•li•an•cy** (-yən-sē). **1.** Extreme brightness. **2.** Sharpness and clarity of musical tone. **3.** Splendor; magnificence. **4.** Exceptional clarity and agility of intellect or invention.

bril•liant (brĭl'yənt) *adj.* **1.** Full of light; shining. **2. a.** Brightly vivid in color. **b.** Designating a color that has a combination of high lightness and strong saturation. **3.** *Music.* Sharp and clear in tone. **4.** Glorious; splendid; magnificent. **5.** Superb; excellent; wonderful. Used also as a general term of approval. **6.** Marked by extraordinary powers of intellect or invention. —See Synonyms at **bright, intelligent.**
∼*n.* **1.** A cut for precious gems, especially diamonds, having 58 facets and shaped like two cones joined at their bases with the top one cut off close to the base. **2.** A precious stone having this cut. [French *brillant,* present participle of *briller,* to shine, from Italian *brillare.*†] **—bril•liant•ly** *adv.* **—bril•liant•ness** *n.*

bril•lian•tine (brĭl'yən-tēn') *n.* **1.** An oily, perfumed preparation for the hair. **2.** A glossy fabric made from cotton and worsted or cotton and mohair. [French *brillantine,* from *brillant,* BRILLIANT.]

brim (brĭm) *n.* **1.** The rim or uppermost edge of a cup or other vessel. **2.** A projecting rim or edge: *the brim of a hat.* **3.** A border or edge, especially one surrounding a body of water.
∼*v.* **brimmed, brimming, brims.** —*tr.* To fill to the brim. —*intr.* To be full to the brim; be filled. Used with *with.* **—brim over.** To overflow: *brim over with happiness.* [Middle English *brimme,* from Germanic; akin to Middle High German *brem.*]

brim•ful, brim•full (brĭm'fo͝ol') *adj.* Completely full.

brim•stone (brĭm'stōn') *n.* **1.** *Obsolete.* **Sulfur** *(see).* Now used chiefly in the phrase *fire and brimstone.* **2.** A bright yellow butterfly, *Gonepteryx rhamni,* common in northern temperate regions of Eurasia. **3.** A very common moth, *Opisthograptis luteolata,* of Europe and temperate Asia. [Middle English *brimston,* Late Old English *brynstān,* probably "burning stone," from *bryne,* burning.] **—brim•ston•y** *adj.*

brin (brĭn) *n.* Any of the ribs of a fan. [French *brin*†.]

Brin•di•si (brĭn'dĭ-zē). Ancient name **Brun•di•si•um** (brŭn-dĭz'ē-əm). Port in the Apulia region of southeastern Italy, on the Adriatic coast. In ancient times it was an important center of trade with the eastern Mediterranean, and it was also the point of departure for the Crusades of the Middle Ages.

brin•dle (brĭnd'l) *adj.* Brindled.
∼*n.* **1.** A brindled color. **2.** A brindled animal.

brin•dled (brĭnd'əld) *adj.* Tawny or grayish with streaks or spots of a darker color. [Variant of earlier *brinded, brended,* from Middle English *brende,* perhaps from Scandinavian; akin to Old Norse *brandr,* piece of burning wood.]

brine (brīn) *n.* **1.** Water saturated with or containing large amounts of a salt, especially of sodium chloride. **2. a.** The water of a sea or ocean. **b.** A large body of salt water. **3.** Salt water used for preserving and pickling foods.
∼*tr.v.* **brined, brining, brines.** To immerse or pickle in brine. [Middle English *brine,* Old English *brȳne*†, from Germanic.]

Bri•nell hardness (brĭ-nĕl') *n.* The relative hardness of metals and alloys, determined by forcing a steel ball into a test piece under standard conditions and measuring the surface area of the resulting indentation to calculate the relevant Brinell number. [After Johann A. *Brinell* (1849–1925), Swedish engineer.]

Brinell number *n. Abbr.* **Bhn.** The numerical value assigned to the Brinell hardness of metals and alloys. It is calculated by dividing the load on the ball in kilograms by the area of the indentation in square millimeters.

brine shrimp *n.* Any of various small crustaceans of the genus *Artemia.* [So called because they have been observed living in highly saline water.]

bring (brĭng) *tr.v.* **brought** (brôt), **bringing, brings. 1.** To take with oneself to a place; convey or carry along: *brought enough money with him.* **2.** To carry as an attribute or contribution: *brought years of experience to her new post.* **3.** To lead or cause to come to a specified state, situation, or location: *brought to ruin; brought tears to our eyes.* **4.** To succeed in persuading; induce: *His confession brought others to confess.* **5.** To cause to occur as a consequence or concomitant: *Floods brought death to the valley.* **6.** To cause to become apparent to the mind; recall: *bring back memories.* **7.** *Law.* To advance or set forth (charges or evidence, for example) in a court. **8.** To sell for; fetch. **—bring about.** To cause to happen. **—bring around** (or **round**). **1.** To cause to recover consciousness. **2.** To cause to adopt an opinion or course of action. **—bring down the house.** *Informal.* To cause wild or general applause. **—bring forth. 1.** To give rise to; effect; produce. **2.** *Archaic.* To give birth to. **—bring forward. 1.** To present; cite in argument: *bring forward an opinion.* **2.** *Accounting.* To carry (a sum) from one page or column to another. **—bring in. 1.** To give or submit (a verdict). **2.** To produce or yield (profits or income). **—bring off.** To accomplish successfully. **—bring on. 1.** To give rise to; cause. **2.** To cause to appear: *bring on the dessert.* **—bring out. 1.** To reveal or expose. **2.** To produce or publish. **3.** To encourage; especially, to encourage (a shy person) to speak out or participate. **—bring over.** To win over. **—bring to. 1.** To cause to recover consciousness. **2.** To cause (a ship) to turn into the wind and lose headway. **—bring up. 1.** To take care of and educate (a child); rear. **2.** To introduce into discussion; mention. **3.** To vomit or cough up. [Bring, brought, brought; Middle English *bringen, broughte, brought,* Old English *bringan, brōhte, brōht,* from Germanic *brengen* (unattested).] **—bring•er** *n.*

bring down *tr.v.* **1.** To cause to fall, come down, or collapse. **2.** To reduce; lower. **3.** *Slang.* To cause to feel disappointed or depressed.

bring•down (brĭng'doun') *n.* Something that disturbs or disappoints.

bring•ing-up (brĭng'ĭng-ŭp') *n.* The care, training, and education of a child; upbringing.

brink (brĭngk) *n.* **1. a.** The upper edge of a steep or vertical declivity: *the brink of a cliff.* **b.** The margin of land bordering a body of water. **2.** The verge of something: *on the brink of discovery.* —See Synonyms at **border.** [Middle English *brinke, brenk,* akin to Middle Dutch *brink*†, slope.]

brink•man•ship (brĭngk'mən-shĭp') *n.* Also **brinks•man•ship** (brĭngks'-). The practice of seeking advantage by forcing a dangerous situation to crisis point in the hope that one's opponent will back down first. [BRINK + (GAMES)MANSHIP.]

brin•y (brī'nē) *adj.* **-ier, -iest.** Of, pertaining to, or resembling brine; salty.
∼*n. Slang.* The sea. **—brin•i•ness** *n.*

bri•o (brē'ō) *n.* Vigor; vivacity. [Italian, "vivacity," from Gaulish *brigo-* (unattested), might, strength.]

bri•oche (brē-ôsh', -ŏsh') *n.* A soft, light-textured roll or bun made from eggs, butter, flour, and yeast. [French, from Old French, from *brier,* dialectal form of *broyer,* to knead, from Germanic.]

bri•o•lette (brē'ə-lĕt') *n.* A pear-shaped gem, especially a diamond, cut with long triangular facets. [French, *bri(ll)olette,* probably an irregular diminutive of *brillant,* BRILLIANT.]

bri•quette, bri•quet (brĭ-kĕt') *n.* A block of compressed coal dust or charcoal, used for fuel and kindling. [French *briquette,* from *brique,* BRICK.]

bri•sance (brĭ-zäns') *n.* The shattering effect of a sudden release of energy, as in an explosion. [French, from *brisant,* present participle of *briser,* to break, from Vulgar Latin *brisāre,* from Gaulish.] **—bri•sant** *adj.*

Bris•bane (brĭz'bən, -bān'). Capital of the state of Queensland, Australia, a port and transport hub on the Brisbane River near its mouth on Moreton Bay and the third-largest city in Australia. The city began as a penal colony (1824), was incorporated as a town (1834), and was named after Sir Thomas Brisbane, the governor of New South Wales (1821–25).

brisk (brĭsk) *adj.* **brisker, briskest. 1.** Moving or acting quickly; lively; energetic: *a brisk walk.* **2.** Sharp or abrupt in speech or manner: *a brisk greeting.* **3.** Stimulating and invigorating: *a brisk wind.* **4.** Pleasantly zestful: *a brisk tea.* —See Synonyms at **nimble.** [Probably a variant of BRUSQUE.] **—brisk•ly** *adv.* **—brisk•ness** *n.*

bris•ket (brĭs'kĭt) *n.* **1.** The chest of an animal. **2.** The ribs and meat from this part. [Middle English *brusket,* probably from a Scandinavian compound akin to Old Norse *brjōst,* breast + *ket*†, meat.]

bris•ling (brĭz'lĭng, brĭs'-) *n.* A fish, the **sprat** *(see),* which is usually preserved and canned. [From Norwegian and Danish.]

bris•tle (brĭs'əl) *n.* A short, coarse, stiff hair or hairlike part.
∼*v.* **bristled, -tling, -tles.** —*intr.* **1.** To raise the bristles, as an angry, excited, or frightened animal does: *The dog bristled with fear.* **2.** To react with hostility or anger. **3.** To stand erect like bristles: *His hair bristled.* **4.** To be covered or thick with or as if with bristles: *The path bristled with thorns.* —*tr.* **1.** To furnish or supply with bristles; put bristles on. **2.** To make bristly; ruffle; disturb. [Mid-

dle English *bristil, brustel,* from *brust,* bristle, Old English *byrst.*] —**bris·tly** *adj.*

bris·tle·cone pine (brĭs′əl-kōn′) *n.* A small pine tree, *Pinus aristata,* native to the Rocky Mountains, that has the longest life span of any known conifer. Its annual rings are used in archaeological dating.

bris·tle·tail (brĭs′əl-tāl′) *n.* Any of various wingless insects of the order Thysanura, such as the silverfish, having bristlelike posterior appendages.

bristle worm *n.* A type of worm, the **polychaete** *(see).*

Bris·tol (brĭs′təl). City, port, and administrative center of Avon, in southwestern England, on the lower Avon River 11 kilometers (7 miles) from its mouth on the Bristol Channel. It has been a trading depot since the 12th century and is now a center of nuclear and aeronautical engineering works.

Bristol board *n.* A smooth, heavy pasteboard of fine quality. Also called "Bristol paper."

Bristol Channel. An inlet of the Atlantic Ocean, *c.* 137 kilometers (85 miles) long, broadening out from the mouth of the Severn River and separating Wales from southwestern England.

Bristol fashion *adj. British.* In good order; neat; tidy. Used especially in the phrase *all shipshape and Bristol fashion.* —**Bristol fashion** *adv.*

brit, britt (brĭt) *n.* **1.** The young of herring and similar fish. **2.** Minute marine organisms, such as crustaceans of the genus *Calanus,* that are a major source of food for many fish and whales. [Perhaps from Cornish *brȳthel,* mackerel.]

Brit (brĭt) *n. Informal.* A British person.

Brit. Britain; British.

Brit·ain (brĭt′n). *Abbr.* **Br., Brit.** See **Great Britain.**

bri·tan·ni·a (brĭ-tăn′yə, -tăn′ē-ə) *n.* Also **Britannia.** A white alloy of tin with copper, antimony, and sometimes bismuth and zinc. It is used in the manufacture of tableware and light bearings. Also called "britannia metal." [From **BRITANNIA.**]

Bri·tan·nia (brĭ-tăn′yə, -tăn′ē-ə) *n.* **1.** The ancient Roman province in Great Britain. **2.** *Poetic.* Great Britain. **3.** A female personification of Great Britain or the British Empire.

Bri·tan·nic (brĭ-tăn′ĭk) *adj.* British. Used chiefly in the phrase *His* (or *Her*) *Britannic Majesty.*

britch·es (brĭch′ĭz) *pl.n. Informal.* Breeches. —**too big for one's britches.** *Informal.* Overconfident; cocky; arrogant.

Brit·i·cism (brĭt′ə-sĭz′əm) *n.* Also **Brit·ish·ism** (brĭt′ĭsh-ĭz′əm). A word, phrase, or idiom characteristic of or peculiar to English as it is spoken in Great Britain.

Brit·ish (brĭt′ĭsh) *adj. Abbr.* **B., Br., Brit. 1.** Of, pertaining to, or characteristic of Great Britain, the United Kingdom, or the Commonwealth. **2.** Of, pertaining to, or characteristic of the ancient Britons.
~*n.* **1.** *Used with a plural verb.* The people of Great Britain. Preceded by *the.* **2. British English** *(see).* **3.** The language spoken by the ancient Britons.

British Ant·arc·tic Territory (ănt-ärk′tĭk, -är′tĭk). Area in the extreme Southern Hemisphere, bounded by latitude 60° S and longitudes 20° W and 80° W. It includes the South Orkney Islands, Graham Land (on Antarctica), and the South Shetland Islands (parts of which are claimed by Argentina) and has been a colony administered from the Falkland Islands since 1962. Most of the small islands in the region are uninhabited, except for a transient population manning research stations.

British Anti-Lew·is·ite (ăn′tē-lōō′ĭ-sīt′, -lyōō′-) *n.* A drug, **BAL** *(see).*

British Cameroons. See **Cameroon.**

British Co·lum·bi·a (kə-lŭm′bē-ə). *Abbr.* **B.C.** The westernmost province of Canada, bordering on the Pacific Ocean and stretching to the Yukon in the north. The capital is Victoria, on Vancouver Island, but the largest city is Vancouver. The province is almost entirely mountainous, with the Rocky Mts. in the east and the Coast Mts. in the west. Timber and pulp and paper manufacture are its leading industries, but mining of silver, copper, gold, iron ore, lead, and zinc is also important. The silver mine at Kimberley is the largest in the world, and Kimberley also has the world's largest reserves of lead and zinc. —**British Co·lum·bi·an** *n. & adj.*

British Commonwealth of Nations. See the **Commonwealth.**

British East Af·ri·ca (ăf′rĭ-kə). Collectively, the former British territories in eastern Africa, including Kenya, Uganda, Tanganyika, and Zanzibar.

British Empire. Collectively, all geographical and political units formerly under British control, including dominions, colonies, dependencies, trust territories, and protectorates.

British English *n.* The English language as spoken, pronounced, and written in Britain, as compared with the English spoken elsewhere.

Brit·ish·er (brĭt′ĭsh-ər) *n. Informal.* A native or inhabitant of Great Britain or a person of British origin.

British Guiana. See **Guyana.**

British Honduras. See **Belize.**

British In·di·a (ĭn′dē-ə). The part of the Indian subcontinent exclusive of the Indian states, under direct British administration until 1947. See **India.**

British In·di·an Ocean Territory (ĭn′dē-ən). British colony in the west Indian Ocean since 1965. The main islands include Diego Garcia, which has a U.S. base.

British Isles. A group of islands off the northwestern coast of Europe, comprising Great Britain, Ireland, and adjacent smaller islands.

British Movement *n.* A modern British fascist splinter group, noted for its virulent racism.

British North A·mer·i·ca (ə-měr′ə-kə). *Abbr.* **B.N.A.** Formerly, the British possessions in North America north of the United States; specifically, Canada.

British Somaliland. See **Somaliland.**

British thermal unit *n. Abbr.* **btu, B.th.u.** The quantity of heat required to raise the temperature of one pound of water by one degree Fahrenheit.

British Vir·gin Islands (vûr′jĭn). A British colony in the West Indies, in the eastern Caribbean. The colony, comprising *c.* 30 islands, lies east of Puerto Rico and the U.S. Virgin Islands. Its capital is Road Town, on Tortola Island.

British West Af·ri·ca (ăf′rĭ-kə). *Abbr.* **B.W.A.** The former British possessions in western Africa, including Nigeria, Gambia, Sierra Leone, and the Gold Coast and the trust territories of Togoland and Cameroons.

British West In·dies (ĭn′dēz). *Abbr.* **B.W.I.** The former name for the islands of the West Indies that were colonies or self-governing colonies of the United Kingdom.

Brit·on (brĭt′n) *n.* **1.** A native or inhabitant of Britain. **2.** One of a Celtic people who inhabited Britain before the Roman invasion.

britt. Variant of **brit.**

Brit·ta·ny (brĭt′n-ē). *French* **Bre·tagne** (brə-tän′yə). Region and former province of northwest France, between the English Channel and the Bay of Biscay. It has a deeply indented rocky coast with deep natural harbors at Brest and St. Malo.

Brit·ta·ny spaniel (brĭt′n-ē) *n.* A large spaniel of a breed originating in France. [After **BRITTANY.**]

Brit·ten (brĭt′n), **(Edward) Benjamin, Baron** (1913–76). British composer. His reputation rests chiefly on his vocal compositions, which fall into two main categories: song cycles such as *Les Illuminations* (1939) and the *Serenade* for tenor, horn, and string orchestra (1943); and the operas, including *Peter Grimes* (1945), *Albert Herring* (1947), and *Death in Venice* (1973).

brit·tle (brĭt′l) *adj.* **1.** Likely to break; fragile: *brittle porcelain.* **2. a.** Difficult to deal with; touchy; snappish: *a brittle disposition.* **b.** Lacking warmth or friendliness. —See Synonyms at **fragile.**
~*n.* A confection of caramelized sugar to which nuts are added: *peanut brittle.* [Middle English *brotel, britel,* Old English *brytel* (unattested), from Germanic.] —**brit·tle·ness** *n.*

brittle star *n.* Any of various marine organisms of the class Ophiuroidea, related to and resembling the starfish but having long, slender, whiplike arms.

Brix scale (brĭks) *n.* A density scale used in the sugar industry. A Brix hydrometer has a scale calibrated in units equivalent to the percentage of sugar in a pure sugar solution. [After A.F.W. *Brix,* 19th-century German inventor.]

Br·no (bûr′nō). *German* **Brünn** (brün). An industrial city in central Czechoslovakia. The Bren gun was developed there.

bro. brother.

broach¹ (brōch) *n.* **1.** A tapered and serrated tool used to shape or enlarge a hole. **2.** The hole made by such a tool. **3.** A spit for roasting meat. **4.** A narrow mason's chisel. **5.** A gimlet for tapping or broaching casks. **6.** Variant of **brooch.**
~*tr.v.* **broached, broaching, broaches. 1. a.** To begin to talk about: *broach a subject.* **b.** To announce: "*Ernest broached his plans for spending the next year or two*" (Samuel Butler). **2.** To pierce in order to draw off liquid: *broach a keg.* **3.** To draw off (a liquid) by piercing a hole in a cask, keg, or other container. **4.** To shape or enlarge (a hole) with a broach. **5.** To open and start using the contents of (a box, for example). —See Synonyms at **vent.** [Middle English *broche,* pointed rod or pin, from Old French, a spit, from Vulgar Latin *brocca* (unattested), a spike.] —**broach·er** *n.*

broach² *v.* **broached, broaching, broaches.** *Nautical.* —*tr.* To cause to veer broadside to the wind and waves. —*intr.* To veer broadside to the wind and waves. Used with *to.* [18th century : origin obscure.]

broad (brôd) *adj.* **broader, broadest. 1. a.** Extending a considerable distance from side to side. **b.** Of the specified extent from side to side; in breadth: *six feet broad.* **2.** Large in expanse; spacious: *a broad lawn.* **3.** Open to view; clear: *broad daylight.* **4.** Extensive in scope; generalized: *a broad rule.* **5.** Liberal; tolerant. **6.** Covering the essentials; comprehensive, but not detailed: *a broad outline of the problem.* **7.** Plain and clear; obvious: *a broad hint.* **8.** Outspoken; unrestrained. **9.** Vulgar; crude: *a broad joke.* **10.** Strongly marked by regional pronunciation: *a broad accent.* **11.** *Phonetics.* Designating a vowel that is pronounced with the tongue placed low and flat and with the oral cavity wide open, especially as when the *a* in *bath* is pronounced like the *a* in *bard.*
~*n.* **1.** The broad part of something. **2.** *Slang.* A woman or girl.
~*adv.* Fully; completely: *broad awake.* [Middle English *brood,* Old English *brād,* from Common Germanic *braithaz* (unattested). For noun sense 2, compare obsolete *broadwife* (abroad + wife), female slave separated from her husband, who was owned by a different master.] —**broad·ly** *adv.*

broad arrow *n.* **1.** An arrow with a wide, barbed head. **2.** A wide arrowhead mark identifying British government property and, formerly, prison clothing.

broad·ax, broad·axe (brôd′ăks′) *n., pl.* **-axes.** An ax with a wide, flat head and a short handle; battle-ax.

broad·band (brôd′bănd′) *adj.* Designating a wide band of electromagnetic frequencies: *broadband communications.* —**broad·band** *n.*

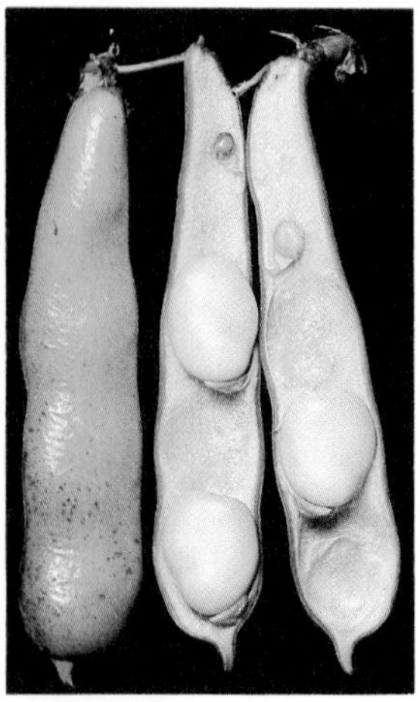

broad bean *The seeds of this plant, also known as fava bean, have been used as a vegetable for centuries. The plant, which is thought to have been introduced into northern Europe by the Romans, was an important crop in the Middle Ages.*

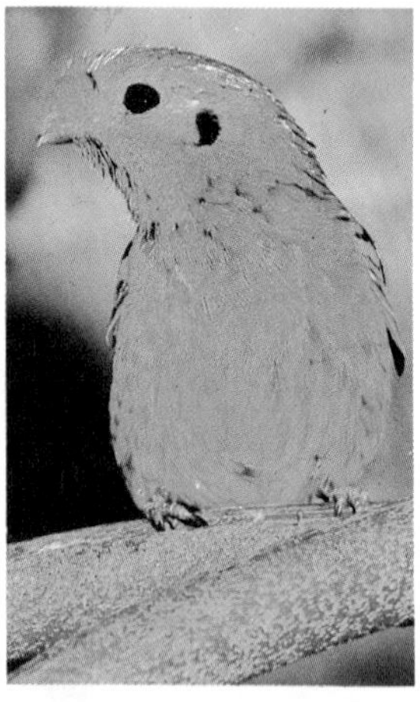

broadbill *The brightly colored broadbill is native to the tropical forests of Africa and Asia. Most of its 14 species live on insects, but the Malaysian green broadbill (above) feeds on fruit.*

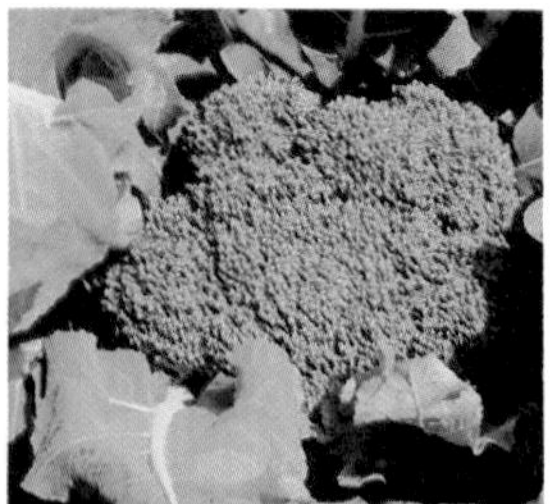

broccoli *The flower head of a green, or sometimes purple, edible plant of the same genus as the cabbage.*

broad bean *n.* **1.** A plant, *Vicia faba,* native to the Old World, cultivated for its edible pods and seeds. **2.** The somewhat flattened seed of this plant. Also called "fava bean," "horse bean."
broad·bill (brôd′bĭl′) *n.* **1.** Any of various birds of the family Eurylaimidae, of Africa and tropical Asia, having a short, wide bill and brightly colored plumage. **2.** Any of several other broad-billed birds, such as the shoveler. **3.** The **swordfish** *(see).*
broad·brim (brôd′brĭm′) *n.* **1.** A hat with a broad, flat brim, as those worn by Quakers. **2. Broadbrim.** *Informal.* A member of the Society of Friends; a Quaker.
broad·cast (brôd′kăst′, -käst′) *v.* **-cast** or **-casted, -casting, -casts.** —*tr.* **1.** To transmit (a program or signal) by radio or television. **2.** To make known over a wide area: *broadcast rumors.* **3.** To sow (seed) over a wide area, especially by hand. —*intr.* **1.** To transmit a radio or television program. **2.** To participate in a radio or television program.
~*n.* **1.** Transmission of a radio or television program or signal. **2.** A radio or television program, or the duration of such a program. **3.** The act of scattering seed.
~*adj.* Scattered over a wide area.
~*adv.* In a scattered manner; far and wide. [BROAD (adverb), "widely" + CAST (past participle).] —**broad·cast·er** *n.*
Broad Church *n.* Those members of the Anglican Communion favoring liberalism in matters of doctrine and ritual. Compare **High Church, Low Church.** —**Broad-Church** (brôd′chûrch′) *adj.* —**Broad-Church·man** *n.*
broad·cloth (brôd′klôth′, -klŏth′) *n.* **1.** A densely textured woolen cloth with a plain or twill weave and a lustrous finish. **2.** A closely woven silk, cotton, or synthetic fabric with a narrow crosswise rib.
broad·en (brôd′n) *v.* **-ened, -ening, -ens.** —*tr.* To make broad or broader. —*intr.* To become broad or broader.
broad gauge *n.* A railway track with a width between the rails greater than the standard gauge of 56½ inches.
broad-gauge (brôd′gāj′) *adj.* **1.** Having a broad gauge. **2.** *Informal.* Having a wide scope; liberal.
broad jump *n.* A **long jump** *(see).*
broad·leaf (brôd′lēf′) *n.* Any of various tobacco plants having broad leaves.
broad-leaved (brôd′lēvd′) *adj.* Also **broad-leaf** (-lēf′), **broad-leafed** (-lēft′). Having relatively broad leaves, as evergreens such as the rhododendron and holly, rather than needles.
broad·loom (brôd′lo͞om′) *adj.* Designating carpet woven on a wide loom and measuring from 1.3 meters (4½ feet) to 5.5 meters (18 feet) in width.
~*n.* A broadloom carpet.
broad-mind·ed (brôd′mīn′dĭd) *adj.* Having or arising from liberal or tolerant views. —**broad-mind·ed·ly** *adv.* —**broad-mind·ed·ness** *n.*
broad·ness (brôd′nĭs) *n.* The state, quality, or aspect of being broad. Compare **breadth.**
broad seal *n.* The official public seal of a state or nation.
Broads, the (brôdz). Region of inland waterways in East Anglia, chiefly in Norfolk but extending also into Suffolk. A great number of wide, shallow lakes are connected by the Yare and Bure rivers and their tributaries. The region is a wildlife sanctuary and recreational boating center.
broad·sheet (brôd′shēt′) *n.* See **broadside** (sense 4).
broad·side (brôd′sīd′) *n.* **1.** The side of a ship above the water line. **2. a.** All the guns on one side of a warship. **b.** Their simultaneous discharge. **3.** An explosive verbal attack or denunciation. **4. a.** A large sheet of paper printed on one side. **b.** Something, as an advertisement, printed on a broadside. **5.** Any broad, unbroken surface.
~*adv.* With the side turned to a given object.
broadside ballad *n.* A rhymed popular tale of romance, adventure, or crime, printed on a broadsheet and sold by hawkers from the 16th to the 19th century.
broad-spec·trum (brôd′spĕk′trəm) *adj.* Widely applicable or effective: *a broad-spectrum drug.*
broad·sword (brôd′sôrd′, -sōrd′) *n.* A cutting sword with a wide blade.
broad·tail (brôd′tāl′) *n.* **1.** A breed of sheep, the **karakul** *(see).* **2.** The pelt of a newborn or prematurely born karakul lamb, having a flat surface with wavy markings. Compare **Persian lamb.**
Broad·way[1] (brôd′wā′). A thoroughfare in New York City and New York State. The longest street in the world, it begins at the southern tip of Manhattan Island and extends *c.* 242 kilometers (150 miles) north to Albany.
Broadway[2] *n.* **1.** The principal theater district of New York City, located on or near Broadway (thoroughfare). **2.** The American legitimate stage: *a career in television and on Broadway.* Compare **off-Broadway.** —**Broad·way** *adj.*
Brob·ding·nag·i·an (brŏb′dĭng-năg′ē-ən, -dĭg-năg′-) *adj.* **1.** Gigantic; enormous. **2.** On a large scale; enlarged. [After *Brobdingnag,* the land of giants visited by Gulliver in *Gulliver's Travels* (1726), by Jonathan Swift.]
bro·cade (brō-kād′) *n.* A heavy fabric interwoven with a rich, raised design.
~*tr.v.* **brocaded, -cading, -cades.** To weave with a raised design. [Earlier *brocado,* from Spanish or Portuguese, from Italian *broccato,* embossed fabric, from *brocco,* twisted thread, shoot, from Vulgar Latin *brocca* (unattested), a spike, from Latin *brocchus,* in *brocci dentes,* "projecting teeth."]
broc·a·tel, broc·a·telle (brŏk′ə-tĕl′) *n.* A very heavy fabric resembling brocade, but with a more highly raised design. [French *brocatelle,* from Italian *broccatello,* diminutive of *broccato,* BROCADE.]
broc·co·li (brŏk′ə-lē) *n.* **1.** A plant, *Brassica oleracea italica,* closely related to the cabbage and the cauliflower, having a branched, greenish or purplish flower head. Also called "sprouting broccoli." **2.** The flower heads of this plant, eaten as a vegetable before the tightly clustered buds have opened. [Italian, plural of *broccolo,* cabbage sprout, diminutive of *brocco,* shoot. See **brocade.**]
broch (brŏk, brŭk, brŏch, brŭch) *n.* An ancient, round, dry-stone tower of a type found in northern Scotland, formerly used as a fortified dwelling. [From Old Norse *borg,* castle.]
bro·ché (brō-shā′) *adj.* Woven with a raised pattern or design; brocaded. [French, past participle of *brocher,* to stitch, from *broche,* knitting needle, spit, from Old French, a spit, from Vulgar Latin *brocca* (unattested), a spike. See **brocade.**]
bro·chette (brō-shĕt′) *n.* **1.** A small spit or skewer upon which meat, fish, or vegetables are roasted or grilled. **2.** A dish cooked on a brochette. [French, from Old French, diminutive of *broche,* spit. See **broché.**]
bro·chure (brō-sho͝or′) *n.* A small pamphlet or booklet, especially one providing information about a service or product. [French, "a stitching" (from the former loose stitching of the pages), from *brocher,* to stitch.]
brock (brŏk) *n. British.* A badger. [Old English *broc,* from Celtic *brokko-* (unattested), badger.]
Brock·en (brŏk′ən). A large granite dome in western East Germany, the highest peak (1,142 meters; 3,747 feet) in the Harz Mountains. The peak is the legendary site of the witches' sabbath, held on Walpurgis Night.
brock·et (brŏk′ĭt) *n.* **1.** A two-year-old stag with its first horns. **2.** Any of several small deer of the genus *Mazama,* of South America, having short, unbranched horns. [Middle English *broket,* from Old North French *brocard,* from *broque,* the horn of an animal, any pointed implement, variant of Old French *broche,* a spit.]
bro·de·rie an·glaise (brō′də-rē ŏn′glĕz, -glāz) *n.* Embroidery incorporating perforated patterns on fine white linen, cotton, or the like. [French, "English embroidery."]
bro·gan (brō′gən) *n.* A heavy, ankle-high work shoe. [Irish-Gaelic *brōgan,* diminutive of *brōg,* BROGUE (shoe).]
Bro·glie (brô-glē′), **Louis Victor, 7th Duc de** (1892–). French physicist. In 1927 he demonstrated by experiments that particles exhibit wavelike properties, thus establishing the field of wave mechanics. For this contribution to modern quantum theory he was awarded the Nobel Prize in physics (1929).
brogue[1] (brōg) *n.* A strong regional accent; especially, a strong Irish accent. [From BROGUE (shoe), with reference to the shoes of Irish and Scottish peasants.]
brogue[2] *n.* **1.** A heavy shoe of untanned leather, formerly worn in Scotland and Ireland. **2.** A strong oxford shoe, usually with ornamental perforations. [Irish and Scottish Gaelic *brōg,* from Old Irish *brōc,* shoe, apparently from Old Norse *brōk,* trousers.]
broi·der (broi′dər) *tr.v.* **-dered, -dering, -ders.** *Obsolete.* To ornament with needlework; embroider. —**broi·der·y** *n.*
broil[1] (broil) *v.* **broiled, broiling, broils.** —*tr.* **1.** To expose to great heat. **2.** To cook by direct radiant heat; grill. —*intr.* To become broiled.
~*n.* **1.** The act or condition of broiling. **2.** Something broiled. [Middle English *broillen, brulen,* from Old French *brul(l)er,* earlier *brusler,* to burn, from Vulgar Latin *brustulāre* (unattested), perhaps from Germanic.]
broil[2] *n.* A rowdy argument; a brawl.
~*intr.v.* **broiled, broiling, broils.** To engage in a brawl. [From obsolete *broil,* to confound, disturb, from Middle English *broilen,* from Old French *brouiller,* perhaps from *breu,* broth.]
broil·er (broi′lər) *n.* **1.** One who broils. **2. a.** A small electric oven used for broiling. **b.** The part of a stove used for broiling. **3.** A tender young chicken suitable for broiling.
broke (brōk). Past tense and *nonstandard* past participle of **break.**
~*adj. Informal.* Having no money.
bro·ken (brō′kən). Past participle of **break.**
~*adj.* **1.** Shattered or snapped into two or more pieces. **2.** Disregarded; not honored: *a broken promise.* **3.** Fragmentary; incomplete: *a broken set of books.* **4.** Disorganized; routed: *broken troops.* **5.** Intermittently stopping and starting; discontinuous. **6.** Varying abruptly, as in pitch: *broken sobs.* **7.** Spoken imperfectly: *broken English.* **8.** Topographically rough; uneven: *broken ground.* **9.** Subdued; humbled: *a broken spirit.* **10.** Tamed and trained: *a broken stallion.* **11.** Weakened; exhausted: *broken health.* **12. a.** Crushed by grief: *a broken heart.* **b.** Utterly demoralized: *a broken man.* **13.** Financially ruined; bankrupt. **14.** In which the marriage partners or parents are separated or divorced: *a broken home.* **15.** Not functioning. —**bro·ken·ly** *adv.*
bro·ken-down (brō′kən-doun′) *adj.* **1.** Out of working order. **2.** Debilitated; infirm.
bro·ken·heart·ed (brō′kən-här′tĭd) *adj.* Extremely sad, as through the loss of a loved one.
Bro·ken Hill (brō′kən). Town in New South Wales, Australia, near the border with South Australia. It is named after a humped range of mountains, part of the Main Barrier Range. The town has one of the world's richest deposits of silver.
broken wind *n.* A disease of horses, the **heaves** *(see).*
bro·ker (brō′kər) *n.* **1.** One who acts as an agent for others in negotiating contracts, purchases, or sales in return for a fee or commis-

sion. **2.** A stockbroker. [Middle English, peddler, pawnbroker, go-between, from Norman French *brocour*†.]

bro·ker·age (brō′kər-ĭj) *n.* **1.** The business of a broker. **2.** A fee or commission paid to a broker.

brol·ly (brŏl′ē) *n., pl.* **-lies.** *British Informal.* An umbrella.

bro·mate (brō′māt′) *n.* A salt or ester of bromic acid.
~*tr.v.* **bromated, -mating, -mates. 1.** To treat (a substance) chemically with a bromate. **2.** Loosely, to combine (a substance) chemically with bromine. [Probably German *Bromat* : BROM(O)- + -ATE.]

brome-grass (brōm′grăs′) *n.* Any grass of the genus *Bromus*, especially *B. mollis*, having spikelets in loose, often drooping clusters. Also called "brome." [New Latin *Bromus*, from Latin *bromos*, oats, from Greek *bromos*†.]

bro·me·li·ad (brō-mē′lē-ăd′) *n.* Any of various mostly epiphytic plants of the tropical American family Bromeliaceae, which includes the pineapple, Spanish moss, and many species grown as house plants. Typically, bromeliads have a rosette of fleshy, strap-shaped leaves producing a long, central, often brightly colored spike of flowers. [From New Latin *Bromelia* (type genus), after Olaf *Bromelius* (1639–1705), Swedish botanist.]

bro·mic acid (brō′mĭk) *n.* A corrosive, colorless, unstable liquid, HBrO₃, used in making dyes and pharmaceuticals. [French *bromique* : BROM(O)- + -IC.]

bro·mide (brō′mīd′) *n.* **1.** Any chemical compound in which the element bromine has a valence of one, either as a negative ion or as an atom linked to another by a covalent bond. **2.** A sedative, **potassium bromide** *(see).* **3. a.** A commonplace remark or notion; a platitude. **b.** A tiresome person; bore. **4.** A photographic print on paper that has been treated with bromine and silver. **5.** A photographic print on bromide paper of a typeset page of a book, magazine, or the like, to which artwork is attached before filming and platemaking. —See Synonyms at **cliché.** [BROM(INE) + -IDE.] —**bro·mid·ic** (brō-mĭd′ĭk) *adj.*

bro·mi·nate (brō′mĭ-nāt′) *tr.v.* **-nated, -nating, -nates.** To combine (a substance) with bromine or a bromine compound. —**bro·mi·na·tion** *n.*

bro·mine (brō′mēn′) *n. Symbol* **Br** A heavy, volatile, corrosive, reddish-brown, nonmetallic liquid element, having a highly irritating vapor. It is used in producing gasoline antiknock mixtures, fumigants, dyes, and photographic chemicals. Atomic weight 79.909, atomic number 35, melting point -7.2°C, boiling point 58.78°C, specific gravity 3.119, valences 1, 3, 5, 7. [French *brome*, from Greek *brōmos*†, stench + -INE.]

bro·mism (brō′mĭz′əm) *n.* Also **bro·min·ism** (brō′mə-nĭz′əm). Poisoning from overuse of bromides. Symptoms include skin eruptions, headache, sleepiness, apathy, and loss of strength. [Probably French *bromisme* : BROM(O)- + -ISM.]

bromo- *prefix.* Indicates bromine as the principal element in a chemical compound; for example, **bromoacetone.** [Probably from French *brome*, BROMINE.]

bro·mo·ac·e·tone (brō′mō-ăs′ə-tōn′) *n.* Also **brom·ac·e·tone** (brō-măs′ə-tōn′). A colorless liquid, CH₂BrCOCH₃, used as a constituent of tear gas. Also called "bromomethane." [BROMO- + -ACETONE.]

bro·mo·form (brō′mə-fôrm′, -fôrm′) *n.* A heavy, colorless liquid, CHBr₃, having a sweet taste and odor resembling chloroform, used in laboratory separations of minerals.

bron·chi. Plural of **bronchus.**

bron·chi·a (brŏng′kē-ə) *pl.n. Singular* **-chium** (-kē-əm). *Anatomy.* Bronchial tubes smaller than the bronchi and larger than bronchioles. [Late Latin, from Greek *bronkhia*, plural of *bronkhion*, diminutive of *bronkhos*, windpipe, BRONCHUS.]

bron·chi·al (brŏng′kē-əl) *adj.* Of or pertaining to the bronchi, the bronchia, or the bronchioles. —**bron·chi·al·ly** *adv.*

bronchial asthma *n.* A usually allergic asthma of the bronchi.

bronchial tube *n. Anatomy.* A bronchus or any of its branches.

bron·chi·ec·ta·sis (brŏng′kē-ĕk′tə-sĭs) *n. Pathology.* Chronic dilation of the bronchial tubes, with cough and formation of mucus and pus. [New Latin : BRONCH(O)- + *ectasis*, dilation, from Greek *ektasis*, stretching.]

bron·chi·ole (brŏng′kē-ōl′) *n. Anatomy.* Any of the fine, thin-walled, tubular extensions of a bronchus.

bron·chi·tis (brŏng-kī′tĭs) *n.* Chronic or acute inflammation of the mucous membrane of the bronchial tubes. Symptoms include coughing and breathing difficulties. [New Latin : BRONCH(O)- + -ITIS.] —**bron·chi·tic** (brŏng-kĭt′ĭk) *adj.*

broncho-, bronch- *prefix.* Indicates the bronchi or bronchial tubes; for example, **bronchoscope, bronchitis.** [Late Latin, from Greek *bronkh(o)-*, from *bronkhos*, windpipe, BRONCHUS.]

bron·cho·dil·a·tor (brŏng′kō-dī′lā′tər) *n.* Any of various drugs that relax bronchial muscles and therefore widen the air passages, used to treat asthma, bronchitis, and other breathing difficulties.

bron·cho·pneu·mo·ni·a (brŏng′kō-nōō-mōn′yə, -nyōō-mōn′yə) *n.* Inflammation of the lungs spreading from and following infection of the bronchial tubes.

bron·cho·scope (brŏng′kə-skōp′) *n.* A slender tubular instrument with a small light on the end for inspection of the interior of the bronchial tubes. [BRONCHO- + -SCOPE.]

bron·chus (brŏng′kəs) *n., pl.* **-chi** (-kī′, -kē′). *Anatomy.* Either of two main branches of the trachea, having walls thickened with cartilage and branching into smaller air passages, leading directly to the lungs. [New Latin, from Greek *bronkhos*, trachea, windpipe, throat.]

bron·co (brŏng′kō) *n., pl.* **-cos.** A wild or semiwild horse of western North America. [Mexican Spanish, from Spanish, rough, wild.]

bron·co-bust·er (brŏng′kō-bŭs′tər) *n.* A cowboy who breaks wild horses to the saddle.

Bron·të (brŏn′tē), **Charlotte** (1816–55), **Emily** (1818–48), and **Anne** (1820–49). British novelists and poets, daughters of the Anglo-Irish clergyman and writer, Patrick Brunty, or Brontë, who was the curate at Haworth, Yorkshire, after 1820. In 1846 their first publication was issued, a volume of verse entitled *Poems by Currer, Ellis and Acton Bell.* In 1847 Charlotte published *Jane Eyre*, Emily *Wuthering Heights*, and Anne *Agnes Grey.* Anne's *The Tenant of Wildfell Hall* was published in 1848. Charlotte published *Shirley* in 1849 and *Villette* in 1853. Their brother, **(Patrick) Branwell** (1817–48), was an artist.

bron·to·sau·rus (brŏn′tə-sôr′əs) *n.* Also **bron·to·saur** (brŏn′tə-sôr′). A very large, plant-eating dinosaur of the genus *Apatosaurus* (or *Brontosaurus*), of the Late Jurassic period, having a long neck and tail and a small head. [New Latin *Brontosaurus* : Greek *brontē*, thunder + -SAUR.]

Bronx, the (brŏngks). Borough of New York City, the only one on the mainland. It is chiefly residential, except for the waterfront, which is crowded with warehouses and factories.

Bronx cheer *n. Slang.* An expression of derision or contempt, a **raspberry** *(see).*

bronze (brŏnz) *n.* **1. a.** Any of various alloys of copper and tin, sometimes with traces of other metals. **b.** Any of various alloys of copper, with or without tin, and antimony, phosphorus, or other components. **2.** A work of art made of bronze. **3.** A bronze medal. **4.** Metallic yellowish to olive brown.
~*tr.v.* **bronzed, bronzing, bronzes. 1.** To give the appearance of bronze to. **2.** To give a suntanned appearance to. [French, from Italian *bronzo*, perhaps from Persian *birinj*, copper.] —**bronze** *adj.* —**bronz·y** *adj.*

Bronze Age *n.* A period of human culture between the Stone Age and the Iron Age, characterized by weapons and implements made of bronze. See feature, next page.

bronze diabetes *n.* Hemochromatosis *(see).*

Bronze Star *n.* A U.S. Army decoration awarded for heroism or meritorious achievement in ground combat.

brooch, broach (brōch, brōōch) *n.* An ornament worn on the clothing, attached by means of a pin and catch. [Middle English *broche*, brooch, BROACH (n.).]

brood (brōōd) *n.* **1.** The young of certain animals, such as birds or fish; especially, a group of young birds or fowl hatched at one time and cared for by the same mother. **2.** The children in one family. **3.** A group with a common origin or purpose: *a brood of trouble-makers.*
~*v.* **brooded, brooding, broods.** —*tr.* To sit on or hatch (eggs). —*intr.* **1.** To sit on or hatch eggs. **2.** To hover enveloping: *"that gentle heat that brooded on the waters"* (Thomas Browne). **3.** To ponder moodily; sulk.
~*adj.* Kept for breeding: *a brood mare.* [Middle English *brood*, Old English *brōd*, from Germanic *bro-* (unattested), heat.] —**brood·ing·ly** *adv.*

brood·er (brōō′dər) *n.* **1.** One that broods. **2.** A heated enclosure in which young chickens, other fowl, or young livestock are raised.

brood·y (brōō′dē) *adj.* **-ier, -iest. 1.** Moody; meditative. **2.** Inclined to sit on eggs to hatch them. Said of hens and other poultry.

brook¹ (brōōk) *n.* A small, natural freshwater stream. [Middle English *brook*, *broke*, Old English *brōc*.]

brook² *tr.v.* **brooked, brooking, brooks.** To put up with; bear; tolerate. Usually used in the negative: *I can't brook rudeness.* [Middle English *brouken*, *broken*, enjoy, to use (as food), to stomach, Old English *brūcan*.]

Brooke (brōōk), **Rupert Chawner** (1887–1915). British poet. His first volume of verse, *Poems*, was published in 1911. His *1914 and Other Poems* was published in 1915. The romantic patriotic lyricism of his war sonnets differs sharply in mood from the angry poems of the other leading war poets, Wilfred Owen and Siegfried Sassoon.

Brooke-bor-ough (brōōk′bûr-ō, -bə-rə), **Sir Basil Stanlake Brooke, 1st Viscount** (1888–1973). Northern Irish politician. After serving in the Special Constabulary in its struggle against the I.R.A., he was a member of the Northern Irish Assembly at Stormont (1929–68), serving as minister of agriculture (1933–41), minister of commerce (1941–45), and prime minister (1943–63). An outspoken opponent of Irish reunification and a fierce upholder of Protestant ascendancy in Northern Ireland, he was raised to the peerage (1952).

brook·ite (brōōk′īt′) *n.* A red-brown to black titanium dioxide mineral with characteristic orthorhombic crystals. [After Henry J. *Brooke* (1771–1857), English mineralogist.]

brook lamprey *n.* Any of several usually small lampreys that live mostly in brooks.

brook·let (brōōk′lĭt) *n.* A small brook.

brook·lime (brōōk′līm′) *n.* Either of two closely related trailing plants, *Veronica americana*, of North America, and *V. beccabunga*, native to Eurasia, growing in moist places and having small blue flowers resembling the speedwell. [Variant (influenced by LIME) of Middle English *brokelemke* : *broke*, BROOK + *lemke*, a kind of brooklime, Old English *hleomoce*.]

Brook·lyn (brōōk′lĭn). Borough of New York City, occupying the southwestern part of Long Island. It is both a residential and industrial borough, and in population it is the city's largest. It includes

bromeliad *The bromeliad family of plants is native to tropical America and the West Indies. The family contains more than 1,000 species, including the pineapple and the torch bromeliad shown here.*

brooch *A Victorian mosaic brooch. The earliest brooches were functional as well as decorative; they were used to fasten clothing.*

Bronze Age

THE METAL THAT BROUGHT THE STONE AGE TO AN END

Craftsmen who smelted copper with tin produced bronze for tools and weapons

It is thought that bronze was invented about 3000 B.C. in the city states of Mesopotamia. There, because the land was fertile through irrigation, there was no need for all the inhabitants to be occupied in food production. Craftsmen could be fed by the labors of their fellow men and had time to experiment; when they mixed tin and copper in their smelting furnaces, they produced bronze.

Bronze is much harder than copper. It was easily cast into hard tools and weapons that could be recast if they broke, straightened if they bent, and sharpened

again and again. The new alloy eventually replaced stone for all agricultural tools and for weapons: the Stone Age had been succeeded by the Bronze Age.

The first bronze casts were made in flat molds carved out of stones or pressed into sand. Very early in the Bronze Age, casts were made in one-piece clay molds; these had to be broken for the cast to be taken out. Soon, molds were being prepared in two pieces, which were tied together with string or held by dowels during the casting and could be used more than once. Ax heads, daggers, sword blades, and shield mounts

were made in either one-piece or two-piece molds.

For making finely modeled figures and small, intricate horse trappings a complex "lost wax" method was devised. It used less metal but required more skill. The object to be cast was modeled in clay and covered first with a layer of wax, then with a thick layer of clay in which two holes were made. Molten bronze was poured through one hole; it melted and forced out the wax through the other hole. A layer of bronze thus replaced the layer of wax and hardened to give a hollow cast.

METHODS OF MAKING SOLID CASTS

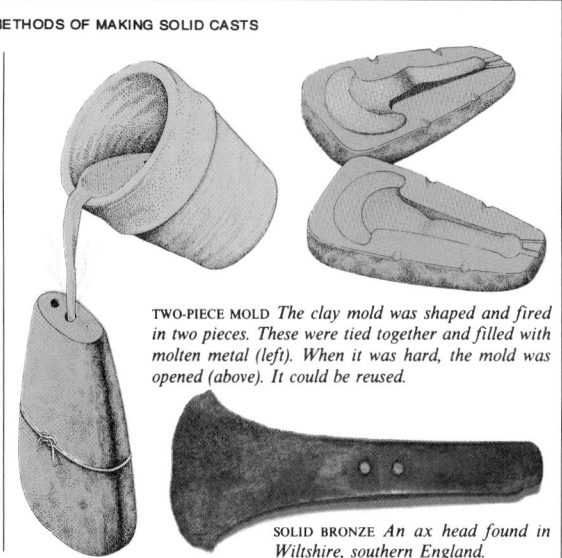

TWO-PIECE MOLD *The clay mold was shaped and fired in two pieces. These were tied together and filled with molten metal (left). When it was hard, the mold was opened (above). It could be reused.*

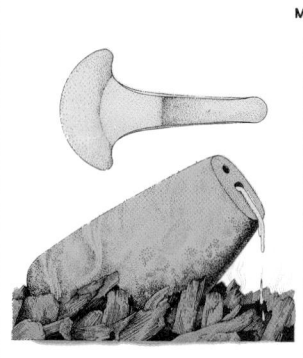

ONE-PIECE MOLD *A beeswax model (top) of the object being cast, an ax head for example, was thickly encased in clay. This was fired to harden it (bottom). The beeswax melted and ran out. The mold was filled with molten bronze, and when the metal was hard, the mold was broken off.*

SOLID BRONZE *An ax head found in Wiltshire, southern England.*

HOLLOW BRONZE *This head of Sargon of Akkad, king of Mesopotamia 4,300 years ago, was made by the lost-wax process— the method still used for fine detail, as in the headdress and beard.*

---

broom Common broom, Sarothamnus scoparius, is found throughout western Europe and temperate North America on sandy, acid soils. It grows up to 2 meters (6 feet) tall, bearing masses of golden flowers in early summer. Under its former name, Planta genista, broom was the badge of the English royal house of Plantagenet, who took their name from the plant.

Coney Island, famous for its beach and amusement park.
Brooks (brŏŏks), **Van Wyck** (1886–1963). U.S. literary historian, critic, and translator. He wrote many books on the literary history of America, including *The Flowering of New England* (1936), for which he won a Pulitzer Prize. His several volumes of memoirs were collected and published posthumously as *An Autobiography.*
brook trout *n.* A freshwater game fish, *Salvelinus fontinalis,* of eastern North America. Also called "speckled trout."
brook·weed (brŏŏk′wēd′) *n.* Either of two related plants, *Samolus valerandi* of Europe and *S. floribundus* of North America, both having small white flowers and growing in moist areas. Also called "water pimpernel."
broom (brŏŏm, brŏŏm) *n.* **1.** A sweeping implement consisting traditionally of a bundle of twigs or straw bound to a stick, but now usually of synthetic bristles fastened to a long handle. **2.** Any shrub of the genus *Sarothamnus (Cytisus),* especially *S. scoparius,* native to Eurasia, having compound leaves and usually yellow flowers. **3.** Any of several similar or related shrubs, especially of the genus *Genista.*
~*tr.v.* **broomed, brooming, brooms.** To sweep with a broom. [Middle English *broom,* broom made of broom twigs, broom plant, Old English *brōm,* broom plant.] —**broom·y** *adj.*
broom·corn (brŏŏm′kôrn′, brŏŏm′-) *n.* A grass, *Sorghum vulgare technicum,* having flower clusters with stiff, branching stalks that are used to make brooms and brushes.
broom moss *n.* Any moss of the genus *Dicranum,* especially *D. scoparium,* having leaves turned to one side along the stem.
broom·rape (brŏŏm′rāp′, brŏŏm′-) *n.* Any of several leafless, parasitic plants of the genus *Orobanche,* having yellow, purple, or reddish-brown flowers and living on the roots of other plants. [Partial translation of New Latin *rapum genistae,* "tuber of Genista (a genus of broom)" (from the resemblance of one of the parasitic growths to a tuber on the roots of broom).]
broom·stick (brŏŏm′stĭk′, brŏŏm′-) *n.* The long handle of a broom.
bros. brothers.
brose (brōz) *n.* A kind of oatmeal porridge eaten in Scotland. [Scottish form of BREWIS.]
broth (brôth, brŏth) *n., pl.* **broths** (brôths, brôthz, brŏths, brŏthz). **1.** The water in which meat, fish, or vegetables have been boiled; stock. **2.** A thin, clear soup based on stock, to which rice, barley, meat, or vegetables may be added. **3.** A nutrient medium for the

culture of microorganisms and tissues. [Middle English, Old English, from Germanic.]
broth·el (brŏth′əl, brŏ′thəl) *n.* A house of prostitution. [Shortened from *brothel-house,* from Middle English *brothel,* worthless person, prostitute, from Old English *brēothan,* fall into ruin.]
broth·er (brŭth′ər) *n., pl.* **brothers** or archaic **brethren** (brĕth′rən). *Abbr.* **b., B., br., bro. 1.** A male having the same mother and father as another person (*full brother*), having one parent in common with another person (*half brother*), having one parent in common with another person, by marriage rather than by blood (*stepbrother*), or having the same father and mother after adoption (*foster brother*). **2.** One who shares a common ancestry, allegiance, character, or purpose with another or others, specifically: **a.** A kinsman. **b.** A fellow man. **c.** A fellow member, as of a trade union or profession. **d.** A close male friend; a comrade: "*Such a gallant set of fellows! Such a band of brothers!*" (Lord Nelson). **e.** *Informal.* Friend; fellow. Used as a term of address. **3.** *Ecclesiastical. Abbr.* **Br. a.** A member of a men's religious order who is not in holy orders, but engages in the work of the order. **b.** A lay member of a religious order of men. **c. Brother.** A form of address for such a person: *Brother Luke.* **4.** A black man or boy. Used as a term of address, especially by fellow blacks, to express solidarity. Compare **sister.**
~*interj.* Used to express annoyance, disgust, or the like. [Middle English, Old English *brōthor,* from Germanic.]
broth·er·hood (brŭth′ər-hŏŏd′) *n.* **1.** The state or relationship of being a brother or brothers. **2.** The quality of being brotherly; fellowship. **3.** *Abbr.* **B.** An association of men united for common purposes; a union, society, or similar organization. **4.** All the members of a specific profession or trade.
broth·er-in-law (brŭth′ər-ĭn-lô′) *n., pl.* **brothers-in-law. 1.** The brother of one's husband or wife. **2.** The husband of one's sister. **3.** The husband of the sister of one's husband or wife.
Brother Jon·a·than (jŏn′ə-thən) *n. British Archaic.* **1.** A personification of the people or government of the United States. **2.** An American. Also called "Jonathan." [Originally applied by British soldiers to American patriots during the American War of Independence (probably from the frequent use of Old Testament first names in the New England colonies).]
broth·er·ly (brŭth′ər-lē) *adj.* **1.** Characteristic of or befitting brothers; fraternal. **2.** Kind; generous; affectionate: *brotherly love.* —**broth·er·li·ness** *n.* —**broth·er·ly** *adv.*

Brothers of the Christian Schools *pl.n.* The official name for the **Christian Brothers** *(see)*.

Brough (brŭf), **Althea Louise** (1923–). U.S. tennis player. Between 1948 and 1955 she won nine Wimbledon titles (four singles, three ladies' doubles, and two mixed doubles). With Margaret Osborne DuPont she formed the most successful doubles partnership in history. They were undefeated in the U.S. championships between 1942 and 1950.

brough·am (brōōm, brōō'əm, brō'əm) *n.* **1.** A closed four-wheeled carriage with an open driver's seat in front. **2.** A car with an open driver's seat. **3.** An obsolete electrically powered car resembling a coupé. [After Henry Peter BROUGHAM.]

Brougham (brōōm, brōm), **Henry Peter, 1st Baron of Brougham and Vaux** (1778–1868). British politician and educational reformer, born in Scotland. A member of Parliament from 1810, he defended Queen Caroline in the divorce proceedings brought by George IV (1820) and, as Lord Chancellor (1830–34), played an important role in the passing of the 1832 Reform Act. He is remembered equally for his lifelong campaign against slavery, his great part in the extension of education, and his role as legal reformer.

brought. Past tense and past participle of **bring.**

brou·ha·ha (brōō'hä-hä') *n.* An uproar; a hubbub. [French (imitative).]

Brou·wer (brou'wər), **Adriaen** (c. 1606–38). Flemish genre and landscape painter, the pupil of Hals. He is famous for his lively treatment of everyday peasant life and for his mastery of landscape.

brow (brou) *n.* **1.** *Anatomy.* **a.** The part of the face between the eyes and the hairline; the forehead. **b.** The **eyebrow** *(see).* **2.** A facial expression; countenance: *"Speak you this with a sad brow?"* (Shakespeare). **3.** The edge of a steep place; the top of a slope or hill. —See Synonyms at **border.** [Middle English *brow,* Old English *brū,* eyelash, eyelid, eyebrow, from Germanic.]

brow·beat (brou'bēt') *tr.v.* **-beat, -beaten** (-bēt'n), **-beating, -beats.** To intimidate or bully with an overbearing manner.

brown (broun) *n.* **1.** *Abbr.* **br.** Any of a group of colors between red and yellow in hue that are medium to low in lightness, and low to moderate in saturation. **2.** Any of various butterflies of the family Satyridae, such as the mountain ringlets and the heaths. In this sense, also called "satyr." —*adj.* **browner, brownest. 1.** *Abbr.* **br.** Of the color brown. **2.** Deeply sun-tanned. —*v.* **browned, browning, browns.** —*tr.* To make brown; specifically, to cook until brown. —*intr.* To become brown. [Middle English *broun, brown,* Old English *brūn.*] —**brown·ish** *adj.* —**brown·ness** *n.*

Brown (broun), **Sir Arthur Whitten** (1886–1948). British aviator. On July 14, 1919, with Sir John William Alcock, he made the first nonstop flight across the Atlantic Ocean.

Brown, Ford Madox (1821–93). British painter, born in France. He trained in Paris and Rome before settling in England (1845). He was closely associated with the pre-Raphaelites, but was never a member of the brotherhood. He painted chiefly historical subjects and scenes from contemporary life, of which the most famous is *Work* (1863).

Brown, John (1800–59). U.S. abolitionist commemorated in the song, "John Brown's Body Lies Amouldering in the Grave." A leading campaigner against slavery in the South, he enlisted men (1857) to give escaped slaves armed protection in a mountain stronghold. On October 16, 1859, they captured the U.S. arsenal at Harpers Ferry, Virginia. In the subsequent fighting his men were defeated, and Brown was hanged on December 2.

Brown, Lancelot (1716–83). British landscape gardener, known as "Capability Brown" from his habit of assuring his patrons of the great capabilities of their estates. He broke with the convention of geometrically laid-out gardens and planned parks and gardens in imitation of a natural landscape, as at Blenheim and Chatsworth. George III appointed him gardener at Hampton Court (1764).

Brown, Robert (1773–1858). British botanist. He discovered and named the nucleus of the cell, but he is most famous for his investigation of the sexual behavior of plants. It was the microscopic observation of pollination that brought about his discovery (1827) of the irregular movement of pollen grains. This observation led to the general physical concept known as Brownian motion.

brown algae *n.* Dark brown to olive green, chiefly marine algae of the division Phaeophyta, which includes the rockweeds and the kelps.

brown bagging *n.* **1.** The practice of taking one's own liquor into a restaurant or club, where setups are available. **2.** The practice of taking one's lunch to work, usually in a brown paper bag. —**brown bagger** *n.*

brown bear *n.* **1.** A very large bear, *Ursus arctos,* of Alaska and northern Eurasia, having brown to yellowish fur. Compare **grizzly bear, Kodiak bear. 2.** A brown variety of the American black bear.

brown Bet·ty (bĕt'ē) *n.* A baked pudding consisting of apples, raisins, and spices covered with bread crumbs, sugar, and butter.

brown bread *n.* **1.** A bread made of a dark flour, such as graham or whole-wheat. **2.** A steamed bread made of cornmeal, flour, and molasses.

brown coal *n.* A type of coal, **lignite** *(see).*

Browne (broun), **Charles Farrar,** known as "Artemus Ward" (1843–67). U.S. humorist and lecturer. His pieces, using backwoods characters and comic misspellings, chronicled the fictional adventures of an itinerant showman. In his writings on current events,

Browne often lampooned insincerity and sentimentality.

Browne, Hablot Knight (1815–82). British illustrator and caricaturist, who worked under the pseudonym "Phiz." Dickens invited him to illustrate *Pickwick Papers* (1836), and thereafter he illustrated a number of Dickens's novels.

Browne, Sir Thomas (1605–82). English writer. He was an eminent physician, but his most successful, enduring work was *Religio Medici* (1642), in which he attempted to reconcile the faith of a Christian with the growing body of scientific knowledge.

brown earth *n.* A type of soil, typically found where there is a mild climate and moderate rainfall, usually supporting deciduous forest.

brown fat *n.* Adipose tissue whose oxidation is a major source of heat in mammals.

Brown·i·an motion (brou'nē-ən) *n.* The random motion of microscopic particles suspended in a liquid or gas, caused by collision with molecules of the surrounding medium. Also called "Brownian movement." [After Robert BROWN, who described it.]

brown·ie (brou'nē) *n.* **1.** *Folklore.* A small sprite supposed to do helpful work at night, especially domestic chores. **2.** A small bar of rich, usually chocolate cake often with nuts. [Diminutive of BROWN. The sprite was thought of as a "wee brown man."]

Brownie *n.* A member of a junior branch of the Girl Scouts from 7 to 9 years of age. [From BROWNIE (sprite).]

Brownie point *n.* Credit considered as earned, especially by favorably impressing a superior. [From the practice of awarding points for achievement by Brownies in the Girl Scouts.]

Brown·ing (brou'nĭng), **Elizabeth Barrett** (1806–61). British poet. Her first volume of verse, *Poems* (1844), was read by Robert Browning; he subsequently married her and took her to live in Italy (1846), where she wrote *Sonnets from the Portuguese* (1850). Her verse novel *Aurora Leigh* was published in 1857.

Browning, Robert (1812–89). British poet. He published his first poem, *Pauline,* in 1833. After his initial visit to Italy, he wrote *Sordello* (1840) and *Pippa Passes* (1841). The collection *Bells and Pomegranates* was published in 1846, the year that he married Elizabeth Barrett in secret. For the next 15 years they lived together in Italy, where Browning wrote *Christmas Eve and Easter Day* (1850) and the collection *Men and Women* (1855). After Elizabeth's death (1861), he returned to England. *The Ring and the Book* (1868–69) is considered his masterpiece, but he is more widely known for his dramatic monologues, such as *My Last Duchess, Andrea del Sarto,* and *The Italian in England.*

Browning automatic rifle *n. Abbr.* **BAR** A .30 caliber air-cooled, automatic or semiautomatic, gas-operated, magazine-fed rifle used in World Wars I and II. [After John Moses *Browning* (1855–1926), U.S. firearms designer.]

Browning machine gun *n.* A .30 or .50 caliber automatic machine gun capable of firing ammunition at a rate of more than 500 rounds per minute.

brown·out (broun'out') *n.* A partial extinguishing or dimming of lights in a city, especially as a defensive measure against enemy bombardment or as a means of conserving electricity. [After BLACKOUT.]

brown rat *n.* A common and very destructive rodent pest, *Rattus norvegicus,* found in both town and country. Also called "common rat," "Norway rat."

brown rice *n.* Unpolished rice grains, retaining the germ and the yellowish outer layer containing the bran.

brown rot *n.* **1.** A disease of ripe fruits that is caused by fungi of the genus *Sclerotinia.* **2.** A disease of citrus trees that is caused by fungi of the genus *Phytophthora.*

Brown Shirts *pl.n.* A Nazi militia, Sturmabteilung *(see).*

brown·stone (broun'stōn') *n.* **1.** A brownish-red sandstone once widely used as a building material, especially for façades of houses. **2.** A house faced with such stone, especially in New York City. —**brown·stone** *adj.*

brown study *n.* A state of deep thought, melancholy, or reverie.

brown sugar *n.* **1. a.** Unrefined or partially refined sugar. **b.** Loosely, any sugar that is brown in color. **2.** *Slang.* A coarse, low-grade variety of heroin from Southeast Asia.

Brown Swiss *n.* One of a hardy breed of dairy cattle that originated in Switzerland.

brown thrasher *n.* A North American bird, *Toxostoma rufum,* having a reddish-brown back and a dark-streaked breast.

brown trout *n.* A freshwater fish, *Salmo trutta,* native to Europe, having yellow-brown sides with black and red spots, the latter circled by pale rings. Compare **sea trout.**

browse (brouz) *v.* **browsed, browsing, browses.** —*intr.* **1.** To look through or inspect something, such as a book or goods in a shop, in a leisurely and casual way. **2.** To feed on leaves, young shoots, and other vegetation. —*tr.* **1.** To nibble; crop. **2.** To graze on. —*n.* **1.** An instance of browsing. **2.** Young twigs, leaves, and tender shoots of plants or shrubs that animals eat. [From Old French *broust, brost,* shoot, twig, from Germanic.] —**brows·er** *n.*

Bru·beck (brōō'bĕk), **Dave,** full name David Warren Brubeck (1920–). U.S. jazz pianist and composer. He was trained from the age of four as a classical pianist and studied composition under Milhaud and Schoenberg, but later turned entirely to jazz, forming an octet in 1946 and a successful quartet in 1951.

Bruce, Robert the. See Robert I.

bru·cel·lo·sis (brōō'sə-lō'sĭs) *n.* A contagious disease of certain livestock caused by bacteria of the genus *Brucella* and transmissible to humans, for example through infected milk. Symptoms in humans

brown bear *Living throughout the Northern Hemisphere, brown bears eat almost anything, including roots, fruit, mice, and deer. They also hunt fish, flipping salmon from streams with their paws.*

include fever, headache, weakness, and painful joints and in animals, abortions. Also called "Malta fever," "Mediterranean fever," "undulant fever," and in animals "contagious abortion." [New Latin : *Brucella,* after Sir David *Bruce* (1855–1931), Australian bacteriologist and physician + -OSIS.]

bru·cine (broo'sēn', -sĭn) *n.* A poisonous white crystalline alkaloid, $C_{23}H_{26}O_4N_2 \cdot 2H_2O$, derived from nux vomica seeds. [After James *Bruce* (1730–94), Scottish explorer in Africa.]

Bruck·ner (brook'nər), **Anton** (1824–96). Austrian composer and organist. He did not write his first important work until he was in his forties, and it was not until his sixties that he became famous. His most important works are the nine symphonies and large choral works, especially the three masses and the *Te Deum.*

Brue·gel or **Breu·ghel** (broi'gəl), **Jan** (1568–1625). Flemish painter, second son of Pieter the Elder. He painted landscapes and often put figures or landscape backgrounds into other artists' paintings, including some of Rubens. His reputation now rests mainly on his paintings of still lifes, especially flowers.

Bruegel, Pieter the Elder (c. 1530–69). Foremost of a family of Flemish painters, he was one of the first painters to treat landscape as a worthy subject of itself. He is best known for his genre paintings, especially of peasant scenes, in which he combined minute observation of the Flemish tradition with the somewhat fantastical manner of Hieronymus Bosch.

Bruegel, Pieter the Younger (c. 1564–c. 1638). Flemish painter, son of Pieter the Elder. Many of his paintings are copies of his father's works. Owing to the scarcity of the latter's originals, Pieter the Younger is much better represented in museums and galleries.

Bruges (broozh). *Flemish* **Brug·ge** (broog'ə). Industrial city in northwestern Belgium, connected to the port of Zeebrugge on the North Sea by a canal. It was founded in the 9th century and in the 13th century was a leading member of the Hanseatic League. In the High Middle Ages, at the zenith of its prosperity, it was one of the most important wool-processing towns and commercial hubs of Europe.

bru·in (broo'ĭn) *n.* A name for bear, used especially in folktales and children's stories. [Dutch *bruin,* "brown."]

bruise (brooz) *v.* **bruised, bruising, bruises.** —*tr.* **1.** To damage the underlying tissue or bone of (part of the body) without breaking the skin. **2.** To damage or mar (fruit, for example). **3.** To pound into fragments; crush. **4.** To hurt psychologically; offend. —*intr.* To become discolored, as the skin does after a hard blow. ~*n.* An area of skin discoloration, caused by the escape of blood from ruptured capillaries following a blow; a contusion. [Middle English *brusen, brisen,* to crush, mangle, from Old English *brȳsan* and Old French *bruisier†,* to break, crush.]

bruis·er (broo'zər) *n. Slang.* A rough-looking, powerfully built man.

bruit (broot) *tr.v.* **bruited, bruiting, bruits.** To spread (a rumor, for example); report. Used with *about* or *abroad.* ~*n.* **1.** *Medicine.* An abnormal sound heard in the body during auscultation, especially a heart murmur. **2.** *Archaic.* A rumor. **3.** *Archaic.* A din; a clamor. [Middle English, noise, from Old French, from the past participle of *bruire,* to roar, from Vulgar Latin *brūgere* (unattested), variant of Latin *rugīre,* to roar.]

bru·mal (broo'məl) *adj. Archaic.* Of, pertaining to, or characteristic of winter; wintry. [Latin *brūmālis,* from *brūma,* winter solstice, "the shortest day," from *brevima* (unattested), the shortest, from *brevis,* short.]

brume (broom) *n.* Heavy fog or mist; dense vapor. [French, mist, winter, from Old French, from Old Provençal *bruma,* from Latin *brūma.* See **brumal.**] —**bru·mous** *adj.*

brum·ma·gem (brŭm'ə-jəm) *adj.* Cheap and showy; tawdry. ~*n.* Any cheap and gaudy imitation, especially of jewelry. [Dialect

---

Brueghel

THE PAINTER WHO "SPOKE" WITH HIS BRUSH

Brueghel's lively scenes are crowded with comment

The lively peasant scenes and crowded landscapes of Pieter Brueghel's canvases opened up a new door for the Flemish school of painters. Brueghel looked in on his subjects; there is satire and social comment in his compositions. Satire in the silly grin on the bride's face in *Peasant Wedding* (about 1567); social comment in the hungry looks of the musicians.

Little is known of Brueghel. It is not known where he was born, but it was between 1525 and 1530. By 1551 he was a master of the Painters' Guild at Antwerp. He visited Italy and on his return painted some impressive landscapes. He satirized sin and drunkenness in *The Fall of the Rebel Angels* (1562) and *Peasant Dance* (1566), and produced two masterpieces on biblical themes, *Procession to Calvary* and *Massacre of the Innocents* (1566). A religious subject is embedded in the 16th-century detail in many of his works.

For a time after his death in Brussels in 1569, Brueghel's work seems to have been neglected, yet his observation of everyday life and his rapid, fluent style of brushwork were taken up by the Flemish painters who followed him. Among them were his sons, Pieter the Younger (c. 1564–1638), and Jan (1568–1625), known as Velvet Brueghel for his silky landscapes and detailed still-life paintings.

PEASANT WEDDING *Brueghel's observation of daily life shines through this vivid picture. All his characters say something about themselves: the bridegroom spooning his food thoughtfully, the friar and magistrate talking seriously, the little boy licking his plate.*

form of BIRMINGHAM, England (with reference to counterfeit coins made there in the 17th century).]

Brum·mell (brŭm′əl), **George Bryan,** known as "Beau Brummell" (1778–1840). British dandy and socialite. He became the close friend of the Prince of Wales and set the male fashion—dark, simply tailored clothes, trousers rather than breeches, and elaborate neckwear—of the prince's society at Brighton. He was a leader of society in London, but gambling forced him deeply into debt and he fled to France (1816) to escape his creditors. He never returned to England and died, after years of penniless squalor, in an insane asylum at Caen.

brunch (brŭnch) *n. Informal.* A meal eaten late in the morning as a combination of breakfast and lunch. [*breakfast* + *lunch*.]

Brundisium. See **Brindisi.**

Bru·nei, State of (br○○′nī). Sultanate and former self-governing British protectorate on the northern coast of Borneo. It is split into two sections, each of which is an enclave within Malaysian territory. The only British dependency inhabited by Malays not to have entered the Federation of Malaysia (1963), it became fully independent at the end of 1983. The economy is largely dependent on the export of oil. Area, 5,800 square kilometers (2,226 square miles). Population, 213,000. Capital, Bandar Seri Begawan. See map at **Malaysia.**

Brunei Town. See **Bandar Seri Begawan.**

Bru·nel (br○○-nĕl′), **Isambard Kingdom** (1806–59). British civil engineer, son of Sir Marc. He was an engineer with the Great Western Railway and also helped build railways in Australia, Italy, and India. He worked with his father in the construction of the Thames Tunnel, but he is most famous for his design and construction of the three great ocean steamships, the *Great Western* (1838), which was the first transatlantic steamship, the *Great Britain* (1845), and the *Great Eastern* (1858).

Brunel, Sir Marc Isambard (1769–1849). British engineer and inventor, born in France. A royalist, he came to the United States in 1793 to escape the Reign of Terror and began his career as a civil engineer. By 1799 he had settled in England, where he patented a number of inventions, including a knitting machine. His greatest engineering achievement was the design and construction of the Thames Tunnel, which was completed in 1843.

Bru·nel·les·chi (br○○′nə-lĕs′kē), **Filippo** (1377–1446). Italian architect, the most celebrated of the 15th century Florentine Renaissance. He reintroduced Roman forms of perspective and methods of construction, but his greatest architectural feat, the dome of Florence cathedral (completed after his death), is in Gothic style. See feature, next page.

bru·net (br○○-nĕt′) *adj.* **1.** Of a dark complexion or coloring. **2.** Having dark brown or black hair or eyes. —*n.* A person with brown hair. [French, from Old French, from *brun,* brown, from Germanic.]

bru·nette (br○○-nĕt′) *adj.* Having dark or brown hair. —*n.* A girl or woman with dark or brown hair.

Brun·hild (br○○n′hĭlt). *Norse Mythology.* A legendary queen of Iceland who is won as a bride by Gunther in the *Nibelungenlied.*

Brünn. See **Brno.**

Brun·ner (br○○n′ər), **Emil** (1889–1966). Swiss Protestant theologian. With Karl Barth he was one of the foremost opponents of the rational, liberal school of modern theology and resolute in his insistence upon the importance of revelation in the relationship between God and humankind. Among his most influential writings were *The Divine Human Encounter* (1938) and *Christianity and Civilization* (1948–49).

Brünn·hil·de (br○○n-hĭl′də). The heroine of Wagner's opera *Ring of the Nibelung,* a Valkyrie who is placed in a circle of fire by Wotan and is eventually released by Siegfried.

Bru·no (br○○′nō), **Giordano** (*c.* 1548–1600). Italian philosopher and cosmologist. He entered the Dominican order at the age of 15, but left it (1576) when he was charged with heresy and thereafter traveled throughout Europe. He was delivered to the Inquisition by the Venetian authorities (1592) and, after refusing to recant, was burned at the stake (1600) for immoral conduct, blasphemy, and heresy. His most important works were the series of dialogues in which he argued for the indivisibility of all matter and all forms and in which he extended Copernican thought to state that the universe is an infinite series of solar systems.

Bruno of Co·logne (kə-lōn′), **Saint** (*c.* 1030–1101). German monk, the founder of the Carthusian order. He was ordained a priest, but was deprived of his offices when he exposed the malpractices of an archbishop. In 1084 he retired with six fellow monks to the mountains of the Grande Chartreuse in southern France and founded a monastery.

Bruns·wick (brŭnz′wĭk). German **Braun·schweig** (broun′shvīk′). Former duchy and West German state, mostly in present-day West Germany but extending also into East Germany. The city of Brunswick, the former capital, is located on the Oker River.

brunt (brŭnt) *n.* **1.** The main impact or force, as of a blow or attack. Used especially in the phrase *bear the brunt of.* **2.** *Obsolete.* A violent attack. [Middle English *brunt*†.]

Brusa. See **Bursa.**

brush[1] (brŭsh) *n.* **1.** Any of various devices consisting of bristles, fibers, or other flexible material fastened into a handle, for such uses as scrubbing, polishing, applying paint, or grooming the hair. Often used in combination: *a toothbrush; a hairbrush.* **2.** An act of using such an implement. **3.** A light touch in passing; a graze. **4.** A

brief, often unpleasant, contact or encounter: *had several brushes with the law.* **5.** The bushy tail of a fox, used especially as a hunting trophy. **6.** The art or profession of painting. Preceded by *the.* **7.** *Electricity.* A yielding or sliding connection completing a circuit between a fixed and a moving, especially rotating, conductor. —*v.* **brushed, brushing, brushes.** —*tr.* **1.** To use a brush on, so as to clean, polish, paint, or groom. **2.** To apply with or as if with motions of a brush. **3.** To remove with or as if with motions of a brush. **4.** To dismiss or rebuff abruptly or curtly. Used with *aside* or *off: brushed the matter aside.* **5.** To touch lightly in passing; graze against. —*intr.* **1.** To use or apply a brush. **2.** To move past something so as to touch it lightly. —**brush up.** To refresh or improve one's knowledge of or skill at performing. [Middle English *brusshe,* from Old French *broisse, brosse,* perhaps from *broce,* BRUSH (brushwood).] —**brush·er** *n.* —**brush·y** *adj.*

brush[2] *n.* **1. a.** A dense growth of bushes or shrubs. **b.** Land covered by such a growth. **2.** Sparsely populated woodland. **3.** Cut or broken branches. [Middle English *brusch(e),* from Norman French *brousse,* from Old French *broce,* from Vulgar Latin *bruscia* (unattested).] —**brush·y** *adj.*

brush discharge *n.* A faintly visible, relatively slow, crackling discharge of electricity without sparking.

brushed (brŭsht) *adj.* Of or designating knitted or woven fabrics that have a nap produced by brushing during manufacture.

brush fire *n.* A fire in low-growing, scrubby trees and brush.

brush-off (brŭsh′ôf′, -ŏf′) *n.* An abrupt dismissal or snub; a rejection.

brush·wood (brŭsh′wŏŏd′) *n.* **1.** Cut or broken-off branches. **2. a.** Dense undergrowth. **b.** An area covered by such growth.

brush·work (brŭsh′wûrk′) *n.* **1.** Work done with a brush. **2.** The manner in which a painter applies paint with the brush.

brusque, brusk (brŭsk) *adj.* Abrupt and curt in manner or speech; discourteously blunt. —See Synonyms at **gruff.** [French *brusque,* lively, fierce, harsh, from Italian *brusco,* sour, sharp, butcher's broom (as noun), from Vulgar Latin *bruscum*†.] —**brusque·ly** *adv.* —**brusque·ness** *n.*

brus·que·rie (brŭs′kə-rē′) *n.* Brusqueness; curtness.

Brus·sels (brŭs′əlz). French **Bru·xelles** (brü-sĕl′). Capital of Belgium, in Brabant province on the Senne River. Officially a bilingual (Flemish and French) city, it is the executive headquarters of the European Economic Community.

Brussels carpet *n.* A machine-made carpet consisting of small, colored woolen loops that form a heavy, patterned pile.

Brussels lace *n.* **1.** Fine needlepoint or bobbin lace worked in floral patterns. **2.** Net lace with an appliqué design, formerly made by hand but now usually made by machine.

Brussels sprout *n.* **1.** A variety of cabbage, *Brassica oleracea* or *B. gemmifera,* having a stout stem studded with budlike heads resembling miniature cabbages. **2. Brussels sprouts.** The small edible heads of this plant. Also called "sprouts."

brut (br○○t) *adj.* Very dry. Said of wines, especially champagne. Compare **sec.** [French, raw, rough, from Old French, from Latin *brūtus,* heavy.]

bru·tal (br○○t′l) *adj.* **1.** Characteristic of a brute; cruel; inhumane. **2.** Crude or unfeeling in manner or speech; insensitive. **3.** Harsh; unrelenting; merciless: *brutal criticism.* —**bru·tal·ly** *adv.*

bru·tal·ism *n.* A style of architecture that uses stark, geometric lines and large areas of unrelieved concrete to create an impression of monolithic strength. —**bru·tal·ist** *n.*

bru·tal·i·ty (br○○-tăl′ə-tē′) *n., pl.* **-ties. 1.** The state or quality of being brutal. **2.** A brutal act.

bru·tal·ize (br○○t′l-īz′) *tr.v.* **-ized, -izing, -izes. 1.** To make brutal. **2.** To treat brutally. —**bru·tal·i·za·tion** *n.*

brute (br○○t) *n.* **1.** Any animal other than a human being; a beast. **2. a.** *Informal.* A brutal person. **b.** *Informal.* A person who is much disliked. —*adj.* **1.** Of or pertaining to beasts; animal: *"None of the brute creation requires more than food and shelter"* (Henry Thoreau). **2.** Characteristic of a brute: **a.** Entirely physical or instinctive: *brute force.* **b.** Lacking reason or intelligence. **3.** Savage; cruel. **4.** Gross; coarse. [Middle English, from Old French *brut,* rough. See **brut.**] —**brut·ism** *n.*

bru·ti·fy (br○○t′ə-fī) *v.* **-fied, -fying, -fies.** —*tr.* To brutalize. —*intr.* To become brutalized.

brut·ish (br○○t′ĭsh) *adj.* **1.** Of or characteristic of a brute. **2.** Crude in feeling or manner. **3.** Sensual; carnal. —**brut·ish·ly** *adv.* —**brut·ish·ness** *n.*

Bru·tus (br○○t′əs), **Marcus Junius** (*c.* 85–42 B.C.). Roman republican statesman and soldier. He joined Cassius in the successful plot to assassinate Caesar (44) and began to rally forces for the coming war against Mark Antony and Octavian. In Macedonia in 42 the opposing armies met; Brutus committed suicide after his defeat at the Battle of Philippi on October 23.

Bruxelles. See **Brussels.**

Bry·an (brī′ən), **William Jennings** (1860–1925). U.S. lawyer and Democratic politician. He was secretary of state in Woodrow Wilson's administration (1913–15). Many of the reforms of which he was a principal advocate—income tax, women's suffrage, prohibition—were later adopted.

Bry·ant (brī′ənt), **William Cullen** (1794–1878). U.S. poet and newspaper editor. After establishing himself as a fine nature poet in such works as "Thanatopsis," "Rizpah," and "Autumn Woods," he became the editor of the New York *Evening Post,* a position he held

Brunelleschi

THE FOUNDER OF RENAISSANCE ARCHITECTURE
Adapting classical architecture to produce a new style

The Renaissance style of architecture began in Florence, inspired by Filippo Brunelleschi (1377–1446), who lived at a time when Italians regarded the period of the Roman Empire as Italy's golden age. They believed that reviving their glorious past would bring about a new golden era. Brunelleschi did not copy the architecture of classical Rome, but adapted it to Gothic building techniques and produced a new style that influenced western architecture until the 20th century.

Brunelleschi worked as a sculptor in gold before turning to architecture and engineering. When the Florentines wished to complete their cathedral with a large dome, it was Brunelleschi who solved the problem of how to build it. Begun in 1420, the dome is second in size only to the Pantheon in Rome. It is unbuttressed, but supported by a chain of timber and iron at its base, and the drum it rests on is stabilized by

three semidomes below. The dome itself is strengthened by Gothic-arch ribs, and with them Brunelleschi combined two techniques of classical Rome—brickwork laced firmly together in a herringbone pattern and upper courses of tufa for lightness.

His other buildings—all in Florence—include the Foundling Hospital, which he began about 1419. The arcade was designed with mathematical precision as a row of square bays topped by a row of arches half the area of the squares.

Brunelleschi was an outstanding mathematician and geometrician who was as much interested in the construction of a building as in its aesthetic qualities. He worked out the mathematical rules governing perspective with a single vanishing point. These were eagerly adopted by Renaissance painters, who could now give a more realistic three-dimensional look to their work.

PAZZI CHAPEL *Built in the cloisters of Santa Croce, in the style of a Roman temple, the chapel (left and above) shows Brunelleschi's mathematical planning. Its square, domed nave is flanked by transepts half as wide as the nave. The choir and the porch at either end are a quarter the area of the nave; each is domed inside. The chapel was begun in about 1429 but was completed with a makeshift roof after Brunelleschi died.*

bryony *The white brýony and black bryony, both European plants, are entirely unrelated but are similar in appearance, and both bear poisonous red berries and yellow flowers. The white bryony (above) has paler flowers. The two types get their names from the color of their roots.*

for 49 years while continuing to write poetry.

Bryn·hild (brĭn′hĭld′). *Norse Mythology.* A Valkyrie in the *Volsunga Saga* who is revived from an enchanted sleep by Sigurd.

bryo– *prefix.* Indicates moss; for example, **bryophyte.** [New Latin, from Greek *bruon,* moss, akin to Greek *bruein,* to swell. See **embryo.**]

bry·ol·o·gy (brī-ŏl′ə-jē) *n.* The study of mosses and liverworts. [BRYO- + -LOGY.] —**bry·o·log·i·cal** *adj.*

bry·o·ny (brī′ə-nē) *n., pl.* **-nies.** Either of two European plants, the **black bryony** or the **white bryony** (*both of which see*). [Latin *bryōnia,* from Greek *bruōnia,* akin to Greek *bruein,* to swell. See **embryo.**]

bry·o·phyte (brī′ə-fīt′) *n.* Any plant of the major botanical division Bryophyta, which includes the mosses and liverworts. Bryophytes have stems and leaves but lack true roots and vascular tissue. [New Latin *Bryophyta* : BRYO- + -PHYTE.] —**bry·o·phyt·ic** *adj.*

bry·o·zo·an (brī′-ə-zō′ən) *n.* Any of various small aquatic animals of the phylum Bryozoa that reproduce by budding and form moss-like or branching colonies. Also called "polyzoan." [New Latin *Bryozoa,* plural of *bryozoon* : BRYO- + -ZOON.] —**bry·o·zo·an** *adj.*

Bryth·on (brĭth′ən, -ŏn′) *n.* **1.** An ancient Celtic Briton of Cornwall, Wales, or Cumbria. **2.** One who speaks a Brythonic language.

Bry·thon·ic (brĭ-thŏn′ĭk) *adj.* Of, pertaining to, or characteristic of the Brythons or their language.
~*n.* The branch of the Celtic languages that includes Welsh, Breton, and Cornish.

B.S. 1. Bachelor of Science. **2.** balance sheet. **3.** bill of sale.

B.S.A. 1. Bachelor of Science in Agriculture. **2.** Boy Scouts of America.

B.S.Ed. Bachelor of Science in Education.

bsh. bushel.

bsk. basket.

Bt. baronet.

B.Th. Bachelor of Theology.

Btu British thermal unit.

bu bushel.

bu. 1. bureau. **2.** bushel.

bub (bŭb) *n. Informal.* Fellow. Used as a term of affectionate address. [From *bubby,* possibly a baby-talk variant of BROTHER.]

bub·ble (bŭb′əl) *n.* **1.** A thin transparent film of liquid, generally spherical, enclosing an accumulation of gas: *a soap bubble.* **2.** A small globule of gas trapped in a liquid or solid, as in a carbonated drink or in hardened glass. **3.** A sound made by or as if by the forming and bursting of bubbles. **4.** Anything insubstantial, groundless, or ephemeral, such as a scheme that comes to nothing. **5.** A glass or plastic dome, usually transparent.
~*v.* **bubbled, -bling, -bles.** —*intr.* **1.** To form or give off bubbles, as a boiling liquid does. **2.** To move or flow with a gurgling sound. **3.** To display irrepressible activity or animation. —*tr.* To cause to form bubbles. [Middle English *bobelen* (imitative).]

bubble and squeak *n. Chiefly British.* Leftover cabbage and mashed potatoes fried together, sometimes with meat added. [From the sounds it makes in cooking.]

bubble bath *n.* **1.** A perfumed liquid preparation added to bath water in order to make it foam. **2.** A bath to which such a preparation has been made.

bubble cap *n.* A perforated or slotted cap forming part of the plates of a distillation column that promotes the mixing of the condensate and the vapor.

bubble chamber *n. Physics.* An apparatus for detecting the paths of charged particles, or inferring the paths of electrically neutral particles, by examination of trails of bubbles that form on ions produced in a superheated liquid. Compare **cloud chamber.**

bubble gum *n.* Chewing gum that can be blown into bubbles.

bubble memory *n.* A computer memory in which information is stored in the form of binary digits represented by the presence or absence of magnetic bubbles.

bub·bler (bŭb′lər) *n.* A drinking fountain in which the water flows through a small vertical nozzle.

bub·bly (bŭb′lē) *adj.* **-blier, -bliest. 1.** Containing bubbles; effervescent. **2.** Lively; vivacious.
~*n. Informal.* Champagne.

Bu·ber (bōō′bər), **Martin** (1878–1965). Austrian-born philosopher and theologian. Much of his writing was devoted to interpreting the mysticism of the Chassidim, but he was also greatly influenced by the Christian existentialism of Kierkegaard. His highly personal interpretation of the direct dialogue between God and man, expressed in *I and Thou* (1923), was much drawn upon by contemporary Christian writers.

bu·bo (bōō′bō, byōō′-) *n., pl.* **-boes.** An inflamed swelling of a lymphatic gland, especially in the area of the armpit or groin. [Middle English, from Medieval Latin *bubo,* from Greek *boubōn,* groin, swollen gland.] —**bu·bon·ic** (bōō-bŏn′ĭk, byōō-) *adj.*

bubonic plague *n.* A contagious, often fatal epidemic disease caused by the bacterium *Pasteurella pestis,* transmitted by fleas from infected rats and characterized by chills, fever, vomiting, diarrhea, and buboes.

bu·bon·o·cele (bōō-bŏn′ə-sēl′, byōō-) *n.* An incomplete hernia of the groin; a partial inguinal hernia. [Greek *boubōn,* groin + -CELE.]

buc·cal (bŭk′əl) *adj.* Of or pertaining to the cheeks or mouth. [Latin *bucca,* cheek.]

buc·ca·neer (bŭk′ə-nîr′) *n.* A pirate, especially one of the freebooters who preyed upon Spanish shipping in the West Indies during the 17th century. [French *boucanier,* pirate, "one who cures meat on a barbecue frame" (as done by 17th-century French pirates), from *boucaner,* to cure meat, from *boucan,* barbecue frame, from Tupi *mukem.*]

buc·ca·neer·ing (bŭk′ə-nîr′ĭng) *adj.* Showing boldness and enterprise, often to the point of recklessness or unscrupulousness.

buc·ci·na·tor (bŭk′ə-nā′tər) *n.* A muscle of the cheek, important in chewing. [Latin, from *buccinare,* to blow a trumpet, from *buccina,* trumpet.]

Bu·ceph·a·lus (byōō-sĕf′ə-ləs). The war horse of Alexander the Great. [Latin *Būcephalus,* from Greek *Boukephalos,* "ox-headed" : *bous,* ox + -CEPHALOUS.]

Buch·an (bŭk′ən), **Sir John, 1st Baron Tweedsmuir** (1875–1940). British writer and politician. He was member of Parliament for the Scottish universities (1927–35), then was appointed governor general of Canada and raised to the peerage. He wrote a number of historical works, but his fame rests chiefly on his novels, especially *The Thirty-Nine Steps* (1915).

Bu·chan·an (byōō-kăn′ən, bə-), **James** (1791–1868). 15th president of the United States (1857–61). When he took office the tensions between the North and South were already rising. Although personally opposed to slavery, he sought to defend it under the Constitution. He attempted to quell the conflict between the states, but was unable to stop the secession of South Carolina on December 20, 1860.

Bu·cha·rest (bōō′kə-rĕst′, byōō′-). Romanian **Bu·cu·reş·ti** (bōō′-kōō-rĕsht′, -rĕsh′tē). Capital and largest city of Romania, in the southeastern region of Walachia, on the Dîmboviţa River. Founded in the 14th century the town was a fortress and a trading center on the trade route to Constantinople. It became the capital of Walachia in 1698 and, after the union of Walachia and Moldavia, the capital of Romania in 1861.

Bu·chen·wald (bōō′kən-wôld′). A village in southwestern East Germany, in the Buchenwald Forest near Weimar. It was the site of a

Nazi concentration camp in World War II.

Buch·man (bo͝ok′mən, bŭk′-), **Frank Nathan Daniel** (1878–1961). U.S. evangelist, founder of the Moral Rearmament movement. A Lutheran minister, he preached "world-changing through life-changing" to Oxford undergraduates (1921). The movement emphasized the importance of purity, honesty, selflessness, and love, allied with reliance upon God.

Buch·man·ism (bo͝ok′mən-ĭz′əm, bŭk′-) *n.* The doctrine of **Moral Rearmament** *(see).* **—Buch·man·ite** *n.*

Buch·ner (bo͝oKH′nər), **Eduard** (1860–1917). German chemist, famous for his discovery (1896) that the alcoholic fermentation of sugars is caused not by the yeast cells themselves but by enzymes in the yeast. In 1903 he discovered zymase, the part of the enzyme system that produces fermentation. He was awarded the Nobel Prize for chemistry (1907).

Büch·ner (büKH′nər), **Georg** (1813–37). German playwright, one of the early founders of the school of social realism in the theater. He wrote only three plays, *Danton's Death* (1835), *Leonce and Lena* (1836), and the fragmentary *Woyzeck* (1836).

buck¹ (bŭk) *n., pl.* **bucks** or collectively **buck** (for senses 1, 2). **1.** The adult male of some animals, such as the deer or hare. Also used adjectivally: *a buck rabbit.* **2.** A male antelope. Often used in combination. **3.** *Informal.* **a.** A robust or high-spirited young man. **b.** A fop. [Middle English *bukke,* Old English *buc,* stag, and *bucca,* he-goat, from Old Norse.]

buck² *v.* **bucked, bucking, bucks.** *—intr.* **1.** To jump upward suddenly with a humped back. Used of a horse or mule. **2.** To be obstinately opposed. Often used with *at* or *against.* *—tr.* **1.** To throw (a rider or burden) by bucking. Often used with *off.* **2.** To oppose or resist stubbornly: *buck the system.* **—buck up.** *Informal.* To summon one's courage or spirits; pull oneself together.
~*n.* An act of bucking. [From BUCK (deer).] **—buck·er** *n.*

buck³ *n.* **1.** A sawhorse. **2.** A leather-covered frame used for gymnastic vaulting. [Short for SAWBUCK.]

buck⁴ *n. Slang.* A dollar. [Short for BUCKSKIN (a unit of trade with the American Indians).]

buck⁵ *n.* A counter or marker formerly placed before a poker player to mark him as the next dealer. **—pass the buck.** To shift responsibility or blame to someone else. [Short for earlier *buckhorn knife,* from its use for this purpose.]

Buck (bŭk), **Pearl Sydenstricker** (1892–1973). U.S. novelist, whose fiction deals mainly with life in China, where she lived until 1924. She wrote more than 85 books, including *The Good Earth* (1931), which won a Pulitzer Prize. She won the Nobel Prize for literature (1938).

buck and wing *n.* A fast solo tap dance with much springing of the legs and clicking of the heels.

buck·a·roo, (bŭk′ə-ro͞o′) *n., pl.* **-roos.** A cowboy. [Variant of Spanish *vaquero,* VAQUERO, from *vaca,* a cow, from Latin *vacca.*]

buck·bean (bŭk′bēn′) *n.* A plant, the **bogbean** *(see).* [Translation of Dutch *boksboon.*]

buck·board (bŭk′bôrd′, -bōrd′) *n.* A four-wheeled open carriage with the seat attached to a flexible board extending from the front to the rear axle. [From obsolete *buck,* body of a wagon, "trunk of a body," belly, Old English *būc,* from Germanic.]

buck·et (bŭk′ĭt) *n.* **1.** A cylindrical vessel with a semicircular handle and an open top used for holding or carrying liquids or solids; a pail. **2.** Any of various machine compartments that receive and convey material, such as the scoop of a steam shovel. **3.** A bucketful. **4. buckets.** *Informal.* Large quantities: *She's got buckets of money.* **5.** *Computer Science.* A region on a direct-access storage device from which data can be read. **—kick the bucket.** *Informal.* To die. [Referring to the death throes of a slaughtered animal, from obsolete *bucket,* beam (from which freshly killed animals were suspended).]
~*v.* **bucketed, -eting, -ets.** *—tr.* **1.** To hold, carry, or put in a bucket. **2.** To ride (a horse) long and hard. *—intr.* **1.** To move or proceed rapidly and jerkily. **2.** To make haste; hustle. [Middle English *buket, boket,* from Norman French *buket,* bucket, tub, perhaps from Old English *būc,* belly, pitcher.]

buck·et·ful (bŭk′ĭt-fo͝ol′) *n., pl.* **-fuls** or **bucketsful.** The amount that a bucket will hold.

bucket seat *n.* A seat with a rounded or molded back, as in sports cars and airplanes.

bucket shop *n.* **1.** A fraudulent brokerage operation that accepts orders to buy or sell shares or commodities but delays executing the orders on the gamble that prices will change adversely to the interests of the customer, so that it can pocket what the customer thinks he has lost. **2.** *Chiefly British.* An unlicensed travel agency that buys airline tickets in bulk and sells them to the public at a discount. [Originally a place where small amounts of commodity gambling transactions took place and where the customer could buy alcoholic drink in buckets.]

buck·eye (bŭk′ī′) *n.* **1.** Any of several North American trees of the genus *Aesculus,* having compound leaves and erect clusters of white or reddish flowers. See **horse chestnut. 2.** The glossy brown nut of any of these trees. [BUCK (male deer) + EYE, referring to the appearance of the nut.]

buck fever *n. Informal.* Nervous excitement felt by a novice hunter at the first sight of game.

buck·horn (bŭk′hôrn′) *n.* The material of a buck's horn used for making handles for knives or other implements.

buck·hound (bŭk′hound′) *n.* A hound used for hunting deer.

Buck·ing·ham (bŭk′ĭng-əm, -hăm′), **George Villiers, 1st Duke of** (1592–1628). English courtier, statesman, and favorite of James I. He was murdered by John Felton, a discharged officer nursing a grievance.

Buckingham, George Villiers, 2nd Duke of (1628–87). English courtier and statesman, son of the 1st duke. A staunch Royalist during the Civil War, he fled to Holland (1648) and became a leading adviser to the exiled Charles II. On the restoration of Charles II (1660) he rose to prominence as a leading member of the royal administration, known as the Cabal. Financial malpractice and open philandering led to his dismissal from office (1674).

Buckingham Palace. The official London residence of the British sovereign, situated at the western end of St James's Park between Birdcage Walk and the Mall.

Buck·ing·ham·shire (bŭk′ĭng-əm-shîr, -shər). Also **Buck·ing·ham** (bŭk′ĭng-əm) or **Bucks** (bŭks). County in central England, almost entirely agricultural. It has extensive parklands and a great number of country estates, of which the most famous is Cliveden. The county town is Aylesbury.

buck·ish (bŭk′ĭsh) *adj. Archaic.* Foppish; dandified. **—buck·ish·ly** *adv.* **—buck·ish·ness** *n.*

buck·le¹ (bŭk′əl) *n.* **1.** A clasp, especially a metal frame with one or more movable tongues for fastening the two ends of a strap or belt. **2.** An ornament that resembles such a clasp.
~*v.* **buckled, -ling, -les.** *—tr.* To fasten or secure with a buckle. *—intr.* To become fastened or attached with a buckle. **—buckle down.** To apply oneself with determination. [Middle English *bocle,* from Old French *boucle,* metal ring, buckle, from Latin *buccula,* cheek strap of a helmet, diminutive of *bucca,* cheek.]

buckle² *v.* **-led, -ling, -les.** *—intr.* **1.** To bend, warp, or crumple under pressure or heat. **2.** To give way; collapse: *struts buckling under the stress.* *—tr.* To cause to bend, warp, or crumple. **—buckle under.** To surrender to another's authority; yield.
~*n.* A bend, bulge, or other distortion. [Middle English *boclen,* from Old French *boucler,* "to fasten with a buckle," from *boucle,* BUCKLE.]

buck·ler (bŭk′lər) *n.* **1.** A small round shield either carried or worn on the arm. **2.** A means of protection; a defense.
~*tr.v.* **bucklered, -lering, -lers.** To shield with or as if with a buckler; protect. [Middle English *boc(e)ler,* from Old French *bocler, boucler,* from *boucle,* boss on a shield, BUCKLE.]

buckler fern *n.* A shield fern *(see).*

Buck·ley (bŭk′lē), **William Frank, Jr.** (1925–). U.S. editor and author. In 1955 he founded and became editor of the *National Review.* Many of his works, including *Up From Liberalism* (1959), and his strong debating style have established him as an intellectual force in American conservatism. He also writes mystery novels such as *Saving the Queen* (1976) and *Marco Polo, If You Can* (1983).

buck·ling (bŭk′lĭng) *n. British.* A smoked herring. [German *Bückling,* bloater.]

buck·o (bŭk′ō) *n., pl.* **-oes. 1.** *Slang.* A swaggering bully. **2.** *Chiefly Irish.* A young man; a lad. Often used as a term of address. [From BUCK (young man).]

buck·ram (bŭk′rəm) *n.* **1.** A coarse cotton fabric heavily sized with glue, used for stiffening garments and in bookbinding. **2.** *Obsolete.* Stiffness; formality.
~*adj.* Made of buckram or resembling it in stiffness.
~*tr.v.* **buckramed, -raming, -rams.** To stiffen with buckram. [Middle English *bokram,* a fine linen, from Old French *boquerant,* obscurely from BOKHARA, from where the fine linen was once imported.]

Bucks. See **Buckinghamshire.**

buck·saw (bŭk′sô′) *n.* A wood-cutting saw, usually set in an H-shaped frame. [From BUCK (sawhorse).]

buck·shee (bŭk′shē) *n. British Slang.* **1.** A windfall or gratuity. **2.** An extra ration.
~*adj.* Free of charge; gratis. [Variant of BAKSHEESH.]

buck·shot (bŭk′shŏt′) *n.* A large lead shot for shotgun shells. [Originally the distance at which a buck could be shot.]

buck·skin (bŭk′skĭn′) *n.* **1.** The skin of a male deer. **2.** A strong, grayish-yellow leather once made from deerskins but now usually made from sheepskins. **3. buckskins.** A pair of breeches or shoes made from this leather.
~*adj.* Made of buckskin.

buck·thorn (bŭk′thôrn′) *n.* Any of various shrubs or trees of the genera *Rhamnus, Frangula,* or *Hippophaë*; especially, *R. catharticus,* native to Eurasia, with small greenish flowers, black berries, and often thorny branches. See **sea buckthorn.**

buck·tooth (bŭk′to͞oth′) *n., pl.* **-teeth** (-tēth′). A prominent, projecting upper front tooth. [From BUCK (deer).] **—buck·toothed** *adj.*

buck·wheat (bŭk′hwēt′) *n.* **1.** Any plant of the genus *Fagopyrum*; especially, *F. esculentum,* native to Asia, having fragrant white or pink flowers and small triangular seeds. **2.** The edible seeds of this plant, often ground into flour. [Partial translation of Middle Dutch *boecweite,* "beech wheat" (because its seeds resemble beech nuts) : *boek,* beech + *weite,* wheat.]

bu·col·ic (byo͞o-kŏl′ĭk) *adj.* **1.** Of or characteristic of shepherds and flocks; pastoral. **2.** Of or characteristic of the countryside or its people; rustic. —See Synonyms at **rural.**
~*n.* **bucolics.** A collection of pastoral poems. [Latin *būcolicus,* from Greek *boukolikos,* from *boukolos,* cowherd : *bous,* cow + *-kolos,* herd.] **—bu·col·i·cal·ly** *adv.*

Bucureşti. See **Bucharest.**

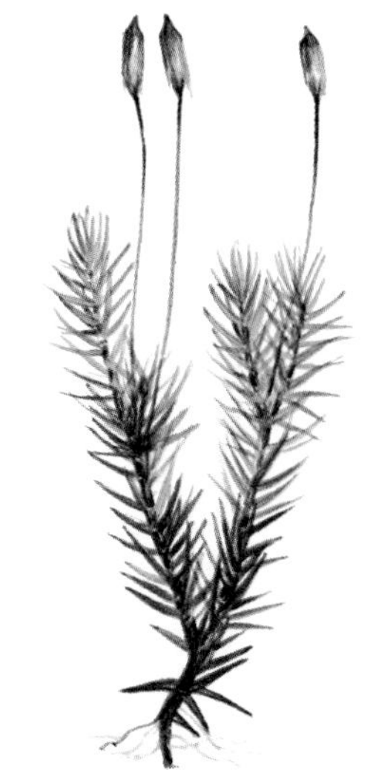

bryophyte *There are about 24,000 species of primitive green plants in the phylum* Bryophyta, *including mosses. This is* Polytrichum commune, *once used for stuffing mattresses and making brooms.*

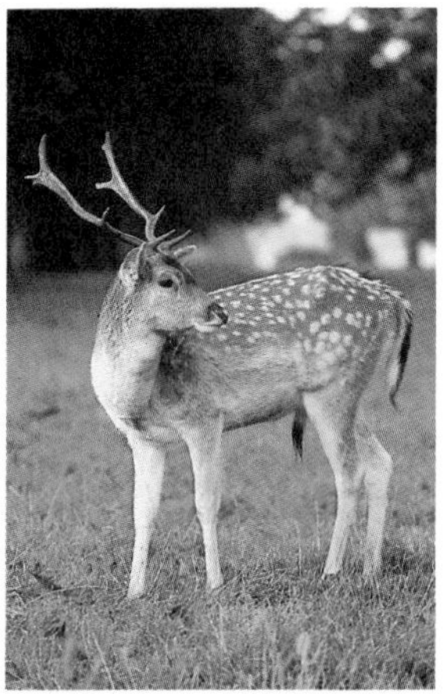

buck *Male deer are generally called bucks, although the male red deer is called a stag. This is a fallow buck in its summer coat.*

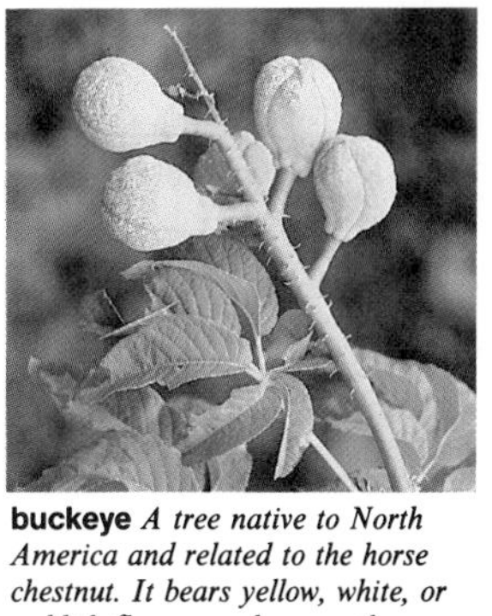

buckeye *A tree native to North America and related to the horse chestnut. It bears yellow, white, or reddish flowers and a smooth, rounded fruit.*

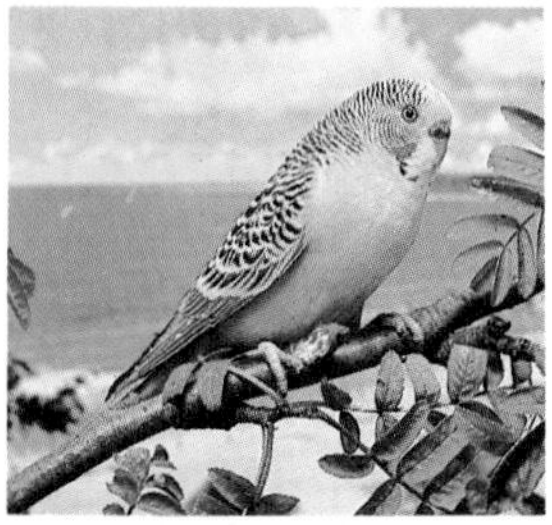

budgerigar *A small parakeet that lives in large flocks in the dry outback of Australia. Budgerigars are naturally green, but types with many other colors have been bred in captivity.*

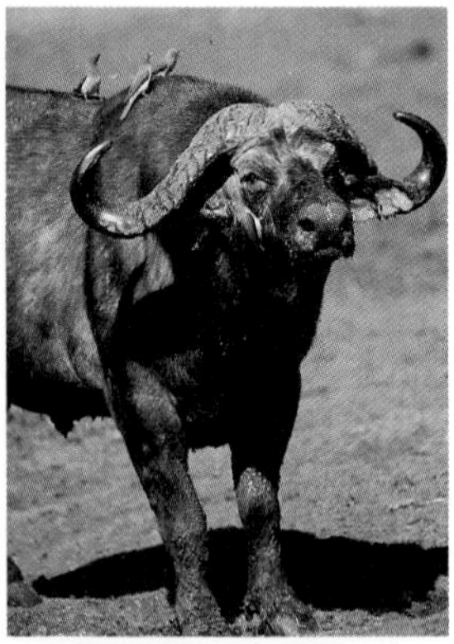

buffalo *The African buffalo, a grazing animal, weighs nearly a ton when fully grown. The birds on this buffalo's back are tick birds, also known as oxpeckers, which feed on the animal's insect parasites.*

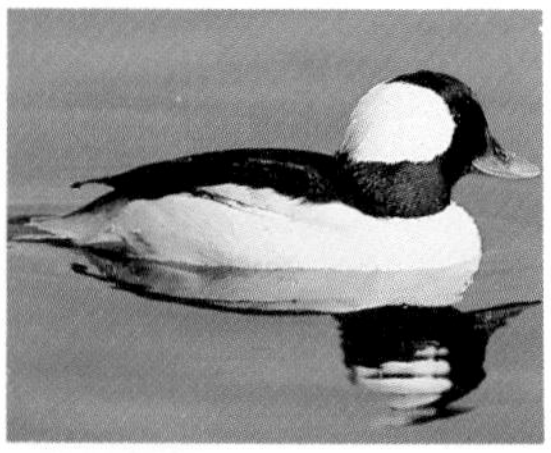

bufflehead *Old woodpecker holes are a favorite nesting place for the bufflehead. The duck, which is native to North America, lays up to a dozen eggs at a time.*

bud¹ (bŭd) *n.* **1.** *Botany.* **a.** An outgrowth on a stem or branch, often enclosed in protective scales, comprising a shortened stem and immature leaves or floral parts. **b.** The stage or condition of having buds. **c.** A partially opened flower. **2.** *Biology.* **a.** An asexually produced outgrowth, as on a polyp, that develops into a mature, complete organism. **b.** Any small, rounded organic part resembling a plant bud: *taste buds.* **—nip in the bud.** To stop (an idea, plan, or the like) in its initial stages.
~v. **budded, budding, buds.** *—intr.* **1.** To put forth or produce a bud or buds. **2.** To begin to develop or grow from or as if from a bud. *—tr.* **1.** To cause to put forth buds. **2.** To graft a bud onto (a plant). [Middle English *budde,* bud, perhaps from Low German *but,* perhaps from Old French *boter,* to push forth, from Germanic.] **—bud·der** *n.*

bud² *n.* Fellow; mister. Used as an informal term of address. [Short for BUDDY.]

Bu·da·pest (bo͞o′də-pĕst′). Capital and largest city of Hungary, on the Danube River in the northern part of the country. It was formed (1873) by the union of Buda and Óbuda on the right bank of the Danube with Pest on the left bank. Buda was the capital of Hungary from 1361 to 1541, when it was captured by the Ottoman Turks. In 1686 both Buda and Pest passed to the control of the Austro-Hungarian Empire. The city was the site of the counterrevolutionary uprising of 1956.

Bud·dha¹ (bo͞o′də, bo͝od′ə), born Gautama Siddhartha (*c.* 563–*c.* 483 B.C.). Indian mystic, the founder of Buddhism. He was the son of a prince of the Sakya clan in northern India and was brought up sheltered from the world, but at the age of about 29 he left the palace to wander about the world, deserting his wife and son. He studied yoga, then devoted himself to fasting and extreme asceticism. He is said to have gained perfect spiritual enlightenment at Buddh Gaya at the age of 35. Having thereby become the first Buddha, he lectured at Sarnath to five ascetic companions who became the first Buddhist disciples. He spent the rest of his life traveling through India preaching Buddhism to all listeners, regardless of caste. When he died, he was cremated and his ashes were distributed among eight Buddhist communities, who enshrined them in stupas.

Buddha² *n.* **1.** In Buddhism, one who has achieved a state of perfect spiritual enlightenment. **2.** A representation or likeness of Gautama Buddha. [Sanskrit, "awakened," past participle of *bōdhati,* he awakes, becomes aware.]

Buddh Ga·ya, Bodh Ga·ya (bo͝od′ gə-yä′). Village in Bihar state, east-central India. It was here, according to traditional belief, that Buddha gained enlightenment while sitting under a bo tree.

Bud·dhism (bo͞o′dĭz′əm, bo͝od′ĭz′əm) *n.* **1.** The doctrine, attributed to Gautama Buddha, that suffering is inseparable from existence but that inward extinction of the self and of worldly desire culminates in a state of spiritual enlightenment beyond both suffering and existence. **2.** The religion represented by the many groups, especially numerous in Asia, that profess varying forms of this doctrine and venerate Gautama Buddha. **—Bud·dhist** *n.* & *adj.* **—Bud·dhis·tic, Bud·dhis·ti·cal** *adj.*

bud·ding (bŭd′ĭng) *adj.* Beginning to develop; promising.

bud·dle (bŭd′l) *n.* An inclined trough on which ore is separated from waste by washing with running water.

bud·dlei·a (bŭd′lē-ə, bŭd-lē′ə) *n.* A shrub of the genus *Buddleia,* the **butterfly bush** *(see).* [After Adam *Buddle* (died 1715), British botanist.]

bud·dy (bŭd′ē) *n., pl.* **-dies.** *Informal.* A good friend. Often used as a term of address.
~adj. Informal. Of, pertaining to, or representing a close, warm relationship between two tough men: *a buddy movie.* [Probably from a baby-talk variant of BROTHER.]

bud·dy-bud·dy (bŭd′ē-bŭd′ē) *adj. Informal.* Showing great outward friendship.

buddy system *n.* An informal arrangement in which persons are paired, as for mutual safety or assistance.

budge¹ (bŭj) *v.* **budged, budging, budges.** *—intr.* **1.** To move or stir slightly. **2.** To alter a position or attitude. *—tr.* **1.** To cause or persuade to move slightly. **2.** To cause to alter a position or attitude. [Earlier *bouge,* from Old French *bouger, bougier,* from Vulgar Latin *bullicāre* (unattested), from Latin *bullīre,* to boil.]

budge² *n.* Fur, usually lambskin, treated to be worn with the wool outward.
~adj. Archaic. Extremely formal; solemn; pompous. [Middle English *bugee, bogey*†.]

Budge (bŭj), **(John) Donald** (1915–). U.S. tennis player, the first to win the Grand Slam (Wimbledon, French, U.S., and Australian titles) in one year (1938). He won all three titles (men's singles, men's doubles, and mixed doubles) at both Wimbledon and Forest Hills (1937, 1938).

budg·er·i·gar (bŭj′ə-rē-gär′) *n.* A parakeet, *Melopsittacus undulatus,* native to Australia, having green plumage in the wild. It is a popular cage bird and breeders have raised many different-colored varieties. Also *informal* "budgie." [Native Australian name : *budgeri,* good + *gar,* cockatoo.]

budg·et (bŭj′ĭt) *n.* **1.** An itemized summary of probable expenditures and income for a given period, usually embodying a systematic plan for meeting expenses. **2.** The total sum of money allocated for a particular purpose or time period.
~v. **budgeted, -eting, -ets.** *—tr.* **1.** To plan in advance the expenditure of (money or time, for example). **2.** To enter or plan for in a budget. [Middle English *bouget,* wallet, from Old French *bougette,* diminutive of *bouge,* leather bag, from Latin *bulga,* from Gaulish.] **—budg·et·ar·y** *adj.*

budg·ie (bŭj′ē) *n. Informal.* A budgerigar.

Bue·nos Ai·res (bwā′nəs âr′ēz, ĭr′ēz, bō′nəs). The capital, chief port, and largest city of Argentina, at the mouth of the Río de la Plata. Situated at the edge of the pampas, an intensely cultivated agricultural region, and connected by rivers to Brazil, Uruguay, and Paraguay, the city is one of the world's busiest ports. It is also one of the most heavily industrialized cities in South America. It was founded in 1536 by Spanish colonists and has been the capital since 1862.

buff¹ (bŭf) *n.* **1.** A soft, thick, undyed leather made chiefly from the skins of buffalo, elk, or oxen. **2.** The color of this leather; pale creamy yellow to light yellowish brown. **3.** *Informal.* The bare skin. Used chiefly in the phrase *in the buff.* **4.** A polishing implement covered with a soft material, such as velvet or leather.
~adj. **1.** Made of buff. **2.** Of the color of buff.
~tr.v. **buffed, buffing, buffs. 1.** To polish or shine with a buff. **2.** To give (leather, for example) the velvety surface of buff, as with sandpaper. [Originally "buffalo," from Old French *buffle,* from Vulgar Latin *būfalus* (unattested), BUFFALO.]

buff² *tr.v.* **buffed, buffing, buffs.** To deaden the shock of.
~n. A buffet; a blow. [As verb, from obsolete *buff,* "to sound as a soft body when struck" (perhaps imitative); as noun, from Middle English *buffe,* from Old French, BUFFET.]

buff³ *n. Informal.* One who is enthusiastic and knowledgeable about a specified subject: *an opera buff.* [Originally a New York volunteer fireman, hence an enthusiast, from the firemen's buff uniforms.]

buf·fa·lo (bŭf′ə-lō′) *n., pl.* **-loes** or **-los** or collectively **buffalo. 1.** Any of several oxlike Old World mammals of the family Bovidae, having massive curved horns and humped backs, such as *Syncerus caffer* of Africa or the **water buffalo** *(see).* **2.** A related North American animal, the **bison** *(see).* [Portuguese *bufalo,* from Vulgar Latin *būfalus* (unattested), from Latin *būbalus,* from Greek *boubalos,* African antelope, buffalo, probably from *bous,* cow, ox.]

Buf·fa·lo (bŭf′ə-lō′). The second-largest city of New York State, in the west on Lake Erie and the Buffalo and Niagara rivers. Buffalo is an important Great Lakes port, especially for grain distribution, and has flour and steel mills, automobile factories, and other diversified manufactures.

buffalo berry *n.* **1.** Either of two North American shrubs, *Shepherdia argentea* of *S. canadensis,* having small yellowish flowers and red or yellowish berries. **2.** The berry of a buffalo berry.

Buffalo Bill. See William Frederick **Cody.**

buffalo bug *n.* Also **buffalo beetle.** The **carpet beetle** *(see).*

buffalo fish *n.* Any of several North American freshwater fishes of the genus *Ictiobus,* having a humped back.

buffalo gnat *n.* The **black fly** *(see).*

buffalo grass *n.* A short grass, *Buchloë dactyloides,* of the plains east of the Rocky Mountains.

buffalo robe *n.* The dressed skin of the North American bison, used as a lap robe, cape, or blanket.

buff·er¹ (bŭf′ər) *n.* An implement used to shine or polish, such as a soft cloth or a buffing wheel.

buffer² *n.* **1.** Something that lessens or absorbs the shock of an impact; especially, either of a pair of spring-loaded or hydraulically mounted steel pads attached to both ends of railway rolling stock and at the end of a railway line to reduce the shock of collision. **2.** One that protects by intercepting or moderating adverse pressures or influences. **3.** Something interposed between two rival powers, lessening the danger of conflict. Often used adjectivally: *a buffer zone.* **4.** *Chemistry.* An ionic solution capable of maintaining the relative concentrations of hydrogen and hydroxyl ions in a solution by neutralizing, within limits, added acids or bases. Also called "buffer solution." **5.** *Computer Science.* A memory device used for the temporary storage of data. **6.** *Electronics.* A circuit used to join two other circuits so as to minimize the reactance between them.
~tr.v. **buffered, -ering, -ers.** *Chemistry.* To treat (a solution) with a buffer.

buf·fet¹ (bə-fā′, bo͞o-) *n.* **1.** A large sideboard with drawers and cupboards. **2. a.** A counter or table from which meals or refreshments are served. **b.** A restaurant having such a counter. **3.** A meal at which guests serve themselves from various dishes displayed on a table or sideboard. Also used adjectivally: *a buffet lunch.* [French *buffet*†.]

buf·fet² (bŭf′ĭt) *n.* **1.** A blow or cuff with the hand. **2.** A blast of wind or the impact of a wave. **3.** A blow; a setback.
~v. **buffeted, -feting, -fets.** *—tr.* **1.** To strike against forcefully or repeatedly; batter. **2.** To contend with; struggle against. *—intr.* **1.** To struggle; contend. **2.** To force one's way by struggling. [Middle English, from Old French, diminutive of *buffe,* blow (imitative).] **—buf·fet·er** *n.*

Buf·fet (bo͞o-fā′), **Bernard** (1928–). French painter. His many works, including *The Horrors of War* and *The Angel of Destruction,* express disillusionment and misery.

buff·ing wheel *n.* A wheel covered with a soft material, such as velvet or leather, for shining and polishing metal.

buf·fle·head (bŭf′əl-hĕd′) *n.* A small North American duck, *Bucephala albeola,* having black and white plumage and a densely feathered, rounded head. Also called "butterball." [From obsolete *buffle,* a buffalo (from the duck's large head), from Old French. See **buff** (leather).]

Buddhism

THE EIGHTFOLD PATH TO ENLIGHTENMENT
Compassion and meditation in the quest for Nirvana

Buddhists try to emulate the life of Siddhartha Gautama—the Buddha—who founded the religion and philosophical system named after him in northeast India in the 6th century B.C.

According to tradition, Gautama was brought up in luxury and protected from all unpleasant sights during his early life. But one day he encountered in succession first an old man, then a sick man, and, finally, a corpse. These meetings made him aware of the sufferings of mankind and the impermanence of life, and he determined to leave his comforts and set out on a quest for spiritual truth.

Buddhism teaches Four Noble Truths: that the world is full of suffering; that suffering is caused by human desires; that suffering stops when desires are renounced; and that the Eightfold Path is the way to achieve this. The Eightfold Path consists of eight principles of behavior that make up the road to enlightenment: right understanding, right resolve, right speech, right action, right livelihood, right effort, right mindfulness, and right meditation.

Nirvana, the Buddhist's ultimate goal, is the ultimate state of blessedness, to which enlightenment gives entry. It is viewed in different ways by the two main Buddhist schools. The Hinayana school—the older, more conservative form of Buddhism—regards Nirvana as the means by which the individual is liberated from earthly existence. The Mahayana school, on the other hand, asserts that the disciple who gains enlightenment remains in the world, as a *Bodhisattva*, to help others along the path. The followers of Hinayana are chiefly found in Sri Lanka, Burma, Thailand, Laos, and Kampuchea; the Mahayana has most support in Tibet, Mongolia, China, Korea, and Japan. Today there are some 500 million Buddhists in the Far East, and a growing number in the West.

BUDDHIST SHRINE *The Swayambhunath Temple, near Katmandu in Nepal, is a typical example of Buddhist architecture.*

WHEEL OF BECOMING *The Bhavachakra, or Wheel of Becoming, is an image of the earthly existence from which the Buddhist seeks liberation; it is held by the demon of impermanence. The six segments represent the six possible states into which beings may be reborn: (clockwise from bottom) titans, hungry ghosts, humans, gods, demons, and animals.*

---

buf·fo (boo'fō) *n., pl.* **-fi** (-fē). A male singer of comic opera roles. ~*adj.* Characteristic of a buffo; comic. [Italian, "puff of wind," from *buffare,* to puff. See **buffoon.**]

Buf·fon (boo-fôn'), **Georges-Louis Leclerc, Comte de** (1707–88). French biologist. In his 44-volume *Natural History* (1749) and *Epochs of Nature* (1778), he contributed greatly to the development of modern science by stressing a materialist, geological explanation of the world's origin and history. Buffon also wrote a *Discourse on Style* (1753), an analysis of literary expression that features the famous phrase, "the style is the man."

buf·foon (bə-foon') *n.* **1.** A clown; a jester: *a court buffoon.* **2.** A witless person given to making coarse jokes. [French *bouffon,* from Italian *buffone,* from *buffare,* to puff (imitative).] —**buf·foon·er·y** *n.*

bug (bŭg) *n.* **1.** Any of various wingless or four-winged insects of the order Hemiptera, and especially the suborder Heteroptera, having mouthparts adapted for piercing and sucking. **2.** Broadly, any insect or similar organism. **3.** *Informal.* **a.** A disease-producing microorganism. **b.** A disease so caused, often spreading as a minor epidemic. **4.** A mechanical, electrical, or other systemic defect or difficulty, as in a computer system. **5.** *Slang.* An enthusiast or devotee; a buff; *a hi-fi bug.* **6.** *Informal.* A small hidden microphone or other device used for eavesdropping or surveillance. ~*tr. v.* **bugged, bugging, bugs.** *Informal.* **1. a.** To annoy; pester. **b.** To worry; prey on: *That memory bugged me over the years.* **2.** To fit (a room, for example) with concealed electronic surveillance equipment. [17th century : origin obscure.]

Bug¹ (boog). Also **Western Bug.** A river rising in the southwestern Ukraine, west European U.S.S.R. It flows northward 770 kilometers (480 miles) through Poland to the Vistula River near Warsaw.

Bug² Also **Southern Bug.** A river rising in the southwestern Ukraine, west European U.S.S.R. It flows 790 kilometers (490 miles) generally southeast to the Black Sea. It is navigable for *c.* 160 kilometers (100 miles) above its mouth.

bug·a·boo (bŭg'ə-boo') *n., pl.* **-boos.** **1.** A bugbear. **2.** A steady source of concern. [Perhaps from Celtic; akin to Cornish *buccaboo,* the devil. Compare **bugbear** and **bogle.**]

Bu·gan·da (boo-găn'də, byoo-). A former kingdom in East Africa, occupying the northern shores of Lake Victoria in present-day Uganda. It was ruled by the Ganda tribe until it became a British protectorate (1900). It was merged with Uganda when Uganda became an independent state (1962).

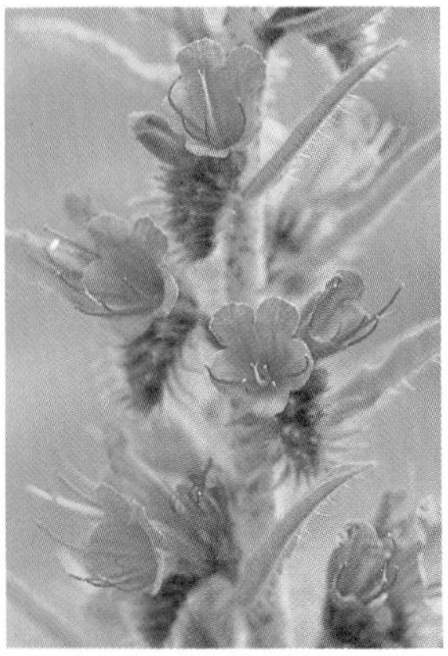

bugloss *The name of this wildflower is derived from two Greek words meaning "ox-tongued"—a reference to the shape and texture of its leaves. It grows on sandy soils throughout Europe and in the eastern United States.*

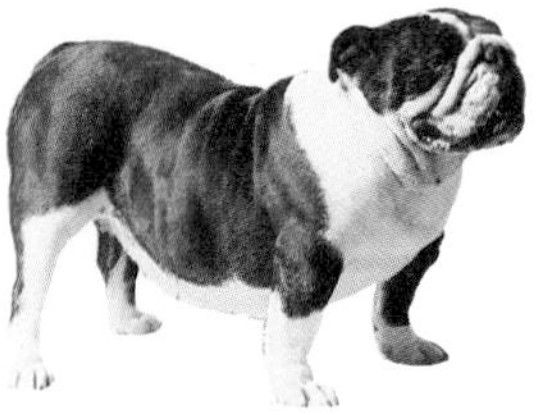

bulldog *This English breed of mastiff—noted for its tenacity—was once used to bait bulls.*

PRONUNCIATION KEY

ă, pat; ā, pay; âr, care;
ä, father, are; b, bib;
ch, church; d, deed; ĕ, pet;
ē, be; f, fife; g, gag; h, hat;
hw, which; ĭ, pit; ī, pie;
îr, pier; j, judge; k, kick;
l, lid, needle; m, mum;
n, no, sudden; ng, thing;
ŏ, pot; ō, toe; ô, paw, for;
oi, noise; ou, out; o͝o, book;
o͞o, boot; p, pop; r, roar;
s, sauce; sh, ship, dish;
t, tight; th, thin, path;
th, this, bathe; ŭ, cut; ûr, fur;
v, valve; w, with; y, yes;
z, zebra, size; zh, vision;
ə, about, item, edible,
gallop, circus, peaceful

IN FOREIGN WORDS:

à, *Fr.* ami; œ, *Fr.* feu, *Ger.* schön; ü, *Fr.* tu, *Ger.* über; KH, *Ger.* ich, *Scot.* loch; N, *Fr.* bon; y', *Fr.* Compiègne

STRESS MARKS:

Primary stress: ′
in·cite′ (ĭn-sīt′)
Secondary stress: ′
in′sight′ (ĭn′sīt′)

bug·bane (bŭg′bān′) *n.* Any of several plants of the genus *Cimicifuga;* especially, *C. americana* of eastern North America, having clusters of small white flowers supposed to repel insects.

bug·bear (bŭg′bâr′) *n.* **1.** An object of obsessive, but often groundless, dread. **2.** *Archaic.* A goblin reputed to eat naughty children. [Obsolete *bug,* from Middle English *bugge;* akin to Welsh *bwg(a),* ghost, and Cornish *buccaboo,* the devil.]

bug-eyed (bŭg′īd′) *adj. Slang.* Agog, as with amazement.

bug·ger[1] (bŭg′ər) *n.* **1.** *Slang.* A contemptible or disreputable person. **2.** A fellow; a chap.

bugger[2] *n. Informal.* A person who plants an electronic eavesdropping or surveillance device. [BUG + -ER[1].]

bug·gy[1] (bŭg′ē) *n., pl.* **-gies. 1.** A small, light, horse-drawn carriage. **2.** A baby carriage. [18th century : origin obscure.]

buggy[2] *adj.* **-gier, -giest. 1.** Infested with bugs. **2.** *Slang.* Crazy. **—bug·gi·ness** *n.*

bug·house (bŭg′hous′) *n. Slang.* An insane asylum. [From BUGGY (crazy).]

bu·gle[1] (byo͞o′gəl) *n.* **1.** A brass wind instrument somewhat shorter than a trumpet, and without keys or valves. **2.** A hunting horn. ~*intr. v.* **bugled, -gling, -gles.** To play a bugle. [Middle English *bugle,* buffalo, horn, bugle, from Old French, from Latin *būculus,* diminutive of *bōs,* ox.] **—bu·gler** *n.*

bugle[2] *n.* A tubular glass or plastic bead used to trim clothing. Also called "bugle bead." [16th century : origin obscure.]

bugle[3] *n.* Any of several plants of the genus *Ajuga,* especially *A. reptans,* native to Eurasia, having spikes or dense clusters of small blue or white flowers. Also called "bugleweed." [Middle English, from Old French, from Late Latin *bugula,* perhaps from Latin *bugillō,* from Gaulish.]

bu·gle·weed (byo͞o′gəl-wēd′) *n.* **1.** A plant of the genus *Lycopus,* especially *L. virginicus,* having small, whitish flowers and an aromatic odor. **2.** A plant, the **bugle** *(see).* [Perhaps from its tubular flowers.]

bu·gloss (byo͞o′glŏs′, -glôs′) *n.* Any of several plants of the genera *Lycopsis, Echium,* and *Anchusa,* especially *L. arvensis,* having hairy stems and leaves and clusters of blue flowers. See **alkanet, viper's bugloss.** [Middle English *buglosse,* from Old French, from Latin *būglōssa,* from Greek *bouglōssos,* "ox-tongued" (from the broad, rough leaves) : *bous,* ox + *glōssa,* tongue.]

buhl, boule, boulle (bo͞ol) *n.* **1.** A style of furniture decoration in which elaborate designs are inlaid with tortoiseshell, ivory, and metals of various colors. **2.** A piece of furniture so decorated. [After André C. *Boulle* (1642–1732), French cabinetmaker.]

buhr·stone, burr·stone (bûr′stōn′) *n.* A tough limestone impregnated with silica, from which millstones were formerly made. [Variant of *bur(r)stone* : perhaps BUR + STONE.]

build (bĭld) *v.* **built** (bĭlt) or *archaic* **builded, building, builds.** —*tr.* **1.** To form by combining materials or parts; erect; construct. **2.** To develop and give form to according to a definite plan or process; fashion; mold; create. **3.** To establish and strengthen; create and add to: *build a savings account.* **4.** To establish a basis for; found or ground: *build an argument on fact.* **5.** *Card Games.* To accumulate combinations or sequences of (cards) according to suit or number. —*intr.* **1.** To construct something or have something constructed: *"Each of the three architects built in a different style"* (Dwight Macdonald). **2.** To be a builder. **3.** To develop an idea, argument, theory, or the like. Used with *on* or *upon.* **4.** *Card Games.* To accumulate combinations or sequences of cards. **5.** To progress toward a maximum, as of intensity, excitement, or the like. **—build in.** To construct as an integral or permanent part of.
~*n.* The physical make-up of a person or thing: *an athletic build.* [Middle English *bilden,* Old English *byldan,* from *bold,* a dwelling.]

build·er (bĭl′dər) *n.* **1.** One that builds; especially, a person who contracts for and supervises the construction of a building. **2.** An abrasive or filler used in a soap or a detergent.

build·ing (bĭl′dĭng) *n.* **1.** *Abbr.* **bldg.** Something that is built; a structure; an edifice. **2.** The act, process, or occupation of constructing.

build up *tr.v.* **1.** To renew the strength or health of. **2.** To construct or develop in stages or by degrees; create and add to: *build up a business.* **3.** To magnify (a person or thing) by extravagant praise or publicity. **4.** To fill up (an area) with buildings.

build-up, build·up (bĭld′ŭp′) *n.* **1.** The act of amassing or increasing. **2.** *Informal.* Extravagant praise; widely favorable publicity, especially by a systematic campaign. **3.** The result of building up: *the build-up of tension; the build-up of traffic.*

built. Past tense and past participle of **build.**
~*adj.* Having a physique or physical make-up of the specified type: *well built; heavily built.*

built-in (bĭlt′ĭn′) *adj.* **1.** Constructed as part of a larger unit; not detachable: *a built-in cabinet.* **2.** Forming a permanent or essential element or quality: *a built-in escape clause.*

built-up (bĭlt′ŭp′) *adj.* **1.** Occupied by or covered with many buildings. **2.** Made by fastening several layers or sections one on top of the other: *a built-up roof.*

Bu·jum·bu·ra (bo͞o′jəm-bo͝or′ə). Capital and largest city of Burundi, eastern Africa, situated on Lake Tanganyika.

Bu·kha·ra (bo͞o-kär′ə, -här′ə). Also **Bo·kha·ra** (bō-). A city in Uzbek S.S.R., central Asian U.S.S.R., in the Zeravshan River valley. It is one of the oldest cultural and trading centers of Asia and was the capital of the khanate, or state, of Bukhara during its heyday from the 16th to the 19th century.

Bukhara rug *n.* Also **Bokhara rug.** A kind of rug, usually having a black and white pattern of large and small octagons on a red, brownish-red, or sometimes tan ground.

Bu·kha·rin (bo͞o-KHär′ĭn) **Nikolai Ivanovich** (1888–1938). Soviet politician, theoretician, and editor of *Pravda* (1915–29). In 1923 he became a full member of the Politburo and in the power struggle that followed Lenin's death (1924) supported Stalin. Later his advocacy of gradual agricultural collectivization and industrialization lost him major posts in the party (1929). He was executed for treason after the last of the Moscow "show trials" (1938).

Bu·la·wa·yo (bo͞o′lə-wä′yō, -wā′ō). Industrial city on the western border of Zimbabwe, on the Matsheumlope River. It is the second-largest city in Zimbabwe and was founded in 1893 when it was moved five kilometers (three miles) south of its old site, which was the seat of the last king of the Ndebele.

bulb (bŭlb) *n.* **1.** *Botany.* A modified underground stem, such as that of the onion or tulip, usually surrounded by scalelike modified leaves and containing stored food for the undeveloped shoots of the new plant enclosed within it. **2.** Loosely, an underground stem resembling this, such as a corm, rhizome, or tuber. **3.** Any plant that grows from a bulb. **4.** A rounded projection or part of something: *the bulb of a syringe.* **5.** An incandescent lamp or its glass housing. Also called "light bulb." **6.** *Anatomy.* Any of various rounded, enlarged, or bulb-shaped structures, especially the **medulla oblongata** *(see).* [Latin *bulbus,* bulb, onion, from Greek *bolbos*†, name of various bulbous plants.]

bul·bar (bŭl′bər, -bär′) *adj. Anatomy.* Of, pertaining to, or characteristic of a bulb, especially of the medulla oblongata: *bulbar poliomyelitis.*

bul·bil (bŭl′bĭl′) *n. Botany.* A small bulblike part growing above ground on a flower stalk or in a leaf axil. [French *bulbille,* diminutive of *bulbe,* BULB.]

bul·bous (bŭl′bəs) *adj.* **1.** Resembling a bulb in shape. **2.** *Botany.* Bearing bulbs or growing from a bulb.

bul·bul (bo͝ol′bo͝ol′) *n.* **1.** Any of various chiefly tropical Old World songbirds of the family Pycnonotidae, having grayish or brownish plumage. **2.** A songbird, thought to be a nightingale, often mentioned in Persian poetry. [Persian, from Arabic.]

Bulg. Bulgaria.

Bul·ga·nin (bo͝ol-gä′nĭn, -găn′ĭn), **Nikolai Alexandrovich** (1895–1975). Soviet politician. He rose to prominence during the Stalinist purges of the mid-1930s, later distinguishing himself as an administrator during World War II. After the war he was appointed a full member of the Politburo and deputy premier. In 1955 he replaced Malenkov as premier, but was dismissed by Khrushchev (1958) for his participation in the so-called anti-Party group.

Bul·gar·i·a (bŭl-gâr′ē-ə, bo͝ol-). *Abbr.* **Bulg.** Republic in the Balkan Peninsula of southeastern Europe, bordered on the west by Yugoslavia, on the north by Romania, on the east by the Black Sea, and on the south by Turkey and Greece. The center of the country is crossed from west to east by the Balkan Mts. Between these and the Danube, which forms most of the northern boundary, lies a broad, fertile plateau. Although the country has been considerably industrialized since 1945, agriculture remains the leading sector of the economy. Bulgaria is famous for its cultivation of damask roses, used to make attar of roses for perfumes. From the late 14th to the early 20th century, Bulgaria was ruled by Turkey. In 1946 it became a people's republic within the Soviet bloc. Area, 110,911 square kilometers (42,823 square miles). Population, 8,900,000. Capital, Sofia.

Bul·gar·i·an (bŭl-gâr′ē-ən, bo͝ol-) *adj.* Of, pertaining to, or characteristic of Bulgaria, its inhabitants, or their language.
~*n.* Also **Bul·gar** (bŭl′gər, bo͝ol′-) (for sense 1). **1.** A native or inhabitant of Bulgaria. **2.** The Slavonic language spoken by Bulgarians.

bulge (bŭlj) *n.* **1.** A protruding part; an outward curve or swelling. **2.** The rounded lower section of a ship's hull. **3.** *Slang.* An advantage.
~*v.* **bulged, bulging, bulges.** —*tr.* To cause to curve outward. —*intr.* **1.** To swell up or outward; grow larger or rounder. **2.** To be swollen because full: *a bulging wallet.* [Middle English, wallet, pouch, from Old French *bouge,* from Latin *bulga,* leather bag, probably from Gaulish.] **—bulg·i·ness** *n.* **—bulg·y** *adj.*

Bulge, Battle of the. The last major German counteroffensive of World War II, launched December 16, 1944, and repulsed by January 21, 1945. [So called because the line of combat formed a large bulge deep into Belgium.]

bul·gur, bul·ghur (bo͝ol′go͝or′, bŭl′gər) *n.* A cereal food prepared by boiling and drying coarsely ground wheat. [Turkish *burgul.*]

bu·lim·i·a (byo͞o-lĭm′ē-ə) *n.* Insatiable appetite. [New Latin, from Greek *boulimia* : *bous,* ox, cow + *limos,* hunger, famine.]

bulimia ner·vos·a (nûr-vō′sə) *n.* A psychological illness, often found in combination with **anorexia nervosa** *(see),* in which bouts of compulsive eating are followed by self-induced and ultimately involuntary vomiting. [New Latin, "nervous bulimia."]

bulk (bŭlk) *n.* **1.** Size, mass, or volume, especially when very large. **2. a.** A distinct mass or portion of matter, especially a large one. **b.** The body of a human being or animal, especially a large and corpulent body. **3.** The major portion or greater part of something: *"the great bulk of necessary work can never be anything but painful"* (Bertrand Russell). **4.** Thickness of paper or cardboard in relation to weight. **5.** *Abbr.* **blk.** A ship's hold or the cargo stowed there. **6.** Any substance that stimulates the action of the intestines; roughage. **—in bulk. 1.** Unpackaged; loose. **2.** In large numbers, amounts, or volume. **—v. bulked, bulking, bulks.** *—intr.* **1.** To appear to be, in terms of size, volume, or importance; loom: *"shopkeeping naturally bulks large among London occupations"* (G.D.H. Cole and Raymond Postgate). **2.** To grow or increase in size or importance. Usually used with *up.* **3.** To cohere or form a mass: *Certain paper pulps bulk well.* *—tr.* To gather together into a mass. [Middle English *bulke, bolke,* heap, mass, body, from Old English *bulki,* cargo.]

bulk buy *n.* A product bought in bulk. **—bulk-buy** *v.*

bulk density *n.* The mass of a substance divided by its volume when it is present in bulk. For example, the bulk density of coal is lower than its true density because of the air spaces between lumps.

bulk·head (bŭlk′hĕd′) *n.* **1.** Any of the upright partitions dividing a ship into compartments and serving to prevent the spread of leakage or fire. **2.** A wall or embankment constructed in a mine or tunnel to protect against earth slides, fire, water, or gas. **3.** A horizontal or sloping structure providing access to a cellar stairway or to an elevator shaft. [From BULK (ship's hold).]

bulk modulus *n.* A measure of the elasticity of a substance equal to the ratio of the stress applied to the resulting change in volume.

bulk·y (bŭl′kē) *adj.* **-i·er, -i·est. 1.** Extremely large; massive. **2.** Difficult to carry; unwieldy. **—bulk·i·ly** *adv.* **—bulk·i·ness** *n.*

bull¹ (bŏŏl) *n.* **1. a.** An adult male bovine mammal. **b.** The uncastrated adult male of domestic cattle. **2.** The male of certain other mammals, such as the elephant and whale. **3.** An exceptionally large, strong, and aggressive man. **4.** *Stock Market.* A person who buys stocks or shares in a market in anticipation of a rise in prices or who tries by speculative purchases to effect such a rise, in order to sell later at a profit. Compare **bear. 5. Bull.** The constellation and sign of the zodiac, **Taurus** (*see*). **6.** *Slang.* A policeman or detective. **7.** *Slang.* Empty, foolish, or boastful talk; nonsense. **—take the bull by the horns.** To deal with a problem directly and resolutely. **—v. bulled, bulling, bulls.** *—tr.* **1.** *Stock Market.* To engage in speculative buying so as to raise the price of (stocks) or prices in (a market). **2.** To push; force. *—intr.* **1.** *Stock Market.* To rise in price. **2.** To push ahead or through forcefully. *—adj.* **1.** Male; masculine. **2.** Resembling a bull; large and strong. **3.** *Stock Market.* Characterized by rising prices: *a bull market.* Compare **bear.** [Middle English *bule, bole,* from Old English *bula,* from Old Norse *boli.* Stock Market senses, 18th century : term introduced to contrast with BEAR as descriptions of the two different types of speculators.]

bull² *n.* **1.** An official document issued by the pope and sealed with a bulla. **2.** The bulla itself. [Middle English *bulle,* from Old French *bulle,* from Medieval Latin *bulla,* seal, BULLA.]

Bull, John. See John Bull.

bul·la (bŏŏl′ə) *n., pl.* **bullae** (bŏŏl′ē). **1.** A round seal affixed to a papal bull. **2.** *Pathology.* A large blister or vesicle. Compare **bleb.** [Both senses, Medieval Latin, from Latin, bubble, seal.]

bul·lace (bŏŏl′ĭs) *n.* A plum, the **damson** (*see*). [Middle English *bolas,* from Old French *buloce, beloce,* sloe, probably from Medieval Latin *bolluca‡.*]

bul·late (bŏŏl′āt′, bŭl′-) *adj.* Having a puckered or blistered appearance: *bullate leaves.* [New Latin *bulla,* bubble, from Latin.]

bull-bait·ing (bŏŏl′bā-tĭng) *n.* The setting of dogs upon bulls, once a popular sport in England.

bull·bat (bŏŏl′băt′) *n.* See **nighthawk** (sense 1). [From its roaring sound in flight.]

bull·dog (bŏŏl′dôg′, -dŏg′) *n.* **1.** A short-haired dog of a breed characterized by a large head, strong, square jaws with dewlaps, and a stocky body. **2.** A short-barreled revolver or pistol of a large caliber. **3.** *British.* A proctor's assistant at the universities of Oxford or Cambridge. *—adj.* Resembling or having the qualities of a bulldog; stubborn; tenacious. *—tr.v.* **bulldogged, -dogging, -dogs.** *Western U.S.* To throw (a steer) by seizing its horns and twisting its neck until it falls.

bulldog ant *n.* A large Australian ant of the genus *Myrmecia* measuring up to one inch long having powerful jaws and a painful sting. Also called "bull ant."

bull·doze (bŏŏl′dōz′) *tr.v.* **-dozed, -dozing, -dozes. 1.** To clear, dig up, or move with a bulldozer. **2.** *Slang.* To coerce by intimidation; bully. [Perhaps BULL + DOSE.]

bull·doz·er (bŏŏl′dō′zər) *n.* **1.** A tractor with a vertical metal scoop in front for moving earth and rocks, used especially to grade or clear land. **2.** An overbearing or bullying person.

bul·let (bŏŏl′ĭt) *n.* **1.** A spherical or pointed cylindrical metallic projectile that is fired from a pistol, rifle, or other relatively small firearm. **2.** Such a projectile in a metal casing; a cartridge. **3.** Any object of similar shape, action, or effect. **4.** *Printing.* A heavy dot (•) used to call attention to a particular passage. **—bite the bullet.** *Informal.* To endure a painful or difficult situation bravely and stoically. [French *boulette,* diminutive of *boule,* ball, from Old French, from Latin *bulla,* bubble, ball.]

bul·le·tin (bŏŏl′ə-tən, -tĭn) *n.* **1.** A brief, authoritative statement on a matter of public interest for immediate broadcast or publication. **2.** A brief, periodically broadcast summary of the news. **3.** A periodical published by an organization or society. *—tr.v.* **bulletined, -tining, -tins.** To inform by bulletin. [French, probably from Old French *bullette,* from *bulle,* BULL (document).]

bulletin board *n.* A board mounted on a wall, on which notices are posted.

bul·let·proof (bŏŏl′ĭt-prŏŏf′) *adj.* Impenetrable by bullets. *—tr.v.* **bulletproofed, -proofing, -proofs.** To make impenetrable by bullets.

bull fiddle *n.* A double bass (*see*).

bull·fight (bŏŏl′fīt′) *n.* A public spectacle, especially in Spain and Latin America, in which a fighting bull is engaged in a series of traditional maneuvers culminating usually with the matador's ceremonial execution of the bull by sword. **—bull·fight·er** *n.* **—bull·fight·ing** *n.*

bull·finch (bŏŏl′fĭnch′) *n.* **1.** A European bird, *Pyrrhula pyrrhula,* having a short, thick bill and, in the male, a red breast, black head, wings, and tail, and a gray and white back. **2.** Any of several other similar finches. [From its thick neck.]

bull·frog (bŏŏl′frôg′, -frŏg′) *n.* Any of several large frogs, chiefly of the genus *Rana;* especially, *R. catesbeiana,* of North America, having a characteristic deep, resonant croak.

bull·head (bŏŏl′hĕd′) *n.* **1.** Any of several North American freshwater catfishes of the genus *Ictalurus.* **2.** Any of several fishes of the family Cottidae, such as the **sculpin** and the **miller's thumb** (both of which see).

bull·head·ed (bŏŏl′hĕd′ĭd) *adj.* Very stubborn; obstinate; headstrong. **—bull·head·ed·ly** *adv.* **—bull·head·ed·ness** *n.*

bull·horn (bŏŏl′hôrn′) *n.* An electric megaphone that amplifies the volume of a voice or other sounds. Also *chiefly British* "loudhailer."

bul·lion (bŏŏl′yən) *n.* **1.** Gold or silver considered with respect to quantity rather than value. **2.** Gold or silver in the form of bars, ingots, or plates. **3.** A heavy lace trimming made of twisted gold or silver threads. [Middle English, from Norman French, "mint," perhaps variant of Old French *bouillon,* "a boiling," from *bouillir,* to BOIL.]

bull·ish (bŏŏl′ĭsh) *adj.* **1.** Like a bull; brawny or bull-headed. **2. a.** Causing, expecting, or characterized by rising stock-market prices. Compare **bearish. b.** Optimistic or confident. **—bull·ish·ly** *adv.* **—bull·ish·ness** *n.*

bull mastiff *n.* A heavy-set dog of a breed developed from the bulldog and the mastiff.

bull·necked (bŏŏl′nĕkt′) *adj.* Having a short, thick neck.

bul·lock (bŏŏl′ək) *n.* **1.** A castrated bull; a steer. **2.** A young bull. [Middle English *bullok,* Old English *bulluc,* diminutive of *bula,* BULL.]

bull·pen (bŏŏl′pĕn′) *n.* **1.** A pen for confining bulls. **2.** *Informal.* A place for the temporary detention of prisoners. **3.** *Baseball.* **a.** An area where relief pitchers warm up during a game. **b.** The relief pitchers of a team collectively.

bull·ring (bŏŏl′rĭng′) *n.* A circular arena for bullfights.

bull·roar·er (bŏŏl′rôr′ər, -rōr′ər) *n.* A small wooden slat attached to a string that makes a roaring noise when whirled.

Bull Run (bŏŏl′ rŭn). A small stream in northeastern Virginia, near Washington, D.C. It was the site of two Civil War battles (July 21, 1861, and August 29–30, 1862) in which the Confederates defeated Union troops. The battles are also known as the First and Second Battles of Manassas, after a small town nearby.

bull session *n.* *Informal.* An informal group discussion.

bull's-eye, bull's eye (bŏŏlz′ī′) *n.* **1. a.** The small central circle on a target. **b.** A shot that hits this circle. **2.** Anything that precisely achieves a desired goal. **3.** A thick, circular piece of glass set in a roof, pavement, ship's deck, or the like, to admit light. **4.** Any circular opening or window. **5. a.** A plano-convex lens used to concentrate light. **b.** A lantern or lamp having such a lens. **6.** *Nautical.* A small round or oval wooden pulley. **7.** A piece of round, hard candy.

bull snake *n.* Any of several nonvenomous North American snakes of the genus *Pituophis,* having yellow and brown or black markings. Some species are also called "gopher snake."

bull terrier *n.* A dog of a breed developed by crossing a bulldog and

bullfinch *Pyrrhula pyrrhula, the bullfinch, is native to Europe and lives on a diet of berries, buds, and seeds. It is sometimes considered a pest because of the damage it does to fruit trees. This is an adult male of the species; the female has broadly similar plumage but a brown instead of a pink chest.*

bullfrog *These large frogs are noted for their low, resonant mating call that can be heard up to 800 meters away (about half a mile). Their powerful hind legs, which enable them to jump 7.5 meters (25 feet) in a single leap, are eaten as a delicacy in some countries. Bullfrogs are found in North and South America, Africa, India, and Australia—this is an Australian species.*

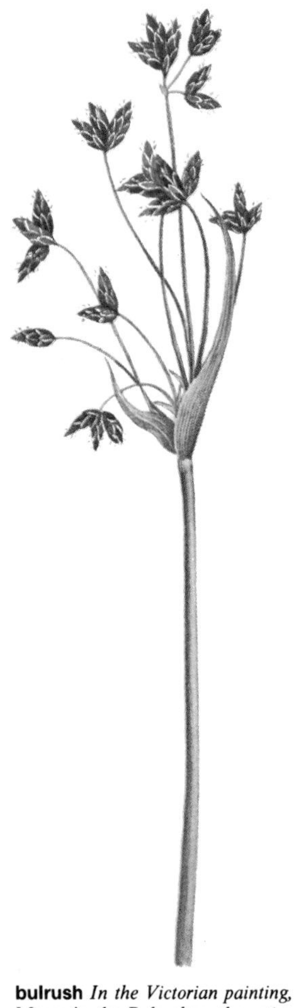

bulrush *In the Victorian painting,* Moses in the Bulrushes, *the artist showed the tall, cigar-shaped reed mace* (Typha latifolia); *but the true bulrush was the sedge grass* Scirpus lacustris, *shown here. Since then the name bulrush has gone into common usage for reed mace, and* Scirpus lacustris *no longer has a common name.*

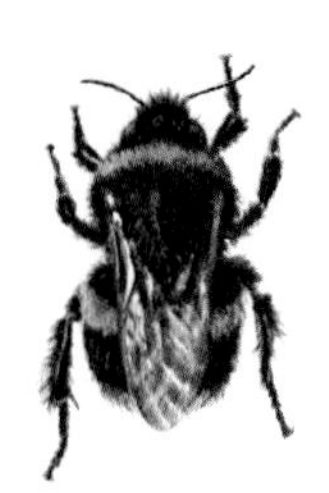

bumblebee *Distinguished by their furry, yellow-banded bodies, bumblebees live in colonies that last only one year. The queen bee, shown here, lays eggs that produce female workers who look after her and the nest. Male bees develop from eggs laid by the workers.*

the now extinct white English terrier, having a short, usually white coat and a tapering muzzle.

bull thistle *n.* A coarse weed, *Cirsium vulgare,* native to Eurasia, having spiny stems and leaves and purple flowers. [From its large head.]

bull tongue *n.* A heavy plow with a single shovel, used chiefly in cotton fields.

bull·whip (bo͝ol'hwĭp') *n.* A long, plaited rawhide whip with a knotted end.
~*tr.v.* **bullwhipped, -whipping, -whips.** To whip with a bullwhip.

bul·ly[1] (bo͝ol'ē) *n., pl.* **-lies.** **1.** A person who is habitually cruel or overbearing toward smaller or weaker people. **2.** *Archaic.* A hired ruffian. **3.** *Obsolete.* A pimp. **4.** *Obsolete.* A fine fellow. **5.** *Obsolete.* A sweetheart.
~*v.* **bullied, -lying, -lies.** —*tr.* To intimidate with superior size or strength. —*intr.* To behave like a bully.
~*adj. Informal.* **1.** Excellent; splendid. **2.** Dashing; gallant.
~*interj.* Used to express admiration or approval: *bully for you.* [Originally "sweetheart," probably from Middle Dutch *boele,* lover, from Middle High German *buole,* perhaps of baby-talk origin.]

bully[2] *n.* Canned or pickled beef. [French *bouilli,* boiled (beef), from the past participle of *bouillir,* to BOIL.]

bully off *intr.v. British.* Formerly, to start or restart a game of hockey. Two players hit each other's sticks and then the ground three times before trying to hit the ball.

bul·ly-off (bo͝ol'ē-ôf', -ŏf') *n. British.* The former procedure for starting or restarting a game of hockey.

bul·ly·rag (bo͝ol'ē-răg') *tr.v.* **-ragged, -ragging, -rags.** Also **bal·ly·rag** (băl'-). To mistreat or intimidate by bullying or teasing.

bully tree *n.* A tropical American tree, the **balata** *(see).* [By folk etymology, variant of BALATA.]

Bü·low (byo͞o'lō), **Bernard Heinrich Martin, Prince von** (1849–1929). German politician, chancellor of the German Empire (1900–09). His chancellorship was marked by an aggressive foreign policy.

bul·rush (bo͝ol-rŭsh') *n.* **1.** Any of various grasslike sedges of the genus *Scirpus,* growing in wet places. **2.** A marsh plant, the **reed mace** *(see).* **3.** In the Old Testament, the **papyrus** *(see).* [Middle English *bulrish* : perhaps *bule,* BULL (in the sense "large") + *rish,* RUSH.]

bul·wark (bo͝ol'wərk, bŭl'-, -wôrk') *n.* **1.** A wall or wall-like structure raised as a defensive fortification; a rampart. **2.** Anything serving as a principal defense against attack or encroachment: *a bulwark against oppression.* **3.** A breakwater. **4.** *Usually* **bulwarks.** The part of a ship's side that is above the upper deck.
~*tr.v.* **bulwarked, -warking, -warks.** **1.** To fortify with a bulwark. **2.** To provide defense or protection for. [Middle English *bulwerke,* from Middle High German *bolwerc* : *bole,* plank + *werc,* WORK.]
Synonyms: *barricade, bastion, breastwork, earthwork, parapet, rampart.*

Bulwer-Lytton, Edward. See **Lytton, 1st Baron.**

bum[1] (bŭm) *n.* **1.** A tramp; hobo. **2.** A person who avoids work and seeks to live off others. **3.** An incompetent or disagreeable person. **4.** One who is devoted to a specified activity: *ski bums.* **—on the bum.** *Slang.* **1.** Living as a tramp. **2.** Sponging or cadging.
~*v.* **bummed, bumming, bums.** *Informal.* —*intr.* **1.** To live by begging and scavenging from place to place. Often used with *around.* **2.** To loaf. —*tr.* To acquire by begging or sponging.
~*adj. Slang.* **1.** Of poor quality; worthless: *a bum deal.* **2.** Disabled; malfunctioning: *a bum shoulder.* [From earlier *bummer,* a loafer, probably from German *bummler,* from *bummeln*†, to loaf.]

bum[2] *intr.v.* **bummed, bumming, bums.** *Chiefly British.* To make a humming sound; drone.

bum[3] *n. Chiefly British Slang.* The buttocks. [Middle English *bom*†.]

bum·bail·iff (bŭm-bā'lĭf) *n. British.* Formerly, a court officer who pursued debtors. Used derogatorily. [From BUM (buttocks), since he pursues and catches from behind.]

bum·ble[1] (bŭm'bəl) *v.* **-bled, -bling, -bles.** —*intr.* To speak or behave in a clumsy or faltering manner. —*tr.* To bungle; botch. [Variant of BUNGLE.] **—bum·bler** *n.* **—bum·bling·ly** *adv.*

bumble[2] *intr.v.* **-bled, -bling, -bles.** To make a humming or droning sound; buzz.
~*n.* A droning sound; a buzz. [Middle English *bomblen* (imitative).]

bum·ble·bee (bŭm'bəl-bē') *n.* Any of various large, hairy bees of the genus *Bombus.* [BUMBLE + BEE.]

bum·boat (bŭm'bōt') *n.* A small boat used to peddle provisions and small wares to ships anchored offshore. [Probably Dutch *bom*†, a kind of fishing boat + BOAT.]

Bu·mi·put·ra (bo͞o'mə-po͞o'trə) *n.* Any of the indigenous natives of Malaysia. **—Bu·mi·put·ra** *adj.*

bum·mer (bŭm'ər) *n. Slang.* **1. a.** A bad reaction to a hallucinogenic drug. **b.** A disagreeable person, event, or situation. **2.** A failure.

bump (bŭmp) *v.* **bumped, bumping, bumps.** —*tr.* **1.** To strike or collide with. **2.** To cause to knock against an obstacle. **3.** To knock to a new position; displace; dislodge. **4.** *Informal.* To displace by right of seniority or authority. —*intr.* **1.** To hit or knock with force. Often used with *against* or *into.* **2.** To proceed with jerks and jolts. Often used with *along.* **3.** To thrust the pelvis forward in a sensual way when dancing. Used chiefly in the phrase *bump and grind.* **—bump into.** To meet by chance. **—bump off.** *Slang.* To murder or kill.
~*n.* **1. a.** A light blow, collision, or jolt. **b.** The noise caused by this; a thud. **2.** A slight swelling or lump. **3.** A raised part on a generally even surface. **4.** One of the natural protuberances of the human skull. **5.** A sudden violent upward air current striking an airplane in flight. **6.** A sensual forward thrust of the pelvis when dancing.

bump·er[1] (bŭm'pər) *n.* **1.** One that bumps. **2.** Either of two metal or rubber structures, typically horizontal bars, attached to the front and rear of a motor vehicle to absorb the impact of a collision. **3.** A similar protective device on other objects.

bumper[2] *n.* **1.** A drinking vessel filled to the brim. **2.** Something unusually or extraordinarily large.
~*tr.v.* **bumpered, -ering, -ers.** **1.** To fill to the brim. **2.** To propose a toast to.
~*adj.* Unusually good, large, or abundant: *a bumper crop.* [Perhaps from BUMP (lump, hence something large).]

bumper sticker *n.* A sticker bearing a printed message for display on a vehicle's bumper.

bum·per-to-bum·per (bŭm'pər-tə-bum'pər) *adj.* Traveling close together, with bumpers almost touching. Said of motor vehicles. **—bum·per-to-bum·per** *adv.*

bump·kin (bŭmp'kĭn, bŭm'-) *n.* Also **bum·kin** (bŭm'-) (for sense 2). **1.** An awkward, untutored rustic. **2.** A short spar projecting from the deck of a ship. Used to extend a sail or secure a block or stay. [Perhaps originally "Dutchman," probably from Dutch *boomken,* "little tree," squat person, diminutive of *boom,* tree, from Middle Dutch.]

bump·tious (bŭmp'shəs) *adj.* Crudely arrogant and self-assertive in behavior; pushy. [Perhaps a blend of BUMP and FRACTIOUS.] **—bump·tious·ly** *adv.* **—bump·tious·ness** *n.*

bump·y (bŭm'pē) *adj.* **-ier, -iest.** **1.** Covered with bumps or protuberances: *a bumpy road.* **2.** Involving jerks and jolts: *a bumpy ride.* **—bump·i·ly** *adv.* **—bump·i·ness** *n.*

bum's rush *n. Slang.* Forcible ejection or dismissal. [From BUM (tramp).]

bun (bŭn) *n.* **1.** A small bread roll, often sweetened or spiced. **2.** A small round sweet bread roll, often made with dried fruit. **3.** A roll of hair worn at the back of a woman's head. [Middle English *bunne*†.]

Bu·na (bo͞o'nə, byo͞o'-) *n.* A trademark for a type of synthetic rubber made by polymerization of butadiene and sodium.

bunch (bŭnch) *n.* **1.** A group of like items growing, fastened, or placed together; a cluster or tuft. **2.** *Informal.* A small group of things or people. **3.** A lump or swelling.
~*v.* **bunched, bunching, bunches.** —*tr.* **1.** To gather or form into a cluster or tuft. **2.** To gather together in a group. **3.** To gather (fabric) into folds. —*intr.* **1.** To form a cluster or tuft. **2.** To gather together in a group; cluster. **3.** To be gathered up in folds. Used of fabric. [Middle English *bunche*†.] **—bunch·y** *adj.*

bunch·ber·ry (bŭnch'bĕr'ē) *n., pl.* **-ries.** A plant, the **dwarf cornel** *(see).*

Bunche (bŭnch), **Ralph Johnson** (1904–71). U.S. civil servant and political scientist. He was the first black to become a divisional head in the Department of State (1946). At the United Nations (1946–71) he carried out detailed research into colonial administration and race relations and was awarded the Nobel Peace Prize (1950) for his work as principal secretary of the UN Palestine Commission.

bunch·flow·er (bŭnch'flou'ər) *n.* A bog plant, *Melanthium virginicum,* of the eastern United States, having narrow leaves and a branching cluster of greenish flowers.

bun·co (bŭng'kō) *n., pl.* **-cos.** Also **bun·ko,** *pl.* **-kos.** *Informal.* A swindle; a confidence trick.
~*tr.v.* **buncoed, -coing, -cos.** Also **bunko, -koed, -koing, -kos.** *Informal.* To swindle; cheat. [Spanish *banca,* name of a card game, "bank" (in gambling), from Italian *banca,* BANK (financial establishment).]

buncombe. Variant of **bunkum.**

bund[1] (bŭnd) *n.* **1.** In India and the Far East, an embankment or dyke. **2.** A street running along a harbor or waterway. [Hindi *band,* from Persian.]

bund[2] (bo͝ond, bŭnd) *n.* **1.** A confederation or league. **2. Bund.** A pro-Nazi German-American organization of the 1930's. [German *Bund,* "league."] **—bund·ist** *n.*

Bun·des·rat, Bun·des·rath (bo͝on'dəs-rät') *n.* **1.** The upper house of the federal legislative body of West Germany, made up of ministers from each of the states. **2.** The federal council of certain countries, as of Switzerland and Austria. **3.** Formerly, a federal legislative council composed of representatives from the 26 states of the German Empire. [*Bundes,* genitive of BUND + *Rat,* council.]

Bun·des·tag (bo͝on'dəs-täg') *n.* The lower house of the federal legislative body of West Germany, elected by universal suffrage. [German : *Bundes,* genitive of BUND + *-tag,* meeting.]

bun·dle (bŭnd'l) *n. Abbr.* **bdl.** **1.** A number of objects bound, wrapped, or otherwise held together. **2.** Anything wrapped or tied up for carrying; a package. **3.** *Biology.* A cluster or strand of specialized cells. **4.** *Botany.* A **vascular bundle** *(see).* **5.** *Slang.* A large sum of money.
~*v.* **bundled, -dling, -dles.** —*tr.* **1.** To tie, wrap, fold, or otherwise secure together. **2.** To dispatch or cause to move quickly and unceremoniously; hustle. Usually used with *off* or *into.* **3.** To dress warmly. Used with *up.* —*intr.* To sleep in the same bed while fully clothed, a custom formerly practiced by engaged couples in early New England. [Middle English *bundel,* probably from Middle

Dutch, sheaf of papers, bundle.] —**bun·dler** *n.*

bung (bŭng) *n.* **1.** A stopper for a cask, flask, or the like. **2.** The hole itself; a bunghole.
~*tr.v.* **bunged, bunging, bungs. 1.** To close (a bunghole) with a cork or stopper. **2.** *Informal.* To beat up; bruise; maul. Often used with *up.* [Middle English *bunge,* from Middle Dutch *bonghe,* perhaps variant of *bonne,* perhaps from Late Latin *puncta,* hole, from the feminine past participle of Latin *pungere,* to prick.]

bun·ga·low (bŭng′gə-lō′) *n.* A small cottage, usually of one story. [Earlier *bungale,* perhaps from Gujarati *bangalo,* from Hindi *baṅglā,* "of Bengal."]

bung·hole (bŭng′hōl′) *n.* The hole in a cask, keg, or barrel through which liquid is poured in or drained out.

bun·gle (bŭng′gəl) *v.* **-gled, -gling, -gles.** —*intr.* To work or act ineptly or inefficiently. —*tr.* To manage (a task) badly; botch.
~*n.* A clumsy or inept job or performance. [Perhaps from Scandinavian, akin to Swedish (dialectal) *bangla,* to work ineffectually.] —**bun·gler** *n.*

bun·gling (bŭng′glĭng) *adj.* Performing clumsily or ineptly; incompetent. —See Synonyms at **awkward.** —**bun·gling·ly** *adv.*

Bu·nin (bōō′nĭn, -nyĭn), **Ivan Alexeyevich** (1870–1953). Russian writer. He gained international recognition with his novel *The Village* (1910), but he is best known for his short stories, especially *The Gentleman from San Francisco* (1915). He was awarded the Nobel Prize for literature (1933).

bun·ion (bŭn′yən) *n.* A painful, inflamed swelling at the bursa of the big toe. [Probably from earlier *bunny, bony,* swelling, from Old French *buigne†,* bump on the head.]

bunk[1] (bŭngk) *n.* **1.** A narrow bed attached like a shelf against a wall. **2.** Either of a pair of narrow beds stacked one on top of the other. Also called "bunk bed." **3.** *Informal.* Any place for sleeping. ~*intr.v.* **bunked, bunking, bunks. 1.** To sleep in a bunk. **2.** To go to bed. [Possibly short for BUNKER.]

bunk[2] *n. Slang.* Nonsense. [Short for BUNKUM.]

bun·ker (bŭng′kər) *n.* **1.** A bin or tank for fuel storage, as on a ship. **2.** A sand trap serving as an obstacle on a golf course. **3.** A fortified underground defensive position, with an overground projection for gun emplacements.
~*tr.v.* **bunkered, -kering, -kers. 1.** To store (fuel) in a bunker. **2.** To drive (a golf ball) into a bunker. [Earlier Scottish *bonker†.*]

Bun·ker Hill (bŭng′kər). Height in Charlestown, Boston, Massachusetts. The Battle of Bunker Hill (June 17, 1775), the first major engagement of the American Revolution, actually took place on nearby Breed's Hill. The British were victorious, but the American defense of the hill raised morale and stiffened colonial resistance.

bunk·house (bŭngk′hous′) *n.* Sleeping quarters on a ranch or in a camp.

bunk·mate (bŭngk′māt′) *n.* A person with whom one shares rough sleeping quarters.

bunko. Variant of **bunco.**

bun·kum, bun·combe (bŭng′kəm) *n.* Empty or meaningless talk, especially by a politician; claptrap. [After *Buncombe* County, North Carolina, from a remark made in about 1820 by its congressman, Felix Walker, who made a fatuous speech, calling it "a speech for Buncombe."]

bun·ny (bŭn′ē) *n., pl.* **-nies.** A rabbit. Used especially by and to children. [From dialectal *bun†,* squirrel.]

bunny hug *n.* A dance in ragtime rhythm popular in the United States during the early part of the 20th century.

bun·rak·u (bōōn-rä′kōō, bōōn′rä′-) *n.* **1.** The traditional Japanese puppet theater. **2.** One of the two schools of Japanese puppet theater. [Japanese : *bun,* literary composition + *raku,* easy.]

buns (bŭnz) *pl.n. Slang.* The buttocks. [From dialectal *bun,* hind part of a rabbit or squirrel, from Scottish Gaelic, stump, bottom.]

Bun·sen (bŭn′sən), **Robert Wilhelm** (1811–99). German chemist. He did important work in the analysis of gases and was a joint discoverer, with Gustav Kirchhoff (1824–87), of the elements caesium and rubidium. He also invented several pieces of laboratory equipment.

Bunsen burner *n.* A small laboratory burner consisting of a vertical metal tube connected to a gas source, and producing a hot flame from a mixture of gas and air let in through adjustable holes at the base. [After Robert Wilhelm BUNSEN, its inventor.]

bunt[1] (bŭnt) *v.* **bunted, bunting, bunts.** —*tr.* **1.** To butt (something) with or as if with the horns or head. **2.** *Baseball.* To bat (a pitched ball) with a half swing, and with the upper hand supporting the middle of the bat, so that the ball rolls slowly in front of the infielders. —*intr. Baseball.* To bunt a pitch.
~*n.* A butt with or as if with the horns or head. **2.** *Baseball.* **a.** The act of bunting. **b.** A bunted ball. [Probably from Celtic, akin to Breton *bounta,* to butt.]

bunt[2] *n.* **1.** *Nautical.* The middle section of a square sail. **2.** The sagging middle part of a fishnet. [Perhaps from Middle Low German *bunt,* bundle.]

bunt[3] *n.* A disease of wheat, rye, and other cereal grasses, caused by fungi of the genus *Tilletia* and resulting in sooty black spores in place of normal seeds. [18th century : origin obscure.]

bunt·ing[1] (bŭn′tĭng) *n.* **1.** A light cotton or woolen cloth used for making flags. **2.** Flags collectively. **3.** Long, variously colored strips of cloth or material used for festive decoration. [18th century : origin obscure.]

bunting[2] *n.* Any of various birds of the family Fringillidae, such as the **snow bunting** (*see*), having short,ʼ cone-shaped bills and brown-

ish or grayish plumage. [Middle English *buntynge†.*]

bunting[3] *n.* A snug-fitting, hooded sleeping bag for infants. [Origin unknown.]

bunt·line (bŭnt′lĭn, -līn′) *n. Nautical.* A rope attached to a square sail when it is being hauled up for furling.

Bu·ñu·el (bōō-nyōō-ĕl′), **Luis** (1900–). Spanish film director. In the 1920's he collaborated with Dali in making a number of surrealist films, notably *Un Chien Andalou* (1929), but he is most highly regarded for his studies of social manners and social conditions, such as *Belle de Jour* (1966) and *The Discreet Charm of the Bourgeoisie* (1972).

bun·ya (bŭn′yə) *n.* Also **bun·ya-bun·ya** (bŭn′yə-bŭn′yə). An evergreen tree, *Araucaria bidwilli,* native to Australia, having sharp-pointed, close-set leaves and large cones. [From a native Australian language.]

Bun·yan (bŭn′yən), **John** (1628–88). English writer and preacher. As a Puritan, he served in the Parliamentary army from 1644 to 1646 during the Civil War. He was imprisoned (1660–72) for unlicensed preaching. *The Pilgrim's Progress from This World to That Which Is to Come* was published in two parts in 1678 and 1684.

Bun·yan·esque (bŭn′yə-nĕsk′) *adj.* **1.** Of, pertaining to, or suggestive of the allegorical writings of John Bunyan. **2. a.** Of, pertaining to, or suggestive of the stories about Paul Bunyan. **b.** Of astonishingly large size.

buoy (bōō′ē, boi) *n.* **1.** *Nautical.* A float moored in water as a warning of danger under the surface or as a marker for a channel. See **bell buoy. 2.** A device made of cork or other buoyant material for keeping a person afloat. In this sense, also called "lifebuoy."
~*tr.v.* **buoyed, buoying, buoys. 1.** *Nautical.* To mark with a buoy. **2.** To keep afloat. **3.** To uplift the spirits of; cheer; hearten. Used with *up.* [Middle English *boye,* probably from Old French *boie,* perhaps from Old High German *bouhhan.*]

buoy·ance (boi′əns, bōō′yəns) *n.* Buoyancy.

buoy·an·cy (boi′ən-sē, bōō′yən-) *n.* **1. a.** The tendency or capacity to remain afloat in a liquid or to rise in air or gas. **b.** The upward force of a fluid upon a floating or immersed object. **2.** The ability to recover quickly from setbacks. **3.** Lightness of spirit; cheerfulness.

buoy·ant (boi′ənt, bōō′yənt) *adj.* Having or marked by buoyancy. [Spanish *buoyante,* present participle of *boyar,* to float, from *boya,* buoy, from Old French *boie,* BUOY.] —**buoy·ant·ly** *adv.*

bu·pres·tid (byōō-prĕs′tĭd) *n.* Any of various often brightly colored beetles of the family Buprestidae, many of which are destructive wood borers as larvae.

bur[1], burr (bûr) *n.* **1. a.** The rough, prickly, or spiny fruit husk, seed pod, or flower of various plants, such as the chestnut or the burdock. **b.** A plant producing burs. **2.** A person or thing that clings persistently. **3.** Any of various rotary cutting tools designed to be attached to a drill. [Middle English *burre,* probably from Scandinavian, akin to Old Swedish *borre.*]

bur[2]. 1. Variant of **burr** (rough edge). **2.** Variant of **burr** (guttural trill). **3.** Variant of **burr** (washer).

Bur. 1. bureau. **2.** Burma.

bu·ran (bōō-rän′) *n.* Also **bu·ra** (-rä′). A violent windstorm of the steppes of Russia, accompanied in summer by dust and in winter by snow. [Russian, *burya,* from Turkic; akin to Turkish and Kazan Tatar *buran.*]

Bur·bage (bûr′bĭj), **Richard** (c. 1567–1619). English actor, the foremost tragedian of his age. As the leading player in Shakespeare's company, the Chamberlain's Men, he was the first to play the title roles in *Hamlet, King Lear, Othello,* and *Richard III.*

Bur·bank (bûr′băngk). A city in southern California, in the Greater Los Angeles area. Aircraft manufacturing is the major industry. Several motion-picture and television studios are here.

Burbank, Luther (1849–1926). U.S. biologist and plant breeder. He applied Mendel's laws of heredity to create new varieties of plants. Besides the Burbank potato, he produced hundreds of new varieties of fruit and roses and a spineless cactus for use as cattle fodder.

bur·ble (bûr′bəl) *n.* **1.** A rushing or bubbling sound. **2.** A rapid, excited flow of speech. **3.** *Aviation.* A separation in the boundary layer of air about a moving streamlined body, causing a breakdown in the smooth airflow and resulting in turbulence.
~*intr.v.* **burbled, -bling, -bles. 1.** To bubble; gurgle. **2.** To speak quickly and excitedly. [Middle English *burblen,* to flow with a bubbling sound (imitative).]

bur·bot (bûr′bət) *n., pl.* **-bots** or collectively **burbot.** A freshwater fish, *Lota lota,* of the Northern Hemisphere, related to and resembling the cod. [Middle English *borbot,* from Old French *bourbotte, bourbete,* from *bourbeter,* to burrow in the mud, from *bourbe†,* mud.]

Burck·hardt (bōōrk′härt), **Jacob Christoph** (1818–97). Swiss historian, one of the founders of the modern school of history-writing. His great achievement was to direct historians away from an almost exclusive concentration on political and military events to a consideration of wider cultural history, as in his work *The Civilization of the Renaissance in Italy* (1860).

bur cucumber *n.* **1.** A climbing vine, *Sicyos angulatus,* of eastern North America, having lobed leaves, small greenish flowers, and bristly, egg-shaped fruit. **2.** The fruit of the bur cucumber.

bur·den[1] (bûr′dn) *n.* Also *archaic* **bur·then** (bûr′thən). **1. a.** Something that is carried. **b.** Something that is difficult to bear physically or emotionally. **2.** A responsibility or duty. **3. a.** The amount of cargo that a vessel can carry. **b.** The weight of the cargo carried by a vessel at one time. **4.** The carrying of heavy loads: *a beast of burden.*

~*tr.v.* **burdened, -dening, -dens.** Also *archaic* **burthen. 1.** To load or overload. **2.** To weigh down; oppress. [Middle English *burden, burthen,* Old English *byrthen.*]

burden² *n.* **1.** The chorus or refrain of a musical composition. **2.** A recurring idea or theme. **3.** The bass accompaniment to a song. **4.** The drone of a bagpipes. [Variant (influenced by BURDEN, load) of BOURDON, from the idea of the burden being carried along by the melody.]

burden of proof *n.* The responsibility of giving proof for a disputed charge or allegation. [Translation of Latin *onus probandi.*]

bur·den·some (bûrd′n-səm) *adj.* Heavy; hard to bear; onerous. —**bur·den·some·ly** *adv.* —**bur·den·some·ness** *n.*
    Synonyms: *arduous, demanding, exacting, harsh, onerous, oppressive, rigorous.*

bur·dock (bûr′dŏk′) *n.* Any of several coarse, weedy plants of the genus *Arctium,* native to Eurasia, having large, heart-shaped leaves, purplish flowers surrounded by hooked bristles, and prickly fruits. [BUR + DOCK (plant).]

bu·reau (byŏor′ō) *n., pl.* **-reaus** or **bureaux** (byŏor′ōz). **1.** A chest of drawers. **2.** *Chiefly British.* A writing desk or writing table with drawers. **3.** *Abbr.* **Bur, bu. a.** A government department or subdivision of a department. **b.** An office, usually of a large organization, that performs a specific duty: *a news bureau.* **c.** A business or office that offers information of a specified kind: *a travel bureau.* [French, bureau, woolen material used to cover writing desks, from Old French, *burel,* from *bure,* dark brown, from Latin *burrus,* bright red, from Greek *purros,* red.]

bu·reauc·ra·cy (byŏo-rŏk′rə-sē) *n., pl.* **-cies. 1. a.** Government administration through departments staffed by civil servants or similar officials. **b.** The officials in these departments. **2.** A form of administration in which authority is diffused among numerous offices and there is adherence to inflexible rules of operation. **3.** Any administration in which the need to follow complex procedures impedes effective action. [French *bureaucratie.*]

bu·reau·crat (byŏor′ə-krăt′) *n.* **1.** An official of a bureaucracy. **2.** Any official who insists on rigid adherence to rules, forms, and routines. —**bu·reau·crat·ic** *adj.* —**bu·reau·crat·i·cal·ly** *adv.*

bu·reau·crat·ese (byŏor′ə-krə-tēz′, -tēs′) *n.* A style of language used especially by bureaucrats that is characterized by jargon and euphemism.

bu·reau·cra·tize (byŏo-rŏk′rə-tīz′) *tr.v.* **tized, -tizing, -tizes.** To bring under bureaucratic influence or control. —**bu·reau·crat·i·za·tion** *n.*

bu·rette, bu·ret (byŏo-rĕt′) *n.* A uniform-bore glass tube with fine graduations and a stopcock at the bottom, used especially in laboratory procedures for accurate dispensing and measurement of liquids. [French, originally "cruet," from Old French, cruet for sacramental wine, from *buire,* pitcher, variant of *buie,* from Frankish *būk* (unattested).]

burg (bûrg) *n.* **1.** A fortified town. **2.** *Informal.* A city or town. [Old English *burg, burh.*]

bur·gage (bûr′gĭj) *n.* A tenure in England and Scotland under which property of the king or a lord in a town was held in return for a yearly rent or other services. [Middle English, from Medieval Latin *burgāgium,* from *burgus,* fortified town, from Old English *burg,* BURG.]

bur·gee (bûr′jē, bər-jē′) *n.* A small distinguishing flag displayed by a ship or yacht. [Perhaps originally *burgee's flag,* from Channel Islands French *bourgeais,* shipowner, from Old French *burgeis,* owner, BURGESS.]

bur·geon (bûr′jən) *intr.v.* **-geoned, -geoning, -geons.** Also **bourgeon. 1.** To put forth new buds, leaves, or greenery; begin to sprout, grow, or blossom. **2.** To emerge and develop rapidly; flourish.

~*n.* Also **bour·geon.** A bud, sprout, or newly developing growth. [Middle English *burgenen,* from *burjon,* a bud, from Old French, from Vulgar Latin *burriō* (stem *burriōn-*) (unattested), from Late Latin *burra,* wool (probably from the down on some buds).]

    Usage: The verb *burgeon* and its past participle *burgeoning,* used as an adjective, are properly restricted to the actual or figurative sense of "to bud or sprout," or "to emerge and develop": *the burgeoning talent of the young Mozart.* They are not mere substitutes for the more general *expand, grow,* or *thrive.*

burg·er (bûr′gər) *n.* A hamburger *(see).*

bur·gess (bûr′jĭs) *n.* **1.** A freeman or citizen of an English borough. **2.** Formerly, a member of the English Parliament, representing a town, borough, or university. **3.** A member of the lower house of the colonial legislature of either Virginia or Maryland. [Middle English *burgeis,* from Old French, from Vulgar Latin *burgensis* (unattested), from Late Latin *burgus,* fortified place, from Germanic.]

Bur·gess (bûr′jĭs), **Anthony** (1917-). British novelist and essayist. His fame rests chiefly on his novels, in which he exhibits a flamboyant range and command of language. His most successful novels have been *A Clockwork Orange* (1962), *Nothing Like the Sun* (1964), and *End of the World News* (1982).

burgh (bûrg) *n.* A chartered town or borough in Scotland. Compare **borough.** [Scottish, variant of BOROUGH.] —**burgh·al** *adj.*

burgh·er (bûr′gər) *n.* **1. a.** A member of the mercantile class of a medieval city. **b.** A citizen of a medieval city. **2.** A solid citizen. [Either German *Bürger,* from Middle High German *burgære,* from Old High German *burgāri,* town-dweller, from *burg,* fortified place;

or Dutch *burger,* from Middle Dutch *burgher,* from Middle High German *burgære.*]

Burgh·ley or **Bur·leigh** (bûr′lē), **William Cecil, 1st Baron** (1520-98). English statesman, Elizabeth I's most important administrator and chief spokeman in the House of Commons. He had great influence in guiding Elizabeth to a middle religious course between the extreme Puritans and the Roman Catholics.

bur·glar (bûr′glər) *n.* One who commits burglary; a housebreaker. [Norman French *burgler,* from Medieval Latin *burgulator,* probably from Medieval Latin *burg-* (unattested), plunder.]

bur·glar·i·ous (bər-glâr′ē-əs) *adj.* Pertaining to burglary.

bur·glar·ize (bûr′glə-rīz′) *tr.v.* **-ized, -izing, -izes.** To commit burglary in. —See Synonyms at **rob.**

bur·glar·proof (bûr′glər-prŏof′) *adj.* Secure against burglary.

bur·gla·ry (bûr′glə-rē) *n., pl.* **-ries.** The crime or an act of breaking into and entering premises with intent to commit a felony.

bur·gle (bûr′gəl) *v.* **-gled, -gling, -gles.** *Informal.* —*tr.* To burglarize. —*intr.* To commit burglary. [Back-formation from BURGLAR.]

bur·go·mas·ter (bûr′gə-măs′tər, -mäs′tər) *n.* In the Netherlands, Flanders, Austria, and Germany, the principal magistrate of a city or town, comparable to a mayor. [Partial translation of Dutch *burgemeester : burg,* town + MASTER.]

bur·go·net (bûr′gə-nĭt, bûr′gə-nĕt′) *n.* A light steel helmet with a peak and hinged flaps covering the cheeks. [French *bourguignotte,* feminine of *bourguignot,* "of Burgundy," from *Bourgogne,* Burgundy.]

bur·goo (bûr′gŏo, bər-gŏo′) *n., pl.* **-goos. 1.** Thick oatmeal gruel, originally served to sailors. **2.** *Southern U.S.* **a.** A thick, spicy soup or stew of meat and vegetables. **b.** A picnic or gathering where this dish is served. [Perhaps from Arabic *burghul,* from Turkish *bulgur,* "bruised grain."]

Bur·gos (bŏor′gōs). A city in northern Spain, on a mountainous plateau near the Arlanzón River. It was founded in *c.* 884 and was the capital of the kingdom of Castile from 1035 to 1087. It was the headquarters of the Nationalists during the Spanish Civil War of 1936-39. Its limestone cathedral (13th to 16th centuries) is one of the finest examples of Gothic architecture in Europe.

Bur·goyne (bər-goin′), **John,** called "Gentleman Johnny" (1722-1792). British officer. A major general in the American Revolution, he captured Fort Ticonderoga on July 6, 1977. His army was defeated by an American force at the Battle of Saratoga on October 17, 1777. He also wrote several plays, including *The Heiress* (1786).

bur·grave (bûr′grāv′) *n.* **1.** In medieval Germany, the appointed governor of a town or military fortress. **2.** The hereditary lord of a German town and its surroundings. [Middle High German *burcgrāve : burc,* fortress, from Old High German *burg + grāve,* count.]

Bur·gun·dy¹ (bûr′gən-dē). *French* **Bour·gogne** (bŏor-gôn′y′). A historic region of eastern France. The region was first organized into a kingdom by the Burgundii tribe from Savoy in the late 5th century. The great age of Burgundian influence and power began (1364) when John II gave the duchy to his son Philip the Bold, who thus initiated the royal Valois-Bourgogne line. By the 15th century Burgundy had added most of present-day Belgium, Luxembourg, and the Netherlands to its territory and had become the most powerful duchy in France. Its historical importance and independence came to an end in the late 15th century, when Mary of Burgundy married the Emperor Maximilian I and so transferred Burgundy to the Hapsburgs. Today Burgundy is famous for its wines, produced in the Chablis district, the mountains of the Côte d'Or, and the Saône and Rhône river valleys.

Burgundy² *n., pl.* **-dies. 1. a.** Any of various red or white wines produced in Burgundy. **b.** Any of various similar full-bodied wines produced elsewhere. **2. burgundy.** A dark grayish or blackish purple to dark purplish red or reddish brown.

bur·i·al (bĕr′ē-əl) *n.* The interment of a dead body or an instance of this. [Middle English *biriel, buryel,* grave, singular of *buriels,* Old English *byrgels.*] —**bur·i·al** *adj.*

bu·rin (byŏor′ĭn, bûr′-) *n.* **1.** A pointed steel cutting tool used in engraving or in carving stone. **2.** The style or technique of an engraver's work. **3.** *Archaeology.* A primitive flint tool with a head like that of a chisel. [French, perhaps from Italian *burino.*]

burke (bûrk) *tr.v.* **burked, burking, burkes. 1.** To murder by suffocation so as to leave the body intact and suitable for dissection. **2.** To suppress quietly and unceremoniously. [After William *Burke* (1792-1829), Irish murderer executed in Edinburgh, for this crime.]

Burke (bûrk), **Edmund** (1729-97). British political writer and politician. As a member of Parliament from 1765, he played a major part until the French Revolution in developing liberal policy for the Whigs and in formulating the constitutional notion of party responsibility and a loyal opposition (1770). He pleaded on behalf of the American colonists' appeal for independence and in the 1780's led the campaign to reduce the influence of the Crown. The outbreak of the French Revolution caused him to abandon the Whigs and support Pitt.

Burke, Martha Jane, known as "Calamity Jane" (c. 1852-1903). U.S. frontierswoman who has become a legend of the Wild West. Often dressing in men's clothes, she is reputed to have been a crack shot and a skilled horsewoman.

Burkina Faso. See Upper Volta.

burl (bûrl) *n.* **1.** A knot, lump, or slub in yarn or cloth. **2.** A large, rounded growth on the trunk or branch of a tree. **3.** The strongly marked wood from such a growth, especially walnut, usually cut into thin pieces and used as veneer.

~*tr.v.* **burled, burling, burls.** To dress or finish (fabric) by removing burls or loose threads. [Middle English *burle,* from Old French *bourle,* diminutive of *bourre,* coarse wool, from Late Latin *burra*†, wool.] **—burl·er** *n.*

bur·lap (bûr′lăp′) *n.* A coarsely woven cloth made of fibers of jute, flax, or hemp, used to make bags, to reinforce linoleum, and in interior decoration. [17th century : origin obscure.]

Burleigh, 1st Baron. See **Burghley.**

bur·lesque (bər-lĕsk′) *n.* **1.** A literary or dramatic work that makes a subject appear ridiculous by treating it in an incongruous style, as by presenting a lofty subject with vulgarity, or the inconsequential with mock dignity. **2.** Any ludicrous or mocking imitation; a travesty. **3.** A variety show characterized by broad, ribald comedy, dancing, and striptease.

~*v.* **burlesqued, -lesquing, -lesques.** —*tr.* To imitate mockingly: *"always bringing junk . . . home, as if he were burlesquing his role as provider"* (John Updike). —*intr.* To use the methods or techniques of burlesque.

~*adj.* **1.** Mockingly and ludicrously imitative. **2.** Of, pertaining to, or characteristic of theatrical burlesque, especially in its ribald aspects. [French, from Italian *burlesco,* from *burla,* joke, ridicule, from Vulgar Latin *burrula* (unattested), diminutive of Late Latin *burra,* trifle, bit of nonsense, perhaps from *burra,* wool, shaggy garment.] **—bur·lesque·ly** *adv.* **—bur·les·quer** *n.*

bur·ley, Bur·ley (bûr′lē) *n., pl.* **-leys.** A light-colored tobacco grown chiefly in Kentucky. [Probably from *Burley,* a proper name.]

bur·ly (bûr′lē) *adj.* **-lier, -liest.** Heavy, strong, and muscular; thickset. [Middle English *burli, borlich,* stately, probably from Old English *būrlic* (unattested), exalted.] **—bur·li·ly** *adv.* **—bur·li·ness** *n.*

Bur·ma (bûr′mə). *Abbr.* **Bur.** A republic in Southeast Asia. It is bordered on the west by the Indian Ocean, on the north by Bangladesh and India, and on the east by China, Laos, and Thailand. On both its northern and eastern borders it is cut off from its neighbors by large mountain ranges, between which lies the fertile Irrawaddy River valley, whose crops make Burma one of the world's largest producers of rice. Burma was made a province of British India (1886); it gained its independence in 1948. Area, 676,552 square kilometers (261,218 square miles). Population, 32,900,000. Capital and largest city, Rangoon. See map, next page.

bur marigold *n.* Any of various plants of the genus *Bidens,* having yellow flowers and pointed seeds that cling to fur and clothing. Also called "beggar-ticks," "sticktight."

Bur·mese (bər-mēz′, -mēs′) *adj.* Also **Bur·man** (bûr′mən). Of, pertaining to, or characteristic of Burma, its people, their language, or their culture.

~*n., pl.* **Burmese.** Also **Bur·man** (for sense 1) *pl.* **-mans.** **1.** A native or inhabitant of Burma. **2.** The Sino-Tibetan language spoken in Burma.

Burmese cat *n.* A cat of a breed resembling the Siamese but having a dark-brown or blue-gray coat.

burn[1] (bûrn) *v.* **burned** or **burnt** (bûrnt), **burning, burns.** —*tr.* **1. a.** To cause to undergo combustion. **b.** To destroy or consume with fire. **2.** To damage or injure the surface of by fire, heat, or a heat-producing agent: *He burned the toast.* **3.** *Slang.* To kill or execute. **4.** To produce by fire or heat: *burn a clearing in the brush.* **5.** To use as a fuel. **6.** To impart a sensation of intense heat to: *The chili burned his mouth.* **7.** To brand (an animal). **8.** To harden or impart a finish to by subjecting to intense heat; fire. **9.** To let (oneself or part of one's body) become sunburned. **10.** *Slang.* **a.** To defeat in a contest, especially by a narrow margin. **b.** To swindle or deceive; cheat. **11.** *Slang.* To execute in the electric chair; electrocute. —*intr.* **1.** To be on fire; undergo combustion; flame. **2.** To emit heat or light by or as if by means of fire. **3.** To be destroyed, injured, damaged, or changed by or as if by fire: *The house burned down.* **4.** To feel or look hot: *Her cheeks burned.* **5.** To be consumed with strong emotion. **6.** *Slang.* To be executed in the electric chair; be electrocuted. **—burn in.** To darken part of (a photographic print) by exposing unmasked areas. **—burn off.** To remove stubble from (land) by burning. **—burn up.** *Informal.* To make or become very annoyed; enrage.

~*n.* **1.** An injury produced by fire, heat, light, chemicals, electricity, or radiation. **2.** A burned place or area. **3.** The process or result of firing or burning, as in the manufacture of bricks. **4.** A sunburn. **5.** *Aerospace.* One firing of a rocket. [Middle English *bernen, burnen,* from Old English *beornan, byrnan* (intransitive) and *bærnan.*]

Usage: *burn, scorch, singe, sear, char, parch.* These verbs mean to injure or alter by heat. *Burn* can apply to the effect of exposure to any source of heat. *Scorch* usually refers to contact with flame or heated metal and involves superficial (surface) burning that discolors, damages texture, or makes brittle. *Singe* specifies superficial and momentary burning of edges through nearness to the heat source. *Sear* applies to surface burning of organic tissue, as by branding, cauterizing, or application of intense flames, as to meat. *Char* pertains to the reduction of a burning substance to carbon, or to any blackening or disintegration due to fire. *Parch* emphasizes surface drying and, often, fissuring by long exposure to flame or sun.

burn[2] *n. Chiefly Scottish.* A small stream; a brook. Often used in Scottish place names: *Bannockburn.* [Middle English *burn, burne,* Old English *burn, burna,* spring, fountain; from Germanic.]

burn·back (bûrn′băk′) *n. Australian.* The deliberate burning off of strips of land in order to prevent bushfires.

burn·er (bûr′nər) *n.* **1.** One that burns something. **2.** The part of a stove, furnace, or lamp that is lit to produce a flame. **3.** A device in which something is burned: *an oil burner.*

bur·net (bər-nĕt′, bûr′nĭt) *n.* Any of several plants of the genus *Sanguisorba,* having cucumber-flavored leaves and clusters of small white, red, or greenish flowers. [Middle English, dark brown (from the brownish-red flowers), from Old French *burnete, brunette,* BRUNETTE.]

Bur·net (bər-nĕt′, bûr′nĭt), **Sir Frank Macfarlane** (1899–). Australian virologist. For his work in the development of immunity against influenza and his research with P.B. Medawar into the tolerance of the body to the introduction of foreign living tissues, he shared with Medawar the Nobel Prize for medicine (1960).

burnet rose *n.* A Eurasian wild rose, *Rosa pimpinellifolia,* having cream or sometimes pink flowers and dark purple or black fruits.

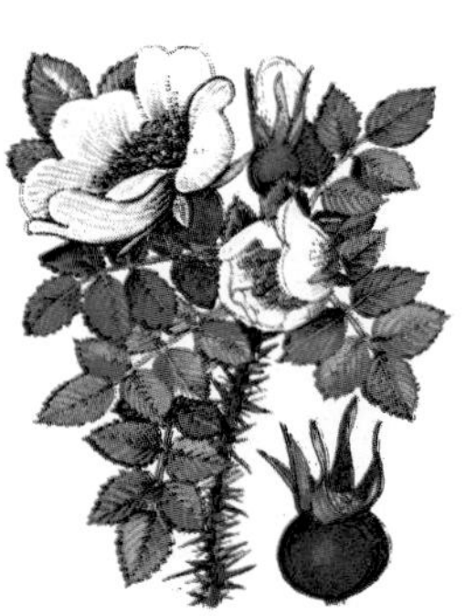

burnet rose *A European wild rose that grows on heaths and coastal sand dunes. Apart from its white summer flowers, it can be identified by its spiny stem and by its berries, which are blue-black instead of red as in other wild roses.*

Bur·nett (bər-nĕt′), **Frances Eliza Hodgson** (1849–1924). U.S. writer, born in England. She lived in the United States after 1865 and became world-famous for her children's books, especially *Little Lord Fauntleroy* (1886) and *The Secret Garden* (1911).

Bur·ney (bûr′nē), **Fanny** (1752–1840). British diarist and novelist. Her diaries, begun in 1768 and continuing for more than 70 years, are a witty, sophisticated, and stylish record of the manners of the polished English society of her day.

burn·ing (bûr′nĭng) *adj.* **1.** Characterized by intense emotion; passionate. **2.** Of immediate import; urgent; pressing: *burning issues.* **—burn·ing·ly** *adv.*

burning bush *n.* **1.** Any of several plants or shrubs having foliage that turns bright red, such as the **summer cypress** *(see).* **2.** The **gas plant** *(see).* [So called from the burning bush in Exodus 3:2.]

burning glass *n.* A convex lens used to focus the sun's rays and produce heat, especially for ignition. Also called "sunglass."

bur·nish (bûr′nĭsh) *tr.v.* **-nished, -nishing, -nishes.** To polish or smooth by or as if by rubbing.

~*n.* A smooth, glossy finish or appearance; luster. [Middle English *burnischen,* from Old French *burnir* (present stem *burniss-*), variant of *brunir,* "to make brown," burnish, from *brun,* brown, shining, from Germanic.] **—bur·nish·er** *n.*

bur·noose, bur·nous (bər-no͞os′) *n.* A long hooded cloak worn by Arabs and Moors. [French, from Arabic *burnus,* from Greek *birros,* cloak.]

burn out *intr.v.* **1.** To stop burning or functioning from lack of fuel. Used of a fire, engine, or rocket. **2.** To wear out or become inoperative as a result of heat or friction. **3.** To become exhausted, especially as a result of long-term stress, overwork, or dissipation.

burn·out (bûrn′out′) *n.* **1.** A failure in a device attributable to burning, excessive heat, or friction. **2.** *Aerospace.* The termination of rocket or jet-engine operation because of fuel exhaustion or shutoff.

Burns (bûrnz), **Robert** (1759–96). Scottish poet. His first volume, *Poems, Chiefly in the Scottish Dialect* (1786) won him wide popularity through the humanity of its verse and the use of the Lallans dialect.

burn·sides (bûrn′sīdz′) *pl.n.* Mutton-chop whiskers and a moustache, worn with the chin clean-shaven. [After Ambrose E. *Burnside* (1824–81), U.S. general, who wore them.]

burnt (bûrnt). Alternate past tense and past participle of **burn.**

~*adj.* **1.** Affected by or as if by burning; scorched. **2.** Treated by fire or calcined for a particular purpose. Said of bricks, certain pigments, or minerals, for example.

burnt offering *n.* An offering, such as a slaughtered animal, burnt on an altar as a religious sacrifice.

burnt orange *n.* A deep rust-colored orange. **—burnt-or·ange** *adj.*

burnt orchid *n.* An orchid, *Orchis ustulata,* having dark maroon flowers resembling those of the lady orchid.

burnt-out (bûrnt′out′) *adj.* Exhausted; spent; extinguished.

burnt sienna *n.* **1.** A reddish-brown pigment prepared by calcining raw sienna. **2.** Dark reddish orange. Also called "sienna."

burn-up (bûrn′ŭp′) *n. Chiefly British Informal.* A fast ride in a car or on a motorcycle.

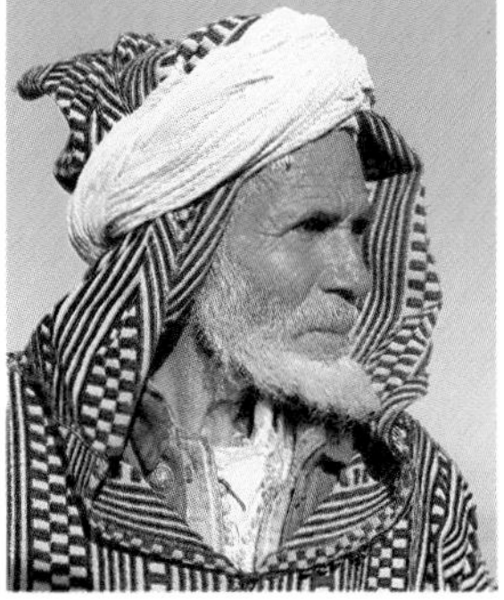

burnoose *Arabs, like this Berber tribesman from North Africa, wear hooded cloaks to keep out the sun, sand, and the chill of desert nights.*

bur oak *n.* A timber tree, *Quercus macrocarpa,* of eastern North America, having acorns enclosed within a deep, fringed cup.

bu·roo (bə-ro͞o′) *n., pl.* **-roos.** *Scottish & Irish Informal.* A social-security office. **—on the buroo.** Receiving unemployment benefits; on the dole. [From BUREAU.]

burp (bûrp) *n. Informal.* A belch.

~*v.* **burped, burping, burps.** *Informal.* —*intr.* To belch. —*tr.* To cause (a baby) to bring up wind after feeding. [Imitative.]

Bur·pee (bûr′pē). American family of horticulturalists and seedsmen, including **Washington Atlee** (1858–1915), founder of W. Atlee Burpee & Co., the world's largest mail-order seed company. His son **David** (1893–1980) headed the company after his father's death. The company's success was partially due to the family's constant experimentation, which produced many new strains of flowers and vegetables.

burp gun *n.* A portable, lightweight machine gun.

burr[1], bur (bûr) *n.* **1.** A rough edge or area remaining on metal or other material after it has been cast, cut, or drilled. **2.** Any rough protuberance; especially, a burl on a tree. **3.** A part in a surgical drill used for cutting into teeth or bone.

~*tr.v.* **burred, burring, burrs.** **1.** To form a rough edge on. **2.** To remove a rough edge or edges from. [Middle English *burre,* rough edge, BUR.]

burr[2], bur *n.* **1.** A rough trilling of the letter *r,* as in Scottish pro-

nunciation. **2.** Any similar pronunciation or speech sound. **3.** A buzzing or whirring sound.
~*v.* **burred, burring, burrs.** —*tr.* To pronounce with a burr. —*intr.* **1.** To speak with a burr. **2.** To make a buzzing or whirring sound. [Imitative, associated with BUR, from its roughness.] —**bur·ry** *adj.*

burr³, bur *n.* **1.** A washer that fits around the smaller end of a rivet. **2.** A blank punched from a sheet of metal. [Variant of obsolete *burrow*†.]

burr⁴. Variant of **bur.**

Burr (bûr), **Aaron** (1756-1836). U.S. vice president (1801-05), soldier, and adventurer. In a duel on July 11, 1804, he mortally wounded his lifelong rival, Alexander Hamilton. Burr fled and began scheming to found an independent country in Mexico and several Western states. He was tried for treason but acquitted for lack of evidence.

bur reed *n.* Any of various marsh plants of the genus *Sparganium*, having narrow leaves and round, prickly fruit.

bur·ri·to (boo-rē'tō, bə-) *n.* A flour tortilla wrapped around a filling, as beef, beans, or cheese. [American Spanish, from Spanish, little donkey, diminutive of *burro*, burro.]

bur·ro (bûr'ō, boor'ō) *n., pl.* **-ros.** A small donkey, especially one used as a pack animal. [Spanish, from *borrico*, donkey, from Late Latin *burricus*†, small horse.]

Bur·roughs (bûr'ōz), **Edgar Rice** (1875-1950). U.S. novelist. He wrote many science-fiction and jungle tales, but is most famous for creating the character of Tarzan in *Tarzan of the Apes* (1914).

Burroughs, William (1914–). U.S. novelist. He became a cult figure of the beat generation after the publication of *The Naked Lunch* (1959), with its kaleidoscopic treatment of the brutality of contemporary life.

bur·row (bûr'ō) *n.* **1.** A hole or tunnel dug in the ground by a small

burying beetle *This beetle is also called the sexton beetle because it buries carrion, digging away the soil from beneath dead birds and small mammals in order to lay its eggs near the carcass. It is common throughout temperate latitudes.*

animal, such as a rabbit or a mole, for habitation or refuge. **2.** Any similar narrow or snug place.
~*v.* **burrowed, -rowing, -rows.** —*intr.* **1.** To dig a burrow. **2.** To live or hide in a burrow. **3.** To move or progress through something as if by digging or tunneling. —*tr.* **1.** To make by or as if by tunneling or digging: *burrowed his way through the hedge; burrow a hole.* **2.** To dig a burrow in or through. **3.** To hide or seclude (oneself) in a burrow. [Middle English *borow*, probably a variant of BOROUGH.] —**bur·row·er** *n.*

burrowing owl *n.* A small, long-legged owl, *Speotyto cunicularia*, of American prairies, that nests in burrows dug by animals such as the prairie dog or rabbit.

burrstone. Variant of **buhrstone.**

bur·ry (bûr'ē) *adj.* **-rier, -riest. 1.** Like a bur; prickly. **2.** Full of or covered with burs.

bur·sa (bûr'sə) *n., pl.* **-sae** (-sē) or **-sas.** A saclike body cavity, especially one located between joints or at points of friction between moving structures. [New Latin, from Medieval Latin, bag, PURSE.]

Bur·sa (bûr'sə). Formerly **Bru·sa** (broo'sə). An industrial town and market center in northwest Turkey. It dates from the 3rd century B.C., when it was founded by Prusias I, king of Bithynia. Its baths have been famous since ancient times, and its importance as a silk-manufacturing center dates from the Middle Ages. It was the capital of the Ottoman Empire from 1326 to 1413.

bur·sal (bûr'səl) *adj.* **1.** *Anatomy.* Of or functioning as a bursa. **2.** *Archaic.* Pertaining to the public revenue; fiscal.

bur·sar (bûr'sər, -sär') *n.* **1.** A treasurer or similar official in charge of funds and accounting, as at a school, college, or university. **2.** A scholarship student at a Scottish university. [Sense 1, Medieval Latin *bursārius*, from *bursa*, PURSE; sense 2, French *boursier*, from *bourse*, purse, from Medieval Latin *bursa*.]

bur·sa·ry (bûr'sə-rē) *n., pl.* **-ries. 1.** A treasury, especially of a public institution or religious order. **2.** A scholarship, allowance, or award granted to a student at a school or university, especially at a Scottish university. [Medieval Latin *bursāria*, from *bursa*, purse.] —**bur·sar·i·al** *adj.*

burse (bûrs) *n.* **1.** *Ecclesiastical.* A flat cloth case for carrying the piece of linen, or corporal, that is used in celebrating the Eucharist. **2.** A foundation or fund for providing bursaries.

bur·seed (bûr'sēd) *n.* A plant, the **stickseed** (see).

bur·si·form (bûr'sə-fôrm') *adj. Anatomy.* Shaped like a pouch or sac. [Medieval Latin *bursa*, bag, purse + -FORM.]

bur·si·tis (bər-sī'tis) *n.* Inflammation of a bursa, especially of one of the shoulder, elbow, or knee joints. [New Latin : BURS(A) + -ITIS.]

burst (bûrst) *v.* **burst, bursting, bursts.** —*intr.* **1.** To come open or fly apart suddenly or violently, especially from internal pressure. **2.** To be full to the point of almost breaking open; swell: *a bag bursting with goodies.* **3.** To come forth, emerge, or arrive suddenly and in full force: *burst into the room; burst into flames.* **4.** To give sudden utterance or expression, especially to an emotion or feeling. Used with *into* or *out: burst into song; burst out laughing.* —*tr.* **1.** To cause or experience the rupture or bursting apart of: *burst a blood vessel.* **2.** To bring or force into a breached or opened state: *burst open the door.* **3.** *Computer Science.* To separate (a continuous roll of print-out) into individual sheets. —See Synonyms at **break.**
~*n.* **1.** A sudden breaking open or flying apart; an explosion. **2.** The result of bursting; a breach or rupture. **3.** A sudden, vehement outbreak or occurrence: *"blow with the strength of a hurricane in fitful bursts"* (Joseph Conrad). **4.** An abrupt, intense increase or spurt: *a burst of speed.* **5.** *Military.* **a.** The explosion of a projectile or bomb on impact or in the air. **b.** The number of bullets fired from an automatic weapon by one pull of the trigger. [Middle English *bersten*, Old English *berstan*, from Germanic.]

burst·er (bûr'stər) *n. Computer Science.* An offline device used to burst computer print-out.

burthen. *Archaic.* Variant of **burden.**

bur·ton (bûr'tn) *n. Nautical.* A light tackle having double or single blocks, used to hoist or tighten rigging. [Earlier *Breton (takles)*, *Brytton (takles)*, probably from BRETON.]

Bur·ton (bûr'tn), **Richard,** born Richard Jenkins (1925-84). Welsh-born actor. He was known as much for his tempetuous lifestyle, including his two marriages to actress Elizabeth Taylor, as for the variety of roles he played, ranging from Shakespeare to modern works such as *Who's Afraid of Virginia Woolf?* by Edward Albee.

Burton, Sir Richard Francis (1821-90). British explorer and orientalist. Disguised as a Pathan, he journeyed to the heart of Arabia. In 1858 he and John Hanning Speke (1827-64) became the first white men to explore the interior of Somaliland and to see Lake Tanganyika. His best-known work is his translation of *The Arabian Nights* (1885-1888).

Burton, Robert, pen name Democritus Junior (1577-1640). English clergyman and author. He was vicar of St. Thomas's at Oxford (1616-40). He is chiefly known for *The Anatomy of Melancholy*, a treatise on the causes, symptoms, and cure of melancholy that is a lively depiction of the everyday life of his time.

Bur·ton-up·on-Trent (bûr'tn-ə-pŏn-trĕnt'). Town in Staffordshire, west-central England, on the Trent River. It is a center for brewing, which was introduced by monks who founded a Benedictine abbey on the site in 1002.

Bu·run·di (boo-roon'dē). A republic in east-central Africa, between Rwanda and Tanzania on the northeastern extremity of Lake Tanganyika. The capital is Bujumbura, the only large town in the coun-

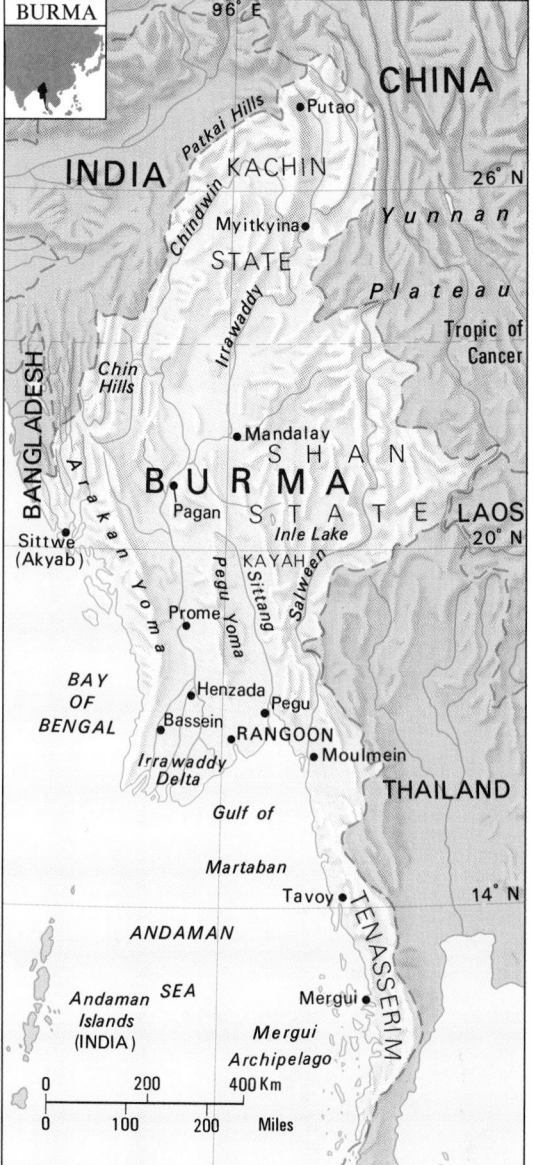

BURMA

96° E

CHINA

INDIA

KACHIN

Patkai Hills • Putao

26° N

Myitkyina•

STATE

Y u n n a n

Chindwin

Irrawaddy

P l a t e a u

Tropic of Cancer

BANGLADESH

Chin Hills

Arakan Yoma

•Mandalay

S H A N

B U R M A

STATE LAOS

Pagan

Inle Lake

20° N

KAYAH

Pegu Yoma

Sittang

Salween

Prome•

Sittwe• (Akyab)

BAY OF BENGAL

•Henzada

Bassein•

•Pegu

RANGOON

•Moulmein

Irrawaddy Delta

THAILAND

Gulf of Martaban

Tavoy•

14° N

T E N A S S E R I M

ANDAMAN

SEA

Andaman Islands (INDIA)

Mergui•

Mergui

Archipelago

0   200   400 Km

0   100   200 Miles

try. The western edge of the country is in the East African Rift Valley; the eastern parts are dominated by mountains. Burundi, one of the poorest nations in the world, exports coffee, but most of the people live by subsistence agriculture. It was part of Belgian-ruled Ruanda-Urundi until 1962, when it gained its independence (Ruanda becoming Rwanda and Urundi becoming Burundi). Following a military coup in 1966, Burundi became a republic. Area, 27,834 square kilometers (10,747 square miles). Population, 4,000,000. See map at **Tanzania.**

bur·weed (bûr′wēd) *n.* Any of various plants that bear burs, such as the burdock.

bur·y (bĕr′ē) *tr.v.* **-ied, -ying, -ies. 1.** To place in the ground; conceal by covering over with earth. **2.** To place (a dead body) in a grave, a tomb, or in the sea; inter. **3.** To cover from view; hide: *buried her head in her hands.* **4.** To embed; immerse or sink. **5.** To occupy (oneself) with deep concentration. **6.** To put an end to; forget; abandon. **—See Synonyms at hide.** [Middle English *berien, burien,* Old English *byrgan,* from Germanic.] **—bur·i·er** *n.*

Bur·y (bĕr′ē). A town in the metropolitan county of Greater Manchester, in northern England. It was the site of a Saxon settlement and, since the introduction of wool weaving by Flemish immigrants in the mid-14th century, has been a textile center.

Bur·yat Autonomous Soviet Socialist Republic (bŏŏr-yät′, bŏŏr′-ē-ät). A constituent republic of the Soviet Union, lying north of Mongolia between Lake Baikal and the Yablonovy Mts. It is largely mountainous, with dense forests and many rivers and lakes rich in fish. Timber and mining are the main economic activities.

burying beetle *n.* Any of various black or black and orange beetles of the genus *Necrophorus,* that bury dead mice and other small animals, on which they feed and lay their eggs. Also called "sexton beetle."

Bury St. Ed·munds (sənt ĕd′mŭndz, sänt). Town in Suffolk, east-central England. It is the market and processing center for a rich agricultural region. In 903 the remains of St. Edmund, the martyred Saxon king, were interred here in a monastery, founded *c.* 630, that later became a famous shrine and Benedictine abbey.

bus (bŭs) *n., pl.* **buses** or **busses. 1.** A long motor vehicle, sometimes with two decks, used as a means of public transport, usually along a fixed route. Also called "omnibus." **2.** *Informal.* A large car or airplane. **3.** A four-wheeled cart for carrying dishes in a restaurant. **4.** *Electricity.* A **bus bar** (see). **—miss the bus.** To miss an opportunity; arrive too late. **~v. bused** or **bussed, busing** or **bussing, buses** or **busses. —tr.** To transport in a bus, especially to schools in different areas in order to encourage racial integration. **—intr. 1.** To travel in a bus. **2.** To work as a bus boy or bus girl. [Short for OMNIBUS.]

Usage: **Bus** is now well established as a transitive verb. It has the general meaning of "to transport (passengers)" and the specialized meaning of "to transport (schoolchildren) to achieve racial integration."

bus. business.

bus bar *n.* **1.** A conducting bar that carries heavy currents to supply several electric circuits. **2.** A conducting bar in a computer used to carry data from one part to another. Also called "bus."

bus boy *n.* A restaurant employee who clears away dirty dishes and serves as a waiter's assistant.

bus·by (bŭz′bē) *n., pl.* **-bies.** A tall, fur hat with a plume and a bag hanging at one side worn in certain regiments of the British Army, especially the hussars. [18th century : origin obscure.]

bus girl *n.* A girl or woman restaurant employee who clears away dirty dishes and serves as a waiter's assistant.

bush¹ (bŏŏsh) *n.* **1.** Any low, branching, woody plant, usually smaller than a tree; a shrub. **2.** A thick growth of shrubs; a thicket. **3. a.** Land covered with a dense growth of shrubs. **b.** Land remote from settled or cultivated areas, especially in Australia, New Zealand, Canada, or Africa. Usually preceded by *the.* **4.** A fox's tail. **5. a.** A clump of ivy formerly used as the sign of a tavern. **b.** *Obsolete.* A tavern. **—beat around** (or **about) the bush.** To delay in getting to the point. **~v. bushed, bushing, bushes. —intr. 1.** To grow or branch out like a shrub or bush. **2.** To extend in a bushy growth. **—tr.** To decorate, protect, or support with shrubs or bushes. [Middle English *busshe,* Old English *bysc* (unattested); akin to Old Norse *buski,* Old French *bosc,* all of Germanic origin.]

bush² *tr.v.* **bushed, bushing, bushes.** To furnish or line with a bush. [From Middle Dutch *busse,* bush of a wheel, wheel box, from Late Latin *buxis,* BOX.]

bush baby *n.* Any of several small nocturnal primates of the genera *Galago* and *Euoticus,* having dense, woolly fur, large, round eyes, prominent ears, and a long tail. Also often called "galago."

bush Baptist *n.* *Australian Informal.* A person who has strong religious beliefs but who does not belong to any particular sect.

bush bean *n.* A shrubby plant, *Phaseolus vulgaris humilis,* a variety of the string bean.

bush·buck (bŏŏsh′bŭk′) *n.* An African antelope, *Tragelaphus scriptus,* having a reddish-brown coat with white markings and twisted horns. Also called "harnessed antelope." [Translation of Afrikaans *bosbok.*]

bush clover *n.* Any of various plants or shrubs of the genus *Lespedeza,* having compound leaves with three leaflets and clusters of purple or yellowish flowers.

bush·craft (bŏŏsh′krăft′, -kräft′) *n.* *Australian.* Experience or knowledge of life or survival in the bush.

bush cricket *n.* A grasshopper of the family Tettigoniidae having long, threadlike antennae and tarsi feet divided into four segments.

bushed (bŏŏsht) *adj.* **1.** *Informal.* Extremely tired; exhausted. **2.** *Chiefly Australian & Canadian.* Lost or confused. [Probably from BUSH (wilderness).]

bush·el¹ (bŏŏsh′əl) *n.* *Abbr.* **bu, bu., bsh. 1. a.** A unit of volume or capacity in the U.S. Customary System, used in dry measure and equal to 4 pecks or 2,150.42 cubic inches. **b.** A unit of volume or capacity in the British Imperial System, used in dry and liquid measure, and equal to 2,219.36 cubic inches. **2.** A container with the capacity of this unit. **3.** *Informal.* A large amount; a great deal. [Middle English *busshel, boyschel,* from Old French *boissiel,* from *boisse,* one sixth of a bushel, from Gaulish *bostia†* (unattested), handful.]

bush·el² *tr.v.* **-eled** or **-elled, -eling** or **-elling, -els.** To alter or mend (clothing). [German *bosseln,* to mend, do small jobs, probably from Middle High German *bōzeln,* to knock, tap repeatedly, from *bōzen,* to knock, shove, from Old High German *bōzan.*]

bush fly *n.* Any of the small and irritating flies that swarm about humans and animals in the bush.

bush hammer *n.* A hammer used for dressing stone, having a flat face with small pyramidal projections.

bush honeysuckle *n.* Any of several North American shrubs of the genus *Diervilla,* having yellow flowers that turn reddish.

bush-house (bŏŏsh′hous′) *n.* *Chiefly Australian.* **1.** A house or hut in the bush. **2.** A shed or hut in a garden.

Bu·shi·do, bu·shi·do (bŏŏ′shē-dō′) *n.* The traditional code of the Japanese samurai, stressing self-discipline, bravery, and simple living. [Japanese *bushidō,* "the way of the warrior."]

bush·ie, bush·y (bŏŏsh′ē) *n., pl.* **-ies.** *Australian & New Zealand.* A person who lives in the bush, especially a person who is unsophisticated and ignorant of city life.

bush·ing (bŏŏsh′ĭng) *n.* **1.** A fixed or removable metal lining used to constrain, guide, or reduce friction. **2.** An insulating lining for an aperture through which a wire or other conductor passes. **3.** An adapter threaded to permit joining of pipes with different diameters. [From earlier *bush,* (metal lining).]

bush jacket *n.* A light, belted jacket with four patch pockets.

bush·law·yer (bŏŏsh′loi′ər) *n.* *Australian & New Zealand.* **1.** A layman who pretends or claims to have knowledge of the law. **2.** Loosely, an argumentative person.

bush league *n.* *Baseball Slang.* A minor league.

bush-league (bŏŏsh′lēg′) *adj.* *Slang.* **1.** *Baseball.* Of or belonging to a minor league **2.** Second-rate. **—bush-lea·guer** *n.*

Bush·man (bŏŏsh′mən) *n., pl.* **-men** (-mĭn). **1.** A member of a nomadic Negroid people of southwestern Africa, characteristically of short stature. **2.** Any of several Khoisan languages spoken by this people. **3. bushman.** *Chiefly Australian.* A person who lives in or knows the ways of life in the bush. [Translation of Afrikaans *boschjesman.*]

bush·mas·ter (bŏŏsh′măs′tər, -mäs′tər) *n.* A large, venomous snake, *Lachesis muta,* of tropical America, having brown and grayish markings.

Bush·nell (bŏŏsh′nəl), **David,** known as "father of the submarine" (1742–1824). U.S. inventor. In 1775 he designed a man-propelled submarine for use against British ships in the Revolution. A foot-operated valve in the keel let in water for submerging; two hand-operated pumps removed the water for ascending. The device proved ineffectual against the enemy and was ridiculed as "Bushnell's Turtle."

bush oyster *n.* *Australian Informal.* A testicle, usually of a sheep, that is cooked and eaten.

bush pig *n.* A wild pig, *Potamochoerus porcus,* of southern Africa, having long tufts of hair on the face and ears. [Translation of Afrikaans *bosvark.*]

bush pilot *n.* A pilot who flies a small airplane to and from areas inaccessible to larger aircraft or other means of transportation.

bush poppy *n.* The **tree poppy** (see).

bush·rang·er (bŏŏsh′rān′jər) *n.* **1.** A backwoodsman **2.** *Australian.* An outlaw living in the bush.

bush-sick (bŏŏsh′sĭk′) *adj.* *Chiefly Australian.* Of or designating livestock that are rapidly losing energy and weight due to mineral deficiencies in the soil. **—bush-sick·ness** *n.*

bush telegraph *n.* **1.** Word of mouth as a means by which rumors or gossip is rapidly spread. Also called "bush wire." **2.** Formerly, a means of disseminating information, especially amongst primitive tribes, as by beating drums.

bush-tit (bŏŏsh′tĭt′) *n.* Either of two small, long-tailed songbirds, *Psaltriparus minimus* or *P. melanotis,* of western North America, having predominantly gray plumage.

bush·veldt, bush·veld (bŏŏsh′fĕlt′, -vĕlt′) *n.* In South Africa, open country or veld whose flora consists predominantly of scrub or thorny bush.

bush week *n.* *Australian Informal.* **1.** A fictitious week during which bush dwellers come to town. **2.** A set of circumstances in which a person is easily duped: *What do you think this is—bush week?*

bush·whack (bŏŏsh′hwăk′) *v.* **-whacked, -whacking, -whacks. —intr. 1.** To make one's way through thick woods by cutting away bushes and branches. **2.** To travel through the woods, as in scouting. **3.** To fight as a guerrilla in the back country or bush. **—tr.** To attack suddenly from a place of concealment; ambush. [Back-formation from BUSHWHACKER.]

bush baby *Often called galagos, bush babies are small nocturnal primates of the African woodlands. They are tree-dwelling creatures and are able to make huge leaps from branch to branch.*

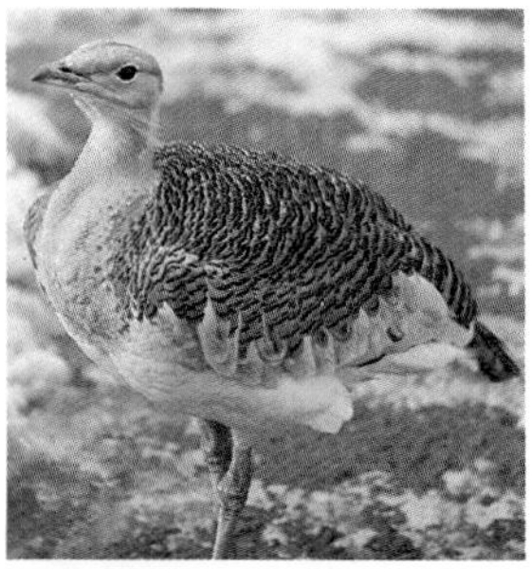

bustard *The great bustard is the largest European land bird. It lives on open steppes and plains and can weigh as much as 14 kilograms (31 pounds), with a wingspan of up to 2.25 meters (7½ feet).*

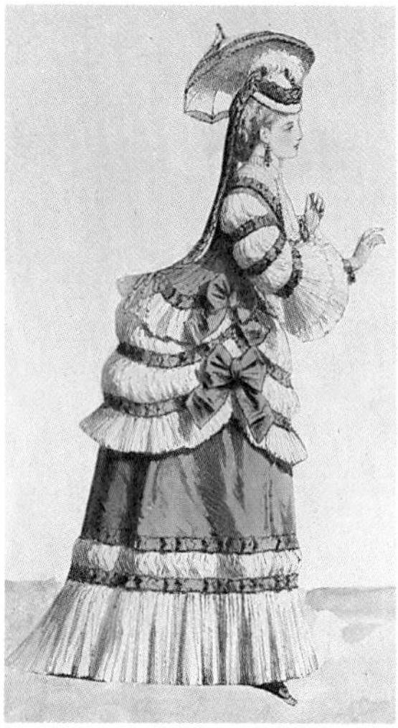

bustle *Material used to push out a skirt from the back of the waist. Bustles, which first became fashionable in the 14th century, were fashioned from foxes' tails, kitchen dusters, down cushions, and wire cages. This one dates from the mid-19th century.*

bush·whacked (bo͝osh′hwăkt′) *adj. Austrialian.* Bushed.
bush·whack·er (bo͝osh′hwăk′ər) *n.* **1.** One that bushwhacks. **2.** A woodsman. **3.** A guerrilla, especially a Confederate in the American Civil War. [BUSH + *whacker,* one who whacks, from WHACK.]
bush·y (bo͝osh′ē) *adj.* **-ier, -iest. 1.** Overgrown or thick with bushes. **2.** Shaggy and thick. **3.** Variant of **bushie.** **—bush·i·ly** *adv.* **—bush·i·ness** *n.*
bus·i·ly (bĭz′ə-lē) *adv.* In a busy manner.
busi·ness (bĭz′nĭs) *n. Abbr.* **bus. 1.** The occupation, work, or trade in which a person is engaged. **2.** Commercial, industrial, or professional dealings; the buying and selling of goods or services. **3.** Any commercial establishment, such as a store or factory. **4.** Volume or amount of commercial trade: *We're doing very good business.* **5.** Commercial policy or practice. **6.** One's rightful or proper concern or interest; responsibility: *Mind your own business.* **7.** Serious work or endeavor, especially pertaining to one's job: *went to Tokyo on business.* **8.** An affair or matter: *tired of this silly business.* **9.** Incidental actions performed by an actor on the stage to fill a pause between lines or to provide dramatic effect. Also called "stage business." **—get down to business.** To begin in earnest. **—mean business.** To be in dead earnest. [Middle English *bissinesse,* diligence, state of being busy, Old English *bisig,* BUSY.]
Usage: *business, industry, commerce, trade, traffic.* These nouns apply to forms of activity that have the objective of supplying commodities. *Business* pertains broadly to all gainful activity, though it usually excludes the professions and farming. *Industry* is the production and manufacture of goods and commodities, especially on a large scale, and *commerce* and *trade,* the exchange and distribution of commodities. Often *commerce* is applied to exchange of commodities for money, as within a country, while *trade* refers to exchange of commodities for commodities, as between countries. *Traffic* may suggest illegal trade, as in narcotics.
business administration *n.* A college or university course of studies that offers instruction in business principles and practices.
business card *n.* A small card that conveys information about a business or a business representative.
business end *n. Informal.* The end of something, such as a gun, knife, or the like, that actually performs the function for which the whole instrument has been designed.
business hours *pl.n.* The hours of the day during which a business, such as a store, bank, or the like, conducts business.
busi·ness·like (bĭz′nĭs-līk′) *adj.* **1.** Methodical; systematic; efficient. **2.** Purposeful; earnest.
busi·ness·man (bĭz′nĭs-măn′) *n., pl.* **-men** (-mĕn′). A man engaged in business, especially at an executive level.
business person *n.* A person engaged in business.
busi·ness·wom·an (bĭz′nĭs-wo͝om′ən) *n., pl.* **-women** (-wĭm′ĭn). A woman engaged in business, especially at an executive level.
bus·ing, bus·sing (bŭs′ĭng) *n.* The transportation of children by bus to schools outside their neighborhoods, especially as a means of achieving racial integration.
busk[1] (bŭsk) *n.* **1.** A thin, flexible strip of wood, whalebone, plastic, or metal sewn in a woman's undergarment as stiffening. **2.** *Regional.* A corset. [French *busc,* from Italian *busco,* splinter, from Germanic.]
busk[2] *intr.v.* **busked, busking, busks.** *British.* To entertain by singing, playing music, or dancing, especially in streets and public places, in return for money. [Perhaps from obsolete French *busquer,* to look for, seek.] **—busk·er** *n.*
busk[3] *tr.v.* **busked, busking, busks.** *Chiefly Scottish.* To make ready; prepare. [Middle English *busken,* from Old Norse *būask,* reflexive of *būa,* to prepare.]
bus·kin (bŭs′kĭn) *n.* **1.** A foot and leg covering reaching halfway to the knee, resembling a laced half-boot. **2.** A thick-soled laced half boot, worn by actors of tragedies in ancient Greece. Compare **sock. 3.** *Formal & Poetic.* Tragedy. Usually preceded by *the.* [Old French *bouzequin, brousequin,* akin to Spanish *borzeguí,* Italian *borzacchino*†.]
bus·man (bŭs′mən) *n., pl.* **-men** (-mĭn). One who operates a bus.
bus·man's holiday (bŭs′mənz) *n. Informal.* A holiday on which a person engages in recreation similar to his usual work. [A bus driver might go for a drive on a holiday.]
Bu·so·ni (bo͞o-zō′nē), **Gerruccio Benvenuto** (1866–1924). Italian composer, conductor, and pianist. He achieved great fame as a pianist in the flamboyant manner of Liszt and was a prolific composer, though few of his works are played today.
buss (bŭs) *v.* **bussed, bussing, busses.** *Regional.* —*tr.* To kiss with a loud smacking sound. —*intr.* To kiss loudly.
∼*n. Regional.* A smacking kiss. [From earlier *bass;* akin to French *baiser,* Latin *basiare.*]
bus·ses. 1. Alternate plural of **bus. 2.** Alternate third person singular of **bus.**
bus shelter *n.* A structure at a bus stop designed to protect waiting passengers from wind and rain.
bus·stop (bŭs′stŏp′) *n.* A place on a bus route, usually marked, where passengers alight from or board buses.
bust[1] (bŭst) *n.* **1. a.** A woman's bosom. **b.** *Archaic.* The human chest. **2.** A piece of sculpture representing a person's head, shoulders, and upper chest. [French *buste,* from Italian *busto,* piece of sculpture, origin obscure.]
bust[2] *v.* **busted** or **bust, busting, busts.** *Informal.* —*tr.* **1.** To burst or break. **2.** To break up (a trust or monopoly). **3.** To break or tame (a horse) **4.** To cause to become bankrupt or short of money. **5.** To reduce the rank of; demote. **6.** To hit or punch. **7.** To place under arrest. —*intr.* **1.** To burst or break. **2.** To become bankrupt or short of money.
∼*n.* **1.** A failure; a flop. **2.** A state of bankruptcy. **3.** A time or period of widespread financial depression. Compare **boom. 4.** A punch or blow. **5.** A spree. **6.** An arrest. [Variant of BURST.]
Bus·ta·man·te (bo͞os′tə-män′tē), **Sir William Alexander** (1884-1977). Jamaican politician, the first prime minister of independent Jamaica (1962–67). As a trade union leader he led the campaign for Jamaican independence and formed the Jamaica Labour Party (1943).
bus·tard (bŭs′tərd) *n.* Any of various large terrestrial Old World birds of the family Otididae, frequenting open, grassy regions. Bustards have long, strong legs, a stout body, and brown, mottled plumage. [Middle English *bustarde,* possibly from Norman French *bustarde* (unattested), blend of Old French *bistarde* and *oustarde,* both perhaps from Latin *avis tarda,* "slow bird" : *avis,* bird + *tarda,* feminine of *tardus,* slow (see **tardy**).]
bus·tee, bus·ti (bŭs′tē) *n.* A slum or shantytown in India.
bust·er (bŭs′tər) *n. Slang.* **1.** One who destroys or breaks up: *a crimebuster.* **2.** One who breaks horses; a broncobuster. **3.** Something especially large or remarkable. **4.** A spree. **5.** *Often* **Buster.** A man or boy. Used in direct address.
bus·tle[1] (bŭs′əl) *v.* **-tled, -tling, -tles.** —*intr.* To hurry energetically and busily. —*tr.* To cause to hurry.
∼*n.* Excited activity; commotion; stir. [Probably a variant of obsolete *buskle,* frequentative of dialectal *busk,* to prepare, from Middle English *busken,* from Old Norse *buāsk* : *būa,* to prepare + *-sk,* reflexive ending.]
bustle[2] *n.* **1.** A frame or pad worn, especially in the 19th and early 20th centuries, to support and extend the rear of a woman's skirt. **2.** A bow, peplum, or gathering of material at the back of a skirt below the waist. [Perhaps from German *Buschel*†, a bunch, pad.]
bust·y (bŭs′tē) *adj.* **-ier, -iest.** *Informal.* Full-bosomed.
bu·sul·fan (byo͞o-sŭl′fən) *n.* A drug, $C_6H_{14}O_6S_2$, that destroys cancer cells and is used mainly to treat certain forms of leukemia. [Blend of BUTANE and SULFONYL.]
bus·y (bĭz′ē) *adj.* **-ier, -iest. 1.** Actively engaged in some form of work; occupied. **2.** Crowded with activity: *a busy morning.* **3.** Meddlesome; prying. **4.** Temporarily in use. Said of a telephone line. **5.** Cluttered with minute and distracting detail: *a busy design.*
∼*tr.v.* **busied, -ying, -ies.** To make busy; occupy. Often used reflexively. [Middle English *bisy, busy,* Old English *bysig, bisig,* akin to Middle Low German *besich*†.] **—bus·y·ness** *n.*
Usage: *busy, industrious, diligent, assiduous, sedulous.* All these words suggest active or sustained effort to accomplish something. *Busy* primarily applies to one engaged in present activity, without definite implication of kind, continuity, or duration of activity. *Industrious* implies continuing activity and a natural inclination to be so engaged. *Diligent* suggests intense activity in the accomplishment of a specific goal; often it implies keen interest in work of one's choosing. *Assiduous* emphasizes sustained devotion to work. *Sedulous* adds to assiduity the sense of earnest, persistent, painstaking labor.
bus·y·bod·y (bĭz′ē-bŏd′ē) *n., pl.* **-ies.** A person who meddles or pries into the affairs of others.
busy Liz·zie (lĭz′ē) *n.* A fast-growing hybrid plant of the genus *Impatiens,* having red, pink, white, or orange flowers, widely cultivated as a house plant.
busy signal *n.* A series of sharp buzzing tones heard over the telephone when the number dialed is in use.
bus·y·work (bĭz′ē-wûrk′) *n.* Activity that takes up time but does not necessarily yield productive results.
but (bŭt, *unstressed* bət) *conj.* **1.** On the contrary. **2.** Contrary to expectation; however; yet. **3.** Except; save. —See Usage note below. **4.** With the exception that; except that. Used to introduce a dependent clause with *that* expressed: *They should have resisted but that they lacked courage.* **5.** Without the result that: *It never rains but it pours.* **6.** Other than: *I have no choice but to leave.* **7.** That. Often used after a negative: *There's no doubt but he'll win.* **8.** That . . . not. Used after a negative or question: *There never is a change made but someone complains.* **9.** Who . . . not; which . . . not: *None came to him but were treated well.* **10.** *Archaic.* Unless; if not: *"Beshrew me but I love her heartily"* (Shakespeare). **11.** *Archaic & Nonstandard.* Than: *"No sooner acquainted my brother, but he immediately wanted to propose it"* (Henry Fielding).
∼*prep.* With the exception of; barring; save: *none but the brave.* **—but for.** Were it not for: *But for luck, he would still be poor.*
∼*adv.* **1.** No more than; just: *but a month to live.* **2.** Only; simply: *If I had but known.* **3.** *Informal.* Really: *rich, but rich!* **—all but.** Nearly; almost: *His poem is all but finished.*
∼*n.* An objection, restriction, or exception: *no ifs, ands, or buts.* [Middle English *bute, but* (conjunction and adverb), Old English *būtan, būte* (conjunction and preposition).]
Usage: *But* is used to mean "except" in sentences like *No one but John can read it.* Some traditionalists have suggested that *but* is a conjunction in this use and so should be followed by nominative pronouns like *I* and *he* when the phrase in which it occurs is the subject of the sentence. But this use of *but* is perhaps better thought of as a preposition, since the verb always agrees with the subject preceding *but;* we say *no one but the boys has left* (not *have left*), and traditionalists themselves do not say *everyone but I am leaving,* which is clearly ungrammatical. Accordingly, this use of *but* should

properly be accompanied by pronouns in the objective case, like *me* and *him*: *Everyone but me has received an answer.* *But* is redundant when used in combination with *however,* as in *But the army, however, went on with its own plans* (eliminate either *but* or *however*). *But* is often used in informal speech together with a negative in sentences like *It won't take but an hour.* The construction should be avoided in formal style; write *It won't take an hour. But what* is informal in sentences like *I don't know but what we'll get there before the boys do.* In writing, substitute *whether* or *that* for *but. But* is also informal when used in place of *than* in sentences like *It no sooner started but it stopped* (in writing, use *than*). *But* is usually not followed by a comma. Write *Kim wanted to go, but we didn't want to,* not *Kim wanted to go, but, we didn't want to,* which is incorrect. *But* can be used to begin a sentence, even in formal style. But it should not be followed by a comma here either. See also Usage notes at **doubt** and **than.**

but– *prefix.* Indicates a chemical compound containing four carbon atoms; for example, **butane.** [From BUTYRIC.]

bu·ta·di·ene (byo͞o'tə-dī'ēn', -dī-ēn') *n.* A colorless, highly flammable gaseous hydrocarbon, C_4H_6, obtained from petroleum and used in the manufacture of synthetic rubber. [BUTA(NE) + DI- + -ENE.]

bu·tane (byo͞o'tān') *n.* Either of two isomers of a gaseous hydrocarbon, C_4H_{10}, produced synthetically from petroleum and used as a household fuel, refrigerant, and aerosol propellant, and in the manufacture of synthetic rubber.

bu·ta·no·ic acid (byo͞o'tə-nō'ĭk) *n.* **Butyric acid** *(see).*

bu·ta·nol (byo͞o'tə-nôl', -nōl') *n.* **1.** An alcohol, C_4H_9OH, derived naturally from the bacterial fermentation of grain and used as a solvent for resins, in plasticizers, hydraulic fluids, and as a dehydrating agent. **2.** An isomeric alcohol derived from the cracking of petroleum or natural gas and used as a solvent in varnishes, lacquers, and paint removers.

bu·ta·none (byo͞o'tə-nōn') *n.* A colorless, flammable ketone, C_4H_8O, used in lacquers, paint removers, cements and adhesives, celluloid, and cleaning fluids. Also called "methyl ethyl ketone."

butch (bo͝och) *n. Slang.* A woman who is masculine in appearance or manner; sometimes used of a lesbian assuming a pseudo-masculine role.
~*adj. Informal.* **1.** Sturdily masculine in appearance. **2.** Assuming exaggeratedly masculine ways or appearance. Said of both male and female homosexuals. [From a boy's nickname, *Butch,* perhaps ultimately from BUTCHER.]

butch·er (bo͝och'ər) *n.* **1.** One who slaughters and prepares animals for food or market. **2.** One who sells meat. **3.** One guilty of cruel or pointless killing. **4.** A vender of candy, magazines, and the like on a train. **5.** One who performs a task very unskillfully.
~*tr.v.* **butchered, -ering, -ers. 1.** To slaughter or dress (animals) for market. **2.** To kill cruelly or pointlessly. **3.** To spoil by botching; bungle. [Middle English *bo(u)cher,* from Norman French, from Old French *bouchier,* from *boc,* he-goat.] **—butch·er·er** *n.*

butch·er·bird (bo͝och'ər-bûrd') *n.* Any of various birds that impale their prey on thorns; especially, a **shrike** *(see).*

butcher knife *n.* A heavy-duty knife about 8 inches long with a broad blade.

butch·ers¹ (bo͝och'ərz) *n. British Slang.* A look; a glance. [Short for *butcher's hook,* rhyming slang for *look.*]

butchers² *adj.* Also **butcher's hook.** *Australian Informal.* Unwell; crook. **—go butcher's (or hook) at.** To become angry with.

butcher's broom *n.* A shrub, *Ruscus aculeatus,* native to Europe, having stiff, prickle-tipped, flattened stems resembling true leaves. [Formerly used as a broom by butchers.]

butch·er·y (bo͝och'ə-rē) *n., pl.* **-ies. 1.** The trade of a butcher. **2.** A slaughterhouse. **3.** *South African.* A butcher's shop, where meat is sold. **4.** Wanton or cruel killing; carnage.

Bute (byo͞ot). Also **Bute·shire** (byo͞ot'shîr, -shər). Former county of Scotland, absorbed in 1975 into Strathclyde.

Bute, John Stuart, 3rd Earl of (1713–92). British politician. From 1751 he was tutor to the heir to the throne, later George III. In 1761 he was appointed secretary of state and helped bring about the defeat of the elder Pitt (1762). Bute succeeded Pitt as chief minister of the crown and worked to conclude peace with France (1763).

Bu·te·nandt (bo͞o'tə-nänt'), **Adolf Friedrich** (1903–). German chemist. Known especially for his work on sex hormones, he declined his share of the 1939 Nobel Prize for chemistry, following a Nazi edict prohibiting acceptance.

bu·te·o (byo͞o'tē-ō') *n., pl.* **-os.** Any of various hawks of the genus *Buteo,* characterized by broad wings and broad, rounded tails. [New Latin, genus name, from Latin *buteo,* a kind of hawk or falcon.]

Bu·the·le·zi (bo͞o'tə-lā'zē) **(Mangosuthu) Gatsha** (1928–). Chief Minister of KwaZulu—one of the national states created as homelands for South Africa's blacks—and a prominent spokesman on South African racial and political affairs.

but·ler (bŭt'lər) *n.* A male head servant in a household, in charge of the table and the wine cellar. [Middle English *buteler,* servant in charge of the wine cellar, from Old French *bouteillier,* a bottle bearer, from *bouteille, botele,* BOTTLE.]

But·ler (bŭt'lər), **Nicholas Murray** (1862–1947). U.S. educator. Widely known for his theories on education and the training of teachers, he helped organize the School of Education at Columbia University. Butler worked widely for international peace and shared the Nobel Peace Prize (1931) with Jane Addams.

Butler, Samuel¹ (1612–80). English satirical poet. His reputation rests on one long poem, *Hudibras* (1663–78), a mock-heroic satire on the Puritans.

Butler, Samuel² (1835–1902). British novelist. He first gained literary notice with his novel, *Erewhon* (1872), a trenchant satire on English life and laws. Perhaps his greatest achievement was the semiautobiographical novel *The Way of All Flesh* (1903).

butler's pantry *n.* A serving and storage room between the kitchen and the dining room.

butt¹ (bŭt) *v.* **butted, butting, butts.** *—tr.* To hit or push against with the head or horns; ram. *—intr.* **1.** To hit or push something with the head or horns. **2.** To project forward or out. **—butt in.** *Informal.* To interfere or meddle; intrude.
~*n.* A push or blow with the head or horns. [Middle English *butten,* from Norman French *buter, boter,* from Germanic.]

butt² *v.* **butted, butting, butts.** *—tr.* To attach the ends of; abut. ~*intr.* To be joined at the ends.
~*n.* **1. a.** The act of joining two objects end to end. **b.** A **butt joint** *(see).* **2.** A **butt hinge** *(see).* [From BUTT (end).]

butt³ *n.* **1.** A person or thing serving as an object of ridicule or contempt. **2.** A target. **3. butts.** A target range. **4.** A mound of earth, a wall, or another obstacle behind a target for stopping the shot. **5.** *Obsolete.* A limit; goal. [Middle English *butte,* target, from Old French *but*†.]

butt⁴ *n.* **1.** The larger or thicker end of something: *the butt of a rifle.* **2.** An unburned end, as of a cigarette. **3.** A short or broken remnant; a stub. **4.** *Slang.* A cigarette. **5.** *Informal.* The buttocks; the rear end. [Middle English *but, butte,* thicker end, from Germanic.]

butt⁵ *n.* **1.** A large cask. **2.** A unit of volume equal to 126 U.S. gallons. [Middle English, from Norman French *but,* variant of Old French *bot, bout,* from Late Latin *buttis.* See **bottle.**]

butte (byo͞ot) *n.* A hill rising abruptly above the surrounding area and having sloping sides and a flat top. [French, from Old French *but,* BUTT (mound behind targets).]

Butte (byo͞ot). A city in southwestern Montana. Butte was established as a gold-mining camp (1862), then became a silver center, and gained importance when copper was discovered (*c.* 1880). The city has a mining museum and offers tours of nearby mines.

but·ter¹ (bŭt'ər) *n.* **1.** A soft, yellowish or whitish emulsion of butterfat, water, air, and sometimes salt, churned from milk or cream and processed for use in cooking and as a food. **2.** Any of various similar substances, especially: **a.** A spread made from fruit, nuts, or other foods, as *apple butter.* **b.** A vegetable fat having a nearly solid consistency at ordinary temperatures, as **cocoa butter** *(see).* **3.** *Informal.* Flattery.
~*tr.v.* **buttered, -tering, -ters. 1.** To put butter on or in. **2.** *Informal.* To flatter. Usually used with *up.* [Middle English *buter(e),* Old English *butere,* from West Germanic, from Latin *būtȳrum,* from Greek *bouturon,* "cow cheese" : *bous,* cow + *turos,* cheese.]

butt·er² (bŭt'ər) *n.* One that butts with the head or horns.

but·ter-and-eggs (bŭt'ər-ən-ĕgz') *n. Used with a singular or plural verb.* A North American plant, *Linaria vulgaris,* having numerous narrow leaves and a spike of spurred pale-yellow and orange flowers. Also called "toadflax."

but·ter·ball (bŭt'ər-bôl') *n.* **1.** A ball of butter. **2.** *Informal.* A fat or chubby person. **3.** A duck, the **bufflehead** *(see).*

butter bean *n.* **1.** The **wax bean** *(see).* **2.** *Regional.* The **lima bean** *(see).* [From the yellow pods of the wax bean.]

but·ter·bur (bŭt'ər-bûr') *n.* Any of several plants of the genus *Petasites,* having woolly leaves and fragrant whitish or purple flowers. [Its leaves are said to have been used to wrap butter.]

but·ter·cup (bŭ'tər-kŭp') *n.* Any of various plants of the genus *Ranunculus,* characteristically having glossy yellow flowers, especially the meadow buttercup, *R. acris,* native to Europe, but widely introduced elsewhere.

but·ter·fat (bŭt'ər-făt') *n.* The oily content of milk from which butter is made, consisting largely of the glycerides of oleic, stearic, and palmitic acids.

but·ter·fin·gers (bŭt'ər-fĭng'gərz) *n. Plural in form, used with a singular verb.* A clumsy or awkward person who drops things. **—but·ter·fin·gered** *adj.*

but·ter·fish (bŭt'ər-fĭsh') *n., pl.* **-fishes** or collectively **butterfish. 1.** A marine food fish, *Poronotus triacanthus,* of the North American Atlantic coast, having a flattened body. **2.** Any of various similar or related fishes. [From its slippery mucous coating.]

but·ter·fly (bŭt'ər-flī') *n., pl.* **-flies. 1.** Any of various diurnal insects of the order Lepidoptera, characteristically having slender bodies, knobbed antennae, and four broad, usually colorful wings that are closed over the back at rest. **2.** A frivolous pleasure-seeker: *a social butterfly.* **3.** The **butterfly stroke** *(see).* **4. butterflies.** *Informal.* Nervous tremors in the stomach. [Middle English *butterflie,* from Old English *buttorflēoge* : *buter(e),* BUTTER + FLY, perhaps from the belief that butterflies steal butter.] See feature, next page.

butterfly bird *n.* A bird, the **wall creeper** *(see).*

butterfly bush *n.* Any of several shrubs of the genus *Buddleia,* cultivated for their clusters of purplish or white flowers. Also called "buddleia."

butterfly fish *n.* Any of various tropical marine fishes of the family Chaetodontidae, having brightly colored flattened bodies.

butterfly nut *n.* A **wing nut** *(see).*

butterfly pea *n.* A twining vine, *Clitoria mariana,* of the eastern United States, having compound leaves and pale-blue flowers.

butterfly stroke *n.* A swimming stroke, a variation of the breast stroke, in which both arms are drawn upward out of the water and

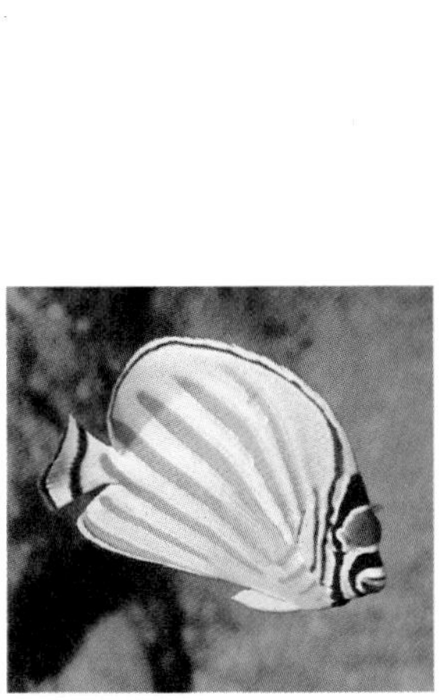

butterfly fish *These small tropical fish have deep, flattened bodies, a single dorsal fin, and a small mouth with brushlike teeth.*

PRONUNCIATION KEY

ă, pat; ā, pay; âr, care; ä, father, are; b, bib; ch, church; d, deed; ĕ, pet; ē, be; f, fife; g, gag; h, hat; hw, which; ĭ, pit; ī, pie; îr, pier; j, judge; k, kick; l, lid, needle; m, mum; n, no, sudden; ng, thing; ŏ, pot; ō, toe; ô, paw, for; oi, noise; ou, out; o͝o, book; o͞o, boot; p, pop; r, roar; s, sauce; sh, ship, dish; t, tight; th, thin, path; *th*, this, bathe; ŭ, cut; ûr, fur; v, valve; w, with; y, yes; z, zebra, size; zh, vision; ə, about, item, edible, gallop, circus, peaceful

IN FOREIGN WORDS:

à, *Fr.* ami; œ, *Fr.* feu, *Ger.* schön; ü, *Fr.* tu, *Ger.* über; KH, *Ger.* ich, *Scot.* loch; N, *Fr.* bon; y', *Fr.* Compiègne

STRESS MARKS:

Primary stress: ′ in·cite′ (ĭn-sīt′)
Secondary stress: ′ in′sight′ (ĭn′sīt′)

butterfly

THE FLY-BY-DAYS

Scales of bright pigment make delicate wings of incomparable beauty

There are about 10,000 known species of butterflies in the world and, together with moths, they make up the order of insects known as Lepidoptera. This order gets its name from the Greek words *lepis* (scale) and *pteron* (wing). Butterflies fly during the day, while most species of moths fly at night.

A butterfly's wing is covered with thousands of minute scales, arranged in an overlapping pattern like slates on a roof. The dust that rubs so easily off a butterfly when it is handled is, in fact, composed of these scales. Seen under a microscope, each scale is a tiny flattened bag with a short stem that fits into a socket in the wing

membrane. Some of the scales are filled with varied pigments and form the vivid patterns on the wings. Others contain no pigment but are grooved and polished on the outside so that they reflect light and color.

The beautiful coloring of butterflies' wings seems to serve as visual signaling. It may be that, as in some tropical fish and birds, the patterns help in finding or identifying a mate. In some species, however, the colors seem to be for defense, warning birds that the insect is distasteful or poisonous, or distracting predators toward less vulnerable parts of the body—by means of a bright tail spot, for example.

LARVA *The wanderer butterfly of Papua, New Guinea, emerges from the egg as a caterpillar, or larva.*

COCOON *The larva hangs from a twig and, from special glands, spins a fine thread around itself to form a sealed cocoon.*

CHRYSALIS *The silky cocoon hardens into a chrysalis—a protective case. Inside it the larva becomes a dormant pupa.*

TRANSFORMED *The pupa develops wings and legs while its turquoise chrysalis becomes clear and soft enough to split.*

EMERGENCE *The fully formed butterfly breaks free from its soft chrysalis and waits for its crumpled wings to dry.*

ADULT *The new adult wanderer butterfly is poised to spread its wings in flight for the first time.*

BRIEF LIFE *A butterfly is a beautiful adult for only a few weeks—even days—in a year-long life cycle.*

forward with a simultaneous up-and-down kick of the feet.

butterfly table *n.* A small, drop-leaf table, the leaves of which have brackets shaped like a butterfly's wings.

butterfly valve *n.* **1.** A disk turning on a diametrical axis inside a pipe, used as a throttle valve or damper. **2.** A valve composed of two semicircular plates hinged on a common spindle, used to permit flow in one direction only. [Its action somewhat resembles that of a butterfly's wings.]

butterfly weed *n.* A North American plant, *Asclepias tuberosa,* having flat-topped clusters of bright-orange flowers. Also called "orange milkweed," "pleurisy root."

but·ter·milk (bŭt'ər-mĭlk') *n.* **1.** The sour liquid that remains after the butterfat has been removed from whole milk or cream by churning. **2.** Milk soured with certain microorganisms.

butter muslin *n.* A coarse loosely woven cotton gauze. [Formerly used for wrapping butter.]

but·ter·nut (bŭt'ər-nŭt') *n.* **1.** A tree, *Juglans cinerea,* of eastern North America, having compound leaves and egg-shaped nuts. Also called "white walnut." **2.** The edible, oily nut of this tree. **3.** The hard, grayish-brown wood of this tree. **4.** The bark of this tree, or an extract obtained from it, formerly used as a laxative. **5.** A brownish color or dye obtained from butternut bark **6. butternuts.** Clothing dyed with butternut extract. **7.** *Informal.* A Confederate soldier or partisan in the Civil War. **8.** The **souari nut** *(see).* [From the oiliness of the nut. Sense 7, from homemade uniforms dyed with butternut extract.]

butternut squash *n.* A small, yellowish, pear-shaped winter squash, with orange to yellow flesh.

but·ter·scotch (bŭt'ə-skŏch') *n.* **1.** A syrup, sauce, or flavoring made by melting butter, brown sugar, and sometimes artificial flavorings. **2.** A hard, sticky sweet made from these ingredients. [Perhaps originally made in Scotland.]

but·ter·weed (bŭt'ər-wēd') *n.* **1.** A plant, *Senecio glabellus,* of the southern and central United States, having yellow flowers. **2.** The **horseweed** *(see).* [From its yellow flowers.]

but·ter·wort (bŭt'ər-wûrt', -wôrt') *n.* Any plant of the genus *Pinguicula;* especially, *P. vulgaris,* of wet places, having violet-blue, spurred flowers and fleshy, greasy leaves. [From the oiliness of the leaves.]

but·ter·y¹ (bŭt'ə-rē) *adj.* **1.** Resembling, containing, or spread with butter. **2.** *Informal.* Effusively and insincerely flattering. —**but·ter·i·ness** *n.*

buttery² *n., pl.* **-ies.** *Chiefly British.* **1.** A pantry or wine cellar. **2.** A room or bar in colleges and universities where students can buy provisions. [Middle English *boteri, buttrie,* from Old French *boterie,* from *bot,* BUTT (cask).]

butt hinge *n.* A hinge composed of two plates attached to abutting surfaces of a door and door jamb and joined by a pin. Also called "butt." [From BUTT (abut).]

but·tin·sky, but·tin·ski (bŭ-tĭn'skē) *n., pl.* **-skies.** *Slang.* An interfering busybody. [One who *butts in* + *-sky,* surname suffix.]

butt joint *n.* A joint formed by two abutting surfaces placed squarely together. Also called "butt." [From BUTT (abut).]

but·tock (bŭt'ək) *n.* **1. a.** Either of the two rounded fleshy parts on the lower rear part of the human torso. **b.** The analogous part of the body of certain mammals. **2. buttocks.** These two parts together; the bottom. [Middle English, from Old English *buttuc,* end, ridge, strip of land.]

but·ton (bŭt'n) *n.* **1.** A fastener, usually disk-shaped, used to join two parts of a garment by fitting through a buttonhole or loop. **2.** Such an object used for decoration. **3.** Any of various objects of similar appearance, especially: **a.** A control switch, as on a bell or machine. **b.** In fencing, the tip of a foil. **c.** A fused metal or glass globule. **4.** Any of various knoblike organic structures, especially: **a.** The head of a small mushroom. **b.** The tip of a rattlesnake's tail. **5.** A round flat emblem bearing a design or printed information and pinned to the front of a garment. **6.** *Slang.* The end of the chin. —*v.* **buttoned, -toning, -tons.** —*tr.* **1.** To furnish with a button or buttons. **2.** To fasten with a button or buttons. Often used with *up.* —*intr.* **1.** To admit of being fastened with a button or buttons. Often used with *up.* **2.** *Informal.* To become uncommunicative. Used with *up.* [Middle English *boton,* from Old French *bouton,* bud, button, from *bouter,* to strike against, thrust, pierce, of Germanic origin.] —**but·ton·er** *n.* —**but·ton·y** *adj.*

But·ton (bŭt'n), **Richard Totten,** known as "Dick" (1929–). U.S. figure skater. In 1946 he became the youngest person ever to win the U.S. senior ice-skating championship. By 1948 he held all five major figure-skating titles in the world, including the Olympic gold medal. He won another Olympic championship in 1952. Button now organizes ice shows and is a television sports commentator.

but·ton·ball (bŭt'n-bôl') *n.* A North American tree, the **sycamore** *(see).* [From its button-shaped fruit.]

but·ton·bush (bŭt'n-boŏosh') *n.* A North American shrub, *Cephalanthus occidentalis,* having spherical clusters of small white flowers.

but·ton·down (bŭt'n-doun') *adj.* **1.** Having the ends of the collar fastened down by buttons: *a button-down shirt.* **2.** Also **buttoned-down** (bŭt'nd-). Conservative, conventional, or unimaginative: *buttoned-down diplomacy.*

but·ton·hole (bŭt'n-hōl') *n.* **1.** A slit in a garment or piece of fabric for fastening a button. **2.** *Chiefly British.* A flower worn in a buttonhole on the lapel of a coat or jacket. —*tr.v.* **buttonholed, -holing, -holes. 1.** To make a buttonhole in.

2. To sew with a buttonhole stitch. **3.** To accost and detain in conversation. —**but·ton·hol·er** *n.*

buttonhole stitch *n.* A loop stitch that forms a reinforced edge, as around a buttonhole. Also called "close stitch."

but·ton·hook (bŭt′n-hŏŏk′) *n.* A small hook for buttoning shoes or gloves.

but·ton·mold (bŭt′n-mōld′) *n.* A piece of wood, plastic, or metal that is covered with fabric to form a button.

but·ton·quail (bŭt′n-kwāl′) *n.* Any of various small, quaillike birds of the family Turnicidae, occurring in warm grassland regions of the Old World.

but·tons (bŭt′nz) *n., pl.* **buttons.** *Informal.* A pageboy, especially in a pantomime. [From the buttons on his jacket.]

button snakeroot *n.* **1.** A plant, the blazing star *(see)*. **2.** A plant, the **rattlesnake master** *(see)*. [Probably from its button-like umbels.]

but·ton·wood (bŭt′n-wŏŏd′) *n.* A North American tree, the **sycamore** *(see)*. [From the buttonlike fruit.]

butt plate *n.* A metal plate on the butt end of a gunstock.

but·tress (bŭt′rĭs) *n.* **1.** A structure, usually brick or stone, built against a wall for support or reinforcement. See **flying buttress. 2.** Anything resembling a buttress, such as a projecting part of a hill. **3.** A horny growth on the heel of a horse's hoof. **4.** Anything that serves to support, prop, or reinforce. —*tr.v.* **buttressed, -tressing, -tresses. 1.** To support or reinforce with a buttress. **2.** To sustain, prop, or bolster: *buttress an argument with evidence.* [Middle English *butres, boteras,* from Old French *bouterez,* shortened from *(ars) bouterez,* thrusting (arch), from *bouter,* to strike against.]

buttress root *n.* A root growing from and supporting the trunk of a tree, as in the mangrove.

butt shaft *n.* A blunt, unbarbed arrow.

butt weld *n.* A welded butt joint.

butt·weld (bŭt′wĕld′) *tr.v.* **-welded, -welding, -welds.** To join by a butt weld.

but·ty¹ (bŭt′ē) *n., pl.* **-ties.** *Chiefly Welsh.* A miner's mate. [Perhaps from BOOTY, as in the phrase *play booty,* to share takings.]

butty² *n., pl.* **-ties.** *Northern English.* A sandwich or a slice of buttered bread: *a jam butty.* [From BUTTER.]

bu·tut (bōō′tōōt′) *n.* A coin equal to ¹⁄₁₀₀ of the dalasi of the Gambia. See feature at **currency.** [From a native Gambian language.]

bu·tyl (byōōt′l, byōō′tĭl) *n.* A hydrocarbon radical, C_4H_9, with the structure of butane and valence 1.

butyl alcohol *n.* Any of four isomeric alcohols widely used as solvents and in organic synthesis, each having the formula $C_4H_9OH.$

bu·ty·lene (byōōt′l-ēn′) *n.* Any of three gaseous isomeric ethylene hydrocarbons, $C_4H_8,$ used principally in making synthetic rubbers.

butyl rubber *n.* A synthetic rubber produced by copolymerization of a butylene (98 percent) with isoprene or butadiene (2 percent), outstanding in gaseous impermeability and used in tires, insulation, and as a binder fuel in solid propellants for rockets.

bu·ty·ra·ceous (byōō′tə-rā′shəs) *adj.* Resembling butter in appearance, consistency, or chemical properties; buttery. [Latin *būtȳrum,* BUTTER + -ACEOUS.]

bu·tyr·al·de·hyde (byōō′tə-răl′də-hīd′) *n.* A transparent, extremely flammable liquid, $CH_3(CH_2)_2CHO,$ used in synthesizing resins. [BUTYR(IC) + ALDEHYDE.]

bu·ty·rate (byōō′tə-rāt′) *n.* A salt or ester of butyric acid. [BUTYR(IC) + -ATE.]

bu·tyr·ic (byōō-tĭr′ĭk) *adj.* **1.** Of, pertaining to, containing, or derived from butter. **2.** Of, pertaining to, or derived from butyric acid.

butyric acid *n.* Either of two colorless isomeric acids, $C_3H_7COOH,$ occurring in animal milk fats and used in disinfectants, emulsifying agents, and pharmaceuticals.

bu·ty·rin (byōō′tə-rĭn) *n.* Any one of three isomeric glyceryl esters of butyric acid, naturally present in butter. [Earlier *butirine,* from French : Latin *būtȳrum,* BUTTER + -INE.]

bux·om (bŭk′səm) *adj.* **1.** Full-bosomed and plump. Said of a woman. **2.** *Archaic.* Lively; blithe; vivacious. **3.** *Obsolete.* Obedient; yielding. [Earlier, flexible, gay, comely, Middle English *buhsum, buxum,* obedient, humble, bending, from Old English *gebūhsum* (unattested), easy to bend, pliable, from *būgan,* to bend.] —**bux·om·ly** *adv.* —**bux·om·ness** *n.*

Bux·te·hu·de (bŏŏks′tə-hōō′də), **Dietrich** (1637–1707). Danish composer and organist. As church organist at Lübeck (1668–1707), he gained the admiration of Handel and Bach.

Bux·ton (bŭks′tən). Town in Derbyshire, central England, in the Peak District. It is *c.* 305 meters (1,000 feet) above sea level, overlooking the Wye River; the oldest section of the town is on a hill above the modern section. Buxton is a year-round resort, with mineral springs and baths.

buy (bī) *v.* **bought, bought** or *regional* **boughten, buying, buys.** —*tr.* **1.** To acquire in exchange for money or its equivalent; purchase. **2.** To be a means of obtaining or procuring: *Money buys power.* **3.** To acquire by sacrifice, exchange, or trade. **4.** To bribe. **5.** *Slang.* To accept the truth, merit, or feasibility of. —*intr.* To purchase goods; act as a purchaser: *to buy in bulk.* —**buy in** (or **into**). **1.** To purchase (a supply of something) for future use. **2.** To purchase shares or an interest in (a company, for example). **3.** *Slang.* To pay money in exchange for joining (a social or business group). —**buy off.** To bribe in order to proceed

without interference, or to be exempted from an obligation or from prosecution. —**buy out.** To purchase the controlling stock, business rights, or interests of. —**buy up.** To purchase all that is available of.

~*n.* Anything bought or capable of being bought; a purchase, especially something that is underpriced: *a good buy.* [Buy, bought (past tense), bought (past participle); Middle English *byen* (earlier *byggen*), *bo(g)hte, (i)bo(g)ht,* Old English *bycgan, bohte, geboht,* from Germanic *bugjan* (unattested).] —**buy·a·ble** *adj.*

Usage: Buy, as a noun denoting a purchase or bargain, is appropriate only to commercial usage. Its use in a more general context (as in *luxury gained at the expense of liberty is never a good buy*) is considered by many to be unacceptable in written usage.

buy·er (bī′ər) *n.* **1.** One who buys goods; a customer. **2.** A purchasing agent, especially one who buys for a company or store.

buyers' market *n. Economics.* A market condition characterized by low prices, occurring when the supply of commodities exceeds market demand. Compare **sellers' market.**

Buys Bal·lot's law (bīs′bə-lŏts′) *n. Meteorology.* The principle that in the northern hemisphere an observer standing with his back to the wind has a lower atmospheric pressure on his left. In the southern hemisphere the pressure is lower on his right. [After C.H.D. *Buys Ballot,* 19th-century Dutch meteorologist.]

buzz¹ (bŭz) *v.* **buzzed, buzzing, buzzes.** —*intr.* **1.** To make a low droning or vibrating sound like that of a bee. **2.** To talk excitedly in low tones. **3.** To move quickly and busily; bustle. —*tr.* **1.** To cause to buzz: *hornets buzzing their wings.* **2.** To spread (gossip). **3.** *Informal.* To fly low over: *The plane buzzed the control tower.* **4.** To signal (a person) with a buzzer. **5.** *Informal.* To telephone (a person). —**buzz off.** *Informal.* To go away. Usually used in the imperative.

~*n.* **1.** A rapidly vibrating, humming, or droning sound. **2.** A low murmur, as of many hushed voices speaking at once: *a buzz of talk.* **3.** *Informal.* A telephone call. **4.** *Slang.* A pleasant euphoric feeling, as induced by drugs; a high. [Middle English *bussen* (attested only in the verbal noun *bussyng*), to drone (imitative).]

buzz² *tr.v.* **buzzed, buzzing, buzzes.** *Chiefly British Regional.* To drink (a bottle or cup) to the last drop. [From BUZZ (sound).]

buz·zard (bŭz′ərd) *n.* **1.** Any of various North American vultures, such as the **turkey buzzard** *(see)*. **2.** Any hawk of the genus *Buteo,* having broad wings and a broad tail. **3.** An avaricious or unpleasant person. [Middle English *busard,* from Old French, alteration of *buson,* from Latin *būteō* (stem *būteōn-*).]

Buz·zards Bay (bŭz′ərdz). Inlet of the Atlantic Ocean, *c.* 48 kilometers (30 miles) long and from 8 to 16 kilometers (5 to 10 miles) wide, in southeastern Massachusetts. It is connected with Cape Cod Bay by the Cape Cod Canal. Its shoreline is very irregular.

buzz bomb *n.* A robot bomb *(see)* of World War II. [From the buzzing noise made by its pulsejet engine.]

buzz·er (bŭz′ər) *n.* Any of various electric signaling devices that make a buzzing sound, such as a doorbell.

buzz saw *n.* A circular saw *(see)*. [From the sound it makes.]

buzz session *n.* An informal group discussion, as in a workshop or classroom.

buzz word *n. Informal.* A catchword; a jargon word, often one used to convey an impression of specialized knowledge. [From the meaninglessness or frequency of the word in question.]

B.V. Blessed Virgin.

B.V.M. Blessed Virgin Mary.

bvt. brevet; brevetted.

B.W.A. British West Africa.

bwa·na (bwä′nə) *n. East African.* A boss or employer. Often used as a term of respectful address. [Swahili, from Arabic *abūna,* our father.]

B.W.I. British West Indies.

bx. box.

by¹ (bī) *prep.* **1.** Next to; close to: *the window by the door.* **2.** Passing along or through: *He came by the back road.* **3.** Up to and beyond; past: *He drove by the house.* **4.** In the period of; during: *sleeping by day.* **5.** Not later than: *by five o'clock.* **6.** Used to indicate: **a.** Rate or amount: *letters by the thousand.* **b.** Units: *paid by the hour.* **7.** To the extent of: *shorter by two inches.* **8. a.** According to: *by his own admission.* **b.** In accordance with: *play by the rules.* **9.** In the presence or name of. Used in oaths: *swear by the Bible.* **10.** Used to indicate: **a.** A means: *done by machine.* **b.** A creator or originator: *a novel by Dickens.* **c.** The doer of an action: *The window was broken by some children.* **11.** Used to indicate a cause or reason: *thrifty by necessity.* **12.** Used to indicate a sign or piece of evidence: *I knew by his face that he was lying.* **13.** Used to indicate a point of contact: *take by the hand.* **14.** As regards; in respect of: *a plumber by trade.* **15.** As far as it concerns: *It's all right by me.* **16.** In succession to; after: *day by day.* **17.** Used to link certain expressions to be taken together and indicating: **a.** Multiplication or division of quantities. **b.** Coordination of measurements: *a room 12 by 18 feet.* **c.** Alteration of a compass direction: *north by northeast.* —**by the way.** Incidentally.

~*adv.* **1.** On hand; nearby: *stand by.* **2.** Aside; away: *He put it by for later.* **3.** Up to, alongside, and past: *The car raced by.* **4.** Into the past: *as years go by.* —**by and by.** Soon enough; in good time. —**by and large.** Generally; on the whole. [Middle English *by,* Old English *bī, bi, be.*]

Usage: by, through, with. These prepositions indicate the agency or means by which something is accomplished. *By* usually intro-

Byzantium

A CHRISTIAN EMPIRE UNDER CONSTANT THREAT
Politically weak, it displayed enduring cultural strength

Christianity, whose adherents Rome persecuted, was the binding force that enabled Byzantium—the Byzantine Empire—to survive for more than 1,100 years, long after the Roman Empire that gave it birth had perished. Christianity also inspired the art and architecture of Byzantium.

Byzantium owed its wealth to its position astride both north-south and east-west trade routes. It owed its traditions of law and government to Rome and its learning to Greece. But at its heart lay the Christian city of Constantinople. The city, formerly Byzantium, was rebuilt and renamed in 330 by the Roman emperor Constantine, who made it his capital, judging it to be better placed to withstand the barbarian invasions that threatened Rome. The empire, which retained its ancient name, became an increasingly independent entity after 395.

Constantine was the first emperor to see Christianity as a unifying force and to encourage it—fortunately so, for without such a bond the empire would probably have fallen. In the subsequent 11 centuries, Byzantium rarely enjoyed a year's peace. Under a succession of weak emperors, internal conflicts made "Byzantine" a byword for intrigue. Though the empire always included at least parts of the Balkan Peninsula and Turkey, its borders shifted constantly. It was assailed in turn by Goths, Huns, Persians, Avars, Bulgars, Vikings, Slavs, Arabs, Berbers, Turks, Normans, and the Crusaders, who looted Constantinople in 1204. In 1453, the Turkish sultan Mohammed II captured the city—he called it a "monstrous head without a body"—and the empire fell to Islam.

Byzantium's legacy lives on, however. Its own version of Christianity, independent of Rome after 1054, formed the basis of today's Orthodox churches, which claim over 120 million members; it preserved classical literature, an inspiration during the Renaissance; and Justinian's legal code remains the foundation of much European civil law.

THE BYZANTINE EMPIRE *The blue area shows the extent of Byzantium in 550 after Justinian had retaken much of the former Roman Empire fringing the Mediterranean.*

EMPEROR JUSTINIAN *The greatest Byzantine emperor was Justinian (527–565). Backed by his formidable wife Theodora, he retook North Africa from the Vandals and Italy from the Ostrogoths. These gains were temporary, but his power enabled him to leave lasting monuments: gorgeous buildings, such as the Church of St. Sophia, and the codification of a millennium of Roman law. This massive work, the* Corpus Juris Civilis, *has influenced the intellectual, social, and political life of Europe ever since. It is a comprehensive guide to Roman law and the basic document of civil law throughout Europe today.*

GREEK FIRE *During the 7th century, when Arabs swept to conquest in the Middle East, they besieged Constantinople for five years (673–678). The city was saved by a new flame-throwing weapon. It emitted "Greek fire," an explosive mixture that probably contained sulfur, naphtha, and quicklime. The results were devastating, as this 14th-century painting shows.*

duces directly the agent (person) or agency (power): *named by him*; *struck by lightning*. *Through*, the least direct, is often followed by a person, in the sense of intermediary (*apply through a friend*), or by a word naming a condition as cause or means (*fail through indecision*). *With* is usually followed by an inanimate object denoting physical instrument (*fight with a sword*) or instrumentality (*soothe with kind words*).

by². Variant of **bye**.

by–, bye– *prefix.* Indicates: **1.** Close at hand or near; for example, **bystander**. **2.** Out of the way or aside; for example, **byroad, by-election**. **3.** Secondary or incidental; for example, **by-product**. [Middle English *by-, bi-*, from BY.]

by and by *adv.* At a later time; before long. [Middle English, side by side, again and again, one by one, from BY.]

by-and-by (bī′ən-bī′) *n.* **1.** Some future time or occasion. **2.** The hereafter.

by·bid·der (bī-bĭd′ər) *n.* A person who bids at an auction to raise prices for the owner.

Byb·los (bĭb′ləs). An ancient Phoenician port and the chief city of Phoenicia during the 2nd millennium B.C. It stood northeast of present-day Beirut on the site of modern Jubayl (the biblical Gebal). It was famous for its papyrus.

by-blow (bī′blō′) *n. Archaic.* **1.** An indirect or chance blow. **2.** An illegitimate child; a bastard. [Sense 2 from the idea of a child begotten incidentally or by chance.]

Byd·goszcz (bĭd′gôshch). City, capital of Bydgoszcz province, in north-central Poland on the Brda River, a tributary of the Vistula. One of Poland's major inland ports, it is on the Bydgoszcz Canal (built 1773–74), a part of the Vistula-Oder waterway. Chartered in 1346, the city developed during the Middle Ages around the site of a prehistoric fort. In World War II it was occupied by German forces from 1939 to 1945 and suffered heavy damages.

bye, by (bī) *n.* **1.** A secondary matter; a side issue. **2.** *Sports.* The position of one who draws no opponent for a round in a tournament and so advances to the next round. **3.** *Golf.* One or more holes remaining unplayed at the end of a match. **4.** *Cricket.* A run made off a ball not touched by the batsman. Compare **leg bye. —by the bye** (or **by**). Incidentally; by the way. [From BY (aside, hence, "secondary").]

bye–. Variant of **by-**.

bye-bye (bī′bī′) *interj. Informal.* Goodbye. [Baby-talk form.]

bye-byes (bī′bīz′) *n. Informal.* Sleep; bed. Used especially to children. [From BYE-BYE.]

by-e·lec·tion, bye-e·lec·tion (bī′ĭ-lĕk′shən) *n.* A special election held between regular elections to fill a vacancy in a legislature; especially, in the United Kingdom and other Commonwealth countries, an election to Parliament occurring between general elections.

Byelorussia. See **Belorussian S.S.R.**

Byelorussian. Variant of **Belorussian.**

by·gone (bī′gôn′, -gŏn′) *adj.* Past; gone by; former.
~*n.* A past occurrence. —**let bygones be bygones**. To let past differences be forgotten; be reconciled.

by·lane (bī′lān′) *n.* A side road; a byway.

by·law (bī′lô′) *n.* **1.** A regulation made by a local authority, corporation, or the like, having legal effect only in the area governed by that authority. **2.** A law or rule governing the internal affairs of an organization. [Middle English *bilawe, bylawe*, "village law," probably from Old Norse *bȳr*, village + *lög*, law.]

by·line (bī′līn′) *n.* A line at the head or foot of a newspaper or magazine article with the author's name.
~*tr.v.* **by·lined, -lining, -lines.** To write (an article) under a by-line. —**by·lin·er** *n.*

by·name (bī′nām′) *n.* **1.** A surname. **2.** A nickname.

Byng (bĭng), **George, Viscount Torrington** (1663–1733). English admiral. He persuaded the navy to support William of Orange against James II in 1688 and later repelled the attempted Jacobite invasions of 1708 and 1715. His greatest victory was the defeat of the Spanish fleet in the Strait of Messina (1718).

Byng, John (1704–57). English admiral, son of George Viscount Torrington. After his failure to relieve Menorca from a French siege and his subsequent withdrawal from the island, he was court-martialed and executed for neglect of duty.

BYOB, b.y.o.b. Bring your own bottle.

by-pass, by·pass (bī′păs′, -päs′) *n.* **1.** A road, especially a main road, that passes around or to one side of an obstructed or congested area; a detour. **2.** A pipe or channel to conduct gas or liquid around another pipe or a fixture. **3.** Any means of circumvention. **4.** *Electronics.* A **shunt** (see). **5.** *Medicine.* **a.** An apparatus used to keep the blood circulating and oxygenated while surgery is performed on the heart. **b.** A surgical operation to pass around an obstructed passage, as in an artery or intestine. Also used adjectivally: *by-pass surgery*. **c.** An alternative passage created in such an operation. **d.** A horseshoe-shaped length of tubing worn on the arm by a patient requiring regular treatment on a kidney machine.
~*tr.v.* **by-passed, -passing, -passes.** Also **by·pass. 1.** To go around instead of through; avoid (an obstacle). **2.** To proceed heedless of; ignore or circumvent: *by-passing office procedures*. **3.** To cause (a fluid or electricity, for example) to follow a by-pass.

by-pass engine *n.* A jet engine in which some of the air intake by-passes the combustion zone, flowing directly into or around the main exhaust gas flow to provide additional thrust.

by·past (bī′păst′) *adj.* Past; bygone.

by-path (bī'păth', -päth') *n., pl.* **-paths** (-păthz, -päthz). An indirect or little-used path.

by-play (bī'plā') *n.* Secondary action or speech taking place while the main action proceeds, especially in a play.

by-prod·uct (bī'prŏd'əkt) *n.* **1.** Something, especially something useful, that is produced in the making of something else. **2.** A secondary result; a side effect.

Byrd (bûrd), **Richard Evelyn** (1888–1957). U.S. aviator and polar explorer. In 1926 he made the first flight over the North Pole. Between 1929 and 1956 he led five scientific and exploratory air expeditions to the South Pole, voyages that established the basis of American claims to territory in Antarctica.

Byrd, William (c. 1543–1623). English composer, one of the foremost of early English musicians. The best known of his works today are his settings of the Anglican service and his three Masses.

byre (bīr) *n.* A cowshed or barn. [Middle English *byre,* Old English *bȳre,* stall, hut, perhaps variant of BOWER.]

byr·nie (bûr'nē) *n. Archaic.* A breastplate or a coat or shirt of mail. [Middle English *brinie,* from Old Norse *brynja.*]

by·road (bī'rōd') *n.* A side road; a minor road.

By·ron (bī'rən), **George Gordon, 6th Baron** (1788–1824). British poet, one of the leading figures of the English romantic movement. The first two cantos of *Childe Harold's Pilgrimage,* which appeared in 1812, made him the darling of London society. *Manfred* (1817), in which the full "Byronic hero"—lonely, rebellious, secretive—appeared. His last work, *Don Juan* (1819–24), is considered by many to be the finest satirical and comic poem in the English language. In 1824 he sailed to Greece to help in the nationalist revolt against Turkish rule. He caught a fever and died.

By·ron·ic (bī-rŏn'ĭk) *adj.* Of or characteristic of Byron or his works; especially, adventurous and wildly romantic. **—By·ron·i·cal·ly** *adv.*

bys·sin·o·sis (bĭs'ə-nō'sĭs) *n.* A lung disease affecting textile workers, caused by prolonged exposure to cotton dust and characterized by wheezing. [New Latin, from Greek *bussinos,* of BYSSUS + -OSIS.]

bys·sus (bĭs'əs) *n., pl.* **-suses** or **byssi** (bĭs'ī'). **1.** *Zoology.* A mass of filaments by means of which certain bivalve mollusks, such as mussels, attach themselves to fixed surfaces. **2.** A fine-textured linen of ancient times, used by the Egyptians as wrapping for mummies. [Latin, from Greek *bussos,* flax, linen.]

by·stand·er (bī'stăn'dər) *n.* A person who is present at some event without participating in it.

by·street (bī'strēt') *n.* A small side street; an alley.

by·talk (bī'tôk') *n.* Unimportant talk; small talk.

byte (bīt) *n. Computer Science.* **1.** A group of bits of information, typically six or eight, treated as a unit in a computer process. **2.** The space occupied by a single character in a computer store. [Probably from BIT + BITE.]

By·tom (bī'tôm). City of southwestern Poland, in the Katowice mining region. It is an important industrial center, with factories producing metal products and furniture. The city was chartered in 1254 and held by the Hapsburgs from 1526 until 1742, when it passed to Prussia. It was incorporated into Poland in 1945.

by·way (bī'wā') *n.* **1. a.** A small country road or lane. **b.** An unimportant or partially hidden side road. **2.** A secondary or unexplored field of study.

by·word (bī'wûrd') *n.* **1.** A well-known saying; a proverb. **2.** One that proverbially represents a type, class, or quality. **3.** An object of contempt or notoriety. **4.** A nickname or epithet. [Middle English *biword,* Old English *bīword* (translation of Latin *prōverbium,* PROVERB) : BY + WORD.]

by·work (bī'wûrk') *n.* Work done during one's spare time.

by-your-leave (bī'yər-lēv') *n.* A request for permission. Used chiefly in the phrase *without so much as a by-your-leave.*

byzant. Variant of **bezant.**

By·zan·tine (bĭz'ən-tēn', -tīn', bĭ-zăn'tīn) *adj.* **1.** Of, pertaining to, or characteristic of Byzantium, its inhabitants, or their culture. **2.** Of or designating the style of architecture developed from the 5th century A.D. in Byzantium, characterized by round arches, massive domes, intricate spires and minarets, and extensive use of mosaic. **3.** Of or designating the style of painting and design developed in Byzantium, characterized by formality of design, stylized presentation of figures, rich use of color, especially gold, and generally religious subject matter. **4.** Of the Eastern Orthodox Church or the rites performed in it. **5.** *Sometimes* **byzantine.** Complicated; labyrinthine; devious. **6.** *Sometimes* **byzantine.** Rigid; inflexible. **~***n.* A native or inhabitant of Byzantium.

Byzantine Empire. *Arabic* **Rum** (rōōm). The successor to the Roman Empire, dating from A.D. 330, when Constantine I rebuilt Byzantium, named it Constantinople, and made it the capital of the Roman Empire. It was also called the Eastern Empire, especially after 395, when Honorius became emperor in the east and Arcadius emperor in the west, thus making permanent the split in the Roman Empire. Although its extent varied through the centuries, the core of the empire was always the Balkan Peninsula and Asia Minor. The last Byzantine emperor was Constantine XI Palaeologus, who reigned from 1449–1453. Constantinople fell to the Ottoman Turks in 1453, a defeat that marked the end of the empire.

By·zan·ti·um (bĭ-zăn'shē-əm, -tē-əm). **1.** A Greek city on the site of which Constantine built the city of **Constantinople** *(see)* in A.D. 330. **2.** The Byzantine Empire and its culture.

C

cabbage *Green cabbage is known to have been eaten in the Bronze Age. It is cultivated in most countries of the world.*

c, C (sē) *n., pl.* **c's** or **C's. 1.** The third letter of the modern English alphabet. See feature at **alphabet. 2.** Any of the speech sounds represented by this letter. **3. C** The third best or highest in quality, class, or rank; especially, the third highest mark awarded for academic work. **4.** *Music.* **a.** The first tone in the scale of C major, or the third tone in the relative minor scale. **b.** The key or a scale in which C is the tonic. **c.** A written or printed note representing this tone. **d.** A string, key, or pipe tuned to the pitch of this tone. **5.** Something shaped like the letter **C.**

c, C, c., C. *Note:* As an abbreviation or symbol, *c* may be a small or a capital letter, with or without a period. Established forms or those generally preferred precede the definition. When no form is given, all four forms are in general use in that sense. **1. c** *Physics.* candle. **2. C** *Electricity.* capacitance. **3. c., C.** capacity. **4. c., C.** cape. **5. c** carat. **6. C** The symbol for the element carbon. **7. c., C.** carton. **8. c., C.** case. **9. C.** Catholic. **10. c., C.** *Baseball.* catcher. **11. C** Celsius. **12. C.** Celtic. **13. c., C.** cent. **14. c** centi-. **15. C** centigrade. **16. c., C.** centime. **17. c., C.** century. **18. C.** chancellor. **19. c., C.** chapter. **20. C** *Physics.* charge conjugation. **21. C.** chief. **22. c., C.** church. **23. c.** circa (usually italic *c.*). **24. C.** city. **25. c.** cloudy. **26. C.** companion. **27. c., C.** congius. **28. C.** Congress. **29. C.** Conservative. **30. c, C** *Mathematics.* constant. **31. c., C.** consul. **32. c., C.** copy. **33. c., C.** copyright. **34. c., C.** corps. **35. C** coulomb. **36. C.** court. **37. c** cubic. **38. c.** cup. **39. C** The Roman numeral for 100 [Latin *centum.*] **40.** The third in a series.

Ca The symbol for the element calcium.

CA 1. California (used with Zip Code). **2.** chronological age.

C.A. 1. Central America. **2.** chartered accountant. **3.** chronological age.

C.A.A. Civil Aeronautics Authority.

Caaba. See **Kaaba.**

cab¹ (kăb) *n.* **1.** A taxi (*see*). **2.** The covered compartment of a heavy vehicle or machine, such as a truck or locomotive, in which the operator or driver sits. **3.** Formerly, a one-horse vehicle for public hire. [Short for CABRIOLET.]

cab², kab *n.* A Hebrew measure equal to about two quarts. [Hebrew *qabh,* "hollow vessel."]

ca·bal (kə-băl′) *n.* **1.** A conspiratorial group of plotters or intriguers. **2.** A secret scheme or plot. —See Synonyms at **conspiracy.**

~*intr.v.* **caballed, -balling, -bals.** To form a cabal; plot; conspire. [French *cabale,* from Medieval Latin *cabala,* CABALA. The term was popularized during the reign of Charles II, when it was applied to the ministry of Clifford, Arlington, Buckingham, Ashley, and Lauderdale.]

cab·a·la, cab·ba·la, kab·a·la, kab·ba·la (kăb′ə-lə, kə-bä′lə) *n.* **1.** *Often* Cabala. An occult mystical philosophy of rabbinical origin, widely transmitted in medieval Europe, based on an esoteric interpretation of the Hebrew Scriptures. **2.** Any secret doctrine. [Medieval Latin, from Hebrew *qabbālāh,* received doctrine, tradition, from *qābal,* to receive.] —**cab·a·lism** *n.* —**cab·a·list** *n.*

cab·a·lis·tic (kăb′ə-lĭs′tĭk) *adj.* **1.** Of or pertaining to the Cabala. **2.** Having secret or hidden meaning; occult; mysterious.

cab·al·le·ro (kăb′ə-lâr′ō; *Spanish* kăb′əl-yâr′ō) *n., pl.* **-ros.** In Spanish-speaking countries, a gentleman; a cavalier. [Spanish, from Late Latin *caballārius,* a horse groom, from Latin *caballus,* a horse. See **cavalier.**]

ca·ban·a (kə-băn′ə, -băn′yə) *n.* Also **ca·ba·ña** (kə-bä′nyə). A shelter on a beach used as a bathhouse. [Spanish *cabaña,* from Late Latin *capanna,* hut. CABIN.]

cab·a·ret (kăb′ə-rā′) *n.* **1.** Live entertainment in a restaurant or nightclub, with performances by singers, comedians, dancers, and the like. **2.** A restaurant or nightclub that provides such entertainment. [French, tavern, from Old French, probably of dialect (Walloon) origin.]

cab·bage (kăb′ĭj) *n.* **1.** An edible plant, *Brassica oleracea capitata,* many varieties of which are grown in temperate climates throughout the world, having a short, thick stalk, and a large head formed by tightly overlapping green or reddish leaves. **2.** The head of a cabbage. **3.** An edible leaf bud of the **cabbage palm** (*see*). **4.** *Slang.*

cabriole *The cabriole leg on chairs, cabinets, and tables was used by the ancient Chinese and by the Greeks. It became fashionable in Europe in the late 17th century.*

Money, especially in the form of bills.

~*intr.v.* **cabbaged, -baging, -bages.** To form or grow in a head, as cabbage does. [Middle English *caboche,* from Old North French, variant of Old French *caboce*†, "head."] —**cab·ba·gy** *adj.*

cabbage butterfly *n.* Any of several white butterflies of the genus *Pieris,* having larvae that feed on cabbages and other brassicas.

cabbage moth *n.* A brown-gray moth, *Mamestra brassicae,* whose caterpillars are a horticultural pest.

cabbage palm *n.* A tropical American palm tree, *Roystonea oleracea,* having leaf buds that are edible when young.

cabbage palmetto *n.* See **palmetto.**

cabbage rose *n.* A prickly shrub, *Rosa centifolia,* native to the Caucasus, having large, fragrant, many-petaled pink flowers. It is cultivated in gardens in many varieties.

cab·bage·worm (kăb′ĭj-wûrm′) *n.* Any of several caterpillars that feed on cabbage; especially, the bright green larva of the **cabbage butterfly** (*see*).

cabbage yellow *n.* A disease of cabbage marked by the yellowing of leaves and caused by the fungus *Fusarium conglutinans.*

cab·by, cab·bie (kăb′ē) *n., pl.* **-bies.** *Informal.* A taxi driver.

Cab·ell (kăb′əl), **James Branch** (1879–1958). U.S. essayist and novelist. He wrote many stories and novels that satirized life in Virginia, his home state. *Jurgen* (1919) was his best-known book. He was among the prestigious writers who edited the satirical magazine *American Spectator* (1932–35).

ca·ber (kā′bər, kä′-) *n.* A heavy wooden pole, usually the trunk of a young pine tree, thrown in the air as a trial of strength in Scottish Highland games: *tossing the caber.* [Gaelic *cabar.*]

ca·ber·net sau·vi·gnon (kăb′ər-nā′ sō-vēn-yōn′) *n.* A variety of black grape grown in France and many other countries. It is the main variety used in claret. [French.]

Ca·be·za de Va·ca (kə-bā′zə də vä′kə), **Alvar Núñez** (*c.* 1490–*c.* 1577). Spanish explorer and colonial administrator. After exploring parts of present-day Florida, Texas, and Mexico, he recounted vivid stories of riches and opportunity in the region, thus arousing Spain's interest in southern and southwestern North America.

cab·in (kăb′ĭn) *n.* **1.** A small, roughly or simply built house, cottage, or hut. **2. a.** In a ship, a room used as living quarters by an officer or passenger. **b.** In a boat, an enclosed compartment serving as a shelter or as living quarters. **c.** In an aircraft, the enclosed space for the crew, passengers, or cargo.

~*tr.v.* **cabined, -ining, -ins.** To confine, as in a cabin. [Middle English *cabane,* from Old French, from Old Provençal, from Late Latin *capanna*†, hut, cabin.]

cabin boy *n.* A boy servant aboard a ship.

cabin class *n.* A class of accommodation on some passenger ships, lower than first class and higher than tourist class. —**cab·in-class** *adj. & adv.*

cabin cruiser *n.* See **cruiser** (sense 3).

cab·i·net (kăb′ə-nĭt) *n.* **1.** An upright cupboard or case with shelves, drawers, or compartments for the storage or display of a collection of objects or materials. **2.** A container for a record-player, television set, or the like. **3.** A small or private room set aside for some specific activity. **4.** *Often* **Cabinet.** A powerful advisory and policy-making body appointed by a head of state or prime minister, and comprising those ministers who head the most important government departments.

~*adj.* **1.** Of suitable value, beauty, or size to be kept or displayed in a cabinet: *a cabinet edition.* **2.** Belonging or pertaining to a political cabinet: *a cabinet minister.* **3.** Used for cabinetwork: *teak and other heavy cabinet woods.* [CABIN + -ET, after French *cabinet,* from *cabinet*†, a gambling house.]

cab·i·net·mak·er (kăb′ə-nĭt-mā′kər) *n.* A craftsman specializing in making fine wooden furniture. —**cab·i·net·mak·ing** *n.*

cab·i·net·work (kăb′ə-nĭt-wûrk′) *n.* Finished woodwork made by a cabinetmaker.

ca·ble (kā′bəl) *n.* **1.** A strong, large-diameter, heavy steel or fiber rope. **2.** *Electricity.* A bound or sheathed group of mutually insulated conductors. **3. a.** *Nautical.* A heavy rope or chain for mooring

or anchoring a ship. **b.** A unit of nautical length equal to about 720 feet in the United States and 608 feet in England. Also called "cable's length." **4.** A cablegram. **5.** A **cable stitch** *(see).*
~*v.* **cabled, -bling, -bles.** —*tr.* **1. a.** To send a cablegram to. **b.** To transmit (a message) by telegraph. **2.** To supply or fasten with a cable or cables. —*intr.* To send a cablegram. [Middle English, from Norman French, from Late Latin *capulum,* rope for fastening cattle, from Latin *capere,* to take.]
cable car *n.* A passenger car used on a cableway or cable railway.
ca•ble•cast (kā′bəl-kăst′) *n.* A telecast by cable television. **—ca′ble′cast′** *v.* **—ca′ble•cast′er** *n.*
ca•ble•gram (kā′bəl-grăm′) *n.* An overseas telegram sent by submarine cable.
ca•ble-laid (kā′bəl-lād′) *adj.* Made of three ropes of three strands each, twisted together counterclockwise.
cable railway *n.* A railway on which the cars are suspended on and moved by an endless cable driven by a stationary engine.
cable release *n.* A short length of flexible cable used to operate the shutter of a camera without moving or shaking the camera.
cable stitch *n.* A knitting technique or stitch that produces a twisted rope design. Also called "cable." **—ca•ble-stitch** *adj.*
ca•blet (kā′blĭt) *n.* A cable-laid rope with a circumference of less than 10 inches; a small cable. [Diminutive of CABLE.]
cable television *n.* A television system in which signals are delivered to subscribers' receivers by cable. Also called "cablevision."
ca•ble•vi•sion (kā′bəl-vĭzh′ən) *n.* **Cable television** *(see).*
ca•ble•way (kā′bəl-wā′) *n.* An overhead cable and apparatus for carrying materials, goods, and passengers, normally secured between terminal towers.
cab•man (kăb′mən) *n., pl.* **-men** (-mĭn). The driver of a cab.
cab•o•chon (kăb′ə-shŏn′) *n.* **1.** A highly polished, convex-cut, unfaceted gem. **2.** This style of cutting. [Old French, diminutive of Old North French *caboche, caboce,* head. See **cabbage.**]
ca•boo•dle (kə-bo͞od′l) *n. Informal.* The lot, group, or bunch. Used chiefly in the phrase *the whole kit and caboodle.* [19th century (U.S.) : perhaps contraction of phrase *kit and boodle.*]
ca•boose (kə-bo͞os′) *n.* **1.** The last car on a freight train, having kitchen and sleeping facilities for the train crew. **2.** *Obsolete.* **a.** A ship's galley. **b.** Any of various cast-iron cooking ranges used in such galleys during the early 19th century. **c.** An outdoor oven or fireplace. [Probably from Dutch *kabuis,* ship's supply room or galley, from Middle Low German *kabūse*†.]
Cab•ot (kăb′ət), **John** (*c.* 1425–98). *Italian* **Giovanni Ca•bo•to** (kä-bō′tə). Italian explorer from Genoa who settled in Bristol and led the first English expedition to America. In 1497, under letters patent from Henry VII, he set sail and discovered Newfoundland and Nova Scotia, thinking them to be part of Asia.
cab•o•tage (kăb′ə-täzh′) *n.* **1.** Trade or navigation in coastal waters. **2.** The exclusive right of a country to operate the air traffic within its territory. [French, from *caboter,* to coast, probably from Spanish *cabo,* cape, headland, from Latin *caput,* head.]
Ca•bri•ni (kə-brē′nē), **Saint Frances Xavier,** born Maria Francesca Cabrini, known as "Mother Cabrini" (1850–1917). Italian-born founder of the Missionary Sisters of the Sacred Heart and the first citizen of the United States to be canonized (1946).
cab•ri•ole (kăb′rē-ōl′) *n.* A form of furniture leg, characteristic of Queen Anne and Chippendale furniture, that curves outward and then narrows downward into an ornamental foot. [French, "caper" (from its resemblance to the foreleg of a capering animal). See **capriole.**]
cab•ri•o•let (kăb′rē-ə-lā′) *n.* **1.** A two-wheeled, one-horse vehicle with two seats and a folding top. **2.** A car with a folding roof; a convertible coupé. [French, diminutive of *cabriole,* caper (in allusion to its bounding motion). See **capriole.**]
cab•stand (kăb′stănd′) *n.* A place designated for taxicabs waiting for hire.
ca•ca•o (kə-kā′ō, -kä′ō) *n., pl.* **-os. 1.** An evergreen tropical American tree, *Theobroma cacao,* having yellowish flowers and reddish-brown seed pods. **2.** The seed of this tree, used in making chocolate, cocoa, and cocoa butter. In this sense, also called "cacao bean," "cocoa bean." [Spanish, from Nahuatl *cacahuatl,* cacao tree.]
cacao butter *n.* **Cocoa butter** *(see).*
cach•a•lot (kăsh′ə-lŏt′, kăsh′ə-lō′) *n.* The **sperm whale** *(see).* [French, from Spanish and Portuguese *cachalote*†.]
cache (kăsh) *n.* **1.** A hole or similar hiding place for the concealment and storage of provisions, weapons, or valuables. **2.** A store of goods or articles hidden in a cache.
~*tr.v.* **cached, caching, caches.** To store in a hiding place for future use. —See Synonyms at **hide.** [French, from *cacher,* to hide, from Vulgar Latin *cōacticāre* (unattested), to compress, from Latin *cōactāre,* to constrain, from *cōgere* (past participle *cōactus*), to drive together : *com-,* together + *agere,* to drive.]
ca•chet (kă-shā′) *n.* **1.** A seal on a letter or document. **2.** Distinction; prestige: *social cachet.* **3. a.** A commemorative design stamped on an envelope to mark some postal or philatelic event. **b.** A motto forming part of a postal cancellation. **4.** A kind of wafer capsule formerly used by pharmacists for presenting an unpleasant-tasting drug. [Old French, from *cacher,* to hide, press together. See **cache.**]
ca•chex•i•a (kă-kĕk′sē-ə) *n.* A general wasting of the body or weakening of the brain during any debilitating chronic disease. [Late Latin, from Greek *kakhexia,* bad condition of the body : CAC(O)- + *hexis,* condition, from *ekhein,* to hold, be in a condition.] **—ca•chec•tic** *adj.*
cach•in•nate (kăk′ə-nāt′) *intr.v.* **-nated, -nating, -nates.** To laugh loud, hard, or convulsively; guffaw. [Latin *cachinnāre*†.] **—cach•in•na•tion** *n.*
ca•chou (kă-sho͞o′, kăsh′o͞o) *n.* **1.** An astringent, **catechu** *(see).* **2.** A pastille used to sweeten the breath. [French, from Portuguese *cachu,* from Malayalam *cāccu.*]
ca•chu•cha (kä-cho͞o′chä) *n.* A Spanish solo dance in 3/4 time. [Spanish, origin obscure.]
ca•cique (kə-sēk′) *n.* Also **ca•zique** (-zēk′). **1.** An Indian chief, especially in the Spanish West Indies and other parts of Latin America during colonial and postcolonial times. **2.** A powerful local politician in Latin America or Spain. **3.** Any of various tropical American orioles. [Spanish, of Arawakan origin; akin to Arawak *kassequa,* chief, Taino *cacique.*]
cack•le (kăk′əl) *v.* **-led, -ling, -les.** —*intr.* **1.** To make the shrill, broken cry characteristic of a hen after laying an egg. **2.** To laugh or talk in a similar manner. —*tr.* To utter in cackles.
~*n.* **1.** The act or sound of cackling. **2.** Shrill, brittle laughter. **3.** Foolish chatter. [Middle English *cakelen,* probably from Middle Low German *kakeln* (imitative).] **—cack•ler** *n.*
caco- *prefix.* Indicates bad, incorrect, or unpleasant; for example, **cacography.** [Greek *kako-,* from *kakos,* bad.]
cac•o•dyl (kăk′ə-dĭl′) *n.* **1.** The arsenic group $As(CH_3)_2$. **2.** A poisonous oil, $As_2(CH_3)_4$, with an obnoxious garlicky odor. [Greek *kakōdēs,* bad-smelling : CACO- + *-ōdēs,* from *ozein,* to smell + -YL.] **—cac•o•dyl•ic** *adj.*
cac•o•ë•thes (kăk′ō-ē′thēz) *n.* A mania or irresistible compulsion; a pernicious habit. [Latin, from Greek *kakoēthes,* from the neuter of *kakoēthēs,* ill-disposed, abominable, malignant: CACO- + *ēthos,* custom, disposition.]
cac•o•gen•ics (kăk′ə-jĕn′ĭks) *n.* **Dysgenics** *(see).* [CACO- + -GENIC(S).] **—cac•o•gen•ic** *adj.*
ca•cog•ra•phy (kă-kŏg′rə-fē) *n.* **1.** Bad handwriting. Compare **calligraphy.** **2.** Incorrect spelling. Compare **orthography.** [CACO- + -GRAPHY.]
cac•o•mis•tle (kăk′ə-mĭs′əl) *n.* Also **cac•o•mix•le** (-mĭx′səl) Either of two small, carnivorous mammals, *Bassariscus astutus,* of the southwest United States, or *Jentinkia sumichrasti,* of Central America, related to the raccoons and having grayish or brownish fur and a black-banded tail. Also called "ringtail," "ring-tailed cat." [Mexican Spanish, from Nahuatl *tlacomiztli* : *tlaco,* half + *miztli,* puma.]
ca•coph•o•nous (kə-kŏf′ə-nəs) *adj.* Having a harsh, unpleasant sound; discordant. [Greek *kakophōnos* : CACO- + *phōnē,* sound.] **—ca•coph′o•nous•ly** *adv.*
ca•coph•o•ny (kă-kŏf′ə-nē) *n., pl.* **-nies. 1.** Jarring, discordant sound; dissonance. **2.** The use of harsh-sounding or unharmonious language. Compare **euphony.** [French *cacophonie,* from Greek *kakophōnia,* from *kakophōnos* : CACO- + *phōnē,* sound.]
cac•tus (kăk′təs) *n., pl.* **-tuses** or **-ti** (-tī′). Any of a large group of plants of the family Cactaceae, mostly native to arid regions of the New World. They are characterized by thick, fleshy, often prickly stems that function as leaves and in some species have showy flowers and edible fruit. [New Latin, from Latin, the cardoon, from Greek *kaktos*†.]
Usage: The regular plural of this word, *cactuses,* is increasingly being used in formal contexts in place of *cacti.* In strictly technical usage, *cacti* remains the preferred form.
ca•cu•mi•nal (kă-kyo͞o′mə-nəl) *adj. Phonetics.* Pronounced with the tip of the tongue turned back and up toward the roof of the mouth; retroflex.
~*n. Phonetics.* A cacuminal consonant. [Latin *cacūmen* (stem *cacūmin-*), summit, treetop, point.]
cad (kăd) *n.* An ungentlemanly man. Now usually used humorously. [Short for CADDIE.] **—cad•dish** *adj.* **—cad•dish•ly** *adv.* **—cad•dish•ness** *n.*
ca•das•ter (kə-dăs′tər) *n.* Also **ca•das•tre.** A public record, survey, or map of the value, extent, and ownership of land as a basis of taxation. [French *cadastre,* from Italian *catastro,* variant of Old Italian *catastico,* from Late Greek *katastikhon,* list, from *kata stikhon,* "line by line."] **—ca•das•tral** *adj.*
ca•dav•er (kə-dăv′ər) *n.* A dead body, especially one considered for medical purposes or intended for dissection. [Latin, from *cadere,* to fall, "die."] **—ca•dav•er•ic** *adj.*
ca•dav•er•ine (kə-dăv′ə-rēn′) *n.* A syrupy, colorless fuming ptomaine, $NH_2(CH_2)_5NH_2$, formed from decaying animal flesh.
ca•dav•er•ous (kə-dăv′ər-əs) *adj.* **1. a.** Corpselike. **b.** Sickly pale. **2.** Gaunt and haggard; emaciated: *a cadaverous face.* **—ca•dav•er•ous•ly** *adv.* **—ca•dav•er•ous•ness** *n.*
cad•die, cad•dy (kăd′ē) *n., pl.* **-dies.** A golfer's hired attendant, who carries his clubs.
~*intr.v.* **caddied, -dying, -dies.** To serve as a caddie. [French *cadet,* CADET.]
cad•dis, cad•dice (kăd′ĭs) *n.* A coarse woolen fabric, yarn, or ribbon binding. [Middle English *cadas,* from Old French *cadaz,* from Provençal *cadarz*†.]
caddis fly *n.* Also **caddice fly.** Any of various four-winged insects of the order Trichoptera, found near lakes and streams. [17th century: origin obscure.]
caddis worm *n.* Also **caddice worm.** The aquatic, wormlike larva of the caddis fly, commonly enclosed in a cylindrical case covered with grains of sand, fragments of shell, or the like.

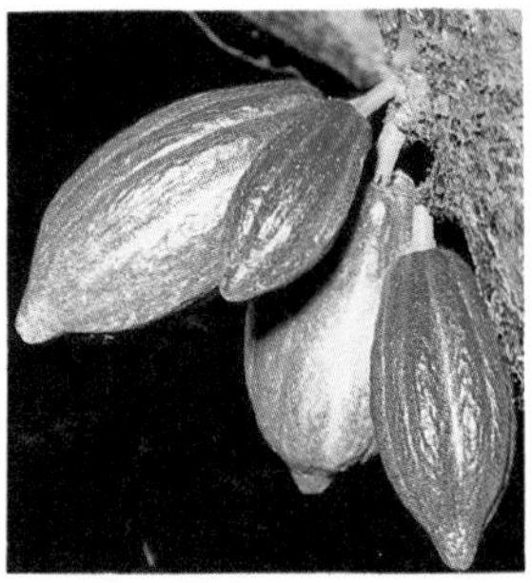
cacao *The reddish seedpods of* Theobroma cacao, *a tropical American tree, produce the beans from which chocolate is made.*

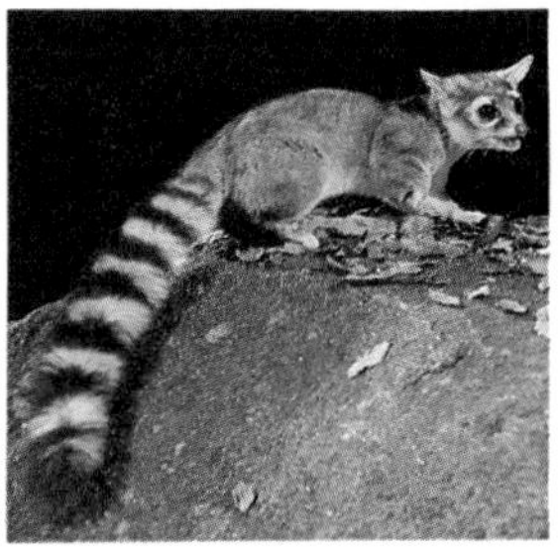
cacomistle *A native of the southwestern United States and Mexico, the cacomistle is a tree-dwelling relative of the raccoon and feeds at night on small animals, fruit, and vegetables.*

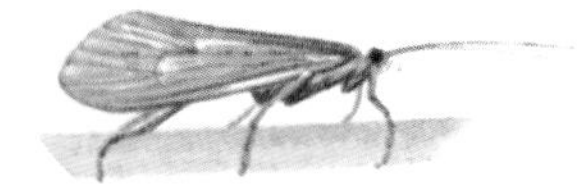
caddis fly *Adult caddis flies, like the one shown here, are nocturnal insects that resemble brownish moths. Some species are used as bait by anglers.*

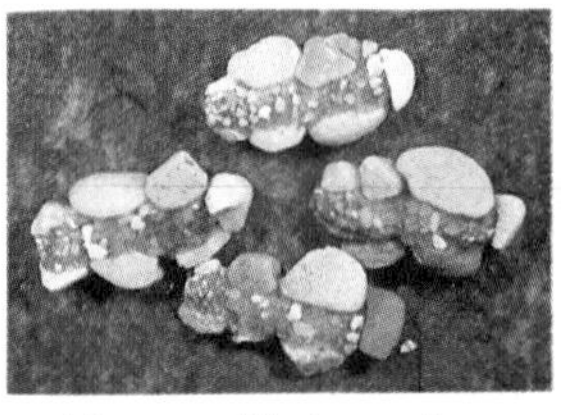
caddis worm *The larvae of many of the 5,000 species of the caddis fly construct portable cases of silk, covered with sand, leaves, and shells. They live in these cases with only their armored heads protruding until they are ready to become adults.*

cad·dy¹ (kăd'ē) *n., pl.* **-dies.** A small box or other container, especially for holding tea. [Originally "a container of one caddy of tea," from Malay *kātī* (weight of 605 grams; 1¹/₃ pounds).)]

caddy². Variant of **caddie.**

cade¹ (kād) *adj.* Left by its mother and raised by hand: *a cade calf.* [Middle English *cad†.*]

cade² *n.* A juniper shrub, *Juniperus oxycedrus,* of the Mediterranean region, the wood of which yields an oily brown liquid *(oil of cade)* used to treat skin ailments. [French, from Old Provençal, from Medieval Latin *catanus,* probably from Gaulish *catános* (unattested).]

Cade (kād), **Jack** (died 1450). English rebel who led an unsuccessful rebellion against Henry VI (1450) and called for the return of Richard Plantagenet, the Duke of York, from Ireland.

-cade *suffix.* Indicates procession or parade; for example, **motorcade.** [From CAVALCADE.]

ca·delle (kə-dĕl') *n.* A small blackish beetle, *Tenebroides mauritanicus,* both the larval and adult forms of which damage stored grain and packaged foods. [French, from Provençal *cadello,* from Latin *catella,* feminine of *catellus, catulus,* offspring.]

ca·dence (kād'ns) *n.* **1.** Balanced, rhythmic flow, as of poetry or oratory. **2.** The measure or beat of movement, as in dancing or marching. **3. a.** A falling inflection of the voice, as at the end of a sentence. **b.** The general modulation of the voice; intonation. **4.** *Music.* A progression of chords moving to a harmonic close or point of rest. —See Synonyms at **rhythm.** [Middle English, from Old French, from Old Italian *cadenza,* from *cadere,* to fall, from Latin.]

ca·dent (kād'nt) *adj.* **1.** Having cadence or rhythm. **2.** *Archaic.* Falling. [Latin *cadēns* (stem *cadent-*), present participle of *cadere,* to fall.]

ca·den·za (kə-dĕn'zə) *n. Music.* **1.** An elaborate ornamental flourish interpolated into an aria or other vocal piece. **2.** An extended, virtuoso section for the soloist near the end of a movement of a concerto. [Italian, CADENCE.]

ca·det (kə-dĕt') *n.* **1.** A student training for service in the armed forces or police force, usually at a college. **2.** A younger son or brother.

~*adj.* Pertaining to or descended from a younger son: *the cadet branch of the family.* [French, from Gascon dialect *capdet,* captain, chief, from Late Latin *capitellum,* "small head," from Latin *caput,* head.] —**ca·det·ship** *n.*

cadge (kăj) *v.* **cadged, cadging, cadges.** *Informal.* —*tr.* To get by begging or pretending to borrow. —*intr.* To beg or borrow something without intent to repay. [Back-formation from *cadger,* carrier, Middle English *cadgear,* from *caggen†,* to carry wares.] —**cadg·er** *n.*

Cá·diz (kə-dĭz', kā'dĭz). Capital of Cádiz province in Spain. Situated at the entrance to the Bay of Cádiz, it is an important seaport, founded by the Phoenicians in *c.* 1100 B.C. After the conquest of the Americas, it was used as a base for the Spanish treasure fleets.

Cad·me·an (kăd-mē'ən) *adj.* Pertaining to, associated with, or resembling Cadmus.

cad·mi·um (kăd'mē-əm) *n.* *Symbol* **Cd** A soft, bluish-white metallic element, occurring primarily in zinc, copper, and lead ores. It is easily cut with a knife and is used in low-friction, fatigue-resistant alloys, solders, dental amalgams, nickel-cadmium accumulators, neutron-absorbing control rods in nuclear reactors, and in rust-proof electroplating. Atomic number 48, atomic weight 112.40, melting point 320.9°C, boiling point 765°C, specific gravity 8.65, valence 2. [New Latin, from Latin *cadmia,* zinc ore, CALAMINE (because cadmium is found together with calamine in the ore).] —**cad·mic** *adj.*

cadmium cell *n.* A photocell of a type having a cadmium electrode that is sensitive to ultraviolet radiation.

cadmium sulfate *n.* A colorless crystalline solid, $CdSO_4$, used as an antiseptic.

cadmium sulfide *n.* An orange or yellow insoluble solid, CdS, used as a pigment in paints *(cadmium yellow).*

Cad·mus (kăd'məs). *Greek Mythology.* A Phoenician prince who killed a dragon and sowed its teeth, from which sprang up an army of men who fought one another until only five survived; with these Cadmus founded the city of Thebes.

cad·re (kăd'rē) *n.* **1.** A nucleus of trained personnel, especially in a military or political organization, around which a larger organization can be built and trained. **2.** A member of such a nucleus. [French, from Italian *quadro,* from Latin *quādrum,* a square, from *quādrus.*]

ca·du·ce·us (kə-dōō'sē-əs, kə-dyōō'-) *n., pl.* **-cei** (-sē-ī'). **1. a.** An ancient herald's wand or staff. **b.** *Greek Mythology.* A winged staff with two serpents twined around it, carried by the messenger-god Hermes. **2.** A similar staff used as the symbol of the medical profession. [Latin *cādūceus,* from Greek (Doric) *karukeion,* from *karux,* herald.] —**ca·du·ce·an** *adj.*

ca·du·ci·corn (kə-dōō'sĭ-kôrn, -dyōō'-) *adj.* Having horns that are shed annually, as certain deer. [Latin *cādūcus,* falling (from *cadere,* to fall) + *cornu,* horn.]

ca·du·ci·ty (kə-dōō'sĭ-tē, kə-dyōō'-) *n.* **1.** The frailty of old age; senility. **2.** Perishability; impermanence. [French *caducité,* from *caduc,* frail, falling, from Latin *cādūcus,* CADUCOUS.]

ca·du·cous (kə-dōō'kəs, kə-dyōō'-) *adj.* **1.** *Biology.* Dropping off or shedding at an early stage of development. Said of the gills of amphibians or the leaves of certain plants. **2.** Not long-lasting; imper-

Caesar *Julius Caesar's likeness appears on the denarius, the principal Roman silver coin. Caesar laid the foundations of the Roman Empire, replacing the Republic that preceded it and profoundly influencing European history. The Russian and German imperial titles of Czar and Kaiser are forms of his name.*

manent; transitory. [Latin *cādūcus,* falling, frail, from *cadere,* to fall.]

cae·cil·i·an (sĭ-sĭl'yən, -sĭl'ē-ən, sĭ-sēl'-) *n.* Any of various legless, burrowing, wormlike amphibians of the order Gymnophiona (formerly Apoda), of tropical regions. [New Latin *Caecilia,* type genus, from Latin *caecilia,* lizard, from *caecus,* blind (in allusion to a lizard's small eyes).]

caecum Variant of **cecum.**

Caed·mon (kăd'mən) (died *c.* A.D. 680). The earliest known English poet, who, according to Bede, was a cowherd at the monastery of Whitby and who, as an old man, was told in a vision to sing "the beginning of all created things." He became a monk and spent the remainder of his days writing songs and poems based on the Scriptures.

Cae·li·an (sē'lē-ən). One of the seven hills of Rome.

Caen (kän). Port and administrative center of the department of Calvados, northwest France, on the Orne River. It first came to prominence under William the Conqueror, who founded the Abbaye aux Hommes where he is buried. His wife Matilda founded the Abbaye aux Dames. Caen was a Huguenot stronghold in the 16th and 17th centuries and saw heavy fighting in World War II. Its industries include machinery, textiles, and cement.

Caer·nar·von or **Caer·nar·fon** (kär-när'vən). County town and port on the south shore of Menai Strait, in Gwynedd, northern Wales. In 1284 Edward I built a castle, reputedly the birthplace of Edward II, the first Prince of Wales. Prince Charles, the 21st Prince of Wales, was invested here (1969).

Caer·nar·von·shire (kär-när'vən-shîr, -shər). Formerly, a county in north Wales, now a part of Gwynedd.

Caer·phil·ly¹ (kär-fĭl'ē). Market and industrial center in Mid Glamorgan, southern Wales, and the home of Caerphilly cheese. Caerphilly Castle, built between the 13th and 14th centuries, is the largest in Wales.

Caerphilly² *n.* A mild, crumbly white cheese originally from Wales. [After CAERPHILLY.]

Cae·sar (sē'zər) *n.* **1.** A surname of the early Roman emperors that after Hadrian became the title of the junior imperial colleague of the **Augustus** (see). **2.** A dictator or autocrat.

Caesar, Gaius Julius (*c.*100-44 B.C.). Roman general, statesman, and writer. During his Gaul campaign, he invaded Britain (55) and returned to Rome a popular hero. He had, however, many political enemies, including Pompey, who persuaded the senate to order Caesar to resign his army command. Instead, Caesar took his legions across the Rubicon River (49) and crushed Pompey at Pharsalus (48). In 47 he pursued his enemies to Egypt where he installed Cleopatra as queen. It is widely believed that Cleopatra later gave birth to his son, Caesarion. Returning to Rome (45), he was given a mandate by the people to rule, as dictator, for life. He introduced many reforms, including the Julian calendar and public libraries. On March 15, 44 B.C. (the ides of March), Caesar was murdered in the senate by a group of republicans, led by Cassius and Brutus, who feared that he was about to establish a monarchy with himself as king.

Cae·sar·e·an, Cae·sar·i·an (sĭ-zâr'ē-ən) *adj.* Pertaining to Julius Caesar or the Caesars.

~*n.* A **Caesarean section** (see).

Caesarean section *n. Sometimes* **caesarian section.** A surgical incision through the abdominal wall and uterus, performed to deliver a baby. Also called "Caesarean." [From an unhistorical tradition that the eponymous ancestor of the Roman family *Caesar* (or Julius *Caesar* himself) was born by this operation, and named *ā caesō mātris ūterē,* "from the *incised* womb of his mother," from *caesus,* past participle of *caedere,* to cut.]

Cae·sa·re·a Pal·es·ti·nae (sē'zə-rē'ə păl'ə-stī'nē, sĕs'ə-, sēz'ə-). Ancient city in Israel, lying south of Haifa. It was founded by Herod the Great in 13 B.C. as a port on the Mediterranean coast. An early center of Christianity, often referred to in the New Testament, Caesarea became the capital of Roman Judaea. The port declined after Muslim occupation (A.D. 638) and, though revived by the Crusaders, was destroyed by the Muslims (1265).

Cae·sar·ism (sē'zə-rĭz'əm) *n.* Military dictatorship. —**Cae·sar·ist** *n.* —**Cae·sar·is·tic** *adj.*

caesar salad *n.* A salad made with lettuce, cheese, croutons, and dressed with raw egg, oil, and lemon juice.

caesium Variant of **cesium.**

caespitose Variant of **cespitose.**

cae·su·ra, ce·su·ra (sĭ-zhōōr'ə, -zyōōr'ə, -zōōr'ə) *n., pl.* **-ras** or **-su·rae** (-zhōōr'ē, -zyōōr'ē, -zōōr'ē). **1.** A pause in a line of verse dictated by sense or natural speech rhythm rather than by meter. It is conventionally indicated by an oblique stroke: "*Drink deep,* / *or taste not the Pierian Spring*" (Alexander Pope). **2.** In Latin and Greek verse, a break in a line caused by the ending of a word within a foot, especially when this coincides with a sense division: "*Arma virumque cano* / *Troiae qui primus ab oris*" (Virgil). **3.** *Music.* A pause or breathing at a point of rhythmic division in a melody. [Latin, "a cutting off," from *caedere,* to cut off.] —**cae·su·ral, cae·su·ric** *adj.*

ca·fé, ca·fe (kă-fā', kə-) *n.* A coffee house, restaurant, or bar. [French, COFFEE.]

ca·fé au lait (kă-fā' ō lā') *n., pl.* **cafés au lait. 1.** Coffee served with hot milk. **2.** A light coffee color. [French, "coffee with milk."]

caf·e·te·ri·a (kăf'ə-tîr'ē-ə) *n.* A restaurant in which the customers are served at a counter and carry their meals to tables. [American

Spanish, coffee shop, from Spanish *cafetero,* coffee maker or seller, from *café,* COFFEE.]

caf·feine, caf·fein (kă-fēn′, kăf′ē-ĭn) *n.* A bitter white alkaloid, C₈H₁₀N₄O₂·H₂O, derived from coffee, tea, and cocoa, and used as a stimulant and diuretic. [German *Kaffein,* from *Kaffee,* COFFEE.]

caf·tan, kaf·tan (kăf′tən, kăf-tăn′) *n.* **1.** In the Near East, a full-length tunic with long sleeves and a sash at the waist, worn under a coat. **2.** A westernized version of this consisting of a loose and often brightly colored waist-length or ankle-length tunic. [Russian *kaftan,* from Turkish *kaftān.*]

cage (kāj) *n.* **1.** A structure for confining birds or animals, enclosed on at least one side by a grating of wires or bars in order to let in air and light. **2. a.** Any enclosure that serves as a means of confining prisoners. **b.** Anything that confines, physically or psychologically. **3.** Any framework having a cagelike appearance or construction. **4.** A rudimentary elevator car, especially one used in a mine. **5.** *Baseball.* **a.** A backstop used for batting practices. **b.** A catcher's mask. **6.** *Basketball.* The basket. **7.** *Hockey.* The goal, made of a network frame.
~*tr.v.* **caged, caging, cages.** To put in a cage; lock up or confine. [Middle English, from Old French, from Latin *cavea,* a hollow, enclosure, from *cavus,* hollow.]

Cage (kāj), **John** (1912–). Avant-garde U.S. composer, whose works include *Sonatas and Interludes,* for a prepared piano with its strings damped by wood and metal (1946–48), *Imaginary Landscape No. 4,* for 12 randomly tuned radios (1951), and *4 minutes 33 seconds,* silence in three movements for any instrument or instruments (1954).

cage bird *n.* A bird of a type that is often kept in a cage.

cage·ling (kāj′lĭng) *n.* A caged bird.

cag·ey, cag·y (kā′jē) *adj.* **-ier, -iest.** *Informal.* Wary; careful; unwilling to disclose information. [20th century (U.S.) : origin obscure.] —**cag·i·ly** *adv.* —**cag·i·ness** *n.*

Ca·glia·ri (käl′yə-rē). Administrative and industrial center of Sardinia, Italy. Also a seaport, it lies at the mouth of the Mannu River on the south side of the island. Founded by the Carthaginians, the city has a Roman amphitheater, a basilica (5th century), a massive Pisan tower (1304), and a university (1606).

Ca·glio·stro (käl-yô′strō), **Alessandro, Conte di,** born Giuseppe Balsamo (1743–95). Italian adventurer who became famous throughout Europe as an alchemist and magician. He died in Italy, following his incarceration for promoting freemasonry.

Cag·ney (kăg′nē), **James** (1899–1986). U.S. actor famous for his portrayals of gangsters, hard characters injected with elements of humanity. His films include *Public Enemy* (1931), *Angels with Dirty Faces* (1938), *The Roaring Twenties* (1939), and *Yankee Doodle Dandy* (1942), for which he won an Academy Award.

ca·hoots (kə-hōōts′) *pl.n. Informal.* Collaboration of a questionable nature. Used in the phrase *in cahoots.* [19th century : origin obscure.]

Cai·a·phas (kā′ə-fəs, kī′-), **Joseph.** Jewish high priest (A.D. *c.* 18–36); president of the council condemning Jesus. Matthew 26.

Caicos. See Turks and Caicos Islands.

cai·man, cay·man (kā′mən, kā-măn′, kī-măn′) *n., pl.* **-mans.** Any of various tropical American crocodilians of the genus *Caiman* and related genera, resembling and closely related to the alligators. [Spanish *caimán,* from Carib *cayman,* perhaps of African origin.]

cain Variant of **kain.**

Cain¹ (kān). The eldest son of Adam and Eve, who killed his brother Abel out of jealousy. Genesis 4. [Latin, from Greek *Kain,* from Hebrew *Qayin,* "creature."]

Cain² *n.* A murderer. —**raise Cain.** *Informal.* To create a great disturbance or uproar; make trouble. [From CAIN.]

–caine *suffix.* Indicates a synthetic alkaloid in anesthetic drugs; for example, **eucaine.** [From (CO)CAINE.]

cai·no·to·pho·bi·a (kā-nō′tə-fō′bē-ə) *n.* An abnormal fear of newness. [Greek *kainotēs,* newness + PHOBIA.]

ca·ique (kä-ēk′) *n.* **1.** A long, narrow rowing boat used in the Middle East. **2.** A small sailing vessel used in the eastern Mediterranean. [French, from Italian *caicco,* from Turkish *kayik.*]

caird (kârd) *n. Scottish.* A traveling tinker or handyman. [Scottish Gaelic *ceard,* artist, craftsman, from Old Irish *cerd,* art, artist.]

cairn (kârn) *n.* A mound of stones erected as a landmark or memorial. [Middle English *carne,* from Celtic *kar-n-, kr-ag-* (both unattested).] —**cairned** *adj.*

cairn·gorm (kârn′gôrm′) *n.* A smoky-brown or yellow variety of quartz, used as a semiprecious gem. Also called "smoky quartz." [After CAIRNGORM MOUNTAINS, where it is found.]

Cairn·gorm Mountains (kärn′gôrm′). Mountain range in northeast Scotland, forming part of the Grampians in Highland Region. A favorite winter sports resort, it includes Ben Macdhui, at 1,309 meters (4,295 feet) the second-highest peak in Scotland. The area was declared a nature reserve for arctic flora and fauna (1954).

Cairns (kârnz). Seaport on Trinity Bay in Queensland, Australia. It serves as an agricultural, timber, and mining region and is a tourist center for the Great Barrier Reef.

Cairn terrier *n.* A small dog of a breed developed in Scotland, having a broad head and a rough, shaggy coat. [So called because it hunts among cairns.]

Cai·ro (kī′rō). *Arabic* **Al Qa·hi·ra** (äl kä′hĭ-rō). Also **Al Fus·tat** (äl fōō-stät′). Capital of Egypt, lying on the east bank of the Nile River. It is the largest city in Africa and the Middle East and is one of the most important cultural, commercial, and political centers of

the Arab world. The pyramids at Giza, 13 kilometers (8 miles) southwest of Cairo, and Egypt's many other monuments and treasures, ensure a busy tourist industry. Other industries include textiles, food processing, plastics, and motor-vehicle assembly. Al Fustat, now Old Cairo, was established by Arab conquerors as a military camp (A.D. 642). Al Qahira was founded by the Fatimids as their capital (968). Saladin built the citadel (*c.* 1176), and extended the city's walls against Crusader attack. Cairo prospered under the Mamelukes, but fell to the Ottoman Turks (1517). Following Napoleon's occupation (1798–1801), it became the capital (1805–49) of a virtually independent kingdom under the pasha Mehemet Ali. The Al Azhar University (970) is reputedly the world's leading center for Koranic studies, and the city is also the headquarters of the Coptic Church of Egypt.

cais·son (kā′sŏn′, -sən) *n.* **1.** A watertight structure within which construction work is carried on. **2.** A watertight float, a **camel** (*see*). **3.** A floating structure used to close off the entrance to a dock or canal lock. **4.** A large box open at the top and one side, designed to fit against the side of a ship and used to repair damaged hulls under water. **5.** *Military.* **a.** A large box used to hold ammunition. **b.** A horse-drawn vehicle, usually two-wheeled, once used to carry ammunition. [French, from Old French *casson,* from Italian *cassa,* chest, box, from Latin *capsa.*]

caisson disease *n.* A disorder in divers and caisson and tunnel workers caused by a too rapid return from high pressure to atmospheric pressure, characterized by pains in the joints, cramps, paralysis, and eventual death unless treated by gradual decompression. Also called "aeroembolism," "the bends," "decompression sickness," "tunnel disease."

Caith·ness (kāth′nĕs′). Former county in northeast Scotland, part of Highland Region since 1975. Mainly infertile moorland and mountains, it sustains sheepherding, fishing, and farming.

cai·tiff (kā′tĭf) *n.* A base coward; a wretch.
~*adj.* Base and cowardly. [Middle English *caitif,* prisoner, captive, wretch, from Old French *caitivus,* from Latin *captīvus,* CAPTIVE.]

caj·e·put, caj·u·put (kăj′ə-pət, -pŏŏt′) *n.* **1.** A tree, *Melaleuca leucadendron,* native to Australia, having whitish flowers and leaves that yield an aromatic medicinal oil. **2.** The oil obtained from this tree. [Malay *kayu puteh : kayu,* tree + *puteh,* white.]

ca·jole (kə-jōl′) *tr.v.* **-joled, -joling, -joles.** To persuade by means of flattery; coax; wheedle. [French *cajoler* †.] —**ca·jol·er** *n.* —**ca·jol·er·y** *n.* —**ca·jol·ing·ly** *adv.*

Ca·jun, Ca·jan (kā′jən) *n.* **1.** A native of Louisiana believed to be descended from the French exiles from Acadia. **2.** The dialect of these people. **3.** Cajun music. [Alteration of ACADIAN.]

Cajun music *n.* A type of folk music originating among the Cajuns, typically using accordions and fiddles.

cake (kāk) *n.* **1.** A sweetened baked mixture of flour, liquid, eggs, and other ingredients, usually in loaf or rounded layer form. **2.** A flat, thin mass of dough or batter, baked or fried, such as a pancake or oatcake. **3.** A patty of fried food, such as a fishcake. **4.** A shaped or molded piece, as of soap. **5.** An aggregate of benefits, especially financial benefits, that are to be divided up or to be distributed: *workers want a larger slice of the cake.* —**go** (or **sell**) **like hot cakes.** To be in great demand; sell in large quantities. —**take the cake.** *Informal.* To win the prize; be outstanding.
~*v.* **caked, caking, cakes.** —*tr.* To cause to dry out and harden around something; encrust. —*intr.* To form a hard, dried-out mass. [Middle English *cake, kake,* from Old Norse *kaka.*]

cakes and ale *n.* Enjoyment of the good things in life.

cake·walk (kāk′wôk′) *n.* **1.** Formerly, a promenade or walk in which those performing the most complex and unusual steps won cakes as prizes. **2. a.** A strutting dance based on this promenade. **b.** The music for this dance. **3.** *Informal.* Something easily done.
~*intr.v.* **cakewalked, -walking, -walks.** To perform a cakewalk.

cal calorie (small).

Cal calorie (large).

cal. **1.** calendar. **2.** caliber.

Cal·a·bar bean (kăl′ə-bär′) *n.* The dark-brown poisonous seed of a woody vine, *Physostigma venenosum,* of tropical Africa. It is the source of the drug **physostigmine** (*see*). Also called "ordeal bean." [After *Calabar,* city in Nigeria.]

cal·a·bash (kăl′ə-băsh′) *n.* **1.** A vine, *Lagenaria siceraria,* native to the Old World, bearing large, hard-shelled gourds. Also called "bottle gourd." **2.** A tropical American tree, *Crescentia cujete,* bearing large, rounded fruit. Also called "bottle gourd." **3.** The hard-shelled fruit of a calabash vine or tree. **4.** A utensil, such as a dish, ladle, or tobacco pipe, made from the fruit of a calabash. [Obsolete French *calabasse,* from Spanish *calabaza*†.]

cal·a·boose (kăl′ə-bōōs′) *n. Slang.* A jail. [Louisiana French *calabouse,* from Spanish *calabozo*†, a dungeon.]

cal·a·bre·se (kăl′ə-brā′zē, -sē) *n.* **1.** An Italian variety of broccoli, *Brassica oleracea italica,* having a branched, greenish flower head. **2.** The flower head of this plant eaten as a vegetable before the green, tightly clustered buds have opened. [Italian, "Calabrian."]

Ca·la·bri·a (kə-lä′brē-ə, -lä′-). Region in Italy comprising the provinces of Cosenza, Cantanzaro, and Reggio di Calabria, forming the "toe of Italy" between the Ionian and Tyrrhenian seas. It is mainly mountainous, with extensive forests. Crotone is an industrial center, but the area is economically underdeveloped. The main sources of income are the cultivation of vines, citrus fruit, and olives, sheep and goat herding, and granite quarrying. Cantanzaro is the capital. —**Ca·la·bri·an** *n. & adj.*

ca·la·di·um (kə-lā'dē-əm) *n.* Any of various tropical plants of the genus *Caladium*, widely cultivated as potted plants for their showy, variegated foliage. [New Latin *Caladium*, from Malay *kĕladi*, araceous plant.]

Ca·lais (kă-lā', kăl'ā). Industrial town and seaport in Pas-de-Calais department, France. It is 35 kilometers (22 miles) east-southeast of Dover, on the shortest crossing between England and France. Calais was conquered by Edward III (1347) after a siege in which six burghers offered their lives for the town, but intervention by Edward's queen, Philippa, saved them. Calais remained in English possession until 1558. It was almost destroyed in World War II during the Dunkirk withdrawal. Industries include fishing, boatbuilding, textiles, and clothing.

cal·a·man·co (kăl'ə-măng'kō) *n., pl.* **-cos** or **-coes**. A glossy woolen fabric with a check pattern on only one side. [16th century : origin obscure.]

cal·a·man·der (kăl'ə-măn'dər) *n.* The hard, black-and-brown-striped wood of certain tropical Asiatic trees of the genus *Diospyros*, used in furniture. [Probably from Dutch *kalamander(hout)*, calamander (wood), perhaps metathetic variant of COROMANDEL COAST.]

cal·a·mine (kăl'ə-mīn', -mĭn) *n.* **1.** A white or sometimes iron- or copper-stained mineral, essentially $Zn_4Si_2O_7(OH)_2 \cdot H_2O$. Also called "hemimorphite." **2.** *Pharmacology.* A pink, odorless, tasteless powder of zinc oxide with a small amount of ferric oxide, dissolved in mineral oils and used in skin lotions. [French, from Medieval Latin *calamīna*, alteration of Latin *cadmia*, from Greek *kadmeia*, "Cadmean (earth)" (first found near Thebes, city founded by Cadmus), from *kadmeios*, of CADMUS.]

cal·a·mint (kăl'ə-mĭnt') *n.* Any of several aromatic plants of the genus *Calamintha*; especially, *S. calamintha*, native to Eurasia, having clusters of purplish or pink flowers. [Middle English *calament*, from Old French, from Medieval Latin *calamentum*, variant of Late Latin *calaminthē*, from Greek *kalaminthē†.*]

cal·a·mite (kăl'ə-mīt) *n.* Any of various extinct treelike Carboniferous plants of the genus *Calamites*, resembling the horsetails, but much larger, and known only as fossils. [New Latin *Calamites*, from Late Greek *kalamitēs*, reedlike, from Greek, of a reed, from *kalamos*, reed.]

ca·lam·i·tous (kə-lăm'ə-təs) *adj.* Causing or involving a disaster. **—ca·lam·i·tous·ly** *adv.* **—ca·lam·i·tous·ness** *n.*

ca·lam·i·ty (kə-lăm'ə-tē) *n., pl.* **-ties. 1.** A disaster, especially one that leads to personal loss and suffering. **2.** Dire distress. —See Synonyms at **disaster.** [Middle English *calamite*, from Old French, from Latin *calamitās* (stem *calamitāt-*).]

Calamity Jane. See Martha Jane **Burke.**

cal·a·mus (kăl'ə-məs) *n., pl.* **-mi** (-mī'). **1.** A plant, the **sweet flag** *(see)*, or its aromatic root. **2.** Any of various tropical Asiatic palms of the genus *Calamus*, from some of which rattan is obtained. **3.** A part of a feather, a **quill** *(see)*. [Latin, reed, cane, from Greek *kalamos.*]

ca·lan·do (kä-län'dō) *adj. Music.* Gradually diminishing in tempo and volume.
~*adv. Music.* In a calando manner. [Italian, from Latin *calandum*, a slackening, from *calāre, chalāre*, to let fall, slacken, from Greek *khalan.*]

cal·an·dri·a (kə-lăn'drē-ə) *n.* A heat exchanger, as in the core of a nuclear reactor, consisting of a vessel with vertical tubes passing through it.

ca·lash (kə-lăsh') *n.* Also **ca·lèche** (kə-lĕsh'). **1.** A carriage with low wheels and a collapsible top. **2.** The top of such a carriage. **3.** A woman's folding bonnet, fashionable in the late 18th century. [French *calèche*, from German *Kalesche*, from Czech *kolesa*, plural of *koleso*, wheel, from *kolo* (stem *koles-*), wheel, from Old Church Slavonic.]

cal·a·thus (kăl'ə-thəs) *n., pl.* **-thi** (-thī'). A vase-shaped basket represented in ancient Greek painting and sculpture. [Latin, from Greek *kalathos†.*]

cal·a·ver·ite (kăl'ə-vâr'īt') *n.* A rare ore of gold, essentially gold telluride, AuTe₂, often containing silver. [After *Calaveras*, county in California, where it was discovered.]

cal·ca·ne·o·cu·boid ligament (kăl-kā'nē-ō-kyōō'boid') *n.* The ligament that connects the calcaneus and the cuboid bones.

cal·ca·ne·us (kăl-kā'nē-əs) *n., pl.* **cal·ca·ne·i** (-nē-ī') *pl.* **-nea** (-nē-ə). The quadrangular bone at the back of the tarsus, forming the projection of the heel. Also called "heel bone." [Latin, "heel," from *calx* (stem *calc-*), heel.] **—cal·ca·ne·al** *adj.*

cal·car (kăl'kär') *n., pl.* **calcaria** (kăl-kâr'ē). *Biology.* An anatomical spur or spurlike projection. [Latin, spur, from *calx* (stem *calc-*), heel.]

cal·car·e·ous (kăl-kâr'ē-əs) *adj.* Composed of, containing, or characteristic of calcium carbonate, calcium, or limestone; chalky. [Latin *calcārius*, from *calx* (stem *calc-*), lime.]

cal·ca·rine fissure (kăl'kə-rīn') *n.* A calcarine sulcus.

calcarine sul·cus (sŭl'kəs) *n.* A sulcus on the occipital lobe of the brain. [CALCAR + -INE.]

cal·ce·i·form (kăl'sē-ə-fôrm') *adj. Botany.* Slipper-shaped; calceolate. [Latin *calceus*, shoe (see **calceolate**) + -FORM.]

cal·ce·o·lar·i·a (kăl'sē-ə-lâr'ē-ə) *n.* Any of various plants of the genus *Calceolaria*, native to tropical America and widely cultivated for their yellow, speckled, slipper-shaped flowers. Also called "slipperwort." [New Latin, from Latin *calceolārius*, shoemaker, from *calceolus*, small shoe. See **calceolate.**]

cal·ce·o·late (kăl'sē-ə-lāt') *adj. Botany.* Shaped like a slipper, as the blossoms of some orchids. [Latin *calceolus*, diminutive of *calceus†*, shoe.]

cal·ces. Alternate plural of **calx.**

calci-, calc– *prefix.* Indicates lime or calcium; for example, **calciferous, calcite.** [Latin *calx* (stem *calc-*), lime, limestone.]

cal·cic (kăl'sĭk) *adj.* Composed of, containing, derived from, or pertaining to calcium or lime.

cal·ci·cole (kăl'sĭ-kōl') *n. Botany.* A plant that thrives in soil rich in lime. [French : CALCI- + -cole, dweller, from Latin -*cola* (see **-colous**).] **—cal·cic·o·lous** *adj.*

cal·ci·co·sis (kăl'sĭ-kō'sĭs) *n.* A pneumoconiosis resulting from the inhalation of calcium carbonate dust. [CALCI- + -cosis (as in *silicosis*).]

cal·cif·er·ol (kăl-sĭf'ə-rôl', -rōl') *n.* One of the forms in which **vitamin D** *(see)* occurs. [*Calciferous* + ergosterol.]

cal·cif·er·ous (kăl-sĭf'ər-əs) *adj.* Of, forming, or containing calcium or calcium carbonate. [CALCI- + -FEROUS.]

cal·cif·ic (kăl-sĭf'ĭk) *adj.* Producing salts of lime, as in the formation of eggshells in birds.

cal·ci·fi·ca·tion (kăl'sə-fĭ-kā'shən) *n.* **1.** Impregnation with calcium or calcium salts, as with calcium carbonate. **2.** Hardening, as of tissue, by such impregnation. **3.** A substance, such as petrified wood, or a part so impregnated.

cal·ci·fuge (kăl'sə-fyōōj') *n.* A plant that does not thrive in lime-rich soil, preferring acid soil. **—cal·cif·u·gal, cal·cif·u·gous** *adj.*

cal·ci·fy (kăl'sə-fī') *v.* **-fied, -fying, -fies.** —*tr.* To make stony or chalky by deposition of calcium salts. —*intr.* To become stony or chalky by deposition of calcium salts. [CALCI- + -FY.]

cal·ci·mine (kăl'sə-mīn') *n.* Also **kal·so·mine.** A white or tinted liquid containing zinc oxide, water, glue, and coloring matter, used as a wash for walls and ceilings. Also *British* "distemper."
~*tr.v.* **calcimined, -mining, -mines.** To cover or wash with calcimine. [Alteration of trademark *Kalsomine.*]

cal·cine (kăl'sīn', kăl-sīn') *v.* **-cined, -cining, -cines.** —*tr.* To heat (a substance) to a high temperature but below the melting or fusing point, causing loss of moisture, reduction, or oxidation. —*intr.* To undergo oxidation as a result of heating. [Middle English *calcinen*, from Old French *calciner*, from Medieval Latin *calcīnāre*, from Latin *calx*, lime. See **calcium.**] **—cal·ci·na·tion** *n.*

cal·cite (kăl'sīt') *n.* A common crystalline form of natural calcium carbonate, the basic constituent of limestone, marble, and chalk. Also called "calcspar." **—cal·cit·ic** *adj.*

cal·ci·ton·in (kăl'sĭ-tō'nĭn) *n.* A hormone secreted by the thyroid that lowers the amount of calcium in the blood to within normal limits. Also called "thyrocalcitonin." [CALCI- + TON(IC) + -IN.]

cal·ci·um (kăl'sē-əm) *n. Symbol* **Ca** A silvery, moderately hard metallic element, constituting approximately three percent of the earth's crust, a basic component of bone, shells, and teeth. It occurs naturally in limestone, gypsum, and fluorite, and its compounds are used to make plaster, quicklime, Portland cement, and metallurgic and electronic materials. Atomic number 20, atomic weight 40.08, melting point 842 to 848°C, boiling point 1,487°C, specific gravity 1.55, valence 2. [New Latin, from Latin *calx* (stem *calc-*), lime, limestone, from Greek *khalix†*, pebble.]

calcium carbide *n.* A grayish-black crystalline compound, CaC₂, obtained by heating pulverized limestone or quicklime with carbon and used to generate acetylene, as a dehydrating agent, and in the manufacture of graphite and hydrogen.

calcium carbonate *n.* A colorless or white crystalline compound, CaCO₃, occurring naturally as chalk, limestone, marble, and other forms and used in a wide variety of manufactured products including commercial chalk, medicines, and toothpastes.

calcium chloride *n.* A white deliquescent compound, CaCl₂, used chiefly as a drying agent, refrigerant, and preservative.

calcium cyanamide *n.* A gray-black compound, Ca(CN)₂, used as a fertilizer and weedkiller. Also called "cyanamide."

calcium fluoride *n.* A white powder, CaF₂, used in emery wheels, carbon electrodes, and cements.

calcium hydroxide *n.* A soft white powder, Ca(OH)₂, used in making mortar, cements, calcium salts, paints, hard rubber products, and petrochemicals. Also called "lime," "slaked lime."

calcium hypochlorite *n.* A white crystalline solid, Ca(OCl)₂, used as a bactericide, fungicide, and bleaching agent.

calcium light *n.* An intense white light produced by incandescent lime, **limelight** *(see).*

calcium oxalate *n.* A white crystalline powder, CaC₂O₄, used to make oxalic acid and found in many plant cells.

calcium oxide *n.* A white caustic lumpy powder, CaO, used as a refractory, as a flux, in manufacturing steel, glassmaking, waste treatment, insecticides, and as an industrial alkali. Also called "lime," "quicklime," "unslaked lime," "calx."

calcium phosphate *n.* Any of several phosphate compounds, especially: **1.** A white crystalline powder, CaHPO₄ or CaHPO₄·2H₂O, used as a food, as a plastic stabilizer, and in glass; dibasic calcium phosphate. **2.** A colorless deliquescent powder, CaH₄(PO₄)₂·H₂O, used in baking powders, as a plant food, plastic stabilizer, and in glass; monobasic calcium phosphate. **3.** A white amorphous powder, Ca₃(PO₄)₂, used in ceramics, rubber, fertilizers, plastic stabilizers, and as a food supplement; tribasic calcium phosphate.

calc-sin·ter (kălk'sĭn'tər) *n.* Natural calcium carbonate, chiefly in the form of stalagmites or stalactites. See **travertine.** [German *Kalksinter : Kalk*, lime + *Sinter*, slag, SINTER.]

calc·spar (kălk′spär′) *n.* **Calcite** *(see).* [Partial translation of Swedish *kalkspar* : *kalk,* lime (see **calcium**) + SPAR (mineral).]

calc-tu·fa (kălk′to͞o′fə, -tyo͞o′fə) *n.* Also **calc-tuff** (-tŭf′). A porous or spongy deposit of calcium carbonate found in calcareous mineral springs. [*Calc*areous + *tufa.*]

cal·cu·la·ble (kăl′kyə-lə-bəl) *adj.* **1.** Capable of being calculated or estimated. **2.** That may be counted or depended on. **—cal·cu·la·bil·i·ty** *n.*

cal·cu·late (kăl′kyə-lāt′) *v.* **-lated, -lating, -lates.** *—tr.* **1.** To ascertain by computation; reckon. **2.** To make an estimate of; evaluate. **3.** To fit or plan for a purpose; design. Usually used in the passive: *His speech was cleverly calculated to stir up ill feeling against the government.* **4.** *Regional.* **a.** To purpose, intend. **b.** To think; suppose. *—intr.* **1.** To execute a mathematical process. **2.** To suppose; think; guess. [Latin *calculāre,* from *calculus,* small stone (used in reckoning), diminutive of *calx* (stem *calc-*), lime, limestone, from Greek *khalix,* pebble.]

Synonyms: *compute, estimate, reckon.*

cal·cu·lat·ed (kăl′kyə-lā′tĭd) *adj.* **1.** Estimated with forethought: *a calculated risk.* **2.** Deliberately planned to achieve a particular purpose. **3.** Determined by mathematical calculation. **—cal·cu·lat·ed·ly** *adv.* **—cal·cu·lat·ed·ness** *n.*

cal·cu·lat·ing (kăl′kyə-lā′tĭng) *adj.* **1.** Performing calculations: *a calculating machine.* **2. a.** Shrewd; crafty. **b.** Coldly scheming or conniving.

cal·cu·la·tion (kăl′kyə-lā′shən) *n.* **1.** The act, process, or result of calculating. **2.** An estimate based upon probabilities. **3.** *Often* **calculations. a.** Deliberation; foresight. **b.** Shrewd scheming. **—cal·cu·la·tive** *adj.*

cal·cu·la·tor (kăl′kyə-lā′tər) *n.* **1.** A mechanical or electronic device for the automatic performance of arithmetical operations. **2.** A person who performs calculations. **3.** A set of mathematical tables used as an aid in calculating.

cal·cu·lous (kăl′kyə-ləs) *adj. Medicine.* Pertaining to, caused by, or having a calculus or calculi.

cal·cu·lus (kăl′kyə-ləs) *n., pl.* **-li** (-lī′) or **-luses. 1.** *Pathology.* An abnormal concretion in the body, usually formed of mineral salts; a stone, as in the gall bladder, kidney, or urinary bladder. **2.** *Mathematics.* **a.** A method of analysis or calculation using a special symbolic notation. **b.** The combined mathematics of **differential calculus** and **integral calculus** *(both of which see).* [Latin, small stone (used in reckoning), reckoning. See **calculate.**]

calculus of variations *n.* The mathematical analysis of the maxima and minima of definite integrals, the integrands of which are functions of independent variables, dependent variables, and the derivatives of one or more dependent variables.

Cal·cut·ta (kăl-kŭt′ə). Capital city of West Bengal state, India. Built on the Hooghly River, it is India's largest city and one of the world's most densely populated. It was founded as a British East India Company trading post (*c.* 1690). Captured by Siraj-ud-Dawlah, the nawab of Bengal (1756), it was retaken by Robert Clive (1757). During the campaign, the nawab confined 146 prisoners overnight in a small guardhouse (see **Black Hole of Calcutta**). Calcutta is the chief port and industrial center of eastern India.

Cal·der (kôl′dər), **Alexander** (1898–1976). U.S. sculptor who created the mobile in Paris in the early 1930's.

cal·de·ra (kăl-dâr′ə, -dĭr′ə) *n.* A large crater formed by the collapse of a volcanic cone, or by a volcanic explosion that removes the top of the original cone. [Spanish, "kettle," "boiler," from Late Latin *caldāria,* CAULDRON.]

Cal·der·ón de la Bar·ca (kăl′də-rôn′ dā lə bär′kə) **Pedro** (1600–81). Spanish author. He was one of the greatest dramatists of Spain's Golden Age (17th century). Among his better known works are *The Surgeon and His Honor* (1635), *Life is a Dream* (1635), and *The Daughter of the Air* (1653).

cal·dron, caul·dron (kôl′drən) *n.* A large kettle or vat for boiling. [Middle English *caud(e)ron, caldron,* from Old North French *caud(e)ron,* from Late Latin *caldāria,* from Latin, warm bath, from *caldārius,* suitable for warming, from *cal(i)dus, warm.*]

Cald·well (kôl′dwĕl′, -dwəl), **Erskine Preston** (1903–). U.S. author. His graphic novels about poverty and degeneration established him as a controversial and highly popular author. *Tobacco Road* (1932), *God's Little Acre* (1933), and *Trouble in July* (1940) are among his most critically successful novels. He also collaborated with his second wife, photographer Margaret Bourke-White, on *You Have Seen Their Faces* (1937) and other titles.

Ca·leb (kā′ləb). A Hebrew leader. He and Joshua were the only two allowed to enter the Promised Land. Numbers 14:24.

calèche. Variant of **calash.**

Cal·e·do·ni·a (kăl′ə-dō′nē-ə, -dōn′yə). The Roman name for Scotland. It was first used by Lucan, the Roman poet (1st century A.D.), to describe Britain north of the Antonine Wall, which reached from the Firth of Forth to the Firth of Clyde. Today Caledonia is chiefly used in the names of many Scottish institutions and in poetry.

Cal·e·do·ni·an (kăl′ə-dō′nē-ən, -yən) *adj.* **1.** *Poetic.* Of or pertaining to Scotland. **2.** *Geology.* Of or pertaining to the mountain-building episode that occurred in the late Silurian and Devonian periods. *~n. Poetic.* A native of Scotland.

cal·en·dar (kăl′ən-dər) *n. Abbr.* **cal. 1.** Any of various systems of reckoning time in which the beginning, length, and divisions of a year are arbitrarily defined or otherwise established. **2.** A table showing the months, weeks, and days in at least one specific year. **3.** A list or schedule, especially one arranged in chronological order, as of court cases awaiting trial, sporting events, or the like: *the next big event in the racing calendar.* **4.** *Library Science.* A chronological list of documents or manuscripts, usually annotated. **5.** *Obsolete.* A guide; an example.
~tr.v. **calendared, -daring, -dars.** To enter on a calendar; list; schedule. [Middle English *calender,* from Norman French, from Medieval Latin *kalendārium,* from Latin, a moneylender's account book (because the monthly interest was due on the calends), from *kalendae,* the CALENDS.] See feature, next page.

calendar month *n.* See **month** (sense 1).

cal·en·der (kăl′ən-dər) *n.* A machine in which paper or cloth is made smooth and glossy by being pressed through rollers.
~tr.v. **calendered, -dering, -ders.** To press in a calender. [French *calendre,* from Medieval Latin *calendra, celendra,* from Latin *cylindrus,* cylinder, roller, from Greek *kulindros,* from *kulindein,* to roll.] **—cal·en·der·er** *n.*

ca·len·dri·cal (kə-lĕn′drĭ-kəl) *adj.* Of, pertaining to, or used in a calendar.

cal·ends (kăl′əndz) *n., pl.* **calends.** Also **kal·ends.** *Used with a singular or plural verb.* In the ancient Roman calendar, the day of the new moon and the first day of the month. [Middle English *kalendes,* from Latin *kalendae.*] **—ca·len·dal** *adj.*

ca·len·du·la (kə-lĕn′jo͞o-lə) *n.* Any plant of the genus *Calendula,* having orange-yellow rayed flowers; especially, the **pot marigold** *(see).* [New Latin *Calendula,* from Medieval Latin *calendula,* marigold, from Latin *kalendae,* CALENDS (perhaps because it was thought to be a cure for menstrual disorders).]

cal·en·ture (kăl′ən-cho͝or′) *n.* A mild, brief, or sometimes persistent tropical fever. [Spanish *calentura,* from *calentar,* to heat, from Latin *calēns* (stem *calent-*), present participle of *calēre,* to be warm.]

calf[1] (kăf, käf) *n., pl.* **calves** (kăvz, kävz). **1.** A young cow or bull. **2.** The young of certain other mammals, such as the elephant or whale. **3.** Calfskin. **4.** A large, floating chunk of ice split from a glacier, iceberg, or floe. **5.** An awkward, callow youth. **—kill the fatted calf.** To prepare a feast of welcome; celebrate in grand style. [Middle English *calf, kelf,* Old English *cealf,* from West Germanic *kalbam* (unattested).]

calf[2] *n., pl.* **calves.** The fleshy, muscular back part of the human leg, between the knee and ankle. [Middle English, from Old Norse *kalfi*†.]

calf's-foot jelly, calves'-foot jelly (kăvz′fo͝ot′, kăvz′-) *n.* A gelatinous food made by boiling calves' feet.

calf·skin (kăf′skĭn′, käf′-) *n.* **1.** The hide of a calf. **2.** *Abbr.* **cf.** Fine leather made from the hide of a calf. In this sense, also called "calf."

Cal·ga·ry (kăl′gə-rē). City of southern Alberta, Canada. Situated at the confluence of the Bow and Elbow rivers, it is the market center for south Alberta and the heart of Canada's petroleum industry. It has a famous annual rodeo, the Calgary Stampede.

Cal·houn (kăl-ho͞on′), **John Caldwell** (1782–1850). U.S. vice president (1824–32) and political philosopher. As a South Carolina senator devoted to protecting the interests of the South, he argued that the citizens of individual states had the right to nullify any federal legislation that they deemed unconstitutional (1832–33). He wrote several theses elucidating his political views.

Cal·i·ban (kăl′ə-băn′) *n.* A man of savage and brutish character. [After a character in Shakespeare's *The Tempest,* perhaps alteration of CARIBAN.]

cal·i·ber (kăl′ə-bər) *n.* Also *chiefly British* **cal·i·bre. 1.** *Abbr.* **cal. a.** The diameter of the inside of a tube. **b.** The diameter of the bore of a gun. **c.** The diameter of a bullet or shell. **2.** Degree of excellence, worth, or distinction. [Old French *calibre,* from Old Italian *calibro,* from Arabic *qālib,* shoemaker's last, probably from Greek *kalapous,* "wooden foot" : *kalon,* wood, firewood, from *kaiein,* to burn + *pous,* foot.]

cal·i·brate (kăl′ə-brāt′) *tr.v.* **-brated, -brating, -brates. 1.** To check, adjust, or standardize systematically the graduations of a quantitative measuring instrument. **2.** To determine the caliber of (a tube). **—cal·i·bra·tion** *n.* **—cal·i·bra·tor** *n.*

ca·li·ces. Plural of **calix.**

ca·li·che (kə-lē′chē; *Spanish* kä-lē′chā) *n.* **1. a.** A crude sodium nitrate occurring naturally in Chile, Peru, and the southwestern United States, used as fertilizer. **b. Sodium nitrate** *(see).* **2.** A hard soil layer cemented by calcium carbonate and found in deserts and other arid or semiarid regions. [American Spanish, from Spanish, chip of limestone, from *cal,* lime(stone), from Latin *calx,* from Greek *khalix,* pebble.]

cal·i·co (kăl′ĭ-kō) *n., pl.* **-coes** or **-cos. 1.** A coarse cloth, usually printed with bright designs. **2.** *British.* A plain white cotton cloth. *~adj.* **1.** Made of calico. **2.** Resembling printed calico; spotted; mottled: *a calico cat.* [Earlier *calicut,* after CALICUT.]

cal·i·co·back (kăl′ĭ-kō-băk′) *n.* The **harlequin bug** *(see).*

calico bush *n.* A shrub, the **mountain laurel** *(see).*

Cal·i·cut (kăl′ə-kət). Also **Ko·zhi·kode** (kō′zhə-kōd′). City on the southwest coast of India. Vasco da Gama made his first landfall in India on the site, where the Portuguese, British, French, and Danes later established trading posts. Finally ceded to Britain (1792), Calicut became the chief port of southern India. It gave its name to calico, its main export in the 17th century.

calif. Variant of **caliph.**

Cal·i·for·nia (kăl′ə-fôrn′yə, -fôr′nē-ə). Pacific state of the United States. The third-largest state and the most populous, it is known as the "Golden State" because of its sunny climate and the discovery of gold in pioneering days. Its forested coastal ranges are noted for

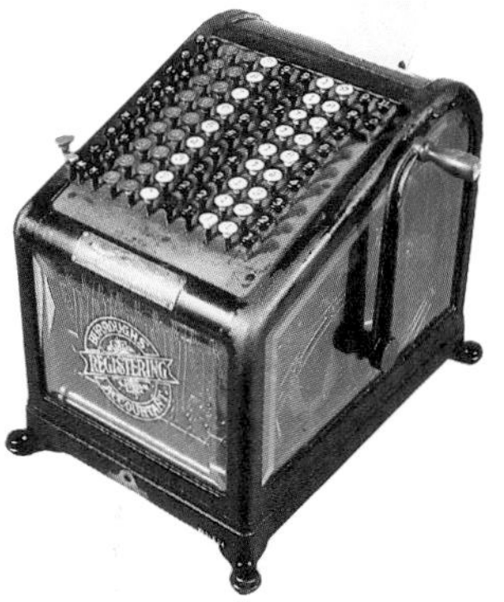

calculator *This Burroughs adding machine, one of the first mechanical calculators, was used by a British bank between 1897 and 1913. Digits were added by pressing the keys and the sum total was given by operating the handle. The machine is now in the Science Museum, London.*

MEASURING THE PASSAGE OF TIME

How cycles of the sun and moon are used to predict events

Almost every society has had to devise a system of measuring time in order to fix dates for annual events such as seasonal or religious festivals. Primitive societies calculated time by so many suns and moons, and the complex calendars of more sophisticated societies are also based on cycles of the sun and moon.

But the lunar and solar cycles are not compatible. The lunar month (the interval between two new moons) averages 29.5 days, 12 lunar months equaling 354 days. The solar year (the time the earth takes to orbit from one vernal equinox to the next) is 365 days 5 hours 48 minutes and 46 seconds (365.24 days), equaling 12.37 lunar months. So calendars based on a lunar year do not keep in step with the seasons.

The Roman Julian calendar of the 1st century B.C. was based on the solar cycle, having an average year of 365.25 days—the fractions of a day were taken up in a 366-day leap year every four years. But by 1582 it was more than 10 days behind the seasons because the time difference between 365.24 and 365.25 days (11 minutes 14 seconds) amounts to 7–8 days over 1,000 years. Pope Gregory XIII therefore deleted 10 days in 1582, and to reduce future error he decreed that centennial years should be leap years only if divisible by 400 (so 1900, for example, was not a leap year but 2000 will be). The Gregorian calendar was adopted in Britain and the American colonies in 1752.

GREGORIAN A widely used calendar matching the seasons with a 365¼-day year.		HEBREW The year 5743 coincided with September 18, 1982–August 10, 1983.		MUSLIM In the Muslim year 1396, Muharram corresponded with January 1976.		CHINESE The ancient Chinese agricultural calendar has 24 seasonal segments each of about a fortnight. The Gregorian dates given are approximate.	
Month	days	Month	days	Month	days	Fortnight	Gregorian dates
January	31	Tishri (September–October)	30	Muharram	30	Li Chun (Spring Begins)	February 5–19
						Yu Shui (Rain Water)	February 19–March 5
February (Leap year 29)	28	Heshvan (October–November) (in some years 30)	29	Safar	29	Jing Zhe (Excited Insects)	March 5–20
						Chun Fen (Vernal Equinox)	March 20–April 4/5
March	31	Kislev (November–December) (in some years 30)	29	Rabī' I	30	Qing Ming (Clear and Bright)	April 4/5–20
						Gu Yu (Grain Rains)	April 20–May 5
April	30	Tevet (December–January)	29	Rabī' II	29	Li Xia (Summer Begins)	May 5–21
						Xiao Man (Grain Fills)	May 21–June 5
May	31	Shevat (January–February)	30	Jumādā I	30	Mang Zhong (Grain in Ear)	June 5–21
						Xia Zhi (Summer Solstice)	June 21–July 7
June	30	Adar (February–March) (in leap year 30)	29	Jumādā II	29	Xiao Shu (Slight Heat)	July 7–23
						Da Shu (Great Heat)	July 23–August 7
July	31	Nisan (March–April)	30	Rajab	30	Li Qiu (Autumn Begins)	August 7–23
						Chu Shu (Limit of Heat)	August 23–September 7
August	31	Iyar (April–May)	29	Sha'ban	29	Bai Lu (White Dew)	September 7–23
						Qui Fen (Autumn Equinox)	September 23–October 8
September	30	Sivan (May–June)	30	Ramadān	30	Han Lu (Cold Dew)	October 8–23
						Shuang Jiang (Frost Descends)	October 23–November 7
October	31	Tammuz (June–July)	29	Shawwāl	29	Li Dong (Winter Begins)	November 7–22
						Xiao Xue (Little Snow)	November 22–December 7
November	30	Av (July–August)	30	Dhū al-Qa'dah	30	Da Xue (Heavy Snow)	December 7–22
						Dong Zhi (Winter Solstice)	December 22–January 6
December	31	Elul (August–September)	29	Dhū al-Hijjah	29 or 30	Xiao Han (Little Cold)	January 6–21
						Da Han (Severe Cold)	January 21–February 5

FOUR CALENDARS IN USE TODAY *The Hebrew and Muslim calendars are based on the lunar year, the Gregorian on the solar year, and the Chinese on lunar and solar cycles. The Hebrew calendar periodically includes an extra month (First Adar), and the Chinese does so occasionally. In the Muslim calendar, an extra day is added to the last month in some years to ensure that the first day of the month coincides with the new moon. The Chinese calendar is banned in China but is still used in parts of Asia.*

their giant redwood trees. The state's products include fruit, wine, natural gas, gold, silver, and copper, while its manufacturing includes aerospace and defense-linked industries. California was colonized by the Spaniards and ceded to the United States in 1848. Sacramento is the capital. —**Cal·i·for·nian** *n. & adj.*

California laurel *n.* An aromatic evergreen tree, *Umbellularia californica*, of the North American Pacific Coast, having yellowish-green fleshy fruit and attractively grained wood. Also called "bay tree," "Oregon myrtle."

California lilac *n.* A shrub, the **blueblossom** *(see).*

California nutmeg *n.* An evergreen tree, *Torreya californica*, having spiny, pointed leaves and purple-streaked, greenish fruit.

California poppy *n.* A plant, *Eschscholtzia californica*, native to the Pacific Coast of North America but widely cultivated, having finely divided bluish-green leaves and orange-yellow flowers.

cal·i·for·ni·um (kăl′ə-fôr′nē-əm) *n. Symbol* **Cf** A synthetic element produced in trace quantities, originally by helium isotope bombardment of curium. All isotopes are radioactive, chiefly by emission of alpha particles. Atomic number 98, mass numbers 244–254, half-

lives varying from 25 minutes to 800 years. [New Latin; discovered at the University of *California* (Berkeley).]

ca·lig·i·nous (kə-lĭj′ə-nəs) *adj.* Dark; gloomy; shadowy. [Old French *caligineux*, from Latin *cālīginōsus*, dark, from *cālīgō†*, darkness.]

Ca·lig·u·la (kə-lĭg′yə-lə), born Gaius Caesar Augustus Germanicus (A.D. 12–41). Roman emperor (37–41). The son of Germanicus Caesar and Agrippina the Elder, he was adopted (A.D. 32) by Tiberius, on whose death he succeeded. He ennobled his favorite horse, claimed to be a manifestation of all the gods, and provoked a riot in Jerusalem by ordering a statue of himself to be erected in the temple. He was assassinated after alienating the army and threatening to execute the members of the senate. As a child, he wore military boots and was dubbed Caligula (little boot) by his father's soldiers.

cal·i·pash (kăl′ə-păsh′, kăl′ə-păsh′) *n.* An edible, gelatinous, greenish substance lying beneath a turtle's upper shell. [Probably alteration of Spanish *carapacho*, CARAPACE.]

cal·i·pee (kăl′ə-pē′, kăl′ə-pē′) *n.* An edible, gelatinous, yellowish substance lying above a turtle's lower shell. [Probably alteration of CALIPASH.]

cal·i·per, cal·li·per (kăl′ə-pər) **1.** *Usually* **calipers.** An instrument consisting essentially of two curved hinged legs, used to measure internal and external dimensions. **2.** A **vernier caliper** *(see).* **3.** *Medical.* Either of a pair of metal rods with straps and attachments for providing support to or exerting tension on a leg.
~*v.* **calipered, -pering, -pers.** —*tr.* To measure with calipers. —*intr.* To determine dimensions by using calipers. [Probably a variant of CALIBRE.]

ca·liph, ca·lif, ka·lif, kha·lif (kā′lĭf, kăl′ĭf) *n.* The secular and religious head of a Muslim state. [Middle English *caliphe, califfe,* from Old French *calife,* from Arabic *khalīfa,* "successor" (of Muhammad), from *khalafa,* to succeed.]

ca·liph·ate (kā′lĭf-āt′, kăl′ĭf-, -ĭt) *n.* The office, jurisdiction, or reign of a caliph.

cal·i·sa·ya (kăl′ə-sā′ə) *n.* The bark of any tree of the genus *Cinchona,* from which quinine is obtained. Also called "calisaya bark," "yellowbark." [Spanish, probably after *Calisaya,* 17th-century Bolivian Indian who taught the Spanish the use of quinine contained in the bark.]

cal·is·then·ics, cal·lis·then·ics (kăl′əs-thĕn′ĭks) *pl.n.* **1.** Simple gymnastic exercises designed to develop muscular tone and to promote physical well-being **2.** *Used with a singular verb.* The practice of such exercises. [CAL(L)I- + Greek *sthenos,* strength (see **sthenia**).] —**cal′is·then′ic** *adj.*

calk[1] (kôk) *n.* A pointed extension on the toe or heels of a horseshoe designed to prevent slipping.
~*tr.v.* **calked, calking, calks. 1.** To supply with calks. **2.** To cut or injure with a calk. [Short for earlier *calkin,* Middle English *kakun,* from Middle Dutch *calcoen,* hoof of a horse, from Old French *calcain,* heel, from Latin *calcāneum, calcāneus,* from *calx*† (stem *calc-*).]

calk[2]. Variant of **caulk.**

call (kôl) *v.* **called, calling, calls.** —*tr.* **1.** To cry out in a loud voice so as to attract attention. **2.** To summon. **3.** To convoke or convene (a meeting). **4.** To summon to a specified vocation or pursuit. **5.** To awaken. **6.** To telephone (someone). **7.** To name. **8.** To estimate as being; consider: *I call that fair.* **9.** To describe as; label: *Nobody calls me a liar.* **10.** *Law.* To bring to action or under consideration: *call a case to court.* **11.** To demand payment of (a loan or bond issue). **12.** *Baseball.* **a.** To stop (a game) because of bad weather or darkness. **b.** To indicate a decision in regard to (a pitch, ball, strike, or player) **13.** *Billiards.* **a.** To predict (the outcome of a shot) before playing **b.** To ask (another player) to do so. **14.** To forecast or predict accurately. **15.** *Poker.* To demand to see the hand of (an opponent) by equaling his bet. **16.** To read aloud (a register or list) to ascertain any absences. **17.** To shout (directions) in rhythm for square dances. —*intr.* **1.** To telephone. **2.** To pay a short visit. **3.** To attract attention by shouting. **4.** To urge one to go: *duty calls.* **5.** *Bridge.* To make a bid. **6.** To guess the result of the toss of a coin or spin of a racket. **7.** To make a characteristic cry. Used chiefly of birds. —**call back. 1.** To telephone in return. **2.** To retract or disavow. —**call down. 1.** To invoke, as from heaven. **2.** *Informal.* To find fault with or berate. —**call for. 1.** To go and get, or stop for. **2.** To be appropriate for; warrant: *This calls for a celebration.* —**call forth.** To evoke. —**call in. 1.** To collect or request payment of. **2.** To take out of circulation: *calling in silver dollars.* **3.** To summon for assistance or consultation: *call in a specialist.* —**call into being.** To create or cause to exist. —**call into question.** To raise doubt about. —**call off. 1.** To cancel or postpone. **2.** To restrain or recall. **3.** To read aloud, as from a list of names. —**call on** or **upon. 1.** To pay a short visit to. **2.** To request or order (someone) to do something. —**call out. 1.** To shout. **2.** To cause to assemble; summon: *call out the guard.*
~*n.* **1.** An act of calling. **2.** A shout or loud cry. **3. a.** The characteristic cry of an animal, especially a bird. **b.** An instrument or sound made to imitate such a cry, used as a lure. **4. a.** Need or occasion: *There was no call for that remark.* **b.** Demand: *There isn't much call for tiepins today.* **5. a.** A claim on a person's time or life: *the call of duty.* **b.** Attraction or appeal: *the call of the wild.* **6.** A short visit; especially, one made as a formality or for business or professional purposes. **7.** A summons or invitation. **8.** A signal, as made by a hunting horn, bugle, or bell. **9.** A vocation, as to the priesthood. **10.** An act of telephoning or instance of being telephoned. **11. a.** A notice summoning actors to rehearsal. **b.** A spoken message telling an actor to be ready to appear on stage. **12.** *Sports.* The decision of an umpire or linesman. **13. a.** *Poker.* A demand to see an opponent's hand. **b.** *Bridge.* A bid or turn to bid. **14.** A demand or request for the payment of a debt. **15.** *Finance.* **a.** A **call option** *(see).* **b.** An unpaid part of the price of a share. **c.** A demand for this outstanding amount. **d.** A demand for the presentation of redeemable bonds or shares. —**on call. 1.** Payable on demand. **2.** Available whenever summoned. —**within call.** Easily summoned; accessible. [Middle English *callen,* Old English *ceallian,* to call, shout, from Old Norse *kalla.*]

cal·la (kăl′ə) *n.* **1.** Any of several tropical or semitropical plants of the genus *Zantedeschia*; especially, *Z. aethiopica,* widely cultivated for its large, showy white spathe that encloses a yellow spadix. Also called "arum lily." **2.** A marsh plant, *Calla palustris,* of the North Temperate Zone, having small, densely clustered greenish flowers partly enclosed in a spreading white spathe. [New Latin *Calla,* probably from Greek *kallaia,* wattle of a cock, from *kallos,* beauty.]

Cal·la·ghan (kăl′ə-hən, -hăn′) **(Leonard) James** (1912–). British Labour prime minister (1976–79). A former clerk who served in the Royal Navy during World War II, he entered Parliament in 1945 and was chancellor of the exchequer from 1964 until his resignation in protest against Wilson's devaluation of the pound (1967). He was home secretary (1967–70) and foreign secretary (1974–76).

Cal·lao (kä-you′, -yä′ō). The major port of Peru, on the Pacific Ocean and now part of Greater Lima. Founded in 1537, it was frequently raided by pirates and adventurers.

Cal·las (kăl′əs, kä′ləs), **Maria,** born Maria Anna Kalogeropoulos (1923–77). U.S.-born Greek coloratura soprano. She made her debut in Athens at the age of 14 in the opera *Cavalleria Rusticana.* She became the prima donna at Milan's La Scala (1950) and made her American debut in Chicago (1954) as Bellini's *Norma.*

call·boy (kôl′boi′) *n.* One who tells actors when it is time for them to go on stage.

call·er[1] (kô′lər) *n.* **1.** Someone or something that calls or cries out. **2.** A person paying a short visit. **3.** A person making a telephone call. **4.** A person who calls numbers at bingo. **5.** In square dancing, a person who calls out the changing sequence of movements.

cal·ler[2] (kăl′ər) *adj. Scottish.* **1.** Fresh. Said of food, especially fish. **2.** Cool and refreshing. Said of a breeze. [Middle English *calour,* earlier *calvur*†.]

call girl *n. Informal.* A prostitute who takes appointments by telephone.

calli- *prefix.* Indicates beauty; for example, **calliopsis.** [Latin, from Greek *kalli-,* from *kallos,* beauty.]

cal·lig·ra·phy (kə-lĭg′rə-fē) *n.* **1.** The art of fine handwriting. **2.** Penmanship; handwriting. Compare **cacography.** [French *calligraphie,* from Greek *kalligraphia* : CALLI- + -GRAPHY.] —**cal·lig·ra·pher, cal·lig·ra·phist** *n.* —**cal·li·graph·ic** (kăl′ə-grăf′ĭk) *adj.*

Cal·lim·a·chus (kə-lĭm′ə-kəs) (*c.* 305–240 B.C.). A poet and scholar of ancient Greece. The fragments of his work that survive include the catalogue of the library of Alexandria and 64 epigrams.

call·ing (kô′lĭng) *n.* **1.** An inner urge; a strong impulse. **2.** An occupation, profession, or career.

calling card *n.* A card bearing one's name and often one's address and telephone number, used for social or business purposes.

cal·li·o·pe (kăl′ē-ōp′, kə-lī′ə-pē′) A musical instrument fitted with steam whistles, played from a keyboard. It is usually heard at carnivals and circuses.

Cal·li·o·pe (kə-lī′ə-pē′). *Greek Mythology.* The Muse of epic poetry. [Latin, from Greek *Kalliopē,* "beautiful-voiced" : CALLI- + *ops,* voice.]

cal·li·op·sis (kăl′ē-ŏp′sĭs) *n.* A plant, the **coreopsis** *(see).* [New Latin, "having a beautiful appearance" : Greek *kallos,* beauty + -OPSIS.]

calliper. Variant of **caliper.**

cal·li·pyg·i·an (kăl′ə-pĭj′ē-ən) *adj.* Also **cal·li·pyg·ous** (-pī′gəs). Having beautifully proportioned buttocks. [Greek *kallipugos* : CALLI- + *pugē,* buttocks.]

callisthenics. Variant of **calisthenics.**

Cal·lis·to (kə-lĭs′tō) *n.* One of the satellites of Jupiter, shown by Voyager 2 to have an extremely smooth, icy surface. [After *Callisto,* in Greek mythology a nymph loved by Zeus.]

call letters *pl.n.* The identifying code letters or numbers of a radio or television transmitting station.

call loan *n.* A loan repayable on demand at any time.

call market *n.* The market for call money.

call money *n.* Money lent by banks, usually to stockbrokers, subject to repayment on demand at any time.

call number *n.* A number used in libraries to classify a book and indicate its place on the shelves.

call option *n.* An agreement in which a trader may, for a commission, buy a quantity of a stock or commodity for a specific price within a limited period of time. Also called "call."

cal·lose (kăl′ōs′) *n.* A complex branched carbohydrate component of plant cell walls. [Latin *callosus,* callous.]

cal·los·i·ty (kă-lŏs′ə-tē, kə-) *n., pl.* **-ties. 1. a.** A calloused area. **b.** The condition of being calloused. **2.** Hard-heartedness; insensitivity. [Middle English *callosite,* from Old French, from Latin *callōsitās* (stem *callōsitāt-*), from *callōsus,* hardened, CALLOUS.]

cal·lous (kăl′əs) *adj.* **1.** Emotionally hardened; insensitive; unfeeling. **2.** Having calluses; toughened. [Middle English, from Old French *calleuse,* from Latin *callōsus,* from *callum, callus,* hard skin, CALLUS.] —**cal·loused** *adj.* —**cal·lous·ly** *adv.* —**cal·lous·ness** *n.*

cal·low (kăl′ō) *adj.* **1.** Immature; inexperienced. **2.** Not yet having feathers; unfledged. Said of birds. [Originally, "bald," hence unfledged, Middle English *calwe,* bald, Old English *calu,* probably from Latin *calvus,* bald.] —**cal·low·ly** *adv.* —**cal·low·ness** *n.*

call rate *n.* The rate of interest charged on call loans.

call sign *n.* A signal, often using code words or letters, used by a radio station to identify itself.

call up *tr.v.* **1.** To summon for military service. **2.** To telephone (someone). **3.** To cause to remember; evoke: *calling up old times.*

call-up (kôl′ŭp′) *n.* **1.** A summons for military service. **2.** Those summoned for military service.

cal·lus (kăl′əs) *n., pl.* **-luses. 1. a.** A localized thickening and enlargement of the horny layer of the skin, resulting from continual pressure or friction; callosity. **b.** The hard bony tissue that develops around the ends of a fractured bone during healing. **2.** *Botany.* The hardened tissue that develops over a wound or cut in a woody stem.
~*intr.v.* **callused, -lusing, -luses.** To form or develop a callus. [Latin *callus, callum*†.]

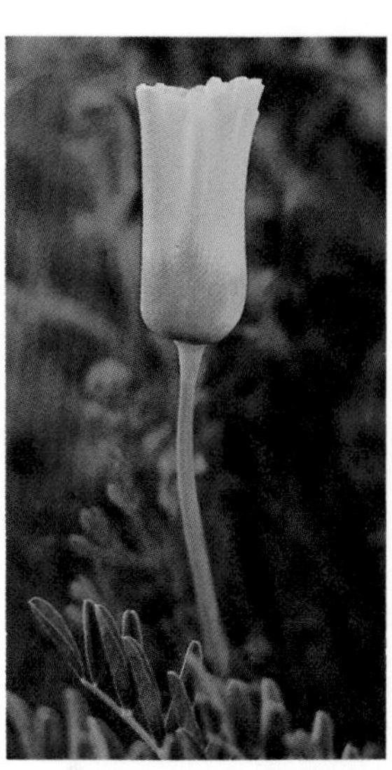

California poppy *A native of the western United States, the California poppy survives even in desert regions. The plant is cultivated as a hardy annual and bears a poppylike flower that closes in dull or cold weather.*

PRONUNCIATION KEY

ă, pat; **ā,** pay; **âr,** care; **ä,** father, are; **b,** bib; **ch,** church; **d,** deed; **ĕ,** pet; **ē,** be; **f,** fife; **g,** gag; **h,** hat; **hw,** which; **ĭ,** pit; **ī,** pie; **îr,** pier; **j,** judge; **k,** kick; **l,** lid, needle; **m,** mum; **n,** no, sudden; **ng,** thing; **ŏ,** pot; **ō,** toe; **ô,** paw, for; **oi,** noise; **ou,** out; **o͝o,** book; **o͞o,** boot; **p,** pop; **r,** roar; **s,** sauce; **sh,** ship, dish; **t,** tight; **th,** thin, path; ***th,*** this, bathe; **ŭ,** cut; **ûr,** fur; **v,** valve; **w,** with; **y,** yes; **z,** zebra, size; **zh,** vision; **ə,** about, item, edible, gallop, circus, peaceful

IN FOREIGN WORDS:

à, *Fr.* ami; **œ,** *Fr.* feu, *Ger.* schön; **ü,** *Fr.* tu, *Ger.* über; **KH,** *Ger.* ich, *Scot.* loch; **N,** *Fr.* bon; **y′,** *Fr.* Compiègne

STRESS MARKS:

Primary stress: ′ **in·cite′** (ĭn-sīt′)
Secondary stress: ′ **in′sight′** (ĭn′sīt′)

calm (käm) *adj.* **calmer, calmest. 1.** Undisturbed by wind. **2.** Free from excitement or agitation. **3.** Not affected by anxiety or qualms. ~*n.* **1.** An absence of disturbance or agitation; peacefulness. **2.** *Meteorology.* A condition of no wind or a wind with a velocity of less than 1 knot; force 0 on the Beaufort scale. **3.** Freedom from anxiety or qualms.
~*v.* **calmed, calming, calms.** —*tr.* To make calm; quiet. Often used with *down.* —*intr.* To become calm or quiet. Often used with *down.* [Middle English *calme,* from Old French, from Late Latin *cauma,* heat of the day, hence, a rest or resting place in the heat of the day, from Greek *kauma,* burning heat, from *kaiein,* to burn.] **—calm·ly** *adv.* **—calm·ness** *n.*
Synonyms: *peaceful, placid, quiet, serene, still, tranquil.*
calm·a·tive (kä′mə-tĭv, kăl′mə-) *adj.* Having relaxing or pacifying properties; sedative.
~*n.* A sedative or tranquilizer. [From CALM (after SEDATIVE).]
cal·o·mel (kăl′ə-məl′, -məl) *n.* A white, tasteless compound, Hg_2Cl_2, used as a purgative. [French, from New Latin *calomelas,* "beautiful black" (calomel, though white, was originally developed from a black powder) : Greek *kalos,* beautiful + *melas,* black.]
cal·o·re·cep·tor (kăl′ə-rĭ-sĕp′tər) *n.* A sensory receptor that detects warmth. [Latin *calor,* heat + RECEPTOR.]
ca·lor·ic (kə-lôr′ĭk, -lŏr′ĭk) *adj.* Of or pertaining to heat or calories. ~*n.* A hypothetically indestructible, uncreatable, highly elastic, self-repellent, all-pervading fluid, formerly thought responsible for the production, possession, and transfer of heat.
cal·o·rie (kăl′ə-rē) *n.* **1.** *Abbr.* **cal** Any of several approximately equal units of heat, each measured as the quantity of heat required to raise the temperature of 1 gram of water by 1°C from a standard initial temperature, especially from 3.98°C, 14.5°C, or 19.5°C, at 1 atmosphere pressure. Also called "gram calorie," "small calorie." **2.** *Abbr.* **cal** The unit of heat equal to $^1/_{100}$ the quantity of heat required to raise the temperature of 1 gram of water from 0 to 100°C at 1 atmosphere pressure. Also called "mean calorie." **3.** *Abbr.* **Cal** The unit of heat equal to the amount of heat required to raise the temperature of 1 kilogram of water by 1°C at 1 atmosphere pressure. Also called "kilocalorie," "kilogram calorie," "large calorie." **4.** The unit of heat equal to 4.184 joules. Also called "thermochemical calorie." The calorie has been replaced by the joule for all scientific purposes and some nonscientific uses. The calories used to express the energy value of foods are kilocalories (sense 3): 1 kilocalorie is equal to 4,184 joules. [French, from Latin *calor,* heat.]
cal·o·rif·ic (kăl′ə-rĭf′ĭk) *adj.* Pertaining to or generating heat or calories. [French *calorifique,* from Latin *calorificus* : *calor,* heat + -FIC.]
calorific value *n.* The quantity of heat, usually expressed in joules per kilogram, that will be produced by the complete combustion of a given mass of a fuel.
cal·o·rim·e·ter (kăl′ə-rĭm′ə-tər) *n.* **1.** An apparatus for measuring heat. **2.** The part of such an apparatus, usually a sample container, in which the heat measured causes a change of state. [Latin *calor,* heat + -METER.]
cal·o·rim·e·try (kăl′ə-rĭm′ə-trē) *n.* The measurement of the quantity of heat evolved or absorbed by a chemical reaction, change of state, or formation of a solution. **—cal·o·ri·met·ri·cal** (kăl′ə-rĭ-mĕt′rĭ-kəl) *adj.*
ca·lotte (kə-lŏt′) *n.* A skullcap, especially one worn by Roman Catholic clergymen. [French, diminutive of Old French *cale,* cap, from Germanic.]
ca·loy·er (kə-loi′ər, kăl′ə-yər) *n.* A monk of the Eastern Orthodox Church. [French, from obsolete Italian *caloiero,* from Medieval Greek *kalogēros,* venerable, "handsome old man" : Greek *kalos,* beautiful + *gēras,* old age.]
cal·pac, cal·pack, kal·pak (kăl′păk′, kăl-păk′) *n.* A large black cap, usually of sheepskin or felt, worn in Turkey, Armenia, and other Near Eastern regions. [Turkish *kalpāk.*]
calque (kălk) *n. Linguistics.* **1.** A form of semantic borrowing in which a word is given a special extended meaning by analogy with that of a word having the same basic meaning in another language. **2.** A **loan translation** *(see).*
~*tr.v.* **calqued, calquing, calques.** To model (the meaning of a word) upon that of an analogous word in another language. [French, tracing, imitation, close copy, from *calquer,* to trace, copy, from Italian *calcar,* to press, from Latin *calcāre,* to trample, stamp, from *calx,* a heel.]
cal·trop, cal·trap (kăl′trəp) *n.* **1.** *Military.* An iron ball with four projecting spikes so arranged that when three of the spikes were on the ground, the fourth pointed upward. It was formerly used to delay the advance of mounted and unmounted troops. Also called "crowfoot." **2.** Any of several plants having spiny burs or bracts, as members of the genus *Tribulus.* See **water chestnut.** [Middle English *cal(ke)trap(pe),* from Old French *chauchetrap,* iron ball with spikes, and Old English *calcatrippe,* spiny plant, brambles, both from Medieval Latin *calcatrappa, calcatrippa,* "foot trap" : Latin *calcāre,* to tread, from *calx,* heel + Medieval Latin *trappa,* trap, from Germanic.]
cal·u·met (kăl′yə-mĕt′, -mət, kăl′yə-mĕt′) *n.* A long-stemmed, ornamented pipe used by North American Indians for ceremonial purposes. Also called "peace pipe." [Canadian French, from French (Normandy dialect), variant of French *chalumeau,* a straw, from Late Latin *calamellus,* little reed, from *calamus,* a reed, from Greek *kalamos.*]

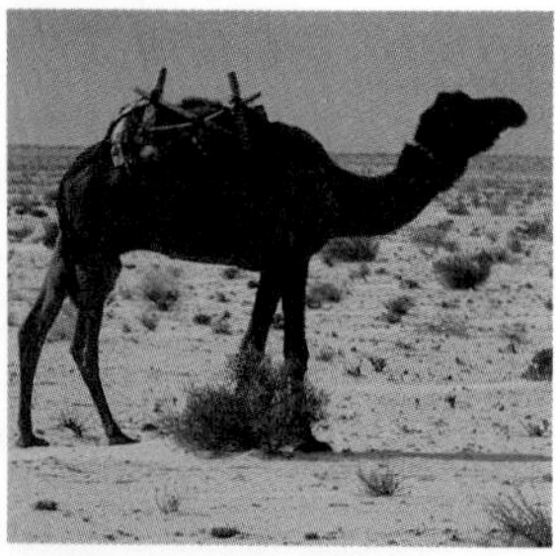
camel *Although camels can survive long periods without water, they have a correspondingly gargantuan thirst. A full-grown camel can drink up to 120 liters (27 gallons) at a time. The two-humped Bactrian camel, found in central Asia, is used for carrying loads in cold mountainous regions, while the single-humped dromedary (above) is better adapted to riding and load carrying in hot deserts. The humps of both types contain deposits of fat, which act as a food reserve.*

ca·lum·ni·ate (kə-lŭm′nē-āt′) *tr.v.* **-ated, -ating, -ates.** To make false and damaging statements about; slander. —See Synonyms at **malign.** [Latin *calumniārī,* from *calumnia,* CALUMNY.] **—ca·lum·ni·a·tion** *n.* **—ca·lum·ni·a·tor** *n.*
ca·lum·ni·ous (kə-lŭm′nē-əs) *adj.* Also **ca·lum·ni·a·to·ry** (-ə-tôr′ē, -tōr′ē). Containing or implying calumny; slanderous; defamatory. **—ca·lum·ni·ous·ly** *adv.*
cal·um·ny (kăl′əm-nē) *n., pl.* **-nies. 1.** A false statement, maliciously or knowingly made to injure someone's reputation. **2.** The utterance of such statements; slander. [Middle English, from Old French *calomnie,* from Latin *calumnia,* "trickery," "deception," from *calvī,* to deceive, trick.]
cal·u·tron (kăl′yə-trŏn′) *n. Physics.* A device for separating isotopes by deflecting ions in electric and magnetic fields. It is similar in action to a large mass spectrometer.
cal·va·dos (kăl′və-dōs′) *n.* A French brandy made from apples. [French, after *Calvados,* department in Normandy where it was originally made.]
cal·var·i·um (kăl-vâr′ē-əm) *n., pl.* **-iums** or **-ia** (-ē-ə). *Anatomy.* The top, rounded part of the skull. Also called "skullcap." [Late Latin, skull. See **Calvary.**]
cal·va·ry (kăl′vər-ē) *n., pl.* **-ries. 1.** A sculptured depiction of the Crucifixion. **2.** A spiritual ordeal. [After CALVARY.]
Cal·va·ry (kăl′və-rē). The hill outside the ancient city of Jerusalem where Jesus was crucified. [Middle English *Calvarie,* Old English *Calvarie,* from Late Latin *Calvāria,* from Latin *calvāria,* skull (translation of Greek *kranion,* translation of Aramaic *gulgūtha,* GOLGOTHA), from *calva,* scalp, from *calvus,* bald.]
Calvary cross *n. Heraldry.* A Latin cross set on three steps.
calve (kăv, käv) *v.* **calved, calving, calves.** —*intr.* **1.** To give birth to a calf. **2.** To break up and lose a mass of ice. Used of a glacier or an iceberg. —*tr.* **1.** To give birth to (a calf). **2.** To set loose (a mass of ice). [Middle English *calven,* Old English *cealfian,* from *cealf,* CALF (young cow).]
calves. Plural of **calf.**
calves'-foot jelly. Variant of **calf's-foot jelly.**
Cal·vin (kăl′vĭn), **John** (1509–64). French Protestant reformer and theologian who, after breaking with the Roman Catholic Church (1533), settled in Geneva (1541). Although he was never ordained into the priesthood, his brand of theology, published in his book *Institutes* and known today as Presbyterianism, had a profound effect on the Christian world.
Cal·vin·ism (kăl′vĭn-ĭz′əm) *n.* **1.** The religious doctrines of John Calvin, which emphasize the supremacy of the Scriptures in the revelation of truth, the omnipotence of God, the sinfulness of man, the salvation of the elect by God's grace alone, and a rigid moral code. **2.** Agreement with or advocacy of such doctrines. **—Cal·vin·ist** *n.* **—Cal·vin·is·tic** *adj.*
calx (kălks) *n., pl.* **calxes** or **calces** (kăl′sēz′). **1.** The crumbly residue left after a mineral or metal has been calcined or roasted. **2.** Lime; chalk. **3. Calcium oxide** *(see).* [Latin, lime, limestone, from Greek *khalix,* pebble.]
ca·ly·cine (kā′lə-sīn′, kăl′ə-) *adj.* Of, pertaining to, or resembling a calyx.
ca·ly·cle (kā′lə-kəl, kăl′ə-) *n.* **1.** *Botany.* An **epicalyx** *(see).* **2.** *Biology.* A calyculus. [French *calicule,* from Latin *calyculus,* diminutive of *calyx,* bud, CALYX.] **—ca·lyc·u·late** (kə-lĭk′yə-lāt′, -lĭt) *adj.*
ca·lyc·u·lus (kə-lĭk′yə-ləs) *n., pl.* **-li** (-lī′). *Biology.* A small cup-shaped structure. Also called "calycle." [Latin, CALYCLE.] **—ca·lyc·u·lar** *adj.*
ca·lyp·so[1] (kə-lĭp′sō) *n., pl.* **-sos.** An orchid, *Calypso bulbosa,* of the North Temperate Zone, having a pinkish flower with a slipper-shaped lip. [After CALYPSO.]
calypso[2] *n., pl.* **-sos** or **-soes. 1.** A type of song originating in the West Indies, notably in Trinidad, characterized by improvised lyrics on topical or broadly humorous subjects and a syncopated rhythm. **2.** A dance to calypso music. [After CALYPSO.]
Ca·lyp·so (kə-lĭp′sō). *Greek Mythology.* A sea nymph who delayed Odysseus on her island, Ogygia, for seven years. [Latin, from Greek *Kalupsō,* "she who conceals," from *kaluptein,* to cover, conceal.]
ca·lyp·tra (kə-lĭp′trə) *n. Botany.* **1.** The protective cap covering the spore case of a moss or related plant. **2.** Any similar hoodlike or caplike structure. [New Latin, from Greek *kaluptra,* veil, covering, from *kaluptein,* to cover, conceal.] **—ca·lyp·trate** (kə-lĭp′trāt′) *adj.*
ca·lyp·tro·gen (kə-lĭp′trə-jən) *n. Botany.* A layer of actively dividing cells at the end of a root tip, from which the root cap is formed.
ca·lyx (kā′lĭks, kăl′ĭks) *n., pl.* **-lyxes** or **calyces** (kā′lə-sēz′, kăl′ə-). **1.** The outer protective covering of a flower, consisting of a series of leaflike, usually green segments called sepals. Compare **corolla. 2.** A cuplike or funnel-shaped animal structure, such as one of those forming part of the kidney. [Latin, from Greek *kalux.*]
cam (kăm) *n.* An eccentric or multiply curved wheel mounted on a rotating shaft and used to produce variable or reciprocating motion in another engaged or contacted part. [Perhaps from French *came,* from German *Kamm,* "comb," from Old High German *kamb.*]
ca·ma·ra·de·rie (kä′mə-rä′də-rē, kăm′ə-răd′ə-) *n.* Good will and lighthearted rapport between or among friends; comradeship. [French, from *camarade,* COMRADE.]
Ca·margue, La (lä kə-märg′, kä-). Island in the delta of the Rhône River, Bouches-du-Rhône department, southern France. Much of the once predominantly marshy land has been reclaimed and now supports livestock including cattle, bulls for the bullrings of Spain, Portugal, and France, and horses.

cam·a·ril·la (kăm′ə-rĭl′ə, -rē′ə) n. A group of confidential advisers; a cabal. [Spanish, "small room," from *cámara*, room, from Late Latin *camera*, from Latin, arched roof, from Greek *kamara*, vault.]

cam·as, cam·ass (kăm′əs) n. Also **quam·ash** (kwŏm′ăsh′). 1. Any of several North American plants of the genus *Camassia*; especially, *C. quamash*, of western North America, having a showy cluster of blue or white flowers and an edible bulb. 2. The **death camas** (*see*). [Chinook jargon *kamass*.]

cam·ber (kăm′bər) n. 1. a. A slightly arched surface, as of a road, a ship's deck, or an airfoil. b. The condition of having an arched surface. 2. A setting of the front wheels of an automotive vehicle so that they are closer together at the bottom than at the top. ～v. **cambered, -bering, -bers.** —tr. To give a slight arch to. —intr. To arch slightly. [Middle English *ca(u)mber*, curved, from Old French *cambre*, from Latin *camur(us)*†, curved inward.]

Cam·ber·well beauty (kăm′bər-wĕl′, -wəl) n. A butterfly, the **mourning cloak** (*see*). [After *Camberwell*, a district of south London.]

cam·bist (kăm′bĭst) n. 1. A manual giving exchange rates of different currencies and equivalents of different weights and measures. 2. A dealer in or expert on international exchange. [French *cambiste*, from Italian *cambista*, from *cambio*, exchange, from *cambiare*, to exchange, from Late Latin *cambiāre*.] —**cam·bis·try** n.

cam·bi·um (kăm′bē-əm) n. A layer of cells in the stems and roots of vascular plants that gives rise to phloem and xylem and thus increases the girth of the plant. [New Latin, "that which changes into new layers," from Medieval Latin, exchange, from Latin *cambiāre*, to exchange.] —**cam·bi·al** adj.

Cambodia. See **Kampuchea.** —**Cam·bo·di·an** (kăm-bō′dē-ən) n. & adj.

cam·bo·gi·a (kăm-bō′jē-ə) n. A resin, **gamboge** (*see*). [New Latin, variant of GAMBOGE.]

Cam·brai (käm-brā′). Industrial town in northeast France. Famous for the cambric cloth that originated here in the 16th century, it still has a large cloth-dyeing and bleaching industry.

Cam·bri·a (kăm′brē-ə). The Latin name for Wales. [Latin, from Welsh *Cymru*, from Old Welsh *kombroges* (unattested), Welshmen, "compatriots" : *kom-*, with + *bro*, border, region.]

Cam·bri·an¹ (kăm′brē-ən) adj. Of or pertaining to Wales; Welsh. ～n. A Welshman.

Cambrian² adj. Of, belonging to, or pertaining to the geologic time, system of rocks, and sedimentary deposits of the first period of the Paleozoic era, characterized by warm seas and desert land areas. ～n. Geology. The Cambrian period. Preceded by *the.* [After CAMBRIA (Wales), where rocks and fossils of this period were found.]

cam·bric (kăm′brĭk) n. A finely woven white linen or cotton fabric. [Earlier *cameryk*, from Flemish *Kameryk*, CAMBRAI, where it was first made.] —**cam·bric** adj.

cambric tea n. A drink, especially for children, that is made of hot water, milk, sugar, and usually a small amount of tea. [So called because it is thin and white like CAMBRIC.]

Cam·bridge¹ (kăm′brĭj). City on the Cam River in Cambridgeshire. An important market center for East Anglia and the administrative center of the county, the city is best known for its university, which dates back to 1284.

Cambridge². City on the Charles River, opposite Boston, in Massachusetts, the seat of America's oldest university, Harvard (established 1636), and the Massachusetts Institute of Technology.

Cam·bridge·shire (kăm′brĭj-shîr, -shər). County in East Anglia, England. Consisting mainly of low-lying fens, it is chiefly agricultural and includes the former county of Huntingdonshire, the Soke of Peterborough, parts of west Suffolk, and the Isle of Ely. The chief towns, Cambridge, Peterborough, and Wisbech, have industries that include brickmaking, cement, electronics, and printing.

came¹ (kām) n. A slender, grooved lead bar used to hold together the panes in stained-glass or latticework windows. [Perhaps Scottish *calm*, casting mold.]

came². Past tense of **come.**

cam·el (kăm′əl) n. 1. A humped, long-necked ruminant mammal of the genus *Camelus*, domesticated in Old World desert regions as a beast of burden and as a source of wool, milk, and meat. See **Bactrian camel, dromedary.** 2. A device used to raise a sunken or submerged vessel. In this sense, also called "caisson." 3. A light fawn or brownish yellow. [Middle English, from Old English, from Latin *camēlus*, from Greek *kamēlos*, from Semitic; akin to Hebrew and Phoenician *gāmāl*, Arabic *jamal*.]

cam·el·back (kăm′əl-băk′) adj. Having a shape characterized by a hump or upward curve.

cam·el·eer (kăm′ə-lîr′) n. A person who drives or rides a camel.

camel hair. Variant of **camel's hair.**

ca·mel·lia (kə-mēl′yə) n. 1. Any of several shrubs or trees of the genus *Camellia*, native to Asia; especially, *C. japonica*, having shiny evergreen leaves and showy, usually white, pink, or red flowers. 2. The flower of a camellia. Also called "japonica." [New Latin; first described by George Joseph *Kamel* (1661-1706), Moravian Jesuit missionary.]

ca·mel·o·pard (kə-mĕl′ə-pärd′) n. 1. Archaic. A giraffe. 2. Heraldry. A bearing resembling a giraffe, but represented with long curved horns. [Medieval Latin *camēlopardus*, from Latin *camēlopardalis*, from Greek *kamēlopardalis* : *kamēlos*, CAMEL + *pardalis*, variant of *pardos*, PARD (leopard), so called because the giraffe has a head like a camel's and the spots of a leopard.]

Ca·mel·o·par·da·lis (kə-mĕl′ō-pär′də-lĭs) n. A constellation in the Northern Hemisphere near Ursa Major and Cassiopeia. [New Latin, from Latin.]

Cam·e·lot (kăm′ə-lŏt) n. 1. The legendary place where King Arthur held court with his Knights of the Round Table. 2. A place, time, or circumstance marked by idealized beauty, peacefulness, and enlightenment.

camel's hair n. Also **camel hair.** 1. The soft, fine hair of a camel or a substitute for it. 2. A soft, heavy cloth, usually light tan, made chiefly of camel's hair. —**camel's-hair** (kăm′əlz-hâr′) adj.

Cam·em·bert¹ (kăm′əm-bâr′). Village in Normandy, northwest France, famous for the cheese of the same name, originally made here.

Camembert² n. A creamy, mold-ripened cheese that softens on the inside as it matures.

cam·e·o (kăm′ē-ō′) n., pl. **-os.** 1. a. A technique of engraving in relief on a gem, stone, or shell, especially one with layers of different hues, cut so the raised design is of one color and the background of another. Compare **intaglio.** b. A gem, stone, or shell so cut. 2. A medallion with a profile cut in raised relief. 3. A brief literary work or dramatic sketch. 4. A brief but dramatic appearance of a prominent actress or actor in a single scene in a television play or in a film. In this sense, also called "cameo role." ～tr.v. **cameoed, -oing, -os.** 1. To make into or like a cameo. 2. To portray in sharp, delicate relief, as in a literary composition. [Middle English *cameu*, from Italian *cam(m)eo* and Old French *camaïeu*, perhaps from Arabic *qamā′īl*, plural of *qum′ūl*, flower bud.]

cameo ware n. Pottery having raised figures on a background of contrasting color.

cam·er·a (kăm′ər-ə, kăm′rə) n., pl. **-eras** or **-erae** (-ə-rē) (for sense 4). 1. Any apparatus for taking photographs, generally consisting of a lightproof enclosure having an aperture with a shuttered lens through which the image of an object is focused and recorded on a photosensitive film or plate. 2. The part of a television transmitting apparatus that receives the primary image on a light-sensitive cathode tube and transforms it into electrical impulses. 3. A **camera obscura** (*see*). 4. A room or chamber; specifically, a judge's private office. —**in camera.** 1. In court with only the judge and litigants or their representatives present. 2. In private; privately. [Late Latin, room, from Latin, arched roof, from Greek *kamara*, vault.] See feature, next page.

cam·er·al (kăm′ər-əl) adj. 1. Pertaining to a judge's chamber or to the judicial affairs that take place there. 2. Pertaining to public finance and state business or to a council that manages such matters. [Medieval Latin *camerālis*, from *camera*, office, department of state, CAMERA.]

camera lu·ci·da (lōō′sĭ-də) n. An optical device that projects a virtual image of an object onto a plane surface, especially for tracing. [New Latin, "light chamber" : CAMERA + Latin *lūcīda*, feminine of *lūcīdus*, LUCID.]

cam·er·a·man (kăm′ər-ə-măn′, kăm′rə-) n., pl. **-men** (-mĕn′). A man who operates a motion-picture or television camera.

camera ob·scu·ra (ŏb-skyŏŏr′ə, əb-) n. A darkened chamber in which the real image of an object is received through a small opening or lens and focused in natural color onto a facing surface. Also called "camera." [New Latin, "dark chamber" : CAMERA + Latin *obscūra*, feminine of *obscūrus*, OBSCURE.]

cam·er·a·shy (kăm′ər-ə-shī′, kăm′rə-) adj. Reluctant or nervous about being photographed.

camera tube n. The part of a television camera that converts the optical image into electrical signals.

cam·er·a·wom·an (kăm′ər-ə-wŏŏm′ən, kăm′rə-) n., pl. **-women** (-wĭm′ĭn). A woman who operates a motion picture or television camera.

cam·er·lin·go (kăm′ər-lĭng′gō) n., pl. **-gos.** Also **cam·er·len·go** (-lĕng′gō). Roman Catholic Church. The cardinal who manages the pope's secular affairs. [Italian *camarlingo*, from Germanic *kamarling* (unattested), "chamber servant" : *kamar* (unattested), room, from Late Latin *camera*, CAMERA + -LING.]

Cam·er·on (kăm′ər-ən), **Julia Margaret** (1815-79). British photographer noted for her pioneering work in artistic portrait photography. Tennyson, Darwin, and the actress Ellen Terry were among her subjects.

Cam·e·roon (kăm′ə-rōōn′). Country in west-central Africa. Originally the German colony of Kamerun, the country was divided between Britain and France (1919). It became a United Nations trust territory after World War II. French Cameroons was granted independence (1960) as the Cameroon Republic and was joined by the southern part of the British Cameroons (when the remainder of the British territory joined Nigeria) to form the Federal Republic of Cameroon (1961). In 1974 it became the United Republic of Cameroon. Its population of more than 150 different ethnic groups is mainly occupied in agriculture, with coffee, cocoa, and timber the main exports. Offshore oil deposits and large reserves of bauxite are being exploited. The main city and port is Douala. Area, 475,442 square kilometers (183,521 square miles). Population, 8,500,000. Capital, Yaoundé. See map, page 261.

cam·i·knick·ers (kăm′ə-nĭk′ərz) pl.n. British. An undergarment worn by women that consists of a pair of underpants combined with a camisole top. [camisole + knickers.]

cam·i·on (kăm′ē-ən, kȧ-myôn′) n. 1. A low, sturdy wagon. 2. a. A truck. b. A bus. [French, from Old French *chamion*†.]

ca·mi·sa (kə-mē′sə) n. Southwestern U.S. A shirt or chemise. [Spanish, from Late Latin *camīsia*, shirt.]

camellia Camellia reticulata *is one of the ornamental flowering species belonging to the Theaceae family of evergreen shrubs and trees. Camellias are native to India, China, and Japan.*

camera

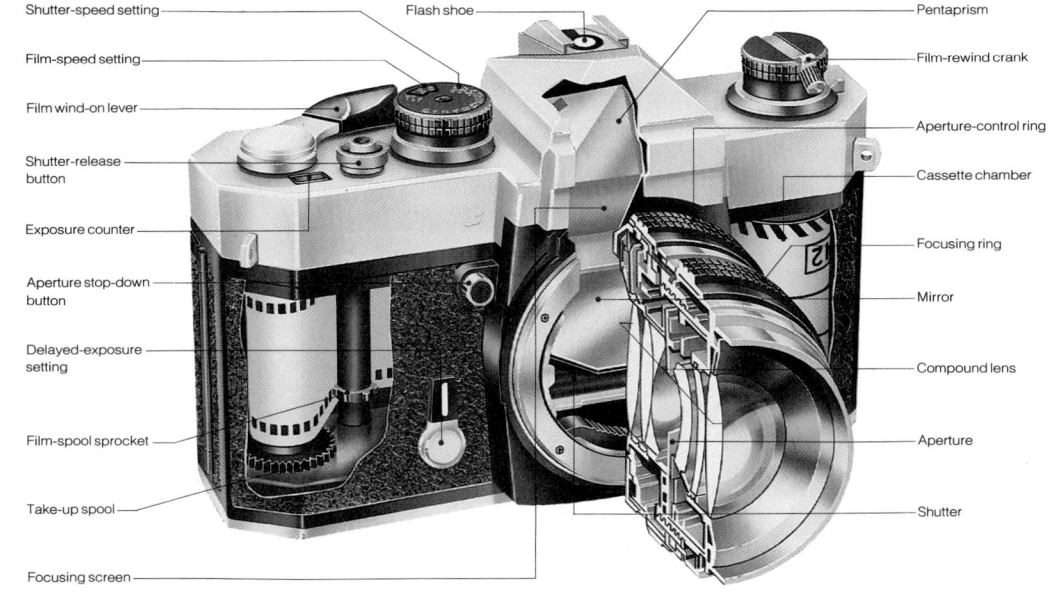

FOUR MAIN TYPES OF CAMERA
Different ways of seeing what the camera will record

In the VIEWFINDER CAMERA, the light image is focused on the film through the lens, but the eye of the photographer receives the image through the viewfinder, which is above the lens. The image received by the eye is slightly different from the image fixed on the film; some models of camera have a built-in adjustment to allow for this. The SINGLE-LENS REFLEX CAMERA (below) receives an image virtually identical to that fixed on the film, because a mirror and prism inside the camera reflect to the eye the image entering the lens. In the TWIN-LENS REFLEX CAMERA, the picture is taken through the lower lens, and the image is reflected by a mirror from the upper lens to a viewing screen on the top of the camera. Because the photographer looks into the camera from above, it need not be held at eye level. As in the viewfinder camera, there can be a slight difference between what the eye sees and the image fixed on the film through the lens. In the VIEW CAMERA, the eye receives the image directly through the lens.

Shutter-speed setting — Film-speed setting — Film wind-on lever — Shutter-release button — Exposure counter — Aperture stop-down button — Delayed-exposure setting — Film-spool sprocket — Take-up spool — Focusing screen

Flash shoe — Pentaprism — Film-rewind crank — Aperture-control ring — Cassette chamber — Focusing ring — Mirror — Compound lens — Aperture — Shutter

THE 35 MM SINGLE-LENS REFLEX CAMERA *The lens reverses the image of the scene before it. The mirror and pentaprism turn it the right way around and show it on the focusing screen for the photographer to view through the eyepiece (at the back of the camera) and adjust with the focusing ring. The aperture and shutter speeds are set to suit the lighting. When the shutter-release button is pressed, the mirror moves to block light from the eyepiece and the shutter opens to expose the film for the set time.*

---

camouflage *Like some other insects,* Gastropacha quercifolia *has a remarkable ability to merge with its surroundings. While it rests during the day, its folded wings look like a dead leaf.*

---

cam·i·sa·do (kăm'ə-sä'dō, -sā'dō) n., pl. **-dos.** Archaic. A surprise attack by night. [Probably from obsolete Spanish *camisada,* "shirted" (because attackers wore white shirts over armor for identification), from *camisa,* shirt, CAMISA.]

ca·mise (kə-mēz', -mēs') n. A loose shirt, shift, or tunic. [Arabic *qamīs,* from Late Latin *camīsia,* shirt.]

cam·i·sole (kăm'ə-sōl') n. **1.** A woman's sleeveless undergarment. **2.** A short negligee. [French, from Old Provençal *camisolla,* diminutive of *camisa,* shirt, from Late Latin *camīsia.*]

Cam·lan (kăm'lən) n. The legendary battlefield where King Arthur was mortally wounded.

cam·let (kăm'lĭt) n. **1.** A kind of rich cloth of Oriental origin, supposed to have been made formerly of camel's hair and silk, and later made of goat's hair and silk or other combinations. **2.** A garment made from this cloth. [Middle English *chamelet,* from Old French *c(h)amelot,* from Arabic *ḥamlat.*]

Ca·mões (kə-moinsh'), **Luis Vaz de.** Also **Cam·o·ëns** (kăm'ō-ĕnz) (1524–80). Portuguese poet and soldier noted for his book *Os Lusíadas* (1572), possibly the greatest of all Portuguese literary works.

camomile. Variant of **chamomile.**

Ca·mor·ra (kə-môr'ə, -mōr'ə) n. **1.** A Neapolitan secret society organized about 1820 and notorious for practicing violence and blackmail. Compare **Mafia. 2. camorra.** An unscrupulous, clandestine group. [Italian, perhaps from *camorra†,* a kind of smock (said to have been worn by members of this society).] **—Ca·mor·rism** n. **—Ca·mor·rist** n. & adj.

cam·ou·flage (kăm'ə-fläzh', -fläj') n. **1. a.** The method or result of concealing personnel or material from an enemy by making them appear to be part of the natural surroundings. **b.** The materials or techniques used for such concealment: *Heavy nets were an effective camouflage for the planes.* **2. a.** The condition of an animal that is concealed from predators or prey by means of protective coloration or shape. **b.** The protective coloration or shape of an animal. **3.** A means of concealment or deception; dissimulation: *She used a sweet smile as camouflage for her anger.*
~v. camouflaged, -flaging, -flages. —tr. To conceal by camouflage: *The decorator camouflaged the unattractive view with colorful curtains.* **—intr.** To use camouflage. [French, from *camoufler,* to

disguise, from Italian *camuffare†,* to disguise, trick.]

camp¹ (kămp) n. **1. a.** A place where a body of people, such as soldiers, miners, or sportsmen, are temporarily lodged in tents, huts, or other makeshift shelters. **b.** The shelters in such a place. **c.** The persons using such shelters. **2.** A place where enemy aliens, political prisoners, and the like are detained. **3.** A place consisting of more or less permanent shelters, as cabins or tents, used for vacationing or other recreational purposes. **4.** Military service; army life: *recruits getting used to the routine in camp.* **5.** A group of persons, parties, or states favorable to a common cause, doctrine, or political system: *the socialist camp.*
~adj. 1. Pertaining to or used in a camp or camping. **2.** Being portable and usually collapsible: *a camp bed.*
~intr.v. camped, camping, camps. 1. To make or set up a camp. **2.** To live in or as if in a camp: *We camped in the apartment until the electricity was connected and the furniture arrived.* **—camp out.** To sleep in the open. [French, from Italian *campo,* from Latin *campus†,* open field.]

camp² n. **1. a.** An affectation or appreciation of manners and tastes commonly thought to be outlandish, vulgar, or banal. **b.** Behavior exhibiting such affectation or appreciation. **2.** Banality or artificiality when appreciated for its humor.
~adj. 1. Theatrical, affected, or exaggerated in manner or style. **2.** Effeminately homosexual. Said of a man. **3.** In the style of an effeminate man; mannered.
~intr.v. camped, camping, camps. To act in a theatrical or effeminate manner. Used in the phrase *camp it up.* [20th century : origin obscure.] **—camp·i·ly** adv. **—camp·i·ness** n. **—camp·y** adj.

cam·paign (kăm-pān') n. **1.** A series of military operations undertaken to achieve a specific objective within a given area. **2.** An operation undertaken, as by means of propaganda, to attain some political, social, commercial, or personal goal: *We launched a campaign to raise funds for the hospital.*
~intr.v. campaigned, -paigning, -paigns. To engage or serve in a campaign: *Many of the city's businessmen campaigned for the mayor's re-election.* [French *campagne,* from Old French, battlefield, from Italian *campania,* from Late Latin *campānia,* countryside, from *campus,* field.] **—cam·paign·er** n.

Cam·pa·nia (kăm-pān′yə). Region in southern Italy spanning the provinces of Avellino, Benevento, Caserta, Napoli, and Salerno, with the islands of Capri, Ischia, Porcida, and the Pontine Islands. It joined Italy (1861) as part of the kingdom of Naples. The excavated Roman towns of Pompeii and Herculaneum and the region's many resorts give it a large tourist trade.

cam·pa·ni·le (kăm′pə-nē′lē) *n., pl.* **-les** (-lēz) or **-li** (-lē). A bell tower, especially one near but not attached to a church. [Italian, from *campana*, bell, from Late Latin *campāna*, bell (made of metal produced in Campania), from Latin *campānus*, of Campania.]

cam·pa·nol·o·gy (kăm′pə-nŏl′ə-jē) *n.* The art or study of bell ringing. [New Latin *campanologia* : Late Latin *campāna*, bell (see **campanile**) + -LOGY.] —**cam·pa·nol·o·gist** *n.*

cam·pan·u·la (kăm-păn′yə-lə) *n.* Any of various plants of the genus *Campanula*, which includes the bellflowers. [New Latin, diminutive of Late Latin *campāna*, bell. See **campanile**.]

cam·pan·u·late (kăm-păn′yə-lĭt, -lāt′). Also **cam·pan·i·form** (kăm-păn′ə-fôrm′). Bell-shaped: *campanulate flowers*. [New Latin *campanula*, small bell.]

Camp·bell (kăm′bəl), **Donald** (1921–67). Son of Sir Malcolm, he set the land speed record in a gas-turbine four-wheeled car on July 17, 1964, at Lake Eyre Salt Flats, Australia, reaching a top speed of 648.7 km/h (403.1 mph). Later that year he achieved the water speed record of 444.89 km/h (276.33 mph) at Dumbleyung Lake, Australia. Finally, during an attempt on the water speed record, his jet-powered boat *Bluebird* was wrecked and he was killed, having reached a speed of 527.8 km/h (328 mph), which is still the fastest time recorded.

Campbell, (Ignatius) Royston Dunnachie (1901–57). South African poet and satirist, who spent part of his working life in England, where he was associated with the Bloomsbury Group. He also translated several important French, Spanish, and Portuguese literary works into English.

Campbell, Sir Malcolm (1885–1948). British motor engineer who held the land speed record nine times between 1924 and 1935 and the water speed record three times between 1937 and 1939. His fastest time on land was 483 km/h (301 mph), and on water he reached a top speed of 227 km/h (141 mph).

Campbell, Mrs Patrick, born Beatrice Stella Tanner (1865–1940). Leading British actress, who played the original Eliza in *Pygmalion*, a part written especially for her by George Bernard Shaw. She also played roles in Shakespeare and Ibsen with great success.

Camp Da·vid (dā′vĭd). The official country retreat of the President of the United States, in the Appalachian Mountains, Maryland. It was here (1978) that President Jimmy Carter mediated at a meeting between Anwar el-Sadat, the Egyptian president, and Menachem Begin, the prime minister of Israel, to produce the framework for a peace treaty between their two countries. Signed by both parties (March 1979), the treaty was known as the Camp David Agreement. Technically, Camp David becomes the White House whenever the President is in residence.

camp·er (kăm′pər) *n.* **1.** A person who camps outdoors or who attends a camp for recreation. **2. a.** A compact vanlike vehicle resembling an automobile-and-trailer combination, designed to serve as a dwelling and used for camping or on long motor trips. **b.** A porta-

ble shelter resembling the top part of a trailer, made to be mounted on a pickup truck to form such a vehicle.

cam·pes·tral (kăm-pĕs′trəl) *adj.* Of, pertaining to, or growing in uncultivated land or open fields. [Latin *campester*, of the fields, from *campus*, field.]

camp·fire (kămp′fīr′) *n.* **1.** An outdoor fire in a camp, used for warmth or cooking. **2.** A meeting held around a campfire.

camp follower *n.* **1.** A civilian who follows a military unit from place to place to sell goods or services, especially sexual services. **2.** One who sympathizes with but does not belong to a main body or group.

cam·phene (kăm′fēn′) *n.* A colorless crystalline compound, $C_{10}H_{16}$, used in the manufacture of synthetic camphor and insecticides.

cam·phor (kăm′fər) *n.* A volatile crystalline compound, $C_{10}H_{16}O$, obtained from the wood of the camphor tree or synthesized and used as an insect repellent, in the manufacture of film, plastics, lacquers, and explosives, and medicinally as a stimulant, expectorant, and diaphoretic. [Middle English *ca(u)mfre*, from Old French *camphre*, from Medieval Latin *camphora*, from Arabic *kāfūr*, from Sanskrit *karpūram*.] —**cam·phor·ic** (kăm-fôr′ĭk, -fŏr′ĭk) *adj.*

cam·phor·ate (kăm′fə-rāt′) *tr.v.* **-ated, -ating, -ates.** To treat, fill, or saturate with camphor.

camphorated oil *n.* A liniment containing camphor and vegetable oil, used as a counterirritant.

camphor tree *n.* An evergreen tree, *Cinnamomum camphora*, native to eastern Asia, having aromatic wood that is a source of camphor.

cam·pi·on (kăm′pē-ən) *n.* Any of various plants of the genus *Lychnis*, or related genera, having red, pink, or white flowers. [Probably from *campion*, obsolete variant of CHAMPION; applied first to *lychnis coronaria*, "crowning lychnis" (whose leaves were formerly used to make crowns for athletic champions).]

Cam·pi·on (kăm′pē-ən), **Saint Edmund** (1540–81). English Jesuit martyr. Ordained an Anglican deacon, he was converted to Roman Catholicism (1571) in Douai. He was executed in England for circulating anti-Anglican literature (1581) and was canonized in 1970.

Campion, Thomas (1567–1620). English composer, poet, and physician. The *Poemata* and his *Masques* are among his best-known works.

camp meeting *n.* An evangelistic gathering held in a tent or outdoors and often lasting several days.

cam·po (kăm′pō, käm′-) *n., pl.* **-pos.** A large, grassy plain in South America with occasional bushes and small trees. [Portuguese, from Latin *campus*.]

camp·site (kămp′sīt′) *n.* An area suitable or used for camping or pitching tents.

camp·stool (kămp′stōōl′) *n.* A light folding stool.

cam·pus (kăm′pəs) *n., pl.* **-puses.** **1.** The grounds of a school, college, or university, especially when situated away from an urban center. **2.** A field in ancient Rome used for various events, such as games, military exercises, and public meetings. [Latin *campus*, field, plain (sense 1, first used at Princeton University).]

Cam·ranh Bay (kăm′rän′). Natural harbor in the South China Sea on the coast of southern Vietnam, 20 kilometers (12 miles) wide, and protected by two peninsulas. It was a naval, military, and air base during the Vietnam War.

cam·shaft (kăm′shăft′) *n.* An engine shaft fitted with a cam or cams, especially one used to operate the valves of an internal-combustion engine.

Ca·mus (kä-mü′), **Albert** (1913–60). French existentialist novelist. A member of the Algerian Communist Party (1934–35), he edited the French Resistance magazine *Combat* during the Nazi occupation of France. Among his best-known works are *The Stranger* (translated 1946) and *The Plague* (translated 1948). In 1957 he was awarded the Nobel Prize for literature.

cam·wood (kăm′wōōd′) *n.* **1.** An African tree, *Baphia nitida*, whose hard red-brown wood has been used as the source of a red dye. **2.** The wood of this tree.

can¹ (kăn; *unstressed* kən) *v.* Past tense **could** (kōōd), present tense **can** or *archaic* **canst** (kănst) (for second person singular). Used as an auxiliary, followed by an infinitive without *to,* or with the infinitive understood. It can indicate: **1. a.** Ability to do or perform: *I can meet you today.* **b.** With verbs of sense perception, ability plus achievement: *At last I can see the sun.* **2.** Possession of a specified power, right, or means: *Only the judge can save her from prison.* **3.** Possession of a specified capacity, faculty, or skill: *He can tune the harpsichord as well as play it.* **4.** Possibility or likelihood: *I wonder if she can be alive after all these years.* **5. a.** Right or sanction: *You can't drive without a license.* **b.** Permission granted according to one's conscience or feelings. Usually used in the negative: *I can't let you take such a risk.* **c.** A requesting or granting of permission: *Can I be excused? No, you cannot.* [Can, could; Middle English *can, coude* (also *couthe*), Old English *can* (also *con*), *cūthe*, first and third person present and past indicative of *cunnan*, to know how, from Germanic.]

Usage: In formal English, a clear distinction is maintained between *can* and *may*: the former refers to ability (*I can sing*), the latter to permission or possibility (*You may sing now. Tomorrow I may sing again*). In informal English, however, the use of *can* to refer to permission is becoming more frequent, and it is now heard even in relatively formal contexts. *May*, correspondingly, is becoming more restricted in its use, and usually implies a clear distinction in status between speaker and person referred to (*You may go. She may leave now*). In negative statements and questions, *mayn't* tends

campanile *These bell towers are usually freestanding and generally near a church or town hall. Dating from 1329, this one in St. Mark's Square (Piazza San Marco) in Venice, Italy, was rebuilt in 1902.*

[Map: CAMEROON — showing L. Chad, CHAD, NIGERIA, Maroua, Garoua, N'Gaoundéré, CAMEROON, C.A.E., Sanaga, Mt Cameroon 4070m, Limbe, MALABO, Douala, Bioko, YAOUNDÉ, EQUATORIAL GUINEA, Mbini, Principe, SÃO TOMÉ AND PRINCIPE, São Tomé, Annobón (EQ. GUIN.), GABON, CONGO, Equator, Km 0–400, Miles 0–200, 10° E, 10° N]

to be avoided, on account of its awkwardness, but the uncontracted form *may not* is also quite cumbersome, especially in questions (*Why may I not buy that book?*). As a consequence, forms using *can* are increasingly replacing *may*: *Why can't I. . . ?*

can² (kăn) *n.* **1.** A metal container, open or with a lid, used for holding oil, gasoline, or the like. **2. a.** An airtight container in which foods are preserved. **b.** A cylindrical airtight metal container for cold drinks: *a beer can.* **c.** The contents of such a container. **3.** *Slang.* **a.** A jail or prison. **b.** A toilet or rest room. **c.** The buttocks. **—in the can.** Recorded and edited; completed. Said of film.
~*tr.v.* **canned, canning, cans. 1.** To seal (vegetables, meat, fruit, drinks, or jam) in a can or jar for future use. **2.** *Slang.* To make a recording of. **3.** *Slang.* **a.** To dismiss from employment or school. **b.** To stop or dispense with: *can the chatter.* [Middle English *canne,* Old English *canne,* from Common Germanic *kannōn-* (unattested).]

Canada goose *Though a native of Canada, this goose now lives wild throughout the Northern Hemisphere. It feeds mainly on grass but also on aquatic plants.*

can. 1. canon. **2.** canto.

Can. Canada; Canadian.

Ca·na (kā'nə). Village in northern Palestine, 6.5 kilometers (4 miles) northeast of Nazareth, where Jesus performed his first miracle by changing water into wine. John 2:1, 11.

Ca·naan (kā'nən). The name given to ancient Palestine before it was occupied by the Jews. Covering an area approximately equal to that of Israel, western Jordan, and southern Syria, it was referred to in the Bible as the land promised by God to the Israelites.

Ca·naan·ite (kā'nə-nīt') *n.* **1.** One of the Semitic inhabitants of the ancient land of Canaan before its conquest by the Israelites. **2.** The Semitic language of this people. **—Ca·naan·it·ic** (-ĭtĭk) *adj.*

Can·a·da (kăn'ə-də). *Abbr.* **Can.** A country occupying (with the exception of Alaska) the northern part of North America. The second-largest country in the world, it has six different time zones, ten provinces, two territories (the Northwest Territories and the Yukon), and two main languages (English and French). The population, concentrated in the southeast, includes Europeans (the main ethnic group), about 250,000 Indians, mostly living on reservations, and 17,000 Eskimos. The Canadian coast was reached by John Cabot who sailed from Bristol (1497), but it was Samuel de Champlain who founded the first permanent settlement at Port Royal (1605) and the settlement on the site of present-day Quebec (1608). Quebec, known as New France, became a royal province of the French crown (1663). With the British Hudson's Bay Company establishing fur-trading posts and strongholds in the Hudson Bay area, a seven-year war broke out between the British and the French (1756). In 1763 Canada was ceded to Britain. With the British North American Act (1867) the Dominion of Canada, a federation of the provinces of Lower Canada (Quebec), Upper Canada (Ontario), New Brunswick, and Nova Scotia, was formed. Between then and 1905, Rupert's Land (Northwest Territories) was acquired from the Hudson's Bay Company, and Manitoba, British Columbia, Prince Edward Island, Alberta, and Saskatchewan became part of the federation. The Statute of Westminster (1931) confirmed and defined Canada as an independent constitutional monarchy equal in status to Britain in the Commonwealth. Since Newfoundland joined the federation (1949), Canada has had ten provinces, in spite of the autonomist Parti Québecois in the largely French-speaking province of Quebec. Fishing is Canada's oldest industry, and modern and effective farming methods produce spring wheat, oats, barley, and hay. Manufacturing industries include paper, motor vehicles, iron, steel, and food processing. Canada is rich in mineral resources and exports natural gas, petroleum, iron ore, nickel, zinc, copper, gold, and uranium. With forests covering a third of the country, Canada supplies the world with wood pulp, newsprint, and timber. The traditional fur trade still flourishes. Area, 9,976,139 square kilometers (3,851,809 square miles). Population, 24,100,000. Capital, Ottawa. **—Ca·na·di·an** (kə-nā'dē-ən) *n. & adj.*

canary *Introduced into Europe in the 16th century as a cage bird, the canary takes its name from its native land—the Canary Islands. In its wild state it is mainly gray-green.*

Canada balsam *n.* **1.** A viscous, yellowish, transparent resin obtained from the balsam fir and used as a mounting cement for microscopic specimens. **2.** A tree, the **balsam fir** *(see).*

Canada goose *n.* A common wild goose, *Branta canadensis,* originally of North America but introduced into Britain in the 17th century, having grayish plumage, a black neck and head, and a white face patch.

Canada thistle *n.* A plant, **creeping thistle** *(see).*

Canadian bacon *n.* Cured rolled bacon from the loin of a pig.

Canadian French *n.* The French language as spoken and written in Canada, chiefly in Quebec and the Maritime Provinces.

ca·naille (kə-nī', -năl') *n.* The masses of common people; rabble or riffraff. [French, from Italian *canaglia,* "pack of dogs," from *cane,* dog, from Latin *canis.*]

ca·nal (kə-năl') *n.* **1.** A man-made waterway or artificially improved river used for irrigation, shipping, or travel. **2.** *Anatomy.* A tube or duct. **3.** *Astronomy.* One of the faint, hazy markings resembling straight lines on the surface of Mars.
~*tr.v.* **canalled** or **-naled, -nalling** or **-naling, -nals. 1.** To dig an artificial waterway through. **2.** To provide with a canal or canals. [Middle English, tube, from Latin *canālis,* channel, from *canna,* reed, from Greek *kanna.*]

Can·a·let·to (kăn'ə-lĕt'ō), **Antonio,** born Giovanni Antonio Canal or Canale (1697–1768). Venetian painter famous for his views of Venice and London. Canaletto was a master of light, flickering colors, and shadows, and his works influenced landscape artists for generations.

can·a·lic·u·lus (kăn'ə-lĭk'yə-ləs) *n., pl.* **-li** (-lī'). *Anatomy.* A small bodily channel, as a tear duct. [Latin, diminutive of *canālis,* CANAL.] **—can·a·lic·u·lar** *adj.*

can·a·li·za·tion (kăn'ə-lī-zā'shən) *n.* **1.** The act or an instance of canalizing. **2.** A system of canals.

can·a·lize (kăn'ə-līz') *tr.v.* **-lized, -lizing, -lizes. 1.** To furnish with, build, or convert into a canal or canals. **2.** To channel into a particular direction; provide an outlet for.

canal rays *pl.n.* Positively charged ions formed in a gas by electrical discharge and attracted to the cathode of the discharge tube. Not in current technical use. [Translation of German *Kanalstrahlen* (because the ions pass through fissures in the cathode).]

Canal Zone. Territory extending 8 kilometers (5 miles) on either side of the Panama Canal. It is administered by the United States under a 1977 treaty. The canal is scheduled to come under Panamanian control in 2000.

can·a·pé (kăn'ə-pā', -pē) *n.* A biscuit or small, thin piece of bread or toast spread with cheese, meat, or relish and served as an appetizer. [French, "couch" ("seat" for the relish), from Medieval Latin *canapeum.* See **canopy.**]

ca·nard (kə-närd') *n.* A false or unfounded and especially a deliberately misleading story or item of news. [French, "duck" (from the expression *vendre des canards à moitié,* "to half-sell ducks," swindle, deceive), from Old French *canart,* duck, from *caner,* to cackle (imitative).]

ca·nar·y (kə-nâr'ē) *n., pl.* **-ies. 1.** A songbird, *Serinus canaria,* native to the Canary Islands, that is greenish to yellow and has long been bred as a cage bird. **2.** *Slang.* A stool pigeon; informer. **3.** A sweet white wine, similar to Madeira, from the Canary Islands. **4.** A lively 16th-century French and English court dance. **5.** A light to moderate or vivid yellow. [French *canari* (bird), *canarie* (wine, dance), from Old Spanish *canario,* "of the Canary Islands," from *Islas Canarias,* CANARY ISLANDS, from Latin *Canaria,* from *Canis,* dog (one of the islands was famous among the Romans for its breed of large dogs).]

canary grass *n.* A grass, *Phalaris canariensis,* native to Europe, having straw-colored seeds used to feed birds.

Ca·nar·y Islands (kə-nâr'ē). Also **Ca·nar·ies** (-ēz). *Spanish* **Is·las Ca·nar·i·as** (ēz'läs kə-när'ē-äs). Group of volcanic islands in the North Atlantic Ocean, 96 kilometers (60 miles) off the northwest coast of Africa. It comprises two provinces of Spain, each named after their capitals: Las Palmas de Gran Canaria has the islands of Fuerteventura, Lanzarote, Gran Canaria, and six unhabited islands; Santa Cruz de Tenerife contains the islands of Tenerife, La Palma, Gomera, and Hierro. The islands were once possessions of Ferdinand and Isabella of Aragon-Castile (1476). After a treaty between Portugal and Aragon-Castile (1479), they became wholly subject to Spain. Having a mild climate, the islands are popular as a winter resort. With the help of irrigation, citrus fruits, bananas, tomatoes, peaches, onions, and potatoes are grown for export.

ca·nas·ta (kə-năs'tə) *n.* **1.** A card game for two to six players, related to rummy and requiring two packs of cards. **2.** A meld of seven cards in this game. [Spanish, "basket" (from the use of two packs, or a "basketful," of cards), from *canasto, canastro,* basket, from Latin *canistrum,* CANISTER.]

ca·nas·ter (kə-năs'tər) *n.* Tobacco made from dried leaves that have been roughly shredded. [Spanish *canastro,* basket (referring to the rush baskets in which the tobacco was shipped). See **canister.**]

Ca·nav·er·al, Cape (kə-năv'ər-əl). Known 1963–73 as **Cape Ken·ne·dy** (kĕn'ə-dē). Cape on the east coast of Florida. It is the site of NASA's Kennedy Manned Space Flight Center, the key launching site for all U.S. space missions.

Can·ber·ra (kăn'bĕr'ə, -bər-ə). Capital of Australia. Situated on the Molongo River in the Australian Capital Territory, it was founded in 1824, chosen as capital (1908), and planned by the U.S. architect Walter Burley Griffin (1876–1937). It is the site of the Australian National University.

can·can (kăn'kăn') *n.* An exuberant dance, popular especially in 19th-century France, performed by women and marked by high kicking. [French, earlier (16th century) "noise," "uproar," of obscure origin.]

can·cel (kăn'səl) *v.* **-celed, -celing, -cels.** Also *chiefly British* **-celled, -celling, -cels.** —*tr.* **1.** To call off (an event, appointment, or the like), usually without rescheduling: *They canceled the picnic because of rain.* **2.** To cross out with lines or other markings. **3. a.** To annul, revoke, or invalidate. **b.** To mark or perforate (a postage stamp or check, for example) to indicate that it may not be used again. **4.** To equalize or make up for; neutralize; offset. Usually followed by *out.* **5.** *Mathematics.* **a.** To remove (a common factor) from the numerator and denominator of a fractional expression. **b.** To remove (a common factor or term) from both members of an equation or inequality. **6.** *Printing.* To omit or delete. —*intr.* To balance or neutralize one another: *two forces that canceled out.* **—See Synonyms at erase, nullify.**
~*n.* **1. a.** The omission or deletion of typed or printed matter. **b.** The matter omitted or deleted or its replacement. **2.** A part of a book used as a substitute for an original part of the book. [Middle English *cancellen,* from Old French *canceller,* from Latin *cancellāre,* to make like a lattice, cross out, from *cancellī,* lattice, diminutive of *cancer, carcer,* jail.] **—can·cel·a·ble** *adj.* **—can·cel·er** *n.*

can·cel·late (kăn-sĕl'ĭt, kăn'sə-lāt') *adj.* Also **can·cel·lat·ed** (kăn'sə-lā'tĭd), **can·cel·lous** (kăn'sə-ləs, kăn-sĕl'əs). **1.** *Anatomy.* Having a coarse netlike or spongy structure. Said of bone. **2.** *Botany.* In the form of a network, as the vein pattern of a leaf. [Latin *cancellātus,*

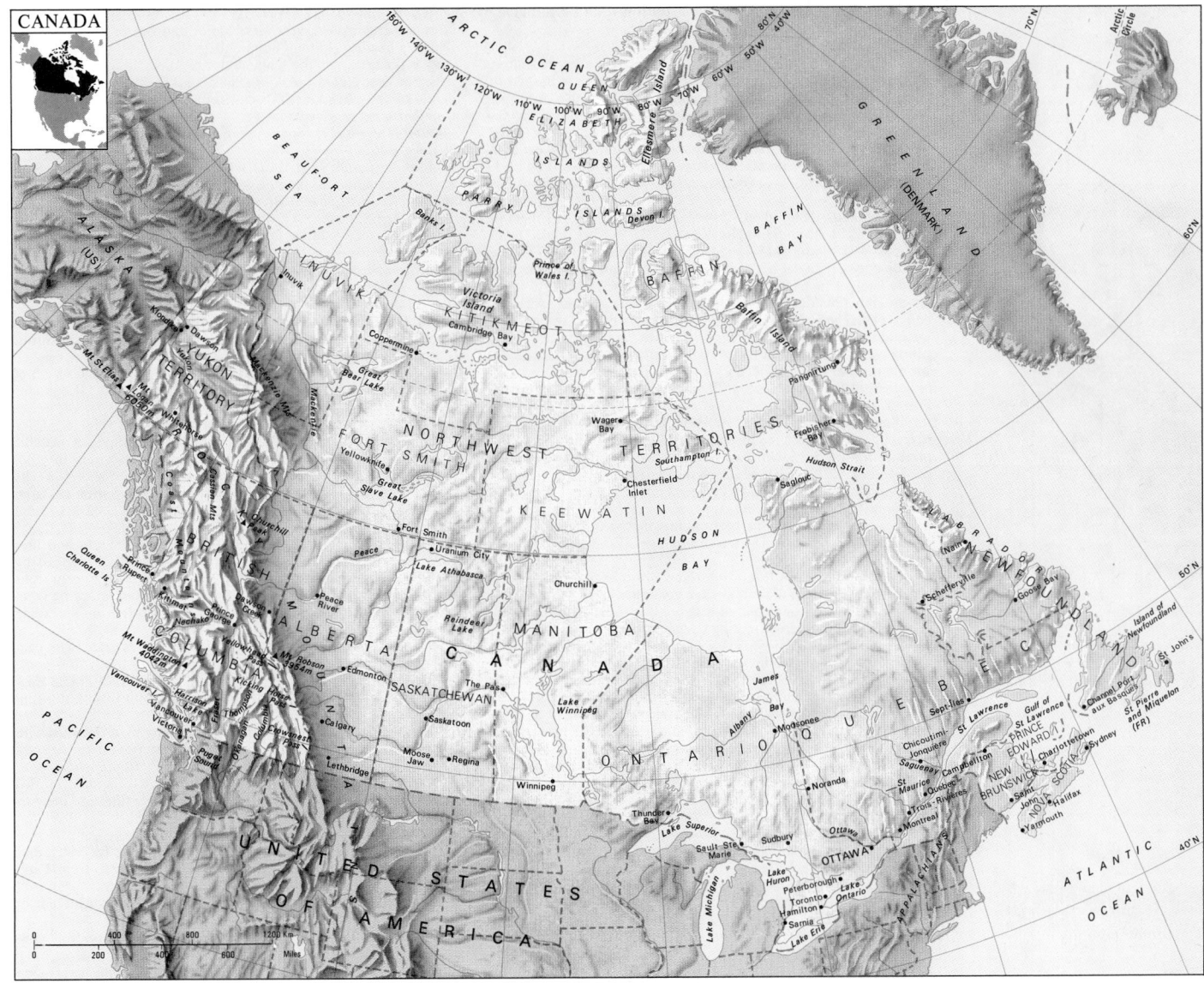

CANADA

past participle of *cancellāre*, to make like a lattice. See **cancel**.]
can·cel·la·tion (kăn′sə-lā′shən) *n.* **1.** The act of canceling. **2.** Marks or perforations indicating canceling. **3.** Something that has been canceled. **4.** Something, such as a ticket or hotel room, that becomes available after a reservation has been canceled.
can·cer (kăn′sər) *n.* **1. a.** Any of various malignant neoplasms, caused by abnormal division of cells, that invade surrounding tissues and often spread to other parts of the body through the blood or lymph. **b.** The pathological condition characterized by such growths. **2.** A pernicious, spreading evil. [Latin *cancer*, crab, creeping ulcer (formed after Greek *karkinōma*, CARCINOMA).] —**can·cer·ous** *adj.*
Can·cer (kăn′sər) *n.* **1.** A constellation in the Northern Hemisphere near Leo and Gemini. **2. a.** The fourth sign of the **zodiac** (*see*). Also called the "Crab." **b.** One born under this sign. [Middle English, from Latin *cancer*, crab.]
can·croid (kăng′kroid′) *adj.* **1.** Similar to a cancer. **2.** Similar to a crab.
~*n.* A skin cancer. [Latin *cancer* (stem *cancr-*), crab, CANCER + -OID.]
can·de·la (kăn-dĕl′ə) *n. Abbr.* **cd** A unit of luminous intensity equal to 1/60 of the luminous intensity per square centimeter of a blackbody radiating at the temperature of solidification of platinum (2,046°K). Also called "candle," "standard candle." [Latin *candēla*, CANDLE.]
can·de·la·bra (kăn′də-lä′brə, -lăb′rə, -lā′brə) *n., pl.* **-bras.** A candelabrum. —See Usage note at **candelabrum.**
can·de·la·brum (kăn′də-lä′brəm, -lăb′rəm, -lā′brəm) *n., pl.* **-bra** (-brə) or **-brums.** A large decorative candlestick having several arms or branches. [Latin *candēlābrum*, from *candēla*, CANDLE.]
  Usage: Two different usage trends have affected this word. First, its original Latin-based plural, *candelabra*, has been in conflict with a later English-based plural, *candelabrums*, considered to be incorrect in formal speech or writing. Secondly, *candelabra* has increasingly come to be used as a singular form, from which a new

English-based plural form has derived: *I bought a new candelabra today; The candelabras need cleaning.* This second development is widespread in all but the most formal and technical contexts.
can·dent (kăn′dənt) *adj.* Having a white-hot glow; incandescent. [Latin *candēns* (stem *candent-*), present participle of *candēre*, to shine, glow, be white.]
can·des·cence (kăn-dĕs′əns) *n.* The state of being white hot; incandescence. [Latin *candēscēns*, present participle of *candēscere*, inceptive of *candēre*, to shine, glow, be white.] —**can·des·cent** *adj.* —**can·des·cent·ly** *adv.*
Candia. See **Iráklion.**
can·did (kăn′dĭd) *adj.* **1.** Without pretense or reserve; straightforward and open. **2.** Without prejudice; impartial. **3.** Not posed or rehearsed: *a candid snapshot.* —See Synonyms at **frank.**
~*n.* An unposed informal photograph. [French *candide*, from Latin *candidus*, glowing, white, pure, guileless, from *candēre*, to glow, be white.] —**can·did·ly** *adv.* —**can·did·ness** *n.*
can·di·da (kăn′dĭ-də) *n.* Any of the pathogenic yeastlike fungi of the genus *Candida.* [New Latin *Candida*, genus name, from Latin, feminine of *candidus*, white.]
can·di·date (kăn′də-dāt′, -dĭt) *n.* **1.** A person who seeks or is nominated for an office, prize, honor, or the like. **2.** A person who seems likely to gain a certain position or undergo a certain fate. **3.** Something that seems likely to be chosen: *The book is a candidate for the award.* [Latin *candidātus*, "(Roman candidate) clothed in a white toga," from *candidus*, white, CANDID.] —**can·di·da·cy** (kăn′-də-də-sē), **can·di·da·ture** (kăn′də-də-chōōr′, -chər) *n.*
candid camera *n.* Any small, easily operated camera with a fast lens for taking unposed or informal photographs.
can·di·di·a·sis (kăn′də-dī′ə-sĭs) *n.* Infection with a fungus of the genus *Candida*, usually affecting moist areas of the body. Also called "moniliasis." [New Latin *Candida* (genus name), from Latin *candidus*, white + -IASIS.]
can·died (kăn′dēd) *adj.* Permeated, covered, encrusted, or cooked with sugar: *candied fruit.*

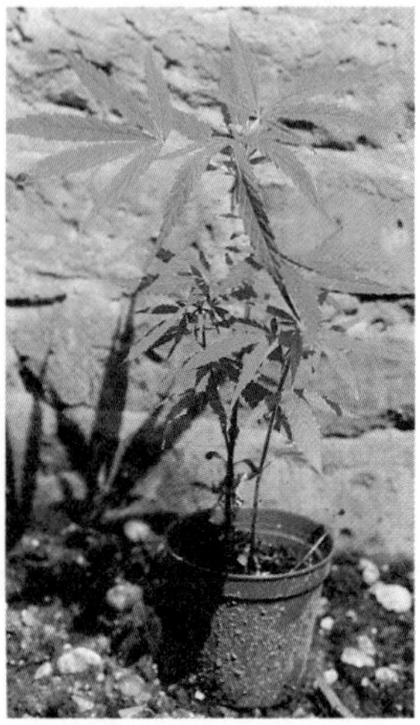

cannabis *Also known as hemp,* Cannabis sativa *is the plant from which hashish and marijuana are derived. It is a native of Asia and its possession in most Western countries is prohibited.*

Can·di·ot (kăn′dē-ŏt′) *adj.* Also **Can·di·ote** (-ōt′). Of or pertaining to Candia (Iráklion) or Crete.
~*n.* A native or inhabitant of Crete.

can·dle (kăn′dəl) *n.* **1.** A solid mass, usually a cylinder, of tallow, wax, or other fatty substance, containing a wick that is burned to provide light. **2.** Something resembling a candle in use or shape. **3. a.** *Physics.* An obsolete unit of luminous intensity, originally defined in terms of a wax candle with standard composition and equal to 1.02 candelas. Also called "international candle." **b.** A **candela** *(see).* **—burn the candle at both ends.** To exhaust oneself by leading too hectic a life. **—not hold a candle to.** To be not nearly as good as.
~*tr.v.* **candled, -dling, -dles.** To examine (an egg) for freshness in front of a light. [Middle English *candel,* Old English *candel,* from Latin *candēla,* from *candēre,* to shine.] **—can·dler** *n.*

can·dle·ber·ry (kăn′dəl-bĕr′ē) *n., pl.* **-ries.** A shrub or tree, the **wax myrtle** *(see),* or its fruit. [From the wax in the berry.]

can·dle·fish (kăn′dəl-fĭsh′) *n., pl.* **candlefish** or **-fishes.** An oily, edible fish, *Thaleichthys pacificus,* of northern Pacific waters, formerly dried and used as a torch. Also called "eulachon."

can·dle-foot (kăn′dəl-fo͝ot′) *n.* A **foot-candle** *(see).*

can·dle·hold·er (kăn′dəl-hōl′dər) *n.* A candlestick.

can·dle·light (kăn′dəl-līt′) *n.* **1.** Illumination from a candle or candles. **2.** Dusk; twilight.

Can·dle·mas (kăn′dəl-məs) *n.* A church festival celebrated on February 2 as the feast of the purification of the Virgin Mary and the presentation of the infant Jesus in the temple. [Middle English *candelmasse,* Old English *candelmæsse* : CANDLE + -MAS (candles for church use were blessed at the feast).]

can·dle·nut (kăn′dəl-nŭt′) *n.* **1.** A tree, *Aleurites moluccana,* of tropical Asia and Polynesia, bearing nuts that yield an oil used in paints and varnishes. **2.** The nut of this tree. [From the use of the oily nuts as candles.]

can·dle·pin (kăn′dəl-pĭn′) *n.* **1.** A slender bowling pin used in a variation of the game of tenpins. **2. candlepins.** *Used with a singular verb.* A bowling game played with a ball smaller than that used in tenpins and a different scoring system.

can·dle·pow·er (kăn′dəl-pou′ər) *n.* Luminous intensity of a light source expressed in standard candles.

can·dle·stick (kăn′dəl-stĭk′) *n.* A holder, often ornamental, with a cup or spike for a candle.

can·dle·wick (kăn′dəl-wĭk′) *n.* **1.** The wick of a candle. **2. a.** Soft, heavy cotton thread similar to that used to make wicks for candles. **b.** Embroidery made of tufts of candlewick.

can·dle·wood (kăn′dəl-wo͝od′) *n.* **1.** A tree, the **ocotillo** *(see).* **2.** The resinous wood of this or similar trees. [After the use of the wood for torches and as a substitute for candles.]

can·dor (kăn′dər) *n.* Also *chiefly British* **can·dour. 1.** Frankness of expression; sincerity; straightforwardness. **2.** Freedom from prejudice; impartiality. [Latin *candor,* whiteness, purity, frankness, from *candēre,* to glow, be white.]

can·dy (kăn′dē) *n., pl.* **-dies. 1.** A rich, sweet confection, as one made with sugar or corn syrup, often flavored and combined with fruits or nuts. **2.** A single piece of such confection.
~*v.* **candied, -dying, -dies.** —*tr.* **1.** To reduce to sugar crystals. **2.** To cook, preserve, saturate, or coat with sugar or syrup. —*intr.* **1.** To crystallize. Used of sugar. **2.** To become coated with sugar or syrup. [Short for *sugar candy,* from French *sucre candi,* from Arabic *sūkkar qandī,* from *qand,* sugar, from Persian, from Sanskrit *khanda,* sugar in lumps.]

Candy. See **Kandy.**

can·dy-striped (kăn′dē-strīpt′) *adj.* Having stripes, usually of bright colors, against a plain background.

candy strip·er (strī′pər) *n.* A usually teenage volunteer nurse's aide in a hospital. [From the resemblance of the volunteer's red and white striped uniform to a candy cane.]

can·dy·tuft (kăn′dē-tŭft′) *n.* Any of various plants of the genus *Iberis,* cultivated for their clusters of white, red, or purplish flowers. [*Candy,* obsolete variant of *Candia,* Crete + TUFT.]

cane (kān) *n.* **1. a.** A slender, jointed stem, woody but usually flexible, as of bamboo, rattan, or certain palm trees. **b.** Any plant having such a stem. **c.** Such stems, or strips of such stems, used for wickerwork. **2.** A grass, *Arundinaria gigantea,* of the southeastern United States, having long stiff stems and often forming canebrakes. **3.** The long, woody stem of the raspberry, blackberry, certain roses, or similar plants. **4. Sugar cane** *(see).* **5.** A stick used as an aid in walking or carried as an accessory. **6.** A rod used for flogging, especially in schools.
~*tr.v.* **caned, caning, canes. 1.** To make, supply, or repair with cane. **2.** To hit or beat with a cane. [Middle English, from Old French, from Latin *canna,* from Greek *kanna,* reed.] **—can·er** *n.*

Ca·ne·a or **Ka·ne·a** (kə-nē′ə). *Greek* **Khan·iá** (KHän-yä′). Capital of the Greek island of Crete and of the Canea *nome* (province) in the northwest of the island. It prospered under the Venetians between the 13th and the 17th century until it was taken by the Turks in 1645. The Venetian fortifications and town walls can still be seen.

cane·brake (kān′brāk′) *n.* A dense thicket of cane.

ca·nes·cent (kə-nĕs′ənt) *adj.* **1.** *Biology.* Covered with whitish or grayish down; hoary. **2.** Turning white or grayish. [Latin *cānēscēns* (stem *cānēscent-*), present participle of *cānēscere,* to grow white, turn gray, from *cānēre,* to be white or gray, from *cānus,* white, gray.] **—ca·nes·cence** *n.*

cane sugar *n.* A sugar yielded by sugar cane, **sucrose** *(see).*

Ca·nes Ve·nat·i·ci (kā′nēz vī-năt′ə-sī′) *n.* A constellation in the Northern Hemisphere near Ursa Major and Boötes, under the Big Dipper's handle. [Latin, "hunting dogs."]

cangue (kăng) *n.* An old Chinese device for punishing petty criminals, consisting of a heavy wooden yoke enclosing the neck and hands of the offender. [French, from Portuguese *canga,* a yoke, from Vietnamese *gong.*]

Ca·nic·u·la (kə-nĭk′yə-lə) *n.* A star, **Sirius** *(see).* [Latin, diminutive of *canis,* dog.]

ca·nic·u·lar (kə-nĭk′yə-lər) *adj.* **1.** Of or pertaining to the Dog Star. **2.** Of or pertaining to the dog days in July and August.

canikin. Variant of **cannikin.**

ca·nine (kā′nīn′) *adj.* **1.** Of or pertaining to dogs. **2.** Of, pertaining to, or characteristic of the family Canidae, which includes the dogs, wolves, and foxes. **3.** Of or designating one of the conical teeth located between the incisors and the first bicuspids.
~*n.* **1.** A canine animal. **2.** A canine tooth. Also called "eyetooth." [Latin *canīnus,* from *canis,* dog.]

Ca·nis Ma·jor (kā′nĭs mā′jər) *n.* A constellation in the Southern Hemisphere near Puppis and Lepus. It contains the star Sirius. [Latin, "the larger dog."]

Canis Mi·nor (mī′nər) *n.* A constellation in the equatorial region of the Southern Hemisphere near Hydra and Monoceros. It contains the star Procyon. [Latin, "the smaller dog."]

can·is·ter (kăn′ĭ-stər) *n.* **1.** A container, usually of thin metal, for holding dry foods, chemicals, and the like. **2.** *Military.* A metallic cylinder that when fired from a gun bursts and scatters the shot packed inside it. Also called "canister shot," "case shot." **3.** The part of a gas mask containing a filter for removing poison gas from the air. [Latin *canistrum,* reed basket, from Greek *kanastron,* from *kanna,* reed.]

can·ker (kăng′kər) *n.* **1.** An ulcerous sore of the mouth and lips. **2.** An area of dead or decaying tissue in a plant surrounded by healthy wood or bark. **3.** Any of several animal diseases characterized by chronic inflammation of affected parts and attacking especially the ears of dogs and cats. **4.** Any source of spreading corruption or debilitation.
~*v.* **cankered, -kering, -kers.** —*tr.* **1.** To attack or infect with canker. **2.** To cause to decay or become corrupt. —*intr.* To become infected with or as if with canker. [Middle English, from Old English *cancer* and Old Northern French *cancre,* both from Latin *cancer,* CANCER.]

can·ker·ous (kăng′kər-əs) *adj.* **1.** Of, pertaining to, or infected with a canker; ulcerous. **2.** Causing canker; ulcerating.

canker sore *n.* A small, painful ulcer, usually of the mouth.

can·ker·worm (kăng′kər-wûrm′) *n.* The larva of either of two moths, *Paleacrita vernata* or *Alsophila Pometaria,* that are destructive to fruit and shade trees.

can·na (kăn′ə) *n.* Any of various tropical plants of the genus *Canna,* having broad leaves and showy red or yellow flowers for which they are widely grown for ornament. [New Latin *Canna,* from Latin *canna,* reed, CANE.]

can·na·bi·di·ol (kăn′ə-bĭ-dī′ôl′, -ōl′) *n.* A chemical constituent of cannabis, $C_{21}H_{29}(OH)_2$.

can·na·bin (kăn′ə-bĭn) *n.* A resinous material extracted from cannabis. [CANNAB(IS) + -IN.]

can·na·bis (kăn′ə-bĭs) *n.* **1.** A plant of the genus *Cannabis,* **hemp** *(see).* **2.** A preparation made from the dried flowering tops of the hemp plant, and smoked, chewed, or drunk for its euphoric or relaxing effect. See **marijuana, hashish.** [New Latin, from Latin, hemp, from Greek *kannabis.*] **—can·na·bic** *adj.*

canned (kănd) *adj.* **1.** Preserved and sealed in a can. **2.** *Informal.* Recorded or taped: *"So if television is to have canned laughter, how about canned tears?"* (Jack Paar).

can·nel (kăn′əl) *n.* A type of bituminous coal that burns brightly with much smoke. Also called "cannel coal." [From *cannel coal,* dialectal form for *candle coal* (from its bright flame).]

can·nel·lo·ni (kăn′ə-lō′nē) *n.* An Italian pasta dish of large-sized macaroni stuffed with a meat or cheese mixture, baked, and served with tomato sauce or cream sauce. [Italian, plural of *cannellone,* from *cannello,* diminutive of *canna,* reed, CANE.]

can·ne·lure (kăn′ə-lo͝or′, -əl-yo͝or′) *n.* A groove or fluting, especially that around the cylindrical part of a bullet. [French, from *canneler,* to make a groove, channel, from *canne,* CANE.]

can·ner (kăn′ər) *n.* Someone or something that cans.

can·ner·y (kăn′ə-rē) *n., pl.* **-ies.** An establishment where meat, vegetables, or other foods are canned.

Cannes (kăn). Resort and port in Alpes-Maritimes department, southern France. It has been a fashionable French Riviera resort since Lord Brougham (1778–1868) built a villa here. It has the oldest monastery in Western Europe (on the Île St. Honorat). Each spring Cannes hosts an international film festival.

can·ni·bal (kăn′ə-bəl) *n.* **1.** A person who eats the flesh of human beings. **2.** Any animal that feeds on others of its own kind. [Spanish *Canibales* (plural), variant (recorded by Columbus) of *Caribes,* the man-eating Caribs of Cuba and Haiti.] **—can·ni·bal·ism** *n.* **—can·ni·bal·is·tic** *adj.*

can·ni·bal·ize (kăn′ə-bə-līz′) *tr.v.* **-ized, -izing, -izes. 1. a.** To remove serviceable parts from (damaged aircraft, cars, or other machinery) for use in the repair of other equipment. **b.** To extract material from (a book or magazine, for example) for use in another work. **2.** To deprive (an organization) of personnel or equipment for use in another organization. [Originally, "to eat human flesh," from CANNIBAL.] **—can·ni·bal·i·za·tion** *n.*

can·ni·kin, can·i·kin (kăn′ĭ-kĭn) *n.* A little can or cup. [Dutch *kanneken,* diminutive of CAN.]

Can·ning (kăn′ĭng), **George** (1770–1827). British statesman, remembered for his achievements as foreign secretary (1807–09, 1822–27). After resigning (1809) over Viscount Castlereagh's handling of the Napoleonic Wars, he was wounded in the thigh by Castlereagh in a duel. During his second term as foreign secretary, he liberalized Tory politics, withdrew from Emperor Alexander I of Russia's Holy Alliance, and supported the rebellion of the Spanish-American colonies (1823) and the Greeks in their struggle for freedom from the Turks (1825–27). In 1827 he became prime minister, but half the cabinet and over 40 ministers refused to serve under him. He resigned, in failing health, after four months.

Can·niz·za·ro (kä′nē-zär′ō), **Stanislao** (1826–1910). Italian chemist whose ideas are the basis of much of modern chemistry. He expanded on Avogadro's work in distinguishing between molecular and atomic weights and employed Avogadro's hypothesis to solve the problem of representing compounds by formulas.

can·non (kăn′ən) *n., pl.* **cannon** or **-nons.** **1.** A weapon used for firing projectiles that consist of a heavy metal tube mounted on a carriage. **2. a.** A heavy firearm larger than 0.60 caliber. See **gun, howitzer, mortar.** **b.** An automatic gun mounted on an aircraft. **3.** The loop at the top of a bell by which the bell is suspended. **4.** A round bit for a horse. **5. a.** The section of leg containing the cannon bone. **b.** The cannon bone. **6.** *Chiefly British.* A shot in billiards in which the cue ball strikes two other balls in succession.
∼v. **cannoned, -noning, -nons.** *—tr.* To bombard or batter with cannon. *—intr.* **1.** To fire cannon. **2.** *Chiefly British.* To make a cannon shot in billiards. **3.** *Chiefly British.* To crash into with violence; collide. Used with *into.* [Middle English *canon,* from Old French, from Italian *cannone,* "large tube, barrel," from *canna,* reed, tube, CANE.]

can·non·ade (kăn′ə-nād′) *v.* **-aded, -ading, -ades.** *—tr.* To assault or bombard with heavy artillery fire. *—intr.* To deliver heavy artillery fire.
∼n. An extended, usually heavy, discharge of artillery. [French *canonade,* discharge of artillery, from Italian *cannonata,* from *cannone,* CANNON.]

can·non·ball (kăn′ən-bôl′) *n.* **1.** A round projectile fired from a cannon. **2.** A jump into water made with the arms grasping the upraised knees. **3.** Something moving with great speed, as a fast train. **4.** A fast low serve in tennis.
∼intr.v. **cannonballed, -balling, -balls.** **1.** To travel rapidly in the manner of a cannonball: *The truck cannonballed down the highway.* **2.** To make a cannonball jump into water.

cannon bone *n.* The bone located between the back of the knee and the fetlock of a horse or ruminant, made up of fused, elongated metatarsals or metacarpals. [So called from its shape.]

can·non·eer (kăn′ə-nîr′) *n.* A gunner or artilleryman. [Old French *canonier,* from *canon,* CANNON.] **—can·non·eer·ing** *n.*

cannon fodder *n.* Soldiers considered as expendable material of warfare. [Translation of German *Kanonenfutter.*]

can·non·ry (kăn′ən-rē) *n., pl.* **-ries.** **1.** Artillery; cannons collectively. **2.** Artillery fire.

cannon shot *n.* **1.** Ammunition for a cannon. **2.** A shot or shots fired by cannon. **3.** The firing distance of a cannon.

can·not (kăn′ŏt′, kə-nŏt′, kă-) *v.* The negative form of **can.** —See Usage note at **can.**

can·nu·la, can·u·la (kăn′yə-lə) *n., pl.* **-las** or **-lae** (-lē′). A tube inserted into a bodily cavity to drain fluid or insert medication. [New Latin, from Latin, diminutive of *canna,* a reed, tube, CANE.]

can·nu·lar (kăn′yə-lər) *adj.* Cannulate.

can·nu·late (kăn′yə-lāt′) *tr.v.* **-lated, -lating, -lates.** To insert a cannula into.
∼adj. Tubular; hollow. **—can·nu·la·tion** *n.*

can·ny (kăn′ē) *adj.* **-nier, -niest.** **1.** Shrewd and prudent, especially in looking after one's own interests. **2.** Cautious in spending money; thrifty. **3.** *Chiefly Scottish.* **a.** Pleasant; attractive. **b.** Gentle; mild. [From CAN (to know how, be able).] **—can·ni·ly** *adv.* **—can·ni·ness** *n.*

ca·noe (kə-no͞o′) *n.* A light, slender boat with pointed ends, propelled by paddles.
∼v. **canoed, -noeing, -noes.** *—tr.* To carry or send by canoe, especially as a sport or hobby. *—intr.* To travel in or propel a canoe. [Earlier *canoa,* from Spanish, from Arawakan (recorded by Columbus), from Cariban.] **—ca·noe·ist** *n.*

can of worms *n. Informal.* A complicated situation or problem that is likely to become more complicated with any attempt to resolve it.

can·on¹ (kăn′ən) *n. Abbr.* **can.** **1.** An ecclesiastical law or code of laws established by a church council. **2.** A secular law, rule, or code of law. **3.** A basis for judgment; a standard; a criterion. **4.** The books of the Bible officially recognized as the Holy Scripture. **5.** *Often* **Cannon.** The part of the Mass beginning after the Sanctus and ending just before the Lord's Prayer. **6.** The calendar of saints accepted by the Roman Catholic Church. **7.** An authoritative list, as of the works of an author. **8.** *Music.* A composition or passage in which the same melody is repeated by one or more voices, overlapping in time in the same or a related key. See **fugue, round.** **9.** *Printing.* A size of type, 48-point. [Middle English *cano(u)n,* from Old English and Old French *canon,* both from Late Latin *canōn,* from Latin, measuring line, rule, model, from Greek *kanōn,* rod, rule.]

canon² *n.* **1.** A member of a chapter of priests serving in a cathedral or collegiate church. **2.** A member of certain religious communities living under a common rule and bound by vows. [Middle English *cano(u)n,* from Norman French *canunie,* from Late Latin *canōnicus,* one living under a rule, from *canōn,* CANON (rule).]

cañon. Variant of **canyon.**

can·on·ess (kăn′ə-nĭs) *n.* A member of a religious community of women, living under a common rule but not bound by vows.

ca·non·i·cal (kə-nŏn′ĭ-kəl) *adj.* Also **ca·non·ic** (-ĭk). **1.** Of, pertaining to, required by, or abiding by canon law. **2.** Of or appearing in the Biblical canon. **3.** Authoritative; officially approved; orthodox. **4.** *Music.* Having the form of a canon. **5.** Of, pertaining to, or belonging to a cathedral chapter. **—ca·non·i·cal·ly** *adv.* **—can·on·ic·i·ty** (kăn′ə-nĭs′ə-tē) *n.*

canonical form *n.* **1.** *Mathematics.* A diagonal matrix (one in which all nondiagonal elements are zero), obtained by transformations on a given matrix. **2.** The simplest form of something.

canonical hours *pl.n.* **1.** *Ecclesiastical.* **a.** A special set of prayers, prescribed by canon law, normally to be recited at specific times of the day. They are matins (with lauds), prime, terce, sext, nones, vespers, and complin. **b.** The times of day set aside for these prayers. **2.** *British.* The hours between 8 A.M. and 6 P.M., during which marriages may legally take place in parish churches.

ca·non·i·cals (kə-nŏn′ĭ-kəlz) *pl.n.* The dress prescribed by canon law for officiating clergy.

ca·non·i·cate (kə-nŏn′ĭ-kāt′, -kĭt) *n.* The office or dignity of a canon; canonry. [Medieval Latin *canōnicātus,* from Late Latin *canōnicus,* a canon, from *canōn,* CANON (rule).]

can·on·ist (kăn′ə-nĭst) *n.* A person skilled in canon law. **—can·on·is·tic, can·on·is·ti·cal** *adj.*

can·on·ize (kăn′ə-nīz′) *tr.v.* **-ized, -izing, -izes.** **1.** To declare (a deceased person) to be a saint and entitled to be fully honored as such. Compare **beatify.** **2.** To include in the Biblical canon. **3.** To approve as being within canon law. **4.** To glorify; exalt. **—can·on·i·za·tion** *n.* **—can·on·iz·er** *n.*

canon law *n.* The body of officially established rules governing the faith and practice of the members of a Christian church.

can·on·ry (kăn′ən-rē) *n., pl.* **-ries.** **1.** The position or benefice of one who is an ecclesiastical canon. **2.** Canons collectively.

Ca·no·pic (kə-nō′pĭk, -nŏp′ĭk) *adj.* Designating an ancient Egyptian vase, urn, or jar used to hold the remains of the dead. [Latin *Canopicus,* from *Canopus,* ancient Egyptian port east of Alexandria.]

Ca·no·pus (kə-nō′pəs) *n.* A star in the constellation Carina, 650 light-years from Earth, the second-brightest star in the sky. [Latin, from Greek *Kanōpos*†.]

can·o·py (kăn′ə-pē) *n., pl.* **-pies.** **1.** A cloth covering fastened or held horizontally above a person or an object for protection or ornamentation. **2.** *Architecture.* An ornamental, rooflike projection, as over an altar, pulpit, or the like. **3.** A high covering: *a vast canopy of foliage.* **4. a.** The transparent, movable enclosure over the cockpit of an aircraft. **b.** The hemispherical fabric surface of a parachute.
∼tr.v. **canopied, -pying, -pies.** To overhang with a canopy; form a canopy over: *Mist canopied the landscape.* [Middle English *canape, canope,* from Medieval Latin *canopeum,* (couch with a) mosquito net, from Greek *kōnōpeion,* from *kōnōps,* gnat.]

ca·no·rous (kə-nôr′əs, -nōr′əs, kăn′ər-əs) *adj.* Agreeable to the ears; melodious. [Latin *canōrus,* from *canor,* tune, melody, from *canere,* to sing.] **—ca·no·rous·ly** *adv.* **—ca·no·rous·ness** *n.*

Ca·nos·sa (kə-nŏs′ə). A village in north-central Italy, in the Apennines. In January 1077 the Holy Roman Emperor Henry IV did penance here to obtain a pardon from his excommunication by Pope Gregory VII.

Ca·no·va (kə-nō′və), **Antonio** (1757–1822). Italian neoclassical sculptor whose works include *The Tomb of Clement XIII* (1792) and *Pauline Borghese as Venus Victrix* (1807).

canst (kănst). *Archaic.* The second person singular present tense of **can.** Used with *thou.*

cant¹ (kănt) *n.* **1.** Angular deviation from a vertical or horizontal plane or surface; inclination; slant; slope. **2. a.** A thrust or motion that tilts something. **b.** The tilt caused by such a motion. **3.** An outer corner, as of a building. **4.** A slanted edge or surface.
∼v. **canted, canting, cants.** *—tr.* **1.** To set at an oblique angle; cause to slant or tilt. **2.** To give a slanting edge to; bevel. **3.** To change the direction of suddenly. *—intr.* **1.** To tilt to one side; slant. **2.** To take an oblique direction or course; swing around. Used of a ship. [Middle English, side, edge, ultimately from Latin *cant(h)us,* iron tire, rim of a wheel, from Celtic.]

cant² *n.* **1.** Hypocritically pious language. **2.** Platitudes uttered mindlessly. **3.** The special vocabulary peculiar to the members of a group on the fringe of society, such as thieves, for example; argot. **4.** The special terminology understood among the members of a profession, discipline, or class, but obscure to the general population; jargon. **5.** Whining speech, as used by beggars.
∼intr.v. **canted, canting, cants.** **1.** To speak in a whining, pleading tone. **2.** To speak tediously or sententiously; moralize. **3.** To use special jargon or argot. [Perhaps from Norman French *cant,* musical sound, singing, whining speech of beggars (sense perhaps derived from original application to the singing of religious mendicants), from *canter,* to sing, tell, from Latin *cantāre,* frequentative of *canere,* to sing.] **—cant·ing·ly** *adv.*

can't (kănt, känt). Contraction of *cannot.* —See Usage note at **can.**

can·ta·bi·le (kän-tä′bə-lā′) *adv. Music.* In a smooth, lyrical, flowing

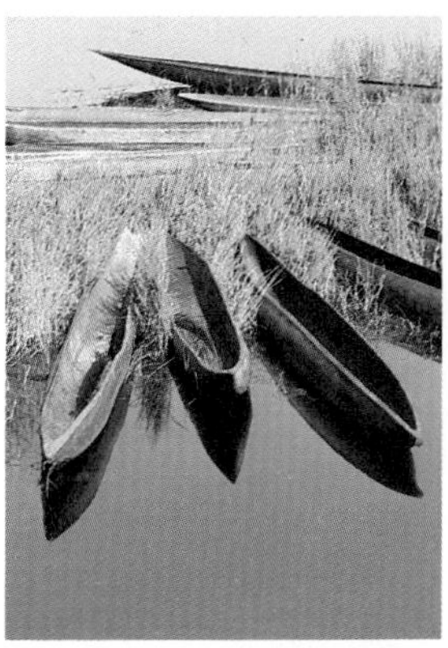

canoe *Primitive canoes—like these in New Guinea—are made by hollowing out the center of a log and are called dugouts.*

PRONUNCIATION KEY

ă, pat; ā, pay; âr, care; ä, father, are; b, bib; ch, church; d, deed; ĕ, pet; ē, be; f, fife; g, gag; h, hat; hw, which; ĭ, pit; ī, pie; îr, pier; j, judge; k, kick; l, lid, needle; m, mum; n, no, sudden; ng, thing; ŏ, pot; ō, toe; ô, paw, for; oi, noise; ou, out; o͝o, book; o͞o, boot; p, pop; r, roar; s, sauce; sh, ship, dish; t, tight; th, thin, path; *th,* this, bathe; ŭ, cut; ûr, fur; v, valve; w, with; y, yes; z, zebra, size; zh, vision; ə, about, item, edible, gallop, circus, peaceful

IN FOREIGN WORDS:

à, *Fr.* ami; œ, *Fr.* feu, *Ger.* schön; ü, *Fr.* tu, *Ger.* über; KH, *Ger.* ich, *Scot.* loch; N, *Fr.* bon; y′, *Fr.* Compiègne

STRESS MARKS:

Primary stress: ′ **in·cite′** (ĭn-sīt′)
Secondary stress: ′ **in′sight′** (ĭn′sīt′)

style. Used as a direction to the performer.
~*n. Music.* A cantabile passage or movement. [Italian, from Late Latin *cantābilis,* singable, from Latin *cantāre,* frequentative of *canere,* to sing.] —**can·ta·bi·le** *adj.*

Can·ta·bri·an Mountains (kăn-tā′brē-ən). Mountain range in the north of Spain stretching *c.* 480 kilometers (300 miles) east to west along the Bay of Biscay. Its highest peak is Torre de Cerredo (2,642 meters; 8,668 feet).

Can·ta·brig·i·an (kăn′tə-brĭj′ē-ən) *adj.* **1.** Of or pertaining to Cambridge in England or Cambridge in Massachusetts. **2.** Of or pertaining to Cambridge University.
~*n.* **1.** A native or resident of Cambridge. **2.** A student or graduate of Cambridge University. [Medieval Latin *Cantabrigia,* CAMBRIDGE.]

can·ta·la (kăn-tä′lə) *n.* **1.** A century plant, *Agave cantula,* native to tropical America, cultivated for its coarse, tough fiber. **2.** The fiber of the cantala. [Origin unknown.]

can·ta·loupe, can·ta·loup (kăn′tə-lōp′) *n.* **1.** A variety of melon, *Cucumis melo cantalupensis,* having fruit with a ribbed, rough rind and aromatic orange flesh. **2.** Any of several similar melons. **3.** The fruit of any of these plants. [French *cantaloup,* from Italian *cantalupo,* first grown at *Cantalupo,* a papal villa.]

can·tan·ker·ous (kăn-tăng′kər-əs) *adj.* Ill-tempered and quarrelsome. [Perhaps from Middle English *contekour,* rioter, brawler, from *contek,* quarrel, strife, from Norman French *contek*†.] —**can·tan·ker·ous·ly** *adv.* —**can·tan·ker·ous·ness** *n.*

can·ta·ta (kən-tä′tə) *n.* A vocal and instrumental composition comprising choruses, arias, and recitatives. [Italian *(aria) cantata,* "sung (aria)," from *cantare,* to sing, from Latin *cantāre.* See cant (jargon).]

can·teen (kăn-tēn′) *n.* **1.** An institutional recreation hall or cafeteria. **2.** A temporary or mobile eating place, especially one set up in an emergency. **3. a.** A store for on-base military personnel. **b.** *Chiefly British.* A recreational club for soldiers. **4. a.** A mess kit. **b.** A box divided into compartments containing a set of cooking gear. **5.** A flask for drinking water of the kind carried by soldiers. [French *cantine,* from Italian *cantina,* a wine cellar, from *canto,* edge, from Latin *cant(h)us.* See cant (angle).]

can·ter (kăn′tər) *n.* **1.** A horse's gait, slower than the gallop but faster than the trot, in which a three-beat rhythm commences on the inside leg. **2.** A ride at this gait.
~*v.* **cantered, -tering, -ters.** —*intr.* To move or ride at a canter. —*tr.* To make (a horse) go at a canter. [18th century : short for *Canterbury gallop, trot,* or the like, supposedly the slow pace at which mounted pilgrims rode to Canterbury in the Middle Ages.]

Can·ter·bur·y (kăn′tər-bĕr′ē). City at the foot of the North Downs, on the Stour River, in east Kent, England. The 11th- to 16th-century cathedral, where Thomas Becket was martyred (1170), dominates the city and is the seat of the archbishop and primate of the Anglican Communion. The original cathedral, founded by St. Augustine (597), was destroyed by fire (1067). The shrine erected to commemorate the canonization of Becket was a focal point for pilgrims for three centuries and inspired Chaucer's *Canterbury Tales.*

Can·ter·bur·y bells (kăn′tər-bĕr′ē) *n. Used with a singular or plural verb.* A plant, *Campanula medium,* native to Europe, widely cultivated for its bell-shaped, violet-blue flowers. [The flowers resemble the bells on the horses of Canterbury pilgrims.]

can·thar·i·des (kăn-thăr′ə-dēz′) *pl.n. Singular* **can·tha·ris** (kăn′thər-ĭs). *Used with a singular or plural verb.* A toxic preparation of the crushed, dried bodies of the beetle *Lytta vesicatoria* (or *Cantharis vesicatoria*), formerly used as a counterirritant for skin blisters and as an aphrodisiac. Also called "Spanish fly." [Latin, plural of *cantharis,* from Greek *kantharis,* blister beetle, from *kantharos*†, dung beetle.]

can·thi·tis (kăn-thī′tĭs) *n.* Inflammation of the canthus.

cant hook *n.* A wooden pole with a hinged hook near the end, used for moving logs, similar to a **peavey** *(see)* but with a blunt end. [From CANT (angle).]

can·thus (kăn′thəs) *n., pl.* **-thi** (-thī′). The corner at either side of the eye, formed by the meeting of the upper and lower eyelids. [Late Latin, from Greek *kanthos*†.]

can·ti·cle (kăn′tĭ-kəl) *n.* A song or chant; specifically, a nonmetrical hymn with words taken directly from a Biblical text. [Middle English, from Latin *canticulum,* diminutive of *cantus,* song, from *canere,* to sing.]

Canticle of Canticles *n.* In the Douay Bible, the **Song of Solomon** *(see).*

can·ti·le·na (kăn′tə-lā′nə, -lē′nə) *n. Music.* A sustained, smooth-flowing melodic line. [Italian.]

can·ti·le·ver (kăn′tə-lē′vər, -lĕv′ər) *n.* **1.** A projecting beam or other structure supported only at one end. **2.** A beam or other part projecting beyond a fulcrum and supported by a balancing part or a downward force exerted by the fulcrum. **3.** A bracket or block supporting a balcony or cornice.
~*v.* **cantilevered, -vering, -vers.** —*tr.* To build as a cantilever. —*intr.* To extend outward as or like a cantilever. [17th century : origin obscure.]

cantilever bridge *n.* A bridge formed by two projecting beams or trusses that are joined in the center by a connecting part and are supported on piers and anchored by counterbalancing parts.

can·til·late (kăn′tə-lāt′) *v.* **-lated, -lating, -lates.** —*tr.* To chant or recite in a musical monotone, as in Jewish or other rituals. —*intr.* To recite in a musical monotone. [Latin *cantillāre,* to sing in a low

voice, hum, from *cantāre,* frequentative of *canere,* to sing.] —**can·til·la·tion** *n.*

can·ti·na (kăn-tē′nə) *n. Southwestern U.S.* An establishment that serves liquor; a bar or saloon. [Spanish, CANTEEN.]

cant·ing (kăn′tĭng) *adj. Heraldry.* Of, pertaining to, or being a visual allusion to the owner's or bearer's name.

can·tle (kăn′tl) *n.* **1.** The rear part of a saddle. **2.** A corner or portion, especially when cut off from something, such as a piece of land or cheese; a slice. [Middle English *cantel,* from Norman French, diminutive of *cant,* corner, CANT.]

can·to (kăn′tō) *n., pl.* **-tos.** *Abbr.* **can.** Any of the principal divisions of a long poem. [Italian, from Latin *cantus,* song, from *canere,* to sing.]

can·ton (kăn′tən, -tŏn′) *n.* **1. a.** A small territorial division of a country; especially, any of the constituent states of Switzerland. **b.** A subdivision of an arrondissement in France. **2.** *Heraldry.* A small, square division of a shield, usually in the upper right corner. **3.** A division of a flag, usually rectangular, occupying the upper corner next to the staff.
~*tr.v.* (kăn′tən, -tŏn′ *for sense 1;* kăn-tōn′, -tŏn′ *for sense 2*) **cantoned, -toning, -tons.** **1.** To divide into parts, especially into cantons or territorial districts. **2.** To assign quarters to (troops); billet. [French, corner, subdivision, from Old French *canton,* augmentative of *canto,* CANT (corner).] —**can·ton·al** (kăn′tə-nəl, kăn-tōn′əl) *adj.*

Canton. See Guangzhou.

Can·ton crepe (kăn′tŏn′) *n.* A soft fabric of silk or similar material with a finely crinkled texture. It is similar to crêpe de Chine but heavier. [After CANTON, China, where it was originally made.]

Can·ton·ese (kăn′tə-nēz′, -nēs′) *n., pl.* **Cantonese. 1.** The dialect of Chinese spoken in Guangdong province in southern China. **2.** A native or inhabitant of Guangdong province in southern China. —**Can·ton·ese** *adj.*

Canton flannel *n.* Flannelette. [After CANTON, China.]

can·ton·ment (kăn-tōn′mənt, kăn-tŏn′-) *n.* **1.** A group of more or less temporary buildings for housing troops. **2.** The assignment of troops to temporary quarters.

Canton ware *n.* Ceramic ware, including blue-and-white enameled porcelain, exported from China, especially during the 18th and 19th centuries. [After CANTON, China.]

can·tor (kăn′tər) *n.* **1.** The official soloist or chief singer of the liturgy in a synagogue. **2.** The person who leads a church choir or congregation in singing; a precentor. [Latin, singer, from *canere,* to sing.] —**can·to·ri·al** (kăn-tôr′ē-əl, -tōr′ē-əl) *adj.*

Can·tor (kăn′tôr), **Georg** (1845–1918). Russian mathematician, noted for setting the concept of infinity on a mathematical foundation. Born in St. Petersburg, he moved to Germany with his family in 1856. His main achievements were in applying ideas of symbolic logic to sets of numbers and formulating his theory of sets. Attacked by many of his contemporaries, he had a breakdown (1884) and died in an asylum.

can·trip (kăn′trĭp) *n. Scottish.* **1.** A magic spell; a witch's trick. **2.** A mischievous trick; a prank. [18th century : origin obscure.]

can·tus fir·mus (kăn′təs fîr′məs, fûr′məs) *n.* A plainsong melody serving as the basis of a polyphonic composition by the addition of contrapuntal voices, as in 15th-century polyphony. [Medieval Latin, "fixed melody."]

canula. Variant of **cannula.**

Ca·nute or **Cnut** (kə-nōōt′, -nyōōt′) (c. 994–1035). Danish King of England (from 1016), Denmark (from 1019), and Norway (from 1028). He repelled Viking attacks on England and temporarily subjugated Malcolm II and the Scots (1028). To prove to flatterers that even his powers were limited, he is reputed to have taken his court to the seashore and commanded the incoming waves to recede.

can·vas (kăn′vəs) *n.* **1.** A heavy, coarse, closely woven fabric of cotton, hemp, or flax, used for making tents and sails. **2. a.** A piece of such material on which a painting, especially an oil painting, is executed. **b.** A painting of this kind. **3.** Sailcloth. **4. a.** A sail. **b.** Sails collectively. **5. a.** A tent. **b.** Tents collectively. **c.** A circus tent. **6.** A fabric of coarse open weave, used as a foundation for needlework. **7.** The floor of a ring in which boxing or wrestling takes place. **8.** A covering made of canvas to enclose the section at the front or back of a racing boat in order to keep out water. —**under canvas. 1.** In a tent or tents. **2.** With sails spread. [Middle English *canevas,* from Norman French, from Vulgar Latin *cannabāceus* (unattested), "made of hemp," from Latin *cannabis,* hemp, from Greek *kannabis.*]

can·vas·back (kăn′vəs-băk′) *n.* A North American duck, *Aythya valisneria,* having a reddish-brown head and neck and a whitish back.

canvas duck *n.* A fabric made of lightweight cotton or linen.

can·vass (kăn′vəs) *v.* **-vassed, -vassing, -vasses.** —*tr.* **1. a.** To go through (a region) or go to (persons) to solicit votes, orders, subscriptions, or the like. **b.** To conduct a survey of (public opinion) on a given subject; poll. **2.** To examine carefully or discuss thoroughly; scrutinize. —*intr.* **1.** To solicit political support, sales orders, or opinions. **2.** To make a thorough examination or conduct a detailed discussion.
~*n.* **1. a.** A solicitation of votes, sales orders, or opinions. **b.** A survey of public opinion. **2.** An examination or discussion. [From CANVAS, probably from the idea of "tossing a person in a canvas sheet," hence to agitate, harangue.] —**can·vass·er** *n.*

can·yon (kăn′yən) *n.* Also **ca·ñon.** A narrow chasm with steep cliff walls, usually formed by running water; a gorge. [American Spanish *cañon*, from Spanish, pipe, tube, conduit, augmentative of *caña*, tube, cane, from Latin *canna*, a reed, from Greek *kanna*.]

Can·yon·lands National Park (kăn'yən-lăndz'). A national park covering 104,344 hectares (257,640 acres) in southeastern Utah. The park is in a desert region and has deep canyons, unusual rock pinnacles and arches, and high mesas.

can·zo·ne (kăn-zō'nĕ, känt-sō'nä) *n., pl.* **-nes** (-nĕz, -näz) or **-ni** (-nē). **1.** A poetic form that was the dominant lyric genre of 13th-century Italy, consisting of a sequence of equal stanzas with various standard rhyme schemes developed as a synthesis of pre-existing Provençal forms by Dante and others. **2.** A polyphonic song form evolving from this and resembling the madrigal in style. [Italian, from Latin *cantiō* (stem *cantiōn-*), song, from *canere*, to sing.]

can·zo·net (kăn'zə-nĕt') *n.* Also **can·zo·net·ta** (-nĕt'ə). A short, lighthearted song or air. [Italian *canzonetta*, diminutive of CAN-ZONE.]

caou·tchouc (kou'chŏŏk', -chŏŏk') *n.* Natural **rubber** *(see).* [French, from obsolete Spanish *cauchuc*, from Quechua.]

cap (kăp) *n.* **1.** A covering for the head, usually soft and close-fitting and often having a visor. **2.** A special head covering worn to indicate rank, occupation, or membership in a particular group: *a cardinal's cap.* **3.** Any of numerous objects that cover, protect, or seal: *a bottle cap.* **4.** *Architecture.* The capital of a column. **5.** The top part, or pileus, of a fungus such as a mushroom or toadstool. **6. a.** A percussion cap *(see).* **b.** A small explosive charge enclosed in paper for use in a toy gun. **7.** An academic mortarboard. Used especially in the phrase *cap and gown.* **8.** *British.* **a.** *Sports.* A token award made to a player on each appearance for a special team, especially an international football or cricket team. **b.** A sportsman awarded a cap. **9.** Any of several sizes of writing paper. See **foolscap.** **10.** Something that limits or restrains: *put a cap on government spending.* —**set one's cap for.** To attempt to attract and win (a man) as a lover or husband.
~*tr.v.* **capped, capping, caps. 1.** To put a cap on: *Engineers capped the oil well to contain the fire.* **2.** To lie over or on top of; serve as a cap for; cover: *Snow capped the hills.* **3.** To apply the finishing touch to; complete: *cap a meal with dessert.* **4.** To surpass; outdo. **5.** *British.* To name (a sportsman) as member of a special team. [Middle English *cappe*, Old English *cæppe*, from Late Latin *cappa*, hood, probably from Latin *caput*, head.]

cap. 1. capacity. **2.** capital (city). **3.** capital letter.

ca·pa·bil·i·ty (kā'pə-bĭl'ə-tē) *n., pl.* **-ties. 1.** The quality of being capable; physical, mental, or moral capacity; ability. **2.** Potential ability: *live up to one's capabilities.* **3.** The capacity to be used, treated, or developed for a specific purpose.

ca·pa·ble (kā'pə-bəl) *adj.* **1.** Having capacity or ability; competent; efficient; able: *a capable administrator.* **2.** Having the required mental or physical capacity; qualified. Used with *of.* **3.** Open; susceptible. Used with *of: an error capable of remedy.* [French, from Old French, from Late Latin *capābilis,* "able to hold," from *capere,* to hold.] —**ca·pa·ble·ness** *n.* —**ca·pa·bly** *adv.*

ca·pa·cious (kə-pā'shəs) *adj.* Able to contain a large quantity; spacious; roomy. [Latin *capāx* (stem *capāc-*), able to hold, from *capere,* to hold, contain.] —**ca·pa·cious·ly** *adv.* —**ca·pa·cious·ness** *n.*

ca·pac·i·tance (kə-păs'ə-təns) *n. Symbol* **C** **1.** The ratio of charge to potential on an electrically charged, isolated conductor. **2.** The ratio of the electric charge transferred from one to the other of a pair of conductors to the resulting potential difference between them. Formerly called "capacity." **3. a.** The property of a circuit element that permits it to store charge. **b.** The part of a circuit exhibiting capacitance. [CAPACIT(Y) + -ANCE.] —**ca·pac·i·tive** *adj.* —**ca·pac·i·tive·ly** *adv.*

ca·pac·i·tate (kə-păs'ə-tāt') *tr.v.* **-tated, -tating, -tates.** To render fit; make qualified; enable. —**ca·pac·i·ta·tion** *n.*

ca·pac·i·tor (kə-păs'ə-tər) *n.* An electric circuit element used to store charge temporarily, consisting typically of two metallic plates separated by a dielectric. Formerly called "condenser."

ca·pac·i·ty (kə-păs'ə-tē) *n., pl.* **-ties.** *Abbr.* **c., cap. 1.** The ability to receive, hold, or absorb. **2.** A measure of this ability; volume. **3.** The maximum amount that can be contained: *a trunk filled to capacity.* **4.** The maximum or optimum amount of production: *factories operating below capacity.* **5.** The ability to learn or retain knowledge. **6.** The ability to do something; faculty; aptitude. Used with *of, for,* or an infinitive: *a capacity for self-expression.* **7.** The quality of being suitable for or receptive to specified treatment: *the capacity of elastic to be stretched.* **8.** The position in which one functions; a role: *in her capacity as hostess.* **9.** Legal qualification or authority: *the capacity to make an arrest.* **10.** *Electricity.* **a.** *Obsolete.* Capacitance. **b.** A measure of the electric output of a generator. —See Synonyms at **ability.**
~*adj.* As large or numerous as possible: *a capacity crowd on opening night.* [Middle English *capacite,* from Old French, from Latin *capācitās* (stem *capācitāt-*), from *capāx,* CAPACIOUS.]

cap-a-pie, cap-à-pie (kăp'ə-pē') *adv.* From head to foot. [Old French *(de) cap a pie,* from Old Provençal *de cap a pe : cap,* head, from Latin *caput* + *pe,* foot, from Latin *pēs.*]

ca·par·i·son (kə-păr'ə-sən) *n.* **1.** A cover, usually ornamental, placed over a horse's saddle or harness; trappings. **2.** Richly ornamented clothing; finery.
~*tr.v.* **caparisoned, -soning, -sons.** To equip with a caparison. [Old French *caparaçon,* from Spanish *caparazón,* saddle blanket, "mantle with hood," probably from *capa,* CAPE (garment).]

cape¹ (kāp) *n.* A sleeveless garment fastened at the throat and worn hanging over the shoulders. [French, from Old Provençal *cape* and Spanish *capa,* both from Late Latin *cappa,* hood, cloak, from Latin *caput,* head.]

cape² *n. Abbr.* **c., C.** A point or head of land projecting into a sea or other body of water; a promontory. Compare **peninsula.** [Middle English *cap,* from Old French, from Old Provençal, from Latin *caput,* head.]

Cape, Cape of. For names of actual capes, see the specific element of the name, as **Hatteras, Cape; Good Hope, Cape of; Cod, Cape.** Other names beginning with *Cape* are entered under **Cape,** as **Cape Province.**

Cape Bret·on Island (kăp brĕt'n). Island forming northern Nova Scotia, eastern Canada. A causeway links it to the mainland.

Cape Coast. Town on the Gulf of Guinea, Ghana. The capital of the British colony of the Gold Coast until 1877, it was formerly known as Cape Coast Castle after the castle built by the Swedes (1652). The Dutch followed the Swedes as the colonial power before handing it over to the British (1664). Cocoa is its chief export.

Cape Cod Canal (kŏd). A sea level canal, 28.2 kilometers (17.5 miles) long, at the base of Cape Cod in Massachusetts. It was built (1910-14) with private funds and purchased by the U.S. government in 1927. The canal can accommodate oceangoing vessels and cuts the distance between New York and Boston by 121 kilometers (75 miles).

Cape Cod National Seashore. A scenic area, *c.* 18,060 hectares (44,600 acres), on Cape Cod in southeastern Massachusetts. It includes beaches, sand dunes, heathlands, marshes, freshwater ponds, and historic sites.

Cape colored *n.* A South African of mixed racial descent who lives in or near the Cape Peninsula.

Cape cowslip *n.* Any of various bulbous South African plants of the genus *Lachenalia,* having clusters of drooping red, green, or yellow flowers and widely cultivated as a potted plant.

Cape gooseberry *n.* A plant, *Physalis peruviana,* native to tropical America, having yellow flowers and edible yellow berries.

Cape jasmine *n.* A species of **gardenia** *(see).*

cap·e·lin (kăp'ə-lĭn, kăp'lĭn) *n.* Also **cap·lin** (kăp'lĭn). A small, edible marine fish, *Mallotus villosus,* of northern Atlantic and Pacific waters, related to and resembling the smelts. [French, from Provençal, "smelt," CHAPLAIN.]

Ca·pel·la (kə-pĕl'ə) *n.* A double star in Auriga, the brightest star in the constellation, approximately 46 light-years from Earth. [New Latin, from Latin, diminutive of *capra,* she-goat, from *caper,* goat.]

Cape Province. Officially, Province of the Cape of Good Hope. *Abbr.* **C.P.** Largest and most southerly province of South Africa. The first settlers (1652) were Dutch. Ceded to Britain (1814), it became Cape Colony (Crown Colony of the Cape of Good Hope) and joined the Union of South Africa as a province (1910). It produces diamonds, copper, asbestos, manganese, iron ore, fruit, and vegetables. Its capital is Cape Town.

ca·per¹ (kā'pər) *n.* **1.** A playful leap or hop; a skip. **2.** A wild escapade. **3.** A criminal plot or enterprise.
~*intr.v.* **capered, -pering, -pers.** To leap or frisk about; frolic; gambol. [Short for CAPRIOLE.] —**ca·per·er** *n.*

caper² *n.* **1.** A spiny, trailing shrub, *Capparis spinosa,* of the Mediterranean region. **2. a.** A pickled flower bud of this shrub, having a pungent taste and used as a condiment. **b.** Any similar pickled bud or pod. [From earlier *capres* (mistaken as plural), Middle English *caperis,* from Latin *kapparis*†.]

cap·er·cail·lie (kăp'ər-kāl'yē, -kā'lē) *n.* Also **cap·er·cail·zie** (-kāl'zē). A large grouse, *Tetrao urogallus,* of northern Europe, having dark plumage and, in the male, a fanlike tail. [Scottish Gaelic *capalcoille,* "horse of the wood" : *capall,* horse, probably from Latin *caballus* + *coille,* forest, probably from Old Irish *caill.*]

Ca·per·na·um (kə-pûr'nē-əm). Ancient town on the northern shore of the Sea of Galilee, Israel. Closely associated with Christ's teachings, it is the scene of many Biblical events.

cape·skin (kāp'skĭn') *n.* Soft leather made from sheepskin. [After CAPE PROVINCE, where it was originally made.]

Ca·pet (kā'pĭt, kā-pā'). Dynasty of French kings (987-1328) descended from **Robert the Strong** (died 866), including **Hugh Capet** (*c.* 940-99) who was elected king in 987, permanently removing the Carolingians from power, and ruled until his death. Their gradual expansion of territory and centralization of power initiated the movement toward a unified France.

Ca·pe·tian (kə-pē'shən) *adj.* Pertaining or belonging to the Capet dynasty. —**Ca·pe·tian** *n.*

Cape Town. Legislative capital of South Africa and the capital city of Cape Province. Founded by Jan van Riebeeck (1652) as a supply post on the Atlantic coast for the Dutch East India Company, it is the oldest white settlement in South Africa. The chief seaport and second-largest city in the country (after Johannesberg), it is an important commercial and industrial center producing chemicals, textiles, and motor vehicles.

Cape Verde (vûrd). Portuguese **Ca·bo Ver·de** (kä'bŏŏ vĕr'dĭ). Country occupying an archipelago in the North Atlantic Ocean. Settled by the Portuguese in the mid-15th century, the ten islands and five islets became a Portuguese colony in 1495, an overseas province in 1951, and independent in 1975. The islands, of volcanic origin, have a poor economy based on subsistence farming. Area, 4,033 square kilometers (1,557 square miles). Population, 300,000. Capital, Praia. See map at **Atlantic Ocean.**

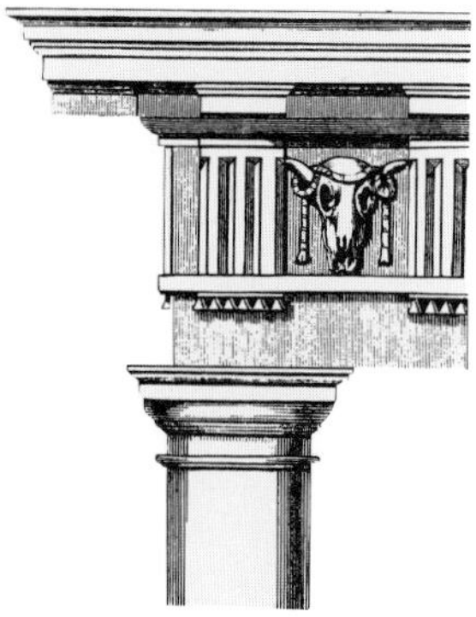

capital *A column was first designed with a capital for a practical purpose: to concentrate the load of the roof above onto the column. But the capital soon became a focus for decoration. Designs range from the simplicity of this Roman Doric capital to the elaborate Corinthian and Gothic capitals.*

Cape York Peninsula (yôrk). Northern part of Queensland, Australia, situated between the Gulf of Carpentaria and the Coral Sea. The low-lying peninsula, tipped by Cape York, the most northerly point of the Australian mainland, supplies bauxite to Australia's aluminium industries.

cap·ful (kăp′fo͝ol′) *n., pl.* **-fuls.** The amount a cap will hold.

cap gun *n.* A cap pistol.

caph. Variant of **kaph.**

Cap-Ha·ï·tien (kăp-hā′shən, kå-på-ē-syăɴ′). Also **Le Cap** (lə kăp′). Seaport and resort on the north coast of Haiti. Under French rule, it was the capital of the colony until superseded by Port-au-Prince.

ca·pi·as (kā′pē-əs) *n. Law.* A writ authorizing an officer to arrest the person named in it. [Middle English, from Latin *capias,* "you are to arrest" (first word of the writ), from *capere,* to seize, take.]

cap·il·lar·i·ty (kăp′ə-lăr′ə-tē) *n., pl.* **-ties.** The interaction between contacting surfaces of a liquid and a solid that, as a result of surface tension, distorts the liquid surface from a planar shape.

cap·il·lar·o·scope (kăp′ə-lăr′ə-skōp′) *n.* A microscope used in capillaroscopy. [CAPILLAR(Y) + -SCOPE.]

cap·il·la·ros·co·py (kăp′ə-lə-rŏs′kə-pē) *n.* The diagnostic examination of the capillaries. [CAPILLAR(Y) + -SCOPY.]

cap·il·lar·y (kăp′ə-lĕr′ē) *adj.* **1.** Pertaining to or resembling a hair; fine and slender. **2.** Having a very small internal diameter. Said of tubes. **3.** *Anatomy.* In, of, or pertaining to the capillaries. **4.** *Physics.* Of or pertaining to capillarity.
~*n., pl.* **capillaries. 1.** *Anatomy.* Any of the minute blood vessels that connect the arteries and veins. **2.** A tube with a small internal diameter. [Latin *capillāris,* from *capillus*†, hair.]

capillary attraction *n.* The force that results in the raising of the surface molecules of a liquid in contact with a solid surface, when the attraction between the solid and the liquid molecules is greater than that between the liquid molecules themselves.

capillary repulsion *n.* The force that results in the lowering of the surface molecules of a liquid in contact with a solid surface, when the attraction between the solid and the liquid molecules is less than that between the liquid molecules themselves.

cap·i·tal[1] (kăp′ə-təl) *n.* **1.** *Abbr.* **cap.** A town or city that is the official seat of government in a state, nation, or other political entity. **2.** Wealth in the form of money or property, owned, used, or accumulated in business by an individual, partnership, or corporation. **3.** Any form of material wealth used or available for use in the production of more wealth. **4. a.** *Accounting.* The remaining assets of a business after all liabilities have been deducted; net worth. **b.** The funds contributed to a business by the owners or stockholders. **5.** Capitalists considered as a group or class. **6.** Any asset or advantage. **7.** A **capital letter** *(see).*
~*adj.* **1.** First and foremost; chief; principal. **2.** Of, pertaining to, or being a political capital. **3.** First-rate; excellent: *a capital fellow.* **4.** Extremely serious; fatal: *a capital blunder.* **5.** Involving death or calling for the death penalty: *a capital crime.* **6.** Of or pertaining to monetary capital. **7.** Designating an upper-case letter. [Middle English, from Old French, from Latin *capitālis,* "of the head," important, chief, from *caput,* head.]

capital[2] *n. Architecture.* The top part, or head, of a pillar or column. [Middle English *capitale,* from Norman French *capitel,* from Late Latin *capitellum,* "small head," from Latin *caput,* head.]

capital account *n.* **1.** An account stating the amount of funds and assets invested in a business by the owners or stockholders, including retained earnings; the owner's interest in the firm. **2.** *Accounting.* A statement of the net worth of a business enterprise at a given time.

capital assets *pl.n.* Long-term assets, as land, buildings, or shares belonging to an individual.

capital expenditure *n.* Funds spent for additions or improvements to plant or equipment.

capital gain *n.* Profit acquired by the sale of capital assets.

capital goods *pl.n.* Goods used in the production of commodities. Also called "producer goods." Compare **consumer goods.**

cap·i·tal·ism (kăp′ə-tə-lĭz′əm) *n.* **1.** An economic system characterized by a free competitive market with private and corporate ownership of production and distribution means, in which development is proportionate to the accumulation and reinvestment of profits. **2.** A political or social system regarded as being based on this. Compare **socialism.**

cap·i·tal·ist (kăp′ə-tə-lĭst) *n.* **1.** An investor of capital in business; especially, one having a major financial interest in an important enterprise. **2.** *Informal.* Any person of great wealth. **3.** A supporter of capitalism.
~*adj.* Capitalistic.

cap·i·tal·is·tic (kăp′ə-tə-lĭs′tĭk) *adj.* **1.** Of or pertaining to capitalism or capitalists. **2.** Favoring or practicing capitalism. **—cap·i·tal·is·ti·cal·ly** *adv.*

cap·i·tal·i·za·tion (kăp′ə-tə-lə-zā′shən) *n.* **1.** The act, practice, or result of capitalizing. **2. a.** The total value of shares in a business firm; the total investment of shareholders. **b.** The authorized or outstanding stock or bonds in a corporation. **3.** The process of converting anticipated future income into present value. **4.** The use of capital letters in printing or writing.

cap·i·tal·ize (kăp′ə-tə-līz′) *v.* **-ized, -izing, -izes.** *—tr.* **1.** To utilize as capital; convert into capital. **2.** To supply with capital or investment funds. **3.** To authorize the issue of a certain amount of capital stock of (a business). **4.** To convert (debt) into capital stock or shares. **5.** To estimate the present value of (a stock, annuity, or real estate, for example). **6.** *Accounting.* To include (expenditures) in business accounts as assets instead of expenses. **7. a.** To write or print in upper-case letters. **b.** To begin (a word) with an upper-case letter. *—intr.* To turn something to advantage; exploit an opportunity. Often used with *on*: *capitalize on an opponent's error.* **—cap·i·tal·iz·a·ble** *adj.* **—cap·i·tal·iz·er** *n.*

capital letter *n. Abbr.* **cap.** An upper-case letter; a letter written or printed in a size larger than and often in a form differing from its corresponding lower-case letter. Also called "capital."

capital levy *n.* A tax on capital assets or real property.

capital punishment *n.* The infliction of the death penalty for the commission of crimes.

capital ship *n.* A warship, such as a battleship or aircraft carrier, of the largest class.

capital stock *n.* **1.** The total amount of stock authorized for issue by a corporation. **2.** The total stated or par value of the permanently invested capital of a corporation.

cap·i·tate (kăp′ə-tāt′) *adj.* **1.** *Zoology.* Enlarged or globular at an end, as some tentacles and bones. **2.** *Botany.* Forming a headlike mass or dense cluster. Said of certain flowers. [Latin *capitātus,* having a head, from *caput* (stem *capit-*), head.]

cap·i·ta·tion (kăp′ə-tā′shən) *n.* **1.** A tax fixed at an equal sum per person; a per capita or poll tax. **2.** A payment or fee of a fixed amount per person. [Late Latin *capitātiō* (stem *capitātiōn-*), from *caput* (stem *capit-*), head, person.] **—cap·i·ta·tive** (kăp′ə-tā′tĭv) *adj.*

cap·i·tol (kăp′ə-təl) *n.* **1. Capitol.** The ancient temple of Jupiter on the Capitoline Hill in Rome. **2.** The building in which a state legislature assembles. **3. Capitol.** The building in Washington, D.C., occupied by the Congress of the United States. [Middle English *Capitol(ie),* Jupiter's temple in Rome, from Latin *Capitōlium,* probably "the chief (temple)," from *caput* (stem *capit-*), head.]

Cap·i·to·line (kəp′ə-tə-līn) *adj.* Of or pertaining to the Roman Capitol or to the Capitoline Hill.

Capitoline Hill. The highest of the seven hills of Rome.

Capitol Reef National Park. An area of 13,355 hectares (33,000 acres) in south-central Utah. The park contains cliff dwellings, petrified trees, and highly colored sandstone cliffs.

ca·pit·u·lar (kə-pĭch′ə-lər) *adj.* **1.** Pertaining or belonging to a chapter, especially an ecclesiastical chapter: *capitular clergy.* **2.** Of or pertaining to a capitulum. [Medieval Latin *capitulāris,* from *capitulum,* (ecclesiastical) chapter, from Late Latin, division (of a book), chapter. See **capitulate.**] **—ca·pit·u·lar·ly** *adv.*

ca·pit·u·lar·y (kə-pĭch′ə-lĕr′ē) *n., pl.* **capitularies. 1.** A member of an ecclesiastical or similar chapter. **2. capitularies.** Ordinances or a set of them; especially, those promulgated by Charlemagne and his successors.

ca·pit·u·late (kə-pĭch′ə-lāt′) *intr.v.* **-lated, -lating, -lates. 1.** To surrender under specified conditions; come to terms. **2.** To give up all resistance; acquiesce. —See Synonyms at **yield.** [Originally "to propose or make terms (of surrender)," from Medieval Latin *capitulāre,* to draw up under heads or chapters, from Late Latin *capitulum,* chapter, from Latin, heading, from *caput,* head.] **—ca·pit·u·lant** *n.* **—ca·pit·u·la·tor** *n.*

ca·pit·u·la·tion (kə-pĭch′ə-lā′shən) *n.* **1. a.** The act of capitulating; surrender. **b.** A document containing the terms of surrender. **2.** An enumeration of the main parts of a subject; a summary. —See Synonyms at **surrender. —ca·pit·u·la·to·ry** *adj.*

ca·pit·u·lum (kə-pĭch′ə-ləm) *n., pl.* **-la** (-lə). **1.** *Botany.* A dense, headlike cluster of stalkless flowers, seen in the daisy and related plants. **2.** *Anatomy.* A small knob or head-shaped part, such as the end of a bone or the knoblike tip of an insect's antenna. [New Latin, from Latin, diminutive of *caput,* head.]

caplin. Variant of **capelin.**

ca·po[1] (kā′pō) *n., pl.* **-pos.** A small movable bar placed across the fingerboard of a guitar or other similar instrument for altering the pitch of all the strings simultaneously. [Italian *capo (di tasto),* "cap (of the keys)," from Latin *caput,* head.]

ca·po[2] (kā′pō, kăp′ō) *n., pl.* **capos.** The head of an organized crime syndicate or one of its branches. [Italian, head, chief.]

ca·pon (kā′pŏn′, -pən) *n.* A rooster castrated when young to improve the quality of its flesh for food. Compare **poulard.** [Middle English *capon,* Old English *capūn* and Norman French *capon,* both from Latin *capō* (stem *cāpōn-*).]

Ca·pone (kə-pōn′) **Alphonse,** "Al" and also known as "Scarface." (1899–1947). Italian-born U.S. gangster. He ruled the Chicago underworld ruthlessly, as in the St. Valentine's Day Massacre (1929), when he had seven members of Bugs Moran's gang shot to death. Never successfully prosecuted for any of his gangland crimes, he was finally convicted of tax evasion and sent to Alcatraz prison (1931).

cap·o·ral (kăp′ər-əl, kăp′ə-răl′) *n.* A strong, dark cigarette and pipe tobacco. [French *(tabac de) caporal,* "corporal's tobacco" (superior to *tabac de soldat,* private soldier's tobacco), from Italian *caporale,* corporal, from *capo,* head, chief, from Latin *caput,* head.]

ca·pote (kə-pōt′) *n.* A long cloak or coat, usually hooded. [French, from Old French *cape,* CAPE (cloak).]

Ca·po·te (kə-pō′tē), **Truman** (1924–84). U.S. novelist and journalist best known for the book *In Cold Blood* (1966). *Breakfast at Tiffany's* (1958) enjoyed great success as a film.

Capp (kăp), **Al,** born Alfred Gerald Caplin (1909–79). U.S. cartoonist who created the Li'l Abner comic strip, first published in the New York *Mirror* (1934). His characters satirized events and personalities of the time.

Cap·pa·do·ci·a (kăp′ə-dō′shē-ə, -shə). An ancient region of eastern Asia Minor, now forming the central part of Turkey. —**Cap·pa·do·cian** adj. & n.

cap pistol n. A toy pistol with a hammer action that detonates a mildly explosive cap.

cap·puc·ci·no (kăp′ə-chē′nō, kä′pə-) n., pl. -nos. 1. Espresso coffee mixed or topped with steamed milk or cream. 2. A cup of such coffee. [Italian, Capuchin (alluding to the white hood).]

Ca·pra (kăp′rə), **Frank** (1897–). U.S. film director, born in Italy, whose comedies dealt with the individual's battles against corruption. His successful films included *Platinum Blonde* (1932), *It Happened One Night* (1934), *Mr. Smith Goes to Washington* (1939), and *It's a Wonderful Life* (1946).

cap·re·o·late (kăp′rē-ə-lāt′, kə-prē′-) adj. Biology. Having or like tendrils. [Latin *capreolus*, wild goat, wooden prop (suggesting horns) supporting tendrils of vines.]

Ca·pri (kə-prē′, kä′prē). Small island in the Bay of Naples, Italy. Warm and picturesque, it has been a tourist resort since Roman times. It has the remains of Emperor Tiberius's villas and the Blue Grotto, discovered in 1826.

cap·ric acid (kăp′rĭk) n. Chemistry. A white crystalline compound, $C_{10}H_{20}O_2$, derived from coconut oil by fractional distillation. It is chiefly used in the manufacture of esters for artificial fruit flavors and perfumes, and as a base for plasticizers and resins. Also called "decanoic acid." [Latin *caper*, goat (from the unpleasant odor of the acid).]

ca·pric·cio (kə-prē′chō, -chē-ō′) n., pl. -cios. Music. An instrumental work with an improvisatory style and a free form. [Italian, CAPRICE.]

ca·pric·cio·so (kə-prē′chō′sō) adv. Music. Lively and free. Used as a direction. [Italian, from *capriccio*, CAPRICE.] —**ca·pric·cio·so** adj.

ca·price (kə-prēs′) n. 1. An impulsive change of mind. 2. An inclination to make such changes. 3. Music. A capriccio. [French, from Italian *capriccio*, "head with hair standing on end," hence horror, whim (in sense influenced by *capra*, goat, from Latin *caper*) : *capo*, head, from Latin *caput* + *riccio*, hedgehog, from Latin *ērīcius*, from *ēr*, hedgehog.]

> **Synonyms:** *fancy, notion, vagary, whim.*

ca·pri·cious (kə-prĭsh′əs, -prē′shəs) adj. Characterized by or subject to whim; impulsive and unpredictable; fickle. —**ca·pri·cious·ly** adv. —**ca·pri·cious·ness** n.

Cap·ri·corn (kăp′rĭ-kôrn′) n. 1. a. The tenth sign of the **zodiac** (see). Also called the "Goat." b. One born under this sign. 2. Variant of **Capricornus.**

Cap·ri·cor·nus (kăp′rĭ-kôr′nəs) n. Also **Cap·ri·corn** (kăp′rĭ-kôrn′). A constellation in the equatorial region of the Southern Hemisphere, near Aquarius and Sagittarius. [Latin (translation of Greek *aigokeros*, "goat-horned") : *caper*, goat + *cornū*, horn.]

cap·ri·fi·ca·tion (kăp′rə-fĭ-kā′shən) n. A method of assuring pollination of the edible fig by allowing certain wasps to carry pollen from the flowers of the caprifig to those of the edible variety. [Latin *caprifĭcātiō* (stem *caprifĭcātiōn-*), from *caprifĭcāre*, to ripen figs by caprification, from *caprifĭcus*, CAPRIFIG.]

cap·ri·fig (kăp′rə-fĭg′) n. A wild variety of fig, *Ficus carica sylvestris*, of the eastern Mediterranean region, used in the caprification of the edible fig. [Middle English *caprifige*, *caprificus*, from Latin *caprifĭcus*, "goat fig" : *caper*, goat + *ficus*, FIG.]

cap·rine (kăp′rīn′) adj. Of or like a goat. [Middle English, from Latin *caprīnus*, from *caper* (stem *capr-*), he-goat.]

cap·ri·ole (kăp′rē-ōl′) n. 1. An upward leap in dressage made by a trained horse without going forward and with all feet off the ground. 2. A leap or jump in ballet.
—*intr.v.* **caprioled, -oling, -oles.** To perform a capriole. [French, from Italian *capriola*, "leap of a goat," from *capriolo*, wild goat, roebuck, from Latin *capreolus*, diminutive of *caper*, goat.]

ca·pro·ic acid (kə-prō′ĭk, kă-) n. A liquid fatty acid, $C_6H_{12}O_2$, found in animal fats and oils and used in the manufacture of pharmaceuticals and flavors. [Latin *caper* (stem *capr-*), goat (referring to its smell).]

capsaicin. Variant of **capsicin.**

cap screw n. A screw with a head that has a shaped groove, usually six-sided, and is turned by a wrench that fits into this groove.

Cap·si·an (kăp′sē-ən) adj. Of or designating a Paleolithic culture of northern Africa and southern Europe. [French *capsien*, after *Capsa*, ancient name of *Gafsa*, Tunisia, near which remains of the culture were found.]

cap·si·cin (kăp′sə-sĭn) n. Also **cap·sa·i·cin** (kăp-sā′ə-sĭn). A peppery, reddish-brown liquid, $C_{18}H_{27}O_3N$, obtained from plants of the genus *Capsicum* and used in flavoring vinegar and pickles and medicinally as an irritant. [CAPSIC(UM) + -IN.]

cap·si·cum (kăp′sĭ-kəm) n. 1. Any of various tropical plants of the genus *Capsicum*. See **pepper.** 2. The dried fruit of pungent varieties of *C. frutescens*, used medicinally as a gastric stimulant and counterirritant. [New Latin, probably from Latin *capsa*, box (from its podlike fruit). See **capsule.**]

cap·sid[1] (kăp′sĭd) n. Any bug of the family Miridae (formerly Capsidae), especially one that feeds on and damages crop plants. [New Latin *Capsus* (former genus name).]

capsid[2] n. The proteinaceous covering of a virus particle. [French *capside*, from Latin *capsa*, box.]

cap·size (kăp′sīz, kăp-sīz′) v. **-sized, -sizing, -sizes.** —*intr.* To overturn. Used typically of a boat or ship. —*tr.* To cause to capsize. [18th century : origin obscure.]

cap·stan (kăp′stən, -stăn) n. 1. Nautical. An apparatus consisting of a vertical cylinder rotated manually by a lever (*capstan bar*) or by motor, used for hoisting weights by winding in a cable. 2. Electronics. A small cylindrical pulley used to regulate the speed of magnetic tape in a tape recorder. [Middle English, from Old Provençal *cabestan, cabestran*, from *cabestre*, rope noose, from Latin *capistrum*, halter, from *capere*, to take, seize.]

capstan lathe n. A lathe fitted with a rotatable head capable of holding a number of different tools.

capstan screw n. A screw with a number of radial holes through the head, turned by a bar that fits through one of these holes.

cap·stone (kăp′stōn) n. Also **cope·stone** (kōp′-). 1. The top stone of a structure or wall. Compare **coping.** 2. The crowning or final stroke; the culmination; the acme.

cap·su·lar (kăp′sə-lər, -syə-lər) adj. Of, pertaining to, or characteristic of a capsule.

cap·su·late (kăp′sə-lāt′, -lĭt, kăp′syə-) adj. Also **cap·su·lat·ed** (-lā′tĭd). In or formed into a capsule. —**cap·su·la·tion** n.

cap·sule (kăp′səl, -sool) n. 1. Pharmacology. A soluble container, usually of gelatin, enclosing a dose of an oral medicine. 2. A seal or airtight cap, as for the mouth of a bottle. 3. Anatomy. A fibrous, membranous, or fatty envelope enclosing an organ or part, such as the sac surrounding the kidney. 4. Microbiology. A mucopolysaccharide layer enveloping certain bacteria. 5. Botany. a. A dry fruit that contains two or more seeds that are released when it splits open. b. The spore case of a moss or other bryophyte. 6. A pressurized modular compartment of an aircraft or spacecraft, especially one designed to accommodate a crew or to be ejected if required.
~*adj.* Condensed into a small or brief unit; concise; compact: *a capsule description.*
~*tr.v.* **capsuled, -suling, -sules.** 1. To enclose in or furnish with a capsule. 2. To devise or present in a very brief form; condense or summarize. [French, from Latin *capsula*, diminutive of *capsa*, box, chest.]

cap·sul·ize (kăp′sə-līz′) *tr.v.* **-ized, -izing, -izes.** To capsule. —**cap·sul·i·za·tion** n.

Capt. captain.

cap·tain (kăp′tən) n. 1. One who commands, leads, or guides others, specifically: a. The officer in command of a ship, aircraft, or spacecraft. b. A precinct chief in a police or fire department. c. The designated leader of a team or crew in sports. 2. Abbr. **Capt.** a. A commissioned officer in the Army, Air Force, or Marine Corps who ranks below a major and above a first lieutenant. b. A commissioned officer in the Navy who ranks below a commodore or rear admiral and above a commander. 3. A figure in the forefront; a leader: *a captain of industry.* 4. A headwaiter.
~*tr.v.* **captained, -taining, -tains.** 1. To act as captain of (a team, for example). 2. To command or direct. [Middle English *capitane, captein*, from Old French *capitain(e)*, from Late Latin *capitāneus*, chief, from Latin *caput*, head.] —**cap·tain·cy** n. —**cap·tain·ship** n.

cap·tan (kăp′tən, -tăn′) n. An agricultural fungicide, $C_9H_8Cl_3NO_2S$. [Short for MERCAPTAN.]

cap·tion (kăp′shən) n. 1. A title, short explanation, or description accompanying an illustration or photograph. 2. A subtitle in a film. 3. A title or heading, as of a document or chapter in a book. 4. Law. The part of a legal document that states the time, place, and authority of its execution.
~*tr.v.* **captioned, -tioning, -tions.** To furnish a caption for. [Originally "arrest," hence record of execution of a commission, from Middle English *capcioun*, arrest, seizure, from Latin *captiō* (stem *captiōn-*), from *capere*, to seize, take.]

cap·tious (kăp′shəs) adj. 1. Marked by a disposition to find fault and make petty criticisms; carping. 2. Intended to entrap or confuse: *a captious question.* [Middle English *capcious*, from Old French *captieux*, from Latin *captiōsus*, "ensnaring," from *captiō*, seizure, CAPTION.] —**cap·tious·ly** adv. —**cap·tious·ness** n.

cap·ti·vate (kăp′tə-vāt′) *tr.v.* **-vated, -vating, -vates.** 1. To fascinate or hold the attention of by special charm, interest, or beauty. 2. Archaic. To capture. [Late Latin *captivāre*, to capture, from Latin *captīvus*, CAPTIVE.] —**cap·ti·va·tion** n. —**cap·ti·va·tor** n.

cap·tive (kăp′tĭv) n. 1. One that is forcibly confined, restrained, or subjugated, such as a prisoner. 2. One who is enslaved by a strong emotion or passion.
~*adj.* 1. Held as prisoner. 2. Under restraint or control. 3. Captivated; enraptured. 4. Obliged to be present: *a captive audience.* 5. Forced to buy from a particular source: *a captive market.* [Middle English *captif*, from Latin *captīvus*, from *capere*, to seize.]

cap·tiv·i·ty (kăp-tĭv′ə-tē) n., pl. **-ties.** The state or a period of being captive.

cap·tor (kăp′tər, -tôr′) n. One who takes or keeps someone or something captive. [Late Latin, from Latin *capere*, to seize.]

cap·ture (kăp′chər) *tr.v.* **-tured, -turing, -tures.** 1. To take captive; seize or catch by force or craft. 2. To win possession or control of, as in a contest. 3. To succeed in preserving in a fixed form: *capture a likeness in a painting.*
~n. 1. The act of capturing; seizure. 2. One that is seized, caught, or won; a catch or prize. 3. Physics. a. The phenomenon whereby an atomic nucleus absorbs a subatomic particle, especially an orbiting electron, often with the subsequent emission of radiation. b. The phenomenon whereby an atom, molecule, or positive ion takes up an extra electron. [French, from Old French, from Latin *captūra*, from *capere*, to seize.]

captured rotation n. Astronomy. An orbit of a satellite in which the

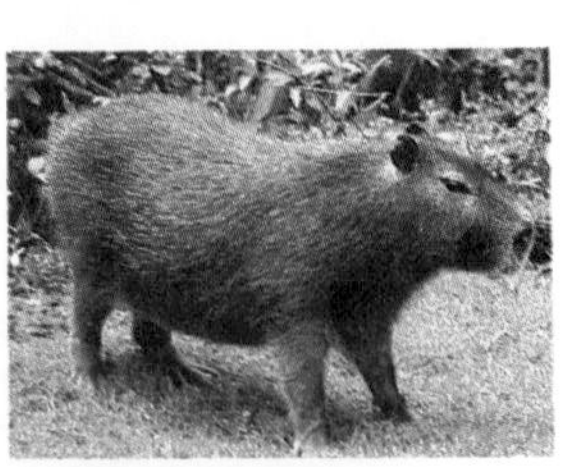

capybara *An aquatic rodent related to the guinea pig family and found in South America. It is the world's largest rodent, growing to a length of about 1.2 meters (4 feet) and weighing up to 50 kilograms (110 pounds).*

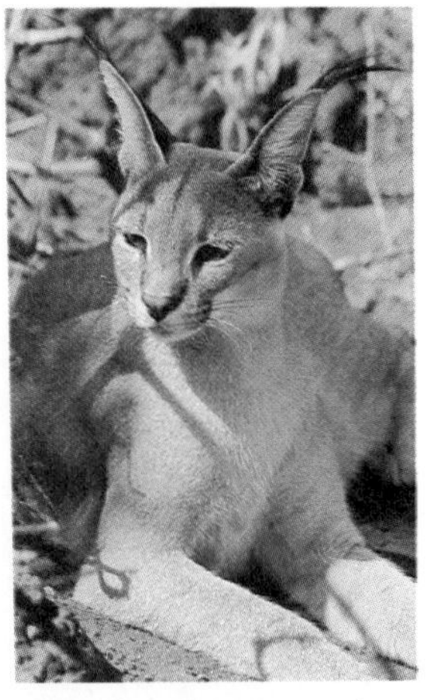

caracal *A wild cat native to the drier parts of Africa and western Asia. Caracals normally live alone and hunt by night and are fast enough to knock a low-flying bird out of the air.*

satellite's orbital period is equal to its rotation period. This means that the satellite always points the same hemisphere to its primary, as in the case of the Moon in relation to Earth. Also called "synchronous rotation."

Cap·u·a (kăp′yo͞o-ə). Market town in Campania, southern Italy, near Naples. It rose to prominence under the Romans when it was linked to Rome by the Appian Way.

ca·puche (kə-po͞och′, -po͞osh′) *n.* A hood on a cloak; especially, the long, pointed cowl worn by a Capuchin monk. [Italian *cappuccio,* from *cappa,* hood, from Late Latin, hood, cloak, from Latin *caput,* head.]

cap·u·chin (kăp′yə-chĭn, kə-pyo͞o′-, -shĭn) *n.* **1. Capuchin.** A monk belonging to the Order of Friars Minor Capuchins, an independent branch of the Franciscans, founded in 1525, and licensed in 1619. **2.** A hooded cloak worn by women. **3.** Any of several long-tailed monkeys of the genus *Cebus,* of Central and South America, many of which have hoodlike tufts of hair on the head. In this sense, also called "sapajou." [French, from Old French, from Italian *cappuccino,* "hooded one," from *cappuccio,* CAPUCHE.]

cap·y·ba·ra (kăp′ə-bä′rə, -băr′ə) *n.* A large, short-tailed, semi-aquatic rodent, *Hydrochoerus hydrochaeris,* of tropical South America, often attaining a length of four feet. [Portuguese *capibara,* from Tupi.]

car (kär) *n.* **1.** An automobile; motor car. **2.** A conveyance, such as a streetcar, with wheels that run along tracks. **3.** *Archaic.* A chariot. **4.** A boxlike enclosure, such as an elevator car, for passengers on a conveyance. [Middle English *car(re),* cart, wagon, from Norman French, from Vulgar Latin *carra* (unattested), variant of Latin *carrus,* two-wheeled wagon.]

car. carat.

car·a·bao (kăr′ə-bou′, kä′rə-) *n., pl.* **-baos.** The **water buffalo** *(see).* [Visayan *karabáw,* akin to Malay *karbaw.*]

car·a·bid (kăr′ə-bĭd, kə-răb′ĭd) *n.* Any of various black carnivorous beetles of the family Carabidae.

~adj. Of or belonging to the Carabidae. [New Latin *Carabidae,* from Latin *cārabus,* from Greek *karabos*†, crayfish, horned beetle.]

carabin, carabine. Variants of **carbine.**

car·a·bi·neer, car·a·bi·nier (kăr′ə-bə-nîr′) *n.* Also **car·bi·neer** (kär′-bə-). A soldier armed with a carbine.

ca·ra·bi·nie·re (kăr′ə-bən-yâr′ā, kä′rə-) *n, pl.* **-nieri** (-yâr′ē). An Italian policeman under military command. [Italian.]

car·a·cal (kăr′ə-kăl′) *n.* A wild cat, *Lynx caracal,* of Africa and southern Asia, having short, fawn-colored fur and long, tufted ears. Also called "desert lynx." [French, from Turkish *kara kūlāk,* "black ear" : *kara,* black + *kūlāk,* ear.]

Car·a·cal·la (kăr′ə-kăl′ə) (A.D. 188–217). Roman emperor from the age of 23. He was obsessed with and sought to imitate Alexander the Great. However his bloody, undisciplined rule of the empire left only a legacy of infamy. He was assassinated by the order of the commander of the imperial guard and next emperor, Macrinus (A.D. 164–218).

ca·ra·ca·ra (kä′rə-kä′rə, -kə-rä′) *n.* Any of several large, carrion-eating or predatory birds of the subfamily Caracarinae, of South and Central America and the southern United States, related to the hawks and falcons. [Spanish *caracara* and Portuguese *caracará,* from Tupi *caracara* (imitative).]

Ca·ra·cas (kə-rä′kəs, -răk′əs). Capital of Venezuela. In a basin at 1,000 meters (3,280 feet) above sea level, it is connected to its port and airport at La Guaira by a tunneled motorway 18 kilometers (11 miles) long. Caracas was founded by the Spanish in 1567. It now earns much of its wealth from oil.

carack. Variant of **carrack.**

car·a·cole (kăr′ə-kōl′) *n.* Also **car·a·col** (-kŏl′). A half turn to either side performed by a horse in dressage.

~intr.v. **caracoled, -coling, -coles.** To perform a caracole or caracoles. [French, from Spanish *caracol*†, snail, winding stair.]

car·a·cul (kăr′ə-kəl) *n.* **1.** The loosely curled fur of a karakul lamb. **2.** Variant of **karakul.**

ca·rafe (kə-răf′, -räf′) *n.* **1.** A glass bottle for serving water or wine at the table; a decanter. **2.** The amount a carafe will hold. [French, from Italian *caraffa,* from Spanish *garaffa,* from Arabic *gharrāfa,* from *gharafa,* to dip.]

car·a·mel (kăr′ə-məl, -mĕl′, kär′məl) *n.* **1.** A smooth, chewy candy made with sugar, butter, cream or milk, and flavoring. **2.** Burnt sugar, used for coloring and sweetening foods. [French, from Old Spanish, probably from Late Latin *calamellus,* diminutive of Latin *calamus,* reed, cane, from Greek *kalamos.*]

car·a·mel·ize (kăr′ə-mə-līz′, kär′mə-) *v.* **-ized, -izing, -izes.** *—tr.* To convert (sugar) into caramel. *—intr.* To change into caramel. **—car·a·mel·i·za·tion** *n.*

ca·ran·gid (kə-răn′jĭd, -răng′gĭd) *n.* Any of various fishes of the family Carangidae, which includes the jacks, pilot fish, and pompanos, having a compressed body and forked tail.

~adj. Of or belonging to the Carangidae. [New Latin *Carangidae* : *Caranx* (stem *Carang-*) (genus), from French *carangue,* mackerel, from Spanish *caranga*† + -IDAE.]

car·a·pace (kăr′ə-pās′) *n.* **1.** *Zoology.* A hard bony or chitinous outer covering, such as the fused dorsal plates of a turtle or the portion of the exoskeleton covering the head and thorax of a crustacean. **2.** A protective covering similar to a carapace. [French, from Spanish *carapacho.*]

car·at (kăr′ət) *n.* **1.** *Abbr.* **c, car.** A unit of weight for precious stones, equal to 200 milligrams. **2.** Variant of **karat.** [French, from Old French, from Medieval Latin *carratus,* from Arabic *qīrāṭ,* small weight, carat, from Greek *keration,* "little horn," carob fruit, carat, diminutive of *keras,* horn.]

Ca·ra·vag·gio (kăr′ə-vä′jō), born Michelangelo Merisi (*c.* 1565–1610). Italian baroque painter, born in Caravaggio, Lombardy. Refusing to conform to the tradition of earlier European art with its idealized religious figures, he chose instead to use peasants and street people as the models for many of his sacred subjects. The altarpiece *Death of the Virgin* and the painting *Supper at Emmaus* are examples of his work. His mastery of light and shade influenced Velázquez and Rembrandt. He fled from Rome in 1606 after killing a man in a dispute over a tennis match, and his final years were spent in exile in Naples, Malta, and Sicily.

car·a·van (kăr′ə-văn′) *n.* **1.** A company of travelers journeying together, especially across a desert. **2.** A single file of vehicles or pack animals. **3.** A large covered vehicle, as one used by gypsies; van. **4.** *Chiefly British.* An unmotorized furnished vehicle, often attached as a trailer to a car or truck and used as living quarters, a temporary office, or a vacation home. [French *caravane* or Italian *caravana, carovana,* from Persian *kārwān*†.]

car·a·van·sa·ry (kăr′ə-văn′sə-rē) *n., pl.* **-ries.** Also **car·a·van·se·rai** (-sə-rī′). **1.** In the Near or Far East, an inn built around a large court for accommodating caravans at night. **2.** Any large inn or hostelry. [Persian *kārwānsarāī* : *kārwān,* CARAVAN + *sarāī,* palace, inn.]

car·a·vel, car·a·velle (kăr′ə-vĕl′) *n.* Also **car·vel** (kär′vəl, -vĕl′). A small, light sailing ship of the kind used by the Spanish and Portuguese in the 15th and 16th centuries. [French *caravelle, carvelle,* from Portuguese *caravela,* diminutive of *cáravo,* ship, from Latin *cārabus,* from Greek *karabos*†, crayfish, light ship.]

car·a·way (kăr′ə-wā′) *n.* **1.** A plant, *Carum carvi,* native to Eurasia, having finely divided leaves and clusters of small, whitish flowers. **2.** The pungent, aromatic seeds of this plant, used in baking and cooking. [Middle English *car(a)way,* probably from Old Spanish *alcarahueya* and Medieval Latin *carvi,* both from Arabic *alkarāwiyā,* probably from Greek *karon*†, cumin.]

carb·an·i·on (kär-băn′ī′ən, -ī′ŏn′) *n.* A negatively charged organic ion, such as H_3C^-, having one more electron than the corresponding free radical. [CARBO- + AN- + ION.]

car·bide (kär′bīd′) *n.* **1.** A binary carbon compound consisting of carbon and a more electropositive element. **2. Calcium carbide** *(see).* [CARB(O)- + -IDE.]

car·bine (kär′bīn′, -bēn′) *n.* Also **car·a·bin** (kăr′ə-bĭn), **car·a·bine** (-bīn′, -bēn′). A light shoulder rifle with a short barrel, originally for cavalry use. [French *carabine,* carbine, carabineer, from Old French *carabin,* cavalryman, soldier armed with a musket, probably derisively from *escarrabin,* "one who lays out plague corpses," variant of *escarabilh, scarabée,* dung beetle, from Latin *scarabeus,* a beetle. See **scarab.**]

carbineer, carabinier. Variants of **carabineer.**

car·bi·nol (kär′bə-nôl′, -nōl′) *n.* **1.** Wood alcohol, **methanol** *(see).* **2.** An alcohol derived from methanol by substitution of one or more hydrogen atoms by other hydrocarbon groups. [German *Karbinol* : CARB(O)- + -IN + -OL.]

carbo-, carb- *prefix.* Indicates carbon; for example, **carbohydrate, carbolic acid.** [French, from *carbone,* CARBON.]

car·bo·hy·drate (kär′bō-hī′drāt′) *n.* Any of a group of chemical compounds, including sugars, starches, and cellulose, containing carbon, hydrogen, and oxygen only, with the ratio of hydrogen to oxygen atoms usually 2:1.

car·bo·lat·ed (kär′bə-lā′tĭd) *adj.* Containing or treated with carbolic acid.

car·bol·ic acid (kär-bŏl′ĭk) *n.* An organic compound, **phenol** *(see).* [CARB(O)- + -OL + -IC.]

car·bon (kär′bən) *n.* **1.** *Symbol* **C** A naturally abundant nonmetallic element that occurs in many inorganic and in all organic compounds, exists in amorphous, graphitic, and diamond forms, and is capable of chemical self-bonding to form an enormous number of chemically, biologically, and commercially important molecules. Atomic number 6; atomic weight 12.01115; sublimes above 3,500°C; boiling point 4,827°C; specific gravity of amorphous carbon 1.8 to 2.1, of diamond 3.15 to 3.53, of graphite 1.9 to 2.3; valences 2, 3, 4. **2. a.** A sheet of carbon paper. **b.** A copy made by using carbon paper. **3.** *Electricity.* **a.** Either of two rods through which current flows to form an arc in lighting or in welding. **b.** A carbonaceous electrode in an electric cell.

~adj. **1.** Of, pertaining to, or like carbon. **2.** Treated with carbon. [French *carbone,* from Latin *carbō* (stem *carbōn-*), charcoal.] **—car·bon·ous** *adj.*

carbon 14 *n.* A naturally radioactive carbon isotope with atomic mass 14 and half-life 5,700 years, used in dating ancient carbon-containing objects. Also called "radiocarbon."

car·bo·na·ceous (kär′bə-nā′shəs) *adj.* Consisting of, containing, pertaining to, or yielding carbon.

car·bo·nade, car·bon·nade (kär′bə-näd′) *n.* A rich stew of beef, onions, and beer, of Belgian origin. [French.]

car·bo·na·do¹ (kär′bə-nā′dō, -nä′dō) *n., pl.* **-does** or **-dos.** A piece of scored and broiled fish, poultry, or meat.

~tr.v. **carbonadoed, -doing, -dos. 1.** To score and broil (fish, poultry, or meat). **2.** *Archaic.* To slice; slash; chop. [Spanish *carbonada,* from *carbón,* charcoal, coal, from Latin *carbō,* CARBON.]

carbonado² *n., pl.* **-does.** A form of opaque or dark-colored diamond, chiefly Brazilian, used for drills. Also called "black diamond," "bort." [Portuguese, "carbonated," from *carbone,* carbon, from French, CARBON.]

carbon arc *n.* An electric arc produced by a carbon electrode, as in an arc lamp or welder.

Car·bo·na·ri (kär′bə-nä′rē) *pl.n. Singular* **Car·bo·na·ro** (-rō). The members of a secret society originally organized in Naples in the early 19th century to establish a liberal, unified Italian republic. [Italian, "charcoal burners," name adopted by members of the society apparently after disguising themselves as such after being driven into hiding in the forest of the Abruzzi.] **—Car·bo·na·rism** *n.* **—Car·bo·na·rist** *n. & adj.*

car·bon·ate (kär′bə-nāt′) *tr.v.* **-ated, -ating, -ates. 1.** To add carbon dioxide gas to (a cold drink, for example) to produce fizz. **2.** To burn to carbon; carbonize. **3.** To change into a carbonate.
~*n.* (-nāt′, -nĭt). A salt or ester of carbonic acid. **—car·bon·a·tion** *n.* **—car·bon·a·tor** *n.*

carbonated water *n.* **Soda water** *(see).*

carbon bisulfide *n.* **Carbon disulfide** *(see).*

carbon black *n.* Any of various finely divided forms of carbon derived from the incomplete combustion of natural gas or petroleum oil and used principally in rubber and ink.

carbon copy *n.* **1.** *Abbr.* **C.C., c.c.** A replica, as of a letter, made by using carbon paper. **2.** *Informal.* A close copy or reproduction; duplicate.

carbon cycle *n.* **1.** *Astrophysics.* The **carbon-nitrogen cycle** *(see).* **2.** *Biology.* The cycle of natural processes in which atmospheric carbon in the form of carbon dioxide is converted by photosynthesis in plants to carbohydrates that are eaten and metabolized by animals and ultimately returned to the atmosphere as carbon dioxide through respiration or decomposition.

carbon dating *n.* Determination of the approximate age of carbon-containing objects by the use of the radiation rate of carbon 14.

carbon dioxide *n.* A colorless, odorless, incombustible gas, CO_2, formed during respiration, combustion, and organic decomposition and used in food refrigeration, carbonated beverages, inert atmospheres, fire extinguishers, and aerosols.

carbon dioxide snow *n.* Solid carbon dioxide, used as a refrigerant.

carbon disulfide *n.* A clear flammable liquid, CS_2, used to manufacture viscose rayon and cellophane, as a solvent for fats, rubber, resins, waxes, and sulfur, and in matches, fumigants, and pesticides. Also called "carbon bisulfide."

carbon fiber *n.* A fine filament of almost pure crystalline carbon made by heating stretched textile threads and extensively used in composite plastic and metal materials, as for aircraft parts.

car·bon·ic acid (kär-bŏn′ĭk) *n.* A weak, unstable acid, H_2CO_3, present only in solutions of carbon dioxide in water.

carbonic acid gas *n.* Carbon dioxide.

Car·bon·if·er·ous (kär′bə-nĭf′ər-əs) *adj.* **1.** *Geology.* Of, belonging to, or designating a period of the Paleozoic era following the Devonian and preceding the Permian. It was characterized by swamp formation and deposition of plant remains that later hardened into coal. **2. carboniferous.** Producing or containing coal or carbon.
~*n. Geology.* The Carboniferous period. Preceded by *the.*

car·bo·ni·um (kär-bō′nē-əm) *n.* A positively charged organic ion, such as H_3C^+, having one electron fewer than a corresponding free radical and behaving chemically as if the positive charge were localized on the carbon atom.

car·bon·i·za·tion (kär′bə-nə-zā′shən) *n.* **1.** The process of carbonizing. **2.** The decomposition by destructive distillation of bituminous coal to obtain coke and other by-products.

car·bon·ize (kär′bə-nīz′) *tr.v.* **-ized, -izing, -izes. 1.** To reduce or convert to carbon, as by partial burning. **2.** To coat or combine with carbon. **—car·bon·iz·er** *n.*

carbon microphone *n.* A type of microphone in which an electric current passes through a diaphragm with carbon powder packed behind it. Sound waves vibrate the diaphragm, producing a varying pressure on the carbon and changing its electrical resistance.

carbon monoxide *n.* A colorless, odorless, highly poisonous gas, CO, formed by the incomplete combustion of carbon or any carbonaceous material.

car·bon-ni·tro·gen cycle (kär′bən-nī′trə-jən) *n.* A chain of thermonuclear reactions in which nitrogen isotopes are formed in intermediate stages and carbon acts essentially as a catalyst to convert four protons into one helium nucleus. The sequence is thought to generate significant amounts of energy in certain classes of stars. Also called "carbon cycle," "nitrogen cycle."

carbon paper *n.* A lightweight paper faced on one side with a dark waxy pigment that is transferred by the impact of typewriter keys or by writing pressure to any copying surface, such as paper.

carbon process *n.* A photographic printing process using permanent pigments, such as carbon, contained in a sensitized tissue or film of gelatin.

carbon steel *n.* A type of steel composed mainly of iron with added carbon. Compare **alloy steel.**

carbon tetrachloride *n.* A poisonous, nonflammable, colorless liquid, CCl_4, used as a solvent.

car·bon·yl (kär′bə-nĭl′, -nēl′) *n.* **1.** The bivalent radical CO. **2.** A metal compound containing the CO group bound directly to a metal atom or ion. **—car·bon·yl·ic** (kär′bə-nĭl′ĭk) *adj.*

carbonyl chloride *n.* A poisonous gas, **phosgene** *(see).*

Car·bo·run·dum (kär′bə-rŭn′dəm) *n.* A trademark for a silicon carbide abrasive.

car·box·yl (kär-bŏk′səl) *n.* A univalent radical, COOH, characteristic of all organic acids. [CARB(O)- + OX(Y)- + -YL.]

car·box·yl·ase (kär-bŏk′sə-lās′, -lāz′) *n.* An enzyme that produces an aldehyde and carbon dioxide from certain acids.

car·box·yl·ic acid (kär′bŏk-sĭl′ĭk) *n. Chemistry.* An organic acid with the general formula RCOOH, where R is an organic group. See **fatty acid.**

car·boy (kär′boi′) *n.* A large glass or plastic bottle, usually encased in a protective basket or crate and often used to hold corrosive liquids. [Persian *qarāba,* from Arabic *qarrābah.*]

car·bun·cle (kär′bŭng′kəl) *n.* **1.** An extensive skin eruption, resembling a boil but much larger and having multiple openings, usually caused by infection with *Staphylococcus aureus.* Compare **boil. 2.** *Obsolete.* A deep-red precious stone, especially the garnet, unfaceted and convex. [Middle English, from Old French, from Latin *carbunculus,* small glowing ember, tumor, diminutive of *carbō* (stem *carbōn-*), charcoal, ember.] **—car·bun·cled** *adj.* **—car·bun·cu·lar** (kär-bŭng′kyə-lər) *adj.*

car·bu·ret (kär′bə-rāt′, kär′byə-, -rĕt′) *tr.v.* **-reted** or **-retted, -reting** or **-retting, -rets.** To combine or mix with carbon or hydrocarbons in order to increase available fuel energy. [From obsolete *carbure(t),* carbide, from French *carbure,* from Latin *carbō,* CARBON.]

car·bu·re·tor (kär′bə-rā′tər, kär′byə-) *n.* Also *chiefly British* **car·bu·ret·tor, car·bu·ret·ter** (-rĕt′ər). A device used in internal-combustion engines to produce an efficient explosive vapor of fuel and air. [From CARBURET.]

car·bu·rize (kär′bə-rīz′, kär′byə-) *tr.v.* **-rized, -rizing, -rizes.** To treat (iron or steel, for example) with carbon. [CARBUR(ET) + -IZE.] **—car·bu·ri·za·tion** *n.*

car·byl·a·mine (kär-bĭl′ə-mēn′, kär′bĭl-ăm′ēn′) *n.* A type of chemical compound, an **isocyanide** *(see).*

car·ca·jou (kär′kə-jo͞o′, -zho͞o′) *n. Canadian.* An animal, the **wolverine** *(see).* [Canadian French, from Algonquian *karkajou.*]

car·cass (kär′kəs) *n.* Also *archaic* **car·case. 1.** The dead body of an animal or bird, especially one slaughtered and gutted. **2.** The body of a human being. Used humorously or derogatorily. **3.** Something from which the substance or character is gone: *the carcass of a once-glorious empire.* **4.** A framework or basic structure, as of a ruined building. [French *carcasse,* from Old French *c(h)arcois*†.]

Car·cas·sonne (kär′kə-sôn′, -sŏn′). Capital of Aude department on the Canal du Midi and the Aude River in southwest France. It includes an old fortified medieval hill town (La Cité) and a modern town (Ville Basse).

Car·che·mish (kär′kə-mĭsh′). Ancient city on the Euphrates River, in southern Turkey. A Hittite stronghold until the empire's collapse in the 12th century B.C., it survived as an independent kingdom until taken by the Assyrians under Sargon (717 B.C.). It was the scene of the Egyptians' defeat at the hands of Nebuchadnezzar II and the Babylonians (605 B.C.).

car·cin·o·gen (kär-sĭn′ə-jən, kär′sə-nə-jĕn′) *n.* A cancer-causing substance. [Greek *karkinos,* cancer, crab + -GEN.] **—car·cin·o·gen·ic** (kär′sə-nə-jĕn′ĭk) *adj.*

car·ci·no·ma (kär′sə-nō′mə) *n., pl.* **-mas** or **-mata** (-mə-tə). A malignant tumor arising in epithelial tissue. [Latin *carcinōma,* cancerous ulcer, from Greek *karkinōma,* from *karkinos,* cancer, crab.] **—car·ci·no·ma·toid** (kär′sə-nō′mə-toid′, -nŏm′ə-toid′), **car·ci·nom·a·tous** (-nŏm′ə-təs, -nō′mə-təs) *adj.*

car·ci·no·ma·to·sis (kär′sə-nō′mə-tō′sĭs) *n.* The existence of carcinomas at many bodily sites. [New Latin : Latin *carcinōma* (stem *carcinōmat-*), CARCINOMA + -OSIS.]

card[1] (kärd) *n.* **1.** A small, flat piece of stiff paper, thin pasteboard, or plastic, usually rectangular, with numerous uses, as: **a.** Any of a set bearing significant numbers, symbols, and figures, used in numerous games and in fortunetelling. See **cards. b.** One used to send messages; especially, a postcard. **c.** One printed with a suitable illustration and greeting and sent in an envelope, as for Christmas. **d.** A card or membership card, bearing a person's name and other information and used for purposes of identification or classification. **e.** One used for cataloguing information in a file, such as a reference card. **f.** A **credit card** *(see).* **2.** A notice or advertisement printed on cardboard. **3.** *Sports.* A list of events or competitors, such as a **scorecard** *(see).* **4.** A **compass card** *(see).* **5.** *Computer Science.* A **punch card** *(see).* **6.** *Informal.* An amusing or eccentric person. **—have a card up one's sleeve.** To have a secret resource or plan held in reserve.
~*tr.v.* **carded, carding, cards. 1.** To furnish with or attach to a card. **2.** To list on a card; catalogue. **3.** *Informal.* To check the identification of, especially in order to verify legal age. [Middle English *carde,* from Old French *carte,* from Latin *charta,* leaf of papyrus, from Greek *khartēs,* probably from Egyptian.]

card[2] *n.* **1.** A wire-toothed brush or comblike machine used to disentangle fibers, as of wool, prior to spinning. **2.** A similar device used to raise the nap on a fabric.
~*tr.v.* **carded, carding, cards.** To comb out or brush with a card. [Middle English *carde,* from Old French, from *carder,* to card, from Old Provençal *cardar,* from Vulgar Latin *caritāre* (unattested), from Latin *cārere,* to card.] **—card·er** *n.*

Card. *Roman Catholic Church.* cardinal.

car·da·mom, car·da·mum (kär′də-məm) *n.* Also **car·da·mon** (-mən). **1. a.** A tropical Asiatic perennial plant, *Elettaria cardamomum,* having large, hairy leaves and capsular fruit. **b.** The fruit and seeds of this plant, used as a condiment and in medicine. **2. a.** An East Indian plant, *Amomum cardamomum.* **b.** The fruit and seeds

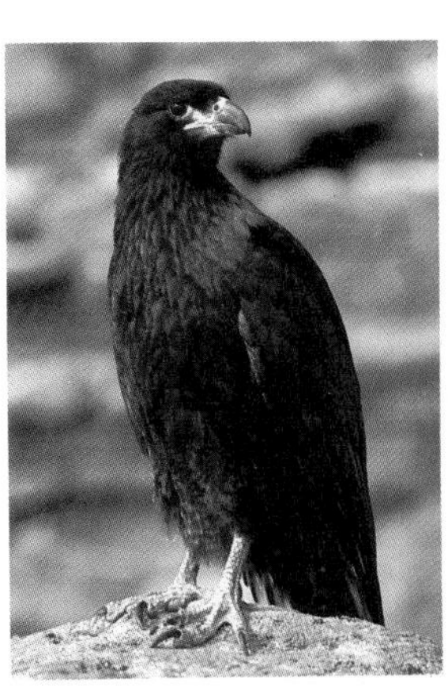

caracara *Native to Central and South America, the caracara, a type of hawk, spends much of its life on the ground, where its long legs enable it to run swiftly. It feeds on carrion, small animals, and birds. This is the striated caracara.*

PRONUNCIATION KEY

ă, pat; ā, pay; âr, care; ä, father, are; b, bib; ch, church; d, deed; ĕ, pet; ē, be; f, fife; g, gag; h, hat; hw, which; ĭ, pit; ī, pie; îr, pier; j, judge; k, kick; l, lid, needle; m, mum; n, no, sudden; ng, thing; ŏ, pot; ō, toe; ô, paw, for; oi, noise; ou, out; o͝o, book; o͞o, boot; p, pop; r, roar; s, sauce; sh, ship, dish; t, tight; th, thin, path; *th*, this, bathe; ŭ, cut; ûr, fur; v, valve; w, with; y, yes; z, zebra, size; zh, vision; ə, about, item, edible, gallop, circus, peaceful

IN FOREIGN WORDS:

à, *Fr.* ami; œ, *Fr.* feu, *Ger.* schön; ü, *Fr.* tu, *Ger.* über; KH, *Ger.* ich, *Scot.* loch; N, *Fr.* bon; y′, *Fr.* Compiègne

STRESS MARKS:

Primary stress: ′ in·cite′ (ĭn-sīt′)
Secondary stress: ′ in′sight′ (ĭn′sīt′)

of this plant, used as an inferior substitute for true cardamom seed. [Latin *cardamōmum,* from Greek *kardamōmon* : *kardamon†,* cress + *amōmon†,* an Indian spice.]

card·board (kärd'bôrd', -bōrd') *n.* A thin, stiff pasteboard made of paper pulp, used for making cartons and boxes.
~*adj.* **1.** Made of cardboard. **2.** Superficial; two-dimensional: *cardboard characters.*

card-car·ry·ing (kärd'kăr'ē-ĭng) *adj.* **1.** Being an enrolled member, especially of a political organization: *a card-carrying Communist.* **2.** Being strongly identified with or devoted to a group, as of persons with shared ideals: *a card-carrying liberal.*

card catalog *n.* An alphabetical listing, especially of books in a library, made with a separate card for each item.

car·di·a (kär'dē-ə) *n.* The opening of the esophagus into the stomach. [New Latin, from Greek *kardia,* heart, cardiac orifice of the stomach.]

car·di·ac (kär'dē-ăk') *adj.* **1.** Of, near, or pertaining to the heart. **2.** Of or pertaining to the cardia.
~*n.* A person with a heart disorder. [Latin *cardiacus,* from Greek *kardiakos,* from *kardia,* heart.]

cardiac arrest *n.* The cessation of effective pumping of blood by the heart, resulting in loss of consciousness, absence of the pulse, and cessation of breathing.

cardiac massage *n.* A procedure to restore circulation in an individual by rhythmic manual compression either of the chest or of the heart through an opening in the chest wall.

cardiac muscle *n.* The striated muscle of the heart.

car·di·al·gi·a (kär'dē-ăl'jē-ə, -jə) *n.* **1. Heartburn** *(see).* **2.** Pain in or close to the heart. [New Latin, from Greek *kardialgia* : CARDI(O)- + -ALGIA.]

Car·diff (kär'dĭf). Capital of Wales, situated in South Glamorgan on the Taff River. Cardiff is the administrative center of South and Mid Glamorgan. With the expansion of the South Wales coal and iron mines in the 19th century, Cardiff grew from a small market town into one of the world's leading coal exporters. It was chosen as the capital of Wales only in 1955. After World War II the port declined, and Tiger Bay, the quayside area, is now a residential suburb. Industries include general shipping, ship repairs, steel, engineering, chemicals, and cement.

car·di·gan (kär'dĭ-gən) *n.* A sweater or knitted jacket worn by both sexes and opening down the front. [After the Earl of CARDIGAN.]

Car·di·gan (kär'dĭ-gən). Town on the Teifi River, Dyfed, south Wales, noted for its salmon and sea-trout angling. It was the county town of the former county of Cardiganshire.

Car·di·gan (kär'dĭ-gən), **James Thomas Brudenell, 7th Earl of** (1797–1868). British cavalry officer. He is remembered chiefly for leading the suicidal Charge of the Light Brigade at Balaclava (1854) in the Crimean War.

Car·di·gan·shire (kär'dĭ-gən-shîr, -shər). Also **Car·di·gan** Former county in Wales, which became part of the county of Dyfed (1974).

Car·din (kär-dăn'), **Pierre** (1922–). French fashion designer who made his mark in the 1950's with his slim-line coats, large collars, and Eastern-influenced designs.

car·di·nal (kärd'n-əl, kärd'nəl) *adj.* **1.** Of foremost importance; pivotal. **2.** Of a dark to deep or vivid red color.
~*n.* **1.** *Abbr.* **Card.** *Roman Catholic Church.* A member of the Sacred College or College of Cardinals. Members are appointed by the pope and elect a new pope when the Holy See is vacated. **2.** A dark to deep or vivid red. **3.** A North American bird, *Richmondena cardinalis,* having a crested head, a short, thick bill, and bright red plumage in the male. **4.** A short, hooded cloak, originally of scarlet cloth, worn by women in the 18th century. **5.** A **cardinal number** *(see).* [Middle English, from Old French, from Late Latin *cardinālis,* from Latin, principal, of a hinge, from *cardō†* (stem *cardin-*), hinge.]

car·di·nal·ate (kärd'n-ə-lĭt, kärd'nə-, -lāt') *n.* Also **car·di·nal·ship** (-shĭp'). *Roman Catholic Church.* **1.** The College of Cardinals. **2.** The position, rank, dignity, or term of a cardinal.

cardinal beetle *n.* A bright red European beetle of the genus *Pyrodehroa,* especially *P. coccinea* and *P. serraticornis,* whose coloration and unpleasant taste help to protect it from predatory birds.

cardinal flower *n.* A plant, *Lobelia cardinalis,* of eastern North America, having a terminal cluster of brilliant scarlet flowers.

cardinal number *n.* **1.** A number, such as 3 or 11 or 412, used to indicate quantity but not order. Compare **ordinal number.** **2.** A symbol denoting the size of a transfinite set.

cardinal point *n.* Any of the four principal directions on a compass: north, south, east, or west.

cardinal sins *pl.n.* The **seven deadly sins** *(see).*

cardinal virtues *pl.n.* The four qualities of justice, prudence, fortitude, and temperance. Also called "natural virtues."

cardio–, cardi– *prefix.* Indicates the heart; for example, **cardiogram, cardioid.** [Greek *kardi(o)-,* from *kardia,* heart.]

car·di·o·ac·cel·er·a·tor (kär'dē-ō'ăk-sĕl'ə-rā'tər) *n.* An agent that increases the heart rate.

car·di·o·gen·ic (kär'dē-ō-jĕn'ĭk, -jē'nĭk) *adj.* Having origin in a cardiac condition.

car·di·o·gram (kär'dē-ə-grăm') *n.* **1.** The curve traced by a cardiograph, used in the diagnosis of heart defects. **2.** An **electrocardiogram** *(see).* [CARDIO- + -GRAM.]

car·di·o·graph (kär'dē-ə-grăf', -gräf') *n.* **1.** An instrument used to record the mechanical movements of the heart. **2.** An **electrocardiograph** *(see).* [French *cardiographe* : CARDIO- + -GRAPH.] —**car·**

di·og·ra·pher (kär'dē-ŏg'rə-fər) *n.* —**car·di·o·graph·ic** (kär'dē-ə-grăf'ĭk), **car·di·o·graph·i·cal** *adj.* —**car·di·o·graph·i·cal·ly** *adv.* —**car·di·og·ra·phy** (kär'dē-ŏg'rə-fē) *n.*

car·di·oid (kär'dē-oid') *n.* A heart-shaped plane curve, the locus of a fixed point on a circle that rolls on the circumference of another circle with the same radius. [CARDI(O)- + -OID.]

car·di·ol·o·gy (kär'dē-ŏl'ə-jē) *n.* The medical study and treatment of the diseases and functioning of the heart. [CARDIO- + -LOGY.] —**car·di·ol·o·gist** *n.*

car·di·o·meg·a·ly (kär'dē-ō-mĕg'ə-lē) *n. Pathology.* **Megalocardia** *(see).* [CARDIO- + -megaly, from MEGALO-.]

car·di·o·pul·mo·nar·y (kär'dē-ō-pŏŏl'mə-nĕr'ē) *adj.* Of or pertaining to the heart and the lungs.

car·di·o·res·pir·a·to·ry (kär'dē-ō-rĕs'pər-ə-tôr'ē, -rĭ-spîr'ə-tôr'ē, -tōr'ē) *adj.* Of or pertaining to the heart and the respiratory system.

car·di·o·vas·cu·lar (kär'dē-ō-văs'kyə-lər) *adj.* Pertaining to or involving the heart and the blood vessels.

car·di·tis (kär-dī'tĭs) *n.* Inflammation of the heart.

car·doon (kär-dōōn') *n.* A plant, *Cynara cardunculus,* of southern Europe, closely related to the artichoke and having spiny leaves, purple flowers, and an edible leafstalk. [French *cardon,* from Provençal, from Late Latin *cardō* (stem *cardōn-*), thistle, from Latin *carduus,* thistle, artichoke.]

Car·do·zo (kär-dō'zō), **Benjamin Nathan** (1870–1938). U.S. jurist, justice of the Supreme Court (1932–38), and author. Appointed to the Supreme Court by Herbert Hoover, he blended his confidence in the Constitution and concern for social inadequacies into a broader interpretation of the role of federal government.

card reader *n. Computer Science.* A device for reading data from punched cards into a computer or storage device.

cards (kärdz) *n. Usually used with a singular verb.* **1.** Any game played with cards, such as bridge, whist, or poker, usually in packs of 52 cards divided into four suits: spades, hearts, diamonds, and clubs. **2.** The playing of such games. —**in the cards.** Likely to occur; probable. —**play one's cards right.** To carry out one's plans in the cleverest possible manner. —**put** or **lay one's cards on the table.** To make an open and honest declaration of one's position.

card·sharp (kärd'shärp') *n.* Also **card·sharp·er** (-shar'pər). A person expert in cheating at cards. —**card·sharp·ing** *n.*

card vote *n.* A method of voting, used especially at European trade-union conferences, in which the vote of each delegate counts for a specific number of his constituents.

care (kâr) *n.* **1.** Mental distress and uncertainty; worry. **2.** Mental suffering; grief. **3.** An object or source of worry, attention, or solicitude: *The preparation of meals was my particular care.* **4.** Caution in avoiding harm or danger; heedfulness: *handle with care.* **5.** Protection; supervision; charge: *in the care of a nurse.* **6.** Attentiveness to detail; painstaking application: *The report should be prepared with great care.* —**(in) care of.** *Abbr.* **c/o, c.o.** At the address of. Used in addressing letters and other mail. —**take care.** To act cautiously or prudently. —**take care of.** To look after or deal with.
~*v.* **cared, car·ing, cares.** —*intr.* **1.** To have a strong feeling or opinion; be concerned or interested: *The senator cares about human rights.* **2.** To have a fondness, regard, liking, or attachment: *I care for her deeply. They don't care for classical music.* **3.** To have an objection; mind: *I won't care if you borrow my car.* **4.** To look after; provide care: *an agency that cares for the homeless.*
~*tr.* **1.** To be concerned to the degree of: *I don't care a damn.* **2.** To be inclined; wish: *We don't care to attend the party.* [Middle English *care,* Old English *caru, cearu.*]

ca·reen (kə-rēn') *v.* **-reened, -reening, -reens.** —*intr.* **1.** To lean to one side; sway or heel, in the manner of a ship sailing in the wind. **2.** *Nautical.* To turn a ship on its side for cleaning, caulking, or repairing. **3.** To move rapidly and erratically. —*tr. Nautical.* **1.** To cause to lean to one side; tilt. **2.** To lean (a ship) on one side for cleaning, caulking, or repairing. [French *(en) carène,* "(on) the keel," from Old French *carene,* keel, from Old Italian *carena,* from Latin *carīna,* keel of a ship, nutshell.] —**ca·reen·er** *n.*

Usage: Both *careen* and *career* may refer to rapid and uncontrolled movement, the similarity in their form having promoted their use as synonyms. Many people try to maintain a distinction in meaning between the words, restricting *career* to forward movement, and *careen* to leaning and tilting, as in nautical usage. *Careen* is generally accepted in informal contexts, however, in statements such as *The car careened across the icy pavement.*

ca·reen·age (kə-rē'nĭj) *n.* **1.** A place for careening ships. **2.** The careening of ships. **3.** The charge for careening.

ca·reer (kə-rîr') *n.* **1.** An occupation, especially one with the possibility of advancement; a profession that lasts most of one's working lifetime. **2.** A path, course, or progress through life or history; especially, the course of a working life. **3.** Rapid progress; swift movement; speed. Often used with *full:* "*My hasting days fly on with full career.*" (Milton).
~*adj.* Engaged in a specified occupation as a chosen career: *a career diplomat.*
~*intr.v.* **careered, -reering, -reers.** To move or run at full speed; go headlong; rush. —See Usage note at **careen.** [French *carrière,* racecourse, course, career, from Old French, from Old Provençal *carriera,* street, from Medieval Latin *(via) carrāria,* (road) for vehicles, from Latin *carrus,* a kind of vehicle.]

ca·reer·ism (kə-rîr'ĭz'əm) *n.* The practice of seeking one's professional advancement by all possible means. —**ca·reer·ist** *n. & adj.*

care·free (kâr′frē′) *adj.* Free of worries and responsibilities.

care·ful (kâr′fəl) *adj.* **1.** Cautious in thought, speech, or action; circumspect; prudent. **2.** Thorough; painstaking; conscientious: *careful investigation.* **3.** Solicitous; protective. Used with *of.* **4.** *Chiefly British Informal.* Frugal, often to the point of meanness. —**care·ful·ly** *adv.* —**care·ful·ness** *n.*

care·less (kâr′lĭs) *adj.* **1.** Inattentive; negligent. **2.** Marked by or resulting from lack of thought, thoroughness, or planning: *a careless mistake.* **3.** Inconsiderate: *a careless remark.* **4.** Unconcerned; unmindful: *careless about her health.* **5.** Unstudied; effortless: *careless grandeur.* —**care·less·ly** *adv.* —**care·less·ness** *n.*

Synonyms: *heedless, lax, negligent, thoughtless.*

ca·ress (kə-rĕs′) *n.* A gentle touch or gesture of fondness, tenderness, or love.

~*tr.v.* **caressed, -ressing, -resses. 1.** To touch or stroke in an affectionate or loving manner. **2.** To touch or stroke gently. [French *caresse,* from Italian *carezza,* endearment, from *caro,* dear, from Latin *cārus.*] —**ca·ress·er** *n.* —**ca·ress·ing·ly** *adv.*

car·et (kăr′ĭt) *n.* A proofreading symbol used to indicate where something is to be inserted in printed or written matter. [Latin, "there is lacking," from *carēre,* to cut off, be without.]

care·tak·er (kâr′tā′kər) *n.* **1.** A person employed to look after or take charge of goods, property, or a person; a custodian. **2.** One taking charge temporarily. Also used adjectivally: *a caretaker government.*

care·worn (kâr′wôrn′, -wōrn′) *adj.* Showing the effects of anxiety; weary from worry. —See Synonyms at **haggard.**

car·fare (kär′fâr′) *n.* Fare charged a passenger.

car·go (kär′gō) *n., pl.* **-goes** or **-gos.** The freight carried by a ship, airplane, or other vehicle. [Spanish *cargo, carga,* load, cargo, from *cargar,* to load, from Late Latin *carricāre,* from Latin *carrus,* a kind of vehicle.]

cargo cult *n.* A religious cult, existing mainly in the South Pacific islands of Melanesia, based on a belief that suitable actions will bring the future arrival from boats and airplanes of rich and desirable goods.

Car·ib (kăr′ĭb) *n., pl.* **-ibs** or collectively **Carib. 1.** A member of a group of American Indian peoples of northern South America and the Lesser Antilles. **2.** Any of the languages of these peoples. —**Car·ib** *adj.*

Car·ib·be·an (kăr′ə-bē′ən, kə-rĭb′ē-ən) *n.* A Carib Indian.

~*adj.* **1.** Of, pertaining to, or originating in the Caribbean Sea and its islands. **2.** Of or pertaining to the Carib or their language.

Caribbean Sea. Part of the western Atlantic Ocean, separated from the main section of the ocean by the West Indies. This tropical sea, covering 2,590,000 square kilometers (1,000,000 square miles), has been an important shipping route since the opening of the Panama Canal in 1914. It takes its name from the original inhabitants of the area, the Caribs.

car·i·bou (kăr′ə-bo͞o′) *n., pl.* **-bous** or collectively **caribou.** A deer, *Rangifer tarandus,* of arctic regions of the New World, having antlers in both sexes. It also occurs in northern Europe and Asia, where it is called a reindeer. [Canadian French, probably from Algonquian.]

car·i·ca·ture (kăr′ĭ-kə-cho͝or′) *n.* **1.** A representation, especially pictorial, in which the subject's distinctive features or peculiarities are deliberately exaggerated or distorted to produce a comic or grotesque effect. **2.** The process or art of creating such representations. **3.** An imitation or copy so inferior as to be absurd.

~*tr.v.* **caricatured, -turing, -tures.** To represent or imitate in or as if in a caricature; satirize. [French, from Italian *caricatura,* caricature, "exaggeration," from *caricare,* to load, from Late Latin *carricāre,* from Latin *carrus,* a kind of vehicle.] —**car·i·ca·tur·ist** *n.*

Synonyms: *lampoon, parody, satire, spoof, takeoff.*

car·ies (kâr′ēz) *n.* Decay of a bone or a tooth. [Latin *cariēs,* caries, decay.]

car·il·lon (kăr′ə-lŏn′, -lən) *n.* **1.** A set of chromatically tuned bells that are housed in a tower and are usually played from a keyboard. **2.** A stop on an organ that produces a bell-like sound. **3.** A composition written or arranged for or played on a carillon.

~*intr.v.* **carillonned, -lonning, -lons.** To play a carillon. [French, variant of Old French *carignon, quarregnon,* from Vulgar Latin *quadriniō* (stem *quadriniōn-*) (unattested), set of four bells, variant of Late Latin *quaterniō,* set of four, from *quaternī,* four each, from *quater,* four times.]

car·il·lon·neur (kăr′ə-lə-nûr′) *n.* A person who plays a carillon.

ca·ri·na (kə-rī′nə, -rē′nə) *n., pl.* **-nae** (-nē). *Biology.* A keel-shaped ridge, such as that on the breastbone of a bird or in the petals of certain flowers. [New Latin, from Latin *carīna,* keel.]

Ca·ri·na (kə-rī′nə, -rē′nə) *n.* A constellation in the Southern Hemisphere near Vela containing the star Canopus. [Latin, "the Keel."]

car·i·nate (kăr′ə-nāt′, -nĭt) *adj.* Also **car·i·nat·ed** (-nā′tĭd). *Biology.* Having or shaped like a keel; ridged.

Carinthia. See **Kärnten.**

car·i·o·ca (kăr′ē-ō′kə) *n.* **1.** A South American ballroom dance that originated in Rio de Janeiro. **2.** The music for this dance. **3. Carioca.** A native or resident of Rio de Janeiro. [Portuguese *Carioca,* from Tupi.]

car·i·o·gen·ic (kăr′ē-ō-jĕn′ĭk) *adj.* Producing caries, especially of the teeth. [CARIES + -GENIC.]

car·i·ole, car·ri·ole (kăr′ē-ōl′) *n.* **1.** A small, open, one-horse vehicle with two wheels. **2.** A light, covered cart. [French *carriole,* from Old Provençal *carriola,* diminutive of *carri,* chariot, from Vulgar Latin *carrium* (unattested), from Latin *carrus,* a kind of vehicle.]

car·i·ous (kâr′ē-əs) *adj.* Having caries; decayed. Said of teeth and bones. —**car·i·os·i·ty** (kăr′ē-ŏs′ə-tē) **car·i·ous·ness** *n.*

car·line[1] (kär′lən, -līn′) *n.* A thistlelike Eurasian plant, *Carlina vulgaris,* having spiny leaves and flower heads surrounded by slender, raylike, straw-colored bracts. [French, from Medieval Latin *carlina,* perhaps variant of *cardina* (through association with *Carolus* (*Magnus*), Charlemagne, from Latin *cardo,* thistle.]

car·line[2], **car·lin** (kär′lən) *n. Scottish.* **1.** A woman, especially an old woman. **2.** A witch. [See **carling.**]

car·ling (kär′lĭng, -lĭn) *n. Nautical.* Any of the short timbers running fore and aft that connect the transverse beams supporting the deck of a ship. [French *carlingue,* from Old French *cal(l)ingue,* probably from Old Norse *kerling,* "old woman," from *karl,* man.]

Car·lisle (kär-līl′, kär′līl′). City and administrative center of Cumbria, England, on the Eden River. Once a Roman fortress, it was destroyed by the Danes in 875 and rebuilt (1092) by William Rufus. Mary, Queen of Scots was imprisoned in its 11th-century castle.

Carl·ist (kär′lĭst) *n.* In Spain, a supporter of Don Carlos, the pretender to the throne, or his heirs. —**Carl·ism** *n.* —**Carl·ist** *adj.*

car·load (kär′lōd′) *n.* The amount a car carries or is able to carry.

Carlovingian. Variant of **Carolingian.**

Car·low (kär′lō). A largely agricultural county in Leinster, southeast Republic of Ireland. Carlow is the chief town.

Carls·bad Caverns National Park (kärlz′băd). Area of 18,935 hectares (46,753 acres) in southeastern New Mexico, in the Guadalupe Mts. These limestone caves, discovered *c.* 1900, began forming 60 million years ago when ground water began dissolving the rock. There are remarkable stalactite and stalagmite formations.

Carlsruhe. See **Karlsruhe.**

Car·lyle (kär-līl′), **Thomas** (1795-1881). Scottish historian and essayist, well known for a literary style characterized by complex syntax and rich vocabulary. His book *Sartor Resartus* (1833–34), a blend of fiction, autobiography, and philosophy, was followed by *The French Revolution* (1837). His other works include *Past and Present* (1843), an attack on England's social and political ills.

car·man (kär′mən) *n., pl.* **-men** (-mĭn). **1.** A man who drives a car or cart. **2.** A driver or conductor, as of a streetcar.

Car·mar·then (kər-mär′*th*ən, kär-). One of the oldest towns in Wales, on the Towey River in Dyfed, south Wales. It was once the site of a Roman fort.

Car·mar·then·shire (kər-mär′*th*ən-shîr, -shər, kär-). Former county in southwest Wales. It became part of Dyfed in 1974.

Car·mel (kär-mĕl′). Also **Car·mel-by-the-Sea** (-bī-thə-sē′). Village in western California, on Carmel Bay at the southern end of the Monterey peninsula. It is known as a writers' and artists' community and is popular with tourists.

Car·mel (kär′məl), **Mount.** A limestone ridge, 546 meters (1,791 feet) at its highest, in northwest Israel. It was the scene of Elijah's struggle with the priests of Baal. The religious order of the Carmelites was founded here in the 12th century.

Car·mel·ite (kär′mə-līt′) *n.* **1.** A monk or mendicant friar belonging to the order of Our Lady of Mt. Carmel, founded at Mt. Carmel in about 1155. Also called "White Friar." **2.** A member of a community of nuns of this order, founded in 1452. —**Car·mel·ite** *adj.*

Car·mi·chael (kär′mī-kəl), **Hoagland Howard,** known as "Hoagie" (1899–1981). U.S. songwriter. He wrote his first successful song, "Riverboat Shuffle," while in college. He moved to New York City in the 1920's and dedicated himself to music. He wrote many popular songs, such as "Stardust" (1929) and "Georgia on My Mind" (1931).

car·min·a·tive (kär-mĭn′ə-tĭv, kär′mə-nā′-) *adj.* Inducing expulsion of gas from the stomach and intestines.

~*n.* A carminative drug. [Middle English, from Medieval Latin *carminātīvus,* from *carmināre* (past participle *carminātus*), to card wool, comb out impurities, from Latin *carmen,* a card for wool, from *cārere,* to card.]

car·mine (kär′mĭn, -mīn′) *n.* **1.** A deep vivid red color with a purplish tinge. **2.** A crimson pigment derived from **cochineal** *(see).*

~*adj.* Vivid red or purplish red. [French *carmin,* from Medieval Latin *carminium* : Arabic *qirmiz,* KERMES + Latin *minium,* MINIUM.]

Car·nac (kär′năk). Small coastal village in Brittany, France, famous for its prehistoric standing stones extending in parallel rows for c. 5 kilometers (3 miles).

car·nage (kär′nĭj) *n.* **1.** Massive slaughter, as in war; massacre. **2.** *Obsolete.* Corpses, especially of men killed in battle: *a battlefield bloody with carnage.* [Old French, from Medieval Latin *carnāticum,* slaughter of animals, from Latin *carō* (stem *carn-*), flesh, meat.]

car·nal (kär′nəl) *adj.* **1.** Pertaining to the desires and appetites of the flesh or body; sensual. **2.** Worldly or earthly; temporal. [Middle English, from Medieval Latin *carnālis,* from Latin *carō* (stem *carn-*), flesh.] —**car·nal·i·ty** (kär-năl′ə-tē) *n.* —**car·nal·ly** *adv.*

carnal knowledge *n.* Sexual intercourse.

car·nall·ite (kär′nə-līt′) *n.* A white, brownish, or reddish mineral, $KMgCl_3 \cdot 6H_2O$, that is used in the manufacture of potassium salts. [German *Carnallit,* after Rudolf von Carnall (1804–74), German mining engineer.]

car·nas·si·al (kär-năs′ē-əl) *adj.* Adapted for tearing apart flesh. Said of teeth.

~*n.* A carnassial tooth, either the last upper premolar or the first lower molar in carnivorous mammals. [French *carnassier,* carnivorous, from Provençal, from *carnasso,* meat in abundance, from *carn,* flesh, from Latin *carō* (stem *carn-*), flesh.]

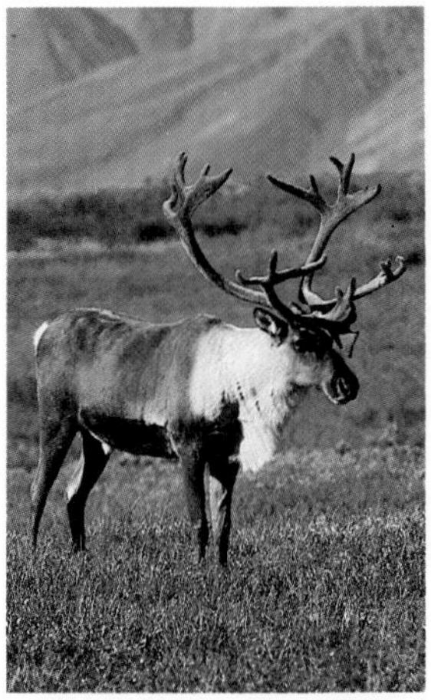

caribou *This North American deer is the same species as the reindeer of Europe and Asia. The thick hair and furry muzzle protect it against cold, and, unlike other deer, both sexes have antlers.*

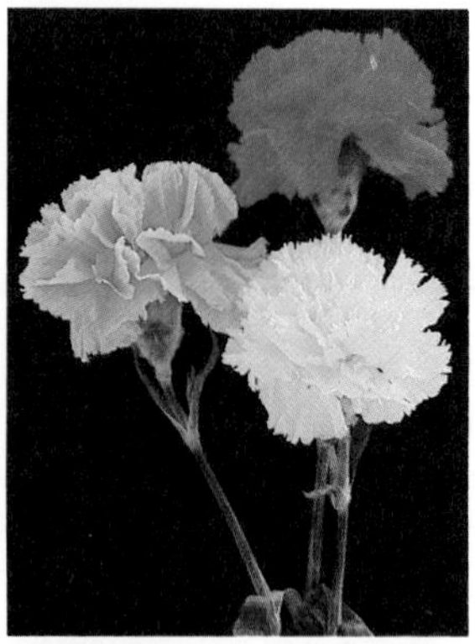

carnation *A species of the genus* Dianthus, *a group of annual or perennial herbs and flowers that also includes sweet William.*

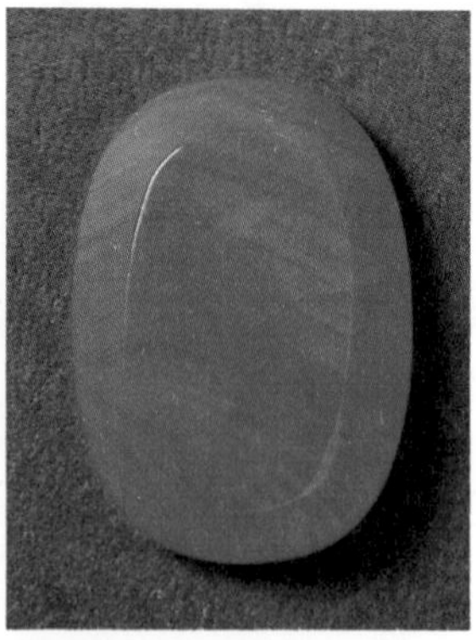

carnelian *Although this translucent semiprecious stone is found in many parts of the world, it is commercially exploited mainly in Brazil and Uruguay.*

car·na·tion (kär-nā′shən) *n.* **1. a.** A plant, *Dianthus caryophyllus,* native to Eurasia, widely cultivated for its fragrant, variously colored flowers with fringed petals. **b.** The flower of this plant. **2.** A flesh-colored tint once used in painting. [French, flesh-colored, carnation, from Italian *carnagione,* complexion, from *carne,* flesh, from Latin *carō* (stem *carn-*), flesh.]

car·nau·ba (kär-nô′bə, -nou′bə) *n.* **1.** A palm tree, *Copernica cerifera,* of tropical South America. **2.** A hard wax obtained from the leaves of this tree, used as a polish and in candles. In this sense, also called "carnauba wax." [Portuguese, probably of Tupi origin.]

Car·neg·ie (kär′nə-gē, kär-nĕg′ē) **Andrew** (1835–1919). Scottish-born U.S. industrialist and philanthropist. Arriving in the United States as a penniless young boy, he became one of the world's richest men and gave millions of dollars to charities in the United States and in the United Kingdom.

car·nel·ian (kär-nēl′yən) *n.* Also **cor·nel·ian** (kôr-). A reddish or reddish-brown variety of chalcedony, used in jewelry. [Middle English *corneline,* from Old French, probably "cherry-colored," from *cornelle,* CORNEL (cherry).]

car·net (kär-nā′) *n.* A permit or customs license allowing a motor vehicle to be imported or driven across certain national frontiers. [French, "notebook."]

carney. Variant of **carny.**

car·ni·val (kär′nə-vəl) *n.* **1.** The season just before Lent, celebrated by processions, dancing, merrymaking, and feasting. See **Mardi gras. 2.** A time of revelry; a festival. **3.** A traveling amusement show. **4.** *Australian.* A large-scale sporting event: *a surfing carnival.* [Italian *carnevale,* from Old Italian *carnelevare,* "the putting away of flesh," Shrovetide, from Medieval Latin *carnelevāmen* : Latin *carō* (stem *carn-*), flesh + *levāre,* to raise, remove.]

car·ni·vore (kär′nə-vôr′, -vōr′) *n.* **1.** *Zoology.* Any animal belonging to the order Carnivora, which includes predominantly flesh-eating mammals such as dogs, cats, bears, and weasels. **2.** Any flesh-eating or predatory organism, such as a bird of prey or an insectivorous plant. [French, from Latin *carnivorus,* CARNIVOROUS.]

car·niv·o·rous (kär-nĭv′ər-əs) *adj.* **1.** Belonging or pertaining to the order Carnivora. **2.** Flesh-eating or predatory. **3.** *Botany.* Capable of trapping and absorbing insects or other small organisms; insectivorous. Said of plants such as the pitcher plant and the Venus's-flytrap. [Latin *carnivorus* : *carō* (stem *carn-*), flesh + -VOROUS.] **—car·niv·o·rous·ly** *adv.* **—car·niv·o·rous·ness** *n.*

Car·not (kär-nō′), **Nicolas Léonard Sadi** (1796–1832). French physicist, engineer, and soldier who founded the science of thermodynamics. His investigations on the motive power of heat established that heat and work are reversible conditions. The Carnot cycle and Carnot's principle are described in his study *Réflexions sur la Puissance Motrice du Feu* (1824).

Carnot, Lazare Nicolas Marguerite (1753–1823). Father of Sadi Carnot and statesman and military engineer whose book *De la Défense de Places Fortes* (1810) became a classic study on fortifications.

Carnot cycle *n. Physics.* The thermodynamic cycle of an ideal heat engine, consisting of an adiabatic compression, an isothermal expansion, an adiabatic expansion, and an isothermal compression, the sequence restoring the initial conditions of the system. [After N.L.S. CARNOT.]

car·no·tite (kär′nə-tīt′) *n.* A yellow uranium ore with composition $K_2(UO_2)_2(VO_4)_2H_2O$. [French, after M.A. *Carnot* (died 1920), French inspector general of mines.]

Carnot's principle *n. Physics.* The principle that the efficiency of a perfect heat engine does not depend on the substance used. [After N.L.S. CARNOT.]

car·ny (kär′nē) *n., pl.* **-nies.** Also **car·ney** *pl.* **-neys.** *Slang.* **1.** A carnival. **2.** A person who works with a carnival.

car·ob (kăr′əb) *n.* **1.** An evergreen tree, *Ceratonia siliqua,* of the Mediterranean region, having compound leaves and edible pods. Also called "algarroba," "locust." See **St. John's bread. 2.** The edible pod of the carob tree, used as animal fodder and to make a preparation resembling chocolate. [Obsolete French *caro(u)be,* from Medieval Latin *carrūbium,* from Arabic *kharrūbah.*]

ca·roche (kə-rōch′, -rōsh′) *n.* A stately carriage of the 16th and 17th centuries. [French *carroche,* from Old Italian *carroccio,* augmentative of *carro,* vehicle, from Latin *carrus.*]

car·ol (kăr′əl) *v.* **-oled, -olings, -ols.** Also *chiefly British* **-olled, -olling.** *—tr.* **1.** To celebrate in song. **2.** To sing (something) joyously. *—intr.* **1.** To sing in a joyous manner; warble. **2.** To go from house to house singing Christmas carols.
~n. **1.** A song of praise or joy, especially one celebrating the birth of Christ. **2.** An old round dance often accompanied by singing. [Middle English *carolen,* from Old French *caroler,* of obscure origin.] **—car·ol·er** *n.*

Car·ol II (kăr′əl) (1893–1953). King of Romania. Because of his love for a commoner, Magda Lupescu, he renounced his right to succession (1925) in favor of his son Michael, who became king in 1927. He returned to his country in 1930 and was proclaimed king, but his reign lasted only until 1940. After failure to prevent Nazi domination of the kingdom, he abdicated and settled in Mexico.

Car·o·le·an (kăr′ə-lē′ən) *adj.* Caroline. [Medieval Latin *Carolus,* Charles.]

Car·o·li·na (kăr′ə-lī′nə). An English colony in southern North America, first settled in 1653 and divided into what became North and South Carolina in 1729. The colonies and present-day states of North and South Carolina are called **the Carolinas.**

Car·o·line (kăr′ə-līn′, -lĭn) *adj.* **1.** Of or pertaining to the life and times of Charles I or Charles II of England. **2.** Of or pertaining to Charlemagne or his time. [New Latin *Carolinius,* from Medieval Latin *Carolus,* CHARLES.]

Car·o·line Islands (kăr′ə-līn′). Also **Car·o·lines** (-līnz′). Archipelago in the western Pacific Ocean, comprising four main groups: Ponape, Truk, Yap, and Palau. Formerly part of the U.S. Trust Territory of the Pacific Islands (1947–80), all but Palau joined the Federated States of Micronesia. Palau was renamed Belau and became an independent republic (1981).

Car·o·lin·gi·an (kăr′ə-lĭn′jē-ən, -jən) *adj.* Also **Car·lo·vin·gi·an** (kär′lə-vĭn′jē-ən, -jən). Related to, designating, or belonging to the Frankish dynasty that was founded by Pepin the Short in 751 and that lasted until 987 in France and 911 in Germany.
~n. Also **Car·lo·vin·gi·an.** A member of this dynasty. [French *Carolingien,* variant of *Carlovingien,* probably a blend of Medieval Latin *Carolus,* Charles, and *Mérovingien,* MEROVINGIAN.]

car·om (kăr′əm) *n.* **1. a.** A shot in billiards in which the cue ball successively strikes two other balls. **b.** A similar shot in related games, such as pool. **2.** A collision followed by a rebound.
~v. **caromed, -oming, -oms.** *—intr.* **1.** To collide with and rebound: *The boat caromed off the dock.* **2.** To make a carom, as in billiards. *—tr.* To cause to carom. [Earlier *carambole,* from Spanish *carambola,* a kind of fruit, from Portuguese, from Marathi *karambal*†.]

Ca·ro's acid (kä′rōz) *n.* A strong acid, **peroxysulfuric acid** *(see).* [After Heinrich *Caro* (1834–1910), German chemist.]

car·o·tene (kăr′ə-tēn′) *n.* Also **car·o·tin** (-tĭn). An orange-yellow to red hydrocarbon, $C_{40}H_{56}$, existing in six isomeric forms, occurring in many plants as a pigment. Three of the isomers may be converted to vitamin A in the liver. [German *Karotin* : Latin *carōta,* CARROT + -ENE.]

ca·rot·e·noid, ca·rot·i·noid (kə-rŏt′n-oid′) *n.* Any of a class of yellow to deep red pigments, such as the carotenes, occurring in many vegetable oils and some animal fats.

ca·rot·id (kə-rŏt′ĭd′) *n.* Either of the two major arteries in the neck that carry blood to the head.
~adj. Of or pertaining to either of these arteries. [French *carotide,* from Greek *karōtides,* from *karoun,* to stupefy (it was once thought that pressure on the carotids causes stupor).]

ca·rous·al (kə-rou′zəl) *n.* A jovial, riotous drinking party; boisterous merrymaking; revelry.

ca·rouse (kə-rouz′) *n.* A carousal.
~intr.v. **caroused, -rousing, -rouses.** To drink excessively; go on a drinking spree. [Old French *carrousse,* from *(boire) carous,* (to drink) all out, from German *garaus (trinken)* : *gar,* quite, entirely + *aus,* out.] **—ca·rous·er** *n.*

car·ou·sel, car·rou·sel (kăr′ə-sĕl′, -zĕl′) *n.* **1.** A tournament in which knights or horsemen engaged in various exercises and races. **2.** A **merry-go-round** *(see).* **3.** A rotating conveyor system, as for delivering luggage in an airport. [French *carrousel,* probably from Italian dialectal *carosello*†, a kind of tournament.]

carp[1] (kärp) *intr.v.* **carped, carping, carps.** To find fault and complain constantly; harp on petty grievances; grumble. Often used with *at.* [Middle English *carpen,* from Old Norse *karpa,* to boast.] **—carp·er** *n.* **—carp·ing·ly** *adv.*

carp[2] *n., pl.* **carps** or collectively **carp. 1.** An edible freshwater fish, *Cyprinus carpio,* frequently bred in ponds and lakes. **2.** Any of various other fishes of the family Cyprinidae. [Middle English *carpe,* from Old French, from Late Latin *carpa*†.]

-carp *suffix. Botany.* Indicates fruit or similar reproductive structure; for example, **mesocarp.** [New Latin *-carpium,* from Greek *-karpion,* from *karpos,* fruit.]

Car·pac·cio (kär-pä′chō, -chē-o) **Vittore,** born Vittore Scarpazza (*c.* 1460–*c.* 1525). Venetian painter noted for his views of the city and his narrative cycles. Influenced by Gentile and Giovanni Bellini, his works include the cycle *Scenes from the Life of St. Ursula* and *The Miracle of the Cross.*

car·pal (kär′pəl) *adj. Anatomy.* Of, pertaining to, or near the carpus.
~n. Any bone of the carpus. [New Latin *carpalis,* from Greek *karpos,* wrist.]

car park *n. Chiefly British.* A parking lot.

Car·pa·thi·an Mountains (kär-pā′thē-ən). Also **Car·pa·thi·ans** (-ənz). Mountain range extending through central and eastern Europe in an arc 1,400 kilometers (900 miles) long. It forms part of the Czechoslovak-Polish border, crosses the southwest Ukrainian S.S.R. into Romania, and swings back to the Danube at the Iron Gate on the Romanian-Yugoslavian frontier. Sparsely inhabited, it is a resort area and rich in mineral deposits.

car·pe di·em (kär′pĕ dē′ĕm′, -əm, dī′-) *n.* The admonition to seize the pleasures of the moment without thought for the future. [Latin, "seize the day."]

car·pel (kär′pəl) *n. Botany.* The central, ovule-bearing female organ of a flower, consisting of an ovary, style, and stigma. Carpels may be separate or fused to form a single pistil. [New Latin *carpellum,* from Greek *karpos,* fruit.] **—car·pel·lar·y** (kär′pə-lĕr′ē) *adj.*

car·pel·late (kär′pə-lāt′, -lĭt) *adj. Botany.* Having carpels.

Car·pen·tar·ia (kär′pən-târ′ē-ə). **Gulf of.** A large inlet of the Arafura Sea between Arnhem Land and Cape York Peninsula in north Australia. It is approximately 480 kilometers (300 miles) west to east and 595 kilometers (370 miles) north to south.

car·pen·ter (kär′pən-tər) *n.* One whose occupation is constructing

and repairing wooden objects and structures, especially large solid ones, such as ships or houses.
~v. carpentered, -tering, -ters. *—tr.* To make, build, or repair (wooden objects or structures). *—intr.* To work as a carpenter. [Middle English, from Norman French, from Latin *carpentārius (artifex),* carriage(-maker), from adjective, from *carpentum,* two-wheeled vehicle, wagon, from Celtic.] **—car·pen·try** (kär′pən-trē) *n.*
carpenter moth *n.* Any of various moths of the family Cossidae, the larvae of which are harmful to the wood of various trees.
Car·pen·tier (kär-pôn-tyā′), **Georges** (1894–1975). French boxer who held the world light-heavyweight title (1920–22). His fight against Jack Dempsey (1921) was the first to realize a million dollars in takings.
car·pet (kär′pĭt) *n.* **1. a.** A thick, heavy covering for a floor, usually made of wool or synthetic fibers. **b.** The fabric used for this. **2.** A surface similar to a carpet in texture or appearance: *a carpet of leaves and pine needles.* **—on the carpet.** *Informal.* In the position of being reprimanded by one in authority.
~tr.v. carpeted, -peting, -pets. To cover with or as if with a carpet: *The pool was carpeted with green sponge"* (Rachel Carson). [Middle English *carpete,* from Old French *carpite,* from Old Italian *carpita,* from *carpire,* to pluck, tear, from Latin *carpere.*]
car·pet·bag (kär′pĭt-băg′) *n.* An old-fashioned kind of traveling bag made of carpet fabric.
car·pet·bag·ger (kär′pĭt-băg′ər) *n.* **1.** A politician who for political interest seeks to represent an area with which he has no personal connections. **2.** A Northerner who went to the South after the Civil War for political or financial advantage. Compare **scalawag.** **—car·pet·bag·ger·y, car·pet·bag·gism** *n.*
carpet beetle *n.* Any of various small beetles of the genera *Anthrenus* and *Attagenus,* having larvae injurious to fabrics, furs, and other plant and animal products. Also called "buffalo bug."
car·pet·ing (kär′pĭ-tĭng) *n.* **1.** Material or fabric used for making carpets. **2.** Carpets.
carpet shark *n.* Any of certain sharks of the family Orectolobidae, having a back patterned in brown and white and a fringe of fleshy growths around the sides of the head.
carpet snake *n.* A nonvenomous Australian snake, *Morelia variegata,* marked on its back with a pattern resembling that of a Persian carpet.
carpetsweeper *n.* A hand-operated household implement with a revolving brush, used for sweeping carpets.
car·pet·weed (kär′pĭt-wēd′) *n.* A low-growing weedy plant, *Mollugo verticillata,* forming dense mats and having whorled leaves and small greenish-white flowers.
carpo– *prefix.* Indicates fruit or similar reproductive structure; for example, **carpogonium, carpology.** [Greek *karpos,* fruit.]
car·po·go·ni·um (kär′pə-gō′nē-əm) *n., pl.* **-nia** (-nē-ə). *Botany.* The female reproductive structure of red algae, comprising a swollen base enclosing the ovum and a long neck along which the male gametes pass. [New Latin : CARPO- + -GONIUM.] **—car·po·go·ni·al** *adj.*
car·pol·o·gy (kär-pŏl′ə-jē) *n.* The area of botany concerned with fruits and seeds. [CARPO- + -LOGY.]
car·po·met·a·car·pus (kär′pō-mĕt′ə-kär′pəs) *n.* A bone in a bird's wing made up of the metacarpal bones and some of the carpal bones fused together. [CARPO- + META- + CARPUS.]
car·pool (kär′pōōl′) *n.* **1.** An arrangement whereby several commuters travel together in one car. **2.** A group, as of commuters, participating in a car-pool.
car·poph·a·gous (kär-pŏf′ə-gəs) *adj.* Feeding on fruit; fruit-eating. [Greek *karpophagos* : CARPO- + -PHAGOUS.]
car·po·phore (kär′pə-fôr′, -fōr′) *n. Botany.* **1.** The elongated part of the axis of certain flowers to which the carpels and stamens are attached. **2.** A fruiting body or the stalk of a fruiting body in certain fungi. [CARPO- + -PHORE.]
car·port (kär′pôrt′, -pōrt′) *n.* A roof projecting from the side of a building, used as a shelter for a motor vehicle.
car·po·spo·ran·gi·um (kär′pə-spə-răn′jē-əm) *n., pl.* **-gia** (-jē-ə). A specialized sporangium in red algae, in which carpospores are formed. [New Latin : CARPO- + SPORANGIUM.]
car·po·spore (kär′pə-spôr′, -spōr′) *n. Botany.* A nonmotile haploid or diploid spore formed within the carposporangium of red algae.
–carpous *suffix.* Indicates a specified number or kind of fruit; for example, **polycarpous, monocarpic.** [New Latin *-carpus,* from Greek *karpos,* fruit.]
car·pus (kär′pəs) *n., pl.* **-pi** (-pī′). *Anatomy.* **1. a.** The **wrist** *(see).* **b.** The bones of the wrist. **2.** Any joint corresponding to the wrist in quadrupeds. [New Latin, from Greek *karpos,* wrist.]
car·rack, car·ack (kär′ək) *n.* A type of merchant ship used in the 14th, 15th, and 16th centuries; a galleon. [Middle English *caryk, carrake,* from Old French *caraque,* from Old Spanish *carraca,* from Arabic *qarāqīr,* plural of *qurqūr,* carrack.]
car·ra·geen, car·ra·gheen (kär′ə-gēn′) *n.* A seaweed, **Irish moss** *(see).* [After *Carragheen,* Ireland, where it flourishes.]
Car·ran·tuo·hill (kär′ən-tōō′əl). Mountain in Macgillicuddy's Reeks in County Kerry, Republic of Ireland. At 1,041 meters (3,414 feet), it is Ireland's highest peak.
Car·ran·za (kə-răn′zə, -rän′-), **Venustiano** (1859–1920). Mexican revolutionary statesman. He became the first president of the new Mexican Republic after the overthrow of dictator Porfirio Diaz (1911). After he tried to engineer the election of his chosen successor, an armed rebellion forced him to flee the capital. He was be-

trayed and murdered while hiding in the mountains.
Car·ra·ra (kə-rär′ə). City in north-central Italy, famous for the white marble quarried nearby that was favored by Michelangelo.
car·rel (kär′əl) *n.* Also **car·rell.** A small separate enclosure, especially in a library, used for private study. [Variant of CAROL (in obsolete sense "small enclosure").]
Car·rel (kə-rĕl′, kär′əl), **Alexis** (1873–1944). French surgeon and biologist, who worked in the United States (1905–39). For his development of a method of suturing blood vessels, he was awarded the Nobel Prize in physiology and medicine in 1912.
car·riage (kär′ĭj; kär′ē-ĭj *for sense 6b) n.* **1.** A four-wheeled, horse-drawn passenger vehicle, often of an elegant design. **2.** *Chiefly British.* A railroad car for passengers. **3.** A baby carriage; perambulator. **4.** A wheeled support or frame for moving a heavy object, such as a cannon. **5.** A moving part of a machine for holding or shifting another part, as on a lathe. **6. a.** The act or process of transporting or carrying. **b.** The cost of or charge for transporting. **7.** The manner of holding and moving one's head and body; posture or bearing. **—See Synonyms at bearing.** [Middle English *cariage,* from Old North French, from *carier,* to transport in a vehicle, CARRY.]
carriage dog *n.* The **Dalmatian** *(see).*
carriage trade *n.* Wealthy patrons, as of a restaurant.
car·rick bend (kär′ĭk) *n. Nautical.* A type of knot used to fasten two cables or hawsers together. [From obsolete *carrick,* carrack, from Middle English *caryk,* CARRACK.]
carrick bitt *n. Nautical.* Either of the two posts that support the windlass on a ship's deck. [See **carrick bend.**]
car·ri·er (kär′ē-ər) *n.* **1.** One that transports or conveys. **2.** An organization or individual that deals in transporting passengers or goods. **3.** A mechanism or device by which something is conveyed or conducted. **4.** *Medicine.* A person or animal that shows no symptoms of a disease but transmits it directly or indirectly to others or, in the case of a hereditary disease, to offspring. **5.** *Pathology.* A **vector** *(see).* **6.** *Electronics.* **a.** A **carrier wave** *(see).* **b.** A charge-carrying entity, especially an electron or a hole in a semiconductor. **7.** An **aircraft carrier** *(see).* **8. a.** *Chemistry.* A support, such as alumina or asbestos, for a solid catalyst. **b.** A molecule or ion that transports an atom or group between molecules. **c.** The solid that adsorbs a dyestuff in the formation of a lake. **d.** An inert substance containing a radioactive isotope, used to introduce the isotope into a system for tracer studies.
carrier bag *n. Chiefly British.* A large plastic or paper bag used especially for carrying shopping.
carrier pigeon *n.* A **homing pigeon** *(see),* especially one trained to carry messages.
carrier wave *n.* A radio wave or other electromagnetic wave that can be modulated in frequency, amplitude, phase, or otherwise to transmit speech, music, images, or other signals.
carriole. Variant of **cariole.**
car·ri·on (kär′ē-ən) *n.* Dead and decaying flesh.
~adj. 1. Of or similar to carrion. **2.** Carrion-eating. [Middle English *carion, caroine,* from Norman French *caroine,* from Vulgar Latin *carōnia* (unattested), from Latin *carō* (stem *carn-*), flesh.]
carrion crow *n.* A common scavenging and predatory crow, *Corvus corone,* of Europe and Asia, resembling the rook but having a pure black bill.
carrion flower *n.* **1.** A climbing vine, *Smilax herbacea,* of eastern North America, having clusters of small, greenish flowers with an odor of decaying flesh. **2.** Any of several other plants having flowers with an unpleasant odor.
Car·roll (kär′əl), **Charles,** known as "Carroll of Carrollton" (1737–1832). U.S. Revolutionary leader. Barred from entering Maryland colonial politics because he was a Roman Catholic, he became active in the movement for independence from Great Britain. He signed the Declaration of Independence in July 1776.
Carroll, John (1735–1813). U.S. Jesuit clergyman and cousin of Charles Carroll. He was named the first Roman Catholic bishop in the United States (1789) and the first archbishop of Baltimore (1808). He actively promoted missions to the Indians and founded what is now Georgetown University (1791).
Carroll, Lewis. See Charles Lutwidge **Dodgson.**
car·rot (kär′ət) *n.* **1.** A widely cultivated plant, *Daucus carota sativa,* having finely divided leaves, flat clusters of small white flowers, and an edible, yellow-orange root. **2.** The long, tapering root of this plant, eaten as a vegetable. **3.** Something offered as a means of persuasion; an incentive. [Old French *carotte,* from Latin *carōta,.* from Greek *karōton.*]
car·rot-and-stick (kär′ət-ən-stĭk′) *adj.* Combining a promised reward with a threat or punishment: *a carrot-and-stick approach to getting things done.*
car·rot·y (kär′ə-tē′) *adj.* **1.** Similar to a carrot, especially in color. **2.** Having orange-red hair.
carrousel. Variant of **carousel.**
car·ry (kär′ē) *v.* **-ried, -rying, -ries.** *—tr.* **1.** To bear or convey from one place to another; transport: *carry cargo.* **2.** To make known, take, bring, or communicate (a message, for example). **3.** To serve as a means for the conveyance or transmission of; transmit: *Flies carry disease.* **4.** To hold or bear while moving: *The plane carried us to safety.* **5. a.** To hold or be capable of holding: *The car carries four people.* **b.** To sustain the weight of; support. **6.** To support or sustain the responsibility of. **7.** To keep or have on one's person. **8.** To be pregnant with. **9. a.** To hold and move (the body or a part of it) in a specified way. **b.** To behave or conduct (oneself) in a specified

carrion crow *Native to Europe and Asia, the carrion crow feeds mainly on the ground and eats almost anything, including the eggs and young of other birds.*

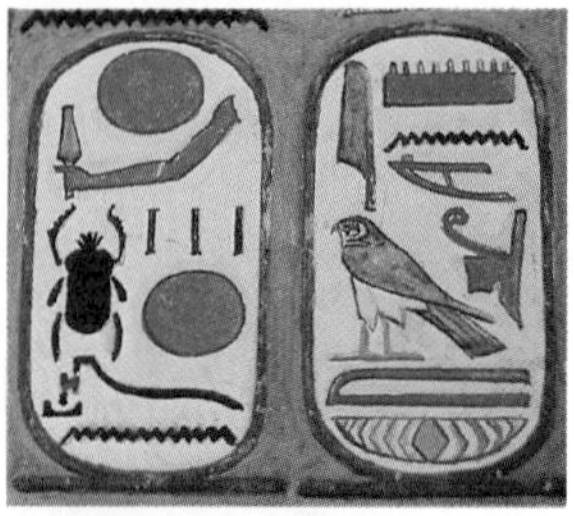

cartouche *In ancient Egypt these oblong or oval frames enclosed the name of the pharaoh, spelled out in pictorial hieroglyphics. They were often inscribed on Egyptian monuments, but smaller cartouches were also used as royal seals.*

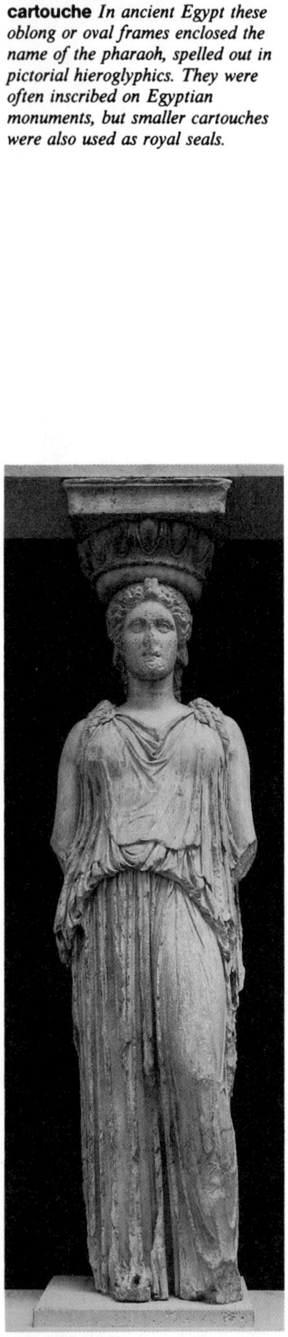

caryatid *A sculptured female figure used as a column. This example is from the Acropolis at Athens. It was carved in about 415 B.C.*

manner. **10.** To extend or continue in a certain direction or to a given point or degree: *carry a joke too far.* **11.** To cause to move; drive; impel. **12.** To take or seize, especially by force; capture: *"The Turks carried the defenses of Jebel Subh"* (T.E. Lawrence). **13.** To gain victory, support, or acceptance for; especially, to secure the adoption of (a motion or bill). **14.** To be successful in; win. **15.** To include as part of a publication, broadcast, or the like. **16.** To sway; move; gain the interest of: *Her enthusiasm carried the audience.* **17.** To have as a customary, necessary, or characteristic attribute or accompaniment: *an appliance carrying a five-year guarantee; a critic whose views carry a lot of weight.* **18.** To involve necessarily as a condition, consequence, effect, or the like: *The crime carried a five-year sentence.* **19.** To keep in stock; offer for sale: *carry a large selection of china and glass.* **20.** *Mathematics.* To transfer (a number) from one column of digits for inclusion in the calculations of another. **21.** To include in another set of accounts: *carry a loss over to the following year.* **22.** To make up for the deficiencies of (a colleague, for example). **23.** To yield (a crop, for example). **24.** To support or sustain (livestock): *An acre can carry 60 sheep.* **25.** *Golf.* To cover (a distance) or advance beyond (a point or object) in one stroke. **26.** In hunting, to keep and follow (a scent). —*intr.* **1.** To act as a bearer: *She used to fetch and carry for her old aunt.* **2.** To reach; cover a distance or range: *a soprano voice that carries to the back of the hall; guns that carry for 500 feet.* **3.** To be accepted or approved: *The motion carried by a wide margin.* —See Synonyms at **convey.** **—carry away.** To move emotionally or excite greatly: *carried away by his beauty.* **—carry forward. 1.** To progress with: *carried forward the program.* **2.** *Accounting.* To transfer (an entry) to the next column, page, book, or to another account. **—carry off. 1.** To cause the death of: *carried off by a fever.* **2.** To handle or cope with (a situation, for example) successfully. **3.** To win (a prize or award, for example). **—carry through. 1.** To accomplish; complete. **2.** To enable to endure; sustain: *Fortitude carried her through the ordeal.*

~*n., pl.* **carries. 1.** The act or process of carrying. **2. a.** The range of a gun or projectile. **b.** The distance traveled by a ball, especially a golf ball. **3.** *Football.* The act or an instance of rushing with the ball. [Middle English *carien,* from Old North French *carier,* to transport in a vehicle, from *car(re),* vehicle, from Latin *carrus.*]

car·ry·all (kăr'ē-ôl') *n.* **1. a.** A covered one-horse carriage with two seats. **b.** A closed automobile with two lengthwise seats facing each other. **2.** A large bag, basket, or pocketbook.

car·ry·cot (kăr'ē-kŏt') *n. Chiefly British.* A portable bed for a baby, usually made from canvas stretched over a metal frame or occasionally from wickerwork.

carrying charge *n.* The interest charged on the balance owed when paying in installments.

car·ry·ings-on (kăr'ē-ĭngz-ŏn', -ôn') *pl.n.* **1.** Behavior that is regarded as improper or frivolous: *Grandmothers do not generally hold with the carryings-on of the young.* **2.** Noisy or excitable behavior.

carry on *tr.v.* To conduct; continue the process or activities of: *will carry on the business in my absence.* —*intr.v.* **1. a.** To persevere; continue: *carry on in the face of disaster.* **b.** To resume after stopping: *carry on where you left off.* **2.** *Informal.* To have a usually illicit sexual involvement: *Mrs. Brown is carrying on with the mailman.* **3.** To behave in an excited or foolish manner; act hysterically or childishly.

car·ry·on (kăr'ē-ŏn', -ôn') *n.* An item, such as luggage, that is small or compact enough to be carried aboard an airplane by a passenger. **—car·ry·on** *adj.*

carry out *tr.v.* **1.** To put into practice or effect; accomplish. **2.** To follow or obey: *carry out orders.*

car·ry·out (kăr'ē-out') *n.* Food or drink intended to be consumed away from the premises where it is prepared or sold. **—car·ry·out** *adj.*

carry over *tr.v.* **1.** *Accounting.* To transfer (an entry) to another column, page, book, or account. **2.** To continue at another time; put off: *carry over a problem until the next meeting.*

car·ry·o·ver (kăr'ē-ō'vər) *n.* **1.** A part or quantity, as of goods or commodities, left over or held for future use. **2.** *Accounting.* A sum transferred to a new column, page, book, or account.

carse (kärs) *n. Scottish.* An alluvial plain beside a river or an estuary. [Middle English, of obscure origin.]

car·sick (kär'sĭk) *adj.* Suffering nausea from vehicular motion. **—car·sick·ness** *n.*

Car·son (kär'sən), **Christopher,** known as "Kit" (1808–68). U.S. trapper, guide, and Indian agent. An almost legendary figure among the Indian fighters and heroes of the West, he was a guide of John C. Frémont's three expeditions in the 1840's and became a national hero during the Mexican War.

Carson, Rachel Louise (1907–64). U.S. marine and genetic biologist and science writer. Her *The Sea Around Us* (1951) deals with the biology, chemistry, history, and geography of the sea. *Silent Spring* (1962) is a condemnation of the use of pesticides.

Carson City. The capital (since 1864) of Nevada, in the western part of the state. It became important (1859) after the discovery of gold and silver at the Comstock Lode.

cart (kärt) *n.* **1.** A two-wheeled vehicle usually drawn by a horse or other animal and used for transporting goods. **2.** A light, open two-wheeled vehicle pulled by a pony, horse, or dog. **3.** A small, light vehicle moved by hand, as a grocery cart.

~*tr.v.* **carted, carting, carts. 1. a.** To convey in a cart. **b.** To convey laboriously, as in a cart; lug. **2.** To remove or transport (a person or thing) in an unceremonious manner or by force. Often used with *away* or *off*: *He was carted off to jail.* [Middle English *carte, cart,* partly from Old English *cræt,* partly from Old Norse *kartr.*] **—cart·a·ble** *adj.* **—cart·er** *n.*

cart·age (kär'tĭj) *n.* **1.** The act or process of transporting by cart. **2.** The cost of transporting by cart or other means.

Car·ta·ge·na¹ (kär'tə-gā'nə, -jē'-). Capital of the Bolívar department on Colombia's Caribbean coast. The Spanish built a fortified stronghold here (1533) to export precious metals.

Cartagena². A fortified naval base and seaport on the Mediterranean Sea, in the Spanish province of Murcia. The Carthaginian leader Hasdrubal founded it *c.* 225 B.C.

Carte, Richard D'Oyly. See **D'Oyly Carte.**

carte blanche (kärt blänsh') *n.* Unrestricted power to act at one's own discretion; unconditional authorization. [French, "blank card."]

car·tel (kär-tĕl') *n.* **1.** A combination of independent business organizations formed to regulate production, pricing, and marketing of goods by the members. **2.** An official agreement between governments at war, especially one concerning the exchange of prisoners. **3.** In some European countries, a political group united in a common cause; a bloc. [German *Kartell,* from French *cartel,* from Italian *cartello,* diminutive of *carta,* CARD.]

Car·ter (kär'tər), **Howard** (1874–1939). British archaeologist who excavated ancient Egyptian tombs, including that of the pharaoh Tutankhamen (1922–32).

Carter, James Earl, Jr., known as "Jimmy" (1924–). 39th president of the United States (1977–81). A Democrat, he was twice elected senator for Georgia (1962, 1964) and governor of Georgia (1970–74). He was elected president in the wake of the Watergate scandal. After promising a more "open" style of government, he lost popularity because of the failure of his economic measures and the lack of confidence in his social reforms. He was also hurt politically by his handling of the hostage crisis in Iran (November 1979–January 1981). First he appeared to do nothing, then he ordered an abortive mission aimed at rescuing the hostages (April 1980). Eight servicemen were killed and five injured in the raid when a helicopter and cargo plane collided. His main achievements were to cut national energy consumption and to negotiate the Camp David Agreement between Egypt and Israel (1979).

Car·te·sian (kär-tē'zhən) *adj.* **1.** Of or pertaining to Descartes or to the philosophy or methods of Descartes. **2.** Of or forming a Cartesian coordinate.

~*n.* A person who follows the philosophy or methods of Descartes. **—Car·te·sian·ism** *n.*

Cartesian coordinate *n.* A coordinate in a Cartesian coordinate system.

Cartesian coordinate system *n. Mathematics.* **1.** A rectangular coordinate system, usually in two or three dimensions, in which the location of a point in rectangular space is identified by its distance from the mutually perpendicular axes. **2.** A three-dimensional coordinate system in which the coordinates of a point are its distances from each of three intersecting, often mutually perpendicular planes along lines parallel to the intersection of the other two.

Car·thage (kär'thĭj). Ancient city-state in North Africa on the Bay of Tunis, near modern Tunis. Founded by the Phoenicians (9th century B.C.), it became the center of Carthaginian power in the western Mediterranean from the 6th century B.C. Its trading empire included colonies in Senegal and Guinea, and it grew rich on the sale of slaves, ivory, and gold from the tropics of Africa. The three Punic Wars with Rome resulted in the complete destruction of Carthage (146 B.C.). In 44 B.C. Julius Caesar refounded the city, and it became the commercial, cultural, and administrative center of Roman Africa. The Vandals took it (A.D. 439) and made it their capital. Carthage was recaptured by the Byzantines (534), but virtually destroyed by Arabs (698). Only a few Punic and Roman ruins survive. **—Car·tha·gin·i·an** (kär'thə-jĭn'ē-ən) *adj. & n.*

cart·horse (kärt'hôrs') *n.* A large, heavily built horse bred for pulling carts or similar vehicles.

Car·thu·sian (kär-thōō'zhən) *n. Roman Catholic Church.* A member of a contemplative order of monks founded in 1084 in Chartreuse, France, by St. Bruno. **—Car·thu·sian** *adj.*

Car·tier (kär-tyā', kär'tē-ā'), **Jacques** (1491–1557). French explorer. King Francis I of France commissioned him to explore the northern lands of the New World. His explorations of the St. Lawrence River and the surrounding region gave rise to France's future claims to Canada.

Car·ti·er-Bres·son (kär-tyā'brĕ-sôN'), **Henri** (1908–). French photographer and pioneer of photojournalism. He took up photography in 1931 and worked with the film director Jean Renoir (1936–39). Imprisoned by the Nazis (1940–43), he escaped and set up underground photographic units. He is the author of many photographic books, including *The Decisive Moment* (1952).

car·ti·lage (kär'tə-lĭj) *n.* A tough fibrous connective tissue attached at the joints between bones. It is a major constituent of the young vertebrate skeleton that is largely converted to bone with maturation. Also called "gristle." [Latin *cartilāgo* (stem *cartilāgin-*).]

cartilage bone *n.* A bone developed from cartilage. Compare **membrane bone.**

car·ti·lag·i·nous (kär'tə-lăj'ə-nəs) *adj.* **1.** Of or pertaining to cartilage. **2.** Having a skeleton consisting mainly of cartilage.

cartilaginous fish *n.* Any fish of the class Chondrichthyes, which includes the sharks, skates, and rays, having a skeleton entirely or mainly made up of cartilage.

cart·load (kärt′lōd′) *n.* The amount that is or that can be carried in a cart.

car·to·gram (kär′tə-grăm′) *n.* A presentation of statistical data in geographical distribution using lines, dots, and other marks on a map. [French *cartogramme* : *carte,* map, CARD + -GRAM.]

car·tog·ra·phy (kär-tŏg′rə-fē) *n.* The art or technique of making maps or charts. [French *cartographie* : *carte,* map, CARD + -GRAPHY.] —**car·tog·ra·pher** *n.* —**car·to·graph·ic** (kär′tə-grăf′ĭk), **car·to·graph·i·cal** *adj.*

car·to·man·cy (kär′tə-măn′sē) *n.* The telling of fortunes using playing cards, such as the tarot pack. [French *cartomancie* : *carte,* CARD + -*mancie,* -MANCY.]

car·ton (kärt′n) *n.* **1.** *Abbr.* **C., c., ctn.** A cardboard box or other container, especially: **a.** A box closed by flaps on the top or on one end, used for transporting goods. **b.** A container for liquids: *a milk carton.* **2.** The contents of a carton. [French, from Italian *cartone,* pasteboard, from *carta,* CARD.]

car·toon (kär-tōōn′) *n.* **1.** A drawing in a newspaper, magazine, or the like, often accompanied by a caption that depicts a humorous situation or makes a satirical comment on a subject of current public interest. **2.** A preliminary sketch similar in size to the work, as a fresco, mosaic, or tapestry, that is to be copied from it. **3.** An **animated cartoon** *(see).* **4.** A **comic strip** *(see).* [Italian *cartone,* pasteboard, CARTON.] —**car·toon·ist** *n.*

car·touche, car·touch (kär-tōōsh′) *n.* **1.** *Architecture.* A scroll-like tablet used either to provide space for an inscription or for ornamental purposes. **2.** In ancient Egyptian hieroglyphics, an oval or oblong figure that encloses characters expressing the names or epithets of royal or divine personages. **3.** A case containing the combustible materials in some varieties of fireworks. **4.** An elaborate or decorative frame, as a panel on a map for displaying the title and scale. **5.** *Obsolete.* A cartridge. [French, cartridge, from Italian *cartoccio,* from *carta,* paper, card. See **carton.**]

car·tridge (kär′trĭj) *n.* **1. a.** A tubular metal or cardboard-and-metal case containing the propellant powder and primer of small arms ammunition or shotgun shells. **b.** Such a case loaded with shotgun pellets. **c.** Such a case fitted with a projectile, such as a bullet, for use in rifles, small arms, machine guns, or the like. **2. a.** A small modular unit of equipment, especially: **a.** A removable case containing the stylus and electric conversion circuitry in a phonograph pickup. **b.** A cassette for use in tape recorders, video recorders, and the like. **c.** A case with photographic film that can be loaded directly into a camera. **d.** A disposable ink reservoir for a pen. [From earlier *cartage,* variant of French CARTOUCHE (cartridge).]

cartridge belt *n.* A belt for carrying ammunition, with loops or pockets for cartridges or clips of cartridges.

cartridge clip *n.* A metal container or frame for holding cartridges to be loaded into an automatic rifle or pistol.

car·tu·lar·y (kär′chə-lĕr′ē) *n., pl.* -**ies.** Also **char·tu·lar·y** (kär′-). A collection of deeds or charters; especially, a register of titles to all the property of an estate or monastery. [Medieval Latin *c(h)artulārium,* from Latin *chartula,* little paper, diminutive of *charta,* leaf of papyrus. See **card.**]

cart·wheel (kärt′hwēl′) *n.* **1.** The wheel of a cart. **2.** A somersault or handspring in which the body turns over sideways with the arms and legs spread like the spokes of a wheel.

cart·wright (kärt′rīt′) *n.* A person who makes carts.

car·un·cle (kär′ŭng′kəl, kə-rŭng′-) *n.* **1.** A fleshy, naked outgrowth, such as a fowl's wattles. **2.** *Botany.* An excrescence on a seed at or near the hilum. [Obsolete French *caruncule,* from Latin *caruncula,* diminutive of *carō* (stem *carn-*), flesh.] —**ca·run·cu·lar** (kə-rŭng′kyə-lər) *adj.* —**ca·run·cu·late** (kə-rŭng′kyə-lĭt, -lāt′), **ca·run·cu·lat·ed** (-lā′tĭd) *adj.*

Ca·ru·so (kə-rōō′sə), **Enrico** (1873–1921). Italian tenor opera singer who made his debut at the Teatro Nuovo, Naples (1894). His final performance was with the Metropolitan Opera, New York (1920), when he ruptured a blood vessel in his throat while singing. He died of related complications. His most popular roles included Canio in *Pagliacci;* Rodolpho in *La Bohème;* and the Duke in *Rigoletto.*

car·va·crol (kär′və-krôl′, -krŏl′) *n.* A liquid phenol, $C_{10}H_{14}O$, used in flavorings and fungicides. [From New Latin *carvi,* specific epithet of *Carum carvi,* caraway + Latin *acr-,* sharp + -OL.]

carve (kärv) *v.* **carved, carving, carves.** —*tr.* **1. a.** To divide into pieces or slices by cutting: *carve a chicken.* **b.** To divide by parceling out: *carve up an estate.* **2.** To cut into a desired shape; fashion by cutting: *carve the wood into a figure.* **3.** To produce or form by or as if by cutting: *carve initials in the bark; carved out a career.* **4.** To decorate by carving. —*intr.* **1.** To engrave or cut figures as a hobby or trade. **2.** To disjoint, slice, and serve meat or poultry. —*n.* An act or stroke of slicing or carving. [Middle English *kerven, carven,* Old English *ceorfan.*] —**carv·er** *n.*

carvel. Variant of **caravel.**

car·vel-built (kär′vəl-bĭlt′, kär′vĕl′-) *adj.* Designating a boat or ship built with the hull planks lying flush or edge to edge, rather than overlapping. Compare **clinker-built.**

car·vel joint (kär′vəl, -vĕl′) *n.* A joining of wood planks so that they lie flush or edge to edge.

carv·en (kär′vən) *adj.* Produced, formed, or decorated by carving; carved.

Carver (kär′vər), **George Washington** (c. 1864–1943). U.S. bota-

Cartier-Bresson

THE MAN WHO TURNED PHOTOJOURNALISM INTO AN ART FORM
His spontaneous, unposed pictures brought a new realism to photography

Soon after World War II, the French photographer Henri Cartier-Bresson traveled the world with his camera—and the documentary pictures that he took established photojournalism as a creative medium. His subjects were not posed or rehearsed, and he captured public events at their crucial, historical moments. He covered the assassination of the Indian leader Mohandas Gandhi in 1948, and in 1949 he recorded the proclamation in Beijing (Peking) of the People's Republic of China under the leadership of Mao Ze-dong (Tse-t'ung).

Cartier-Bresson was born at Chanteloup in 1908. He studied to be a painter and took up photography when he was 23. His first magazine pictures were published in Paris in 1932. In 1936 he worked as an assistant to the renowned

French film director Jean Renoir. He later made a powerful documentary film about the Spanish Civil War of 1936–39.

Cartier-Bresson wrote, "For me, the camera is a sketch book. It is an instrument of intuition and spontaneity." In *The Decisive Moment,* published in 1952, he explained the meaning and technique of his work. He strives to remain unnoticed while taking a photograph and covers the shiny parts of his Leica camera with black tape so that his subjects will not be distracted. In his 50 years as a photographer he has produced some 10 books of photographs and his work has been exhibited and published throughout the world. His candid pictures of everyday life have been extremely influential in the development of other photographers.

SUNDAY ON THE BANKS OF THE MARNE *Cartier-Bresson's photograph of picnickers in 1938 typifies his unposed pictures of everyday life. He said they were like a diary—"a daily record of images."*

nist, agricultural chemist, and educator. In his laboratory at Tuskegee Institute, Alabama, he produced hundreds of peanut products, including soap, wood stains, and even shaving cream. His research prompted southern farmers to raise peanuts, which became an important cash crop in the region.

carv·ing (kär′vĭng) *n.* **1.** The cutting of material such as wood or stone to form a figure or design. **2.** A figure or design formed by carving.

carving knife *n.* A knife with a long blade for slicing meat.

Car·y (kâr′ē), **(Arthur) Joyce Lunel** (1888–1957). British novelist. His major works, *The Horse's Mouth* (1944) and *Prisoner of Grace* (1952), deal with the classic themes of conflict between the generations, the individual and society, and the artist and the middle classes.

car·y·at·id (kăr′ē-ăt′ĭd) *n., pl.* -**ids** or -**ides** (-ĭ-dēz′). *Architecture.* A supporting column sculptured in the form of a woman in classical Greek dress. Compare **telamon.** [Latin *Caryātidēs* (plural), from Greek *Karuatidēs,* caryatids, priestesses of Artemis at *Karuai,* village in Laconia.]

caryo-. Variant of **karyo-.**

car·y·op·sis (kăr′ē-ŏp′sĭs) *n., pl.* -**ses** (-sēz) or -**sides** (-sĭ-dēz′) *Botany.* A one-seeded dry fruit, such as a grain of barley or wheat, having its outer coat fused to the seed coat. [New Latin : CARY(O)- + -OPSIS.]

ca·sa·ba, cas·sa·ba (kə-sä′bə) *n.* A variety of **winter melon** *(see)* having a yellow rind and sweet, whitish flesh. [From *Kasaba,* former name of Turgutlu, Turkey.]

Ca·sa·blan·ca (kăs′ə-blăngk′ə, käz′-). *Arabic* **Dar-al-Beida** (där-ăl′bā′də). Seaport on the Atlantic coast of Morocco. It was founded by the Portuguese in the early 16th century. Taken by the French in 1907, it remained for many years a center of French influence in Africa. It is now Morocco's largest city.

Ca·sals (kə-sälz′), **Pablo** (1876–1973). Spanish cellist, conductor, and composer. He founded the Barcelona Orchestra (1919), but left Spain in 1939 after Franco came to power. He was acclaimed as one of the greatest interpreters of Bach's unaccompanied cello suites and the cello concertos of Dvořák, Elgar, and Schumann.

Ca·sa·no·va (kăz′ə-nō′və, kăs′-), **Giovanni Giacomo, Chevalier de Seingalt** (1725–98). Italian adventurer and legendary lover. After being expelled from a seminary for immoral conduct, he lived in many European cities and worked as a violinist, a spy, a writer, and a librarian. His adventures are chronicled in his memoirs.

Casanova *n.* An ostentatiously promiscuous man; libertine.

casava. Variant of **cassava.**

Cas·bah (kăz′bä′, käz′-) *n.* Also **Kas·bah.** **1.** The citadel and palace of a sovereign in northern Africa. **2.** The native quarter in any of several cities in northern Africa. [French, from dialectal Arabic *qaṣbah*, from Arabic *qaṣabah*, fortress.]

cas·cade (kăs-kād′) *n.* **1. a.** A waterfall or a series of small waterfalls over steep rocks. **b.** Anything that falls loosely or freely: *a cascade of flowers.* **2.** *Physics.* An analogous structure or phenomenon, as: **a.** A cosmic-ray shower generated by the successive alternate production of electron–positron pairs by pair production and of photons by bremsstrahlung, continuing until the energy of each single particle is below the threshold for pair production. **b.** A process occurring in an electrical discharge in a gas by which at least one member of an ion pair is accelerated by the field to sufficiently high energy to produce another pair of ions in a collision. **c.** An **avalanche** *(see)*, as in a Geiger counter. **3.** *Electricity.* A series of components or networks, the output of each of which serves as the input for the next. **4.** *Chemistry.* A series of compressed gases of successively lower boiling points, the expansion of which produces successively lower temperatures. This arrangement is used to liquefy gases.
~*intr.v.* **cascaded, -cading, -cades.** To fall from one level to another in a continuous series; fall loosely or freely. [French, from Italian *cascata,* from *cascare,* to fall, from Vulgar Latin *casicāre* (unattested), from Latin *cadere* (past participle *cāsus*).]

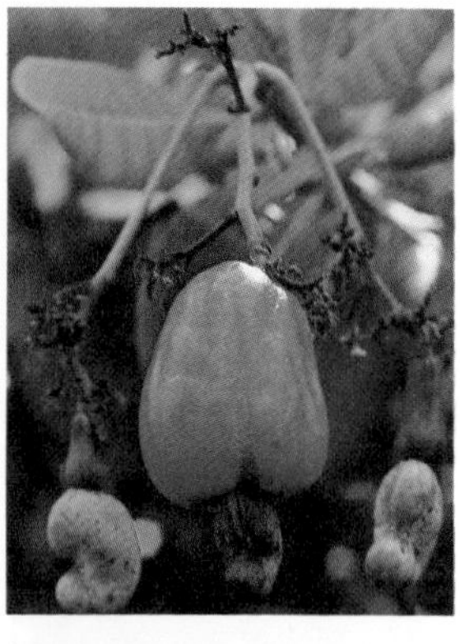
cashew *The edible kidney-shaped nuts grow beneath the reddish, fleshy fruit of the cashew tree, a small evergreen native to tropical America.*

Cascade Range. Mountain chain, *c.* 1,125 kilometers (700 miles) long, extending from southern British Columbia to northern California, where it joins the Sierra Nevada. Many of its highest peaks, including Mt. Ranier, are volcanic cones covered with snowfields and glaciers.

cas·car·a (kăs-kăr′ə) *n.* **1.** The cascara buckthorn. **2.** Cascara sagrada. [Spanish *cáscara,* bark, from *cascar,* to break, break off, from Vulgar Latin *quassicāre* (unattested), from Latin *quassāre,* from *quatere* (past participle *quassus*), to shake.]

cascara buckthorn *n.* A shrub or tree, *Rhamnus purshiana,* of northwestern North America, the bark of which is the source of cascara sagrada.

cascara sa·gra·da (sə-grä′də) *n.* The dried bark of the cascara buckthorn, used as a stimulant, cathartic, and laxative.

cas·ca·ril·la (kăs′kə-rĭl′ə) *n.* **1.** A shrub, *Croton eluteria,* of the West Indies, having bitter, aromatic bark. **2.** The bark of this shrub, used as a tonic. In this sense, also called "cascarilla bark." [Spanish, diminutive of *cáscara,* bark. See **cascara.**]

case[1] (kās) *n.* **1.** An instance or exemplification of the existence or occurrence of something. **2. a.** An occurrence of disease or disorder: *He had a bad case of pneumonia.* **b.** A client, as of a doctor, psychiatrist, lawyer, or social worker. **3. a.** A particular set of circumstances or state of affairs: *will make an exception in this case.* **b.** The actual situation; the truth: *It simply isn't the case.* **4.** A set of circumstances subject to or requiring investigation, especially for a formal or official body: *a detective's most famous case.* **5.** A set of reasons, arguments, or supporting facts offered in justification of a statement, action, situation, or thing: *the case for legalized abortion.* **6.** A question or problem; a matter: *a case of honor.* **7.** *Law.* **a.** An action or suit. **b.** Just grounds for legal action. **c.** The facts or evidence offered in support of a claim. **8.** *Informal.* A peculiar or eccentric person. **9.** *Linguistics.* **a.** The syntactic relationship of a noun, pronoun, or adjective to the other words of a sentence, indicated in inflected languages typically by endings and in noninflected languages by word order or prepositions. **b.** The form or position of a word that indicates this relationship. **c.** Such forms, positions, or relationships collectively. —See Synonyms at **example.** **—in any case.** Regardless of what occurred or will occur. **—in case. 1.** As a preventive measure: *I took along a sandwich just in case.* **2.** If. **—in case of.** In the event of; if there should happen: *In case of fire, sound the alarm.* [Middle English *cas,* an occurrence, from Old French, from Latin *cāsus,* fall, event, occurrence, from the past participle of *cadere,* to fall.]

case[2] *n.* **1. a.** A container or receptacle. **b.** A suitcase. **2. a.** A decorative or protective covering or cover. **b.** A glass box for exhibiting items of interest; showcase. **3.** *Abbr.* **C., c., cs.** A box with its contents, especially when of a standard quantity; for example, a case of wine usually contains 12 bottles. **4.** A set or pair, as of pistols. **5.** The frame or framework of a window, door, or stairway. **6.** *Printing.* A shallow, compartmented tray for storing type or type matrices. **7.** A cover of stiff boards ready to be attached to a book.
~*tr.v.* **cased, casing, cases. 1.** To put into, cover, or protect with or as if with a case. **2.** *Slang.* To examine carefully, as in planning a crime: *cased the bank before the robbery.* [Middle English, from Old North French *casse,* from Latin *capsa,* chest, case.]

ca·se·ate (kā′sē-āt′) *intr.v.* **-ated, -ating, -ates.** To undergo caseation. [Latin *cāseus,* CHEESE.]

ca·se·a·tion (kā′sē-ā′shən) *n.* **1.** The production of cheese from casein in the coagulation of milk. **2.** The degeneration of dead bodily tissue into a cheeselike substance. [From CASEATE.]

case·book (kās′bo͝ok′) *n.* **1.** A book containing a record of medical or legal cases. **2.** A book containing source materials in a specific area that is used as a reference and in teaching.

case ending *n.* A letter or letters added to the stem of a noun, pronoun, or adjective in inflected languages to indicate case.

case·hard·en (kās′härd′n) *tr.v.* **-ened, -ening, -ens. 1.** To harden the surface of (iron or steel) by high-temperature shallow infusion of carbon followed by quenching. **2.** To harden the spirit or emotions of; make callous. [From CASE (covering).]

case history *n.* An organized set of facts relevant to the development of an individual or group under study or treatment, especially in social work, psychiatry, or medicine.

ca·sein (kā′sēn′, -sē-ĭn) *n.* A white, tasteless, odorless protein, precipitated from milk by rennin. It is the basis of cheese and is used to make plastics, adhesives, paints, and foods. [Probably French *caséine* : Latin *cāseus,* CHEESE + -IN.]

case knife *n.* **1.** A knife kept in a sheath or case. **2.** A table knife.

case law *n.* Law based on judicial decision and precedent rather than statute.

case load *n.* The number of cases for which a social worker, doctor, or similar professional person is responsible at any one time.

case·mate (kās′māt′) *n.* *Military.* **1.** On a warship, a fortified enclosure for artillery. **2.** A recess in a rampart with openings, or embrasures, from which artillery can be fired. [Old French, from Italian *casamatta,* perhaps from Greek *khasmata,* plural of *khasma,* gap, CHASM.] **—case·mat·ed** *adj.*

case·ment (kās′mənt) *n.* **1. a.** A window frame that opens outward or inward by means of hinges along one side. **b.** A window with such frames. **2.** A case or covering. [Middle English *casement*†.] **—case·ment·ed** *adj.*

Case·ment (kās′mənt), **Sir Roger David** (1864–1916). British consular official and Irish nationalist. He retired to Ireland in 1912, and with the outbreak of World War I he attempted to obtain German help for the Irish nationalist cause. Caught returning to Ireland in a German submarine, he was convicted for treason and hanged.

ca·se·ous (kā′sē-əs) *adj.* Resembling cheese. [Latin *cāseus,* CHEESE.]

ca·sern, ca·serne (kə-zûrn′) *n.* A military barracks. [French *caserne,* from Old French, small room for the night watch, from Old Provençal *cazerna,* group of four persons, from Vulgar Latin *quaderna* (unattested), from Latin *quater,* four times.]

Ca·ser·ta (kə-zĕr′tə). A market town in southern Italy, and capital of Caserta province. In the 19th century it was the center of operations for Giuseppe Garibaldi's campaigns for the unification of Italy. The German forces in Italy in World War II surrendered to the Allied Command at Caserta (1945).

case shot *n.* **1.** A **canister** *(see).* **2.** The shot in a canister. **3.** A shrapnel shell.

case study *n.* A detailed analysis of an individual or group, especially as a model of medical, psychological, or social phenomena.

case·work (kās′wûrk′) *n.* The part of a social worker's duties dealing with the problems of a particular case. **—case·work·er** *n.*

case·worm (kās′wûrm′) *n.* An insect larva, such as a caddis worm, that constructs a protective case around its body.

cash[1] (kăsh) *n.* **1.** Ready money; currency or coins. **2.** Payment for goods or services in money or by check, as opposed to credit.
~*tr.v.* **cashed, cashing, cashes.** To exchange for or convert into ready money: *cash a check.* **—cash in. 1.** To withdraw from a venture by or as if by settling one's account. **2.** *Slang.* To die. **—cash in on.** To take advantage of. [Old French *casse,* money box, CASE (box).]

cash[2] *n., pl.* **cash.** Any of various Oriental coins of small denomination; especially, a copper and lead coin with a square hole in its center. [Portuguese *caixa,* from Tamil *kācu,* a small copper coin, from Sanskrit *karṣa*†, a certain weight.]

cash-and-car·ry (kăsh′ən-kăr′ē) *n.* The practice of selling for cash on the spot and usually removal by the purchaser.
~*adj.* Sold in accordance with the policy of cash-and-carry.

cash·book (kăsh′bo͝ok′) *n.* A book in which a record of cash receipts and expenditures is kept.

cash·box (kăsh′bŏks′) *n.* A receptacle, especially a compartmented metal box with a lid, in which to keep cash.

cash crop *n.* A crop grown especially for sale, often to another country, and usually constituting an important source of income.

cash discount *n.* *Abbr.* **c.d.** A reduction in the price of an item for sale allowed if payment is made within a stipulated period.

cash·ew (kăsh′o͞o, kə-sho͞o′) *n.* **1.** A widely cultivated tropical American evergreen tree, *Anacardium occidentale,* bearing kidney-shaped nuts that protrude from a fleshy receptacle. **2.** The nut of this tree, edible when roasted. In this sense, also called "cashew nut." [Portuguese *cajú, acajú,* from Tupi *acajú.*]

cash flow *n.* The movement of money into and out of a business. **—cash-flow** *adj.*

cash·ier[1] (kă-shîr′) *n.* **1.** The person in a bank or business concern in charge of paying and receiving money. **2.** An employee whose major function is to handle cash transactions for any of various business operations, such as a restaurant or supermarket. [Dutch *cassier,* from French *caissier,* from *caisse,* money box, from Old French *casse,* CASE (box).]

cashier[2] *tr.v.* **-shiered, -shiering, -shiers.** To dismiss from a position of command or responsibility, as in the armed forces, especially for disciplinary reasons. [Dutch *casseren,* from Old French *casser,* to discharge, annul, from Latin *quassāre,* to shake, break in pieces, from *quassus,* past participle of *quatere,* to shake.]

cashier's check *n.* A check drawn by a bank on its own funds and signed by the bank's cashier.

cash·mere (kăzh′mîr′, kăsh′-) *n.* **1.** Fine, downy wool growing beneath the outer hair of the Cashmere goat. **2.** A soft fabric made of wool from this goat or of similar fibers.

Cashmere. See **Kashmir.**

Cashmere goat *n.* Also **Kashmir goat.** A goat native to the Himalayan regions of India and Tibet and prized for its wool.

cash register *n.* A machine that tabulates the amount of sales transactions, displays the amount of each, has a tape for making a permanent and cumulative record of them, and has a drawer in which cash may be kept.

cas·ing (kā′sĭng) *n.* **1.** Something that encases; an outer cover. **2.** The cleaned intestines of cattle, sheep, or pigs used for encasing processed meat. **3.** The frame or framework for a window or door. **4.** A metal pipe or tube used as a lining for water, oil, or gas wells. **5.** The outer covering of a pneumatic tire.

ca·si·no (kə-sē′nō) *n., pl.* **-nos. 1.** A public room or building for entertainment, especially for gambling. **2.** Variant of **cassino. 3.** A summer or country house in Italy. [Italian, diminutive of *casa,* house, from Latin *casa*†, hut, cottage.]

cask (kăsk, käsk) *n. Abbr.* **ck. 1.** A barrel of any size. **2.** The quantity contained in a barrel. [Spanish *casco,* helmet, cask, perhaps from *cascar,* to crack, break, from Vulgar Latin *quassicāre* (unattested), to shake, break, from Latin *quassāre.*]

cas·ket (kăs′kĭt, kä′skĭt) *n.* **1.** A small case or chest for jewels or other valuables. **2.** A coffin.
—*tr.v.* **-keted, -keting, -kets.** To enclose in a casket. [Middle English, from Old French *cassette.* See **cassette.**]

Cas·par (kăs′pər). Also **Gas·par** (găs-pär′). One of the three Magi who traveled to see the infant Jesus.

Cas·par·i·an strip (kă-spăr′ē-ən, kă-spä′rē-ən) *n. Botany.* A band of thickening in the walls of certain cells in the plant stem surrounding the conducting tissues, forming a ring impervious to liquids and gases. Also called "Casparian band."

Cas·pi·an Sea (kăs′pē-ən). The world's largest inland sea. It lies between southeast Europe and Asia and covers 393,898 square kilometers (152,084 square miles). It is slowly shrinking due to dam construction on the Volga River, which feeds the lake. Its fisheries produce the world's finest caviar.

casque (kăsk) *n.* **1.** A helmet or other piece of armor for the head. **2.** *Zoology.* A helmetlike structure or protuberance. [French, from Spanish *casco,* CASK.] **—casqued** (kăskt) *adj.*

cassaba. Variant of **casaba.**

Cas·san·dra[1] (kə-săn′drə). *Greek Mythology.* A daughter of Priam, King of Troy, endowed with the gift of prophecy but fated by Apollo never to be believed.

Cassandra[2] *n.* A prophet of doom, especially one whose prophecies go unheeded. [After CASSANDRA.]

cas·sa·reep (kăs′ə-rēp′) *n.* The boiled juice of the cassava root, used as a condiment. [Earlier *casserepo,* of Cariban origin.]

cas·sa·tion (kă-sā′shən, kə-) *n.* Abrogation; annulment. [Middle English *cassacioun,* from Old French *cassation,* from *casser,* to annul. See **cashier** (dismiss).]

Cas·satt (kə-săt′), **Mary** (1845–1926). U.S. painter. She is noted for her studies of mothers and their children and was associated with the French impressionist movement.

cas·sa·va, ca·sa·va (kə-sä′və) *n.* **1.** Any of various tropical American plants of the genus *Manihot,* having a large starchy root. Also called "manioc." **2.** A starch derived from the root of the cassava, used to make tapioca and as a staple food in the tropics. [Spanish *cazabe,* cassava, from Taino *caçábi.*]

Cas·se·grain·i·an telescope (kăs′ə-grā′nē-ən) *n.* A reflecting telescope in which a concave primary mirror reflects incident light to a convex secondary mirror that in turn reflects the light back through a central hole in the primary mirror onto the focal plane. [After N. *Cassegrain,* 17th-century French physician, who invented it.]

Cassel. See **Kassel.**

cas·se·role (kăs′ə-rōl′) *n.* **1.** A dish, usually of earthenware, glass, or cast iron, in which food is both baked and served. **2.** Food prepared and served in such a dish. **3.** *Chemistry.* A small-handled, deep porcelain crucible used for heating and evaporating.
—*tr.v.* **casseroled, -roling, -roles.** To cook in a casserole. [French, saucepan, from Old French, from *casse,* ladle, dripping pan, from Old Provençal *cassa,* from Medieval Latin *cattia,* dipper, from Greek *kuathion,* small ladle, diminutive of *kuathos*†, ladle.]

cas·sette (kə-sĕt′, kă-) *n.* **1.** A case containing reeled magnetic tape, a pickup reel, and guide and feed mechanisms that is used instead of separate reels in certain tape recorders, tape players, and video recorders. **2.** A lightproof camera cartridge, for daylight loading of photographic film. [French, small box, from Old French, diminutive of *casse,* CASE (box).]

cas·sia (kăsh′ə) *n.* **1.** Any of various chiefly tropical trees, shrubs, and plants of the genus *Cassia,* having compound leaves, usually yellow flowers, and long pods. See **senna. 2.** A tree, *Cinnamomum cassia,* of tropical Asia, having bark similar to cinnamon but of inferior quality. **3.** The bark of *Cinnamomum cassia,* used as a spice. In this sense, also called "cassia bark." [Middle English *cassia,* Old English *cassia,* from Latin *cas(s)ia,* a kind of plant, from Greek *kas(s)ia,* from Hebrew *kesi'ah,* bark resembling cinnamon.]

cassia oil *n.* An oil derived from the bark of the tree *Cinnamomum cassia* and used in medicine and as a flavor.

cas·si·mere (kăz′ə-mîr′, kăs′-) *n.* A twilled fabric, **kerseymere** *(see).* [From *Cassimere,* variant of KASHMIR.]

Cas·si·ni's division (kə-sē′nēz) *n.* A gap 2,500 miles across in the ring structure of Saturn. The Voyager missions have shown that it contains some ring particles that themselves are arranged in ring formations. [After Gian Domenico *Cassini* (1625–1712), Italian astronomer.]

cas·si·no, ca·si·no (kə-sē′nō) *n.* A card game for two to four players in which cards on the table are matched by cards in the hand. [From CASINO.]

Cas·si·no (kə-sē′nō). Town in Latium, central Italy. During World War II the town and the Benedictine monastery of Monte Cassino were destroyed (1944).

Cas·si·o·pe·ia (kăs′ē-ə-pē′ə) *n.* A W-shaped constellation in the Northern Hemisphere near Camelopardalis and Cepheus.

Cas·sir·er (kə-sîr′ər, kä-), **Ernst** (1874–1945). German philosopher. Primarily a Kantian, he was concerned with concept formation and the mind's functions as they pertain to cultural values. *The Philosophy of Symbolic Forms* (translated 1953–57) is his major work.

cas·sis (kə-sēs′, kă-) *n.* **1.** A European bush, *Ribes nigrum,* that bears black currants. **2.** A cordial made from the berries of the cassis. [French, black currant.]

cas·sit·er·ite (kə-sĭt′ə-rīt′) *n.* A red-brown or black mineral, SnO_2, that is the chief ore of tin. Also called "tinstone." [French *casitérite,* from Greek *kassiteros,* tin, from Elamite *kassi-ti-ra,* "coming from the land of the Kassi," an Elamite people.]

Cas·sius Lon·gi·nus (kăsh′əs lŏn-jī′nəs), **Gaius** (died 42 B.C.). Roman general and politician. He was a leading member of the conspiracy to assassinate Julius Caesar. After the defeat of the Republican forces at Philippi, he committed suicide.

Cas·si·ve·lau·nus (kăs′ĭ-və-lô′nəs). King of the Catuvellauni, a people from north of the Thames River who temporarily resisted Julius Caesar's invasion of southeast Britain (54 B.C.) but finally agreed on peace terms with the Romans.

cas·sock (kăs′ək) *n.* A long garment, usually black, reaching to the feet and worn by members of the clergy, choristers, and others assisting in church services. [Old French *casaque,* from Persian *kazagand*†, padded jacket.]

cas·sou·let (kăs′ə-lā′) *n.* A stew originating in France made of beans, sausages, and goose, pork, or duck. [French, diminutive of dialectal *cassolo,* CASSEROLE (saucepan).]

cas·so·war·y (kăs′ə-wĕr′ē) *n., pl.* **-ies.** Any of several large, flightless birds of the genus *Casuarius,* of northern Australia, New Guinea, and adjacent islands, having a large, bony projection on the top of the head, coarse dark plumage, and a brightly colored head, neck, and wattles. [Malay *kĕsuari.*]

cast (kăst, käst) *v.* **cast, casting, casts.** —*tr.* **1.** To throw, especially with violence or force; hurl; toss; fling. **2.** To throw off or away. **3.** To shed; molt. **4.** To throw forth or drop (a fishing net or anchor, for example). **5. a.** To throw to the ground, as in wrestling. **b.** To overthrow; defeat. **6.** To put or place, especially with haste or violence. **7.** To throw aside; dismiss; discard: *cast one's doubts aside.* **8.** To deposit or register (a vote). **9.** To turn or direct (one's eyes). **10.** To cause (light, for example) to fall upon or over something or in a certain direction. **11.** *Archaic.* To bestow; confer. Used with *upon.* **12. a.** To draw (lots). **b.** To throw (dice). **13.** To express, utter, or give rise to (doubt or criticism, for example): *cast aspersions on his ability.* **14.** To cause (hounds) to scatter and circle in search of a lost scent. **15. a.** To choose actors for (a play or film). **b.** To assign a certain role to (an actor). **c.** To assign an actor to (a part). **16. a.** To form (liquid metal or plaster, for example) into a particular shape by pouring into a mold. **b.** To produce (an object) in this way. **17.** To arrange in some system. **18.** To contrive; formulate: *cast a spell.* **19.** To calculate or compute; add up (a column of figures). Often used with *up.* **20.** To calculate astrologically: *cast a horoscope.* **21.** To warp; twist. **22.** *Printing.* To stereotype or electroplate. **23.** *Nautical.* To turn (a ship); change to the opposite tack. —*intr.* **1.** To throw; especially, to throw out a lure or bait at the end of a fishing line. **2. a.** To add a column of figures; make calculations. **b.** To calculate horoscopes, tides, or the like. **3.** To receive form or shape in a mold. **4.** To spread out and search for a lost scent. Used of hunting hounds. **5.** *Nautical.* **a.** To veer to leeward from a former course; fall off. **b.** To put about; tack. **6.** To choose the actors for a play, film, or the like. **7.** To become warped. —See Synonyms at **throw. —cast about. 1.** To search or look for. **2.** To devise means; contrive; scheme. **—cast back.** To refer or direct to something past: *cast your mind back to last summer.* **—cast down.** To make dejected or disappointed. **—cast on.** To make the first row of stitches in knitting. **—cast out.** To drive out by force; expel.
—*n.* **1. a.** The act of casting or throwing. **b.** The distance thrown. **2. a.** The throwing of a fishing line or net into the water. **b.** The line or net thrown. **c.** *Chiefly British.* The leader with flies or baited hooks attached. **3. a.** A throw of dice. **b.** The number thrown. **c.** A stroke of fortune or fate; one's lot. **4. a.** A slight squint in the eye. **b.** A turning of the eye; a glance in a particular direction. **5.** A quantity or thing thrown off, out, or away, such as the mass of waste and earth excreted by an earthworm, the skin shed by an insect, or a mass of feathers, bones, and other matter ejected from the crop of an owl. **6. a.** The addition of a column of figures; a calculation. **b.** A conjecture or forecast. **7. a.** The act of casting or founding. **b.** The amount of molten material poured into a mold at a single operation. **c.** Something formed by this means. **8. a.** An

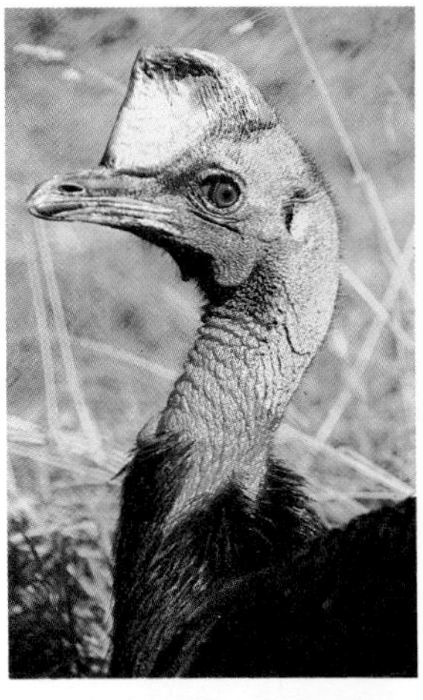

cassowary *A close relative of the emu, the cassowary—of which there are several species—is a flightless bird found in Australia and New Guinea. It can grow up to 150 centimeters (5 feet) tall and has long powerful legs with sharp claws. This is* Casuarius unappendiculatus.

PRONUNCIATION KEY

ă, pat; ā, pay; âr, care;
ä, father, are; b, bib;
ch, church; d, deed; ĕ, pet;
ē, be; f, fife; g, gag; h, hat;
hw, which; ĭ, pit; ī, pie;
îr, pier; j, judge; k, kick;
l, lid, needle; m, mum;
n, no, sudden; ng, thing;
ŏ, pot; ō, toe; ô, paw, for;
oi, noise; ou, out; ŏŏ, book;
ōō, boot; p, pop; r, roar;
s, sauce; sh, ship, dish;
t, tight; th, thin, path;
th, this, bathe; ŭ, cut; ûr, fur;
v, valve; w, with; y, yes;
z, zebra, size; zh, vision;
ə, about, item, edible,
gallop, circus, peaceful

IN FOREIGN WORDS:

à, *Fr.* ami; œ, *Fr.* feu, *Ger.* schön; ü, *Fr.* tu, *Ger.* über;
KH, *Ger.* ich, *Scot.* loch;
N, *Fr.* bon; y′, *Fr.* Compiègne

STRESS MARKS:

Primary stress: ′
in·cite′ (ĭn-sīt′)
Secondary stress: ′
in′sight′ (ĭn′sīt′)

impression formed in a mold or matrix; a mold. **b.** *Geology.* A three-dimensional replica or solidified impression, as of ripple marks or footprints; especially, a fossil formed by a mineral substance that has filled a hole left by an object, such as a shell, that has been dissolved out of a rock or earth mass. **9.** The form in which something is made or constructed; an arrangement; a disposition. **10.** The actors in a play, film, or the like. **11.** A rigid dressing, usually made of gauze and plaster of Paris, for immobilizing a broken bone, an arthritic joint, or part or all of the spine. Also called "plaster cast." **12. a.** A slight trace of color. **b.** A tinge or shade of any quality. **13.** Outward form or aspect; appearance. **14.** A sort; a type. **15.** An inclination; a tendency. **16.** A distortion or twist. **17.** A pair of hawks released by a falconer at one time. **18.** The circling of hounds to pick up a scent. [Middle English *casten,* to throw, from Old Norse *kasta†.*]

cas·ta·nets (kăs′tə-něts′) *pl.n.* A pair of slightly concave shells of ivory or hardwood, held in the palm of the hand by a connecting cord over the thumb and clapped together with the fingers as a rhythmical accompaniment to dancing. [Spanish *castañeta,* from *castaña,* chestnut, from Latin *castanea,* CHESTNUT.]

cast away *tr.v.* **1.** To shipwreck; strand. Usually used in the passive. **2.** To throw away; squander.

cast·a·way (kăst′ə-wā′, käst′-) *n.* **1.** One who has been shipwrecked. **2.** An outcast. —**cast·a·way** *adj.*

caste (kăst, käst) *n.* **1.** One of the four major hereditary classes into which Hindu society is divided. Each caste is distinctly separated from the others by restrictions placed upon occupation and marriage. See **Brahman, Kshatriya, Vaisya, Sudra. 2.** Any social class separated from others by distinctions of hereditary rank, profession, or the like. **3.** A social system or principle of organization based on these distinctions. Also used adjectively: *a caste system.* **4.** The social position or status conferred by such a system: *lose caste.* **5.** *Zoology.* In social insects, any of the various kinds of specialized individuals, such as drones or workers. [Spanish and Portuguese *casta,* caste, race, breed, from the feminine of *casto,* pure, chaste, from Latin *castus.*]

Cas·tel Gan·dol·fo (käs-těl′ gän-dôl′fō). Village on the shore of Lake Albano, central Italy, where the pope has his summer residence.

cas·tel·lan (kăs′tə-lən) *n.* The governor or keeper of a castle. [Middle English *castelain,* from Norman French, from Latin *castellānus,* "of a castle," from *castellum,* CASTLE.]

cas·tel·lat·ed (kăs′tə-lā′tĭd) *adj.* Furnished with turrets and battlements in the style of a castle. [Medieval Latin *castellātus,* past participle of *castellāre,* to fortify as a castle, from Latin *castellum,* CASTLE.] —**cas·tel·la·tion** *n.*

cast·er (kăs′tər, kä′stər) *n.* Also **cas·tor** (for senses 2, 3). **1.** A person or thing that casts. **2. a.** A small container, as of silver or glass, having a perforated top and used for sprinkling sugar or spices. **b.** A stand, often rotating, for holding condiment containers such as casters and cruets. **3.** A small wheel on a swivel attached to the underside of a piece of furniture or other heavy object to make it easier to move.

caster sugar *n. Chiefly British.* A very finely granulated white sugar.

cas·ti·gate (kăs′tə-gāt′) *tr.v.* **-gated, -gating, -gates. 1.** To punish or chastise. **2.** To criticize severely. —See Synonyms at **punish.** [Latin *castīgāre,* to correct, punish : *castus,* pure + *agere,* to do, make.] —**cas·ti·ga·tion** *n.* —**cas·ti·ga·tor** *n.*

Cas·ti·glio·ne (kä′stē-lyō′nə), **Baldassare** (1478–1529). Italian courtier, writer, and humanist. He is best known for *Il Cortegiano* (1528), which describes the perfect courtier.

Cas·tile (kăs-tēl′). *Spanish* **Cas·til·la** (kä-stēl′yä). Region in the high plateau of central Spain. Stretching from the Bay of Biscay in the north to Sierra Morena in the south, it became an independent kingdom in 1035. In 1230 it joined the kingdom of León, and in 1479 after the marriage of Isabella of Castile and Ferdinand II of Aragon, the nucleus of modern Spain was established. The name Castile probably derives from the number of castles that were built here against the Moorish invasions.

Cas·tile soap (kăs-tēl′) *n.* Also **castile soap.** A fine, hard, white, odorless soap made with olive oil and sodium hydroxide.

Cas·til·ian (kăs-tĭl′yən) *n.* **1.** The dialect of Spanish spoken in Castile, now the standard and official form of the Spanish language in Spain. **2.** A native or inhabitant of Castile. —**Cas·til·ian** *adj.*

cast·ing (kăs′tĭng, kä′stĭng) *n.* **1.** The act or process of one that casts. **2.** That which is cast in a mold, as a metal piece. **3.** That which is cast off or out, as skin or earth excreted by worms; a cast.

casting vote *n.* The vote of a presiding officer in an assembly or committee, given to decide a question when the votes of the members are tied.

cast iron *n.* A hard, brittle nonmalleable iron-carbon alloy containing 2.0 to 4.5 percent carbon, 0.5 to 3 percent silicon, and lesser amounts of sulfur, manganese, and phosphorus.

cast-i·ron (kăst′ī′ərn, käst′-) *adj.* **1.** Made of cast iron. **2.** Rigid; inflexible: *a cast-iron rule.* **3.** Tough; resilient: *a cast-iron stomach.* **4.** Unquestionable; indisputable: *a cast-iron alibi.*

cas·tle (kăs′əl, kä′səl) *n.* **1.** A fortified building or group of buildings designed to defend a town, route, or territory, especially in medieval Europe. **2.** A former stronghold of this kind converted to residential use; a mansion. **3.** A place that provides security or refuge; a stronghold. **4. a.** A small defensive tower on the deck of a medieval warship. Compare **forecastle. b.** A small tower carried on

the back of an elephant in war. **5.** *Chess.* The rook *(see).* —**castle in the air** or **in Spain.** An aspiration that is unlikely to be realized; daydream.

~*v.* **castled, -tling, -tles.** —*tr.* **1.** To place in or as if in a castle. **2.** *Chess.* To move (the king) from his own square two squares to one side and then, in the same move, bring the rook from that side to the square immediately past the king. —*intr. Chess.* To move the king and rook by castling. [Middle English *castel,* from Old English *castel,* from Late Latin *castellum,* village, from Latin *castellum,* castle, diminutive of *castrum,* fortified place.]

cas·tled (kăs′əld, kä′səld) *adj.* Castellated; fortified.

Cas·tle·reagh (kăs′əl-rā′), **Robert Stewart, Viscount,** also called "2nd Marquis of Londonderry" (1769–1822). British statesman. As the Irish chief secretary he was able to quell the 1798 rebellion and form a political union with Great Britain in 1800, thereby protecting Ireland from the threat of French invasion.

cast off *tr.v.* **1.** To discard or reject. **2.** To set loose; especially, to detach (a boat) from its moorings. **3.** To estimate the space (a manuscript) will occupy when set into type. **4.** To loop (a knitted stitch or stitches) over the next, thus leaving a short finished edge. —*intr.v.* **1.** To finish the last row in a strip of knitting by looping each stitch in turn over the next. **2.** To detach a boat from its moorings.

cast-off (kăst′ôf′, -ŏf′, käst′-) *adj.* Discarded; rejected: *The little boy hated wearing his big brother's cast-off clothes.*

cast-off (kăst′ôf′, -ŏf′, käst′-) *n.* **1.** Someone or something that has been discarded, especially an item of clothing. **2.** *Printing.* A calculation of the amount of space a manuscript will occupy when set into type.

cas·tor¹ (kăs′tər, kä′stər) *n.* **1.** An oily, brown, odorous substance obtained from glands in the groin of the beaver and used as a perfume fixative. **2.** A beaver hat. [Middle English, beaver, from Latin, from Greek *kastōr,* beaver.]

castor². Variant of **caster.**

Cas·tor (kăs′tər, kä′stər) *n.* A double star in the constellation Gemini, the brightest star in the group, approximately 46 light-years from Earth.

Castor and Pol·lux (pŏl′əks). *Greek Mythology.* The twin sons of Leda, one by Tydareus, the other by Zeus. They were transformed by Zeus into the constellation Gemini so that they would not be separated. Also called "Dioscuri."

castor bean *n.* **1.** The castor-oil plant. **2.** The very poisonous seed of the castor bean.

castor oil *n.* A colorless or yellowish oil extracted from castor-oil plant seeds and used as a laxative and a fine lubricant. [Probably from a mistaken connection with the substance CASTOR.]

cas·tor-oil plant (kăs′tər-oil′, kä′stər-) *n.* A large evergreen plant, *Ricinus communis,* native to tropical Africa and Asia, with lobed, bronze- or purple-flushed leaves, grown for ornament and for the commercial extraction of castor oil from its poisonous seeds.

cas·trate (kăs′trāt′) *tr.v.* **-trated, -trating, -trates. 1.** To remove the testicles of; geld. **2.** To remove the ovaries of; spay. **3.** To deprive of strength or vigor. **4.** To bowdlerize. [Latin *castrāre.*] —**cas·tra·tion** *n.*

cas·tra·to (kä-strä′tō) *n., pl.* **-ti** (-tē) or **-tos.** A male singer castrated in boyhood so as to retain a soprano or alto voice. [Italian, "castrated (one)."]

Cas·tries (kä-strē, käs′trēs′). Capital and the chief port of St. Lucia, in the Windward Islands, the West Indies.

Cas·tro (kăs′trō), **Fidel,** born Fidel Castro Ruz (1927–). Cuban statesman and prime minister. He overthrew the corrupt regime of the dictator Fulgencio Batista and became the head of the Cuban government in February 1959. He seized U.S. and other foreign-owned property and established a socialist state. Under Castro, Cuba has become one of the leading Third World countries. —**Cas·tro·ism** *n.* —**Cas·tro·ist** *n.*

cast steel *n.* Carbon steel that has been cast into shape rather than wrought.

cas·u·al (kăzh′ōō-əl) *adj.* **1.** Resulting from or occurring by chance; accidental. **2.** Occurring at irregular intervals; occasional. **3. a.** Without ceremony; informal or relaxed. **b.** Suitable for informal occasions: *casual clothes.* **4.** Showing little interest; nonchalant: *a casual manner.* **5.** Not serious or thorough; superficial: *a casual inspection.* **6.** Not close or intimate: *a casual acquaintance.* **7.** Pertaining to or associated with accidents. —See Synonyms at **chance.**

~*n.* **1.** A person who works at irregular intervals. **2.** A soldier temporarily attached to a unit while awaiting permanent assignment. **3.** Casual clothing or footwear. [Middle English *casuel,* from Old French, from Late Latin *cāsuālis,* from Latin *cāsus,* fall, chance, CASE.] —**cas·u·al·ly** *adv.* —**cas·u·al·ness** *n.*

cas·u·al·ty (kăzh′ōō-əl-tē) *n., pl.* **-ties. 1.** An unfortunate accident, especially one involving loss of life. **2.** One who is injured or killed in an accident. **3.** One injured, killed, captured, or missing in action against an enemy: *We suffered heavy casualties in the invasion.* **4.** A person or thing that has suffered injury, loss, or destruction as the result of a particular occurrence or circumstance: *one of the casualties of the recent cabinet reshuffle.* [Middle English *casuelte,* from *casuel,* CASUAL.]

cas·u·a·ri·na (kăzh′ōō-ə-rī′nə) *n.* Any of various tropical trees of the genus *Casuarina,* which includes the beefwoods. [New Latin, from Malay *kĕsuari,* CASSOWARY (from the resemblance of its twigs to the drooping feathers of the cassowary).]

castle

FORTRESS RESIDENCE OF THE MIDDLE AGES

A castle defended a route or territory as well as housing a lord and his family

The castle of medieval Europe was both a fortress and the private residence of the lord who owned it. Earlier, the Roman fortress, unlike the castle, was built for occupation by a garrison, and the defense works of Anglo-Saxon Britain, known as burhs, consisted of little more than ditches and timber stockades. It was the Normans, in the 10th century, who built private fortresses, which spread with the Norman conquests throughout the countries of western Europe.

The Norman motte-and-bailey castle was a two-story wooden tower on a steep-sided, flat-topped mound (the motte), round or oval at its base. The motte was surrounded by a ditch filled with water or sharpened stakes. At the foot of the motte was an enclosed courtyard called a bailey.

In the 12th century, stone walls replaced the stockades of the motte-and-bailey, and the keep, or donjon (a stone tower, three or more stories high), became the focal point of the castle. Concentrically planned castles, having a series of walls one within the other, were introduced in the 13th century. Castles as fortresses did not survive the introduction of firearms in the 15th and 16th centuries, and some (Windsor Castle, for example) became private or royal residences.

CONCENTRIC CASTLE *Defenders in the keep could shoot over the heads of the men on the lower outer walls. Walls, towers, and turrets were fortified with battle-* *ments—parapets indented with openings called crenels, or embrasures. Archers shot through these and sought protection behind the merlons between them. The gate-* *house was protected by a tower—the barbican—and a portcullis, a grating of iron-plated oak. A drawbridge was raised or lowered from inside the gatehouse.*

---

cas·u·ist (kăzh′ōō-ĭst) *n.* **1.** One who argues plausibly but falsely; a sophist. **2.** One who determines what is right and wrong in matters of conscience or conduct. [French *casuiste,* from Spanish *casuista,* from Latin *cāsus,* chance, CASE.]

cas·u·is·tic (kăzh′ōō-ĭs′tĭk) *adj.* Also **cas·u·is·ti·cal** (-tĭ-kəl). Of or pertaining to casuists or casuistry. —**cas·u·is·ti·cal·ly** *adv.*

cas·u·ist·ry (kăzh′ōō-ĭ-strē) *n.* **1.** Plausible but false reasoning; sophistry. **2.** The determination of right and wrong in questions of conduct or conscience by the application of general principles of ethics. [From CASUIST.]

ca·sus bel·li (kā′səs bĕl′ī′, kä′səs bĕl′ē′) *n.* An act or event that justifies or leads directly to a declaration of war. [Latin, "occasion of war."]

cat (kăt) *n.* **1. a.** A carnivorous mammal, *Felis catus* (or *F. domesticus*), domesticated since early times as a catcher of rats and mice and as a pet and existing in several distinctive breeds and varieties. **b.** Any of the other animals of the family Felidae, which includes the lion, tiger, lynx, and leopard. **c.** The fur of a domestic cat. **2.** A spiteful woman. **3.** A cat-o'-nine-tails. **4.** A catfish. **5.** *Nautical.* **a.** A cathead. **b.** A device for raising an anchor to the cathead. **c.** A catboat. **6.** *Slang.* A man. —**let the cat out of the bag.** To let a secret be known. —**play cat and mouse with.** To play with, tease, or keep in suspense in an unkind way. —**rain cats and dogs.** To rain heavily. See feature, next page.

~*tr.v.* **catted, catting, cats. 1.** To flog with a cat-o'-nine-tails. **2.** To hoist (an anchor) to the cathead. [Middle English *cat(te),* Old English *cat(t),* from Common Germanic *kattuz* (unattested).]

CAT (kăt) *n.* Computerized axial tomography.

cat. catalogue.

cata– *prefix.* Indicates: **1.** Reversing of a process; for example, **cataplasia. 2.** Lower in position or down from; for example, **cataphyll, catadromous.** [In borrowed Greek compounds *kata-* indicates: 1. Down, as in **catabolism.** 2. Down from, as in **catalepsy.** 3. Off or away, as in **catalectic.** 4. Against, as in **category.** 5. Wrongly or overly, as in **catachresis.** 6. According to, as in **catechize.** 7. Completely or thoroughly, as in **catalogue.** Greek *kata-,* from *kata,* down, down from, according to.]

ca·tab·o·lism (kə-tăb′ə-lĭz′əm) *n.* The metabolic change of complex into simple molecules with the release of energy; destructive metabolism. Compare **anabolism.** [Greek *katabolē,* a throwing down, from *kataballein,* to throw down : *kata-,* down + *ballein,* to throw.] —**cat·a·bol·ic** (kăt′ə-bŏl′ĭk) *adj.* —**cat·a·bol·i·cal·ly** *adv.*

ca·tab·o·lite (kə-tăb′ə-līt′) *n.* A substance produced in the process of catabolism. [CATABOL(ISM) + -ITE.]

ca·tab·o·lize (kə-tăb′ə-līz′) *v.* **-lized, -lizing, -lizes.** —*tr.* To break down (complex molecules) by metabolic processes. —*intr.* To undergo catabolism.

cat·a·caus·tic (kăt′ə-kô′stĭk) *adj.* Designating a caustic curve or surface formed by reflected light rather than refracted light. ~*n.* A catacaustic curve or surface. Compare **diacaustic.**

cat·a·chre·sis (kăt′ə-krē′sĭs) *n., pl.* **-ses** (-sēz′). **1. a.** Strained use of a word or phrase, as for rhetorical effect. **b.** A deliberately paradoxical figure of speech. **2.** Incorrect use of a word. [Latin *catachrēsis,* from Greek *katakhrēsis,* excessive use, misuse, from *katakhrēsthai,* to misuse, use up : *kata-,* wrongly + *khrēsthai,* to use.] —**cat·a·chres·tic** (kăt′ə-krĕs′tĭk) *adj.*

cat·a·cla·sis (kăt′ə-klā′sĭs) *n., pl.* **-ses** (-sēz′). *Geology.* The process in which rocks are deformed by mechanical shearing, or in which selected rock minerals are granulated. [CATA- + -CLASIS.] —**cat·a·clas·tic** (kăt′ə-klăs′tĭk) *adj.*

cat·a·clysm (kăt′ə-klĭz′əm) *n.* **1.** A violent and sudden change in the earth's crust. **2.** Any violent or destructive upheaval, especially one that brings fundamental change. **3.** A devastating flood. —See Synonyms at **disaster.** [French *cataclysme,* from Latin *cataclysmos,* deluge, flood, from Greek *kataklusmos,* from *katakluzein,* to deluge, inundate : *kata-,* down + *kluzein,* to wash.] —**cat·a·clys·mic** (kăt′ə-klĭz′mĭk), **cat·a·clys·mal** (-məl) *adj.*

cat·a·comb (kăt′ə-kōm′) *n.* **1.** *Usually* **catacombs.** A series of underground chambers or tunnels with recesses for graves, especially those in Rome. **2.** An underground cemetery. [From Old French *catacombe,* a subterranean chamber, probably from Old Italian *catacomba,* from Late Latin *catacumba†.*]

cat·a·di·op·tric (kăt′ə-dī-ŏp′trĭk) *adj.* Pertaining to or designating an optical instrument, such as a telescope, that uses lenses and

cat

HUNTERS BY STEALTH

Success in catching prey has spread wildcats around the globe

From the domestic cat to the lion, all feline species catch their prey by stealth. They stalk it and pounce on it, or lie in wait to ambush it, rather than run it down over long distances as dogs do. Cats are strong, speedy, and agile, and their good vision, hearing, and sense of smell make them formidable hunters by night or day. Success in hunting means that wildcats are found on every continent except Australasia and the Antarctic.

Black leopard (panther)
Far East, especially Indonesia
Length 2.4 meters
(8 feet)

Ocelot
Central and
South America
Length 1.45
meters
(4 feet 10
inches)

Snow Leopard
Central Asia
Length 2.3 meters
(7 feet 8 inches)

Leopard
Africa and Asia
Length 2.4 meters (8 feet)

African wildcat
Africa
Length 75 centimeters
(2 feet 6 inches)

Bobcat
North America
Length 90 centimeters
(3 feet)

**European
wildcat**
Europe and
West Asia
Length 80 centimeters
(2 feet 8 inches)

Lynx
Poland,
Scandinavia,
Siberia
Length 1.4 meters
(4 feet 8 inches)

Domestic cat
Worldwide
Length 65 centimeters
(2 feet 2 inches)

Golden cat
Africa and Southeast Asia
Length 1.25 meters
(4 feet 2 inches)

Puma
North and South America
Length 2.4 meters (8 feet)

Lion
Africa, rarely India
Length 3.75 meters
(12 feet 3 inches)

Tiger
Asia
Length 3.8 meters
(12 feet 6 inches)

All lengths represent an average, measuring from the nose to the tip of the tail

mirrors in its operation. [CATA- + DIOPTRIC.]

ca·tad·ro·mous (kə-tăd′rə-məs) *adj.* Migrating down river to breed in marine waters, as some fishes do. Compare **anadromous.** [CATA- + -DROMOUS.]

cat·a·falque (kăt′ə-fălk′, -fôlk′) *n.* The raised structure upon which a coffin rests, as during a state funeral. [French, from Italian *catafalco†.*]

Cat·a·lan (kăt′l-ăn′, -ən) *adj.* Of or pertaining to Catalonia, its people, language, or culture.
~*n.* **1.** A native or inhabitant of Catalonia. **2.** The Romance language of Catalonia.

cat·a·lase (kăt′l-ās′, -āz′) *n.* An enzyme that catalyzes the decomposition of hydrogen peroxide into water and oxygen. [CATAL(YSIS) + -ASE.]

cat·a·lec·tic (kăt′l-ěk′tĭk) *adj.* Designating a verse that lacks part of the last foot. [Late Latin *catalēcticus,* from Greek *katalēktikos,* incomplete, from *katalēgein,* to leave off : *kata-,* off, away + *lēgein,* to leave off, stop.]

cat·a·lep·sy (kăt′l-ěp′sē) *n.* A condition marked by muscular rigidity, lack of awareness of environment, and lack of response to external stimuli that is often associated with encephalitis, schizophrenia, and hysteria. [Learned respelling of earlier *catalency,* from Middle English *cathalempsia,* from Medieval Latin *catalepsia,* from Late Latin *catalēpsis,* from Greek *katalēpsis,* "a seizing," from *katalambanein,* to seize : *kata-,* down from + *lambanein,* to take.] —**cat·a·lep·tic** (kăt′l-ěp′tĭk) *adj.*

Catalina Island. See **Santa Catalina.**

catalo. Variant of **cattalo.**

cat·a·logue, cat·a·log (kăt′l-ôg′, -ŏg′) *n. Abbr.* **cat. 1. a.** A systematized list, usually in alphabetical order, often with descriptions of the listed items. **b.** A publication, such as a book, containing such a list. **2.** A card catalog. **3.** A series of related or similar things: *a catalogue of disasters.*
~*v.* **-logued, -loguing, -logues** or **cataloged, -loging, -logs.** —*tr.* **1.** To list in a catalogue; make a catalogue of. **2.** To add (a new item) to an existing catalogue. —*intr.* To make a catalogue. [Middle English *cateloge,* from Old French *catalogue,* from Late Latin *catalogus,* an enumeration, from Greek *katalogos,* from *katalegein,* to recount, enumerate : *kata-,* thoroughly + *legein,* to gather, speak.] —**cat·a·logu·er** *n.*

Cat·a·lo·nia (kăt′l-ōn′yə, -ō′nē-ə). *Spanish* **Ca·ta·lu·ña** (kä′tə-lōō′nyä). A mountainous, industrialized region of northeast Spain, extending from the Pyrenees along the Mediterranean coast. It is an autonomous region comprising the provinces of Barcelona, Gerona, Lérida, and Tarragona.

ca·tal·pa (kə-tăl′pə, -tôl′pə) *n.* Any of several chiefly North American trees of the genus *Catalpa,* having large leaves, showy clusters of whitish flowers, and long, slender pods. Also called "Indian bean." [Creek *kutuhlpa,* "head with wings" (from the shape of its flowers).]

ca·tal·y·sis (kə-tăl′ə-sĭs) *n.* The action of a catalyst in modifying the rate of a chemical reaction. [Greek *katalusis,* dissolution, from *kataluein,* to dissolve : *kata-,* down + *luein,* to loosen, release.] —**cat·a·lyt·ic** (kăt′l-ĭt′ĭk) *adj.* —**cat·a·lyt·i·cal·ly** *adv.*

cat·a·lyst (kăt′l-ĭst) *n.* **1.** *Chemistry.* A substance that modifies, and especially increases, the rate of a chemical reaction without being consumed or chemically changed in the process. **2.** One that precipitates a process or event, especially without being involved in or changed by the consequences. [From CATALYSIS (by analogy with ANALYST and ANALYSIS).]

catalytic converter *n.* A reaction chamber, typically containing a finely divided platinum-iridium catalyst, into which exhaust gases from an automotive engine are passed together with excess air so that carbon monoxide and hydrocarbon pollutants are oxidized to carbon dioxide and water.

catalytic cracker *n.* An oil-refinery unit in which catalytic **cracking** *(see)* of petroleum is performed.

cat·a·lyze (kăt′l-īz′) *tr.v.* **-lyzed, -lyzing, -lyzes.** To modify the rate of (a chemical reaction) by catalysis. —**cat·a·lyz·er** *n.*

cat·a·ma·ran (kăt′ə-mə-răn′) *n.* **1.** A boat with two parallel hulls. **2.** A raft of logs or floats lashed together. [Tamil *kaṭṭumaram* : *kaṭṭu-,* to tie + *maram,* tree, timber.]

cat·a·me·ni·a (kăt′ə-mě′nē-ə) *n. Physiology.* Menstruation. [New Latin, from Greek *katamēnia,* neuter plural of *katamēnios,* monthly : *kata-,* according to + *mēn,* month.] —**cat·a·me·ni·al** *adj.*

cat·a·mite (kăt′ə-mīt′) *n.* A boy kept by a pederast. [Latin *catamītus,* from *Catamītus,* Ganymede, from Greek *Ganumēdēs,* GANYMEDE (cupbearer of the gods).]

cat·a·mount (kăt′ə-mount′) *n.* Also **cat·a·moun·tain** (kăt′ə-moun′tən). Any of various wild felines, as a mountain lion. [Short for *catamountain,* variant of earlier *cat of the mountain.*]

Ca·ta·nia (kə-tä′nyə). Capital city of Catania province in Sicily, situated at the foot of Mt. Etna.

cat·a·pho·re·sis (kăt′ə-fə-rē′sĭs) *n. Chemistry.* **Electrophoresis** *(see).* [New Latin : CATA- + -PHORESIS.] —**cat·a·pho·ret·ic** (kăt′ə-fə-rĕt′ĭk) *adj.* —**cat·a·pho·ret·i·cal·ly** *adv.*

cat·a·phyll (kăt′ə-fĭl′) *n. Botany.* A modified or rudimentary leaf, such as a bud scale. [CATA- + -PHYLL (translation of German *Niederblatt,* "lower leaf").]

cat·a·pla·sia (kăt′ə-plā′zhə, -zhē-ə) *n.* Degenerative reversion of cells or tissue to a less differentiated form. [New Latin : CATA- + -PLASIA.] —**cat·a·plas·tic** (kăt′ə-plăs′tĭk) *adj.*

cat·a·plasm (kăt′ə-plăz′əm) *n. Medicine.* A **poultice** *(see).* [Old

French *cataplasme,* from Late Latin *cataplasma,* from Greek *kataplasma,* from *kataplassein,* to plaster over : *kata-,* thoroughly + *plassein,* to mold.]

cat·a·plex·y (kăt′ə-plĕk′sē) *n.* A sudden temporary paralysis; especially, the hypnotic state assumed by animals when shamming death. [From Greek *kataplēxis* : *kata-,* CATA- + *plēxis,* from *plēssein,* to strike.] **—cat·a·plec·tic** (kăt′ə-plĕk′tĭk) *adj.*

cat·a·pult (kăt′ə-pŭlt′, -po͝olt′) *n.* **1.** An ancient military machine for hurling missiles, as stones. **2.** A mechanism for launching aircraft without a runway, as from the deck of a ship. **3.** A slingshot.
~*v.* **catapulted, -pulting, -pults.** —*tr.* **1. a.** To hurl or launch from or as if from a catapult. **b.** To shoot at with a catapult. **2.** To bring or move suddenly or abruptly: *catapulted to fame by the success of her first novel.* —*intr.* To become catapulted; spring up abruptly. [Old French *catapulte,* from Latin *catapulta,* from Greek *katapaltēs, katapeltēs* : *kata-,* down + *pallein,* to sway, brandish.]

cat·a·ract (kăt′ə-răkt′) *n.* **1. a.** A very large waterfall, especially one with a sheer drop. **b.** A series of rapids on a stretch of river. **2.** A great downpour. **3.** *Pathology.* Opacity of the lens or capsule of the eye, causing partial or total blindness. [Middle English *cataracte,* floodgate, from Old French, portcullis, cataract (of the eye), from Latin *catarractēs,* waterfall, portcullis, from Greek *katar(rh)aktēs,* "a down-swooping," from *katarassein,* to dash down : *kata-,* down + *rassein,* to strike.]

ca·tarrh (kə-tär′) *n.* Inflammation of mucous membranes, especially of the nose and throat, causing excessive secretion of phlegm or mucus. [Old French *catarrhe,* from Late Latin *catarrhus,* from Greek *katarrhous,* a flowing down, from *katarrhein,* to flow down : *kata-,* down + *rhein,* to flow.] **—ca·tarrh·al** *adj.*

cat·arrh·ine (kăt′ə-rīn′) *adj.* Of or designating a group of primates that includes the Old World monkeys, higher apes, and man, characterized by close-set nostrils directed forward or downward.
~*n.* A catarrhine primate. [New Latin *Catarrhina,* from Greek *katarrhin,* hook-nosed : *kata-,* down + *rhis* (stem *rhin-*), nose.]

ca·tas·ta·sis (kə-tăs′tə-sĭs) *n., pl.* **-ses** (-sēz′). **1.** In classical tragedy, the intensified part of the action directly preceding the catastrophe. **2.** The climax of a play. [Greek *katastasis,* settlement, establishment, from *kathistanai,* to set in order, bring down : *kata-,* down + *histanai,* to set, place.]

ca·tas·tro·phe (kə-tăs′trə-fē) *n.* **1.** A great and sudden calamity causing extreme, often widespread ruin or destruction; a disaster. **2.** A sudden violent change in the earth's surface; a cataclysm. **3.** A complete failure; fiasco. **4.** The dénouement of a play, especially a classical tragedy. —See Synonyms at **disaster.** [Greek *katastrophē,* from *katastrephein,* to turn down, overturn : *kata-,* down + *strephein,* to turn.] **—cat·a·stroph·ic** (kăt′ə-strŏf′ĭk) *adj.* **—cat·a·stroph·i·cal·ly** *adv.*

catastrophe theory *n.* A mathematical theory applied to a wide range of phenomena that show different structures or sudden discontinuous changes, such as biological differentiation, mechanical failure, social conflict, and the like. It depends on representation of different states of the system by geometrical shapes, and on topological analysis of shape and changes of shape.

ca·tas·tro·phism (kə-tăs′trə-fĭz′əm) *n. Geology.* The theory that geological changes in the past were caused by sudden catastrophic disturbances. The theory is also used to account for extinction of plant and animal species. Compare **uniformitarianism.**

cat·a·to·ni·a (kăt′ə-tō′nē-ə) *n.* A condition associated with schizophrenia and certain organic brain disorders and characterized by catalepsy and negativism. [New Latin, from German *Katatonie* : CATA- + -TONIA.] **—cat·a·ton·ic** (kăt′ə-tŏn′ĭk) *adj. & n.*

cat·bird (kăt′bûrd′) *n.* **1.** Any of various Australian bowerbirds of the generus *Ailuroedus.* **2.** A North American songbird, *Dumetella carolinensis,* having predominantly slate-gray plumage. [After one of its calls, resembling the mewing of a cat.]

catbird seat *n.* A position of power or prominence.

cat·boat (kăt′bōt′) *n.* A broad-beamed sailing boat carrying a single sail on a mast stepped well forward. Also called "cat."

cat·bri·er (kăt′brī′ər) *n.* Any of several thorny vines of the genus *Smilax,* especially *S. rotundifolia,* having heart-shaped leaves, small green flowers, and blackish berries.

cat burglar *n.* A burglar who enters buildings by climbing to the upper stories.

cat·call (kăt′kôl′) *n.* A harsh or shrill call expressing disapproval or derision. **—cat·call** *v.*

catch (kăch) *v.* **caught** (kôt), **catching, catches.** —*tr.* **1.** To capture or seize, especially after a chase. **2.** To take by trapping or snaring. **3.** To come upon suddenly, unexpectedly, or accidentally. **4. a.** To lay hold of forcibly or suddenly; grasp: *caught my arm.* **b.** To grab so as to stop the motion of: *tried to catch the ball.* **5. a.** To reach; especially, to reach and overtake. **b.** To reach in time to board, attend, or otherwise make use of: *catch a plane; caught the last mail.* **6. a.** To entangle; grip. **b.** To cause to become suddenly or accidentally hooked, entangled, or the like. **7.** To hit; strike: *a punch that caught him in the stomach.* **8.** To check (oneself) in some sort of action. **9.** To become subject to, as by exposure or contagion; contract: *caught a cold.* **10.** To become affected by: *caught the joyous mood of the festival.* **11.** To take or get suddenly, momentarily, or quickly: *caught a glimpse of the President.* **12. a.** To grasp mentally; comprehend. **b.** To grasp by the senses; apprehend: *I didn't quite catch his last remark.* **13.** To apprehend and reproduce accurately, especially by artistic means; capture: *a novel that catches the flavor of the period.* **14.** To attract and fix; arrest: *catch the waiter's attention.* **15.** *Informal.* To watch or listen to (a theatrical performance, for example). —*intr.* **1.** To become held, entangled, or fastened. **2.** To be communicable or infectious; spread. **3.** To take fire; kindle and burn. **4.** To act as catcher in baseball. **—catch at. 1.** To try to catch; snatch or grab at. **2.** To clutch at gratefully or eagerly. **—catch it.** *Informal.* To receive some form of punishment or scolding. **—catch on.** *Informal.* **1.** To understand or perceive. **2.** To become popular. **—catch one's breath. 1.** To rest so as to be able to go on. **2.** To cease breathing briefly. **—catch out.** To detect (someone) in a mistake. **—catch up. 1.** To lift up suddenly; grab; snatch. **2.** To entangle: *caught up in some barbed wire.* **3. a.** To come up from behind and draw level. **b.** To reach the same level or amount. Used with *with*: *When will the supply catch up with the demand?* **c.** To have an expected, usually undesirable effect, especially after a lapse of time. Used with *with*: *Years of riotous living finally caught up with him.* **4.** To cause to become involved, often unwillingly. Used in the passive: *caught up in the scandal.* **5. a.** To deal with an accumulation of work or the like. Used with *on* or *with*: *catch up on one's correspondence.* **b.** To become acquainted with the latest information. Used with *on* or *with*: *catch up on the gossip.* **6.** To absorb completely; engross. Used in the passive: *He is caught up in his work.*
~*n.* **1.** The act of catching; a taking and holding. **2.** Something that catches, especially a device for fastening or for checking motion. **3.** Something that is caught. **4.** The amount caught. **5.** A choking or stoppage of the breath or voice. **6.** *Informal.* One worth catching, especially as a partner in marriage. **7.** *Informal.* A tricky or unsuspected drawback or condition. **8.** A snatch or fragment. **9.** *Music.* A type of round for three or more voices, popular especially in the 17th and 18th centuries. **10. a.** The grabbing and holding of a thrown, kicked, or batted ball before it hits the ground. **b.** A game of throwing and catching a ball. [Catch, caught, caught; Middle English *cacchen, cauhte, cauht,* to chase, catch, from Old North French *cachier,* to hunt, from Vulgar Latin *captiāre* (unattested), from Latin *captāre,* to chase, strive to seize, from *capere* (past participle *captus*), to take, seize.]

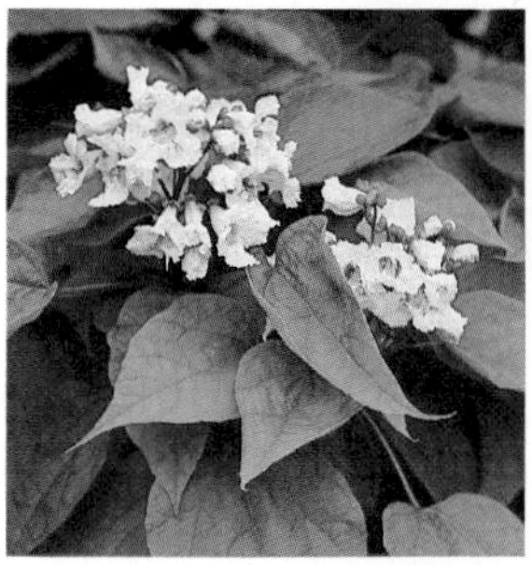

catalpa *Native to Asia and South America, but widely grown in North America as well, the catalpa tree flowers in summer. It is also called the Indian bean.*

catch·all (kăch′ôl′) *n.* **1.** A receptacle for a variety of odds and ends. **2.** Something, such as a phrase or law, that covers a variety of situations. **—catch·all** *adj.*

catch-as-catch-can (kăch′əz-kăch-kăn′) *n.* A style of wrestling in which a contestant is permitted to hold his opponent below the waist and to trip and tackle.
~*adj.* Using any available means or opportunity.

catch crop *n.* **1.** A crop grown between two staple crops in consecutive seasons. **2.** A crop grown between the rows of a staple crop.

catch·er (kăch′ər) *n.* One that catches, especially in baseball.

catch·fly (kăch′flī′) *n., pl.* **-flies.** Any of several plants of the genus *Silene* and related genera, having white, pink, or red flowers with characteristically sticky stems and calyxes.

catch·ing (kăch′ĭng) *adj. Informal.* **1.** Infectious. **2.** Attractive; alluring.

catch·ment (kăch′mənt) *n.* **1.** A catching or collecting of water. **2. a.** A structure, such as a basin, for collecting or draining water. **b.** The amount of water collected. **3.** A **catchment area** *(see).*

catchment area *n.* The geographical area from which people are drawn to an institution, as a hospital.

catch·pen·ny (kăch′pĕn′ē) *adj.* Designed and made to sell without concern for quality; cheap. **—catch·pen·ny** *n.*

catch phrase *n.* A word or phrase that is often repeated in popular use; slogan.

catch·pole, catch·poll (kăch′pōl′) *n.* A sheriff's officer, especially one who arrests debtors. [Middle English *cacchepol,* Old English *cæccepol,* from Old North French *cachepol,* "chicken chaser" : *cachier,* variant of Old French *chacier,* to hunt, CHASE + *poul, pol,* rooster, from Latin *pullus,* young animal, young fowl.]

Catch-22 (kăch′twĕn′tē-to͞o′) *n.* A paradox or predicament in which seeming alternatives actually cancel each other out, leaving no means of escape from a dilemma. [After *Catch-22* (1961), a novel by Joseph Heller (born 1923).]

catchup. Variant of **ketchup.**

catch·weight (kăch′wāt′) *adj. Sports.* Having no weight restriction. Used especially in wrestling.

catch·word (kăch′wûrd′) *n.* **1.** A catch phrase, especially one associated with a political party. **2.** *Printing.* **a.** A word placed at the head of a column or page, as in a dictionary or encyclopedia, to indicate the first or last entry on the page. **b.** The first word of a page printed at the bottom of the preceding page.

catch·y (kăch′ē) *adj.* **-ier, -iest. 1.** Catching one's attention or interest; striking. **2.** Easily remembered and quickly popular.

cat·e·che·sis (kăt′ə-kē′sĭs) *n., pl.* **-ses** (-sēz′). Instruction of catechumens. [Late Latin *catēchēsis,* from Greek *katēkhēsis,* from *katēkhein,* to CATECHIZE.] **—cat·e·chet·ic** (kăt′ə-kĕt′ĭk), **cat·e·chet·i·cal** *adj.*

cat·e·chin (kăt′ə-kĭn′) *n.* A soluble yellow solid substance, $C_{15}H_{14}O_6$, derived from catechu and used in tanning and dyeing. [CATECH(U) + -IN.]

cat·e·chism (kăt′ə-kĭz′əm) *n.* **1.** A short book giving, in question-and-answer form, a brief summary of the basic principles of a religion, especially Christianity. **2.** A book of similar form giving instruction in other subjects. **3.** A question-and-answer examination, as of a political candidate. [Late Latin *catēchismus,* from Late Greek *katēkhismos,* from *katēkhizein,* to CATECHIZE.] **—cat·e·chis·mal** (kăt′ə-kĭz′məl) *adj.*

PRONUNCIATION KEY

ă, pat; ā, pay; âr, care;
ä, father, are; b, bib;
ch, church; d, deed; ĕ, pet;
ē, be; f, fife; g, gag; h, hat;
hw, which; ĭ, pit; ī, pie;
îr, pier; j, judge; k, kick;
l, lid, needle; m, mum;
n, no, sudden; ng, thing;
ŏ, pot; ō, toe; ô, paw, for;
oi, noise; ou, out; o͝o, book;
o͞o, boot; p, pop; r, roar;
s, sauce; sh, ship, dish;
t, tight; th, thin, path;
th, this, bathe; ŭ, cut; ûr, fur;
v, valve; w, with; y, yes;
z, zebra, size; zh, vision;
ə, about, item, edible,
gallop, circus, peaceful

IN FOREIGN WORDS:

à, *Fr.* ami; œ, *Fr.* feu, *Ger.* schön; ü, *Fr.* tu, *Ger.* über; KH, *Ger.* ich, *Scot.* loch; N, *Fr.* bon; y′, *Fr.* Compiègne

STRESS MARKS:

Primary stress: ′
in·cite′ (ĭn-sīt′)
Secondary stress: ′
in′sight′ (ĭn′sīt′)

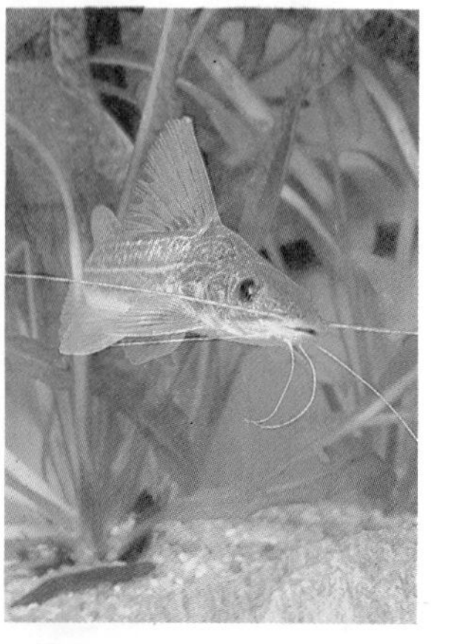

catfish *The catfish group contains a large number of species of freshwater fish identified by their catlike whiskers. The barbels beneath the chin help the fish to locate food on riverbeds.*

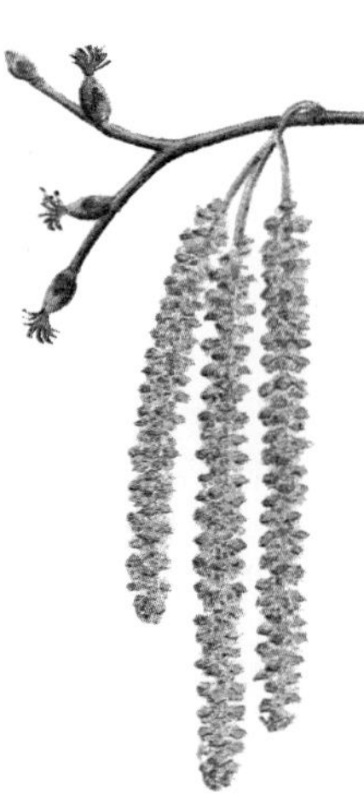

catkin *Many plants produce the long tassellike flower spikes known as catkins. The yellow catkins shown here are the male flowers of the alder tree. The small red blooms are the tree's female flowers.*

cat·e·chist (kăt'ə-kĭst) *n.* A person who catechizes, especially one who instructs catechumens in preparation for baptism. [Late Latin *catēchista,* from Late Greek *katēkhistēs,* from *katēkhizein,* to CATECHIZE.] **—cat·e·chis·tic** (kăt'ə-kĭs'tĭk), **cat·e·chis·ti·cal** *adj.*

cat·e·chize (kăt'ə-kīz') *tr.v.* **-chized, -chizing, -chizes. 1.** To instruct orally in the principles of a religious creed by means of questions and answers. **2.** To question searchingly or persistently. [Late Latin *catēchizāre,* from Late Greek *katēkhizein,* from Greek *katēkhein,* to teach by word of mouth : *kata-,* according to + *ēkhein,* to sound, from *ēkhē,* sound.] **—cat·e·chi·za·tion** *n.* **—cat·e·chiz·er** *n.*

cat·e·chol (kăt'ə-kôl', -kōl') *n.* A colorless crystalline derivative of phenol, $C_6H_4(OH)_2$, used as a photographic developer. [CATECH(U) + -OL.]

cat·e·cho·la·mine (kăt'ə-kō'lə-mēn', -kô'lə-mēn') *n.* Any of a group of amine derivatives of catechol that have important physiological effects on the central nervous system and include epinephrine, norepinephrine, and dopamine.

cat·e·chu (kăt'ə-cho͞o') *n.* Any of several water-soluble, resinous, astringent substances used in tanning and dyeing, as that obtained from a tree, *Acacia catechu,* of southern Asia, or from a woody vine, *Uncaria gambier,* of Malaya. Also called "cachou," "cutch." [Probably from Malay *kachu,* probably from Dravidian, akin to Malayalam *kāccu,* CACHOU.]

cat·e·chu·men (kăt'ə-kyo͞o'mən) *n.* One who is being taught the principles of Christianity; a neophyte. [Middle English *cathecumyn,* from Old French *cathecumene,* from Late Latin *catēchūmenus,* from Greek *katēkhoumenos,* present passive participle of *katēkhein,* to CATECHIZE.]

cat·e·gor·i·cal (kăt'ə-gôr'ĭ-kəl, -gŏr'ĭ-kəl) *adj.* Also **cat·e·gor·ic** (-ĭk). **1.** Without exception or qualification; absolute. **2.** Of, concerning, or included in a category. **—cat·e·gor·i·cal·ly** *adv.*

categorical imperative *n.* In Kant's ethical system, an absolute and universally binding moral law derived from pure reason. Compare **hypothetical imperative.**

cat·e·go·rize (kăt'ə-gə-rīz') *tr.v.* **-rized, -rizing, -rizes.** To put into a category; classify. **—cat·e·go·ri·za·tion** *n.*

cat·e·go·ry (kăt'ə-gôr'ē, -gōr'ē) *n., pl.* **-ries. 1.** A specifically defined division in a system of classification; a class. **2.** *Logic.* Any of the basic classifications into which all knowledge can be placed. [Late Latin *catēgoria,* accusation, predicament, category of predicables, from Greek *katēgoria,* from *katēgorein,* to accuse : *kata-,* against + *-agorein,* to speak publicly, from *agora,* assembly.]

ca·te·na (kə-tē'nə) *n., pl.* **-nae** (-nē') or **-nas.** A closely linked series, especially of commentaries on the Bible by church fathers. [Latin *catēna*†, chain.]

cat·e·nar·y (kăt'ə-nĕr'ē, kə-tē'nə-rē) *n., pl.* **-ies. 1.** The curve theoretically formed by a perfectly flexible, uniformly dense and thick, inextensible cable suspended from two points. **2.** Anything having the shape of this curve. **3.** The overhead wire system of an electric railway. [New Latin *catenaria,* from Latin *catēnāria,* feminine of *catēnārius,* of a chain, from *catēna*†, chain.] **—cat·e·nar·y** *adj.*

catenary bridge *n.* A suspension bridge hanging from chains or cables.

cat·e·nate (kăt'ə-nāt') *tr.v.* **-nated, -nating, -nates.** To connect in a series of ties or links; form into a chain. [Latin *catēnāre,* from *catēna*†, chain.] **—cat·e·na·tion** *n.*

cat·e·noid (kăt'ə-noid') *n.* A geometrical solid generated by rotating a catenary about its axis.

ca·ten·u·late (kə-tĕn'yə-lĭt, -lāt') *adj. Biology.* Consisting or formed of chainlike links. [From Latin *catēnula,* little chain, diminutive of Latin *catēna*†, chain.]

ca·ter (kā'tər) *v.* **-tered, -tering, -ters.** *—intr.* **1.** To provide food or entertainment, usually for large dinners, banquets, and receptions. **2.** To provide anything wished for or needed: *He read books that catered to his appetite for adventure.* **3.** To behave with special thoughtfulness: *catered to the unhappy invalid.* *—tr.* To provide food or entertainment for: *catering a banquet.* [From obsolete *cater,* a buyer of provisions, caterer, from Middle English *catour,* short for *acatour,* from Norman French, from *acater,* to buy, from Vulgar Latin *accaptāre* (unattested), to buy, procure, from Latin *acceptāre,* to ACCEPT.]

cat·er·an (kăt'ər-ən) *n.* A former robber of the Scottish highlands. [Middle English, probably from Scottish Gaelic *ceathairneach.*]

cat·er·cor·nered (kăt'ər-kôr'nərd, kăt'ē-) *adj.* Also **cat·ty·cor·nered** (kăt'ē-). Diagonal. [From obsolete *cater,* four at dice, from Middle English, from Old French *quatre,* four, from Latin *quattuor.*] **—cat·er·cor·nered** *adv.*

ca·ter·er (kā'tər-ər) *n.* One that caters; specifically, a person or company whose business is to supply and serve food and drinks for large social gatherings, banquets, and the like.

cat·er·pil·lar (kăt'ər-pĭl'ər, kăt'ə-) *n.* **1. a.** The wormlike, often brightly colored hairy or spiny larva of a butterfly or moth, having many legs and biting jaws. **b.** Any of various similar insect larvae. **2. Caterpillar.** A trademark for a tractor or bulldozer equipped with a pair of endless chain treads. [Middle English *catyrpel,* probably from Old French *catepelose,* "hairy cat" : *cate,* female cat, from Late Latin *catta,* CAT + *pelose, pelouse,* feminine of *pelous,* hairy, from Latin *pilōsus,* from *pilus,* hair.]

cat·er·waul (kăt'ər-wôl') *intr.v.* **-wauled, -wauling, -wauls. 1.** To cry or screech like a sexually aroused cat. **2.** To have a noisy argument. *~n.* **1.** The cry of a sexually aroused cat. **2.** Any similar cry. [Middle English *caterw(r)awen,* perhaps from Low German *katerwaulen* : *kater,* tomcat, from Common Germanic *kattuz* (unattested), CAT + *waulen,* to screech (perhaps imitative).]

cat·fish (kăt'fĭsh') *n., pl.* **-fishes** or collectively **catfish.** Any of numerous scaleless, chiefly freshwater fishes of the order Siluriformes, characteristically having whiskerlike barbels extending from the upper jaw.

cat·gut (kăt'gŭt') *n.* A tough, thin cord or thread made from the dried intestines of certain animals (usually sheep, but not cat), used for stringing musical instruments and tennis rackets and for surgical ligatures. [16th century : origin obscure.]

cath. cathedral.

Cath·ar (kăth'är') *n., pl.* **Cath·ars** or **Cath·a·ri** (kăth'ə-rī'). An adherent of Catharism.

Cath·a·rism (kăth'ə-rĭz'əm) *n.* The teachings of an ascetic sect of Gnostic heretics that existed in Europe between the 10th and 14th centuries, whose adherents regarded all matter as the creation of an evil deity opposed to God. **—Cath·a·rist** *adj. & n.*

ca·thar·sis (kə-thär'sĭs) *n., pl.* **-ses** (-sēz'). **1.** *Medicine.* Purgation, especially for the digestive system. **2.** A purifying or figurative cleansing or release of the emotions, especially as experienced by the audience of a drama. **3.** *Psychoanalysis.* **a.** A technique used to relieve tension and anxiety by bringing repressed material to consciousness. **b.** The result of this process; abreaction. [New Latin, from Greek *katharsis,* from *kathairein,* to purge, purify, from *katharos*†, pure.]

ca·thar·tic (kə-thär'tĭk) *adj.* Inducing catharsis; purgative; cleansing.
~n. A cathartic agent, especially a laxative. [Late Latin *catharticus,* from Greek *kathartikos,* from *kathairein,* to purge, purify.]

Ca·thay (kă-thā'). *Archaic & Poetic.* China. [Medieval Latin *Cataya, Kitai,* from Old Turkic *Qitar, Qitan,* name of a Turkic tribe that invaded the north of China in the 10th century and subsequently ruled China as the Liao Dynasty (A.D. 907–1101).]

cat·head (kăt'hĕd') *n.* A beam projecting outward from the bow of a ship and used as a support to lift the anchor. [CAT (nautical) + HEAD.]

ca·thec·tic (kə-thĕk'tĭk) *adj.* Of or pertaining to cathexis.

ca·the·dra (kə-thē'drə) *n., pl.* **-drae** (-drē). **1.** The official chair or throne of a bishop. **2.** The office or see of a bishop. See **ex cathedra. 3.** The official chair of an office or position, as of a professor. [Latin, chair, from Greek *kathedra,* seat : *kata-,* down + *hedra,* seat.]

ca·the·dral (kə-thē'drəl) *n. Abbr.* **cath.** The principal church of a bishop's see and one that contains his throne.
~adj. Of or pertaining to a cathedral. [Originally *cathedral church,* from Middle English *cathedral,* of a cathedra, from Old French, from Late Latin *cathedrālis,* from Latin *cathedra,* CATHEDRA.]

ca·thep·sin (kə-thĕp'sĭn) *n.* Any of a group of enzymes, found in animals, that digest proteins. [Greek *kathepsein,* "to boil down," soften.]

Cath·er (kăth'ər), **Willa Sibert** (1873–1947). U.S. author. Growing up in frontier Nebraska, she experienced the trials of pioneer and small-town life that became dominant themes in her works, including *O Pioneers!* (1913), *The Song of the Lark* (1915), and her Pulitzer Prize winner *One of Ours* (1922).

Cath·e·rine II (kăth'rĭn, -ər-ĭn), known as "Catherine the Great" (1729–96). German-born empress of Russia. When her husband, Peter III, succeeded to the throne (1762), Catherine deposed Peter, who was later murdered, and seized the crown. She had schools built, encouraged public health, extended education for women, and promoted religious tolerance. During her reign Russia's frontiers were extended to include most of Poland, the Crimea, and tracts of land bordering the Black Sea.

Catherine de Me·di·ci (də mĕd'ə-chē) (1519–89). Wife of Henry II of France. She ruled France as regent during the minority of her son, Charles IX (1560–63) and, unofficially, until Charles' death (1574). Her plotting was largely responsible for the massacre of Protestants on St. Bartholemew's Day, 1572.

Catherine of Ar·a·gon (ăr'ə-gŏn') (1485–1536). The first wife of Henry VIII of England and mother of Mary I. Henry's insistence on a divorce from her (1533) caused his break with Roman Catholicism and the beginning of the English Reformation.

Catherine of Bra·gan·za (brə-găn'zə) (1638–1705). Portuguese princess and wife of Charles II of England. She married Charles in 1662, but her staunch Roman Catholicism and her failure to produce an heir led to unpopularity with the English people.

cath·er·ine wheel (kăth'ər-ĭn, kăth'rĭn) *n.* **1.** A circular firework that rotates around a pin; pinwheel. **2.** A circular window with ribs radiating from its center. [After St. *Catherine* of Alexandria (died c. A.D. 307), who was condemned to be tortured on a wheel.]

cath·e·ter (kăth'ə-tər) *n. Medicine.* A slender, flexible tube of metal, rubber, or plastic inserted into a body channel, such as a vein, to introduce or remove fluid. [Late Latin *cathetēr,* from Greek *kathetēr,* something inserted, from *kathienai,* let fall, send down : *kata-,* down + *hienai,* to send.]

cath·e·ter·ize (kăth'ə-tə-rīz') *tr.v.* **-ized, -izing, -izes.** To introduce a catheter into (a bodily passage). **—cath·e·ter·i·za·tion** *n.*

cath·e·tom·e·ter (kăth'ə-tŏm'ə-tər) *n.* An instrument that measures vertical distances, especially small differences in the level of liquids in tubes. [*catheto-* (see **catheter**) + -METER.]

ca·thex·is (kə-thĕk'sĭs) *n., pl.* **-es** (-sēz'). The concentration of emotional energy upon some object or idea. [New Latin (adopted to translate German *Besetzung,* the term used by Freud), from Greek *kathexis,* a holding, retention, from *katekhein,* to hold fast : *kata-,* down + *ekhein,* to have, hold.]

cath·ode (kăth′ōd′) *n.* **1.** Any negatively charged electrode, as of an electrolytic cell, storage battery, or electron tube. **2.** The positively charged terminal of a primary cell or of a storage battery that is supplying current. [Greek *kathodos,* way down, descent : *kata-,* down + *hodos,* way.] **—ca·thod·ic** (kă-thŏd′ĭk) *adj.* **—ca·thod·i·cal·ly** *adv.*

cathode ray *n.* A stream of electrons emitted by the cathode in an electrical discharge tube.

cath·ode-ray tube (kăth′ōd-rā′) *n.* A vacuum tube, as one used in television sets, in which a hot cathode emits electrons that are accelerated as a beam through a relatively high voltage anode, further focused or deflected electrostatically or electromagnetically, and allowed to fall on a fluorescent screen to produce a visible spot of light.

cath·o·lic (kăth′ə-lĭk, kăth′lĭk) *adj.* **1.** Universal; general; all-inclusive. **2.** Broad and comprehensive in interests, sympathies, or the like; liberal. [Old French *catholique,* from Late Latin *catholicus,* from Greek *katholikos,* from *katholou,* in general : *kata-,* according to + *holou,* neuter genitive of *holos,* whole.] **—ca·thol·i·cal·ly** (kə-thŏl′ĭ-kə-lē, -ĭk-lē) *adv.*

Cath·o·lic (kăth′ə-lĭk, kăth′lĭk) *adj. Abbr.* **C. 1.** Of, pertaining to, or designating the universal Christian church. **2.** Of, pertaining to, or designating the ancient undivided Christian church. **3.** Of, pertaining to, or designating any of those churches that have claimed to be representatives of the ancient undivided church, especially the Roman Catholic Church. **4.** Of, pertaining to, or designating the Western Church as opposed to the Eastern Orthodox Church.
~*n. Abbr.* **C.** A member of any Catholic church; specifically, a Roman Catholic.

Catholic Apostolic Church *n.* A religious sect founded in England in 1832 and based on the principles of the Rev. E. Irving, whose liturgies follow those of the Roman Catholic, Eastern Orthodox, and Anglican churches.

Catholic Church *n.* The **Roman Catholic Church** *(see).*

Ca·thol·i·cism (kə-thŏl′ə-sĭz′əm) *n.* The faith, doctrine, system, and practice of a Catholic church, especially the Roman Catholic Church. See **Roman Catholicism.**

cath·o·lic·i·ty (kăth′ə-lĭs′ə-tē) *n.* **1.** The condition or quality of being catholic; liberality; broad-mindedness. **2.** General prevalence or acceptance; universality. **3. Catholicity.** Roman Catholicism.

ca·thol·i·cize (kə-thŏl′ə-sīz′) *v.* **-cized, -cizing, -cizes.** *—tr.* **1.** To make catholic. **2.** To convert to Catholicism. *—intr.* To become catholic. **2.** To be converted to Catholicism.

ca·thol·i·con (kə-thŏl′ə-kŏn′) *n.* A universal remedy; a panacea. [French, from Medieval Latin, from Greek *katholikon,* neuter of *katholikos,* CATHOLIC.]

Cat·i·line (kăt′l-īn′) (*c.* 108–62 B.C.). Roman politician and conspirator. He led an unsuccessful revolt against the Roman Republic while Cicero was a consul. His movement died with him and most of his followers in a battle at Pistoria (Pistoia, Italy).

cat·i·on (kăt′ī′ən) *n.* An ion having a positive charge and, in electrolytes, characteristically moving toward a negative electrode. Compare **anion.** [Greek *kation,* neuter of *katiōn,* present participle of *katienai,* to go down : *kata-,* down + *ienai,* to go.] **—cat·i·on·ic** (kăt′ī-ŏn′ĭk) *adj.*

cation exchange *n.* A chemical process used in water softening in which cations of like charge are exchanged equally between a solid, as zeolite, and a solution, as water.

cat·kin (kăt′kĭn) *n. Botany.* A dense, often drooping flower cluster, such as that of a birch, consisting of small, scalelike flowers. Also called "ament." [Translation of obsolete Dutch *katteken,* "little cat" (the cluster resembles a kitten's tail).]

cat·like (kăt′līk′) *adj.* Like a cat; especially, stealthy and silent.

Cat·lin (kăt′lĭn), **George** (1796–1872). U.S. painter. In 1824, after seeing a convention of North American Indians in Philadelphia, he dedicated his life and talent to preserving and publicizing Indian culture with his artwork. His hundreds of paintings, sketches, and etchings are a reliable, detailed record of Indian life and customs.

cat nap *n.* A short nap; a light sleep.

cat·nip (kăt′nĭp′) *n.* A hairy, aromatic blue-flowered plant, *Nepeta cataria,* native to Eurasia, to which cats are attracted.

Ca·to the Elder (kā′tō), **Marcus Porcius** (234–149 B.C.). Roman statesman who wrote the first history of Rome. Opposing luxury and decadence, he attempted, as censor, to restore simplicity to Roman life. After a mission to Africa (153) he was convinced that Rome would always be threatened by Carthage and reportedly ended all his speeches in the Senate, whatever the subject, with *Delenda est Carthago* ("Carthage must be destroyed").

Cato the Younger, Marcus Porcius (95–46 B.C.). Roman politician and great-grandson of Cato the Elder. A conservative opponent of Julius Caesar's political ambitions, he supported Pompey against Caesar in the civil war (49–46 B.C.).

cat-o'-nine-tails (kăt′ə-nīn′tālz′) *n.* A whip consisting of nine knotted cords fastened to a handle, formerly used for flogging. [So called because it leaves marks like the scratches of a cat.]

ca·top·tric (kə-tŏp′trĭk) *adj.* Of or pertaining to mirrors and reflected images. [Greek *katoptrikos,* from *katoptron,* mirror : *kata-,* against + *optos,* visible.] **—ca·top·trics** *n.*

CAT scan *n.* A cross-sectional picture produced by a CAT scanner.

CAT scanner *n.* A device that makes cross-sectional x-rays of the body using computerized axial tomography.

CAT scanning *n.* The act or process of using a CAT scanner.

cat's cradle *n.* A child's game in which an intricately looped string is transferred from the hands of one player to the next, resulting in a succession of different loop patterns.

cat scratch disease *n.* Also **cat scratch fever.** A viral disease transmitted to humans following a skin injury, such as a cat scratch, and characterized by fever and glandular swelling.

cat's-ear (kăts′îr′) *n.* Any of various European plants of the genus *Hypochoeris,* having yellow dandelionlike flowers.

cat's-eye (kăts′ī′) *n.* **1.** Any of various semiprecious gems displaying a band of reflected light that shifts position as the gem is turned. **2.** A colored reflector attached to the back of a vehicle to indicate its presence on the road at night.

cat's-foot (kăts′fo͝ot′) *n.* A small European plant, *Antennaria dioica,* having woolly flowers that form a cluster resembling a cat's paw.

Cats·kill Mountains (kăt′skĭl). Mountain range in New York State, west of the Hudson River and at the north end of the Appalachians. The well-forested mountains, rising to 1,281 meters (4,203 feet) at Slide Mt., provide water and resort areas for New York.

cat's-paw, cats·paw (kăts′pô′) *n.* **1.** A person used by another as a dupe or tool. **2.** A light breeze that ruffles small areas of a water surface. **3.** *Nautical.* A hitch in the bight of a rope, on which a tackle is hooked. ["These he useth as the Monkey did the cat's paw to scrape the nuts out of the fire." M. Hawke, *Killing Is Murder* (1657).]

catsup. Variant of **ketchup.**

cat·tail (kăt′tāl′) *n.* Any of several marsh plants of the genus *Typha,* especially *T. latifolia,* having long straplike leaves and a dense cylindrical head of minute brown flowers. Also called "reed mace."

cat·ta·lo (kăt′l-ō′) *n., pl.* **-loes** or **-los.** Also **cat·a·lo.** A hardy, fertile hybrid breed resulting from a cross between the American buffalo and domestic cattle. [CAT(TLE) + (BUFF)ALO.]

Cattegat. See **Kattegat.**

cat·ter·y (kăt′ə-rē) *n, pl.* **-ies.** A place where cats are bred or boarded.

cat·tle (kăt′l) *pl.n.* **1.** Various animals of the genus *Bos,* especially those of the domesticated species *B. taurus,* raised in many breeds for meat and dairy products. **2.** Human beings, especially when viewed as a mob. [Middle English *catel,* personal property, livestock, from Old North French, from Medieval Latin *capitāle,* property, from Latin, neuter of *capitālis,* chief, primary, from *caput,* head.]

cattle cake *n. Chiefly British.* Concentrated cattle food made up into cake-shaped slabs.

cattle grid *n. Chiefly British.* A ditch covered by a grid of parallel bars that prevents livestock from crossing but allows the passage of vehicles and pedestrians.

cat·tle·man (kăt′l-mən, -măn′) *n., pl.* **-men** (-mĭn, -mĕn′). A man who tends or rears cattle.

cattle plague *n.* **Rinderpest** *(see).*

cattle prod *n.* An electric prod for driving cattle.

catt·ley·a (kăt′lē-ə) *n.* Any orchid of the genus *Cattleya,* having showy rose-purple or white flowers. [New Latin, after William *Cattley* (died 1832), British patron of botany.]

cat·ty[1], **cat·tie** (kăt′ē) *n., pl.* **-ties.** A unit of weight used in China and Southeast Asia generally equivalent to 1 1/3 pounds avoirdupois. [Malay *kati.*]

catty[2] *adj.* **-tier, -tiest.** Subtly cruel or malicious; spiteful: *a catty remark.* **—cat·ti·ly** *adv.* **—cat·ti·ness** *n.*

catty-cornered. Variant of **cater-cornered.**

Ca·tul·lus (kə-tŭl′əs), **Gaius Valerius** (*c.* 84–54 B.C.). Roman lyric poet whose best-known poems tell of his love, from the beginning to the final disillusionment, for Lesbia, an aristocratic Roman woman whose real name was Clodia.

cat·walk (kăt′wôk′) *n.* A narrow platform or pathway, as along the sides of a bridge.

cat whisker *n.* **1.** A fine, pointed wire formerly used to make electrical contact in a crystal radio receiver. **2.** A wire used to make contact with a semiconductor.

Cau·ca·sian (kô-kā′zhən, -kăzh′ən) *n.* **1.** A member of the Caucasoid ethnic division; especially, a white person. **2.** A native or inhabitant of the Caucasus. **3.** The group of languages spoken in the area of the Caucasus that are neither Indo-European nor Altaic, including Circassian and Georgian.
~*adj.* **1.** Of or pertaining to the Caucasus, its people, or their languages and culture. **2.** Caucasoid.

Cau·ca·soid (kô′kə-soid′) *adj. Anthropology.* **1.** Of, pertaining to, or designating a major ethnic division of the human species having certain distinctive physical characteristics such as skin color varying from very light to brown and fine hair ranging from straight to wavy or curly. This division is considered to include groups of peoples indigenous to or inhabiting Europe, northern Africa, southwestern Asia, and the Indian subcontinent, and persons of this ancestry in other parts of the world. **2.** Of, pertaining to, or characteristic of Caucasoids.
~*n.* A member of the Caucasoid ethnic division.

Cau·ca·sus (kô′kə-səs). Also **Cau·ca·sia** (kō-kā′zhə, -shə). Historic region between the Black and Caspian seas, southwest U.S.S.R. Its earliest inhabitants, before 2000 B.C., were Caucasoid peoples, and today, after many invasions, more than 40 languages are spoken, including Circassian, Armenian, Georgian, and Azerbaijani. It is divided in two by the **Caucasus Mts.,** whose highest peak is Mt. Elbrus (5,633 meters; 18,481 feet), the highest mountain in Europe.

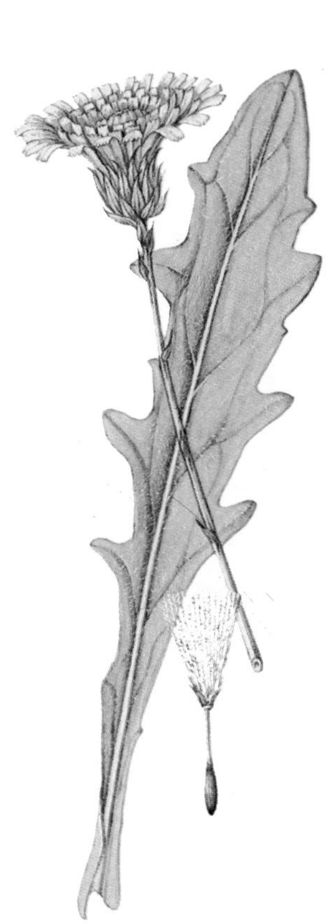

cat's-ear Hypochoeris radicata *is one of many wildflowers that belong to the daisy family. The flower heads, up to 4 centimeters (1 1/2 inches) across, decorate the pastures and woodlands of Europe and North America, but the plants are regarded as weeds by gardeners.*

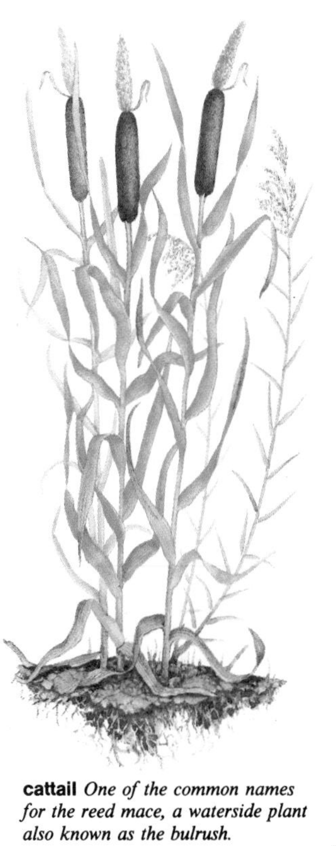

cattail *One of the common names for the reed mace, a waterside plant also known as the bulrush.*

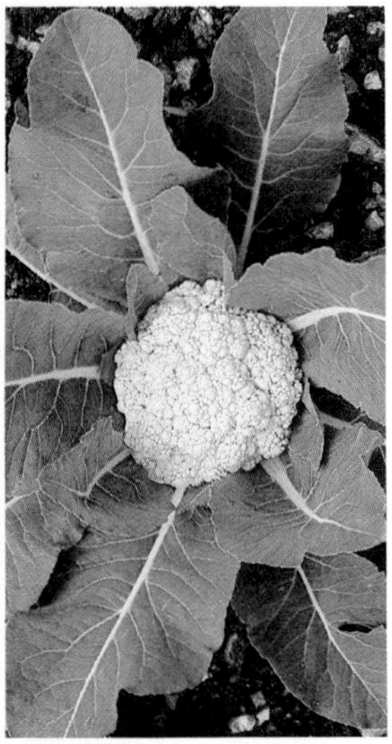

cauliflower *A flowering vegetable, of which only the white head is normally eaten.*

cau·cus (kô′kəs) *n., pl.* **-cuses** or **-cusses. 1.** *Chiefly British.* A group of activists within a political party, sometimes considered as unrepresentative or undemocratic. **2. a.** A closed meeting of the members of a political party within a legislative body to decide upon questions of policy and the selection of candidates for office. **b.** These members as a group.
～*intr.v.* **-cused** or **-cussed, -cusing** or **-cussing, -cuses** or **-cusses.** To assemble in or hold a caucus. [Perhaps from Algonquian *caucauasu,* counselor (a term recorded by Capt. John Smith).]

cau·dad (kô′dăd′) *adv. Anatomy.* Toward the tail or posterior part of the body. Compare **cephalad.** [Latin *cauda*†, tail + -AD.]

cau·dal (kôd′l) *adj.* **1.** *Anatomy.* Of, at, or near the tail or hind parts; posterior. **2.** *Zoology.* Of, pertaining to, or resembling the tail. [New Latin *caudalis,* from Latin *cauda*†, tail.] **—cau·dal·ly** *adv.*

caudal fin *n.* The tail fin of a fish.

cau·date (kô′dāt′) *adj.* Also **cau·dat·ed** (-dā′tĭd). Having a tail or a taillike part. [New Latin *caudatus,* from Latin *cauda*†, tail.]

caudate nucleus *n.* A large ganglion in the lateral ventricle of the brain that functions in motor control.

cau·dex (kô′dĕks′) *n., pl.* **-dices** (-də-sēz′) or **-dexes.** *Botany.* **1.** The thickened base of the stem of some perennial plants. **2.** A woody, trunklike stem, such as that of a tree fern. [Latin *caudex, cōdex*†, stem, tree trunk.]

cau·di·llo (kou-*thē*l′yō, -*thē*′yō) *n., pl.* **-llos.** In Spanish-speaking countries, a military leader who sets himself up as a dictator. [Spanish, chieftain, from Late Latin *capitellum,* small head, diminutive of *caput,* head.]

cau·dle (kôd′l) *n.* A warm beverage formerly given to invalids, consisting of wine or ale mixed with sugar, eggs, bread, and various spices. [Middle English *caudel,* from Old North French *caudel, chaudel,* from *chaud,* warm, from Latin *cal(i)dus.*]

caught. Past tense and past participle of **catch.**

caul (kôl) *n.* **1.** A portion of the membrane that surrounds a fetus, which is sometimes found on the head at birth and considered a sign of good luck. **2.** The large omentum covering the intestines. [Middle English *calle,* probably from Old French *cale,* cap, from Germanic.]

cauldron. Variant of **caldron.**

cau·les·cent (kô-lĕs′ənt) *adj. Botany.* Having a stem showing above the ground. [Latin *caulis,* stem.]

cau·li·cle (kô′lĭ-kəl) *n. Botany.* A small stem. [Latin *cauliculus,* diminutive of *caulis,* stem.]

cau·li·flow·er (kô′lĭ-flou′ər, kŏl′ĭ-) *n.* **1.** A plant, *Brassica oleracea botrytis,* related to the cabbage and broccoli and having an enlarged, crowded flower head. **2.** The compact, whitish flower head of this plant, eaten as a vegetable. [Earlier *colie-florie,* probably from Italian *caoli-fiori,* plural of *cavolo-fiore,* "flowered cabbage" : *cavolo,* cabbage, from Late Latin *caulus,* variant of Latin *caulis,* stem + *fiore,* flower, from Latin *flōs* (stem *flōr-*).]

cauliflower ear *n.* An ear swollen and deformed by repeated blows, as in boxing.

cau·line (kô′līn′) *adj. Botany.* Of, having, or growing on a stem. [New Latin *caulinus,* from Latin *caulis,* stalk, stem.]

caulk, calk (kôk) *tr.v.* **caulked, caulking, caulks** or **calked, calking, calks. 1.** *Nautical.* To make (a boat) watertight by packing seams with oakum or tar. **2.** To make (pipes, for example) watertight or airtight by filling in cracks. [Middle English *ca(u)lken,* from Old North French *cauquer,* to trample, tread, from Latin *calcāre,* from *calx* (stem *calc-*), a heel.] **—caulk·er** *n.*

cau·ri (kou′rē) *n., pl.* **-ris.** A monetary unit of Guinea, equal to 1/100 of a syli. See feature at **currency.**

caus·al (kô′zəl) *adj.* **1.** Pertaining to, constituting, or involving a cause: *a number of causal factors.* **2.** Expressing a cause or reason.
～*n.* A word or grammatical element that expresses a cause or reason. **—caus·al·ly** *adv.*

cau·sal·gia (kô-zăl′jə, -jē-ə) *n.* A burning pain felt in a limb along the course of a peripheral nerve that has been injured. It may be accompanied by changes in the appearance of the skin. [New Latin, from Greek *kausos,* fever, burning + -ALGIA.] **—cau·sal·gic** (kô-zăl′jĭk) *adj.*

cau·sal·i·ty (kô-zăl′ə-tē) *n., pl.* **-ties. 1.** The relationship between cause and effect. **2.** A causal agency, force, or quality.

cau·sa·tion (kô-zā′shən) *n.* **1.** The act or process of causing. **2.** The relationship between cause and effect.

caus·a·tive (kô′zə-tĭv) *adj.* **1.** Functioning as a cause; effective. **2.** Designating a verb or verbal affix that expresses causation. In the phrase *to fell a tree, fell* is a causative verb.
～*n.* A word or form expressing causation. **—caus·a·tive·ly** *adv.*

cause (kôz) *n.* **1.** That which produces an effect, result, or consequence; the person, event, or condition responsible for an action or result. **2.** A basis for an action or decision; ground; reason; motive. **3.** Good or sufficient reason or ground. **4.** A goal, principle, or concern that is actively pursued: *the cause of mental health.* **5.** The interests of a person or group engaged in a struggle: *"The cause of America is in great measure the cause of all mankind"* (Thomas Paine). **6.** *Law.* **a.** A ground for legal action. **b.** A lawsuit. **7.** A subject under debate or discussion.
～*tr.v.* **caused, causing, causes.** To be the cause of; make happen; bring about. [Middle English, from Old French, from Latin *causa*†, reason, purpose, motive, lawsuit.] **—caus·a·ble** *adj.* **—cause·less** *adj.* **—caus·er** *n.*
Usage: *cause, reason, occasion.* These nouns denote things or prior conditions that bring about, or are associated with, certain effects. A *cause,* singly or as one of a series, must exist for an effect logically to occur: *Deficiency in vitamin C is the cause of scurvy. Reason* refers to what explains the occurrence or nature of an effect in terms of human thought rather than objective or external factors: *There was no reason to leave.* An *occasion* is the situation or time that permits existing causes to come into play: *The occasion for the robbery was the absence of the regular night watchman.*

cause cé·lè·bre (kōz′ sā-lĕb′r′) *n., pl.* **causes célèbres** (*pronounced as singular*). **1.** A celebrated legal case. **2.** A controversial issue arousing heated public debate and partisanship. [French, "celebrated case."]

cause list *n. Law.* A list of cases awaiting trial.

cau·se·rie (kōz-rē′, kō′zə-rē′) *n.* **1.** An informal talk or chat. **2.** A short, conversational piece of writing. [French, from *causer,* to talk.]

cause·way (kôz′wā′) *n.* **1.** A raised roadway, as across water or marshland. **2.** A paved highway. [Middle English *caucewei* : *cauce,* from Old North French *cauciee,* from Vulgar Latin *calciāta* (unattested), paved (as with limestone), from Latin *calx* (stem *calc-*), limestone, small stone, from Greek *khalix,* small stone + *wei,* WAY.]

caus·tic (kô′stĭk) *adj.* **1.** Able to burn, corrode, dissolve, or otherwise eat away by chemical action. **2.** Marked by sharp and bitter wit; cutting: *"Her new clothes were the subject of caustic comment"* (Willa Cather). **3.** *Optics.* Of or designating a curve or surface of revolution formed by rays of an initially parallel beam of light after they have been reflected or refracted by an optical system that does not bring the rays to a single focus. —See Usage note at **sarcastic.**
～*n.* **1.** A caustic material or substance. **2.** A caustic curve or surface. [Latin *causticus,* from Greek *kaustikos,* from *kaiein,* to burn.] **—caus·ti·cal·ly** *adv.* **—caus·tic·i·ty** (kô-stĭs′ə-tē) *n.*

caustic lime *n.* **Calcium hydroxide** *(see).*

caustic potash *n.* **Potassium hydroxide** *(see).*

caustic soda *n.* **Sodium hydroxide** *(see).*

cau·ter·ize (kô′tə-rīz′) *tr.v.* **-ized, -izing, -izes.** To burn or sear with a cautery. [Old French *cauteriser,* from Late Latin.] **—cau·ter·i·za·tion** *n.*

cau·ter·y (kô′tə-rē) *n., pl.* **-ies. 1.** A caustic agent or a very hot or very cold instrument used, especially in the treatment of wounds, to destroy abnormal tissue. **2.** The act or result of using a cautery; cauterization. [Latin *cautērium,* branding iron, from Greek *kautērion,* from *kaiein,* to burn.]

cau·tion (kô′shən) *n.* **1. a.** Forethought to avoid danger or harm. **b.** An instinctive avoidance of risks and danger. **2.** A warning; an admonishment. **3.** *British Law.* An official warning, given to a person suspected of or arrested for a crime, that if he chooses to speak, anything he says may be set down and used in evidence. **4.** *Informal.* Someone or something that is striking or amusing.
～*tr.v.* **cautioned, -tioning, -tions. 1.** To warn, especially against danger; put on guard. **2.** *British Law.* To give a caution to (a person suspected of a crime). —See Synonyms at **warn.** [Middle English *caucion,* from Old French *caution,* from Latin *cautiō* (stem *cautiōn-*), a guarding, from *cavēre* (past participle *cautus*), to watch, take heed.]

cau·tion·ar·y (kô′shə-nĕr′ē) *adj.* **1.** Of, pertaining to, or being a caution. **2.** Giving or serving as a warning.

caution money *n. British.* Money deposited as a surety, as for example against possible debts or damage.

cau·tious (kô′shəs) *adj.* **1.** Showing or practicing caution; wary; careful. **2.** Showing prudence and deliberation; guarded; tentative: *cautious optimism.* **—cau·tious·ly** *adv.* **—cau·tious·ness** *n.*

cav. cavalry.

cav·al·cade (kăv′əl-kād′, kăv′əl-kād′) *n.* **1.** A ceremonial procession, especially of horsemen or horse-drawn carriages. **2.** A colorful procession or display. **3.** A succession: *a cavalcade of stars.* [French, from Italian *cavalcata,* from *cavalcare,* to ride on horseback, from Vulgar Latin *caballicāre* (unattested), from Latin *caballus,* horse.]

Cav·al·can·ti (kăv′əl-kăn′tē), **Guido** (*c.* 1255–1300). Florentine poet whose major themes were love and emotional suffering. A friend of Dante, he died in exile, banished for his political meddlings.

cav·a·lier (kăv′ə-lîr′) *n.* **1.** A gentleman accomplished in arms and horsemanship. **2.** A gallant courtly gentleman, especially one escorting a lady. **3. Cavalier.** A supporter of Charles I of England in his struggles against the Parliamentarians; a Royalist.
～*adj.* **1.** Showing arrogant self-assurance; offhand: *He dismissed my objection with a cavalier wave of his hand.* **2.** Carefree and gay. **3. Cavalier.** Of or pertaining to the Cavaliers. [French, from Italian *cavaliere,* from Late Latin *caballārius,* horseman, rider, from Latin *caballus,* horse.] **—cav·a·lier·ly** *adv.*

Cavalier poets *pl.n.* A group of English poets, including Lovelace and Suckling, associated with the court of Charles I.

ca·val·la (kə-văl′ə) *n., pl.* **-las** or **cavalla.** Also **ca·val·ly** (-văl′ē) *pl.* **-lies** or **cavally. 1.** Any of various tropical marine food fishes of the family Carangidae. **2.** The **king mackerel** *(see).* [Spanish *caballa,* horse mackerel, from Late Latin, feminine of Latin *caballus,* horse.]

cav·al·ry (kăv′əl-rē) *n., pl.* **-ries.** *Abbr.* **cav. 1.** Troops mounted on horseback. **2.** A highly mobile army unit using armored vehicles, helicopters, and the like. [French *cavallerie,* from Italian *cavalleria,* cavalry, chivalry, from *cavaliere,* CAVALIER.]

cav·al·ry·man (kăv′əl-rē-mən) *n., pl.* **-men** (-mĭn). A soldier in the cavalry.

Cav·an (kăv′ən). County in the Republic of Ireland, in Ulster. It is a predominantly hilly region, infertile and boggy with many lakes. The county town is also named Cavan.

cav·a·ti·na (kăv′ə-tē′nə, kä′və-) *n. Music.* **1.** A short operatic solo in a simple style. **2.** An instrumental piece or movement in a simple style. [Italian.]

cave (kāv) *n.* **1.** A hollow beneath the earth's surface, often having an opening in the side of a hill or cliff. **2.** *British.* A dissident group formally seceding from a political party. ~*v.* **caved, caving, caves.** —*tr.* To hollow out. —*intr.* To explore caves. [Middle English, from Old French, from Latin *cava*, from the neuter plural of *cavus*, hollow.]

ca·ve·at (kä′vē-ăt′, kăv′ē-, kä′vē-ät′) *n.* **1.** *Law.* A formal application filed by an interested party to a court or officer, requesting the postponement of proceedings until he is heard. **2.** A warning or caution. ~*v.* **caveated, -ating, -ats.** —*intr. Law.* To enter a caveat. —*tr. Slang.* To do or say (something) with an accompanying warning or caution. [Latin, let him beware, from *cavēre,* to beware, take care.]

caveat emp·tor (ĕmp′tôr′) *n.* The principle in commerce that the buyer alone is responsible for assessing the quality of a purchase before buying it. [Latin, "let the buyer beware."]

cave·fish (kāv′fĭsh′) *n., pl.* **fishes** or collectively **cavefish.** Any of various freshwater fishes of the family Amblyopsidae, of subterranean waters, having rudimentary eyes. Also called "blindfish."

cave in *intr.v.* **1.** To fall in; collapse, as from being undermined. **2.** *Informal.* To cease resistance. —*tr.v.* To cause to collapse.

cave-in (kāv′ĭn′) *n.* **1.** An act of caving in. **2.** A place where a structure, such as a mineshaft, has caved in.

Cav·ell (kăv′əl), **Edith** (1865–1915). British nurse who remained in Brussels after the German occupation (1915) helping to smuggle Allied troops to the Dutch border. Caught by the Germans, she was executed by firing squad.

cave·man (kāv′măn′) *n., pl.* **-men** (-mĕn′). **1.** A prehistoric man who lived in caves. **2.** *Informal.* A man who is crude or brutal, especially toward women.

cav·en·dish (kăv′ən-dĭsh) *n. British.* Tobacco that has been sweetened and molded into plugs or cakes. [Perhaps from the name of the first manufacturer.]

Cav·en·dish (kăv′ən-dĭsh), **Henry** (1731–1810). English physicist and chemist who discovered (1766) the properties of hydrogen and later established that water was a compound of hydrogen and oxygen. Using the universal gravitational constant, he measured the density of the earth in 1798.

cave painting *n.* **1.** A painting made by prehistoric man on a cave wall. **2.** Prehistoric art found on cave walls.

cav·er (kā′vər) *n.* One who explores caves.

cav·ern (kăv′ərn) *n.* **1.** A large cave. **2.** Something resembling a cavern in depth, hollowness, or darkness. ~*tr.v.* **caverned, -erning, -erns.** **1.** To enclose in or as if in a cavern. **2.** To hollow. Used with *out.* [Middle English *caverne,* from Old French, from Latin *caverna,* from *cavus,* hollow.]

cav·er·nic·o·lous (kăv′ər-nĭk′ə-ləs) *adj.* Inhabiting caverns or caves.

cav·ern·ous (kăv′ər-nəs) *adj.* **1.** Filled with caverns. **2.** Like a cavern in depth, vastness, or darkness. **3.** Filled with cavities; porous. —**cav·ern·ous·ly** *adv.*

cav·es·son (kăv′ĭ-sən) *n.* A strong noseband used when breaking in difficult horses. [French *caveçon,* from Italian *cavezzone,* augmentative of *cavezza,* halter, from Medieval Latin *capitium,* head covering, from Latin *caput* (stem *capit-*), head.]

ca·vet·to (kə-vĕt′ō) *n., pl.* **-vetti** (-vĕt′ē) or **-tos.** A concave molding for cornices, shaped like a circular quadrant. [Italian, from *cavo,* hollow, from Latin *cavus.*]

cav·i·ar, cav·i·are (kăv′ē-är′, kä′vē-) *n.* The roe of a large fish, especially a sturgeon, that is salted, seasoned, and eaten as a delicacy. [Earlier *caviari, cavialy,* probably from French *caviar,* from Italian *caviaro,* from Turkish *kāvyār.*]

cav·il (kăv′əl) *intr.v.* **-iled, -iling, -ils.** Also *chiefly British* **-illed, -illing.** To raise unnecessary or trivial objections; carp. Used with *at, about,* or *with.* ~*n.* A captious or trivial objection. [French *caviller,* from Latin *cavillārī,* to satirize, criticize, from *cavilla,* a jeering.] —**cav·il·er** *n.*

cav·ing (kā′vĭng) *n.* The exploration of caves as a sport or scientific pursuit.

cav·i·tar·y (kăv′ə-tĕr′ē) *adj.* Of, pertaining to, or marked by cavitation in the body.

cav·i·ta·tion (kăv′ĭ-tā′shən) *n.* **1.** The sudden formation and collapse of low-pressure bubbles in liquids by means of mechanical forces, such as those resulting from rotation of a marine propeller. **2.** The formation of cavities in tissue or an organ, especially as a result of disease. [From CAVITY.]

cav·i·ty (kăv′ĭ-tē) *n., pl.* **-ties.** **1.** A hollow or hole. **2.** A hollow area within the body: *a sinus cavity.* **3.** A pitted area in a tooth caused by **caries** (*see*). —See Synonyms at **hole.** [French *cavité,* Old French *cavete,* from Late Latin *cavitās,* hollowness, from Latin *cavus,* hollow.]

cavity resonator *n. Electronics.* A microwave device containing an enclosed space in which an oscillating electromagnetic field can be maintained. The dimensions of the cavity determine the frequency of the oscillations. Also called "rhumbatron."

cavity wall *n.* A wall, usually of masonry, consisting of two layers separated by an air space for insulation.

ca·vort (kə-vôrt′) *intr.v.* **-vorted, -vorting, -vorts.** **1.** To bound or prance about in a sprightly manner; caper. **2.** To make merry; frolic. [Perhaps variant of CURVET.]

Ca·vour (kə-voor′), **Count Camillo Benso di** (1810–61). Italian liberal statesman who helped to unify Italy. Prime minister of Sardinia-Piedmont (1852–59, 1860–61) he made various alliances to oust the Austrians from Italy and with Giuseppi Garibaldi, created the kingdom of Italy under the king of Sardinia-Piedmont, Victor Emmanuel II.

ca·vy (kā′vē) *n., pl.* **-vies.** Any of various short-tailed or apparently tailless South American rodents of the family Caviidae, which includes the guinea pig. [New Latin *Cavia,* probably from Galibi *cabiai.*]

caw (kô) *n.* The hoarse, raucous sound uttered by a crow or similar bird. ~*intr.v.* **cawed, cawing, caws.** To utter a caw. [Imitative.]

Cawnpore. See Kanpur.

Cax·ton (kăk′stən), **William** (c. 1422–91). The first English printer and publisher, formerly a cloth merchant. *Recuyell of the Historyes of Troye* (c. 1475) was the first book printed in English. He set up his own press (1476) at Westminster where he published and printed *Canterbury Tales* (1478) and the first illustrated English book, an encyclopedia, *Myrrour of the Worlde* (1481).

cay (kē, kā) *n.* A small, low islet composed largely of coral or sand; a key. [Spanish *cayo,* probably from Old French *quai, cay,* QUAY.]

Cay·enne (kī-ĕn′, kā-). The capital and chief seaport of French Guiana, situated on the coast of the Île de Cayenne. The French founded it in 1643, and it was a penal colony (1854–1938).

cay·enne pepper (kī-ĕn′, kā-) *n.* A condiment made from the very pungent fruit of a variety of the plant *Capsicum frutescens.* Also called "cayenne," "red pepper." [Earlier *kian, chian* (influenced by CAYENNE), from Tupi *kyinha.*]

cayman. Variant of **caiman.**

Cay·man Islands (kā-măn′, kā′mən). A group of three low-lying coral islands in the Caribbean Sea approximately 320 kilometers (200 miles) northwest of Jamaica. The largest, Grand Cayman, includes Georgetown, the capital. Little Cayman and Cayman Brac make up the rest of this British colony. Columbus discovered the islands in 1503.

Ca·yu·ga (kə-yōō′gə, kī-) *n., pl.* **-gas** or collectively **Cayuga.** **1.** A member of an American Indian people formerly living around Cayuga and Seneca lakes in central New York. **2.** The Iroquoian language spoken by this people. —**Ca·yu·ga** *adj.*

Cayuga Lake. The longest of the Finger Lakes in west-central New York. It is 61 kilometers (38 miles) long and 1.6 to 5.6 kilometers (1 to 3.5 miles) wide.

cay·use (kī-yōōs′, kī′yōōs′) *n. Western U.S.* A horse; especially, an Indian pony. [After the CAYUSE Indians.]

Cay·use (kī-yōōs′, kī′yōōs′) *n., pl.* **-uses** or collectively **Cayuse.** **1.** A member of an American Indian people of Oregon. **2.** The Sahaptin language of this tribe. —**Cay·use** *adj.*

cazique. Variant of **cacique.**

Cb The symbol for the element columbium.

CB (sē-bē′) *n., pl.* **CB's. Citizens band** (*see*).

CBC **1.** Canadian Broadcasting Corporation. **2.** complete blood count.

C.B.D. cash before delivery.

C.B.E. Commander of the (Order of the) British Empire.

CBS Columbia Broadcasting System.

cc cubic centimeter.

cc. chapters.

c.c., C.C. carbon copy.

C.C.A. Circuit Court of Appeals.

CCC **1.** Civilian Conservation Corps. **2.** Commodity Credit Corporation.

C clef *n. Music.* A clef sign used to form any of three clefs, soprano, alto, or tenor, by locating middle C on, respectively, the lowest line of the staff, the middle line, or the fourth (next to the highest) line.

cd *Physics.* candela.

Cd The symbol for the element cadmium.

c.d. cash discount.

C.D. **1.** civil defense. **2.** compact disc.

CDC Center for Disease Control.

Cdr. commander.

Ce The symbol for the element cerium.

C.E. **1.** chemical engineer. **2.** chief engineer. **3.** civil engineer. **4.** common era.

ce·a·no·thus (sē′ə-nō′thəs) *n.* A shrub of the North American genus *Ceanothus,* often grown for ornament. [New Latin, from Greek *keanōthos,* a type of thistle.]

cease (sēs) *v.* **ceased, ceasing, ceases.** —*tr.* To put an end to; discontinue. —*intr.* **1.** To come to an end; stop. **2.** To desist; discontinue. Often used with *from.* ~*n.* Pause or end. Used in the phrase *without cease.* [Middle English *ces(s)en,* from Old French *cesser,* from Latin *cessāre,* to delay, stop, frequentative of *cēdere* (past participle *cessus*), to CEDE.]

cease-fire (sēs′fīr′) *n.* **1.** An order to cease firing. **2.** A suspension of active hostilities; a truce.

cease·less (sēs′lĭs) *adj.* Without stop; endless. —See Synonyms at **continual.** —**cease·less·ly** *adv.*

Ceau·şes·cu (chou-shĕs′koo), **Nicolae** (1918–). Romanian statesman. As Romania's first president (1974–) he has maintained close

cave painting *Some prehistoric paintings, such as this one discovered at Lascaux in France, are at once realistic and highly stylized. Painting in the caves at Lascaux began in about 15,000 B.C.*

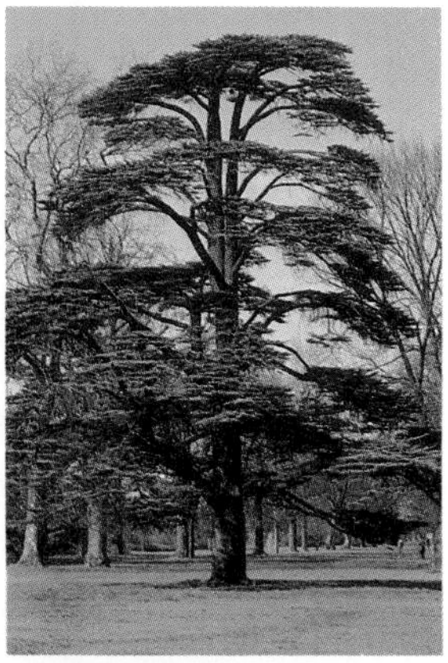

cedar of Lebanon *These trees, native to the mountains of Lebanon, Syria, and Asia Minor, yield a hard and durable timber. In biblical times, they became a symbol of longevity.*

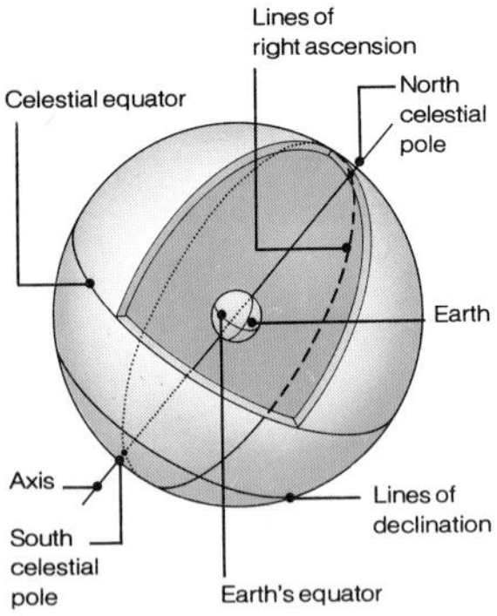

celestial sphere *The imaginary celestial sphere, with the observer at its center, is used to identify the position of a heavenly body.*

political ties with the U.S.S.R., but restricted its interference in Romania's national affairs.

Čechy. See **Bohemia.**

Cecil, William. See William Cecil, 1st Baron **Burghley.**

ce·cum, cae·cum (sē′kəm) *n., pl.* **-ca** (-kə). **1.** A cavity with only one opening. **2.** *Anatomy.* The large blind pouch forming the beginning of the large intestine. [New Latin, from Latin *(intestinum) caecum,* blind (intestine), from *caecus,* blind.]

ce·dar (sē′dər) *n.* **1.** Any of several coniferous evergreen trees of the genus *Cedrus,* native to the Old World and having spreading branches and barrel-shaped cones, as the **cedar of Lebanon** *(see).* **2.** Any of various similar evergreen trees, mostly of the genera *Thuja, Chamaecyparis,* and *Juniperus.* **3.** The durable, aromatic, often reddish wood of a cedar. [Middle English *cedre,* from Old French, from Latin *cedrus,* cedar, juniper, from Greek *kedros*†.]

cedar of Lebanon *n.* A tall evergreen tree, *Cedrus libani,* of Asia Minor, having level spreading branches, short dark needles, and fragrant hard wood. [Translation of Late Latin *cedrus libani* (translation of Hebrew *arzē Ləbānōn*).]

Cedar Rapids. A city of east-central Iowa, on the Cedar River. A thriving commercial and industrial city, Cedar Rapids is a distribution and rail center for an extensive agricultural area. Its museum has a collection of paintings by Grant Wood.

cedar waxwing *n.* A North American bird, *Bombycilla cedrorum,* having a crested head and predominantly brown plumage. [Probably so called because it eats the berries of the red cedar.]

cede (sēd) *tr.v.* **ceded, ceding, cedes. 1.** To surrender possession of officially or formally. **2.** To yield; grant. —See Synonyms at **relinquish.** [French *céder,* from Latin *cēdere,* to withdraw, yield.]

ce·di (sā′dē) *n., pl.* **cedi** or **-dis. 1.** The basic monetary unit of Ghana, equal to 100 pesewas. See feature at **currency. 2.** A note worth one cedi.

ce·dil·la (sĭ-dĭl′ə) *n.* A mark (̧) placed beneath the letter *c* in the spelling of French, Portuguese, and older Spanish to indicate that the letter is to be pronounced (s), as in the French word *garçon.* The cedilla is also used for various purposes in Turkish and Romanian spelling. [Obsolete Spanish *cedilla,* diminutive of *ceda,* the letter zee, from Late Latin *zēta,* ZETA (so called because a small *z* was formerly used to make a hard *c* sibilant).]

cei·ba (sā′bə) *n.* Any of various large tropical trees of the genus *Ceiba,* which includes the silk-cotton tree, the source of the fiber kapok. [New Latin, from Spanish, probably from Arawakan.]

ceil (sēl) *tr.v.* **ceiled, ceiling, ceils. 1.** To make a ceiling for. **2.** To provide (a ship) with interior planking. [Middle English *celen,* perhaps a back-formation from CEILING.]

cei·lidh (kā′lē) *n.* An Irish or Scottish social gathering with traditional music, dancing, and storytelling. [Gaelic.]

ceil·ing (sē′lĭng) *n.* **1.** The interior upper surface of a room. **2.** The planking applied to the interior framework of a ship. **3.** A maximum limit, especially on wages or prices. **4.** Any of various vertical boundaries, especially of atmospheric visibility, cloud-cover altitude, or operable aircraft altitude. [Middle English *celing*†.]

ceil·om·e·ter (sē-lŏm′ə-tər) *n.* A photoelectric instrument for ascertaining cloud heights. [CEIL(ING) + -METER.]

cel·a·don (sĕl′ə-dŏn′) *n.* **1.** A pale to very pale green. **2.** A kind of pottery with a pale grayish-green glaze that was originally produced in China. [French *céladon,* from *Céladon,* wan character in Honoré d'Urfé's *L'Astrée* (1607–19).] —**cel·a·don** *adj.*

cel·a·don·ite (sĕl′ə-də-nīt′) *n.* A soft mica having a green hue and a high iron content.

Ce·lae·no[1] (sĭ-lē′nō). *Greek Mythology.* One of the **Pleiades** *(see).*

Celaeno[2] *n.* One of the six stars in the Pleiades cluster visible to the naked eye. [After CELAENO.]

cel·an·dine (sĕl′ən-dīn′, -dēn′) *n.* **1.** A plant, *Chelidonium majus,* native to Eurasia, having deeply divided leaves, yellow flowers, and yellow-orange juice. Also called "swallowwort." **2.** The **lesser celandine** *(see).* [Middle English *celidoine,* from Old French, from Medieval Latin *celidonia,* from Latin *chelidonia, chelidonium,* from Greek *khelidonion,* from *khelidōn,* swallow (the ancients associated the plant with the habits of the swallow).]

-cele[1] *suffix.* Indicates a tumor or hernia; for example, **cystocele.** [From Greek *kēlē*†, tumor.]

-cele[2], **-coel, -coele** *suffix.* Indicates a hollow chamber; for example, **hematocele, blastocoel, blastocoele.**

Celebes. See **Sulawesi.**

cel·e·brant (sĕl′ə-brənt) *n.* **1.** The priest officiating at the celebration of the Eucharist or other religious ceremony. **2.** A person who participates in a celebration.

cel·e·brate (sĕl′ə-brāt′) *v.* **-brated, -brating, -brates.** —*tr.* **1.** To mark or observe (a special day or event) with ceremonies of respect, festivity, or rejoicing. **2.** To perform (a religious ceremony). **3.** To extol; praise. —*intr.* **1.** To observe an occasion with appropriate ceremony, festivity, or merrymaking. **2.** To perform a religious ceremony. —See Synonyms at **observe.** [Latin *celebrāre,* to frequent, fill, celebrate, from *celeber,* numerous, much frequented.] —**cel·e·bra·tion** *n.* —**cel·e·bra·tor** *n.*

cel·e·brat·ed (sĕl′ə-brā′tĭd) *adj.* Famous.

ce·leb·ri·ty (sə-lĕb′rə-tē) *n., pl.* **-ties. 1.** A famous person. **2.** Notoriety or renown; fame. [Latin *celebritās* (stem *celebritāt-*), from *celeber,* numerous.]

ce·le·ri·ac (sə-lîr′ē-ăk′, sə-lĕr′-) *n.* A variety of celery, *Apium graveolens rapaceum,* cultivated for its edible, turniplike root. [Unexplained derivative of CELERY.]

ce·ler·i·ty (sə-lĕr′ə-tē) *n.* Swiftness of action or motion; speed. [Middle English *celerite,* from Old French, from Latin *celeritās,* from *celer,* swift.]

cel·er·y (sĕl′ə-rē) *n., pl.* **-ies.** A plant, *Apium graveolens dulce,* native to Eurasia and widely cultivated for its edible stalks and its small seeds, used as seasoning. [French *céleri,* from Italian (Lombardy dialect) *seleri,* plural of *selero,* from Late Latin *selīnum,* from Greek *selinon*†, celery.]

ce·les·ta (sə-lĕs′tə) *n.* Also **ce·leste** (sə-lĕst′). A musical instrument having a keyboard and metal plates struck by hammers that produce bell-like tones. [French *célesta,* coined from *céleste,* celestial, from Latin *caelestis,* CELESTIAL.]

ce·les·tial (sə-lĕs′chəl) *adj.* **1.** Of or pertaining to the sky or the heavens. **2.** Of, from, or suggestive of heaven; divine or spiritual: *celestial beings.* **3.** Supreme in nature or kind; heavenly: *celestial happiness.* **4.** Of or pertaining to the Chinese people or to the former Chinese Empire. [Middle English, from Old French, from Latin *caelestis,* from *caelum*†, sky, heaven.]

celestial body *n.* Any object occurring naturally in space, especially a planet, star, or comet.

Celestial Empire *n.* The Chinese Empire. [Translation of Chinese *tiān cháo,* literally "celestial dynasty" (from the belief that the emperors were sons of Heaven).]

celestial equator *n.* A great circle on the celestial sphere in the same plane as the earth's equator. Also called "equinoctial," "equinoctial circle," "equinoctial line."

celestial globe *n.* A model of the celestial sphere showing the stars and other celestial bodies.

celestial guidance *n.* The guiding of missiles or spacecraft by reference to the positions of one or more celestial bodies.

celestial horizon *n.* See **horizon** (sense 2c).

celestial latitude *n.* The angular distance of a celestial body north (counted positive) or south (counted negative) of the ecliptic, measured on the great circle through the body and the poles of the ecliptic.

celestial longitude *n.* The angular distance of a celestial body from the vernal equinox, measured eastward along the ecliptic to its intersection with the great circle through the body and the poles of the ecliptic. Also called "longitude."

celestial mechanics *n. Used with a singular verb.* The science of the motion of celestial bodies under the influence of gravitational forces.

celestial navigation *n.* Ship or aircraft navigation based on the positions of celestial bodies. Also called "astronavigation."

celestial pole *n.* Either of two diametrically opposite points at which the extensions of the earth's axis intersect the celestial sphere.

celestial sphere *n.* An imaginary sphere of infinite extent with the earth at its center. The stars, planets, and other heavenly bodies appear to be located on its imaginary surface.

cel·es·tite (sĕl′ĭ-stīt′, sə-lĕs′tīt′) *n.* A white, red-brown, or light-blue strontium ore, essentially strontium sulfate, $SrSO_4$. [German *Zölestin,* from Latin *caelestis,* CELESTIAL (from its blue color).]

ce·li·ac, coe·li·ac (sē′lē-ăk′) *adj.* Of or relating to the abdomen. [Latin *coeliacus,* from Greek *koiliakos,* from *koilia,* abdomen, from *koilos,* hollow.]

celiac disease *n.* A chronic nutritional disturbance of infants and young children, caused by improper absorption of fats and resulting in malnutrition, distended abdomen, and diarrhea.

cel·i·ba·cy (sĕl′ə-bə-sē) *n.* The condition of being unmarried or sexually abstinent, especially by reason of religious vows. [Latin *caelibātus,* celibacy, from *caelebs*† (stem *caelib-*), unmarried.]

cel·i·bate (sĕl′ə-bĭt) *n.* One who remains unmarried, especially by religious vow, or abstains from sexual intercourse.
∼*adj.* **1.** Unmarried. **2.** Not having sexual intercourse; chaste. [From Latin *caelebs*† (stem *caelib-*), unmarried.]

cell (sĕl) *n.* **1.** A small, narrow room, as in a prison or monastic institution. **2.** Any small and humble dwelling. **3.** A small religious house dependent on a larger one, such as a priory within an abbey. **4.** The primary organizational unit of a subversive or revolutionary political group, consisting of a few members usually living or working in the same place. **5.** A small group of Christian lay persons working for the propagation of the faith. **6.** *Biology.* The smallest structural unit of an organism that is capable of independent functioning, consisting of one or more nuclei, cytoplasm, various organelles, and inanimate matter, all surrounded by a semipermeable plasma membrane. Plant cells have cellulose outer cell walls. **7.** *Biology.* A small, enclosed cavity or space, such as a compartment in a honeycomb or within a plant ovary, or an area bordered by veins in an insect's wing. **8. a.** A single unit for electrolysis or for conversion of chemical into electric energy, usually consisting of a container with electrodes and an electrolyte. **b.** A single unit that converts radiant energy into electric energy: *a solar cell.* **9.** *Computer Science.* The smallest unit of data, capable of storing a single bit in part of a computer memory.
∼*v.* **celled, celling, cells.** —*tr.* To store in a honeycomb. —*intr.* To live in a cell. [Middle English *celle,* from Old French, from Latin *cella,* cella, storeroom, chamber.]

cel·la (sĕl′ə) *n., pl.* **cellae** (sĕl′ē′). The inner room of an ancient Greek or Roman temple. [Latin *cella,* cella, CELL.]

cel·lar (sĕl′ər) *n.* **1.** A room used for storage, usually beneath the ground or under a building. **2. a.** A dark, cool room for storing wines. **b.** A stock of wines. **3.** *Informal.* The lowest level, especially in the standing of an athletic team.

~*tr.v.* **cellared, -laring, -lars.** To store in a cellar. [Middle English *celer*, from Norman French, from Late Latin *cellārium*, storehouse, larder, from Latin *cella*, storeroom, CELL.]

cel·lar·age (sĕl′ər-ĭj) *n.* **1.** A fee charged for storage in a cellar. **2.** The amount of storage space in a cellar. **3. a.** A cellar. **b.** Cellars collectively.

cel·lar·er (sĕl′ər-ər) *n.* The member of a monastic community responsible for the maintenance of adequate supplies of food and drink. [Middle English *celerer*, from Norman French, from Late Latin *cellāriārius*, from *cellārium*, CELLAR.]

cel·lar·et, cel·lar·ette (sĕl′ə-rĕt′) *n.* A cabinet used for storing bottles of wine. [Diminutive of CELLAR.]

cell division *n.* The process by which a cell divides and multiplies. See amitosis, meiosis, mitosis.

celled (sĕld) *adj.* Having cells of the specified type or number. Used in combination: *single-celled.*

Cel·li·ni (chə-lē′nē), **Benvenuto** (1500–71). Italian goldsmith and sculptor, famous also for his *Autobiography*, which described court life in Rome, Florence, and Paris and the siege of Rome (1527). *Perseus*, at the Loggia dei Lanzi, Florence, is considered his masterpiece as a sculptor.

cell membrane *n.* A plasma membrane *(see).*

cel·lo (chĕl′ō) *n.*, *pl.* **-los.** A four-stringed instrument of the violin family, pitched lower than the viola but higher than the double bass and held upright between the knees. Also called "violoncello." [Short for VIOLONCELLO.] **—cel·list** (chĕl′ĭst) *n.*

cel·loi·din (sə-loid′n) *n.* A pure pyroxylin in which specimens being sectioned for microscopic examination are embedded. [CELL(U-LOSE) + -OID + -IN.]

cel·lo·phane (sĕl′ə-fān′) *n.* A thin, flexible, transparent cellulose material made from wood pulp and used as a moistureproof wrapping. [CELL(ULOSE) + -PHANE.]

cel·lu·lar (sĕl′yə-lər) *adj.* **1.** Of, pertaining to, or resembling a cell. **2.** Consisting of or containing a cell or cells. **3.** Containing a number of small compartments or cavities. Said of rock. **—cel·lu·lar·i·ty** (sĕl′yə-lăr′ə-tē) *n.*

cel·lu·lase (sĕl′yə-lās′, -lāz′) *n.* Any of several enzymes, found in fungi, bacteria, and lower animals, that hydrolyze cellulose. [CELLUL(OSE) + -ASE.]

cel·lule (sĕl′yōol) *n.* Biology. A small cell. [French, monk's cell, from Latin *cellula*, small apartment, diminutive of *cella*, CELL.]

cel·lu·lite (sĕl′yə-līt′) *n.* A fatty deposit, found particularly around the thighs and buttocks and the tops of the arms. [CELLUL(E) + -ITE.]

cel·lu·li·tis (sĕl′yə-lī′tĭs) *n.* Inflammation of subcutaneous tissue, causing pain and fever. [New Latin : Latin *cellula*, cell (see **cellule**) + -ITIS.]

cel·lu·loid (sĕl′yə-loid′) *n.* A colorless, flammable material made from nitrocellulose and camphor and used for toys, toilet articles, and photographic film. [Originally a trademark.]

cel·lu·lose (sĕl′yə-lōs′, -lōz′) *n.* A polysaccharide, $(C_6H_{10}O_5)_x$, of high tensile strength, the main constituent of plant cell walls and used in the manufacture of many fibrous products, including paper, textiles, and explosives. [French, from *cellule*, biological cell, CELLULE.] **—cel·lu·lo·sic** (sĕl′yə-lō′sĭk, -zĭk) *adj.*

cellulose acetate *n.* A cellulose resin used in lacquers, photographic film, transparent sheeting, and cigarette filters.

cellulose nitrate *n.* A tough thermoplastic, nitrocellulose *(see).*

cell wall *n.* The rigid outermost layer of a plant cell, consisting of cellulose and other polysaccharides.

celom. Variant of **coelom.**

Cel·si·us (sĕl′sē-əs, -shəs) *adj. Abbr.* **C** Of or pertaining to a temperature scale that registers the freezing point of water as 0°C and the boiling point as 100°C under normal atmospheric pressure. Also called "centigrade." The designation *Celsius* has been official since 1948, but *centigrade* remains in common use. [After Anders *Celsius* (1701–44), Swedish astronomer who devised the scale.]

celt (sĕlt) *n.* A prehistoric axlike tool. [Late Latin *celtis, celtes†*, chisel, a possible misreading of *certe*, surely, in a disputed text of the Vulgate (Job 19:24) (influenced in form by CELT).]

Celt (kĕlt, sĕlt) *n.* **1.** A member of an ancient people of western and central Europe, including the Britons, the Irish, and the Gauls. **2.** A speaker or a descendant of speakers of a Celtic language. [French *Celte*, singular of *Celtes*, from Latin *Celtae*, from Greek *Keltoi†*.]

Celt·ic (kĕl′tĭk, sĕl′-) *n. Abbr.* **C., Celt.** A subfamily of the Indo-European family of languages, subdivided into the Brythonic branch, consisting of Cornish, Welsh, and Breton, and the Goidelic branch, consisting of Irish Gaelic, Scottish Gaelic, and Manx. ~*adj.* Of or pertaining to the Celtic people and languages.

Celtic Church *n.* The Church as it existed throughout the British Isles until the late 6th century and as it remained, at variance with the Church of Rome, in Wales and Ireland for some time.

Celtic cross *n.* An upright cross superimposed on a circle.

Celt·i·cism (kĕl′tə-sĭz′əm, sĕl′-) *n.* A Celtic custom or idiom.

Celt·i·cist (kĕl′tə-sĭst, sĕl′-) *n.* A specialist in Celtic culture or Celtic languages.

Celtic Sea. A section of the Atlantic Ocean bounded by southern Ireland, Wales, Cornwall, Brittany, and southwest England.

cem·ba·lo (chĕm′bə-lō′) *n.*, *pl.* **-los.** A harpsichord. [Italian, short for *clavicembalo*, from Medieval Latin *clāvicymbalum* : Latin *clāvis*, key + *cymbalum*, CYMBAL.] **—cem·ba·list** *n.*

ce·ment (sĭ-mĕnt′) *n.* **1.** Any of various construction adhesives, consisting essentially of powdered, calcined rock and clay materials,

---

cell division

THE BUILDING BLOCKS OF LIFE
Every living organism grows from a single cell

All growth is the result of cells splitting in two, a process triggered by the genetic instructions carried in the core, or nucleus, of each cell in the form of DNA (deoxyribonucleic acid). In single-celled animals such as amoebas, this division, or "mitosis," results in two separate but identical individuals. But in multicelled plants and animals, the process is more complex.

In humans, for example, the mother's ovum, which is a single cell just visible to the naked eye, begins to divide soon after conception. It becomes two, then four, then eight, then sixteen cells, and so on. The cells are identical at first. But as growth continues, the cluster of cells forms a hollow ball with two distinct layers—an inner endoderm and an outer ectoderm. Later a third layer, the mesoderm, forms between the two.

Eventually, ectoderm cells give rise to skin or nerve tissue. Endoderm cells develop into glands, the digestive system, and the lungs. Mesoderm cells become blood, bone, and muscle. But every cell still carries within it the genetic blueprint for the entire individual. At birth a baby contains 20 trillion cells, and the number increases to about 50 trillion by adulthood. Then, apart from the replacement of blood cells and of tissue such as skin—which is renewed by cell division every few days—and the repair of wounds with scar tissue, all growth stops.

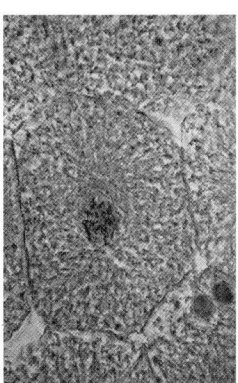

PROPHASE *Strands of chromosomes in the nucleus darken as they duplicate themselves before splitting.*

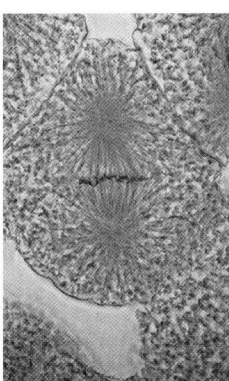

METAPHASE *Minute fibers draw the strands, which contain the cell's genetic instructions, into a line.*

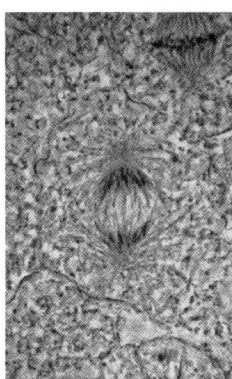

ANAPHASE *The fibers contract, pulling the strands apart into two identical sets of chromosomes.*

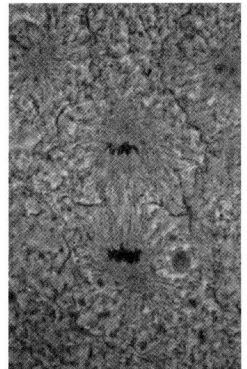

EARLY TELOPHASE *The separated sets—seen here more than 300 times lifesize—gather into clusters.*

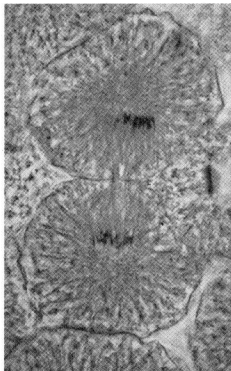

LATE TELOPHASE *Cell walls form around the two new nuclei to complete the hour-long process of division.*

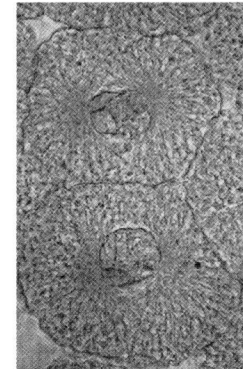

INTERPHASE *Chromosome strands spread through the nucleus until a new division begins 10–20 hours later.*

---

that form a paste with water and can be molded or poured to set as a solid mass, especially when mixed with sand and aggregate to form concrete. See **Portland cement, hydraulic cement. 2.** Any substance that hardens to act as an adhesive; glue. **3.** Any of various substances used in dentistry to form fillings or fix crowns in place. **4.** *Geology.* A chemically precipitated substance that binds particles of clastic rocks. **5. Cementum** *(see).* ~*v.* **cemented, -menting, -ments.** —*tr.* **1.** To bind with or as if with cement. **2.** To cover or coat with cement. **3.** To make firm and united; bind closely: *cement a friendship.* —*intr.* To become cemented. [Middle English *siment, cyment*, from Old French *ciment*, from Latin *caementum*, rough quarried stone, and its plural *caementa*, marble chips (used to make lime), from *caedere*, to cut, hew.] **—ce·ment·er** *n.*

ce·men·ta·tion (sē′mĕn-tā′shən) *n.* **1.** The process or result of cementing. **2.** A metallurgical coating process in which iron or steel is immersed in a powder of another metal, such as zinc, chromium, or aluminum, and heated to a temperature below the melting point of

centaur *For the ancient Greeks the mythical centaurs—half men, half horses—represented lawlessness, animal passions, and barbarism. They were often pictured, as here, being ridden by Eros, the god of love—an allusion to their amorous nature.*

either. **3.** A similar process in which wrought iron is heated in a bed of charcoal to produce steel.

ce·ment·ite (sĭ-mĕn′tīt′) *n.* A hard, brittle iron carbide, Fe_3C, formed in steel with more than 0.85 percent carbon.

cement mixer *n.* A **concrete mixer** *(see).*

ce·ment·um (sĭ-mĕn′təm) *n.* A bony substance that covers the root of a tooth and anchors the tooth in the socket. [New Latin, from Latin *caementum,* rough stone, CEMENT.]

cem·e·ter·y (sĕm′ə-tĕr′ē) *n., pl.* **-ies.** A place for burying the dead; graveyard. [Middle English *cimitery,* from Late Latin *coemētērium,* from Greek *koimētērion,* sleeping room, burial place, from *koiman,* to put to sleep.]

cen. **1.** central. **2.** century.

cen–, ceno–. Variants of **coeno-.**

cen·a·cle (sĕn′ə-kəl) *n.* **1.** A small social group that meets to discuss shared interests; especially, a literary clique. **2.** A small dining room, usually on an upper floor. **3.** A retreat house. [Middle English, from Old French, from Late Latin *cēnāculum,* dining room, the Cenacle of the Last Supper, from Latin *cēna,* dinner.]

–cene *suffix.* Indicates a recent geological period; for example, **Miocene.** [From Greek *kainos,* new, fresh.]

cen·o·bite, coen·o·bite (sĕn′ə-bīt′, sē′nə-) *n.* A member of a monastic community. [Late Latin *coenobīta,* from *coenobium,* convent, from Greek *koinobion,* life in community : *koinos,* common + *bios,* life.] **—cen·o·bit·ic** (sĕn′ə-bĭt′ĭk, sē′nə-), **cen·o·bit·i·cal** (-ĭ-kəl) *adj.*

ce·no·gen·e·sis, coe·no·gen·e·sis (sē′nō-jĕn′ə-sĭs, sĕn′ō-) *n.* The environmentally determined development of characteristics or structures in an organism. [Greek *kainos,* new + GENESIS.] **—ce·no·ge·net·ic** (sē′nō-jə-nĕt′ĭk, sĕn′ō-) *adj.*

ce·no·spe·cies (sē′nə-spē′shēz, sĕn′ə-) *n., pl.* **cenospecies.** Any of a group of species that are capable of interbreeding: *Donkeys and horses are cenospecies.* [From Greek *koinos,* common + SPECIES.]

cen·o·taph (sĕn′ə-tăf′, -täf′) *n.* A monument erected in honor of a dead person or persons whose remains lie elsewhere. [French *cénotaphe,* from Latin *cenotaphium,* from Greek *kenotaphion,* empty tomb : *kenos,* empty + *taphos,* tomb.]

Ce·no·zo·ic (sē′nə-zō′ĭk, sĕn′ə-) *adj.* Of, belonging to, or designating the latest era of geological time, which includes the Tertiary and Quaternary periods and is characterized by the evolution of mammals, birds, plants, modern continents, and glaciation.
~n. Geology. The Cenozoic era. Preceded by *the.* [Greek *kainos,* new, fresh + -ZOIC.]

cense (sĕns) *tr.v.* **censed, censing, censes. 1.** To perfume with incense. **2.** To offer incense to. [Middle English *censen,* short for *encensen,* to burn incense, from Old French *encenser,* from *encens,* INCENSE (noun).]

cen·ser (sĕn′sər) *n.* A vessel in which incense is burned, especially at religious ceremonies. Also called "thurible." [Middle English *censer,* from Old French *censier,* short for *encensier,* from *encens,* INCENSE (noun).]

cen·sor (sĕn′sər) *n.* **1.** An authorized examiner of literature, plays, films, or other material, who may prohibit what he considers morally, politically, or otherwise objectionable. **2.** An official, as in the armed forces or a prison, who examines personal mail and official dispatches to remove any information considered secret or improper. **3.** Any person who condemns or censures. **4.** In ancient Rome, either of two officials responsible for supervising the public census and public behavior and morals. **5.** *Psychoanalysis.* The agent responsible for censorship.
~tr.v. **censored, -soring, -sors.** To examine and expurgate. [Latin *cēnsor,* from *cēnsēre,* to assess, estimate, judge.] **—cen·so·ri·al** (sĕn-sôr′ē-əl, sĕn-sōr′-) *adj.*

cen·so·ri·ous (sĕn-sôr′ē-əs, sĕn-sōr′-) *adj.* **1.** Tending to reprimand or censure; highly critical. **2.** Expressing censure. [Latin *cēnsōrius,* of a censor, from *cēnsor,* CENSOR.] **—cen·so·ri·ous·ly** *adv.* **—cen·so·ri·ous·ness** *n.*

cen·sor·ship (sĕn′sər-shĭp′) *n.* **1.** The act or process of censoring. **2.** The office or authority of a Roman censor. **3.** A program or policy of censoring. **4.** *Psychoanalysis.* The inhibition, by either ego or superego, of conscious awareness of painful feelings or ideas.

cen·sur·a·ble (sĕn′shər-ə-bəl) *adj.* Deserving censure. **—cen·sur·a·ble·ness, cen·sur·a·bil·i·ty** *n.* **—cen·sur·a·bly** *adv.*

cen·sure (sĕn′shər) *n.* An expression of disapproval or severe criticism: *passed a vote of censure.*
~tr.v. **censured, -suring, -sures.** To criticize severely; express strong disapproval of; blame. —See Synonyms at **criticize.** [Latin *cēnsūra,* censorship, the office of a censor, from *cēnsor,* CENSOR.] **—cen·sur·er** *n.*

cen·sus (sĕn′səs) *n.* An official, periodic enumeration of population that usually also includes the collection of related demographic information. [Latin *cēnsus,* registration of citizens, from *cēnsēre,* to assess, tax.]

census taker *n.* One who gathers information for a census.

cent (sĕnt) *n. Abbr.* **c., C., ct. 1. a.** *Symbol* **¢** A monetary unit equal to $^{1}/_{100}$ of the U.S. dollar. **b.** A monetary unit equal to $^{1}/_{100}$ of the dollar of various other countries, such as Australia, Canada, New Zealand, Hong Kong, and Zimbabwe. **c.** A monetary unit equal to $^{1}/_{100}$ of various standard monetary units, such as the leone of Sierra Leone, the rand of South Africa, the rupee of Sri Lanka, and the yuan of China. **d.** A monetary unit equal to $^{1}/_{100}$ of the shilling of Kenya, Tanzania, Uganda, and Somalia. See feature at **currency. 2.** A coin or note worth one cent. [Old French, "hundred," from Latin *centum,* hundred.]

cent. **1.** centime. **2.** central. **3.** century.

cen·taur (sĕn′tôr′) *n.* **1.** *Greek Mythology.* One of a race of monsters, born of Ixion, having the head, arms, and trunk of a man and the body and legs of a horse. **2. Centaur.** Variant of **Centaurus.** [Middle English *Centaur,* from Latin *Centaurus,* from Greek *Kentauros*†, originally the name of a primitive Thessalian tribe.]

Cen·tau·rus (sĕn-tôr′əs) *n.* Also **Cen·taur** (sĕn′tôr′). A constellation in the Southern Hemisphere near Vela and Lupus. [Latin, CENTAUR.]

cen·tau·ry (sĕn′tôr′ē) *n., pl.* **-ries. 1.** Any of several plants of the genus *Centaurium,* native to Eurasia; especially, *C. umbellatum,* having clusters of rose-purple flowers. **2.** A plant of the genus *Centaurea,* which includes the cornflower and knapweed. [Middle English *centaure,* from Old French *centauree,* from Late Latin *centaurea,* variant of Latin *centaureum,* from Greek *kentaureion,* centaury, from *Kentauros,* CENTAUR (its medicinal properties were supposedly discovered by the centaur Chiron, a physician).]

cen·ta·vo (sĕn-tä′vō) *n., pl.* **-vos. 1. a.** A monetary unit equal to $^{1}/_{100}$ of the Portuguese escudo. **b.** A monetary unit equal to $^{1}/_{100}$ of the standard monetary unit of various countries in Central and South America, such as the cruzeiro of Brazil or the peso of Mexico. **c.** A monetary unit equal to $^{1}/_{100}$ of the escudo of Cape Verde. See feature at **currency. 2.** A coin worth one centavo. [Spanish, "a hundredth," from Latin *centum,* hundred.]

cen·te·nar·i·an (sĕn′tə-nâr′ē-ən) *n.* A person who is one hundred years old or older. [From Latin *centēnārius,* CENTENARY.] **—cen·te·nar·i·an** *adj.*

cen·ten·a·ry (sĕn-tĕn′ə-rē, sĕn′tə-nĕr′ē) *adj.* **1.** Of or pertaining to a 100-year period. **2.** Of or pertaining to a 100th anniversary.
~n., pl. **centenaries. 1.** A 100-year period. **2.** A centennial. [Latin *centēnārius,* of a hundred, from *centēnī,* a hundred each, from *centum,* hundred.]

cen·ten·ni·al (sĕn-tĕn′ē-əl) *adj.* **1.** Of, pertaining to, or existing for a 100-year period. **2.** Occurring once every 100 years. **3.** Of or pertaining to a 100th anniversary.
~n. **1.** A 100th anniversary. **2.** A celebration of a centennial. [Latin *centum,* hundred + (BI)ENNIAL.] **—cen·ten·ni·al·ly** *adv.*

cen·ter (sĕn′tər) *n.* Also *chiefly British* **cen·tre.** *Abbr.* **ctr. 1.** A point equidistant or at the average distance from all points on the sides or outer boundaries of anything. **2.** *Geometry.* **a.** A point equidistant from the vertexes of a regular polygon. **b.** A point equidistant from all points on the circumference of a circle or on the surface of a sphere. **3.** A point around which something revolves; an axis. **4.** A part of an object that is surrounded by the rest; a core: *a chocolate with a soft center.* **5.** An area that is roughly in the middle of a larger area: *the center of town.* **6. a.** The main area in which a particular activity is concentrated: *the center of the steel industry.* **b.** An area of special influence: *a center of power.* **c.** A place used for a specified purpose or activity: *an arts center.* **7.** A person or thing that is the chief object of attention, interest, activity, or emotion. **8.** A person, object, or group occupying a middle position. **9.** A political group or a set of policies representing a compromise between the right and the left. **10.** In some team sports, a player who holds a middle position on the field, court, or forward line. **11.** A collection of nerve cells in the central nervous system that controls a particular function: *the respiratory center.* **12.** A small conical hole made in a piece of work with a center punch in order to center a drill within it accurately. **13.** A bar with a conical point used to support work, as during turning in a lathe.
~v. **centered, -tering, -ters.** Also *chiefly British* **centre, -tred, -tring, -tres.** *—tr.* **1.** To place in or on a center. **2.** To concentrate at a center. **3.** To pass (a football) from the line to a back. *—intr.* To have a center; be concentrated: *The dispute centered on the issue of overtime rates.*
~adj. Also *chiefly British* **centre.** Being at the center; middle. [Middle English, from Old French, from Latin *centrum,* center, stationary point of a compass, from Greek *kentron,* sharp point, needle, from *kentein,* to prick.]

center bit *n.* A drill bit having a sharp center point, used in carpentry for boring holes.

cen·ter·board (sĕn′tər-bôrd′, -bōrd′) *n. Nautical.* A flat board or metal plate that can be lowered through the bottom of a sailing boat to prevent drifting and provide stability.

center field *n. Baseball.* **1.** The middle part of the outfield, behind second base. **2.** The position of center field. **—center fielder** *n.*

cen·ter·fold (sĕn′tər-fōld′) *n.* An illustration that fills the center spread of a magazine or newspaper.

center of gravity *n.* **1.** *Abbr.* **c.g.** The point in or near a body at which the gravitational potential energy of the body is equal to that of a single particle of the same mass located at that point and through which the resultant of the gravitational forces on the component particles of the body acts. **2.** The point of greatest importance, most concentrated activity, or the like; the focal point.

center of mass *n.* The point in a body or system of bodies through which all external forces may be considered to act and at which the entire mass is apparently concentrated. Also called "barycenter."

cen·ter·piece (sĕn′tər-pēs′) *n.* **1.** Something in a central position; especially a decorative object or arrangement placed at the center of a table. **2.** A part or item intended as the principal or most impressive feature: *the centerpiece of the party's manifesto.*

center punch *n.* A tool with a sharp point used in metalwork to mark centers or center lines on pieces to be drilled.

cen·tes·i·mal (sĕn-tĕs′ə-məl) *adj.* Of, pertaining to, or characterized

PRONUNCIATION KEY

ă, pat; ā, pay; âr, care; ä, father, are; b, bib; ch, church; d, deed; ĕ, pet; ē, be; f, fife; g, gag; h, hat; hw, which; ĭ, pit; ī, pie; îr, pier; j, judge; k, kick; l, lid, needle; m, mum; n, no, sudden; ng, thing; ŏ, pot; ō, toe; ô, paw, for; oi, noise; ou, out; ŏŏ, book; ōō, boot; p, pop; r, roar; s, sauce; sh, ship, dish; t, tight; th, thin, path; *th,* this, bathe; ŭ, cut; ûr, fur; v, valve; w, with; y, yes; z, zebra, size; zh, vision; ə, about, item, edible, gallop, circus, peaceful

IN FOREIGN WORDS:

à, *Fr.* ami; œ, *Fr.* feu, *Ger.* schön; ü, *Fr.* tu, *Ger.* über; KH, *Ger.* ich, *Scot.* loch; N, *Fr.* bon; y′, *Fr.* Compiègne

STRESS MARKS:

Primary stress: ′
in·cite′ (ĭn-sīt′)
Secondary stress: ′
in′sight′ (ĭn′sīt′)

by division into hundredths. [From Latin *centēsimus,* hundredth, from *centum,* hundred.] —**cen·tes·i·mal·ly** *adv.*

cen·tes·i·mo (sĕn-tĕs'ə-mō'; *Italian* chän-tä'zē-mō') *n., pl.* **-mi** (-mē). A monetary unit equal to ¹/₁₀₀ of the lira of Italy and the shilling of Somalia. See feature at **currency.** [Italian, "hundredth," from Latin *centēsimus,* CENTESIMAL.]

cen·tés·i·mo (sĕn-tĕs'ə-mō'; *Spanish* sĕn-tĕ'sē-mō') *n., pl.* **-mos.** A monetary unit equal to ¹/₁₀₀ of the balboa of Panama, the escudo of Chile, and the nuevo peso of Uruguay. See feature at **currency.** [Spanish, "hundredth," from Latin *centēsimus,* CENTESIMAL.]

cen·te·sis (sĕn-tē'sĭs) *n., pl.* **-ses** (-sēz'). The surgical puncture of a membrane or body cavity, usually for diagnostic purposes. [Greek *kentēsis,* act of pricking, from *kentein,* to prick.]

centi-, cent– *prefix. Abbr.* **c** Indicates a hundred or hundredth; for example, **centinewton, centiliter.** [French, from Latin *centum,* hundred.]

cen·ti·grade (sĕn'tĭ-grād') *adj.* **1.** Consisting of or divided into 100 degrees. **2.** *Abbr.* **C** Designating the **Celsius** temperature scale. [French : CENTI- + GRADE.]

cen·ti·gram (sĕn'tĭ-grăm') *n. Abbr.* **cg** One hundredth (10⁻²) of a gram.

cen·tile (sĕn'tīl, -tĭl) *n.* **Percentile** *(see).*

cen·ti·li·ter (sĕn'tə-lē'tər) *n. Abbr.* **cl** One hundredth (10⁻²) of a liter. [French : CENTI- + LITER.]

cen·til·lion (sĕn-tĭl'yən) *n.* **1.** In British and German usage, the cardinal number represented by one followed by 600 zeros, usually written 10⁶⁰⁰. **2.** In U.S. and French usage, the cardinal number represented by one followed by 303 zeros, usually written 10³⁰³. [CENTI- + (MI)LLION.]

cen·time (sän'tēm'; *French* säN-tēm') *n. Abbr.* **c., C., cent. 1. a.** A monetary unit equal to ¹/₁₀₀ of the French franc. **b.** A monetary unit equal to ¹/₁₀₀ of the franc of various other countries, such as Belgium, Luxembourg, and Switzerland. See feature at **currency. 2.** A coin worth one centime. [French, from *cent,* hundred. See **cent.**]

cen·ti·me·ter (sĕn'tə-mē'tər, sän'-) *n. Abbr.* **cm** A unit of length equal to one hundredth (10⁻²) of a meter or 0.3937 inch. [French *centimètre* : CENTI- + -METER.]

cen·ti·me·ter-gram-sec·ond system (sĕn'tə-mē'tər-grăm'sĕk'ənd) *n. Abbr.* **cgs, CGS** A coherent system of units for mechanics, electricity, and magnetism, in which the basic units of length, mass, and time are the centimeter, gram, and second.

cén·ti·mo (sĕn'tə-mō') *n., pl.* **-mos. 1.** A monetary unit equal to ¹/₁₀₀ of various standard monetary units, such as the bolívar of Venezuela, the colón of Costa Rica, and the peseta of Spain. See feature at **currency. 2.** A coin worth one céntimo. [Spanish *céntimo,* from French *centime,* CENTIME.]

cen·ti·new·ton (sĕn'tə-nōō'tən, -nyōō'tən) *n. Abbr.* **cN** One hundredth (10⁻²) of a newton.

cen·ti·pede (sĕn'tə-pēd') *n.* Any of various wormlike arthropods of the class Chilopoda, having numerous body segments, each with a pair of legs, the front pair modified into venomous biting organs. Compare **millipede.** [Latin *centipeda* : CENTI- + -PEDE.]

cen·ti·poise (sĕn'tə-poiz') *n. Abbr.* **cP** One hundredth (10⁻²) of a poise.

cent·ner (sĕnt'nər) *n.* **1.** A unit of weight corresponding to the hundredweight, equal to 50 kilograms (110.23 pounds), used in several European countries. **2.** An assaying unit equal to one dram. [German *Zentner,* from Old High German *centenāri,* from Medieval Latin *centēnārius,* weighing a hundred pounds, from Latin, CENTENARY.]

cen·to (sĕn'tō) *n., pl.* **-tos.** A literary work pieced together from the works of several authors. [Latin *centō,* patchwork, cento.]

cen·tral (sĕn'trəl) *adj. Abbr.* **cen., cent. 1.** At, in, near, or being the center. **2.** Of, pertaining to, or constituting that from which other things proceed or upon which they depend: *central government.* **3.** Of great importance; essential: *the central theme of the book.* **4.** Easily reached from various points: *tried to find a central location for the new store.* **5.** Of or being a single source controlling all components of a mechanical system: *installed central air conditioning.* **6.** *Anatomy & Physiology.* **a.** Of or pertaining to the central nervous system. **b.** Of or pertaining to a centrum. **7.** *Phonetics.* Pronounced with the tongue in a neutral position, as *e* in *mister.* —*n.* **1.** A telephone exchange. **2.** An operator at a telephone exchange. [Latin *centrālis,* from *centrum,* CENTER.] —**cen·tral·ly** *adv.*

Central African Republic. Formerly **U·ban·gi-Sha·ri** (ōō-băng'-gē-shär'ē, yōō-). A country in Central Africa. Known from 1976 to 1979 as the Central African Empire, it was, from 1894 to 1960, Ubangi-Shari, one of the four territories of French Equatorial Africa. It was granted independence in 1960, and in 1966 a coup brought Jean Bédel Bokassa to power. In 1976 he had himself crowned Emperor Bokassa I. Following allegations of corruption and massacres, he fled, and the short-lived empire became once again the Central African Republic. The country, one of the world's poorest, is covered by savanna. More than 90 percent of its workers are subsistence farmers, but the republic does export diamonds, uranium, cotton, and coffee. Area, 622,984 square kilometers (240,472 square miles). Population, 2,300,000. Capital, Bangui. See map at **Chad.**

Central America. *Abbr.* **C.A.** See **Americas, the.**

Central A·mer·i·can States (ə-mĕr'ĭ-kən). The countries that comprise Central America, south of Mexico and north of Colombia.

central angle *n.* An angle having radii as sides and the center of a circle as its vertex.

central dogma *n.* The hypothesis of biochemical genetics that genetic information is carried only one way in the cell, from DNA to RNA to protein.

Central European Time *n. Abbr.* **CET, C.E.T.** The standard time adopted by some countries of Central Europe, Western Europe, and Africa. It is one hour ahead of Greenwich Mean Time. See map at **Time Zone.**

central heating *n.* A method of or apparatus for heating the rooms of a building, as a house or office, by means of water-filled radiators or hot-air vents connected to a central boiler or heat source.

Central Intelligence Agency *n. Abbr.* **CIA** The coordinating agency for the intelligence and espionage activities of the U.S. government.

cen·tral·ism (sĕn'trə-lĭz'əm) *n.* The act or policy of concentrating control, as of the making of decisions, in a central authority or organization. —**cen·tral·ist** *n.* —**cen·tral·is·tic** *adj.*

cen·tral·i·ty (sĕn-trăl'ə-tē) *n.* **1.** The state or quality of being central. **2.** The tendency to be or remain at the center.

cen·tral·ize (sĕn'trə-līz') *v.* **-ized, -izing, -izes.** —*tr.* **1.** To draw into or toward a center; consolidate. **2.** To bring under a single, central authority. —*intr.* To come together at a center; concentrate. —**cen·tral·i·za·tion** *n.* —**cen·tral·iz·er** *n.*

central nervous system *n. Abbr.* **CNS** The portion of the vertebrate nervous system consisting of the brain and spinal cord. Compare **autonomic nervous system.**

Central Powers *pl.n.* The alliance comprising Germany, Austria-Hungary, Bulgaria, and Turkey in World War I.

central processing unit *n. Abbr.* **CPU** The central part of a computer, in which all the logical and arithmetical operations are performed.

Central Region. Since 1975 a Scottish local government region formed from Clackmannan, most of Stirlingshire, south Perthshire, and a small part of West Lothian. Extending from the Grampian Mts. to the Central Lowlands, it includes the Forth River valley. Stirling is the county town.

Central Standard Time *n. Abbr.* **CST, C.S.T.** The local civil time of the 90th meridian west of Greenwich, England, observed in the central United States, Canada, and Mexico and in some countries of Central America. It is six hours behind Greenwich Mean Time. See map at **Time Zone.** Also called "Central Time."

Central Sudanic *n.* A group of African languages of the Chari-Nile family, spoken in Chad, Central African Republic, Congo, Sudan, and Uganda.

centre. *Chiefly British.* Variant of **center.**

cen·tric (sĕn'trĭk) *adj.* Also **cen·tri·cal** (-trĭ-kəl). **1.** At, of, or having a center. **2.** *Physiology.* Of or originating at a nerve center. [Greek *kentrikos,* from *kentron,* CENTER.] —**cen·tri·cal·ly** *adv.* —**cen·tric·i·ty** (sĕn-trĭs'ə-tē) *n.*

–centric *suffix.* Indicates possession of a specified center; for example, **anthropocentric.**

cen·trif·u·gal (sĕn-trĭf'yə-gəl, -trĭf'ə-gəl) *adj.* **1.** Moving or directed away from a center or axis. Compare **centripetal. 2.** Operated by means of centrifugal force. **3.** *Physiology.* Transmitting impulses away from the central nervous system; efferent. **4.** *Botany.* Developing outward from a center or axis. Said of certain inflorescences. [New Latin *centrifugus* : Latin *centrum,* CENTER + *fugere,* to flee.] —**cen·trif·u·gal·ly** *adv.*

centrifugal force *n.* The component of apparent force on a body in curvilinear motion, as observed from that body, that is directed away from the center of curvature or axis of rotation; the equilibrant of centripetal force.

cen·tri·fuge (sĕn'trə-fyōōj') *n.* Any apparatus consisting essentially of a compartment spun about a central axis, used to separate con-

centipede *Unlike the millipede, which has two pairs of legs on each body segment, the centipede has only a single pair of legs to each segment. It is also armed with venomous fangs for killing prey. Centipedes are found in most temperate and tropical countries and may grow up to 200 millimeters (8 inches) in length.*

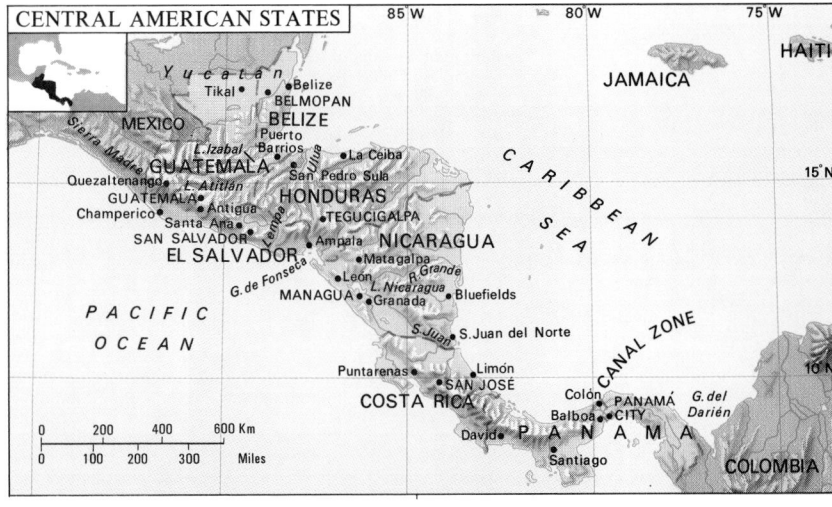

CENTRAL AMERICAN STATES

tained materials of different density or to simulate gravity with centrifugal force.

~*tr.v.* **centrifuged, -fuging, -fuges.** To separate, dehydrate, or test by means of a centrifuge. [French, from New Latin *centrifugus,* CENTRIFUGAL.] —**cen·trif·u·ga·tion** (sĕn-trĭf′yə-gā′shən, -trĭf′ə-) *n.*

cen·tri·ole (sĕn′trē-ōl′) *n. Genetics.* Either of two tiny cylindrical organelles in most animal cells that form the poles of the spindle during mitosis. [Latin *centrum,* CENTER + -OLE.]

cen·trip·e·tal (sĕn-trĭp′ə-təl) *adj.* **1.** Directed or moving toward a center or axis. Compare **centrifugal. 2.** Operated by means of centripetal force. **3.** *Physiology.* Transmitting impulses toward the central nervous system; afferent. **4.** *Botany.* Developing inward toward the center or axis. Said of some forms of inflorescence. [New Latin *centripetus* : Latin *centrum,* CENTER + -PETAL.] —**cen·trip·e·tal·ly** *adv.*

centripetal force *n.* The component of force acting on a body in curvilinear motion that is directed toward the center of curvature or axis of rotation.

cen·trism (sĕn′trĭz′əm) *n.* A political philosophy of avoiding extremes by taking a position in the center.

cen·trist (sĕn′trĭst) *n.* One taking a position in the political center; a moderate. [CENTR(O)- + -IST.]

centro-, centr– *prefix.* Indicates center; for example, **centromere, centrist.** [Greek *kentron,* CENTER.]

cen·tro·bar·ic (sĕn′trə-băr′ĭk) *adj.* Of or relating to the center of gravity. [Late Greek *kentrobarikos,* from Greek *kentrobarikē,* the theory of the center of gravity : *kentron,* CENTER + *bareos,* genitive of *baros,* weight.]

cen·tro·cli·nal (sĕn′trə-klī′nəl) *n. Geology.* Designating a rock formation in which the strata slope down and inward toward a central point or area. [CENTRO- + -CLINE.]

cen·troid (sĕn′troid′) *n.* The center of mass of an object having constant density. [CENTR(O)- + -OID.]

cen·tro·mere (sĕn′trə-mîr′) *n. Genetics.* The region of a chromosome to which the spindle is attached during mitosis. [CENTRO- + -MERE.]

cen·tro·some (sĕn′trə-sōm′) *n. Genetics.* A small mass of differentiated cytoplasm containing the centriole. [CENTRO- + -SOME (body).] —**cen·tro·so·mic** (sĕn′trə-sō′mĭk, -sŏm′ĭk) *adj.*

cen·tro·sphere (sĕn′trə-sfîr′) *n. Genetics.* The mass of cytoplasm surrounding the centriole in a centrosome.

cen·trum (sĕn′trəm) *n., pl.* **-trums** or **-tra** (-trə). The major part of a vertebra, exclusive of the bases of the neural arch. [Latin, CENTER.]

cen·tum (kĕn′təm) *adj.* Of, pertaining to, or designating those Indo-European languages that retained the velar *k* and the labiovelar *kw* of primitive Indo-European. Compare **satem.** [From Latin *centum,* hundred (chosen as a typical word in which initial *c* represents initial Indo-European *k*).]

cen·tu·ple (sĕn′tə-pəl, sĕn-tōō′pəl, -tyōō′pəl) *adj.* Multiplied by a hundred; hundredfold.

~*tr.v.* **centupled, -pling, -ples.** To increase a hundredfold; multiply by a hundred. [French, from Late Latin *centuplus* : Latin *centum,* hundred + *-plus,* "-fold."]

cen·tu·pli·cate (sĕn-tōō′plĭ-kāt′, sĕn-tyōō′-) *tr.v.* **-cated, -cating, -cates.** To multiply by one hundred.

~*adj.* (-kĭt, -kāt′). Hundredfold. [Latin *centuplicāre,* from *centuplex,* hundredfold : *centum,* hundred + *-plex,* "-fold."] —**cen·tu·pli·ca·tion** (sĕn-tōō′plĭ-kā′shən, sĕn-tyōō′-) *n.*

cen·tu·ri·on (sĕn-tŏŏr′ē-ən, sĕn-tyŏŏr′-) *n.* An officer commanding a century in the Roman army. [Middle English *centurioun,* from Old French *centurion,* from Latin *centuriō* (stem *centuriōn-*), from *centuria,* CENTURY.]

cen·tu·ry (sĕn′chə-rē) *n., pl.* **-ries.** *Abbr.* **c., C., cen., cent. 1.** A period of 100 years. **2.** Each of the successive periods of 100 years before or since the advent of the Christian era. **3.** A unit of the Roman army, originally consisting of 100 men. **4.** One of the 193 groups into which the Roman people were divided for purposes of electing the consuls and other state officials. **5.** A group of 100 things. [Latin *centuria,* a group of a hundred, from *centum,* hundred.]

century plant *n.* Any of several fleshy plants of the genus *Agave,* some species of which bloom only once in 10 to 20 years and then die; especially, *A. americana,* having large grayish leaves and greenish flowers.

ce·orl (chā′ôrl′) *n.* In Anglo-Saxon England, a freeman of the lowest class. Also called "churl." [Old English *ceorl,* CHURL.]

cepe, cep (sĕp) *n.* An edible mushroom, *Boletus edulis,* having a brown shiny cap. [French *cèpe,* from dialect (Gascon) *cep,* from Latin *cippus,* stake.]

ceph·a·lad (sĕf′ə-lăd′) *adv. Anatomy.* Toward the head or anterior section. Compare **caudad.** [CEPHAL(O)- + -AD.]

ceph·al·al·gia (sĕf′ə-lăl′jə, -jē-ə) *n.* Pain in the head; headache. [CEPHAL(O)- + -ALGIA.]

ce·phal·ic (sə-făl′ĭk) *adj.* **1.** Of or relating to the head or skull. **2.** Located on, in, or near the head. [Old French *cephalique,* from Latin *cephalicus,* from Greek *kephalikos,* from *kephalē,* head.]

–cephalic *suffix.* Indicates head or skull; for example, **orthocephalic.** [From Greek *-kephalos,* -CEPHALOUS.]

cephalic index *n.* The ratio of the maximum width of the head to its maximum length, multiplied by 100. Compare **cranial index.**

ceph·a·lin (sĕf′ə-lĭn) *n.* A phosphatide derived from the brain and spinal cord, usually of cattle, and used as a homeostatic agent. [CEPHAL(O)- + -IN.]

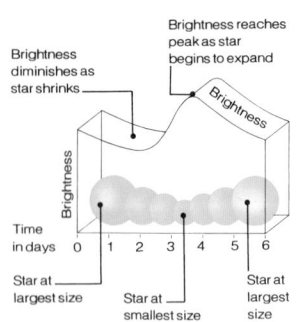

Cepheid variable *Delta Cephei, after which Cepheid variable stars are named, was discovered in 1784. It contracts and expands over a period of 5 days 9 hours. Such stars are used in the calculation of distances in the universe.*

ceph·a·li·za·tion (sĕf′ə-lə-zā′shən) *n. Zoology.* The gradually increasing concentration of nervous tissue and feeding and sensory organs at the head end during animal evolution. [CEPHAL(O)- + -IZ(E) + -ATION.]

cephalo-, cephal– *prefix.* Indicates head; for example, **cephalopod, cephalad.** [Latin, from Greek *kephalo-,* from *kephalē,* head.]

ceph·a·lo·chor·date (sĕf′ə-lə-kôr′dāt′) *adj.* Of or belonging to the subphylum Cephalochordata, which includes primitive forerunners of the vertebrates such as the lancelet.

~*n.* A cephalochordate animal. [New Latin *Cephalochordata* : CEPHALO- + CHORDATE.]

ceph·a·lo·pod (sĕf′ə-lə-pŏd′) *n.* Any of various mollusks of the class Cephalopoda, such as an octopus or nautilus, having a beaked head, an internal shell in some species, and prehensile tentacles. ~*adj.* Also **ceph·a·lop·o·dous** (sĕf′ə-lŏp′ə-dəs). Of, pertaining to, or belonging to the Cephalopoda. [New Latin *Cephalopoda* : CEPHALO- + -POD.] —**ceph·a·lop·o·dan** (sĕf′ə-lŏp′ə-dən) *n. & adj.*

ceph·a·lo·spo·rin (sĕf′ə-lə-spôr′ĭn, -spōr′ĭn) *n.* Any of a group of antibiotics, derived from the mold *Cephalosporium* and used to treat a wide variety of infections. [New Latin *Cephalosporium* : CEPHALO- + SPORE.]

ceph·a·lo·tho·rax (sĕf′ə-lə-thôr′ăks′, -thōr′ăks′) *n.* The anterior section of arachnids and many crustaceans, consisting of the fused head and thorax.

–cephalous *suffix.* Indicates a head; for example, **hydrocephalous.** [New Latin *-cephalus,* from Greek *-kephalos,* from *kephalē,* head.]

–cephalus *suffix.* Indicates an abnormality of the head; for example, **hydrocephalus.** [New Latin *-cephalus,* -CEPHALOUS.]

–cephaly *suffix.* Indicates a head; for example, **megalocephaly.** [From Greek *-kephalos,* -CEPHALOUS.]

Ce·phe·id variable (sē′fē-ĭd, sĕf′ē-) *n.* Either of two classes of intrinsically variable stars with exceptionally regular periods of light pulsation. Also called "Cepheid." [From CEPHEUS.]

Ce·pheus (sē′fyōōs, sē′fē-əs, sĕf′ē-) *n.* A constellation in the Northern Hemisphere near Cassiopeia and Draco. [Latin *Cēpheus,* from Greek *Kēpheus,* a mythical king.]

ce·ra·ceous (sə-rā′shəs) *adj.* Waxy or waxlike. [Latin *cēra* (see **cerate**) + -ACEOUS.]

ce·ram·al (sə-răm′əl) *n.* **Cermet** *(see).* [CERAM(IC) + AL(LOY).]

ce·ram·ic (sə-răm′ĭk) *n.* **1.** Any of various hard, brittle, heat-resistant and corrosion-resistant materials made by firing a nonmetallic mineral, as clay, at a high temperature. **2. a.** An object made of ceramic. **b. ceramics.** *Used with a singular verb.* The art or technique of making objects of ceramic, especially from fired clay or porcelain. [Probably French *céramique,* "of pottery," from Greek *keramikos,* from *keramos,* potter's clay, earthenware.] —**ce·ram·ic** *adj.* —**ce·ram·ist** *n.*

ce·rar·gy·rite (sə-rär′jə-rīt′) *n.* A gray to yellow mineral, AgCl, used as a source of silver. Also called "horn silver." [From Greek *keras,* horn + *arguros,* silver + -ITE.]

ce·ras·tes (sə-răs′tēz) *n., pl.* **cerastes.** Either of the two species of desert-dwelling, venomous snakes of the genus *Cerastes,* especially the **horned viper** *(see).* [Middle English, from Latin *cerastēs,* from Greek *kerastēs,* horned (serpent), from *keras,* horn.]

ce·rate (sîr′āt′) *n.* A hard, oily, fat- or wax-based solid, sometimes medicated, formerly applied to the skin directly or on dressings. [Latin *cērātum,* a wax plaster, wax salve, from *cēra,* wax, akin to Greek *kēros*†, wax.]

ce·rat·o·dus (sə-răt′ə-dəs) *n., pl.* **-duses.** Any of various extinct lungfishes of the genus *Ceratodus,* of the Triassic and Cretaceous periods. [New Latin *Ceratodus,* "horn-tooth" : Greek *keras* (stem *kerat-*), horn + *odous,* tooth.]

cer·a·toid (sĕr′ə-toid′) *adj.* Hornlike. [Greek *keratoeidēs* : *keras* (stem *kerat-*), horn + -OID.]

Cer·ber·us (sûr′bər-əs). *Greek & Roman Mythology.* A three-headed dog guarding the entrance of Hades. [Latin, from Greek *Kerberos*†.] —**Cer·be·re·an** (sûr′bə-rē′ən) *adj.*

cer·car·i·a (sər-kâr′ē-ə) *n., pl.* **-iae** (-ē-ē′) or **-as.** The parasitic larva of a trematode worm, having a tail that disappears in the adult stage. [New Latin, "the tailed one" : Greek *kerkos,* tail + *-aria,* from *-arius,* -ARY.] —**cer·car·i·al** *adj.*

cer·co·pi·the·coid (sûr′kə-pĭ-thē′koid′, -pĭth′ə-koid′) *adj.* Of or belonging to the family Cercopithecidae, which includes Old World monkeys such as the baboons, mandrills, macaques, and langurs. ~*n.* A member of the Cercopithecidae. [Latin *cercopithēcus,* long-tailed ape, from Greek *kerkopithēkos* : *kerkos,* tail + *pithēkos,* ape + -OID.]

cere[1] (sîr) *tr.v.* **cered, cering, ceres.** To wrap (a corpse, for example) in or as if in cerecloth. [Middle English *ceren,* to cover with wax, from Old French *cirer,* from Latin *cērāre,* from *cēra,* wax. See **cerate.**]

cere[2] *n.* A fleshy or waxlike swelling at the base of the upper part of the beak in certain birds, such as parrots and some birds of prey. [Middle English *sere,* from Old French *cire,* from Medieval Latin *cēra,* from Latin, wax. See **cerate.**] —**cered** (sîrd) *adj.*

ce·re·al (sîr′ē-əl) *n.* **1.** An edible grain, such as wheat, oats, or corn. **2.** A grass producing such a grain. **3.** A food prepared from such a grain, especially one eaten at breakfast. [Latin *cereālis,* of grain, "of Ceres," from *Cerēs,* CERES.] —**ce·re·al** *adj.*

cer·e·bel·lum (sĕr′ə-bĕl′əm) *n., pl.* **-lums** or **-bella** (-bĕl′ə). The structure of the brain responsible for regulation and coordination of complex voluntary movement, lying below the occipital lobes of the cerebral hemispheres. [Medieval Latin, from Latin, diminutive of *cerebrum,* brain.] —**cer·e·bel·lar** (sĕr′ə-bĕl′ər) *adj.*

cer·e·bral (sĕr′ə-brəl, sə-rē′-) *adj.* **1.** Of or pertaining to the brain or cerebrum. **2.** Appealing to or involving the workings of the intellect, rather than of the emotions. —**ce·re·bral·ly** *adv.*

cerebral cortex *n.* The extensive outer layer of gray matter of the cerebral hemispheres, largely responsible for higher nervous functions. Also called "mantle," "pallium."

cerebral hemisphere *n.* Either hemisphere of the cerebrum of the brain, divided by a deep groove running lengthwise.

cerebral palsy *n.* Impaired muscular power and coordination and weakness of the limbs resulting from brain damage usually occurring at or before birth.

cer·e·brate (sĕr′ə-brāt′) *intr.v.* **-brated, -brating, -brates.** To use the power of reason; think. [Back-formation from CEREBRATION.]

cer·e·bra·tion (sĕr′ə-brā′shən) *n.* The action of thinking; thought. [From Latin *cerebrum,* CEREBRUM.]

cerebro-, cerebr- *prefix.* Indicates the brain or cerebrum; for example, **cerebral, cerebration.**

cer·e·bro·side (sĕr′ə-brə-sīd′, sə-rē′-) *n.* Any of a group of lipids found in the brain and other nerve tissue, yielding on decomposition a fatty acid, an unsaturated amino alcohol, and a sugar. [CEREBR(UM) + -OS(E) + -IDE.]

cer·e·bro·spi·nal (sĕr′ə-brō-spī′nəl, sə-rē′brō-) *adj.* Of or pertaining to the brain and spinal cord. [CEREBR(UM) + SPINAL.]

cerebrospinal fluid *n.* The serumlike fluid that bathes the ventricles of the brain and the cavity of the spinal cord.

cerebrospinal meningitis *n.* An acute, infectious, epidemic meningitis that is caused by the bacterium *Neisseria meningitidis* and is often fatal. Also called "spinal meningitis," "cerebrospinal fever."

cer·e·bro·vas·cu·lar (sĕr′ə-brō-văs′kyə-lər, sə-rē′brō-) *adj.* Of or pertaining to the blood vessels supplying the brain or to the blood they carry.

cerebrovascular accident *n.* A sudden interruption of the supply of blood to the brain, caused by rupture (as in a cerebral hemorrhage) or blocking of a cerebral artery and resulting in a stroke.

cer·e·brum (sĕr′ə-brəm, sə-rē′-) *n., pl.* **-brums** or **-bra** (-brə). The large rounded structure of the brain occupying most of the cranial cavity, divided into two cerebral hemispheres and joined at the bottom by the corpus callosum. [Latin, brain.]

cere·cloth (sîr′klôth′, -klŏth′) *n.* Cloth coated with wax, formerly used for wrapping the dead. [Earlier *cered cloth,* waxed cloth. See **cerate.**]

cere·ment (sîr′mənt) *n. Often* **cerements.** Cerecloth. [French *cirement,* from *cirer,* to wax. See **cerate.**]

cer·e·mo·ni·al (sĕr′ə-mō′nē-əl) *adj.* Of, appropriate to, or characterized by ceremony; formal; ritual.
~*n.* **1.** The ceremonies to be observed on an official or religious occasion; a rite. **2.** The observance of these ceremonies. —**cer·e·mo·ni·al·ism** *n.* —**cer·e·mo·ni·al·ist** *n.* —**cer·e·mo·ni·al·ly** *adv.*
Usage: The similarity in form between *ceremonial* and *ceremonious* often leads to a confusion of senses, but a clear distinction is maintained in standard English. *Ceremonial* relates primarily to what involves or is involved in ceremony: *ceremonial occasions, ceremonial dress. Ceremonious* stresses formality and display, often in the unfavorable sense of pompousness: *He met me at the door and delivered a ceremonious greeting.*

cer·e·mo·ni·ous (sĕr′ə-mō′nē-əs) *adj.* Having, showing, or indicative of a fondness for ceremony; rigidly or elaborately formal. —See Usage note at **ceremonial.** —**cer·e·mo·ni·ous·ly** *adv.* —**cer·e·mo·ni·ous·ness** *n.*

cer·e·mo·ny (sĕr′ə-mō′nē) *n., pl.* **-nies.** **1. a.** A formal act or set of acts performed as prescribed by ritual, custom, or etiquette. **b.** Such acts collectively; pomp. **2.** A conventional social gesture or act without intrinsic purpose. **3.** Strict observance of formalities or etiquette. —**stand on ceremony.** To insist on or behave with excessive formality. [Middle English *ceremonie,* from Old French, from Latin *caerimōnia†,* sacredness, religious rite.]

Če·ren·kov radiation (chə-rĕng′kôf′) *n. Physics.* The light emitted by a beam of high-energy particles passing through transparent, nonconducting material at a speed greater than the speed of light in that medium. [After Pavel A. *Čherenkov* (1904–), Russian physicist.]

Ce·res¹ (sîr′ēz). *Roman Mythology.* The goddess of agriculture; identified with the Greek goddess Demeter. [Latin *Cerēs.*]

Ceres² *n.* The first asteroid to be discovered (1801), having an orbit between Mars and Saturn. [After CERES.]

ce·re·us (sîr′ē-əs) *n.* Any of several tall tropical American cacti of the genus *Cereus* or other genera, such as the **night-blooming cereus** (see). [New Latin, "candle" (from the shape), from Latin, taper, from *cēra,* wax. See **cerate.**]

ce·ric (sîr′ĭk, sĕr′-) *adj.* Of, pertaining to, or containing cerium, especially with valence 4.

ceric oxide *n.* A pale yellow-white powder, CeO₂, used in ceramics, to polish glass, and to sensitize photosensitive glass.

ce·rise (sə-rēs′, -rēz′) *n.* Purplish pink. [French, from Old French, CHERRY.] —**ce·rise** *adj.*

ce·ri·um (sîr′ē-əm) *n. Symbol* **Ce** A lustrous, iron-gray, malleable metallic rare-earth element that occurs chiefly in the mineral monazite, exists in four allotropic states, is a constituent of lighter flint alloys, and is used in various metallurgical and nuclear applications. Atomic number 58, atomic weight 140.12, melting point

795°C, boiling point 3,468°C, specific gravity 6.67 to 8.23, valences 3, 4. [New Latin, after the asteroid CERES, discovered shortly before the element.]

cer·met (sûr′mĕt′) *n.* A material consisting of processed ceramic particles bonded with metal and used in high-strength and high-temperature applications. Also called "ceramal." [CER(AMIC) + MET(AL).]

CERN (sûrn) *n.* The research center of the European Organization for Nuclear Research in Geneva. [French *Conseil Européen Pour Recherches Nucléaires.*]

cer·nu·ous (sûr′nyōō-əs) *adj. Botany.* Hanging downward; drooping; nodding. [Latin *cernuus†.*]

ce·ro·plas·tics (sîr′ō-plăs′tĭks, sĕr′ō-) *n. Used with a singular verb.* The art of modeling in wax. [Latin *cēra,* wax (see **cerate**) + PLASTICS.] —**ce·ro·plas·tic** *adj.*

ce·ro·tic acid (sə-rŏt′ĭk, -rōt′ĭk) *n.* An acid, C₂₅H₅₁COOH, occurring in waxes, such as beeswax and carnauba wax. [From Latin *cērōtum,* wax plaster, from Greek *kērōton,* from *kēros,* wax. See **cerate.**]

ce·ro·type (sîr′ə-tīp′, sĕr′ə-) *n.* The process of preparing a printing surface for electrotyping by first engraving on a wax-coated metal plate. [Greek *kēros,* wax (see **cerate**) + -TYPE.]

ce·rous (sîr′əs) *adj.* Of, pertaining to, or containing cerium, especially with valence 3. [CER(IUM) + -OUS.]

cert. certificate; certification; certified.

cer·tain (sûr′tn) *adj.* **1.** Definitely known; determined beyond doubt. **2. a.** Sure; destined; bound: *certain to be a best seller.* **b.** Sure to happen; inevitable: *At such speeds, an accident would mean certain death.* **3.** Confident or convinced; having no doubt about something. **4.** Sound; dependable; unerring. **5.** Of a particular but unspecified character or identity: *has a certain rustic charm; a certain well-known politician.* **6.** Designating a person not known or previously mentioned: *a certain Mr. Harvey.* **7.** Some but not much; limited: *to a certain degree.* —See Synonyms at **sure.**
~*pron.* An indefinite but limited number; some. —**for certain.** Definitely; without doubt. [Middle English, from Old French, from Vulgar Latin *certānus* (unattested), from Latin *certus,* past participle of *cernere,* to decide, determine.]
Usage: Because *certain* implies an absolute lack of doubt, purists have criticized such constructions as *more certain, most certain, quite certain, fairly certain, very certain,* and so on. But such qualifications are widespread in all styles and dialects and would generally be considered to be standard.

cer·tain·ly (sûr′tn-lē) *adv.* **1.** Undoubtedly; indeed. **2.** By all means; of course. **3.** Admittedly.

cer·tain·ty (sûr′tn-tē) *n., pl.* **-ties.** **1.** The fact, quality, or state of being certain. **2.** A clearly established fact. **3.** Something that is bound to happen.
Synonyms: assurance, certitude, conviction.

cer·tes (sûr′tēz, sûrts) *adv. Archaic.* Certainly; truly; verily. [Middle English, from Old French, from Vulgar Latin *certās* (unattested), from Latin *certus,* CERTAIN.]

cer·ti·fi·a·ble (sûr′tə-fī′ə-bəl) *adj.* **1.** Capable of being certified. **2.** Fit to be declared insane. —**cer·ti·fi·a·bly** *adv.*

cer·tif·i·cate (sər-tĭf′ĭ-kĭt) *n. Abbr.* **cert., ct. 1.** A document testifying to the truth of a given fact, such as a person's date of birth or ownership of shares. **2. a.** A document issued to a person completing a course of study. **b.** A document certifying that a person may officially practice in certain professions.
~*tr.v.* **(-kāt′) certificated, -cating, -cates.** To furnish with, testify to, or authorize by a certificate. [Middle English *certificat,* from Old French, from Medieval Latin *certificātum,* from the neuter past participle of Late Latin *certificāre,* to CERTIFY.]

certificate of deposit *n.* A certificate from a bank stating that the named person has a specified sum on deposit.

cer·ti·fi·ca·tion (sûr′tə-fī-kā′shən) *n. Abbr.* **cert. 1.** The act of certifying or certificating. **2.** The state of being certified. **3.** A certified statement.

cer·ti·fied (sûr′tə-fīd′) *adj. Abbr.* **cert. 1.** Guaranteed in writing; vouched for; endorsed. **2.** Holding a certificate. **3.** Declared legally insane.

certified check *n.* A check guaranteed by a bank to be covered by sufficient funds on deposit.

certified mail *n.* Uninsured first-class mail whose delivery is recorded by having the addressee sign for it.

certified public accountant *n. Abbr.* **C.P.A.** A public accountant who has received a certificate stating that he has met a state's legal requirements.

cer·ti·fy (sûr′tə-fī′) *v.* **-fied, -fying, -fies.** —*tr.* **1. a.** To confirm formally as true, accurate, or genuine, especially in writing. **b.** To guarantee as meeting a standard. **2.** To acknowledge in writing on the face of (a check) that the signature of the maker is genuine and that there are sufficient funds on deposit for its payment. **3.** To issue a license or certificate to. **4.** To declare legally insane. —*intr.* To testify: *certify to the facts.* —See Synonyms at **approve.** [Middle English *certifien,* from Old French *certifier,* from Late Latin *certificāre,* to make certain : Latin *certus,* CERTAIN + *facere,* to make.] —**cer·ti·fi·er** *n.*

cer·ti·o·rar·i (sûr′shē-ə-râr′ē, -rä′rē) *n. Law.* A writ from a higher court to a lower one requesting a transcript of the proceedings of a case for review. [Medieval Latin *certiorārī volumus,* "we wish to be informed" (words used in the writ), from *certiorāre,* to inform, certify, from *certior,* comparative of *certus,* CERTAIN.]

cer·ti·tude (sûr′tə-tōōd′, -tyōōd′) *n.* Complete assurance. —See Synonyms at **certainty.** [Middle English, from Late Latin *certitūdō,* from Latin *certus,* CERTAIN.]

ce·ru·le·an (sə-rōō′lē-ən) *adj.* Sky-blue; azure. [Latin *caeruleus,* dark-blue, azure, from *caelum,* sky. See **celestial.**]

ce·ru·men (sə-rōō′mən) *n.* A yellowish waxy secretion of the external ear; earwax. [New Latin, from Latin *cēra,* wax. See **cerate.**]

ce·ruse (sə-rōōs′, sîr′ōōs′) *n.* **White lead** *(see).* [Middle English, from Old French, from Latin *cērussa,* perhaps from Greek *kēroessa* (unattested), white wax cosmetic, from *kēroun,* to wax, from *kēros,* wax. See **cerate.**]

ce·rus·site (sə-rŭs′īt′) *n.* Natural lead carbonate, PbCO₃, a lead ore. [German *Zerussit* : Latin *cērussa,* CERUSE + -ITE.]

Cer·van·tes Sa·a·ve·dra (sər-văn′tĕz sä′ə-vä′drə), **Miguel de** (1547–1616). Spanish writer. He is best known for *Don Quixote* (1605–15), the story of a middle-aged landowner who equips himself as a knight in armor and sets out into the world with his cunning squire, Sancho Panza, to right the wrongs of mankind.

cer·ve·lat (sûr′və-lät′, -lăt′) *n.* A kind of spiced smoked sausage made from pork or a mixture of beef and pork. [Obsolete French, from Italian *cervellata.*]

cer·vi·cal (sûr′vĭ-kəl) *adj. Anatomy.* Pertaining to the neck or the cervix. [New Latin *cervicalis,* from Latin *cervīx* (stem *cervic-*), CERVIX.]

cervical smear *n.* A specimen of material taken from the cervix of the uterus and examined for the presence of cancer.

cer·vi·ci·tis (sûr′vĭ-sī′tĭs) *n.* Inflammation of the cervix of the uterus. [New Latin : CERVIX + -ITIS.]

cer·vine (sûr′vīn′) *adj.* Pertaining to, resembling, or characteristic of a deer. [Latin *cervīnus,* from *cervus,* deer.]

cer·vix (sûr′vĭks) *n., pl.* **-vixes** or **-vices** (sûr′və-sēz′, sər-vī′sēz′). *Anatomy.* **1.** The neck. **2.** Any neck-shaped anatomical structure; especially, the narrow outer end of the uterus. [Latin *cervīx,* neck.]

Cesarean. Variant of **Caesarean.**

ce·si·um, cae·si·um (sē′zē-əm) *n. Symbol* **Cs** A soft, silvery-white ductile metal, liquid at room temperature, the most electropositive and alkaline of the elements, used in photoelectric cells and to catalyze hydrogenation of some organic compounds. Atomic number 55, atomic weight 132.905, melting point 28.5°C, boiling point 690°C, specific gravity 1.87, valence 1. [New Latin, from Latin *caesius,* bluish gray (from its blue spectral lines).]

cesium clock *n.* A form of atomic clock based on the frequency of the radiation absorbed in changing the state of cesium nuclei in a magnetic field. It is used in the definition of the second.

Československo. See **Czechoslovakia.**

ces·pi·tose, caes·pi·tose (sĕs′pĭ-tōs′) *adj.* Growing in dense tufts. or turflike clumps; matted. [New Latin *caespitosus,* from Latin *caespes,* turf.]

cess¹ (sĕs) *n.* Any of various taxes, especially one formerly levied in Britain, Ireland, and British India. [Variant of *sess,* from obsolete *assess* (noun). See **assess.**]

cess² *n. Irish.* Luck: *Bad cess to him!* [Perhaps from CESS (tax).]

ces·sa·tion (sĕ-sā′shən) *n.* A ceasing; a discontinuance. [Middle English *cessacioun,* from Latin *cessātiō* (stem *cessātiōn-*), from *cessāre,* to CEASE.]

ces·ser (sĕs′ər) *n. Law.* The end, as of a term or annuity; ceasing. [Norman French and Old French, from *cesser,* to CEASE.]

ces·sion (sĕsh′ən) *n.* The act or an instance of giving up or ceding something to which one has a claim; especially, a surrendering of territory to another country by treaty. [Middle English, from Old French, from Latin *cessiō* (stem *cessiōn-*), from *cēdere* (past participle *cessus*), to yield.]

ces·sion·ar·y (sĕsh′ə-nĕr′ē) *n., pl.* **-ies.** One to whom a cession is made; a transferee; an assignee.

cess·pool (sĕs′pōōl′) *n.* **1.** A covered hole or pit for receiving sediment or drained sewage. **2.** A filthy or disgusting place. Also called "cesspit." [Variant (influenced by POOL) of earlier *cesperalle,* drainpipe, from Middle English *suspiral,* from Old French *souspirail,* breathing hole, from *sou(s)pirer,* to breathe, SUSPIRE.]

ces·tode (sĕs′tōd′) *n.* Any flatworm of the class Cestoda, including tapeworms. [New Latin *Cestoda,* variant of *Cestoidea,* "ribbon-shaped ones" : Latin *cestus,* CESTUS (belt) + -OID.]

ces·tus¹ (sĕs′təs) *n., pl.* **-ti** (-tī′). A woman's belt or girdle, especially as formerly worn by a bride. [Latin *cestus,* girdle, belt, from Greek *kestos.*]

cestus² *n., pl.* **-tuses.** A covering for the hand, made of leather straps weighted with iron or lead, worn by ancient Roman boxers. [Latin *caestus, cestus,* boxing glove, from *caedere,* to strike.]

cesura. Variant of **caesura.**

CET, C.E.T. Central European Time.

ce·ta·cean (sĭ-tā′shən) *adj.* Of or belonging to the order Cetacea, which includes fishlike aquatic mammals such as the whale and porpoise.
~*n.* Any mammal of the order Cetacea. [New Latin *Cetacea,* from the neuter plural of *cetaceus,* of whales : Latin *cētus,* whale, from Greek *kētos*† + -ACEAN.] —**ce·ta·ceous** (sĭ-tā′shəs) *adj.*

ce·tane (sē′tān′) *n.* A colorless liquid, C₁₆H₃₄, used as a solvent and in standardized hydrocarbons to determine the cetane number of diesel fuels. [Latin *cētus,* whale (so called because it belongs to a series of compounds found in sperm whale oil) + -ANE.]

cetane number *n.* The performance rating of a diesel fuel, expressed as the percentage of cetane that must be mixed with liquid methylnaphthalene to produce the same ignition performance as

the diesel fuel being rated. Also called "cetane rating." Compare **octane number.**

cete (sēt) *n.* A company of badgers. [Probably from Latin *coetus, coitus,* meeting, reunion, assembly, COITUS.]

ce·ter·is par·i·bus (kā′tər-ĭs păr′ə-bəs, sĕt′ər-īs) *adv.* With all other factors or things being the same. [New Latin, with other things equal.]

ce·tol·o·gy (sĭ-tŏl′ə-jē) *n.* The zoology of whales and related aquatic mammals. [Latin *cētus,* whale (see **cetacean**) + -LOGY.] —**ce·to·log·i·cal** (sē′tə-lŏj′ĭ-kəl) *adj.* —**ce·tol·o·gist** *n.*

Ce·tus (sē′təs) *n.* A constellation in the equatorial region of the Southern Hemisphere near Aquarius and Eridanus. [Latin *cētus,* whale. See **cetacean.**]

ce·tyl alcohol (sēt′l) *n.* A waxy alcohol, C₁₆H₃₃OH, used in cosmetics and pharmaceutical products. Also called "hexadecanol."

Cé·vennes (sā-vĕn′). A mountain range at the extreme southeast of the Massif Central, France. Its highest peak is Mont Mézenc at 1,754 meters (5,753 feet). It is the source of many rivers, including the Allier, the Loire, the Lot, and the Tarn.

Ceylon. See **Sri Lanka.**

Cey·lon moss (sĭ-lŏn′) *n.* A red seaweed, *Gracilaria lichenoides,* of the East Indies, used for making agar.

Cé·zanne (sā-zăn′), **Paul** (1839–1906). French painter whose works led to the development of cubism and abstract art. His most famous paintings include a celebrated view of Mont Sainte-Victoire and *The Card Players.*

Cf The symbol for the element californium.

cf. **1.** calfskin. **2.** compare (Latin *confer*).

c.f., C.F. cost and freight.

C/F *Accounting.* carried forward.

CFAFr. franc communauté financière africaine.

c.f.i., C.F.I. cost, freight, and insurance.

cg centigram.

c.g. **1.** center of gravity. **2.** consul general.

C.G. **1.** coast guard. **2.** commanding general. **3.** consul general.

cgs, CGS centimeter-gram-second (system of units).

ch chain (measurement).

ch. **1.** chaplain. **2.** chapter. **3.** chief. **4.** church.

Ch. **1.** chaplain. **2.** chief. **3.** China; Chinese. **4.** church.

c.h., C.H. **1.** clearing-house. **2.** courthouse. **3.** customhouse.

Cha·blis (shă-blē′, shä-, shäb′lē) *n.* A very dry white Burgundy wine produced in the region of Chablis, in east-central France.

cha-cha (chä′chä) *n.* **1.** A rhythmic ballroom dance that originated in Latin America. **2.** The music for the cha-cha.
~*intr.v.* **cha-chaed, -chaing, -chas.** To dance the cha-cha. [American Spanish *cha-cha-cha.*]

chac·ma (chăk′mə) *n.* A grayish-black baboon, *Chaeropithecus ursinus* (or *Papio ursinus*), of southern and eastern Africa. [Hottentot.]

cha·conne (shä-kôn′, -kŏn′, -kūn′) *n.* **1.** A slow and stately dance of the 18th century. **2.** The music for this dance. **3.** A musical form consisting of variations on a repeated harmonic pattern. Compare **passacaglia.** [French, from Spanish *chacona* (perhaps imitative of the castanets used for the music).]

chad (chăd) *n.* The small disks of paper, card, or the like removed by punching from paper tape or computer cards. [Perhaps alteration of CHAFF (rubbish).]

Chad (chăd). *French* **Tchad** (chäd). A landlocked country in north-central Africa, formerly a territory of French Equatorial Africa (1897–1960). The Sahara covers its northern half. Its population is predominately Muslim in the north with Bantu peoples in the south, a cultural rift reflected from 1965 in costly civil war. In 1980 fighting broke out between the factions of Hissené Habré and Col. Goukouni Oueddei, and Oueddei was aided by Libyan troops sent by Col. Muammar el-Qaddafi, who declared a union of the two countries (1981). The Libyans withdrew, and an Organization of African Unity peace-keeping force entered Chad (1982). When this failed, Habré's troops took the capital, and Oueddei fled into exile. Chad is one of the world's poorest countries and relies on foreign aid. Most of its people live as subsistence farmers, but some cotton is exported and oil has been discovered. Area, 1,284,000 square kilometers (495,624 square miles). Population, 4,300,000. Capital, N'djamena. —**Chad·i·an** *n. & adj.*

Chad, Lake. A shallow lake in north-central Africa, partitioned between Chad, Cameroon, Nigeria, and Niger. It is watered by the Shari, and has no outlet. It reaches 20,700 square kilometers (7,990 square miles) in extent during the wet season between May and October, but shrinks to half that size by April. The lake was first sighted by Europeans in 1823.

cha·dor (chŭd′ər, chä′dôr) *n.* A garment worn by women in some Muslim countries, especially India and Iran, made from a long, usually black cloth covering the upper body, head, and part of the face. [Hindi, from Persian *chaddar.*]

Chad·wick (chăd′wĭk), **Sir James** (1891–1974). British physicist who discovered the neutron (1932), pointing the way to the fission process that, in turn, led to the atom bomb. He was awarded the Nobel Prize for physics (1935).

chae·ta (kē′tə) *n., pl.* **-tae** (-tē′). *Zoology.* A bristle, or seta, on the body of annelid worms, such as the earthworms, used in locomotion. [New Latin, from Greek *khaitē,* long hair.]

chae·tog·nath (kē′tŏg-năth′) *n.* Any of various marine worms of the phylum Chaetognatha, which includes the arrow worms. [New

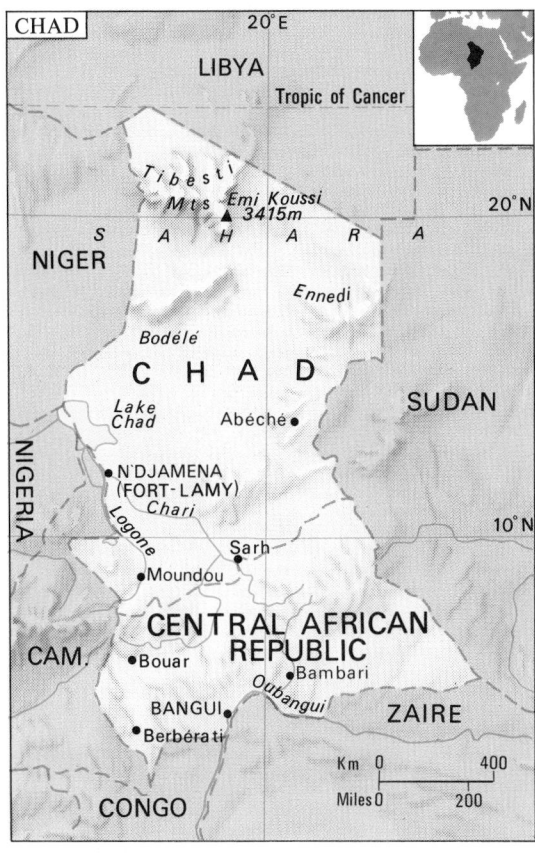

CHAD

LIBYA
Tropic of Cancer
20° E

Tibesti
Mts ▲ Emi Koussi
3415m
20° N

NIGER
S A H A R A
Ennedi

Bodélé

C H A D
SUDAN

Lake
Chad
Abéché ●

N'DJAMENA
(FORT-LAMY)
Chari
10° N

Logone
Sarh ●

● Moundou

CENTRAL AFRICAN
REPUBLIC

CAM.
● Bouar
● Bambari

BANGUI ●
● Berbérati
ZAIRE

Km 0   400
Miles 0   200

CONGO

Latin *Chaetognatha*, "bristle-jaw" (so named from the spines at the jaws) : CHAETA + *gnathos*, jaw.]

chafe (chāf) *v.* **chafed, chafing, chafes.** —*tr.* **1.** To wear away or irritate by rubbing. **2.** To annoy; vex. **3.** To heat or warm by rubbing. —*intr.* **1.** To cause friction; rub. **2.** To become worn or sore from rubbing. **3.** To be or become irritated, impatient, or frustrated. ~*n.* **1.** Warmth, wear, or soreness produced by friction. **2.** Annoyance; irritation; vexation. [Middle English *chaufen*, from Old French *chauf(f)er*, to warm (by rubbing), from Vulgar Latin *calefāre* (unattested), variant of Latin *calefacere* : *calēre*, to be warm + *facere*, to make.]

cha·fer (chā′fər) *n.* Any of various beetles of the family Scarabaeidae, such as the cockchafer. [Middle English *cheaffer*, Old English *ceafor*.]

chaff¹ (chāf) *n.* **1.** The husks of grain after separation from the seed. **2.** Finely cut straw or hay used as fodder. **3.** Trivial or worthless matter. **4.** Strips of metal foil released in the atmosphere to inhibit radar. [Middle English *chaf(f)*, Old English *ceaf*.]

chaff² *v.* **chaffed, chaffing, chaffs.** —*tr.* To make fun of good-naturedly; tease. —*intr.* To engage in good-natured teasing. ~*n.* Good-natured teasing; banter. [Probably a blend of CHAFF (trivia) and CHAFE (to irritate).] —**chaff·er** *n.*

chaf·fer (chǎf′ər) *intr.v.* **-fered, -fering, -fers. 1.** To bargain or haggle. **2.** To bandy words; chatter. ~*n.* A bargaining or haggling. [Middle English *chaffare, cheapfare*, trade, merchandise, Old English *ceapfaru*, "bargain journey." See **cheap, fare**.] —**chaf·fer·er** *n.*

chaf·finch (chǎf′ǐnch) *n.* A small European songbird, *Fringilla coelebs*, having predominantly reddish-brown plumage and black and white wings. [Middle English *chaffynche*, Old English *ceaffinc* : CHAFF + FINCH.]

chafing dish *n.* A dish set above a heating device, used to cook or maintain the warmth of food at the table.

Cha·gall (shə-gäl′), **Marc** (1887–1985). Russian-born artist noted for his brilliant colors and dreamlike, fanciful imagery. Among his works is a huge painting, completed in 1964, for the ceiling of the Paris Opera House.

Cha·gas disease (shä′gəs) *n.* A South American form of trypanosomiasis caused by the protozoan *Trypanosoma cruzi*, which is carried by a bloodsucking insect. [First described by Carlos *Chagas* (1879–1934), Brazilian physician.]

cha·grin (shə-grĭn′) *n.* A feeling of embarrassment, annoyance, or humiliation caused by failure or disappointment. ~*tr.v.* **chagrined, -grining, -grins.** To cause to feel chagrin; discomfit. Usually used in the passive. [French, sadness, from *chagrin†*, sad.]

chain (chān) *n.* **1. a.** A connected, flexible series of links, usually of metal, used for binding, connecting, or other purposes. **b.** Such a set of links, often of precious metal and with pendants attached,

worn as an ornament or symbol of office. **2.** Anything that restrains or confines. **3. chains.** Bonds, fetters, or shackles. **4. chains.** Captivity or oppression; bondage. **5.** A number of events or processes that form a continuous or interconnected series: *a chain of coincidences.* **6.** A number of establishments, such as stores, restaurants, or theaters, under common ownership or management. **7.** A mountain range. **8.** *Chemistry.* A group of atoms bonded in a spatial configuration resembling a chain. **9. a.** A measuring instrument for surveying, consisting of 100 linked pieces of iron or steel. **b.** *Abbr.* **ch** The length of this instrument as a unit of length, equal to 100 links or 66 feet. Also called "Gunter's chain." **10. a.** A similar instrument used in engineering. **b.** *Abbr.* **ch** The length of this instrument used as a unit of length, equal to 100 feet. Also called "engineer's chain." —See Synonyms at **series.** ~*tr.v.* **chained, chaining, chains.** To bind or confine with or as if with a chain or chains: *The spectators of the football game were chained to their seats by excitement.* [Middle English *chayne, cheyne*, from Old French *chaine, chaeine*, from Latin *catēna*, CATENA.]

Chain (chān), **Sir Ernst Boris** (1906–79). British biochemist, born in Germany. He worked with Sir Howard Florey on antibiotic substances produced by various microorganisms and isolated and purified penicillin. With Sir Alexander Fleming, who discovered penicillin, Chain and Florey were jointly awarded the Nobel Prize for discovering the healing properties of the antibiotic (1945).

chain gang *n.* A group of convicts chained together and set to outdoor labor.

chain letter *n.* A letter instructing the recipient to send out multiple copies, so that its circulation increases in a geometrical progression as long as the instructions are followed.

chain mail *n.* Flexible armor of joined metal links or scales.

chain·man (chān′mən) *n., pl.* **-men** (-mĭn). In surveying, either of the two people who hold the measuring chain.

chain printer *n.* A printer used in computer systems in which the type is arranged in a continuous chain.

chain pump *n.* A pump that lifts water by means of containers, attached to an endless chain, that pass under water and up over a wheel.

chain-re·act (chān′rē-ăkt′) *intr.v.* **-acted, -acting, -acts.** To undergo a chain reaction.

chain reaction *n.* **1.** A series of events each of which induces or otherwise influences its successor. **2.** *Physics.* A self-sustaining series of nuclear reactions; especially, a fission reaction in which neutrons are released and cause other nuclei to split, leading to a succession of fissions and an increasing number of neutrons. **3.** *Chemistry.* A series of reactions in which one product of a reacting set is a reactant in the following set.

chain rule *n.* A mathematical theorem used in the differentiation of a function of a function. If y is a function of x and u is a function of y, then $du/dx = (du/dy) (dy/dx)$.

chain saw *n.* A power saw with teeth linked in an endless chain.

chain-smoke (chān′smōk′) *v.* **-smoked, -smoking, -smokes.** —*intr.* To smoke cigarettes or cigars in a continuous succession. —*tr.* To smoke (cigarettes or cigars) in a continuous succession. —**chain smoker** *n.*

chain stitch *n.* A decorative stitch in which loops are connected like the links of a chain. —**chain-stitch** (chān′stĭch′) *v.*

chain store *n.* Any of a group of retail shops under the same ownership.

chair (châr) *n.* **1. a.** A piece of furniture consisting of a seat, legs, back, and often arms, designed to accommodate one person. **b.** Any of various types of seats designed for a particular purpose. Used in combination: *a deck chair; a sedan chair.* **2. a.** A seat of office, authority, or dignity, such as that of a bishop. **b.** A professorship. **3.** The office or position of a person having authority. **4.** A person who holds such an office or position; especially, one who presides over a meeting. **5.** A metal block for supporting and holding railroad tracks in position. **6.** *Slang.* The electric chair. —**take the chair.** To preside as chairman at a meeting. ~*tr.v.* **chaired, chairing, chairs. 1.** To preside over (a meeting). **2.** To install in a position of authority, especially as a presiding officer. **3.** *British.* To carry (a person) aloft in triumph, usually in a chair. [Middle English *chaiere, chare*, from Old French *chaiere*, bishop's chair, from Latin *cathedra*, chair, from Greek *kathedra*, seat : *kata-*, down + *hedra*, seat.]

chair car *n.* A parlor car.

chair lift *n.* A cable-suspended, power-driven chair assembly used to transport people up or down mountains. See **ski lift.**

chair·man (châr′mən) *n., pl.* **-men** (-mĭn). *Abbr.* **chm. 1.** A person who presides over an assembly, meeting, committee, or board. **2.** Formerly, one employed to carry a sedan chair. —See Usage note at **-person.** ~*tr.v.* **-manned, -manning, -mans.** To act as chairman of.

chair·man·ship (châr′mən-shĭp′) *n.* The office or term of a chairman.

chair·per·son (châr′pûr′sən) *n.* A person who presides over an assembly, meeting, or board. —See Usage note at **-person.**

chair·wom·an (châr′wo͝om′ən) *n., pl.* **-women** (-wĭm′ən). A woman who presides over an assembly, meeting, or board. —See Usage note at **-person.**

chaise (shāz) *n.* **1.** Any of various light, open carriages, often with a collapsible hood; especially, a two-wheeled carriage drawn by one

chalice *The chalice has been used in the Christian church to celebrate the Eucharist since ancient times. At first it was usually made out of glass, semiprecious stone, or horn, but after Christianity was recognized by the Roman Empire in the fourth century, gold and silver became the usual materials, and chalices were often adorned with precious stones and carvings.*

chambered nautilus *A spiraling series of chambers fills the curves of a nautilus shell. The nautilus—a mollusk related to squids and octopuses—occupies the large outer chamber and fills the others with gas to control its buoyancy.*

horse. **2.** A **post chaise** *(see).* [French, chair, seat, from Old French, variant of *chaiere,* CHAIR.]

chaise longue (shāz lông′) *n., pl.* **chaise longues** or **chaises longues** *(pronounced as singular).* A reclining chair with a seat long enough to support the outstretched legs of the sitter. [French, "long chair."]

chak·ra (chŭk′rə) *n.* In yoga philosophy, one of the seven centers of spiritual energy in the human body. [Sanskrit, wheel.]

chalah. Variant of **challah.**

cha·la·za (kə-lā′zə, -lăz′ə) *n., pl.* **-zae** (-zē′) or **-zas. 1.** *Zoology.* Either of the two spiral bands of tissue in an egg, connecting the yolk to the lining membrane. **2.** *Botany.* The part of an ovule that is opposite the micropyle and that serves as a point of attachment for the integuments and the nucellus. [New Latin, from Greek *khalaza,* hailstone, small cyst.]

cha·la·zi·on (kə-lā′zē-ən, -ŏn′) *n., pl.* **-zi·a** (-zē-ə). A cyst in the eyelid formed by a blocked and swollen sebaceous gland. [New Latin, diminutive of Greek *khalaza,* small cyst, hailstone, CHALAZA.]

chal·can·thite (kăl-kăn′thīt′, kăl′kən-) *n.* A blue mineral, $CuSO_4 \cdot 5H_2O$, that occurs in some copper ores. [Latin *chalcanthum,* copper sulfate solution, from Greek *khalkanthon* : *khalkos,* CHALCO- + *anthos,* flower.]

chal·ced·o·ny (kăl-sĕd′n-ē) *n., pl.* **-nies.** A translucent to transparent milky or grayish quartz, SiO_2, with distinctive microscopic crystals arranged in slender fibers in parallel bands. [Middle English *calcedonie,* from Late Latin *chalcēdonius,* from Greek *khalkēdōn,* a mystical stone (Revelation 21:19), perhaps after *Khalkēdōn,* Chalcedon, town in Asia Minor.] **—chal·ce·don·ic** (kăl′sĭ-dŏn′ĭk) *adj.*

chal·cid (kăl′sĭd) *n.* Any of various minute wasps of the superfamily Chalcidoidea, of which the larvae of many species are parasitic on the larval stages of other insects. Also called "chalcid wasp." [New Latin *Chalcis* (genus), "copper (fly)" (from its metallic color and sheen), from Greek *khalkos,* copper.]

Chal·cid·i·ce (kăl-sĭd′ĭ-sē). *Greek* **Khal·ki·dhi·kí** (käl′kə-*thĭ*-kē′). Mountainous peninsula of northeast Greece. It terminates in the three parallel promontories of Kassandra, Sithonia, and Akte. The latter is the site of Mt. Athos, a monastic center of the Greek Orthodox Church.

Chal·cis (kăl′sĭs). *Greek* **Khal·kis** (käl′kĭs). The principal town on the island of Euboea in eastern Greece. A prosperous city-state from the 8th century B.C., its traders established settlements in Italy, Sicily, Syria, and mainland Greece.

chalco-, chalc- *prefix.* Indicates copper or bronze; for example, **Chalcolithic.** [Greek *khalkos,* copper.]

chal·co·cite (kăl′kə-sīt′) *n.* An important copper ore, essentially Cu_2S. [French *chalcos(ine)* : Greek *khalkos,* copper + -ITE.]

Chal·co·lith·ic (kăl′kə-lĭth′ĭk) *adj. Archaeology. Sometimes* **chalcolithic.** Of or relating to a period of man's development in which both stone and copper implements were in use.
~*n.* The Chalcolithic period. Preceded by *the.* [CHALCO- + -LITH.]

chal·co·py·rite (kăl′kə-pī′rīt′) *n.* An important copper ore, essentially $CuFeS_2$. Also called "copper pyrites." [New Latin *chalcopyrites* : Greek *khalkos,* copper + PYRITES.]

chal·co·sis (kăl-kō′sĭs) *n.* Copper poisoning, sometimes with the formation of copper deposits in the tissues. [Greek *khalkos,* copper + -OSIS.]

Chal·de·a or **Chal·dae·a** (kăl-dē′ə). Area of southern Babylonia that produced the last Babylonian dynasty, the so-called Chaldean or neo-Babylonian dynasty. It achieved supremacy under Nabopolassar (626–605 B.C.) and reached its height under Nebuchadnezzar II, who extended the kingdom to include Syria and Palestine and rebuilt Babylon. The Persians destroyed the empire in 539 B.C.

Chal·de·an, Chal·dae·an (kăl-dē′ən) *n.* Also **Chal·dae·an, Chal·dee** (kăl′dē′). **1.** A member of an ancient Semitic people who ruled in Babylonia. **2.** The Semitic language of the Chaldeans. **3.** A person versed in occult learning; an astrologer, soothsayer, or sorcerer. **—Chal·da·ic** (kăl-dā′ĭk) *n. & adj.* **—Chal·de·an** *adj.*

Chal·dee (kăl′dē′) *n.* **1. Biblical Aramaic** *(see).* **2.** Variant of **Chaldean.**

chal·dron (chôl′drən) *n.* A unit of dry measure, as for coke, coal, or lime, equal to 32 to 36 bushels, formerly used in England. [Old French *chauderon,* augmentative of *chaudiere,* kettle, from Late Latin *caldāria,* CALDRON.]

cha·let (shă-lā′, shăl′ā) *n.* **1.** A house with a gently sloping overhanging roof, common in Switzerland and other Alpine regions. **2.** The hut of a herdsman in the Alps. **3.** A small, often wooden cottage, as one for vacationers, built in the style of a chalet. [French, from Swiss French, cabin, perhaps a diminutive of *cala* (unattested), stone shelter, from a Mediterranean root *cal-,* "stone."]

Cha·leur Bay (shə-lŏŏr′). Inlet of the Gulf of St. Lawrence, *c.* 135 kilometers (85 miles) long and from 24 to 40 kilometers (15 to 25 miles) wide, between northern New Brunswick and the Gaspé Peninsula of eastern Quebec. It is a famous fishing ground for cod, herring, mackerel, and salmon.

Cha·lia·pin (shə-lyä′pĭn), **Feodor Ivanovich** (1873–1938). Russian opera singer. He is best known for his bass performances as Boris Godunov and Mephistopheles.

chal·ice (chăl′ĭs) *n.* **1.** A cup for the consecrated wine of the Eucharist. **2.** A cup or goblet. **3.** A cup-shaped blossom. [Middle English, from Norman French, from Latin *calix,* cup, goblet.]

chal·i·co·there (kăl′ĭ-kə-thîr′) *n.* Any of various extinct ungulate mammals of the Eocene to Pleistocene epochs, having distinctive three-clawed, three-toed feet. [New Latin *Chalicotherium* (genus), "fossil beast" : Greek *khalix,* stone, pebble (see **calcium**) + Greek *thērion,* diminutive of *thēr,* beast.]

chalk (chôk) *n.* **1.** A soft, compact calcium carbonate, $CaCO_3$, a type of limestone, with varying amounts of silica, quartz, feldspar, or other mineral impurities, generally gray-white or yellow-white and derived chiefly from the remains of small marine organisms. **2.** A piece of chalk or chalklike substance, often calcium sulfate, frequently colored, used for marking on a blackboard or other surface. **3.** A mark or picture made with chalk. **4.** A reckoning, as of credit given; tally. **—by a long chalk.** *British Informal.* By a wide margin: *This isn't the last you'll see of them by a long chalk.*
~*tr.v.* **chalked, chalking, chalks. 1.** To mark, draw, or write with chalk. **2.** To smear or cover with chalk. **3.** To treat (soil, for example) with chalk. **—chalk up. 1.** To earn or score: *chalk up points.* **2.** To credit: *Chalk that up to experience.*
~*adj.* Made with or consisting of chalk. [Middle English *chalk,* Old English *cealc,* from Latin *calx,* stone, pebble, from Greek *khalix.*] **—chalk·i·ness** *n.* **—chalk·y** *adj.*

chalk·board (chôk′bôrd′, -bōrd′) *n.* A panel, usually green or black, for writing on with chalk; blackboard.

chalk·stone (chôk′stōn′) *n. Medicine.* A **tophus** *(see).*

chalk stripe *n.* A striped fabric in two colors such that thin stripes of one color alternate with thick stripes of the other. Compare **pinstripe. —chalk-stripe** (chôk′strīp′) *adj.*

chal·lah, cha·lah, hal·lah (KHä′lə) *n.* A yeast-leavened white egg bread, usually in a braided loaf, traditionally eaten by Jews on the Sabbath, holidays, and ceremonial occasions. [Hebrew *ḥallāh.*]

chal·lenge (chăl′ənj) *n.* **1. a.** A call to engage in a contest or fight. **b.** Any act or statement likely to produce conflict or confrontation: *a challenge to the government's authority.* **2.** A demand for an explanation or justification. **3.** A sentry's call for identification. **4. a.** The quality of requiring full use of one's abilities, energy, or resources: *a career that offers plenty of challenge.* **b.** An undertaking having this quality. **5.** *Law.* A formal objection, especially to the qualifications of a juror or jury. **6. a.** A test of immunity following immunization treatment. **b.** A dose of the antigen or substance administered in such a test.
~*v.* **challenged, -lenging, -lenges.** —*tr.* **1.** To call to engage in a contest or fight. **2.** To call into question; dispute: *a book that challenges established beliefs.* **3.** To order to halt and be identified. **4.** *Law.* To object formally to (a juror or jury, for example). **5.** To claim; call for: *events that challenge our attention.* **6.** To present a challenge to; stimulate: *a problem that challenges the imagination.* **7.** To test (a patient or laboratory animal) for immunity following immunization treatment. —*intr.* To make or give voice to a challenge. [Middle English *c(h)alenge,* accusation, challenge, from Old French *c(h)alenge,* from Latin *calumnia,* trickery, false accusation, from *calvī,* to deceive.] **—chal·lenge·a·ble** *adj.*

chal·leng·er (chăl′ən-jər) *n.* **1.** One that challenges. **2.** One who takes part in a sporting contest against the holder of a title or championship.

chal·leng·ing (chăl′ən-jĭng) *adj.* Calling for full use of one's abilities and resources; difficult but stimulating.

chal·lis (shăl′ē) *n.* A light fabric usually printed and made of wool, cotton, or rayon. [Perhaps from the surname *Challis.*]

chal·one (kăl′ōn′, kā′lōn′) *n.* Any of a group of internal secretions that inhibit a metabolic process. [Greek *khalōn,* present participle of *khalan,* to slacken, let down.]

cha·lyb·e·ate (kə-lĭb′ē-ĭt, -lē′bē-ĭt) *adj.* **1.** Impregnated with or containing salts of iron. **2.** Tasting like iron. Said of mineral water.
~*n.* Water or medicine containing iron in solution. [New Latin *chalybeatus,* from Latin *chalybs,* steel, from Greek *khalups* (stem *khalub-*), from *Khalups*†, the Chalybes, ancient people in Asia Minor famous for their work in iron and steel.]

cham (kăm) *n. Archaic.* A Tatar or Mogul khan. [French, from Persian *khān,* from Turkish, KHAN.]

Cha·mae·leon, Cha·me·leon (kə-mēl′yən, -mē′lē-ən) *n.* A constellation in the southern polar region near Apus and Mensa. [Latin *chamaeleōn,* chameleon.]

cham·ae·phyte (kăm′ə-fīt′) *n.* A plant whose winter buds are situated close to the soil surface. [Greek *khamai,* on the ground + -PHYTE.]

cham·ber (chām′bər) *n.* **1.** A room where a person of authority, rank, or importance receives visitors. **2. a.** A hall for the meeting of an assembly, especially a legislative assembly. **b.** A legislative, judicial, or deliberative assembly. **3. a.** A room in a house, especially a bedroom. **b. chambers.** *Chiefly British.* A suite of rooms in an office building. **4.** *Usually* **chambers.** An office to which a judge withdraws, as for consultations with attorneys, and in which some legal matters can be dealt with. **5.** A place where state or municipal funds are received and held; a treasury. **6.** An enclosed space or compartment, as one in the body or in a piece of machinery; a cavity. **7. a.** An enclosed space in the bore of a gun that holds the charge. **b.** The part of a cylinder of a revolver that receives the cartridge.
~*tr.v.* **chambered, -bering, -bers. 1.** To put in or as if in a chamber; enclose; confine. **2.** To furnish with a chamber. [Middle English *chambre,* from Old French, from Late Latin *camera, camara,* from Latin, vault, arched roof, from Greek *kamara.*]

chambered nautilus *n.* A cephalopod mollusk, *Nautilus pompilius,* of the Pacific and Indian oceans, having a partitioned shell lined with a pearly layer. Also called "pearly nautilus."

cham·ber·lain (chām′bər-lən) *n.* **1.** An official who manages the household of a sovereign or nobleman; a chief steward. **2.** An official who receives the rents and fees of a municipality; a treasurer. **3.** *Roman Catholic Church.* A papal attendant, usually honorary. [Middle English *chamberleyn,* from Old French *chamberlenc,* from Frankish *kamerling* (unattested), bedchamber servant : CHAMBER + -LING.]

Chamberlain (chām′bər-lĭn), **(Arthur) Neville** (1869–1940). As Conservative prime minister (1937–40), he advocated a policy of appeasement toward the fascist regimes of Europe. In the hope of preventing war, he visited Hitler three times in 1938 before reaching the Munich Agreement that recognized Hitler's annexation of the Sudetenland. Germany's subsequent invasion of Czechoslovakia forced Chamberlain to abandon his policy. In September 1939 he declared war on Germany after Hitler's invasion of Poland. He resigned as prime minister and joined Churchill's war cabinet (May 1940).

Chamberlain, Owen (1920–). U.S. physicist, who contributed to the development of the atom bomb. In 1955 he and Emilio Segrè discovered the antiproton by bombarding a copper target with high-energy protons. They were awarded the Nobel Prize in physics (1959).

Cham·ber·lin (chām′bər-lĭn), **Thomas Chrowder** (1843–1928). U.S. geologist, who with the astronomer Forest Ray Moulton (1872–1952) proposed the planetismal hypothesis (1906) of the formation of the planets in the solar system.

cham·ber·maid (chām′bər-mād′) *n.* A female servant who cleans and cares for bedrooms, now chiefly in hotels.

chamber music *n.* Music appropriate for performance in a private room or small concert hall and composed for a small group of instruments.

chamber of commerce *n. Abbr.* **C. of C.** An association of business persons and merchants for the promotion of business interests in its community. Also called "board of trade."

chamber orchestra *n.* A small orchestra, usually with only one instrument to a part, playing chamber music.

chamber pot *n.* A portable vessel used in a bedroom as a toilet.

Cham·bers (chām′bərz), **(Jay David) Whittaker** (1901–61). U.S. journalist. For some 15 years after 1924 Chambers was a member of the Communist Party, but in 1938 or 1939 he left the party. In 1948 he testified before the House Committee on Un-American Activities, implicating Alger Hiss as a fellow party worker. His autobiography, *Witness,* was published in 1952.

Cham·bé·ry (shäN-bā-rē′). Capital of Savoie department in the French Alps. It is popular with tourists.

cham·bray (shăm′brā′) *n.* A fine, lightweight fabric woven with white threads across a colored warp. [After CAMBRAI.]

cha·me·leon (kə-mēl′yən, -mē′lē-ən) *n.* **1.** Any of various tropical Old World lizards of the family Chamaeleontidae, characterized by their ability to change color. **2.** A lizard, the **anole** *(see).* **3.** A changeable or inconstant person. **4. Chameleon.** Variant of **Chamaeleon.** [Middle English *camelion,* from Latin *chamaeleōn,* from Greek *khamaileōn,* "ground lion" : *khamai,* on the ground + *leōn,* LION.] **—cha·me·le·on·ic** (kə-mē′lē-ŏn′ĭk) *adj.*

cham·fer (chăm′fər) *tr.v.* **-fered, -fering, -fers. 1.** To cut off the edge or corner of; bevel. **2.** To cut a groove in; flute.
~*n.* **1.** A flat surface made by cutting off the edge or corner of something, such as a block of wood. **2.** A furrow or groove, as in a piece of wood. [Perhaps a back-formation from *chamfering,* from French *chanfrein,* a bevel, from Old French *chanfrein(t),* past participle of *chanfraindre,* to break the edge off : *chant,* edge, rim, from Latin *canthus,* iron ring of a wheel, from Celtic + *fraindre,* to break, from Latin *frangere.*]

cham·ois (shăm′ē; shăm-wä′ *for sense 1 only*) *n., pl.* **chamois** (shăm′ēz; shăm-wä′ *for sense 1 only).* Also **cham·my, sham·my** (for sense 2) *pl.* **-mies. 1.** A hoofed mammal, *Rupricapra rupricapra,* of mountainous regions of Europe, having upright horns with backward-hooked tips. **2. a.** The soft leather made from the hide of this animal or others such as deer or sheep. **b.** A piece of such leather, used for polishing windows and the like. **3.** A moderate to grayish yellow. [Old French, probably from Late Latin *camox*†.]

cham·o·mile, cam·o·mile (kăm′ə-mīl′) *n.* **1.** Any of various plants of the genus *Anthemis*; especially, *A. nobilis,* an aromatic plant native to Eurasia, with finely dissected leaves and white flowers. **2.** Any of several similar plants of the genus *Matricaria*; especially *M. chamomilla,* native to Eurasia. [Middle English, from Old French *camomile,* from Late Latin *chamomilla,* from Greek *khamaimēlon,* "earth-apple" (referring to the apple scent of the flowers).]

Cha·mo·nix (shă-mô-nē′). Tourist resort in the Haute-Savoie department of the French Alps. It is close to Mont Blanc and is a winter sports center.

champ[1] (chămp) *v.* **champed, champing, champs.** Also **chomp** (chŏmp), **chomped, chomping, chomps.** *—tr.* To bite or chew upon noisily or impatiently. *—intr.* To work the jaws and teeth vigorously. **—champ at the bit.** To be impatient or frustrated at being held back. [Probably imitative.]

champ[2] *n. Informal.* A champion.

cham·pagne (shăm-pān′) *n.* **1. a.** A sparkling white wine produced in the Champagne region of France. **b.** A wine that is similar to champagne but is produced elsewhere. **2.** A pale orange yellow to grayish yellow.
~*adj.* Of, pertaining to, or being champagne.

Cham·pagne (shăm-pān′). Ancient province of northeast France, now chiefly in Marne department. The sparkling wine that takes its name from the province was first produced around 1700.

cham·paign (shăm-pān′) *n.* A stretch of level and open country; a plain.
~*adj.* Pertaining to or like a champaign; level and open. [Middle English *champayn,* from Old French *champagne,* from Late Latin *campānia,* from Latin *Campānia,* Campagna (province in central Italy), from *campus,* plain, field. See **camp, campaign.**]

cham·pak, cham·pac (chăm′păk′, chŭm′pŭk) *n.* A tree, *Michelia champaca,* of India and the East Indies, having yellow flowers and yielding a camphorlike substance and an oil used in perfumes. [Hindi *campak,* from Sanskrit *campaka,* of Dravidian origin.]

cham·pers (shăm′pərz) *n. British Slang.* Champagne. [CHAMP(AGNE) + -ERS (humorous suffix).]

cham·per·ty (chăm′pər-tē) *n., pl.* **-ties.** *Law.* An illegal sharing in the proceeds of a lawsuit by an outside party who has promoted it. [Middle English *champartie,* from Norman French, from Old French *champart,* division of farm produce : *champ,* field, from Latin *campus* (see **camp**) + *part,* PART.]

cham·pi·gnon (shăm-pĭn′yən) *n.* Any of various edible mushrooms, especially the common species *Agaricus campestris.* [French, from Old French *champigneul,* probably from Vulgar Latin *(fungus) campāniolus* (unattested), "(fungus) growing in the fields," from Late Latin *campānia,* countryside, CHAMPAIGN.]

cham·pi·on (chăm′pē-ən) *n.* **1.** One that holds first place or wins first prize in a contest, especially in sports. **2.** One who fights for, defends, or supports a cause or another person: *champion of the oppressed.* **3.** One who fights; a warrior.
~*tr.v.* **championed, -oning, -ons. 1.** To fight as champion of; defend; support: *"championed the government and defended the system of taxation"* (Samuel Chew). **2.** *Obsolete.* To defy or challenge. **—**See Synonyms at **support.**
~*adj.* Holding first place or prize; superior to all others: *She was the champion chess player in her class.* [Middle English *champi(o)un,* from Old French *champion,* from Medieval Latin *campiō* (stem *campiōn-*), warrior, from Latin *campus,* field. See **camp.**]

cham·pi·on·ship (chăm′pē-ən-shĭp′) *n.* **1.** The position or title of a champion. **2.** Defense or support; advocacy. **3.** *Often* **championships.** A competition or series of competitions to determine a winner.

Cham·plain, Lake (shăm-plān′). A lake, 201 kilometers (125 miles) long and from .8 to 22.5 kilometers (.5 to 14 miles) wide, forming part of the border between New York and Vermont. Lake Champlain is a link in the Hudson River–St. Lawrence waterway. There are many resorts in the scenic region.

Champlain, Samuel de (*c.* 1567–1635). French explorer. In 1605 he founded the colony of Port Royal, and three years later he founded Stadacona, on the site of present-day Quebec.

champ·le·vé (shäN′lə-vā′) *n.* A technique of decorating silver and other metals in which hollowed-out areas are filled with colored enamel. [From French *champ,* field, flat surface + *levé,* raised area.] **—champ·le·vé** *adj.*

Cham·pol·lion (shäN-pô-lyôN′), **Jean François** (1790–1832). French Egyptologist. In 1821, working from the Rosetta stone, he became the first person to decipher Egyptian hieroglyphics.

chance (chăns, chäns) *n.* **1. a.** The abstract nature or quality shared by unexpected, random, or unpredictable events; contingency. **b.** This quality regarded as a cause of such events; luck. **2. a.** A possibility: *There's just a chance that the letter has gone astray.* **b.** *Often* **chances.** Likelihood; probability: *What are the chances of our catching the plane?* **3. a.** An opportunity. **b.** A risk or gamble. **c.** A raffle or lottery ticket. **4. a.** An unexpected, random, or unpredicted event. **b.** A fortuitous event.
~*v.* **chanced, chancing, chances.** *—intr.* To happen by chance; occur by accident. *—tr.* To take the risk or hazard of. Often used in the phrase *chance it.* **—**See Synonyms at **happen. —chance on (or upon).** To find or meet accidentally; happen upon.
~*adj.* Occurring as or in consequence of chance. [Middle English, from Old French, from Vulgar Latin *cadentia* (unattested), "a fall," happening, from Latin *cadere,* to fall.]
Synonyms: *casual, desultory, haphazard, random.*

chan·cel (chăn′səl, chän′-) *n.* The space around the altar of a church for the clergy and choir, often enclosed by a lattice or railing. [Middle English *chauncel,* from Old French *chancel,* from Late Latin *cancellus,* altar, from Latin *cancellī,* grating, lattice, plural diminutive of *cancer,* lattice.]

chan·cel·ler·y, chan·cel·lor·y (chăn′sə-lə-rē, -slə-rē, chän′-) *n., pl.* **-ies. 1.** The rank or position of a chancellor. **2.** The office or department of a chancellor or the building in which it is located. **3.** The official place of business of an embassy, consulate, or legation. [Middle English *chancelerie,* from Old French, from *chancelier,* CHANCELLOR.]

chan·cel·lor (chăn′sə-lər, -slər, chän′-) *n. Abbr.* **C. 1.** Any of various officials of high rank; especially: **a.** A secretary to a king or nobleman. **b.** *Chiefly British.* The chief secretary of an embassy. **c.** The chief minister of state in some European countries, such as West Germany. **2. a.** *Chiefly British.* The honorary or titular head of a university. **b.** The president of certain American universities. **3.** An Episcopal bishop's administrative officer who is responsible especially for matters of canon law. [Middle English *cha(u)nceler,* from Norman French *chanceler,* from Old French *chancelier,* from Late

chameleon *A lizard that lives in trees and bushes in Africa and Asia. It is famous for its ability to change color to blend in with its surroundings. The skull is crested and the tongue is at least half as long as the animal itself—and in some species longer.*

chamois *Chamois are mountain antelopes native to Europe and the eastern Mediterranean. Their specially adapted rubbery hoof pads make them sure-footed even on slippery rocks. Adult males live apart from the herd for most of the year; but during the November breeding season they rejoin the herd, drive out the young males, and fight among themselves for possession of the females.*

Latin *cancellārius,* secretary, doorkeeper, from *cancellus,* grating, CHANCEL.] —**chan·cel·lor·ship** *n.*

Chancellor of the Exchequer *n.* The senior finance minister in the British Cabinet.

Chan·cel·lors·ville (chăn'səl-ərz-vĭl', -slərz-vĭl', chăn'-). Village in northeastern Virginia, site of a major Civil War battle (May 2-4, 1863) in which the Confederate Army under Robert E. Lee defeated a Union force that was double its size. Gen. Stonewall Jackson was killed in the battle.

chance-med·ley (chăns'mĕd'lē, chăns'-) *n.* **1.** *Law.* An action, especially manslaughter, that is largely but not wholly accidental. **2.** A random or haphazard action. [Middle English, from Norman French *chance medlée,* "mixed chance" : Old French *chance,* CHANCE + *medlee,* past participle of *medler,* to MEDDLE.]

chanc·er (chăn'sər, chän'-) *n. British Informal.* One who risks doing something, especially something likely to incur disapproval, in the hope of avoiding loss or discovery.

chan·cer·y (chăn'sə-rē, chän'-) *n., pl.* **-ies. 1.** *Often* **Chancery.** One of the five divisions of the High Court of Justice in Great Britain, presided over by the Lord High Chancellor. **2. a.** A court of equity. Also called "court of chancery." **b.** The proceedings and practice of a court of equity. **3.** *British.* The political section of a diplomatic mission. **4.** *Ecclesiastical.* A diocesan office controlling archives and legal matters. **5.** An office of public record; an archive. **6.** A chancellery. —**in chancery. 1.** *Law.* In litigation or pending in a court of chancery. **2.** *Wrestling.* Having the head locked firmly in an opponent's arm and held against his chest. **3.** *Informal.* In an embarrassing or hopeless predicament. [Middle English *chancerie,* contraction of *chancelerie,* CHANCELLERY.]

chan·cre (shăng'kər) *n.* A dull-red, hard, insensitive lesion that is the first manifestation of syphilis. [French, from Latin *cancer,* ulcer, CANCER.] —**chan·crous** *adj.*

chan·croid (shăng'kroid') *n.* A soft, nonsyphilitic, usually venereal lesion of the genital region, caused by infection with the bacterium *Haemophilus ducreyi.* Also called "soft sore." [French *chancroïde* : CHANCR(E) + -OID.]

chanc·y (chăn'sē, chän'-) *adj.* **-ier, -iest.** *Informal.* Uncertain or hazardous.

chan·de·lier (shăn'də-lîr') *n.* A branched fixture that holds a number of light bulbs or candles, and is usually suspended from a ceiling. [French, from Old French, from Vulgar Latin *candēlārum* (unattested), from Latin *candēlābrum,* CANDELABRUM.]

chan·delle (shăn-dĕl') *n.* A sudden, steep climbing turn of an aircraft, executed to alter flight direction and gain altitude simultaneously. [French, "candle," from Old French. See **chandler.**] —**chan·delle** *v.*

Chan·di·garh (chŭn'dē-gər). The joint capital of Punjab and Haryana states in northern India, situated below the foothills of the Himalayas. It was planned as the new Punjabi capital when Lahore became part of Pakistan (1947). The city, opened in 1953, was laid out in spacious rectangular blocks by a European team of architects under Le Corbusier.

chan·dler (chănd'lər, chänd'-) *n.* **1.** A person who makes or sells candles. **2.** A dealer in specified goods or equipment: *a ship's chandler.* [Middle English *chandeler,* from Old French *chandelier,* from *c(h)andelle,* candle, from Latin *candēla,* CANDLE.]

Chan·dler (chănd'lər), **Raymond** (1888-1959). U.S. novelist noted for creating the character Philip Marlowe, a cynical and incorruptible private eye. His works include *The Big Sleep* (1939), *Farewell My Lovely* (1940), and *The Long Goodbye* (1953).

Chandler wobble *n.* A small periodic variation in the location of the geographic poles on the Earth's surface. It has an interval of about 14 months. [After Seth Carlo *Chandler* (1846-1913), U.S. astronomer.]

chan·dler·y (chănd'lə-rē, chänd'-) *n., pl.* **-ies.** The stock or business of a chandler.

Chan·dra·se·khar (chŭn'drə-shā'kər), **Subrahmanyan** (1910-). Indian-born U.S. astronomer noted for his work on the evolution of stars, especially the small, low-mass white dwarfs.

Cha·nel (shə-nĕl'), **Gabrielle,** known as "Coco" (1883-1971). French fashion designer, noted for her classic dresses and suits and later for her range of perfumes, particularly Chanel No. 5. She retired in 1939, but returned to work in 1954.

Cha·ney (chā'nē), **Lon** (1883-1930). U.S. actor. The son of deaf-mute parents, he developed his pantomime skill at an early age. With this skill and his mastery of make-up he brought eerily sensitive, human qualities to horribly ugly monsters in movies such as *The Hunchback of Notre Dame* (1923) and *The Phantom of the Opera* (1925).

Changan. See **Xi'an.**

Ch'ang Chiang. See **Chang Jiang.**

Ch'ang-chou or **Changchow.** See **Changzhou.**

Chang·chun or **Ch'ang-ch'un** (chäng'chʊn'). *Japanese* **Hsin·king** (shĭn'jĭng'). Capital of Jilin province in northeast China. It grew in the early years of this century as a key station on the Chinese Eastern Railway, connecting the Trans-Siberian Railway with lines to Vladivostok and Port Arthur (now part of Lü-da).

Chang·de or **Ch'ang-te** (chäng'dʊ'). City of Hunan province, southeast China, on the Yüan River. The center of a "rice bowl," it was formerly a treaty port.

change (chănj) *v.* **changed, changing, changes.** —*tr.* **1. a.** To cause to be different; alter. **b.** To give a completely different form or appearance to; transform. **2.** To give and receive reciprocally;

interchange. **3.** To exchange for or replace by another, usually of the same kind or category: *change one's name.* **4.** To lay aside or leave for another; switch: *change sides.* **5.** To transfer from (one vehicle) to another: *change planes.* **6.** To give or receive the equivalent of (money) in lower denominations or in foreign currency. **7.** To engage a higher or lower (gear) in a motor vehicle. **8.** To put fresh clothes or coverings on: *change a baby.* —*intr.* **1.** To become different or altered. **2.** To go from one phase to another. Used of the Moon. **3.** To pass from one state or position to another according to an established pattern: *Wait till the traffic lights change before you cross the street.* **4.** To transfer from one vehicle, as a train or airplane, to another. **5.** To put on other clothing: *She changed for dinner.* **6.** To become deeper in pitch. Used of the voice. —**change hands.** To pass from one owner to another. —**change off. 1.** To alternate with another person in performing a task. **2.** To perform two tasks at once by alternating or a single task by alternate means. ~*n.* Also **'change** (for sense 9). **1. a.** The process or condition of changing. **b.** An instance of changing; an alteration or modification: *make a few changes.* **c.** The replacing of one thing for another; substitution. **2.** A transition from one state, condition, or phase to another: *the change of seasons.* **3. a.** Something different; a substitution. **b.** Variety; novelty: *ate early for a change.* **4.** A different or fresh set of clothing, especially one kept in reserve. **5.** The money of smaller denomination given or received in exchange for money of higher denomination. **6.** The balance of money returned when an amount given is more than what is due. **7.** Any coins, especially when of low value. **8.** A pattern or order in which bells are rung. **9.** A market or exchange where business is transacted. —**ring the changes. 1.** To ring bells with every possible variation. **2.** To do or say something familiar or routine in a new and different way. [Middle English *changen,* from Old French *changier,* from Late Latin *cambiāre,* probably from Celtic.] —**chang·er** *n.* —**change·less** *adj.*

Synonyms: *alter, convert, modify, transform, transmute, vary.*

change·a·ble (chān'jə-bəl) *adj.* **1.** Liable to change. **2.** Capable of being altered. **3.** Changing color or appearance when seen from different angles or in different lights: *changeable taffeta.* —**change·a·bil·i·ty, change·a·ble·ness** *n.* —**change·a·bly** *adv.*

change·ful (chānj'fəl) *adj.* Likely to change; variable.

change·ling (chānj'lĭng) *n.* **1.** A child believed to have been secretly exchanged for another, especially by fairies. **2.** *Archaic.* A changeable, fickle person.

change of life *n.* The **menopause** *(see).*

change over *intr.v.* To make a complete change; convert to a new system, position, or attitude: *The accounting department changed over to computers.*

change·o·ver (chānj'ō'vər) *n.* A conversion, as to a different method, attitude, or system.

change ringing *n.* The ringing of a set of chimes or bells with every possible unrepeated variation.

Chang Jiang or **Ch'ang Chiang** (chäng' jē-äng'). Also **Yang·tze Kiang** (yăng'tsĕ' jē-äng', kē-äng') or **Yang·tze.** Longest river of China. Rising in the Kunlun Shan in southwestern Qinghai province, it flows some 5,520 kilometers (3,430 miles) southeastward along the Tibet-Sichuan border and then mainly eastward to enter the East China Sea at Shanghai through a delta.

Chang·sha (chäng'shä'). Capital of Hunan province, south China, on the Xiang Jiang River. This historic trade center is set in rice-growing country and is famous for its handicrafts. Industries include engineering and chemicals and zinc and lead mining.

Ch'ang-te. See **Changde.**

Chang·zhou or **Ch'ang-chou** or **Chang-chow** (chäng'jō'). Formerly (until 1949) **Wu·tsin** (wōō'jĭn'). City in southern Jiangsu province, eastern China. It lies on the Grand Canal and is an agricultural and industrial center.

chan·nel¹ (chăn'əl) *n.* **1.** The bed of a stream or river. **2.** The deeper part of a river or harbor; especially, a deep navigable passage. **3.** A broad strait, especially one that connects two seas: *the English Channel.* **4.** A tubular passage for liquids. **5.** A course or passage through which something may be moved or directed: *a channel of thought.* **6.** *Often* **channels.** A means of communication or access, especially one that is officially recognized: *went through the proper channels.* **7.** *Electronics.* **a.** A specific frequency band for the transmission and reception of electromagnetic signals, as of television signals. **b.** Loosely, a television station: *What channel is it on?* **c.** A thin layer of semiconductor between the source and the drain of a field-effect transistor. **d.** Any path along which signals, data, or the like can travel. **8.** A trench, furrow, or groove. **9.** A rolled metal bar with a bracket-shaped section. Also called "channel bar," "channel iron." **10.** *Computer Science.* Any of the rows of punched holes in a punched-paper tape used to store information. ~*tr.v.* **channeled, channeling, channels.** Also *chiefly British* **channelled, -nelling. 1.** To make or cut channels in: *"No more shall trenching war channel her fields."* (Shakespeare). **2.** To form a channel or flute in. **3.** To direct or guide along some desired course. [Middle English *chanel,* from Old French, from Latin *canālis,* CANAL.]

channel² *n. Nautical.* A wood or steel ledge projecting from a sailing vessel's sides to spread the shrouds and keep them clear of the gunwales. [Earlier *chainwale* : CHAIN (fastening) + WALE (plank).]

Chan·nel Islands (chăn'əl). *Abbr.* **C.I.** An island group in the English Channel. They were settled by the Vikings and formed part of the duchy of Normandy, being united with the English crown in 1066. When England lost mainland Normandy in the 15th century, the islands remained possessions of the Crown. They have a measure of autonomy; British laws do not apply until approved by their own legislative bodies. The islands were occupied by the Germans in World War II. Jersey and Guernsey are famous for potato and tomato crops, woolen sweaters, and pedigreed cattle. Tourism is a major industry.

chan·nel·ize (chăn′ə-līz′) *tr.v.* **-ized, -izing, -izes.** To channel. —**chan·nel·i·za·tion** *n.*

chan·son de geste (shäɴ-sôɴ′ də zhĕst′) *n., pl.* **chansons de geste** (*pronounced as singular*). A genre of Old French epic poem falling into cycles of poems celebrating the deeds of heroic or historical figures. [French, "song of heroic deeds."]

chant (chănt, chänt) *n.* Also *archaic* **chaunt** (chônt, chänt). **1.** A short, simple melody in which a number of syllables or words are sung on each note. **2.** A psalm or canticle sung in this manner. **3.** A repetitive rhythmic intonation of words or slogans, as by political demonstrators, striking workers, or spectators at a football game. **4.** A singsong way of speaking. ~*v.* **chanted, chanting, chants.** —*tr.* To sing or intone as a chant. —*intr.* **1.** To sing; especially, to sing chants. **2.** To intone words or slogans in a repetitive, rhythmic manner. [Middle English *chanten*, to sing, from Old French *chanter*, from Latin *cantāre*, from *canere*.]

chant·er (chănt′ər, chän′-) *n.* **1.** A person who chants; especially, a chorister or precentor. **2.** The pipe on a set of bagpipes on which the melody is played.

chan·te·relle (shăn′tə-rĕl′, shän′-) *n.* An edible yellow mushroom, *Cantharellus cibarius,* having a pleasant fruity odor. [French, from New Latin *cantharella,* "little cup" (from its shape), diminutive of Latin *cantharus,* drinking vessel, from Greek *kantharos*†.]

chan·teuse (shän-tœz′) *n.* A woman singer, especially a nightclub singer. [French, feminine of *chanteur,* singer, from *chanter,* to sing, CHANT.]

chan·tey (shăn′tē, chăn′-) *n., pl.* **-teys.** Also **chan·ty,** *pl.* **-ties.** A song that is sung by sailors to the rhythm of their motions while working. [Probably from French *chantez,* imperative of *chanter,* to sing, CHANT.]

chan·ti·cleer (chăn′tə-klîr′, shăn′-) *n.* A cock or rooster. [Middle English *Chantecleer,* from Old French *Chantecler* (the cock in *Reynard the Fox*) : *chanter,* to CHANT + *cler,* CLEAR.]

Chan·til·ly (shăn-tĭl′ē). Town in the Oise department of northern France. It was known in the 17th and 18th centuries for fine chantilly lace, no longer made there.

chan·try (chăn′trē, chän′-) *n., pl.* **-tries.** *Ecclesiastical.* **1.** In medieval times, an endowment to cover expenses for the saying of masses and prayers, usually for the soul of the founder of the endowment. **2.** An altar or chapel endowed for this purpose. [Middle English *chaunterie,* from Old French *chanterie,* from *chanter,* to CHANT.]

chanty. Variant of **chantey.**

Cha·nu·kah, Cha·nuk·kah, Ha·nu·kah, Ha·nuk·kah (ᴋʜä′nə-kə, hä′-) *n.* A Jewish festival beginning on the 25th day of the month of Kislev and lasting eight days. It commemorates the victory of the Maccabees over the Syrians in 165 B.C. and the rededication of the Temple at Jerusalem. Also called "Feast of Lights," "Feast of Dedication." [Hebrew *ḥanukkāh,* "dedication," from *ḥānakh,* he dedicated.]

Cha·nute (shə-nōōt′), **Octave** (1832-1910). U.S. engineer and aviation pioneer, born in France. After establishing himself as a civil engineer he studied aerodynamics; designed, improved, and flew many gliders; and encouraged the Wright brothers' experiments, greatly advancing man's quest for powered flight.

chao (dou) *n.* Also **hao** (hou). A monetary unit of Vietnam equal to 1/10 of a dong. See feature at **currency.** [Vietnamese.]

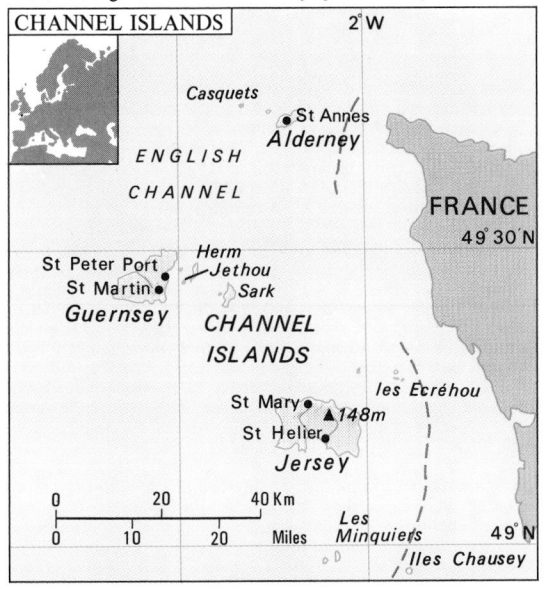

Chao Phra·ya (chou prī′ə). River in north Thailand. It flows some 365 kilometers (225 miles) north to south, passing through Krung Thep (Bangkok) and emptying into the Gulf of Thailand.

cha·os (kā′ŏs) *n.* **1.** A condition of total disorder or confusion. **2.** *Often* **Chaos.** The disordered state of unformed matter and infinite space supposed to have existed prior to the ordered universe according to some religious cosmological views. **3.** *Obsolete.* A vast abyss or chasm. [Latin, from Greek *khaos,* empty space, chaos.] —**cha·ot·ic** (kā-ŏt′ĭk) *adj.* —**cha·ot·i·cal·ly** *adv.*

chap[1] (chăp) *v.* **chapped, chapping, chaps.** —*tr.* To cause (the skin) to split or roughen, especially as a result of cold or exposure. —*intr.* To split or become rough and sore. ~*n.* A sore roughening of the skin, caused especially by cold or exposure. [Middle English *chappen,* perhaps of Low German origin, akin to Middle Low German *kappen,* to chop off.]

chap[2] *n. Informal.* A man or boy; a fellow. [Short for CHAPMAN.]

chap. chapter.

cha·pa·re·jos, cha·pa·ra·jos (shăp′ə-rā′ōs) *pl.n. Southwestern U.S.* Heavy leather trousers worn by cowboys, **chaps** (*see*). [Probably from Mexican Spanish *chaparreras* (influenced by Spanish *aparejo,* equipment), from *chaparro,* CHAPARRAL.]

chap·ar·ral (shăp′ə-răl′) *n.* A dense thicket of shrubs and small trees, especially in the southwestern United States and Mexico, that is similar to the maquis of southern Europe. [Spanish, from *chaparro,* evergreen oak, probably from Basque *txapar,* diminutive of *saphar,* thicket.]

cha·pat·ti, cha·pa·ti (chə-pä′tē, -pät′ē) *n.* In the cookery of India, a thin flat cake of coarse unleavened bread. [Hindi.]

chap·book (chăp′bŏōk′) *n.* A small book or pamphlet containing poems, ballads, stories, or religious tracts. [Originally, "a book sold by chapmen" : CHAP(MAN) + BOOK.]

chape (chāp, chăp) *n.* A metal tip or mounting on a scabbard or sheath. [Middle English, from Old French, cape, from Late Latin *cappa,* hood, "head covering," from Latin *caput,* head.]

cha·peau (shă-pō′) *n., pl.* **-peaux** (-pōz′) or **-peaus** (-pōz′). A hat. [French, from Old French *chapel,* from Vulgar Latin *cappellus* (unattested), diminutive of Late Latin *cappa,* head covering. See **chape.**]

chap·el (chăp′əl) *n.* **1.** A place of Christian worship that is smaller than and subordinate to a church. **2.** A place of worship in a college, hospital, or other institution. **3.** A recess or room in a church that has its own altar and is set apart for special or small services. **4. a.** In England and Wales, a place of worship for those not connected with or not members of the established church. **b.** In Scotland, a Roman Catholic church. **5.** The services held in a chapel. **6. a.** An association of workers in a print shop. **b.** *Obsolete.* A printing house or print shop. ~*adj. Chiefly British.* Belonging to a Nonconformist church. Compare **church.** [Middle English, from Old French *chapele,* from Medieval Latin *cappella,* originally a shrine containing the cape of St. Martin of Tours, diminutive of Late Latin *cappa,* cape. See **chape.**]

chap·er·on, chap·er·one (shăp′ə-rōn′) *n.* A person, especially an older or married woman, who for propriety supervises a group of young unmarried people or accompanies a young unmarried woman in public. ~*tr.v.* **chaperoned, -oning, -ons.** To act as chaperon to or for. —See Synonyms at **accompany.** [French, "hood," protection, protectress, from Old French, from *chape,* CHAPE.] —**chap·er·on·age** (shăp′ə-rō′nĭj) *n.*

chap·i·ter (chăp′ə-tər) *n. Architecture.* The capital of a column. [Middle English *chapitre,* from Latin *capitulum.* See **chapter.**]

chap·lain (chăp′lən) *n. Abbr.* **ch., Ch. 1.** A clergyman attached to a chapel. **2.** A clergyman attached to a hospital, prison, university, or other institution. **3.** A clergyman attached to a military unit or on board a ship. [Middle English *chapeleyn,* from Old French *chapelain,* from Medieval Latin *cappellānus,* from *cappella,* CHAPEL.] —**chap·lain·cy** (chăp′lən-sē), **chap·lain·ship** (-shĭp′) *n.*

chap·let (chăp′lĭt) *n.* **1.** A wreath or garland for the head. **2.** A string of beads; especially, a string of prayer beads having one third the number of a rosary's beads. **3.** *Architecture.* A small molding carved in a way resembling a string of beads. [Middle English *chapelet,* from Old French, diminutive of *chapel,* CHAPEAU.] —**chap·let·ed** *adj.*

Chap·lin (chăp′lĭn), **Sir Charles Spencer,** known as "Charlie" (1889-1977). British film star, director, producer, choreographer, and composer, knighted in 1975. His early films, in which he created a tramp in baggy trousers with a bowler hat and twirling cane, made him an immediate success. His productions included *The Kid* (1920), *The Gold Rush* (1924), *City Lights* (1931), *Modern Times* (1936), and *The Great Dictator* (1940). His later films include *Monsieur Verdoux* (1947), in which he played a murderer; and *Limelight* (1952), in which he portrayed an aging music-hall comic. A victim of the McCarthy anti-Communist witch-hunt of the early 1950's, he left the United States for Switzerland in 1952.

chap·man (chăp′mən) *n., pl.* **-men** (-mĭn). *Archaic.* A dealer or merchant, especially a peddler. [Middle English *chapman,* Old English *cēapman* : *cēap,* trade (see **cheap**) + MAN.]

Chapman (chăp′mən), **George** (c. 1560-1634). English poet, dramatist, and scholar noted for his translations of Homer's *Iliad* (1598-1611) and *Odyssey* (1616), which later prompted John Keats to compose his sonnet *On First Looking Into Chapman's Homer.*

Chapman, John, known as "Johnny Appleseed" (c. 1775-1845). U.S. pioneer and hero of many legends. Born in New England, he

chanterelle *An edible fungus with the color and smell of apricot. It is found in woodlands, particularly beech woods, from July to December.*

MAP:

CHANNEL ISLANDS   2° W

Casquets

St Annes
Alderney

E N G L I S H

C H A N N E L

FRANCE
49° 30′ N

Herm
St Peter Port
St Martin   *Jethou*
Sark
Guernsey   CHANNEL

ISLANDS

les Écréhou
St Mary   ▲148m
St Helier
Jersey

0   20   40 Km
0   10   20   Miles
Les Minquiers   49° N
Îles Chausey

settled in the Ohio River valley after 1800, traveling widely over the countryside to plant apple seeds and prune the young trees.

chap·pal (chŭp′əl, chăp′-) *n.* A type of Indian sandal, usually made of leather. [Hindi.]

chap·pie (chăp′ē) *n. Chiefly British Informal.* A fellow; chap.

chaps (chăps, shăps) *pl.n.* Heavy leather trousers without a seat, worn over ordinary trousers by cowboys to protect their legs. Also called "chaparejos." [Short for Mexican Spanish *chaparreras,* CHAPAREJOS.]

chap·ter (chăp′tər) *n. Abbr.* **chap., ch., c., C. 1.** Any of the main divisions of a book or other piece of writing, usually numbered or titled. **2.** A distinct period or sequence of connected events, as in history or in a person's life. **3.** *British.* A numbered division of a session of Parliament relating to a specific Act of Parliament. **4.** *Ecclesiastical.* **a.** An assembly of the canons of a cathedral or collegiate church. **b.** The canons collectively. **5.** *Ecclesiastical.* An assembly of the members or representatives of a religious community or knightly order. **6.** A local branch of an organization, as a college fraternity or a club. [Middle English *chapitre,* from Old French, from Late Latin *capitulum,* from Latin, small head, chapiter, from *caput,* head.]

chapter and verse *n.* The exact source or authority for a statement or action. [Referring to citing the chapter and verses of books of the Bible.]

chapter house *n.* **1.** A building in which the chapter of a cathedral or monastery assembles. **2.** A house in which a chapter of a fraternity or sorority lives and holds its meetings.

char[1] (chär) *v.* **charred, charring, chars.** —*tr.* **1.** To burn the surface of; scorch. **2.** To reduce to charcoal by incomplete combustion. —*intr.* To become charred. **—See Usage note at burn.**
∼*n.* A substance that has been charred; charcoal. [Back-formation from CHARCOAL.]

char[2] *n., pl.* **chars** or collectively **char.** Also **charr.** Any of several fishes of the genus *Salvelinus,* related to the trout; especially, the widely distributed *S. alpinus.* [17th century : origin obscure.]

char[3] *n.* **1.** A chore or odd job, especially a household task. **2.** A charwoman.
∼*intr.v.* **charred, charring, chars. 1.** To do small jobs, tasks, or chores. **2.** To work as a charwoman. [Middle English *char(re),* piece of work, Old English *cerr,* piece of work, a turning, from *cierran,* to turn, from Germanic.]

char·a·banc (shăr′ə-băng′) *n., pl.* **-bancs.** *Chiefly British.* A large bus or coach, often used for sightseeing, group outings, or the like. [French *char à bancs,* "carriage with benches."]

char·a·cin (kăr′ə-sĭn) *n.* Also **char·a·cid** (-sĭd). Any of numerous chiefly tropical freshwater fishes of the family Characidae, related to the carp, many of which are popular aquarium fishes. [New Latin *Characinidae* (earlier family name) : *Charax* (genus), from Greek *kharax* (stem *kharak-*), a kind of fish, pointed stake + -IDAE.]

char·ac·ter (kăr′ək-tər) *n.* **1.** The combination of qualities or features that distinguishes one person, group, or thing from another. **2.** One such distinguishing feature or attribute; a characteristic. **3.** The moral or ethical nature of a person or group. **4.** Moral or ethical strength; integrity and fortitude. **5.** The quality of being distinctive or outstanding: *an old house of great character.* **6.** Status; capacity; role: *in his character as a father.* **7.** *Informal.* **a.** A person: *There's some character at the door asking to see you.* **b.** A person who is amusing or eccentric. **8.** A person portrayed in a drama, novel, or other artistic piece. **9.** A statement regarding an employee's competence and dependability; reference. **10.** A symbol or mark used in a writing system, as a letter of the alphabet. **11.** *Printing.* A letter, punctuation mark, numeral, or the like, cast in type and usually occupying a fixed amount of space. **12.** A style of printing or writing. **13.** *Computer Science.* **a.** One of a set of symbols, as letters or numbers, arranged to express information. **b.** The multi-bit code representing a character. **14.** *Genetics.* A structure, function, or attribute determined by a gene or group of genes. **—See Synonyms at disposition, quality, type. —in** (or **out of**) **character.** Consistent (or inconsistent) with the usual nature of a person.
∼*adj.* **1.** Specializing in roles portraying odd, eccentric, or unusual personality types: *a character actor.* **2.** Calling for the abilities of such an actor: *a character part.*
∼*tr.v.* **charactered, -tering, -ters.** *Archaic.* **1.** To portray, describe, or represent. **2.** To write, print, engrave, or inscribe. [Learned respelling of Middle English *caracter,* from Old French *caractere,* from Latin *charactēr,* character, mark, instrument for branding, from Greek *kharaktēr,* engraved mark, brand, from *kharassein,* to brand, sharpen, from *kharax* (stem *kharak-*), pointed stake.]

character assassination *n.* The malicious slandering of the reputation of a person, especially a public figure.

char·ac·ter·is·tic (kăr′ək-tə-rĭs′tĭk) *adj.* Pertaining to, indicating, or constituting a distinctive character, quality, or disposition; typical.
∼*n.* **1.** A distinguishing feature or attribute. **2.** *Mathematics.* The integral part of a logarithm as distinguished from the mantissa: *6 is the characteristic of the logarithm 6.3214.* **—char·ac·ter·is·ti·cal·ly** *adv.*

Synonyms: *distinctive, individual, peculiar, typical.*

char·ac·ter·i·za·tion (kăr′ək-tər-ə-zā′shən) *n.* **1.** The act of characterizing; especially, a description of the qualities or peculiarities of a person or thing. **2.** The creation or delineation of a character or characters on the stage, in a film, or in writing, especially by imitating or describing actions, gestures, or speech.

char·ac·ter·ize (kăr′ək-tə-rīz′) *tr.v.* **-ized, -izing, -izes. 1.** To describe the qualities or peculiarities of: *characterized him as ruthless.* **2.** To be a distinguishing trait or mark of.

char·ac·ter·less (kăr′ək-tər-lĭs) *n.* Without any distinguishing or interesting features or qualities.

character sketch *n.* A brief portrayal or summary of a person's qualities, distinguishing features, idiosyncrasies, or the like.

char·ac·ter·y (kăr′ək-tə-rē, kə-răk′-) *n., pl.* **-ies. 1.** The use of characters or symbols to express or convey thought and meaning. **2.** Such characters or symbols collectively.

cha·rade (shə-rād′) *n.* **1. a. charades.** A game in which a word or phrase is acted out syllable by syllable until it is guessed by the other players or team. **b.** An episode or word in this game. **2.** A readily perceived pretense; travesty. [French, from Provençal *charrado,* chat, from *charra,* to chat (imitative).]

char·broil (chär′broil′) *tr.v.* **-broiled, -broiling, -broils.** To broil over charcoal: *charbroiled our steaks.* [CHAR[1] + BROIL.]

char·coal (chär′kōl′) *n.* **1.** A black, porous carbonaceous material produced by the destructive distillation of wood and used as a fuel, filter, and absorbent. **2.** A drawing pencil or crayon made from this substance. **3.** A drawing executed with such a pencil or crayon. **4.** A dark smoky gray to black.
∼*tr.v.* **charcoaled, -coaling, -coals.** To draw, write, or blacken with charcoal. [Middle English *charcole* : perhaps Old French *charbon,* charcoal (see **carbon**) + COAL.]

charcoal rot *n.* A disease of plants that is caused by a fungus, *Macrophomina phaseoli,* and that results in black, decayed tissue.

Char·cot (shär-kō′), **Jean Martin** (1825–93). French physiologist noted for his research into the nervous system. Sigmund Freud was one of his students.

char·cu·te·rie (shär-ko͞o′tə-rē′) *n.* **1.** Cooked meats, as ham and sausages. **2.** A shop selling charcuterie. [French, from *charcutier,* seller of cooked meat, from Old French, from *chair cuite,* "cooked meat" : *chair,* from Latin *caro* (stem *carn-*), flesh + *cuite,* past participle of *cuire,* from Latin *coquere,* to cook.]

chard (chärd) *n.* A variety of beet, *Beta vulgaris cicla,* having large leaves used as a vegetable. Also called "Swiss chard," "leaf beet." [French *carde,* edible stalks of the cardoon, from Old French, cardoon, from Late Latin *cardō,* from Latin *carduus,* artichoke.]

Chardin, Pierre Teilhard de. See **Teilhard de Chardin.**

char·don·nay (shär′də-nā′) *n.* A variety of white grape used for making fine white Burgundy wine. [French.]

Cha·rente (shə-räNT′). River in western France. It rises in the foothills of the Massif Central and flows 354 kilometers (220 miles) through Angoulême and Rochefort to the Bay of Biscay.

charge (chärj) *v.* **charged, charging, charges.** —*tr.* **1.** To place a burden on; entrust with a duty, responsibility, task, or obligation. **2.** To command, instruct, or urge with authority: *The judge charged the court to be silent.* **3.** To blame or accuse; impute something to. Often used with *with*: *charged with murder.* **4.** To set or ask (a given amount) as a price. **5.** To hold financially liable; demand payment from: *Customers will be charged for any breakage.* **6.** To postpone payment on (a service or purchase) by recording as a debt: *charge the dress to my account.* **7.** To attack by rushing violently toward: *The soldiers charged the fort.* **8.** To load (a gun or other firearm). **9.** To fill fully: *His mind was charged with ideas.* **10.** *Electricity.* **a.** To cause formation of a net electric charge on or in (a conductor, for example). **b.** To energize (a storage battery). Often used with *up*: *charge up the battery.* **11. a.** To cause to be saturated; impregnate: *The air was charged with perfume.* **b.** To fill so as to intensify: *The argument was charged with emotion.* **12.** *Heraldry.* To depict a heraldic charge on. —*intr.* To make an attack by rushing forward: *The cows charged toward the gate.* —See Synonyms at **command.**
∼*n.* **1. a.** Care or custody: *children in the charge of their teacher.* **b.** Supervision; a position of responsibility or authority: *Who's in charge here?* **2.** An obligation or responsibility. **3.** A person or thing entrusted to one's care or management. **4.** An order, command, or injunction. **5.** An address, given by a judge to a jury at the end of a trial, of instruction about such matters as legal points and the weight of evidence. **6.** An accusation or indictment: *a charge of conspiracy to defraud.* **7.** *Abbr.* **chg.** The price set or demanded for an article or service: *bank charges.* **8.** Expense: *gave the banquet at his own charge.* **9.** *Abbr.* **chg.** A debt or an entry in an account recording a debt. **10.** A rushing, forceful attack. **11.** The maximum quantity of anything that an apparatus or container can hold at one time. **12.** The quantity of explosive with which a firearm is loaded for one shot. **13.** *Electricity.* **a.** The intrinsic property of matter responsible for all electric phenomena, in particular for the force of the electromagnetic interaction, occurring in two forms arbitrarily designated *negative* and *positive.* **b.** A measure of this property. **c.** The net measure of this property possessed by a body or contained in a bounded region of space. **14.** *Heraldry.* A device, figure, or emblem depicted on a shield. **15.** *Informal.* A feeling of pleasant excitement; thrill: *We got a real charge out of the movie.* —See Synonyms at **price.** [Middle English *chargen,* to load, from Old French *charger,* from Late Latin *carricāre,* from Latin *carrus,* CAR.]

charge·a·ble (chär′jə-bəl) *adj.* **1.** That may be or is suitable to be charged, as to an account. **2.** Liable to be accused.

charge account *n.* A credit arrangement in which a customer receives purchases or services prior to payment.

charge conjugation *n. Symbol* **C** *Physics.* **1.** A mathematical op-

PRONUNCIATION KEY

ă, pat; ā, pay; âr, care;
ä, father, are; b, bib;
ch, church; d, deed; ĕ, pet;
ē, be; f, fife; g, gag; h, hat;
hw, which; ĭ, pit; ī, pie;
îr, pier; j, judge; k, kick;
l, lid, needle; m, mum;
n, no, sudden; ng, thing;
ŏ, pot; ō, toe; ô, paw, for;
oi, noise; ou, out; o͝o, book;
o͞o, boot; p, pop; r, roar;
s, sauce; sh, ship, dish;
t, tight; th, thin, path;
th, this, bathe; ŭ, cut; ûr, fur;
v, valve; w, with; y, yes;
z, zebra, size; zh, vision;
ə, about, item, edible,
gallop, circus, peaceful

IN FOREIGN WORDS:

à, *Fr.* ami; œ, *Fr.* feu, *Ger.* schön; ü, *Fr.* tu, *Ger.* über;
KH, *Ger.* ich, *Scot.* loch;
N, *Fr.* bon; y′, *Fr.* Compiègne

STRESS MARKS:

Primary stress: ′
in·cite′ (ĭn-sīt′)
Secondary stress: ′
in′sight′ (ĭn′sīt′)

erator that changes the sign of the charge and of the magnetic moment of every particle in the system to which it is applied. **2.** Loosely, the theoretical conversion of matter to antimatter or of antimatter to matter.

char·gé d'af·faires (shär-zhā′ də-fâr′) *n., pl.* **chargés d'affaires** (-zhā′, -zhāz′). **1.** A governmental official temporarily placed in charge of diplomatic affairs while the ambassador or minister is absent. **2.** A low-ranking diplomat representing his government in a country to which no higher-ranking diplomat has been appointed. [French, "(one) charged with affairs."]

charge density *n.* The electric charge per unit area or per unit volume of a body or of a region of space.

charge hand *n. British.* A workman, usually below the rank of foreman, who is in charge of a particular section or group of workers.

charge nurse *n.* A nurse in charge of a hospital ward.

charg·er[1] (chär′jər) *n.* **1.** One that charges. **2.** A powerful horse trained for battle; a cavalry horse. **3.** An instrument that charges or replenishes storage batteries.

charger[2] *n.* A large, shallow dish; a platter. [Middle English *chargeour,* from Norman French, probably from CHARGE, "to fill."]

charge sheet *n.* A document kept in a police station listing persons arrested and the charges made against them.

Char·ing Cross (chăr′ĭng). District in the London borough of the City of Westminster, where Whitehall and the Strand once met. There, in about 1290, Edward I set up the last of a series of crosses in memory of his queen, Eleanor. The cross was destroyed during the English Civil War, but another was erected (1865) in front of Charing Cross Station, a major railway terminus.

Cha·ri-Nile (shä′rē-nīl′) *n.* A family of languages spoken in eastern and central Africa, including the East and Central Sudanic languages.

char·i·ot (chăr′ē-ət) *n.* **1.** An ancient horse-drawn two-wheeled vehicle used in war, races, and processions. **2.** A light four-wheeled carriage used for ceremonial occasions or for pleasure. —*v.* **charioted, -oting, -ots.** —*tr.* To convey or drive in a chariot. —*intr.* To ride in or drive a chariot. [Middle English, from Old French, augmentative of *char,* vehicle, from Latin *carrus,* CAR.]

char·i·o·teer (chăr′ē-ə-tîr′) *n.* **1.** A person who drives a chariot. **2. Charioteer.** The constellation **Auriga** *(see).*

cha·ris·ma (kə-rĭz′mə) *n., pl.* **-mata** (-mə-tə). Also **char·ism** (kăr′ĭz-əm). **1.** An exceptional ability to attract and influence others; marked personal charm or magnetism. **2.** *Theology.* A divinely inspired gift or power, such as the ability to heal or to perform miracles. [Greek *kharisma,* favor, divine gift, from *kharizesthai,* to favor, from *kharis,* grace, favor.]

char·is·mat·ic (kăr′ĭz-măt′ĭk) *adj.* **1.** Of, pertaining to, or marked by charisma. **2.** *Theology.* Inspired or bestowed by the Holy Spirit. **3.** Of, pertaining to, or following a charismatic movement. —*n.* A follower of a charismatic group or movement. —**char·is·mat·i·cal·ly** *adv.*

charismatic movement *n.* A movement among various Christian churches, seeking to reassert the influence of the Holy Spirit in the world and reviving certain practices of the early Church, such as the ministry of healing and speaking in tongues.

char·i·ta·ble (chăr′ə-tə-bəl) *adj.* **1.** Generous in giving money or other help to the needy. **2.** Mild or tolerant in judging others; lenient. **3.** Of, for, or concerned with charity: *a charitable organization.* —**char·i·ta·ble·ness** *n.* —**char·i·ta·bly** *adv.*

char·i·ty (chăr′ə-tē) *n., pl.* **-ties. 1.** The provision of help or relief to the poor. **2.** An institution, organization, or fund established to help the needy or carry out other socially useful work. **3.** Something that is given to help the needy; alms. **4.** An act or feeling of benevolence, good will, or affection. **5.** Indulgence or forbearance in judging others; leniency: *The teacher showed charity toward the less gifted students.* **6.** *Theology.* **a.** The benevolence of God toward man. **b.** The love of man for his fellow men; brotherly love. [Middle English *charite,* Christian love, from Old French, from Latin *cāritās* (stem *cāritāt-*), love, regard, from *cārus,* dear.]

cha·ri·va·ri (shĭv′ə-rē′, shĭv′ə-rē′) *n., pl.* **-ris.** Also **chiv·a·ree, shiv·a·ree.** A noisy mock serenade to newlyweds. [French, from Late Latin *caribaria,* headache, from Greek *karēbaria,* "heavy head" : *karē, kara,* head + *barus,* heavy.]

char·kha, char·ka (chûr′kə, chär′-) *n.* In India, a spinning wheel, especially one used for cotton. [Hindi *carkha,* from Persian *charkha,* wheel.]

char·la·dy (chär′lā′dē) *n., pl.* **-dies.** *British.* A charwoman *(see).*

char·la·tan (shär′lə-tən) *n.* A person who claims to possess knowledge or skill that he does not have; quack. [French, from Italian *ciarlatano,* from *ciarlare,* to chatter, babble (as when peddling quack remedies), probably imitative.] —**char·la·tan·ic** (shär′lə-tăn′ĭk) *adj.* —**char·la·tan·ism** *n.*

Char·le·magne (shär′lə-mān′), also called "Charles the Great" (c. 742–814). King of the Franks (768–814) and founder of the first empire in Western Europe since the fall of Rome. The elder son of King Pepin the Short, he built an empire that encompassed the entire heartland of Western Europe, stretching from the Danube River to the Pyrenees, from Rome to the North Sea. Pope Leo III crowned him emperor on Christmas Day, 800. Charlemagne's court at Aix-la-Chapelle became the center of a cultural rebirth in Europe, known as the Carolingian Renaissance.

Charles (chärlz), **Prince Philip Arthur George** (1948–). The eldest son of Elizabeth II and heir to the British throne. He was invested as Prince of Wales (1969). He was educated at Gordonstoun and Cambridge and later served in the Royal Navy and RAF. He married Lady Diana Spencer (1981).

Charles, Ray (1930–). U.S. singer and pianist. Blind from the age of six, he became an outstanding blues singer.

Charles I (1600–49). King of England, Scotland, and Ireland (1625–49) and son of James I. His clashes with Parliament on constitutional issues led to the English Civil War. Conflict with three successive parliaments (1625, 1626, and 1628-9) on the issue of his right to raise taxes without parliamentary consent led to 11 years' rule without Parliament. His arbitrary rule, High Church leanings, and indulgence in the Roman Catholic faith of his wife, Henrietta Maria, culminated in an attempt to force Archbishop William Laud's Anglican prayer book on Presbyterian Scotland and led to the Bishops' Wars against Scotland (1639-40). Charles summoned a parliament that refused him financial support unless grievances were discussed. This so-called Short Parliament (April–May 1640) was dissolved, but a new one was summoned in November after a military defeat by the Scots. The Long Parliament vigorously opposed Charles, and, following the failure of his attempt to have five of its members arrested for treason (January 1642), the king raised his standard against Parliament on August 22. The Battle of Naseby (1645) was decisive, and Charles surrendered to the Scots at Newark in the following year. In January 1647 he was handed over to Parliament. In November he escaped to the Isle of Wight, where he secretly enlisted the Scots against Parliament, a move that failed. Charles was tried for treason and executed in January 1649.

Charles II (1630–85). King of England, Scotland, and Ireland (1660–85). Exiled during the Commonwealth, Charles was invited to return in 1660. Seeking to free the monarchy from financial dependence on Parliament, he negotiated the secret Treaty of Dover (1670) with Louis XIV, agreeing to help the French against the Dutch. Parliament responded with the Test Act (1673) excluding Dissenters and Roman Catholics from office. Fear of Roman Catholicism came to a head with the Popish Plot (1678), which fabricated a plan to place Charles's brother and heir, later James II, on the throne. Charles resisted parliamentary attempts to exclude James from the succession and from 1681 ruled without Parliament.

Charles V (1500–58). Holy Roman Emperor (1519–56). The son of Philip of Burgundy, he inherited Burgundy with its Dutch possessions on his father's death in 1506, succeeded to the throne of Spain in 1516, and was elected Holy Roman Emperor on the death of his grandfather, Maximilian I.

Charles XIV, King of Sweden and Norway, born Jean Baptiste Jules Bernadotte (1763-1844). French Revolutionary general and king of Sweden and Norway (1818-44). He served brilliantly under Napoleon Bonaparte in the Italian campaign (1796-97) and became minister of war (1799) and marshal of the empire (1804). Sweden was in need of an heir to the throne and approached Bernadotte. With Napoleon's support, he accepted, and was elected crown prince in 1810. In 1814 he marched into Denmark and forced the Danes to cede Norway to Sweden; both countries became united under the same crown. His reign was peaceful and marked by internal improvements, such as the building of the Göta Canal. He was the founder of the present Swedish royal dynasty.

Charles Mar·tel (mär-těl′) (c. 689-741). Frankish ruler and illegitimate son of Pepin of Herstal, mayor of the palace of the eastern Frankish kingdom of Austrasia. He was the grandfather of Charlemagne.

Charles's law *n. Physics.* The law that the volume of a fixed mass of gas held at a constant pressure varies directly with the absolute temperature. Also called "Gay-Lussac's law." [After Jacques *Charles* (1746–1823), French physicist.]

Charles's Wain (wān) *n.* A constellation, the **Big Dipper** *(see).*

Charles·ton[1] (chärl′stən). City in South Carolina, on the southeastern coast, on a peninsula between the Ashley and Cooper rivers. It was founded in 1670 and is a major port and industrial center.

Charleston[2]. The capital and largest city of West Virginia, in the west-central part of the state. It is an important transportation, manufacturing, and trading center.

Charleston[3] *n.* A fast dance in 4/4 time, characterized by kicks out to the side from the knees, and first popular during the 1920s. [After CHARLESTON, South Carolina.]

char·ley horse (chär′lē) *n. Informal.* A cramp or muscular stiffness caused by injury or excessive exertion. [Origin unknown.]

Char·lie (chär′lē) *n. British Slang.* **1.** A fool. **2. Charlies.** A woman's breasts. [Unexplained use of *Charlie,* diminutive of *Charles.*]

char·lock (chär′lək, -lŏk′) *n.* A weedy plant, *Brassica kaber,* native to Eurasia, having hairy stems, foliage, and yellow flowers. Also called "wild mustard." [Middle English *cherlok, carlok,* Old English *cerlic*†.]

char·lotte (shär′lət) *n.* **1.** A cold dessert, **Charlotte russe** *(see).* **2.** A dessert, served either hot or cold, consisting of a mold of sponge cake or bread with a filling of fruits, whipped cream, custard, or the like. [French, from the name *Charlotte.*]

Char·lotte A·ma·lia (shär′lət ə-mäl′yə). Capital of the U.S. Virgin Islands, on St. Thomas Island.

Char·lot·ten·burg (shär-lŏt′ən-bûrg′). A residential area of West Berlin in West Germany. Once a city in its own right, it contains a 17th-century castle with museum and art gallery.

charlotte russe (rōos) *n.* A cold dessert of whipped cream or a custard mixture set in a mold lined with ladyfingers. Also called "charlotte." [French, "Russian charlotte."]

chariot *A detail of an Athenian black-figure vase, depicting a light racing chariot. The vase was made in about 550 B.C.*

Charolais *A heavy, milky white French-bred cow. Charolais cattle are extensively crossed with animals such as Holsteins to produce quick-maturing beef calves from dairy herds.*

chateau *Azay-le-Rideau, a 16th-century French moated castle. Some chateaux are more modest manor houses.*

Char·lottes·ville (shär′ləts-vĭl′). A city of central Virginia, in a piedmont area known for its apples. The University of Virginia is in Charlottesville. Monticello, Thomas Jefferson's home, is nearby.

Char·lotte·town (shär′lət-toun′). Capital city of Prince Edward Island province, Canada. It was the site of the conference (1864) that laid the foundations of the confederation of Canada in 1867.

charm¹ (chärm) *n.* **1.** The power or quality of pleasing, attracting, or fascinating. **2.** A particular quality or feature that fascinates or attracts: *The painting's charm is its simplicity.* **3.** A trinket or small ornament worn on a bracelet or other piece of jewelry. **4.** Anything that is worn for its supposed magical effect, as in warding off evil; an amulet. **5.** Any action or formula thought to have magical power. **6.** A chanting of a magic word or verse; an incantation. **7.** *Physics.* A quantum property of one of the quarks whose conservation explains the absence of certain strange-particle decay modes and that accounts for the longevity of the particle.
~*v.* **charmed, charming, charms.** —*tr.* **1.** To attract or delight greatly or irresistibly; fascinate. **2.** To act upon with or as if with magic; bewitch. —*intr.* **1.** To be alluring or pleasing. **2.** To act as an amulet or charm. **3.** To employ spells. [Middle English *charme,* chant, magic spell, from Old French, from Latin *carmen,* song, incantation.] **—charm·less** *adj.*

charm² *n.* **1.** *Archaic.* A confused sound of voices or bird calls. **2.** A company of finches. [Middle English *cherme* (influenced by *charme,* incantation, CHARM), Old English *cirm, cierm,* clamor, cry, of imitative origin.]

charmed (chärmd) *adj.* **1.** Affected or protected by or as if by a charm: *a charmed life.* **2.** *Physics.* Exhibiting the property of charm.

charmed circle *n.* A very exclusive group.

charm·er (chär′mər) *n.* **1.** One who charms or has the power to charm. **2.** A sorcerer.

charm·ing (chär′mĭng) *adj.* **1.** Having charm or a pleasant manner. **2.** Delightful; appealing.
~*interj.* Used ironically to express indignation or distaste. **—charm·ing·ly** *adv.*

char·mo·ni·um (chär-mō′nē-əm) *n. Physics.* Any of various elementary particles consisting of a charmed quark and the antiparticle of a quark. [CHARM + *-onium,* pseudoscientific suffix representing typical technical words (*ammonium, plutonium,* and so on).]

char·nel (chär′nəl) *n.* A charnel house.
~*adj.* Resembling or suggesting a charnel house; sepulchral; deathlike. [Middle English, from Old French, from Medieval Latin *carnāle,* from Late Latin *carnālis,* carnal, from Latin *carō* (stem *carn-*), flesh.]

charnel house *n.* A building, room, or vault in which the bones or bodies of the dead are placed.

Char·o·lais (shăr′ə-lā′) *n.* Any of a French breed of large white beef cattle.

Char·on (kâr′ən). *Greek Mythology.* The ferryman who conveyed the dead to Hades over the river Styx.

char·poy (chär′poi′) *n.* A light bedstead used especially in India. [Urdu *chārpāī.*]

char·qui (chär′kē) *n.* Cured or jerked meat, especially beef. Also called "jerky." [Spanish, from Quechua *ch'arki.*]

charr. Variant of **char** (fish).

chart (chärt) *n.* **1. a.** A map showing coastlines, water depths, or other information of use to navigators. **b.** A map of the sky showing the positions of the stars. **2.** An outline map on which special information, such as weather data, can be plotted. **3.** A sheet presenting information in the form of graphs, tables, or other figures. **4.** A **graph** *(see).* **5. charts.** A list, as of phonograph records, whose members are ranked in accordance with popularity or sales.
~*tr.v.* **charted, charting, charts. 1.** To make a chart of. **2.** To plan in detail. **3.** To record (progress, for example). [Old French *charte,* from Latin *charta,* papyrus leaf, paper, CARD.]

char·ta·ceous (kär-tā′shəs) *adj.* Resembling paper; papery. [Late Latin *chartāceus,* from Latin *charta,* papyrus leaf, paper. See **card.**]

char·ter (chär′tər) *n.* **1.** A document issued by a sovereign, legislative body, or other authority, creating a public or private corporation, such as a city, college, or bank, and defining its privileges and purposes. **2.** A written grant from the sovereign power of a country conferring certain rights and privileges upon a person, a corporation, or the people. **3.** *Often* **Charter.** A document outlining the principles, functions, and organization of a corporate body; constitution. **4.** A document claiming or asserting certain rights. **5.** A special privilege or immunity. **6.** A charter party. **7. a.** The hiring or leasing of an aircraft, vessel, or land vehicle. **b.** An agreement for such a hiring or leasing. **8.** A written instrument given as evidence of agreement, transfer, or contract; a deed.
~*tr.v.* **chartered, -tering, -ters. 1.** To grant a charter to; establish by charter. **2.** To hire or lease by charter. **3.** To hire (a vehicle). [Middle English *chartre,* from Old French, from Latin *chartula,* diminutive of *charta,* papyrus leaf, CARD.] **—char·ter·er** *n.*

char·ter·age (chär′tər-ĭj) *n.* **1.** The act or business of chartering, especially of ships. **2.** The fee charged by a ship broker.

charter colony *n.* A British colony in America, as Massachusetts, Connecticut, or Rhode Island, that was created by a royal charter exempting it from direct interference by the Crown.

chartered accountant *n. Abbr.* **C.A.** *Chiefly British.* A member of an institute of accountants granted a royal charter.

charter flight *n.* A flight by a specially chartered aircraft; especially, one providing cheap fares for members of the chartering group.

char·ter·house (chär′tər-hous′) *n.* A Carthusian monastery. [Middle English, altered (by assimilation to HOUSE) from Norman French *Chartrous,* (La Grande) Chartreuse. See **Carthusian.**]

charter member *n.* An original member or founder of an organization.

charter party *n.* A contract for the commercial leasing of a vessel or space on a vessel.

Chart·ism (chär′tĭz′əm) *n.* The principles and practices of a movement of social and political reformers, chiefly workingmen, active in England from 1838 to 1848. Their views were stated in the People's Charter, published in 1838. **—Chart·ist** *n.* & *adj.*

Chartres (shärt, shär′trə). Capital of the Eure-et-Loir department of northwest France, on the Eure River. Its 13th-century cathedral is one of the masterpieces of Gothic architecture and is famous for its magnificent statuary and stained glass.

char·treuse (shär-tro͞oz′, -tro͞os′, -trœz′) *n.* **1.** Either of two liqueurs, green or yellow, made from herbs and spices by the Carthusian monks. **2.** Strong to brilliant greenish yellow to moderate or strong yellow green. [French, first made at *la Grande Chartreuse,* Carthusian monastery near Grenoble.] **—char·treuse** *adj.*

chartulary. Variant of **cartulary.**

char·wom·an (chär′wo͝om′ən) *n., pl.* **-women** (-wĭm′ĭn). *Chiefly British.* A woman hired to do cleaning or similar work in an office or home. [CHAR (chore) + WOMAN.]

char·y (châr′ē) *adj.* **-ier, -iest. 1.** Careful; wary. **2.** Fastidious; finicky. **3.** Shy: *chary of meeting people.* **4.** Sparing: *chary of compliments.* [Middle English *charig, charry,* cherished, dear, Old English *cearig,* sorrowful, from Germanic *karō* (unattested), CARE.] **—char·i·ly** *adv.* **—char·i·ness** *n.*

Cha·ryb·dis (kə-rĭb′dĭs). *Greek Mythology.* A whirlpool off the Sicilian coast, opposite the cave of **Scylla** *(see).*

chase¹ (chās) *v.* **chased, chasing, chases.** —*tr.* **1.** To pursue in order to catch or overtake. **2.** To follow (game) in order to capture or kill; hunt. **3. a.** To try to obtain. **b.** *Informal.* To pursue and force one's attentions on (a woman, for example). **4.** To put to flight; drive. Often used with *away, out,* or *off.* —*intr.* **1.** To go or follow in pursuit. **2.** *Informal.* To go hurriedly; rush. Often used with *after* or *off.*
~*n.* **1.** The act of chasing; pursuit. **2.** The sport of hunting. Preceded by *the.* **3.** That which is hunted or pursued; a quarry. **4.** *Chiefly British.* **a.** A privately owned, unenclosed game preserve. **b.** The right to hunt or keep game on the land of others. **—give chase.** To pursue; chase. [Middle English *chacen, chasen,* from Old French *chasser, chacier,* from Vulgar Latin *captiāre* (unattested), from Latin *captāre,* to seize, frequentative of *capere,* to take.]

chase² *n. Printing.* A rectangular steel or iron frame into which type is locked for printing or plate making. [Probably from French *châsse,* a case, from Latin *capsa,* box, CASE.]

chase³ *n.* **1. a.** A groove cut in any object; a slot. **b.** A trench or channel for drainpipes or wiring. **c.** A longitudinal groove for a tenon or tongue. **2.** The part of a gun that contains the bore.
~*tr.v.* **chased, chasing, chases. 1.** To decorate (metal) by engraving or embossing. **2. a.** To groove; indent. **b.** To cut or finish (the thread of a screw). [Old French *chas,* "enclosure," from Latin *capsus,* from *capsa,* box, CASE.]

chas·er¹ (chā′sər) *n.* **1.** One that chases or pursues. **2.** A gun on the bow or stern of a ship, used during pursuit or flight. Also called "chase gun." **3.** *Informal.* A drink, as of water or beer, taken after hard liquor.

chaser² *n.* **1.** One who decorates metal by engraving or embossing. **2.** A steel tool for cutting or finishing screw threads.

chasm (kăz′əm) *n.* **1.** A deep cleft or crack in the earth's surface; an abyss or narrow gorge. **2.** A sudden and considerable interruption of continuity; a gap; a hiatus. **3.** Any marked difference of opinion, interests, loyalty, or the like. [Latin *chasma,* from Greek *khasma,* akin to *khainein,* to gape.] **—chas·mal** (kăz′məl) *adj.*

chas·sé (shă-sā′) *n.* A dance movement consisting of one or more quick, gliding steps with the same foot always leading.
~*intr.v.* **chasséd, -séing, -sés.** To make or perform a chassé. [French, from the past participle of *chasser,* to CHASE.]

chasse·pot (shăs′pō′) *n.* A type of breech-loading rifle introduced into the French army in 1866. [French, after Antoine *Chassepot* (1833–1905), French gunsmith.]

chas·seur (shă-sûr′) *n.* **1.** A soldier; especially, one of certain light cavalry or infantry troops of the French army, trained for rapid maneuvers. **2.** A huntsman. **3.** A uniformed footman.
~*adj.* Served with a sauce of mushrooms and white wine: *chicken chasseur.* [French, "huntsman," from *chasser,* to CHASE.]

Chas·si·dim, Has·si·dim (KHä-sē′dĭm) *pl.n. Singular* **Chas·sid, Has·sid** (KHä′sĭd). A sect of Jewish mystics founded in Poland (about 1750) in opposition to the formalistic Judaism of the period and to ritual laxity. [Hebrew *ḥasīdhīm,* "pious ones," from *ḥāsīdh,* pious.] **—Chas·si·dic** (KHə-sĭd′ĭk, -sē′dĭk) *adj.* **—Chas·si·dism** *n.*

chas·sis (shăs′ē, chăs′ē) *n., pl.* **chassis** (-ēz). **1.** The rectangular steel frame, supported on springs and attached to the axles, that holds the body and engine of an automotive vehicle. **2.** The landing gear of an aircraft, including the wheels, floats, and other structures that support the aircraft on land or water. **3.** The frame on which a casement gun carriage moves forward and backward. **4.** The framework to which the functioning parts of a radio, television, record player, tape recorder, or other electronic equipment are attached. [French *châssis,* from Old French *chassis,* from Vulgar Latin *capsī-*

cium (unattested), from Latin *capsa,* box, CASE.]

chaste (chāst) *adj.* **chaster, chastest. 1.** Morally pure in thought and conduct; decent and modest. **2. a.** Not having experienced sexual intercourse; virginal. **b.** Abstaining from unlawful sexual intercourse. **c.** Abstaining from all sexual activity; celibate. **3.** Pure or simple in design or style; not ornate, extreme, or artificial. [Middle English, from Old French, from Latin *castus,* morally pure.] —**chaste·ly** *adv.* —**chaste·ness** *n.*

chas·ten (chā′sən) *tr.v.* **-tened, -tening, -tens. 1.** To punish, either physically or morally; chastise. **2.** To restrain; moderate. **3.** To refine; purify: *chasten one's style.* [From obsolete *chaste* (verb), from Middle English *chasten, chastien,* from Old French *chastier,* from Latin *castigāre,* to CASTIGATE.] —**chas·ten·er** *n.*

chaste tree *n.* A shrub, *Vitex agnus-castus,* of southern Europe, often cultivated for its spikes of lilac-blue flowers. [Translation of New Latin *agnus castus,* by folk etymology (influenced by Latin *agnus,* lamb) from Greek *agnos*† (confused with *hagnos,* holy, chaste).]

chas·tise (chăs-tīz′) *tr.v.* **-tised, -tising, -tises. 1.** To punish, usually by beating. **2.** To criticize severely. **3.** *Archaic.* To purify. —See Synonyms at **punish.** [Middle English *chastisen,* variant of *chastien,* to CHASTEN.] —**chas·tise·ment** (chăs-tīz′mənt, chăs·tīz′-) *n.* —**chas·tis·er** *n.*

chas·ti·ty (chăs′tə-tē) *n.* **1.** The state or quality of being chaste or pure. **2. a.** Celibacy. **b.** Virtuousness. **c.** Virginity. [Middle English *chastete,* from Old French, from Latin *castitās* (stem *castitāt-*), from *castus,* CHASTE.]

chastity belt *n.* Any of various devices worn by medieval women to prevent sexual intercourse.

chas·u·ble (chăz′ə-bəl, chăzh′ə-, chăs′ə-) *n.* A long, sleeveless vestment worn over the alb by the priest at Mass. [French, from Old French, from Late Latin *casubla,* hooded garment, irregularly from Latin *casula,* cloak (literally, little house, cottage), diminutive of *casa,* house.]

chat (chăt) *intr.v.* **chatted, chatting, chats.** To converse in an easy, informal, or familiar manner. —**chat up.** *British Informal.* To engage (a person) in friendly or flirtatious conversation, especially so as to win personal favor or strike up a sexual relationship.
~*n.* **1.** An informal or familiar conversation. **2.** Any of several birds known for their chattering call, such as: **a.** Any of several Old World birds of the genus *Saxicola.* See **stonechat, whinchat. b.** A North American bird, *Icteria virens,* having a yellow breast and a greenish back. This species is also called "yellow-breasted chat." **c.** Any of several Australian wrens of the genus *Ephthianura.* [Middle English *chatten,* short for *chatteren,* to CHATTER.]

cha·teau, châ·teau (shă-tō′) *n., pl.* **-teaux** (-tōz′). **1.** A French castle or manor house. **2.** A country house; especially, one resembling a French castle. [French *château,* from Old French *chastel,* from Latin *castellum,* CASTLE.]

cha·teau-bot·tled (shă-tō′bŏt′ld) *adj.* Designating a wine coming from the vineyards attached to a chateau and bottled within its domain.

Châ·teau·bri·and (shă-tō′brē-än′) *n. Sometimes* **châteaubriand. 1.** A double-thick tender center cut of beef tenderloin. **2.** A cut of Châteaubriand in which a pocket is cut and filled with various seasonings before grilling. [Probably invented by the chef of the Vicomte de CHATEAUBRIAND.]

Chateaubriand, François René, Vicomte de (1768–1848). French author and diplomat and a leading figure in the early romantic movement in France. His 12 volumes of memoirs, *Mémoires d'Outre-tombe,* were published after his death.

chat·e·lain (shăt′ə-lān′) *n.* The keeper of a castle; a castellan. [Middle English *chateleyn,* from Old French *chastelain,* from Latin *castellānus,* from *castellum,* CASTLE.]

chat·e·laine (shăt′ə-lān′) *n.* **1.** The lady or mistress of a castle, chateau, or large, fashionable household. **2.** A clasp or chain worn at the waist for holding keys, a purse, or a watch.

Chat·ham Islands (chăt′əm). Small Pacific island group forming part of New Zealand. They were discovered in 1791. Sheep farming is the main occupation. See map at **Pacific Ocean.**

cha·toy·an·cy (shə-toi′ən-sē) *n.* The quality or state of being chatoyant.

cha·toy·ant (shə-toi′ənt) *adj.* Having a changeable luster.
~*n.* A chatoyant stone or gemstone, such as the cat's-eye. [French, present participle of *chatoyer,* gleam like a cat's eyes, from *chat,* CAT.]

chat show *n. Chiefly British.* A talk show.

Chat·ta·noo·ga (chăt′ə-nōō′gə). City in southeast Tennessee on the Tennessee River. It is a major rail terminus, celebrated in the song "Chattanooga Choo Choo."

chat·tel (chăt′l) *n.* **1.** *Law.* An article of personal, movable property. **2.** A slave. [Middle English *chatel,* property, goods, from Old French. See **cattle.**]

chattel mortgage *n.* A mortgage on personal property as security for an obligation or debt.

chat·ter (chăt′ər) *intr.v.* **-tered, -tering, -ters. 1.** To utter a rapid series of short, inarticulate, speechlike sounds. Used of a bird or animal. **2.** To talk rapidly or incessantly, especially on a trivial subject; jabber. **3.** To click together quickly, as the teeth do from cold. **4.** To vibrate or rattle while in operation, as a power tool does. —See Synonyms at **speak.**
~*n.* **1.** Idle or trivial talk. **2.** The jabbering of an animal or bird. **3.** A rattling or clicking, as of the teeth. **4.** A rattling or vibration,

---

CHARTRES CATHEDRAL: A SPLENDOR OF MEDIEVAL ART

Its windows preserve pictures showing local life of 700 years ago

Unsurpassed stained glass, superb sculpture, and fine high-Gothic architecture make the 13th-century Chartres Cathedral one of the outstanding medieval cathedrals of Europe. The light cast through its 173 stained glass windows, including the great western rose window, gives a twilight radiance dominated by red and deep, vivid blue—the unique "Chartres blue." Many of the windows were donated by medieval guilds, and pictures of the donors' trades and crafts are worked into the designs.

The cathedral replaced one that was destroyed by fire in 1194; the most sacred relic, said to be the Virgin's tunic, survived the fire and inspired the rebuilding. The use of flying buttresses allowed the building of thinner walls and more windows than had been possible in previous cathedrals. The windows cover some 2,000 square meters (22,000 square feet). The Royal Portal (1145–55) at the west front, a remainder from the earlier building, has fine examples of the sculpture of its period.

The northern tower was given a new spire after the old one was destroyed by lightning in 1506. It does not compare with the southern tower, one of the most beautiful in Europe.

GOTHIC GRANDEUR *Few cathedrals have the unity of design of the great 13th-century high-Gothic cathedral of Notre Dame at Chartres, most of it built within 30 years (1194–1220). Only the ornamented north tower and eastern St. Piat Chapel are later exterior work.*

NORTH PORCH CARVINGS *The Old Testament figures in the central bay of the porch include Abraham about to sacrifice Isaac (second left) and King David carrying a spear (extreme right).*

STAINED GLASS *Pisces is one sign of the zodiac depicted on the left side of a south ambulatory window. On the right side there are scenes showing seasonal labors performed during that month.*

---

as of a power tool in operation. [Middle English *chat(t)eren* (imitative).] —**chat·ter·er** *n.*

chat·ter·box (chăt′ər-bŏks′) *n.* An extremely talkative person.

chatter mark, chat·ter·mark (chăt′ər-märk′) *n.* **1.** A riblike marking on wood or metal, caused by vibration of a cutting tool. **2.** *Geology.* Any of a series of short scars on a glaciated rock surface.

Chaucer *A portrait of the 14th-century poet taken from an illustration in an early manuscript of his best-known work,* The Canterbury Tales.

Chat·ter·ton (chăt′ər-tən), **Thomas** (1752–70). English poet. As a youth he fooled readers by ascribing his works to a 15th-century monk, Thomas Rowley. Although some of his works were published under his own name, he was unable to support himself with writing. Starving and dejected, he took his life at the age of 18. His work and example greatly influenced the romantic poets.

chat·ty (chăt′ē) *adj.* **-tier, -tiest. 1.** Given to informal conversation. **2.** Marked by a familiar, conversational style: *a chatty letter.* **—chat·ti·ly** *adv.* **—chat·ti·ness** *n.*

Chau·cer (chô′sər), **Geoffrey** (*c.* 1342–1400). English poet, considered the father of English poetry. He was also a diplomat and customs official, traveling widely in Europe under Richard II. *The Book of the Duchess* (1369), written in honor of the wife of John of Gaunt, was his first work, followed by others including the *Parliament of Fowls* and *Troilus and Criseyde.* His *Canterbury Tales,* a collection of stories supposedly told by a party of pilgrims traveling from London to Canterbury, is his most famous work.

Chau·ce·ri·an (chô-sîr′ē-ən) *adj.* Of, pertaining to, or characteristic of Chaucer or his writings.
∼*n.* A scholar specializing in the study of Chaucer.

chaud·froid (shō-frwä′) *n.* **1.** A jellied white or brown sauce used as an aspic for cold meats or fish. **2.** Molded cold meat or fish dishes garnished with a chaudfroid sauce. [French, "hot-cold."]

chauf·feur (shō′fər, shō-fûr′) *n.* One employed to drive a private or official car.
∼*v.* **chauffeured, -feuring, -feurs.** *—tr.* To serve as a driver for. *—intr.* To serve as a chauffeur. [French, stoker, from *chauffer,* to warm. See **chafe.**]

chaul·moo·gra (chôl-mo͞o′grə) *n.* Any of several trees of tropical Asia, especially *Taraktogenos kurzii* and those of the genus *Hydnocarpus,* having seeds that yield an oil formerly used in treating leprosy. [Bengali *cāulmugrā* : *cāul,* rice + *mugrā,* hemp.]

chaunt. *Archaic.* Variant of **chant.**

chausses (shōs) *pl.n.* Medieval armor of mail for the legs and feet. [Middle English *chauces,* from Old French, from Medieval Latin *calcia,* clothing for the leg, from Latin *calceus,* shoe. See **calceate.**]

chau·vin·ism (shō′və-nĭz′əm) *n.* **1.** Militant devotion to and glorification of one's country; fanatical patriotism. **2.** Prejudiced belief in the superiority of one's own group: *male chauvinism.* [French *chauvinisme,* after Nicolas *Chauvin,* veteran of the First Republic and Empire noted for his patriotic fervor, popularized as a character in the play *La Cocarde tricolore* (1831).] **—chau·vin·ist** *n.* **—chau·vin·is·tic** (shō′və-nĭs′tĭk) *adj.* **—chau·vin·is·ti·cal·ly** *adv.*

Chá·vez (chä′vĕz), **Cesar Estrada** (1927–). U.S. labor organizer. In 1962 he founded the National Farm Workers Association and organized the workers of California's prime agricultural areas. In 1968 he launched a two-year nationwide boycott of California grapes, which led to important concessions by the grape growers.

chaw (chô) *v.* **chawed, chawing, chaws.** *Regional. —intr.* To chew. *—tr.* To chew (something). **—chaw** *n.*

Cha·yef·sky (chī-ĕf′skē, chä-), **Paddy** (1923–81). U.S. playwright and screenwriter. Considered one of the most successful early television writers, he depicted the unglamorous drama of everyday life. Many of his television dramas were made into movies. He earned Academy Awards for *Marty* (1955) and *Hospital* (1971).

cha·yo·te (chä-yō′tā) *n.* **1.** A tropical American vine, *Sechium edule,* bearing edible squashlike fruit. **2.** The fruit of the chayote. [Spanish, from Nahuatl *chayotli.*]

cha·zan, chaz·zan, haz·zan (KHä′zən) *n.* A cantor in a synagogue. [Late Hebrew *ḥazzān,* officer, cantor.]

Ch.E. chemical engineer.

cheap (chēp) *adj.* **cheaper, cheapest. 1.** Relatively low in cost; inexpensive. **2.** Charging low prices: *a cheap restaurant.* **3.** Worth more than the price paid. **4.** Involving little effort or loss: *a cheap victory.* **5.** Of small value. **6.** Of poor quality; shoddy. **7.** Not worthy of respect; vulgar; despicable. **8.** Ashamed or abashed. **9.** *Economics.* **a.** Obtainable at a low rate of interest. **b.** Devalued, as in buying power.
∼*adv.* Inexpensively. [Middle English *chep,* sale, bargain, purchase, Old English *cēap,* from West Germanic *kaupaz* (unattested), trader, from Latin *caupō,* innkeeper.] **—cheap·ly** *adv.* **—cheap·ness** *n.*

cheap·en (chē′pən) *v.* **-ened, -ening, -ens.** *—tr.* **1.** To make cheap or cheaper. **2.** To lower in estimation; degrade. *—intr.* To become cheap or cheaper. **—cheap·en·er** *n.*

cheap·ie (chē′pē) *n. Informal.* Something that is cheap and often of poor quality.

cheap-jack (chēp′jăk′) *adj.* **1.** Selling overpriced goods of poor quality. **2.** Of poor quality; worthless. [CHEAP + JACK (fellow), originally a hawker or dealer in shoddy goods.]

cheap·o (chē′pō) *adj. Informal.* Cheap.

cheap shot *n. Informal.* An unjust action or statement, especially one directed at a vulnerable target, as a public figure.

Cheap·side (chēp′sīd′). Street in the City of London. It was the central market area of medieval London. St. Mary le Bow, built here by Christopher Wren in 1680, is the church of Bow Bells.

cheap·skate (chēp′skāt′) *n. Informal.* A stingy person; a miser. [CHEAP + SKATE (chap).] **—cheap·skate** *adj.*

cheat (chēt) *v.* **cheated, cheating, cheats.** *—tr.* **1.** To deceive by trickery; swindle. **2.** To mislead; fool. **3.** To elude; escape: *cheat death. —intr.* **1.** To act dishonestly to gain some advantage: *cheat at cards.* **2.** To act fraudulently. **3.** *Informal.* To be unfaithful, especially to one's spouse: *cheating on his wife.*
∼*n.* **1.** A fraud or swindle. **2.** One who cheats. **3.** *Law.* The fraudulent acquisition of another's property. [Middle English *cheten,* to revert, short for *acheten,* variant of *escheten,* from *eschete,* ESCHEAT.] **—cheat·er** *n.* **—cheat·ing·ly** *adv.*

check (chĕk) *n.* Also *chiefly British* **cheque** (for sense 10). **1.** An abrupt stopping or interruption of motion or progress; a halt or delay. **2.** Restraint or control. **3.** Someone or something that restrains or controls: *I tried to put a check on my emotions.* **4.** An inspection or examination, as to assess or verify accuracy, efficiency, attendance, or the like. **5.** A standard of comparison used in such an inspection; a test. **6. a.** A pattern of small squares, as on a chessboard. **b.** Any of the squares of such a pattern. **c.** A fabric patterned with such squares. **7.** A small crack or fault, especially in a piece of timber. **8.** *Chess.* **a.** A move that directly attacks an opponent's king but does not constitute a checkmate. **b.** The position or tactical condition of a king so attacked. **9.** A ticket or slip of identification: *a baggage check.* **10.** A written order to a bank to pay the amount specified from funds on deposit; draft. **11.** A bill in a restaurant or bar. **12.** A mark indicating verification or approval. **13.** A gambling chip or counter. **—in check.** Under restraint; in control.
∼*interj.* **1.** *Chess.* A declaration made to an opponent that his king is in check. **2.** *Informal.* Used to express affirmation.
∼*v.* **checked, checking, checks.** *—tr.* **1.** To arrest the motion or progress of abruptly; halt. **2.** To hold in restraint; curb. **3.** To slow the growth of; retard. **4.** To rebuke or rebuff. **5. a.** To test or examine, as for accuracy or efficiency. **b.** To ascertain or verify: *I'll just check that I've locked the door.* **6.** *Chess.* To move so as to put (an opponent's king) under direct attack. **7.** *Ice Hockey.* To impede (an opponent in control of the puck). **8.** To put a check mark on or next to. **9.** To deposit for temporary safekeeping, as in a cloakroom. *—intr.* **1.** To come to an abrupt halt; stop. **2.** To make an examination or investigation, as to verify something or to assess accuracy. Often used with *up, on,* or *upon.* **3.** To correspond accurately; agree. **4.** To pause to relocate a scent. Used of hunting dogs. **5.** *Chess.* To place an opponent's king in check. **—**See Synonyms at **restrain, delay.** [Middle English *chek,* attack, quarrel, check at chess, from Old French *eschec, eschac,* from Arabic *shāh,* king, check at chess, from Persian, king.] **—check·a·ble** *adj.*

check·book (chĕk′bo͝ok′) *n.* A book containing blank checks issued by a bank.

checked (chĕkt) *adj.* **1.** Having a pattern of squares. **2.** Held in check; restrained. **3.** Situated in a stopped or closed syllable: *a checked vowel.*

check·er (chĕk′ər) *n.* Also *chiefly British* **cheq·uer. 1.** One of the disks used in the game of checkers. **2. a.** A pattern of checks or squares. **b.** One of the squares in such a pattern. **3.** One who checks, examines, or supervises. **4.** A person who processes purchases at a check-out, as in a supermarket.
∼*tr.v.* **checkered, -ering, -ers.** Also *chiefly British* **cheq·uer. 1.** To mark into a pattern of squares. **2.** To diversify, as in color or character; variegate. [Middle English, from *cheker,* chessboard, from Old French *eschequier,* from *eschec,* CHECK.]

check·er·ber·ry (chĕk′ər-bĕr′ē) *n., pl.* **-ries. 1.** A plant, the **wintergreen** *(see).* **2.** The red, edible, spicy berry of this plant. [CHECKER (a name for the fruit of the service tree) + BERRY.]

check·er·bloom (chĕk′ər-blo͞om′) *n.* A plant, *Sidalcea malvaeflora,* of California, with long clusters of rose-pink flowers. [CHECKER, the wild service tree + BLOOM.]

check·er·board (chĕk′ər-bôrd′, -bōrd′) *n.* A game board divided into 64 squares of two alternating colors on which chess and checkers are played.

check·ers (chĕk′ərz) *n.* Also *chiefly British* **cheq·uers.** *Used with a singular verb.* A game played on a checkerboard by two players each using 12 pieces.

check in *intr.v.* To register on one's arrival, as at work or an airport. *—tr.v.* To register (passengers or luggage, for example) on arrival.

check-in (chĕk′ĭn′) *n.* **1.** The act of checking in, as at an airport. **2.** The place or time at which one checks in.

checking account *n.* A bank account in which checks may be written against amounts on deposit.

check·list (chĕk′lĭst′) *n.* A list against which items can be compared, verified, or identified.

check·mate (chĕk′māt′) *tr.v.* **-mated, -mating, -mates. 1.** *Chess.* To attack (an opponent's king) in such manner that no escape or defense is possible, thus ending the game. **2.** To defeat completely.
∼*n.* **1.** *Abbr.* **chm.** *Chess.* **a.** A move that constitutes an inescapable and indefensible attack on an opponent's king. **b.** The position of a king so attacked. **2.** Utter defeat.
∼*interj. Chess.* A call declaring the checkmate of an opponent's king. [Middle English *chekmate,* from Old French *eschec mat,* from Persian *shāh māt,* the king is dead.]

check·off (chĕk′ôf′, -ŏf′) *n.* The collection of dues from members of a union by authorized deduction from their wages.

check out *intr.v.* **1.** To pay one's bill and depart, as from a hotel. **2.** To record one's departure, as from a workplace.
∼*tr.v.* To process through a check-out, as in a supermarket.

check-out (chĕk′out′) *n.* **1.** The act, time, or place of checking out, as at a supermarket or hotel. **2.** A test, as of a machine, for proper functioning. **3.** An investigation or inspection.

check·point (chĕk′point′) *n.* A place where people or vehicles are stopped for inspection.

check·rein (chĕk′rān′) *n.* **1.** A short rein connected from a horse's bit to the saddle to keep the horse from lowering its head. Also called "bearing rein." **2.** A rein joining the bit of one of a span of horses to the driving rein of the other horse.

check·room (chĕk'rōōm', -rōōm') *n.* A place where items, as clothing or packages, can be stored temporarily.

check·row (chĕk'rō') *n.* A row, as of corn, in which the distance between plants is the same as the distance between adjacent rows to permit cross cultivation.
~*tr.v.* **checkrowed, -rowing, -rows.** To plant in checkrows.

checks and balances *pl.n.* The system of maintaining a balance of power between various branches of a government.

check·up (chĕk'ŭp') *n.* **1.** A thorough examination, as for verification or accuracy. **2.** A physical examination.

Ched·dar¹ (chĕd'ər). Town in Somerset in southwest England, in the valley of the Axe River. Cheddar cheese was first produced here in the 17th century. Cheddar Gorge, cutting through the Mendip Hills to the east, has limestone caverns and rare flora.

Ched·dar² (chĕd'ər) *n. Sometimes* **cheddar.** Any of several types of smooth, hard cheese varying in flavor from mild to extra sharp. [After CHEDDAR, where it was originally made.]

cheek (chĕk) *n.* **1.** The fleshy part of either side of the face below the eye and between the nose and ear. **2.** Something resembling this in shape or position, as either of two sides of something. **3.** *Informal.* A buttock. **4.** Sauciness; impudence. —See Synonyms at **te·merity.** —**cheek by jowl.** Side by side; close. —**turn the other cheek.** To submit to unjust or unkind treatment without retaliating.
~*tr.v.* **cheeked, cheeking, cheeks.** *Informal.* To speak impudently to. [Middle English *che(e)ke,* Old English *cēce, cēace,* from Germanic *kækōn-* (unattested).]

cheek·bone (chĕk'bōn') *n.* A bone in the upper cheek, the **zygomatic bone** *(see).*

cheek pouch *n.* A pouch inside the mouth of many rodents and certain other animals, used for holding food.

cheek·y (chē'kē) *adj.* **-ier, -iest.** Saucy; impudent; brazen. —**cheek·i·ly** *adv.* —**cheek·i·ness** *n.*

cheep (chēp) *n.* A faint, shrill sound like that of a young bird; a chirp.
~*v.* **cheeped, cheeping, cheeps.** —*tr.* To utter with a chirp. —*intr.* To chirp; peep. [Imitative.] —**cheep·er** *n.*

cheer (chîr) *n.* **1.** Gaiety; animation. **2.** A shout of approval, encouragement, or congratulation. **3.** Something that gives joy or comfort; encouragement. **4.** Food or drink; refreshment.
~*v.* **cheered, cheering, cheers.** —*tr.* **1. a.** To fill with joy. **b.** To comfort. Often used with *up.* **2.** To encourage with or as if with cheers; urge. Often used with *on.* **3.** To salute or acclaim with cheers; applaud. —*intr.* **1.** To shout cheers; applaud. **2.** To become cheerful. Often used with *up.* [Middle English *chere,* cheer, disposition, countenance, face, from Old French *ch(i)ere,* face, from Late Latin *cara,* from Greek *karē, kara,* head.] —**cheer·er** *n.* —**cheer·ing·ly** *adv.*

cheer·ful (chîr'fəl) *adj.* **1.** Being in good spirits; happy. **2.** Promoting cheer; pleasant. —See Synonyms at **glad.** —**cheer·ful·ly** *adv.* —**cheer·ful·ness** *n.*

cheer·i·o (chîr'ē-ō') *interj. Chiefly British Informal.* **1.** Used as a farewell or greeting. **2.** Used as a toast. [From CHEER.]

cheer·lead·er (chîr'lē'dər) *n.* One who leads group cheering, especially at sporting events.

cheer·less (chîr'lĭs) *adj.* **1.** Lacking cheer; gloomy. **2.** Pessimistic; in low spirits. —**cheer·less·ly** *adv.* —**cheer·less·ness** *n.*

cheers (chîrz) *interj.* Used as a toast.

cheer·y (chîr'ē) *adj.* **-ier, -iest.** In good spirits; cheerful. —**cheer·i·ly** *adv.* —**cheer·i·ness** *n.*

cheese¹ (chēz) *n.* **1. a.** A solid or semisolid food prepared from the pressed curd of milk. **b.** A molded mass of this substance. **2.** Something like cheese in shape, smell, or consistency. [Middle English *chese,* Old English *cēse,* from Germanic *kasjus* (unattested), from Latin *cāseus†*.] See feature, next page.

cheese² *tr.v.* **cheesed, cheesing, cheeses.** *Slang.* To stop. —**cheese it.** *Slang.* Look out; get away fast. [Origin unknown.]

cheese³ *n. Slang.* An important person: *He thinks he's a big cheese.* [Perhaps from Urdu *chīz,* thing, from Persian.]

cheese·burg·er (chēz'bûr'gər) *n.* A hamburger topped with melted cheese.

cheese·cake (chēz'kāk') *n.* **1.** A cake made of sweetened cottage cheese or cream cheese, eggs, milk, sugar, and flavoring. **2.** *Slang.* Photographs, as in advertisements, of attractive women scantily clothed. Compare **beefcake.**

cheese·cloth (chēz'klôth', -klŏth') *n.* A coarse, loosely woven cotton gauze, originally used for wrapping cheese.

cheesed off (chēzd) *adj. British Slang.* Annoyed; fed up. [From CHEESE (to stop).]

cheese mite *n.* A white mite, *Tyrophagus longior,* sometimes found in moldy cheese, on which it feeds.

cheese·par·ing (chēz'pâr'ĭng) *n.* Stinginess; parsimony.
~*adj.* Miserly; stingy.

chees·y (chē'ze) *adj.* **-ier, -iest. 1. a.** Resembling cheese. **b.** Containing cheese. **2.** *Slang.* Of poor quality; shoddy: *That was a cheesy movie.* —**chees·i·ly** *adv.* —**chees·i·ness** *n.*

chee·tah (chē'tə) *n.* A long-legged, swift-running feline mammal, *Acinonyx jubatus,* of Africa and southwestern Asia, having black-spotted, tawny fur and partially retractile claws. It is sometimes trained to pursue game. Also called "hunting leopard." [Hindi *cītā,* from Sanskrit *citrakāya,* tiger : *citra,* speckled + *kāya,* body.]

Chee·ver (chē'vər), **John** (1912-82). U.S. author. In many of his more than 100 short stories and five novels he humorously and compassionately depicted life in the American suburbs. He won America's most respected literary awards, including a Pulitzer Prize for *The Stories of John Cheever* (1978).

chef (shĕf) *n.* A cook; especially, the chief cook of a large kitchen staff. [French, CHIEF.]

chef-d'oeu·vre (shā-dœ'vr', -dûrv') *n., pl.* **chefs-d'oeuvre** (pronounced as singular). A masterpiece, especially in literature or art. [French, "chief work."]

chef's salad *n.* A green salad that usually includes raw vegetables, hard-boiled egg, and julienne strips of cheese and meat.

chei·lo·sis (kī-lō'sĭs) *n.* Inflammation and cracking of the lips, a symptom of riboflavin (Vitamin B_2) deficiency and other nutritional disorders. [New Latin, from Greek *kheilos,* lip + -OSIS.]

cheiro–. Variant of **chiro–.**

Che·ka (chā'kä, -kə, chĕk'ə) *n.* The Soviet security service organized in 1918 by Lenin. Reorganized many times, it acquired in 1954 the designation **KGB** *(see).* [Russian, short for *Chrezvychaynaya Komissiya,* "extraordinary commission."]

Che·khov (chĕk'ôf'), **Anton Pavlovich** (1860-1904). Russian playwright and short-story writer. Between 1898 and 1904 he had four plays produced at the Moscow Art Theatre: *The Seagull, Uncle Vanya, The Three Sisters,* and *The Cherry Orchard.* All are now acknowledged masterpieces.

Chekiang. See **Zhejiang.**

che·la (kē'lə) *n., pl.* **-lae** (-lē). A pincerlike claw of arthropods, as of a lobster, crab, or similar crustacean. [New Latin, from Latin *chēlē,* from Greek *khēlē†,* claw.]

che·late (kē'lāt') *adj.* **1.** *Zoology.* Having or characteristic of a chela. **2.** *Chemistry.* Of or pertaining to a heterocyclic ring containing a metal ion attached by coordinate bonds to at least two nonmetal ions in the same molecule.
~*tr.v.* **chelated, -lating, -lates.** To form a ring compound by joining a chelating agent to (a metal ion). —**che·late** *n.* —**che·la·tion** (kē-lā'shən) *n.*

che·lic·er·a (kə-lĭs'ər-ə) *n., pl.* **-erae** (-ə-rē') Either of the first pair of appendages near the mouth of a spider or other arachnid, often modified for grasping food. [New Latin : CHELA + Greek *keras,* horn.] —**che·lic·er·ate** (kə-lĭs'ə-rāt') *adj.*

che·li·form (kē'lə-fôrm') *adj.* Shaped like a chela; pincerlike.

Chel·li·an, Chel·le·an (shĕl'ē-ən) *adj. Archaeology.* Abbevillian. [French *chelléen,* of *Chelles,* site near Paris where some archaeological specimens were found.]

Chelms·ford (chĕmz'fərd, chĕlmz'-). City in Essex in southeast England, the administrative center of the county. Marconi began the world's first broadcasting service here (1920).

cheloid. Variant of **keloid.**

che·lo·ni·an (kə-lō'nē-ən) *adj. Zoology.* Of or belonging to the Chelonia, an order of reptiles that includes the turtles and tortoises.
~*n.* A member of the Chelonia. [New Latin *Chelonia,* from Greek *khelōnē,* tortoise.]

Chel·sea (chĕl'sē). District in the west London royal borough of Kensington and Chelsea, on the north bank of the Thames, popular since the 18th century with writers and artists. It is now a fashionable residential and shopping area.

chem–, chemi–. Variants of **chemo–.**

chem. chemical; chemist; chemistry.

chem·i·cal (kĕm'ĭ-kəl) *adj. Abbr.* **chem. 1.** Of, used in, or pertaining to chemistry. **2.** Of, employing, or pertaining to the properties or actions of chemicals.
~*n.* A substance produced by or used in a chemical process. [Earlier *chimical,* from *chimic,* an alchemist, from New Latin *chimicus,* from Medieval Latin *alchimicus,* from *alchimia, alchymia,* ALCHEMY.] —**chem·i·cal·ly** *adv.*

chemical bond *n.* Any of several forces or mechanisms, especially the **ionic bond, covalent bond, coordinate bond,** and **metallic bond** *(all of which see),* by which atoms or ions are bound in a molecule or crystal.

chemical engineering *n.* The technology of large-scale chemical and chemical materials production. —**chemical engineer** *n.*

chemical equation *n.* A representation of a chemical reaction using the chemical symbols of the elements taking part. The amount of substance of the reactants and products is usually given in moles.

Chemical Mace *n.* A trademark for a mixture of organic chemicals used in aerosol form as a weapon to disable with intense burning eye pain, blepharospasm, acute bronchitis, and respiratory irritation. Also called "Mace."

chemical reaction *n.* An interaction between substances involving changes in the outer electron structure and energy content of their molecules, atoms, or ions.

chemical warfare *n.* Warfare using chemicals other than explosives, especially irritants, asphyxiants, contaminants, poisons, and incendiaries, as direct weapons.

chemical weathering *n.* The wearing away of rocks or soil; **leaching** or **corrosion** *(both of which see).*

chem·i·lu·mi·nes·cence (kĕm'ə-lōō'mə-nĕs'əns, kē'mə-) *n.* The emission of light as a result of a chemical reaction at environmental temperatures.

che·min de fer (shə-măn' də fâr') *n.* A gambling game that is a variation of baccarat. [French, "road of iron," railroad.]

che·mise (shə-mēz') *n.* **1.** A woman's loose, shirtlike undergarment. **2.** A dress, a **shift** *(see).* [Middle English, from Old French, shirt,

cheetah *The cheetah, which is native to Africa and southwest Asia, is the world's fastest mammal. It can sprint at up to 110 kilometers (70 miles) per hour in pursuit of prey such as antelope. Unlike other big cats, the cheetah cannot retract its claws; instead they remain extended, helping it to grip the ground as it runs.*

THE MAGIC OF CURDS AND WHEY

How curdled milk is turned into Camembert and Caerphilly

All cheese begins as milk—mostly cows' milk, although it can be the milk of ewes or goats—and it was being eaten about 3000 B.C. in the ancient civilization of Sumer, Mesopotamia. Cheese is made by adding rennet—a preparation derived from a calf's stomach—to milk to produce curds and whey. The curds are drained of whey (which is used as a protein-rich animal feed), heated, salted, and pressed into drum-shaped molds. The cheeses are then ripened—sometimes for years. Variations of this method, together with the amount of fermentation that takes place during ripening, determine the final flavor and texture. Blue cheeses, such as Stilton, Danish Blue, and Gorgonzola, get their distinctive veining from bacteria allowed to grow on and into the cheeses.

HARD AND MEDIUM CHEESES

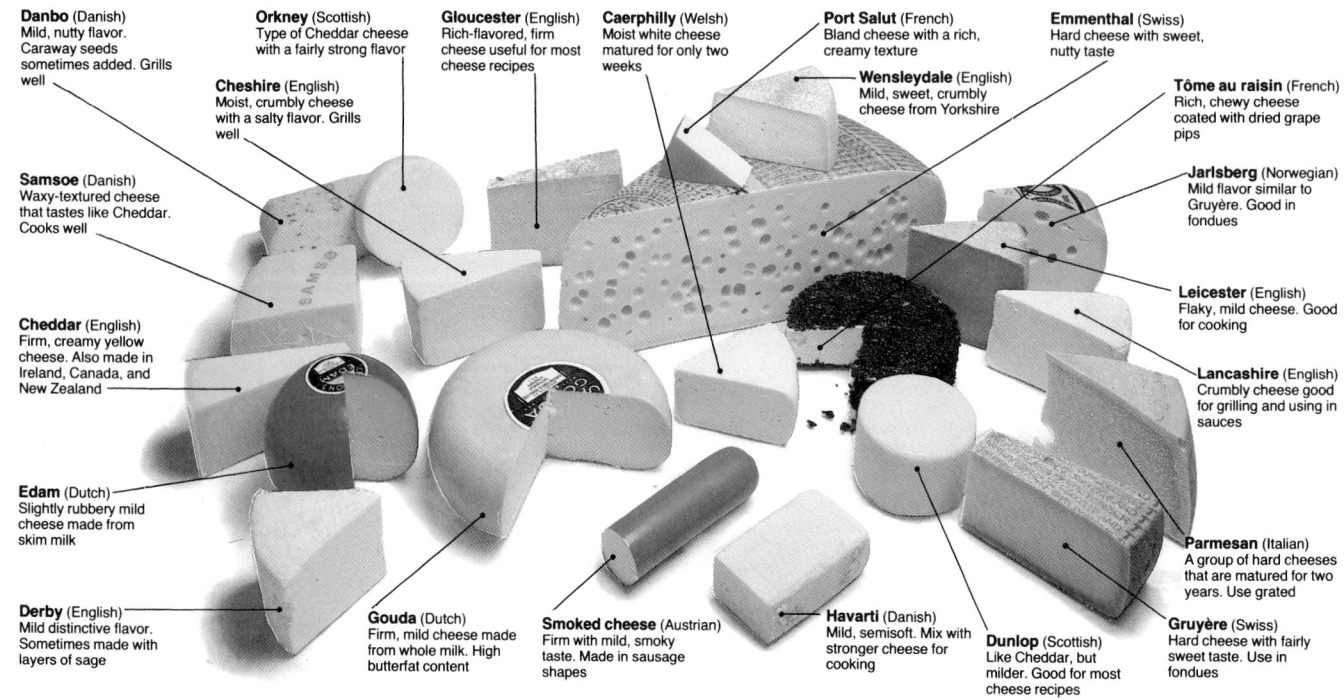

Danbo (Danish) Mild, nutty flavor. Caraway seeds sometimes added. Grills well

Orkney (Scottish) Type of Cheddar cheese with a fairly strong flavor

Gloucester (English) Rich-flavored, firm cheese useful for most cheese recipes

Caerphilly (Welsh) Moist white cheese matured for only two weeks

Port Salut (French) Bland cheese with a rich, creamy texture

Emmenthal (Swiss) Hard cheese with sweet, nutty taste

Cheshire (English) Moist, crumbly cheese with a salty flavor. Grills well

Wensleydale (English) Mild, sweet, crumbly cheese from Yorkshire

Tôme au raisin (French) Rich, chewy cheese coated with dried grape pips

Samsoe (Danish) Waxy-textured cheese that tastes like Cheddar. Cooks well

Jarlsberg (Norwegian) Mild flavor similar to Gruyère. Good in fondues

Cheddar (English) Firm, creamy yellow cheese. Also made in Ireland, Canada, and New Zealand

Leicester (English) Flaky, mild cheese. Good for cooking

Lancashire (English) Crumbly cheese good for grilling and using in sauces

Edam (Dutch) Slightly rubbery mild cheese made from skim milk

Parmesan (Italian) A group of hard cheeses that are matured for two years. Use grated

Derby (English) Mild distinctive flavor. Sometimes made with layers of sage

Gouda (Dutch) Firm, mild cheese made from whole milk. High butterfat content

Smoked cheese (Austrian) Firm with mild, smoky taste. Made in sausage shapes

Havarti (Danish) Mild, semisoft. Mix with stronger cheese for cooking

Dunlop (Scottish) Like Cheddar, but milder. Good for most cheese recipes

Gruyère (Swiss) Hard cheese with fairly sweet taste. Use in fondues

BLUE-VEINED AND CREAM CHEESES

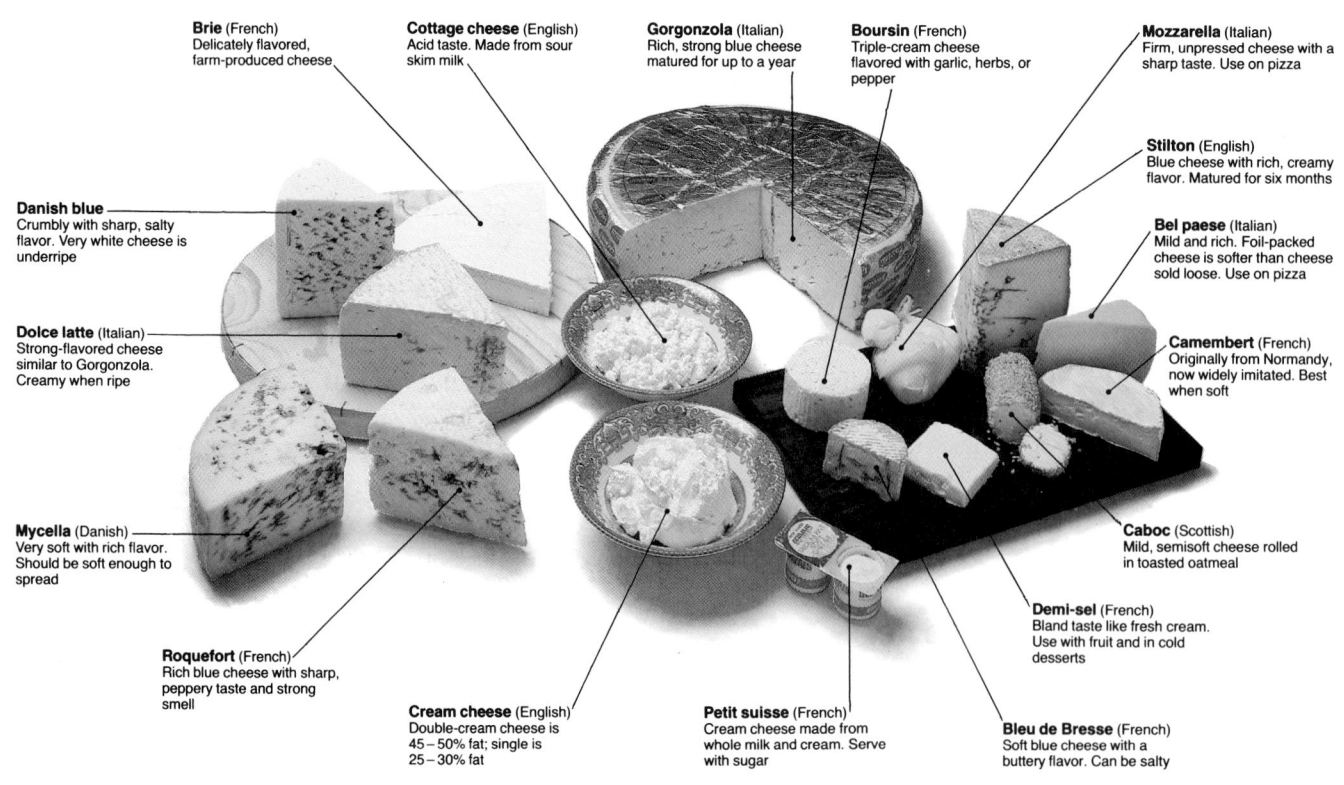

Brie (French) Delicately flavored, farm-produced cheese

Cottage cheese (English) Acid taste. Made from sour skim milk

Gorgonzola (Italian) Rich, strong blue cheese matured for up to a year

Boursin (French) Triple-cream cheese flavored with garlic, herbs, or pepper

Mozzarella (Italian) Firm, unpressed cheese with a sharp taste. Use on pizza

Danish blue Crumbly with sharp, salty flavor. Very white cheese is underripe

Stilton (English) Blue cheese with rich, creamy flavor. Matured for six months

Bel paese (Italian) Mild and rich. Foil-packed cheese is softer than cheese sold loose. Use on pizza

Dolce latte (Italian) Strong-flavored cheese similar to Gorgonzola. Creamy when ripe

Camembert (French) Originally from Normandy, now widely imitated. Best when soft

Mycella (Danish) Very soft with rich flavor. Should be soft enough to spread

Caboc (Scottish) Mild, semisoft cheese rolled in toasted oatmeal

Demi-sel (French) Bland taste like fresh cream. Use with fruit and in cold desserts

Roquefort (French) Rich blue cheese with sharp, peppery taste and strong smell

Cream cheese (English) Double-cream cheese is 45–50% fat; single is 25–30% fat

Petit suisse (French) Cream cheese made from whole milk and cream. Serve with sugar

Bleu de Bresse (French) Soft blue cheese with a buttery flavor. Can be salty

from Late Latin *camīsia,* linen shirt, nightgown.]

chem·i·sette (shĕm′ĭ-zĕt′) *n.* **1.** A short, sleeveless underbodice, formerly worn by women. **2.** A blouse front formerly worn by women to fill in the neckline of a dress. [French, diminutive of CHEMISE.]

chem·i·sorb (kĕm′ĭ-sôrb′) *tr.v.* **-sorbed, -sorbing, -sorbs.** Also **chem·o·sorb** (kĕm′ə-). To take up and chemically bind (a substance) on the surface of another substance. [CHEMI- + (AB)SORB.] **—chem·i·sorp·tion** (kĕm′ĭ-sôrp′shən) *n.*

chem·ist (kĕm′ĭst) *n. Abbr.* **chem. 1.** A scientist specializing in chemistry. **2.** *Chiefly British.* A pharmacist. **3.** *Obsolete.* An alchemist. [Earlier *chimist,* from New Latin *chimista,* short for Medieval Latin *alchymista,* ALCHEMIST.]

chem·is·try (kĕm′ĭ-strē) *n., pl.* **-tries.** *Abbr.* **chem. 1.** The science of the composition, structure, properties, and reactions of matter, especially of atomic and molecular systems. **2.** The composition, structure, properties, and reactions of a substance. **3.** Spontaneous interaction, as between two individuals: *the chemistry of love.* [Earlier *chimistrie,* from *chimist,* CHEMIST.]

chemo–, chemi–, chem– *prefix.* Indicates chemicals or chemical reactions; for example, **chemisorb, chemosmosis, chemotaxis.** [CHEM(ICAL) + -O-.]

chem·o·pro·phy·lax·is (kĕm′ō-prō′fə-lăk′sĭs, kē′mō-) *n.* The use of chemicals to prevent infectious disease. **—chem·o·pro·phy·lac·tic** *adj.*

chem·o·re·cep·tion (kĕm′ō-rĭ-sĕp′shən, kē′mō-) *n.* The reaction of a sense organ to a chemical stimulus. **—chem·o·re·cep·tive** *adj.* **—chem·o·re·cep·tiv·i·ty** *n.*

chem·o·re·cep·tor (kĕm′ō-rĭ-sĕp′tər, kē′mō-) *n.* A nerve ending or sense organ, such as a taste bud, sensitive to chemical stimuli.

chem·os·mo·sis (kĕm′ŏz-mō′sĭs, kĕm′ŏs-) *n.* The phenomenon of ionic or molecular transport across a membrane. **—chem·os·mot·ic** (kĕm′ŏz-mŏt′ĭk, kĕm′ŏs-) *adj.*

chem·o·sphere (kĕm′ə-sfîr′, kē′mə-) *n.* The region of the atmosphere between 20 and 120 miles altitude in which photochemical reactions initiated by solar radiation occur.

che·mo·sur·ger·y (kē′mō-sûr′jə-rē, kĕm′ō-) *n.* The combined use of surgery and chemotherapy to remove tumors of the skin.

chem·o·syn·the·sis (kĕm′ō-sĭn′thə-sĭs, kē′mō-) *n.* The synthesis of organic substances from carbon dioxide by certain bacteria using the energy of chemical reactions. **—chem·o·syn·thet·ic** (kĕm′ō-sĭn-thĕt′ĭk, kē′mō-) *adj.* **—chem·o·syn·thet·i·cal·ly** *adv.*

chem·o·tax·is (kĕm′ō-tăk′sĭs, kē′mō-) *n.* Characteristic orientation or motion of a freely moving living organism in response to a chemical substance. [New Latin : CHEMO- + -TAXIS.] **—chem·o·tac·tic** (kĕm′ō-tăk′tĭk, kē′mō-) *adj.* **—chem·o·tac·ti·cal·ly** *adv.*

chem·o·ther·a·py (kĕm′ō-thĕr′ə-pē, kē′mō-) *n.* The treatment of disease with chemicals; especially, the use of drugs rather than radiotherapy to treat cancer. **—chem·o·ther·a·peu·tic** (kĕm′ō-thĕr′ə-pyōō′tĭk, kē′mō-) *adj.* **—chem·o·ther·a·pist** *n.*

chem·ot·ro·pism (kĕm-ŏt′rə-pĭz′əm) *n.* Growth of an organism, especially a plant, in response to chemical stimuli. [German *Chemotropismus* : CHEMO- + -TROPISM.] **—chem·o·trop·ic** (kĕm′ō-trŏp′ĭk, -trō′pĭk, kē′mo-) *adj.*

chem·ur·gy (kĕm′ər-jē, kĕ-mûr′-) *n.* The development of new industrial chemical products from organic raw materials, especially from those of agricultural origin. [CHEM(O)- + -URGY.] **—chem·ur·gic** (kĕ-mûr′jĭk), **chem·ur·gi·cal** *adj.*

Cheng-chou, Chengchow. See **Zhengzhou.**

Cheng·du or **Cheng·tu** (chĕng′dōō′) or **Ch'eng-too.** Capital of Sichuan province in central China and one of the country's largest and oldest cities, founded before 770 B.C. It lies on the Min Jiang, an irrigation system more than 2,000 years old.

Ché·nier (shā-nyā′), **André Marie de** (1762–94). French poet. He is considered the greatest 18th-century French poet, although the vast majority of his work was not published until 25 years after his death by guillotine during the last days of the Reign of Terror.

che·nille (shə-nēl′) *n.* **1.** A soft, tufted cord of silk, cotton, or worsted used in embroidery or for fringing. **2.** Fabric made of this cord.
~*adj.* Of, made of, or resembling chenille: *a chenille bedspread.* [French, "caterpillar," from Latin *canīcula,* diminutive of *canis,* dog (from its hairy pile).]

Chen·nault (shə-nôlt′), **Claire Lee** (1890-1958). U.S. aviator and air-force officer. While commandant of the 19th Pursuit Group, Hawaii, he studied aerial combat strategies and the effectiveness of paratroops. He was named brigadier general in 1942 and led the U.S. Army Air Forces in China until his resignation in 1945.

che·no·pod (kē′nə-pŏd′, kĕn′ə-) *n.* Any plant of the goosefoot family, Chenopodiaceae, which includes spinach and beets as well as many common weeds. [New Latin *Chenopodiaceae,* from *Chenopodium* (genus) : Greek *khēn,* goose + -PODIUM.] **—che·no·po·di·a·ceous** (kē′nə-pō′dē-ā′shəs, kĕn′ə-) *adj.*

cheong·sam (chông′säm′) *n.* A light tight-fitting dress with a high collar and a slit skirt, typically worn by Chinese women. [Cantonese *cheung saam,* "long gown."]

Che·ops (kē′ŏps) (2590–2567 B.C.). Also **Khu·fu** (kōō′fōō′). Egyptian king. The second king of the fourth dynasty (*c.* 2613–*c.* 2494), he is renowned as the builder of the Great Pyramid at Giza, the largest single manmade structure at that time.

cheque. *Chiefly British.* Variant of **check** (sense 10).

cheque card *n. Chiefly British.* A **bankcard** *(see).*

chequer. *Chiefly British.* Variant of **checker.**

Cheq·uers (chĕk′ərz). The country residence of the prime minister of Great Britain, near Princes Risborough, Buckinghamshire. It was given to the nation by Lord Lee of Fareham (1917).

Cher·bourg (shâr′bŏŏrg′). Port in the Manche department of northwest France on the Cotentin Peninsula. It serves cross-Channel lines to Southampton.

cher·i·moy·a (chĕr′ə-moi′ə) *n.* **1.** A tropical American tree, *Annona cherimola,* having yellow flowers and edible fruit with white, soft, aromatic pulp. **2.** The fruit of this tree. [American Spanish *chirimoya,* from Quechua *chirimuya.*]

cher·ish (chĕr′ĭsh) *tr.v.* **-ished, -ishing, -ishes. 1.** To hold dear; treat with affection and tenderness. **2.** To keep fondly in mind; cling to: *We cherished the memory of our trip.* —See Synonyms at **appreciate.** [Middle English *cherissen, cherishen,* from Old French *cherir* (present stem *cheriss-*), from *cher,* dear, from Latin *cārus.*] **—cher·ish·er** *n.* **—cher·ish·ing·ly** *adv.*

cherished number plate *n. Chiefly British.* A **vanity plate** *(see).*

Cher·nen·ko (chûr-nyĕng′kō), **Konstantin Ustinovich** (1911–85). Soviet politician, president of the U.S.S.R. (1984–85).

cher·no·zem (chĕr′nə-zĕm′, -zhôm′) *n.* A black soil, rich in humus, ypical of cool to temperate semiarid regions, such as the grasslands of European Russia. Also called "black earth." [Russian, contraction of *chërnaya zemlya,* "black earth" : *chërnyĭ,* black + *zemlya,* earth.]

Cher·o·kee (chĕr′ə-kē′, chĕr′ə-kē′) *n., pl.* **-kees** or collectively **Cherokee. 1. a.** A tribe of North American Indians that formerly inhabited North Carolina and northern Georgia and are now settled in Oklahoma. **b.** A member of this tribe. **2.** The Iroquoian language of the Cherokee. **—Cher·o·kee** *adj.*

Cherokee rose *n.* A climbing rose, *Rosa laevigata,* of Chinese origin, having large, white, fragrant flowers.

che·root (shə-rōōt′, chə-) *n.* A cigar with square-cut ends. [Tamil *curuṭṭu, śurruṭṭu,* from *śuruḷ,* a curl.]

cher·ry (chĕr′ē) *n., pl.* **-ries. 1. a.** Any of several trees of the genus *Prunus,* having small, fleshy, globe-shaped or heart-shaped fruit with a small, hard stone; especially, *P. avium,* the common wild cherry, and *P. cerasus,* the sour cherry. **b.** The fruit or wood of any of these trees. **2.** A moderate or strong red to purplish red.
~*adj.* **1.** Of the color cherry: *She bought a cherry dress.* **2.** Made from the wood of a cherry tree: *a cherry highboy.* [Middle English *chery,* from Old Northern French *cherise,* variant of Old French *cerise,* from Vulgar Latin *ceresia* (unattested), from Latin *cerasus,* cherry tree, from Greek *kerasos*†.]

cherry Prunus "Kanzan," *an ornamental Japanese cherry tree, which is widely grown for its spectacular spring blossoms. The fruit on ornamental cherries are insignificant.*

cherry brandy *n.* A liqueur made from brandy and crushed cherry stones.

cherry laurel *n.* An evergreen European shrub, *Prunus laurocerasus,* having white flowers and blackish fruits.

cherry picker *n.* Any of various large, usually mobile cranes having a long, maneuverable obliquely vertical boom often supporting a work platform.

cherry pie *n. Chiefly British.* A widely cultivated garden heliotrope, *Heliotropium peruvianum.*

cherry plum *n.* A tree, the **myrobalan** *(see).*

cherry tomato *n.* A variety of the common tomato, *Lycospermum esculentum cerasiforme,* having small red or yellow fruit.

chert (chûrt) *n.* Any of various microscopically crystalline mineral varieties of silica, usually occurring in bands or layers of modules in sedimentary rocks. [17th century : origin obscure.]

cher·ub (chĕr′əb) *n., pl.* **-ubim** (-ə-bĭm′, -yə-bĭm′) for senses 1, 2) or **-ubs** (for senses 3, 4). **1.** A winged celestial being. Genesis 3:24. **2.** In medieval angelology, any of the second order of angels. See **angel. 3.** A representation of an angelic cherub, portrayed as a winged child with a chubby, rosy face. **4.** A delightful or innocent-looking child. [Hebrew *kərūbh.*] **—che·ru·bic** (chə-rōō′bĭk) *adj.* **—che·ru·bi·cal·ly** *adv.*

Che·ru·bi·ni (kĕr′ə-bē′nē, kā′rōō-), **(Maria) Luigi Carlo Zenobio Salvatore** (1760–1842). Italian composer. His 29 operas helped form the transition between classicism and romanticism. He did most of his composing in France, where he was appointed director of the Paris Conservatoire in 1822.

cher·vil (chûr′vəl) *n.* **1.** An aromatic plant, *Anthriscus cerefolium,* native to Eurasia, having leaves used in soups and salads. **2.** Any of several related plants, especially *Chaerophyllum bulbosum,* having an edible root. [Middle English *cherville,* Old English *cerfille,* from West Germanic *kervila* (unattested), from Latin *chaerephylla,* from Greek *khairephullon* : *khairein,* to delight in + *phullon,* leaf.]

Ches. Cheshire.

Ches·a·peake Bay (chĕs′ə-pēk′). An inlet 320 kilometers (200 miles) long on the eastern seaboard of Virginia and Maryland. Baltimore is its main port.

Cheshire cat *A colored version of Tenniel's drawing that appeared in Lewis Carroll's* Alice's Adventures in Wonderland.

Chesapeake Bay retriever *n.* A hunting dog of a breed developed in the United States, having a thick, short, brownish coat.

Chesh·ire (chĕs′ər, -îr). *Abbr.* **Ches.** County in western England, bounded by the Welsh border to the west and Merseyside to the north. It is noted for dairy produce, including Cheshire cheese. Extensive salt beds supply an important chemical industry. Chester is the administrative center.

Cheshire cat *n.* In *Alice's Adventures in Wonderland,* by Lewis Carroll, a cat that faded until only its grin remained visible.

Chesh·ire cheese (chĕsh′ər) *n.* A fairly hard, crumbly English cheese made from cow's milk. [From CHESHIRE.]

chess¹ (chĕs) *n.* A board game for two players, each possessing an initial force of a king, a queen, two bishops, two knights, two rooks, and eight pawns, all maneuvered following individual rules of movement with the objective of checkmating the opposing king. [Middle English *ches,* short for Old French *esches,* plural of *eschec,* CHECK (at chess).]

chess² *n.* One of the floorboards of a pontoon bridge. [Middle English *ches,* tier, from Old French *chasse,* frame, from Latin *capsa,* box.]

chess·board (chĕs'bôrd', -bōrd') *n.* A board used in playing chess, marked with 64 squares.

ches·sel (chĕs'əl) *n.* A mold used in the manufacture of cheese. [Probably CHEESE + WELL.]

chess·man (chĕs'măn', -mən) *n., pl.* **-men** (-mĕn', -mĭn). Any of the pieces used in playing the game of chess. Also called "chess piece."

chest (chĕst) *n.* **1.** The part of the body between the neck and the abdomen, enclosed by the ribs and the breastbone. **2. a.** A sturdy box with a lid and often a lock, used for storage and protection of articles. **b.** A chest of drawers; dresser. **c.** A small closet or cabinet with shelves. **3. a.** The treasury of a public institution. **b.** The funds kept there. **4. a.** A box for the shipping of certain goods, such as tea. **b.** The quantity packed in such a box. [Middle English *chest,* Old English *cest, cist,* box, from West Germanic *kistā* (unattested), from Latin *cista,* from Greek *kistē.*] **—chest·ed** *adj.*

Ches·ter (chĕs'tər). City and administrative center of Cheshire, on the Dee River. The Romans, who built a fort here to command the river crossing into Wales, called it Deva. It has an 11th-century cathedral.

ches·ter·field (chĕs'tər-fēld') *n.* **1.** A single-breasted or double-breasted overcoat, usually with concealed buttons and a velvet collar. **2.** A large, overstuffed sofa with straight armrests of the same height as the back. [After an Earl of *Chesterfield* of the 19th century.]

Ches·ter·ton (chĕs'tər-tən), **Gilbert Keith** (1874–1936). British author, poet, and literary critic. His works include studies of *Robert Browning* (1903) and *Charles Dickens* (1906). His skills as a writer of mystery and fantasy were shown in *The Napoleon of Notting Hill Gate* (1904) and *The Man Who Was Thursday* (1908). In 1911 he published the first of his popular Father Brown stories, featuring a Roman Catholic priest as a detective.

Chester White *n.* A white hog of a breed that originated in Chester County, Pennsylvania.

chest·nut (chĕs'nŭt', -nət) *n.* **1. a.** Any of several trees of the genus *Castanea,* of the Northern Hemisphere, bearing nuts enclosed in a prickly bur. **b.** The nut of any of these trees, edible when cooked. **c.** The hard wood of these trees, used in furniture and as a building material. **2.** The horse chestnut *(see).* **3.** A grayish brown to rich reddish brown. **4.** A reddish-brown horse. **5.** A small, hard callus on the inner surface of a horse's foreleg. **6.** *Informal.* Anything lacking freshness or originality, as a joke, song, or story. ~*adj.* **1.** Of the color chestnut: *chestnut hair.* **2.** Of or pertaining to chestnut: *chestnut purée.* [Earlier *chesten nut :* Middle English *chesten, chasteine,* chestnut, from Old French *chastaigne,* from Latin *castanea,* from Greek *kastanea†* + NUT.]

chestnut blight *n.* A disease of the native American chestnut tree that is caused by a fungus, *Endothia parasitica,* and that results in cankers on the trunk and branches and eventual death.

chestnut soil *n.* A dark brown, friable type of chernozem found in arid areas of steppe that have little grass.

chest of drawers *n.* A piece of furniture consisting of a set of drawers that fit in a frame.

chest register *n.* The lowest register of the human voice. Also called "chest voice."

chest·y (chĕs'tē) *adj.* **-ier, -iest.** *Informal.* **1.** Having a large or well-developed chest. **2.** Arrogant; proud; conceited. **—chest·i·ness** *n.*

Chet·nik (chĕt'nĭk) *n., pl.* **-niks** or **Chetnici** (chĕt-nēt'sē). A Serbian guerrilla fighter, especially in World War II. [Serbian *četnik,* from *četa†,* troop.]

chet·rum (chĕ'trəm, chĕt'rəm) *n.* A monetary unit of Bhutan equal to ¹/₁₀₀ of a ngultrum. See feature at **currency.** [Native word in Bhutan.]

che·val-de-frise (shə-văl'də-frēz') *n., pl.* **che·vaux-de-frise** (shə-vō'-). **1.** A defensive obstacle composed of barbed wire or spikes attached to a wooden frame. **2.** An obstacle in the form of jagged glass or spikes set in the masonry on the top of a wall. [French, "Frisian horse." It was first used in Friesland to compensate for a lack of cavalry.]

che·val glass (shə-văl') *n.* A long mirror mounted on swivels in a frame. [French *cheval,* support, "horse."]

chev·a·lier (shĕv'ə-lîr') *n.* **1.** A member of certain orders of knighthood or merit, such as the Legion of Honor in France. **2.** A knight. **3.** A chivalrous, gallant man. [Middle English *chevaler,* from Old French *chevalier,* from Late Latin *caballārius,* horseman, CAVALIER.]

Che·va·lier (shə-văl'yə), **Maurice** (1888–1972). French singer and film actor. His career began in cabaret, but he moved to Hollywood to take part in screen musicals in the 1930's. *Gigi* (1958) is his best-known film.

che·ve·lure (shəv-lür') *n.* A head of hair. [Old French, from Latin *capillātūra,* the hair, from *capillus,* hair.]

che·vet (shə-vā') *n.* The rounded east end of a church, usually with apses. [French, "pillow," from Latin *capitium,* from *caput,* head.]

Chev·i·ot (shĕv'ē-ət, chĕv'-) *n.* **1.** A sheep of a breed with short, thick wool, originally bred in the Cheviot Hills. **2. cheviot.** A woolen fabric with a coarse twill weave, used chiefly for suits and overcoats and originally made from the wool of the Cheviot sheep.

Cheviot Hills. Range of hills bordering England and Scotland. The

Cheviot *The fleece of this sheep, which was first bred in the Cheviot hills of northern England, is used for carpets, tweeds, and flannel. Both crossbred and purebred flocks are also reared for meat.*

Cheviot (816 meters; 2,677 feet) is the highest peak.

chev·ron (shĕv'rən) *n.* **1.** A badge or insignia consisting of parallel stripes meeting at an angle, worn on the sleeve of a policeman or a noncommissioned officer in the armed forces and indicating rank, merit, or length of service. **2.** *Heraldry.* A device shaped like an inverted V. **3.** A V-shaped pattern, especially a kind of architectural molding. [Middle English, from Old French, beam, rafter, from Vulgar Latin *capriō* (unattested), from Latin *capra,* feminine of *caper,* goat.]

chev·ro·tain (shĕv'rə-tān') *n.* Any of several small, hornless ruminants of the genera *Hyemoschus* and *Tragulus* of central Africa and southeastern Asia. The males have tusklike upper canine teeth. Also called "mouse deer." [French *chevrotin,* from Old French, diminutive of *chevrot,* kid, diminutive of *chevre,* goat, from Latin *capra.* See **chevron.**]

chevy. Variant of **chivvy.**

chew (chōō) *v.* **chewed, chewing, chews.** *—tr.* To bite and grind with the teeth; masticate. *—intr.* To make a crushing and grinding motion with the teeth. **—chew out.** *Slang.* To scold or reprimand. **—chew over.** To meditate upon; ponder. **—chew the fat** (or **rag**). To talk casually or idly; chat. **—chew up.** To grind, crush, or damage with or as if with the teeth: *heavy trucks that chew up the road.* ~*n.* **1.** The act of chewing. **2.** Something held in the mouth and chewed: *a chew of tobacco.* [Middle English *chewen,* Old English *cēowan.*] **—chew·er** *n.*

chewing gum *n.* A sweetened, flavored preparation with a rubbery texture for chewing, usually made of chicle.

chew·y (chōō'ē) *adj.* **-ier, -est.** Of a texture that requires chewing: *a chewy caramel.*

Chey·enne¹ (shī-ăn', -ĕn'). Capital of Wyoming, in the southeast part of the state. It was founded (1867) as a station of the Union Pacific Railway and became a cattle center.

Cheyenne² *n., pl.* **-ennes** or collectively **Cheyenne. 1. a.** A tribe of North American Indians that formerly inhabited central Minnesota and North and South Dakota and are now settled in Montana and Oklahoma. **b.** A member of this tribe. **2.** The Algonquian language of the Cheyenne. [Canadian French, from Dakota *šahíyena.*] **—Chey·enne** *adj.*

Cheyne-Stokes respiration (chān'stōks') *n.* An abnormal type of respiration, seen particularly in comatose patients, characterized by alternating shallow and deep breathing. [After John *Cheyne* (1777–1836), Scottish physician, and William *Stokes* (1804–78), Irish physician.]

chez (shā) *prep.* *French.* At the home or place of business of.

chg. charge.

chi, khi ((kī)) *n.* The 22nd letter in the Greek alphabet, written X, χ. Transliterated in English as *ch* or *kh,* and sometimes as *h,* especially for Modern Greek words. See feature at **alphabet.** [Greek *khi.*]

Chiang Ch'ing. See **Jiang Qing.**

Chiang-hsi. See **Jiangxi.**

Chiang Kai-shek. Jiang Jieshi.

Chiang-su. See **Jiangsu.**

Chi·an·ti (kē-än'tē, -än'tē) *n.* **1.** A fruity dry red wine produced in the Monte Chianti region of Tuscany in Italy. **2.** A wine similar to Chianti.

chiao (tyou) *n., pl.* **chiao.** A monetary unit equal to ¹/₁₀ of the yuan of the People's Republic of China. See feature at **currency.** [Chinese (Mandarin) *jiao³.*]

chi·a·ro·scu·ro (kē-är'ə-skŏŏr'ō, -skyŏŏr'ō) *n., pl.* **-ros. 1.** The technique of using light and shade in pictorial representation. **2.** The arrangement of light and dark elements in a pictorial work of art. **3.** The use of contrast in literary works. [Italian : *chiaro,* light, clear, from Latin *clārus,* clear + *oscuro,* dark, from Latin *obscūrus.*] **—chi·a·ro·scu·rist** *n.*

chi·as·ma ((kī-ăz'mə) *n., pl.* **-mata** (-mə-tə) or **-mas.** Also **chi·asm** (kī'ăz'əm). **1.** *Anatomy.* A crossing or intersection of two tracts, such as that of the two optic nerves in the brain. **2.** *Genetics.* A point of contact between homologous chromosomes, considered the cytological manifestation of crossing over. [New Latin, from Greek *khiasma,* cross, from *khiazein,* to mark with the letter CHI.] **—chi·as·mal, chi·as·mic, chi·as·mat·ic** (kī'ăz-măt'ĭk) *adj.*

chi·as·mus (kī-ăz'məs) *n., pl.* **-mi** (-mī'). A rhetorical inversion of the second of two parallel structures, as *He went onward, but home went she.* [New Latin, from Greek *khiasmos,* from *khiazein,* to mark with the letter CHI.]

chi·as·to·lite (kī-ăs'tə-līt') *n.* A mineral variety of andalusite with carbonaceous impurities symmetrically arranged along the longer axis of the crystal. In cross-section the crystals show a black cross, hence the name. Also called "macle." [German *Chiastolith :* Greek *khiastos,* crossed, past participle of *khiazein,* to mark with the letter CHI + -LITE.]

Chib·cha (chĭb'chə) *n., pl.* **-chas** or collectively **Chibcha. 1.** A member of an extinct Indian people once inhabiting Colombia. **2.** The extinct language of this people.

Chib·chan (chĭb'chən) *n.* **1.** A South American or Central American Indian ethnic stock including the Chibcha. **2.** The language spoken by these people. ~*adj.* Of or pertaining to this ethnic stock or language.

chi·bouk, chi·bouque (chĭ-bŏŏk', shĭ-) *n.* A Turkish tobacco pipe with a long stem and a red clay bowl. [French *chibouque,* from Turkish *çubuk, çibuk,* tube.]

chic (shēk) *adj.* **1.** Sophisticated; stylish. **2.** Dressed smartly and fashionably; elegant.

~n. 1. Sophistication in dress and manner; elegance. 2. The quality of being fashionable; stylishness. [French, perhaps from German *Schick,* skill, Middle High German *schicken†,* to arrange, prepare.] —**chic·ly** *adv.*

Chi·ca·go (shə-kä′gō, -kô′-). Second-largest city in the United States and a major port on the Illinois shore of Lake Michigan. During the Prohibition years (1919-33), it became a notorious center of gangsterism and corruption. Chicago is a vital focus of industry, trade, finance, and communications.

chi·cane (shĭ-kān′, chĭ-) *v.* **-caned** *or* **-caning, -canes.** —*tr.* **1.** To trick; deceive. **2.** To quibble over; cavil. —*intr.* To use tricks or chicanery. ~*n.* **1.** Chicanery. **2.** In bridge or whist, a hand without trumps. **3.** In automobile racing, an obstacle on the track intended to slow the cars down. [French *chicaner,* from Old French *chicaner†,* to quibble.] —**chi·can·er** *n.*

chi·can·er·y (shĭ-kā′nə-rē, chĭ-) *n., pl.* **-ies. 1.** Deception by trickery or sophistry. **2.** A trick; a subterfuge.

Chi·ca·no (chĭ-kä′nō, shĭ-) *n., pl.* **-nos.** A Mexican-American. [American Spanish *Chicano,* variant of *Mejicano,* a Mexican, from *Méjico,* MEXICO.] —**Chi·ca·no** *adj.*

Chich·es·ter (chĭch′ĭ-stər). City in southern England, the administrative center of West Sussex. Laid out by the Romans, it prospered in the medieval wool trade. Parts of its ancient walls and gates survive.

Chichester, Sir Francis Charles (1901-77). British pilot and yachtsman. He made the first long-distance seaplane flight (1931) and won the first solo transatlantic yacht race (1960). He was the first person to sail round the world alone (1966-67).

chi-chi (shē′shē) *adj.* **1.** Elaborate; fussy; frilly. **2.** Pretentiously fashionable; precious. [French.]

chick (chĭk) *n.* **1. a.** A young chicken. **b.** The young of any bird. **2.** A child. **3.** *Slang.* A girl or young woman. [Middle English *chike,* short for CHICKEN.]

chick·a·dee (chĭk′ə-dē′) *n.* Any of several small, plump North American birds of the genus *Parus,* having predominantly gray plumage and a dark-crowned head. [Imitative of its cry.]

Chick·a·saw (chĭk′ə-sô′) *n., pl.* **-saws** *or collectively* **Chickasaw. 1.** A member of a North American Indian people, originally of Mississippi, later removed to Oklahoma. **2.** The Muskhogean language of this tribe. —**Chick·a·saw** *adj.*

chick·en (chĭk′ən) *n.* **1.** A young bird, especially of the common domestic fowl. **2.** The flesh of the common domestic fowl. **3.** Any of various birds similar or related to the common domestic fowl, such as the **prairie chicken** *(see).* —**count one's chickens before they are hatched.** To rely on an outcome that is still uncertain. ~*adj. Slang.* Cowardly; timid. ~*intr.v.* **chickened, -ening, -ens.** *Slang.* To act in a cowardly manner; lose one's nerve. Usually used with *out.* [Middle English *chiken,* Old English *cīcen,* from Germanic.]

chicken feed *n. Slang.* A trifling amount of money.

chicken hawk *n.* Any of various hawks that prey on or have the reputation of preying on chickens.

chick·en-heart·ed (chĭk′ən-här′tĭd) *adj.* Cowardly; timid.

chick·en-liv·ered (chĭk′ən-lĭv′ərd) *adj.* Cowardly; timid.

chicken louse *n.* A louse, *Menopon pallidum* (or *gallinae*), parasitic on domestic fowl.

chicken pox *n.* An acute contagious viral disease, usually of children, characterized by skin eruption, slight fever, and mild constitutional symptoms. Also called "varicella." [Perhaps alluding to the mildness of the disease.]

chicken wire *n.* A light-gauge galvanized wire fencing, usually made with hexagonal mesh.

chick·pea (chĭk′pē′) *n.* **1.** A bushy plant, *Cicer arietinum,* grown in the Mediterranean region and central Asia and bearing edible seeds. **2.** Any of the pealike seeds of this plant, widely used as food. Also called "garbanzo." [Earlier *chich-pease* : Middle English *chiche,* chickpea, from Old French, from Latin *cicer†* + *pease,* PEA.]

chick·weed (chĭk′wēd′) *n.* Any of various plants of the genera *Cerastium* and *Stellaria;* especially, *S. media,* a weedy plant with white flowers. [So called because it is eaten by chickens.]

chic·le (chĭk′əl) *n.* The coagulated juice of the sapodilla, used as the main ingredient of chewing gum. [Spanish, from Nahuatl *chictli.*]

chic·o·ry (chĭk′ə-rē) *n., pl.* **-ries. 1.** A widely cultivated plant, *Cichorium intybus,* having usually blue flowers, and leaves used in salads. **2.** The root of this plant, dried, roasted, and ground for mixing with coffee or as a coffee substitute. See **endive.** [Middle English *cicoree,* from Old French, from Latin *cichorium,* from Greek *kikhora†.*]

chide (chīd) *v.* **chided** *or* **chid** (chĭd), **chided** *or* **chid** *or* **chidden** (chĭd′n), **chiding, chides.** —*intr.* To scold; rebuke. —*tr.* To state one's disapproval to so as to correct or improve; scold: *chided the child for being sloppy.* [Middle English *chiden,* Old English *cīdan,* from *cīd†,* strife.] —**chid·er** *n.* —**chid·ing·ly** *adv.*

chief (chēf) *n. Abbr.* **C., ch., Ch. 1.** One who is highest in rank or authority; a leader: *a meeting of party chiefs.* **2.** The head man of a tribe or clan. **3.** *Slang.* A boss. **4.** *Heraldry.* The upper section of a shield. —**in chief. 1.** Having the highest or most important position: *the commander in chief.* **2.** Chiefly. ~*adj.* **1.** Highest in rank, authority, or office. **2.** Principal; most important. ~*adv. Archaic.* Chiefly. [Middle English *chief, chef,* from Old

French, from Vulgar Latin *capum* (unattested), from Latin *caput,* head.]

Synonyms: *foremost, leading, main, primary, principal.*

chief constable *n.* In Britain, a high-ranking police officer in command of a regional police force.

chief·dom (chēf′dəm) *n.* The office or domain of a chief, especially of a tribal leader.

Chief Justice *n. Abbr.* **C.J.** The presiding judge of a court of several judges, especially the Supreme Court of the United States.

chief·ly (chēf′lē) *adv.* **1.** Above all; especially. **2.** Mostly; mainly. ~*adj.* Of, befitting, or similar to a chief.

chief of staff *n. Abbr.* **C.S. 1.** The senior staff officer of a major military formation. **2.** *Often* **Chief of Staff.** The commanding officer of the U.S. Army, Navy, or Air Force.

chief petty officer *n.* The highest rank of noncommissioned officer in the navy or coast guard.

Chief Rabbi *n.* The religious leader of the Jewish community within a country.

chief·tain (chēf′tən) *n.* The leader of a clan or tribe. [Middle English *chieftaine, cheftaine,* from Old French *chevetain,* from Late Latin *capitāneus,* from Latin *caput,* head.]

chiff-chaff (chĭf′chăf′) *n.* A small European warbler, *Phylloscopus collybita,* with brownish-gray plumage. [Imitative of its cry.]

chif·fon (shĭ-fŏn′, shĭf′ŏn′) *n.* **1.** A fabric of sheer silk or rayon. **2.** *Often* **chiffons.** Ribbons, laces, or other ornamental accessories for women's clothing. ~*adj.* **1.** Of or relating to chiffon. **2.** Having a light and fluffy consistency. Said of food. [French, "rag," from *chiffe,* old rag, variant of Old French *chipe,* from Middle English *chip,* CHIP.]

chif·fo·nier, chif·fon·nier (shĭf′ə-nîr′) *n.* A narrow, high chest of drawers, often with a mirror attached. [French *chiffonnier,* "bureau for rags," from CHIFFON.]

chig·ger (chĭg′ər) *n.* **1.** Any of various small six-legged larvae of mites of the family Trombidiidae, causing intensely irritating itching when lodged on the skin. Also called "chigoe," "jigger," "harvest bug," "harvest mite." **2.** A flea, the **chigoe** *(see).* [Variant of CHIGOE.]

chi·gnon (shēn-yŏn′, shēn′yŏn′) *n.* A roll or knot of hair worn at the back of the head or nape of the neck by women. [French, variant of Old French *chaignon,* chain, from Vulgar Latin *catēniō* (unattested), from Latin *catēna,* CATENA.]

chig·oe (chĭg′ō, chē′gō) *n.* **1.** A small tropical flea, *Tunga penetrans,* of which the fertile female burrows under the skin, causing intense irritation and sores that may become severely infected. Also called "chigger," "jigger," "sand flea." **2.** A flea, the **chigger** *(see).* [Cariban *chigo.*]

Chihli, Gulf of. See **Bo Hai.**

Chi·hua·hua¹ (chĭ-wä′wä, -wə). Capital of Chihuahua state in northern Mexico. It is situated in a valley of the Sierra Madre.

Chihuahua² *n.* A very small dog of a breed originating in Mexico, having pointed ears and a smooth coat. [After CHIHUAHUA, Mexico.]

chil·blain (chĭl′blān′) *n.* An inflammation followed by itchy irritation on the hands, feet, or ears, resulting from exposure to moist cold. [CHIL(L) + BLAIN.] —**chil·blained** *adj.*

child (chīld) *n., pl.* **children** (chĭl′drən). **1.** Any person between birth and puberty. **2. a.** An unborn infant; a fetus. **b.** An infant; a baby. **3.** One who is childish or immature. **4.** A son or daughter. **5. children.** In Biblical usage, members of a tribe; descendants. **6.** A person or thing considered as the product of a specified influence or phenomenon: *a child of nature.* —**with child.** Pregnant. [Child, children; Middle English *child(e), childre(ns),* Old English *cild, cildra,* from Common Germanic *kiltham* (unattested).] —**child·less** *adj.* —**child·less·ness** *n.*

child·bear·ing (chīld′bâr′ĭng) *n.* The process of pregnancy and childbirth. Also used adjectively: *of childbearing age.*

child·bed (chīld′bĕd) *n.* The state of a woman in childbirth.

childbed fever *n.* **Puerperal fever** *(see).*

child·birth (chīld′bûrth′) *n.* The process of giving birth to a child; parturition.

child care *n.* Professional supervision, as by a local authority, of the welfare of children, especially in the absence or failure of parental supervision.

childe (chīld) *n. Archaic.* A young man of noble birth. [Middle English *child(e),* CHILD.]

Chil·ders (chĭl′dərz), **Robert Erskine** (1870-1922). Irish nationalist. He was active in the cause of Irish Home Rule and became a Sinn Fein deputy in the Irish Assembly (1921). He acted as publicity director for the I.R.A. during the Irish civil war. Arrested in 1922 for carrying arms, he was tried and shot. His son, **Erskine Hamilton Childers** (1905-74), became Irish president (1973-74).

child·hood (chīld′hood′) *n.* The time or state of being a child.

child·ish (chīl′dĭsh) *adj.* **1.** Of, similar to, or suitable for a child. **2.** Foolishly immature. —**child·ish·ly** *adv.* —**child·ish·ness** *n.*

Usage: *Childish* applied to adults is almost invariably a term of reproach but lacks such connotation when applied to children. *Childlike* is generally favorable on all age levels, suggesting endearing traits characteristic of children.

child·like (chīld′līk′) *adj. Also rare* **child·ly** (-lē). Like or befitting a child, as in innocence or guilelessness. —See Usage note at **childish.**

child·mind·er (chīld′mīn′dər) *n. Chiefly British.* A **baby sitter** *(see).*

child·proof (chīld′proof′) *adj.* Safe against tampering by children.

chil·dren. Plural of **child.**

chicory *This native of Europe is now grown worldwide. Its roots are dried, roasted, and ground, then added to coffee to strengthen its flavor.*

Children of Israel *pl.n.* The Jews.

child's play *n. Informal.* **1.** Anything that is very easy to do. **2.** A trivial matter.

Chil·e (chĭl′ē). A long, narrow country on the western seaboard of South America. The Spaniards colonized it from 1541, and the country declared its independence in 1818. After World War I cut off its markets and sources of manufactured goods, economic chaos ensued, and the military intervened in the government several times. Salvador Allende's Marxist coalition was elected (1970) and instituted sweeping reforms and nationalization, but inefficiency and costly welfare schemes brought economic collapse and street violence. The armed forces staged a bloody coup in 1973, and under the harshly repressive regime of President Augusto Pinochet Ugarte, the economy revived. A referendum in 1980 confirmed Pinochet in office until 1989, but too rapid economic growth brought more instability. Chile has large energy resources: oil and gas in Patagonia, hydroelectric power in the Andes, and coal. The fertile central valley is its economic heartland, with industries concentrated around Concepción and Santiago. Exports include copper, iron ore, and nitrates, wood products, and fruit and wine. Area, 756,945 square kilometers (292,181 square miles). Population, 11,200,000. Capital, Santiago. —**Chil·e·an** *adj. & n.*

chil·e con car·ne, chil·i con car·ne (chĭl′ē kŏn kär′nē) *n.* A highly spiced dish made of red peppers, meat, and usually beans. Also called "chili." [Spanish, "chili with meat."]

Chile saltpeter *n. Chemistry.* **Sodium nitrate** (see).

chil·i, chil·e, chil·li (chĭl′ē) *n., pl.* **-ies, -es, -lies. 1. a.** The very pungent red fruit of several varieties of a woody plant, *Capsicum frutescens.* **b.** A condiment made from the dried fruits of this plant. In both senses, also called "chili pepper." **2.** Chile con carne (see). [Spanish *chile, chilli,* from Nahuatl *chilli.*]

chil·i·ad (kĭl′ē-ăd′, -əd) *n.* **1.** A group containing 1,000 elements. **2.** One thousand years. [Late Latin *chīliās* (stem *chīliad-*), from Greek *khilias,* thousand, from *khilioi,* thousand.]

chil·i·asm (kĭl′ē-ăz′əm) *n.* **Millenarianism** (see). [New Latin *chiliasmus,* from Greek *khiliasmos,* from *khilias,* CHILIAD.] —**chil·i·ast** (kĭl′ē-ăst′) *n.* —**chil·i·as·tic** (kĭl′ē-ăs′tĭk) *adj.*

chili sauce *n.* A spiced sauce made with chilies and tomatoes.

chill (chĭl) *n.* **1.** A moderate but penetrating coldness. **2. a.** A sensation of coldness, marked by shivering. **b.** An illness characterized by this: *catch a chill.* **3.** A checking or dampening of enthusiasm, spirit, or joy. **4.** A sudden numbing fear or dread.
~*adj.* **1.** Chilly. **2.** Depressing; discouraging.
~*v.* **chilled, chilling, chills.** —*tr.* **1.** To affect with cold. **2.** To discourage; dispirit. **3.** To cool, as in a refrigerator: *Serve the wine chilled.* **4.** *Metallurgy.* To harden (a metallic surface) by rapid cooling. —*intr.* **1.** To be seized with cold. **2.** To become cold: *jelly that chills quickly.* **3.** *Metallurgy.* To become hard by rapid cooling. [Middle English *chile, chele,* frost, Old English *c(i)ele.*] —**chill·ing·ly** *adv.* —**chill·ness** *n.*

chill·er (chĭl′ər) *n.* One that chills or frightens; a thriller.

Chil·lon (shĭ-lŏn′, shĭl′ən). Castle in Switzerland, at the east end of Lake Geneva, near Montreux. Byron's poem *The Prisoner of Chillon* (1816) describes the fate of François de Bonnivard (1496–1570), a Genevan patriot imprisoned here (1530–36).

chill·y (chĭl′ē) *adj.* **-ier, -iest. 1.** Cool or cold enough to cause shivering. **2.** Seized with cold; shivering. **3.** Distant and cool; unfriendly. —**chill·i·ly** *adv.* —**chill·i·ness** *n.*

chi·lo·pod (kī′lə-pŏd′) *n.* Any of various arthropods of the class Chilopoda, which includes the centipedes. [New Latin *Chilopoda,* "foot jaws" (the foremost pair of legs are jawlike appendages) : Greek *kheilos,* lip + -POD.]

Chil·tern Hills (chĭl′tərn). Also **Chil·terns** (-tərnz). Range of chalk hills in south-central England, running northeast from the Thames at the Goring Gap to the Bedfordshire-Hertfordshire border.

Chiltern Hundreds *pl.n. British.* A now merely formal office applied for by Members of Parliament when they wish to resign from the House of Commons. [After a Crown manor in the CHILTERN HILLS (the administration of which would require resignation from the House of Commons).]

chi·mae·ra (kĭ-mîr′ə, kī-) *n.* **1.** Any deep-sea cartilaginous fish of the order *Chimaeriformes* having a smooth-skinned tapering body and a whiplike tail. See **rabbitfish. 2.** Variant of **chimera.**

chime (chīm) *n.* **1.** An apparatus for striking a bell or bells to produce a musical sound. **2.** *Often* **chimes.** A set of bells tuned to a scale and used as an orchestral instrument or in a clock. **3.** A single bell. **4.** The musical sound produced by a bell or bells. **5.** Agreement; accord.
~*v.* **chimed, chiming, chimes.** —*intr.* **1.** To sound with a harmonious ring when struck. **2.** To make a musical sound by striking a chime. **3.** To agree; harmonize. Usually used with *with.* —*tr.* **1.** To produce (music) by striking bells. **2.** To strike (a bell) to produce music. **3.** To make known (the hour) by chiming. —**chime in. 1.** To break into a conversation, especially to express agreement. **2.** To accord harmoniously. [Middle English *chime, chimbe,* cymbal, chime, perhaps from Old French *chimbe,* from Latin *cymbalum,* CYMBAL.] —**chim·er** *n.*

chi·me·ra, chi·mae·ra (kĭ-mîr′ə, kī-) *n.* **1. Chimera.** *Greek Mythology.* A fire-breathing she-monster usually represented as a composite of a lion, a goat, and a serpent. **2.** A creation of the imagination; an impossible and foolish fancy. **3.** *Biology.* **a.** An organism, especially a cultivated plant, containing tissues from at least two distinct genetic types, often because of grafting. **b.** An animal or plant pro-

chili *Mature chilies on display in an African market. Fresh or dried, they are used in cooking.*

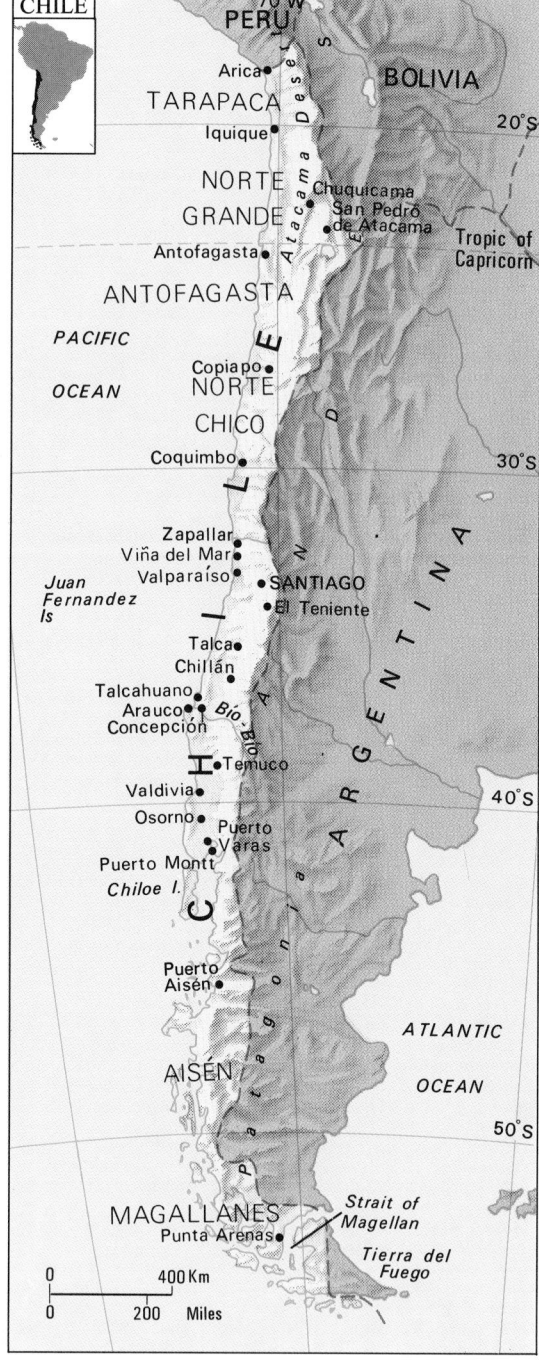

CHILE

duced by genetic engineering, in which DNA from two distinct parent species is artificially combined to produce an individual with a double chromosome complement. [Latin *Chimaera,* from Greek *khimaira,* chimera, "she-goat."]

chi·mere (shə-mîr′, chə-) *n.* A long black or scarlet robe, often with lawn sleeves, worn over a rochet by Anglican bishops. [Middle English, perhaps from Medieval Latin *chimēra,* "sheepskin" (see **chimera**); akin to Spanish *zamarra,* sheepskin cloak.]

chi·mer·i·cal (kī-měr′ĭ-kəl, -mîr′ĭ-kəl, kĭ-) *adj.* Also **chi·mer·ic** (-měr′ĭk, -mîr′ĭk). **1.** Like a chimera; imaginary; unreal. **2.** Given to unrealistic fantasies. —**chi·mer·i·cal·ly** *adv.*

chim·ney (chĭm′nē) *n., pl.* **-neys. 1.** A passage through which smoke and gases escape from a fire or furnace; a flue. **2. a.** The usually vertical structure containing a flue. **b.** The part of such a structure that rises above a roof. **3.** A glass tube for enclosing the flame of a lamp. **4.** Anything resembling a chimney, such as a narrow cleft in a mountain by which a climber may ascend. **5.** The vent of a volcano. [Middle English *chimenee,* from Old French *cheminee,* from Late Latin *caminata,* from Latin *camīnus,* furnace, from Greek *kaminos†.*]

chimney breast *n.* The projection of a chimney from the walls surrounding it.

chimney corner *n.* A recessed seat inside or next to a large, old-fashioned fireplace.

chim·ney·piece (chĭm'nē-pēs') *n.* **1.** The mantel of a fireplace. **2.** A decoration over a fireplace.

chimney pot *n.* A pipe placed on the top of a chimney to improve the draft.

chimney stack *n.* **1.** The part of a chimney rising above the roof of a building; stack. **2.** The masonry enclosing a number of flues.

chimney sweep *n.* Also **chimney sweeper.** A worker employed to clean soot from chimneys. Also called "sweep."

chimney swift *n.* A small, dark, swallowlike North American bird, *Chaetura pelagica,* that frequently nests in chimneys.

chimp (chĭmp) *n. Informal.* A chimpanzee.

chim·pan·zee (chĭm'păn-zē', chĭm-păn'zē) *n.* An anthropoid ape, *Pan troglodytes,* of tropical Africa, having dark hair, gregarious, somewhat arboreal habits, and a high degree of intelligence. [French *chimpanzé,* from Kongo.]

chin (chĭn) *n.* The central forward portion of the lower jaw. **—take it on the chin.** To undergo misfortune or defeat.
~*v.* **chinned, chinning, chins.** **—***tr.* **1.** To pull (oneself) up with the arms while grasping an overhead horizontal bar until the chin is level with the bar. **2.** To place (a violin) under the chin. **—***intr.* **1.** *Informal.* To chatter. **2.** To chin oneself. [Middle English *chin,* Old English *cin(n),* from Germanic.]

Chin. China; Chinese.

Ch'in or **Qin** (chĭn). A dynasty that ruled China from 221 to 206 B.C.

chi·na (chī'nə) *n.* **1.** High-quality porcelain or ceramic ware, originally made in China. **2.** Any porcelain ware. **3.** Tableware, as plates and cups, of porcelain or earthenware. **—chi·na** *adj.*

Chi·na (chī'nə). *Abbr.* **Ch., Chin.** Officially, People's Republic of China. The world's most populous and third-largest country, lying in East Asia. Its heartland is formed by three great river systems running west to east: the Huang He in the north, the Chang Jiang and the Xi Jiang in the south. The country also includes the barren plateau of Tibet and deserts in the north and west. China is the home of the oldest surviving civilization, traditionally dated from the first emperor (c. 2700 B.C.) on the North China Plain. Bronzework had already evolved and a form of writing was in use. Under the Chou (Zhou) dynasty (c. 1027–221 B.C.), Confucian and Taoist thought spread. The Ch'in (Qin) dynasty (221–206 B.C.) founded the first unified empire and linked up the sections of the Great Wall against nomadic invasion. The Han dynasty (206 B.C.–A.D. 220) made great advances, and frontiers were extended, the "silk road" to Rome was opened up, and Buddhism introduced. The empire fell into decay, but was reunited by the Sui (581). Under the T'ang (618–960) a golden age in the arts and great expansion in trade occurred. The Song (960–1279) were removed by the Mongols, who set up the Yuan dynasty at Beijing (Peking), which Marco Polo visited. During the native Ming dynasty (1368–1644) the first European seafarers reached China. The Manchus, a northern people, set up the (Ch'ing) Qing dynasty (1644–1911), under which the 18th century was a period of relative stability, but in the later Ch'ing (Qing) isolation and stagnation led to backwardness. China was defeated in the Opium War (1839–42), by Japan (1895), was humiliated in the Boxer Rising (1900), and was forced to accept treaty ports for foreign trade. After a popular revolution, Sun Zhong-shan inaugurated a republic (1912), but civil war between the nationalist Guomindang and the Chinese Communist Party broke out. Japanese encroachments from 1931 led to war (1937), and an uneasy alliance against the invader. After World War II a civil war (1946–49) established the People's Republic under chairman Mao Ze-dong, and the nationalists fled to Taiwan. China made great strides in modernization and social and economic development, but Soviet aid ceased (1960) after an ideological break between the two countries, and Mao launched the Cultural Revolution (1966). In 1971 China was admitted to the United Nations, from which Taiwan was expelled. Mao's failing health led to a period of confusion during which the Gang of Four, led by his wife Jiang Qing, made a bid for power. Mao died in 1976, and was succeeded by Hua Guo-feng. Under Hua and Deng Xiao-ping modernization was resumed, and relations with the West and Japan greatly improved. Chinese agriculture, the basis of the economy, is organized on a commune system and is traditionally dependent on rice. Cotton and tea are grown for export. Pigs are widely farmed. Coal, mined in most provinces, is the main mineral product, and China is also a leading producer of oil, natural gas, iron ore, and antimony. Steel, machinery, and fertilizers are the major manufacturing industries, and fishing is important. Some 94 percent of China's vast population is Han Chinese, a Sinitic group of the Mongoloid race. There are over 20 cities with more than a million inhabitants, the largest by far being Shanghai, which is also the main port. Area, 9,596,961 square kilometers (3,704,427 square miles). Population, 1,000,000,000. Capital, Beijing (Peking).

China aster *n.* A plant, *Callistephus chinensis,* native to China, widely cultivated for its variously colored asterlike flowers.

chi·na·ber·ry (chī'nə-bĕr'ē) *n., pl.* **-ries. 1.** A spreading tree, *Melia azedarach,* native to Asia, widely grown for its white or purple flower clusters. Also called "China tree," "azedarach." **2.** A soapberry tree, *Sapindus marginatus* (or *S. saponaria*), of the West Indies, Mexico, and the southwestern United States. **3.** The fruit of either of these trees.

chi·na·graph pencil (chī'nə-grăf') *n.* A type of colored pencil that can write on surfaces such as china or glass.

Chi·na·man (chī'nə-mən) *n., pl.* **-men** (-mĭn). A Chinese man. An offensive term.

Chi-nan. See Jinan.

chimpanzee *Thought to be the primates most closely related to man, chimpanzees are highly intelligent apes found in the forests of West Africa. They are one of the few tool-using animals and will use sticks to dig up ants for food.*

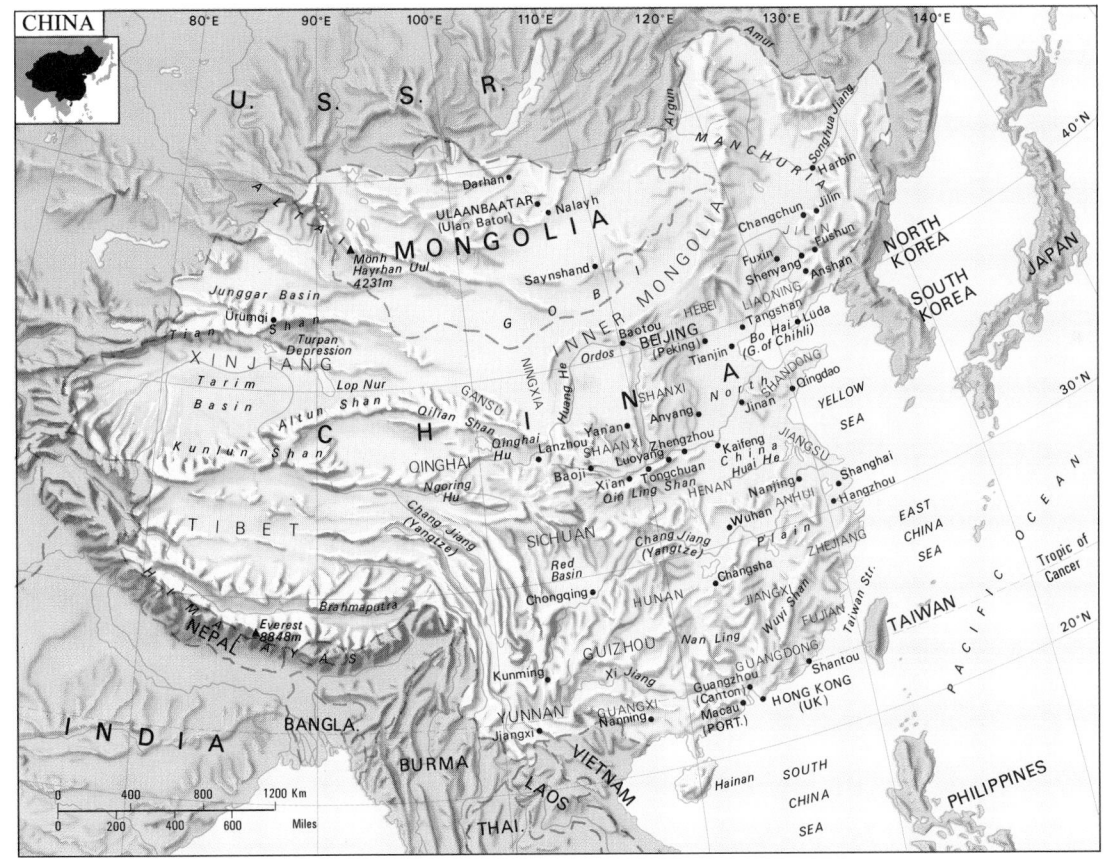

chinchilla *A rodent native to South America, the chinchilla is farmed worldwide for its blue-gray fur.*

chinoiserie *A decorative style, seen here on a 19th-century willow pattern plate. In Britain, the Chinese-derived style had two vogues: after about 1775 it faded away, but it returned with the building of the Brighton Pavilion between 1815 and 1821.*

China rose *n.* **1.** A shrub, *Rosa chinensis,* that has fragrant red or pink flowers and is the original ancestor of many cultivated hybrid roses. **2.** A dwarf, red-flowered rose, *Rosa semperflorens.*

Chi·na·town (chī′nə-toun′) *n.* A district of a city inhabited mainly by Chinese people.

chi·na·ware (chī′nə-wâr′) *n.* Porcelain or similar ware.

chinch (chĭnch) *n. Regional.* A bedbug. [Spanish *chinche,* from Latin *cīmex* (stem *cīmic-*), bug.]

chinch bug *n.* **1.** A small black and white European insect, *Ischnodemus sabuleti,* that is very destructive to grains and grasses. **2.** A similar American insect, *Blissus leucopterus.*

chin·che·rin·chee (chĭn′chə-rĭn-chē′, chĭng′kə-) *n.* A bulbous plant, *Ornithogalum thyrsoides,* of southern Africa, having long clusters or spikes of white or yellow flowers. [Imitative of the squeaky sound made by its stalks.]

chin·chil·la (chĭn-chĭl′ə) *n.* **1. a.** A squirrellike rodent, *Chinchilla laniger,* native to the mountains of South America and widely bred in captivity for its soft pale gray fur. **b.** The fur of this animal. **2.** A thick, twilled cloth of wool and cotton, used for overcoats. **3.** *Often* **Chinchilla. a.** A breed of domesticated rabbit having a thick bluish-gray coat. **b.** A breed of long-haired cat having silvery-white fur. [Spanish, perhaps from Aymara.]

chin-chin (chĭn′chĭn′) *interj. British.* Used as a toast or expression of farewell. [Pidgin English, from Chinese *qǐng qǐng,* "please please."]

Chin·co·teague pony (shĭng′kə-tēg′, chĭng′-) *n.* A type of small, inbred North American horse that runs wild on certain islands off the Virginia coast. [From *Chincoteague* Island, Virginia, where the breed developed.]

chine[1] (chīn) *n.* **1.** The backbone; the spine. **2.** A cut of meat containing part of the backbone. **3.** A ridge or crest. **4.** The line of intersection between the side and bottom of a boat.
~*tr.v.* **chined, chining, chines.** To separate the backbone from the ribs of (a piece of meat). [Middle English *chyne,* from Old French *eschine,* probably from Germanic.]

chine[2] *n. British Regional.* A deep, narrow cleft in a cliff wall. [Old English *cinu,* cleft, chink, from Germanic.]

Chi·nese (chī-nēz′, -nēs′) *adj. Abbr.* **Ch., Chin.** Of or pertaining to China, its culture, people, or languages.
~*n., pl.* **Chinese. 1. a.** A native or inhabitant of China. **b.** A person of Chinese ancestry. **2.** A branch of the Sino-Tibetan language family that consists of the various dialects spoken in China. **3.** Any of the dialects spoken by the Chinese people.
Usage: This is the normal term for someone of Chinese origin, other forms being generally considered derogatory or nonstandard. Many people find *a Chinese* and other singular uses awkward and somewhat formal and prefer an adjectival construction—*a Chinese man came in.*

Chinese anise *n.* A tree, the **star anise** *(see),* or its fruit.

Chinese cabbage *n.* **1.** A Chinese plant, *Brassica pekinensis,* related to the common cabbage, having a cylindrical head of crisp, edible leaves. **2.** A plant similar to Chinese cabbage, **pak choi** *(see).*

Chinese calendar *n.* The lunar calendar of the Chinese people, supposed to have begun in 2397 B.C. Years are reckoned in cycles of 60, each year having a name that is a combination of two characters derived schematically from two series of signs, the celestial and the terrestrial. Months are reckoned also in cycles of 60 that are renewed every 5 years, and each month consists of 28 to 30 days. See feature at **calendar.**

Chinese checkers *n.* A game that is played on a board with a six-pointed star in which marbles or pegs are transferred, via holes or depressions in the board, from one point of the star to the point opposite it.

Chinese Chippendale *n.* Chippendale furniture characterized by certain Oriental influences.

Chinese date *n.* A tree, the **jujube** *(see),* or its fruit.

Chinese evergreen *n.* A plant, *Aglaonema simplex,* of tropical Asia, that has glossy, pointed leaves and is widely grown as a house plant. Also called "Japanese leaf."

Chinese gooseberry *n.* A plant, the **kiwi** *(see),* or its fruit.

Chinese houses *n. Used with a singular or plural verb.* A plant, *Collinsia bicolor,* of California, having showy white or rose-purple flowers.

Chinese lantern *n.* **1.** A decorative, collapsible lantern of thin, brightly colored paper. **2.** One of the papery, inflated seed cases of the **winter cherry** *(see).*

Chinese lantern plant *n.* The **winter cherry** *(see).*

Chinese puzzle *n.* **1.** A very intricate puzzle. **2.** Any very difficult problem.

Chinese red *n.* **Vermilion** *(see).*

Chinese restaurant syndrome *n.* A group of symptoms, including dizziness, facial pressure, sweating, and headache, that may occur after the ingestion of food containing large amounts of monosodium glutamate.

Chinese Revolution *n.* **1.** The revolution of 1911–12 in which the Republic of China was founded. **2.** The revolution culminating in the proclamation of the People's Republic of China (1949).

Chinese sacred lily *n.* A variety of the polyanthus narcissus, *Narcissus tazetta orientalis,* that has fragrant yellow and white flowers and is frequently grown as a house plant.

Chinese Turkestan. See **Xinjiang Uigur Zizhiqu.**

Chinese white *n.* A paint pigment, **zinc oxide** *(see).*

Chinese windlass *n. Machinery.* A **differential windlass** *(see).*

Chinese wood oil *n.* **Tung oil** *(see).*

Ch'ing or **Qing** (chĭng). A Manchu dynasty that in 1644 took Beijing from the Ming and became the last ruling dynasty of China.

Ch'ing-hai. See **Qinghai.**

Chingiz Khan. See **Genghis Khan.**

chink[1] (chĭngk) *n.* A crack or fissure; a narrow opening.
~*tr.v.* **chinked, chinking, chinks. 1.** To make chinks in. **2.** To fill chinks in. [Perhaps variant of earlier *chine,* from Middle English *chine,* crack, Old English *cinu, cine.*]

chink[2] *n.* A short, metallic sound.
~*v.* **chinked, chinking, chinks.** —*tr.* To strike (something) and make a chink. —*intr.* To make a chink. [Imitative.]

chin·less (chĭn′lĭs) *adj.* Having a small or receding chin.

chinless wonder *n. British Informal.* An upper-class man, especially a stupid or ineffectual one.

Chin-men. See **Jinmen.**

Chinnereth, Sea of. See **Galilee, Sea of.**

chi·no (chē′nō, shē′-) *n., pl.* **-nos. 1.** A coarse, twilled cotton fabric used for uniforms and sports clothes. **2. chinos.** Boys' and men's trousers of this material. [American Spanish *chino*†, "toasted" (from its original tan color).]

chi·noi·se·rie (shēn′wäz-rē′) *n.* **1.** A style, especially of the 17th and 18th centuries, primarily in the decorative arts, in which Chinese motifs, such as the willow tree, are employed. **2.** An object in this style. [French.]

Chi·nook (shĭ-nŏŏk′, chĭ-) *n., pl.* **-nooks** or collectively **Chinook. 1.** A member of a North American Indian people formerly inhabiting the Columbia River basin in Oregon and speaking one of the Chinookan languages. **2.** The language of this people. **3. chinook.** A moist, warm wind blowing from the sea on the Oregon and Washington coasts. **4. chinook.** A warm, dry wind that descends from the eastern slopes of the Rocky Mountains, causing a rapid rise in temperature.

Chi·nook·an (shĭ-nŏŏk′ən, chĭ-) *n.* A North American Indian language family of Washington and Oregon.

Chinook jargon *n.* A language combining simple English, French, Chinookan, and other North American Indian dialects, formerly used by Indians and fur traders of the Pacific Northwest.

Chinook salmon *n.* A salmon, *Oncorhynchus tshawytscha,* of northern Pacific waters, valued as a food fish.

chintz (chĭnts) *n.* A printed and glazed cotton fabric, usually of bright colors. [Variant of earlier *chints,* plural of *chint,* from Hindi *chīṇt,* from Sanskrit *chitra* many-colored, bright.]

chintz·y (chĭnt′sē) *adj.* **-ier, -iest. 1.** Of, pertaining to, or decorated with chintz. **2.** Characterized by a bright, fussy, flowery style that attempts to evoke an old-fashioned atmosphere. **3. a.** Gaudy; trashy. **b.** Cheap: *too chintzy to pay for my coffee.*

chin·wag (chĭn′wăg′) *n. Slang.* A gossip or conversation.

chip (chĭp) *n.* **1.** A small piece broken or cut off. **2.** A crack or other mark caused by chipping. **3. a.** A small disk or counter used in gambling to represent money. **b.** *Slang.* Money: *They won the lottery and are in the chips now.* **4.** *Electronics.* A minute square of a thin semiconducting material, such as silicon or germanium, doped and otherwise processed to have specific electrical characteristics; especially, such a square before attachment of electrical leads and packaging as an electronic component or integrated circuit. **5. a.** A thin, brittle slice of a food, usually fried in deep fat: *a potato chip.* **b. chips.** *Chiefly British.* French-fried potatoes. **6.** A chip shot in golf. **7.** Wood, palm leaves, straw, or similar material cut and dried for weaving. **8.** A fragment of dried animal dung used as fuel. **—chip off the old block.** *Informal.* One who resembles a parent, especially in behavior. **—have a chip on one's shoulder.** To behave in an aggressive, challenging, truculent manner, especially owing to sensitivity about one's imagined social inferiority.
~*v.* **chipped, chipping, chips.** —*tr.* **1.** To break a small piece from: *fell and chipped a tooth.* **2.** To chop or cut with an implement, especially an ax. **3.** To shape or carve by cutting or chopping. **4.** To hit (a golf ball) with a short, lofted stroke. —*intr.* **1.** To become broken off. **2.** To play a chip shot in golf. **—chip in.** *Informal.* **1.** To contribute money, labor, or the like. **2.** To interject; interrupt. [Middle English *chip,* Old English *cipp*†, beam, piece cut off a beam.]

chip basket *n. Chiefly British.* **1.** A wire basket for holding food during deep-frying. **2.** A basket made of thin woven strips of split wood.

chip·board (chĭp′bôrd′, -bōrd′) *n.* A hard, flat material made from sawdust and wood chips compressed and bound with resin.

chip·munk (chĭp′mŭngk′) *n.* A small rodent, *Tamias striatus,* of eastern North America, or any of several similar rodents of the genus *Eutamias,* of western North America and northern Asia, resembling a squirrel but smaller and having a striped back. [Variant of earlier *chitmunk,* from Algonquian.]

chip·o·la·ta (chĭp′ə-lä′tə) *n.* A small sausage with a spicy flavor. [French, from Italian *cipollata,* "onion-flavored (dish or mixture)," from *cipolla,* onion.]

Chip·pen·dale (chĭp′ən-dāl′) *adj.* Of, pertaining to, or designating a type of furniture characterized by flowing lines and rococo ornamentation. [After Thomas CHIPPENDALE (1718–79).]

Chip·pen·dale (chĭp′ən-dāl′), **Thomas** (1718–79). British furniture maker whose name is associated with elegant mid-18th century taste. His son, **Thomas Chippendale** (*c.* 1749–1822), expanded the business to include fabrics and wallpaper.

chip·per (chĭp′ər) *adj. Informal.* Active; cheerful; brisk; pert. [Perhaps from northern English dialect *kipper,* active, cheerful.]
chip·py (chĭp′ē) *n., pl.* **-pies.** *Slang.* A prostitute. [From *chip,* chirp (imitative).]
chip shot *n.* A short, lofted golf stroke used in approaching the green.
Chi·rac (shîr′ăk, shē-răk′), **Jacques** (1932–). French politician and prime minister (1974–76). A Gaullist, he served as prime minister in the government of Giscard d'Estaing, but resigned (1976), reorganizing Gaullist forces in the Rassemblement des Français pour la République.
chi·ral (kī′rəl) *adj.* Of or pertaining to the handedness or chirality of an asymmetric molecule. [Greek *kheir,* hand.]
chi·ral·i·ty (kī-răl′ĭ-tē) *n. Chemistry.* The concept of left or right-handedness applied to stereoisometric molecules. A figure representing the configuration of a molecule is said to have chirality if its image in a plane mirror cannot be superimposed on it.
chi-rho (kī′rō′, kē′-) *n.* A monogram and symbol for Christ, consisting of the superimposed Greek letters chi (X) and rho (P). [CHI + RHO, first two letters of Greek *khristos,* CHRIST.]
chiro–, cheiro– *prefix.* Indicates of or with the hand; for example, **chiropractic.** [Latin, from Greek *kheir,* hand.]
Chi·ri·co (kîr′ĭ-kō′), **Giorgio de** (1888–1978). Italian painter, born in Greece. He produced distinctive canvases that feature enigmatically arranged statues and objects set against semideserted backgrounds of Italian architecture. He founded the Italian metaphysical school of painting (1917).
chi·rog·ra·phy (kī-rŏg′rə-fē) *n.* Penmanship. [French *chirographie* : CHIRO- + -GRAPHY.] **—chi·rog·ra·pher** *n.* **—chi·ro·graph·ic** (kī′rə-grăf′ĭk), **chi·ro·graph·i·cal** *adj.*
chi·ro·man·cy (kī′rə-măn′sē) *n.* The art or practice of foretelling a person's future by studying the palm of the hand; palmistry. [CHIRO- + -MANCY.] **—chi·ro·man·cer** *n.*
Chi·ron (kī′rŏn′). *Greek Mythology.* The wise centaur who tutored Achilles, Nestor, and Asclepius.
chi·rop·o·dy (kə-rŏp′ə-dē, shə-) *n. Medicine.* **Podiatry** *(see).* [CHIRO- + -PODY.] **—chi·rop·o·dist** *n.*
chi·ro·prac·tic (kī′rə-prăk′tĭk) *n.* A system of therapy in which disease is considered the result of neural malfunction and manipulation of the spinal column and other bodily structures is the preferred method of treatment. [CHIRO- + Greek *praktikos,* effective, PRACTICAL.] **—chi·ro·prac·tor** (kī′rə-prăk′tər) *n.*
chi·rop·ter·an (kī-rŏp′tər-ən) *n.* Also **chi·rop·ter** (kī′rŏp′tər). Any flying mammal of the order Chiroptera, which includes the bats. [New Latin *Chiroptera* : CHIRO- + -PTER + -AN.] **—chi·rop·ter·an** *adj.*
chirp (chûrp) *v.* **chirped, chirping, chirps.** *—intr.* **1.** To utter a short, high-pitched sound, like that of a small bird or grasshopper. **2.** To speak in a quick, sprightly manner. *—tr.* To utter with a short, high-pitched sound.
~n. A short, high-pitched sound; a tweet. [Middle English *chirpen* (attested only in gerund *chirpinge*), to chirp, twitter (imitative).] **—chirp·er** *n.*
chirp·y (chûr′pē) *adj.* **-ier, -iest.** *Informal.* Cheerful; bright; in a good or lively mood. **—chirp·i·ly** *adv.* **—chirp·i·ness** *n.*
chirr (chûr) *intr.v.* **chirred, chirring, chirrs.** To make a harsh, trilled sound, as a cricket does. [Imitative.] **—chirr** *n.*
chir·rup (chûr′əp, chĭr′-) *v.* **-ruped, -ruping, -rups.** *—intr.* To utter a series of chirps; make a light, tremulous sound. *—tr.* To sound with chirps. [Variant of CHIRP.] **—chir·rup** *n.*
chis·el (chĭz′əl) *n.* A metal tool with a sharp, beveled edge, used to cut and shape stone, wood, or metal.
~v. **chiseled, -eling, -els.** Also *chiefly British* **-elled, -elling.** *—tr.* **1.** To shape or cut with or as if with a chisel. **2.** *Slang.* To cheat or swindle. *—intr.* **1.** To use a chisel. **2.** *Slang.* To use unethical methods; cheat. [Middle English, from Old North French, from Vulgar Latin *cīsellus, caesellus* (both unattested), diminutive formation from *caedere* (past participle *caesus*), to cut.] **—chis·el·er** *n.*
Chis·holm (chĭz′əm), **Shirley Anita St. Hill** (1924–). U.S. politician. Concerned with education and social reform, she used her straightforward manner and genuine interest to earn the trust of her constituents. She served as New York State assemblywoman (1965–67) and as a U.S. congresswoman (1969–81). Her campaign slogan also served as the title of her book *Unbought and Unbossed* (1970).
chi-square test (kī′skwâr′) *n. Statistics.* A test used in relation to a hypothesis concerning the discrepancy between observed and expected results. The result of the test, the *chi-square distribution,* is calculated as the sum of the squares of observed values minus expected values divided by the expected values.
chit[1] (chĭt) *n.* **1.** A statement of an amount owed for food and drink; check. **2.** *Chiefly British.* A small slip of paper, as one carrying a memo. [Short for earlier *chitty,* from Hindi *ciṭṭhi,* note, pass, from Sanskrit *chitra,* mark.]
chit[2] *n.* A child, girl, or young woman, especially one thought to be impertinent. [Middle English *chitte*†, young animal.]
chi·tal (chē′təl) *n.* The **axis deer** *(see).* [Hindi *cītal,* from Sanskrit *citrala,* spotted, from *chitra,* bright, variegated.]
chit·chat (chĭt′chăt′) *n.* **1.** Casual, light conversation. **2.** Gossip. [Dissimilated reduplication of CHAT.] **—chit·chat** *v.*
chi·tin (kīt′n, kī′tĭn) *n.* A semitransparent horny substance, primarily a mucopolysaccharide, forming the principal component of arthropod exoskeletons and the cell walls of certain fungi. [French *chitine,* from New Latin CHITON (mollusk).] **—chi·tin·ous** *adj.*
chi·ton (kīt′n, kī′tŏn′) *n.* **1.** A tunic worn by men and women in ancient Greece. **2.** Any of various marine mollusks of the class Amphineura, especially of the genus *Chiton,* living on rocks and having shells consisting of eight overlapping transverse plates. [New Latin, mollusk (with tuniclike shell), from Greek *khiton,* tunic, from Semitic, akin to Hebrew *kəthōnet.*]
Chit·ta·gong (chĭt′ə-gŏng′). Port and city in Bangladesh, near the mouth of the Karnaphuli River. It is the southern terminus of all the country's major land, river, and air routes, and Bangladesh's second-largest industrial center, processing cotton, jute, and tea.
chi·tar·ro·ne (kē′tə-rō′nā) *n., pl.* **-ni** (-nē). A large baroque lute. [Italian, augmentative of *chittara,* lute, GUITAR.]
chit·ter·lings (chĭt′lĭnz) *pl.n.* Also **chit·lins, chit·lings.** The small intestines of pigs, cooked and eaten as food. [Middle English *chiterling,* perhaps diminutive of Old English *cieter* (unattested), intestines.]
Chiu-lung. See **Jiulong.**
chiv·al·rous (shĭv′əl-rəs) *adj.* Also **chi·val·ric** (shĭ-văl′rĭk, shĭv′əl-). **1. a.** Having the qualities of gallantry and honor attributed to an ideal knight. **b.** Courteous, considerate, and protective, especially to women. Said of men. **2.** Of or pertaining to chivalry. **—chiv·al·rous·ly** *adv.* **—chiv·al·rous·ness** *n.*
chiv·al·ry (shĭv′əl-rē′) *n., pl.* **-ries. 1. a.** The medieval institution of knighthood. **b.** The principles and customs of this institution. **2. a.** The qualities idealized by knighthood, as bravery, courtesy, honor, and readiness to help the weak. **b.** The manifestation of any of these qualities. **3.** A group of knights. [Middle English *chivalrie,* from Old French *chevalerie,* knightliness, from *chevalier,* knight, from Late Latin *caballārius,* horseman, CAVALIER.]
chivaree. Variant of **charivari.**
chive (chīv) *n.* **1.** A plant, *Allium schoenoprasum,* native to Eurasia, having rose-pink flowers and hollow, grasslike leaves. **2. chives.** The leaves of this plant, used as a seasoning. [Middle English *cyve, cheve,* from Old French *cive,* from Latin *cēpa,* onion, perhaps akin to Greek *kapia*†, onions.]
chiv·vy, chiv·y (chĭv′ē) *tr.v.* **-vied, -vying, -vies** or **-ied, -ying, -ies.** Also **chev·y** (chĕv′ē) **-ied, -ying, -ies.** *Chiefly British.* To cause to act or move more quickly; chase or harass. [English dialectal *chevy,* short for *chevy chase,* confusion, pursuit, from *Chevy Chase,* name of a Middle English ballad about the battle of Otterburn (1388), which arose from a hunt *(chase)* near the CHEVIOT HILLS.]
chla·myd·e·ous (klə-mĭd′ē-əs) *adj. Botany.* Having a floral envelope. [Latin *chlamys* (stem *chlamyd-*), mantle, CHLAMYS.]
chla·myd·o·spore (klə-mĭd′ə-spôr′, -spōr′) *n.* A thick-walled fungus spore derived from a hyphal cell; a resting spore. [Latin *chlamys* (stem *chlamyd-*), mantle, CHLAMYS + SPORE.]
chlam·ys (klā′mĭs, klăm′ĭs) *n., pl.* **-myses** or **chlamydes** (klăm′ə-dēz′). A short mantle fastened at the shoulder, worn by men in ancient Greece. [Latin *chlamys,* from Greek *khlamus*†.]
chlo·as·ma (klō-ăz′mə) *n., pl.* **-mata** (-mə-tə). A brown patch on the skin, usually on the face, that may occur during pregnancy and the menopause. [New Latin, from Late Greek *khloasma,* greenness, from *khloazein,* to be green, from *khloos,* green color.]
chlor·ac·ne (klôr-ăk′nē, klōr-) *n.* An acnelike skin disorder caused by prolonged exposure to chlorinated hydrocarbons.
chlo·ral (klôr′əl, klōr′-) *n.* A colorless, mobile, oily liquid, CCl_3CHO, a penetrating lung irritant, used to manufacture DDT and chloral hydrate. [French : CHLOR(O)- + AL(COHOL).]
chloral hydrate *n.* A colorless crystalline compound, $CCl_3CH(OH)_2$, used medicinally as a sedative and hypnotic.
chlor·am·bu·cil (klôr-ăm′byə-sĭl, klōr-) *n.* A drug, $C_{14}H_{19}Cl_2NO_2$, administered orally in the treatment of cancers.
chlo·ra·mine (klôr′ə-mēn′, klōr′-) *n.* Any of several compounds containing nitrogen and chlorine; especially, an unstable colorless liquid, NH_2Cl, used to make hydrazine. [CHLOR(O)- + AM(MONIA) + -INE.]
chlo·ram·phen·i·col (klôr′ăm-fĕn′ĭ-kôl′, -kōl′, klōr′-) *n.* An antibiotic, $C_{11}H_{12}O_2N_2Cl_2$, derived from the soil bacterium *Streptomyces venezuelae* or produced industrially by chemical synthesis. [CHLOR(O)- + AM(IDE) + PHE(NO)- + NI(TRO)- + (GLY)COL.]
chlo·rate (klôr′āt′, klōr′-) *n.* The inorganic group ClO_3 or a compound containing it. [CHLOR(O)- + -ATE.]
chlor·dane (klôr′dān′, klōr′-) *n.* Also **chlor·dan** (-dăn′). An amber-colored, odorless viscous liquid, $C_{10}H_6Cl_8$, used as an insecticide. [CHLOR(O)- + (IN)D(ENE) + -ANE.]
chlor·di·az·e·pox·ide (klôr′dī-ăz′ə-pŏk′sīd′, klōr′-) *n.* A drug used as a sedative and mild tranquilizer.
chlo·rel·la (klə-rĕl′ə) *n.* Any of various minute green algae of the genus *Chlorella,* widely used in studies of photosynthesis. [New Latin *Chlorella* : CHLOR(O)- + *-ella,* diminutive suffix.]
chlo·ren·chy·ma (klə-rĕng′kə-mə) *n.* Plant tissue containing chlorophyll. [CHLOR(OPHYLL) + -ENCHYMA.]
chlo·ric (klôr′ĭk, klōr′-) *adj.* Of, pertaining to, or containing chlorine, especially with a valence of 5. [CHLOR(O)- + -IC.]
chloric acid *n.* A strongly oxidizing unstable acid, $HClO_3{\cdot}7H_2O$.
chlo·ride (klôr′īd′, klōr′-) *n.* Any binary compound of chlorine. [CHLOR(O)- + -IDE.] **—chlo·rid·ic** (klə-rĭd′ĭk) *adj.*
chlo·rin·ate (klôr′ə-nāt′, klōr′-) *tr.v.* **-ated, -ating, -ates.** To treat or combine with chlorine or with a chlorine compound. **—chlo·ri·na·tion** *n.* **—chlo·ri·na·tor** *n.*
chlorinated lime *n.* A white powder of varying composition, as

chiton *A tunic worn by the men and women of ancient Greece. The women's version was ankle length but the chiton normally worn by men, like the one shown here, barely reached the knees. Chitons worn by slaves were designed to leave the right arm bare and part of the chest exposed.*

chive *Although* Allium schoenoprasum *is cultivated for salads and flavoring, it also grows wild—up to 40 centimeters (16 inches) tall.*

CaCl (ClO) • 4H$_2$O, produced by chlorinating slaked lime and used as a bleach.

chlo·rine (klôr'ēn', klōr'-, -ĭn) *n. Symbol* **Cl** A highly irritating, greenish-yellow gaseous halogen, capable of combining with nearly all other elements, produced principally by electrolysis of sodium chloride and used widely to purify water, as a disinfectant, a bleaching agent, and in the manufacture of many important compounds including chloroform and carbon tetrachloride. Atomic number 17, atomic weight 35.45, freezing point –100.98°C, boiling point –34.0°C, specific gravity 1.56 (–33.6°C), valences 1, 3, 5, 7. [CHLOR(O)- + -INE.]

chlo·rite[1] (klôr'īt', klōr'-) *n.* A generally green or black secondary mineral, (Mg, Fe), Al (Al, Si$_3$)O$_{10}$ (OH)$_9$, often formed by metamorphic alteration of primary dark rock minerals. [Latin *chlorītis*, a green precious stone, from Greek *khlōritis*, from *khlōros*, greenish yellow.]

chlorite[2] *n.* The inorganic group ClO$_2$ or a compound containing it. [CHLOR(O)- + -ITE.]

chloro–, chlor– *prefix.* Indicates: **1.** The color green; for example, **chlorosis**. **2.** The presence of chlorine; for example, **chloroform**, **chlorate**. [Greek *khlōros*, greenish yellow.]

chlo·ro·a·ce·tic acid (klôr'ō-ə-sē'tĭk, -sĕt'ĭk, klōr'-) *n.* Also **chlor·a·ce·tic acid** (klôr'ə-sē'tĭk, -sĕt'ĭk, klōr'-) *n.* **1.** A colorless crystalline solid, CH$_2$ClCOOH, prepared by chlorinating acetic acid and used as an intermediate. **2.** A colorless liquid, CHCl$_2$COOH, used in the manufacture of dyes. **3.** A deliquescent crystalline solid, **trichloroacetic acid** *(see).*

chlo·ro·ben·zene (klôr'ō-bĕn'zēn', -bĕn-zēn', klōr'-) *n.* A colorless, volatile flammable liquid, C$_6$H$_5$Cl, used to prepare phenol, DDT, aniline, and as a general solvent.

chlo·ro·eth·ene (klôr'ō-ĕth'ēn', klōr'-) *n.* **Vinyl chloride** *(see).*

chlo·ro·form (klôr'ə-fôrm', klōr'-) *n.* A clear, colorless, heavy liquid, CHCl$_3$, used in refrigerants, propellants, and resins and as an anesthetic.
~*tr.v.* **chloroformed, -forming, -forms. 1.** To anesthetize or kill with chloroform. **2.** To apply chloroform to. [CHLORO- + FORM(YL).]

chlo·ro·hy·drin (klôr'ō-hī'drĭn, klōr'-) *n.* An aliphatic organic chemical compound that is both an alkyl chloride and an alcohol, frequently containing a single chlorine atom and a single hydroxyl group on adjacent carbon atoms. [CHLORO- + HYDR(O)- + -IN.]

Chlo·ro·my·ce·tin (klôr'ō-mī-sēt'n, klōr'-) *n.* A trademark for **chloramphenicol** *(see).*

chlo·ro·phyll, chlo·ro·phyl (klôr'ə-fĭl', klōr'-) *n.* Any of a group of related green pigments found in plants that trap energy from sunlight for use in photosynthesis, especially: **1.** *Chlorophyll a*, a waxy blue-black microcrystalline green-plant pigment, C$_{55}$H$_{72}$MgN$_4$O$_5$, with a characteristic blue-green alcohol solution. **2.** *Chlorophyll b*, a similar green-plant pigment, C$_{55}$H$_{70}$MgN$_4$O$_6$, having a brilliant green alcohol solution. [French *chlorophylle* : CHLORO- + -PHYLL.]

chlo·ro·pic·rin (klôr'ə-pĭk'rĭn, klōr'-) *n.* An oily colorless liquid, CCl$_3$NO$_2$, used to make poison gas, in dyestuffs, disinfectants, insecticides, and fumigants. Also called "nitrochloroform," "vomiting gas." [CHLORO- + PICR(O)- + -IN.]

chlo·ro·plast (klôr'ə-plăst', klōr'-) *n.* Also **chlo·ro·plas·tid** (klôr'-ə-plăs'tĭd, klōr'-). *Botany.* A plastid containing chlorophyll in photosynthetic plants. [CHLORO- + -PLAST.]

chlo·ro·prene (klôr'ə-prēn', klōr'-) *n.* A colorless liquid, C$_4$H$_5$Cl, used as the monomer of neoprene rubber. [CHLORO- + (ISO)-PRENE.]

chlor·o·quine (klôr'ə-kwīn', -kwēn', klōr'-) *n.* A drug, C$_{18}$H$_{26}$ClN$_3$, used mainly in the treatment and prevention of malaria.

chlo·ro·sis (klə-rō'sĭs) *n.* **1.** *Botany.* An abnormal condition of plants, characterized by absence of or deficiency in green pigment and caused by lack of light, mineral deficiency, or genetic disorders. **2.** *Pathology.* An iron-deficiency anemia chiefly affecting girls at puberty and characterized by greenish skin color. Also called "greensickness." [CHLOR(O)- + -OSIS.]

chlo·rous (klôr'əs, klōr'-) *adj.* Of, pertaining to, or containing chlorine, especially with a valence of 3.

chlor·prom·a·zine (klôr-prŏm'ə-zēn', -prō'mə-zēn', klōr-) *n.* An oily liquid, C$_{17}$H$_{19}$ClN$_2$S, derived from phenothiazine and used as a sedative, tranquilizer, and antiemetic. [CHLOR(O)- + PRO(PYL) + METH(YL) + AZINE.]

chlor·tet·ra·cy·cline (klôr'tĕt-rə-sī'klēn', klōr'-) *n.* An antibiotic, C$_{22}$H$_{23}$ClN$_2$O$_8$, obtained from the soil bacterium *Streptomyces aureofaciens* and used for treating a variety of infections.

chm. 1. chairman. **2.** *Chess.* checkmate.

cho·a·na (kō'ə-nə) *n., pl.* **-nae** (-nē'). *Anatomy.* A funnel-shaped opening; especially, either of the two internal openings of the nose into the pharynx. [Greek *khoanē*, funnel, from *khein*, to pour.]

cho·an·o·cyte (kō-ăn'ə-sīt') *n. Biology.* One of the flagellated cells that line the body cavity of a sponge. Also called "collar cell." [Greek *khoanē*, funnel, from *khein*, to pour + -CYTE.]

cho·cho (chō'chō) *n.* The cucumberlike fruit of the vine *Sechium edule*, eaten especially in the West Indies, Australia, and New Zealand. [Brazilian native name *chuchy.*]

chock (chŏk) *n.* **1.** A block or wedge placed under something, such as a boat, barrel, or wheel, to keep it from moving. **2.** *Nautical.* A heavy fitting of metal or wood with two jaws curving inward, through which a rope or cable may be run.
~*tr.v.* **chocked, chocking, chocks.** To fit, secure, or wedge with a chock or chocks.

~*adv.* As completely or as closely as possible. [17th century : origin obscure.]

chock-a-block (chŏk'ə-blŏk') *adj.* **1.** Completely full; jammed: *chock-a-block with cars.* **2.** *Archaic.* Drawn so close as to have the blocks touching. Said of a ship's hoisting tackle. —**chock-a-block** *adv.*

chock-full (chŏk'fŏŏl', chŭk'-) *adj.* Completely filled; stuffed. Used with *of.* [Middle English *chokkeful*, probably from CHOCK (to ram tight with chocks).]

choc·o (chŏk'ō, chō'kō) *n., pl.* **-os.** *Australian Slang.* During World War II, a military recruit. [Shortened from *chocolate soldier.*]

choc·o·late (chô'kə-lĭt, chŏk'lĭt, chŏk'ə-lĭt, chŏk'lĭt) *n.* **1.** Husked, roasted, and ground cacao seeds, often combined with a sweetener or flavoring agent. **2.** A candy or beverage made from chocolate. **3.** A grayish to deep reddish brown. [Spanish, from Aztec *xocolatl* : *xococ*, bitter + *atl*, water.] —**choc·o·late** *adj.*

choc·o·late-box (chô'kə-lĭt-bŏks', chŏk'lĭt-, chŏk'ə-lĭt-, chŏk'lĭt) *adj.* Pretty in a sentimental way. Usually said of pictures.

choc·taw (chŏk'tô) *n.* In figure-skating, a turn from either outer edge of one skate to the opposite edge of the other. [After CHOCTAW.]

Choc·taw (chŏk'tô) *n., pl.* **-taws** or collectively **Choctaw. 1.** A member of a North American Indian people, formerly living in southern Mississippi and Alabama, now settled in Oklahoma. **2.** The Muskhogean language of this tribe.

chog·yal (chŏg'yäl') *n.* The traditional title of the ruler of Sikkim.

choice (chois) *n.* **1.** The act of choosing; selection; election. **2.** The power, right, or liberty of choosing; option. **3.** The person or thing chosen. **4. a.** A sufficient number or variety from which to choose. **b.** A supply chosen with care. **5.** The best part; the pick. **6.** An alternative.
~*adj.* **choicer, choicest. 1.** Of fine quality; select; excellent. **2.** Selected with care. **3.** Appealing to refined taste. [Middle English *chois*, from Old French, from *choisir*, to CHOOSE.]
   Synonyms: alternative, option, preference, selection.

choir (kwīr) *n.* **1. a.** An organized body of singers, especially one performing church music or singing in a church. **b.** The part of a church used by such singers. **2.** *Architecture.* The part of a cruciform church between the nave and the main altar. Compare **chancel. 3. a.** A musical group or band. **b.** A section of a musical group or band.
~*intr.v.* **choired, choiring, choirs.** To sing in chorus. [Earlier *quier, quire*, Middle English *quere*, from Old French *cuer*, from Medieval Latin *chorus*, CHORUS.]

choir·boy (kwīr'boi') *n.* A boy member of a choir.

choir loft *n.* A gallery for a church choir.

choke (chōk) *v.* **choked, choking, chokes.** —*tr.* **1.** To interfere with or terminate the normal breathing of (a person, for example), especially by constricting or breaking the windpipe or by polluting the air. **2.** To stop by or as if by strangling; silence; suppress. Often used with *off, down,* or *back: choke back tears.* **3.** To reduce the air intake of (a carburetor), thereby enriching the fuel mixture. **4.** To check or slow down the movement, growth, or development of (plants, for example). **5.** To block up or obstruct by filling or crowding; clog; congest. **6.** To fill completely; jam; pack. Often used with *up.* **7.** To cause to be temporarily overcome with strong emotion. Usually used in the passive. —*intr.* **1.** To become suffocated; have difficulty in breathing, swallowing, or speaking. **2.** To be blocked up or obstructed.
~*n.* **1.** The act or sound of choking. **2.** That which constricts or chokes; a narrow part, such as the chokebore of a gun. **3.** A device used in an internal-combustion engine to enrich the fuel mixture by reducing the flow of air to the carburetor. **4.** *Electronics.* A coil of wire with a high impedance used to smooth the output of a rectifier or prevent the passage of high frequencies. **5.** The inner part of a globe artichoke, composed of small inedible hairs. [Middle English *choken, cheken*, short for *achoken, acheken*, Old English *āceocian*, from Germanic *kēkōn-* (unattested), CHEEK.]

choke-bore (chōk'bôr', -bōr') *n.* **1.** A shotgun bore that narrows toward the muzzle to prevent wide scattering of the shot. **2.** A gun with a chokebore.

choke-damp (chōk'dămp') *n.* A gaseous mixture, **blackdamp** *(see).* [So called because it causes suffocation in mines.]

chok·er (chō'kər) *n.* **1.** One that chokes. **2. a.** A necklace or band that fits closely round the throat. **b.** A high, tight collar.

cho·key (chō'kē) *n., pl.* **-keys.** *British Slang.* Prison. [Hindi *chaukī*, (police) station, shed.]

cho·lan·gi·og·ra·phy (kō-lăn'jē-ŏg'rə-fē) *n.* Examination by x-ray of the bile ducts in order to detect obstruction or the presence of stones. [CHOLE- + ANGIO- + -GRAPHY.] —**cho·lan·gi·o·graph·ic** (kō-lăn'jē-ə-grăf'ĭk) *adj.*

chole-, chol– *prefix.* Indicates gall or bile; for example, **cholecyst**, **choline.** [Greek *kholē*, bile, gall.]

cho·le·cal·cif·er·ol (kō'lĭ-kăl-sĭf'ə-rôl', -rōl') *n.* One of the forms in which **Vitamin D** *(see)* occurs.

cho·le·cyst (kō'lĭ-sĭst', kōl'ə-) *n.* The gallbladder. [New Latin *cholecystis* : CHOLE- + CYST.]

cho·le·cys·tec·to·my (kō'lĭ-sĭ-stĕk'tə-mē, kŏl'ə-) *n., pl.* **-mies.** Surgical removal of the gallbladder.

chol·er (kŏl'ər, kō'lər) *n.* **1.** *Archaic.* **a.** One of the four humors of the body thought in the Middle Ages to cause anger and bad temper when present in excess; yellow bile. **b.** Biliousness. **2.** Anger; irritability. [Middle English *colre, coler(a)*, from Old French *colere*, from Latin *cholera,* bilious diarrhea, from Greek *kholera,* from *kholē,* bile, gall.]

chol·er·a (kŏl′ər-ə) *n.* An acute infectious epidemic disease caused by the bacterium *Vibrio comma,* characterized by watery diarrhea, vomiting, cramps, suppression of urine, and collapse. [Latin *cholera,* bilious diarrhea. See **choler.**] —**chol·er·a·ic** (kŏl′ə-rā′ĭk) *adj.* —**chol·er·oid** (kŏl′ə-roid′) *adj.*

chol·er·ic (kŏl′ər-ĭk, kə-lĕr′ĭk) *adj.* Bad-tempered; irascible. —**chol·er·i·cal·ly, chol·er·ic·ly** *adv.*

cho·les·ter·ol (kə-lĕs′tə-rôl′, -rōl′) *n.* A glistening white soapy crystalline substance, $C_{27}H_{45}OH$, the most common animal sterol, a precursor of a form of Vitamin D and an essential tissue constituent, occurring notably in bile, gallstones, the brain, blood cells, plasma, egg yolk, and seeds. Also called "cholesterin." [CHOLE- + Greek *stereos,* hard, solid + -OL (so called because it was first found in gallstones).]

cho·li (chō′lē) *n.* A short-sleeved woman's bodice worn mainly by women in India. [Hindi *coli.*]

cho·lic acid (kō′lĭk) *n.* An abundant crystalline bile acid, $C_{24}H_{40}O_5$. [Greek *kholikos,* bilious, from *kholē,* bile.]

cho·line (kō′lēn′) *n.* A natural amine, $C_5H_{15}NO_2$, sometimes classed in the vitamin B complex and a precursor of various phospholipids and acetylcholine. [CHOL(E)- + -INE (from its function in preventing fat accumulation in the liver).]

cho·lin·er·gic (kō′lə-nûr′jĭk) *adj.* 1. Activated by or capable of liberating **acetylcholine** (*see*). Said of certain nerve fibers. 2. Having physiological effects similar to acetylcholine. [(ACETYL)CHOLIN(E) + Greek *ergon,* work + -IC.]

cho·lin·es·ter·ase (kō′lə-nĕs′tə-rās′, -rāz′) *n.* An enzyme that hydrolyzes acetylcholine to form acetic acid and choline. Also called "acetylcholinesterase." [CHOLIN(E) + ESTERASE.]

chol·la (choi′ə) *n.* Any of several very spiny cacti of the genus *Opuntia,* characterized by cylindrical stem segments. See **prickly pear.** [Mexican Spanish, from Spanish *cholla,* head, possibly from Old French *cholle,* head, from Germanic.]

chomp. Variant of **champ** (bite).

Chom·sky (chŏm′skē), **Noam** (1928–). U.S. language theorist whose works revolutionized the study of linguistics. He argues that the structure of language is determined by the structure of the human mind, and that human language differs radically from the way animals communicate or machines may be programmed. —**Chomsky·an** *adj. & n.*

chon (chŏn) *n., pl.* **chon.** A coin equal to ¹/₁₀₀ of the won, the monetary unit of South Korea. See feature at **currency.** [Korean.]

chon·dri·fy (kŏn′drə-fī′) *v.* **-fied, -fying, -fies.** —*tr.* To change into cartilage. —*intr.* To become cartilage. [CHONDRI- + -FY.] —**chon·dri·fi·ca·tion** *n.*

chon·dri·o·some (kŏn′drē-ə-sōm′) *n. Biology.* A **mitochondrion** (*see*). [CHONDRI- + -SOME.]

chon·drite (kŏn′drīt′) *n.* A stone of meteoric origin characterized by chondrules. [CHONDR(O)- + -ITE.] —**chon·drit·ic** (kŏn-drĭt′ĭk) *adj.*

chondro-, chondr-, chondri- *prefix.* Indicates: 1. Cartilage; for example, **chondroma, chondrify.** 2. Granule or chondrule; for example, **chondrite.** [Greek *khondros,* granule, cartilage.]

chon·dro·cra·ni·um (kŏn′drō-krā′nē-əm) *n., pl.* **-ums** or **-nia** (-nē-ə). The embryonic cartilaginous cranium, especially as distinguished from the **osteocranium** (*see*).

chon·dro·ma (kŏn-drō′mə) *n., pl.* **-mas** or **-mata** (-mə-tə). A benign cartilaginous tumor. [New Latin : CHONDR(O)- + -OMA.]

chon·drule (kŏn′drōōl′) *n. Geology.* A small round granule of mineral or glass embedded in some meteorites. [CHONDR(O)- + -ULE.]

Chong·qing, Ch'ung-ch'ing, or **Chung·king** (chŏōng′chĭng′, -kĭng′). City and river port in Sichuan province of central China, on the Chang Jiang. It was made capital of China (1937–46) during the war with Japan. Coal and iron are mined nearby.

choose (chōōz) *v.* **chose** (chōz), **chosen** (chō′zən), **choosing, chooses.** —*tr.* 1. To decide upon and pick out from a number of possible alternatives; select. 2. To prefer to others. 3. To want; desire: *choose to go.* —*intr.* 1. To make a choice; select; decide. [Choose, Middle English *chosen,* Old English *cēosan* (later *ceōsan*). Chose, chosen; Middle English *chosen* (past plural), *chosen,* both from the infinitive *chosen.* All from Germanic *kiusan* (unattested).] —**choos·er** *n.*

Synonyms: *elect, pick, select.*

choos·y, choos·ey (chōō′zē) *adj.* **-ier, -iest.** Unwilling to settle for less than the best; hard to please. —**choos·i·ness** *n.*

chop¹ (chŏp) *v.* **chopped, chopping, chops.** —*tr.* 1. To cut by striking with a heavy, sharp tool, such as an ax. 2. To make by chopping. 3. To cut into bits; mince: *chop onions.* 4. *Sports.* To hit or hit at with a short, swift downward stroke. 5. To cut short: *chopped off the sentence midway.* —*intr.* 1. To make heavy, cutting strokes. 2. To move roughly or suddenly.
~*n.* 1. The act of chopping. 2. A swift, short cutting blow or stroke. 3. A chopped-off piece; especially, a cut of meat, usually taken from the rib, shoulder, or loin and containing a bone. 4. A short, irregular motion of waves. 5. *Australian Slang.* A share, as of winnings. —**get the chop.** *British Slang.* To be dismissed from one's job. [Middle English *choppen,* variant of *chappen,* CHAP (to split).]

chop² *intr.v.* **chopped, chopping, chops.** To change direction suddenly, as a ship in the wind; swerve. [Originally, "to exchange," from Middle English *choppen,* variant of *chappen, chepen* to barter,

trade, Old English *cēapian,* ultimately from Latin *caupō,* innkeeper; akin to CHEAP.]

chop³ *n.* 1. An official stamp or permit in the Far East. 2. Quality: *a painter of the first chop.* [Hindi *chhāp†,* seal.]

chop-chop (chŏp′chŏp′) *adv. Informal.* Quickly. [Pidgin English, from Cantonese *gap gap,* "quickly," reduplication of *gap,* corresponding to Mandarin *ji,* urgent.]

chop·house (chŏp′hous′) *n.* A restaurant that specializes in serving chops and steaks.

Chopin (shō′păn′), **Frédéric François** (1810–49). Polish pianist and composer, of French parentage. He became a celebrated figure in the romantic age and was known for his affair with the novelist George Sand, with whom he lived for nine years. His music, written chiefly for the piano, drew inspiration from the romance and melancholy of traditional Polish dance music.

chop·log·ic (chŏp′lŏj′ĭk) *n.* Cunning but fallacious argument. —**chop·log·ic** *adj.*

chop·per (chŏp′ər) *n.* 1. One that chops. 2. A butcher's cleaver. 3. A device that interrupts an electric current or beam of radiation. 4. A motorcycle, especially one that is customized. 5. *Slang.* A helicopter. 6. **choppers.** *Slang.* Teeth, especially false teeth.

chop·py (chŏp′ē) *adj.* **-pier, -piest.** 1. Abruptly shifting or breaking, as waves: *choppy seas.* 2. Marked by abrupt transitions; jerky: *choppy prose.*

chops (chŏps) *pl.n.* The jaws, cheeks, or jowls of an animal or human being. [Origin unknown.]

chop·sticks (chŏp′stĭks′) *pl.n.* A pair of slender sticks made of wood, ivory, or plastic and used as eating utensils by the Chinese, Japanese, and some other Asian peoples. [Pidgin English *chop,* fast (see **chopchop**) + STICK(S), a loose translation of Cantonese *kuàizi,* "fast ones."]

chop su·ey (chŏp sōō′ē) *n.* A Chinese-style dish consisting of small pieces of meat or chicken cooked with bean sprouts and other vegetables and served with rice. [Cantonese *tsaap sui,* corresponding to *zá sui,* "mixed pieces."]

cho·ra·gus (kə-rā′gəs) *n., pl.* **-gi** (-jī′). 1. In Greek drama: **a.** The leader of the chorus. **b.** An elected official supervising the production of dramatic performances in the festival of Dionysus at Athens. 2. The leader of a choir. [Latin, from Greek *khoragos* : *khoros,* CHORUS + -*agos,* leader, from *agein,* to lead.] —**cho·rag·ic** *adj.*

cho·ral (kôr′əl, kōr′-) *adj.* 1. Of or pertaining to a chorus or choir. 2. Written for performance by a chorus.
~*n.* Variant of **chorale.** [Medieval Latin *chorālis,* from *chorus,* CHORUS.] —**cho·ral·ly** *adv.*

cho·rale, cho·ral (kə-rāl′, -răl′) *n.* 1. A Protestant hymn tune. 2. A harmonized hymn, especially one for organ: *a Bach chorale.* 3. A chorus or choir. [German *Choral(gesang),* "choral (song)," from Medieval Latin *chorālis,* CHORAL.]

chorale prelude *n. Music.* A composition for the organ, chiefly in baroque style, characterized by an elaborate contrapuntal structure based on the melody of a hymn or chorale.

chord¹ (kôrd, kōrd) *n.* 1. A combination of three or more usually concordant notes sounded simultaneously. 2. An emotional feeling or response: *Her words struck a sympathetic chord.* [Alteration (influenced by Latin *chorda,* string, CORD) of Middle English *cord,* agreement, harmony, short for ACCORD.]

chord² *n.* 1. *Geometry.* A line segment that joins two points on a curve. 2. *Aviation.* An imaginary straight line connecting the leading and trailing edges of an airfoil. 3. *Archaic.* The string of a musical instrument. 4. *Engineering.* A part of a truss, especially a member lying along the top or the bottom. [16th century : respelling (influenced by Latin *chorda,* string) of CORD.]

chord³. Variant of **cord.**

chord·al (kôrd′l) *adj. Music.* 1. Relating to or consisting of a harmonic chord. 2. Giving prominence to harmonic rather than contrapuntal structure: *chordal music.*

chor·date (kôr′dāt′, -dĭt) *n. Zoology.* Any of numerous animals belonging to the phylum Chordata, which includes all vertebrates and certain marine animals having a notochord, such as the lancelets.
~*adj. Zoology.* Of or belonging to the Chordata. [New Latin *Chordata,* from *chorda,* notochord, from Latin, CORD.]

chor·do·phone (kôr′də-fōn′) *n.* Any musical instrument producing its sound through the vibration of strings.

chore (chôr, chōr) *n.* 1. A routine or minor task. 2. An unpleasant or burdensome task. —See Synonyms at **task.** [Variant of CHARE, CHAR.]

-chore *suffix.* Indicates a plant distributed by a specified agency; for example, **anemochore, zoochore.** [Greek *khōrein,* to move, spread abroad.]

cho·re·a (kə-rē′ə, kō-) *n.* Any of various nervous disorders marked by uncontrollable and irregular movements of the muscles of the arms, legs, and face, one of which is "St. Vitus' dance." Also *informally* "jerks." [Latin *chorea,* dance, from Greek *khoreia,* choral dance, from *khoros,* dance, CHORUS.]

cho·re·o·graph (kôr′ē-ə-grăf′, -gräf′, kōr′-) *v.* **-graphed, -graphing, -graphs.** —*tr.* To create the choreography of (a ballet or other stage work). —*intr.* To serve as a choreographer. [Back-formation from CHOREOGRAPH.]

cho·re·og·ra·pher (kôr′ē-ŏg′rə-fər, kōr′-) *n.* One who creates, arranges, or directs dances, especially ballets.

cho·re·og·ra·phy (kôr′ē-ŏg′rə-fē, kōr′-) *n.* 1. The art of creating and arranging ballets or dances. 2. The steps and movements of a dance or ballet. **3.** The art and technique of dance notation. **4.** The art of dancing. [French *chorégraphie* : Greek *khoreios*, of a dance, from *khoros*, dance, CHORUS + -GRAPHY.] —**chor·e·o·graph·ic** (kôr′-ē-ə-grăf′ĭk, kōr′-) *adj.* —**cho·re·o·graph·i·cal·ly** *adv.*

chor·i·amb (kôr′ē-ămb′, kōr′-) *n., pl.* **-ambs.** Also **cho·ri·am·bus** (kôr′ē-ăm′bəs, kōr′-) *pl.* **-bi** (-bī′) or **-buses.** In Greek and Latin verse, a metrical foot consisting of a trochee followed by an iamb, much employed in Aeolic poetry and in the choric odes of tragedy. [Late Latin *choriambus*, from Greek *khoriambos* : *khoreios*, of a chorus, hence trochee, from *khoros*, CHORUS + *iambos*, IAMBUS.] —**chor·i·am·bic** *adj.*

chor·ic (kôr′ĭk, kōr′-, kŏr′-) *adj.* Of, pertaining to, or in the style of a singing or speaking chorus. Used with reference to Greek poetry or drama: *choric dance.* [Late Latin *choricus*, from Greek *khorikos*, from *khoros*, CHORUS.]

cho·rine (kôr′ēn′, kōr′-) *n. Slang.* A chorus girl.

cho·ri·on (kôr′ē-ŏn′, kōr′-) *n.* The outer membrane enclosing the embryo in reptiles, birds, and mammals. Compare **amnion.** [Greek *khorion*, afterbirth.] —**cho·ri·on·ic** *adj.*

chor·is·ter (kôr′ĭs-tər, kōr′-, kŏr′-) *n.* A choir singer; especially, a choirboy. [Learned respelling of Middle English *queristre*, from Norman French *cueristre* (unattested), from Medieval Latin *chorista*, from *chorus*, CHORUS.]

cho·ri·zo (chə-rē′zō, -sō) *n.* A spicy pork sausage, traditionally made in Spain. [Spanish.]

cho·rog·ra·phy (kə-rŏg′rə-fē) *n.* **1.** The technique of mapping a region or district. **2.** *Archaic.* A description or map of a region. [Latin *chōrographia*, from Greek *khōrographia* : *khōros*, place, + -GRAPHY.] —**cho·rog·ra·pher** *n.* —**cho·ro·graph·ic** (kôr′ə-grăf′ĭk, kōr′-), **cho·ro·graph·i·cal** *adj.* —**cho·ro·graph·i·cal·ly** *adv.*

cho·roid (kôr′oid′, kōr′-) *n.* The dark brown vascular coat of the eye between the sclera and the retina. —*adj.* Also **cho·ri·oid** (kôr′ē-oid′, kōr′-). *Anatomy.* **1.** Resembling the chorion. **2.** Resembling the corium. **3.** Of or pertaining to the choroid. [Greek *khoroeidēs*, scribal error for *khorioeidēs*, resembling an afterbirth : *khorion*, afterbirth, CHORION + -OID.]

choroid plexus *n.* A network of blood vessels in the ventricles of the brain that secretes cerebrospinal fluid.

cho·rol·o·gy (kə-rŏl′ə-jē) *n.* **1.** The study of the geographical distribution of plants and animals. **2.** The study of geographical features and their relationship within a particular region. [German *Chorologie* : Greek *khoros*, place + *-logie*, -LOGY.]

chor·tle (chôr′tl) *intr.v.* **-tled, -tling, -tles.** To chuckle throatily: *"He chortled in his joy"* (Lewis Carroll). —*n.* A snorting, joyful chuckle. [Blend of CHUCKLE and SNORT, coined by Lewis Carroll.] —**chor·tler** *n.*

cho·rus (kôr′əs, kōr′-) *n., pl.* **-ruses. 1.** *Music.* **a.** A composition in four or more parts written for a large number of singers. **b.** A song refrain in which the audience joins the soloist. **c.** A solo section in jazz based on the main melody and played by a member of the group. **d.** A body of singers who perform choral compositions. **e.** A body of singers or dancers who support the soloists and leading actors in an opera, musical, or revue. **2. a.** In drama or poetry recitation, a group of persons who speak or sing a given part or composition in unison. **b.** In Elizabethan drama, an actor who recites the prologue and epilogue to a play and sometimes comments on the action. **c.** The lines spoken by this actor. **3.** In Greek poetry and drama: **a.** A ceremonial dance performed to the singing of odes. **b.** The portion of a drama consisting of choric dance and ode. **c.** The body of actors whose choric performance comments upon and accompanies the action of the play. **4. a.** Any speech, song, or other utterance made in concert by many people. **b.** Any simultaneous utterance by a number of persons or animals: *the dawn bird chorus.* —**in chorus.** With simultaneous utterance; all together. —*v.* **chorused, -rusing, -ruses.** —*tr.* To sing or utter in chorus. —*intr.* To speak or sing in chorus. [Latin *chorus*, from Greek *khoros*, dance, chorus.]

chorus girl *n.* A girl who dances in a theatrical chorus.

chose¹. Past tense of **choose.**

chose² (shōz) *n. Law.* An item of personal property; a chattel. [French, "thing," from Old French, from Latin *causa*, thing, CAUSE.]

cho·sen (chō′zən). Past participle of **choose.** —*adj.* **1.** Selected or preferred above others. **2.** *Theology.* Elect. —*n., pl.* **chosen. 1.** One of the elect. **2.** The elect collectively. Preceded by *the.*

Cho·sen (chō′sĕn′) **1.** A name traditionally designating Korea since the 2nd millennium B.C. **2.** See **Korea.**

chosen people *pl.n.* The Israelites regarded as the people chosen to receive God's revelation. Nehemiah 9:8.

Choson. See **Korea.**

cho·ta (chō′tə) *adj. Indian.* Small; lesser in size or importance. [Hindi.]

chott. Variant of **shott.**

Chou or **Zhou** (jō). A dynasty that ruled China from *c.* 1027 to 221 B.C., enlarging the empire and promoting philosophy.

Chou En-Lai. See **Zhou En-Lai.**

chough (chŭf) *n.* A crowlike Old World bird of the genus *Pyrrhocorax*, especially *P. pyrrhocorax*, having black plumage and red legs. [Middle English *choge, chowe*, from Germanic, proably imitative; akin to Old English *cēo*, jackdaw, jay, Middle Dutch *cauwe*, chough (imitative).]

choux pastry (shōō) *n.* A light glossy pastry made with eggs, typi-

cally used for making eclairs. [Partial translation of French *pâte choux*, "cabbage dough" (from its round shape), plural of *chou*, cabbage.]

chow¹ (chou) *n.* Also **chow chow.** A heavy-set dog of a breed originating in China, having a long, dense, reddish-brown or black coat and a blackish tongue. [Pidgin English, perhaps from Cantonese *gao*, dog.]

chow² *n. Slang.* Food. [Pidgin English, probably from Cantonese *chaau*, to fry, cook.]

chow·chil·la (chou′chĭl′ə) *n.* The **auctioneer-bird** (see).

chow-chow (chou′chou′) *n.* A relish consisting of chopped vegetables pickled in mustard. [Pidgin English.]

chow·der (chou′dər) *n.* A thick soup or stew containing fish or shellfish, especially clams, and vegetables, often in a milk base. [French *chaudière*, stew pot, from Old French, from Late Latin *caldāria*, caldron, from Latin *caldārius*, suitable for heating, from *caldus, calidus*, hot.]

chow mein (chou′ mān′) *n.* A Chinese-style dish consisting of any of various combinations of stewed vegetables and meat, served over fried noodles. [Cantonese *chaau min* or Mandarin *chāo mian* : *chāo*, to shallow fry + *mian*, noodles.]

Chr. Christ; Christian.

chres·ard (krĕs′ərd) *n.* Water present in the soil and available for plant absorption. [Greek *khrēsis*, use, from *khrēsthai*, to use + *ardein†*, to water.]

chres·tom·a·thy (krĕs-tŏm′ə-thē) *n., pl.* **-thies.** A selection of literary passages, used in studying literature or a language. [Greek *khrēstomatheia*, "useful learning" : *khrēstos*, useful, from *khrēsthai*, to use + *-matheia*, learning, from *manthanein*, to learn.] —**chres·to·math·ic** (krĕs′tə-măth′ĭk) *adj.*

Chré·tien de Troyes (krā-tyăn′ də trwä′) (*c.* 1135–*c.* 1183). French poet and author of the earliest surviving Arthurian romances, including *Lancelot, Knight of the Barrow.*

chrism (krĭz′əm) *n.* **1.** A mixture of oil and balsam consecrated by a bishop and used for anointing in various church sacraments, such as baptism and confirmation. **2.** A sacramental anointing, especially upon confirmation into the Eastern Orthodox Church. [Middle English *crisme*, Old English *crisma*, from Late Latin *chrisma*, from Greek *khrisma*, ointment, from *khriein*, to anoint.] —**chris·mal** (krĭz′məl) *adj.* —**chris·ma·tion** (krĭz-mā′shən) *n.*

chris·om (krĭz′əm) *n.* **1.** A white cloth or robe worn by an infant at baptism. **2.** *Archaic.* An infant wearing a baptismal robe; a baby. [Middle English *crisom*, variant of *crisma*, CHRISM.]

Christ (krīst) *n. Abbr.* **Chr. 1.** The Anointed; the Messiah, as foretold by the prophets of the Old Testament. **2.** See **Jesus. 3.** *Christian Science.* "The divine manifestation of God, which comes to the flesh to destroy incarnate error" (Mary Baker Eddy). —*interj. Slang.* Used as an oath to express surprise, irritation, or the like. [Middle English *Crist*, Old English *Crist*, from Latin *Christus*, from Greek *Khristos*, "the anointed (one)," from *khriein*, to anoint.] —**Christ·li·ness** *n.* —**Christ·ly** *adj.*

Chris·ta·del·phi·an (krĭs′tə-dĕl′fē-ən) *n.* A member of a Christian sect, founded in the United States by Dr. John Thomas (1805–71) in the mid-19th century, that believes in the **millennium** (see) and rejects the doctrine of the Trinity. [From CHRIST + Greek *adelphos*, brother.] —**Chris·ta·del·phi·an** *adj.*

Christ·church¹ (krīst′chûrch′). Capital of Canterbury province in New Zealand, situated on the Banks Peninsula in the eastern part of South Island.

Christchurch². Coastal resort in Dorset in southern England, at the mouths of the Stour and Avon rivers.

christ·cross (krĭs′krôs′, -krŏs′) *n. Archaic.* The cross, used as a signature by someone who cannot write. [From *Christ's cross.*]

chris·ten (krĭs′ən) *tr.v.* **-tened, -tening, -tens. 1.** To baptize into a Christian church. **2.** To give a name to at baptism. **3.** To name and dedicate ceremonially: *christen a ship.* **4.** *Informal.* To use for the first time. [Middle English *cristen, cristnen*, Old English *cristnian*, from *Cristen*, CHRISTIAN.]

Chris·ten·dom (krĭs′ən-dəm) *n.* **1.** Christians collectively. **2.** The Christian world. **3.** *Obsolete.* Christianity. [Middle English *Cristendom*, Old English *Cristendōm* : *Cristen*, CHRISTIAN + -DOM.]

chris·ten·ing (krĭs′ə-nĭng) *n.* The Christian sacrament of baptism, including the bestowal of a name upon an infant.

Chris·tian (krĭs′chən) *adj.* **1.** Professing belief in Jesus as Christ or following the religion based on his teachings. **2.** Pertaining to or derived from Jesus or his teachings. **3.** Manifesting the qualities or spirit of Christ; Christlike. **4.** Pertaining to or characteristic of Christianity or its adherents. **5.** *Informal.* Neighborly, decent, or generous. —*n.* **1.** *Abbr.* **Chr.** One who professes belief in Jesus as the Christ or follows the religion based on his teachings. **2.** One who lives according to the teachings of Jesus. **3.** *Informal.* A kind or generous human being. [Middle English *Cristen, Christen*, Old English *Crīsten*, from Latin *Christiānus*, believer in Christ, from Greek *Khristianos*, from *Khristos*, CHRIST.] —**Chris·tian·ly** *adj. & adv.*

Chris·tian X (krĭs′chən) (1870–1947). King of Denmark (1912–47), notable for his passive resistance to the German occupation of his country during World War II. He rejected Nazi demands for anti-Jewish legislation (1942) and was kept in confinement until 1945.

Christian Brothers *pl.n.* An order of Roman Catholic laymen concerned with education of the poor. Also officially called "Brothers of the Christian Schools."

Christian era *n.* The period beginning with the birth of Jesus (con-

Christianity

CHRISTIANITY, THE WORLDWIDE RELIGION

Almost a quarter of the world's people embrace the teachings of Christ

The traditional basis of the Christian faith is that in Jesus Christ, God himself—in the person of his eternal son—became man, lived and taught on earth, died on the cross, and rose from the dead, all for the salvation of mankind. Today more than 1.2 billion people are professedly Christian and are associated, however loosely, with a Christian denomination. The belief that forgiveness of sins and eternal life are found only in Christ remains at the heart of the Christian allegiance.

Christianity arose in Roman-occupied Palestine 2,000 years ago, when Jesus was proclaimed by his disciples after his death as the awaited Messiah, or Deliverer, of his people. This claim, and repudiation of the need to accept Jewish Law completely to gain salvation, led to the final breach between Christians and Jews. Although rooted in the Old Testament, Christianity developed in the Greco-Roman world, which largely determined its thought and culture.

THE CRUCIFIXION *The 15th-century Italian artist Stefano da Zevio painted this death of Christ (above). On the left are Mary, the mother of Jesus, Mary Magdalene, and Mary, the mother of James and John. On the right, Roman soldiers cast lots for Christ's robes.*

THE RESURRECTION *The miracle of Christ's resurrection causes three of his disciples to faint and a fourth to cover his eyes. Painted by Piero della Francesca around 1460, the fresco (right) can be seen in his hometown of Borgo San Sepolcro in central Italy.*

---

ventionally in A.D. 1). Dates in this era are marked A.D., and dates before it, B.C. Also called "common era."

chris·ti·a·ni·a (krĭs′tə-ä′nē-ə, krĭs′chē-än′ē-ə) *n.* A ski turn in which the body is swung around with the skis parallel, to change direction or to make a stop. Also called "christie," "christy." [Norwegian, after CHRISTIANIA.]

Christiania. See **Oslo.**

Chris·ti·an·i·ty (krĭs′chē-ăn′ə-tē) *n., pl.* **-ties. 1.** The Christian religion, founded on the teachings of Jesus. **2.** Christians as a group; Christendom. **3.** The state or fact of being a Christian.

Chris·tian·ize (krĭs′chə-nīz′) *v.* **-ized, -izing, -izes.** —*tr.* **1.** To convert to Christianity. **2.** To instill with Christian principles and qualities. —*intr. Rare.* To adopt Christianity. —**Chris·tian·i·za·tion** *n.* —**Chris·tian·iz·er** *n.*

Christian name *n.* A name other than a surname given to a person at birth or when christened.

Christian Science *n. Abbr.* **C.S.** The church and the religious system founded by Mary Baker Eddy, emphasizing healing through spiritual means as an important element of Christianity, and teaching pure divine goodness as underlying the scientific reality of existence. Also officially called "Church of Christ, Scientist." —**Christian Scientist** *n.*

chris·tie (krĭs′tē) *n.* A ski turn, the **christiania** *(see).*

Chris·tie (krĭs′tē), **Dame Agatha Mary Clarissa** (1890–1976). British author of detective fiction. Her play *The Mousetrap* (1952) set a world record for the longest continuous run in one theater.

Chris·ti·na (krĭs-tē′nə) (1626–89). Swedish queen (1632–54; crowned 1644). The sole heir of King Gustavus II, she was crowned at the age of 18. Highly intelligent and a great patron of the arts, she confused much of Europe when she abdicated the throne, converted to Roman Catholicism, and spent most of the rest of her life in Rome.

Christ Jesus. See **Jesus.**

Christ·like (krīst′līk′) *adj.* Having the spiritual qualities or attributes of Christ. —**Christ·like·ness** *n.*

Christ·mas (krĭs′məs) *n.* **1.** December 25, a holiday celebrated by Christians as the anniversary of the birth of Jesus. **2.** The Christian church festival extending from December 24 (Christmas Eve) to January 6 (Epiphany). In this sense, also called "Christmastide." [Middle English *Cristesmasse,* Old English *Crīstesmæsse* : *Crīstes,* genitive of *Crīst,* CHRIST + *mæsse,* -MAS.]

Christmas berry *n.* A shrub, the **toyon** *(see).*

Christmas box *n.* In Britain, a small gift, usually of money, given at Christmas to those who provide services, such as postmen.

Christmas cactus *n.* A spineless, epiphytic cactus, *Zygocactus truncatus,* of South America, cultivated as a house plant for its showy red flowers. Also called "crab cactus."

Christmas disease *n.* A type of hemophilia that is caused by a deficiency of the plasma thromboplastin component. [After Stephen *Christmas,* the first patient in whom the disease was diagnosed and studied.]

Christmas Eve *n.* The evening or the day before Christmas.

Christmas fern *n.* The dagger fern *(see).*

Christmas Island¹. A coral atoll just north of the equator in the central North Pacific Ocean. It is a territory of Kiribati.

Christmas Island². An island territory of Australia, in the Indian Ocean southwest of Java. Phosphates are mined here.

Christmas pudding *n.* A **plum pudding** *(see).*

Christmas rose *n.* An evergreen plant, *Helleborus niger,* native to Europe, having white or pinkish-green flowers that bloom in late autumn or winter. Also called "hellebore."

Christmas stocking *n.* A stocking hung up by children on Christmas Eve, to be filled with presents by Santa Claus.

Christ·mas·sy, Christ·mas·y (krĭs′mə-sē) *adj. Informal.* Characteristic of Christmas.

Christ·mas·tide (krĭs′məs-tīd′) *n.* See **Christmas** (sense 2).

Christmas tree *n.* An evergreen or artificial tree decorated with lights and ornaments during the Christmas season.

Chris·tol·o·gy (krĭs-tŏl′ə-jē) *n., pl.* **-gies. 1.** The study of Christ's person, qualities, and deeds. **2.** Any doctrine or theory based on Christ or his teachings. —**Chris·to·log·i·cal** (krĭs′tə-lŏj′ĭ-kəl) *adj.*

Chris·to·pher (krĭs′tə-fər), **Saint** *(fl. c.* 3rd century A.D.). Christian martyr. Often depicted as a giant who converted to Christianity and thereafter devoted himself to carrying travelers across a river, he is

Christmas rose *A clump of Helleborus niger, or Christmas rose—so named because its flowers, which resemble wild roses, bloom in winter.*

the patron saint of travelers and, with the advent of the automobile, motorists.

Christ's-thorn (krīsts'thôrn') *n.* Any of several plants of the Near East, such as the jujube or *Paliurus spina-christi,* having spiny thorns and popularly believed to have been used for Christ's crown of thorns.

chris·ty (krĭs'tē) *n., pl.* **-ties.** A ski turn, the **christiania** *(see).*

chro·ma (krō'mə) *n.* That aspect of color in the Munsell color system by which a sample appears to differ from a gray of the same lightness or brightness. Chroma corresponds to **saturation** *(see)* of the perceived color. [Greek *khrōma,* color.]

chro·mate (krō'māt') *n.* A salt or ester of chromic acid. [CHROM(O)- + -ATE.]

chro·mat·ic (krō-măt'ĭk) *adj.* **1. a.** Pertaining to colors or color. **b.** Pertaining to color perceived to have a saturation greater than zero. **2.** *Music.* **a.** Of, pertaining to, or based on the chromatic scale. **b.** Pertaining to chords or harmonies based on nonharmonic notes. [Greek *khrōmatikos,* from *khrōma,* color, modification of musical note.] —**chro·mat·i·cal·ly** *adv.* —**chro·mat·i·cism** (krō-măt'ə-sĭz'əm) *n.*

chromatic aberration *n.* Color distortion in an image produced by a lens because of the focusing of light of different wavelengths by the lens at different points.

chro·ma·tic·i·ty (krō'mə-tĭs'ə-tē) *n.* The aspect of color that includes consideration of its dominant wavelength and purity.

chro·mat·ic·ness (krō-măt'ĭk-nĭs) *n. Physics.* Hue and saturation considered together as an attribute of color.

chro·mat·ics (krō-măt'ĭks) *n. Used with a singular verb.* The scientific study of color. Also called "chromatology." —**chro·ma·tist** (krō'mə-tĭst) *n.*

chromatic scale *n. Music.* A scale consisting of 12 semitones.

chro·ma·tid (krō'mə-tĭd) *n. Genetics.* Either of two daughter strands of a duplicated chromosome while still joined by a single centromere. [CHROMAT(O)- + -ID.]

chro·ma·tin (krō'mə-tən) *n. Genetics.* A complex of nucleic acids and proteins in the nucleus of a cell, characterized by intense staining with basic dyes. [CHROMAT(O)- + -IN.]

chromato-, chromat- *prefix.* Indicates: **1.** Color, staining, or pigmentation; for example, **chromatophore, chromatid. 2.** Chromatin; for example, **chromatolysis.** [Greek *khrōma* (stem *khrōmat-),* color.]

chro·mat·o·gram (krō-măt'ə-grăm') *n.* **1.** The absorbent column or strip of material containing the stratographically differentiated constituents separated from a solution or mixture by chromatography. **2.** A graph or graphlike diagram indicating quantitatively the substances present in a chromatographic analysis. [CHROMATO- + -GRAM.]

chro·ma·tog·ra·phy (krō'mə-tŏg'rə-fē) *n.* Any of several methods of separating chemical substances for analysis in which the substance is passed through a selectively absorbent medium such as treated filter paper *(paper chromatography)* or a column of powder *(column chromatography).* [CHROMATO- + -GRAPHY.] —**chro·ma·tog·ra·pher** *n.* —**chro·mat·o·graph·ic** (krō-măt'ə-grăf'ĭk, krō'mə-tə-) *adj.*

chro·ma·tol·o·gy (krō'mə-tŏl'ə-jē) *n.* Chromatics *(see).* —**chro·ma·to·log·i·cal** (krō'mə-tə-lŏj'ĭ-kəl), **chro·ma·to·log·ic** *adj.* —**chro·ma·tol·o·gist** (krō'mə-tŏl'ə-jĭst) *n.*

chro·ma·tol·y·sis (krō'mə-tŏl'ə-sĭs) *n. Biology.* The disintegration of chromatin within a cell. [CHROMATO- + -LYSIS.]

chro·mat·o·phore (krō-măt'ə-fôr', -fōr') *n. Biology.* A pigment-containing or pigment-producing cell; especially, a pigment-containing animal cell, as in certain lizards, that by expansion or contraction can change the overall color of the skin. Also called "pigment cell." [CHROMATO- + -PHORE.] —**chro·ma·to·phor·ic** (krō'mə-tə-fôr'ĭk, -fōr'ĭk) *adj.*

chrome (krōm) *n.* **1. a.** Chromium. **b.** Anything plated with a chromium alloy. **2.** A pigment containing chromium. —*tr.v.* **chromed, chroming, chromes. 1.** To plate with chromium. **2.** To tan or dye with a chromium compound. [French, from Greek *khrōma,* color (from the brilliant colors of the chromium compounds).]

-chrome *suffix.* Indicates pigment, color, or colored; for example, **autochrome.** [Greek *khrōma,* color.]

chrome alum *n.* A violet-red crystalline compound, $CrK(SO_4)_2 \cdot 12H_2O$, used in tanning, as a mordant, and in photography.

chrome green *n.* **1.** Any of a class of green pigments consisting of chrome yellow and iron blue in various proportions. **2.** Very dark yellowish green to moderate or strong green.

chrome red *n.* A light orange to red pigment consisting of basic lead chromate with varying proportions of $PbCrO_4$ and PbO.

chrome steel *n.* Any of various hard, rustproof steels that contain chromium. Also called "chromium steel."

chrome yellow *n.* Lead chromate, $PbCrO_4$, a yellow pigment often combined with lead sulfate, $PbSO_4$, for lighter hues.

chro·mic (krō'mĭk) *adj.* Of, pertaining to, or containing chromium, especially with valence 3.

chromic acid *n.* **1.** A corrosive, oxidizing acid, H_2CrO_4, known only in solution. **2.** The anhydride of this acid, CrO_3, a purplish crystalline material that reacts explosively with reducing agents and is used in chromium plating and to color glass and rubber.

chromic oxide *n.* A bright green, crystalline powder, Cr_2O_3, used in metallurgy and as a paint pigment.

chro·mi·nance (krō'mə-nəns) *n.* The quality of light that creates the sensation of color and is determined by comparing it with a reference source of the same brightness and of known chromaticity. [CHROMO- + LUMINANCE.]

chro·mite (krō'mīt') *n.* **1.** A widely distributed black to brownish-black chromium ore, $FeCr_2O_4$. **2.** A salt of chromous acid. [CHROM(O)- + -ITE.]

chro·mi·um (krō'mē-əm) *n. Symbol* **Cr** A lustrous, hard, steel-gray metallic element, resistant to tarnish and corrosion, and found primarily in chromite. It is used as a catalyst, to harden steel alloys, to produce stainless steels, in corrosion-resistant decorative platings, and as pigment in glass. Atomic number 24, atomic weight 51.996, melting point 1,890°C, boiling point 2,482°C, specific gravity 7.18, valences 2, 3, 6. [New Latin, from French *chrome,* CHROME.]

chromium steel *n.* Chrome steel.

chromo-, chrom- *prefix.* Indicates: **1.** Color, colored, staining, or pigment; for example, **chromophore, chromosome. 2.** Chromium or chromic acid; for example, **chromate.** [Greek *khrōma,* color.]

chro·mo·dy·nam·ics (krō'mō-dī-năm'ĭks) *n. Used with a singular verb.* The physics of the relationship between quarks and of the nature of the strong interaction, color, and the exchange of gluons. Also called "quantum chromodynamics."

chro·mo·gen (krō'mə-jən) *n.* **1.** *Chemistry.* A substance capable of chemical conversion into a pigment or dye. **2.** *Biology.* A strongly pigmented or pigment-generating organ, organelle, or microorganism. [CHROMO- + -GEN.] —**chro·mo·gen·ic** (krō'mə-jĕn'ĭk) *adj.*

chro·mo·lith·o·graph (krō'mō-lĭth'ə-grăf', -gräf') *n.* A colored print produced by chromolithography.

chro·mo·li·thog·ra·phy (krō'mō-lĭ-thŏg'rə-fē) *n.* The art or process of printing color pictures from a series of stone or zinc plates by lithography. —**chro·mo·li·thog·ra·pher** *n.* —**chro·mo·lith·o·graph·ic** (krō'mō-lĭth'ə-grăf'ĭk) *adj.*

chro·mo·mere (krō'mə-mîr') *n.* One of the serially aligned chromatin granules forming a chromosome. [CHROMO- + -MERE.]

chro·mo·ne·ma (krō'mə-nē'mə) *n., pl.* **-mata** (-mə-tə). The coiled threadlike core of a chromosome. [CHROMO- + Greek *nēma,* thread.] —**chro·mo·ne·mal** (krō'mə-nē'məl), **chro·mo·ne·mat·ic** (krō'mə-nī-măt'ĭk), **chro·mo·ne·mic** (krō'mə-nē'mĭk) *adj.*

chro·mo·phore (krō'mə-fôr', -fōr') *n.* A molecular group capable of selective light absorption resulting in coloration of aromatic compounds. [CHROMO- + -PHORE.] —**chro·mo·phor·ic** (krō'mə-fôr'ĭk, -fōr'ĭk) *adj.*

chro·mo·plast (krō'mə-plăst') *n. Botany.* A colored plastid containing a pigment other than or in addition to chlorophyll. [CHROMO- + -PLAST.]

chro·mo·pro·tein (krō'mō-prō'tēn', -prō'tē-ĭn) *n.* A substance consisting of a protein forming a complex with a pigmented group.

chro·mo·scope (krōm'mə-skōp') *n. Electronics.* A device used in sonar systems that displays information about objects detected by the sonar beam on a screen, in colors whose shade and intensity vary according to the density of the object.

chro·mo·some (krō'mə-sōm') *n.* Any of a number of threadlike structures in the cell nuclei of plants and animals, consisting of DNA, RNA, and protein, that carry genetic information in the form of genes and are responsible for the determination and transmission of hereditary characteristics. [CHROMO- + -SOME (body).] —**chro·mo·so·mal** (krō'mə-sō'məl) *adj.* —**chro·mo·so·mal·ly** *adv.*

chro·mo·sphere (krō'mə-sfîr') *n.* **1.** An incandescent, transparent layer of gas, primarily hydrogen, several thousand miles in depth, that lies above and surrounds the photosphere of the sun but is distinctly separate from the corona. **2.** A similar gaseous layer around a star. [CHROMO- (from its rosy color) + SPHERE.] —**chro·mo·spher·ic** (krō'mə-sfîr'ĭk, -sfĕr'ĭk) *adj.*

chro·mous (krō'məs) *adj.* Of, pertaining to, or containing chromium, especially with valence 2.

chro·myl (krō'məl) *adj.* Of or designating a chemical compound that contains the divalent radical CrO_2. [CHROM(O)- + -YL.]

chro·nax·y, chro·nax·ie (krō'năk'sē) *n., pl.* **-ies.** Also **chro·nax·i·a** (krō-năk'sē-ə). The time interval necessary to stimulate a muscle or nerve fiber electrically, using twice the minimum current needed to elicit a threshold response. [French *chronaxie* : CHRON(O)- + Greek *axia,* value, from *axios,* worthy.]

chron·ic (krŏn'ĭk) *adj.* **1.** Of long duration; continuing; constant. **2.** Prolonged or developing slowly. Said of certain diseases. Compare **acute. 3.** Subject to a disease or habit for a long time; inveterate. [French *chronique,* from Latin *chronicus,* from Greek *khronikos,* pertaining to time, from *khronos*†, time.] —**chron·i·cal·ly** *adv.* —**chro·nic·i·ty** (krō-nĭs'ə-tē) *n.*

chron·i·cle (krŏn'ĭ-kəl) *n.* A chronological record of events. —*tr.v.* **chronicled, -cling, -cles.** To record in, or in the form of, a chronicle. [Middle English *cronicle,* from Norman French, from Old French *cronique,* from Latin *chronica,* from Greek *(biblia) khronika,* "chronological (books)," from *khronikos,* chronological. See **chronic.**] —**chron·i·cler** (krŏn'ĭ-klər) *n.*

Chron·i·cles (krŏn'ĭ-kəlz) *pl.n. Abbr.* **Chron.** Either of two books in the Old Testament, I and II Chronicles.

chrono-, chron- *prefix.* Indicates time; for example, **chronaxy, chronometer.** [Greek *khronos,* time. See **chronic.**]

chron·o·bi·ol·o·gy (krŏn'ō-bī-ŏl'ə-jē) *n.* The branch of biology concerned with biorhythms.

chron·o·gram (krŏn'ə-grăm') *n.* **1.** The record produced by a chronograph. **2.** An inscribed phrase in which certain letters can be read as Roman numerals indicating a specific date. [CHRONO- + -GRAM.] —**chron·o·gram·mat·ic** (krŏn'ə-grə-măt'ĭk) *adj.* —**chron·o·gram·mat·i·cal·ly** *adv.*

chron·o·graph (krŏn′ə-grăf′, -gräf′) *n.* An instrument that registers or graphically records time intervals such as the duration of an event. [CHRONO- + -GRAPH.] —**chron·o·graph·ic** (krŏn′ə-grăf′ĭk) *adj.* —**chron·o·graph·i·cal·ly** *adv.*

chron·o·log·i·cal (krŏn′ə-lŏj′ĭ-kəl, krō′nə-) *adj.* Also **chron·o·log·ic** (-lŏj′ĭk). *Abbr.* **chron., chronol.** **1.** Arranged in order of time of occurrence. **2.** In accordance with or relating to chronology. —**chron·o·log·i·cal·ly** *adv.*

chronological age *n. Abbr.* **CA, C.A.** The number of years a person has lived, used in psychometrics as a comparison standard for various performance measures. Compare **mental age.**

chro·nol·o·gy (krə-nŏl′ə-jē) *n., pl.* **-gies.** *Abbr.* **chron., chronol.** **1.** The determination of dates and the sequence of events. **2.** The arrangement of events in time. **3.** A chronological list or table. [CHRONO- + -LOGY.] —**chro·nol·o·gist** *n.*

chro·nom·e·ter (krə-nŏm′ə-tər) *n.* An exceptionally precise clock, watch, or other timepiece. [CHRONO- + -METER.] —**chron·o·met·ric** (krŏn′ə-mĕt′rĭk, krō′nə-) —**chron·o·met·ri·cal** *adj.* —**chron·o·met·ri·cal·ly** *adv.*

chro·nom·e·try (krə-nŏm′ə-trē) *n.* The scientific measurement of time. [CHRONO- + -METRY.]

chro·non (krō′nŏn) *n.* A unit of time equal to about 10^{-24} second, the time taken for a photon to traverse an electron. [CHRONO- + -ON.]

chron·o·scope (krŏn′ə-skōp′, krō′nə-) *n.* An optical instrument for measuring minute time intervals. [CHRONO- + -SCOPE.] —**chron·o·scop·ic** (krŏn′ə-skŏp′ĭk, krō′nə-) *adj.*

–chroous *suffix.* Indicates colored; for example, **isochroous.** [Greek *khrōs,* flesh, complexion, color.]

chrys·a·lid (krĭs′ə-lĭd) *n. Entomology.* A chrysalis.
~*adj.* Also **chry·sal·i·dal** (krĭ-săl′ə-dəl) Pertaining to or resembling a chrysalis.

chrys·a·lis (krĭs′ə-lĭs) *n., pl.* **-lises** or **chrysalides** (krĭ-săl′ə-dēz′). **1.** *Entomology.* A pupa; especially, the pupa of a moth or butterfly, enclosed in a firm case or cocoon. **2.** A state of incomplete development; a transitional stage. [Latin *chrȳsallis,* from Greek *khrusallis,* the golden pupa of a butterfly, from *khrusos,* gold. See **chryso-**.]

chry·san·the·mum (krĭ-săn′thə-məm) *n.* **1.** Any of various plants of the genus *Chrysanthemum,* the cultivated forms of which have showy flowers of various sizes and colors, especially red, yellow, white, and brown. **2.** The flower of any of these plants. [Latin *chrȳsanthemum,* from Greek *khrusanthemon,* "gold flower" : CHRYS(O)- + *anthemon,* flower, from *anthos,* flower.]

chrys·a·ro·bin (krĭs′ə-rō′bən) *n.* A medicine obtained from a deposit found in the wood of the araroba tree and formerly used to treat certain chronic skin conditions. [CHRYS(O)- (from its golden color) + (AR)AROB(A) + -IN.]

chrys·el·e·phan·tine (krĭs′ĕl-ə-făn′tēn′, -tĭn′) *adj.* Made of or overlaid with gold and ivory. Said especially of ancient Greek statues. [Greek *khruselephantinos* : CHRYS(O)- + *elephantinos,* of ivory, from *elephas,* ivory (see **elephant**).]

chryso-, chrys– *prefix.* Indicates gold or the color of gold; for example, **chrysotile, chrysarobin.** [Greek *khrusos,* gold, from Semitic; akin to Hebrew *ḥarūz,* gold.]

chrys·o·ber·yl (krĭs′ə-bĕr′əl) *n.* A green to yellow vitreous mineral, $BeAl_2O_4$, used as a gemstone. [Latin *chrȳsobēryllus* : CHRYSO- + BERYL.]

chrys·o·lite (krĭs′ə-līt′) *n.* A mineral, **olivine** *(see).* [Middle English *crisolite* : CHRYSO- + -LITE.]

chrys·o·prase (krĭs′ə-prāz′) *n.* An apple-green chalcedony used as a gemstone. [Middle English *crisopase,* from Old French *crisopace, crisopras,* from Latin *chrȳsoprasus,* from Greek *khrusoprasos,* "gold green" : CHRYSO- + *prason,* leek.]

Chrys·o·stom (krĭs′əs-təm), **Saint John** (*c.* 347-407). Greek Church Father, archbishop of Constantinople (398-404). He earned the name of *Chrysostom* (golden-mouthed) by preaching in Antioch.

chrys·o·ther·a·py (krĭs′ō-thĕr′ə-pē) *n.* The treatment of certain diseases, especially rheumatoid arthritis, with gold compounds.

chrys·o·tile (krĭs′ə-tīl′) *n.* A fibrous mineral variety of serpentine used as a variety of commercial asbestos. Also called "white asbestos." [CHRYSO- + Greek *tilos,* something plucked, fine hair, from *tillein†,* to pluck.]

chthon·ic (thŏn′ĭk) *adj.* Also **chtho·ni·an** (thō′nē-ən). Pertaining to the gods and spirits of the underworld. [Greek *khthonios,* under the earth, from *khthōn,* earth.]

chub (chŭb) *n., pl.* **chubs** or collectively **chub.** **1.** Any of various freshwater fishes of the family Cyprinidae, related to the carps and minnows, especially a Eurasian species, *Leuciscus cephalus.* **2.** Any of various North American fishes, such as a whitefish of the genus *Coregonus* or a marine fish of the genus *Kyphosus.* [15th century : origin obscure.]

chub·by (chŭb′ē) *adj.* **-bier, -biest.** Rounded and plump. —See Synonyms at **fat.** [Probably from CHUB, from the plumpness of the fish.] —**chub·bi·ness** *n.*

Chuchiang. See **Zhujiang.**

chuck¹ (chŭk) *tr.v.* **chucked, chucking, chucks.** **1.** To pat or squeeze fondly or playfully, especially under the chin. **2.** *Informal.* To throw; toss. **3.** *Informal.* To throw out; discard. Often used with *out.* **4.** *Informal.* To expel forcibly; eject. Used with *out: chucking out the troublemakers.*
~*n.* **1.** An affectionate pat or squeeze under the chin. **2.** *Informal.* A throw, toss, or pitch. [Perhaps from Old French *choquer, chuquer,* to strike, SHOCK.]

chuck² *n.* **1.** A cut of beef extending from the neck to the ribs and including the shoulder blade. **2.** *Western U.S. Slang.* Food. **3.** A clamp with adjustable jaws that holds a tool, or the material being worked, in a machine such as a drill or a lathe. [Variant of CHOCK (wedge).]

chuck³ *intr.v.* **chucked, chucking, chucks.** To make a clucking sound. [Imitative.] —**chuck** *n.*

chuck⁴ *n. Informal.* A woodchuck.

chuck·le (chŭk′əl) *intr.v.* **-led, -ling, -les.** To laugh quietly or to oneself.
~*n.* A quiet laugh of mild amusement or satisfaction. [Probably frequentative of CHUCK (to make a clucking sound).]

chuck·le·head (chŭk′əl-hĕd′) *n. Informal.* A stupid and gauche person; a blockhead. —**chuck·le·head·ed** *adj.*

chuck wagon *n.* A wagon equipped with food and utensils, as in lumber camp.

chuck·wal·la (chŭk′wŏl′ə) *n.* A lizard, *Sauromalus obesus,* of the southwestern United States and Mexico, related to the iguana. [Mexican Spanish *chacahuala,* from Shoshonean *tcaxxwal.*]

chuck-will's-wid·ow (chŭk′wĭlz-wĭd′ō) *n.* A bird, *Caprimulgus carolinensis,* of the southern and central United States, resembling but larger than the whippoorwill. [Imitative of its song.]

chu·fa (chōō′fə) *n.* A sedge, *Cyperus esculentus,* native to warm regions of the Old World, having edible, nutlike tubers. [Spanish, fluff, nonsense, from Old Spanish, from *chufar, chuflar,* to hiss at, laugh at, from Vulgar Latin *sufilāre* (unattested), variant of Latin *sībilāre,* to whistle at, hiss down.]

chuff (chŭf) *n.* A short, usually repeated, puffing sound.
~*intr.v.* **chuffed, chuffing, chuffs.** To make a regular puffing sound. Used especially of steam trains. [Imitative.]

chug (chŭg) *n.* A dull, low sound, usually short and repeated, made by or as if by a laboring engine.
~*intr.v.* **chugged, chugging, chugs.** **1.** To make such sounds. **2.** To travel or move while making such sounds. Often used with *along.* [Imitative.]

chu·kar (chə-kär′) *n.* An Old World partridge, *Alectoris graeca,* having a black-striped brownish plumage and red legs and bill. [Hindi *chakor,* from Sanskrit *cakōra.*]

Chuk·chi (chōōk′chē) *n., pl.* **-chis** or collectively **Chukchi.** Also **Chuk·chee,** *pl.* **-chees** or collectively **Chukchee.** **1.** A member of a Mongoloid people of northeastern Siberia. **2.** The language of this people, noted for being pronounced differently by men and women.

Chukiang. See **Zhujiang.**

chuk·ka (chŭk′ə) *n.* A short, ankle-length boot, usually made of suede, having two pairs of eyelets. Also called "chukka boot." [From CHUKKER (polo players wear a kind of chukka boot).]

chuk·ker, chuk·kar (chŭk′ər) *n.* One of the periods of play, lasting 7 to 7½ minutes, in a polo match. [Hindi *cakkar,* circle, turn, from Sanskrit *cakra-,* wheel.]

chum¹ (chŭm) *n.* An intimate friend or companion.
~*v.* **chummed, chumming, chums.** —*intr.* To be or become an intimate friend of. Often used with *up* or *up with.* —*tr. Scottish.* To accompany; escort. [17th century : Oxford University slang, probably from *chamber fellow,* "roommate."]

chum² *n.* Bait usually consisting of oily fish ground up and scattered on the water.
~*intr.v.* **chummed, chumming, chums.** To fish with chum. [Origin unknown.]

chum·my (chŭm′ē) *adj.* **-mier, -miest.** *Informal.* Intimate; friendly; amicable. —See Synonyms at **familiar.** —**chum·mi·ly** *adv.* —**chum·mi·ness** *n.*

chump (chŭmp) *n.* **1.** *Informal.* A blockhead; a dolt. **2.** A blunt end of something, such as a piece of wood. [Probably a blend of CHUNK and LUMP or STUMP.]

chump chop *n. British.* A chop, especially of pork or lamb, cut from between the leg and loin.

Ch'ung-ch'ing, Chungking. See **Chongqing.**

chunk (chŭngk) *n.* **1.** A thick mass or piece of something: *a chunk of bread.* **2.** *Informal.* A fair or substantial amount. [Probably a nasalized variant of CHUCK (cut of beef).]

chunk·y (chŭng′kē) *adj.* **-ier, -iest.** **1.** Short; thickset; stocky. **2.** In chunks. **3.** Being or knitted with thick wool: *a chunky sweater.* —**chunk·i·ness** *n.*

church (chûrch) *n. Abbr.* **Ch., C., ch., c.** **1. Church.** The body of all Christians throughout the world. **2.** A building for public worship, especially Christian worship. **3.** A congregation. **4.** Public divine worship in a church; a religious service. **5.** *Usually* **Church.** A specified Christian denomination: *the Presbyterian Church.* **6.** Ecclesiastical power as distinguished from secular power. **7.** The clerical profession; the clergy. **8.** *Christian Science.* "The structure of Truth and Love" (Mary Baker Eddy). See feature, next page.
~*tr.v.* **churched, churching, churches.** To conduct church services for; especially, to perform a religious service for (a woman after childbirth).
~*adj.* **1.** Of or pertaining to the church; ecclesiastical. **2.** *Chiefly British.* Being a member of the Anglican church. Compare **chapel.** [Middle English *chirche,* Old English *cirice,* from West Germanic *kirika* (unattested), from Late Greek *kurikon,* variant of *(dōma) kuriakon,* the Lord's (house), from Greek *kuriakos,* of the Lord, from *kurios,* lord.]

church·go·er (chûrch′gō′ər) *n.* One who attends church regularly. —**church·go·ing** *adj. & n.*

Church·ill¹ (chûr′chĭl). River, 1,610 kilometers (1,000 miles) long,

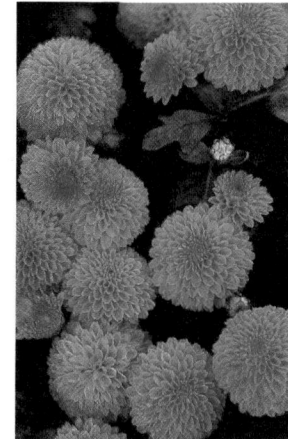

chrysalis *The intermediate stage between caterpillar and adult in the life cycle of butterflies and moths. The metamorphosis is usually completed within a protective case, or cocoon. When it has taken place, the adult may split the case and chew its way out or it may emerge after secreting a fluid that softens the covering.*

chrysanthemum *Found in temperate and northern regions, the chrysanthemum genus contains more than 200 species and a large number of garden varieties. The blooms vary in shape and formation, from a daisylike flower to a pompom of tightly packed petals such as the variety "Fairie" shown here.*

church

A CHRISTIAN HOUSE OF WORSHIP

Three main designs: basilica, Greek cross, and cruciform

The earliest churches were private homes where the first Christians, a small, often persecuted minority, met to worship. With the spread of Christianity such meetings became more common. Private homes were adapted into community houses for use as meeting places. Only after the Roman emperor Constantine officially recognized Christianity in A.D. 313 were the first churches specifically built as places for public Christian worship.

Naturally, early designs were modeled on existing public halls or Roman basilicas. The basilican plan consists of a nave flanked on each side by one or two aisles. Rows of columns separate the aisles from the nave. The aisles are lower in height than the nave, so the nave can be lit by rows of windows built into its

upper walls (the clerestory, or clear story).

Crucifixion was a common form of execution for criminals in ancient Rome so the cross did not quickly become a Christian symbol—it would have seemed as gruesome a choice as a hangman's noose might today. The crucifix did eventually emerge from these shadows, and buildings were erected to reflect its powerful symbolism.

The eastern remnant of imperial Rome became the empire of Byzantium and the Greek cross plan of architecture originated there. Churches of this type have a square, domed central area from which four wings extend.

The Latin cross, or cruciform shape, that was adopted elsewhere has different proportions. The

longest arm of the Latin cross is the nave, which usually points west. Shorter transepts to the north and south cross the top of the nave and the short eastern arm is extended as the chancel. The complete structure is truly cruciform.

There are round churches based on the original basilican plan and others based on the rectangular design of the mosque al-Aqsa in Jerusalem. When the Crusaders took Jerusalem in 1099, the mosque was believed to be the Temple of Solomon and replicas were constructed by the powerful Knights Templars all over Europe.

In the 20th century architects have not been constrained by any particular design but have used a variety of plans.

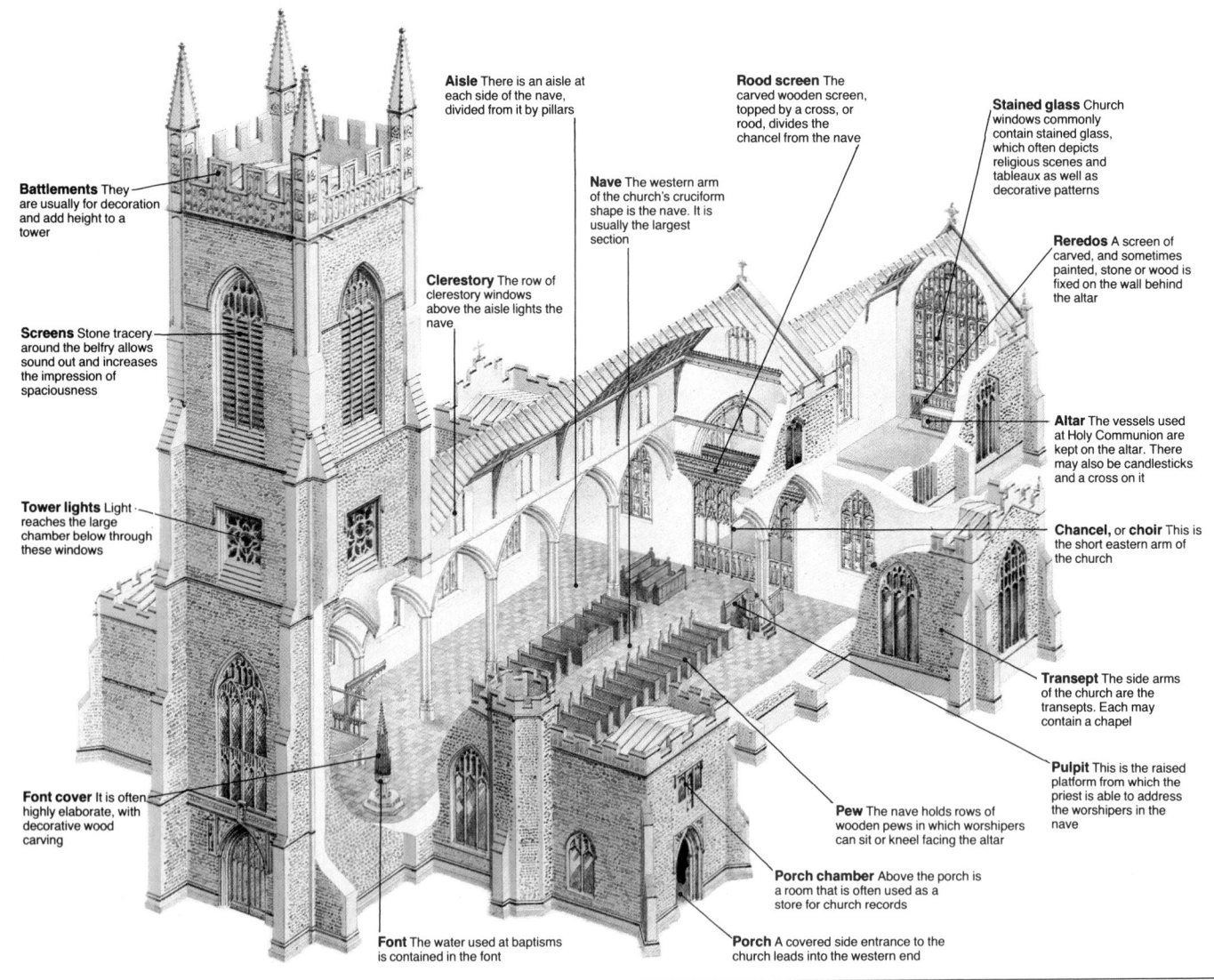

Aisle There is an aisle at each side of the nave, divided from it by pillars

Rood screen The carved wooden screen, topped by a cross, or rood, divides the chancel from the nave

Stained glass Church windows commonly contain stained glass, which often depicts religious scenes and tableaux as well as decorative patterns

Battlements They are usually for decoration and add height to a tower

Nave The western arm of the church's cruciform shape is the nave. It is usually the largest section

Reredos A screen of carved, and sometimes painted, stone or wood is fixed on the wall behind the altar

Clerestory The row of clerestory windows above the aisle lights the nave

Screens Stone tracery around the belfry allows sound out and increases the impression of spaciousness

Altar The vessels used at Holy Communion are kept on the altar. There may also be candlesticks and a cross on it

Tower lights Light reaches the large chamber below through these windows

Chancel, or choir This is the short eastern arm of the church

Transept The side arms of the church are the transepts. Each may contain a chapel

Pulpit This is the raised platform from which the priest is able to address the worshipers in the nave

Font cover It is often highly elaborate, with decorative wood carving

Pew The nave holds rows of wooden pews in which worshipers can sit or kneel facing the altar

Porch chamber Above the porch is a room that is often used as a store for church records

Font The water used at baptisms is contained in the font

Porch A covered side entrance to the church leads into the western end

in western Canada. It flows from Saskatchewan to Hudson Bay.

Churchill². River in eastern Canada. It flows some 970 kilometers (600 miles) through Labrador into the Atlantic Ocean.

Churchill, Lord Randolph Henry Spencer (1849–95). British statesman and father of Winston Churchill. He was leader of the so-called Fourth Party, a group of Conservative M.P.'s who pressed for social and constitutional reform.

Churchill, Sir Winston Leonard Spencer (1874–1965). British statesman and author. He became a Conservative M.P. (1900), but joined the Liberals over tariff reform (1904). He held office in several Liberal governments and Lloyd George's coalition government, but rejoined the Conservative Party (1924). As Chancellor of the Exchequer (1924–29) he forcefully opposed the General Strike

(1926). With the rise of Nazism in Germany he urged British rearmament and on the outbreak of war (1939) became first lord of the admiralty and succeeded Neville Chamberlain as prime minister, heading the coalition government (1940–45). He was returned as prime minister (1951) and knighted (1953). He published several volumes including *The Second World War* (1948–53) and was awarded the Nobel Prize for literature (1953). He resigned as prime minister in 1955, subsequently publishing his major study, *A History of the English Speaking Peoples* (1956–58).

church·ly (chûrch′lē) *adj.* Of, pertaining to, or fit for a church. —**church·li·ness** *n.*

church·man (chûrch′mən) *n., pl.* **-men** (-mĭn). **1.** A clergyman; a priest. **2.** A male member of a church. **—church·man·ly** *adj.* **—church·man·ship** *n.*

Church militant *n.* The Church on earth viewed as fighting against evil. Compare **Church triumphant.**

Church of Christ, Scientist *n.* The official name of the Christian Science Church. See **Christian Science.**

Church of England *n. Abbr.* **C. of E.** The episcopal and liturgical national church of England, which withdrew its recognition of papal authority in the 16th century. See **Anglican Communion.**

Church of Jesus Christ of Latter-day Saints *n.* The official name of the Mormon Church. See **Mormon.**

Church of Rome *n.* The **Roman Catholic Church** *(see).*

Church of Scotland *n.* The established Presbyterian church in Scotland.

Church Slavonic *n.* The literary language of Slavonic manuscripts written after the early 11th century, still used as a liturgical language in the Eastern Orthodox Church.

church text *n. Printing.* **Black letter** *(see).*

Church triumphant *n.* That part of the Church that has overcome evil and reached heaven. Compare **Church militant.**

church·war·den (chûrch′wôrd′n) *n.* **1.** In the Anglican Church, a lay officer chosen annually by the vicar or the congregation to handle the secular and legal affairs of the parish. **2.** One of two elected chief lay officers of the vestry in the Episcopal Church. **3.** A clay pipe with a long stem.

church·wom·an (chûrch′wo͝om′ən) *n., pl.* **-women** (-wĭm′ĭn). A female member of a church.

church·yard (chûrch′yärd′) *n.* A yard adjacent to a church, often used as a graveyard.

chu·rin·ga (chə-rĭng′gə) *n., pl.* **-gas** or collectively **churinga.** An Australian aboriginal sacred amulet. [From a native Australian language.]

churl (chûrl) *n.* **1.** A rude, boorish person. **2.** A miser; a niggard. **3. a.** A **ceorl** *(see).* **b.** A medieval English peasant. [Middle English *churl, cherl,* man, husband, Old English *ceorl,* man, free man of the lowest rank, from West Germanic *kerl-* (unattested), man.]

churl·ish (chûr′lĭsh) *adj.* **1. a.** Rude; surly. **b.** Boorish. **2.** Difficult to work: *churlish soil.* **—churl·ish·ly** *adv.* **—churl·ish·ness** *n.*

churn (chûrn) *n.* **1.** A vessel or device in which cream or whole milk is agitated to separate the oily globules used to make butter. **2.** *British.* A large can used to carry milk.

∼v. **churned, churning, churns.** *—tr.* **1.** To stir or agitate (milk or cream) in a churn in order to make butter. **2.** To make by the agitation of milk or cream: *churn butter.* **3.** To shake or agitate vigorously. *—intr.* **1.** To make butter by operating a churn. **2.** To move with great agitation: *My stomach churned at the prospect.* **—churn out.** To produce in large quantities, as if mechanically and usually at the expense of quality. [Middle English *chirne, cherine,* Old English *cyrin, cyrn,* from Germanic *kernjōn* (unattested).] **—churn·er** *n.*

churn·ing (chûr′nĭng) *n.* The amount of butter churned at one time.

churr (chûr) *n.* The sharp, whirring or trilling sound made by some insects and birds. [Imitative.] **—churr** *v.*

chute (sho͞ot) *n.* **1.** An inclined trough, passage, or channel down which things may pass. **2.** A waterfall or rapid. **3.** *Informal.* A parachute. [French, a fall, from Old French *cheoite,* feminine past participle of *cheoir,* to fall, from Vulgar Latin *cadēre* (unattested), from Latin *cadere.*]

chut·ney (chŭt′nē) *n.* A pungent relish made of fruit, vinegar, spices, and herbs. [Hindi *caṭnī*†.]

chutz·pah (KHo͝ots′pə) *n. Slang.* Brazenness; gall. [Yiddish.]

Chu·vash (cho͞o-väsh′) *n., pl.* **-vashes** or collective **Chuvash. 1.** A member of a Tatar people living chiefly in the Chuvash A.S.S.R. **2.** The Turkic language of this people. [Russian, from Chuvash *čă-vaš,* akin to Turkish *yavaş,* gentle.]

Chuvash Autonomous Soviet Socialist Republic. A part of the Russian Soviet Federative Socialist Republic, in the west-central U.S.S.R. Its capital is Cheboksary.

chyle (kīl) *n.* A thick white or pale-yellow fluid, consisting of lymph and finely emulsified fat, that is taken up by the lacteals from the intestine in digestion. [Latin *chȳlus,* juice, from Greek *khulos,* from *khein,* to pour.] **—chy·la·ceous** (kī-lā′shəs), **chy·lous** (kī′ləs) *adj.*

chy·lo·mic·ron (kī′lō-mī′krŏn′) *n.* Any of the microscopic fat particles present in the blood after fat has been digested and absorbed from the small intestine. [From *chylo-,* CHYLE + Greek *mikron,* particle, from *mikros,* small.]

chyme (kīm) *n.* The thick semifluid mass of partly digested food in the stomach that passes into the duodenum. [Late Latin *chȳmus,* from Greek *khumos,* juice, from *khein,* to pour. See **chyle.**] **—chy·mous** (kī′məs) *adj.*

chy·mo·sin (kī′mə-sĭn) *n.* An enzyme, **rennin** *(see).* [CHYM(E) + -OS(E) + -IN.]

chy·mo·tryp·sin (kī′mə-trĭp′sĭn) *n.* A protein-digesting enzyme secreted by the pancreas in an inactive form, which is activated by trypsin. [CHYM(E) + TRYPSIN.]

Ci curie.

C.I. Channel Islands.

CIA Central Intelligence Agency.

Cia·no (chä′nō), **Conte Galeazzo** (1903–44). Italian fascist statesman. He became an influential figure after marrying Benito Mussolini's daughter Edda in 1930. Having urged Italy to join the Axis powers in World War II, he later favored a separate peace with the Allies and was among those who forced Mussolini's resignation. He was captured, tried for treason, and executed on Mussolini's order.

ciao (chou) *interj.* Used informally to express greeting or farewell. [Italian.]

Ciar·di (chär′dē), **John Anthony** (1916–86). U.S. poet and author. In his clear, simple poems and works of literary criticism, including *How Does a Poem Mean?* (1960), he was concerned with making poetry more accessible to adults and children. He also produced a much-heralded translation of Dante's *Divine Comedy* (1954–70).

ci·bo·ri·um (sĭ-bôr′ē-əm, sĭ-bōr′-) *n., pl.* **-boria** (-bôr′ē-ə, -bōr′ē-ə) A covered receptacle for holding the consecrated wafers of the Eucharist. [Medieval Latin *cibōrium,* from Latin, drinking vessel, from Greek *kibōrion,* the seed vessel of the Indian lotus, hence, a cup made from this, probably from Semitic.]

ci·ca·da (sĭ-kā′də, -kä′də) *n., pl.* **-das** or **-dae** (-dē′). Any of various insects of the family Cicadidae, having a broad head, membranous wings, and, in the male, a pair of resonating organs that produce a characteristic high-pitched, droning sound. [Latin *cicāda,* probably of Mediterranean origin.]

cic·a·trix (sĭk′ə-trĭks′, sĭ-kā′trĭks) *n., pl.* **cicatrices** (sĭk′ə-trī′sēz, sĭ-kā′trə-sēz′). Also **cic·a·trice** (sĭk′ə-trəs). **1.** Recently formed connective tissue on a healing wound; scar tissue. **2.** *Botany.* A scar left where a leaf or a branch has been detached. [Middle English *cicatrice,* from Latin *cicātrix*†.] **—cic·a·tri·cial** (sĭk′ə-trĭsh′əl), **ci·cat·ri·cose** (sĭ-kăt′rĭ-kōs′) *adj.*

cic·a·trize (sĭk′ə-trīz′) *v.* **-trized, -trizing, -trizes.** *—tr.* To heal by the forming of a scar. *—intr.* To become healed or closed by the forming of a scar.

cic·e·ly (sĭs′ə-lē) *n., pl.* **-lies.** See **sweet cicely.** [Middle English *ciceli, seseli,* from Latin *seselis,* from Greek *seselis*†.]

cic·e·ro (sĭs′ə-rō′) *n., pl.* **-ros.** *Printing.* A unit of measurement for type, slightly larger than the pica, used in Europe. [After an edition (1458) of Cicero, in which it was first used.]

Cic·e·ro (sĭs′ə-rō′), **Marcus Tullius** (106–43 B.C.). Roman orator and statesman, a leading figure during the last years of the republic. **—Cic·e·ro·ni·an** (sĭs′ə-rō′nē-ən) *adj.*

cic·e·ro·ne (sĭs′ə-rō′nē) *n., pl.* **-nes** or **-ni** (-nē). A guide who conducts sightseers. [Italian *cicerone,* originally "a learned antiquarian," from *Cicerone,* CICERO.]

cich·lid (sĭk′lĭd) *n.* Any of various tropical freshwater fishes of the family Cichlidae, many of which are popular as aquarium fish.

∼adj. Of or belonging to the Cichlidae. [New Latin *Cichlidae,* from *Cichla,* type genus, from Greek *kikhlē,* thrush, also, a sea fish.]

ci·cis·be·o (chē′chĭz-bā′ō) *n. pl.* **-bei** (-bā′-ē′). *Italian.* The male lover or companion of a married woman, especially in the 18th century. [Italian : origin obscure.]

Cid, The. See **El Cid.**

C.I.D. Criminal Investigation Department (Scotland Yard).

-cide *suffix.* Indicates: **1.** Killer of; for example, **insecticide. 2.** Murder or killing of; for example, **genocide, regicide.** [French, from Latin *-cīda,* killer, and *-cīdium,* killing, from *caedere,* to kill.]

ci·der (sī′dər) *n.* Also *chiefly British* **cy·der.** The juice pressed from apples or, formerly, from other fruit, and used to produce a beverage or vinegar. [Middle English *cidre, sidre,* from Old French *sidre, cisdre,* from Medieval Latin *sīcera,* from Greek (Septuagint) *sikera,* strong drink, from Hebrew *shēkār.*]

c.i.f. cost, insurance, freight.

cig (sĭg) *n. Informal.* A cigarette.

ci·gar (sĭ-gär′) *n.* A small, compact roll of tobacco leaves prepared for smoking. [Spanish *cigarro.*]

cig·a·rette (sĭg′ə-rĕt′) *n.* A small roll of finely cut tobacco for smoking, usually enclosed in a wrapper of thin paper. [French *cigarette,* diminutive of *cigare,* from Spanish *cigarro,* CIGAR.]

cigarette holder *n.* A thin tube with a mouthpiece for holding a cigarette while smoking it.

cigarette paper *n.* A thin piece of gummed paper in which tobacco is rolled to make a cigarette.

cig·a·ril·lo (sĭg′ə-rĭl′ō) *n., pl.* **-los.** A small, narrow cigar. [Spanish, diminutive of *cigarro,* CIGAR.]

ci·lan·tro (sĭ-lăn′trō) *n.* The parsleylike leaves of fresh coriander, used in Oriental cookery. [Spanish, coriander, from Late Latin *coliandrum,* from Latin *coriandrum,* CORIANDER.]

cil·i·a (sĭl′ē-ə) *pl.n. Singular* **-ium** (-ē-əm). **1.** Microscopic hairlike growths extending from the surface of a cell or organism. Their rhythmical beating causes movement of the cell or of the surrounding medium. **2.** The eyelashes. [New Latin, plural of *cilium,* eyelash, hairlike process, from Latin, the lower eyelid.]

cil·i·ar·y (sĭl′ē-ĕr′ē) *adj.* **1.** Of, pertaining to, or resembling cilia. **2.** Of or pertaining to the ciliary body.

ciliary body *n.* The thickened part of the vascular tunic of the eye that connects the choroid with the iris.

cil·i·ate (sĭl′ē-ĭt, -āt′) *adj.* Also **cil·i·at·ed** (sĭl′ē-ā′tĭd). **1.** Having cilia. **2.** Of or belonging to the protozoan class Ciliata.

∼n. Any of various protozoans of the class Ciliata, having numerous cilia. [New Latin *Ciliata,* plural of *ciliatus,* having cilia, from CILIA.]

cil·ice (sĭl′ĭs) *n.* **1.** A coarse cloth; haircloth. **2.** A garment made from this cloth. [French, from Latin *cilicium,* from Greek *kilikion,* coarse cloth made of Cilician goats' hair, from *Kilikia,* Cilicia.]

Ci·li·cian Gates (sə-lĭsh′ən). *Turkish* **Kü·lek Bo·ğa·zi** (kyo͞o-lĕk′ bō-gä′zē). Mountain pass through the Taurus Mountains of southern Turkey.

cil·i·o·late (sĭl′ē-ə-lāt′) *adj.* Having minute cilia. [New Latin *ciliolum,* minute cilium, from *cilium,* singular of CILIA.]

churn *This type of butter churn, commonly called a tumbling churn because of its end-over-end motion, was developed in 1880. The slatted frame, called a diaphragm, was set loosely inside the barrel to increase the agitation of the cream.*

cicada *Male cicadas attract females by means of special drumlike organs at the base of their abdomens. Muscles vibrate the stretched membranes of these organs to produce a shrill noise. The sound is related to temperature—the hotter the weather, the louder the noise.*

cichlid *Because of their bright colors, cichlids are popular in aquariums. They are found mainly in slow-moving rivers and in lakes in Africa and South America. This is* Hemichromis bimaculatus *of Lake Tanganyika.*

cinquefoil *So called because of its five-lobed leaves, this plant was used as a medicine by the ancient Greeks. In the Middle Ages in Britain, it was hung over doorways to ward off witches.*

Ci·ma·bu·e (chē'mä-bōō'ā), **Giovanni Cenni de Peppi** (*c.* 1240–*c.* 1302). Florentine artist, considered the originator of the Italian Renaissance in painting. He worked within the tradition of Byzantine art, but introduced a new expressiveness and sense of three-dimensional reality.

cim·ba·lom (sĭm'bə-ləm) *n.* A type of dulcimer, used especially in Hungary. [Hungarian, from Italian (see **cembalo**).]

ci·met·i·dine (sī-mĕt'ĭ-dēn', -dīn') *n.* A drug that reduces acid secretion in the stomach and is used to treat peptic ulcers and other digestive disorders.

ci·mex (sī'mĕks') *n., pl.* **cimices** (sĭm'ĭ-sēz'). Any insect of the genus *Cimex,* which includes the bedbugs. [New Latin *Cimex,* from Latin *cīmex*†, bedbug.]

Cim·me·ri·an (sĭ-mîr'ē-ən) *adj.* Gloomy; dark.
~*n.* One of a mythical people described by Homer as inhabiting a land of perpetual darkness.

C in C, C-in-C commander in chief.

cinch (sĭnch) *n.* **1.** A girth for a pack or saddle. **2.** A firm grip. **3.** *Slang.* **a.** Something easy to accomplish. **b.** A certainty.
~*v.* **cinched, cinching, cinches.** —*tr.* **1.** To put a saddle girth on. **2.** To get a tight grip on. **3.** To make certain of: *cinch a victory.* —*intr.* To tighten a saddle girth. Often used with *up.* [Spanish *cincha,* "girdle," from Latin *cingula,* from *cingere,* to gird.]

cin·cho·na (sĭng-kō'nə, sĭn-chō'nə) *n.* **1.** Any of various trees and shrubs of the genus *Cinchona,* native to South America, whose bark yields quinine and other medicinal alkaloids. **2.** The dried bark of any of these trees. In this sense, also called "Peruvian bark." **3.** Any drug derived from this bark. [New Latin, after Francisca Henriquez de Ribera, countess of *Chinchón* (1576–1639), who introduced it into Europe after recovering from a fever through the use of cinchona bark.] **—cin·chon·ic** (sĭng-kŏn'ĭk, sĭn-chŏn'ĭk) *adj.*

cin·cho·nine (sĭng'kə-nēn') *n.* An alkaloid, $C_{19}H_{22}N_2O$, derived from the bark of various cinchona trees and used as an antimalarial agent.

cin·cho·nism (sĭng'kə-nĭz'əm) *n.* A pathological condition resulting from an overdose of cinchona, marked by deafness, headache, giddiness, and dimming eyesight.

Cin·cin·nat·i (sĭn'sə-năt'ē, -năt'ə). A city of extreme southwestern Ohio, on the Ohio River. Founded in 1788, the city is a river port and an important industrial, commercial, and cultural center for an extensive area in southern Ohio and northern Kentucky.

Cin·cin·na·tus (sĭn'sə-năt'əs), **Lucius Quinctius** (*c.* 519–*c.* 438 B.C.). A peasant farmer, twice called to assume the dictatorship of Rome during crises. He was regarded as a model of simple virtue, especially because of his refusal to accept permanent dictatorship.

cinc·ture (sĭngk'chər) *n.* **1.** A belt; a girdle. **2.** Something that encompasses or surrounds.
~*tr.v.* **cinctured, -turing, -tures.** To gird or encompass. [Latin *cinctūra,* girdle, from *cingere* (past participle *cinctus*), to gird.]

cin·der (sĭn'dər) *n.* **1.** A burned or partly burned substance, such as coal or wood, that is not reduced to ashes, but is incapable of further combustion. **2.** A partly charred substance that can burn further, but without flame; an ember. **3. cinders.** Ashes. **4. cinders.** *Geology.* Volcanic **scoria** *(see).* **5.** *Metallurgy.* **Slag** *(see).*
~*tr.v.* **cindered, -dering, -ders.** To burn or reduce to cinders. [Middle English *cinder, sinder,* Old English *sinder,* (iron) slag, dross.] **—cin·der·y** *adj.*

Cin·der·el·la (sĭn'də-rĕl'ə) *n.* **1.** A person or thing that achieves recognition after a period of obscurity. **2.** A person or thing whose worth or beauty remains unrecognized. [After the fairy-tale character who, with the help of a fairy godmother, escaped from a life of drudgery and married a prince.]

cine- *prefix.* Indicates motion pictures or film-making; for example, **cinecamera.**

cin·e·aste (sĭn'ē-ăst) *n.* A person who is enthusiastic and knowledgable about motion pictures; a film buff. [French : CINE- + *enthousiaste,* enthusiast.]

cin·e·cam·e·ra (sĭn'ə-kăm'rə) *n.* A motion-picture camera.

cin·e·ma (sĭn'ə-mə) *n.* **1.** A motion picture. **2.** A motion-picture theater. **3. a.** Motion pictures collectively. **b.** The motion-picture industry. **4.** The art of making motion pictures. [French *cinéma,* shortened from *cinématographe,* CINEMATOGRAPH.]

Cin·e·ma·Scope (sĭn'ə-mə-skōp') *n.* A trademark for a process using an anamorphic lens to create films that can be projected onto a wide, curved screen.

cin·e·ma·theque (sĭn'ə-mə-tĕk') *n.* A small theater showing experimental, artistic, and less commercially successful films. [French, originally "film library" : CINEMA + *bibliothèque,* library.]

cin·e·mat·ic (sĭn'ə-măt'ĭk) *adj.* **1.** Of, in, or relating to motion pictures: *her stage and cinematic performances; cinematic art.* **2.** Peculiar to or characteristic of motion pictures: *a vivid, highly cinematic movie.* **—cin·e·mat·i·cal·ly** *adv.*

cin·e·mat·o·graph (sĭn'ə-măt'ə-grăf, -gräf) *n. British.* A camera or projector used in cinematography. [French *cinématographe* : Greek *kinēma* (stem *kinēmat-*), motion, from *kinein,* to move + -GRAPH.] **—cin·e·mat·o·graph·ic** (sĭn'ə-măt'ə-grăf'ĭk) *adj.* **—cin·e·mat·o·graph·i·cal·ly** *adv.*

cin·e·ma·tog·ra·phy (sĭn'ə-mə-tŏg'rə-fē) *n.* The practice or technique of making motion pictures. **—cin·e·ma·tog·ra·pher** *n.*

ci·né·ma vér·i·té (sē'nā-mä' vĕr'ē-tā') *n.* A style of film-making that tries to achieve an effect of realism and spontaneity by techniques such as the use of hand-held cameras and minimal editing of sound and image. [French, "cinema truth."]

cin·e·ol, cin·e·ole (sĭn'ē-ōl') *n.* **Eucalyptol** *(see).* [New Latin *cina*†, wormseed + Latin *oleum,* OIL.]

cin·e·ra·di·og·ra·phy (sĭn'ə-rā'dē-ŏg'rə-fē) *n.* Also **cin·e·mat·o·ra·di·og·ra·phy** (sĭn'ə-măt'ə-rā'dē-ŏg'rə-fē). A radiographic investigation of an organ or part in which a film is made from a series of successive x-rays to show the organ in motion.

cin·e·rar·i·a (sĭn'ə-râr'ē-ə) *n.* A plant, *Senecio cruentis,* native to the Canary Islands but widely cultivated as a house plant, having flat clusters of blue or purplish daisylike flowers. [New Latin, from the feminine of Latin *cinerārius,* of ashes (from the ash-colored down on its leaves). See **cinerarium.**]

cin·e·rar·i·um (sĭn'ə-râr'ē-əm) *n., pl.* **-ia** (-ē-ə) A place for keeping the ashes of a cremated body. [Latin, from *cinerārius,* of ashes, from *cinis* (stem *ciner-*), ashes.] **—cin·er·ar·y** (sĭn'ə-rĕr'ē) *adj.*

ci·ne·re·ous (sĭ-nîr'ē-əs) *adj.* **1.** Consisting of or like ashes. **2.** Of the color of ashes; gray tinged with black. [Latin *cinereus,* from *cinis,* ashes.]

cin·gu·lum (sĭng'gyə-ləm) *n., pl.* **-la** (-lə). *Biology.* A girdlelike structure or band. [New Latin, from Latin, girdle, from *cingere,* to gird.] **—cin·gu·late** (sĭng'gyə-lĭt) **cin·gu·la·ted** (-lā'tĭd) *adj.*

Cin·na (sĭn'ə), **Lucius Cornelius** (died 84 B.C.). Roman consul, expelled by Sulla (87). Joining forces with Marius, he captured Rome, forcing Sulla's exile. He restored order as consul (86–84), but was killed by his own troops.

cin·na·bar (sĭn'ə-bär') *n.* **1.** A heavy reddish mineral form of mercuric sulfide, HgS, that is the principal ore of mercury. **2.** Red mercuric sulfide used as a pigment; vermilion. **3.** Bright red; vermilion. [Middle English *cynoper, cynabare,* from Old French *cenobre,* from Latin *cinnābaris,* from Greek *kinnabari,* of Oriental origin.]

cin·nam·ic acid (sə-năm'ĭk) *n.* A white insoluble organic acid, $C_6H_5CH{:}CHCOOH$, existing in two isomeric forms and used in perfumes.

cin·na·mon (sĭn'ə-mən) *n.* **1.** Either of two trees, *Cinnamomum zeylanicum* or *C. loureirii,* of tropical Asia, having very aromatic bark. **2.** The yellowish-brown bark of either of these trees, dried and often ground, used as a spice. **3.** Any of several trees yielding a spice similar to this, such as cassia. **4.** A deep reddish brown. [Middle English *sinamome, cynamone,* from Old French *cinnamome,* from Latin *cinna(mo)mum, cinnamon,* from Greek *kinna(mō)mon,* from Hebrew *qinnāmown.*] **—cin·nam·ic** (sĭ-năm'ĭk), **cin·na·mon·ic** (sĭn'ə-mŏn'ĭk) *adj.*

cinnamon bear *n.* The American black bear during the phase when its color is reddish-brown.

cinnamon stone *n.* A mineral, **essonite** *(see).*

cinque (sĭngk, săngk) *n.* The number five, in cards or dice. [Middle English *cink,* from Old French *cinq,* from Latin *quīnque.*]

cin·que·cen·to (chĭng'kwĭ-chĕn'tō) *n.* The 16th century, especially in Italian art and architecture. [Italian, short for *(mil) cinquecento,* "(one thousand) five hundred."]

cinque·foil (sĭngk'foil', săngk'-) *n.* **1.** Any of various plants of the genus *Potentilla,* having compound leaves, often with five lobes. Also called "five-finger." **2.** *Architecture.* A design having five sides composed of converging arcs, usually used as a frame for glass or a panel. [Middle English *cincfoil,* from Old French *cincfoille,* from Latin *quīnquefolium,* "five leaves" (translation of Greek *pentaphullon*) : *quīnque,* five + *folium,* a leaf.]

Cinque Ports (sĭngk). An association of ports in southeast England, formed in the 11th century to defend the English Channel coast. There were five original members: Sandwich, Dover, Hythe, Romney, and Hastings. Winchelsea and Rye joined later.

Cintra. See **Sintra.**

CIO, C.I.O. Congress of Industrial Organizations.

ci·pher, cy·pher (sī'fər) *n.* **1.** The mathematical symbol (0) denoting absence of quantity; zero. **2.** Any Arabic numeral or figure; a number. **3.** The Arabic system of numerical notation. **4.** A person or thing without influence or value; a nonentity. **5. a.** Any system of secret writing in which units of text of regular length, usually letters, are arbitrarily transposed or substituted according to a predetermined key. Compare **code. b.** The key to such a system. **6.** A message in cipher. **7.** A design combining or interweaving letters or initials; a monogram. **8.** The continuous sounding of a pipe in an organ resulting from mechanical failure.
~*v.* **ciphered, -phering, -phers.** —*intr.* To solve problems in arithmetic; calculate. —*tr.* **1.** To put (a message) in secret writing; encipher. **2.** To solve (a problem) by means of arithmetic. [Middle English *cifre,* zero, from Old French, from Medieval Latin *cifra,* from Arabic *ṣifr.*]

cir., circ. 1. circular. **2.** circulation. **3.** circumference.

cir·ca (sûr'kə) *prep. Abbr.* **ca, c.** About. Used before approximate dates or figures. [Latin *circā,* from *circum,* round about, from *circus,* circle.]

cir·ca·di·an (sər-kā'dē-ən) *adj. Biology.* Exhibiting approximately 24-hour periodicity: *circadian rhythm.* See **biorhythm.** [Latin *circā,* about, CIRCA + *diēs,* day.]

Cir·cas·sia (sər-kăsh'ə, -kăsh'ē-ə). Region of the southwestern U.S.S.R., northwest of the Caucasus Mts.

Cir·cas·sian (sər-kăsh'ən, -kăsh'ē-ən) *n.* Also **Cir·cas·sic** (-kăs'ĭk). **1.** An inhabitant of Circassia; especially, a member of a Caucasian people inhabiting Circassia, noted for their striking physical beauty. **2.** The North Caucasian language of this people.
~*adj.* Of or pertaining to Circassia, its people or their language.

Circassian walnut *n.* The mottled or veined light-brown wood of the English walnut, used especially in decorative cabinetwork.

Cir·ce (sûr′sē). An enchantress described in Homer's *Odyssey* who detains Odysseus for a year and turns his men into swine.

Cir·ce·an (sûr′sē-ən, sər-sē′ən) *adj.* Dangerously and deceptively beautiful; bewitching. [From CIRCE.]

cir·ci·nate (sûr′sə-nāt′) *adj.* 1. Ring-shaped. 2. Rolled up from the tip, as a young fern frond or a butterfly's tongue. [Latin *circinātus,* from *circināre,* to make circular, from *circinus,* pair of compasses, from *circus,* CIRCLE.] —**cir·ci·nate·ly** *adv.*

Cir·ci·nus (sûr′sə-nəs) *n.* A constellation in the Southern Hemisphere near Musca and Triangulum Australe. [Latin *circinus,* a pair of compasses. See **circinate.**]

cir·cle (sûr′kəl) *n.* 1. A plane curve with the property that all points on the curve are equidistant from a given fixed point, the center. See **great circle, small circle.** 2. A planar region bounded by such a curve. 3. a. Anything shaped like a circle, such as a region or halo: *the Arctic Circle.* b. A group of things or people in a circle. 4. A circular course, circuit, or orbit. 5. An upper curved section or tier of seats in a theater: *dress circle.* 6. A series or process that finishes at its starting point or continuously repeats itself; a cycle. 7. *Sometimes* **circles.** A group of people sharing an interest, activity, achievement, or the like: *publishing circles; circle of friends.* 8. *Archaeology.* A ring of megalithic stones, such as Stonehenge, often thought to have some religious significance. 9. A sphere of influence or interest; a domain. 10. *Logic.* A fallacy in reasoning in which the premise is used to prove the conclusion, and the conclusion used to prove the premise. Also called "vicious circle." 11. In field hockey, a **striking circle** *(see).* —**come full circle.** To arrive back at a starting point. —**go** (or **run**) **around in circles.** To expend effort fruitlessly.
~*v.* **circled, -cling, -cles.** —*tr.* 1. To make or form a circle around; enclose. 2. To move in a circle around. —*intr.* To move in circles; revolve: *Crows circled overhead.* —See Synonyms at **turn.** [Middle English *cercle,* from Old French, from Latin *circulus,* diminutive of *circus,* ring.] —**cir·cler** (sûr′klər) *n.*

Synonyms: clique, club, coterie, set, society.

cir·clet (sûr′klĭt) *n.* A small circle; especially, a circular ornament worn on the head. [Middle English *cerclett,* band, from Old French, diminutive of *cercle,* CIRCLE.]

cir·cuit (sûr′kĭt) *n.* 1. a. A closed, usually circular, curve. b. The area enclosed by such a curve. 2. a. Any path or route, the complete traversal of which without local change of direction requires returning to the starting point. b. The act of following such a path. c. A journey made on such a path or route. 3. *Electricity.* a. A closed path followed or capable of being followed by an electric current. b. Any configuration of electrically or electromagnetically connected components or devices. See **closed circuit, open circuit.** 4. a. A regular or accustomed course from place to place, such as that of a judge or salesman; a round. b. The area or district thus covered; especially, a territory under jurisdiction of a judge, in which he holds periodic court sessions. 5. An administrative unit of the Methodist Church. 6. An association of theaters, usually under a single management, in which plays, acts, or motion pictures move from one to another for presentation. 7. An association of teams or clubs, especially for the playing of a particular sport.
~*v.* **circuited, -cuiting, -cuits.** —*tr.* To make a circuit of. —*intr.* To move about in a circuit. [Middle English, from Old French, from Latin *circuitus,* from *circuīre, circumīre,* to go round : *circum-,* round + *īre,* to go.]

circuit breaker *n.* An automatic switch that stops the flow of electric current in a suddenly overloaded or otherwise abnormally stressed electric circuit.

circuit court *n.* In some states, the lowest court of record, in some instances holding sessions in different places.

circuit diagram *n.* A diagram representing the interconnections between elements of an electrical or electronic circuit.

circuit element *n.* A resistor, capacitor, inductor, transistor, or other device used in constructing electrical circuits.

circuit judge *n.* A judge who holds a circuit court.

cir·cu·i·tous (sər-kyōō′ə-təs) *adj.* Being or taking a roundabout, lengthy course. [Medieval Latin *circuitōsus,* from Latin *circuitus,* CIRCUIT.] —**cir·cu·i·tous·ly** *adv.* —**cir·cu·i·tous·ness, cir·cu·i·ty** *n.*

circuit rider *n.* A minister who travels from church to church in a circuit, especially in a rural or frontier area.

cir·cuit·ry (sûr′kə-trē) *n.* 1. The design of or a detailed plan for an electric circuit. 2. Electric circuits collectively.

cir·cu·lar (sûr′kyə-lər) *adj. Abbr.* **cir., circ.** 1. Of or pertaining to a circle. 2. a. Having the shape of a circle. b. Having a shape approximately that of a circle; round. 3. Moving in or forming a circle. 4. Circuitous; indirect; roundabout. 5. a. Addressed or distributed to a large number of persons. b. Using the premise to prove the conclusion, which is used in turn to prove the premise: *a circular argument.* 6. *Mathematics.* a. Having a base in the shape of a circle: *a circular cone.* b. Designating a helix in which the distance from the curve to the axis is constant.
~*n.* A printed advertisement, directive, or notice intended for distribution. [Middle English, from Norman French, from Old French *circulier,* from Late Latin *circulāris,* from *circulus,* CIRCLE.] —**cir·cu·lar·i·ty** (sûr′kyə-lăr′ĭ-tē) *n.* —**cir·cu·lar·ly** *adv.*

circular file *n. Informal.* A wastepaper basket. Used humorously.

circular function *n. Mathematics.* A trigonometric function *(see).*

cir·cu·lar·ize (sûr′kyə-lə-rīz′) *tr.v.* **-ized, -izing, -izes.** 1. To make circular. 2. To distribute circulars to. —**cir·cu·lar·i·za·tion** (sûr′kyə-lə-rĭ-zā′shən) *n.* —**cir·cu·lar·iz·er** *n.*

circular measure *n.* The measure of angles in **radians** *(see).*

circular mil *n. Abbr.* **c.m.** A unit of cross-sectional measurement, especially of wire, equal to the area of a circle with a diameter of one mil.

circular polarization *n. Physics.* A type of polarization of electromagnetic radiation in which the plane of polarization rotates at a uniform rate about the direction of propagation of the radiation.

circular saw *n.* A power-driven saw consisting of a toothed steel disk rotated at high speed. Also called "buzz saw."

cir·cu·late (sûr′kyə-lāt′) *v.* **-lated, -lating, -lates.** —*intr.* 1. To move in or flow through a circle or circuit. 2. To move around, as from person to person, or place to place. 3. To move about or flow freely; be diffused, as air. 4. To spread widely among persons or places; disseminate. —*tr.* To cause to move about or be distributed. [Latin *circulāre,* from *circulus,* CIRCLE.] —**cir·cu·la·tive** (sûr′kyə-lə-tĭv, -lā′tĭv) *adj.* —**cir·cu·la·tor** *n.* —**cir·cu·la·tor·y** (sûr′kyə-lə-tôr′ē, -tōr′ē) *adj.*

circulating decimal *n. Mathematics.* A **repeating decimal** *(see).*

circulating library *n.* A lending library.

circulating medium *n.* Currency or coin that can be exchanged for goods without endorsement.

cir·cu·la·tion (sûr′kyə-lā′shən) *n. Abbr.* **cir., circ.** 1. Movement in a circle or circuit. 2. The movement of blood around the body through the arteries and veins as a result of the heart's pumping action. 3. Any movement or passage through a system of vessels, as of water through pipes or sap through a plant. 4. Free movement or passage. 5. The passing of something, as money or news, from place to place or from person to person. 6. The condition of being passed about and widely known; distribution. 7. The distribution of printed material, especially copies of newspapers or magazines, among readers. 8. The number of copies sold or distributed of a given or an average issue of a publication.

circulatory system *n.* The system of vessels by which blood is circulated throughout the body by the heart.

circum– *prefix.* Indicates around or on all sides; for example, **circumlunar.** [Latin, from *circum,* around, from *circus,* circle.]

cir·cum·am·bi·ent (sûr′kəm-ăm′bē-ənt) *adj.* Surrounding; enclosing. [Latin *circumambiēns* (stem *circumambient-*) : CIRCUM- + AMBIENT.] —**cir·cum·am·bi·ence, cir·cum·am·bi·en·cy** *n.*

cir·cum·cen·ter (sûr′kəm-sĕn′tər) *n. Mathematics.* The center of a circumscribed circle.

cir·cum·cir·cle (sûr′kəm-sûr′kəl) *n. Mathematics.* A circumscribed circle.

cir·cum·cise (sûr′kəm-sīz′) *tr.v.* **-cised, -cising, -cises.** 1. a. To remove the foreskin of (a male). b. To remove the clitoris of (a female). c. To perform the religious rite of circumcision for. 2. To purify spiritually: *"Circumcise yourselves to the Lord"* (Jeremiah 4:4). [Middle English *circumcisen,* from Latin *circumcīdere* (past participle *circumcīsus*), "to cut round" (translation of Greek *peritemnein*) : CIRCUM- + *caedere,* to cut.] —**cir·cum·cis·er** *n.*

cir·cum·ci·sion (sûr′kəm-sĭzh′ən) *n.* 1. *Medicine.* The act of circumcising. 2. A religious ceremony in which someone is circumcised. 3. Spiritual purification.

cir·cum·fer·ence (sər-kŭm′fər-əns) *n. Abbr.* **cir., circ.** 1. a. The boundary line of a circle. b. The boundary line of any closed figure; a perimeter. 2. The length of such a boundary. [Middle English, from Old French, from Latin *circumferentia,* from *circumferēns,* present participle of *circumferre,* to carry around : CIRCUM- + *ferre,* to carry.] —**cir·cum·fer·en·tial** (sər-kŭm′fə-rĕn′shəl) *adj.*

cir·cum·flex (sûr′kəm-flĕks′) *n.* A mark (ˆ) used over a letter in certain languages, such as French, or in phonetic keys, to indicate quality of pronunciation, such as lengthening of a vowel.
~*adj.* Marked with a circumflex.
~*tr.v.* **circumflexed, -flexing, -flexes.** To mark with a circumflex. [Latin *circumflexus,* "a bending around," from *circumflectere,* to bend round : CIRCUM- + *flectere,* to bend, to FLEX.]

cir·cum·fuse (sûr′kəm-fyōōz′) *tr.v.* **-fused, -fusing, -fuses.** 1. To pour or diffuse around; spread. 2. To surround, as with liquid; suffuse. [Latin *circumfundere* (past participle *circumfūsus*), to pour around : CIRCUM- + *fundere,* to pour.] —**cir·cum·fu·sion** *n.*

cir·cum·lo·cu·tion (sûr′kəm-lō-kyōō′shən) *n.* 1. The use of prolix and indirect language. 2. Evasion in speech or writing. 3. A roundabout expression. [Middle English *circumlocucioun,* from Latin *circumlocūtiō* (stem *circumlocūtiōn-*), from *circumloquī,* "to speak in a roundabout way" : CIRCUM- + *loquī,* to speak.] —**cir·cum·loc·u·to·ry** (sûr′kəm-lŏk′yə-tôr′ē, -tōr′ē) *adj.*

cir·cum·lu·nar (sûr′kəm-lōō′nər) *adj.* Revolving around or surrounding the moon.

cir·cum·nav·i·gate (sûr′kəm-năv′ĭ-gāt′) *tr.v.* **-gated, -gating, -gates.** To sail or fly completely around. [Latin *circumnāvigāre* : CIRCUM- + *nāvigāre,* NAVIGATE.] —**cir·cum·nav·i·ga·tion** (sûr′kəm-năv′ĭ-gā′shən) *n.* —**cir·cum·nav·i·ga·tor** *n.*

cir·cum·nu·tate (sûr′kəm-nōō′tāt′, -nyōō′tāt′) *intr.v.* **-tated, -tating, -tates.** *Botany.* To exhibit circumnutation. [CIRCUM- + Latin *nūtāre,* to nod, sway.]

cir·cum·nu·ta·tion (sûr′kəm-nōō-tā′shən, -nyōō-tā′shən) *n. Botany.* An elliptical or spiral direction of growth shown by certain plant parts, such as the apex of a growing tendril.

cir·cum·po·lar (sûr′kəm-pō′lər) *adj.* 1. Located or found in one of the polar regions. 2. *Astronomy.* Designating a star that from a given observer's latitude does not go below the horizon.

cir·cum·scis·sile (sûr′kəm-sĭs′əl) *adj. Botany.* Splitting or opening along a transverse circular line: *a circumscissile seed capsule.* [CIR-

cithara *A Greek statue of a woman playing the cithara, similar in construction to the lyre. The statue was carved in about 200* B.C.

CUM- + Latin *scissilis,* capable of being cut, from *scissus* (see **scission**).]

cir·cum·scribe (sûr'kəm-skrīb') *tr.v.* **-scribed, -scribing, -scribes. 1.** To draw a line around; encircle. **2.** To confine within bounds; limit; restrict. **3.** To determine the limits of. **4.** *Geometry.* To enclose (a geometric figure) within another geometric figure, so that the enclosed object touches but does not intersect with the enclosing figure. —See Synonyms at **limit.** [Middle English *circumscriben,* from Latin *circumscrībere* : CIRCUM- + *scrībere,* to write.] **—cir·cum·scrib·a·ble** *adj.* **—cir·cum·scrib·er** *n.*

cir·cum·scrip·tion (sûr'kəm-skrĭp'shən) *n.* **1. a.** The act of circumscribing. **b.** The state of being circumscribed. **2.** Something that circumscribes. **3.** A circumscribed space; a limited area. **4.** A circular inscription, as on a coin or medallion. **—cir·cum·scrip·tive** *adj.* **—cir·cum·scrip·tive·ly** *adv.*

cir·cum·spect (sûr'kəm-spĕkt) *adj.* Taking into account all circumstances or consequences; prudent. [Middle English, from Latin *circumspectus,* past participle of *circumspicere,* to look round, take heed : CIRCUM- + *specere,* to look.] **—cir·cum·spec·tion** (sûr'kəm-spĕk'shən) *n.* **—cir·cum·spect·ly** *adv.*

cir·cum·stance (sûr'kəm-stăns') *n.* **1.** One of the conditions or facts attending an event and having some bearing upon it; a determining or modifying factor. **2.** One of the conditions or facts that determine or that must be considered in the determining of a course of action. **3.** The sum of determining factors beyond willful control: *a victim of circumstance.* **4.** *Usually* **circumstances.** Financial status or means: *living in reduced circumstances.* **5.** Additional or accessory information; detail. **6.** Formal display; ceremony: *pomp and circumstance.* —See Synonyms at **occurrence. —under no circumstances.** In no case; never. **—under** (or **in**) **the circumstances.** Given these conditions; such being the case. [Middle English, from Old French, from Latin *circumstantia,* accessory details, from *circumstāns,* present participle of *circumstāre,* to stand around, be accessory : CIRCUM- + *stāre,* to stand.]

cir·cum·stanced (sûr'kəm-stănst') *adj.* Placed in specified circumstances, especially with regard to finance.

cir·cum·stan·tial (sûr'kəm-stăn'shəl) *adj.* **1.** Of, pertaining to, or dependent upon circumstances. **2.** Of no primary significance; incidental; inessential. **3.** Complete and particular; full of detail. **—cir·cum·stan·ti·al·i·ty** (sûr'kəm-stăn'shē-ăl'ə-tē) *n.* **—cir·cum·stan·tial·ly** *adv.*

circumstantial evidence *n. Law.* Evidence not bearing directly on the fact in dispute, but on various attendant circumstances from which the judge or jury might infer the occurrence of the fact in dispute.

cir·cum·stan·ti·ate (sûr'kəm-stăn'shē-āt') *tr.v.* **-ated, -ating, -ates.** To support or verify with detailed evidence or proof. **—cir·cum·stan·ti·a·tion** *n.*

cir·cum·val·late (sûr'kəm-văl'āt') *tr.v.* **-lated, -lating, -lates.** To surround with a rampart or other defensive barrier.
~*adj.* (sûr'kəm-văl'āt', -văl'ĭt). Surrounded by or as if by a rampart. [Latin *circumvallāre* : CIRCUM- + *vallāre,* to wall, from *vallum,* wall.] **—cir·cum·val·la·tion** *n.*

cir·cum·vent (sûr'kəm-vĕnt') *tr.v.* **-vented, -venting, -vents. 1.** To surround and entrap (an enemy, for example). **2.** To overcome by artful maneuvering; outwit. **3.** To avoid by or as if by passing around. [Latin *circumvenīre* (past participle *circumventus*) : CIRCUM- + *venīre, to come.*] **—cir·cum·vent·er, cir·cum·ven·tor** *n.* **—cir·cum·ven·tion** *n.* **—cir·cum·ven·tive** *adj.*

cir·cum·vo·lu·tion (sər-kŭm'və-lo͞o'shən, sûr'kəm-vō-) **1.** An act or instance of turning, coiling, or folding about a center core or axis. **2.** A single turn, coil, or fold; convolution. [Middle English *circumvolucioun,* from Medieval Latin *circumvolūtiō* (stem *-volūtion-*), from Latin *circumvolvere* (past participle *circumvolūtus*), CIRCUMVOLVE.]

cir·cum·volve (sûr'kəm-vŏlv') *v.* **-volved, -volving, -volves.** *—intr.* To revolve. *—tr.* To cause to revolve. [Latin *circumvolverse* : CIRCUM- + *volvere,* to roll.]

cir·cus (sûr'kəs) *n.* **1.** A public entertainment consisting typically of a variety of performances by acrobats, clowns, and trained animals. **2.** A traveling company that performs such entertainments. **3.** A circular arena, surrounded by tiers of seats and often covered by a tent, in which such entertainments are performed. **4.** A roofless, oval enclosure surrounded by tiers of seats and used in ancient times for public spectacles. **5.** *British.* An open circular place where several streets intersect. **6.** *Informal.* A place or activity given over to rowdy or noisy disorder. [Latin *circus,* ring, CIRCLE.]

cire per·due (sēr' pĕr-dü') *n.* A technique used in casting bronze, the **lost wax process** *(see).* [French, "lost wax."]

cirque (sûrk) *n.* A steep, bowl-shaped hollow, often containing a small lake, occurring at the upper end of some mountain valleys. Also called "corrie" in Scotland, "cwm" in Wales. [French, from Latin *circus,* ring, CIRCLE.]

cir·rate (sĭr'āt') *adj.* Also **cir·rose** (sĭr'ōs'), **cir·rous** (sĭr'əs). Having or of the nature of a cirrus or cirri. [Latin *cirrātus,* curled, from *cirrus,* curl, CIRRUS.]

cir·rho·sis (sĭ-rō'sĭs) *n.* **1.** A chronic disorder of the liver, in which normal tissue is replaced by fibrous tissue similar to scar tissue, caused for example by alcoholism or hepatitis. **2.** Interstitial inflammation of any tissue or organ. [New Latin, "orange-colored disease" (from the color of the diseased liver) : Greek *kirrhos*†, orange tawny + -OSIS.] **—cir·rhot·ic** (sĭ-rŏt'ĭk) *adj.*

cir·ri·pede (sĭr'ə-pēd') *n.* Also **cir·ri·ped** (sĭr'ə-pĕd') Any of various crustaceans of the subclass Cirripedia, which includes the barnacles and similar organisms that attach themselves to objects or become parasitic in the adult stage. [New Latin *Cirripedia,* "the cirrus-footed ones" : CIRR(US) + *-ped.*] **—cir·ri·ped** *adj.*

cir·ro·cu·mu·lus (sĭr'ō-kyo͞om'yə-ləs) *n.* A high-altitude cloud composed of a series of small, regularly arranged cloudlets in the form of ripples or grains. [New Latin : CIRR(US) + CUMULUS.]

cir·ro·stra·tus (sĭr'ō-strā'təs, -străt'əs) *n.* A high-altitude, thin, hazy, veil-like cloud, usually covering the sky and often producing a halo effect around the sun. [New Latin : CIRR(US) + STRATUS.]

cir·rus (sĭr'əs) *n., pl.* **cirri** (sĭr'ī'). **1.** A high-altitude cloud composed of narrow bands or patches of thin, generally white, fleecy parts. **2.** *Botany.* A mass of coherent spores that are discharged through an ostiole. **3.** *Zoology.* A slender, flexible appendage, such as a tentacle. [New Latin, from Latin *cirrus*†, curl, filament, tuft.]

cis– *prefix.* **1.** Indicates location on this or the near side; for example, **cislunar. 2.** *Chemistry.* Indicates an isomer in which two atoms or groups in a molecule occupy positions on the same side of a line, usually a chemical bond, or a center. Compare **trans-.** [Latin, from *cis,* on this side of.]

Cis·al·pine Gaul (sĭs-ăl'pīn' gôl). The part of ancient Gaul south of the Alps of northern Italy.

cis·at·lan·tic (sĭs'ət-lăn'tĭk) *adj.* On this (the speaker's) side of the Atlantic. [CIS- + ATLANTIC]

Cis·cau·ca·sia (sĭs'kô-kā'zhə, -shə). Also **North Cau·ca·sia** (kô-kā'zhə, -shə). A steppeland region in the southwestern U.S.S.R.

cis·co (sĭs'kō) *n., pl.* **-coes** or **-cos** or collectively **cisco.** Any of several North American whitefish, especially the **lake herring** *(see)* of the Great Lakes. [Canadian French *ciscoette,* from Ojibwa *pemitewiskawet,* oily-skinned fish.]

cis·lu·nar (sĭs-lo͞o'nər) *adj.* Of or pertaining to the region between the earth and the moon. Compare **translunar.**

cis·mon·tane (sĭs-mŏn'tān') *adj.* On this (the speaker's) side of the mountains. [French *cismontain,* from Latin *cismontānus* : CIS- + *montānus,* of the mountains, MONTANE.]

cis·soid (sĭs'oid') *n. Mathematics.* A type of geometric curve with a cusp and two branches, both asymptotic to a straight line. Its equation is $x^3 = y^2(2a - x)$, with the cusp at the origin and the asymptote being the line $x = 2a$.
~*adj.* Lying between the concave sides of two curves. Compare **sistroid.** [Greek *kissoeidēs,* ivy-shaped, from *kissos,* ivy.]

cissy. *British.* Variant of **sissy.**

cist (kĭst, sĭst) *n.* Also **kist** (kĭst). A Neolithic stone coffin. [Welsh, "chest," from Latin *cista,* basket, wicker receptacle, from Greek *kistē.*]

Cis·ter·cian (sĭ-stûr'shən) *n.* A member of a contemplative monastic order founded by reformist Benedictines in France in 1098.
~*adj.* Of, pertaining to, or belonging to this order. [French *Cistertien,* from Medieval Latin *Cistercium,* Cîteaux, near Dijon, site of the original abbey.]

cis·tern (sĭs'tərn) *n.* **1.** A receptacle for holding water or other liquid, especially, a water tank in the roof of a house or connected to a toilet. **2.** *Anatomy.* A cisterna. [Middle English *cisterne,* from Old French, from Latin *cisterna,* water tank, from *cista,* box, from Greek *kistē,* basket.] **—cis·ter·nal** (sĭ-stûr'nəl) *adj.*

cis·ter·na (sĭ-stûr'nə) *n., pl.* **-nae** (-nē'). Any fluid-containing sac or space in the body of an organism. Also called "reservoir." [New Latin, from Latin, CISTERN.]

cis-trans isomerism (sĭs'trănz') *n. Chemistry.* A type of isomerism in which two atoms or groups in a molecule can occupy positions on the same side (*cis*) or opposite sides (*trans*) of a line or center. It is found especially in organic compounds containing double bonds and in inorganic square and octahedral coordination complexes. Also called "geometrical isomerism." **—cis-trans isomer** *n.*

cis·tron (sĭs'trŏn') *n.* A unit of genetic function: a section of DNA controlling the production of a single polypeptide chain of a protein molecule. [From *cis-trans* + -ON (molecular unit).]

cit. **1.** citation. **2.** cited. **3.** citizen.

cit·a·del (sĭt'ə-dəl, -dĕl') *n.* **1.** A fortress in a commanding position in or near a city. **2.** Any stronghold or fortified place; a bulwark. **3.** A Salvation Army meeting hall. [French *citadelle* or Italian *citadella,* diminutive of obsolete *cittade,* city, from Latin *cīvitās,* citizenry, state, CITY.]

ci·ta·tion (sī-tā'shən) *n. Abbr.* **cit. 1.** The act of citing. **2.** A quoting of an authoritative source for substantiation. **3.** A source so cited; a quotation. **4.** *Law.* A reference to previous court decisions or authoritative writings. **5.** An official commendation for meritorious action, especially in military service. **6.** A summons, especially one calling for appearance in court. **—ci·ta·to·ry** (sī'tə-tôr'ē, -tōr'ē) *adj.*

cite (sīt) *tr.v.* **cited, citing, cites. 1.** To quote as an authority or example. **2.** To mention or bring forward as support, illustration, or proof. **3.** To commend (a unit or individual in the armed forces) in dispatches, for meritorious action. **4.** To summon before a court of law. **5.** *Archaic.* To call to action; rouse. [Middle English *citen,* to summon, from Old French *citer,* from Latin *citāre,* frequentative of *ciēre,* to set in motion, summon.]

cith·a·ra (sĭth'ə-rə, kĭth'-) *n.* An ancient musical instrument resembling the lyre. [Latin, from Greek *kithara*†.]

cith·er (sĭth'ər, *sĭth'-*) *n.* Also **cith·ern** (sĭth'ərn, *sĭth'-*). A musical instrument, a **cittern** *(see).* [French *cithare,* from Latin *cithara,* CITHARA.]

cit·i·fied (sĭt'ĭ-fīd') *adj.* Having customs, manners, fashions, or other characteristics attributed to city people.

cit·i·fy (sĭt'ĭ-fī') *tr.v.* **-fied, -fying, -fies. 1.** To cause to become like a city; make urban. **2.** To cause to acquire the styles or manners of city people. **—cit·i·fi·ca·tion** (sĭt′ĭ-fĭ-kā′shən) *n.*

cit·i·zen (sĭt′ə-zən) *n. Abbr.* **cit. 1.** A person owing loyalty to and entitled by birth or naturalization to the protection of a given nation. **2.** A resident of a city or town, especially one entitled to vote and enjoy other privileges there. [Middle English *citisein,* from Norman French *citesein,* variant of Old French *citeien,* from *cite,* CITY.] **—cit·i·zen·ly** *adj.*

cit·i·zen·ry (sĭt′ə-zən-rē) *n., pl.* **-ries.** Citizens collectively.

citizen's arrest *n.* An arrest made by an ordinary member of the public, in accordance with the right of any citizen to arrest someone who has committed an arrestable offense or a breach of the peace.

citizens band *n.* A range of radio frequencies officially allocated for radio communications between private individuals. Often used adjectivally: *citizens band radio.* Also called "CB."

cit·i·zen·ship (sĭt′ĭ-zən-shĭp′) *n.* The status of a citizen with its attendant duties, rights, and privileges.

Ci·tlal·té·petl (sē′tläl-tā′pĕt-l). An extinct volcanic peak in southern Mexico, situated between Mexico City and Veracruz. At 5,699 meters (18,697 feet) it is Mexico's highest peak.

cit·ral (sĭt′răl′) *n.* A free-flowing pale yellow liquid, $C_{10}H_{16}O$, derived from lemon-grass oil and used in perfumery and as a flavoring. It exists in two isomeric forms: the cis-isomer (**geranial**) and the trans-isomer (**neral**). [CITR(US) + -AL (aldehyde).]

cit·rate (sĭt′rāt′) *n.* A salt or ester of citric acid.

cit·ric (sĭt′rĭk) *adj.* Of or obtained from citrus fruits.

citric acid *n.* A colorless translucent crystalline acid, $C_6H_8O_7$, principally derived by fermentation of carbohydrates or from lemon, lime, and pineapple juices, and used to prepare citrates, in flavorings, and in metal polishes.

citric acid cycle *n.* The **Krebs cycle** *(see).*

cit·ri·cul·ture (sĭt′rĭ-kŭl′chər) *n.* The cultivation of citrus fruits. [*citrus* + *culture.*] **—cit·ri·cul·tur·ist** (sĭt′rĭ-kŭl′chə-rĭst) *n.*

cit·rine (sĭt′rĭn, -rēn′) *n.* **1.** A pale-yellow variety of quartz, resembling topaz. **2.** The greenish-yellow color of a lemon. [Middle English, from Old French *citrin,* from Medieval Latin *citrīnus,* from Latin *citrus,* citron tree, CITRUS.] **—cit·rine** *adj.*

cit·ron (sĭt′rən) *n.* **1.** A tree, *Citrus medica,* native to Asia, having lemonlike fruit with a thick, aromatic rind. **2.** The fruit of this tree. **3.** A variety of watermelon, *Citrullus vulgaris citroides,* having fruit generally considered inedible and a hard rind used as flavoring. In this sense, also called "citron melon." **4.** The preserved or candied rind of either of these fruits, used especially in baking. **5.** Grayish green yellow. [French, from Old French, from Latin *citrus*†, citron tree.] **—cit·ron** *adj.*

cit·ron·el·la (sĭt′rə-nĕl′ə) *n.* **1.** A tropical Eurasian grass, *Cymbopogon nardus,* having bluish-green, lemon-scented leaves. Also called "citronella grass." **2.** A light yellow, aromatic oil obtained from this grass and used in insect repellents and perfumery. Also called "citronella oil." [New Latin, from French *citronnelle,* lemon oil, diminutive of *citron,* CITRON.]

cit·ron·el·lal (sĭt′rə-nĕl′ăl′) *n.* A colorless mixture of isomeric liquids, $C_9H_{17}CHO$, the chief constituent of citronella oil. [CITRONELL(A) + -AL (aldehyde).]

cit·rus (sĭt′rəs) *adj.* Also **cit·rous. 1.** Of or pertaining to trees or shrubs of the genus *Citrus,* many of which bear edible fruit such as the orange, lemon, lime, and grapefruit. **2.** Of or characteristic of the fruits of these trees or shrubs.
~n., pl. **citruses** or collectively **citrus.** A citrus tree or shrub. [New Latin, from Latin *citrus*†, citron tree, citrus tree.]

Città del Vaticano. See **Vatican City.**

cit·tern (sĭt′ərn) *n.* A 16th-century guitar with a pear-shaped body. Also called "cither." [Variant (assimilated to GITTERN or CITHERN).]

cit·y (sĭt′ē) *n., pl.* **-ies.** *Abbr.* **C. 1.** A town of significant size. **2.** In the United States, an incorporated municipality with definite boundaries and legal powers set forth in a charter granted by the state. **3.** In Canada, a municipality of high rank, usually determined by population but varying according to province. **4.** In Great Britain, a large incorporated town, usually the seat of a bishop, with its title conferred by the Crown. **5.** In various other countries, a large town, designated as a city according to population, the presence of a cathedral, or other factors. **6.** The inhabitants of a city as a group. **7.** An ancient Greek city-state. **—the City.** The commercial and financial district of London, in which the stock exchange and the Bank of England are situated.
~adj. Of, in, or belonging to a city. [Middle English *cite,* from Old French, from Latin *cīvitās* (stem *cīvitat-*), citizenry, state, (later) city, from *cīvis,* citizen.]

city editor *n.* **1.** A newspaper editor responsible for handling local news and reporters' assignments. **2.** In Great Britain, the editor who handles commercial and financial news.

city fathers *pl.n.* The members of the governing body of a city.

city hall *n.* **1.** The building housing the administrative offices of a municipal government. **2.** The officials of a municipal government.

city manager *n.* An administrator appointed by a city council to manage the affairs of the municipality.

city slicker *n. Informal.* A person with the sophisticated or smooth manners traditionally associated by rural people with city dwellers. Often used derogatorily.

cit·y-state (sĭt′ē-stāt′) *n.* A sovereign state consisting of an independent city and its surrounding territory, especially as in ancient Greece.

Ciu·dad Bo·lí·var (syōō-däd′ bō-lē′vär). Seaport on the Orinoco River in eastern Venezuela, renamed Bolívar in 1849.

Ciudad Re·al (rā-äl′). Town in New Castile province in south-central Spain, founded in the 13th century.

Ciudad Trujillo. See **Santo Domingo.**

civ. civil; civilian.

civ·et (sĭv′ĭt) *n.* **1.** Any of various catlike mammals of the family Viverridae, of Africa and Asia, having spotted or blotched fur and anal scent glands that secrete a fluid with a musky odor. Also called "civet cat." **2.** This fluid, used in the manufacture of perfumes. **3.** The fur of a civet. [French *civette,* from Old French, from Italian *zibetto,* from Arabic *zabād.*]

civ·ic (sĭv′ĭk) *adj.* Of, pertaining to, or belonging to a city, to a citizen, or to citizenship; municipal or civil. [Latin *cīvicus,* from *cīvis,* citizen.] **—civ·i·cal·ly** *adv.*

civic center *n.* A building or complex containing the municipal offices of a city, often with other facilities such as a hall.

civ·ics (sĭv′ĭks) *n. Used with a singular verb.* **1.** The study of the rights and duties of a citizen. **2.** The branch of political science that deals with civic affairs.

civies. Variant of **civvies.**

civ·il (sĭv′əl) *adj. Abbr.* **civ. 1.** Of, pertaining to, or befitting citizens or the citizen as an individual. **2.** Of or pertaining to citizens and their relations with one another or with the state. **3.** Of ordinary citizens or ordinary community life, as distinguished from the military or the ecclesiastical. **4.** Of or in accordance with organized society and government; civilized. **5.** Observing or befitting accepted social usages; proper; polite. **6.** Designating or according to legally recognized divisions of time: *a civil year.* **7.** *Law.* **a.** Of or in accordance with Roman civil law or with its medieval and modern derivatives. **b.** Pertaining to the rights of private individuals and to legal proceedings concerning these rights. Used to distinguish a court, proceeding, or rule that is not criminal, military, or international. —See Synonyms at **polite.** [Middle English, from Old French, from Latin *cīvīlis,* from *cīvis,* citizen.] **—civ·il·ly** *adv.*

civil day *n.* A **mean solar day** *(see).*

civil death *n. Law.* Formerly, the total deprivation of civil rights resulting from conviction for treason or other serious offenses.

civil defense *n. Abbr.* **C.D. 1.** The activities of an organized body of civilian volunteers to protect life and property in the case of a natural disaster or an attack by an enemy. **2.** These civilian volunteers.

civil disobedience *n.* The refusal to obey civil laws that are regarded as unjust, usually by employing methods of passive resistance to bring about political change.

civil engineer *n. Abbr.* **C.E.** An engineer trained in the design and construction of public works.

ci·vil·ian (sə-vĭl′yən) *n. Abbr.* **civ.** A person following the pursuits of civil life, as distinguished from one serving in the armed forces.
~adj. Of or pertaining to civilians or civil life; nonmilitary. [Middle English, practitioner of civil law, jurist, from *civile,* civil law, from Latin, from *(jūs) cīvīle,* from *cīvīlis,* CIVIL.]

ci·vil·i·ty (sə-vĭl′ə-tē) *n., pl.* **-ties. 1.** Politeness; courtesy. **2.** A courteous act or utterance.

civ·i·li·za·tion (sĭv′ə-lə-zā′shən) *n.* **1.** A condition of human society marked by an advanced stage of development in the arts and sciences and by corresponding social, political, and cultural complexity. **2.** Those nations or peoples regarded as having arrived at this stage. **3.** The type of culture and society developed by a particular group, nation, or region, or by any of these in some particular epoch. **4.** The act or process of civilizing or of reaching a civilized state. **5.** The state of being cultured or having good taste. **6.** Populated areas, especially urban areas, and the conveniences associated with them.

civ·i·lize (sĭv′ə-līz′) *tr.v.* **-lized, -lizing, -lizes. 1.** To bring out of a primitive or savage state into a more developed one. **2.** To educate or enlighten. **—civ·i·liz·a·ble** *adj.* **—civ·i·liz·er** *n.*

civ·i·lized (sĭv′ə-līzd′) *adj.* **1.** Having a highly developed society and culture. **2.** Of, pertaining to, or characteristic of a people or nation so developed. **3.** Polite or cultured; refined.

civil law *n.* **1.** The body of law dealing with the rights of private citizens in a particular state or nation, as distinguished from criminal law, military law, or international law. Compare **criminal law. 2.** The law of ancient Rome, especially that which applied to private citizens. **3.** Any system of law having its origin in Roman law, as distinguished from common law or canon law.

civil liberty *n.* A liberty legally guaranteeing to the individual a right, such as free speech, thought, or action, limited only insofar as its use must not interfere with the rights of others.

civil list *n.* In Great Britain, the yearly provision by Parliament of funds for the personal and household expenses of the monarch.

civil marriage *n.* A marriage ceremony performed by a civil official, such as a registrar.

civil rights *pl.n.* Rights belonging to a person by virtue of his or her status as a citizen or as a member of civil society. Also used adjectivally to designate efforts to win political, economic, and social equality for U.S. blacks: *the civil rights movement.*

civil servant *n.* A person employed in the civil service.

civil service *n. Abbr.* **C.S. 1.** All branches of government administration that are not legislative, judicial, military, or naval. **2.** Collectively, the persons employed by these branches of the government.

civil time *n.* **Mean solar time** *(see).*

civil war *n.* A war between factions or regions of one country.

Civil War *n.* **1.** In the United States, the war between the Union (the

civet *The scent glands of these catlike meat eaters are used in the manufacture of some perfumes. Civets, which also eat fruit and nuts, are native to the tropical forests of Southeast Asia, India, and Africa. They are related to the mongoose.*

PRONUNCIATION KEY
ă, pat; ā, pay; âr, care;
ä, father, are; b, bib;
ch, church; d, deed; ĕ, pet;
ē, be; f, fife; g, gag; h, hat;
hw, which; ĭ, pit; ī, pie;
îr, pier; j, judge; k, kick;
l, lid, needle; m, mum;
n, no, sudden; ng, thing;
ŏ, pot; ō, toe; ô, paw, for;
oi, noise; ou, out; ŏŏ, book;
ōō, boot; p, pop; r, roar;
s, sauce; sh, ship, dish;
t, tight; th, thin, path;
th, this, bathe; ŭ, cut; ûr, fur;
v, valve; w, with; y, yes;
z, zebra, size; zh, vision;
ə, about, item, edible, gallop, circus, peaceful

IN FOREIGN WORDS:
à, *Fr.* ami; œ, *Fr.* feu, *Ger.* schön; ü, *Fr.* tu, *Ger.* über;
KH, *Ger.* ich, *Scot.* loch;
N, *Fr.* bon; y′, *Fr.* Compiègne

STRESS MARKS:
Primary stress: ′
in·cite′ (ĭn-sīt′)
Secondary stress: ′
in′sight′ (ĭn′sīt′)

North) and the Confederacy (the South) from 1861 to 1865. Also called "War Between the States," "War of Secession." **2.** In Great Britain, the war between the Parliamentarians and the Royalists from 1642 to 1652. Also called the "Great Rebellion."

Ci·vi·ta·vec·chia (chē'vē-tä-věk'yə). Fishing port on the west coast of central Italy. The old town was founded by Trajan, and Roman baths survive. Michelangelo designed the citadel.

civ·vies, civ·ies (sĭv'ēz) *pl.n. Slang.* Civilian clothes, as distinguished from military dress. [Short for CIVILIAN.]

Civ·vy Street (sĭv'ē) *n. Slang.* Civilian life.

C.J. **1.** chief justice. **2.** corpus juris.

ck. cask.

cl centiliter.

Cl The symbol for the element chlorine.

cl. **1.** class; classification. **2.** clause. **3.** clearance. **4.** clergyman. **5.** closet. **6.** cloth.

c.l. **1.** carload. **2.** *Sports.* center line. **3.** common law.

clab·ber (klăb'ər) *n.* Sour, curdled milk.
~*v.* **clabbered, -bering, -bers.** —*tr.* To cause to curdle. —*intr.* To become curdled. [Short for earlier *bonnyclabber,* from Irish : *bainne,* milk, from Middle Irish *banne,* a drop + *clabair†,* thick sour milk.]

clach·an (klăкн'ən) *n. Scottish.* A village or hamlet. [Scottish Gaelic, from *clach,* stone.]

clack (klăk) *v.* **clacked, clacking, clacks.** —*intr.* **1.** To make an abrupt, dry sound, as by the collision of two wooden surfaces. **2.** To chatter thoughtlessly or at length. **3.** To cackle or cluck, as a hen does. —*tr.* To cause to make an abrupt, dry sound.
~*n.* **1.** A clacking sound. **2.** Something that makes a clacking sound. **3.** Thoughtless, prolonged talk; chatter. [Middle English *clacken,* from Old Norse *klaka* (imitative).] —**clack·er** *n.*

Clack·man·nan (klăk-măn'ən). Also **Clack·man·nan·shire** (-shîr, -shər). Former county in central Scotland, the smallest in the country. In 1975 it became Clackmannan district in Central Region.

clack valve *n.* A hinged or ball valve that permits fluids to flow in only one direction.

Clac·to·ni·an (klăk-tō'nē-ən) *adj. Archaeology.* Of or pertaining to a lower Paleolithic culture of northwestern Europe. [From *Clacton-on-Sea,* southeast England, site of the discovery of artifacts from which the culture was classified.]

clad¹ (klăd) *tr.v.* **clad, cladding, clads.** To sheathe or cover (a metal) with a metal, as for decoration or protection. [Middle English *cladden,* from *cladde,* past participle of *clathen, clothen,* CLOTHE.]

clad². Alternate past tense and past participle of **clothe.**

clad–, clado– *prefix.* Indicates a sprout or branch; for example, **cladistics.** [Greek *klados,* branch.]

clad·ding (klăd'ĭng) *n.* **1.** A metal coating bonded onto another metal. **2.** A protective or insulating layer fixed to the outside of a building or other structure.

clade (klăd) *n.* A group of organisms that share a common ancestor. [Greek *klados,* branch.]

cla·dist (klă'dĭst) *n.* One who practices cladistics.

cla·dis·tics (klə-dĭs'tĭks) *n. Used with a singular verb.* A method of scientific classification in which organisms are placed in the same taxonomic group when they share features thought to indicate recent common ancestry. [CLADE + -ISTICS.] —**cla·dis·tic** *adj.*

cla·doc·er·an (klə-dŏs'ər-ən) *n.* Any of various small aquatic crustaceans of the order Cladocera, which includes the water fleas.
~*adj.* Of or belonging to the Cladocera. [New Latin *Cladocera* : Greek *klados,* branch, shoot + *keras,* horn.]

clad·ode (klăd'ōd') *n.* A leaflike plant stem, a **cladophyll** (*see*).

cla·do·gram (klăd'ə-grăm') *n.* A diagram used in cladistics to show the relationships between organisms, consisting of a series of branches that repeatedly divide into two, each point of branching representing divergence from a common ancestor. [CLADE + -GRAM.]

clad·o·phyll (klăd'ə-fĭl') *n.* A branch or portion of a stem that resembles a leaf. Also called "cladode," "phylloclade." [New Latin *cladophyllum* : Greek *klados,* twig + *phullon,* leaf, -PHYLL.]

clag (klăg) *v.* **clagged, clagging, clags.** —*tr.* **1.** To clog. **2.** To stick; adhere. —*intr.* **1.** To become clogged. **2.** To become stuck.
~*n.* A clog or clot. [Middle English *claggen,* to daub with mud, from Scandinavian; akin to Danish *klagge,* mud.] —**clag·gy** *adj.*

claim (klām) *v.* **claimed, claiming, claims.** —*tr.* **1.** To demand as one's due; assert one's right to. **2.** To take by or as if by right: *He claimed the reward.* **3.** To state to be true; assert or maintain. **4.** To deserve or call for; require. **5.** To demand (money) under an insurance policy, as after an accident. —*intr.* To make a claim, especially an insurance claim.
~*n.* **1.** A demand for something as one's rightful due; affirmation of a right. **2.** A basis for demanding something; a title or right. **3.** Something claimed in a formal or legal manner; especially, a tract of land staked out by a miner or prospector. **4. a.** A sum of money demanded, as after an accident, in accordance with an insurance policy or other formal arrangement. **b.** A demand for such money. **5.** A statement of something as a fact; an assertion of truth. —**lay claim to.** To assert one's right to or ownership of. [Middle English *claimen,* from Old French *clamer* (present stem *claim-*), to cry, appeal, from Latin *clāmāre,* to call.] —**claim·a·ble** *adj.* —**claim·er** *n.*

claim·ant (klā'mənt) *n.* A person making a claim.

Clair (klâr), **René** (1898–1981). French film director. As an early exponent of sound productions, he directed the classics *Sous les Toits de Paris* (1929) and *Le Million* (1931).

clair·au·di·ence (klâr-ô'dē-əns) *n.* The supposed faculty of hearing things outside the normal range of perception. [French *clair,* CLEAR + AUDIENCE, by analogy with CLAIRVOYANCE.] —**clair·au·di·ent** *n. & adj.*

clair de lune (klâr' də lōōn') *n.* **1.** A pale, grayish-blue glaze applied to various kinds of Chinese porcelain. **2.** The color of this glaze. [French, "moonlight."] —**clair-de-lune** *adj.*

clair·schach, clar·sach (klâr'shôкн) *n.* An ancient Irish harp. [Middle English *clareschaw,* from Scottish Gaelic *clārsach†.*]

Clair·vaux (klâr-vō'). Village in the Aube department of northeast France. Its abbey, founded by St. Bernard of Clairvaux in 1115, became the most influential center of the Cistercian order.

clair·voy·ance (klâr-voi'əns) *n.* **1.** The supposed power to see or know things that are out of the natural range of human perception. **2.** Acute intuitive insight or perceptiveness. [French *clairvoyant,* "clear-seeing" : *clair,* clear, from Latin *clārus* + *voyant,* present participle of *voir,* to see, from Latin *vidēre.*] —**clair·voy·ant** *n. & adj.*

clam¹ (klăm) *n.* **1.** Any of various usually burrowing marine and freshwater bivalve mollusks, including members of the genera *Venus, Mya,* and others, many of which are edible. See quahog. **2.** The soft, tasty, edible flesh of such a mollusk. **3.** *Informal.* An uncommunicative person.
~*intr.v.* **clammed, clamming, clams.** To hunt for clams. —**clam up.** To cease talking or remain silent. [Shortened from *clamshell,* "bivalve that shuts tight like a clamp," from CLAM (clamp).]

clam² *n.* A clamp or vise. [Middle English, Old English *clamm,* bond, fetter.]

cla·mant (klā'mənt) *adj.* **1.** Clamorous; loud. **2.** Urgent; compel-

---

Civil War

THE CONFLICT THAT SPLIT THE UNITED STATES

Deeply divided along many lines, the Union was restored at terrible cost

Well over a century after the last gunfire, the American Civil War (1861–65) is more likely to arouse dispute than bring consensus. Long before the Confederate shelling of Fort Sumter, South Carolina, opened the shooting war, sectional rivalries had already split families, friendships, churches, political parties—and the nation itself.

A divided nation played cruel tricks with allegiances. Mary Todd, the wife of President Abraham Lincoln (1809–65), had three brothers who fought and died for the South. Robert E. Lee (1807–70), more respected in the Confederacy than even its president, Jefferson Davis (1808–89), was offered command of the Union forces but became a Rebel because he would not fight against his native Virginia. Before the war, Lee had captured the abolitionist zealot John Brown (1800–59). Brown was hanged and the poem "John Brown's Body" and a Southern melody combined to become a marching song of Union troops. With lyrics (1862) by Julia Ward Howe (1819–1910), it became "The Battle Hymn of the Republic."

Lincoln's Emancipation Proclamation made slaves free as of January 1, 1863, in states "in rebellion"—but not in loyal border states. His priority was to "save the Union," and alienating loyal states would not help that cause. Worn down by the North's industrial and manpower edge, the South began to fold in 1864. On April 9, 1865, Lee surrendered to Ulysses S. Grant (1822–85) at Appomattox Court House, Virginia. Five days later, screaming "the South is avenged!" John Wilkes Booth assassinated Lincoln. The last Confederate force gave up on May 26. Counting deaths from disease (about 315,000), some 530,000 perished in the war—more Americans than died in World Wars I and II combined.

NEAR THE END *Prisoners from the Front by Winslow Homer shows three captured Confederate soldiers, with and without uniforms, confronting a Union officer. On assignment for* Harper's Weekly, *Homer competed with photographers to bring images of the war to the Northern homefront.*

ling. [Latin *clāmāns* (stem *clāmant*-), present participle of *clāmāre*, to cry out.]

clam·a·to·ri·al (klăm'ə-tôr'ē-əl, -tōr'ē-əl) *adj. Ornithology.* Of or pertaining to the American flycatchers, a group of perching and singing birds. [New Latin *clamatores*, plural of Latin *clāmātor*, shouter, from *clāmāre*, to cry out.]

clam·bake (klăm'bāk') *n.* **1.** A seashore picnic where clams, fish, and other foods are baked in layers on buried hot stones. **2.** *Informal.* A party, especially a noisy and lively one.

clam·ber (klăm'ər, klăm'bər) *intr.v.* **-bered, -bering, -bers.** To climb with difficulty, especially on all fours; scramble. —*n.* The act of clambering. [Middle English *clambren*, from Old Norse *klembra*, originally, "to grip."] —**clam·ber·er** *n.*

clam chowder *n.* Any of various soups made from shelled clams, salt pork, potatoes, and onions.

clam·my (klăm'ē) *adj.* **-mier, -miest. 1.** Disagreeably moist and usually cold. **2.** Humid; damp. Said of weather. [Middle English, from *clammen*, to stick, smear, Old English *clǣman*.] —**clam·mi·ly** *adv.* —**clam·mi·ness** *n.*

clam·or (klăm'ər) *n.* Also *chiefly British* **clam·our. 1.** A loud outcry or shouting; hubbub. **2.** A vehement expression of discontent or protest; a public outcry. **3.** Any loud and sustained noise; din; blare. —See Synonyms at **noise.** —*v.* **clamored, -oring, -ors.** Also *chiefly British* **clam·our.** —*intr.* **1.** To make a clamor. **2.** To make vigorous demands or complaints. —*tr.* To exclaim insistently and noisily. [Middle English *clamour*, from Old French, from Latin *clāmor*, from *clāmāre*, to cry out.] —**clam·or·er** *n.*

clam·or·ous (klăm'ər-əs) *adj.* Making, full of, or characterized by clamor. —**clam·or·ous·ly** *adv.* —**clam·or·ous·ness** *n.*

clamp (klămp) *n.* Any of various devices used to join, grip, support, or compress mechanical or structural parts. —*tr.v.* **clamped, clamping, clamps.** To fasten, grip, or support with or as if with a clamp. [Middle English, from Middle Dutch *clampe*.]

clamp down *intr.v.* To repress, restrict, or prohibit something not approved of. Used with *on*. —**clamp-down** (klămp'doun') *n.*

clamp·er (klăm'pər) *n.* A spiked plate attached to the sole of a shoe to prevent slipping on ice.

clam·shell (klăm'shĕl') *n.* **1.** The shell of a clam. **2.** A dredging bucket made of two hinged jaws. **3.** Either of a pair of doors in an airplane that open outward and away from each other.

clam·worm (klăm'wûrm') *n.* Any of various segmented marine worms of the genus *Nereis;* especially, *N. virens,* swimming by means of paired, paddlelike appendages. Also called "ragworm."

clan (klăn) *n.* **1.** A traditional social unit in Scotland, consisting of a number of families claiming a common ancestor and following the same hereditary chieftain. **2.** In some tribal societies, a division of a tribe tracing descent from a common ancestor. **3.** Any numerous group of relatives, friends, or associates. [Middle English, from Scottish Gaelic *clann*, children, family, from Latin *planta*, shoot, PLANT.]

clan·des·tine (klăn-dĕs'tən) *adj.* Concealed, usually for some secret or illicit purpose. —See Synonyms at **secret.** [French *clandestin*, from Old French, from Latin *clandestīnus*, from *clam*, in secret (after *intestīnus*, inward, INTESTINE).] —**clan·des·tine·ly** *adv.* —**clan·des·tine·ness, clan·des·ti·ni·ty** (klăn'dĕs-tĭn'ə-tē) *n.*

clang (klăng) *n.* **1.** A loud, metallic, resonant sound. **2.** The strident call of a crane or goose. —*v.* **clanged, clanging, clangs.** —*intr.* To make a clang. —*tr.* To cause to clang. [Latin *clangere*, to resound (imitative).]

clang·er (klăng'ər) *n. Slang.* An embarrassing or tactless blunder. [Imitative, also influenced by Latin *clangor*, resounding noise.]

clan·gor (klăng'ər, klăng'gər) *n.* Also *chiefly British* **clan·gour.** A clang or repeated clanging; a loud ringing; a din. [Latin, from *clangere*, CLANG.] —**clangor** *v.* —**clan·gor·ous** *adj.* —**clan·gor·ous·ly** *adv.*

clank (klăngk) *n.* A metallic sound, sharp and hard but not as resonant as a clang. —*v.* **clanked, clanking, clanks.** —*intr.* To make a clank. —*tr.* To cause to clank. [Imitative.]

clan·nish (klăn'ĭsh) *adj.* **1.** Of, pertaining to, or characteristic of a clan. **2.** Inclined to cling together in a group and exclude outsiders. —**clan·nish·ly** *adv.* —**clan·nish·ness** *n.*

clans·man (klănz'mən) *n., pl.* **-men** (-mĭn). A person belonging to a clan.

clans·wom·an (klănz'wŏŏm'ən) *n., pl.* **-women** (-wĭm'ĭn). A woman belonging to a clan.

clap¹ (klăp) *v.* **clapped, clapping, claps.** —*intr.* **1.** To strike the palms of the hands together with a sudden, explosive sound, as in applauding. **2.** To come together suddenly with a sharp noise. —*tr.* **1.** To strike (the hands, for example) together with a brisk movement and an abrupt, loud sound. **2.** To applaud (actors, for example) by clapping the hands. **3.** To strike lightly but firmly with the open hand, as in greeting: *clapped him on the shoulder.* **4.** To put or place quickly or firmly: *clapped him in jail.* **5.** To flap (the wings). —**clap eyes on.** *Informal.* To catch sight of. —**clap hold of.** *Informal.* To grip. —*n.* **1. a.** The act or sound of clapping the hands. **b.** A loud, sharp, or explosive noise, especially that made by thunder. **2.** A sharp blow with the open hand; a slap. [Middle English *clappen*, from Old English *clappian*, to throb, beat, from Germanic *klap-* (unattested), imitative.]

clap² *n. Slang.* Gonorrhea. [Old French *clapoir*, venereal sore; akin

to *clapier*, brothel, and Old Provençal *clapt*, heap of stones.]

clap·board (klăb'ərd, klăp'bôrd', -bōrd') *n.* A long, narrow board with one edge thicker than the other, overlapped to cover the outer walls of frame houses. Also called "weatherboard." —*tr.v.* **clapboarded, -boarding, boards.** To cover with clapboards. [Partial translation of Middle Dutch *clapholt : clappen,* to crack, split, akin to Old English *clappian,* to CLAP + *holt,* board, wood.]

cla·po·tis (klə-pō'tĭs) *n.* A type of wave formation in which standing waves that have no horizontal motion of crests are formed by the approach of waves to a sea wall, breakwater, or other barrier. [French, from *clapoter,* (of a liquid) agitate with waves.]

clap·per (klăp'ər) *n.* **1.** A person or thing that claps. **2.** The part of a bell that strikes the side. **3.** **clappers.** A rattle consisting of two pieces of wood that strike together to make a clapping sound. **4.** *Slang.* The tongue.

clap·per·board (klăp'ər-bôrd, -bōrd) *n.* A device used in filmmaking consisting of two hinged pieces of wood that are held before the camera bearing the scene number and clapped together to allow the synchronization of the soundtrack and the image.

clap·per·claw (klăp'ər-klô') *tr.v.* **-clawed, -clawing, -claws.** *Archaic.* **1.** To claw or scratch. **2.** To berate or revile. [Probably CLAPPER + CLAW.]

clapper rail *n.* A North American marsh bird, *Rallus longirostris,* having brownish plumage, a long bill, and a clattering cry.

clap·trap (klăp'trăp') *n. Informal.* Pretentious, insincere, or empty language. [CLAP + TRAP ("a trick to win applause").]

claque (klăk) *n.* **1.** A group of persons hired to applaud at a performance. **2.** Any group of adulating or fawning admirers. [French, from *claquer,* to clap (imitative).]

clar·a·bel·la (klăr'ə-bĕl'ə) *n.* An eight-foot organ stop producing soft, sweet tones. [Latin *clāra,* feminine of *clārus,* CLEAR + *bella,* feminine of *bellus,* pretty.]

Clare (klâr). A county in Munster province on the Atlantic coast of the Irish Republic. It is a farming district, with salmon fisheries in the Shannon estuary.

Clare, John (1793–1864). British poet, known for his lyrical evocations of the English countryside. His works, which include *The Shepherd's Calendar* (1827) and *The Rural Muse* (1835), sold poorly and he was destitute. After 1841 he spent his life in a mental hospital, where he produced some of his best poetry.

clar·ence (klăr'əns) *n.* A four-wheeled closed carriage with seats for four passengers. [After the Duke of *Clarence* (1765–1837), later William IV.]

clar·en·don (klăr'ən-dən) *n. Printing.* A variety of boldface roman type. [After the *Clarendon* Press, printing house of Oxford University.]

Clare of As·si·si (klâr; ə-sē'sē, -zē), **Saint** (1194–1253). Italian nun, who founded the first Franciscan order of nuns, the Poor Clares. She has become the patron saint of television because she is said to have once witnessed a mass celebrated far away.

clar·et (klăr'ət) *n.* **1. a.** The dry red table wine from the Bordeaux region of France. **b.** Any of various similar red wines made elsewhere. **2.** Dark or grayish purplish red. [Middle English, from Old French, from Medieval Latin *(vīnum) clārātum,* "clarified (wine)," from Latin *clārāre,* to make clear, purify, from *clārus,* CLEAR.] —**clar·et** *adj.*

claret cup *n.* A chilled mixed drink of red wine with spirits, fruit, and other ingredients.

clar·i·fy (klăr'ə-fī') *v.* **-fied, -fying, -fies.** —*tr.* **1.** To make clear or easier to understand; elucidate. **2.** To make clear by removing impurities, often by heating gently: *clarify butter.* —*intr.* To become clear. [Middle English *clarifien,* from Old French *clarifier,* from Late Latin *clārificāre : Latin clārus,* CLEAR + *facere,* to make.] —**clar·i·fi·ca·tion** (klăr'ə-fĭ-kā'shən) *n.* —**clar·i·fi·er** *n.*

clar·i·net (klăr'ə-nĕt') *n.* Also *rare* **clar·i·o·net** (klăr'ē-ə-nĕt'). **1.** A woodwind instrument having a straight, cylindrical tube with a flaring bell and a single-reed mouthpiece, played by means of finger holes and keys. **2.** An eight-foot organ stop producing a sound suggestive of a clarinet. [French *clarinette,* from Italian *clarinetto,* diminutive of *clarino,* trumpet, from Latin *clārus,* CLEAR.] —**clar·i·net·ist, clar·i·net·tist** *n.*

cla·ri·no (klə-rē'nō) *n., pl.* **-nos.** *Music.* **1.** The high register of the trumpet, especially in baroque music. **2.** A high, trumpetlike organ stop. [Italian, trumpet, probably from Spanish *clarin.*]

clar·i·on (klăr'ē-ən) *n.* **1.** A medieval trumpet with a shrill, clear tone. **2.** The sound made by this instrument or any sound resembling it. **3.** An organ stop with a high, shrill tone. —*adj.* Shrill and clear: *a clarion call to resistance.* [Middle English *clarioun,* from Medieval Latin *clāriō* (stem *clāriōn-*), trumpet, from Latin *clārus,* CLEAR.]

clar·i·ty (klăr'ə-tē) *n.* **1.** Clearness. **2.** Plainness; lucidity: *clarity of style.* [Middle English *clarite,* from Latin *clāritās,* from *clārus,* CLEAR.]

Clark (klärk), **George Rogers** (1752–1818). U.S. military leader and frontiersman. During the American Revolution he led a band of less than 200 men on many successful raids against hostile Indians and British troops. His efforts contributed to England's concession of the Northwest Territory to the United States in 1783.

Clark, Kenneth Mackenzie, Baron (1903–83). British art critic and historian. *The Gothic Revival* (1929) was the first of his many influential books, and *The Nude* (1955) perhaps his most famous.

Clark, William (1770–1838). U.S. explorer and soldier. With Meriwether Lewis, he explored the American northwest in search of a land passage to the Pacific (1804–06). During the expedition he studied the flora and fauna and carefully mapped the region, helping to open the area to settlers. He was the brother of George Rogers Clark.

Clark cell *n. Physics.* A former standard voltaic cell with an emf of 1.4345 volts (15°C). It has a zinc cathode in zinc sulfate and a mercury anode in mercury sulfate. [After Josiah L. *Clark* (1822–98), English engineer.]

clark·i·a (klär′kē-ə) *n.* Any of several annual plants of the genus *Clarkia,* of western North America, especially *C. pulchella,* which is cultivated for its red, purple, and white flowers. [New Latin, after William CLARK, who discovered it.]

clarsach. Variant of **clairschach.**

clart (klärt) *n. Northern British.* A dirty or sticky smear. [Middle English, origin obscure.] —**clart·y** *adj.*

clar·y (klâr′ē) *n., pl.* -**ies.** Any of several European plants of the genus *Salvia,* especially *S. sclarea,* an aromatic herb with bluish-white flowers. Also called "clary sage." [Middle English *clarye, sclarey,* from Old French *sclaree,* from Medieval Latin *sclarea†.*]

-**clase** *suffix.* Indicates a mineral with a specified cleavage; for example, **plagioclase.** [French, from Greek *klasis,* a breaking, from *klan,* to break.]

clash (klăsh) *v.* **clashed, clashing, clashes.** —*intr.* **1.** To collide with a loud, harsh noise. **2.** To conflict, as in a fight, contest, or debate; be in opposition. **3.** To create an unpleasant visual impression when combined. Used of colors. **4.** To occur at the same time; coincide: *The date of the meeting clashes with my dental appointment.* —*tr.* To strike together with a harsh, metallic noise.
—*n.* **1.** A loud, resounding, metallic noise, such as that made by two objects colliding. **2.** A conflict, opposition, or disagreement. **3.** An inharmonious grouping, for example of colors. —See Synonyms at **discord.** [Imitative.]

clasp (klăsp) *n.* **1.** A fastening, such as a hook or buckle, used to hold two objects or parts together. **2. a.** An embrace; a hug. **b.** A grip or grasp of the hand. **3.** A small metal bar attached to a military decoration indicating the action for which it was awarded. —*tr.v.* **clasped, clasping, clasps.** **1.** To fasten with or as if with a clasp. **2.** To hold in a tight grasp; embrace. **3.** To grip firmly in or with the hand. [Middle English *claspe,* from *claspen, clapsen,* to grip, grasp, perhaps from Old English *clyppan,* to embrace.] —**clasp·er** *n.*

clas·pers (klăs′pərz, kläs-) *pl.n.* A pair of appendages, found in male insects and certain fish, that are specialized for the introduction of sperm into the female reproductive tract.

clasp knife *n.* A pocketknife with a single blade.

class (klăs, kläs) *n. Abbr.* **cl. 1. a.** A set, collection, group, or configuration containing members having or thought to have at least one attribute in common; a kind; a sort. **b.** *Statistics.* Any interval in a **frequency distribution** (*see*). See **set** (in mathematics). **2.** Any division of people or objects by quality, rank, or grade. **3.** A social stratum whose members share similar economic, social, and cultural characteristics. **4. a.** The division of society into relative strata or ranks: *discrimination on grounds of class.* **b.** Social rank or caste, especially high rank. **5. a.** A group of pupils or students studying the same subject or following the same course. **b.** The period during which such a group meets. **c.** A group of students graduating in the same year. **6.** *Biology.* A taxonomic category ranking below a phylum (animals) or division (plants) and above an order. **7.** The quality of accommodation on a public vehicle: *travel in first class.* **8.** *Informal.* Good taste in manner or dress; stylishness: *a girl with class.*
—*tr.v.* **classed, classing, classes.** To arrange, group, or rate according to qualities or characteristics; assign to a class; classify. [French *classe,* from Late Latin *classis,* from Latin, one of the six divisions of the Roman people, army, fleet.]

class. 1. classic; classical. **2.** classification; classified; classify.

class action *n.* A legal action undertaken on behalf of all unnamed persons having the same interest in the alleged wrong as the named plaintiffs.

class-con·scious (klăs′kŏn′shəs) *adj.* Aware of belonging to a particular socioeconomic class, often to the extent of being hostile to or envious of other classes. —**class-con·scious·ness** *n.*

clas·sic (klăs′ĭk) *adj.* **1.** Of the highest rank or class. **2.** Serving as an outstanding representative of its kind; model. **3.** Having lasting significance or recognized worth. **4.** *Abbr.* **class.** Pertaining to ancient Greek or Roman literature or art; classical. **5. a.** Of or in accordance with established principles and methods in the arts and sciences. **b.** Having a simple and harmonious design unaffected by passing fashions. **6.** Of lasting historical or literary significance. **7.** *Informal.* Of a well-known or traditional type; remarkably typical: *a classic mistake.*
—*n.* **1.** An artist, author, or work generally considered to be of the highest rank or excellence. **2. classics.** The literature of ancient Greece and Rome. **3.** Something considered to be typical or traditional. **4.** A traditional, usually annual, sporting event: *The World Series is the fall classic of baseball.*
   Usage: Classic and *classical* are sometimes interchangeable when used as adjectives, as in such phrases as *classic/classical design* or *look. Classical* is more common in senses pertaining to ancient Greek or Roman culture. *Classic* has a more general range of use, including the broad sense of "highest rank or excellence": *a classic story; Edward Lear's classic limericks.* In this sense it would be different from *a classical story,* in that there is not necessarily any

implication of historical origins. *Classic* has also undergone considerable semantic development in recent years, with its meaning of "typical," "appropriate," and its widespread ironic use in informal speech: *That's classic!* See also Usage note at **-ic, -ical.**

clas·si·cal (klăs′ĭ-kəl) *adj. Abbr.* **class. 1. a.** Of, pertaining to, or in accordance with the precedents of ancient Greek and Roman art, architecture, and literature. **b.** Learned in or studying Greek and Roman art, architecture, or literature. **2.** Of or concerning the most artistically developed stage of a civilization: *Chinese classical poetry.* **3.** *Music.* **a.** Pertaining to or designating the European music, such as that of Haydn and Mozart, of the latter half of the 18th century. **b.** Designating any music in the educated European tradition, as distinguished from popular or folk music. **4.** Conventional and authoritative rather than new or experimental. **5.** Showing artistic restraint and respect for principles of traditional design. **6.** Of or pertaining to nonrelativistic or nonquantum physics: *classical mechanics.* —See Usage note at **classic.** —**clas·si·cal·ism, clas·si·cal·ness** *n.* —**clas·si·cal·ly** *adv.*

Classical Greek *n.* The forms of Greek used in classical literature, chiefly Attic-Ionic, Doric, and Aeolic.

Classical Latin *n.* The form of Latin used in classical literature. Compare **Vulgar Latin.**

clas·si·cism (klăs′ə-sĭz′əm) *n.* **1.** Aesthetic attitudes and principles based on the culture, art, architecture, and literature of ancient Greece and Rome and characterized by emphasis on form, simplicity, proportion, and restraint. **2.** Classical scholarship. **3.** A Greek or Latin form or idiom.

clas·si·cist (klăs′ə-sĭst) *n.* A student of classics.

clas·si·fi·a·ble (klăs′ə-fī′ə-bəl) *adj.* Capable of being classified.

clas·si·fi·ca·tion (klăs′ə-fĭ-kā′shən) *n. Abbr.* **cl., class. 1.** The act or result of classifying. **2.** A category in which something may be classified. **3.** In South Africa, any of various racial groups as distinguished in law. **4.** *Biology.* The systematic grouping of organisms into categories based on shared characteristics or traits; taxonomy. **5.** The designation of information as officially secret. **6.** One of a series of degrees of availability for conscription assigned to men by a selective service system. —**clas·si·fi·ca·to·ry** (klăs′ə-fĭ-kə-tôr′ē, -kə-tōr′ē) *adj.*

class·i·fied (klăs′ə-fīd′) *adj.* **1.** Arranged in classes or categories. **2.** Designated as secret and available only to authorized persons.

classified advertisement *n.* An advertisement in a newspaper, usually brief and in small type. Also called "classified."

clas·si·fy (klăs′ə-fī′) *tr.v.* **-fied, -fying, -fies. 1.** To arrange or organize according to class or category. **2.** In South Africa, to assign to or register under any of the various racial groups. **3.** To designate (a document, for instance) as secret and available only to authorized persons: *The report was classified top secret.* [Latin *classis,* CLASS + -FY.] —**clas·si·fi·er** *n.*

clas·sis (klăs′ĭs) *n., pl.* **classes** (klăs′ēz′). *Ecclesiastical.* **1.** In certain Reformed churches, a governing body of pastors and elders having jurisdiction over local churches. **2.** The district or churches governed by such a body. [New Latin, from Latin, division, CLASS.]

class·less (klăs′lĭs) *adj.* **1.** Not divided economically or socially; lacking class distinctions. **2.** Not belonging to any particular social class.

class mark *n. Statistics.* The numerical value given for computational convenience to a statistical observation falling within a number of intervals. Also called "mark."

class·mate (klăs′māt′, kläs′-) *n.* A member of the same class at school.

class·room (klăs′rōōm′, -rŏŏm′, kläs′-) *n.* A room in which classes are conducted in a school.

class struggle *n.* Conflict between social classes; especially, in Marxist theory, the conflict for economic and political power between an exploiting class, as the capitalist bourgeoisie, and an exploited class, as the proletariat. Also called "class war."

class·y (klăs′ē, kläs′ē) *adj.* **-ier, -iest.** *Informal.* Stylish; elegant. —**class·i·ness** *n.*

clast (klăst) *n. Geology.* A fragment of rock. [Greek *klastos,* fragmented, from *klân,* to break.]

-**clast** *suffix.* Indicates one that breaks or destroys; for example, **osteoclast, iconoclast.** [Medieval Latin *-clastēs,* from Medieval Greek *-klastēs,* breaker, from *klân,* to break.]

clas·tic (klăs′tĭk) *adj.* **1.** Separable into parts or having removable sections: *a clastic anatomical model.* **2.** *Geology.* Made up of fragments; fragmental. **3.** *Biology.* Dividing into parts. [Greek *klastos,* broken, from *klân,* to break.]

clath·rate (klăth′rāt′, klăth′-) *adj. Biology.* Having a latticelike structure or appearance.
—*n. Chemistry.* An inclusion complex in which atoms or molecules of one substance are trapped within the crystal structure of another. Also called "clathrate compound." [Latin *clāthrātus,* past participle of *clāthrāre,* to provide with a lattice, from *clāthrī, clātra,* lattice, from Greek *klēithra,* from *klēithron,* door bar, from *kleiein,* to close.]

clat·ter (klăt′ər) *n.* **1.** A loud rattling sound or sounds. **2.** A loud disturbance; a commotion.
—*v.* **clattered, -tering, -ters.** —*intr.* **1.** To make a clatter; move with a clatter. —*tr.* To cause to clatter. [Middle English *clatren,* Old English *clatrian* (attested in gerund, *clatrung*) (imitative).] —**clat·ter·er** *n.*

Claude Lor·rain (klōd lô-răɴ′), born Claude Gellée (1600–82). French landscape painter, who settled in Rome. He produced luminous landscapes and coastal scenes suffused with golden light.

Clau·di·an (klô′dē-ən), born Claudius Claudianus (*c.* A.D. 370–404). Roman poet, considered the last in the classical tradition. He is best known for his epic *The Rape of Proserpine.*

clau·di·ca·tion (klô′dĭ-kā′shən) *n.* A halt in one's walk; a limp; lameness. [Middle English *claudicacioun*, from Latin *claudicātiō* (stem *claudicātiōn-*), from *claudicāre*, to limp, from *claudus†*, lame.]

Clau·di·us I (klô′dē-əs) (10 B.C.–A.D. 54). Roman emperor (A.D. 41–54) and historian. Physically disabled and considered weak in the head, he was excluded from public life until Caligula made him consul (37). When Caligula was murdered (41), Claudius became emperor and proved a sound, efficient ruler.

claus·al (klô′zəl) *adj.* 1. Of the nature of a clause. 2. Of or pertaining to clauses.

clause (klôz) *n. Abbr.* **cl.** 1. A group of words containing a subject and a predicate that forms part of a compound or complex sentence. See **subordinate clause, main clause.** 2. A section of a legal document, contract, or the like; a distinct article, stipulation, or provision in a document. [Middle English, from Old French, from Medieval Latin *clausa,* close of a rhetorical period, conclusion of a legal argument, hence section of a law, from *claudere* (past participle *clausus*), to close.]

Clau·se·witz (klou′zə-vĭts), **Karl von** (1780–1831). Prussian general and military theorist. In his *On War* he argued for the mobilization of the national effort in a concept of total warfare that dominated Prussian and German military strategy up to World War I.

Clau·si·us (klou′zē-ŏŏs), **Rudolph Julius Emanuel** (1822–88). German molecular physicist, who formulated the second law of thermodynamics (1850) that "heat cannot of itself pass from a colder to a hotter body." He developed the concept of entropy and a kinetic theory of gases.

claustral. Variant of **cloistral.**

claus·tro·pho·bi·a (klôs′trə-fō′bē-ə) *n.* A pathological fear of confined spaces. [New Latin : Latin *claustrum,* enclosed place, CLOIS-TER + -PHOBIA.]

claus·tro·pho·bic (klôs′trə-fō′bĭk) *adj.* 1. Suffering from claustrophobia; fearful of confined spaces. 2. Uncomfortably confined or crowded: *a claustrophobic little room.*

cla·vate (klā′vāt′) *adj.* Having one end thickened; club-shaped; claviform. [New Latin *clavatus,* from Latin *clāva,* club.] —**cla·vate·ly** *adv.*

clave. *Archaic.* 1. Past tense of **cleave** (to split). 2. Past tense of **cleave** (to cling).

cla·ver (klā′vər) *intr.v.* **-vered, -vering, -vers.** *Scottish.* To gossip or talk idly.
~*n. Scottish.* Gossip; idle talk. [Scottish Gaelic *clabaire†,* babbler.]

clav·i·chord (klăv′ĭ-kôrd′) *n.* An early musical keyboard instrument with a soft sound produced by brass pins (tangents) striking horizontal strings. [Medieval Latin *clāvichordium* : Latin *clāvis,* key + *chorda,* CHORD.]

clav·i·cle (klăv′ĭ-kəl) *n.* 1. In human beings, either of the two bones connecting the upper part of the breastbone with the shoulder blades. Also called "collarbone." 2. The corresponding structure in the pectoral girdle of certain other vertebrates. [Medieval Latin *clāvicula,* diminutive of Latin *clāvis,* key (referring to the shape).] —**cla·vic·u·lar** (klā-vĭk′yə-lər) *adj.* —**cla·vic·u·late** (klā-vĭk′yə-lāt′) *adj.*

clav·i·corn (klăv′ĭ-kôrn′) *adj.* Belonging to or designating a group of beetles of the section Clavicornia, having club-shaped antennae, including the ladybugs and grain beetles. [New Latin *Clavicornia* (family name) : Latin *clāva,* club + Latin *cornū,* horn.]

cla·vier (klə-vîr′, klā′vē-ər, klăv′ē-ər) *n.* 1. A keyboard. 2. Any stringed keyboard instrument, such as a harpsichord or piano. [German *Klavier,* piano, from French *clavier,* keyboard, from Old French *clavier,* key-bearer, from Latin *clāvis,* key.]

clav·i·form (klăv′ə-fôrm′) *adj.* Club-shaped; clavate. [Latin *clāva,* club + -FORM.]

claw (klô) *n.* 1. a. A sharp, often curved, nail on the toe of a mammal, reptile, or bird. b. The foot of a mammal, reptile, or bird having such nails. 2. a. A chela or similar pincerlike structure on the limb of a crustacean or other arthropod. b. A limb terminating in such a structure. 3. Anything resembling a claw, such as the cleft end of a hammerhead. 4. *Botany.* The narrowed basal part of certain petals or sepals.
~*v.* **clawed, clawing, claws.** —*tr.* To scratch, tear, grab, or pull with or as if with claws. —*intr.* To make scratching or digging motions with or as if with claws. [Middle English *clawe,* Old English *clawu,* from Germanic.]

claw hammer *n.* A hammer having a head with one end forked for removing nails.

claw hatchet *n.* A hatchet having one end of the head forked.

clay (klā) *n.* 1. A fine-grained, firm, natural material, plastic when wet, that consists primarily of hydrated silicates of aluminum and is widely used in making bricks, tiles, and pottery. 2. Any earth that forms a paste with water and hardens when heated or dried. 3. Moist earth; mud. 4. The human body as distinct from the spirit. Used in literary or poetic contexts. [Middle English *cley, clay,* Old English *clæg,* from Germanic.] —**clay·ey** (klā′ē), **clay·ish** *adj.*

Clay, Cassius Marcellus. See Muhammad **Ali.**

Clay (klā), **Henry** (1777–1852). U.S. statesman. A U.S. congressman and senator, his efforts to reconcile the free and slave states through the Missouri Compromise (1820), the compromise tariff of 1833, and the Compromise of 1850 earned him the nickname "the Great Compromiser." He ran unsuccessfully for president in 1824, 1832, and 1844.

clay court *n.* A tennis court having a surface made of clay or a synthetic substance resembling clay.

clay mineral *n.* Any of a group of hydrated silicates, mainly of aluminum and magnesium, present in clays and responsible for their plastic properties.

clay·more (klā′môr′, -mōr′) *n.* A large, double-edged broadsword formerly used by Scottish Highlanders. [Gaelic *claidheamh mōr,* "great sword" : *claidheamh,* sword + *mōr,* great.]

clay·pan (klā′păn′) *n.* 1. *Geology.* A layer of compact clay beneath the surface soil, causing poor drainage and waterlogging. 2. In Australia, a hollow or slight depression in the ground that has a bottom of clay and holds water after rain.

clay pigeon *n.* A clay disk thrown or propelled into the air as a flying target to be shot at for sport. Also called "bird."

clay·to·ni·a (klā-tō′nē-ə) *n.* Any North American or eastern Siberian succulent plant of the genus *Claytonia,* many of which are cultivated as ornamentals. [After John *Clayton* (1693-1773), U.S. botanist.]

–cle *suffix.* Indicates small size; for example, **particle.** [Middle English, from Old French, from Latin *-culus.*]

clean (klēn) *adj.* **cleaner, cleanest.** 1. Free from dirt, stains, or impurities; unsoiled. 2. a. Free from foreign matter; unadulterated. b. Not infected: *a clean wound.* 3. Producing little radioactive fallout or contamination. 4. a. Without imperfections or blemishes; regular; perfect: *a clean line.* b. Well-formed or elegant; streamlined. 5. Free from clumsiness; deft; adroit: *a clean throw.* 6. Without restrictions or encumbrances: *a clean bill of health.* 7. Entire; thorough; complete: *a clean sweep.* 8. Having few alterations or corrections; legible: *a clean page.* 9. Blank: *a clean page.* 10. Morally pure; unsullied; sinless. 11. Not ribald or obscene. 12. Honest; fair, as in sports: *a clean fighter.* 13. *Slang.* a. Possessing no hidden drugs, weapon, stolen goods, or the like. b. Innocent of a crime. 14. Having or showing no record or history of crimes, offenses, or misdeeds: *a clean past.* 15. In religious and biblical contexts: a. Free from defilement. b. Not prohibited by dietary law. 16. Fresh; pleasantly sharp: *a clean taste.* 17. *Informal.* Able to control urination and defecation.
~*adv.* 1. In a clean manner; cleanly. 2. *Informal.* Entirely; wholly; thoroughly. —**come clean.** *Slang.* To admit the truth; confess.
~*v.* **cleaned, cleaning, cleans.** —*tr.* 1. To rid of dirt or other impurities. 2. To remove (dirt or impurities) from something. 3. To prepare (fowl or other food) for cooking. —*intr.* To undergo or perform the act of ridding of dirt and impurities. —**clean out.** 1. To rid of dirt, rubbish, or impurities. 2. To rid or empty of contents or occupants. 3. To drive or force out. 4. *Informal.* To deprive completely of money or material wealth: *The robbery cleaned them out.* 5. *Informal.* To exhaust (a supply of goods or money).
~*n.* An act or instance of cleaning. [Middle English *clene,* Old English *clǣne,* from West Germanic *klaini* (unattested).] —**clean·a·ble** *adj.* —**clean·ness** *n.*

clean-cut (klēn′kŭt′) *adj.* 1. Clearly and sharply defined or outlined. 2. Wholesome; neat and well-dressed.

clean·er (klē′nər) *n.* 1. A person who is employed to clean houses, offices, and the like. 2. A machine, device, or chemical agent that cleans.

clean·ers (klē′nərz) *n. Used with a singular or plural verb.* A commercial establishment providing a dry-cleaning service. —**take to the cleaners.** *Slang.* 1. To swindle or rob. 2. To take all the money or possessions of; ruin. 3. To subject to withering criticism.

clean·ly (klēn′lē) *adj.* **-lier, -liest.** Habitually and carefully neat and clean.
~*adv.* (klēn′lē). 1. In a clean manner. 2. Smoothly; deftly or easily: *cut the wood cleanly.* —**clean·li·ness** *n.*

cleanse (klĕnz) *tr.v.* **cleansed, cleansing, cleanses.** 1. To free from dirt, defilement, or guilt; purge or clean. 2. To clean (a wound). 3. To use a cleanser on. [Middle English *clensen,* Old English *clǣnsian.*]

cleans·er (klĕn′zər) *n.* 1. One that cleans. 2. A detergent, powder, or other chemical agent that removes dirt, grease, or stains. 3. A skin lotion or cream that is used to clean the face.

clean-shav·en (klēn-shā′vən) *adj.* 1. Having the beard or hair shaved off. 2. Having recently shaved.

clean up *intr.v.* 1. To rid a place of dirt or disorder. 2. To make oneself clean, neat, or presentable. 3. *Informal.* To finish; conclude. 4. *Informal.* To make a large profit. —*tr.v.* 1. To clean and make tidy (a room or oneself, for example); remove dirt or debris from. 2. *Informal.* To rid (a town, for example) of corruption.

clean·up (klēn′ŭp′) *n.* 1. A thorough cleaning or tidying. 2. *Informal.* The process of ridding a place of corruption or dishonesty. 3. *Informal.* The final often routine tasks that complete a project. 4. *Informal.* A large profit.

clear (klîr) *adj.* **clearer, clearest.** 1. Free from anything that dims, obscures, or darkens; unclouded. 2. Free from flaw, blemish, or impurity. 3. Free from impediment, obstruction, or hindrance; open. 4. Plain or evident. 5. Easily perceptible to the eye or ear; distinct. 6. Free of guilt; untroubled: *a clear conscience.* 7. a. Free from doubt or confusion; certain; sure. b. Logical and incisive: *a clear thinker.* 8. Free from qualification or limitation; absolute: *a clear winner.* 9. Resonant; ringing, as certain sounds. 10. Freed from contact or connection; disengaged. Used with *of: We are now clear of danger.* 11. Free from roughness or protrusions, as timber.

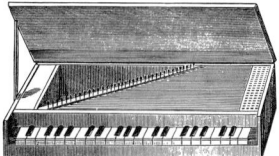

clavichord *The clavichord was originally designed for organists to practice on. The basic clavichord, illustrated here, consists of a single keyboard, but there are examples with two keyboards and a pedal board—reproducing on a small scale the effect of an organ with two manuals.*

clematis *There are approximately 200 species of* Clematis *found in temperate regions. The climbing species (vines) are the most common, and this hybrid variety is known as "The President."*

12. Freed from burden or obligation. **13.** Without charges or deductions; net: *She earns a clear $15,000.* **14.** Transparent: *clear soup.* **15.** Not cloudy or raining. Said of weather. **16.** Empty: *a clear desk; a clear ship.* **17.** In show jumping, having incurred no penalties: *a clear round.* **—in the clear.** Free from burdens, dangers, difficulties, or suspicion.
~*adv.* **1.** Distinctly; clearly. **2.** *Informal.* All the way; completely; entirely: *He slept clear through the night.* **3.** Out of the way; completely away: *stand clear of the doors.*
~*v.* **cleared, clearing, clears.** —*tr.* **1.** To make clear, light, or bright. **2.** To rid of impurities, blemishes, muddiness, or foreign matter. **3.** To free from confusion, doubt, or ambiguity; make plain or intelligible. **4. a.** To rid of obstructions or entanglements: *clear the road of snow.* **b.** To make (a way, path, clearing, or the like) by removing obstacles or entanglements: *clear a space in the snow.* **c.** To remove or get rid of (obstacles or entanglements): *clear snow from the road.* **5.** To free from a legal charge or imputation of guilt; acquit. **6.** To pass by, under, or over without contact. **7.** To settle (a debt). **8.** To gain (a given amount) as net profit or earnings. **9. a.** To pass (a check or other bill of exchange) through a clearing-house. **b.** To pass (a check) through the banking system and debit and credit the relevant accounts. **10.** To free (a ship or cargo) from legal detention at a harbor by fulfilling the customs and harbor requirements. **11.** To free (the throat) of phlegm by coughing. **12.** To empty; remove objects from: *clear the cupboard.* **13.** To leave; evacuate: *If the fire alarm goes off, everyone must clear the building.* **14.** To declare (a person) fit to see secret or classified documents or to take part in confidential matters. **15.** To pass through by complying with or satisfying certain conditions: *clear customs.* **16.** *Sports.* To kick, hit, throw, or carry (a ball or puck) away from the defended goal. **17.** *Computer Science.* To remove (stored data) from a storage device. **18.** To make (a microscope specimen) transparent by immersing in a fluid such as xylene. —*intr.* **1.** To become clean, fair, or bright. **2.** To exchange checks and bills or settle accounts, through a clearing-house. **3.** To pass through the banking system and be debited and credited to the relevant accounts. Used of a check. **4.** To be enabled to pass through by satisfying certain conditions; especially, to comply with customs regulations. **5.** To become empty or unblocked. **6.** To stop raining or become less cloudy; brighten. **7.** To go away; disappear. Used of fog, mist, rain, or the like. **—clear off.** *Informal.* To go away; leave quickly. Often used in the imperative. **—clear up. 1.** To make clear. **2.** To become fair and sunny after having been cloudy. **3.** To rid of confusion or mystery; explain. [Middle English *clere,* from Old French *cler,* from Latin *clārus,* bright, clear.] **—clear·a·ble** *adj.* **—clear·er** *n.* **—clear·ly** *adv.* **—clear·ness** *n.*
clear-air turbulence (klîr′âr′) *n. Abbr.* **CAT** A type of turbulence encountered by aircraft at high altitudes, caused by waves formed at the interface between two unmixed air layers.
clear·ance (klîr′əns) *n.* **1.** The act of clearing. **2.** A space cleared; a clearing. **3.** *Abbr.* **cl.** The amount by which a moving object clears something. **4.** An intervening distance or space enabling free play, such as that between machine parts. **5.** Permission for an aircraft, ship, or other vehicle to proceed, as after an inspection of equipment or cargo or during certain traffic conditions. **6.** Official certification of blamelessness, trustworthiness, or suitability. **7.** A sale, generally at reduced prices, to dispose of old merchandise. **8.** *Abbr.* **cl.** The passage of checks and other bills of exchange through a clearing-house.
clear·cole (klîr′kōl′) *n.* A primer or size that contains whiting. **—clear·cole** *v.*
clear-cut (klîr′kŭt′) *adj.* **1.** Distinctly and sharply defined or outlined. **2.** Plain; evident.
clear-eyed (klîr′īd′) *adj.* **1. a.** Having sharp, bright eyes. **b.** Keen-sighted. **2.** Mentally acute or perceptive.
clear-head·ed (klîr′hĕd′ĭd) *adj.* Having a clear, orderly mind; sensible. **—clear-head·ed·ly** *adv.* **—clear-head·ed·ness** *n.*
clear·ing (klîr′ĭng) *n.* **1.** A tract of land within a wood or other overgrown area from which the trees and other obstructions have been removed. **2.** In banking, the exchange among banks of checks, drafts, and notes, and the settlement of differences arising from it.
clear·ing-house (klîr′ĭng-hous′) *n. Abbr.* **c.h., C.H.** An office where banks exchange checks and drafts and settle accounts.
clear out *tr.v.* To tidy or empty by removing rubbish or unwanted articles. —*intr.v. Informal.* To leave. **—clear·out** (klîr′out′) *n.*
clear-sight·ed (klîr′sī′tĭd) *adj.* **1.** Having sharp, clear vision. **2.** Discerning. **—clear-sight·ed·ly** *adv.* **—clear-sight·ed·ness** *n.*
clearstory. Variant of **clerestory.**
clear·wing (klîr′wĭng′) *n.* Any of various moths of the family Sesiidae (or Aegeriidae), having scaleless, transparent wings and resembling wasps.
cleat (klēt) *n.* **1.** A strip of wood or iron used to strengthen or support the surface to which it is attached. **2.** A piece of iron, rubber, or leather attached to the underside of a shoe to preserve the sole or prevent slipping. **3.** A piece of metal or wood having projecting arms or ends on which a rope can be wound or secured. **4.** A wedge-shaped piece of wood or other material fastened onto something such as a spar to act as a support or to prevent slipping. **5.** A spurlike device used in gripping a tree or pole in climbing. **6.** *Mining.* A joint or system of joints developed in a coal seam.
~*tr.v.* **cleated, cleating, cleats. 1.** To supply or support with a cleat or cleats. **2.** *Nautical.* To secure (a rope, for example) to or with a cleat. [Middle English *clete,* Old English *clēat* (unattested), lump, wedge.]
cleav·age (klē′vĭj) *n.* **1.** The act of splitting or cleaving. **2.** The state of being split or cleft; a fissure or division. **3.** *Mineralogy.* The splitting of a crystal, or the tendency to split, along definite crystalline planes *(cleavage planes),* yielding smooth surfaces. **4.** *Zoology.* The process of cell division that produces a blastula (hollow ball of cells) from a fertilized ovum. Also called "segmentation." **5.** *Informal.* The hollow or line between a woman's breasts, especially that exposed by a low neckline.
cleave¹ (klēv) *v.* **cleft** (klĕft) or **cleaved** or **clove** (klōv) or *archaic* **clave** (klāv), **cleft** or **cleaved** or **cloven** (klō′vən) or *archaic* **clove, cleaving, cleaves.** —*tr.* **1.** To split or separate, as with an ax. **2.** To make or accomplish as if by cutting: *cleave a path through the forest.* **3.** To pierce or penetrate. —*intr.* **1.** To split or separate, especially along a natural line of division. **2.** To make one's way; penetrate; pass. Used with *through.* **—See Synonyms at tear.** [Cleave, clove, cloven; Middle English *cleven, clave, cloven,* Old English *clēofan, clēaf* (past singular), *clofen.* The weak form *cleft,* Middle English *cleved, cleft,* from the infinitive *cleven.*]
cleave² *intr.v.* **cleaved** or *archaic* **clave** (klāv) or **clove** (klōv), **cleaved, cleaving, cleaves.** *Archaic.* **1.** To adhere, cling, or stick fast. Used with *to.* **2.** To be faithful. Used with *to*: *"Cleave to that which is good"* (Romans 12:9). [Middle English *clevien,* Old English *cleofian.*]
cleav·er (klē′vər) *n.* A heavy, axlike knife or hatchet used especially by butchers.
cleav·ers (klē′vərz) *n., pl.* **-ers.** Any of several plants of the genus *Galium*; especially, *G. aparine,* having small white flowers and prickly stems and fruits. This species is also called "goose grass." [Middle English *clivre* (probably influenced by *clivres,* claws), Old English *clīfe,* "the clinging plant," from *cleofian,* CLEAVE (cling.]
cleek (klēk) *n.* **1.** A number-one golf iron, having very little loft to the club face. **2.** *Scottish.* A large hook. [Middle English *cleche, cleike,* "grasping," from *clechen,* to grasp, seize, Old English *clǣcan* (unattested), probably akin to CLUTCH (verb).]
clef (klĕf) *n.* A symbol on a musical staff, indicating the pitch of the notes. See **alto clef, bass clef, treble clef.** [French, key, musical key, from Old French, from Latin *clāvis,* key.]
cleft (klĕft). A past tense and past participle of **cleave** (to split).
~*adj.* **1.** Divided; split; separated. **2.** *Botany.* Having deeply divided lobes or divisions: *a cleft leaf.*
~*n.* **1.** A crack; a crevice; a split. **2.** A split or indentation between two parts, as of the chin. **3.** A **rill** *(see)* on the moon's surface. [Middle English *clift,* rift, fissure, Old English *geclyft.*]
cleft palate *n.* A congenital fissure in the roof of the mouth, often associated with a cleft in the upper lip (a harelip).
cleg (klĕg) *n.* A horsefly. [Old Norse *kleggi.*]
clei·do·ic egg (klī-dō′ĭk) *n.* An egg with a tough shell that limits water loss but permits gas exchange, characteristic of reptiles, birds, and insects. [Greek *kleidoun,* to lock in, from *kleis* (stem *kleid-*), key.]
cleis·tog·a·mous (klī-stŏg′ə-məs) *adj.* Also **cleis·to·gam·ic** (klī′stə-găm′ĭk). *Botany.* Characterized by self-fertilization in an unopened, budlike state, as in the violet. [Greek *kleistos,* closed + -GAMOUS.] **—cleis·tog·a·mous·ly** *adv.* **—cleis·tog·a·my** (klī-stŏg′ə-mē) *n.*
cleis·to·the·ci·um (klī′stə-thē′sē-əm) *n. Botany.* In fungi, a type of ascocarp in which the ascospores are completely enclosed and released by decay of its wall. [Greek *kleistos,* closed + New Latin *-thecium,* case, from Greek *thēkē,* case.]
Cle·land (klē′lənd), **John** (1709–89). English author, best known for the racy novel *Fanny Hill* (1749).
clem·a·tis (klĕm′ə-tĭs) *n.* Any of various northern temperate plants or vines of the genus *Clematis,* many of which are cultivated as ornamentals, having white or variously colored flowers and plumelike seeds. See **traveler's-joy.** [New Latin *Clematis,* from Latin *clēmatis,* from Greek *klēmatis,* from *klēma,* twig.]
Cle·men·ceau (klĕm′ən-sō′), **Georges** (1841–1929). French statesman and prime minister (1906–09, 1917–20), whose polemical style earned him the nickname "the Tiger." He played a key role in negotiating the Treaty of Versailles (1919).
clem·en·cy (klĕm′ən-sē) *n., pl.* **-cies. 1.** Mildness of temper, especially toward an offender or enemy; leniency; mercy. **2.** Mildness, especially of weather. —See Synonyms at **mercy.**
Clem·ens (klĕm′ənz), **Samuel Langhorne,** pen name "Mark Twain" (1833–1910). U.S. author and humorist. Influenced by his early years on the Mississippi River, he brought his unmatched humor and sarcasm to southern life in such works as *The Adventures of Tom Sawyer* (1876), *Life on the Mississippi* (1883), and *The Adventures of Huckleberry Finn* (1884).
clem·ent (klĕm′ənt) *adj.* **1.** Lenient or merciful in disposition. **2.** Mild. Said of weather or climate. [Middle English, from Latin *clēmēns*† (stem *clēment-*), gentle.] **—clem·ent·ly** *adv.*
clem·en·tine (klĕm′ən-tēn, -tīn) *n.* A type of citrus fruit resembling a tangerine, possibly a hybrid between a tangerine and an orange. [French *clémentine,* probably from the feminine name.]
clench (klĕnch) *tr.v.* **clenched, clenching, clenches. 1.** To bring together (hands or teeth) tightly; close up: *clenched his fist in anger.* **2.** To grasp or grip tightly. **3.** To clinch (a nail or bolt, for example). **4.** *Nautical.* To fasten with a clinch.
~*n.* **1.** A tight grip or grasp. **2.** Anything that clenches or holds fast, such as a mechanical device. **3.** *Nautical.* A kind of knot, a

clinch *(see).* [Middle English *clenchen,* Old English *beclencan.*]

cle·o·me (klē-ō′mē) *n.* Any of various mostly tropical plants of the genus *Cleome;* especially, *C. spinosa,* cultivated for its clusters of white or purplish flowers with long, conspicuous stamens. Also called "spiderflower." [New Latin *Cleome*†.]

Cle·on (klē′ŏn′) (died 422 B.C.). Athenian statesman and orator, known for his vigorous opposition to Sparta and its allies in the Peloponnesian War.

Cle·o·pat·ra VII (klē′ə-păt′rə, -pä′trə) (69–30 B.C.). Queen of Egypt (51–49 B.C., 48–30 B.C.), noted for her beauty and charisma. Her lovers included Julius Caesar and Mark Antony.

clepe (klēp) *tr.v.* **cleped** (klēpt, klĕpt) or **clept, cleping, clepes.** Also *past participle* **ycleped** or **yclept** (i-klĕpt′, i-klĕpt′). *Archaic.* To call by the name of; name. [Middle English *clepen,* to speak, call out, Old English *cleopian, clipian*†, to call out, call by name.]

clep·sy·dra (klĕp′sə-drə) *n., pl.* **-dras** or **-drae** (-drē′). An ancient device that measured time by marking the regulated flow of water through a small opening. Also called "water clock." [Latin, from Greek *klepsudra,* "water stealer" (from the "stealthy" flow of the water) : *kleps-,* stem of *kleptein,* to steal + *hudōr,* water.]

clere·sto·ry, clear·sto·ry (klîr′stôr′ē, -stōr′ē) *n., pl.* **-ries. 1.** The upper part of the nave, transepts, and choir of a church, containing windows. **2.** Any similar windowed wall or construction used for light and ventilation. [Middle English : *clere,* lighted, CLEAR + STORY (of a building).]

cler·gy (klûr′jē) *n., pl.* **-gies.** The body of women and men ordained for religious service. Compare **laity.** [Middle English *clergie,* from Old French (influenced by *clerge,* body of clerks), from *clerc,* ecclesiastic, CLERK.]

cler·gy·man (klûr′jē-mən) *n., pl.* **-men** (-mĭn). *Abbr.* **cl.** A male member of the clergy.

clergyman's throat *n.* Hoarseness after a long period of talking, especially as suffered by professional speechmakers.

cler·gy·wom·an (klûr′jē-wo͝om′ən) *n., pl.* **-women** (-wĭm′ĭn). A female member of the clergy.

cler·ic (klĕr′ĭk) *n.* A member of the clergy. [Medieval Latin *clēricus,* CLERK.]

cler·i·cal (klĕr′ĭ-kəl) *adj.* **1. a.** Of or pertaining to clerks or office workers. **b.** Of, pertaining to, or designating office work such as filing and correspondence. **2.** Of, pertaining to, or characteristic of the clergy or a member of the clergy. **3.** Advocating clericalism.
∼*n.* **1.** A member of the clergy. **2. clericals.** The distinctive garb of a member of the clergy. **3.** A person or party advocating clericalism. **—cler·i·cal·ly** *adv.*

clerical collar *n.* A stiff white collar in the shape of a band fastening at the back of the neck, worn by clergymen.

cler·i·cal·ism (klĕr′ĭ-kəl-ĭz′əm) *n.* A policy of supporting the power or influence of the clergy in secular matters. **—cler·i·cal·ist** *n.*

cler·i·hew (klĕr′ə-hyo͞o′) *n.* A humorous rhyming quatrain about a person whose name generally serves as one of the rhymes. [After Edmund *Clerihew* BENTLEY, writer who invented it.]

cler·i·sy (klĕr′ə-sē) *n.* Educated people as a class; the literati. [German *Klerisei,* from Medieval Latin *clēricia,* the clergy, from Late Latin *clēricus,* CLERK.]

clerk (klûrk; *British* klärk) *n.* **1.** A person who works in an office performing such tasks as keeping records, attending to correspondence, or filing. **2.** A person who keeps the records and performs the regular business of a court or legislative body. **3.** A person who works at a service or sales counter; as in a store. **4.** *Anglican Church.* A lay minister who helps the parish clergyman to perform his duties. **5.** *Archaic.* A clergyman. **6.** *Archaic.* **a.** A literate person. **b.** A scholar.
∼*intr.v.* **clerked, clerking, clerks.** To work or serve as a clerk. [Middle English, from Old English and Old French *clerc,* from Late Latin *clēricus,* a cleric, from Greek *klērikos,* belonging to inheritance, cleric (with reference to the Levites whose only inheritance was the Lord), from *klēros,* allotment, inheritance.] **—clerk·dom** *n.* **—clerk·ship** *n.*

clerk·ly (klûrk′lē) *adj.* **-lier, -liest. 1.** Of or pertaining to a clerk or clerks. **2.** *Archaic.* Scholarly. **—clerk·li·ness** *n.*

Cleve·land[1] (klēv′lənd). A small county in northeast England, formed in 1974 from parts of southern Durham and northern Yorkshire. Its center is the industrial region of Teeside.

Cleveland[2]. A city of northeastern Ohio, a port of entry on Lake Erie at the mouth of the Cuyahoga River. The city was laid out in 1796 and grew rapidly after the opening of the Ohio and Erie Canal in 1827 and the arrival of the railroad in 1851. It is a leading oil and steel center.

Cleveland, (Stephen) Grover (1837–1908). 22nd and 24th U.S. president (1885–89, 1893–97). Recognized as an honest, independent president, he lost his bid for re-election in 1888 primarily because he advocated a lower tariff. He was re-elected in in 1892 to a politically trying term highlighted by the repeal of the Sherman Silver Purchase Act (1893).

clev·er (klĕv′ər) *adj.* **cleverer, cleverest. 1.** Mentally quick and original; bright. **2.** Nimble with the hands; dexterous. **3.** Showing quick-wittedness; ingenious: *a clever story.* **4.** *Informal.* Superficial or contrived. **5.** *Regional.* Handy; suitable. —See Synonyms at **intelligent.** [Probably from Middle English *cliver,* dexterous, perhaps from Scandinavian; akin to Old Norse *kleyfr.*] **—clev·er·ly** *adv.* **—clev·er·ness** *n.*
Synonyms: *cunning, ingenious, shrewd.*

clev·is (klĕv′ĭs) *n.* A U-shaped metal piece with holes in each end through which a pin or bolt is run, used for attaching a drawbar to a plow, for example. [Probably plural of *clevi,* "cleft instrument," from Scandinavian, akin to Old Norse *klofi,* cleft, fissure.]

clew[1] (klo͞o) *n.* **1.** *Archaic.* A ball of yarn or thread. **2.** *Greek Mythology.* The ball of thread used by Theseus as a guide through the labyrinth of Minos on Crete. **3. clews.** The cords by which a hammock is suspended. **4.** *Nautical.* **a.** One of the two lower corners of a square sail. **b.** The lower aft corner of a fore-and-aft sail.
∼*tr.v.* **clewed, clewing, clews. 1.** To roll or coil into a ball. **2.** *Nautical.* To raise the lower corners of (a square sail) by means of clew lines. Used with *up.* [Middle English *clewe(n),* Old English *cliewen, clewe(n).*]

clew[2]. Variant of **clue.**

clew line *n.* A rope for raising the clew of a sail up to the yard or mast.

cli·an·thus (klē-ăn′thəs) *n.* Any of several plants of the genus *Clianthus,* native to Indochina, Australia, and New Zealand, having showy clusters of elongated scarlet flowers.

cli·ché (klē-shā′) *n.* **1.** A trite or overused expression or idea. **2.** *Printing.* A stereotype or electrotype plate. [French, "stereotyped," from *clicher,* to stereotype (imitative of the sound made when the matrix is dropped into the molten metal to make a stereotype plate).]
Synonyms: *banality, bromide, commonplace, truism.*

cli·chéd (klē-shād′) *adj.* Hackneyed; trite.

click (klĭk) *n.* **1.** A brief, sharp, nonresonant sound: *the click of a door latch.* **2.** A mechanical device that snaps into position, such as a detent or pawl. **3.** *Phonetics.* An oral ingressive speech sound, common in some African languages, produced by drawing air into the mouth and clicking the tongue. Also called "suction stop."
∼*v.* **clicked, clicking, clicks.** —*intr.* **1.** To produce one or a series of clicks. **2.** *Slang.* **a.** To become a success. **b.** To establish an immediate rapport. **c.** To become clear; fall into place. —*tr.* To cause to click. [Imitative.] **—click·er** *n.*

click beetle *n.* Any of various beetles of the family Elateridae, characterized by the ability to right itself from an overturned position by flipping into the air with a clicking sound. Also called "snapping beetle," "skipjack."

click languages *pl.n.* A set of African languages employing the phonetic click, including the **Khoisan** *(see)* family and the Nguni group.

cli·ent (klī′ənt) *n.* **1.** One for whom services, usually professional services, are rendered. **2.** A customer or patron. **3.** One dependent on the patronage of another. **4.** One receiving the attention and care of a social worker or doctor. [Middle English, from Old French, from Latin *cliēns* (stem *client-*), dependent, follower, earlier *cluēns,* from *cluere,* to follow, obey.] **—cli·en·tal** (klī-ĕn′təl) *adj.* **—cli·ent·ship** *n.*

cli·en·tele (klī′ən-tĕl′, klē-äN-tĕl′) *n.* Customers, patrons, or clients of a restaurant, professional person, or the like, considered collectively. [French *clientèle,* from Latin *clientēla,* from *cliēns,* CLIENT.]

client state *n.* A country that is economically or politically dependent on a larger or more powerful country.

cliff (klĭf) *n.* A high, steep, or overhanging face of rock. [Middle English *clif,* Old English *clif,* from Germanic *klibam* (unattested).] **—clif·fy** *adj.*

cliff dweller *n.* **1.** A member of certain prehistoric Indian tribes of the southwestern United States who lived in caves in the sides of cliffs. **2.** *Slang.* A person who lives in a large apartment house, especially in a city. **—cliff-dwel·ling** *adj.*

cliff·hang·er (klĭf′hăng′ər) *n.* **1.** A situation of great suspense occurring usually at the end of a chapter in a book, scene in a film, or episode in a serial. **2.** A serial in which each episode ends in suspense. **3.** A situation, as in a competition or election, in which the outcome is uncertain until the very end. **—cliff·hang·ing** *adj.*

cliff swallow *n.* A North American swallow, *Petrochelidon pyrrhonota,* that builds a bottle-shaped mud nest on the face of a cliff or bluff or under the eaves of a roof.

cli·mac·ter·ic (klī-măk′tər-ĭk, klī′măk-tĕr′ĭk) *n.* **1. a.** The **menopause** *(see).* **b.** A corresponding period in the male, marked by a reduction in sexual activity. **2.** *Archaic.* A critical period or year in a person's life when major changes in health or fortune take place. **3.** *Botany.* The increase in respiration rate associated with fruit ripening and senescence. **4.** Any critical period.
∼*adj.* Also **cli·mac·ter·i·cal** (klī′măk-tĕr′ĭ-kəl) Pertaining to a critical stage, period, or year. [Latin *clīmactēricus,* from Greek *klimaktērikos,* from *klimaktēr,* rung of a ladder, crisis, from *klimax,* ladder. See **climax.**]

cli·mac·tic (klī-măk′tĭk) *adj.* Pertaining to or constituting a climax. **—cli·mac·ti·cal·ly** *adv.*

cli·ma·gram, cli·mo·gram (klī′mə-grăm′) *n.* A **climograph** *(see).*

climagraph. Variant of **climograph.**

cli·mate (klī′mĭt) *n.* **1.** The meteorological conditions, including temperature, rainfall, and wind, that characteristically prevail in a particular region. **2.** A region having particular meteorological conditions. **3.** A prevailing set of attitudes or opinions in human affairs: *the political climate.* [Middle English *climat,* from Old French, from Late Latin *clīma,* climate, zone of latitude, from Greek *klima,* sloping surface of the earth.] **—cli·mat·ic** (klī-măt′ĭk), **cli·ma·tal** (klī′mə-təl), **cli·mat·i·cal** *adj.* **—cli·mat·i·cal·ly** *adv.*

cli·mat·o·graph (klī-măt′ə-grăf′, -gräf′) *n. Meteorology.* A circular graph showing the yearly variations of average temperature (as dis-

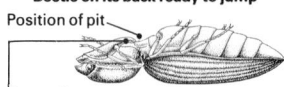

Beetle on its back ready to jump
Position of pit
Peg on first segment of body pulled out of pit by body-arching muscle
Section through head and pit
Peg notch engaged with pit lip
Armor-plated pit withstands continual jarring
Body-arching muscle
Peg-moving muscle

click beetle *When adult click beetles fall onto their backs, their special click mechanism (above), between their head and body, enables them to regain their feet and escape predators. When triggered, the mechanism can catapult them up to 300 millimeters (12 inches) into the air. The beetles' larvae, known as wireworms, are serious crop pests, living underground for up to five years and feeding on plant roots.*

PRONUNCIATION KEY

ă, pat; ā, pay; âr, care; ä, father, are; b, bib; ch, church; d, deed; ĕ, pet; ē, be; f, fife; g, gag; h, hat; hw, which; ĭ, pit; ī, pie; îr, pier; j, judge; k, kick; l, lid, needle; m, mum; n, no, sudden; ng, thing; ŏ, pot; ō, toe; ô, paw, for; oi, noise; ou, out; o͝o, book; o͞o, boot; p, pop; r, roar; s, sauce; sh, ship, dish; t, tight; th, thin, path; *th,* this, bathe; ŭ, cut; ûr, fur; v, valve; w, with; y, yes; z, zebra, size; zh, vision; ə, about, item, edible, gallop, circus, peaceful

IN FOREIGN WORDS:

à, *Fr.* ami; œ, *Fr.* feu, *Ger.* schön; ü, *Fr.* tu, *Ger.* über; KH, *Ger.* ich, *Scot.* loch; N, *Fr.* bon; y′, *Fr.* Compiègne

STRESS MARKS:

Primary stress: ′ in·cite′ (ĭn-sīt′)
Secondary stress: ′ in′sight′ (ĭn′sīt′)

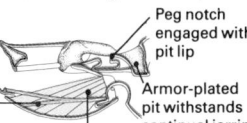

tance from center) against time of year (as angular position). [CLI-MATE + -GRAPH.]

cli·ma·tol·o·gy (klī'mə-tŏl'ə-jē) *n.* The meteorological study of climate. [CLIMAT(E) + -LOGY.] —**cli·ma·to·log·ic** (klī'mə-tə-lŏj'ĭk), **cli·ma·to·log·i·cal** *adj.* —**cli·ma·tol·o·gist** (klī'mə-tŏl'ə-jĭst) *n.*

cli·max (klī'măks') *n.* **1. a.** The point of greatest intensity, excitement, or interest in any series or progression of events; the culmination. **b.** Such a point in a literary or dramatic work. **2.** An orgasm. **3.** *Rhetoric.* **a.** A series of statements or ideas in an ascending order of force or intensity. **b.** The final statement in such a series. **4.** The stage in ecological development or evolution in which the community of organisms becomes stable. —See Synonyms at **summit.** ~*v.* **climaxed, -maxing, -maxes.** —*intr.* To reach a climax. —*tr.* To bring to a climax. [Latin, rhetorical climax, from Greek *klimax,* ladder.]

climax community *n.* *Ecology.* The mature or stabilized stage in a successional series of communities, usually associated with maximum complexity, when dominant species are completely adapted to environmental conditions, as in tropical rain forests.

climb (klīm) *v.* **climbed** or *archaic* **clomb** (klŏm), **climbing, climbs.** —*tr.* To move up or mount, especially by using the hands and feet; ascend. —*intr.* **1.** To rise to a higher position; move upward: *The sun climbed in the sky.* **2.** To rise slowly or with effort in rank, status, or fortune. **3.** To slant or slope upward. **4.** To grow in an upward direction, as some plants do, by twining about or clinging to another object for support. **5.** To move in a specified direction by or as if by clambering: *climbed out of the window.* —See Synonyms at **rise.** ~*n.* **1.** An act of climbing; an ascent. **2.** A place to be climbed. [Climb, clomb; Middle English *climben, clomb,* Old English *climban, clamb* (or *clomb*).] —**climb·a·ble** *adj.*

Usage: Both *up* and *down* are used with this verb in standard English. *Climb up* has been said to contain an unnecessary element, in that climbing implies ascent. By the same token, *climb down* is said to be self-contradictory, but both uses are well established.

climb down *intr.v.* **1.** To move downward by using the limbs. **2.** To retreat in an argument or dispute; back down. ~*tr.v.* To descend by using the limbs. —See Usage note at **climb.**

climb-down (klīm'doun') *n.* An act of yielding or backing down in an argument or dispute.

climb·er (klī'mər) *n.* **1.** Something or someone that climbs; especially, a person who climbs mountains. **2.** *Informal.* A person seeking to gain a higher social or professional position. Used derogatorily. **3.** A plant that grows upward by clinging to or twining about something.

climbing frame *n.* A structure, usually of metal tubing, for children to climb on.

climbing irons *pl.n.* Iron bars with spikes or spurs attached, which are strapped to a shoe or boot and used in climbing telegraph poles, trees, or ice slopes.

clime (klīm) *n.* *Poetic.* Climate or region. [Middle English, region of the earth, zone, from Late Latin *clīma,* CLIMATE.]

-clinal *suffix.* Indicates a slope or inclination; for example, **anticlinal, synclinal.** [-CLINE + -AL.]

cli·mo·graph, cli·ma·graph (klī'mə-grăf', -gräf') *n.* *Meteorology.* A graph in which one climatic feature at a location is plotted against another, for example temperature against humidity. Also called "climagram," "climogram." [CLIMATE + -GRAPH.]

clin-. Variant of **clino-.**

cli·nan·dri·um (klĭ-năn'drē-əm) *n., pl.* **-dria** (-drē-ə). *Botany.* A hollow containing the anther in the upper part of the column of an orchid. [New Latin, "stamen bed" : CLIN(O)- + -*andrium,* "stamen," from Greek *anēr* (stem *andr-*), man.]

clinch (klĭnch) *v.* **clinched, clinching, clinches.** —*tr.* **1.** To fix or secure (a nail or bolt, for example) by bending down or flattening the end that has been driven through something. **2.** To fasten together in this way. **3.** To settle definitely and conclusively; make final. **4.** *Nautical.* To fasten with a clinch. —*intr.* **1.** In boxing and wrestling, to hold the opponent's body with one or both arms to prevent or hinder his movements. **2.** *Informal.* To embrace. ~*n.* **1.** The act of clinching. **2.** Something that clinches, such as a clinched nail or clamp. **3.** The clinched part of a nail, bolt, rivet, or the like. **4.** In boxing and wrestling, the act or an instance of clinching. **5.** *Nautical.* A knot in a rope made by a half hitch with the end of the rope fastened back by seizing. Also called "clench." **6.** *Informal.* An amorous or romantic embrace. [Variant of CLENCH.]

clinch·er (klĭn'chər) *n.* **1.** One that clinches; specifically, a tool for clinching nails or bolts. **2.** *Informal.* A decisive point, fact, or remark, as in an argument.

clincher-built. Variant of **clinker-built.**

cline (klīn) *n.* **1.** *Ecology.* A continuous variation in form within members of a species or population, resulting from gradual changes or transitions in the environment over a wide range. **2.** Loosely, a continuum. [Greek *klinein,* to slope, lean.]

-cline *suffix.* Indicates slope; for example, **anticline, syncline.** [Greek *klinein,* to slope.]

cling (klĭng) *intr.v.* **clung** (klŭng), **clinging, clings. 1.** To hold fast or adhere to something, as by grasping, sticking, or entwining. **2. a.** To stay near; remain close. **b.** To resist separation. **3.** To hold on, often stubbornly; remain attached: *cling to old-fashioned ideas.* [Cling, clung (past tense), clung (past participle); Middle English *clingen, clong* (past singular), *clungen* (past plural), *clungen,* Old English *clingan, clang, clungon, clungen.*] —**cling·er** *n.*

cling·fish (klĭng'fĭsh) *n., pl.* **-fishes** or collectively **clingfish.** Any of various small marine fishes of the family Gobiesocidae, having an adhesive disk under the front part of the body, by which it fastens itself to rocks and seaweed.

clinging vine *n.* A person who shows excessive dependence on his or her spouse.

cling peach *n.* A clingstone peach.

cling·stone (klĭng'stōn') *n.* A fruit, especially a peach, having pulp that adheres partially to the stone. Compare **freestone.** —**cling·stone** *adj.*

cling·y (klĭng'ē) *adj.* **-gier, -giest.** Tending to cling: *a clingy dress.*

clin·ic (klĭn'ĭk) *n.* **1.** An establishment, often a department of a hospital specializing in a particular branch of medicine, devoted to the treatment and care of outpatients. **2.** A medical establishment run by several specialists working cooperatively. **3.** A private hospital or nursing home. **4.** A group meeting or seminar devoted to the study of problems in a particular field, or offering to teach certain skills to those who attend: *a tennis clinic.* [French *clinique,* originally "a bedridden person," from Greek *klinikē,* medical treatment at sickbed, from *klinikos,* "of a bed," doctor who visits bedridden persons, from *klinē,* bed.]

-clinic *suffix.* Indicates: **1.** Inclination or slope; for example, **isoclinic. 2.** A specified number of oblique axial intersections; for example, **triclinic.** [-CLINE + -IC.]

clin·i·cal (klĭn'ĭ-kəl) *adj.* **1.** Pertaining to or connected with a clinic. **2.** Of or pertaining to direct observation and treatment of patients: *a clinical lecture.* **3.** Analytical; highly objective; rigorously scientific: *clinical details.* **4.** Suggestive of a hospital or clinic; austere; antiseptic: *a clinical style of decor.* ~*n.* A class in which medical students are instructed in the examination and treatment of patients at the bedside. —**clin·i·cal·ly** *adv.*

clinical thermometer *n.* A thermometer used to measure body temperature; especially, a small mercury-in-glass thermometer designed with a narrowing in the base so that the mercury column stays in position when the instrument is removed from the body.

cli·ni·cian (klĭ-nĭsh'ən) *n.* A doctor, psychologist, or psychiatrist specializing in clinical studies or practice. [French *clinicien,* from *clinique,* CLINIC.]

clink¹ (klĭngk) *n.* A soft, sharp, ringing sound. ~*v.* **clinked, clinking, clinks.** —*intr.* To make a clink. —*tr.* To cause to clink. [Middle English, from Middle Dutch *klinken.*]

clink² *n.* *Slang.* Prison. [16th century (as *the Clink,* name of former prison near London) : origin obscure.]

clink·er (klĭng'kər) *n.* **1.** The incombustible residue, fused into irregular lumps, that remains after the combustion of coal. **2.** A partially vitrified brick or a mass of bricks fused together. **3.** An extremely hard burned brick. **4.** Vitrified matter expelled by a volcano. **5.** *Slang.* A conspicuous mistake or failure. ~*intr.v.* **clinkered, -ering, -ers.** To form clinker while burning. [Earlier *clincart, klincard,* from obsolete Dutch *klinckaerd,* "one that clinks" (from its clinking sound when struck), from Middle Dutch *klinken, clinken,* CLINK.]

clink·er-built (klĭng'kər-bĭlt') *adj.* Also **clinch·er-built** (klĭn'chər-). Built with overlapping planks or boards. Said of ships or boats. Compare **carvel-built.** [From *clinker,* a fastening or clinching with nails, from Middle English *clinken,* probably variant of *clenchen,* CLENCH.]

clink·stone (klĭngk'stōn') *n.* *Mineralogy.* **Phonolite** (see).

clino-, clin- *prefix.* Indicates slope or slant; for example, **clinometer, clinandrium.** [New Latin, from Greek *klinein,* to slope, *klinē,* bed.]

cli·nom·e·ter (klĭ-nŏm'ə-tər, klī-) *n.* An instrument for measuring the angle of an incline, as of an embankment. Also called "inclinometer." [CLINO- + -METER.] —**cli·no·met·ric** (klī'nə-mĕt'rĭk), **cli·no·met·ri·cal** *adj.* —**cli·nom·e·try** (klī-nŏm'ə-trē) *n.*

cli·no·stat (klī'nō-stăt') *n.* *Botany.* An apparatus used to study plant growth, consisting of a rotating disk to which the plant is attached. Rotation ensures that all parts of the plant receive identical stimulation, for example from light or gravity. [CLINO- + -STAT.]

clin·quant (klĭng'kənt; *French* klăN-käN') *adj.* *Archaic.* Adorned with gold or silver. ~*n.* *Archaic.* Imitation gold leaf; tinsel. [French, "glistening," from *clinquer,* to glitter, clink, from Middle Dutch *clinken,* CLINK.]

clint (klĭnt) *n.* *Geology.* Any of a number of irregularly shaped blocks making up a type of flat, exposed limestone formation. [Middle English, perhaps from Scandinavian; akin to Danish and Swedish *klint,* Old Norse *klettr,* cliff.]

clin·to·ni·a (klĭn-tō'nē-ə) *n.* Any plant of the genus *Clintonia,* having narrow leaves, white, greenish-yellow, or purplish flowers, and usually blue berries. [New Latin, after DeWitt *Clinton* (1765–1828), U.S. statesman.]

Cli·o (klī'ō). *Greek Mythology.* The Muse of history. [Latin *Clīō,* from Greek *Kleiō,* "teller," from *kleiein, kleein,* to tell, praise.]

cli·o·met·rics (klī'ə-mĕt'rĭks) *n.* Used with a singular verb. The use of statistics in the study of history. —**cli·o·met·ric** *adj.*

clip¹ (klĭp) *tr.v.* **clipped, clipping, clips. 1.** To cut off or cut out with or as if with scissors or shears: *clip an article from a newspaper; clipped three seconds off the record.* **2.** To make shorter by cutting; trim. **3.** To cut off the edge of: *clip a coin.* **4. a.** To cut short (a word or words) by leaving out letters or syllables. **b.** To enunciate with clarity and precision: *clip one's speech.* **5.** *British.* To punch a hole in (a ticket). **6.** *Informal.* To hit with a sharp blow. **7.** *Slang.* To cheat or overcharge.

~n. **1.** The act of clipping. **2.** A short extract from a film or videotape. **3. a.** The wool shorn at one shearing. **b.** A season's shearing. **4.** *Informal.* A quick, sharp blow: *a clip on the ear.* **5.** *Informal.* A brisk pace. **6. clips.** A pair of shears or clippers. [Middle English *clippen,* from Old Norse *klippa*†, to cut short.]

clip² *n.* **1.** A device for holding things together; a clasp. **2.** A piece of jewelry fastened by a clip; a brooch. **3.** A **cartridge clip** *(see).* *~tr.v.* **clipped, clipping, clips. 1.** To fasten with a clip. **2.** *Football.* To block (an opponent who is not carrying the ball) illegally from the rear. [Middle English *clipp,* from *clippen,* to embrace, fasten, Old English *clyppan.*]

clip·board (klĭp′bôrd, -bōrd′) *n.* A small writing board with a spring clip at the top for holding papers or a writing pad.

clip joint *n. Slang.* A restaurant or place of public entertainment where customers are overcharged or otherwise defrauded.

clip-on (klĭp′ŏn′) *adj.* Designating an article that is attached by means of a clip: *clip-on earrings; a clip-on bow tie.*

clip·per (klĭp′ər) *n.* **1.** One who cuts, clips, or shears. **2. clippers.** An instrument or tool for cutting, clipping, or shearing: *nail clippers.* **3.** A sharp-bowed sailing vessel of the mid-19th century, having tall masts and sharp lines and built for great speed. Also called "clipper ship." **4.** *Electronics.* A **limiter** *(see).*

clip·ping (klĭp′ĭng) *n.* **1.** Something that is cut off or out: *nail clippings.* **2.** An item cut out of a newspaper.

clique (klēk, klĭk) *n.* An exclusive group of friends or associates; coterie. —See Synonyms at **circle.** [French, from Old French, probably "a group of applauders," from *cliquer,* to click, clap, applaud (imitative).]

cli·quish (klē′kĭsh, klĭk′ĭsh) *adj.* Also **cli·quey, cli·quy** (klē′kē, klĭk′ē). Of, like, or characteristic of a clique; exclusive. **—cli·quish·ly** *adv.* **—cli·quish·ness** *n.*

cli·tel·lum (klī-tĕl′əm, klĭ-) *n., pl.* **-tella** (-tĕl′ə). A swollen, glandular, saddlelike region in the epidermis of certain annelid worms, such as the earthworm, serving to bind worms together during copulation. [New Latin, from Latin *clītellae,* packsaddle.]

clit·o·rid·ec·to·my *n.* The ritualistic mutilation of the clitoris, as performed on prepubertal girls in certain cultures. [New Latin *clitoris* (stem *clitorid-*), CLITORIS + -ECTOMY.]

clit·o·ris (klĭt′ə-rĭs, klī-tôr′əs) *n.* A part of the female genitalia lying above the vagina and urethra, consisting of a small, highly sensitive, erectile organ, which plays a major role in the female orgasm. [New Latin, from Greek *kleitoris,* "little hill," diminutive of *kleitor-* (unattested), hill, from *klinein,* to incline.] **—clit·o·ral** (klĭt′ə-rəl) *adj.*

Clive of Plas·sey (klīv; plăs′ē), **Robert, Baron,** also known as "Clive of India" (1725–74). British soldier and statesman, famous for securing British interests in India.

clo·a·ca (klō-ā′kə) *n., pl.* **-cae** (-sē′, -kē′). **1.** *Zoology.* The cavity into which the intestinal, genital, and urinary tracts open in vertebrates such as fish, reptiles, birds, and some primitive mammals. **2.** A sewer. [Latin *cloāca,* sewer, canal.] **—clo·a·cal** (klō-ā′kəl) *adj.*

cloak (klōk) *n.* **1.** A loose outer garment, usually sleeveless. **2.** Anything that covers or conceals.
~tr.v. **cloaked, cloaking, cloaks. 1.** To cover with a cloak. **2.** To cover up; hide; conceal. —See Synonyms at **hide.** [Middle English *cloke,* from Old French *cloque,* bell, "bell-shaped garment." See **clock.**]

cloak-and-dagger (klōk′ən-dăg′ər) *adj.* Concerned with or suggestive of melodramatic intrigue.

cloak·room (klōk′ro͝om′, -ro͞om′) *n.* **1.** A room where coats and other articles may be left temporarily, as in a school or theater. **2.** A private lounge for members of a legislative chamber.

clob·ber¹ (klŏb′ər) *tr.v.* **-bered, -bering, -bers.** *Slang.* **1.** To strike violently and repeatedly; batter or maul. **2.** To defeat completely. **3.** To criticize or condemn harshly. [20th century : origin obscure; perhaps akin to *club* (to beat).]

clobber² *n. British Slang.* **1.** Belongings; equipment. **2.** Clothes. [19th century : origin obscure.]

cloche (klōsh, klŏsh) *n.* **1.** A semicylindrical or bell-shaped cover, usually of glass, used to protect young plants. **2.** A close-fitting woman's hat with a bell-like shape. [French, bell, from Old French, bell, CLOCK.]

clock¹ (klŏk) *n.* **1.** An instrument for measuring or indicating time; especially, a mechanical device, larger than a watch, with a numbered dial and moving hands or pointers. **2.** Any of various scientific devices for the accurate measurement or standardization of time. **3.** *Informal.* Any of various instruments that indicate measurement by a dial and pointer or by a digital display, such as a speedometer or the meter on a taxi. **4.** An electronic circuit that produces regular pulses. See **clock pulse. 5.** A **time clock** *(see).* **6.** *Botany.* The downy flower head of a dandelion that has gone to seed. **—put the clock back. 1.** To revert to outmoded practices or ideas; regress. **2.** To revert to a former, preferable, and idealized state of affairs. See feature, next page.
~v. **clocked, clocking, clocks.** *—tr.* **1.** To record the time or speed of, as with a stopwatch. **2.** To register or record (a distance traveled, a speed attained, or the like). Used with *up.* **3.** *Electronics.* To regulate (a circuit) with clock pulses. *—intr.* **1.** To register the time of arrival at work. Used with *in*: *She clocked in early.* **2.** To register the time of departure from work. Used with *out.* [Middle English *clok,* from Middle Dutch *clocke,* bell, clock, from Old French *cloche, cloque,* bell, from Late Latin *clocca* (imitative).] **—clock·er** *n.*

clock² *n.* An embroidered or woven decoration on the side of a stocking or sock. [Perhaps originally "a bell-shaped ornament," from Middle Dutch *clocke,* bell, CLOCK.]

clock pulse *n.* One of a series of regular electrical pulses used to drive an electronic circuit such as a computer logic circuit.

clock radio *n.* An appliance that combines an alarm clock with a radio that can be set to start playing at a particular time.

clock-watch·er (klŏk′wŏch′ər) *n.* A person who continually checks the time while at work. **—clock-watch·ing** *n.*

clock·wise (klŏk′wīz′) *adv.* In the same direction as the rotating hands of a clock. **—clock·wise** *adj.*

clock·work (klŏk′wûrk′) *n.* A mechanism of gears driven by a wound spring, as in a mechanical clock, toy, or the like. **—like clockwork.** With machinelike regularity and precision; perfectly. **—clock·work** *adj.*

clod (klŏd) *n.* **1.** A lump of earth or clay. **2.** Earth or soil. **3.** A dull, ignorant, or stupid person; an oaf. **4.** A cut of the shoulder of beef. [Middle English *clodde,* Old English *clod-* (only in compounds), variant of *clott,* lump.] **—clod·dish** *adj.* **—clod·dish·ness** *n.*

clod·hop·per (klŏd′hŏp′ər) *n.* **1.** A clumsy, coarse person; a lout or bumpkin. **2. clodhoppers.** Big, heavy shoes. [Originally "farmer" : CLOD (earth) + HOPPER.] **—clod·hop·ping** *adj.*

clog (klŏg) *n.* **1.** A heavy wooden or wooden-soled shoe. **2.** A block or other weight attached to the leg of an animal to hinder movement. **3.** *Archaic.* An obstacle or hindrance.
~v. **clogged, clogging, clogs.** *—tr.* **1.** To block up; obstruct. **2.** To impede or encumber; hamper. *—intr.* **1.** To become obstructed or choked up. **2.** To thicken or stick together; coagulate. **3.** To do a clog dance. [Middle English *clog, clogge*†, block of wood.] **—clog·gy** *adj.*

clog dance *n.* A dance performed wearing clogs and characterized by heavy, stamping steps.

cloi·son·né (kloi′zə-nā′; *French* klwä-zô-nā′) *n.* **1.** A kind of enamelware in which the surface decoration is formed by different colors of enamel separated by thin strips of metal. **2.** The process or method of producing such enamelware.
~adj. Of or designating this ware or method. [French, past participle of *cloisonner,* to partition, from Old French *cloison,* partition, from Vulgar Latin *clausiō* (unattested), enclosure, from Latin *claudere,* to close.]

clois·ter (kloi′stər) *n.* **1.** Sometimes **cloisters.** A covered walk with an open colonnade on one side, running along the walls of buildings that face a quadrangle. **2.** A place devoted to religious seclusion; especially, a monastery or convent. **3.** Life in a monastery or convent. Preceded by *the.*
~tr.v. **cloistered, -tering, -ters. 1.** To shut away from the world in or as if in a cloister; seclude. **2.** To furnish (a building) with a cloister. [Middle English *cloistre,* from Old French, variant of *clostre* (influenced by *cloison,* partition, CLOISONNÉ), from Medieval Latin *claustrum,* from Latin, enclosed place, from *claudere,* to close.]

clois·tral (kloi′strəl) *adj.* Also **claus·tral** (klôs′trəl). Of, resembling, or suggesting a cloister; secluded. [Middle English *claustral,* from Medieval Latin *claustrālis,* from *claustrum,* CLOISTER.]

clomb. *Archaic.* Past tense and past participle of **climb.**

clomp (klŏmp) *intr.v.* **clomped, clomping, clomps.** To walk heavily; clump. [Variant of CLUM.]

clone (klōn) *n.* **1.** A group of genetically identical cells descended from a single common ancestor. **2.** One or more organisms descended asexually from a single ancestor. **3.** An exact copy of a person or thing; a duplicate.
~v. **cloned, cloning, clones.** *—intr.* To create a genetic duplicate of an individual organism through asexual reproduction, as by stimulating a single cell or taking cuttings of plants. *—tr.* **1.** To duplicate (an organism) asexually by cloning. **2.** To create (a new organism) in this way. **3.** To create a duplicate of. [Greek *klōn,* twig, shoot.] **—clon·al** (klō′nəl) *adj.* **—clon·al·ly** *adv.*

clonk (klŏngk) *n.* A dull, metallic sound.
~v. **clonked, clonking, clonks.** *—intr.* To make a clonk. *—tr.* **1.** To cause to clonk. **2.** *Informal.* To hit; punch.

clo·nus (klō′nəs) *n., pl.* **-nuses.** A convulsion characterized by rapidly alternating muscular contraction and relaxation. [New Latin, from Greek *klonos,* agitation, turmoil.] **—clo·nic** (klō′nĭk, klŏn′ĭk) *adj.* **—clo·nic·i·ty** (klō-nĭs′ə-tē, klŏ-), **clo·nism** (klō′nĭz′əm, klŏn′ĭz′əm) *n.*

clop (klŏp) *n.* The sound of a horse's hoof striking a paved surface.
~intr.v. **clopped, clopping, clops.** To make or move with this sound. [Imitative.]

close (klōs) *adj.* **closer, closest. 1.** Separated by only a small distance; not far off in space or time; near. **2.** Near in relationship: *close relatives.* **3.** Having all elements or parts near to each other; compact; dense: *a close weave.* **4.** Near the surface; short: *a close haircut.* **5.** Nearly even; decided by a narrow margin: *a close finish.* **6.** Fitting tightly. **7.** Not deviating substantially from an original or model: *a close resemblance.* **8.** Complete; thorough; rigorous: *a close examination.* **9.** Bound by mutual interests, loyalties, or affection: *close friends.* **10.** Enclosed or confined. **11.** Confined to specific persons or groups; restricted: *a close secret.* **12.** Heavily guarded; allowing no means of escape: *under close arrest.* **13.** Secretive in manner; reticent. **14.** Not generous; miserly. **15.** Airless; stuffy; oppressive. **16.** *Phonetics.* Spoken with the tongue near the palate. Said of vowels. —See Synonyms at **familiar, stingy.**
~v. (klōz) **closed, closing, closes.** *—tr.* **1.** To shut. **2.** To bar or obstruct: *The road is closed for repairs.* **3.** To bring together all the

cloisonné *The Hope-Beresford Cross, a 9th-century Byzantine icon now in the Victoria and Albert Museum, London. Each section of the design is made of enamel, separated from the adjoining sections by thin strips of metal.*

cloister *In medieval monasteries, cloisters were the places where the elders studied and younger monks were educated.*

PRONUNCIATION KEY

ă, pat; ā, pay; âr, care; ä, father, are; b, bib; ch, church; d, deed; ĕ, pet; ē, be; f, fife; g, gag; h, hat; hw, which; ĭ, pit; ī, pie; îr, pier; j, judge; k, kick; l, lid, needle; m, mum; n, no, sudden; ng, thing; ŏ, pot; ō, toe; ô, paw, for; oi, noise; ou, out; o͝o, book; o͞o, boot; p, pop; r, roar; s, sauce; sh, ship, dish; t, tight; th, thin, path; *th,* this, bathe; ŭ, cut; ûr, fur; v, valve; w, with; y, yes; z, zebra, size; zh, vision; ə, about, item, edible, gallop, circus, peaceful

IN FOREIGN WORDS:

à, *Fr.* ami; œ, *Fr.* feu, *Ger.* schön; ü, *Fr.* tu, *Ger.* über; KH, *Ger.* ich, *Scot.* loch; N, *Fr.* bon; y′, *Fr.* Compiègne

STRESS MARKS:

Primary stress: ′
in·cite′ (ĭn-sīt′)
Secondary stress: ′
in′sight′ (ĭn′sīt′)

SEVEN CENTURIES OF IMPROVING TIMEKEEPING

Precision that has increased with the advance of technology

The mechanical clock was invented in Europe in the 13th century. Its driving power was a falling weight on a cord, and the escapement—the method of converting the power into a regular beat or tick—was a swinging spindle, or verge. The clocks were used in churches and monasteries. They could be regulated by moving a weight on a bar known as the foliot bar, but the system was inaccurate. A keeper had to correct the clock by a sundial every few days. Nevertheless the verge escapement remained in use for 550 years.

In the early 15th century the energy stored in a wound-up spiral mainspring was first used as the driving force for clocks. It made possible light, portable clocks—and also pocket watches. The rate at which the spring turned the wheels was kept steady by a fusee and chain.

The first practical pendulum clock was designed by a Dutchman, Christian Huygens, about 1656. It was based on the observation that no matter how far a certain pendulum swings, each swing takes the same length of time. Such absolute regularity gave much greater accuracy to clocks. The pendulum replaced the foliot bar in large clocks. Huygens's pendulum mechanism was improved by the invention of the anchor escapement about 1670. It limited the swing to a narrow arc and led to grandfather clocks.

Later Huygens invented the spiral balance wheel. This replaced the swinging foliot bar in small clocks and watches and could make them accurate to within 2 minutes a day. Combined with the lever escapement invented about 1754, it became the regulating device of modern mechanical clocks and watches, still in use alongside electric and quartz-crystal timepieces.

VERGE ESCAPEMENT

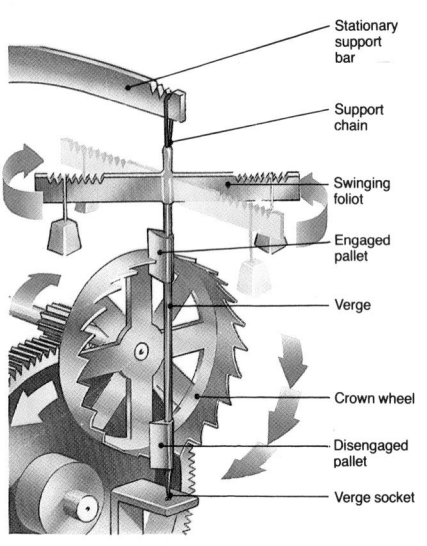

The turning crown wheel, powered by a falling weight, is checked as its teeth engage with one pallet after the other. As the teeth escape the pallets, the foliot swings to and fro, regulating the turning of the crown wheel.

FUSEE AND CORD OR CHAIN

Mainspring fully wound

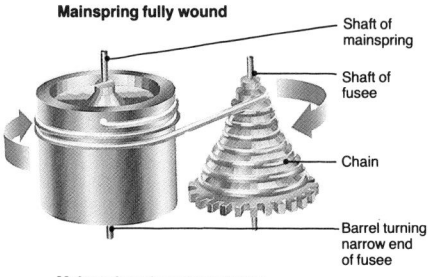

Mainspring almost run down

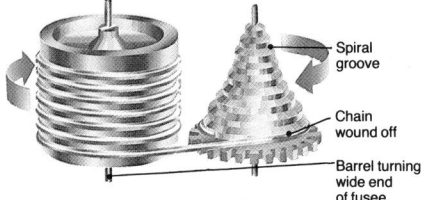

The fully wound mainspring inside the barrel makes it turn the fusee's narrow end. As the spring runs down it loses force, but compensates by turning the fusee's wider end, driving the mechanism at the same rate.

ANCHOR ESCAPEMENT

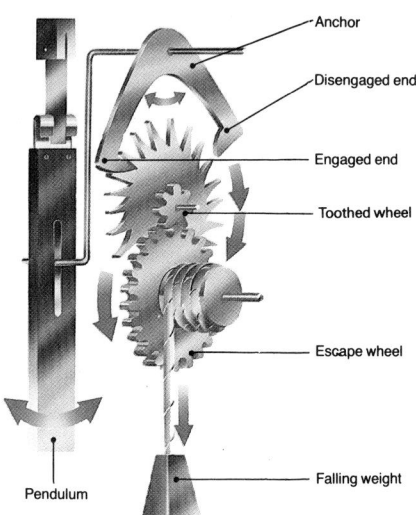

The anchor rocks with each pendulum swing; alternately its ends halt the toothed wheel and through it the escape wheel, which is turned by the weight. Each swing lets the mechanism move forward one tooth, or "tick."

LEVER ESCAPEMENT

Right motion

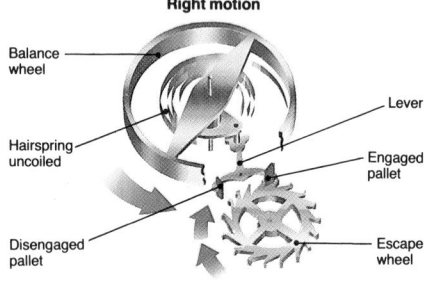

Left motion

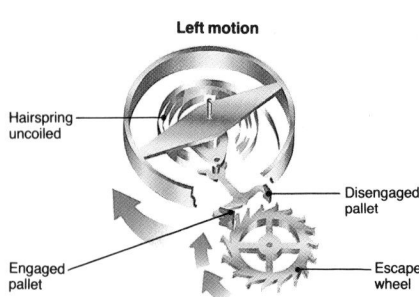

The balance wheel oscillates five times a second and keeps the hairspring coiling and uncoiling. This rocks the lever; the pallets, one after another, halt the escape wheel so that it turns one tooth, or "tick," at a time.

QUARTZ-CRYSTAL CLOCK

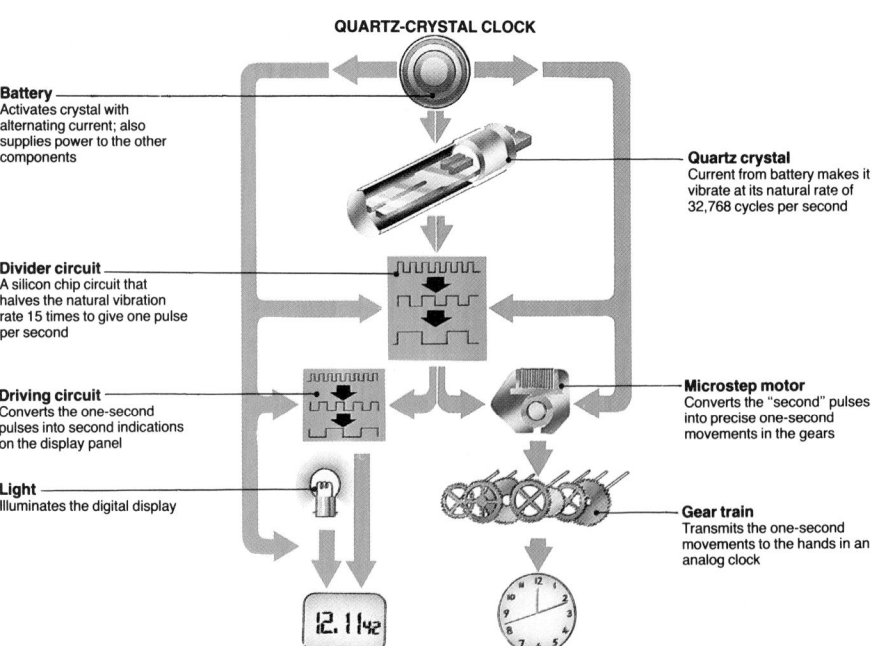

The battery makes the crystal oscillate at its natural rate of 32,768 cycles per second. The divider circuit converts the vibration rate to one per second. A driving circuit or a motor converts these vibrations into one-second "ticks," which are then transmitted to the digital display or the clock face.

elements of; end; finish. **4.** To bring to an end, temporarily or permanently, the operations of (a business establishment, factory, or the like). **5.** To settle (an account) finally, by withdrawing any money credited to it and settling outstanding debts. **6.** To join or unite; bring into contact: *close a circuit.* **7.** *Archaic.* To enclose on all sides. —*intr.* **1.** To become shut. **2.** To finish or conclude. **3.** To cease operations, temporarily or permanently. **4.** To engage at close quarters; begin to fight. Used with *with.* **5.** To reach an agreement; come to terms. Used with *with.* **6.** To have a specified value at the end of the day's trading: *Gold closed at 520 dollars an ounce.* —See Synonyms at **complete.** —**close in.** To surround and advance upon, so as to eliminate the possibility of escape. Often used with *on* or *upon.*

~*n.* (klōz *for senses 1,2,3;* klōs *for senses 4,5*). **1.** A conclusion; a finish. **2.** The concluding part of a musical phrase or theme; a cadence. **3.** *Archaic.* A fight at close quarters. **4.** An enclosed place, especially land surrounding a cathedral. **5.** *Chiefly British.* **a.** A narrow passage or alley leading to the back of a house or to the common stairway of an apartment building. **b.** A cul-de-sac.

~*adv.* (klōs). Closely. —**close on.** Approximately; practically. [Middle English *clos,* from Old French, from Latin *clausus,* past participle of *claudere,* to close.] —**close·ly** (klōs′lē) *adv.* —**close·ness** (klōs′nĭs) *n.* —**clos·er** (klō′zər) *n.*

close call (klōs) *n. Informal.* A narrow escape.

closed (klōzd) *adj.* **1.** Having complete boundaries; enclosed. **2.** Blocked or barred to passage or entry. **3.** Having explicitly limited membership; restricted; exclusive. **4.** *Phonetics.* Ending in a consonant. Said of a syllable. **5.** *Geometry.* **a.** Of or pertaining to a curve, such as a circle, having no end points. **b.** Of or pertaining to a surface having no boundary curves.

closed book *n. Informal.* A person or matter that is not known or understood.

closed-cap·tioned (klōzd′kăp′shənd) *adj.* Broadcast with captions that appear only on the screens of specially equipped receivers: *A closed-captioned television program for the hearing-impaired.*

closed chain *n.* A chemical **ring** *(see).* Compare **open chain.**

closed circuit *n.* **1.** A television transmission circuit with a limited number of reception stations and no broadcasting facilities. **2.** An electric circuit providing an uninterrupted, endless path for the flow of current. Compare **open circuit.**

close down (klōz) *intr.v.* **1.** To stop or cease operations entirely. **2.** To end transmission for the day. Used of a radio or television station. —**close-down** (klōz′doun′) *n.*

closed season (klōzd) *n.* The period in the year when the law prohibits the killing for sport of certain animals, birds, and fish. Compare **open season.**

closed shop *n.* A business or industrial establishment in which the employers have a contractual agreement with a particular trade union to employ only members of that union. Compare **open shop, union shop.**

close-fist·ed (klōs′fĭs′tĭd) *adj.* Miserly; tight-fisted.

close-grained (klōs′grānd′) *adj.* Dense or compact in structure or texture: *close-grained wood.*

close harmony (klōs) *n.* A singing arrangement in which the three upper parts lie close together, usually within an octave.

close-hauled (klōs′hôld′) *adv. Nautical.* With sails trimmed flat for sailing as close to the wind as possible. —**close-hauled** *adj.*

close-knit (klōs′nĭt′) *adj.* Bound together by social or cultural ties: *a close-knit village community.*

close-mouthed (klōs′mou*th*d′, -moutht′) *adj.* Not disposed to talk; reticent; taciturn.

close out (klōz) *tr.v.* To dispose of (goods), usually at greatly reduced prices.

close-out (klōz′out′) *n.* A sale in which all remaining goods are disposed of, usually at greatly reduced prices.

close packing (klōs) *n.* An arrangement of objects, such as spheres or atoms in a crystal, such that the total occupies the minimum possible volume. In the close packing of equal spheres each sphere has 12 near neighbors. —**close packed** *adj.*

close quarters (klōs) *pl.n.* Close range; close proximity. Used chiefly in the phrase *at close quarters.*

close shave (klōs) *n. Informal.* A narrow escape.

close stitch (klōs) *n.* The **buttonhole stitch** *(see).*

clos·et (klŏz′ĭt, klô′zĭt) *n. Abbr.* **cl.** **1.** A small room, cabinet, or recess for storing linens or supplies, hanging clothes, or the like. **2.** *Archaic.* A small private chamber for studying, meditating, praying, or the like. **3.** A water closet; a toilet. —**come out of the closet.** To give up concealing proclivities, opinions, or affiliations considered undesirable by others.

~*tr.v.* **closeted, -eting, -ets.** To enclose or shut up in a private room, as for discussion or meditation. Usually used reflexively.

~*adj.* **1.** Concealed; confidential: *a closet liberal.* **2.** Based upon theory and speculation rather than practice: *closet plans.* [Middle English, from Old French, diminutive of *clos,* enclosure, from Medieval Latin *clausum,* from Latin *clausus,* enclosed, CLOSE.]

close up (klōz) *tr.v.* **1.** To close entirely. **2.** To bring nearer together. —*intr.v.* To come nearer together.

close-up (klōs′ŭp′) *n.* **1.** A picture, such as a film or television shot, taken at close range. **2.** A close or intimate view or description.

clos·trid·i·um (klŏs-trĭd′ē-əm) *n., pl.* **-tridia** (-trĭd′ē-ə). Any of various rod-shaped, spore-forming, chiefly anaerobic bacteria of the genus *Clostridium,* including some of the nitrogen-fixing bacteria found in soil and those causing botulism and tetanus. [New Latin, "small spindle," from Greek *klōstēr,* spindle, from *klōthein,* to spin. See **Clotho.**]

clo·sure (klō′zhər) *n.* **1.** The act of closing or the condition of being closed. **2.** Something that closes or shuts. **3.** A finish; a conclusion. **4.** *Geology.* The vertical distance from the highest point of a structure and the lowest surrounding contour. **5.** *Mathematics.* The property of an algebraic structure, such as a group, by which combinations of elements produce other elements that belong to the set. **6.** Variant of **cloture.**

~*tr.v.* **closured, -suring, -sures.** To end (a debate) by cloture. [Middle English, from Old French, from Latin *clausūra,* from *clausus,* enclosed, CLOSE.]

clot (klŏt) *n.* **1.** A thick, viscous, or coagulated mass or lump, as of blood. **2.** *British Slang.* A stupid person; blockhead.

~*v.* **clotted, clotting, clots.** —*intr.* To form into clots. —*tr.* To cause to clot; fill or cover with clots. [Middle English *clot,* Old English *clott,* lump.]

cloth (klôth, klŏth) *n., pl.* **cloths** (klôths, klô*th*z, klŏths, klŏ*th*z). **1.** *Abbr.* **cl.** Fabric or material formed by weaving, knitting, pressing, or felting natural or synthetic fibers. **2.** A piece of fabric or material used for a specific purpose. Often used in combination: *tablecloth; dishcloth.* **3.** *Nautical.* **a.** Canvas. **b.** A sail. **4.** Professional attire or mode of dress. —**the cloth.** The clergy. [Middle English *cloth,* Old English *clāth,* from Germanic.] —**cloth** *adj.*

cloth·bound (klôth′bound′, klŏth′-) *adj.* Designating a book bound in boards and covered with cloth.

cloth-cap (klôth′kăp′, klŏth′-) *adj. British.* Of or considered as characteristic of the working class: *a cloth-cap mentality.*

clothe (klō*th*) *tr.v.* **clothed** or **clad** (klăd), **clothing, clothes. 1.** To put clothes on; dress. **2.** To cover as if with clothes. [Middle English *clothen, clathen,* Old English *clāthian,* from *clāth,* CLOTH.]

clothes (klōz; klō*th*z) *pl.n.* **1.** Articles of dress; garments. **2. Bedclothes** *(see).* [Middle English, from Old English *clāthas,* plural of *clāth,* CLOTH.]

clothes·horse (klōz′hôrs′, klō*th*z′-) *n.* **1.** A frame on which clothes are hung to dry or air. **2.** A person considered to be excessively concerned with dress.

clothes·line (klōz′līn′, klō*th*z′-) *n.* A cord, rope, or wire on which clothes are hung to dry or air.

clothes moth *n.* Any of various moths of the family Tineidae, the larvae of which feed on wool, hair, fur, and feathers.

clothes·pin (klōz′pĭn′, klō*th*z′-) *n.* A clip of wood or plastic for fastening clothes to a clothesline. Also *British* "clothespeg."

clothes tree *n.* An upright pole or stand with hooks or pegs on which to hang garments.

cloth·ier (klō*th*′yər, klō′*th*ē-ər) *n.* One who deals in clothing, especially men's clothing.

cloth·ing (klō′*th*ĭng) *n.* **1.** Clothes collectively; attire. **2.** A covering.

Clo·tho (klō′thō). *Greek Mythology.* One of the three **Fates** *(see).* She spins the thread of life. [Greek *klōthō,* "spinner," from *klōthein,* to spin, akin to *kalathos,* CALATHUS.]

cloth of gold *n.* Silk or woolen cloth interwoven with gold threads.

clot·ted cream (klŏt′ĭd) *n.* Thick cream made by scalding milk.

clo·ture (klō′chər) *n.* Also **clo·sure** (klō′zhər). A parliamentary procedure by which debate is ended and an immediate vote is taken on the matter under discussion.

~*tr.v.* **clotured, -turing, -tures.** To close (a parliamentary debate) by cloture. [French *clôture,* variant of Old French *closure,* CLOSURE.]

cloud (kloud) *n.* **1.** A visible body of very fine droplets of water or particles of ice dispersed in the atmosphere above the earth's surface at various altitudes ranging up to several miles. **2.** Any visible mass in the air, as of steam, smoke, or dust. **3.** A large mass of things moving in the air; a swarm. **4.** Anything that darkens, threatens, or fills with gloom. **5.** A dark region or blemish on a polished stone or gem. **6.** An appearance of dimness or milkiness, as in glass or a liquid. —**have one's head in the clouds.** To be impractical; live in a world of fantasy. —**under a cloud.** Under suspicion or out of favor.

~*v.* **clouded, clouding, clouds.** —*tr.* **1.** To cover with or as if with clouds; darken; dim. **2.** To make gloomy, sullen, or troubled. —*intr.* To become cloudy or overcast. Often used with *over* or *up.* [Middle English *cloud,* hill, mass of earth, cloud, Old English *clūd,* rock, hill.] —**cloud·less** *adj.* See feature, next page.

cloud·ber·ry (kloud′bĕr′ē) *n., pl.* **-ries. 1.** A creeping plant, *Rubus chamaemorus,* of northern regions, having white flowers and edible fruit. **2.** The reddish-orange fruit of this plant.

cloud·burst (kloud′bûrst′) *n.* A sudden rainstorm; a downpour.

cloud chamber *n.* A device for detecting charged subatomic particles by the formation of small droplets of liquid along the paths of the particles as they pass through supersaturated vapor. The droplets condense on ions produced by the particles. Compare **bubble chamber.**

cloud-cuck·oo-land (kloud′ko͝o′ko͞o-lănd′) *n.* An ideal realm of imagination or fantasy. Often used derogatorily. [Translation of Greek *Nephelokokkugia* (*nephelē,* cloud + *kokkux,* cuckoo), a comic utopia in Aristophanes' comedy *The Birds* (414 B.C.).]

cloud nine *n. Informal.* A state of great happiness. Used in the phrase *on cloud nine.* [Originally *on cloud seven;* the phrase is perhaps related to *in the seventh heaven* (in some Jewish and Muslim literature the seventh and final heaven is the abode of God).]

cloud seeding *n.* A technique of stimulating rainfall, especially by distributing quantities of dry-ice crystals or silver iodide smoke

cloudberry *A wild relative of the blackberry and raspberry that grows in damp patches on exposed moors of northern regions. White flowers produce amber berries in late summer.*

PRONUNCIATION KEY

ă, pat; ā, pay; âr, care;
ä, father, are; b, bib;
ch, church; d, deed; ĕ, pet;
ē, be; f, fife; g, gag; h, hat;
hw, which; ĭ, pit; ī, pie;
îr, pier; j, judge; k, kick;
l, lid, needle; m, mum;
n, no, sudden; ng, thing;
ŏ, pot; ō, toe; ô, paw, for;
oi, noise; ou, out; o͝o, book;
o͞o, boot; p, pop; r, roar;
s, sauce; sh, ship, dish;
t, tight; th, thin, path;
th, this, bathe; ŭ, cut; ûr, fur;
v, valve; w, with; y, yes;
z, zebra, size; zh, vision;
ə, about, item, edible, gallop, circus, peaceful

IN FOREIGN WORDS:

à, *Fr.* ami; œ, *Fr.* feu, *Ger.* schön; ü, *Fr.* tu, *Ger.* über; KH, *Ger.* ich, *Scot.* loch; N, *Fr.* bon; y′, *Fr.* Compiègne

STRESS MARKS:

Primary stress: ′
in·cite′ (ĭn-sīt′)
Secondary stress: ′
in′sight′ (ĭn′sīt′)

TEN TYPES OF CLOUDS AND WHAT THEY MEAN

How tomorrow's rain and snow are stored in reservoirs in the sky

Moisture from the world's seas, rivers, plants, and soil is constantly evaporating. As a result, large quantities of water rise unseen from the earth into the atmosphere. When air rises it cools and its capacity to hold the invisible water vapor is reduced until the air becomes saturated. Further cooling then causes the formation of tiny water particles and—at low temperatures—of ice crystals, which develop into various types of clouds. A vast number of cloud particles must join together to form a drop of rain, hail, or snow large enough to fall to earth. Clouds are classified according to appearance and height.

CIRRUS *High-level ice-crystal clouds, often a sign of bad weather to come*

NIMBOSTRATUS *A solid mass of low clouds means that rain is imminent*

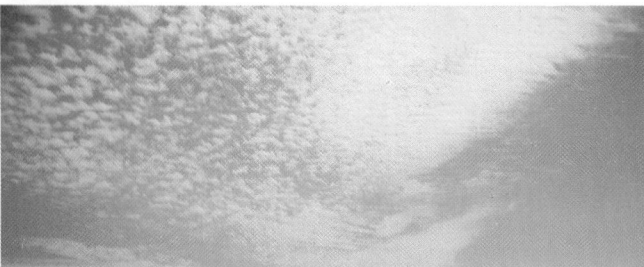

CIRROCUMULUS *High-level rippling clouds on the edge of unsettled weather*

STRATOCUMULUS *Low rolls, usually associated with dry, overcast weather*

CIRROSTRATUS *High milky clouds, often bringing rain within 12 hours*

STRATUS *Low, shapeless, foggy clouds that often bring drizzle*

ALTOCUMULUS *Midlevel banded masses, usually breaking up to give sunny periods*

CUMULUS *Fluffy cauliflowers of low cloud associated with sunny spells*

ALTOSTRATUS *Midlevel thin gray sheet that can develop into rain clouds*

CUMULONIMBUS *Tall, towering thunderheads appearing before a thunderstorm*

through clouds. Also informally called "rainmaking."

cloud·y (klou′dē) *adj.* **-ier, -iest. 1.** *Abbr.* **c.** Full of or covered with clouds; overcast. **2.** Of or like a cloud or clouds. **3.** Marked with indistinct masses or streaks: *cloudy marble.* **4.** Not transparent; milky. Said of liquids. **5.** Obscure; vague. **6.** Troubled; gloomy. **—cloud·i·ly** *adv.* **—cloud·i·ness** *n.*

clout (klout) *n.* **1.** A blow, especially with the fist. **2.** *Slang.* A long, powerful hit in baseball. **3.** *Informal.* Power, prestige, or influence; pull: *political clout.* **4.** An archery target. **5.** *Archaic & Regional.* A piece of cloth. **6.** A short nail with a wide flat head. Also called "clout nail."
~*tr.v.* **clouted, clouting, clouts. 1.** To hit with much force. **2.** *Archaic & Regional.* To patch. [Middle English *clout,* from Old English *clūt* (noun), lump, piece of material, patch, *clūtian,* to patch.]

clove[1] (klōv) *n.* **1.** An East Indian evergreen tree, *Eugenia aromatica,* of which the aromatic unopened flower buds are used, whole or ground, as a spice. **2.** The small dried flower bud of this tree. [Middle English *clowe (of gilofre),* "nail-shaped bud (of clove)," from Old French *clou (de girofle)* : *clou,* nail, from Latin *clāvus* + *girofle,* clove tree (see **gillyflower**).]

clove[2] *n.* Any of the small sections of a separable bulb, such as that of garlic. [Middle English *clove,* Old English *clufu.*]

clove[3]. **1.** Alternate past tense and *archaic* past participle of **cleave** (to split). **2.** *Archaic.* Past tense of **cleave** (to cling).

clove hitch *n.* A knot used to secure a line to a spar, post, or other object, consisting of two turns with the second held under the first. [*Clove,* from CLOVEN (split).]

clo·ven (klō′vən). Alternate past participle of **cleave** (to split).
~*adj.* Split; divided.

cloven foot *n.* A cloven hoof. **—clo·ven-foot·ed** *adj.*

cloven hoof *n.* **1.** A divided or cleft hoof, as in deer or cattle. **2.** The symbol of Satan, who is often depicted with such hooves. **—clo·ven-hoofed** (klō′vən-ho͝oft′, -ho͞oft′) *adj.*

clove pink *n.* A plant, *Dianthus caryophyllus,* having pink flowers from which the garden carnations have been bred.

clo·ver (klō′vər) *n.* **1.** Any plant of the genus *Trifolium,* having compound leaves with usually three leaflets and tight heads of small flowers. Many species provide valuable pasturage. **2.** Any of several related plants, such as the sweet clover, or **melilot** *(see).* **—in clover.** Living a carefree life of ease, comfort, or prosperity. [Middle English *clover, claver,* Old English *clǣfre,* clover, from Germanic *klaibrōn* (unattested).]

clo·ver·leaf (klō′vər-lēf′) *n., pl.* **-leaves** (-lēvz′) or **-leafs.** A highway interchange in the shape of a four-leafed clover at which two roads crossing each other on different levels are provided with curving access and exit ramps, enabling vehicles to go in any of four directions.

Clo·vis (klō′vĭs) (*c.* A.D. 466–511). King of the Franks (481–511), the greatest of the early Merovingian dynasty, who united Gaul as a single kingdom and set up his capital in Paris. His name, Gallicized as "Louis," was given to 18 later French monarchs.

clown (kloun) *n.* **1.** A buffoon or jester, often wearing outlandish clothes and make-up, who entertains by jokes, antics, and tricks, in a circus, play, or other presentation. **2.** A person who acts the fool or behaves in a comic way. **3.** An ignorant or boorish person. **4.** *Archaic.* A rustic or peasant. See feature, next page.
~*intr.v.* **clowned, clowning, clowns. 1.** To behave in a silly, clownlike fashion. Often used with *around.* **2.** To perform as a clown. [Probably from Scandinavian, akin to Icelandic *klunni,* clumsy person.] **—clown·ish** *adj.* **—clown·ish·ly** *adv.* **—clown·ish·ness** *n.*

cloy (kloi) *v.* **cloyed, cloying, cloys.** *—tr.* To supply with too much of something, especially with something too rich or sweet; surfeit. *—intr.* To cause a feeling of surfeit. [Short for obsolete *accloy,* to nail, hence, to clog, satiate, Middle English *acloien,* to obstruct, hamper, from Old French *encloer,* to nail, from Vulgar Latin *inclāvāre* (unattested) : Latin *in,* in + *clāvāre,* to nail, from *clāvus,* nail.] **—cloy·ing** *adj.* **—cloy·ing·ly** *adv.* **—cloy·ing·ness** *n.*

club[1] (klub) *n.* **1.** A stout, heavy stick, usually thicker at one end than at the other, suitable for use as a weapon; a cudgel. **2.** A bat or stick used in certain games to drive a ball; especially, a stick with a curved head used in golf. **3.** *Botany.* A club-shaped structure or organ. **4. a.** The black symbol appearing on one of the four suits of playing cards, in the shape of a trefoil or cloverleaf. **b.** A card bearing this symbol. See **clubs. 5.** *Nautical.* A spar.
~*tr.v.* **clubbed, clubbing, clubs. 1.** To strike or beat with or as with a club. **2.** To gather or combine (hair, for example) into a clublike mass; tangle: *clubbed roots.* [Middle English *clubbe,* from Old Norse *klubba,* billet, club.]

club[2] *n.* **1. a.** A group of people organized for a common purpose; especially, a group that meets regularly. **b.** An association of people formed for social purposes, having premises providing meals, accommodation, and other facilities. **c.** *Sports.* An association that organizes and provides teams, matches, facilities, and events, in a particular game or sport: *a tennis club; a golf club.* **2.** The room, building, or other facilities used by such a group or association. —See Synonyms at **circle.**
~*v.* **clubbed, clubbing, clubs.** *—tr.* To contribute for a joint or common purpose. *—intr.* To join or combine for a common purpose. Used with *together*: *They clubbed together to buy her a farewell present.* [Probably from CLUB (to gather into a mass).]

club·ba·ble (klŭb′ə-bəl) *adj. Informal.* Suited to membership in a social club; sociable.

club car *n.* A railroad passenger car equipped with lounge chairs, tables, a buffet or bar, and other extra comforts.

club chair *n.* An upholstered easy chair with arms and a low back.

club·foot (klŭb′fo͝ot′) *n., pl.* **-feet** (-fēt). **1.** Congenital deformity of the foot, marked by a misshapen appearance often resembling a club. Also called "talipes." **2.** A foot so deformed. **—club·foot·ed** *adj.*

club·house (klŭb′hous′) *n.* A building occupied by a club.

club·man (klŭb′mən, -măn′) *n., pl.* **-men** (-mĭn, -mĕn′). A man who is an active member of a fashionable club or clubs.

club moss *n.* Any of various erect or creeping mosslike plants of the genus *Lycopodium,* having tiny, scalelike, overlapping leaves and reproducing by spores. Some species are also called "ground pine." Also called "lycopodium." [After the club-shaped strobiles on some species.]

club root *n.* A disease of cabbage and related plants, caused by a fungus of the genus *Plasmodiophora,* and resulting in large, distorted swellings on the roots.

clubs (klŭbz) *n. Used with a singular or plural verb.* One of the four suits of playing cards, distinguished by black trefoil figures printed on the face of each card.

club sandwich *n.* A sandwich, usually of three slices of toast, with a filling of various meats, tomato, lettuce, and dressing.

club soda *n.* An effervescent, unflavored water used in various alcoholic and nonalcoholic drinks.

club steak *n.* **Delmonico steak** *(see).*

cluck (klŭk) *v.* **clucked, clucking, clucks.** *—intr.* To utter a cluck or clucks. *—tr.* To express by clucking: *He clucked his disapproval.*
~*n.* **1. a.** The characteristic sound made by a hen when brooding or calling her chicks. **b.** Any sound resembling this. **2.** *Informal.* A stupid or foolish person: *a dumb cluck.* [Imitative.]

clue, clew (klo͞o) *n.* Anything that guides or directs in the solution of a problem or mystery. **—not have a clue.** *Informal.* To be ignorant or incapable.
~*tr.v.* **clued, clueing** or **cluing, clues.** Also **clew, clewed, clewing, clews.** To give (someone) guiding information. Used with *in.* [Variant of CLEW (ball of yarn).]

Clum·ber spaniel (klŭm′bər) *n.* A dog of a breed developed in England, having short legs and a silky, predominantly white coat. [After *Clumber,* a country estate in Nottinghamshire.]

clump (klŭmp) *n.* **1.** A clustered mass; a lump. **2.** A thick grouping, as of plants. **3.** A heavy dull sound; a thud, as of footsteps.
~*v.* **clumped, clumping, clumps.** *—intr.* **1.** To walk with a heavy dull sound. **2.** To form clumps. *—tr.* **1.** To gather into or form clumps of. **2.** To cause (blood cells or bacteria for example) to form clumps. [Low German *klump,* from Middle Low German *klumpe.*] **—clump·y** *adj.*

clum·sy (klŭm′zē) *adj.* **-sier, -siest. 1.** Lacking physical coordination, skill, or grace; awkward. **2.** Awkwardly made; unwieldy. **3.** Gauche; inept: *a clumsy excuse; a clumsy compliment.* —See Synonyms at **awkward.** [From obsolete *clumse,* to be numb with cold, Middle English *clumsen,* probably from Scandinavian, akin to Swedish dialectal *klumsen,* benumbed, from Germanic *klum-* (unattested).] **—clum·si·ly** *adv.* **—clum·si·ness** *n.*

clung. Past tense and past participle of **cling.**

clunk (klŭngk) *n.* **1.** A heavy blow. **2.** A dull, hollow sound; thump. [Imitative.]

clunk·er (klŭng′kər) *n.* **1.** An old, broken-down car or other machine. **2.** A failure; flop.

Clu·ny (klo͞o′nē). Town in Saône-et-Loire department of east-central France, on the Grosne River. The Cluniac order of Benedictine monks was established here in 910 at an abbey which survives to this day.

clu·pe·id (klo͞o′pē-ĭd)) *n.* Any of various fishes of the family Clupeidae, which includes herrings, sardines, and sprats. [New Latin *Clupeidae,* from Latin *clupea*†, a kind of small fish.] **—clu·pe·id** *adj.*

clus·ter (klŭs′tər) *n.* **1.** Any configuration of elements gathered or occurring closely together; a group; a bunch. **2.** Two or more successive consonants in a word; for example, *cl* and *st* in the word *cluster.* **3.** *Astronomy.* A group of stars or galaxies moving together.
~*v.* **clustered, -tering, -ters.** *—intr.* To gather or grow in clusters. *—tr.* To cause to grow or form into clusters. [Middle English *cluster,* Old English *clyster, cluster*†.]

cluster bomb *n.* A bomb consisting of a collection of **fragmentation bombs** *(see)* that are dispersed on impact.

cluster fly *n.* A fly of the family Calliphoridae that gathers with others of its kind in crevices or corners of buildings.

cluster pine *n.* A tree, the **pinaster** *(see).*

clutch[1] (klŭch) *v.* **clutched, clutching, clutches.** *—tr.* **1.** To grasp and hold tightly. **2.** To seize or snatch. *—intr.* To attempt to grasp or seize. Used with *at.*
~*n.* **1.** The hand, claw, talon, paw, or the like, used in the act of grasping. **2.** A tight grasp. **3.** *Usually* **clutches.** Control or power: *She had them in her clutches.* **4.** *Machinery.* **a.** Any of various devices for engaging and disengaging two working parts of a shaft or of a shaft and a driving mechanism, as in a car. **b.** The pedal, lever, or other apparatus that activates such a device. **—in the clutch.** *Informal.* In a crucial or critical situation. [Middle English *clicchen, clucchen,* Old English *clyccan,* from Germanic *klukjan* (unattested).]

clutch[2] *n.* **1.** The number of eggs produced or incubated by one bird or in one nest at one time. **2.** A brood of chickens. **3.** *Informal.* A group of people or things.

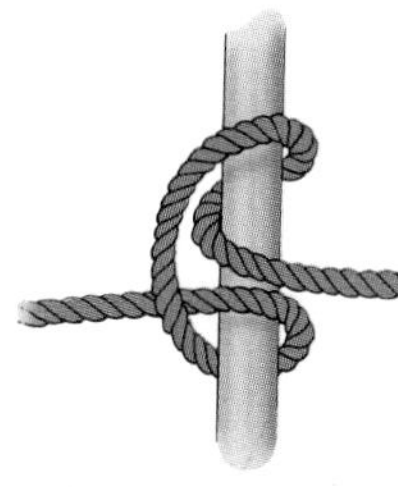

clove hitch *This is made of two adjustable loops that jam together, fastening the rope securely. It is often used for mooring boats.*

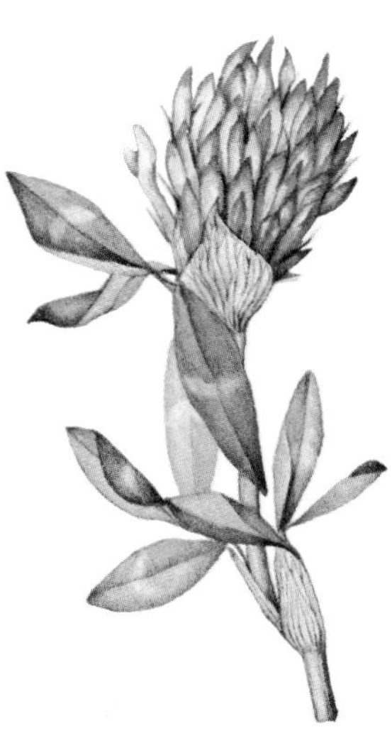

clover *An inconspicuous meadow plant that can absorb nitrogen from the air. Red clover (above) is often grown and plowed into the ground in order to enrich it with nitrogen, a vital plant food.*

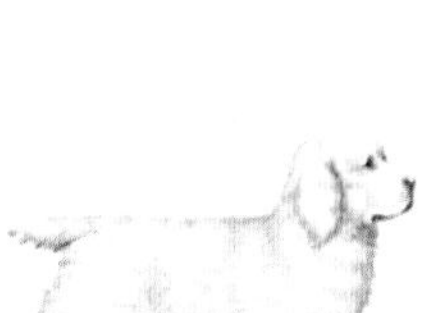

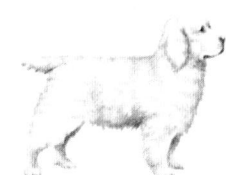

Clumber spaniel *This English breed of sporting dog was developed at Clumber Park in Nottingham. It is one of the largest types of spaniel and, like other spaniels, was originally used to retrieve and flush out game animals such as pheasants, ducks, and rabbits.*

~*tr.v.* **clutched, clutching, clutches.** To hatch (chicks). [18th century : variant of dialectal *cletch,* from Middle English *clecken,* to hatch, give birth, from Old Norse *klekja*†.]

clutch bag *n.* A small handbag without a strap or handles.

clut·ter (klŭt′ər) *n.* **1.** A confused or disordered state or collection; a jumble. **2.** *Archaic.* A confused noise; a clatter. **3.** *Electronics.* Noise, echoes, or other unwanted signals on a radar display.

~*tr.v.* **cluttered, -tering, -ters.** To litter or pile in a disordered state. Used with *up.* [Middle English *clotteren,* to clot, coagulate, heap, from *clot,* lump, CLOT.]

Clw·yd (klōō′ĭd). County in northeast Wales, formed in 1974 from Flintshire and parts of Denbighshire and Merionethshire. It is bounded by England to the east. Upland pastures, rising to 690 meters (2,265 feet) at Foel Wen in the south are broken by the fertile valleys of the Clwyd and Dee rivers, where sheep and cattle are farmed. Its county town is Mold.

Clyde (klīd). River in western Scotland. It rises in the Southern Uplands and flows 170 kilometers (106 miles) northwest through Glasgow and Clydebank to the sea at the Firth of Clyde, an inlet of the Atlantic Ocean.

Clyde·bank (klīd′băngk′). Town in the Strathclyde Region, on the lower Clyde River. Many ocean liners were built in its shipyards, including the *Queen Mary* and *Queen Elizabeth.*

Clydes·dale (klīdz′dāl′) *n.* **1.** A large, powerful draft horse of a breed developed in the Clyde valley in Scotland. **2.** A type of small terrier.

clyp·e·ate (klĭp′ē-īt) *adj.* Also **clyp·e·i·form** (klĭp′ē-ə-fôrm).
1. Shaped like a round shield. **2.** Having a clypeus.

clyp·e·us (klĭp′ē-əs) *n., pl.* **-ei** (-ē-ī′). *Biology.* A shieldlike structure, especially a plate on the front of the head of an insect. [New Latin, from Latin *clipeus, clupeus*†, round shield.] —**clyp′e·al** *adj.*

clys·ter (klĭs′tər) *n. Medicine. Rare.* An enema. [Middle English *clister,* from Old French *clistere,* from Latin *clystēr,* from Greek *klustēr,* "liquid for washing out," from *kluzein,* to wash out.]

Cly·tem·nes·tra (klī′təm-nĕs′trə). *Greek Mythology.* The wife of Agamemnon and mother of Orestes and Electra. With her lover Aegisthus she murdered Agamemnon and was killed by her son in revenge.

cm centimeter; centimeters.

Cm The symbol for the element curium.

c.m. **1.** circular mil. **2.** court-martial.

CMA certified medical assistant.

Cmdr. commander.

C.M.G. Companion (of the Order) of St. Michael and St. George.

cml. commercial.

cN centinewton.

C/N credit note.

CND Campaign for Nuclear Disarmament.

cni·dar·i·an (nī-dâr′ē-ən) *n.* Any of various aquatic invertebrates of the Cnidaria, a chiefly marine subphylum of the Coelenterata that includes the jellyfish, sea anemones, and corals.
~*adj.* Of or belonging to the Cnidaria. [New Latin *Cnidaria,* from Greek *knidē,* nettle.]

Cnossos. See **Knossos.**

CNS central nervous system.

Cnut. See **Canute.**

Co The symbol for the element cobalt.

CO Colorado (with Zip Code).

co– *prefix.* Indicates: **1.** Joint, jointly, together, or mutually; for example, **co-education, cooperate, copilot. 2.** Same, similar; for example, **coconscious. 3.** Complement of an angle; for example, **cosine, coaltitude.** [In borrowed Latin compounds, *co-* is the reduced form of *com-* (see **com-**), used before *h, gn,* and usually before vowels, as in COHERE, COGNATE, and COALESCE.]

co., Co. 1. company. **2.** county.

c.o. 1. care of. **2.** *Accounting.* carried over. **3.** cash order.

C.O. 1. commanding officer. **2.** conscientious objector.

c/o care of.

co·ac·er·vate (kō-ăs′ər-vāt′) *n. Chemistry.* A cluster of droplets separated out of a lyophilic colloid. [Latin *coacervātus,* past participle of *coacervāre,* to heap together : *co-,* together + *acervāre,* to heap, ACERVATE.]

Clydesdale *A tall and powerful workhorse once widely used for plowing and for pulling heavy farm wagons and brewers' drays.*

---

clown

THE FOOL WHO IS SUFFERED GLADLY

A tradition of buffoonery that goes back to ancient Greece

Clowns are mostly found today in the circus, but the professional buffoon has a long tradition behind him. He was seen on the stages of ancient Greece and Rome, and as the Old Vice (attendant on the Devil) in medieval religious drama.

From Italian Renaissance comedy—the *commedia dell'arte*—came Punch and Pierrot and the comic character of 19th-century English pantomime. A character called Clown in pantomime was mainly the creation of the London actor Joseph Grimaldi

(1779–1837), who played in pantomime from the age of four.

In Grimaldi's honor the present-day circus clown, who has inherited many of his characteristics, is known as "Joey." He has as his butt the "Auguste," according to some an 1870's invention of the French circus, but attributed by some others to Tom Belling in a Berlin circus in 1864. The Auguste is a shambling figure with a bulbous red nose and a fright wig, who interrupts and ruins all Clown's tricks and trips over anything in his way.

AUGUSTE *Coco, who performed with Bertram Mills's Circus in Britain for 30 years, was an Auguste, the clown who does everything wrong and often has buckets of water thrown over him.*

WHITE-FACED CLOWN *In the Cirque de Paris, a white-faced clown plays to the audience on a clarinet, before his performance is wrecked by the clumsy assistance of an Auguste.*

co·ac·er·va·tion (kō-ăs'ər-vā'shən) *n.* The process of becoming a coacervate.

coach (kōch) *n.* **1.** A large, closed horse-drawn carriage with four wheels. **2.** A railway carriage. **3.** *Chiefly British.* A motor bus. **4.** Economy-class seating on a train or airplane. **5.** A person who trains athletes or sports teams. **6.** A private tutor employed to prepare a student for an examination. ~*v.* **coached, coaching, coaches.** —*tr.* **1.** To teach or train; tutor. **2.** To transport by coach. —*intr.* **1.** To act as a coach. **2.** To ride in a coach. —See Synonyms at **teach.** [French *coche,* from German *Kutsche,* from Hungarian *kocsi,* after *Kocs,* a town in Hungary, where such carriages originated. Sense 6: 19th-century university slang use of *coach* (carriage).] —**coach·er** *n.*

coach-built (kōch'bĭlt') *adj.* Designating a vehicle body built specially by craftsmen.

coach dog *n.* The **Dalmatian** (*see*). [Formerly trained as a fashionable pet to run behind a coach.]

coach·ing inn (kō'chĭng) *n.* An inn where the horses pulling a long-distance coach could be changed for a fresh team.

coach·man (kōch'mən) *n., pl.* **-men** (-mĭn). **1.** A person who drives a horse-drawn coach. **2.** A type of artificial fishing fly.

coach·wood (kōch'wŏŏd') *n.* An Australian tree yielding closely grained wood suitable for making furniture.

coach·work (kōch'wûrk') *n.* The bodywork of a motor vehicle.

co·ac·tion (kō-ăk'shən) *n.* **1.** Joint action. **2.** *Archaic.* Compulsion. [Middle English *coaccioun,* from Old French *coaction,* from Latin *coactiō,* from *cōgere* (past participle *cōactus*), to drive together, force. See **coagulum.**] —**co·ac·tive** *adj.* —**co·ac·tive·ly** *adv.*

co·ad·ju·tant (kō-ăj'ə-tənt) *adj.* Helping each other. ~*n.* A coworker; an assistant.

co·ad·ju·tor (kō'ə-jōō'tər, kō-ăj'ə-tər) *n. Abbr.* **coad. 1.** The assistant to a bishop. **2.** Any coworker; an assistant. [Middle English *coadjutour,* from Old French *coadjuteur,* from Latin *coadjūtor* : *cō-,* together + *adjūtor,* assistant, from *adjuvāre,* to assist, AID.]

co·ad·u·nate (kō-ăj'ə-nĭt, -nāt') *adj.* Closely joined by growing together; connate. [Late Latin *coadūnāre* : *cō-,* together + *adūnāre,* to unite to : Latin *ad-,* to + *ūnāre,* to unite, from *ūnus,* one.] —**co·ad·u·na·tion** (kō-ăj'ə-nā'shən) *n.* —**co·ad·u·na·tive** (kō-ăj'ə-nā'tĭv, -nə-tĭv) *adj.*

co·ag·u·lant (kō-ăg'yə-lənt) *n.* An agent that causes coagulation. —**co·ag·u·lant** *adj.*

co·ag·u·lase (kō-ăg'yə-lās', -lāz') *n.* An enzyme, such as thrombin, that causes blood clotting. [COAGUL(ATE) + -ASE.]

co·ag·u·late (kō-ăg'yə-lāt') *v.* **-lated, -lating, -lates.** —*tr.* To cause transformation of (a liquid or solid, such as blood) into a soft, semisolid, or solid mass. —*intr.* To become such a mass. [Middle English *coagulaten,* from Latin *coāgulāre,* to curdle, from COAGULUM.] —**co·ag·u·la·ble** (kō-ăg'yə-lə-bəl) *adj.* —**co·ag·u·la·bil·i·ty** (kō-ăg'yə-lə-bĭl'ə-tē) *n.* —**co·ag·u·la·tion** (kō-ăg'yə-lā'shən) *n.* —**co·ag·u·la·tive** (kō-ăg'yə-lā'tĭv, -lə-tĭv) *n.* —**co·ag·u·la·tor** *n.*

coagulation factor *n.* Any factor in the blood or plasma that contributes to the clotting of blood.

co·ag·u·lum (kō-ăg'yə-ləm) *n., pl.* **-la** (-lə). A coagulated mass; a clot; a curd. [Latin *coāgulum,* from *cōgere,* to drive together, condense : *cō-,* together + *agere,* to drive.]

coal (kōl) *n.* **1.** A natural dark brown to black solid used as a fuel, formed from fossilized plants, and consisting of carbon with various organic and some inorganic compounds. **2.** A piece of this substance. **3.** A glowing or charred piece of coal, wood, or other solid fuel; an ember. —**haul** (or **drag**) **over the coals.** To reprimand; scold. —**take coals to Newcastle.** To take something to a place where it is already plentiful. ~*v.* **coaled, coaling, coals.** —*tr.* To provide (a ship, for example) with coal. —*intr.* To take on coal. [Middle English *cole,* Old English *col,* coal, live coal.]

coal bunker *n.* A place for storing coal outside a house or in a ship.

coal·er (kō'lər) *n.* A ship that transports coal.

co·a·lesce (kō'ə-lĕs') *intr.v.* **-lesced, -lescing, -lesces. 1.** To grow together; fuse. **2.** To come together so as to form one whole; unite. —See Synonyms at **mix.** [Latin *coalēscere,* to grow together : *cō-,* together + *alēscere,* to grow, inceptive of *alere,* to nourish.] —**co·a·les·cence** (kō'ə-lĕs'əns) *n.* —**co·a·les·cent** (kō'ə-lĕs'ənt) *adj.*

coal·face (kōl'fās') *n.* The exposed seam in a mine from which the coal is cut.

coal·field (kōl'fēld') *n.* An area with large deposits of coal.

coal·fish (kōl'fĭsh') *n., pl.* **-fishes** or collectively **coalfish.** An edible deep-water marine fish, *Gadus virens,* closely related to the cod, with a blackish back and chin barbel. Also called "coley," "saithe."

coal gas *n.* **1.** A gaseous mixture produced by the destructive distillation of bituminous coal and formerly used as a commercial fuel. **2.** The gaseous mixture released by burning coal.

coal·i·fy (kō'lə-fī') *v.* **-fied, -fying, -fies.** —*tr.* To cause (plant material) to form coal. —*intr.* To form coal. Used of plant material. —**coal·i·fi·ca·tion** (kō'lə-fĭ-kā'shən) *n.*

co·a·li·tion (kō'ə-lĭsh'ən) *n.* **1.** An alliance, especially a temporary one, of factions, parties, or nations. **2.** A combination or fusion into one body. [French, from Medieval Latin *coalitiō* (stem *coalitiōn-*), from Latin *coalescere,* COALESCE.] —**co·a·li·tion·ist** *n.*

coal measures *pl.n. Geology.* **1. Coal Measures.** A stratigraphic unit equivalent to the uppermost division of the Pennsylvanian or Upper Carboniferous periods. **2.** Strata of the Carboniferous period containing coal deposits.

coal oil *n.* **1.** An oil formed during the distillation of coal. **2. Kerosene** (*see*).

Coal·port (kōl'pôrt', -pōrt') *n.* An antique type of translucent bone china, decorated with brightly colored patterns on a white base. [After *Coalport,* Shrewsbury, England, where it was made.] —**Coalport** *adj.*

Coal·sack (kōl'săk') *n.* **1.** A dark nebula near the Southern Cross, appearing as a hole in the Milky Way. **2.** A similar dark region of the sky, the Northern Coalsack, near the Northern Cross.

coal scuttle *n.* A metal container, usually with a handle, in which coal is kept by a hearth.

coal tar *n.* A viscous black liquid obtained by the destructive distillation of coal, used as a raw material for many dyes, drugs, medications, and organic chemicals and for waterproofing, paints, roofing, and insulation materials. —**coal-tar** (kōl'tär') *adj.*

coal-tar pitch *n.* A heavy black pitch produced by the distillation of coal tar, used as a binder in smokeless fuels and in road surfacing.

coam·ing (kō'mĭng) *n.* A raised rim or curb around an opening in a ship's deck or in the roof of a building, designed to keep out water. [17th century : origin obscure.]

co·an·chor (kō-ăng'kər) *n.* A newscaster who anchors a news broadcast with another or others. —**co·an·chor** *v.*

co·ap·ta·tion (kō'ăp-tā'shən) *n.* The adjustment of parts to each other; especially, the joining of broken bones or the edges of a wound. [Late Latin *coaptātiō* (stem *coaptātiōn-*), a careful fitting together, from Latin *co-,* together + *aptāre,* to fit.]

co·arc·tate (kō-ärk'tāt') *adj. Entomology.* Describing an insect pupa in which the final larval cuticle remains to form a hardened shell around the body. [Latin *coarctātus,* past participle of *coarctāre, coartāre,* to press tightly : *co-,* together + *artāre,* to press, from *artus,* narrow, tight.] —**co·arc·ta·tion** (kō'ärk-tā'shən) *n.*

coarse (kôrs, kōrs) *adj.* **coarser, coarsest. 1.** Of low, common, or inferior quality. **2. a.** Lacking in delicacy or refinement. **b.** Obscene or improper. Said of language. **3.** Consisting of large particles; not fine in texture. **4.** Rough; harsh. [Middle English *co(a)rs,* ordinary, coarse, probably from *co(u)rs,* COURSE ("the usual practice").] —**coarse·ly** *adv.* —**coarse·ness** *n.*

Synonyms: crass, gross, obscene, ribald, vulgar.

coarse fish *n. British.* Any freshwater fish that does not belong to the salmon or trout families. —**coarse fishing** *n.*

coarse-grained (kôrs'grānd', kōrs'-) *adj.* **1.** Having a rough or coarse texture. **2.** Not refined; indelicate; crude.

coars·en (kôr'sən, kōr'sən) *v.* **-ened, -ening, -ens.** —*intr.* To become coarse. —*tr.* To make coarse.

coast (kōst) *n.* **1.** The land next to the sea; the seashore. **2.** *Obsolete.* The frontier or border of a country. **3.** The act of sliding or coasting; a slide. **4.** A hill or other slope down which one may coast, as on a toboggan. —**the Coast.** The Atlantic or Pacific coast of the United States. —**the coast is clear.** *Informal.* There are no dangers or hindrances. ~*v.* **coasted, coasting, coasts.** —*intr.* **1. a.** To move along without power, as a freewheeling car does. **b.** To progress effortlessly, at an unhurried pace. **2.** To slide down a slope, as on a sled. **3.** To sail near or along a coast. —*tr.* To sail or move along the coast or border of. [Middle English *cost,* from Old French *coste,* from Latin *costa,* rib, side.] —**coast·al** (kōs'təl) *adj.*

coast·er (kōs'tər) *n.* **1.** A ship engaged in coastal trade. **2.** A disk placed under a bottle or glass to protect a table top. **3.** A small tray or stand, often wheeled, for passing a wine decanter around a table, for example. **4.** A sled or toboggan for coasting.

coaster brake *n.* A brake in the hub of the rear wheel of a bicycle, engaged by pedaling backward.

coast guard *n.* **1.** *Abbr.* **C.G.** The military or naval coastal patrol of a nation, responsible for the protection of life and property at sea, coastal defense, and enforcement of customs, immigration, and navigation laws. **2.** A member of a coast guard; coastguardsman.

coast·guards·man (kōst'gärdz'mən) *n., pl.* **-men** (-mĭn). A member of a coast guard.

coast·line (kōst'līn') *n.* The shape or boundary of a coast.

Coast Mountains. Range of western British Columbia and southeastern Alaska, extending c. 1,610 kilometers (1,000 miles) northward from the Cascade Range. The mountains have been heavily eroded by glaciers and slope steeply to the Pacific Ocean, where the shoreline is deeply indented by fjords.

Coast Ranges. The mountain ranges along the Pacific coast of North America, extending from southeastern Alaska to Lower California. North of San Francisco the ranges are thickly forested; the southern parts are dry and covered with brush and grass.

coast·ward (kōst'wərd) *adj.* Directed toward a coast. ~*adv.* Also **coast·wards** (kōst'wərdz). Toward the coast.

coast·wise (kōst'wīz') *adj.* Following the coast. ~*adv.* By way of or along the coast.

coat (kōt) *n.* **1.** An outer garment covering the body from the shoulders to the waist or below, worn primarily for protection from cold or bad weather. **2. a.** A woman's garment extending to just below the waist and usually forming the top part of a suit. **b.** The jacket of a man's suit. **3.** A natural integument or outer covering, such as the fur of an animal. **4.** A layer of some material covering something else; a coating: *a coat of dust; a coat of paint.* ~*tr.v.* **coated, coating, coats. 1.** To provide or cover with a coat. **2.** To cover with a layer, as of paint or chocolate. [Middle English *cote,* from Old French, from Frankish *kotta* (unattested), from West Germanic *kotta* (unattested).]

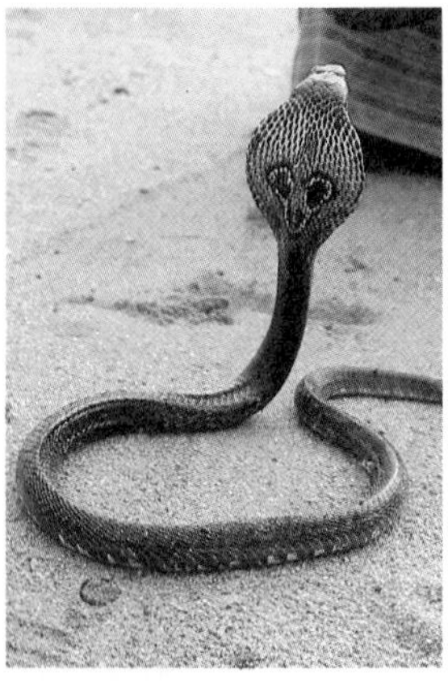

cobra *The Indian cobra (above) has a larger hood than the African varieties. Some species can spit venom, at a distance and with great accuracy, into the eyes of an approaching aggressor.*

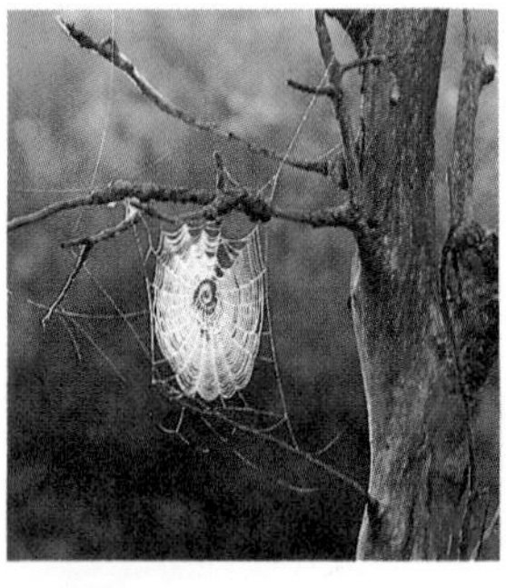

cobweb *Spider's cobweb spun in a dead tree. Cobwebs are made of silk exuded from the spider's body. But only the central trap is sticky; the supporting threads are dry.*

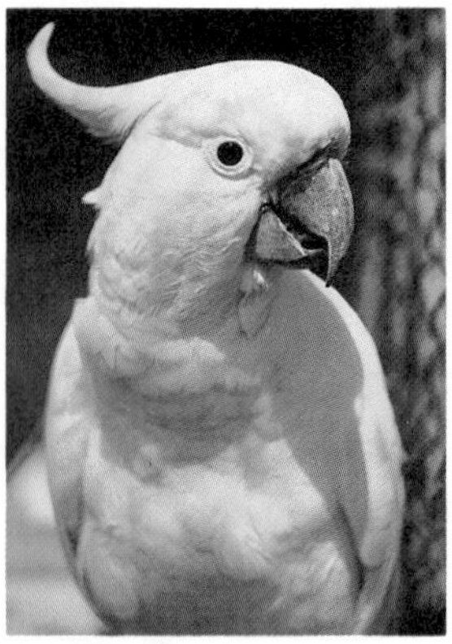

cockatoo *There are 16 species in this group of crested parrots, all native to Australia and nearby islands. They range in color from pink and black to white and yellow; this is the sulfur-crested cockatoo.*

coat·ed (kō'tĭd) *adj.* **1.** Having an outer layer, coat, or covering. **2.** Having a highly polished surface suitable for halftone printing: *coated paper.* **3.** *Optics.* Having a thin layer to minimize reflection; bloomed. Said of a lens.

co·a·ti (kō-ä'tē) *n.* Any of several omnivorous mammals of the genus *Nasua,* of South and Central America and the southwestern United States, related to and resembling the raccoon but having a longer snout and tail. Also called "coatimundi." [Portuguese *coatí,* from Tupi *coatí, coatim,* "belt-nosed" : *cua,* belt, band + *tim,* nose.]

co·a·ti·mun·di (kō-ä'tē-mŭn'dē) *n.* The **coati** *(see).*

coat·ing (kō'tĭng) *n.* **1.** A layer of any substance spread over a surface for protection or decoration. **2.** Cloth for making coats.

coat of arms *n.* **1.** A tabard or surcoat blazoned with heraldic bearings. **2.** The heraldic bearings of a family, city, or the like, usually represented on an escutcheon or shield and accompanied by a crest and motto.

coat of mail *n., pl.* **coats of mail.** An armored coat made of chain mail, interlinked rings, or overlapping metal plates.

coat·tails (kōt'tālz') *pl.n.* The long divided part at the back of a formal or dress coat. **—on (someone's) coattails.** Benefiting from someone else's advancement.

co-au·thor (kō-ô'thər) *n.* A collaborating or joint author.
~tr.v. **co-authored, -thoring, -thors.** To be a co-author of.

coax[1] (kōks) *v.* **coaxed, coaxing, coaxes.** *—tr.* **1.** To persuade or try to persuade by pleading or flattery; cajole; wheedle. **2.** To obtain by persistent persuasion. *—intr.* To use persuasion or inducement. —See Synonyms at **urge.** [Earlier *coaks, cokes,* to fool, from *cokes*†, fool.] **—coax·er** *n.* **—coax·ing·ly** *adv.*

co·ax[2] (kō'ăks') *n.* A **coaxial cable** *(see).*

co·ax·i·al (kō-ăk'sē-əl) *adj.* Having or mounted on a common axis.

coaxial cable *n.* A high-frequency cable used for telephone, telegraph, or television transmission, consisting of a conducting metal tube enclosing and insulated from a central conducting wire core.

cob[1] (kŏb) *n.* **1.** The central core of an ear of corn; corncob. **2.** A male swan. Compare **pen. 3.** A thick-set, stocky, short-legged horse. **4.** A tree, the **cobnut** *(see),* or its edible nut. [Middle English *cobbe*†, lump, round object.]

cob[2] *n.* A mixture of clay and straw formerly used as a building material. [17th century : origin obscure.]

co·balt (kō'bôlt') *n. Symbol* **Co** A hard, brittle metallic element, found associated with nickel, silver, lead, copper, and iron ores and resembling nickel and iron in appearance. It is used chiefly for magnetic alloys, high-temperature alloys, and in the form of its salts for blue glass and ceramic pigments. Atomic number 27, atomic weight 58.9332, melting point 1,495°C, boiling point 3,100°C, specific gravity 8.9, valences 1, 2, 3. [German *Kobalt, Kobold,* from Middle High German *kobolt,* an underground goblin (cobalt was thought to be injurious to silver ores).]

cobalt-60 *n.* A radioactive isotope of cobalt with mass number 60 and exceptionally intense gamma-ray activity, used in radiotherapy, metallurgy, and materials testing.

cobalt blue *n.* **1.** A blue to green pigment consisting of a variable mixture of cobalt and aluminum oxides. **2.** Vivid or strong greenish blue. **—co·balt-blue** *adj.*

cobalt bomb *n.* **1.** An apparatus for producing a beam of gamma rays from a cobalt-60 source, used in medical radiation treatment. **2.** A nuclear weapon designed to release large amounts of radioactive cobalt-60 into the atmosphere.

co·bal·tic (kō-bôl'tĭk) *adj.* Of or containing cobalt. Said especially of chemical compounds containing cobalt with valence 3.

co·bal·tite (kō'bôl-tīt') *n.* Also **co·balt·ine** (-tēn'). A silver-white to gray mineral, CoAsS, that is an important cobalt ore and is used in ceramics.

co·bal·tous (kō-bôl'təs) *adj.* Of or containing cobalt. Said especially of chemical compounds containing cobalt with valence 2.

cob·ber (kŏb'ər) *n. Australian.* Comrade; mate. [Origin unknown.]

Cob·bett (kŏb'ĭt), **William** (1763–1835). British radical author known for his *Weekly Political Register* (1802–35). His *Rural Rides* (1830) described horseback tours of England, charting the decline of traditional values and liberties with industrialization.

cob·ble[1] (kŏb'əl) *n.* **1.** A cobblestone. **2. cobbles.** Coal in lumps about the size of cobblestones.
~tr.v. **cobbled, -bling, -bles.** To pave with cobblestones. [Back-formation from COBBLESTONE.]

cobble[2] *tr.v.* **-bled, -bling, -bles. 1.** To make or mend (boots or shoes). **2.** To put together quickly and roughly: *She cobbled together a speech.* [Probably back-formation from COBBLER.]

cob·bler[1] (kŏb'lər) *n.* **1.** One who mends boots and shoes. **2.** *Archaic.* A clumsy worker; bungler. [Middle English *cobelere*†.]

cobbler[2] *n.* **1.** A deep-dish fruit pie with a thick upper crust. **2.** An iced drink made of wine or liqueur, sugar, and citrus fruit. [Perhaps from COBBLER (mender).]

cob·ble·stone (kŏb'əl-stōn') *n.* A naturally rounded stone, formerly used for paving streets and walls. Also called "cobble." [Middle English *cobelston* : *cobel-,* probably diminutive of *cobbe,* COB (lump) + STONE.]

Cob·den (kŏb'dən), **Richard** (1804–65). British economist and a leading spokesman for free trade. He was a supporter of the Anti-Corn-Law League (1838–46), which brought about the repeal of protectionist legislation.

co·bel·lig·er·ent (kō'bə-lĭj'ər-ənt) *n.* A nation associated with another or others in waging war.

co·bi·a (kō'bē-ə) *n.* A large game fish, *Rachycentron canadum,* of tropical and subtropical seas. [Origin obscure.]

co·ble (kō'bəl) *n. British.* A small, flat-bottomed fishing boat with a lugsail on a raking mast. [Old English *cobel,* from Celtic; akin to Old Breton *caubal.*]

Coblenz. See **Koblenz.**

cob·nut (kŏb'nŭt') *n.* **1.** A European hazel tree, *Corylus avellana grandis.* **2.** The large, edible nut of this tree. Also called "cob."

CO·BOL (kō'bôl') *n.* A computer language based on English words and phrases, used for various business applications. [*CO*mmon *B*usiness *O*riented *L*anguage.]

co·bra (kō'brə) *n.* Any of several venomous snakes of the genus *Naja* and related genera, of Asia and Africa, capable of expanding the skin of the neck to form a flattened hood. [Short for Portuguese *cobra (de capello),* "snake (with a hood)," from Latin *colubra,* feminine of *coluber*†, snake.]

cob·web (kŏb'wĕb') *n.* **1.** The web spun by a spider to catch its prey. **2.** A single thread of such a web. **3.** Something resembling a cobweb in fineness or flimsiness. **4. cobwebs. a.** Any musty accumulation, especially as a result of disuse or neglect. **b.** Confusion; disorder: *cobwebs in the brain.*
~tr.v. **cobwebbed, -webbing, -webs.** To cover with or as if with cobwebs. [Middle English *coppeweb* : *coppe,* spider, Old English *(āttor)coppe* + WEB.] **—cob·web·by** *adj.*

co·ca (kō'kə) *n.* **1.** A South American tree, *Erythroxylon coca,* having leaves that contain cocaine and related alkaloids. **2.** The dried leaves of this shrub or related plants, chewed by people of the Andes as a stimulant. [Spanish, from Quechua *kúka, cuca.*]

co·caine (kō'kān', kō-kān') *n.* A colorless or white crystalline narcotic alkaloid, $C_{17}H_{21}NO_4$, extracted from coca leaves and used as a stimulant or local anesthetic. [COCA + -INE.]

co·cain·ism (kō-kā'nĭz'əm) *n.* The habitual use of cocaine.

coc·cid (kŏk'sĭd) *n.* An insect of the family Coccidae, which includes the scale insects and mealybugs. [New Latin *Coccidae,* from *Coccus* (genus), from Greek *kokkos,* kermes berry, pit.]

coc·cid·i·o·sis (kŏk-sĭd'ē-ō'sĭs) *n.* A disease of many animals, including cattle, pigs, sheep, dogs, cats, and poultry, but rarely of humans, resulting from an infection of the digestive tract by parasitic protozoa of the order Coccidia. [New Latin : *Coccidia,* from COCCUS + -OSIS.]

coc·cus (kŏk'əs) *n., pl.* **cocci** (kŏk'sī', kŏk'ī'). **1.** A bacterium with a spherical or spheroidal shape. Compare **bacillus, spirillum. 2.** *Botany.* A division that contains a single seed and splits apart from a many-lobed fruit. [New Latin, from Greek *kokkos,* kermes berry, pit.] **—coc·coid** (kŏk'oid'), **coc·cal** (kŏk'əl) *adj.*

-coccus *suffix.* Indicates a microorganism that is spheroidal in shape; for example, **streptococcus.** [New Latin, from COCCUS.]

coc·cyx (kŏk'sĭks) *n., pl.* **coccyges** (kŏk-sī'jēz, kŏk'sə-jēz'). In humans and certain apes, a small bone at the base of the spinal column, consisting of several fused rudimentary vertebrae, which represents a vestigial tail. [New Latin, from Greek *kokkux,* cuckoo, coccyx (bone shaped like the cuckoo's beak) (imitative).] **—coc·cyg·e·al** (kŏk-sĭj'ē-əl) *adj.*

Co·chin[1] (kō'chĭn, kōch'ĭn). Port on the Malabar Coast of southwest India. It was the first European settlement in India, colonized by the Portuguese from 1502.

Cochin[2] *n.* A large domestic fowl of a breed developed in Asia, having thickly feathered legs. Also called "Cochin China." [After COCHIN CHINA.]

Cochin Chi·na (chī'nə). The European name for a historic region of central and southern Vietnam. French Cochin China (1862–67) was a territory surrounding Saigon and the Mekong delta. It was subsequently incorporated into the French Union of Indochina (1887–1945) and now forms part of Vietnam.

coch·i·neal (kŏch'ə-nēl', kōch'ə-nēl') *n.* **1.** A tropical American scale insect, *Dactylopius coccus,* that feeds on certain species of cacti. Also called "cochineal insect." **2.** A brilliant red dye, used especially in cooking, made by drying and pulverizing the bodies of the females of this insect. **3.** Vivid red. [French *cochenille,* from Spanish *cochinilla,* from Latin *coccinus,* scarlet, from Greek *kokkinos,* from *kokkos,* kermes berry.] **—coch·i·neal** *adj.*

Co·chise (kō-chēs', -chēz') (*c.* 1812–74). U.S. Indian leader. An Apache chief, he was falsely imprisoned for kidnapping a white child. When he escaped, hostilities began between Indians and U.S. troops. He and his warriors took refuge in the Dragoon Mts. until 1872, when a treaty relegated the Apaches to an Arizona reservation.

coch·le·a (kŏk'lē-ə) *n., pl.* **-leae** (-lē-ē'). A spiral tube of the inner ear resembling a snail shell and containing nerve endings essential for hearing. [New Latin, from Latin, snail shell, from Greek *kokhlias,* from *kokhlos,* land snail.] **—coch·le·ar** (kŏk'lē-ər) *adj.*

cochlear nerve *n.* The nerve connecting the cochlea to the brain, responsible for the nerve impulses relating to hearing. It is a division of the **acoustic nerve** *(see).*

coch·le·ate (kŏk'lē-ĭt, -āt') *adj.* Also **coch·le·at·ed** (-ā'tĭd). Shaped like a snail shell; spirally twisted. [Latin *cochleātus,* from *cochlea,* snail. See **cochlea.**]

Coch·ran (kŏk'rən), **Jacqueline** (1910–80). U.S. aviator and businesswoman. In the 1930's she studied aviation and founded a cosmetics company. During World War II she trained women as auxiliary pilots for English and American armed forces. She was the first woman to break the sound barrier (1953).

cock[1] (kŏk) *n.* **1.** The adult male of the domestic fowl; rooster. **2. a.** The male of various other birds. **b.** The male of certain other animals, such as the lobster and the salmon. **3.** A weathervane in the shape of a cock; a weathercock. **4.** A valve by which the flow of a liquid or gas can be regulated. **5. a.** The hammer in a firearm. **b.** Its position when ready for firing. **6.** A tilting or turning upward. *~v.* **cocked, cocking, cocks.** *—tr.* **1.** To set the hammer of (a firearm) in a position ready for firing. **2.** To tilt or turn (the ears, for example) up or to one side, usually in a jaunty or alert manner. *—intr.* **1.** To cock the hammer of a firearm. **2.** To turn or stick up. *~adj.* Male. Said of birds and, sometimes, other animals: *a cock lobster.* [Middle English, Old English *cocc,* probably from Medieval Latin *coccus* (imitative).]

cock² *n.* A cone-shaped pile of straw or hay.
~tr.v. **cocked, cocking, cocks.** To arrange (straw or hay) in such piles. [Middle English *cok,* Old English *cocc* (attested only in place names), perhaps from Scandinavian.]

cock·ade (kŏk-ād′) *n.* A rosette or knot of ribbon worn especially on the hat as a badge. [Originally *cockard,* from French *cocarde,* jauntily tilted hat, from Old French *coquard,* strutting, vain, from *coq,* COCK.] **—cock·ad·ed** (kŏk-ā′dĭd) *adj.*

cock-a-doo·dle-doo (kŏk′ə-do͝od′l-do͞o′) *n.* A representation of the characteristic crow of a cock. [Imitative.]

cock-a-hoop (kŏk′ə-ho͞op′, -ho͝op′) *adj.* **1.** In a state of elation or exultation. **2.** Boastful. **3.** Askew. [From the expression *set cock a hoop,* perhaps "to set a cock on a hoop or measure of grain."] **—cock-a-hoop** *adv.*

Cock·aigne, Cock·ayne (kŏ-kān′) *n.* An imaginary land of easy and luxurious living. [Middle English *cockayne,* from Old French *(pais de) quoquaigne,* "(land of) delicacies," probably from Middle Low German *kōkenje,* small fancy sugar cake, diminutive of *kōke,* cake.]

cock-a-leek·ie, cock·ie·leek·ie (kŏk′ə-lē′kē) *n.* A cream soup of Scottish origin, made with leeks and chicken.

cock·a·lo·rum (kŏk′ə-lôr′əm, -lōr′əm) *n.* **1.** A little man with an unduly high opinion of himself. **2.** Boastful talk. **3.** A children's jumping game like leapfrog. [Pseudo-Latin : COCK ("strutting leader") + Latin *-orum,* genitive plural ending.]

cock-and-bull story (kŏk′ən-bo͝ol′) *n.* An absurd or highly improbable tale. [Originally a rambling animal fable about a cock changed into a bull.]

cock·a·tiel (kŏk′ə-tēl′) *n.* A crested parrot, *Nymphicus hollandicus,* of Australia, having gray and yellow plumage. Also called "quarrion." [Dutch *kaketielje,* probably from Portuguese *cacatilha,* diminutive of *cacatua,* COCKATOO.]

cock·a·too (kŏk′ə-to͞o′) *n., pl.* **-toos.** Any of various parrots of the genus *Cacatuinae* and related genera, of Australia and adjacent areas, characterized by a long, erectile crest. [Dutch *kaketoe,* from Malay *kakatua.*]

cock·a·trice (kŏk′ə-trĭs, -trīs′) *n.* A mythical serpent reputed to be hatched from a cock's egg and supposed to have the power of killing by its glance. Compare **basilisk.** [Middle English *cocatrice,* basilisk, crocodile, from Old French *cocatris,* from Medieval Latin *cocātrix,* variant of Late Latin *calcātrix,* "the tracker" (translation of Greek *ikhneumōn,* ICHNEUMON), from *calcāre,* to track, from *calx,* heel.]

cock·boat (kŏk′bōt′) *n.* A small rowing boat kept on a ship. [Middle English *cokbote* : *cok,* cockboat, from Old French *coque, coche,* probably from Late Latin *caudica,* canoe (made from the trunk of a tree), from Latin *caudex,* trunk of a tree + BOAT.]

cock·chaf·er (kŏk′chā′fər) *n.* Any of various Old World beetles of the Scarabaeidae family; especially, *Melolontha melolontha,* the larvae of which often destroy plant roots. Also called "May bug." [COCK (bird) + CHAFER (so called probably from its large size).]

Cock·croft (kŏk′krôft′, -krŏft′) **Sir John Douglas** (1897–1967). British pioneer of atomic physics. He invented, with E.T.S. Walton, the first machine to split the atom (1932). He contributed to the wartime development of the atomic bomb and was director of the Atomic Energy Research Establishment at Harwell (1946–59). He and Walton were awarded the 1951 Nobel Prize for physics.

Cockcroft-Walton accelerator *n.* An early linear particle accelerator consisting of an ion source and a series of cylindrical high-voltage electrodes to accelerate the ions on to a target. It was used in producing the first artificial disintegration of an atomic nucleus. Also called "Cockcroft-Walton generator." [After Sir John Douglas COCKCROFT and Ernest Thomas Sinton WALTON, the inventors.]

cock·crow (kŏk′krō′) *n.* The time of day when the cock crows; early morning; dawn.

cocked hat (kŏkt) *n.* A hat with the brim turned up in two or three places; especially, a three-cornered hat; a tricorn. **—knock into a cocked hat.** *Informal.* To defeat or nullify utterly.

cock·er¹ (kŏk′ər) *n.* **1.** A cocker spaniel. **2.** A person who keeps or trains fighting cocks.

cocker² *tr.v.* **-ered, -ering, -ers.** To pamper, spoil, or coddle. [Middle English *cokerenägger.*]

cock·er·el (kŏk′ər-əl) *n.* A young rooster. [Middle English *cokerelle,* diminutive of COCK.]

cocker spaniel *n.* A dog of a breed originally developed in England, having long, drooping ears and a variously colored silky coat. [Originally used for hunting woodcocks.]

cock-eyed (kŏk′īd′) *adj.* **1.** Cross-eyed. **2.** *Slang.* **a.** Crooked; askew. **b.** Foolish; ridiculous; absurd. **c.** Drunk.

cock·fight (kŏk′fīt′) *n.* A fight between gamecocks that are often fitted with metal spurs. **—cock·fight·ing** *adj.* & *n.*

cock·horse (kŏk′hôrs′) *n.* A rocking horse.

cockieleekie. Variant of **cock-a-leekie.**

cock·le¹ (kŏk′əl) *n.* **1.** Any of various bivalve mollusks of the family Cardiidae, especially *Cardium edule,* having rounded or heart-shaped shells with radiating ribs. **2.** The shell of any of these mollusks; a cockleshell. **3.** A wrinkle or pucker. **4.** A small and shallow boat. **—the cockles of one's heart.** One's innermost feelings.
~v. **cockled, -ling, -les.** *—tr.* To cause to wrinkle or pucker. *—intr.* To become wrinkled or puckered. [Middle English *cokille,* from Old French *coquille,* shell, from Vulgar Latin *conchīllia* (unattested), variant of Latin *conchȳllium,* from Greek *konkhullion,* diminutive of *konkhē,* mussel, conch.]

cockle² *n.* Any of several plants often growing as weeds in grain fields, especially the corn cockle. [Middle English *cok(k)el,* Old English *coccel,* from Medieval Latin *cocculus* (unattested), diminutive of Latin *coccus,* kermes berry.]

cock·le·bur (kŏk′əl-bûr′) *n.* **1.** Any of several coarse weeds of the genus *Xanthium,* especially *X. spinosum,* bearing prickly burs. **2.** The bur of any of these plants.

cock·le·shell (kŏk′əl-shĕl′) *n.* **1. a.** The shell of a cockle. **b.** A shell similar to that of a cockle. **2.** A small, light boat.

cock·loft (kŏk′lôft′, -lŏft) *n.* A small loft. [16th century : perhaps COCK (fowl) + LOFT, from its use as a roosting place.]

cock·ney (kŏk′nē) *n., pl.* **-neys. 1.** *Often* **Cockney.** A native of the East End of London or adjacent areas. **2.** The dialect or accent of cockneys.
~adj. Of or like cockneys or their dialect. [Middle English *cokeney,* "cock's egg," pampered brat, effeminate youth, townsman (of London) : *cokene,* genitive plural of *cok,* COCK + *ey,* egg, Old English *ǣg.*]

cock of the north *n.* The **brambling** *(see).*

cock-of-the-rock (kŏk′əv-*thə*-rŏk′) *n., pl.* **cocks-of-the-rock.** Either of two South American birds, *Rupicola rupicola* or *R. peruviana,* having a distinctive crest and bright-orange or reddish plumage in the male. [From its habit of nesting on rocks.]

cock of the walk *n.* **1.** The leader or most important person in a group. **2.** An overbearing or domineering person.

cock·pit (kŏk′pĭt′) *n.* **1.** A pit or enclosed space for cockfights. **2.** A site of many battles. **3. a.** In old warships, a section used as quarters for junior officers and as a station for the wounded during a battle. **b.** In small decked vessels, an area from which the vessel is steered. **4. a.** The space for the pilot, and sometimes passengers, in the fuselage of a small aircraft. **b.** The space set apart for the pilot and crew in a large airliner; the flight deck. **5.** The place where the driver of a racing car sits.

cock·roach (kŏk′rōch′) *n.* Any of various oval, flat-bodied insects of the family Blattidae, several species of which are common household pests. [Earlier *cacarootch,* from Spanish *cucaracha*†.]

cocks·comb (kŏks′kōm′) *n.* Also **cox·comb** (for senses 2, 4). **1.** The comb of a rooster. **2.** The cap of a jester, decorated to resemble this. **3.** Any of several plants of the genus *Celosia*; especially, *C. argentea cristata,* having a showy crested or rolled flower cluster. **4.** A pretentious fop.

cocks·foot (kŏks′fo͝ot′) *n., pl.* **-foots.** A perennial grass, *Dactylis glomerata,* sown as a pasture grass in North America and South Africa. [From its appearance.]

cock·shy (kŏk′shī′) *n., pl.* **-shies.** *British.* **1.** A target aimed at in throwing contests. **2.** The throw itself. **3.** A target for abuse or ridicule. [In the earliest form of this game, the contestants shied or threw sticks at a cock.]

cock·spur (kŏk′spûr′) *n.* **1.** A small, thorny North American tree, *Crataegus crus-galli,* having white flowers and small red fruit. **2.** An annual grass, *Echinochloa crus-galli,* widely distributed in warm temperate and tropical areas. [From the resemblance of its thorn to a cock's spur.]

cock·sure (kŏk′sho͝or′) *adj.* Too sure of oneself or one's opinions; overconfident. [16th century : perhaps from *cock,* euphemistic for GOD + SURE.] **—cock·sure·ly** *adv.* **—cock·sure·ness** *n.*

cock·tail¹ (kŏk′tāl′) *n.* **1.** Any of various mixed alcoholic drinks, often served chilled, consisting usually of a spirit combined with fruit juices or other ingredients, such as bitters or vermouth. **2.** An appetizer typically consisting of seafood or mixed fruits: *a prawn cocktail.* **3.** A mixture of medicinal drugs in drinkable form.
~adj. **1.** Of, pertaining to, or served with cocktails: *cocktail sausages.* **2.** Suitable for wear on semiformal occasions: *a cocktail dress.* [19th-century : apparently from COCKTAIL (horse), but the connection is obscure.]

cocktail² *n.* A horse that has had its tail docked. [Earlier, "docked tail (of horse)," from COCK (fowl) + TAIL.]

cocktail party *n.* A party, usually in the early evening, at which cocktails are served.

cock-up (kŏk′ŭp′) *n.* **1.** *British Slang.* **a.** A blunder. **b.** Something that has been bungled; a mess. **2.** *Archaic.* A hat or cap with upturned front.

cock·y (kŏk′ē) *adj.* **-ier, -iest.** *Informal.* Cheerfully self-assertive or self-confident; conceited. Said especially of or about males. **—cock·i·ly** *adv.*

co·co (kō′kō) *n., pl.* **-cos. 1.** A tree, the **coconut palm** *(see).* **2.** Its fruit, the coconut.
~adj. Made of fibers from the coconut shell: *coco matting.* [Spanish, from Portuguese *coco,* goblin, grimace (referring to the base of the coconut shell, which resembles a face).]

co·coa (kō′kō) *n.* **1.** A powder made from cocoa beans after they have been roasted, ground, and freed of most of their fatty oil. **2.** A

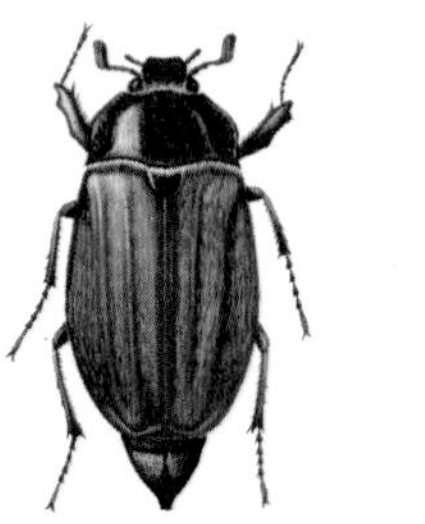

cockchafer *Also known as the May bug, this large beetle can be up to 25 millimeters (1 inch) long.*

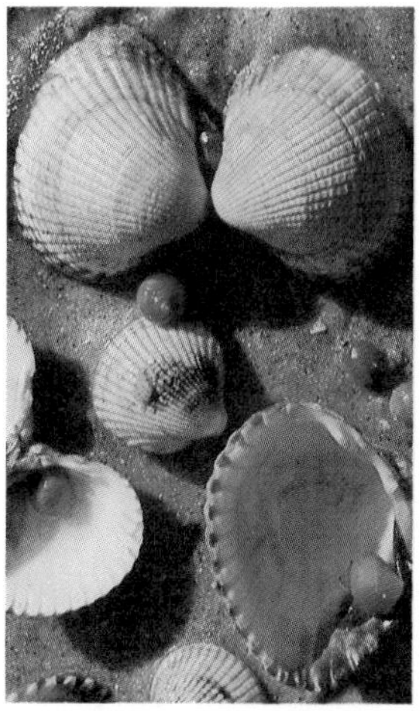

cockle *These edible shellfish live under the sand, completely buried except for the tips of the feeding tubes through which they siphon plankton. The tidal zones of some beaches may contain over 1,000 cockles per square meter. Their shells—some still hinged—become visible only when they are washed up on beaches after the animals die.*

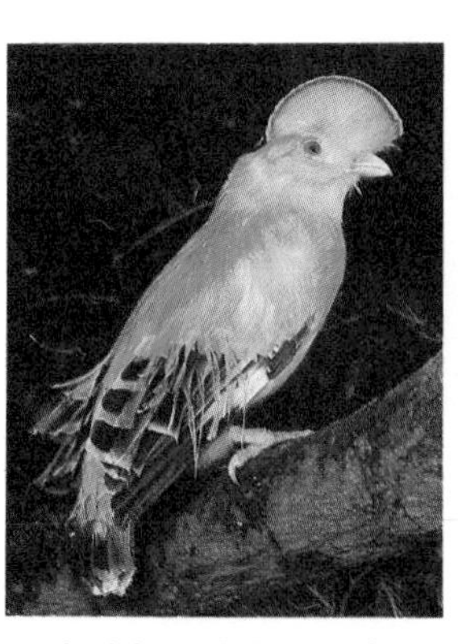

cock-of-the-rock *In tropical rain forests, the brightly colored male cock-of-the-rock struts and postures on communal mating grounds known as leks. The females have plain brown plumage.*

beverage made by combining this powder with water or milk and sugar. **3.** Moderate brown to reddish brown. [Variant of CACAO, by confusion with COCO (nut).] —**co·coa** *adj.*

cocoa bean *n.* The seed of the cacao.

cocoa butter *n.* A yellowish-white, waxy solid obtained from cocoa beans and used in the manufacture of pharmaceuticals, confections, and soap. Also called "cacao butter."

coco de mer (kō'kō də mĕr') *n.* **1.** A Seychelles palm tree, *Lodoicea maldivica*, bearing a large fruit that contains a two-lobed edible nut. **2.** The nut of this palm. [French, "sea coconut."]

co·con·scious (kō'kŏn'shəs) *adj.* Being aware or conscious of the same things.
~*n.* Also **co·con·scious·ness** (ko'kŏn'shəs-nĭs). *Psychiatry.* Mental processes outside the realm of conscious activity or awareness, as with schizophrenic individuals.

co·co·nut, co·coa·nut (kō'kə-nŭt', -nət) *n.* The fruit of the coconut palm, a large seed with a thick, hard shell that encloses edible white meat and has a milky fluid, *coconut milk,* filling the hollow center.

coconut butter *n.* A solid form of coconut oil used for making soap, candles, and other products.

coconut crab *n.* The **robber crab** *(see).*

coconut matting *n.* A type of coarse matting made from the outer fibers of the coconut.

coconut oil *n.* The oil obtained from the white flesh of the coconut, used especially in the manufacture of soaps and cosmetics.

coconut palm *n.* A tall palm tree, *Cocos nucifera,* native to the East Indies, bearing coconuts as fruit. Also called "coco," "coco palm," "coconut tree."

coconut shy *n. British.* A sideshow at a fair in which balls are thrown at coconuts to knock them off their stands and win a prize.

co·coon (kə-kōōn') *n.* **1.** A covering of silk or similar fibrous material spun by the larvae of moths and other insects as protection for their pupal stage. **2.** Any similar protective covering or structure, such as that of a spider or earthworm. **3.** A protective plastic coating placed over stored inactive military or naval equipment.
~*v.* **cocooned, -cooning, -coons.** —*tr.* To cover or envelop in, or as if in, a cocoon. —*intr.* To form a cocoon. [French *cocon,* from Provençal *coucoun,* from *coco,* eggshell, hence, cocoon, from Latin *coccum, coccus,* kermes berry, from Greek *kokkos.*]

co·co·pan (kō'kō-păn') *n.* In South Africa, a small truck on a mine railway. [Possibly from Zulu *nqukumbana,* small cart.]

Co·cos Islands (kō'kəs). Also **Kee·ling Islands** (kē'lĭng). A group of coral island territories of Australia in the eastern Indian Ocean. They were discovered in 1609 and settled from 1826.

co·cotte (kō-kôt') *n.* **1.** A prostitute or demimondaine. **2.** A small dish used for baking individual portions, especially of egg dishes. [French, originally a baby's word for hen, from *coq,* cock.]

co·co·yam (kō'kō-yăm') *n.* A tropical plant, the **taro** *(see).*

Coc·teau (kŏk-tō'), **Jean** (1889-1963). French artist, poet, and dramatist. His works, including *Orphée* (1950) and *La Machine Infernale* (1934), show a fascination with dreams and myths.

Co·cy·tus (kō-kī'təs) *n. Greek Mythology.* One of the six rivers of Hades. [Latin, from Greek *Kōkutos,* "river of lamentation," from *kōkuein,* to wail, lament.]

cod¹ (kŏd) *n., pl.* **cods** or collectively **cod.** Any of various marine fishes of the family Gadidae; especially, *Gadus morhua* (or *G. callarias*), an important food fish of Northern Atlantic waters and a source of cod-liver oil. Also called "codfish." [Middle English, perhaps from COD (bag), from its shape.]

cod² *n. British Slang.* Nonsense. [Shortened from CODSWALLOP.]

cod³ *n.* **1.** *Regional.* A husk or pod. **2.** *Obsolete.* A bag. **3.** *Archaic.* The scrotum. [Middle English *cod,* Old English *codd,* bag, husk.]

Cod, Cape (kŏd). A low, sandy peninsula 105 kilometers (65 miles) long in Massachusetts Bay. It encloses Cape Cod Bay, where the Pilgrims first landed in America (1620). Cape Cod is a popular resort area.

COD, C.O.D. **1.** cash on delivery. **2.** collect on delivery.

Cod. codex.

co·da (kō'də) *n.* **1.** *Music.* A passage added on to the end of a movement or composition that brings it to a formal close. **2.** In ballet, the closing part of a pas de deux. [Italian, "tail," from Latin *cōda, cauda.*]

cod·dle (kŏd'l) *tr.v.* **-dled, -dling, -dles.** **1.** To cook in water just below boiling point. **2.** To treat indulgently; pamper. —See Synonyms at **pamper.** [Variant of CAUDLE.] —**cod·dler** *n.*

code (kōd) *n.* **1. a.** A systematically arranged and comprehensive collection of laws. **b.** Any systematic collection of regulations and rules of procedure or conduct: *the military code.* **2.** A generally accepted set of principles: *a code of conduct.* **3.** A system of signals used to represent letters or numbers in transmitting messages. **4.** A system of symbols, letters, or words given certain arbitrary meanings, used for transmitting messages requiring secrecy or brevity. Compare **cipher.** **5.** A system of symbols used to identify something for classification or selection. See **genetic code.**
~*v.* **coded, coding, codes.** —*tr.* **1.** To systematize and arrange (laws and regulations) into a code; codify. **2.** To encode. **3.** To carry the genetic information for (a specific amino acid, for example). —*intr.* To be or carry genetic information. Used with *for.* [Middle English, from Old French, from Latin *cōdex,* CODEX.] —**cod·er** *n.*

co·deine (kō'dēn', kō'dē-ĭn) *n.* An alkaloid narcotic, $C_{18}H_{21}NO_3$, derived from opium or morphine, used for relieving coughing, as an analgesic, and as a hypnotic. [French *codéine* : Greek *kōdeia,* pop-

pyhead, from *koos,* hollow place, cavity + -INE.]

Code Na·po·lé·on (kōd' nȧ-pô-lā-ôN') *n.* The code of French civil law, prepared under the direction of Napoleon Bonaparte between 1804 and 1807.

co·dex (kō'dĕks') *n., pl.* **codices** (kō'də-sēz', kŏd'ə-). *Abbr.* **Cod.** A manuscript volume, especially of the Scriptures or of a classic work. [Latin *cōdex, caudex,* tree trunk, board, writing tablet, book (of laws).]

Co·dex Ju·ris Ca·non·i·ci (kō'dĕks' jŏŏr'ĭs kə-nŏn'ə-sī') *n.* The code of law that has governed the Roman Catholic Church since 1918. [Latin, "book of canon laws."]

cod·fish (kŏd'fĭsh') *n., pl.* **-fishes** or collectively **codfish.** The **cod** *(see).*

codg·er (kŏj'ər) *n. Informal.* An old man; especially, an eccentric one. Used in the phrase *old codger.* [Perhaps a variant of *cadget.* See **cadge.**]

cod·i·cil (kŏd'ə-sĭl) *n.* **1.** *Law.* A supplement or appendix to a will. **2.** Any supplement or appendix. [Middle English, from Old French *codicille,* from Latin *cōdicillus,* diminutive of *cōdex,* CODEX.] —**cod·i·cil·la·ry** (kŏd'ə-sĭl'ə-rē) *adj.*

cod·i·fy (kŏd'ə-fī', kō'də-) *tr.v.* **-fied, -fying, -fies.** **1.** To reduce to a code: *codify laws.* **2.** To arrange or systematize. —**cod·i·fi·ca·tion** (kŏd'ə-fĭ-kā'shən) *n.* —**cod·i·fi·er** *n.*

cod·ling¹ (kŏd'lĭng) *n.* Also **cod·lin** (-lĭn). *British.* **1.** A long, tapering apple. **2.** An unripe apple. [Middle English *querdlyng,* from Norman French *quer de lion,* "lion's heart," from its elongated shape.]

codling² *n., pl.* **-lings** or collectively **codling.** A young cod.

codling moth *n.* Also **codlin moth.** A small grayish moth, *Laspreyresia pomonella,* the larvae of which are destructive to various fruits, especially apples.

cod·lins-and-cream (kŏd'lĭnz-ən-krēm') *n.* A Eurasian plant, *Epilobium hirsutum,* having hairy stems and leaves and purple-red flowers in a stalked spike. [From CODLING (apple).]

cod-liver oil (kŏd'lĭv'ər) *n.* An oil obtained from the livers of cod and containing a rich supply of vitamins A and D.

co·do·main (kō'dō-mān') *n. Mathematics.* The **range** *(see)* of a function.

co·don (kō'dŏn') *n. Genetics.* A sequence of three adjacent nucleotides on a DNA molecule that specifies the insertion of an amino acid in a specific structural position during protein synthesis. [COD(E) + -ON.]

cod·piece (kŏd'pēs') *n.* A pouch at the crotch of the tight-fitting breeches worn by men in the 15th and 16th centuries. [Middle English : COD (bag, scrotum) + PIECE.]

co·driv·er (kō'drī'vər) *n.* One who takes turns with another to drive a car, especially in a race or rally.

cods·wal·lop (kŏdz'wŏl'əp) *n. British Slang.* Nonsense, especially when put forward as a serious statement. [20th century : origin obscure.]

Co·dy (kō'dē), **William Frederick,** known as "Buffalo Bill." (1846-1917). U.S. frontiersman and showman, who from 1883 toured the United States and Europe with his Wild West Show.

co·ed, co·ed (kō'ĕd') *n. Informal.* A woman student attending a co-educational school, college, or university.
~*adj. Informal.* Co-educational. [Short for *co-educational student.*]

co·ed·u·ca·tion (kō'ĕj-ōō-kā'shən) *n.* The system of education in which both male and female pupils or students attend the same institution or classes. —**co·ed·u·ca·tion·al** *adj.*

co·ef·fi·cient (kō'ə-fĭsh'ənt) *n.* **1.** *Mathematics.* **a.** A numerical factor of an elementary algebraic term, such as 4 in the term 4*x.* **b.** The product of all but one of the factors of an expression, the product being regarded as a distinct entity with respect to the excluded factor and to a designated operation. See **correlation coefficient.** **2.** A numerical measure of a physical or chemical property that is constant for a system under specified conditions. [New Latin *coefficiens* : CO- (together) + EFFICIENT.]

coefficient of self-induction *n.* **Self-inductance** *(see).*

coel- *prefix.* Indicates a cavity within a body or bodily organ; for example, **coelenterate.** [New Latin, from Greek *koilos,* hollow.]

-coel, -coele. Variants of **-cele** (hollow chamber).

coe·la·canth (sē'lə-kănth') *n.* Any of various fishes of the order Coelacanthiformes, known only in fossil form until a living species, *Latimeria chalumnae,* of African marine waters, was identified in 1938. [New Latin *coelacanthus,* "hollow-spined" : COEL- + Greek *akanthos,* spine, thorn, from *akantha,* thorny plant.] —**coe·la·can·thine** (sē'lə-kăn'thĭn', -thĭn) *adj.* —**coe·la·can·thous** (sē'lə-kăn'thəs) *adj.*

coe·len·ter·ate (sĭ-lĕn'tə-rāt', -rĭt) *n.* Any invertebrate animal of the phylum Coelenterata, characterized by a radially symmetrical body with a saclike internal cavity, and including the jellyfishes, hydras, sea anemones, and corals. See **cnidarian, ctenophore.**
~*adj.* Of or belonging to the Coelenterata. [New Latin *coelenterata,* "hollow-intestined ones" : COEL- + ENTER(ON) + -ATE.] —**coe·len·ter·ic** (sĭ-lĕn'tĕr'ĭk) *adj.*

coe·len·ter·on (sĭ-lĕn'tə-rŏn', -rən) *n., pl.* **-tera** (-tər-ə). *Zoology.* The saclike body cavity of a coelenterate. [New Latin : COEL- + ENTERON.]

coeliac. Variant of **celiac.**

coe·lom, ce·lom (sē'ləm) *n., pl.* **-loms** or **-lomata** (sĭ-lō'mə-tə). The body cavity in all animals higher than the coelenterates and certain primitive worms, formed by the splitting of the mesoderm into two

coconut palm *This tall Indonesian palm tree bears the hard-shelled seed used for oil, confectionery, and beauty preparations. One tree may produce 50 or more coconuts a year.*

layers. [German *Koelom,* from Greek *koilōma,* cavity, from *koilos,* hollow.]

coe·lo·stat (sē′lə-stăt′) *n. Astronomy.* A movable mirror that rotates slowly so as to compensate for the earth's rotation, used to direct light from a fixed region of the sky into a telescope or other optical instrument. [COEL- + -STAT.]

coeno-, ceno- *prefix.* Also **coen-, cen-.** Indicates common; for example, **coenurus.** [New Latin, from Greek *koino-,* from *koinos,* common.]

coenobite. Variant of **cenobite.**

coen·o·bi·um (sē-nō′bē-əm) *n. Botany.* A colony of motile cells formed by certain green algae. [New Latin, from Greek *koinobion,* convent : *koinos,* common + *bios,* life.]

coe·no·cyte (sē′nə-sīt′) *n. Botany.* An organism consisting of a multinucleate protoplasmic mass resulting from nuclear division without the formation of a new cell wall or membrane, as in slime molds and certain fungi and algae. [COENO- + -CYTE.] **—coe·no·cyt·ic** (sē′nə-sīt′ĭk) *adj.*

coenogenesis. Variant of **cenogenesis.**

coe·no·sarc (sē′nə-särk′) *n.* The system of tissues connecting the polyps of compound zoophytes such as corals. [COENO- + Greek *sarx* (stem *sark-*), flesh.]

coe·nu·rus (sĭ-nyŏŏr′əs) *n., pl.* **-nuri** (-nyŏŏr′ī′). The encysted larval stage of a tapeworm, *Taenia multiceps* (or *Multiceps multiceps*), that attacks the central nervous system of ruminant animals. [New Latin, "having a common tail" (because it has many heads and only one tail) : COEN(O)- + -UR(O)US.]

co·en·zyme (kō-ĕn′zīm′) *n.* A heat-stable organic molecule that must be loosely associated with certain enzymes for them to function.

co·e·qual (kō-ē′kwəl) *adj.* Equal with one another, as in rank or size. **~***n.* An equal. **—co·e·qual·i·ty** (kō′ē-kwŏl′ə-tē) *n.* **—co·e·qual·ly** *adv.*

co·erce (kō-ûrs′) *tr.v.* **-erced, -ercing, -erces. 1.** To force to act or think in a given manner; compel: *The suspect was coerced into confessing.* **2.** To dominate, restrain, or control forcibly. **3.** To achieve by means of force; enforce: *coerce an agreement.* **—See Synonyms at force.** [Middle English *cohercen,* from Old French *cohercier,* from Latin *coercēre,* to constrain : *cō-,* together + *arcēre,* to restrain, confine.] **—co·erc·er** *n.* **—co·er·ci·ble** *adj.*

co·er·cion (kō-ûr′shən) *n.* **1.** The act or practice of coercing. **2.** A government or power that coerces. **—co·er·cion·ar·y** (kō-ûr′shə-nĕr′ē) *adj.*

co·er·cive (kō-ûr′sĭv) *adj.* Characterized by or inclined to coercion. **—co·er·cive·ly** *adv.* **—co·er·cive·ness** *n.*

coercive force *n. Physics.* The external magnetic field strength required to demagnetize a given sample.

co·er·civ·i·ty (kō′ər-sĭv′ə-tē) *n. Physics.* The external magnetic field strength required to demagnetize a given sample that has been magnetized to saturation.

co·es·sen·tial (kō′ĭ-sĕn′shəl) *adj. Theology.* Having the same nature or essence. **—co·es·sen·ti·al·i·ty** (kō′ĭ-sĕn′shē-ăl′ə-tē), **co·es·sen·tial·ness** *n.* **—co·es·sen·tial·ly** *adv.*

co·e·ta·ne·ous (kō′ĭ-tā′nē-əs) *adj.* Of equal age, duration, or period; contemporary. [Latin *coaetāneus* : *co-,* same + *aetās,* age.] **—co·e·ta·ne·ous·ly** *adv.* **—co·e·ta·ne·ous·ness** *n.*

co·e·ter·nal (kō′ĭ-tûr′nəl) *adj.* Equally eternal; eternally existing with one another. **—co·e·ter·nal·ly** *adv.* **—co·e·ter·ni·ty** (kō′ĭ-tûr′nĭ-tē) *n.*

Coeur de Lion. See **Richard I.**

co·e·val (kō-ē′vəl) *adj.* Originating or existing during the same period of time; lasting through the same era. [Latin *coaevus* : *cō-,* same + *aevum,* age.] **—co·e·val** *n.* **—co·e·val·ly** *adv.*

co·ex·ist (kō′ĭg-zĭst′) *intr.v.* **-isted, -isting, -ists. 1.** To exist together, at the same time or in the same place. **2.** To exist together in peace.

co·ex·is·tence (kō′ĭg-zĭs′təns) *n.* **1.** The condition of existing together: *"excitement in coexistence with an overbalance of pleasure"* (Wordsworth). **2.** The concurrent but separate existence of two or more nations of great ideological disparity. **—co·ex·is·tent** *adj.*

co·ex·ten·sive (kō′ĭk-stĕn′sĭv) *adj.* Extending over the same space or time; having the same scope. **—co·ex·ten·sive·ly** *adv.*

co·fac·tor (kō′făk′tər) *n.* **1.** *Mathematics.* A determinant associated with a given element of a matrix, formed by removing the row and column containing this element. **2.** *Biochemistry.* A nonprotein portion of certain enzymes, essential for their activity, such as a coenzyme or a metal ion, as of sodium or potassium.

C. of C. chamber of commerce.

C. of E. Church of England.

cof·fee (kô′fē, kŏf′ē) *n.* **1.** Any of several trees of the genus *Coffea,* native to eastern Asia and Africa, bearing berries containing beans used in the preparation of a beverage; especially, *C. arabica,* the chief commercial source of these beans. **2. a.** The seeds or beans of the coffee tree. **b.** Such beans roasted and ground. **3. a.** An aromatic, mildly stimulating beverage prepared from ground coffee beans. **b.** A cup of coffee. **4.** Moderate to dark yellowish brown. **~***adj.* **1.** Of, pertaining to, or accompanied by the drink coffee: *a coffee hour.* **2.** Having the color coffee. [Italian *caffè,* from Turkish *kahve,* from Arabic *qahwah.*]

coffee cake *n.* A sweet cake to be eaten with coffee, often containing nuts or raisins and topped with icing.

coffee cup *n.* A usually small cup from which coffee is drunk.

coffee house, cof·fee·house (kô′fē-hous′, kŏf′ē-) *n.* An establishment serving coffee and other refreshments, popular especially in the 17th and 18th centuries as a rendezvous for fashionable people.

coffee mill *n.* A device for grinding roasted coffee beans.

cof·fee·pot (kô′fē-pŏt′, kŏf′ē-) *n.* A pot for making or serving coffee.

coffee shop *n.* A small restaurant in which light meals are served.

coffee table *n.* A long, low table, often placed before a sofa.

coffee tree *n.* **1.** Any tree of the genus *Coffea,* producing coffee beans. **2.** The Kentucky coffee tree *(see).*

cof·fer (kô′fər, kŏf′ər) *n.* **1. a.** A chest. **b.** A strongbox. **2. coffers.** Funds; a treasury. **3.** A decorative sunken panel in a soffit, ceiling, dome, or vault. **4.** A cofferdam. **~***tr.v.* **coffered, -fering, -fers. 1.** To supply with decorative sunken panels. **2.** To put in a coffer. [Middle English *cof(f)re,* box, chest, from Old French, from Latin *cophinus,* basket. See **coffin.**]

cof·fer·dam (kô′fər-dăm′, kŏf′ər-) *n. Engineering.* **1.** A temporary watertight enclosure built in the water and pumped dry to expose the bottom so that construction, as of piers, may be undertaken. **2.** A watertight chamber attached to a ship's side to facilitate repairs below the water line.

cof·fin (kô′fĭn, kŏf′ĭn) *n.* **1.** An oblong box in which a corpse is buried or cremated. **2.** A horse's hoof. **3.** A thick, usually lead, container for transporting radioactive materials. **~***tr.v.* **coffined, -fining, -fins.** To place in or as if in a coffin. [Middle English, box, basket, from Old French *cofin,* from Latin *cophinus,* from Greek *kophinus†,* basket, measure of capacity.]

coffin bone *n.* The bone inside the hoof of a horse or similar animal.

cof·fle (kô′fəl, kŏf′əl) *n.* A file of animals, prisoners, or slaves, chained together in transit. [Arabic *qāfilah,* caravan.]

C. of S. chief of staff.

cog¹ (kŏg) *n.* **1.** Any of a series of teeth on the rim of a wheel which by engagement transmit motive force to a corresponding wheel or toothed rack. **2.** A cogwheel. **3.** A subordinate member within a given organization. **~***tr.v.* **cogged, cogging, cogs.** To roll (steel ingots) to convert into blooms. [Middle English *cogge,* probably from Scandinavian, akin to Swedish *kugge.*]

cog² *v.* **cogged, cogging, cogs.** *Archaic Slang.* **—***tr.* To load or manipulate (dice) fraudulently. **—***intr.* To cheat, especially at dice. [16th century : origin obscure.]

cog³ *n.* A tenon projecting from a wooden beam and fitting into a mortise in another beam to form a joint. **~***tr.v.* **cogged, cogging, cogs.** To join with such tenons. [19th century : origin obscure.]

cog. cognate.

co·gent (kō′jənt) *adj.* **1.** Forcibly convincing. **2.** Compelling; powerful. [Latin *cōgens* (stem *cogent-*), present participle of *cōgere,* to force, drive together : *cō-,* together + *agere,* to drive.] **—co·gen·cy** (kō′jən-sē) *n.* **—co·gent·ly** *adv.*

cog·i·tate (kŏj′ə-tāt′) *v.* **-tated, -tating, -tates.** **—***intr.* To take long and careful thought; meditate; ponder. **—***tr.* To think carefully about; consider intently. [Latin *cōgitāre* : *cō-* (intensive) + *agitāre,* to turn in mind, consider, AGITATE.] **—cog·i·ta·ble** (kŏj′ə-tə-bəl) *adj.* **—cog·i·ta·tor** *n.*

cog·i·ta·tion (kŏj′ə-tā′shən) *n.* **1.** Thoughtful consideration; meditation. **2.** A serious thought; a reflection.

cog·i·ta·tive (kŏj′ə-tā′tĭv) *adj.* Meditative. **—cog·i·ta·tive·ly** *adv.* **—cog·i·ta·tive·ness** *n.*

cog·i·to (kŏg′ĭ-tō) *n. Philosophy.* The principle that establishes a person's existence from the fact of his thinking and awareness. [Latin, "I think" (abstracted from Descartes' phrase, *cogito, ergo sum,* "I think, therefore I am").]

co·gnac (kōn′yăk′, kŏn′-, kôn′-) *n.* A brandy produced in the vicinity of Cognac in western France.

Co·gnac (kōn′yăk′, kŏn′-). Town in the Charente department of western France, on the Charente River. Only brandy produced in a limited area around the town can be called cognac.

cog·nate (kŏg′nāt′) *adj. Abbr.* **cog. 1.** Related by blood; having a common ancestor; maternal one. **2.** *Linguistics.* Akin. Said especially of languages or of words in different languages derived from the same root. **3.** Related or analogous in nature, character, or function. **~***n. Abbr.* **cog.** A person or thing cognate with another. [Latin *cōgnātus* : *cō-,* same + *gnātus,* born, from *gnāscī, nāscī,* to be born.] **—cog·na·tion** (kŏg-nā′shən) *n.*

cog·ni·tion (kŏg-nĭsh′ən) *n.* **1.** The mental process or faculty by which knowledge is acquired. **2.** That which comes to be known, as through perception, reasoning, or intuition; knowledge. [Middle English *cognicioun,* from Latin *cognitiō* (stem *cognition-*), from *cognōscere,* to get to know, learn : *cō-* (intensive) + *gnōscere,* to know.] **—cog·ni·tion·al** *adj.*

cog·ni·tive (kŏg′nə-tĭv) *adj.* Of, pertaining to, or constituting cognition: *cognitive processes such as perception and comparison.*

cog·ni·za·ble (kŏg′nə-zə-bəl, kŏg-nī′-) *adj.* **1.** Knowable or perceptible. **2.** Within a court's jurisdiction. **—cog·ni·za·bly** *adv.*

cog·ni·zance (kŏg′nə-zəns) *n.* **1.** Conscious knowledge or awareness. **2.** The range of what one can know or understand. **3.** *Law.* **a.** The examination of a case by a court. **b.** The right or power of a court's jurisdiction. **4.** *Heraldry.* A crest or badge worn to distinguish the bearer. **—take cognizance of.** To take notice of; acknowledge. [Middle English *co(g)nisaunce,* from Old French *conoissance,* from *conoistre,* to know, from Latin *cognōscere,* to learn. See **cognition.**]

coffee *The coffee tree* Coffea arabica *yields the seeds (above) used to make coffee. A native of Asia and Africa, the tree was introduced into Brazil in 1727 and that country is now the world's leading coffee producer.*

cog·ni·zant (kŏg'nə-zənt) *adj.* **1.** Fully informed; conscious. Used with *of.* **2.** *Philosophy.* Having cognition. [From COGNIZANCE.]

cog·nize (kŏg-nīz', kŏg'nīz') —*tr.v.* **-nized, -nizing, -nizes.** *Philosophy.* To have cognition of. [Back-formation from COGNIZANCE, by analogy with *recognize,* and so on.]

cog·no·men (kŏg-nō'mən) *n., pl.* **-mens** or **-nomina** (-nŏm'ə-nə). **1.** A family name; a surname. **2.** The third and usually last name of a citizen of ancient Rome, such as *Caesar* in *Caius Julius Caesar.* Compare **nomen, praenomen. 3.** Any name, especially a descriptive nickname. [Latin *cōgnōmen,* "additional name" (formed after *cognōscere,* to learn) : *cō-,* together + *nōmen,* name.] —**cog·nom·i·nal** (kŏg-nŏm'ə-nəl) *adj.*

co·gno·scen·te (kŏn'yō-shĕn'tē) *n., pl.* **-ti** (-tē). A person of expert knowledge or superior taste; a connoisseur. [Obsolete Italian, "the knowing one," from Latin *cognōscēns* (stem *cognōscent-*), present participle of *cognōscere,* to get to know. See **cognition.**]

cog·no·vit (kŏg-nō'vĭt) *n. Law.* A written admission by a defendant of his liability, made to avoid the expense of a trial. [Latin, "he has acknowledged," from *cognōscere,* to get to know, recognize, acknowledge. See **cognition.**]

cog railway *n.* A railway designed to operate on steep slopes, having locomotives with a center cogwheel that engages with a cogged center rail to provide traction. Also called "rack railway."

cog·wheel (kŏg'hwēl') *n.* Any of a set of cogged wheels within a given mechanism.

co·hab·it (kō-hăb'ĭt) *intr.v.* **-ited, -iting, -its.** To live together in a sexual relationship when not legally married. Used with *with.* [Late Latin *cohabitāre : cō-,* together + *habitāre,* to inhabit.] —**co·hab·it·ant, co·hab·it·ee** *n.* —**co·hab·i·ta·tion** *n.*

Co·han (kō'hăn'), **George Michael** (1878–1942). U.S. singer, songwriter, and playwright. Perhaps best remembered for his patriotic hits "Over There" (1917) and "You're a Grand Old Flag" (1906), he also wrote many successful musical comedies, including *The Yankee Prince* (1909), *Broadway Jones* (1912), and *American Born* (1925).

co·here (kō-hîr') —*intr.v.* **-hered, -hering, -heres.** **1.** To stick or hold together. **2.** To be logically or contextually connected or consistent. [Latin *cohaerēre : cō-,* together + *haerēre,* to cling to.]

co·her·ence (kō-hîr'əns, kō-hĕr'-) *n.* Also **co·her·en·cy** (-ən-sē). The quality or state of logical or orderly relationship of parts; consistency; logical or contextual congruity.

Usage: Standard English makes a clear distinction between *coherence* and *cohesion. Coherence* refers to the logical or orderly relationship of parts, especially in speech or writing. *Cohesion* refers to the literal sticking together of objects or substances, or figuratively to a close connection established between people.

co·her·ent (kō-hîr'ənt, kō-hĕr'-) *adj.* **1.** Sticking together; cohering. **2.** Marked by an orderly or logical relation of parts that allows comprehension or recognition: *coherent speech.* **3.** *Physics.* Of or pertaining to waves with a continuous relationship among phases. **4.** Designating or pertaining to a system of units of measurement in which a small number of basic units are defined from which all others in the system are derived by multiplication or division only. —**co·her·ent·ly** *adv.*

co·he·sion (kō-hē'zhən) *n.* **1.** The process or condition of cohering; a becoming or remaining united, especially in a tangible or explicit way. **2.** *Physics.* The mutual attraction by which the elements of a body are held together. Compare **adhesion. 3.** *Botany.* The congenital joining of two parts, such as flower petals. —See Usage note at **coherence.** [Latin *cohaesus,* past participle of *cohaerēre,* COHERE.]

co·he·sive (kō-hē'sĭv, -zĭv) *adj.* Showing or producing cohesion or unity. —**co·he·sive·ly** *adv.* —**co·he·sive·ness** *n.*

co·hort (kō'hôrt') *n.* **1.** Any of the ten divisions of a Roman legion, consisting of 300 to 600 men. **2.** A group or band united in some struggle. **3.** *Informal.* An associate. [Middle English, from Old French *cohorte,* from Latin *cohors* (stem *cohort-*), enclosed yard, company of soldiers, multitude.]

co·ho salmon (kō'hō) *n.* A food and game fish, *Oncorhyncus kisutch,* native to the North Pacific coasts and introduced in the Great Lakes. Also called "silver salmon." [*Coho,* probably from an American Indian language.]

co·hune (kō-hōōn') *n.* A tropical American palm tree, *Attalea cohune,* having long featherlike leaves and oily nuts. Also called "cohune palm." [American Spanish, from Mosquito *ókhún.*]

coif (koif) *n.* **1.** A tight-fitting cap worn under a veil, as by nuns. **2. a.** A white skullcap formerly worn by English lawyers and sergeants at law. **b.** The office or rank of sergeant at law. —*tr.v.* (koif; *also* kwôf *for sense 2*) **coifed, coifing, coifs. 1.** To cover with or as if with a coif. **2.** To arrange or dress (the hair, especially of women). [Middle English *coyfe,* from Old French *coiffe, coife,* from Late Latin *cofia†.*]

coif·feur (kwä-fœr') *n. Feminine* **coif·feuse** (kwä-fœz'). A hairdresser. [French, from COIF.]

coif·fure (kwä-fyōor') *n.* A way of arranging the hair; a woman's hairstyle. —*tr.v.* **coiffured, -furing, -fures.** To arrange or dress (women's hair). [French, from *coiffer,* to COIF.]

coign (koin) *n.* A projecting corner, a **quoin** (*see*). [Variant of COIN (quoin).]

coil (koil) *n.* **1.** A series of connected spirals or concentric rings formed by gathering or winding: *a coil of rope.* **2.** An individual spiral or ring within such a series. **3.** A spiral pipe or series of spiral pipes, as in a radiator. **4.** *Electricity.* **a.** A wound spiral of two or more turns of insulated wire, used to introduce inductance into a

circuit or to provide a magnetic field. **b.** Any device of which such a spiral is the major component. **5.** An **intrauterine device** (*see*) shaped like a coil. **6.** A transformer in a gasoline engine that supplies the high voltage to the spark plugs through the distributor. ~*v.* **coiled, coiling, coils.** —*tr.* **1.** To wind in loops, spirals, or concentric rings. **2.** To wind into a shape resembling a coil. —*intr.* **1.** To form coils. **2.** To move in a spiral course. **3.** To move in a sinuous way. [Middle English *coilen,* to collect, cull, from Old French *coillir,* from Latin *colligere : com-,* together + *legere,* to gather.] —**coil·er** *n.*

coil spring *n.* A spring formed from a helical coil of wire.

Co·im·bra (kō-ĭm'brə). City in central Portugal, situated on the Mondego River. It has the oldest university in the country and a fine Romanesque cathedral.

coin (koin) *n.* **1.** A small piece of metal, usually flat and circular, authorized by a government for use as money. **2.** Metal money collectively. **3.** *Architecture.* A corner or cornerstone. —*tr.v.* **coined, coining, coins. 1. a.** To make (coins) from metal; mint; strike: *coin silver dollars.* **b.** To make coins from (metal): *coin gold.* **2.** To invent (a word or phrase). [Middle English *coyne,* wedge, design stamped on a coiner's die, coin, from Old French *coing,* coin, wedge, from Latin *cuneus†,* wedge.] —**coin·a·ble** *adj.* —**coin·er** *n.*

coin·age (koi'nĭj) *n.* **1.** The act or process of making coins. **2. a.** Metal currency. **b.** A system of metal currency. **3. a.** A coined word or phrase. **b.** The invention of new words.

co·in·cide (kō'ĭn-sīd') *intr.v.* **-cided, -ciding, -cides. 1. a.** To occupy the same position simultaneously. **b.** To have identical dimensions. **2.** To happen at the same time or during the same period. **3.** To correspond exactly; be identical. **4.** To concur; agree. —See Synonyms at **agree.** [Medieval Latin *coincidere : cō-,* together + *incidere,* to happen.]

co·in·ci·dence (kō-ĭn'sə-dəns, -dĕns') *n.* **1.** The state or fact of coinciding. **2.** An accidental sequence of events that appear to have a causal relationship. —**co·in·ci·dent** *adj.*

coincidence gate *n. Electronics.* A circuit or device that produces an output only when both its input terminals receive pulses within a specific short interval; a **gate** (*see*).

co·in·ci·den·tal (kō-ĭn'sə-dĕn'təl) *adj.* Occurring as or resulting from coincidence. —**co·in·ci·den·tal·ly** *adv.*

coin-op (koin'ŏp') *n.* A self-service laundry in which the machines are operated by the insertion of coins. Also called "coin-op laundry."

co·in·sur·ance (kō'ĭn-shōōr'əns) *n.* **1.** Insurance held jointly with another or others. **2.** A form of insurance in which a person insures property for less than its full value and agrees to be responsible for the difference. —**co·in·sure** *v.* —**co·in·sur·er** *n.*

Coin·treau (kwän'trō) *n.* A trademark for a colorless liqueur made from brandy and oranges.

coir (koir) *n.* The fiber obtained from the husk of a coconut, used in making rope and matting. [Malayalam *kāyar,* cord.]

co·i·tus (kō'ə-təs) *n.* Also **co·i·tion** (kō-ĭsh'ən). Sexual intercourse. [Latin *coitus,* "meeting," from *coīre,* to come together : *cō-,* together + *īre,* to go.] —**co·i·tal** *adj.*

coitus in·ter·rup·tus (kō'ə-təs ĭn'tə-rŭp'təs) *n.* Sexual intercourse deliberately interrupted by withdrawal of the penis prior to ejaculation. [Latin, "interrupted intercourse."]

coke¹ (kōk) *n.* **1.** The solid carbonaceous residue obtained from coal after removal of volatile material by destructive distillation, used as fuel. **2.** A similar material formed in different ways; especially, the layer of carbon formed within an engine as a result of incomplete combustion of the fuel. ~*v.* **coked, coking, cokes.** —*tr.* To convert or change into coke. —*intr.* To become coke. [Middle English *coke†.*]

coke² *n. Slang.* Cocaine.

Coke *n.* A trademark for Coca-Cola, a soft drink.

Coke (kōōk, kōk), **Sir Edward** (1552–1634). English jurist. As the chief justice of the court of common pleas (1606–16) he ruled that the common law was the supreme law, even when the Crown disagreed. His bill of liberties (1628), which became the Petition of Right, melded ancient English legal precedents into a charter that limited the royal prerogative.

col (kŏl) *n.* **1.** A pass between two peaks or a gap in a ridge. **2.** *Meteorology.* A region of intermediate pressure between two anticyclones and two depressions. [French, from Old French, neck, from Latin *collum.*]

col. 1. collect; collected; collector. **2.** college; collegiate. **3.** colonial; colony. **4.** color. **5.** column.

Col. 1. Colombia. **2.** colonel. **3.** Colossians (New Testament).

col–¹. Variant of **com–.** Used before *l.*

col–². Variant of **colo–.**

co·la¹, ko·la (kō'lə) *n.* **1.** Either of two African trees, *Cola nitida* or *C. acuminata,* cultivated in the tropics for their seeds. See **cola nut. 2.** A soft carbonated drink flavored with an extract from cola nuts. [Probably a variant of Mandingo *kolo,* nut.]

co·la². Alternative plural of **colon.**

col·an·der (kŭl'ən-dər, kŏl'-) *n.* A bowl-shaped kitchen utensil with a perforated bottom for draining off liquids and rinsing food. [Middle English *colyndore, culatre,* from Old Provençal *colador* (unattested), from Vulgar Latin *cōlātor* (unattested), from Latin *cōlāre,* to strain, from *cōlum,* sieve, filter.]

cola nut, kola nut *n.* The seed of the cola tree, containing caffeine and theobromine and yielding an extract used in carbonated drinks and in pharmaceutical products.

co·lat·i·tude (kō'lăt'ĭ-tōōd', -tyōōd') *n. Astronomy.* The complement of the celestial latitude; (90°-*β*), where *β* is the celestial latitude.

Col·bert (kôl-bâr', kōl'-), **Claudette,** born Lily Claudette Chauchoin (1905-). French film actress, later a U.S. citizen. She made her name with vivacious performances in comedies such as *It Happened One Night* (1934).

Colbert, Jean-Baptiste (1619-83). French statesman and leading adviser to Louis XIV. To encourage trade, he reformed taxes, centralized the administration, and improved road and canal networks. He also developed the French navy and codified laws.

col·can·non (kŏl-kăn'ən) *n.* An Irish dish of mashed potatoes and cabbage. [Irish Gaelic *cal ceannan,* "white-headed cabbage" : *cal,* cabbage, from Old Irish, from Latin *caulis* + *ceannan,* whiteheaded, from *ceann,* head.]

Col·ches·ter (kōl'chĭs-tər). Town in Essex in southeast England, on the Colne River. Parts of the old Roman town, called Camulodunum, have been excavated, and relics are displayed in a fine Norman castle.

col·chi·cine (kŏl'chə-sēn', kŏl'kə-) *n.* A poisonous alkaloid, $C_{22}H_{25}NO_6$, used experimentally to induce chromosome doubling and medicinally to treat gout. [German *Kolchizin,* from New Latin *colchicum,* COLCHICUM.]

col·chi·cum (kŏl'chĭ-kəm, kŏl'kĭ-) *n.* **1.** Any of various bulbous plants of the genus *Colchicum,* such as the **autumn crocus** (see). **2.** The dried seeds or corms of the autumn crocus, a source of colchicine. [New Latin, from Latin, a poisonous root, from Greek *Kolkhikon,* from *Kolkhikos,* of Colchis, belonging to the witch Medea of Colchis, from *Kolkhis, Colchis,* ancient region on the Black Sea.]

col·co·thar (kŏl'kə-thər, -thär') *n.* A brownish-red iron oxide obtained as a residue after heating ferrous sulfate, used in glass polishing and as a pigment. [French *colcotar,* from Spanish, from Arabic *qolqoṭār.*]

cold (kōld) *adj.* **colder, coldest. 1. a.** Having a low or lower than usual temperature. **b.** Lacking heat: *the cold light of the moon.* **2.** Feeling no warmth; uncomfortably chilled. **3.** Designating a color or tone that suggests little warmth, such as pale gray. **4.** Served without heating after being processed or cooked: *cold cereal; cold chicken.* **5.** *Informal.* **a.** Unconscious; insensible: *knocked cold.* **b.** Dead. **6.** Not affected by emotion; objective: *cold logic.* **7.** Without appeal to the senses or feelings; depressing: *cold decor.* **8.** Not affectionate or friendly: *a cold reception.* **9.** Without sexual desire; frigid. **10.** Unenthusiastic; apathetic: *The prospect left him cold.* **11.** Without freshness; faint; weak. Said of a scent in hunting. **12.** *Informal.* In guessing and searching games, far removed from the object sought. —*adv. Informal.* **1.** Completely; thoroughly: *turned our offer down cold.* **2.** Without preparation or rehearsal. —*n.* **1.** The relative lack of warmth. **2.** The sensation resulting from lack of warmth. **3.** A viral infection characterized by inflammation of the mucous membranes of the respiratory passages and accompanying fever, chills, coughing, and sneezing. **4.** A condition of low air temperature; cold weather. —**out in the cold.** Neglected; ignored. [Middle English *cold, cald,* Old English *ceald,* from Germanic.] —**cold·ly** *adv.* —**cold·ness** *n.*

cold-blood·ed (kōld'blŭd'ĭd) *adj.* **1.** Ruthless; unfeeling; heartless. **2.** *Zoology.* Having a body temperature that varies with the external environment; poikilothermic. **3.** *Informal.* Likely to feel the cold. —**cold·blood·ed·ly** *adv.* —**cold·blood·ed·ness** *n.*

cold cathode *n.* An electrode from which electrons are emitted at ambient temperatures as a result of a high surface potential gradient.

cold chisel *n.* A chisel made of hardened, tempered steel and used for cutting cold metal.

cold comfort *n.* Something that gives little consolation or cheer.

cold cream *n.* An emulsion for cleansing and softening the skin.

cold cuts *pl.n.* Slices of assorted cold meats.

cold desert *n.* **1.** A polar area with no vegetation. **2.** A tundra. **3.** A high plateau in a continental interior, cut off from moist maritime influences.

cold-drawn (kōld'drôn') *adj.* Designating a metal wire, bar, or the like that has been pulled through a die without heating to reduce its thickness or change its toughness or appearance.

cold duck *n.* An alcoholic drink combining champagne and burgundy. [Translation of German *Kalte Ente,* a drink made from a mixture of wines.]

cold feet *n. Informal.* Failure of nerve.

cold frame *n.* A structure consisting of a frame with a glass top, used for protecting young plants from the cold.

cold front *n.* The leading portion of a cold atmospheric air mass moving into the base of and eventually replacing a warm air mass.

cold-heart·ed (kōld'här'tĭd) *adj.* Unkind; stern.

cold light *n.* **1.** Light producing little or no heat. **2.** Light emitted by a process other than incandescence.

cold pack *n.* **1.** *Medicine.* A therapeutic pack consisting of a cold, damp sheet, used to lower body temperature. **2.** A canning process in which uncooked food is packed in cans, then sterilized by heat.

cold rubber *n.* A durable, strong, synthetic rubber polymerized at low temperatures.

cold shoulder *n. Informal.* Deliberately unkind or unfriendly treatment; a snub. Preceded by *the.*

cold-shoul·der (kōld'shōl'dər) *tr.v.* **-dered, -dering, -ders.** *Informal.* To give (someone) the cold shoulder; slight; snub.

cold snap *n.* A sudden, brief spell of cold weather.

cold sore *n.* A small sore on the lips that often accompanies a fever or cold and is caused by a viral infection; a fever blister. Also called "fever blister," "herpes simplex."

cold storage *n.* **1.** The protective storage of foods, furs, or the like in a refrigerated place. **2.** *Informal.* A state of temporary suspension.

Cold·stream (kōld'strēm'). Town in Borders Region in southeast Scotland, on the Tweed River. The regiment of Coldstream Guards, for which it is famous, was first formed here in 1660.

cold sweat *n.* A reaction to extreme nervousness, characterized by a cold, moist skin.

cold turkey *n. Informal.* Immediate, complete withdrawal from something on which one has become dependent, such as an addictive drug. [Originally, a blunt statement, with reference to a plain ungarnished dish of cold meat; hence, a "blunt" withdrawal from drugs.]

cold type *n.* Typesetting, such as photocomposition, done without the casting of metal.

cold war *n.* **1.** A state of political tension and rivalry between nations, stopping short of actual full-scale war. **2. Cold War.** The state of such rivalry existing between the Soviet and Western blocs, following World War II. —**cold warrior** *n.*

cold wave *n.* **1.** An abrupt onset of unusually cold weather brought by a cold air mass following a depression. **2.** A form of permanent wave in which the hair is set by chemicals rather than heat. See **perm.**

cold-weld (kōld'wĕld') *tr.v.* **-welded, -welding, -welds.** To join (two metals) together without heat by forcing their surfaces together under pressure.

cold-work (kōld'wûrk') *tr.v.* **-worked, -working, -works.** To shape or form (metal) in the absence of heat.

cole (kōl) *n. Rare.* Any of various plants of the genus *Brassica,* such as the cabbage or rape. Also called "colewort." [Middle English *col, coole,* Old English *cāl, caul,* from Latin *caulis,* plant stalk, cabbage.]

Cole (kōl), **Nat "King"** (1919-65). U.S. singer and pianist. In 1937 he formed the King Cole Trio, which drew enthusiastic crowds on the jazz circuit. In 1943 he began recording a string of hits, including "Nature Boy," "The Christmas Song," and "Mona Lisa," making him one of the most popular recording artists of the 1940's and 1950's.

Cole, Thomas (1801-48). U.S. painter, born in England. The acknowledged leader of the Hudson River School, America's first native painting movement, he traveled the country capturing nature on canvas. Later he created religious and symbolic works, including *Course of Empire* (1835-36) and *The Voyage of Life* (1839).

co·lec·to·my (kə-lĕk'tə-mē) *n., pl.* **-mies.** Surgical removal of part or all of the colon. [COL(O)- + -ECTOMY.]

cole·man·ite (kōl'mə-nīt') *n.* A natural white or colorless hydrated calcium borate, $Ca_2B_6O_{11} \cdot 5H_2O$, a principal source of borax. [After William T. *Coleman* (1824-93), U.S. pioneer, owner of the mine where it was discovered.]

co·le·op·ter·an (kō'lē-ŏp'tər-ən, kŏl'ē-) *n.* Also **co·le·op·ter·on** (-tə-rŏn'). Any insect of the order Coleoptera, characterized by forewings modified to form tough protective covers for the hind wings, and including the beetles. —*adj.* Also **co·le·op·ter·ous** (-tər-əs) Of or belonging to the Coleoptera. [New Latin *Coleoptera,* "sheath-winged ones," from Greek *koleopteros,* sheath-winged : *koleon,* sheath + -PTEROUS.] —**co·le·op·ter·ist** *n.*

co·le·op·tile (kō'lē-ŏp'tĭl, kŏl'ē) *n. Botany.* A leaflike structure in grasses and similar monocotyledons, forming a protective sheath around the plumule. [New Latin *coleoptilum,* "sheathed plume" : Greek *koleon,* sheath + *ptilon,* plume, down.]

co·le·o·rhi·za (kō'lē-ə-rī'zə, kŏl'ē-) *n., pl.* **-zae** (-zē). *Botany.* A protective sheath around the embryonic root of grasses and similar monocotyledons. [New Latin, "root sheath" : Greek *koleon,* sheath + *rhiza,* root.]

Cole·ridge (kōl'rĭj), **Samuel Taylor** (1772-1834). British poet and critic. With William Wordsworth he published *Lyrical Ballads* (1798), which contained *The Rime of the Ancient Mariner,* his best-known poem. Other works include the visionary poem "Kubla Khan" (published 1816) and the critical and philosophical *Biographia Literaria* (1817).

cole·slaw (kōl'slô') *n.* Also **cole slaw.** A salad consisting mainly of finely shredded raw cabbage with a dressing. Also called "slaw." [Dutch *koolsla* : *kool,* cabbage, from Middle Dutch *côle,* from Latin *caulis* + *sla,* short for *salade,* SALAD.]

Col·et (kŏl'ĭt), **John** (*c.* 1466-1519). English humanist theologian and champion of Renaissance scholarship within the Catholic Church. He founded St. Paul's School, London (1509), to promote classical as well as scriptural learning.

Co·lette (kô-lĕt'), born Sidonie Gabrielle Claudine Colette (1873-1954). French novelist, famous especially for her sensuous and idyllic evocations of childhood and nature. Her works include *Gigi* (1944) and the series of *Claudine* books.

co·le·us (kō'lē-əs) *n.* Any of various plants of the genus *Coleus,* of Eurasia and Africa, cultivated for their showy leaves, which are often marked with red, yellow, or white. [New Latin *Coleus,* from Greek *koleos, koleon,* sheath (from the way its filaments are joined).]

colchicum *A crocuslike flower whose blooms appear in autumn, the autumn crocus,* Colchicum autumnale, *is found in meadowland.*

cole·wort (kōl'wûrt', -wôrt') n. A plant, **cole** (see).

co·ley (kō'lē) n., pl. **coleys** or collectively **coley.** Any of several edible fishes, especially the **coalfish** (see). [Probably shortened from *coalfish.*]

col·ic (kŏl'ĭk) n. **1.** Acute, paroxysmal pain in the abdomen, caused by spasm, obstruction, or distension of the intestine. **2.** Severe abdominal pain in infants, usually resulting from accumulation of gas in the alimentary canal. [Middle English *colike,* from Old French *colique,* from Latin *cōlicus,* from Greek *kōlikos,* suffering in the colon, from *kōlon,* variant of *kolon,* COLON (intestine).] —**col·ick·y** (kŏl'ĭ-kē) adj.

col·i·cin (kō'lĭ-sən, kŏl'ə-) n. A protein produced by some strains of coliform bacteria such as *Escherichia coli* that is lethal to other strains of the same species. [New Latin, *coli* (specific name of the bacterium) + -*c*- (connective) + -IN.]

co·li·form bacteria (kō'lə-fôrm', kŏl'ə-) pl.n. A group of rod-shaped bacteria most commonly occurring in the intestines of man and other vertebrates, some of which can cause disease. [COL(ON) + -FORM.]

col·i·se·um, col·os·se·um (kŏl'ə-sē'əm) n. A large amphitheater for public entertainment or assemblies. [After the COLOSSEUM in Rome.]

Coliseum. See **Colosseum.**

co·lis·tin (kə-lĭs'tĭn, kō-) n. An antibiotic produced by the bacterium *Bacillus colistinus* that is used mainly in treating gastrointestinal infections. [New Latin *colistinus* (specific name of the bacterium).]

co·li·tis (kō-lī'tĭs) n. Inflammation of the mucous membrane of the colon. [New Latin : COL(O)- + -ITIS.]

coll. 1. collateral. **2.** collect; collection; collector. **3.** college; collegiate. **4.** colloquial; colloquialism.

coll–. Variant of **collo–.**

col·lab·o·rate (kə-lăb'ə-rāt') intr.v. **-rated, -rating, -rates. 1.** To work together, especially in a joint intellectual or artistic effort. **2.** To cooperate treasonably, especially with an enemy occupying one's country. [Late Latin *collabōrāre* : Latin *com-,* together + *labōrāre,* to work, from *labor,* labor.] —**col·lab·o·ra·tion** n. —**col·lab·o·ra·tor** n.

col·lab·o·ra·tion·ist (kə-lăb'ə-rā'shən-ĭst) n. A person who collaborates with an occupying enemy. —**col·lab·o·ra·tion·ism** n.

col·lage (kō-läzh') n. **1.** An artistic composition of materials and objects pasted over a surface. **2.** Such compositions as an art form. **3.** An assemblage of images or sounds on a theme. [French, from *coller,* to glue, paste, from *colle,* glue, from Vulgar Latin *colla* (unattested), from Greek *kolla.*]

col·la·gen (kŏl'ə-jən) n. A fibrous protein occurring in bone, cartilage, and connective tissue. [Greek *kolla,* glue + -GEN.] —**col·la·gen·ic** (kŏl'ə-jĕn'ĭk), **col·lag·e·nous** (kə-lăj'ə-nəs) adj.

col·lap·sar (kə-lăp'sär') n. A star which has collapsed under its own gravitational force; a black hole.

col·lapse (kə-lăps') v. **-lapsed, -lapsing, -lapses.** —intr. **1.** To fall down or inward suddenly; cave in. **2.** To break down suddenly in health or strength; lose consciousness or energy. **3.** To suffer a complete loss of power, effectiveness, or the like: *Opposition to the proposals has collapsed.* **4.** To fold compactly. —tr. To cause to collapse.
~n. **1.** The act of falling down or inward, as from external pressure or loss of supports. **2.** An abrupt failure of function, strength, or health. [Back-formation from *collapsed,* from Latin *collāpsus,* past participle of *collābī,* to fall together, fall in ruin : *com-,* together + *lābī,* slide, fall.] —**col·laps·i·ble, col·laps·a·ble** adj. —**col·laps·i·bil·i·ty** n.

col·lar (kŏl'ər) n. **1.** The part of a garment that encircles the neck. **2.** A necklace, choker, or similar ornament for the neck. **3.** A restraining or identifying band of leather or metal put around the neck of an animal. **4.** The cushioned part of a harness that presses against the shoulders of a draft animal. **5.** Biology. An encircling structure or bandlike marking suggestive of a collar. **6.** Any of various ringlike devices or parts used to limit, guide, or secure a machine part. —**hot under the collar.** Informal. Angry; annoyed.
~tr.v. **collared, -laring, -lars. 1.** To furnish with a collar. **2.** To seize by the collar. **3.** Informal. To seize or detain. [Middle English *coler,* from Norman French, from Latin *collāre,* necklace, collar, from *collum,* neck.]

collar beam n. A timber beam connecting the midpoints of the sloping rafters of a pitched roof.

col·lar·bone (kŏl'ər-bōn') n. Anatomy. The **clavicle** (see).

collar cell n. Biology. A **choanocyte** (see).

col·lard (kŏl'ərd) n. **1.** A variety of kale, *Brassica oleracea acephala,* having a crown of edible leaves. **2.** collards. The leaves of this plant used as a vegetable. [Variant of COLEWORT.]

col·lared dove n. A common European dove, *Streptopelia decaocto,* having a pale, brownish-gray plumage with a black band around the back of the neck.

collat. collateral.

col·late (kə-lāt', kŏl'āt', kō'lāt') tr.v. **-lated, -lating, -lates. 1.** To examine and compare carefully (texts) in order to note points of difference and agreement. **2.** In bookbinding, to examine (gathered signatures) in order to arrange them in proper sequence before binding. **3.** To verify the order and completeness of (the pages of a volume). **4.** To assemble in proper numerical or logical sequence. **5.** Ecclesiastical. To admit (a cleric) to a benefice. [Latin *collātus* (past participle of *conferre,* to bring together) : *com-,* together + *lātus,* "carried."] —**col·la·tor** (kə-lā'tər, kŏl'ā-tər, kō'lā'-) n.

col·lat·er·al (kə-lăt'ər-əl) adj. Abbr. **coll., collat. 1.** Situated or running side by side; parallel. **2.** Coinciding in tendency or effect; concomitant; accompanying. **3.** Serving to support or corroborate: *collateral evidence.* **4.** Of a secondary nature; subordinate. **5.** Finance. Of, designating, or guaranteed by a security pledged against the performance of an obligation: *a collateral loan.* **6.** Descended from the same ancestor, but through a different line: *a collateral branch of the family.* In this sense, compare **lineal.**
~n. **1.** Finance. Property acceptable as security for a loan or other obligation. **2.** A collateral relative. [Middle English, from Medieval Latin *collaterālis* : *com-,* together + *laterālis,* of the side, LATERAL.] —**col·lat·er·al·ly** adv.

col·la·tion (kə-lā'shən, kō-, kŏ-) n. **1.** The act or process of collating. **2.** A description of the material aspects of a book. **3.** In the Roman Catholic Church, a light meal permitted on fast days. **4.** Any light meal. [Middle English, from Old French, from Latin *collātiō* (stem *collātiōn-*), a bringing together (see **collate).** Senses 3, 4 : from the custom in Benedictine monasteries of reading from Cassian's *Collationes Patrum (Lives of the Fathers)* before taking a light meal on fast days.]

col·league (kŏl'ēg') n. A fellow member, typically of a profession, staff, or academic faculty; an associate. —See Synonyms at **partner.** [French *collègue,* from Old French, from Latin *collēga,* one chosen to serve with another : *com-,* together + *lēgāre,* to choose.] —**col·league·ship** n.

col·lect[1] (kə-lĕkt') v. **-lected, -lecting, -lects.** —tr. **1.** To bring together in a group; assemble. **2.** To accumulate as a hobby or for study. **3.** To obtain payment of (rents or taxes, for example). **4.** To recover control of. **5.** To call for; go and fetch. **6.** Informal. To win or receive (money, for example). —intr. **1.** To gather together; congregate. **2.** To take in payments or donations. —See Synonyms at **gather.**
~adj. With payment to be made by the receiver: *a collect phone call.*
~adv. So that the receiver is charged: *phone collect.* [Middle English *collecten,* from Latin *colligere* (past participle *collectus*), to gather together : *com-,* together + *legere,* to gather.] —**col·lect·i·ble, col·lect·a·ble** adj.

col·lect[2] (kŏl'ĭkt, -ĕkt') n. Ecclesiastical. A brief formal prayer used in various Western liturgies before the epistle at Mass or Holy Communion and varying with the day. [Middle English *collecte,* from Old French, from Medieval Latin *collēcta,* from *ōrātiō ad collēctam,* "prayer at the congregation," from Late Latin *collēcta,* assembly, from Latin *collēctus,* collected. See **collect**[1].]

col·lec·ta·ne·a (kŏl'ĕk-tā'nē-ə) pl.n. A selection of passages from one or more authors; an anthology. [Latin, "things collected," from *collēctāneus,* collected, from *collēctus.* See **collect**[1].]

col·lect·ed (kə-lĕk'tĭd) adj. **1.** Self-possessed; composed. **2.** Brought or placed together from various sources: *the collected poems of W.H. Auden.* —See Synonyms at **cool.** —**col·lect·ed·ly** adv. —**col·lect·ed·ness** n.

col·lec·tion (kə-lĕk'shən) n. Abbr. **coll. 1.** The act or process of collecting. **2.** A group of things that have been brought together, especially: **a.** A set of like objects collected as a hobby or for exhibition: *a postcard collection.* **b.** A set of literary works assembled in a single volume: *a collection of short stories.* **c.** A range of clothes exhibited by a fashion designer. **3.** An accumulation; deposit. **4. a.** A collecting of money, as in church. **b.** The sum collected. **5.** A removal of letters for delivery from a mailbox.

col·lec·tive (kə-lĕk'tĭv) adj. **1.** Formed by collecting; assembled or accumulated into a whole. **2.** Of, pertaining to, characteristic of, or made by a number of individuals taken or acting as a group: *a collective decision.*
~n. **1.** A collective enterprise, such as a **workers' cooperative** (see), or the persons working in it. **2.** A group of people working together for mutual support or advancement: *a women's collective.* **3.** Grammar. A collective noun. —**col·lec·tive·ly** adv. —**col·lec·tive·ness** n.

collective bargaining n. Negotiation between trade-union representatives and employers to determine wages, hours, rules, and working conditions.

collective farm n. A farm or a group of farms organized as a unit, managed and worked cooperatively by a group of workers, typically under government supervision. See also **kibbutz, kolkhoz.**

collective fruit n. Botany. A **multiple fruit** (see).

collective noun n. Grammar. A noun, such as *family* or *committee,* that denotes a collection of persons or things regarded as a unit.
Usage: A collective noun takes a singular verb when it refers to the collection as a whole and a plural verb when it refers to the members of the collection as separate persons or things: *The orchestra was playing,* but *The orchestra have all gone home.* A collective noun should not be treated as both singular and plural in the same construction. Thus: *The family is determined to press its* (not *their) claim.*

col·lec·tiv·ism (kə-lĕk'tə-vĭz'əm) n. The principle or system of ownership and control of the means of production and distribution by the people collectively. —**col·lec·tiv·ist** adj. & n.

col·lec·tiv·i·ty (kŏl'ĕk-tĭv'ə-tē, kə-lĕk'-) n. **1.** The condition or quality of being collective. **2.** The people as a whole.

col·lec·tiv·ize (kə-lĕk'tə-vīz') tr.v. **-ized, -izing, -izes.** To organize (an economy, industry, or enterprise) on the basis of collectivism. —**col·lec·tiv·i·za·tion** n.

col·lec·tor (kə-lĕk'tər) n. **1.** A person or thing that collects. **2.** Abbr.

col., coll. A person employed to collect taxes, duties, or other payments. **3.** A person who collects things as a hobby, such as stamps. **4.** Formerly, the chief administrative officer of a district in British India. **5. a.** *Electricity.* A conducting contact between moving and stationary parts of an electric circuit. **b.** *Electronics.* The output terminal of a three-terminal semiconducting device, especially of a transistor. **—col·lec·tor·ship** *n.*

col·leen (kŏl′ēn′, kŏ-lēn′) *n.* An Irish girl. [Irish *cailīn,* diminutive of *caile,* girl, from Old Irish *calé,* probably from Latin *pellex,* concubine, akin to Greek *pallakē,* Sanskrit *pallavaki,* of non-Indo-European origin.]

col·lege (kŏl′ĭj) *n. Abbr.* **col., coll. 1. a.** An institution offering courses in higher education that grants the bachelor's degree in liberal arts or science or both. **b.** Any of the undergraduate divisions or schools of a university offering courses or granting degrees in a particular field. **c.** A technical or professional school, often affiliated with a university, offering the bachelor's or master's degree: *a teachers' college.* **d.** The building or buildings occupied by any such school. **e.** *Chiefly British.* A self-governing body of scholars incorporated within a university. **f.** In France, an institution for secondary education not supported by the state. **2.** A company or assemblage; especially, a body of persons having a common purpose, common professional interests, or common duties: *a college of surgeons.* **3.** A body of clergymen living together on an endowment. [Middle English, from Old French, from Latin *collēgium,* corporate institution, partnership, from *collēga,* COLLEAGUE.]

College of Arms *n.* A royal corporation in Britain that deals with matters of heraldry. Also called "Heralds' College."

College of Cardinals *n. Roman Catholic Church.* A body comprising all the cardinals that elects the pope, assists him in governing the church, and administers the Holy See when vacant. Also called "Sacred College."

col·le·gi·al·i·ty (kə-lē′jē-ăl′ĭ-tē) *n.* **1.** Shared authority among colleagues. **2.** *Roman Catholic Church.* The principle that the bishops, together with the pope, share collectively the responsibility of ruling the Church.

col·le·gian (kə-lē′jən, -jē-ən) *n.* A student or recent graduate of a college.

col·le·giate (kə-lē′jĭt, -jē-ĭt) *adj.* Also **col·le·gi·al** (kə-lē′jē-əl, -jəl). *Abbr.* **col., coll. 1.** Of, pertaining to, or resembling a college. **2.** Of, for, or typical of college students. **3.** Of or pertaining to a collegiate church. [Medieval Latin *collēgiātus,* from Latin *collēgium,* COLLEGE.]

collegiate church *n.* **1.** A Roman Catholic or Anglican church other than a cathedral, having a chapter of canons and presided over by a dean or provost. **2. a.** A church in the United States associated with others under a common body of pastors. **b.** An association of such churches. **3.** In Scotland, a church served by two or more ministers at the same time.

col·le·gi·um (kə-lē′jē-əm) *n., pl.* **-gia** (-jē-ə) or **-giums.** An executive council or committee of equally empowered members; specifically, one supervising an industry, commissariat, or other organization in the U.S.S.R. [Russian *kollegya,* from Latin *collēgium,* COLLEGE.]

col·lem·bo·lan (kə-lĕm′bə-lən) *n.* Any small wingless insect of the order Collembola; a springtail. [New Latin *Collembola,* from Greek *kolla,* glue + *embolon,* wedge, peg (referring to a projecting pouch characteristic of all members of the order).] **—col·lem·bo·lan** *adj.*

col·len·chy·ma (kə-lĕng′-kə-mə) *n. Botany.* Supportive tissue of plants, consisting of elongated, approximately rectangular cells with cell walls thickened with cellulose and pectin. [New Latin, "glue tissue" : COLL(O)- + -ENCHYMA.] **—col·len·chym·a·tous** (kŏl′ən-kĭm′ə-təs) *adj.*

Col·les' fracture (kŏl′ĭs) *n.* A fracture of the wrist, at the lower end of the radius, in which the hand is displaced backwards. [After Abraham *Colles* (died 1843), Irish surgeon.]

col·let (kŏl′ĭt) *n.* **1.** A cone-shaped sleeve used for holding circular or rodlike machine pieces. **2.** A metal collar used in watchmaking to join one end of a balance spring to the balance staff. **3.** A circular flange or rim, as in a ring, into which a gem is set.
~*tr.v.* **colleted, -leting, -lets.** To set in or supply with a collet. [French, diminutive of *col,* neck, collar, from Latin *collum,* neck.]

col·lide (kə-līd′) *intr.v.* **-lided, -liding, -lides. 1.** To come together with violent, direct impact. **2.** To meet in opposition; clash; conflict. [Latin *collīdere* : *com-,* together + *laedere,* to strike, injure.]

col·lie (kŏl′ē) *n.* A large dog of a breed originating in Scotland and widely used as a sheep dog, having long hair and a long, narrow muzzle. [Scottish, possibly from *colly,* "black like coal" (its original color), from *coll,* variant of COAL.]

col·li·er (kŏl′yər) *n. British.* **1.** A coal miner. **2.** A coal ship. [Middle English *colier,* from *col, cole,* COAL.]

col·lier·y (kŏl′yər-ē) *n., pl.* **-ies.** *British.* A coal mine.

col·li·gate (kŏl′ĭ-gāt′) *tr.v.* **-gated, -gating, -gates. 1.** To tie together. **2.** *Logic.* To bring (isolated observations) together by an explanation or hypothesis that applies to them all. [Latin *colligāre* : *com-,* together + *ligāre,* to tie.] **—col·li·ga·tion** *n.*

col·li·ga·tive (kŏl′ĭ-gā′tĭv) *adj.* Designating the physical properties of a substance that depend on the concentrations of molecules, atoms, or ions present rather than on their nature: *colligative properties.*

col·li·mate (kŏl′ə-māt′) *tr.v.* **-mated, -mating, -mates. 1.** To make parallel; line up. **2.** To adjust the line of sight of (a transit, telescope, or other optical device). [New Latin *collimare,* to adjust, misreading of Latin *collīneāre,* to direct in a straight line : *com-* (intensive) + *līneāre,* to make straight, from *līnea,* LINE.] **—col·li·ma·tion** *n.*

col·li·ma·tor (kŏl′ə-mā′tər) *n.* **1.** Any device capable of collimating radiation, such as a long narrow tube in which strongly absorbing or reflecting walls permit only radiation travelling parallel to the tube axis to traverse the entire length. **2.** A small telescope attached to a larger one as an aid to adjusting its line of sight.

col·lin·e·ar (kō-lĭn′ē-ər, kə-) *adj.* **1.** Lying on the same line. **2.** Containing a common line; coaxial. [COM- + LINEAR.]

col·lins (kŏl′ənz) *n.* A tall iced drink made with gin, vodka, rum, or other spirits, and lemon or lime juice, soda water, and sugar. [20th century : origin obscure.]

Collins *n. Chiefly British Informal.* A letter written to thank a host for his hospitality. [After William *Collins,* a character in Jane Austen's *Pride and Prejudice* (1813).]

Col·lins (kŏl′ənz), **Michael** (1890–1922). Irish nationalist. He took part in the Easter Rising in Dublin (1916) and was elected a Sinn Fein member of the Dáil (1919). He helped to negotiate the establishment of the Irish Free State (1921) but was killed in an ambush by republican opponents.

Collins, (William) Wilkie (1824–89). British novelist, a pioneer of the mystery story, best remembered for *The Woman in White* (1860) and *The Moonstone* (1868).

col·lin·si·a (kə-lĭn′zē-ə) *n.* Any of various North American plants of the genus *Collinsia,* having blue-and-white or purplish flowers.

col·li·sion (kə-lĭzh′ən) *n.* **1.** A direct, violent striking together; crash. **2.** A clash of ideas or interests; a conflict. **3.** *Physics.* A dynamic event consisting of the interaction between two or more bodies, usually of very brief duration, resulting in a change of momentum of at least one participating body. [Middle English, from Latin *collīsiō* (stem *collīsion-*), from *collīdere,* COLLIDE.]

collision course *n.* A course, as of moving objects or ideas, that will end in collision or conflict if continued unchanged.

collo-, coll- *prefix.* Indicates: **1.** Glue; for example, **collenchyma. 2.** Colloid; for example, **collotype.** [New Latin, from Greek *kolla,* glue.]

col·lo·cate (kŏl′ō-kāt′) *v.* **-cated, -cating, -cates.** —*tr.* To place together or in proper order; arrange. —*intr. Linguistics.* To occur habitually and naturally together; for example, *quick* collocates with *temper,* but *fast* does not. [Latin *collocāre* : *com-,* together + *locāre,* to place, LOCATE.]

col·lo·ca·tion (kŏl′ō-kā′shən) *n.* **1. a.** The act of collocating. **b.** The state of being collocated. **2.** An arrangement or juxtaposition; especially, a group of words habitually occurring together.

col·lo·di·on (kə-lō′dē-ən) *n.* Also **col·lo·di·um** (kə-lō′dē-əm). A highly flammable, colorless or yellowish syrupy solution of **pyroxylin** *(see)* in ether and alcohol, used to hold surgical dressings, as a coating for certain skin diseases, and for making photographic plates. [New Latin *collodium,* from Greek *kollōdēs,* gluelike, from *kolla,* glue.]

col·logue (kə-lōg′) *intr.v.* **-logued, -loguing, -logues.** *British Regional.* To confer secretly; conspire. [Probably from obsolete verb *colleague,* to be a colleague, ally, conspire (influenced by Latin *colloquī,* to converse), from Old French *colleguer,* from Latin *colligāre,* to tie together, COLLIGATE.]

col·loid (kŏl′oid′, kŏ′loid′) *n.* **1.** *Chemistry.* **a.** A suspension of finely divided particles in a continuous medium (a gaseous, liquid, or solid substance), such as an atmospheric fog, a paint, or foam rubber, containing suspended particles that are approximately 1 to 1,000 nanometers in size, do not settle out of the medium rapidly, and are not readily filtered. **b.** The particulate matter so suspended. See **sol, gel, emulsion, foam. 2.** *Physiology.* A clear gelatinous secretion of the thyroid gland. Also called "thyroid colloid." **3.** *Pathology.* Gelatinous material resulting from tissue degeneration.
~*adj.* Also **col·loi·dal** (kə-loid′l, kŏ-). Of, pertaining to, or having the nature of a colloid. [French *colloïde* : COLL(O)- + -OID.]

col·lop (kŏl′əp) *n.* **1.** A small portion or slice, especially of meat. **2.** A roll of flesh on the body. [Middle English *coloppe, colhoppe*†.]

col·lo·qui·al (kə-lō′kwē-əl) *adj. Abbr.* **coll., colloq. 1.** Characteristic of or appropriate to the spoken language or to writing that seeks its effect; informal in diction or style of expression. **2.** Pertaining to conversation; conversational. [From COLLOQUY.] **—col·lo·qui·al·ly** *adv.* **—col·lo·qui·al·ness** *n.*

col·lo·qui·al·ism (kə-lō′kwē-əl-ĭz′əm) *n. Abbr.* **coll., colloq. 1.** Colloquial style or quality. **2.** A colloquial expression.

col·lo·qui·um (kə-lō′kwē-əm) *n., pl.* **-ums** or **-quia** (-kwē-ə). An academic seminar on some broad field of study, usually led by a different lecturer at each meeting. [Latin *colloquium,* COLLOQUY.]

col·lo·quy (kŏl′ə-kwē) *n., pl.* **-quies. 1.** A conversation, especially one that is formal or mannered. **2.** A written dialogue. [Latin *colloquium,* conversation, from *colloquī,* to converse : *com-,* together + *loquī,* to speak.]

col·lo·type (kŏl′ə-tīp′) *n.* **1.** A printing process utilizing a glass plate with a gelatin surface carrying the image to be reproduced. Also called "photogelatin process." **2.** A print made by this process. [COLLO- + -TYPE.]

col·lude (kə-lo͞od′) *intr.v.* **-luded, -luding, -ludes.** To be in collusion; act together secretly. [Latin *collūdere* : *com-,* together + *lūdere,* to play, deceive, from *lūdus,* game.] **—col·lud·er** *n.*

col·lu·sion (kə-lo͞o′zhən) *n.* **1.** Secret agreement between two or more persons for a deceitful or fraudulent purpose. **2.** A secret agreement between the parties in a lawsuit to obtain a specific verdict. —See Synonyms at **conspiracy.** [Middle English *collucioun,*

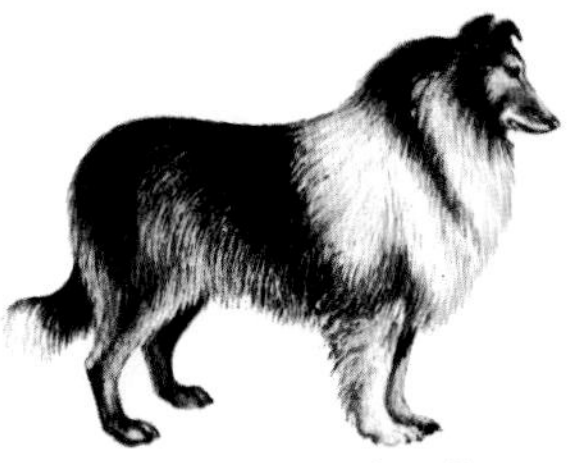

collie *The initiative and intelligence of the collie—one of the oldest breeds of sheepdog—make it a popular working dog for farmers. This is a rough collie, named for its thick shaggy coat.*

from Old French *collusion,* from Latin *collūsiō* (stem *collūsiōn-*), from *collūdere,* COLLUDE.]

col·lu·sive (kə-lōō′sĭv, -zĭv) *adj.* Secretly arranged for fraudulent purposes. —**col·lu·sive·ly** *adv.* —**col·lu·sive·ness** *n.*

col·lu·vi·um (kə-lōō′vē-əm) *n., pl.* **-via** (-vē-ə) or **-ums.** A loose deposit of rock debris accumulated at the base of a cliff or slope. [Latin *colluvium, colluviō,* collection of filth, washings, from *colluere,* to wash thoroughly, wash out : *com-* (intensive) + *lavere,* to wash.] —**col·lu·vi·al** *adj.*

col·lyr·i·um (kə-lĭr′ē-əm) *n., pl.* **-ums** or **-ia** (-ē-ə). A medicinal lotion applied to the eye; eyewash. [Latin, from Greek *kollurion,* poultice, diminutive of *kollura†,* roll of bread.]

col·ly·wob·bles (kŏl′ē-wŏb′əlz) *pl.n. Informal.* **1.** A pain in the stomach, especially due to nervousness. **2.** A state of nervous apprehension. [19th century : fanciful coinage, from COLIC + WOBBLE.]

colo-, col- *prefix.* Indicates the colon; for example, **colostomy, colitis.** [New Latin, from Latin *colon,* COLON (intestine).]

col·o·bo·ma (kŏl′ə-bō′mə) *n., pl.* **-ma·ta** (-mə-tə). A lesion or fissure of the eye or eyelid. [New Latin, from Greek *kolobōma,* a mutilation, from *koloboun,* to mutilate, from *kolobos,* cut, docked.]

col·o·bus (kŏl′ə-bəs) *n.* Any Old World monkey of the genus *Colobus* of West and Central Africa, having a long tail, long silky fur, and short thumbs. [New Latin, from Greek *kolobos,* cut short (referring to its reduced thumb).]

col·o·cynth (kŏl′ə-sĭnth′) *n.* **1.** A vine, *Citrullus colocynthis,* of the Mediterranean region, bearing a small, bitter fruit. **2.** The fruit of this plant, used as a cathartic. Also called "bitter apple." [Latin *colocynthis,* from Greek *kolokunthis,* from *kolokunthē†,* round gourd.]

co·log·a·rithm (kō-lŏg′ə-rĭth′əm) *n.* The logarithm of the reciprocal of a number, expressed with a positive mantissa.

co·logne (kə-lōn′) *n.* A scented liquid made of alcohol and various fragrant oils. Also called "cologne water," "eau de cologne." [French *eau de cologne,* "water of COLOGNE."]

Cologne. See **Köln.**

Co·lom·bi·a (kə-lŭm′bē-ə). *Abbr.* **Col.** Country in northwest South America. It was settled by the Spaniards in 1510. In 1740 it became part of the viceroyalty of New Granada, which was liberated from Spain by Simón Bolívar (1819). By 1903 Colombia had its present boundaries and had suffered 27 civil wars. Land and other reforms were slow, and strife led to military intervention (1953). However, agreements in 1957 and 1974 left Colombia a fragile democracy. The country, formerly dependent on coffee, is diversifying, and coffee now accounts for about half its exports. With industrialization Colombia has become an importer instead of an exporter of oil. It also has large reserves of coal and emeralds. Area, 1,138,914 square kilometers (439,735 square miles). Population, 27,500,000. Capital, Bogotá. —**Co·lom·bi·an** *adj. & n.*

Co·lom·bo (kə-lŭm′bō). Capital of Sri Lanka, a port on the west coast of the island near the mouth of the Kelani River. It is noted for gem cutting and ivory carving.

Colombo, Cristoforo. See Christopher **Columbus.**

co·lon¹ (kō′lən) *n., pl.* **-lons** or **-la** (-lä) (for sense 2). **1. a.** A punctuation mark (:) used after a word introducing a quotation, explanation, example, or series, and after the salutation of a formal letter. **b.** The sign (:) used between numbers or groups of numbers, as in

ratios (1:2), biblical references (Genesis 4:1-5), or expressions of time (8:45 A.M.). **2.** A section of a rhythmical period in Greek and Latin verse, consisting of two to six feet and having one principal accent. [Latin *colon,* unit of verses, from Greek *kōlon,* "limb."]

co·lon² (kō′lən) *n., pl.* **-lons** or **-la** (-lə). The section of the large intestine extending from the cecum to the rectum. [Middle English, from Latin, from Greek *kolont,* large intestine.] —**co·lon·ic** (kə-lŏn′ĭk) *adj.*

co·lón (kə-lōn′) *n., pl.* **-lóns** (-lōnz′) or *Spanish* **colónes** (kə-lō′nās′). **1. a.** The basic monetary unit of Costa Rica, equal to 100 céntimos. **b.** The basic monetary unit of El Salvador, equal to 100 centavos. **2.** A coin or note worth one colón. See feature at **currency.** [Spanish *colón,* after *Cristóbal Colón,* Christopher Columbus.]

Colón, Archipiélago de. See **Galápagos Islands.**

Colón, Cristóbal. See Christopher **Columbus.**

colo·nel (kûr′nəl) *n. Abbr.* **Col. 1. a.** An officer in the U.S. Army, Air Force, or Marine Corps ranking immediately above a lieutenant colonel and below a brigadier general. **b.** An officer of similar rank in other military or paramilitary organizations. **2.** An honorary title awarded by some states of the United States. [French, from Italian *colonnello,* "commander of a column," diminutive of *colonna,* column (of soldiers), from Latin *columna.*] —**colo·nel·cy, colo·nel·ship** *n.*

Colonel Blimp (blĭmp) *n.* A pompous reactionary, especially an army officer or government official. [After *Colonel Blimp,* character in cartoons by Sir David Low (1891–1963).]

co·lo·ni·al (kə-lō′nē-əl) *adj. Abbr.* **col. 1.** Of, pertaining to, possessing, or inhabiting a colony or colonies. **2.** *Often* **Colonial. a.** Of or pertaining to the 13 British colonies that became the original United States of America. **b.** Of or pertaining to the colonial period in the United States. **3.** *Often* **Colonial.** Designating an architectural style prevalent in the American colonies in the 17th and 18th centuries. —*n.* An inhabitant of a colony, especially a settler or one descended from settlers. —**co·lo·ni·al·ly** *adv.*

co·lo·ni·al·ism (kə-lō′nē-ə-lĭz′əm) *n.* A policy by which a nation maintains or extends its control over foreign dependencies. —**co·lo·ni·al·ist** *n. & adj.*

colonic irrigation *n.* The washing out of the contents of the large intestine by injecting large quantities of fluid through the rectum.

col·o·nist (kŏl′ə-nĭst) *n.* **1.** An original settler or founder of a colony. **2.** An inhabitant of a colony.

col·o·ni·za·tion (kŏl′ə-nə-zā′shən) *n.* The act or process of establishing a colony or colonies.

col·o·nize (kŏl′ə-nīz′) *v.* **-nized, -nizing, -nizes.** —*tr.* **1. a.** To establish a colony or colonies in. **b.** To migrate to and settle in; occupy as a colony. **c.** To establish in a colony. **2.** To register party supporters as votes in (a district) so as to influence an election there. —*intr.* **1.** To set up or form a colony. **2.** To settle in a colony or colonies. —**col·o·niz·er** *n.*

col·on·nade (kŏl′ə-nād′) *n. Architecture.* A series of columns placed at regular intervals. [French, from Italian *colonnato,* from *colonna,* column, from Latin *columna.*] —**col·on·nad·ed** *adj.*

col·o·ny (kŏl′ə-nē) *n., pl.* **-nies. 1.** A group of emigrants or their descendants who settle in a distant land but remain subject to or intimately connected with the parent country. **2.** A territory thus settled. **3.** *Abbr.* **col.** Any region politically controlled by a distant country; a dependency. **4. Colony.** Any of the 13 British colonies that became the original United States of America. **5. a.** A group of people with the same interests or ethnic origin, concentrated in a particular area. **b.** The area or place occupied by such a group. **6.** An area or institution in which a specified group of people is kept apart from others: *a leper colony; a penal colony.* **7.** *Biology.* **a.** A group of the same kind of animals or plants living or growing together. **b.** A group of individuals structurally connected and functioning as a single unit, as in sponges and corals. **8.** *Microbiology.* A visible growth of microorganisms in a nutrient medium. [Middle English *colonie,* from Old French, from Latin *colōnia,* farm, settlement, from *colōnus,* farmer, settler, from *colere,* to cultivate, inhabit.]

col·o·phon (kŏl′ə-fŏn′, -fən) *n.* **1.** An inscription placed at the end of a book, giving facts pertaining to its publication. **2.** A publisher's emblem or trademark placed usually on the title page of a book. [Latin *colophōn,* from Greek *kolophōn,* summit, finishing.]

co·loph·o·ny (kə-lŏf′ə-nē) *n.* **Rosin** (*see*). [Latin *Colophonia rēsina,* "resin of *Colophon*" (ancient city in Lydia).]

col·or (kŭl′ər) *n.* Also *chiefly British* **col·our.** *Abbr.* **col. 1.** That aspect of things that is caused by differing qualities of the light reflected or emitted by them. It may be defined in terms of the observer (sense a) or by the light (sense b): **a.** The appearance of objects or light sources described in terms of the individual's perception of them, involving hue, lightness, and saturation for objects, and hue, brightness, and saturation for light sources. **b.** The characteristics of light by which the individual is made aware of objects or light sources through the receptors of the eye, described in terms of dominant frequency, luminance, and purity. **2.** Any of the gradations of this aspect, conventionally divided into shades as, for example, red, green, or brown. See **primary color, secondary color. 3.** A dye, pigment, paint, or other substance that imparts color. **4. a.** A redness of complexion, considered as a sign of normal health. **b.** A reddening of the face, as from indignation or embarrassment. **5.** The skin pigmentation of a person not classed as a Caucasian, especially that of a Negro. **6. colors. a.** An identifying

colobus *Unlike other primates, these African monkeys have almost no thumb. They spend most of their lives in trees, feeding on leaves, and descend to the ground only to lick salt from the earth.*

COLOMBIA

Caribbean Sea

70° W

Barranquilla
Cartagena

CANAL
ZONE

PANAMA

PACIFIC

OCEAN

Medellín

Manizales

Cúcuta

VENEZUELA

10° N

Bucaramanga

BOGOTÁ

Meta

C O L O M B I A

Cali

Equator

Caqueta

ECUADOR

PERU

BRAZIL

400 Km

200 Miles

flag or banner, as of a country, organization, or military unit. **b.** A ceremony of lowering or raising military colors. **7. colors. a.** Any distinguishing symbol, badge, ribbon, or mark: *the colors of a college.* **b.** *British.* Such a badge or ribbon awarded for representing one's school, for example at sport. **8.** Character or nature: *appear in one's true colors.* **9.** Outward, often deceptive, appearance. Used chiefly in the phrase *under color of.* **10.** Appearance of truth or authenticity; plausibility. **11. colors.** An opinion or position: *Stick to your colors.* **12.** Variety of effect or expression. **13.** Picturesque and authentic detail, as in a film or novel, for example. **14.** Vitality; exuberance: *She loved the color of Mediterranean life.* **15.** In art, the use or effect of color as distinct from form. **16.** *Music.* Tonal quality. **17.** *Printing.* The amount, shade, or tone of ink used. **18.** *Law.* An apparent or prima-facie right, pretext, or ground. **19.** A particle or bit of gold found in auriferous gravel or sand. **20.** *Physics.* A hypothetical property associated with quark theory. Each quark may exist in any of three states designated red, blue, and green. The combination of certain color and quark types produces the various baryons and mesons. **—with flying colors.** With great success.
∼*v.* **colored, -oring, -ors.** —*tr.* **1.** To impart color to or change the color of. **2.** To give a distinctive character or quality to; modify or influence. **3.** To misrepresent, especially by distortion or exaggeration. —*intr.* **1.** To take on color or become colored. **2.** To change color. **3.** To become red in the face, as from embarrassment or indignation. [Middle English, from Old French, from Latin *color.*] **—col·or** *adj.* **—col·or·er** *n.*

col·or·a·ble (kŭl′ər-ə-bəl) *adj.* **1.** Seemingly true or genuine. **2.** Feigned; pretended. **—col·or·a·bil·i·ty, col·or·a·ble·ness** *n.* **—col·or·a·bly** *adv.*

Col·o·ra·do[1] (kŏl′ə-rä′dō, -răd′ə). State in the west-central United States, where the Rocky Mts. meet the Great Plains. The Rockies contain reserves of molybdenum, uranium, and oil. Denver is the capital.

Colorado[2]. River in the southwestern United States. It rises in the Rocky Mts. of Colorado and flows 2,336 kilometers (1,450 miles) southwest through Utah and Arizona, reaching the sea in Mexico at the Gulf of California. It supplies the Hoover Dam.

Colorado beetle *n.* A small black-and-yellow striped beetle, *Leptinotarsa decemlineata,* native to Central America but now widespread in Europe, that is a major pest of potatoes. Also called "Colorado potato beetle," "potato beetle." [After COLORADO, where it first became a major pest of potatoes.]

Colorado Springs. A city of central Colorado, at the foot of Pikes Peak. It is a year-round vacation center and health resort and has thriving industries. The U.S. Air Force Academy is nearby.

col·or·ant (kŭl′ər-ənt) *n.* Anything that colors or modifies the color of something else, especially a dye, pigment, ink, or paint.

col·or·a·tion (kŭl′ə-rā′shən) *n.* Arrangement of colors.

col·or·a·tu·ra (kŭl′ər-ə-to͝or′ə, -tyo͝or′ə) *n.* **1.** Florid ornamental trills and runs in vocal music. **2.** Music characterized by such ornamentation. **3.** A singer, especially a soprano, specializing in this. [Obsolete Italian, "coloring," from Late Latin *colōrātūra,* from Latin *colōrāre,* to COLOR.]

col·or-blind (kŭl′ər-blīnd′) *adj.* **1.** Partially or totally unable to distinguish certain colors. See **deuteranopia, protanopia, tritanopia.** **2. a.** Not subject to racial prejudices. **b.** Not recognizing racial distinctions. **—color blindness** *n.*

col·or·breed (kŭl′ər-brēd′) *tr.v.* **-bred** (-brĕd′), **breeding, -breeds.** To breed (plants or animals) selectively to produce new or desired colors. **—col·or·bred** *adj.*

color code *n.* A method of distinguishing items, such as parts, components, wires, or resistors, using distinctive colors for identification. **—col·or-cod·ed** (kŭl′ər-kō′dĭd) *adj.*

col·ored (kŭl′ərd) *adj.* **1.** Having color. **2.** Distorted or biased, as by irrelevant or incorrect information.
∼*n. Often* **Colored.** In South Africa, a person of racially mixed descent belonging to a population grouping that is distinct from Asians, blacks, and whites.

col·or·fast (kŭl′ər-făst′, -fäst′) *adj.* Having color that will not run or fade with washing or wear. Said of fabrics. **—col·or·fast·ness** *n.*

color filter *n.* A photographic filter used to increase contrast or in taking photographs through haze.

col·or·ful (kŭl′ər-fəl) *adj.* **1.** Full of color; abounding in colors. **2.** Characterized by rich variety; vivid; distinctive. **—col·or·ful·ly** *adj.* **—col·or·ful·ness** *n.*

color guard *n.* The ceremonial escort for the flag, as of a country or an organization.

col·or·if·ic (kŭl′ə-rĭf′ĭk) *adj.* **1.** Producing or imparting color. **2.** Of or pertaining to color.

col·or·im·e·ter (kŭl′ə-rĭm′ə-tər) *n.* **1.** Any of various instruments used to determine or specify colors, as by comparison with spectroscopic or visual standards. **2.** An instrument that measures the concentration of a known solution constituent by comparison with colors of standard solutions of that constituent. **—col·or·i·met·ric** (kŭl′ər-ə-mĕt′rĭk) *adj.* **—col·or·i·met·ri·cal·ly** *adv.* **—col·or·im·e·try** *n.*

color index *n.* **1.** *Astronomy.* The numerical difference between the apparent photographic magnitude and the apparent visual magnitude of a star, as an indication of its color and temperature. **2.** *Geology.* The percentage of dark and colored minerals in a rock, calculated on the basis of its total mineral content.

col·or·ing (kŭl′ər-ĭng) *n.* **1.** The art, manner, or process of applying color. **2.** Any substance used to color something. **3.** Appearance with regard to color. **4.** The arrangement of or patterns created by colors. **5.** A false or misleading appearance.

col·or·ist (kŭl′ər-ĭst) *n.* An artist skilled in achieving special effects with color. **—col·or·is·tic** *adj.*

col·or·less (kŭl′ər-lĭs) *adj.* **1.** Without color. **2.** Weak or dull in color; pallid. **3.** Lacking animation, variety, or distinction; uninteresting; dull. **4.** Without bias; neutral; objective. **—col·or·less·ly** *adv.* **—col·or·less·ness** *n.*

color phase *n.* **1.** A seasonal variation in the color of the fur or feathers of some animals, especially those living in arctic regions. **2.** Variation in the color of animals of the same species.

color scheme *n.* An arrangement of colors, especially one planned for a certain effect, as in interior decorating.

Co·los·sae (kə-lŏs′-ē). An ancient city in western Asia Minor, the seat of a congregation to which St. Paul addressed the Epistle to the Colossians. **—Co·los·sian** (kə-lŏsh′ən) *adj.* & *n.*

co·los·sal (kə-lŏs′əl) *adj.* **1.** Enormous in size or extent; gigantic. **2.** *Informal.* Great in degree; enormous: *a colossal waste of time.* —See Synonyms at **enormous.** [French, from Latin *colossus,* COLOSSUS.] **—co·los·sal·ly** *adv.*

colosseum. Variant of **coliseum.**

Col·os·se·um, Col·i·se·um (kŏl′ə-sē′əm). An amphitheater in Rome built by Vespasian and Titus (A.D. *c.* 75–80). [Latin, from *colossēus,* huge, from *colossus,* COLOSSUS.] See feature, next page.

Co·los·sians (kə-lŏsh′ənz, -lŏs′ē-ənz) *n.* *Used with a singular verb. Abbr.* **Col.** A book of the New Testament, an epistle of Saint Paul to the Christians of Colossae.

co·los·sus (kə-lŏs′əs) *n., pl.* **-lossi** (-lŏs′ī′) or **-suses. 1.** A huge statue. **2.** Any person or thing of outstanding size or importance. [Latin, from Greek *kolossos,* probably of Mediterranean origin.]

Colossus of Rhodes (rōdz). A huge statue of Apollo, about 36 meters (120 feet) high, built about 280 B.C. and later destroyed by an earthquake. It was set at the entrance to the harbor of Rhodes and was one of the Seven Wonders of the World.

co·los·to·my (kə-lŏs′tə-mē) *n., pl.* **-mies.** The surgical construction of an artificial excretory opening from the colon onto the surface of the abdomen. [COLO- + -STOMY.]

co·los·trum (kə-lŏs′trəm) *n.* The first secretion of the mammary glands immediately after childbirth, lasting for a few days and consisting of serum, white blood cells, and antibodies. Also called "foremilk." [Latin *colostrum, colostra*†.]

colour. *Chiefly British.* Variant of **color.**

-colous *suffix.* Indicates habitat in or among; for example, **arenicolous.** [Latin *-cola,* inhabitant.]

col·pi·tis (kŏl-pī′tĭs) *n.* **Vaginitis** *(see).* [New Latin : Greek *kolpos,* bosom, womb, vagina + -ITIS.]

col·por·tage (kŏl′pôr′tĭj, -pōr′tĭj) *n.* The work of a colporteur.

col·por·teur (kŏl′pôr′tər, -pōr′tər) *n.* A peddler of devotional literature. [French, from Old French *comporteur* (influenced by *col,* neck), from *comporter,* to peddle, COMPORT.]

col·po·scope (kŏl′pə-skōp′) *n.* A speculum that is used to examine the tissues of the vagina and the cervix of the uterus. [Greek *kolpos,* womb, vagina + -SCOPE.] **—col·pos·co·py** (kŏl-pŏs′kə-pē) *n.*

colt (kōlt) *n.* **1.** A young male horse. **2. a.** A youthful or inexperienced person; a novice or beginner. **b.** *Sports.* An inexperienced player; a player on a junior team. **3.** A rope whip formerly used for shipboard discipline. [Middle English *colt,* Old English *colt,* young ass or camel, perhaps from Scandinavian; akin to Swedish dialectal *kult, kulter*†, half-grown animal, boy.]

Colt *n.* A trademark for a type of revolver invented by Samuel Colt.

Colt (kōlt) **Samuel** (1814–62). U.S. firearms inventor and manufacturer. He developed the revolver, the first single-barrel, multishot pistol (1836). Colt used assembly-line techniques, interchangeable parts, and quality control to efficiently manufacture the guns, which played an important part in the settling of the West.

col·ter, coul·ter (kōl′tər) *n.* A blade or wheel on a plow for making vertical cuts in the sod. [Middle English *culter, colter,* from Old English *culter* and Old French *coltre,* both from Latin *culter,* knife, plowshare.]

colt·ish (kōl′tĭsh) *adj.* **1.** Of or like a colt. **2.** Lively and playful; frisky. **—colt·ish·ly** *adv.* **—colt·ish·ness** *n.*

Col·trane (kōl′trān′, kōl′-), **John William** (1912–67). U.S. musician and composer. He brought his mastery of the saxophone to several jazz bands. His controversial, occasionally violent style and his incorporation of the music of India into his work made him a respected and much-imitated musician.

colts·foot (kōlts′fo͝ot′) *n., pl.* **-foots.** A plant, *Tussilago farfara,* native to the Old World, having yellow, daisylike flowers that appear before the heart-shaped leaves. [From the shape of its leaves.]

col·u·brid (kŏl′ə-brĭd, kŏl′yə-) *n.* Any of numerous chiefly nonvenomous snakes of the family Colubridae, which includes the garter snake.
∼*adj.* Of or belonging to the Colubridae. [New Latin *Colubridae,* from Latin *coluber,* snake.]

col·u·brine (kŏl′ə-brīn′, kŏl′yə-) *adj.* **1.** Of or like a snake. **2.** Of or belonging to the Colubrinae, a subfamily of nonvenomous colubrid snakes. [Latin *colubrīnus,* from *coluber,* snake.]

co·lu·go (kə-lo͞o′gō) *n., pl.* **-gos.** A mammal, the **flying lemur** *(see).* [Malay.]

Co·lum·ba (kə-lŭm′bə) *n.* A constellation in the Southern Hemisphere near Caelum and Puppis. Also called the "Dove." [New Latin, from Latin *columba,* dove.]

Columba, Saint (521–97). Irish saint and missionary. He founded a

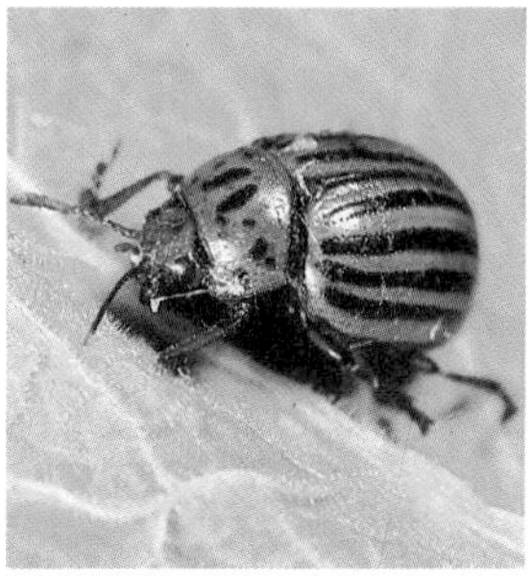

Colorado beetle *A devastating pest of potato crops, this insect spread eastward as the settlers moved west across the United States.*

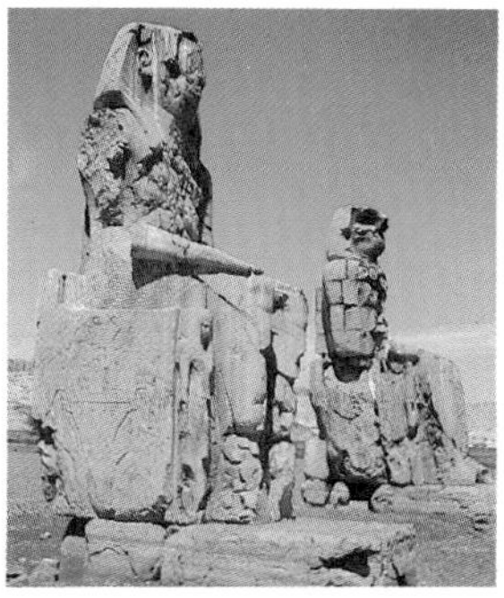

colossus *Some 20 meters (70 feet) tall, these Colossi of Memnon are statues of the Egyptian pharaoh Amenhotep III.*

PRONUNCIATION KEY

ă, pat; ā, pay; âr, care;
ä, father, are; b, bib;
ch, church; d, deed; ĕ, pet;
ē, be; f, fife; g, gag; h, hat;
hw, which; ĭ, pit; ī, pie;
îr, pier; j, judge; k, kick;
l, lid, needle; m, mum;
n, no, sudden; ng, thing;
ŏ, pot; ō, toe; ô, paw, for;
oi, noise; ou, out; o͝o, book;
o͞o, boot; p, pop; r, roar;
s, sauce; sh, ship, dish;
t, tight; th, thin, path;
th, this, bathe; ŭ, cut; ûr, fur;
v, valve; w, with; y, yes;
z, zebra, size; zh, vision;
ə, about, item, edible,
gallop, circus, peaceful

IN FOREIGN WORDS:

ȧ, *Fr.* ami; œ, *Fr.* feu, *Ger.* schön; ü, *Fr.* tu, *Ger.* über;
KH, *Ger.* ich, *Scot.* loch;
N, *Fr.* bon; y′, *Fr.* Compiègne

STRESS MARKS:

Primary stress: ′
in·cite′ (ĭn-sīt′)
Secondary stress: ′
in′sight′ (ĭn′sīt′)

Colosseum

THEATER OF DEATH WHERE 2,000 GLADIATORS MIGHT FIGHT ON A SINGLE ROMAN HOLIDAY
The Colosseum remains as a monument to the ingenuity of Roman engineering

The Colosseum is a four-storied complex of arches and arcades 48 meters (157 feet) high, with 80 arches around the exterior. It was constructed with a soundness that has endured for almost two millennia and is a striking monument to the skills of Roman engineers.

Overall the Colosseum is 189 meters (620 feet) long and 156 meters (513 feet) across, by far the largest of the Roman amphitheaters that, despite centuries of vandalism, still stand. Its present name was not used until the Middle Ages; it derives not from the amphitheater's dimensions but perhaps from those of the colossal statue of Nero that used to stand nearby.

Mortal combat between men, or men and beasts, was the dramatic form most often staged in the vast Roman amphitheaters. Gladiatorial combat was intro-

duced in 264 B.C., when the consul Decimus Junius Brutus held games for his father's funeral in the tradition of the ancient Etruscan funeral rites. These fights to the death provided blood to give strength to the deceased. Contests gradually became celebrations of imperial Roman victories but ostensibly remained tributes to the dead until Julius Caesar's games of 46 B.C.

Gladiators drawn from the ranks of slaves, criminals, and prisoners of war were trained in special schools and then made to fight lions, panthers, bears, bulls, and other beasts that had been goaded into savagery by fear and hunger.

The emperor Nero (A.D. 37–68) sent Christians into the arena to face wild beasts, but such persecution was

unusual until the 2nd century A.D., when it became commonplace.

Gladiatorial combats and the "hunting" of wild animals were first held in a closed-off part of the Forum, the public marketplace. From 80 B.C. stone buildings were constructed throughout the Roman world, from Caerleon in Wales to Aspendos in Turkey, to house the increasingly popular spectacles. By the late 1st century A.D., when the Colosseum was built in Rome, they were held once or twice a week as a diversion for the people. Five thousand wild animals were killed on the day in A.D. 80 when the Colosseum was inaugurated by the emperor Titus, son of its originator Vespasian. On a single public holiday 2,000 gladiators might be scheduled to fight.

STRUCTURE OF THE COLOSSEUM *A Roman amphitheater was usually built into the side of a hill, which gave structural support. The Colosseum is unusual in being freestanding and is a story higher than any other. The arena was open to the sky with only a giant canvas awning to shield it when necessary from the sun. Cells beneath the arena accommodated beasts and performers. The spectators entered through the ground-floor arches, the gladiators and the emperor through underground corridors. The imperial throne, set on a podium and surrounded by seats for officers of state, was just behind the wall, 4.5 meters (15 feet) high, that encircles the arena.*

church and monastery on the island of Iona (563). This became the center of evangelical activity in Scotland, from which the northern Picts were converted.

col·um·bar·i·um (kŏl′əm-bâr′ē-əm) *n., pl.* **-ia** (-ē-ə). **1. a.** A vault with niches for urns containing ashes of the dead. **b.** Any of the niches in such a vault. **2.** A dovecote. [Middle English *columba(i)re,* dovecote, from Latin *columbārium,* from *columba,* dove.]

Co·lum·bi·a¹ (kə-lŭm′bē-ə) *n. Poetic.* A feminine personification of the United States. [After Christopher COLUMBUS.]

Columbia². River in western Canada and the northwestern United States. It rises in British Columbia and flows 1,950 kilometers (1,210 miles) southwest to the Pacific in Oregon. For much of its length it forms the border between the states of Washington and Oregon.

Columbia³. The capital of South Carolina, in the central part of the state on the Congaree River. It is an important trade and commercial center in the heart of a rich farm region. Most of the original city was burned on February 17, 1865, by Gen. William T. Sherman's soldiers.

Columbia, District of. See **District of Columbia.**

col·um·bine (kŏl′əm-bīn′) *n.* Any of several plants of the genus *Aquilegia,* having variously colored flowers with five conspicuously spurred petals. [Middle English, from Medieval Latin *(herba) columbīna,* from Latin *columbīnus,* dovelike (from the resemblance of the inverted flower to a cluster of five doves), from *columba,* dove.]

Columbine *n.* In pantomime, the partner or sweetheart of Harlequin.

co·lum·bite (kə-lŭm′bīt′) *n.* A black mineral, essentially (Fe,

Mn)(Nb, Ta)₂O₆, used as a source of niobium and tantalum. [CO-LUMB(IUM) + -ITE.]

co·lum·bi·um (kə-lŭm′bē-əm) *n. Symbol* **Cb** The element **niobium** *(see).* [New Latin, after *Columbia* (name of a personification of the United States), because it was discovered in a mineral found in Connecticut.] —**co·lum·bic** *adj.*

Co·lum·bus (kə-lŭm′bəs). The capital of Ohio, in the central part of the state, on the Scioto River. It is a port of entry and a major industrial and trade center in a rich farm region. Its early growth was stimulated in the early 1800's by the Ohio and Erie Canal, the National Road, and the arrival of the railroad.

Columbus, Christopher (1451–1506). *Italian* **Cristoforo Co·lom·bo** (kō-lōm′bō). *Spanish* **Cristóbal Co·lón** (kō-lôn′). Italian explorer in the service of Spain, the first modern European to discover America. Believing that the earth was not flat, Columbus concluded that it must be possible to reach the east by sailing westward. He reached the Bahamas (1492) and discovered Puerto Rico, Jamaica, and other islands (1493–96). On a third voyage (1498–1500) he reached Trinidad and the mouth of the Orinoco in South America. Having set up colonies in the New World, he was charged with mismanaging them and returned to Spain in chains (1500). On a fourth voyage (1502–04), he landed at Honduras, Costa Rica, and Panama.

col·u·mel·la (kŏl′yə-mĕl′ə, kŏl′ə-) *n., pl.* **-mellae** (-mĕl′ē). Any of several small, columnlike structures in various plants and animals, such as the central part of the sporangium of certain fungi and mosses. [New Latin, from Latin, diminutive of *columna,* COLUMN.] —**col·u·mel·lar** *adj.*

col·umn (kŏl′əm) *n. Abbr.* **col. 1.** A pillar consisting of a base, a cylindrical shaft, and a capital, used as a support or standing alone as a monument. **2.** Anything resembling a pillar in form or function: *a column of smoke.* **3.** Any of two or more vertical sections of printed lines lying side by side on a page and separated by a rule or blank space. **4.** A section of a newspaper or magazine that regularly contains an article by a particular writer or is devoted to a particular subject: *the personal column.* **5.** A vertical row of numbers on a page. **6.** A formation, as of troops, vehicles, ships, or aircraft, in which the elements follow one behind the other. **7.** *Botany.* An organ in an orchid flower formed by the fusion of stamens and style. [Middle English *columpne,* from Old French *colomne,* from Latin *columna.*] **—co·lum·nar** (kə-lŭm′nər), **col·umned** (kŏl′əmd) *adj.*

co·lum·ni·a·tion (kə-lŭm′nē-ā′shən) *n.* The use or arrangement of columns in a building.

column inch *n.* A unit used to measure advertising space in newspapers or magazines, one column wide and one inch deep.

col·um·nist (kŏl′əm-nĭst, -ə-mĭst) *n.* A writer of a regular column in a newspaper or periodical.

co·lure (kə-lo͝or′, -lo͝or′, kō′-) *n. Astronomy.* Either of two great circles passing through the celestial poles on the celestial sphere: one passing through the equinoxes (*equinoctial colure*) and the other through the solstices (*solstitial colure*). [Middle English, from Late Latin, from Greek *kolouros,* "dock-tailed," truncated (because the view of the lower part of the circles is cut short) : *kolos,* docked + *oura,* tail.]

col·za (kŏl′zə, kōl′-) *n.* A plant, **rape** *(see).* [French, from Dutch *koolzaad,* "cabbage seed."]

COM (kŏm) *n.* A process that enables computer output to be presented directly in the form of photographic film or fiche. [*C*omputer *O*utput on *M*icrofilm.]

com– *prefix.* Indicates with, together, jointly; for example, **commeasure, commingle.** [In borrowed Latin compounds, *com-* indicates: 1. With, together, joint, jointly, mutually, collectively, as in **compose, compact.** 2. Altogether, comprehensively, inclusively, intensively, as in **comfort, combust.** 3. Same, similar, as in **concord, consubstantial.** 4. Together in mind, mentally, as in **compute, comprehend.** (The semantic function of *com-* is often so indistinct as to be indefinable, as in **concave.**) Before *l* and *r, com-* is assimilated to *col-* and *cor-;* before *h, gn,* and usually before vowels, it is reduced to *co-* (hence English **co-**); before all other consonants except *b, p,* and *m,* it becomes *con-. Com-* is the preverbal form of the Old Latin preposition *com,* which in classical Latin became *cum,* with.]

com. 1. comedy; comic. **2.** commerce; commercial. **3.** committee.

Com. 1. commander. **2.** commission; commissioner. **3.** committee. **4.** commodore. **5.** communist.

co·ma¹ (kō′mə) *n., pl.* **-mas.** A state of deep, prolonged unconsciousness, usually the result of injury, disease, or poison. [New Latin, from Greek *kōma,* deep sleep, lethargy.]

coma² *n., pl.* **-mae** (-mē). **1.** *Astronomy.* The nebulous luminescent cloud containing the nucleus and constituting the major portion of the head of a comet. **2.** *Botany.* A tuft of hairs, as on some seeds. **3.** *Optics.* The distorted image of a point source, appearing as a diffuse, pear-shaped spot. It is the result of errors in an optical system. [Latin, hair, from Greek *komē*†.] **—co·mal** *adj.*

Co·ma Ber·e·ni·ces (kō′mə bĕr′ə-nī′sēz) *n.* A constellation in the northern sky near Boötes and Leo. It contains the coma cluster of galaxies. Also called "Berenice's Hair."

Co·man·che (kə-măn′chē) *n., pl.* **-ches** or collectively **Comanche. 1.** A member of a Uto-Aztecan-speaking North American Indian people, formerly ranging over the western plains from Wyoming to Texas, now living in Oklahoma. **2.** The language of this people. **—Co·man·che** *adj.*

Co·man·che·an (kə-măn′chē-ən) *adj.* Of, belonging to, or designating the geologic time, system of rocks, or sedimentary deposits of the Mesozoic era between the Jurassic and the Upper Cretaceous. *~n.* The Comanchean period. [After *Comanche,* a county in Texas.]

Co·ma·neci (kōm′ə-nēch), **Nadia** (1961–). Romanian gymnast. She became Olympic champion at the Montreal Olympic Games (1976).

co·mate (kō′māt′) *adj.* Also **co·mose** (-mōs′). *Botany.* Having or resembling a tuft of hairs. [Latin *comātus,* from *coma,* hair, from Greek *komē.*]

co·ma·tose (kō′mə-tōs′, kŏm′ə-) *adj. Pathology.* **1.** Of, pertaining to, or affected with coma; unconscious. **2.** Lethargic or torpid. **—co·ma·tose·ly** *adv.*

co·mat·u·lid (kə-măch′o͝o-lĭd) *n.* Also **co·mat·u·la** (-lə) *pl.* **-lae** (-lē′). Any of several marine invertebrates of the order Crinoidea, including the feather stars, that are attached to a surface by a stalk when young but are free-swimming as adults. [New Latin *Comatulidae* (former designation), from Late Latin *comātulus,* with neatly curled hair, from Latin *comātus,* having hair, COMATE.]

comb (kōm) *n.* **1.** A thin, toothed strip of plastic, bone, rubber, or other material, used to smooth, arrange, or fasten the hair. **2.** Something resembling a comb in shape or use, such as: **a.** A card for dressing and cleansing wool or other fibers. **b.** A toothed part, as in a shearing device, guiding hair or fleece toward the blade. **3.** A **currycomb** *(see).* **4.** The fleshy crest or ridge that grows on the crown of the head of domestic fowl and other birds and is most prominent in the male. **5.** Something suggesting a fowl's comb in appearance or position. **6.** A **honeycomb** *(see).*
~v. **combed, combing, combs.** *—tr.* **1.** To dress or arrange with or as if with a comb. **2.** To card (wool or other fibers). **3.** To search thoroughly; look through. *—intr.* To roll and break. Used of waves. **—comb out.** To isolate and get rid of (something unwanted). [Middle English *comb,* Old English *comb, camb.*]

comb. 1. combination. **2.** combining.

com·bat (kəm-băt′, kŏm′băt′) *v.* **-bated, -bating, -bats.** Also *chiefly British* **-batted, -batting.** *—tr.* **1.** To fight against; contend with; oppose in battle. **2.** To oppose vigorously; resist. *—intr.* To engage in fighting; contend; struggle. Used with *with* or *against*: *combat against laziness.* **—**See Synonyms at **oppose.**
~n. (kŏm′băt′). Fighting, especially armed battle; strife. Also used adjectivally: *combat troops.* **—**See Synonyms at **conflict.** [Old French *combattre,* from Vulgar Latin *combattere* (unattested), to fight with : Latin *com-,* with + *battuere,* beat.]

com·bat·ant (kəm-băt′ənt, kŏm′bə-tənt) *n.* One taking part in armed combat. **—com·bat·ant** *adj.*

combat fatigue *n.* A nervous disorder, usually temporary but sometimes leading to a permanent neurosis, brought on by the exhaustion and stress of combat or similar situations, and characterized by deep anxiety, depression, irritability, and other related symptoms. Also called "battle fatigue." Compare **shell shock.**

com·bat·ive (kəm-băt′ĭv) *adj.* Eager or disposed to fight. **—com·bat·ive·ly** *adv.* **—com·bat·ive·ness, com·ba·tiv·i·ty** *n.*

comb·er (kō′mər) *n.* **1.** One that combs. **2.** A long, cresting wave of the sea; breaker.

com·bi·na·tion (kŏm′bə-nā′shən) *n. Abbr.* **comb. 1. a.** The act of combining. **b.** The state of being combined. **2.** Something resulting from combining; a compound; an aggregate: *passed the exam through a combination of luck and hard work.* **3.** An alliance or association of persons or parties for a common purpose. **4.** A sequence of numbers or letters used to open a combination lock. **5.** A one-piece undergarment consisting of an undershirt or chemise and drawers. **6.** *Mathematics.* One or more elements selected from a set without regard to order of selection. **7.** *Chemistry.* The union of two or more compounds, as a result of chemical reaction, to form another compound. **—com·bi·na·tion·al** *adj.*

combination lock *n.* A lock that will open only when its dial is turned through a predetermined sequence of positions identified on the dial face by numbers or letters.

com·bi·na·tive (kŏm′bə-nā′tĭv, kəm-bī′nə-tĭv) *adj.* **1.** Of, pertaining to, or resulting from combination. **2.** Tending, serving, or able to combine.

com·bi·na·to·ri·al (kŏm′bə-nə-tôr′ē-əl, -tōr′-, kəm-bī′nə-) *adj.* **1.** Pertaining to or involving combinations. **2.** *Mathematics.* Pertaining to the arrangement and manipulation of combinations and permutations and mathematical elements in sets: *combinatorial analysis.*

com·bi·na·tor·ics (kŏm′bə-nə-tôr′ĭks, -tōr′-, kəm-bī′nə-) *n.* Combinatorial mathematics.

com·bine (kəm-bīn′) *v.* **-bined, -bining, -bines.** *—tr.* **1.** To bring into a state of unity; join; merge; blend. **2.** To possess or exhibit in combination. *—intr.* **1.** To become united; coalesce. **2.** To join forces for a common purpose; enter into an alliance. **3.** *Chemistry.* To form a chemical compound. **—**See Synonyms at **join, mix.**
~n. (kŏm′bīn′). **1.** An association of persons or firms united for commercial interests, such as control of prices. **2.** A combine harvester. **3.** A combination. [Middle English *combinen,* from Old French *combiner,* from Late Latin *combīnāre* : Latin *com-,* together + *bīnī,* two at a time.] **—com·bin·er** *n.*

com·bine harvester (kŏm′bīn′) *n.* A harvesting machine that cuts, threshes, and cleans grain. Also called "combine."

comb·ings (kō′mĭngz) *pl.n.* Hairs, wool, or other material removed with a comb.

combining form *n. Grammar.* A word element that can form new words by combining with complete words, other combining forms, or sometimes with affixes; for example, **-logy,** as in **gynecology; macro-,** as in **macrochemistry; Sino-,** as in **Sino-Soviet.**

combining weight *n.* **Equivalent weight** *(see).*

comb jelly *n.* A marine organism, a **ctenophore** *(see).*

com·bo (kŏm′bō) *n., pl.* **-bos. 1.** *Informal.* A small group of musicians, usually jazz musicians. **2.** *Slang.* The result or product of combining; combination. [Short for COMBINATION.]

com·bust (kəm-bŭst′) *adj. Astrology.* Not visible because of proximity to the sun. Said of a star or planet.
~v. **combusted, -busting, -busts.** *—tr.* To cause to burn. *—intr.* To burn; undergo combustion. [Middle English, "burned," from Old French, from Latin *combustus,* past participle of *combūrere,* to burn up (infixed *b* probably influenced by *ambūrere,* to burn up) : *com-* (intensive) + *ūrere,* to burn.] **—com·bus·tive** *adj.*

com·bus·ti·ble (kəm-bŭs′tə-bəl) *adj.* **1.** Capable of igniting and burning. **2.** Easily aroused or excited.
~n. A combustible substance. **—com·bus·ti·bil·i·ty** *n.* **—com·bus·ti·bly** *adv.*

com·bus·tion (kəm-bŭs′chən) *n.* **1.** The act or process of burning. **2.** *Chemistry.* A chemical change, especially oxidation, accompanied by the production of heat and light. [Middle English, from Old French, from Late Latin *combustiō* (stem *combustiōn-*), from Latin *combustus.* See **combust.**]

combustion chamber *n.* An enclosure in which combustion, especially of a fuel or propellant, is initiated and controlled.

com·bus·tor (kəm-bŭs′tər) *n.* The combustion system of a jet engine or gas turbine, consisting of a combustion chamber together with its igniter and fuel injection system.

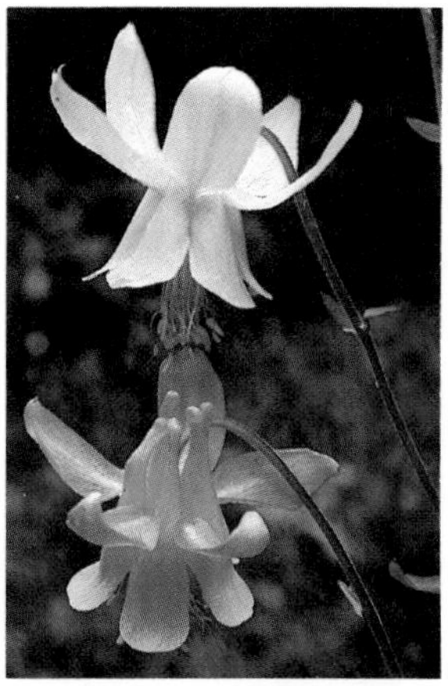

columbine *This group of hardy border plants with funnel-shaped flowers is related to the buttercup. The Latin name for the group is* Aquilegia.

PRONUNCIATION KEY

ă, pat; ā, pay; âr, care; ä, father, are; b, bib; ch, church; d, deed; ĕ, pet; ē, be; f, fife; g, gag; h, hat; hw, which; ĭ, pit; ī, pie; îr, pier; j, judge; k, kick; l, lid, needle; m, mum; n, no, sudden; ng, thing; ŏ, pot; ō, toe; ô, paw, for; oi, noise; ou, out; o͝o, book; o͞o, boot; p, pop; r, roar; s, sauce; sh, ship, dish; t, tight; th, thin, path; *th*, this, bathe; ŭ, cut; ûr, fur; v, valve; w, with; y, yes; z, zebra, size; zh, vision; ə, about, item, edible, gallop, circus, peaceful

IN FOREIGN WORDS:

å, *Fr.* ami; œ, *Fr.* feu, *Ger.* schön; ü, *Fr.* tu, *Ger.* über; KH, *Ger.* ich, *Scot.* loch; N, *Fr.* bon; y′, *Fr.* Compiègne

STRESS MARKS:

Primary stress: ′ in·cite′ (ĭn-sīt′)
Secondary stress: ′ in′sight′ (ĭn′sīt′)

comdg. commanding.
Comdr. commander.
Comdt. commandant.
come (kŭm) *v.* **came** (kām), **come, coming, comes.** —*intr.* **1. a.** To advance toward the speaker or toward a specified place; approach. **b.** To advance in a specified manner. **2.** To arrive as a result of moving or making progress. **3.** To reach a particular point in a series or as a result of orderly progression. **4.** To move into view; appear. **5.** To occur in time. **6. a.** To arrive at a particular result or end: *come to an understanding.* **b.** To arrive at or reach a particular state or condition: *came to like him; didn't come to any harm.* **c.** To move or be brought to a particular position: *The bus came to an abrupt halt.* **7.** To extend; reach: *hair coming to the waist.* **8.** To exist at a particular point or place: *The letter* T *comes before* U. **9. a.** To happen: *How did you come to know that?* **b.** To happen as a result: *This comes of your carelessness.* **10.** To be allotted or given: *On my death the jewels will come to you.* **11.** To occur in the mind: *An idea came to her.* **12. a.** To issue forth: *A loud scream came from the next room.* **b.** To descend; originate: *comes of an old Scottish family.* **c.** To be derived. **13.** To be a native or have been a resident of. **14.** To be moving toward a concluding or culminating stage; develop; evolve: *The project is coming along very well.* **15.** To become: *The knot came loose.* **16.** To be available or obtainable: *Houses here don't come cheap; It comes in two sizes.* **17.** To prove or turn out to be: *His wish came true.* **18.** To be achieved or mastered as specified: *Math comes easily to some people.* **—come about. 1.** To occur; take place; happen. **2.** *Nautical.* To change tack. **—come across. 1.** To encounter or find by chance. **2.** To leave an impression: *He comes across as a very pushy young man.* **3.** *Slang.* To do or give what is wanted. **—come again. 1.** To come or go back; return. **2.** *Informal.* To repeat what one has just said. Used in the imperative. **—come along. 1.** To improve; progress; advance. **2.** To appear; arrive: *Don't just take the first job that comes along.* **—come around** (or **round**). **1.** To recover; revive. **2.** To change one's opinion or position. **—come at. 1.** To attack; rush at. **2.** To obtain; get. **—come between.** To cause the separation or estrangement of. **—come by.** To acquire or get, especially by chance. **—come clean.** To confess all. **—come down on** (or **upon**). **1.** To descend upon; attack. **2.** *Informal.* To criticize; scold. **—come forward.** To volunteer one's services. **—come in. 1.** To turn out to be: *Some matches would come in handy.* **2.** To become popular or fashionable. **3.** To be received as income. **4.** To finish a race: *My horse came in last as usual.* **5.** To rise; flow. Used of the tide. **—come in for.** *Informal.* **1.** To be eligible for. **2.** To get; receive; acquire. **—come into.** To inherit. **—come off. 1.** To happen; occur. **2.** To acquit oneself. **3.** To have an intended effect; succeed. **—come off it.** *Informal.* To stop talking nonsense. Used in the imperative. **—come out. 1.** To be disclosed or made public. **2.** To declare oneself openly to be something, especially a homosexual or lesbian. **3.** To make a formal social debut. **4.** To result; end up. **5.** *Chiefly British.* To go on strike. **6.** To become available; be published: *His new book is coming out next month.* **7.** To be developed successfully. Used of photographic film: *Our holiday photos didn't come out.* **—come out with. 1.** To disclose publicly; declare. **2.** To put into words; say. **—come over. 1.** To seize; possess: *Strange feelings came over me.* **2.** To change sides. **3.** *Informal.* To visit. **—come through. 1.** To recover; survive. **2.** *Informal.* To do as expected. **3.** To become manifest: *His love of nature comes through in his paintings.* **—come to. 1.** To recover consciousness. **2.** To amount to. **3.** To be a matter of; concern: *When it comes to fixing things, he's in a class of his own.* **4.** *Nautical.* **a.** To bring a ship's bow into the wind. **b.** To anchor. **—come to grips with.** To face squarely: *came to grips with the problem.* **—come up. 1.** To be regurgitated. **2.** To manifest itself; arise: *Something came up and we couldn't go.* **—come up against. 1.** To struggle or do battle with. **2.** To encounter (a problem, for example). **—come upon. 1.** To meet by accident. **2.** To attack. **—come up to. 1.** To reach or extend to; meet. **2.** To equal. **—come up with.** *Informal.* To propose; produce. **—how come.** *Informal.* Why. Used interrogatively.
∼*interj.* Used to express anger, impatience, or remonstrance: *Come now, that's enough.*
∼*prep.* As from; by: *Come next Friday, our financial problems will be solved.* [Come, came, come; Middle English *comen* or *cumen* (infinitive), *com* or *cam* (past singular), *comen* or *camen* (past plural), *comen* or *cumen* (past participle), Old English *cuman, cōm, c(w)ōmon, cumen,* from Germanic.]
come back *intr.v.* **1.** To return to popularity; become fashionable again. **2.** To return to memory. **3.** To retort. Usually used with *at.*
come·back (kŭm′băk′) *n.* **1.** A return to former prosperity or status. **2.** A retort; a piece of repartee. **3.** A recourse; a means of redress.
Com·e·con (kŏm′ē-kŏn′, kŏm′ĭ-) *n.* An association of Communist states for economic cooperation. Its members include the U.S.S.R. and its European allies, Cuba, Mongolia, and Vietnam. [*Co*uncil for *M*utual *Econ*omic Assistance.]
co·me·di·an (kə-mē′dē-ən) *n.* **1.** A professional entertainer who tells jokes, does impersonations, or performs various other comic acts. **2.** An actor in comedy. **3.** A comedy writer. **4.** An amusing person; clown.
co·me·dic (kə-mē′dĭk) *adj.* Of or relating to comedy.
co·me·di·enne (kə-mē′dē-ĕn′) *n.* A female professional entertainer who tells jokes, does impersonations, or performs various other comic acts. [French.]
com·e·do (kŏm′ə-dō′) *n., pl.* **-dos** or **-do·nes** (-dō′nēz). A **blackhead** *(see).* Used in technical contexts. [New Latin, from Latin *comedo,* glutton, from *comedere,* to eat up : *com-* (intensive) + *edere,* to eat.]
come down *intr.v.* **1.** To lose status or wealth. **2.** To become ill. Used with *with*: *come down with measles.* **3.** To move to a lower position; drop. **4.** To reach a decision about a matter: *They came down on the side of the union.* **5.** To be transmitted through history; be passed down. Often used with *to.* **6.** To amount to. Used with *to*: *It comes down to this.* **7.** *Slang.* To come out of a drug-induced state.
come·down (kŭm′doun′) *n.* **1.** A decline or drop to a lower status or level. **2.** *Informal.* A disappointment.
com·e·dy (kŏm′ĭ-dē) *n., pl.* **-dies.** *Abbr.* **com. 1.** A play, film, or other work that is humorous in its treatment of theme and character and usually has a happy ending. **2.** Any literary composition with humorous themes or characters. **3.** The branch of literature dealing with comedies. **4.** The art or technique of composing or acting in comedy. **5.** A comic element of literature or life. **6.** A comic occurrence. [Middle English *comedie,* from Old French, from Latin *cōmoedia,* from Greek *kōmōidia,* from *kōmōidos,* originally "a singer in the revels" : *kōmos*†, revel + *ōidos, aoidēs,* singer, from *aeidein,* to sing.]
comedy of manners *n.* A comedy satirizing fashionable society.
come-hith·er (kŭm′hĭ*th*′ər) *adj.* Seductive; alluring.
come·ly (kŭm′lē) *adj.* **-lier, -liest. 1.** Having a pleasing appearance; attractive. —See Synonyms at **beautiful. 2.** Suitable; proper; seemly: *comely behavior.* [Middle English *comli, comeli(ch),* Old English *cȳmlic,* lovely, splendid, from *cȳme*†, beautiful.] **—come·li·ness** *n.*
Co·me·ni·us (kə-mē′nē-əs), **John Amos** (1592–1671). *Czech* **Jan Ko·men·ský** (kô′mən-skē). Czech theologian and educational reformer, who believed that science exalted divine majesty rather than threatened it. He held that learning should be by observation rather than through authoritarian dogma.
come on *intr.v.* **1.** To make progress; improve; develop. **2.** To enter or appear, as on a theater stage. **3.** To begin: *I feel a cold coming on.* **4.** *Informal.* To try to attract; allure. —*tr.v.* To find or encounter; happen on.
come-on (kŭm′ŏn′, -ôn′) *n.* Something offered to allure or attract; an inducement.
com·er (kŭm′ər) *n.* **1.** One that arrives or comes. Usually used in combination: *a latecomer; a newcomer.* **2.** *Informal.* One showing great promise.
co·mes·ti·ble (kə-mĕs′tə-bəl) *adj.* Edible.
∼*n.* **comestibles.** Food. [Old French, from Medieval Latin *comestibilis,* from Latin *comedere* (past participle *comestus*), to eat up : *com-* (intensive) + *edere,* eat.]
com·et (kŏm′ĭt) *n. Astronomy.* A celestial body, observed only in that part of its orbit that is relatively close to the sun, having a head consisting of a solid nucleus surrounded by a nebulous coma, an elongated curved vapor tail arising from the coma when sufficiently close to the sun, and thought to consist chiefly of ammonia, methane, carbon dioxide, and water. [Middle English *comete,* Old English *comēta,* from Latin *comēta, comētēs,* from Greek *(astēr) komētēs,* "long-haired (star)," from *koman,* to wear long hair, from *komē*†, hair.] **—com·et·ar·y** (kŏm′ə-tĕr′ē), **co·met·ic** (kə-mĕt′ĭk) *adj.*
come·up·pance (kŭm′ŭp′əns) *n. Informal.* Punishment or retribution that one deserves; one's just deserts. [From phrase *come up,* sense development obscure.]
com·fit (kŭm′fĭt, kŏm′-) *n.* A sugar-coated sweet. [Middle English *confit,* from Old French, from Latin *confectum,* "preparation," from Latin *conficere,* to prepare : *com-* (intensive) + *facere,* to make.]
com·fort (kŭm′fərt) *tr.v.* **-forted, -forting, -forts. 1.** To soothe in time of grief or fear; console. **2.** To ease physically; relieve of pain or discomfort. —See Synonyms at **relieve.**
∼*n.* **1.** A state of ease or well-being; freedom from pain or anxiety. **2.** Relief; consolation; solace. **3.** A source of consolation or support. **4.** A source of physical well-being: *home comforts.* **5.** Capacity to give physical ease and well-being: *enjoying the comfort of his favorite chair.* —See Synonyms at **rest.** [Middle English *comforten,* from Old French *conforter,* from Late Latin *confortāre,* to strengthen : Latin *com-* (intensive) + *fortis,* strong.] **—com·fort·ing·ly** *adv.*
com·fort·a·ble (kŭm′fər-tə-bəl, kŭmf′tər-bəl) *adj.* **1.** Providing or giving comfort. **2.** Being in a state of comfort; at ease. **3.** *Informal.* **a.** Providing adequately for one's material needs: *a comfortable income.* **b.** Having an adequate income. **—com·fort·a·ble·ness** *n.* **—com·fort·a·bly** *adv.*
***Synonyms:** cozy, restful, snug.*
com·fort·er (kŭm′fər-tər) *n.* **1.** One that comforts. **2. Comforter.** The Holy Spirit. **3.** A quilted bedcover. **4.** *Chiefly British.* A woolen neck scarf.
comfort station *n.* A public toilet or rest room.
com·frey (kŭm′frē) *n., pl.* **-freys.** Any of several usually hairy or bristly plants of the genus *Symphytum,* native to the Old World, having clusters of blue, purplish, or white flowers. [Middle English *conferie,* from Old French *cumfirie, confire,* from Latin *conferva,* a water plant, "healer," from *confervēre,* to boil together, heal : *com-,* together + *fervēre,* to boil.]
com·fy (kŭm′fē) *adj.* **-fier, -fiest.** *Informal.* Comfortable.
com·ic (kŏm′ĭk) *adj. Abbr.* **com. 1.** Of, characteristic of, or pertaining to comedy. **2.** Of or pertaining to comic strips. **3.** Amusing; humorous.

PRONUNCIATION KEY
ă, pat; ā, pay; âr, care;
ä, father, are; b, bib;
ch, church; d, deed; ĕ, pet;
ē, be; f, fife; g, gag; h, hat;
hw, which; ĭ, pit; ī, pie;
îr, pier; j, judge; k, kick;
l, lid, needle; m, mum;
n, no, sudden; ng, thing;
ŏ, pot; ō, toe; ô, paw, for;
oi, noise; ou, out; o͝o, book;
o͞o, boot; p, pop; r, roar;
s, sauce; sh, ship, dish;
t, tight; th, thin, path;
th, this, bathe; ŭ, cut; ûr, fur;
v, valve; w, with; y, yes;
z, zebra, size; zh, vision;
ə, about, item, edible,
gallop, circus, peaceful

IN FOREIGN WORDS:
à, *Fr.* ami; œ, *Fr.* feu, *Ger.* schön; ü, *Fr.* tu, *Ger.* über;
KH, *Ger.* ich, *Scot.* loch;
N, *Fr.* bon; y′, *Fr.* Compiègne

STRESS MARKS:
Primary stress: ′
in·cite′ (ĭn-sīt′)
Secondary stress: ′
in′sight′ (ĭn′sīt′)

~*n. Abbr.* **com. 1. a.** A comedian. **b.** A person who is comical. **2. a. comics.** Comic strips. **b.** A comic book. **c. comics.** The part of a newspaper devoted to comic strips. **3.** Something that provokes humor in art or life. [Latin *cōmicus,* from Greek *kōmikos,* from *kōmos,* revelry, merrymaking. See **comedy.**]

com·i·cal (kŏm′ĭ-kəl) *adj.* **1.** *Obsolete.* Of or pertaining to comedy. **2.** Provoking mirth; funny; amusing. —**com·i·cal·i·ty** (kŏm′ĭ-kăl′-ə-tē), **com·i·cal·ness** *n.* —**com·i·cal·ly** *adv.*

comic book *n.*

comic opera *n.* An opera or operetta with a humorous plot, spoken dialogue, and, usually, a happy ending.

comic strip *n.* A narrative series of cartoons.

com·ing (kŭm′ĭng) *adj.* **1.** Approaching; next. **2.** *Informal.* Showing promise of fame or success; up-and-coming. ~*n.* Arrival; advent.

com·ing-out (kŭm′ĭng-out′) *n. Informal.* A social debut. Also used adjectivally: *a coming-out party.*

Com·in·tern (kŏm′ĭn-tûrn) *n.* The Third **International** *(see)* or, especially, its executive committee in Moscow. [*Communist International.*]

com·i·ti·a (kə-mĭsh′ē-ə, -mĭsh′ə) *n., pl.* **comitia.** A popular assembly in ancient Rome having legislative or electoral duties. [Latin, plural of *comitium,* meeting place : *com-,* together + *īre* (past participle *itus*), to go.] —**co·mi·tial** (kə-mĭsh′əl) *adj.*

com·i·ty (kŏm′ə-tē) *n., pl.* **-ties.** *Formal.* Civility; courtesy. [Latin *cōmitās,* from *cōmis,* courteous.]

comity of nations *n.* **1.** Courteous recognition accorded by one nation to the laws and institutions of another. **2.** The nations observing such courtesy.

comm. 1. commerce. **2.** commission; commissioner. **3.** commonwealth. **4.** communication.

com·ma (kŏm′ə) *n.* **1.** A punctuation mark (,) used to indicate a separation of ideas or of elements within the structure of a sentence, and, in some countries, to precede a decimal fraction. **2.** A pause or separation; caesura. **3.** Any of several butterflies of the genus *Polygonia,* having wings with brownish coloring and irregularly notched edges. [Latin, from Greek *komma,* a cut, section, clause, from *koptein,* to cut.]

comma bacillus *n.* A bacillus, *Vibrio comma,* that causes Asiatic cholera. [From its commalike shape.]

comma fault *n. Grammar.* Improper use of a comma between independent clauses not joined by a conjunction.

com·mand (kə-mănd′, -mänd′) *v.* **-manded, -manding, -mands.** —*tr.* **1.** To direct with authority; give orders to. **2.** To have control or authority over; rule. **3.** To have at one's disposal: *The country commands enormous mineral resources.* **4.** To deserve and receive as due; require: *His bravery commanded respect.* **5.** To dominate by position; overlook. —*intr.* **1.** To give commands. **2.** To exercise authority as a commander; be in control. ~*n.* **1.** The act of commanding or giving orders. **2.** An order so given. **3.** The authority to command. **4.** The possession and exercise of authority to command: *using all the skill at his command.* **5.** Ability to control; mastery: *an impressive command of the language.* **6.** Dominance by location; extent of view. **7. a.** The jurisdiction of a commander. **b.** *Military.* A unit, post, or region under the control of one officer. **c.** *U.S. Air Force.* A unit consisting of a specified number of wings, generally three or more, under the authority of an officer. **8.** *British.* An invitation from the reigning monarch. **9.** *Computer Science.* An instruction. Also used adjectivally: *a command file.* [Middle English *com(m)aunden,* from Norman French *comaunder,* from Old French *comander,* from Late Latin *commandāre,* to COMMEND.]
   Synonyms: bid, charge, direct, enjoin, instruct, order.

com·man·dant (kŏm′ən-dănt′, -dänt′) *n. Abbr.* **Comdt. 1.** A commanding officer of a military organization. **2.** *South African.* A lieutenant-colonel.

com·man·deer (kŏm′ən-dîr′) *tr.v.* **-deered, -deering, -deers. 1.** To force into military service. **2.** To seize (property) for military use; confiscate. **3.** *Informal.* To take arbitrarily or by force. [Afrikaans *kommandeer,* from French *commander,* to COMMAND.]

com·mand·er (kə-măn′dər, kə-män′-) *n.* **1.** A person who commands; leader. **2. a.** *Abbr.* **Comdr., Cdr., Com., Cmdr.** An officer in the U.S. Navy who ranks next above a lieutenant commander and next below a captain. **b.** The chief commissioned officer of a military unit, regardless of his rank. **3.** A chief or an officer in certain knightly or fraternal orders.

commander in chief *n., pl.* **commanders in chief. 1.** *Often* **Commander in Chief.** *Abbr.* **CINC, C in C.** The supreme commander of all the armed forces of a nation. **2.** The officer commanding a major armed force.

com·mand·er·y (kə-măn′dər-ē, kə-män′-) *n., pl.* **-ies. 1.** The district or office of a commander, especially of an order of knights. **2.** A lodge or local branch of certain fraternal orders.

com·mand·ing (kə-măn′dĭng, kə-män′-) *adj.* **1.** *Abbr.* **comdg.** Having command; controlling. **2.** Impressive. **3.** Dominating, as by height or position. —**com·mand·ing·ly** *adv.*

commanding officer *n. Abbr.* **C.O.** An officer in charge of any military unit.

com·mand·ment (kə-mănd′mənt, kə-mänd′-) *n.* **1.** A command; edict. **2.** *Sometimes* **Commandment.** Any of the **Ten Commandments** *(see).*

command module *n.* The portion of a spacecraft in which the astronauts live and operate controls during a flight.

com·man·do (kə-măn′dō, kə-män′-) *n., pl.* **-dos** or **-does. 1. a.** A small fighting force specially trained for making quick, destructive raids against enemy-held areas. Also used adjectivally: *a commando unit.* **b.** A member of such a force. **2. a.** Originally, in South Africa, an organized force of Boer troops. **b.** A raid made by such a force. [Afrikaans *kommando,* from Dutch *commando,* unit of troops, from Spanish *comando,* from *comandar,* to command, from Vulgar Latin *commandāre* (unattested), COMMAND.]

command performance *n.* A theatrical performance, entertainment, or the like, given at the request of a head of state.

command post *n. Abbr.* **C.P.** The field headquarters used by the commander of a military unit.

com·meas·ure (kə-mĕzh′ər) *tr.v.* **-ured, -uring, -ures.** To coincide

---

comet

REGULAR VISITORS FROM SPACE

Long trails of gas and dust lit up by the sun

More than 1,600 comets have been recorded, but only a few are visible with the naked eye. A comet is a ball of gas and dust with a starlike nucleus; probably space debris, it spins around the sun in an elongated orbit and can be seen from earth for only a short part of its journey. As it nears the sun, the comet shines by reflected sunlight, the gas warms up and evaporates, and a streaming tail of gas and dust is formed—always pointing away from the sun.

Orbits may take a few years or thousands of years. Encke's comet has the shortest-known orbital period —just over three years. Halley's comet, a bright comet visible to the naked eye for a few months every 76 years, was the first for which an orbital period was calculated. It was used by Edmund Halley (1656–1742), the English astronomer, as proof of Newton's theory of gravitation. In 1687 Newton had published his theories and calculations on the laws of motion that govern all bodies, including comets. Halley had observed a comet in 1682. Using Newton's equations, he calculated that its orbital period was 76 years. He then found records of a great comet in 1607 and 1531, and predicted its return in 1758. It actually appeared in December 1758 and was named after him.

At once it became clear that many previous sightings had been made. In 1301, the Italian painter Giotto used the comet later to become known as Halley's as a model for the Star of Bethlehem. Its appearance in 1066 was recorded in the Bayeux Tapestry. Chinese astronomers noted it in 240 B.C. It returned in the winter of 1985–86 and could be seen at its best in early 1986. Gravitational pulls from other planets can slightly shorten or lengthen the orbital period.

STREAKING THROUGH SPACE *The glowing tail, millions of miles long, streams behind Halley's comet as it is photographed passing Venus. On its appearance in 1986, the comet was more difficult to see than in 1910, but a space probe monitored it.*

with; be coextensive with. [COM- + MEASURE.] —**com·meas·ur·a·ble** adj.

com·me·dia dell'ar·te (kə-mā′dē-ə dĕl-är′tē) n. A type of comedy developed in Italy in the 16th century, characterized by improvisation from a plot outline and by the use of stock characters. [Italian, "comedy of art."]

comme il faut (kô mĕl fō′) adj. French. As one or it should be; proper.

com·mem·o·rate (kə-mĕm′ə-rāt′) tr.v. **-rated, -rating, -rates.** 1. To honor the memory of (a person or event) in speech or writing, or with a ceremony. 2. To serve as a memorial to. —See Synonyms at **observe.** [Latin commemorāre, to call to mind clearly : com- (intensive) + memorāre, to remind, speak of, from memor, mindful.] —**com·mem·o·ra·tor** n.

com·mem·o·ra·tion (kə-mĕm′ə-rā′shən) n. 1. The act of commemorating. 2. Something that commemorates. 3. A commemorative celebration.

com·mem·o·ra·tive (kə-mĕm′ər-ə-tĭv, -ə-rā′tĭv) adj. 1. Serving to commemorate. 2. Issued to commemorate a notable person or event. Said of coins, stamps, or the like.
~n. Anything that commemorates.

com·mence (kə-mĕns′) v. **-menced, -mencing, -mences.** —tr. To begin; start. —intr. To come into existence; have a beginning. —See Synonyms at **begin.** [Middle English commencen, from Old French comencer, from Vulgar Latin cominitiāre (unattested) : Latin com- (intensive) + initiāre, to INITIATE.] —**com·menc·er** n.

com·mence·ment (kə-mĕns′mənt) n. 1. A beginning; start. 2. A ceremony at which academic degrees or diplomas are conferred.

com·mend (kə-mĕnd′) tr.v. **-mended, -mending, -mends.** 1. To represent as worthy, qualified, or desirable; recommend. 2. To express approval of; praise. 3. To commit to the care of another; entrust. —See Synonyms at **praise.** [Middle English commenden, from Latin commendāre, to commit to one's charge, commend, recommend : com- (intensive) + mandāre, to entrust.] —**com·mend·a·ble** adj. —**com·mend·a·bly** adv. —**com·mend·er** n.

com·men·da·tion (kŏm′ən-dā′shən) n. 1. The act of commending; recommendation; approval. 2. An award or honor: a commendation for bravery. —**com·men·da·to·ry** (kə-mĕn′də-tôr′ē, -tōr′ē) adj.

com·men·sal (kə-mĕn′səl) adj. 1. Rare. Eating at the same table. 2. Biology. Pertaining to or characterized by commensalism.
~n. 1. Rare. A mealtime companion. 2. Biology. An organism participating in commensalism. [Middle English, from Medieval Latin commensālis : Latin com-, together + mēnsa, table.] —**com·men·sal·ly** adv.

com·men·sal·ism (kə-mĕn′səl-ĭz′əm) n. Biology. A relationship in which two or more organisms live in close association, and in which one may derive some benefit, but in which neither harms or is parasitic on the other. Compare **symbiosis.**

com·men·su·ra·ble (kə-mĕn′sər-ə-bəl, -shər-ə-bəl) adj. 1. Able to be measured by a common standard or in units having the same dimensions. 2. Properly proportioned; commensurate. 3. Mathematics. Exactly divisible by the same unit an integral number of times. Said of two quantities. [Late Latin commēnsūrābilis : com-, same + mēnsūrābilis, measurable, from mēnsūrāre, to measure, from Latin mēnsūra, MEASURE.] —**com·men·su·ra·bil·i·ty** n. —**com·men·su·ra·bly** adv.

com·men·su·rate (kə-mĕn′sə-rĭt, -shə-rĭt) adj. 1. Of the same size, extent, or duration; coextensive. 2. Corresponding in scale or measure; proportionate: a salary commensurate with the job's responsibilities. 3. Having a common measure or standard; commensurable. [Late Latin commēnsūrātus : com-, same + mēnsūrātus, past participle of mēnsūrāre, to MEASURE.] —**com·men·su·rate·ly** adv.

com·ment (kŏm′ĕnt) n. 1. a. A remark, as in criticism or observation. b. A brief statement of fact or opinion, especially one that expresses a personal reaction or attitude. 2. Usually **comments.** A written note intended as an explanation, illustration, or criticism of a passage in a book or other writing; an annotation. 3. Talk; gossip: caused a lot of comment. 4. Something that exemplifies; an illustration: The incident was a sad comment on our times.
~intr.v. **commented, -menting, -ments.** To make a comment; remark. Often used with on. [Middle English, from Latin commentum, contrivance, interpretation, from commentus, past participle of comminīscī, to contrive by thought.]

com·men·tar·y (kŏm′ən-tĕr′ē) n., pl. **-ies.** 1. A series of annotations, explanations, or interpretations of a literary text. 2. Often **commentaries.** An expository treatise or essay; exegesis. 3. A series of descriptive observations of an event, especially a sports event, as it happens in a radio or television broadcast. 4. An illustration; comment. 5. Often **commentaries.** A personal narrative; memoir. —**com·men·tar·i·al** (kŏm′ən-târ′ē-əl) adj.

com·men·tate (kŏm′ən-tāt′) v. **-tated, -tating, -tates.** —tr. To make a commentary on. —intr. To serve as commentator; make a commentary, especially for a film or a radio or television broadcast. Used with on.

com·men·ta·tor (kŏm′ən-tā′tər) n. 1. An author of commentaries, especially on current or political events. 2. A person who makes radio or television commentaries.

com·merce (kŏm′ərs) n. 1. Abbr. **com., comm.** The buying and selling of goods, especially on a large scale, as between cities or nations; business; trade. 2. Intellectual exchange or social intercourse. 3. Sexual intercourse. —See Usage note at **business.**

[Old French, from Latin commercium : com- (collective) + merx (stem merc-), merchandise.]

com·mer·cial (kə-mûr′shəl) adj. Abbr. **com., cml.** 1. a. Of, pertaining to, or engaged in commerce. b. Suitable for commerce; profitable: valuable minerals in commercial quantities. 2. Produced in large quantities for use by industry; unrefined. Said especially of chemicals. 3. a. Viewed purely in terms of financial returns: The play was a commercial success. b. Having profit, success, or immediate results as chief aim: a commercial painter. 4. Financed by advertising revenue: commercial television.
~n. An advertisement on radio or television.

commercial bank n. A privately owned bank, usually with a large umber of branches, the principal functions of which are to operate deposit and current accounts and to make short-term loans.

com·mer·cial·ism (kə-mûr′shə-lĭz′əm) n. 1. The practices, methods, aims, and spirit of commerce or business. 2. An attitude that emphasizes or overemphasizes tangible profit or success. —**com·mer·cial·ist** n. —**com·mer·cial·is·tic** adj.

com·mer·cial·ize (kə-mûr′shə-līz′) tr.v. **-ized, -izing, -izes.** 1. To make commercial; apply methods of business to. 2. a. To exploit, do, or make mainly for financial gain. b. To sacrifice the quality of for profit. —**com·mer·cial·i·za·tion** n.

commercial paper n. Any of various short-term negotiable papers originating in business transactions.

commercial traveler n. A traveling salesman (see).

commercial vehicle n. A vehicle used for transporting merchandise by road.

com·mi·na·tion (kŏm′ə-nā′shən) n. 1. A formal denunciation; a threatening. 2. In the Anglican liturgy, a recital of God's judgment and anger against sinners, read on Ash Wednesday. [Middle English comminacioun, from Old French commination, from Latin comminātiō (stem comminātiōn-), from comminārī, to threaten : com- (intensive) + minārī, threaten, from minae, threats.] —**com·min·a·to·ry** (kə-mĭn′ə-tôr′ē, -tōr′ē, kŏm′ĭ-nə-) adj.

com·min·gle (kə-mĭng′gəl) v. **-gled, -gling, -gles.** —intr. To blend together; mix. —tr. To mix together; combine.

com·mi·nute (kŏm′ə-nōōt′, -nyōōt′) tr.v. **-nuted, -nuting, -nutes.** To reduce to powder; pulverize; triturate. [Latin comminuere : com- (intensive) + minuere, to lessen.] —**com·mi·nu·tion** n.

com·mis·er·ate (kə-mĭz′ə-rāt′) v. **-ated, -ating, -ates.** —tr. To feel or express sorrow or pity for; sympathize with. —intr. To feel or express sympathy. [Latin commiserārī : com-, with + miserārī, to pity, from miser, wretched, pitiable.] —**com·mis·er·a·tive** adj. —**com·mis·er·a·tive·ly** adv. —**com·mis·er·a·tor** n.

com·mis·er·a·tion (kə-mĭz′ə-rā′shən) n. A feeling or expression of sorrow or sympathy for the distress of another; compassion. —See Synonyms at **pity.**

com·mis·sar (kŏm′ĭ-sär′) n. 1. An official of the Communist Party charged with the teaching of political principles and the enforcement of party loyalty. 2. Formerly, the head of a commissariat in the U.S.S.R. [Russian kommissar, from French commissaire, COMMISSARY.]

com·mis·sar·i·at (kŏm′ə-sâr′ē-ĭt) n. 1. a. A department of an army in charge of providing food and other supplies for the troops. b. The officers in charge of this. 2. A food supply. 3. Formerly, any major government department in the U.S.S.R. [Russian kommissariat, from French and Medieval Latin commissariatus, from commissārius, COMMISSARY.]

com·mis·sar·y (kŏm′ə-sĕr′ē, -sâr′ē) n., pl. **-ies.** 1. A person to whom a special duty is given by a higher authority; a representative, deputy. 2. a. A supermarket for the use of soldiers in a camp, employees, diplomatic personnel, or the like. b. A cafeteria on a film set or in a television studio. 3. Formerly, an army officer in charge of supplying provisions. [Middle English commissarie, from Medieval Latin commissārius, commissioner, agent, from committere, to entrust, commission, COMMIT.] —**com·mis·sar·y·ship** n.

com·mis·sion (kə-mĭsh′ən) n. 1. a. An act of committing or giving authority to carry out a particular task or duty, or granting certain powers; an entrusting. b. A document conferring such an authority. 2. The authority, duty, or task conferred in this way. 3. The state of being authorized to perform certain functions. 4. Abbr. **Com., comm.** A group of people lawfully authorized to perform certain duties or functions, such as a government agency. 5. A committing or perpetrating: commission of a crime. 6. A fee or percentage allowed to a salesman or agent for his services. 7. Abbr. **Com., comm.** a. An official document issued by a government, conferring the rank of a commissioned officer in the armed forces. b. The rank and powers so conferred. —**in** (or **out of**) **commission.** 1. In (or out of) active service. Said of a ship. 2. In (or out of) working condition or use.
~tr.v. **commissioned, -sioning, -sions.** 1. To grant a commission to. 2. To place an order for. 3. Nautical. To put (a ship) into active service. [Middle English commissioun, from Old French commission, from Latin commissiō (stem commissiōn-), from committere (past participle commissus), COMMIT.] —**com·mis·sion·al, com·mis·sion·ar·y** (kə-mĭsh′ə-nĕr′ē) adj.

com·mis·sion·aire (kə-mĭsh′ə-nâr′) n. Chiefly British. A uniformed doorman. [French commissionnaire, from Old French commission, COMMISSION.]

commissioned officer n. Any officer in the armed forces who holds a commission and ranks as a second lieutenant or above in the U.S. Army, Air Force, or Marine Corps, or as an ensign or above in the U.S. Navy or Coast Guard. Compare **noncommissioned officer, warrant officer.**

com·mis·sion·er (kə-mĭsh′ən-ər) *n. Abbr.* **Com., Comr., comm.** **1.** A person authorized by a commission to perform certain duties. **2.** A member of a commission. **3.** An official in charge of a particular department: *commissioner of police.* **4.** *Sports.* An official selected by an athletic association or league to exercise judicial or regulatory power: *a baseball commissioner.* —**com·mis·sion·er·ship** *n.*

commission merchant *n.* A person who buys and sells goods for others on a commission basis.

commission plan *n.* A type of municipal government in which legislative and administrative functions and powers are vested in an elected commission rather than in a mayor and city council.

com·mis·sure (kŏm′ə-shoor′) *n.* **1.** A line or place at which two things are joined; seam; juncture. **2.** *Anatomy.* **a.** A tract of nerve fibers passing from one side to the other of the spinal cord or brain. **b.** The angle or corner of such structures as the lips, eyelids, or cardiac valves. **3.** *Botany.* A surface by which adhering carpels, leaf lobes, or other parts are joined. [Middle English, from Latin *commissūra,* from *committere,* COMMIT.] —**com·mis·su·ral** (kŏm′-ə-shoor′əl, kə-mĭsh′ər-əl) *adj.*

com·mit (kə-mĭt′) *tr.v.* **-mitted, -mitting, -mits. 1.** To do, perform, or perpetrate (especially something bad or wrong): *commit a murder.* **2.** To place in trust or charge; consign; entrust. **3.** To place officially in confinement or custody; especially, to place in a mental institution. **4.** To consign for future use or reference or for preservation: *commit a poem to memory.* **5.** To put in some place to be kept safe or be disposed of: *commit old love letters to the flames.* **6. a.** To pledge (oneself) to a position on some issue. **b.** To bind or obligate, as by a pledge. **c.** To assign for a particular purpose; pledge. **7.** To refer (a bill, for example) to a committee. [Middle English *committen,* from Latin *committere,* to join, connect, entrust : *com-,* together + *mittere,* to send, put.] —**com·mit·ta·ble** *adj.*

Synonyms: assign, confide, consign, entrust.

com·mit·ment (kə-mĭt′mənt) *n.* Also **com·mit·tal** (kə-mĭt′l) (for senses 1, 2, 3, 8). **1. a.** The act of committing; a giving in charge or entrusting. **b.** The state of being committed. **2.** Official consignment, as to a prison or mental hospital. **3.** *Law.* A court order authorizing consignment to a prison; a mittimus. **4. a.** A pledge to do something. **b.** Something pledged. **5.** An engagement by contract involving financial obligation. **6.** The state of being bound emotionally or intellectually to some way of thinking or course of action: *a deep commitment to liberal policies.* **7.** A perpetration, as of a crime. **8.** The act of referring a legislative bill to a committee.

com·mit·tee (kə-mĭt′ē) *n. Abbr.* **com., Com. 1.** A group of people, usually appointed from a larger body, delegated to perform a function, such as investigating, considering, or acting on a matter. **2.** *Law.* Formerly, a person to whom the care of an estate or incompetent person is committed; a trustee; guardian. —**in committee.** Under consideration by a committee. Said of a legislative measure. [Middle English *committe,* trustee, from *committen,* COMMIT.]

com·mit·tee·man (kə-mĭt′ē-mən, -măn′) *n., pl.* **-men** (-mĭn, -měn′). A committee member.

committee of the whole *n.* The whole membership of a legislative body sitting as a committee to consider the details of a proposal.

com·mit·tee·wom·an (kə-mĭt′ē-wŏom′ən) *n., pl.* **-women** (-wĭm′ĭn). A female committee member.

com·mix (kə-mĭks′, kŏ-) *v.* **-mixed, -mixing, -mixes.** *Rare.* —*tr.* To mix together. —*intr.* To mix; blend. [Middle English, back-formation from *commixt,* from Latin *commixtus,* past participle of *commiscēre,* to mix together : *com-,* together + *miscēre,* mix.]

com·mix·ture (kə-mĭks′chər, kŏ-) *n.* **1.** The act or process of mixing together. **2.** The result of this; a mixture.

com·mode (kə-mōd′) *n.* **1.** A low cabinet or chest of drawers, often elaborately decorated and usually on legs or short feet. **2.** Formerly: **a.** A movable stand or cupboard containing a washbowl. **b.** A chair containing a concealed chamber pot. **3.** A toilet. **4.** A woman's ornate lace headdress, fashionable around 1700. [French, "convenient," from Latin *commodus,* COMMODIOUS.]

com·mo·di·ous (kə-mō′dē-əs) *adj.* **1.** Spacious; roomy. **2.** *Archaic.* Convenient; suitable. [Middle English, from Old French *commodieux,* from Medieval Latin *commodiōsus,* from Latin *commodus,* convenient, "(conforming) with (due) measure" : *com-,* with + *modus,* measure.] —**com·mo·di·ous·ly** *adv.* —**com·mo·di·ous·ness** *n.*

com·mod·i·ty (kə-mŏd′ə-tē) *n., pl.* **-ties. 1.** Anything useful or that can be turned to commercial or other advantage. **2.** *Economics.* **a.** An article of trade or commerce that can be transported, especially an agricultural or mining product. **b.** Any economic unit that can be exchanged, such as a service or a product. **3.** *Obsolete.* **a.** Convenience; profit; expediency: "*kings break faith upon commodity*" (Shakespeare). **b.** A quantity of goods. [Middle English *commodite,* profit, income, property, from Old French *commodite,* from Latin *commoditās* (stem *commoditāt-*), advantage, convenience, from *commodus,* convenient, COMMODIOUS.]

com·mo·dore (kŏm′ə-dôr′, -dōr′) *n. Abbr.* **Com., COMO, Como. 1.** *U.S. Navy.* Formerly, an officer ranking below rear admiral and above captain. This rank was abolished in 1899 but temporarily restored during World War II. **2.** *British Navy.* An unofficial designation for a captain temporarily in command of a fleet division or squadron. **3. a.** The senior captain of a naval squadron or merchant fleet. **b.** The presiding officer of a yacht club. [Dutch *komandeur,* commander, from French *commandeur,* commander.]

com·mon (kŏm′ən) *adj.* **-moner, -monest. 1.** Belonging equally to two or more; shared by all alike; joint: *common interests.* **2.** Pertaining to the community as a whole; public: *the common good.* **3.** Generally known: *common knowledge.* **4.** Widespread; prevalent; general. **5.** Of frequent or habitual occurrence; usual. **6.** Most widely known or occurring most frequently; ordinary: *the common crow.* **7.** Without special designation, status, or rank: *a common sailor.* **8.** Not distinguished by superior or other characteristics; average: *the common spectator.* **9.** Of no special quality; standard; plain: *common courtesy.* **10.** Of mediocre or inferior quality; not costly or rare: *common cloth.* **11.** Vulgar; unrefined; coarse. **12.** Of variable length; either short or long. Said of a syllable in verse. **13.** *Grammar.* **a.** Either masculine or feminine in gender. **b.** Representing one or all the members of a class; not designating a unique entity. **14.** *Anatomy.* Having several branches: *common bile duct.* —See Usage note at **mutual.** ~*n.* **1. commons.** The common people; commonalty. **2. commons.** *Used with a singular or plural verb. British.* **a.** The political class comprising the commoners. **b.** The parliamentary representatives of this class. **c. Commons.** The House of Commons. **3.** *Sometimes* **commons.** A tract of land belonging to or used by a community as a whole. **4.** *Law.* The right of a person to use the lands or waters of another, as for fishing or grazing cattle. **5.** *Sometimes* **Common.** A church service used for a particular class of festivals. **6. commons.** *Used with a singular verb.* A building or hall for dining. —**in common.** Equally with or by all; jointly. [Middle English *commun(e),* from Old French, from Latin *commūnis.*] —**com·mon·ness** *n.*

Synonyms: familiar, ordinary, prevalent.

com·mon·age (kŏm′ə-nĭj) *n.* **1.** The right to pasture animals on common land. **2.** The use of this right. **3.** The state of being held in common. **4.** That which is held in common, especially land.

com·mon·al·i·ty (kŏm′ən-ăl′ə-tē) *n.* **1.** The state of being held in common or shared by numerous people or things. **2.** An object or attribute so shared. **3.** A common occurrence. **4.** The common people; commonalty.

com·mon·al·ty (kŏm′ən-əl-tē) *n., pl.* **-ties. 1.** The common people, as opposed to the upper classes. **2.** A body corporate; corporation. **3.** An entire group or body. [Middle English *communalte,* from Old French *comunalte,* from Medieval Latin *commūnālitās* (stem *commūnālitat-*), from *commūnālis,* COMMUNAL.]

common blue *n.* A blue butterfly, *Polyommatus icarus,* of the temperate Old World, the male of which is bright violet-blue and the female of which is dark brown.

common carrier *n.* A carrier by land, water, or air which is prepared to accept any passengers or goods that require transport. Compare **private carrier.**

common cold *n.* A respiratory viral infection, characterized by sneezing, nasal congestion, coughing, and inflammation of the nasal mucous membranes.

common denominator *n.* **1.** A quantity into which all the denominators of a set of fractions may be evenly divided. **2.** A quality or belief common to all the members of a particular group, and considered to characterize them as a group.

common divisor *n.* A quantity that is a factor of two or more quantities. Also called "common factor," "common measure."

com·mon·er (kŏm′ə-nər) *n.* **1.** One of the common people. **2.** One who is not a noble. **3.** In certain British universities and public schools, a student who does not hold a scholarship or similar award.

common era *n. Abbr.* **C.E.** The **Christian era** (see).

common fraction *n.* A **simple fraction** (see).

common gender *n.* Gender that may refer to either masculine or feminine categories; for example, *child, person.* Compare **natural gender, grammatical gender.**

common ground *n.* Points of agreement between the parties in a discussion providing a basis for argument or negotiation.

common law *n. Abbr.* **c.l. 1.** The system of laws originated and developed in England, based on court decisions, on the doctrines implicit in those decisions, and on customs and usages, rather than on codified written laws. Compare **statute law. 2.** The part of a system of laws of any state or nation that is of a general and universal application. —**com·mon-law** *adj.*

common-law marriage *n.* **1.** In English law, a marriage contracted in circumstances not allowing an official ceremony. **2.** A marriage existing by mutual agreement between a man and a woman without a civil or religious ceremony.

common logarithm *n.* A logarithm to the base 10. Compare **natural logarithm.**

com·mon·ly (kŏm′ən-lē) *adv.* **1.** Generally; ordinarily. **2.** In a common manner.

Common Market *n.* **1.** The **European Economic Community** (see). **2.** *Usually* **common market.** Any economic union between countries in which trade barriers are removed.

common measure *n.* **1.** *Music.* **Common time** (see). **2.** A **common divisor** (see).

common meter *n.* A form of stanza used in hymns and carols, consisting of four lines, alternately of eight and six syllables.

common multiple *n.* A quantity that is a multiple of each of two or more given quantities.

common noun *n. Grammar.* A noun that represents one or all of the members of a class; for example, *book, woman.* Compare **proper noun.**

Commonwealth

THE BAND OF NATIONS THAT GREW OUT OF THE BRITISH EMPIRE

A billion people of many languages, cultures, and political systems

The Commonwealth grew out of the old British Empire, as former colonies achieved their independence and joined together in a loose association for consultation and cooperation.

As the British Commonwealth, it developed gradually between 1919 and 1949, the Statute of Westminster (1931) referring to the self-governing dominions of Australia, Canada, New Zealand, and South Africa as "freely associated members." In April 1949, membership was broadened to include republics (notably India) prepared to acknowledge the British reigning monarch as head of the Commonwealth, and "British" was dropped from the title. The Republic of Ireland withdrew in 1949, South Africa in 1961 because of its apartheid policy, and Pakistan in 1972 in protest against the recognition of East Pakistan as Ban-

gladesh. In 1982, the admission of the Maldives brought membership to 47 nations.

The Commonwealth has no formal constitution. Members accept the Singapore Declaration of Commonwealth Principles (1971) calling for individual liberty, international peace and cooperation, free and fair international trade for a more equitable international society, and opposition to all forms of racial oppression. A Commonwealth Secretariat was established in London in 1965. Heads of government meet every two years, with the emphasis on informal sessions and private discussion. Commonwealth Day is the second Monday in March, and the Commonwealth Games are held every four years; the 1986 venue was Edinburgh, Scotland.

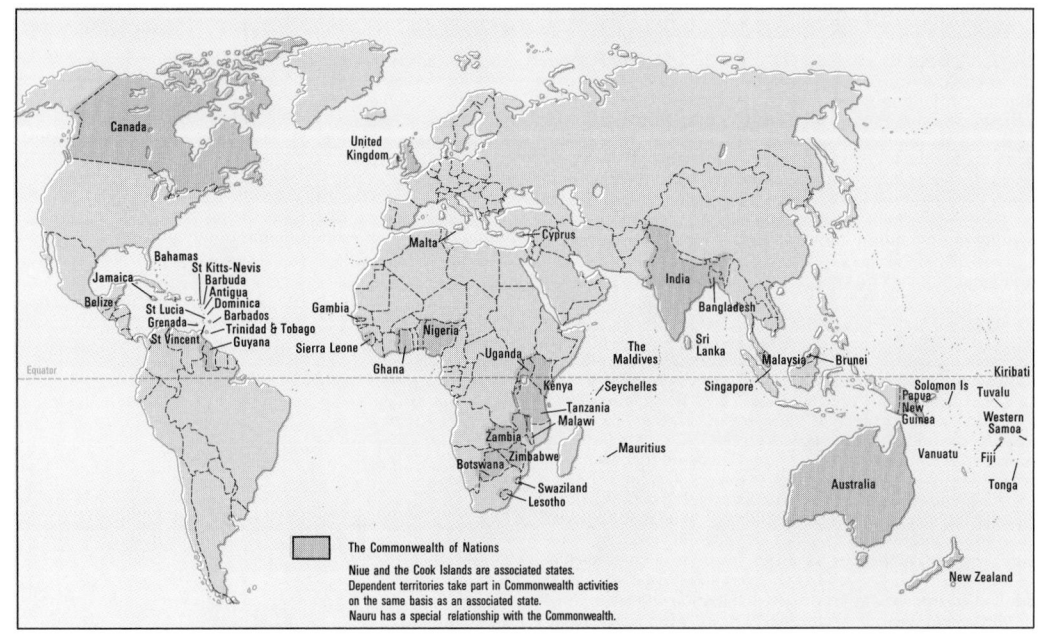

The Commonwealth of Nations

Niue and the Cook Islands are associated states.
Dependent territories take part in Commonwealth activities on the same basis as an associated state.
Nauru has a special relationship with the Commonwealth.

com·mon·place (kŏm′ən-plās′) *adj.* Ordinary; uninteresting; common. —See Synonyms at **trite.**

~*n.* **1.** A trite or obvious remark; platitude. **2.** Something ordinary or common. **3.** A passage in a book marked for reference or entered in a commonplace book. —See Synonyms at **cliché.** [Translation of Latin *locus commūnis,* translation of Greek *koinos topos,* "common place," literary passage of universal application.] —**com·mon·place·ness** *n.*

commonplace book *n.* A personal journal in which quotable passages, literary excerpts, and comments are written.

common pleas *n.* A Court of Common Pleas (see).

Common Prayer *n.* **1.** The liturgy for public worship in the Church of England. **2.** The **Book of Common Prayer** (see).

common rat *n.* The brown rat (see).

common room *n.* A sitting room or lounge in an educational or similar institution.

common salt *n.* **1.** Salt (see). **2.** Sodium chloride (see). **3.** Table salt (see).

common sense *n.* **1.** Native good judgment. **2.** A set of general unexamined assumptions as distinguished from specially acquired concepts. [Translation of Latin *sensus commūnis* and Greek *koinē aisthēsis,* total perception of the five senses.] —**com·mon·sense, com·mon-sense** (kŏm′ən-sĕns′) *adj.*

common stock *n.* Ordinary capital shares of a corporation that have exclusive residual claim on the net assets and net income of the corporation after all prior claims have been paid. Also called "equity stock."

common time *n. Music.* A meter having four quarter notes to the measure. It is written ⁴/₄. Also called "common measure."

com·mon·weal (kŏm′ən-wēl′) *n.* **1.** The public good. **2.** *Archaic.* A commonwealth.

com·mon·wealth (kŏm′ən-wĕlth′) *n.* **1.** The people of a nation or state; the body politic. **2.** *Abbr.* **comm.** A nation or state governed by the people; republic. **3. Commonwealth. a.** The official title of some U.S. states, including Kentucky, Virginia, Massachusetts, and Pennsylvania. **b.** The official title of Puerto Rico, indicating its special status as a self-governing, autonomous political unit voluntarily

associated with the United States. **4.** *Obsolete.* The public welfare. Also *archaic* "commonweal." —**the Commonwealth. 1.** The political community consisting of the United Kingdom, its dependencies, and certain former colonies that are now sovereign nations. Also officially called the "Commonwealth of Nations," formerly the "British Commonwealth of Nations." **2. a.** The period of republican government in Britain between 1649 and 1660. **b.** The parts of this period that preceded (1649–53) and followed (1659–60) Oliver Cromwell's personal protectorship. **c.** The form or forms of government during these periods. Also called the "Commonwealth of England." **3. Australia** *(see).*

com·mo·tion (kə-mō′shən) *n.* **1.** Violent or turbulent motion; agitation. **2.** Political disturbance or insurrection; disorder. **3.** A confused noise, suggesting upheaval; tumult. [Middle English *commocioun,* from Old French *commotion,* from Latin *commōtiō* (stem *commōtiōn-*), from *commovēre* (past participle *commōtus*), to move violently : *com-* (intensive) + *movēre,* to move.] —**com·mo·tion·al** *adj.*

com·move (kə-mōōv′) *tr.v.* **-moved, -moving, -moves.** To agitate; disturb; excite. [Middle English *commeven, comm(o)even,* from Latin *commovēre.* See **commotion.**]

com·mu·nal (kə-myōōn′əl, kŏm′yə-nəl) *adj.* **1.** Of or pertaining to a commune or community. **2.** Of, pertaining to, or shared by the people of a community or members of a group; common: *communal washing facilities.* **3.** Of or concerning different and opposed communities, especially in India: *communal riots between Hindus and Muslims.* [French, from Old French *comunal,* from Medieval Latin *commūnālis,* from *commūna, commūnia,* **COMMUNE** (community).] —**com·mu·nal·i·ty** (kŏm′yə-năl′ə-tē) *n.* —**com·mu·nal·ly** *adv.*

com·mu·nal·ism (kə-myōōn′əl-īz′əm, kŏm′yə-nəl-) *n.* **1.** A theory or system of government in which virtually autonomous local communities are loosely bound in a federation. **2.** Belief in or practice of communal ownership, as of goods and property. **3.** Strong devotion to the interests of one's own cultural or ethnic group rather than those of society as a whole. —**com·mu·nal·ist** *n.* —**com·mu·nal·is·tic** *adj.*

com·mu·nal·ize (kə-myōōn′əl-īz′, kŏm′yə-nəl-) *tr.v.* **-ized, -izing,**

-izes. To convert into municipal or community property.
Com·mu·nard (kŏm′yə-närd′) *n.* **1.** A member or supporter of the **Paris Commune** (*see*). **2. communard.** A member of a commune. [French, from *commune*, COMMUNE (division).]
com·mune¹ (kə-myōōn′) *intr.v.* **-muned, -muning, -munes. 1.** To have close or intimate rapport or communication. Often used with *with.* **2.** To receive Communion. ~*n.* (kŏm′yōōn′). Intimate conversation or communion. [Middle English *communen*, to distribute, share, communicate, from Old French *comuner*, from *comun*, *commun*, COMMON. Sense 2 of verb : back-formation from COMMUNION.]
com·mune² (kŏm′yōōn′) *n.* **1.** The smallest local political division of France, Belgium, Italy, and Switzerland, governed by a mayor and municipal council. **2. a.** A local community organized legally for promoting local interests. **b.** A municipal corporation in the Middle Ages. **3.** A small, often rural community whose members have common interests and in which property is often shared or owned jointly. **4.** The people of a commune. **—the Commune. 1.** The revolutionary committee that governed Paris from 1789 to 1795. **2.** The **Paris Commune** (*see*). [French, from Medieval Latin *commūnia*, community, from Latin *commūnis*, public, COMMON.]
com·mu·ni·ca·ble (kə-myōō′nĭ-kə-bəl) *adj.* **1.** Able to be communicated or transmitted. **2.** Talkative. **3.** *Medicine.* Liable to be readily passed on from one person to another; infectious. Said of a disease. **—com·mu·ni·ca·bil·i·ty, com·mu·ni·ca·ble·ness** *n.* **—com·mu·ni·ca·bly** *adv.*
com·mu·ni·cant (kə-myōō′nĭ-kənt) *n.* **1.** A person who receives, or is entitled to receive, Communion. **2.** One who communicates. ~*adj.* Communicating.
com·mu·ni·cate (kə-myōō′nə-kāt′) *v.* **-cated, -cating, -cates.** *—tr.* **1.** To make known; impart: *communicate information.* **2.** To transmit (a disease, for example). *—intr.* **1.** To share or convey information. **2. a.** To have an interchange, as of ideas. **b.** To have mutual sympathy or good mutual understanding. **3.** To express oneself in such a way that one is readily and clearly understood. **4.** To receive Communion. **5.** To be connected or form a connecting passage. [Latin *commūnicāre*, "to make common," make known, from *commūnis*, COMMON.] **—com·mu·ni·ca·tor** *n.*
com·mu·ni·ca·tion (kə-myōō′nə-kā′shən) *n. Abbr.* **comm. 1.** The act of communicating; transmission. **2.** The exchange of thoughts, messages, or the like, as by speech, signals, or writing. **3.** Something communicated. **4. communications.** A means of communicating, especially: **a.** A system for sending and receiving messages, as by mail, telephone, or telegram. **b.** Any method by which human beings pass information to one another, including publishing, broadcasting, and telecommunications. **c.** *Military.* A network of routes for sending messages and transporting troops and supplies. **5.** Any connective passage or channel. **6. communications.** The art and technology of communicating in all its forms.
communications satellite *n.* A satellite used to aid communications, as by reflecting a radio signal. Also called "comsat."
com·mu·ni·ca·tive (kə-myōō′nə-kā′tĭv, -nĭ-kə-tĭv) *adj.* **1.** Inclined to communicate readily; talkative. **2.** Of communication.
com·mun·ion (kə-myōōn′yən) *n.* **1.** A possessing or sharing in common; participation. **2.** The act of communing; the sharing of thoughts or feelings; close rapport: *in communion with nature.* **3. a.** A religious or spiritual fellowship. **b.** A body of Christians with a common religious faith who practice the same rites; a denomination. **4. a. Communion.** The Eucharist (*see*). **b.** The consecrated elements of the Eucharist. **c.** The part of the Mass in which the sacrament of the Eucharist is received. [Middle English *communioun*, from Old French *communion*, from Late Latin *commūnio* (stem *commūnion-*), the Eucharist, from Latin, participation by all, from *commūnis*, COMMON.]
com·mu·ni·qué (kə-myōō′nə-kā′, kə-myōō′nə-kā′) *n.* An official announcement made to the press and public. [French, from *communiquer*, to inform, announce, from Latin *commūnicāre*, COMMUNICATE.]
com·mu·nism (kŏm′yə-nĭz′əm) *n.* **1.** A social system characterized by the absence of classes and by common ownership of the means of production and subsistence. **2. a.** A political, economic, and social doctrine aiming at the establishment of such a society. **b.** *Often* **Communism.** The Marxist-Leninist doctrine of revolutionary struggle toward this goal, the political movement representing it, or, loosely, socialism as practiced in countries ruled by communist parties. **c. Communalism. 3.** Loosely, left-wing activity aiming at revolution. [French *communisme*, from *commun*, COMMON.]
Communism Peak. The highest mountain in the U.S.S.R., situated in the south in the Pamir range of the Tadzhik Soviet Socialist Republic. It rises to 7,495 meters (24,590 feet) above sea level.
com·mu·nist (kŏm′yə-nĭst) *n.* **1.** *Often* **Communist.** *Abbr.* **Com.** A member of a Marxist-Leninist party. **2.** A supporter of such a party or movement. **3.** A communalist. **4.** A Communard. **5.** Any radical viewed as a subversive or revolutionary. ~*adj. Often* **Communist.** Pertaining to, characteristic of, or resembling communism or communists.
com·mu·nis·tic (kŏm′yə-nĭs′tĭk) *adj.* Of, characteristic of, or inclined to communism. **—com·mu·nis·ti·cal·ly** *adv.*
Communist International *n.* The Third **International** (*see*).
Communist Manifesto *n.* A pamphlet, issued in 1848 by Karl Marx and Friedrich Engels, constituting the first statement of the principles of modern Communism.
Communist Party *n. Abbr.* **C.P.** A Marxist-Leninist party, usually

one originally belonging to the Third **International** (*see*).
com·mu·ni·tar·i·an (kə-myōō′nə-târ′ē-ən) *n.* A member or supporter of a communistic community.
com·mu·ni·ty (kə-myōō′nə-tē) *n., pl.* **-ties. 1. a.** A group of people living in the same locality or under the same local government. **b.** The district or locality in which they live. **2.** A social group or class having common characteristics. **3.** Any group having common interests: *the scientific community.* **4.** Joint participation or common ownership: *community of property.* **5.** Similarity or identity: *a community of interests.* **6.** Society as a whole; the public. Preceded by *the.* **7.** *Ecology.* **a.** A group of plants and animals living in a specific region under relatively similar conditions, and interacting with each other through food webs and other relationships. **b.** The region in which they live. [Middle English *communite*, from Old French *comunete*, from Latin *commūnitās* (stem *commūnitat-*), from *commūnis*, COMMON.]
community center *n.* A meeting place used by members of a community for social, cultural, or recreational purposes.
community chest *n.* A welfare fund financed by private contributions for aiding various charitable organizations.
com·mu·nize (kŏm′yə-nīz′) *tr.v.* **-nized, -nizing, -nizes. 1.** To make public all the property of a community. **2.** To convert to Communist principles or control. [From Latin *commūnis*, COMMON.] **—com·mu·ni·za·tion** *n.*
com·mut·a·ble (kə-myōō′tə-bəl) *adj.* **1.** Capable of being commuted; interchangeable. **2.** *Law.* Capable of being reduced in length or severity. Said of a sentence. **—com·mut·a·bil·i·ty** *n.*
com·mu·tate (kŏm′yə-tāt′) *tr.v.* **-tated, -tating, -tates. 1.** To reverse the direction of (an alternating electric current) each half-cycle. **2.** To convert (an alternating electric current) into a direct current. [Back-formation from COMMUTATION.]
com·mu·ta·tion (kŏm′yə-tā′shən) *n.* **1.** A substitution, exchange, or interchange. **2. a.** The substitution of one kind of payment for another. **b.** The payment substituted. **3.** The travel of a commuter. **4.** *Electricity.* **a.** The conversion of alternating to direct electric current. **b.** The reversing of current direction. **5.** *Law.* A reduction of a penalty to a less severe one. [Middle English, from Old French, from Latin *commutātiō* (stem *commutātiōn-*), from *commutāre*, COMMUTE.]
commutation ticket *n.* A ticket issued at a reduced rate by a railroad, bus, or other transportation company for passage over a given route for a specified number of trips.
com·mu·ta·tive (kŏm′yə-tā′tĭv, kə-myōō′tə-tĭv) *adj.* **1.** Pertaining to, involving, or characterized by substitution, interchange, or exchange. **2.** *Mathematics & Logic.* Independent of the order of terms. Said of a combining operation, such as multiplication.
commutative group *n. Mathematics.* An algebraic group in which the result of multiplying one member by another is independent of the order of the members. Also called "Abelian group."
commutative law *n. Mathematics & Logic.* The law that certain operations, such as addition, multiplication, and conjunction, are independent of the order of the terms to which they are applied.
com·mu·ta·tor (kŏm′yə-tā′tər) *n.* A cylindrical arrangement of insulated metal bars connected to the coils of an electric motor or generator to provide a unidirectional current from the generator or a reversal of current into the coils of the motor.
com·mute (kə-myōōt′) *v.* **-muted, -muting, -mutes.** *—tr.* **1.** To substitute; exchange; interchange. **2.** To convert; change; transform. **3.** To change (a penalty, debt, or payment) to a less severe one. *—intr.* **1. a.** To compensate. **b.** To serve as a substitute. **2.** To pay in gross, usually at a reduced rate, rather than in individual payments. **3.** To travel as a commuter. **4.** *Mathematics & Logic.* To satisfy or engage in a commutative operation. [Middle English *commuten*, from Latin *commutāre*, to exchange : *com-*, mutually + *mutāre*, to change.]
com·mut·er (kə-myōō′tər) *n.* A person who travels regularly from one place to another, especially between work and home.
Co·mo, Lake (kō′mō). Lake in Lombardy in north Italy, in the southern margin of the Alps. It is a popular tourist center.
Com·o·ros (kŏm′ə-rōz′). Country consisting of the Comoro archipelago (except Mayotte Island), in the Indian Ocean. Most people are of mixed African, Arab, and Malay descent. The islands became a French colony (1912) and a French overseas territory in 1947. In 1974 all the islands except Mayotte voted for independence, which was attained in 1975. The islands export vanilla, sisal, copra, coffee, and perfume oils. Area, 2,200 square kilometers (849 square miles). Population, 300,000. Capital, Moroni. See map at **Madagascar.**
comose. Variant of **comate.**
comp¹ (kŏmp) *intr.v.* **comped, comping, comps.** *Music.* To play a jazz accompaniment, as on a piano or guitar.
comp² *n. Informal.* Something, as a theater ticket, given free of charge. [Short for COMPLIMENTARY.]
comp. 1. comparative. **2.** complete. **3.** composer. **4.** composite; composition; compositor. **5.** compound. **6.** comprehensive. **7.** comprising.
com·pact¹ (kəm-păkt′, kŏm-, kŏm′păkt′) *adj.* **1.** Closely and firmly united or packed together; dense. **2.** Packed into or arranged within a relatively small space. **3.** Expressed briefly and concisely. **4.** Designating a car that is small and inexpensive to run. ~*tr.v.* (kəm-păkt′). **compacted, -pacting, -pacts. 1.** To press or join firmly together; condense; consolidate. **2.** To make or compose by pressing or joining together. ~*n.* (kŏm′păkt′). **1.** A small case containing a mirror, face powder,

and a powder puff. **2.** A small economical car. [Middle English, from Latin *compactus,* past participle of *compingere,* to join together : *com-,* together + *pangere,* to fasten.] **—com·pact·er** *n.* **—com·pac·tion** *n.* **—com·pact·ly** *adv.* **—com·pact·ness** *n.*

com·pact² (kŏm′păkt′) *n.* An agreement or covenant. [Latin *compactum,* from *compactus,* past participle of *compacīscī,* to agree together : *com-,* together + *pacīscī,* to agree.]

compact disc *n. Abbr.* **C.D.** A compact laser disc for reproducing recorded sound when it is played on a specially designed record player.

com·pac·tor (kəm-păk′tər, kŏm′păk′-) *n.* An apparatus that compresses refuse into relatively small packs for handy disposal.

com·pa·dre (kəm-pä′drā) *n. Southwestern U.S.* A friend or close companion. [Spanish, godfather, from Medieval Latin *compater,* "joint father," godfather : Latin *com-,* with, + *pater,* father.]

com·pan·der, com·pan·dor (kəm-păn′dər, kŏm-) *n. Electronics.* A system for reducing the noise level of a channel by compressing the volume range of the signal at the transmitter or recorder and restoring it to its original value at the receiving or reproducing device. [*Com*pression + Ex*pander.*]

com·pan·ion¹ (kəm-păn′yən) *n.* **1. a.** A person who accompanies or associates with another; comrade. **b.** One who lives with another as an intimate, but without formal legal ties. **2.** A person employed to assist, live with, or travel with another. **3.** Any of two or more matching or complementary things; mate; match. Also used adjectivally: *a companion volume.* **4.** A guidebook or handbook. **5.** *Abbr.* **C.** A member of the lowest rank or grade in certain orders of knighthood. **6.** The fainter part of a double star.
~tr.v. **companioned, -ioning, -ions.** *Rare.* To be a companion to; associate with; accompany. [Middle English *compai(g)noun,* from Old French *compaignon,* from Vulgar Latin *compāniō* (stem *compāniōn-*), "one who eats bread with another" : Latin *com-,* together + *pānis,* bread.]

companion² *n.* **1.** A raised frame on the open deck of a ship, containing windows to light the cabins or closed deck below. **2.** A companionway. [Obsolete Dutch *kompanje,* quarterdeck, from Old French *compagne,* from Italian *(camera della) compagna,* ship's storeroom, perhaps related to COMPANION (comrade).]

com·pan·ion·a·ble (kəm-păn′yə-nə-bəl) *adj.* Suited to be a good companion; sociable; friendly. **—com·pan·ion·a·bly** *adv.*

com·pan·ion·ship (kəm-păn′yən-shĭp′) *n.* The relationship existing between companions; fellowship.

com·pan·ion·way (kəm-păn′yən-wā′) *n.* A stairway leading from a ship's deck to the cabins or deck below.

com·pa·ny (kŭm′pə-nē) *n., pl.* **-nies. 1.** A group of people; an assembly; gathering. **2.** People assembled for a social purpose. **3.** A guest or guests. **4. a.** Companionship; fellowship. **b.** A source of companionship: *She'll be company for you.* **c.** A person's companions: *bad company.* **5.** A social environment; society: *she's rather shy in company.* **6.** A business enterprise; firm. **7.** *Abbr.* **co., Co.** A partner or partners not specifically named in a firm's title: *John Rogers and Company.* **8.** A troupe of dancers or dramatic or musical performers: *a repertory company.* **9.** *Military.* A subdivision of a regiment or battalion, usually under the command of a captain. **10.** A ship's crew and officers. **11.** A medieval guild. **—keep company.** To associate, as in courtship. **—keep someone company.** To accompany. **—part company.** To end an association or friendship.
~v. **companied, -nying, -nies.** *Archaic.* *—tr.* To accompany or associate with. *—intr.* To keep company; associate. [Middle English *compaignie,* from Old French *compagnie,* from *compain,* COMPANION.]

compar. comparative.

com·pa·ra·ble (kŏm′pər-ə-bəl) *adj.* **1.** Able to be compared; similar or equivalent. **2.** Worthy of comparison. **—com·pa·ra·bil·i·ty, com·pa·ra·ble·ness** *n.* **—com·pa·ra·bly** *adv.*

com·par·a·tist (kəm-păr′ə-tĭst) *n.* A person who employs the comparative method, as in linguistics.

com·par·a·tive (kəm-păr′ə-tĭv) *adj. Abbr.* **comp., compar. 1.** Pertaining to, based on, or involving comparison: *comparative studies.* **2.** Estimated by comparison; relative: *a comparative failure.* **3.** *Grammar.* Expressing or involving the intermediate degree of comparison of adjectives and adverbs. Compare **positive** and **superlative.**
~n. Grammar. **1.** The comparative degree. **2.** An adjective or adverb expressing the comparative degree; for example, *brighter* is the comparative of *bright; more keenly* is the comparative of *keenly.* **—com·par·a·tive·ly** *adv.*

comparative linguistics *n.* The study of two languages or linguistic varieties which are usually synchronous, with the emphasis on common features or divergence from a common source. Compare **historical linguistics.**

com·pa·ra·tor (kŏm′pə-rā′tər, kəm-păr′ə-tər) *n.* **1.** Any of various devices for comparing an aspect of an object, such as shape, color, or brightness, with a standard. **2.** An electrical device containing a circuit for comparing two signals.

com·pare (kəm-pâr′) *v.* **-pared, -paring, -pares.** *—tr.* **1.** To represent as similar, equal, or analogous; liken. Used with *to.* **2.** *Abbr.* **cf., cp.** To examine in order to note similarities or differences. Used with *with* or *and.* **3.** *Grammar.* To form the positive, comparative, or superlative degrees of (an adjective or adverb). *—intr.* **1.** To be worthy of comparison; be considered as similar or equal. Used with *with*: *Nothing can compare with real silk.* **2.** To draw comparisons.
~n. Comparison: *a musician beyond compare.* [Middle English *comparen,* from Old French *comparer,* from Latin *comparāre,* to pair, match, from *compar,* like, equal : *com-,* mutually + *pār,* equal.] **—com·par·er** *n.*
Usage: In formal usage, *compare to* and *compare with* have different interpretations. In the sense "represent as similar," *compare to* is usual: *He compared the meeting to a battlefield.* In the sense "examine in order to note similarities and differences," *compare with* is usual: *He compared Shelley's poetry with Wordsworth's.*

com·par·i·son (kəm-păr′ə-sən) *n.* **1.** A comparing or being compared; a statement or estimate of similarities and differences. **2.** The quality of being capable or worthy of being compared; similarity; likeness. **3.** *Grammar.* The modification or inflection of an adjective or adverb to denote the three degrees (positive, comparative, and superlative). [Middle English *comparisoun,* from Old French *comparaison,* from Latin *comparātiō* (stem *comparātiōn-*), from *comparāre,* COMPARE.]

com·part (kəm-pärt′) *tr.v.* **-parted, -parting, -parts.** To divide into parts or compartments; partition. [Italian *compartire,* from Late Latin *compartīrī,* to divide, share with : *com-,* with + *partīrī,* to share, from *pars* (stem *part-*), a part.]

com·part·ment (kəm-pärt′mənt) *n.* **1.** Any of the parts or spaces into which an area is subdivided. **2.** Any separate room, section, or chamber: *a storage compartment.* **3.** Any separate part or division. **4.** A separate section of a railroad car. [French, *compartiment,* from Italian, *compartire,* from Late Latin *compartīrī,* to divide, share with : *com-,* with + *partīrī,* to share, from *pars* (stem *part-*), a part + -MENT.]

com·part·men·tal·ize (kŏm′pärt-mĕn′təl-īz′, kəm-pärt′-) *tr.v.* **-ized, -izing, -izes.** To divide or partition into compartments or categories. **—com·part·men·tal·i·za·tion** *n.*

com·pass (kŭm′pəs, kŏm′-) *n.* **1. a.** A device used to determine geographical direction, usually consisting of a magnetic needle horizontally mounted or suspended and free to pivot until aligned with the magnetic field of the earth. **b.** Any other device for determining geographical direction, such as a **radio compass** or a **gyrocompass** *(both of which see).* **2.** *Sometimes* **compasses.** A V-shaped device for drawing circles or circular arcs, consisting of a pair of rigid, hinged arms, one of which is equipped with a pen or pencil and the other with a sharp point providing a central anchor or pivot about which the drawing arm is turned. Also called "pair of compasses." **3.** An enclosing line or boundary; circumference. **4.** An enclosed space or area. **5.** A range or scope; extent. **6.** *Music.* The range of a voice or instrument; register.
~tr.v. **compassed, -passing, -passes. 1.** To go around; circle. **2.** *Literary.* To surround; encircle. **3.** To understand; comprehend. **4.** To achieve; obtain; accomplish. **5.** To contrive, especially by scheming or plotting. —See Synonyms at **reach.** [Middle English *compas,* measure, circle, compasses, compass, from Old French, from *compasser,* to measure (with compasses), from Vulgar Latin *compassāre* (unattested), "to measure off by steps" : Latin *com-* (intensive) + *passus,* PACE.] **—com·pass·a·ble** *adj.*

compass *Seamen of the 12th century are the first known to have used a compass for navigation. It was simply a magnetized needle floating in a bowl of water. Decorative compass cards such as the one in this compass were common in the 18th and 19th centuries. A similar highly decorative device showing directions was usually included on a map or chart of the time, and is known as a compass rose.*

compass card *n.* A freely pivoting circular disk carrying the magnetic needles of a compass and marked with the 32 points of the compass and the 360 degrees of the circle.

com·pas·sion (kəm-păsh′ən) *n.* A deep feeling of pity for the suffering of another, and an inclination to give aid or support, or to show mercy. —See Synonyms at **pity.** [Middle English *compassioun,* from Old French *compassion,* from Late Latin *compassiō* (stem *compassiōn-*), from *compatī* (past participle *compassus*), to sympathize with : *com-,* with + *patī,* to suffer.]

com·pas·sion·ate (kəm-păsh′ən-ĭt) *adj.* Feeling or showing pity or compassion; sympathetic. —See Synonyms at **kind. —com·pas·sion·ate·ly** *adv.* **—com·pas·sion·ate·ness** *n.*

compass plant *n.* **1.** A tall plant, *Silphium laciniatum,* of central North America, having yellow flowers and lower leaves that tend to align in a north-south plane. Also called "rosinweed." **2.** Any of several similar plants.

compass rose *n.* A circle resembling a compass card, often decorated, printed onto a chart or map to indicate the points of the compass relative to the land depicted in the map or chart.

compass saw *n.* A handsaw with a narrow blade for making curved cuts.

compass window *n.* A bay window that has a rounded rather than square projection.

com·pat·i·ble (kəm-păt′ə-bəl) *adj.* **1.** Capable of living or performing in harmonious, consistent, or congenial combination with another or others. **2.** Capable of efficient integration and operation with each other or with other elements in a system. Said of pieces of machinery, electronic equipment, or the like. **3.** Capable of forming a chemically or biochemically stable system. **4.** *Botany.* Capable of being successfully grafted. Said of plants. **5.** Of or pertaining to a television system in which color broadcasts can be received in black and white by sets incapable of color reception. [Middle English, from Old French, from Medieval Latin *compatibilis,* from Late Latin *compatī,* to sympathize with. See **compassion.**] **—com·pat·i·bil·i·ty, com·pat·i·ble·ness** *n.* **—com·pat·i·bly** *adv.*

com·pa·tri·ot (kəm-pā′trē-ət, -ŏt′) *n.* **1.** A fellow countryman or countrywoman. **2.** *Informal.* A colleague. [French *compatriote,* from Late Latin *compatriōta* : *com-,* together + *patriōta,* PATRIOT.] **—com·pa·tri·ot·ic** *adj.*

com·peer (kəm-pîr′, kŏm′pîr′) *n.* **1.** A person of equal status, ability, or rank; a peer or equal. **2.** A comrade, companion, or associate. [Middle English *comper*, from Old French, from Latin *compār* : *com-*, with + *pār*, an equal, PEER.]

com·pel (kəm-pĕl') *tr.v.* **-pelled, -pelling, -pels. 1.** To force, drive, or constrain. **2.** To obtain or bring about by or as if by force; exact: *compel obedience; compel respect.* **3.** *Archaic.* To gather or unite by force; herd. —See Synonyms at **force.** [Middle English *compellen*, from Old French *compeller*, from Latin *compellere*, "to drive (cattle) together," force : *com-*, together + *pellere*, drive.] —**com·pel·la·ble** *adj.* —**com·pel·la·bly** *adv.* —**com·pel·ler** *n.*

com·pel·la·tion (kŏm'pə-lā'shən, kŏm'pĕl-ā'-) *n. Rare.* **1.** An addressing or designating by name or title. **2.** The name or title used; an appellation. [Latin *compellātiō* (stem *compellātiōn-*), from *compellāre*, to accost, address.]

com·pel·ling (kəm-pĕl'ĭng) *adj.* **1.** Forceful. **2.** Worthy of serious attention or interest; convincing. —**com·pel·ling·ly** *adv.*

com·pen·di·ous (kəm-pĕn'dē-əs) *adj.* Containing or stating briefly and concisely all the essentials of something; terse; succinct. —See Synonyms at **concise.** [Middle English, from Latin *compendiōsus*, from *compendium*, COMPENDIUM.] —**com·pen·di·ous·ly** *adv.* —**com·pen·di·ous·ness** *n.*

com·pen·di·um (kəm-pĕn'dē-əm) *n., pl.* **-ums** or **-dia** (-dē-ə). **1.** A short, complete summary; an abridgment. **2.** *British.* A collection of useful information. [Latin, "that which is weighed together," gain, saving, abridgment, from *compendere*, to weigh together : *com-*, together + *pendere*, to weigh.]

com·pen·sa·ble (kəm-pĕn'sə-bəl) *adj.* Entitled to compensation; capable of being compensated.

com·pen·sate (kŏm'pən-sāt') *v.* **-sated, -sating, -sates.** —*tr.* **1.** To make up for or offset; counterbalance. **2.** To make equivalent or satisfactory reparation to; recompense or reimburse. **3.** To provide (a pendulum, for example) with a mechanism to offset the effects of variations such as expansion. —*intr.* **1.** To provide or serve as a substitute or counterbalance. **2.** *Biology & Psychology.* To make up for a failing, defect, or unwanted effect by cultivating some other characteristic: *compensated for his lack of height by an aggressive manner.* [Latin *compensāre*, to weigh one thing against another, counterbalance : *com-*, mutually, reciprocally + *pensāre*, frequentative of *pendere*, to weigh.] —**com·pen·sa·tive** (-sā'tĭv, kəm-pĕn'sə-tĭv), **com·pen·sa·to·ry** (kəm-pĕn'sə-tôr'ē, -tōr'ē) *adj.* —**com·pen·sa·tor** *n.*

com·pen·sa·tion (kŏm'pən-sā'shən) *n.* **1. a.** The act of compensating or making amends. **b.** The state of being compensated. **2.** Something given or received as an equivalent or as reparation for a loss, service, or debt; a recompense; an indemnity. **3.** *Biology.* The counterbalancing of any functional defect in one organ by the supplementary development or activation of another organ or another part of the defective structure. **4.** *Psychology.* Behavior designed to compensate for real or imagined defects. —**com·pen·sa·tion·al** *adj.*

com·pere (kŏm'pâr') *n. British.* The master of ceremonies of a television program, variety show, cabaret, or the like. [Old French "godfather" : *com-* (joint) + *père*, father.] —**com·pere** *v.*

com·pete (kəm-pēt') *intr.v.* **-peted, -peting, -petes.** To strive or contend with another or others for profit, prize, position, or the necessities of life; vie. —See Synonyms at **rival.** [Latin *competere*, "to strive together" : *com-*, together + *petere*, to seek, strive.]

com·pe·tence (kŏm'pə-təns) *n.* Also **com·pe·ten·cy** (-tən-sē). **1.** The state or quality of being capable or competent; adequate skill or ability. **2.** Sufficient means for a comfortable existence. **3.** *Law.* The quality or condition of being legally qualified, eligible, or admissible; legal authority, qualification, or jurisdiction. **4.** *Linguistics.* The knowledge underlying an individual's ability to speak or understand a language. Compare **langue, performance. 5.** The ability possessed by embryonic cells at an early stage of development to differentiate into any of various types of cells. —See Synonyms at **ability.**

com·pe·tent (kŏm'pə-tənt) *adj.* **1.** Properly or well qualified; having adequate skill or ability; capable. **2.** *Law.* Legally qualified or fit; admissible. **3.** Rightly or properly belonging; permissible. Used with *to.* **4.** Adequate for the purpose; suitable. **5.** Able to differentiate in any of various ways. Said of embryonic cells at an early stage of development. [Middle English, from Old French, from Latin *competēns* (stem *competent-*), present participle of *competere*, to be competent, COMPETE.] —**com·pe·tent·ly** *adv.*

com·pe·ti·tion (kŏm'pə-tĭsh'ən) *n.* **1. a.** The action of competing with another or others for profit, prize, position, or the necessities of life; rivalry. **b.** The person or persons competing; one's competitors considered collectively. **2. a.** A contest, match, or other trial of skill or ability. **b.** A series of such contests. **3.** The rivalry between two or more businesses striving for the same customer or market: *Competition tends to keep prices down.* **4.** *Ecology.* The struggle between organisms in a community for scarce resources.

com·pet·i·tive (kəm-pĕt'ĭ-tĭv) *adj.* **1.** Of, involving, or determined by competition. **2.** Comparatively low in price. **3.** Having an urge to compete; inclined to rivalry. —**com·pet·i·tive·ly** *adv.* —**com·pet·i·tive·ness** *n.*

com·pet·i·tor (kəm-pĕt'ə-tər) *n.* Someone or something that competes; rival. —See Synonyms at **opponent.**

Com·piègne (kôⁿ-pyĕn'y'). Town in the Oise department of northern France, on the Oise River. The Armistice that ended World War I (1918) was signed in a railroad car in Compiègne forest, and Hitler insisted that the same coach be used to conclude the agreement by which France fell to the Germans (1940).

com·pi·la·tion (kŏm'pə-lā'shən) *n.* **1.** The act of collecting or compiling. **2.** Something compiled, such as a set of data, a report, or an anthology.

com·pile (kəm-pīl') *tr.v.* **-piled, -piling, -piles. 1.** To gather (facts, literature, or other material) into one book or corpus. **2.** To put together or compose (a book, outline, or other collection) from materials gathered from several sources. **3.** *Computer Science.* To convert to machine language. [Middle English *compilen*, from Old French *compiler*, from Latin *compīlāre*, "to heap together," plunder, plagiarize : *com-*, together + *pīlāre*, to plunder, "pile up (booty)," from *pīla*, "pile," PILLAR.]

com·pil·er (kəm-pī'lər) *n.* **1.** A person who compiles something. **2.** *Computer Science.* A computer program that converts from a high-level language into machine language. Each language needs its own compiler for each type of computer.

com·pla·cen·cy (kəm-plā'sən-sē) *n.* Also **com·pla·cence** (-səns). **1. a.** A feeling of contentment or satisfaction; gratification. **b.** Equanimity, sometimes excessive, in the face of real or potential problems. **2.** Self-satisfaction; smugness.

com·pla·cent (kəm-plā'sənt) *adj.* **1.** Having or showing complacency. **2.** Complaisant. [Originally "pleasing," from Latin *complacēns* (stem *complacent-*), present participle of *complacēre*, to please : *com-* (intensive) + *placēre*, to please.] —**com·pla·cent·ly** *adv.*

com·plain (kəm-plān') *intr.v.* **-plained, -plaining, -plains. 1.** To express feelings of pain, dissatisfaction, or resentment. **2.** To describe one's pains, problems, or dissatisfactions. Used with *of.* **3.** To make a formal accusation or report a grievance officially: *complained to the police about the neighbor's dog.* —See Synonyms at **object.** [Middle English *compleinen*, from Old French *complaindre*, from Vulgar Latin *complangere* (unattested) : Latin *com-* (intensive) + *plangere*, to lament.] —**com·plain·er** *n.*

com·plain·ant (kəm-plā'nənt) *n. Law.* A person who makes a complaint or files a formal charge, as in a court of law; plaintiff.

com·plaint (kəm-plānt') *n.* **1.** An expression of pain, dissatisfaction, resentment, discontent, or grief. **2.** A cause or reason for complaining; grievance. **3.** A cause of physical pain; malady; illness. **4.** A literary outpouring of grief, typically a poem lamenting lost love. **5.** *Law.* A formal allegation made by the plaintiff in a civil action. [Middle English *compleint(e)*, from Old French *complainte*, from *complaint*, past participle of *complaindre*, COMPLAIN.]

com·plai·sance (kəm-plā'səns, -zəns) *n.* Willing compliance with the wishes of others; obligingness.

com·plai·sant (kəm-plā'sənt, -zənt, kŏm'plā-zănt') *adj.* Showing a desire or willingness to please; cheerfully obliging. [French, pleasing, agreeable, from Old French, present participle of *complaire*, to please, from Latin *complacēre*. See **complacent.**] —**com·plai·sant·ly** *adv.*

com·pleat (kəm-plēt') *adj. Archaic.* Complete: "*The Compleat Angler*" (Izaak Walton). Often used humorously.

com·plect (kəm-plĕkt') *tr.v.* **-plected, -plecting, -plects.** To join by weaving or twining together; interweave. [Latin *complectī, complectere* : *com-*, together + *plectere*, to entwine.]

com·plect·ed (kəm-plĕk'tĭd) *adj. Regional.* Complexioned. Used only in combination: *dark-complected.* [Irregularly from COMPLEXION.]

com·ple·ment (kŏm'plə-mənt) *n.* **1.** Something that completes, makes up a whole, or perfects. **2.** The quantity or number needed to make up a whole. **3.** Either of two parts that complete the whole or mutually complete each other. **4.** The full quantity, allowance, or amount; a complete set. **5.** *Geometry.* An angle related to another so that the sum of their measures is 90 degrees. **6.** *Grammar.* A word or words used after a verb to complete a predicate construction; for example, *their best player* acts as the complement in the sentence *They considered her their best player.* **7.** An interval in music that completes an octave when added to a given interval. **8.** The full crew of officers and men required to man a ship. **9.** *Biochemistry.* The heat-sensitive substance found in normal blood serum that helps to destroy pathogenic bacteria and other materials. In this sense, also formerly called "alexin."

~*tr.v.* (kŏm'plə-mĕnt') **complemented, -menting, -ments.** To add or serve as a complement to. [Middle English, from Latin *complēmentum*, from *complēre*, to COMPLETE.]

Usage: Complement and *compliment* are often confused because of their identical pronunciations, as are the adjectival pair *complementary* and *complimentary.* The former has the sense of completion, the latter the sense of praising.

com·ple·men·tal (kŏm'plə-mĕn'təl) *adj.* Complementary. —**com·ple·men·tal·ly** *adv.*

com·ple·men·ta·ry (kŏm'plə-mĕn'tə-rē, -mĕn'trē) *adj.* **1.** Forming or serving as a complement; completing. **2.** Complementing each other; supplying what is needed to make whole or complete. **3.** *Genetics.* Producing effects when in combination that are different from those produced separately. Said of genes. —**com·ple·men·ta·ri·ness** *n.*

complementary angles *pl.n.* Two angles whose sum is 90 degrees.

complementary color *n.* Either of a pair of colors, such as blue-green and red, that appear as white or gray when mixed in the correct proportions.

complement fixation *n. Biochemistry.* The joining of a complement to the antigen-antibody pair for which it is specific. It is used as a test for the presence of specific antigens and antibodies and hence used in the diagnosis of certain infections.

com·plete (kəm-plēt') *adj. Abbr.* **comp. 1.** Having all necessary or

normal parts; entire; whole. **2.** *Botany.* Having all characteristic floral parts, including sepals, petals, stamens, and a pistil. **3.** Brought to a satisfactory conclusion; ended: *Work on the new bridge is almost complete.* **4.** Thorough; exhaustive: *a complete report on the accident.* **5.** Total; absolute: *a complete stranger.* **6.** Fully supplied or equipped: *comes complete with its own instruction manual.* **7.** *Archaic.* Skilled; accomplished.
~*tr.v.* **completed, -pleting, -pletes. 1.** To make whole or complete. **2.** To fill in (a form). **3.** To conclude. [Middle English *complet(e),* from Old French, from Latin *complētus,* past participle of *complēre,* to fill up : *com-* (intensive) + *plēre,* to fill.] **—com·plete·ly** *adv.* **—com·plete·ness** *n.* **—com·ple·tive** *adj.*

Synonyms: *close, conclude, end, finish, terminate.*

Usage: In formal English, anything that is *complete* is absolutely so. It is therefore incorrect to use such qualifying words as *more, most, very, quite,* and so on, unless the implication is one of comprehensiveness of scope or thoroughness of treatment (where degrees of completeness are felt to exist), as in *Her report is a more complete account of the situation than is mine.*

com·ple·tion (kəm-plē′shən) *n.* **1.** The act of concluding, perfecting, or making entire. **2.** The state of being completed. **3.** Accomplishment; realization; fulfillment.

com·plex (kəm-plĕks′, kŏm′plĕks′) *adj.* **1.** Consisting of interconnected or interwoven parts; composite; compound. **2.** Involved or intricate, as in structure; complicated. **3.** *Grammar.* **a.** Pertaining to or designating a word consisting of at least one bound form, such as *slowly.* **b.** Pertaining to a **complex sentence** *(see).* **4.** *Mathematics.* Of, pertaining to, or designating a number or variable that has both a real and an imaginary part.
~*n.* (kŏm′plĕks′). **1.** A whole composed of intricate or interconnected parts. **2.** *Psychology.* A connected group of repressed ideas that compel characteristic or habitual patterns of thought, feeling, and action. **3.** *Informal.* An exaggerated or obsessive concern or fear. **4.** A group of buildings designed for a particular purpose or supplying a variety of related facilities: *an apartment complex; an industrial complex.* **5.** *Chemistry.* **a.** A complex ion. **b.** Any compound in which two molecules or groups are linked to each other by a coordinate bond. [Latin *complexus,* past participle of *complectī, complectere,* to entwine : *com-,* together + *plectere,* to twine, plait.] **—com·plex·ly** *adv.* **—com·plex·ness** *n.*

Synonyms: *complicated, intricate, involved, knotty.*

complex conjugate *n. Mathematics.* A complex number that differs from another complex number only by the reversal of the sign of the imaginary part. For example, $a + bi$ has as complex conjugate $a - bi$.

complex fraction *n.* A fraction in which the numerator or denominator or both contain fractions, such as $^{1}/_{5/6}$. Also called "compound fraction."

com·plex·i·fy (kəm′plĕks′ĭ-fī, kŏm′-) *v.* **-fied, -fying, -fies.** —*tr.* To make more complex. —*intr.* To become more complex. **—com·plex·i·fi·ca·tion** *n.*

complex ion *n. Chemistry.* An ion or radical in which several groups or ions are attached to a central atom by coordinate bonds. Also called "complex," "coordination compound."

com·plex·ion (kəm-plĕk′shən) *n.* **1.** The natural color, texture, and appearance of the skin, especially on the face. **2.** General character, aspect, or appearance. **3.** In medieval physiology, the combination of the four humors of cold, heat, moistness, and dryness in specific proportions, thought to control the temperament and the constitution of the body. [Middle English *complexioun,* physical constitution, temperament, from Old French *complexion,* from Medieval Latin *complexiō* (stem *complexiōn-*), "combination of corporeal humors," from Latin, connection, combination, from *complexus.* See **complex.**] **—com·plex·ion·al** *adj.*

com·plex·ioned (kəm-plĕk′shənd) *adj.* Of or having a specified complexion. Used in combination: *fair-complexioned.*

com·plex·i·ty (kəm-plĕk′sə-tē) *n., pl.* **-ties. 1.** The state or condition of being intricate or complex. **2.** Something intricate or complex.

complex number *n.* A number consisting of a real and imaginary part, usually expressed in the form $a + bi$ where a and b are real numbers and i is the imaginary unit such that $i^2 = -1$.

complex plane *n.* A plane that has complex numbers as its points.

complex salt *n.* A salt containing one or more complex ions.

complex sentence *n. Grammar.* A sentence containing one main clause and one or more subordinate clauses; for example, the sentence *When the rain stops, we'll leave* is a complex sentence. Compare **simple sentence.**

complex variable *n.* An expression of the form $x + iy$, where x and y are real variables and $i^2 = -1$.

com·pli·ance (kəm-plī′əns) *n.* Also **com·pli·an·cy** (-ən-sē). **1.** The act of yielding to a wish, request, or demand; acquiescence. **2.** A disposition or tendency to yield to others. **3. a.** *Mechanics.* The extension or displacement of a loaded structure per unit load. **b.** Flexibility. Not in technical usage.

com·pli·ant (kəm-plī′ənt) *adj.* Also *archaic* **com·pli·a·ble** (kəm-plī′ə-bəl). Yielding; submissive. —See Synonyms at **obedient.** [COMPL(Y) + -ANT.] **—com·pli·ant·ly** *adv.*

com·pli·ca·cy (kəm-plĭk′ə-sē) *n., pl.* **-cies.** *Rare.* **1.** The state of being complicated. **2.** A complication.

com·pli·cate (kŏm′plĭ-kāt′) *tr.v.* **-cated, -cating, -cates. 1.** To make complex, intricate, or perplexing. **2.** To combine so as to produce a more complex result. **3.** *Pathology.* To aggravate (an existing disease).
~*adj.* (kŏm′plə-kĭt). **1.** *Biology.* Folded longitudinally one or several times, as certain leaves or the wings of some insects are. **2.** *Archaic.* Complex; intricate; involved. [Latin *complicāre,* to fold together : *com-,* together + *plicāre,* to fold.]

com·pli·cat·ed (kŏm′plə-kā′tĭd) *adj.* Containing intricately combined or involved parts; not easily understood or untangled. —See Synonyms at **complex.** **—com·pli·cat·ed·ly** *adv.* **—com·pli·cat·ed·ness** *n.*

com·pli·ca·tion (kŏm′plə-kā′shən) *n.* **1.** The act of complicating. **2.** A confused or intricate relationship of parts. **3.** Any factor, condition, or event that is complicated or that complicates. **4.** *Pathology.* A condition occurring during the course of or as a consequence of another disease and often aggravating it.

com·plice (kŏm′plĭs) *n. Obsolete.* An associate or accomplice. [Middle English, from Old French, from Latin *complex,* closely connected, hence a confederate : *com-,* together + *-plex,* -fold.]

com·plic·i·ty (kəm-plĭs′ə-tē) *n., pl.* **-ties. 1.** The state of being an accomplice in a wrongful act. **2.** *Rare.* Complexity.

com·pli·er (kəm-plī′ər) *n.* A person who complies or yields.

com·pli·ment (kŏm′plə-mənt) *n.* **1.** An expression of praise, admiration, or congratulation. **2.** A formal act of civility, courtesy, or respect. **3.** *Usually* **compliments.** A formal or ceremonious greeting or expression of regards: *Please give my compliments to your parents.* **4.** *Archaic.* A gift presented for services rendered; gratuity.
~*tr.v.* **complimented, -menting, -ments. 1.** To pay a compliment to. **2.** To show fondness, regard, or respect for (someone) by giving a gift or performing a favor. —See Usage note at **complement.** [French, from Spanish *cumplimiento,* from *cumplir,* to complete, behave properly, be courteous, from Latin *complēre,* to fill up : *com-* (intensive) + *plēre,* to fill.]

com·pli·men·ta·ry (kŏm′plə-mĕn′tər-ē, -trē) *adj.* **1.** Expressing, using, or resembling a compliment. **2.** Given free of charge to repay a favor, as an act of courtesy, or for publicity purposes. **—com·pli·men·ta·ri·ly** *adv.*

com·pline, com·plin (kŏm′plĭn) *n. Ecclesiastical.* **1.** The last of the seven **canonical hours** *(see).* **2.** The time of day set aside for this prayer, usually just before retiring to bed. [Middle English *compline,* from Old French *complie,* from Medieval Latin *(hōra) complēta,* "completed (hour)," from Latin *complētus,* past participle of *complēre,* COMPLETE.]

com·ply (kəm-plī′) *intr.v.* **-plied, -plying, -plies. 1.** To act in accordance with a command, request, rule, wish, or the like. Used with *with.* **2.** *Obsolete.* To be courteous or obedient. [Italian *complire,* from Spanish *cumplir,* to complete, do what is proper, be courteous, from Latin *complēre,* to fill up : *com-* (intensive) + *plēre,* to fill.]

com·po (kŏm′pō) *n., pl.* **-pos.** Any of various combined substances, such as mortar or plaster, formed by mixing ingredients. [Short for COMPOSITION.]

com·po·nent (kəm-pō′nənt) *n.* **1.** A constituent part of a complex whole, especially of a mechanical or electrical device. **2.** *Mathematics.* Any of a set of two or more vectors having a sum equal to a given vector. **3.** *Chemistry.* Any of the minimum number of substances required to specify completely the composition of all phases of a chemical system.
~*adj.* Being or functioning as a component; constituent. [Latin *compōnens* (stem *compōnent-*), present participle of *compōnere,* to place together : *com-,* together + *pōnere,* to put.]

com·po·ny (kəm-pō′nē, kŏm-) *adj. Heraldry.* Composed of a row of squares in alternating tinctures. [Old French *componé,* "made of pieces," from *compon, copon,* piece. See **coupon.**]

com·port (kəm-pôrt′) *v.* **-ported, -porting, -ports.** —*tr.* To conduct or behave (oneself) in a specified manner. —*intr.* To agree, correspond, or harmonize. Used with *with.* [Old French *comporter,* to support, conduct, from Latin *comportāre,* to bring together, later to support : *com-,* together + *portāre,* to carry, bear.] **—com·port·ment** *n.*

com·pose (kəm-pōz′) *v.* **-posed, -posing, -poses.** —*tr.* **1.** To make up or be the constituent parts of; constitute or form. —See Usage note at **comprise.** **2.** To make or create by putting together parts or elements. **3.** To create or produce (a literary or musical piece). **4.** To make (oneself) calm or tranquil; quiet. **5.** To settle (arguments or differences); reconcile. **6. a.** To arrange aesthetically or artistically (the constituents of a painting, for example). **b.** To put in order; arrange (one's thoughts, for example). **7.** *Printing.* To arrange or set (type or matter to be printed). —*intr.* **1.** To create literary or musical pieces. **2.** *Printing.* To set type. [Middle English, from Old French *composer* : *com-,* together, from Latin + *poser,* to place, from Latin *pausāre,* to cease, repose, hence to place, from *pausa,* a pause, from Greek *pausis,* from *pauein,* to stop.]

com·posed (kəm-pōzd′) *adj.* Calm; serene; self-possessed. —See Synonyms at **cool.** **—com·pos·ed·ly** (kəm′pō′zĭd-lē) *adv.* **—com·pos·ed·ness** (kəm′pō′zĭd-nĭs) *n.*

com·pos·er (kəm-pō′zər) *n. Abbr.* **comp.** A person who composes, especially one who composes music.

composing stick *n. Printing.* Especially formerly, a small shallow tray, usually metal and with an adjustable end, in which a compositor sets type before it is placed in the galley.

com·pos·ite (kəm-pŏz′ĭt) *adj. Abbr.* **comp. 1.** Made up of distinct components; compound. **2.** *Mathematics.* Having factors; factorable. **3.** *Botany.* Of, belonging to, or characteristic of the Compositae, a large plant family characterized by flower heads consisting of both **ray flowers** and **disk flowers** *(both of which see),* as in the daisy, of disk flowers only, as in wormwood, or of ray flowers only, as in

PRONUNCIATION KEY

ă, pat; ā, pay; âr, care;
ä, father, are; b, bib;
ch, church; d, deed; ĕ, pet;
ē, be; f, fife; g, gag; h, hat;
hw, which; ĭ, pit; ī, pie;
îr, pier; j, judge; k, kick;
l, lid, needle; m, mum;
n, no, sudden; ng, thing;
ŏ, pot; ō, toe; ô, paw, for;
oi, noise; ou, out; o͝o, book;
o͞o, boot; p, pop; r, roar;
s, sauce; sh, ship, dish;
t, tight; th, thin, path;
th, this, bathe; ŭ, cut; ûr, fur;
v, valve; w, with; y, yes;
z, zebra, size; zh, vision;
ə, about, item, edible, gallop, circus, peaceful

IN FOREIGN WORDS:
à, *Fr.* ami; œ, *Fr.* feu, *Ger.* schön; ü, *Fr.* tu, *Ger.* über; KH, *Ger.* ich, *Scot.* loch; N, *Fr.* bon; y′, *Fr.* Compiègne

STRESS MARKS:
Primary stress: ′
in·cite′ (ĭn-sīt′)
Secondary stress: ′
in′sight′ (ĭn′sīt′)

the dandelion. **4. Composite.** *Architecture.* Pertaining to or designating the Composite order.
~*n.* **1.** A composite structure or entity. **2.** A complex material, such as wood or fiberglass, in which two or more distinct, structurally complementary substances, especially metals, ceramics, glasses, and polymers, combine to produce some structural or functional properties not present in any individual component. **3.** A composite plant.
~*tr.v.* **composited, -iting, -ites.** To make composite or into something composite. [Latin *compositus,* past participle of *compōnere,* to put together : *com-,* together + *pōnere,* to put.] **—com·pos·ite·ly** *adv.* **—com·pos·ite·ness** *n.*

composite number *n.* An integer exactly divisible by at least one number other than itself or 1.

Composite order *n. Architecture.* A late Roman style of capital formed by superimposing Ionic volutes on a Corinthian capital.

com·po·si·tion (kŏm′pə-zĭsh′ən) *n. Abbr.* **comp. 1.** A putting together of parts or elements to form a whole; a combining. **2.** The manner in which such parts are combined or related; constitution; make-up. **3.** The result or product of composing; mixture; compound. **4.** The arrangement of artistic parts so as to form a unified whole. **5.** The art or act of composing a literary or musical work. **6.** Any work of art, literature, or music, or its structure and arrangement. **7. a.** An essay; especially, one written as a school exercise. **b.** An exercise or class in writing poetry or prose. **8.** *Linguistics.* The formation of compound words from separate words. **9.** *Printing.* Typesetting. **10.** *Law.* **a.** A settlement whereby the creditors of a debtor about to enter bankruptcy agree to accept partial payment in lieu of full payment for debts. **b.** The sum thus agreed upon. **11.** *Archaic.* Settlement by mutual agreement or compromise. [Middle English *composicioun,* from Old French *composition,* from Latin *compositiō* (stem *compositiōn-*), from *compōnere,* to put together, arrange : *com-,* together + *pōnere,* to put.] **—com·po·si·tion·al** *adj.*

composition of forces *n.* The finding or determination of a vector that is the resultant of a given set of forces.

com·pos·i·tor (kəm-pŏz′ə-tər) *n. Abbr.* **comp.** *Printing.* A typesetter. **—com·pos·i·to·ri·al** (kəm-pŏz′-ə-tôr′ē-əl, -tōr′-) *adj.*

com·pos men·tis (kŏm′pəs mĕn′tĭs) *adj.* Of sound mind; sane. [Latin, having control of one's mind.]

com·post (kŏm′pōst) *n.* **1.** A mixture of decaying organic matter, such as leaves and manure, used as fertilizer. **2.** A composition; mixture.
~*tr.v.* **composted, -posting, -posts. 1.** To fertilize with compost. **2.** To change (vegetable matter) to compost. [Middle English, stew, compote, from Old French *composte,* stewed fruit, and *compost,* mixture, respectively from Latin *composita* and *compositum,* feminine and neuter of *compositus,* put together, COMPOSITE.]

com·po·sure (kəm-pō′zhər) *n.* Self-possession; calmness; tranquillity. —See Synonyms at **equanimity.** [From COMPOSE.]

com·pote (kŏm′pōt; *French* kôN-pôt′) *n.* **1.** Fruit stewed or cooked in syrup. **2.** A long-stemmed dish for holding fruit, nuts, or candy. [French, from Old French *composte,* stewed fruit, COMPOST.]

com·pound¹ (kŏm-pound′, kəm-) *v.* **-pounded, -pounding, -pounds.** *—tr.* **1.** To combine; mix. **2.** To produce or create by combining ingredients or parts. **3.** *Pharmacology.* To mix (drugs) according to prescription. **4.** To settle (a debt, for example) by agreeing on an amount less than the claim; adjust. **5.** To compute (compound interest). **6.** *Law.* To agree, for payment or other consideration, not to prosecute: *compound a felony.* **7.** To add to or intensify (a difficulty, an error, or the like). *—intr.* **1.** To come to terms; agree. **2.** To settle or compromise with a creditor. —See Synonyms at **mix.**
~*adj.* (kŏm′pound, kŏm-pound′). Consisting of two or more substances, ingredients, elements, or parts.
~*n.* (kŏm′pound). *Abbr.* **comp., cpd. 1.** A combination of two or more elements or parts. **2.** *Linguistics.* **a.** A word formed either from other words, for example *racehorse,* or by the addition or combination of affixes or combining forms, for example *geography* or *isometric.* **b.** An intonational pattern exhibiting a primary stress and a terminal juncture. **c.** A verb form, in any of various tenses, the passive mood, or the like, consisting of a main verb and at least one auxiliary verb; for example, *may have been eaten.* **d.** In transformational grammar, a sequence of words not connected by a functional element in surface structure but functioning as a grammatical unit in deep structure. **3.** *Chemistry.* A pure, macroscopically homogeneous substance consisting of atoms or ions of two or more different elements in definite proportions, and usually having properties unlike those of its constituent elements. [Middle English *compounen,* from Old French *compon(d)re,* from Latin *compōnere,* to put together : *com-,* together + *pōnere,* to put.] **—com·pound·a·ble** *adj.* **—com·pound·er** *n.*

com·pound² (kŏm′pound) *n.* **1.** In the Orient, an enclosure for a factory or group of European residences. **2.** In South Africa, living quarters, usually inside an enclosure, for black workers. **3.** A large enclosed area inside a prison, concentration camp, or the like. [Portuguese *campon* or Dutch *kampoeng,* from Malay *kampong,* village, cluster of buildings.]

com·pound-com·plex sentence (kŏm′pound-kŏm′plĕks) *n.* A sentence consisting of at least two coordinate main clauses and one or more subordinate clauses.

compound engine *n.* **1.** A steam engine in which the steam is expanded in two or more stages in different cylinders. **2.** A gas or diesel engine in which the exhaust gases are used to drive a turbine-powered supercharger.

compound eye *n.* The eye of most insects and some crustaceans, composed of many light-sensitive elements, each with its own refractive system and each forming a portion of an image.

compound flower *n.* A flower head of a composite plant, such as a daisy, consisting of numerous small flowers appearing as a single bloom.

compound fraction *n. Mathematics.* A **complex fraction** *(see).*

compound fracture *n.* A fracture in which broken bone lacerates soft tissue.

compound interest *n.* Interest computed on the accumulated unpaid interest as well as on the original principal. Compare **simple interest.**

compound leaf *n.* A leaf consisting of two or more separate leaflets borne on a single leafstalk.

compound microscope *n.* A microscope consisting of an objective and an eyepiece, that is, two lenses or lens systems, at opposite ends of an adjustable tube.

compound number *n.* A quantity, such as 10 pounds 5 ounces or 3 feet 4 inches, involving different units of measure.

compound pendulum *n.* See **pendulum.**

compound sentence *n.* A sentence of two or more coordinate main clauses, often joined by a conjunction or conjunctions, as *The problem was difficult, but I finally found the answer.*

compound tense *n. Grammar.* A tense in which the verb is expressed by means of at least one auxiliary; for example, the present perfect tense of "go," *I have gone,* as opposed to the simple past tense, *I went.* Compare **simple tense.**

compound time *n. Music.* Time in which each beat in a bar is divisible into thirds, sixths, and so on; for example, 6/8 time.

com·pra·dor, com·pra·dore (kŏm′prə-dôr′) *n.* Formerly, in China and certain other Asian countries, a native agent for a foreign business. [Portuguese, "buyer," from Late Latin *comparātor,* from Latin *comparāre,* provide, buy, prepare : *com-* (collectively) + *parāre,* to prepare.]

com·pre·hend (kŏm′prĭ-hĕnd′) *tr.v.* **-hended, -hending, -hends. 1.** To grasp mentally; understand or fathom. **2.** To take in; include; embrace. —See Synonyms at **apprehend, include.** [Middle English *comprehenden,* from Latin *comprehendere,* to grasp mentally : *com-,* together in mind, mentally + *prehendere,* to seize, grasp.]

com·pre·hen·si·ble (kŏm′prĭ-hĕn′sə-bəl) *adj.* Capable of being comprehended or understood; intelligible. **—com·pre·hen·si·bil·i·ty, com·pre·hen·si·ble·ness** *n.* **—com·pre·hen·si·bly** *adv.*

com·pre·hen·sion (kŏm′prĭ-hĕn′shən) *n.* **1.** The act of or capacity for comprehending or understanding. **2.** Comprehensiveness. **3.** *Logic.* The attributes making up a concept; intension. **4.** An exercise designed to test students' powers of comprehension.

com·pre·hen·sive (kŏm′prĭ-hĕn′sĭv) *adj.* **1.** Including or comprehending much; large in scope or content. **2.** Marked by or showing extensive understanding: *comprehensive knowledge.* **3.** Designating a type of motor-vehicle insurance that provides wide-ranging cover.
~*n.* **1.** Often **comprehensives.** *Informal.* Examinations covering the entire field of major study, given in the final undergraduate or graduate year of college. **2.** An advertising layout showing all the elements planned for an advertisement but not ready for actual reproduction. **—com·pre·hen·sive·ly** *adv.* **—com·pre·hen·sive·ness** *n.*

com·press (kəm-prĕs′) *tr.v.* **-pressed, -pressing, -presses.** To press together or force into a smaller space; condense; compact. —See Synonyms at **contract.**
~*n.* (kŏm′prĕs′). *Medicine.* **1.** A soft pad of gauze or other material, either hot or cold, dry or moistened with water or medication, applied to a part of the body to alleviate pain or reduce inflammation. **2.** A soft pad of gauze or other material applied with force to reduce bleeding. **3.** A machine for compressing, especially for baling cotton. [Middle English *compressen,* from Old French *compresser,* from Late Latin *compressāre,* frequentative of Latin *comprimere* (past participle *compressus*), to press together : *com-,* together + *premere,* to press.] **—com·press·i·bil·i·ty, com·press·i·ble·ness** *n.* **—com·press·i·ble** *adj.*

com·pressed (kəm-prĕst′) *adj.* **1.** Pressed together or into less space; made compact. **2.** *Biology.* Flattened laterally or lengthwise. Said of certain seed pods or the bodies of many fish.

compressed air *n.* Air under greater than atmospheric pressure, especially when used to power a mechanical device or provide a portable supply of oxygen.

compressed air illness *n.* **Decompression sickness** *(see).*

com·pres·sion (kəm-prĕsh′ən) *n.* **1. a.** The act or process of compressing. **b.** The state of being compressed. **2. a.** The process by which the working substance in a heat engine, such as the vapor mixture in the cylinder of an internal-combustion engine, is compressed. **b.** The engine cycle during which this process occurs.

com·pres·sion-ig·ni·tion engine (kəm-prĕsh′ən-ĭg-nĭsh′ən) *n.* A **diesel-engine** *(see).*

compression ratio *n.* The ratio of the volume of the combustion chamber of an internal-combustion engine with the piston at the bottom of its stroke to the volume when the piston has reached the top of its stroke.

compression wave or **compressional wave** *n.* A wave, as of sound, propagated by means of the compression of an elastic medium.

com·pres·sive (kəm-prĕs′ĭv) *adj.* Compressing or capable of compressing. **—com·pres·sive·ly** *adv.*

Composite order *A combination by the Romans of the scrolls (or volutes) of the Greeks' Ionic order and the acanthus leaves of the Corinthian order. The Composite style appeared in the first century A.D.*

compound eye *The horsefly (genus* Tabanus, *above), like other insects and crustaceans, has eyes made up of many separate elements that are effectively individual eyes. Each element transmits a single spot of light, so that the insect sees the world as a shifting mosaic of dots.*

com·pres·sor (kəm-prĕs′ər) n. **1.** A device or machine for compressing a gas. **2.** The part of a gas turbine that compresses the air before it enters the combustion chambers. **3.** *Electronics.* A device for reducing the variation in signal amplitude in a communication channel. **4.** *Anatomy.* Any muscle that acts to compress an organ or part. **5.** *Medicine.* An instrument used for holding down a tissue or part of the body.

com·prise (kəm-prīz′) tr.v. **-prised, -prising, -prises. 1.** To consist of; be composed of. **2.** To include; contain. **3.** To constitute; make up. —See Synonyms at **include.** [Middle English *comprisen,* from Old French *comprendre* (past participle *compris*), to comprehend, include, from Latin *comprehendere,* to grasp mentally : *com-,* together, in mind, mentally + *prehendere,* to seize.] —**com·pris·a·ble** adj.

Usage: The traditional rule states that the whole *comprises* the parts; the parts *compose* the whole. In strict usage: *The Union comprises fifty states. Fifty states compose* (or *constitute* or *make up*) *the Union.* While this distinction is still maintained by many writers, *comprise* is increasingly used, especially in the passive, in place of *compose: The Union is comprised of fifty states.* This last example is considered unacceptable by many.

com·pro·mise (kŏm′prə-mīz′) n. **1.** A settlement of differences in which each side makes concessions. **2.** Anything resulting from such a settlement. **3.** Something midway between different things or courses of action, combining certain of their qualities. Also used adjectively: *a compromise proposal.* **4.** Loosely, a concession, especially one involving one's principles or integrity: *She had to make a lot of compromises to keep this job.* ~v. **compromised, -mising, -mises.** —*tr.* **1.** To settle by concessions. **2.** To expose or make liable to scandal, suspicion, or disrepute. **3.** To make concessions damaging to (one's interests, principles, or integrity). —*intr.* To make a compromise. [Middle English *compromis,* from Old French, from Latin *comprōmissum,* from *comprōmittere,* to promise mutually (to abide by an arbiter's decision) : *com-,* mutually + *prōmittere,* to PROMISE.] —**com·pro·mis·er** n.

Comp·tom·e·ter (kŏmp-tŏm′ə-tər) n. A trademark for a high-speed calculating and adding machine.

Comp·ton (kŏmp′tən), **Arthur Holly** (1892–1962). U.S. physicist, noted for his research into radiation. In 1923 he discovered the Compton effect, an important step toward the development of quantum mechanics. He was awarded the Nobel Prize for physics with C.T.R. Wilson (1927).

Comp·ton-Bur·nett (kŏmp′tən-bər-nĕt′), **Dame Ivy** (1892–1969). British novelist. She is best remembered for a series of popular novels about life in the wealthy households of England, at the turn of the century.

Compton effect n. The increase in wavelength of electromagnetic radiation, especially of an x-ray or gamma-ray photon, scattered by an electron. [After A.H. COMPTON, who discovered it.]

comptroller. Variant of **controller** (sense 2).

com·pul·sion (kəm-pŭl′shən) n. **1.** The act of compelling or forcing; coercion; constraint. **2.** The state of being compelled. **3.** *Psychology.* **a.** An irresistible impulse to act in a certain way, regardless of the rationality of the motivation. **b.** An act or acts performed in response to such an impulse. [Middle English *compulsioun,* from Old French *compulsion,* from Late Latin *compulsiō* (stem *compulsiōn-*), from Latin *compellere* (past participle *compulsus*), COMPEL.]

com·pul·sive (kəm-pŭl′sĭv) adj. **1.** Having the power to or tending to compel. **2.** *Psychology.* Acting from or constituting compulsion or obsession: *a compulsive gambler.* —**com·pul·sive·ly** adv. —**com·pul·sive·ness** n.

com·pul·so·ry (kəm-pŭl′sə-rē) adj. **1.** Obligatory; required; enforced. **2.** Employing or exerting compulsion; coercive; compelling. [Medieval Latin *compulsōrius,* from Latin *compellere,* to COMPEL.] —**com·pul·so·ri·ly** adv. —**com·pul·so·ri·ness** n.

com·punc·tion (kəm-pŭngk′shən) n. **1.** A strong uneasiness caused by a sense of guilt; remorse. **2.** A slight uneasiness or feeling of regret. —See Synonyms at **qualm.** [Middle English, from Old French *componction,* from Late Latin *compunctiō* (stem *compunctiōn-*), "prick of conscience," from Latin, puncture, from *compungere,* to prick hard : *com-* (intensive) + *pungere,* to prick, sting.] —**com·punc·tious** adj. —**com·punc·tious·ly** adv.

com·pur·ga·tion (kŏm′pər-gā′shən) n. *Law.* The former practice, especially in the Middle Ages, of clearing an accused person of a charge by having a number of people swear to a belief in his innocence or good character. [Late Latin *compurgātiō* (stem *compurgātiōn-*), from Latin *compurgāre,* to purify completely : *com-* (intensive) + *purgāre,* to purify.] —**com·pur·ga·tor** n.

com·pu·ta·tion (kŏm′pyōō-tā′shən) n. **1.** The act, process, or method of computing. **2.** The result of computing.

com·pute (kəm-pyōōt′) v. **-puted, -puting, -putes.** —*tr.* To determine by mathematics, especially by numerical methods or with the aid of a computer. —*intr.* **1.** To determine an amount or number. **2.** To perform mathematical or logical calculations. Used of a computer. —See Synonyms at **calculate.** ~n. Computation; calculation. Used in the phrase *beyond compute.* [Latin *computāre,* to reckon together : *com-,* together in mind, mentally + *putāre,* to think, reckon.] —**com·put·a·bil·i·ty** n. —**com·put·a·ble** adj.

com·put·er (kəm-pyōō′tər) n. One that computes; specifically, an electronic machine that performs high-speed mathematical or logical calculations or that assembles, stores, correlates, or otherwise processes and prints information derived from coded data in accordance with a predetermined **program** *(see).* See **digital computer, analog computer.**

com·pu·ter·ese (kəm-pyōō′tə-rēz′, -rēs′) n. The technical language or jargon of the computer profession.

com·put·er·ize (kəm-pyōō′tə-rīz′) tr.v. **-ized, -izing, -izes. 1.** To perform (an operation) or process (information) with an electronic computer or system of computers. **2.** To furnish with a computer or computer system. —**com·put·er·i·za·tion** n.

com·put·er·ized axial tomography (kəm-pyōō′tə-rīzd′) n. *Abbr.* **CAT** A radiological technique for examining the soft tissues of the body. X-ray slices are recorded by a **CAT scanner** *(see)* and integrated by computer to give a three-dimensional image of the tissue or organ.

computer language n. A code used to provide data and instructions to computers; a code for programming computers.

computer typesetting n. A method of setting type using the output of a computer to drive the typesetting machine.

Comr. commissioner.

com·rade (kŏm′răd, -rĭd, kŭm′-) n. **1.** A friend, associate, or companion. **2.** A person who shares one's interests, occupation, or activities. **3.** *Often* **Comrade.** A fellow member; especially, a fellow member of a Communist or socialist party. [Earlier *camerade, cumrade,* from Old French *camarade,* roommate, soldier sharing the same room, from Spanish *camarada,* from *camara,* room, from Late Latin *camera,* from Latin, arched roof, from Greek *kamara,* vault.] —**com·rade·ship** n.

com·sat (kŏm′săt′) n. A **communications satellite** *(see).*

Comte (kônt), **(Isidore) Auguste (Marie François)** (1798–1857). French philosopher and the founder of modern sociology, a term he coined. He believed that intellectual life had developed through three stages: theological, metaphysical, and positivist. Sociology, he held, formed the apex of a hierarchy of sciences and would help to build a better future.

Com·tism (kŏm′tĭz-əm) n. The philosophy of Auguste Comte; positivism. —**Com·tist** (kŏm′tĭst) adj. & n.

Co·mus (kō′məs). In Roman mythology, a god or the spirit of revelry. [Latin, from Greek *Kōmos,* personification of *kōmos,* revel, festival procession. See **comedy.**]

con¹ (kŏn) n. *Informal.* One that votes or argues against. Used in the phrase *pros and cons.* [Middle English, short for *contra,* against, from Latin *contrā.*]

con² tr.v. **conned, conning, cons. 1.** To study, peruse, or examine carefully. **2.** To learn or commit to memory. [Middle English *connen, cunnen,* to know how, be able, master, Old English *cunnan.*] —**con·ner** n.

con³, conn tr.v. **conned, conning, cons.** *Nautical.* To direct the steering or course of (a ship). ~n. *Nautical.* **1.** The station or post of the person who cons. **2.** The act or process of conning. [Earlier *cond, cund,* from Middle English *conduen, condien,* to guide, from Old French *conduire,* to conduct, from Latin *condūcere,* "to bring together" : *com-,* together + *dūcere,* to lead.]

con⁴ tr.v. **conned, conning, cons.** *Slang.* To swindle or defraud by first winning the confidence of; dupe. ~n. *Slang.* A swindle; trick. [Short for CONFIDENCE TRICK.]

con⁵ n. *Slang.* A convict.

con. **1.** concerto. **2.** *Law.* conclusion. **3.** connection. **4.** consolidate; consolidated.

Con. **1.** conformist. **2.** Conservative. **3.** consul.

Con·a·kry (kŏn′ə-krē). Capital and chief port of Guinea, situated on Tombo Island off the west coast of Africa. It is connected by a causeway to the mainland.

con a·mo·re (kŏn ä-mō′rā) adv. *Music.* Lovingly; tenderly. Used as a direction. [Italian, "with love."]

Conan Doyle, Sir Arthur. See Sir Arthur Conan **Doyle.**

Co·nant (kō′nənt), **James Bryant** (1893–1978). U.S. educator, diplomat, and author. In addition to his duties as president of Harvard (1933–53) and U.S. ambassador to West Germany (1955–57), he wrote many books on education, including *Education for a Classless Society* (1951), and *The American High School Today* (1959).

co·na·tion (kō-nā′shən) n. *Psychology.* The aspect of mental processes or behavior directed toward action or change and including impulse, desire, volition, and striving. [Latin *cōnātiō* (stem *cōnātiōn-*), endeavor, effort, from *cōnātus,* past participle of *cōnārī,* to endeavor.] —**co·na·tion·al** adj.

co·na·tive (kŏn′ə-tĭv, kō′nə-) adj. **1.** *Psychology.* Of, pertaining to, or involving conation. **2.** *Grammar.* Being or designating a verb, verb form, verbal aspect, or affix in certain inflected languages, such as Russian, that expresses an attempt to perform an action that is not necessarily achieved. ~n. A conative linguistic form.

co·na·tus (kō-nā′təs) n., pl. **conatus.** Any natural tendency, impulse, or directed effort. [Latin *cōnātus* (stem *cōnātus,* endeavor, effort, from the past participle of *cōnārī,* to endeavor. See **conation.**]

con bri·o (kŏn brē′ō) adv. *Music.* With spirit and vigor. Used as a direction. [Italian, "with vigor."]

conc. concentrate; concentrated.

con·cat·e·nate (kŏn-kăt′ə-nāt′) tr.v. **-nated, -nating, -nates.** To connect or link in a series or chain. ~adj. (-nĭt, -nāt′). Connected or linked in a series. [Late Latin *concatēnāre* : *com-,* together + *catēnāre,* to link, chain, from Latin *catēna,* CATENA.] —**con·cat·e·na·tion** n.

computer

A DIGITAL COMPUTER SYSTEM
How the equipment stores, retrieves, and processes information

The chief components of the multipurpose, and most widely used, digital computer are a central processing unit (CPU), consisting of control and arithmetic/logic sections, that processes information (data); a main memory unit (the ROM in the illustration) in which information is held while being processed; and devices that respectively feed information into the CPU (input) and provide the user with the results of the computation (output). These components are termed hardware. Information such as details of employees' salaries is held on magnetic tape in the back-up memory store and can be obtained by the CPU when it is required.

Programs, sets of instructions to the computer, are called software. They are required to convert the information into the binary notation in which the computer operates, and computer languages, such as BASIC, FORTRAN, ALGOL, and COBOL, translate the programs into a form comprehensible to the computer.

The programs are stored in the main memory unit. The output required, the total salary bill, for example, can be displayed on a visual display unit (VDU) or printed out. An operator may communicate directly with the computer using the VDU and keyboard.

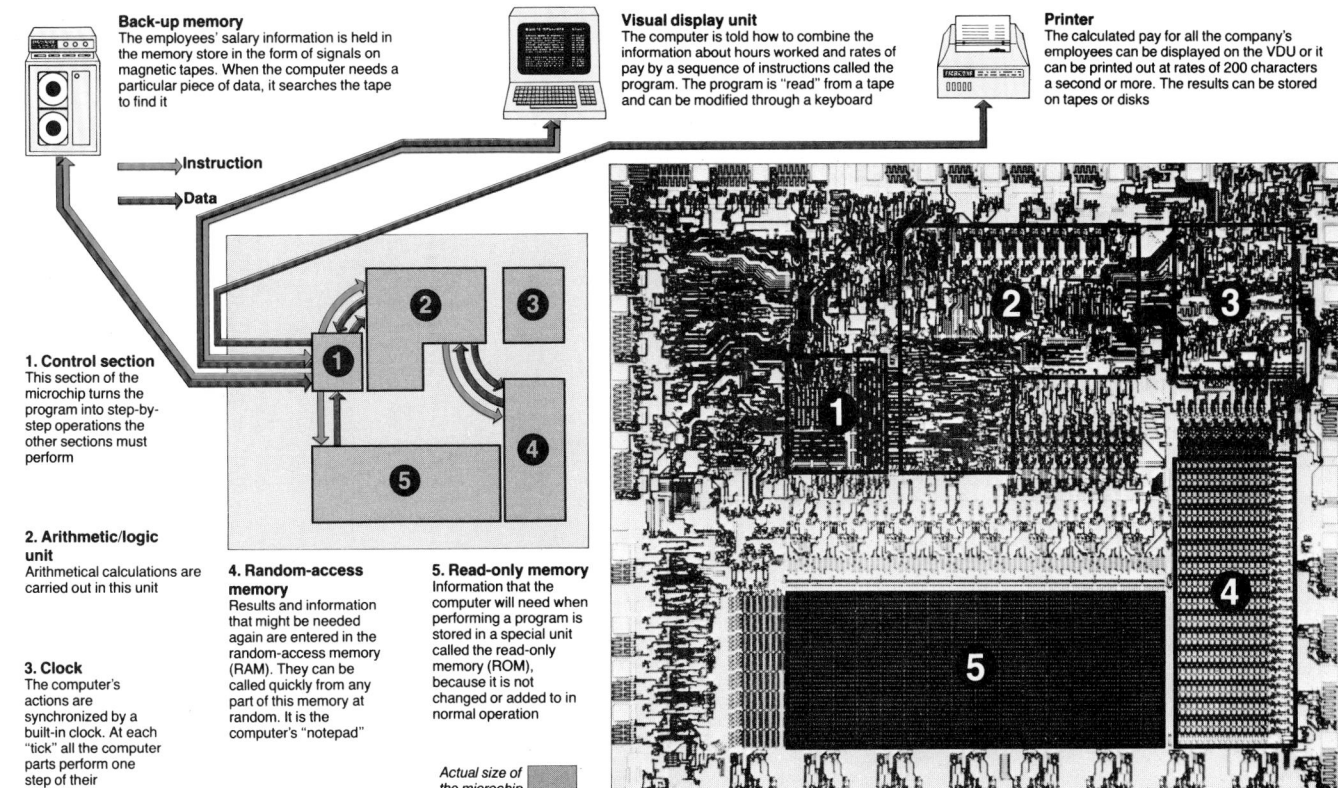

Back-up memory
The employees' salary information is held in the memory store in the form of signals on magnetic tapes. When the computer needs a particular piece of data, it searches the tape to find it

Visual display unit
The computer is told how to combine the information about hours worked and rates of pay by a sequence of instructions called the program. The program is "read" from a tape and can be modified through a keyboard

Printer
The calculated pay for all the company's employees can be displayed on the VDU or it can be printed out at rates of 200 characters a second or more. The results can be stored on tapes or disks

→ Instruction
→ Data

1. Control section
This section of the microchip turns the program into step-by-step operations the other sections must perform

2. Arithmetic/logic unit
Arithmetical calculations are carried out in this unit

3. Clock
The computer's actions are synchronized by a built-in clock. At each "tick" all the computer parts perform one step of their operations

4. Random-access memory
Results and information that might be needed again are entered in the random-access memory (RAM). They can be called quickly from any part of this memory at random. It is the computer's "notepad"

5. Read-only memory
Information that the computer will need when performing a program is stored in a special unit called the read-only memory (ROM), because it is not changed or added to in normal operation

Actual size of the microchip

MICROPROCESSOR *An entire computer can be etched onto a single silicon chip called a microprocessor. In this payroll computing system, the chip is housed in a visual display unit (VDU). The program is fed in from magnetic tapes, which also provide additional memory storage (back-up memory). Employees' wages can be displayed on the VDU and also printed out on paper by a printer linked to the microprocessor. The computer can list the employees' names in any given order.*

---

con·cave (kŏn-kāv′) *adj.* Curved like a section of the inner surface of a sphere: *a concave mirror.* Compare **convex.** ~*n.* A concave surface, structure, or line. [Middle English, from Old French, from Latin *concavus,* vaulted, hollow : *com-* (intensive) + *cavus,* hollow.] —**con·cave·ly** *adv.* —**con·cave·ness** *n.*

con·cav·i·ty (kŏn-kăv′ə-tē) *n., pl.* **-ties. 1.** The condition or state of being concave. **2.** A concave surface or structure.

con·ca·vo-con·cave (kŏn-kā′vō-kŏn-kāv′) *adj.* Concave on both surfaces, as certain lenses are.

con·ca·vo-con·vex (kŏn-kā′vō-kŏn-vĕks′) *adj.* **1.** Concave on one side and convex on the other; convexo-concave. **2.** Designating a lens with greater concave than convex curvature.

con·ceal (kən-sēl′) *tr.v.* **-cealed, -cealing, -ceals. 1.** To prevent from being noticed or discovered: *couldn't conceal her disgust.* **2.** To keep out of sight; hide: *a concealed entrance.* —See Synonyms at **hide.** [Middle English *concelen,* from Old French *conceler,* from Latin *concēlāre* : *com-* (intensive) + *cēlāre,* to hide.] —**con·ceal·a·ble** *adj.* —**con·ceal·er** *n.* —**con·ceal·ment** *n.*

con·cede (kən-sēd′) *v.* **-ceded, -ceding, -cedes.** —*tr.* **1.** To acknowledge as true, just, or proper; admit. **2.** To yield or grant (a privilege or right, for example). **3.** To allow an opponent to score (a goal, points, or the like). —*intr.* **1.** To make a concession. **2.** To admit defeat, as in an election. —See Synonyms at **acknowledge.** [French *concéder,* from Latin *concēdere,* to yield : *com-* (intensive) + *cēdere,* to go away, withdraw.] —**con·ced·ed·ly** *adv.* —**con·ced·er** *n.*

con·ceit (kən-sēt′) *n.* **1.** A high, often exaggerated, opinion of one's own abilities, worth, or personality; vanity. **2.** An ingenious, fanciful, or witty thought or expression. **3. a.** A far-fetched or exaggerated metaphor. **b.** The use of such metaphors. **c.** A poem or verse constructed entirely around an elaborate conceit. **4.** *Archaic.* A thought or idea; opinion. ~*tr.v.* **conceited, -ceiting, -ceits.** *Obsolete.* **1.** To imagine or consider. **2.** *Regional.* To take a fancy to. [Middle English *conceite,* concept, notion, from *conceiven,* to CONCEIVE (by analogy with DECEIVE, DECEIT).]

con·ceit·ed (kən-sē′tĭd) *adj.* **1.** Holding too high an opinion of oneself; vain. **2.** *Regional.* Inclined to be fanciful or whimsical. —**con·ceit·ed·ly** *adv.* —**con·ceit·ed·ness** *n.*

con·ceiv·a·ble (kən-sē′və-bəl) *adj.* Capable of being conceived or imagined; possible. —**con·ceiv·a·bil·i·ty, con·ceiv·a·ble·ness** *n.* —**con·ceiv·a·bly** *adv.*

con·ceive (kən-sēv′) *v.* **-ceived, -ceiving, -ceives.** —*tr.* **1. a.** To become pregnant with. **b.** To begin or induce the conception of: *a test-tube baby conceived outside the womb.* **2. a.** To form in the mind; become possessed by: *conceived an instant dislike for her.* **b.** To formulate; devise: *conceive a plan.* **3.** To apprehend mentally; imagine or understand. Often followed by a clause. **4.** To think or consider. Often followed by a clause. —*intr.* **1.** To form an idea. Used with *of.* **2.** To become pregnant. [Middle English *conceiven,* from Old French *conceivre,* from Latin *concipere,* to take to oneself, hence to be impregnated, to take into the mind : *com-,* comprehensively + *capere,* to take.] —**con·ceiv·er** *n.*

con·cel·e·brate (kən-sĕl′ə-brāt′) *intr.v.* **-brated, -brating, -brates.** To take part in a concelebration. [Latin *concelebrāre* : *com-,* together + *celebrāre,* to CELEBRATE.]

con·cel·e·bra·tion (kən-sĕl′ə-brā′shən) *n.* The celebration of the Eucharist by two or more clergymen.

con·cen·ter (kŏn-sĕn′tər) *v.* **-tered, -tering, -ters.** —*tr.* To direct toward a common center. —*intr.* To come together at a common

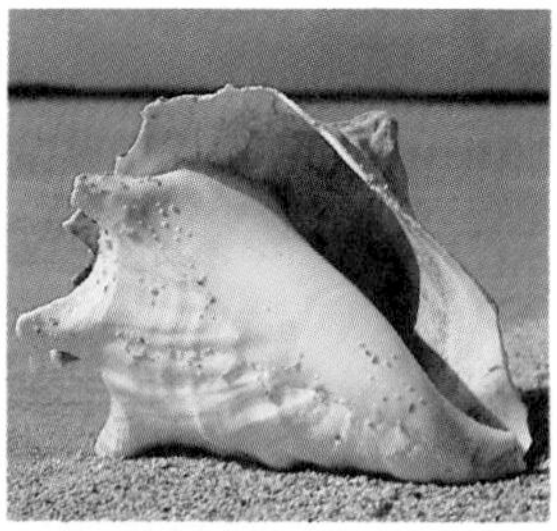

conch *In Greek mythology, the sea god Triton used the shell of the trumpet conch,* Charonia tritonis, *as his horn. Although conches are still sometimes used as musical instruments, they are now mainly valued as the material from which cameos are carved. Conches are large edible snails—sometimes weighing over 2 kilograms (4½ pounds) without their shells—and are found around the world in warm coastal waters. This shell is from a Caribbean species.*

center. [French *concentrer,* to CONCENTRATE.]

con•cen•trate (kŏn′sən-trāt′) *v.* **-trated, -trating, -trates.** *—tr.* **1.** To direct or draw toward a common center, purpose, or the like; focus: *tried to concentrate her mind on her work.* **2.** *Chemistry.* To increase the concentration of (a solution or mixture). *—intr.* **1.** To converge toward a center. **2. a.** To focus one's thoughts or attention. Often used with *on* or *upon.* **b.** To keep one's attention closely on a matter at hand.
~n. Abbr. **conc.** *Chemistry.* A product of concentration.
~adj. Abbr. **conc.** Concentrated. [French *concentrer* : *com-,* same + *center,* CENTER.] **—con•cen•tra•tor** *n.*

con•cen•tra•tion (kŏn′sən-trā′shən) *n.* **1.** The act or process of concentrating or the condition of being concentrated. **2.** A concentrated mass; an accumulation. **3.** Closely directed thoughts or attention. **4.** *Chemistry.* The amount of a given substance in a unit amount of another substance, usually expressed as the number of moles of solute in a liter or a cubic decimeter of solvent.

concentration camp *n.* An internment camp of a type first used by the British in the Boer War, where prisoners of war, enemy aliens, and political prisoners are confined and sometimes, as in those of Nazi Germany, subjected to brutal treatment. [Referring to the *concentration* of large numbers of such prisoners in one area.]

con•cen•tric (kən-sĕn′trĭk) *adj.* Having a common center. Compare **eccentric.** [Middle English *concentrik,* from Old French *concentrique,* from Medieval Latin *concentricus* : Latin *com-,* same + *centrum,* CENTER.] **—con•cen•tri•cal•ly** *adv.* **—con•cen•tric•i•ty** (kŏn′sĕn-trĭs′ĭ-tē) *n.*

con•cept (kŏn′sĕpt) *n.* **1.** A general idea or understanding, especially one derived from specific instances or occurrences. **2.** A thought or notion, especially one that is abstract or theoretical. **3. a.** A way of thinking about something. **b.** The structure or design of something, considered in the abstract. —See Synonyms at **idea.** [Late Latin *conceptus,* a thing conceived, thought, from past participle of *concipere,* to take to oneself, CONCEIVE.]

con•cep•ta•cle (kən-sĕp′tə-kəl) *n.* A cavity in certain algae and fungi that opens to the exterior and contains reproductive structures. [French, from Latin *conceptāculum,* from *concipere,* to receive, contain, CONCEIVE.]

con•cep•tion (kən-sĕp′shən) *n.* **1. a.** The fertilization of an egg cell by a sperm in the uterus to form an embryo capable of survival and maturation in normal conditions. **b.** The entity so formed; an embryo. **2.** A beginning. **3.** The ability to form mental concepts; invention. **4.** That which is mentally conceived; a concept, plan, design, idea, or thought. —See Synonyms at **idea.** [Middle English *concepcioun,* from Old French *conception,* from Latin *conceptiō* (stem *conceptiōn-*), from *concipere,* to take to oneself, CONCEIVE.] **—con•cep•tion•al** *adj.*

con•cep•tive (kən-sĕp′tĭv) *adj.* Able to conceive mentally.

con•cep•tu•al (kən-sĕp′cho͞o-əl) *adj.* Of or pertaining to concepts or mental conception. **—con•cep•tu•al•ly** *adv.*

conceptual art *n.* Art that is intended to convey an idea or concept to the perceiver and need not involve the creation or appreciation of a traditional art object such as a painting or sculpture.

con•cep•tu•al•ism (kən-sĕp′cho͞o-əl-ĭz′əm) *n. Philosophy.* The doctrine that universals, or abstract concepts, exist only within the mind and have no external or substantial reality. **—con•cep•tu•al•ist** *n.* **—con•cep•tu•al•is•tic** *adj.*

con•cep•tu•al•ize (kən-sĕp′cho͞o-əl-īz′) *v.* **-ized, -izing, -izes.** *—tr.* To form concepts or a concept of. *—intr.* To form concepts, theories, or ideas. **—con•cep•tu•al•i•za•tion** *n.*

con•cern (kən-sûrn′) *v.* **-cerned, -cerning, -cerns.** *—tr.* **1. a.** To pertain or relate to. **b.** To be of interest or importance to; affect. **2.** To engage or involve the mind or interests of. Used reflexively or in the passive: *concern oneself with trivia.* **3.** To cause anxiety or uneasiness in; trouble. *—intr. Obsolete.* To be of importance.
~n. **1. a.** A matter that relates to or affects one. **b.** Something of interest or importance. **2.** Regard for or interest in someone or something: *concern for her well-being.* **3.** A matter about which one is concerned. **4.** Anxiety; worry. **5.** A business establishment or enterprise; a company. —See Synonyms at **anxiety.** [Middle English *concernen,* from Old French *concerner,* from Medieval Latin *concernere,* to relate to, involve with, from Latin, to mix in a sieve (before sifting) : *com-,* together + *cernere,* to sift.]

con•cerned (kən-sûrnd′) *adj.* **1.** Interested or affected; involved. **2.** Anxious; troubled; disturbed.

con•cern•ing (kən-sûr′nĭng) *prep.* With reference to; regarding; about.

con•cern•ment (kən-sûrn′mənt) *n.* **1.** A matter that concerns one; an affair. **2.** Reference, relation, or importance. **3.** Anxiety; worry.

con•cert (kŏn′sûrt) *n.* **1.** A musical performance in which a number of singers or players participate. **2.** Agreement in purpose, feeling, or action. **—in concert. 1.** All together; in agreement. **2.** Playing or singing live, at a concert.
~adj. Pertaining to, playing in, or designed for concerts.
~tr.v. (kən-sûrt′) **concerted, -certing, -certs. 1.** To plan or arrange by mutual agreement. **2.** To contrive or devise. [French, from Italian *concerto,* from Old Italian *concertare*†, to bring into agreement, harmonize.]

con•cert•ed (kən-sûr′tĭd) *adj.* **1.** Planned or accomplished together; combined: *a concerted effort.* **2.** *Music.* Arranged in parts for voices or instruments. **—con•cert•ed•ly** *adv.*

concert grand *n.* The largest type of grand piano, being roughly 2.8 meters (9 feet) in length.

con•cer•ti•na (kŏn′sər-tē′nə) *n.* A small, hexagonal accordion with bellows, and buttons for keys. [CONCERT + Italian *-ina* (feminine diminutive suffix).]

con•cer•ti•no (kŏn′chĕr-tē′nō) *n., pl.* **-nos** or **-ni** (-nē). *Music.* **1.** A short concerto. **2.** The solo instrument group in a concerto grosso. [Italian, diminutive of *concerto,* concerto, CONCERT.]

con•cer•tize (kŏn′sər-tīz′) *intr.v.* **-tized, -tizing, -tizes.** To give, or perform in, concerts.

con•cert•mas•ter (kŏn′sərt-măs′tər, -mäs′tər) *n.* The first violinist and assistant conductor in a symphony orchestra.

con•cer•to (kən-chĕr′tō) *n., pl.* **-tos** or **-ti** (-tē). *Abbr.* **con.** A composition for an orchestra and one or more solo instruments, typically in three movements. [Italian, CONCERT.]

concerto gros•so (kən-chĕr′tō grō′sō) *n., pl.* **concerti grossi** (kən-chĕr′tē grō′sē). A composition for a small group of solo instruments and a full orchestra. [Italian, "great concerto."]

concert pitch *n.* **1.** *Music.* A pitch to which orchestral instruments are tuned with the A above middle C at 440 hertz. Also called "international pitch." **2.** *Informal.* The state of being ready and tensely alert.

con•ces•sion (kən-sĕsh′ən) *n.* **1.** The act of conceding, granting, or yielding. **2.** Any thing or point so conceded. **3.** Something granted by a government or controlling authority, such as a right to land or exploration, to be used for a specific purpose. **4. a.** The right to operate a subsidiary business within a larger establishment. **b.** The space allotted for such a business. [Middle English, from Old French, from Latin *concessiō* (stem *concessiōn-*), from *concēdere* (past participle *concessus*), to CONCEDE.]

con•ces•sion•aire (kən-sĕsh′ən-âr′) *n.* Also **con•ces•sion•er** (-sĕsh′ən-ər). The operator or holder of a concession.

con•ces•sion•ar•y (kən-sĕsh′ən-ĕr′ē) *adj.* Of the nature of or granted by a concession.

con•ces•sive (kən-sĕs′ĭv) *adj.* **1.** Of the nature of or containing a concession; tending to concede. **2.** *Grammar.* Expressing concession, as the conjunction *although.* [Latin *concessīvus,* from *concessus,* past participle of *concēdere,* to CONCEDE.]

conch (kŏngk, kŏnch) *n., pl.* **conchs** (kŏngks) or **conches** (kŏn′chĭz). **1.** Any of various tropical marine gastropod mollusks of the genus *Strombus* and other genera, having large, often brightly colored spiral shells and, in some species, edible flesh. **2.** The shell of any of these mollusks, used for ornament, in making cameos, or as a horn. **3.** A concha. [Middle English *conche, conk,* from Latin *concha,* from Greek *konkhē.*]

con•cha (kŏng′kə) *n., pl.* **-chae** (-kē). **1.** *Anatomy.* A shell-like structure, such as the external ear. **2.** *Architecture.* The half dome over an apse. [Latin, CONCH.]

con•chif•er•ous (kŏng-kĭf′ər-əs) *adj.* **1.** Having or forming a shell. **2.** Containing shells. Said of certain rocks. [CONCH(O)- + -FEROUS.]

con•chi•o•lin (kŏng-kī′ə-lĭn, kŏn-) *n.* A fibrous protein, $C_{32}H_{98}N_2O_{11}$, that is the principal constituent of mollusk shells. [From CONCH.]

concho–, conch–, conchi– *prefix.* Indicates shell; for example, **conchology.** [Greek *konkho-,* from *konkhē,* shell.]

con•choid (kŏng′koid′) *n.* In geometry, a curve having two branches with a common asymptote, so that a line from a fixed point that intersects both branches is of constant length between the asymptote and either branch. [CONCH + -OID (referring to the shape of the curve).]

con•choi•dal (kŏng-koid′l) *adj.* Of or designating rocks, such as flint or obsidian, having bivalve shell-like surfaces when fractured. [Greek *konkhoeidēs,* shell-like : CONCH(O)- + -OID.]

con•chol•o•gy (kŏng-kŏl′ə-jē) *n.* The study of mollusks and their shells. [CONCHO- + -LOGY.] **—con•cho•log•i•cal** (kŏng′kə-lŏj′ĭ-kəl) *adj.* **—con•chol•o•gist** (kŏng-kŏl′ə-jĭst) *n.*

con•ci•erge (kŏn′sē-ûrzh; *French* kôɴ-syârzh′) *n.* A person who attends the entrance of a building and acts as caretaker. [French, from Old French *cumcerges,* from Vulgar Latin *conservius* (unattested), variant of Latin *conservus,* a fellow slave : *com-,* together + *servus,* slave.]

con•cil•i•ar (kən-sĭl′ē-ər) *adj.* Of or pertaining to a council, especially an ecclesiastical council.

con•cil•i•ate (kən-sĭl′ē-āt′) *tr.v.* **-ated, -ating, -ates. 1.** To overcome the distrust or animosity of; win over; placate; soothe. **2.** To gain, win, or secure (favor, friendship, or goodwill, for example) by friendly overtures. **3.** To reconcile. —See Synonyms at **pacify.** [Latin *conciliāre,* to bring together, unite, from *concilium,* union, gathering, meeting.] **—con•cil•i•a•ble** (kən-sĭl′ē-ə-bəl) *adj.* **—con•cil•i•a•tor** *n.* **—con•cil•i•a•to•ry** (kən-sĭl′ē-ə-tôr′ē, -tōr′ē) *adj.*

con•cil•i•a•tion (kən-sĭl′ē-ā′shən) *n.* **1.** The act or process of conciliating; placation; propitiation. **2.** The process of settling differences between employers and employees through the good offices of a third party but without resort to arbitration. —See Synonyms at **mediation.**

con•cin•ni•ty (kən-sĭn′ə-tē) *n., pl.* **-ties. 1.** A skillful, harmonious arrangement of parts. **2.** Elegance of literary style. [Latin *concinnitās,* from *concinnus,* placed fitly together, from *concinnāre,* to place fitly together, arrange in good order : *com-,* together + *cinnus*†, a mixed drink.]

con•cise (kən-sīs′) *adj.* Expressing much in few words; short and to the point; succinct. [Latin *concīsus,* past participle of *concīdere,* to cut up : *com-* (intensive) + *caedere,* to cut.] **—con•cise•ly** *adv.* **—con•cise•ness** *n.*

Synonyms: *compendious, epigrammatic, laconic, pithy, succinct, summary, terse.*

con·ci·sion (kən-sĭzh′ən) *n.* **1.** The quality of being concise; terseness; brevity; succinctness. **2.** *Archaic.* A cutting apart or off. [Middle English *concisioun,* from Latin *concīsiō* (stem *concīsiōn-*), from *concīsus,* CONCISE.]

con·clave (kŏn′klāv, kŏng′-) *n.* **1.** A confidential or secret meeting. **2. a.** The private rooms in which the cardinals of the Roman Catholic Church meet to elect a pope. **b.** The meeting so held. [Middle English, from Old French, from Latin *conclāve,* "room locked with a key": *com-,* together + *clāvis,* key.]

con·clude (kən-klo͞od′) *v.* **-cluded, -cluding, -cludes.** *—tr.* **1.** To bring to an end; wind up; finish. **2.** To arrive finally at (an agreement or settlement); settle: *conclude a peace treaty.* **3.** To infer or deduce. **4.** To determine; decide. *—intr.* **1.** To come to an end; close. **2.** To form a final judgment; come to a decision or an agreement. —See Synonyms at **complete, decide.** [Middle English *concluden,* from Latin *conclūdere,* to shut up closely: *com-* (intensive) + *claudere,* to shut.] **—con·clud·er** *n.*

con·clu·sion (kən-klo͞o′zhən) *n.* **1.** The close or termination of something; the end; the finish. **2.** The closing or last part, as of a speech, paper, or the like, often containing a summing up. **3.** A final outcome or result: *Their election victory was a foregone conclusion.* **4.** A judgment, inference, or decision reached after deliberation. **5.** A final arrangement or settlement, as of a treaty. **6.** *Law. Abbr.* **con. a.** The close of a plea or deed. **b.** An **estoppel** *(see).* **7.** *Logic.* **a.** In a syllogism, the proposition that must follow from the major and minor premises. **b.** The proposition concluded from one or more premises; a deduction. **—try conclusions with.** *Archaic.* To engage in a contest or argument. [Middle English *conclusioun,* from Old French *conclusion,* from Latin *conclūsiō* (stem *conclūsiōn-*), from *conclūdere,* to shut up closely, CONCLUDE.]

con·clu·sive (kən-klo͞o′sĭv) *adj.* Serving to put an end to doubt or question; decisive; final. —See Synonyms at **valid.** **—con·clu·sive·ly** *adv.* **—con·clu·sive·ness** *n.*

con·coct (kən-kŏkt′) *tr.v.* **-cocted, -cocting, -cocts. 1.** To prepare by mixing ingredients, as in cookery. **2.** To invent or fabricate; contrive: *concoct a plausible story.* [Latin *concoquere* (past participle *concoctus*), to cook together: *com-,* together + *coquere,* to cook.] **—con·coct·er, con·coc·tor** *n.* **—con·coc·tion** *n.* **—con·coc·tive** *adj.*

con·com·i·tance (kən-kŏm′ə-təns) *n.* Also **con·com·i·tan·cy** (-tən-sē) *pl.* **-cies. 1.** Occurrence together or in connection with another; accompaniment. **2.** A concomitant. **3.** *Theology.* The coexistence of the body and blood of Christ in each element of the Eucharist.

con·com·i·tant (kən-kŏm′ə-tənt) *adj.* Existing or occurring concurrently as an attendant feature or circumstance; accompanying. —See Synonyms at **contemporary.**
~n. A concomitant state, circumstance, or thing. [Latin *concomitāns* (stem *concomitant-*), present participle of *concomitārī,* to accompany, from *com-,* together + *comitārī,* to accompany, from *comes* (stem *comit-*), companion.]

con·cord (kŏn′kôrd, kŏng′-) *n.* **1.** Harmony or agreement of interests or feelings; concurrence; accord. **2.** A treaty establishing peaceful relations. **3.** *Grammar.* Agreement between words in person, number, gender, or case. **4.** A harmonious combination of simultaneously sounded notes; consonance. Compare **discord.** [Middle English, from Old French *concorde,* from Latin *concordia,* from *concors,* "of the same mind": *com-,* same, mutually + *cors* (stem *cord-*), the heart, mind.]

Con·cord¹ (kŏng′kərd) *n.* A city of eastern Massachusetts, on the Concord River. It is the site of the Revolutionary War Battle of Concord (April 19, 1775). There are many fine old houses in the city.

Concord². The capital of New Hampshire, in the south-central part of the state on the Merrimack River. The city is famous for its granite and also has varied industries.

con·cor·dance (kən-kôr′dəns) *n.* **1.** A state of agreement; harmony; concord. **2.** An index of all the words in a text or corpus of texts, showing every contextual occurrence of a word.

con·cor·dant (kən-kôr′dənt) *adj.* Harmonious; agreeing; corresponding. [Middle English *concordaunt,* from Old French *concordant,* from Latin *concordāns* (stem *concordant-*), present participle of *concordāre,* to agree, from *concors,* agreed. See **concord.**] **—con·cor·dant·ly** *adv.*

con·cor·dat (kən-kôr′dăt) *n.* A formal agreement; especially, an agreement between the pope and a government for the regulation of church affairs. [French, from Medieval Latin *concordātum,* from Latin *concordāre,* to agree. See **concordant.**]

Con·corde (kŏn′kôrd, kŏng′-) *n.* An Anglo-French supersonic airliner, capable of flying at speeds greater than Mach 2. [French, *concord,* unity, referring to Anglo-French cooperation in producing it.]

Concord grape *n.* A variety of grape having purple-black fruit with a bluish bloom. [Discovered (1846) at CONCORD, Massachusetts.]

con·course (kŏn′kôrs, -kōrs, kŏng′-) *n.* **1.** A great crowd; throng; multitude. **2.** A coming, moving, or flowing together. **3. a.** A large open space for the gathering or passage of crowds, as in a railroad station. **b.** A broad thoroughfare. [Middle English, from Old French *concours,* from Latin *concursus,* from the past participle of *concurrere,* to run together: *com-,* together + *currere,* to run.]

con·cres·cence (kən-krĕs′əns) *n.* The uniting, especially the grow-

ing together, of related parts, as of physical particles or anatomical structures. [Latin *concrēscentia,* from *concrēscēns* (stem *concrēscent-*), present participle of *concrēscere,* to grow together: *com-,* together + *crēscere,* to grow.]

con·crete (kŏn-krēt′, kŏn′krēt) *adj.* **1.** Pertaining to an actual, specific thing or instance; not general; particular. **2.** Existing in reality or in real experience; perceptible by the senses; real. **3.** Designating a material object or thing as opposed to an abstraction or quality. **4.** Formed by the coalescence of separate particles or parts into one mass; solid. **5.** Made of concrete. —See Synonyms at **real.**
~n. (kŏn′krēt, kŏn-krēt′). **1.** A construction material consisting of sand, gravel, pebbles, broken stone, or the like in a mortar or cement matrix. **2.** A mass formed by the coalescence of particles.
~v. (kŏn′krēt, kŏn-krēt′) **concreted, -creting, -cretes.** *—tr.* **1.** To form into a mass by coalescence or cohesion of particles. **2.** To build, treat, or cover with concrete. *—intr.* To coalesce; solidify. [Middle English *concret,* from Old French, from Latin *concrētus,* past participle of *concrēscere,* to grow together, harden: *com-,* together + *crēscere,* to grow.] **—con·crete·ly** *adv.* **—con·crete·ness** *n.*

concrete mixer *n.* A machine with a revolving drum in which cement, sand, gravel, and water are combined into concrete. Also called "cement mixer."

concrete noun *n.* A noun designating a material object as opposed to an abstract idea or quality. Compare **abstract noun.**

concrete poetry *n.* Poetry in which the physical representation or arrangement of the words conveys or adds meaning.

con·cre·tion (kən-krē′shən) *n.* **1.** The act or process of growing together or becoming united in one mass; coalescence. **2.** A solid or concrete mass. **3.** *Geology.* A rounded or irregular mass of mineral matter found in sedimentary rock. **4.** *Pathology.* A solid mass of inorganic material formed in a cavity or tissue of the body; a calculus. **—con·cre·tion·ar·y** (kən-krē′shə-nĕr′ē) *adj.*

con·cret·ism (kən-krē′tĭz′əm) *n.* The theory or practice of concrete poetry. **—con·cret·ist** *n.*

con·cre·tize (kŏn′krĭ-tīz′) *tr.v.* **-tized, -tizing, -tizes.** To render concrete; make real or specific. **—con·cre·ti·za·tion** *n.*

con·cu·bi·nage (kŏn-kyo͞o′bə-nĭj) *n.* **1.** Cohabitation without legal marriage. **2.** The state of being a concubine.

con·cu·bine (kŏng′kyə-bīn′, kŏn′-) *n.* **1.** A woman who cohabits with and is supported by a man without being married to him. **2.** In certain polygamous societies, a secondary wife, usually of inferior legal and social status. [Middle English, from Old French, from Latin *concubīna,* "one to sleep with": *com-,* together + *cubāre,* to lie down.] **—con·cu·bi·nar·y** *adj.*

con·cu·pis·cence (kŏn-kyo͞o′pə-səns) *n.* **1.** Sexual desire; lust. **2.** Any abnormally strong desire. [Latin *concupīscēns,* present participle of *concupīscere,* inceptive of *concupere,* to have a strong desire for: *com-* (intensive) + *cupere,* to desire.] **—con·cu·pis·cent** *adj.*

con·cur (kən-kûr′) *intr.v.* **-curred, -curring, -curs. 1.** To have the same opinion; agree. **2.** To act together; cooperate. **3.** To occur at the same time; coincide. —See Synonyms at **assent.** [Middle English *concurren,* from Latin *concurrere,* to run together: *com-,* together + *currere,* to run.]
Usage: *Concur in* is generally used to express approval or joint action: *concur in a plan. Concur with* expresses agreement: *concur with her view.*

con·cur·rence (kən-kûr′əns) *n.* **1.** Agreement in opinion; accord. **2.** Cooperation or combination, as of agents, causes, circumstances, or events. **3.** Simultaneous occurrence; coincidence. **4.** In geometry, the intersection of three or more lines. **5.** *Rare.* Competition; rivalry. **6.** *Law.* A power or claim held jointly.

con·cur·rent (kən-kûr′ənt) *adj.* **1. a.** Happening at the same time or place. **b.** Intended to run simultaneously. **2.** Operating in conjunction. **3.** Meeting at or tending to meet at the same point. **4.** In accordance or agreement; harmonious. **5.** Exercising equal authority or having the same jurisdiction. —See Synonyms at **contemporary.** [Middle English, from Old French, from Latin *concurrēns* (stem *concurrent-*), present participle of *concurrere,* to run together, CONCUR.] **—con·cur·rent·ly** *adv.*

concurrent resolution *n.* A resolution adopted by both houses of a bicameral legislature that does not have the force of law and does not require the signature of the chief executive. Compare **joint resolution.**

con·cuss (kən-kŭs′) *tr.v.* **-cussed, -cussing, -cusses. 1.** To injure by concussion. **2.** *Rare.* To shake or agitate; disturb severely. [Late Latin *concutere* (past participle *concussus*), to shake violently: Latin *com-* (intensive) + *-cutere,* from *quatere,* to shake, dash.]

con·cus·sion (kən-kŭsh′ən) *n.* **1.** An injury of a soft structure, especially of the brain, resulting from a violent blow and usually causing loss of consciousness. **2.** Any violent jarring shock. **—con·cus·sive** (kən-kŭs′ĭv) *adj.*

Con·dé (kôn-dā′), **Louis I** (1530–69). French prince of a branch of the Bourbon dynasty. He was leader of the Huguenots during the French Wars of Religion.

Condé, Louis II, also known as "the Great Condé" (1621–86). Great-grandson of Louis Condé I. He was a brilliant general who won famous victories for France during the Thirty Years' War.

con·demn (kən-dĕm′) *tr.v.* **-demned, -demning, -demns. 1.** To express disapproval of; censure; criticize. **2. a.** To pronounce judgment against; sentence. **b.** To force into an undesirable state; doom. **3.** To demonstrate the guilt of; convict. **4.** To judge or declare to be unfit for use or consumption, usually by official order:

$$nC_6H_{12}O_6 \rightarrow (C_6H_{10}O_5)_n + nH_2O$$

glucose starch water

condensation *In this example of the chemical reaction known as condensation, glucose, a sugar, changes to starch, releasing water in the process.*

condemn an old building. —See Synonyms at **criticize.** [Middle English *condem(p)nen,* from Old French *condem(p)ner,* from Latin *condemnāre* : *com-* (intensive) + *damnāre,* to damage, condemn, from *damnum,* damage, fine.] —**con·dem·na·ble** *adj.* —**con·demn·er** *n.*

con·dem·na·tion (kŏn′dĕm-nā′shən) *n.* **1.** The act of condemning. **2.** The state of being condemned. **3.** Severe reproof; strong censure. **4.** A reason or occasion for condemning. —**con·dem·na·to·ry** (kŏn′dĕm′nə-tôr′ē, -tōr′ē) *adj.*

con·demned cell (kən-dĕmd′) *n.* The prison cell of a person who has been condemned to death.

con·den·sate (kən-dĕn′sāt′) *n.* A liquid formed by condensation. [Latin *condēnsātus,* past participle of *condēnsāre,* to CONDENSE.]

con·den·sa·tion (kŏn′dən-sā′shən) *n.* **1.** The act of condensing. **2.** The state of being condensed. **3.** A product of condensing, especially, abridgment. **4.** *Physics.* **a.** The physical process by which a liquid is removed from a vapor or vapor mixture. **b.** The liquid so removed; a condensate, especially water droplets forming on cold glass as air cools. **5.** *Chemistry.* A chemical reaction in which water or another simple substance is released by the combination of two or more molecules. **6.** *Psychoanalysis.* The process by which a single idea or word is invested with the emotional content of a group of ideas.

condensation trail *n.* A **vapor trail** *(see).*

con·dense (kən-dĕns′) *v.* **-densed, -densing, -denses.** —*tr.* **1.** To reduce the volume of; compress. **2.** To abridge (a literary work, for example). **3. a.** To form a condensate from (a vapor, for example). **b.** To subject (a vapor, for example) to condensation. —*intr.* **1.** To become more compact. **2.** To undergo condensation. —See Synonyms at **contract.** [Middle English *condensen,* from Old French *condenser,* from Latin *condēnsāre* : *com-* (intensive) + *dēnsāre,* to make dense, from *dēnsus,* dense.] —**con·dens·a·bil·i·ty** *n.* —**con·dens·a·ble** *adj.*

con·densed (kən-dĕnst′) *adj.* **1. a.** Made more compact. **b.** Abridged: *a condensed book.* **2.** *Printing.* Narrower than normal in proportion to its height. Said of type. Compare **expanded.** **3.** *Botany.* Having stalkless or nearly stalkless flowers tightly crowded together. Said of certain inflorescences.

condensed milk *n.* Cow's milk with sugar added, and reduced by evaporation to a thick consistency. Compare **evaporated milk.**

con·dens·er (kən-dĕn′sər) *n.* **1.** One that condenses. **2.** *Physics.* An apparatus used to condense vapor. **3.** *Electricity.* A **capacitor** *(see).* **4.** A mirror, lens, or combination of lenses used to gather light and direct it upon an object or projection lens.

con·de·scend (kŏn′dĭ-sĕnd′) *intr.v.* **-scended, -scending, -scends.** **1.** To come down voluntarily to the level of inferiors with whom one is dealing; deign. **2.** To behave in a patronizing manner. [Middle English *condescenden,* from Old French *condescendre,* from Medieval Latin *condēscendere,* to stoop to : Latin *com-* (intensive) + *dēscendere,* to descend : *dē-,* down + *scandere,* to climb.] —**con·de·scend·er** *n.*

con·de·scen·dence (kŏn′dĭ-sĕn′dəns) *n.* **1.** *Scottish Law.* A list of facts or grounds presented by the plaintiff. **2.** Condescension.

con·de·scend·ing (kŏn′dĭ-sĕn′dĭng) *adj.* Showing or assuming an air of superiority; patronizing. —**con·de·scend·ing·ly** *adv.*

con·de·scen·sion (kŏn′dĭ-sĕn′shən) *n.* **1. a.** The act of condescending. **b.** An instance of this. **2.** Patronizing behavior or manner.

con·dign (kən-dīn′) *adj.* Deserved; adequate; merited. Said of punishment or censure. [Middle English *condigne,* from Old French, from Latin *condignus,* wholly worthy : *com-* (intensive) + *dignus,* worthy.] —**con·dign·ly** *adv.*

Con·dil·lac (kôɴ′-dē-yăk′), **Étienne Bonnot de** (1715–80). French philosopher, a leading figure in the Enlightenment. He developed John Locke's view that all knowledge derives from the senses.

con·di·ment (kŏn′də-mənt) *n.* A seasoning for food, such as mustard, vinegar, or a spice. [Middle English, from Old French, from Latin *condīmentum,* from *condīre,* to season, preserve by pickling, perhaps variant of *condere,* to bring together, store up.] —**con·di·men·tal** *adj.*

con·di·tion (kən-dĭsh′ən) *n.* **1.** The particular mode or state of being of a person or thing, especially: **a.** State of health. **b.** State of readiness or preparation: *out of condition for the race.* **c.** State of repair or fitness for use. **d.** Rank or social position. **2.** A disease or ailment: *a heart condition.* **3.** Something indispensable to the appearance or occurrence of something else; a prerequisite: *The Moon's atmosphere lacks the essential conditions for supporting human life.* **4.** Something required as prerequisite to the fulfillment or performance of something else; stipulation. **5.** Something that restricts or modifies something else; qualification. **6.** *Usually* **conditions.** The existing or external circumstances: *poor driving conditions.* **7.** *Grammar.* The dependent clause of a conditional sentence. **8.** *Logic.* A proposition upon which another proposition depends; the antecedent of a conditional proposition. **9.** *Law.* **a.** A provision making the effect of a legal instrument contingent upon the occurrence of some uncertain future event. **b.** The event itself. —See Synonyms at **state.**

~*tr.v.* **conditioned, -tioning, -tions.** **1.** To make conditional; govern. Often used in the passive. **2.** To render fit; put into the desired condition. **3. a.** *Psychology.* To cause to respond in a specific manner to a specific stimulus. **b.** To accustom (a person) to adopt or conform to certain attitudes, modes of behavior, or the like. **4.** To treat with conditioner: *conditioned his hair.* [Middle English *condicioun,* from Old French *condicion,* from Latin *conditiō* (stem *conditiōn-*), agreement, stipulation, probably (irregularly) from *condīcere,* to talk together, agree : *com-,* together + *dīcere,* to talk.]

con·di·tion·al (kən-dĭsh′ən-əl) *adj.* **1.** Imposing, depending on, or containing a condition or conditions. **2.** *Grammar.* Stating or implying a condition. **3.** *Psychology.* Brought about by conditioning. ~*n. Grammar.* A mood, tense, clause, or word expressing a condition. —**con·di·tion·al·i·ty** *n.* —**con·di·tion·al·ly** *adv.*

conditional probability *n.* The probability that an event will take place provided that some other event has occurred or will occur.

con·di·tioned (kən-dĭsh′ənd) *adj.* **1.** Subject to or dependent upon conditions or stipulations. **2. a.** Physically fit; in good physical condition. **b.** Prepared for a specific action or process. **3.** *Psychology.* Exhibiting or trained to exhibit a conditioned response.

conditioned response *n. Psychology.* A response, elicited by conditioning, to a stimulus that does not really cause it. Also called "conditioned reflex."

conditioned stimulus *n. Psychology.* A stimulus rendered capable of eliciting a response like that of a specific **unconditioned stimulus** *(see)* by conditioning.

con·di·tion·er (kən-dĭsh′ən-ər) *n.* **1.** A person or thing that conditions. **2.** An additive or application that improves the condition of something: *a soil conditioner; a hair conditioner.*

con·di·tion·ing (kən-dĭsh′ən-ĭng) *n. Psychology.* The process of altering behavior by modifying the stimuli associated with it. In *classical conditioning* the stimulus that normally causes the response is paired with a different stimulus until a conditioned response is elicited by the second stimulus alone. In *operant,* or *instrumental, conditioning* the response is modified by reinforcement (reward or punishment).

con·dole (kən-dōl′) *v.* **-doled, -doling, -doles.** —*intr.* To mourn or express sympathy with someone in pain, grief, or misfortune. Used with *with.* —*tr. Archaic.* To commiserate with or grieve over. [Late Latin *condolēre,* to feel another's pain : Latin *com-,* together + *dolēre,* to feel pain, grieve.] —**con·do·la·to·ry** (kən-dō′lə-tôr′ē, -tōr′ē) *adj.* —**con·dol·er** *n.*

con·do·lence (kən-dō′ləns) *n.* **1.** Sympathy with a person in pain, grief, or misfortune. **2. condolences.** A formal declaration of such sympathy. —See Synonyms at **pity.** —**con·do·lent** *adj.*

con·dom (kŏn′dəm) *n.* A sheath, usually made of thin rubber, designed to cover the penis during sexual intercourse, for contraception or as protection against venereal disease. [18th century : origin obscure.]

con·do·min·i·um (kŏn′də-mĭn′ē-əm) *n.* **1. a.** Joint sovereignty; especially, the joint rule of a territory by two or more states. **b.** The territory so governed. **2. a.** An apartment building in which the apartments are owned individually. **b.** An apartment in such a building. Also informally called "condo." [New Latin : CON- + DOMINIUM.]

con·do·na·tion (kŏn′dō-nā′shən) *n.* **1.** The condoning or overlooking of an offense. **2.** *Law.* A forgiving by a wife or husband of an offense by the other, especially adultery.

con·done (kən-dōn′) *tr.v.* **-doned, -doning, -dones.** To forgive, overlook, or disregard (an offense) without protest or censure. —See Synonyms at **forgive.** [Latin *condōnāre,* to give up, forgive : *com-* (intensive) + *dōnāre,* to give away, from *dōnum,* gift.] —**con·don·er** *n.*

con·dor (kŏn′dôr, -dər) *n.* **1.** Either of two very large, black and white New World vultures, *Vultur gryphus* of the Andes or *Gymnogyps californianus* of the mountains of California. **2.** Any of several gold coins of some South American countries bearing the figure of a condor. [Spanish *cóndor,* from Quechua *kúntur.*]

con·dot·tie·re (kŏn′dō-tyâr′ā) *n., pl.* **-tieri** (-tyâr′ē). **1.** A leader of mercenary soldiers in Europe between the 14th and 16th centuries. **2.** A mercenary soldier. [Italian, leader, from *condotto,* conduct, leadership, from Latin *conductum,* from *condūcere,* to lead together, CONDUCT.]

con·duce (kən-do͞os′, -dyo͞os′) *intr.v.* **-duced, -ducing, -duces.** To contribute or lead to a particular end or result. Used with *to* or *toward.* [Middle English *conducen,* from Latin *condūcere,* to lead together, be useful, contribute : *com-,* together + *dūcere,* to lead.] —**con·duc·er** *n.*

con·du·cive (kən-do͞o′sĭv, -dyo͞o′sĭv) *adj.* Conducing; promoting; contributive. Used with *to.* —See Synonyms at **favorable.** —**con·du·cive·ness** *n.*

con·duct (kən-dŭkt′) *v.* **-ducted, -ducting, -ducts.** —*tr.* **1.** To direct the course of; manage; carry out: *conduct an opinion poll.* **2.** To guide or escort: *conduct a tour.* **3.** To direct or guide (an orchestra or other musical group), with movements of the hands or a baton. **4.** To serve as a medium or channel for conveying; transmit (heat or electricity, for example). **5.** To behave. Used reflexively. —*intr.* **1.** To act as a conductor. **2.** To be capable of transmitting heat, electricity, or other forms of energy. —See Synonyms at **accompany.**

~*n.* (kŏn′dŭkt). **1.** The way a person acts; behavior. **2.** The act of directing or controlling; management; administration. **3.** *Obsolete.* A guide or escort. [Middle English *conducten,* from Medieval Latin *condūcere,* to escort, from Latin, to lead together : *com-,* together + *dūcere,* to lead.] —**con·duct·i·bil·i·ty** *n.* —**con·duct·i·ble** *adj.*

Synonyms: *control, direct, manage, oversee, supervise.*

con·duc·tance (kən-dŭk′təns) *n.* A measure of a material's ability to conduct electric charge, the real part of the complex representation of **admittance** *(see).*

con·duc·tim·e·try (kŏn′dŭk-tĭm′ĭ-trē) *n.* The study of chemical

PRONUNCIATION KEY

ă, pat; ā, pay; âr, care;
ä, father, are; b, bib;
ch, church; d, deed; ĕ, pet;
ē, be; f, fife; g, gag; h, hat;
hw, which; ĭ, pit; ī, pie;
îr, pier; j, judge; k, kick;
l, lid, needle; m, mum;
n, no, sudden; ng, thing;
ŏ, pot; ō, toe; ô, paw, for;
oi, noise; ou, out; o͝o, book;
o͞o, boot; p, pop; r, roar;
s, sauce; sh, ship, dish;
t, tight; th, thin, path;
th, this, bathe; ŭ, cut; ûr, fur;
v, valve; w, with; y, yes;
z, zebra, size; zh, vision;
ə, about, item, edible, gallop, circus, peaceful

IN FOREIGN WORDS:

à, *Fr.* ami; œ, *Fr.* feu, *Ger.* schön; ü, *Fr.* tu, *Ger.* über; KH, *Ger.* ich, *Scot.* loch; N, *Fr.* bon; y′, *Fr.* Compiègne

STRESS MARKS:

Primary stress: ′
in·cite′ (ĭn-sīt′)
Secondary stress: ′
in′sight′ (ĭn′sīt′)

analyses that involve titrations based on changes in the electrical conductance of a solution.

con·duc·tion (kən-dŭk'shən) n. The transmission or conveying of something through a medium or passage, especially: **1.** The transmission of electric charge or heat through a conducting medium without perceptible motion of the medium itself. **2.** The transmission of a nerve impulse along a nerve fiber.

con·duc·tive (kən-dŭk'tĭv) adj. Exhibiting conductivity.

con·duc·tiv·i·ty (kŏn'dŭk-tĭv'ə-tē) n. Symbol σ **1.** A measure of the ability of a material to conduct an electric charge, the reciprocal of **resistivity** (see). See **thermal conductivity. 2.** The ability or power to conduct or transmit.

con·duc·tor (kən-dŭk'tər) n. **1.** A person who conducts or leads. **2.** The person in charge of a railroad train, bus, or streetcar. **3.** One who conducts an orchestra or other musical ensemble. **4.** Physics. A substance or medium that conducts heat, sound, or an electric current. **5.** A lightning rod. **—con·duc·tor·ship** n.

con·duc·tress (kən-dŭk'trəs) n. A woman who works as a bus or train conductor.

con·duit (kŏn'dĭt, -dōō-ĭt) n. **1.** A channel or pipe for conveying water or other fluids. **2.** A tube or duct for enclosing electric wires or cable. **3.** Archaic. A fountain. [Middle English, from Old French, conveyance, from Medieval Latin conductus, escort, transportation, from Latin, past participle of condūcere, to lead together, CONDUCT.]

con·du·pli·cate (kŏn-dōō'plə-kĭt, kŏn-dyōō'-) adj. Botany. Folded in half lengthwise. Said especially of unopened leaves. [Latin conduplicātus, past participle of conduplicāre, to double, fold together : com-, together + duplicāre, to double, DUPLICATE.] **—con·du·pli·ca·tion** n.

con·dyle (kŏn'dīl) n. A rounded articulatory prominence at the end of a bone. [French, from Latin condylus, knuckle, from Greek kondulos†.] **—con·dy·lar** adj. **—con·dy·loid** adj.

con·dy·lo·ma (kŏn-də-lō'mə) n., pl. **-mas** or **-mata** (-mə-tə). A wartlike growth near the anus or external genitalia, usually a result of venereal infection. [New Latin, from Greek kondulōma : kondulos, knuckle, CONDYLE + -OMA.] **—con·dy·lom·a·tous** adj.

Con·dy's fluid (kŏn'dīz) n. A solution of potassium permanganate, used especially as a disinfectant or in the treatment of snakebites. [After Henry Bollman Condy, 19th-century British chemist.]

cone (kōn) n. **1.** Geometry. **a.** A surface generated by a straight line, the generator, passing through a fixed point, the vertex, and moving along the intersection with a fixed curve, the directrix. **b.** The surface generated by such a generator passing through a vertex lying on the perpendicular axis of a circular directrix. **2. a.** The figure formed by such a surface bound, or regarded as bound, by its vertex and a plane section taken anywhere above or below the vertex. **b.** Anything having the shape of this figure. **3. a.** A conical, spheroidal, or cylindrical structure borne by certain trees, such as the pines, firs, and hemlocks, consisting of clusters of stiff, overlapping, woody scales, between which are the naked ovules. **b.** Any similar structure, such as the fruit of the magnolia or hop or the reproductive structure of pteridophytes. Also called "strobilus." **4.** A photoreceptor in the retina of the eye that is sensitive to color and bright light. Compare **rod. 5.** Any of various gastropod mollusks of the family Conidae, of tropical seas, having a conical, often vividly marked shell. Also called "cone shell." **6.** A volcanic peak having a wide base.

~tr.v. coned, con·ing, cones. To shape like a cone or cone segment. [French cône, from Latin cōnus, from Greek kōnos.]

cone-flow·er (kōn'flou'ər) n. Any of various North American plants of the genera Rudbeckia, Ratibida, and Echinacea, having rayed flowers with a conelike center of tubular florets.

cone·nose (kōn'nōz') n. Any of several assassin bugs; especially, Triatoma sanguisuga, of the southern and western United States and Mexico, having sucking mouth-parts and capable of inflicting a painful, toxic bite. Also called "cone-nosed bug."

coney. Variant of **cony.**

Co·ney Island (kō'nē). A beach resort and amusement area of Brooklyn, New York, on the southwestern tip of Long Island.

conf. conference.

con·fab (kŏn'făb') n. Informal. A confabulation; chat.

~intr.v. (kən-făb', kŏn'făb') **confabbed, -fabbing, -fabs.** Informal. To talk informally; confabulate.

con·fab·u·late (kən-făb'yə-lāt') intr.v. **-lated, -lating, -lates. 1.** To talk informally; chat. **2.** Psychiatry. To replace fact with fantasy in memory. [Latin confābulārī : com-, together + fābulārī, to talk, from fābula, story, conversation, from fārī, to speak.] **—con·fab·u·la·tion** n. **—con·fab·u·la·tor** n. **—con·fab·u·la·to·ry** (kən-făb'yə-lə-tôr'ē, -tōr'ē) adj.

con·fect (kən-fĕkt') tr.v. **-fected, -fecting, -fects. 1.** To put together; make. **2.** To make into a confection or preserve.

~n. (kŏn'fĕkt'). A candy or other sweet confection. [Middle English confecten, from Latin conficere (past participle confectus), to prepare : com- (intensive) + facere, to make.]

con·fec·tion (kən-fĕk'shən) n. **1.** The act or a product of compounding, mixing, or preparing. **2.** A sweet preparation, such as candy or preserves. **3.** A sweetened medicinal compound. **4.** Especially formerly, a stylish article of women's clothing.

con·fec·tion·ar·y (kən-fĕk'shən-ĕr'ē) adj. Pertaining to or resembling confections or their preparation.

con·fec·tion·er (kən-fĕk'shən-ər) n. One who makes or sells confections, especially sweets.

confectioners' sugar n. Finely pulverized sugar with some cornstarch added.

con·fec·tion·er·y (kən-fĕk'shən-ĕr'ē) n., pl. **-ies.** Also **con·fec·tion·ar·y** (for sense 3). **1.** Candies and other confections collectively. **2.** The art or occupation of a confectioner. **3.** A confectioner's shop.

con·fed·er·a·cy (kən-fĕd'ər-ə-sē) n., pl. **-cies. 1.** A union of persons, parties, or states; alliance; league. **2.** A combination for unlawful practices; conspiracy. **3. Confederacy.** The Confederate States of America. [Middle English confederacie, from Norman French, from Latin confoederātiō, union, from confoederāre, to unite. See **confederate.**]

con·fed·er·ate (kən-fĕd'ər-ĭt) n. **1.** A member of a confederacy; an ally. **2.** One who assists in a plot; an accomplice. **3. Confederate.** Formerly, a supporter of the Confederate States of America. **—See** Synonyms at **partner.**

~adj. 1. United in a confederacy; allied. **2. Confederate.** Of or pertaining to the Confederate States of America.

~v. (kən-fĕd'ə-rāt') **confederated, -ating, -ates. —tr.** To form into a confederacy. **—intr.** To unite into, or become part of, a confederacy. [Middle English confederat, from Latin confoederātus, from past participle of confoederāre, to unite in a league : com-, together + foederāre, to unite, from foedus, league.] **—con·fed·er·a·tive** adj.

Confederate rose n. The **cotton rose** (see).

Confederate States of America n. Abbr. **C.S.A.** The confederation of 11 Southern states that seceded from the United States (1860–65), comprising Alabama, Arkansas, Florida, Georgia, Louisiana, Mississippi, North Carolina, South Carolina, Tennessee, Texas, and Virginia. Also called the "Confederacy," "Southern Confederacy."

con·fed·er·a·tion (kən-fĕd'ə-rā'shən) n. Abbr. **confed. 1.** An act of confederating or a state of being confederated. **2.** A group of confederates, especially of states or nations, united for a common purpose; a league. Compare **federation. —con·fed·er·a·tion·ism** n. **—con·fed·er·a·tion·ist** n.

con·fer (kən-fûr') v. **-ferred, -ferring, -fers. —tr. 1.** To bestow (an honor or degree, for example). Used with on or upon. **2.** Obsolete. To compare. **—intr.** To hold a conference; compare views; consult together. [Latin conferre, to bring together, contribute, bestow : com-, together + ferre, to bring, bear.] **—con·fer·ment, con·fer·ral** n. **—con·fer·ra·ble** adj. **—con·fer·rer** n.

con·fer·ee, con·fer·ree (kŏn'fə-rē') n. **1.** A participant in a conference. **2.** One upon whom something is conferred.

con·fer·ence (kŏn'fə-rəns, -frəns) n. Abbr. **conf. 1. a.** A meeting for consultation or discussion. **b.** An exchange of views. **c.** A meeting of committees to settle differences between two legislative bodies. **2.** A formal meeting, especially one held annually, at which delegates representing different states or organizations, or different branches of the same organization, discuss and debate matters of common interest. **3.** In the Methodist and some other Protestant churches, the annual assembly of clerical and lay members that constitutes the governing body of such churches. **4.** An association for mutual benefit. **5.** The act of conferring, as of a degree; bestowal or conferral. **—in conference.** Taking part in a meeting or discussion. [Old French, from Medieval Latin conferentia, from Latin conferēns (stem conferent-), present participle of conferre, to CONFER.] **—con·fer·en·tial** adj.

conference call n. A conference by telephone in which several persons participate by means of a central switching unit.

con·fer·va (kən-fûr'və) n., pl. **-vae** (-vē) or **-vas.** Any of various bright green, threadlike freshwater algae, especially any of the genus Tribonema. [New Latin, from Latin conferva, COMFREY.] **—con·fer·void** n. & adj.

con·fess (kən-fĕs') v. **-fessed, -fessing, -fesses. —tr. 1.** To disclose or acknowledge (something damaging or inconvenient to oneself). **2.** To concede the truth or validity of; admit. **3.** To acknowledge belief or faith in. **4. a.** To make known (one's sins), especially to a priest for absolution. **b.** To confess thus the sins of (oneself). **c.** To hear the confession of. Used of a priest. **—intr. 1.** To admit or acknowledge a crime or deed. Sometimes used with to. **2.** To tell one's sins to a priest. **—See** Synonyms at **acknowledge.** [Middle English confessen, from Old French confesser, from Late Latin confessāre, frequentative of confitērī (past participle confessus), to acknowledge : com- (intensive) + fatērī, to admit.]

con·fess·ed·ly (kən-fĕs'ĭd-lē) adv. By one's own admission; admittedly.

con·fes·sion (kən-fĕsh'ən) n. **1.** The act or an instance of confessing; acknowledgment; avowal; admission. **2.** A formal declaration of guilt. **3.** The disclosure of sins to a priest for absolution. **4.** An avowal of belief in the doctrines of a particular faith. Also called "confession of faith." **5.** A church or group of worshipers adhering to a particular creed.

con·fes·sion·al (kən-fĕsh'ən-əl) adj. Of, pertaining to, or resembling confession.

~n. 1. A small enclosed stall in a church, in which a priest hears confessions. **2.** The act or practice of confessing to a priest.

con·fes·sor (kən-fĕs'ər) n. **1.** A priest who hears confession and gives absolution. **2.** One who confesses. **3.** One who confesses faith in Christianity in the face of persecution but does not suffer martyrdom: King Edward the Confessor.

con·fet·ti (kən-fĕt'ē) n. Used with a singular verb. Small pieces of colored paper thrown during festive celebrations, especially at the bride and groom after a wedding. [Italian, plural of confetto, con-

condor With a wingspan of up to about 2.75 meters (10 feet), the condors of the Andes and the California condor (above) are among the world's largest flying birds. Both are vultures of mountain regions; the California condor is one of the world's rarest birds.

fection, from Medieval Latin *confectum,* from Latin *confectus,* past participle of *conficere,* to put together, prepare, CONFECT.]

con·fi·dant (kŏn'fə-dănt', -dänt', kŏn'fə-dănt', -dänt') *n.* One to whom secrets or private matters are confided. [French *confident,* from Italian *confidente,* from Latin *confīdēns* (stem *confīdent-*), present participle of *confīdere,* to CONFIDE.]

con·fi·dante (kŏn'fə-dănt', -dänt', kŏn'fə-dănt', -dänt) *n.* A woman to whom secret or private matters are confided. [French *confidente,* feminine of *confident,* CONFIDANT.]

con·fide (kən-fīd') *v.* **-fided, -fiding, -fides.** —*tr.* **1.** To tell (something) in confidence. **2.** To entrust (something) to another. —*intr.* To tell private matters to another in confidence. Used with *in.* —See Synonyms at **commit.** [Middle English *confiden,* from Old French *confider,* from Latin *confīdere* : *com-* (intensive) + *fīdere,* to trust.] —**con·fid·er** *n.*

con·fi·dence (kŏn'fə-dəns) *n.* **1.** Trust in a person or thing. **2.** A trusting relationship in which secrets may be imparted: *took us into her confidence.* **3.** Something confided, such as a secret. **4.** A feeling of assurance or certainty, especially in oneself and one's capabilities. —**in confidence.** As a secret. —See Synonyms at **trust.**

confidence game *n.* A swindle in which the victim is defrauded after his confidence has been won. Also *informal* "con game."

confidence interval *n.* A statistical range, bounded by confidence limits, with a stipulated probability that a given parameter lies within the range.

confidence limit *n.* One of the two values reasonably chosen to specify the limits of a confidence interval.

confidence man *n.* One who swindles by using a confidence game. Also *informal* "con man."

con·fi·dent (kŏn'fə-dənt) *adj.* **1.** Having or indicating assurance or certainty, as of success. **2.** Having confidence in oneself; self-assured. **3.** Very bold; presumptuous. **4.** *Obsolete.* Confiding; trustful. —See Synonyms at **sure.**
—*n.* A confidant. [Latin *confīdēns* (stem *confīdent-*), present participle of *confīdere,* to CONFIDE.] —**con·fi·dent·ly** *adv.*

con·fi·den·tial (kŏn'fə-dĕn'shəl) *adj.* **1.** Done or communicated in confidence; told in secret. **2.** Entrusted with the confidence of another; intimate: *a confidential secretary.* **3.** Denoting trust or intimacy: *a confidential tone of voice.* —**con·fi·den·ti·al·i·ty** (kŏn'fə-dĕn'shē-ăl'ə-tē), **con·fi·den·tial·ness** *n.* —**con·fi·den·tial·ly** *adv.*

con·fid·ing (kən-fī'dĭng) *adj.* Trusting; unsuspicious. —**con·fid·ing·ly** *adv.* —**con·fid·ing·ness** *n.*

con·fig·u·ra·tion (kən-fĭg'yə-rā'shən) *n.* **1. a.** The arrangement of the parts or elements of something. **b.** The form of a figure as determined by the arrangement of its parts; outline; contour. **2.** *Psychology.* A gestalt *(see).* **3.** *Chemistry.* Conformation *(see).* [Late Latin *configūrātiō* (stem *configūrātiōn-*), from Latin *configūrāre,* "to form together," fashion after : *com-,* together + *figūrāre,* to form, from *figūra,* shape, FIGURE.] —**con·fig·u·ra·tive, con·fig·u·ra·tion·al** *adj.* —**con·fig·u·ra·tion·al·ly** *adv.*

con·fig·u·ra·tion·ism (kən-fĭg'yə-rā'shə-nĭz'əm) *n.* **Gestalt psychology** *(see).*

con·fine (kən-fīn') *v.* **-fined, -fining, -fines.** —*tr.* **1.** To keep within bounds; restrict. **2.** To shut within an enclosure; imprison. **3.** To keep (a woman who is about to give birth) in bed. Used in the passive. —*intr. Archaic.* To border; be adjacent. —See Synonyms at **limit.**
—*n.* (kŏn'fīn' *for senses 1, 3;* kən-fīn' *for sense 2*). **1.** *Usually* **confines.** A border or limit; boundary. **2.** *Archaic.* Confinement. **3.** *Obsolete.* A place of confinement. —See Synonyms at **boundary.** [Old French *confiner,* from *confin,* boundary, limit, from Latin *confīne,* from *confīnis,* having the same border : *com-,* together + *fīnis,* border, end.] —**con·fin·a·ble, con·fine·a·ble** *adj.* —**con·fin·er** *n.*

con·fine·ment (kən-fīn'mənt) *n.* **1.** The act of confining or the state of being confined. **2.** The state of being confined prior to and during childbirth. **3.** *Physics.* The theory that the attractive force between two quarks increases as the quarks are pulled apart as a result of the exchange of gluons, used to explain why quarks cannot be found as free particles.

con·firm (kən-fûrm') *tr.v.* **-firmed, -firming, -firms. 1.** To assure the certainty or validity of; corroborate; verify. **2.** To make more firm; strengthen: *She confirmed my suspicions.* **3.** To make valid or binding by a formal or legal act; ratify. **4.** To administer the religious rite of confirmation to. [Middle English *confirmen,* from Old French *confirmer,* from Latin *confirmāre* : *com-* (intensive) + *firmāre,* to make firm, strengthen, from *firmus,* firm.] —**con·firm·a·ble** *adj.* —**con·firm·er** *n.*
Synonyms: *authenticate, corroborate, establish, prove, ratify, substantiate, validate, verify.*

con·fir·ma·tion (kŏn'fər-mā'shən) *n.* **1.** An act of confirming. **2.** That which confirms; corroboration or verification. **3.** A rite admitting a baptized person to full membership in a church. —**con·firm·a·to·ry** (kən-fûr'mə-tôr'ē, -tōr'ē), **con·firm·a·tive** (kən-fûr'mə-tĭv) *adj.*

con·firmed (kən-fûrmd') *adj.* Firmly established in a given state or habit, and unlikely to change; inveterate: *a confirmed bachelor.* —**con·firm·ed·ly** (kən-fûr'mĭd-lē) *adv.*

con·fis·ca·ble (kən-fĭs'kə-bəl) *adj.* Subject to confiscation.

con·fis·cate (kŏn'fĭs-kāt') *tr.v.* **-cated, -cating, -cates. 1.** To seize (private property) for a public treasury, especially by way of penalty. **2.** To seize by or as by authority.
—*adj.* **1.** Confiscated; appropriated. **2.** Having lost property through confiscation. [Latin *confiscāre,* to lay up in a chest, confiscate : *com-* (collective) + *fiscus,* chest, the treasury.] —**con·fis·ca·tion** *n.* —**con·fis·ca·tor** *n.*

Con·fit·e·or (kən-fēt'ē-ôr) *n. Roman Catholic Church.* A prayer in which confession of sins is made. [Latin, "I confess" (first word of the prayer).]

con·fla·grant (kən-flā'grənt) *adj.* Burning intensely; blazing. [Latin *conflagrāns* (stem *conflagrant-*), present participle of *conflagrāre,* to burn up. See **conflagration.**]

con·fla·gra·tion (kŏn'flə-grā'shən) *n.* A large, blazing, and destructive fire. [Latin *conflagrātiō* (stem *conflagrātiōn-*), from *conflagrāre,* to burn up : *com-* (intensive) + *flagrāre,* to burn, blaze.]

con·flate (kən-flāt') *tr.v.* **-flated, -flating, -flates.** To fuse or blend into a single unit (especially two versions of a text).

con·fla·tion (kən-flā'shən) *n.* **1.** A combining, as of two variant texts into one text. **2.** A product of this; especially, a text or reading arrived at by fusing material from different sources. [Middle English *conflacioun,* from Late Latin *conflātiō* (stem *conflātiōn-*), from *conflāre,* "to blow together," combine two readings : *com-,* together + *flāre,* to blow.]

con·flict (kŏn'flĭkt) *n.* **1.** A prolonged battle; a struggle. **2.** The clash of opposing ideas or forces; disagreement; opposition. **3.** *Psychology.* Inner struggle resulting from the opposition of irreconcilable impulses, desires, or tendencies. **4.** A crashing together; collision. —See Synonyms at **discord.**
—*intr.v.* (kən-flĭkt') **conflicted, -flicting, -flicts. 1.** To come into opposition; collide; differ. **2.** To fight; do battle. [Middle English, from Latin *conflīctus,* from the past participle of *conflīgere,* to clash together, contend : *com-,* together + *flīgere,* to strike.] —**con·flic·tion** *n.* —**con·flic·tive** *adj.*
Synonyms: *affray, combat, contest, fight, melee, scuffle.*

con·flic·ting (kən-flĭk'tĭng) *adj.* Mutually incompatible or contradictory: *conflicting ideologies; conflicting reports.* —**con·flic·ting·ly** *adj.*

con·flu·ence (kŏn'flōō-əns) *n.* Also **con·flux** (-flŭks). **1.** A flowing together, as of two or more streams. **2.** The point of juncture of such streams. **3.** A gathering together; crowd.

con·flu·ent (kŏn'flōō-ənt) *adj.* **1.** Flowing together; blended into one. **2.** *Pathology.* Merging together so as to form a mass. Said of sores in a rash. **3.** *Anatomy.* Coalesced. Said for example of two originally separate bones.
—*n.* **1.** A confluent stream. **2.** A tributary. [Middle English, from Latin *confluēns* (stem *confluent-*), present participle of *confluere,* to flow together : *com-,* together + *fluere,* to flow.]

con·fo·cal (kŏn-fō'kəl) *adj.* Having the same focus or foci.

con·form (kən-fôrm') *v.* **-formed, -forming, -forms.** —*intr.* **1.** To come to have the same form or character as another or each other. **2.** To act or be in accord or agreement; comply. Used with *to* or *with.* **3.** To act in accordance with current customs or modes. **4.** To comply with the usages of an established church, especially the Church of England. —*tr.* **1.** To make similar. **2.** To bring into agreement or correspondence. Often used reflexively. —See Synonyms at **agree.** [Middle English *conformen,* from Old French *conformer,* from Latin *conformāre,* "to have the same form" : *com-,* same, similar + *formāre,* to shape, from *forma,* form, shape.] —**con·form·er** *n.*

con·form·a·ble (kən-fôrm'ə-bəl) *adj.* **1.** In harmony or agreement; corresponding; similar. Often used with *to.* **2.** Quick to comply; submissive. **3.** *Geology.* Designating strata that are parallel to each other without interruption. —**con·form·a·bil·i·ty, con·form·a·ble·ness** *n.* —**con·form·a·bly** *adv.*

con·for·mal (kən-fôr'məl) *adj.* **1.** *Mathematics.* Designating a depiction of a surface or region upon another surface so that all angles between intersecting curves remain unchanged. **2.** Of, pertaining to, or designating a map projection in which angles around any point are true, and at any point the scale is the same in any direction, so that small areas are rendered with true shape. [Late Latin *conformālis,* having the same form : Latin *com-,* same, similar + *formālis,* having a form, FORMAL.] —**con·for·mal·ly** *adv.*

con·for·mance (kən-fôr'məns) *n.* Conformity.

con·for·ma·tion (kŏn'fər-mā'shən) *n.* **1.** The structure or outline of something as determined by the arrangement of its parts. **2.** The act of conforming or state of being conformed; adjustment; adaptation. **3.** *Chemistry.* The shape of a molecule or an atom as determined by the three-dimensional arrangement of its constituents. Also called "configuration."

conformation theory *n. Chemistry.* The theory that the stability and reactivity of a molecule can be predicted from its three-dimensional structure, especially with respect to the conformation of organic molecules and their substituents.

con·form·ist (kən-fôr'mĭst) *n.* **1.** One who conforms to current standards or customs. **2.** *Abbr.* **Con.** One who complies with the usages of an established church, especially the Church of England. Compare **dissenter, nonconformist.** —**con·form·ism** *n.*

con·form·i·ty (kən-fôr'mə-tē) *n., pl.* **-ties.** Also **con·form·ance** (-fôr'məns). **1.** Similarity in form or character; correspondence; agreement. **2.** Action or behavior in correspondence with current customs, rules, or styles. **3.** Compliance with the usages of an established church, especially the Church of England.

con·found (kən-found', kŏn'-) *v.* **-founded, -founding, -founds. 1.** To cause to become confused or disordered; bewilder. **2.** To mix up (incompatible elements or ideas). **3.** To fail to distinguish; confuse; mix up. **4.** To cause to be ashamed; abash. **5.** To defeat;

overthrow. **6.** To damn. Used in mild oaths: *Confound it!* —See Synonyms at **puzzle.** [Middle English *confounden,* from Old French *confondre,* from Latin *confundere,* to pour together, mix up : *com-,* together + *fundere,* to pour.] **—con·found·er** *n.*

con·found·ed (kən-foun′dĭd, kŏn-) *adj.* **1.** Confused; befuddled. **2.** Damned. Used as a mild oath: *a confounded fool.* **—con·found·ed·ly** *adv.* **—con·found·ed·ness** *n.*

con·fra·ter·ni·ty (kŏn′frə-tûr′nə-tē) *n., pl.* **-ties.** An association of men united by profession or in some common purpose, usually of a religious or charitable nature. [Middle English *confraternite,* from Old French, from Medieval Latin *confrāternitās* (stem *confrāternitāt-*), from *confrāter,* colleague, CONFRERE.]

con·frere (kŏn′frâr) *n.* A fellow member of a fraternity or profession; a colleague. [Middle English, from Old French, from Medieval Latin *confrāter,* colleague, fellow member : Latin *com-,* together + *frāter,* brother.]

con·front (kən-frŭnt′) *tr.v.* **-fronted, -fronting, -fronts. 1.** To come face to face with; stand in front of. **2.** To face with hostility or defiance. **3.** To bring close together for comparison; compare. **4.** To cause to meet or face: *confronted them with the evidence of their guilt.* **5.** To come up against; encounter. [Old French *confronter,* from Medieval Latin *confrontāre,* to have a common border : Latin *com-,* together + *frōns* (stem *front-*), forehead, FRONT.] **—con·front·er** *n.*

con·fron·ta·tion (kŏn′frən-tā′shən) *n.* The act of confronting or state of being confronted; especially, a condition or stance of conflict and rivalry rather than of conciliation. **—con·fron·ta·tion·al** *adj.* **—con·fron·ta·tion·ist** *adj. & n.*

Con·fu·cian (kən-fyōō′shən) *adj.* Of, pertaining to, or characteristic of Confucius, his teachings, or his followers.
~*n.* One who adheres to the teachings of Confucius.

Con·fu·cian·ism (kən-fyōō′shən-ĭz′əm) *n.* The ethical system based on the teachings of Confucius, emphasizing personal virtue, devotion to family (including the spirits of one's ancestors), and justice. **—Con·fu·cian·ist** *n.*

Con·fu·cius (kən-fyōō′shəs) (*c.* 551–479 B.C.). *Chinese* **Kong-zi** (kōōng′dzə), **Kong-fu-zi** (-fōō′dzə). Chinese philosopher, who was a statesman and adviser to various feudal lords. When none would implement his philosophy of perfecting one's own moral character, he became a teacher. Many books and sayings have been attributed to him, but few can be authenticated.

con·fuse (kən-fyōōz′) *tr.v.* **-fused, -fusing, -fuses. 1.** To disturb the thought process, perceptions, or purpose of; perplex. **2.** To assemble without order or sense; jumble. **3.** To make less distinct; blur: *confuse an important issue.* **4.** To fail to distinguish between; mix up: *confuse a word with a near synonym.* [Back-formation from Middle English *confused,* from Old French *confus,* from Latin *confūsus,* past participle of *confundere,* to mix up, CONFOUND.] **—con·fus·ed·ly** (kən-fyōō′zĭd-lē) *adv.* **—con·fus·ed·ness** *n.* **—con·fus·er** *n.* **—con·fus·ing·ly** *adv.*

con·fu·sion (kən-fyōō′zhən) *n.* **1.** The act of confusing or state of being confused. **2.** Disorder; jumble. **3.** Distraction; bewilderment. **—con·fu·sion·al** *adj.*

con·fu·ta·tion (kŏn′fyōō-tā′shən) *n.* **1.** An act of confuting. **2.** Something that confutes. **—con·fu·ta·tive** (kən-fyōō′tə-tĭv) *adj.*

con·fute (kən-fyōōt′) *tr.v.* **-futed, -futing, -futes.** To prove conclusively to be wrong or in error: *confute a theory.* [Latin *confūtāre,* to check, restrain.] **—con·fut·a·ble** *adj.* **—con·fut·er** *n.*

cong. *Pharmacology.* congius.

Cong. 1. Congregational. **2.** Congress; Congressional.

con·ga (kŏng′gə) *n.* **1.** A dance of Latin-American origin in which the dancers form a long, winding line. **2.** Music for this dance.
~*intr.v.* **congaed, -gaing, -gas.** To dance the conga. [American Spanish *(danza) Conga,* "the Congo (dance)," from CONGO.]

conga drum *n.* A tall, narrow bass drum beaten with the hands.

con game *n. Slang.* A **confidence game** *(see).*

con·gé (kôN-zhā′, kŏn′jā′) *n.* Also **con·gee** (kŏn′jē). **1.** Formal or authoritative permission to depart. **2.** An abrupt dismissal. **3. a.** *Archaic.* A formal bow. **b.** A leave-taking. **4.** *Architecture.* A kind of concave molding.
~*intr.v.* **congéed, -géeing, -gées.** *Archaic.* **1.** To take ceremonious leave. **2.** To make a formal bow. [French, from Old French *congie,* from Latin *commeātus,* "a going to and fro," from *commeāre,* to go to and fro : *com-,* mutually, back and forth + *meāre,* to go.]

con·geal (kən-jēl′) *v.* **-gealed, -gealing, -geals.** —*intr.* **1.** To solidify, as by freezing. **2.** To coagulate; jell. —*tr.* To cause to solidify or coagulate. [Middle English *congelen,* from Old French *congeler,* from Latin *congelāre,* to freeze solid : *com-,* together + *gelāre,* to freeze.] **—con·geal·a·ble** *adj.* **—con·geal·er** *n.* **—con·geal·ment** *n.* **—con·ge·la·tion** (kŏn′jə-lā′shən) *n.*

con·gee (kŏn′jē) *intr.v.* **-geed, -geeing, -gees.** *Archaic.* **1.** To take ceremonious leave. **2.** To make a formal bow.
~*n.* Variant of **congé.** [Middle English *congeien,* from Old French *congier,* from *congie,* leave of absence, CONGÉ.]

con·ge·ner (kŏn′jə-nər, kən-jē′-) *n.* **1.** A member of the same kind, class, or group. **2.** An organism belonging to the same genus as another or others. [Latin, of the same race : *com-,* same + *genus* (stem *gener-*), race, kind.] **—con·ge·ner·ic** (kŏn′jə-nĕr′ĭk), **con·gen·er·ous** (kən-jĕn′ər-əs) *adj.*

con·gen·i·al (kən-jēn′yəl) *adj.* **1.** Having the same tastes, habits, or temperament; sympathetic. **2.** Agreeably suited to one's needs or tastes; pleasant. **3.** Of a pleasant disposition; friendly and sociable. [CON- (same) + GENIAL.] **—con·ge·ni·al·i·ty** (kən-jē′nē-ăl′ə-tē), **con·gen·ial·ness** *n.* **—con·gen·ial·ly** *adv.*

con·gen·i·tal (kən-jĕn′ə-təl) *adj.* **1.** Existing at birth but not hereditary: *a congenital defect.* **2.** Having a specified character as if by nature: *a congenital thief.* —See Synonyms at **innate.** [Latin *congenitus,* born together with : *com-,* together + *genitus,* born, past participle of *gignere,* to beget.] **—con·gen·i·tal·ly** *adv.*

con·ger eel (kŏng′gər) *n.* Any of various large marine eels of the family Congridae; especially, *Conger oceanicus,* of Atlantic waters. [Middle English *congre,* from Old French, from Latin *conger, congrus,* from Greek *gongros,* of Mediterranean origin.]

con·ge·ries (kən-jîr′ēz, kŏn′jə-rēz′) *n. Used with a singular verb.* A collection of things heaped together; an aggregation. [Latin *congeriēs,* heap, pile, from *congerere,* to bring together, CONGEST.]

con·gest (kən-jĕst′) *v.* **-gested, -gesting, -gests.** —*tr.* **1.** To overfill or overcrowd; clog. **2.** *Pathology.* To cause excessive accumulation of blood in (a vessel or organ). **3.** To block (the nose). Used of mucus. —*intr.* To become congested. [Latin *congerere* (past participle *congestus*), to bring together, heap up : *com-,* together + *gerere,* to carry.] **—con·ges·tive** *adj.*

con·ges·tion (kən-jĕs′chən) *n.* **1. a.** An excessive accumulation of blood in a body part. **b.** An excessive accumulation of mucus in the nose. **2.** An overcrowded condition, especially as caused by traffic.

con·gi·us (kŏn′jē-əs) *n., pl.* **-gii** (-jē-ī′). *Abbr.* **c., C., cong.** *Pharmacology.* A gallon. [Middle English, from Latin *congius,* perhaps from Greek *konkhos,* conch, shell.]

con·glo·bate (kŏn-glō′bāt′, kŏng′glō-) *v.* **-bated, -bating, -bates.** Also **con·globe** (kŏn-glōb′), **-globed, -globing, -globes.** —*intr.* To become a globe or globule. —*tr.* To gather into a globe or ball.
~*adj.* Shaped like or formed into a ball. [Latin *conglobāre* : *com-,* together + *globāre,* to make into a globe, from *globus,* globe.] **—con·glo·ba·tion** *n.*

con·glom·er·ate (kən-glŏm′ə-rāt′) *v.* **-ated, -ating, -ates.** —*tr.* To collect into a cohesive mass. —*intr.* To form into an adhering or rounded mass.
~*n.* (kən-glŏm′ər-ĭt). **1.** A collected heterogeneous mass; a cluster. **2.** *Geology.* A rock consisting of pebbles and gravel embedded in a loosely cementing material. Also called "pudding stone." **3.** A business corporation made up of a number of different companies that operate in widely diversified fields.
~*adj.* (kən-glŏm′ər-ĭt). **1.** Gathered into a cohesive mass; clustered. **2.** *Geology.* Made up of cemented heterogeneous material. [Latin *conglomerāre,* to roll together : *com-,* together + *glomerāre,* to roll into a ball, from *glomus,* ball.] **—con·glom·er·at·ic** (kən-glŏm′ə-răt′ĭk) *adj.*

con·glom·er·a·tion (kən-glŏm′ə-rā′shən) *n.* **1.** The process of conglomerating or state of being conglomerated. **2.** A collection or cohesive mass of miscellaneous things.

con·glu·ti·nant (kən-glōōt′tə-nənt) *adj. Medicine.* Promoting adhesion, as of the lips of a wound. [Latin *conglūtināns* (stem *conglūtinant-*), present participle of *conglūtināre,* to glue together, CONGLUTINATE.]

con·glu·ti·nate (kən-glōōt′tə-nāt′) *v.* **-nated, -nating, -nates.** —*intr.* **1.** To become stuck or glued together; adhere. **2.** *Medicine.* To become reunited. Used of bones or tissues. —*tr.* **1.** To stick or glue together. **2.** *Medicine.* To cause (bones or tissues) to reunite. [Middle English *conglutinaten,* from Latin *conglūtināre,* to glue together : *com-,* together + *glūtināre,* to glue, from *glūten,* glue.] **—con·glu·ti·na·tion** *n.* **—con·glu·ti·na·tive** (kən-glōōt′tə-nā′tĭv, -nə-tĭv) *adj.*

Con·go[1] (kŏng′gō). Country in west-central Africa. Oil from offshore fields and timber are the main exports. The Portuguese encountered the powerful Kongo kingdom in the 15th and 16th centuries. The area was claimed by France and in 1910 became the Middle Congo, a territory of French Equatorial Africa. In 1960 it was granted independence as the Republic of the Congo (Brazzaville). The country became Africa's first Marxist state in 1970. In 1977 the military junta assumed control. Area, 342,000 kilometers (132,047 square miles). Population, 1,500,000. Capital, Brazzaville. See map, next page.

Congo[2]**.** See **Zaire (river).**

Congo, Democratic Republic of the. See **Zaire.**

congo eel *n.* An eellike amphibian, *Amphiuma means,* of the southeastern United States, having two pairs of tiny, nonfunctioning legs.

Con·go·lese (kŏng′gə-lēz′) *adj.* Of or pertaining to the region of the Congo and the two Congo republics or their inhabitants.
~*n., pl.* **Congolese.** An inhabitant of the region of the Congo or of either of the two Congo republics.

Congo peacock *n.* A variety of **peacock** *(see).*

Congo red *n.* A brownish-red powder, $C_{32}H_{22}N_6O_6S_2Na_2$, used as a diagnostic and chemical indicator, a dye, and a biological stain.

con·grat·u·late (kən-grăch′ōō-lāt′) *tr.v.* **-lated, -lating, -lates. 1.** To express pleasure at the success or good fortune of: *congratulated him on his promotion.* **2.** To take pride in (oneself) for an achievement. [Latin *congrātulārī,* to rejoice with someone : *com-,* with + *grātulārī,* to express one's joy, rejoice, from *grātus,* pleasing.] **—con·grat·u·la·tor** (kən-grăch′ōō-lā′tər) *n.*

con·grat·u·la·tion (kən-grăch′ōō-lā′shən) *n.* **1.** The act of congratulating. **2. congratulations.** Acknowledgment of the success or good fortune of another. Often used as an interjection.

con·grat·u·la·to·ry (kən-grăch′ōō-lə-tôr′ē, -tōr′ē) *adj.* Conveying or expressing congratulations: *a congratulatory telegram.*

con·gre·gant (kŏng′grə-gənt) *n.* A member of a congregation.

con·gre·gate (kŏng′grə-gāt′) *v.* **-gated, -gating, -gates.** —*intr.* To come together in a crowd; assemble. —*tr.* To bring together in a

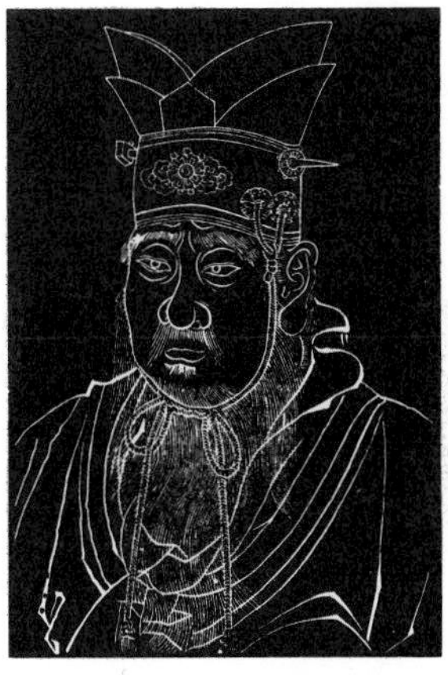

Confucius *The social and moral teachings of this Chinese philosopher, who was born in the sixth century B.C., became after his death the philosophical underpinning of classical Chinese civilization. The teachings emphasize a network of mutual duties binding families, friends, and nations.*

crowd or an assembly; collect. [Middle English *congregaten*, from Latin *congregāre*, to assemble : *com-*, together + *gregāre*, to flock together, from *grex* (stem *greg-*), herd, flock.] —**con·gre·ga·tive** *adj.* —**con·gre·ga·tor** *n.*

con·gre·ga·tion (kŏng′grə-gā′shən) *n.* **1.** An act of congregating. **2.** A body of assembled people or things; a gathering. **3. a.** A group of people gathered for religious worship. **b.** The members of a specific religious group who regularly worship at a particular church. **4.** *Roman Catholic Church.* **a.** A religious institute in which only simple vows, not solemn vows, are taken. **b.** Any of several committees of the **Curia** (see). **5.** *Chiefly British.* An assembly of the senior members of a university.

con·gre·ga·tion·al (kŏng′grə-gā′shən-əl) *adj.* **1.** Of or pertaining to a congregation. **2.** Congregational. *Abbr.* **Cong.** Of or pertaining to Congregationalism or Congregationalists.

Congregational Church *n.* An evangelical Protestant denomination practicing Congregationalism and, since 1957, merged with the United Church of Christ.

con·gre·ga·tion·al·ism (kŏng′grə-gā′shən-əl-ĭz′əm) *n.* **1.** A type of church government in which each local congregation is self-governing. **2.** Congregationalism. The system of government and religious beliefs of the Congregational Church, in which each member church is self-governing. —**con·gre·ga·tion·al·ist, Con·gre·ga·tion·al·ist** *n. & adj.*

Congregation of the Holy Office *n.* The official name for the **Holy Office** (see).

con·gress (kŏng′grĭs) *n.* **1.** A formal assembly of representatives, as of various nations or of an association, to discuss problems and policy. **2.** The national legislative bodies of certain nations, especially of republics. **3.** Congress. *Abbr.* **Cong., C. a.** The national legislative body of the United States, consisting of the Senate and the House of Representatives. **b.** The two-year session of this legislature between elections of the House of Representatives. **4.** A coming together; a meeting. **5.** Sexual intercourse. [Middle English *congresse*, a coming together, from Latin *congressus*, from *congredī*, to come together : *com-*, together + *gradī*, to go.]

con·gres·sion·al (kən-grĕsh′ən-əl) *adj.* **1.** Of or pertaining to a congress. **2.** Congressional. *Abbr.* **Cong.** Of or pertaining to the Congress of the United States.

congressional district *n.* Any of the districts of each state of the United States, entitled to one representative in Congress.

Congressional Medal of Honor *n.* The **Medal of Honor** (see).

con·gress·man (kŏng′grĭs-mən) *n., pl.* -**men** (-mĭn). *Sometimes* **Congressman.** A member of the U.S. Congress, especially of the House of Representatives.

con·gress·wom·an (kŏng′grĭs-wŏom′ən) *n., pl.* -**women** (-wĭm′ĭn). *Sometimes* **Congresswoman.** A female member of the U.S. Congress, especially of the House of Representatives.

Con·greve (kŏn′grĕv, kŏng′-), **William** (1670–1729). English dramatist, brought up in Ireland. He is best known for his witty comedies, including *Love for Love* (1695) and *The Way of the World* (1700).

con·gru·ence (kŏng′grōō-əns, kən-grōō′əns) *n.* Also **con·gru·en·cy** (kən-grōō′ən-sē). **1.** Agreement; conformity. **2.** *Mathematics.* **a.** The state of being congruent. **b.** A mathematical statement that two quantities are congruent.

con·gru·ent (kŏng′grōō-ənt, kən-grōō′ənt) *adj.* **1.** Corresponding; congruous. **2.** *Mathematics.* **a.** Coinciding exactly when superim-

posed: *congruent triangles.* **b.** Having a difference divisible by a modulus: *congruent numbers.* [Middle English, from Latin *congruēns* (stem *congruent-*), present participle of *congruere*†, to meet together, agree.] —**con·gru·ent·ly** *adv.*

con·gru·i·ty (kən-grōō′ə-tē) *n., pl.* -**ties**. **1.** The quality or fact of being congruous. **2.** A point of agreement. **3.** *Geometry.* Exact coincidence when superimposed.

con·gru·ous (kŏng′grōō-əs) *adj.* Corresponding in character or kind; appropriate; harmonious. [Latin *congruus*, from *congruere*†, to meet together, agree.]

con·ic (kŏn′ĭk) *adj.* Also **con·i·cal** (kŏn′ĭ-kəl). **1.** Shaped like a cone. **2.** Pertaining to a cone. ~*n.* *Mathematics.* A conic section. [New Latin *conicus*, from Greek *kōnikos*, from *kōnos*, CONE.]

conic projection *n.* In cartography, a method of projecting pictures of parts of the earth's spherical surface onto a tangent cone, which is then flattened to a plane surface having concentric circles as parallels of latitude and radiating lines from the apex as meridians. Also called "conical projection."

conic section *n.* One of a group of plane curves, including the circle, ellipse, hyperbola, and parabola, generated by: **1.** An intersection of a right circular cone and a plane. **2.** The plane locus of a point that moves so that the ratio of its distance to a fixed point to its distance from a fixed line is a positive constant. **3.** A graph of the general quadratic equation in two variables.

co·nid·i·o·phore (kə-nĭd′ē-ə-fôr′, -fōr′) *n.* A specialized hyphal filament in certain fungi, bearing conidia. [CONIDI(UM) + -PHORE.]

co·nid·i·um (kə-nĭd′ē-əm) *n., pl.* -**ia** (-ē-ə). An asexual spore in certain fungi that is produced at the tip of a conidiophore. [New Latin (diminutive), from Greek *konis*, dust.] —**co·nid·i·al** *adj.*

con·i·fer (kŏn′ə-fər, kō′nə-) *n.* Any tree of the order Coniferales, typically evergreen and bearing cones, including the pine, spruce, and fir. [New Latin *Coniferae* (family name), from Latin *cōnifer*, cone-bearing : *cōnus*, CONE + -FER.] See feature, pages 372–373.

co·nif·er·ous (kō-nĭf′ər-əs) *adj.* **1.** Bearing cones. **2.** Of or composed of conifers.

co·ni·ine (kō′nē-ēn′) *n.* A poisonous, colorless liquid alkaloid, $C_8H_{17}N$, obtained from the poison hemlock and formerly used in the treatment of spasmodic disorders. Also called "Z-propylpiperidine." [German *Koniin* : CONIUM + -IN.]

co·ni·um (kō′nē-əm) *n.* Any of several poisonous plants of the genus *Conium*, including the **poison hemlock** (see). [New Latin *Conium*, from Late Latin *cōnium*, poison hemlock, from Greek *kōneion*, perhaps from *kōnos*, cone (from its indented, pinnatifid leaves suggesting pine cones).]

con·i·za·tion (kŏn′ə-zā′shən) *n.* Surgical removal of a cone of tissue, especially from the cervix of the uterus. [CON(E) + -IZ(E) + -ATION.]

conj. 1. conjugation. **2.** *Grammar.* conjunction; conjunctive. **3.** *Astronomy.* conjunction.

con·jec·tur·al (kən-jĕk′chər-əl) *adj.* **1.** Involving conjecture. **2.** Inclined to conjecture. —**con·jec·tur·al·ly** *adv.*

con·jec·ture (kən-jĕk′chər) *v.* -**tured, -turing, -tures.** —*tr.* To infer from inconclusive evidence; guess. —*intr.* To make a conjecture. ~*n.* **1.** Inference based on inconclusive or incomplete evidence; guesswork. **2.** An opinion or conclusion based on incomplete evidence. [Middle English, from Old French, from Latin *conjectūra*, conclusion, interpretation, from *conjicere*, "to throw together," put together mentally, conjecture, interpret : *com-*, together + *jacere*, to throw.] —**con·jec·tur·a·ble** *adj.* —**con·jec·tur·a·bly** *adv.* —**con·jec·tur·er** *n.*

Synonyms: *guess, infer, presume, speculate, surmise.*

con·join (kən-join′) *v.* -**joined, -joining, -joins.** —*tr.* To join together; connect; unite. —*intr.* To become joined or connected. [Middle English *conjoinen*, from Old French *conjoindre*, from Latin *conjungere* : *com-*, together + *jungere*, to join.] —**con·join·er** *n.*

con·joint (kən-joint′) *adj.* **1.** Joined together; connected; associated. **2.** Of, pertaining to, or involving two or more associated parties; joint. [Middle English, from Old French, past participle of *conjoindre*, to CONJOIN.] —**con·joint·ly** *adv.*

con·ju·gal (kŏn′jə-gəl) *adj.* Of or pertaining to marriage or the marital relationship. [Old French, from Latin *conjugālis*, from *conjux* (stem *conjug-*), a spouse, from *conjungere*, to join together (in marriage) : *com-*, together + *jungere*, to join.] —**con·ju·gal·i·ty** (kŏn′jə-găl′ə-tē) *n.* —**con·ju·gal·ly** *adv.*

conjugal rights *pl.n.* A right to sexual intercourse with one's husband or wife.

con·ju·gant (kŏn′jə-gənt) *n.* Either of a pair of organisms, cells, or gametes undergoing conjugation. [Latin *conjugāns* (stem *conjugant-*), present participle of *conjugāre*, to CONJUGATE.]

con·ju·gate (kŏn′jə-gāt′) *v.* -**gated, -gating, -gates.** —*tr.* *Grammar.* To give the inflectional forms of (a verb) in a fixed order according to person, number, tense, mood, and voice. —*intr.* **1.** *Biology.* To undergo conjugation. **2.** *Grammar.* To inflect or admit of inflection. Used of a verb. ~*adj.* (kŏn′jə-gĭt). **1.** Joined together, especially in a pair or pairs; coupled. **2.** *Mathematics & Physics.* Inversely or oppositely related with respect to one of a group of otherwise identical properties; especially, designating either or both of a pair of complex numbers differing only in the sign of the imaginary term. **3.** *Geometry.* Designating two angles that together have a sum of 360°. **4.** Having the same derivation and usually a related meaning: *conjugate words.* ~*n.* (kŏn′jə-gĭt). **1.** One of two or more conjugate words. **2.** *Mathe-*

CONGO

15 E

C.A.E.

CAMEROON

Impfondo

Zaïre

Sangha

Oubangui

Equator

GABON

C O N G O

Gamboma

Bateke Plateau

Kouilou

Niari

Congo

ZAIRE

BRAZZAVILLE

Pointe Noire

CABINDA (ANGOLA)

Km 0 — 200
Miles 0 — 100

matics & Physics. Either of a pair of conjugate quantities. [Middle English *conjugat,* joined, from Latin *conjugātus,* past participle of *conjugāre,* to yoke or join together : *com-,* together + *jugāre,* to yoke, from *jugum,* yoke.] **—con·ju·ga·tive** (kŏn′jə-gā′tĭv) *adj.* **—con·ju·ga·tor** (kŏn′jə-gā′tər) *n.*

con·ju·gat·ed (kŏn′jə-gā′tĭd) *adj. Chemistry.* **1.** Designating a double bond that is separated from another double bond in a molecule by one single bond. **2.** Designating a molecule or compound containing two or more double bonds that alternate with single bonds. **3.** Formed by the combination of two compounds.

conjugated protein *n.* A compound consisting of a protein attached to a nonprotein group, such as a lipid or a carbohydrate.

con·ju·ga·tion (kŏn′jə-gā′shən) *n. Abbr.* **conj. 1.** *Grammar.* **a.** The inflection of a particular verb. **b.** A presentation of the complete set of inflected forms of a verb. **c.** A class of verbs having the same type of inflected forms. Compare **declension. 2.** *Biology.* **a.** A process of sexual reproduction in ciliate protozoans, certain algae, and some bacteria, in which two individuals of the same species temporarily couple and exchange genetic material. **b.** Chromosome pairing in the first meiotic division. **c.** The fusion of gamete nuclei; karyogamy. **d.** The union of sex cells; syngamy. **—con·ju·ga·tion·al** *adj.* **—con·ju·ga·tion·al·ly** *adv.*

conjugation tube *n.* A slender protoplasmic tube formed between two algae undergoing conjugation, through which exchange of gametes between the individuals occurs.

con·junct (kən-jŭngkt′, kŏn′jŭngkt) *adj.* **1.** Joined together; united. **2.** Associated with another; joint. **3.** *Music.* Pertaining to progression by intervals no larger than a major second. Compare **disjunct.** [Middle English, from Latin *conjunctus,* past participle of *conjungere,* to join together : *com-,* together + *jungere,* to join.] **—con·junct·ly** (kən-jŭngkt′lē) *adv.*

con·junc·tion (kən-jŭngk′shən) *n.* **1.** The act of joining or state of being joined; combination. **2.** Simultaneous occurrence; coincidence. **3.** *Abbr.* **conj.** *Grammar.* A part of speech consisting of words that connect other words, phrases, clauses, or sentences. Some English conjunctions are *and, but, because.* See **coordinate conjunction, copulative conjunction, correlative conjunction, subordinate conjunction. 4.** *Abbr.* **conj.** *Astronomy.* The position of two celestial bodies on the celestial sphere when they have the same celestial longitude. **5.** *Logic.* **a.** A compound proposition in which the components are joined by the word *and,* which is true only if both or all the components are true. **b.** The relationship between the components of such a proposition. **—con·junc·tion·al** *adj.* **—con·junc·tion·al·ly** *adv.*

con·junc·ti·va (kŏn′jŭngk-tī′və) *n., pl.* **-vas** or **-vae** (-vē). The mucous membrane that lines the inner surface of the eyelid and covers the exposed surface of the eyeball. [Middle English, from Medieval Latin *(membrāna) conjunctīva,* "the connective (membrane)," from Late Latin *conjunctīvus,* CONJUNCTIVE.] **—con·junc·ti·val** *adj.*

con·junc·tive (kən-jŭngk′tĭv) *adj.* **1.** Joining; connective. **2.** Joined together; combined. **3.** *Abbr.* **conj.** *Grammar.* **a.** Designating or used as a conjunction. **b.** Serving to connect elements of meaning and construction in a sentence, as *and* and *but.*
∼*n. Abbr.* **conj.** *Grammar.* A connective word, especially a conjunction. [Late Latin *conjunctīvus,* from Latin *conjunctus,* CONJUNCT.] **—con·junc·tive·ly** *adv.*

con·junc·ti·vi·tis (kən-jŭngk′tə-vī′tĭs) *n. Pathology.* Inflammation of the conjunctiva. [New Latin : CONJUNCTIV(A) + -ITIS.]

con·junc·ture (kən-jŭngk′chər) *n.* **1.** A combination of circumstances or events. **2.** A critical set of circumstances; a crisis.

con·ju·ra·tion (kŏn′jŏŏ-rā′shən) *n.* **1.** Threat of conjuring. **2.** A solemn invocation. **3.** A magic spell or incantation. **4.** Magic; legerdemain.

con·jure (kŏn′jər; *in tr. sense 1* kən-jŏŏr′) *v.* **-jured, -juring, -jures.** —*tr.* **1.** To call upon or entreat solemnly, especially by an oath. **2.** To summon (a devil or spirit) by incantation or magic spell. **3.** To cause or effect by or as by magic. —*intr.* **1.** To practice magic; especially, to perform tricks using sleight of hand. **2.** To summon a devil by incantation or magic spell. **—conjure up. 1.** To bring into existence as if by magic. **2.** To bring to the mind's eye; evoke. [Middle English *conjuren,* from Old French *conjurer,* from Medieval Latin *conjūrāre,* to invoke with oaths or incantations, from Latin, to swear together, conspire : *com-,* together + *jūrāre,* to swear.]

con·jur·er, con·ju·ror (kŏn′jər-ər) *n.* One who practices magic tricks or sleight of hand, especially as an entertainer.

conk[1] (kŏngk) *n. Slang.* **1.** The head. **2.** A blow on the head.
∼*tr.v.* **conked, conking, conks.** *Slang.* To hit on the head. **—conk out. 1.** To fail suddenly: *The motor conked out.* **2.** To tire or fall asleep. **3.** To faint. [Probably alteration of CONCH.]

conk[2] *n.* The hard, shelflike fruiting body of a tree fungus. [Probably alteration of CONCH.]

conk[3] *tr.v.* **conked, conking, conks.** To straighten (kinky hair), usually by a chemical method. [Perhaps alteration of *congolene,* a substance for straightening hair.] **—conk** *n.*

con·ker (kŏng′kər) *n. British.* **1.** The brown shiny nut of the horse chestnut *(see).* **2. conkers.** A children's game in which each player swings a horse chestnut on a string and tries to break one held by the opponent. [From dialect *conker,* snail shell (later replaced by horse chestnuts in the game), perhaps (through influence of CONQUER) an alteration of CONCH.]

con man *n. Slang.* A **confidence man** *(see).*

con moto (kŏn mō′tō) *adv. Music.* With movement; in a spirited manner. Used as a direction. [Italian.]

conn. Variant of **con** (to steer).

Conn. Connecticut.

Con·nacht (kŏn′əKHt, -ət). Formerly **Con·naught** (-ôt). Province in the northwest of the Republic of Ireland. It consists of counties Galway, Leitrim, Mayo, Roscommon, and Sligo.

con·nate (kŏn′āt′) *adj.* **1.** Part of or existing in someone or something from birth; inborn; innate. **2.** Coexisting since birth or origin; cognate; related. **3.** *Biology.* Congenitally or firmly united. Said of similar parts or organs. [Late Latin *connātus,* past participle of *connascī,* to be born together : *com-,* together + Latin *nascī,* to be born.] **—con·nate·ly** *adv.* **—con·nate·ness** *n.*

con·nat·u·ral (kə-năch′ər-əl) *adj.* **1.** Innate; congenital; natural. **2.** Related or similar in nature; cognate. [Medieval Latin *connātūrālis* : *com-,* together + Latin *nātūrālis,* NATURAL.] **—con·nat·u·ral·ly** *adv.* **—con·nat·u·ral·ness** *n.*

con·nect (kə-nĕkt′) *v.* **-nected, -necting, -nects.** —*tr.* **1.** To join or fasten together; link; unite. **2.** To associate or consider as related. **3.** To establish communication between, especially by telephone. **4.** To join to a communications circuit. —*intr.* **1.** To be or become joined or united. **2.** To operate so that passengers can easily transfer from one route to another: *The trains connect at Chicago.* **3.** *Sports.* To make a successful hit, kick, or shot; make contact. **4.** *Informal.* To be successful; have the desired effect. —See Synonyms at **join.** [Middle English *connecten,* from Latin *connectere* : *com-,* together + *nectere,* to bind, tie.] **—con·nect·ed·ly** *adv.* **—con·nect·a·ble, con·nect·i·ble** *adj.* **—con·nec·tor** (kə-nĕk′tər), **con·nect·er** *n.*

Con·nect·i·cut (kə-nĕt′ə-kət). *Abbr.* **Conn** State in the northeastern United States, in New England. Connecticut was one of the original 13 states. Its capital is Hartford.

con·nect·ing rod (kə-nĕk′tĭng) *n.* **1.** A rod linking rotating parts of a machine in reciprocating motion. **2.** Such a rod connecting the crankshaft of an internal-combustion engine to a piston. Also called "piston rod."

con·nec·tion (kə-nĕk′shən) *n.* Also *British* **con·nex·ion.** *Abbr.* **con. 1.** The act of joining or state of being joined; union. **2.** Anything that joins, relates, or connects; a bond; a link. **3. a.** The fact of being related or associated: *wanted in connection with a series of robberies.* **b.** A point of relationship or association: *What was her connection with the deceased?* **4.** The logical ordering of words or ideas; coherence. **5.** The relation of a word or idea to the surrounding text; context. **6.** A person with whom one is associated, especially by professional or family ties: *has some useful connections in New York.* **7. a.** The meeting of various means of transportation for the transfer of passengers. **b.** A connecting train, plane, or the like: *missed my connection.* **8.** A line of communication between two points in a telephone system. **9.** A point of contact in an electrical circuit: *a loose connection.* **10.** A religious organization or denomination. **11.** *Slang.* **a.** A dealer in illegal drugs. **b.** A major supply route for illegal drugs. **—in this connection.** Relating to the matter at hand. **—con·nec·tion·al** *adj.*

con·nec·tive (kə-nĕk′tĭv) *adj.* Serving or tending to connect.
∼*n.* **1.** Anything that connects. **2.** *Grammar.* A word, such as a conjunction, that connects words, phrases, clauses, and sentences. **3.** *Botany.* The tissue of a stamen that forms the division between the two lobes of an anther. **—con·nec·tive·ly** *adv.* **—con·nec·tiv·i·ty** (kŏn′ĕk-tĭv′ə-tē) *n.*

connective tissue *n.* Tissue arising chiefly from the embryonic mesoderm, consisting typically of a jellylike matrix in which are embedded collagen and elastic fibers, fat cells, fibroblasts, and mast cells. It forms the supporting and connecting structures of the body and occurs in tendons, ligaments, cartilage, and bone.

Con·ne·ma·ra (kŏn′ə-mär′ə). Region of County Galway in the west of the Republic of Ireland, between the Atlantic Ocean and Mask and Corrib loughs.

con·ning tower (kŏn′ĭng) *n.* **1.** A raised, enclosed observation post in a submarine, also usually used as a means of entrance and exit. **2.** The armored pilothouse of a warship. [From CON (to steer).]

con·nip·tion (kə-nĭp′shən) *n. Informal.* A fit of anger or hysteria. [19th century : origin obscure.]

con·niv·ance (kə-nī′vəns) *n.* **1.** The act of conniving. **2.** *Law.* Knowledge of, and tacit consent to, the commission of an illegal act by another.

con·nive (kə-nīv′) *intr.v.* **-nived, -niving, -nives. 1.** To feign ignorance of a wrong, thus implying tacit encouragement or consent. Usually used with *at.* **2.** To cooperate secretly or conspire. Used with *with.* [French *conniver,* from Latin *connivēre, cōnivēre,* to close the eyes, be indulgent.] **—con·niv·er** *n.*

con·ni·vent (kə-nī′vənt) *adj. Biology.* Converging and touching, but not fused together. Said especially of stamens or an insect's wings. [Latin *connivēns* (stem *connivent-*), present participle of *connivēre,* "to bend together," close the eyes, CONNIVE.]

con·nois·seur (kŏn′ə-sûr′) *n.* A person with informed and astute discrimination, especially concerning the arts or matters of taste. [Obsolete French, from Old French *connoisseor,* from *connoistre,* to know, from Latin *cognōscere,* to get acquainted with, know thoroughly : *co-,* together + *gnōscere, nōscere,* to know.] **—con·nois·seur·ship** *n.*

Con·nors (kŏn′ərz), **James Scott,** known as "Jimmy" (1952–). U.S. tennis player. He twice won both the U.S. and the Wimbledon men's singles titles (1974, 1982) and also won the U.S. title in 1976, 1978, and 1983.

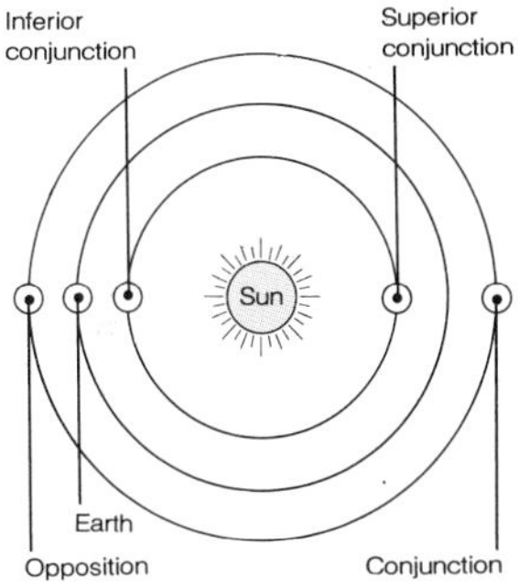

conjunction *Two heavenly bodies are said to be in conjunction when they align with the sun. The diagram shows the two conjunctions of the planet Mercury with Earth. When Mercury lies on the opposite side of the sun from Earth, it is known as a superior conjunction. When it lies between the sun and Earth, it is called an inferior conjunction.*

conifer

TREES THAT FLOURISHED IN THE WORLD'S ANCIENT FORESTS
Conifers thrive in extreme conditions and at high altitudes

Conifers, or cone-bearing trees, flourished in the prehistoric forests in which dinosaurs lived, and their descendants are found over one third of the earth's land surface. They grow in subtropical and temperate areas; on dry, hot mountainsides; and in the moister, colder zones up to and beyond the Arctic Circle.

Unlike broad-leaved trees, which have flowers pollinated by wind or insects, the narrow-leaved conifers reproduce when some of the wind-borne pollen grains from male cones—carrying the male cells—alight on the female cones and fertilize them. The rest of the pollen grains may be blown miles away, sometimes in

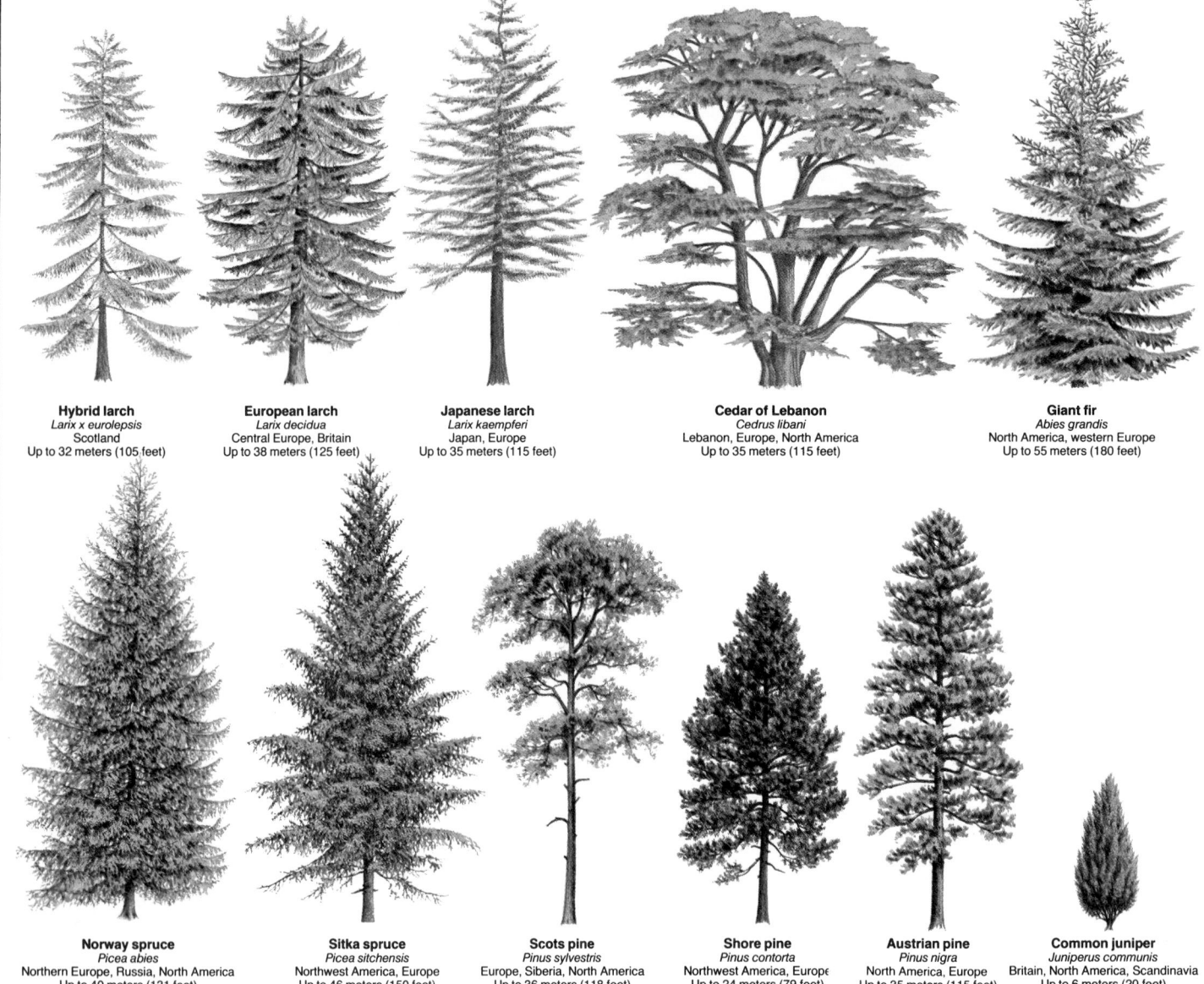

Hybrid larch
Larix x eurolepsis
Scotland
Up to 32 meters (105 feet)

European larch
Larix decidua
Central Europe, Britain
Up to 38 meters (125 feet)

Japanese larch
Larix kaempferi
Japan, Europe
Up to 35 meters (115 feet)

Cedar of Lebanon
Cedrus libani
Lebanon, Europe, North America
Up to 35 meters (115 feet)

Giant fir
Abies grandis
North America, western Europe
Up to 55 meters (180 feet)

Norway spruce
Picea abies
Northern Europe, Russia, North America
Up to 40 meters (131 feet)

Sitka spruce
Picea sitchensis
Northwest America, Europe
Up to 46 meters (150 feet)

Scots pine
Pinus sylvestris
Europe, Siberia, North America
Up to 36 meters (118 feet)

Shore pine
Pinus contorta
Northwest America, Europe
Up to 24 meters (79 feet)

Austrian pine
Pinus nigra
North America, Europe
Up to 35 meters (115 feet)

Common juniper
Juniperus communis
Britain, North America, Scandinavia
Up to 6 meters (20 feet)

con·no·ta·tion (kŏn′ə-tā′shən) *n.* **1.** An act or instance of connoting. **2. a.** The configuration of suggestive or associative implications constituting the general sense of an abstract expression beyond its literal, explicit sense. **b.** A secondary meaning suggested by a word in addition to its literal meaning. **3.** *Logic.* The total of the attributes constituting the meaning of a term; intension. **—con·no·ta·tive** (kŏn′ə-tā′tĭv, kə-nō′tə-tĭv) *adj.* **—con·no·ta·tive·ly** *adv.*

con·note (kə-nōt′) *tr.v.* **-noted, -noting, -notes. 1.** To suggest or imply in addition to literal meaning: *The word "safari" connotes adventure.* **2.** To involve as a condition or consequence. —See Usage note at **denote.** [Medieval Latin *connotāre,* "to mark in addition" : Latin *com-,* together with + *notāre,* to mark, note, from *nota,* a mark, note.]

con·nu·bi·al (kə-nōō′bē-əl, -nyōō′-) *adj.* Of marriage or the married state; conjugal. [Latin *connūbiālis,* from *connūbium,* marriage : *com-,* together + *nūbere,* to marry.] **—con·nu·bi·al·i·ty** (kə-nōō′bē-ăl′ə-tē, -nyōō′-) *n.* **—con·nu·bi·al·ly** *adv.*

co·no·dont (kō′nə-dŏnt′) *n.* Any of various small, toothlike Paleozoic fossils of unknown origin. [Greek *kōnos,* cone + -ODONT.]

co·noid (kō′noid′) *adj.* Also **co·noid·al** (kō-noid′l). Shaped like a cone.

~*n.* **conoid. 1.** Something that is shaped like a cone. **2.** A geometric surface obtained when a parabola, ellipse, or hyperbola is rotated about one axis. [CON(E) + OID.]

con·quer (kŏng′kər) *v.* **-quered, -quering, -quers.** —*tr.* **1.** To defeat or subdue by force, especially by force of arms. **2.** To gain or secure control of by or as if by force of arms. **3.** To overcome or surmount by physical, mental, or moral force: *conquer one's fear of flying.* **4.** To climb (a mountain) successfully. —*intr.* To be victorious; win. —See Synonyms at **defeat.** [Middle English *conqueren,* from Old French *conquerre,* from Vulgar Latin *conquaerere* (unattested), variant of Latin *conquīrere,* to search for, procure, win : *con-* (intensive) + *quaerere,* to seek.] **—con·quer·a·ble** *adj.*

billowing, yellow clouds. There are more than 500 species of conifers, including pines, junipers, yews, cedars, monkey puzzles, spruces, firs, and the different kinds of larch, one of the few cone-bearing trees to shed its leaves each year.

Conifers vary in size from small shrubs to the spectacular coast redwoods and giant sequoias of the United States. Some of these are more than 3,000 years old and include the world's most massive living object—the giant sequoia "General Sherman," which is 85.4 meters (280 feet) tall and weighs about 2,020 tons. It has enough timber to make 5 billion matches. The world's tallest tree—at 111.6 meters (366 feet 2 inches) is a coast redwood.

Although most conifers are spread throughout the Northern Hemisphere, a few coniferous trees are found in the Southern Hemisphere. They include the ornamental bunya pine that grows in eastern Australia, and the totara yellowwood, kauri, and red pine of New Zealand.

The conifer's soft wood is used to make posts, poles, crates, boxes, and cabinets; and the trees are a valuable source of resins, oils, tars, and turpentines. The wood pulp provides paper for newsprint.

Noble fir
Abies procera
North America, western Europe
Up to 46 meters (150 feet)

Douglas fir
Pseudotsuga menziesii
North America, Europe, Australasia
Up to 100 meters (330 feet)

Coast redwood
Sequoia sempervirens
Northwest America
Up to 111.6 meters (366 feet)

Monkey puzzle
Araucaria araucana
South America, Europe
Up to 24 meters (79 feet)

Common yew
Taxus baccata
Europe, North America, Asia
Up to 20 meters (60 feet)

Leyland cypress
x Cupressocyparis leylandii
Europe, North America
Up to 30 meters (98 feet)

Totara pine
Podocarpus totara
New Zealand
Up to 38 meters (125 feet)

Kauri pine
Agathis australis
New Zealand
Up to 46 meters (150 feet)

Rimu, or Red pine
Dacrydium cupressinum
New Zealand
Up to 24 meters (79 feet)

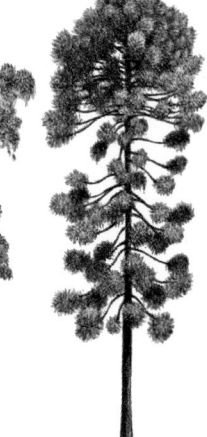

Bunya-bunya pine
Araucaria bidwillii
Australia
Up to 43 meters (141 feet)

con·quer·or (kŏng′kər-ər) *n.* Someone who conquers. **—the Conqueror. William I** of England *(see).*

con·quest (kŏn′kwĕst, kŏng′-) *n.* **1.** The act or process of conquering. **2.** Something acquired by conquering, especially territory. **3.** A successful amorous exploit: *boasting about his latest conquest.* **4.** Someone whose love or favor has been captured. **—the Conquest.** The **Norman Conquest** *(see).* [Middle English *conquest(e),* from Old French, from Vulgar Latin *conquaesītus* (unattested), past participle of *conquaerere* (unattested), to CONQUER.]

con·qui·an (kŏng′kē-ən) *n.* A card game resembling rummy, for two players. Also called "cooncan." [(Mexican) Spanish *con quién,* with whom?]

con·quis·ta·dor (kŏn-kēs′tə-dôr′, -kwĭs′-) *n., pl.* **conquistadores** (kŏn-kēs′tə-dôr′ās, -dôr′ēz, -kwĭs′-) or **-dors.** A conqueror; specifically, any of the Spanish conquerors of Central and South America, especially Mexico and Peru, in the 16th century. [Spanish, from *conquistar,* to conquer, from Medieval Latin *conquestāre,* frequentative of Vulgar Latin *conquaerere* (unattested). See **conquer.**]

Con·rad (kŏn′răd), **Joseph,** born Teodor Jósef Konrad Korzeniowski (1857-1924). Polish-born novelist who became a major English literary figure. His masterpieces include *Lord Jim* (1900), *The Heart of Darkness* (1902), and *Under Western Eyes* (1911).

cons. **1.** consigned; consignment. **2.** consonant. **3.** constable. **4.** constitution; constitutional. **5.** construction.

Cons. **1.** Constable. **2.** Consul.

con·san·guin·e·ous (kŏn′săng-gwĭn′ē-əs) *adj.* Also **con·san·guine** (kŏn-săng′gwĭn). Of the same lineage or origin; especially, related by blood. [Latin *consanguineus : com-,* joint + *sanguineus,* of blood, SANGUINE.] **—con·san·guin·e·ous·ly** *adv.*

con·san·guin·i·ty (kŏn′săng-gwĭn′ə-tē) *n.* **1.** Blood relationship. **2.** Any close connection or affinity.

con·science (kŏn′shəns) *n.* **1.** The faculty of recognizing the distinction between right and wrong in regard to one's own conduct, together with the feeling that one ought not to do wrong: *the voice* *of conscience.* **2.** A feeling or consciousness of conformity to one's own sense of right conduct: *a clear conscience.* **3.** *Archaic.* Consciousness. —**in (all) conscience. 1.** In fairness; reasonably. **2.** To be sure; certainly. —**on one's conscience.** Causing remorse. [Middle English, from Old French, from Latin *conscientia,* from *consciēns* (stem *conscient-*), present participle of *conscīre,* to be conscious, know well : *com-* (intensive) + *scīre,* to know.] —**conscience-less** *adj.*

conscience clause *n.* A clause in a law that recognizes or exempts persons whose moral scruples forbid compliance.

conscience money *n.* Money paid to atone for some concealed dishonest or morally wrong act.

con·science-strick·en (kŏn'shəns-strĭk'ən) *adj.* Feeling guilty or remorseful about something one has done or failed to do.

con·sci·en·tious (kŏn'shē-ĕn'shəs) *adj.* **1.** Governed by or accomplished according to conscience; scrupulous. **2.** Thorough and painstaking; careful and diligent. —See Synonyms at **meticulous.** [French *conscientieux,* from Medieval Latin *conscientiōsus,* from Latin *conscientia,* CONSCIENCE.] —**con·sci·en·tious·ly** *adv.* —**con·sci·en·tious·ness** *n.*

conscientious objector *n.* *Abbr.* **CO, C.O.** One who on the basis of religious or moral principles refuses to bear arms or participate in military service.

con·scion·a·ble (kŏn'shən-ə-bəl) *adj.* *Obsolete.* Conscientious. [From *conscions,* obsolete variant of CONSCIENCE + -ABLE.]

con·scious (kŏn'shəs) *adj.* **1. a.** Having an awareness of one's own existence, sensations, and thoughts and of one's environment. **b.** Having a particular preception; aware: *conscious of having offended her.* **2.** Not asleep or stuporous; awake: *conscious after surgery.* **3.** Subjectively known and felt: *She spoke with conscious pride.* **4.** Intentionally conceived or done; deliberate: *a conscious insult.* **5.** Having or showing self-consciousness: *conscious of her limp.* **6.** Concerned about or interested in something. Often used in combination: *fashion-conscious.*
~*n.* The component of waking awareness perceptible by an individual at any given instant. Preceded by *the.* [Latin *conscius,* knowing with others, participating in knowledge, aware of : *com-,* with + *scīre,* to know.] —**con·scious·ly** *adv.*

Usage: *Conscious, subconscious, preconscious,* and *unconscious.* These are psychological terms referring to aspects of the workings of the mind. *Conscious* refers to mental processes, such as thoughts or emotional reactions, of which a person is aware. *Subconscious* pertains to thoughts or feelings outside the immediate awareness either wholly or partly. *Preconscious* refers to mental processes that are outside the consciousness, but are easily brought into the conscious mind. *Unconscious* alludes to all mental processes that a person is not aware of, including thoughts or feelings that have been forgotten or repressed, and also images, instincts, desires, and the like. It is often used interchangeably with *subconscious.*

con·scious·ness (kŏn'shəs-nĭs) *n.* **1.** The state or condition of being conscious. **2.** The essence or totality of attitudes, opinions, and sensitivities held or thought to be held by an individual or group: *national consciousness.* **3.** The conscious. **4.** A critical awareness of one's own indentity and situation.

con·scious·ness-rais·ing (kŏn'shəs-nĭs-rā'zĭng) *n.* A process whereby one achieves greater personal or social awareness.

con·script (kŏn'skrĭpt) *n.* One who is compulsorily enrolled for service in the armed forces; a draftee.
~*adj.* (kŏn'skrĭpt). Enrolled compulsorily; drafted.
~*tr.v.* (kən-skrĭpt') **conscripted, -scripting, -scripts. 1.** To enroll compulsorily for military service; draft. **2.** To force into service. [Old French, enlisted, from Latin *conscriptus,* past participle of *conscrībere,* to write together, enter in a list, enrol : *com-,* together + *scrībere,* to write.]

con·scrip·tion (kən-skrĭp'shən) *n.* Compulsory enrollment for military service.

con·se·crate (kŏn'sə-krāt') *tr.v.* **-crated, -crating, -crates. 1.** To make, declare, or set apart as sacred: *consecrate a church.* **2. a.** To change (the bread and wine of the Eucharist) into the body and blood of Christ, according to the doctrines of the Roman Catholic Church. **b.** To sanctify (bread and wine) to be taken as a memorial of Christ, according to the beliefs of the Reformed churches. **3.** To initiate (a priest) into the order of bishops. **4.** To dedicate to some service or goal: *consecrated her life to helping the poor.* **5.** To make venerable: *a tradition consecrated by time.* —See Synonyms at **devote.**
~*adj.* Dedicated to a sacred purpose; sanctified. [Middle English *consecraten,* from Latin *consecrāre* : *com-* (intensive) + *sacrāre,* to make sacred, from *sacer,* sacred.] —**con·se·cra·tive** (kŏn'sə-krā'tĭv) *adj.* —**con·se·cra·tor** (kŏn'sə-krā'tər) *n.* —**con·se·cra·to·ry** (kŏn'sə-krə-tôr'ē, -tôr'ē) *adj.*

con·se·cra·tion (kŏn'sə-krā'shən) *n.* **1.** The act, process, or ceremony of consecrating. **2.** The state of being consecrated.

con·se·cu·tion (kŏn'sə-kyōō'shən) *n.* **1.** A sequence or succession. **2.** The relation of consequent to antecedent; deduction; inference. [Latin *consecūtiō* (stem *consecūtiōn-*), sequence, from *consequī,* to follow up. See **consequent.**]

con·sec·u·tive (kən-sĕk'yə-tĭv) *adj.* **1.** Following successively without interruption. **2.** Marked by logical sequence. **3.** *Music.* Designating harmonic intervals of a similar kind. **4.** *Grammar.* Expressing a consequence. [French *consécutif,* Medieval Latin *consecūtīvus,* from Latin *consequī,* to follow up. See **consequent.**] —**con·sec·u·tive·ly** *adv.* —**con·sec·u·tive·ness** *n.*

con·sen·su·al (kən-sĕn'shōō-əl) *adj.* **1.** Based on or involving mutual consent or consensus. **2.** *Physiology.* Responding to reflex stimulation. Said especially of certain reflex actions by parts of the body that respond to stimulation of another part. [From CONSENSUS (after SENSUAL).] —**con·sen·su·al·ly** *adv.*

con·sen·sus (kən-sĕn'səs) *n.* Collective opinion or concord; general agreement or accord; a majority view. Also used adjectivally: *consensus politics.* [Latin, from *consentīre,* to agree, CONSENT.]

Usage: The phrase *consensus of opinion* is widely used in informal speech and writing, and is sometimes used in formal speech. But people aware of the definition of *consensus* (which already contains the notion of "opinion") avoid the phrase, on the grounds that it contains a redundant element.

con·sent (kən-sĕnt') *intr.v.* **-sented, -senting, -sents. 1.** To give assent or permission; accede; agree. **2.** *Archaic.* To agree in opinion; be of the same mind. —See Synonyms at **assent.**
~*n.* **1.** Voluntary acceptance or allowance of what is planned or done by another; permission. **2.** Agreement as to opinion or a course of action: *by common consent.* [Middle English *consenten,* from Old French *consentir,* from Latin *consentīre,* to feel together, agree : *com-,* together + *sentīre,* to feel.] —**con·sent·er** *n.*

con·sen·ta·ne·ous (kŏn'sĕn-tā'nē-əs) *adj.* **1.** Manifesting agreement; accordant. **2.** Done by common consent; unanimous. [Latin *consentāneus,* from *consentīre,* to feel together, CONSENT.] —**con·sen·ta·ne·i·ty** (kŏn'sĕn-tə-nē'ə-tē), **con·sen·ta·ne·ous·ness** *n.* —**con·sen·ta·ne·ous·ly** *adv.*

con·sen·tient (kən-sĕn'shənt) *adj.* United in agreement; of the same opinion.

con·se·quence (kŏn'sə-kwĕns', -kwəns) *n.* **1.** That which rationally or naturally follows from an action or condition; an effect; a result: *He must face the consequences of his thoughtlessness.* **2.** A logical result or inference. **3.** Importance in rank: *someone of consequence.* **4.** Significance: *a matter of little consequence.* —**in consequence** As a result; hence. —See Synonyms at **effect, importance.**

con·se·quent (kŏn'sə-kwĕnt', -kwənt) *adj.* **1. a.** Following as a natural effect, result, or conclusion: *a reduction in taxes with a consequent loss of revenue; a water shortage consequent to the drought.* **b.** Following as a logical conclusion. **2.** Logically correct or consistent. **3.** *Geology.* Having a position or direction relating to or resulting from the original slope of the earth's surface: *consequent rivers. In this sense, compare* **obsequent, subsequent.**
~*n.* **1.** Anything that follows something else, usually with causal relation. **2.** An outcome or result. **3.** *Logic.* The second part of a conditional proposition, whose truth is dependent on the truth of the antecedent. **4.** *Mathematics.* The second term of a ratio. [Middle English, from Old French, from Latin *consequēns* (stem *consequent-*), present participle of *consequī,* to follow up, accompany : *com-,* together + *sequī,* to follow.]

Usage: The usual prepositions following the adjectival sense of this word are *on* or *upon. To* is also common, but this usage increases the likelihood of confusion with *subsequent to. Consequent* usually implies a causal or logical relationship with what has gone before; *subsequent* has no such meaning, being equivalent to "after."

con·se·quen·tial (kŏn'sə-kwĕn'shəl) *adj.* **1.** Following as an effect, result, or conclusion; resultant; consequent. **2.** Having important consequences; significant. **3.** Self-important; pompous. —**con·se·quen·ti·al·i·ty** (kŏn'sə-kwĕn-shē-ăl'ə-tē), **con·se·quen·tial·ness** *n.* —**con·se·quen·tial·ly** *adv.*

con·se·quent·ly (kŏn'sə-kwĕnt'lē, -kwənt-) *adv.* As a result; therefore.

con·ser·van·cy (kən-sûr'vən-sē) *n., pl.* **-cies. 1.** Conservation, especially of natural resources. **2.** *British.* A commission supervising fisheries and navigation.

con·ser·va·tion (kŏn'sər-vā'shən) *n.* **1.** The act of conserving; preservation from loss, depletion, waste, or harm. **2.** The systematic preservation of the environment, especially of natural resources such as topsoil, forests, and waterways. —**con·ser·va·tion·al** *adj.*

con·ser·va·tion·ist (kŏn'sər-vā'shən-ĭst) *n.* One who practices or advocates the preservation of natural resources and the protection of wildlife and the environment.

conservation law *n.* **1.** *Physics.* A law stating that a given quantity, such as mass, energy, or charge, cannot be created or destroyed regardless of changes of distribution of that quantity within a system. **2.** A law by which a government seeks to prohibit certain actions in order to preserve a natural amenity or resource.

conservation of energy *n.* *Physics.* An exact conservation law stating that the total energy of an isolated system remains constant regardless of changes within the system.

conservation of mass *n.* *Physics.* The classical principle that the total mass of an isolated system is unchanged by interaction of its parts.

conservation of momentum *n.* *Physics.* An exact conservation law stating that the total linear or angular momentum of an isolated system remains constant regardless of changes within the system.

con·ser·va·tism (kən-sûr'və-tĭz'əm) *n.* **1.** The disposition in politics or culture to maintain the existing order and to resist or oppose change or innovation. **2.** The principles and practices of persons or groups so disposed. **3. Conservatism.** The principles and practices of the Conservative Party.

con·ser·va·tive (kən-sûr'və-tĭv) *adj.* **1.** Tending to favor the preservation of the existing order; averse to and distrustful of change. **2. Conservative.** *Abbr.* **Con.** Belonging to, supporting, or character-

istic of the Conservative Party of the United Kingdom. **3. Conservative.** Adhering to or characteristic of Conservative Judaism. **4.** Marked by moderation; prudent; cautious: *a conservative estimate.* **5.** Traditional in manner or style; not showy. **6.** Tending to conserve; conserving; preservative.
~*n.* **1.** A conservative person; especially, one who supports or belongs to a conservative political party. **2. Conservative.** *Abbr.* **C.** A member or supporter of the Conservative Party. —**con·ser·va·tive·ly** *adv.* —**con·ser·va·tive·ness** *n.*
Conservative Judaism *n.* A branch of Judaism that holds a modified view of the sanctity of the Torah and is flexible in its submission to the authority of the Rabbinical Law, accepting some liturgical and ritual changes in the light of the needs of modern life. Compare **Orthodox Judaism, Reform Judaism.**
Conservative Party *n.* The major right-wing political party of the United Kingdom, which supports private enterprise and privatization and opposes state control and nationalization.
con·ser·va·tor (kən-sûr′və-tər) *n.* **1.** Someone who preserves from injury or violation; a protector. **2.** A custodian of an art gallery or museum. **3.** *Law.* A guardian; a keeper.
con·ser·va·to·ry (kən-sûr′və-tôr′ē, -tōr′ē) *n., pl.* **-ries. 1.** A glass-enclosed room or greenhouse, usually forming part of a dwelling, in which plants are grown and displayed. **2.** A school of music or dramatic art.
con·serve (kən-sûrv′) *tr.v.* **-served, -serving, -serves. 1.** To protect from loss or wasteful depletion; preserve. **2.** To preserve (fruits) with sugar.
~*n.* (kŏn′sûrv). *Often* **conserves.** A jam containing whole fruit or whole pieces of fruit, especially one made of a mixture of fruits. [Middle English *conserven,* from Old French *conserver,* from Latin *conservāre* : *com-* (intensive) + *servāre,* to keep, preserve.] —**con·serv·a·ble** *adj.* —**con·serv·er** *n.*
con·sid·er (kən-sĭd′ər) *v.* **-ered, -ering, -ers.** —*tr.* **1.** To deliberate upon; examine; study. **2.** To regard as; think or deem to be: *considered him a fool.* **3.** To believe, especially after deliberation; judge: *considers waste criminal.* **4.** To take into account; make allowance for: *Consider that he's just a beginner.* **5.** To have regard for; pay attention to: *Consider her feelings.* **6.** To regard highly; esteem. **7.** To think about as possible or acceptable: *refused to consider the other possibilities.* —*intr.* To think carefully; reflect. [Middle English *consideren,* from Old French *considerer,* from Latin *consīderāre,* to observe (originally a term of augury meaning "to observe the stars carefully").] —**con·sid·er·er** *n.*
  Synonyms: account, deem, reckon, regard.
con·sid·er·a·ble (kən-sĭd′ər-ə-bəl) *adj.* **1.** Fairly large in amount, extent, or degree: *a man of considerable influence.* **2.** Worthy of consideration; important; significant: *a considerable poet.*
~*n. Informal.* A considerable amount, extent, or degree. —**con·sid·er·a·bly** *adv.*
con·sid·er·ate (kən-sĭd′ər-ĭt) *adj.* **1.** Having regard for the needs or feelings of others. **2.** Characterized by careful thought; deliberate. —See Synonyms at **thoughtful.** [Latin *consīderātus,* past participle of *consīderāre,* to be considerate, CONSIDER.] —**con·sid·er·ate·ly** *adv.* —**con·sid·er·ate·ness** *n.*
con·sid·er·a·tion (kən-sĭd′ə-rā′shən) *n.* **1.** Careful thought; deliberation. **2.** A factor to be considered in forming a judgment or decision: *Health is the major consideration.* **3.** Thoughtful concern for others; solicitude. **4.** Payment given in exchange for a service rendered. **5.** A thought produced by considering; a thoughtful opinion. **6.** *Law.* Something promised, given, or done that has the effect of making an agreement a legally enforceable contract. **7.** High regard. —**in consideration of. 1.** In view of; on account of. **2.** In return for.
con·sid·ered (kən-sĭd′ərd) *adj.* **1.** Reached after deliberation or careful thought. **2.** Regarded; esteemed.
con·sid·er·ing (kən-sĭd′ər-ĭng) *prep.* In view of; taking into consideration.
~*adv. Informal.* With all things considered: *He does well, considering.*
~*conj. Informal.* In view of the fact that; inasmuch as: *Considering he's only six, he reads very well.*
con·sign (kən-sīn′) *tr.v.* **-signed, -signing, -signs. 1.** To give over to the care of another; entrust. **2.** To turn over permanently; commit irrevocably. **3.** To ship (goods) to an agent for sale, custody, or use. —See Synonyms at **commit.** [Middle English *consignen,* to certify by a seal, from Old French *consigner,* from Latin *consignāre* : *com-* (intensive) + *signāre,* to seal, from *signum,* seal, mark.] —**con·sign·a·ble** *adj.* —**con·sig·na·tion** (kŏn′sĭg-nā′shən) *n.* —**con·sig·nor** (kŏn′sī-nôr′, kən-sī′nər), **con·sign·er** *n.*
con·sign·ee (kŏn′sī-nē′, kən-sī′nē) *n.* A person to whom goods are consigned.
con·sign·ment (kən-sīn′mənt) *n. Abbr.* **cons. 1.** The consigning of goods or cargo, especially to an agent for sale or custody. **2.** That which is consigned; a shipment of goods. —**on consignment.** Sent to a dealer who pays only for what is sold.
con·sist (kən-sĭst′) *intr.v.* **-sisted, -sisting, -sists. 1.** To be made up or composed. Used with *of.* **2.** To have a basis; lie; rest. Used with *in.* **3.** To be compatible; accord. [Old French *consister,* from Latin *consistere,* to stand still, exist : *com-* (intensive) + *sistere,* to cause to stand, place.]
con·sis·ten·cy (kən-sĭs′tən-sē) *n., pl.* **-cies.** Also **con·sis·tence** (-təns). **1.** Agreement or logical coherence among things or parts. **2.** Compatibility or agreement among successive acts, ideas, or

events. **3.** Degree or texture of firmness, density, or viscosity.
con·sis·tent (kən-sĭs′tənt) *adj.* **1.** In agreement; compatible; not contradictory. Often used with *with.* **2.** Constantly conforming to the same principles, course of action, or standards. [Latin *consistens* (stem *consistent-*), present participle of *consistere,* to stand firmly, CONSIST.] —**con·sis·tent·ly** *adv.*
con·sis·to·ry (kən-sĭs′tər-ē) *n., pl.* **-ries. 1.** *Roman Catholic Church.* A gathering, either of cardinals alone *(secret consistory),* or with others present *(public consistory),* presided over by the pope for the solemn promulgation of papal acts, such as the appointment of cardinals or bishops or the canonization of a saint. **2.** In certain Reformed churches, a governing body of a local congregation, composed of the ministers and elders. **3.** In Lutheran churches, a court appointed to regulate ecclesiastical affairs. **4.** In the Anglican Church, a diocesan court presided over by the bishop's chancellor or commissary. **5.** The meeting place, or the meeting itself, of any such body. **6.** A council or tribunal. [Middle English *consistorie,* from Old French, from Medieval Latin *consistōrium,* from Late Latin, place of assembly, from Latin *consistere,* to take one's place (at a meeting), stand, CONSIST.] —**con·sis·to·ri·al** (kŏn′sĭs-tôr′ē-əl, -tōr′-), **con·sis·to·ri·an** *adj.*
con·so·ci·ate (kən-sō′shē-āt′) *v.* **-ated, -ating, -ates.** —*tr.* To bring into friendly association. —*intr.* To come into friendly association. ~*adj.* (kən-sō′shē-ĭt). Associated; united. ~*n.* (kən-sō′shē-ĭt). An associate; a companion; a partner. [Middle English *consociat,* associated, from Latin *consociātus,* past participle of *consociāre,* to associate, join : *com-,* together + *sociāre,* to join, from *socius,* ally, companion.]
con·so·ci·a·tion (kən-sō′sē-ā′shən, -shē-) *n.* **1.** The act of consociating. **2.** A subdivision of an ecological association having one dominant species of plant.
con·so·la·tion (kŏn′sə-lā′shən) *n.* **1. a.** The act or an instance of consoling. **b.** The state of being consoled. **2.** Someone or something that consoles; a comfort. —**con·sol·a·to·ry** (kən-sŏl′ə-tôr′ē, -tōr′ē, -sōl′ə-) *adj.*
consolation prize *n.* A prize given to a competitor who loses.
con·sole¹ (kən-sōl′) *tr.v.* **-soled, -soling, -soles.** To comfort in time of grief, disappointment, or trouble; solace. [French *consoler,* from Old French, from Latin *consōlārī* : *com-* (intensive) + *sōlārī,* to comfort.] —**con·sol·a·ble** *adj.* —**con·sol·er** *n.* —**con·sol·ing·ly** *adv.*
con·sole² (kŏn′sōl) *n.* **1.** A decorative bracket for supporting a cornice, shelf, bust, or other object. **2.** A console table. **3.** The desklike part of an organ that contains the keyboard, stops, and pedals. **4.** A cabinet for a radio, television set, or record player, designed to stand on the floor. **5.** A panel housing the controls for electrical, electronic, or mechanical equipment; especially, the control panel of a computer. [French, short for *consolateur,* a carved human figure used to support cornices, from Latin *consōlātor,* one that consoles, hence a support, from *consōlārī,* to CONSOLE.]
con·sole table (kŏn′sōl) *n.* **1.** A table supported by decorative consoles fixed to a wall. **2.** A small table, often with curved legs resembling consoles, designed to be set against a wall.
con·sol·i·date (kən-sŏl′ə-dāt′) *v.* **-dated, -dating, -dates.** —*tr.* **1.** To make firm or coherent; form into a compact mass; solidify. **2.** To make strong or secure; strengthen: *consolidated their empire.* **3.** To unite into one system or body; combine; merge. —*intr.* To become solidified or united. —See Synonyms at **join.** [Latin *consolidāre* : *com-* (intensive) + *solidāre,* to make solid or firm, from *solidus,* solid.] —**con·sol·i·da·tor** (kən-sŏl′ə-dā′tər) *n.*
consolidated school *n.* A public school, usually rural, for pupils from several adjacent districts.
con·sol·i·da·tion (kən-sŏl′ə-dā′shən) *n.* **1.** The act of consolidating or the state of being consolidated. **2.** The process of combining or uniting, as of separate corporations into a single new corporation. **3.** *Geology.* The process by which a loose deposit is compressed and cemented into solid rock.
con·sols (kŏn′sōlz, kən-sōlz′) *pl.n.* The perpetual governmental securities of Great Britain. Also called "bank annuities." [Short for *consolidated annuities.*]
con·so·lute (kŏn′sə-loot′) *adj.* Designating two or more liquids that are mutually soluble in all proportions. [Latin *consolūtus* : *con-,* together + *solūtus,* past participle of *solvere,* to dissolve.]
con·som·mé (kŏn′sə-mā′) *n.* A clear soup made of meat, fish, or vegetable stock or a combination of these. [French, "concentrate," from Old French *consommer,* to consume, from Latin *consummāre* : *com-* (intensive) + *summa,* SUM.]
con·so·nance (kŏn′sə-nəns) *n.* **1.** Agreement; harmony; accord. **2. a.** Correspondence or recurrence of sounds. **b.** In poetry, a similarity or recurrence of terminal consonants but not of vowels in two or more syllables, words, or lines, as in *rain* and *tone.* Compare **assonance. 3.** *Music.* A simultaneous combination of sounds conventionally regarded as pleasing and final in effect. Compare **dissonance.**
con·so·nant (kŏn′sə-nənt) *adj.* **1.** In agreement or accord: *remarks consonant with his beliefs.* **2.** Corresponding in sound. **3.** Harmonious in sound. **4.** Consonantal.
~*n. Abbr.* **cons. 1.** *Phonetics.* A speech sound produced by a partial or complete obstruction of the air stream by any of various constrictions of the speech organs. **2.** A letter or character representing such a sound, such as *p, t, g, k;* a letter that is not a vowel. [Middle English from Old French, from Latin *(littera) consonāns* (stem *consonant-*), "(letter) sounded with (a vowel)," from the pres-

ent participle of *consonāre*, to sound at the same time, harmonize, agree : *com-*, together + *sonāre*, to sound.] —**con·so·nant·ly** *adv.*

con·so·nan·tal (kŏn'sə-năn'təl) *adj.* **1.** Of, relating to, or having the nature of a consonant. **2.** Containing a consonant or consonants. —**con·so·nan·tal·ly** *adv.*

con sor·di·no (kŏn sôr-dē'nō) *adv. Music.* Using the mute. Used as a direction. [Italian.]

con·sort (kŏn'sôrt) *n.* **1.** A husband or wife; especially, the spouse of a monarch. **2.** A companion or partner. **3.** A ship accompanying another. **4. a.** *Archaic.* A harmonious combination of voices or musical instruments. **b.** A group of singers or instrumentalists. ~*v.* (kən-sôrt') **consorted, -sorting, -sorts.** —*intr.* **1.** To keep company; associate, especially with undesirable characters. **2.** To be in accord or agreement. —*tr.* To bring together; associate. [Middle English, from Old French, from Latin *consors* (stem *consort-*), "one who shares the same fate," companion, partner : *com-*, together + *sors*, fate, share.]

con·sor·ti·um (kən-sôr'tē-əm, -shē-əm, -shəm) *n., pl.* **-tia** (-tē-ə, -shē-ə, -shə). **1.** An association of business organizations or financial institutions for carrying out a project requiring extensive financial resources, especially in international finance. **2.** Any association or partnership. **3.** *Law.* A married person's right to the company, help, and affection of his or her spouse. [Latin, fellowship, participation, from *consors*, partner, companion, CONSORT.]

con·spe·cif·ic (kŏn'spĭ-sĭf'ĭk) *adj. Biology.* Of the same species.

con·spec·tus (kən-spĕk'təs) *n.* **1.** A general survey of a subject. **2.** An outline or synopsis. [Latin, "view," "survey," from the past participle of *conspicere*, to observe (see **conspicuous**).]

con·spic·u·ous (kən-spĭk'yōō-əs) *adj.* **1.** Easy to notice; obvious. **2.** Attracting attention by being unusual or remarkable. [Latin *conspicuus*, from *conspicere*, to look at closely, observe : *com-* (intensive) + *specere*, to look.] —**con·spic·u·ous·ly** *adv.* —**con·spic·u·ous·ness** *n.*

conspicuous consumption *n.* Showy extravagance pursued in order to enhance one's prestige in society.

con·spir·a·cy (kən-spîr'ə-sē) *n., pl.* **-cies. 1.** An agreement to perform together an illegal, treacherous, or evil act. **2.** A combining or acting together, as if by evil design: *a conspiracy of natural forces.*

3. *Law.* An agreement between two or more persons to commit a crime or to accomplish a legal purpose through illegal action. [Middle English *conspiracie*, from Norman French, variant of Old French *conspiration*, from Latin *conspīrātiō*, from *conspīrāre*, to CONSPIRE.]

    Synonyms: cabal, collusion, intrigue, plot.

conspiracy of silence *n.* A secret agreement that nothing should be said on a particular matter, usually in order to promote or protect the interests of the conspirators.

con·spir·a·tor (kən-spîr'ə-tər) *n.* A person engaged in a conspiracy; a plotter.

con·spir·a·to·ri·al (kən-spîr'ə-tôr'ē-əl, -tōr'-) *adj.* Pertaining to or suggestive of conspirators or a conspiracy: *gave me a conspiratorial wink.* —**con·spir·a·to·ri·al·ly** *adv.*

con·spire (kən-spîr') *v.* **-spired, -spiring, -spires.** —*intr.* **1.** To plan together with another or others secretly, especially to commit an illegal or evil act. **2.** To combine or act together, especially to do harm: *factors that conspired against his re-election.* —*tr.* To plan or plot secretly. [Middle English *conspiren*, from Old French *conspirer*, from Latin *conspīrāre*, "to breathe together," agree, unite, plot : *com-*, together + *spīrāre*, to breathe, blow.] —**con·spir·er** *n.* —**con·spir·ing·ly** *adv.*

con spi·ri·to (kŏn spîr'ĭ-tō') *adv. Music.* With spirit and vigor. Used as a direction.

const. 1. constable. **2.** constant. **3.** constitution. **4.** construction.

Const. 1. constable. **2.** constitution.

con·sta·ble (kŏn'stə-bəl, kŭn'-) *n. Abbr.* **cons., Cons., const., Const. 1.** A peace officer with less authority and smaller jurisdiction than a sheriff, empowered to serve writs and warrants and to make arrests. **2.** In medieval monarchies, an officer of high rank, usually serving as military commander in the ruler's absence. **3.** The governor of a royal castle. **4.** *British.* A policeman. [Middle English, from Old French, from Late Latin *comes stabulī*, "count of the stable" : Latin *comes*, companion, count + *stabulī*, genitive of *stabulum*, STABLE.] —**con·sta·ble·ship** *n.*

Con·sta·ble (kŭn'stə-bəl, kŏn'-), **John** (1776–1837). British landscape painter. His direct observations of nature and free use of broken color were original and influential. *The Hay Wain* (1821) is his best-known work.

con·stab·u·lar·y (kən-stăb'yə-lĕr'ē) *n., pl.* **-ies. 1.** The body of constables of a district or city. **2.** The district under the jurisdiction of a constable. **3.** An armed police force organized like a military unit. ~*adj.* Also **con·stab·u·lar** (-lər). Of or pertaining to constables or to constabularies.

Constance. See **Konstanz.**

Con·stance, Lake (kŏn'stəns). German **Bo·den·see** (bō'dən-zā'). Alpine lake on the border between West Germany, Austria, and Switzerland.

con·stan·cy (kŏn'stən-sē) *n.* **1.** Steadfastness in purpose or loyalty; faithfulness. **2.** An unchanging quality or state.

con·stant (kŏn'stənt) *adj.* **1. a.** Continuous; unremitting: *constant noise.* **b.** Continually recurring; persistent: *a constant worry.* **2.** Unchanging in nature, value, or extent; invariable. **3.** Steadfast in purpose, loyalty, or affection; faithful. —See Synonyms at **continual, faithful, steady.** ~*n.* **1.** A thing that is unchanging or invariable. **2.** *Abbr.* **const.** *Symbol* **c, C. a.** A quantity taken to have a fixed value in a specific mathematical context. **b.** An experimental or theoretical condition, factor, or quantity that occurs or is regarded as invariant in specific circumstances. [Middle English, from Old French, from Latin *constāns* (stem *constant-*), present participle of *constāre*, to stand together, remain steadfast : *com-*, together + *stāre*, to stand.] —**con·stant·ly** *adv.*

Con·stant (kôn-stôn'), **Benjamin** (1767–1830). French writer and political figure who wrote pamphlets defending the French Revolution, but opposed Napoleon and went into exile (1803). He had a long affair with Madame de Staël that he used as the basis for his novel *Adolphe* (1816).

con·stant·an (kŏn'stən-tăn') *n.* An alloy of copper nickel, used chiefly in electrical instruments because of its constant resistance. [Coined from CONSTANT.]

Con·stan·tine II (kŏn'stən-tēn). (1940–). King of Greece (1964–67). He went into exile after a right-wing coup by army officers (1967). Greece became a republic (1973).

Constantine the Great (c. A.D. 285–337). Roman emperor who ruled the Western Roman Empire (312–24) and became sole emperor (324–37). He adopted the Christian faith (312) and suspended the persecution of Christians. He rebuilt Constantinople (modern Istanbul) as the new Rome (330).

Con·stan·ti·no·ple (kŏn'stăn-tə-nō'pəl). Formerly **By·zan·ti·um** (bĭ-zăn'shē-əm, -tē-əm). Capital of the Byzantine Empire (330–1453) and of Turkey (1453–1923). The city was founded by Greeks in 667 B.C., captured by Roman forces in A.D. 196, and rebuilt by Constantine (330), who changed its name to Constantinople. The city enjoyed a golden age under Justinian the Great (532–62), when the church of Hagia Sophia was built. Constantinople finally fell to the Ottoman Turks (1453) and, as their capital, expanded across the Bosporus. Hagia Sophia became a mosque. In 1923 the Turkish capital was moved to Ankara and Constantinople was renamed Istanbul (1930).

Constanz. See **Konstanz.**

con·sta·ta·tion (kŏn'stə-tā'shən) *n.* **1.** The act of ascertaining or verifying. **2.** A statement or fact that has been ascertained.

Constable

RURAL SCENES FROM BOYHOOD MADE CONSTABLE A PAINTER

The artist who tried to capture nature's serenity

So influenced was John Constable (1776–1837) by his native Suffolk that the rural vistas of his boyhood became the theme of his paintings. "These scenes made me a painter, and I am grateful," he once declared. He became the greatest exponent of the English Picturesque style of painting.

Constable painted landscapes at a time when the function of artists was to represent man. He hoped to elevate the genre by replacing its conventions with what he himself called the "light-dews-breezes-bloom-and-freshness" of nature. He saw himself as a "natural" artist, but he is counted among the Romantics. His paintings exemplify the Romantic preference for color to express nature's changing moods, rather than the neoclassical ideal of purity of form and elegance of composition.

The somber moods that lowering storm clouds imposed on the landscape depressed him, and he preferred to paint nature in its more serene moments.

WEYMOUTH BAY *In this landscape painted about 1817, and in many others, Constable sought to capture in pigment scudding clouds and their shad-ows, and the transient reflections of light on water. His work anticipated Impressionism by more than 50 years.*

[French, from *constater,* to verify, from Latin *constat,* it is certain.]

con·stel·late (kŏn′stə-lāt′) *v.* **-lated, -lating, -lates.** —*tr.* To cause to form a group or cluster. —*intr.* To form a group or cluster. [Back-formation from CONSTELLATION.]

con·stel·la·tion (kŏn′stə-lā′shən) *n.* **1.** *Astronomy.* **a.** Any of 88 scientifically arbitrary groupings of stars as seen from Earth, considered to resemble and named after various mythological characters, inanimate objects, and animals. **b.** An area of the celestial sphere occupied by such a group. **2.** *Astrology.* The position of the stars at the time of one's birth, regarded as determining one's character or fate. **3.** A brilliant gathering or assemblage. **4.** A set or configuration of objects, properties, or individuals, especially a structurally or systematically related grouping. [Middle English *constellacioun,* from Old French *constellation,* from Late Latin *constellātiō* (stem *constellātiōn-*), group of stars : Latin *com-,* together + *stellātus,* starred, from *stella,* star.] —**con·stel·la·to·ry** (kən-stĕl′ə-tôr′ē, -tōr′ē) *adj.*

con·ster·nate (kŏn′stər-nāt′) *tr.v.* **-nated, -nating, -nates.** To fill with consternation. Usually used in the passive. [Latin *consternāre,* to stretch out, overcome, perplex : *com-* (intensive) + *sternere,* to spread out.]

con·ster·na·tion (kŏn′stər-nā′shən) *n.* Sudden confusion, amazement, or frustration.

con·sti·pate (kŏn′stə-pāt′) *tr.v.* **-pated, -pating, -pates.** **1.** To cause constipation in. **2.** To repress; restrain. [Latin *constīpāre,* to press or crowd together (in Medieval Latin, "to confine the bowels") : *com-,* together + *stīpāre,* to press, cram.]

con·sti·pa·tion (kŏn′stə-pā′shən) *n.* Difficult, incomplete, or infrequent evacuation of the bowels.

con·stit·u·en·cy (kən-stĭch′o͞o-ən-sē) *n., pl.* **-cies.** **1. a.** The body of voters represented by an elected legislator or executive. **b.** The district represented. **2.** Any group of supporters or people whose wishes must be considered.

con·stit·u·ent (kən-stĭch′o͞o-ənt) *adj.* **1.** Serving as part of a whole; component. **2.** Authorized to make or amend a constitution. **3.** Empowered to elect representatives.
∼*n.* **1.** Someone represented by an elected official. **2.** Someone represented by another; a client. **3.** A constituent part; a component. **4.** *Grammar.* Any of the functional elements into which a construction or compound may be divided by analysis, being either immediate, as *He/ works on the railroad,* or ultimate, as *He/work/s/on/the/rail/road.* [Latin *constituēns* (stem *constituent-*), present participle of *constituere,* to CONSTITUTE.] —**con·stit·u·ent·ly** *adv.*

con·sti·tute (kŏn′stə-to͞ot′, -tyo͞ot′) *tr.v.* **-tuted, -tuting, -tutes.** **1. a.** To be the elements or parts of; make up; compose: *Ten members constitute a quorum.* **b.** To be equivalent or tantamount to: *Does this constitute a precedent?* **2.** To give legal form to (an assembly, court, or the like). **3.** To establish formally; found (an institution, for example). **4.** To set up; enact (a law, for example). **5.** To appoint to an office or task; designate. [Middle English *constituten,* from Latin *constituere,* to cause to stand, set, fix : *com-* (intensive) + *statuere,* to set up.] —**con·sti·tut·er, con·sti·tu·tor** *n.*

con·sti·tu·tion (kŏn′stə-to͞o′shən, -tyo͞o′-) *n. Abbr.* **cons., const., Const.** **1.** The act or process of constituting or establishing. **2.** The composition of something made of a number of parts; make-up. **3.** A person's physical make-up as it relates to his or her characteristic state of health: *a strong constitution.* **4. a.** The system of fundamental laws and principles that prescribes the nature, functions, and limits of a government or other institution. **b.** The document in which this system is recorded. **5.** In former times, a decree or enactment. —**the Constitution.** The Constitution of the United States, adopted in 1787 and put into effect in 1789.

con·sti·tu·tion·al (kŏn′stə-to͞o′shən-əl, -tyo͞o′-) *adj. Abbr.* **cons.** **1.** Of or proceeding from the basic structure or nature of a person or thing; essential. **2.** Contained in or consistent with a constitution. **3.** Regulated by or operating under a constitution. **4.** For the sake of one's general health.
∼*n.* A walk taken for the sake of one's health. —**con·sti·tu·tion·al·i·ty** *n.* —**con·sti·tu·tion·al·ly** *adv.*

con·sti·tu·tion·al·ism (kŏn′stə-to͞o′shən-əl-ĭz′əm, -tyo͞o′-) *n.* **1.** Government in which power is distributed and limited by a system of laws that must be obeyed by the rulers. **2.** Advocacy of such government. —**con·sti·tu·tion·al·ist** *n.*

constitutional monarchy *n.* A monarchy in which the powers of the ruler are restricted to those granted under the constitution and laws of the nation.

con·sti·tu·tive (kŏn′stə-to͞o′tĭv, -tyo͞o′-) *adj.* **1.** Making a thing what it is; essential. **2.** Having power to institute, establish, or enact. —**con·sti·tu·tive·ly** *adv.*

constitutive enzyme *n.* An enzyme that is always present in a cell, being synthesized at a constant rate regardless of substrate.

constr. construction.

con·strain (kən-strān′) *tr.v.* **-strained, -straining, -strains.** **1. a.** To compel by physical, moral, or circumstantial force; oblige. **b.** To bring about by compulsion; enforce. **2.** To keep within close bounds; confine. **3.** To check the freedom or mobility of; restrain. —See Synonyms at **force.** [Middle English *constreinen,* from Old French *constraindre,* from Latin *constringere,* to draw or bind tightly together : *com-,* together + *stringere,* to draw tight.] —**con·strain·a·ble** *adj.* —**con·strain·er** *n.*

con·strained (kən-strānd′) *adj.* **1.** Resulting from constraint; restrained. **2.** Forced; unnatural: *a constrained smile.* —**con·strain·ed·ly** (kən-strā′nĭd-lē) *adv.*

con·straint (kən-strānt′) *n.* **1.** The threat or use of force to prevent, restrict, or dictate the action or thought of others. **2.** The state or sense of being restricted to a given course of action or inaction. **3.** Something that restricts, limits, or regulates. **4.** A lack of ease; embarrassed reserve or reticence. [Middle English *constreint(e),* from Old French *constrainte,* from *constraindre,* to CONSTRAIN.]

con·strict (kən-strĭkt′) *tr.v.* **-stricted, -stricting, -stricts.** **1.** To make smaller or narrower, as by shrinking or contracting. **2.** To squeeze or compress by or as if by narrowing or tightening. **3.** To limit; inhibit. —See Synonyms at **contract.** [Latin *constringere* (past participle *constrictus*), to draw or bind tightly together, CONSTRAIN.] —**con·stric·tive** *adj.* —**con·stric·tive·ly** *adv.*

con·stric·tion (kən-strĭk′shən) *n.* **1. a.** The act or process of constricting. **b.** The condition of being constricted. **2.** A feeling of pressure or tightness. **3.** A constricted or narrow part.

con·stric·tor (kən-strĭk′tər) *n.* **1.** Something that constricts. **2.** *Anatomy.* A muscle that compresses an organ or causes narrowing of a duct or passage. **3.** Any of various snakes, such as a python or boa, that coil around and crush their prey.

con·stringe (kən-strĭnj′) *tr.v.* **-stringed, -stringing, -stringes.** To cause to shrink or contract. [Latin *constringere,* to CONSTRAIN.] —**con·strin·gen·cy** *n.* —**con·strin·gent** *adj.*

con·struct (kən-strŭkt′) *tr.v.* **-structed, -structing, -structs.** **1.** To form by assembling parts; build; erect. **2.** To create (an argument or sentence, for example) by systematically arranging ideas or expressions; devise with the mind. **3.** *Mathematics.* To draw (a geometric figure) according to specific requirements, usually with instruments limited to a ruler and compass.
∼*n.* (kŏn′strŭkt). Something synthesized or constructed from simple elements, especially a concept. [Latin *construere* (past participle *constructus*), to pile up together, build : *com-,* together + *struere,* to pile up.] —**con·struc·tor** (kən-strŭk′tər), **con·struct·er** *n.* —**con·struct·i·ble** *adj.*

con·struc·tion (kən-strŭk′shən) *n. Abbr.* **cons., const., constr.** **1. a.** The act or process of constructing. **b.** The business or work of building. Also used adjectivally: *the construction industry.* **2.** That which is constructed; a structure or building. **3.** The way in which a thing is put together; structure. **4.** The interpretation or explanation given to an action or statement. **5.** *Grammar.* The particular arrangement of words in a phrase, clause, or sentence. —**con·struc·tion·al** *adj.* —**con·struc·tion·al·ly** *adv.*

con·struc·tive (kən-strŭk′tĭv) *adj.* **1.** Serving to advance a good purpose; helpful. **2.** Of or pertaining to construction; structural. **3.** *Law.* Based on an interpretation; inferred but not directly expressed. —**con·struc·tive·ly** *adv.* —**con·struc·tive·ness** *n.*

con·struc·tiv·ism (kən-strŭk′tĭ-vĭz′əm) *n.* Also **Constructivism.** A movement in modern art that developed in Russia around 1920, in which glass, sheet metal, and other industrial materials are used to create nonrepresentational, often geometric objects. —**con·struc·tiv·ist** *adj.* & *n.*

con·strue (kən-stro͞o′) *v.* **-strued, -struing, -strues.** —*tr.* **1.** *Grammar.* **a.** To analyze the structure of (a clause or sentence). Compare **parse.** **b.** To use syntactically: *The noun "fish" can be construed as singular or plural.* **2.** To deduce and explain the meaning of; especially, to put a particular construction or interpretation upon: *construed his remark as offensive.* **3.** To translate, especially aloud. —*intr.* **1.** To analyze grammatical structure. **2.** To be capable of grammatical analysis. Used of a phrase or sentence.
∼*n.* (kŏn′stro͞o). An interpretation or translation. [Middle English *construen,* from Late Latin *construere,* from Latin, to CONSTRUCT.]

con·sub·stan·tial (kŏn′səb-stăn′shəl) *adj.* Having the same substance, nature, or essence. [Middle English *consubstancial,* from Late Latin *consubstantiālis* : Latin *com-,* same + *substantiālis,* SUBSTANTIAL.]

con·sub·stan·ti·ate (kŏn′səb-stăn′shē-āt′) *v.* **-ated, -ating, -ates.** —*tr.* To unite in one common substance, nature, or essence. —*intr.* To become united in one common substance. [New Latin *consubstantiare* : *com-,* together + SUBSTANTIATE.]

con·sub·stan·ti·a·tion (kŏn′səb-stăn′shē-ā′shən) *n. Theology.* The Lutheran doctrine that the body and blood of Christ coexist with the elements of bread and wine during the Eucharist. Compare **transubstantiation.**

con·sue·tude (kŏn′swĭ-to͞od′, -tyo͞od′) *n. Chiefly Law.* Custom; usage; habit. [Middle English, from Latin *consuētūdo,* from *consuēscere,* to accustom : *com-* (intensive) + *suēscere,* to become accustomed.] —**con·sue·tu·di·nar·y** (kŏn′swĭ-to͞o′də-nĕr′ē, -tyo͞o′-) *adj.*

con·sul (kŏn′səl) *n. Abbr.* **c., C., Con., Cons.** **1.** An official appointed by a government to reside in a foreign city and represent its commercial interests and give assistance to its citizens there. **2.** Either of the two chief magistrates of the Roman Republic, elected for a term of one year. **3.** Any of the three chief magistrates of the French Republic from 1799 to 1804. [Middle English, Roman magistrate, from Old French, from Latin *consul,* akin to *consulere,* to CONSULT.] —**con·su·lar** (kŏn′sə-lər) *adj.* —**con·sul·ship** *n.*

con·su·late (kŏn′sə-lĭt) *n.* **1.** The official premises occupied by a consul. **2.** The office or term of office of a consul. **3.** Government by, or the period of government by, consuls. [Middle English *consulat,* from Old French, from Latin *consulātus,* from *consul,* CONSUL.]

consul general *n., pl.* **consuls general.** *Abbr.* **c.g., C.G.** A consular officer of the highest rank.

con·sult (kən-sŭlt′) *v.* **-sulted, -sulting, -sults.** —*tr.* **1. a.** To seek the advice or opinion of: *consult an attorney.* **b.** To refer to: *consult*

PRONUNCIATION KEY
ă, pat; ā, pay; âr, care;
ä, father, are; b, bib;
ch, church; d, deed; ĕ, pet;
ē, be; f, fife; g, gag; h, hat;
hw, which; ĭ, pit; ī, pie;
îr, pier; j, judge; k, kick;
l, lid, needle; m, mum;
n, no, sudden; ng, thing;
ŏ, pot; ō, toe; ô, paw, for;
oi, noise; ou, out; o͝o, book;
o͞o, boot; p, pop; r, roar;
s, sauce; sh, ship, dish;
t, tight; th, thin, path;
th, this, bathe; ŭ, cut; ûr, fur;
v, valve; w, with; y, yes;
z, zebra, size; zh, vision;
ə, about, item, edible,
gallop, circus, peaceful

IN FOREIGN WORDS:
à, *Fr.* ami; œ, *Fr.* feu, *Ger.* schön; ü, *Fr.* tu, *Ger.* über; KH, *Ger.* ich, *Scot.* loch; N, *Fr.* bon; y′, *Fr.* Compiègne

STRESS MARKS:
Primary stress: ′
in·cite′ (ĭn-sīt′)
Secondary stress: ′
in′sight′ (ĭn′sīt′)

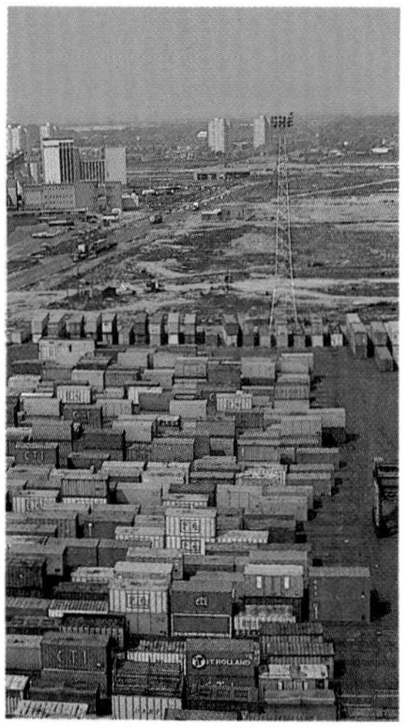
container *Rows of containers fill a dockyard in London. Containers were introduced in the 1960's to speed the movement of freight and make it easier to transfer goods between ships, trains, airplanes, and trucks.*

a directory. **2.** To have an eye to; consider: *consult a checkbook balance before buying.* —*intr.* **1.** To exchange views; confer. Often used with *with.* **2.** To give expert advice as a professional. [Old French *consulter,* from Latin *consultāre,* frequentative of *consulere*†, to take counsel.]

con·sul·tan·cy (kən-sŭl′tən-sē) *n., pl.* **-cies.** The business or position of a consultant.

con·sul·tant (kən-sŭl′tənt) *n.* **1.** A person who gives expert or professional advice. **2.** A person who consults another. **3.** A specialist physician who is asked to confirm a diagnosis.

con·sul·ta·tion (kŏn′səl-tā′shən) *n.* **1.** The act or procedure of consulting. **2.** A conference at which advice is given or views are exchanged.

con·sul·ta·tive (kən-sŭl′tə-tĭv) *adj.* Of or pertaining to consultation; advisory.

con·sult·ing (kən-sŭl′tĭng) *adj.* Acting in an advisory capacity in a specialized field: *a consulting engineer.*

consulting room *n.* A room in which a doctor sees patients.

con·sume (kən-so͞om′) *v.* **-sumed, -suming, -sumes.** —*tr.* **1.** To eat or drink up; ingest. **2.** To use up; expend: *consume fuel.* **3.** To waste; squander. **4.** To destroy totally, especially by fire. **5.** To absorb completely; engross: *consumed with curiosity.* —*intr.* To be destroyed or expended; waste away. [Middle English *consumen,* from Old French *consumer,* from Latin *consūmere,* to take completely, consume : *com-* (intensive) + *sūmere,* to take up.] —**con·sum·a·ble** *adj.* & *n.*

con·sum·ed·ly (kən-so͞o′mĭd-lē) *adv.* Excessively.

con·sum·er (kən-so͞o′mər) *n.* **1.** One that consumes. **2.** *Economics.* One who acquires goods or services; a buyer. **3.** *Ecology.* An organism, such as an animal or insectivorous plant, that feeds on other organisms. Compare **producer.**

consumer credit *n. Economics.* Credit granted to a consumer, permitting the individual to own or use goods while making payments on them.

consumer goods *pl.n. Economics.* Goods, such as food, clothing, or household appliances, that directly satisfy human wants, as distinguished from those used in the production of other goods. Compare **capital goods.**

con·sum·er·ism (kən-so͞o′mə-rĭz′əm) *n.* **1.** Protection of the interests of the consumer, as through fair advertising, improved safety standards, and honest packaging. **2.** *Economics.* The theory that a progressively greater consumption of goods is economically desirable. —**con·sum·er·ist** *n.* & *adj.*

consumer price index *n.* An index of prices used to measure the change in the cost of basic goods and services in comparison with a fixed base period. Also called "cost-of-living index."

consumer research *n.* Investigation into what purchasers of goods and services buy and what they require.

con·sum·mate (kŏn′sə-māt′) *tr.v.* **-mated, -mating, -mates.** **1.** To bring to completion, perfection, or fulfillment; conclude: *consummate a business transaction.* **2.** To fulfill (a marriage) with the first act of sexual intercourse after the ceremony.
~*adj.* (kən-sŭm′ĭt, kŏn′sə-mĭt). **1.** Supremely accomplished or skilled: *a consummate artist.* **2.** Completely perfect: *consummate happiness.* **3.** Total, utter: *a consummate bore.* [Middle English *consummaten,* from Latin *consummāre,* to bring together, sum up : *com-,* together + *summa,* a SUM.] —**con·sum·mate·ly** *adv.* —**con·sum·ma·tive** (kŏn′sə-mā′tĭv, kən-sŭm′ə-tĭv), *adj.* —**con·sum·ma·tor** (kŏn′sə-mā′tər) *n.*

con·sum·ma·tion (kŏn′sə-mā′shən) *n.* **1.** The act of consummating, especially the consummating of a marriage. **2.** An ultimate end or goal.

con·sump·tion (kən-sŭmp′shən) *n.* **1. a.** The act or process of consuming. **b.** The state of being consumed. **2.** The amount consumed. **3.** *Economics.* The using up of consumer goods and services. **4.** A wasting away of the body, especially as caused by tuberculosis of the lungs. [Middle English *consumpcioun,* from Old French *consumption,* from Latin *consūmptiō,* from *consūmere,* to CONSUME.]

con·sump·tive (kən-sŭmp′tĭv) *adj.* **1.** Tending to consume; wasteful; destructive. **2.** Pertaining to or afflicted with consumption, especially tuberculosis of the lungs.
~*n.* A person afflicted with tuberculosis of the lungs.

cont. **1.** containing. **2.** contents. **3.** continent; continental. **4.** continue; continued. **5.** contract. **6.** contraction.

con·tact (kŏn′tăkt) *n.* **1. a.** The coming together of objects or surfaces so that there is no space between them. **b.** The fact or relation of not being separated by space or another object. **2.** The state of being in communication: *in contact with the doctor.* **3.** An acquaintance who might be of use; a connection. **4.** *Electricity.* **a.** A connection between two conductors that permits a flow of current. **b.** A part or device that makes or breaks such a connection. **5.** *Medicine.* A person exposed to a contagious disease and potentially able to transmit it. **6.** A contact lens.
~*v.* (kŏn′tăkt, kən-tăkt′) **contacted, -tacting, -tacts.** —*tr.* **1.** To bring into contact. **2.** To communicate with: *Contact your lawyer.* —*intr.* To be in or come into contact.
~*adj.* (kŏn′tăkt). **1.** Of, sustaining, or making contact. **2. a.** Caused or transmitted by contact: *a contact skin rash.* **b.** Activated or operating by means of contact: *a contact insecticide.* [Latin *contāctus,* from the past participle of *contingere,* to touch, border upon, attain to : *com-,* together + *tangere,* to touch.] —**con·tac·tu·al** (kən-tăk′cho͞o-əl) *adj.* —**con·tac·tu·al·ly** *adv.*

contact dermatitis *n.* Inflammation of the skin caused by direct contact with an irritating substance, especially a chemical.

contact flight *n.* Aircraft navigation by visual reference to the horizon or to landmarks. Also called "contact flying."

contact lens *n.* A thin corrective lens fitted over the cornea.

contact print *n.* A photographic print made by exposing a photosensitive surface that is in direct contact with the negative.

con·ta·gion (kən-tā′jən) *n.* **1.** Disease transmission by direct or indirect contact. **2.** A disease that is or may be so transmitted. **3.** A contagium. **4.** A harmful or corrupting influence. **5.** The tendency to spread, as of an idea or emotional state: *the contagion of laughter.* [Middle English *contagioun,* from Old French *contagion,* from Latin *contāgiō* (stem *contāgiōn-*), from *contingere,* to touch, touch with pollution, CONTACT.]

con·ta·gious (kən-tā′jəs) *adj.* **1.** Transmissible by direct or indirect contact; communicable. Said of certain diseases. **2.** Carrying or capable of carrying disease. **3.** Spreading or tending to spread from one to another; catching. Compare **infectious.** —**con·ta·gious·ly** *adv.* —**con·ta·gious·ness** *n.*

contagious abortion *n.* **Brucellosis** *(see)* of cattle.

con·ta·gi·um (kən-tā′jē-əm) *n., pl.* **-gia** (-jē-ə). The direct cause, such as a virus, of a communicable disease. [Latin, from *contāgiō,* CONTAGION.]

con·tain (kən-tān′) *tr.v.* **-tained, -taining, -tains.** **1.** To have within; enclose. **2.** To have as component parts; comprise; include. **3.** To be able to hold; have capacity for. **4.** *Mathematics.* To be exactly divisible by. **5.** To hold or keep within limits; restrain; confine: *contain one's emotions.* **6.** To prevent the expansion of (a country or power bloc, for example), as by encircling it with hostile alliances. [Middle English *conteinen,* from Old French *contenir,* from Latin *continēre,* to hold together, enclose, contain : *com-,* together + *tenēre,* to hold.] —**con·tain·a·ble** *adj.*
Synonyms: *accommodate, hold.*

con·tain·er (kən-tā′nər) *n.* **1.** One that contains; especially, something used for holding or carrying, such as a box. **2.** A large, usually rectangular, receptacle used for transporting cargo.

con·tain·er·ize (kən-tā′nər-īz′) *tr.v* **-ized, -izing, -izes.** To package (cargo) in large, standardized containers to facilitate shipping and handling. —**con·tain·er·i·za·tion** *n.*

container ship *n.* A ship specially designed for transporting containerized cargo.

con·tain·ment (kən-tān′mənt) *n.* The act of containing; especially, the act or policy of keeping a hostile power or bloc within existing limits of influence.

con·tam·i·nant (kən-tăm′ə-nənt) *n.* Something that contaminates.

con·tam·i·nate (kən-tăm′ə-nāt′) *tr.v.* **-nated, -nating, -nates.** **1.** To make impure or corrupt by contact or mixture. **2.** To expose to radioactivity. [Middle English *contaminaten,* from Latin *contāmināre.*] —**con·tam·i·na·tive** *adj.* —**con·tam·i·na·tor** (kən-tăm′ə-nā′tər) *n.*

con·tam·i·na·tion (kən-tăm′ə-nā′shən) *n.* **1. a.** The act or process of contaminating. **b.** The state of being contaminated. **2.** One that contaminates; an impurity. **3.** The alteration of a word form through association with a related form. For example, *miniscule* is a contamination of *minuscule* through association with *miniature.*

con·tan·go (kən-tăng′gō) *n., pl.* **-gos.** **1.** On the London Stock Exchange, an arrangement whereby the settlement for the delivery of stock is carried forward from one account to the next. **2.** The fee paid for this postponement. [19th century : arbitrary coinage apparently based on *continuation.*]

contd. continued.

conte (kôNt) *n., pl.* **contes** (kôNt). A short story; especially, a tale of adventure. [French, from Old French *conter, compter,* COUNT (to relate).]

con·temn (kən-tĕm′) *tr.v.* **-temned, -temning, -temns.** To view with contempt; despise. [Middle English *contempnen,* from Old French *contem(p)ner,* from Latin *contemnere* : *com-* (intensive) + *temnere*†, to despise.] —**con·temn·er** (kən-tĕm′ər, -tĕm′nər) *n.*

con·tem·plate (kŏn′təm-plāt′) *v.* **-plated, -plating, -plates.** —*tr.* **1.** To look at pensively: *comtemplate the stars.* **2.** To ponder or consider thoughtfully. **3.** To have in mind as a purpose; intend: *contemplate marriage.* **4.** To regard as possible; take seriously. —*intr.* To engage in serious thought, especially about spiritual matters; meditate. —See Synonyms at **see.** [Latin *contemplārī,* to observe carefully (originally a term of augury) : *com-* (intensive) + *templum,* open space marked out by augurs for observation.] —**con·tem·pla·tor** *n.* —**con·tem·pla·tion** *n.*

con·tem·pla·tive (kən-tĕm′plə-tĭv, kŏn′təm-plā′-) *adj.* **1.** Disposed to or characterized by contemplation. **2.** Devoted to religious contemplation. —See Usage note at **pensive.**
~*n.* **1.** A person given to contemplation. **2.** A member of a religious order dedicated to meditation. —**con·tem·pla·tive·ly** *adv.* —**con·tem·pla·tive·ness** *n.*

con·tem·po·ra·ne·ous (kən-tĕm′pə-rā′nē-əs) *adj.* Originating, existing, or happening during the same period of time: *The reign of Philip II was contemporaneous with that of Elizabeth I.* —See Synonyms at **contemporary.** [Latin *contemporāneus* : *com-,* same + *tempus* (stem *tempor-*), time.] —**con·tem·po·ra·ne·i·ty** (kən-tĕm′pə-rə-nē′ə-tē, -nā′ə-tē), **con·tem·po·ra·ne·ous·ness** *n.* —**con·tem·po·ra·ne·ous·ly** *adv.*

con·tem·po·rar·y (kən-tĕm′pə-rĕr′ē) *adj.* **1.** Belonging to the same period of time: *a fact documented by two contemporary sources.* **2.** Of about the same age. **3. a.** Belonging to the present time; current. **b.** Very modern; up-to-date.

~n., pl. **-ies. 1.** One belonging to the same period of time as another. **2.** A person of about the same age as another. **3.** A modern. [Medieval Latin *contemporārius* : Latin *com-*, together + *tempus* (stem *tempor-*), time (see **temporal**).]

Synonyms: *coincident, concomitant, concurrent, contemporaneous, simultaneous, synchronous.*

Usage: When *contemporary* is used in reference to something in the past, its meaning is not always clear. *Contemporary critics of Shakespeare* may mean critics in his time or critics in our time. When the context does not make the meaning clear, misunderstanding may be avoided by using such phrases as "critics in Shakespeare's time" or "modern critics."

con·tem·po·rize (kən-tĕm′pə-rīz′) *tr.v.* **-rized, -rizing, -rizes.** To relate in time; synchronize. [From CONTEMPORARY (after TEMPORIZE).]

con·tempt (kən-tĕmpt′) *n.* **1.** Reproachful disdain, as for something vile or dishonorable; bitter scorn. **2.** The state of being scorned, despised, or dishonored: *hold someone in contempt.* **3.** Open disrespect or willful disobedience of the authority of a court of law or a legislative body. Also called "contempt of court." [Middle English, from Latin *contemptus*, from the past participle of *contemnere*, to CONTEMN.]

con·tempt·i·ble (kən-tĕmp′tə-bəl) *adj.* Deserving contempt; despicable. —**con·tempt·i·bil·i·ty, con·tempt·i·ble·ness** *n.* —**con·tempt·i·bly** *adv.*

con·temp·tu·ous (kən-tĕmp′chōō-əs) *adj.* Manifesting or feeling contempt; scornful; disdainful: *contemptuous of her wealth.* —**con·temp·tu·ous·ly** *adv.* —**con·temp·tu·ous·ness** *n.*

con·tend (kən-tĕnd′) *v.* **-tended, -tending, -tends.** —*intr.* **1.** To strive, as in battle; fight. **2.** To compete, as in a contest; vie. **3.** To strive in controversy or debate; dispute. —*tr.* To maintain or assert. —See Synonyms at **discuss.** [Middle English *contenden*, from Old French *contendre*, from Latin *contendere*, to strain, strive with : *com-*, with + *tendere*, to stretch, strain, strive.]

con·tend·er (kən-tĕn′dər) *n.* One who takes part in a contest, as for a championship or political office.

con·tent¹ (kŏn′tĕnt) *n.* **1.** *Abbr.* **cont.** *Usually* **contents.** That which is contained in a receptacle: *the content of a drawer.* **2. a.** *Sometimes* **contents.** The subject matter, as of a book or speech. **b. contents.** The chapter or other division headings of a book or document: *table of contents.* **3.** The meaning or significance of a literary or artistic work, as distinguished from its form. **4.** Ability to receive and hold; capacity. **5.** The amount held; volume. **6.** The proportion of a specified substance: *a high fat content.* [Middle English, from Medieval Latin *contentum*, from Latin *contentus*, past participle of *continēre*, to CONTAIN.]

con·tent² (kən-tĕnt′) *adj.* **1.** Not desiring more than what one has; satisfied. **2.** Resigned to circumstances. —*tr.v.* **contented, -tenting, -tents.** To make content or satisfied. —**content oneself with.** To limit oneself to: *He contented himself with one slice of cake.* —*n.* **1.** Contentment; satisfaction. **2.** *British.* An affirmative vote or voter in the House of Lords. [Middle English, from Old French, from Latin *contentus*, restrained, satisfied, past participle of *continēre*, to restrain, CONTAIN.]

con·tent·ed (kən-tĕn′tĭd) *adj.* Satisfied with things as they are; content. —**con·tent·ed·ly** *adv.* —**con·tent·ed·ness** *n.*

con·ten·tion (kən-tĕn′shən) *n.* **1.** A verbal struggling; dispute; controversy. **2.** A striving to win in competition; a state of rivalry. **3.** An assertion put forward in argument. —See Synonyms at **discord.** [Middle English *contencioun*, from Old French *contention*, from Latin *contentiō* (stem *contentiōn-*), from *contendere*, CONTEND.]

con·ten·tious (kən-tĕn′shəs) *adj.* Given to contention; quarrelsome. **2.** Involving or likely to cause contention; controversial. —See Synonyms at **belligerent.** —**con·ten·tious·ly** *adv.* —**con·ten·tious·ness** *n.*

con·tent·ment (kən-tĕnt′mənt) *n.* The state of being contented; satisfaction.

con·ter·mi·nous (kən-tûr′mə-nəs) *adj.* Also **co·ter·mi·nous** (kō-). **1.** Having a boundary in common; contiguous. **2.** Contained in the same boundaries; coextensive. [Latin *conterminus* : *com-*, together + *terminus*, boundary, limit.] —**con·ter·mi·nous·ly** *adv.*

con·tes·sa (kŏn-tĕs′ə) *n.* An Italian countess. [Italian.]

con·test (kŏn′tĕst) *n.* **1.** A struggle for superiority or victory between rivals. **2.** A dispute; a debate. **3.** Any competition; especially, one in which entrants perform separately and are rated by judges. —See Synonyms at **conflict.** —*v.* (kən-tĕst′, kŏn′tĕst) **contested, -testing, -tests.** —*tr.* **1.** To compete or strive for: *Six candidates contested the seat at the last election.* **2.** To attempt to disprove or invalidate; dispute; challenge: *contest a will.* —*intr.* To struggle or contend; contend. —See Synonyms at **oppose.** [Old French *conteste*, from *contester*, from Latin *contestārī*, bring in (a lawsuit) by calling witnesses (from both parties) : *com-*, together + *testārī*, to bear witness, from *testis*, a witness.] —**con·test·a·ble** *adj.* —**con·test·er** *n.*

con·tes·tant (kən-tĕs′tənt) *n.* **1.** One who takes part in a contest; a competitor. **2.** One who contests something, such as an election or a will.

con·tes·ta·tion (kŏn′tĕs-tā′shən) *n.* Controversy; disputation.

con·text (kŏn′tĕkst) *n.* **1.** The part of a written or spoken statement that surrounds a particular word or passage and can clarify its meaning. **2.** The circumstances in which something occurs or exists; background or setting. [Middle English, from Latin *contextus*,

coherence, sequence of words, from the past participle of *contexere*, to join together, weave : *com-*, together + *texere*, to join, weave, plait.]

con·tex·tu·al (kən-tĕks′chōō-əl) *adj.* Of, pertaining to, or depending upon the context. —**con·tex·tu·al·ly** *adv.*

con·tex·tu·al·ize (kən-tĕks′chōō-əl-īz′) —*tr.v.* **-ized, -izing, -izes.** To place (a word, an idea, or an activity, for example) in an appropriate context. —**con·tex·tu·al·i·za·tion** *n.*

con·tex·ture (kən-tĕks′chər) *n.* **1.** The act of weaving or assembling parts. **2.** An arrangement of interconnected parts; a structure. —**con·tex·tur·al, con·tex·tured** *adj.*

con·ti·gu·i·ty (kŏn′tĭ-gyōō′ə-tē) *n., pl.* **-ties. 1.** The state of being contiguous. **2.** A continuous mass or series.

con·tig·u·ous (kən-tĭg′yōō-əs) *adj.* **1.** Sharing an edge or boundary; touching. **2.** Nearby; neighboring; adjacent. **3.** Adjacent in time; immediately preceding or following. [Latin *contiguus*, from *contingere*, to touch on all sides, CONTACT.] —**con·tig·u·ous·ly** *adv.* —**con·tig·u·ous·ness** *n.*

con·ti·nence (kŏn′tə-nəns) *n.* **1.** Self-restraint; moderation. **2.** Control of the bodily functions of urination and defecation. **3.** Partial or complete abstention from sexual activity. —See Synonyms at **abstinence.**

con·ti·nent¹ (kŏn′tə-nənt) *n.* **1.** *Abbr.* **cont.** One of the principal land masses of the earth, usually regarded as including Africa, Antarctica, Asia, Australia, Europe, North America, and South America. **2.** *Archaic.* A thing that holds or retains. —**the Continent.** The mainland of Europe. [Latin *(terra) continēns* (stem *continent-*), "continuous (land)," from the present participle of *continēre*, to hold together, continue. See **continent** (adjective).]

continent² *adj.* **1.** Self-restrained; moderate. **2.** Able to control the bodily functions of urination and defecation. **3.** Partially or completely abstaining from sexual activity. [Middle English, from Old French, from Latin *continēns* (stem *continent-*), present participle of *continēre*, to hold together, CONTAIN.] —**con·ti·nent·ly** *adv.*

con·ti·nen·tal (kŏn′tə-nĕn′təl) *adj.* **1.** Of, pertaining to, or characteristic of a continent. **2.** *Usually* **Continental.** Of or relating to the mainland of Europe; European. **3. Continental.** Of or pertaining to the American colonies during and immediately after the Revolutionary War. —*n. Usually* **Continental. 1.** An inhabitant of the mainland of Europe; a European. **2. Continental.** A soldier in the Continental Army during the Revolutionary War. **3.** A piece of paper money issued by the Continental Congress during the Revolutionary War. —**con·ti·nen·tal·ly** *adv.*

continental breakfast *n.* A light meal consisting of rolls, usually with butter and jam, and coffee.

Continental Congress *n.* Either of two American legislative assemblies that governed the United States during the Revolutionary era. The first convened in 1774 to voice grievances against Great Britain. The second, convening in 1775, established the Continental Army and served as both the legislative and the executive arm of the government until the Constitution took effect in 1789.

continental divide *n.* **1.** An extensive stretch of high ground from each side of which the river systems of a continent flow in opposite directions. **2. Continental Divide.** In North America, such a stretch formed by the crests of the Rocky Mountains. In this sense, also called "Great Divide."

continental drift *n.* The theory that the earth's continents are not fixed in position but move slowly over the surface of the earth, their present positions resulting from the break-up of a single landmass about 200 million years ago. See **plate tectonics.**

continental shelf *n.* A generally shallow, flat submerged portion of a continent, extending to a point of steep descent to the ocean floor.

con·tin·gence (kən-tĭn′jəns) *n.* **1.** A joining or touching. **2.** The condition of contingency.

con·tin·gen·cy (kən-tĭn′jən-sē) *n., pl.* **-cies. 1. a.** An event that may occur but that is not certain or intended; a possibility. **b.** A possibility that must be prepared against; a future emergency. Sometimes used adjectivally: *a contingency fund.* **2.** The condition of being dependent upon chance; uncertainty; fortuitousness. **3.** Something incidental to something else. **4.** *Statistics.* The degree of association between theoretical and observed frequencies of certain types of variable.

con·tin·gent (kən-tĭn′jənt) *adj.* **1.** Likely but not certain to occur; possible. **2.** Dependent upon conditions or events not yet established; conditional. Often used with *on* or *upon.* **3.** Happening by chance or accident; fortuitous. **4.** *Philosophy.* Neither necessarily true nor necessarily false. Said of a proposition. —*n.* **1.** A contingency. **2.** A share or quota, as of troops, contributed to a general effort. **3.** A representative group forming part of a larger group. [Middle English, from Old French, from Latin *contingēns* (stem *contingent-*), present participle of *contingere*, to touch on all sides, happen, CONTACT.] —**con·tin·gent·ly** *adv.*

con·tin·u·al (kən-tĭn′yōō-əl) *adj.* **1.** Repeated regularly and frequently; recurring often: *continual interruptions.* **2.** Continuing indefinitely; unending; incessant: *a source of continual worry.* —**con·tin·u·al·ly** *adv.*

Synonyms: *ceaseless, constant, continuous, eternal, incessant, interminable, perennial, perpetual.*

con·tin·u·ance (kən-tĭn′yōō-əns) *n.* **1.** The act or fact of continuing. **2.** The time during which something exists or lasts; duration. **3.** A continuation; a sequel. **4.** *Law.* Adjournment to a future date.

Usage: *Continuance*, except in its legal sense, and *continuation* are sometimes interchangeable; but usually the former emphasizes the duration of a condition (*a machine's continuance in working order*), whereas the latter stresses prolongation or resumption of action (*the continuation of the story*).

con·tin·u·ant (kən-tĭn′yōō-ənt) *n. Phonetics.* A consonant, such as *s, z,* or *f,* that may be prolonged as long as the breath lasts without a change in quality. Compare **stop.** [French, from Latin *continuāns* (stem *continuant-*), present participle of *continuāre,* to CONTINUE.]

con·tin·u·a·tion (kən-tĭn′yōō-ā′shən) *n.* **1. a.** The act or fact of continuing. **b.** The state of being continued.—See Usage note at **continuance. 2.** A part by which something is carried on or extended; a supplement or sequel.

con·tin·u·a·tive (kən-tĭn′yōō-ā′tĭv) *adj.* **1.** Serving to continue or cause continuation. **2.** *Grammar.* Expressing continuation. Said of a word or clause.
~*n.* Something that expresses or causes continuation.—**con·tin·u·a·tive·ly** *adv.*

con·tin·u·a·tor (kən-tĭn′yōō-ā′tər) *n.* One that continues; especially, a person who resumes the work of another.

con·tin·ue (kən-tĭn′yōō) *v.* **-ued, -uing, -ues.**—*intr.* **1.** To exist over a prolonged period; last; persist. **2.** To exist over an extended space; extend. **3.** To remain in the same state, capacity, or place. **4.** To go on after an interruption; resume.—*tr.* **1.** To carry forward; keep up; persist in. **2.** To carry further in time, space, or development; extend. **3.** To carry on after an interruption; resume. **4.** *Law.* To postpone (a trial or other legal proceeding). [Middle English *continuen,* from Old French *continuer,* from Latin *continuāre,* from *continuus,* continuous, from *continēre,* to hold together, be continuous, CONTAIN.]—**con·tin·u·a·ble** *adj.*—**con·tin·u·er** *n.*

continuing education *n.* **1.** An educational program that brings participants up to date in a particular field. **2.** A course of study designed for part-time adult students.

con·ti·nu·i·ty (kŏn′tə-nōō′ə-tē, -nyōō′-) *n., pl.* **-ties. 1.** The state or quality of being continuous. **2.** An uninterrupted succession; an unbroken course. **3. a.** A detailed script or scenario consulted to avoid errors and prevent discrepancies from shot to shot in a film. **b.** Spoken matter serving to link parts of a radio or television program so that no break occurs.

con·tin·u·o (kən-tĭn′yōō-ō) *n., pl.* **-os.** A bass part, typically played on a stringed or keyboard instrument, in which numerals indicate the successive chords, the actual notes played being left to the performer. Also called "basso continuo," "figured bass." [Italian, "continuous."]

con·tin·u·ous (kən-tĭn′yōō-əs) *adj.* **1.** Extending or prolonged without interruption or cessation; unceasing. **2.** *Mathematics.* Designating a function in which no sudden changes in value occur as the variable increases or decreases gradually. **3.** *Grammar.* **Progressive** *(see).*—See Synonyms at **continual.** [Latin *continuus,* from *continēre,* to hold together, CONTINUE.]—**con·tin·u·ous·ly** *adv.*—**con·tin·u·ous·ness** *n.*

continuous assessment *n.* Assessment of a student's work throughout a course, as opposed, for example, to assessment based solely on a final examination.

continuous creation *n.* The hypothesis that the universe did not start at a particular instant but has been continuously created throughout time. This hypothesis is a part of the **steady-state theory** *(see).*

continuous spectrum *n. Physics.* A spectrum having no breaks, especially a spectrum of radiation distributed over an uninterrupted range of wavelengths.

con·tin·u·ous-wave (kən-tĭn′yōō-əs-wāv′) *adj. Abbr.* **cw, CW** Emitting or capable of emitting continuously; not pulsed. Said especially of lasers.

con·tin·u·um (kən-tĭn′yōō-əm) *n., pl.* **-tinua** (-tĭn′yōō-ə) or **-tinuums.** **1.** A continuous extent, succession, or whole, no part of which can be distinguished from neighboring parts except by arbitrary division. **2.** *Mathematics.* A set having the same number of points as all the real numbers in an interval. [Latin, neuter of *continuus,* CONTINUOUS.]

con·tort (kən-tôrt′) *v.* **-torted, -torting, -torts.**—*tr.* To twist or bend severely out of shape.—*intr.* To become twisted into a strained shape or expression: *His face contorted with pain.*—See Usage note at **distort.** [Latin *contorquēre* (past participle *contortus*), to twist together : *com-,* together + *torquēre,* to twist.]—**con·tor·tion** *n.*—**con·tor·tive** *adj.*

con·tort·ed (kən-tôr′tĭd) *adj.* **1.** Twisted or strained out of shape. **2.** *Botany.* Twisted or bent upon itself.—**con·tort·ed·ly** *adv.*—**con·tort·ed·ness** *n.*

con·tor·tion·ist (kən-tôr′shən-ĭst) *n.* An acrobat who can twist his body into extraordinary positions.—**con·tor·tion·is·tic** *adj.*

con·tour (kŏn′tōōr) *n.* **1.** The outline of a figure, body, or mass; shape. **2.** A line that represents such an outline. **3.** Often **contours.** A surface, especially of a curving form. **4.** A **contour line** *(see).*—See Synonyms at **form.**
~*tr.v.* **contoured, -touring, -tours. 1.** To make or shape the outline of; represent in contour. **2.** To build (a road, for example) to follow the contour of the land.
~*adj.* **1.** Following the contour lines of uneven terrain to limit erosion of topsoil: *contour plowing.* **2.** Shaped to fit the outline or form of something. [French, from Italian *contorno,* from *contornare,* to go around, draw in outline : *con-* (intensive), from Latin *con-, com-* + *tornare,* to turn in a lathe, from Latin *tornāre,* from *tornus,* lathe, from Greek *tornos.*]

contour feather *n.* Any of the outermost feathers of a bird, forming the visible body contour and plumage.

contour line *n.* An imaginary line, or its representation on a contour map, joining points of equal elevation.

contour map *n.* A map showing elevations and surface configuration by means of contour lines.

contr. 1. contract. **2.** contraction. **3.** contralto.

con·tra (kŏn′trə) *prep.* **1.** Against. Used chiefly in the phrase *pro and contra.* **2.** Contrary to the view or evidence of: *They believe, contra recent opinion polls, that they can win the election.* [Latin.]

contra– *prefix.* Indicates: **1.** Against, opposing, or contrary; for example, **contradistinction, contraindicate. 2.** Pitched next below a specified musical instrument; for example, **contrabassoon.** [Middle English, from Latin *contrā-,* from *contrā,* against.]

con·tra·band (kŏn′trə-bănd′) *n.* **1.** Goods prohibited by law or treaty from being imported or exported. **2. a.** Illegal traffic in such goods; smuggling. **b.** Smuggled goods. **3.** *International Law.* Goods that may be confiscated by a belligerent if supplied to another belligerent by a neutral. Also called "contraband of war." **4.** During the Civil War, an escaped slave who fled to or was taken behind Union lines. [French *contrebande,* from Italian *contrabbando : contra-,* against, from Latin *contrā-* + *bando,* proclamation, from Late Latin *bannus, bannum.*]—**con·tra·band** *adj.*—**con·tra·band·ist** *n.*

con·tra·bass (kŏn′trə-bās′) *n. Music.* A **double bass** *(see).*
~*adj. Music.* Pitched an octave below the normal bass range. [Obsolete Italian *contrabasso : contra-,* pitched below, from Latin *contrā-,* against + *basso,* low, bass, from Late Latin *bassus.*]—**con·tra·bass·ist** *n.*

con·tra·bas·soon (kŏn′trə-bə-sōōn′) *n.* The largest and lowest-pitched of the double-reed wind musical instruments, sounding an octave below the bassoon. Also called "double bassoon."

con·tra·cep·tion (kŏn′trə-sĕp′shən) *n.* Prevention of conception; birth control. [CONTRA- + (CON)CEPTION.]

con·tra·cep·tive (kŏn′trə-sĕp′tĭv) *adj.* Capable of preventing conception.
~*n.* A contraceptive agent or device, such as a condom.

con·tract (kŏn′trăkt′) *n. Abbr.* **contr., cont. 1.** An agreement between two or more parties, especially one that is written and enforceable by law. **2.** The writing or document containing such an agreement. **3.** The branch of law dealing with contracts. **4.** An agreement by which property is transferred; a conveyance. **5.** Marriage as a formal agreement; betrothal. **6.** In the game of bridge: **a.** The last and highest bid of one hand. **b.** The number of tricks thus bid. **7.** *Slang.* An arrangement to kill someone for a fee.
~*v.* (kən-trăkt′, kŏn′trăkt′) **contracted, -tracting, -tracts.**—*tr.* **1.** To enter into by contract; establish or settle by formal agreement. **2. a.** To acquire or incur (a debt, for example). **b.** To catch (a disease). **3.** To reduce in size by drawing together; shrink. **4.** To pull together; wrinkle. **5.** To shorten (a word or words) by omitting or combining some of the letters or sounds: *to contract "I am" to "I'm."*—*intr.* **1.** To enter into or make a contract. **2.** To become reduced in size by or as if by being drawn together.—**contract out.** To arrange to purchase (services, for example) by contract. [Middle English, from Old French, from Latin *contractus,* from the past participle of *contrahere,* to draw together, bring about, enter into an agreement : *com-,* together + *trahere,* to draw.]—**con·tract·i·bil·i·ty** *n.*—**con·tract·i·ble** *adj.*
Synonyms: *compress, condense, constrict, contract, shrink.*

contract bridge *n.* A form of auction bridge in which tricks in excess of the contract may not count toward game. Compare **auction bridge.**

con·trac·tile (kən-trăk′təl) *adj.* Capable of contracting or causing contraction.—**con·trac·til·i·ty** (kŏn′trăk-tĭl′ə-tē) *n.*

contractile root *n.* A specialized root formed by certain bulbs and corms that pulls the bulb or corm down to the appropriate depth in the soil.

contractile vacuole *n.* A vesicle found in many protozoa that expels water to the exterior and so regulates osmosis.

con·trac·tion (kən-trăk′shən) *n. Abbr.* **cont., contr. 1.** The act of contracting or the state of being contracted. **2.** *Grammar.* **a.** A shortened word or words formed by omitting or combining some of the letters or sounds; for example, *isn't* for *is not.* **b.** The formation of such a word. **3.** *Physiology.* The shortening and thickening of functioning muscle, especially that which occurs in childbirth. **4.** *Medicine.* Any abnormal, often irreversible, shrinking or shortening of a body or part. **5.** *Physics.* A decrease in size caused by a reduction in temperature.

con·trac·tor (kŏn′trăk′tər, kən-trăk′tər) *n.* **1.** One who agrees to furnish materials or perform services at a specific price, especially in the building trade. **2.** Something that contracts, especially a muscle.

con·trac·tu·al (kən-trăk′chōō-əl) *adj.* Of, connected with, or having the nature of a contract.

con·trac·ture (kən-trăk′chər) *n.* A drawing together, as of muscle or scar tissue, resulting in distortion or deformity.

contradance. Variant of **contredanse.**

con·tra·dict (kŏn′trə-dĭkt′) *v.* **-dicted, -dicting, -dicts.**—*tr.* **1.** To assert or express the opposite of (a statement). **2.** To deny the statement or assertions of. **3.** To be contrary to; be inconsistent with: *His actions contradict his beliefs.*—*intr.* To utter a contradictory statement.—See Synonyms at **deny.** [Latin *contrādīcere,* to speak against : *contrā-,* against + *dīcere,* to speak.]—**con·tra·dict·a·ble** *adj.*—**con·tra·dict·er, con·tra·dic·tor** *n.*

con·tra·dic·tion (kŏn′trə-dĭk′shən) *n.* **1. a.** The act of contradicting.

b. The state of being in disagreement or opposition. **2.** A statement that contradicts; a denial. **3.** Inconsistency or discrepancy. **4.** Something that contains contradictory elements: *a contradiction in terms.*

con·tra·dic·tious (kŏn′trə-dĭk′shəs) *adj.* Tending to contradict; argumentative.

con·tra·dic·to·ry (kŏn′trə-dĭk′tə-rē) *adj.* **1.** Involving or having the nature of a contradiction; mutually inconsistent. **2.** Given to contradicting. —See Synonyms at **opposite.**
~*n., pl.* **contradictories.** *Logic.* Either of two propositions related in such a way that it is impossible for both to be true or both to be false. Compare **contrary.** —**con·tra·dic·to·ri·ly** *adv.* —**con·tra·dic·to·ri·ness** *n.*

con·tra·dis·tinc·tion (kŏn′trə-dĭ-stĭngk′shən) *n.* Distinction by contrast or opposing qualities. —**con·tra·dis·tinc·tive** *adj.* —**con·tra·dis·tinc·tive·ly** *adv.*

con·tra·dis·tin·guish (kŏn′trə-dĭ-stĭng′gwĭsh) *tr.v.* **-guished, -guishing, -guishes.** To distinguish by contrasting qualities.

con·trail (kŏn′trāl′) *n.* A visible trail of water droplets or ice crystals sometimes forming in the wake of an aircraft or rocket. Also called "vapor trail." [CON(DENSATION) + TRAIL.]

con·tra·in·di·cate (kŏn′trə-ĭn′də-kāt′) *tr.v.* **-cated, -cating, -cates.** To indicate the inadvisability of: *An allergic reaction contraindicates the use of penicillin.* —**con·tra·in·di·cant** (kŏn′trə-ĭn′də-kənt) *n.* —**con·tra·in·di·ca·tion** *n.*

con·tral·to (kən-trăl′tō) *n., pl.* **-tos** or **-ti** (-tē). *Abbr.* **contr.** *Music.* **1.** The lowest female voice or voice part, intermediate in range between soprano and tenor. **2.** A woman having such a voice. [Italian : *contra-*, pitched below, from Latin *contrā-*, against + ALTO.]

con·tra·po·si·tion (kŏn′trə-pə-zĭsh′ən) *n.* An opposite position; opposition; antithesis.

con·trap·tion (kən-trăp′shən) *n.* A mechanical contrivance; a device or gadget. [Humorous blend of CONTRIVE and TRAP + -TION.]

con·tra·pun·tal (kŏn′trə-pŭn′tl) *adj. Music.* Of, pertaining to, or incorporating counterpoint. [From Italian *contrapunto* : *contra-*, against + *punto,* POINT.] —**con·tra·pun·tal·ly** *adv.*

con·tra·pun·tist (kŏn′trə-pŭn′tĭst) *n.* A specialist in contrapuntal music.

con·tra·ri·e·ty (kŏn′trə-rī′ə-tē) *n., pl.* **-ties.** **1.** The quality or condition of being contrary. **2.** Something contrary; a discrepancy or inconsistency. [Middle English, from Old French *contrarieté,* from Late Latin *contrārietās* (stem *contrārietāt-*), from *contrārius,* CONTRARY.]

con·trar·i·ous (kən-trâr′ē-əs) *adj. Archaic.* Perverse; contrary; adverse. [Middle English, from Medieval Latin *contrāriōsus,* from *contrārius,* CONTRARY.] —**con·trar·i·ous·ly** *adv.*

con·trar·i·wise (kŏn′trĕr′ē-wīz′, kən-trâr′ē-) *adv.* **1.** From a contrasting point of view. **2.** In the opposite way or reverse order. **3.** Contrarily; perversely.

con·tra·ry (kŏn′trĕr′ē; *in sense 4 also* kən-trâr′ē) *adj.* **1.** Opposed, as in character or purpose; completely different: *contrary beliefs.* **2.** Opposite in direction or position. **3.** Adverse; unfavorable: *contrary winds.* **4.** Given to acting or speaking in opposition to others; obstinate; willful. —**contrary to.** In opposition to; despite: *contrary to my request, she left early.* —See Synonyms at **opposite.**
~*n., pl.* **contraries.** **1.** That which is contrary; the opposite. **2.** Either of two contrary, opposing, or incompatible things or conditions. **3.** *Logic.* A proposition related to another in such a way that if the latter is true, the former must be false, but if the latter is false, the former is not necessarily true. In this sense, compare **contradictory.** —**by contraries.** In opposition to what is expected. —**on the contrary.** Quite the opposite; in complete disagreement; conversely. —**to the contrary.** To a contrasting or opposite effect: *in the absence of any evidence to the contrary.*
~*adv.* In opposition; contrariwise. [Middle English *contrarie,* from Old French *contraire,* from Latin *contrārius,* from *contrā,* against.] —**con·tra·ri·ly** *adv.* —**con·tra·ri·ness** *n.*
Synonyms: *adverse, obstinate, perverse, stubborn, wayward, willful.*

con·trast (kən-trăst′) *v.* **-trasted, -trasting, -trasts.** —*tr.* To set in opposition or compare in order to show differences: *contrast one style of writing with another.* —*intr.* To show differences or differing qualities when compared.
~*n.* (kŏn′trăst′). **1.** The act of contrasting or the state of being contrasted. Often used in the phrases *by contrast, in contrast with,* and *in contrast to.* **2.** A striking dissimilarity between things compared. **3.** Something that shows a striking dissimilarity when compared to something else. **4.** In a work of art, the use of opposing elements, such as colors, forms, or lines, in proximity to produce an effect. **5.** The extent of difference between the light and dark areas of a photographic image or television picture. [French *contrester, contraster,* to contrast, resist, from Italian *contrastare,* from Medieval Latin *contrāstāre* : Latin *contrā-*, against + *stāre,* to stand.] —**con·trast·a·ble** *adj.* —**con·trast·ing·ly** *adv.*
Usage: As a verb, *contrast* is usually followed by *with.* As a noun the usual preposition is *between* (*the contrast between X and Y*), but *with* and *to* are also used (*the contrast with last year; as a contrast to his father.*). The phrase *in contrast* is usually followed by *with,* but *to* is also used, especially when the notion of opposition is being stressed.

con·tras·tive (kən-trăs′tĭv) *adj.* Tending to or resulting in contrast. —**con·tras·tive·ly** *adv.*

con·trast·y (kŏn′trăs′tē) *adj. Photography.* Having or producing sharp contrasts between light and dark.

con·tra·sug·gest·ible (kŏn′trə-səg-jĕs′tə-bəl) *adj. Psychology.* Tending to do or believe the opposite in response to a suggestion.

con·tra·vene (kŏn′trə-vēn′) *tr.v.* **-vened, -vening, -venes.** **1.** To act or be counter to (especially laws or regulations); violate; infringe. **2.** To oppose in argument. [Old French *contravenir,* from Late Latin *contrāvenīre,* to come against, oppose : Latin *contrā-*, against + *venīre,* to come.] —**con·tra·ven·er** *n.*

con·tra·ven·tion (kŏn′trə-vĕn′shən) *n.* An act of contravening; a violation; an infringement.

con·tre·danse, con·tra·dance (kŏn′trə-dăns′, -däns′; *French* kôN-trə-däNs′) *n.* **1.** A folk dance performed in two lines with the partners facing each other. **2.** The music for such a dance. [French, from English COUNTRY DANCE (influenced by French *contre,* against, opposite, because the partners face each other).]

con·tre·temps (kŏn′trə-täN′; *French* kôN-trə-täN′) *n., pl.* **contretemps** (-täNz′; *French* -täN′). **1.** An inopportune or embarrassing occurrence; a mishap. **2.** An argument or confrontation. [French : *contre-*, against, from Latin *contrā-* + *temps,* time, from Latin *tempus.*]

con·trib·ute (kən-trĭb′yo͞ot) *v.* **-uted, -uting, -utes.** —*tr.* **1.** To give or supply in common with others; give to a common fund or for a common purpose. **2.** To submit (an article, for example) for inclusion in a publication. —*intr.* **1.** To make a contribution. **2.** To act as a significant factor; play an important part. Used with *to*: *We have all contributed to his failure.* **3.** To submit material for publication. [Latin *contribuere,* to bring together, unite, collect : *com-*, together + *tribuere,* to allot, grant (see **tribute**).] —**con·trib·ut·a·ble** *adj.* —**con·trib·u·tive** *adj.* —**con·trib·u·tive·ly** *adv.* —**con·trib·u·tive·ness** *n.*

con·tri·bu·tion (kŏn′trə-byo͞o′shən) *n.* **1.** The act of contributing. **2.** Something contributed, as a piece of writing submitted to a publication or money donated to a cause. **3.** An impost or levy for a special, especially military, purpose.

con·trib·u·tor (kən-trĭb′yə-tər) *n.* One who contributes; especially, one who contributes articles or features to a newspaper or magazine.

con·trib·u·to·ry (kən-trĭb′yə-tôr′ē, -tōr′ē) *adj.* **1.** Pertaining to or involving a contribution. **2.** Contributing toward a result. **3.** Designating an employees' pension fund to which both employer and employee make contributions. **4.** Subject to an impost or levy.
~*n., pl.* **contributories.** One that contributes.

contributory negligence *n. Law.* Carelessness on the part of the injured party as a factor in causing the injury suffered.

con·trite (kən-trīt′, kŏn′trīt′) *adj.* **1.** Humbled by guilt and repentant for one's sins; penitent; remorseful. **2.** Arising from contrition: *contrite resolutions.* [Middle English *contrit,* from Old French, from Medieval Latin *contrītus,* "broken in spirit," repentant, from Latin, past participle of *conterere,* to bruise, grind : *com-* (intensive) + *terere,* to rub, grind.] —**con·trite·ly** *adv.* —**con·trite·ness** *n.*

con·tri·tion (kən-trĭsh′ən) *n.* **1.** Sincere remorse for wrongdoing. **2.** *Theology.* Repentance for sin, as *perfect contrition,* repentance with a sincere desire to amend, arising from pure love of God, or *imperfect contrition,* repentance arising from a motive less than the pure love of God. Compare **attrition.**

con·tri·vance (kən-trī′vəns) *n.* **1. a.** The act or manner of contriving. **b.** The ability to contrive; inventiveness. **2.** Something contrived, such as a mechanical device or a clever plan.

con·trive (kən-trīv′) *v.* **-trived, -triving, -trives.** —*tr.* **1.** To plan or devise with cleverness or ingenuity. **2.** To plot with evil intent; scheme: *contrived his murder.* **3.** To invent or fabricate, especially by improvisation: *had to contrive excuses on the spur of the moment.* **4.** To manage or succeed in, as by scheming. —*intr.* To plot or scheme. [Middle English *contreven, controven,* from Old French *controver,* from Late Latin *contropāre,* to represent figuratively, compare : Latin *com-*, together + *tropus,* figure of speech, trope, from Greek *tropos,* turn, manner, style.] —**con·triv·a·ble** *adj.* —**con·triv·er** *n.*

con·trived (kən-trīvd′) *adj.* Achieved by artifice; artificial; unnatural. —**con·triv·ed·ly** (kən-trī′vĭd-lē) *adv.*

con·trol (kən-trōl′) *tr.v.* **-trolled, -trolling, -trols.** **1. a.** To exercise authority or a dominating influence over; direct: *control an empire.* **b.** To regulate; operate: *This button controls the lights.* **2.** To hold in restraint; check: *could not control her anger.* **3.** To reduce the severity or spread of: *control an outbreak of measles.* **4.** To verify or regulate (a scientific experiment) by conducting a parallel experiment in which the variable to be tested is absent or held constant, or by comparing with some other standard. —See Synonyms at **conduct.**
~*n.* **1.** Authority or ability to regulate, direct, restrain, or dominate: *under the control of the local authority; lost control of her temper; remained in control of the project.* **2.** An act or means of regulating or verifying; a check or curb: *go through passport control; price controls.* **3. a.** A standard of comparison for checking or verifying the results of an experiment. **b.** An individual or group used as a standard of comparison in a control experiment. Also used adjectivally: *a control group.* **4.** Any of a set of instruments used to operate, regulate, or guide a machine or vehicle. Also used adjectivally: *control panel.* **5.** The organization, personnel, and equipment used in directing a space flight: *control mission.* **6.** In spiritualism, a spirit presumed to act through a medium. [Middle English *controllen,* from Old French *cont(r)eroller,* from Medieval Latin *contrārotulāre,* to check by a counter roll or duplicate register, from

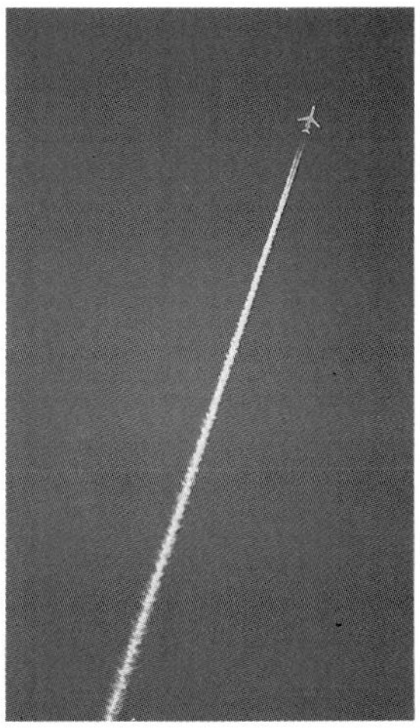

contrail *Water vapor from the exhaust of a Boeing 727 condenses in the chill of high-altitude air to form a white contrail of water droplets and ice crystals behind the jet. The same condensation principle is at work in the creation of clouds.*

contrārotulus, counter roll, duplicate register : Latin *contrā-,* against, opposite + *rotulus,* roll, "little wheel," from *rota,* wheel.] —**con·trol·la·bil·i·ty** *n.* —**con·trol·la·ble** *adj.*

control chart *n. Statistics.* A graph of a quantitative characteristic of a manufacturing process, usually determined from small, periodically repeated samples and evaluated with respect to control limits rendered as parallel horizontal lines above and below a line representing the expected or average value of the characteristic.

control experiment *n.* An experiment designed to check or verify a parallel experiment or as part of a set of experiments testing the effects of a variable or variables, in which the variable factors are controlled so that the effects of changing one at a time can be observed.

con·trolled response (kən-trōld′) *n.* A response to a military attack by limited military means in an effort to avoid nuclear war.

con·trol·ler (kən-trō′lər) *n.* Also **comp·trol·ler** (kən-trō′lər) (for sense 2). **1.** One who controls. **2.** An officer who audits accounts and supervises the financial affairs of a corporation or government body. **3.** A regulating mechanism, as in a vehicle or electrical device.

control rod *n. Physics.* One of a number of rods that can be moved into or out of the core of a nuclear reactor, used to control the rate of the reaction. They are made of a material that absorbs neutrons, such as boron.

control stick *n.* A lever used in small aircraft to control the angle of the elevators and ailerons; a joystick.

control surface *n.* A movable airfoil, especially a rudder, aileron, or elevator, used to control or guide an aircraft, guided missile, or rocket.

control tower *n.* A usually glass-enclosed tower at an airport from which air traffic is controlled by radio.

con·tro·ver·sial (kŏn′trə-vûr′shəl) *adj.* **1.** Subject to, surrounded by, or likely to produce controversy. **2.** Fond of controversy; disputatious. —**con·tro·ver·sial·ist** *n.* —**con·tro·ver·sial·ly** *adv.*

con·tro·ver·sy (kŏn′trə-vûr′sē) *n., pl.* **-sies. 1.** A dispute or debate, especially a lengthy and public one, between sides holding opposing views. **2.** Disputation; contention: *an affair surrounded by controversy.* —See Synonyms at **argument.** [Middle English *controversie,* from Latin *contrōversia,* from *contrōversus,* turned against, disputed : *contrō-,* variant of *contrā-,* against + *versus,* past participle of *vertere,* to turn.]

con·tro·vert (kŏn′trə-vûrt′) *tr.v.* **-verted, -verting, -verts. 1.** To raise arguments against; voice opposition to; deny. **2.** To argue or dispute about; debate. [From CONTROVERSY (by analogy with CONVERT, REVERT).] —**con·tro·vert·i·ble** *adj.*

con·tu·ma·cious (kŏn′tŏŏ-mā′shəs, -tyŏŏ-) *adj.* Obstinately disobedient or rebellious; insubordinate. —**con·tu·ma·cious·ly** *adv.* —**con·tu·ma·cious·ness** *n.*

con·tu·ma·cy (kŏn′tŏŏ-mə-sē, -tyŏŏ-) *n., pl.* **-cies. 1.** Obstinate or contemptuous resistance to authority. **2.** Willful disobedience to a court order. [Middle English *contumacie,* from Latin *contumācia,* from *contumāx,* stubborn, disobedient.]

con·tu·me·ly (kŏn′tŏŏ-mə-lē, -tyŏŏ-, kən-tŏŏ′mə-lē, -tyŏŏ′-) *n., pl.* **-lies. 1.** Rudeness or contempt in behavior or speech; insolence. **2.** An insulting remark or act. [Middle English *contumelie,* from Old French, from Latin *contumēlia,* insult, reproach.] —**con·tu·me·li·ous** (kŏn′tŏŏ-mē′lē-əs, -tyŏŏ-) *adj.* —**con·tu·me·li·ous·ly** *adv.*

con·tuse (kən-tŏŏz′, -tyŏŏz′) *tr.v.* **-tused, -tusing, -tuses.** To injure without breaking the skin; bruise. [Middle English *contusen,* from Old French *contuser,* from Latin *contundere* (past participle *contūsus*), to beat, pound : *com-* (intensive) + *tundere,* to beat.]

con·tu·sion (kən-tŏŏ′zhən, -tyŏŏ′-) *n.* An injury in which the skin is not broken; a bruise.

co·nun·drum (kə-nŭn′drəm) *n.* **1.** A riddle in which a fanciful question is answered by a pun. **2.** A puzzling problem or question admitting of no satisfactory solution. [16th century : perhaps originally a mock-Latin university slang word.]

con·ur·ba·tion (kŏn′ər-bā′shən) *n.* A large urban sprawl including smaller towns that have spread and joined together. [CON- + Latin *urbs,* city (see **urban**) + -ATION.]

con·va·lesce (kŏn′və-lĕs′) *intr.v.* **-lesced, -lescing, -lesces.** To return to health after illness, particularly by resting; recuperate. [Latin *convalēscere* : *com-* (intensive) + *valēscere,* to grow strong, from *valēre,* to be strong or well.]

con·va·les·cence (kŏn′və-lĕs′əns) *n.* **1.** Gradual return to health and strength after illness, particularly by resting. **2.** The period needed for this.

con·va·les·cent (kŏn′və-lĕs′ənt) *n.* One who is regaining health and strength after illness. —**con·va·les·cent** *adj.*

con·vect (kən-vĕkt′) *v.* **-vected, -vecting, -vects.** —*tr.* To transfer (heat) by convection. —*intr.* To undergo convection.

con·vec·tion (kən-vĕk′shən) *n.* **1.** The act or process of transmitting or conveying. **2.** *Physics.* **a.** Heat transfer by fluid motion between regions of unequal density that result from nonuniform heating. Also called "natural convection." **b.** Fluid motion caused by an external force such as a fan. Also called "forced convection." **3.** *Meteorology.* The transfer of heat or other atmospheric properties by massive motion within the atmosphere, especially by such motion directed upward. [Late Latin *convectiō* (stem *convectiōn-*), from *convehere,* to carry together, bring along : *com-,* together + *vehere,* to carry.] —**con·vec·tion·al** *adj.* —**con·vec·tive** *adj.* —**con·vec·tive·ly** *adv.*

con·vec·tor (kən-vĕk′tər) *n.* A heating unit typically having an enclosed electrically heated element from which warm air circulates by natural convection.

con·vene (kən-vēn′) *v.* **-vened, -vening, -venes.** —*intr.* To assemble, usually for an official or public purpose; meet formally. —*tr.* **1.** To cause to come together or assemble; convoke. **2.** To summon to appear, as before a court of law. [Middle English *convenen,* from Old French *convenir,* to come together, meet, hence agree, be suitable, from Latin *convenīre* : *com-,* together + *venīre,* to come.] —**con·ven·a·ble** *adj.*

con·ven·er, con·ve·nor (kən-vē′nər) *n.* A person, usually elected, who convenes or is the chairperson of a meeting, committee, or the like.

con·ven·ience (kən-vēn′yəns) *n.* **1.** The quality of being convenient; suitability or handiness. **2.** Personal comfort or advantage: *for the passenger's convenience.* **3.** A suitable time: *Call at your convenience.* **4.** Something that increases comfort or makes work less difficult, as an appliance or service. **5.** *Chiefly British.* A lavatory.

convenience food *n.* Packaged food requiring minimal preparation.

con·ven·ien·cy (kən-vēn′yən-sē) *n., pl.* **-cies.** *Archaic.* Convenience.

con·ven·ient (kən-vēn′yənt) *adj.* **1.** Suited or favorable to one's comfort, purpose, or needs. **2.** Easy to reach; accessible. **3.** *Obsolete.* Fitting and proper; appropriate. [Middle English, from Latin *conveniēns* (stem *convenient-*), present participle of *convenīre,* to be suitable. See **convene.**] —**con·ven·ient·ly** *adv.*

con·vent (kŏn′vənt, -vĕnt′) *n.* **1.** A community, especially of nuns, bound by vows to a religious life under a superior. **2.** The building or buildings occupied by such a community; especially, a nunnery. **3.** A convent school. [Middle English *covent,* from Old French, from Medieval Latin *conventus,* from Latin, a coming together, assembly, from *convenīre,* to come together, CONVENE.]

convent school *n.* A school in which the teaching staff are nuns.

con·ven·ti·cle (kən-vĕn′tĭ-kəl) *n.* **1.** A religious meeting, especially a secret or illegal one, such as those held by dissenters in England and Scotland in the 16th and 17th centuries. **2.** A building used for such a meeting. [Middle English, from Latin *conventiculum,* a place of meeting, diminutive of *conventus,* assembly, CONVENT.] —**con·ven·ti·cler** *n.*

con·ven·tion (kən-vĕn′shən) *n.* **1.** A formal assembly or meeting of members, representatives, or delegates of a group, such as a political party or trade union. **2.** The body of persons attending such an assembly. **3.** An agreement or compact; especially, an international agreement, less formal than a treaty, dealing with a specific subject, as the treatment of war prisoners. **4.** General agreement on or acceptance of certain practices or attitudes. **5.** A practice or procedure widely established in a group, especially in social matters; a custom. **6.** A widely used and accepted device or technique, as in drama, literature, or painting. **7.** In card games, a prearranged method of bidding or play that conveys information to partners. [Middle English *convencioun,* from Old French *convention,* from Latin *conventiō* (stem *conventiōn-*), assembly, agreement, from *convenīre,* to come together, CONVENE.]

con·ven·tion·al (kən-vĕn′shən-əl) *adj.* **1.** Developed, established, or approved by general usage; customary. **2.** Conforming to or rigidly following established practice or accepted standards; not adventurous or spontaneous. **3.** Marked by or dependent upon convention to the point of artificiality; stereotyped; trite. **4.** *Art.* Represented in simplified or abstract form. **5.** *Law.* Based upon mutual consent or agreement; contractual. **6.** Of or having to do with an assembly. **7.** Using means other than nuclear power: *conventional warfare.* —**con·ven·tion·al·ly** *adv.*

conventional current *n.* An electric current that flows from a positive point to a negative, as distinguished from the actual current, which is a flow of electrons in the opposite direction.

con·ven·tion·al·ism (kən-vĕn′shən-əl-ĭz′əm) *n.* **1.** Advocacy of or adherence to existing conventions. **2.** *Philosophy.* The view that principles and laws, especially in science, are formulated and adopted according to convention and conventional ways of interpreting evidence rather than purely by reason. —**con·ven·tion·al·ist** *n.*

con·ven·tion·al·i·ty (kən-vĕn′shən-ăl′ə-tē) *n., pl.* **-ties. 1.** The state, quality, or character of being conventional. **2.** A conventional act, principle, or practice. **3.** Adherence to convention.

con·ven·tion·al·ize (kən-vĕn′shən-əl-īz′) *tr.v.* **-ized, -izing, -izes.** To make conventional. —**con·ven·tion·al·i·za·tion** *n.*

conventional wisdom *n.* A body of established, received ideas accepted uncritically.

con·ven·tion·eer, con·ven·tion·er (kən-vĕn′shə-nîr′) *n.* One who attends a convention.

con·ven·tu·al (kən-vĕn′chŏŏ-əl) *n.* **1.** A member of a convent. **2. Conventual.** A member of a branch of the Franciscan order that permits the accumulation and possession of common property. —**con·ven·tu·al** *adj.*

con·verge (kən-vûrj′) *v.* **-verged, -verging, -verges.** —*intr.* **1.** To approach the same point from different directions; tend toward a meeting or intersection. **2.** To tend or move toward union or toward a common conclusion or result. **3.** *Mathematics.* To approach a limit. Compare **diverge.** —*tr.* To cause to converge. [Late Latin *convergere,* to incline together : Latin *com-,* together + *vergere,* to bend, turn, incline.]

con·ver·gence (kən-vûr′jəns) *n.* Also **con·ver·gen·cy** (-jən-sē), *pl.* **-cies. 1.** The act, condition, quality, or fact of converging. **2.** *Mathematics.* The property or manner of approaching a limit such as a point, line, surface, or value. **3.** The point or degree of converging. **4.** *Physiology.* The coordinated turning of the eyes inward to focus on a nearby point. **5.** *Biology.* The adaptive evolution of superficially similar structures, such as the wings of birds and insects, in unrelated species subjected to similar environments. Also called "convergent evolution." **6.** *Meteorology.* A condition characterized by a horizontal net inflow of air over a region, which may be compensated by an upward air current giving rise to clouds and rain. **—con·ver·gent** *adj.*

convergent thinking *n. Psychology.* A type of thinking characterized by the use of logical reasoning to arrive at a single correct solution to a problem. Compare **divergent thinking.**

con·vers·a·ble (kən-vûr′sə-bəl) *adj.* Easy to talk to; affable. **—con·vers·a·ble·ness** *n.*

con·ver·sant (kən-vûr′sənt, kŏn′vər-) *adj.* Familiar, as by study or experience: *conversant with Roman history.* [Middle English *conversaunt,* from Old French *conversant,* from Latin *conversāns* (stem *conversant-*), present participle of *conversārī,* to associate with, CONVERSE.] **—con·ver·sance, con·ver·san·cy** *n.* **—con·ver·sant·ly** *adv.*

con·ver·sa·tion (kŏn′vər-sā′shən) *n.* **1.** An informal spoken exchange of thoughts and feelings; a talk. **2.** *Archaic.* Close acquaintance or association. **3.** *Archaic.* Manner of life; behavior. **4.** *Archaic.* Sexual intercourse. **—make conversation.** To talk for the sake of politeness.

con·ver·sa·tion·al (kŏn′vər-sā′shən-əl) *adj.* **1.** Of, pertaining to, or in the style of conversation; informal. **2.** Adept at or given to conversation. **—con·ver·sa·tion·al·ly** *adv.*

con·ver·sa·tion·al·ist (kŏn′vər-sā′shən-əl-ĭst) *n.* Also **con·ver·sa·tion·ist** (-shən-ĭst). One given to or skilled at conversation.

conversation piece *n.* **1.** A type of painting, especially popular in the 18th century, depicting a group of fashionable people. **2.** An unusual object that arouses comment or interest.

con·ver·sa·zi·o·ne (kŏn′vər-sät′sē-ō′nē) *n., pl.* **-nes** or **-ni** (-nē). A meeting for conversation or for discussion, especially of the arts. [Italian, "conversation."]

con·verse¹ (kən-vûrs′) *intr.v.* **-versed, -versing, -verses. 1.** To engage in spoken exchange of thoughts and feelings; talk. **2.** *Archaic.* To consort; associate. —See Synonyms at **speak.**
~n. (kŏn′vûrs′). Spoken interchange of thoughts and feelings; conversation. [Middle English *conversen,* to dwell, associate with, from Old French *converser,* from Latin *conversārī,* to associate with : *com-,* with + *versārī,* to live, occupy oneself, from *versāre,* frequentative of *vertere,* to turn.]

con·verse² (kən-vûrs′, kŏn′vûrs′) *adj.* Reversed, as in position, order, or action; contrary.
~n. (kŏn′vûrs′). **1.** Something that is contrary; the opposite. **2.** *Logic.* A proposition obtained by conversion. [Latin *conversus,* past participle of *convertere,* to turn around. See **convert.**] **—con·verse·ly** (kən-vûrs′lē) *adv.*

con·ver·sion (kən-vûr′zhən, -shən) *n.* **1.** The act of converting or the state of being converted. **2.** Something that has been changed from one use or form to another. **3.** A change in which one adopts a new religion. **4.** A change from one belief, opinion, or practice to another. **5.** *Law.* **a.** The unlawful appropriation of another's property. **b.** The changing of real property to personal property or vice versa. **6.** *Finance.* The exchange of one type of security or currency for another. **7.** *Logic.* The interchange of the subject and predicate of a proposition. **8.** *Football.* A successful attempt for an extra score after making a touchdown. **9.** *Psychiatry.* The symbolic manifestation of repressed ideas or impulses in motor or sensory abnormalities such as paralysis. Also called "conversion hysteria." **10.** *Physics.* The process in which an atomic nucleus in an excited state of energy changes to a lower state, the energy being taken up by an orbiting electron that is ejected from the atom. Also called "internal conversion." **11.** The act or result of converting a quantity in one system of units into another system of units, as meters into feet and inches. [Middle English *conversioun,* from Old French *conversion,* from Latin *conversiō* (stem *conversiōn-*), from *convertere,* to turn about, CONVERT.] **—con·ver·sion·al, con·ver·sion·ar·y** *adj.*

conversion factor *n.* A numerical factor used to multiply or divide a quantity in order to convert it from one system of units into another.

con·vert (kən-vûrt′) *v.* **-verted, -verting, -verts.** *—tr.* **1.** To change into another form, substance, state, or product; transform; transmute: *convert water into ice.* **2.** To persuade or induce to adopt a particular religion, belief, or practice. **3. a.** To change from one use to another; adapt to a new or different purpose: *converted the bedroom into a study.* **b.** To make structural alterations to (a building). **4.** To exchange for something of equal value. **5.** *Finance.* To exchange (a security or bond, for example) by substituting an equivalent in another form. **6.** To express (a quantity) in alternative units. **7.** *Logic.* To transform (a proposition) by conversion. **8.** *Law.* **a.** To appropriate without right (another's property) to one's own use. **b.** To change (property) from real to personal, from joint to separate, or vice versa. *—intr.* **1.** To be converted or convertible; undergo a change: *a sofa that converts into a bed.* **2.** *Football.* To make a conversion. —See Synonyms at **change.**
~n. (kŏn′vûrt′). One who has been converted, especially from one religion or belief to another. [Middle English *converten,* from Old French *convertir,* from Medieval Latin *convertere,* to convert religiously, from Latin, to turn around, transform : *com-* (intensive) + *vertere,* to turn.]

con·vert·er, con·ver·tor (kən-vûr′tər) *n.* **1.** One that converts. **2.** A furnace in which pig iron is converted into steel by the Bessemer process. **3. a.** A device that changes electric current from one kind to another, especially one that converts direct current into alternating current. **b.** A radio device that changes one frequency to another. **c.** A device that transforms information from one code to another. **4.** A converter reactor.

converter reactor *n.* A nuclear reactor designed to change one type of nuclear fuel into another. Also called "converter." Compare **breeder reactor.**

con·vert·i·ble (kən-vûr′tə-bəl) *adj.* **1.** Capable of being converted. **2.** Having a top that may be folded back or removed: *a convertible automobile.* **3.** *Finance.* Capable of being lawfully exchanged for gold or another currency: *dollars convertible into pounds.*
~n. **1.** A convertible automobile. **2.** Something that can be converted. **—con·vert·i·bil·i·ty, con·vert·i·ble·ness** *n.* **—con·vert·i·bly** *adv.*

con·vert·i·plane, con·vert·a·plane (kən-vûr′tə-plān′) *n.* An airplane that is designed to fly vertically as well as forward. [CONVERTI(BLE) + (AIR)PLANE.]

con·vex (kŏn′vĕks′, kən-vĕks′) *adj.* **1.** Having a surface or boundary that curves or bulges outward, as the exterior of a sphere. Compare **concave. 2. a.** Thicker at the center than at the edges. Said of a lens. **b.** Having a convex reflecting surface. Said of a mirror. **3.** *Mathematics.* Designating a set in which the line segment between any two points is also contained in the set. [Latin *convexus,* arched, convex.] **—con·vex·ly** *adv.*

con·vex·i·ty (kən-vĕk′sə-tē) *n., pl.* **-ties. 1.** The state of being convex. **2.** A convex surface, body, part, or line.

con·vex·o-con·cave (kən-vĕk′sō-kən-kāv′) *adj.* **1. Concavo-convex** *(see).* **2.** *Optics.* Having greater convex than concave curvature. Said of a lens.

con·vex·o-con·vex (kən-vĕk′sō-kən-vĕks′) *adj.* Convex on both sides; doubly convex; biconvex.

con·vey (kən-vā′) *tr.v.* **-veyed, -veying, -veys. 1.** To take or carry from one place to another; transport. **2.** To serve as a medium of transmission for; conduct; transmit. **3.** To communicate or make known: *"a look intended to convey sympathetic comprehension"* (Saki). **4.** *Law.* To transfer ownership of or title to. **5.** *Obsolete.* To steal. [Middle English *conveien,* from Old French *conveier,* from Medieval Latin *conviāre,* to go with, escort : Latin *com-,* with + *via,* way.] **—con·vey·a·ble** *adj.*

Synonyms: *bear, carry, convey, transfer, transmit, transport.*

con·vey·ance (kən-vā′əns) *n.* **1.** The act of transporting, transmitting, or communicating. **2.** A means of conveying; especially, a vehicle such as a bus. **3.** *Law.* **a.** The transfer of title to property from one person to another. **b.** The document by which this transfer is effected.

con·vey·anc·ing (kən-vā′ən-sĭng) *n.* **1.** The branch of legal practice dealing with the conveyance of property. **2.** An act or instance of conveying property. **—con·vey·anc·er** *n.*

con·vey·or, con·vey·er (kən-vā′ər) *n.* **1.** One that conveys. **2.** Any mechanical contrivance, especially a conveyor belt, that transports materials.

conveyor belt *n.* A continuous moving belt, usually driven by rollers, that transports objects or packages from one place to another, as on an assembly line in a factory. Also called "belt."

con·vict (kən-vĭkt′) *tr.v.* **-victed, -victing, -victs. 1.** To find or prove (someone) guilty of an offense, especially by the verdict of a court. **2.** To convince (someone) of his own guilt or sinfulness.
~n. (kŏn′vĭkt′). **1.** A person found or declared guilty of an offense or crime. **2.** A person serving a sentence of imprisonment. [Middle English *convicten,* from Latin *convincere* (past participle *convictus*), to prove guilty, CONVINCE.]

con·vic·tion (kən-vĭk′shən) *n.* **1.** The act or process of finding or proving guilty of an offense. **2.** The state or an instance of being convicted: *a string of previous convictions.* **3.** The act or process of convincing. **4.** The state of being convinced or persuaded. **5.** A fixed or strong belief. **6.** The quality of being convincing; plausibility: *His defense of government policy doesn't carry much conviction.* —See Synonyms at **certainty, opinion. —con·vic·tion·al** *adj.*

con·vince (kən-vĭns′) *tr.v.* **-vinced, -vincing, -vinces.** To bring by argument and evidence to belief; cause to believe something; persuade: *convinced him to tell the truth; I am convinced that he is evil; convince them of our sincerity.* —See Synonyms at **persuade.** [Latin *convincere,* to overcome, refute, prove guilty : *com-* (intensive) + *vincere,* to conquer, overcome.] **—con·vince·ment** *n.* **—con·vinc·er** *n.* **—con·vin·ci·ble** *adj.*

con·vinc·ing (kən-vĭn′sĭng) *adj.* **1.** Persuading or satisfying by evidence or argument. **2.** Believable; plausible: *a convincing story.* —See Synonyms at **valid. —con·vinc·ing·ly** *adv.* **—con·vinc·ing·ness** *n.*

con·viv·i·al (kən-vĭv′ē-əl) *adj.* **1.** Fond of feasting, drinking, and good company; sociable; jovial. **2.** Appropriate to or of the nature of a festive occasion; warm and friendly: *a convivial atmosphere at the office party.* —See Synonyms at **jolly.** [Late Latin *convīviālis,* from Latin *convīvium,* "a living together," banquet : *com-,* together + *vīvere,* to live.] **—con·viv·i·al·i·ty** (kən-vĭv′ē-ăl′ə-tē) *n.* **—con·viv·i·al·ly** *adv.*

con·vo·ca·tion (kŏn′vō-kā′shən) *n.* **1.** The act of convoking or calling together. **2.** A group of people assembled by summons. **3.** *Anglican Church.* A clerical assembly similar to a synod, but assembling only when called. **4.** *Episcopal Church.* **a.** An assembly of the clergy and representative laity of a section of a diocese.

PRONUNCIATION KEY

ă, pat; ā, pay; âr, care;
ä, father, are; b, bib;
ch, church; d, deed; ĕ, pet;
ē, be; f, fife; g, gag; h, hat;
hw, which; ĭ, pit; ī, pie;
îr, pier; j, judge; k, kick;
l, lid, needle; m, mum;
n, no, sudden; ng, thing;
ŏ, pot; ō, toe; ô, paw, for;
oi, noise; ou, out; ŏŏ, book;
ōō, boot; p, pop; r, roar;
s, sauce; sh, ship, dish;
t, tight; th, thin, path;
th, this, bathe; ŭ, cut; ûr, fur;
v, valve; w, with; y, yes;
z, zebra, size; zh, vision;
ə, about, item, edible,
gallop, circus, peaceful

IN FOREIGN WORDS:

à, *Fr.* ami; œ, *Fr.* feu, *Ger.* schön; ü, *Fr.* tu, *Ger.* über; KH, *Ger.* ich, *Scot.* loch; N, *Fr.* bon; y′, *Fr.* Compiègne

STRESS MARKS:

Primary stress: ′
in·cite′ (ĭn-sīt′)
Secondary stress: ′
in′sight′ (ĭn′sīt′)

b. The district represented at such an assembly. **5.** In certain British universities, a deliberative or legislative assembly, typically composed of graduates of the university. Compare **senate**, **congregation.** —**con·vo·ca·tion·al** *adj.*

con·voke (kən-vōk′) *tr.v.* **-voked, -voking, -vokes.** To cause to assemble; convene. [Old French *convoquer*, from Latin *convocāre*, to call together, summon : *com-*, together + *vocāre*, to call.] —**con·vok·er** *n.*

con·vo·lute (kŏn′və-lōōt′) *adj.* Rolled or folded together with one part over another; twisted; coiled.
~*v.* **convoluted, -luting, -lutes.** —*tr.* To coil or wind around. —*intr.* To coil up. [Latin *convolūtus*, past participle of *convolvere*, to CONVOLVE.] —**con·vo·lute·ly** *adv.*

con·vo·lut·ed (kŏn′və-lōō′tĭd) *adj.* **1.** Exhibiting convolutions; coiled; twisted. **2. a.** Intricate; complicated. **b.** Difficult to understand because lengthy, roundabout, or tortuous: *a convoluted explanation.*

con·vo·lu·tion (kŏn′və-lōō′shən) *n.* **1. a.** A coiling or twisting together. **b.** An entangling or interlacing, so as to make intricate. **2.** Any of the convex folds of the surface of the brain. See **gyrus.** **3.** *Mathematics.* A function that measures how the shape of one function affects another, defined by the integral of the product $g(t)f(x-t)$ with respect to the variable t.

con·volve (kən-vŏlv′) *v.* **-volved, -volving, -volves.** —*tr.* To roll together; coil up. —*intr.* To form convolutions. [Latin *convolvere*, to roll together, enwrap : *com-*, together + *volvere*, to roll.]

con·vol·vu·lus (kən-vŏl′vyə-ləs) *n., pl.* **-luses** (-lī′). Any of several trailing or twining plants of the genus *Convolvulus,* which includes the bindweeds. [New Latin *Convolvulus,* from Latin *convolvere,* bindweed, from *convolvere,* to interweave, CONVOLVE.]

con·voy (kŏn′voi′, kən-voi′) *tr.v.* **-voyed, -voying, -voys.** To accompany on the way for protection, either by sea or land; escort.
~*n.* (kŏn′voi′). **1.** An accompanying and protecting force; a convoying vessel, fleet, or troop. **2.** That which is convoyed, such as ships or troops. **3.** The act of convoying. **4.** A group, as of vehicles, traveling together. [Middle English *convoyen, conveien,* from Old French *convoier, conveier,* to CONVEY.]

con·vul·sant (kən-vŭl′sənt) *n.* A drug or other agent that produces convulsions. —**con·vul·sant** *adj.*

con·vulse (kən-vŭls′) *tr.v.* **-vulsed, -vulsing, -vulses. 1.** To shake or agitate violently. **2.** To cause to shake with laughter. **3.** To affect with irregular and involuntary muscular contractions; throw into convulsions. [From Latin *convellere* (past participle *convulsus*), to pull violently, wrest : *com-* (intensive) + *vellere,* to pull.]

con·vul·sion (kən-vŭl′shən) *n.* **1.** A violent involuntary contraction or series of contractions of the muscles. **2.** An uncontrolled fit of laughter. **3.** A violent turmoil.

con·vul·sion·ar·y (kən-vŭl′shən-ĕr′ē) *adj.* Of, pertaining to, affected with, or of the nature of convulsions.
~*n., pl.* **convulsionaries.** A person affected with convulsions, especially as a result of religious fervor.

con·vul·sive (kən-vŭl′sĭv) *adj.* **1.** Marked by or of the nature of convulsions. **2.** Having or producing convulsions. —**con·vul·sive·ly** *adv.* —**con·vul·sive·ness** *n.*

Con·wy (kŏn′wē). Formerly **Con·way** (-wā). Town in Gwynedd, near the mouth of the Conwy River in northwest Wales.

co·ny (kō′nē, kŭn′ē) *n., pl.* **-nies.** Also **co·ney** *pl.* **-neys. 1.** A rabbit, especially the Old World species *Oryctolagus cuniculus.* **2.** The fur of a rabbit. **3.** A mammal, the **pika** (see). **4.** In the Old Testament, a mammal, the **hyrax** (see). Deuteronomy 14:7. [Middle English *coni(n)g, cunin,* from Old French *conin, conil,* from Latin *cunīculus,* rabbit.]

coo (kōō) *v.* **cooed, cooing, coos.** —*intr.* **1.** To utter the characteristic murmuring sound of a dove or pigeon, or a sound resembling this. **2.** To talk amorously or fondly in murmurs. Usually used in the phrase *bill and coo.* —*tr.* To utter gently or amorously, as with a murmuring sound.
~*n., pl.* **coos.** The murmuring sound made by a dove or pigeon, or a sound resembling this.
~*interj. Chiefly British.* Used to express surprise, admiration, or amazement. [Imitative.] —**coo·er** *n.*

coo·ee (kōō′ē) *n., pl.* **-ees.** Also **coo·ey** *pl.* **-eys.** A prolonged shrill cry used as a signal by the Australian aborigines and later adopted by the settlers.

cook (kŏŏk) *v.* **cooked, cooking, cooks.** —*tr.* **1.** To prepare for eating by applying heat, as by boiling, frying, or baking. **2.** To subject to heat. **3.** *Informal.* To falsify (accounts, records, or statistics). Used chiefly in the phrase *cook the books.* —*intr.* **1.** To prepare food for eating by applying heat. **2.** To undergo cooking. **3.** *Slang.* To happen, develop, or take place: *What's cooking in town?* —**cook up.** *Informal.* To fabricate; concoct: *cook up an excuse.*
~*n.* A person who prepares food for eating. [Middle English *coken,* from *cok(e),* a cook, Old English *cōc,* from Vulgar Latin *cōcus* (unattested), from Latin *cocus, coquus,* from *coquere,* to cook.]

Cook (kŏŏk), **James,** known as "Captain Cook" (1728–79). British explorer and navigator. From 1768–71 in his ship *Endeavour,* Cook charted the coasts of New Zealand, reached eastern Australia, landed at Botany Bay, and skirted the Great Barrier Reef. On the voyage he conquered scurvy by providing fresh vegetables for his crew. His second voyage (1772–75) reached as far south as the Antarctic Circle, charting Easter Island and most of the major island groups in the South Pacific. On his third voyage (1776–79) he dis-

covered the Sandwich (now Hawaiian) Islands and charted the Bering Strait.

Cook, Mount. *Maori* **A·o·rang·i** (ä-ō-räng′gē). The highest mountain in New Zealand, on the west of South Island in the Southern Alps. It is 3,763 meters (12,346 feet) high.

cook·book (kŏŏk′bŏŏk′) *n.* A book containing recipes and other information about the preparation of food.

cook·er (kŏŏk′ər) *n.* **1.** An appliance or utensil used for cooking: *a pressure cooker.* **2.** A person employed to operate a cooking apparatus in the commercial preparation of food and drink. **3.** *British.* A stove.

cook·er·y (kŏŏk′ər-ē) *n.* **1.** The art or practice of preparing food. **2.** A place for cooking.

cookery book *n. British.* A cookbook.

cook·house (kŏŏk′hous′) *n.* A place or building where the cooking is done, as on a ranch.

cook·ie, cook·y (kŏŏk′ē) *n., pl.* **-ies. 1.** A small, usually flat cake made from sweet dough. **2.** *Scottish.* A bun. [Dutch *koekje,* diminutive of *koek,* cake, from Middle Dutch *koeke.*]

cook·ing (kŏŏk′ĭng) *adj.* **1.** Used in or for cooking: *cooking utensils.* **2.** Suitable primarily for use in cooking: *cooking sherry; cooking apples.*

Cook Islands. An associated state of New Zealand, in the southwest Pacific Ocean. Discovered by Captain Cook (1773), the group comprises 15 islands, including Rarotonga, with Avarua the administrative center.

cook·out (kŏŏk′out′) *n.* An outing or gathering at which a meal is cooked and served outdoors.

Cook Strait. Sea channel between North Island and South Island, New Zealand, 26 to 145 kilometers (16 to 90 miles) wide.

cook·ware (kŏŏk′wâr′) *n.* Utensils used in cooking.

cool (kōōl) *adj.* **cooler, coolest. 1.** Moderately cold; neither warm nor very cold. **2.** Reducing discomfort in hot weather; allowing a feeling of coolness: *a cool blouse.* **3.** Not excited; calm; controlled: *a cool head in a crisis.* **4.** Showing dislike, disdain, or indifference; unenthusiastic; not cordial: *a cool greeting.* **5.** Calmly audacious; impudent: *gave him a cool look and walked away.* **6.** Designating or characteristic of colors, such as blue and green, that produce the impression of coolness. **7.** Marked by a quietly self-possessed, unruffled attitude. **8.** *Slang.* **a.** Excellent; first-rate. **b.** Acceptable; O.K.: *Tonight, if that's cool with you.* **9.** *Informal.* Without exaggeration; entire; full: *He lost a cool million.*
~*v.* **cooled, cooling, cools.** —*tr.* **1.** To make less warm. Often used with *down* or *off.* **2.** To make less ardent, intense, or zealous; calm. —*intr.* **1.** To become less warm. Often used with *down* or *off: We cooled off with a swim.* **2.** To become less ardent, intense, or zealous; become calm. Often used with *down* or *off.* —**cool it.** *Slang.* Calm down; relax. —**cool one's heels.** To be kept waiting.
~*n.* **1.** A cool atmosphere: *the cool of early morning.* **2.** The state or quality of being cool. **3.** *Slang.* Composure: *lose one's cool.* [Middle English *col,* Old English *cōl,* from Germanic.] —**cool·ly** *adv.* —**cool·ness** *n.*
   Synonyms: *collected, composed, detached, imperturbable, nonchalant, unruffled.*

coo·la·bah, coo·li·bah (kōō′lə-bä′) *n.* An Australian eucalyptus tree, *Eucalyptus microtheca,* found near rivers. [From a native Australian language.]

cool·ant (kōō′lənt) *n.* An agent that produces cooling; especially, a fluid that draws off heat by circulating through a machine or by bathing a mechanical part. [COOL + -ant, by analogy with *lubricant.*]

cool·er (kōō′lər) *n.* **1.** A device or container that cools something or keeps it cool. **2.** Anything that cools, such as an iced drink. **3.** *Slang.* Jail.

Coo·ley's anemia (kōō′lēz) *n.* **Thalassemia** (see). [After Thomas B. Cooley (1871–1945), U.S. pediatrician.]

cool-head·ed (kōōl′hĕd′ĭd) *adj.* Not easily excited or flustered.

Coo·lidge (kōō′lĭj), **(John) Calvin** (1872–1933). U.S. Republican statesman and 30th president (1923–29). He succeeded Warren Harding (1923) and helped to restore public trust after the scandals of his predecessor's administration.

coo·lie, coo·ly (kōō′lē) *n., pl.* **-lies.** In India and the Far East, an unskilled laborer. [Hindi *kulī, qulī,* perhaps from *Kulī, Kolī,* an aboriginal tribe of Gujarat, India.]

cool·ing-off period (kōō′lĭng-ôf′, -ŏf′) *n.* A break during negotiations to allow time for the parties in a dispute to calm down and take stock of their positions.

Coomassie. See **Kumasi.**

coomb (kōōm) *n. British.* A short valley, especially in coastal areas. [Old English *cumb,* probably from Celtic.]

coon (kōōn) *n. Informal.* A raccoon. [Short for RACCOON.]

coon·can (kōōn′kăn′) *n.* A card game. **conquian** (see).

coon·hound (kōōn′hound′) *n.* A smooth-coated black and tan hound of a breed developed in the southeastern United States to hunt raccoons.

coon's age *n. Slang.* A long time.

coon·skin (kōōn′skĭn′) *n.* **1.** The pelt of the raccoon. **2.** An article made of coonskin, such as a hat. —**coon·skin** *adj.*

coon·tie (kōōn′tē) *n.* An evergreen plant, *Zamia floridana,* of southern Florida, having underground stems that yield a starch resembling arrowroot. [Mikasuki (Seminole) *kuntie,* flour.]

coop (kōōp) *n.* **1.** An enclosure or cage, as for poultry or small

animals. **2.** *Slang.* Any place of confinement. **—fly the coop.** *Slang.* To escape.
~*tr.v.* **cooped, cooping, coops.** To confine in a limited space. Usually used with *up.* [Middle English *c(o)upe,* wicker basket, chicken coop, probably from Middle Low German *kūpe,* basket, cask, tub, barrel.]

co-op (kō′ŏp′, kō-ŏp′) *n.* A cooperative.

coop·er (ko͞o′pər) *n.* One who makes or repairs wooden tubs and casks.
~*v.* **coopered, -ering, -ers.** *—tr.* To make or repair (wooden tubs and casks). *—intr.* To work as a cooper. [Middle English *couper,* probably from Middle Low German *kūper,* from *kūpe,* cask, COOP.]

Coop·er (ko͞o′pər), **Gary,** born Frank James Cooper (1901–61). U.S. film actor, who specialized in "strong, silent" hero roles in Hollywood westerns, such as the classic *High Noon* (1952).

Cooper, James Fenimore (1789–1851). U.S. novelist. He is best remembered for his novels of frontier life, such as *The Last of the Mohicans* (1826).

coop·er·age (ko͞o′pər-ĭj) *n.* A cooper's work, shop, or products.

co·op·er·ate (kō-ŏp′ə-rāt′) *intr.v.* **-ated, -ating, -ates. 1.** To work or act together toward a common end or purpose. **2.** To adopt a helpful and willing attitude. **3.** To practice economic cooperation. [Latin *cooperārī* : *co-,* together + *operārī,* to work, from *opus,* work.] **—co·op·er·a·tor** (kō-ŏp′ə-rā′tər) *n.*

co·op·er·a·tion (kō-ŏp′ə-rā′shən) *n.* **1.** The act of cooperating. **2.** Help or a helpful attitude: *We need your cooperation.* **3.** An association of persons for mutual benefit. **—co·op·er·a·tion·ist** *n.*

co·op·er·a·tive (kō-ŏp′ər-ə-tĭv, -ŏp′rə-, -ə-rā′tĭv) *adj.* **1.** Done in cooperation with others: *a cooperative effort.* **2.** Marked by willingness to cooperate: *a cooperative patient.* **3.** Of, pertaining to, or functioning as a cooperative: *a cooperative farm.*
~*n.* An enterprise, such as a farm, factory, shop, or set of houses or dwellings, that is collectively owned and operated for mutual benefit. Also called "co-op." **—co·op·er·a·tive·ly** *adv.* **—co·op·er·a·tive·ness** *n.*

Cooper pair *n. Physics.* A pair of interacting electrons responsible for carrying the electric current in a superconductor. [After Leon N. *Cooper* (born 1930), U.S. physicist.]

Coo·pers Creek (ko͞o′pərz). Intermittent watercourse in eastern Australia. It flows 1,420 kilometers (880 miles) southwest from the Great Dividing Range into Lake Eyre.

co-opt (kō-ŏpt′, kō′ŏpt′) *tr.v.* **-opted, -opting, -opts. 1.** To elect as a fellow member of a group. **2.** To appoint summarily. **3.** To preempt; appropriate. **4.** To absorb or take over, especially by assimilation into an established group or culture. [Latin *cooptāre* : *cō-,* together + *optāre,* to choose, elect.] **—co-op·ta·tion** (kō′ŏp-tā′shən), **co-op·tion** *n.* **—co-op·ta·tive** (kō-ŏp′tə-tĭv), **co-op·tive** *adj.*

co·or·di·nate (kō-ôr′də-nĭt, -nāt′) *n.* **1.** One that is equal in importance, rank, or degree. **2.** *Mathematics.* **a.** Any of a set of numbers that determines the location of a point in a space of a given dimension. **b.** Any of a set of two or more magnitudes used to determine the position of a point, line, curve, or plane. **3. coordinates.** Items of clothing or accessories designed to match and be worn together.
~*adj.* (kō-ôr′də-nĭt, -nāt′). **1.** Of equal importance, rank, or degree; not subordinate. **2.** Of or involving coordination. **3.** Of or based on coordinates.
~*v.* (kō-ôr′də-nāt′) **coordinated, -nating, -nates.** *—tr.* **1.** To place in the same order, class, or rank. **2.** To arrange in the proper relative position. **3.** To bring together in a common and harmonious action or effort. **4.** *Chemistry.* To cause (an atom, ion, or the like) to form a coordinate bond. *—intr.* **1.** To work together harmoniously. **2.** *Chemistry.* To form a coordinate bond. [Back-formation from COORDINATION.] **—co·or·di·nate·ly** *adv.* **—co·or·di·nate·ness** *n.* **—co·or·di·na·tive** *adj.* **—co·or·di·na·tor** (kō-ôr′də-nā′tər) *n.*

coordinate bond *n.* A covalent chemical bond in which both electrons forming the bond are supplied by one atom. Also called "semipolar bond," "dative bond."

coordinate conjunction *n.* Also **coordinating conjunction.** *Grammar.* A conjunction that connects parallel grammatical elements; for example, *or* in *She doesn't know whether she's coming or going.* Compare **subordinate conjunction.**

coordinate geometry *n.* A branch of geometry, **analytical geometry** *(see).*

coordinate system *n. Mathematics.* A method of specifying the positions of points in space by reference to fixed points, lines, or planes. See **Cartesian coordinates, cylindrical coordinates, polar coordinates.**

co·or·di·na·tion (kō-ôr′də-nā′shən) *n.* **1.** The act of coordinating. **2.** The state of being coordinated; harmonious adjustment or interaction. **3.** *Physiology.* The coordinated functioning of muscles or groups of muscles in the execution of a complex task. [French, from Late Latin *coōrdinātiō* (stem *coōrdinātiōn-*), arrangement in the same order : Latin *cō-,* same + *ōrdinātiō,* arrangement, from *ōrdināre,* to arrange in order, from *ōrdō,* order.]

coordination compound *n.* A chemical compound or complex ion formed by joining independent molecules or ions to a central metallic atom. Also called "coordination complex."

coot (ko͞ot) *n.* **1.** Any of several dark-gray aquatic birds of the genus *Fulica;* especially *F. americana* of the New World, and *F. atra* of the Old World. **2.** A duck, the **scoter** *(see).* **3.** *Informal.* A foolish old man. [Middle English *cote,* probably from Middle Dutch *coet, cuut*†.]

coo·tie (ko͞o′tē) *n. Slang.* A body louse. [Perhaps from Malay *kutu.*]

cop[1] (kŏp) *n.* **1.** A cone-shaped or cylindrical roll of yarn or thread wound on a spindle. **2.** *Archaic.* A summit or crest. [Middle English *cop, coppe,* summit, top, tip, Old English *copp,* from Late Latin *cuppa,* from Latin *cūpa,* tub.]

cop[2] *n. Informal.* A policeman.
~*tr.v.* **copped, copping, cops.** *Slang.* **1.** To seize; catch. **2.** To steal. **— cop a plea.** *Slang.* To plead guilty to a lesser charge so as to avoid having to stand trial on a more serious one. [Probably from obsolete *cap,* to arrest, from Old French *caper,* to seize.]

cop. copyright.

co·pa·cet·ic, co·pa·set·ic (kō′pə-sĕt′ĭk) *adj. Slang.* Excellent; first-rate. [20th century : origin obscure.]

co·pai·ba (kō-pī′bə, -pā′-) *n.* A transparent, yellowish, viscous resin from South American trees of the genus *Copaifera,* used in varnishes and tracing papers. [Spanish, from Portuguese *copaíba,* from Tupi *copaiba.*]

co·pal (kō′pəl) *n.* A brittle, aromatic, yellow to red resin of recent or fossil origin, obtained from various tropical trees and used in varnishes. [Spanish, from Nahuatl *copalli,* resin.]

Co·pán (kō-pän′). A ruined city of the ancient Maya on the Copán River in western Honduras, discovered by the Spanish in the early 16th century. Copán, second largest of the great Maya cities, flourished from *c.* 300 B.C.–A.D. 900.

co·par·ce·nar·y (kō-pär′sə-nĕr′ē) *n., pl.* **-ies. 1.** *Law.* Joint ownership of inherited property. Also called "parcenary." **2.** Any joint ownership. **—co·par·ce·nar·y** *adj.*

co·par·ce·ner (kō-pär′sə-nər) *n. Law.* Any of two or more persons sharing an undivided inheritance. Also called "parcener."

co·part·ner, co-part·ner (kō-pärt′nər) *n.* A partner, as in a business enterprise; an associate. **—co·part·ner·ship** *n.*

cope[1] (kōp) *intr.v.* **coped, coping, copes. 1.** To contend or struggle successfully. Used with *with: coping with career and family.* **2.** To contend with difficulties and attempt to overcome them. Often used with *with.* [Middle English *co(u)pen,* to contend with, join in battle with, from Old French *couper,* to strike, from *coup,* a blow, from Late Latin *colpus,* from Latin *colaphus,* from Greek *kolaphos.*]

cope[2] *n.* **1.** A long cloaklike ecclesiastical vestment worn over the alb or surplice. **2.** Any covering resembling a cloak or mantle.
~*tr.v.* **coped, coping, copes.** To provide (a wall, for example) with coping. [Middle English *cope,* Old English *(cantel)cāp,* from Late Latin *cāpa, cappa,* cloak, hood, from Latin *caput,* head.]

copeck. Variant of **kopeck.**

Co·pen·ha·gen (kō′pən-hā′gən, -hä′-). *Danish* **Kø·ben·havn** (kœ′bən-houn′). The capital of Denmark, on the Baltic coast of Sjaelland opposite the coast of southern Sweden.

co·pe·pod (kō′pə-pŏd′) *n.* Any of numerous small marine and freshwater crustaceans of the subclass *Copepoda.* [New Latin *Copepoda,* "oar-footed ones" : Greek *kōpē,* oar handle, oar + POD.]

cop·er (kō′pər) *n. British.* A horse dealer. [From obsolete *cope,* to buy, exchange, from Low German; akin to Dutch *koopen,* German *kaufen,* to buy.]

Co·per·ni·can system (kō-pûr′nə-kən) *n.* The description of the solar system published by Copernicus in 1543, with the sun at the center and the planets moving around it in, as originally formulated, circular orbits and epicycles. Compare **Ptolemaic system.**

Co·per·ni·cus (kō-pûr′nə-kəs, kə-), **Nicolaus** (1473–1543). *Polish* **Mikolaj Ko·per·nik** (kô-pĕr′nĭk). Polish astronomer. The difficulties he encountered in trying to calculate the position of the planets within the framework of the well-established Ptolemaic system led him to reject Ptolemy's belief that the heavenly bodies moved around the earth and to place the sun at the center of the universe. **—Co·per·ni·can** *adj.*

cope·stone (kōp′stōn′) *n.* **1.** A **capstone** *(see).* **2.** A coping stone.

cop·i·er (kŏp′ē-ər) *n.* **1.** Any of various office machines that make copies. **2.** A copyist or transcriber. **3.** An imitator.

co·pi·lot, co-pi·lot (kō′pī′lət) *n.* The second or relief pilot of an aircraft.

cop·ing (kō′pĭng) *n.* The top part of a wall or roof, usually slanted. [From COPE (vestment).]

coping saw *n.* A narrow, short-bladed saw with a thin blade in a U-shaped frame, used for cutting designs in wood.

coping stone *n.* A stone used in or as a coping.

co·pi·ous (kō′pē-əs) *adj.* **1.** Yielding or containing plenty; affording ample supply. **2.** Large in quantity; abundant. **3.** Abounding in matter, thoughts, or words; wordy. [Middle English, from Old French *copieux,* from Latin *cōpiōsus,* from *cōpia,* abundance.] **—co·pi·ous·ly** *adv.* **—co·pi·ous·ness** *n.*

co·pla·nar (kō-plā′nər) *adj.* Lying or occurring in the same plane.

Cop·land (kōp′lənd), **Aaron** (1900–). U.S. pianist and composer. His works include the ballets *Rodeo* (1942) and *Appalachian Spring* (1944) and his highly acclaimed *Third Symphony* (1946).

Cop·ley (kŏp′lē), **John Singleton** (1738–1815). U.S. painter. A member of a Loyalist Boston family, he earned a reputation as a fine portraitist, painting such colonial dignitaries as Paul Revere and John Hancock. When the Revolution seemed imminent he went overseas (1774) and settled in England, where he continued to paint until his death.

co·pol·y·mer (kō-pŏl′ə-mər) *n.* A polymer of two or more different monomers. **—co·pol·y·mer·ic** (kō-pŏl′ə-mĕr′ĭk) *adj.*

co·pol·y·mer·ize (kō-pŏl′ə-mə-rīz′) *v.* **-ized, -izing, -izes.** *—tr.* To polymerize (different monomers) together. *—intr.* To react to form a copolymer. **—co·pol·y·mer·i·za·tion** *n.*

cop out *intr.v. Slang.* **1.** To evade a difficult question, situation, or

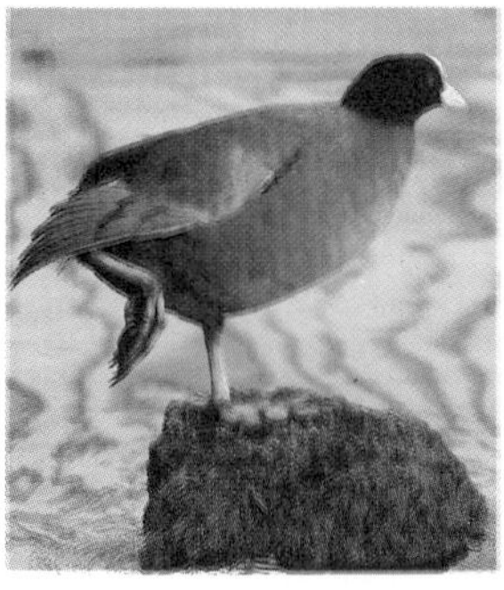

coot *A bird of lakes and ponds, found on all continents except Australia and Antarctica. It has lobed, not webbed, feet and swims and dives to feed on water plants.*

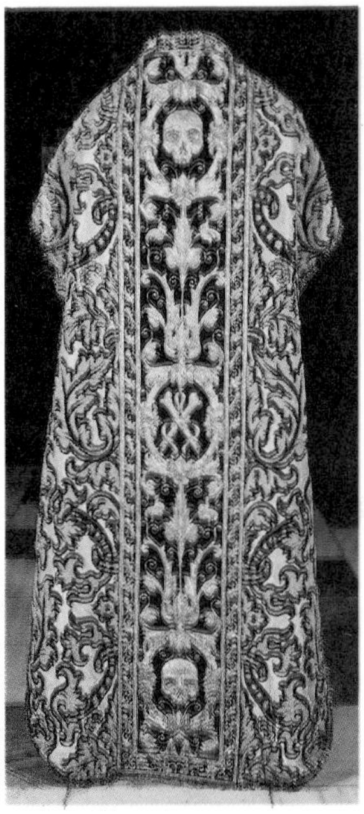

cope *A full-length and often richly embroidered church vestment.*

commitment. **2.** To back down, as on a promise. **3.** To compromise one's principles. [From COP (to seize).]

cop-out (kŏp′out′) *n. Slang.* An act of copping out; a failure to commit oneself or abide by one's principles.

cop·per[1] (kŏp′ər) *n.* **1.** *Symbol* **Cu** A ductile, malleable, reddish-brown metallic element that is an excellent conductor of heat and electricity and is widely used for electrical wiring, water piping, and corrosion-resistant parts either pure or in alloys such as brass and bronze. Atomic number 29, atomic weight 63.54, melting point 1,083°C, boiling point 2,595°C, specific gravity 8.96, valences 1, 2. **2.** A coin of low value made of copper or a copper alloy. **3.** *Chiefly British.* A large boiler made of copper or often of iron, especially one used for laundry. **4.** Any of various small butterflies of the subfamily Lycaeninae, having predominantly copper-colored wings.
~tr.v. **coppered, -pering, -pers.** To coat or finish with a layer of copper. [Middle English, Old English *coper, copor,* from Common Germanic *kupar* (unattested), from Late Latin *cuprum,* from Latin *Cyprium (aes),* "(copper) of Cyprus" (Cyprus was known in ancient times as the source of the best copper).] **—cop·per·y** *adj.*

copper[2] *n. Slang.* A policeman. [From COP (to seize).]

cop·per·as (kŏp′ər-əs) *n.* A greenish, crystalline, hydrated ferrous sulfate, $FeSO_4 \cdot 7H_2O$, used in the manufacture of fertilizers and inks and in water purification. [Middle English *coperose,* from Old French *co(u)perose,* from Medieval Latin *cup(e)rosa,* probably short for *aqua cup(e)rosa,* "copper water."]

copper beech *n.* A variety of the European beech, *Fagus sylvatica,* having copper-colored or purple leaves.

Cop·per·belt (kŏp′ər-bĕlt′). A region of central Africa, extending in an arc from southeastern Zaire into northern Zambia. It has the largest copper deposits in Africa.

cop·per·head (kŏp′ər-hĕd′) *n.* **1.** A venomous snake, *Agkistrodon contortrix* (or *Ancistron contortrix*), of the eastern United States, having reddish-brown markings. **2. Cooperhead.** A Northerner who sympathized with the South during the Civil War.

Cop·per·mine (kŏp′ər-mīn′). River, 845 kilometers (525 miles) long, in central Mackenzie district, Northwest Territories, Canada. It flows northwest to the Arctic Ocean. Its many falls give it great hydroelectric power potential.

copper nickel *n.* A nickel ore, **niccolite** *(see).*

cop·per·plate (kŏp′ər-plāt′) *n.* **1.** A copper printing plate, engraved or etched to form a recessed pattern of the matter to be printed. **2.** A print or engraving made by using such a plate. **3.** An ornate, cursive handwriting style based on copperplate engraved models and characterized by a slant to the right, regular loops, and vertical strokes thicker than horizontal strokes.

copper pyrites *n.* A copper ore, **chalcopyrite** *(see).*

cop·per·smith (kŏp′ər-smĭth′) *n.* **1.** A worker or manufacturer of objects in copper. **2.** A brightly colored bird, *Megalaima haemacephala,* of southeastern Asia, having a ringing, metallic call.

copper sulfate *n.* A poisonous crystalline copper salt, $CuSO_4$, used in agriculture, textile dyeing, leather treatment, electroplating, and the manufacture of germicides. It is white when anhydrous; the hydrate, $CuSO_4 \cdot 5H_2O$, is blue and is also called "blue vitriol."

cop·pice (kŏp′ĭs) *n. Chiefly British.* A thicket or copse. [From Old French *copeïz,* from Vulgar Latin *colpaticium* (unattested), from *colpare* (unattested), to cut, from Medieval Latin *colpus,* blow. See **cope** (to contend).]

cop·ra (kŏp′rə) *n.* Dried coconut meat from which coconut oil is extracted. [Portuguese, from Malayalam *koppara.*]

copro– *prefix.* Indicates dung or excrement; for example, **coprolite.** [From Greek *kopros,* dung.]

cop·ro·lite (kŏp′rə-līt′) *n.* Fossilized excrement. [COPRO- + -LITE.] **—cop·ro·lit·ic** (kŏp′rə-lĭt′ĭk) *adj.*

cop·rol·o·gy (kŏp-rŏl′ə-jē) *n.* Scatology. [COPRO- + -LOGY.]

cop·roph·a·gous (kŏp-rŏf′ə-gəs) *adj.* Feeding on excrement: *coprophagous insects.* [New Latin *coprophagus,* from Greek *koprophagos* : COPRO-´ + -PHAGOUS.] **—cop·roph·a·gy** (kŏp-rŏf′ə-jē) *n.*

cop·ro·phil·i·a (kŏp′rə-fĭl′ē-ə) *n.* An abnormal attraction to fecal matter. [New Latin : COPRO- + -PHILIA.]

copse (kŏps) *n.* A thicket of small trees or shrubs, especially one grown for periodic cutting. [Short for COPPICE.]

Copt (kŏpt) *n.* **1.** A native of Egypt descended from ancient Egyptian stock. **2.** A member of the Coptic Church. [French *Copte,* from New Latin *Coptus,* from Arabic *quft, qubt,* the Copts, from Coptic *gyptios,* from Greek *Aiguptios,* from *Aiguptos,* EGYPT.]

cop·ter (kŏp′tər) *n. Informal.* A helicopter.

Cop·tic (kŏp′tĭk) *n.* The Afro-Asiatic language of the Copts, used today only in the liturgy of the Coptic Church. **—Cop·tic** *adj.*

Coptic Church *n.* The Christian church of Egypt, adhering to the Monophysite doctrine.

cop·u·la (kŏp′yə-lə) *n., pl.* **-las** or **-lae** (-lē). **1.** A verb, such as *feel, become, seem,* or any form of *be,* that identifies the predicate of a sentence with the subject. In the sentence *The child seems unhappy,* the copula is *seems.* **2.** *Logic.* The word or set of words that serves as a link between the subject and predicate of a proposition. [Latin *cōpula,* link, bond.] **—cop·u·lar** (kŏp′yə-lər) *adj.*

cop·u·late (kŏp′yə-lāt′) *intr.v.* **-lated, -lating, -lates.** To engage in sexual intercourse. [Latin *cōpulāre,* to fasten together, link, from *cōpula,* link, bond.] **—cop·u·la·tion** *n.*

cop·u·la·tive (kŏp′yə-lā′tĭv, -lə-tĭv) *adj.* **1.** Joining or uniting. **2.** *Grammar.* **a.** Serving to connect coordinate words or clauses: *a copulative conjunction.* **b.** Serving as a copula: *a copulative verb.* **3.** Of or pertaining to copulation.
~n. Grammar. A copulative word or group of words. **—cop·u·la·tive·ly** *adv.*

copulative conjunction *n.* Any of various conjunctions that serve to connect words or word groups in a coordinate relationship; for example, the conjunction *and.*

co·punc·tal (kō-pŭngk′təl) *adj. Mathematics.* Having a point in common. Said of three or more intersecting planes or surfaces.

cop·y (kŏp′ē) *n., pl.* **-ies.** **1.** An imitation or reproduction of something original; a duplicate. **2.** One specimen or example of a printed text or picture: *an autographed copy of a novel.* **3.** *Abbr.* **c., C. a.** Manuscript or other material to be printed. **b.** Text, especially advertising material, as distinct from graphic material. **4.** Suitable source material, as for a newspaper story: *Celebrities make good copy.*
~v. **copied, -ying, -ies.** *—tr.* **1.** To make a copy or copies of; transcribe or reproduce. **2.** To follow as a model or pattern; imitate. *—intr.* **1.** To make one or more copies or reproductions. **2.** To cheat, as in an examination, by copying another's work. **3.** To admit of being reproduced. —See Synonyms at **imitate.** [Middle English *copie,* from Old French, from Medieval Latin *cōpia,* transcript, right of reproduction, from Latin, abundance, power.]

cop·y·book (kŏp′ē-bo͝ok′) *n.* **1.** A book of models, especially of penmanship, for imitation. **2.** A book for copies, as of documents.
~adj. Unoriginal; trite: *a copybook phrase.*

copy boy *n.* An employee in a newspaper office who carries copy and runs errands.

cop·y·cat (kŏp′ē-kăt′) *n. Informal.* One who imitates, especially in a slavish way. **—cop·y·cat** *adj.*

copy desk *n.* The desk in a newspaper office where copy is edited and prepared for printing.

cop·y·ed·it (kŏp′ē-ĕd′ĭt) *tr.v.* **-ited, -iting, -its.** To correct and prepare (a manuscript or other material) for printing. **—copy editor** *n.*

cop·y·graph (kŏp′ē-grăf′, -gräf′) *n.* A **hectograph** *(see).*

cop·y·hold (kŏp′ē-hōld′) *n.* **1.** Formerly in England, tenure based on the customs of the local manor. **2.** Land held in this way.

cop·y·hold·er (kŏp′ē-hōl′dər) *n.* **1.** An assistant who reads manuscript aloud to a proofreader. **2.** A device that holds copy in place for the typesetter. **3.** Formerly, one holding land by copyhold.

cop·y·ist (kŏp′ē-ĭst) *n.* One who makes written copies.

cop·y·read·er (kŏp′ē-rē′dər) *n.* One who edits and corrects newspaper copy for publication.

cop·y·right (kŏp′ē-rīt′) *n. Abbr.* **c., C., cop.** The right granted by law to an author, composer, playwright, publisher, or distributor, to exclusive publication, production, sale, or distribution of a literary, musical, dramatic, or artistic work. In the United States, this right extends for a period of 28 years, with the privilege of renewal for an additional 28 years.
~adj. Also **cop·y·right·ed.** Protected by copyright.
~tr.v. **copyrighted, -righting, -rights.** To secure a copyright for. **—cop·y·right·a·ble** *adj.* **—cop·y·right·er** *n.*

copy typist *n.* One who types out written rather than dictated material. Compare **audiotypist.**

cop·y·writ·er (kŏp′ē-rī′tər) *n.* One who writes advertising or publicity copy. **—cop·y·writ·ing** *n.*

coq au vin (kōk′ ō văN′) *n.* Chicken cooked in red wine, with mushrooms, onions, and garlic. [French, "cock in wine."]

co·quet (kō-kĕt′) *intr.v.* **-quetted, -quetting, -quets.** **1.** To play the coquette; flirt. **2.** To trifle; dally. [French *coqueter,* to flirt, from *coquet,* flirtatious man. See **coquette.**]

co·quet·ry (kō′kĭ-trē, kō-kĕt′rē) *n., pl.* **-ries.** Dalliance; flirtation. [French *coquetterie,* from COQUETTE.]

co·quette (kō-kĕt′) *n.* A woman who flirts with men. [French, feminine of *coquet,* flirtatious man, diminutive of *coq,* cock, from Old French *coc,* from Late Latin *coccus,* from Latin *coco,* cackle. See **cock.**] **—co·quet·tish** *adj.* **—co·quet·tish·ly** *adv.* **—co·quet·tish·ness** *n.*

co·quil·la nut (kō-kēl′yə, -kē′yə) *n.* The nut of a South American palm tree, *Attalea funifera,* having a hard oval shell used for decorative carving or turning. [Portuguese *coquilho,* diminutive of *côco,* COCO.]

co·quille (kō-kēl′) *n.* A scallop-shaped dish or a scallop shell in which various seafood dishes are browned and served. [French, variant (influenced by *coque,* shell) of Latin *conchylia,* plural of *conchylium,* mussel, from Greek *konkhulion,* mussel, cockle, diminutive of *konkhē,* CONCH.]

co·qui·na (kō-kē′nə) *n.* **1.** Any of various small bivalve mollusks of warm marine waters, having variously colored, often striped or banded shells. **2.** A soft porous limestone, essentially of shell and coral fragments, used as construction material. [Spanish, shellfish, cockel, irregular diminutive of concha, shell, mussel, from Latin, CONCH.]

co·qui·to (kō-kē′tō) *n., pl.* **-tos.** A Chilean palm tree, *Jubaea spectabilis,* whose sap gives a sweet edible syrup. [Spanish, diminutive of *coco,* coco palm, from Portuguese *côco,* COCO.]

cor. **1.** corner. **2.** cornet. **3.** coroner. **4.** corpus. **5.** correction. **6.** correspondence; correspondent; corresponding.

Cor. Corinthians (New Testament).

cor·a·ci·i·form (kôr′ə-sī′ə-fôrm′) *adj.* Of, belonging to, or pertaining to the Coraciiformes, an order of birds that includes the kingfishers, hornbills, hoopoes, and bee-eaters. [From New Latin *Coracias* (genus), from Greek *korakias,* chough.]

cor·a·cle (kôr′ə-kəl, kŏr′-) *n.* A small, rounded boat made of waterproof material stretched over a wicker or wooden frame. Also *Scot-*

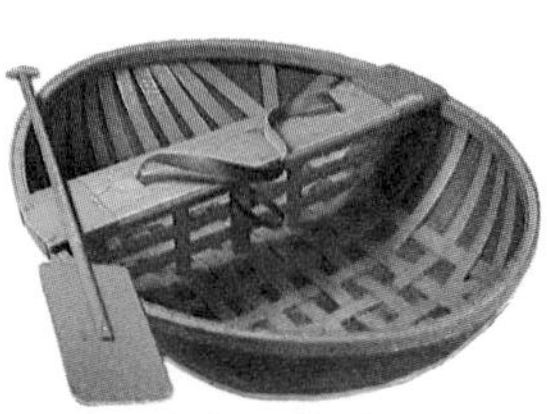

coracle *A light and highly maneuverable fishing boat still found in parts of Britain and Ireland. Coracles are made from a wicker or wood frame covered in leather or tarred cloth. The design dates back to prehistoric times.*

PRONUNCIATION KEY

ă, pat; ā, pay; âr, care;
ä, father, are; b, bib;
ch, church; d, deed; ĕ, pet;
ē, be; f, fife; g, gag; h, hat;
hw, which; ĭ, pit; ī, pie;
îr, pier; j, judge; k, kick;
l, lid, needle; m, mum;
n, no, sudden; ng, thing;
ŏ, pot; ō, toe; ô, paw, for;
oi, noise; ou, out; o͝o, book;
o͞o, boot; p, pop; r, roar;
s, sauce; sh, ship, dish;
t, tight; th, thin, path;
th, this, bathe; ŭ, cut; ûr, fur;
v, valve; w, with; y, yes;
z, zebra, size; zh, vision;
ə, about, item, edible,
gallop, circus, peaceful

IN FOREIGN WORDS:

à, *Fr.* ami; œ, *Fr.* feu, *Ger.* schön; ü, *Fr.* tu, *Ger.* über; KH, *Ger.* ich, *Scot.* loch; N, *Fr.* bon; y′, *Fr.* Compiègne

STRESS MARKS:

Primary stress: ′
in·cite′ (ĭn-sīt′)
Secondary stress: ′
in′sight′ (ĭn′sīt′)

tish & *Irish* "currach." [Earlier *corougle,* from Welsh *corwgl, cwrwgl.* See **currach.**]

cor·a·coid (kôr′ə-koid′, kŏr′-) *n.* A paired cartilage bone projecting from the scapula toward the sternum in teleost fish and quadrupeds. In mammals it is reduced to a peg, the *coracoid process.* [New Latin *coracoides,* "(bone) shaped like a crow's beak," from Greek *korakoeidēs,* like a raven : *korax,* raven + -OID.] **—cor·a·coid** *adj.*

cor·al (kôr′əl, kŏr′-) *n.* **1.** Any of numerous chiefly colonial marine coelenterates of the class Anthozoa, characterized by calcareous skeletons massed in a wide variety of shapes, and often forming reefs or islands. **2.** The often hard, rocklike structure formed by such organisms. **3.** The material forming such a structure; especially, the red-orange, pinkish, or white stony substance secreted by corals of the genus *Corallium,* used to make jewelry and ornaments. **4.** An object made of coral. **5.** Deep or strong pink to moderate red or reddish orange. [Middle English, from Old French, from Latin *corallium,* from Greek *korallion,* probably of Semitic origin, akin to Hebrew *gōrāl,* a pebble.] **—cor·al** *adj.*

cor·al·bells (kôr′əl-bĕlz′, kŏr′-) *n. Used with a singular or plural verb.* A plant, *Heuchera sanguinea,* of the western United States, widely cultivated for its clusters of small, bell-shaped red flowers.

cor·al·ber·ry (kôr′əl-bĕr′ē, kŏr′-) *n.* **1.** A North American shrub, *Symphoricarpos orbiculatus,* having red or purplish fruit. **2.** The fruit of this shrub.

cor·al·line (kôr′ə-lĭn, -līn′, kŏr′-) *adj.* **1.** Of, consisting of, or producing coral. **2.** Resembling coral; especially, coral-colored.
∼*n.* **1.** A corallike animal, such as certain polyzoans or hydrozoans. **2.** Any of various red algae, especially of the genus *Corallina,* covered with a calcareous substance and forming stony deposits.

cor·al·loid (kôr′ə-loid′, kŏr′-) *adj.* Resembling coral.

coral reef *n.* A marine ridge or mound consisting chiefly of compacted coral together with algal material and biochemically deposited magnesium and calcium carbonates.

cor·al·root (kôr′əl-ro͞ot′, -ro͝ot′, kŏr′-) *n.* Any of several saprophytic orchids of the genus *Corallorhiza,* having small yellow-green or purplish flowers and branched roots that resemble coral.

Cor·al Sea (kôr′əl, kŏr′-). A region of the South Pacific Ocean, between northeast Australia and the New Britain–New Caledonia island chain. It contains the Great Barrier Reef, the largest coral reef in the world.

coral snake *n.* Any of various venomous snakes of the genus *Micrurus,* of tropical America and the southern United States, characteristically having brilliant red, black, and yellow banded markings.

cor an·glais (kôr än-glā′) *n., pl.* **cors anglais** (kôrz). A musical instrument, the **English horn** *(see).* [French, "English horn."]

cor·beil (kôr′bəl, kôr-bā′) *n.* Also **cor·beille** (kôr-bā′). A sculptured basket of flowers or fruit used as an architectural ornament. [French *corbeille,* from Late Latin *corbicula,* diminutive of Latin *corbis,* basket.]

cor·bel (kôr′bəl) *n.* A bracket of stone, wood, brick, or other building material, projecting from the face of a wall and generally used to support a cornice or an arch.
∼*tr.v.* **corbeled** or **-belled, -beling** or **-belling,** or **-bels.** To provide with or support by a corbel or corbels. [Middle English, from Old French, diminutive of *corp,* raven (early corbels were wedge-shaped, like ravens' beaks), from Latin *corvus.*]

cor·bel·ing (kôr′bəl-ĭng) *n.* An overlapping arrangement of bricks or stones in which each course extends farther out from the vertical of the wall than the course below.

cor·bie (kôr′bē) *n. Scottish.* A raven, crow, or rook. [Middle English, diminutive of Old French *corb,* from Latin *corvus,* crow.]

corbie gable *n.* A gable roof with corbie-steps.

cor·bie-step (kôr′bē-stĕp′) *n.* Also **corbel step.** Any of a series of steps or steplike projections on the top of a gable wall. [From Middle English *corbie,* raven (the steps being accessible only to birds), from Old French *corbin,* from Latin *corvīnus,* ravenlike.]

cor·bi·na (kôr-bē′nə) *n.* Also **cor·vi·na** (-vē′nə). A game fish, *Menticirrhus undulatus,* of North American Pacific coastal waters. [Spanish *corvina,* from *corvino,* ravenlike (from its color), from Latin *corvīnus,* from *corvus,* raven.]

Corbusier, Le. See **Le Corbusier.**

Corcyra. See **Corfu.**

cord (kôrd) *n.* Also **chord** (for sense 5 only). **1.** A string or small rope of twisted strands or fibers. **2.** An insulated, flexible electric wire fitted with a plug or plugs. **3.** An influence, feeling, or force that binds or restrains. **4.** The hangman's rope. **5.** An anatomical structure resembling a cord: *spinal cord; umbilical cord.* **6.** A raised rib on the surface of cloth, as on corduroy. **7.** A fabric with such ribs. **8. cords.** Trousers made of corduroy. **9.** A unit of quantity for cut fuel wood, equal to 128 cubic feet in a stack measuring 4 by 4 by 8 feet.
∼*tr.v.* **corded, cording, cords. 1.** To fasten or bind with a cord or cords. **2.** To pile (wood) in cords. [Middle English, from Old French *corde,* from Latin *chorda,* catgut, cord, from Greek *khordē.*] **—cord·er** *n.*

cord·age (kôr′dĭj) *n.* **1.** The ropes in the rigging of a ship. **2.** The amount of wood in an area, as measured in cords.

cor·date (kôr′dāt′) *adj. Biology.* Having a heart-shaped outline: *a cordate leaf.* [New Latin *cordatus,* from Latin *cor* (stem *cord-*), heart.] **—cor·date·ly** *adv.*

Cor·day (kôr-dā′), **Charlotte,** born Marie Anne Charlotte Corday d'Armont (1768–93). French noblewoman who assassinated Jean Paul Marat (1793). Of an impoverished Norman aristocratic family, she sympathized with the Girondins in the French Revolution. She was guillotined in 1793.

cord·ed (kôr′dĭd) *adj.* **1.** Furnished with or made of cords. **2.** Bound with cords. **3.** Ribbed or twilled, as corduroy. **4.** Stacked in cords, as firewood. **5.** Standing out like tightened cords. Said of muscles.

cor·dial (kôr′jəl) *adj.* **1.** Warm and sincere; hearty. **2.** Serving to invigorate; stimulating; reviving.
∼*n.* **1.** A stimulant. **2.** A **liqueur** *(see).* [Middle English, of the heart, from Medieval Latin *cordiālis,* from Latin *cor* (stem *cord-*), heart.] **—cor·di·al·i·ty** (kôr′jē-ăl′ə-tē, -jăl′-), **cor·dial·ness** *n.* **—cor·dial·ly** *adv.*

cor·di·er·ite (kôr′dē-ə-rīt′) *n.* A dichroic violet-blue to gray mineral silicate of magnesium, aluminum, and sometimes iron. Also called "dichroite," "iolite." [French, after Pierre L.A. *Cordier* (1777–1861), French geologist who first described it.]

cor·di·form (kôr′də-fôrm′) *adj.* Heart-shaped. [French *cordiforme* : Latin *cor* (stem *cord-*), heart + -FORM.]

cor·dil·le·ra (kôr′dĭl-yâr′ə, kôr-dĭl′ər-ə) *n.* A series of broadly parallel mountain ranges; especially, the principal mountain system of a large land mass. [Spanish, from *cordilla,* diminutive of *cuerda,* cord, chain, from Latin *chorda,* CORD.] **—cor·dil·le·ran** *adj.*

Cor·dil·ler·as (kôr′dĭl-yâr′əz). The entire chain of mountain ranges of western North, Central, and South America. The Cordilleras extend from northern Alaska to Cape Horn and include the Rocky Mts., the Sierra Nevada, and the Andes.

cord·ite (kôr′dīt′) *n.* A smokeless explosive powder consisting of nitrocellulose, nitroglycerin, and petrolatum dissolved in acetone, dried, and extruded in cords. [From CORD.]

cord·less (kôrd′lĭs) *adj.* Operated by battery.

cór·do·ba (kôr′də-bə) *n.* The basic monetary unit of Nicaragua, equal to 100 centavos. [After Francisco de *Córdoba* (*c.* 1475–1526), Spanish explorer.]

Cór·do·ba[1] (kôr′də-bə). Capital of Córdoba province, southern Spain, on the Guadalquivir River. As a Moorish capital (756–1031) it was a brilliant cultural center.

Córdoba[2]. Capital of Córdoba province in central Argentina. It lies on the Primero River, and was founded in 1573.

cor·don (kôr′dən) *n.* **1.** A line of troops, military posts, ships, or the like, stationed around an area to enclose or guard it. **2.** A cord or braid worn as a fastening or an ornament. **3.** A ribbon, worn usually diagonally across the chest as a badge of honor or a decoration. **4.** *Architecture.* An ornamental band of stone or masonry, a **string-course** *(see).* **5.** *Horticulture.* A fruit tree trained and pruned to grow along wires or other supports.
∼*tr.v.* **cordoned, -doning, -dons.** To form a cordon around (an area) so as to prevent movement in or out. Often used with *off.* [French, from Old French, diminutive of *corde,* CORD.]

cor·don bleu (kôr-dôɴ′ blœ′) *n., pl.* **cordons bleus** *(pronounced as singular).* **1.** The blue ribbon worn as a decoration by members of the Order of the Holy Ghost, the highest order of French chivalry under the Bourbon monarchy. **2.** A person highly distinguished in his field; especially, a master chef.
∼*adj.* Of the highest standard of cooking. [French, "blue ribbon."]

cor·don sa·ni·taire (kôr-dôɴ′ sä-nē-târ′) *n., pl.* **cordons sanitaires** *(pronounced as singular).* **1.** A chain of buffer states organized around a nation considered ideologically dangerous or potentially hostile. **2.** Any physical or figurative barrier devised so as to keep off some potential danger. [French, "quarantine line."]

cor·do·van (kôr′də-vən) *n.* A fine leather made originally at Córdoba, Spain, first of goatskin but now more frequently of split horsehide. Also called "cordovan leather."
∼*adj.* Made of this leather. [Spanish *cordobán,* from CÓRDOBA, Spain.]

Cor·do·van (kôr′də-vən) *n.* An inhabitant or native of Córdoba. [Spanish *Cordován,* from *Córdova,* CÓRDOBA, Spain.] **—Cor·do·van** *adj.*

cor·du·roy (kôr′də-roi′, kôr′də-roi′) *n.* **1.** A durable cut-pile fabric, usually made of cotton, with vertical ribs or wales. **2. corduroys.** Corduroy trousers; cords.
∼*adj.* **1.** Made of or resembling corduroy. **2.** Made of logs laid together transversely: *a corduroy road.*
∼*tr.v.* **corduroyed, -roying, -roys.** To build (a road) of logs laid together transversely. [Probably from CORD (ribbed cloth) + obsolete *duroy, deroy*†, a coarse woolen fabric.]

cord·wood (kôrd′wo͝od′) *n.* Wood piled or sold in cords.

core (kôr, kōr) *n.* **1.** The hard or fibrous central part of certain fruits, such as the apple or pear, containing the seeds. **2. a.** The innermost or most important part of anything; the heart; the center; the essence. **b.** A group or body forming the essential basis of something, as of an organization. **3.** *Electricity.* A soft iron rod in the coil of an electromagnet or transformer that intensifies and provides a path for the magnetic field produced by the windings. **4.** A mass of dry sand placed within a mold to provide openings or shape to a casting. **5.** The base, usually of soft or inferior wood, to which veneer woods are glued. **6.** *Computer Science.* **a.** Any of the tiny magnetic rings used to store a bit of information in a computer memory. Also called "magnetic core." **b.** A computer memory made up of such magnetic rings. **7.** The central part of the earth lying below the mantle. **8. a.** The central part of any planet that is differentiated into layers. **b.** The central part of a star, in which the energy is produced. **9.** *Physics.* The part of a nuclear reactor in

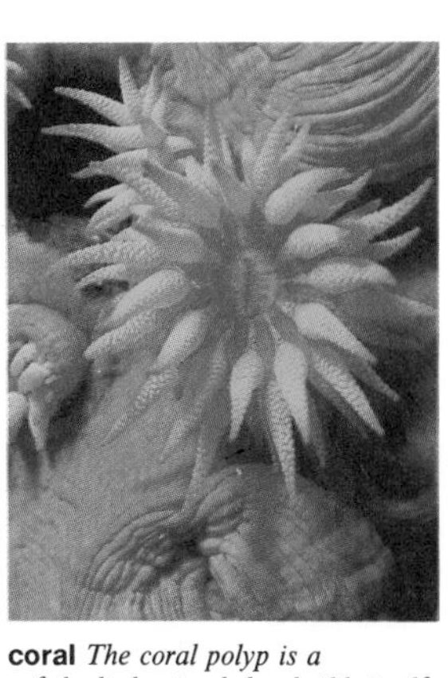

coral *The coral polyp is a soft-bodied animal that builds itself a protective, chalky skeleton into which it can withdraw. Its flowerlike tentacles usually emerge only at night to feed on tiny fish and plankton. When corals live together in large colonies, their skeletons accumulate to form reefs. Australia's Great Barrier Reef, which is some 1,930 kilometers (1,200 miles) long, is composed of the skeletons of billions of polyps, each only a few millimeters across.*

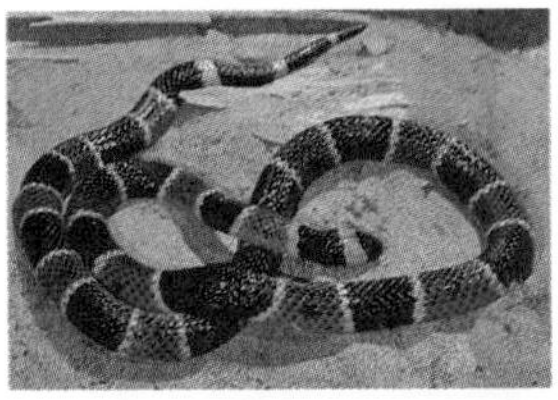

coral snake *Although this relative of the cobra is highly venomous, it seldom attacks man. Coral snakes, which are native to the tropical regions of the Americas and to the southern United States, live mostly under cover or in a burrow, emerging to feed on small animals.*

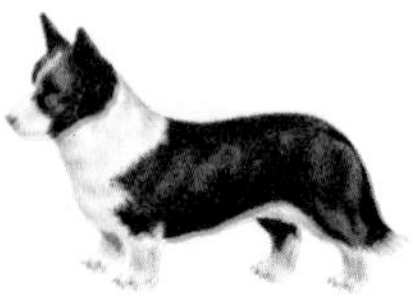

corgi *The Welsh corgi was originally a farm dog, bred to herd cattle by nipping at their heels. This is a Cardigan corgi, which has a long tail.*

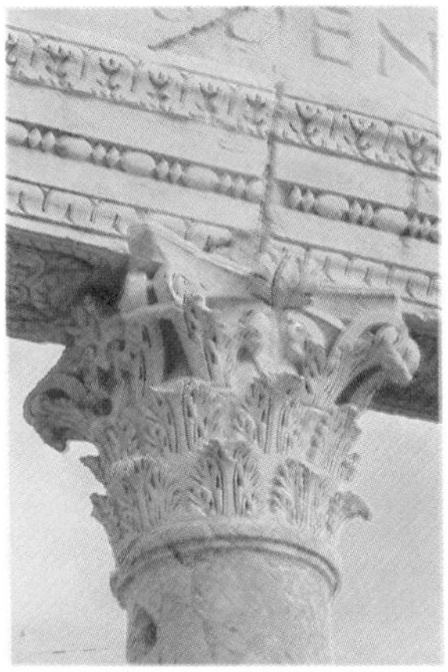

Corinthian order *This is the most richly ornamented style of pillar capital in ancient Greek architecture—an inverted, bell-shaped cluster of acanthus leaves.*

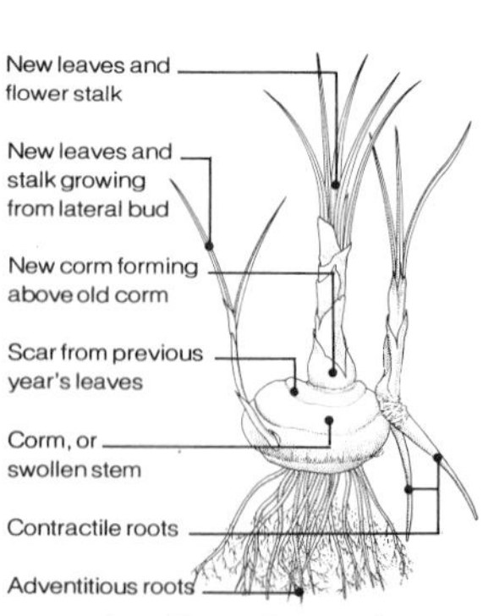
New leaves and flower stalk
New leaves and stalk growing from lateral bud
New corm forming above old corm
Scar from previous year's leaves
Corm, or swollen stem
Contractile roots
Adventitious roots

corm *A swollen underground stem, such as that of the gladiolus, which stores food from one season to the next.*

which the reaction occurs, containing the fuel and control rods. **10.** *Geology.* A cylindrical sample of the earth's crust obtained by a hollow drill or piston.
~*tr.v.* **cored, coring, cores.** To remove the core of: *core apples.* [Middle English *core, coor*†.] **—cor•er** *n.*

core dump *n.* A listing in the form of a print-out or a display on a screen of the data stored in a computer core.

core-dump (kôr′dŭmp′, kōr′-) *tr.v.* **-dumped, -dumping, -dumps.** To print out or display (the data in a computer core).

corelate. *Chiefly British.* Variant of **correlate.**

co•re•lig•ion•ist (kō′rĭ-lĭj′ə-nĭst) *n.* One having the same religion as another.

Co•rel•li (kə-rĕl′ē), **Arcangelo** (1653–1713). Italian composer and violinist and an important innovator of violin technique in the baroque era. As a composer he is best remembered for his 12 *concerti grossi,* which shaped the development of the concerto.

co•re•op•sis (kôr′ē-ŏp′sĭs) *n.* Any of several plants of the genus *Coreopsis,* having daisylike yellow or variegated flowers. Also called "tickseed" and sometimes "calliopsis." [New Latin, "resembling a bedbug" (from the shape of the seed) : Greek *koris,* bedbug + -OPSIS.]

co•re•spon•dent (kō′rĭ-spŏn′dənt) *n. Law.* A person cited as having committed adultery with the defendant (respondent) in a divorce suit. **—co•re•spon•den•cy** *n.*

corf (kôrf) *n., pl.* **corves** (kôrvz). *British.* A wagon, tub, or basket used in a mine. [Middle English, basket, from Middle Dutch *corf* or Middle Low German *korf,* probably from Latin *corbis*†.]

Cor•fam (kôr′făm′) *n.* A trademark for a synthetic leather, used especially for shoes.

Cor•fu (kôr′fo͞o, -fyo͞o). *Ancient* **Cor•cy•ra** (kôr-sī′rə). *Greek* **Kér•ky•ra** (kər-kîr′ə). Island in the Ionian Sea off northwest Greece. It is probably the Scheria of Homer. The island passed through the hands of Rome, Byzantium, Sicily, and Venice and was under British protection from 1815 to 1864, when it was ceded to Greece. Corfu's beaches attract many tourists.

cor•gi (kôr′gē) *n.* A dog belonging to either of two long-bodied, short-legged breeds, the *Cardigan corgi* or the *Pembroke corgi.* Also called "Welsh corgi." [Welsh : *cor,* dwarf + *ci,* dog.]

co•ri•a•ceous (kôr′ē-ā′shəs) *adj.* Of or like leather, especially in texture; tough. [Late Latin *coriāceus,* from Latin *corium,* leather, hide.]

co•ri•an•der (kôr′ē-ăn′dər, kōr′-) *n.* **1.** A herb, *Coriandrum sativum,* widely cultivated for its aromatic seeds. **2.** The dried ripe seeds of this plant, used especially to flavor food. [Middle English *coriandre,* from Old French, from Latin *coriandrum,* from Greek *koriandron, koriannon,* perhaps of Mediterranean origin.]

Cor•inth (kôr′ĭnth, kŏr′-). *Greek* **Kó•rin•thos** (kôr′ĭn-thôs′). Port in southern Greece, on the Isthmus of Corinth. It became rich and influential in the 7th and 6th centuries B.C. as the region's leading pottery producer and maritime power, but it was later overshadowed by Athens. Medieval exports included currants, which get their name from the city.

Corinth, Isthmus of. A neck of land, *c.* 32 kilometers (20 miles) long and 6.5 to 13 kilometers (4 to 8 miles) wide, connecting the Peloponnese to the rest of Greece. It is between the Gulf of Corinth, an inlet of the Ionian Sea, and the Saronic Gulf.

Co•rin•thi•an (kə-rĭn′thē-ən) *adj.* **1.** Of or pertaining to ancient Corinth. **2.** Given to luxury; licentious; profligate. **3.** Elegantly or elaborately ornate. **4.** Pertaining to the Corinthian order.
~*n.* **1.** A native or inhabitant of Corinth. **2.** A wealthy amateur sportsman, especially a yachtsman. **3.** A man-about-town. **4. Corinthians.** *Abbr.* **Cor.** Either of two epistles addressed by Saint Paul to the Christian community at Corinth, each forming a book of the New Testament. In this sense, also called "Epistle to the Corinthians."

Corinthian order *n.* The most ornate of the three classical orders of architecture, characterized by a slender fluted column having an ornate bell-shaped capital decorated with acanthus leaves. Compare **Doric order, Ionic order.**

Cor•i•o•la•nus (kôr′ē-ō-lā′nəs), **Gaius Marcius** (5th century B.C.). Roman general, commemorated in Shakespeare's play *Coriolanus.* Of noble birth, he is alleged to have won his name at the siege of Corioli in the war against the Volsci (493 B.C.).

Cor•i•o•lis force (kôr′ē-ō′lĭs) *n. Physics.* A fictitious force used mathematically to describe motion relative to a noninertial, uniformly rotating frame of reference. It is used, for example, to describe the motion of air relative to the rotating earth. [After Gaspard G. de *Coriolis* (1792–1843), French mathematician.]

co•ri•um (kôr′ē-əm, kōr′-) *n., pl.* **coria** (-ə). The **dermis** *(see).* [New Latin, from Latin, skin, hide.]

cork (kôrk) *n.* **1.** The light, porous, elastic outer bark of the cork oak, used widely in industry and the arts. **2.** Something made of cork, especially a bottle stopper. **3.** A bottle stopper made of other material, such as plastic or rubber. **4.** A small float used on a fishing line or net to buoy up the line or to indicate when a fish bites. **5.** *Botany.* Cork cambium.
~*tr.v.* **corked, corking, corks.** **1.** To stop or seal with or as if with a cork. **2.** To hold back; restrain or check. Usually used with *up.* **3.** To blacken with burnt cork. [Middle English, from Dutch *kurk* or Low German *korck,* from Spanish *alcorque,* cork sole or shoe, probably from Spanish Arabic *al-qūrq.*]

Cork[1] (kôrk). A county in Munster in the southwest of the Republic of Ireland. Its hills are scattered with fortified castles, including the 15th-century Blarney Castle, famous for the Blarney Stone.

Cork[2]. The administrative center of County Cork at the mouth of the Lee River in the southwest of the Republic of Ireland. It is Ireland's second-largest city.

cork•age (kôr′kĭj) *n.* A charge exacted at a restaurant for opening and serving bottles of wine or other alcoholic beverages not bought on the premises.

cork•board (kôrk′bôrd′, -bōrd′) *n.* A construction and insulating sheet material made of compressed and baked granules of cork.

cork cambium *n. Botany.* A layer of continually dividing cells situated near the surface of woody plant stems and roots, which forms cork to the outside and secondary cortical cells to the inside. Also called "cork," "phellem."

corked (kôrkt) *adj.* **1.** Sealed with a cork. **2.** Designating wine that has been impaired in taste by a poor or decaying cork. **3.** Blackened by burnt cork. **4.** *British Slang.* Drunk.

cork•er (kôr′kər) *n.* **1.** One that inserts corks, as in bottles. **2.** *Slang.* Someone or something that is remarkable or astounding. **3.** *Slang.* An unanswerable fact or argument.

cork•ing (kôr′kĭng) *adj. Informal.* Excellent; splendid; fine. [From CORK (verb), probably influenced in meaning by CORKER.] **—cork•ing** *adv.*

cork oak *n.* An evergreen oak tree, *Quercus suber,* of the Mediterranean region, having a porous outer bark that is the source of cork. Also called "cork tree."

cork•screw (kôrk′skro͞o′) *n.* A device for drawing corks from bottles, consisting typically of a pointed metal spiral attached to a handle.
~*adj.* Resembling a corkscrew in shape; spiral; helical.
~*v.* **corkscrewed, -screwing, -screws.** —*tr.* To cause to move in a spiral or winding course. —*intr.* To move spirally.

cork•wood (kôrk′wo͝od′) *n.* **1.** A small tree or shrub, *Leitneria floridana,* of the southeastern United States, having a very light wood that is used for fishing-net floats. **2.** Any of several other trees having light, porous wood. **3.** The wood of these.

cork•y (kôr′kē) *adj.* **-ier, -iest.** **1.** Of or like cork. **2.** *Informal.* Lively; buoyant. **3.** Tasting of cork; corked. **—cork•i•ness** *n.*

corm (kôrm) *n. Botany.* An underground stem, such as that of the gladiolus, similar to a bulb but having papery, rather than fleshy, scale leaves. [New Latin *cormus,* from Greek *kormos,* a trimmed tree trunk, from *keirein,* to shear.]

cor•mel (kôr′məl) *n. Botany.* A young corm that arises at the base of a fully developed corm.

cor•mo•phyte (kôr′mə-fīt′) *n.* Any of a former botanical division, Cormophyta, consisting of plants having roots, stems, and foliage. [New Latin *Cormophyta* : Greek *kormos,* tree trunk (see **corm**) + -PHYTE.] **—cor•mo•phyt•ic** (kôr′mə-fĭt′ĭk) *adj.*

cor•mo•rant (kôr′mər-ənt) *n.* **1.** Any of several widely distributed aquatic birds of the genus *Phalacrocorax,* especially *P. carbo,* having dark plumage, webbed feet, a hooked bill, and a distensible pouch. **2.** A greedy or rapacious person. [Middle English *cormeraunt,* from Old French *cormoran, cormaran, cormareng* : *corp,* raven, from Latin *corvus* + *marenc,* of the sea, from Latin *marīnus,* MARINE.]

corn[1] (kôrn) *n.* **1. a.** Any of several varieties of a tall, widely cultivated cereal plant, *Zea Mays,* bearing seeds or kernels on large ears. **b.** The seeds or kernels of this plant, used for food or fodder, and yielding an edible oil. **c.** The ears of this plant. Also called "Indian corn," "maize." **2.** *British.* **a.** Any of several cereal plants producing edible seed, especially when the main crop of a region, such as wheat in England and oats in Scotland. **b.** The seeds of such a plant or crop; grain. **3. a.** A single seed of a cereal plant; a grain. **b.** A seed or fruit of various other plants. **4.** *Informal.* Corn whiskey. **5.** *Slang.* Anything considered trite, dated, or unduly sentimental.
~*tr.v.* **corned, corning, corns.** **1. a.** To preserve and season with granulated salt. **b.** To preserve in brine. **2.** To feed (animals) with corn or grain. [Middle English *corn,* Old English *corn.*]

corn[2] *n.* A horny painful thickening of the skin, usually on or near a toe, resulting from pressure or friction. [Middle English *corne,* from Old French *corne,* corn on the foot, horn, from Latin *cornū,* horn.]

Corn. Cornwall.

corn•ball (kôrn′bôl′) *n. Slang.* An unsophisticated or overly sentimental person. **—corn•ball** *adj.*

Corn Belt. A region of the midwestern United States, stretching across Ohio, Indiana, Illinois, Iowa, Minnesota, South Dakota, Missouri, Kansas, and Nebraska, where the chief products are corn and corn-fed livestock.

corn borer *n.* **1.** The larva of a moth, *Pyrausta nubilalis,* native to the Old World, that feeds on and destroys corn and other plants. **2.** Any of various similar insect larvae that infest corn.

corn bread, corn•bread (kôrn′brĕd′) *n.* A bread made of cornmeal.

corn•cake, corn cake (kôrn′kāk′) *n.* A bread made with white cornmeal cooked either as small cakes on a griddle or oven-baked in a pan. Also called "johnnycake."

corn•cob (kôrn′kŏb′) *n.* **1.** The hard core of an ear of corn to which the kernels are attached. **2.** A corncob pipe.

corncob pipe *n.* A pipe with a bowl made of a dried corncob.

corn cockle *n.* A plant, *Agrostemma githago,* native to Europe, having red flowers and growing in grain fields and by roadsides.

corn•crake (kôrn′krāk′) *n.* A common Old World bird, *Crex crex,* having brownish plumage and frequenting cornfields and meadows.

corn•dodg•er (kôrn′dŏj′ər) *n.* A corncake either baked, pan-fried, or broiled. [CORN + DODGER.]

cor•ne•a (kôr′nē-ə) *n.* The transparent anterior portion of the outer fibrous coat of the vertebrate eye, a uniformly thick, nearly circular, convex structure that refracts light onto the lens. [Medieval Latin *cornea (tēla),* "horny (tissue)," from Latin, feminine of *corneus,* horny, from *cornū,* horn.] **—cor·ne·al** *adj.*

corn earworm *n.* The large, destructive larva of a moth, *Heliothis armigera,* that feeds on corn and many other plants. Also called "bollworm."

corned beef *n.* A type of beef preserved with salt and spices.

Cor·neille (kôr-nā′), **Pierre** (1606–84). French playwright, the pioneer of French classical drama. His plays, including *Le Cid* (*c.* 1637) and *Horace* (1640), dramatize grand moral themes within measured and elegant verse.

cor·nel (kôr′nəl) *n.* Any of various plants of the genus *Cornus,* which includes the dogwoods. [German *Kornel(beere), Kornel(baum),* cornel (berry), cornel (tree), from Old High German *kornul-,* from Medieval Latin *corna* (unattested), from Latin *cornus*†, cornel tree.]

cornelian. Variant of **carnelian.**

cor·nel·ian cherry (kôr-nēl′yən) *n.* A shrub or small tree, *Cornus mas,* native to Eurasia, having very small yellow flowers and bright-red edible fruit. [From CORNEL.]

Cor·nell (kôr-nĕl′), **Katharine** (1893–1974). U.S. actress and producer. She made her Broadway debut in 1921 and that same year won acclaim for her starring role in *A Bill of Divorcement.* One of her most popular roles was Elizabeth Barrett Browning in *The Barretts of Wimpole Street,* which first opened in 1931.

cor·ne·ous (kôr′nē-əs) *adj.* Made of horn or a hornlike substance; horny. [Latin *corneus,* from *cornū,* horn.]

cor·ner (kôr′nər) *n. Abbr.* **cor. 1.** The position at which two lines or surfaces meet. **2.** The immediate interior or exterior region of the angle formed at this position, bounded by the two lines or surfaces. **3.** The point or place where the sides of roads, streets, or walls join, meet, or intersect. **4.** A threatening or embarrassing position, especially one from which escape is difficult or impossible: *backed into a corner.* **5.** Any part, quarter, or region: *from every corner of the globe.* **6.** A remote, secluded, or secret place, area, or part. **7.** A guard or decoration fitted on various kinds of corners, as of a bookbinding. **8.** A speculative monopoly of a stock or commodity created by purchasing all or most of the available supply in order to raise its price. **9.** In boxing and wrestling, either of two diagonally opposite corners of the ring in which opponents rest between rounds. **—cut corners. 1.** To take the shortest route around obstacles, often dangerously or illegally. **2.** To reduce expenses; economize. **—turn the corner.** To get over or come through the worst part of an illness, financial difficulty, or the like; pass the critical point.

~v. **cornered, -nering, -ners.** *—tr.* **1.** To furnish with corners. **2.** To place or drive into a corner. **3.** To get a corner in (a stock or commodity). *—intr.* **1.** To get a corner in a stock or commodity. **2.** To turn, as at a corner.

~adj. **1.** On or at a corner. **2.** Designed for or used in a corner. [Middle English, from Old French *cornere, corniere,* from Vulgar Latin *cornārium* (unattested), from Latin *cornū,* horn, extremity.]

cor·ner·stone (kôr′nər-stōn′) *n.* **1.** A stone at the corner of a building uniting two intersecting walls; a quoin. **2.** Such a stone ceremonially laid and often inscribed with the date of construction. **3.** The indispensable and fundamental basis of something: *Free speech is the cornerstone of a democracy.*

cor·net (kôr-nĕt′ *for sense 1;* kôr′nĭt *for senses 2–6) n.* **1.** *Abbr.* **cor.** A musical wind instrument of the trumpet class, having three valves operated by pistons. **2.** A piece of paper twisted into a cone and used to hold small wares such as candy and nuts. **3.** *British.* A wafer, usually cone-shaped, topped with ice cream. **4.** A large white headdress worn by certain nuns. **5.** A headdress, often cone-shaped, worn by women in the late Middle Ages. **6. a.** Formerly, the fifth commissioned officer in a British cavalry troop. **b.** The standard carried by such an officer. [Middle English, from Old French, diminutive of *corn,* horn, from Latin *cornū.*]

cor·net·cy (kôr′nĭt-sē) *n., pl.* **-cies.** Formerly, the rank or commission of a cornet cavalry officer.

cor·net·ist, cor·net·tist (kôr-nĕt′ĭst) *n.* One who plays a cornet.

corn-fed (kôrn′fĕd′) *adj.* **1.** Fed on corn. **2.** Well-fed and healthy, but provincial and unsophisticated.

corn·field (kôrn′fēld′) *n.* A field planted with corn.

corn·flakes (kôrn′flāks′) *pl.n.* A crisp, flaky, commercially prepared cold cereal made from coarse cornmeal.

corn·flour (kôrn′flou′ər) *n. British.* Cornstarch.

corn·flow·er (kôrn′flou′ər) *n.* A garden plant, *Centaurea cyanus,* native to Eurasia, having blue, purple, pink, or white flowers. Also called "bachelor's-button," "bluebottle." [So called because it is found in cornfields.]

corn·husk (kôrn′hŭsk′) *n.* The leafy husk surrounding an ear of corn. Also called "corn shuck."

cor·nice (kôr′nĭs) *n.* **1.** *Architecture.* **a.** A horizontal molded projection that crowns or completes a building or wall. **b.** The uppermost part of an entablature. **2.** A molding at the top of the walls of a room, between the walls and ceiling. **3.** An ornamental horizontal molding or frame used to conceal curtain rods, picture hooks, or other devices. **4.** An overhanging mass of snow at a precipice.

~tr.v. **corniced, -nicing, -nices.** To supply, decorate, or finish with, or as with, a cornice. [French *corniche,* from Italian *cornice,* perhaps from Latin *cornix* (stem *cornic-*), crow, also influenced by Greek *korōnis,* curved line, coping stone, from *korōnē,* anything curved, from *korōnos,* curved.]

cor·niche (kôr-nēsh′) *n.* A coast road, often along the side of a cliff. [French. See **cornice.**]

cor·nic·u·late (kôr-nĭk′yə-lāt′, -lĭt) *adj.* Having horns or hornlike projections. [Latin *corniculātus,* from *corniculum,* little horn, diminutive of *cornū,* horn.]

Cor·ning (kôr′nĭng). City in southern New York State, on the Chemung River in a dairy and vineyard region. It is famous for its glassworks dating from 1868 and its glass museum.

Cor·nish (kôr′nĭsh) *adj.* Of or pertaining to Cornwall in southwest England, its inhabitants, or their language.

~n. The Brythonic Celtic language of Cornwall, extinct since the late 18th century. **—Cor·nish·man** *n.*

Cornish hen *n.* See **Rock Cornish hen.**

Corn Laws *pl.n.* A series of British laws in force before 1846 regulating the grain trade and restricting imports of grain.

corn lily *n.* Any of several bulbous plants of the genus *Ixia,* native to southern Africa, having variously colored lilylike flowers.

corn marigold *n.* A Eurasian plant, *Chrysanthemum segetum,* having yellow or white daisylike flowers.

corn·meal, corn meal (kôrn′mēl′) *n.* Meal ground from corn.

corn pone (pōn) *n. Southern U.S.* Corn bread made without milk or eggs. Also called "pone."

corn poppy *n.* An Old World plant, *Papaver rhoeas,* having bright-red flowers, frequently a weed in cultivated fields. Also called "Flanders poppy."

corn rose *n. British.* Any of several red-flowered plants growing in grain fields, such as the corn poppy or the corn cockle.

corn·row (kôrn′rō′) *tr.v.* To style (hair) by dividing into sections and braiding in parallel rows close to the scalp. **—corn·row** *n.*

corn rule *n. Chemistry.* A rule for indicating the optical activity of amino acids with the formula $RCH(NH_2)(COOH)$. If the molecule were observed along the H–C direction, the COOH, R, and NH_2 groups would be arranged clockwise in dextrorotatory acids and counterclockwise in levorotatory acids. [From *COOH R* NH_2.]

corn salad *n.* Any of several plants of the genus *Valerianella;* especially, *V. locusta* (or *V. olitoria*), native to Europe, having small bluish flowers and leaves that are used in salad. Also called "lamb's-lettuce." [So called because it is found in cornfields.]

corn shuck *n.* A **cornhusk** *(see).*

corn silk *n.* The silky styles that appear as a tuft or tassel at the tip of an ear of corn.

corn·stalk (kôrn′stôk′) *n.* A stalk or stem of corn.

corn·starch (kôrn′stärch′) *n.* A starch made from corn and used as a thickener in cooking.

corn sugar *n.* **Dextrose** *(see).*

corn syrup *n.* A syrup prepared from corn, containing glucose combined with dextrin and maltose.

cor·nu (kôr′nyo͞o, -no͞o) *n., pl.* **-nua** (-nyo͞o-ə, -no͞o-ə). *Anatomy.* A structure resembling a horn. [Latin *cornū,* horn.] **—cor·nu·al** *adj.*

cor·nu·co·pi·a (kôr′nə-kō′pē-ə) *n.* **1.** A goat's horn overflowing with fruit, flowers, and corn, signifying prosperity; a horn of plenty. **2.** An overflowing store; an abundance. **3.** Any cone-shaped receptacle or ornament. [Late Latin *cornūcōpia,* horn of plenty, from Latin *cornū cōpiae* : *cornū,* horn + *cōpiae,* genitive of *cōpia,* plenty.] **—cor·nu·co·pi·an** *adj.*

cor·nute (kôr-no͞ot′, -nyo͞ot′) *adj.* Also **cor·nut·ed** (kôr-no͞o′tĭd, -nyo͞o′tĭd). **1.** Horn-shaped. **2.** Having horns or horn-shaped anatomical processes. [Latin *cornūtus,* horned, from *cornū,* horn.]

Corn·wall (kôrn′wôl′). *Abbr.* **Corn.** County in the extreme southwest of England. At its extremity is Land's End, the westernmost point of the English mainland. Tin was mined in Cornwall in ancient times and is still mined in a number of places. Following the Roman and Saxon invasions of Britain, Cornwall became a bastion of Celtic culture and its language, of Celtic origin, has never entirely disappeared. Truro is the administrative center, and Penzance the largest town.

Corn·wal·lis (kôrn-wŏl′ĭs), **Charles, 1st Marquess** (1738–1805). British soldier and statesman who commanded British forces in South Carolina during the American Revolution. His surrender at Yorktown on October 19, 1781, marked the final British defeat. As governor general of India (1786–93) he introduced a series of land reforms to secure administrative control of India for the East India Company.

corn whiskey *n.* Whiskey distilled from corn.

corn·y (kôr′nē) *adj.* **-ier, -iest.** *Informal.* **1.** Trite or mawkishly sentimental: *a corny love story.* **2.** Lacking subtlety; unsophisticated: *corny jokes.* [From CORN (from the supposedly unsophisticated humor of farmers).]

co·rol·la (kə-rŏl′ə) *n. Botany.* The inner envelope of a flower, consisting of fused or separate petals. Compare **calyx.** [New Latin, from Latin, diminutive of *corōna,* garland, CORONA.]

cor·ol·lar·y (kôr′ə-lĕr′ē, kŏr′-) *n., pl.* **-ies. 1.** A proposition that follows with little or no additional proof from one already proved. **2.** A deduction or inference. **3.** A natural consequence or effect; a result.

~adj. Consequent or resultant. [Middle English *corolarie,* from Latin *corollārium,* money paid for a garland, gratuity, from *corolla,* small garland, diminutive of *corōna,* garland, CORONA.]

Cor·o·man·del Coast (kôr′ə-măn′dĕl). The southern reaches of India's eastern seaboard, from Point Calimere to the mouth of the Krishna River. It is lashed by rough seas and monsoons.

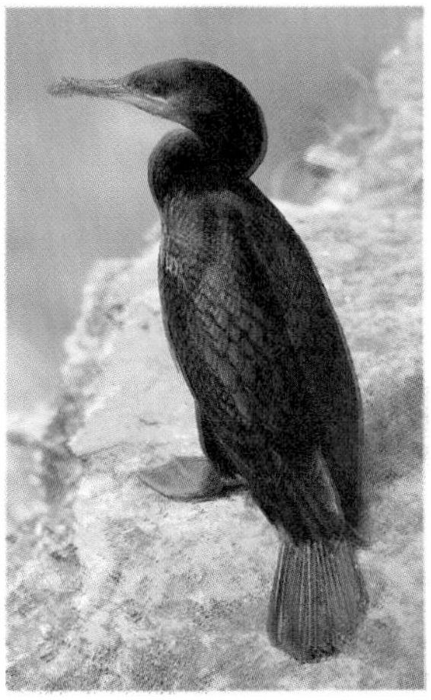

cormorant *In Japan, these diving birds—which are found in coastal waters in most parts of the world—have been used by fishermen for centuries. The birds are trained to dive for fish from boats and to return with their catch; tight leather collars prevent them from swallowing the fish. The cormorant's plumage is not oiled to resist water, and between hunting expeditions the bird often perches with its wings spread out to dry.*

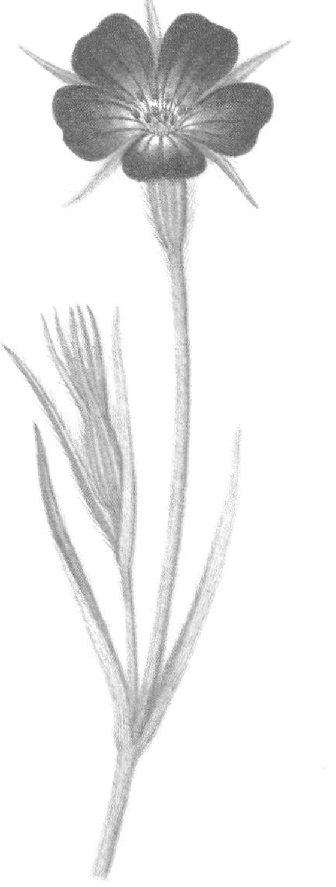

corn cockle Agrostemma githago *was once a common weed in northern European cornfields. But, since it grew among the corn, it lowered the quality of the flour; with improved methods of agriculture, this wildflower is becoming less common.*

co·ro·na (kə-rō′nə) *n., pl.* **-nas** or **-nae** (-nē). **1.** *Astronomy.* **a.** A faintly colored luminous ring around a celestial body visible through a haze or thin cloud, especially such a ring around the moon or sun, caused by diffraction of light from small suspended ice crystals in the upper atmosphere. **b.** The luminous irregular envelope of highly ionized gas outside the chromosphere of the sun. **2.** *Architecture.* The top projecting part of a cornice. **3.** A cigar having a long tapering body and blunt ends. **4.** A circular chandelier hanging from the ceiling of a church. **5.** *Anatomy.* A crownlike or upper part or structure, such as the top of the head. **6.** *Botany.* A crownlike part of a flower, usually between the petals and stamens, but sometimes an appendage of the corolla, as in daffodils. Also called "crown." **7.** *Electricity.* A faint glow enveloping the high-field electrode in a **corona discharge** *(see),* often accompanied by streamers directed toward the low-field electrode. [Latin *corōna,* garland, crown, from Greek *korōnē,* something curved, kind of crown, from *korōnos,* curved.]

Corona Aus·tra·lis (ô-strā′lĭs) *n.* A constellation in the Southern Hemisphere near Telescopium and Sagittarius. Also called the "Southern Crown."

Corona Bo·re·al·is (bôr′ē-ăl′ĭs, -ā′lĭs, bōr′ē-) *n.* A constellation containing the Corona Borealis cluster of galaxies, in the Northern Hemisphere near Hercules and Boötes. Also called the "Northern Crown."

co·ro·nach (kôr′ə-nəкн, kŏr′-) *n.* In Ireland or the Highlands of Scotland, a Gaelic funeral dirge. [Irish *coranach* and (Scottish) Gaelic *corranach* : *comh-,* together + *rānach,* a crying.]

Co·ro·na·do (kôr′ə-nä′dō, kŏr′-), **Francisco Vásquez de** (1510–54). Spanish explorer and colonial administrator. The governor of a Mexican province, he was intrigued by stories of immeasurable wealth to the north. He led an expedition through present-day southwest America in search of gold (1540), but was considered a failure when he returned to Mexico with only stories of the Grand Canyon and other natural wonders discovered on the journey.

corona discharge *n.* An electrical discharge characterized by a corona and occurring when one of two electrodes in a gas has a shape such that the electric field strength close to its surface is significantly greater than that between the electrodes.

co·ro·na·graph, co·ro·no·graph (kə-rō′nə-grăf′, -gräf′) *n. Astronomy.* A type of refracting telescope designed for study of the sun's corona, having a central disk to block light from the sun's surface. **—co·ro·na·graph·ic** *adj.*

cor·o·nal (kôr′ə-nəl, kŏr′-) *n.* **1.** A garland, wreath, or circlet. **2.** *Anatomy.* The coronal suture. **3.** *Phonetics.* A coronal speech sound.

~*adj.* **co·ro·nal** (kə-rō′nəl, kôr′ə-nəl, kŏr′-) **1.** Of or pertaining to a coronal. **2.** *Anatomy.* Of, designating, or having the direction of the coronal suture. **3.** *Phonetics.* Articulated with the blade of the tongue raised. [Middle English, from Old French *coronal,* from Latin *corōnālis,* of a crown, from CORONA.]

coronal suture *n.* The line of union of the two parietal bones with the frontal bone of the skull. Also called "coronal."

cor·o·nar·y (kôr′ə-nĕr′ē, kŏr′-) *adj.* **1.** Encircling. Said of arteries, ligaments, nerves, and the like that encircle a structure. **2.** Of or pertaining to the coronary arteries. **3.** Loosely, of or pertaining to the heart.

~*n., pl.* **coronaries.** A coronary thrombosis. [Latin *corōnārius,* of a wreath or garland, from *corōna,* garland, crown, CORONA.]

coronary artery *n.* Either of the two arteries that originate in the aorta and supply blood to the heart.

coronary occlusion *n.* The partial or complete obstruction of blood flow in a coronary artery, as by a blood clot or spasm.

coronary thrombosis *n.* The obstructing of a coronary artery by a blood clot, often leading to destruction of heart muscle and causing severe pain in the chest.

cor·o·na·tion (kôr′ə-nā′shən, kŏr′-) *n.* The act or ceremony of crowning a sovereign or a sovereign's consort. [Middle English *coronacioun,* from Old French *coronation,* from Medieval Latin *corōnātiō* (stem *corōnātiōn-*), from Latin *corōnāre* (past participle *corōnātus*), to crown, from CORONA.]

cor·o·ner (kôr′ə-nər, kŏr′-) *n. Abbr.* **cor.** A public officer, normally a physician, whose primary function is to investigate by inquest any death that may not have been from natural causes. [Middle English, officer charged with maintaining the record of the Crown's pleas, from Norman French *corouner,* from *coro(u)ne,* CROWN.] **—cor·o·ner·ship** *n.*

coroner's jury *n.* A group of people summoned to a coroner's inquest to determine the cause of the death under investigation.

cor·o·net (kôr′ə-nĕt′, kŏr′-) *n.* **1.** A small crown worn by princes and other nobles below the rank of sovereign. **2.** A chaplet or headband decorated with gold or jewels. **3.** The upper margin of a horse's hoof. [Middle English *coronette,* from Old French, diminutive of *coro(u)ne,* CROWN.]

Co·rot (kō-rō′), **Jean Baptiste Camille** (1796–1875). French landscape painter. His early informal sketches of the Italian countryside are today among his most highly regarded works, though they were never exhibited in his lifetime. His larger compositions are somewhat more mannered, characterized by soft contours and muted, silvery tones.

corp. corporation.

cor·po·ra. Plural of **corpus.**

cor·po·ral[1] (kôr′pər-əl) *adj.* Of the body; bodily. [Middle English *corporal, corporel,* from Old French, from Latin *corporālis,* from

corpus (stem *corpor-*), body.] **—cor·po·ral·i·ty** (kôr′pə-răl′ə-tē) *n.* **—cor·po·ral·ly** *adv.*

Usage: The similarity in form between *corporal* and *corporeal* sometimes leads to confusion. *Corporal* means simply "of the body" and is used in many phrases where the physical form of the body is involved (*corporal punishment, corporal needs*). *Corporeal* adds the implication of "bodily as opposed to spiritual or intangible" (*corporeal substance*). For *body* in the sense of "group of people united for some common end," the related adjective is *corporate.*

corporal[2] *n. Abbr.* **Cpl.** A noncommissioned officer of the lowest rank in the U.S. Army, Air Force, or Marine Corps. [Obsolete French, variant (probably influenced by *corporal,* bodily, as if meaning "leader of a body of troops") of CAPORAL.]

corporal[3] *n.* Also **cor·po·ra·le** (kôr′pə-rā′lē). *Ecclesiastical.* A white linen cloth on which the consecrated elements are placed during the celebration of the Eucharist. [Middle English *corporale,* from Old French *corporal,* from Medieval Latin *corporāle,* from the neuter of Latin *corporālis,* of the body, CORPORAL.]

corporal punishment *n.* Physical punishment, such as beating.

cor·po·rate (kôr′pər-ĭt) *adj.* **1.** Formed into a corporation; incorporated. **2.** Of a corporation. **3.** United or combined into one body; collective. **4.** Considered as, pertaining to, or shared by a united body. **—See Usage note at corporal. 5.** Variant of **corporative.** [Latin *corporātus,* past participle of *corporāre,* to make into a body, from *corpus* (stem *corpor-*), CORPUS.] **—cor·po·rate·ly** *adv.*

cor·po·ra·tion (kôr′pə-rā′shən) *n. Abbr.* **corp. 1.** A body of persons granted a charter legally recognizing them as a separate entity having its own rights, privileges, and liabilities distinct from those of its members. Also called "body corporate." **2.** Such a body created for purposes of government, especially that of a city. **3.** Any group of people acting as one body. **4.** *Informal.* A potbelly.

cor·po·ra·tive (kôr′pə-rā′tĭv, -pər-ə-tĭv) *adj.* Also **cor·po·rate** (kôr′pər-ĭt). **1.** Of, pertaining to, or associated with a corporation. **2.** Of or designating a government or political system in which the principal economic functions, such as banking, industry, labor, and government, are organized as corporate entities with some official status. **—cor·po·rat·ism** *n.*

cor·po·re·al (kôr-pôr′ē-əl, -pōr′-) *adj.* **1.** Of, pertaining to, or characteristic of the body. **2.** Of a material rather than spiritual nature; tangible. **—See Usage note at corporal.** [From Latin *corporeus,* of the body, from *corpus* (stem *corpor-*), CORPUS.] **—cor·po·re·al·ly** *adv.* **—cor·po·re·al·ness** *n.*

cor·po·re·i·ty (kôr′pə-rē′ə-tē) *n.* Also **cor·po·re·al·i·ty** (kôr′pə-rē-ăl′ə-tē). The state of being material or corporeal; physical existence.

cor·po·sant (kôr′pə-zănt′, -sănt′) *n.* A luminous electrical phenomenon, **St. Elmo's fire** *(see).* [Portuguese *corpo-santo,* "holy body."]

corps (kôr, kōr) *n., pl.* **corps** (kôrz, kōrz). **1.** *Abbr.* **c., C.** *Military.* **a.** A separate branch or department of the armed forces having a specialized function. **b.** A tactical unit of ground combat forces, composed of two or more divisions and auxiliary service troops. **2.** A body of persons acting together or associated in a common calling or purpose. [French, from Latin *corpus,* body, CORPUS.]

corps de bal·let (kôr′ də bă-lā′) *n.* The dancers in a ballet troupe who perform as a group and have no solo parts. [French, "ballet troupe."]

corpse (kôrps) *n.* A dead body, especially of a human being. [Middle English *corps, cors,* from Old French, from Latin *corpus,* body.]

cor·pu·lence (kôr′pyə-ləns) *n.* Fatness; obesity. [Middle English, from Latin *corpulentia,* from *corpulentus,* from *corpus,* body, CORPUS.]

cor·pu·lent (kôr′pyə-lənt) *adj.* Large in body; obese. **—See Synonyms at fat. —cor·pu·lent·ly** *adv.*

cor·pus (kôr′pəs) *n., pl.* **-pora** (-pər-ə). *Abbr.* **cor. 1.** A large collection of writings or other artistic compositions of a specific kind or having a specific theme; especially, the complete body of work of an author. **2.** *Anatomy.* **a.** A structure constituting the main part of an organ. **b.** Any distinct mass or body. **3.** The principal or capital, as distinguished from the interest or income, of a fund, estate, investment, or the like. **4.** A human or animal body, especially when dead. [Middle English, from Latin, body, substance.]

corpus cal·lo·sum (kə-lō′səm) *n., pl.* **corpora callosa** (-sə). *Anatomy.* A wide arched band of white matter connecting the cerebral hemispheres of the brain at the base of the longitudinal fissure. [New Latin, "callous body."]

Cor·pus Chris·ti (kôr′pəs krĭs′tē). A city of southern Texas, on Corpus Christi Bay, an inlet of the Gulf of Mexico. The city is a petroleum and natural gas center, with much heavy industry and a large shrimp fleet.

Corpus Christi *n. Roman Catholic Church.* A festival celebrated in honor of the Eucharist on the first Thursday after Trinity Sunday. [Middle English, from Medieval Latin, "body of Christ."]

cor·pus·cle (kôr′pə-səl, -pŭs′əl) *n.* **1.** *Biology.* A cell, such as an erythrocyte or leucocyte, that is capable of free movement in a fluid or matrix, as distinguished from a cell fixed in tissue. **2.** *Anatomy.* The encapsulated ending of a secondary nerve. **3.** A discrete particle such as a photon or electron. **4.** Any minute globular particle. [Latin *corpusculum,* diminutive of CORPUS.] **—cor·pus·cu·lar** (kôr-pŭs′kyə-lər) *adj.*

corpuscular theory *n. Physics.* The theory that light consists of streams of small particles. Compare **wave theory.** See **light.**

corpus de·lic·ti (dĭ-lĭk′tī) *n.* **1.** *Law.* **a.** The material substance upon which a crime has been committed. **b.** The material evidence of the fact that a crime has been committed, such as the discovered corpse of a murder victim. **2.** Loosely, the victim's corpse in a murder case. [New Latin, "body of the crime."]

corpus ju·ris (jŏŏr′ĭs) *n. Abbr.* **C.J.** The collective or comprehensive body of all the laws of a nation or state. [Late Latin, "body of law."]

Corpus Juris Ca·non·i·ci (kə-nŏn′ə-sī′) *n. Roman Catholic Church.* The body of decrees and canons constituting the standard of ecclesiastical law until replaced in 1918 by Codex Juris Canonici. [Late Latin, "body of canon law."]

Corpus Juris Ci·vil·is (sĭ-vĭl′ĭs) *n.* The body of civil or Roman law comprising the Digest, the Institutes, the Code, and the Novels, assembled and issued (529–535) during Justinian's reign and forming the basis of most continental European law. [Latin, "body of civil law."]

corpus lu·te·um (lōō′tē-əm) *n., pl.* **corpora lutea** (-ə). A yellow mass of endocrine cells in a ruptured mature Graafian follicle of the ovary, formed after the release of an ovum. It secretes the hormone progesterone, which maintains pregnancy. [New Latin, "yellowish body."]

corpus stri·a·tum (strī-ā′təm) *n., pl.* **corpora striata** (-tə). Either of two gray-and-white, striated ganglionic masses of the brain stem in the lower lateral wall of each cerebral hemisphere. [New Latin, "striated body."]

corr. 1. correction. **2.** correspondence; correspondent.

cor·rade (kə-rād′) *v.* **-raded, -rading, -rades.** —*tr.* To wear away by friction of objects such as sand and gravel moving by gravity or carried in waves, running water, wind, or ice. —*intr.* To be worn away in this way. [Latin *corrādere*, to scrape together : *com-*, together + *rādere*, to scrape.] —**cor·ra·sion** (kə-rā′zhən) *n.* —**cor·ra·sive** (kə-rā′sĭv, -zĭv) *adj.*

cor·ral (kə-rǎl′) *n.* **1.** An enclosure for confining livestock. **2.** An enclosure formed by a circle of wagons for defense against attack while encamped. —*tr.v.* **corralled, -ralling, -rals. 1.** To drive into and hold in a corral. **2.** To arrange (wagons) in a corral. **3.** *Informal.* To seize; capture. [Spanish and Portuguese, possibly of Hottentot origin. See also **kraal**.]

cor·rect (kə-rĕkt′) *tr.v.* **-rected, -recting, -rects. 1.** To remove the errors or mistakes from. **2.** To indicate or mark the errors of. **3.** To admonish or punish for the purpose of improving. **4.** To remove, remedy, or counteract (a malfunction, for example). **5.** To adjust so as to meet a standard or other required condition. —*adj.* **1.** Free from error or fault; true or accurate. **2.** Conforming to accepted standards; proper: *correct behavior.* [Middle English *correcten*, from Latin *corrigere* (past participle *correctus*), to make straight, correct : *com-* (intensifier) + *regere*, to lead straight, rule.] —**cor·rect·a·ble, cor·rect·i·ble** *adj.* —**cor·rect·ly** *adv.* —**cor·rect·ness** *n.* —**cor·rec·tor** *n.*

    Synonyms: amend, rectify, redress, reform, remedy, revise.

cor·rec·tion (kə-rĕk′shən) *n. Abbr.* **cor., corr. 1.** The act or process of correcting. **2.** That which is offered or substituted for a mistake, fault, or abnormality; an improvement. **3.** Punishment intended to rehabilitate or improve. **4.** An amount or quantity that is added or subtracted by way of correcting. **5.** A decline in stock market prices or activity following a rise. —**cor·rec·tion·al** *adj.*

cor·rec·ti·tude (kə-rĕk′tə-tōōd′, -tyōōd′) *n.* The state or quality of being correct, especially in manners and behavior; propriety.

cor·rec·tive (kə-rĕk′tĭv) *adj.* Tending or intended to correct. —*n.* Something that corrects. —**cor·rec·tive·ly** *adv.*

Cor·reg·gio (kə-rĕj′ō, -rĕj′ē-ō), born Antonio Allegri da Correggio (*c.* 1494–1534). Italian painter, a master of the High Renaissance, whose name derived from his home town in northern Italy. He produced devotional pictures that include *Holy Night* and frescoes, such as those in the convent of San Paolo, Parma (1518).

Cor·reg·i·dor (kə-rĕg′ə-dôr′). An island at the entrance to Manila Bay, in the Philippines. It was the site of a World War II battle (April 9–May 6, 1942), after whtch the Philippines were surrendered to the Japanese. The island was recaptured in March 1945 and is now a national shrine.

correl. correlative.

cor·re·late (kôr′ə-lāt′, kŏr′-) *v.* **-lated, -lating, -lates.** Also chiefly *British* **co·re·late.** —*tr.* **1.** To put or bring into causal, complementary, parallel, or reciprocal relation: *correlate data from several sources.* **2.** To establish or demonstrate as having a correlation: *correlated drug abuse and crime.* —*intr.* To be related by a correlation. —*adj.* (kôr′ə-lĭt, -lāt′, kŏr′-) Related by a correlation; especially, having corresponding characteristics. —*n.* (kôr′ə-lĭt, -lāt′, kŏr′-) Either of two entities related by a correlation; a correlative. [Back-formation from CORRELATION.]

cor·re·la·tion (kôr′ə-lā′shən, kŏr′-) *n.* **1.** A causal, complementary, parallel, or reciprocal relationship; especially, a structural, functional, or qualitative correspondence between two comparable entities: *a correlation between recession and unemployment.* **2.** *Statistics.* **a.** The simultaneous increase or decrease in value of two numerically valued random variables. Also called "positive correlation." **b.** The simultaneous increase in the value of one and decrease in the value of the other of two numerically valued random variables. Also called "negative correlation." **3.** The act of correlating or the condition of being correlated. [Medieval Latin *correlātiō* (stem *correlātiōn-*): *com-*, together + *relātiō*, relation, from Latin *relātus*, "carried back" (see **relate**).] —**cor·re·la·tion·al** *adj.*

correlation coefficient *n. Statistics.* A measure of the interdependence of two random variables that ranges in value from −1 to +1,

indicating perfect negative correlation at −1, absence of correlation at 0, and perfect positive correlation at +1.

cor·rel·a·tive (kə-rĕl′ə-tĭv) *adj. Abbr.* **correl. 1.** Related; corresponding. **2.** Reciprocally related. —*n. Abbr.* **correl. 1.** Either of two related entities; a correlate. **2.** *Grammar.* A correlative word or expression. —**cor·rel·a·tive·ly** *adv.* —**cor·rel·a·tive·ness, cor·rel·a·tiv·i·ty** *n.*

correlative conjunction *n. Grammar.* Either of a pair of conjunctions indicating a reciprocal or complementary grammatical relation. *Neither* and *nor* are correlative conjunctions.

cor·re·spond (kôr′ĭ-spŏnd′, kŏr′-) *intr.v.* **-sponded, -sponding, -sponds. 1.** To be in agreement, harmony, or conformity; be consistent or compatible: *Our goals correspond.* **2.** To be similar or equivalent in some way, such as character, meaning, or function. Used with *to* or *with: English "good-by" corresponds to French "adieu."* **3.** To communicate by letter, usually over a period of time. —See Synonyms at **agree.** [Old French *correspondre*, from Medieval Latin *correspondēre* : *com-*, together, mutually + *respondēre*, RESPOND.]

cor·re·spon·dence (kôr′ə-spŏn′dəns, kŏr′-) *n. Abbr.* **cor., corr., corresp. 1.** The act, fact, or state of agreeing or conforming. **2.** Similarity or analogy. **3. a.** Communication by the exchange of letters. **b.** The letters written or received.

correspondence principle *n. Physics.* The principle that predictions of quantum theory approach those of classical physics in the limit of large quantum numbers.

correspondence school *n.* A school that offers instruction by mail, sending lessons and examinations to students at home.

cor·re·spon·dent (kôr′ə-spŏn′dənt, kŏr′) *n. Abbr.* **cor., corr. 1.** One who communicates by means of letters. **2.** Someone employed by a newspaper, magazine, or broadcasting company to supply news or articles from a distant place or on a specific subject: *a foreign correspondent.* **3.** A person who writes letters to a newspaper or magazine. **4.** A person or firm having regular business relations with another, especially at a distance. **5.** A thing that corresponds to something else. —*adj.* Corresponding; consistent. —**cor·re·spon·dent·ly** *adv.*

cor·re·spon·ding (kôr′ə-spŏn′dĭng, kŏr′-) *adj. Abbr.* **cor. 1.** Agreeing or conforming; consistent. **2.** Analogous or equivalent. —**cor·re·spon·ding·ly** *adv.*

corresponding angle *n. Mathematics.* Either of a pair of angles formed when two lines are cut by a third (the transversal). The pairs of corresponding angles are angles that lie on the same side of each line and the same side of the transversal. If the two lines are parallel, the corresponding angles are equal.

cor·re·spon·sive (kôr′ə-spŏn′sĭv, kŏr′-) *adj.* Corresponding. —**cor·re·spon·sive·ly** *adv.*

cor·ri·da (kô-rē′də) *n.* A bullfight. [Spanish, "a running," from the feminine past participle of *correr*, to run, from Latin *currere*.]

cor·ri·dor (kôr′ĭ-dər, -dôr′, kŏr′-) *n.* **1.** A narrow hallway, passageway, or gallery, generally with rooms or apartments opening onto it. **2.** A similar passageway alongside the compartments of a train. **3.** A tract of land forming a passageway, such as that which allows an inland country access to the sea through another country. **4.** A lane for the passage of aircraft. [French, from Italian *corridore*, "a run," from *correre*, to run, from Latin *currere*.]

cor·rie (kôr′ē, kŏr′ē) *n. Scottish.* A cirque (see). [Scottish Gaelic *coire*, cauldron, hollow.]

cor·ri·gen·dum (kôr′ə-jĕn′dəm, kŏr′-) *n., pl.* **-da** (-də). **1.** An error to be corrected, especially a printer's error. **2. corrigenda.** A list of errors shown with their corrections in a book or other publication. [Latin, gerundive of *corrigere*, to CORRECT.]

cor·ri·gi·ble (kôr′ə-jə-bəl, kŏr′-) *adj.* Capable of being corrected, reformed, or improved. [Middle English, from Old French, from Medieval Latin *corrigibilis*, from Latin *corrigere*, to CORRECT.] —**cor·ri·gi·bil·i·ty** *n.* —**cor·ri·gi·bly** *adv.*

cor·ri·val (kə-rī′vəl, kō-) *n.* A rival or opponent. —*adj.* Rival or opposing. [Old French *corrival*, from Latin *corrivālis*, joint rival : *com-*, together + *rīvālis*, RIVAL.] —**cor·ri·val·ry** *n.*

cor·ro·bo·rant (kə-rŏb′ər-ənt) *adj. Archaic.* **1.** Corroborating. **2.** Strengthening. —*n. Archaic.* Something that corroborates.

cor·rob·o·rate (kə-rŏb′ə-rāt′) *tr.v.* **-rated, -rating, -rates.** To strengthen or support (other evidence); attest the truth or accuracy of. —See Synonyms at **confirm.** [Latin *corrōborāre* : *com-* (intensive) + *rōborāre*, to strengthen, from *rōbur*, hard kind of oak, strength.] —**cor·rob·o·ra·tion** *n.* —**cor·rob·o·ra·tor** *n.*

cor·rob·o·ra·tive (kə-rŏb′ə-rā′tĭv, -ər-ə-tĭv) *adj.* Also **cor·rob·o·ra·to·ry** (kə-rŏb′ər-ə-tôr′ē, -tōr′ē) Confirming or tending to confirm. —**cor·rob·o·ra·tive·ly** *adv.*

cor·rob·o·ree (kə-rŏb′ə-rē) *n. Australian.* **1.** An aboriginal dance festival held at night to celebrate tribal victories or other events. **2.** Any large or noisy celebration. [Native Australian *korobra*.]

cor·rode (kə-rōd′) *v.* **-roded, -roding, -rodes.** —*tr.* **1.** To eat away or wear away gradually, especially by chemical action. **2.** To impair steadily; slowly destroy. —*intr.* To be eaten or worn away; become corroded. [Middle English *corroden*, from Latin *corrōdere*, to gnaw to pieces : *com-* (intensive) + *rōdere*, to gnaw.] —**cor·rod·ent** *n.* —**cor·rod·i·ble** (kə-rō′sə-bəl) *adj.*

cor·ro·sion (kə-rō′zhən) *n.* **1.** The act or process of corroding; especially, the wearing away of metals. **2.** A substance, such as rust, resulting from such a process. **3.** The condition produced by such a process. **4.** *Geology.* The wearing down of rocks by chemical means

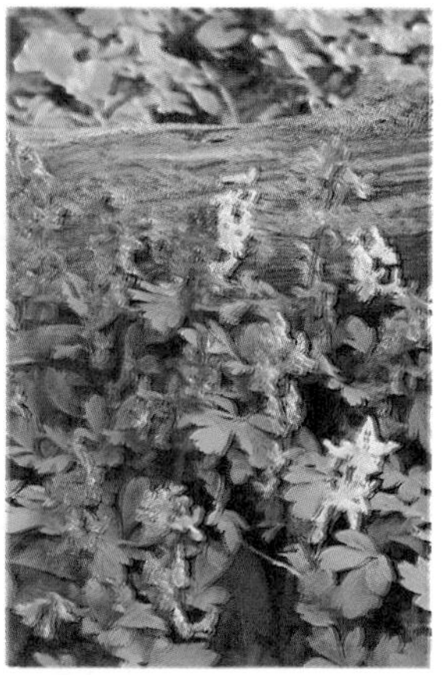

corydalis *There are about 20 species in the* Corydalis *genus. This is* Corydalis cava, *a European species that grows to about 150 millimeters (6 inches) high and flowers between February and May.*

PRONUNCIATION KEY

ă, pat; ā, pay; âr, care; ä, father, are; b, bib; ch, church; d, deed; ĕ, pet; ē, be; f, fife; g, gag; h, hat; hw, which; ĭ, pit; ī, pie; îr, pier; j, judge; k, kick; l, lid, needle; m, mum; n, no, sudden; ng, thing; ŏ, pot; ō, toe; ô, paw, for; oi, noise; ou, out; o͝o, book; o͞o, boot; p, pop; r, roar; s, sauce; sh, ship, dish; t, tight; th, thin, path; *th*, this, bathe; ŭ, cut; ûr, fur; v, valve; w, with; y, yes; z, zebra, size; zh, vision; ə, about, item, edible, gallop, circus, peaceful

IN FOREIGN WORDS:

à, *Fr.* ami; œ, *Fr.* feu, *Ger.* schön; ü, *Fr.* tu, *Ger.* über; KH, *Ger.* ich, *Scot.* loch; N, *Fr.* bon; y', *Fr.* Compiègne

STRESS MARKS:

Primary stress: ′
in·cite′ (ĭn-sīt′)
Secondary stress: ′
in′sight′ (ĭn′sīt′)

such as solution or oxidation. Also called "chemical weathering." **5.** Slow destruction, as of a relationship. [Middle English *corosioun,* from Old French *corrosion,* from Late Latin *corrōsiō* (stem *corrōsiōn-*), from Latin *corrōsus,* past participle of *corrōdere,* to CORRODE.]

cor·ro·sive (kə-rō′sĭv) *adj.* **1. a.** Capable of corroding. **b.** Inclined to produce corrosion. **2.** Spiteful, malicious, or malevolent. **3.** Insidiously destructive.
~*n.* A corrosive substance. **—cor·ro·sive·ly** *adv.* **—cor·ro·sive·ness** *n.*

corrosive sublimate *n. Chemistry.* An inorganic compound, **mercuric chloride** *(see).*

cor·ru·gate (kôr′ə-gāt′, kŏr′-) *v.* **-gated, -gating, -gates.** *—tr.* To shape into folds or parallel and alternating ridges and grooves. *—intr.* To become corrugated. [Latin *corrūgāre,* to make full of wrinkles : *com-,* together + *rūgāre,* to wrinkle, from *rūga,* wrinkle.] **—cor·ru·gat·ed** *adj.* **—cor·ru·ga·tion** *n.*

corrugated iron *n.* A structural sheet steel, usually galvanized, shaped in parallel grooves and ridges for rigidity.

cor·rupt (kə-rŭpt′) *adj.* **1.** Morally debased and perverted; depraved. **2.** Marked by or guilty of venality and dishonesty, especially bribery: *a corrupt mayor.* **3.** Decaying; putrid. **4.** Infected; contaminated; unclean. **5.** Containing errors or alterations, as a text: *a corrupt translation.*
~*v.* **corrupted, -rupting, -rupts.** *—tr.* **1.** To destroy or subvert the honesty or integrity of, especially by bribery. **2.** To ruin morally; pervert. **3.** To taint; contaminate; infect. **4.** To cause to become rotten; spoil. **5.** To change the original form of (a text, language, or the like). **6.** *Computer Science.* To change (stored data) so that it cannot be used. *—intr.* To become corrupt. [Middle English, from Old French, from Latin *corruptus,* past participle of *corrumpere,* break to pieces, destroy, ruin : *com-,* completely + *rumpere,* to break.] **—cor·rupt·er, cor·rup·tor** (kə-rŭp′tər) *n.* **—cor·rup·tive** *adj.* **—cor·rupt·ly** *adv.* **—cor·rupt·ness** *n.*

cor·rupt·i·ble (kə-rŭp′tə-bəl) *adj.* Capable of being corrupted, as by bribery or depravity. **—cor·rupt·i·bil·i·ty, cor·rupt·i·ble·ness** *n.* **—cor·rupt·i·bly** *adv.*

cor·rup·tion (kə-rŭp′shən) *n.* **1.** The act or result of corrupting. **2.** The state of being corrupt. **3.** An altered or debased form of a word or text. **4.** *Archaic.* Anything that corrupts; a corrupting influence.

cor·rup·tion·ist (kə-rŭp′shən-ĭst) *n.* One who defends or practices corruption.

cor·sage (kôr-säzh′) *n.* **1.** A small bouquet of flowers worn by a woman at the shoulder or waist or on the wrist. **2.** The bodice or waist of a dress. [Middle English, from Old French, torso, bust, from *cors, corps,* body, from Latin *corpus,* CORPUS.]

cor·sair (kôr′sâr′) *n.* **1.** A privateer, especially along the Barbary Coast of North Africa. **2.** A swift pirate ship. **3.** A pirate. [Old French *corsaire,* pirate, from Old Provençal *corsari,* from Old Italian *corsaro,* from Medieval Latin *cursārius,* from *cursus,* plunder, from Latin, "a run," from the past participle of *currere,* to run.]

corse (kôrs) *n. Archaic.* A corpse. [Middle English *cors,* CORPSE.]

corse·let (kôrs′lĭt *for sense 1;* kôr′sə-lĕt′ *for sense 2*) *n.* Also **cors·let** (for sense 1 only). **1.** Body armor; especially, a breastplate. **2.** A one-piece undergarment consisting of a light corset and a brassiere. [Old French *corselet,* diminutive of *cors,* body. See **corpse.**]

cor·set (kôr′sĭt) *n.* **1.** A close-fitting undergarment, often reinforced by elastic or stays, worn especially by women to support and shape the waistline, hips, and abdomen. **2.** A medieval outer garment, especially a laced jacket or bodice.
~*tr.v.* **corseted, -seting, -sets.** To enclose in or as if in a corset; fit a corset on. [Middle English, from Old French, diminutive of *cors,* body. See **corpse.**]

cor·se·tière (kôr′sə-tyâr′) *n. Masculine* **corsetier** (kôr′sə-tyā′). A maker, fitter, or seller of corsets. [French, from CORSET.]

Cor·si·ca (kôr′sĭ-kə). A rugged Mediterranean island forming two departments of France. Napoleon Bonaparte was born here. The landscape and poor communications have contributed to a tradition of banditry. Sheep and goats are raised, and vines, olives, lemons, and tobacco are grown. Ajaccio is the capital and Bastia the largest city. **—Cor·si·can** *adj. & n.*

cor·tege, cor·tège (kôr-tĕzh′, -tāzh′) *n.* **1. a.** A ceremonial procession. **b.** A funeral procession. **2.** A train of attendants; a retinue, as of a distinguished person. [French *cortège,* from Italian *corteggio,* from *corteggiare,* to pay honor, court, from *corte,* court, from Latin *cohors* (stem *cohort-*), enclosure, court.]

Cor·tes (kôr′tĕs) *n.* The legislative assembly of Spain. [Spanish, plural of *corte,* COURT.]

Cor·tés or **Cor·tez** (kôr-tĕz′), **Hernán** or **Hernando** (1485–1547). Spanish soldier and explorer who won Aztec Mexico for Spain. With an army of native Tlaxcalans he reached the Aztec capital, Tenochtitlán, in 1519 and took their ruler, Montezuma, hostage. In his absence the Aztecs rebelled and drove the Spaniards out. Cortés besieged the city (1521) and razed it to the ground. Appointed governor of New Spain, he reorganized land tenure and launched expeditions to Central America (1524–26).

cor·tex (kôr′tĕks′) *n., pl.* **-tices** (-tə-sēz′) or **-texes. 1.** *Anatomy.* The outer layer of an organ or part, as of the kidney, adrenal gland, cerebrum, or cerebellum. **2.** *Botany.* **a.** A layer of tissue in roots and stems lying between the epidermis and the vascular tissue. **b.** An external layer such as bark or rind. [Latin, bark, shell, rind.]

cor·ti·cal (kôr′tĭ-kəl) *adj.* **1.** Of, pertaining to, or consisting of cortex. **2.** Of, pertaining to, associated with, or depending on the cerebral cortex. [New Latin *corticalis,* from Latin *cortex* (stem *cortic-*), bark, shell, CORTEX.] **—cor·ti·cal·ly** *adv.*

cor·ti·cate (kôr′tĭ-kĭt, -kāt′) *adj.* Also **cor·ti·cat·ed** (-kā′tĭd). Having a bark, rind, or similar specialized outer layer. [Latin *corticātus,* covered with bark, from *cortex* (stem *cortic-*), bark, CORTEX.]

cortico–, cortic– *prefix.* Indicates cortex; for example, **corticosteroid.** [Latin *cortex* (stem *cortic-*), CORTEX.]

cor·tic·o·lous (kôr-tĭk′ə-ləs) *adj. Biology.* Growing or living on tree bark. [French *corticicole* : CORTI(CO)- + -COLOUS.]

cor·ti·co·ster·oid (kôr′tĭ-kō-stĕr′oid′, -stîr′-) *n.* Also **cor·ti·coid** (kôr′tĭ-koid′). Any of the steroid hormones of the adrenal cortex.

cor·ti·co·ster·one (kôr′tĭ-kŏs′tə-rōn′, kôr′tĭ-kō-stĕr′ōn′, -stîr′ōn′) *n.* A corticosteroid, $C_{21}H_{30}O_4$, that induces hyperglycemia and depositing of glycogen in the liver. [CORTICO- + STER(OL) + -ONE.]

cor·ti·co·tro·pin (kôr′tĭ-kō-trō′pĭn) *n.* Also **cor·ti·co·tro·phin** (-trō′fĭn). An anterior pituitary hormone, **ACTH** *(see).* [CORTICO- + -TROP(IC) + -IN.]

cor·ti·sol (kôr′tə-sôl′, -sōl′) *n.* A corticosteroid, **hydrocortisone** *(see).* [CORTIS(ONE) + -OL.]

cor·ti·sone (kôr′tə-sōn′, -zōn′) *n.* A corticosteroid, $C_{21}H_{28}O_5$, active in carbohydrate metabolism and used to treat rheumatoid arthritis, adrenal insufficiency, certain allergies, diseases of connective tissue, and gout. [Short for CORTICOSTERONE.]

co·run·dum (kə-rŭn′dəm) *n.* An extremely hard mineral, aluminum oxide, sometimes containing iron, magnesia, or silica, occurring in gem varieties such as ruby and sapphire and in a common gray, brown, or blue form used chiefly in abrasives. [Tamil *kuruntam,* probably ultimately from Sanskrit *kuruvinda*†, ruby.]

cor·us·cate (kôr′əs-kāt′, kŏr′-) *intr.v.* **-cated, -cating, -cates. 1.** To give forth flashes of light; sparkle; glitter; scintillate. **2.** To make a brilliant display, as of wit. [Latin *coruscāre,* to thrust, vibrate, glitter.] **—co·rus·cant** (kə-rŭs′kənt) *adj.* **—cor·us·ca·tion** *n.*

cor·vée (kôr-vā′) *n.* **1.** A day of unpaid labor, as on roads, required of a vassal by his feudal lord. **2.** Labor exacted by a local authority for little or no pay or instead of taxes, used especially in the maintenance of roads. [Middle English *corve,* from Old French, from Late Latin *(opera) corrogāta,* "(works) collected," feminine past participle of Latin *corrogāre,* to summon together, collect : *com-,* together + *rogāre,* to ask.]

corves. Plural of **corf.**

cor·vette (kôr-vĕt′) *n.* **1.** A fast, lightly armed warship, smaller than a destroyer. **2.** Formerly, a warship, smaller than a frigate, usually armed with one tier of guns. [French, from Old French, probably from Middle Dutch *corf,* basket, kind of small ship, CORF.]

corvina. Variant of **corbina.**

cor·vine (kôr′vīn′, -vĭn) *adj.* Of, resembling, or characteristic of crows, ravens, or related birds. [Latin *corvīnus,* from *corvus,* raven.]

Cor·vus (kôr′vəs) *n.* A constellation in the Southern Hemisphere near Crater and Virgo. [New Latin, from Latin, raven.]

Cor·y·bant (kôr′ə-bănt′, kŏr′-) *pl.* **-bants** or **Corybantes** (kôr′ə-băn′tēz, kŏr′-). *Greek Mythology.* A priest of the ancient Phrygian goddess Cybele whose rites were celebrated with music and ecstatic dances. [Latin *Corybas* (stem *Corybant-*), from Greek *Korubas,* probably of Phrygian origin.] **—Cor·y·ban·tian, Cor·y·ban·tic** *adj.*

co·ryd·a·lis (kə-rĭd′ə-lĭs) *n.* Any of various plants of the genus *Corydalis,* having finely lobed leaves and spurred two-lipped yellow, cream, or pinkish flowers. [New Latin, from Greek *korudallis,* crested lark (the shape of the flowers resembles the bird's spur), variant of *korudos.*]

Cor·y·don (kôr′ə-dən, -dŏn′, kŏr′-). A conventional name for a shepherd in many pastoral poems. [Latin, from Greek *Korudōn*†, proper name.]

cor·ymb (kôr′ĭmb, -ĭm, kŏr′-) *n. Botany.* A flat-topped flower cluster in which the individual stalks grow upward from various points of the main stem to approximately the same height. [French *corymbe,* from Latin *corymbus,* cluster, from Greek *korumbos,* uppermost point, cluster of fruits or flowers.] **—co·rym·bose** (kə-rĭm′bōs′, kôr′ĭm-bōs′, kŏr′-), **co·rym·bous** (kə-rĭm′bəs) *adj.* **—co·rym·bose·ly** *adv.*

cor·y·phae·us (kôr′ə-fē′əs, kŏr′-) *n., pl.* **-phaei** (-fē′ī′). **1.** The leader of the chorus in ancient Greek drama. **2.** Any leader or spokesman. [Latin *coryphaeus,* leader, chief, from Greek *koruphaios,* leader, leader of the chorus, from *koruphē,* head, top.]

cor·y·phée (kôr′ə-fā′) *n.* A ballet dancer ranking above the ordinary members of the corps de ballet but below the principal soloists. [French, from Latin *coryphaeus,* leader, CORYPHAEUS.]

co·ry·za (kə-rī′zə) *n.* An acute inflammation of the nasal mucous membrane marked by discharge of mucus, sneezing, and watering of the eyes; a head cold. [Late Latin *coryza,* from Greek *koruza*†, catarrh.]

cos[1] (kôs, kŏs) *n.* A lettuce, **romaine** *(see).* [After Cos, Aegean island where it originated.]

cos[2] cosine.

Cos (kŏs, kôs). *Greek* **Kos.** Greek island in the Dodecanese group. It joined the Delian League in the 5th century B.C. and was a seat of learning.

COS, C.O.S. cash on shipment.

Co·sa Nos·tra (kō′zə nōs′trə, kō′sə) *n.* A crime syndicate active throughout the United States, hierarchic in structure and comprising locally independent units known as families. It is believed to have an important relationship with the Sicilian Mafia. [Italian, "our thing," "our enterprise."]

co·se·cant (kō-sē′kănt′, -kənt) *n. Abbr.* **cosec, csc** *Trigonometry.* The **secant** *(see)* of the complement of a directed angle or arc.

cosech hyperbolic cosecant.

co·seis·mal (kō-sīz′məl, -sīs′-) *adj.* Also **co·seis·mic** (-mĭk). Pertaining to or designating a line connecting the points on a map that indicate the places simultaneously affected by an earthquake shock. ~*n.* A coseismal line. [CO- (together) + SEISM(O)- + -AL.]

co·set (kō′sĕt′) *n. Mathematics.* A set associated with a subgroup of a group and formed by the products of elements of the group and elements of the subgroup.

Cos·grave (kŏs′grāv), **William Thomas** (1880–1965). Irish statesman. A Sinn Fein supporter, he fought in the Easter Rising (1916) and was imprisoned. Released the next year, he was elected to the Dáil and served in the illegal Republican ministry (1918–21). He was the first president of the Irish Free State (1922–32).

cosh[1] (kŏsh) *n. British.* **1.** A heavy stick, such as a truncheon or bludgeon, used as a weapon. **2.** An attack with such a weapon. ~*tr.v.* **coshed, coshing, coshes.** *British.* To bludgeon. [19th century : origin obscure.]

cosh[2] hyperbolic cosine.

cosh·er (kŏsh′ər) *tr.v.* **-ered, -ering, -ers.** To coddle; pamper. [19th century : origin obscure.]

co·sign (kō-sīn′, kō′sīn′) *tr.v.* **-signed, -signing, -signs. 1.** To sign (a document) jointly with another or others. **2.** To endorse (a signature), as for a loan or mortgage. —**co·sign·er** *n.*

co·sig·na·to·ry (kō-sĭg′nə-tôr′ē, -tōr′ē) *adj.* Signed jointly with another or others. ~*n., pl.* **cosignatories.** One who signs a document jointly with another or others; a cosigner.

co·sine (kō′sīn′) *n. Abbr.* **cos 1.** In a right-angled triangle, the function of an acute angle that is the ratio of the adjacent side to the hypotenuse. **2.** A trigonometric function of an angle, given by the *X*-coordinate of the end of a line of unit length drawn from the origin at the stated angle to the positive *X*-axis. [CO- + SINE.]

cosine rule *n. Mathematics.* The rule that in any triangle $a^2 = b^2 + c^2 - 2bc \cos A$, where *a*, *b*, and *c* are the lengths of the sides and *A* is the angle opposite side *a*.

cos lettuce (kôs, kŏs) *n.* **Romaine** *(see).*

cos·met·ic (kŏz-mĕt′ĭk) *n.* A preparation, such as a skin cream or lipstick, designed to beautify the body, especially the face, by direct application. ~*adj.* **1.** Serving to beautify the body, especially the face. **2.** Serving to improve or modify the appearance of the body, especially the face: *cosmetic surgery.* **3.** Decorative or superficial only; not having any significant effect or function: *Fenders on cars are now essentially cosmetic.* [French *cosmétique,* from adjective, "of adornment," from Greek *kosmētikos,* skilled in arranging, from *kosmētos,* well ordered, from *kosmein,* to arrange, from *kosmos,* order, COSMOS.] —**cos·met·i·cal·ly** *adv.*

cos·me·ti·cian (kŏz′mə-tĭsh′ən) *n.* A person whose occupation is manufacturing, selling, or applying cosmetics.

cos·me·tol·o·gy (kŏz′mə-tŏl′ə-jē) *n.* The study or art of cosmetics and their use. [French *cosmétologie : cosmétique,* COSMET(IC) + -LOGY.] —**cos·me·tol·o·gist** *n.*

cos·mic (kŏz′mĭk) *adj.* Also **cos·mi·cal** (kŏz′mĭ-kəl). **1. a.** Of or pertaining to the entire universe. **b.** Of or pertaining to the universe as distinct from the earth and its atmosphere or, sometimes, from the solar system. **2.** Infinitely or inconceivably extended, as in space or time; vast: *an issue of cosmic dimensions.* **3.** *Rare.* Harmonious; orderly. [Greek *kosmikos,* of the universe, from *kosmos,* COSMOS.] —**cos·mi·cal·ly** *adv.*

cosmic background *n.* The **microwave background** *(see).*

cosmic censorship *n. Astronomy.* The principle that, in a black hole, the point at which the density could become infinite (the singularity) can never be observed because of a surrounding spherical boundary (the event horizon) that prevents the passage of information.

cosmic dust *n.* Fine solid particles of matter in interstellar space.

cosmic radiation *n.* Streams of ionizing radiation; cosmic rays.

cosmic ray *n.* Any of a number of high-energy ionizing particles or photons that can be observed moving through the earth's atmosphere or reaching the surface of the earth. Cosmic rays originate as primary radiation from space (mainly protons and atomic nuclei with some electrons) which interacts with atoms in the atmosphere to produce secondary radiation (pions, muons, electrons, and gamma rays).

cosmic year *n.* The time required for the sun to make one complete revolution about the center of the galaxy (about 220 million years). Also called "galactic year."

cosmo-, cosm- *prefix.* Indicates world or universe; for example, **cosmology.** [Greek *kosmos,* COSMOS.]

cos·mo·chem·is·try (kŏz′mō-kĕm′ĭs-trē) *n.* The branch of astronomy concerned with the chemical composition of the universe. —**cos·mo·chem·i·cal** *adj.*

cos·mo·drome (kŏz′mə-drōm′) *n.* A Soviet spacecraft-launching center. [COSMO- + -DROME.]

cos·mo·gen·ic (kŏz′mə-jĕn′ĭk) *adj.* Of or produced by cosmic rays. [COSMO- + -GENIC.]

cos·mog·o·ny (kŏz-mŏg′ə-nē) *n., pl.* **-nies. 1.** The astrophysical study of the evolution of the universe. **2.** A specific theory or model of this evolution. [Greek *kosmogonia,* the creation of the world : COSMO- + *gonos,* creation.] —**cos·mo·gon·ic** (kŏz′mə-gŏn′ĭk), **cos·mo·gon·i·cal** *adj.* —**cos·mog·o·nist** (kŏz-mŏg′ə-nĭst) *n.*

cos·mog·ra·phy (kŏz-mŏg′rə-fē) *n., pl.* **-phies. 1.** The study of the constitution of nature. **2.** A description of the world or universe. [Greek *kosmographia,* description of the world : COSMO- + -GRAPHY.] —**cos·mog·ra·pher** *n.* —**cos·mo·graph·ic** (kŏz′mə-grăf′ĭk), **cos·mo·graph·i·cal** *adj.*

cos·mol·o·gy (kŏz-mŏl′ə-jē) *n.* **1.** A branch of philosophy dealing with the origin, processes, and structure of the universe. **2. a.** The astrophysical study of the structure and constituent dynamics of the universe. **b.** A specific theory or model of such structure and dynamics. See **big-bang theory, steady-state theory.** [New Latin *cosmologia :* COSMO- + -LOGY.] —**cos·mo·log·ic** (kŏz′mə-lŏj′ĭk), **cos·mo·log·i·cal** *adj.* —**cos·mo·log·i·cal·ly** *adv.* —**cos·mol·o·gist** (kŏz-mŏl′ə-jĭst) *n.*

cos·mo·naut (kŏz′mə-nôt′) *n.* An astronaut, especially a Soviet astronaut. [Russian *kosmonavt :* COSMO- + Greek *nautēs,* sailor.]

cos·mo·pol·i·tan (kŏz′mə-pŏl′ə-tən) *adj.* **1. a.** At home in or familiar with many parts of the world or many spheres of interest. **b.** Sophisticated and broadminded. **2.** Inhabited by or composed of many races of people with differing cultural backgrounds. **3.** Common to the whole world. **4.** *Biology.* Growing or occurring in all or most parts of the world; widely distributed. ~*n.* A person who has lived or traveled in many parts of the world and is free from provincial or national prejudices. [French *cosmopolitain,* from Old French, from Greek *kosmopolitēs,* COSMOPOLITE.] —**cos·mo·pol·i·tan·ism** *n.*

cos·mop·o·lite (kŏz-mŏp′ə-līt′) *n.* **1.** A cosmopolitan. **2.** *Biology.* A cosmopolitan organism. [Greek *kosmopolitēs,* citizen of the world : COSMO- + *politēs,* citizen, from *polis,* city.] —**cos·mop·o·lit·ism** *n.*

cos·mo·ra·ma (kŏz′mə-rä′mə, -răm′ə) *n.* A series of scenes and pictures from all over the world viewed through an eyehole using mirrors, lenses, or the like. [COSM(O)- + (PAN)ORAMA.] —**cos·mo·ram·ic** (kŏz′mə-răm′ĭk) *adj.*

cos·mos (kŏz′məs, -mōs′, -mŏs′) *n.* **1.** The universe regarded as an orderly, harmonious whole. **2.** Any system regarded as ordered, harmonious, and whole. **3.** Harmony and order as distinct from chaos. **4.** Any of various tropical American plants of the genus *Cosmos,* having variously colored rayed flowers; especially, *C. bipinnatus,* widely cultivated as a garden plant. [Greek *kosmos,* order, the universe, the world.]

cos·mo·tron (kŏz′mə-trŏn) *n. Physics.* A large synchrotron designed to produce high-energy protons. [COSMO- + -TRON.]

Cos·sack (kŏs′ăk) *n.* A member of a people of the southern Soviet Union in Europe and adjacent parts of Asia, noted as cavalrymen, especially under the czars. —**Cos·sack** *adj.*

cos·set (kŏs′ĭt) *tr.v.* **-seted, -seting, -sets.** To pamper; spoil. ~*n.* A pet; especially, a pet lamb. [Noun ("pet lamb"), from Norman French *cozet, coscet,* from Old English *cotsǣta,* cottager.]

cost (kôst) *n.* **1.** An amount paid or required in payment for a purchase or for the production or upkeep of something, often measured in terms of effort and time expended. **2.** A loss or sacrifice. **3. costs.** *Law.* The charges fixed for litigation, usually payable by the losing party. —See Synonyms at **price.** ~*v.* **cost, costing, costs.** —*intr.* To require a specified payment, expenditure, effort, or loss. —*tr.* **1.** To estimate or determine the cost of. **2.** *Informal.* To be costly to. [Middle English, from Old French, from *coster,* to cost, from Latin *constāre,* to stand with, stand at a particular price : *com-,* with + *stāre,* to stand.]

cos·ta (kŏs′tə) *n., pl.* **-tae** (-tē). *Biology.* A rib or a riblike part, such as the midrib of a leaf or a thickened anterior vein or margin of an insect's wing. [Latin, rib.] —**cos·tal** *adj.*

Cos·ta Bra·va (kŏs′tə brä′və). The Mediterranean coastline in eastern Spain, stretching from Barcelona to the French border. It is a popular tourist area.

cost accountant *n.* An accountant who keeps records of all the costs of production and distribution of an enterprise. —**cost accounting** *n.*

co·star, co-star (kō′stär′) *n.* A starring actor or actress given equal status with another or others in a play or film. ~*v.* (kō′stär′) **costarred, -starring, -stars.** —*intr.* To act as a costar. —*tr.* To present or feature as a costar.

cos·tard (kŏs′tərd, kôs′-) *n.* **1.** An English variety of apple tree or the fruit of this tree. **2.** *Archaic Slang.* The head. [Middle English, from Norman French, "ribbed one" (from its appearance), from *coste,* rib, from Latin *costa.*]

Cos·ta Ri·ca (kŏs′tə rē′kə). Country in Central America. Its heartland is a broad, upland plateau amid volcanic ranges. The country was discovered by Christopher Columbus (1502) and became a territory of Spain. Its native Indian population almost disappeared under colonial rule, and the people are now of Spanish or mixed descent. Costa Rica became independent in 1821. In 1948 it abolished its army to make military coups impossible. Attempts are being made to stimulate industrial growth and tourism, but the economy is chiefly agricultural, and coffee and bananas are still the leading exports. Area, 50,700 square kilometers (19,575 square miles). Population, 2,300,000. Capital, San José. See map at **Central American States.**

cost benefit analysis *n.* An analysis that takes into account the losses or benefits in economic and social welfare that will be incurred if a particular project is undertaken.

cost-effective (kôst′ĭ-fĕk′tĭv) *adj.* Of or resulting in a profit or return that justifies the initial outlay.

cos·ter·mon·ger (kŏs′tər-mŭng′gər, -mŏng′gər, kôs′-) *n. British.* One who sells fruit, vegetables, fish, or other goods from a cart, barrow, or stall in the streets, especially in London. Also called "coster." [Originally *costardmonger,* "apple seller" : COSTARD + MONGER.]

cos·tive (kŏs′tĭv) *adj.* **1. a.** Constipated. **b.** Causing constipation. **2.** Slow; sluggish. **3.** Stingy. [Middle English *costif,* from Old French *costive,* past participle of *costiver,* to bind, constipate, from Latin *constīpāre,* to CONSTIPATE.]

cost·ly (kôst′lē) *adj.* **-li·er, -li·est. 1.** Of high price or value; expensive. **2.** Entailing loss or sacrifice. **—cost·li·ness** *n.*
  Synonyms: *dear, expensive, invaluable, precious, priceless, valuable.*

cost·mar·y (kôst′mâr-ē, kôst′-) *n.* A herb, *Chrysanthemum balsamita,* native to Asia, having aromatic foliage sometimes used as seasoning. [Middle English *costmarie* : *cost,* costmary, Old English *cost,* from Latin *costum,* from Greek *kostos,* from Arabic *kust* + *Mary* (so named because regarded as sacred to the Virgin Mary).]

cost of living *n.* The average cost of those goods and services considered necessary to provide a person with a basic or average standard of living.

cost-of-living adjustment (kôst′əv-lĭv′ĭng) *n.* An adjustment made in wages that corresponds with a change in the cost of living.

cost-of-living index *n.* The **consumer price index** *(see).*

cost-plus (kôst′plŭs′, kôst′-) *adj.* Of or designating a method of calculating prices based on the cost of production plus a fixed rate of profit.

cost price *n.* The price at which a merchant or retailer buys goods.

cost-push (kôst′pŏŏsh′) *adj.* Designating a type of inflation in which increased production costs, as from higher wages, tend to drive up prices. Compare **demand-pull.**

cos·trel (kŏs′trəl) *n. Archaic.* A flat, pear-shaped drinking vessel with loops for attachment to the belt of the user. [Middle English, from Old French *costerel,* perhaps from *costier,* "that which is at the side," from *coste,* side, rib, from Latin *costa.*]

cos·tume (kŏs′tōōm, -tyōōm, kŏs-tōōm′, -tyōōm′) *n.* **1.** A complete style of dress including clothes, accessories, and often hairstyle, characteristic of a particular country, period, or people. **2.** A set of clothes worn for a play, film, fancy-dress ball, or the like, designed to give the wearer the appearance of the role that he or she is playing. **3.** A woman's suit. **4.** A set of clothes appropriate for a usually specified occasion or season, such as a swimming costume. ~*tr.v.* **costumed, -tuming, -tumes. 1.** To put a costume on; dress. **2.** To furnish a costume or costumes for (a play or film, for example). [French, from Italian, custom, dress, from Latin *consuētūdō* (stem *consuētūdin-*), CUSTOM.]

costume drama *n.* A stage or television play, or a film, set in a specific era, in which the actors wear the appropriate dress of the period.

costume jewelry *n.* Inexpensive jewelry made from cheap materials such as glass, diamante, or the like.

cos·tum·er (kŏs-tōō′mər, -tyōō′mər) *n.* Also **cos·tum·i·er** (kŏs-tōōm′yər, -tyōōm′yər; *French* kôs-tü-myā′). A person or company that makes or supplies costumes.

cosy. Variant of **cozy.**

cot[1] (kŏt) *n.* A narrow bed, especially a camp bed. [Anglo-Indian, from Hindi *khāṭ,* bedstead, couch, from Sanskrit *kháṭvā,* from Dravidian, akin to Tamil *kaṭṭil.*]

cot[2] *n.* **1.** A shelter or protective covering, especially a cote. **2.** A small house; a cottage. [Middle English *cot(e),* Old English *cot.*]

co·tan·gent (kō-tăn′jənt) *n. Abbr.* **ctn** *Trigonometry.* The tangent of the complement of a directed angle or arc. **—co·tan·gen·tial** *adj.*

cot death *n. Chiefly British.* **Crib death** *(see).*

cote[1] (kōt) *n.* **1.** A small shed or shelter for sheep or birds. **2.** *Regional.* A cottage; a hut. [Middle English *cote,* Old English *cote.*]

cote[2] *tr.v.* **coted, coting, cotes.** *Archaic.* To go round by the side of; pass. [Origin obscure.]

Côte d'A·zur (kōt′də-zōōr′). The Mediterranean coast of France, especially its eastern end. It is part of the Riviera.

co·ten·ant (kō-tĕn′ənt) *n.* One of two or more tenants sharing common property. [CO- + TENANT.] **—co·ten·an·cy** *n.*

co·te·rie (kō′tə-rē) *n.* A small, usually select, group of persons who associate frequently, especially because of shared artistic interests. Sometimes used derogatorily. —See Synonyms at **circle.** [French, from Old French, an association of peasant tenants, probably from *cotier,* cottager, from *cote* (unattested), cottage, perhaps from Middle English *cot,* COT (cottage).]

coterminous. Variant of **conterminous.**

coth hyperbolic cotangent.

co·thur·nus (kō-thûr′nəs) *n., pl.* **-ni** (-nī′). Also **co·thurn** (kō′thûrn, kō-thûrn′). A buskin or thick-soled boot worn by actors of classical tragedy. [Latin, from Greek *kothornos,* perhaps from Lydian.]

co·ti·dal (kō-tīd′l) *adj.* **1.** Of or pertaining to a coincidence of the tides. **2.** Designating lines on a map that join places at which high or low tides occur simultaneously.

co·til·lion, co·til·lon (kō-tĭl′yən, kə-) *n.* **1.** A lively dance originating in France in the 18th century, with varied, intricate patterns and steps. **2.** A quadrille. **3.** A formal ball. [French *cotillon,* peasant dress, country dance, from Old French, petticoat, diminutive of *cote,* COAT.]

co·to·ne·as·ter (kə-tō′nē-ăs′tər) *n.* Any of various Old World shrubs of the genus *Cotoneaster,* having small white or pinkish flowers and frequently cultivated for their showy red fruit. [New Latin *Cotoneaster,* from Latin *cotōneum,* QUINCE.]

Co·to·pax·i (kō′tō-păk′sē). One of the highest active volcanos in the world, in the Andes Mts. of northern Ecuador. It has erupted periodically since the first recorded outburst in 1532 and rises to 5,896 meters (19,457 feet).

cot·quean (kŏt′kwēn′) *n. Archaic.* **1.** A vulgar woman; a hussy. **2.** A man who does domestic work considered more suitable for women. [COT (cottage) + QUEAN.]

Cots·wold (kŏts′wōld, -wəld) *n.* A sheep of a breed known for its long wool and originally developed in the Cotswolds.

Cots·wolds (kŏts′wōldz, -wəldz). Also **Cotswold Hills.** Range of limestone hills in southwest England, chiefly in Gloucestershire.

cot·ta (kŏt′ə) *n., pl.* **cottae** (kŏt′ē) or **-tas.** A short ecclesiastical surplice, often sleeveless or short-sleeved. [Medieval Latin, from West Germanic *kotta,* COAT.]

cot·tage (kŏt′ĭj) *n.* **1.** A small house, typically in the suburbs or the country. **2.** A small summer house used during vacations. [Middle English *cotage,* from *cot(e),* COT (cottage).] **—cot·tag·ey** *adj.*

cottage cheese *n.* A soft, white cheese made of strained and seasoned curds of skimmed milk.

cottage industry *n.* A cottage industry, such as weaving or sewing, carried out in the home by individual workers rather than in a factory.

cottage loaf *n. British.* A loaf of bread made of two round masses, with the smaller on top of the larger.

cottage piano *n.* An upright, usually small, piano of the 19th century.

cottage pie *n.* **Shepherd's pie** *(see).*

cottage pudding *n.* Plain cake covered with a sweet sauce.

cot·tag·er (kŏt′ĭj-ər) *n.* A person, especially a farm laborer, who lives in a cottage.

cottage tulip *n.* A type of tall-stemmed garden tulip, usually having pointed petals.

cot·ter (kŏt′ər) *n.* **1.** A bolt, wedge, key, or pin inserted through a slot in order to hold parts together. **2.** A cotter pin. [17th century : shortened from dialectal *cotterel†.*]

cotter pin *n.* A split cotter inserted through holes in two or more pieces and bent at the ends to fasten and prevent excessive sliding and rotation.

Cot·ti·an Alps (kŏt′ē-ən). A section of the western Alps between northwestern Italy and southeastern France. Its highest elevation is Mt. Viso (3,844 meters; 12,602 feet).

cot·ti·er (kŏt′ē-ər) *n.* **1.** In Ireland in former times, a peasant renting and cultivating a small piece of land directly from its owner, the rate having been fixed by public competition. **2.** A cottager. [Middle English, from Old French *cotier,* cottager, from *cote* (unattested), cottage, perhaps from Middle English *cot,* COT (cottage).]

cot·ton (kŏt′n) *n.* **1.** Any of various plants or shrubs of the genus *Gossypium,* cultivated in warm climates for the fiber surrounding their seeds. **2.** The soft, white, downy fiber attached to the seeds of the cotton plant, used in making textiles and other products. **3.** Cotton plants collectively. **4.** The crop of these plants. **5.** Thread or cloth manufactured from cotton fiber. **6.** Any of various soft, downy substances found in other plants. ~*adj.* Of, pertaining to, or made from cotton. ~*intr.v.* **cottoned, -toning, -tons.** *Informal.* To take a liking; become friendly. Used with *to.* **—cotton up to.** *Informal.* To flatter; make overtures to. [Middle English *cotoun,* from Old French, from Arabic (dialectal) *qoṭon,* variant of Arabic *quṭn.*]

cotton batting *n.* See **batting** (sense 2).

cotton candy *n.* **Spun sugar** *(see).*

cotton flannel *n.* A soft, warm, napped fabric woven of cotton.

cotton gin *n.* A machine that separates the seeds, seed hulls, and other small objects from the fibers of cotton. Also called "gin."

cotton grass *n.* Any of various grasslike bog plants of the genus *Eriophorum* that grow in colder north temperate zones, having densely tufted, cottony flower heads.

cotton leafworm *n.* The larva of a New World moth, *Alabama argillacea,* that feeds on and destroys cotton leaves.

cot·ton·mouth (kŏt′n-mouth′) *n.* A snake, the **water moccasin** *(see).* [Its mouth is lined with a white cottony substance.]

cotton rose *n.* **1.** A Chinese shrub, *Hibiscus mutabilis,* cultivated in warm regions for its white or pink flowers that turn deep red. Also called "Confederate rose." **2.** The **cudweed** *(see).*

cotton rust *n.* A disease of the cotton plant caused by the fungus *Puccinia stakmani* that produces yellowish discolorations on the leaves.

cot·ton·seed (kŏt′n-sēd′) *n., pl.* **-seeds** or collectively **cottonseed.** The seed of cotton, used as a source of oil and meal.

cottonseed meal *n.* Meal made from the residue of cottonseed after the oil has been removed, used as animal feed and fertilizer.

cottonseed oil *n.* A yellowish to dark red oil obtained by crushing cottonseed and used in cooking and as salad oil and in the manufacture of paints, soaps, and other products.

cotton stainer *n.* Any of various small, flat, red insects of the genus *Dysdercus,* that pierce cotton bolls and stain the fibers.

cot·ton·tail (kŏt′n-tāl′) *n.* Any of several New World rabbits of the genus *Sylvilagus,* having grayish or brownish fur and a tail with a white underside.

cotton tree *n.* A spiny tropical tree, *Bombax Malabaricum,* having seeds surrounded by a cottonlike fiber.

cot·ton·weed (kŏt′n-wēd′) *n.* Any of various plants covered with cottony down or having cottonlike tufts.

cot·ton·wood (kŏt′n-wŏŏd′) *n.* Any of several softwood trees of the genus *Populus,* having seeds with cottonlike tufts; especially, *P. deltoides,* of eastern and central North America.

cotton *Mexican Indians used the plant's natural fiber to weave clothes as early as 2400* B.C.

cotton wool *n.* **1.** Cotton in its natural or raw state. **2. Absorbent cotton** *(see).*

cot·ton·y (kŏt′n-ē) *adj.* **1.** Of or resembling cotton; downy; fluffy. **2.** Covered with fibers resembling cotton; nappy.

cot·ton·y-cush·ion scale (kŏt′n-ē-ko͝osh′ən) *n.* A scale insect, *Icerya purchasi,* that attacks citrus trees.

cot·y·le·don (kŏt′ə-lēd′n) *n.* **1.** *Botany.* A simple leaf of a plant embryo, being in some species the first or one of the first to appear from the sprouting seed and that acts to store food in many seeds. Also called "seed leaf." See **dicotyledon, monocotyledon. 2.** *Anatomy.* A lobule of the placenta, especially of ruminants. [Latin *cotylēdon,* navelwort, from Greek *kotulēdōn,* cup-shaped hollow, navelwort, from *kotulē*†, anything hollow, cup.] **—cot·y·le·don·al, cot·y·le·do·nous** *adj.*

cot·y·loid (kŏt′ə-loid′) *adj.* Also **cot·y·loi·dal** (kŏt′ə-loi′dəl) *Anatomy.* **1.** Shaped like a cup. **2.** Of or relating to the acetabulum. [Greek *kotuloeidēs,* cup-shaped : *kotulē,* anything hollow, cup (see **cotyledon**) + -OID.]

couch (kouch) *n.* **1. a.** A long piece of upholstered furniture with a back and arms that more than one person may sit on; a sofa. **b.** A bed, especially one with a headrest and low back, used by a psychoanalyst's patients, for example. **2. a.** The frame or floor on which grain, usually barley, is spread in malting. **b.** A layer of grain, usually barley, spread to germinate. **3.** Couch grass. **4.** In papermaking, a board or felt blanket on which sheets of paper are laid to dry. **5.** *Archaic.* The lair of a wild beast.
~*v.* **couched, couching, couches.** —*tr.* **1.** *Archaic.* To cause to lie down. Usually used passively. **2.** To express in a certain context or style. **3.** To embroider by laying thread flat on a surface and fastening by stitches at regular intervals. **4.** To spread (grain) on a frame or floor to germinate, as in malting. **5.** To lower (a spear, lance, or the like) to the position of attack. **6.** *Medicine.* To remove (a cataract) by downward and backward displacement of the lens. —*intr.* **1.** To lie in ambush or concealment; lurk. **2.** *Archaic.* **a.** To lie down; recline. **b.** To crouch. **3.** To be in a heap or pile. Used especially of leaves for decomposition or fermentation. [Middle English *couche,* from Old French, from *coucher,* to lay down, from Latin *collocāre,* to place together, put : *com-,* together + *locāre,* to place, LOCATE.] **—couch·er** *n.*

couch·ant (kou′chənt) *adj. Heraldry.* Lying down with the head raised. Used after the noun: *a lion couchant.* [Middle English, from Old French, present participle of *coucher,* to lay down, COUCH.]

cou·chette (ko͞o-shĕt′) *n. British.* A folding bunk in a railroad sleeping car. [French, diminutive of *couche,* bed, COUCH.]

couch grass *n.* A grass, *Agropyron repens,* having whitish-yellow rootstocks by means of which it multiplies rapidly, becoming a troublesome weed. Also called "couch," "quack grass," "twitch grass." [Originally *quitch grass,* Middle English *quicche* (unattested), Old English *cwice;* perhaps akin to *cwicu,* alive, QUICK.]

couch·ing (kou′chĭng) *n.* Embroidery work in which heavy thread is attached at intervals to a material with minute stitches. [Middle English, from *couchen,* to embroider, COUCH.]

cou·dé (ko͞o-dā′) *adj. Astronomy.* Of or pertaining to a system of deflecting light from the primary mirror of a reflecting telescope into the eyepiece. [French, "bent like an elbow," past participle of *couder,* to bend at right angles, from *coude,* elbow, from Latin *cubitum,* elbow, CUBIT.]

cou·gar (ko͞o′gər) *n.* The **mountain lion** *(see).* [French *couguar,* from Portuguese *cuguardo,* from Tupi *suasuarana,* "like a deer" (from its color) : *suasú,* deer + *ran, rā,* similar to.]

cough (kôf, kŏf) *v.* **coughed, coughing, coughs.** —*intr.* **1.** To expel air from the lungs suddenly and noisily. **2.** To make a noise like coughing. —*tr.* To expel or utter with a cough. Usually used with *up* or *out.* **—cough up.** *Slang.* To hand over (money, information, or the like) reluctantly.
~*n.* **1.** A sudden and noisy effort to expel the air from the lungs. **2.** An illness marked by coughing. [Middle English *coughen,* Old English *cohhian* (unattested), from an imitative root *kokh-.*]

cough drop *n.* A small, often medicated and sweetened lozenge taken to ease coughing or soothe a sore throat.

cough syrup *n.* A sweetened, medicated liquid taken to relieve coughing.

could. Past tense of **can,** but often used as an auxiliary verb for various shades of associated meanings indicating: **1.** Possibility: *This could be a world record.* **2.** Advice: *You could always take a taxi if you're in a hurry.* **3.** A polite appeal or request: *Could I ask you a favor?* **4.** Condition: *If you could just be more tolerant, people would like you better.*

could·n't (ko͝od′ənt). Contraction of *could not.*

couldst. *Archaic.* The second person singular past tense of *can.* Used with *thou.*

cou·lee, cou·lée (ko͞o′lē) *n.* **1.** A sheet of solidified lava. **2.** A stream of molten lava. **3.** In the western United States and Canada: **a.** A deep gulch or ravine formed by rainstorms or melting snow, often dry in summer. **b.** A stream in such a gulch. [Canadian French *coulée,* from French, a flow, a flow of lava, from the past participle of *couler,* to flow, from Latin *cōlāre,* to strain, filter, from *cōlum,* a sieve.]

cou·lisse (ko͞o-lēs′) *n.* **1.** A grooved piece of timber in which a frame or panel slides. **2.** *Theater.* **a.** Any of the side scenes in the wings of a stage; a stage flat. **b.** The space between two side scenes. **3.** A body of unofficial dealers on a stock exchange, especially the Paris Stock Exchange. [French, groove, corridor (see **portcullis**); sense 3, after the dealers' corridors in the Paris Bourse.]

cou·loir (ko͞ol-wär′) *n.* A deep mountainside gorge or gully, especially in the Alps. [French, colander, passageway, ravine, from *couler,* to slide, flow. See **coulee.**]

cou·lomb (ko͞o′lŏm′, -lōm′) *n. Abbr.* **C** A meter-kilogram-second unit of electrical charge equal to the quantity of charge transferred in one second by a steady current of one ampere. [After Charles A. de COULOMB.]

Cou·lomb (ko͞o-lôɴ′), **Charles Augustin de** (1736–1806). French physicist who pioneered research into magnetism and electricity and formulated Coulomb's law.

Coulomb field *n.* An electric field equivalent to one that would be produced by a point charge, substituted for a charged body so that the force due to the body at every point is described by Coulomb's law.

Coulomb force *n.* An attractive or repulsive electrostatic force described by Coulomb's law.

cou·lomb·me·ter, cou·lom·e·ter (ko͞o-lŏm′ə-tər) *n.* A **voltameter** *(see).*

cou·lomb·met·ric, cou·lo·met·ric (ko͞o′lə-mĕt′rĭk) *adj. Chemistry.* Of or pertaining to measurement of electric current. Said of techniques involving electrolysis, as in a voltameter, or electrolyte conduction, as in certain types of titration. **—cou·lomb·met·ri·cal·ly** *adv.*

Coulomb potential *n.* The potential at any point in a Coulomb field.

Coulomb scattering *n.* The scattering of a charged particle from another charged particle, especially from an atomic nucleus, principally or exclusively as a result of Coulomb forces.

Coulomb's law *n.* The principle that the force between two charged particles is directly proportional to the product of their charges and inversely proportional to the square of the distance between them.

cou·lom·e·try (ko͞o-lŏm′ĭ-trē) *n.* An analytical method for determining the amount of a substance released during electrolysis in which the number of coulombs used is measured. [COULO(MB) + -METRY.]

coulter. Variant of **colter.**

cou·ma·rin (ko͞o′mə-rĭn) *n.* A toxic fragrant organic compound, $C_9H_6O_2$, present in many plants including sweet clover and tonka beans. It is usually produced synthetically and used in perfumery. [French *coumarine,* from *coumarou,* tonka bean tree, from Spanish *coumarú,* from Tupi *cumaru, comaru.*] **—cou·ma·ric** *adj.*

coun·cil (koun′səl) *n.* **1.** An assembly of persons called together for consultation, deliberation, or discussion. **2. a.** A body of people elected or appointed to serve in an administrative, legislative, or advisory capacity. **b.** Such a body elected to serve as a local government authority. **3.** The discussion or deliberation that takes place in a council. **4.** An assembly of church officials and theologians convened for regulating matters of doctrine and discipline. **5.** The **Sanhedrin** *(see).* [Middle English *co(u)nceil,* from Norman French *concilie, cuncile,* assembly, from Latin *concilium,* meeting, assembly.]
Usage: Identity of pronunciation and relatedness of meaning between *council* and *counsel, councilor* and *counselor,* lead to regular spelling confusions. *Council* refers to a deliberative assembly; *councilor* to its member. *Counsel* may be either noun or verb, referring to advice and guidance in general; *counselor* or, in law, *counsel,* refers to the person who provides it.

coun·cil·man (koun′səl-mən) *n., pl.* **-men** (-mĭn). A councilor.

coun·cil·or, coun·cil·lor (koun′sə-lər) *n.* A member of a council, especially the local governing body of a city or town. —See Usage note at **council.**

coun·sel (koun′səl) *n., pl.* **-sels** or **counsel** (for sense 5). **1.** The exchanging of opinions and ideas; consultation; discussion. **2.** Advice or guidance, especially as given by a knowledgeable or qualified person. **3.** A deliberate resolution; a plan; a scheme. **4.** A private purpose or opinion: *keep one's own counsel.* **5.** A lawyer, group of lawyers, or others giving legal advice; especially, an attorney engaged to conduct a case in court. —See Usage notes at **council, lawyer.**
~*v.* **counseled** or **-selled, -seling** or **-selling, -sels.** —*tr.* **1.** To give counsel to; advise. **2.** To give professional help to on social or psychological problems. **3.** To urge the adoption of; recommend. —*intr.* To give or take counsel or advice. —See Usage note at **council.** [Middle English *counseil, conseil,* from Old French *conseil,* from Latin *consilium,* deliberation, consultation, akin to *consulere,* to CONSULT.]

coun·sel·or, coun·sel·lor (koun′sə-lər) *n.* **1. a.** A person who gives counsel; an adviser. **b.** Such a person employed to advise on personal or other problems as a social service. **2.** A lawyer, especially one appearing in court. Also called "counselor-at-law." **3.** A high-ranking diplomat. **4.** A person supervising children at a summer camp. —See Usage notes at **council, lawyer. —coun·se·lor·ship** *n.*

count¹ (kount) *v.* **counted, counting, counts.** —*tr.* **1.** To find out the total number of units by listing the individual units. **2.** To recite numerals in ascending order up to and including: *count three before firing.* **3.** To include in a reckoning; take account of: *ten dogs, counting the puppies.* **4.** To believe or consider to be; deem: *He counts himself lucky.* —*intr.* **1.** To recite or list numbers in order or enumerate items by units or groups: *count by tens; count to three.* **2.** To have importance, especially when a judgment is being made: *His ill-health counted against him.* **3.** To have a specified value or importance; amount. Usually used with *for: His opinions count for*

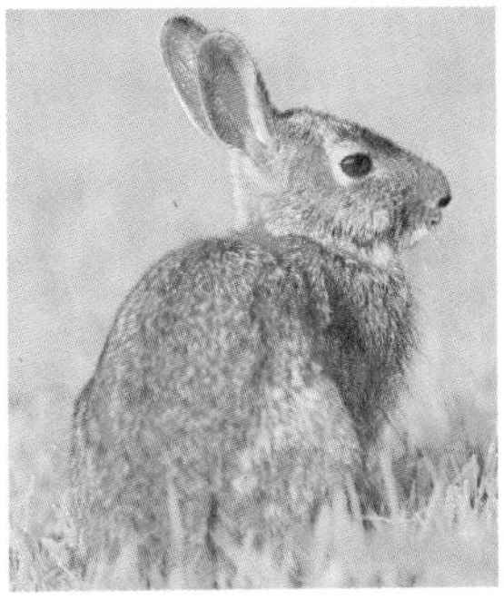

cottontail *The North American cottontail often relies on its ability to "freeze" in order to escape danger. Unlike the European rabbit, it does not dig itself an underground burrow. Its name is derived from the white fur on the underside of its tail.*

PRONUNCIATION KEY

ă, pat; ā, pay; âr, care;
ä, father, are; b, bib;
ch, church; d, deed; ĕ, pet;
ē, be; f, fife; g, gag; h, hat;
hw, which; ĭ, pit; ī, pie;
îr, pier; j, judge; k, kick;
l, lid, needle; m, mum;
n, no, sudden; ng, thing;
ŏ, pot; ō, toe; ô, paw, for;
oi, noise; ou, out; o͝o, book;
o͞o, boot; p, pop; r, roar;
s, sauce; sh, ship, dish;
t, tight; th, thin, path;
th, this, bathe; ŭ, cut; ûr, fur;
v, valve; w, with; y, yes;
z, zebra, size; zh, vision;
ə, about, item, edible,
gallop, circus, peaceful

IN FOREIGN WORDS:

à, *Fr.* ami; œ, *Fr.* feu, *Ger.* schön; ü, *Fr.* tu, *Ger.* über;
KH, *Ger.* ich, *Scot.* loch;
ɴ, *Fr.* bon; y′, *Fr.* Compiègne

STRESS MARKS:

Primary stress: ′
in·cite′ (ĭn-sīt′)
Secondary stress: ′
in′sight′ (ĭn′sīt′)

little. **4.** *Music.* To keep time by counting beats. **5.** *Informal.* To rely. Used with *on.* —See Synonyms at **rely.** —**count in.** To include. —**count off.** To separate into groups by or as if by counting. —**count out. 1.** To exclude or discount. **2.** To count to ten and thereupon declare beaten (a boxer who has fallen to the floor). ~*n.* **1.** The act of counting or calculating. **2.** A number reached by counting. **3.** A reckoning; an accounting. **4.** *Law.* Any of the separate and distinct charges in an indictment. **5.** A counting from one to ten seconds, during which time a boxer who is down must rise or be declared the loser. [Middle English *counten,* from Old French *conter, compter,* from Latin *computāre;* see **compute.**]

count² *n. Abbr.* **Ct.** In some European countries, a nobleman whose rank corresponds to that of an earl in Britain. [Middle English *counte,* from Old French *conte, comte,* from Late Latin *comes* (stem *comit-*), occupant of any state office, from Latin, companion.]

count·a·ble (kount′ə-bəl) *adj.* **1.** Capable of being counted. **2.** *Mathematics.* Capable of being put in a one-to-one correspondence with the positive integers. **3.** *Grammar.* Designating nouns that can be preceded by the indefinite article or a cardinal number and take a plural; for example, *cat* and *bag* are countable. Compare **noncountable.** —**count·a·bly** *adv.*

count·down (kount′doun′) *n.* **1.** The act or process of counting backward aloud to indicate the time elapsing before an imminent deadline that will initiate an event or operation. **2.** *Aerospace.* The act or process of making a timed scheduled series of successive checks during the preparation of a missile or space vehicle for launching. **3.** The time leading up to an important event.

coun·te·nance (koun′tə-nəns) *n.* **1.** Aspect; appearance; especially, the expression of the face. **2.** The face or facial features. **3.** Support or approval in general. **4.** Composure; bearing; self-control. —**out of countenance.** Visibly disconcerted or embarrassed. ~*tr.v.* **countenanced, -nancing, -nances.** To give approval to; condone. [Middle English *contenaunce,* behavior, demeanor, from Old French *contenance,* from *contenir,* to behave, CONTAIN.] —**coun·te·nanc·er** *n.*

count·er¹ (koun′tər) *adj.* Contrary; opposing. ~*n.* **1.** One that is counter; an opposite; a contrary. **2.** *Boxing.* A blow given while receiving or parrying another. **3.** *Fencing.* A parry in which one foil follows the other in a circular fashion. **4.** A stiff piece of leather around the heel of a shoe. **5.** The portion of a ship's stern extending from the water line to the end of the curved part. **6.** The part of a horse's chest between the shoulders and under the neck. **7.** The depression between the raised lines of a typeface. ~*v.* **countered, -ering, -ers.** —*tr.* **1.** To meet or return (a blow) by another blow. **2.** To oppose; act counter to. **3.** To respond to by retaliating in kind. —*intr.* **1.** To give a return blow while receiving or parrying one, as in boxing. **2.** To retaliate. ~*adv.* In a contrary manner or direction. [Middle English *countre,* from Old French *contre,* from Latin *contrā,* contrary to, against.]

counter² *n.* **1.** A table or similar flat surface on which money is counted, business is transacted, or food is served. **2.** A piece, as of wood or ivory, used for keeping a count or a place in games. **3.** An imitation coin; a token. —**under the counter.** In an underhand way. [Middle English *contour,* from Old French *comptouer, conteoir,* from Medieval Latin *computātōrium,* place of accounts, from Latin *computāre,* to COUNT.]

counter³ *n.* **1.** A person who counts. **2.** Any electronic or mechanical device that automatically counts occurrences or repetitions of phenomena or events. **3.** *Physics.* An apparatus that detects individual particles or photons.

counter– *prefix.* Indicates: **1.** Opposition, as in direction or purpose; for example, **countermarch, counteract. 2.** Reciprocation; for example, **countersign. Note:** Many compounds other than those entered here may be formed with *counter-*. In forming compounds, *counter-* is normally joined to the following element without a space or hyphen: *counterrevolution.* The adjective *counter* is written as a separate word, as in *Counter Reformation* or *counter word,* but except for these examples it is hardly ever used in an attributive position. Rather, the preference is for forming a compound with *counter-,* as evidenced by the entries that follow. [Middle English *countre-,* from Norman French, from Old French *contre-,* from Latin *contrā,* opposite to, COUNTER.]

coun·ter·act (koun′tər-ăkt′) *tr.v.* **-acted, -acting, -acts.** To oppose and mitigate the effects of by contrary action; check. —See Synonyms at **neutralize.** —**coun·ter·ac·tion** *n.* —**coun·ter·ac·tive** *adj.* —**coun·ter·ac·tive·ly** *adv.*

coun·ter·at·tack (koun′tər-ə-tăk′) *n.* A return attack. ~*v.* **counterattacked, -tacking, -tacks.** —*intr.* To deliver a counterattack. —*tr.* To make a counterattack against.

coun·ter·at·trac·tion (koun′tər-ə-trăk′shən) *n.* A rival or alternative attraction.

coun·ter·bal·ance (koun′tər-băl′əns, koun′tər-băl′əns) *n.* **1.** Any force or influence equally counteracting another. **2.** A weight that acts to balance another; counterpoise. ~*tr.v.* (koun′tər-băl′əns, koun′tər-băl′əns) **counterbalanced, -ancing, -ances. 1.** To act as a counterbalance to; counterpoise. **2.** To oppose with an equal force; offset.

coun·ter·change (koun′tər-chānj′) *tr.v.* **-changed, -changing, -changes. 1.** To exchange; transpose. **2. a.** To make checkered. **b.** *Heraldry.* To reverse (colors and metals) on a field so that color comes next to metal and metal next to color.

coun·ter·charge (koun′tər-chärj′) *n.* A charge in opposition to a charge made by another.

~*v.* (koun′tər-chärj′) **countercharged, -charging, -charges.** —*tr.* To bring a charge against (one's accuser). —*intr.* To make a countercharge.

coun·ter·check (koun′tər-chĕk′) *n.* **1.** Something that serves to check or verify something else. **2.** Something that confirms or denies the correctness of a previous check. **3. a.** A restraint that reinforces another check. **b.** A restraint that counteracts another check. ~*tr.v.* (koun′tər-chĕk′) **counterchecked, -checking, -checks. 1.** To oppose or check by a counteraction. **2.** To check again.

coun·ter·claim (koun′tər-klām′) *n.* A claim made in opposition to a claim made by another. ~*v.* (koun′tər-klām′) **counterclaimed, -claiming, -claims.** —*tr.* To make a counterclaim against. —*intr.* To plead a counterclaim. —**coun·ter·claim·ant** *n.*

coun·ter·clock·wise (koun′tər-klŏk′wīz′) *adv.* Also **con·tra·clock·wise** (kŏn′trə-) In a direction opposite to that of the movement of the hands of a clock. Also *chiefly British* "anticlockwise." —**coun·ter·clock·wise** *adj.*

coun·ter·con·di·tion·ing (koun′tər-kən-dĭsh′ən-ĭng) *n. Psychology.* Conditioning intended to replace a negative response to a stimulus with a positive response.

coun·ter·coup (koun′tər-kōō′) *n.* A coup staged to reverse the effects of a previous coup.

coun·ter·cul·ture (koun′tər-kŭl′chər) *n.* A culture created by or for the alienated young in opposition to traditional lifestyles, values, and assumptions. —**coun·ter·cul·tur·al** *adj.*

coun·ter·cur·rent (koun′tər-kûr′ənt, -kŭr′-) *n.* An opposing current or flow. ~*adj. Chemistry.* Involving or pertaining to an opposing flow. Said of certain analytical or industrial separation techniques.

coun·ter·dem·on·stra·tion (koun′tər-dĕm′ən-strā′shən) *n.* A demonstration held in opposition to another demonstration. —**coun·ter·dem·on·stra·tor** *n.*

coun·ter·es·pi·o·nage (koun′tər-ĕs′pē-ə-näzh′, -nĭj) *n.* Espionage undertaken to detect and counteract enemy espionage.

coun·ter·ex·am·ple (koun′tər-ĕg-zăm′pəl, -zăm′pəl, -ĭg-) *n.* An example that contradicts or disproves a previous one.

coun·ter·feit (koun′tər-fĭt′) *v.* **-feited, -feiting, -feits.** —*tr.* **1.** To make a copy of, usually with the intent to defraud; forge. **2.** To imitate. **3.** To make a presence of; feign. —*intr.* **1.** To carry on a deception; feign; dissemble. **2.** To make imitations or forgeries. ~*adj.* **1.** Made in imitation of what is genuine with the intent to defraud. **2.** Simulated; feigned. —See Synonyms at **artificial.** ~*n.* **1.** A fraudulent imitation or facsimile. **2.** *Obsolete.* A portrait; an image. [Middle English *countrefeten,* from Old French *contrefaire* (past participle *contrefait*), from Medieval Latin *contrāfacere,* to make in contrast to, hence to make in imitation : Latin *contrā-,* opposite to + *facere,* to make.] —**coun·ter·feit·er** *n.*

coun·ter·flow (koun′tər-flō′) *n.* Fluid flow in opposite directions, as in adjacent parts of an apparatus, such as a heat exchanger, or in biological systems, such as the gills of a fish.

coun·ter·foil (koun′tər-foil′) *n.* The part of a check or other commercial paper retained by the issuer as a record of a transaction.

coun·ter·glow (koun′tər-glō′) *n.* **Gegenschein** (see).

coun·ter·in·sur·gen·cy (koun′tər-ĭn-sûr′jən-sē) *n.* Measures taken by a state against the activities of terrorists or other rebels.

coun·ter·in·tel·li·gence (koun′tər-ĭn-tĕl′ə-jəns) *n.* The branch of an intelligence service charged with keeping valuable information from enemy spies, preventing subversion and sabotage, and gathering political and military information.

coun·ter·in·tu·i·tive (koun′tər-ĭn-tōō′ə-tĭv, -tyōō′-) *adj.* Contrary to what is perceived intuitively.

coun·ter·ir·ri·tant (koun′tər-ĭr′ə-tənt) *n. Medicine.* An agent that induces local irritation to counteract general or deep irritation. —**coun·ter·ir·ri·ta·tion** *n.*

coun·ter·man (koun′tər-măn′, -mən) *n., pl.* **-men** (-mĕn′, -mĭn). One who serves at a counter, as in a cafeteria.

coun·ter·mand (koun′tər-mănd′, -mänd′) *tr.v.* **-manded, -manding, -mands. 1.** To cancel or reverse (a command or order). **2.** To recall by a contrary response. ~*n.* An order or command reversing an earlier one. [Middle English *countremaunden,* from Old French *contremander* : COUNTER- + *mander,* to command, from Latin *mandāre.*]

coun·ter·march (koun′tər-märch′) *n.* **1.** A march back or in a reverse direction. **2.** A complete reversal of method or conduct. ~*v.* (koun′tər-märch′) **countermarched, -marching, -marches.** —*tr.* To conduct in a countermarch. —*intr.* To execute a countermarch.

coun·ter·meas·ure (koun′tər-mĕzh′ər) *n.* A measure or action taken to oppose or compensate for another.

coun·ter·mine (koun′tər-mīn′) *n.* **1. a.** A mine or tunnel dug by the defenders of a fortress to intercept and destroy a tunnel made by the besiegers. **b.** A mine or charge of explosive placed so as to explode an enemy's mines. **2.** A counterplot. ~*v.* (koun′tər-mīn′) **countermined, -mining, -mines.** —*tr.* **1.** To make or use a countermine against. **2.** To defeat or frustrate by secret measures. —*intr.* To make or lay down countermines.

coun·ter·move (koun′tər-mōōv′) *n.* A move countering another move.

coun·ter·move·ment (koun′tər-mōōv′mənt) *n.* A movement in an opposing direction.

coun·ter·of·fen·sive (koun′tər-ə-fĕn′sĭv) *n.* A large-scale attack by an army, designed to stop the offensive of an enemy force.

coun·ter·of·fer (koun′tər-ô′fər, -ŏf′ər) n. An offer made in return by one who rejects an unsatisfactory offer.

coun·ter·pane (koun′tər-pān′) n. A coverlet for a bed; a bedspread. [Earlier *counterpoint*, from Middle English, from Old French *contrepointe*, *coultepointe*, from Medieval Latin *culcita puncta*, "stitched quilt" : Latin *culcita*, QUILT + *puncta*, stabbed; see **point.**]

coun·ter·part (koun′tər-pärt′) n. 1. One that closely or exactly resembles another, as in function or relation. 2. **a.** One of two parts that fit and complete each other, such as a seal and its impression. **b.** One that is a natural complement to another.

coun·ter·plot (koun′tər-plŏt′) n. A plot intended to frustrate another plot. ~v. (koun′tər-plŏt′) **counterplotted, -plotting, -plots.** —*tr.* To oppose and frustrate by another plot. —*intr.* To devise a counterplot.

coun·ter·point (koun′tər-point′) n. 1. **a.** Melodic material that is added above or below an existing melody. **b.** The musical technique of combining two or more melodic lines in such a way that they establish a harmonic relationship while retaining their linear individuality. **c.** Music incorporating or consisting of composition in counterpoint. 2. A contrasting but parallel element, item, or theme. ~tr.v. **counterpointed, -pointing, -points.** 2. To compose in counterpoint. 2. To emphasize by means of contrasting detail.

coun·ter·poise (koun′tər-poiz′) n. 1. A counterbalancing weight. 2. Any force or influence that balances or equally counteracts another. 3. The state of being balanced or in equilibrium. ~tr.v. (koun′tər-poiz′) **counterpoised, -poising, -poises.** 1. To oppose with an equal weight; counterbalance. 2. To act against with an equal force or power; offset.

coun·ter·pro·duc·tive (koun′tər-prə-dŭk′tĭv) adj. Tending to hinder rather than serve one's purpose; harmful.

coun·ter·pro·pos·al (koun′tər-prə-pō′zəl) n. A proposal offered to nullify or substitute for a previous one.

coun·ter·ref·or·ma·tion (koun′tər-rĕf′ər-mā′shən) n. A reformation in opposition to previous reformation.

Counter Reformation n. A reform movement within the Roman Catholic Church during the 16th century and the first half of the 17th century organized in reaction to the Protestant Reformation.

coun·ter·rev·o·lu·tion (koun′tər-rĕv′ə-lōō′shən) n. A movement arising in opposition to a revolution and aiming to restore the prerevolutionary state of affairs. —**coun·ter·rev·o·lu·tion·ar·y** adj. & n. —**coun·ter·rev·o·lu·tion·ist** n.

coun·ter·scarp (koun′tər-skärp′) n. The outer wall of a ditch in a fortification.

coun·ter·shaft (koun′tər-shăft′) n. An intermediate shaft between the powered and driven shafts in a belt drive or gear train.

coun·ter·sign (koun′tər-sīn′) tr.v. **-signed, -signing, -signs.** To sign (a previously signed document), as for authentication. ~n. 1. A second or confirming signature, as on a previously signed document; a countersignature. 2. *Military.* A secret sign or signal to be given to a sentry in order to obtain passage; a password. 3. A secret sign or signal given in answer to another.

coun·ter·sig·na·ture (koun′tər-sĭg′nə-chər) n. A signature made in countersigning.

coun·ter·sink (koun′tər-sĭngk′) tr.v. **-sunk** (-sŭngk′), **-sinking, -sinks.** 1. To enlarge the top part of (a hole) so that a screw or bolthead will lie flush with or below the surface. 2. To fit (a screw or bolt) in this way. ~n. *Abbr.* **csk.** 1. A tool for making a countersunk hole. 2. A countersunk hole.

coun·ter·spy (koun′tər-spī′) n. A spy in opposition to enemy espionage.

coun·ter·stain (koun′tər-stān′) n. A dye used to treat microscope specimens that have already been treated with another dye. The stain and the counterstain color different parts of the specimen. ~tr.v. **counterstained, -staining, -stains.** To treat with a counterstain.

coun·ter·ten·or (koun′tər-tĕn′ər) n. 1. An adult male voice with a range above that of tenor. 2. A part written for such a voice. 3. A singer with such a voice.

coun·ter·vail (koun′tər-vāl′, koun′tər-vāl′) v. **-vailed, -vailing, -vails.** —*tr.* 1. To act against with equal force. 2. To compensate for; offset. —*intr.* To avail. Used with *against.* [Middle English *countrevaillen*, to be equal in value, from Old French *contrevaloir* : COUNTER- + *valoir*, to be worth, from Latin *valēre*, to be strong, be worth.]

coun·ter·weigh (koun′tər-wā′) v. **-weighed, -weighing, -weighs.** —*tr.* To cause to counterbalance; counterpoise. —*intr.* To counterbalance.

coun·ter·weight (koun′tər-wāt′) n. A counterbalance. —**coun·ter·weight·ed** adj.

counter word n. A word commonly used without regard to its precise meaning, as *nice* or *awful.*

count·ess (koun′tĭs) n. 1. **a.** In various European countries, the wife or widow of a count. **b.** In Britain, the wife or widow of an earl. 2. A woman holding the title of count or earl in her own right. [Middle English *countes(se)*, from Old French *contesse*, feminine of *conte*, COUNT.]

counting house n. An office in which a business firm carries on operations such as accounting and correspondence. Also called "counting room."

counting number n. Any of the numbers 0, 1, 2, 3, . . . used in counting objects.

count·less (kount′lĭs) adj. Too many to be counted; innumerable; very many. —See Synonyms at **infinite.**

count noun n. A countable (sense 3) noun. Compare **mass noun.**

count palatine n., pl. **counts palatine.** A noble originally exercising certain royal powers within his domain, a **palatine** (see).

coun·tri·fied, coun·try·fied (kŭn′trĭ-fīd′) adj. Resembling or having the characteristics of country life; rural; rustic.

coun·try (kŭn′trē) n., pl. **-tries.** 1. A large tract of land distinguishable by features of topography, biology, or culture. 2. A district outside cities and towns; a rural area. 3. The territory of a nation or state; land. 4. The people of a nation or state. 5. The land of a person's birth or citizenship or to which a person owes allegiance. 6. *Music.* Country music. —See Usage note at **nation.** —**go to the country.** *British.* To dissolve Parliament and hold a general election. ~adj. 1. Of or pertaining to rural areas. 2. Unsophisticated; rustic. [Middle English *cuntree, contre*, from Old French *contree*, from Medieval Latin *(terra) contrāta*, "(land) lying opposite or before one," from *contrātus*, lying opposite, from Latin *contrā*, against, opposite.]

country and western n. Country music (see).

country bumpkin n. A simple country dweller; a yokel; a bumpkin.

country club n. A club in the country or suburbs with facilities for outdoor sports and social activities.

country cousin n. One whose lack of familiarity with the ways of urban life is regarded as laughable by city dwellers.

country-dance n. A folk dance, typically one in which two lines of dancers face each other. —**country-dancing** n.

country gentleman n. 1. The proprietor of a country estate. 2. *Often* **Country Gentleman.** A variety of corn having small, sweet white kernels.

country house n. A mansion or other grand dwelling on a country estate.

coun·try·man (kŭn′trē-mən) n., pl. **-men** (-mĭn). 1. A man from one's own country. 2. A man from a particular region. 3. One who lives in the country and knows the countryside well.

country music n. A style of popular music based on folk music of the rural United States, especially of the southern or southwestern United States. Also called "country," "country and western."

country rock n. *Geology.* An existing rock within which a new rock, such as an igneous intrusion, is formed.

country seat n. 1. An estate in the country. 2. A mansion on such an estate.

coun·try·side (kŭn′trē-sīd′) n. 1. The rural areas of a country. 2. The inhabitants of a rural area.

coun·try·wom·an (kŭn′trē-wŏom′ən) n., pl. **-women** (-wĭm′ən). 1. A woman from one's own country. 2. A woman from a particular region. 3. A woman who lives in the country and knows it well.

coun·ty (koun′tē) n., pl. **-ties.** *Abbr.* **co.** 1. In the United States, an administrative subdivision of a state. In Louisiana, also called "parish." 2. In Great Britain and Ireland a territorial division exercising administrative, judicial, and political functions. 3. The people living in a country. 4. *Obsolete.* **a.** The territory under the jurisdiction of a count or earl. **b.** A count or earl. ~adj. 1. Of or pertaining to a county. 2. *Chiefly British.* Belonging to or characteristic of the landed gentry in its interest in outdoor pursuits such as hunting and riding. [Middle English *co(u)nte*, from Norman French *counté*, from Medieval Latin *comitātus*, territory of a count, from Late Latin, retinue of a count, from *comes* (stem *comit-*), COUNT.]

county palatine n. The domain of a count palatine.

county seat n. A city or town that is the center of government in its county.

county town n. In Great Britain, a county seat. Also called "shire town."

coup (kōō) n., pl. **coups** (kōōz; *French* kōō). 1. A brilliantly executed stratagem; a masterstroke. 2. A coup d'état. [French, from Old French, from Late Latin *colpus*, from Latin *colaphus*, blow, from Greek *kolaphos*, a blow.]

coup de grâce (kōō′ də gräs′) n., pl. **coups de grâce** (pronounced as singular). 1. The mortal or finishing stroke, as delivered to someone mortally wounded. 2. Any finishing or decisive stroke. [Literally, "stroke of mercy."]

coup de main (kōō′ də măn′) n., pl. **coups de main** (pronounced as singular). *French.* A sudden action undertaken to surprise an enemy. [Literally, "stroke of hand."]

coup d'é·tat (kōō′ dā-tä′) n., pl. **coups d'état** (pronounced as singular). A sudden overthrowing of government and seizure of power by others. —See Synonyms at **rebellion.** [Literally, "stroke of state."]

coup de thé·â·tre (kōō′ də tā-ät′r′) n., pl. **coups de théâtre** (pronounced as singular). *French.* An unexpected and dramatic event that overturns some given situation. [Literally, "stroke of theater."]

coup d'oeil (kōō′ dœ′y′) n., pl. **coups d'oeil** (pronounced as singular). *French.* A glance; a quick survey. [Literally, "stroke of eye."]

coupe[1] (kōōp) n. 1. A dessert of ice cream or fruit-flavored ice, variously garnished with nuts, fruit, whipped cream, and the like, served in a special dessert glass. 2. **a.** The stemmed glass in which such a dessert is served. **b.** A shallow, bowl-shaped dessert dish. [French, "cup," from Late Latin *cuppa*, CUP.]

coupe[2]. Variant of **coupé** (a two-door car).

cou·pé (kōō-pā′) n. Also **coupe** (kōōp) (for sense 1). 1. A closed streamlined two-door car. 2. A closed four-wheel carriage with two seats inside and one outside. [French, short for *(carrosse) coupé*, "cut-off (carriage)," from the past participle of *couper,* to cut off, from Old French *coup,* COUP.]

Cou·pe·rin (ko͞o-prăɴ', ko͞o-pə-), **François** (1668–1733). The most famous of a family of French musicians. He was a court organist at Versailles under Louis XIV and wrote songs, chamber music, choral works, and organ pieces.

cou·ple (kŭp'əl) *n.* **1.** Two items of the same kind; a pair. **2.** Something that joins two things together; a connection; a link. **3.** Two people, especially a man and a woman, joined in a stable relationship such as marriage or cohabitation. **4.** Two people engaged in some joint activity, such as dancing. **5.** *Informal.* A few; several: *a couple of days.* **6.** *Physics.* A pair of forces of equal magnitude acting in parallel but opposite directions, capable of causing rotation but not translation. **7.** *Physics.* **a.** A pair of metals or semiconductors in direct contact developing an electromotive force across their junction, as in a thermocouple. **b.** A pair of metals in an electrolyte forming a galvanic cell. Also called "galvanic couple." **8. a.** A pair of hunting dogs. **b.** A double leash joining them.
~*v.* **coupled, -ling, -les.** —*tr.* **1.** To link together; attach; join. **2.** To form into pairs. **3.** To join as man and wife; marry. **4.** To combine. **5.** *Electricity.* To link (two circuits or currents) as by magnetic induction. —*intr.* **1.** To form pairs. **2.** To copulate. **3.** *Physics.* To interact as by electromagnetic interaction. Used of electrons or other elementary particles. [Middle English, pair, bond, from Old French *co(u)ple,* from Latin *cōpula,* bond, link.]
Synonyms: *brace, duo, pair, yoke.*
Usage: In informal usage, the meaning of *couple* has extended so that it is no longer restricted to two, but has the general sense of "a few." As the earlier meaning of "two" is still very much alive, however, the word is often ambiguous. *I've got a couple of dollars in my wallet* does not necessarily mean only two (though it might). On the other hand, *Lend me a couple of dollars* is likely to be interpreted in a precise way.

cou·pler (kŭp'lər) *n.* **1.** A device for coupling. **2.** A device connecting two organ keyboards so that they may be played together. **3.** A device for linking two electronic circuits.

cou·plet (kŭp'lĭt) *n.* **1.** A unit of verse consisting of two successive lines, usually rhyming and having the same meter. **2.** Two similar things; a pair. [Old French *couplet,* diminutive of *co(u)ple,* COUPLE.]

cou·pling (kŭp'lĭng) *n.* **1.** The act of forming couples. **2.** A device for connecting railway carriages or wagons. **3.** The part of the body connecting the hindquarters and forequarters of a four-footed animal. **4.** *Physics.* Interaction between elementary particles, especially between their magnetic moments.

cou·pon (ko͞o'pŏn', kyo͞o'-) *n.* **1.** Any of a number of small, negotiable certificates attached to a bond that represent sums of interest due at stated maturities. **2.** A certificate or detachable part of an advertisement entitling the bearer to certain stated benefits, such as a cash discount or a gift, or for use as an order blank or inquiry form. **3.** Any of a number of detachable slips used when making installment payments. [French, from Old French *colpon,* "a piece cut off," from *colper, couper,* to cut off, from *coup,* a blow. See **coup.**]

cour·age (kûr'ĭj) *n.* **1.** The state or quality of mind or spirit that enables one to face danger and overcome fear. **2.** *Obsolete.* Heart; mind; disposition. [Middle English *corage,* heart as the seat of feeling, courage, from Old French, from Vulgar Latin *corāticum* (unattested), from Latin *cor,* heart.]
Synonyms: *backbone, bravery, fortitude, heroism, mettle, resolution, tenacity, valor.*

cou·ra·geous (kə-rā'jəs) *adj.* Having or characterized by courage; valiant. —See Synonyms at **brave.** —**cou·ra·geous·ly** *adv.* —**cou·ra·geous·ness** *n.*

cou·rante (ko͞o-ränt') *n.* **1.** A French dance of the 17th century, characterized by running and gliding steps to an accompaniment in triple time. **2.** The second movement of the classical suite, typically following the allemande. [French, "running (dance)," from *courir,* to run, from Old French *courre,* from Latin *currere.*]

Cour·bet (ko͝or-bā'), **(Jean Désiré) Gustave** (1819–77). French painter who headed the realist school. He developed an earthy and uncompromising style, as in *Burial at Ornans* (1850), *Bonjour M. Courbet* (1854), and *The Artist's Studio* (1855).

cour·gette (ko͝or-zhĕt') *n. Chiefly British.* A zucchini. [French, diminutive of *courge,* marrow, gourd.]

cour·i·er (ko͝or'ē-ər, kûr'-) *n.* **1.** A messenger employed on urgent business; especially, one working for a parcel delivery service. **2.** An official diplomatic messenger. **3.** A person who carries information back and forth between members of a secret service. **4.** A person employed to make arrangements for and attend to the requirements of travelers. [Middle English, from Old French *courrier,* from Italian *corriere,* "runner," from *correre,* from Latin *currere,* to run.]

cour·lan (ko͝or'lən) *n.* A bird, the **limpkin** *(see).* [French, variant of *courliri,* from Galibi *kurliri.*]

course (kôrs', kōrs, ko͝ors) *n.* **1.** Onward movement in a particular direction; progress; advance. **2.** The direction of continuing movement. **3.** The route or path taken by something that moves, such as a stream. **4. a.** A designated area of land or water on which a race is held or a sport played. **b.** A **golf course** *(see).* **5.** Movement in time; duration: *in the course of a year.* **6.** A mode of action or behavior. **7.** A typical or natural manner of proceeding; customary passage from stage to stage; regular development: *The fad ran its course.* **8.** A systematic or orderly succession regarded as a unit: *a course of treatment.* **9.** *Architecture.* A continuous layer of building material, such as brick or tile, on a wall or roof of a building. **10.** *Education.* **a.** A prescribed body of studies to be followed by students. **b.** The subject matter studied. **11.** A part of a meal served as a unit at one time. **12.** The lowest sail on any mast of a square-rigged ship. **13.** A point on the compass; especially, the one toward which a ship is sailing. **14.** A hunt by hounds pursuing the quarry by sight rather than scent. —See Synonyms at **way.** —**in due course.** In proper order; at the right time. —**lay a course.** *Nautical.* **1.** To go in a particular course or direction without tacking. **2.** To plan some action or project. —**of course. 1.** In the natural order of things; naturally. **2.** Without any doubt; certainly.
~*v.* **coursed, coursing, courses.** —*tr.* **1.** To move swiftly through or over; traverse. **2.** To pursue or hunt, especially with hounds chasing the quarry by sight rather than scent. **3.** To set (hounds) to chase game; send into pursuit. —*intr.* **1.** To proceed on a course; follow a direction. **2. a.** To move swiftly; race. **b.** To run; flow: *"big tears now coursed down her face"* (Iris Murdoch). **3.** To hunt game with hounds. [Middle English *cours, course,* from Old French, from Latin *cursus,* from the past participle of *currere,* to run.]

cours·er¹ (kôr'sər, kōr'-, ko͝or'-) *n.* **1.** A dog trained for coursing. **2.** A person who courses hounds.

courser² *n. Poetic.* A swift horse.

courser³ *n.* Any of various ploverlike birds of the family Glareolidae, found mainly in warm regions of Africa and Asia and characterized by the ability to run fast. [From New Latin *Cursorius* (genus), from Late Latin, "adapted for running," from Latin *cursus,* COURSE (forward movement).]

cours·ing (kôr'sĭng, kōr'-, ko͝or'-) *n.* The sport of hunting with dogs trained to chase game by sight instead of scent.

court (kôrt, kōrt) *n. Abbr.* **C., ct. 1.** An extent of open ground partially or completely enclosed by walls or buildings; a courtyard. **2.** A short street; especially, an alley walled by buildings on three sides. **3.** A large, open section of a building, often with a glass roof or skylight. **4.** Formerly, a mansion or other large building standing in a courtyard. Now used only in proper names. **5.** A level area, marked with appropriate lines, upon which tennis, squash, basketball, or some other game is played. **6.** The place of residence of a sovereign or dignitary; a royal mansion or palace. **7.** The retinue of a sovereign, including the royal family and his personal servants, advisers, ministers, and the like. **8.** A sovereign's governing body, including the council of ministers and state advisers. **9.** A formal meeting called for and presided over by a sovereign. **10. a.** A person or body of persons appointed to hear and submit a decision on legal cases. **b.** The building, hall, or room in which cases are heard and determined. **c.** The regular session of a judicial assembly. **11.** Any similar authorized tribunal having military or ecclesiastical jurisdiction. **12.** The body of directors of a corporation, company, or other organization. —**out of court. 1.** Without a trial. **2.** Being regarded as too trivial, rash, or ridiculous for discussion or consideration. —**pay court to. 1.** To flatter with solicitous overtures in an attempt to obtain something. **2.** To woo.
~*v.* **courted, courting, courts.** —*tr.* **1.** To attempt to gain the favor of by flattery or attention. **2.** To attempt to gain the affections or love of; woo. **3.** To attempt to gain; seek. **4.** To invite, often unwittingly or foolishly: *court disaster.* —*intr.* To be involved in regular social activities with a view to eventual marriage.
~*adj.* Of, pertaining to, or appropriate to a court. [Middle English, from Old French *cort,* from Latin *cohors* (stem *cohort-*), enclosure, court, cohort.]

court bouillon *n.* A light stock made from vegetables, herbs, and white wine, used for poaching fish. [French, "short bouillon."]

court card *n.* A **face card** *(see).* [Folk-etymological alteration of earlier *coat card.*]

cour·te·ous (kûr'tē-əs) *adj.* Characterized by graciousness and good manners; considerate toward others. —See Synonyms at **polite.** [Middle English *curteis, corteis,* having manners befitting a courtly gentleman, from Old French, from *cort,* COURT.] —**cour·te·ous·ly** *adv.* —**cour·te·ous·ness** *n.*

cour·te·san, cour·te·zan (kôr'tə-zən, kōr'-) *n.* A prostitute or kept woman, especially one associating with men of rank or wealth. [Old French *courtisane,* from Old Italian *cortigiana,* "female courtier," from *cortigiano,* courtier, from *corte,* court, from Latin *cohors* (stem *cohort-*), COURT.]

cour·te·sy (kûr'tə-sē) *n., pl.* **-sies. 1.** Polite behavior; gracious manner or manners. **2.** A polite gesture or remark. **3.** Consent or favor; indulgence: *called "doctor" by courtesy.* —**courtesy of. 1.** With the permission of. **2.** Paid for by. [Middle English *curteisie,* from Old French, from *curteis,* COURTEOUS.]

courtesy light *n.* An inside light in a car that is switched on automatically by the opening of a door.

courtesy title *n. British.* A title of nobility having no legal status; for example, the eldest son of the Duke of Bedford is called Marquis of Tavistock during his father's lifetime but is not a peer.

court hand *n.* A style of handwriting formerly used in English legal papers.

court·house (kôrt'hous', kōrt'-) *n. Abbr.* **c.h., C.H.** A building housing judicial courts.

court·i·er (kôr'tē-ər, kōr'-, -tyər) *n.* **1.** An attendant at the court of a sovereign. **2.** One who seeks favor, especially by flattery or obsequious behavior. [Middle English *courteour,* from Norman French, from Old French *corteier,* to be at court, to court, from *cort, court,* COURT.] —**cour·ti·er·ly** *adv.*

court-leet (kôrt'lēt', kôrt'-) *n.* A former court in Britain, a **leet** *(see).*

court·ly (kôrt'lē, kôrt'-) *adj.* **-lier, -liest. 1.** Suitable for a royal court; stately; dignified. **2.** Elegant in manners; polite; refined. **3.** Flattering; obsequious. **—court·li·ness** *n.*

courtly love *n.* A code of chivalrous devotion to an idealized beloved, usually a married lady, that became a regular theme of medieval and Renaissance literature.

court-mar·tial (kôrt'mär'shəl, kôrt'-) *n., pl.* **courts-martial.** *Abbr.* **c.m. 1.** A military or naval court of officers appointed by a commander to try persons for offenses under military law. See **general court-martial, special court-martial, summary court-martial. 2.** A trial by court-martial.
~*tr.v.* **court-martialed** or **-tialled, -tialing** or **-tialling, -tials.** To try by court-martial.

court of appeals *n.* A superior court to which appeals are made on points of law resulting from the judgment of a trial court.

court of chancery *n.* A court with jurisdiction in equity, a **chancery** *(see).*

Court of Claims *n.* A U.S. Federal court that determines claims of a specified sort by individuals against the United States.

Court of Common Pleas *n.* **1.** In some states of the United States, a court having general jurisdiction. **2.** Formerly, a court in Britain to hear civil cases between commoners.

Court of Exchequer *n.* Formerly, a court in Britain with jurisdiction in equity and common law, dealing originally with matters of revenue and later all kinds of cases, now merged with the High Court.

Court of Queen's Bench *n.* A superior court of common law in Britain, now merged with the High Court as the Queen's Bench Division. Called during the reign of a king "Court of King's Bench."

Court of St. James's *n.* The British royal court to which ambassadors are formally accredited.

court plaster *n.* An adhesive plaster formerly used to cover cuts or scratches on the skin. [Originally, referring to the black silk plaster used by ladies at court to make beauty spots.]

Courtrai. See **Kortrijk.**

court·room (kôrt'rōōm', kôrt'-, -rŏom') *n.* A room in which court proceedings are carried on.

court·ship (kôrt'shĭp', kôrt'-) *n.* **1.** The act or period of courting before marriage. **2.** Mating rituals between animals.

court tennis *n.* A form of tennis played in a large indoor court having a specially marked-out floor and high cement walls off which the ball may be played.

court·yard (kôrt'yärd', kôrt'-) *n.* An open space surrounded by walls or buildings, adjoining or within a large building.

cous·cous (kōōs'kōōs') *n.* A North African dish of crushed semolina steamed and served with various meats, spices, and vegetables. [French, from Arabic *kouskous.*]

cous·in (kŭz'ən) *n.* **1.** A child of one's aunt or uncle. Also called "cousin-german," "first cousin," "full cousin." **2.** A relative descended from a common ancestor, such as a grandfather, by two or more steps in a diverging line; for example, one's first cousin's child is one's *first cousin once removed,* and the child of one's parent's first cousin is one's *second cousin.* **3.** *Obsolete.* A person related by descent from a common ancestor, but not a brother or sister. **4.** Loosely, any relative by blood or marriage. **5.** A member of a kindred group or country: *our Canadian cousins.* **6.** A title of address used by a sovereign to a nobleman or to another sovereign. [Middle English *cosin(e),* from Old French *cosin, cousin,* from Latin *consōbrīnus,* maternal first cousin : *com-,* together + *sōbrīnus,* maternal cousin.] **—cous·in·ly** *adj.*

cous·in-ger·man (kŭz'ən-jûr'mən) *n., pl.* **cousins-german.** A first cousin. See **cousin.**

Cou·steau (kōō-stō'), **Jacques Yves** (1910–). French pioneer of underwater exploration. He helped invent the Aqua Lung (1943) and later developed underwater laboratories.

cou·ter (kōō'tər) *n.* A piece of armor protecting the elbow. [Middle English, from Old French *coute* (modern French *coude*), elbow, from Latin *cubitum;* see **cubit.**]

couth (kōōth) *adj.* **1.** Refined; suave; cultured. Used humorously as a back-formation from "uncouth." **2.** *Obsolete.* Friendly; familiar. [Middle English *couth,* familiar, known, Old English *cūth.*]

couth·y, couth·ie (kōō'thē) *adj. Scottish.* Characterized by homeliness or affability. [Middle English. See **couth, uncouth.**]

cou·ture (kōō-tōōr'; *French* kōō-tür') *n.* The business of a couturier, the designing and making of fashionable clothes for women. [French, tailoring, sewing, from Old French *cousture,* from Vulgar Latin *consūtūra* (unattested), from the feminine past participle of Latin *consuere,* to sew together : *com-,* together + *suere,* to sew.]

cou·tu·ri·er (kōō-tōō-ryā'; *French* kōō-tü-ryā') *n. Feminine* **cou·tu·ri·ère** (kōō-tōō-ryâr'; *French* kōō-tü-ryâr') **1.** One who designs, makes, and sells fashionable, usually custom-made, women's clothing. **2.** An establishment engaged in this business. [French, from **COUTURE.**]

cou·vade (kōō-väd') *n.* A practice among certain peoples in which the husband of a woman in labor takes to his bed as if he were bearing the child. [French, "a hatching," from *couver,* to hatch, sit on (eggs), from Latin *cubāre,* to lie down (on).]

cou·vert (kōō-vâr', kōō'-) *n.* **1.** A table setting at a restaurant table. **2.** A **cover charge** *(see).* [French, "cover."]

co·va·lence (kō-vā'ləns) *n.* Also **co·va·len·cy** (-lən-sē). *Chemistry.* The number of electron pairs an atom can share with other atoms in such bonds. **—co·va·lent** *adj.*

covalent bond *n.* A chemical bond formed by the sharing of one or more electrons, especially pairs of electrons, between atoms.

covalent crystal *n. Chemistry.* A crystal in which all the atoms are linked together by covalent bonds.

co·var·i·ance (kō-vâr'ē-əns) *n.* **1.** *Physics.* The principle that the laws of physics have the same form regardless of the system of coordinates in which they are expressed. **2.** *Statistics.* The expected value of the product of the deviations of corresponding values of two variables from their respective means.

co·var·i·ant (kō-vâr'ē-ənt) *adj.* **1.** *Physics.* Expressing, exhibiting, or pertaining to covariance. **2.** *Mathematics.* Varying with another variable quantity in a manner that leaves a specified relationship unchanged.

cove (kōv) *n.* **1.** A small, sheltered bay in the shoreline of a sea, river, or lake. **2. a.** A steep-walled mountain hollow. **b.** A steep-walled semicircular recess, especially one forming the head of a valley. **c.** A cave or cavern. **3.** A concave molding. ~*tr.v.* **coved, coving, coves.** To cause to arch over or curve inwards. [Middle English *cove,* closet, chamber, cave, Old English *cofa.*]

co·vel·lite (kō-vĕl'īt', kō'və-līt') *n.* An indigo-blue mineral form of copper sulfide, CuS; an important source of copper. [After Nicholas *Covelli* (1790–1829), Italian chemist who discovered it.]

cov·en (kŭv'ən, kō'vən) *n.* **1.** An assembly of witches. **2.** A group of 13 witches. [Perhaps from Middle English *covent,* a gathering, **CONVENT.**]

cov·e·nant (kŭv'ə-nənt) *n.* **1.** A binding agreement made by two or more parties; a compact; a contract. **2.** A solemn agreement or vow made by members of a church to defend and support its faith and doctrine. **3.** *Theology.* God's promises to man, as recorded in the Old and New Testaments. **4.** *Law.* **a.** A formal sealed agreement or contract, especially one to pay regular sums, as to a charity or relative. **b.** A particular clause of such a contract. ~*v.* **covenanted, -nanting, -nants.** —*tr.* To promise by a covenant. —*intr.* To enter into a covenant; contract. [Middle English, from Old French, from the present participle of *co(n)venir,* to agree, **CONVENE.**] **—cov·e·nant·al** *adj.* **—cov·e·nant·al·ly** *adv.*

cov·e·nant·ee (kŭv'ə-nən-tē') *n.* The participant in a covenant to whom the promise is made.

cov·e·nant·er (kŭv'ə-nən-tər; *also* kŭv'ə-năn'tər *for sense 2) n.* **1.** One who makes a covenant. **2. Covenanter.** A Scottish Presbyterian who supported either of the agreements (National Covenant, 1638, or Solemn League and Covenant, 1643) intended to defend and extend Presbyterianism.

cov·e·nan·tor (kŭv'ə-nən-tər) *n.* The party to a covenant by whom the obligation expressed in it is to be performed.

Cov·en·try (kŭv'ən-trē). Industrial city in West Midlands, central England. A new cathedral was opened in 1962 and incorporates the ruins of the old, which was bombed in 1942. **—send to Coventry.** To refuse to associate with; ostracize. [*Send to Coventry,* from the sending of Royalist prisoners to Coventry during the English Civil War.]

cov·er (kŭv'ər) *v.* **-ered, -ering, -ers.** —*tr.* **1.** To place something upon, over, or in front of, so as to protect, shut in, or conceal; overlay or spread with something. **2.** To put a covering on; clothe. **3.** To put a cap, hat, or the like on (one's head). **4.** To bring upon (oneself or one's reputation). Used reflexively: *He covered himself in glory.* **5.** To serve as a covering for; occupy the surface of: *Dust covered the table.* **6.** To extend over; occupy: *a farm covering more than 100 acres.* **7.** To copulate with (a female). Used of animals, especially horses. **8.** To sit on (eggs); incubate; brood. **9.** To screen from view or detection; conceal. **10.** To protect or shield from harm, injury, or danger; shelter. **11.** To protect by insurance; insure against a specified risk or loss. **12.** To include; comprise: *a broad category that covers a variety of species.* **13.** To be sufficient to defray (a charge or expense); meet or offset (a liability). **14.** To make provision for; allow for: *This law does not cover such cases.* **15.** To deal with; treat of. **16.** To travel or pass over; traverse. **17.** To have as one's territory or sphere of work: *A single doctor has to cover the whole region.* **18.** To overwhelm; fill. Used in the passive: *covered in confusion.* **19.** *Military.* **a.** To overlook and dominate from a strategic position; have within range. **b.** To protect (a soldier, unit, or position, for example) by occupying a position from which enemy troops can be fired upon. **20.** *Journalism.* To be responsible for securing and reporting the details of (an event or situation): *cover a ball game.* **21.** *Sports.* To be responsible for marking (an opponent) or for defending (an area or position): *cover left field.* **22.** To match (an opponent's stake) in a wager. **23.** *Card Games.* To play a higher-ranking card than (the one previously played). **24.** *Obsolete.* To pardon or remit: *"Thou hast covered all their sins"* (Psalms 85:2). —*intr. Informal.* To act as a substitute or replacement during someone's absence. Often used with *for.* ~*n.* **1.** Something that covers or is laid, placed, or spread over or upon something else, especially: **a.** A blanket or sheet on a bed. **b.** The lid or top of a container. **c.** The binding at the front or back of a book. **d.** The front outer page of a magazine, or its outer front and back pages. **2.** *Military.* Natural or artificial shelter or protection by other armed units: *under a cover of mortar fire.* **3. a.** Vegetation covering an area, often serving to provide shade or prevent erosion. **b.** Undergrowth or other vegetation serving as protective concealment for wild animals. **4. a.** Something that screens or

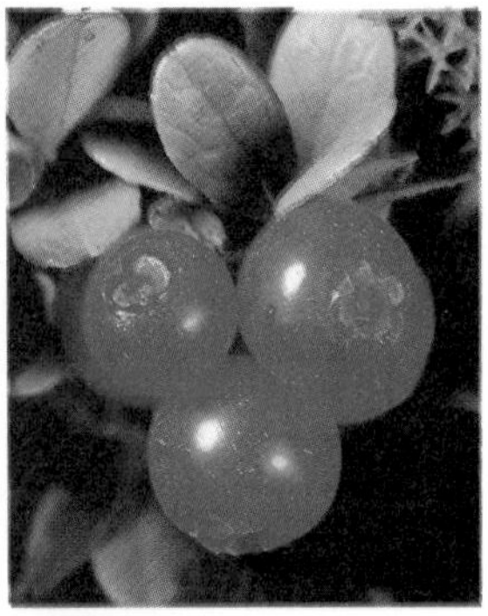

cowberry *This relative of the cranberry is found on boggy wetlands and in the acid woodlands of northern temperate regions. Its dark red bitter fruit ripens in August.*

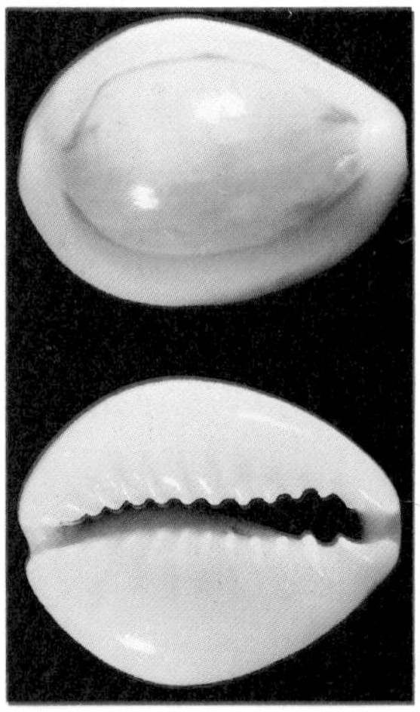

cowry *A marine snail found mainly in the coastal waters of the Indian and Pacific oceans. Unlike most shells, the cowry is glossy outside as well as inside. This is because its mantle—the sheet of tissue that produces the smooth, shiny lining of any mollusk's shell—can be extruded by the cowry to cover the outer surface as well. Cowries are still used as currency in parts of the Pacific, Asia, and West Africa.*

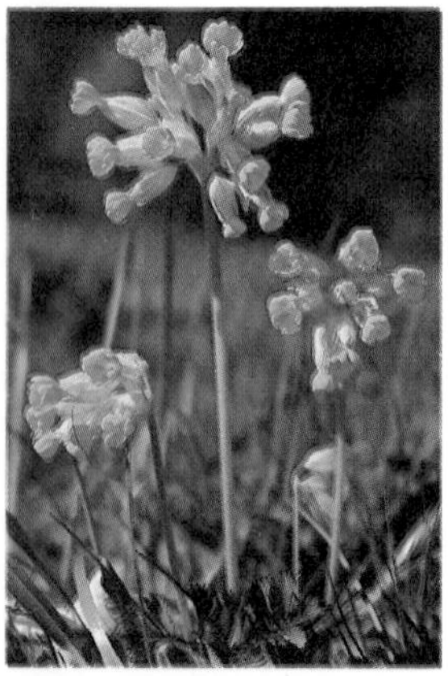

cowslip *Its fragrant yellow flowers were once common in pastures and meadowlands but are now becoming much rarer as old meadows are plowed.*

hides: *a heavy cloud cover.* **b.** Something that conceals or keeps secret, such as a pretext or disguise: *The secret agent's job in the bank is just a cover.* **5.** A table setting for one person. **6.** A **cover charge** *(see).* **7.** *Philately.* **a.** An envelope or wrapper for mail. **b.** An envelope, postcard, or the like bearing a stamp and postal markings of special interest to stamp collectors. **8.** *Finance.* **a.** Funds sufficient to meet an obligation or secure against loss. **b.** See **coverage** (sense 2). **9.** *Mathematics.* A collection of sets associated with a given set such that every point in the given set belongs to at least one other set in the collection. —See Synonyms at **shelter.** —**break cover.** To come out of hiding. —**take cover.** To seek concealment or protection, as from enemy fire. —**under cover. 1.** Operating secretly or under a guise; covert. **2.** Hidden; protected. [Middle English *coveren,* from Old French *covrir,* from Latin *cooperīre,* to cover completely : *co-,* completely + *operīre,* to cover.] —**cov·er·er** *n.*

cov·er·age (kŭv′ər-ĭj) *n.* **1.** The reporting and analysis of a news item. **2.** The extent of protection afforded by an insurance policy. **3.** The amount of funds reserved to meet liabilities. **4.** The way in which a subject is treated. **5.** The range achieved by a transmitter or communication medium.

cov·er·alls (kŭv′ər-ôlz′) *pl.n.* A loose-fitting one-piece garment worn by workmen to protect their clothes.

cover charge *n.* A fixed service charge added to the bill, at a night club, for entertainment or services. Also called "cover," "couvert."

cover crop *n.* A temporary crop planted to protect the soil from erosion in winter and provide humus or nitrogen when plowed under in the spring.

Cov·er·dale (kŭv′ər-dāl′), **Miles** (1488–1568). English Protestant theologian and translator of the Bible (1535).

covered bridge *n.* A bridge protected by a roof.

covered wagon *n.* A large wagon covered with an arched canvas top, used by American pioneers for prairie travel.

cover girl *n.* An attractive female model whose picture appears on magazine colors.

cover glass *n.* A **cover slip** *(see).*

cov·er·ing (kŭv′ər-ĭng) *n.* Something that covers for protection, concealment, or warmth.

covering board *n. Nautical.* A **plank-sheer** *(see).*

covering letter *n.* An explanatory letter enclosed with goods or other documents.

cov·er·let (kŭv′ər-lĭt) *n.* An ornamental cloth covering for a bed; a bedspread.

cover note *n. British.* A temporary document providing the holder with motor insurance until an official policy is issued.

covers versed cosine.

co·ver·sine (kō′vûr′sīn′) *n. Trigonometry.* A **versed cosine** *(see).*

cover slip *n.* A small, usually square, thin piece of glass used to cover a specimen on a microscope slide.

cov·ert (kŭv′ərt, kō′vərt) *adj.* **1.** Concealed; hidden; secret. **2.** *Rare.* Covered or covered over; sheltered. See **feme covert.** —See Synonyms at **secret.**
~*n.* **1.** A covering or cover. **2.** A covered place or shelter; a hiding place. **3.** Thick undergrowth or woodland affording cover for game; cover. **4.** Covert cloth. **5.** *Zoology.* Any of the feathers covering the bases of the longer main feathers of a bird's wings or tail. [Middle English, from Old French, from the past participle of *covrir,* to COVER.] —**cov·ert·ly** *adv.* —**cov·ert·ness** *n.*

covert cloth *n.* A twilled cloth made of woolen or worsted yarn with cotton, silk, or rayon. It has a speckled appearance and is used for clothing. Also called "covert."

cov·er·ture (kŭv′ər-chər) *n.* **1.** A covering; shelter; concealment; disguise. **2.** *Law.* The legal status of a married woman.

cover up *tr.v.* **1.** To put a cover over. **2.** To conceal or attempt to conceal (a crime, for example). —*intr.v.* To conceal or attempt to conceal a crime, scandal, or the like.

cov·er-up (kŭv′ər-ŭp′) *n.* An effort or strategy designed to conceal something, such as a crime or scandal, that could be harmful or embarrassing if known. —**cov·er-up** *adj.*

cov·et (kŭv′ĭt) *tr.v.* **-eted, -eting, -ets. 1.** To desire (that which is another's). **2.** To wish for excessively and culpably; crave. [Middle English *coveiten,* from Old French *coveitier,* from Vulgar Latin *cupiditāre* (unattested), to desire, from Latin *cupiditās,* desire, CUPIDITY.] —**cov·et·a·ble** *adj.* —**cov·et·er** *n.*

cov·et·ous (kŭv′ə-təs) *adj.* **1.** Excessively desirous, especially of someone else's possessions; avaricious; greedy. **2.** Very desirous; eager for acquisition: *covetous of learning.* —**cov·et·ous·ly** *adv.* —**cov·et·ous·ness** *n.*

cov·ey (kŭv′ē) *n., pl.* **-eys. 1.** A family or small flock of partridges. **2.** A small group of people or things. [Middle English *covei(e),* from Old French *covee,* a brood, from *cover, couver,* to hatch, sit on (eggs), from Latin *cubāre,* to lie down (on).]

cov·in (kŭv′ĭn) *n. Law.* A secret arrangement to defraud or injure another person. [Middle English, from Old French *covin(e),* from Medieval Latin *convenium,* "a coming together," agreement, collusion, from Latin *convenīre,* to CONVENE.]

cov·ing (kō′vĭng) *n. Architecture.* **1.** A concave molding, often ready-made, used to form a junction between a ceiling and a wall. **2.** A curved part of a wall where it joins a ceiling.

cow¹ (kou) *n., pl.* **cows** or *archaic* **kine** (kīn). **1.** The mature female of cattle of the genus *Bos.* **2.** The mature female of other animals, such as whales, elephants, or moose. **3.** Broadly, any domesticated bovine. **4.** *Slang.* **a.** A fat or unpleasant woman. **b.** A woman. Used derogatorily. [Cow, kine; Middle English *cou, kin,* Old English *cū, cȳ(e).*]

cow² *tr.v.* **cowed, cowing, cows.** To frighten with threats or a show of force; intimidate. [Originally dialectal (as Scottish *kow*), perhaps ultimately from Old Norse *kūga,* to oppress.]

cow·ard (kou′ərd) *n.* One who lacks courage in the face of danger, pain, or an unpleasant situation; an ignobly frightened or timid person. [Middle English *couherde, coward,* from Old French *couard,* coward, perhaps "one with his tail between his legs," from *coue,* tail, from Latin *cauda,* tail.]

Cow·ard (kou′ərd), **Sir Noël** (1899–1973). British dramatist, composer, and entertainer. He began as an actor and won fame as a playwright, becoming especially noted for his witty and worldly comedies, including *Hay Fever* (1925) and *Private Lives* (1930).

cow·ard·ice (kou′ər-dĭs) *n.* Lack of courage in the face of danger, pain, difficulty, or opposition.

cow·ard·ly (kou′ərd-lē) *adj.* **1.** Lacking courage; ignobly fearful. **2.** Showing cowardice; befitting a coward.
~*adv.* In the manner of a coward; basely; meanly. —**cow·ard·li·ness** *n.*

cow·bane (kou′bān) *n.* **1.** A plant, *Oxypolis rigidior,* of the southeastern and central United States, having poisonous roots and foliage, and clusters of small white flowers. **2.** Any of several related plants, such as the **water hemlock** *(see).*

cow·bell (kou′bĕl′) *n.* A bell hung from a collar around a cow's neck to aid in locating her.

cow·ber·ry (kou′bĕr′ē) *n., pl.* **-ries. 1.** A creeping evergreen shrub, *Vaccinium vitis-idaea,* having pink or reddish flowers and edible, slightly acid red berries. **2.** A berry of this plant. Also called "mountain cranberry," "lingonberry."

cow·bird (kou′bûrd′) *n.* Any of various blackbirds of the genus *Molothrus* and related genera, that lay their eggs in the nests of other birds; especially the common North American species, *M. ater.* [The birds feed on cattle vermin.]

cow·boy (kou′boi′) *n.* **1.** A hired man, especially in the western United States, who tends cattle, as on a ranch, and performs many of his duties on horseback. **2.** In the United States, a performer who demonstrates feats of horsemanship, as at a rodeo. **3.** A figure from the era of the Wild West, conventionally represented as fighting Indians. **4.** *Slang.* A speedy or reckless driver of a motor vehicle. **5.** One of a band of loyalist guerillas that operated between the British and American lines, mostly in Westchester County, New York, during the American Revolution.

cow·catch·er (kou′kăch′ər) *n.* An iron grille or frame that projects from the front of a locomotive and serves to clear the track of obstructions.

cow college *n. Informal.* **1.** An agricultural college. **2.** A college or university considered to be provincial and unsophisticated.

cow·er (kou′ər) *intr.v.* **-ered, -ering, -ers.** To cringe or shrink away, as from cold or in fear. —See Synonyms at **recoil.** [Middle English *couren,* from Middle Low German *kūren*†, lie in wait.]

Cowes (kouz). A town on the Medina River in the north of the Isle of Wight, off southern England. A yachting club was founded here in 1812, and the town stages an international regatta each August.

cow·fish (kou′fĭsh′) *n., pl.* **-fishes** or collectively **cowfish. 1.** Any of various small whales, porpoises, or similar aquatic mammals; especially, a whale of the genus *Mesopledon,* having a pointed snout. **2.** A fish, *Lactophrys quadricornis,* of warm Atlantic waters, having the body encased in a bony covering and hornlike spines over each eye.

cow·girl (kou′gûrl′) *n.* A hired woman, especially in the western United States, who tends cattle and performs many of her duties on horseback.

cow·hand (kou′hănd) *n.* A cowboy.

cow·herd (kou′hûrd′) *n.* A person who herds or tends cattle.

cow·hide (kou′hīd′) *n.* **1. a.** The hide of a cow. **b.** The leather made from this hide. **2.** A strong, heavy, flexible whip, usually made of braided leather.

cowl (koul) *n.* **1. a.** A hood worn by monks. **b.** The hooded robe of a monk or a similar garment. **c.** A loose collar that can be worn as a hood. **2.** A hood-shaped covering used to increase the draught of a chimney. **3.** A cowling.
~*tr.v.* **cowled, cowling, cowls.** To put a cowl on or cover with a cowl. [Middle English *coule,* Old English *cugele, cūle,* from Late Latin *cuculla,* from Latin *cucullus*†, hood.]

cowled (kould) *adj.* **1.** Wearing or supplied with a cowl; hooded. **2.** Having the shape of a cowl.

Cow·ley (kou′lē), **Abraham** (1618–67). English poet and essayist. He published his first volume of poetry, *Poetical Blossoms,* at the age of 15. His best-known work is *Davideis,* an epic poem in four books recounting the Biblical history of King David.

cow·lick (kou′lĭk′) *n.* A projecting tuft of hair on the head that will not lie flat. [It appears to have been licked by a cow.]

cowl·ing (kou′lĭng) *n.* A removable metal covering for the engine of an aircraft or motor vehicle. Also called "cowl."

cow·man (kou′mən) *n., pl.* **-men** (-mĭn). **1.** *British.* A man who tends cows. **2.** The owner of a cattle ranch.

co·work·er (kō′wûrk′ər) *n.* A fellow worker.

cow parsnip *n.* Any of several tall, coarse plants of the genus *Heracleum,* such as *H. Lanatum,* of North America. Also called "masterwart."

cow pat *n.* A mass of cow dung.

cow·pea (kou′pē′) *n.* **1.** A tropical vine, *Vigna sinensis,* bearing long, hanging pods and grown in the southern United States for soil improvement and as animal feed. **2.** The edible, pealike seed of this plant. In this sense, also called "black-eyed pea."

Cow·per (ko͞o′pər, kou′-), **William** (1731–1800). British poet. His best-known works include *Table Talk* (1782) and *On the Loss of the Royal George* (published posthumously).

Cow·per's glands (kou′pərz, ko͞o′pərz) *pl.n.* A pair of small glands lying near the prostate gland that secrete mucus into the male urethra, thus contributing to the semen. [After William *Cowper* (1666–1709), English anatomist who discovered them.]

cow·poke (kou′pōk′) *n. Informal.* A cowboy, as on a ranch.

cow pony *n.* A small, agile horse used in roundups.

cow·pox (kou′pŏks′) *n.* A contagious viral disease of cattle characterized by vesicles on the skin, especially the udder. Inoculation of humans with cowpox virus confers temporary immunity to smallpox. Also called "vaccinia."

cow·punch·er (kou′pŭn′chər) *n. Informal.* A cowboy, as on a ranch.

cow·ry, cow·rie (kou′rē) *n., pl.* **-ries. 1.** Any of various tropical marine mollusks of the family Cypraeidae, having glossy, often brightly marked shells, some of which are used as money in the South Pacific and parts of Africa. **2.** The shell of any of these mollusks. [Hindi *kauṛī,* from Sanskrit *kaparda,* from Dravidian; akin to Tamil *kōṭu,* shell.]

cow shark *n.* Any of several sharks of the family Hexanchidae, of warm and temperate seas.

cow shed *n.* A shed for housing cows.

cow·skin (kou′skĭn′) *n.* **1.** The hide of a cow. **2.** Leather made from this hide.

cow·slip (kou′slĭp′) *n.* An Old World primrose, *Primula veris,* having yellow flowers borne in a cluster. [Middle English *cowslyppe,* Old English *cūslyppe,* "cow dung" (probably because some varieties are found in cow pastures) : *cū,* COW + *slyppe, slypa,* slime, paste.]

cow town *n.* A small town in a cattle-raising area.

cox (kŏks) *n. Informal.* A coxswain.
~*v.* **coxed, coxing, coxes.** *Informal.* —*tr.* To serve as coxswain for (a boat). —*intr.* To act as coxswain.

cox·a (kŏk′sə) *n., pl.* **coxae** (kŏk′sē′) **1.** *Anatomy.* The hip or hip joint. **2.** *Zoology.* The first segment of the leg of an insect or other arthropod, adjoining and attached to the body. [Latin *coxa,* the hip.]

cox·al·gi·a (kŏk-săl′jē-ə) *n.* Pain in or disease of the hip. [New Latin : COX(A) + -ALGIA.] **—cox·al·gic** *adj.*

coxcomb. Variant of **cockscomb** (senses 2, 4).

cox·comb·ry (kŏks′kōm′rē) *n., pl.* **-ries.** Arrogance and pretension in manner or behavior; foolishness; foppery.

cox·i·tis (kŏk-sī′tĭs) *n.* Inflammation of the hip joint. [COX(A) + -ITIS.]

Cox·sack·ie virus (ko͝ok-săk′ē) *n.* Any of a group of enteroviruses, some of which produce a disease resembling poliomyelitis without paralysis. [After *Coxsackie,* a town in New York state; the virus was first identified in a resident of the town.]

Cox's orange pippin (kŏk′sĭs) *n.* A variety of eating apple, having crisp flesh and a red-tinged green skin. Also called "Cox," "Cox's." [19th century : after R. *Cox,* Englishman who propagated it.]

cox·swain (kŏk′sən, kŏk′swān′) *n.* A person who steers a boat or racing shell or has charge of its crew. Also informally called "cox." [Middle English *cok swain* : *cok,* COCKBOAT + *swain,* servant, SWAIN.]

coy (koi) *adj.* **coyer, coyest. 1.** Shy and demure; retiring. **2.** Pretending shyness or modesty; coquettishly shy. **3.** Annoyingly unwilling to commit oneself; affectedly reticent. —See Synonyms at **shy.** [Middle English, from Old French *coi,* shy, quiet, from Vulgar Latin *quētus* (unattested), variant of Latin *quiētus,* QUIET.] **—coy·ly** *adv.* **—coy·ness** *n.*

coy·o·te (kī-ō′tē, kī′ōt) *n.* **1.** A wolflike carnivorous animal, *Canis latrans,* common in desert and prairie regions of western North America. **2.** *Slang.* A contemptible sneak. [Mexican Spanish, from Nahuatl *coyotl.*]

coy·pu (koi′po͞o) *n., pl.* **-pus. 1.** A large, beaverlike South American rodent, *Myocaster coypu,* valued for its fur. **2.** The fur of this animal. Also called "nutria." [American Spanish *coipú,* from Araucanian *kóypu.*]

coz (kŭz) *n. Archaic Informal.* Cousin.

coz·en (kŭz′ən) *v.* **-ened, -ening, -ens.** —*tr.* To deceive, by means of a petty trick or fraud. —*intr.* To act with intent to deceive. [16th century cant : perhaps akin to COUSIN.] **—coz·en·er** *n.*

coz·en·age (kŭz′ən-ĭj) *n.* **1.** The art or practice of cozening; cheating. **2.** A deception; a fraud.

co·zy (kō′zē) *adj.* **-zier, -ziest.** Also **co·sy, -sier, -siest. 1.** Snug and comfortable; warm. **2.** Marked by friendly intimacy. **3.** *Informal.* Marked by close association for devious purposes: *a cozy agreement.* —See Synonyms at **comfortable.**
~*n., pl.* **cozies.** Also **co·sy** *pl.* **-sies.** A padded or knitted covering placed over a teapot, for example, to keep the contents hot. [18th century (Scottish) : origin obscure.] **—coz·i·ly** *adv.* **—coz·i·ness** *n.*

cP centipoise.

cp. compare.

c.p. 1. candle power. **2.** chemically pure.

C.P. 1. Cape Province. **2.** command post. **3.** Communist Party.

CPA, C.P.A. certified public accountant.

cpd. compound.

Cpl. corporal.

C.P.O. chief petty officer.

cps cycles per second.

CPU central processing unit.

CQ (sē′kyo͞o′) *n.* Code letters used at the beginning of radio messages intended for all receivers. [C(all to) Q(uarters).]

Cr The symbol for the element chromium.

cr. 1. credit, creditor. **2.** creek. **3.** crescendo. **4.** crown.

craal. Variant of **kraal.**

crab[1] (krăb) *n.* **1. a.** Any of various predominantly marine crustaceans of the section Brachyura within the order Decapoda, characterized by a broad, flattened cephalothorax covered by a hard shell with the small abdomen concealed beneath it, and five pairs of legs, of which the front pair are large and pincerlike. **b.** The flesh of any edible variety of crab. **2.** Any of various similar related crustaceans, such as the **hermit crab** *(see).* **3.** The **horseshoe crab** *(see).* **4.** The crab louse. **5. Crab.** The constellation and sign of the zodiac, **Cancer** *(see).* **6.** The maneuvering of an aircraft partially into a crosswind in order to compensate for drift. **7.** Any of various machines for handling or hoisting heavy weights. **8. crabs.** *Informal.* The lowest throw, usually a two or three, of a pair of dice. **—catch a crab.** In rowing, to strike the water with an oar in recovering a stroke or to miss it in making one.
~*v.* **crabbed, crabbing, crabs.** —*intr.* **1.** To hunt or catch crabs. **2.** *Nautical.* To drift diagonally or sideways. **3.** To move sideways. —*tr. Aviation.* To direct (an aircraft) partly into a crosswind to eliminate drift. [Middle English *crab(be),* Old English *crabba,* from Germanic.]

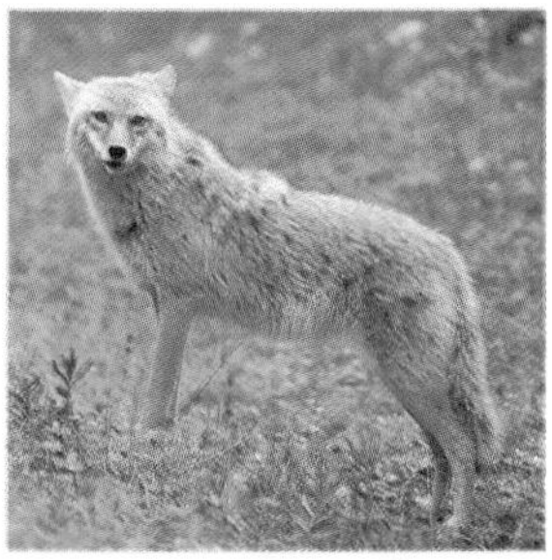

coyote *A wild dog of western North America, with a distinctive, drawn-out howling call.*

crab[2] (krăb) *n.* **1.** The crab apple or its fruit. **2.** A quarrelsome, ill-tempered person.
~*v.* **crabbed** (krăbd), **crabbing, crabs.** *Informal.* —*intr.* To criticize; find fault. —*tr.* **1.** To interfere with and ruin. **2.** To find fault with. [16th century : originally, (of hawks) to claw, fight, from Middle Low German *krabben;* akin to CRAB (crustacean).]

crab apple *n.* **1.** Any of several trees of the genus *Pyrus,* having white, pink, or red flowers and small, sour applelike fruit. **2.** The tart fruit of any of these trees, used for making jelly. [Middle English, perhaps alteration (through influence of CRAB) of earlier *scrab,* probably from Scandinavian.]

Crabbe (krăb), **George** (1754–1832). British poet. His first major poem was *The Village* (1783), in which he portrayed the ugliness of rural life, a theme taken up in subsequent works, including *The Parish Register* (1807) and *The Borough* (1810).

crab·bed (krăb′ĭd) *adj.* **1.** Irritable and perverse in disposition; ill-tempered. **2.** Difficult to understand; complicated. Said of a writer or his style. **3.** Difficult to read. Said of handwriting. [Middle English, partly from *crabbe,* CRAB, referring to the perversity of its gait, and partly from *crabbe,* CRAB (apple), referring to its sourness.] **—crab·bed·ly** *adv.* **—crab·bed·ness** *n.*

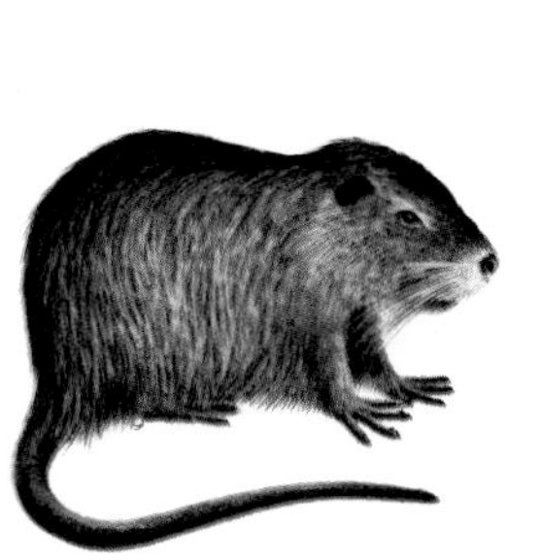

coypu *A South American rodent found in marshes and rivers.*

crab·ber (krăb′ər) *n.* **1.** A person whose occupation is fishing for crabs. **2.** The boat used in fishing for crabs.

crab·by (krăb′ē) *adj.* **-bier, -biest.** Irritable; bad-tempered.

crab cactus *n.* A **Christmas cactus** *(see).*

crab·grass (krăb′grăs′, -gräs′) *n.* Any of various coarse grasses of the genus *Digitaria,* that tend to spread and displace other grasses in lawns.

crab louse *n.* A body louse, *Phthirus pubis,* that generally infests the pubic region and causes severe itching.

Crab Nebula *n.* An expanding nebula of dust and gas about 5,000 light-years away in the constellation Taurus. It contains a pulsar and is the remnant of a supernova recorded in 1504. [So called from its shape.]

crabs (krăbz) *n. Informal.* Infestation by crab lice.

crab·stick (krăb′stĭk′) *n.* **1.** A stick made of crab-apple wood. **2.** A bad-tempered person.

crack (krăk) *v.* **cracked, cracking, cracks.** —*intr.* **1.** To break with a sharp, snapping sound. **2.** To make such a sound; snap. **3.** To break without dividing into parts; split slightly. **4.** To change sharply in pitch or timbre, as from hoarseness or emotion. Used of the voice. **5. a.** To break down; fail; give out. **b.** To give in to pressure. **6.** *Chemistry.* To decompose into simpler compounds. Used especially of large-molecule hydrocarbons from petroleum, which are broken by heat or catalysis to smaller molecules suitable for use as fuel. —*tr.* **1.** To cause to make a sharp, snapping sound; snap: *crack the whip.* **2.** To cause to break or split slightly or completely. **3.** To break with a sharp, snapping sound: *crack an egg.* **4.** To strike with a sudden, sharp sound. **5.** To break open or into. **6.** To discover the solution to, especially after considerable effort: *crack a problem.* **7.** To cause (the voice) to crack. **8.** *Informal.* To tell (a joke). **9.** To impair or diminish (a reputation, for example). **10.** *Chemistry.* To reduce (petroleum, for example) to simpler compounds by cracking. **11.** *Informal.* To open and drink (a bottle of wine, can of beer, or the like). —See Synonyms at **break. —cracked up to be.** *Informal.* Praised or lauded as; believed to be. **—get cracking.** *Informal.* To set about something promptly.
~*n.* **1.** A sharp, snapping sound, such as the report of a firearm. **2.** A partial split or break; a flaw; a fissure. **3.** A slight, narrow space: *The window was open a crack.* **4.** A sharp, resounding blow. **5.** A mental or physical impairment; a defect. **6.** A cracking vocal tone or sound, as in hoarseness. **7.** *Informal.* An attempt; a chance: *gave him a crack at the job.* **8.** *Informal.* **a.** A flippant or sarcastic remark. **b.** A humorous remark; a joke. **9.** A moment; an instant: *at the crack of dawn.* —See Synonyms at **joke.**
~*adj.* Excelling in skill or achievement; superior; first-rate: *a crack*

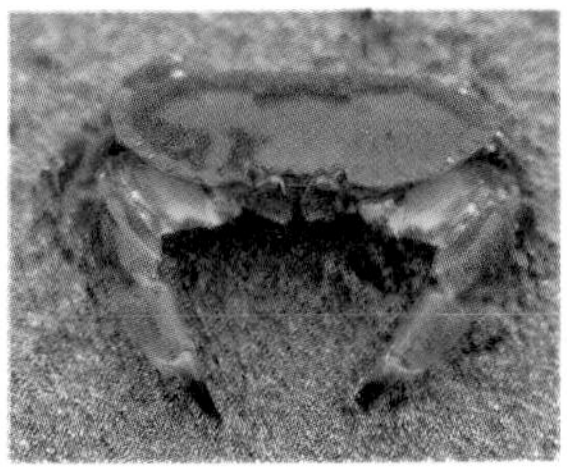

crab *Edible crabs, like the species shown here, can grow to about 250 millimeters (10 inches) across. As a crab grows, it molts, shedding its old shell and forming a new one.*

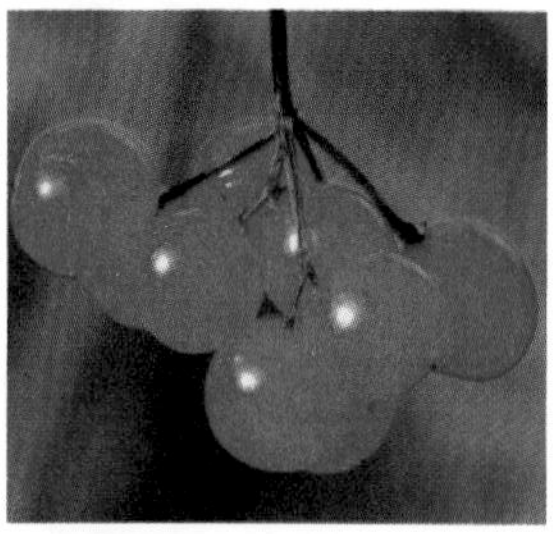

cranberry *The berries of this marsh plant are made into a piquant sauce served with turkey or venison. This is the fruit of the North American high-bush cranberry.*

PRONUNCIATION KEY

ă, pat; ā, pay; âr, care; ä, father, are; b, bib; ch, church; d, deed; ĕ, pet; ē, be; f, fife; g, gag; h, hat; hw, which; ĭ, pit; ī, pie; îr, pier; j, judge; k, kick; l, lid, needle; m, mum; n, no, sudden; ng, thing; ŏ, pot; ō, toe; ô, paw, for; oi, noise; ou, out; o͝o, book; o͞o, boot; p, pop; r, roar; s, sauce; sh, ship, dish; t, tight; th, thin, path; *th*, this, bathe; ŭ, cut; ûr, fur; v, valve; w, with; y, yes; z, zebra, size; zh, vision; ə, about, item, edible, gallop, circus, peaceful

IN FOREIGN WORDS:

à, *Fr.* ami; œ, *Fr.* feu, *Ger.* schön; ü, *Fr.* tu, *Ger.* über; KH, *Ger.* ich, *Scot.* loch; N, *Fr.* bon; y', *Fr.* Compiègne

STRESS MARKS:

Primary stress: ′
in·cite′ (ĭn-sīt′)
Secondary stress: ′
in′sight′ (ĭn′sīt′)

marksman. [Middle English *craken,* Old English *cracian,* to resound, from Germanic.]

crack·brain (krăk′brān′) *n.* A foolish or insane person. **—crack·brained** *adj.*

crack down *intr.v.* To become more demanding, severe, or strict. Often used with *on*: *crack down on student absences.*

crack·down (krăk′doun′) *n.* Sudden punitive action.

cracked (krăkt) *adj.* **1.** Having a crack or cracks. **2.** *Informal.* Crazy; foolish.

cracked stem *n.* A disease of the celery plant caused by a deficiency of boron and characterized by cracking of the stalks.

cracked wheat *n.* A cereal, **bulgur** *(see).*

crack·er (krăk′ər) *n.* **1.** A thin, crisp wafer or biscuit, usually made of unleavened, unsweetened dough. **2.** A firecracker. **3.** A small cardboard cylinder covered with decorative paper and containing a joke, a small toy, or the like and a weak explosive that makes a sharp popping noise when a paper strip is pulled at one or both ends and torn. **4.** *Chemistry.* A piece of apparatus in an oil refinery for cracking petroleum. **5.** A poor white person of the rural southeastern United States. Used disparagingly. **6.** One that cracks.

crack·er-bar·rel (krăk′ər-băr′əl) *adj.* Resembling or characteristic of the extended informal discussions carried on by persons habitually assembled at a general store; homespun and unsophisticated: *cracker-barrel theories.* [Cracker barrels were common fixtures in country stores.]

crack·er·jack (krăk′ər-jăk′) *adj. Slang.* Of excellent quality or ability; fine.
∼*n. Slang.* Someone or something with excellent skills or abilities. [From CRACK (proficient) + JACK (man).]

crack·ers (krăk′ərz) *adj. Chiefly British Slang.* Insane; crazy.

crack·ing (krăk′ĭng) *n. Chemistry.* Thermal decomposition, sometimes with catalysis, of a complex substance; especially, such decomposition of petroleum to extract low-boiling fractions, such as gasoline.
∼*adj. British Informal.* Very good: *had a cracking time.* **—crack·ing** *adv.*

crack·le (krăk′əl) *v.* **-led, -ling, -les.** —*intr.* To make a succession of slight sharp, snapping noises, as a small fire may. —*tr.* **1.** To crush (paper, for example) with such sounds. **2.** To cause (china, for example) to become covered with a network of fine cracks.
∼*n.* **1.** The act or sound of crackling. **2.** A network of fine cracks on the surface of glazed pottery, china, or glassware. **3.** Ware bearing this network of cracks. Also called "crackleware." [Frequentative of CRACK.]

crack·le·ware (krăk′əl-wâr′) *n.* Ceramic ware made with a surface network of cracks.

crack·ling (krăk′lĭng) *n.* **1.** A succession of slight sharp, snapping noises. **2.** The crisp browned rind of roasted pork. **3. cracklings.** The crisp bits that remain of pork fat after rendering.

crack·ly (krăk′lē) *adj.* Likely to crackle; crisp.

crack·nel (krăk′nəl) *n.* **1.** A hard, crisp biscuit. **2. cracknels.** Crisp bits of fried pork fat. [Middle English *crak(e)nel,* probably from Old French *craquelin,* from Middle Dutch *krākelinc,* from *krāken,* to crack.]

crack·pot (krăk′pŏt′) *n. Informal.* An eccentric person, especially one espousing bizarre ideas. **—crack·pot** *adj.*

crack up *intr.v. Informal.* **1.** To have a mental or physical breakdown. **2.** To laugh boisterously. **3.** To crash; collide.

crack·up (krăk′ŭp′) *n. Informal.* **1.** A mental or physical breakdown. **2.** A collision.

Cracow. See **Kraków.**

-cracy *suffix.* Indicates government or rule; for example, **aristocracy, mobocracy.** [Old French *-cratie,* from Late Latin *-cratia,* from Greek *-kratia,* from *kratos,* strength, power.]

cra·dle (krād′l) *n.* **1.** A small, low bed for an infant, often furnished with rockers. **2.** A place of origin; a birthplace. **3.** A framework of wood or metal used to support something, such as a ship undergoing construction or repair. **4.** A framework used to protect an injured limb. **5.** The part of a telephone upon which the handset rests. **6. a.** A frame projecting above a scythe, used to catch grain as it is cut so that it can be laid flat. **b.** A scythe equipped with such a frame. **7.** A low, flat framework that rolls on casters, for use by a mechanic working beneath a motor vehicle. **8.** A movable platform suspended by cables down the side of a building or ship, used by painters, window-cleaners, and the like. **9.** A boxlike device fitted with rockers, used for washing gem- or gold-bearing dirt. **10.** A metal frame inserted under bedclothes to keep them from touching an injured part of the body.
∼*v.* **cradled, -dling, -dles.** —*tr.* **1.** To place into, rock, or hold in or as if in a cradle. **2.** To care for or nurture in infancy. **3.** To reap (grain) with a cradle. **4.** To place or support (a ship) in a cradle. **5.** *Mining.* To wash (gem- or gold-bearing dirt) in a cradle. —*intr. Rare.* **1.** To lie in or as if in a cradle. **2.** To reap grain with a cradle. [Middle English *cradel;* probably akin to Old High German *kratto,* basket.] **—cra·dler** *n.*

cradle cap *n.* Crusting of the scalp occurring in young babies. It is a type of seborrhoea.

cra·dle·snatch *v.* **-snatched, -snatching, -snatches.** —*tr.* To take (a much younger person) as a lover or spouse. —*intr.* To practice cradlesnatching. **—cra·dle·snatch·er** *n.*

cra·dle·song (krād′l-sông′, -sŏng′) *n.* A lullaby.

craft (krăft, kräft) *n., pl.* **crafts** or **craft** (for sense 5). **1.** Skill or ability in something, especially in handiwork or the arts; proficiency; expertness. **2.** Skill in evasion or deception; cunning; guile. **3.** An occupation, art, or trade, especially one requiring manual dexterity. **4.** The membership of such an occupation or trade; a guild. **5.** A boat, ship, aircraft, or spacecraft.
∼*tr.v.* **crafted, crafting, crafts. 1.** To make by hand. **2.** To make, produce, or create with painstaking skill and attention to detail. [Middle English *craft,* strength, skill, device, Old English *cræft,* from West Germanic *kraftaz, krab-taz* (both unattested), strength.]

-craft *suffix.* Indicates work, art, or practice of; for example, **woodcraft, stagecraft.** [From CRAFT.]

crafts·man (krăfts′mən, kräfts′-) *n., pl.* **-men** (-mĭn). **1.** A skilled worker who practices a craft by occupation. **2.** An artist considered with regard to technical skill. **—crafts·man·ly** *adj.* **—crafts·man·ship** *n.*

craft union *n.* A trade union limited in membership to workers engaged in the same type of work. Compare **industrial union.**

craft·y (krăf′tē, kräf′-) *adj.* **-ier, -iest. 1.** Skilled in underhandedness and deception; shrewd; cunning. **2.** *Archaic.* Skillful; ingenious; dexterous. —See Synonyms at **sly. —craft·i·ly** *adv.* **—craft·i·ness** *n.*

crag[1] (krăg) *n.* A steeply projecting mass of rock forming part of a rugged cliff or headland. [Middle English, from Celtic *kar-n-, krag-* (both unattested). See **cairn.**]

crag[2] *n. Geology.* **1.** A shelly deposit of sandstone, found especially in East Anglia. **2.** Strata containing this deposit. [18th century : perhaps specialized use of CRAG[1].]

crag·gy (krăg′ē) *adj.* **-gier, -giest.** Also **crag·ged** (krăg′ĭd). **1.** Having crags; steep and rugged. **2.** Uneven; rugged: *craggy features.* **—crag·gi·ly** *adv.* **—crag·gi·ness** *n.*

crake (krāk) *n.* Any of several birds of the family Rallidae, such as the corncrake, or a marsh bird of the genus *Porzana.* [Middle English *crak, crake,* crow, raven, from Old Norse *krāka* (imitative).]

cram (krăm) *v.* **crammed, cramming, crams.** —*tr.* **1.** To force, press, or squeeze into an insufficient space; stuff. **2.** To fill too tightly. **3.** To gorge with food. **4.** *Informal.* To prepare (a person) hastily or revise and study (a subject) intensively for an examination. —*intr.* **1.** To gorge oneself with food. **2.** *Informal.* To make a concentrated last-minute review of a given academic subject, as in studying for an examination.
∼*n.* **1.** The act of, or condition resulting from, cramming. **2.** *Informal.* The knowledge acquired by cramming. [Middle English *crammen,* Old English *crammian* from Germanic.]

cram·bo (krăm′bō) *n., pl.* **-boes. 1.** A word game in which a player or team must find and express a rhyme for a word or line presented by the opposing player or team. **2.** Doggerel. [Obsolete *crambe,* "stale cabbage," tedious repetition, from Latin *crambē (repetīta),* "cabbage (served up again)" (expression used by Juvenal), from Greek *krambē.*]

cram-full (krăm′fo͝ol′) *adj.* Filled to the maximum; stuffed.

cramp[1] (krămp) *n.* **1.** A sudden involuntary muscular contraction causing severe pain, often occurring in the calf or foot as the result of overexertion, chill, or salt loss. **2.** A temporary partial paralysis of habitually or excessively used muscles: *writer's cramp.* **3.** Sharp, persistent pains in the abdomen.
∼*tr.v.* **cramped, cramping, cramps.** To affect or cause to be affected with or as if with a cramp. [Middle English *crampe,* from Old French, probably from Old High German *krampho.*]

cramp[2] *n.* **1.** A bar, usually of steel, with right-angle bends at both ends, used for permanently holding together stones, timber, and other building materials. Also called "cramp iron." **2.** A frame with an adjustable part to hold pieces together; a clamp. **3.** Anything that compresses or restrains. **4.** A confined position or part.
∼*tr.v.* **cramped, cramping, cramps. 1.** To hold together with a cramp. **2.** To confine; restrict; hamper. [Middle English, from Middle Dutch *crampe,* hook, from Germanic; akin to CRAMP[1].]

cramped (krămpt) *adj.* **1.** Restricted; contracted; narrowed. **2.** Difficult to read or decipher: *cramped handwriting.*

cramp·fish (krămp′fĭsh′) *n., pl.* **-fishes** or collectively **crampfish.** The **electric ray** *(see).* [From CRAMP, pain, from its ability to give electric shocks.]

cram·pon (krăm′pən) *n.* Also **cram·poon** (krăm-po͞on′) **1.** Either of a hinged pair of curved metal bars for raising heavy objects, such as stones or timber. **2.** An iron spike or spiked frame attached to the sole of a boot to prevent slipping when climbing or walking on ice. [Old French *crampon,* perhaps from Frankish *kramp* (unattested), hook; akin to CRAMP[2].]

cran (krăn) *n.* A British unit of capacity for fresh herring, equal to 37.5 imperial gallons in volume. [18th century : from Gaelic *crann*†.]

Cra·nach (krăn′ək), **Lucas,** also known as "Cranach the Elder," (1472–1553). German painter and engraver. His works include a famous *Adam and Eve,* as well as portraits of Elector John Frederick, Martin Luther, and others. His work was carried on by his son, **Lucas Cranach the Younger** (1515–86).

cran·age (krā′nĭj) *n.* **1.** The hire, loan, or use of a crane. **2.** The amount of money charged or paid for such use.

cran·ber·ry (krăn′bĕr′ē, -bər-ē) *n., pl.* **-ries. 1.** A slender, trailing North American shrub, *Vaccinium macrocarpon,* growing in damp ground and bearing tart red berries. **2.** The edible berry of this plant, often made into a sauce or jelly. **3.** Any of various similar or related plants, especially the European species *V. oxycoccus.* [Partial translation of (American colonial) Low German *kraanbere,* "crane-berry" (from the stamens which resemble a beak).]

cranberry bush *n.* The **high-bush cranberry** *(see).*

crane (krān) *n.* **1.** Any of various large wading birds of the family Gruidae, having a long neck, long legs, and a long bill. **2.** Loosely, a similar bird, such as a heron. **3.** A machine for hoisting and moving heavy objects by means of cables attached to a movable boom. **4.** A movable arm on which a film or television camera is mounted.
~*v.* **craned, craning, cranes.** —*tr.* **1.** To hoist or move with or as if with a crane. **2.** To strain and stretch (the neck). —*intr.* **1.** To stretch one's neck for a better view. **2. a.** To balk and lean forward, as a horse does before jumping. **b.** To hesitate. [Middle English *crane,* Old English *cran,* from Germanic; akin to Latin *grus.*]

Crane (krān), **Hart,** born Harold Hart Crane (1899–1932). U.S. poet. His mature work is characterized by a passionate spiritual affirmation of America's democratic potential.

Crane, Stephen (1871–1900). U.S. novelist. He won fame with *The Red Badge of Courage* (1895), set in the Civil War.

crane fly *n.* Any of various flies of the family Tipulidae, having a slender body, long delicate wings, and long legs. Also *chiefly British* "daddy longlegs."

cranes·bill (krānz'bĭl') *n.* Any of various plants of the genus *Geranium* with fruits ending in a long, straight, pointed beak. See **wild geranium.**

cra·ni·al (krā'nē-əl) *adj.* Of or pertaining to the skull. [From CRANIUM.]

cranial index *n.* The ratio of the maximum width to the maximum length of the cranium, multiplied by 100. Compare **cephalic index.**

cranial nerve *n.* Any of several nerves that arise in pairs from the brainstem and reach the periphery through openings in the skull.

cra·ni·ate (krā'nē-ĭt, -nē-āt) *adj.* Having a skull.
~*n.* Any animal having a skull; a vertebrate. [CRANI(O)- + -ATE.]

cra·ni·ec·to·my (krā'nē-ĕk'tə-mē) *n., pl.* **-mies.** The surgical removal of a portion of the cranium.

cranio–, crani– *prefix.* Indicates cranium or cranial; for example, **craniology, craniate.** [From CRANIUM.]

cra·ni·o·ce·re·bral (krā'nē-ō-sə-rē'brəl, -sĕr'ə-brəl) *adj.* Of or pertaining to the cranium and the brain.

cra·ni·ol·o·gy (krā'nē-ŏl'ə-jē) *n.* The scientific study of the characteristics of the skull, such as size and shape, especially in humans. [CRANIO- + -LOGY.] **—cra·ni·o·log·i·cal** (krā'nē-ə-lŏj'ĭ-kəl) *adj.* **—cra·ni·o·log·i·cal·ly** *adv.* **—cra·ni·ol·o·gist** *n.*

cra·ni·om·e·ter (krā'nē-ŏm'ə-tər) *n.* An instrument for measuring skulls. [CRANIO- + -METER.] **—cra·ni·o·met·ric, cra·ni·o·met·ri·cal** *adj.* **—cra·ni·om·e·try** *n.*

cra·ni·o·sa·cral system (krā'nē-ō-săk'rəl, -sā'krəl) *n.* The **parasympathetic nervous system** *(see).*

cra·ni·ot·o·my (krā'nē-ŏt'ə-mē) *n., pl.* **-mies.** *Surgery.* **1.** The cutting or removal of part of the skull to relieve pressure or to expose the brain for examination. **2.** The cutting or breaking of the skull of a dead fetus to reduce its size for removal when normal delivery is not possible. [CRANIO- + -TOMY.]

cra·ni·um (krā'nē-əm) *n., pl.* **-ums** or **-nia** (-nē-ə). **1.** The skull of a vertebrate. **2.** The portion of the skull enclosing the brain comprising eight bones connected by immovable joints. [Medieval Latin *crānium,* from Greek *kranion.*]

crank¹ (krăngk) *n.* **1.** A device for transmitting rotary motion, consisting of a handle or arm attached at right angles to a shaft. **2.** A turn of speech; a verbal conceit. **3.** A peculiar or eccentric idea or action. **4.** *Informal.* **a.** A bad-tempered person. **b.** An eccentric.
~*v.* **cranked, cranking, cranks.** —*tr.* **1.** To start or operate (an engine, for example) by turning a crank. **2.** To make into the shape of a crank; twist; bend. **3.** To provide with a crank. —*intr.* **1.** To turn a crank. **2.** To twist; wind. **—crank out.** To produce, especially mechanically and rapidly: *cranks out memo after memo.* **—crank up.** To cause to start or to get started as if by turning a crank: *cranking up a massive publicity campaign.* [Middle English *crank,* Old English *cranc* (only in *crancstæf,* a weaving instrument), perhaps from *crincan,* to curl, twist, variant of *cringan,* to fall in a battle.]

crank² *adj. Nautical.* Liable to capsize; unstable. [Short for earlier *crank-sided*†, lopsided.]

crank³ *adj. Regional.* Lively, cheerful; spirited. [Middle English *cranket.*]

crank·case (krăngk'kās') *n.* The metal case enclosing the crankshaft and associated parts in a reciprocating engine.

crank·pin (krăngk'pĭn') *n.* A bar or cylinder in the arm of a crank to which a reciprocating member or connecting rod is attached.

crank·shaft (krăngk'shăft', -shäft') *n.* A shaft that turns or is turned by a crank.

crank·y¹ (krăng'kē) *adj.* **-ier, -iest.** **1.** *Informal.* Odd; eccentric. **2.** *Informal.* Ill-tempered; peevish. **3.** Full of bends and turns; crooked. **4.** Unreliable; mechanically faulty. [Perhaps from obsolete cant *crank,* a rogue pretending sickness; akin to Dutch *krank,* ill, weak.] **—crank·i·ly** *adv.* **—crank·i·ness** *n.*

crank·y² (krăng'kē) *adj.* **-ier, -iest.** **1.** *Nautical.* Liable to capsize. **2.** Rickety; loose; shaky.

Cran·mer (krăn'mər), **Thomas** (1489–1556). English churchman, Archbishop of Canterbury (1533–53). A leading reformer, he worked on the English Prayer Books (1549 and 1552). He was burned at the stake during the Catholic reaction under Mary I.

cran·ny (krăn'ē) *n., pl.* **-nies.** A small opening, as in a wall or rock face; a crevice; a fissure. [Middle English *crani,* from Old French *cran, cren,* notch, perhaps from Late Latin *crēna.*] **—cran·nied** *adj.*

crape. Variant of **crepe.**

crape·hang·er (krāp'hăng'gər) *n.* A morose, gloomy, or pessimistic person.

crape jasmine (krāp) *n.* A fragrant shrub, *Tabernaemontana coronaria,* of India, cultivated in warm regions for its white flowers. [From the crinkled lobes of the corolla.]

crape myrtle *n.* An Oriental shrub, *Lagerstroemia indica,* widely cultivated in warm climates for its showy flowers.

crap·pie (krăp'ē) *n., pl.* **-pies.** Either of two edible North American freshwater fishes, *Pomoxis nigromaculatus* (the black crappie), or *P. annularis,* (the white crappie), related to the sunfishes. [Canadian French *crapet*†.]

craps (krăps) *n. Usually used with a singular verb.* A gambling game played with two dice in which a first throw of 7 or 11 wins, a first throw of 2, 3, or 12 loses the bet, and a first throw of any other number (a point) must be repeated to win before a 7 is thrown, which loses both the bet and the dice. [Louisiana French, from French *crabs, craps,* from obsolete English slang *crabs,* the lowest throw at hazard, plural of CRAB.]

crap·shoot·er (krăp'sho͞o'tər) *n.* One who plays craps.

crap·u·lence (krăp'yo͞o-ləns) *n.* **1.** Sickness caused by excessive eating or drinking. **2.** Excessive indulgence; intemperance. [Late Latin *crāpulentus,* drunk, from Latin *crāpula,* intoxication, from Greek *kraipalē,* intoxication, hangover.] **—crap·u·lent, crap·u·lous** *adj.*

cra·que·lure (kră-klo͝or') *n.* A pattern of tiny cracks on an old or deteriorated painting or its varnish. [French, from *craqueler,* to crackle, from *craquer,* to crack (imitative).]

crash¹ (krăsh) *v.* **crashed, crashing, crashes.** —*intr.* **1.** To fall or break noisily; smash. **2. a.** To collide. **b.** To undergo sudden damage or destruction on impact. **3.** To make a sudden loud noise. **4.** To move noisily or so as to cause damage. **5.** To fail suddenly, as a business or an economy might. **6.** *Computer Science.* To break down as a result of a malfunction of hardware or software. Used of computers and storage disks. **7.** *Slang.* To lodge temporarily; stay over: *Can I crash at your place tonight?* —*tr.* **1.** To cause to crash. **2.** To dash to pieces; smash. **3.** *Informal.* To join or enter without invitation; gate-crash. **—crash out.** *Slang.* To fall asleep; collapse with tiredness.
~*n.* **1.** A sudden loud noise, as of something breaking. **2.** A sudden accidental wrecking, smashing, or collision, especially of a car, train, or aircraft. **3.** A sudden business failure. **4.** *Computer Science.* An instance of crashing.
~*adj.* **1.** *Informal.* Of or characterized by an intensive effort to produce or accomplish something: *a crash program.* **2.** Abrupt or violent: *a crash tackle.* [Middle English *crashen* (imitative).] **—crash·er** *n.*

crash² *n.* **1.** A coarse, light, unevenly woven fabric of cotton or linen, used for towels and curtains. **2.** Starched reinforced fabric used to strengthen a book binding or the spine of a bound book. [Russian *krashenina,* a kind of colored linen, from *krashenie,* coloring, from *krasit',* to color, from *krasa,* beauty.]

crash barrier *n.* A barrier set up between traffic lanes, around racetracks, and the like, to limit the damage in the event of an accident.

crash cymbal *n.* A cymbal that produces an especially loud crashing sound when struck.

crash dive *n.* **1.** A rapid submerging of a submarine, especially in an emergency. **2.** A steep, uncontrolled fall to earth by an aircraft. **—crash-dive** *v.*

crash helmet *n.* A padded helmet, as worn by motorcyclists and pilots, to protect the head.

crash·ing (krăsh'ĭng) *adj. Informal.* **1.** Complete; utter; absolute: *a crashing bore.* **2.** Out of the ordinary; exceptional; unusual: *a crashing celebration.*

crash-land (krăsh'lănd') *v.* **-landed, -landing, -lands.** —*tr.* To land (an aircraft) in emergency conditions so as to minimize damage. —*intr.* To crash-land an aircraft. **—crash landing** *n.*

crash pad *n.* **1.** A padded area inside cars or other vehicles for protecting occupants in the event of an accident, sudden stop, or the like. **2.** *Slang.* A temporary lodging.

crash truck *n.* A truck specially designed and equipped to rescue victims of an airplane crash. Also called "crash wagon."

crash·wor·thy (krăsh'wûr'thē) *adj.* Capable of withstanding the effects of a crash: *new models of crashworthy cars.* **—crash·wor·thi·ness** *n.*

cra·sis (krā'sĭs) *n., pl.* **-ses** (-sēz'). Vowel contraction at the beginning and end of two adjacent words. [New Latin, from Greek *krasis,* "a mixture."]

crass (krăs) *adj.* **crasser, crassest.** **1.** Grossly ignorant; unfeeling; stupid. **2.** *Rare.* Thick; coarse. —See Synonyms at **coarse, stupid.** [Latin *crassus*†, fat, gross, dense.] **—crass·ly** *adv.* **—crass·ness** *n.*

Cras·sus (krăs'əs), **Marcus Licinius** (*c.* 115–53 B.C.). Roman politician and general. A wealthy and politically powerful man, he joined Julius Caesar and Pompey in the first triumvirate to challenge the senate's power (60). Hungry for military glory, he invaded Parthia and was killed in battle.

–crat *suffix.* Indicates a participant in or supporter of a class or form of government; for example, **democrat, technocrat.** [French *-crate,* from Greek *-kratēs,* from *-kratia,* -CRACY.]

cratch (krăch) *n.* **1.** A frame for holding fodder, used for feeding farm animals out of doors. **2.** *Archaic.* A manger. [Middle English, from Old French *creche,* crib, CRÈCHE.]

crate (krāt) *n.* **1.** A container for storing or transporting objects,

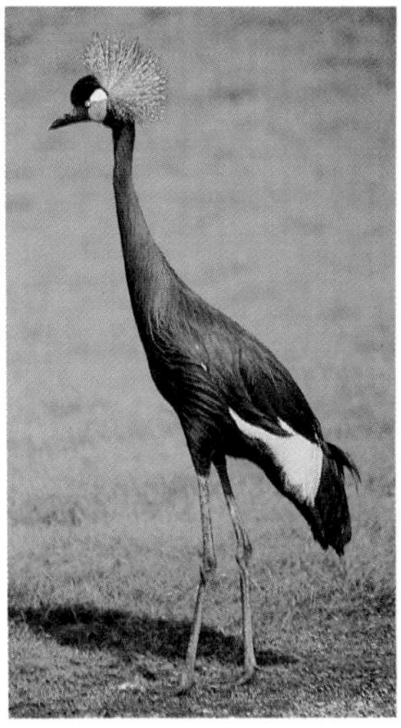

crane *Many of the 14 species of crane are marsh waders, but some—like this African crowned crane—also live on dry plains.*

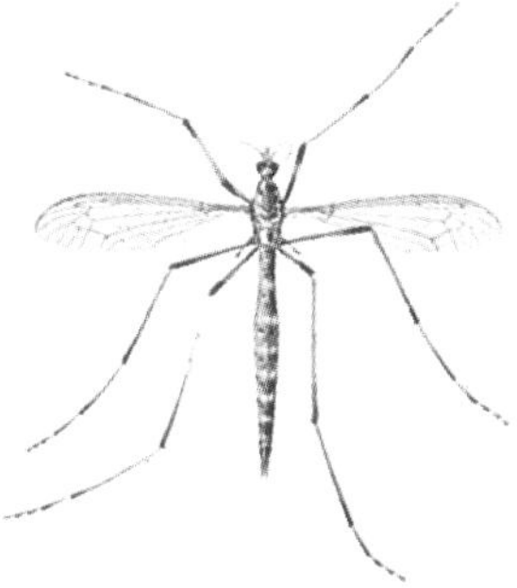

crane fly *Crane flies are found all over the world and can have a wingspan of up to 60 millimeters (2½ inches).*

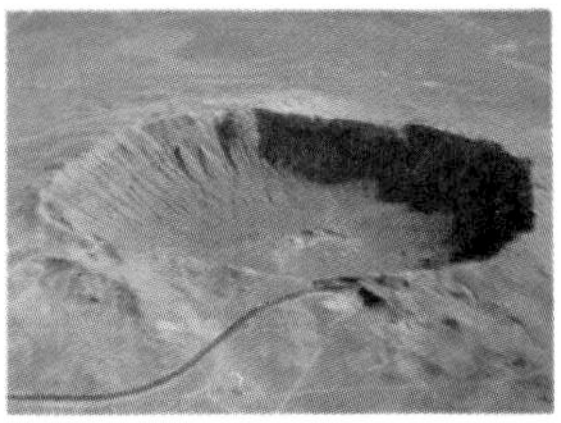

crater *Most natural craters are volcanic, but some have been created by the impact of meteorites. The one shown here is Meteor Crater, near Winslow in the Arizona desert. Made between 5,000 and 50,000 years ago, it is about 1,200 meters (4,000 feet) across and some 180 meters (600 feet) deep.*

usually consisting of a slatted wooden case or box or a wicker basket. **2.** *Slang.* An old, rickety vehicle, especially a car or aircraft.
~tr.v. **crated, crating, crates. 1.** To pack into a crate. Often used with *up.* **2.** To transport (goods) in a crate. [Latin *crātis,* wickerwork, hurdle.] **—crat•er** *n.*

cra•ter (krā′tər) *n.* **1.** A bowl-shaped depression at the mouth of a volcano or geyser. **2.** Any of numerous round, bowl-shaped depressions with raised rims covering the surface of the moon and various planets. **3.** Any bowl-shaped pit, especially when formed by an exploded projectile or by the impact of a meteor. **4.** A wide, two-handled bowl used in ancient Greece and Rome for mixing wine and water.
~tr.v. **cratered, -tering, -ters.** To cause craters to form on (the moon or a planet, for example). [Latin *crātēr,* bowl, crater, from Greek *kratēr,* mixing vessel.]

Cra•ter (krā′tər) *n.* A constellation in the Southern Hemisphere near Hydra and Corvus.

Crater Lake National Park. An area of *c.* 64,918 hectares (160,290 acres) in southwestern Oregon, in the Cascade Range. Crater Lake, 52 square kilometers (20 square miles), is the second-deepest lake in North America. It was created when the top of a prehistoric volcano was blown off by a violent eruption. The lake was discovered in 1853 by prospectors, who called it Deep Blue Lake because of the intense blue color of the water.

cra•ton, kra•ton (krā′tŏn′) *n.* A large part of the Earth's crust which has not been significantly deformed for many millions of years. Also called "shield."

cra•vat (krə-văt′) *n.* **1.** A small, light scarf, often of silk, worn round the neck and knotted at the front, usually by men. **2.** A necktie. [French *cravate,* originally a neckband worn by Croatian mercenaries in the service of France, from *Cravate,* a Croatian, from Flemish *Krawaat,* from Serbo-Croatian *Hrvat,* a CROAT.]

crave (krāv) *v.* **craved, craving, craves.** *—tr.* **1.** To have an intense desire for. **2.** To need urgently; require. **3.** To beg earnestly for; implore. *—intr.* To have an eager or intense desire. —See Synonyms at **beg.** [Middle English *craven,* Old English *crafian,* to beg, demand, from West Germanic *krabjan* (unattested), to demand, from the stem of *krab-taz* (unattested), strength.] **—crav•er** *n.* **—crav•ing•ly** *adv.*

cra•ven (krā′vən) *adj.* Characterized by abject fear; cowardly.
~n. A coward. [Middle English *cravant,* perhaps from Old French *crevant,* dying, from *crever,* to burst, die, from Latin *crepāre,* to crack, burst.] **—cra•ven•ly** *adv.* **—cra•ven•ness** *n.*

crav•ing (krā′vĭng) *n.* A consuming desire; a longing; a yearning.

craw (krô) *n.* **1.** The crop of a bird. **2.** The stomach of an animal. **—stick in one's craw.** To be unacceptable or offensive. [Middle English *crawe,* Old English *craga* (unattested). from Germanic.]

craw•fish (krô′fĭsh′) *intr.v.* **-fished, -fishing, -fishes.** *Informal.* To withdraw from an undertaking.
~n. Variant of **crayfish.**

Craw•ford (krô′fərd), **Joan,** born Lucille Le Sueur (1908–77). U.S. film actress. She specialized in portraying tough-minded and ambitious women in films such as *The Women* (1939) and *Mildred Pierce* (1945), for which she won an Academy Award.

crawl[1] (krôl) *intr.v.* **crawled, crawling, crawls. 1.** To move slowly on the hands and knees or by dragging the body along the ground; creep. **2.** To advance slowly, feebly, or laboriously: *Time crawls.* **3.** To proceed or act servilely. **4.** To be or feel as if covered with crawling things: *her flesh crawled in horror. The place was crawling with journalists.* **5.** To swim the crawl.
~n. **1.** The action of crawling. **2.** A rapid swimming stroke consisting of alternating overarm strokes and a flutter kick. See **Australian crawl.** [Middle English *craulen,* from Old Norse *krafla,* to crawl, creep.] **—crawl•ing•ly** *adv.*

crawl[2] *n.* A pen in shallow water, as for confining fish or turtles. [Dutch *kraal,* KRAAL.]

crawl•er (krô′lər) *n.* **1.** One that crawls, especially an insect. **2.** *Chiefly British Slang.* A toady; a fawning flatterer. —See Synonyms at **sycophant. 3.** A tractor with caterpillar tracks instead of wheels. **4. crawlers.** A one-piece garment worn by a baby. Compare **creeper** (sense 8).

crawl•space (krôl′spās′) *n.* A low or narrow space, as in the walls of a building, that gives workers access to plumbing or wiring equipment.

crawl•y (krô′lē) *adj.* **-ier, -iest.** *Informal.* **1.** Creepy. **2.** Feeling as if insects are crawling over one's skin.

cray•fish (krā′fĭsh′) *n., pl.* **-fishes** or collectively **crayfish.** Also **craw•fish** (krô′-). **1.** Any of various mostly freshwater crustaceans of the genera *Cambarus* and *Astacus,* resembling a lobster but considerably smaller. **2.** Broadly, a similar crustacean, such as the **spiny lobster** *(see).* [Alteration (influenced by FISH) of earlier *crevis, cravis,* Middle English *crevise,* from Old French, from Frankish *krabītja* (unattested), CRAB.]

cray•on (krā′ən, -ŏn′) *n.* **1.** A stick or pencil of colored wax, charcoal, or chalk, used for drawing. **2.** A drawing made with crayons.
~tr.v. **crayoned, -oning, -ons.** To draw, color, or decorate with crayons. [French, crayon, pencil, from *craie,* chalk, from Latin *crēta*†.] **—cray•on•ist** *n.*

craze (krāz) *v.* **crazed, crazing, crazes.** *—tr.* **1.** To cause to become mentally deranged or obsessed; make insane. **2.** To produce a network of fine cracks in (a ceramic, metal, or painted surface). *—intr.* **1.** To become mentally deranged or obsessed; go insane. **2.** To become covered with fine cracks.
~n. **1.** A short-lived popular fashion; a rage; a fad. **2.** A pattern of fine cracks. [Middle English *crasen,* to shatter, render insane, from Old Norse *krasa* (unattested), to shatter (probably imitative).]

cra•zy (krā′zē) *adj.* **-zier, -ziest. 1.** *Informal.* Affected with or suggestive of madness; insane. **2.** *Informal.* Departing from proportion or moderation, especially: **a.** Possessed by enthusiasm or excitement. **b.** Immoderately fond; infatuated. **c.** Not sensible; impractical. **3.** Rickety or dilapidated.
~n., pl. **-zies.** *Slang.* A mad or eccentric person. [From CRAZE.] **—cra•zi•ly** *adv.* **—cra•zi•ness** *n.*

crazy bone *n. Informal.* The **funny bone** *(see).*

Crazy Horse (*c.* 1849–1877). Sioux Indian chief. Resisting U.S. settlement in Dakota, he joined Sitting Bull at Little Bighorn and led the force that defeated Gen. George A. Custer's cavalry (1876). He surrendered (1877), but was killed while in custody.

crazy quilt *n.* **1.** A patchwork quilt of pieces of cloth of various shapes, colors, and sizes, arranged in no definite pattern. **2.** A disorderly mixture; a hodgepodge.

C-re•ac•tive protein (sē′rē-ăk′tĭv) *n.* A globulin that occurs in the blood in certain acute illnesses, such as rheumatic fever. [C(ARBOHYDRATE POLYSACCHARIDE) + REACTIVE.]

creak (krēk) *v.* **creaked, creaking, creaks.** *—intr.* **1.** To make a grating or squeaking sound. **2.** To move with such a sound or sounds. *—tr.* To cause to make a creaking sound.
~n. A grating or squeaking sound. [Middle English *creken* (imitative).] **—creak•ing•ly** *adv.*

creak•y (krē′kē) *adj.* **-ier, -iest. 1.** Tending or liable to creak. **2.** Dilapidated; decrepit. **3.** Suspect; unreliable: *a creaky argument.* **—creak•i•ly** *adv.* **—creak•i•ness** *n.*

cream (krēm) *n.* **1.** The yellowish fatty component of unhomogenized milk that tends to accumulate at the surface. **2.** The color of cream; pale yellow to yellowish white. **3.** Any of various substances resembling cream, such as certain cosmetics. **4.** The choicest part: *the cream of the crop.* **5.** A soup, dessert, or other dish containing cream or resembling cream in consistency.
~v. **creamed, creaming, creams.** *—intr.* **1.** To form cream. **2.** To form foam or scum at the top. *—tr.* **1.** To allow the cream to separate from (milk). **2.** To remove the cream from; skim. **3. a.** To select or remove the best part from. **b.** To select or remove (the best part) of something. Used with *off.* **4.** To beat (butter and sugar, for example) into a creamy consistency. **5.** To prepare or cook (a vegetable, for example) in or with a cream sauce. **6.** To add or apply cream or a similar substance to. **7.** *Slang.* To defeat overwhelmingly. [Middle English *creme, creime,* from Old French *cresme, craime,* blends of Late Latin *chrisma,* ointment, CHRISM, and Late Latin *crāmum*†, cream.] **—cream** *adj.*

cream cheese *n.* A soft white cheese made of cream and milk.

cream•cups (krēm′kŭps′) *n. Used with a singular or plural verb.* A plant, *Platystemon californicus,* of the southwestern United States, having long-stemmed, cream-colored or light-yellow flowers.

cream•er (krē′mər) *n.* **1.** A machine or device for separating cream from milk. **2.** A small jug or pitcher for cream. **3.** A refrigerator in which milk is placed to form cream.

cream•er•y (krē′mə-rē) *n., pl.* **-ies.** An establishment where dairy products are prepared or sold.

cream of tartar *n.* A chemical compound used in cookery, **potassium bitartrate** *(see).*

cream puff *n.* **1.** A shell of light pastry filled with whipped cream, custard, or ice cream. **2.** *Slang.* A sissy; an effeminate man.

cream sauce *n.* A white sauce made by heating a mixture of flour and butter and adding milk or cream.

cream soda *n.* A sweet soft drink flavored with vanilla.

cream•y (krē′mē) *adj.* **-ier, -iest.** Rich in cream or resembling cream. **—cream•i•ly** *adv.* **—cream•i•ness** *n.*

crease (krēs) *n.* **1.** A line made by pressing, folding, or wrinkling. **2.** *Cricket.* Any of the lines marking off the positions of the bowler and batsman or the space bounded by these lines. **3.** *Hockey.* The rectangular area marked off in front of each goal cage. **4.** *Lacrosse.* The circular area around each goal.
~v. **creased, creasing, creases.** *—tr.* **1.** To make a fold or wrinkle in. **2.** To graze with a bullet; wound superficially. *—intr.* To become wrinkled or creased. [Earlier *creast,* from Middle English *crest,* ridge, CREST.] **—creas•er** *n.* **—creas•y** *adj.*

cre•ate (krē-āt′) *v.* **-ated, -ating, -ates.** *—tr.* **1. a.** To cause to exist; bring into being; originate. **b.** To make or produce (something, especially an artistic work). **2.** To give rise to; bring about; produce: *Her remark created a stir.* **3.** To invest with office or title; appoint. **4.** To be first to portray and give character to (a role or part).
~adj. Poetic. Created. [Middle English *createn* from Latin *creāre.*]

cre•a•tine (krē′ə-tēn, -tĭn) *n.* Also **cre•a•tin** (-tĭn). A nitrogenous organic acid, $C_4H_9N_3O_2$, found, combined with phosphoric acid, mainly in the muscle tissue of many vertebrates and acting in muscular contraction. [Greek *kreas* (stem *kreat-*), flesh + -INE.]

creatine phosphate *n.* An organic compound, **phosphocreatine** *(see).*

cre•at•i•nine (krē-ăt′ə-nēn) *n.* The creatine anhydride $C_4H_7N_3O$, a normal metabolic waste. [CREATIN(E) + -INE.]

cre•a•tion (krē-ā′shən) *n.* **1. a.** The act of creating. **b.** The fact or process of being created. **2. Creation.** God's primal act of bringing the world into existence. Usually preceded by *the.* **3. a.** The world or universe and all things in it. **b.** All creatures or a class of creatures: *all creation.* **4.** An original product of human invention or imagination; a work. **5.** A specially designed garment or other article of fashion. **—cre·a·tion·al** *adj.*

cre·a·tion·ism (krē-ā′shən-ĭz′əm) *n.* **1.** The doctrine ascribing the origin of all matter and living forms as they now exist to distinct acts of creation by God. Compare **evolutionism. 2.** The doctrine that each human soul is a distinct and new creation by God. Compare **infusionism, traducianism. —cre·a·tion·ist** *n.*

cre·a·tive (krē-ā′tĭv) *adj.* **1.** Having the ability or power to create things. **2.** Creating; productive. Often used with *of.* **3.** Characterized by originality and expressiveness; imaginative. **4.** Stimulating to the imagination: *creative tension.* **5.** Extending its scope beyond normal limits, often for questionable purposes: *creative accounting.* **—cre·a·tive·ly** *adv.* **—cre·a·tiv·i·ty, cre·a·tive·ness** *n.*

cre·a·tor (krē-ā′tər) *n.* **1.** One that creates. **2. Creator.** God.

crea·ture (krē′chər) *n.* **1.** Anything created. **2.** A living being, especially an animal. **3.** A human being. Often used with a suggestion of pity or contempt. **4.** One dependent upon or subservient to another; a tool. **—crea·tur·al, crea·ture·ly** *adj.*

creature comforts *pl.n.* Material possessions that help ensure bodily comfort.

crèche (krĕsh) *n.* **1.** A representation of the Nativity scene. **2.** A foundling hospital. **3.** *Chiefly British.* A day nursery for very young children, in a place of work or study. [French, from Old French, from Vulgar Latin *creppja* (unattested), from Germanic *krippja* (unattested), manager, CRIB.]

Cré·cy, Battle of (krā-sē′) *n.* The first major land battle of the Hundred Years' War, fought near Crécy-en-Ponthieu in Somme department, northern France (August 26, 1346). English longbowmen outdistanced French crossbowmen and inflicted a crushing defeat on the French.

cre·dence (krēd′ns) *n.* **1.** Acceptance as true or valid; belief. **2.** Claim to acceptance; trustworthiness. **3.** Recommendation; credential: *a letter of credence.* **4.** *Ecclesiastical.* A small shelf or table to hold the bread and wine used in the Eucharist. In this sense, also called "credence table." [Middle English, from Old French, from Medieval Latin *crēdēntia,* belief, trust, hence a table holding food for tasting in order to detect poison, from Latin *crēdere,* to believe.]

cre·den·dum (krē-dĕn′dəm) *n., pl.* **-da** (-də). *Ecclesiastical.* An article or matter of faith. [Latin *crēdundum,* from the neuter gerundive of *crēdere,* to believe.]

cre·den·tial (krĭ-dĕn′shəl) *n.* **1.** That which entitles one to confidence, credit, or authority. **2. credentials. a.** A letter attesting one's right to credit, confidence, or authority. **b.** Written evidence of qualifications. [From Medieval Latin *crēdentiālis,* giving authority, from *crēdentia,* trust, CREDENCE.]

cre·den·za (krĭ-dĕn′zə) *n.* A cupboard or sideboard, especially one without legs, sometimes used as a credence table. [Italian, from Medieval Latin *crēdentia,* CREDENCE (table).]

cred·i·bil·i·ty (krĕd′ə-bĭl′ə-tē) *n.* Worthiness of belief.

credibility gap *n.* **1.** An inability to carry conviction because of previous failure to live up to promises; especially, the improbability of official claims and pronouncements when viewed against the apparent facts. **2.** Public scepticism about official claims.

cred·i·ble (krĕd′ə-bəl) *adj.* **1.** Capable of being believed; believable; plausible. **2.** Worthy of confidence; reliable. [Middle English, from Latin *crēdibilis,* from *crēdere,* to believe, entrust.] **—cred·i·ble·ness** *n.* **—cred·i·bly** *adv.*

Usage: *Credible, credulous,* and *creditable* are sometimes confused. *Credible* means "believable": *a credible story. Credulous* is used to refer to someone who is disposed to believe too readily: *a credulous person. Creditable* has nothing to do with the notion of belief; it means "deserving commendation": *a creditable result.*

cred·it (krĕd′ĭt) *n. Abbr.* **cr. 1.** Belief or confidence in the truth of something; trust. **2.** The quality or state of being trustworthy or credible. **3.** A reputation for sound character or quality; standing; repute. **4.** A source of honor or distinction: *He is a credit to his family.* **5.** Approval for some act, ability, or quality; praise. **6.** Influence based on the good opinion or confidence of others. **7. credits. a.** An acknowledgment of sources or contributors as in the production of a film, play, or book. **b.** A list appearing at the beginning or end of a film or broadcast, naming all those who have taken part. **8.** *Education.* **a.** Official certification that a student has successfully completed a course of study. **b.** A unit of study so certified. **c.** A distinction awarded for a high mark in a course of study. **9.** Reputation for solvency and integrity, entitling a person to be trusted in buying or borrowing. **10. a.** Confidence in a buyer's ability and intention to fulfill financial obligations at some future time. **b.** The commercial practice which allows such future payments. **c.** The time allowed for payment for anything sold on trust. **11.** *Accounting.* **a.** The acknowledgment of payment by a debtor by entry of the sum in an account. **b.** The right-hand side of an account on which such amounts are entered. **c.** An entry on this side. **d.** The sum of such entries. Compare **debit. 12.** The positive balance or amount remaining in a person's account. **13.** An amount placed by a bank, store, or the like, at the disposal of a client, against which he may draw. **—on credit.** With payment to be made at some time in the future.

~*tr.v.* **credited, -iting, -its. 1.** To believe; trust: *"she refused steadfastly to credit the reports of his death"* (Agatha Christie). **2.** *Archaic.* To bring honor or distinction to. **3. a.** To give credit to (a person) for something. Used with *with: credit him with the invention.* **b.** To ascribe (something) to a person; attribute. Used with *to: credit the invention to him.* **4.** *Accounting.* **a.** To give credit for (a sum paid). **b.** To give credit to (a payer). **c.** To make an entry in the right-hand side of (an account). Compare **debit. 5.** *Education.* To give or award credits to (a student). —See Synonyms at **attribute.** [French, from Italian *credito,* from Latin *crēditum,* "something entrusted," loan, from the past participle of *crēdere,* to believe, entrust.]

cred·it·a·ble (krĕd′ĭ-tə-bəl) *adj.* **1.** Deserving commendation. **2.** Capable of being credited or assigned. —See Usage note at **credible. —cred·it·a·bil·i·ty, cred·it·a·ble·ness** *n.* **—cred·it·a·bly** *adv.*

credit bureau *n.* An organization to which business firms apply for credit information on prospective customers. Also called "credit agency."

credit card *n.* A card issued by banks and business concerns authorizing the holder to buy goods or services on credit.

credit limit *n.* The maximum amount of credit to be extended to a customer. Also called "credit line," "line of credit."

credit line *n.* **1.** A line of copy acknowledging the source or origin of a news report, published article, film, or other work. **2.** A credit limit.

cred·i·tor (krĕd′ə-tər) *n.* A person or firm to whom money or its equivalent is owed. Compare **debtor.**

credit rating *n.* An estimate of the amount of credit that can be extended to a company or individual without undue risk.

credit squeeze *n.* **1.** The restriction by government of the availability of credit facilities by means of regulations limiting bank loans, overdrafts, and the like. **2.** A period of such restriction.

credit union *n.* A cooperative organization that makes loans to its members at low interest rates.

credit·wor·thy (krĕd′ĭt-wûr′*thē*) *adj.* Designating a person or company to whom credit may be safely extended. **—cred·it·wor·thi·ness** *n.*

cre·do (krē′dō, krā′-) *n., pl.* **-dos. 1.** A statement of belief; a creed. **2.** *Often* **Credo. a.** The **Apostles' Creed** or the **Nicene Creed** *(both of which see).* **b.** A musical setting for either of these. [Latin *crēdo,* "I believe," the first word of the Apostles' Creed, from *crēdere,* to believe.]

cre·du·li·ty (krĭ-do͞o′lə-tē, -dyo͞o′lə-tē) *n.* A disposition to believe too readily; gullibility. [Middle English *credulite,* from Old French, from Latin *crēdulitās* (stem *crēdulitāt-*), from *crēdulus,* CREDULOUS.]

cred·u·lous (krĕj′o͞o-ləs, krĕd′yo͞o-) *adj.* **1.** Disposed to believe too readily; gullible. **2.** Arising from or characterized by credulity. —See Usage note at **credible.** [Latin *crēdulus,* from *crēdere,* to believe.] **—cred·u·lous·ly** *adv.* **—cred·u·lous·ness** *n.*

Cree (krē) *n., pl.* **Crees** or collectively **Cree. 1.** A member of a North American Indian people formerly living in Ontario, Manitoba, and Saskatchewan. **2.** The Algonquian language of this people. [Shortened from Canadian French *Christianaux,* by folk etymology from Ojibwa *Kenistenoag,* earlier *Kilistino* (unattested), tribal name.]

creed (krēd) *n.* **1.** A formal statement of religious belief; a confession of faith. **2.** An authoritative statement of certain articles of Christian faith that are considered essential; for example, the Apostles' Creed or the Nicene Creed. **3.** Any statement or system of belief, principles, or opinions. [Middle English *crede,* Old English *crēda,* from Latin *crēdo,* "I believe."] **—creed·al** *adj.*

creek (krēk, krĭk) *n.* **1.** A small stream, often a shallow or intermittent tributary to a river; a brook. **2.** *British.* A small tidal inlet in a shoreline. **—up the creek.** *Slang.* In a difficult or unfortunate position. [Middle English *creke, crike,* possibly from Old Norse *kriki,* a bend, nook.]

Creek (krēk) *n., pl.* **Creeks** or collectively **Creek. 1.** A member of any of several confederated American Indian peoples, formerly inhabiting parts of Georgia, Alabama, and northern Florida. **2.** Any of the languages of these peoples, of the Muskhogean family of languages.

creel (krēl) *n.* **1.** A wicker basket, especially one used by anglers for carrying fish. **2.** A wickerwork trap for fish or lobsters. **3.** A frame for holding bobbins or spools in a spinning machine. [Middle English (Scottish) *crel, crelle*†.]

Cree·ley (krē′lē), **Robert** (1926–). U.S. poet and author. The editor of the *Black Mountain Review* (1954–57), he has also written prose fiction, including the novel *The Island* (1963).

creep (krēp) *intr.v.* **crept** (krĕpt), **creeping, creeps. 1.** To move with the body close to the ground, as a reptile does. **2.** To move stealthily, cautiously, or very slowly. **3.** To behave obsequiously; fawn. **4.** *Botany.* To grow along a surface, rooting at intervals or clinging by means of suckers or tendrils. **5.** To slip out of place from pressure or wear; shift gradually. **6.** *Metallurgy.* To undergo slow deformation as a result of applied stress or high temperature. **7.** To have a tingling sensation: *made my flesh creep.*

~*n.* **1.** The action of creeping; a creeping motion or progress. **2.** *Slang.* An obnoxious or insignificant person. **3.** *Metallurgy.* A slow flow of metal when under high temperature or great stress. **4.** *Geology.* The slow movement of rock debris and soil, lubricated by rainwater, down a slope. **5.** Any slow deformation of an object, or slow distortion of the relative positions of two or more objects. **—the creeps.** *Informal.* A sensation of fear or repugnance, as if things were crawling on one's skin. [Creep: Middle English *crepen,* Old English *crēopan.* Crept: Middle English *creped, crept,* analogous formation from the infinitive *crepen.*]

creep·er (krē′pər) *n.* **1.** One that creeps. **2. creepers.** *Slang.* Shoes with thick soft soles. **3.** *Botany.* A plant having stems that grow along a surface, either rooting at intervals or clinging for support. **4. a.** Any of various birds that creep about in bushes looking for

PRONUNCIATION KEY

ă, pat; ā, pay; âr, care; ä, father, are; b, bib; ch, church; d, deed; ĕ, pet; ē, be; f, fife; g, gag; h, hat; hw, which; ĭ, pit; ī, pie; îr, pier; j, judge; k, kick; l, lid, needle; m, mum; n, no, sudden; ng, thing; ŏ, pot; ō, toe; ô, paw, for; oi, noise; ou, out; o͝o, book; o͞o, boot; p, pop; r, roar; s, sauce; sh, ship, dish; t, tight; th, thin, path; *th*, this, bathe; ŭ, cut; ûr, fur; v, valve; w, with; y, yes; z, zebra, size; zh, vision; ə, about, item, edible, gallop, circus, peaceful

IN FOREIGN WORDS:

à, *Fr.* ami; œ, *Fr.* feu, *Ger.* schön; ü, *Fr.* tu, *Ger.* über; KH, *Ger.* ich, *Scot.* loch; N, *Fr.* bon; y′, *Fr.* Compiègne

STRESS MARKS:

Primary stress: ′ **in·cite′** (ĭn-sīt′)
Secondary stress: ′ **in′sight′** (ĭn′sīt′)

food. **b.** A **treecreeper** (see). **5.** A grappling device for dragging lakes and rivers. **6.** A small platform on wheels for working underneath a car; a cradle. **7.** Usually **creepers.** A metal frame with spikes, attached to a shoe or boot to prevent slipping. **8. creepers.** A one-piece suit for a baby.

creeping bent grass n. A perennial grass, *Agrostis stolonifera,* of temperate regions.

creeping eruption n. An intensely irritating skin disease caused by larvae burrowing beneath the skin and characterized by spreading eruptions in the form of reddish lines.

creeping Jen·ny, creeping Jen·nie (jĕn′ē) n. Any of several creeping or trailing plants, such as **moneywort** (see).

creeping thistle n. A perennial plant, *Cirsium arrense,* having brushlike lilac flowers with purple bracts, found in waste places. Also called "Canada thistle."

creep·y (krē′pē) adj. **-ier, -iest. 1.** Creeping; slow-moving. **2.** Informal. Inducing or having a sensation of repugnance or fear, as of insects crawling on one's skin. **—creep·i·ness** n.

creese. Variant of **kris.**

cre·mains (krĭ-mānz′) pl.n. The ashes that remain after cremation of a corpse. [Blend of CREMATED and REMAINS.]

cre·mate (krē′māt′, krĭ-māt′) tr.v. **-mated, -mating, -mates.** To burn (a corpse) to ashes. [Latin *cremāre,* to burn, consume by fire.] **—cre·ma·tion** n.

cre·ma·tor (krē′mā′tər, krĭ-mā′tər) n. **1.** One that cremates. **2.** Chiefly British. A furnace used for cremating.

cre·ma·to·ri·um (krē′mə-tôr′ē-əm, -tōr′ē-əm) n., pl. **-ums** or **-toria** (-tôr′ē-ə, -tōr′ē-ə). A crematory.

crem·a·to·ry (krē′mə-tôr′ē, -tōr′ē, krĕm′ə-) adj. Of or pertaining to cremation.

—n., pl. **crematories.** A furnace, building, or place for the cremation of corpses. [New Latin *crematorium,* from Latin *cremāre,* CREMATE.]

crème brû·lée (krĕm brōō′lā) n. A rich, soft cream or custard dessert coated with a layer of hard caramelized sugar. [French, "burnt cream."]

crème caramel (krĕm) n. A solid but soft baked custard with a caramel sauce. [French "cream caramel."]

crème de ca·ca·o (krĕm′ də kə-kā′ō, kə-kä′ō) n. A sweet liqueur with a chocolate flavor. [French, "cream of cacao."]

crème de la crème (krĕm də lä krĕm′) n. **1.** The essence of excellence. **2.** The very best of a given kind. [French, "cream of the cream."]

crème de menthe (krĕm də mäɴt′) n. A sweet green or white liqueur, well flavored with mint. [French, "cream of mint."]

Cre·mo·na¹ (krĭ-mō′nə). A city on the Po River in Lombardy in northern Italy, famous for the making of fine stringed instruments.

Cremona² n. Any of the fine violins or other stringed instruments made in Cremona, from the 16th to the 18th century, especially by the Amati family, Antonio Stradivari, or Giuseppe Guarneri.

cre·nate (krē′nāt′) adj. Also **cre·nat·ed** (-nā′tĭd). Biology. Having a margin with rounded or scalloped projections: *a crenate leaf.* [New Latin *crenatus,* probably from Late Latin *crēna†,* notch.] **—cre·nate·ly** adv.

cre·na·tion (krĭ-nā′shən) n. **1.** A rounded projection; a crenature. **2.** The condition or fact of being crenate.

cren·a·ture (krĕn′ə-chŏŏr, krĕn′-) n. **1.** A crenation. **2.** A notch between crenations, as on a leaf.

cren·e·lat·ed (krĕn′ə-lā′tĭd) adj. Also chiefly British **cren·el·lat·ed** **1.** Having battlements. **2.** Having square indentations: *a crenelated molding.* [French *crenel,* a crenelation, from Old French, perhaps from Vulgar Latin *crenellus* (unattested), diminutive of Late Latin *crēna,* notch.] **—cren·e·la·tion** n.

cren·u·late (krĕn′yə-lĭt, -lāt) adj. Also **cren·u·lat·ed** (-lā′tĭd). Having minutely notched or scalloped projections: *a crenulate shell.* [New Latin *crenulatus,* from *crenula,* perhaps diminutive of Late Latin *crēna,* notch.] **—cren·u·la·tion** n.

cre·o·dont (krē′ə-dŏnt′) n. Any of various extinct carnivorous mammals of the suborder Creodonta, of the Paleocene to Pliocene epochs. [New Latin *Creodonta,* "flesh-toothed ones" : Greek *kreas,* flesh + -ODONT.]

Cre·ole (krē′ōl′) n. **1.** Any person of European descent born in the West Indies or Spanish America. **2.** A person descended from or culturally related to the original French settlers of the southern United States, especially Louisiana. **3.** The French patois spoken by these people. **4.** A person descended from or culturally related to the Spanish and Portuguese settlers of the Gulf States. **5.** A person of Negro descent born in the West Indies or Spanish America, as distinguished from a Negro brought from Africa. Also called "Creole Negro." **6.** Any person of mixed European and Negro ancestry who speaks a Creole dialect. **7.** Often **creole.** A creolized language.

—adj. **1.** Of, relating to, or characteristic of creole or the Creoles. **2. creole.** Cooked with a spicy sauce containing tomatoes, onions, and peppers. [French *créole,* from Spanish *criollo,* from Portuguese *crioulo,* slave born in his master's house, from *criar,* to bring up, from Latin *creāre,* to create, beget.]

cre·o·lize (krē′ə-līz′) tr.v. **-lized, -lizing, -lizes.** To establish as a creolized language. **—cre·o·li·za·tion** n.

creolized language n. Any of several mixed languages of a kind that develops through contact between two language communities, incorporating the basic vocabulary of the dominant or colonial language with the grammar and an admixture of words from the sub-

ordinate or indigenous language. It then becomes the native tongue of the indigenous people. Compare **pidgin.**

Cre·on (krē′ŏn). In Greek legend, King of Thebes, successor to his nephew Oedipus and uncle of Antigone.

cre·o·sol (krē′ə-sôl′) n. A colorless to yellow aromatic liquid, $C_8H_{10}O_2$, that is a constituent of creosote and is obtained from beechwood tar. [CREOS(OTE) + -OL.]

cre·o·sote (krē′ə-sōt′) n. **1.** A colorless to yellowish oily liquid, obtained by the distillation of wood tar, especially from beechwood, and formerly used to treat chronic bronchitis. **2.** A yellowish to greenish-brown oily liquid obtained from coal tar and used as a wood preservative and disinfectant.

—tr.v. **creosoted, -soting, -sotes.** To treat or paint (wood or other material) with creosote. [German *Kreosot,* "flesh preserver" (from its antiseptic qualities) : Greek *kreas,* flesh + *sōtēr,* preserver, from *sōzein,* to preserve, save, from *saos,* safe.]

creosote bush n. A resinous shrub, *Larrea tridentata,* of the western United States and Mexico, exuding an odor like that of creosote. Also called "greasewood."

crepe, crêpe (krāp) n. Also **crape** (for senses 1-4). **1.** A light, soft, thin fabric of silk, cotton, wool, or other fiber, with a crinkled surface. **2.** A black band of this fabric, originally displayed or worn on the sleeve or hat as a sign of mourning. **3.** Crepe paper. **4.** Crepe rubber. **5.** A very thin pancake.

—tr.v. **creped, creping, crepes.** Also **crêpe, crape.** To cover or drape with crepe. [French *crêpe,* from Old French *crespe,* crisp, curly, from Latin *crispus.*] **—crep·y, crep·ey** adj.

crêpe de Chine (krāp′ də shĕn′, krĕp′) n. A silk crepe used for women's dresses and blouses. [French, "crepe of China."]

crepe hair n. False hair used in theatrical make-up for making artificial beards, sideburns, and the like.

crepe myrtle. Variant of **crape myrtle.**

crepe paper n. Crinkled tissue paper, resembling crepe, used for decorations. Also called "crepe."

crepe rubber n. A white or yellowish natural or synthetic rubber with a crinkled texture, used for shoe soles. Also called "crepe."

crêpe su·zette (krāp sōō-zĕt′; French krĕp sü-zĕt′) n., pl. **crêpe suzettes.** A thin pancake usually rolled with hot orange or tangerine sauce and served with a flaming brandy or curaçao sauce. [French : CREPE (pancake) + *Suzette,* pet form of the name *Suzanne.*]

crep·i·tate (krĕp′ə-tāt′) intr.v. **-tated, -tating, -tates.** To make a creaking or rattling sound; crackle. [Latin *crepitāre,* to crackle, frequentative of *crepāre* (past participle *crepitus*), to crack, creak.] **—crep·i·ta·tion** n.

cre·pi·tus (krĕp′ə-təs) n. **1.** A rattling sound heard in the chest of someone suffering from a lung disease such as pneumonia. **2.** A grating sound produced by the rubbing together of the two edges of a broken bone. [Latin, from *crepāre,* to creak.]

crept. Past tense and past participle of **creep.**

cre·pus·cu·lar (krĭ-pŭs′kyə-lər) adj. **1.** Of or like twilight; hazy; dim. **2.** Zoology. Becoming active at twilight or before sunrise. Said of certain insects and birds. [From Latin *crepusculum,* twilight, from *creper,* dusky, dark.]

cres·cen·do (krə-shĕn′dō, -sĕn′dō) n., pl. **-dos** or **-di** (-dē). Abbr. **cr., cresc., cres. 1.** A gradual increase in the volume or intensity of sound. **2.** The direction or symbol indicating this in music. The sign < is displayed above the notes. **3.** A musical passage played in a crescendo. Compare **decrescendo.**

—adj. Abbr. **cresc., cres.** Gradually increasing in volume or intensity.

—adv. Abbr. **cresc., cres.** With a crescendo. Often used as a direction.

—intr.v. **crescendoed, -doing, -dos.** To increase gradually in volume. [Italian, "increasing," from *crescere,* to increase, from Latin *crēscere,* to grow.]

cres·cent (krĕs′ənt) n. **1.** The figure of the moon as it appears in its first or last quarters, with concave and convex edges terminating in points. **2.** Something shaped like this. **3.** Often **Crescent. a.** The Turkish emblem. **b.** Turkish or Muslim power. Often preceded by *the.* **4.** British. Abbr. **Cres.** A crescent-shaped street, often lined with Georgian houses. **5.** Heraldry. A crescent moon, especially with horns pointing upward, indicating a second son.

—adj. **1.** Crescent-shaped. **2.** Increasing; waxing, as does the moon. [Middle English *cressaunt,* from Old French *creissant,* waxing, increasing, from Latin *crēscēns* (stem *crēscent-*), present participle of *crēscere,* to increase, grow.] **—cres·cen·tic** adj.

cre·sol (krē′sôl′) n. Any of three isomeric phenols, $CH_3C_6H_4OH$, found in coal tar and used in resins and as a disinfectant. [Variant of CREOSOL.]

cress (krĕs) n. Any of various plants of the cabbage family, such as those of the genera *Cardamine* and *Arabis,* having pungent leaves often used in salads and as a garnish. See **watercress, garden cress.** [Middle English *cresse,* Old English *cresse, cærse.*]

cres·set (krĕs′ĭt) n. A metal cup, often suspended on a pole, containing burning oil or pitch and used as a torch. [Middle English, from Old French *cresset, craisset,* from *craisse,* oil, grease, from Vulgar Latin *crassia* (unattested), animal fat, from Latin *crassus,* fat, thick.]

Cres·si·da (krĕs′ĭ-də). In medieval romances and in Shakespeare, a Greek lady who first returns the love of the Trojan Troilus but later forsakes him for the Greek Diomedes.

crest (krĕst) n. **1.** A tuft, ridge, or similar projection on the head of

creeping Jenny Also known as moneywort and creeping Charlie. The plant is native to Europe but is grown in North America as well.

a bird or other animal. **2. a.** A plume used as decoration on top of a helmet. **b.** A helmet. **c.** The ridge or raised part on a helmet. **3.** *Heraldry.* An emblem placed above the shield on a coat of arms and also used by itself on seals, stationery, and the like. **4. a.** The top of something, as a mountain or wave; a peak; a summit. **b.** A ridge. **5.** The ridge of an animal's neck or the mane growing on it. **6.** The ridge of a bone. **7.** *Architecture.* Cresting. —*v.* **crested, cresting, crests.** —*tr.* **1.** To serve as or decorate or furnish with a crest. **2.** To reach the crest of (a hill, for example). —*intr.* To form into a crest, as a wave might. [Middle English *creste,* from Old French, from Latin *crista,* crest, plume.] —**crest·ed** *adj.* —**crest·less** *adj.*

crest·fall·en (krĕst'fô'lən) *adj.* Dejected; dispirited; depressed. —**crest·fall·en·ly** *adv.*

crest·ing (krĕs'tĭng) *n. Architecture.* An ornamental ridge, as on top of a wall or roof.

cre·syl·ic (krĭ-sĭl'ĭk) *adj. Chemistry.* Of or pertaining to creosote or cresol. [CRES(OL) + -YL + -IC.]

Cre·ta·ceous (krĭ-tā'shəs) *adj.* **1.** Of, belonging to, or designating the geological time, system of rocks, and sedimentary deposits of the third and last period of the Mesozoic era, characterized by the deposition of chalk, the development of flowering plants, and the disappearance of dinosaurs. **2. cretaceous.** Of, containing, or resembling chalk. —*n. Geology.* The Cretaceous period. Preceded by *the.* [Latin *crētāceus : crēta†,* chalk, clay (see also **crayon**) + -ACEOUS.]

Cretain mullein *n.* A plant, *Celsia cretica,* native to the Mediterranean region, having hairy foliage and yellow flowers splotched with purple.

Crete (krēt). Greek **Krí·ti** (krē'tē). The largest of the Greek islands, lying southeast of the mainland between the Mediterranean and Aegean seas. The Minoan civilization flourished in the mountainous island *c.* 3500–1400 B.C. and was celebrated in Greek mythology through the legends of King Minos, the Labyrinth, and the Minotaur. Modern excavations at Knossos have shown it to have been an advanced Bronze Age culture and a sea power. The civilization perished in the 15th century B.C., partly, it is thought, because of a catastrophic eruption. Crete was subsequently occupied by Romans, Byzantines, Muslims, Venetians, and Turks. It was ceded to Greece (1913) following unrest between its Christian and Muslim populations. In the World War II Battle of Crete (1941) Germany won the island through the world's first major airborne landing, using paratroops and troop-carrying gliders to defeat an Allied force that had been evacuated here from Greece. Crete was liberated in 1945. Sheep and goats are raised, and grapes, olives, and citrus fruits grown. Canea (Khaniá) is the capital; Iráklion, the chief port and center of the tourist industry. —**Cre·tan** *n. & adj.*

cre·tic (krē'tĭk) *n. Prosody.* A metrical foot consisting of one long syllable followed by a short and long syllable. [From Latin *crēticus,* from Greek *krētikos,* "Cretan (foot)," from *Krētē,* Crete.]

cre·tin (krē'tĭn, krĕt'n) *n.* **1.** One afflicted with cretinism. **2.** A fool; an idiot. [French *crétin,* idiot, from Swiss French *crestin,* CHRISTIAN, hence human being (an idiot being nonetheless human).] —**cre·tin·oid** *adj.* —**cre·tin·ous** *adj.*

cre·tin·ism (krē'tĭn-ĭz'əm) *n.* A condition caused by congenital deficiency of thyroid hormone and characterized by dwarfism and mental retardation.

cre·tonne (krĭ-tŏn', krē'tŏn') *n.* A heavy unglazed cotton, linen, or rayon fabric, colorfully printed and used for curtains and chair covers. [French, first made in *Creton,* village in Normandy.]

cre·vasse (krə-văs') *n.* **1.** A deep fissure, as in a glacier; a chasm. **2.** A crack in a dike or embankment. —*tr.v.* **crevassed, -vassing, -vasses.** To make crevasses in; fissure. [French, from Old French *crevace,* CREVICE.]

Crève·coeur (krĕv-kœr'), **Michel Guillaume Jean de** (1735–1813). French agriculturalist, author, and diplomat. A naturalized U.S. citizen, he farmed with his family in New York State until the American Revolution began. Returning to Europe, he published, among other works, *Letters from an American Farmer* (1782), a book of 12 essays that provided insight into American life.

crev·ice (krĕv'ĭs) *n.* A narrow crack or opening; a cleft. [Middle English *crevice, crevace,* from Old French *crevace,* from *crever,* to split, from Latin *crepāre,* to rattle, crack.] —**crev·iced** *adj.*

crew¹ (krōō) *n.* **1.** *Nautical.* **a.** All personnel manning a ship. **b.** All of a ship's personnel except the officers. **2.** All personnel manning an aircraft in flight. **3.** Any group of people working together; a team. **4.** A company; a crowd. Often used derogatorily. **5.** A team of oarsmen. —*v.* **crewed, crewing, crews.** —*tr.* To be a member of the crew on (a ship, aircraft, or boat in rowing). —*intr.* To work as a member of a crew. [Middle English *creue,* military reinforcement, from Old French *creue,* an increase, from the feminine past participle of *creistre,* to grow, from Latin *crēscere.*]

crew². A past tense of **crow** (sense 1).

crew cut *n.* A close-cropped man's haircut. [Oarsmen formerly had this kind of haircut.] —**crew-cut** *adj.*

crew·el (krōō'əl) *n.* A loosely twisted worsted yarn used for embroidery, crochet, and the like. [Middle English *crulel.*]

crew neck *n.* A round, slightly raised neckline on a sweater. [After the style of sweaters worn by boat crews.]

crew sock *n.* A warm usually ribbed sock. [From its use by oarsmen.]

crib (krĭb) *n.* **1. a.** A child's bed; a cradle. **b.** A cot. **2.** A small building, bin, or box for storing grain. **3.** A rack or trough for fodder; a manger. **4.** A cattle stall. **5.** A small, crude cottage or room. **6.** A framework to support or strengthen a mine or shaft. **7.** A representation of the Nativity scene. **8.** *Informal.* **a.** A petty theft. **b.** Plagiarism. **9.** *Chiefly British Informal.* A translation or summary of a text, used by students, usually illicitly, as an aid in understanding the text or in answering examination questions. Also called "pony." **10.** *Cribbage.* A set of cards made up from discards by each player, used by the dealer. —*v.* **cribbed, cribbing, cribs.** —*tr.* **1.** To confine in or as in a crib. **2.** To furnish with a crib. **3.** *Informal.* To steal (something, especially an idea); plagiarize. **4.** To reinforce a mine or shaft with a wooden framework. —*intr. Informal.* To use a crib or copy from a neighbor in lessons or examinations; cheat. [Middle English *crib,* manger, stall, basket, Old English *cribb,* manger.] —**crib·ber** *n.*

crib·bage (krĭb'ĭj) *n.* A card game for from two to four players, in which the object is to score a given number of points with certain combinations of cards. [Perhaps from CRIB (noun), "basket," hence discard pile.]

crib·bing (krĭb'ĭng) *n.* **1.** A supporting framework, as of timber lining a shaft; a crib. **2.** Crib-biting.

crib·bit·ing (krĭb'bī'tĭng) *n.* A harmful habit of horses of biting at the edge of a feed trough or other object and swallowing air at the same time. —**crib-bite** *v.* —**crib-bit·er** *n.*

crib death *n.* The sudden and unexplained death of a baby during sleep. Also called "sudden infant death syndrome," and *chiefly British* "cot death."

cri·bel·lum (krĭ-bĕl'əm) *n. pl.* **-la** (-lə). An additional, sievelike, silk-spinning organ possessed by certain spiders, located between the spinnerets. [New Latin, diminutive of Latin *crībrum,* sieve.]

crib·ri·form (krĭb'rə-fôrm') *adj. Anatomy.* Perforated like a sieve. [Latin *crībrum,* sieve + -FORM.]

crib·work (krĭb'wûrk') *n.* A structural framework made of logs stacked one above the other, with the logs in each layer at right angles to those in the layer below, used in constructing mines, foundations, and the like.

cri·ce·tid (krī-sē'tĭd, -sĕt'ĭd) *n.* Any of various small rodents of the family Cricetidae, which includes muskrats and gerbils. [New Latin *Cricetidae,* family name, from *Cricetus,* hamster genus, of Slavic origin.] —**cri·ce·tid** *adj.*

Crich·ton (krī'tən), **James** (1560–82). Scottish prodigy whose accomplishments as a scholar, poet, linguist, and athlete earned him the nickname "the Admirable Crichton." In Italy after 1579, he was in the service of the Duke of Mantua until he was killed during a nocturnal brawl by the duke's son.

crick¹ (krĭk) *n.* A painful cramp or muscle spasm, as in the back or neck. —*tr.v.* **cricked, cricking, cricks.** To cause a crick by turning or wrenching. [Middle English *crike, crykke†.*]

crick² (krĭk) *n. Regional.* A creek.

Crick (krĭk), **Francis Harry Compton** (1916–). British biophysicist who, with the U.S. geneticist James D. Watson, pioneered the study of DNA, proposing a spiral model for the molecular structure of DNA (1953). Crick subsequently investigated protein synthesis in the DNA molecule. He was awarded the Nobel Prize for medicine with Watson and Maurice Wilkins (1962).

crick·et¹ (krĭk'ĭt) *n.* **1.** Any of various insects of the family Gryllidae, having long antennae and legs adapted for leaping. The males of many species produce a shrill, chirping sound by rubbing their front wings together. **2.** Any of various similar insects, such as the bush cricket, or the mole cricket. [Middle English *criket,* from Old French *criquet,* from *criquer,* to click, creak (imitative).]

cricket² *n.* A field game, popular in Britain and many of its former colonies, played with bats and a ball on a large field with a 22-yard pitch between the wickets. The object is to score more runs than the opposing team. A full game consists of two innings by each team and can last up to five days. —**not cricket.** *Informal.* Unfair; unsporting. —*intr.v.* **cricketed, -eting, -ets.** To play cricket. [16th century : origin obscure.] —**crick·et·er** *n.*

cricket³ *n.* A small, low wooden stool. [Origin obscure.]

cri·coid (krī'koid) *n. Anatomy.* A ring-shaped cartilage of the lower larynx. [Greek *krikoeidēs,* ring-shaped : *krikos,* ring + -OID.] —**cri·coid** *adj.*

cri de coeur (krē də kœr') *n., pl.* **cris de coeur.** A cry from the heart; a heartfelt appeal or utterance. [French, "cry from the heart."]

cri·er (krī'ər) *n.* **1.** One that cries. **2.** A person who shouts out public announcements; especially, a **town crier** *(see).* **3.** A hawker who advertises his wares by shouting.

crime (krīm) *n.* **1.** An act committed or omitted in violation of a law forbidding or commanding it, and for which punishment is imposed upon conviction. **2.** Unlawful activity in general. **3.** Any serious wrongdoing or offense. **4.** *Informal.* An unjust or senseless act or condition. [Middle English, from Old French, from Latin *crīmen,* verdict, judgment, crime.]

Cri·me·a (krī-mē'ə). A peninsula and autonomous region of the Ukrainian S.S.R., in the southwest U.S.S.R. In 1475 the Crimea was conquered by the Ottoman Turks and was governed as a tributary Tatar khanate until annexed by Russia in 1783. At the outset of the Crimean War (1853) much of the Tatar population was deported. After 1944 the remaining Tatars were exiled, accused of collaborating with occupying German troops (1941–43) during World War II.

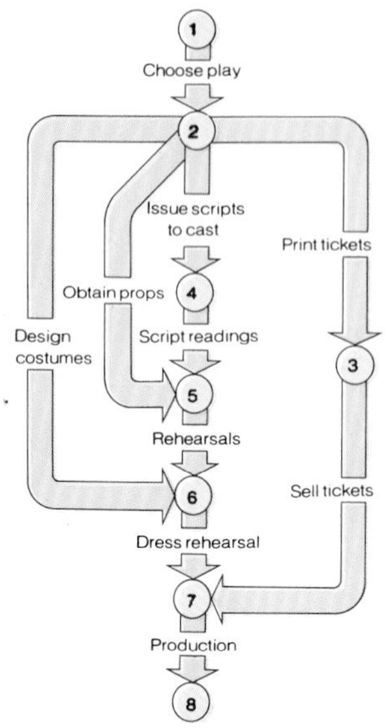

critical-path analysis *Critical-path network showing the preparation of a theatrical production. Delays matter only when they are on, or when they reach, the critical path down the center.*

Simferopol is the capital; Sevastopol the major port. **—Cri·me·an** *adj.*

Crimean War *n.* A war (1853–56) conducted mainly in the Crimea, in which Britain, France, Turkey, and Piedmont defeated Russia.

crime pas·si·o·nel (krĕm′ päs′ē-ə-nĕl′) *n., pl.* **crimes passionels** *(pronounced as singular).* A crime prompted by the heat of passion, usually unpremeditated and often connected with sexual jealousy. Also called "crime of passion." [French, "passionate crime."]

crim·i·nal (krĭm′ə-nəl) *adj. Abbr.* **crim.** **1.** Of, involving, or having the nature of crime. **2.** Pertaining to the administration of penal law as distinguished from civil law. **3.** Guilty of crime. **4.** *Informal.* Regrettable; senseless: *a criminal waste of space.*
~n. **1.** A person who has committed or been legally convicted of a crime. **2.** A person who habitually commits crime, usually theft. [Middle English, from Old French *criminel,* from Late Latin *crīminālis,* from Latin *crīmen* (stem *crīmin-*), CRIME.] **—crim·i·nal·ly** *adv.*

criminal conversation *n. Law.* Adultery.

crim·i·nal·i·ty (krĭm′ə-năl′ə-tē) *n., pl.* **-ties.** **1.** The state, quality, or fact of being criminal. **2.** A criminal action or practice.

criminal law *n.* Law involving crime and its punishment. Compare **civil law.**

crim·i·nate (krĭm′ə-nāt′) *tr.v.* **-nated, -nating, -nates.** **1.** To implicate in a crime; incriminate. **2.** To charge with a crime; accuse. **3.** To condemn as criminal; censure. [Latin *crīmināri,* to accuse, from *crīmen,* accusation, CRIME.] **—crim·i·na·tion** *n.* **—crim·i·na·tive, crim·i·na·to·ry** *adj.* **—crim·i·na·tor** *n.*

crim·i·nol·o·gy (krĭm′ə-nŏl′ə-jē) *n.* The study of crime, criminals, and criminal behavior. See **penology.** [Italian *criminologia* : CRIME + -LOGY.] **—crim·i·no·log·i·cal** *adj.* **—crim·i·no·log·i·cal·ly** *adv.* **—crim·i·nol·o·gist** *n.*

crimp¹ (krĭmp) *tr.v.* **crimped, crimping, crimps.** **1.** To press into small, regular folds or ridges; pleat; corrugate. **2.** To bend or mold (leather) into shape. **3.** To gash (the flesh of a raw fish, for example) to make it crisper and firmer when cooked. **4.** To form (hair) into tight curls or waves. **5.** To bend the edges of (metal) before joining. **6.** To hamper; obstruct.
~n. **1. a.** The act of crimping. **b.** Something that has been crimped. **2.** *Usually* **crimps.** Tightly curled or waved hair. **3.** The natural curliness of wool fibers. **4.** A fold or bend in sheet metal to provide stiffness or form a joint. **—put a crimp in.** *Informal.* To obstruct; hamper. [Middle English *crimpen,* to wrinkle, shrivel, Old English *gecrympan,* to curl.] **—crimp·er** *n.* **—crimp·y** *adj.*

crimp² *n.* Formerly, a person who procured men to serve as sailors or soldiers by tricking or coercing them.
~tr.v. **crimped, crimping, crimps.** To procure (sailors or soldiers) by trickery or coercion. [17th century : origin obscure.]

crimp·y (krĭm′pē) *adj.* **-ier, -iest.** Full of crimps; wavy.

crim·son (krĭm′zən) *n.* A deep to vivid purplish red to vivid red.
~v. **crimsoned, -soning, -sons.** *—intr.* **1.** To become crimson. **2.** To blush. *—tr.* To make crimson. [Middle English *cremesin,* from Old Spanish, from Arabic *qirmizī,* from *qirmiz,* kermes insect (from which red dye was obtained).] **—crim·son** *adj.*

cringe (krĭnj) *intr.v.* **cringed, cringing, cringes.** **1.** To shrink back, as with fear, revulsion, or distaste. **2.** To behave in a servile manner; fawn. —See Synonyms at **recoil.**
~n. An act or instance of cringing. [Middle English *crengen,* probably ultimately from Old English *cringan,* to fall dead.]

crin·gle (krĭng′gəl) *n. Nautical.* A small ring or eyelet of rope or metal fastened to the edge of a sail. [Low German *kringel,* diminutive of *kring,* ring, circle, from Middle Low German *krink, kring.*]

cri·nite (krī′nīt′, krī′-) *adj. Biology.* Covered with delicate hairs or hairlike tufts. [Latin *crīnītus,* past participle of *crīnīre,* to provide with hair, from *crīnis,* hair.]

crin·kle (krĭng′kəl) *v.* **-kled, -kling, -kles.** *—intr.* **1.** To form into wrinkles or ripples. **2.** To make a soft, crackling sound; rustle. *—tr.* To cause to wrinkle or rustle.
~n. **1.** A wrinkle or ripple; a fold. **2.** A rustling sound. [Middle English *crinkelen,* akin to Middle Dutch *crinkelen.*] **—crin·kly** *adj.*

crin·kle·root (krĭng′kəl-ro͞ot′, -ro͝ot′) *n.* A woodland plant, *Dentaria diphylla,* of eastern north America, having fleshy rootstocks and clusters of white or pinkish flowers. Also called "pepperroot," "toothwort."

cri·noid (krī′noid′) *n.* Any of various marine invertebrates of the class Crinoidea, which includes the sea lilies and feather stars, characterized by feathery, radiating arms and a stalk by which they are attached to a surface.
~adj. **1.** Of or belonging to the Crinoidea. **2.** Resembling a lily in shape. [New Latin *Crinoidea* : Greek *krinon,* lily + -OID.]

crin·o·line (krĭn′ə-lĭn) *n.* **1.** A coarse, stiff cotton fabric, formerly made of horsehair and linen, used to line and stiffen garments. **2.** A petticoat made of this fabric. **3.** A **hoop skirt** *(see).* [French, from Italian *crinolino* : *crino,* horsehair, from Latin *crīnis,* hair + *lino,* flax, from Latin *līnum.*] **—crin·o·line** *adj.*

cri·num (krī′nəm) *n., pl.* **-nums.** Any of several mostly tropical plants of the genus *Crinum,* having long, strap-shaped leaves and clusters of lilylike flowers. Also called "crinum lily." [New Latin *Crinum,* from Greek *krinon*†, lily.]

cri·ol·lo (krē-ō′lō) *n., pl.* **-los.** **1.** A native of Latin America of Spanish descent. Compare **Creole.** **2.** Any of various domestic animals belonging to South American breeds. **3.** A high-grade type of cocoa. [Spanish, "native, local." See **Creole.**] **—cri·ol·lo** *adj.*

cri·o·sphinx (krī′ə-sfĭngks′) *n., pl.* **-sphinxes** or **sphinges** (-sfĭn′jēz). A sphinx with the head of a ram. [Greek, *krios,* ram + SPHINX.]

cripes (krīps) *interj.* Used to express surprise or dismay. [Euphemistic for *Christ!*]

crip·ple (krĭp′əl) *n.* **1.** One who is partly disabled or lame. **2.** One who is deficient in a specified way: *an emotional cripple.*
~tr.v. **crippled, -pling, -ples.** **1.** To make into a cripple. **2.** To disable or damage. [Middle English *crepel,* Old English *crypel,* from Germanic; akin to CREEP.] **—crip·pler** *n.*

Crip·ple Creek (krĭp′əl). A city of central Colorado, in the Rocky Mts. near Pikes Peak. After 1891 it was the center of a thriving gold-producing area, but declined as the deposits were exhausted. New veins were found in the 1930's.

Cripps (krĭps), **Sir (Richard) Stafford** (1889–1952). British statesman. As a Labour M.P. he helped form the Socialist League and was an advocate of the Popular Front alliance with the Communists. In World War II he was ambassador to Moscow (1940–42).

cri·sis (krī′sĭs) *n., pl.* **-ses** (-sēz′). **1. a.** A crucial point or situation in the course of anything; a turning point. **b.** An unstable condition in political, international, or economic affairs in which an abrupt or decisive change is impending. **2.** *Medicine.* A sudden change in the course of an acute disease, either toward improvement or deterioration. **3.** The point in a story or drama at which hostile forces are at their most tense state of opposition. [Latin, from Greek *krisis,* turning point, from *krinein,* to separate, decide.]

crisis center *n.* **1.** A place used as headquarters during an emergency for organizing relief work. **2.** A place providing advice or psychological support, as, for example, to victims of rape or assault.

crisp (krĭsp) *adj.* **crisper, crispest.** **1.** Firm but easily broken or crumbled; brittle. **2.** Firm and fresh: *crisp celery.* **3.** Brisk; invigorating; bracing. **4.** Animated; stimulating. **5.** Terse; pithy; sharp. **6.** Well defined; neat. **7.** Having small curls, waves, or ripples. —See Synonyms at **incisive.**
~v. **crisped, crisping, crisps.** *—tr.* To make crisp. *—intr.* To become crisp.
~n. *Chiefly British.* A potato chip. [Middle English, curly, from Old English, from Latin *crispus,* crisped, curly.] **—crisp·ly** *adv.* **—crisp·ness** *n.*

cris·pate (krĭs′pāt′) *adj.* Also **cris·pat·ed** (-pā′tĭd). Crimped, curled, or tightly waved. [Latin *crispātus,* from *crispāre,* to curl, from *crispus,* curly, CRISP.]

cris·pa·tion (krĭs-pā′shən) *n.* **1. a.** The act of crisping or curling. **b.** The state of being crisped or curled. **2.** A slight involuntary contraction or constriction, as of the skin. **3.** A minute undulation on the surface of a liquid, produced by vibration.

crisp·er (krĭs′pər) *n.* One that crisps; especially, a compartment in a refrigerator, used for storing vegetables to keep them fresh.

crisp·y (krĭs′pē) *adj.* **-ier, -iest.** Crisp. **—crisp·i·ly** *adv.* **—crisp·i·ness** *n.*

cris·sa. Plural of **crissum.**

criss·cross (krĭs′krôs′, -krŏs′) *v.* **-crossed, -crossing, -crosses.** *—tr.* **1.** To mark with crossing lines. **2.** To move crosswise through or over. *—intr.* To move crosswise or in a crossing direction.
~n. **1.** A mark or pattern made of crossing lines. **2.** A game, **tick-tacktoe** *(see).*
~adj. Crossing one another or marked by crossings.
~adv. In a crisscross manner; in crossing directions. [Variant of CHRISTCROSS.]

cris·sum (krĭs′əm) *n., pl.* **crissa** (krĭs′ə). *Zoology.* The feathers or area surrounding a bird's cloacal opening. [New Latin, from Latin *crissāre, crisāre,* to move the haunches.] **—cris·sal** *adj.*

cris·ta (krĭs′tə) *n., pl.* **-tae** (-tē). *Biology.* A crest or ridge; especially, any of the infoldings of the inner membrane of a mitochondrion, or a sensory structure in the semicircular canal of the ear. [Latin, CREST.]

cris·tate (krĭs′tāt′) *adj.* Also **cris·tat·ed** (-tā′tĭd). Having or forming a crest. [Latin *cristātus,* from *crista,* tuft, crest.]

cris·to·bal·ite (krĭs-tō′bə-līt′) *n.* A white mineral form of silica, SiO_2, found in volcanic rocks. [From German, after Cerro San *Cristóbal,* Mexico, where it was discovered.]

crit. critic; critical; criticism.

cri·te·ri·on (krī-tîr′ē-ən) *n., pl.* **-teria** (-tîr′ē-ə) or **-rions.** A standard, rule, or test on which a judgment or decision can be based. [Greek *kritērion,* a means for judging, standard, from *kritēs,* a judge, umpire, from *krinein,* to separate, choose.]

Usage: *Criteria* is a plural form only. It should not be substituted for the singular *criterion.*

crit·ic (krĭt′ĭk) *n.* **1.** One who forms and expresses judgments of the merits and faults of anything. **2.** *Abbr.* **crit.** A professional specialist in the explication and judgment of literary or artistic works. **3.** A person who finds fault; a severe judge. **4.** *Obsolete.* A critique; a criticism. [Latin *criticus,* from adjective, "decisive," from Greek *kritikos,* able to discern, critical, from *kritos,* separated, chosen, from *krinein,* to separate, choose.]

crit·i·cal (krĭt′ĭ-kəl) *adj. Abbr.* **crit.** **1.** Inclined to judge severely; given to censuring. **2.** Characterized by careful and exact evaluation and judgment. **3.** Of, pertaining to, or characteristic of critics or criticism: *critical acclaim.* **4.** Forming or of the nature of a crisis; crucial. **5.** Fraught with danger or risk; perilous. **6.** Designating materials and products essential to some condition or project but in short supply. **7.** *Medicine.* Of or pertaining to a crisis. **8.** *Mathematics.* Of or pertaining to a point at which a curve has a maximum, minimum, or point of inflection. **9.** *Chemistry & Physics.* Of or pertaining to a condition causing an abrupt change in a quality, property, or phenomenon. **—go critical.** To produce a self-sustaining nuclear reaction, as when becoming operational. Used especially of a nuclear power station. **—crit·i·cal·i·ty** *n.* **—crit·i·cal·ly** *adv.*

Synonyms: *acute, crucial, serious.*

critical angle *n.* **1.** *Optics.* The smallest angle of incidence at which a light ray passing from one medium to another less refractive medium can be totally reflected from the boundary between the two. **2.** *Aviation.* The **stalling angle** *(see).*

critical apparatus *n.* An **apparatus criticus** *(see).*

critical constants *pl.n. Physics.* Constants, such as critical temperature, pressure, and volume, that characterize the critical point of a given substance.

critical mass *n.* The smallest mass of a fissionable material that will sustain a nuclear chain reaction.

crit·i·cal-path analysis (krĭt′ĭ-kəl-păth′, -päth′) *n.* A technique for finding the best way of completing a complex process in the minimum time by analyzing alternative combinations of stages.

critical point *n.* **1.** *Physics.* The condition in which the liquid and vapor phases of a pure stable substance have the same density. Also called "critical state." **2.** *Mathematics.* **a.** A maximum, minimum, or point of inflection. **b.** A point at which the derivative of a function is zero or infinite.

critical pressure *n.* The least applied pressure required at the critical temperature to liquefy a gas.

critical speed *n. Physics.* The speed above which fluid flow changes from smooth laminar flow to turbulent flows.

critical state *n. Physics.* See **critical point** (sense 1).

critical temperature *n.* The temperature above which a gas cannot be liquefied, regardless of the pressure applied.

critical volume *n.* The volume of one mole of a substance at its critical point.

crit·ic·as·ter (krĭt′ĭ-kăs′tər) *n.* A petty or inferior critic.

crit·i·cism (krĭt′ə-sĭz′əm) *n. Abbr.* **crit. 1.** The act of making judgments or criticizing. **2. a.** The passing of unfavorable judgment; censure; disapproval. **b.** An instance of this; a critical comment or observation. **3.** The art, skill, or profession of making discriminating judgments and evaluations, especially of literary or other artistic works. **4.** A review or other article expressing such judgment and evaluation; a critique. **5.** The detailed investigation of the origin and history of literary documents, especially in order to produce the most authentic possible text. Also called "textual criticism."

crit·i·cize (krĭt′ə-sīz′) *v.* **-cized, -cizing, -cizes.** *—tr.* **1.** To judge the merits and faults of; analyze and evaluate. **2.** To judge with severity; find fault with; censure. *—intr.* **1.** To find fault. **2.** To act as a critic. **—crit·i·ciz·a·ble** *adj.* **—crit·i·ciz·er** *n.*

Synonyms: *blame, censure, condemn, denounce, reprehend.*

cri·tique (krĭ-tēk′) *n.* **1.** A critical review or commentary, especially one dealing with a literary or other artistic work. **2.** A critical discussion of some specified topic. **3.** The art of criticism.
~*tr.v.* **critiqued, -tiquing, -tiques.** To write a critique of; review. [French, from Greek *kritikē,* the art of criticism, from *kritikos,* critical. See **critic.**]

crit·ter (krĭt′ər) *n. Regional.* **1.** A creature, especially a domestic animal. **2.** A person. [Variant of CREATURE.]

croak (krōk) *v.* **croaked, croaking, croaks.** *—intr.* **1.** To utter the low, hoarse sound characteristic of frogs and crows. **2.** To speak with a low, hoarse voice. **3.** To talk discontentedly or dolefully. **4.** *Slang.* To die. *—tr.* **1.** To utter by croaking. **2.** *Slang.* To kill.
~*n.* A croaking sound. [Middle English *croken* (imitative).] **—croak·i·ly** *adv.* **—croak·y** *adj.*

croak·er (krō′kər) *n.* **1. a.** A croaking animal. **b.** A person who grumbles or habitually predicts evil. **2.** Any of various chiefly marine fishes of the family Sciaenidae, that make croaking sounds.

Croat (krōt, krō′ăt) *n.* **1.** A Slavonic native or inhabitant of Croatia. **2.** The language of the Croats; Croatian.

Cro·a·tia (krō-ā′shə). *Serbo-Croatian* **Hr·vat·ska** (hûr-vät′skä). The second-largest of the six republics of Yugoslavia, in the northwest of the country. The Croats, a Slav people, occupied the area in the 7th century. In 1102 it became associated with the Hungarian crown and largely remained so until the collapse of Austria-Hungary (1918), when the Kingdom of Serbs, Croats, and Slovenes (later Yugoslavia) was formed. Zagreb is the capital.

Cro·a·tian (krō-ā′shən) *adj.* Of or pertaining to Croatia, the Croats, their language, or their culture.
~*n.* **1.** A Croat. **2.** A form of the Serbo-Croatian language written using the Latin alphabet.

Cro·ce (krō′chā), **Benedetto** (1866–1952). Italian philosopher and political figure. He was minister of education (1920–21), and under Fascist rule he used his review *La Critica* (founded 1903) for veiled attacks on Mussolini's regime. He became a leader of the regrouped Liberal Party (1943) and its president (1947).

cro·ce·in (krō′sē-ĭn) *n.* Any of various red or orange acid azo dyes. [Latin *croceus,* saffron-colored, from *crocus,* saffron, CROCUS + -IN.]

cro·chet (krō-shā′) *v.* **-cheted** (-shād′), **-cheting** (-shā′ĭng), **-chets** (-shāz′). *—intr.* To make a piece of needlework by looping thread with a hooked needle. *—tr.* To make or decorate (a fabric) by looping thread with a hooked needle.
~*n.* A kind of needlework made by crocheting. [French, a hook, from Old French, diminutive of *croc(he),* a hook, from Frankish *krōk* (unattested).]

cro·cid·o·lite (krō-sĭd′ə-līt′) *n.* A fibrous, lavender-blue or greenish mineral, a sodium iron silicate that is used as a commercial form of asbestos. Also called "blue asbestos." [German *Krokydolith,* "fibrous stone" : Greek *krokus* (stem *krokud-*), nap of cloth + -LITE.]

crock¹ (krŏk) *n.* **1.** An earthenware vessel. **2.** A piece of broken earthenware; a potsherd. [Middle English *crokke,* Old English *crocc(a).*]

crock² *n. British Regional.* **1.** Soot. **2.** Coloring matter that rubs off from poorly dyed cloth.
~*v.* **crocked, crocking, crocks.** *British Regional. —tr.* To stain with or as with crock. *—intr.* To give off soot or color. [Possibly from CROCK (pot, hence "soot on a cooking pot").]

crock³ *n. Chiefly British Informal.* One that is worn-out, decrepit, or impaired, especially a car.
~*v.* **crocked, crocking, crocks.** *Chiefly British Informal. —intr.* To get sick; become weak or disabled. Often used with *up. —tr.* To cause to collapse; disable. Sometimes used with *up.* [Middle English *crok,* perhaps from Scandinavian.]

crocked (krŏkt) *adj. Slang.* Drunk. [Perhaps from CROCK (to become disabled).]

crock·er·y (krŏk′ə-rē) *n.* Plates, cups, and the like collectively; china or earthenware.

crock·et (krŏk′ĭt) *n. Architecture.* An ornamental device, usually in the form of a cusp or curling leaf, placed along outer angles of pinnacles and gables, especially in the Gothic style. [Middle English *croket,* from Old North French *croquet,* variant of Old French *crochet,* hook. See **crochet.**]

Crock·ett (krŏk′ĭt), **David,** known as "Davy" (1786–1836). U.S. frontiersman and political figure who cultivated the image of a shrewd, homespun backwoodsman. He became a congressman (1827–31, 1833–35) and later joined the Texas revolutionaries fighting against Mexico. He died at the siege of the Alamo.

croc·o·dile (krŏk′ə-dīl′) *n.* **1.** Any of various large aquatic reptiles of the genus *Crocodylus* and related genera, of tropical regions, having thick, armorlike skin and long, tapering jaws. **2.** Broadly, any crocodilian reptile, such as an alligator, cayman, or gavial. **3.** Leather made from crocodile skin. [Middle English *cocodril,* from Old French, from Medieval Latin *cocodrillus,* from Latin *crocodīlus,* from Greek *krokodilos,* "worm of the pebbles" (from its habit of basking in the sun) : *krokē*†, pebbles + *drilos*†, worm.]

crocodile clip *n.* A small spring clip with long-toothed jaws, used to make temporary electrical connections.

crocodile tears *pl.n.* False tears; an insincere display of grief. [From the belief that crocodiles weep after eating their victims.]

croc·o·dil·i·an (krŏk′ə-dĭl′ē-ən, -dĭl′yən) *n.* Any of various reptiles of the order Crocodilia, which includes the alligators, crocodiles, caymans, and gavials. [New Latin *Crocodylia,* from Latin *crocodīlus,* CROCODILE.] **—croc·o·dil·ian** *adj.*

croc·oi·site (krŏk′wə-zīt′) *n.* Crocoite. [German *Krokoisit,* from French *crocoise,* from Greek *krokoeis,* saffron-colored, from *krokos,* saffron.]

croc·o·ite (krŏk′ō-īt′, krō′kō-) *n.* A rare orange to reddish mineral of lead chromate, $PbCrO_4$, found in oxidized lead deposits. [German *Krokoit,* alteration of *Krokoisit,* crocoisite.]

cro·cus (krō′kəs) *n., pl.* **-cuses** or **-ci** (-sī). **1.** Any plant of the genus *Crocus,* widely cultivated in gardens, and having showy, variously colored flowers and grasslike leaves. **2.** Grayish to light reddish purple. **3.** A red variety of iron oxide, Fe_2O_3, used in the form of an abrasive powder for polishing. [New Latin *Crocus,* from Latin *crocus,* saffron, from Greek *krokos,* from Semitic, akin to Hebrew *karkōm.*]

Croe·sus (krē′səs) (died *c.* 546 B.C.). Last king of Lydia (*c.* 560–546). He allied himself with Babylonia and Egypt and extended his kingdom, building a legendary prosperity on commerce.

croft (krôft, krŏft) *n. British.* **1.** A small enclosed field or pasture. **2.** An agricultural smallholding, especially in the Highlands and islands of Scotland. [Middle English *croft,* Old English *croft.*]

croft·er (krôf′tər, krŏf′-) *n. British & Scottish.* A person who rents or owns a croft, especially in Scotland.

crois·sant (krwä-säN′) *n.* A rich, crescent-shaped roll of leavened dough or puff pastry. [French, from Old French *croissant, creissant,* CRESCENT.]

Croix de Guerre (krwä′ də gâr′) *n.* A French military decoration for bravery in battle. [French, "cross of war."]

Cro-Mag·non (krō-măg′nən, -măn′yən) *adj.* Of, relating to, or designating an early form of modern man, *Homo sapiens sapiens,* inhabiting Europe in the late Palaeolithic era, characterized by a tall stature and known from skeletal parts found in the Cro-Magnon cave in southern France. **—Cro-Magnon** *n.*

crom·lech (krŏm′lĕk′) *n.* **1.** A prehistoric monument consisting of monoliths encircling a mound. **2.** A **dolmen** *(see).* [Welsh : *crom,* feminine of *crwn,* arched + *llech,* flat stone.]

Cromp·ton (krŏmp′tən) **Samuel** (1753–1827). British inventor of the spinning mule (1779), which combined the principles of Hargreaves's spinning jenny and Arkwright's water frame.

Crom·well (krŏm′wĕl′, -wəl, krŭm′-), **Oliver** (1599–1658). English soldier and statesman, lord protector of England (1653–58). A Puritan and critic of Charles I, he founded the New Model Army (1644). Originally working for reconciliation between army, Crown, and Parliament, he eventually sided with the army. During the second Civil War (1648) he came to support demands for Charles's execution (1649). As lord lieutenant of Ireland (1649–50), he ruthlessly suppressed rebellion and defeated the royalist rising of Scots at Worcester (1651). In 1653 he dismissed the governing Rump Parliament, and after the failure of the Barebones Parliament he

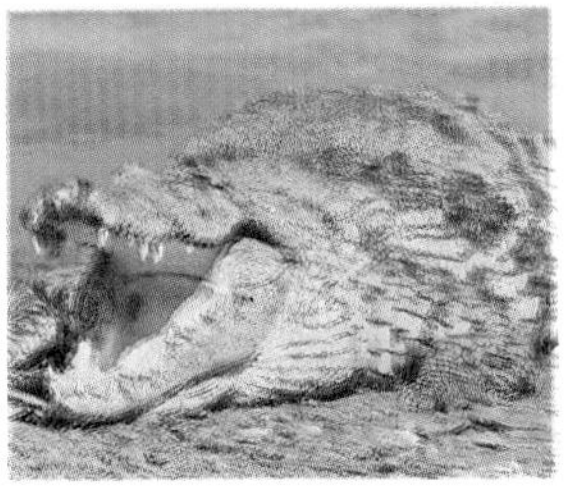

crocodile *The largest and among the oldest living reptiles, crocodiles have existed since the time of the dinosaurs, 150 million years ago. Some species can grow to more than 6.5 meters (20 feet) long.*

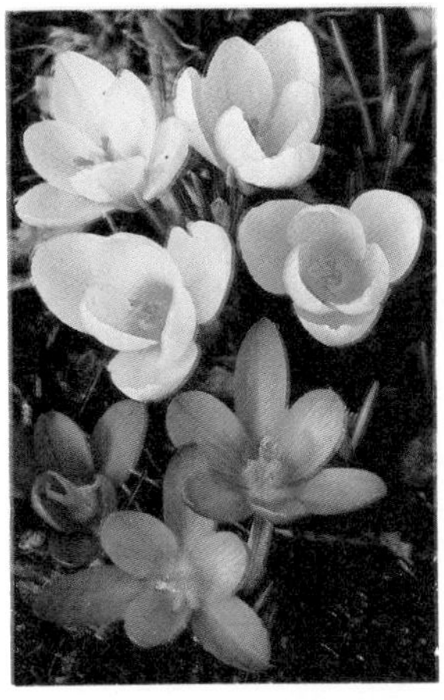

crocus *These low-growing plants—of which there are more than 70 species and numerous varieties—flower in the Northern Hemisphere between August and April.*

PRONUNCIATION KEY

ă, pat; ā, pay; âr, care;
ä, father, are; b, bib;
ch, church; d, deed; ĕ, pet;
ē, be; f, fife; g, gag; h, hat;
hw, which; ĭ, pit; ī, pie;
îr, pier; j, judge; k, kick;
l, lid, needle; m, mum;
n, no, sudden; ng, thing;
ŏ, pot; ō, toe; ô, paw, for;
oi, noise; ou, out; ŏŏ, book;
ōō, boot; p, pop; r, roar;
s, sauce; sh, ship, dish;
t, tight; th, thin, path;
th, this, bathe; ŭ, cut; ûr, fur;
v, valve; w, with; y, yes;
z, zebra, size; zh, vision;
ə, about, item, edible, gallop, circus, peaceful

IN FOREIGN WORDS:

à, *Fr.* ami; œ, *Fr.* feu, *Ger.* schön; ü, *Fr.* tu, *Ger.* über; KH, *Ger.* ich, *Scot.* loch; N, *Fr.* bon; y′, *Fr.* Compiègne

STRESS MARKS:

Primary stress: ′
in·cite′ (ĭn-sīt′)
Secondary stress: ′
in′sight′ (ĭn′sīt′)

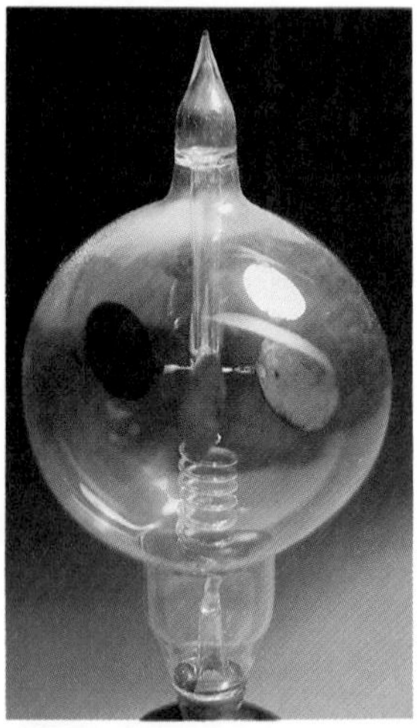

Crookes radiometer *The British physicist Sir William Crookes believed that electromagnetic radiation, such as light, caused the vanes in the bulb shown here to turn, but it is now known that the force of the radiation alone is too feeble. In fact, the dark sides of the vanes are warmed by absorbing more energy than the white sides; and the air molecules in the bulb gather on these warmer sides, causing a relative "breeze."*

PRONUNCIATION KEY

ă, pat; ā, pay; âr, care;
ä, father, are; b, bib;
ch, church; d, deed; ĕ, pet;
ē, be; f, fife; g, gag; h, hat;
hw, which; ĭ, pit; ī, pie;
îr, pier; j, judge; k, kick;
l, lid, needle; m, mum;
n, no, sudden; ng, thing;
ŏ, pot; ō, toe; ô, paw, for;
oi, noise; ou, out; o͝o, book;
o͞o, boot; p, pop; r, roar;
s, sauce; sh, ship, dish;
t, tight; th, thin, path;
th, this, bathe; ŭ, cut; ûr, fur;
v, valve; w, with; y, yes;
z, zebra, size; zh, vision;
ə, about, item, edible, gallop, circus, peaceful

IN FOREIGN WORDS:

à, *Fr.* ami; œ, *Fr.* feu, *Ger.* schön; ü, *Fr.* tu, *Ger.* über; KH, *Ger.* ich, *Scot.* loch; N, *Fr.* bon; y', *Fr.* Compiègne

STRESS MARKS:

Primary stress: ′
in·cite′ (ĭn-sīt′)
Secondary stress: ′
in′sight′ (ĭn′sīt′)

accepted leadership of a kingless protectorate. As lord protector he pursued a vigorous foreign policy against Spain and conquered Jamaica (1655). At home he tried to restrain the excess of Puritan zeal but was beset by constitutional difficulties.

Cromwell, Richard (1626–1712). Son of Oliver, he succeeded him briefly as lord protector (1658–59) before the restoration of the monarchy under Charles II.

Cromwell, Thomas, Earl of Essex (*c.* 1485–1540). English lawyer and statesman who devised the legislation that made the English church independent of Rome, culminating in the Act of Supremacy (1534). From 1536 he supervised the dissolution of the monasteries. He lost favor, was accused of treason, and was executed.

Cromwell current *n.* A Pacific Ocean current at the equator, flowing eastward from the Hawaiian to the Galapagos islands. [After Townsend *Cromwell* (1922–1958), American oceanographer.]

Crom·wel·li·an (krŏm-wĕl′ē-ən, krŭm-) *adj.* Of, pertaining to, or characteristic of Oliver Cromwell or his time; especially, austere or puritanical.

crone (krōn) *n.* A withered old woman. [Middle English, from Middle Dutch *caroonje, croonje,* old ewe, dead body, from Old North French *carogne,* CARRION.]

Cro·nin (krō′nĭn), **Archibald Joseph** (1896–1981). British novelist, born in Scotland. A former physician, he published his first novel *Hatter's Castle* in 1931. Later titles include *The Keys of the Kingdom* (1941) and *The Minstrel Boy* (1975).

Cron·je (krôn-yä), **Piet Arnoldus** (*c.* 1840–1911). South African Boer general. He commanded the siege of Potchefstroom (1881) and headed the force that captured the Jameson Raiders (1896). In 1899 he was appointed general in command of the Boers' western forces, fighting off a major British assault at Magersfontein. He surrendered at Paardeburg (1900) and remained in captivity on St. Helena until the end of the war.

Cron·os, Kron·os (krō′nəs). *Greek Mythology.* A Titan who ruled the universe until dethroned by his son Zeus; identified with the Roman god Saturn.

cro·ny (krō′nē) *n., pl.* **-nies. 1.** A close friend or companion. **2.** An associate in some dishonest or questionable activity. [Earlier *chrony* (Cambridge University slang), "old companion," from Greek *khronios,* long-lasting, from *khronos,* time.]

cro·ny·ism (krō′nē-ĭz′əm) *n.* Favoritism shown to cronies, without regard for their qualifications, as in political appointments to office.

crook (kro͝ok) *n.* **1.** Something that is bent or curved; a hook or hooked part. **2.** An implement or tool that has a bent or curved part, such as a bishop's crosier or a shepherd's staff. **3.** A curve or bend; a turn. **4.** *Informal.* A person who makes a living by dishonest methods; a thief.
∼*v.* **crooked, crooking, crooks.** —*tr.* To give a crook to or make a crook in; curve; bend. —*intr.* To become crooked. [Middle English *crok,* from Old Norse *krōkr,* a hook.]

crook·back (kro͝ok′băk′) *n. Archaic.* A hunchback. —**crook·backed** *adj.*

crook·ed (kro͝ok′ĭd) *adj.* **1.** Having bends, curves, or angles; not straight. **2.** *Informal.* Dishonest or unscrupulous; fraudulent. **3.** Misshapen; deformed. —**crook·ed·ly** *adv.* —**crook·ed·ness** *n.*

Crookes (kro͝oks), **Sir William** (1832–1919). British chemist and physicist. He discovered the element thallium (1861) and invented the radiometer. He pioneered research into cathode rays and produced a shield to protect the eyes of glassworkers.

Crookes dark space *n.* A small dark region near the cathode in a luminous gas discharge. [After Sir William CROOKES.]

Crookes glass *n.* A type of glass containing cerium, which cuts down the transmission of ultraviolet radiation. It is used in sunglasses and protective goggles. [After Sir William CROOKES.]

Crookes radiometer *n.* A device consisting of a small, evacuated glass bulb containing a set of four light, vertical metal vanes, each blackened on one side and mounted on a vertical, rotating spindle. When light or other radiation falls on the tube, the vanes rotate. The rate of rotation depends on the intensity of the radiation. [After Sir William CROOKES.]

Crookes tube *n.* A low-pressure discharge tube used to study the properties of cathode rays. [After Sir William CROOKES.]

crook·neck (kro͝ok′nĕk′) *n.* A type of squash having a long, curved neck and yellow flesh.

croon (kro͞on) *v.* **crooned, crooning, croons.** —*intr.* **1.** To sing or hum softly; murmur. **2.** To sing popular songs in a soft, sentimental manner. **3.** *British Regional.* **a.** To wail or cry softly, as when lamenting. **b.** To utter a deep, loud sound; roar. —*tr.* To sing by crooning.
∼*n.* A soft singing, humming, or murmuring. [Middle English *croynen,* to boom, sing, from Middle Dutch *krōnen,* to groan, lament (imitative).] —**croon·er** *n.*

crop (krŏp) *n.* **1.** Cultivated plants or agricultural produce, such as grain, vegetables, or fruit. **2.** The quantity or quality of such produce of a particular season, place, or kind. **3.** A group, quantity, or supply appearing at one time: *this year's crop of students.* **4.** A short haircut. **5.** An animal hide, tanned and complete. **6. a.** A short whip used in horseback riding, with a loop serving as a lash. **b.** The stock of a whip. **7.** *Zoology.* **a.** A pouchlike enlargement of a bird's esophagus, in which food is stored or partially digested. **b.** A similar organ in earthworms, insects, and other invertebrates. **8.** The mark produced by cropping the ears of a domestic animal.
∼*v.* **cropped, cropping, crops.** —*tr.* **1.** To cut or bite off the stems or top of (a plant). **2.** To cut (hair, for example) very short. **3.** To clip (an animal's ears or a photograph, for example). **4.** To reap; harvest. **5.** To cause to grow or yield a crop or crops. —*intr.* To plant, grow, or yield a crop or crops. —**crop out.** To project above the ground. Used of rock formations. —**crop up.** To appear or develop unexpectedly. [Middle English *crop,* Old English *cropp,* cluster, bunch, ear of corn, from Germanic.]

crop-dust·ing (krŏp′dŭs′tĭng) *n.* The spraying of crops with an insecticidal or fungicidal dust, usually from a light aircraft. —**crop·dust** *v.* —**crop·dust·er** *n.*

crop-eared (krŏp′îrd′) *adj.* **1.** Having the ears cropped. **2.** With the hair cut so short that the ears show.

crop·per¹ (krŏp′ər) *n.* **1.** A person, animal, or machine that crops. **2.** A person who works land in return for a share of the yield; a sharecropper. **3.** *Informal.* A plant that yields a crop of the specified type: *a generous cropper; a late cropper.*

cropper² *n.* **1.** A heavy fall; a tumble. **2.** A disastrous failure; a fiasco. —**come a cropper. 1.** To fall heavily. **2.** To fail miserably; come to grief. [From the phrase *neck and crop,* "completely," perhaps from CROP (to cut off).]

crop rotation *n.* A method of maintaining and renewing soil fertility by the successive planting of different crops on the same land.

cro·quet (krō-kā′) *n.* **1.** An outdoor game in which the players drive wooden balls through a series of loops using long-handled mallets. **2.** The act of driving away an opponent's croquet ball by hitting one's own ball when the two are in contact.
∼*v.* **croqueted** (-kād′), **-queting** (-kā′ĭng), **-quets** (-kāz′). —*tr.* To drive away (an opponent's ball) with a croquet. —*intr.* To croquet an opponent's ball. [Perhaps dialect form of French *crochet,* a hook. See **crochet.**]

cro·quette (krō-kĕt′) *n.* A small cake of savory minced or molded food, coated with bread crumbs and deep-fried. [French, from *croquer,* to crunch, crack (imitative).]

cro·qui·gnole (krō′kĭn-yōl′) *n.* A kind of permanent wave in which the hair is wound around metal rods. [French, a biscuit, perhaps from *croquer,* to crunch. See **croquette.**]

Cros·by (krôz′bē, krŏz′-), **Bing,** born Harry Lillis Crosby (1904–77). U.S. singer, actor, and entertainer. He popularized a new, softer, and more relaxed style of singing and starred with Bob Hope in the *Road* series of comedy films.

cro·sier, cro·zier (krō′zhər) *n.* **1.** A staff with a crook at the end, carried by or before an abbot, bishop, or archbishop as a symbol of office. Also called "pastoral staff." **2.** *Botany.* A coiled tip of a plant stalk, as of a young fern frond. [Middle English *crocer,* from Old French *crossier,* staff-bearer, from *crosse,* bishop's staff, from Germanic.]

cross (krôs, krŏs) *n.* **1.** A structure, mark, or pattern formed typically by the intersection of two lines of equal length or two lines at right angles. **2.** An upright post with a transverse piece near the top, upon which condemned persons were executed in ancient times. **3.** Any of several representations of the cross upon which Jesus was crucified. **4.** A sign made by tracing the outline of a cross with the right hand upon the forehead and chest as a devotional act. **5.** A crucifix. **6. a.** Any of various symbolic or ornamental figures or structures in the form of a cross or modified cross, such as a medal or emblem. **b.** A monument in the form of a cross, often at a central place in a town or village. **7.** A source of trouble or sorrow; an affliction: *She too has her cross to bear.* **8.** A mark (X) used as a signature or to indicate an error, point of intersection, and the like. **9.** A pipe fitting with four branches in the form of a cross, used as a junction for intersecting pipes. **10.** *Biology.* **a.** A plant or animal produced by crossbreeding; a hybrid. **b.** The process of crossbreeding; hybridization. **11.** A combination of the qualities of two things or people. **12.** *Slang.* A swindle or fraud; especially, a contest whose outcome has been dishonestly prearranged. **13.** *Sports.* **a.** In boxing, a punch launched from the side, usually the right. **b.** In soccer, a shot that sends the ball across the pitch: *a long cross to the center.* —**the Cross. 1.** The cross upon which Jesus was crucified. **2.** Christianity; the Christian religion.
∼*v.* **crossed, crossing, crosses.** —*tr.* **1.** To go across; pass from one side of to the other. **2.** To carry or convey across. **3.** To extend or pass across, through, or over; intersect. **4.** To make or put a line across. **5.** To lay across or over; place crosswise: *cross one's legs.* **6.** To make the sign of the cross upon (oneself) or over (another) as a sign of devotion. **7.** To encounter in passing: *His path crossed mine.* **8.** To thwart or obstruct; interfere with: *Do not cross me.* **9.** *Biology.* To crossbreed or cross-fertilize (plants or animals). —*intr.* **1.** To lie or pass across each other; intersect. **2.** To move or extend from one side to another. **3.** To encounter each other in passing: *Our paths crossed.* **4.** *Biology.* To crossbreed or cross-fertilize. **5.** To be in the mail simultaneously. Used of two letters addressed to each other's senders. —**cross off** or **out.** To cancel or eliminate by or as if by drawing a line or lines through.
∼*adj.* **1.** Lying or passing crosswise; intersecting. **2.** Contrary or counter; opposing. **3.** Showing ill humor; annoyed. **4.** Crossbred; hybrid. [Middle English *cros,* Old English *cros,* from Old Irish *cross,* from Latin *crux* (stem *cruc-*), perhaps from Phoenician.] —**cross·er** *n.* —**cross·ly** *adv.* —**cross·ness** *n.*

cross·bar (krôs′bär′, krŏs′-) *n.* A horizontal beam or bar, as on a hurdle, on a bicycle, or on goalposts.

cross·beam (krôs′bēm′, krŏs′-) *n.* A beam that links or rests on two supports.

cross bedding *n. Geology.* The formation of laminations within a stratum at a different angle to that of the main bed. Also called "current bedding," "false bedding."

cross·bench (krôs'běnch', krŏs'-) n. British. A bench in Parliament occupied by members who belong to neither government nor opposition. —**cross·bench·er** n.

cross·bill (krôs'bĭl', krŏs'-) n. Any of several birds of the genus Loxia, having bills whose upper and lower parts curve and cross at their narrow tips.

cross·bones (krôs'bōnz', krŏs'-) n. See skull and crossbones.

cross·bow (krôs'bō', krŏs'-) n. A medieval weapon consisting of a bow fixed crosswise on a wooden stock, with grooves on the stock to direct the arrow or other projectile. —**cross·bow·man** n.

cross·breed (krôs'brēd', krŏs'-) v. **-bred** (-brĕd'), **-breeding, -breeds.** —tr. 1. To mate individuals of different varieties or breeds; hybridize. 2. To produce (a hybrid) by crossbreeding. —intr. To mate so as to produce a hybrid; interbreed.
~n. A hybrid produced by crossbreeding. Also called "intercross."

cross·check (krôs'chĕk', krŏs'-) tr.v. **-checked, -checking, -checks.** To verify by comparing with supplementary data.
~n. (krôs'chĕk', krŏs'-). An act of crosschecking.

cross·coun·try (krôs'kŭn'trē, krŏs'-) adj. 1. Moving or directed across open country, rather than following roads. 2. From one side of a country to the opposite side.
~n. A long running race over open country. —**cross·coun·try** adv.

cross·cul·tur·al (krôs'kŭl'chər-əl, krŏs'-) adj. Dealing with or involving two or more different cultures: a cross-cultural study of marriage customs.

cross·cur·rent (krôs'kûr'ənt, krŏs'-) n. 1. A current flowing across another current. 2. A conflicting movement, tendency, or inclination.

cross·cut (krôs'kŭt', krŏs'-) v. **-cut, -cutting, -cuts.** —tr. 1. To cut across transversely. 2. In film-making, to intercut. —intr. To cut or run crosswise.
~adj. 1. Used or constructed for cutting crosswise: a crosscut saw. 2. Cut on the bias or across the grain.
~n. 1. A course or cut going crosswise. 2. A path more direct than the main path; a short cut. 3. Mining. A level driven so that it intersects a vein of ore.

cross·dres·ser (krôs'drĕs'ər, krŏs'-) n. A transvestite (see). —**cross·dres·sing** n.

crosse (krôs, krŏs) n. A lacrosse stick. [French, from Old French crosse, staff. See crosier.]

crossed line n. A telephone connection between two callers in which another call can be heard.

cross·ex·am·ine (krôs'ĭg-zăm'ĭn, krŏs'-) v. **-ined, -ining, -ines.** —tr. 1. To question (someone) closely, especially in order to check the resulting answers against answers previously made. 2. Law. To question (a witness already examined by the opposing side). —intr. To question a person closely. —**cross·ex·am·i·na·tion** n. —**cross·ex·am·in·er** n.

cross·eye (krôs'ī', krŏs'ī') n. An eye defect in which one or both eyes turn toward the nose. See strabismus. —**cross·eyed** adj.

cross·fer·ti·li·za·tion (krôs'fûr't'l-ə-zā'shən, krŏs'-) n. 1. Biology. The union of gametes from different individuals, usually of the same species. Cross-fertilization in plants is also called "allogamy." 2. An interchange, as of ideas or methods, between different groups. —**cross·fer·tile** adj.

cross·fer·ti·lize (krôs'fûr't'l-īz', krŏs'-) v. **-lized, -lizing, -lizes.** —tr. To fertilize by means of cross-fertilization. —intr. To be fertilized by means of cross-fertilization.

cross·file (krôs'fīl', krŏs'-) intr.v. **-filed, -filing, -files.** To register as a candidate in the primaries of more than one political party. —**cross·fil·er** n.

cross·fire (krôs'fīr', krŏs'-) n. 1. Military. Lines of fire from two or more positions crossing one another at or near a single objective. 2. Any situation in which things originating from different sources meet in conflict. 3. A heated exchange of conflicting ideas.

cross·grained (krôs'grānd', krŏs'-) adj. 1. Having an irregular, transverse, or diagonal grain. 2. Stubborn; contrary.

cross hair n. Either of two fine strands of wire crossed in the focus of an eyepiece of an optical instrument and used as a calibration or sighting reference.

cross·hatch (krôs'hăch', krŏs'-) tr.v. **-hatched, -hatching, -hatches.** In drawing, to shade with two or more sets of intersecting parallel lines. —**cross·hatch·ing** n.

cross·head (krôs'hĕd', krŏs'-) n. 1. Engineering. A beam that connects the piston rod to the connecting rod of a reciprocating engine. 2. Printing. A subheading.
~adj. 1. Designating a screw that has a cross-shaped notch in its head. 2. Designating a screwdriver designed to fit such a screw.

cross·in·dex (krôs'ĭn'dĕks, krŏs'-) v. **-dexed, -dexing, -dexes.** —tr. To furnish (an index) with cross-references. —intr. To furnish cross-references.

cross·ing (krôs'ĭng, krŏs'-) n. 1. A place at which roads, lines, or tracks intersect; an intersection. 2. A place at which something, such as a river or road, may be crossed. 3. An act or instance of crossing, especially in a ship: a rough crossing from Bar Harbor to Yarmouth. 4. The intersection of the nave and transept in a cruciform church. 5. The act of crossbreeding.

crossing over n. The exchange of genetic material between homologous chromosomes during the formation of gametes. Also called "crossover."

cross·jack (krôs'jăk', krŏs'-) n. The square sail below the lowest mizzenmast spar on a ship. [CROSS + JACK (flag).]

cross·leg·ged (krôs'lĕg'ĭd, krŏs'-) adj. With one leg crossed over the other. —**cross·leg·ged** adv.

cross·let (krôs'lət, krŏs'-) n. Heraldry. A cross with a smaller cross at each of the four tips. [16th century croslet, diminutive of CROSS.]

cross·link (krôs'lĭngk', krŏs'-) n. Chemistry. A short chain of atoms joined across two long chains in certain types of polymer.
~v. **cross·linked, -linking, -links.** Chemistry. —tr. To cause the formation of cross-links in (a polymer). —intr. To polymerize with cross-links.

cross matching n. The process by which blood compatibility between donor and recipient is tested before transfusion.

cros·sop·te·ryg·i·an (krŏ-sŏp'tə-rĭj'ē-ən) n. A member of the Crossopterygii, a group of mostly extinct bony fishes including the coelacanths, believed to have been the possible ancestors of terrestrial vertebrates. [New Latin Crossopterygii, "the fringed-winged ones" : Greek krossoi†, fringe + Greek pterux, wing, from pteron, feather, wing.] —**cros·sop·te·ryg·i·an** adj.

cross·o·ver (krôs'ō'vər, krŏs'-) n. 1. A place at which or the means by which a crossing is made. 2. A short connecting track by which a train can be transferred from one line to another. 3. Genetics. a. A crossing over (see). b. A character combination resulting from crossing over.

cross·patch (krôs'păch', krŏs'-) n. Informal. A peevish, irascible person. [CROSS (angry) + obsolete patch, jester, probably from Italian pazzo†.]

cross·piece (krôs'pēs', krŏs'-) n. A transverse piece, such as a beam in a building.

cross·ply (krôs'plī', krŏs'-) adj. Designating car tires that have fabric cords lying crosswise to stiffen the sidewalls.
~n. A cross-ply tire.

cross·pol·li·na·tion (krôs'pŏl-ə-nā'shən, krŏs'-) n. The transfer of pollen from the stamens of a flower of one plant to the stigma of a flower of another plant, either naturally by insects or wind, or artificially by hand. —**cross·pol·li·nate** v. —**cross·pol·li·na·tor** n.

cross product n. Mathematics. A vector product (see).

cross·pur·pose (krôs'pûr'pəs, krŏs'-) n. A conflicting or contrary purpose; mutual misunderstanding. —**be at cross-purposes.** To have or act under a misunderstanding of each other's purposes.

cross·ques·tion (krôs'kwĕs'chən, krŏs'-) tr.v. **-tioned, -tioning, -tions.** To cross-examine; question closely.
~n. A question asked in the process of cross-examination.

cross·re·fer (krôs'rĭ-fûr', krŏs'-) v. **-ferred, -ferring, -fers.** —tr. 1. To refer (the reader) from one part or passage to another. 2. To refer (one item or section in a text) to another. —intr. To make a cross-reference.

cross·ref·er·ence (krôs'rĕf'ər-əns, -rĕf'rəns, krŏs'-) n. A reference from one part of a book, index, catalogue, or file to another part containing related information.
~tr.v. **cross·referenced, -encing, -ences.** To supply (a text) with cross-references.

cross·road (krôs'rōd', krŏs'-) n. 1. A road that intersects another road. 2. crossroads. a. A place where two or more roads meet. b. A place where different cultures meet. c. A crucial point or place.

cross·ruff (krôs'rŭf', -rŭf', krŏs'-) n. A series of plays in card games such as bridge and whist where partnership hands alternately trump the other's lead.
~v. **crossruffed, -ruffing, -ruffs.** —intr. To perform a crossruff or a series of crossruffs. —tr. To trump (one's partner's lead or a lead from the dummy) in alternating plays.

cross section n. 1. A section formed by a plane cutting through an object, usually at right angles to an axis. 2. A piece so cut or a graphic representation of such a piece. 3. Physics. A measure of the probability of occurrence of a particular atomic or nuclear reaction. 4. A representative sample meant to be typical of the whole. —**cross·sec·tion·al** adj.

cross·slide (krôs'slīd', krŏs'-) n. The part of a lathe that moves the tool post at right angles to the bed of the lathe.

cross·stitch (krôs'stĭch', krŏs'-) n. 1. In sewing and embroidery, a double stitch forming an X. 2. Needlework made with this stitch.
~v. **cross·stitched, -stitching, -stitches.** —tr. To make or embroider with cross-stitches. —intr. To work in cross-stitch.

cross·sub·si·dize v. **-dized, -dizing, -dizes.** —tr. To give financial support to (an unprofitable section of a firm or similar operation) from the profits of another. —intr. To cross-subsidize a financial operation. —**cross·sub·si·dy** n.

cross·talk (krôs'tôk', krŏs'-) n. 1. Noise or garbled sounds heard on a telephone or other electronic receiver, caused by interference from another channel. 2. British. Exchange of repartee; witty conversation.

cross·tie (krôs'tī', krŏs'-) n. 1. A transverse beam or rod serving as a support or connection. 2. A wood, concrete, or metal beam that connects and supports the rails of a railroad.

cross·town (krôs'toun', krŏs'-) adj. Running across a city or town; specifically, running across the principal direction of traffic flow: a cross-town bus. —**cross·town** adv.

cross·tree (krôs'trē', krŏs'-) n. Nautical. Either of the two horizontal crosspieces at the upper ends of the lower masts in fore-and-aft-rigged vessels, serving to spread the shrouds.

cross·vine (krôs'vīn', krŏs'-) n. A woody vine, Bignonia capreolata, of the southeastern United States, having large, trumpet-shaped, reddish flowers. Also called "bignonia." [So called because a cross

crossbill The crossed tips of this bird's beak enable it to extract the seeds from pinecones. This is a male European crossbill, Loxia curvirostra.

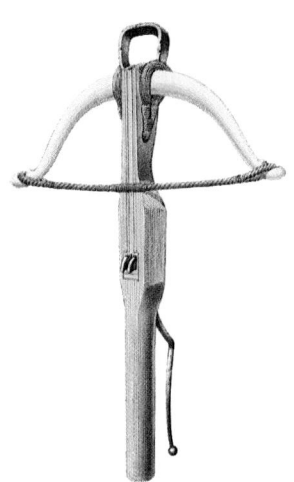

crossbow First developed in China before 200 B.C., these powerful weapons were introduced to Europe in the 10th century A.D. Their wooden or iron bolts could pierce chain mail at a range of more than 350 meters (400 yards), but they could not be reloaded as quickly as a longbow.

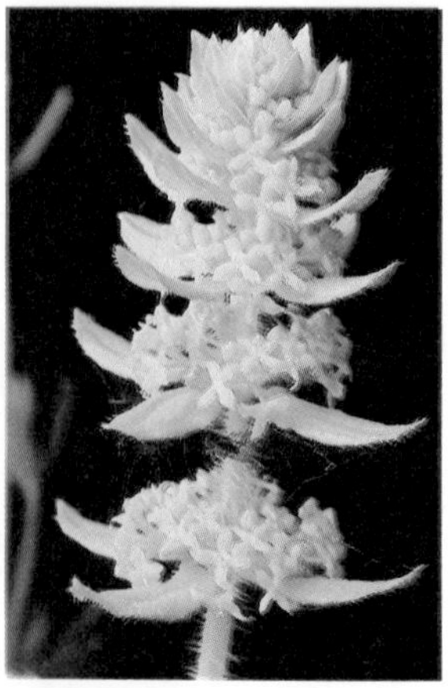

crosswort Galium cruciata, *the crosswort, is found in open woodland and hedgerows in Europe. Its honey-scented flowers grow in the angle between leaves and stem.*

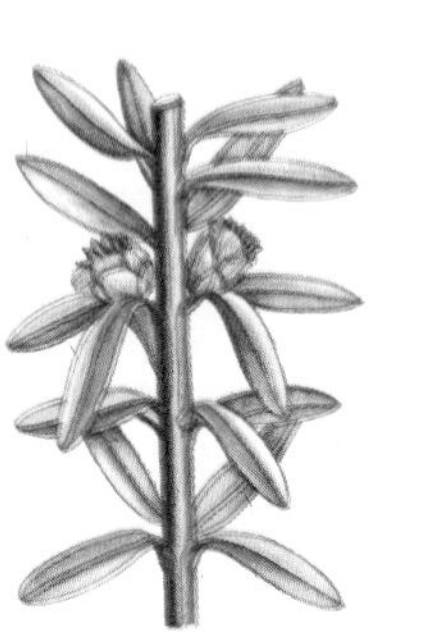

crowberry Empetrum nigrum, *the crowberry, grows throughout the Northern Hemisphere's cooler regions on boggy grasslands and mountain slopes. Its name may be derived from its edible black berries—the color of crows.*

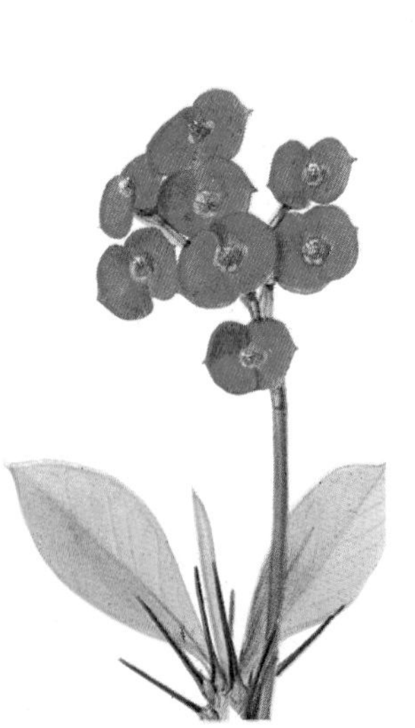

crown-of-thorns *The family Euphorbiaceae is one of the largest families of flowering plants. It includes both the tree from which rubber is harvested,* Hevea brasiliensis, *and this Madagascan plant, the crown-of-thorns* (Euphorbia splendens).

is found in a cross section of the stem.]

cross·way (krôs'wā', krŏs'-) *n.* A crossroad.

crossways. Variant of **crosswise.**

cross·wind (krôs'wĭnd', krŏs'-) *n.* A wind blowing more or less at right angles to a given direction, as to an aircraft's line of flight.

crosswise (krôs'wīz', krŏs'-) *adv.* Also **cross·ways** (-wāz'). Transversely; across; diagonally.

cross·word puzzle (krôs'wûrd', krŏs'-) *n.* A puzzle in which an arrangement of numbered squares has to be filled with words running across and down in answer to correspondingly numbered clues.

cross·wort (krôs'wôrt', krŏs'-) *n.* A herbaceous perennial plant, *Galium cruciata,* having small yellow flowers borne at the leaf bases.

crotch (krŏch) *n.* **1.** The angle, or region of the angle, formed by the junction of parts or members, as by two branches, limbs, steps, or legs. **2.** The fork of a pole or other support. [Perhaps a variant of Middle English and Old French *croche,* hook. See **crochet.**] —**crotched** *adj.*

crotch·et (krŏch'ĭt) *n.* **1.** A small hook or hooklike structure. **2.** An odd, whimsical, or stubborn notion. **3.** *Music.* A **quarter note** *(see).* [Middle English *crochet,* small hook, from Old French. See **crochet.**]

crotch·et·y (krŏch'ĭ-tē) *adj.* **1.** Irritable; snappish. **2.** Capriciously stubborn or eccentric; perverse. —**crotch·et·i·ness** *n.*

cro·ton (krōt'n) *n.* **1.** Any of various chiefly tropical plants, shrubs, or trees of the genus *Croton.* See **croton oil. 2.** Any of various tropical plants of the genus *Codiaeum;* especially, *C. variegatum pictum,* frequently grown as a house plant for its showy, varicolored foliage. [New Latin *Croton,* from Greek *krotōn*†.]

croton oil *n.* A yellowish-brown, violently cathartic oil obtained from the seeds of a tree, *Croton tiglium,* of southeastern Asia.

crouch (krouch) *v.* **crouched, crouching, crouches.** —*intr.* **1.** To bend low with the limbs pulled close to the body. **2.** To bend servilely or timidly; cringe. —*tr.* To cause to bend low, as in fear or humility.
∼*n.* The act or posture of crouching. [Middle English *cro(u)chen,* from Old French *crochir,* to be bent, from *croc(he),* a hook. See **crochet.**] —**crouch·ing·ly** *adv.*

croup[1] (kro͞op) *n.* A disorder affecting the throat in children, characterized by difficulty in breathing and a harsh cough and associated with inflammation and obstruction of the larynx. [Probably imitative of coughing.] —**croup·ous, croup·y** *adj.*

croup[2], **croupe** (kro͞op) *n.* The rump of certain animals, especially the horse. [Middle English *croupe,* from Old French, from Frankish *kruppa* (unattested).]

crou·pi·er (kro͞o'pē-ər, -pē-ā') *n.* An attendant at a gaming table who deals the cards and collects and pays bets. [French, originally "rider on the rump (behind a rider)," from *croupe,* rump, CROUP.]

crou·ton (kro͞o'tŏn', kro͞o-tŏn') *n.* A small crisp cube of toasted or fried bread, often served in soup. [French *croûton,* from *croûte,* crust, from Old French *crouste,* from Latin *crusta,* CRUST.]

crow[1] (krō) *n.* **1.** Any of several large, glossy, black birds of the genus *Corvus,* having a characteristic raucous call; especially, *C. brachyrhynchos,* of North America. **2.** Loosely, any similar bird. **3.** A crowbar. —**as the crow flies.** In a straight line. —**eat crow.** *Informal.* To be forced into a humiliating situation, as from having been in error. [Middle English *croue,* Old English *crāwe,* akin to *crāwan,* to CROW.]

crow[2] (krō) *intr.v.* **crowed** or **crew** (kro͞o) (for sense 1), **crowing, crows. 1.** To utter the shrill cry characteristic of a cock. **2. a.** To boast, especially over the misfortune of another. **b.** To exult. **3.** To make a sound expressive of pleasure or well-being, like that of a baby. —See Synonyms at **boast.**
∼*n.* **1.** The shrill cry of a cock. **2.** An inarticulate sound expressive of pleasure or delight. [Middle English *crouen,* Old English *crāwan* (imitative).]

Crow (krō) *n., pl.* **Crows. 1.** A member of a North American Indian people, formerly inhabiting the region between the Platte and Yellowstone rivers and now settled in southeastern Montana. **2.** The Siouan language of the Crow.

crow·bar (krō'bär') *n.* A straight bar of iron or steel, with the working end shaped like a forked chisel, used as a lever. Also called "crow." [From the resemblance of the forked end to a crow's foot.]

crow·ber·ry (krō'bĕr'ē) *n., pl.* **-ries. 1.** A low-growing evergreen shrub, *Empetrum nigrum,* of cool regions of the Northern Hemisphere, having small, purplish flowers and black, berrylike fruit. **2.** Any of several similar or related plants, such as the **bearberry** *(see).* **3.** The fruit of any of these plants.

crow blackbird *n.* The **grackle** *(see).*

crowd[1] (kroud) *n.* **1. a.** A large number of people gathered together; a throng. **b.** The mass of spectators, as at a football match. **2.** Ordinary people; people in general. Used with *the.* **3.** A specified social group; a clique: *the usual crowd; the arty crowd.* **4.** A large number of things grouped or considered together.
∼*v.* **crowded, crowding, crowds.** —*intr.* **1.** To throng; congregate closely. **2.** To advance by shoving. —*tr.* **1.** To press, cram, or force tightly together; compress. **2.** To fill or occupy to overflowing. **3.** *Informal.* To put pressure on; harass. —**crowd (on) sail.** *Nautical.* To spread a large amount of (sail) to increase speed. [Middle English *crouden, crowden,* to crowd, press, Old English *crūdan,* to hasten.] —**crowd·ed·ness** *n.* —**crowd·er** *n.*

crowd[2] (kroud, kro͝od) *n.* An ancient Celtic musical instrument, stringed and played with a bow. [Middle English *croud, crouth,* from Welsh *crwth.*]

crowd puller *n. Informal.* A very popular person, event, or the like, that is assured of a large audience.

crow·foot (krō'fo͝ot') *n., pl.* **-foots** (for senses 1, 2) or **-feet** (-fēt) (for sense 3). **1.** Any of various plants of the genus *Ranunculus,* related to the buttercups, such as *R. aquatilis* and *R. sceleratus,* having small, inconspicuous yellow flowers and divided leaves. **2.** Loosely, any of various other plants having leaves or other parts resembling a bird's foot. **3.** *Military.* A defensive device, **caltrop** *(see).* **4.** *Nautical.* **a.** A block used in supporting the middle section of an awning. **b.** A set of small lines passed through holes of a batten or fitting to help support the backbone of an awning.

crown (kroun) *n.* **1.** An ornamental circlet or head covering, often made of precious metal set with jewels, and worn as a symbol of sovereignty. **2.** The power, position, or empire of a monarch. **3. a.** A decorative garland or wreath worn on the head as a symbol of victory, honor, or distinction. **b.** A championship title in a sport: *Borg's fifth Wimbledon crown.* **4.** Distinction or reward for achievement: *the crown of martyrdom.* **5.** Anything resembling a crown in shape, such as a badge, emblem, or heraldic bearing. **6.** A coin stamped with a crown or crowned head on the reverse side. **7. a.** A former British coin worth 5 shillings (25 pence). **b.** Any of several European coins with a name that means crown, such as the koruna, krona, and krone. **8. a.** The top or highest part of the head. **b.** The head itself. **9.** The top or upper part of a hat. **10.** The highest point of anything, especially: **a.** The summit of a hill or mountain. **b.** The highest point of a curved structure or surface, such as an arch or a cambered road. **11.** The highest or most outstanding state or point; the culmination: *the crown of her athletic career.* **12.** The most outstanding attribute or exemplar; the chief ornament. **13.** *Dentistry.* **a.** The part of a tooth that is covered by enamel and projects beyond the gum line. **b.** A gold, porcelain, or plastic substitute for the natural crown of a tooth. **14.** The lowest part of the shank of an anchor, where the arms are joined to it. **15. a.** The upper part of a tree, including the leaves and living branches. **b.** The part of a plant, usually at ground level, between the root and the stem. **c.** A flower part, the **corona** *(see).* **16.** The crest of an animal, especially of a bird. **17.** The portion of a cut gem above the girdle. —**the Crown. 1.** The monarch as the head of state or sovereign governing power. **2.** The power, position, or empire of a monarch.
∼*tr.v.* **crowned, crowning, crowns. 1.** To put a crown or garland upon the head of. **2.** To invest with regal power; make a monarch of; enthrone. **3.** To confer honor, dignity, or reward on. **4. a.** To cover or occupy the top of. **b.** To surmount or be the highest part of. **5.** To form the crown, top, or chief ornament of. **6.** To bring to completion or successful conclusion; complete; consummate. **7.** To put a crown on (a tooth). **8.** In checkers, to make (a piece that has reached the last row) into a king by placing another piece upon it. **9.** *Informal.* To hit on the head. [Middle English *crowne, coroune,* from Old French *corone,* from Latin *corōna,* garland, from Greek *korōnē,* anything curved, from *korōnos,* curved.] —**crown** *adj.*

crown canopy *n.* The canopy or cover formed by the upper branches of trees in a forest. Also called "crown cover."

crown cap *n.* An airtight bottle top for beer and soft drink bottles, consisting of a lined metal disk with its edge crimped over the mouth of the bottle.

crown colony *n.* A British colony in which the sovereign has control of legislation, usually administered by an appointed governor.

Crown Derby *n.* A fine porcelain, marked with a crown, made in Derby, England, in the late 18th and early 19th centuries.

crown gall *n.* A disease of plants caused by a bacterium, *Agrobacterium tumefaciens,* and characterized by warty, usually woody growths on roots and stems, especially near the soil line.

crown glass *n.* **1.** A clear soda-lime-silica optical glass with low refraction. Compare **flint glass. 2.** A form of window glass made by whirling a glass bubble to make a flat circular disk with a lump in the center formed by the craftsman's rod. —**crown-glass** *adj.*

crown graft *n.* A horticultural graft in which the scion is grafted onto the crown of the stock.

crown imperial *n.* A garden plant, *Fritillaria imperialis,* with a terminal cluster of orange bell-shaped flowers.

crown jewels *pl.n.* The jewels belonging to the regalia of a sovereign or royal family, used on state occasions.

crown lens *n.* The crown-glass element in an achromatic lens.

crown-of-thorns (kroun'əv-thôrnz') *n.* **1.** A spiny, vinelike desert plant, *Euphorbia splendens* (or *E.milii*), often grown as a potted plant for its flowers, which have scarlet bracts. **2.** A starfish, *Acanthaster planci,* that is covered with spines and feeds on living coral.

crown prince *n.* The male heir apparent to a throne.

crown princess *n.* **1.** The wife of a crown prince. **2.** A female heir apparent to a throne.

crown roast *n.* Two or more rib sections of veal, pork, or especially lamb, secured together at the ends to form a circle and roasted.

crown saw *n.* A cylindrical saw with teeth on the bottom edge of the cylinder.

crow's-foot (krōz'fo͝ot') *n., pl.* **-feet** (-fēt'). **1. crow's-feet.** The wrinkles at the outer corner of the eye, common in many adults. **2.** A three-pointed embroidery stitch used as finishing, as at the end of a seam. **3.** The set of ropes or strands of a rope attached to a single rope, used in sailing, ballooning, and the like.

crow's-nest (krōz'nĕst') *n.* **1.** A small lookout platform with a high protective railing and wind screen, located near the top of a ship's mast. **2.** Any similar lookout platform located ashore.

Croy·don (kroid′n). Borough of Greater London since 1965; it was formerly an important market town in Surrey.

croze (krōz) *n.* **1.** The groove at the ends of the staves of a barrel or cask into which the head is set. **2.** A cooper's tool, used as a plane, for making this groove. [French *creux*, from Old French *crues*, socket, groove, perhaps from Gallo-Roman *crosus*† (unattested).]

crozier. Variant of **crosier.**

CRT cathode-ray tube.

cru (krōō) *n.* A wine produced by certain superior French vineyards. [French, growth, from *crû*, past participle of *croître*, to grow.]

cru·ces. Alternate plural of **crux.**

cru·cial (krōō′shəl) *adj.* **1.** Of supreme importance in determining an outcome; critical; decisive: *a crucial election.* **2.** *Informal.* Very important or significant. **3.** Having the form of a cross; cross-shaped. —See Synonyms at **critical.** [French, from Latin *crux* (stem *cruc-*), CROSS.] —**cru·cial·ly** *adv.*

cru·ci·ate (krōō′shē-āt′) *adj.* **1.** Cross-shaped. **2.** Overlapping or crossing, as the wings of some insects when at rest. [New Latin *cruciatus*, from Latin *crux*, CROSS.]

cru·ci·ble (krōō′sə-bəl) *n.* **1.** A vessel made of a refractory substance, such as graphite or porcelain, used for melting and calcining materials at high temperatures. **2.** The bottom of an ore furnace, in which the molten metal collects. **3.** A severe test or trial. [Middle English *crusible*, from Medieval Latin *crucibulum*, perhaps originally a lamp kept burning in front of a crucifix, from Latin *crux*, CROSS.]

crucible steel *n.* A high-grade steel made by fusing low-carbon steel with charcoal or cast iron in a graphite crucible and used in tools and dies.

cru·ci·fer (krōō′sə-fər) *n.* **1.** One who bears a cross in a religious procession. **2.** *Botany.* Any plant of the family Cruciferae, such as a mustard or cress, having four-petaled flowers suggestive of a cross. [Late Latin : Latin *crux*, CROSS + -FER.] —**cru·cif·er·ous** *adj.*

cru·ci·fix (krōō′sə-fĭks′) *n.* A cross with an image of Christ on it. [Middle English, from Old French, from Late Latin *crucifixus*, from the past participle of *crucifigere*, CRUCIFY.]

cru·ci·fix·ion (krōō′sə-fĭk′shən) *n.* **1.** The action of putting to death on a cross. **2.** A representation, as in painting or carving, of Christ on the Cross. —**the Crucifixion.** The crucifying of Christ on Calvary.

cru·ci·form (krōō′sə-fôrm′) *adj.* Cross-shaped.
~*n.* A cross-shaped geometric curve having four branches forming similar asymptotes with two mutually perpendicular pairs of lines. [Latin *crux* (stem *cruc-*), CROSS + -FORM.]

cru·ci·fy (krōō′sə-fī′) *tr.v.* **-fied, -fying, -fies.** **1.** To put to death by nailing or binding to a cross. **2.** To mortify or subdue (the passions, for example). **3.** To torment; torture, especially mentally. **4. a.** *Slang.* To defeat overwhelmingly, as in a sporting contest. **b.** *Informal.* To criticize or ridicule mercilessly. [Middle English *crucifien*, from Old French *crucifier*, from Late Latin *crucifigere* : Latin *crux* (stem *cruc-*), CROSS + *figere*, to fasten.] —**cru·ci·fi·er** *n.*

cruck (krŭk) *n.* *Architecture.* Either of a pair of sloping timbers, often curved, that help support a roof. [19th century : variant of CROOK (noun).]

crud (krŭd) *n.* *Slang.* **1.** A coating or incrustation of filth or refuse. **2.** A contemptible or disgusting person or thing. **3.** Nonsense; rubbish. **4.** Any disease, imaginary or real, especially one affecting the skin. [Middle English *crudde*, CURD.] —**crud·dy** *adj.*

crude (krōōd) *adj.* **cruder, crudest.** **1.** In an unrefined or natural state; raw. **2.** *Archaic.* Unripe; immature. **3.** Lacking finish, tact, or polish. **4.** Not carefully, skillfully, or completely made; rough. **5.** *Statistics.* Not corrected, analyzed, or tabulated. Said of data. **6.** Undisguised or unadorned; blunt. **7.** Offensive and tasteless; vulgar.
~*n.* **Crude oil** *(see).* [Middle English, from Latin *crūdus*, bloody, raw.] —**crude·ly** *adv.* —**crude·ness, cru·di·ty** *n.*

crude oil *n.* **Petroleum** *(see)* in its unrefined state.

cru·el (krōō′əl) *adj.* **-eler** or **-eller, -elest** or **-ellest.** **1.** Disposed to inflict pain or suffering. **2.** Causing suffering; painful: *a cruel hoax.* [Middle English, from Old French, from Latin *crūdēlis*, morally unfeeling, cruel; akin to *crūdus*, bloody, CRUDE.] —**cru·el·ly** *adv.*
Synonyms: *barbarous, ferocious, inhuman, pitiless, ruthless, sadistic, vicious.*

cru·el·ty (krōō′əl-tē) *n., pl.* **-ties.** **1.** The quality or condition of being cruel. **2.** Something that causes pain or suffering, such as a cruel action or remark. **3.** *Law.* Behavior that damages or endangers the physical or mental health of a spouse and constitutes grounds for divorce.

cru·et (krōō′ĭt) *n.* **1. a.** A small glass bottle for holding vinegar or oil. **b.** A small container for other condiments, such as a saltcellar, a pepperbox, or a mustard bowl. **2.** A pair or set of cruets, often on a tray or rack. **3.** Either of two small vessels used for wine and water at the Eucharist. [Middle English, from Norman French *cruet*, diminutive of Old French *crue*, flask, from Germanic.]

Cruik·shank (krŏŏk′shangk), **George** (1792–1878). British caricaturist and illustrator, best remembered for his illustrations of Dickens and other novelists. His own collections include his *Comic Almanack* (1835–53).

cruise (krōōz) *v.* **cruised, cruising, cruises.** —*intr.* **1.** To sail or travel about, as for pleasure or reconnaissance. **2.** To travel at a speed (*cruising speed*) that provides maximum operating efficiency

for a sustained period. **3.** *Informal.* To wander about the street, frequent bars, and so on, in search of a sexual partner. —*tr.* **1.** To cruise or journey over. **2.** *Slang.* To appraise sexually.
~*n.* A sea voyage for pleasure, usually in a liner stopping at numerous ports. [Perhaps Dutch *kruisen*, to sail to and fro, from Middle Dutch *crucen*, to cross, from *crūce*, a cross, from Latin *crux*, CROSS.]

cruise missile *n.* A subsonic, long-range guided missile armed with a nuclear warhead, which can fly low toward its target to avoid radar detection and which uses inbuilt computerized navigation equipment.

cruis·er (krōō′zər) *n.* **1.** One that cruises. **2.** Any of a class of fast warships of medium tonnage with a long cruising radius and less armor and firepower than a battleship. **3.** A large motorboat whose cabin is equipped with living facilities. Also called "cabin cruiser," "cruising yacht." **4.** *Informal.* A police **squad car** *(see).*

cruising radius *n.* The longest distance a ship or aircraft can go

cruck *A wooden frame used in medieval house building. The crucks form a supporting triangle from the roof ridge to the outer walls.*

crow

THE WORLDWIDE SUCCESS OF CROWS
One family with 100 thriving branches

Crows are found throughout the world in a wide range of habitats. They are large birds, up to 660 millimeters (26 inches) long, with rounded bills and usually black, glossy plumage. Often they are recognized by their harsh call, or caw. They are omnivorous. The crow family, Corvidae, has about 100 species. Of these 30 belong to the genus *Corvus*, the most common being the carrion crow of Eurasia and the American crow. The common name of 18 other *Corvus* species includes the word crow, but the rook, jackdaw, and raven also belong to the genus *Corvus*. The magpie and jay are close relatives from other branches of the vast Corvidae family.

JACKDAW
Corvus monedula

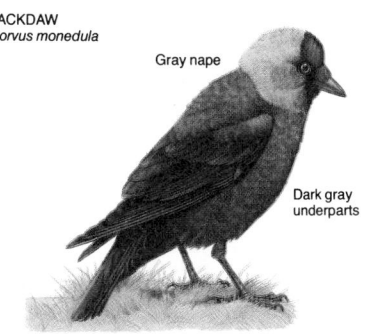

Gray nape

Dark gray underparts

Distinguished by its white iris and gray nape, the jackdaw is small, only 330 millimeters (13 inches) long, and a skilled aerobat. Its reputation as a thief is exaggerated: it is less likely than other crows to rob the nests of other birds.

RAVEN
Corvus corax

Stout bill

Shaggy throat feathers

Glossy black plumage

Wordsworth's "blithe croakers of death" were so long persecuted for pecking at corpses on the gibbet that ravens have retreated to the wilds. These—the largest of the world's perching birds, 660 millimeters (26 inches) long—feed on carrion but also hunt and forage.

CARRION CROW
Corvus corone corone

Heavy rounded bill

Glossy black plumage

ROOK
Corvus frugilegus

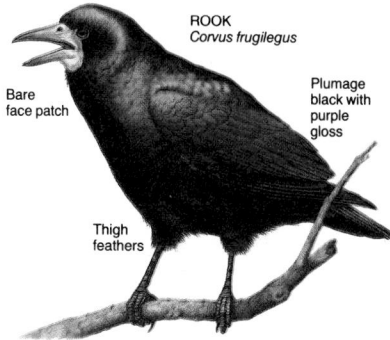

Bare face patch

Plumage black with purple gloss

Thigh feathers

Migrating from woodlands, carrion crows make their homes in cities and suburbs, scavenging on refuse and nesting on posts and pylons as well as in trees. They feed on grain and root crops and on the eggs and young of other birds. Length: 470 millimeters (18 inches).

Unlike crows, which nest alone, rooks live gregariously in rookeries consisting of anything from a few to several thousand nests, built usually in clusters of trees. A native of farmland, the rook is 460 millimeters (18 inches) long and distinguished by a bare face patch.

and return at cruising speed without refueling.

crul·ler (krŭl′ər) *n.* A small cake of sweet dough fried in deep fat, usually ring-shaped or twisted. [Dutch *krulle*, from *krullen*, to curl, from *krul*, curly, from Middle Dutch *crulle*.]

crumb (krŭm) *n.* **1.** A small piece broken or fallen from cake, bread, or other baked goods. **2.** Any small fragment or scrap. **3.** The soft inner portion of bread. Compare **crust. 4.** *Slang.* A contemptible, untrustworthy, or loathsome person.
—*v.* **crumbed, crumbing, crumbs.** —*tr.* **1.** To break into small pieces or crumbs; crumble. **2.** In cookery, to cover or prepare with breadcrumbs; bread. —*intr.* To break apart in crumbs. [Middle English *crome*, Old English *cruma*.]

crum·ble (krŭm′bəl) *v.* **-bled, -bling, -bles.** —*tr.* To break or cause to break into small parts or crumbs. —*intr.* To fall into tiny pieces; disintegrate. —See Synonyms at **decay.**
—*n. British.* A baked dessert of stewed fruit topped with a sweet, crumblike mixture of flour, fat, and sugar. [Earlier *crimble*, from Middle English *cremelen*, perhaps from Old English *gecrymian*, from *cruma*, CRUMB.]

crum·bly (krŭm′blē) *adj.* **-blier, -bliest.** Easily crumbled.

crum·horn, krumm·horn (krŭm′hôrn′) *n.* A medieval musical instrument, with a deep pitch, curving tube, and double reed. [From German *Krummhorn*, "carved horn."]

crum·mie (krŭm′ē) *n. Scottish.* A cow with crooked horns. [From Scottish *crum(b)*, crooked, Middle English *croumb*, Old English *crumb*.]

crum·my (krŭm′ē) *adj.* **-mier, -miest.** Also **crumb·y, -ier, -iest.** *Slang.* Inferior, worthless, or unpleasant. [From CRUMB.]

crump (krŭmp) *v.* **crumped, crumping, crumps.** —*tr.* **1.** To crush or crunch with the teeth. **2.** To bombard or strike heavily with a crunching or thudding sound. —*intr.* To make a crunching sound.
—*n.* **1.** A crunching sound. **2.** The sound of a bomb or shell exploding [Imitative.]

crum·pet (krŭm′pĭt) *n. Chiefly British.* **1.** A light, round teacake with holes in the top, made from a yeast batter, which is poured into special rings *(crumpet rings)* and cooked on one side on a heated baking sheet or a griddle and often toasted. **2.** *Slang.* Women collectively when considered sexually attractive. [Probably from Middle English *crompid (cake)*, "curled cake," from *crampen, crumpen*, to curl, from *crump, crumb*, crooked, Old English *crump*.]

crum·ple (krŭm′pəl) *v.* **-pled, -pling, -ples.** —*tr.* **1.** To crush together or press into wrinkles; rumple. —*intr.* **1.** To become wrinkled; shrivel. Often used with *up.* **2.** To collapse; break down.
—*n.* An irregular fold, crease, or wrinkle. [Frequentative of obsolete *crump*, to curl up, from Middle English *crampen*. See **crumpet.**]

crunch (krŭnch) *v.* **crunched, crunching, crunches.** —*tr.* **1.** To chew with a noisy crackling sound. **2.** To crush, grind, or walk on noisily. —*intr.* **1.** To chew noisily with a crackling sound. **2.** To move with a crushing sound. **3.** To produce a crushing sound.
—*n.* **1.** The act or sound of crunching. **2. a.** A decisive confrontation. **b.** A critical situation.
—*adj.* Decisively important; crucial: *a crunch issue.* [Earlier *craunch* (imitative), assimilated to *munch*.]

crup·per (krŭp′ər) *n.* **1.** A leather strap looped under a horse's tail and attached to a harness or saddle to keep it from slipping forward. **2.** The rump of a horse. [Middle English *crouper, cropier*, from Old French *cropiere*, from *croupe*, rump, CROUP.]

cru·ral (krŏŏr′əl) *adj.* Of or pertaining to the leg, shank, or thigh. [Latin *crūrālis*, from *crūs* (stem *crūr-*), leg, CRUS.]

crus (krŏŏs, krŭs) *n., pl.* **crura** (krŏŏr′ə). **1.** The section of the leg or hind limb between the knee and foot; the shank. **2.** A leglike part. [Latin *crūs*†, leg.]

cru·sade (krŏŏ-sād′) *n.* **1.** Often **Crusade. a.** Any of the military expeditions undertaken by European Christians in the 11th, 12th, and 13th centuries to recover the Holy Land from the Muslims. **b.** Any holy war undertaken with papal sanction: *the Albigensian Crusade.* **2.** Any vigorous concerted movement for a cause or against an abuse.
—*intr.v.* **crusaded, -sading, -sades.** To engage in a crusade. [Earlier forms: (a) *croisade*, from Old French, variant of *croisée*, from the past participle of *croiser*, to bear the cross, from *crois*, cross, from Latin *crux*; (b) *crusado*, from Spanish *cruzada*, from *cruzar*, to bear the cross, from *cruz*, cross, from Latin *crux*, CROSS.] —**crusad·er** *n.*

cruse (krŏŏz, krŏŏs) *n.* A small jar or pot for holding water, wine, or oil. [Middle English *crouse*, perhaps from Middle Dutch *cruyse*, pot.]

crush (krŭsh) *v.* **crushed, crushing, crushes.** —*tr.* **1.** To press between opposing bodies so as to break, injure, or damage. **2. a.** To obtain juice from (a fruit). **b.** To obtain (juice) by crushing fruit thus. **3.** To crumple or rumple. **4.** To break, pound, or grind into small fragments or powder. **5.** To press upon, shove, or crowd. **6.** To put down; subdue. **7.** To overwhelm or humiliate, as in an argument or contest. **8.** To oppress severely: *Debt was crushing them.* —*intr.* **1.** To be or become crushed. **2.** To proceed or move by crowding or pressing. —See Synonyms at **break.**
—*n.* **1.** The act of crushing; extreme pressure. **2.** The state of being crushed. **3.** A great crowd or throng. **4.** A drink prepared from crushed fruit, or one made to taste like this. **5.** *Informal.* **a.** An infatuation. Usually used with *on.* **b.** The person who is the object of such an infatuation. [Middle English *crushen*, from Old French *croissir*, probably from Vulgar Latin *cruscīre*† (unattested).]
—**crush·a·ble** *adj.* —**crush·er** *n.*

crush barrier *n. Chiefly British.* A safety barrier, often temporary, used to hold back a crowd.

Crusoe, Robinson. See **Robinson Crusoe.**

crust (krŭst) *n.* **1.** The hard outer portion or surface area of bread. Compare **crumb. 2.** A piece of bread consisting mostly of this part. **3.** A pastry shell, as of a pie or tart. **4.** Any hard, crisp covering or surface. **5.** A hard deposit produced by maturing wine on the interior of bottles. **6. a.** *Geology.* The solid exterior portion of the earth that lies above the Mohorovičić discontinuity. **b.** The outermost solid layer of a planet or moon. **7.** The hard outer covering or integument of certain plants and animals, such as lichens and crustaceans. **8.** *Pathology.* A coating or dry outer layer, as of pus or blood; a scab. **9.** *Informal.* Insolence; audacity; gall.
—*v.* **crusted, crusting, crusts.** —*tr.* **1.** To cover with a crust; encrust. **2.** To form (dough) into a crust. —*intr.* **1.** To become covered with a crust. **2.** To harden into a crust. [Middle English *cruste*, from Old French *crouste*, from Latin *crusta*†, shell.]

crus·ta·cean (krŭ-stā′shən) *n.* Any of various predominantly aquatic arthropods of the class Crustacea, including lobsters, crabs, shrimps, and wood lice, characteristically having a segmented body, a chitinous exoskeleton, and paired, jointed limbs. [From New Latin *crustacea*, "the shelled ones," from *crustaceus*, CRUSTACEOUS.] —**crus·ta·cean** *adj.*

crus·ta·ceous (krŭ-stā′shəs) *adj.* **1.** Having, resembling, or constituting a hard crust or shell. **2.** Crustacean. [New Latin *crustaceus* : Latin *crusta*, shell, CRUST + -ACEOUS.]

crus·tal (krŭs′təl) *adj.* Of or pertaining to a crust, especially that of the earth or the moon.

crust·y (krŭs′tē) *adj.* **-ier, -iest. 1.** Like or having a crust. **2.** Surly or short-tempered. —See Synonyms at **gruff.** —**crust·i·ness** *n.*

crutch (krŭch) *n.* **1.** A staff or support used by the lame or infirm as an aid in walking, usually having a crosspiece to fit under the armpit and often used in pairs. **2.** Any device similar to this in form or function. **3.** A forked support for the boom of a sailing vessel when the sails are furled. **4.** Anything or anyone depended upon for support; a prop. **5.** The human crotch.
—*tr.v.* **crutched, crutching, crutches.** To support on or as on crutches. [Middle English *crucche*, Old English *crycc*, from Germanic.]

crux (krŭks, krŏŏks) *n., pl.* **cruxes** or **cruces** (krŏŏ′sēz). **1.** A crucial or vital moment; a critical point. **2.** The basic or essential feature: *the crux of our argument.* **3.** A puzzling problem. [Latin, CROSS.]

Crux (krŭks) *n.* A constellation in the Southern Hemisphere near Centaurus and Musca. Also called "Southern Cross."

crux an·sa·ta (ăn-sā′tə) *n.* An ansate cross *(see).*

cru·zei·ro (krŏŏ-zā′rō, -rŏŏ) *n., pl.* **-ros. 1.** The basic monetary unit of Brazil, equal to 100 centavos. **2.** A coin worth one cruzeiro. [Portuguese, "(coin) bearing the figure of a cross," from *cruz*, cross, from Latin *crux*, CROSS.]

cry (krī) *v.* **cried, crying, cries.** —*intr.* **1.** To make inarticulate sobbing sounds expressing grief, sorrow, or pain. **2.** To produce moisture from the eyes; shed tears; weep. **3.** To call aloud; shout. Often used with *out.* **4.** To utter a characteristic sound or call. Used of an animal. **5.** To withdraw from an undertaking or back out of an agreement or promise. Used with *off.* —*tr.* **1.** To utter loudly. **2.** To proclaim or announce (especially goods for sale) in public. **3.** To beg for; beseech; implore: *cry forgiveness.* **4. a.** To bring into a specified condition by weeping: *cry oneself to sleep.* **b.** To weep or shed (tears). **5.** To belittle or disparage. Used with *down.* **6.** To break or withdraw from a promise, agreement, or undertaking. Used with *off.* **7.** To praise highly; extol. Used with *up.* —**cry out for.** To be in urgent need of; demand.
—*n., pl.* **cries. 1.** A loud utterance of some emotion, such as fear or anger. **2.** Any loud exclamation or utterance; a shout; a call. **3.** A fit of weeping. **4.** An urgent entreaty or appeal. **5.** A public or general demand or complaint; a clamor; an outcry. **6.** An advertising of wares by calling out. **7.** A rallying call or signal as in a battle or election campaign. **8.** A political slogan. **9.** The characteristic call or utterance of an animal or bird. **9.** A pack of hounds. —**a far cry. 1.** A very different state of affairs. **2.** A long way. —**in full cry.** In hot pursuit, as hounds hunting. [Middle English *crien*, from Old French *crier*, from Latin *quirītāre*, to cry out, to implore the aid of the citizens, from *Quirītēs*, plural of *Quirīs*†, a Roman citizen.]
Synonyms: blubber, moan, sob, wail, weep, whimper.

cry·ba·by (krī′bā′bē) *n., pl.* **-bies.** A person who cries or complains frequently with little cause.

cry·ing (krī′ĭng) *adj.* Demanding or requiring immediate action or remedy: *a crying shame; a crying need.*

crymotherapy. Variant of **cryotherapy.**

cryo– *prefix.* Indicates cold, freezing, or frost; for example, **cryometer.** [From Greek *kruos*†, icy cold, frost.]

cry·o·bi·ol·o·gy (krī′ō-bī-ŏl′ə-jē) *n.* The study of the effects of very low temperatures on living organisms.

cry·o·gen (krī′ə-jən) *n.* A refrigerant used to obtain very low temperatures. [CRYO- + -GEN.]

cry·o·gen·ics (krī′ə-jĕn′ĭks) *n.* The science of low-temperature phenomena. [From CRYO- + -GENIC.] —**cry·o·gen·ic** *adj.*

cry·o·lite (krī′ə-līt′) *n.* A white, vitreous natural fluoride of aluminum and sodium, Na_3AlF_6, used chiefly as an electrolyte in aluminum refining and in the production of glass, enamel, and ceramics. Also called "Greenland spar." [CRYO- + -LITE.]

cry·om·e·ter (krī-ŏm′ə-tər) *n.* A thermometer capable of measuring very low temperatures. [CRYO- + -METER.]

cry·on·ics (krī-ŏn′ĭks) *n. Used with a singular verb.* The process of freezing and storing a dead human body to prevent tissue decomposition so that at some time in the future the individual might be brought back to life when new medical cures have been developed. [CRY(O)- + *-onics*, as in *bionics.*] —**cry·on·ic** *adj.*

cry·o·plank·ton (krī′ō-plangk′tən) *n. Biology.* Minute organisms living in snow, ice, or perpetually icy waters.

cry·o·scope (krī′ə-skōp′) *n.* An instrument used to measure the freezing point of a substance. [Back-formation from CRYOSCOPY.]

cry·os·co·py (krī-ŏs′kə-pē) *n.* The study of the freezing points of solutions. [CRYO- + -SCOPY.] —**cry·o·scop·ic** (krī′ə-skŏp′ĭk) *adj.*

cry·o·stat (krī′ə-stăt′) *n.* An apparatus used to maintain constant low temperature. [CRYO- + -STAT.]

cry·o·sur·ger·y (krī′ō-sûr′jə-rē) *n.* Surgery performed by local or general application of extreme cold to destroy unwanted tissue.

cry·o·ther·a·py (krī′ō-thĕr′ə-pē) *n.* Also **cry·mo·ther·a·py** (krī′mō-). The use of low temperatures in medical therapy.

cry·o·tron *n.* A small electronic switch that is based on the phenomenon of superconductivity. It works at the temperature of liquid helium, switching the conducting wire from a superconducting state to a nonsuperconducting state. [CRYO- + -TRON.]

crypt (krĭpt) *n.* **1.** An underground vault or chamber, especially one beneath a church that is used as a burial place. **2.** *Anatomy.* Any of various small pits, recesses, glandular cavities, or follicles in the body. [Latin *crypta,* from Greek *kruptē,* from *kruptos,* hidden, from *kruptein,* to hide.]

cryp·ta·nal·y·sis (krĭp′tə-năl′ə-sĭs) *n., pl.* **-ses** (-sēz). The analysis and deciphering of cryptograms, ciphers, codes, or other secret writings. [CRYPT(OGRAM) + ANALYSIS.] —**cryp·tan·a·lyst** *n.* —**cryp·tan·a·lyt·ic** *adj.*

cryp·tes·the·sia (krĭp′təs-thē′zhə, -zhē-ə) *n. Psychology.* A term describing the various modes of supposed paranormal perception, such as clairvoyance. [New Latin : CRYPT(O)- + ESTHESIA.]

cryp·tic (krĭp′tĭk) *adj.* Also **cryp·ti·cal** (-tĭ-kəl). **1.** Hidden; concealed. **2. a.** Mysterious; enigmatic. **b.** Intentionally obscure. **3.** Having esoteric or hidden meaning; mystifying. **4.** *Biology.* Tending to conceal or camouflage: *cryptic coloring.* [Late Latin *crypticus,* from Greek *kruptikos,* from *kruptos,* hidden. See **crypt.**]

crypto-, crypt- *prefix.* Indicates hidden or secret; for example, **cryptoclastic.** [New Latin, from Greek *kruptos,* hidden, from *kruptein,* to hide.]

cryp·to·clas·tic (krĭp′tō-klăs′tĭk) *adj.* Composed of microscopic fragments. Said of rocks.

cryp·to·crys·tal·line (krĭp′tō-krĭs′tə-lĭn) *adj.* Having a microscopic crystalline structure. Said of rocks and minerals.

cryp·to·gam (krĭp′tə-găm′) *n. Botany.* In former classification systems, any of the flowerless and seedless plants that reproduce by spores, such as fungi, algae, mosses, and ferns. Compare **phanerogam.** [French *cryptogame,* from New Latin *cryptogamia* : CRYPTO- + -GAMY.] —**cryp·to·gam·ic, cryp·tog·a·mous** *adj.*

cryp·to·gen·ic (krĭp′tə-jĕn′ĭk) *adj.* Also **cryp·tog·e·nous** (krĭp-tŏj′ə-nəs). Of obscure or unknown origin. Said of diseases.

cryp·to·gram (krĭp′tə-grăm′) *n.* **1.** Something written in code or cipher; a cryptograph. **2.** A figure having a secret or occult significance. [French *cryptogramme* : CRYPTO- + -GRAM (written).] —**cryp·to·gram·mic** *adj.*

cryp·to·graph (krĭp′tə-grăf′, -gräf′) *n.* **1.** A cryptogram. **2.** A system of secret or cipher writing; a cipher. **3. a.** A device for translating plain text into cipher. **b.** A device for deciphering codes and ciphers. [Back-formation from CRYPTOGRAPHY.]

cryp·tog·ra·phy (krĭp-tŏg′rə-fē) *n.* **1.** The art or process of writing in or deciphering secret code. **2.** Any system of secret writing. [New Latin *cryptographia* : CRYPTO- + -GRAPHY.] —**cryp·tog·ra·pher, cryp·tog·ra·phist** *n.* —**cryp·to·graph·ic** *adj.* —**cryp·to·graph·i·cal·ly** *adv.*

cryp·tol·o·gy (krĭp-tŏl′ə-jē) *n.* **1.** The study of the use of secret codes or ciphers; cryptography. **2.** Cryptanalysis. [CRYPTO- + -LOGY.]

cryp·to·me·ri·a (krĭp′tə-mîr′ē-ə) *n.* An evergreen tree, *Cryptomeria japonica,* native to Japan, having short, inward-curving needles and soft, durable, fragrant wood. Also called "Japanese cedar." [New Latin : CRYPTO- + Greek *meros,* part, -MERE.]

cryp·to·nym (krĭp′tə-nĭm′) *n.* A secret name. [French *cryptonyme* : CRYPT(O)- + -ONYM.] —**cryp·ton·y·mous** (krĭp-tŏn′ə-məs) *adj.*

crypt·or·chism (krĭp-tôr′kĭz′əm) *n.* Also **crypt·or·chi·dism** (-kĭ-dĭz′əm). The condition of the testes failing to descend into the scrotum at puberty. [CRYPTO- + Greek *orkhis* (stem *orchid-*), testicle + -ISM.]

cryp·to·zo·ite (krĭp′tə-zō′īt′) *n.* A sporozoite such as a malarial parasite as it exists in its host's tissues prior to invasion of the red blood cells. [CRYPTO- + (SPORO)ZOITE.]

cryst. **1.** crystalline. **2.** crystallography.

crys·tal (krĭs′təl) *n.* **1. a.** A three-dimensional atomic, ionic, or molecular structure consisting of periodically repeated, identically constituted, congruent unit cells. **b.** The unit cell of such a structure. **2.** A body, such as a piece of quartz, having such a structure, often characterized by external planar faces visible without magnification. **3.** An oscillator, detector, or other electronic device based on crystalline piezoelectricity, magnetism, semiconductivity, or other electric properties. **4. a.** A high-quality clear, colorless glass. **b.** An object, especially a vessel or ornament, made of such glass. **c.** Such objects collectively. **5.** A clear glass or plastic protective cover for the face of a watch or clock.

~*adj.* **1.** Of, pertaining to, made of, or based on crystal. **2.** Desig-

nating an electronic device operated by a crystal. **3.** Clear; transparent. [Middle English *cristal,* from Old French, from Latin *crystallum,* rock crystal, crystal, from Greek *krustallos†.*]

crystal ball *n.* A glass globe used in crystal gazing.

crystal counter *n.* A high-energy radiation detector in which particles strike a crystal, causing a brief increase in conductivity.

crystal detector *n.* A rectifying detector used especially in early radio receivers and consisting of a semiconducting crystal in point contact with a fine metal wire.

crystal gazing *n.* A foretelling or attempt to foretell the future by or as if by seeing future events in a crystal ball. —**crystal gazer** *n.*

crystall. crystallography.

crystallo-. Variant of **crystallo-.**

crystal lattice *n.* A regular network of fixed points about which the ions, atoms, or molecules forming a crystal vibrate.

crys·tal·lif·er·ous (krĭs′tə-lĭf′ər-əs) *adj.* Also **crys·tal·lig·er·ous** (-lĭj′ər-əs). Producing or containing crystals.

crys·tal·line (krĭs′tə-lĭn) *adj.* **1.** *Abbr.* **cryst.** Pertaining to or made of crystal or crystals. **2.** Pertaining to crystals or their structure. **3.** Resembling crystal; transparent. [Middle English *cristalin,* from Old French, from Latin *crystallinus,* from Greek *krustallinos,* from *krustallos,* CRYSTAL.] —**crys·tal·lin·i·ty** *n.*

crystalline lens *n.* The **lens** (see) of the vertebrate eye.

crys·tal·lite (krĭs′tə-līt′) *n.* Any of numerous minute rudimentary, crystalline bodies found in glassy igneous rocks. [German *Kristallit* : CRYSTALL(O)- + -ITE.] —**crys·tal·lit·ic** (krĭs′tə-lĭt′ĭk) *adj.*

crys·tal·lize (krĭs′tə-līz′) *v.* -lized, -lizing, -lizes. —*tr.* **1.** To cause to form crystals or to assume a crystalline structure. **2.** To give a definite and permanent form to. **3.** To coat with sugar. —*intr.* **1.** To assume a crystalline form. **2.** To take on a definite and permanent form. [CRYSTALL(O)- + -IZE.] —**crys·tal·liz·a·bil·i·ty** *n.* —**crys·tal·liz·a·ble** *adj.* —**crys·tal·li·za·tion** *n.* —**crys·tal·liz·er** *n.*

crystallo-, crystall- *prefix.* Indicates crystal; for example, **crystallography, crystalloid.** [Greek *krustallos,* CRYSTAL.]

crys·tal·log·ra·phy (krĭs′tə-lŏg′rə-fē) *n. Abbr.* **cryst., crystall.** The science of the structure, form, and properties of crystals. [French *crystallographie,* from New Latin *crystallographia* : CRYSTALLO- + -GRAPHY.] —**crys·tal·log·ra·pher** *n.* —**crys·tal·lo·graph·ic, crys·tal·lo·graph·i·cal** *adj.* —**crys·tal·lo·graph·i·cal·ly** *adv.*

crys·tal·loid (krĭs′tə-loid′) *n.* **1.** *Chemistry.* A water-soluble crystalline substance capable of diffusion through a semipermeable membrane. **2.** *Botany.* Any of various minute crystalline protein particles, found in certain plant cells, especially oily seeds. ~*adj.* Also **crys·tal·loi·dal** (krĭs′tə-loid′l). Resembling or having the properties of a crystal or crystaloid. [CRYSTALL(O)- + -OID.]

crystal pickup *n.* A record-player pickup that uses a piezoelectric crystal to convert stylus vibrations into electric impulses. Compare **magnetic pickup.**

crystal set *n.* An early radio receiver using a crystal detector.

crystal system *n.* Any of seven classifications into which crystals fall, depending on their symmetry: cubic, tetragonal, hexagonal, trigonal (sometimes regarded as a subsystem of hexagonal), orthorhombic, monoclinic, and triclinic.

crystal violet *n.* **Gentian violet** (see).

Cs The symbol for the element cesium.

cs. case.

c/s cycles per second.

C.S. **1.** chief of staff. **2.** Christian Science; Christian Scientist. **3.** civil service.

C.S.A. Confederate States of America.

csc cosecant.

CSC, C.S.C. Civil Service Commission.

csch hyperbolic cosecant.

CS gas *n.* A tear gas, *ortho*-chlorobenzylidine malonitrile $C_6H_4ClCH: C(CN)_2$, used in the control of civil disturbances. It causes tears, salivation, and breathing difficulties. [*CS,* after Ben Carson and Roger Staughton, its U.S. inventors.]

csk. **1.** cask. **2.** countersink.

CST, C.S.T. Central Standard Time.

CT Connecticut (with a Zip Code).

ct. **1.** carat. **2.** cent. **3.** certificate. **4.** court.

Ct. count (title).

C.T. Central Time.

cte·nid·i·um (tĭ-nĭd′ē-əm) *n., pl.* **-ia** (-ē-ə). *Zoology.* A comblike structure, such as the respiratory apparatus of a mollusk or a row of spines in some insects. [New Latin : Greek *kteis* (stem *kten-*), a comb.]

cte·noid (tĕn′oid′, tē′noid′) *adj. Biology.* Having narrow segments or spines resembling the teeth of a comb: *fishes with ctenoid scales.* [Greek *ktenoeidēs,* like a comb : *kteis* (stem *kten-*), comb + -OID.]

cte·no·phore (tĕn′ə-fôr′, -fōr′) *n.* Any of various marine coelenterate animals of the subphylum Ctenophora, having transparent, gelatinous bodies bearing eight rows of locomotive cilia used for locomotion. Also called "comb jelly." [New Latin *Ctenophora* : Greek *kteis* (stem *kten-*), a comb + -PHORE.] —**cte·noph·o·ran** *adj.*

ctn cotangent.

ctn. carton.

ctr. center.

Cu The symbol for the element copper [Latin *cuprum*].

cu. cubic.

cub (kŭb) *n.* **1.** The young of certain carnivorous animals, such as the bear, wolf, or lion. **2.** An inexperienced, awkward, or ill-mannered youth. **3.** A novice or learner, particularly in journalism.

crystal *This naturally formed piece of rock crystal is a variety of quartz.*

Also used adjectivally: *a cub reporter*. **4. Cub.** A **Cub Scout** (see). [16th century : origin obscure.]

Cu·ba (kyōō′bə). Country in the Caribbean Sea and the largest island in the West Indies. Cuba was discovered by Columbus (1492) and was a Spanish colony until 1898. Then it became nominally independent under the United States, which reserved the right to intervene in its affairs until 1934. From 1935 the dictator Fulgencio Batista dominated Cuba until he was overthrown by Fidel Castro (1959). Cuba began to import Soviet arms and a U.S.-backed attempt to topple the regime resulted in disaster at the Bay of Pigs (1961). The Soviet installation of rocket bases caused a U.S. naval blockade and acute international tension until the missiles were withdrawn. From the 1970's Cuba has supplied troops to help liberation movements in Africa. Sugar remains the mainstay of the economy, while nickel and tobacco are also exported. Area, 114,524 square kilometers (44,206 square miles). Population, 9,7000,000. Capital, Havana. —**Cu·ban** *adj. & n.*

cub·age (kyōō′bĭj) *n.* Cubic content or volume.

Cuba li·bre, cuba li·bre (lē′brə) *n.* An iced drink of rum, a cola beverage, and lemon or lime juice. [American Spanish, "free Cuba."]

Cuban heel *n.* A moderately high heel, tapering only very slightly, for a boot or shoe.

cu·ba·ture (kyōō′bə-chŏŏr′) *n.* Also **cub·age** (kyōō′bĭj). **1.** The determination of the cubic contents of a solid. **2.** Cubic contents. [CUB(E) + (QUADR)ATURE.]

cub·by (kŭb′ē) *n., pl.* **-bies.** A small room; a cubbyhole. [From obsolete English *cub*, a stall, perhaps from Dutch *kub, kubbe,* trap, basket, from Middle Dutch *cubbe.*]

cub·by·hole (kŭb′ē-hōl′) *n.* **1.** A snug or cramped space or room. **2.** A small compartment. **3.** A small cupboard.

cube (kyōōb) *n.* **1.** *Geometry.* A regular solid having six congruent square faces. **2.** Anything having such a shape. **3.** *Mathematics.* The third power of a number or quantity; the result of multiplying something by itself twice: *27 is the cube of 3.*
~*tr.v.* **cubed, cubing, cubes. 1.** To raise (a quantity or number) to the third power. **2.** To determine the cubic contents of. **3.** To form or cut into cubes or the shape of a cube; dice. **4.** To tenderize (meat) by breaking the fibers with superficial cuts in a pattern of squares. [French, from Latin *cubus*, a dice, cube, from Greek *kubos.*]

cu·bé, cu·be (kyōō′bā′, kyōō-bā′) *n.* **1.** Any of various tropical American shrubs or plants, especially of the genus *Lonchocarpus,* whose roots yield the chemical compound rotenone. **2.** An extract from the roots of these plants, used as a fish poison and insecticide. [American Spanish *cubé†.*]

cu·beb (kyōō′bĕb′) *n.* **1.** A treelike woody vine, *Piper cubeba,* of southeastern Asia, bearing brownish berries. **2.** Its dried, unripe, spicy fruit, used medicinally as a stimulant and diuretic and sometimes smoked in cigarettes. [Middle English *cubibe,* from Old French *cubebe,* from Medieval Latin *cubēba,* from Arabic *kabābah.*]

cube root *n.* The number that when cubed produces a given number: *3 is the cube root of 27.*

cube steak *n.* A thin round or square slice of beef made tender by cubing, usually pan-broiled.

cu·bic (kyōō′bĭk) *adj.* **1. a.** Having the shape of a cube. **b.** Having a shape similar to or approximating that of a cube. **2.** *Abbr.* **c, cu. a.** Having three dimensions. **b.** Having a volume equal to a cube whose edge is of a stated length: *a cubic foot.* **3.** *Mathematics.* Of the third power, order, or degree. **4.** *Crystallography.* Isometric.
~*n. Mathematics.* A cubic expression, curve, or equation.

cu·bi·cal (kyōō′bĭ-kəl) *adj.* **1.** Cubic. **2.** Of or pertaining to volume.

—**cu·bi·cal·ly** *adv.* —**cu·bi·cal·ness** *n.*

cu·bi·cle (kyōō′bĭ-kəl) *n.* **1.** A small sleeping compartment, especially one partitioned off from a larger room. **2.** Any small compartment or partitioned-off part: *a shower cubicle.* [Latin *cubiculum,* sleeping chamber, from *cubāre,* to lie down, sleep.]

cubic measure *n.* A unit, such as a cubic meter or a cubic foot, or a system of units used to measure volume or capacity.

cu·bi·form (kyōō′bə-fôrm′) *adj.* Having the shape of a cube.

cub·ism (kyōō′bĭz′əm) *n. Often* **Cubism.** A movement in painting and sculpture, initiated in Paris in the early 20th century by Picasso and Braque, that emphasized the structure of objects by combining lines, planes, and geometrical shapes to represent several viewpoints of an object simultaneously. [French, from CUBE (from a remark by Henri Matisse concerning the "small cubes" that predominated in a painting by Georges Braque).] —**cub·ist** *adj. & n.* —**cu·bis·tic** *adj.* —**cu·bis·ti·cal·ly** *adv.*

cu·bit (kyōō′bĭt) *n.* An ancient unit of linear measure, originally equal to the length of the forearm from the tip of the middle finger to the elbow, or from 17 to 22 inches. [Middle English *cubite,* from Latin *cubitum,* cubit, elbow.]

cu·bi·tal (kyōō′bĭ-təl) *adj.* **1.** Of, pertaining to, or situated near the forearm or elbow. **2.** Of or pertaining to measurement by cubits.

cu·boid (kyōō′boid) *adj.* Also **cu·boi·dal** (kyōō-boid′l). **1.** Having the shape or approximate shape of a cube. **2.** *Anatomy.* Designating the bone on the side of the tarsus between the calcaneus and the fourth and fifth metatarsal bones of the foot.
~*n.* **1.** *Anatomy.* The cuboid bone. **2.** *Geometry.* A rectangular parallelepiped.

Cub Scout *n.* A member of the junior division of the Boy Scouts.

cu·chi·fri·to (kōō′chĭ-frē′tō) *n., pl.* **-tos.** A small deep-fried cube of pork. [American Spanish : *cuchi,* pig (from Spanish *cochino*) + Spanish *frito,* past participle of *freir,* to fry (from Latin *frigere*).]

Cu·chul·ain, Cu·chul·ainn (kōō-kŭl′ĭn). *Celtic Mythology.* A tribal hero of Ulster who single-handedly defended it against the rest of Ireland.

cuck·ing stool (kŭk′ĭng) *n.* A former instrument of punishment for prostitutes or dishonest tradesmen, consisting of a chair in which the offender was tied and exposed to public derision or ducked in water. Compare **ducking stool.** [Middle English *cucking stol,* "excreting stool" : *cucking,* present participle of *cukken,* to defecate, from Old Norse *kúka* (unattested) + *stol,* STOOL.]

cuck·old (kŭk′əld) *n.* A man whose wife has committed adultery.
~*tr.v.* **cuckolded, -olding, -olds.** To make a cuckold of. [Middle English *cukeweld, cokewold,* from Norman French *cucuald* (unattested), variant of Old French *cucualt,* pejorative form of *cucu,* cuckoo (perhaps because cuckoos leave their eggs in the nests of other birds).] —**cuck·old·ry** *n.*

cuck·oo (kōō′kōō, kōōk′ōō) *n., pl.* **-oos. 1. a.** A European bird, *Cuculus canorus,* having grayish plumage and a characteristic two-note call. It lays its eggs in the nests of other birds. **b.** Any of various related birds of the family Cuculidae. **2.** The call or cry of a cuckoo. **3.** A foolish person; a simpleton.
~*v.* **cuckooed, -ooing, -oos.** —*tr.* To repeat again and again. —*intr.* To utter or imitate a cuckoo's call.
~*adj. Informal.* Crazy; foolish. [Middle English *cuccu* (imitative).]

cuck·oo·bud (kōō′kōō-bŭd′, kōōk′ōō-) *n. Archaic.* A yellow-flowered plant, probably the buttercup: *"cuckoo-buds of yellow hue/ Do paint the meadows with delight"* (Shakespeare).

cuckoo clock *n.* A wall clock having a mechanical cuckoo announcing intervals of time.

cuck·oo·flow·er (kōō′kōō-flou′ər, kōōk′ōō-) *n.* **1.** A plant, *Cardamine pratensis,* of the North Temperate Zone, having white or rose-pink flowers. Also called "lady's-smock." **2.** A plant, the **ragged robin** (see).

cuck·oo·pint (kōō′kōō-pĭnt′, kōōk′ōō-) *n.* A European plant, *Arum maculatum,* having arrow-shaped leaves and a spadix enclosed in a purple-spotted spathe. Also called "lords-and-ladies." [Short for obsolete *cuckoo-pintle,* from Middle English *cokkupyntel* : *cokku, cuccu,* CUCKOO + *pintel,* penis, PINTLE (from the shape of the spadix).]

cuckoo shrike *n.* Any songbird of the family Campephagidae, of the Old World tropics, having long pointed wings and mainly gray plumage.

cuckoo spit *n.* A frothy mass of liquid secreted on plant stems as a protective covering by nymphs of the froghopper. Also called "frog spit," "toad spit."

cu·cu·li·form (kyōō′kə-lə-fôrm′) *adj.* Of or belonging to the order Cuculiformes, which includes the cuckoos and related birds. [New Latin *Cuculiformes* : Latin *cuculus,* cuckoo (imitative) + -FORM.]

cu·cul·late (kyōō′kə-lāt′, kyōō-kŭl′āt′) *adj.* Having the shape of a cowl or hood: *cucullate sepals.* [Medieval Latin *cucullātus,* from Latin *cucullus,* cap, hood. See cowl.] —**cu·cul·late·ly** *adv.*

cu·cum·ber (kyōō′kŭm′bər) *n.* **1.** A vine, *Cucumis sativus,* cultivated for its edible fruit. **2.** The usually cylindrical fruit of this vine, having a hard green rind and firm, white, succulent flesh. [Middle English *cucumer, cocumber,* from Old French *cocombre,* from Latin *cucumis,* of Mediterranean origin.]

cucumber mosaic *n.* A viral disease of the cucumber plant that produces a variegated spotting of the leaves and fruit.

cucumber tree *n.* **1.** A tree, *Magnolia acuminata,* of eastern and central North America, having cup-shaped greenish-yellow flowers and brown or scarlet cucumber-shaped fruit. **2.** A tree, *Averrhoa bilimbi,* of eastern Asia, having reddish-purple flowers and edible

cubism *The cubist movement, with its emphasis on geometrical shapes and structure rather than the ordinary appearance of objects, broke away from the largely representational tradition of art and opened the way for modern abstract art. This oil on canvas,* Still Life with Bottles and Knife, *was painted in 1912 by the Spanish artist Juan Gris (1887–1927), who spent most of his adult life in Paris and was a neighbor and friend of Picasso.*

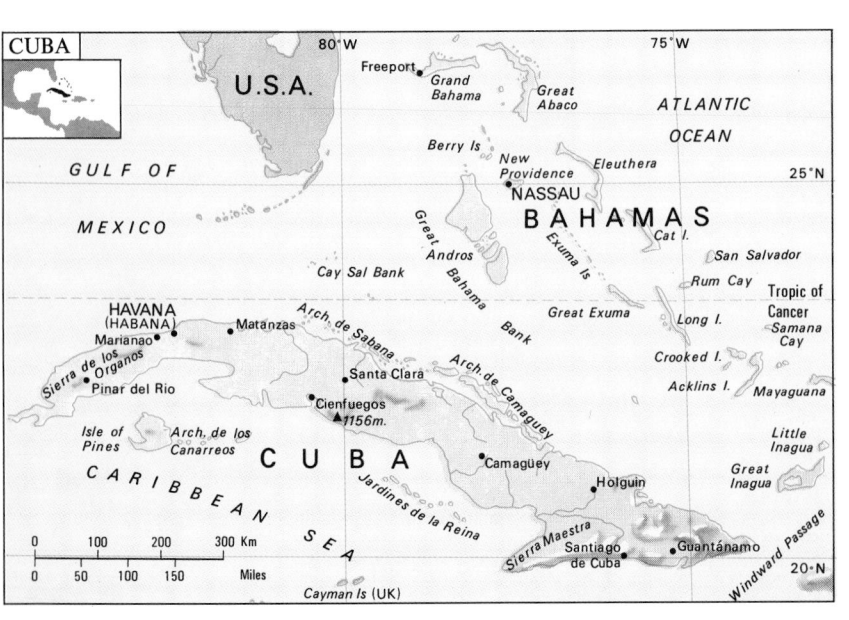

fruit that resemble small cucumbers.
cu·cu·mi·form (kyo͞o-kyo͞o′mə-fôrm′) *adj.* Having the shape of a cucumber. [Latin *cucumis,* CUCUMBER + -FORM.]
cu·cur·bit (kyo͞o-kûr′bĭt) *n.* **1.** A gourd-shaped flask forming the body of an alembic, formerly used in distillation. **2.** Any of various vines of the family Cucurbitaceae, which includes the squash, pumpkin, and cucumber. [Middle English *cucurbite,* from Old French, from Latin *cucurbita,* GOURD.]
Cú·cu·ta (ko͞o′ko͞o-tä′). City of northeastern Colombia, near the border with Venezuela. Founded in 1733, Cúcuta is an industrial city and the center of a region producing coffee, oil, and minerals. The city was rebuilt after an earthquake in 1875.
cud (kŭd) *n.* Food regurgitated from the first stomach to the mouth of a ruminant and chewed again. **—chew the cud.** *Informal.* To ponder. [Middle English *cud(de),* Old English *cwudu, cudu,* from Germanic; akin to Old High German *kuti,* glue.]
cud·bear (kŭd′bâr′) *n.* A purplish-red coloring substance derived from certain lichens, especially of the genera *Rocella* and *Lecanora.* [From the name of Dr. *Cuthbert* Gordon, 18th-century Scottish chemist who patented the substance.]
cud·dle (kŭd′l) *v.* **-dled, -dling, -dles.** *—tr.* To fondle in the arms; hug tenderly. *—intr.* To nestle; snuggle. Often followed by *up.* *∼n.* The act of cuddling; a hug or embrace. [16th century : origin obscure.] **—cud·dle·some** *adj.* **—cud·dly** *adj.*
cud·dy[1] (kŭd′ē) *n., pl.* **-dies. 1.** A small cabin or the cook's galley on a ship. **2.** A small room or cupboard. [Origin obscure.]
cuddy[2] *n., pl.* **-dies.** *Scottish.* **1.** A donkey. **2.** A fool; dolt. [Perhaps from *Cuddy,* nickname for *Cuthbert.*]
cudg·el (kŭj′əl) *n.* A short, heavy club. **—take up the cudgels.** To join in a dispute, especially in defense of a participant.
∼tr.v. **cudgeled, -eling, -els.** Also *chiefly British* **-elled, -elling.** To beat or strike with a cudgel. **—cudgel one's brains.** To think hard. [Middle English *cuggel,* Old English *cycgel.*] **—cudg·el·er** *n.*
cudg·el-play (kŭj′əl-plā′) *n.* **1.** A sporting contest with cudgels. **2.** The art of fighting with cudgels.
cud·weed (kŭd′wēd′) *n.* **1.** Any of various woolly plants of the genus *Gnaphalium,* having clusters of whitish or yellow buttonlike flowers. **2.** Any of several similar or related plants, especially a European plant, *Filago germanica.*
cue[1] (kyo͞o) *n.* **1.** In billiards and pool, the long, tapered rod used to propel the ball. **2.** A queue of hair; a long braid.
∼v. **cued, cuing, cues. 1.** To strike (a ball) with a cue. **2.** To braid or twist (hair) into a cue. *—intr.* To strike a ball with a cue. [French *queue,* "tail" (from the shape of the cue), from Old French *coue,* from Latin *cauda,* tail.]
cue[2] *n.* **1. a.** A word or bit of stage action signaling the beginning of another action or speech. **b.** Any guide to a performer, such as a musician or singer, that serves as a signal for subsequent action. **2.** A hint or reminder; a prompting. **3.** *Psychology.* A perceived signal for action, especially one that produces an operant response. **—on cue.** Precisely at the right moment. **—take one's cue from.** To imitate the style of behavior of.
∼tr.v. **cued, cuing, cues.** To give (an actor or other performer) a cue. [16th century : origin obscure.]
cue[3] *n.* The letter *q.*
cue ball *n. Billiards.* The ball that is hit directly with the cue.
Cuen·ca (kwĕng′kä). City of south-central Ecuador, at an altitude of *c.* 2,440 meters (8,000 feet). Founded in 1557, Cuena is the commercial center of a rich agricultural basin. It is known as "the Marble City" because of its many fine buildings.
Cuer·na·va·ca (kwâr′nə-vä′kə). City of southern Mexico, the capital of Morelos state. The city has flour mills and beverage, textile, and cement industries. It is also a popular tourist and health resort, with beautiful churches, monasteries, a formal garden, and a palace built by Hernán Cortés.
cues·ta (kwĕs′tə) *n.* A land elevation with a gentle slope on one side and a much steeper one on the other. [Spanish, sloping side, from Latin *costa,* side.]
cuff[1] (kŭf) *n.* **1. a.** The bottom of a sleeve. **b.** A fold or band used as trimming at the bottom of a sleeve. **2.** The turned-up fold at the bottom of a trouser leg. **3.** A band of linen, lace, or other fabric attached about the wrist, either under or over a sleeve. **4.** The part of a gauntlet that extends over the wrist. **5.** *Informal.* A **handcuff** *(see).* **—off the cuff.** *Informal.* Extemporaneously. **—on the cuff.** *Informal.* **1.** Without immediate payment; on credit. **2.** Without payment; gratis. [Middle English *cuffe†,* glove, mitten.]
cuff[2] *tr.v.* **cuffed, cuffing, cuffs.** To strike with the open hand; slap. *∼n.* A blow or slap with the open hand. [16th century : perhaps imitative.]
cuff links *pl.n.* A pair of linked buttons, used to fasten the cuffs of a shirt.
Cufic. Variant of **Kufic.**
cui·rass (kwĭ-răs′) *n.* **1.** A piece of armor for protecting the breast and back. **2.** The breastplate alone. **3.** *Zoology.* A protective covering of bony plates, scales, or shell.
∼tr.v. **cuirassed, -rassing, -rasses.** To protect with a cuirass. [Middle English *curace,* cuirass (especially one of leather), from Old French *cuirasse,* from Vulgar Latin *coriāca* (unattested), "leather buckler," from Latin *coriāceus,* of leather, from *corium,* hide, skin.]
cui·ras·sier (kwîr′ə-sîr′) *n.* Formerly, a horse soldier in European armies whose equipment included the cuirass.
cuir bouil·li (kwîr′ bo͞ol′yē) *n.* Leather soaked and left to harden, used as an early form of armor. [French, "boiled leather."]
Cui·se·naire (kwē′zə-nâr′) *n.* A trademark for a set of colored rods used to teach arithmetic.
cui·sine (kwĭ-zēn′) *n.* **1.** A characteristic manner or style of preparing food. **2.** Food prepared by a hotel, restaurant, or the like. [French, from Late Latin *coquīna,* a kitchen, cookery, from *coquere,* to cook.]
cuisine min·ceur (mᴀɴ-sœr′) *n.* A style of French cooking that seeks to minimize the use of rich ingredients such as flour, butter, and cream. [French, "slenderness cuisine."]
cuisse (kwĭs) *n.* Also **cuish** (kwĭsh). A piece of plate armor worn to protect the thigh. [Back-formation from Middle English *cussues, cushies,* from Old French *cuissaux,* plural of *cuissel,* from *cuisse,* thigh, from Latin *coxa,* thigh, hip.]
Cu·kor (kyo͞o′kər, -kôr, ko͞o′-), **George Dewey** (1899–1983). U.S. filmmaker. In his 50-year career, he used his skillful rapport with actresses and actors and his attention to detail to direct some of Hollywood's finest films, including *Little Women* (1933), *The Philadelphia Story* (1940), and *Adam's Rib* (1949). In 1964 he earned an Academy Award for his direction of *My Fair Lady.*
Cul·bert·son (kŭl′bərt-sən), **Ely** (1891–1955). U.S. contract bridge authority. He helped popularize contract bridge through his widely reported dominance of international matches and several books on the subject, including *The Contract Bridge Blue Book* (1930). He was also active in peace movements.
culch, cultch (kŭlch) *n.* **1.** A natural bed for oysters, consisting of gravel or crushed shells to which oyster spawn may adhere. **2.** The spawn of the oyster. **3.** Rubbish or refuse. [Perhaps from Old French *culche, couche,* bed, COUCH.]
cul-de-sac (kŭl′dĭ-săk′, ko͝ol′-) *n., pl.* **cul-de-sacs. 1.** A dead-end street; a road closed at one end. **2.** *Anatomy.* A saclike cavity or tube open only at one end. [French, "bottom of the sack," blind alley.]
-cule *suffix.* Indicates smallness; for example, **molecule.** [French, from New Latin *-cula,* diminutive suffix from Latin *-culus, -cula, -culum.* See also **-cle.**]
Culebra Cut. See **Gaillard Cut.**
cu·let (kyo͞o′lĭt) *n.* **1.** The flat face of a gem cut as a brilliant. **2.** One of the plates of medieval armor covering the lower back. [French, diminutive of *cul,* the rump, from Latin *cūlus.*]
cu·lex (kyo͞o′lĕks) *n., pl.* **-lices** (-lə-sēz′). Any of various mosquitoes of the genus *Culex,* which includes the house mosquito, *C. pipiens.* [New Latin, from Latin *culex†,* gnat.]
Cu·lia·cán (kyo͞o′lyä-kän′). City of western Mexico, capital of Sinaloa state. Founded in 1531, it is located on a hot coastal plain that produces tropical fruits, sugar cane, cotton, beans, and corn; cattle raising is also important. In the Spanish colonial period the city was a point of departure for northern expeditions, including that of Francisco Coronado (1540).
cu·li·cide (kyo͞o′lə-sīd′) *n.* A chemical used to destroy mosquitoes or gnats. [Latin *culex* (stem *culic-*), gnat + -CIDE.]
cu·li·nar·y (kyo͞o′lə-nĕr′ē, kŭl′ə-) *adj.* Of or pertaining to a kitchen or to cookery. [Latin *culīnārius,* from *culīna,* kitchen, deformed variant of *coquīna,* cook.] **—cu·li·nar·i·ly** *adv.*
cull (kŭl) *tr.v.* **culled, culling, culls. 1.** To pick out from others; select. **2.** To gather; collect. **3. a.** To remove and kill (weak or surplus animals in a herd or flock). **b.** To search through (a herd or flock) in order to remove and kill weak or surplus animals.
∼n. **1.** The act of culling. **2.** The amount culled. **3.** Something picked out from others; especially, something rejected because of inferior quality. [Middle English *coilen,* from Old French *cuillir,* from Latin *colligere,* to COLLECT.] **—cull·er** *n.*
Cul·len (kŭl′ən), **Countée** (1903–46). U.S. poet. Cullen established his reputation as a lyric poet with his first book, *Color* (1925). He also published a novel, *One Way to Heaven* (1932), several more books of verse, and an anthology of black poetry, *Caroling Dusk* (1927).
cullender. Variant of **colander.**
cul·let (kŭl′ĭt) *n.* Scraps of broken or waste glass gathered for remelting. [Perhaps variant of earlier *collet,* from French *collet,* "little neck" (the neck of glass broken off a newly blown vessel), diminutive of *col,* neck, from Old French, from Latin *collum.*]
cul·lis (kŭl′ĭs) *n., pl.* **-lises.** A gutter or groove in a roof. [Middle English *colis,* from Old French *coleïs,* channel, from *coler,* to pour, strain, from Latin *cōlāre,* to filter, strain, from *cōlum,* a sieve.]
Cul·lod·en Moor (kə-lŏd′n, -lō′dən). Moorland near Inverness in northeastern Scotland. It was the site of a battle in which the Jacobite forces of Charles Edward Stuart were defeated by an army commanded by the Duke of Cumberland (1746). The battle marked the final defeat of the Jacobite cause and was followed by savage repression in the Highlands.
culm[1] (kŭlm) *n.* The jointed stem of a grass or sedge. [Latin *culmus,* stalk.]
culm[2] *n.* **1.** Waste from anthracite coal mines, consisting of fine coal, coal dust, and dirt. **2. a.** *Often* **Culm.** *Geology.* A Lower Carboniferous formation consisting of shale and sandstone. Also called "culm measures." **b.** Inferior anthracite coal. [Middle English *colme,* coal dust, perhaps akin to *col,* COAL.]
cul·mi·nant (kŭl′mə-nənt) *adj.* Culminating; highest.
cul·mi·nate (kŭl′mə-nāt′) *intr.v.* **-nated, -nating, -nates. 1.** To reach the highest point or degree; come to full effect; climax. Usually used with *in.* **2.** *Astronomy.* To cross the meridian of the observer; reach the highest point above an observer's horizon. Used of stars and other celestial bodies. [Late Latin *culmināre,* from Latin *cul-*

cuckoo *There are about 130 species of the cuckoo family distributed worldwide. Most are parasitic, laying their eggs in the nests of other birds. The young European cuckoo, seen here, is often reared in a reed warbler's nest.*

cuckoopint *In springtime, cuckoopint (*Arum maculatum*) is a common sight in the hedgerows of the Northern Hemisphere. The poisonous red berries that appear later can be fatal to humans if eaten. Cuckoopint is just one of many local names for this flower. An alternate name is lords-and-ladies.*

men (stem *culmin-*), top, summit.] —**cul·mi·na·tion** *n.*

cu·lottes (kōō-lŏts′, kyōō-) *pl.n.* A woman's full trousers, usually knee-length, cut to resemble a skirt. [French, breeches, diminutive of *cul*, backside, from Latin *cūlus.*] —**cu·lotte** *adj.*

cul·pa (kŭl′pə, kŏŏl′-) *n. Law.* Fault; misconduct. [Latin.]

cul·pa·ble (kŭl′pə-bəl) *adj.* Responsible for wrong or error; deserving censure. [Middle English *coupable*, from Old French, from Latin *culpābilis*, from *culpāre*, to blame, from *culpa*, CULPA.] —**cul·pa·bil·i·ty** *n.* —**cul·pa·ble·ness** *n.* —**cul·pa·bly** *adv.*

Cul·pep·er (kŭl′pĕp′ər), **Nicholas** (1616–54). English herbalist and physician. He set up as an apothecary in 1640 and in 1649 angered the London College of Physicians by producing a popular translation from Latin of their official *Pharmocopoeia.* He is best remembered for *Culpeper's Herbal*, describing properties of herbs.

cul·prit (kŭl′prĭt) *n.* **1.** A person guilty of a fault or crime. **2.** A person charged with an offense or crime. [From the 17th-century legal phrase "*Culprit*, how will you be tried?", perhaps a mistake for Norman French "*Culpable. Prit d'averrer . . .*," "Guilty. (I am) ready to prove . . . ," the prosecutor's response to a plea of not guilty, which might have been abbreviated as "*Cul. prit, etc.*" : CULPABLE + *prit, prist*, ready, from Latin *praestus* (see **presto**).]

cult (kŭlt) *n.* **1.** A system or community of religious worship and ritual, especially one focusing upon a single deity or spirit. **2. a.** Obsessive devotion or veneration for a person, principle, or ideal. **b.** The object of such devotion. **3. a.** An exclusive group of persons sharing an esoteric interest. **b.** The object of such an interest. **4.** Any fashion or fad. Often used derogatorily. ~*adj.* Pertaining to or characteristic of a cult: *a cult figure.* [French *culte*, from Latin *cultus*, cultivation, a laboring, worship, from the past participle of *colere*, to CULTIVATE.] —**cult·ic** *adj.* —**cult·ism** *n.* —**cult·ist** *n. & adj.*

cultch. Variant of **culch.**

cul·ti. Alternate plural of **cultus.**

cul·ti·gen (kŭl′tə-jən) *n.* An organism, especially a cultivated plant such as maize, of a kind not known to have a wild or uncultivated counterpart. [CULTI(VATED) + -GEN.]

cul·ti·va·ble (kŭl′tə-və-bəl) *adj.* Also **cul·ti·vat·a·ble** (-vā′tə-bəl). Capable of being cultivated. —**cul·ti·va·bil·i·ty** *n.*

cul·ti·var (kŭl′tə-vär′, -vâr′) *n.* A horticulturally or agriculturally derived variety of a plant, as distinguished from a natural variety. [*Culti*vated + *var*iety.]

cul·ti·vate (kŭl′tə-vāt′) *tr.v.* **-vated, -vating, -vates. 1. a.** To improve and prepare (land), as by plowing or fertilizing, for raising crops; till. **b.** To loosen or dig (soil) around growing plants. **2.** To grow or tend (a plant or crop). **3.** To promote the growth of (a biological culture, for example). **4.** To nurture; foster. **5.** To form and refine, as by education. **6.** To seek the acquaintance or goodwill of. [Medieval Latin *cultīvāre*, from *(terra) cultīva*, tilled (land), from *cultīvus*, tilled, from Latin *cultus*, past participle of *colere*, to till, cultivate.]

cul·ti·vat·ed (kŭl′tə-vā′tĭd) *adj.* **1.** Cultured; refined. **2.** Specially nurtured or improved by cultivation. Said of plants.

cul·ti·va·tion (kŭl′tə-vā′shən) *n.* **1. a.** The act of cultivating. **b.** The state of being cultivated. **2.** Refinement; social polish. —See Usage Note at **culture.**

cul·ti·va·tor (kŭl′tə-vā′tər) *n.* **1.** One who cultivates. **2.** An implement or machine for loosening the earth and destroying weeds around growing plants.

cul·trate (kŭl′trāt′) *adj.* Also **cul·trat·ed** (-trā′tĭd). Sharp-edged and pointed; knifelike: *a cultrate beak.* [Latin *cultrātus*, knifelike, from *culter* (stem *cultr-*), knife.]

cul·tur·al (kŭl′chər-əl) *adj.* **1.** Of or relating to culture, especially social, intellectual, or artistic pursuits. **2.** Obtained by specialized breeding, as certain plant varieties are.

cultural anthropology *n.* The scientific study of human culture based on archaeological, ethnologic, ethnographic, linguistic, social, and psychological data and methods of analysis. Compare **physical anthropology.**

Cultural Revolution *n.* A political movement in China (1966–68), thought to have been launched by Mao Ze-dong, aimed at overthrowing entrenched bureaucracy and rekindling revolutionary fervor and ideals.

cul·ture (kŭl′chər) *n.* **1.** Social and intellectual formation. **2.** The totality of socially transmitted behavior patterns, arts, beliefs, institutions, and all other products of human work and thought characteristic of a community or population. **3.** A style of social and artistic expression peculiar to a society or class. **4. a.** Intellectual and artistic activity. **b.** Intellectual and social refinement resulting from such activity. **5.** The cultivation of the soil; tillage. **6.** The breeding of animals or growing of plants, especially to produce improved stock. **7.** *Biology.* **a.** The growing of microorganisms in a nutrient medium for scientific research or medical use. **b.** Such a growth or colony, as of bacteria. ~*tr.v.* **cultured, -turing, -tures. 1.** To cultivate. **2.** To develop (microorganisms or tissues, for example) in a culture medium. [Middle English, cultivation, tillage, from Old French, from Latin *cultūra*, from *cultus*, cultivation. See **cultivate.**]

Usage: culture, cultivation, breeding, refinement, gentility, taste. These nouns are applied to personal achievement in the development of intellect, manners, and aesthetic appreciation. *Culture*, which overlaps the others, implies enlightenment attained through close association with and appreciation of the highest level of civilization. *Cultivation* usually refers to the self-improvement or self-

development by which a person acquires culture. *Breeding* is the development of good character and behavior, and is especially revealed in manners, poise, and sensitivity to the feelings of others. *Refinement*, the highest product of breeding, stresses aversion to coarseness; sometimes it may imply a delicacy of feeling associated with fastidiousness. *Gentility* is sometimes still synonymous with refinement or good birth; in modern usage it may suggest extreme elegance in behavior or manners. *Taste* is the capacity for recognizing and appreciating what is aesthetically superior.

cul·tured (kŭl′chərd) *adj.* **1.** Cultivated; refined. **2.** Produced under artificial and controlled conditions.

cultured pearl *n.* A pearl made to grow in the shell of an oyster or clam by inserting a small bead of mother-of-pearl, around which layers of nacre are deposited.

culture medium *n.* A substance, such as agar or blood, on which colonies of microorganisms, such as bacteria, are grown.

culture shock *n.* Severe and often distressing feelings of disorientation and isolation felt by a person on coming into contact with a completely alien society or foreign way of life.

culture vulture *n.* A person whose interest in art, literature, and the like is considered excessive or overzealous.

cul·tus (kŭl′təs) *n., pl.* **-tuses** or **-ti** (-tī). A religious cult. [New Latin, from Latin *cultus*, worship, CULT.]

cul·ver (kŭl′vər) *n. Poetic.* A dove; a pigeon. [Middle English *culver*, Old English *culufre*, from Vulgar Latin *columbra* (unattested), from Latin *columbula*, diminutive of *columba*, dove.]

Cul·ver City (kŭl′vər). City of southern California, a residential suburb of Los Angeles. It is a center of the motion-picture industry, which began in the city around 1915. The city's chief commercial products are electronic and aerospace equipment.

cul·ver·in (kŭl′vər-ĭn) *n.* **1.** A type of early musket. **2.** A heavy cannon used in the 16th and 17th centuries. [Middle English, from Old French *coulevrine*, "serpentine," from *couleuvre*, snake, from Vulgar Latin *colobra* (unattested), from Latin *colubra*, feminine of *coluber*, snake.] —**cul·ver·i·neer** *n.*

Cul·ver's root (kŭl′vərz) *n.* **1.** A North American plant, *Veronicastrum virginicum*, having spikes of small white or purplish flowers. **2.** The root of this plant, formerly used as a cathartic and emetic. [After a Dr. *Culver*, 18th-century U.S. physician.]

cul·vert (kŭl′vərt) *n.* **1.** A sewer or drain crossing under a road or embankment. **2.** A pipe or channel for an electric cable. [18th century : origin obscure.]

cum (kŏŏm, kŭm) *prep.* Together with; plus. Used in combination to indicate a dual nature or function: *her attic-cum-studio.* [Latin, with.]

Cu·mae (kyōō′mē). An ancient city of south-central Italy, near modern-day Naples. It was the earliest-known Greek colony in Italy, founded *c.* 750 B.C. At one time Cumae was a great power, with a number of colonies. It fell to the Samnites (late 5th century B.C.), later adopted Roman culture and civilization, and finally declined as neighboring cities rose to power.

Cu·ma·ná (kōō′mä-nä′). City of northeastern Venezuela, on the Manzanares River near its mouth on the Gulf of Cariaco, an inlet of the Caribbean Sea. Founded in 1521 to exploit nearby pearl fisheries, the city was frequently raided by the Dutch and British in the 16th and 17th centuries.

cum·ber (kŭm′bər) *tr.v.* **-bered, -bering, -bers. 1.** To weigh down; burden. **2.** To hamper; obstruct. ~*n.* A hindrance; an encumbrance. [Middle English *combren*, perhaps from Old French *combrer*, from *combret*†, hindrance.]

Cum·ber·land[1] (kŭm′bər-lənd). Former county of northwest England. Since 1974 it has been a part of the new county of Cumbria.

Cumberland[2]. A river rising in southeastern Kentucky and flowing 1,105 kilometers (687 miles) through Kentucky and Tennessee to the Ohio River in western Kentucky.

Cumberland, William Augustus, Duke of (1721–65). British general, the third son of George II. Made commander in chief of the British army (1745), he crushed the Jacobite Rebellion at the Battle of Culloden (1746).

Cumberland Gap. A natural passage through the Cumberland Mts., at the junction of the borders of Kentucky, Virginia, and Tennessee. Daniel Boone's Wilderness Road traversed the Gap. It was a strategic point during the Civil War, held alternately by Union and Confederate forces.

cum·ber·some (kŭm′bər-səm) *adj.* **1.** Clumsy; unwieldy. **2.** Burdensome; onerous. —See Synonyms at **heavy.** —**cum·ber·some·ly** *adv.* —**cum·ber·some·ness** *n.*

cum·brance (kŭm′brəns) *n.* **1.** An encumbrance. **2.** Trouble. [Middle English *cumbraunce*, from *cumbren*, to CUMBER.]

Cum·bri·a (kŭm′brē-ə). County in northwest England, formed (1974) from Cumberland and Westmoreland with parts of Yorkshire and Lancashire. It encompasses the Lake District and the Cumbrian Mts., which rise to 977 meters (3,205 feet) at Scafell Pikes, the highest point in England. Carlisle is the administrative center. —**Cum·bri·an** *adj. & n.*

cum·brous (kŭm′brəs) *adj.* Cumbersome. [Middle English, from *cumbren*, to CUMBER.]

cum gra·no sa·lis (kŏŏm grä′nō sä′lĭs, kŭm grä′no sā′lĭs) *adv. Latin.* With a grain of salt; with skepticism.

cum·in, cum·min (kŭm′ĭn) *n.* **1.** An Old World plant, *Cuminum cyminum*, having finely divided leaves and small white or pinkish flowers. **2.** The aromatic seeds of this plant, used as a condiment. [Middle English *comin*, from Old French *cumin*, from Latin *cumī-*

num, from Greek *kuminon,* from Semitic, akin to Hebrew *kammōn,* Akkadian *kamūnu.*]

cum lau·de (ko͝om lou'də, lou'dē, kŭm lô'dē) *adv.* With praise. Used on university and college diplomas to designate the third-highest degree of academic distinction. Compare **magna cum laude, summa cum laude.** [New Latin.]

cum·mer·bund (kŭm'ər-bŭnd') *n.* A broad, pleated sash worn round the waist in men's formal dress. [Hindi *kamarband,* from Persian, loinband, waistband : *kamar,* loins, waist + *band,* band.]

Cum·mings (kŭm'ĭngz), **Edward Estlin,** known as "e e cummings" (1894–1962). U.S. poet, noted for his lyricism and unconventional use of punctuation and typography. He won fame through the bizarre format of his poetry, in which the visual impact of eccentric typography underlines the content.

cumquat. Variant of **kumquat.**

cum·shaw (kŭm'shô) *n.* A tip; a gratuity; a present. [Pidgin English, from Chinese dialect (Amoy) *kam sia,* to thank.]

cumul–. Variant of **cumulo–.**

cu·mu·late (kyo͞om'yə-lāt') *v.* **-lated, -lating, -lates.** —*tr.* **1.** To accumulate. **2.** To combine into one unit; merge. **3.** To expand by an increment in new material. —*intr.* To become massed. [Latin *cumulāre,* from *cumulus,* heap.] **—cu·mu·la·tion** *n.*

cu·mu·la·tive (kyo͞om'yə-lā'tĭv, -yə-lə-tĭv) *adj.* **1.** Increasing or enlarging by successive addition. **2.** Acquired by or resulting from accumulation. **3.** *Finance.* **a.** Of or pertaining to interest or a dividend that increases if not paid when due. **b.** Designating shares that entitle holders to be paid arrears of dividend before any other payment is made to ordinary shareholders. **4.** *Law.* Designating additional or supporting evidence. **5.** *Statistics.* **a.** Of, pertaining to, or designating the sum of the frequencies of experimentally determined values of a random variable that are less than or equal to a given value. **b.** Of, pertaining to, or designating experimental error that increases in magnitude with each successive measurement. **—cu·mu·la·tive·ly** *adv.* **—cu·mu·la·tive·ness** *n.*

cumulative voting *n.* A system of voting, used, for example, by shareholders, in which each voter has as many votes as there are representatives to be elected and may give them all to one candidate or distribute them among several candidates.

cu·mu·li (kyo͞om'yə-lī'). Plural of **cumulus.**

cumuli–. Variant of **cumulo–.**

cu·mu·li·form (kyo͞om'yə-lə-fôrm') *adj. Meteorology.* Having the shape of a cumulus cloud. [CUMUL(US) + -FORM.]

cumulo–, cumuli–, cumul– *prefix.* Indicates cumulus; for example, **cumulonimbus.** [From CUMULUS.]

cu·mu·lo·nim·bus (kyo͞om'yə-lō-nĭm'bəs) *n., pl.* **-buses** or **-bi** (-bī'). *Meteorology.* An extremely dense cumulus cloud developed vertically to a great height, usually producing heavy rains, thunderstorms, or hailstorms. [New Latin : CUMUL(US) + NIMBUS.]

cu·mu·lus (kyo͞om'yə-ləs) *n., pl.* **-li** (-lī'). **1.** *Meteorology.* A dense, white, flat-based cloud with a multiple rounded top and a well-defined outline, occurring at heights of 2,000 to 3,000 feet, and usually formed by the ascent of thermally unstable air masses. Also called "cumulus cloud." **2.** A pile, mound, or heap. [New Latin, from Latin, heap, mass.] **—cu·mu·lous** *adj.*

cunc·ta·tion (kŭngk'tā'shən) *n.* Delay; procrastination. [Latin *cūnctātiō* (stem *cunctātion-),* from *cūnctātus,* past participle of *cūnctārī,* to delay.] **—cunc·ta·tive** *adj.* **—cunc·ta·tory** *adj.* **—cunc·ta·tor** *n.*

cu·ne·al (kyo͞o'nē-əl) *adj.* Wedge-shaped. [New Latin *cunealis,* from Latin *cuneus,* wedge. See **coin.**]

cu·ne·ate (kyo͞o'nē-ĭt, -āt') *adj.* Wedge-shaped. Said especially of leaves that are narrow and triangular, and taper toward the base. [Latin *cuneātus,* from *cuneus,* wedge. See **coin.**] **—cu·ne·ate·ly** *adv.*

cu·ne·i·form (kyo͞o'nē-ə-fôrm', kyo͞o-nē'-) *adj.* **1.** Wedge-shaped. **2.** Designating: **a.** The wedge-shaped characters used in ancient Sumerian, Akkadian, Assyrian, Babylonian, and Persian writing. **b.** Documents, stone tablets, or inscriptions written or engraved in such characters. **3.** *Anatomy.* Designating any of the three wedge-shaped bones in the tarsus of the foot.
∼*n.* **1.** Cuneiform writing. **2.** A cuneiform bone. [French *cunéiforme* : Latin *cuneus,* wedge (see **coin**) + -FORM.]

Cu·ne·ne or **Ku·ne·ne** (ko͞o'nā-nə). River of southern Africa. It rises in central Angola and flows some 1,200 kilometers (about 750 miles) to the Atlantic, its lower course forming much of the Angola-Namibia border.

cun·ner (kŭn'ər) *n.* A marine fish, *Tautogolabrus adspersus,* of North American Atlantic waters. [Origin unknown.]

cun·ning (kŭn'ĭng) *adj.* **1.** Shrewd; crafty; artful. **2.** Executed with or exhibiting ingenuity. —See Synonyms at **clever, sly.**
∼*n.* **1.** Skill in deception; craftiness; guile. **2.** Skill or adeptness in performance; adroitness; dexterity. [Middle English *conning,* perhaps from the present participle of *connen,* to know, Old English *cunnan.*] **—cun·ning·ly** *adv.* **—cun·ning·ness** *n.*

Cun·ning·ham (kŭn'ĭng-hăm', -əm) **Merce** (1919–). U.S. choreographer, a pioneer of experimental ballet. He danced with Martha Graham's company (1939–45) and from 1942 often worked with the avant-garde composer John Cage.

Cu·no·be·li·nus (kyo͞o'nō-bə-lī'nəs) (died *c.* A.D. 42). *English* **Cym·be·line** (sĭm'bə-lēn). Ancient British ruler, chief of a tribe who ruled a territory corresponding to modern Hertfordshire.

cup (kŭp) *n.* **1.** A small, rounded, open container, typically with a flat bottom and a handle, used for drinking. **2. a.** Such a container and its contents. **b.** The contents alone. **3.** *Abbr.* **c. a.** A measure equal to ½ pint, 8 fluid ounces, or 16 tablespoons. **4.** The bowl of a drinking vessel. **5.** The chalice or the wine used in the celebration of the Eucharist. **6.** An ornamental cup-shaped vessel, usually two-handed, given to commemorate an event or as a prize or trophy. **7.** A sporting contest, often an elimination competition lasting several rounds, played for a cup as the prize. Also used adjectivally: *cup final; cup winner.* **8.** Either of the two rounded, hollow parts of a brassiere that contain or support the breasts. **9.** *Golf.* A hole or the metal container inside a hole. **10.** Any of various beverages, usually combining wine, fruit, and spices. **11.** Anything resembling a cup. **12.** *Biology.* A cuplike structure or organ. **13.** A lot or portion to be suffered or enjoyed. **—in one's cups.** Drunk. **—not one's cup of tea.** *Informal.* Not to one's taste; not agreeable.
∼*tr.v.* **cupped, cupping, cups. 1.** To place in or as if in a cup. **2.** To shape like a cup: *cup one's hand.* **3.** *Medicine.* To practice cupping on. [Middle English *cuppe,* Old English *cuppe,* from Late Latin *cuppa*†, drinking vessel.]

cup·bear·er (kŭp'bâr'ər) *n.* One who serves wine, as in a royal household.

cup·board (kŭb'ərd) *n.* A cabinet or recessed portion of a room enclosed by a door, usually with shelves for storing food, crockery, and the like.

cupboard love *n. British.* Love shown or simulated in order to gain material goods or advantages.

cup·cake (kŭp'kāk') *n.* A small cake baked in a cup-shaped container.

cu·pel (kyo͞o'pəl, kyo͞o-pĕl') *n.* **1.** A shallow, porous vessel used in assaying to separate precious metals from less valuable elements. **2.** The bottom or receptacle in a silver-refining furnace.
∼*tr.v.* **cupeled** or **cupelled, -peling** or **-pelling, -pels.** To separate from base metals in a cupel. [French *coupelle,* diminutive of *coupe,* cup, from Late Latin *cuppa,* CUP.] **—cu·pel·er** *n.*

cu·pel·la·tion (kyo͞o'pə-lā'shən) *n.* A refining process for nonoxidizing metals, such as silver and gold, in which the components of a metallic mixture oxidized at high temperatures are separated by absorption into the walls of a cupel.

cup·ful (kŭp'fo͝ol') *n., pl.* **-fuls** or **cupsful. 1.** The amount a cup will hold. **2.** *Cooking.* A measure of capacity equal to ½ pint, 8 ounces, or 16 tablespoons.

cu·pid (kyo͞o'pĭd) *n.* A representation of the god Cupid as a winged boy holding a bow and arrow.

Cu·pid (kyo͞o'pĭd). The Roman god of love, identified with the Greek Eros. [Latin *Cupīdō,* personification of *cupīdō,* desire, from *cupere,* to desire.]

cu·pid·i·ty (kyo͞o-pĭd'ə-tē) *n.* Avarice; greed; strong desire for gain. [Middle English *cupidite,* from Old French, from Latin *cupiditās* (stem *cupiditāt-),* from *cupidus,* desiring, from *cupere,* to desire.]

cu·po·la (kyo͞o'pə-lə) *n.* **1. a.** A domed roof or ceiling. **b.** A small, usually domed structure surmounting a roof. **2.** A cylindrical vertical type of blast furnace used for remelting metals, usually iron, before casting. Also called "cupola furnace." **3.** A protective revolving dome on the guns of a warship. **4.** *Geology.* A small dome-shaped igneous intrusion. [Italian *cupola,* from Late Latin *cūpula,* diminutive of Latin *cūpa,* tub, vat.]

cup·ping (kŭp'ĭng) *n.* A therapeutic process, rarely used in modern medicine, in which glass cups (*cupping glasses*), partially evacuated by heating, are locally applied to the skin in order to draw blood toward or through the surface.

cup plant *n.* A coarse North American plant, *Silphium perfoliatum,* having yellow-rayed flowers. Also called "rosinweed." [From the cup formed around its stem by its leaves.]

cu·pre·ous (kyo͞o'prē-əs) *adj.* Of, resembling, or containing copper; coppery. [Late Latin *cupreus,* from *cuprum,* COPPER.]

cu·pric (kyo͞o'prĭk) *adj.* Of or containing divalent copper. [Late Latin *cuprum,* COPPER.]

cu·prif·er·ous (kyo͞o-prĭf'ər-əs) *adj.* Yielding copper. [Late Latin *cuprum,* COPPER + -FEROUS.]

cu·prite (kyo͞o'prīt') *n.* A natural red copper ore, essentially Cu_2O. [German *Kuprit* : Late Latin *cuprum,* COPPER + -ITE.]

cupro–, cupri–, cupr– *prefix.* Indicates copper; for example, **cupronickel, cupriferous.** [Late Latin *cuprum,* copper.]

cu·pro·nick·el (ko͞o'prō-nĭk'əl, kyo͞o'-) *n.* An alloy of copper with up to 40 percent of nickel, highly resistant to corrosion.

cu·prous (kyo͞o'prəs) *adj.* Of, pertaining to, or containing univalent copper. [Late Latin *cuprum,* COPPER.]

cu·pu·la (kyo͞o'pyə-lə) *n., pl.* **-lae** (-lē). *Anatomy.* A cup-shaped or domed structure, such as the apex of the cochlea. [New Latin, CUPULE.]

cu·pu·late (kyo͞o'pyə-lāt', -lĭt) *adj.* Also **cu·pu·lar** (-lər). **1.** Resembling a small cup; cup-shaped. **2.** Having or bearing a cupule.

cu·pule (kyo͞o'pyo͞ol') *n. Biology.* A cup-shaped part, structure, or indentation; especially, the cuplike base of an acorn. [New Latin *cupula,* from Late Latin *cūpula,* little cask or tub, diminutive of Latin *cūpa,* a tub, vat.]

cur (kûr) *n.* **1.** A dog considered to be inferior, vicious, or undesirable; a mongrel. **2.** A base or cowardly person. [Middle English *curre,* short for *kur(dogge),* "growling dog," perhaps from Old Norse *kurra,* to growl.]

cur. 1. currency. **2.** current.

cur·a·ble (kyo͝or'ə-bəl) *adj.* Capable of being healed or cured. **—cur·a·bil·i·ty, cur·a·ble·ness** *n.* **—cur·a·bly** *adv.*

cu·ra·çao (kyo͝or'ə-sō', -sou', ko͝or'-) *n.* A liqueur flavored with the peel of the sour Curaçao orange. [From CURAÇAO.]

cuneiform *One of the earliest forms of writing. Its wedge-shaped characters have been found, baked into tablets of clay, in Mesopotamia. This tablet dates from about 1250* B.C.

Cupid *The Roman winged god of love. Legend says he fires his arrows of love while blindfolded. This Roman statue of him dates from the second century* A.D.

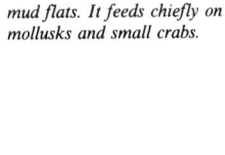

curlew *A common wader found worldwide on marshes and coastal mud flats. It feeds chiefly on mollusks and small crabs.*

PRONUNCIATION KEY

ă, pat; ā, pay; âr, care;
ä, father, are; b, bib;
ch, church; d, deed; ĕ, pet;
ē, be; f, fife; g, gag; h, hat;
hw, which; ĭ, pit; ī, pie;
îr, pier; j, judge; k, kick;
l, lid, needle; m, mum;
n, no, sudden; ng, thing;
ŏ, pot; ō, toe; ô, paw, for;
oi, noise; ou, out; o͝o, book;
o͞o, boot; p, pop; r, roar;
s, sauce; sh, ship, dish;
t, tight; th, thin, path;
th, this, bathe; ŭ, cut; ûr, fur;
v, valve; w, with; y, yes;
z, zebra, size; zh, vision;
ə, about, item, edible, gallop, circus, peaceful

IN FOREIGN WORDS:

à, *Fr.* ami; œ, *Fr.* feu, *Ger.* schön; ü, *Fr.* tu, *Ger.* über; KH, *Ger.* ich, *Scot.* loch; N, *Fr.* bon; y', *Fr.* Compiègne

STRESS MARKS:

Primary stress: ′
in·cite′ (ĭn-sīt′)
Secondary stress: ′
in′sight′ (ĭn′sīt′)

Cu·ra·çao (kyo͝or′ə-sō′, ko͞o′rä-sä′ō). The largest island in the Netherlands Antilles group, in the south Caribbean Sea. It was discovered and settled by Spain (1499) and occupied by the Dutch in the 17th century. It received autonomy under the Dutch Crown (1954). Willemstad is the administrative center.

cu·ra·cy (kyo͝or′ə-sē) *n., pl.* **-cies.** The office, duties, or term of office of a curate.

curagh, curragh. Variants of **currach.**

cu·ra·re, cu·ra·ri (ko͞o-rär′ē, kyo͞o-) *n.* **1.** A resinous substance obtained from several species of South American trees. It is used medicinally as a muscle relaxant and by some South American Indians as an arrow poison. **2.** Any of the trees from which this substance is obtained. [Portuguese and Spanish, from Carib *kurari.*]

cu·ra·rine (kyo͞o-rär′ĭn, -ēn′) *n.* A poisonous alkaloid, $C_{19}H_{26}N_2O$, obtained from curare. [CURAR(E) + -INE.]

cu·ra·rize (kyo͞o-rär′īz′) *tr.v.* **-rized, -rizing, -rizes. 1.** To poison with curare. **2.** To treat with curare so as to paralyze the motor nerves. **—cu·ra·ri·za·tion** *n.*

cu·ras·sow (kyo͝or′ə-sō′) *n.* Any of several long-tailed, crested tropical American birds of the family Cracidae, related to the pheasants and domestic fowl. [Variant of CURAÇAO (island).]

cu·rate (kyo͝or′ĭt) *n.* **1.** A clergyman who assists or deputizes for a rector or vicar. **2.** A clergyman who has charge of a parish. [Middle English *curat,* from Medieval Latin *cūrātus,* "one having a (spiritual) cure or charge," from *cūra,* CURE.]

cur·a·tive (kyo͝or′ə-tĭv) *adj.* **1.** Serving or tending to cure. **2.** Of or relating to the cure of disease.
~n. Something that cures; a remedy. **—cur·a·tive·ly** *adv.* **—cur·a·tive·ness** *n.*

cu·ra·tor (kyo͞o-rā′tər, kyo͝or′ə-tər) *n.* The administrative director of a museum, library, zoo, or other similar institution. [Middle English *curatour,* from Old French *curateur,* from Latin *cūrātōr,* overseer, manager, from *cūrāre,* to take care of, from *cūra,* care, CURE.] **—cu·ra·to·ri·al** *adj.* **—cu·ra·tor·ship** *n.*

curb (kûrb) *n.* Also *British* **kerb** (sense 2). **1.** Anything that checks or restrains. **2.** A concrete border or row of joined stones forming part of a gutter along the edge of a street. **3.** A chain or strap serving, with the bit, to restrain a horse. **4.** A **curb exchange** *(see).*
~tr.v. **curbed, curbing, curbs. 1.** To check, restrain, or control. **2.** To place a curb on (a horse). **3.** To lead (a dog) off the sidewalk into the gutter so that it can eliminate waste. —See Synonyms at **restrain.** [Middle English, from Old French *courber,* from Latin *curvāre,* bend, CURVE.] **—curb·er** *n.*

curb broker *n.* A broker on a curb exchange.

curb exchange *n.* A market dealing in securities not listed on the regular stock exchange. Also called "curb."

curb·ing (kûr′bĭng) *n.* **1.** The material used to construct a curb. **2.** A row of curbstones; a curb.

curb roof *n.* A roof having two slopes on each side, the lower slope being the steeper.

curb·stone (kûrb′stōn′) *n.* Also *British* **kerb·stone.** A stone or row of stones that constitutes a curb.

cur·cu·li·o (kər-kyo͞o′lē-ō′) *n., pl.* **-os.** Any of several American weevils of the family Curculionidae, many of which are destructive to fruit and other plants. [New Latin, from Latin *curculiō*†, weevil.]

cur·cu·ma (kûr′kyə-mə) *n.* Any of various Old World tropical plants of the genus *Curcuma,* having aromatic rootstocks. *C. longa* provides **turmeric** *(see).* [New Latin, from Arabic *kurkum,* saffron.]

curd (kûrd) *n.* **1.** *Often* **curds.** The coagulated part of milk, formed by the action of rennet or acid and used especially to make cheese. **2.** Any coagulation resembling this. **3.** The edible whitish flower head of the cauliflower.
~v. **curded, curding, curds.** *—tr.* To form into curd; cause to thicken; curdle. *—intr.* To become curd; curdle; coagulate. [Middle English *curd, crudde*†.] **—curd·y** *adj.*

curd cheese *n.* A soft, mild cheese made from skimmed milk curds.

cur·dle (kûrd′l) *v.* **-dled, -dling, -dles.** *—intr.* **1.** To congeal; become curd; coagulate. **2.** To go sour. *—tr.* **1.** To cause to congeal or change into curd. **2.** To make sour. [Frequentative of CURD.]

cure (kyo͝or) *n.* **1.** Restoration of health; recovery from disease. **2.** A method or course of medical treatment used to restore health. **3. a.** An agent, such as a drug, that restores health; a remedy. **b.** A remedy for a harmful or troublesome condition: *a cure for unemployment.* **4.** *Ecclesiastical.* Spiritual charge or care of souls, as of a priest for his congregation. Also called "cure of souls." **5.** The office or duties of a curate. **6.** The act or process of preserving a product such as fish, meat, or tobacco.
~v. **cured, curing, cures.** *—tr.* **1.** To restore to health; heal. **2.** To get rid of; remedy: *cure an evil.* **3.** To preserve (meat, fish, or the like), as by salting or smoking. **4.** To prepare, preserve, or finish (a substance) by a chemical or physical process. **5.** To vulcanize (rubber). *—intr.* **1.** To effect a cure or recovery. **2.** To be prepared, preserved, or finished by a chemical or physical process. [Middle English, care, spiritual charge, cure, from Old French, from Latin *cūra,* care, charge, healing.] **—cure·less** *adj.* **—cur·er** *n.*

cu·ré (kyo͞o-rā′, kyo͝or′ā′) *n. French.* A parish priest.

cure-all (kyo͝or′ôl) *n.* That which cures all diseases or evils; a panacea.

cu·ret·tage (kyo͝or′ə-täzh′, kyo͞o-rĕt′ĭj) *n.* Surgical scraping of a bodily cavity, as of the uterus, with a curette. Also called "curettement." See **D & C.** [French, from CURETTE.]

cu·rette, cu·ret (kyo͞o-rĕt′) *n.* A surgical instrument shaped like a scoop or spoon, used to remove dead tissue or growths from a bodily cavity. [French, from *curer,* to clean, from Old French, from Latin *cūrāre,* from *cūra,* CURE.]

cu·rette·ment (kyo͞o-rĕt′mənt) *n.* **Curettage** *(see).*

cur·few (kûr′fyo͞o) *n.* **1.** An order or regulation enjoining most people or specific members of the population to retire from the streets or from public premises at a prescribed hour. **2.** A similar medieval regulation requiring fires to be extinguished. **3. a.** The period during which any such regulation is in effect. **b.** The signal, such as a bell, announcing a curfew. **c.** The hour at which a curfew comes into effect. [Middle English *curfeu, coeverfu,* from Old French *cuevrefeu,* "a covering of the fire" : *co(u)vrir,* to COVER + *feu,* fire, from Latin *focus,* hearth (see **fuel**).]

cu·ri·a (kyo͝or′ē-ə) *n., pl.* **curiae** (kyo͝or′ē-ē′). **1. a.** The Senate or any of the various buildings in which it met in republican Rome. **b.** The place of assembly of high councils in various Italian cities under Roman administration. **2.** The ensemble of central administrative and governmental services in imperial Rome. **3.** *Often* **Curia.** The central administration governing the Roman Catholic Church. **4.** In medieval Europe: **a.** A feudal assembly or council. **b.** A royal court of justice. [Latin *cūria,* curia, council.] **—cu·ri·al** *adj.*

cu·rie (kyo͝or′ē, kyo͞o-rē′) *n. Abbr.* **Ci** A unit of radioactivity, the amount of any nuclide that undergoes exactly 3.7×10^{10} radioactive disintegrations per second. [After Marie CURIE.]

Cu·rie (kyo͝or′ē), **Marie,** born Maria Sklodowska (1867–1934). Polish chemist, famous for her discovery of radium (1898). She studied science in Paris and in 1895 married **Pierre Curie** (1859–1906), a French professor of physics. From 1896 the Curies investigated radioactivity and laid the foundations of nuclear physics. They were awarded the Nobel Prize for physics jointly with Henri Becquerel (1903). After her husband's death, Marie Curie continued her work and was awarded a second Nobel Prize, this time in chemistry for her discovery of radium and polonium and their properties (1911).

Curie law *n.* The law that magnetic susceptibility varies inversely with thermodynamic temperature in a paramagnetic substance. Also called "Curie's law." [After Pierre CURIE.]

Curie point *n.* A transition temperature marking a change in the magnetic properties of a substance, especially the change from ferromagnetism to paramagnetism. Also called "Curie temperature." [After Pierre CURIE.]

Cu·rie-Weiss law (kyo͝or′ē-wīs′, -vīs′, kyo͞o-rē′-) *n.* The law that the magnetic susceptibility of a paramagnetic substance above the Curie point varies inversely with the excess of temperature above that point. [After Pierre CURIE and Pierre *Weiss* (1865–1940), French physicist.]

cu·ri·o (kyo͝or′ē-ō′) *n., pl.* **-os.** A curious or unusual object of art or bric-a-brac. [Short for CURIOSITY.]

cu·ri·o·sa (kyo͝or′ē-ō′sə, -zə) *pl.n.* Books, writings, or objects dealing with unusual, especially pornographic, topics; erotica. [New Latin, from Latin *cūriōsa,* neuter plural of *cūriōsus,* CURIOUS.]

cu·ri·os·i·ty (kyo͝or′ē-ŏs′ə-tē) *n., pl.* **-ties. 1. a.** A desire to know or learn, especially about something new or strange. **b.** Excessive interest or eagerness to know; inquisitiveness. **2.** That which arouses interest, as by being novel or extraordinary. **3.** Strangeness; novelty. Also used adjectivally: *curiosity value.*

cu·ri·ous (kyo͝or′ē-əs) *adj.* **1.** Eager to acquire information or knowledge. **2.** Unduly inquisitive; prying; nosy. **3.** Interesting because of novelty or rarity; singular; odd. **4.** *Obsolete.* Accomplished with skill or ingenuity. [Middle English, from Old French *curios,* from Latin *cūriōsus,* careful, diligent, inquisitive, from *cūra,* care, CURE.] **—cu·ri·ous·ly** *adv.* **—cu·ri·ous·ness** *n.*
Usage: *curious, inquisitive, snoopy, nosy, intrusive.* These adjectives apply to persons who show a marked desire for information or knowledge. *Curious* more often implies a legitimate desire to enlarge one's knowledge, but can suggest a less commendable urge to concern oneself in others' affairs. *Inquisitive* frequently suggests excessive curiosity and the asking of many questions. *Snoopy* implies an unworthy motive and underhandedness in implementing it. *Nosy* suggests excessive curiosity and impertinence in an adult; applied to a child, it may refer less unfavorably to habitual curiosity. *Intrusive* stresses unwarranted and unwelcome concern with another's affairs.

Cu·ri·ti·ba (ko͞o-rē-tē′bä). Capital of Paraná state, in southeastern Brazil. It is a commercial and processing center for an expansive agricultural and ranching area. The city was founded in 1654 and grew rapidly in the late 19th and early 20th centuries when German, Italian, and Slavic immigrants began to develop the surrounding hinterland.

cu·ri·um (kyo͝or′ē-əm) *n. Symbol* **Cm** A silvery, metallic, synthetic, radioactive, transuranic element having 13 isotopes with mass numbers from 238 to 250 and half-lives from 64 minutes to 16.4 million years. Atomic number 96. [New Latin, after Marie and Pierre CURIE.]

curl (kûrl) *v.* **curled, curling, curls.** *—tr.* **1.** To twist (the hair, for example) into ringlets or coils. **2.** To form into the spiral or curved shape of a ringlet or coil. *—intr.* **1.** To form ringlets or coils. **2.** To assume a spiral or curved shape. Often used with *up.* **3.** To move in a curve or spiral. **4.** To play the game of curling. **—curl up. 1.** To assume a position with the legs drawn up. **2.** To make oneself comfortable.
~n. **1.** Something with a spiral or coiled shape. **2.** A coil or ringlet of hair. **3. a.** The act of curling. **b.** The state of being curled. **4.** *Mathematics.* The vector product of the del operator and a vector function. Compare **divergence.** [Middle English *curlen, crullen,*

from *crulle,* curly, from Middle Dutch.]

curl·er (kûr′lər) *n.* **1.** One that curls. **2.** A pin, roller, or the like on which hair is wound for curling. **3.** A player of the game of curling.

cur·lew (kûrl′yo͞o, kûr′lo͞o′) *n.* Any of several brownish, long-legged shore birds of the genus *Numenius,* having long, slender, downward-curving bills. [Middle English *curleu,* from Old French *courlieu* (imitative).]

Cur·ley (kûr′lē), **James Michael** (1874–1958). U.S. political leader. He was mayor of Boston (1914–18, 1922–26, 1930–34, 1946–50) and governor of Massachusetts (1935–37); he also served in the U.S. House of Representatives (1911–14, 1943–47). Widely known for his flamboyant control of Boston's political machine, he was the inspiration for Edwin O'Connor's novel *The Last Hurrah* (1956).

curl·i·cue, curl·y·cue (kûr′lĭ-kyo͞o′) *n.* A fancy twist or curl, such as a flourish made with a pen. [CURLY + CUE (rod).] **—curl·i·cued, curl·y·cued** *adj.*

curl·ing (kûr′lĭng) *n.* A game originating in Scotland and played on ice, in which two four-man teams slide heavy, flat, round stones *(curling stones)* toward a fixed mark in the center of a circle.

curling iron *n.* Also **curling irons.** A scissorlike metal device, usually rod-shaped, that is heated and used to curl individual locks of hair.

curl paper *n.* A piece of soft paper on which a lock of hair is rolled up in order to make it curl.

curl·y (kûr′lē) *adj.* **-ier, -iest. 1.** Having curls. **2.** Having the tendency to curl. **3.** Having a wavy grain. Said of wood: *curly maple.* **—curl·i·ly** *adv.* **—curl·i·ness** *n.*

curly top *n.* A disease of plants caused by a virus, *Ruga verrucosans,* and resulting in severe stunting of plants.

cur·mudg·eon (kər-mŭj′ən) *n.* **1.** A surly person. **2.** A miser. [16th century : origin obscure.] **—cur·mudg·eon·ly** *adj.*

cur·rach, cur·agh, cur·ragh (kûr′əKH, kûr′ə) *n. Scottish & Irish.* A kind of boat, a **coracle** *(see).* [Middle English *currok,* from Scottish Gaelic *curach* and Irish Gaelic *currach*; akin to Welsh *corwgl, cwrwgl*†.]

cur·rant (kûr′ənt) *n.* **1.** A small, dried seedless grape of the Mediterranean region, used in cooking. **2.** Any of various shrubs of the genus *Ribes,* bearing clusters of red, black, or greenish fruit. See **black currant, red currant. 3.** The small, sour fruit of any of these plants, used chiefly for making jam and jelly. [Middle English *raysons of coraunce,* from Norman French *raisins de corauntz,* grapes of CORINTH (from where they were originally exported).]

cur·ra·wong (kûr′ə-wông, -wŏng) *n.* Any Australian bird of the genus *Strepera,* usually having a black plumage with white markings. Also called "bell magpie." [From a native Australian name.]

cur·ren·cy (kûr′ən-sē) *n., pl.* **-cies. 1.** *Abbr.* **cur.** Any form of money in actual use as a medium of exchange. **2.** A passing from hand to hand; circulation. **3.** Common acceptance; prevalence. [Medieval Latin *currentia,* "a flowing," from Latin *currēns* (stem *current-*), present participle of *currere,* to run. See **current.**] See feature, next page.

cur·rent (kûr′ənt) *adj.* **1. a.** Belonging to the time now passing; now in progress. **b.** Most recent: *the current issue.* **2.** Passing from one to another; circulating, as money does. **3.** Commonly accepted; prevalent. —See Synonyms at **prevailing.**

~*n.* **1.** A steady and smooth onward movement, as of water. **2.** The part of any body of liquid or gas that has a continuous movement in a specific direction: *a river current.* **3.** A general tendency, movement, or course. **4.** *Symbol* **i, I** *Electricity.* **a.** A flow of electric charge. **b.** The amount of electric charge flowing past a specific circuit point per unit time. In this sense, also called "electric current." —See Synonyms at **tendency.** [Middle English *curraunt,* from Old French *corant,* present participle of *courre,* to run, from Latin *currere.*] **—cur·rent·ly** *adv.* **—cur·rent·ness** *n.*

current assets *pl.n.* Cash or other assets convertible into cash at short notice.

current bedding *n.* **Cross bedding** *(see).*

current density *n. Symbol* **J 1.** *Electricity.* The ratio of the magnitude of current flowing in a conductor to the cross-sectional area perpendicular to the current flow. **2.** *Physics.* The number of subatomic particles per unit time crossing a unit area in a designated plane perpendicular to the direction of motion of the particles.

current events *pl.n.* **1.** Topical news, usually of serious issues such as politics or international affairs. **2.** Discussion of such news, as on television. Also used adjectivally: *current events programs.* Also called "current affairs."

current ratio *n.* The arithmetic ratio of current assets to liabilities.

cur·ri·cle (kûr′ĭ-kəl) *n.* A light, open two-wheeled vehicle, drawn by two horses abreast. [Latin *curriculum,* a running, racecourse, racing chariot. See **curriculum.**]

cur·ric·u·lum (kə-rĭk′yə-ləm) *n., pl.* **-la** (-lə) or **-lums. 1.** All the courses of study offered by an educational institution. **2.** A particular course of study, often in a special field. [New Latin, from Latin, a running, course, from *currere,* to run.] **—cur·ric·u·lar** *adj.*

cur·ric·u·lum vi·tae (kə-rĭk′yə-ləm vī′tē, ko͝o-rĭk′o͞o-lo͝om wē′tī′) *n., pl.* **curricula vitae.** *Abbr.* **c.v.** A short résumé of one's educational background and career, as for a prospective employer. [Latin, the course of one's life.]

currie. Variant of **curry.**

cur·ri·er (kûr′ē-ər) *n.* One who curries something, especially leather. [Middle English *curr(e)iour,* from Old French, from Latin *coriārius,* a tanner, from *corium,* leather.]

Cur·ri·er (kŭr′ē-ər, kŭr′-), **Nathanial** (1813–88). U.S. lithographer. With his business partner James Merritt Ives, he produced more than 7,000 prints depicting American life and tradition. The prints, each signed "Currier & Ives," are now valued collector's items.

cur·ri·er·y (kûr′ē-ə-rē) *n., pl.* **-ies.** The trade, work, or shop of a leather currier.

cur·rish (kûr′ĭsh) *adj.* Of or like a cur; snarling; bad-tempered. **—cur·rish·ly** *adv.*

cur·ry[1] (kûr′ē) *tr.v.* **-ried, -rying, -ries. 1.** To groom (a horse) with a currycomb. **2.** To prepare (tanned hides) for use by soaking, coloring, or other processes. **—curry favor.** To seek or gain favor by fawning or flattery. [Middle English *curreien,* from Old French *co(n)reer,* to prepare, equip, from Vulgar Latin *conrēdāre* (unattested) : *com-* (intensive), with + *rēdāre* (unattested), to prepare, from Germanic. Sense 2 is partly a back-formation from CURRIER.]

curry[2] *n., pl.* **-ries.** Also **cur·rie. 1.** A dish that originated in India, consisting of meat, fish, or vegetables prepared and cooked in a sauce made of various spices that give it a hot or piquant flavor. **2.** Curry powder or curry paste. **3.** A dish seasoned with curry powder or curry paste.

~*tr.v.* **curried, -rying, -ries. 1.** To make a curry of. **2.** To season with curry. [Tamil *kari,* sauce.]

Cur·ry (kûr′ē), **John Anthony** (1949–). British ice skater, who brought the expressiveness of ballet to his art. He won the Olympic, European, and World figure-skating championships in a single season (1976). Curry has since toured extensively with his ice-dancing companies.

Curry, John Steuart (1897–1946). U.S. painter. He is noted for his vigorous depictions of the rural American scene, especially for his murals and oil paintings of Kansas, including *Baptism in Kansas* and *Tornado over Kansas.*

cur·ry·comb (kûr′ē-kōm′) *n.* A comb with metal teeth, used for grooming horses.

~*tr.v.* **currycombed, -combing, -combs.** To groom with a currycomb.

curry paste *n.* A condiment prepared from pungent spices, as in curry powder, blended with oil, tomatoes, onions, and the like.

curry powder *n.* A blended condiment prepared from turmeric and other pungent spices such as cumin, coriander, and chili.

curse (kûrs) *n.* **1.** An appeal to a supernatural power for evil or injury to befall someone or something. **2.** The evil or injury thus invoked. **3.** Someone or something accursed. **4.** That which brings or causes evil; a scourge. **5.** Any profane oath or obscenity. **6.** *Ecclesiastical.* A censure, ban, or anathema. **7.** *Informal.* Menstruation. Preceded by *the.*

~*v.* **cursed** or **curst, cursing, curses.** —*tr.* **1.** To invoke evil, calamity, or injury upon; damn. **2.** To swear at; abuse profanely. **3.** To bring harm upon; afflict. **4.** *Ecclesiastical.* To put under ban or anathema; excommunicate. —*intr.* To utter curses; swear. [Middle English *curs(e),* Old English *curs*†.] **—curs·er** *n.*

curs·ed (kûr′sĭd, kûrst) *adj.* Also **curst** (kûrst). **1.** Deserving to be cursed; wicked; detestable. **2.** Damned; under a curse. **—curs·ed·ly** *adv.* **—curs·ed·ness** *n.*

cur·sive (kûr′sĭv) *adj.* Designating writing or printing in which the letters are joined together; flowing.

~*n.* **1.** A cursive character or letter. **2.** A manuscript written in cursive characters. **3.** *Printing.* A kind of type that imitates handwriting. [Medieval Latin *(scripta) cursīva,* "flowing (script)," from Latin *cursus,* past participle of *currere,* to run.]

cur·sor (kûr′sər) *n.* **1.** The point of a measuring or calculating instrument that slides; especially, the movable window on a slide rule. **2.** A visual indicator, such as a movable point of light, that is used to indicate a specific position on a visual display unit, such as where a deletion or insertion is to be made. [Latin, "runner," from *currere* (past participle stem *curs-*), to run.]

cur·so·ri·al (kûr-sôr′ē-əl, -sōr′ē-əl) *adj. Zoology.* Adapted to or specialized for running: *cursorial birds; cursorial legs.* [Late Latin *cursōrius,* of running. See **cursory.**]

cur·so·ry (kûr′sə-rē) *adj.* Hasty and superficial; not thorough. See Synonyms at **superficial.** [Late Latin *cursōrius,* of running, from Latin *cursor,* a runner, from *cursus.* See **cursive.**] **—cur·so·ri·ly** *adv.* **—cur·so·ri·ness** *n.*

curst. 1. Variant of **cursed. 2.** Alternate past tense and past participle of **curse.**

curt (kûrt) *adj.* **1.** Rudely brief or abrupt, as in speech or manner. **2.** Terse; concise. **3.** Shortened. —See Synonyms at **gruff.** [Latin *curtus,* cut short.] **—curt·ly** *adv.* **—curt·ness** *adj.*

cur·tail (kər-tāl′) *tr.v.* **-tailed, -tailing, -tails.** To reduce by or as if by cutting short. [Variant of obsolete *curtal,* to dock the tail of a horse, from CURTAL.] **—cur·tail·er** *n.* **—cur·tail·ment** *n.*

curtail step *n.* The widened step or steps at the foot of a flight of stairs. [Origin obscure.]

cur·tain (kûrt′n) *n.* **1.** A piece of cloth or similar material hanging in a window or other opening as a decoration, shade, or screen. **2.** *Theater.* **a.** A hanging barrier that rises at the beginning of a scene and falls at the end of a scene. **b.** A line, speech, or situation in a play that occurs at the very end or just before the curtain falls. **3.** The part of a rampart or parapet connecting two bastions or gates. **4.** Any barrier to visibility: *a curtain of fog.* **5.** Any barrier, such as a restriction on communication. **6. curtains.** *Informal.* The end; ruin.

~*tr.v.* **curtained, -taining, -tains. 1.** To shut off with or as if with a curtain. Often used with *off.* **2.** To provide with curtains. [Middle English *curtin(e),* from Old French, from Late Latin *cortīna,* enclo-

curassow *The turkeylike curassow lives in flocks in the forests of tropical America. The birds are sometimes kept as pets by villagers.*

COUNTRY	BASIC UNIT	SUBDIVISION	ABBREV.
Afghanistan	afghani	100 puls	Af.
Albania	lek	100 quintars or qindarka	Lk.
Algeria	dinar	100 centimes	D.A.
Angola	kwanza	100 lwei	Kw.
Antigua and Barbuda	E. Caribbean dollar	100 cents	E.C. $.
Argentina	peso	100 centavos	Arg. $.
Australia	dollar	100 cents	A. $.
Austria	schilling	100 groschen	A. Sch.
Bahamas	dollar	100 cents	Ba. $.
Bahrain	dinar	1,000 fils	B.D.
Bangladesh	taka	100 paise or poisha	Tk.
Barbados	dollar	100 cents	Bds. $.
Belgium	franc	100 centimes	B. Fr.
Belize	dollar	100 cents	Bz. $.
Benin	CFAFr.*	100 centimes	CFAFr.
Bermuda	dollar	100 cents	Bda. $.
Bhutan	ngultrum	100 tikchungs or chetrum	N.
Bolivia	peso	100 centavos	B. $.
Botswana	pula	100 thebe	P.
Brazil	cruzado	100 centavos	Cr.
Brunei	dollar	100 sen	Br. $.
Bulgaria	lev	100 stotinki	Lv.
Burkina Faso	CFAFr.*	100 centimes	CFAFr.
Burma	kyat	100 pyas	K.
Burundi	franc	100 centimes	Bu. Fr.
Cameroon	CFAFr.*	—	CFAFr.
Canada	dollar	100 cents	C. $.
Cape Verde	escudo	100 centavos	C. V. Esc.
Cayman Islands	dollar	100 cents	C.I. $.
Central African Republic	CFAFr.*	100 centimes	CFAFr.
Chad	CFAFr.*	—	CFAFr.
Chile	peso	100 centavos	Ch. $.
China	yuan	10 jiao or 100 fen	Y.
Colombia	peso	100 centavos	Col. $.
Comoros	CFAFr.*	100 centimes	CFAFr.
Congo	CFAFr.*	—	CFAFr.
Costa Rica	colón	100 céntimos	C.R. ₡.
Cuba	peso	100 centavos	Cub. $.
Cyprus	pound	100 cents	C. £.
Czechoslovakia	koruna or crown	100 halers or haleru	Kčs.
Denmark	krone	100 øre	D. Kr.
Djibouti	franc	100 centimes	Dj. Fr.
Dominica	E. Caribbean dollar	100 cents	E.C. $.
Dominican Republic	peso	100 centavos	D.R. $.
East Germany	Mark	100 pfennig	M.
Eastern Caribbean	dollar	100 cents	E.C. $.
Ecuador	sucre	100 centavos	Su.
Egypt	pound	100 piasters or 1,000 millièmes	E.£.
El Salvador	colón	100 centavos	E.S. ₡.
Equatorial Guinea	franc	100 centimes	CFAFr.
Ethiopia	birr	100 cents	Br.
Fiji	dollar	100 cents	F. $.
Finland	markka	100 penniä	F. Mk.
France	franc	100 centimes	Fr.
Gabon	CFAFr.*	—	CFAFr.
Gambia	dalasi	100 bututs	Di.
Ghana	cedi	100 pesewas	₵.
Greece	drachma	100 lepta	Dr.
Grenada	E. Caribbean dollar	100 cents	E.C. $.
Guatemala	quetzal	100 centavos	Q.
Guinea	syli	100 cauris	Sy.
Guinea-Bissau	peso	100 centavos	G.B. P.
Guyana	dollar	100 cents	G. $.

COUNTRY	BASIC UNIT	SUBDIVISION	ABBREV.
Haiti	gourde	100 centimes	Gde.
Honduras	lempira or peso	100 centavos	La.
Hong Kong	dollar	100 cents	H.K. $.
Hungary	forint	100 fillér	Ft.
Iceland	króna (plural = krónur)	100 aurar	I. Kr.
India	rupee	100 paise	I.R.
Indonesia	rupiah	100 sen	Rp.
Iran	rial	100 dinars	Rl.
Iraq	dinar	20 dirhams or 1,000 fils	I.D.
Ireland, Republic of	pound or punt Eirennach	100 pence or pighne	I. £.
Israel	shekel	100 new agorot	Sk.
Italy	lira	100 centesimi	L.
Ivory Coast	CFAFr.*	100 centimes	CFAFr.
Jamaica	dollar	100 cents	J. $.
Japan	yen	100 sen	¥
Jordan	dinar	1,000 fils	J.D.
Kampuchea	riel	100 sen	K. RL.
Kenya	shilling	100 cents	K. Sh.
Kuwait	dinar	10 dirhams or 1,000 fils	K.D.
Laos	kip	100 at(s)	Kp.
Lebanon	pound	100 piasters	L.£.
Lesotho	loti (plural = maloti)	100 lisente	Lo. or Mo.
Liberia	dollar	100 cents	L. $.
Libya	dinar	1,000 dirhams	L.D.
Luxembourg	franc	100 centimes	L. Fr.
Madagascar	franc	—	Mg. Fr.
Malawi	kwacha	100 tambala	M. K.
Malaysia	dollar or ringgit	100 cents or sen	Ma. $.
Maldives	rufiyaa	100 laaris	Mv.R.
Mali	CFAFr.*	100 centimes	M. Fr.
Malta	Maltese lira	100 cents or 1,000 mils	L. M.
Mauritania	ouguiya	5 khoums	U.
Mauritius	rupee	100 cents	M. R.
Mexico	peso	100 centavos	Mex. $.
Mongolia	tugrik	100 möngö	Tug.
Morocco	dirham	100 centimes	Dh.
Mozambique	metical	100 centavos	Mt.
Nepal	rupee	100 pice or paisa	N.R.
Netherlands	guilder or florin	100 cents	Gld or Fl.
Netherlands Antilles	guilder or florin	100 cents	N.A. Gld or Fl.
New Zealand	dollar	100 cents	N.Z. $.
Nicaragua	córdoba	100 centavos	C. $.
Niger	CFAFr.*	100 centimes	CFAFr.
Nigeria	naira	100 kobo	₦
North Korea	won	100 jun	N.K.W.
Norway	krone	100 øre	N. Kr.
Oman	rial Omani	1,000 baiza	O.R.
Pakistan	rupee	100 paisa	P.R.
Panama	balboa	100 cents or centésimos	Ba.
Papua New Guinea	kina	100 toea	Ka.
Paraguay	guaraní	100 céntimos	₲.
Peru	sol	100 centavos	S.
Philippines	peso	100 centavos	P.P.
Poland	zloty	100 groszy	Zl.
Portugal	escudo	100 centavos	Esc.
Qatar	Qatar riyal	100 dirhams	Q.R.
Rumania	leu (plural = lei)	100 bani	—
Rwanda	franc	100 centimes	Rw. Fr.
St. Lucia	E. Carib. dollar	100 cents	E.C. $.

COUNTRY	BASIC UNIT	SUBDIVISION	ABBREV.
St. Vincent and the Grenadines	E. Caribbean dollar	—	E.C. $.
São Tomé and Principe	dobra	100 centavos	Db.
Saudi Arabia	riyal or rial	100 halalah	S.A. R.
Senegal	CFAFr.*	100 centimes	CFAFr.
Seychelles	rupee	100 cents	S.R.
Sierra Leone	leone	100 cents	Le.
Singapore	dollar	100 cents	S. $.
Solomon Islands	dollar	100 cents	S.I. $.
Somalia	shilling	100 cents or centesimi	So. Sh.
South Africa	rand	100 cents	R.
South Korea	won	100 chon	S.K. W.
South Yemen	dinar	1,000 fils	Y.D.
Spain	peseta	100 céntimos	Pa.
Sri Lanka	rupee	100 cents	S.L. R.
Sudan	pound	100 piasters or 1,000 millièmes	S. £.
Surinam	guilder or florin	100 cents	S. Gld. or S. Fl.
Swaziland	lilangeni (plural = emalangeni)	100 cents	Li. or Ei.
Sweden	krona	100 öre	S. Kr.
Switzerland	franc	100 centimes or rappen	S. Fr.
Syria	pound	100 piasters	Sy. £.
Taiwan	New Taiwan dollar	100 cents	N.T. $.
Tanzania	shilling	100 cents	T. Sh.
Thailand	baht	100 satang	Bt.
Togo	CFAFr.*	100 centimes	CFAFr.
Tonga	pa'anga	100 seniti	T. $.
Trinidad and Tobago	dollar	100 cents	T.T. $.
Tunisia	dinar	1,000 millièmes	T.D.
Turkey	lira or pound	100 kurus or piasters	T.L.
Uganda	shilling	100 cents	U. Sh.
United Arab Emirates	dirham	100 fils	U.A.E. Dh.
United Kingdom	pound	100 pence	£.
United States	dollar	100 cents	$.
Uruguay	nuevo peso	100 centésimos	Urug. N.$.
U.S.S.R.	rouble	100 kopecks or kopeks	Rub.
Vanuatu	vatu	100 cents	V.
Venezuela	bolívar	100 céntimos	B.
Vietnam	dong	10 hao or 100 xu	D.
Western Samoa	talà or dollar	100 sene or cents	W.S. $.
West Germany	deutsche mark	100 pfennig	D.M.
Yemen	riyal	100 fils	Y.R.
Yugoslavia	dinar	100 para	Yu. D. or Ju. D.
Zaire	zaire	100 makuta or 10,000 sengi	Z.
Zambia	kwacha	100 ngwee	K.
Zimbabwe	dollar	100 cents	Z. $.

*Franc communauté financière africaine

USING FOREIGN CURRENCY AT HOME *Some smaller countries use other currencies besides their own. For instance, the Solomon Islands in the southwest Pacific use as legal tender the Australian dollar as well as their own. A few sovereign states use only foreign money—in San Marino and Vatican City, for example, the currency in use is the Italian lira.*

sure, curtain, translation of Greek *aulaia,* from *aulē,* court.]

curtain call *n.* The appearance of a performer or performers at the end of a performance in response to applause.

curtain lecture *n.* A private reprimand given to a husband by his wife, so called from the curtained beds in which such scoldings once took place.

curtain raiser *n.* **1.** A short entertainment presented before the principal dramatic production. **2.** Any preliminary event.

curtain speech *n.* **1.** A talk given in front of the curtain at the conclusion of a theatrical performance. **2.** The final speech of a play or of an act of a play.

cur·tal (kûr′təl) *n. Obsolete.* **1.** An animal with a docked tail. **2.** Anything cut short or docked.
~*adj. Obsolete.* **1.** Cut short or docked, as an animal's tail may be. **2.** Wearing a short frock: *a curtal friar.* [Old French *courtault,* horse with a cropped tail or mane, from *court,* short, from Latin *curtus,* shortened.]

curtal ax *n. Archaic.* A cutlass. [Variant (influenced by CURTAL and AX) of earlier *curtelace, coutelace,* CUTLASS.]

cur·tate (kûr′tāt′) *adj.* Shortened; abbreviated. [Latin *curtātus,* past participle of *curtāre,* to shorten, from *curtus,* short, CURT.]

cur·te·sy (kûr′tə-sē) *n., pl.* **-sies.** The life tenure which by common law is held by a man over the property of his deceased wife if children with rights of inheritance were born during the marriage. [Middle English *courteisie,* curtesy, COURTESY.]

cur·ti·lage (kûr′tə-lĭj) *n. Law.* The enclosed land surrounding a house or dwelling. [Middle English, from Old French *courtillage,* from *courtil,* little court, diminutive of *cort,* COURT.]

Cur·tiss (kûr′tĭs), **Glenn Hammond** (1878–1930). U.S. aviation pioneer. He developed and refined the first plane to complete a one-kilometer flight (1908), the first seaplane (1911), and the aileron (1911). He founded the Curtiss Aeroplane & Motor Company that produced thousands of biplanes for army and navy flight schools.

curt·sy (kûrt′sē) *n., pl.* **-sies.** Also **curt·sey,** *pl.* **-seys.** A gesture of respect or reverence made by women by bending the knees with one foot forward and lowering the body.
~*intr.v.* **curtsied, -sying, -sies.** Also **curt·sey, -seyed, -seying, -seys.** To make a curtsy. [Variant of COURTESY.]

cu·rule (kyo͝or′o͞ol) *adj.* Privileged to sit in a curule chair; of superior rank. [Latin *curūlis,* "of a chariot," of a curule chair (originally a throne mounted on a chariot), from *currus,* a chariot, from *currere,* to run.]

curule chair *n.* A seat with heavy, curved legs and no back, reserved for the use of the highest officials in ancient Rome. Also called "curule seat."

cur·va·ceous (kûr-vā′shəs) *adj.* **1.** Curving. **2.** *Informal.* Of, pertaining to, or designating a woman having a full or voluptuous figure; shapely. [CURV(E) + -ACEOUS.] **—cur·va·ceous·ly** *adv.*

cur·va·ture (kûr-və-cho͝or) *n.* **1. a.** An act of curving. **b.** The state of being curved. **2.** *Mathematics.* **a.** The ratio of the change in tangent inclination over a given arc to the length of the arc. Also called "average curvature." **b.** The limit of this ratio as the length of the arc approaches zero. **3.** *Medicine.* A curving or bending, especially an abnormal one: *curvature of the spine.* [Latin *curvātūra,* from *curvātus,* past participle of *curvāre,* to bend, from *curvus,* curved.]

curve (kûrv) *n.* **1. a.** A line that deviates from straightness in a smooth, continuous fashion. **b.** A surface that deviates from a flat plane in a smooth, continuous fashion. **2.** A curved part, object, or region, such as a part of the human body. **3. a.** A line representing data on a graph. **b.** A trend derived from or as if from such a graph. **4.** *Mathematics.* **a.** The graph of a function on a coordinate plane. **b.** The intersection of two surfaces in three dimensions.
~*v.* **curved, curving, curves.** —*intr.* To move in or take the shape of a curve. —*tr.* To cause to curve. [From earlier *curve (line),* "curved (line)," from Middle English *curve,* curved, from Latin *curvus.*] **—curv·ed·ly** *adv.* **—curv·ed·ness** *n.* **—curv·y** *adj.*

curve ball *n.* **1.** *Baseball.* A pitched ball that veers or breaks to the left when thrown with the right hand and to the right when thrown with the left hand. **2.** *Slang.* A trick or deception.

cur·vet (kûr′vĭt) *n. Dressage.* A light leap by a horse, in which both hind legs leave the ground just before the forelegs are set down.
~*v.* **curvetted** or **-veted, -vetting** or **-veting, -vets.** —*intr.* **1.** To leap in a curvet. **2.** To prance; frolic. —*tr.* To cause to leap in a curvet. [Italian *corvetta,* "curving leap," from Old Italian, diminutive of *corva,* a curve, from Latin *curva,* feminine of *curvus,* curved, bent.]

cur·vi·lin·e·ar (kûr′və-lĭn′ē-ər) *adj.* Also **cur·vi·lin·e·al** (-əl). Formed, bounded, or characterized by curved lines. [Latin *curvus,* curved (see **curve**) + LINEAR.] **—cur·vi·lin·e·ar·ly** *adv.*

Cur·wen (kûr′wən), **John** (1816–80). British educator. He devised a method of teaching music by using the tonic sol-fa system of notation invented (*c.* 1812) by another music teacher, Sarah Ann Glover (1785–1867).

cus·cus (kŭs′kəs) *n.* Any of several marsupials of the genus *Phalanger,* of New Guinea and adjacent areas, having protruding eyes, a yellow nose, and a long, prehensile tail. [New Latin, probably from the native New Guinean name.]

cu·sec (kyo͞o′sĕk) *n.* A unit of volumetric flow of liquids, equal to one cubic foot per second. [CU(BIC) + SEC(OND).]

Cush[1] (kŭsh, ko͝osh). The eldest son of Ham. Genesis 10:6.

Cush[2], **Kush** (kŭsh, ko͝osh). **1.** A legendary ancient region of northeastern Africa where the Biblical descendants of Cush settled, often identified with Ethiopia. **2.** An ancient kingdom of Nubia in northern Sudan. It flourished from the 11th century B.C. until the 4th century A.D. when its capital, Merowe, fell to the Ethiopians.

cu·shaw (kə-shô′) *n.* A squash, *Cucurbita moschata,* having variably shaped, often crook-necked fruit. [Earlier *coscushaw,* from some Algonquian language of North Carolina or Virginia.]

Cush·ing (ko͝osh′ĭng), **Caleb** (1800–79). U.S. politician, lawyer, and diplomat. As special envoy to China (1843–45), he negotiated a treaty that opened five ports ot U.S. trade and establsihed the principle of extraterritoriality for U.S. citizens in China. He later served as U.S. attorney general (1853–57) and minister to Spain (1874–77).

Cush·ing's disease (ko͝osh′ĭngz) *n.* A disease resulting from excess corticosteroid hormones in the body, characterized by obesity, high blood pressure, and loss of minerals from the bones. Also called "Cushing's syndrome." [After Harvey *Cushing* (1869–1939), U.S. neurologist.]

cush·ion (ko͝osh′ən) *n.* **1.** A pad or pillow with a soft filling, used for resting or reclining against or on. **2.** Anything resilient used as a rest, support, or shock absorber. **3.** Something that provides protection against harmful or distressing effects: *Her savings were a cushion against inflation.* **4.** The rim bordering the playing area on a billiard table. **5.** A pillow used in lacemaking. **6.** An **air cushion** *(see).*
~*tr.v.* **cushioned, -ioning, -ions.** **1.** To provide with a cushion. **2.** To place or seat on a cushion. **3.** To cover or hide with or as if with a cushion. **4.** To protect against or absorb the shock or adverse effects of something. [Middle English *cuisshen,* from Old French *coissin,* from Vulgar Latin *coxīnus* (unattested), "hip rest," cushion, from Latin *coxa,* hip.] **—cush·ion·y** *adj.*

Cush·it·ic, Kush·it·ic (ko͞o-shĭt′ĭk) *n.* A group of Hamitic languages, including Somali and other languages spoken in Somalia and Ethiopia.
~*adj.* Of or pertaining to this group of languages.

Cush·man (ko͝osh′mən), **Charlotte Saunders** (1816–76). U.S. actress. She made her debut in Boston in 1835, then appeared in New York and Philadelphia (1837–44) before traveling to London, where she disciplined and polished her talents as an actress who had the ability to move audiences passionately. She lived in Europe until 1870, but returned frequently to tour America, where she was acclaimed as the leading actress of her day.

cush·y (ko͝osh′ē) *adj.* **-ier, -iest.** *Slang.* Comfortable; undemanding: *a cushy job.* [Anglo-Indian, from Hindi *khūsh,* from Persian *khōsh*†, pleasant.]

cusk (kŭsk) *n., pl.* **cusk** or **cusks.** A food fish, *Brosme brosme,* of North Atlantic coastal waters. [Probably variant of earlier *tusk,* from Norn.]

cusk eel *n.* Any of various eellike, chiefly marine fishes of the family Ophidiidae.

cusp (kŭsp) *n.* **1.** A point or pointed end. **2.** *Anatomy.* **a.** A prominence or projection on the chewing surface of a tooth. **b.** A fold or flap of a heart valve. **3.** *Geometry.* A point at which a curve crosses itself and at which the two tangents to the curve coincide. In this sense, also called "spinode." **4.** *Architecture.* The pointed figure formed by two intersecting arcs or foils. **5.** *Astronomy.* Either point of: **a.** A crescent moon. **b.** A satellite or inferior planet in a similar phase. **6.** *Astrology.* The transitional first or last part of a house or sign. [Latin *cuspis*†, a point, spear.]

cus·pate (kŭs′pāt) *adj.* Also **cus·pat·ed** (-pāt′ĭd), **cusped** (kŭspt). **1.** Having a cusp or cusps. **2.** Shaped like a cusp.

cus·pid (kŭs′pĭd) *n.* A tooth having one point; a canine tooth. [Back-formation from BICUSPID.]

cus·pi·date (kŭs′pə-dāt) *adj.* Also **cus·pi·dat·ed** (-dā′tĭd), **cus·pi·dal** (-dəl). **1.** Having a cusp or cusps. **2.** *Biology.* Terminating in or tipped with a sharp point: *a cuspidate leaf.* [Latin *cuspidātus,* from the past participle of *cuspidāre,* to make pointed, from *cuspis* (stem *cuspid-*), point, CUSP.]

cus·pi·da·tion (kŭs′pə-dā′shən) *n. Architecture.* Decoration with cusps.

cus·pi·dor (kŭs′pə-dôr′) *n.* A **spittoon** *(see).* [Portuguese, from *cuspir,* to spit, from Latin *conspuere,* to spit upon : *com-* (intensive), with + *spuere,* to spit.]

cuss (kŭs) *v.* **cussed, cussing, cusses.** *Informal.* —*intr.* To curse. —*tr.* To shout curses at.
~*n. Informal.* **1.** A curse. **2.** An odd or perverse creature. [Variant of CURSE.]

cuss·ed (kŭs′ĭd) *adj. Informal.* **1.** Cursed. **2.** Perverse; obstinate. **3.** Irritating; vexatious. **—cuss·ed·ly** *adv.* **—cuss·ed·ness** *n.*

cus·tard (kŭs′tərd) *n.* **1. a.** A thick, sweet, yellow sauce for desserts and puddings, made of sweetened milk and eggs, heated together and sometimes thickened with cornflour. **b.** A similar preparation made with sweetened milk and custard powder. **2.** A dessert of milk, sugar, sometimes cream, eggs, and usually flavoring, baked until set. [Middle English *crustade,* a kind of pie, from Norman French *crustade* (unattested), from *crute,* CRUST.]

custard apple *n.* **1.** A tropical American tree, *Annona reticulata,* bearing large, heart-shaped fruit. **2.** The fruit of this tree, having edible, fleshy pulp. **3.** Any of several related trees or fruit; especially, the **papaw** *(see).* [So called because its pulp resembles custard.]

Cus·ter (kŭs′tər), **George Armstrong** (1839–76). U.S. cavalry officer, made a brigadier general at the age of 23. Facing Sioux opposition under Sitting Bull and Crazy Horse, he rashly divided his force and led a party of 264 men to annihilation by an over-

cuscus *Up to 60 centimeters (2 feet) long, these monkeylike marsupials live in the forests of New Guinea, northern Australia, and the Indonesian island of Sulawesi (Celebes).*

custard apple *The fruit of a group of trees native to the American tropics. The yellow pulp looks and tastes like custard.*

PRONUNCIATION KEY

ă, pat; ā, pay; âr, care; ä, father, are; b, bib; ch, church; d, deed; ĕ, pet; ē, be; f, fife; g, gag; h, hat; hw, which; ĭ, pit; ī, pie; îr, pier; j, judge; k, kick; l, lid, needle; m, mum; n, no, sudden; ng, thing; ŏ, pot; ō, toe; ô, paw, for; oi, noise; ou, out; o͝o, book; o͞o, boot; p, pop; r, roar; s, sauce; sh, ship, dish; t, tight; th, thin, path; *th,* this, bathe; ŭ, cut; ûr, fur; v, valve; w, with; y, yes; z, zebra, size; zh, vision; ə, about, item, edible, gallop, circus, peaceful

IN FOREIGN WORDS:

à, *Fr.* ami; œ, *Fr.* feu, *Ger.* schön; ü, *Fr.* tu, *Ger.* über; KH, *Ger.* ich, *Scot.* loch; N, *Fr.* bon; y′, *Fr.* Compiègne

STRESS MARKS:

Primary stress: ′ **in·cite′** (ĭn-sīt′)
Secondary stress: ′ **in′sight′** (ĭn′sīt′)

whelmingly larger Indian force at Little Bighorn (1876). The site of his defeat is marked by the Custer Battlefield National Monument, a national cemetery.

cus·to·di·al (kŭs-tō′dē-əl) *adj.* **1.** Of or pertaining to guarding or guardianship. **2.** Involving or necessitating imprisonment.

cus·to·di·an (kŭs-tō′dē-ən) *n.* **1.** One who has charge of something; a warder or caretaker. **2.** A keeper, especially of a public building, art collection, or the like. **—cus·to·di·an·ship** *n.*

cus·to·dy (kŭs′tə-dē) *n., pl.* **-dies. 1.** The act or right of guarding, especially such a right granted by a court to a guardian of a minor. **2.** The state of being kept or guarded. **3.** The state of being detained or held under guard, especially by the police. [Middle English *custodie,* from Latin *custōdia,* from CUSTOS.]

cus·tom (kŭs′təm) *n.* **1.** A practice followed as a matter of course among a people or society; a conventional mode or form of action. **2.** A habitual practice of an individual. **3.** *Law.* A common tradition or usage so long established that it has the force or validity of law. **4. a.** Habitual patronage, as of a store or business. **b.** Collectively, those who patronize a store or business; customers. **5.** Tribute, service, or rent paid by a feudal tenant to his lord. —See Synonyms at **habit.**
~adj. Made to the specifications of an individual purchaser: *a custom car.* [Middle English *custume,* from Old French *costume,* from Latin *consuētūdō,* a being accustomed, from *consuēscere,* to accustom : *com-* (intensive), with + *suēscere,* to become accustomed.]

cus·tom·a·ble (kŭs′təm-ə-bəl) *adj.* Subject to tariffs.

cus·tom·ar·y (kŭs′tə-mĕr′ē) *adj.* **1.** Commonly practiced or used as a matter of course; usual. **2.** Based on custom or tradition rather than written law or contract. —See Synonyms at **usual.**
~n., pl. **customaries.** A written record of the customary laws of a community. **—cus·tom·ar·i·ly** *adv.* **—cus·tom·ar·i·ness** *n.*

cus·tom-built (kŭs′təm-bĭlt′) *adj.* Built according to the specifications of the buyer.

cus·tom·er (kŭs′təm-ər) *n.* **1.** A person or organization that buys goods or services. **2.** *Informal.* A person with whom one must deal: *a tough customer.*

custom·house (kŭs′təm-hous′) *n., pl.* **-houses** (-hou′zĭz). *Abbr.* **c.h., C.H.** A government building or office where customs are collected and ships are cleared for entering or leaving the country.

cus·tom·ize (kŭs′tə-mīz′) *tr.v.* **-ized, -izing, -izes.** To alter (a standard car model, for example) to the tastes of the buyer.

cus·tom-made (kŭs′təm-mād′) *adj.* Made according to the specifications of an individual purchaser.

cus·toms (kŭs′təmz) *n. Used with a singular or plural verb.* **1.** A duty or tax imposed on imported and, less commonly, exported goods. Also called "customs duty." **2.** The government department authorized to collect such duties. **3. a.** The procedure for inspecting goods and baggage entering a country. **b.** The place, as at an airport or frontier, where this inspection takes place.

customs union *n.* An international association organized to eliminate customs restrictions on goods exchanged between member nations and to establish a uniform tariff policy toward nonmember nations.

cus·tos (kŭs′tōs) *n., pl.* **custodes** (kŭs-tō′dēz). **1.** A guardian or keeper; a custodian. **2.** A superior in certain monastic orders. [Middle English, from Latin *custōs*†, guard, protector.]

cus·tu·mal (kŭs′cho͞o-məl, -tyo͞o-məl) *n.* A written record of the customs of a monastery or community. [Medieval Latin *custumāle,* from the neuter of *custumālis,* customary, from Old French *custume,* from *custome,* CUSTOM.]

cut (kŭt) *v.* **cut, cutting, cuts.** *—tr.* **1.** To penetrate with a sharp edge; strike a narrow opening in. **2.** To separate into parts with or as if with a sharp-edged instrument; sever: *cut cloth with scissors.* **3.** To sever the edges or outer extensions of; shorten; trim. **4.** To reap; harvest. **5.** To fell by sawing; hew. Often used with *down.* **6.** To have (a new tooth) grow through the gums. **7.** To form or shape by severing or incising: *a doll cut from paper.* **8.** To form by penetrating, probing, or digging. **9.** To separate or dissociate from a main body; detach: *cut off a chicken drumstick.* **10.** To pass through or across; cross. **11.** *Card Games.* To divide (a pack of cards) in two, as before dealing. **12. a.** To curtail the size, extent, or duration of; abridge. **b.** To reduce; diminish: *cut expenditure.* **13.** To lessen the strength of; dilute: *cut whiskey with water.* **14.** To dissolve by breaking down the fat of: *Soap cuts grease.* **15.** To injure the feelings of; hurt keenly. **16.** *Informal.* To deliberately fail to attend: *cut a class.* **17.** *Informal.* To cease; stop. **18. a.** *Sports.* To strike (a ball) with a slicing stroke so that it spins irregularly or is deflected. **b.** *Cricket.* To hit (a ball), usually with the bat held horizontally, on the off side in a direction between third man and cover. **19.** To perform: *cut a caper.* **20.** To terminate (a scene in a film). **21.** To record a performance on (a phonograph record). **22.** To edit (film or audio tape). **23.** *Informal.* To switch off (a car engine, for example). **24.** *Geometry.* To meet across (a line or curve). **25.** To castrate. *—intr.* **1.** To make an incision or separation. **2.** To allow incision or severing: *Butter cuts easily.* **3.** To use a sharp-edged instrument. **4.** To grow through the gums. Used of new teeth. **5.** To penetrate so as to cause injury. **6. a.** To change direction abruptly: *cut to the left.* **b.** *Cricket.* To turn abruptly on pitching. Used of a bowled ball. **7.** To go directly and often hastily: *cut across the field.* **8.** To divide a pack of cards into two parts in order, for example, to make a decision on the basis of the card or cards displayed. **9.** *Geometry.* To intersect. Used of lines. **10.** To stop filming or recording. Often used in the imperative. **—cut back. 1.** To shorten by cutting; prune. **2.** To reduce or decrease: *cut back production.* **—cut corners.** To do something quickly or cheaply to the detriment of quality; skimp. **—cut down to size.** To deflate the self-importance of. **—cut loose.** To become independent; break free. **—cut no ice with.** To fail to have an effect on; make no impression on. **—cut one's teeth on.** To gain early experience from. **—cut short.** To stop before the end; abbreviate.
~n. **1.** The act of incising, severing, or separating. **2.** The result of cutting; an incision; especially, a smallish wound or gash. **3.** A part that has been severed from a main body: *a cut of beef.* **4.** A passage or channel resulting from excavating or probing. **5. a.** An elimination or excision of a part: *a cut in a speech.* **b.** The eliminated part. **6. a.** A reduction: *a salary cut.* **b.** *Often* **cuts.** Reduction in government expenditure. **7.** The style in which hair or a garment is cut. **8.** *Informal.* A share of profits or earnings. **9.** *Informal.* **a.** A wounding remark; an insult. **b.** A snub. **10.** *Chemistry.* A fraction obtained by distilling. **11.** *Printing.* **a.** An engraved block or plate. **b.** A print made from such a block. **12.** *Sports.* A stroke played by cutting. **13.** *Card Games.* The act of dividing a pack of cards into two parts, as before dealing. **14.** A sharp transition between shots or scenes in a film. **15.** A **power cut** *(see).* **—a cut above.** A little better than. [Middle English *cutten, kitten,* probably from late Old English *cyttan* (unattested), akin to Icelandic *kuta,* to cut with a knife, of North Germanic origin.]

cut-and-dried (kŭt′ən-drīd′) *adj.* **1.** Prepared and arranged in advance; settled. **2.** Ordinary; routine; lacking spontaneity.

cu·ta·ne·ous (kyo͞o-tā′nē-əs) *adj.* Of, pertaining to, or affecting the skin. [New Latin *cutaneus,* from Latin *cutis,* skin.] **—cu·ta·ne·ous·ly** *adv.*

cutaneous anaphylaxis *n.* Anaphylaxis characterized by a violent skin reaction upon contact with the sensitizing substance.

cut·a·way (kŭt′ə-wā′) *n.* **1.** A diagram, as of a building or machine, that shows the interior by omitting the outer shell. **2.** A man's formal daytime coat, with front edges sloping diagonally from the waist and forming tails at the back. Also called "cutaway coat."

cut back *tr.v.* **1.** To prune severely; shorten (the stem of a plant, for example). **2.** To reduce; curtail. *—intr.v.* To make reductions; economize. Used with *on.*

cut·back (kŭt′băk′) *n.* **1.** A decrease; a curtailment: *a cutback in production.* **2.** A **flashback** *(see).* **3.** A sharp reversal of direction, as of a ballcarrier in football.

cutch (kŭch) *n.* A resinous substance, **catechu** *(see).* [Malay *kachu,* CATECHU.]

cut down *intr.v.* To reduce consumption, expenditure, or the like. Used with *on.* *—tr.v.* To kill, especially suddenly.

cut-down (kŭt′doun′) *n.* **1.** An act of cutting down; a reduction. **2.** Something reduced in size or extent.
~adj. Shortened; abridged.

cute (kyo͞ot) *adj.* **cuter, cutest. 1.** Delightfully pretty or dainty. **2.** Obviously contrived to charm; affected. **3.** Shrewd; clever. [Short for ACUTE.] **—cute·ly** *adv.* **—cute·ness** *n.*

cut glass *n.* Glassware shaped or decorated by cutting instruments or abrasive wheels. **—cut-glass** *adj.*

cut-grass (kŭt′grăs′, -gräs′) *n.* Any of several swamp and marsh grasses of the genus *Leersia,* having leaves with very rough margins.

Cuth·bert (kŭth′bərt), **Saint** (*c.* A.D. 635–687). English saint and missionary, who converted the Northumbrians to Christianity. His allegedly uncorrupted body was moved from the island of Farne for burial in Durham Cathedral in the 10th century.

cu·ti·cle (kyo͞o′tĭ-kəl) *n.* **1.** The strip of hardened skin at the base of a fingernail or toenail. **2.** The epidermis. **3.** *Zoology.* The noncellular, often horny protective outer covering in many invertebrates. **4.** *Botany.* The protective layer of cutin covering the epidermis of plants. [Latin *cutīcula,* diminutive of *cutis,* skin.] **—cu·tic·u·lar** *adj.*

cut·ie, cut·ey (kyo͞o′tē) *n., pl.* **-ies.** *Slang.* An attractive or charming person.

cut in *intr.v.* **1.** To move in front of another car too sharply, thus endangering or inconveniencing another motorist. **2.** To interrupt. **3.** To interrupt a dancing couple in order to dance with one of them. **4.** To take another player's place in a card game. *—tr.v.* *Informal.* To share with; give a share to: *cut him in.*

cut-in (kŭt′ĭn′) *n.* An inserted shot, often a still close-up, interrupting the continuity of the main action of a motion picture.

cu·tin (kyo͞o′tĭn) *n.* *Botany.* A waxlike, water-repellent material present in the walls of some plant cells, and forming the cuticle that covers the epidermis. [Latin *cut(is),* skin + -IN.]

cu·tin·ize (kyo͞o′tə-nīz′) *v.* **-ized, -izing, -izes.** *Botany.* *—tr.* To coat or impregnate with cutin. *—intr.* To become coated or impregnated with cutin. **—cu·tin·i·za·tion** *n.*

cu·tis (kyo͞o′tĭs) *n.* *Anatomy.* The **dermis** *(see).* [Latin *cutis,* skin.]

cut·lass, cut·las (kŭt′ləs) *n.* A short, heavy sword with a curved single-edged blade, once used as a weapon by sailors. [Variant of earlier *coutelace,* from Old French *coutelas,* from *coutel,* knife, from Latin *cultellus,* diminutive of *culter,* knife.]

cutlass fish *n.* Any of several marine fishes of the genus *Trichiurus,* having a long, narrow body and a pointed tail.

cut·ler (kŭt′lər) *n.* A person who makes, repairs, or sells knives, cutlery, or other cutting instruments. [Middle English, from Old French *coutelier,* from *coutel,* knife. See **cutlass.**]

cut·ler·y (kŭt′lĕr-ē) *n.* **1.** Cutting instruments and tools. **2.** Implements used as tableware. **3.** The occupation of a cutler.

cut·let (kŭt′lĭt) *n.* **1.** A thin slice of meat, usually veal or lamb, cut

PRONUNCIATION KEY

ă, pat; ā, pay; âr, care; ä, father, are; b, bib; ch, church; d, deed; ĕ, pet; ē, be; f, fife; g, gag; h, hat; hw, which; ĭ, pit; ī, pie; îr, pier; j, judge; k, kick; l, lid, needle; m, mum; n, no, sudden; ng, thing; ŏ, pot; ō, toe; ô, paw, for; oi, noise; ou, out; o͝o, book; o͞o, boot; p, pop; r, roar; s, sauce; sh, ship, dish; t, tight; th, thin, path; *th,* this, bathe; ŭ, cut; ûr, fur; v, valve; w, with; y, yes; z, zebra, size; zh, vision; ə, about, item, edible, gallop, circus, peaceful

IN FOREIGN WORDS:

à, *Fr.* ami; œ, *Fr.* feu, *Ger.* schön; ü, *Fr.* tu, *Ger.* über; KH, *Ger.* ich, *Scot.* loch; N, *Fr.* bon; y′, *Fr.* Compiègne

STRESS MARKS:

Primary stress: ′ **in·cite′** (ĭn-sīt′)
Secondary stress: ′ **in′sight′** (ĭn′sīt′)

from the leg or ribs of an animal. **2.** A piece of fish cut across or widthwise, from between the head and middle part of the body of a large fish such as cod or halibut. **3.** A flat, cutlet-shaped croquette of chopped meat or fish. [French *côtelette,* from Old French *costelette,* diminutive of *coste,* rib, from Latin *costa,* rib.]
cut off *tr.v.* **1.** To detach by severing. **2.** To discontinue; stop. **3.** To interrupt or intercept. **4.** To separate; isolate. **5.** To disinherit. **6.** To disconnect (a power supply, for example).
cut-off (kŭt'ôf', -ŏf') *n.* **1.** A designated limit or point of termination. **2.** A new channel cut by a river across the neck of an oxbow lake. **3. a.** A checking or cutting off of a flow of steam, water, or other fluid. **b.** The device that cuts off.
~adj. Of or pertaining to a cut-off: *a cut-off point.*
cut-offs, cut·offs (kŭt'ôfs', -ŏfs') *pl.n.* Pants, as blue jeans, made into shorts by cutting off part of the legs.
cut out *tr.v.* **1.** To shape or fashion by cutting. **2.** To remove the background from behind a figure (as in a photograph or painting). **3.** *Informal.* To be temperamentally suited or fitted: *cut out for city life.* **4.** *Informal.* To cease or give up: *cut out cigarettes.* **5.** To outdo or take the place of (a rival). *—intr.v.* **1.** To cease functioning; switch off. **2.** To leave or be excluded from a card game.
cut-out (kŭt'out') *n.* **1.** Something cut out or intended to be cut out. **2.** *Electricity.* A device that interrupts, bypasses, or disconnects a circuit or circuit element, especially as a safety measure.
cut·o·ver (kŭt'ō'vər) *adj.* Cleared of trees.
cut·purse (kŭt'pûrs') *n. Archaic.* A pickpocket. [Originally one who cut off purses that were attached to a girdle.]
cut-rate (kŭt'rāt') *adj.* Sold or on sale at a reduced price.
cut·ter (kŭt'ər) *n.* **1.** One who cuts, especially in tailoring or hairdressing. **2.** A device or machine that cuts. **3.** *Nautical.* **a.** A single-masted fore-and-aft-rigged sailing vessel with a running bowsprit, a mainsail, and two or more headsails. Compare **sloop. b.** A ship's boat, powered by a motor or oars, and used for transporting stores or passengers. **c.** A small, lightly armed motorboat used by the Coast Guard. **4.** A small sleigh, usually seating one person and drawn by a single horse.
cut·throat (kŭt'thrōt') *n.* **1.** One who cuts throats; a murderer. **2.** *Chiefly British.* A razor having a long blade that folds into the handle. Also called "cutthroat razor."
~adj. **1.** Cruel; murderous. **2.** Relentless or merciless in competition. **3.** *Games & Sports.* Of or designating a form of game in which each of three players acts and scores for himself.
cut time *n. Music.* A kind of measure, **alla breve** *(see).*
cut·ting (kŭt'ĭng) *adj.* **1.** Capable of or designed for incising, shearing, or severing. **2.** Sharply penetrating; piercing and cold. **3.** Bitterly sarcastic or insulting. **—**See Synonyms at **incisive.**
~n. **1.** A part cut off from a main body. **2.** An excavation made through high ground in the construction of a road, railway, or the like. **3.** *Chiefly British.* An article, story, or other item cut out from a newspaper or magazine. **4.** The editing of film or audio tape. **5.** *Horticulture.* **a.** A twig, leaf, or plant part removed in order to form roots and propagate a new plant. **b.** Propagation by means of cuttings.
cut·tle (kŭt'l) *n. Rare.* A cuttlefish. [Middle English *codel,* Old English *cudele.* See **ku-** in Appendix.*]
cut·tle·bone (kŭt'l-bōn') *n.* The calcareous internal shell of a cuttlefish, used as a dietary supplement for cage birds or ground into powder for use as a polishing agent.
cut·tle·fish (kŭt'l-fĭsh') *n., pl.* **-fishes** or collectively **cuttlefish.** Any of various squidlike cephalopod marine mollusks of the genus *Sepia,* having ten arms and a calcareous internal shell, and secreting a dark, inky fluid. Also called "cuttle." [Middle English *codel,* Old English *cudele;* akin to *cod,* bag (see **codpiece**), referring to its ink sac.]
cut up *tr.v.* **1.** To divide into pieces. **2.** To inflict lacerations upon. **3.** *Informal.* To criticize severely. *—intr.v. Informal.* To behave mischievously.
cut·up (kŭt'ŭp') *n. Informal.* A mischievous person; prankster.
cut·wa·ter (kŭt'wô'tər) *n.* **1.** The forward part of a ship's prow. **2.** The wedge-shaped end of a bridge pier, designed to divide the current and break up ice floes.
cut·work (kŭt'wûrk') *n.* Openwork embroidery in which the ground fabric is cut away from the design.
cut·worm (kŭt'wûrm') *n.* The larva of any of various moths of the family Noctuidae, feeding on a wide variety of plants. [So called because many species eat through stems of plants.]
Cu·vier (ko͞o'vē-ā', kyo͞o'-), **Georges, Baron** (1769–1832). French naturalist, chiefly remembered for his pioneer work in comparing fossil remains with the anatomy of existing species. His main work was *The Animal Kingdom* (1817).
Cuy·a·ho·ga (kī'ə-hō'gə). River, c. 130 kilometers (80 miles), of northeastern Ohio. It flows southwest through the city of Cuyahoga Falls, a suburb of Akron, then north of Lake Erie, forming part of Cleveland harbor.
Cuz·co (ko͞os'kō). City in southern Peru, in the Andes. The capital of the Inca empire before the Spanish conquests, it contains the ruins of many impressive Inca temples.
c.v. curriculum vitae.
CVA cerebrovascular accident.
cvt. *Finance.* convertible.
cw, CW continuous wave.
cwm (ko͞om) *n. Welsh.* **1.** A valley. **2.** A steep hollow, a **cirque** *(see).*
CWO chief warrant officer.
c.w.o. cash with order.
CWS Chemical Warfare Service.
cwt. hundredweight.
-cy *suffix.* Indicates: **1.** A quality or condition; for example, **bankruptcy, infancy. 2.** Office or rank; for example, **baronetcy, magistracy.** [Middle English *-cie,* from Old French, from Latin *-cia, -tia,* and Greek *-kiā, -tiā,* both abstract noun suffixes.]
cy·an (sī'ăn) *n.* Greenish blue; one of the subtractive primary colors; a complement of red. [Greek *kuanos,* CYANO-.]
cy·an·a·mide (sī-ăn'ə-mĭd) *n.* Also **cy·an·a·mid. 1.** An irritating caustic acidic crystalline compound, $NCNH_2$, prepared by continuous carbonation of calcium cyanamide in water. **2.** A compound, **calcium cyanamide** *(see).* **3.** A salt or ester of cyanamide. [French : CYAN(O)- + AMIDE.]
cy·a·nate (sī'ə-nāt', -nət) *n.* A salt or ester of cyanic acid. [CYAN(O)- + -ATE.]
cy·an·ic (sī-ăn'ĭk) *adj.* **1.** Pertaining to or containing cyanogen. **2.** Blue or bluish. [CYAN(O)- + -IC.]
cyanic acid *n.* A poisonous, unstable, highly volatile organic acid, HOCN, used to prepare certain cyanates.
cy·a·nide (sī'ə-nīd') *n.* Also **cy·an·id** (-nĭd). Any of various salts or esters of hydrogen cyanide containing a CN group; especially, the extremely poisonous compounds **potassium cyanide** and **sodium cyanide** *(both of which see).*
~tr.v. **cyanided, -niding, -nides. 1.** To treat (a metal surface) with cyanide to produce a hard surface. **2.** To treat (an ore) with cyanide to extract gold or silver. [CYAN(O)- + -IDE.]
cyanide process *n.* A process of extracting gold or silver from ores treated with a solution of sodium or calcium cyanide.
cy·a·nine (sī'ə-nīn) *n.* Any of various blue dyes, used to extend the range of color sensitivity of photographic emulsions. [CYAN(O)- + -INE.]
cyanite. Variant of **kyanite.**
cyano-, cyan- *prefix.* Indicates: **1.** A blue or dark-blue coloring; for example, **cyanine, cyanic. 2.** *Chemistry.* Cyanide or cyanogen; for example, **cyanate, cyanotype.** [German *zyan-,* from Greek *kuanos,* dark-blue enamel, the color blue, from an unknown language of Asia Minor.]
cy·a·no·ac·ry·late (sī'ə-nō-ăk'rə-lāt', sī-ăn'ō-) *n.* An industrial and medical adhesive with an acrylic base.
cy·a·no·co·bal·a·min (sī'ə-nō'kō-bôl'ə-mĭn) *n.* **Vitamin B_{12}** *(see).* [CYANO- + COBAL(T) + (VIT)AMIN.]
cy·an·o·gen (sī-ăn'ə-jən) *n. Chemistry.* A colorless, flammable, highly poisonous gas, C_2N_2, used as a rocket propellant, fumigant, military weapon, and in welding. [French *cyanogène* : CYANO- + -GEN.]
cyano group *n.* The univalent radical CN, found in simple and complex cyanide compounds.
cy·a·no·hy·drin (sī'ə-nō-hī'drĭn, sī-ăn'ō-) *n. Chemistry.* Any of a class of organic compounds containing both CN and OH groups attached to the same carbon atom. [CYANO- + HYDRO- + -IN.]
cy·a·nosed (sī'ə-nōzd') *adj. Pathology.* Afflicted with cyanosis. [From CYANOSIS.]
cy·a·no·sis (sī'ə-nō'sĭs) *n. Pathology.* A bluish discoloration of the skin, resulting from inadequate oxygenation of the blood. [New Latin, from Greek *kuanōsis,* dark blue : CYAN(O)- + -OSIS.] **—cy·a·not·ic** (sī'ə-nŏt'ĭk) *adj.*
cy·an·o·type (sī-ăn'ə-tīp') *n.* A **blueprint** *(see).*
cy·a·nu·ric acid (sī'ə-no͝or'ĭk, -nyo͝or'ĭk) *n.* A white crystalline acid, $C_3N_3(OH)_3$, that decomposes with heating to form cyanic acid. [CYAN(O)- + URIC ACID.]
Cyb·e·le (sĭb'ə-lē, kĭb'ə-lā). The Phrygian goddess of nature and mother of all living things.
cy·ber·nate (sī'bər-nāt') *v.* **-nated, -nating, -nates.** *—tr.* To control (an industrial process) automatically by computer. *—intr.* To become so controlled. [From CYBERNET(ICS) + -ATE.] **—cy·ber·na·tion** *n.*
cy·ber·net·ics (sī'bər-nĕt'ĭks) *n. Used with a singular verb.* The theoretical study of control processes in electronic, mechanical, and biological systems; especially, the mathematical analysis of the flow of information in such systems. [Coined by Norbert Wiener from Greek *kubernētēs,* pilot, governor, from *kubernan,* to steer, guide, GOVERN.] **—cy·ber·net·ic** *adj.* **—cy·ber·net·i·cist** *n.*
cy·borg (sī'bôrg') *n.* A human individual who has some of his vital bodily processes controlled by cybernetically operated devices. [CYB(ERNETIC) + ORG(ANISM).]
cy·cad (sī'kăd) *n.* Any seed-bearing gymnosperm plant of the family Cycadaceae, resembling a palm tree but surmounted by fernlike leaves. [New Latin *Cycas* (stem *Cycad-*), genus name, from Greek *kukas,* manuscript error for *koïkas,* accusative plural of *koïx,* doom palm, perhaps from Egyptian.] **—cy·cad·a·ceous** *adj.*
cycl-. Variant of **cyclo-.**
Cyc·la·des (sĭk'lə-dēz). *Greek* **Ki·klá·dhes** (kē-klä'*th*ēz). A group of more than 200 Greek islands, in the Aegean Sea southeast of the mainland. They include Naxos, the largest, Paros, and Delos. Hermoupolis, on Syros, is the capital.
cyc·la·mate (sī'klə-māt', sĭk'lə-) *n.* A salt of cyclamic acid; especially, either of two very sweet crystalline compounds, **sodium cyclamate** *(see)* and calcium cyclamate, $C_{12}H_{24}N_2O_6S_2Ca$.
cyc·la·men (sī'klə-mən, sĭk'lə-, -mĕn') *n.* Any of several plants of the genus *Cyclamen,* widely cultivated for their showy white, pink, or red flowers with reflexed petals. [New Latin, from Greek *kuklaminos,* probably from *kuklos,* a circle (from the bulbous roots).]

cuttlefish *Fossil evidence shows that this ancient genus of shellfish has existed in its present form for more than 20 million years, characterized by its cuttlebone, a type of internal, calcified shell, containing a network of hollow chambers. By regulating the amount of gas or water in these chambers, the cuttlefish controls its buoyancy, so that it can rise close to the surface to feed or sink to the seabed where it lives. Sepia is both its genus name and the word used for the brownish pigment that is obtained from its dried ink sac.*

$$CH_3CN + 2H_2 \rightarrow CH_3.CH_2.NH_2$$
methyl cyanide — hydrogen — ethylamine

cyanide *All cyanide compounds are highly poisonous, but some are useful too. Organic cyanides, for instance, such as methyl cyanide, are combined with hydrogen to form ethylamine—used in the manufacture of detergents.*

cycad *Cycads, which originated some 160 million years ago, are among the most primitive seed-bearing plants still in existence. They are slow-growing plants that resemble palm trees. But, unlike palms, they have no flowers. Instead they bear their seeds in cones that, in some species, can be 1 meter (3.3 feet) long and weigh more than 35 kilograms (77 pounds).*

cyc·la·mic acid (sĭk'lə-mĭk', sī'klə-) *n.* A sour-sweet crystalline acid, $C_6H_{13}NO_3S$.

cy·clase (sī'klās', -klāz') *n.* An enzyme that acts as a catalyst in the cyclization of a compound.

cy·cle (sī'kəl) *n.* **1.** A time interval in which a characteristic, especially regularly repeated, event or sequence of events occurs. **2. a.** A single complete execution of a periodically repeated phenomenon. **b.** A periodically repeated sequence of events. **c.** The time taken for the phenomenon or sequence to be completed. **3.** The orbit of a celestial body. **4.** A long period of time; an age; an eon. **5. a.** The aggregate of traditional legends, stories, or tales concerning a central theme or hero: *the Arthurian cycle.* **b.** A series of poems or songs on the same theme. **6.** A bicycle, tricycle, or the like. **7.** *Botany.* A circular arrangement of flower parts such as petals or sepals. *~intr.v.* **cycled, -cling, -cles. 1.** To occur in or pass through a cycle. **2.** To move in or as if in a circle. **3.** To ride a bicycle, tricycle, or similar vehicle. [French, from Late Latin *cyclus,* from Greek *kuklos,* circle.]

cy·cler·y (sī'kəl-rē) *n.* A shop for the sale and service of bicycles.

cy·clic (sī'klĭk, sĭk'lĭk) *adj.* Also **cy·cli·cal** (sī'klĭ-kəl, sĭk'lĭ-). **1. a.** Of, relating to, or characterized by cycles. **b.** Recurring or moving in cycles. **2.** *Chemistry.* Of or pertaining to compounds having atoms arranged in a ring or closed-chain structure. **3.** *Botany.* **a.** Having parts arranged in a whorl. **b.** Forming a whorl. **4.** *Geometry.* Designating a polygon whose vertices lie on the circumference of a circumscribing circle: *a cyclic quadrilateral.* **—cy·cli·cal·ly** *adv.*

cyclic AMP *n. Biochemistry.* A cyclic form of adenosine monophosphate that has an important role in regulating metabolic processes, including the action of many hormones, in animals and humans.

cyclic GMP *n.* A cyclic nucleotide of guanosine believed to act as an antagonist to cyclic AMP in cellular processes.

cyclic pitch lever *n.* A helicopter control lever that alters the angle of attack of individual rotor blades, causing the aircraft to move forward, backward, or sideways.

cy·clist (sī'klĭst) *n.* Also **cy·cler** (-klər). One who rides a bicycle, motorcycle, or similar vehicle.

cy·cli·za·tion (sī'klə-zā'shən) *n.* The formation of rings in a hydrocarbon.

cyclo-, cycl– *prefix.* Indicates: **1.** Circle; for example, **cyclometer, cyclorama. 2.** A cyclic compound; for example, **cyclohexane.** [Greek *kuklos,* circle, CYCLE.]

cy·clo·al·kane (sī'klō-ăl'kān') *n.* **Cycloparaffin** (*see*).

cy·clo·hex·ane (sī'klō-hĕk'sān') *n.* An extremely flammable, colorless, mobile liquid, C_6H_{12}, obtained from petroleum and benzene and used as a solvent, paint and varnish remover, and in the manufacture of nylon.

cy·clo·hex·i·mide (sī'klō-hĕk'sə-mīd, -mĭd) *n. Chemistry.* A compound, $C_{15}H_{23}NO_4$, that is used as an agricultural fungicide.

cy·cloid (sī'kloid') *adj.* **1.** Resembling a circle. **2.** *Zoology.* Thin, rounded, and smooth-edged; disklike. Said of fish scales, such as those of the salmon. **3.** *Psychiatry.* Designating a person suffering from **cyclothymia** (*see*). *~n. Geometry.* The curve traced by a point on the circumference of a circle that rolls on a straight line. [French *cycloïde,* from Greek *kukloeidēs* : CYCL(O)- + -OID.] **—cy·cloi·dal** *adj.*

cy·clom·e·ter (sī-klŏm'ə-tər) *n.* **1.** An instrument that records the revolutions of a wheel in order to indicate distance traveled. **2.** An instrument that measures circular arcs. [CYCLO- + -METER.] **—cy·clo·met·ric** *adj.* **—cy·clom·e·try** *n.*

cy·clone (sī'klōn') *n.* **1.** *Meteorology.* **a.** A type of tropical atmospheric disturbance characterized by masses of air rapidly circulating clockwise in the southern and counterclockwise in the northern hemisphere, about a low-pressure center, usually accompanied by stormy, often destructive, weather. **b.** Formerly, a **depression** (sense 4). **2.** Loosely, any violent, rotating windstorm, such as a **tornado** (*see*). [Probably from Greek *kuklōma,* coil, wheel, from *kuklos,* circle, CYCLE.] **—cy·clon·ic** (sī-klŏn'ĭk), **cy·clon·i·cal** *adj.*

cyclone cellar *n.* An underground shelter in or adjacent to a house, used for protection from cyclones, tornadoes, or the like. Also called "storm cellar."

cy·clo·par·af·fin (sī'klō-păr'ə-fĭn) *n.* Any of a class of hydrocarbons, including cyclopropane, cyclopentane, and cyclohexane, in which at least three carbon atoms per molecule are joined in a ring structure and each such carbon in the ring is bonded to two hydrogen atoms or alkyl groups. Also called "cycloalkane."

cy·clo·pe·an (sī'klə-pē'ən, sī-klō'pē-ən) *adj.* **1.** *Often* **Cyclopean.** Pertaining to or suggestive of the Cyclopes. **2.** Pertaining to or designating a primitive style of masonry characterized by the use of massive stones of irregular shape and size.

cy·clo·pe·di·a, cy·clo·pae·di·a (sī'klə-pē'dē-ə) *n.* An encyclopedia. **—cy·clo·pe·dic** *adj.* **—cy·clo·pe·dist** *n.*

cy·clo·pen·tane (sī'klə-pĕn'tān, sĭk'lə-) *n.* A colorless flammable liquid, C_5H_{10}, derived from petroleum and used as a solvent and motor fuel.

cy·clo·ple·gi·a (sī'klə-plē'jē-ə) *n.* Loss of ability to focus vision because of paralysis of the ciliary muscles of the eye. [New Latin : CYCLO- + -PLEGIA.]

cy·clo·pro·pane (sī'klə-prō'pān') *n.* A highly flammable, explosive, colorless gas, C_3H_6, used as an anesthetic.

Cy·clops (sī'klŏps). *pl.* **Cyclopes** (sī-klō'pēz), **Cyclopses, Cyclops.** *Greek Mythology.* **1.** Any of the three one-eyed Titans who forged thunderbolts for Zeus. **2.** Any of a race of one-eyed giants, reputedly descended from these Titans, inhabiting the island of Sicily.

cy·clo·ram·a (sī'klə-răm'ə, -rä'mə) *n.* **1.** A large composite picture placed on the interior walls of a cylindrical room so as to appear in natural perspective to a spectator standing in the center. **2.** A large curtain or wall, usually concave, placed or hung at the rear of a stage. [CYCL(O)- + (PAN)ORAMA.] **—cy·clo·ram·ic** *adj.*

cy·clo·ser·ine (sī'klō-sĕr'ēn') *n.* An antibiotic active against a wide range of bacteria, used chiefly in the treatment of tuberculosis and infections of the urinary tract.

cy·clo·sis (sī-klō'sĭs) *n., pl.* **-ses** (-sēz'). The circulatory motion of protoplasm or organelles within certain cells and one-celled animals. [New Latin, from Greek *kuklōsis,* a surrounding, from *kukloun,* to surround, from *kuklos,* a circle, CYCLE.]

cy·clo·stome (sī'klə-stōm') *n.* Any of various primitive eellike vertebrates of the class Agnatha, such as the lamprey, lacking jaws and true teeth and having a circular, sucking mouth. [New Latin *Cyclostomi,* "round-mouths" and *Cyclostomata,* "round-mouthed" : CYCLO- + -STOME.] **—cy·clos·to·mate, cy·clo·stom·a·tous** *adj.*

cy·clo·style (sī'klō'stīl') *n.* A device consisting of a pen with a small toothed wheel producing a stencil from which copies can be made. *~tr.v.* **cyclostyled, -styling, -styles.** To produce (copies) using a cyclostyle. [CYCLO- + Latin *stylus,* writing implement.]

cy·clo·thyme (sī'klə-thīm') *n. Psychiatry.* A person afflicted with cyclothymia.

cy·clo·thy·mi·a (sī'klə-thī'mē-ə) *n. Psychiatry.* A form of depressive psychosis characterized by alternating periods of activity and excitement and periods of inactivity and depression. [New Latin, from German *Zyklothymie* : CYCLO- + -THYMIA.]

cy·clo·thy·mic (sī'klə-thī'mĭk) *adj.* Of or characterized by cyclothymia. *~n.* A cyclothyme.

cy·clo·tron (sī'klə-trŏn') *n. Physics.* A circular particle accelerator capable of generating particle energies between a few million and several tens of millions of electron volts, in which charged particles generated at a central source are accelerated spirally outward in a plane at right angles to a fixed magnetic field by an alternating electric field. [CYCLO- + -TRON.]

cyder. *Chiefly British.* Variant of **cider.**

cy·e·sis (sī-ē'sĭs) *n., pl.* **-ses** (-sēz). Pregnancy; gestation. [New Latin, from Greek *kuēsis,* from *kuein,* to be pregnant, to swell.]

cyg·net (sĭg'nĭt) *n.* A young swan. [Middle English *sygnett,* diminutive of Old French *cygne,* swan, from Latin *cycnus, cygnus,* from Greek *kuknos.*]

Cyg·nus (sĭg'nəs) *n.* A constellation in the Northern Hemisphere near Lacerta and Lyra in the Milky Way. Also called "Northern Cross," "Swan." [Latin *cygnus,* swan. See **cygnet.**]

cyl·in·der (sĭl'ən-dər) *n. Abbr.* **cyl. 1.** *Geometry.* **a.** A surface generated by a straight line moving parallel to a fixed straight line and intersecting a plane curve. **b.** The portion of such a surface bounded by two parallel planes and the regions of the planes bounded by the surface. **c.** A solid consisting of two parallel planes bounded by two identical closed curves, usually circles. **2.** Any cylindrical container or object. **3. a.** The chamber in which the piston of a reciprocating engine moves. **b.** The chamber of a pump from which fluid is expelled by a piston. **4.** The rotating chamber of a revolver that holds the cartridges. **5.** Any of the rotating cylinders in a printing press that carry the paper or the curved printing plate, or receive the ink or impression. **6.** *Archaeology.* A cylindrical stone or clay object with an engraved design or inscription. *~tr.v.* **cylindered, -dering, -ders.** To press or furnish with a cylinder. [Old French *cylindre,* from Latin *cylindrus,* from Greek *kulindros,* roller, cylinder, from *kulindein,* to revolve, roll.]

cylinder block *n.* The casting containing the cylinders and cooling channels of an internal-combustion engine.

cylinder head *n.* The closed, often detachable, end of a cylinder or cylinders in an internal-combustion engine.

cy·lin·dri·cal (sə-lĭn'drĭ-kəl) *adj.* Also **cy·lin·dric** (-drĭk). *Abbr.* **cyl. 1.** Having the shape of a cylinder, especially of a circular cylinder. **2.** Of or pertaining to a cylinder. **3.** Of or pertaining to the coordinate system, or to any of three coordinates in it, formed by two polar coordinates in a plane and a rectangular coordinate measured perpendicularly from the plane. **—cy·lin·dri·cal·i·ty** *n.* **—cy·lin·dri·cal·ly** *adv.*

cylindrical projection *n.* A map projection in which points on the globe are projected onto a cylinder placed at a tangent to or intersecting its surface, which is then opened and laid flat.

cyl·in·droid (sĭl'ĭn-droid') *n.* A cylindrical surface or solid that is elliptical in cross section. *~adj.* Resembling a cylinder.

cylix. Variant of **kylix.**

cy·ma (sī'mə) *n., pl.* **-mae** (-mē') or **-mas. 1.** *Architecture.* A molding for a cornice, having a partly concave and partly convex curve in profile. A *cyma recta* has the concave curve uppermost, a *cyma reversa* the convex. **2.** *Botany.* A cyme. [Greek *kuma,* anything swollen, waved molding, from *kuein,* to swell, be pregnant.]

cy·ma·ti·um (sī-mā'shē-əm) *n., pl.* **-tia** (-shē-ə). **1.** A cyma. **2.** The topmost molding of a classical cornice. [Latin *cymatium,* from Greek *kumation,* diminutive of *kuma,* moulding, CYMA.]

cym·bal (sĭm'bəl) *n.* **1.** One of a pair of concave brass plates that are struck together as percussion instruments. **2.** A single brass plate, sounded by hitting with a drumstick and often part of a set of drums. [Middle English, from Old French *symbale,* from Latin *cymbalum,* from Greek *kumbalon,* from *kumbē,* hollow of a vessel, a cup.] **—cym·bal·ist** *n.*

Cymbeline. See **Cunobelinus.**

cym·bid·i·um (sǐm-bǐd′ē-əm) *n.* Any orchid of the genus *Cymbidium,* cultivated as ornamentals for their sprays of long-lasting flowers. [New Latin, from Greek *kumbē,* cup.]

cyme (sīm) *n. Botany.* An often flat-topped flower cluster that blooms from the center toward the edges, and whose main axis always terminates in a flower. Also called "cyma." [New Latin *cyma,* from Latin *cȳma,* young cabbage sprout, from Greek *kuma,* anything swollen, CYMA.] —**cy·mif·er·ous** *adj.*

cy·mene (sī′mēn′) *n. Chemistry.* Any of three colorless isomeric liquid hydrocarbons, C₁₀H₁₄, obtained chiefly from the essential oils of various plants and used in the manufacture of synthetic resins. [French *cymène,* from Greek *kuminon,* CUMIN.]

cym·ling (sĭm′lĭng) *n.* Also **cym·lin** (-lĭn), **sim·lin.** A greenish-white, flat, round squash with a scalloped edge. Also called "pattypan squash." [Probably variant of SIMNEL.]

cy·mo·gene (sī′mə-jēn′) *n.* A flammable gaseous fraction of petroleum, chiefly butane. [CYM(ENE) + -GENE.]

cy·moid (sī′moid′) *adj.* Resembling a cyma or cyme. [CYM(E) or CYM(A) + -OID.]

cy·mo·phane (sī′mə-fān′) *n.* A variety of chrysoberyl having an undulating luster. [French : Greek *kuma,* undulation, CYMA + -PHANE.]

cy·mose (sī′mōs′, sī-mōs′) *adj. Botany.* **1.** Pertaining to or resembling a cyme. **2.** Bearing a cyme or cymes. [CYM(E) + -OSE.] —**cy·mose·ly** *adv.*

Cym·ric, Kym·ric (kĭm′rĭk, sĭm′rĭk) *adj.* Of or pertaining to the Cymry or their languages, especially Welsh. ~*n.* **1.** The Welsh language. **2.** The Brythonic branch of the Celtic languages, including Welsh, Breton, and Cornish.

Cymru. See **Wales.**

Cym·ry, Cym·ri, Kym·ry (kĭm′rē, sĭm′rē) *n.* **1.** The Welsh. **2.** The branch of the Celtic people to which the Welsh, the Cornish, and the Bretons belong.

Cyn·e·wulf (kĭn′ə-wŏolf′) (c. A.D. 800). Anglo-Saxon poet, probably Northumbrian. He was the author of four poems that survive in 10th-century manuscripts: *Juliana, Elene, The Ascension,* and *The Fates of the Apostles.*

cyn·ic (sĭn′ĭk) *n.* **1. a.** One who believes that people are insincere and motivated by selfishness and who consequently expects the worst of human behavior. **b.** A scornful or mocking person. **2. Cynic.** A member of a sect, founded by Antisthenes of Athens, of ancient Greek philosophers who believed virtue to be the only good and self-control to be the only means of achieving virtue. ~*adj.* **1.** *Rare.* Cynical. **2. Cynic.** Of or pertaining to the Cynics or their doctrines. [Latin *cynicus,* from Greek *kunikos,* "doglike," currish (perhaps mistaken by the Greeks from the first part of *kunosarge,* the gymnasium where Antisthenes taught), from *kuōn* (stem *kun-*), dog.]

cyn·i·cal (sĭn′ĭ-kəl) *adj.* **1. a.** Scornful or skeptical of the motives or virtue of others. **b.** Bitterly mocking; sneering. **2.** Showing contempt for accepted morality or values: *a cynical cover-up by the authorities.* **3. Cynic.** Of or pertaining to the Cynics or their doctrines. —**cyn·i·cal·ly** *adv.* —**cyn·i·cal·ness** *n.*

cyn·i·cism (sĭn′ə-sĭz′əm) *n.* **1.** A cynical attitude or character. **2.** A cynical comment or act. **3. Cynic.** The beliefs and doctrines of the Cynics.

cy·no·sure (sī′nə-shŏor′, sĭn′ə-) *n.* **1.** An object or person that serves as a focal point of attention and admiration. **2.** Anything that serves to guide. [French, Ursa Minor, "the guiding star," from Latin *cynosūra,* from Greek *kunosoura,* "the dog's tail," Ursa Minor : *kunos,* genitive of *kuōn,* dog + *-ura,* plural of *-urus,* -UROUS.] —**cy·no·sur·al** *adj.*

Cyn·thi·a¹ (sĭn′thē-ə). *Greek Mythology.* Artemis, goddess of the moon. [Artemis was born on Mount *Cynthus,* on the island of Delos, Greece.]

Cynthia² *n. Poetic.* The moon or its personification.

CYO Catholic Youth Organization.

cypher. Variant of **cipher.**

cy·press (sī′prəs) *n.* **1.** Any evergreen coniferous tree of the genus *Cupressus,* having small, scalelike leaves and rounded cones. **2.** Any similar and related tree of the genus *Chamaecyparis,* such as *C. lawsoniana,* (Lawson's cypress). Also called "false cypress." **3.** Any of various other trees, such as the **swamp cypress** *(see).* **4.** The wood of any of these trees. **5.** Cypress branches used as a symbol of mourning. [Middle English *cipres,* from Old French, from Late Latin *cypressus,* from Greek *kuparissos,* of Mediterranean origin.]

cypress spurge *n.* A plant, *Euphorbia cyparissias,* native to Eurasia, having densely crowded, narrow leaves, and clusters of yellow-green flowers. [Probably because its narrow leaves suggest the needles of the cypress.]

cypress vine *n.* A tropical American vine, *Quamoclit pennata,* having finely divided compound leaves and scarlet flowers.

Cyp·ri·an (sĭp′rē-ən) *adj.* **1.** Of or pertaining to Cyprus, its people, their customs, or their language. **2.** Characteristic of or resembling the ancient worship of Aphrodite on Cyprus; licentious; wanton. ~*n.* **1.** A **Cypriot** *(see).* **2.** *Often* **cyprian.** *Obsolete.* A wanton person, especially a prostitute.

cy·pri·nid (sĭp′rə-nĭd) *n.* Any of numerous freshwater fishes of the family Cyprinidae, which includes the minnows, carps, and tench. [New Latin *Cyprinidae* : *Cyprinus* (genus name), from Latin *cyprīnus,* a carp, from Greek *kuprinos,* from *kupros,* "the henna plant,"

from Semitic, akin to Hebrew *kōpher* + -ID.] —**cy·pri·nid** *adj.*

cy·prin·o·dont (sī-prĭn′ə-dŏnt′, sĭ-prī′nə-) *n.* Any of various soft-finned fishes of the family Cyprinodontidae, which includes the killifishes, and many species popular in home aquariums. [New Latin *Cyprinodon* : Latin *cyprinus,* carp (see **cyprinid**) + -ODONT.]

cyp·ri·noid (sĭp′rə-noid′, sī-prī′-) *adj.* Of, pertaining to, or resembling a carp or related fish. [New Latin *Cyprinoidea* : *Cyprinus,* genus (see **cyprinid**) + -OID.] —**cyp·ri·noid** *n.*

Cyp·ri·ot, Cyp·ri·ote (sĭp′rē-ōt) *n.* **1.** A native or inhabitant of Cyprus. Also called "Cyprian." **2. a.** The ancient Greek dialect of Cyprus, belonging to the Arcado-Cyprian branch. **b.** The dialect of Modern Greek spoken in Cyprus. —**Cyp·ri·ot** *adj.*

cyp·ri·pe·di·um (sĭp′rə-pē′dē-əm) *n.* Any orchid of the genus *Cypripedium,* which includes the lady's-slippers. [New Latin, probably "Venus' slipper" : Late Latin *Cypris,* Venus, from Greek *Kupris,* Aphrodite, from *Kupros,* CYPRUS (supposedly her birthplace) + New Latin *-pedium,* probably a variant of Greek *pedilon,* sandal.]

cy·prot·er·one (sī-prŏt′ə-rōn′) *n.* A hormone that inhibits the secretion of androgen. [Probably Latin *Cypris,* Venus (from Greek *Kupris,* from *Kupros,* Cyprus) + (TESTOS)TERONE.]

Cy·prus, (sī′prəs). *Turkish* **Ki·bris** (kē′brĭs). *Greek* **Ky·pros** (kē′prôs). Island state in the east Mediterranean Sea. Dominated in turn by ancient Egypt, Assyria, Greece, Persia, the Romans, and Byzantium, it fell to the Ottoman Empire (1571) and passed to Britain (1878). Some Greek Cypriots sought *enosis* ("union") with Greece, and violence erupted in 1931 and again in 1955 under the EOKA movement. The island became an independent Commonwealth republic (1960), but violence between Greeks and Turks (the latter making up 18 percent of the population) continued. President Makarios was temporarily overthrown (1974) by an army coup supported by Greece, and Turkey invaded the north. The island was partitioned, the northern part becoming known internally as the Turkish Federated State of Cyprus. Economic recovery in the south led to resumed exports of clothing, copper, vegetables, fruit, and wine, and a renewed tourist industry. Area, 9,251 square kilometers (3,572 square miles). Population, 630,000. Capital, Nicosia. See map at **Turkey.**

cyp·se·la (sĭp′sə-lə) *n., pl.* **-lae** (-lē′). *Botany.* A small dry fruit that resembles an achene but does not separate from its calyx, characteristic of composite plants. [New Latin, from Greek *kupselē,* hollow vessel, chest.]

Cy·ra·no de Ber·ge·rac (sîr′ə-nō də bûr′zhə-răk′), **Savinien de** (1619–55). French dramatist and novelist, whose spirited dramas *Le Pédant Joué* (c. 1654) and *La Mort d'Agrippine* (1653) ran counter to the classical taste of his day. He was the subject of Edmond Rostand's play *Cyrano de Bergerac* (1897), which depicted him as a chivalric duelist with a comically long nose.

Cyr·e·na·ic (sîr′ə-nā′ĭk, sīr′-) *adj.* **1.** Of or pertaining to Cyrenaica or its major city, Cyrene. **2.** Of or pertaining to the hedonistic school of philosophy founded in Cyrene by Aristippus, who believed that pleasure is the only good in life. ~*n.* **1.** A native or inhabitant of Cyrenaica or Cyrene. **2.** A disciple of the Cyrenaic school of philosophy.

Cy·re·na·i·ca (sîr′ə-nā′ĭ-kə, sîr′-). Region of eastern Libya, extending from the Mediterranean coast into the desert.

Cy·re·ne (sī-rē′nē). Ancient city in northeast Libya. Founded by Greeks (c. 630 B.C.), it became the chief city of Cyrenaica.

Cyr·il (sîr′əl), **Saint** (827–69). Macedonian missionary to the Slavs, the alleged inventor of the Cyrillic alphabet. From 863 he and his brother St. Methodius (825–84) worked among the Khazars of Moravia, translating the scriptures into the local language through an adaptation of the Greek alphabet.

Cy·ril·lic (sə-rĭl′ĭk) *adj.* **1.** Of or pertaining to St. Cyril, the 9th-century missionary to the Moravians. **2.** Of or designating the Cyrillic alphabet. ~*n.* The Cyrillic alphabet.

Cyrillic alphabet *n.* An old alphabet ascribed to St. Cyril, presently used in modified form for Russian, Bulgarian, Serbo-Croat, Macedonian, and certain languages of the U.S.S.R., such as Ukranian. Also called "Cyrillic."

Cy·rus II (sī′rəs), called "the Great" (died 529 B.C.). King of Persia (550–529 B.C.) and founder of the Achaemenid empire. Having seized the empire of the Medes, he went on to conquer Lydia, the Ionian cities, and Babylon with its subject states in Syria. He was tolerant in religious matters, permitting the worship of native gods and allowing the Jews to return to Jerusalem (537).

cyst (sĭst) *n.* **1.** *Pathology.* An abnormal membranous sac containing a liquid or semisolid substance. **2.** *Anatomy.* Any sac or vesicle in the body. **3.** *Biology.* A capsulelike membrane enclosing certain organisms in a resting stage. [New Latin *cystis,* from Greek *kustis,* bladder, pouch.]

cyst–. Variant of **cysto–.**

cys·tec·to·my (sĭ-stĕk′tə-mē) *n., pl.* **-mies. 1.** Surgical excision of the gallbladder or of a portion of the urinary bladder. **2.** Surgical removal of a cyst.

cys·te·ine (sĭs′tē-ēn′, -tē-ĭn) *n.* An amino acid, C₃H₇NO₂S, found in most proteins, especially in keratin. [From CYSTINE.]

cys·tic (sĭs′tĭk) *adj.* **1.** Of, pertaining to, or like a cyst. **2.** Having or containing a cyst or cysts. **3.** Enclosed in a cyst. **4.** *Anatomy.* Pertaining to the gallbladder or urinary bladder.

cys·ti·cer·coid (sĭs′tə-sûr′koid) *n.* The larval stage of certain tapeworms, like a cysticercus but having the scolex completely filling the enclosing sac. [CYSTICERC(US) + -OID.]

cypress *The bald cypress (above), which is so called because it is deciduous, is native to the swamplands of the southern United States. Woody humps around the tree's base carry oxygen down to its waterlogged roots.*

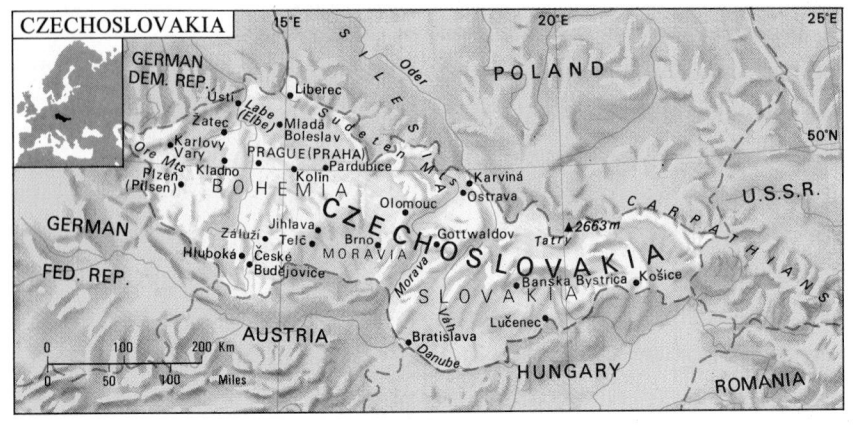

CZECHOSLOVAKIA

cys·ti·cer·co·sis (sĭs'tə-sər-kō'sĭs) *n.* The condition of being infested with cysticerci. [CYSTICERC(US) + -OSIS.]

cys·ti·cer·cus (sĭs'tə-sûr'kəs) *n., pl.* **-ci** (-sī') The larval stage of many tapeworms, consisting of a scolex, or head, enclosed in a fluid-filled sac. [New Latin, "bladder tail" : CYST(O)- + Greek *kerkos,* tail.]

cystic fibrosis *n.* A congenital disease of mucous and sweat glands throughout the body, usually developing during childhood and causing pancreatic insufficiency and pulmonary disorders.

cys·tine (sĭs'tēn) *n.* A white crystalline compound, $C_6H_{12}N_2O_4S_2$, the principal sulfur-containing amino acid of protein. [CYST(O)- + -INE.]

cys·ti·tis (sĭs-tī'tĭs) *n.* Inflammation of the urinary bladder. [New Latin : CYST(O)- + -ITIS.]

cysto-, cyst- *prefix.* Indicates a bladder or cyst; for example, **cystocele, cystoid.** [Greek *kustis,* bladder.]

cys·to·carp (sĭs'tə-kärp') *n. Botany.* A structure consisting of fertile filaments and carpospores, developed after fertilization of the carpogonium in red algae. [CYSTO- + -CARP.]

cys·to·cele (sĭs'tə-sēl') *n.* A hernia of the bladder. [CYSTO- + -CELE (hernia).]

cys·toid (sĭs'toid') *n.* A structure resembling a cyst but lacking an enclosing membrane. [CYST(O)- + -OID.] —**cys·toid** *adj.*

cys·to·lith (sĭs'tə-lĭth) *n.* **1.** *Botany.* A mineral concretion, usually calcium carbonate, formed in the cellulose wall of certain plant cells. **2.** *Pathology.* A urinary calculus. [CYSTO- + -LITH.]

cys·to·scope (sĭs'tə-skōp') *n.* A tubular instrument fitted with a light and used to examine the urinary bladder and ureter. [CYSTO- + -SCOPE.] —**cys·to·scop·ic** (sĭs'tə-skŏp'ĭk) *adj.*

cys·tos·co·py (sĭs-tŏs'kə-pē) *n.* Examination of the urinary bladder using a cystoscope in order to detect and remove polyp, take tissue specimens, or the like. [CYSTO- + -SCOPY.]

cys·tot·o·my *n.* Surgical cutting of the urinary bladder, usually through the abdominal wall. [CYSTO- + -TOMY.]

-cyte *suffix.* Indicates a cell; for example, **leucocyte.** [New Latin *-cyta,* from Greek *kutos,* hollow vessel.]

Cy·the·ra (sə-thîr'ə). Greek **Kí·thi·ra** (kē'thîr-ə). Greek island, southernmost of the Ionian Islands, in the Mediterranean off the southern Peloponnese. In ancient times it was the chief center of the cult of Aphrodite.

Cytherea. See **Aphrodite.**

cyto-, cyt- *prefix.* Indicates cell; for example, **cytokinesis, cytology.** [Greek *kutos,* hollow vessel.]

cy·to·chem·is·try (sī'tō-kĕm'ĭs-trē) *n.* The chemistry of plant and animal cells. —**cy·to·chem·i·cal** *adj.*

cy·to·chrome (sī'tō-krōm') *n.* Any of a class of compounds containing iron and protein, important for oxidation-reduction reactions in cells. [CYTO- + -CHROME.]

cytochrome oxidase *n.* An oxidizing enzyme that functions in cell respiration by reacting with oxygen in the reduced state.

cy·to·gen·e·sis (sī'tō-jĕn'ə-sĭs) *n.* Also **cy·tog·e·ny** (sī-tŏj'ə-nē). The formation and development of cells. [CYTO- + -GENESIS.] —**cy·to·ge·net·ic** (sī'tō-jə-nĕt'ĭk) *adj.*

cy·to·ge·net·ics (sī'tō-jə-nĕt'ĭks) *n. Used with a singular verb.* The study of heredity by cytological and genetic methods, particularly involving the study of chromosomes. —**cy·to·ge·net·i·cal** *adj.* —**cy·to·ge·net·i·cal·ly** *adv.* —**cy·to·ge·net·i·cist** *n.*

cy·to·ki·ne·sis (sī'tō-kĭ-nē'sĭs, -kī-nē'sĭs) *n.* The cleavage of cytoplasm during cell division. [New Latin : CYTO- + -KINESIS.]

cy·to·ki·nin (sī'tə-kī'nĭn) *n.* Any of various growth regulators that promote cell division in plants.

cy·tol·o·gy (sī-tŏl'ə-jē) *n. Abbr.* **cytol.** The branch of biology dealing with the study of the formation, structure, and function of cells. [CYTO- + -LOGY.] —**cy·to·log·i·cal** *adj.* —**cy·to·log·i·cal·ly** *adv.* —**cy·tol·o·gist** *n.*

cy·tol·y·sin (sī-tŏl'ə-sĭn) *n.* A substance capable of destroying an animal cell partially or completely. [CYTOLYS(IS) + -IN.]

cy·tol·y·sis (sī-tŏl'ə-sĭs) *n.* The dissolution of a cell. [New Latin : CYTO- + -LYSIS.] —**cy·to·lyt·ic** *adj.*

cy·to·me·gal·ic (sī'tō-mə-găl'ĭk) *adj.* Pertaining to or characterized by greatly enlarged cells.

cy·to·meg·a·lo·vi·rus (sī'tə-mĕg'ə-lō-vī'rəs) *n.* Any of a group of viruses that cause cellular enlargement and also cause a disease of infants characterized by circulatory dysfunction and microcephaly.

cy·to·path·ic (sī'tə-păth'ĭk) *adj.* Of or pertaining to pathologic changes in cells.

cy·toph·a·gy (sī-tŏf'ə-jē) *n.* The devouring of other cells by the phagocytes. [CYTO- + -PHAGY.] —**cy·to·phag·ic, cy·toph·a·gous** *adj.*

cy·to·pho·tom·e·try (sī'tə-fō-tŏm'ə-trē) *n.* The photometric study of a cell. —**cy·to·pho·to·met·ric** (sī'tə-fō-tə-mĕt'rĭk) *adj.*

cy·to·plasm (sī'tə-plăz'əm) *n.* The protoplasm outside a cell nucleus. [CYTO- + -PLASM.] —**cy·to·plas·mic** *adj.* —**cy·to·plas·mi·cal·ly** *adv.*

cy·to·plast (sī'tə-plăst') *n.* The cytoplasm within a single cell. [CYTO- + -PLAST.] —**cy·to·plas·tic** *adj.*

cy·to·sine (sī'tō-sēn', -zēn', -sən) *n.* A pyrimidine base, $C_4H_5N_3O$, that is an essential constituent of both RNA and DNA. [CYT(O)- + -OS(E) + -INE.]

cy·to·tax·on·o·my (sī'tō-tăk-sŏn'ə-mē) *n.* The classification of organisms based on cellular structure, especially on the comparative morphology of chromosomes. —**cy·to·tax·o·nom·ic** *adj.* —**cy·to·tax·on·o·mist** *n.*

cy·to·tech·nol·o·gist (sī'tə-tĕk-nŏl'ə-jĭst) *n.* A technician who is trained in the medical examination and identification of cellular abnormalities.

cy·to·tox·ic *adj.* Destructive to cells. Said particularly of drugs that destroy cancer cells and are used in chemotherapy. [CYTO- + TOXIC.] —**cy·to·tox·ic·i·ty** *n.*

czar (zär) *n.* Also **tsar, tzar.** **1.** A king or emperor, especially one of the former emperors of Russia. **2.** A tyrant; autocrat. **3.** *Informal.* One in authority; leader: *a czar in finance.* [Polish, from Russian *tsar',* from old Russian *tsĭsarĭ,* from Gothic *kaisar,* from Latin *Caesar,* emperor, CAESAR.] —**czar'dom** *n.*

Usage: Czar is the most common form in American usage and virtually the only one employed in the extended senses *(any tyrant* or, informally, *one in authority).* But *tsar* is preferred by most scholars of Slavic studies as a more accurate transliteration of the Russian, and is often found in scholarly writing with reference to one of the Russian emperors.

czar·das, csar·das (chär'däsh) *n.* **1.** An intricate Hungarian dance characterized by variations in tempo. **2.** Music for this dance. [Hungarian *csárdás.*]

czar·e·vitch (zär'ə-vĭch) *n.* The eldest son of a czar. [Polish, from Russian *tsarevich* : *tsar',* CZAR + *-evich,* masculine patronymic suffix.]

cza·rev·na (zä-rĕv'nə) *n.* **1.** The daughter of a czar. **2.** The wife of a czarevitch. [Polish, from Russian *tsarevna* : *tsar',* CZAR + *-evna,* feminine patronymic suffix.]

cza·ri·na (zä-rē'nə) *n.* Also **cza·rit·za** (zä-rĭt'sə). The wife of a czar; an empress of Russia. [Polish, from Russian *tsarina* : *tsar',* CZAR + *-ina,* feminine suffix.]

czar·ism (zär'ĭz'əm) *n.* The system of government in Russia under the czars; absolute monarchy; autocracy. —**czar'ist** *adj.*

Czech (chĕk) *n.* **1.** A native or inhabitant of Czechoslovakia; especially, a Bohemian or Moravian. **2.** The West Slavonic language of these people. Formerly called "Bohemian."

Czech·o·slo·vak·i·a (chĕk'ə-slō-vä'kē-ə, -väk'ē-ə). *Abbr.* **Czech.** *Czech* **Čes·ko·slo·ven·sko** (chĕs'kô-slô'vĕn-skô). Country in central Europe. Czechoslovakia was created (1918) out of the former Austrian territories of Bohemia and Moravia, with parts of Silesia. Ruthenia was added in 1920. The nation's name derives from the two main language groups: Czech in the west and Slovak in the east. Czechoslovakia developed in the interwar years under the democratic leadership of Tomáš Masaryk and Eduard Beneš. Tensions grew among its component nationalities, especially the German-speakers in the areas known as the Sudetenland, and the region was ceded to Germany by the Munich Agreement (1938). Hitler occupied the rest of the country (1939). After World War II the country fell within the Soviet orbit. Ruthenia was ceded to the U.S.S.R., and by 1948 the Communist Party was in control. In 1968 a liberal program was introduced by the new secretary of the Communist Party, Alexander Dubček. The experiment ended when Warsaw Pact tanks invaded and Dubček was ousted. He was succeeded by Gustáv Husák, who supervised a return to rigid pro-Soviet orthodoxy. Czechoslovakia is a highly industrialized country, producing iron and steel, machinery, cars, textiles, glass, and ceramics. Cereals, sugar beet, potatoes, and hops are the chief crops, and timber is an important product. Czechslovakia depends heavily on the U.S.S.R. for its oil. Area, 127,868 square kilometers (49,370 square miles). Population, 15,300,000. Capital, Prague. —**Czech·o·slo·vak, Czech·o·slo·va·ki·an** *adj. & n.*

Czer·ny (chĕr'nē), **Karl** (1791–1857). Austrian pianist and composer. A disciple of Ludwig van Beethoven and the teacher of Franz Liszt, he is most remembered and respected for his piano studies, including the *School of Velocity* and the *School of the Left Hand,* which have been toiled over by generations of beginning pianists.

D

d, D (dē) *n., pl.* **d's** or **D's. 1.** The fourth letter of the modern English alphabet. See feature at **alphabet. 2.** Any of the speech sounds represented by this letter. **3. D** The lowest passing grade given to a student in a school or college. **4. D** *Music.* **a.** The second tone in the scale of C major, or the fourth tone of the relative minor scale. **b.** The key or a scale in which D is the tonic. **c.** A written or printed note representing this tone. **d.** A string, key, or pipe tuned to the pitch of this tone.

d, D, d., D. *Note:* As an abbreviation or symbol, *d* may be a small or a capital letter, with or without a period. Established forms or those generally preferred precede the definition. When no form is given, all four forms are in general use in that sense. **1. d.** dam (mother). **2. d.** date. **3. d.** daughter. **4. d** day. **5. D.** December. **6. d** deci-. **7. D, D.** Democrat; Democratic. **8. D.** department. **9. d., D.** deputy. **10. D.** Deus. **11. D** The symbol for deuterium. **12. d** *Physics.* deuteron. **13. d** dextro-. **14. d.** died. **15. D.** *Optics.* diopter. **16. D.** doctor (in academic degrees). **17. D.** Dominus. **18. D.** Don (title). **19. d., D.** dose. **20. d., D.** drachma. **21. D.** duchess. **22. D.** duke. **23. D.** Dutch. **24. D** The Roman numeral for 500. **25. d.** *British.* penny (Latin *denarius*). **26.** The fourth in a series.

d– *prefix. Chemistry.* Indicates a dextrorotatory compound. Usually written in italics; for example, "*d*-glucose." Compare **l–.**

D– *prefix. Chemistry.* Indicates an optically active compound with a molecular structure derived from or related to the structure of dextrorotatory glyceraldehyde; for example, "D-alanine." Compare **L–.** An isomer designated D– may itself be dextrorotatory (*d*–) but is not necessarily so.

–'d *suffix.* Indicates: **1.** Contraction of *had, should, would,* or *did,* as in *Who'd you see?* **2.** Contraction of *-ed,* as in *martyr'd.*

da¹ (dä) *n. Informal.* Father. [Of baby-talk origin.]

da² deca-.

Da. Danish.

D.A. district attorney.

dab¹ (dăb) *v.* **dabbed, dabbing, dabs.** *—tr.* **1.** To apply with short, poking strokes. **2.** To cover or press on lightly with or as if with something moist. **3.** To strike or hit lightly, as with a quick pat of the hand. *—intr.* **1.** To touch or poke gingerly at something. **2.** To tap gently; pat. *~n.* **1. a.** A small amount. **b.** A small mass or lump of a moist substance: *a dab of jam.* **2.** A quick, light pat, as with the hand. **3.** *Chiefly British Slang.* A fingerprint. [Middle English *dabben,* probably from Middle Dutch *dabben,* to tap (imitative).]

dab² *n.* Any of various small flatfishes, chiefly of the genera *Limanda* and *Hippoglossoides,* related to and resembling the flounders. [15th century : origin obscure.]

dab³ *n. British Informal.* An expert. [17th century : origin obscure.]

dab·ber (dăb'ər) *n.* **1.** One that dabs. **2.** *Printing.* A cushioned pad used with a brayer by printers and engravers to apply ink.

dab·ble (dăb'əl) *v.* **-bled, -bling, -bles.** *—tr.* **1.** To splash or spatter, as with a liquid. **2.** To move (a part of the body) in water. *—intr.* **1.** To splash liquid gently and playfully. **2.** To undertake something superficially or without serious intent: *dabble in antiques.* **3.** To bob forward and under in shoal water so as to feed off the bottom. [Probably from Dutch *dabbelen,* frequentative of *dabben,* to strike, tap, from Middle Dutch; see DAB.]

dab·bler (dăb'lər) *n.* **1.** One who dabbles; dilettante. **2.** A duck of the genus *Anas* that feeds near the surface of the water or on land, including the mallard, teal, and widgeon. Compare **diving duck.**

dab·chick (dăb'chĭk') *n.* Any of various small grebes of the genus *Podiceps.* [Earlier *dapchick, dopchick* : *dop-,* probably from Middle English *doppe,* diving bird, Old English *-doppa* + CHICK.]

dab hand *n. British Informal.* An expert; a skillful person: *a dab hand at sewing.*

da ca·po (dä kä'pō, də) *adv. Abbr.* **D.C.** *Music.* From the beginning. Used as a direction to repeat a passage: *da capo al fine.* [Italian.]

Dac·ca or **Dha·ka** (dăk'ə). Capital of Bangladesh, on a branch of the Dhaleswari River in the south of the country. Formerly the capital of Mogul Bengal (1608–1704), it came under British rule and was the capital of the province of East Bengal and Assam (1905–12). After Indian independence (1947), Dacca was made the capital of East Pakistan (1956), which became Bangladesh in 1971.

dace (dās) *n., pl.* **daces** or collectively **dace.** Any of various small freshwater fishes of the family Cyprinidae, related to and resembling the minnows. [Middle English *dars, dase,* from Old French *dars,* probably from *dart,* DART (from its swift motion).]

da·cha (dä'chə) *n.* A Russian country house; a villa. [Russian *dacha,* gift, portion, land (granted by a prince), country or holiday house.]

Da·chau (dä'kou'). Town in southeast West Germany, near Munich in Bavaria. A Nazi concentration camp was built here in 1935, and an estimated 70,000 inmates died.

dachs·hund (däks'hŏŏnt', däks'hŏŏnd') *n.* A small dog of a breed developed in Germany for hunting badgers, having a long body with a usually short-haired brown or black and brown coat, drooping ears, and very short legs. [German *Dachshund* : *Dachs,* badger + *Hund,* dog.]

Da·cia (dä'shə). An ancient name for the area roughly corresponding to modern Romania. **—Da·cian** *adj. & n.*

da·coit, da·koit (də-koit') *n.* A member of any of the robber bands of India and Burma who live in the hills and attack in armed gangs, usually on horseback. [Hindi *ḍakait,* from *ḍākā,* "gang-robbery," from Sanskrit *daṣṭaka†,* crowded.]

da·coit·y (də-koi'tē) *n., pl.* **-ties.** Gang robbery in India or Burma. [Hindi *dakaiti.* See **dacoit.**]

Da·cron (dä'krŏn', däk'rŏn') *n.* A trademark for a synthetic polyester textile fiber resistant to stretching and wrinkling.

dac·tyl (dăk'təl) *n.* Also **dac·ty·lus** (-tə-ləs), *pl.* **-li** (-lī') (for sense 2). **1.** *Prosody.* **a.** In accentual verse, a metrical foot consisting of one accented syllable followed by two unaccented. **b.** In quantitative verse, one long syllable followed by two short. **2.** *Zoology.* A finger, toe, or similar part or structure; digit. [Middle English *dactil,* from Latin *dactylus,* from Greek *daktulos†,* finger, hence dactyl (the three syllables of which correspond to the three joints of a finger).] **—dac·tyl·ic** (-tĭl'ĭk) *adj. & n.* **—dac·tyl·i·cal·ly** *adv.*

dactylo–, dactyl– *prefix.* Indicates finger or toe; for example, **dactylogram.** [Greek *daktulos,* finger, DACTYL.]

dac·tyl·o·gram (dăk-tĭl'ə-grăm') *n.* A fingerprint. [DACTYLO- + -GRAM.]

dac·ty·log·ra·phy (dăk'tə-lŏg'rə-fē) *n.* The study of fingerprints as a method of identification. [DACTYLO- + -GRAPHY.] **—dac·ty·log·ra·pher** *n.* **—dac·ty·lo·graph·ic** (dăk'tə-lō-grăf'ĭk) *adj.*

dac·ty·lol·o·gy (dăk'tə-lŏl'ə-jē) *n.* The use of the fingers and hands to communicate, as in the manual alphabet. [DACTYLO- + -LOGY.]

dad (dăd) *n.* **1.** *Informal.* A father. **2.** *Slang.* A term of address used to an older male person other than one's father. [Of baby-talk origin.]

Da·da, da·da (dä'dä) *n.* Also **Da·da·ism** (-ĭz'əm). A western European artistic and literary movement (1916–24) that reacted against traditional cultural aesthetic values by emphasizing irrationality. [French *dada,* hobbyhorse, from baby talk (a name arbitrarily adopted first as the title of a Dadaist review of 1916).] **—Da·da·ist** *n.* **—Da·da·is·tic** *adj.* See feature, next page.

Dadd (dăd), **Richard** (1817–86). British painter. Of unstable temperament, he murdered his father and produced much of his best work in a lunatic asylum. He is known for his extraordinarily dense and intricate fantasy scenes of fairies, goblins, and sprites.

dad·dy (dăd'ē) *n., pl.* **-dies.** *Informal.* Father; dad. Used familiarly, especially by children. [Diminutive of DAD.]

daddy long·legs (lông'lĕgz', lŏng'-) *n., pl.* **daddy longlegs. 1.** Any of various arachnids of the order Phalangida, having a small, rounded body and long, slender legs. Also called "harvestman." **2.** *Chiefly British.* An insect, the **crane fly** (*see*).

da·do (dä'dō) *n., pl.* **-does. 1.** *Architecture.* The section of a pedestal between the base and crown. **2.** The lower portion of the wall of a room, decorated differently from the upper section, as with panels. *~tr.v.* **dadoed, -doing, -does.** To provide with a dado. [Italian, a die, cube, probably from Latin *datum,* gift, pawn (chessman), from the past participle of *dare,* to give.]

dabchick *The smallest of the grebe family, the dabchick is common on densely vegetated lakes in Europe, Asia, and Africa. The male (above left) has a red neck only during the breeding season in summer; at other times of the year, its plumage is brown, buff, and white. The female has similar but duller markings.*

dado *The crisscross-painted plaster decoration on this wall extends down to a paneled dado.*

Dada

ART CREATED FROM CHANCE

Dada—French for "hobbyhorse"—was a name picked at random

Dada was born in Zurich in 1916 when a nightclub, the Cabaret Voltaire, was opened to operate as an agency for progressive and émigré artists. The movement's purpose was not to create a new style but to escape from artistic conventions and to explore materials and modes of communication not previously deemed suitable for the arts. An artist could use materials found by chance or arranged at random. The very name Dada, French for "hobbyhorse," was picked at random from a dictionary.

Leading figures in this "anti-art" movement were Jean Arp, Richard Hülsenbeck, and Tristan Tzara. The movement became international through artists such as Marcel Duchamps, Man Ray, and Francis Picabia in New York, André Breton and a literary cell in Paris, and Kurt Schwitters and Max Ernst in Germany. In the Berlin group, John Heartfield was perfecting the new form of photomontage that he later used for vivid anti-Nazi propaganda.

In 1924 Dada merged with surrealism.

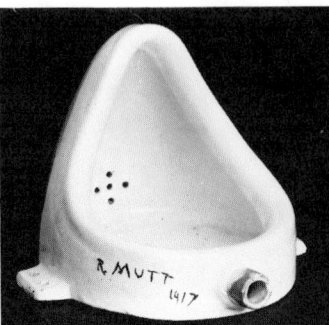

EXHIBIT REJECTED *Marcel Duchamp tried, and failed, to exhibit this urinal in New York in 1917. He called it* Fountain *and said it was a "ready-made" work of art.*

PAPER COLLAGE Hair Navel Picture *was done by the German Kurt Schwitters, who said an artist could mold paper into pictures "provided he is capable of molding a picture." In the subtlety of their colors, his works are widely seen as transcending Dada.*

dae·dal (dēd′l) *adj.* **1.** Ingenious and complex in design or function; intricate. **2.** Finely or skillfully made or employed; artistic. [Latin *daedalus,* from Greek *daidalos,* skillful.]

Daed·a·lus (dĕd′l-əs; *British* dēd′l-əs). *Greek Mythology.* A sculptor and inventor, father of Icarus and builder of the Labyrinth. —**Dae·da·li·an, Dae·da·le·an** (dĭ-dā′lē-ən, -dāl′yən) *adj.*

daemon. Variant of **demon.**

daf·fa·dil·ly, daf·fo·dil·ly (dăf′ə-dĭl′ē) *n., pl.* **-lies.** *Regional.* A daffo-

dil. Also called "daffadowndilly," "daffydowndilly."

daf·fo·dil (dăf′ə-dĭl) *n.* **1.** A bulbous plant, *Narcissus pseudonarcissus,* having usually yellow flowers with a trumpet-shaped central crown. **2.** Its flower. **3.** Brilliant to vivid yellow. [Probably from Dutch *de affodil,* the asphodel : *de,* the + *affodil,* from Medieval Latin *affodilus,* from Latin *asphodelus,* ASPHODEL.]

daf·fy (dăf′ē) *adj.* **-fier, -fiest.** *Informal.* Silly; foolish; zany. [Obsolete English *daff,* fool, Middle English *daffe,* probably related to *dafte,* gentle, foolish, DAFT.]

daft (dăft, däft) *adj.* **1.** Mad; crazy. **2.** Foolish; stupid. [Middle English *dafte,* gentle, modest, foolish, Old English *gedæfte,* mild, meek.] —**daft·ly** *adv.* —**daft·ness** *n.*

Da·fydd ap Gruf·fydd (dä′wĭth ăp grĭf′ĭth, dä′-) (died 1283). The last native Prince of Wales (1282–83), he fought his brother Llywelyn ap Gruffydd for the title, claiming it when his brother died (1282). He was captured by the English under Edward I and executed.

Dafydd ap Gwil·ym (gwĭl′əm) (c. 1320–c. 1380). Welsh poet. He was influenced by the troubadours of Europe and wrote in a tone more personal than the conventions of his day. He also popularized a new metrical form adopted by later bardic writers.

dag (dăg) *n.* **1.** A lock of matted or dung-coated wool. **2.** A loosely hanging end or shred. [Middle English *dagge†,* shred, tag.]

dag decagram.

Da·gan (dä′gän). The Babylonian god of the earth, considered by some to be identified with Baal.

Da·ge·stan Autonomous Soviet Socialist Republic (dăg′ə-stän′, däg′ə-stän′). A part of the R.S.F.S.R., U.S.S.R., bordered on the east by the Caspian Sea. It was annexed by Russia in 1813. Though comprising over 30 different nationalities, the population is chiefly Muslim. Its capital is the Caspian port of Makhachkala.

dag·ga (dăg′ə) *n. South African.* Indian hemp used as a narcotic; cannabis. [Afrikaans, from Hottentot *dachab.*]

dag·ger (dăg′ər) *n.* **1.** A short pointed weapon with sharp edges, used for stabbing. **2.** Something that agonizes, torments, or wounds. **3.** *Printing.* **a.** An **obelisk** (see). **b.** A **double dagger** (see). —**at daggers drawn.** Hostile; ready for confrontation. —**look daggers.** To glare angrily or hatefully.
~*tr.v.* **daggered, -gering, -gers. 1.** To stab with a dagger. **2.** To mark with a dagger. [Middle English *daggere,* from obsolete *dag,* to pierce, influenced by Old French *dague,* from Old Provençal or Old Italian *daga,* perhaps from Vulgar Latin *daca* (unattested), "Dacian knife," feminine of Latin *Dācus,* Dacian, from DACIA.]

dagger fern *n.* An evergreen North American fern, *Polystichum acrostichoides,* having dense clusters of lance-shaped fronds. Also called "Christmas fern."

dag·lock (dăg′lŏk′) *n.* A lock of wool; a dag.

Da·gon (dä′gŏn′). The chief god of the ancient Philistines and later the Phoenicians, represented as half man and half fish. [Middle English, from Latin, from Greek *Dagōn,* from Hebrew *Dāgōn,* "small fish," diminutive of *dāg,* fish.]

Da·guerre (də-gâr′), **Louis Jacques Mandé** (1787–1851). French inventor of a photographic method in which sunlight formed a permanent image on a copper plate treated with silver iodide.

da·guerre·o·type (də-gâr′ə-tīp′) *n.* **1.** An early photographic process with the impression made on a light-sensitive silver-coated metallic plate and developed by mercury vapor. **2.** A photograph made by this process.
~*tr.v.* **daguerreotyped, -typing, -types.** To photograph by this process. [After Louis DAGUERRE.] —**da·guerre·o·typ·er** *n.* —**da·guerre·o·typ·y** *n.*

dah (dä) *n.* A dash in Morse code. Compare **dit.**

da·ha·be·ah, da·ha·bee·yah, da·ha·bi·ah (dä′hə-bē′ə) *n.* A houseboat used on the Nile, having sails and sometimes an engine. [Arabic *dahabīya,* "the golden" (that is, gilded barge), originally with reference to those used by Egyptian rulers.]

Dahl (däl), **Roald** (1916–). British author, born in Wales of Norwegian parents. He has written suspense stories and children's books, such as *Charlie and the Chocolate Factory* (1964).

dahl·i·a (dăl′yə, däl′-, dāl′-) *n.* **1.** Any of several plants of the genus *Dahlia,* native to Mexico and Central America, having tuberous roots and showy, variously colored flowers; especially, any of the horticultural forms derived from *D. pinnata* and *D. juarezii.* **2.** The flower of any of these plants. [New Latin *Dahlia;* named in honor of Anders *Dahl,* 18th-century Swedish botanist.]

Dahomey. See **Benin.**

da·hoon (də-hoōn′) *n.* An evergreen shrub or small tree, *Ilex cassine,* of the southeastern United States, having red fruit. [Origin unknown.]

Dail Ei·reann (dô′əl â′rən). The lower legislative house of the Irish parliament. Also called "Dáil." See **Oireachtas.** [Irish : *dáil,* assembly, from Old Irish *dál* + *Éireann,* genitive of *Éire,* Ireland, from Old Irish *Ériu,* "land."]

dai·ly (dā′lē) *adj.* Of, pertaining to, occurring, or published every day or every weekday.
~*n., pl.* **dailies. 1.** A daily publication, especially a newspaper. **2.** *British.* A servant, especially a cleaning woman, who lives off the premises.
~*adv.* Each day; day after day. [Middle English *daili,* Old English *dæglīc,* from *dæg,* DAY.]

daily double *n. Horse Racing.* A bet won by choosing both winners of two specified races on one day.

dai·mio, dai·myo (dī′myō) *n., pl.* **daimio, daimyo, -mios,** or **-myos.**

A hereditary nobleman in feudal Japan. [Japanese *daimyō,* "great name."]

daimon. Variant of **demon.**

dain•ty (dān'tē) *adj.* **-tier, -tiest. 1.** Delicately beautiful or charming; exquisite: *"No dainty rhymes or sentimental love verses for you, terrible year"* (Walt Whitman). **2.** Delicious; choice. **3.** Of refined taste or manners. **4.** Too fastidious; fussy.
~*n., pl.* **dainties.** Something delicious; a delicacy. [Middle English *deinte,* delicious, pleasant, from *deinte,* pleasure, delicacy, from Old French *deintie,* from Latin *dīgnitās* (stem *dīgnitāt-*), dignity, worth, from *dīgnus,* worthy.] **—dain•ti•ly** *adv.* **—dain•ti•ness** *n.*

dai•qui•ri (dī'kə-rē, dăk'ə-rē) *n., pl.* **-ris.** An iced cocktail of rum, lime or lemon juice, and sugar. [After *Daiquirí,* Cuba, source of the rum originally used in this drink.]

Dairen. See **Lü-da.**

dair•y (dâr'ē) *n., pl.* **-dairies. 1.** A commercial establishment that processes or sells milk and milk products. **2.** A place where milk and cream are stored and processed, such as a specially equipped building on a farm. **3. a.** A dairy farm. **b.** The herd of cattle on a dairy farm. **4.** The dairy business; dairying. **5.** Dairy products, as distinguished from meat, with reference to Jewish religious dietary laws. [Middle English *daierie,* from *daie,* dairymaid, Old English *dǣge,* dough-kneader.] **—dair•y** *adj.*

dairy cattle *pl.n.* Cows bred and raised for milk rather than meat.

dairy farm *n.* A farm for producing milk and milk products.

dair•y•ing (dâr'ē-ĭng) *n.* **1.** The business of a dairy. **2.** Dairy farming. **—dair•y•ing** *adj.*

dair•y•maid (dâr'ē-mād') *n.* A woman or girl who works in a dairy.

dair•y•man (dâr'ē-mən) *n., pl.* **-men** (-mĭn). **1.** A man who works in a dairy. **2.** A dairy manager or owner.

da•is (dā'ĭs, dās) *n., pl.* **-ises** (-ĭ-sĭz). A raised platform, as in a lecture hall or dining hall, used by speakers, dignitaries, or the like. [Middle English *deis,* from Old French, table, platform, from Latin *discus,* dish, quoit, DISK.]

dai•sy (dā'zē) *n., pl.* **-sies. 1.** Any of several related plants having rayed flowers; especially, in North America, a widely naturalized Eurasian plant, *Chrysanthemum leucanthemum,* having flowers with a yellow center and white rays. This species is also called "oxeye daisy," "white daisy." **2.** A low-growing European plant, *Bellis perennis,* having flowers with pink or white rays. This species is the daisy of literary tradition. Also called "English daisy," "bachelor's-button." **3.** The flower of any of these plants. **4.** *Slang.* Something excellent or notable. [Middle English *daisie, dayeseye,* Old English *dægesēage,* "day's eye" (the flower of some species opens to reveal a yellow disk in the morning and closes again in the evening) : *dæges,* genitive of *dæg,* DAY + *ēage,* eye.]

daisy fleabane *n.* Any of several plants of the genus *Erigeron,* especially *E. annuus,* a weedy North American plant having numerous small flowers with white or pinkish rays.

daisy wheel *n.* A printing device, used especially in the printing machines attached to computers and word processors, consisting of printing characters fixed at the end of spokes on a wheel.

dak (dăk) *n.* In India, the post or mail. [Hindi and Marathi.]

Da•kar (də-kär'). Capital of Senegal, a port on Cape Verde Peninsula. A fort was built here by the French in 1857, and the city was the capital of French West Africa (1904–59).

dak bungalow *n.* In India, a place providing lodging for travelers.

Da•kin's solution (dā'kənz) *n.* A dilute solution of sodium hypochlorite in water, used as a surgical disinfectant. [Developed by Henry Drysdale *Dakin* (1880–1952), British biochemist.]

dakoit. Variant of **dacoit.**

Da•ko•ta[1] (də-kō'tə) *n., pl.* **-tas** or collectively **Dakota. 1.** A member of any of a large group of Siouan-speaking people of North American Plains Indians, commonly called Sioux, now living on reservations in North and South Dakota, Minnesota, and Montana. **2.** The Siouan language of these Indians. **—Da•ko•tan** *adj.* & *n.*

Dakota[2]**.** See **James** (river of North Dakota).

Dakota[3]**.** A U.S. territory (established 1861) comprising present-day North and South Dakota and much of Wyoming and Montana. It was reduced in size by the creation of the Montana Territory (1864) and Wyoming Territory (1868). The area was further divided (1889) into two new states, North and South Dakota. The two states are known as **the Dakotas.**

dal. Variant of **dhal.**

Da•la•dier (də-lä'dē-ā'), **Edouard** (1884–1970). French statesman and prime minister (1933, 1934, 1938–40). Daladier signed the Munich Agreement (1938) for France. He was arrested after France fell to the Germans in 1940 and remained in captivity until 1945.

Da•lai La•ma (dä-lī' lä'mə) *n.* The traditional ruler and highest priest of the Buddhist religion in Tibet and Mongolia. The position is not hereditary or elective, but said to be held by the same individual in successive incarnations. Also called "Grand Lama." [Tibetan : Mongolian *dalai,* ocean, great + Tibetan *bla-ma,* superior one, a Buddhist monk, LAMA.]

dal•a•pon (dăl'ə-pŏn) *n.* A selective weedkiller used on unwanted grasses. [Probably *di-* + *alpha* + *propionic* acid.]

da•la•si (də-lä'sē) *n.* The basic monetary unit of Gambia, equivalent to 100 bututs. See feature at **currency.** [Native name in Gambia.]

dale (dāl) *n.* A valley. [Middle English *dale,* Old English *dæl.*]

d'A•lem•bert (dȧ-lăN-bâr'), **Jean le Rond** (1717–83). French mathematician and philosopher, who defined the laws of dynamics governing equilibrium and centrifugal force, known as d'Alembert's principle. A friend of Voltaire and Diderot, he contributed to the *Encyclopédie.*

dales•man (dālz'mən) *n., pl.* **-men** (-mĭn). A person who lives in a dale, especially in northern Yorkshire, England.

da•leth (dä'lĭth) *n.* The fourth letter of the Hebrew alphabet. See feature at **alphabet.** [Hebrew *dāleth,* from *dālt,* door, daleth.]

Da•li (dä'lē). **Salvador** (1904–). Spanish painter. He went to Paris in 1929 and joined the surrealist movement. Influenced by Freud's psychoanalytic theories of the unconscious, he painted disturbing images whose quasi-photographic finish heightens their disquieting effect, as in *Persistence of Memory* (1931).

Dal•las (dăl'əs). City on the Trinity River in northeast Texas. It grew on the site of Peter's Colony (founded 1841), becoming Dallas in 1845. The town prospered as a cotton center and expanded after 1915 with the discovery of oil nearby, becoming the largest city in Texas.

dal•li•ance (dăl'ē-əns) *n.* **1.** Frivolous spending of time; dawdling. **2.** Amorous play; flirtation.

Dal•lis grass (dăl'əs, -ĭs) *n.* A South American grass, *Paspalum dilatatum,* grown for pasturage in the southern United States. [*Dallis,* probably alteration of DALLAS.]

dal•ly (dăl'ē) *v.* **-lied, -lying, -lies.** *—intr.* **1.** To play amorously; flirt: *"Sylvester dallied about Lena until he began to make mistakes in his work"* (Willa Cather). **2.** To trifle; toy. **3.** To waste time; dawdle. *—tr.* To waste (time). Used with *away.* [Middle English *dalien,* from Old French *dalier*†, to chat.] **—dal•li•er** *n.* **—dal•ly•ing•ly** *adv.*

Dal•ma•tia (dăl-mā'shə). The southern part of Yugoslavia's coastline. The region is mountainous and the population mostly Croatian. It was dominated by Venice from the 15th to 18th century, then fell to Austria. Italy claimed Dalmatia in World War I, but it joined the Kingdom of Serbs, Croats, and Slovenes (1918), which became Yugoslavia (1929). During World War II much of it was held by Italy but was subsequently restored to Yugoslavia. Dalmatia's scenic coastline attracts many tourists, and the region produces wines and liqueurs. Split is the chief town.

Dal•ma•tian (dăl-mā'shən) *n.* **1.** A dog of a breed believed to have originated in Dalmatia, having a short, smooth, white coat covered with black or dark brown spots. Also called "coach dog," "carriage dog." **2.** A native or inhabitant of Dalmatia.
~*adj.* Of or pertaining to Dalmatia or its inhabitants.

dal•mat•ic (dăl-măt'ĭk) *n.* **1.** *Roman Catholic Church.* A wide-sleeved garment formerly worn over the alb by the deacon at the celebration of High Mass and now worn by bishops and other prelates. **2.** A similar garment worn by an English monarch as a coronation robe. [Middle English *dalmatik,* from Old French *dalmatique,* from Late Latin *dalmatica (vestis),* "Dalmatian (garment)" (originally of Dalmatian wool), from *dalmaticus,* of DALMATIA.]

dal se•gno (däl săn'yo) *adv. Abbr.* **d.s., D.S.** *Music.* From the sign. Used as a direction to repeat from the place marked by the sign (§) to a designated point. [Italian.]

Dal•ton (dôlt'n), **John** (1766–1844). British chemist, whose pioneer work on the properties of gases led to his discovery in 1803 that the atoms of chemical elements differed in weight and to his formulation of the atomic theory.

dal•to•ni•an (dôl-tō'nē-ən) *adj.* Also **Dal•to•ni•an** (especially for sense 1). **1.** Of or pertaining to John Dalton or his atomic theory. **2.** Of or pertaining to daltonism.

dal•ton•ism (dôlt'n-ĭz'əm) *n.* Also **Dal•ton•ism. 1.** Red-green colorblindness. **2.** Any form of colorblindness. [After John DALTON, who was colorblind.] **—dal•ton•ic** (dôl-tŏn'ĭk) *adj.*

Dalton plan *n.* An educational system in which pupils learn by completing long-term study projects. [After *Dalton,* Massachusetts, where the plan was introduced.]

Dalton's law *n. Chemistry.* The principle that the pressure of a mixture of gases is the sum of the partial pressures of the components of the mixture. Also called "Dalton's law of partial pressures." [After John DALTON.]

dam[1] (dăm) *n.* **1.** A barrier constructed across a waterway to control the flow or raise the level of water. **2.** A natural barrier, such as an ice dam, across a watercourse. **3.** A body of water controlled by such a barrier. **4.** Any obstruction or hindrance.
~*tr.v.* **dammed, damming, dams. 1.** To construct a dam across; hold back by means of a dam. **2.** To obstruct or restrain; confine. Usually used with *up.* —See Synonyms at **hinder.** [Middle English, probably from Middle Low German *dam,* from Germanic *dammjan* (unattested), to impede, dam.]

dam[2] *n.* **1.** *Abbr.* **d.** A female parent of a quadruped, such as a sheep or horse. **2.** *Archaic.* A mother. [Middle English, variant of DAME.]

dam decameter.

dam•age (dăm'ĭj) *n.* **1.** Harm done to a person or thing, usually reducing usefulness, value, soundness, or standing. **2. damages.** *Law.* Money paid or ordered to be paid as compensation for injury or loss. **3.** *Informal.* Cost; price: *What's the damage?*
~*v.* **damaged, -aging, -ages.** *—tr.* To cause injury to; impair; harm. *—intr.* To suffer or be susceptible to damage. —See Synonyms at **injure, ruin.** [Middle English, from Old French, from *dam(me),* loss, damage, from Latin *damnum,* loss, harm, fine.] **—dam•age•a•ble** *adj.* **—dam•ag•ing•ly** *adv.*

da•man (dăm'ən) *n. Rare.* The hyrax, a small mammal of Africa and Asia Minor. [Arabic *damān (Isrā'īl),* "sheep of Israel."]

Da•man (də-män'). *Portuguese* **Da•mão** (dä-mouN'). Region of northwest India, on the eastern shore of the Gulf of Khambar

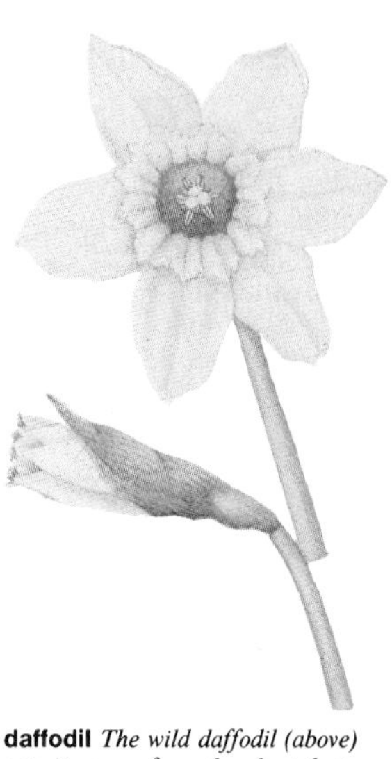

daffodil *The wild daffodil (above) gets its name from the plant that grew in the meadows of the nether world in Greek mythology. The Greeks called the plant* asphodelos, *which later became affadyl and then daffodil.*

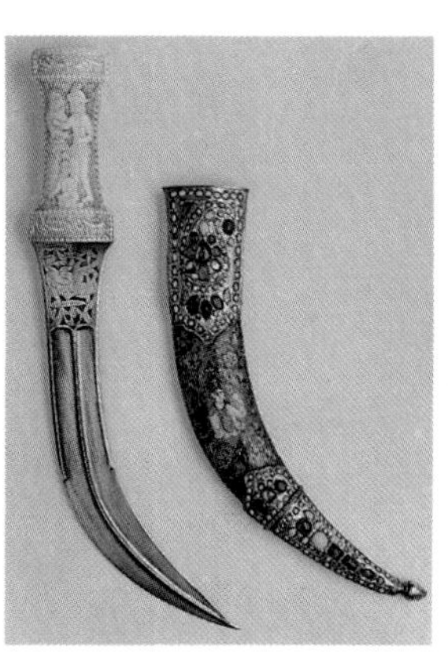

dagger *A 19th-century Persian dagger, with ivory handle and jeweled scabbard, now in the Victoria and Albert Museum, London.*

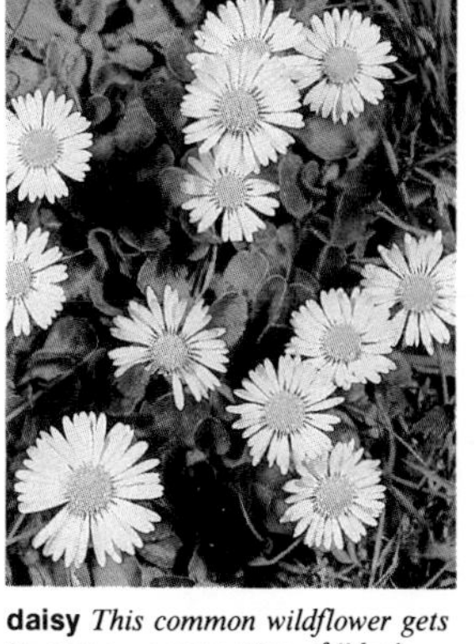

daisy *This common wildflower gets its name—a corruption of "day's eye"—from its habit of opening and closing with the sun.*

damascene *Detail from an iron damascened plaque, made in Milan in the mid-16th century. The wavy-patterned style gets its name from its resemblance to the ornamentation used by medieval Arab weavers and metalworkers in the Syrian capital, Damascus.*

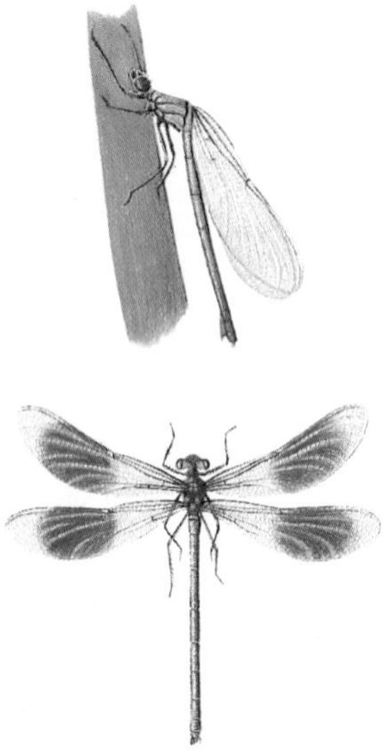

damselfly *These fragile relatives of the dragonflies live near streams and prey on tiny insects. In this species, the banded agrion, the males have dark blue bands on their wings; the females (top) do not.*

PRONUNCIATION KEY

ă, pat; ā, pay; âr, care; ä, father, are; b, bib; ch, church; d, deed; ĕ, pet; ē, be; f, fife; g, gag; h, hat; hw, which; ĭ, pit; ī, pie; îr, pier; j, judge; k, kick; l, lid, needle; m, mum; n, no, sudden; ng, thing; ŏ, pot; ō, toe; ô, paw, for; oi, noise; ou, out; o͝o, book; o͞o, boot; p, pop; r, roar; s, sauce; sh, ship, dish; t, tight; th, thin, path; *th*, this, bathe; ŭ, cut; ûr, fur; v, valve; w, with; y, yes; z, zebra, size; zh, vision; ə, about, item, edible, gallop, circus, peaceful

IN FOREIGN WORDS:

à, *Fr.* ami; œ, *Fr.* feu, *Ger.* schön; ü, *Fr.* tu, *Ger.* über; KH, *Ger.* ich, *Scot.* loch; N, *Fr.* bon; y', *Fr.* Compiègne

STRESS MARKS:

Primary stress: ′ **in·cite′** (ĭn-sīt′)
Secondary stress: ′ **in′sight′** (ĭn′sīt′)

(Cambay). It was a Portuguese territory from the 16th century and was occupied by India in 1961. It now forms part of the territory of Goa, Daman, and Diu.

damar. Variant of **dammar.**

dam·as·cene (dăm′ə-sēn′, dăm′ə-sēn′) *tr.v.* **-cened, -cening, -cenes.** To decorate (metal) with wavy patterns of inlay, usually of gold or silver, or etching.
~*n.* Work decorated by damascening.
~*adj.* Of or pertaining to damascening or damask. [Middle English, from Old French *damasquiner,* "to decorate in the manner of Damascus blades or steel," from *damasquin,* of Damascus, from Italian *damaschino,* from Latin *Damascēnus,* from Greek *Damaskēnos,* from *Damaskos,* DAMASCUS.] **—dam·a·scen·er** *n.*

Dam·a·scene (dăm′ə-sēn′) *n.* A native or inhabitant of Damascus.
~*adj.* Of or pertaining to Damascus or its inhabitants.

Da·mas·cus (də-măs′kəs). *French* **Da·mas** (də-mä′). *Arabic* **Ash Sham** (ăsh shăm′) or **Di·mash** (dĭ-măsh′). Capital of Syria, on the Barada River in the southwest of the country. A city of great antiquity, it is mentioned in the Bible. Damascus fell to the Arabs (635) and was the capital of the Islamic empire under the Umayyad caliphs (661–750). A Saracen stronghold in the Crusades, the city was in Ottoman hands (1516–1918) and then occupied by the French before becoming the capital of independent Syria (1941). The city was once famous for its blades and armor and still produces fine metalware, textiles, glass, and leather goods.

Damascus steel *n.* An early form of steel having wavy markings, developed in Near Eastern countries, especially Persia, and used chiefly in sword blades. Also called "damask steel."

dam·ask (dăm′əsk) *n.* **1.** A rich patterned fabric of cotton, linen, silk, or wool. **2.** A fine, twilled table linen. **3.** Damascus steel. **4.** The wavy pattern on Damascus steel.
~*tr.v.* **damasked, -asking, -asks. 1.** To damascene. **2.** To decorate or weave with rich patterns.
~*adj.* **1.** Of or from Damascus. **2.** Made from damask or Damascus steel. [Middle English *damask (cloth),* from Medieval Latin *(pannus de) damasco,* "(cloth of) Damascus."]

damask rose *n.* A rose, *Rosa damascena,* native to Asia, having fragrant red or pink flowers that are used as a source of attar. [Medieval Latin *rosa Damascēna,* from Latin *Damascēnus,* of DAMASCUS, its supposed place of origin.]

dame (dām) *n.* **1.** A title formerly given to a woman in authority or to the mistress of a household. Now only used in expressions such as *Dame Fortune.* **2.** A married woman; matron. **3.** Slang. A woman; female. **4.** *British.* **a.** *Archaic.* The legal title of the wife or widow of a knight or baronet. **b.** A title of a woman, equivalent to that of a knight. **5.** *Obsolete.* A schoolmistress. [Middle English, from Old French, from Latin *domina,* feminine of *dominus,* master, lord.]

dame school *n.* Formerly, a small local school run by an elderly woman, usually for children of primary school age.

dame's rocket *n.* A plant, *Hesperis matronalis,* native to Europe, having clusters of fragrant purple or white flowers. Also called "dame's violet," "damewort." [Translation of its Latin name.]

Da·mien (dā′mē-ən), **Father,** born Joseph de Veuster Damien (1840–89). Belgian Roman Catholic missionary who volunteered in 1873 to supervise Hawaii's leper colony on Molokai Island. He died there of leprosy.

dam·mar, da·mar, dam·mer (dăm′ər) *n.* Any of various hard resins obtained from Indo-Malayan trees of the genera *Agathis* and *Shorea,* used in varnishes and lacquers. [Malay *damar,* resin.]

damn (dăm) *v.* **damned, damning, damns.** —*tr.* **1.** To pronounce an adverse judgment upon; criticize adversely. **2.** To bring about the failure of; ruin. **3.** To condemn as harmful, illegal, or immoral: *damn gambling and strong drink.* **4.** *Theology.* To condemn to everlasting punishment or a similar fate. **5.** To swear at by using the word "damn"; curse. —*intr.* To swear; curse.
~*interj.* Used to express anger, irritation, or disappointment.
~*n.* **1.** The saying of "damn"; a curse. **2.** *Informal.* The least valuable bit; a jot: *don't give a damn; not worth a damn.*
~*adj.* Damned.
~*adv.* *Informal.* Damned. Used as an intensive. [Middle English *dam(p)nen,* from Old French *dam(p)ner,* from Latin *damnāre,* to inflict loss upon, condemn, from *damnum,* loss, damage.]

dam·na·ble (dăm′nə-bəl) *adj.* **1.** Deserving condemnation; odious; hateful. **2.** Disagreeable; unpleasant: *damnable weather.* **—dam·na·ble·ness** *n.* **—dam·na·bly** *adv.*

dam·na·tion (dăm-nā′shən) *n.* **1.** The act of damning or condition of being damned. **2.** *Theology.* **a.** Condemnation to everlasting punishment; doom. **b.** Everlasting punishment. **3.** Failure or ruination incurred by adverse criticism.
~*interj.* Used to express anger or annoyance.

dam·na·to·ry (dăm′nə-tôr′ē, -tōr′ē) *adj.* Threatening with damnation; condemning; damning.

damned (dămd) *adj.* **1.** Condemned, especially to eternal punishment; doomed. **2.** *Informal.* **a.** Deserving condemnation; detestable. Used as an expression of irritation or disappointment: *This damned weather!* **b.** Absolute; utter. Used as an intensive: *a damned fool.* **3.** *Informal.* Used as an expression of surprise or refusal: *I'm damned if I'll lend him my car!*
~*adv.* *Informal.* Very; extremely: *a damned poor excuse.*
~*n.* *Theology.* Souls doomed to eternal punishment.

damned·est (dăm′dĭst) *adj.* *Informal.* Most extraordinary: *the damnedest thing I've ever heard.* **—do one's damnedest.** To do all one possibly can.

dam·ni·fy (dăm′nə-fī′) *tr.v.* **-fied, -fying, -fies.** *Law.* To cause loss or damage to. [Old French *damnifier,* from Late Latin *damnificāre,* from Latin *damnificus,* causing loss, harmful : *damnum,* loss, harm + *-ficus,* -FIC.] **—dam·ni·fi·ca·tion** *n.*

damn·ing (dăm′ĭng) *adj.* **1.** That condemns or criticizes: *a damning review.* **2.** That incriminates or gives proof of guilt: *damning evidence.* **—damn·ing·ly** *adv.*

Dam·o·cles (dăm′ə-klēz′). A member of the court of Dionysius the Elder, tyrant of Syracuse, who was forced by Dionysius to sit at a banquet under a sword suspended by a single hair to demonstrate the precariousness of a king's fortunes. **—Dam·o·cle·an** *adj.*

Da·mon and Pyth·i·as (dā′mən; pĭth′ē-əs). *Roman Mythology.* Two friends so devoted that Damon pledged his life as a hostage for the condemned Pythias.

dam·o·sel, dam·o·zel (dăm′ə-zĕl′) *n.* Also **dam·oi·selle** (dăm′ə-zĕl′). *Archaic.* A damsel. [Variant of DAMSEL.]

damp (dămp) *adj.* **damper, dampest. 1.** Slightly wet; moist; humid. **2.** *Archaic.* Dejected. —See Synonyms at **wet.**
~*n.* **1. a.** Moisture; humidity; mist. **b.** Moisture on the inside walls of a building caused by condensation, by rain entering through an outside wall, or by water seeping up from the ground *(rising damp).* **2.** Foul or poisonous gas that sometimes pollutes the air in mines. See **afterdamp, blackdamp, firedamp. 3.** *Archaic.* Lowness of spirits; depression. **4.** A restraint or check; discouragement.
~*tr.v.* **damped, damping, damps. 1.** To make damp or moist; moisten. **2.** To cut off the flow of air to (a fire) to reduce combustion. Often used with *down.* **3.** To restrain or check; discourage. Often used with *down.* **4.** To provide (the strings of a keyboard instrument) with dampers as a means of deadening the sound. **5.** *Physics.* To decrease the amplitude of (an oscillation or wave). **—damp off.** *Botany.* To be affected by **damping off** *(see).* [Middle English, poison gas, chokedamp, from Middle Low German and Middle Dutch, smoke, vapor, from Germanic *damp-* (unattested).] **—damp·ish** *adj.* **—damp·ly** *adv.* **—damp·ness** *n.*

damp course *n.* A strip of plastic or layer of other waterproof material placed between two courses of bricks close to the ground in a wall in order to prevent rising damp. Also called "dampproof course."

damp·en (dăm′pən) *v.* **-ened, -ening, -ens.** —*tr.* **1.** To moisten; make damp. **2.** To deaden; depress: *dampen one's spirits.* —*intr.* To become wet or moist. **—damp·en·er** *n.*

damp·er (dăm′pər) *n.* **1.** One that damps, restrains, or depresses. **2.** An adjustable plate in the flue of a furnace or stove for controlling the draft. **3.** *Music.* **a.** A device in various keyboard instruments for deadening the vibrations of the strings. **b.** A mute for various brass instruments. **4.** Any device that eliminates or progressively diminishes oscillations. **5.** *Australian.* An unleavened bread made from flour and water and cooked in an open fire. **—put a damper on.** *Informal.* To suppress; discourage.

Dam·pi·er (dăm′pē-ər), **William** (1652–1715). British pirate who later became an explorer and circumnavigated the globe, which he described in his *Voyage Round the World* (1697). In 1699 he was sent to the South Seas and discovered the Dampier Archipelago off northwest Australia.

damping off *n.* A disease of planted seeds or very young seedlings caused by fungi, particularly those of the genus *Pythium,* and resulting in death of the newly sprouted plants due to softening and collapse of the stem base.

dampproof (dămp′pro͞of′) *adj.* Resistant to damp.
~*tr.v.* **dampproofed, -proofing, -proofs.** To make dampproof, especially by providing a damp course.

dam·sel (dăm′zəl) *n.* A young woman or girl; maiden. [Middle English *damisele,* from Old French *dameisele,* from Vulgar Latin *dominicella* (unattested), diminutive of Latin *domina,* lady, DAME.]

dam·sel·fish (dăm′zəl-fĭsh′) *n., pl.* **-fishes** or collectively **damselfish.** Any of various small tropical marine fishes of the family Pomacentridae, having laterally compressed, usually brightly colored bodies. Also called "demoiselle."

dam·sel·fly (dăm′zəl-flī′) *n., pl.* **-flies.** Any of various slender-bodied, often brightly colored insects of the order Odonata, related to the dragonflies but differing in having wings that are folded together over the back when at rest. Also *rarely* "demoiselle."

dam·son (dăm′zən, -sən) *n.* **1.** A plum tree, *Prunus institia* (or *P. domestica institia*), native to Eurasia, cultivated since ancient times for its edible fruit. Also called "bullace." **2.** The oval, bluish-black, juicy plum borne by this tree. Also called "damson plum." [Middle English *damascene, damson,* from Latin *(prūnum) Damascēnum,* "(plum) of Damascus."]

dan (dän, dăn) *n.* *Sometimes* **Dan. 1.** In the oriental martial arts such as judo, any of twelve levels of proficiency at the grade of **black belt** *(see).* **2.** One who has achieved such a level. [Japanese.]

Dan[1] (dăn) *n.* **1.** The fifth son of Jacob. Genesis 30:6. **2.** One of the 12 tribes of Israel, descended from Dan.

Dan[2] *n.* *Obsolete.* A title of honor equivalent to *master* or *sir:* *"Dan Chaucer, well of English undefiled"* (Spenser). [Middle English *Dan, Daunz,* "master," "mister," originally a title of respect for a monk or priest, from Old French *Dan, Danz,* from Medieval Latin *Domnus,* contracted from Latin *dominus,* master, lord.]

Dan. 1. Daniel (Old Testament). **2.** Danish.

Da·na (dā′nə), **Richard Henry** (1815–82). U.S. lawyer and author. He wrote *Two Years Before the Mast* (1840), a popular description of his experience as a sailor voyaging from Boston to California. As a lawyer he specialized in maritime law and persuaded the Supreme Court to sanction the Union blockade of Southern ports (1861).

Dan·a·e, Dan·a·ë (dăn′ə-ē′). *Greek Mythology.* The mother of Perseus by Zeus, who visited her in the form of a shower of gold during her imprisonment by her father.

Dan·a·id, Dan·a·ïd (dăn′ē-ĭd) *n.* Any of the Danaides.

Da·na·i·des, Da·na·ï·des (də-nā′ə-dēz′) *pl.n. Greek Mythology.* The fifty daughters of Danaus who, with one exception, murdered their bridegrooms on their wedding night and were condemned in Hades to fill sieves with water. [Greek, from *Danaos,* DANAUS.] **—Dan·a·id·e·an** (dăn′ē-ĭd′ē-ən) *adj.*

Da Nang (də năng′). Formerly **Tou·rane** (to͞o-rän′). City and port on the South China Sea coast of Vietnam. A U.S. airforce base was sited here during the Vietnam War. The chief product is textiles.

Dan·a·us, Dan·a·üs (dăn′ē-əs). *Greek Mythology.* A king of Argos, father of the Danaides.

dance (dăns, däns) *v.* **danced, dancing, dances.** *—intr.* **1.** To move rhythmically, usually to music, using prescribed or improvised steps and gestures. **2. a.** To leap or skip about excitedly; caper; frolic. **b.** To move lightly or nimbly. **3.** To bob up and down. **4.** To be a dancer by profession. *—tr.* **1.** To engage in or perform (a dance). **2.** To cause to dance. **3.** To bring to a specified state or condition by dancing: *She danced him off his feet.* **—dance attendance.** To wait upon another attentively; lavish attentions on someone.

∼n. **1.** A series of rhythmical motions and steps, usually to music. **2.** A particular set of such prescribed movements. **3.** The art of dancing. Often preceded by *the.* **4.** A party or gathering of people for dancing. **5.** One round or turn of dancing. **6.** An act of dancing; a dance performance. **7.** A musical or rhythmical accompaniment composed or played for dancing. [Middle English *dansen, dauncen,* from Old French *danser,* from Vulgar Latin *dansāre*†.] **—danc·er** *n.* **—danc·ing·ly** *adv.*

dance·a·ble (dăns′ə-bəl, däns′-) *adj.* Suitable for dancing. Said of music.

Dance of Death *n.* In the art, music, and literature of medieval Europe, the concept of death as all-powerful, represented by a dance in which the living are led off to their graves in order of rank. Also called "danse macabre."

D and C *n.* **Dilation and curettage** *(see).*

dan·de·li·on (dăn′də-lī′ən) *n.* **1.** A plant, *Taraxacum officinale,* native to Eurasia and widely naturalized as a weed having many-rayed yellow flowers and deeply notched basal leaves that are sometimes used in salads. **2.** Any of several similar, related plants. [Middle English *dent-de-lion,* from Old French, translation of Medieval Latin *dēns leōnis,* "lion's tooth" (from its sharply indented leaves) : Latin *dēns* (stem *dent-*), tooth + *leōnis,* genitive of *leō,* LION.] **—dan·de·li·on** *adj.*

dan·der[1] (dăn′dər) *n. Informal.* Temper. **—get one's dander up.** *Informal.* To become angry or roused to vigorous action. [19th century : origin obscure.]

dander[2] *n.* Scurf from the coat of various animals, such as dogs, cats, or horses, often of an allergenic nature. [Short for DANDRUFF.]

dander[3] *n. Scottish.* A saunter; a stroll.

∼intr.v. **dandered, -dering, -ders.** *Scottish.* To go for a stroll. [19th century : origin obscure.]

Dan·die Din·mont (dăn′dē dĭn′mŏnt′) *n.* A small terrier of a breed having a rough grayish or brownish coat and short legs. [After *Dandie Dinmont,* owner of two such dogs in *Guy Mannering* (1815), a novel by Sir Walter Scott.]

dan·di·fy (dăn′də-fī′) *tr.v.* **-fied, -fying, -fies.** To dress up or make resemble a dandy or fop. **—dan·di·fi·ca·tion** *n.*

dan·di·prat (dăn′dē-prăt′) *n.* **1.** *Archaic.* A little, insignificant, or contemptible fellow. **2.** A small 16th-century English coin. [16th century : origin obscure.]

dan·dle (dănd′l) *tr.v.* **-dled, -dling, -dles.** To move (a small child) up and down, usually on the knees or in the arms. [16th century : perhaps related to Italian *dandolare,* to dandle, swing (expressive formation).] **—dan·dler** *n.*

dan·druff (dăn′drəf) *n.* A scaly, whitish scurf formed on and shed from the scalp, often caused by seborrhea. [16th century : unexplained first element + *-ruff,* perhaps from Middle English *roufe,* scab, from Old Norse *hrufa.*]

dan·dy[1] (dăn′dē) *n., pl.* **-dies.** **1.** A man who affects extreme elegance in his clothes and manners. **2.** *Informal.* Something very good or agreeable. **3.** *Nautical.* A **yawl** *(see).*

∼adj. **dandier, -diest.** **1.** Like or dressed like a dandy; foppish. **2.** *Informal.* Fine; good. [Perhaps short for *jack-a-dandy,* pert person, fop : JACK (person) + A- (of) + *dandy,* probably from *Dandy,* Scottish nickname for the name *Andrew.*] **—dan·dy·ism** *n.*

dandy[2] *n. Pathology.* **Dengue** *(see).* Also called "dandy fever." [West Indian, variant of DENGUE.]

dandy-brush (dăn′dē-brŭsh) *n.* A stiff brush used for grooming horses.

dandy roll *n.* Also **dandy roller.** *Printing.* A cylinder of wire gauze pressed on drained but moist paper pulp before it starts through the rollers. It produces watermarks in the paper. [From DANDY (fine, neat).]

Dane (dān) *n.* A native or inhabitant of Denmark or a person of Danish ancestry. [Middle English *Dan* (replacing *Dene,* from Old English *Dene,* the Danes), from Old Norse *Danr.*]

Dane·geld (dān′gĕld′) *n.* Also **Dane·gelt** (-gĕlt′). A tax levied in England from the 10th to the 12th century, initially to finance protection against Danish invasion. It was later continued as a land tax. [Middle English (modeled upon some Scandinavian compound such as Old Danish *Danegjeld*) : *Dane,* genitive plural of *Dan,* DANE + *geld,* tribute, payment, Old English *gield.*]

Dane·law, Dane·lagh (dān′lô′) *n.* **1.** The body of law established by the Danish invaders and settlers in northeastern England in the 9th and 10th centuries. **2.** The area of northern and eastern England under jurisdiction of this law, roughly encompassing present-day Yorkshire, the east Midlands, and East Anglia. [Middle English *Dene laue,* Old English *Dena lagu,* "Danes' law" : *Dena,* genitive of *Dene,* the Danes + *lagu,* law.]

dane·wort (dān′wûrt′, -wôrt′) *n.* A Eurasian shrub, *Sambucus ebulus,* similar and related to the elder.

dan·ger (dān′jər) *n.* **1.** Exposure or vulnerability to harm or evil; risk; peril. **2.** A source or instance of risk or peril. **3.** *Obsolete.* Power, especially power to harm. **—on (or off) the danger list.** In (or out of) serious danger of death. [Middle English *daunger,* power, dominion, peril, damage, from Old French *dangier, dongier,* from Vulgar Latin *dom(i)niārium* (unattested), authority, from Latin *dominium,* sovereignty, from *dominus,* lord, master.]

Synonyms: *hazard, jeopardy, peril, risk.*

danger money *n. Chiefly British.* A payment made, in addition to basic wages, for work involving risk or danger.

dan·ger·ous (dān′jər-əs) *adj.* **1.** Involving or fraught with danger; perilous. **2.** Able or apt to do harm. **—dan·ger·ous·ly** *adv.* **—dan·ger·ous·ness** *n.*

dan·gle (dăng′gəl) *v.* **-gled, -gling, -glings.** *—intr.* **1.** To hang loosely and swing or sway to and fro. **2.** To hover around someone; follow; be a hanger-on. Usually used with *after.* *—tr.* **1.** To cause to dangle. **2.** To offer (something enticing) as an inducement or temptation.

∼n. **1.** The act of dangling. **2.** Something that is dangled. [Perhaps from Danish *dangle* or Swedish *dangla,* from Germanic *dang-* (unattested).] **—dan·gler** *n.* **—dan·gly** *adj.*

dan·gle·ber·ry (dăng′gəl-bĕr′ē) *n., pl.* **-ries.** **1.** A shrub, *Gaylussacia frondosa,* of eastern North America, having small, greenish-purple flowers and bluish-black fruit. **2.** The sweet, edible fruit of this shrub. Also called "tangleberry."

dangling participle *n. Grammar.* A participle that lacks clear connection with the word it modifies. In the sentence *Working at my desk, the sudden noise startled me, Working at my desk* is a dangling participle. The connection between the participle and the word it modifies may be clarified by revision: *Working at my desk, I was startled by the sudden noise.*

Dan·iel[1] (dăn′yəl). An Old Testament prophet during the Babylonian captivity whose faith protected him from death in a lions' den.

Daniel[2] *n. Abbr.* **Dan.** The book in the Old Testament containing the story and prophecies of Daniel.

Dan·iell (dăn′yəl), **John Frederic** (1790–1845). British chemist. In 1836 he invented the Daniell cell and the dewpoint hygrometer, which measures atmospheric humidity.

Daniell cell *n.* An electric cell in which the anode is a zinc rod in sulfuric acid and the cathode is a copper rod in copper sulfate solution, the two electrodes being separated by a porous partition. It has an emf of about 1.1 volts. [After J. F. DANIELL.]

da·ni·o (dā′nē-ō′) *n., pl.* **-os.** Any of various small, often brightly colored freshwater fishes of the genera *Danio* and *Brachydanio,* native to Asia and popular as aquarium fish. [New Latin *Danio*†.]

Dan·ish (dā′nĭsh) *adj. Abbr.* **Dan., Da.** Of or pertaining to Denmark, the Danes, their language, or their culture.

∼n. **1.** *Abbr.* **Dan., Da.** The North Germanic language of the Danes. **2.** *Informal.* A Danish pastry. [Middle English *Danish,* Old English *Denisc,* from *Dene,* the Danes.]

Danish blue *n.* A pungent, soft, blue-veined white cheese.

Danish pastry *n.* A sweet, buttery pastry made with raised dough, often filled with fruit and topped with icing, nuts, or other decoration. Also *informally* "Danish."

Dan·ite (dăn′īt′) *n.* A descendant of Dan. Judges 13:2.

∼adj. Of or pertaining to the Hebrew tribe descended from Dan.

dank (dăngk) *adj.* **danker, dankest.** Unpleasantly damp; chilly and wet: *a dank cellar.* —See Synonyms at **wet.** [Middle English *dank*†.] **—dank·ly** *adv.* **—dank·ness** *n.*

Danmark. See **Denmark.**

D'An·nun·zio (dä-no͞on′tsyō), **Gabriele** (1863–1938). Italian writer and nationalist. His first novel, *The Child of Pleasure,* appeared in 1898. In the same year his play, *City of Death,* written for Sarah Bernhardt, was first performed. He became a leading nationalist. In 1919 he headed an unofficial Italian expedition to seize the Dalmatian port of Fiume (now Rijeka) and held the city for 15 months in defiance of his government. He encouraged Mussolini's movement, helping to set up a Fascist seamen's union.

Da·no-Nor·we·gian (dā′nō-nôr-wē′jən) *n.* A form of the Norwegian language, **Bokmål** *(see).*

danse ma·ca·bre (däns má-kä′br′) *n.* The **dance of death** *(see).*

dan·seur (däɴ-sœr′) *n., pl.* **-seurs** (-sœr′). A male ballet dancer. [French, from Old French, from *danser,* to DANCE.]

dan·seuse (däɴ-sœz′) *n. pl.* **-seuses** (-sœz′). A female ballet dancer. [French, see **danseur.**]

Dan·te A·li·ghie·ri (dän′tā äl′ə-gyā′rē) (1265–1321). Italian poet. Son of a noble burgher family in Florence, he remained in exile from the city after political rivals took over in 1302. He wrote *La Vita Nuova* (1292), the story of his boyhood love for a girl named

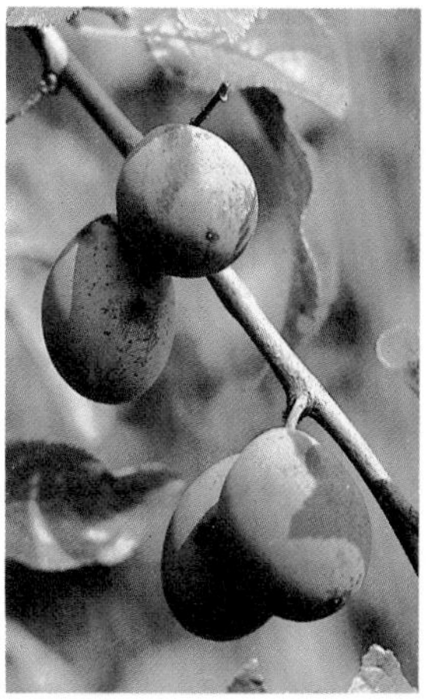

damson *A small blue plum. It gets its name from Damascus in Syria, where it was first cultivated.*

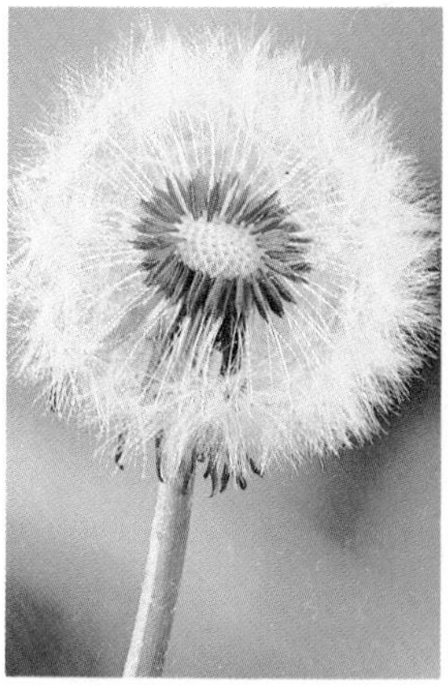

dandelion *The fluffy seed head of this plant is a favorite in the folklore of children everywhere, serving to tell the time or predict the number of one's future children by counting the seeds left after one or more puffs.*

Beatrice. *La Divina Commedia (The Divine Comedy)* he dates from a vision in 1300. It describes his progress through Hell and Purgatory (guided by Virgil) and Heaven (guided by Beatrice).

Dan·te·an (dăn'tē-ən, dăn-tē'ən) *adj.* **1.** Of or pertaining to Dante or his writings: *Dantean scholarship.* **2.** Dantesque.
~*n.* A scholar specializing in the life and writings of Dante.

Dan·tesque (dăn-tĕsk') *adj.* Resembling or having the visionary literary style of Dante.

dan·tho·ni·a (dăn-thō'nē-ə) *n.* Any grass of the genus *Danthonia,* of the Southern Hemisphere. See **wallaby grass.** [New Latin, after E. Danthoine, 19th-century French botanist.]

Dan·ton (däN-tôN'), **Georges Jacques** (1759–94). French lawyer and revolutionary leader. He took part in the storming of the Bastille in 1789, became minister of justice in 1792, and a member of the Committee for Public Safety. Danton supported the execution of Louis XVI in 1793, but the next year he joined the Jacobin moderates, opposing the Reign of Terror. Robespierre brought him before the revolutionary tribunal in 1794, and he was guillotined.

Da·nu (thä'nōō). *Irish Mythology.* The goddess of death and mother of the gods. [Irish, akin to Welsh *Don†.*]

Dan·ube (dăn'yōōb). German **Do·nau** (dō'nou). Czech **Du·naj** (dōō'nī). Serbo-Croatian **Du·nav** (dōō'näv). Romanian **Du·nă·rea** (dōō'nə-ryä). Hungarian **Du·na** (dōō'nô). The largest river in Europe, exceeding the Volga in volume though not in length. It rises in the Black Forest of southwestern West Germany and flows 2,850 kilometers (1,770 miles) through central and southeastern Europe into the Black Sea in Romania. During the Middle Ages it was the chief route from Central Europe to Constantinople (Istanbul), and it remains a major trade artery. It passes through three European capitals, Vienna, Budapest, and Belgrade, and is connected to the Rhine, Main, Oder, and Tisza rivers by canals. —**Dan·u·bi·an** (dăn-yōōb'ē-ən) *adj.*

Danzig. See **Gdańsk.**

Dao. Variant of **Tao.**

Daoism. Variant of **Taoism.**

dap (dăp) *intr.v.* **dapped, dapping, daps. 1.** To fish by letting a baited hook fall gently on the water. **2.** To dip lightly or quickly into water, as a bird does. **3.** To skip or bounce, especially over the surface of water. [Probably alteration of DAB (to strike lightly), influenced by DIP.]

daph·ne (dăf'nē) *n.* Any of several shrubs of the genus *Daphne,* native to Eurasia, cultivated for their glossy evergreen foliage and clusters of bell-shaped flowers. See also **spurge laurel.** [New Latin *Daphne,* from Latin *daphnē,* laurel, from Greek. See **Daphne.**]

Daph·ne (dăf'nē). *Greek Mythology.* A nymph who chose to be turned into a laurel in order to escape from Apollo. [Latin *Daphnē,* from Greek, from *daphnē,* laurel, probably related to Latin *laurus,* LAUREL.]

daph·ni·a (dăf'nē-ə) *n., pl.* **daphnia.** Any of various small freshwater crustaceans of the genus *Daphnia,* some species of which are commonly used as food for aquarium fish. See also **water flea.** [New Latin *Daphnia,* perhaps from Latin *Daphnē,* DAPHNE.]

Da Pon·te (də pŏn'tā), **Lorenzo** (1749–1838). Italian author. He wrote the librettos for Mozart's operas *The Marriage of Figaro* (1786), *Don Giovanni* (1787), and *Così fan Tutti* (1790).

dap·per (dăp'ər) *adj.* **1.** Neatly dressed; trim. **2.** Small, compact, and active. [Middle English *dapyr,* elegant, probably from Middle Low German or Middle Dutch *dapper,* quick, nimble.] —**dap·per·ly** *adv.* —**dap·per·ness** *n.*

dap·ple (dăp'əl) *n.* **1. a.** Mottled or spotted marking, as on a horse's coat. **b.** An individual spot. **2.** An animal, especially a horse, with a mottled or spotted coat.
~*tr.v.* **dappled, -pling, -ples.** To mark or mottle with spots: *Sunlight dappled the lawn.*
~*adj.* Also **dap·pled** (-əld). Spotted or mottled. [Probably from DAPPLE-GRAY.]

dap·ple-gray (dăp'əl-grā') *adj.* Gray with a mottled pattern of darker gray markings.
~*n.* A dapple-gray horse. [Middle English *dappel-grey,* perhaps alteration (influenced by Old Norse *depill,* a spot) of *appel-grey* (unattested), "apple-gray," probably from Old Norse *apalgrār : apall-, epli,* apple + *grār,* gray.]

Dapsang. See **Godwin-Austin, Mt.**

dap·sone (dăp'sōn', -zōn') *n.* An antimicrobial agent, $C_{12}H_{12}N_2OS$, used against leprosy. [Contraction of *diaminodiphenyl sulfone,* a drug used to treat leprosy.]

DAR, D.A.R. Daughters of the American Revolution.

darb (därb) *n. Canadian Slang.* Something considered especially excellent or outstanding. [Perhaps variant of DAB (expert).]

dar·by¹ (där'bē) *n., pl.* **-bies.** A tool for smoothing a plaster surface. [After DERBY, England.]

darby² *n. British Slang.* A handcuff. [Originally *darbies* (plural), alluding to the phrase *Father Darby's bands,* a harsh binding agreement between a moneylender and a debtor.]

Dar·by and Joan (där'bē; jōn) *n.* An elderly married couple who live a placid, harmonious life together and are seldom seen apart. [After the elderly couple in a popular 18th-century English ballad.]

Dard (därd) *n., pl.* **Dards** or collectively **Dard.** A member of any of various Indo-European peoples speaking a Dardic language.

Dar·dan (därd'n) *n.* Also **Dar·da·ni·an** (där-dā'nē-ən). A Trojan. [After DARDANUS.] —**Dar·dan** *adj.*

Dar·da·nelles (därd'n-ĕlz'). Ancient name **Hel·les·pont** (hĕl'ĭs-pŏnt'). A strait linking the Aegean Sea with the Sea of Marmara

and separating Europe from Asia Minor. It was the site of the Dardanelles campaign (1915–16) of World War I. Allied landings were made at Gallipoli and Suvla Bay to try to secure the straits and open a route to Russia, forcing Turkey from the war. The attempt failed with the loss of many lives.

Dar·da·nus (därd'n-əs). *Greek Mythology.* The son of Zeus and Electra and founder of Troy.

Dar·dic (där'dĭk) *n.* The group of Indic languages of the upper Indus Valley.

dare (dâr) *v.* **dared** or *archaic* **durst** (dûrst), **daring, dare** or **dares.** —*tr.* **1.** To have the courage or boldness required for. Often used with an infinitive, with or without *to: No one dared oppose the dictator's wishes.* **2.** To challenge (a person) to do something requiring boldness: *I dare you to climb that tree.* —*intr.* To be courageous or bold enough to do or try something. —**dare say.** Also **dare·say.** To consider very likely or almost certain. Used only in the first person.
~*n.* A challenge, especially to give proof of bravery; an act of taunting or defying. [*Dare, durst;* Middle English *dar, dorste* (also *durste*), Old English *dear, dorste* (also *durste*), first and third person present and past indicative of *durran,* to venture, dare.] —**dar·er** *n.*

Dare (dâr), **Virginia** (1587–*c.* 87). First child born to English parents in America. She disappeared with the other members of the second colony on Roanoke Island, called the "Lost Colony."

dare·dev·il (dâr'dĕv'əl) *n.* One who is recklessly bold.
~*adj.* Recklessly bold. —**dare·dev·il·ry, dare·dev·il·try** *n.*

Dar-el-Beida. See **Casablanca.**

Dar es Sa·laam (där' ĕs sə-läm'). City of Tanzania, an Indian Ocean port. It was founded by the sultan of Zanzibar (1862), and its name means "haven of peace." The German East Africa Company made it capital of German East Africa (1891–1916). It was later capital of Tanganyika, then of Tanzania.

darg (därg) *n. Chiefly British Regional.* **1.** A full day's work. **2.** An amount of work to be completed. [Middle English, syncopated form of *daywerk,* day-work.]

dar·ic (dăr'ĭk) *n.* A gold coin of ancient Persia. [Greek *Dār(e)ikos,* probably after *Dāreios,* DARIUS I.]

Da·ri·én (där'ē-ĕn'). Spanish colony founded by Vasco Núñez de Balboa (1510) in what is now Panama, on the west coast of the Gulf of Darién.

Darién, Gulf of. A wide bay of the Caribbean Sea between eastern Panama and northwestern Colombia.

Darién, Isthmus of. See **Panama, Isthmus of.**

dar·ing (dâr'ĭng) *adj.* Willing to take risks; fearless; bold; adventurous. —See Synonyms at **brave, reckless.**
~*n.* Active bravery; boldness; intrepidity. —**dar·ing·ly** *adv.* —**dar·ing·ness** *n.*

dar·i·ole (dăr'ē-ōl') *n.* **1.** A small cream tart made with puff pastry in a circular mold. **2.** The mold itself. [French, from Old French, perhaps a diminutive formation from *dorer,* to gild, from Latin *dēaurāre : dē-* (intensive) + *aurāre,* to gild, from *aurum,* gold.]

Da·ri·us I (də-rī'əs), called "the Great" (*c.* 558–486 B.C.). King of Persia (521–486). He seized the throne after murdering a usurper, then divided the Persian Empire into provinces known as satrapies. Following unrest among subject Greek states, he invaded mainland Greece. A long war ended in defeat of the Persians at Marathon (490).

Dar·jee·ling¹ (där-jē'lĭng). Town in West Bengal, India, in the lower Himalayas. It is a tourist center 2,290 meters (7,500 feet) above sea level, with fine views of mounts Everest and Kangchenjunga. The surrounding district is famous for its tea.

Darjeeling² *n.* A fine variety of black tea from Darjeeling in India. Also called "Darjeeling tea."

dark (därk) *adj.* **darker, darkest.** *Abbr.* **dk. 1.** With very little or no light. **2.** Reflecting only a small fraction of the incident light. **3.** Lacking light or brightness; shaded; obscure: *a dark day.* **4.** Of a shade tending toward black or brown by comparison with *light, pale,* or *white: dark hair; dark green.* **5.** Characterized by or producing gloom; dreary; dismal. **6.** Sullen; threatening: *a dark scowl.* **7.** Hard to understand; obscure. **8.** Concealed; secret; mysterious. **9.** Unenlightened; uncivilized: *a dark era in history.* **10.** Evil or wicked; sinister: *a dark purpose.*
~*n.* **1.** Absence of light. **2.** A place having little light. **3.** Night; nightfall. **4.** A dark hue or color. —**in the dark. 1.** In secret: *things done in the dark.* **2.** In a state of ignorance; uninformed. —**whistle in the dark.** To put on a brave show to hide one's fears. [Middle English *derk,* Old English *deorc;* probably from Germanic.] —**dark·ish** *adj.*

Usage: dark, dim, murky, dusky, obscure, opaque, shady, shadowy. These adjectives indicate the absence of light or clarity. *Dark,* the most widely applicable, can refer to insufficiency of illumination for seeing, to deepness of shade of a color, as *dark brown,* or figuratively to absence of cheer or rectitude: *dark day; dark mood; dark comedy; dark deeds. Dim* suggests lack of clarity of outline of physical things or mental ones, such as memories or recollections, and can also apply to the source of light to indicate insufficiency. *Murky* usually implies darkness such as that produced by smoke or fog; less often it refers to extreme darkness or, figuratively, to unclear, sullen thoughts. *Dusky* applies principally to the dimness characteristic of twilight or to deepness of shade of a color. *Obscure* usually means unclear to the mind or senses but can refer to physical darkness. *Opaque* means incapable of being penetrated by light; figuratively it applies to what is incapable of perceiving reason and to what is unintelligible. *Shady* refers to what is sheltered from light, especially sunlight, or, figuratively, to what is covertly dishonest. *Shadowy* also implies obstructed light but suggests shifting illumination and indistinct vision.

dark adaptation *n.* The physical and chemical adjustments of the eye, including dilation of the pupil, that make vision possible in relative darkness. **—dark·a·dapt·ed** (därk′ə-dăp′tĭd) *adj.*

Dark Ages *n.* **1.** The early part of the Middle Ages from the fall of the Roman Empire in A.D. 476 until the coronation of Charlemagne in A.D. 800. **2.** The entire period from the end of classical civilization to the revival of learning in the West in about A.D. 1000, formerly regarded as a period lacking in cultural development.

Dark Continent *n.* Africa. [So called because its hinterland was largely unknown until the late 19th century.]

dark·en (där′kən) *v.* **-ened, -ening, -ens.** *—tr.* **1.** To shut out the light of; make dark or darker. **2.** To impart a darker hue to; render less white or clear. **3.** To fill with sadness; make gloomy. **4.** To obscure or cloud the meaning of; render vague. **5.** To strike with blindness. *—intr.* **1.** To become dark or darker. **2.** To become dark in color. **3.** To become obscure, vague, or uncertain. **4.** To grow clouded, gloomy, or sullen. **5.** To become blind. **—dark·en·er** *n.*

dark-field microscope (därk′fēld′) *n.* An **ultramicroscope** *(see).*

dark glasses *pl.n.* Glasses with tinted lenses worn to protect the eyes from glare.

dark horse *n.* **1.** A little-known entrant in a horse race, contest, or the like. **2.** One who receives unexpected support as a candidate for the nomination in a political convention. **3.** *Chiefly British.* A secretive person, especially one whose capabilities or talents are not yet revealed.

dark lantern *n.* A lantern whose light can be blocked by a sliding panel or other device.

dar·kle (där′kəl) *intr.v.* **-kled, -kling, -kles.** *Poetic.* **1.** To appear dark or indistinct. **2.** To grow dark. [Back-formation from DARKLING.]

dark·ling (därk′lĭng) *adv. Poetic.* In the dark.
~adj. Poetic. **1.** Being or happening in the dark or the night. **2.** Dim; obscure. [Middle English *derkeling* : DARK + -LING (condition).]

darkling beetle *n.* Any of various nocturnal, black or dark-brown beetles of the widely distributed family Tenebrionidae.

dark·ly (därk′lē) *adv.* **1.** So as to appear dark; in a dark manner. **2. a.** Mysteriously. **b.** In a sinister manner. **3.** Dimly; obscurely; faintly: *"For now we see through a glass, darkly."* (I Corinthians 13:12).

dark·ness (därk′nĭs) *n.* **1.** Total or almost total absence of light. **2.** The quality of being dark in color. **3.** Blindness. **4.** Lack of enlightenment; ignorance. **5.** Evil; wickedness. **6.** Secrecy; concealment. **7.** Lack of clearness; obscurity.

dark·room (därk′ro͞om′, -ro͝om′) *n.* A room in which photographic materials are processed, either in complete darkness or illuminated by sources of light to which the materials are not sensitive.

dark·some (därk′səm) *adj. Poetic.* Dark; darkish; somber.

dark star *n.* A star that is normally obscured or too faint for direct visual observation; especially, the component of an eclipsing binary detectable by spectral analysis or in the eclipse of the bright component.

dar·ling (där′lĭng) *n.* **1.** One who is very dear; a much-loved person. Often used as a term of address. **2.** One that is greatly liked or preferred; a favorite. **3.** A charming or attractive person or thing.
~adj. **1.** Regarded with great affection and tenderness; very dear; beloved. **2.** Regarded with special favor; favorite: *"Metaphysics and poetry . . . are my darling studies."* (S. T. Coleridge). **3.** *Informal.* Charming; amusing; pleasing: *a darling hat.* [Middle English *dereling,* Old English *dēorling* : DEAR + -LING (diminutive).]

Darling. River in New South Wales, in southeast Australia. It flows 2,739 kilometers (1,702 miles) from the Great Dividing Range to join the Murray River.

Darm·stadt (därm′stăt′). City in Hesse in central West Germany. In the 16th to 19th centuries it was the seat of the Hesse-Darmstadt royal house.

darn[1] (därn) *v.* **darned, darning, darns.** *—tr.* To mend by weaving thread or wool across a gap or hole. *—intr.* To mend or repair a hole or garment by darning.
~n. **1.** A hole repaired by darning. **2.** The act of darning. [Perhaps from obsolete *dern,* to hide, Old English *derne, dierne,* concealed, from Germanic.] **—darn·er** *n.*

darn[2] *interj.* Damn. Used euphemistically. **—darn** *adj. & adv.*

darned (därnd) *adj. Informal.* Damned. Used euphemistically and as an intensive: *a darned good player.* **—darned** *adv.*

dar·nel (där′nəl) *n.* Any of several grasses of the genus *Lolium,* native to Europe and Asia; especially, *L. temulentum* or *L. perenne.* [Middle English, akin to French dialect *darnelle*†, cockle.]

darning egg *n.* An egg-shaped object used to hold the shape of material being darned.

darning needle *n.* **1.** A long, large-eyed needle used in darning. **2.** *Informal.* A **dragonfly** *(see).*

Darn·ley (därn′lē), **Henry Stuart, Lord** (1545–67). Scottish earl, who was, by lineage, a possible successor to Elizabeth I of England. He married Mary, Queen of Scots, in 1565, chiefly to cement their joint claims to the throne. He became jealous of his wife's Italian secretary, Rizzio, and connived at his murder in 1566. Darnley himself was found murdered the following year, probably by Mary's lover, the Earl of Bothwell. His son by Mary became James VI of Scotland and the first Stuart king of England.

da·ro·gha (də-rō′gə) *n.* In India, an overseer, manager, or governor. [Urdu.]

Dar·row (dăr′ō), **Clarence Seward** (1857–1938). U.S. lawyer. A renowned defense lawyer, he used meticulous pretrial investigations and remarkable summations to juries to successfully defend Eugene V. Debs (1895), William D. Haywood (1906), and Leopold and Leob (1924), among many others. He opposed William Jennings Bryan in the landmark case of John T. Scopes, called the "Monkey Trial" (1925).

dar·shan (där′shən) *n. Hinduism.* A spiritual feeling experienced in the presence of a holy or revered person. [Hindi, from Sanskrit *darśana,* view.]

dart[1] (därt) *n.* **1.** A slender, pointed missile, often having tail fins, to be thrown by hand or shot, as from a blowgun. **2.** Anything like a dart in shape, use, or effect. **3.** *Zoology.* Any of various slender, pointed structures, such as an insect's sting. **4.** A rapid, sudden movement. **5.** In sewing, a tapered tuck to adjust the fit of a garment.
~v. **darted, darting, darts.** *—intr.* To move suddenly and swiftly. *—tr.* To throw or thrust suddenly or swiftly; shoot. [Middle English, from Old French, from Germanic *darōdhaz* (unattested), spear.]

dart[2] *n. Australian Informal.* A plan or scheme.

dart·board (därt′bôrd, -bōrd) *n.* A circular board divided into numbered segments with a small circle (bull's-eye) at the center, used as the target in the game of darts.

dar·ter (där′tər) *n.* **1.** One that moves suddenly and swiftly. **2.** Any of several long-necked, long-billed birds of the genus *Anhinga,* such as the **water turkey** *(see),* occurring in tropical and subtropical inland waters. **3.** Any of various small, often brightly colored freshwater fishes of the family Percidae, of eastern North America.

dar·tle (därt′l) *tr.v.* **-tled, -tling, -tles.** To thrust or shoot out repeatedly. [Frequentative of *dart,* to pierce with a dart, from Middle English *darten,* from DART.]

Dart·moor (därt′mo͝or′). An expanse of high moorland in southwest Devon, England. Its many tors include High Willhays (621 meters; 2,038 feet), and there are ancient megalithic sites. The prison at Princetown was built (1806–09) for French prisoners of war and later housed American prisoners from the War of 1812. Since 1850 it has held long-term civilian prisoners.

Dartmoor pony *n.* A pony of a breed originating in the Dartmoor region of England.

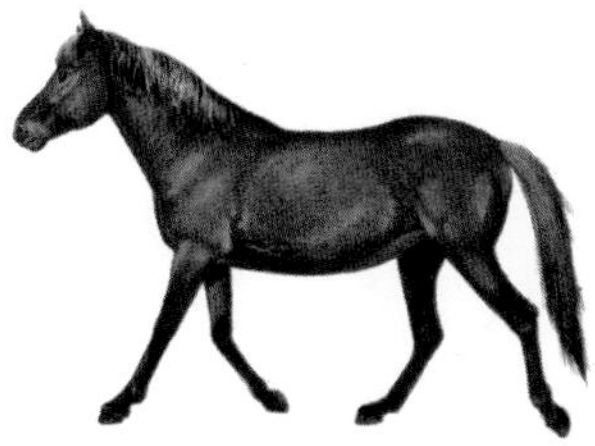

Dartmoor pony *The Dartmoor pony originated in southwest England and was once popular as a packhorse. It is muscular and hardy, standing 12 to 13 hands high at the shoulder (a hand equals 10 centimeters, or 4 inches).*

Dart·mouth (därt′məth). Seaport on the Dart estuary in Devon, southwest England. Richard I's crusaders embarked from here in 1190. In 1905 the Royal Naval College was opened.

darts (därts) *n. Used with a singular verb.* An indoor game in which darts are thrown at a target (a dartboard).

Dar·win (dâr′wĭn). Capital and seaport of Northern Territory, Australia. Founded as Palmerston (1869), it was renamed Port Darwin (1911). The modern city is an important stopover point on international air routes.

Darwin, Charles Robert (1809–82). British naturalist who revolutionized biological theory by putting forward his theory of evolution based on natural selection. His views, formed after his comprehensive observations of fossils and the diverse plant and animal life during his voyage (1831–36) around South America and the Pacific as naturalist on H.M.S. *Beagle,* were published in *On the Origin of Species.* His conclusions conflicted with traditional Christian opinion on the creation of the world and caused much controversy, especially where, as in his *The Descent of Man* (1871), evolutionary theories were applied to human origins.

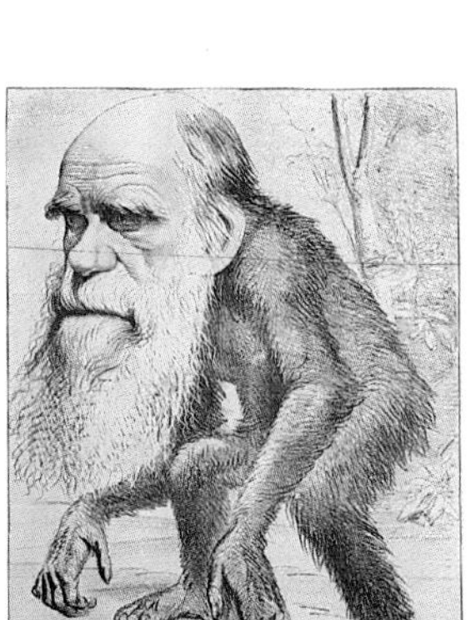

Darwin *A caricature of Charles Darwin from* The Hornet *magazine (1871). Some of Darwin's critics ridiculed the theory of evolution and its claim that man was descended from the apes, preferring to believe instead that all men were descended from Adam and Eve.*

Dar·win·ism (där′wə-nĭz′əm) *n.* A theory of biological evolution developed by Charles Darwin and others. It states that species of plants and animals develop through **natural selection** *(see)* of variations that increase the organism's ability to survive and reproduce. **—Dar·win·ist** *n.* **—Dar·win·is·tic** *adj.*

Darwin's finches *pl.n.* The finches of the subfamily Geospizinae, found only on the Galápagos Islands. Variations in their bill structure and feeding habits provided Charles Darwin with evidence to support his theory of evolution.

dash[1] (dăsh) *v.* **dashed, dashing, dashes.** *—tr.* **1.** To break or smash by striking violently. **2.** To hurl, knock, or thrust with sudden violence: *He was dashed to the ground.* **3.** To splash; bespatter. **4.** To write or execute hastily. Used with *off* or *down.* **5.** To destroy; frustrate: *His dreams were dashed.* **6.** To confound; abash: *She was dashed by the criticism.* **7.** To add an enlivening or altering element to; mix; adulterate: *"Some truth there was, but dash'd and brew'd with lies"* (John Dryden). *—intr.* **1.** To strike violently or with great force; smash. **2.** To move with haste; rush; race.
~n. **1.** A swift, violent blow or stroke. **2.** A splash. **3.** A small amount of an added ingredient: *a dash of salt.* **4.** A quick stroke, as with a pencil or brush. **5.** A sudden movement; a rush. **6.** A foot race run at top speed from the outset, usually less than a quarter-mile long. **7.** Spirited action or style; vigor; verve. **8.** A punctuation mark (—) used in writing and printing. —See Usage note below. **9.** In Morse code and similar codes, the long sound or signal used in combination with the dot, a shorter sound, and silent intervals to represent letters or numbers. [Middle English *daschen, dashen,* perhaps from Scandinavian, akin to Danish *daske,* to beat.]

Usage: The dash as a mark of punctuation has the following uses: 1. To set off a parenthetical clause: *Her face—or so it seemed to me—was never more radiant.* 2. To indicate a break in thought: *Then he ran—the fool.* 3. To mark an omission: *She doesn't give a*

d——. **4.** To mark a summing up: *Study and practice—this is the only solution.* **5.** To do the work of a colon: *Ten were chosen—five girls and five boys.* In modern writing, the dash is not used in combination with the colon or comma, though it may be followed immediately by a period at the end of a sentence. Indiscriminate use of the dash often leads to choppiness and confusion of expression.

dash² *Interj.* Damn. Used euphemistically.

dash³ *n. West African.* A tip or gratuity.
   ~*tr.v.* **dashed, dashing, dashes.** *West African.* To give a tip or gratuity to. [Probably from Fanti.]

dash·board (dăsh′bôrd′, -bōrd′) *n.* A panel under the windshield of a car, aircraft, or the like, containing indicator displays, compartments, and control instruments.

da·sheen (dă-shēn′) *n.* A plant, **taro** *(see).* [Perhaps alteration of French *de Chine,* of China.]

dash·er (dăsh′ər) *n.* **1.** One that dashes. **2.** The plunger of a churn or ice-cream freezer. **3.** *Informal.* A spirited person.

da·shi·ki (dä-shē′kē, də-) *n.* A loose, often brightly colored African tunic, usually worn by men. [Yoruba *danshiki.*]

dash·ing (dăsh′ĭng) *adj.* **1.** Audacious and gallant; bold; spirited. **2.** Marked by showy elegance; splendid: *a dashing new coat.* —**dash·ing·ly** *adv.*

dash·pot (dăsh′pŏt′) *n.* A mechanical device for damping vibration in a machine, consisting of a piston moving in a cylinder of liquid.

dash·y (dăsh′ē) *adj.* **-ier, -iest.** Stylishly showy; dashing.

das·sie (dăs′ē) *n.* A mammal, the **hyrax** *(see).* [Afrikaans, diminutive of *das,* badger, hyrax, from Middle Dutch.]

das·tard (dăs′tərd) *n.* A base, sneaking coward. [Middle English, perhaps from obsolete *dasart,* dull person, influenced by *dotard.*]

das·tard·ly (dăs′tərd-lē) *adj.* Cowardly and mean-spirited; base. —**das·tard·li·ness** *n.*

   Usage: *Dastardly* is employed most precisely when it refers to acts involving cowardice. It is loosely used when it applies to any reprehensible or risky act.

das·y·ure (dăs′ē-yŏŏr′) *n.* Any of various marsupial mammals of the family Dasyuridae, of Australia and adjacent regions, ranging in size and appearance from that of a mouse to that of a dog. See **Tasmanian devil.** [New Latin *Dasyurus* (genus), "hairy-tailed" : Greek *dasus,* hairy, shaggy + -UROUS.]

dat. dative.

da·ta (dā′tə, dăt′ə, dä′tə) *pl.n. Singular* **da·tum** (dā′təm, dăt′əm, dä′təm). **1.** Information; especially, information organized for analysis or used as the basis for a decision. **2.** Numerical information in a form suitable for processing by computer. [Latin, plural of DATUM.]

   Usage: Originally, data was used solely as the plural of *datum,* but it has increasingly come to be used as a singular, in such constructions as *the data is, this data, much data, two items of data.*

da·ta·bank, data bank (dā′tə-băngk′, dăt′ə-) *n.* **1.** A database. **2.** An organization chiefly concerned with building, maintaining, and utilizing a databank.

da·ta·base, data base (dā′tə-bās′, dăt′ə-, dä′tə-) *n.* A store of information; especially, a large store from which information can be selected by computer. Also called "databank."

data capture *n.* The process of converting data into a form in which it can be stored in or processed by a computer, as by keyboarding or optical character recognition (OCR).

data carrier *n.* The medium, as magnetic tape, selected to transport or communicate data.

data processing *n.* **1.** The preparation of information for processing by computers. **2.** The storing or processing of raw data by a computer. —**data processor** *n.*

da·ta·ry (dā′tə-rē) *n., pl.* **-ries.** *Roman Catholic Church.* **1.** The duty, formerly an official office of the curia, of investigating the fitness of candidates for papal benefices. **2.** A cardinal assuming the duty of datary. [Medieval Latin *datārius,* official who dated all papal letters, from Late Latin *data,* DATE (time).]

data set *n.* **1.** An electronic device that provides an interface in the transmission of data to a remote station. **2.** A collection of related computer records. **3.** A modem.

date¹ (dāt) *n. Abbr.* **d. 1.** A particular point or period of time at which something happened or existed or is to happen. **2.** The time during which something lasts; duration. **3.** The time or historical period to which something belongs: *artifacts of a later date.* **4. dates.** The years of a person's birth and death. **5.** The day of the month. **6.** An inscription or statement, as on a coin or letter, indicating when it was made or written. **7.** *Informal.* **a.** An appointment to meet socially at a particular time; especially, one with a member of the opposite sex. **b.** A person so met. —**to date.** Up to the present time; as yet.
   ~*v.* **dated, dating, dates.** —*tr.* **1.** To mark or supply (a letter, for example) with a date. **2.** To assign a date to; determine the date, occurrence, or origin of. **3.** To betray the age of. **4.** *Informal.* **a.** To go out on a date with. **b.** To go on dates regularly with. —*intr.* **1.** To have origin in a particular time or the past. Usually used with *back to* or *from: dates from 500 B.C.* **2.** To become old-fashioned. **3.** *Informal.* To have social engagements with persons of the opposite sex. [Middle English, from Old French, from Medieval Latin *data,* "given," "issued" (used for Latin *datum* in the letter-dating formula, e.g. *datum Romae,* issued at Rome) from Latin *datus,* past participle of *dare,* to give.] —**dat·able, date·able** *adj.* —**dat·er** *n.*

date² *n.* **1.** The sweet, oblong, edible fruit of the **date palm** *(see)* containing a narrow, hard seed. **2.** The date palm. [Middle English, from Old French, from Old Provençal *datil,* from Latin *dactylus,*

from Greek *daktulos,* "finger" (from the shape of the fruit). See **dactyl.**]

dat·ed (dā′tĭd) *adj.* **1.** Marked with or displaying a date. **2.** Old-fashioned; antiquated; outmoded. —**dat·ed·ness** *n.*

date·less (dāt′lĭs) *adj.* **1.** Having no date. **2.** Without limits; endless. **3.** Too old to be dated. **4.** Timeless or eternal.

date line *n. Sometimes* **Date Line.** An imaginary line through the Pacific Ocean roughly corresponding to 180 degrees longitude, to the east of which, by international agreement, the calendar date is one day earlier than to the west. Called in full "International Date Line."

date·line (dāt′līn′) *n.* A phrase at the beginning of a newspaper or magazine article that gives the date and place of its origin.

date palm *n.* A palm tree, *Phoenix dactylifera,* of tropical and subtropical areas, having featherlike leaves and bearing clusters of dates.

date stamp *n.* A device with adjustable numerals and letters for marking a date on documents, goods, and other objects.

date-stamp (dāt′stămp′) *tr.v.* **-stamped, -stamping, -stamps.** To mark a date on with a date stamp.

dating bar *n.* A **singles bar** *(see).*

da·tive (dā′tĭv) *n. Abbr.* **dat. 1.** The grammatical case in certain Indo-European languages, such as Greek, Latin, or Russian, that denotes the indirect object of a verb and the object of any of certain verbs and prepositions. **2.** A form or construction in this case.
   ~*adj.* Also **da·ti·val** (dā-tī′vəl). *Abbr.* **dat.** Designating, pertaining to, or inflected in the dative. [Middle English *datif,* from Latin *(cāsus) datīvus,* "(case) of giving" (translation of Greek *ptōsis dotikē*), from *dare,* to give.] —**da·tive·ly** *adv.*

dative bond *n. Chemistry.* A **coordinate bond** *(see).*

da·to, dat·to (dä′tō) *n., pl.* **-tos. 1.** The chief of a Muslim Moro tribe in the Philippines. **2.** The head man of a barrio or Malay tribe. [Spanish *dato,* from Tagalog *datò,* from Malay *dato',* "grandfather."]

da·tum (dā′təm, dăt′əm, dä′təm) *n., pl.* **-ta** (-tə) or **-tums** (for sense 3). **1.** An assumed, given, measured, or otherwise determined single fact or proposition used to draw a conclusion or make a decision; a single piece of information. —See Usage note at **data.** **2.** The real or assumed point from which any reckoning or scale begins. **3.** A point, line, or level used as a reference, as in surveying or geology. [Latin, "something given," from the neuter past participle of *dare,* to give.]

da·tu·ra (də-tŏŏr′ə, -tyŏŏr′ə) *n.* Any of several plants of the genus *Datura,* including the **thorn apple** *(see),* having large trumpet-shaped flowers. [New Latin *Datura,* from Hindi *dhatūrā,* from Sanskrit *dhattūrā†.*]

daub (dôb) *v.* **daubed, daubing, daubs.** —*tr.* **1.** To cover, coat, or smear with an adhesive substance, such as plaster, mud, or grease. **2.** To apply paint to with hasty or crude strokes. —*intr.* To apply paint or coloring with crude, unskillful strokes.
   ~*n.* **1.** The act or a stroke of daubing. **2.** Any soft adhesive coating material that is daubed on, such as plaster or mud. See **wattle and daub. 3.** A crude or amateurishly inferior painting. [Middle English *dauben,* from Old French *dauber,* from Latin *dēalbāre,* to whitewash : *dē-,* completely + *albāre,* to whiten, from *albus,* white.] —**daub·er** *n.* —**daub·er·y** *n.* —**daub·ing·ly** *adv.* —**daub·y** *adj.*

daube (dōb) *n.* **1.** A method of cooking in which meat, usually beef, is braised in red wine. **2.** A stew so prepared. [French, from Spanish *doba* (unattested), from *dobar†,* to stew.]

Dau·bi·gny (dō-bē-nyē′), **Charles François** (1817–78). French landscape painter whose delight in the fleeting effects of light in the 1850's strongly influenced the young impressionists.

Dau·det (dō-dā′), **Alphonse** (1840–97). French novelist. He wrote *Lettres de mon moulin,* a collection of scenes from Provençal life in 1868. His novels include *Le Petit Chose* (1868) and *Tartarin de Tarascon* (1872).

daugh·ter (dô′tər) *n. Abbr.* **d. 1.** A female child considered in relation to her parents. **2.** A female descendant. **3.** A girl or woman attached to a country, organization, or the like as a child is to a parent: *a daughter of the nation.* **4.** Anything personified or regarded as a female descendant: *regarded Japan as a daughter of Chinese civilization.* Also used adjectivally: *a daughter cell.* **5.** A term of address used to a girl or woman by an older man other than her father, especially a priest. **6.** *Physics & Chemistry.* A particle, nucleus, ion, or the like produced by the decay or breakdown of another entity (the parent). Also used adjectivally: *a daughter nucleus.* [Middle English *doughter,* Old English *dohtor.*] —**daugh·ter·ly** *adj.*

daugh·ter-in-law (dô′tər-ĭn-lô′) *n., pl.* **daughters-in-law.** The wife of one's son.

Daughters of the American Revolution *n. Abbr.* **DAR, D.A.R.** A society of women descended from American patriots of the Revolutionary War, organized in 1890.

Dau·mier (dō-myā′), **Honoré** (1808–79). French caricaturist and painter whose satirical lithographs in *La Caricature* and *Le Charivari* exposed the foibles of contemporary French government and society.

daunt (dônt, dänt) *tr.v.* **daunted, daunting, daunts. 1.** To intimidate. **2.** To discourage; dishearten. [Middle English *daunten,* from Old French *danter, donter,* from Latin *domitāre,* frequentative of *domāre,* to tame, subdue.] —**daunt·er** *n.* —**daunt·ing·ly** *adv.*

daunt·less (dônt′lĭs, dänt′-) *adj.* Incapable of being intimidated or discouraged; fearless; bold. —See Synonyms at **brave.** —**daunt·less·ly** *adv.* —**daunt·less·ness** *n.*

dau·phin (dô′fĭn; *French* dō-fäɴ′) *n.* The eldest son of the king of France. Used as a title from 1349 to 1830. [French, from Old French *dalphin, dalfin,* DOLPHIN. This title (originally borne by the lords of Viennois, whose coat of arms bore three dolphins) was adopted by the French crown princes as a condition when the Viennois province of Dauphiné was ceded to the crown.]

dau·phine (dô-fēn′; *French* dō-fēn′) *n.* Also **dau·phin·ess** (dô′fĭ-nĭs). The wife of the dauphin.

Dau·phi·né (dō-fē-nā′). Region in southeast France, comprising the present departments of Drôme, Hautes-Alpes, and Isère. Before 1343 it was ruled by a count known as a dauphin. It was then sold to Charles of Valois, the future Charles V of France. The king gave the province to his eldest son, and thereafter all eldest sons of the French kings inherited it with the title of dauphin.

DAV, D.A.V. Disabled American Veterans.

Da·vao (dä′vou). City of southeastern Mindanao, Phillippines, at the mouth of the Davao River on Davao Gulf. It is the chief commercial center and major port of the island of Mindanao.

dav·en·port (dăv′ən-pôrt′, -pōrt′) *n.* **1.** A large sofa, often convertible into a bed. **2.** *British.* A small writing desk with drawers and a hinged shelf to write on. [Perhaps from *Davenport,* name of the original manufacturer of the desk.]

Dav·en·port (dăv′ən-pôrt′, -pōrt′). City of east-central Iowa, on the Mississippi River. It is an important rail, commercial, and industrial center. Built on the site of an early trading post, the city prospered after the arrival (1856) of the first railroad to bridge the Mississippi.

Da·vid (dā′vĭd) (died 962 B.C.). King of Judah and Israel, who founded the Jewish royal dynasty at Jerusalem. He was born in Bethlehem and was acclaimed for his legendary boyhood feat of killing the Philistine giant, Goliath. Later outlawed by Saul, he seized the southern kingdom (Judah) on the king's death and gradually subdued the north (Israel), uniting the Israelites. He was succeeded by his son Solomon.

Da·vid (də-vēd), **Jacques Louis** (1748–1825). French painter and leading figure in the neoclassical movement. David welcomed the French Revolution in 1789 and painted pictures including *The Oath of the Horatii* (1785) and *Death of Marat* (1793) to promote republican feeling. He was elected to the national convention in 1792. He survived the downfall of his friend Robespierre to become court painter to Napoleon in 1804. His style became more richly decorative in such paintings as *Napoleon Crowning Josephine* (1805–07). With the fall of Napoleon, David was exiled and died in Brussels.

Da·vid (dā′vĭd), **Saint** (*c.* 520–600). Patron saint of Wales. The primate of the Celtic church in south Wales, set up his seat of government at Mynyw (now St. David's). His feast day is March 1.

David, Star of. A symbol of Judaism, the **Star of David** *(see).*

Da·vid·son (dā′vĭd-sən), **Jo,** born Joseph (1883–1952). U.S. sculptor. He is noted particularly for his portrait busts of contemporary Americans and French leaders, including Woodrow Wilson, Robert M. La Follette, Will Rogers, Marshal Foch, and Clemenceau.

da Vinci, Leonardo. See **Leonardo da Vinci.**

Da·vis (dā′vĭs), **Bette,** born Ruth Elizabeth Davis (1908–). U.S. film actress. She made her screen debut in *The Man Who Played God* (1932) and twice won Academy Awards for her roles in *Dangerous* (1935) and *Jezebel* (1938). She was acclaimed for her role as an old and embittered former child star in *Whatever Happened to Baby Jane?* (1962).

Davis, Sir Colin (1927–). British conductor. He is noted for his interpretations of Mozart and his promotion of the music of Berlioz. He was knighted in 1980.

Davis, Jefferson (1808–89). President of the Confederate States during the Civil War (1861–65). A graduate of West Point Military Academy, he served seven years (1828–35) as a soldier before taking up cotton farming in Mississippi. He was a U.S. senator (1847–51). Back in the senate in 1857, he led the Southern Democrats in upholding slavery and states' rights against federal interference. After the election of Abraham Lincoln (1860), he withdrew his state from the Union (1861). As president of the Confederacy, Davis ordered the offensive that resulted in disaster at Gettysburg (1863). He was captured at Irwinville, Georgia (May 10, 1865) and was imprisoned for two years on a charge of treason.

Davis, Miles (1926–). U.S. jazz trumpeter and composer. Since playing with Charlie Parker in the 1940's he has been one of the most influential musicians in jazz. Important recordings include *Birth of the Cool* (1949–50) and *Bitches Brew* (1970).

Davis, Richard Harding (1864–1916). U.S. journalist, editor, and novelist. As a war correspondent, he covered the Spanish-American War, the Boer War, and the Russo-Japanese War, among others, and became known as the leading reporter of his time. He also wrote vivid short stories, novels, and plays.

Davis, Sammy, Jr. (1925–). U.S. entertainer. An exuberant, talented performer, he has been successful in the recording studio, Broadway productions such as *Mr. Wonderful* (1956), movies, including *Porgy and Bess* (1959), and television specials.

Davis Cup *n.* **1.** A trophy awarded to the nation whose team is the winner of the annual International Lawn Tennis Championship for men. **2.** The competition held for this cup. [After Dwight F. *Davis* (1879–1945), American civic leader and government official who donated the trophy in 1900.]

dav·it (dăv′ĭt, dā′-) *n.* Any of various small cranes, usually one of a pair and made of shaped steel tubing, used on ships to hoist lifeboats, anchors, and cargo. [Middle English *daviot,* from Old French *daviot, daviet,* diminutive of the name *David,* also the name given to a carpenter's tool.]

Da·vos (dä-vôs′). An Alpine town in the Graubünden canton in east Switzerland. It is a tourist center, especially for winter sports.

Da·vy (dā′vē), **Sir Humphry** (1778–1829). British chemist and inventor of the Davy miner's safety lamp. He joined the Royal Institution in London and became a pioneer of electrochemistry. Davy was appointed president of the Royal Society (1820) and gave much encouragement to Michael Faraday.

Davy Jones *n.* The spirit of the sea. [Perhaps *Davy,* nickname for David + *Jones,* alteration of *Jonas, Jonah* (the prophet, with allusion to the whale in Jonah 1:17).]

Davy Jones's locker *n.* The bottom of the sea, especially as the grave of all who perish at sea.

Davy lamp *n.* An early safety oil lamp having a gauze surrounding the flame to prevent ignition of gas, used by coal miners. Also called "davy." [Invented by Sir Humphry DAVY.]

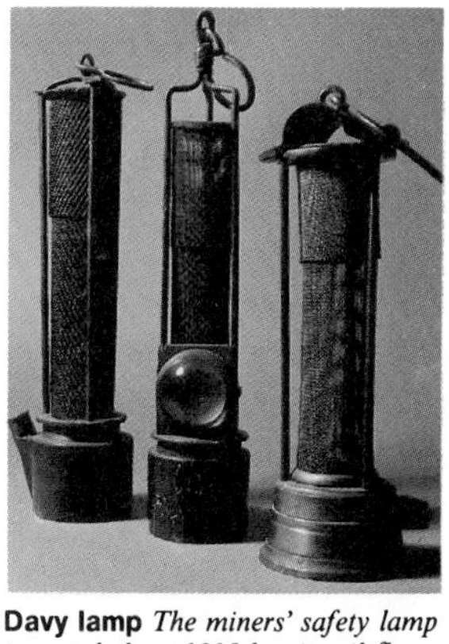

Davy lamp *The miners' safety lamp invented about 1815 has its oil flame surrounded by metal gauze. The metal allows light and air to pass through but conducts heat away so that it does not cause an explosion. The flame changes color in the presence of explosive gas.*

daw (dô) *n.* A bird, the **jackdaw** *(see).* [Middle English *dawe,* probably from Old English *dāwe* (unattested), from West Germanic *dǣgw-* (unattested).]

daw·dle (dôd′l) *v.* **-dled, -dling, -dles.** —*intr.* **1.** To move slowly; loiter; lag behind. **2.** To waste time by trifling; linger. —*tr.* To waste (time) in this manner. Usually used with *away: dawdling away the hours.* [17th century : probably of dialectal origin.] **—daw·dler** *n.* **—daw·dling·ly** *adv.*

Dawes (dôz), **Charles Gates** (1865–1951). U.S. financier and statesman. His report, known as the Dawes Plan (1924), provided a system for Germany to pay reparations for World War I damage. The plan helped the reconstruction of the German economy, and Dawes received the Nobel Peace Prize (1925). He became Republican vice president under Calvin Coolidge (1925–29).

dawn (dôn) *n.* **1.** The time each morning when daylight first appears. **2.** A first appearance; a beginning: *the dawn of history.* ~*intr.v.* **dawned, dawning, dawns. 1.** To begin to become light in the morning. **2.** To begin to appear or develop; emerge. **3.** To begin to be perceived or understood. Used with *on* or *upon*: *"the suspicion dawning on him that he was not a welcome visitor"* (Somerset Maugham). [Middle English *daunen,* probably back-formation from *dauninge,* daybreak, alteration of *dauinge,* Old English *dagung,* from *dagian,* to dawn.]

dawn chorus *n.* The singing of birds when they awaken at first light. Preceded by *the.*

dawn redwood *n.* A Chinese deciduous coniferous tree, *Metasequoia glyptostroboides,* discovered as an extant species after having long been considered extinct. It is often grown for ornament.

Daw·son (dô′sən). A town in Yukon Territory, northwest Canada. It was founded (1896) during the Klondike gold rush and was the territory's capital (1898–1951).

day (dā) *n. Abbr.* **d 1. a.** The period of light between dawn and nightfall; the interval from sunrise to sunset. **b.** The light of day; daylight. **2.** The 24-hour period during which the earth completes one rotation on its axis. See **mean solar day, sidereal day. 3.** The portion of a day devoted to work: *the eight-hour day.* **4.** A day reserved for a certain activity: *a day of rest.* **5.** *Usually* **Day.** A particular day connected with a special event or observance: *Mother's Day.* **6. a.** *Often* **days.** One's lifetime. **b.** The period of activity or prominence in one's lifetime: *a writer who has had his day.* **c.** A period of opportunity: *Every dog has his day.* **7.** *Often* **days.** A period of time; an age; an era: *in Napoleon's day; in days of old.* **8.** A unit of distance traveled in an ordinary day's journey. **9.** The contest or issue at hand: *carry the day.* **10.** *Astronomy.* The period during which a heavenly body completes one turn on its axis. **—call it a day.** *Informal.* **1.** To stop one's work or activity for the day. **2.** To terminate after any period of time. **—day after day.** Continuously; for many days. **—day in, day out.** Every day without fail; continuously. **—late in the day.** At a regrettably late stage. [Middle English *dai, day,* Old English *dæg,* from Germanic.]

Day (dā), **Clarence Shepard, Jr.** (1874–1935). U.S. author. He is best known for his autobiographical works, *God and My Father* (1932) and *Life with Father* (1935; dramatized in a highly successful version by Howard Lindsay and Russel Crouse in 1939), and his posthumous works *Life with Mother* (1937) and *Father and I* (1940).

Dayak. Variant of **Dyak.**

Da·yan (dī-än′), **Moshe** (1915–81). Israeli general and politician. He was chief of the general staff (1953–58) and minister of defense (1967, 1969–74). He became a national hero for directing Israel's victory in the Six-Day War (1967). In 1977 he was made foreign minister, resigning two years later.

day bed *n.* A couch or sofa that can be used as a bed, especially during the day.

day blindness *n. Pathology.* **Hemeralopia** *(see).*

day·book (dā′bo͝ok′) *n.* **1.** *Abbr.* **D.B.** *Bookkeeping.* A book in which daily transactions are recorded. **2.** A diary.

day·boy (dā′boi′) *n. Chiefly British.* A schoolboy who attends a boarding school but lives at home. Compare **boarder.**

day·break (dā′brāk′) *n.* The time each morning when light first appears; dawn.

day care *n.* The providing of daytime supervision, training, medical services, and the like, for children of preschool age or for the elderly or disabled.

day-care (dā′kâr′) *adj.* Of, relating to, or providing day care: *a day-care center.*

day coach *n.* An ordinary passenger car of a railroad train, as

distinguished from other cars with special accommodations.

day·dream (dā′drēm′) *n.* A dreamlike musing or fantasy while awake; idle reverie, especially of the fulfillment of wishes or hopes. ~*intr.v.* **daydreamed** or **-dreamt** (-drĕmt′), **-dreaming, -dreams.** To have daydreams. **—day·dream·er** *n.*

day·flow·er (dā′flou′ər) *n.* Any of various plants of the genus *Commelina,* having blue or purplish flowers that wilt quickly.

day·fly (dā′flī′) *n., pl.* **-flies.** An insect, the **mayfly** (*see*).

day·girl (dā′gûrl′) *n. Chiefly British.* A schoolgirl who attends a boarding school but lives at home. Compare **boarder.**

Day-Glo (dā′glō′) *n.* A trademark for a type of fluorescent paint that glows brightly in daylight.

day hospital *n.* A hospital as for the elderly or mentally ill, in which patients receive medical supervision but do not stay overnight.

day labor *n.* Labor hired and paid by the day. **—day laborer** *n.*

day letter *n.* A telegram sent during the day, usually less expensive but slower than a regular telegram.

day·light (dā′līt′) *n.* **1.** The light of day; direct light of the sun. **2. a.** Daybreak. **b.** Daytime. **3.** Exposure to public notice. **4. daylights.** *Slang.* Sense; wits: *scared the living daylights out of him.* **—see daylight. 1.** To approach the end of a difficult endeavor. **2.** To begin to understand what was formerly obscure.

daylight robbery *n. Chiefly British Informal.* Blatant swindling or overcharging.

day·light-sav·ing time (dā′līt′sā′vĭng) *n. Abbr.* **DST, D.S.T.** Time during which clocks are set one hour or more ahead of standard time to provide more daylight at the end of the working day during late spring, summer, and early autumn.

day lily *n.* **1.** Any of various plants of the genus *Hemerocallis,* native to Eurasia, having sword-shaped leaves and yellow to red funnel-shaped flowers. Also called "hemerocallis." **2.** The **plantain lily** (*see*).

day·long (dā′lông′, -lŏng′) *adj.* Lasting the whole day. ~*adv.* Through the whole day.

day-neutral (dā′nōō′trəl, -nyōō′-) *adj.* Of or designating plants whose ability to flower is not affected by the length of the day.

day nursery *n.* A nursery providing daytime care for children of preschool age.

Day of Atonement *n.* **Yom Kippur** (*see*).

Day of Judgment *n.* The **Judgment Day** (*see*).

day release *n. British.* A system whereby a worker is given regular, paid time off to attend an educational course. Compare **block release.**

day return *n. British.* A ticket, usually at a reduced fare, used when traveling to a place and back again on the same day.

day room *n.* A communal sitting room used for recreation, especially in institutions such as schools, hospitals, and prisons.

days (dāz) *adv.* Regularly or habitually in the daytime: *She prefers working days.*

day sailer *n.* A small sailboat for day trips.

day school *n.* **1.** A private or state school for pupils living at home. Compare **boarding school. 2.** A school that holds classes during the day, as opposed to the evening, or on weekdays, as opposed to Sunday.

day·side (dā′sīd′) *n.* The side of a planet facing the sun.

days·man (dāz′mən) *n., pl.* **-men** (-mĭn). *Rare.* An arbiter or mediator. [Middle English *dayesman* : *dayes,* genitive of DAY (appointed for settlement of dispute) + MAN.]

days of grace *pl. n.* Extra days, usually three, allowed for payment of a note or bill after it has fallen due. [Translation of Latin *diēs grātiae.*]

day·spring (dā′sprĭng′) *n. Poetic.* The early dawn; daybreak.

day·star (dā′stär′) *n.* **1.** The morning star. **2.** *Poetic.* The sun.

day·time (dā′tīm′) *n.* The time between dawn and dark; day. ~*adj.* During the day.

day-to-day (dā′tə-dā′) *adj.* **1.** Occurring daily or on successive days. **2.** Routine or regular; mundane.

Day·ton (dāt′n). A city on the Miami River in southwestern Ohio. It was the home of the aircraft pioneers Orville and Wilbur Wright.

Day·to·na Beach (dā-tō′nə). An Atlantic coastal city in northeast Florida. It is a beach resort, and its hard sands have been the venue for speed trials since 1903. The city is also the site of the Daytona International Speedway.

day-trip (dā′trĭp′) *n.* An excursion to a place and back again completed in one day. **—day-trip-per** *n.*

daze (dāz) *tr.v.* **dazed, dazing, dazes. 1.** To stun, as with a heavy blow or shock; stupefy. **2.** To dazzle, as with strong light. ~*n.* A stunned or bewildered condition: *wandering about in a daze.* [Middle English *dasen,* from Old Norse *dasa* (attested in the reflexive form *dasask,* to become weary).] **—daz′ed·ly** (dā′zəd-lē) *adv.*

daz·zle (dăz′əl) *v.* **-zled, -zling, -zles.** *—tr.* **1.** To dim the vision of; blind temporarily with intense light. **2.** To bewilder, amaze, impress or overwhelm with some dazzling display. *—intr.* **1.** To inspire admiration or wonder: *dazzling wit and repartee.* **2.** To become blinded: *"thy sight is young,/ And thou shalt read when mine begin to dazzle"* (Shakespeare). ~*n.* The act or quality of dazzling: *"the dazzle of league after league of featureless sand"* (T.E. Lawrence). [Frequentative of DAZE.] **—daz′zler** *n.* **—daz′zling·ly** *adv.*

dB, db decibel.

D.B. daybook.

d.b.a. doing business as.

D.B.A. Doctor of Business Administration.

D.B.E. Dame Commander of the Order of the British Empire.

d.b.h. *Forestry.* diameter at breast height.

D.Bib. Douay Bible.

dbl. double.

dc, DC direct current.

D.C. 1. *Music.* da capo. **2.** District of Columbia. **3.** district commissioner. **4.** direct current.

D.C.L. Doctor of Civil Law.

D.C.M. Distinguished Conduct Medal.

D.D. 1. demand draft. **2.** dishonorable discharge. **3.** Doctor of Divinity (Latin *Divinitatis Doctor*).

D-day (dē′dā′) *n.* The unnamed day on which a military offensive or other operation is to be launched; specifically, June 6, 1944, the day on which the Allied forces invaded France during World War II. [*D* (abbreviation for DAY) + DAY.]

D.D.S. Doctor of Dental Science; Doctor of Dental Surgery.

DDT *n.* A colorless contact insecticide, $(ClC_6H_4)_2CHCCl_3$, toxic to man and animals when swallowed or absorbed through the skin. [From *d(ichloro)d(iphenyl)t(richloroethane)*: DI- + CHLORO- + DI- + PHENYL + TRI- + CHLORO- + ETHANE.]

de, De (də) *prep. French.* Of; from. Used in personal names, originally to show place of origin: *Guy de Maupassant.* [French, from Latin *dē,* from.]

DE Delaware (used with a Zip Code).

de- *prefix.* Indicates: **1.** Reversal or undoing; for example, **decode, denationalize. 2.** Removal; for example, **deaminate, delouse. 3.** Degradation, reduction; for example, **declass. 4.** Disparagement; for example, **demean.** *Note:* Many compounds other than those entered here may be formed with *de-.* In forming compounds, *de-* is normally joined with the following element without space or hyphen: *decarbonize.* However, if the second element begins with *e,* it is separated with a hyphen: *de-escalate.* It is also preferable to use the hyphen if the compound brings together three or more vowels: *de-aerate.* In the rare case that the second element begins with a capital letter, it is separated with a hyphen: *de-Americanize.* [In borrowed Latin and French compounds, Latin *dē-* (French *dé-,* Old French *des-*) indicates: **1.** Down, downward, as in **declivity, deject. 2.** Away, away from, off, as in **decide, deprecate. 3.** Reversal, undoing, as in **decrease, destroy. 4.** Removal, riddance, as in **defoliate, decapitate. 5.** Completely, carefully, intensively, as in **denominate, declare. 6.** Pejorative sense, as in **deride, deceive.** Latin *dē-,* from *dē,* from.]

de-ac·ces·sion (dē-ăk-sĕsh′ən) *v.* **-sioned, -sioning, -sions.** *—tr.* To remove (an article) from the collection in a museum or gallery and sell it off in order to raise funds. *—intr.* To remove an article or articles in this way.

de-a·cid·i·fy (dē′ə-sĭd′ə-fī) *tr.v.* **-fied, -fying, -fies.** To remove the acid from or reduce the acid content of. **—de-a·cid·i·fi·ca′tion** *n.*

dea·con (dē′kən) *n.* **1.** In the Anglican, Greek Orthodox, and Roman Catholic churches, a clergyman ranking just below a priest. **2.** In various other Christian churches, a layman who assists the minister in various functions. ~*tr.v.* **deaconed, -coning, -cons.** *Informal.* **1.** To read aloud lines or verses of (a hymn) to help the congregation in singing. **2.** To arrange (fruit and vegetables) for sale so that inferior items are concealed. **3.** To adulterate. [Middle English *dek(e)n,* Old English *dīacon,* from Late Latin *diāconus,* from Greek *diakonos,* "servant."] **—dea·con·ship** *n.*

dea·con·ess (dē′kə-nĭs) *n.* A woman appointed or elected to serve as an assistant in a church.

dea·con·ry (dē′kən-rē) *n., pl.* **-ries. 1.** The office or position of a deacon. **2.** Deacons collectively.

de·ac·ti·vate (dē-ăk′tə-vāt′) *tr.v.* **-vated, -vating, -vates. 1.** To render inactive; especially, to make (a bomb or radioactive sample, for example) harmless or ineffective. **2.** *Military.* To remove from active status. **—de·ac·ti·va′tion** *n.*

dead (dĕd) *adj.* Sometimes **deader, deadest. 1.** No longer alive; lifeless. Compare **brain dead. 2.** Not having the capacity to live; inanimate: *as dead as a stone.* **3. a.** Lacking feeling; numb: *My leg's gone dead.* **b.** Lacking sensitivity; unresponsive: *dead to all our entreaties.* **4.** No longer in existence, use, force, or operation: *a dead language.* **5.** Devoid of animation, interest, or excitement. **6.** Not productive; idle: *dead capital.* **7.** *Informal.* Weary and worn-out; exhausted. **8.** Without brightness or luster. Said of colors. **9.** Without resonance. Said of sounds. **10.** Extinguished: *a dead match.* **11.** Lacking elasticity or resilience. **12.** Suggestive of the finality or absoluteness of death, especially: **a.** Abrupt: *dead stop.* **b.** Complete; utter: *dead silence.* **c.** Exact; unerring: *the dead center.* **13.** *Sports.* Out of play. Said of a ball. **14. a.** Lacking connection to a source of electric current or voltage. **b.** Drained of electric charge; discharged. Said of a battery. **15.** *Printing.* No longer needed for use. Said of type. ~*n.* **1.** A person who has died, or those who have died, collectively. Preceded by *the.* **2.** The period of greatest intensity, as of cold or darkness: *the dead of winter.* ~*adv.* **1.** Absolutely; altogether. **2.** Directly; exactly: *dead ahead.* [Middle English *ded,* Old English *dēad,* from Germanic.] **—dead·ness** *n.*

Usage: *dead, deceased, departed, extinct, lifeless, inanimate.* These adjectives all mean without life. *Dead,* which has the widest use, applies in general to whatever once had physical life, function, or usefulness but no longer has one. *Deceased* refers only to nonliving human beings, as does *departed,* a euphemistic term. *Extinct* can

D-Day

NORMANDY LANDINGS: THE INVASION OF OCCUPIED EUROPE

The Allied offensive that started the reconquest of occupied Europe

The turning point of World War II came in 1944. German forces had finally been forced on the defensive on the Russian front, and the growing demand for a second front to take the offensive against the enemy in western Europe was answered by Operation Overlord—the invasion of Normandy. On June 6, 1944, 156,000 men landed on five beaches between Caen and Cherbourg. This part of the French coast was chosen for its favorable tides and comparatively weak defenses. By feeding the Germans false intelligence reports, the Allies led them to believe that the main assault would be made around Calais. RAF bombers and two American airborne divisions prepared the way by attacking strategic targets. By June 11, the beachheads were completely in Allied hands. Specially designed artificial harbors enabled armored vehicles and heavy guns and artillery to land on the beaches and sustain the invasion.

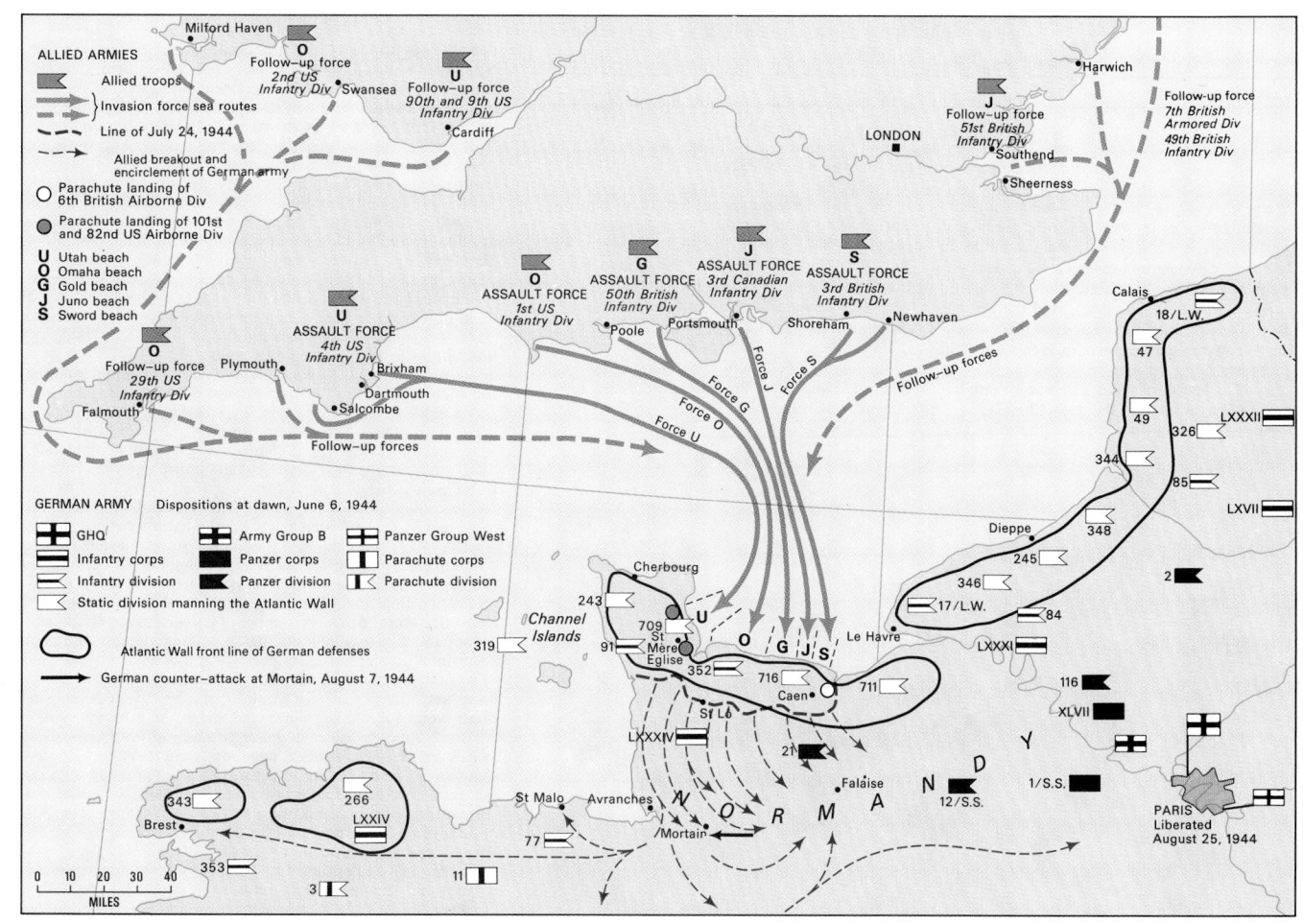

refer to what has no living successors, such as an animal species, or to what is extinguished or inactive, such as a volcano. *Lifeless* applies to what no longer has physical life and to persons or things that lack animation or spirit. *Inanimate* is limited to what has never had physical life.

dead-air space (dĕd'âr') *n.* An unventilated space.

dead ball line *n.* In Rugby football, a line behind the goal line, beyond which the ball is out of play (dead).

dead·beat[1] (dĕd'bēt') *n.* **1.** *Informal.* Someone with no money; a destitute person. **2.** A lazy or lethargic person; a loafer. **3.** A person who does not pay his debts.
~*adj. Informal.* Completely exhausted. [Probably DEAD (completely) + BEAT (exhausted).]

deadbeat[2] *adj.* **1.** *Physics.* Lacking recoil, as the mechanism of a clock. **2.** Stopping without oscillation. [DEAD + BEAT (oscillation).]

dead center *n.* Either of two points in the path of a moving crank and connecting rod at the ends of a stroke when the two lie in a straight line. Also called "dead point."

dead duck *n. Slang.* A failure or a person or thing doomed to failure.

dead·en (dĕd'n) *v.* **-ened, -ening, -ens.** —*tr.* **1.** To render less sensitive, intense, or vigorous: *pills to deaden the pain.* **2.** To make soundproof. **3.** To make less colorful. —*intr.* To become dead or as if dead. —**dead·en·er** *n.*

dead end *n.* **1.** An end of a passage, such as a street or pipe, that affords no outlet or exit. **2.** Any point beyond which no movement or progress can be made; an impasse.

dead-end (dĕd'ĕnd') *adj.* **1.** Not having an exit: *a dead-end street.* **2.** Without opportunity for advancement: *a dead-end job.* **3.** *Infor-*mal. Of or characteristic of the slums or life in the slums: *a dead-end gang.*

dead·en·ing (dĕd'n-ĭng) *n.* Material used for soundproofing.

dead·eye (dĕd'ī') *n.* **1.** *Nautical.* A flat hardwood disk with a grooved perimeter, pierced by three holes through which the lanyards are passed, used to fasten the shrouds. **2.** *Slang.* An expert marksman. [Perhaps because the holes on the disk resemble the empty sockets in a human skull.]

dead·fall (dĕd'fôl') *n.* **1.** A trap for large animals, in which a heavy weight is arranged to fall on and kill or disable the prey. **2.** A mass of fallen timber and tangled brush.

dead hand *n. Law.* **Mortmain** (see). [Middle English *dede hond*, translation of Old French *mortemain*, MORTMAIN.]

dead·head[1] (dĕd'hĕd') *n.* **1.** A vehicle, such as a railway car or airplane, carrying no passengers or freight. **2.** A dull-witted or sluggish person. **3.** *Informal.* A person who uses a free ticket for admittance, accommodation, or entertainment.
~*tr.v.* **deadheaded, -heading, -heads.** *Informal.* To drive (a train, bus, or truck) carrying no passengers or freight.
~*adv. Informal.* Without passengers or freight; empty.

deadhead[2], **dead-head** *v. Chiefly British.* **-headed, -heading, -heads.** —*tr.* To remove the dead flowers from (a plant) to tidy it or prevent seeding. —*intr.* To remove the dead flowers from a plant. —**dead·head·ing** *n.*

dead heart *n. Australian.* The arid interior of Australia.

dead heat *n.* A race in which two or more contestants finish at the same time; a tie.

dead letter *n.* **1.** An unclaimed or undelivered letter that after a period of time is destroyed or returned to the sender by the post office. **2.** A law or directive still formally in effect but no longer valid or enforced.

dead·light (dĕd'līt') *n.* **1.** *Nautical.* **a.** A strong shutter or plate fastened over a ship's porthole or cabin window in stormy weather. **b.** A thick window set in a ship's side or deck. **2.** A skylight made so that it cannot be opened.

dead·line (dĕd'līn') *n.* **1.** A time limit, as for payment of a debt or completion of an assignment. **2.** The time after which copy for a newspaper, periodical, or the like will not be accepted. **3.** A boundary line in a prison that prisoners can cross only at the risk of being shot.

dead load *n.* *Engineering.* The fixed weight of a structure or piece of equipment, such as a bridge on its supports. Also called "dead weight." Compare **live load.**

dead·lock (dĕd'lŏk') *n.* **1.** A stoppage or standstill resulting from the opposition of two unrelenting forces. **2.** A door lock that combines the features of a **Yale lock** and a **mortise lock** (*both of which see*).

~*v.* **deadlocked, -locking, -locks.** —*tr.* To bring to a deadlock. —*intr.* To come to a deadlock.

dead·ly (dĕd'lē) *adj.* **-lier, -liest. 1.** Causing or tending to cause death; lethal. **2.** Suggestive of death; deathly: *deadly white.* **3.** Implacable; mortal: *deadly enemies.* **4.** Destructive in effect. **5.** Absolute; unqualified: *deadly accuracy.* **5.** *Informal.* Extremely dull and boring: *How deadly!* —See Synonyms at **fatal.**

~*adv.* **1.** So as to suggest death. **2.** To an extreme: *deadly earnest.* —**dead·li·ness** *n.*

Usage: *Deadly* (adjective) and *deathly* (adjective) overlap in meaning. But in modern usage *deadly* is largely confined to what causes death or extreme distress (such as disease or boredom) and *deathly* to what resembles or suggests death (such as silence or pallor).

deadly nightshade *n.* **1.** A poisonous plant, *Solanum nigrum,* having small white flowers and black fruit. Also called "black nightshade." **2.** A Eurasian plant, the **belladonna** (*see*).

deadly sins *pl.n.* See **seven deadly sins.**

dead-man's fingers (dĕd'mənz) *n.* *Used with a singular verb.* **1.** A soft coral, *Alcyonium digitatum,* consisting of a colony of flesh-pink, fingerlike polyps. **2.** A fungus, **devil's fingers** (*see*).

dead-man's handle *n.* A safety feature fitted to a train or other vehicle. It is kept depressed to control speed and, when not depressed and contact is broken, it will bring the vehicle to a stop.

dead march *n.* A slow, solemn march played for a funeral.

dead nettle *n.* Any of several weedy plants of the genus *Lamium,* native to the Old World, having nettlelike leaves and clusters of small purplish, white, or yellow flowers. [Because it does not sting.]

dead·pan (dĕd'păn') *adj.* Characterized by a blank or expressionless face or manner. —**dead·pan** *adv.*

dead point *n.* *Machinery.* **Dead center** (*see*).

dead reckoning *n.* **1.** *Navigation.* A method of determining the position of an aircraft or ship without external aids, such as astronomical observations or radio, by calculating from the direction and speed of travel from a known point. **2.** Calculation based on inference or guesswork. [From DEAD (probably "complete," "exact," because it is the closest estimate possible).]

Dead Sea (dĕd). *Arabic* **Bah·ret Lut** (bäh'rĕt loot'). Lake at the outlet of the Jordan River, partitioned between Israel and Jordan to the east. It is the lowest point on the earth's surface, being 396 meters (1,299 feet) below sea level. The surface waters have a salt content nearly nine times the average salinity of the ocean, allowing humans to float like corks. The sea contains no living things and has no outflow, its inflow being lost through evaporation.

Dead Sea Scrolls *pl.n.* A number of parchment scrolls, dated from about 250 B.C. to about A.D. 70, containing Hebrew and Aramaic Scriptural texts and the liturgical writings of an ascetic community. The first scrolls were found in 1947 in caves near the Dead Sea.

dead-set (dĕd'sĕt') *adj.* Determined; resolved: *dead-set on winning.*

dead weight *n.* **1.** The unrelieved weight of a heavy, motionless mass. **2.** An oppressive burden or difficulty affording no advantage whatever. **3.** *Engineering.* A **dead load** (*see*).

dead·wood (dĕd'wood') *n.* **1.** Dead branches or wood on a tree or shrub. **2.** Anything burdensome or superfluous, as useless phrases in writing or unnecessary personnel. **4.** *Nautical.* The vertical planking between the keel of a vessel and the sternpost, serving merely as a reinforcement.

deaf (dĕf) *adj.* **deafer, deafest. 1.** Partially or completely incapable of hearing. **2.** Unwilling or refusing to listen; heedless. [Middle English *de(a)f,* Old English *dēaf,* from Germanic.] —**deaf·ly** *adv.* —**deaf·ness** *n.*

deaf-aid (dĕf'ād') *n.* *British.* A hearing aid (*see*).

deaf·en (dĕf'ən) *tr.v.* **-ened, -ening, -ens. 1.** To make deaf, especially momentarily by a loud noise. **2.** To make soundproof.

deaf·en·ing (dĕf'ən-īng) *adj.* Stunning to the ears; resoundingly loud. —**deaf·en·ing·ly** *adv.*

deaf-mute (dĕf'myoot') *n.* Also **deaf mute.** A person who can neither speak nor hear.

~*adj.* (dĕf-myoot'). Unable to speak or hear.

deal¹ (dēl) *v.* **dealt** (dĕlt), **dealing, deals.** —*tr.* **1.** To give to someone as a share; apportion. **2.** To distribute or pass out among several people. **3.** To administer; deliver (a blow, for example). **4.** *Card Games.* **a.** To distribute (playing cards) among players. **b.** To give (a specific card) to a player while so distributing. —*intr.* **1.** To be occupied or concerned; treat. Used with *in* or *with: a book dealing with the Middle Ages.* **2.** To behave in a specified way toward another or others; have transactions. Used with *with: deal honestly with competitors.* **3.** To take action. Used with *with: The committee will deal with this complaint.* **4.** To do business; trade: *dealing in diamonds.* **5.** *Card Games.* To distribute playing cards. —See Usage note at **distribute.**

~*n.* **1.** The act or a round of apportioning or distributing. **2.** *Card Games.* **a.** The distribution of the playing cards. **b.** The cards so distributed; a hand. **c.** The right or turn of a player to distribute the cards. **d.** The playing of one hand. **3.** An indefinite quantity, extent, or degree: *a great deal of experience.* **4.** An agreement arranged secretly, as in business or politics. **5.** *Informal.* Any agreement or business transaction. **6.** *Informal.* An exchange or bargain. **7.** *Informal.* Treatment received, especially as the result of an agreement: *a raw deal.* **8.** *Slang.* An important issue: *make a big deal out of nothing.* **9.** A program, such as a political platform, that offers

---

Dead Sea Scrolls

THE LIBRARY OF A JEWISH COMMUNITY
Religious texts that survived the ravages of 2,000 years

Early in 1947, a young Bedouin herdsman, searching for a stray lamb on the parched slopes west of the Dead Sea near Qumran, stumbled on some old clay jars in a cave. To his disappointment, they held only ancient scrolls.

However, as scholars deciphered the writings on the scrolls and on thousands of other parchment, papyrus, and copper fragments found in caves nearby, a fascinating story emerged—the story of a Jewish religious community with beliefs similar to those of the early Christians.

The scrolls were the sacred texts of an ancient Jewish sect—probably the Essenes—who were based at Qumran from the 2nd century B.C. to the 1st century A.D. They are thought to have been kept hidden in the caves after about A.D. 68 when the Romans threatened the community during a Jewish revolt.

From the scrolls, scholars have reconstructed the history of Palestine from the 4th century B.C. to A.D. 135 and dated the standardized Old Testament to about A.D. 70.

SACRED SCROLL *The discovery of these fragments from the Book of Exodus helped to confirm the authenticity of the Old Testament tradition. The scrolls are also valuable examples of contemporary Aramaic and Hebrew scripts.*

some specified treatment for those participating; especially, President Franklin Roosevelt's **New Deal** *(see).* [Middle English *delen,* Old English *dǣlan,* to divide, distribute, from Germanic.]

deal² *n.* **1.** A board of fir, pine, or similar wood cut to standard dimensions. **2.** Such boards or planks collectively. **3.** Fir, pine, or similar wood. [Middle English *dele,* from Middle Low German or Middle Dutch *dele.*]

Deal (dēl). Channel port in Kent, southeast England. In the 11th century it became one of the Cinque Ports, and its castle was built by Henry VIII (1539).

deal·er (dē′lər) *n.* **1.** A person or group engaged in buying and selling: *a used-car dealer.* **2.** *Card Games.* The person who distributes the cards. **3.** *Informal.* One who deals in illegal drugs.

deal·fish (dēl′fĭsh′) *n., pl.* **-fishes** or collectively **dealfish.** A marine fish, *Trachipterus arcticus,* of Atlantic waters, resembling the ribbonfishes. [DEAL (plank), from its long, thin body + FISH.]

deal·ing (dē′lĭng) *n.* **1.** *Usually* **dealings.** Transactions or relations with others, usually in business. **2.** Method or manner of conduct in relation to others; treatment: *honest dealing.*

de·am·i·nate (dē-ăm′ə-nāt′) *tr.v.* **-nated, -nating, -nates.** Also **de·am·i·nize** (-nīz′), **-nized, -nizing, -nizes.** To remove an amino group from (an organic compound, especially an amino acid). **—de·am·i·na·tion, de·am·i·ni·za·tion** *n.*

dean¹ (dēn) *n.* **1. a.** An administrative officer in charge of a college, faculty, or division in a university. **b.** In some universities and colleges, a member of the staff who counsels students and supervises the enforcement of rules. **2.** *Ecclesiastical.* The head of the chapter of canons governing a cathedral or collegiate church. **3.** *Chiefly British.* A priest appointed to oversee a group of parishes within a diocese. Also called "rural dean." **4.** *Roman Catholic Church.* **a.** A high-ranking official, usually a cardinal, who runs a department in the Vatican. **b.** The head of the College of Cardinals. **5.** The senior member of any body. [Middle English *deen, den,* from Norman French, from Late Latin *decānus,* "(one) set over ten," from Greek *dekanos,* from *deka,* ten.] **—dean·ship** *n.*

dean², dene. *British.* A valley.

Dean, Forest of (dēn). Woodland region of Gloucestershire in the west of England. Formerly an ancient royal hunting preserve, it became the first of Britain's National Forest Parks (1938).

Dean, James (1931–55). U.S. film actor. He was a youth hero of the rock 'n' roll era, whose screen image was one of moody rebellion. His films include *East of Eden* (1954) and *Rebel Without a Cause* (1955). He was killed in a car crash.

Dean, Jerome Herman, born Jay Hanna Dean, known as "Dizzy" (1911–74). U.S. baseball player. A right-handed pitcher, he played for the St. Louis Cardinals from 1930 to 1937. After his retirement in 1941, Dean became a sportscaster and was noted for his picturesque descriptions of baseball games.

dean·er·y (dē′nə-rē) *n., pl.* **-ies. 1.** The office, jurisdiction, or authority of a dean. **2.** A dean's official residence.

dear¹ (dîr) *adj.* **dearer, dearest. 1.** Beloved; loved; precious. **2.** Highly esteemed or regarded. Used as a conventional form of address at the beginning of a letter: *Dear Sir.* **3. a.** Expensive; costly. **b.** Charging high prices. **4.** Earnest; ardent: *fulfilled his dearest wishes.* **5.** Sweet; lovely: *a dear little kitten.* **6.** *Obsolete.* Noble; worthy. —See Synonyms at **costly.**
~*n.* A greatly loved person; darling. Often used as a term of affectionate address: *my dear.*
~*adv.* **1.** Fondly or affectionately. **2.** At a high cost: *Her mistake will cost her dear.*
~*interj.* Used as a polite exclamation, as of dismay: *Oh dear. Dear me.* [Middle English *dere,* Old English *dēore,* from Germanic *deurjaz* (unattested), worthy, costly, dear.] **—dear·ness** *n.*

dear², dere *adj. Obsolete.* Severe; grievous; dire. [Middle English, *dere,* Old English *dēor*†.]

Dear·born (dîr′bôrn′, -bərn). A city of southeastern Michigan, on the Rouge River adjoining Detroit. It is a manufacturing, warehousing, and distribution center. Greenfield Village, Henry Ford's birthplace, is here.

Dear John letter *n. Informal.* A letter from a woman to her fiancé or lover informing him that their relationship is ended.

dear·ly (dîr′lē) *adv.* **1.** With deep affection; fondly. **2.** At great cost or price. **3.** Earnestly; ardently.

dearth (dûrth) *n.* **1.** Scarcity; lack; paucity. **2.** Shortage of food; famine. [Middle English *dearth(e),* costliness, scarcity, from *dere,* DEAR (expensive).]

dear·y, dear·ie (dîr′ē) *n., pl.* **-ies.** *Informal.* Darling; dear. Used as a term of address.

death (dĕth) *n.* **1. a.** The act of dying; termination of life. Compare **brain death. b.** An instance of dying or killing: *a number of deaths on the road.* **2.** The state of being dead. **3.** *Often* **Death.** A personification of the destroyer of life, usually represented as a skeleton holding a scythe. **4.** Termination; extinction: *the death of imperialism.* **5.** The cause of dying. **6.** A manner of dying: *a hero's death.* **7.** Loss or absence of spiritual life. **8.** *Law.* **Civil death** *(see).* **9.** *Christian Science.* The product of human belief of life in matter. **—be the death of someone.** To irritate or distress someone to an intolerable degree. **—catch one's death (of cold).** *Informal.* To catch a bad cold. **—do (or put) to death.** To kill or execute. **—like death warmed over.** Very ill or looking very ill. **—to death.** To an intolerable degree: *worried to death.* [Middle English *de(e)th,* Old English *dēath,* from Germanic.]

death adder *n.* A venomous Australian snake, *Acanthophis antarcticus,* resembling an adder.

death·bed (dĕth′bĕd′) *n.* **1.** The bed on which a person dies. **2.** The last hours before death. Also used adjectivally: *a deathbed plea.*

death bell *n.* A bell tolled to announce a death. Also called "passing bell."

death·blow (dĕth′blō′) *n.* **1.** A blow or stroke that causes death. **2.** Any fatal event or occurrence.

death camas. Also **death camass.** Any of several plants of the genus *Zygadenus,* of western North America, having grasslike leaves and clusters of greenish-white flowers. [So called because they are poisonous to livestock.]

death camp *n.* An **extermination camp** *(see).*

death cell *n.* A prison cell in which one who is condemned to death awaits execution.

death certificate *n.* An official document, signed by a doctor, giving details of the date, place, and cause of a person's death.

death cup *n.* A deadly poisonous, usually white mushroom, *Amanita phalloides,* having white gills and a prominent bulbous base. Also called "death angel."

death duty *n. British.* A tax on inherited property.

death·ful (dĕth′fəl) *adj.* **1.** Fatal; deadly. **2.** Deathly.

death house *n.* A cell block or other part of a prison in which prisoners condemned to death await execution.

death knell *n.* **1.** A bell tolled to announce a death. **2.** Anything that signals imminent death, as of a person or of hopes or plans.

death·less (dĕth′lĭs) *adj.* Not subject to death; immortal. **—death·less·ly** *adv.* **—death·less·ness** *n.*

death·ly (dĕth′lē) *adj.* **1.** Resembling or characteristic of death. **2.** Causing death; fatal; deadly. **3.** *Poetic.* Of death. —See Usage note at **deadly.**
~*adv.* **1.** In the manner of death. **2.** Extremely; very: *deathly quiet.* **—death·li·ness** *n.*

death mask *n.* A cast of a person's face taken after death.

death penalty *n.* **1.** A sentence of death. **2.** Capital punishment.

death point *n.* An environmental limit, as of temperature, moisture, or radiation, beyond which a specified life form cannot survive.

death rate *n.* **1.** The ratio of total deaths to total population, usually expressed as deaths per 1,000, 10,000, or 100,000 population, in a specified community. Also called "mortality rate." **2.** The number of deaths per 100 persons having the same disease. In this sense, also called "fatality rate."

death rattle *n.* A rare respiratory gurgling or rattling in the throat of a dying person, caused by loss of the cough reflex and by the passage of breath through accumulating mucus in the throat.

death row *n.* A cell block or other part of a prison containing death cells. Also called "death house." **—on death row.** Under sentence of death.

death's-head (dĕths′hĕd′) *n.* The human skull or a representation of it, symbolizing mortality or death.

death's-head moth *n.* A large Eurasian hawk moth, *Acherontia atropos,* having a skull-like marking on the upper part of the thorax.

death squad *n.* Any of several unofficial groups of vigilantes, especially in Latin America, whose members kill criminals, political agitators, or others considered hostile to society.

death tax *n.* An **inheritance tax** *(see).*

death·trap (dĕth′trăp′) *n.* **1. a.** An unsafe building or structure, especially one susceptible to fire. **b.** An unsafe train, motor vehicle, or the like. **2.** Any perilous circumstance or situation.

Death Valley. An arid desert basin in eastern California. It acquired its name after a party crossing the valley in the 1849 gold rush died there. The valley is *c.* 225 kilometers (140 miles) long and is the hottest and deepest spot on the North American continent, 85 meters (282 feet) below sea level. The valley was made a national monument in 1933.

death warrant *n.* **1.** *Law.* An official order authorizing a person's execution. **2.** Anything that destroys hope, joy, or expectation.

death·watch (dĕth′wŏch′) *n.* **1.** A vigil kept beside a dying or dead person. **2. a.** Any of several beetles of the family Anobiidae, especially *Xestobium rufovillosum,* that strike their heads with a hollow, clicking sound against the wood into which they burrow. Also called "deathwatch beetle." **b.** A booklouse that makes a similar sound.

death wish *n. Psychology.* A conscious or unconscious wish for one's own or someone else's death.

Deau·ville (dō′vĭl, dō-vēl′). Coastal resort in the Calvados department of Normandy, northwest France. It has a casino, yachting harbor, and racecourse.

deave (dēv) *tr.v.* **deaved, deaving, deaves.** *British Regional.* To deafen or confuse with noise. [Middle English *deven,* Old English *ādēafian,* from *dēaf,* DEAF.]

deb (dĕb) *n. Informal.* A debutante.

deb. debenture.

de·ba·cle (dĭ-bä′kəl, -băk′əl) *n.* **1.** A sudden, disastrous overthrow or collapse; rout. **2.** The breaking up of ice in a river. **3.** A violent flood. —See Synonyms at **disaster.** [French *débâcle,* from *débâcler,* to unbar, from Old French *desbacler* : *des-,* from Latin *dē-* (removal) + *bacler,* to bar, from Old Provençal *baclar,* from Vulgar Latin *bacclāre* (unattested), from Latin *baculum,* rod, stick.]

de·bag (dē-băg′) *tr.v.* **-bagged, -bagging, -bags.** *British Slang.* To remove the trousers of (someone) as a joke or humiliation.

de·bar (dē-bär′) *tr.v.* **-barred, -barring, -bars. 1.** To exclude or bar; shut out. **2.** To forbid, hinder, or prevent. [Middle English *debar-*

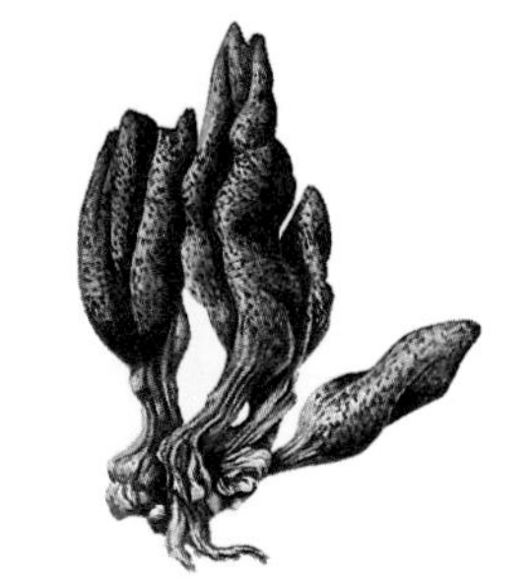

dead-man's fingers *An inedible hard-skinned, black fungus that grows on old tree stumps at all times of the year, sprouting in clusters up to 5 centimeters (2 inches) high.*

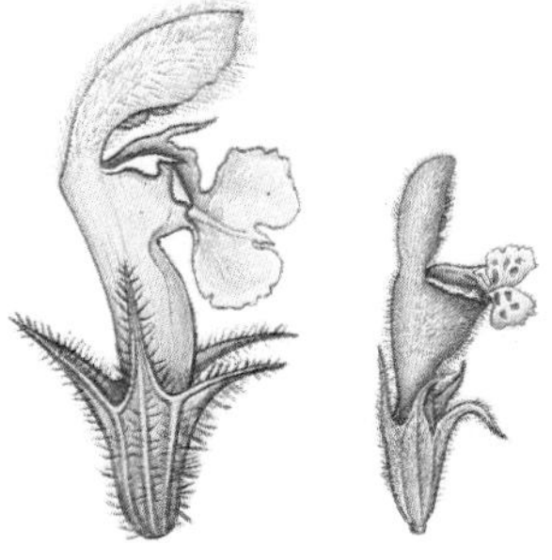

dead nettle *The flower heads of the white dead nettle,* Lamium album *(left), and the red dead nettle,* Lamium purpureum *(right). Both species are common wildflowers in the temperate zones of Europe and Asia. The plants are called "dead nettles" because, though they resemble nettles, they do not sting.*

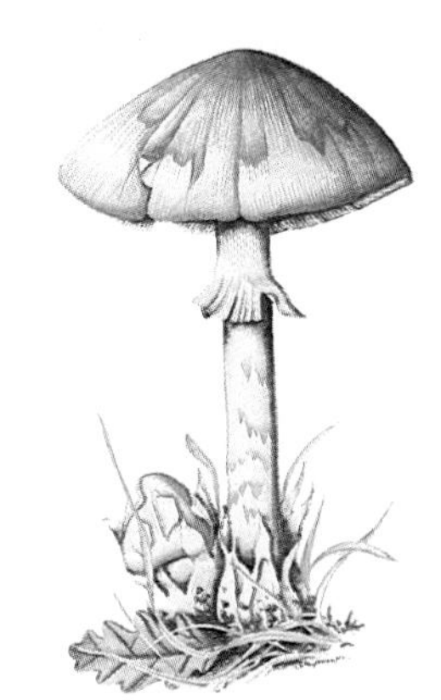

death cup *An aptly named fungus—it is deadly poisonous and there is no known antidote. It is particularly dangerous because it closely resembles the common field mushroom, which is edible; but, when old, the death cup can be recognized by its sickly smell.*

ren, from Old French *desbarrer,* to unbar : *des-,* from Latin *dē-* (removal) + *barrer,* to BAR.] —**de·bar·ment** *n.*

de·bark (dĭ-bärk′) *v.* **-barked, -barking, -barks.** —*tr.* To unload, as from a ship. —*intr.* To disembark. [French *débarquer,* from Old French *debarquer : de-,* from Latin *dē-* (removal) + *barque,* ship, BARK.] —**de·bar·ka·tion** *n.*

de·base (dĭ-bās′) *tr.v.* **-based, -basing, -bases.** 1. To reduce the value of (a coin) by adulterating with base metal. 2. To lower in character, quality, or value; degrade; adulterate. [DE- (down) + BASE (low).] —**de·base·ment** *n.* —**de·bas·er** *n.*

de·bat·a·ble (dĭ-bā′tə-bəl) *adj.* 1. Capable of being argued or discussed. 2. In dispute; questionable. —See Synonyms at **doubtful.** —**de·bat·a·bly** *adv.*

de·bate (dĭ-bāt′) *v.* **-bated, -bating, -bates.** —*intr.* 1. To deliberate; consider. 2. To engage in argument; discuss opposing points. 3. To engage in a formal discussion or argument. 4. *Obsolete.* To fight; quarrel. —*tr.* 1. To dispute or argue about. 2. To discuss or argue (a question, for example) formally, as in a legislative assembly. 3. To deliberate upon; consider. 4. *Obsolete.* To fight or argue for or over. —See Synonyms at **discuss.**
~*n.* 1. a. A discussion involving opposing points as in a legislative assembly. b. An argument; dispute. 2. Deliberation; consideration. 3. A formal argument in which two opposing teams defend and attack a given proposition. 4. *Obsolete.* Conflict; strife; contention. [Middle English *debaten,* from Old French *debattre : de-, des-,* from Latin *dis-,* apart, against each other + *battre,* to fight, beat, from Latin *battere, battuere.*] —**de·bat·er** *n.*

de·bauch (dĭ-bôch′) *v.* **-bauched, -bauching, -bauches.** —*tr.* 1. To corrupt morally; seduce; pervert: *"riches debauched one class with idleness of mind and body"* (Edward Bellamy). 2. *Obsolete.* To cause to forsake allegiance. —*intr.* To indulge in dissipation.
~*n.* An act or period of dissipation. [French *débaucher,* Old French *desbaucher*†.] —**de·bauch·ed·ly** *adv.* —**de·bauch·er** *n.*

deb·au·chee (dĕb′ô-chē′, -shē′, dĭ-bô′chē) *n.* A person who habitually indulges in debauchery; libertine.

de·bauch·er·y (dĭ-bô′chə-rē) *n., pl.* **-ies.** 1. Extreme indulgence in sensual pleasures; intemperance; dissipation. 2. *Archaic.* Seduction from morality, allegiance, or duty.

de·ben·ture (dĭ-bĕn′chər) *n. Abbr.* **deb., deben.** 1. A certificate or voucher acknowledging a debt. 2. An unsecured bond, issued by a civil or governmental corporation or agency and backed only by the credit standing of the issuer. Also called "debenture bond." 3. A customs certificate providing for the payment of a drawback. [Middle English *debentur,* from Latin *dēbentur,* "they are due," from *dēbēre,* to owe.]

de·bil·i·tate (dĭ-bĭl′ə-tāt′) *tr.v.* **-tated, -tating, -tates.** To make feeble; enervate. [Latin *dēbilitāre,* from *dēbilis,* weak.] —**de·bil·i·ta·tion** *n.* —**de·bil·i·ta·tive** *adj.*

de·bil·i·tat·ed (dĭ-bĭl′ə-tā′tĭd) *adj.* Tired; worn-out. —See Synonyms at **weak.**

de·bil·i·ty (dĭ-bĭl′ə-tē) *n.* A state of abnormal bodily weakness; feebleness. [Middle English *debilite,* from Old French, from Latin *dēbilitās,* from *dēbilis,* weak.]

deb·it (dĕb′ĭt) *n. Abbr.* **dr.** *Accounting.* 1. An item of debt as recorded in an account. 2. a. An entry of a sum in the left-hand side of an account, recording money paid out or goods supplied. b. The sum of such entries. Compare **credit.** 3. The left-hand side of an account or ledger where bookkeeping entries are made.
~*tr.v.* **debited, -iting, -its.** 1. To enter (a sum) on the left-hand side of an account or ledger. 2. To charge with a debt. Compare **credit.** [Middle English *debite,* from Old French, from Latin *dēbitum,* DEBT.]

deb·o·nair, deb·o·naire, deb·on·naire (dĕb′ə-nâr′) *adj.* 1. Suave; nonchalant; urbane. 2. Affable; genial. 3. Carefree; jaunty. [Middle English *debonaire,* from Old French, from *de bon aire,* "of good disposition."] —**deb·o·nair·ly** *adv.* —**deb·o·nair·ness** *n.*

Deb·o·rah (dĕb′ər-ə, dĕb′rə). A prophetess and judge of Israel who helped the Israelites free themselves from the Canaanites. Judges 4:4.

de·bouch (dĭ-bōōsh′) *v.* **-bouched, -bouching, -bouches.** —*intr.* 1. *Military.* To march from a narrow or confined area into the open. 2. To emerge or issue, especially into a less restricted space, as a river might. —*tr.* To cause to emerge or issue.
~*n.* A débouché. [French *déboucher : dé-,* from Latin *dē-,* out of + *bouche,* mouth, opening, from Old French, from Latin *bucca,* puffed-out cheek, mouth.]

dé·bou·ché (dā′bōō-shā′) *n.* 1. An opening in military works for the passage of troops. 2. An outlet, as for goods. [French, from *déboucher,* DEBOUCH.]

de·bouch·ment (dĭ-bōōsh′mənt) *n.* 1. The act or an instance of emerging or debouching. 2. A debouchure.

de·bou·chure (dā′bōō-shŏŏr′) *n.* A mouth or opening, especially of a river or channel.

De·brett (də-brĕt′), **John** (1752–1822). British publisher and founder of *Debrett's Peerage and Baronetage.* He took over a directory of the nobility in 1802 and made it into an authoritative guide to the British nobility and royalty.

dé·bride·men′ (dā-brēd-män′, dĭ-brēd′mənt) *n.* The surgical excision of dead and devitalized tissue and the removal of all foreign matter from a wound. [French, from *débrider,* "to unbridle," from Old French *desbrider : des-,* from Latin *dē-* (removal) + *bride,* bridle, from Middle High German *brīdel.*]

de·brief (dē′brēf′) *v.* **-briefed, -briefing, -briefs.** —*tr.* 1. To question or interrogate (a diplomat, spy, or astronaut, for example) to obtain knowledge or intelligence gathered on a mission. 2. To instruct (a government agent or similar employee) not to reveal secret information after his employment has ceased. —*intr.* To answer questions and provide information after returning from a mission.

de·brief·ing (dē-brē′fĭng) *n.* 1. The act or process of being debriefed. 2. The information conveyed during this procedure.

de·bris (də-brē′, dā′brē′) *n.* Also **dé·bris** (dā′brē′). 1. The scattered remains of something broken or destroyed; ruins; fragments. 2. *Geology.* An accumulation of loose material produced by disintegration of rocks. It includes rock fragments, sands, and clays. [French *débris,* from Old French *de(s)brisier,* to break to pieces : *des-,* from Latin *dē-* (intensive) + *brisier,* to break, from (unattested) Vulgar Latin *brīsāre.*]

de Bro·glie (də brŏ′glē), **Louis Victor, Prince** (1892–). French physicist. In 1923 he put forward the hypothesis of wave-particle duality. He was awarded the Nobel Prize (1929).

de Broglie wave *n. Physics.* A wave associated with a particle that represents its wavelike behavior under certain conditions, such as electron diffraction by crystals. The wavelength is given by h/mv, where h is the Planck constant, m is the particle's mass, and v its velocity, interpreted in quantum mechanics as a wave of probability, in which the probability of finding the particle at a given point depends on the square of the wave function. [After Louis Victor DE BROGLIE.]

Debs (dĕbz), **Eugene Victor** (1855–1926). U.S. labor organizer and socialist leader. As president of the American Railway Union (1893) he was instrumental in strikes against the Northern Railroad and the Pullman Company (1894). He was nominated for president by the Socialist Party and ran unsuccessfully for that office five times.

debt (dĕt) *n.* 1. Something owed, such as money, goods, or services. 2. An obligation or liability to pay or render something to someone else. 3. The condition of having such an obligation in debt. 4. *Archaic.* An offense requiring forgiveness or reparation; sin; trespass. [Middle English *det(te),* from Old French *dette,* from Vulgar Latin *dēbita* (unattested), feminine of Latin *dēbitum,* debt, from *dēbitus,* past participle of *dēbēre,* to owe.]

debt of honor *n.* A debt that is morally binding but not legally recoverable, such as a gambling debt.

debt·or (dĕt′ər) *n. Abbr.* **dr.** A person who owes something to another. Compare **creditor.** [Middle English *det(t)our,* from Old French *det(t)or,* from Latin *dēbitor,* from *dēbēre,* to owe.]

de·bug (dē′bŭg′) *tr.v.* **-bugged, -bugging, -bugs.** 1. To remove insects from. 2. To search for and eliminate malfunctioning elements in. 3. To search for and eliminate sources of error in (a computer program, for example). 4. To search for and remove concealed microphones from (a room, for example).

de·bunk (dĭ-bŭngk′) *tr.v.* **-bunked, -bunking, -bunks.** *Informal.* To expose or ridicule the falseness, sham, or exaggerated claims of. [DE- + BUNK (nonsense).] —**de·bunk·er** *n.*

De·bus·sy (də-byōō′sē), **Claude Achille** (1862–1918). French composer. He was the first exponent of musical impressionism, using unusual tone patterns to communicate mood and emotion. His works include *L'Après-midi d'un Faune* (1894) and the opera *Pelléas et Mélisande* (1892–1902).

de·but, dé·but (dĭ-byōō′, dā-, dā′byōō′) *n.* 1. A first public appearance, as of an actor on the stage. 2. The formal presentation of a girl to society. 3. The beginning of a career or course of action. [French *début,* from *débuter,* to make one's debut, "give the first stroke in a game" : *dé-,* from Latin *dē-,* away + *but,* BUTT (target).]

deb·u·tant (dĕb′yōō-tänt′, dĕb′yōō-tänt′, dā′byōō-). A man making a debut, such as a sportsman playing on a team for the first time.

deb·u·tante, dé·bu·tante (dĕb′yōō-tänt′, dĕb′yōō-tänt′, dā′byōō-) *n.* A young lady making a debut into society. Also informally called "deb." [French *débutante,* from *débuter,* to make one's DEBUT.]

dec. 1. deceased. 2. declaration. 3. declension. 4. declination. 5. decrease.

Dec. December.

deca-, dec-, deka-, dek- *prefix. Abbr.* **da** Indicates ten; for example, **decahedron, decane.** [Greek *deka-,* from *deka,* ten.]

dec·ade (dĕk′ād′, dĕ-kād′) *n.* 1. A period of ten years. 2. A group or series of ten. [Middle English, from Old French, from Late Latin *decas* (stem *decad-*) from Greek *dekas,* from *deka,* ten.]

dec·a·dence (dĭ-kā′dəns, dĕk′ə-dəns) *n.* Also **de·ca·den·cy** (-dən-sē) *pl.* **-cies.** 1. A process, condition, or period of deterioration or decline, as in morals or art; decay. 2. *Usually* **Decadence.** The period during which the Decadents flourished. [Old French, from Medieval Latin *dēcadentia,* from Vulgar Latin *dēcadere* (unattested), to DECAY.]

dec·a·dent (dĭ-kā′dənt, dĕk′ə-dənt) *adj.* 1. In a state or condition of decline or decay. 2. Of or pertaining to the Decadents.
~*n.* 1. A person in a condition or process of mental or moral decay. 2. *Usually* **Decadent.** A member of a group of French and English writers of the 19th century who often sought inspiration in the morbid, neurotic, or macabre and tended toward overrefinement of style. [From DECADENCE.] —**de·ca·dent·ly** *adv.*

de·caf·fein·ate (dē-kăf′ə-nāt) *tr.v.* **-ated, -ating, ates.** To remove most of the caffeine from (coffee).

dec·a·gon (dĕk′ə-gŏn′) *n.* A polygon with ten angles and ten sides. [New Latin *decagonum,* from Greek *dekagōnon,* "(one) having ten angles" : DECA- + -GON.] —**de·cag·o·nal** (dĭ-kăg′ə-nəl) *adj.* —**de·cag·o·nal·ly** *adv.*

dec·a·gram, dek·a·gram (dĕk′ə-grăm′) *n. Abbr.* **dag** Ten grams. [French *décagramme* : DECA- + GRAM.]

dec·a·he·dron (dĕk′ə-hē′drən) *n., pl.* **-drons** or **-dra** (-drə). A polyhedron with ten faces. [New Latin : DECA- + -HEDRON.] —**dec·a·he·dral** *adj.*

de·cal (dē′kăl′) *n.* A picture or design transferred by the process of decalcomania (*see*).

de·cal·ci·fy (dē-kăl′sə-fī′) *tr.v.* **-fied, -fying, -fies.** To remove calcium or calcareous matter from (bones or teeth, for example). —**de·cal·ci·fi·ca·tion** *n.* —**de·cal·ci·fi·er** *n.*

de·cal·co·ma·ni·a (dē′kăl-kə-mā′nē-ə) *n.* 1. The process of transferring pictures or designs printed on specially prepared paper to glass, metal, or other material. 2. A picture so transferred; a decal. [French *décalcomanie* : *décalquer*, to transfer by tracing : *dé-*, from, from Latin *dē-* + *calquer*, to trace, from Italian *calcare*, to trace, trample, from Latin, to tread, from *calx* (stem *calc-*), heel (see **calk**) + *manie*, madness, from Late Latin *mania*, MANIA (from its mid-19th-century popularity).]

de·ca·les·cence (dē′kə-lĕs′əns) *n.* In a metal being heated, a sudden slowing in the rate of temperature increase as a result of an endothermic change in crystal structure. [DE- + Latin *calescere*, to become warm, from *calēre*, to be warm.] —**de·ca·les·cent** *adj.*

dec·a·li·ter, dek·a·li·ter (dĕk′ə-lē′tər) *n.* Ten liters.

Dec·a·logue (dĕk′ə-lôg′, -lŏg′) *n.* Also **Dec·a·log, dec·a·logue, dec·a·log.** The **Ten Commandments** (*see*). [Middle English *decalog*, from Old French *decalogue*, from Late Latin *decalogus*, from Greek *dekalogos* : DECA- + *logos*, speech, word.]

dec·a·me·ter, dek·a·me·ter (dĕk′ə-mē′tər) *n. Abbr.* **dam** Ten meters. [DECA- + METER.]

de·camp (dĭ-kămp′) *intr.v.* **-camped, -camping, -camps.** 1. To depart from a camping ground; break camp. 2. To depart secretly or suddenly; run away. [French *décamper*, from Old French *descamper* : *des-*, from Latin *dē-* (reversal) + *camper*, to camp, from *camp*, CAMP.] —**de·camp·ment** *n.*

dec·a·nal (dĕk′ə-nəl, dĭ-kā′nəl) *adj.* 1. Of or pertaining to a dean or deanery. 2. On the south side of a cathedral choir. [Late Latin *decānus*, DEAN.] —**dec·a·nal·ly** *adv.*

dec·ane (dĕk′ān′) *n.* 1. A straight-chain liquid hydrocarbon, $C_{10}H_{22}$, of the alkane series. Also called "normal decane." 2. Any of various isomeric liquid alkanes with the formula $C_{10}H_{22}$. [DEC(A)- + -ANE.]

dec·ane·di·o·ic acid (dĕk′ān-dī-ō′ĭc) *n. Chemistry.* **Sebacic acid** (*see*). [DECANE + DI- + -OIC.]

dec·a·no·ic acid (dĕk′ə-nō′ĭk) *n. Chemistry.* **Capric acid** (*see*). [DECAN(E) + -OIC.]

de·cant (dĭ-kănt′) *tr.v.* **-canted, -canting, -cants.** 1. To pour off (wine, for example) without disturbing the sediment. 2. To pour (a liquid) from one container into another. 3. *Informal.* To transfer (offices, for example) from one location to another. [Medieval Latin *dēcanthāre* : Latin *dē-*, from + *canthus*, rim of a vessel, from Latin, rim of a wheel, tire.] —**de·can·ta·tion** *n.*

de·cant·er (dĭ-kăn′tər) *n.* 1. A decorative bottle used for serving wine or other drinks. 2. A vessel used for decanting.

de·cap·i·tate (dĭ-kăp′ə-tāt′) *tr.v.* **-tated, -tating, -tates.** To cut off the head of; behead. [Late Latin *dēcapitāre* : Latin *dē-* (removal) + *caput*, head.] —**de·cap·i·ta·tion** *n.* —**de·cap·i·ta·tor** *n.*

dec·a·pod (dĕk′ə-pŏd′) *n.* 1. Any crustacean of the order Decapoda, such as a crab, lobster, or shrimp, characteristically having five pairs of walking legs, each pair joined to a segment of the thorax. 2. A cephalopod mollusk, such as a squid or cuttlefish, having ten armlike tentacles. —*adj.* Of or pertaining to the Decapoda or a decapod. [New Latin *Decapoda*, "the ten-footed ones" : DECA- + -POD.] —**de·cap·o·dal** (dĭ-kăp′ə-dəl), **de·cap·o·dan, de·cap·o·dous** *adj.*

De·cap·o·lis (dĭ-kăp′ə-lĭs) A confederacy of 10 originally Greek cities, including Damascus, in the northeastern part of ancient Palestine, established in 63 or 62 B.C. and governed by Rome. [Greek *Dekapolis* : DECA- + *polis*, city.]

de·car·bon·ate (dē-kär′bə-nāt′) *tr.v.* **-ated, -ating, -ates.** To remove carbon dioxide or carbonic acid from —**de·car·bon·a·tion** *n.*

de·car·bon·ize (dē-kär′bə-nīz′) *tr.v.* **-ized, -izing, -izes.** To remove carbon from. —**de·car·bon·i·za·tion** *n.* —**de·car·bon·iz·er** *n.*

de·car·box·y·late (dē-kär-bŏk′sə-lāt′) *v.* **-ated, -ating, -ates.** *Chemistry.* —*tr.* To remove a carboxyl group (−COOH) from (a chemical compound), usually with replacement by hydrogen. —*intr.* To lose a carboxyl group. —**de·car·box·y·la·tion** *n.*

dec·are, dek·are (dĕk′âr′, -är′) *n.* A metric unit of area equal to 10 ares, or 0.2471 acre. [French *décare* : DECA- + ARE.]

dec·a·stere, dek·a·stere (dĕk′ə-stîr′) *n.* Ten steres.

dec·a·syl·la·ble (dĕk′ə-sĭl′ə-bəl) *n.* A word or line of verse having ten syllables. —**dec·a·syl·lab·ic** (dĕk′ə-sə-lăb′ĭk) *adj.*

dec·ath·lon (dĭ-kăth′lən, -lŏn′) *n.* An athletic contest in which contestants participate in ten different events. [French *décathlon* : DECA- + Greek *athlon*, contest (see **athlete**).] —**dec·ath·lete** *n.*

De·ca·tur (dĭ-kā′tər), **Stephen** (1779–1820). U.S. naval officer. He led daring naval missions in the Tripolitan War (1801–05), in the War of 1812 (1812–15), and against the Barbary pirates (1815), and is remembered for his toast, " . . . our country, right or wrong" (1816). He was killed in a duel.

de·cay (dĭ-kā′) *v.* **-cayed, -caying, -cays.** —*intr.* 1. *Biology.* To decompose; rot. 2. *Physics.* To disintegrate or diminish in magnitude. Used of such effects as radioactivity, phosphorescence, and magnetism. 3. *Aerospace.* To decrease in orbit. Used of an artificial satellite. 4. To become a ruin; fall into ruin. 5. *Pathology.* To decline in health or vigor; waste away. 6. To decline from a state of normality, excellence, or prosperity. —*tr.* To cause to decay. —*n.* 1. a. The destruction or decomposition of organic matter as a result of bacterial or fungal action; rot. b. Decaying matter. 2. *Physics.* a. A reduction in or falling away of an effect such as radioactivity. b. A process in which an atomic nucleus disintegrates or emits a particle or gamma ray and transforms into a different nucleus. c. A process in which an elementary particle transforms spontaneously into one or more other particles. Also called "radioactive decay." 3. The decrease in orbital altitude of an artificial satellite owing to conditions such as atmospheric drag. 4. a. A gradual deterioration to an inferior state, as of health or mental capability. b. The state reached in this process. [Middle English *decayen*, from North French *decair*, from Vulgar Latin *dēcadere* (unattested), to fall down, decay : Latin *dē-*, down + *cadere*, to fall.]
Synonyms: crumble, decompose, disintegrate, putrefy, rot, spoil.

decay chain *n.* **Radioactive series** (*see*).

Dec·can¹ or **Dek·kan** (dĕk′ən). India south of the Narmada River. Its population is mostly Dravidian.

Deccan², the. The central plateau of southern India, bounded by the Eastern and Western Ghats. It is an ancient rock shield, and its fertile volcanic soils produce cotton and tea.

decd. deceased.

de·cease (dĭ-sēs′) *intr.v.* **-ceased, -ceasing, -ceases.** To die. —*n.* Death. [Middle English *decesen*, to die, from *deces*, death, from Old French, from Latin *dēcessus*, departure, death, from the past participle of *dēcēdere*, to depart : *dē-*, away + *cēdere*, to go.]

de·ceased (dĭ-sēst′) *adj. Abbr.* **dec., decd.** No longer living; dead. —See Usage note at **dead.** —*n.* A dead person or persons. Preceded by *the.*

de·ce·dent (dĭ-sē′dənt) *n. Law.* A deceased person. [Latin *dēcēdēns* (stem *dēcēdent-*), present participle of *dēcēdere*, to die, DECEASE.]

de·ceit (dĭ-sēt′) *n.* 1. An act of deceiving; misrepresentation; deception. 2. A stratagem; a trick; a wile. 3. A tendency to deceive or habit of deceiving; falseness; deceitfulness. [Middle English *deceit(e)*, from Old French, from Latin *dēcepta*, feminine of *dēceptus*, past participle of *dēcipere*, DECEIVE.]

de·ceit·ful (dĭ-sēt′fəl) *adj.* 1. Given to cheating or deceiving. 2. Misleading; deceptive. —See Synonyms at **dishonest.** —**de·ceit·ful·ly** *adv.* —**de·ceit·ful·ness** *n.*

de·ceive (dĭ-sēv′) *v.* **-ceived, -ceiving, -ceives.** —*tr.* 1. To trick into believing something false; delude; mislead. 2. *Archaic.* To catch by guile; ensnare. —*intr.* To practice deceit. [Middle English *deceiven*, from Old French *deceivre, decevoir*, from Latin *dēcipere*, to take in, deceive : *dē-* (pejorative) + *capere*, to take, seize.] —**de·ceiv·a·bil·i·ty** *n.* —**de·ceiv·a·ble** *adj.* —**de·ceiv·a·bly** *adv.* —**de·ceiv·er** *n.* —**de·ceiv·ing·ly** *adv.*
Synonyms: bamboozle, beguile, betray, delude, double-cross, dupe, fool, hoodwink, mislead, outwit.

de·cel·er·ate (dē-sĕl′ə-rāt′) *v.* **-ated, -ating, -ates.** —*tr.* 1. To decrease the velocity of. 2. To cause (a process, such as a chemical reaction) to slow down. —*intr.* 1. To decrease in velocity. 2. To be slowed down. [DE- + (AC)CELERATE.] —**de·cel·er·a·tor** *n.*

de·cel·er·a·tion (dē-sĕl′ə-rā′shən) *n.* Decrease in velocity.

de·cel·er·om·e·ter (dē-sĕl′ə-rŏm′ə-tər) *n.* Any instrument used to measure decrease in velocity. [DECELER(ATE) + -METER.]

de·cel·er·on (dē-sĕl′ə-rŏn′) *n.* An aileron speed brake used primarily on jet aircraft. [*deceler*ation + *aileron*.]

De·cem·ber (dĭ-sĕm′bər) *n. Abbr.* **Dec., D.** The 12th and last month of the year according to the Gregorian calendar. December has 31 days. See feature at **calendar.** [Middle English *decembre*, from Old French, from Latin *December*, "the tenth month," from *decem*, ten.]

De·cem·brist (dĭ-sĕm′brĭst) *n.* Any of the conspirators or participants in the attempted overthrow of Czar Nicholas I of Russia in December, 1825.

de·cem·vir (dĭ-sĕm′vər) *n., pl.* **-virs** or **-viri** (-və-rī′). A member of a body of ten Roman magistrates; especially, a member of either of two such bodies appointed in 451 and 450 B.C. to draw up a code of laws. 2. A member of any commission or governing body that has ten members. [Middle English, from Latin, singular of *decemvirī*, from *decem virī*, ten men : *decem*, ten + *virī*, plural of *vir*, man.] —**de·cem·vi·ral** *adj.* —**de·cem·vi·rate** *n.*

de·cen·a·ry, de·cen·na·ry (dĭ-sĕn′ə-rē) *adj.* Of or pertaining to a tithing. —*n., pl.* **decenaries.** Also **de·cen·na·ry.** A tithing. [Middle English *decennare*, tithing man, from Medieval Latin *decennārius*, from *decenna*, tithing from Latin *decem*, ten.]

de·cen·cy (dē′sən-sē) *n., pl.* **-cies.** 1. The state or condition of being decent; propriety. 2. Conformity to prevailing standards of propriety or modesty. 3. **decencies.** The things considered necessary for leading a decent life. 4. **decencies.** The proprieties.

de·cen·na·ry¹ (dĭ-sĕn′ə-rē) *adj.* Pertaining to a ten-year period. —*n., pl.* **decennaries.** A decennium; a decade. [Latin *decennis*, of ten years. See **decennium.**]

decennary². Variant of **decenary.**

de·cen·ni·al (dĭ-sĕn′ē-əl) *adj.* 1. Pertaining to or lasting for ten years. 2. Occurring every ten years. —*n.* 1. An anniversary celebrated every ten years. 2. The celebration of such an anniversary. [Latin *decennium*, DECENNIUM.] —**de·cen·ni·al·ly** *adv.*

de·cen·ni·um (dĭ-sĕn′ē-əm) *n., pl.* **-niums** or **-cennia** (-sĕn′ē-ə). A period of ten years; a decade. [Latin, from *decennis*, of ten years : *decem*, ten + *annus*, year.]

de·cent (dē′sənt) *adj.* **1.** Honest and respectable; conforming to recognized standards of morality and propriety. **2.** Proper; fitting. **3.** Free from indelicacy; modest. **4.** Adequate; passable: *a decent salary.* **5.** Kind; obliging; generous. **6.** *Informal.* Properly or modestly dressed. [Latin *decēns* (stem *decent-*), present participle of *decēre,* to be fitting, suit.] **—de·cent·ly** *adv.* **—de·cent·ness** *n.*

de·cen·tral·ize (dē-sĕn′trə-līz′) *v.* **-ized, -izing, -izes.** *—tr.* **1.** To distribute the administrative functions or powers of (a central authority) among regional authorities. **2.** To cause to withdraw from an area of concentration: *decentralize an industry.* *—intr.* To disperse across a greater area or range of authorities. **—de·cen·tral·i·za·tion** *n.*

de·cep·tion (dĭ-sĕp′shən) *n.* **1.** An act of deceiving; the use of deceit. **2.** The fact or state of being deceived. **3.** An act intended to deceive; a trick; a ruse. [Middle English *decepcioun,* from Old French *deception,* from Late Latin *dēceptiō* (stem *dēceptiōn-*), from Latin *dēcipere* (past participle *dēceptus*), DECEIVE.]

de·cep·tive (dĭ-sĕp′tĭv) *adj.* **1.** Intended or tending to deceive. **2.** Likely to confuse; misleading. **—de·cep·tive·ly** *adv.* **—de·cep·tive·ness** *n.*

de·cer·e·brate (dē-sĕr′ə-brāt′) *tr.v.* **-brated, -brating, -brates.** To eliminate the cerebral functions of (an experimental animal) by removing a large part of the brain or cutting across the brain below the cerebrum. [DE- + CEREBR- + -ATE.] **—de·cer·e·bra·tion** *n.*

deci- *prefix. Symbol* **d** Indicates one-tenth; for example, **decimeter.** [French *déci-,* from Latin *decimus,* tenth, from *decem,* ten.]

dec·i·are (dĕs′ē-âr′, -är′) *n.* One-tenth (10^{-1}) of an are.

de·ci·bel (dĕs′ĭ-bəl) *n. Abbr.* **dB, db** A unit used to express relative difference in power, usually between acoustic or electric signals, equal to ten times the common logarithm of the ratio of the two levels. [DECI- + BEL.]

de·cide (dĭ-sīd′) *v.* **-cided, -ciding, -cides.** *—tr.* **1.** To conclude or settle: *He decided which course to follow.* **2.** To influence or determine the conclusion of: *Sheer firepower decided the battle.* **3.** To cause to make a decision: *Your nagging decided me to buy it.* *—intr.* **1.** To pronounce a judgment; announce a verdict. Often used with *for* or *against.* **2.** To make up one's mind. [Middle English *deciden,* from Old French *decider,* from Latin *dēcīdere,* to cut off, determine : *dē-,* off + *cædere,* to cut.] **—de·cid·a·ble** *adj.* **—de·cid·er** *n.*

Synonyms: *conclude, determine, resolve, rule, settle.*

de·cid·ed (dĭ-sī′dĭd) *adj.* **1.** Unquestionable; definite. **2.** Resolute; unhesitating. **—de·cid·ed·ly** *adv.* **—de·cid·ed·ness** *n.*

Usage: *Decided* and *decisive* both have the sense "unquestionable" or "resolute." But *decided* usually means simply "definite," whereas *decisive* emphasizes the notion of decision-making or settling an issue beyond doubt. If one has *a decided advantage,* one is in a very strong position; but if one has a *decisive advantage,* then one is in the strongest possible position and cannot lose.

de·cid·er (dĭ-sī′dər) *n.* In a contest, a round that determines the winner.

de·cid·ing (dĭ-sī′dĭng) *adj.* Settling or able to settle a matter in dispute or doubt; decisive; conclusive: *the deciding vote.*

de·cid·u·a (dĭ-sĭj′o͞o-ə, -sĭd′yo͞o-ə) *n.* A mucous membrane that lines the uterus, modified during pregnancy and cast off during menstruation or at parturition. [New Latin *(membrana) decidua,* "(membrane) that falls off," from Latin *dēcidua,* feminine of *dēciduus,* DECIDUOUS.] **—de·cid·u·al** *adj.*

de·cid·u·ate (dĭ-sĭj′o͞o-ĭt, -sĭd′yo͞o-ĭt) *adj.* **1.** Characterized by or having a decidua. **2.** Characterized by shedding.

de·cid·u·ous (dĭ-sĭj′o͞o-əs, -sĭd′yo͞o-əs) *adj.* **1.** Falling off or shed at a specific season or stage of growth: *deciduous antlers; deciduous leaves.* **2.** Shedding or losing foliage at the end of the growing season: *deciduous trees.* Compare **evergreen. 3.** Not lasting; temporary. [Latin *dēciduus,* from *dēcidere,* to fall off : *dē-,* off + *cadere,* to fall.] **—de·cid·u·ous·ly** *adv.* **—de·cid·u·ous·ness** *n.*

dec·i·gram (dĕs′ĭ-grăm′) *n. Abbr.* **dg** One-tenth (10^{-1}) of a gram.

dec·i·li·ter (dĕs′ə-lē′tər) *n. Abbr.* **dl** One-tenth (10^{-1}) of a liter.

de·cil·lion (dĭ-sĭl′yən) *n.* **1.** The cardinal number represented by 1 followed by 33 zeros, usually written 10^{33}. **2.** *British.* The cardinal number represented by 1 followed by 60 zeros, usually written 10^{60}. [Latin *decem,* ten + (M)ILLION.] **—de·cil·lion** *adj.*

de·cil·lionth (dĭ-sĭl′yənth) *n.* **1.** The ordinal number decillion in a series. **2.** Any of a decillion equal parts. **—de·cil·lionth** *adj. & adv.*

dec·i·mal (dĕs′ə-məl) *n.* **1.** A linear array of integers that represents a fraction, every **decimal place** *(see)* indicating a multiple of a positive or negative power of 10; for example, the decimal .1 = $^1/_{10}$, .003 = $^3/_{1000}$. Also called "decimal fraction." **2.** Any number written using base 10. In this sense, also called "decimal number."

~adj. **1.** Expressed or expressible as a decimal. **2. a.** Based on ten. **b.** Numbered or ordered by tens. **3.** Loosely, not integral; fractional. [Medieval Latin *decimālis,* of tithes, from Latin *decimus,* tenth, from *decem,* ten.] **—dec·i·mal·ly** *adv.*

decimal currency *n.* A system of currency in which the monetary units are divided into or multiplied by further units of 10 or 100.

dec·i·mal·ize (dĕs′ə-mə-līz′) *tr.v.* **-ized, -izing, -izes.** To change to a decimal system. **—dec·i·mal·i·za·tion** *n.*

decimal place *n.* The position of a digit to the right of a decimal point, usually identified by successive ascending ordinal numbers with the digit immediately to the right of the decimal point being first. For example, in the decimal number 1.021, 2 is in the second decimal place.

decimal point *n.* A period, centered dot, or, in some countries, a comma, placed to the left of a decimal fraction. Also called "radix point."

decimal system *n.* **1.** A number system using the base 10. **2.** A measurement system in which all derived units are multiples of ten of basic units. **3.** A classification system using decimals.

dec·i·mate (dĕs′ĭ-māt′) *tr.v.* **-mated, -mating, -mates. 1.** To destroy or kill a large part of. **2. a.** To destroy or kill a tenth of. **b.** Especially in the ancient Roman army, to select by lot and kill one in every ten of, as a punishment for mutiny or cowardice: *decimate a cohort.* [Latin *decimāre,* from *decimus,* tenth, from *decem,* ten.] **—dec·i·ma·tion** *n.* **—dec·i·ma·tor** *n.*

Usage: The earlier meaning of *decimate* is, literally, "to kill one tenth of," but the word is now generally used to mean "to kill many of." This change in usage is still criticized by purists.

dec·i·me·ter (dĕs′ə-mē′tər) *n. Abbr.* **dm** One-tenth (10^{-1}) of a meter. [French *décimètre* : DECI- + METER.]

de·ci·pher (dĭ-sī′fər) *tr.v.* **-phered, -phering, -phers. 1.** To read or interpret (something ambiguous, obscure, or illegible). **2.** To convert from a code or cipher to plain text; decode. [DE- (reversal) + CIPHER (after Old French *deschiffrer*).] **—de·ci·pher·a·ble** *adj.* **—de·ci·pher·er** *n.* **—de·ci·pher·ment** *n.*

de·ci·sion (dĭ-sĭzh′ən) *n.* **1.** The passing of judgment on an issue under consideration. **2.** The act of reaching a conclusion or making up one's mind. **3.** A conclusion or judgment reached or pronounced; a verdict. **4.** Firmness of character or action; determination. **5.** *Boxing.* A victory won on points when no knockout has occurred. [Middle English *decisioun,* from Old French *decision,* from Latin *dēcīsiō* (stem *dēcīsiōn-*), from *dēcīdere,* DECIDE.]

de·ci·sion-mak·er (dĭ-sĭzh′ən-mā′kər) *n.* One who has the responsibility for making decisions; especially, an important administrator in business or government. **—de·ci·sion-mak·ing** *n. & adj.*

de·ci·sive (dĭ-sī′sĭv) *adj.* **1.** Able to settle a matter in dispute or doubt; conclusive. **2.** Characterized by firm decision; resolute; determined. **3.** Beyond doubt; unquestionable. —See Usage note at **decided. —de·ci·sive·ly** *adv.* **—de·ci·sive·ness** *n.*

deck[1] (dĕk) *n. Abbr.* **dk. 1.** *Nautical.* **a.** A platform extending horizontally from one side of a ship to the other. **b.** The space between two such platforms. **2.** Any similar platform or surface, as on a bus. **3.** The roadway on a bridge. **4.** A **tape deck** *(see).* **5.** *Informal.* The floor or ground. **6. a.** A pack of playing cards. **b.** *Computer Science.* A pile of punched computer cards. **7.** A packet of narcotic drugs. **—clear the deck.** To prepare for action. **—hit the deck.** *Slang.* **1.** To fall or drop to the floor or ground. **2.** To get out of bed. **3.** To prepare for action. **—on deck.** *Slang.* **1.** On hand; present. **2.** Waiting to take one's turn.

~tr.v. **decked, decking, decks.** To furnish with a deck. [Middle English *dekke,* from Middle Dutch *dec, decke,* roof, covering.]

deck[2] *tr.v.* **decked, decking, decks.** To clothe with finery; decorate; adorn. Often used with *out: decked out for a party.* [Middle Dutch *dekken,* to cover.]

deck chair *n.* A folding chair, usually with arms and a leg rest, found on the decks of passenger ships and now used generally for sitting outdoors.

deck hand *n.* A member of a ship's crew who works on deck.

deck·house (dĕk′hous′) *n.* A superstructure on the upper deck of a ship.

deck·le, deck·el (dĕk′əl) *n.* **1.** A frame used in making paper by hand to form paper pulp into sheets of a desired size. **2.** A deckle edge. **3.** A device for trimming mechanically made paper to the desired width. [German *Deckel,* diminutive of *Decke,* "a cover," from Old High German *decchī,* from *decchen,* to cover.]

deckle edge *n.* **1.** The rough, crimped edge of handmade paper formed in a deckle. Also called "featheredge." **2.** A similar edge produced by a machine. **—deck·le-edged** (dĕk′əl-ĕjd′) *adj.*

deck tennis *n.* A game in which a small ring or quoit is tossed back and forth over a net.

decl. declension.

de·claim (dĭ-klām′) *v.* **-claimed, -claiming, -claims.** *—intr.* **1.** To deliver an elocutionary recitation. **2.** To speak loudly and vehemently; inveigh. Used with *against.* *—tr.* To utter or recite with rhetorical effect. [Middle English *declamen,* from Latin *dēclāmāre* : *dē-* (intensive) + *clāmāre,* to cry out.] **—de·claim·er** *n.*

dec·la·ma·tion (dĕk′lə-mā′shən) *n.* **1.** An elocutionary recitation. **2. a.** Vehement oratory. **b.** A harangue; a tirade. **3. a.** Correct and expressive delivery of words to a musical accompaniment. **b.** The art or action of reading or reciting a literary text with the proper intonation and expression. [Middle English *declamacioun,* from Latin *dēclāmātiō* (stem *dēclāmātiōn-*), from *dēclāmāre,* DECLAIM.]

de·clam·a·to·ry (dĭ-klăm′ə-tôr′ē, -tōr′ē) *adj.* **1.** Having the quality of a declamation; loudly demanding attention. **2.** Pretentiously rhetorical; meaninglessly bombastic. **—de·clam·a·to·ri·ly** *adv.*

de·clar·a·ble (dĭ-klâr′ə-bəl) *adj.* Such as can or should be declared, as for payment of customs duty.

de·clar·ant (dĭ-klâr′ənt) *n.* **1.** *Law.* One making a declaration. **2.** One who has signed a declaration of intention of becoming a U.S. citizen.

dec·la·ra·tion (dĕk′lə-rā′shən) *n. Abbr.* **dec. 1.** An explicit or formal statement or announcement. **2.** Such a statement in written form. **3.** The act or process of declaring. **4.** A statement of taxable goods or of properties subject to duty. Used especially in the phrase *a customs declaration.* **5.** *Law.* **a.** Formerly, a formal statement by a plaintiff specifying the facts and circumstances constituting the cause of action. **b.** An unsworn statement of facts that may be

PRONUNCIATION KEY

ă, pat; **ā**, pay; **âr**, care;
ä, father, are; **b**, bib;
ch, church; **d**, deed; **ĕ**, pet;
ē, be; **f**, fife; **g**, gag; **h**, hat;
hw, which; **ĭ**, pit; **ī**, pie;
îr, pier; **j**, judge; **k**, kick;
l, lid, needle; **m**, mum;
n, no, sudden; **ng**, thing;
ŏ, pot; **ō**, toe; **ô**, paw, for;
oi, noise; **ou**, out; **o͝o**, book;
o͞o, boot; **p**, pop; **r**, roar;
s, sauce; **sh**, ship, dish;
t, tight; **th**, thin, path;
th, this, bathe; **ŭ**, cut; **ûr**, fur;
v, valve; **w**, with; **y**, yes;
z, zebra, size; **zh**, vision;
ə, about, item, edible, gallop, circus, peaceful

IN FOREIGN WORDS:

à, *Fr.* ami; **œ**, *Fr.* feu, *Ger.* schön; **ü**, *Fr.* tu, *Ger.* über; **KH**, *Ger.* ich, *Scot.* loch; **N**, *Fr.* bon; **y′**, *Fr.* Compiègne

STRESS MARKS:

Primary stress: ′
in·cite′ (ĭn-sīt′)
Secondary stress: ′
in′sight′ (ĭn′sīt′)

admissible as evidence. **6.** *Card Games.* **a.** A bid, especially the final bid of a hand. **b.** An announcement by a player of points made. **7.** *Cricket.* A decision by the captain of the batting side to end an innings before all the batsmen are out.

Declaration of Independence *n.* **1.** A proclamation by the Second Continental Congress declaring the 13 American colonies politically independent from Great Britain, formally adopted on July 4, 1776. **2.** The document in which this proclamation is recorded.

de·clar·a·tive (dĭ-klâr′ə-tĭv) *adj.* Serving to declare or state. **—de·clar·a·tive·ly** *adv.*

de·clar·a·to·ry (dĭ-klâr′ə-tôr′ē, -tōr′ē) *adj.* **1.** Declarative. **2.** *Law.* Explaining a point of law or setting out the rights of the parties.

de·clare (dĭ-klâr′) *v.* **-clared, -claring, -clares.** *—tr.* **1.** To bring into being by announcing officially or formally; decree: *declare war; declare an amnesty.* **2.** To admit to: *declare an interest.* **3.** To pronounce as being in a specified condition: *I declared him fit and well.* **4.** To state with emphasis or authority; affirm: *declare one's loyalty.* **5.** To reveal or manifest; prove: *His face declares his guilt.* **6.** To make a full statement of (dutiable goods, for example). **7.** To announce (a dividend) as payable. **8.** *Bridge.* To designate (a trump suit or no-trump) with the final bid of a hand. **9.** In various card games: **a.** To reveal (cards). **b.** To announce (points scored by such cards). *—intr.* **1.** To make a declaration. **2.** To proclaim one's choice, opinion, or resolution; act. Used with *for* or *against.* **3.** *Cricket.* To decide to end an innings before all one's batsmen are out. —See Synonyms at **assert.** [Middle English *declaren,* from Old French *declarer,* from Latin *dēclārāre,* to make clear : *dē-* (intensive) + *clārāre,* to make clear, from *clārus,* clear.] **—de·clar·ed·ly** *adv.* **—de·clar·er** *n.*

de·class (dē-klăs′, -kläs′) *tr.v.* **-classed, -classing, -classes.** To lower in class or standing; degrade; debase.

dé·clas·sé (dā-klă-sā′) *adj.* Also **de·classed** (dē-klăst′, -kläst′). Lowered in social standing. [French, from *déclasser,* to lower in class : *dé-,* from Latin *dē-,* down + *classe,* CLASS.]

de·clas·si·fy (dē-klăs′ə-fī′) *tr.v.* **-fied, -fying, -fies.** To remove official security classification from (information, documents, and the like); make (information) no longer secret. **—de·clas·si·fi·a·ble** *adj.* **—de·clas·si·fi·ca·tion** *n.*

de·clen·sion (dĭ-klĕn′shən) *n.* **1.** *Abbr.* **dec., decl.** *Linguistics.* **a.** In certain languages, the inflection of nouns, pronouns, and adjectives in such categories as case, number, and gender. **b.** A class of nouns, pronouns, and adjectives with the same or a similar system of inflections, such as the first declension in Latin. Compare **conjugation.** **2.** A descending slope; a descent. **3.** A decline or decrease; deterioration: *empires in their declension.* **4.** A deviation, as from a standard or practice. [Learned respelling of Middle English *declinson,* from Old French *declinaison,* from Late Latin *dēclīnātiō* (stem *dēclīnātiōn-*), grammatical declension, from Latin, DECLINATION.] **—de·clen·sion·al** *adj.*

dec·li·na·tion (dĕk′lə-nā′shən) *n. Abbr.* **dec.** **1.** A sloping or bending downward. **2.** A falling off, especially from prosperity or vigor; a decline. **3.** A deviation, as from a specific direction or standard. **4.** A refusal to accept. **5. Magnetic declination** *(see).* **6.** *Astronomy. Symbol* δ The angular distance to a point on the celestial sphere, measured north or south from the celestial equator along the **hour circle** *(see).* [Middle English *declinacioun,* from Old French *declination,* from Latin *dēclīnātiō* (stem *dēclīnātiōn-*), from *dēclīnāre,* DECLINE.] **—dec·li·na·tion·al** *adj.*

de·cli·na·to·ry (dĭ-klī′nə-tôr′ē, -tōr′ē) *adj.* Involving or conveying declination; expressing refusal.

de·cline (dĭ-klīn′) *v.* **-clined, -clining, -clines.** *—intr.* **1.** To refuse to do or accept something. **2.** To slope downward. **3.** To deteriorate gradually; fail. **4.** To draw to a gradual close; wane. **5.** *Linguistics.* To have inflected forms. Used of nouns, pronouns, and adjectives in certain languages. *—tr.* **1.** To refuse (an offer or request, for example). **2.** To cause to slope downward. **3.** *Linguistics.* In certain languages, to give the inflected forms of (a noun, pronoun, or adjective). Compare **conjugate.** —See Synonyms at **refuse.**
~n. **1.** The process or result of declining; especially, gradual deterioration. **2.** A downward movement. **3.** The period when something is tending toward an end. **4.** A downward slope. **5.** Any disease, such as tuberculosis, that gradually weakens or wastes the body or a bodily part. [Middle English *declinen,* from Old French *decliner,* from Latin *dēclīnāre,* to turn aside, go down, inflect grammatically : *dē-,* away, aside + *clīnāre,* to bend.] **—de·clin·a·ble** *adj.* **—de·clin·er** *n.*

dec·li·nom·e·ter (dĕk′lə-nŏm′ə-tər) *n.* An instrument for measuring magnetic declination. [DECLIN(ATION) + -METER.]

de·cliv·i·tous (dĭ-klĭv′ə-təs) *adj.* Rather steep.

de·cliv·i·ty (dĭ-klĭv′ə-tē) *n., pl.* **-ties.** A descending slope, as of a hill. Compare **acclivity.** [Latin *dēclīvitās,* from *dēclīvis,* sloping down : *dē-,* down + *clīvus,* a slope.]

de·clutch (dē′klŭch′, dĭ-klŭch′) *intr.v.* **-clutched, -clutching, -clutches.** To disengage the clutch of an engine.

de·coct (dĭ-kŏkt′) *tr.v.* **-cocted, -cocting, -cocts.** **1. a.** To extract the flavor, essence, or other desired substance of by boiling. **b.** To steep in hot water. **2.** To concentrate by boiling; boil down. [Middle English *decocten,* from Latin *dēcoquere* (past participle *dēcoctus*), to boil to the dregs : *dē-* (intensive) + *coquere,* to cook.] **—de·coc·tion** *n.*

de·code (dē-kōd′) *tr.v.* **-coded, -coding, -codes.** To convert from code into plain, understandable language; decipher. **—de·cod·er** *n.*

de·coke (dē′kōk′, dĭ-kōk′) *tr.v. British.* To decarbonize (an engine).
~n. An act of decarbonizing.

de·col·late¹ (dĭ-kŏl′āt′) *tr.v.* **-lated, -lating, -lates.** To behead. [Latin *decollāre, decollāt-* : *de-,* off + *collum,* neck.]

de·col·late² (dĕk′ə-lāt′, dē-kŏ′lāt′) *tr.v.* **-lated, -lating, -lates.** To separate out into individual copies. Used of documents produced in multiple copies. [DE- + COLLATE.]

dé·colle·tage (dā′kôl-täzh′) *n.* **1.** A low neckline on a garment. **2.** A décolleté garment. [French, from *décolleter.* See **décolleté.**]

dé·colle·té (dā′kôl-tā′) *adj.* **1.** Having a low neckline: *a décolleté dress.* **2.** Wearing a garment with a low neckline. [French, past participle of *décolleter,* to uncover the neck, cut a low neckline : *dé-* (removal) + *collet,* collar, diminutive of *col,* neck, collar, from Old French, from Latin *collum,* neck.]

de·col·o·nize (dē-kŏl′ə-nīz′) *tr.v.* **-nized, -nizing, -nizes.** To give independence to (a former colony). **—de·col·o·ni·za·tion** *n.*

de·col·or (dē-kŭl′ər) *tr.v.* **-ored, -oring, -ors.** To deprive of color; bleach. **—de·col·or·a·tion** *n.*

de·col·or·ant (dē-kŭl′ər-ənt) *adj.* Able to remove color or to bleach.
~n. A bleaching agent.

de·col·or·ize (dē-kŭl′ər-īz′) *tr.v.* **-ized, -izing, -izes.** To decolor. **—de·col·or·i·za·tion** *n.* **—de·col·or·iz·er** *n.*

de·com·pose (dē′kəm-pōz′) *v.* **-posed, -posing, -poses.** *—tr.* **1.** To separate into component parts or basic elements. **2.** To cause to rot. *—intr.* **1.** To break down into component parts; disintegrate. **2.** To break down into constituent parts by the action of bacteria or decay; putrefy. Used of organic matter. —See Synonyms at **decay.** [French *décomposer* : *dé-* (reversal) + *composer,* to COMPOSE, from Old French.] **—de·com·pos·a·ble** *adj.*

de·com·pos·er (dē′kəm-pōz′ər) *n.* Something that decomposes or causes decomposition; especially, an organism in an ecological community, such as a bacterium or fungus, that breaks down dead organic matter.

de·com·po·si·tion (dē-kŏm′pə-zĭsh′ən) *n.* The act or result of decomposing; especially: **1.** *Chemistry.* Separation into constituents by chemical reaction. **2.** *Biology.* Organic decay. **3.** *Geology.* Chemical breakdown of rock minerals with the resultant disintegration of the rocks themselves.

de·com·pound¹ (dē′kəm-pound′) *tr.v.* **-pounded, -pounding, -pounds.** **1.** To create (compounded things) by combining various elements.
~adj. **1.** Compounded or consisting of things or parts already compound. **2.** Having or consisting of subdivided or compound leaflets: *a decompound leaf.* [DE- (from) + COMPOUND (noun).]

decompound² *tr.v.* **-pounded, -pounding, -pounds.** To decompose. [DE- (reversal) + COMPOUND (verb).]

de·com·press (dē′kəm-prĕs′) *tr.v.* **-pressed, -pressing, -presses.** **1.** To relieve of pressure. **2.** To bring (a person working in a high pressure environment) back to normal air pressure by means of an air lock or a decompression chamber.

de·com·pres·sion (dē′kəm-prĕsh′ən) *n.* **1.** The act or process of decompressing. **2.** Any surgical procedure used to relieve pressure on an organ or part.

decompression chamber *n.* An apparatus in which the air pressure can be artificially varied for the use of divers and others while they gradually readjust from the high pressure of their working environment to normal pressure.

decompression sickness *n. Pathology.* **Caisson disease** *(see).*

de·con·gest·ant (dē′kən-jĕs′tənt) *adj.* Able to relieve congestion, especially in the nasal passages.
~n. A decongestant drug. [DE- + CONGEST + -ANT.]

de·con·se·crate (dē-kŏn′sə-krāt′) *tr.v.* **-crated, -crating, -crates.** To transfer (a church, for example) legally from religious to lay use or ownership. **—de·con·se·cra·tion** *n.*

de·con·tam·i·nate (dē′kən-tăm′ə-nāt′) *tr.v.* **-nated, -nating, -nates.** **1.** To eliminate contamination in. **2.** To make safe by eliminating poisonous or otherwise harmful substances, such as noxious chemicals or radioactive material. **—de·con·tam·i·nant** *n.* **—de·con·tam·i·na·tion** *n.* **—de·con·tam·i·na·tor** *n.*

de·con·trol (dē′kən-trōl′) *tr.v.* **-trolled, -trolling, -trols.** To free from control, especially from government control.

dé·cor, de·cor (dā′kôr′, dā-kôr′) *n.* **1. a.** A decorative style or scheme, as of a room, home, stage setting, or the like. **b.** The decorations and furnishings of a place. **2.** A stage setting; scenery. [French, from *décorer,* to DECORATE, from Latin *decorāre.*]

dec·o·rate (dĕk′ə-rāt′) *tr.v.* **-rated, -rating, -rates.** **1.** To furnish or adorn with fashionable or beautiful things; embellish; ornament. **2.** To confer a medal or other honor upon; present with a decoration. [Latin *decorāre,* from *decus* (stem *decor-*), ornament.]

dec·o·rat·ed (dĕk′ə-rā′tĭd) *adj. Architecture. Often* **Decorated.** Designating a style of English Gothic architecture of the 13th and 14th centuries, characterized by the use of the **ogee** *(see)* and elaborate tracery and carving.

dec·o·ra·tion (dĕk′ə-rā′shən) *n.* **1.** The act, process, technique, or art of decorating. **2.** An object or group of objects used to decorate; an ornament; an embellishment. **3.** A medal, badge, or other emblem of honor.

Decoration Day *n.* **Memorial Day** *(see).*

dec·o·ra·tive (dĕk′ər-ə-tĭv) *adj.* Serving to decorate; ornamental. **—dec·o·ra·tive·ly** *adv.* **—dec·o·ra·tive·ness** *n.*

decorative arts *pl.n.* The arts or crafts, such as pottery or cabinet-making, that produce objects used as decoration or furnishings.

dec·o·ra·tor (dĕk′ə-rā′tər) *n.* An **interior decorator** *(see).*

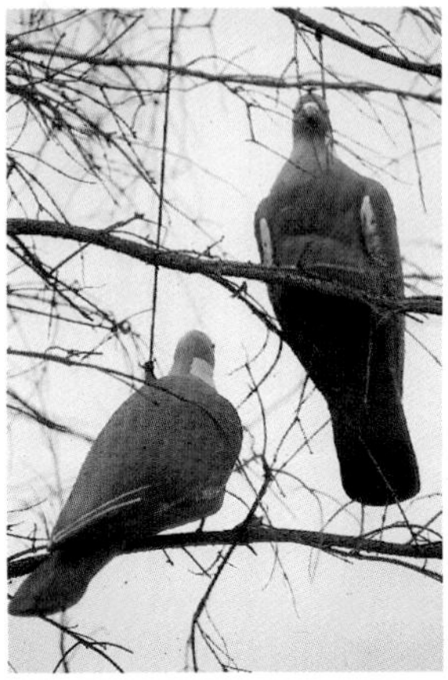

decoy *Two model pigeons hang from wires in a tree. The decoys, which appear to be perching on the branches, fool other birds into thinking that the tree is safe to approach—and lure them within range of the hunter's gun.*

dec·o·rous (dĕk′ər-əs, dĭ-kôr′əs) *adj.* Characterized by or exhibiting decorum; proper. [Latin *decōrus,* from *decor,* seemliness, elegance, beauty.] **—dec·o·rous·ly** *adv.* **—dec·o·rous·ness** *n.*

de·cor·ti·cate (dĭ-kôr′tĭ-kāt′) *tr.v.* **-cated, -cating, -cates. 1.** To remove the cortex from (an organ or structure), especially in surgery. **2.** To remove the bark, husk, or outer layer from; strip; peel. [Latin *dēcorticāre* : *dē-* (removal) + *cortex* (stem *cortic-*), bark.] **—de·cor·ti·ca·tion** *n.* **—de·cor·ti·ca·tor** *n.*

de·co·rum (dĭ-kôr′əm, -kōr′-) *n.* Respect for social convention and good manners; propriety. —See Synonyms at **etiquette.** [Latin *decōrum,* from *decōrus,* DECOROUS.]

de·cou·page, dé·cou·page (dā′ko͞o-päzh′) *n.* **1.** The technique of decorating a surface with paper cutouts. **2.** Something produced by decoupage. [French, from Old French *decouper,* to cut out : *de-,* from Latin *dē-,* away + *couper,* to cut, strike, from *coup,* stroke, COUP.]

de·cou·ple (dē-kŭp′əl) *tr.v.* **-pled, -pling, -ples. 1.** *Electronics.* To reduce or eliminate the coupling of circuits or mechanical parts. **2.** *Physics.* To decrease the seismic effects of (an explosion) by having it take place in an underground cavity. **—de·cou·pler** *n.*

de·coy (dē′koi′, dĭ-koi′) *n.* **1.** An enclosed place, such as a pond or a large trap, into which wildfowl are lured for capture. **2.** A living or artificial bird or other animal used to entice game into a trap or within shooting range. **3.** Someone who leads another into danger, deception, or a trap. **4.** Any means used to mislead or lead into danger.
~v. (dĭ-koi′) **decoyed, -coying, -coys.** *—tr.* To lure into danger or a trap; entrap by or as if by a decoy. *—intr.* To be lured by or as if by a decoy; fall into a trap. —See Synonyms at **lure.** [Perhaps from Dutch *de kooi,* "the cage" : *de,* the + *kooi,* cage, from Middle Dutch *cōie,* from Latin *cavea,* from *cavus,* hollow.] **—de·coy·er** *n.*

de·crease (dĭ-krēs′) *v.* **-creased, -creasing, -creases.** *—intr.* To grow or become gradually less or smaller; diminish gradually; dwindle. *—tr.* To cause to grow or become less or smaller; make less; reduce.
~n. (dē′krēs′) *Abbr.* **dec. 1.** The act or process of decreasing, or the resulting condition. **2.** The amount by which something has been reduced. [Middle English *decresen,* from Old French *de(s)creistre* (present stem *decreiss-*), from Vulgar Latin *discrēscere* (unattested), variant of Latin *dēcrēscere* : *dē-* (reversal) + *crēscere,* to grow, increase.] **—de·creas·ing·ly** *adv.*
Synonyms: *abate, diminish, dwindle, lessen, reduce, shrink, subside.*

de·cree (dĭ-krē′) *n.* **1.** An authoritative order having the force of law. **2.** The judgment of a court of equity, admiralty, probate, or divorce. **3.** *Roman Catholic Church.* **a.** A doctrinal or disciplinary act of an ecumenical council. **b.** An administrative act applying or interpreting articles of canon law.
~v. **decreed, -creeing, -crees.** *—tr.* To ordain, establish, or decide by decree. *—intr.* To issue a decree. [Middle English *decre(t),* from Old French, from Latin *dēcrētum,* from *dēcrētus,* past participle of *dēcernere,* to decide : *dē-* (removal) + *cernere,* to sift.] **—de·cree·a·ble** *adj.* **—de·cre·er** *n.*

de·cree-law (dĭ-krē′lô′) *n.* A decree that has the force of a law enacted by a legislature, but usually issued on the sole authority of an absolute ruler or the executive branch of a government.

dec·re·ment (dĕk′rə-mənt) *n.* **1.** The act or process of decreasing or becoming gradually less. **2.** The amount lost by gradual diminution or waste. **3.** *Mathematics.* The amount by which a variable is decreased; a negative increment. **4.** *Physics.* The ratio of the amplitude of an oscillation to the amplitude after one period, used as a measure of damping. [Latin *dēcrēmentum,* from *dēcrēscere,* to DECREASE.]

de·crep·it (dĭ-krĕp′ĭt) *adj.* Weakened by old age, illness, or hard use; broken-down. —See Synonyms at **weak.** [Middle English, from Old French, from Latin *dēcrepitus,* probably "cracked" : *dē-* (intensive) + *crepitus,* past participle of *crepāre,* to crack, creak.] **—de·crep·it·ly** *adv.*

de·crep·i·tate (dĭ-krĕp′ĭ-tāt′) *v.* **-tated, -tating, -tates.** *—tr.* To roast or calcine (crystals or salts) until they emit a crackling sound or until this sound stops. *—intr.* To crackle when roasted. [Medieval Latin *dēcrepitāre* : Latin *dē-* (intensive) + *crepitāre,* frequentative of *crepāre,* to creak, crack.] **—de·crep·i·ta·tion** *n.*

de·crep·i·tude (dĭ-krĕp′ĭ-to͞od′, -tyo͞od′) *n.* The state of being decrepit; weakness; infirmity.

de·cre·scen·do (dē′krə-shĕn′dō) *n., pl.* **-dos.** *Abbr.* **decresc. 1.** A gradual decrease in force or loudness. **2.** A musical passage marked or performed in a decrescendo. Also called "diminuendo."
~adj. Abbr. **decresc.** Gradually diminishing in force or loudness; diminuendo.
~adv. Abbr. **decresc.** With a decrescendo; diminuendo. [Italian, from Latin *dēcrescendum,* gerund of *dēcrēscere,* to DECREASE.]

de·cres·cent (dĭ-krĕs′ənt) *adj.* Decreasing; waning. Said of the moon. Compare **increscent.** [Latin *dēcrescēns* (stem *dēcrescent-*), present participle *dēcrescere,* to DECREASE.]

de·cre·tal (dĭ-krēt′l) *n. Roman Catholic Church.* **1.** A decree; especially, a letter from the pope giving a decision on some point of canon law. **2. Decretals.** The body of papal laws and decrees forming a part of canon law. [Middle English, from Old French, from Medieval Latin *(epistola) dēcrētālis,* (letter) of decree, from Latin *dēcrētum,* DECREE.] **—de·cre·tal** *adj.*

de·cre·tive (dĭ-krē′tĭv) *adj.* Having the force of a decree.

dec·re·to·ry (dĕk′rə-tôr′ē, -tōr′ē) *adj.* Of or resulting from a decree.

de·crim·i·nal·ize (dē-krĭm′ə-nə-līz′) *tr.v.* **-ized, -izing, -izes.** To cause to be no longer illegal; regulate rather than prohibit: *decriminalize the use of marijuana.* **—de·crim·i·nal·i·za·tion** *n.*

de·cry (dĭ-krī′) *tr.v.* **-cried, -crying, -cries. 1.** To belittle or disparage openly; censure. **2.** To depreciate or devalue (currency, for example) by official proclamation or by rumor. [French *décrier,* from Old French *descrier,* "to cry down" : *des-,* from Latin *dē-,* down + *crier,* to CRY.] **—de·cri·er** *n.*
Synonyms: *belittle, depreciate, disparage.*

de·crypt (dĭ-krĭpt′) *tr.v.* **-crypted, -crypting, -crypts.** To decode a cipher, especially without knowledge of the key. [DE- + CRYPT(OGRAM).] **—de·cryp·tion** *n.*

de·cu·bi·tus ulcer (dĭ-kyo͞o′bə-təs) *n. Medicine.* A **bedsore** *(see).* [Latin *dēcubitus,* past participle of *dēcumbere,* to lie down. See **decumbent.**]

de·cum·bent (dĭ-kŭm′bənt) *adj.* **1.** Reclining; lying down or lying flat; prostrate. **2.** *Botany.* Lying or growing along the ground but turning upward at or near the apex: *decumbent stems.* [Latin *dēcumbēns* (stem *dēcumbent-*), present participle of *dēcumbere,* to lie down : *dē-,* down + *cumbere,* to lie.] **—de·cum·bence, de·cum·ben·cy** *n.*

dec·u·ple (dĕk′yə-pəl) *adj.* Ten times as great; tenfold.
~n. A tenfold amount.
~tr. v. **decupled, -cupling, -cuples.** To multiply by ten or increase tenfold. [Middle English, from Old French, from Late Latin *decuplus* : Latin *decem,* ten + *-plus,* -fold.]

dec·u·plet (dĕk′yə-plət) *n.* A set of ten items of the same type. [From DECUPLE, by analogy with *triplet.*]

de·cu·ri·on (dĭ-kyo͝or′ē-ən) *n.* **1.** A commander in the Roman army in charge of ten men, especially in the cavalry. **2.** A member of the senate of a Roman colony or town. **3.** A member of a council in certain Italian towns. [Latin *decuriō* (stem *decuriōn-*), from *decuria,* company of ten, from *decem,* ten.]

de·cur·rent (dĭ-kûr′ənt) *adj. Botany.* Extending downward from the base along a stem: *decurrent leaves.* [Latin *dēcurrēns* (stem *dēcurrent-*), present participle of *dēcurrere,* to run down : *dē-,* down + *currere,* to run.] **—de·cur·rent·ly** *adv.*

dec·u·ry (dĕk′yə-rē) *n., pl.* **-ries. 1.** A division of the Roman army consisting of ten men. **2.** In ancient times, any group of ten men. [Latin *decuria.* See **decurion.**]

de·cus·sate (dĭ-kŭs′āt′) *v.* **-sated, -sating, -sates.** *—tr.* To intersect so as to form an X. *—intr.* To cross each other; intersect.
~adj. **1.** Intersected or crossed in the form of an X. **2.** *Botany.* Arranged on a stem in opposite pairs at right angles to those above or below. [Latin *decussāre* (past participle *decussātus*), from *decussis,* number ten, symbol X, coin worth ten asses : *decem,* ten + *ās,* AS (coin).] **—de·cus·sate·ly** *adv.*

de·cus·sa·tion (dē′kə-sā′shən) *n.* **1.** A crossing in the shape of an X. **2.** *Anatomy.* An X-shaped crossing of nerve fibers connecting corresponding parts on the two sides of the spinal cord or brain.

de·dans (dē′dəns) *n., pl.* **dedans. 1.** A screened gallery for spectators at the service end of a court-tennis court. **2.** The spectators at a court-tennis match. [French, "inside," "interior," from Old French, "from within" : *de,* from + *dans,* in, within, from Late Latin *deintus* : Latin *dē,* from + *intus,* within.]

ded·i·cate (dĕd′ə-kāt′) *tr.v.* **-cated, -cating, -cates. 1.** To set apart for a deity or for religious purposes; consecrate. **2.** To set apart for some special use; appropriate; devote. **3.** To address or inscribe (a literary work or artistic performance, for example) to someone as a mark of respect or affection. **4.** To commit (oneself) to a particular course of thought or action. **5.** To open (a building, for example) for public use or unveil (a monument), especially with a ceremony. —See Synonyms at **devote.**
~adj. Devoted; dedicated. [Middle English *dedicaten,* from Latin *dēdicāre,* to give out tidings, proclaim : *dē-,* away from oneself + *dicāre,* to say, proclaim.] **—ded·i·cat·ed·ly** *adv.* **—ded·i·ca·tee** (dĕd′ə-kə-tē′) *n.* **—ded·i·ca·tor** *n.*

ded·i·cat·ed (dĕd′ə-kā′tĭd) *adj.* **1.** Devoted to a particular vocation, aim, or cause. **2.** *Computer Science.* Designed to perform one particular function: *a dedicated word processor.*

ded·i·ca·tion (dĕd′ə-kā′shən) *n.* **1. a.** The act of dedicating. **b.** The state of being dedicated. **2.** A note prefixed to a literary, artistic, or musical work dedicating it to someone as a token of affection or esteem. **3.** A rite or ceremony of dedicating. **—ded·i·ca·tive** (dĕd′ə-kā′tĭv), **ded·i·ca·to·ry** (dĕd′ə-kə-tôr′ē, -tōr′ē) *adj.*

de·dif·fer·en·ti·a·tion (dē′dĭf-ə-rĕn′shē-ā′shən) *n. Biology.* The loss of specialized cellular form, especially prior to redifferentiation.

de·duce (dĭ-do͞os′, -dyo͞os′) *tr.v.* **-duced, -ducing, -duces. 1.** To reach (a conclusion) by reasoning. **2.** To infer from a general principle; reason deductively. **3.** To trace the origin or derivation of. [Middle English *deducen,* from Latin *dēdūcere,* to lead away, deduce : *dē-,* away + *dūcere,* to lead.] **—de·duc·i·ble** *adj.*

de·duct (dĭ-dŭkt′) *v.* **-ducted, -ducting, -ducts.** *—tr.* **1.** To take away (a quantity from another); subtract. **2.** To derive by deduction; deduce. *—intr.* To detract; diminish. Usually used with *from: Bad plumbing deducts from the value of the house.* [Latin *dēdūcere* (past participle *dēductus*), to lead or take away, DEDUCE.]

de·duct·i·ble (dĭ-dŭk′tə-bəl) *adj.* **1.** Capable of being deducted. **2.** Allowable as a tax deduction.

de·duc·tion (dĭ-dŭk′shən) *n.* **1.** The act of deducting; subtraction. **2.** That which is or may be deducted: *These expenses are legitimate tax deductions.* **3. a.** The act of deducing; the drawing of a conclusion by reasoning. **b.** *Logic.* The process of reasoning in which a conclusion follows necessarily from the stated premises; inference by reasoning from the general to the specific. **c.** *Logic.* A conclusion reached by this process. In this sense, compare **induction.**

de·duc·tive (dĭ-dŭk'tĭv) *adj.* **1.** Of or based on deduction. **2.** Involving deduction in reasoning. —**de·duc·tive·ly** *adv.*

Dee (dē). River in Grampian Region, northeast Scotland. It flows 140 kilometers (87 miles) from the Grampian Mts. into the North Sea at Aberdeen. *Dee* is an ancient British word for river: there is another one in southern Scotland, one in North Wales, and a fourth in County Limerick in the Republic of Ireland.

Dee, John (1527–1608). English mathematician, astronomer, astrologer, and magician. He wrote a preface to the first English translation of Euclid encouraging the practice of applied geometry. Elizabeth I consulted him as an astrologer.

deed (dēd) *n.* **1.** An act. **2.** A feat; an exploit. **3.** Action or performance in general, especially as distinguished from words: *They were found to be bold in deed as well as in speech.* **4.** *Law.* A document sealed as an instrument of bond, contract, or conveyance, especially one pertaining to property. ~*tr.v.* **deeded, deeding, deeds.** To transfer by means of a deed. [Middle English *dede,* Old English *dǣd.*]

deed poll *n., pl.* **deeds poll.** A deed made by one party, especially by a person changing his name.

dee·jay (dē'jā') *n. Informal.* A disc jockey *(see).* [From the initials *d* and *j.*]

deem (dēm) *v.* **deemed, deeming, deems.** —*tr.* To judge; consider; think: *We deem it advisable to wait.* —*intr.* To have an opinion; suppose. —See Synonyms at **consider.** [Middle English *demen,* Old English *dēman.*]

de·em·pha·size (dē-ĕm'fə-sīz') *tr.v.* **-sized, -sizing, -sizes. 1.** To remove emphasis from. **2.** To reduce the emphasis on.

deep (dēp) *adj.* **deeper, deepest. 1.** Extending to or located at: **a.** An unspecified, usually considerable, distance below a surface. **b.** A specified distance below a surface. **2.** Extending from front to rear, or inward from the outside, for: **a.** An unspecified distance. **b.** A specified distance. **3.** Arising from or penetrating to a depth. **4.** Far distant. **5. a.** Difficult to fathom or understand; obscure. **b.** Learned; understanding; wise. **c.** Cunning; crafty; sly. **6. a.** Profound; intense; extreme. **b.** Profoundly absorbed or immersed. **7.** Dark rather than pale in shade. **8.** Low in pitch; resonant. —**deep down.** *Informal.* In fact rather than in appearance; truthfully. —**go off the deep end.** *Informal.* To act recklessly or hysterically. —**in deep water.** In trouble. ~*n.* **1.** *Sometimes* **Deep.** Any deep place on land or in a body of water, especially in the ocean and over 3,000 fathoms in depth: *the Mindanao Deep.* **2.** The most intense or extreme part. **3.** *Nautical.* A distance estimated in fathoms between successive marks on a sounding line: *by the deep, 11.* —**the deep.** *Poetic.* The ocean. ~*adv.* **1.** Deeply; profoundly. **2.** Well on in time: *worked deep into the night.* —**in deep.** *Informal.* Completely committed. [Middle English *dep,* Old English *dēop,* from Germanic.] —**deep·ly** *adv.* —**deep·ness** *n.*

deep-drawn (dēp'drôn') *adj.* Shaped by forcing through a die while cold. Said of metals.

deep-dyed (dēp'dīd') *adj.* Unmitigated; absolute.

deep·en (dē'pən) *v.* **-ened, -ening, -ens.** —*tr.* To make deep or deeper. —*intr.* **1.** To become deep or deeper. **2.** To become more intensive: *a deepening depression.* —**deep·en·er** *n.*

Deep-freeze (dēp'frēz') *n.* **1.** A trademark for a refrigerator designed to freeze and store food for long periods; a freezer. **2. deepfreeze.** *Informal.* Storage or preservation in, or as if in, a deepfreeze. **3. deepfreeze.** A state of suspended activity. —**deepfreeze** *v.*

deep-fry (dēp'frī') *tr.v.* **-fried, -frying, -fries.** To fry by immersing in a deep pan of fat or oil.

deep-laid (dēp'lād') *adj.* Elaborately worked out and kept secret. Said of a plan or scheme.

deep-root·ed (dēp'rōō'tĭd, -rŏŏt'ĭd) *adj.* Firmly implanted; ingrained.

deep-sea (dēp'sē') *adj.* **1.** Abyssal. **2.** Of or pertaining to distant waters: *deep-sea fishing.*

deep-seat·ed (dēp'sē'tĭd) *adj.* Deeply rooted; ingrained.

deep-six (dēp'sĭks') *tr.v.* **-sixed, -sixing, -sixes.** *Slang.* **1.** To toss overboard. **2.** To toss out; get rid of: *deep-sixed the incriminating papers.*

Deep South *n.* The southeasternmost part of the United States, especially the states of Alabama, Georgia, Louisiana, Mississippi, and South Carolina.

deep space *n.* The regions beyond the moon, encompassing interplanetary, interstellar, and intergalactic space.

deep structure *n. Linguistics.* In the standard theory of transformational grammar, an explicit representation of the parts of a sentence and their relations in a form that allows the sentence's meaning to be understood. For example, the deep structure of the sentence *Children want to play* may be displayed as *Children want (children play).* See **surface structure.**

deep therapy *n.* A type of radiotherapy using penetrating, high-frequency x-rays.

deer (dîr) *n., pl.* **deer. 1.** Any of various hoofed ruminant mammals of the family Cervidae, characteristically having deciduous antlers usually borne only by the males. **2.** Any of various smaller deerlike mammals, such as the mouse deer. [Middle English *der,* animal, beast, deer, Old English *dēor.*]

deer fly *n.* Any of various blood-sucking flies of the genus *Chrysops,*

having dark bars or spots on the wings.

deer·hound (dîr'hound') *n.* A dog of a breed developed in Scotland, resembling a greyhound but larger and having a wiry coat. Also called "Scottish deerhound."

deer ked *n.* A wingless fly, the ked *(see).*

deer lick *n.* A salty spring or patch of ground, to which deer come to lick the salt and other minerals.

deer mouse *n.* Any of various New World mice of the genus *Peromyscus,* having large ears, white feet and underparts, and a long tail. Also called "white-footed mouse." [From its deerlike agility.]

deer·skin (dîr'skĭn') *n.* **1.** Leather made from the hide of a deer. **2.** A garment made from such leather.

deer·stalk·er (dîr'stô'kər) *n.* **1.** A person who stalks deer, usually with the intention of killing them. **2.** A soft cloth hat, with peaks at the front and back and with earflaps that can be tied on its top.

deer's-tongue (dîrz'tŭng') *n.* A tall plant, *Frasera speciosa* of western North America, having whorls of greenish flowers.

deer·weed (dîr'wēd') *n.* Any of several bushlike, yellow-flowered plants of the genus *Lotus,* of southwestern North America, sometimes used as forage in arid regions.

de·es·ca·late (dē-ĕs'kə-lāt') *tr.v.* **-lated, -lating, -lates.** To decrease the scope or intensity of: *de-escalated the war.* —**de·es·ca·la·tion** *n.*

deet (dēt) *n.* A colorless oily liquid, $C_{12}H_{17}NO$, that has a mild odor and is used as an insect repellent. [Pronunciation of *d.t.,* the abbreviation of DIETHYL TOLUAMIDE.]

def. 1. defective. **2.** defendant. **3.** defense. **4.** deferred. **5.** definite. **6.** definition.

de·face (dĭ-fās') *tr.v.* **-faced, -facing, -faces. 1.** To spoil or mar the surface or appearance of; disfigure. **2.** To impair the usefulness, value, or influence of. **3.** To efface or obliterate. [Middle English *defacen,* from Old French *desfacier* : *des-,* from Latin *dē-* (undoing, ruin) + *face,* FACE.] —**de·face·a·ble** *adj.* —**de·face·ment** *n.* —**de·fac·er** *n.*

de fac·to (dē făk'tō) *adv.* In reality or fact; actually. ~*adj.* **1.** Actual. **2.** Actually exercising power. Compare **de jure.** ~*n. Australian & New Zealand.* A lover with whom one lives. [Latin, "from the fact."]

de·fal·cate (dĭ-făl'kāt', -fôl'-, dĕf'əl-) *intr.v.* **-cated, -cating, -cates.** *Law.* To misuse funds; embezzle. [Medieval Latin *dēfalcāre,* to cut off : Latin *dē-,* off + *falx* (stem *falc-*), sickle.] —**de·fal·ca·tion** *n.* —**de·fal·ca·tor** *n.*

def·a·ma·tion (dĕf'ə-mā'shən) *n.* Slander or libel; calumny. —**de·fam·a·to·ry** (dĭ-făm'ə-tôr'ē, -tōr'ē) *adj.*

de·fame (dĭ-fām') *tr.v.* **-famed, -faming, -fames.** To attack the good name of by slander or libel. —See Synonyms at **malign.** [Middle English *diffamen, defamen,* from Old French *diffamer, defamer,* from Latin *diffāmāre* : *dis-* (undoing, ruin) + *fāma,* report, fame.] —**de·fam·er** *n.*

de·fault (dĭ-fôlt') *n.* **1.** A failure to perform a task or fulfill an obligation; especially, failure to meet a financial obligation. **2.** Failure to make a required appearance in court. **3.** The failure of one or more competitors or teams to participate in a contest: *win by default.* **4.** Lack or need. —**go by default.** To be ignored because absent or inconspicuous. —**in default of.** Through the failure, absence, or lack of. ~*v.* **defaulted, -faulting, -faults.** —*intr.* **1.** To fail to do that which is required. **2.** To fail to pay money when it is due. Often used with *on* or *in.* **3.** *Law.* **a.** To fail to appear in court when summoned. **b.** To lose a case by not appearing. **4.** *Sports.* To fail to compete in or complete a scheduled contest. —*tr.* **1.** To fail to perform or pay. **2. a.** To fail to take part in or complete (a contest, for example). **b.** To forfeit (a match, for example) through such failure. **3.** *Law.* **a.** To lose (a case) by failing to take part in it. **b.** To give judgment against (a defendant) because of failure to participate in the case. [Middle English *defaut(e),* from Old French *defaute,* from Vulgar Latin *dēfallita,* from *dēfallīre* (unattested), to fail : *dē-* (intensive) + *fallīre* (unattested), variant of Latin *fallere,* to FAIL.] —**de·fault·er** *n.*

de·fea·sance (dĭ-fē'zəns) *n.* **1.** An annulment or rendering void. **2.** *Law.* The voiding of a contract or deed. **3.** *Law.* A clause within a contract or deed providing for annulment. [Middle English *defesaunce,* from Old French *de(s)fesance,* from *de(s)fesant,* present participle of *de(s)faire,* to destroy, DEFEAT.]

de·fea·si·ble (dĭ-fē'zə-bəl) *adj. Law.* Capable of being annulled or forfeited. —**de·fea·si·bil·i·ty, de·fea·si·ble·ness** *n.*

de·feat (dĭ-fēt') *tr.v.* **-feated, -feating, -feats. 1.** To win a victory over; vanquish. **2.** To prevent the success of; thwart. **3.** *Law.* To annul or make void. ~*n.* **1.** The act of defeating or state of being defeated. **2.** Failure to win; overthrow. **3.** A coming to naught; frustration. **4.** *Law.* A making null and void. [Middle English *defeten,* from Old French *de(s)faire* (past participle *desfait*), from Medieval Latin *disfacere,* to undo, destroy : Latin *dis-* (reversal) + *facere,* to do, make.] —**de·feat·er** *n.*

Synonyms: *beat, conquer, overcome, rout, subdue, subjugate, vanquish.*

de·feat·ism (dĭ-fē'tĭz'əm) *n.* Acceptance of or resignation to the prospect of defeat. —**de·feat·ist** *n.*

def·e·cate (dĕf'ə-kāt') *v.* **-cated, -cating, -cates.** —*intr.* To discharge feces from the bowels. —*tr.* To clarify (a chemical solution). [Latin *dēfaecāre* : *dē-* (removal) + *faex,* dregs, FECES.] —**def·e·ca·tion** *n.* —**def·e·ca·tor** *n.*

de·fect (dē'fĕkt', dĭ-fĕkt') *n.* **1.** The lack of something necessary or

PRONUNCIATION KEY

ă, pat; ā, pay; âr, care;
ä, father, are; b, **bib**;
ch, **church**; d, **deed**; ĕ, pet;
ē, be; f, **fife**; g, **gag**; h, **hat**;
hw, **which**; ĭ, pit; ī, pie;
îr, **pier**; j, **judge**; k, **kick**;
l, lid, needle; m, **mum**;
n, no, sudden; ng, **thing**;
ŏ, pot; ō, toe; ô, **paw**, for;
oi, noise; ou, **out**; o͝o, **book**;
o͞o, boot; p, **pop**; r, roar;
s, sauce; sh, **ship**, **dish**;
t, **tight**; th, **thin**, **path**;
th, **this**, **bathe**; ŭ, cut; ûr, **fur**;
v, valve; w, **with**; y, yes;
z, zebra, size; zh, vision;
ə, about, item, edible,
gallop, circus, peaceful

IN FOREIGN WORDS:

à, *Fr.* ami; œ, *Fr.* feu, *Ger.* schön; ü, *Fr.* tu, *Ger.* über;
KH, *Ger.* ich, *Scot.* loch;
N, *Fr.* bon; y', *Fr.* Compiègne

STRESS MARKS:

Primary stress: ′
in·cite′ (ĭn-sīt′)
Secondary stress: ′
in′sight′ (ĭn′sīt′)

desirable; a deficiency. **2.** An imperfection; a failing; a fault. **3.** *Physics.* An irregularity in a crystal lattice, such as a vacancy or line of missing atoms. —See Synonyms at **blemish**.
~*intr.v.* (dĭ-fĕkt′) **defected, -fecting, -fects. 1.** To desert one's proclaimed allegiance, political party, or the like. **2.** To leave one's country after disowning allegiance to it and take residence in another. [Middle English, from Old French, from Latin *dēfectus,* deficiency, lack, from the past participle of *dēficere,* to remove from, desert, fail, be wanting : *dē-,* away from + *facere,* to do, set.] **—de·fec·tion** *n.* **—de·fec·tor** *n.*

de·fec·tive (dĭ-fĕk′tĭv) *adj. Abbr.* **def. 1.** Lacking perfection; having a defect; faulty. —See Usage note below. **2.** Below average or below an acceptable standard, especially in mental powers. Said of a person. **3.** *Grammar.* Lacking one or more of the inflected forms normal for a particular category of word. In English, *may* is a defective verb.
~*n.* **1.** Something imperfect or damaged. **2.** Someone mentally incapacitated. **—de·fec·tive·ly** *adv.* **—de·fec·tive·ness** *n.*
Usage: The similarity in form and meaning between *defective* and *deficient* sometimes leads to a confusion in usage. *Defective* applies especially to what has a discernible fault and is therefore primarily concerned with quality: *a defective electric light; defective intelligence. Deficient* refers to insufficiency or incompleteness and is basically a quantitative term associated with deficit: *a deficient account; deficient in intelligence.*

defence. *Chiefly British.* Variant of **defense.**

de·fend (dĭ-fĕnd′) *v.* **-fended, -fending, -fends.** —*tr.* **1.** To protect from danger, attack, or harm; shield; guard. **2.** To support or maintain, as by argument or action; justify. **3.** *Law.* **a.** To represent (the defendant) in a civil or criminal case. **b.** To contest (a legal action or claim). **4.** *Sports.* **a.** To protect (oneself or one's goal) against the opposition's attacks. **b.** To compete in order to retain (a title or championship) against a challenger. —*intr.* To make a defense. [Middle English *defenden,* from Old French *defendre,* from Latin *dēfendere,* to ward off.] **—de·fend·a·ble** *adj.* **—de·fend·er** *n.*
Synonyms: *guard, preserve, protect, safeguard, shield.*

de·fen·dant (dĭ-fĕn′dənt) *n. Abbr.* **def.** *Law.* A person against whom an action is brought. Compare **plaintiff.**

Defender of the Faith *n.* A title of English sovereigns, originally conferred upon Henry VIII by Pope Leo X (1521).

de·fen·es·tra·tion (dē-fĕn′ə-strā′shən) *n.* An act of throwing something or someone out of a window. [DE- + FENESTRA + -TION.]

de·fense (dĭ-fĕns′) *n.* Also *chiefly British* **de·fence.** *Abbr.* **def. 1.** The act or policy of defending against attack, danger, or injury; protection. **2.** Anyone or anything that defends or protects. **3.** Military resources and activities designed to discourage or defend against enemy attack: *increased spending on defense.* **4. a.** An argument or set of arguments in support or justification of something. **b.** The speech, document, or the like, in which such arguments are contained. **5.** *Law.* **a.** The defendant's opposition to the complaints or allegations against him. **b.** The defendant and his legal counsel. **6.** *Psychology.* An unconsciously acquired and involuntary mental process such as regression, repression, or projection, that protects one from shame or anxiety. **7.** *Sports.* **a.** The action or policy of defending oneself or one's goal against the opposition's attacks. **b.** The team or those of its players attempting to do this. **c.** The participation in a contest or match against a challenger in order to retain one's title or championship.
~*tr.v.* **defensed, -fensing, -fenses.** *Football.* To act as defense: *defense a play.* **—de·fense·less** *adj.* **—de·fense·less·ly** *adv.* **—de·fense·less·ness** *n.*

defense mechanism *n.* **1.** *Biology.* Any reaction of an organism used in defending itself, as against germs. **2.** *Psychology.* A defense or the psychic structure or mechanism underlying a defense.

de·fen·si·ble (dĭ-fĕn′sə-bəl) *adj.* Capable of being defended, protected, or justified. **—de·fen·si·bil·i·ty, de·fen·si·ble·ness** *n.* **—de·fen·si·bly** *adv.*
Usage: *Defensible* and *defensive* come from the same root but have distinct meanings. *Defensible* means "capable of being defended": *a defensible position. Defensive* means "intended for or providing a defense" and is frequently used with pejorative connotations: *You're very defensive.*

de·fen·sive (dĭ-fĕn′sĭv) *adj.* **1.** Intended or appropriate for defense. **2.** Done for defense; defending. **3.** Of or pertaining to defense. —See Usage note at **defensible.**
~*n.* **1.** A means of defense. **2.** An attitude of defense. **—on the defensive.** Ready to defend or justify oneself. **—de·fen·sive·ly** *adv.* **—de·fen·sive·ness** *n.*

de·fer¹ (dĭ-fûr′) *v.* **-ferred, -ferring, -fers.** —*tr.* **1.** To put off until a future time; postpone. **2.** To postpone the induction of (one eligible for the military draft). —*intr.* To procrastinate; delay. [Middle English *differen,* from Old French *differer,* from Latin *differre* : *dis-,* away + *ferre,* to carry.] **—de·fer·rer** *n.*

defer² *intr.v.* **-ferred, -ferring, -fers.** To comply with or submit to the opinion or decision of another; be deferential. Used with *to.* —See Synonyms at **yield.** [Middle English *deferren,* from Old French *def(f)erer,* from Latin *dēferre,* to carry away, bring to, submit : *dē-,* away + *ferre,* to carry.] **—de·fer·rer** *n.*

def·er·ence (dĕf′ər-əns) *n.* **1.** Submission or courteous yielding to the opinion, wishes, or judgment of another. **2.** Courteous respect. —See Synonyms at **honor.**

def·er·ent¹ (dĕf′ər-ənt) *adj.* Showing deference; deferential.

deferent² *adj.* **1.** Carrying down or away. Said of nerves, blood vessels, and similar channels conveying impulses, fluids, or the like. **2.** Adapted to carry or transport.
~*n. Astronomy.* A circle with the earth at its center, marking the path of the center of a planet's epicycle in the Ptolemaic model of the universe. [Latin *dēferēns* (stem *dēferent-*), present participle of *dēferre,* to bring to, DEFER (to comply).]

def·er·en·tial (dĕf′ə-rĕn′shəl) *adj.* Marked by courteous respect: *"Mr. Bulstrode had also a deferential, bending attitude in listening"* (George Eliot). **—def·er·en·tial·ly** *adv.*

de·fer·ment (dĭ-fûr′mənt) *n.* Also **de·fer·ral** (-fûr′əl). The act or an instance of delaying or putting off; postponement.

de·fer·ra·ble (dĭ-fûr′ə-bəl) *adj.* **1.** Suitable for being postponed: *deferrable plans.* **2.** Eligible for deferment, especially from military service.

de·ferred (dĭ-fûrd′) *adj. Abbr.* **def. 1.** Postponed; delayed. **2.** With benefits or payments withheld until a future date.

de·fer·ves·cence (dē′fûr-vĕs′əns) *n.* The abatement of a fever. [DE- + Latin *fervescere,* inceptive of *fervēre,* to boil, be hot + -ENCE.]

de·fi·ance (dĭ-fī′əns) *n.* **1.** The disposition to defy or resist an opposing force or authority; resolute resistance. **2.** Intentionally provocative behavior or attitude; a challenge. [Middle English *defiaunce,* from Old French *desfiance,* from *desfier,* DEFY.]

de·fi·ant (dĭ-fī′ənt) *adj.* Marked by defiance. **—de·fi·ant·ly** *adv.*

de·fib·ril·la·tion (dē-fĭb′rə-lā′shən) *n. Medicine.* The administration of an electric shock to restore normal heart rhythm in cases of fibrillation. Electrodes from the apparatus used, a *defibrillator,* are placed over the chest wall or directly on the heart.

de·fi·cien·cy (dĭ-fĭsh′ən-sē) *n., pl.* **-cies.** Also *rare* **de·fi·cience** (-fĭsh′əns). **1.** The quality or condition of being deficient. **2.** A lack; a shortage; an insufficiency. **3.** *Genetics.* A **deletion** *(see).*

deficiency disease *n.* A disease caused by the lack of essential substances, especially vitamins, in the diet.

de·fi·cient (dĭ-fĭsh′ənt) *adj.* **1.** Lacking an essential quality or element; incomplete; defective. **2.** Inadequate in amount or degree; insufficient. —See Usage note at **defective.** [Latin *dēficiēns* (stem *dēficient-*), present participle of *dēficere,* to remove from, desert, fail, lack : *dē-,* away + *facere,* to make, do.] **—de·fi·cient·ly** *adv.*

def·i·cit (dĕf′ə-sĭt) *n.* **1.** The amount by which a sum of money falls short of the required or expected amount; a shortage. **2.** *Finance.* An excess of liabilities over assets, or expenditures over income. [French *déficit,* from Latin *dēficit,* it is lacking, from *dēficere,* to lack. See **deficient.**]

deficit spending *n.* Government spending of money obtained by borrowing, resulting in a deficit in the budget.

de fi·de (dā fē′dā′) *adj. Roman Catholic Church.* Designating a doctrine that is an essential part of the faith, especially when so ruled by the pope. [Latin, "of faith."]

def·i·lade (dĕf′ə-lād′) *tr.v.* **-laded, -lading, -lades.** *Military.* To arrange (fortifications) so as to give protection from enfilading and other fire.
~*n.* The act or procedure of defilading or the protection so provided. [DE- + (EN)FILADE.]

de·file¹ (dĭ-fīl′) *tr.v.* **-filed, -filing, -files. 1.** To make filthy or dirty. **2.** To tarnish the luster of; render impure; corrupt. **3.** To profane or sully (a good name or reputation, for example). **4.** To make unclean or unfit for ceremonial use; desecrate. **5.** To violate the chastity of. [Middle English *defilen,* probably alteration (influenced by *filen,* to sully) of *defoulen,* to trample down, injure, from Old French *defouler* : *de-,* from Latin *dē-,* down + *fouler,* to trample, FULL (verb).] **—de·file·ment** *n.* **—de·fil·er** *n.* **—de·fil·ing·ly** *adv.*

defile² *intr.v.* **-filed, -filing, -files. 1.** To march in single file. **2.** To march in files or columns.
~*n.* **1.** A narrow gorge, valley, or other feature of terrain that restricts lateral movement, as of troops. **2.** A marching in line, as of a single column of soldiers or travelers. [French *défiler* : *dé-,* from Latin *dē-,* off, away + *filer,* to march by files, from Old French, to spin, from Late Latin *fīlāre,* from Latin *fīlum,* thread.]

de·fine (dĭ-fīn′) *v.* **-fined, -fining, -fines.** —*tr.* **1.** To state the precise meaning of (a word or sense of a word, for example). **2.** To describe the nature or basic qualities of; explain: *define the properties of a new drug.* **3.** To delineate the outline or form of; make clear: *a shape defined by a line.* **4.** To specify distinctly; fix definitely: *define the weapons to be used in limited warfare.* **5.** To serve to distinguish; characterize. —*intr.* To make a definition. [Middle English *diffinen,* from Old French *definer,* from Vulgar Latin *dēfīnāre* (unattested), variant of Latin *dēfīnīre,* to set bounds to : *dē,* off + *fīnis,* end, boundary.] **—de·fin·a·bil·i·ty** *n.* **—de·fin·a·ble** *adj.* **—de·fin·a·bly** *adv.* **—de·fine·ment** *n.* **—de·fin·er** *n.*

de·fin·i·en·dum (dĭ-fĭn′ē-ĕn′dəm) *n., pl.* **-da** (-də). That which is defined by a definiens. [Latin, neuter of *dēfīniendus,* gerundive of *dēfīnīre,* to set bounds to, DEFINE.]

de·fin·i·ens (dĭ-fĭn′ē-ĕnz′) *n., pl.* **definientia** (dĭ-fĭn′ē-ĕn′shē-ə, -shə). The word or words serving to define another word or expression, as in a dictionary entry. [Latin *dēfīniēns,* present participle of *dēfīnīre,* DEFINE.]

def·i·nite (dĕf′ə-nĭt) *adj.* **1.** Having distinct limits: *definite restrictions on wine and liquor sales.* **2.** Known positively; for certain; sure: *a definite victory.* **3.** Clearly defined; precise; explicit: *a definite statement of the terms of the will.* **4.** *Abbr.* **def.** *Grammar.* Limiting or particularizing. **5.** *Botany.* **a.** Of a specified number not exceeding 20. Said of floral organs, especially stamens. **b.** Determinate. [Middle English *diffinite,* from Latin *dēfīnītus,* past participle of *dēfīnīre,* to determine, DEFINE.] **—def·i·nite·ness** *n.*

Usage: *Definite* and *definitive* both apply to what is precisely defined or explicity set forth. But *definitive* more often refers, in addition, to what is unalterably final, and is not therefore usually interchangeable with *definite.* A *definite decision* is firm and clear-cut, and might come at any time and be provided by anyone. A *definitive decision,* by contrast, usually implies the conclusion of a process of decision-making ("less definite" decisions having previously been made) and suggests that the issues are complex or important and have received the attention of an authority.

definite article *n. Grammar.* The article that restricts or particularizes the noun or noun phrase following it; in English, the article *the.* Compare **indefinite article.**

definite integral *n.* An integral that is calculated between two specified limits, usually expressed in the form $\int_a^b f(x)dx$. The result of performing the integral is a number that represents the area under the curve of function *f(x)* between the limits and the *x*-axis. Compare **indefinite integral.**

def·i·nite·ly (dĕf′ə-nĭt-lē, dĕf′nĭt-lē) *adv.* **1.** In a definite way. **2.** Certainly; undoubtedly.
∼*interj.* Used to express emphatic confirmation.

def·i·ni·tion (dĕf′ə-nĭsh′ən) *n. Abbr.* **def. 1.** The act of stating a precise meaning or significance, as of a word, phrase, or term. **2.** The statement of the meaning of a word, phrase, or term. **3.** The act or an instance of making clear and distinct: *a definition of one's intentions.* **4.** The state of being closely outlined or determined. **5.** A determining of outline, extent, or limits: *the definition of my authority.* **6.** *Telecommunications.* The degree of clarity with which a televised image is received or a radio receives a given station. **7.** *Optics.* The clarity of detail in an optically produced image, as in a photograph, produced by a combination of resolution and contrast. [Middle English *diffinicioun,* from Old French *definition,* from Latin *dēfīnītiō* (stem *dēfīnītiōn-*), from *dēfīnīre,* DEFINE.] **—def·i·ni·tion·al** *adj.* **—def·i·ni·tion·al·ly** *adv.*

de·fin·i·tive (dĭ-fĭn′ə-tĭv) *adj.* **1.** Precisely defining or outlining; explicit. **2.** Determining finally; conclusive; decisive. **3.** Designating a statement or work that can stand as the most complete and authoritative on its subject: *a definitive biography.* **4.** *Zoology.* In a complete, fully developed form. Said especially of parasites. **5.** Issued for permanent rather than commemorative or other use. Said of a postage stamp. —See Usage note at **definite.**
∼*n.* **1.** *Grammar.* A word that defines or limits, such as the definite article or a demonstrative pronoun. **2.** A definitive postage stamp. **—de·fin·i·tive·ly** *adv.* **—de·fin·i·tive·ness** *n.*

de·fin·i·tude (dĭ-fĭn′ə-to͞od′, -tyo͞od′) *n.* The quality of being definite or exact; precision.

def·la·grate (dĕf′lə-grāt′) *v.* **-grated, -grating, -grates.** —*tr.* To cause to burn with great heat and intense light. —*intr.* To burn with great heat and intense light. [Latin *dēflagrāre* : *dē-* (intensive) + *flagrāre,* to burn.] **—def·la·gra·tion** *n.*

de·flate (dĭ-flāt′) *v.* **-flated, -flating, -flates.** —*tr.* **1. a.** To release contained air or gas from. **b.** To collapse by releasing contained air or gas. **2.** To reduce or lessen the confidence, pride, self-esteem, or certainty of. **3.** *Economics.* **a.** To reduce the amount or availability of (currency or credit), effecting a decline in prices. **b.** To produce deflation in (an economy). In these senses, compare **reflate.** —*intr.* To be or become deflated. [DE- (reversal) + (IN)FLATE.] **—de·fla·tor** *n.*

de·fla·tion (dĭ-flā′shən) *n.* **1. a.** The act of deflating. **b.** The state of being deflated. **2.** *Economics.* A reduction in the general price level, brought on by a decrease in the amount of money in circulation or in the total volume of spending. Compare **inflation. 3.** *Geology.* The blowing away of loose rock particles by the wind. **—de·fla·tion·ar·y** *adj.* **—de·fla·tion·ist** *n.*

de·flect (dĭ-flĕkt′) *v.* **-flected, -flecting, -flects.** —*tr.* To cause to swerve or turn aside. —*intr.* To swerve or turn aside. [Latin *dēflectere* : *dē-,* away + *flectere,* to bend, FLEX.] **—de·flect·a·ble** *adj.* **—de·flec·tive** *adj.* **—de·flec·tor** *n.*

de·flec·tion (dĭ-flĕk′shən) *n.* Also *British* **de·flex·ion. 1. a.** The act of deflecting. **b.** The condition of being deflected. **2.** Deviation or the amount of deviation. **3.** The deviation from zero shown by the indicator of a measuring instrument. **4.** The movement of a structure or structural part as a result of stress.

de·flexed (dĭ-flĕkst′, dē′flĕkst′) *adj. Botany.* Bent or turned downward at a sharp angle: *deflexed petals.* [Latin *dēflexus,* past participle of *dēflectere,* DEFLECT.]

deflexion. *British.* Variant of **deflection.**

de·floc·cu·late (dē-flŏk′yə-lāt′) *v.* **-lated, -lating, -lates.** —*tr.* **1.** To disperse (an aggregate, such as clay or soil) into very fine particles. **2.** To prevent or hinder (a suspension or colloid) from forming an aggregate. —*intr.* To be dispersed into very fine particles. **—de·floc·cu·la·tion** *n.*

def·lo·ra·tion (dĕf′lə-rā′shən) *n.* The act of deflowering.

de·flow·er (dē-flou′ər) *tr.v.* **-ered, -ering, -ers. 1.** To strip of flowers. **2.** To rupture the hymen of (a virgin) by sexual intercourse. **3.** To spoil the appearance or nature of; mar. **4.** To destroy the innocence of; violate. [Middle English *deflouren,* from Old French *deflorer,* from Late Latin *dēflōrāre* : Latin *dē-* (removal) + *flōs* (stem *flōr-*), flower.] **—de·flow·er·er** *n.*

De·foe (dĭ-fō′), **Daniel** (1660–1731). English author. He took part in Monmouth's rebellion (1685) and later became a journalist. *Robinson Crusoe,* the most famous of his many novels, was published in 1719. Three major works appeared in 1722 alone: the novels *Moll Flanders* and *The History of Colonel Jack* and the pseudo-documentary *Journal of the Plague Year.*

de·fog (dē-fôg′, -fŏg′) *tr.v.* **-fogged, -fogging, -fogs.** To remove fog from. **—de·fog·ger** *n.*

de·fo·li·ant (dĭ-fō′lē-ənt) *n.* A chemical sprayed or dusted on plants to cause the leaves to fall off.

de·fo·li·ate (dĭ-fō′lē-āt′) *v.* **-ated, -ating, -ates.** —*tr.* **1.** To deprive (a tree or other plant) of leaves. **2.** To cause the leaves of (a tree or other plant) to fall off, especially by the use of a chemical spray or dust. —*intr.* To lose foliage. [Late Latin *dēfoliāre* : Latin *dē,* removal + *folium,* leaf.] **—de·fo·li·ate** (dĭ-fō′lē-ĭt) *adj.* **—de·fo·li·a·tion** *n.* **—de·fo·li·a·tor** *n.*

de·force *tr.v.* **-forced, -forcing, -forces. 1. a.** In English feudal property law, to withhold by force from the rightful owner. **b.** *Law.* To deprive (a rightful owner) of property by force. **2.** In Scots law, to resist an officer of the law in the performance of his duty. [Middle English *deforcen,* from Norman French *deforcer,* variant of Old French *de(s)forcier* : *des-* (reversal) + *forcier,* to force, from Vulgar Latin *fortiāre* (unattested), from Latin *fortis,* strong.] **—de·force·ment** *n.*

de·for·ciant (dē-fôr′shənt, -fōr′-) *n. Law.* One who deforces a rightful owner.

de·for·est (dĭ-fôr′ĭst, -fŏr′-) *tr.v.* **-ested, -esting, -ests.** To cut down and clear away the trees or forests from. **—de·for·es·ta·tion** *n.* **—de·for·est·er** *n.*

De For·est (dĭ fôr′ĭst, fŏr′-), **Lee** (1873–1961). U.S. electrical engineer and inventor. Often called "the Father of Radio," he patented the triode electron tube (1907), which made possible the radio receiver. He received more than 300 patents and greatly contributed to the development of television and radar.

de·form (dĭ-fôrm′) *v.* **-formed, -forming, -forms.** —*tr.* **1.** To spoil the natural form of; misshape. **2.** To deface; disfigure. **3.** To spoil the nature of; pervert. **4.** *Physics.* To alter the shape of by pressure or stress. —*intr.* To become deformed. —See Usage note at **distort.** [Middle English *deformen,* from Old French *deformer,* from Latin *dēformāre* : *dē-* (reversal) + *formāre,* to form, from *forma,* FORM.] **—de·form·a·bil·i·ty** *n.* **—de·form·a·ble** *adj.* **—de·for·ma·tion** (dē′fôr-mā′shən, dĕf′ər-) *n.*

de·formed (dĭ-fôrmd′) *adj.* Misshapen; disfigured.

de·form·i·ty (dĭ-fôr′mĭ-tē) *n., pl.* **-ties. 1.** The state or condition of being deformed. **2.** A bodily malformation, such as a clubfoot or hunchback. **3.** A deformed person or thing. **4.** Gross ugliness or distortion, especially in art or morals.

de·fraud (dĭ-frôd′) *tr.v.* **-frauded, -frauding, -frauds.** To take from or deprive (a person) of property by fraud; swindle. [Middle English *defrauden,* from Old French *defrauder,* from Latin *dēfraudāre* : *dē-* (intensive) + *fraudāre,* to cheat, from *fraus* (stem *fraud-*), FRAUD.] **—de·fraud·a·tion** *n.* **—de·fraud·er** *n.*

de·fray (dĭ-frā′) *tr.v.* **-frayed, -fraying, -frays.** To meet or satisfy (costs or expenses) by payment; pay: *defray the cost of a trip.* [French *défrayer,* from Old French *deffrayer, desfrayer* : *des-* (removal) + *frai* (attested only in the plural *frais*), expense, cost, "damage," from Latin *fractum,* from *fractus,* past participle of *frangere,* to break.] **—de·fray·a·ble** *adj.* **—de·fray·al** *n.*

de·frock (dē-frŏk′) *tr.v.* **-frocked, -frocking, -frocks.** To unfrock.

de·frost (dē-frôst′, -frŏst′) *v.* **-frosted, -frosting, -frosts.** —*tr.* **1.** To remove ice or frost from (a refrigerator, for example). **2.** To cause to thaw. —*intr.* **1.** To become free of ice or frost. **2.** To become unfrozen; thaw.

de·frost·er (dē-frôs′tər, -frŏs′-) *n.* A heating device designed to remove ice or frost or prevent its formation.

deft (dĕft) *adj.* Skillful; adroit. —See Synonyms at **dexterous.** [Middle English *defte,* originally "gentle," "meek," variant of *dafte,* DAFT.] **—deft·ly** *adv.* **—deft·ness** *n.*

de·funct (dĭ-fŭngkt′) *adj.* **1.** Having ceased to live or exist; extinct; dead. **2.** No longer operative, effective, or respected. [Latin *dēfunctus,* past participle of *dēfungī,* to discharge, finish, die : *dē-* (intensive) + *fungī,* to discharge.] **—de·func·tive** *adj.* **—de·funct·ness** *n.*

de·fuse (dē-fyo͞oz′) *tr.v.* **-fused, -fusing, -fuses. 1.** To remove the fuse from (an explosive device). **2.** To make less dangerous, tense, or hostile: *defuse an international crisis.*

de·fy (dĭ-fī′) *tr.v.* **-fied, -fying, -fies. 1.** To confront or stand up to; challenge: *defying convention.* **2.** To resist (an attempt, for example) successfully; withstand, especially in a puzzling way: *"so the plague defied all medicines"* (Daniel Defoe). **3.** To challenge or dare (a person) to perform something considered impossible. [Middle English *defien, diffien,* from Old French *desfier,* from Vulgar Latin *disfīdāre* (unattested), to renounce one's faith : *dis-* (reversal) + *fīdāre* (unattested), variant of Latin *fīdere,* to trust.] **—de·fi·er** *n.*

deg, deg. degree (thermometric).

dé·ga·gé (dā-gȧ-zhā′) *adj.* Free and relaxed in manner; casual. [French, past participle of *dégager,* to disengage, release, from Old French *desgagier,* "to redeem a pledge" : *des-* (reversal) + *gage,* a pledge, gage, from Frankish (unattested) *wadi.*]

de·ga·me (də-gä′mə) *n.* Also **de·ga·mi** (-mē). **1.** A tree, *Calycophyllum candidissimum,* of tropical America, having hard, close-grained, yellowish wood. **2.** The wood of this tree. Also called "lemonwood." [American Spanish *dagame,* a native name.]

de·gas (dē-găs′) *tr.v.* **-gassed, -gassing, -gasses** or **-gases. 1.** To remove poisonous gases from (a place or person). **2.** To evacuate gas from (a substance or device). **—de·gas·ser** *n.*

De·gas (də-gä′), **(Hilaire Germain) Edgar** (1834–1917). French

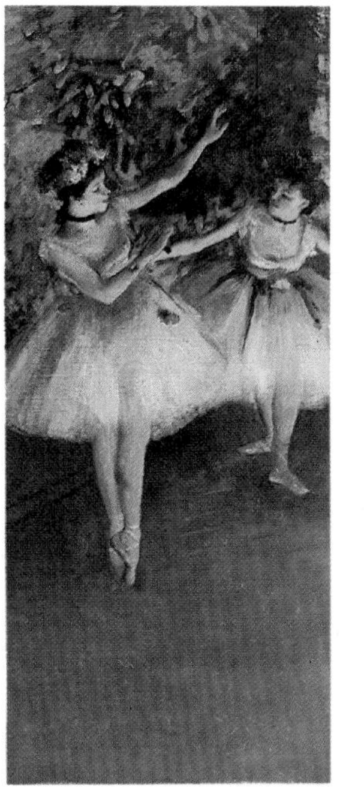

Degas painting *Detail from* Two Dancers on the Stage, *painted in 1874 by the French Impressionist artist Edgar Degas.*

painter and sculptor. He was noted for his portrayal of movement, as in his paintings of ballet dancers.

De Gaulle (də gōl′, gôl′), **Charles André Joseph Marie** (1890–1970). French soldier and statesman, president of France (1959–69). Based in London during World War II, he was made head of the Free French forces in exile and became the acknowledged leader of the Resistance movement in France. He led the provisional government briefly after the liberation (1944–46). With the Algerian crisis (1958), De Gaulle's supporters brought him out of retirement. He was made prime minister, empowered to redraw the constitution, and became president of the new Fifth Republic (1959). Despite violent hostility, he supervised Algeria's path to independence in 1962. He defended the French nuclear deterrent and reduced France's participation in NATO (1966). His leadership was severely tested by strikes and student riots in 1968, and he resigned the following year after proposed constitutional reforms were rejected in a referendum.

de·gauss (dē-gous′) *tr.v.* **-gaussed, -gaussing, -gausses.** To remove or neutralize the magnetic field of (a ship, piece of electronic apparatus, or the like). [DE- + GAUSS.]

de·gen·er·a·cy (dĭ-jĕn′ər-ə-sē) *n., pl.* **-cies. 1.** The state or condition of being degenerate. **2.** The process of degenerating. **3.** *Physics.* The number of quantum states with the same energy. **4.** Degenerate behavior, especially sexual perversion.

de·gen·er·ate (dĭ-jĕn′ə-rāt′) *intr.v.* **-ated, -ating, -ates. 1.** To become degenerate; deteriorate. **2.** *Biology.* To undergo degeneration.
~*adj.* (dĭ-jĕn′ər-ĭt). **1.** Characterized by deterioration; having declined in condition or quality. **2.** Having become debased or depraved; having declined morally. **3.** *Physics.* **a.** Having the same energy. Said of quantum states that are distinct but of equal energy: *degenerate orbitals.* **b.** Designating or pertaining to a semiconductor in which the number of conduction electrons approaches that in a metallic conductor. **c.** Having modes with equal frequencies. Said of a resonance device. **d.** Composed of nuclei and electrons; fully ionized. Said of matter in neutron stars.
~*n.* (dĭ-jĕn′ər-ĭt). **1.** A morally degraded person. **2. a.** A person lacking or having progressively lost normative biological or psychological characteristics. **b.** A person exhibiting antisocial, especially sexually deviant, behavior. [Latin *dēgenerāre,* to fall from one's ancestral quality : *dē-,* away from + *genus* (stem *gener-*), race.] **—de·gen·er·ate·ly** *adv.* **—de·gen·er·ate·ness** *n.* **—de·gen·er·a·tive** (dĭ-jĕn′ər-ə-tĭv) *adj.*

de·gen·er·a·tion (dĭ-jĕn′ə-rā′shən) *n.* **1.** The process of degenerating. **2.** The state or condition of being degenerate. **3.** *Biology.* **a.** The usually irreversible deterioration of specific cells or organs with corresponding functional impairment, caused by injury or disease and often resulting in necrosis or death. **b.** The loss of function of a part or organ over a period of time, as in the evolutionary development of vestigial organs. **4.** *Electronics.* Negative feedback of output power to an input signal in an amplifying circuit.

de·glu·ti·nate (dĭ-glo͞ot′n-āt′) *tr.v.* **-nated, -nating, -nates.** To extract the gluten from (wheat flour, for example). [Latin *dēglūtināre* : *dē* (removal) + *glūtināre,* to glue, from *glūten,* glue.] **—de·glu·ti·na·tion** *n.*

de·glu·ti·tion (dē′glo͞o-tĭsh′ən) *n.* The process or act of swallowing. [French, from Latin *dēglūtīre,* to swallow down : *dē-,* down + *glūtīre,* to swallow.] **—de·glu·ti·to·ry** (dĭ-glo͞o′tə-tôr′ē, -tōr′ē) *adj.*

deg·ra·da·tion (dĕg′rə-dā′shən) *n.* **1.** The act or process of degrading; specifically: **a.** A deposition, removal, or dismissal from rank or office. **b.** A reduction in worth or standing. **2.** A process of transition from a higher to a lower quality or level. **3.** The state or condition of being degraded; deterioration; degeneration. **4.** *Geology.* **a.** A general lowering of the earth's surface by erosion and removal of the eroded material. **b. Denudation** *(see).* **c.** The downward cutting action of a stream as it carves its bed. **5.** The changes in the nature of a soil as its chemicals are washed away. **6.** *Chemistry.* Decomposition of a compound into simpler compounds; especially, decomposition by stages exhibiting well-defined intermediate products. —See Synonyms at **disgrace.**

de·grade (dĭ-grād′) *tr.v.* **-graded, -grading, -grades. 1.** To reduce in grade, rank, or status; especially, to deprive of an office or dignity. **2.** To lower in moral or intellectual character; debase; corrupt. **3.** To reduce, divert, or pervert. **4.** To expose to contempt, dishonor, or disgrace. **5.** To impair or reduce in quality. **6.** *Geology.* To lower or wear down by erosion. Compare **aggrade. 7.** *Chemistry.* To cause (a compound) to undergo degradation. [Middle English *degraden,* from Old French *degrader,* from Late Latin *dēgradāre* : Latin *dē-,* down + *gradus,* rank, step.] **—de·grad·er** *n.* **—de·grad·a·ble** *adj.*
Synonyms: *abase, demean, discredit, humble, humiliate, mortify.*

de·grad·ed (dĭ-grā′dĭd) *adj.* **1.** Reduced in rank, honor, or position. **2.** Reduced in quality or value; distorted; vulgarized: *a degraded level of art.* **3.** Having declined in moral qualities; depraved; degenerate. **4.** Considered as below normal standards of civilization. **—de·grad·ed·ly** *adv.* **—de·grad·ed·ness** *n.*

de·grad·ing (dĭ-grā′dĭng) *adj.* **1.** Giving rise to embarrassment or humiliation; debasing. **2.** *Geology.* Eroding to a lower level; wearing down. **—de·grad·ing·ly** *adv.*

de·grease (dē-grēs′, -grēz′) *tr.v.* **-greased, -greasing, -greases.** To remove the grease from.

de·gree (dĭ-grē) *n.* **1.** One of a series of steps or stages in a process, course of action, progression, or retrogression. **2.** The relative distance, or a step, in a direct hereditary line of descent or ascent. **3.** Relative social or official rank, dignity, or position. **4.** Relative intensity or amount of a quality, attribute, or the like. **5.** Relative condition or extent; capacity; manner. **6.** The extent or measure of a state of being, action, or the like. **7.** *Abbr.* **deg, deg.** *Symbol* ° **a.** A unit division of a temperature scale. **b.** A unit division of various other scales of measurement, such as scales of hardness or relative density. **8.** *Symbol* ° A unit of angular measure equal in magnitude to the central angle subtended by 1/360 of the circumference of a circle. **9.** *Geography.* A unit of latitude or longitude, 1/360 of a great circle. **10.** *Algebra.* **a.** The greatest sum of the exponents of the variables in a term of a polynomial or polynomial equation. **b.** The exponent of the derivative of highest order in a differential equation in standard form; for example, the polynomial $ax^2 + bx + c$ is of the second degree. Compare **order. 11. a.** An academic title given by a college or university to a student who has completed a course of study. **b.** A similar title conferred as an honorary distinction. **12.** *Law.* **a.** A division or classification of a specific crime according to its seriousness. **b.** In Britain, either of the two classifications formerly applied to a felony. **13.** *Grammar.* One of the three forms used in the comparison of adjectives and adverbs. See **positive, comparative, superlative. 14.** *Music.* **a.** One of the seven notes of a diatonic scale. **b.** A space or line of the staff. **15.** Any of the three former classifications of a burn according to seriousness. **—by degrees.** Little by little; gradually. **—to a degree. 1.** To a great extent. **2.** Somewhat. [Middle English *degre,* from Old French, from Vulgar Latin *dēgradus* (unattested), "a step down" : Latin *dē-,* down + *gradus,* a step.]

de·gree-day (dĭ-grē′dā′) *n.* **1.** An indication of the extent of departure of the mean daily temperature from a standard. **2.** A unit used in estimating quantities of fuel and power consumption, based on a daily ratio of consumption and the mean temperature below 65°F (18°C).

degree of freedom *n.* **1.** *Statistics.* Any of the unrestricted, independent random variables that constitute a statistic. **2.** *Mechanics.* Any of the minimum number of coordinates required to specify completely the motion of a mechanical system. **3.** *Thermodynamics.* Any of the independent variables, such as pressure, temperature, or composition, required to specify a system with a given number of phases and components. See **phase rule.**

de·gres·sion (dĭ-grĕsh′ən, dē′-) *n.* **1.** A going down by stages or steps; a descent. **2.** The progressive reduction of the rate of tax on sums below a certain limit. [Middle English *digressioun,* from Medieval Latin *dēgressiō* (stem *dēgressiōn-*), from Latin *dēgredī* (past participle *dēgressus*), to step down : *dē-,* down + *gradī,* to go, step.] **—de·gres·sive** *adj.*

de·gum (dē-gŭm′) *tr.v.* **-gummed, -gumming, -gums.** To free from gum.

de·gust (dĭ-gŭst′, dē′-) *tr.v.* **-gusted, -gusting, -gusts.** To taste with relish or care; savor. [Latin *dēgustāre* : *dē-* (intensive) + *gustāre,* to taste.] **—de·gus·ta·tion** (dē′gŭs-tā′shən) *n.*

de Hav·il·land (də hăv′ə-lənd), **Sir Geoffrey** (1882–1965). British aircraft designer. He taught himself to fly in a plane of his own design (1910). His company produced the Moth biplane (1925), the Mosquito of World War II, and the Comet (1949), which in 1952 became the world's first commercial jet airliner.

de·hisce (dĭ-hĭs′) *intr.v.* **-hisced, -hiscing, -hisces.** To burst or split open along a line or slit, as do the ripe capsules or pods of some plants. [Latin *dēhiscere* : *dē-,* off + *hiscere,* to open, split, inceptive of *hiāre,* to be open, gape.]

de·his·cent (dĭ-hĭs′ənt) *adj.* Opening at pores or by splitting to release seeds within a fruit or pollen from an anther. Compare **indehiscent. —de·his·cence** *n.*

de·horn (dē-hôrn′) *tr.v.* **-horned, -horning, -horns. 1.** To remove the horns from. **2.** To prevent growth in the horns of (cattle, for example), as by cauterization.

Deh·ra Dun (dâr′ə do͞on′). City in Uttar Pradesh, north India. It was founded by a 17th-century Sikh community whose temple (1669) survives. The Indian Military Academy and Forestry Department have their headquarters here.

de·hu·man·ize (dē-hyo͞o′mə-nīz′) *tr.v.* **-ized, -izing, -izes. 1.** To deprive of human qualities or attributes. **2.** To offend human dignity or personality: *dehumanizing conditions.* **3.** To render mechanical and routine. **—de·hu·man·i·za·tion** *n.*

de·hu·mid·i·fy (dē′hyo͞o-mĭd′ə-fī′) *tr.v.* **-fied, -fying, -fies.** To remove atmospheric moisture from; decrease the humidity of. **—de·hu·mid·i·fi·ca·tion** *n.* **—de·hu·mid·i·fi·er** *n.*

de·hy·drate (dē-hī′drāt′) *v.* **-drated, -drating, -drates.** —*tr.* **1.** *Chemistry.* To eliminate water from or make anhydrous. **2.** To remove water from (vegetables, for example) for preservation. **3.** To cause to lose body fluids. —*intr.* **1.** To lose moisture; become dry. **2.** To become dehydrated. **—de·hy·dra·tor** *n.*

de·hy·dra·tion (dē′hī-drā′shən) *n.* **1.** The process of removing water from a substance or compound. **2.** *Pathology.* Excessive loss of water from the body or from an organ or bodily part.

de·hy·dro·gen·ase (dē′hī-drŏj′ə-nās′) *n.* An enzyme that removes hydrogen from a substrate in oxidation-reduction reactions.

de·hy·dro·ge·nate (dē′hī-drŏj′ə-nāt′) *tr.v.* **-nated, -nating, -nates.** *Chemistry.* To remove hydrogen from; dehydrogenize. **—de·hy·dro·ge·na·tion** *n.*

de·hy·dro·ge·nize (dē′hī-drŏj′ə-nīz′) *tr.v.* **-nized, -nizing, -nizes.** To dehydrogenate. **—de·hy·dro·ge·ni·za·tion** *n.*

de·hyp·no·tize (dē-hĭp′nə-tīz′) *tr.v.* **-tized, -tizing, -tizes.** To arouse from a hypnotic state.

PRONUNCIATION KEY

ă, pat; ā, pay; âr, care;
ä, father, are; b, bib;
ch, church; d, deed; ĕ, pet;
ē, be; f, fife; g, gag; h, hat;
hw, which; ĭ, pit; ī, pie;
îr, pier; j, judge; k, kick;
l, lid, needle; m, mum;
n, no, sudden; ng, thing;
ŏ, pot; ō, toe; ô, paw, for;
oi, noise; ou, out; o͝o, book;
o͞o, boot; p, pop; r, roar;
s, sauce; sh, ship, dish;
t, tight; th, thin, path;
th, this, bathe; ŭ, cut; ûr, fur;
v, valve; w, with; y, yes;
z, zebra, size; zh, vision;
ə, about, item, edible, gallop, circus, peaceful

IN FOREIGN WORDS:

à, *Fr.* ami; œ, *Fr.* feu, *Ger.* schön; ü, *Fr.* tu, *Ger.* über;
KH, *Ger.* ich, *Scot.* loch;
N, *Fr.* bon; y′, *Fr.* Compiègne

STRESS MARKS:

Primary stress: ′
in·cite′ (ĭn-sīt′)
Secondary stress: ′
in′sight′ (ĭn′sīt′)

de·ice (dē-īs′) *tr.v.* **-iced, -icing, -ices.** To keep free of ice; remove ice from.

de·ic·er (dē-ī′sər) *n.* **1.** Any device, such as an electric heater, used to keep surfaces free from ice or remove ice after it has formed. **2.** Any compound used to prevent the formation of ice on windows, windshields, and the like.

de·i·cide (dē′ə-sīd′) *n.* **1.** The killing of a god. **2.** One who kills a god. [New Latin *deicida* : Latin *deus*, god, DEITY + -CIDE.]

deic·tic (dīk′tĭk) *adj.* **1.** *Logic.* Directly proving by argument. Compare **elenctic. 2.** *Grammar.* Designating a word, such as *this* or *you,* that specifies the object, person, or time referred to; demonstrative. [Greek *deiktikos*, from *deiktos*, able to show directly, from *deiknunai*, to show.] **—deic·ti·cal·ly** *adv.*

de·if·ic (dē-ĭf′ĭk) *adj.* **1.** Making or tending to make divine. **2.** Divine; godlike. [Old French *deifique*, from Late Latin *deificus* : Latin *deus*, god, DEITY + -FIC.]

de·i·fi·ca·tion (dē′ə-fĭ-kā′shən) *n.* **1.** The act or process of deifying. **2.** The condition of having been deified.

de·i·form (dē′ə-fôrm) *adj.* Embodying the qualities of a god; godlike. [Medieval Latin *deiformis* : *dei-*, genitive of *deus*, god + *-formis*, -FORM.]

de·i·fy (dē′ə-fī′) *tr.v.* **-fied, -fying, -fies. 1.** To raise to divine rank. **2.** To worship, revere, or personify as a god. **3.** To idealize; exalt. [Middle English *deifien*, from Old French *deifier*, from Late Latin *deificāre*, from *deificus*, DEIFIC.] **—de·i·fi·er** *n.*

deign (dān) *v.* **deigned, deigning, deigns. —***intr.* **1.** To think it appropriate or suitable to one's dignity to do something. **2.** To agree in a condescending way to do something. —*tr.* To condescend to give or grant. [Middle English *deinen*, from Old French *deignier*, to regard as worthy, from Latin *dignārī*, from *dignus*, worthy.]

deil (dēl) *n. Scottish.* **1.** A devil. **2.** A mischievous person; imp.

de·in·sti·tu·tion·al·ize (dē-ĭn′stĭ-too′shə-nə-līz′, -tyoo′-) *tr.v.* **-ized, -izing, -izes. 1.** To remove the status of an institution from. **2.** To enable (one who is developmentally disabled or mentally ill, for example) to live away from an institution. **—de·in·sti·tu·tion·al·i·za·tion** *n.*

deip·nos·o·phist (dīp-nŏs′ə-fĭst) *n.* A person who is skilled in dinner-table conversation. [Greek *Deipnosophistai* (plural), title of work by Athenaeus (3rd century) describing learned conversations at banquets: *deipnon*, meal + *sophistai*, wise men (see **sophist**).]

Deir·dre (dîr′drə, -drē) *Irish Mythology.* A princess of Ulster who killed herself after her husband, Naoise, was murdered by King Conchobar, whom she had originally been meant to marry.

de·ism (dē′ĭz′əm) *n.* The belief that the truth of the existence of God can be discovered only by the individual through the evidence of reason and nature without resort to any particular church or to revelation. Compare **pantheism, theism.** [French *déisme*, from Latin *deus*, god.] **—de·ist** *n.* **—de·is·tic** *adj.* **—de·is·ti·cal·ly** *adv.*

de·i·ty (dē′ə-tē) *n., pl.* **-ties. 1.** A god or goddess. **2.** Divinity. **—the Deity.** God. [Middle English *deite*, from Old French, from Late Latin *deitās* (stem *deitāt-*), from Latin *deus*, god.]

deix·is (dīk′sĭs) *n. Grammar.* The use of a deictic word.

dé·jà vu (dā-zhä vü′) *n.* The illusion or feeling of having already experienced something actually being experienced for the first time. [French, "already seen."]

de·ject (dĭ-jĕkt′) *tr.v.* **-jected, -jecting, -jects.** To dishearten; dispirit. [Middle English *dejecten*, from Latin *dējicere* (past participle *dējectus*), to cast down : *dē-*, down + *jacere*, to throw.]

de·jec·ta (dĭ-jĕk′tə) *pl.n.* Excremental matter; feces. [New Latin, from Latin, neuter plural of *dējectus*, past participle of *dējicere*, to cast down, DEJECT.]

de·ject·ed (dĭ-jĕk′tĭd) *adj.* Depressed; disheartened. —See Synonyms at **sad. —de·ject·ed·ly** *adv.* **—de·ject·ed·ness** *n.*

de·jec·tion (dĭ-jĕk′shən) *n.* **1.** A state of depression; melancholy. **2. a.** Evacuation of the bowels. **b.** Excrement. —See Synonyms at **despair.**

de ju·re (dē joor′ē, dā yoo′rā) *adj.* By legal or constitutional right. Compare **de facto.** [Latin, "according to law."]

dek-, deka-. Variants of **deca-.**

dekagram. Variant of **decagram.**

dekaliter. Variant of **decaliter.**

dekameter. Variant of **decameter.**

Dekkan. See **Deccan.**

Dek·ker (dĕk′ər), **Thomas** (*c.* 1572–1632). British dramatist and author. He wrote more than 40 plays, *The Shoemaker's Holiday* (1600) being the best known today.

dek·ko (dĕk′ō) *n., pl.* **-kos.** *British Slang.* A look; a glance. [Hindi *dekho*, imperative of *dekhnā,* to look.]

De Koo·ning (də kō′nĭng, koo′-), **Willem** (1904–). Dutch-born U.S. painter. He emigrated to the United States in 1926 and became connected with action painters. After 1950 he produced a series of female figures with distorted bodies and grimacing faces.

del (dĕl) *n. Symbol* ∇ *Mathematics.* The vector differential operator, having as components in three-dimensional Cartesian coordinates the first partial derivative operators with respect to each coordinate direction. Also called "nabla." [Short for DELTA (because it appears like an inverted delta).]

del. 1. delegate; delegation. **2.** delete.

Del. Delaware.

De·la·croix (dĕl′ə-kwrä′), **(Ferdinand Victor) Eugène** (1798–1863). French painter and leading figure in the romantic movement in art. Delacroix's *Massacre at Chios* caused a sensation when exhibited at the Salon of 1824. Its rich tones and drama were in marked contrast to the sedate canvases of the classicists. Delacroix exalted color and tumult, as in the voluptuous *Death of Sardanapalus* (1827) and *Liberty Leading the People,* celebrating the Revolution of 1830.

de·laine (də-lān′) *n.* A light fabric of wool or cotton and wool. [French *(mousseline) de laine,* "(muslin) of wool," from Latin *lāna,* wool.]

de la Mare (də lə mâr′), **Walter John** (1873–1956). British poet and novelist. He published his first collection of poetry, *Songs of Childhood* (1902), under a pseudonym. *Memoirs of a Midget* (1921) is his best-known novel.

de·lam·i·nate (dē-lăm′ə-nāt) *intr.v.* **-nated, -nating, -nates.** To split into thin layers.

de·lam·i·na·tion (dē-lăm′ə-nā′shən) *n.* **1.** A splitting or separating into layers. **2.** *Embryology.* The splitting of the blastoderm into two layers of cells.

de·late (dĭ-lāt′) *tr.v.* **-lated, -lating, -lates.** *Archaic.* **1.** To report (an offense). **2.** To inform against (a person). [Latin *dēlātus,* past participle of *dēferre,* to bring down, report, indict : *dē-,* down + *ferre,* to bear.] **—de·la·tion** *n.* **—de·la·tor** *n.*

De Lau·ren·tis (dē lô-rĕn′təs), **Dino** (1919–). Italian filmmaker. After a brief acting career, he turned to movie production and collaborated on many critically acclaimed films, including *Bitter Rice* (1949), *Europa '51* (1952), and *War and Peace* (1956).

Del·a·ware¹ (dĕl′ə-wâr′) *n., pl.* **-wares** or collectively **Delaware. 1.** A group of Algonquian-speaking North American Indian tribes, formerly inhabiting the Delaware River valley. **2.** A member of any of these tribes. **3.** Their language. Also called "Lenape," "Leni-Lenape," "Lenni-Lenape." **—Del·a·war·e·an** *n. & adj.*

Delaware² *n.* A variety of grape having sweet light-red fruit. [After the state of DELAWARE.]

Delaware³. *Abbr.* **Del.** The second-smallest of the United States, on the Atlantic seaboard. It covers 5,328 square kilometers (2,057 square miles) on the Delaware River. In 1776 it was one of the 13 founder states of the United States and fought on the Union side in the Civil War (1861–65). Wilmington is the industrial center. Dover is the capital.

Delaware⁴. River, *c.* 450 kilometers (280 miles) long, rising in the Catskill Mts. of southeastern New York and flowing generally south, forming the New York–Pennsylvania, Pennsylvania–New Jersey, and New Jersey–Delaware borders along its course. Its outlet is Delaware Bay, an inlet of the Atlantic Ocean extending 84 kilometers (52 miles) between Delaware and New Jersey. The lower Delaware River south of Trenton, New Jersey (the head of navigation), flows through a highly industrialized area.

De La Warr (dĕl′ə wâr′), **Baron Thomas West** (1577–1618). U.S. colonial administrator, born in England. He organized, fortified, and for two years directly governed the once-troubled Virginia Company colony. The state of Delaware and the Delaware River were named in his honor.

de·lay (dĭ-lā′) *v.* **-layed, -laying, -lays. —***tr.* **1.** To postpone until a later time; defer. **2.** To cause to be late or detained; hinder. —*intr.* To be unduly slow in doing something; linger. ~*n.* **1.** The act of delaying; postponement. **2.** The condition of being delayed; detainment. **3.** The period of time during which one is delayed. **4.** The time interval between any two events. [Middle English *delaien,* from Old French *delaier, deslaier* : *des-,* from Latin *dē-,* off + *laier,* variant of *laissier,* to leave, let, from Latin *laxāre,* to slacken, undo, from *laxus,* slack, loose.] **—de·lay·er** *n.*
    Synonyms: check, detain, retard, slow.

de·layed-ac·tion (dĭ-lād′ăk′shən) *adj.* Also **de·lay-ac·tion** (dĭ-lā′-). **1.** Acting only after a predetermined time interval elapses. **2.** Detonating after impact.

delayed drop *n.* A parachute jump in which the parachutist delays opening the parachute for a certain period of time.

delayed neutron *n.* A neutron emitted by a product of nuclear fission several seconds or minutes after the fission occurs. Compare **prompt neutron.**

delay line *n. Electronics.* Any of various devices used to cause a controlled delay in the passage or action of a signal.

de·le (dē′lē) *n.* A sign indicating that something is to be removed from typeset matter. ~*tr.v.* **deled, -leing, -les. 1.** To take out or delete. **2.** To mark with a dele. Compare **stet.** [Latin *dēle,* imperative singular of *dēlēre,* DELETE.]

de·lec·ta·ble (dĭ-lĕk′tə-bəl) *adj.* Greatly pleasing, especially to the sense of taste; enjoyable. [Middle English, from Old French, from Latin *dēlectābilis,* from *dēlectāre,* to please, DELIGHT.] **—de·lec·ta·bil·i·ty, de·lec·ta·ble·ness** *n.* **—de·lec·ta·bly** *adv.*

de·lec·ta·tion (dē′lĕk-tā′shən) *n.* Pleasure; delight.

del·e·ga·cy (dĕl′ə-gə-sē) *n., pl.* **-cies. 1.** The authority, office, or position of a delegate. **2.** The act of delegating or being delegated. **3.** A body of delegates; a delegation.

del·e·gate (dĕl′ə-gāt′, -gĭt) *n. Abbr.* **del. 1.** A person authorized to act as representative for another or others, especially one elected or appointed to be a representative at a conference. **2. a.** An elected or appointed representative of a U.S. territory in the House of Representatives who is entitled to speak but not vote. **b.** A member of the House of Delegates, the lower house of the Maryland, Virginia, and West Virginia legislatures.
    ~*v.* (dĕl′ə-gāt′) **delegated, -gating, -gates. —***tr.* **1.** To authorize or send (a person) as one's representative. **2.** To commit to one's agent

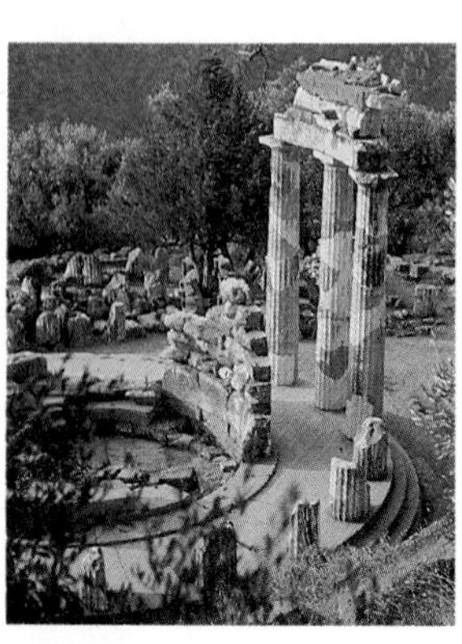

Delphi *The ancient Greeks considered the shrine at Delphi to be the "navel" of the world. This circle of ruined columns is all that remains of the shrine of the Delphic Oracle, dedicated to the god Apollo and built in the fourth century* B.C. *The oracle, the most important center for divination in ancient Greece, was consulted on political and military questions as well as private matters.*

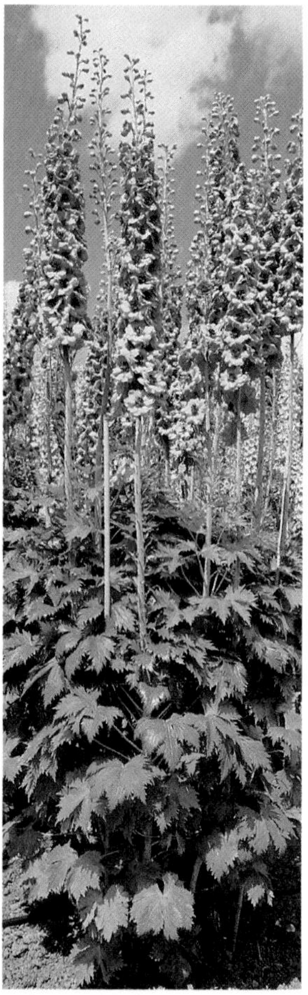

delphinium *"Loch Maree" (above) is a purple-blue perennial variety of this hardy annual, biennial, and perennial garden plant.*

or representative. **3.** To assign (work or duties) to employees or others over whom one has authority. **4.** *Law.* To appoint (one's debtor) as a debtor to one's creditor to replace oneself in satisfying a claim. *—intr.* To assign work or duties to employees or others over whom one has authority: *A manager must know how to delegate effectively.* [Middle English *delegat,* from Medieval Latin *dēlēgātus,* from Latin, past participle of *dēlēgāre,* to send away, dispatch : *dē-,* away + *lēgāre,* to send.]

del·e·ga·tion (dĕl′ə-gā′shən) *n.* **1. a.** The act of delegating. **b.** The condition of being delegated; appointment; deputation. **2.** *Abbr.* **del.** A person or group of persons officially elected or appointed to represent another or others.

de Lesseps, Ferdinand Marie, Vicomte. See **Lesseps.**

de·lete (dĭ-lēt′) *tr.v.* **-leted, -leting, -letes.** *Abbr.* **del.** To strike out or cancel; omit. —See Synonyms at **erase.** [Latin *dēlēre*†, to wipe out, efface.]

del·e·te·ri·ous (dĕl′ə-tîr′ē-əs) *adj.* Having a harmful effect; injurious. [Medieval Latin *dēlētērius,* from Greek *dēlētērios,* from *dēleisthai*†, to harm, injure.] **—del·e·te·ri·ous·ly** *adv.* **—del·e·te·ri·ous·ness** *n.*

de·le·tion (dĭ-lē′shən) *n.* **1.** An act of deleting; an omission or erasing. **2.** A word, passage, or the like that has been deleted from written, printed, or recorded matter. **3.** *Genetics.* A type of mutation in which part of a chromosome is missing. In this sense, also called "deficiency."

delft (dĕlft) *n.* Also **delf** (dĕlf). **1.** A style of glazed earthenware, usually blue and white, originally made in Delft. Also called "delftware." **2.** A piece of pottery in this style. **3.** Any pottery made in imitation of this style.

Delft (dĕlft). Town in South Holland province, southern Netherlands. A fine pottery has been produced here since the late 16th century. The artist Vermeer lived and worked in Delft.

Del·hi (dĕl′ē). Capital of India, on the right bank of the Jumna River, a tributary of the Ganges. Delhi was an ancient capital of Hindu legend. Under its 17th-century Muslim ruler, Shah Jahan, Old Delhi was laid out within defensive walls 9 kilometers (5.5 miles) long. Chief among his monuments are the huge Red Fort (1638–48) and Great Mosque (1644–58). New Delhi was founded under the British in 1912 to replace Calcutta as the capital.

del·i (dĕl′ē) *n., pl.* **-is.** *Informal.* A delicatessen.

De·li·an (dē′lē-ən) *adj.* Of or pertaining to Delos or its inhabitants. *~n.* A native or inhabitant of Delos.

de·lib·er·ate (dĭ-lĭb′ə-rāt′) *v.* **-ated, -ating, -ates.** *—intr.* **1.** To take careful thought; reflect. **2.** To consult with another or others as a process in reaching a decision. *—tr.* To consider (a matter) by carefully weighing alternatives or the like.
~adj. (dĭ-lĭb′ər-ĭt) **1.** Premeditated; intentional. **2. a.** Careful and slow in deciding or determining. **b.** Not rashly or hastily determined: *a deliberate choice.* **3.** Leisurely or slow in motion or manner; not hurried or impulsive. —See Synonyms at **voluntary.** [Latin *dēlīberāre,* to weigh well, ponder : *dē-,* completely + *lībrāre,* to weigh, from *lībra,* a scale, pound.] **—de·lib·er·ate·ly** *adv.* **—de·lib·er·ate·ness** *n.* **—de·lib·er·a·tor** *n.*

de·lib·er·a·tion (dĭ-lĭb′ə-rā′shən) *n.* **1.** The process of deliberating; thoughtful and lengthy consideration. **2.** *Often* **deliberations.** Formal discussion and debate of all sides of an issue. **3.** Thoughtfulness or care in decision or action.

de·lib·er·a·tive (dĭ-lĭb′ə-rā′tĭv, -ər-ə-tĭv) *adj.* **1.** Assembled or organized for deliberation or debate: *a deliberative legislature.* **2.** Characterized by or being the result of deliberation or debate. **3.** *Grammar.* Expressing doubt or deliberation. **—de·lib·er·a·tive·ly** *adv.* **—de·lib·er·a·tive·ness** *n.*

De·libes (də-lēb′), **(Clément Philibert) Léo** (1836–91). French composer. His compositions include the ballet *Coppélia* (1870) and the opera *Lakmé* (1883).

del·i·ca·cy (dĕl′ĭ-kə-sē) *n., pl.* **-cies. 1.** The quality of being delicate. **2.** Frailty of bodily constitution or health. **3.** Sensitivity of perception, feeling, appreciation, or the like; refinement. **4. a.** Consideration of the feelings of others. **b.** Aversion to what is considered morally distasteful or injurious. **5.** A need of taste and tact in treating or handling: *a topic of some delicacy.* **6.** Softness or fineness of touch. **7.** Fineness or keenness of response or reaction. **8.** Something pleasing and appealing, especially a choice food. [Middle English *delicacie,* from *delicat,* DELICATE.]

del·i·cate (dĕl′ĭ-kĭt) *adj.* **1. a.** Exquisitely or pleasingly fine. **b.** Beautiful in a graceful or tender way. **c.** Characterized by precise skill, as in execution or workmanship. **2.** Frail in constitution or health. **3.** Easily broken or damaged. **4.** Requiring tasteful and tactful treatment. **5.** Keen in sense discrimination or perception. **6.** Manifesting extreme sensitivity and distaste toward anything immodest, impolite, or morally reprehensible; squeamish. **7.** Mindful of the feelings of others. **8.** Keenly accurate in response or reaction. **9.** Soft or gentle in touch or skill. **10.** Very subtle in difference or distinction. —See Synonyms at **fragile.** [Middle English *delicat,* from Latin *dēlicātus*†, alluring, charming, dainty.] **—del·i·cate·ly** *adv.* **—del·i·cate·ness** *n.*

del·i·ca·tes·sen (dĕl′ĭ-kə-tĕs′ən) *n.* A shop that sells cooked or prepared foods ready for serving, especially foreign or unusual foods. [German *Delikatessen,* plural of *Delikatesse,* delicacy, from French *délicatesse,* from Italian *delicatezza,* from *delicato,* delicate, dainty, from Latin *dēlicātus,* DELICATE.]

de·li·cious (dĭ-lĭsh′əs) *adj.* **1.** Highly pleasing or agreeable to the senses of taste or smell. **2.** Very pleasant; enjoyable; delightful. [Middle English, from Old French, from Late Latin *dēliciōsus,* pleasing, delightful, from Latin *dēlicia,* pleasure, from *dēlicere,* to entice away, DELIGHT.] **—de·li·cious·ly** *adv.* **—de·li·cious·ness** *n.*

De·li·cious (dĭ-lĭsh′əs) *n.* A variety of red or yellow apple having sweet fruit.

de·lict (dĭ-lĭkt′) *n.* **1.** In civil law, a misdemeanor; tort; an offense. **2.** In Scots and South African law, the branch of law corresponding to the English law of tort. **3.** In Roman law, the obligation to pay or make compensation for any wrong committed. [Latin *dēlictum,* from *dēlictus,* past participle of *dēlinquere,* to fail in duty, offend. See **delinquent.**]

de·light (dĭ-līt′) *n.* **1.** Great pleasure; gratification; joy. **2.** Something that gives great pleasure. —See Synonyms at **ecstasy.**
~v. **delighted, -lighting, -lights.** *—intr.* **1.** To take great pleasure or joy. **2.** To give great pleasure or joy. *—tr.* To please greatly. [Middle English *deliten,* from Old French *deleitier,* from Latin *dēlectāre,* frequentative of *dēlicere,* to allure, entice away : *dē-,* away + *lacere*†, to allure.]

de·light·ed (dĭ-lī′tĭd) *adj.* **1.** Filled with delight. **2.** *Obsolete.* Delightful. **—de·light·ed·ly** *adv.* **—de·light·ed·ness** *n.*

de·light·ful (dĭ-līt′fəl) *adj.* Affording keen satisfaction; greatly pleasing. **—de·light·ful·ly** *adv.* **—de·light·ful·ness** *n.*

de·light·some (dĭ-līt′səm) *adj.* Delightful. **—de·light·some·ly** *adv.* **—de·light·some·ness** *n.*

De·li·lah[1] (dĭ-lī′lə). A Philistine woman who betrayed Samson, her lover, to the Philistines by having his hair shorn as he slept, thus depriving him of his strength. Judges 16.

Delilah[2] *n.* A seductive, treacherous woman. [After DELILAH.]

de·lim·it (dĭ-lĭm′ĭt) *tr.v.* **-ited, -iting, -its.** Also **de·lim·i·tate** (dĭ-lĭm′ə-tāt′) **-tated, -tating, -tates. 1.** To establish the limit or boundaries of; demarcate. **2.** To define: *Their authority is delimited in the constitution.* [French *délimiter,* from Latin *dēlīmitāre* : *dē-,* completely + *līmitāre,* to limit, from *līmes* (stem *līmit-*), LIMIT.] **—de·lim·i·ta·tion** *n.* **—de·lim·i·ta·tive** *adj.*

de·lim·it·er (dĭ-lĭm′ə-tər) *n.* *Computer Science.* A character marking the beginning or end of a unit of data.

de·lin·e·ate (dĭ-lĭn′ē-āt′) *tr.v.* **-ated, -ating, -ates. 1.** To draw or trace the outline of; sketch out. **2.** To represent pictorially; depict. **3.** To depict in words or gestures; portray. [Latin *dēlīneāre* : *dē-,* completely + *līnea,* thread, LINE.] **—de·lin·e·a·tion** *n.* **—de·lin·e·a·tive** *adj.*

de·lin·e·a·tor (dĭ-lĭn′ē-ā′tər) *n.* **1.** One that delineates. **2.** An adjustable pattern used by tailors for cutting garments of various sizes.

de·lin·quen·cy (dĭ-lĭng′kwən-sē) *n., pl.* **-cies. 1.** Negligence or failure in doing what is required. **2.** An offense or minor crime; a misdeed. **3.** A tendency to indulge in antisocial behavior, especially petty crime. See **juvenile delinquency.**

de·lin·quent (dĭ-lĭng′kwənt) *adj.* **1.** Engaging in delinquency. **2.** Failing to do what is required by law or obligation. **3.** Overdue in payment: *a delinquent account.*
~n. **1.** A delinquent person, especially a **juvenile delinquent** *(see).* **2.** A person who neglects or fails to do what law or obligation requires. [Latin *dēlinquēns* (stem *dēlinquent-*), present participle of *dēlinquere,* to fail in duty, offend, "leave undone" : *dē-* (intensive) + *linquere,* to leave.] **—de·lin·quent·ly** *adv.*

del·i·quesce (dĕl′ə-kwĕs′) *intr.v.* **-quesced, -quescing, -quesces. 1.** *Chemistry.* To dissolve and become liquid by absorbing moisture from the air. **2.** *Botany.* **a.** To divide into numerous subdivisions that lack a main axis. **b.** To become fluid or soft on maturing, as do certain fungi. **3.** To melt away or disappear as if by melting. —See Synonyms at **melt.** [Latin *dēliquēscere* : *dē-,* completely + *liquēscere,* to melt, from *liquēre,* to be liquid.]

del·i·ques·cence (dĕl′ə-kwĕs′əns) *n.* **1.** The act or process of deliquescing. **2.** The liquid resulting from the process of deliquescing. **—del·i·ques·cent** *adj.*

de·lir·i·ous (dĭ-lîr′ē-əs) *adj.* **1.** Affected by delirium. **2.** Characteristic of or pertaining to delirium: *delirious speech.* **—de·lir·i·ous·ly** *adv.* **—de·lir·i·ous·ness** *n.*

de·lir·i·um (dĭ-lîr′ē-əm) *n., pl.* **-ums** or **-ia** (-ē-ə). **1.** A state of temporary mental confusion and clouded consciousness resulting from high fever, intoxication, or shock, and characterized by anxiety, tremors, hallucinations, delusions, and incoherence. **2.** A state of uncontrolled excitement or emotion. [Latin *dēlīrium,* from *dēlīrāre,* to deviate from a straight line, be deranged : *dē-,* away from + *līrā,* a furrow.] **—de·lir·i·ant** *adj.*

delirium tre·mens (trē′mənz) *n.* A severe psychotic delirium caused by the withdrawal of alcohol from an alcoholic or similar symptoms occurring when there is severe organic or functional brain disorder. Also informally called "D.T.'s." [New Latin, "trembling delirium."]

del·i·tes·cence (dĕl′ə-tĕs′əns) *n.* **1.** The unexpected disappearance or subsidence of disease symptoms. **2.** An incubation period of an infectious disease. [From Latin *dēlitēscens,* present participle of *dēlitēscere,* to hide away, lurk : *dē-,* away + *latēscere,* inceptive of *latēre,* to be concealed.] **—del·i·tes·cent** *adj.*

De·li·us (dē′lē-əs), **Frederick** (1862–1934). British composer, of German parentage. He emigrated to Florida as an orange planter and was influenced by Negro songs. He moved to France, there composing operas, concertos, orchestral music, songs, and chamber music. His works include *On Hearing the First Cuckoo in Spring* (1912).

de·liv·er (dĭ-lĭv′ər) *v.* **-ered, -ering, -ers.** *—tr.* **1.** To release or rescue from bondage, danger, or evil of any kind; set free. —See Synonyms at **save.** **2. a.** To assist (a female) in giving birth: *The doctor delivered her of twins.* **b.** To assist or aid in the birth of: *The midwife delivered the twins.* **3.** To put into another's possession or power; hand over. **4.** To take to the intended recipient: *deliver groceries.* **5.** To send forth (a blow, for example) by releasing, discharging, or throwing. **6.** To utter or pronounce. **7.** To produce or perform (something promised): *delivered the contract on time.* **—deliver oneself of.** To pronounce; utter. **—deliver the goods.** *Slang.* To perform as desired or promised. *—intr.* **1.** To take goods to the intended recipient: *Our grocer delivers.* **2.** *Informal.* To produce results as promised or expected. [Middle English *deliv(e)ren,* from Old French *delivrer,* from Late Latin *dēlīberāre* : Latin *dē-,* completely + *līberāre,* to set free, from *līber,* free.] **—de·liv·er·a·bil·i·ty** *n.* **—de·liv·er·a·ble** *adj.* **—de·liv·er·er** *n.*

de·liv·er·ance (dĭ-lĭv′ər-əns) *n.* **1.** The act of delivering; especially, rescue from bondage or danger. **2.** The state of being so delivered. **3.** A publicly expressed opinion, such as the verdict of a jury.

de·liv·er·y (dĭ-lĭv′ə-rē) *n., pl.* **-ies.** **1.** The act of delivering or conveying. **2.** That which is delivered. **3.** The act of releasing or rescuing. **4.** The act of giving birth; parturition. **5.** *Law.* The act of transferring possession of an article from one person to another. **6.** A giving up; a surrender. **7. a.** Utterance. **b.** A manner of speaking or singing. **8.** The act or manner of throwing or discharging.

delivery room *n.* A room in a hospital equipped for delivering babies.

dell (dĕl) *n.* A small, secluded wooded valley. [Middle English *del,* Old English *dell,* from Germanic.]

del·la Rob·bi·a (dĕl′ə rō′bē-ə), **Luca** (*c.* 1400–82). Italian sculptor of the early Renaissance. One of his best-known works is a marble relief, *Cantoria,* in the Duomo, Florence. Much of his work was done with enameled terra cotta for which he developed a glazing.

Del·mon·i·co steak (dĕl-mŏn′ĭ-kō′) *n.* A small, often boned, steak from the front section of the short loin of beef. Also called "club steak." [After the *Delmonico* Restaurant, New York City, founded by Lorenzo Delmonico (1813–1881).]

de·lo·cal·ize (dē-lō′kə-līz′) *tr.v.* **-ized, -izing, -izes.** **1.** To remove (something) from its native or usual locality. **2.** To broaden the range or scope of. **3.** *Physics & Chemistry.* To remove (electrons) from a particular position. **—de·lo·cal·i·za·tion** *n.*

De·lorme or **de l'Orme** (də-lôrm′), **Philibert** (*c.* 1510–1570). French architect. He was in charge of work at Fontainebleau, and later commissions included extending the palace of the Tuileries in 1565.

De·los (dē′lŏs). *Greek* **Dhí·los** (*thē′*lôs′). Greek island, virtually uninhabited, in the Aegean. It is the smallest of the Cyclades group, covering an area of barely 3 square kilometers (1 square mile). In Greek myth it was the birthplace of Apollo, and temples dedicated to the god have been excavated on the island.

de·louse (dē-lous′) *tr.v.* **-loused, -lousing, -louses.** To rid (a person or animal) of lice by physical or chemical means.

Del·phi (dĕl′fī′). Ancient site in central Greece, 10 kilometers (6 miles) inland from the Gulf of Corinth. It was the most important sanctuary of Apollo, lying in a secluded glade overlooked by Mt. Parnassus. The site, discovered in 1890, included Apollo's temple, where his oracle was consulted, a theater, and treasuries. The oracle fell into disuse with the rise of Christianity.

Del·phic (dĕl′fĭk) *adj.* Also **Del·phi·an** (-fē-ən). **1.** Of or pertaining to Delphi or to the oracle of Apollo at Delphi. **2.** *Sometimes* **delphic.** Obscure in meaning; ambiguous; oracular.

del·phin·i·um (dĕl-fĭn′ē-əm) *n.* Any plant of the genus *Delphinium*; especially, any of several tall cultivated varieties having spikes of variously colored, especially blue, spurred flowers, such as the larkspur. [New Latin *Delphinium* (genus), from Greek *delphinion,* larkspur, diminutive of *delphis* (stem *delphin-*), DOLPHIN (from the shape of the nectary).]

Del·phi·nus (dĕl-fī′nəs) *n.* A constellation in the Northern Hemisphere near Pegasus and Aquila. [New Latin, from Latin *delphīnus,* DOLPHIN.]

del·ta (dĕl′tə) *n.* **1.** The fourth letter in the Greek alphabet, written Δ, δ, transliterated in English as *d, D.* See feature at **alphabet.** **2. a.** A usually triangular alluvial area at the mouth of a river. **b.** A similar deposit at the mouth of a tidal inlet, caused by tidal currents. **3.** Anything resembling the shape of a triangle. **4.** *Mathematics.* A finite increment in a variable. [Middle English, from Greek, from Semitic; akin to Hebrew *dāleth.*] **—del·ta·ic** (dĕl-tā′ĭk), **del·tic** (dĕl′tĭk) *adj.*

delta ray *n.* An electron ejected from matter by ionizing radiation.

delta wave or **delta rhythm** *n.* A low-frequency brain wave that emanates from the forward portion of the brain during deep sleep in normal adults.

delta wing *n.* An aircraft with sweptback wings that give it the appearance of an isoceles triangle.

del·toid (dĕl′toid′) *n.* A thick, triangular muscle covering the shoulder joint, used to raise the arm from the side.

~adj. **1.** Triangular. **2.** Pertaining to the deltoid. [New Latin *deltoides,* from Greek *deltoeidēs,* triangular : DELTA + -OID.]

de·lude (dĭ-lo͞od′) *tr.v.* **-luded, -luding, -ludes.** **1.** To deceive the mind or judgment of; mislead. **2.** *Obsolete.* To elude or evade. **3.** *Obsolete.* To frustrate the hopes or plans of. —See Synonyms at **deceive.** [Middle English *deluden,* from Latin *dēlūdere,* to play false, deceive : *dē-* (pejorative) + *lūdere,* to play, from *lūdus,* game.] **—de·lud·a·ble** *adj.* **—de·lud·er** *n.* **—de·lud·ing·ly** *adv.*

del·uge (dĕl′yo͞oj) *tr.v.* **-uged, -uging, -uges.** **1.** To overrun with water; flood. **2.** To inundate in overwhelming numbers: *deluged with inquiries.*

~n. **1.** A great flood; a heavy downpour. **2.** Anything that overwhelms as if by a great flood. **—the Deluge.** The great flood that occurred in the time of Noah. Genesis 7–10. [Middle English, from Old French, from Latin *dīluvium,* flood, from *dīluere,* to wash away : *dis-,* apart + *-luere,* from *lavere,* to wash.]

de·lu·sion (dĭ-lo͞o′zhən, -shən) *n.* **1. a.** The act or process of deluding; deception. **b.** The state of being deluded. **2. a.** A mistaken belief or idea. **b.** *Psychiatry.* A false belief, strongly held in spite of invalidating evidence. [Middle English *delusioun,* from Latin *dēlūsio* (stem *dēlūsiōn-*), from *dēlūdere* (past participle *dēlūsus*), DELUDE.] **—de·lu·sion·al** *adj.*

Usage: *Delusion* and *illusion* are seldom interchangeable, though closely related. *Delusion* refers to false belief held without reservation as a result of self-deception, the imposition of another, or mental disorder. It is the stronger term, often associated with harm. *Illusion* is applicable to a false impression, frequently based on fancy or on wishful thinking, or to a false perception (such as an optical illusion) that one eventually recognizes as false.

de·lu·sive (dĭ-lo͞o′sĭv) *adj.* Also **de·lu·so·ry** (-lo͞o′sə-rē). **1.** Tending to deceive or mislead; deceptive. **2.** Having the nature of a delusion; false. **—de·lu·sive·ly** *adv.* **—de·lu·sive·ness** *n.*

de luxe, de·luxe (dĭ-lo͝oks′, dĭ-lŭks′) *adj.* Of special elegance or luxury; superior: *a de luxe model.*

~adv. In an elegant manner; sumptuously. [French, "of luxury."]

delve (dĕlv) *v.* **delved, delving, delves.** *—intr.* **1.** To search deeply and painstakingly. **2.** *Archaic.* To dig the ground, as with a spade. *—tr. Archaic.* To dig (ground) with a spade. [Middle English *delven,* to dig, Old English *delfan.*] **—delv·er** *n.*

Dem. Democrat; Democratic.

de·mag·net·ize (dē-măg′nə-tīz′) *tr.v.* **-ized, -izing, -izes.** To remove magnetic properties from. **—de·mag·net·i·za·tion** *n.* **—de·mag·net·iz·er** *n.*

dem·a·gog·ic (dĕm′ə-gŏj′ĭk) *adj.* Also **dem·a·gog·i·cal** (-ĭ-kəl). Relating to, of the nature of, or characteristic of a demagogue. **—dem·a·gog·i·cal·ly** *adv.*

dem·a·gogue, dem·a·gog (dĕm′ə-gôg′, -gŏg′) *n.* **1.** A leader who obtains power by means of impassioned appeals to the emotions and prejudices of the populace. **2.** A leader of the common people in ancient times. [Greek *dēmagōgos,* popular leader : *dēmos,* common people + *agōgos,* leading, from *agein,* to lead.]

dem·a·gogu·er·y (dĕm′ə-gô′gə-rē, -gŏg′ə-rē) *n.* The practices or rhetoric of a demagogue. Also called "demagogism."

dem·a·go·gy (dĕm′ə-gō′jē, -gô′jē, -gŏj′ē) *n.* **1.** The quality or character of demagogues. **2.** Rule by a demagogue. **3.** Demagogues collectively.

de·mand (dĭ-mănd′, -mänd′) *v.* **-manded, -manding, -mands.** *—tr.* **1.** To ask for urgently or firmly, leaving no chance for refusal or denial. **2.** To claim as a right or due. **3.** To ask to be informed of: *demand the cause of his action.* **4.** To need or require as useful, just, proper, or necessary. **5.** *Law.* **a.** To summon to court. **b.** To claim formally; lay legal claim to. *—intr.* To make a demand.

~n. **1.** The act of demanding. **2.** Something that is demanded. **3. a.** The state of being sought after. **b.** An urgent requirement, need, or claim: *an ever-growing demand for investment.* **4.** *Archaic.* An emphatic question or enquiry. **5.** *Law.* A formal claim. **6.** *Economics.* **a.** The desire to possess something combined with the ability to purchase it. **b.** The amount of any commodity that people are ready and able to buy at a given time for a given price. Compare **supply.** **—in demand.** Much sought after. **—on demand.** Immediately obtainable on presentation or request. [Middle English *demaunden,* from Old French *demander,* to ask, charge with doing, from Latin *dēmandāre,* to give in charge, entrust : *dē-* (intensive) + *mandāre,* to entrust.] **—de·mand·a·ble** *adj.* **—de·mand·er** *n.*

Usage: *Demand* (verb) is commonly followed by a direct object in the form of a word (*demand payment*) or clause (*demand that he go*), or by an infinitive (*demand to know why*). The object is often followed by of or from: demand much of (or from) him. In a parallel construction, demand (noun) is followed by on: make a demand on him.

demand deposit *n.* A bank deposit that can be withdrawn by the depositor immediately and without advance notice.

de·mand·ing (dĭ-măn′dĭng, dĭ-män′-) *adj.* **1.** Making rigorous or excessive demands. **2.** Requiring careful attention or constant effort. —See Synonyms at **burdensome.** **—de·mand·ing·ly** *adv.*

demand note *n.* A bill or draft payable in lawful money on presentation or demand.

de·mand-pull (dĭ-mănd′po͝ol′, dĭ-mänd′-) *adj.* Designating a type of inflation in which increased demand for a limited amount of goods and services tends to drive up prices. Compare **cost-push.**

de·man·toid (dĭ-măn′toid′) *n.* A transparent, green variety of garnet, used as a gem. [German *Demantoid* : *Demant* (obsolete), diamond, from Middle High German *diemant,* from Old French *diamant,* DIAMOND + -OID.]

de·mar·cate (dĭ-mär′kāt′, dē′mär-kāt′) *tr.v.* **-cated, -cating, -cates.** **1.** To set the boundaries of; delimit. **2.** To separate clearly as if by boundaries; discriminate. [Back-formation from DEMARCATION.] **—de·mar·ca·tor** *n.*

de·mar·ca·tion (dē′mär-kā′shən) *n.* **1.** The setting or marking of boundaries or limits. **2.** A separation; a distinction: *a line of demarcation.* **3.** *Chiefly British.* **a.** The practice of strictly differentiating the type of work carried out by members of individual trade unions.

PRONUNCIATION KEY

ă, pat; ā, pay; âr, care;
ä, father, are; b, bib;
ch, church; d, deed; ĕ, pet;
ē, be; f, fife; g, gag; h, hat;
hw, which; ĭ, pit; ī, pie;
îr, pier; j, judge; k, kick;
l, lid, needle; m, mum;
n, no, sudden; ng, thing;
ŏ, pot; ō, toe; ô, paw, for;
oi, noise; ou, out; o͝o, book;
o͞o, boot; p, pop; r, roar;
s, sauce; sh, ship, dish;
t, tight; th, thin, path;
th, this, bathe; ŭ, cut; ûr, fur;
v, valve; w, with; y, yes;
z, zebra, size; zh, vision;
ə, about, item, edible, gallop, circus, peaceful

IN FOREIGN WORDS:

à, *Fr.* ami; œ, *Fr.* feu, *Ger.* schön; ü, *Fr.* tu, *Ger.* über;
KH, *Ger.* ich, *Scot.* loch;
N, *Fr.* bon; y′, *Fr.* Compiègne

STRESS MARKS:

Primary stress: ′
in·cite′ (ĭn-sīt′)
Secondary stress: ′
in′sight′ (ĭn′sīt′)

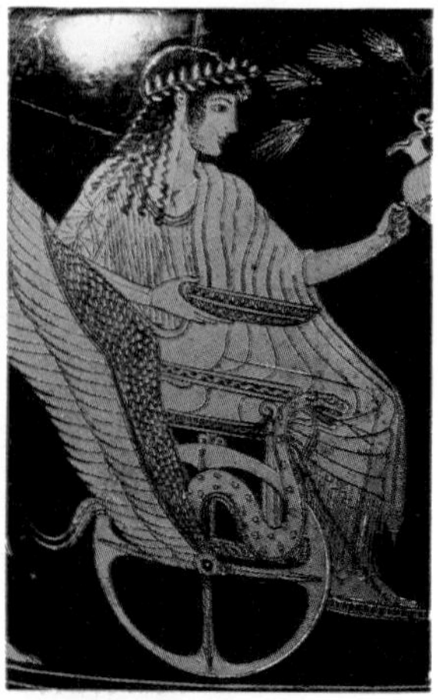

Demeter *The goddess of agriculture sending the gift of corn to mankind—a scene on a Greek vase from about 480 B.C. When Demeter's daughter Persephone was carried off by Hades, god of the netherworld, Demeter in her grief allowed the earth to become barren. Her brother Zeus decided that Persephone should spend six months above ground and six below—the origin, according to Greek mythology, of the seasons.*

PRONUNCIATION KEY
ă, pat; ā, pay; âr, care; ä, father, are; b, bib; ch, church; d, deed; ĕ, pet; ē, be; f, fife; g, gag; h, hat; hw, which; ĭ, pit; ī, pie; îr, pier; j, judge; k, kick; l, lid, needle; m, mum; n, no, sudden; ng, thing; ŏ, pot; ō, toe; ô, paw, for; oi, noise; ou, out; o͝o, book; o͞o, boot; p, pop; r, roar; s, sauce; sh, ship, dish; t, tight; th, thin, path; *th*, this, bathe; ŭ, cut; ûr, fur; v, valve; w, with; y, yes; z, zebra, size; zh, vision; ə, about, item, edible, gallop, circus, peaceful

IN FOREIGN WORDS:
à, *Fr.* ami; œ, *Fr.* feu, *Ger.* schön; ü, *Fr.* tu, *Ger.* über; KH, *Ger.* ich, *Scot.* loch; N, *Fr.* bon; y', *Fr.* Compiègne

STRESS MARKS:
Primary stress: ′ **in·cite′** (ĭn-sīt′)
Secondary stress: ′ **in′sight′** (ĭn′sīt′)

b. An instance of this practice. [Spanish *demarcación,* from *demarcar,* to mark out the boundary : *de-,* completely + *marcar,* to mark, from Italian *marcare,* from Old Italian, from Germanic.]

dé·marche (dā-märsh′) *n.* **1.** An initiative or maneuver; a step. **2.** A diplomatic representation or protest. **3.** A statement or protest addressed to public authorities. [French, from Old French *demarche,* gait, from *demarchier,* to march : *de-,* from + *marchier,* to march, probably of Germanic origin.]

de·ma·te·ri·al·ize (dē′mə-tîr′ē-ə-līz′) *v.* **-ized, -izing, -izes.** —*tr.* To divest of material qualities or characteristics. —*intr.* To lose material character or form; disappear. **—de·ma·te·ri·al·i·za·tion** *n.*

deme (dēm) *n.* **1.** Any of the townships of ancient Attica. **2.** *Ecology.* A local, usually stable population of organisms of the same kind or species. [Greek *dēmos,* common people, deme.]

de·mean¹ (dĭ-mēn′) *tr.v.* **-meaned, -meaning, -means.** To conduct or behave (oneself) in a particular manner.
∼*n. Archaic.* Behavior; demeanor. [Middle English *demeinen,* from Old French *demener* : *de-,* completely + *mener,* to lead, conduct, from Latin *minārе,* to drive (herds), from *minārī,* to threaten, from *minae,* threats.]

demean² *tr.v.* **-meaned, -meaning, -means. 1.** To debase in dignity or stature. **2.** To humble (oneself). —See Synonyms at **degrade.** [DE- (pejorative) + MEAN (base).]

de·mean·or (dĭ-mē′nər) *n.* Also *British* **de·mean·our.** The way in which a person behaves or conducts himself; deportment; manner. —See Synonyms at **bearing.**

de·ment (dĭ-mĕnt′) *tr.v.* **-mented, -menting, -ments.** To make demented. [Late Latin *dēmentāre,* from Latin *dēmēns* (stem *dēment-*), mad : *dē-* (undoing) + *mēns,* mind.]

de·ment·ed (dĭ-mĕn′tĭd) *adj.* **1.** Insane. **2.** Suffering from dementia. **3.** Crazed, as through grief or worry. **—de·ment·ed·ly** *adv.* **—de·ment·ed·ness** *n.*

dé·men·ti (dā′mŏN-tē′) *n., pl.* **démentis** (-tēz, -tē). *French.* An official denial, as of a rumor or news story. Used in diplomacy.

de·men·tia (dĭ-mĕn′shə, -shē-ə) *n.* Deterioration of mental faculties combined with emotional disturbances, resulting from organic brain disorder. See **presenile dementia.** —See Synonyms at **insanity.** [Latin *dēmentia,* madness, from *dēmēns,* mad. See **dement.**]

dementia prae·cox (prē′kŏks′) *n.* **Schizophrenia** *(see).* [New Latin, "premature dementia."]

dem·e·rar·a (dĕm′ə-râr′ə, -rä′rə) *n.* **1.** A type of brown crystallized cane sugar. **2.** A type of blended rum. [After *Demerara,* Guyana, the main source of the sugar.]

Dem·e·ra·ra (dĕm′ə-râr′ə). River in Guyana. It flows 290 kilometers (180 miles) north from the Guiana Highlands to the Atlantic Ocean at Georgetown.

de·mer·it (dĭ-mĕr′ĭt) *n.* **1. a.** A quality or characteristic that deserves blame or censure; a fault. **b.** Absence of merit. **2.** A mark made on one's record by a superior, implying some loss of status or privileges for bad conduct or failure. [Middle English *demerite,* offense, guilt, originally "merit," "desert," from Old French, probably from Latin *dēmerēre,* to deserve : *dē-* (intensive) + *merēre, merērī,* to deserve, MERIT.] **—de·mer·i·tor·i·ous** *adj.* **—de·mer·i·tor·i·ous·ly** *adv.*

de·mer·sal (dĭ-mûr′səl) *adj.* Designating animal life in deep water, as at the bottom of the sea or a lake. [Latin *dēmergere* (past participle *dēmersus*), to plunge: *dē-,* down + *mergere,* to dip.]

de·mesne (dĭ-mān′, -mēn′) *n.* **1.** *Law.* Possession and use of one's own land. **2.** Lands retained by a feudal lord for his own use. **3.** The grounds belonging to a mansion or country house. **4.** An extensive piece of landed property; an estate. **5.** Any district; a territory. **6.** A realm; a domain. [Middle English *demesne, demeine,* from Old French *demaine,* DOMAIN.]

De·me·ter (dĭ-mē′tər). *Greek Mythology.* The goddess of agriculture, fertility, and marriage, identified with the Roman goddess Ceres.

demi– *prefix.* Indicates: **1.** Half; for example, **demisemiquaver. 2.** Less than full status; for example, **demigod.** [French, from *demi,* half, from Medieval Latin *dīmedius,* from Latin *dīmidius,* half, divided in half : *dis-,* apart + *medius,* half.]

dem·i·god (dĕm′ē-gŏd′) *n.* **1. a.** A mythological semidivine being, such as the offspring of a god and a mortal. **b.** An inferior deity; a minor god. **2.** A man with godlike attributes.

dem·i·god·dess (dĕm′ē-gŏd′ĭs) *n.* A woman regarded as a demigod.

dem·i·john (dĕm′ē-jŏn′) *n.* A large, narrow-necked bottle made of glass or earthenware, often encased in wickerwork. [Probably a variant of French *dame-Jeanne,* "Lady Jane," assimilated to DEMI- + the name *John.*]

de·mil·i·ta·rize (dē-mĭl′ə-tə-rīz′) *tr.v.* **-rized, -rizing, -rizes. 1.** To eliminate the military character of. **2.** To prohibit military forces or installations in. **3.** To replace military control of with civilian control. **—de·mil·i·ta·ri·za·tion** *n.*

demilitarized zone *n. Abbr.* **DMZ** A region, defined by diplomatic or political agreement, wherein military forces and installations may not be established.

De Mille (də mĭl′), **Agnes George** (1905–). U.S. choreographer. Among the premier American choreographers of the 1940's and 1950's, she introduduced innovative dance to much of the American public with her choreography of several successful Broadway shows and movies, including *Oklahoma!* (1943) and *Carousel* (1945).

De Mille, Cecil Blount (1881–1959). U.S. film producer and director, known for spectacular epics. He popularized religious and Biblical stories through the cinema with *The Ten Commandments* (1923) and *Samson and Delilah* (1949). His other films include *The Plainsman* (1936), *Union Pacific* (1939), and *The Greatest Show on Earth,* (1952), which won an Academy Award.

dem·i·lune (dĕm′ē-lo͞on′) *n.* **1.** A crescent or half-moon. **2.** *Military.* A crescent-shaped outwork to defend the entrance of a fort. **3.** A crescent-shaped mass of protoplasm found in salivary glands. [French *demi-lune* : DEMI- + *lune,* moon, from Latin *lūna.*]

dem·i·mon·daine (dĕm′ē-mŏn-dān′) *n.* A woman belonging to the demimonde. Also called "demirep."

dem·i·monde (dĕm′ē-mŏnd, dĕm′ē-mŏnd′) *n.* **1.** The social class of those women kept by wealthy lovers or protectors, especially as it existed in the 19th century. **2.** Any group existing on the margin of success or respectability: *the literary demimonde.* Also called "demiworld." [French *demi-monde,* "half-world," coined (1855) by Alexandre Dumas fils to designate "the class of the déclassé."]

de·min·er·al·ize (dē-mĭn′ər-ə-līz′) *tr.v.* **-ized, -izing, -izes.** To remove salts from (a liquid). **—de·min·er·al·i·za·tion** *n.*

de·mi-pen·sion (də-mē′päN-syôN′) *n.* Accommodation in a hotel comprising bed, breakfast, and one main meal. Also *British* "half board." [French, "half-board."]

dem·i·pique (dĕm′ē-pēk′) *n.* A military saddle used during the 18th century, having a pommel about half the height of those on earlier saddles. [Earlier *demipeak* : DEMI- + PEAK.]

dem·i·re·lief (dĕm′ē-rĭ-lēf′) *n. Sculpture.* **Mezzo-relievo** *(see).*

dem·i·rep (dĕm′ē-rĕp′) *n.* A demimondaine.

de·mise (dĭ-mīz′) *n.* **1.** Death. **2.** An ending or failure. **3.** The transfer of an estate by lease or will. **4.** The transfer of a ruler's authority by death or abdication: *demise of the crown.*
∼*v.* **demised, -mising, -mises.** —*tr.* **1.** To transfer (an estate) by will or lease. **2.** To transfer (sovereignty) by abdication or will. —*intr.* **1.** To be transferred by will or descent. **2.** To die. [Middle English *dimise, demise,* transfer of property, from Old French, from feminine past participle of *demettre,* DEMIT.] **—de·mis·a·ble** *adj.*

dem·i·sem·i·qua·ver (dĕm′ē-sĕm′ē-kwā′vər) *n. Chiefly British.* A **thirty-second note** *(see).* [DEMI- + SEMI- + QUAVER (eighth note).]

de·mis·sion (dĭ-mĭsh′ən) *n.* The relinquishment of an office or function. [Middle English *dimissioun,* from Latin *dīmissiō* (stem *dīmissiōn-*), dismissal, from *dīmittere* (past participle *dīmissus*), to send away, DEMIT.]

de·mist (dē′mĭst′) *v.* **-misted, -misting, -mists.** *Chiefly British.* —*tr.* To clear condensation from (a surface, especially a car windshield). —*intr.* To become clear of condensation.

de·mist·er (dē′mĭs′tər) *n. Chiefly British.* A heating device designed to clean condensation from a car windshield or similar surface.

de·mit (dĭ-mĭt′) *v.* **-mitted, -mitting, -mits.** —*tr.* **1.** To relinquish (an office or function). **2.** *Obsolete.* To dismiss. —*intr.* To resign. [Middle English *dimitten,* to release, deliver, Old French *demettre,* from Latin *dīmittere,* to dismiss, renounce, send away : *dis-,* away + *mittere,* to send.]

dem·i·tasse (dĕm′ē-tăs′, -täs′) *n.* **1.** A small coffee cup. **2.** The strong black coffee drunk from such a cup. [French : DEMI- + *tasse,* cup, from Old French, from Arabic *ṭašt,* basin, from Persian *ṭašt*.]

dem·i·urge (dĕm′ē-ûrj′) *n.* **1.** *Often* **Demiurge.** The name used by Plato to designate the deity who fashions the material world. **2.** *Often* **Demiurge.** In Gnostic philosophy, the creator of the material world. **3.** A public magistrate in some ancient Greek states. [Late Latin *dēmiūrgus,* from Greek *dēmiourgos,* "public craftsman" : *dēmios,* public, from *dēmos,* people + *ergon,* work.] **—dem·i·ur·geous, dem·i·ur·gic, dem·i·ur·gi·cal** *adj.* **—dem·i·ur·gi·cal·ly** *adv.*

dem·i·vierge (dĕm′ē-vyĕrzh′) *n.* A woman who engages in sexual activities but who retains her physiological virginity. [French, "half virgin."]

dem·i·volt, dem·i·volte (dĕm′ē-vōlt′) *n. Dressage.* A half-turn performed by a horse on its hind legs.

dem·i·world (dĕm′ē-wûrld′) *n.* **Demimonde** *(see).*

dem·o (dĕm′ō) *n., pl.* **-os.** *Informal.* **1. a.** A demonstration, as of a product or service. **b.** A record or tape recording presented to an agent, concert promoter, or the like to advertise a song or group. **2.** A product, such as an automobile, used for a demonstration and often sold later at a discount.

de·mob (dē-mŏb′) *tr.v.* **-mobbed, -mobbing, -mobs.** *British Informal.* To demobilize.
∼*n. British Informal.* Demobilization.

de·mo·bil·ize (dē-mō′bə-līz′) *v.* **-ized, -izing, -izes.** —*tr.* To discharge from military service or use; disband or dismiss (troops, for example). —*intr.* To be demobilized. **—de·mo·bil·i·za·tion** *n.*

de·moc·ra·cy (dĭ-mŏk′rə-sē) *n., pl.* **-cies. 1.** Government by the people, exercised either directly or through elected representatives. **2.** A political or social unit based upon this form of rule. **3.** A social condition of equality and respect for the individual within the community. **4.** The people considered as a source of political authority. [Old French *democratie,* from Late Latin *dēmocratia,* from Greek *dēmokratia* : *dēmos,* common people + -CRACY.]

dem·o·crat (dĕm′ə-krăt′) *n.* **1.** An advocate of democracy. **2. Democrat.** *Abbr.* **D, D., Dem.** A member or supporter of the Democratic Party. [French *démocrate,* back-formation from *democratie,* DEMOCRACY.]

dem·o·crat·ic (dĕm′ə-krăt′ĭk) *adj.* **1.** Of, characterized by, or advocating democracy. **2.** Pertaining to, encompassing, or promoting the interests of the people. **3.** In favor of or practicing social equality; not snobbish. **4. Democratic.** *Abbr.* **D, D., Dem.** Pertaining to or characteristic of the Democratic Party. **—dem·o·crat·i·cal·ly** *adv.*

Democratic Party *n.* One of the two major political parties in the

United States. It owes its origin to a split in the Democratic-Republican Party under Andrew Jackson in 1828.

Dem·o·crat·ic-Re·pub·li·can Party (dĕm′ə-krăt′ĭk-rĭ-pŭb′lĭ-kən) n. A U.S. political party opposed to the Federalist Party, founded by Thomas Jefferson in 1792 and dissolved in 1828.

de·moc·ra·tize (dĭ-mŏk′rə-tīz′) v. **-tized, -tizing, -tizes.** —tr. To make democratic. —intr. To become democratic. —**de·moc·ra·ti·za·tion** n.

De·moc·ri·tus (dĭ-mŏk′rə-təs) (c. 460–370 B.C.). Greek philosopher and scientist. He developed an atomist theory of the universe, holding that it was made up of minute particles, or atoms, multifariously arranged to account for the differing properties of matter.

dé·mo·dé (dā′mō-dā′) adj. French. Outmoded.

de·mod·u·late (dē-mŏj′ōō-lāt′) tr.v. **-lated, -lating, -lates.** Electronics. To extract (information) from a modulated carrier wave. —**de·mod·u·la·tion** n.

de·mod·u·la·tor (dē-mŏj′ōō-lā′tər) n. A device used in demodulating radio signals. Also called "detector."

dem·o·graph·ics (dĕm′ə-grăf′ĭks, dē′mə-) n. Used with a plural verb. Demographic data that is used especially to identify consumer markets.

de·mog·ra·phy (dĭ-mŏg′rə-fē) n. The study of the characteristics of human populations, such as size, growth, density, distribution, and vital statistics. [French démographie : Greek dēmos, people + -GRAPHY.] —**de·mog·ra·pher** n. —**dem·o·graph·ic** (dĕm′ə-grăf′ĭk), **dem·o·graph·i·cal** adj. —**dem·o·graph·i·cal·ly** adv.

dem·oi·selle (dĕm′wä-zĕl′) n. 1. A young lady or damsel. 2. A small Old World crane, Anthropoides virgo, having gray and black plumage, long black breast feathers, and white plumes at the sides of the head. Also called "demoiselle crane." 3. Rare. A damselfly (see). 4. A damselfish (see). [French, from Old French dameisele, DAMSEL.]

de·mol·ish (dĭ-mŏl′ĭsh) tr.v. **-ished, -ishing, -ishes.** 1. To tear down completely; wreck; level. 2. To do away with completely; put an end to. 3. To destroy or defeat utterly: demolish the prosecution's case. 4. Informal. To eat up completely. —See Synonyms at ruin. [Old French demolir (present stem demoliss-), from Latin dēmōlīrī, to throw down, demolish : dē- (reversal) + mōlīrī, to endeavor, strive, build, from mōlēs, mass.]

dem·o·li·tion (dĕm′ə-lĭsh′ən) n. 1. The act or process of wrecking or destroying; specifically, the destruction, as of a building, by explosives. 2. Military. a. Destruction by explosives. b. demolitions. Explosives used to demolish. [Old French, from Latin dēmōlītiō (stem dēmōlītiōn-), from dēmōlīrī, DEMOLISH.] —**dem·o·li·tion·ist** n.

de·mon (dē′mən) n. Also **dae·mon, dai·mon** (dī′mŏn′) (for senses 3, 4). 1. A devil or evil being; especially, in the New Testament, an unclean spirit that possesses and afflicts a person. 2. A persistently tormenting person, force, or passion. 3. Greek Mythology. An inferior divinity, such as a deified hero. 4. An attendant spirit; a genius. 5. One who is extremely zealous, skillful, or engrossed in a given activity. 6. Australian Slang. A policeman or detective. [Middle English, from Late Latin daemōn, evil spirit, from Latin, spirit, from Greek daimōn, divine power, fate, god.]

demon. Grammar. demonstrative.

de·mon·e·tize (dĭ-mŏn′ə-tīz′, -mŭn′-) tr.v. **-tized, -tizing, -tizes.** 1. To divest (a coin, for example) of monetary value. 2. To stop using (a metal) as a monetary standard. [French démonétiser : dé-, away from + monēta, coin, MONEY.] —**de·mon·e·ti·za·tion** n.

de·mo·ni·ac (dĭ-mō′nē-ăk′) adj. Also **de·mo·ni·a·cal** (dē′mə-nī′ə-kəl). 1. Arising or seeming to arise from possession by a demon. 2. Befitting or suggestive of a devil; fiendish; frenzied. —n. One who is or seems to be possessed by a demon. [Middle English demoniak, from Late Latin daemoniācus, from Greek daimoniakos, from daimonios, of a spirit, from daimōn, DEMON.] —**de·mo·ni·a·cal·ly** adv.

de·mon·ic (dĭ-mŏn′ĭk) adj. 1. Befitting a demon; fiendish. 2. Motivated by a spiritual force or genius; inspired. 3. Showing a frenetic enthusiasm.

de·mon·ism (dē′mə-nĭz′əm) n. 1. Belief in demons. 2. The worship of demons. 3. Demonology. —**de·mon·ist** n.

de·mon·ize (dē′mə-nīz′) tr.v. **-ized, -izing, -izes.** 1. To turn into or as if into a demon. 2. To possess. Used of a demon.

de·mon·ol·o·gy (dē′mə-nŏl′ə-jē) n. 1. The study of demons. Also called "demonism." 2. A treatise on demons or demon worship. —**de·mon·ol·o·gist** n.

de·mon·stra·ble (dĭ-mŏn′strə-bəl) adj. Capable of being shown or proved. —**de·mon·stra·bil·i·ty, de·mon·stra·ble·ness** n. —**de·mon·stra·bly** adv.

de·mon·strant (dĭ-mon′strənt) n. One who participates in a demonstration.

dem·on·strate (dĕm′ən-strāt′) v. **-strated, -strating, -strates.** —tr. 1. To prove or make manifest by reasoning or adducing evidence. 2. To describe or illustrate by experiment or practical application. 3. To manifest or reveal. 4. To display the advantages of (a product, for example) to a prospective buyer, as by operation or explanation. —intr. To present or participate in a demonstration, especially a public rally for a particular cause. [Latin dēmonstrāre, to point out : dē-, completely + monstrāre, to show, from monstrum, divine portent, from monēre, to warn.]

dem·on·stra·tion (dĕm′ən-strā′shən) n. 1. The act of making evident or proving. 2. Conclusive evidence; proof. 3. An illustration or explanation, as of a theory or product, by exemplification and practical application. 4. A manifestation, as of one's feelings. 5. A public display of group opinion, as by a rally or march. 6. A show of military strength.

de·mon·stra·tive (dĭ-mŏn′strə-tĭv) adj. 1. Serving to manifest or prove. 2. Involving or characterized by demonstration. 3. Given to or marked by the open expression of emotion, especially affection. 4. Abbr. demon. Grammar. Designating a word, such as these or then, that specifies or singles out the person, thing, or time referred to. Compare interrogative, relative. —n. Abbr. demon. Grammar. A demonstrative pronoun or adjective. —**de·mon·stra·tive·ly** adv. —**de·mon·stra·tive·ness** n.

dem·on·stra·tor (dĕm′ən-strā′tər) n. 1. One who demonstrates something. 2. A vehicle, domestic appliance, or the like used to demonstrate a product to a potential customer. 3. Chiefly British. A person who demonstrates experiments and other practical work to students in a laboratory. 4. One who takes part in a public demonstration.

dem·o·pho·bi·a (dĕm′ə-fō′bē-ə) n. Abnormal fear of crowds. [Greek dēmos, people, DEMOS + -PHOBIA.] —**dem·o·pho·bic** adj.

de·mor·al·ize (dĭ-môr′əl-īz′, -mŏr′-) tr.v. **-ized, -izing, -izes.** 1. To debase the morals of; corrupt. 2. To undermine the confidence or morale of; dishearten. 3. To put into disorder. —**de·mor·al·i·za·tion** n. —**de·mor·al·iz·er** n.

de·mos (dē′mŏs) n. 1. The people of an ancient Greek state, considered as a social class or as a political entity. 2. The common people; the populace. [Greek dēmos, district, people.]

De·mos·the·nes (dĭ-mŏs′thə-nēz′) (c. 384–322 B.C.). Athenian orator and statesman. He is famous for the Philippics, a series of orations attacking the political ambitions of Philip of Macedon.

de·mote (dĭ-mōt′) tr.v. **-moted, -moting, -motes.** To lower in rank or grade. [DE- (reversal) + (PRO)MOTE.] —**de·mo·tion** n.

de·mot·ic (dĭ-mŏt′ĭk) adj. 1. a. Of or pertaining to the common people; in common use; popular. Said especially of language. b. Of the masses; unsophisticated or unrefined: demotic tastes in food. 2. Of, pertaining to, or written in the simplified form of ancient Egyptian hieratic writing. 3. Demotic. Of or pertaining to Dhimotiki (see). —n. 1. Demotic language. 2. Demotic. The popular form of modern Greek, Dhimotiki (see). [Greek dēmotikos, from dēmotēs, commoner, from dēmos, common people, DEMOS.] —**de·mot·ist** n.

de·mount (dē-mount′) tr.v. **-mounted, -mounting, -mounts.** To remove (a gun or motor, for example) from a position on a mounting or other support. —**de·mount·a·ble** adj.

Demp·sey (dĕmp′sē), **Jack**, born William Harrison Dempsey (1895–1983). U.S. heavyweight boxer; world champion (1919–26).

dempster. Variant of deemster.

de·mul·cent (dĭ-mŭl′sənt) adj. Soothing. —n. A soothing, usually mucilaginous or oily substance, used especially to relieve pain in inflamed or irritated mucous surfaces. [Latin dēmulcēns (stem dēmulcent-), present participle of dēmulcēre, to stroke down, caress, soothe : dē-, down + mulcēre†, to stroke.]

de·mur (dĭ-mûr′) intr.v. **-murred, -murring, -murs.** 1. To take exception; raise objections; object. 2. Law. To enter or interpose a demurrer. 3. To delay. —See Synonyms at object. —n. Also **de·mur·ral** (dĭ-mûr′əl). 1. The act of demurring. 2. An objection. 3. A delay. [Middle English demeoren, demuren, to delay, from French demorer, demurer, from Latin dēmorārī : dē- (intensive) + morārī, to delay, from mora, delay.] —**de·mur·ra·ble** adj.

de·mure (dĭ-myŏŏr′) adj. **-murer, -murest.** 1. Sedate or self-possessed in manner or behavior; reserved. Said especially of women and children. 2. Feigning modesty or shyness. —See Synonyms at shy. [Middle English, from Old French demore, quiet, sedate, "settled," past participle of demorer, to stay, delay, DEMUR.] —**de·mure·ly** adv. —**de·mure·ness** n.

de·mur·rage (dĭ-mûr′ĭj) n. 1. The detention of a ship or other cargo conveyance during loading or unloading beyond the scheduled time of departure. 2. The compensation paid for this detention.

de·mur·rer (dĭ-mûr′ər) n. 1. A person who demurs; an objector. 2. Law. A plea to dismiss a lawsuit on the grounds that although the opposition's statements may be true, they are insufficient to sustain the claim. Compare plea. 3. An objection.

de·my (dĭ-mī′) n., pl. **-mies.** Any of several standard sizes of paper, especially: 1. In Britain, paper measuring 15½ by 20 inches or 17½ by 22½ inches. 2. In the United States, paper measuring 16 by 21 inches. [From DEMI-.]

de·mys·ti·fy (dē-mĭs′tə-fī′) tr.v. **-fied, -fying, -fies.** To make less complex or less ambiguous; make less difficult to understand. —**de·mys·ti·fi·ca·tion** n.

de·my·thol·o·gize (dē′mĭ-thŏl′ə-jīz′) tr.v. **-gized, -gizing, -gizes.** 1. To remove the mythical elements from (a piece of writing) so that the essential meaning may be made clear. 2. To reinterpret mythical elements in (a piece of writing), especially in a way held to be more rational. 3. To do away with the spurious reverence surrounding (a figure or institution).

den (dĕn) n. 1. The shelter or retreat of a wild animal; a lair. 2. A cave considered as a refuge or hiding place. 3. A residence or abode, especially if hidden or squalid: a den of thieves. 4. A small secluded room for study or relaxation. 5. A unit of about eight to ten Cub Scouts. —intr.v. **denned, denning, dens.** To inhabit or hide in a den. [Middle English den(ne), Old English denn, from Germanic.]

Den. Denmark.

de·nar·i·us (dĭ-nâr′ē-əs) n., pl. **-narii** (-nâr′ē-ī′). 1. An ancient Ro-

denarius A Roman denarius minted during the reign of the emperor Augustus (63 B.C.–A.D. 14). The silver coin kept its value and its silver content under Augustus. But later emperors debased the coinage until, by the third century A.D., the denarius was almost worthless.

man silver coin, originally equivalent to four sesterces, or ten bronze asses. **2.** An ancient Roman gold coin valued at 25 silver denarii. [Middle English, from Latin *dēnārius,* from adjective, "consisting of ten," from *dēnī,* by tens.]

den·a·ry (dĕn'ə-rē) *adj.* **1.** Tenfold. **2.** Divided or counted by tens; decimal. [Latin *dēnārius.* See **denarius.**]

de·na·tion·al·ize (dē-năsh'ən-ə-līz') *tr.v.* **-ized, -izing, -izes. 1.** To return (a nationalized industry or service) to private ownership. **2.** To deprive of national rights, status, or characteristics. **—de·na·tion·al·i·za·tion** *n.*

de·nat·u·ral·ize (dē-năch'ər-ə-līz') *tr.v.* **-ized, -izing, -izes. 1.** To make unnatural. **2.** To deprive of the rights of naturalization or citizenship. **—de·nat·u·ral·i·za·tion** *n.*

de·na·tur·ant (dē-nā'chər-ənt) *n.* An evil-tasting chemical substance or vivid coloring that is added to a product to make it unfit for human consumption. [DENATURE + -ANT.]

de·na·ture (dē-nā'chər) *tr.v.* **-tured, -turing, -tures.** Also **de·na·tur·ize** (-chər-īz'), **-ized, -izing, -izes. 1.** To change the nature or natural qualities of. **2.** To render unfit to eat or drink; especially, to add methanol to ethyl alcohol for this purpose. **3.** *Physics.* To add nonfissionable matter to (fissionable material) to prevent use in an atomic weapon. **4.** *Biochemistry.* To cause (a protein) to unfold by subjecting it to a change of temperature, acidity, or the like. **—de·na·tur·a·tion** *n.*

denatured alcohol *n.* Ethyl alcohol made unfit for drinking by the addition of a substance, such as methanol.

de·na·zi·fy (dē-năt'sə-fī', -nät'-) *tr.v.* **-fied, -fying, -fies.** To make or declare free of Nazi influence. **—de·na·zi·fi·ca·tion** *n.*

Den·bigh (dĕn'bē). Formerly county town of Denbighshire, Wales, now in Clwyd. Its castle was built in 1282 for Edward I.

Den·bigh·shire (dĕn'bē-shĭr, -shər). Former county in north Wales. In 1974 it was divided between Clwyd (to the east) and Gwynedd (to the west).

den·dri·form (dĕn'drə-fôrm') *adj.* Having the characteristic form or structure of a tree. [DENDRI- + -FORM.]

den·drite (dĕn'drīt) *n.* **1. a.** A mineral crystallization in a branching or treelike form. **b.** A rock or mineral bearing such a crystal formation. **2.** In a nerve cell, a fine branch of a dendron. [DENDR(O)- + -ITE.]

den·drit·ic (dĕn-drĭt'ĭk) *adj.* Also **den·drit·i·cal** (-ĭ-kəl). **1.** Of, pertaining to, or resembling a dendrite. **2.** Tree-shaped; dendriform. [DENDRIT(E) + -IC.] **—den·drit·i·cal·ly** *adv.*

dendro-, dendri-, dendr- *prefix.* Indicates tree; for example, **dendrology, dendriform, dendrite.** [New Latin, from Greek, from *dendron,* tree.]

den·dro·chro·nol·o·gy (dĕn'drō-krə-nŏl'ə-jē) *n.* The study of the growth rings in trees as an aid in determining and dating past events. **—den·dro·chron·o·log·i·cal** (dĕn'drō-krŏn'ə-lŏj'ĭ-kəl) *adj.*

den·dro·cli·ma·tol·o·gy (dĕn'drō-clī'mə-tŏl'ə-jē) *n.* The determination of past climates and climatic conditions from a study of tree rings.

den·droid (dĕn'droid') *adj.* Also **den·droi·dal** (dĕn-droid'l). Shaped like a tree. [Greek *dendroeidēs* : DENDR(O)- + -OID.]

den·drol·o·gy (dĕn-drŏl'ə-jē) *n.* The botanical study of trees. [DENDRO- + -LOGY.] **—den·dro·log·ic** (dĕn'drə-lŏj'ĭk), **den·dro·log·i·cal** *adj.* **—den·drol·o·gist** *n.*

den·dron (dĕn'drən) *n.* A protoplasmic process of a nerve cell that conducts impulses toward the cell body. [Greek, tree.]

dene¹ (dēn) *n. British Regional.* A sandy tract of land or low hill near the sea. [Probably akin to low German *düne.* See **dune.**]

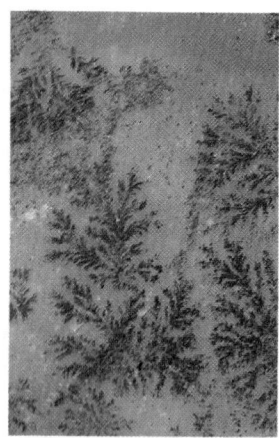

dendrite *These fernlike patterns are formed by impurities in minerals. Here, the dark impurity is manganese oxide; the surrounding stone is flint.*

dene². Variant of **dean** (valley).

De·neb (dĕn'ĕb) *n.* The brightest star in the constellation Cygnus, approximately 1,630 light years from Earth. [Arabic *dhanab,* tail.]

De·neb·o·la (dĭ-nĕb'ə-lə) *n.* The second-brightest star in the constellation Leo. [Arabic *dhanab al- (asad),* "tail of the (lion)."]

den·e·ga·tion (dĕn'ə-gā'shən) *n.* A denial. [Middle English *denegacioun,* from Old French *denegation,* from Latin *dēnegātiō* (stem *dēnegātiōn-*), from *dēnegātus,* past participle of *dēnegāre,* to DENY.]

dene hole *n. Archaeology.* A type of excavation found in chalk soils in Britain and France, consisting of a vertical shaft that widens out into several chambers. [Perhaps from DANE + HOLE.]

den·gue (dĕng'gē, dĕn'gā) *n.* An infectious, virulent, tropical and subtropical viral disease transmitted by mosquitoes and characterized by fever, rash, and severe pains in the joints. Also called "breakbone fever," "dandy." [Spanish, of African origin, akin to Swahili *kidinga.*]

Deng Xiao-ping or **Teng Hsiao-p'ing** (dŭng' shou'pīng') (1904–). Vice premier of the state council of the People's Republic of China (1975–76, 1977–80) and vice chairman of the Chinese Communist Party (1977–). Dismissed during the Cultural Revolution as a "capitalist roader," he was rehabilitated in 1973 and became acting chairman in 1974. Disgraced again in 1976, he was rehabilitated a year later.

de·ni·a·ble (dĭ-nī'ə-bəl) *adj.* Capable of being denied; questionable. **—de·ni·a·bly** *adv.*

de·ni·al (dĭ-nī'əl) *n.* **1.** A negative reply, as to a request; a refusal to comply or satisfy. **2. a.** Refusal to grant the truth of a statement or allegation; contradiction. **b.** An assertion that a statement or allegation is untrue. **3.** A rejection, as of a doctrine or belief. **4.** A disowning or disavowal; repudiation. **5.** Abstinence; self-denial. [From DENY.]

de·nic·o·tin·ize (dē-nĭk'ə-tə-nīz') *tr.v.* **-ized, -izing, -izes.** To remove nicotine from (tobacco, for example).

den·i·er¹ (də-nyâ') *n.* **1.** (also dĕn'yər). A unit of fineness for rayon, nylon, and silk yarns, based on a standard of 50 milligrams per 450 meters of yarn. **2.** (also də-nîr'). A small coin of very low value current in France and western Europe from the 8th century until the French Revolution. [Middle English *denere,* a small coin, from Old French *denier,* from Latin *dēnārius,* DENARIUS.]

de·ni·er² (dĭ-nī'ər) *n.* One who denies.

den·i·grate (dĕn'ĭ-grāt') *tr.v.* **-grated, -grating, -grates. 1. a.** To defame; calumniate. **b.** To belittle; undervalue. **2.** *Rare.* To blacken. [Latin *dēnigrāre* (past participle *dēnigrātus*), to blacken : *dē-,* completely + *nigrāre,* blacken, from *niger,* black.] **—den·i·gra·tion** *n.* **—den·i·gra·tor** *n.*

den·im (dĕn'əm) *n.* **1. a.** A coarse twilled cloth used for jeans, overalls, and work uniforms. **b. denims.** Garments, especially trousers, made of coarse denim. **2.** A finer grade of denim material used in draperies and upholstery. [French *(serge) de Nîmes,* serge of Nîmes.]

Den·is or **Den·ys** (dĕn'ĭs, də-nē'), **Saint** (died A.D. 270). Patron saint of France. He was sent to preach the Gospel to the Gauls and became the first bishop of Paris. He was martyred during the reign of Valerian.

de·ni·tri·fy (dē-nī'trə-fī') *tr.v.* **-fied, -fying, -fies.** To remove nitrogen from (a material or chemical compound), as by bacterial action on soil. **—de·ni·tri·fi·ca·tion** *n.*

de·ni·tri·fy·ing bacteria (dē-nī'trə-fī'ĭng) *pl.n.* The soil bacteria that reduce nitrate to ammonia, including species of *Thiobacillus* and *Escherichia.*

den·i·zen (dĕn'ə-zən) *n.* **1.** An inhabitant; a resident. **2.** *British.* A foreigner permitted certain rights and privileges of citizenship. **3.** *Ecology.* An animal or plant naturalized in a region to which it is not indigenous.
~*tr.v.* **denizened, -zening, -zens.** *British.* To make a denizen of; naturalize. [Middle English *denisein,* from Old French *denzein,* from *deinz,* within, from Late Latin *dēintus,* from within : Latin *dē-,* from + *intus,* within.] **—den·i·zen·a·tion** *n.*

Den·mark (dĕn'märk'). *Abbr.* **Den.** *Danish* **Dan·mark** (dän'märk'). A low-lying kingdom on the Jutland peninsula and islands, in northern Europe. It also has sovereignty over Greenland and the Faeroe Islands. In the 10th century Denmark was unified under the Viking king, Harold Bluetooth (died c. 985), who converted the people to Christianity. His expansionist policy was continued by his successors, who also brought England temporarily into the Danish fold (1013) under King Canute. Norway and Sweden came under the Danish crown in a union cemented at Kalmar in 1397. Sweden broke away (1523), and Denmark later lost Norway to Sweden (1814). It joined the European Economic Community in 1973. The country is intensively farmed and is noted for its beer, bacon, and butter. Its other exports include livestock, fish products, transport equipment, and fine ceramics and glassware. Area, 43,069 square kilometers (16,625 square miles). Population, 5,100,000. Capital, Copenhagen.

den mother *n.* A woman who supervises a den of Cub Scouts.

denom. denomination (religious sect).

de·nom·i·nal (dĭ-nŏm'ə-nəl) *adj.* Formed from a noun or adjective; denominative.

de·nom·i·nate (dĭ-nŏm'ə-nāt') *tr.v.* **-nated, -nating, -nates.** To give a name to; designate. [Latin *dēnōmināre* : *dē-,* completely + *nōmināre,* to name, from *nōmen,* name.] **—de·nom·i·na·ble** (dĭ-nŏm'ə-nə-bəl) *adj.*

de·nom·i·nate number (dĭ-nŏm'ə-nĭt) *n.* A number that designates

DENMARK

[Map of Denmark showing Skagerrak, Skagen, Frederikshavn, Nykøbing, Lim Fjord, Ålborg, Kattegat, Randers, Viborg, JYLLAND (JUTLAND), Århus, DENMARK, Yding Skovhøj 173m, Horsens, Esbjerg, Odense, Fyn (Fünen), COPENHAGEN, Helsingør, Sjælland (Zealand), Store Bælt, Langeland, Lolland, Møn, Nykøbing Falster, Rønne, Bornholm, SWEDEN, Öresund, BALTIC SEA, GERMAN FEDERAL REPUBLIC, GERMAN DEM. REP. Scale: Km 0 50 100 150, Miles 0 50]

a quantity as a multiple of a unit. In the expression *12 feet, 12* is a denominate number.

de·nom·i·na·tion (dǐ-nŏm′ə-nā′shən) *n.* **1.** The act of naming. **2.** A name; a designation. **3.** The name of a class or group; a classification. **4.** A class of units having specific values, as in a system of currency or weights. **5.** *Abbr.* **denom.** A religious grouping with a common organization and name. —See Synonyms at **name.** —**de·nom·i·na·tion·al** *adj.* —**de·nom·i·na·tion·al·ly** *adv.*

de·nom·i·na·tion·al·ism (dǐ-nŏm′ə-nā′shən-ə-lǐz′əm) *n.* **1.** The tendency to separate into religious sects or denominations. **2.** Advocacy of such separation. **3.** Strict adherence to a denomination; sectarianism. —**de·nom·i·na·tion·al·ist** *n.*

de·nom·i·na·tive (dǐ-nŏm′ə-nā′tǐv, -nə-tǐv) *adj.* **1.** Giving or constituting a name; naming; appellative. **2.** *Grammar.* Formed from a noun or adjective.

~*n.* A word, especially a verb, that is derived from a noun or adjective, such as the verb *to bus* from the noun *bus.*

de·nom·i·na·tor (dǐ-nŏm′ə-nā′tər) *n.* The quantity below the line indicating division in a fraction; the quantity that divides the numerator. Compare **numerator.**

de nos jours (də nō zhōōr′) *adj. French.* Of or pertaining to the present time; contemporary. [Literally, "of our days."]

de·no·ta·tion (dē′nō-tā′shən) *n.* **1.** The act of denoting; indication. **2.** A sign, symbol, or reference that denotes; an indicator. **3.** Something signified or referred to; a particular meaning of a symbol. **4.** The explicit meaning of a word, as opposed to its connotation.

de·no·ta·tive (dǐ-nō′tə-tǐv, dē′nō-tā′-) *adj.* **1.** Able to denote; designative. **2.** Explicit. —**de·no·ta·tive·ly** *adv.*

de·note (dǐ-nōt′) *tr.v.* **-noted, -noting, -notes. 1.** To reveal or indicate; mark. **2.** To serve as a symbol or name for; signify. **3.** To refer to specifically; mean explicitly. —See Synonyms at **mean** (convey sense). [French *dénoter,* from Latin *dēnotāre* : *dē-,* completely + *notāre,* mark, from *nota,* NOTE.] —**de·not·a·ble** *adj.* —**de·no·tive** *adj.*

Usage: Denote means "to mark" or "to signify directly." *Connote* means "to suggest or convey to the mind what is not explicit." Thus: *Frost denotes the coming of winter. For us winter connoted the beauty of frost on the windows and the coming of Christmas.* In speaking of words, *denote* is used to indicate the thing a word names, and *connote* to indicate our associations with that thing: *The word* bachelor *denotes an unmarried man and connotes a life of parties and carefree amusement.*

dé·noue·ment, de·noue·ment (dā-nōō-mäɴ′) *n.* **1.** The solution, clarification, or unraveling of the plot of a play or novel. **2.** Any outcome or final solution. [French, "an untying," from Old French *desnouement,* from *desno(u)er,* undo : *des-, de-,* reversing + *no(u)er,* to tie, from Latin *nōdāre,* from *nōdus,* knot.]

de·nounce (dǐ-nouns′) *tr.v.* **-nounced, -nouncing, -nounces. 1.** To condemn openly; censure, especially as evil. **2.** To accuse formally; inform against. **3.** To give formal announcement of the ending of (a treaty). —See Synonyms at **criticize.** [Middle English *denouncen,* from Old French *denoncier,* announce, from Latin *dēnūntiāre,* make an official announcement of : *dē-,* completely + *nūntiāre,* announce, from *nūntius,* messenger.] —**de·nounce·ment** *n.* —**de·nounc·er** *n.*

de nou·veau (də nōō-vō′) *adv. French.* Starting afresh; all over again; anew.

de no·vo (dē nō′vō, dā) *adv. Latin.* Afresh; anew.

dense (dĕns) *adj.* **denser, densest. 1. a.** Having relatively high density. **b.** Crowded closely together; compact. **2.** Thick; impenetrable. **3.** Thickheaded; dull. **4.** Comprehensible only through intellectual effort: *a dense argument.* **5.** *Photography.* Opaque, with good contrast between light and dark areas. Said of a developed negative. —See Synonyms at **stupid.** [Latin *dēnsus.*] —**dense·ly** *adv.* —**dense·ness** *n.*

den·sim·e·ter (dĕn-sĭm′ə-tər) *n.* An instrument used to determine density. [DENSE + -METER.] —**den·si·met·ric** (dĕn′sə-mĕt′rĭk) *adj.*

den·si·tom·e·ter (dĕn′sə-tŏm′ə-tər) *n.* An apparatus for measuring the optical density of a material, such as a photographic negative. [DENSITY + METER.]

den·si·ty (dĕn′sə-tē) *n., pl.* **-ties. 1. a.** The degree or a measure of the degree to which anything is filled or occupied. **b.** The condition or quality of being dense. **2.** *Physics.* **a.** The mass per unit volume of a substance under stipulated or standard conditions of pressure and temperature. **b.** The amount of something per unit measure, especially per unit length, area, or volume. See **charge density, current density, energy density. 3.** *Computer Science.* The number of units of useful information contained within a linear dimension. **4.** The number of inhabitants per unit geographical region. Also called "population density." **5.** The degree of optical opacity of a medium or material, as of a photographic negative. **6.** *Statistics.* A **probability density function** *(see).* Also called "density function." **7.** Thickness of consistency; impenetrability. **8.** Stupidity; dullness.

dent¹ (dĕnt) *n.* **1.** A depression in a surface made by pressure or a blow. **2.** A lessening or weakening effect: *a dent in his confidence.* ~*v.* **dented, denting, dents.** —*tr.* To make a dent in. —*intr.* To become dented. [Middle English *dent,* variant of *dint,* strike, blow, Old English *dynt,* from Germanic *dunti-* (unattested).]

dent² *n.* **1.** A toothlike protuberance, such as that on a gearwheel. **2.** The space between two wires on a loom through which a warp thread is drawn. [French, tooth.]

dent. dental; dentist; dentistry.

den·tal (dĕn′tl) *adj.* **1.** *Abbr.* **dent.** Of, pertaining to, or for the teeth.

2. *Abbr.* **dent.** Of, pertaining to, or for dentistry. **3.** *Phonetics.* Produced with the tip of the tongue near or against the upper front teeth.

~*n. Phonetics.* A dental consonant. [New Latin *dentalis,* from Latin *dēns* (stem *dent-*), tooth.]

dental appliance *n. Dentistry.* A **brace** *(see).*

dental caries *n.* Tooth decay.

dental floss *n.* A strong, usually waxed thread used to clean areas between the teeth. Also called "floss."

dental hygiene *n.* The maintenance of healthy teeth and gums, especially by regular brushing. Also called "oral hygiene."

dental hygienist *n.* A person trained in dental hygiene, who cleans and scales the teeth of dental patients and gives advice on general care. Also called "hygienist."

den·ta·li·um (dĕn-tā′lē-əm) *n., pl.* **-lia** (-lē-ə) or **-liums.** Any tooth shell of the genus *Dentalium.* [New Latin, from Late Latin *dentālis,* of a tooth, DENTAL.]

dental plaque *n.* A film containing bacteria and other substances that forms on the surface of a tooth. Also called "plaque."

dental plate *n.* **1.** A plate fixed to the palate with a fitting used to correct the position of the teeth. **2.** A denture *(see).*

dental surgeon *n.* A dentist *(see).*

dental technician *n.* A person who repairs dentures and makes plaster casts of teeth.

den·tate (dĕn′tāt′) *adj.* Edged with toothlike projections; toothed. [Latin *dentātus,* from *dēns* (stem *dent-*), tooth.] —**den·tate·ly** *adv.*

den·ta·tion (dĕn-tā′shən) *n.* **1.** The condition of being dentate. **2.** A toothlike part or projection.

dent corn *n.* A tall-growing variety of corn, *Zea mays indentata,* having yellow or white kernels that are indented at the tip. Also chiefly British "dent maize."

denti-, dent- *prefix.* Indicates tooth; for example, **dentiform, dentoid.** [Latin *dēns* (stem *dent-*), tooth.]

den·ti·cle (dĕn′tĭ-kəl) *n.* A small tooth or toothlike projection. [Middle English, from Latin *denticulus,* diminutive of *dēns* (stem *dent-*), tooth.]

den·tic·u·late (dĕn-tĭk′yə-lāt′) *adj.* Also **den·tic·u·lat·ed** (-lā′tĭd). **1.** Finely toothed; minutely dentate. **2.** *Architecture.* Having dentils. [Latin *denticulātus,* from *denticulus,* DENTICLE.] —**den·tic·u·late·ly** *adv.* —**den·tic·u·la·tion** *n.*

den·ti·form (dĕn′tə-fôrm′) *adj.* Shaped like a tooth. [DENTI- + -FORM.]

den·ti·frice (dĕn′tə-frĭs) *n.* A substance, such as a powder or paste, for cleaning the teeth; toothpaste or tooth powder. [French, from Latin *dentifricium* : DENTI- + *fricāre,* to rub.]

den·til (dĕn′tĭl) *n. Architecture.* Any of a series of small rectangular blocks forming a molding or projecting beneath a cornice. [Obsolete French *dentille,* from Old French, diminutive of *dent,* tooth, from Latin *dēns* (stem *dent-*), tooth.]

den·ti·la·bi·al (dĕn′tĭ-lā′bē-əl) *adj. Phonetics.* Labiodental. —**den·ti·la·bi·al** *n.*

den·ti·lin·gual (dĕn′tĭ-lĭng′gwəl) *adj. Phonetics.* Interdental. —**den·ti·lin·gual** *n.*

den·tine (dĕn′tēn′) *n.* Also **den·tin** (-tĭn). The calcareous part of a tooth, beneath the enamel, containing the pulp chamber and root canals. [DENT(I)- + -INE.] —**den·ti·nal** *adj.*

den·tist (dĕn′tĭst) *n. Abbr.* **dent.** A person whose profession is dentistry. [French *dentiste,* from *dent,* tooth.]

den·tist·ry (dĕn′tĭ-strē) *n. Abbr.* **dent.** The diagnosis, prevention, and treatment of diseases of the teeth and related structures, including the repair or replacement of defective teeth.

den·ti·tion (dĕn-tĭsh′ən) *n.* **1.** *Biology.* The type, number, and arrangement of teeth, especially in humans and other animals. **2.** The process of cutting new teeth; a teething. [Latin *dentitiō* (stem *dentitiōn-*), from *dentitus,* past participle of *dentīre,* to teethe, from *dēns* (stem *dent-*), tooth.]

dent maize *n. Chiefly British.* **Dent corn** *(see).*

den·toid (dĕn′toid′) *adj.* Toothlike. [DENT(I)- + -OID.]

den·tu·lous (dĕn′chə-ləs) *adj.* Possessing teeth; toothed.

den·ture (dĕn′chər) *n.* **1.** A set of artificial teeth for a single jaw or part of it. Also called "dental plate." **2. dentures.** A set of removable artificial teeth for both jaws. [French, from Old French, from *dent,* tooth.]

de·nu·cle·ar·ize (dē-nōō′klē-ə-rīz′, -nyōō′-) *tr.v.* **-ized, izing, -izes.** To remove nuclear installations from (a country or area).

de·nu·da·tion (dē′nōō-dā′shən, -nyōō-) *n.* **1.** *Geology.* The combined processes of erosion, weathering, and transporting away of the material removed. Also called "degradation." **2.** The act or process of denuding.

de·nude (dǐ-nōōd′, -nyōōd′) *tr.v.* **-nuded, -nuding, -nudes. 1. a.** To strip of covering; make bare. **b.** To divest; deprive completely. **2.** To cause to undergo denudation. —See Synonyms at **strip.** [Latin *dēnūdāre* : *dē-,* thoroughly + *nūdāre,* to make bare, from *nūdus,* NUDE.]

de·nu·mer·a·ble (dǐ-nōō′mər-ə-bəl, dǐ-nyōō′-) *adj.* Capable of being put into one-to-one correspondence with the positive integers; countable. —**de·nu·mer·a·bly** *adv.*

de·nun·ci·ate (dǐ-nŭn′sē-āt′) *tr.v.* **-ated, -ating, -ates.** *Rare.* To denounce. [Latin *dēnūntiāre,* to DENOUNCE.]

de·nun·ci·a·tion (dǐ-nŭn′sē-ā′shən, -shē-ā′shən) *n.* **1.** The act or an instance of denouncing; open condemnation or censure. **2.** The act of accusing another of a crime before a public prosecutor. **3.** A formal declaration of the termination of a treaty.

deodar *In its home in the Himalayan foothills, this species of cedar is known as the Tree of God. Indians regard it as a symbol of fruitfulness and durability. Commercially, its timber is used to make railroad ties and bridges.*

PRONUNCIATION KEY

ă, pat; ā, pay; âr, care;
ä, father, are; b, bib;
ch, church; d, deed; ĕ, pet;
ē, be; f, fife; g, gag; h, hat;
hw, which; ĭ, pit; ī, pie;
îr, pier; j, judge; k, kick;
l, lid, needle; m, mum;
n, no, sudden; ng, thing;
ŏ, pot; ō, toe; ô, paw, for;
oi, noise; ou, out; o͝o, book;
o͞o, boot; p, pop; r, roar;
s, sauce; sh, ship, dish;
t, tight; th, thin, path;
th, this, bathe; ŭ, cut; ûr, fur;
v, valve; w, with; y, yes;
z, zebra, size; zh, vision;
ə, about, item, edible, gallop, circus, peaceful

IN FOREIGN WORDS:

à, *Fr.* ami; œ, *Fr.* feu, *Ger.* schön; ü, *Fr.* tu, *Ger.* über; KH, *Ger.* ich, *Scot.* loch; N, *Fr.* bon; y', *Fr.* Compiègne

STRESS MARKS:

Primary stress: ′
in·cite′ (ĭn-sīt′)
Secondary stress: ′
in′sight′ (ĭn′sīt′)

Den·ver (dĕn′vər). Capital of Colorado, in the north-central part of the state. It lies where the Rocky Mts. meet the Great Plains, a natural stopping point for early 19th-century settlers. The population boomed in 1859 during a gold rush. It is a railroad junction and industrial, tourist, and marketing center.

de·ny (dĭ-nī′) *tr.v.* **-nied, -nying, -nies. 1.** To declare untrue; assert the contrary of; contradict. **2.** To refuse to believe; reject. **3.** To refuse to recognize or acknowledge; disavow; disown. **4.** To refuse to grant; withhold. **—deny oneself.** To abstain from indulging oneself in. [Middle English *denien,* from Old French *denier,* from Latin *dēnegāre* : *dē-,* completely + *negāre,* to say no.]
Synonyms: *contradict, gainsay, refute.*

Denys. See **St. Denis.**

deoch an dor·is (dŏKH′ ən dŏr′ĭs) *n. Scottish & Irish.* A drink, usually of whisky, which is taken before departure. [Gaelic *deoch an doruis,* drink at the door.]

de·o·dand (dē′ə-dănd′) *n.* Formerly in English law, an object that caused the death of a person, either accidentally or intentionally, and that was then confiscated by the Crown to be used for charitable purposes. [Norman French *deodande,* from Latin *Deō dandum,* something to be given to God : *Deus,* God + *dare,* to give.]

de·o·dar (dē′ə-där′) *n.* A tall cedar, *Cedrus deodara,* native to the Himalayas, having drooping branches and wood valued as timber. [Hindi *dē′ odār,* from Sanskrit *devadāru* : *devás,* divine + *dāru,* tree.]

de·o·dor·ant (dē-ō′dər-ənt) *n.* **1.** A substance applied to counteract body odors. **2.** A chemical exposed to or sprayed into the air to counteract staleness. [DE- (removal) + Latin *odor,* odor + -ANT.] **—de·o·dor·ant** *adj.*

de·o·dor·ize (dē-ō′də-rīz′) *tr.v.* **-ized, -izing, -izes.** To disguise or absorb the odor of. **—de·o·dor·i·za·tion** *n.* **—de·o·dor·iz·er** *n.*

De·o gra·ti·as (dē′ō grā′shē-ăs, dā′ō grät′ē-äs′). *Latin.* Thanks be to God.

de·on·tic (dē-ŏn′tĭk) *adj.* **1.** *Logic & Philosophy.* Of or pertaining to such ethical concepts as obligation or commitment. **2.** *Linguistics.* Of or pertaining to the representation in language of obligation and permission, especially through various uses of the modal auxiliaries, for example, *must* and *may.* [Greek *deont-,* participial stem of *dei* (impersonal), it behooves, it is right.]

de·on·tol·o·gy (dē′ŏn-tŏl′ə-jē) *n. Philosophy.* The theory or study of moral obligation or commitment. [Greek *deon* (stem *deont-*), that which is binding or needful (influenced in meaning by *dein,* to bind), from *dei,* it is right + -LOGY.] **—de·on·to·log·i·cal** (dē-ŏn′tə-lŏj′ĭ-kəl) *adj.* **—de·on·tol·o·gist** *n.*

De·o vo·len·te (dē′ō vō-lĕn′tē, dā′ō vō-lĕn′tā) *adv. Abbr.* **D.V.** *Latin.* God willing.

de·ox·i·dize (dē-ŏk′sə-dīz′) *tr.v.* **-dized, -dizing, -dizes.** To remove oxygen, especially chemically combined oxygen, from. **—de·ox·i·di·za·tion** *n.* **—de·ox·i·diz·er** *n.*

deoxy-, desoxy- *prefix.* Indicates that a molecule contains less oxygen than another to which it is related; for example, **deoxyribonucleic acid.**

de·ox·y·cor·ti·co·ster·one (dē-ŏk′sē-kôr′tĭ-kŏs′tə-rōn′) *n.* A steroid hormone, $C_{21}H_{30}O_3$, derived from the adrenal cortex, that regulates water and salt balance and is used to treat adrenal insufficiency.

de·ox·y·gen·ate (dē-ŏk′sə-jə-nāt′) *tr.v.* **-ated, -ating, -ates.** To remove oxygen from. **—de·ox·y·gen·a·tion** *n.*

de·ox·y·ri·bo·nu·cle·ic acid (dē-ŏk′sē-rī-bō-no͞o-klē′ĭk, -nyo͞o-) *n.* Also **des·ox·y·ri·bo·nu·cle·ic acid** (dĕs-). **DNA** *(see).*

de·ox·y·ri·bo·nu·cle·o·tide (dē-ŏk′sē-rī′bō-no͞o′klē-ə-tīd′, -nyo͞o′-) *n.* A nucleotide that contains deoxyribose and is a constituent of DNA. [DEOXYRIBO(SE) + NUCLEOTIDE.]

de·ox·y·ri·bose (dē-ŏk′sē-rī′bōs) *n.* Also **des·ox·y·ri·bose** (dĕs-). A sugar, $C_5H_{10}O_4$, that is a constituent of DNA.

dep. 1. depart; departure. **2.** department. **3.** deponent. **4.** deposit. **5.** depot. **6.** deputy.

Dep. dependency (territorial).

de·part (dĭ-pärt′) *v.* **-parted, -parting, -parts.** —*intr.* **1.** *Abbr.* **dep.** To go away; set forth; leave. **2.** To diverge, as from an established course; deviate: *depart from custom.* —*tr.* To leave. Used especially in the phrase *depart this life.* [Middle English *departen,* divide, from Old French *departir* : *de-,* away + *partir,* to go, divide, from Latin *partīre,* from *pars* (stem *part-*), PART.]

de·part·ed (dĭ-pär′tĭd) *adj.* **1.** Bygone; past. **2.** Dead. —See Usage note at **dead.**

de·part·ment (dĭ-pärt′mənt) *n. Abbr.* **D., dep., dept., dpt. 1.** A distinct division of a large organization, such as a company or shop, having a specialized function and personnel and often housed separately. **2.** *Usually* **Department.** Any of the principal administrative divisions of the government: *the Department of Energy.* **3.** An administrative district in the government of France. **4.** A division of a school, college, or university dealing with a particular field of study. **5.** *Informal.* An area of special knowledge or activity; sphere. [French *département,* from Old French, departure, from *departir,* divide, DEPART.]

de·part·men·tal (dē′pärt-mĕn′təl) *adj.* Pertaining to a department or departments. **—de·part·men·tal·ism** *n.* **—de·part·men·tal·ly** *adv.*

de·part·men·tal·ize (dē′pärt-mĕn′tə-līz′) *tr.v.* **-ized, -izing, -izes.** To organize into departments. **—de·part·men·tal·i·za·tion** *n.*

department store *n.* A large retail establishment offering a wide variety of merchandise and services, and organized into departments according to the kinds of goods sold.

de·par·ture (dĭ-pär′chər) *n. Abbr.* **dep. 1.** The act of leaving; a going away. **2.** A starting out, as on a trip or a new course of action. **3.** A deviation or divergence, as from an established rule, plan, or procedure. **4.** *Nautical.* **a.** The distance sailed due east or west by a ship on its course. **b.** A ship's bearing at the start of a voyage, used as a basis for dead reckoning.

de·pas·ture (dē-păs′chər, -päs′-) *v.* **-tured, -turing, -tures.** *Chiefly British.* —*tr.* **1.** To put out (cattle, for example) to graze. **2.** To empty or denude (a field, for example) by grazing. —*intr.* To graze in a pasture.

de·pend (dĭ-pĕnd′) *intr.v.* **-pended, -pending, -pends. 1.** To rely, as for support or aid. Used with *on* or *upon.* **2.** To be assured; place trust. Used with *on* or *upon.* **3.** To be determined, conditioned, or dependent. Usually used with *on* or *upon*: *It depends upon your taste.* **4.** To hang down. Used with *from.* **5.** *Informal.* To be pending or undecided. —See Synonyms at **rely.** [Middle English *dependen,* from Old French *dependre,* to hang down, from Latin *dēpendēre* : *dē-,* down + *pendēre,* to hang.]
Usage: *Depend,* indicating condition or contingency, is always followed by *on* or *upon*: *It depends (up)on who is in charge.* Omission of the preposition is typical of casual speech.

de·pend·a·ble (dĭ-pĕn′də-bəl) *adj.* Capable of being depended upon; trustworthy. —See Synonyms at **faithful. —de·pend·a·bil·i·ty, de·pend·a·ble·ness** *n.* **—de·pend·a·bly** *adv.*

de·pend·ence, de·pend·ance (dĭ-pĕn′dəns) *n.* **1.** The state or fact of being dependent; especially, subjection to, control by, or reliance upon someone or something else: *drug dependence.* **2.** Trust; reliance. —See Synonyms at **trust.**

de·pend·en·cy, de·pend·an·cy (dĭ-pĕn′dən-sē) *n., pl.* **-cies. 1.** Dependence. **2.** Anything dependent or subordinate. **3.** *Abbr.* **Dep.** A territory under the jurisdiction of another country from which it is separated geographically.

de·pend·ent, de·pend·ant (dĭ-pĕn′dənt) *adj.* **1.** Contingent upon something or someone else. **2.** Subordinate. **3.** Unable to exist or function satisfactorily without the aid or use of someone or something. **4.** Hanging down.
∼n. One who relies on another for support, especially for financial support. **—de·pend·ent·ly** *adv.*

dependent clause *n. Grammar.* A clause that cannot stand alone as a full sentence and that functions as a noun, adjective, or adverb within a sentence. Also called "subordinate clause."

dependent variable *n. Mathematics.* A variable restricted to one or more of a set of values for every value assumed by an independent variable.

de·per·son·al·ize (dē-pûr′sə-nə-līz′) *tr.v.* **-ized, -izing, -izes. 1.** To deprive of personal or individual character. **2.** To render impersonal. **—de·per·son·al·i·za·tion** *n.*

de·phleg·ma·tor (dē-flĕg′mā′tər) *n.* A device used in distillation to condense the higher boiling constituents of a mixed vapor. [DE- + PHLEGM + -ATOR.]

de·pict (dĭ-pĭkt′) *tr.v.* **-picted, -picting, -picts. 1.** To represent in a picture or sculpture. **2.** To represent in words; describe. [Latin *dēpingere* (past participle *dēpictus*) : *dē-,* completely + *pingere,* to picture.] **—de·pic·tion** *n.*

dep·i·late (dĕp′ə-lāt′) *tr.v.* **-lated, -lating, -lates.** To remove hair from (the body). [Latin *dēpilāre* (past participle *dēpilātus*) : *dē-,* completely + *pilāre,* to deprive of hair, from *pilus,* hair.] **—dep·i·la·tion** *n.* **—dep·i·la·tor** *n.*

de·pil·a·to·ry (dĭ-pĭl′ə-tôr′ē, -tōr′ē) *adj.* Capable of removing hair.
∼n., pl. **depilatories.** A liquid or cream used to remove unwanted hair from the body.

de·plane (dē-plān′) *intr.v.* **-planed, -planing, -planes.** To disembark from an airplane.

de·plete (dĭ-plēt′) *tr.v.* **-pleted, -pleting, -pletes. 1.** To reduce or lessen in quantity, value, or effectiveness; exhaust. **2.** To empty. [Latin *dēplēre* (past participle *dēplētus*), to empty : *de-* (reversal) + *plēre,* to fill.] **—de·plet·a·ble** *adj.* **—de·ple·tion** *n.*
Usage: *deplete, drain, enervate, exhaust, impoverish.* These verbs all signify depletion of strength or resources to the point of functional impairment. *Deplete* refers to using up gradually, and only hints at harmful consequences. *Drain* suggests reduction by gradually drawing off, and is stronger in implying harm. *Enervate* refers to weakening of vitality or moral strength. *Exhaust* stresses reduction to a point of no further usefulness in a given activity. *Impoverish* refers to severe reduction of resources or qualities essential to adequate functioning.

de·plor·a·ble (dĭ-plôr′ə-bəl, -plōr′-) *adj.* **1.** Worthy of severe reproach. **2.** Lamentable; grievous. **3.** Wretched; bad. **—de·plor·a·ble·ness, de·plor·a·bil·i·ty** *n.* **—de·plor·a·bly** *adv.*

de·plore (dĭ-plôr′, -plōr′) *tr.v.* **-plored, -ploring, -plores. 1.** To feel or express deep sorrow over; lament. **2.** To feel or express strong disapproval of; censure. [French *déplorer,* from Latin *dēplōrāre* : *dē-,* completely + *plōrāre*†, to wail.]

de·ploy (dĭ-ploi′) *v.* **-ployed, -ploying, -ploys.** —*tr.* **1.** To station (persons or forces) systematically over an area. **2.** *Military.* **a.** To spread out (troops) to form an extended front. **b.** To bring (forces or weapons) into action. **3.** To use or arrange for a particular effect. —*intr.* To be or become deployed. [French *déployer,* from Latin *displicāre,* to scatter : *dis-* (reversal) + *plicāre,* to fold.] **—de·ploy·ment** *n.*

de·plume (dē-plo͞om′) *tr.v.* **-plumed, -pluming, -plumes. 1.** To pluck the feathers from. **2.** To deprive of honor or pride. [Middle English *deplumen,* from Old French *deplumer,* from Medieval Latin *deplumāre* : Latin *de-,* removal + *plūma,* feather.] **—de·plu·ma·tion** *n.*

de·po·lar·i·za·tion (dē-pō′lə-rə-zā′shən) *n.* **1.** An instance or the process of depolarizing. **2.** The sudden diffusion of ions across the membrane of a nerve cell that accompanies the passage of a nerve impulse and produces an action potential.

de·po·lar·ize (dē-pō'lə-rīz') *tr.v.* **-ized, -izing, -izes.** To eliminate or counteract the polarization of.

de·pone (dĭ-pōn') *v.* **-poned, -poning, -pones.** *Archaic.* —*tr.* To testify or declare under oath. —*intr.* To give testimony. [Medieval Latin *dēpōnere,* from Latin, to put down : *dē-,* down + *pōnere,* put.]

de·po·nent (dĭ-pō'nənt) *adj. Abbr.* **dep., dpt.** *Grammar.* Designating a verb of active meaning but passive form, such as certain Latin and Greek verbs.
∼*n. Abbr.* **dep., dpt. 1.** *Grammar.* A deponent verb. **2.** *Law.* A person who testifies under oath, especially in writing. [Late Latin *dēpōnēns* (stem *dēpōnent-*), "laying aside" (in grammar, referring to the idea that the verb has "laid aside" its active form, from Latin, present participle of *dēpōnere,* to put down, lay aside. See **depone.**]

de·pop·u·late (dē-pŏp'yə-lāt') *v.* **-lated, -lating, -lates.** —*tr.* To reduce the population of. —*intr.* To be reduced in population. [Latin *dēpopulāre,* ravage : *dē-,* completely + *populāre,* to ravage, from *populus,* people.] —**de·pop·u·la·tion** *n.* —**de·pop·u·la·tor** *n.*

de·port (dĭ-pôrt', -pōrt') *tr.v.* **-ported, -porting, -ports. 1.** To expel from a country. **2.** To behave or conduct (oneself). —See Synonyms at **banish.** [(Sense 1, from French *déporter*), Old French *deporter,* behave, from Latin *dēportāre,* to carry off, carry away : *dē-,* away, off + *portāre,* to carry.]

de·por·ta·tion (dē'pôr-tā'shən, -pōr-) *n.* Banishment from a country; especially, the expulsion of an undesirable alien.

de·por·tee (dē'pôr-tē', -pōr-) *n.* A deported person.

de·port·ment (dĭ-pôrt'mənt, -pōrt'-) *n.* **1.** Conduct; demeanor. —See Synonyms at **bearing. 2.** Posture; carriage.

de·pos·al (dĭ-pō'zəl) *n.* The act of deposing from office.

de·pose (dĭ-pōz') *v.* **-posed, -posing, -poses.** —*tr.* **1.** To remove from office or a position of power. **2.** *Law.* To declare under oath, especially in writing. —*intr. Law.* To testify, especially in writing. [Middle English *deposen,* from Old French *deposer* : *de-,* away + *poser,* to put, POSE.] —**de·pos·a·ble** *adj.*

de·pos·it (dĭ-pŏz'ĭt) *v.* **-ited, -iting, -its.** —*tr.* **1.** To place carefully or safely in the proper repository. **2.** To lay down or cause to settle, especially in a layer or layers, by a natural process. **3.** To give (money) as partial payment or security. **4.** To entrust (money) to a bank or other institution. —*intr.* To become deposited; precipitate; settle.
∼*n. Abbr.* **dep. 1.** Something entrusted for safekeeping, such as a sum of money in a bank. **2.** The condition of being entrusted for safekeeping. Used chiefly in the phrase *on deposit.* **3.** A partial or initial payment of a cost or debt. **4.** A sum of money given as security for an item acquired for temporary use. **5.** A depository. **6.** Something deposited, especially by a natural process, as: **a.** *Geology.* Material that results from the process of deposition. **b.** *Physiology.* A sediment in a bodily fluid or a localized bodily accretion, as of calcium. **c.** A sediment or precipitate that has settled out of a solution. **7.** A coating or layer formed on a metal surface by electrolysis or by some other process, such as hot dipping. [Latin *dēpōnere* (past participle *dēpositus*), to put aside : *dē-,* aside + *pōnere,* put.] —**de·pos·i·tor** *n.*

deposit account *n. Chiefly British.* A bank account in which the money deposited earns interest and notice of withdrawal is sometimes required.

de·pos·i·tar·y (dĭ-pŏz'ə-tĕr'ē) *n., pl.* **-ies. 1.** A person or group entrusted with the preservation or safekeeping of something. **2.** A repository; a depository.

dep·o·si·tion (dĕp'ə-zĭsh'ən) *n.* **1.** The act of deposing, as from high office. **2.** The act of depositing. **3.** Something deposited; a deposit. **4.** *Law.* Testimony under oath; especially, a written statement by a witness for use in court in his absence. **5.** *Geology.* The laying down of material by natural processes, such as matter transported by wind or water or that resulting from the decay of living matter or organisms. **6. Deposition. a.** The taking down of Christ from the cross. **b.** A work of art depicting this scene.

de·pos·i·to·ry (dĭ-pŏz'ə-tôr'ē, -tōr'ē) *n., pl.* **-ries. 1.** A place where something is deposited for safekeeping; a repository. **2.** A trustee; a depositary.

de·pot (dē'pō, dĕp'ō) *n. Abbr.* **dep. 1.** A railroad or bus station. **2.** A warehouse or storehouse. **3.** *Military.* **a.** A centrally located installation for the storage, repair, or distribution of military equipment and materials. **b.** A station for receiving, classifying, and assembling personnel. [French *dépôt,* from Old French *depost,* from Latin *dēpositum,* deposit, from the neuter past participle of *dēpōnere,* to DEPOSIT.]

de·prave (dĭ-prāv') *tr.v.* **-praved, -praving, -praves.** To deprive of rectitude; debase morally; corrupt. [Middle English *depraven,* from Old French *depraver,* to pervert, from Latin *dēprāvāre* : *dē-,* completely + *prāvus*†, distorted, crooked.] —**dep·ra·va·tion** (dĕp'rə-vā'shən) *n.* —**de·prav·er** *n.*

de·praved (dĭ-prāvd') *adj.* Morally corrupt; debased; perverted. —**de·prav·ed·ly** (dĭ-prā'vĭd-lē) *adv.*

de·prav·i·ty (dĭ-prăv'ə-tē) *n., pl.* **-ties. 1. a.** Moral corruption. **b.** *Theology.* The innate corruption of human nature due to original sin. **2.** A wicked or perverse act.

dep·re·cate (dĕp'rə-kāt') *tr.v.* **-cated, -cating, -cates. 1.** To express disapproval of; protest or plead against. **2.** To depreciate; belittle. —See Usage note below. [Latin *dēprecārī,* to ward off by prayer : *dē-,* away + *precārī,* pray.] —**dep·re·ca·tion** *n.* —**dep·re·ca·tor** *n.*

Usage: Similarity in form and meaning between *deprecate* and *depreciate* has led to a semantic development that is already well established. *Deprecate* means "express disapproval of": *He deprecated the use of force. Depreciate* means "belittle" or "mildly disparage": *depreciated my achievements.* However, examples such as *He deprecated my achievements* and associated forms such as *deprecation, self-deprecatory* are increasingly found and accepted.

dep·re·ca·to·ry (dĭp'rə-kə-tôr'ē, -tōr'ē) *adj.* Also **dep·re·ca·tive** (-kā'tĭv). **1.** Expressing deprecation; disapproving. **2.** Expressing apology, or regret; apologetic.

de·pre·ci·a·ble (dĭ-prē'shē-ə-bəl) *adj.* Liable to depreciation in value.

de·pre·ci·ate (dĭ-prē'shē-āt') *v.* **-ated, -ating, -ates.** —*tr.* **1.** To lessen the price or value of. **2.** To make to seem less in value or importance; belittle. —*intr.* To diminish in value or price. —See Synonyms at **decry** and Usage note at **deprecate.** [Medieval Latin *dēpreciāre,* manuscript error for Late Latin *dēpretiāre* : *dē-,* down from + *pretium,* price.] —**de·pre·ci·a·tor** *n.*

de·pre·ci·a·tion (dĭ-prē'shē-ā'shən) *n.* **1.** A decrease or loss in value because of wear, age, or other cause. **2.** *Accounting.* An allowance made for this loss. **3.** A reduction in the purchasing value of money. **4.** A disparaging; a belittling.

de·pre·ci·a·to·ry (dĭ-prē'shē-ə-tôr'ē, -tōr'ē) *adj.* Also **de·pre·ci·a·tive** (-ā'tĭv). **1.** Diminishing in value. **2.** Disparaging.

dep·re·date (dĕp'rə-dāt') *v.* **-dated, -dating, -dates.** —*tr.* To prey upon; plunder. —*intr.* To commit plunder. [Late Latin *dēpraedārī* : Latin *dē-,* completely + *praedārī,* to plunder, to make booty, from *praeda,* booty. —**dep·re·da·tion** *n.* —**dep·re·da·tor** *n.* —**dep·re·da·to·ry** (dĕp'rə-dā'tə-rē) *adj.*

de·press (dĭ-prĕs') *tr.v.* **-pressed, -pressing, -presses. 1.** To dispirit; sadden. **2.** To press down; lower: *depress a pedal.* **3.** To lower prices in (a stock market). [Middle English *depressen,* from Old French *depresser,* from Latin *deprimere* (past participle *depressus*) : *de-,* down + *premere,* to press.]

de·pres·sant (dĭ-prĕs'ənt) *adj.* **1.** *Medicine.* Serving to lower the rate of vital activities. **2.** Causing dejection; depressing.
∼*n.* **1.** *Medicine.* A depressant drug. **2.** One that causes dejection or gloom.

de·pressed (dĭ-prĕst') *adj.* **1.** Lacking energy and enthusiasm; melancholy; gloomy. **2.** *Botany.* Flattened downward, as if pressed from above. **3.** *Zoology.* Flattened along the dorsal and ventral surfaces. **4.** Sunk below the surrounding region: *the depressed center of a crater.* **5.** Economically and socially disadvantaged; marked by widespread poverty and unemployment: *The resort is a depressed area in the winter.* —See Synonyms at **sad.**

de·pres·sion (dĭ-prĕsh'ən) *n.* **1. a.** The act of depressing. **b.** The condition of being depressed. **2. a.** *Pathology.* An abnormal lowering of the rate of any physiological function or activity, such as heart beat. **b.** *Psychology.* A state of gloom and melancholy often accompanied by feelings of inadequacy and usually by a lack of energy. **3.** An area that is below or has sunk below its surroundings; a hollow. **4.** *Meteorology.* A region of low barometric pressure in high or mid latitudes. Also called "low," "disturbance," and formerly a "cyclone." **5.** *Surveying.* The angular distance below the horizontal plane through the point of observation. **6.** *Astronomy.* The angular distance of a celestial body below the horizon. **7.** *Economics.* **a.** A period of drastic decline in an economy, characterized by decreasing business activity, falling prices, and unemployment. **b. Depression.** The period during the 1930's when such a decline occurred in most industrialized countries. Preceded by *the.* —See Synonyms at **despair.**

Depression glass *n.* Glassware of many colors and patterns produced in large quantities during the 1920's and 1930's. [After the great *Depression,* a period of severe economic hardship during the 1930's.]

de·pres·sive (dĭ-prĕs'ĭv) *adj.* **1.** Causing depression. **2.** *Psychology.* Of or characterized by depression.
∼*n. Psychology.* A person suffering from depression. —**de·pres·sive·ly** *adv.* —**de·pres·sive·ness** *n.*

de·pres·so·mo·tor (dĭ-prĕs'ō-mō'tər) *adj.* Retarding or lessening physiological motor activity: *depressomotor nerves.*
∼*n.* A drug that causes such a retardation.

de·pres·sor (dĭ-prĕs'ər) *n.* **1.** Something that depresses or is used to depress. **2.** A **depressor nerve** *(see).* **3.** Any of several muscles that cause depression or contraction of a part. **4.** Any instrument, such as a tongue depressor, used to depress a part. **5.** *Phonetics.* A consonant that has the effect of lowering the tone of a following vowel.

depressor nerve *n.* A nerve that lowers arterial blood pressure. Also called "depressor."

de·pres·sur·ize (dē-prĕsh'ə-rīz') *tr.v.* **-ized, -izing, -izes.** To reduce the pressure of air or gas within (a sealed container, room, or vehicle). —**de·pres·sur·i·za·tion** *n.*

dep·ri·va·tion (dĕp'rə-vā'shən) *n.* Also **de·priv·al** (dĭ-prī'vəl). **1. a.** The act of depriving. **b.** The condition of being deprived. **2.** Privation. **3.** A taking away of rank or office.

de·prive (dĭ-prīv') *tr.v.* **-prived, -priving, -prives. 1.** To take something away from; dispossess; divest. **2.** To keep from the possession or enjoyment of something; deny. **3.** To take a position from; depose from office. [Middle English *depriven,* from Old French *depriver,* from Medieval Latin *dēprīvāre* : Latin *dē-,* completely + *prīvāre,* to deprive, from *prīvus,* individual, private.] —**de·priv·a·ble** *adj.*

de·prived (dĭ-prīvd') *adj.* **1.** Lacking the financial means, education, family environment, or social ties considered necessary to achieve a fulfilling life: *a deprived childhood.* **2.** Lacking adequate housing, educational facilities, industry, and the like.

de pro•fun•dis (dā' prə-fo͝on'dēs, prō-) *adv. Latin.* Out of the depths of misery or grief.

de•pro•gram (dē-prō'grăm', -grəm) *tr.v.* **-grammed** or **-gramed, -gramming** or **-graming, -grams.** To counteract the effects of previous programming or indoctrination. **—de•pro•gram•mer** *n.*

dept. 1. department. **2.** deputy.

depth (dĕpth) *n.* **1.** The condition or quality of being deep; deepness. **2.** The extent, measurement, or dimension downward, backward, or inward. **3.** *Often* **depths.** A deep part of or place in something. **4.** *Often* **depths.** The middle, inner, or most remote or inaccessible part. **5.** *Often* **depths.** The most profound or intense part or stage: *the depths of despair.* **6.** *Often* **depths.** The severest or worst part: *in the depths of winter.* **7.** Intellectual penetration; profundity. **8.** The range of one's understanding or competence: *out of one's depth.* **9. depths.** An immoral condition; disgrace: *sink to such depths.* **10.** Richness; intensity; darkness: *depth of color.* **11.** Lowness in pitch, as of a voice or musical instrument. **—in depth.** Marked by thorough coverage or treatment: *a study in depth.* [Middle English *depthe,* from DEEP.]

depth charge *n.* Any explosive charge designed for detonation under water, especially such a charge dropped or catapulted from a ship's deck and used against submarines. Also called "depth bomb."

depth of field *n.* The distance in front of and behind an object focused by a camera, microscope, or the like, within which other objects would appear in focus. Compare **depth of focus.**

depth of focus *n.* The amount by which the distance between a camera lens and the film or plate can be varied without altering the sharpness of the image. Compare **depth of field.**

depth perception *n.* Perception of spatial relationships, especially of distances between objects, in three dimensions.

depth psychology *n.* **1.** Any psychology of the unconscious, especially as distinguished from the psychology of conscious behavior. **2.** Loosely, psychoanalysis.

dep•u•rate (dĕp'yə-rāt') *v.* **-rated, -rating, -rates.** *—tr.* To cleanse or purify. *—intr.* To become cleansed or purified. [Medieval Latin *dēpūrāre* : Latin *dē-,* removal + *pūrāre,* to purify, from *pūrus,* pure.] **—dep•u•ra•tion** *n.* **—dep•u•ra•tive** *n. & adj.* **—dep•u•ra•tor** *n.*

dep•u•ta•tion (dĕp'yə-tā'shən) *n.* **1.** A person or group appointed to represent another or others; a delegation. **2. a.** The act of deputing. **b.** The state of being deputed.

de•pute (dĭ-pyo͞ot') *tr.v.* **-puted, -puting, -putes. 1.** To appoint or authorize as an agent or representative. **2.** To appoint to carry out a particular job. **3.** To assign (authority or duties) to another or others; delegate. [Middle English *deputen,* from Old French *deputer,* from Late Latin *dēputāre,* to allot, from Latin, "to cut off," consider : *dē-,* off + *putāre,* to prune, cut, esteem.]

dep•u•tize (dĕp'yə-tīz') *v.* **-tized, -tizing, -tizes.** *—tr.* To appoint as a deputy. *—intr.* To serve as a deputy.

dep•u•ty (dĕp'yə-tē) *n., pl.* **-ties.** *Abbr.* **d., D., dep., dept. 1.** A person named or empowered to act for another. **2.** An assistant exercising full authority in the absence of his superior and equal authority in emergencies. **3.** A representative in a legislative body in certain countries, such as France. **4.** A mining official who is responsible for safety precautions.
~*adj.* Acting as deputy. [Middle English *depute,* from Old French, from the past participle of *deputer,* to DEPUTE.]

De Quin•cey (dĭ kwĭn'sē), **Thomas** (1785–1859). British writer and critic. At Oxford he took opium, ostensibly to cure a toothache, and became addicted to the drug for the rest of his life. He is best known for his *Confessions of an English Opium Eater* (1821).

der. derivation; derivative.

de•rac•i•nate (dĭ-răs'ə-nāt') *tr.v.* **-nated, -nating, -nates. 1.** To pull out by the roots; uproot. **2.** To displace from a natural environment; dislocate. [French *déraciner,* from Old French *desraciner* : *des-, de-* (undoing) + *racine,* root, from Late Latin *radīcīna,* from Latin *rādix* (stem *rādīc-*).] **—de•rac•i•na•tion** *n.*

dé•rac•i•né (dā'rā-sə-nā') *adj.* Uprooted or rootless; having no ties with one's home or origins. [French.] **—dé•rac•i•né** *n.*

de•rail (dē-rāl') *v.* **-railed, -railing, -rails.** *—tr.* To cause (a train) to run off the rails. *—intr.* To run off the rails. [French *dérailler* : *dé-,* off + *rail,* RAIL.] **—de•rail•ment** *n.*

de•rail•leur (dĭ-rā'lər) *n.* A device for changing gear on bicycles. [French, switch (for gears, rails), from *dérailler,* to go off rails, DERAIL.]

De•rain (də-răN'), **André** (1880–1954). French painter, illustrator, and theatrical designer. He was one of the original fauvists, but eventually adopted a more traditional style.

de•range (dĭ-rānj') *tr.v.* **-ranged, -ranging, -ranges. 1.** To disturb the order or arrangement of; disorder; disarrange. **2.** To disturb the normal condition or functioning of; upset. **3.** To disturb the mental stability of; make insane. [French *déranger,* from Old French *desrengier* : *de-* (sense of undoing) + *reng, renc,* line, RANK.]

de•range•ment (dĭ-rānj'mənt) *n.* **1.** Severe mental disorder; insanity. **2.** The act or an instance of deranging. **3.** Disarrangement; confusion; disorder.

der•by (dûr'bē) *n., pl.* **-bies.** A stiff felt hat with a round crown and narrow, curved brim. Also called "bowler." [After DERBY (race).]

Der•by[1] (där'bē *for sense 1;* dûr'bē *for senses 2, 3*) *n.* **1.** A horse race for three-year-olds, held annually at Epsom Downs in Surrey, England. Preceded by *the.* **2.** Any of various other horse races, especially the Kentucky Derby. **3. derby.** Any formal race with a more or less open field of contestants: *a soapbox derby.* [After Edward Smith Stanley (1752–1834), 12th Earl of *Derby,* founder of the English Derby.]

Der•by[2] (där'bē) *n.* A mild cheese originally made in Derby, England, often flavored with sage.

Der•by[3] (där'bē). City at the foot of the Pennines in Derbyshire, central England. The country's first silk mill was founded here in 1719. The making of the porcelain known as Derbyware or Crown Derby was begun by William Duesbury (1725–86) and is still a major concern.

Der•by•shire (där'bē-shîr, -shər). A county in north-central England. The Peak District in the north is largely a national park supporting sheep farming and tourism. Coal is mined around Derby, its administrative center.

dere. Variant of **dear** (dire).

de•reg•u•late (dē-rĕg'yə-lāt') *tr.v.* **1.** To remove rules or restrictions from, especially from governmental restrictions; decontrol: *deregulate the media.* **2.** To remove price controls from: *deregulate air fares.* **—de•reg•u•la•tion** *n.*

der•e•lict (dĕr'ə-lĭkt') *adj.* **1.** Neglectful of duty or obligation; remiss; delinquent. **2.** Deserted by an owner or guardian; abandoned; forsaken. **3.** Dilapidated; falling into ruins; neglected.
~*n.* **1.** An item of abandoned property; especially, a ship abandoned at sea. **2.** A social outcast; a vagrant. **3.** *Law.* Land left dry by a permanent recession of the water line. **4.** One neglectful of duty or obligation. [Latin *dērelictus,* past participle of *dērelinquere,* to abandon : *dē-,* completely + *relinquere,* to leave behind : *re-,* behind + *linquere,* to leave.]

der•e•lic•tion (dĕr'ə-lĭk'shən) *n.* **1.** Willful neglect, as of duty. **2.** Abandonment. **3.** *Law.* **a.** A gaining of land by the permanent recession of the water line. **b.** The land so gained.

de•re•strict (dē'rĭ-strĭkt') *tr.v.* To free from restriction; especially, to free (a road or area) from speed limits. **—de•re•stric•tion** *n.*

Dergue (dûrg) *n.* The ruling council established in Ethiopia after the overthrow of Haile Selassie in 1974.

de•ride (dĭ-rīd') *tr.v.* **-rided, -riding, -rides.** To speak of or treat with contemptuous mirth; scoff at. **—See Synonyms at ridicule.** [Latin *dērīdēre* : *dē-* (pejorative) + *rīdēre,* to laugh at.] **—de•rid•er** *n.* **—de•rid•ing•ly** *adv.*

de ri•gueur (də rē-gœr') *adj.* Required by the current fashion or custom; socially obligatory; proper. [French.]

de•ri•sion (dĭ-rĭzh'ən) *n.* **1. a.** Scoffing; ridicule. **b.** A state of being derided. **2.** An object of ridicule; a laughingstock. [Middle English *derisioun,* from Old French *derision,* from Late Latin *dērīsiō* (stem *dērīsiōn-*), from Latin *dērīsus,* past participle of *dērīdēre,* to DERIDE.] **—de•ris•i•ble** *adj.*

de•ri•sive (dĭ-rī'sĭv) *adj.* **1.** Mocking; scoffing. **2.** Liable to derision; absurd. **—de•ri•sive•ly** *adv.* **—de•ri•sive•ness** *n.*

de•ri•so•ry (dĭ-rī'sə-rē, -zə-rē) *adj.* **1.** Derisive. **2.** So small or inadequate as to be ridiculous: *a derisory pay offer.*

der•i•va•tion (dĕr'ə-vā'shən) *n. Abbr.* **der. 1.** The act or process of deriving. **2.** The condition or fact of being derived. **3.** Something derived; a derivative. **4.** The form or source from which something is derived; the origin; the descent. **5.** The historical origin and development of a word; an etymology. **6.** *Linguistics.* The morphological process by which new words are formed from existing words, chiefly by the addition of affixes to roots, stems, or words. **7.** *Mathematics.* A logical or mathematical process indicating through a sequence of statements that a result, such as a theorem or a formula, necessarily follows from the initial assumptions. **—der•i•va•tion•al** *adj.*

de•riv•a•tive (dĭ-rĭv'ə-tĭv) *adj.* Also **der•i•vate** (dĕr'ə-vāt'). *Abbr.* **der. 1.** Resulting from derivation; derived. **2.** Copied or adapted from others; lacking originality.
~*n.* **1.** Something derived. **2.** *Linguistics.* A word formed from another by derivation. Compare **primitive. 3.** *Mathematics.* The limit, as the increment in the argument of a function approaches zero, of the ratio of the increment in its value to the corresponding increment in the argument; loosely, the instantaneous rate of change of a function with respect to a variable. Also called "differential coefficient." **4.** *Chemistry.* Any compound derived or obtained from known or hypothetical substances and containing essential elements of the parent substance. **—de•riv•a•tive•ly** *adv.*

de•rive (dĭ-rīv') *v.* **-rived, -riving, -rives.** *—tr.* **1.** To obtain or receive from a source. **2.** To arrive at by reasoning; deduce; infer: *derive a conclusion from facts.* **3.** To trace the origin or development of (a word, for example). **4.** *Chemistry.* To produce or obtain (a compound) from another substance by chemical reaction. *—intr.* To issue from a source; originate. [Middle English *deriven,* to conduct water from a source, spring from, from Old French *deriver,* from Latin *dērīvāre,* to draw off, derive : *dē-,* away, off + *rīvus,* stream.] **—de•riv•a•ble** *adj.* **—de•riv•er** *n.*

derived unit *n.* A unit of measurement obtained by multiplying or dividing two or more base units of a system of units without the introduction of numerical factors.

-derm *suffix. Biology.* Indicates skin; for example, **endoderm, echinoderm.** [French *-derme,* from Greek *derma,* skin.]

der•ma[1] (dûr'mə) *n.* Also **derm** (dûrm). *Anatomy.* A layer of skin, the **dermis** *(see).* [New Latin *derma, dermis,* from Greek *derma,* skin.]

derma[2] *n.* Beef or poultry casing stuffed with a seasoned mixture of

PRONUNCIATION KEY

ă, pat; ā, pay; âr, care;
ä, father, are; b, bib;
ch, church; d, deed; ĕ, pet;
ē, be; f, fife; g, gag; h, hat;
hw, which; ĭ, pit; ī, pie;
îr, pier; j, judge; k, kick;
l, lid, needle; m, mum;
n, no, sudden; ng, thing;
ŏ, pot; ō, toe; ô, paw, for;
oi, noise; ou, out; o͝o, book;
o͞o, boot; p, pop; r, roar;
s, sauce; sh, ship, dish;
t, tight; th, thin, path;
th, this, bathe; ŭ, cut; ûr, fur;
v, valve; w, with; y, yes;
z, zebra, size; zh, vision;
ə, about, item, edible,
gallop, circus, peaceful

IN FOREIGN WORDS:

à, *Fr.* ami; œ, *Fr.* feu, *Ger.* schön; ü, *Fr.* tu, *Ger.* über;
KH, *Ger.* ich, *Scot.* loch;
N, *Fr.* bon; y', *Fr.* Compiègne

STRESS MARKS:

Primary stress: '
in•cite' (ĭn-sīt')
Secondary stress: '
in'sight' (ĭn'sīt')

matzo meal or flour, onion, and suet, that is boiled and then roasted. Also called "stuffed derma," "kishke." [Yiddish *derme*, plural of *darm*, intestine, from Middle High German, from Old High German.]

–derma *suffix.* Indicates skin or skin disease; for example, **scleroderma.** [New Latin, from Greek *derma*, skin.]

der·ma·bra·sion (dûr′mə-brā′zhən) *n.* A surgical procedure designed to remove skin imperfections, such as scars or wrinkles, through the abrasion of the frozen epidermis.

der·mal (dûr′məl) *adj.* Also **der·mic** (dûr′mĭk). Of or pertaining to the skin. [DERM(ATO)- + -AL.]

der·ma·ti·tis (dûr′mə-tī′tĭs) *n. Medicine.* Inflammation of the skin. [New Latin : DERMAT(O)- + -ITIS.]

dermato–, derm–, derma–, dermat– *prefix.* Indicates skin; for example, **dermatology, dermal, dermatome, dermatoid.** [Greek, from *derma*, skin.]

der·mat·o·gen (dûr-măt′ə-jən) *n. Botany.* The outer layer of **meristem** (*see*), from which the epidermis is formed.

der·ma·toid (dûr′mə-toid′) *n.* Also **der·moid** (dûr′moid′). Resembling skin; skinlike. [DERMAT(O)- + -OID.]

der·ma·tol·o·gy (dûr′mə-tŏl′ə-jē) *n.* The branch of medicine concerned with the physiology and pathology of the skin and treatment of skin diseases. [DERMATO- + -LOGY.] **—der·ma·to·log·i·cal** (dûr′mə-tə-lŏj′ĭ-kəl) *adj.* **—der·ma·tol·o·gist** *n.*

der·ma·tome (dûr′mə-tōm′) *n.* 1. An area of skin with sensory fibers from a single spinal nerve. 2. An instrument used in cutting thin slices of the skin, as in skin grafting. 3. *Embryology.* The part of a somite that develops into the dermis. [DERMA(TO)- + -TOME.]

der·mat·o·phyte (dûr-măt′ə-fīt′, dûr′mə-tə-) *n.* Any of various fungi that cause skin disease. [DERMATO- + -PHYTE.] **—der·mat·o·phyt·ic** (dûr-măt′ə-fĭt′ĭk) *adj.*

der·ma·to·phy·to·sis (dûr′mə-tō′fī-tō′sĭs) *n.* Any fungal infection of the skin, especially of the feet, such as athlete's foot. [DERMATO-PHYT(E) + -OSIS.]

der·ma·to·plas·ty (dûr′mə-tō-plăs′tē) *n.* The use of skin grafts in plastic surgery to correct defects or replace skin loss. [DERMATO- + -PLASTY.]

der·ma·to·sis (dûr′mə-tō′sĭs) *n., pl.* **-ses** (-sēz′). A skin disease. [DERMAT(O)- + -OSIS.]

–dermatous *suffix.* Having a specified kind of skin; for example, **sclerodermatous.** [From Greek *derma, dermat-*, skin.]

dermic. Variant of **dermal.**

der·mis (dûr′mĭs) *n.* The living part of the skin that forms a thick layer below the epidermis and is made up of connective tissue containing blood and lymph vessels, nerve endings, sweat and sebaceous glands, and smooth muscle. Also called "corium," "derma," "derm." [New Latin, abstracted from EPIDERMIS.]

dermoid. Variant of **dermatoid.**

der·nier cri (dĕr′nyä krē′) *n. French.* The latest thing; the newest fashion. [Literally, "last cry."]

de·ro, der·ro (dĕr′ō) *n., pl.* **-ros.** *Australian Slang.* A vagabond; a tramp. [From DERELICT.]

der·o·gate (dĕr′ə-gāt′) *v.* **-gated, -gating, -gates.** *—intr.* 1. To detract; take away. Used with *from.* 2. To deviate from a standard or expectation; go astray. Used with *from.* *—tr.* To disparage; belittle. [Latin *dērogāre*, repeal, restrict, disparage : *dē-*, away + *rogāre*, ask.] **—der·o·ga·tion** (dĕr′ə-gā′shən) *n.* **—de·rog·a·tive** (dĭ-rŏg′ə-tĭv) *adj.*

de·rog·a·to·ry (dĭ-rŏg′ə-tôr′ē, -tōr′ē) *adj.* Deliberately offensive; detracting or disparaging. **—de·rog·a·to·ri·ly** *adv.* **—de·rog·a·to·ri·ness** *n.*

der·rick (dĕr′ĭk) *n.* 1. A large crane for hoisting and moving heavy objects, consisting of a movable boom equipped with cables and pulleys and connected to the base of an upright stationary beam. 2. A tall framework over the opening of an oil well or other drilled hole, used to support boring equipment or to hoist and lower pipe lengths. [Originally, a gallows, after *Derick*, noted hangman at Tyburn, England *c.* 1600.]

der·ri·ère (dĕr′ē-âr′; French dĕ-ryâr′) *n. Informal.* The buttocks; the rear. [French, "the rear."]

der·ring-do (dĕr′ĭng-dōo′) *n.* Daring spirit and action; valor. [Middle English *durring don*, daring to do (mistaken for a noun phrase by Edmund Spenser and later by Sir Walter Scott) : *durring*, present participle of *durren*, Old English *durran*, to DARE + *don*, to DO.]

der·rin·ger (dĕr′ĭn-jər) *n.* A short-barreled pistol with a large bore. [After Henry *Deringer*, 19th-century U.S. gunsmith who invented it.]

der·ris (dĕr′ĭs) *n.* 1. Any of various woody vines of the genus *Derris*, of tropical Asia, whose roots yield rotenone. 2. The extract from the roots of such plants, which is a powerful insecticide. [New Latin, from Greek, covering, skin.]

derro. Variant of **dero.**

der·ry¹ (dĕr′ē) *n., pl.* **-ries.** A meaningless word used as a refrain or chorus in old songs.

derry² *n. Australian Informal.* A grudge; an aversion: *have a derry on a rival.* [Probably shortened from *derry down*, common refrain in folk songs, with allusion to the phrase *have a down on.*]

Derry. See **Londonderry.**

der·vish (dûr′vĭsh) *n.* A member of any of various Muslim orders of ascetics, some of which practice the achievement of collective ecstasy through whirling dances and the chanting of religious formulas. [Turkish *derviş*, mendicant, from Persian *darvēsh†*.]

Der·went (dûr′wənt). The name of several rivers in England, from a Celtic word meaning "clear water." The longest is in Derbyshire, flowing 96 kilometers (60 miles) into the Trent River.

DES (dē′ē-ĕs′) *n.* **Diethylstilbestrol** (*see*).

De·sai (də-sī′), **Shri Morarji Ranchhodji** (1896–). Indian statesman. A disciple of Mahatma Gandhi, he later came to lead the Congress Party against Indira Gandhi, who as prime minister imprisoned him during a state of emergency. He defeated her in the 1977 elections and as prime minister led the newly formed Janata Party, but resigned in 1979.

de·sal·i·nate (dē-săl′ə-nāt′) *tr.v.* **-nated, -nating, -nates.** To desalinize. **—de·sal·i·na·tion** *n.*

de·sal·in·ize (dē-săl′ə-nīz′) *tr.v.* **-ized, -izing, -izes.** To remove (salts and other chemicals) from sea water or saline water. **—de·sal·i·ni·za·tion** *n.*

de·salt (dē-sôlt′) *tr.v.* **-salted, -salting, -salts.** To desalinize.

des·cant (dĕs′kănt) *n.* Also **dis·cant** (dĭs′-). 1. *Music.* **a.** An ornamental melody or counterpoint sung or played above a musical theme. **b.** The highest part sung in part music. 2. A discussion or discourse on a theme.
~*intr.v.* (dĕs-kănt′) **descanted, -canting, -cants.** Also **dis·cant** (dĭs-kănt′) (for sense 2). 1. To comment at length; discourse. Used with *on* or *upon.* 2. **a.** To sing or play a descant. **b.** To sing melodiously. [Middle English *discant*, from Old North French *descant*, from Medieval Latin *discantus*, refrain : *dis-*, apart + *cantus*, song, from the past participle of *canere*, to sing.] **—des·cant·er** *n.*

descant recorder *n. Music.* A recorder having the highest pitch of those in common use.

Des·cartes (dā-kärt′), **René** (1596–1650). French philosopher. Having rejected all his previously held beliefs, he built his philosophy on the one premise he held to be indisputable, the existence of himself as a thinking subject: "Cogito ergo sum" ("I think, therefore I am"), which he argued in his *Discourse on Method* (1637) and his *Meditations* (1641). As a mathematician, he introduced coordinates and the method of undetermined coefficients.

de·scend (dĭ-sĕnd′) *v.* **-scended, -scending, -scends.** *—intr.* 1. To move from a higher to a lower place, rank, pitch, or the like; come or go down. 2. To slope, extend, or incline downward: *"a rough path descended like a steep stair into the plain"* (J.R.R. Tolkien). 3. To come or be derived from ancestors. 4. To have hereditary derivation. 5. To lower oneself in behavior; stoop. 6. To arrive in an overwhelming manner. Used with *on* or *upon.* 7. To move down toward the horizon. Used of the sun and moon. *—tr.* To move from a higher to a lower part of; go down. [Middle English *descenden*, from Old French *descendre*, from Latin *dēscendere* : *dē-*, down + *scandere*, to climb.] **—de·scend·i·ble, de·scend·a·ble** *adj.*

de·scen·dant (dĭ-sĕn′dənt) *n.* 1. A person, animal, or plant descended from an individual, race, species, or earlier form; an immediate or remote offspring. 2. Anything descended from an earlier form.
~*adj.* Variant of **descendent.**

de·scen·dent, de·scen·dant (dĭ-sĕn′dənt) *adj.* 1. Moving downward; descending. 2. Proceeding by descent from an ancestor. Often used with *from.*

de·scend·er (dĭ-sĕn′dər) *n.* 1. One that descends. 2. *Printing.* **a.** The part of certain letters, such as g, p, or y, that extends below the bottom of most lower-case letters. **b.** Any such letter.

de·scent (dĭ-sĕnt′) *n.* 1. The act or an instance of descending; coming or going down. 2. A way down; downward incline or passage. 3. Hereditary derivation; ancestral extraction; lineage. 4. A generation of a specific lineage. 5. A lowering or decline, as in status or level. 6. A sudden attack; onslaught. 7. *Law.* Transference of property by inheritance. [Middle English *descent*, from Old French, from *descendre*, to DESCEND.]

de·scribe (dĭ-skrīb′) *tr.v.* **-scribed, -scribing, -scribes.** 1. To give a verbal account of; tell about in detail. 2. To transmit a mental image or impression of with words; picture verbally. 3. To trace or draw the figure of; outline: *describe a circle with a compass.* [Latin *dēscrībere*, to copy off, write down : *dē-*, down + *scrībere*, to write.] **—de·scrib·a·ble** *adj.* **—de·scrib·er** *n.*

de·scrip·tion (dĭ-skrĭp′shən) *n.* 1. The act, process, or technique of describing. 2. A statement or account describing someone or something. 3. The act of drawing or tracing a figure. 4. A kind; a sort: *costumes of every description.* [Middle English *descripcioun*, from Old French *description*, from Latin *dēscriptiō* (stem *dēscriptiōn-*), from *dēscriptus*, past participle of *dēscrībere*, to DESCRIBE.]

de·scrip·tive (dĭ-skrĭp′tĭv) *adj.* 1. Involving or characterized by description; serving to describe. 2. Concerned with description or classification rather than explanation: *descriptive science.* 3. *Grammar.* Expressing an attribute of the modified noun; for example, *green* in *green grass.* Said of an adjective or adjectival clause. 4. *Linguistics.* Of or pertaining to descriptive linguistics. **—de·scrip·tive·ly** *adv.* **—de·scrip·tive·ness** *n.*

descriptive geometry *n. Mathematics.* The collection of mathematical techniques used to describe geometric relationships among three-dimensional structures on a plane surface.

descriptive linguistics *n.* The study of a language or languages at a specific stage of development, with emphasis on constructing a complete grammatical analysis rather than on setting standards of usage, examining historical development, or making comparisons among languages.

de·scrip·ti·vism (dĭ-skrĭp′tĭv-ĭz′əm) *n.* 1. *Philosophy.* The doctrine that ethical propositions describe something about the real world and are true or false. Compare **emotivism, prescriptivism.** 2. *Lin-*

derringer *The American gunsmith Henry Deringer (1786–1868) gave his misspelled name to this short and easily concealed pistol—the weapon used to assassinate Abraham Lincoln. Deringer's original design was for a single-shot gun, but it was later modified into a two-shot model: the Remington double derringer shown here.*

desert

DRY AND DESOLATE WASTES

A third of the world's land surface consists of deserts

Deserts are uncultivated, mainly barren regions in which the annual rainfall is less than 250 millimeters (10 inches). There are two main types of desert: hot, arid deserts such as the Sahara and cold deserts such as polar regions.

Hot, arid deserts are the result of high atmospheric pressure combined with slowly descending dry air. They are the world's sunniest regions, where evaporation greatly exceeds rainfall. The cold, polar wastes—which form almost half the world's deserts—are marked by much frozen soil and ice and a lack of tall plants.

Some water-storing plants exist in parts of the hot deserts. Fennel, for instance, grows in cooler crevices in the Sahara, and cacti and agaves grow throughout the deserts of North and Central America.

DESERT DUNES *Ridges or dunes of loose sand, piled by the wind among the prevailing rocks or pebbles, are a feature of hot deserts.*

DESERT FLOWERS *The Atacama Desert of Chile has had droughts lasting for several years. Usually it has a little rain each year. Afterward plants may grow in surface cracks.*

PRONUNCIATION KEY

ă, pat; ā, pay; âr, care;
ä, father, are; b, bib;
ch, church; d, deed; ĕ, pet;
ē, be; f, fife; g, gag; h, hat;
hw, which; ĭ, pit; ī, pie;
îr, pier; j, judge; k, kick;
l, lid, needle; m, mum;
n, no, sudden; ng, thing;
ŏ, pot; ō, toe; ô, paw, for;
oi, noise; ou, out; ŏŏ, book;
ōō, boot; p, pop; r, roar;
s, sauce; sh, ship, dish;
t, tight; th, thin, path;
th, this, bathe; ŭ, cut; ûr, fur;
v, valve; w, with; y, yes;
z, zebra, size; zh, vision;
ə, about, item, edible,
gallop, circus, peaceful

IN FOREIGN WORDS:

à, *Fr.* ami; œ, *Fr.* feu, *Ger.*
schön; ü, *Fr.* tu, *Ger.* über;
KH, *Ger.* ich, *Scot.* loch;
N, *Fr.* bon; y', *Fr.* Compiègne

STRESS MARKS:

Primary stress: ´
in·cite´ (ĭn-sīt´)
Secondary stress: ´
in´sight´ (ĭn´sīt´)

---

guistics. The practice or advocacy of the methods of descriptive linguistics. Compare **prescriptivism**.

de·scry (dĭ-skrī´) *tr.v.* **-scried, -scrying, -scries.** **1.** To discern (something difficult to catch sight of): *through the mists they could descry the long arm of the mountains* (J.R.R. Tolkien). **2.** To discover by careful observation or investigation. —See Synonyms at **see.** [Middle English *descrien,* to cry out, proclaim, catch sight of, from Old French *descrier,* to decry : *des-,* used in pejorative sense, DIS- + *crier,* to CRY.] —**de·scri·er** *n.*

des·e·crate (dĕs´ə-krāt´) *tr.v.* **-crated, -crating, -crates.** To abuse the sacredness of; subject to sacrilege; profane. [DE- + (CON)SECRATE.] —**des·e·crat·er, des·e·cra·tor** *n.* —**des·e·cra·tion** *n.*

de·seg·re·gate (dē-sĕg´rə-gāt´) *v.* **-gated, -gating, -gates.** —*tr.* To abolish racial segregation in (a school, for example). —*intr.* To become desegregated. —**de·seg·re·ga·tion** *n.* —**de·seg·re·ga·tion·ist** *adj. & n.*

de·sen·si·tize (dē-sĕn´sə-tīz´) *tr.v.* **-tized, -tizing, -tizes.** To render

insensitive or less sensitive, as to light or pain. —**de·sen·si·ti·za·tion** *n.* —**de·sen·si·tiz·er** *n.*

Des·e·ret (dĕz´ə-rēt´). A state proposed by the Mormons in 1849 as an independent state or, failing that, a state of the Union. Deseret would have included much of the southwestern United States, with a capital in Salt Lake City.

des·ert¹ (dĕz´ərt) *n.* **1.** A region rendered barren or partially barren by low precipitation (typically less than 250 millimeters or 10 inches a year), or by its exceptionally permeable surface. **2.** A place which lacks aesthetic or cultural appeal: *an architectural desert.* —*adj.* Of, pertaining to, or characteristic of a desert; barren and uninhabited; desolate: *a desert island.* [Middle English, from Old French, from Late Latin *dēsertum,* from Latin, neuter past participle of *dēserere,* to abandon, DESERT.] See feature, next page.

de·sert² (dĭ-zûrt´) *n.* **1.** *Usually* **deserts.** That which is deserved or merited, especially a punishment: *received his just deserts.* **2.** The state or fact of deserving reward or punishment. **3.** *Obsolete.* A good deed. [Middle English *deserte,* from Old French, from *desert,* from *deservir,* to DESERVE.]

de·sert³ (dĭ-zûrt´) *v.* **-serted, -serting, -serts.** —*tr.* **1.** To forsake or leave; abandon: *"his set smile did not once desert him"* (Willa Cather). **2.** To leave (one's post, for example) in violation of orders or oath. —*intr.* To forsake one's duty or post; especially, to be absent without leave from the armed forces with no intention of returning. [French *déserter,* from Late Latin *dēsertāre,* from Latin *dēsertus,* past participle of *dēserere,* to abandon : *dē-,* reversal + *serere,* to join.] —**de·sert·er** *n.*

de·ser·tion (dĭ-zûr´shən) *n.* **1. a.** The act of deserting. **b.** The state of being deserted. **2.** *Law.* Willful abandonment of one's spouse or children, or both, without their consent and with the intention of forsaking all legal obligation.

desert lynx *n.* A wild cat, the **caracal** *(see).*

desert rat *n.* **1.** A **jerboa** *(see).* **2.** *British Informal.* A soldier who served in North Africa during World War II.

de·serve (dĭ-zûrv´) *v.* **-served, -serving, -serves.** —*tr.* To be worthy of; have a right to; merit: *"An American girl of college age . . . deserved instant inspection"* (Kingsley Amis). —*intr.* To be worthy. [Middle English *deserven,* to be entitled to in return for services, deserve, from Old French *deservir,* from Latin *dēservīre,* serve well : *dē-,* completely + *servīre,* to SERVE.]

de·served (dĭ-zûrvd´) *adj.* Merited or earned. Often used in combination: *a well-deserved holiday.* —**de·serv·ed·ly** (dĭ-zûr´vĭd-lē) *adv.* —**de·serv·ed·ness** *n.*

de·serv·ing (dĭ-zûr´vĭng) *adj.* Worthy of reward or praise; meritorious. —*n.* Merit or demerit. —**de·serv·ing·ly** *adv.* —**de·serv·ing·ness** *n.*

de·sex (dē-sĕks´) *tr.v.* **-sexed, -sexing, -sexes.** To remove part or all of the reproductive organs of; spay or castrate.

de·sex·u·al·ize (dē-sĕk´shōō-ə-līz´) *tr.v.* **-ized, -izing, -izes.** **1.** To desex. **2.** To take away the sexual quality of. —**de·sex·u·al·i·za·tion** *n.*

deshabille. Variant of **dishabille.**

De Si·ca (də sē´kə), **Vittorio** (1901–74). Italian film director and actor. Among his best films are *Shoeshine* (1946), *Bicycle Thieves* (1948), and *Umberto D* (1952).

des·ic·cant (dĕs´ĭ-kənt) *n.* A substance, such as calcium oxide or sulfuric acid, that has a high affinity for water and is used as a drying agent to absorb moisture. [Latin *dēsiccāns* (stem *dēsiccant-*), present participle of *dēsiccāre,* to DESICCATE.] —**des·ic·cant** *adj.*

des·ic·cate (dĕs´ĭ-kāt´) *v.* **-cated, -cating, -cates.** —*tr.* **1.** To make thoroughly dry; dry out. **2.** To preserve (foods) by removing the moisture. **3.** To divest of spirit, spontaneity, or animation; make dry or uninteresting. —*intr.* To become dry. —*adj.* Also **des·ic·cat·ed** (-kā´tĭd). Lacking spirit, spontaneity, or animation; arid. [Latin *dēsiccāre* : *dē-,* completely + *siccāre,* to dry up, from *siccus,* dry.] —**des·ic·ca·tion** (dĕs´ĭ-kā´shən) *n.* —**des·ic·ca·tive** (dĕs´ĭ-kā´tĭv) *adj.*

des·ic·ca·tor (dĕs´ə-kā´tər) *n.* **1.** A jar or box, especially one used in laboratories, that contains a desiccant and protects substances from atmospheric moisture. **2.** An apparatus for drying milk, fruit, or other natural products.

de·sid·er·ate (dĭ-sĭd´ə-rāt´) *tr.v.* **-ated, -ating, -ates.** To long for. [Latin *dēsīderāre,* to DESIRE.]

de·sid·er·a·tive (dĭ-sĭd´ə-rā´tĭv) *adj.* **1.** Of or pertaining to desire. **2. a.** Designating a category of verbs in some Indo-European languages, such as Latin, expressing a wish to perform the action denoted by the given verb. **b.** Being a verb, verb form, or affix in this category. —*n.* A desiderative verb.

de·sid·er·a·tum (dĭ-sĭd´ə-rā´təm) *n., pl.* **-ta** (-tə). Something needed and desired. [Latin *desiderātum,* neuter past participle of *dēsīderāre,* to DESIRE.]

de·sign (dĭ-zīn´) *v.* **-signed, -signing, -signs.** —*tr.* **1.** To conceive; invent; contrive. **2.** To form a plan for. **3.** To draw a sketch of. **4.** To have as a goal or purpose; intend. —*intr.* **1.** To make or execute plans. **2.** To create designs. —*n.* **1.** The invention and disposition of the forms, parts, or details of something according to a plan. **2.** A drawing or sketch. **3.** A decorative or artistic work. **4.** A visual composition; pattern. **5.** The art of creating designs. **6.** A plan; project; undertaking. **7.** A reasoned purpose; intention. **8.** *Often* **designs.** A sinister or hostile scheme; crafty plot. Used with *on, upon,* or *against.* [Old French *designer,* from Latin *dēsignāre,* to DESIGNATE.] —**de·sign·a·ble** *adj.*

des·ig·nate (dĕz´ĭg-nāt´) *tr.v.* **-nated, -nating, -nates.** **1.** To indicate or specify; point out. **2.** To give a name or title to; characterize. **3.** To select for a particular duty, office, or purpose; appoint. *~adj.* (dĕz′ĭg-nĭt). Appointed but not yet installed in office. Used after the noun: *the chairwoman designate.* [Latin *dēsignāre,* designate, mark out : *dē-,* out + *signāre,* mark, from *signum,* sign.] **—des·ig·na·tive, des·ig·na·to·ry** (dĕz′ĭg-nə-tôr′ē, -tōr′ē) *adj.* **—des·ig·na·tor** *n.*

des·ig·nat·ed hitter *n. Baseball.* A player designated at the start of a game to bat instead of the pitcher in the lineup.

des·ig·na·tion (dĕz′ĭg-nā′shən) *n.* **1.** The act of designating; marking or pointing out. **2.** Nomination or appointment. **3.** A distinguishing name or mark; title.

de·sign·ed·ly (dĭ-zī′nĭd-lē) *adv.* On purpose; intentionally.

des·ig·nee (dĕz′ĭg-nē′) *n.* A person who has been designated.

de·sign·er (dĭ-zī′nər) *n.* **1.** A person who creates designs, usually commercial designs, as of clothing, fabrics, furniture, or machinery. **2.** A person who has designs; schemer; plotter. *~adj.* Designed by a well-known fashion designer: *a designer dress.*

de·sign·ing (dĭ-zī′nĭng) *adj.* **1.** Conniving; artful; crafty. **2.** Showing or exercising forethought. **—de·sign·ing·ly** *adv.*

des·i·nence (dĕs′ə-nəns) *n.* **1.** A termination; finishing. **2.** *Grammar.* An inflectional ending. [Old French, from Medieval Latin *dēsinentia,* from Latin *dēsinēns,* present participle of *dēsinere,* to cease, leave off : *dē-,* off + *sinere,* to leave.]

de·sir·a·ble (dĭ-zīr′ə-bəl) *adj.* **1.** Worth seeking or deserving preference; pleasing; fine. **2.** Arousing desire, especially sexual desire. **3.** Worth wanting or doing; beneficial; advisable: *a desirable reform.* *~n.* A desirable person or thing. **—de·sir·a·bil·i·ty,** (dĭ-zīr′ə-bĭl′ə-tē), **de·sir·a·ble·ness** *n.* **—de·sir·a·bly** *adv.*

de·sire (dĭ-zīr′) *tr.v.* **-sired, -siring, -sires.** **1.** To wish or long for; want; crave. **2.** To express a wish for. *~n.* **1.** A wish, longing, or craving. **2.** A request as expressed; petition. **3.** Something or someone longed for: *my heart's desire.* **4.** Sexual appetite; lust. [Middle English *desiren,* from Old French *desirer,* from Latin *dēsīderāre.*] **—de·sir·er** *n.*

de·sir·ous (dĭ-zīr′əs) *adj.* Having, expressing, or characterized by desire; desiring. Often used with *of: desirous of quick promotion.* **—de·sir·ous·ly** *adv.* **—de·sir·ous·ness** *n.*

de·sist (dĭ-zĭst′) *intr.v.* **-sisted, -sisting, -sists.** To cease doing something; forbear; abstain. Often used with *from.* [Old French *desister,* from Latin *dēsistere,* cease, stand off : *dē-,* from + *sistere,* to stop, stand.]

desk (dĕsk) *n.* **1.** A piece of furniture typically having a flat or sloping top for writing, and often drawers or other compartments. **2.** A table, counter, or booth at which specified services or functions are performed: *an information desk.* **3.** A department of a large organization, such as a government agency or newspaper, in charge of a specified operation: *city desk.* **4. a.** A music stand in an orchestra. **b.** Two string players using the same music stand in an orchestra. **5.** A bookrest for the service book in a church. [Middle English *deske,* from Medieval Latin *desca,* variant of Italian *desco,* table, from Latin *discus,* quoit, DISK.]

de·skill (dē-skĭl′) *tr.v.* **-skilled, -skilling, -skills.** To remove the need for skilled labor in (an industry), especially by introducing machines and computers: *Printing has been deskilled.*

des·man (dĕs′mən) *n., pl.* **-mans.** Either of two aquatic, insectivorous, molelike mammals, *Desmana moschata* of eastern Europe and western Asia, or *Galemys pyrenaicus* of southwestern Europe, having dense, brownish fur, a long snout, and a flattened, scaly tail. [Short for Swedish *desman(srätta),* musk(rat), from Middle Low German *desem,* musk, from West Germanic *dessem* (unattested), from Medieval Latin *bisamum,* from Semitic, akin to Hebrew *beśem,* mild odor.]

des·mid (dĕs′mĭd) *n.* Any of various green, unicellular freshwater algae of the family Desmidiaceae, often forming chainlike colonies. [New Latin *Desmidiaceae,* from *Desmidium* (genus) : Greek *desmos,* bond, from *dein,* to bind.]

Des Moines (də-moin′). Capital of Iowa, in the south-central part of the state. It is the center of the Corn Belt, a corn-growing and stock-raising region.

des·mo·some (dĕs′mə-sōm) *n. Zoology.* A strengthened area of contact between an epithelial cell and a smooth-muscle cell at which the cell membranes become thickened and fibrils extend into the cytoplasm. [Greek *desmos,* bond, from *dein,* to bind + -SOME (body).]

des·o·late (dĕs′ə-lĭt) *adj.* **1.** Devoid of inhabitants; deserted: *"streets which were usually so thronged now grown desolate"* (Daniel Defoe). **2.** Rendered unfit for habitation; laid waste; devastated. **3.** Dreary; dismal; gloomy. **4.** Without friends or hope; forlorn; lonely. **—See Synonyms at sad.** *~tr.v.* (dĕs′ə-lāt′) **desolated, -lating, -lates.** **1.** To rid or deprive of inhabitants. **2.** To devastate. **3.** To forsake; abandon. **4.** To make lonely, forlorn, or wretched. [Middle English *desolat,* from Latin *dēsōlātus,* past participle of *dēsōlāre,* abandon : *dē-,* completely + *sōlus,* alone.] **—des·o·late·ly** *adv.* **—des·o·late·ness** *n.* **—des·o·lat·er, des·o·la·tor** *n.*

des·o·la·tion (dĕs′ə-lā′shən) *n.* **1.** The act of rendering desolate. **2.** The state of being desolate; ruin. **3.** A wasteland. **4.** Loneliness or misery; wretchedness.

de·sorb (dē-sôrb′, -zôrb′) *v.* **-sorbed, -sorbing, -sorbs.** *Chemistry.* *—intr.* To change from an adsorbed or absorbed state to a liquid or gaseous state. *—tr.* To change (a substance) from an adsorbed or

absorbed state to a liquid or gaseous state. [DE- + (AD)SORB.] **—de·sorp·tion** *n.*

de Soto (dĭ sō′tō), **Hernando** (*c.* 1496-1542). Spanish explorer. After serving under Pizarro in Peru (1531-36), he was appointed governor of Cuba and given royal permission to conquer lands to the north. In 1539 he set out in search of riches with 600 men, landed in present-day Tampa Bay, and explored much of southern North America for two years. He died during the expedition and was laid to rest in his most important discovery, the Mississippi River.

desoxy- Variant of **deoxy-.**

desoxyribonucleic acid. Variant of **deoxyribonucleic acid.**

desoxyribose. Variant of **deoxyribose.**

de·spair (dĭ-spâr′) *intr.v.* **-spaired, -spairing, -spairs.** **1.** To lose all hope; be overcome by a sense of futility or defeat. **2.** To lack trust or confidence, as in a favorable outcome or a person's abilities. Used with *of.* *~n.* **1.** Utter lack of hope. **2.** That which destroys all hope. [Middle English *despeiren,* from Old French *desperer,* from Latin *dēspērāre* : *dē-* (reversal) + *spērāre,* to hope.] **—de·spair·ing·ly** *adv.* **Synonyms:** *dejection, depression, desperation, despondency, discouragement.*

despatch. Variant of **dispatch.**

des·per·a·do (dĕs′pə-rä′dō, -rā′dō) *n.* **-does** or **-dos.** A desperate, dangerous criminal, especially of the western U.S. frontier. [Pseudo-Spanish variant of DESPERATE.]

des·per·ate (dĕs′pər-ĭt) *adj.* **1.** Reckless or violent through despair; driven to take any risk. **2.** Undertaken as a last resort. **3.** Nearly hopeless; critical; grave: *a desperate illness.* **4.** Marked by, arising from, or showing despair; despairing: *the desperate look of hunger.* **5.** In an unbearable situation because of need or anxiety: *an artist desperate for recognition.* **6.** Extreme because of fear, danger, or suffering; very great: *in desperate need.* [Latin *dēspērātus,* past participle of *dēspērāre,* to DESPAIR.] **—des·per·ate·ly** *adv.* **—des·per·ate·ness** *n.*

des·per·a·tion (dĕs′pə-rā′shən) *n.* **1.** The condition of being desperate. **2.** Recklessness arising from despair. **—See Synonyms at despair.**

des·pi·ca·ble (dĕs′pĭ-kə-bəl, dĭ-spĭk′-) *adj.* Deserving of contempt or disdain; mean; vile. [Late Latin *dēspicābilis,* from Latin *dēspicārī,* to despise.] **—des·pi·ca·bil·i·ty, des·pi·ca·ble·ness** *n.* **—des·pi·ca·bly** *adv.*

de·spise (dĭ-spīz′) *tr.v.* **-spised, -spising, -spises.** To regard with contempt or disdain. [Middle English *despisen,* from Old French *despire* (present stem *despis-*), from Latin *dēspicere,* to look down on : *dē-,* down + *specere,* to look.] **—de·spis·er** *n.*

de·spite (dĭ-spīt′) *prep.* In spite of: *won despite overwhelming odds.* *~n.* **1.** Contemptuous defiance. **2.** An act of such defiance; insult; offense. **—in despite of.** In spite of. [Preposition, short for *in despite of,* from Middle English *despit,* spite, from Old French, from Latin *dēspectus,* past participle of *dēspicere,* to DESPISE.]

de·spite·ful (dĭ-spīt′fəl) *adj. Archaic.* Full of malice; spiteful. **—de·spite·ful·ly** *adv.* **—de·spite·ful·ness** *n.*

de·spoil (dĭ-spoil′) *tr.v.* **-spoiled, -spoiling, -spoils.** To deprive of possessions or contents by force; plunder; ravage. [Middle English *despoilen,* from Old French *despoiller,* from Latin *dēspoliāre* : *dē-,* sense of undoing + *spoliāre,* to plunder, from *spolium,* booty, spoil.] **—de·spoil·er** *n.* **—de·spoil·ment** *n.*

de·spo·li·a·tion (dĭ-spō′lē-ā′shən) *n.* The act of despoiling or the condition of being despoiled. [Late Latin *dēspoliātiō* (stem *dēspoliātiōn-*), from Latin *dēspoliātus,* past participle of *dēspoliāre,* to DESPOIL.]

de·spond (dĭ-spŏnd′) *intr.v.* **-sponded, -sponding, -sponds.** To become disheartened. *~n. Archaic.* Despondency. [Latin *dēspondēre,* to despond, promise to give, give up : *dē-,* away + *spondēre,* to promise.] **—de·spond·ing·ly** *adv.*

de·spon·den·cy (dĭ-spŏn′dən-sē) *n., pl.* **-cies.** Also **de·spon·dence** (-dəns). Lowness of spirits from loss of hope, confidence, or courage; dejection. **—See Synonyms at despair.**

de·spon·dent (dĭ-spŏn′dənt) *adj.* Feeling or expressing despondency; disheartened; dejected. [Latin *dēspondēns* (stem *dēspondent-*), present participle of *dēspondēre,* to DESPOND.] **—de·spon·dent·ly** *adv.*

des·pot (dĕs′pət) *n.* **1.** An autocratic ruler; a tyrant. **2.** Any autocratic or domineering person. **3.** A Greek title borne by Byzantine emperors and princes, by Christian rulers in the Balkans under the Turks, and by Eastern Orthodox bishops. [French, from Medieval Latin *despota,* from Greek *despotēs,* lord.] **—des·pot·ic** (dĭ-spŏt′ĭk) *adj.* **—des·pot·i·cal·ly** *adv.*

des·pot·ism (dĕs′pə-tĭz′əm) *n.* **1.** Rule by or as if by a despot; absolute power or authority. **2.** The actions of a despot; tyranny. **3. a.** A government or political system in which the ruler exercises absolute power. **b.** A state so ruled.

des·qua·mate (dĕs′kwə-māt′) *intr.v.* **-mated, -mating, -mates.** *Pathology.* To shed, peel, or come off in scales. Used of skin. [Latin *dēsquāmāre,* removal + *squāma,* scale.] **—des·qua·ma·tion** *n.*

Des·sa·lines (dā-sə-lēn′), **Jean Jacques** (1758-1806). Emperor of Haiti. A former slave, he rose in the slave revolt led by Toussaint L'Ouverture against the French and took over the leadership on Toussaint's capture in 1802. In 1803, with British help, he defeated the French and later declared himself emperor. His tyrannical rule provoked dissent, and he was assassinated.

des·sert (dĭ-zûrt′) *n.* **1.** The last course of a lunch or dinner, consist-

ing of a serving of a sweet food, such as fruit, ice cream, or pastry. **2.** *Chiefly British.* Especially formerly, fresh fruit, nuts, or sweetmeats served after the sweet course of a dinner. [French, from *desservir,* clear the table : *des-, de-,* reversal + *servir,* to SERVE.]
des·sert·spoon (dĭ-zûrt′spo͞on′) *n.* A spoon intermediate in size between a tablespoon and a teaspoon, used for eating dessert. **—des·sert·spoon·ful** *n.*
dessert wine *n.* A wine intended to be drunk with dessert.
de·sta·bil·ize (dē-stā′bə-līz′) *tr.v.* **-ized, -izing, -izes.** To undermine and reduce the effective functioning of (a government or other political authority). **—de·sta·bil·i·za·tion** *n.*
de Stijl (də stīl′, stāl′) *n.* A school of art originating in the Netherlands in 1917 and characterized by the use of rectangular shapes and primary colors. [Dutch, "the style."]
des·ti·na·tion (dĕs′tə-nā′shən) *n.* **1.** The place or point to which someone or something is going or directed. **2.** The ultimate goal or purpose for which anything is created or intended.
des·tine (dĕs′tĭn) *tr.v.* **-tined, -tining, -tines.** **1.** To determine beforehand; preordain to or as if to an inevitable outcome. Usually used with the infinitive: *destined to rule.* **2.** To assign or intend for a specific end, use, or purpose. **3.** To direct toward a given destination. [Middle English *destinen,* from Old French *destiner,* from Latin *dēstināre,* to determine, destine.]
des·tined (dĕs′tĭnd) *adj.* **1.** Preordained; assured through destiny. **2.** Intended for. **3.** Bound for a particular destination.
des·ti·ny (dĕs′tə-nē) *n., pl.* **-nies.** **1.** The inevitable or necessary fate to which a particular person or thing is destined; one's lot. **2.** The preordained or inevitable course of events considered as something beyond human power or control. **3.** The power or agency thought to predetermine events; fate. **4. Destiny.** This power personified or regarded as a goddess. [Middle English *destine,* from Old French *destinee,* from the feminine past participle of *destiner,* to DESTINE.]
des·ti·tute (dĕs′tə-to͞ot′, -tyo͞ot′) *adj.* **1.** Utterly impoverished. **2.** Altogether lacking; devoid. Used with *of*: *destitute of experience.* **3.** *Obsolete.* Abandoned; deserted. —See Synonyms at **poor.** [Middle English *destitut,* from Latin *dēstitūtus,* past participle of *dēstituere,* to set down, desert : *dē-,* down, away from + *statuere,* to place.]
des·ti·tu·tion (dĕs′tə-to͞o′shən, -tyo͞o′shən) *n.* **1.** Extreme want of resources or the means of subsistence; complete poverty. **2.** Any deprivation or lack; deficiency.
des·tri·er (dĕs′trē-ər, -trîr) *n. Archaic.* A war-horse; a charger. [Middle English, from Old French, from Vulgar Latin *dextrārius* (unattested), from Latin *dexter,* right (the squire managed his own horse with his left hand and led his knight's horse with his right).]
de·stroy (dĭ-stroi′) *v.* **-stroyed, -stroying, -stroys.** *—tr.* **1.** To ruin completely; spoil so that restoration is impossible; consume: *The fire destroyed the ancient manuscripts.* **2.** To tear down or break up; raze; demolish. **3.** To do away with; get rid of; put an end to: *a speech that destroyed any chance of a settlement.* **4.** To kill. **5.** To render useless or ineffective. **6.** To subdue or defeat completely; crush. *—intr.* To be destructive or harmful: *"Too much money destroys as surely as too little"* (John Simon). —See Synonyms at **ruin.** [Middle English *destruyen,* from Old French *destruire,* from Vulgar Latin *dēstrūgere* (unattested), from Latin *dēstruere* (past participle *dēstructus*) : *dē-* (reversal) + *struere,* to build, pile up.]
de·stroy·er (dĭ-stroi′ər) *n.* **1.** One that destroys. **2.** A medium-sized, fast warship armed with guns, torpedoes, and depth charges, and noted for its high maneuverability.
destroyer escort *n.* A warship, usually smaller than a destroyer, used to convoy merchant vessels.
destroying angel *n.* Any of several poisonous mushrooms of the genus *Amanita,* especially *A. verna.*

destroying angel *A highly poisonous fungus distinguishable from the edible common field mushroom by its white underside. Many species of this poisonous mushroom flourish in the United States.*

de·struct (dĭ-strŭkt′) *n.* The intentional destruction of a space vehicle, rocket, or missile after launching.
~v. **destructed, -structing, -structs.** *—tr.* To destroy (a defective missile or space vehicle) after launching. *—intr.* To be destroyed deliberately, as a safety measure; self-destruct. Used of a missile or space vehicle. [Back-formation from DESTRUCTION.]
de·struc·ti·ble (dĭ-strŭk′tə-bəl) *adj.* Subject to destruction; capable of being destroyed: *destructible machine parts.* **—de·struc·ti·bil·i·ty, de·struc·ti·ble·ness** *n.*
de·struc·tion (dĭ-strŭk′shən) *n.* **1.** The act of destroying. **2.** The condition or fact of being destroyed. **3.** A cause or means of destroying. [Middle English *destruccioun,* from Old French *destruction,* from Latin *dēstructiō* (stem *dēstructiōn-*), from *dēstructus,* past participle of *dēstruere,* to DESTROY.]
de·struc·tion·ist (dĭ-strŭk′shən-ĭst) *n.* A person who favors destruction, especially of existing social institutions.
de·struc·tive (dĭ-strŭk′tĭv) *adj.* **1.** Tending to destroy; causing or wreaking destruction; ruinous. Often used with *of* or *to*: *destructive to national safety.* **2.** Designed or tending to disprove or discredit; negative; not constructive: *destructive criticism.* **—de·struc·tive·ly** *adv.* **—de·struc·tive·ness** *n.*
destructive distillation *n. Chemistry.* The simultaneous decomposition by heat and distillation of substances such as wood, coal, and oil shale to produce useful by-products such as coke, charcoal, oils, and gases. Also called "dry distillation."
de·struc·tor (dĭ-strŭk′tər) *n.* **1.** A furnace for disposing of rubbish, especially one that generates power from the heat so produced. **2.** A device which causes defective rockets and other space vehicles to explode.
des·ue·tude (dĕs′wə-to͞od′, -tyo͞od′) *n.* The state or condition of disuse: *words fallen into desuetude.* [French *désuétude,* from Latin *dēsuētūdō,* from *dēsuēscere,* to put out of use, become unaccustomed : *dē-* (reversal) + *suēscere,* to become accustomed.]
de·sul·fur·ize (dē-sŭl′fə-rīz′) *tr.v.* **-ized, -izing, -izes.** To eliminate sulfur from. **—de·sul·fu·ri·za·tion** *n.*
des·ul·to·ry (dĕs′əl-tôr′ē, -tōr′ē) *adj.* **1.** Moving or jumping from one thing to another; disconnected; rambling. **2.** Occurring haphazardly; random. —See Synonyms at **chance.** [Latin *dēsultōrius,* of a leaper, from *dēsultor,* a leaper, from *dēsultus,* past participle of *dēsilīre,* to leap down : *dē-,* down + *salīre,* to jump.] **—des·ul·to·ri·ly** *adv.* **—des·ul·to·ri·ness** *n.*
det. **1.** *Military.* detachment. **2.** detail.
de·tach (dĭ-tăch′) *tr.v.* **-tached, -taching, -taches.** **1.** To separate, usually without violence or damage; disconnect. **2.** *Military.* To send (troops or ships, for example) on a special mission. [French *détacher,* from Old French *destachier* : *des-, de-,* apart + *atachier,* variant of *estachier,* to ATTACH.] **—de·tach·a·bil·i·ty** *n.* **—de·tach·a·ble** *adj.* **—de·tach·a·bly** *adv.*
de·tached (dĭ-tăcht′) *adj.* **1.** Standing apart from others; disconnected; separate: *a detached house.* **2.** Free from emotional, intellectual, social, or other involvement; without bias; disinterested. —See Synonyms at **cool, indifferent.**
de·tach·ment (dĭ-tăch′mənt) *n.* **1.** The act or process of disconnecting or detaching; separation. **2.** The state or condition of being separate or apart. **3.** Dissociation from or lack of involvement in worldly affairs or one's environment; aloofness. **4.** Absence of prejudice or bias; disinterest. **5.** *Military.* **a.** The dispatch of troops or ships selected from a larger unit for a special duty or mission. **b.** *Abbr.* **det.** The unit of troops or ships so dispatched. **c.** *Abbr.* **det.** A permanent unit, usually smaller than a platoon, organized for special duties.
de·tail (dĭ-tāl′, dē′tāl) *n. Abbr.* **det.** **1.** An individually considered part, portion, or item; particular. **2.** Such an item considered as trivial or not worth attending to. **3.** Particulars considered separately and in relation to a whole: *careful attention to detail.* **4.** A small or secondary part of a painting, statue, building, or other work of art, especially when considered or represented in isolation. **5.** *Military.* **a.** The selection of one or more troops for a particular duty, usually a fatigue duty. **b.** The personnel so selected. **c.** The duty assigned. **—go into detail.** To discuss the finer points; cover most of the particulars. **—in detail.** With particulars; item by item.
~tr.v. **detailed, -tailing, -tails.** **1.** To report or relate minutely or in detail. **2.** *Military.* To select and dispatch for a particular duty. [French *détail,* from Old French *detail,* piece cut off, from *detailler,* to cut up : *de-,* thoroughly + *tailler,* to cut, from Vulgar Latin *tāliāre* (unattested), to cut off.]
de·tailed (dĭ-tāld′, dē′tāld′) *adj.* Characterized by abundant use of detail or by thoroughness of treatment.
detail man *n.* A representative of a manufacturer of drugs or medical supplies who calls on doctors, pharmacists, and other professional users to promote new drugs and supplies.
de·tain (dĭ-tān′) *tr.v.* **-tained, -taining, -tains.** **1.** To keep from proceeding; delay or retard. **2.** To keep in custody; confine. **3.** *Obsolete.* To retain or withhold. —See Synonyms at **delay.** [Middle English *deteynen,* from Old French *detenir,* from Latin *dētinēre,* to keep back : *dē-,* away + *tenēre,* to hold.] **—de·tain·ment** *n.*
de·tain·ee (dē′tā-nē′, dĭ-tā′-) *n.* A person held in custody: *a political detainee.*
de·tain·er (dĭ-tā′nər) *n. Law.* **1. a.** The unlawful withholding of the property of another. **b.** The detention of a person, especially in custody or confinement. **2.** A writ authorizing the further detention of a person in custody pending action.
de·tect (dĭ-tĕkt′) *tr.v.* **-tected, -tecting, -tects.** **1.** To discover or discern the existence, presence, or fact of. **2.** To find out the true nature of. **3.** *Electronics.* To demodulate. [Middle English *detecten,* from Latin *dētegere* (past participle *dētectus*), to uncover : *dē-* (reversal) + *tegere,* to cover.] **—de·tect·a·ble, de·tect·i·ble** *adj.* **—de·tect·er** *n.*
de·tec·tion (dĭ-tĕk′shən) *n.* **1.** The act of finding out or the fact of being found out; discovery, as of something hidden or obscure. **2.** *Electronics.* Demodulation.
de·tec·tive (dĭ-tĕk′tĭv) *n.* A person, usually a police officer, whose work is investigating crimes and obtaining evidence.
~adj. **1.** Of or pertaining to detectives or their work. **2.** Suited for or used in detection.
de·tec·tor (dĭ-tĕk′tər) *n.* **1.** Any apparatus that detects; especially, a mechanical, electrical, or chemical device that automatically identifies and records or registers a stimulus such as an environmental change in pressure or temperature, an electric signal, or radiation from a radioactive material. **2.** A **demodulator** *(see).*
de·tent (dĭ-tĕnt′) *n. Engineering.* A **pawl** *(see).* [French *détente,* a loosening, a trigger, from Old French *destente,* from *destendre,* to release : *des-, de-,* apart + *tendre,* to stretch, from Latin *tendere.*]
dé·tente (dā-täNt′) *n.* A relaxing or easing, as of tension between nations. [French. See **detent.**]
de·ten·tion (dĭ-tĕn′shən) *n.* **1. a.** The act of detaining. **b.** The state of being detained. **2.** A form of punishment in schools, by which a pupil is made to remain in class after hours. **3.** A keeping in custody or confinement; especially, a period of temporary custody while awaiting trial. [French, from Late Latin *dētentiō* (stem *dētentiōn-*), from Latin *dētentus,* past participle of *dētinēre,* to DETAIN.]
de·ter (dĭ-tûr′) *tr.v.* **-terred, -terring, -ters.** To prevent or discourage (someone) from acting because of fear, doubt, or the like. [Latin

dēterrēre, to frighten from : *dē-,* away from + *terrēre,* to frighten.] **—de·ter·ment** *n.*

de·terge (dĭ-tûrj′) *tr.v.* **-terged, -terging, -terges.** To wash or wipe off; cleanse. [French *déterger,* to cleanse, from Latin *dētergēre,* to wipe off : *dē-,* off, away + *tergēre†,* to wipe.]

de·ter·gen·cy (dĭ-tûr′jən-sē) *n.* Also **de·ter·gence** (-jəns) Cleansing power or quality.

de·ter·gent (dĭ-tûr′jənt) *n.* A cleansing substance, especially one that acts as a wetting agent and emulsifier and is made from a chemical compound such as an alkyl sulfonate, rather than from fats and lye. Compare **soap.**
~adj. Having cleansing power. [Latin *dētergēns* (stem *dētergent-*), present participle of *dētergēre,* to DETERGE.]

de·te·ri·o·rate (dĭ-tîr′ē-ə-rāt′) *v.* **-rated, -rating, -rates.** *—intr.* To decline or grow worse in quality, condition, or value. *—tr.* To lower in quality, condition, or value. [Late Latin *dēteriōrāre,* from Latin *dēterior,* worse, comparative of *dēter* (unattested).] **—de·te·ri·o·ra·tive** *adj.*

de·te·ri·o·ra·tion (dĭ-tîr′ē-ə-rā′shən) *n.* **1.** The act or an instance of deteriorating. **2.** The state or condition of being deteriorated.

de·ter·mi·na·ble (dĭ-tûr′mə-nə-bəl) *adj.* **1.** Capable of being settled, fixed, or determined. **2.** *Law.* Liable to be terminated.

de·ter·mi·nant (dĭ-tûr′mə-nənt) *adj.* Tending or serving to determine; determinative.
~n. **1.** An influencing or determining factor. **2.** *Mathematics.* A square array of quantities, or elements, having a value determined by a rule of combination for the elements and used especially in solving certain classes of simultaneous equations.

de·ter·mi·nate (dĭ-tûr′mə-nĭt) *adj.* **1.** Precisely limited or defined. **2.** Settled; final. **3.** Firm in purpose; resolute. **4.** *Botany.* **a.** Terminating in a flower, and blooming in a sequence beginning with the uppermost or central flower: *a determinate inflorescence.* **b.** Not continuing indefinitely at the tip of an axis: *determinate growth.* [Middle English *determinat,* from Latin *dēterminātus,* past participle of *dētermināre,* to DETERMINE.]

de·ter·mi·na·tion (dĭ-tûr′mə-nā′shən) *n.* **1. a.** The act of making or arriving at a decision. **b.** The decision arrived at; a strong resolve. **2.** The quality of being resolute or firm in purpose; resoluteness. **3. a.** The act of settling a dispute, suit, or other question by an authoritative decision or pronouncement. **b.** The decision or pronouncement made. **4. a.** The ascertaining or establishing of the extent, quality, position, or character of anything. **b.** The result of such ascertaining. **5.** A fixed movement or tendency toward some object or end. **6.** *Logic.* **a.** The rendering of a concept or proposition more definite by further qualification. **b.** The factor or factors that so qualify. **c.** The defining of a concept through its constituent elements.

de·ter·mi·na·tive (dĭ-tûr′mə-nā′tĭv, -nə-tĭv) *adj.* Tending, able, or serving to determine or settle; limiting; deciding.
~n. **1.** Something that determines. **2.** *Grammar.* A determiner. **—de·ter·mi·na·tive·ness** *n.*

de·ter·mine (dĭ-tûr′mĭn) *v.* **-mined, -mining, -mines.** *—tr.* **1. a.** To decide or settle (a dispute, for example) conclusively and authoritatively. **b.** To end or decide by judicial or other final action. **2.** To establish or ascertain definitely, as after consideration, investigation, or calculation. **3.** To cause (someone) to come to a conclusion or resolution. **4.** To influence decisively; be the cause of; regulate. **5.** To give direction to; decide the course of. **6.** To limit in scope or extent; fix the bounds of. **7.** *Mathematics.* In geometry, to fix or define the position, form, or configuration of. **8.** *Logic.* To explain or limit (a concept or notion) by adding or requiring certain features or characteristics. **9.** *Law.* To put an end to; terminate. *—intr.* **1.** To reach a decision; resolve. **2.** *Law.* To come to an end. —See Synonyms at **decide.** [Middle English *determinen,* from Old French *determiner,* from Latin *dētermināre,* to limit : *dē-,* off + *termināre,* to limit, from *terminus,* boundary line.]

de·ter·mined (dĭ-tûr′mĭnd) *adj.* Marked by or showing determination or fixed purpose; resolute; unwavering; firm. **—de·ter·mined·ly** *adv.* **—de·ter·mined·ness** *n.*

de·ter·min·er (dĭ-tûr′mə-nər) *n.* **1.** One that determines. **2.** *Grammar.* A word, such as an article or a possessive adjective, that limits the meaning of a noun or noun phrase and precedes other adjectives that accompany it; for example, in the phrases *the new house, her young daughters,* and *both girls,* the words *the, her,* and *both* are determiners.

de·ter·min·ism (dĭ-tûr′mə-nĭz′əm) *n.* The philosophical doctrine that every event, act, and decision is the inevitable consequence of antecedents, such as physical, psychological, or environmental conditions, that are independent of the individual human will. Compare **free will. —de·ter·min·ist** *n. & adj.* **—de·ter·min·is·tic** *adj.*

de·ter·rence (dĭ-tûr′əns) *n.* **1.** The action or a means of deterring. **2.** A defensive policy or strategy involving the deployment of weapons at a level believed likely to deter potential aggressors.

de·ter·rent (dĭ-tûr′ənt) *n.* **1.** Something that deters: *a deterrent to theft.* **2.** Power of retaliation, especially in the form of weapons, considered as a means of discouraging enemy attack: *a nuclear deterrent.* **—de·ter·rent** *adj.*

de·test (dĭ-tĕst′) *tr.v.* **-tested, -testing, -tests.** To dislike intensely; abhor; loathe. [Latin *dētestārī,* to curse, execrate : *dē-* (pejorative) + *testārī,* to invoke, call to witness, from *testis,* a witness.] **—de·test·er** *n.*

de·test·a·ble (dĭ-tĕs′tə-bəl) *adj.* Deserving abhorrence or execration; odious; abominable. —See Synonyms at **hateful. —de·test·a·**

bil·i·ty, **de·test·a·ble·ness** *n.* **—de·test·a·bly** *adv.*

de·tes·ta·tion (dē′tĕ-stā′shən) *n.* **1.** Strong dislike; hatred or abhorrence. **2.** Someone or something that is detested.

de·throne (dē-thrōn′) *tr.v.* **-throned, -throning, -thrones.** To remove from a throne or high position; depose. **—de·throne·ment** *n.*

det·i·nue (dĕt′ĭ-nyōō′) *n. Law.* **1. a.** An action to recover possession or the value of property wrongfully detained. **b.** The writ authorizing such action. **2.** *Obsolete.* The act of unlawfully detaining personal property. [Middle English *detenewe,* from Old French *detenue,* detention, from the past participle of *detenir,* to DETAIN.]

det·o·na·ble (dĕt′n-ə-bəl) *adj.* Also **det·o·nat·a·ble** (dĕt′n-ā′tə-bəl). Capable of being detonated.

det·o·nate (dĕt′n-āt′) *v.* **-nated, -nating, -nates.** *—intr.* To explode suddenly and violently. Said of a bomb, explosive charge, or the like. *—tr.* To cause to explode. [Latin *dētonāre,* to thunder down : *dē-,* down + *tonāre,* to thunder.] **—de·to·na·tive** (dĕt′ə-nā′tĭv, dē′tə-) *adj.*

det·o·na·tion (dĕt′n-ā′shən) *n.* **1.** The act of detonating or exploding. **2.** A violent explosion.

det·o·na·tor (dĕt′n-ā′tər) *n.* **1.** A device, such as an electric generator, fuse, or percussion cap, used to set off explosives. **2.** An explosive.

de·tour (dē′tŏŏr′, dĭ-tŏŏr′) *n.* **1.** A roundabout way or course; especially, a byroad used temporarily instead of a main route. **2.** Deviation from the direct or shortest road, route, or course of action.
~v. **detoured, -touring, -tours.** *—intr.* To go by a roundabout way. *—tr.* To cause to go by a roundabout way or detour. [French *détour,* from Old French *destour,* from *destorner,* to turn away : *des-, de-,* away + *torner,* to TURN.]

de·tox (dē-tŏks′) *tr.v. Informal.* **-toxed, -toxing, -toxes.** To subject to detoxification.
~n. (dē′tŏks′). A section of a hospital in which patients are detoxified.

de·tox·i·fy (dē-tŏk′sə-fī′) *tr.v.* **-fied, -fying, -fies.** Also **de·tox·i·cate** (-kāt′) **-cated, -cating, -cates.** **1.** To counteract or destroy the toxic properties of. **2.** To remove the effects of poison from. [DE- (reversal) + TOXI(C) + -FY.] **—de·tox·i·fi·ca·tion, de·tox·i·ca·tion** *n.*

de·tract (dĭ-trăkt′) *v.* **-tracted, -tracting, -tracts.** *—intr.* To take away a desirable or valuable quality; diminish. Used with *from.* *—tr.* To distract. [Middle English *detracten,* from Latin *dētrahere* (past participle *dētractus*), to pull down, draw away : *dē-,* away + *trahere,* to pull.]

de·trac·tion (dĭ-trăk′shən) *n.* **1.** A person or thing that detracts. **2.** The act of detracting or taking away; disparagement; depreciation. **—de·trac·tive** *adj.* **—de·trac·tor** *n.*

de·train (dē-trān′) *v.* **-trained, -training, -trains.** *—tr.* To cause to leave a railroad train. *—intr.* To leave a railroad train. **—de·train·ment** *n.*

de·trib·al·ize (dē-trī′bə-līz′) *tr.v.* **-ized, -izing, -izes.** To cause to lose tribal customs or habits, or tribal organization. **—de·trib·al·i·za·tion** *n.*

det·ri·ment (dĕt′rə-mənt) *n.* **1.** Damage, harm, or loss. **2.** Something that causes damage, harm, or loss. [Middle English, from Old French, from Latin *dētrīmentum,* from *dēterere,* to wear away : *dē-,* away + *terere,* to rub.]

det·ri·men·tal (dĕt′rə-mĕnt′l) *adj.* Causing damage or harm; injurious. Often used with *to.* **—det·ri·men·tal·ly** *adv.*

de·trit·ed (dĭ-trī′tĭd) *adj.* **1.** Worn down. **2.** *Geology.* Formed as detritus. [Latin *dētrītus,* past participle of *dēterere,* to wear down. See **detriment.**]

de·tri·tion (dĭ-trĭsh′ən) *n.* The act of wearing away by friction or rubbing. [Medieval Latin *dētrītiō* (stem *dētrītiōn-*), from Latin *dētrītus,* past participle of *dēterere,* to rub away. See **detriment.**]

de·tri·tus (dĭ-trī′təs) *n.* **1.** Loose fragments, particles, or grains that have been formed by the disintegration of rocks. **2.** Any disintegrated matter; debris. [French *détritus,* from Latin *dētrītus,* past participle of *dēterere,* to wear away. See **detriment.**]

De·troit (dĭ-troit′). City in southeastern Michigan, on the Canadian border. It was founded by French settlers in 1701. In the 20th century it became the center of the U.S. automobile industry. It is also a rail and shipping center serving the Great Lakes.

de trop (də trō′) *adj. French.* **1.** Too much; too many; excessive. **2.** Not wanted; superfluous: *I felt distinctly de trop with the honeymoon couple.*

de·trude (dĭ-trōōd′) *tr.v.* **-truded, -truding, -trudes.** To thrust down or away. [Latin *dētrūdere,* to thrust down : *dē-,* down, away + *trūdere,* to thrust.]

de·tu·mes·cence (dē′tōō-mĕs′əns, -tyōō-mĕs′əns) *n.* Contraction following expansion, especially restoration of a swollen organ or part to normal size. [Latin *dētumēscere,* to cease swelling : *dē-* (reversal) + *tumēscere,* to swell up, from *tumēre,* to be swollen.] **—de·tu·mes·cent** *adj.*

Deu·ca·li·on (dōō-kā′lē-ən, dyōō-). *Greek Mythology.* A son of Prometheus who, with his wife Pyrrha, survived a deluge sent by Zeus and became the ancestor of the renewed human race.

deuce¹ (dōōs, dyōōs) *n.* **1. a.** A playing card or side of a die bearing two marks, symbols, or spots. **b.** A cast of the dice totaling two. **2.** *Tennis.* A score in which each player or side has 40 points (or 5 or more games each) and either player or side must win 2 successive points (or games) to win the game (or set). [Old French *deus,* two, from Latin *duōs,* accusative of *duo.*]

deuce² *n. Informal.* Bad luck; the devil.
~interj. Used to express annoyance, impatience, or surprise. Often

preceded by *the* or *what the.* [Probably from Low German *duus,* deuce, two at dice (from the exclamation of the player making the lowest throw), ultimately from Latin *duōs,* two.]

deu·ced (dōō'sĭd, dyōō'sĭd) *adj. Informal.* Darned; confounded; extreme. Not in current usage. [From DEUCE (devil).] —**deu·ced, deu·ced·ly** *adv.*

deuces wild *n.* A variation of certain card games, such as poker, in which each deuce may represent any card the holder chooses.

De·us (dē'əs, dā'ōōs) *n. Abbr.* **D.** *Latin.* God.

de·us ex mach·i·na (dā'ōōs ĕks mä'kĕ-nä', dē'əs ĕks măk'ə-nə) *n.* **1.** A deity in ancient Greek and Roman drama who was brought in by stage machinery to intervene in a difficult situation. **2.** Any unexpected, artificial, or improbable character, device, or event suddenly intervening to resolve a situation or untangle a plot. [New Latin, "god from a machine" (translation of Greek *theos ek mēk-hanēs).]

Deut. Deuteronomy (Old Testament).

deu·ter·a·no·pi·a (dōō'tər-ə-nō'pē-ə, dyōō'-) *n.* A form of color-blindness characterized by confusion of green, bluish red, and neutral. [New Latin : DEUTER(O)- + AN- (lack of) + -OPIA (so called from the blindness to green, which is considered the second of the primary colors).] —**deu·ter·a·nope** *n.*

deu·ter·ide (dōō'tə-rīd, dyōō'-) *n.* A compound of deuterium and another element, analogous to a hydride.

deu·te·ri·um (dōō-tîr'ē-əm, dyōō'-) *n. Symbol* **D** An isotope of hydrogen having an atomic weight of 2.0141. Also called "heavy hydrogen." [New Latin : DEUTER(O)- (because it is the second in the series of possible hydrogen isotopes) + -IUM.]

deuterium oxide *n.* An isotopic form of water with composition D₂O, present in natural water as approximately 1 part in 6,500 and isolated for use as a moderator in certain nuclear reactors. Also called "heavy water."

deutero-, deuter-, deuto- *prefix.* **1.** Indicates second or secondary; for example, **deuterocanonical, deuteranopia, deutoplasm. 2.** *Chemistry.* Indicates the presence of deuterium. [Greek *deuteros,* second.]

deu·ter·o·ca·non·i·cal (dōō'tə-rō-kə-nŏn'ĭ-kəl, dyōō'-) *adj.* **1.** Pertaining to or designating books or sections of books in the New Testament whose authority was once contested but later accepted. **2.** Pertaining to or designating books or sections of books in the Old Testament, considered canonical by Eastern Orthodox Christians and Roman Catholics, and apocryphal by many Protestants. See **Apocrypha.** [DEUTERO- + CANONICAL.]

deu·ter·og·a·my (dōō'tə-rŏg'ə-mē, dyōō'-) *n.* A second legal marriage, after the death or divorce of a first spouse.

Deu·ter·o·I·sa·iah (dōō'tə-rō-ī-zā'ə, dyōō'-) *n.* The name given to the author of chapters 40-66 of Isaiah, who was a Hebrew writer during the Babylonian captivity (597-538 B.C.).

deu·ter·on (dōō'tə-rŏn, dyōō'-) *n. Symbol* **d** The nucleus of a deuterium atom, a composite of a proton and a neutron, regarded as a subatomic particle with unit positive charge. [DEUTER(IUM) + -ON.]

Deu·ter·on·o·my (dōō'tə-rŏn'ə-mē, dyōō'-) *n. Abbr.* **Deut.** The fifth book of the Old Testament, in which the law of Moses is stated completely for the second time. [Middle English, from Late Latin *deuteronomium,* from Greek *deuteronomion,* from the Septuagint mistranslation (Deuteronomy 16:18) of Hebrew *mishnēh hattôrāh hazzō'th,* "a copy of this law," as *deuteronomion (touto),* "(this) second law" : DEUTERO- + *nomos,* law.]

deu·to·plasm (dōō'tə-plăz'əm, dyōō'-) *n.* Also **deu·ter·o·plasm** (-tə-rō-). Food substance or yolk in the cytoplasm of an ovum or other cell. [DEUT(ERO)- + -PLASM.]

Deut·sche Mark, deut·sche·mark (doi'chə märk') *n.* Also **deutsch-mark** (doich'märk). *Abbr.* **DM 1.** The basic monetary unit of West Germany, equal to 100 pfennigs. See feature at **currency. 2.** A coin worth one Deutsche Mark. See **Mark** (money). [German, "German Mark."]

Deutschland. See **Germany.**

deut·zi·a (dōōt'sē-ə, dyōōt'-) *n.* Any of various shrubs of the genus *Deutzia,* cultivated for their clusters of white or pinkish flowers. [New Latin *Deutzia,* after Jean *Deutz* (died *c.* 1784), Dutch patron of botany.]

de·va (dā'və) *n. Sometimes* **Deva.** In Buddhism and Hinduism, any of various gods or divinities. [Sanskrit, god.]

De Va·le·ra (dĕv'ə-lâr'ə, -lûr'ə), **Eamon** (1882-1975). Irish statesman. He was a battalion commander in the 1916 Easter Rising and was imprisoned by the British. He served as president of Sinn Fein (1917-26), prime minister of the Irish Free State (1932-48, 1951-54, 1957-59), and president of the Republic (1959-73).

de·val·u·ate (dē-văl'yōō-āt') *v.* **-ated, -ating, -ates.** Also **de·val·ue** (-văl'yōō). —*tr.* **1.** To lessen or annul the importance or value of. **2.** To lower the exchange value of (currency) against gold or other currencies by government action. Compare **revaluate.** —*intr.* To institute an official reduction in the value of a currency. —**de·val·u·a·tion** *n.*

De·va·na·ga·ri (dā'və-nä'gə-rē) *n.* The alphabet in which Sanskrit and many modern Indian languages are written. [Sanskrit *devānā-garī,* "the divine script of the city" : *deváḥ,* god + *nāgarī,* (script) of the city, from *nāgaram,* town, city, probably from Dravidian.]

dev·as·tate (dĕv'ə-stāt) *tr.v.* **-tated, -tating, -tates. 1.** To reduce to a state of desolation; ravage; lay waste. **2.** *Informal.* To defeat, overwhelm, or confound. —See Synonyms at **ruin.** [Latin *dēvāstāre : dē-* (intensive) + *vāstāre,* to lay waste, from *vāstus,* waste.] —**dev·as·tat·ing·ly** *adv.* —**dev·as·ta·tion** *n.* —**dev·as·ta·tor** *n.*

de·vel·op (dĭ-vĕl'əp) *v.* **-oped, -oping, -ops.** —*tr.* **1.** To expand or realize the potentialities of; bring gradually to a fuller, greater, or better state. **2.** To elaborate or enlarge. **3.** *Music.* To unfold (a theme) with rhythmic and harmonic variations. **4.** To disclose (a plot, for example) gradually. **5.** To bring into being; make active; generate. **6.** To make more available; put to use. **7.** To convert (a tract of land) to a new function, and to increase its value, as by building extensively. **8.** To come to have gradually; acquire. **9.** To become affected with (a disease); contract. **10.** *Photography.* To process (a photosensitive material), especially with chemicals, in order to render a recorded image visible. **11.** *Chess.* To bring (a piece) into play from its starting position. **12.** *Mathematics.* To expand (a function) into a series. —*intr.* **1.** To grow; expand; progress to a more advanced state. **2.** To come gradually into existence or activity. **3.** To be disclosed. **4.** *Biology.* **a.** To progress from earlier to later stages of individual maturation. **b.** To progress from earlier to later or from simpler to more complex stages of evolution. [French *développer,* from Old French *desveloper : des-* (reversal) + *voloper,* to wrap up, perhaps from Celtic *vol-* (unattested), to roll.] —**de·vel·op·a·ble** *adj.*

de·vel·op·er (dĭ-vĕl'ə-pər) *n.* **1.** One that develops; especially, a person who develops property. **2.** *Photography.* A chemical used to render visible the image recorded on a photosensitive surface.

de·vel·op·ing (dĭ-vĕl'ə-pĭng) *adj.* In the process of improving living standards and attaining an economically viable level of industrial production: *developing countries.*

de·vel·op·ment (dĭ-vĕl'əp-mənt) *n.* **1.** The act, process, or result of developing. **2.** A developed state, condition, or form. **3.** Something, such as an event, factor, or piece of information, that has come into existence or been disclosed: *the latest developments in the police corruption scandal.* **4.** A group of dwellings built by the same contractor or in the same scheme. **5.** *Music.* The section of a composition in which a theme is elaborated with rhythmic and harmonic variations. **6.** *Chess.* The moving of pieces from their starting positions, or the state of play resulting from this. —**de·vel·op·men·tal** *adj.* —**de·vel·op·men·tal·ly** *adv.*

de·verb·a·tive (dĭ-vûr'bə-tĭv) *adj.* Also **de·verb·al** (dē-vûr'bəl). *Grammar.* **1.** Designating a word or word form derived from a verb; for example, *variable* is a deverbative adjective derived from the verb *vary.* **2.** Designating an element added to a verb form to produce a derivative; for example, the suffix *-er* in *worker* is a deverbative suffix.
~*n.* Also **deverbal.** *Grammar.* A deverbative word or element.

de·vest (dĭ-vĕst') *tr.v.* **-vested, -vesting, -vests.** *Law.* To take (a title, estate, or right, for example) away from. [Old French *desvestir,* to undress, from Vulgar Latin *disvestire* (unattested) : Latin *dis-* (reversal) + *vestīre,* to dress, from *vestis,* garment.]

De·vi (dä'vē) *n. Hinduism.* The most powerful of the Hindu goddesses, mother and consort of Siva. She combines benevolence with ferocity. See **Durga, Kali, Parvati, Sati.**

de·vi·ant (dē'vē-ənt) *adj.* Differing from a norm or from the accepted standards of society; deviating.
~*n.* A person whose attitude or behavior differs from the norm or from accepted social or moral standards. [Middle English *deviaunt,* from Late Latin *dēviāns* (stem *dēviant-*), present participle of *dēvi-āre,* to DEVIATE.] —**de·vi·ance** *n.*

de·vi·ate (dē'vē-āt') *v.* **-ated, -ating, -ates.** —*intr.* To turn or move increasingly away from a designated norm, as from a specific course or prescribed mode of behavior. —*tr.* To cause to turn aside or differ.
~*n.* (dē'vē-ĭt). A deviant. [Late Latin *dēviāre : Latin *dē-,* away from + *via,* road, way.] —**de·vi·a·tor** *n.*

de·vi·a·tion (dē'vē-ā'shən) *n.* **1.** The act or result of deviating or turning aside. **2.** An abnormality; departure: *That outburst was a deviation from her usual serenity.* **3.** *Statistics.* **a.** The difference, especially the absolute difference, between one of a set of numbers and their mean. **b.** Any variation from a trend. **4.** Divergence from an accepted or dominant policy or ideology. **5.** The deflection of a compass needle due to local magnetic disturbances. —**de·vi·a·tion·ism** *n.* —**de·vi·a·tion·ist** *n.*

de·vice (dĭ-vīs') *n.* **1.** Something devised or constructed for a particular purpose; especially, a machine used to perform one or more relatively simple tasks. **2.** An artistic contrivance in a literary or dramatic work used to achieve a particular effect. **3.** A plan or scheme, especially a malign one. **4.** A decorative design or pattern, such as one used in embroidery. **5.** A graphic symbol, emblem, or design, especially in heraldry. **6.** *Archaic.* The act, state, or power of devising. —**leave to one's own devices.** To allow to do as one pleases. [Middle English *devis, devise,* from Old French *devis,* division, contrivance, invention, and *devise,* difference, design, plan, both from *deviser,* to divide, DEVISE.]

dev·il (dĕv'əl) *n.* **1.** *Often* **Devil.** *Theology.* The major spirit of evil, ruler of Hell, and foe of God, often depicted as a man with horns, a tail, and cloven hoofs; Satan. **2.** A subordinate evil spirit. **3.** A wicked, malevolent, or ill-tempered person or animal. **4.** An unfortunate person or animal; a wretch: *poor devil.* **5.** A person who is energetic, mischievous, daring, or clever. **6.** The personification of something evil or undesirable. **7.** A **printer's devil** (*see*). **8.** Any of various mechanical devices with sharp teeth or spikes, as for tearing up rags. **9.** *Informal.* Anything difficult or hard to manage: *a devil of a job.* **10.** *Christian Science.* The opposite of Truth; error; a lie. —**(caught) between the devil and the deep blue sea.** Having to make a choice between two equally unsatisfactory options. —**give**

the devil his due. To acknowledge the ability or success of an evil or disliked person. **—go to the devil. 1.** To become thoroughly dissipated. **2.** Used as an exclamation of anger or irritation to a person who has annoyed one. **—(let the) devil take the hindmost.** To look after one's own interests and leave others to manage as best they can. **—the devil.** *Informal.* **1.** An exclamation or expletive used to express surprise, anger, disgust, vexation, or the like. **2.** Used as an intensive: *Where the devil is the waiter?* **—talk (or speak) of the devil.** Used when an absent person who has been the subject of conversation suddenly appears. **—the devil to pay.** Trouble to be faced as a result of some action.

~*v.* **deviled, -viling, -vils** or *chiefly British* **devilled, -villing.** —*tr.* **1.** To prepare (food) with pungent seasoning or condiments, such as mustard or cayenne pepper. **2.** To tear up (cloth or rags) in a toothed machine. **3.** To annoy, torment, or harass. —*intr.* To serve as a printer's devil. [Middle English *devel,* Old English *dēofol,* from Late Latin *diabolus,* from Late Greek *diabolos,* from Greek, slanderer, from *diaballein,* to slander, "throw across" : *dia-,* across + *ballein,* to throw.]

dev·il·fish (dĕv′əl-fĭsh′) *n., pl.* **-fishes** or collectively **devilfish. 1.** The **manta** *(see).* **2.** An **octopus** *(see),* or a similar cephalopod.

dev·il·ish (dĕv′ə-lĭsh) *adj.* **1.** Of, resembling, or characteristic of a devil; fiendish: *devilish cruelty.* **2.** *Informal.* Excessive; extreme: *devilish heat.*

~*adv. Informal.* Extremely; very. Not in current usage. **—dev·il·ish·ly** *adv.* **—dev·il·ish·ness** *n.*

dev·il-may-care (dĕv′əl-mā-kâr′) *adj.* Careless; reckless.

dev·il·ment (dĕv′əl-mənt) *n.* Devilish mischief.

devil's advocate *n.* **1.** *Roman Catholic Church.* An official appointed to present arguments against a proposed canonization or beatification. Also officially called "Promoter of the Faith." **2.** A person who opposes an argument with which he does not necessarily disagree, to determine its validity or be provocative. **3.** An adverse critic, especially of a good cause.

devil's bit *n.* A plant, the **blazing star** *(see).* [So called from the ragged bitten-off appearance of the roots.]

devil's darning needle *n. Informal.* A **dragonfly** *(see).*

devil's fingers *n. Usually used with a singular verb.* An ascomycete fungus, *Xylaria polymorpha,* that grows in blackish, club-shaped tufts on the stumps of deciduous trees. Also called "dead-man's fingers."

dev·il's-food cake (dĕv′əlz-fo͝od′) *n.* A rich, dark, dense-textured chocolate cake. [From the contrast with the white color of ANGEL FOOD CAKE.]

Dev·il's Island (dĕv′əlz). *French* **Île du Dia·ble** (ēl dü dyä′blə). Small island in the south Caribbean Sea, off French Guiana. A French penal colony for political prisoners from the late 19th century, it held Alfred Dreyfus (1894–99) and Henri Charrière ("Papillon"), who claimed to have made the first successful escape from it (1941). It was finally closed in 1945.

devil's paintbrush *n.* A plant, the **orange hawkweed** *(see).*

devil's walking stick *n.* A shrub, **Hercules'-club** *(see).*

dev·il·try (dĕv′əl-trē) *n., pl.* **-tries.** Also **dev·il·ry** (-əl-rē). **1.** Wanton or reckless mischief. **2.** Wickedness. **3.** Evil magic.

dev·il·wood (dĕv′əl-wo͝od′) *n.* A tree, *Osmanthus americanus,* of the southeastern United States, having fragrant greenish flowers and hard wood. [Because it is extremely difficult to cut.]

De Vin·ne (də vĭn′ē), **Theodore Low** (1828–1914). U.S. typographer. He was the best-known U.S. printer of his time and did much to advance the cause of good printing through his fine examples of workmanship and his influential writings, including *The Invention of Printing* (1876), *Historic Printing Types* (1886), and *The Practice of Typography* (1900–04).

de·vi·ous (dē′vē-əs) *adj.* **1.** Straying or deviating from the usual, straight, or direct course or way; circuitous; roundabout. **2.** Straying or departing from the correct or proper way; erring. **3.** Done, planned, used, or acting in an underhand manner; not straightforward; shifty: *a devious plot.* [Latin *dēvius,* off the main road : *dē-,* away from + *via,* way.] **—de·vi·ous·ly** *adv.* **—de·vi·ous·ness** *n.*

de·vis·a·ble (dĭ-vī′zə-bəl) *adj.* **1.** *Law.* Capable of being transmitted by will. Said of real property. **2.** Capable of being invented or contrived.

de·vi·sal (dĭ-vī′zəl) *n.* The act of devising.

de·vise (dĭ-vīz′) *tr.v.* **-vised, -vising, -vises. 1.** To form or arrange in the mind; plan; invent; contrive. **2.** *Law.* To transmit or give (real property) by will. **3.** *Obsolete.* To imagine; conceive.

~*n. Law.* **1.** The act of transmitting or giving real property by will. **2.** The property or lands so transmitted. **3.** A will or clause in a will devising real property. [Middle English *devisen,* to divide, distinguish, examine, design, from Old French *deviser,* from Vulgar Latin *dīvīsāre* (unattested), frequentative of Latin *dīvidere* (past participle *dīvīsus*), to divide.] **—de·vis·er** *n.*

de·vi·see (dĭ-vī-zē′) *n. Law.* One to whom property is devised.

de·vi·sor (dĭ-vī′zər) *n. Law.* One who devises property.

de·vi·tal·ize (dē-vīt′l-īz′) *tr.v.* **-ized, -izing, -izes.** To reduce or destroy the vitality of.

de·vit·ri·fy (dē-vĭt′rə-fī′) *tr.v.* **-fied, -fying, -fies. 1.** To deprive of or destroy the glassy quality of. **2.** To treat (material such as glass) so as to cause crystallization, brittleness, and loss of transparency. [French *dévitrifier* : *dé-,* from Latin *dē-* (reversal) + *vitrifier,* VITRIFY.] **—de·vit·ri·fi·ca·tion** *n.*

de·vo·cal·ize (dē-vō′kə-līz′) *tr.v.* **-ized, -izing, -izes.** *Phonetics.* To unvoice (a speech sound). **—de·vo·cal·i·za·tion** *n.*

de·voice (dē-vois′) *tr.v.* **-voiced, -voicing, -voices.** *Phonetics.* To unvoice (a speech sound).

de·void (dĭ-void′) *adj.* Completely lacking; destitute; empty; without. Used with *of.* [Middle English *devoide,* from *devoiden,* to get rid of, from Old French *desvuidier* : *des-,* from Latin *dē-,* completely + *vuidier,* to empty, from Vulgar Latin *vocitāre* (unattested), from *vocitus* (unattested), empty, from Latin *vacāre,* to be empty.]

de·voir (də-vwär′, dĕv′wär′) *n.* **1.** *Usually* **devoirs.** Courteous attentions; compliments; respects: *pay one's devoirs to the host.* **2.** *Archaic.* Duty. [Middle English *dever, devoir,* duty, from Old French *devoir,* "that which is due," from *devoir,* to owe, from Latin *dēbēre.*]

de·vol·a·til·ize (dē-vŏl′ə-tl-īz′) *tr.v.* **-ized, -izing, -izes.** To remove volatile material from. **—de·vol·a·til·i·za·tion** *n.*

dev·o·lu·tion (dĕv′ə-lo͞o′shən) *n.* **1.** A passing down through successive stages. **2.** The passing to a successor of anything, such as properties, rights, or qualities. **3. a.** A delegating of authority or duties to a subordinate or substitute. **b.** The transfer of a certain amount of legislative or executive power from a central to a regional authority. **4.** Biological degeneration, as distinguished from evolution. [Medieval Latin *dēvolūtiō* (stem *dēvolūtiōn-*), from Latin *dēvolvere* (past participle *dēvolūtus*), to roll down, DEVOLVE.] **—dev·o·lu·tion·ar·y** *adj.*

de·volve (dĭ-vŏlv′) *v.* **-volved, -volving, -volves.** —*tr.* To pass on, delegate, or transfer (duty or authority, for example) to a successor or substitute. —*intr.* To fall or be passed on to a substitute or successor; be conferred. Used with *on, to,* or *upon:* "*With this high honor devolves upon you also a corresponding responsibility*" (Lincoln). [Middle English *devolven,* from Latin *dēvolvere,* to roll down : *dē-,* down + *volvere,* to roll.] **—de·volve·ment** *n.*

Dev·on[1] (dĕv′ən). Also **Dev·on·shire** (-shîr, -shər). County in southwest England, spanning the western peninsula between the Bristol Channel and English Channel. The land is hilly, rising to Dartmoor in the south and Exmoor to the northeast. The county is agricultural and famous for its cattle, clotted cream, and cider. The main towns are Exeter, the administrative center, and Plymouth.

Devon[2] *n.* Any of a breed of reddish cattle developed in Devon and raised primarily for beef.

Devon *Devon cattle, which are reared primarily for their beef, get their name from the southwestern English counties of Devon and Somerset, where they were originally bred. They are rarely found elsewhere.*

De·vo·ni·an (dĭ-vō′nē-ən) *adj.* **1.** Of or pertaining to Devon. **2.** *Geology.* Of, belonging to, or designating the geological time or system of rocks of the fourth period of the Paleozoic era, preceded by the Silurian and followed by the Mississippian or Carboniferous period, and characterized by the appearance of forests and amphibians.

~*n.* **1.** A native or inhabitant of Devon. **2.** *Geology.* The Devonian period or system of rocks. Preceded by *the.*

Devonshire cream *n.* A rich yellow clotted cream.

de·vote (dĭ-vōt′) *tr.v.* **-voted, -voting, -votes. 1.** To give or apply (one's time, attention, or self) entirely to a particular activity, pursuit, cause, or person. **2. a.** To dedicate by a vow or solemn act; consecrate. **b.** To set apart; give over to a particular purpose: *a broadcast devoted to Ireland.* **3.** *Rare.* To doom to destruction; curse. [Latin *dēvovēre* (past participle *dēvōtus*), to vow, devote : *dē-,* completely + *vovēre,* to vow.] **—de·vote·ment** *n.*

Synonyms: *consecrate, dedicate, pledge.*

de·vot·ed (dĭ-vō′tĭd) *adj.* **1.** Feeling or displaying strong affection or attachment: *devoted friends.* **2.** Consecrated; dedicated. —See Synonyms at **faithful. —de·vot·ed·ly** *adv.* **—de·vot·ed·ness** *n.*

dev·o·tee (dĕv′ə-tē′, -tā′) *n.* **1.** One ardently devoted or attached to anything; an enthusiast: *a devotee of sports.* **2.** One ardently or fanatically devoted to a religion.

de·vo·tion (dĭ-vō′shən) *n.* **1.** Ardent attachment or affection, as to a person or cause; faithfulness; loyalty. **2.** Religious ardor or zeal; piety. **3.** *Usually* **devotions.** An act of religious observance or prayer, especially when private. **4.** The act of devoting or the state of being devoted. —See Synonyms at **love, fidelity.**

de·vo·tion·al (dĭ-vō′shən-əl) *adj.* **1.** Of or pertaining to devotion. **2.** Used in worship.

~*n.* A short service of worship. **—de·vo·tion·al·ly** *adv.*

de·vour (dĭ-vour′) *tr.v.* **-voured, -vouring, -vours. 1.** To swallow or eat up greedily. **2.** To destroy, consume, or waste. **3.** To take in greedily with the senses or mind: *devour a novel.* **4.** To swallow up; engulf; absorb. [Middle English *devouren,* from Old French *devourer,* from Latin *dēvorāre* : *dē-,* completely + *vorāre,* to swallow, devour.] **—de·vour·er** *n.* **—de·vour·ing·ly** *adv.*

de·vout (dĭ-vout′) *adj.* **1.** Deeply religious; pious. **2.** Expressing reverence or piety. **3.** Sincere; earnest; devoted. [Middle English *devo(u)t,* from Old French *devot,* from Late Latin *dēvōtus,* from Latin, past participle of *dēvovēre,* to vow, DEVOTE.] **—de·vout·ly** *adv.* **—de·vout·ness** *n.*

De Vries (də vrēs′), **Peter** (1910–). U.S. author. With a comic, punning style, he has irreverently described American life in numerous novels such as *No But I Saw the Movie* (1952), *Reuben, Reuben* (1964), and *Slouching Towards Kalamazoo* (1983).

dew (do͞o, dyo͞o) *n.* **1.** Water droplets condensed from the air, usually at night, forming on cool surfaces, such as grass. **2.** Anything resembling or suggestive of dew; something moist, refreshing, or pure. **3.** Any moisture appearing in small drops, as tears.

~*tr.v.* **dewed, dewing, dews.** To wet with or as with dew; moisten; bedew. [Middle English *deu, de(a)w,* Old English *dēaw,* from Germanic.]

DEW distant early warning. See **DEW line.**

de·wan, di·wan (dĭ-wän′, -wôn′) *n.* Any of certain government officials in India, especially a finance minister, or the prime minister of

a state. [Hindi *dīwān,* from Persian *dīvān†,* register, account book, hence office of accounts, council of state. See also **divan.**]

Dew·ar flask (dōō′ər, dyōō′-) *n.* An insulated container used especially to store liquefied gases, having a double wall with evacuated space between the walls and silvered surfaces. [After Sir James *Dewar* (1842–1923), Scottish physicist who invented it.]

dew·ber·ry (dōō′běr′ē, dyōō′-) *n., pl.* **-ries.** **1.** Any of several trailing forms of the blackberry, such as *Rubus hispidus,* of North America, and *R. caesius,* of Europe. **2.** The fruit of any of these plants.

dew·claw (dōō′klô′, dyōō′-) *n.* A vestigial digit, claw, or hoof on the foot of certain mammals. [Because it reaches only the dewy surface of the ground.]

dew·drop (dōō′drŏp′, dyōō′-) *n.* **1.** A drop of dew, or anything that resembles one. **2.** A North American plant, *Dalibarda repens,* having rounded leaves and white flowers.

Dew·ey (dōō′ē, dyōō′ē), **John** (1859–1952). U.S. philosopher and educator, one of the main exponents of philosophical pragmatism. He held that education should be as much concerned with physical and moral welfare as with intellectual development. His writings include *Democracy and Education* (1916), *Reconstruction in Philosophy* (1920), and *Experience and Nature* (1925).

Dewey decimal system *n. Library Science.* A system of classification of books and other publications into ten major categories, each category being further subdivided by number. Also called "Dewey classification." Compare **Library of Congress classification.** [After Melvil *Dewey* (1851–1931), U.S. librarian who devised it in 1876.]

dew·fall (dōō′fôl′, dyōō′-) *n.* **1.** The formation of dew. **2.** The time of evening when dew begins to form. [From the erroneous assumption that dew falls like rain.]

dew·lap (dōō′lăp′, dyōō′-) *n.* **1.** A fold of loose skin hanging from the neck region of certain animals, especially cattle. **2.** A similar pendulous part, such as the wattle of a bird. [Middle English *dewlappe :* DEW + *lappe,* LAP (loose flap).]

DEW line (dōō, dyōō) *n.* A line of radar stations at about the 70th parallel across the North American continent, designed to give advance warning of approaching aircraft and missiles. See **DEW.**

dew point *n.* The temperature at which air becomes saturated and produces dew.

dew pond *n. Chiefly British.* A manmade hollow, usually lined with clay or cement, found on chalk downs. Most of the water in it comes from condensation and rainfall.

dew·worm (dōō′wûrm′, dyōō′-) *n.* Any earthworm found on or near the surface of the ground and used as fishing bait.

dew·y (dōō′ē, dyōō′ē) *adj.* **-i·er, -i·est.** **1.** Wet or moist with or as if with dew. **2.** Pertaining to, resembling, or forming dew. **3.** *Poetic.* Suggestive of dew. **—dew·i·ly** *adv.* **—dew·i·ness** *n.*

dew·y-eyed (dōō′ē-īd′, dyōō′-) *adj.* Characterized by childlike innocence and faith; naive.

dex (děks) *n. Slang.* Dextroamphetamine.

dex·ter (děk′stər) *adj.* **1.** Of or located on the right side. **2.** *Heraldry.* Located on the wearer's right and the observer's left. Compare **sinister.** **3.** *Obsolete.* Auspicious; favorable. [Latin, on the right side.]

Dexter *n.* Any of a breed of small, hardy cattle originating in Ireland. [Perhaps from the surname of the breeder.]

dex·ter·i·ty (děk-stěr′ə-tē) *n.* **1.** Skill in the use of the hands or body; adroitness. **2.** Mental skill or adroitness; cleverness: *"He admired the dexterity with which their host directed the conversation"* (Joyce). **3.** *Rare.* Right-handedness. [French *dextérité,* from Latin *dexteritās* (stem *dexteritāt-*), from *dexter,* skillful, DEXTER.]

dex·ter·ous, dex·trous (děk′strəs) *adj.* **1.** Adroit or skillful in the use of the hands, body, or mind; artful; clever. **2.** Done with dexterity. [Latin *dexter,* skillful, DEXTER.] **—dex·ter·ous·ly** *adv.* **—dex·ter·ous·ness** *n.*
　　Synonyms: *adroit, deft, handy, nimble.*

dex·tral (děk′strəl) *adj.* **1.** Of, pertaining to, or located on the right side; right. **2.** Right-handed. Compare **sinistral.** **3.** *Zoology.* Designating or pertaining to a gastropod shell that has its aperture to the right when facing the observer with the apex upward. [Medieval Latin *dextrālis,* from Latin *dexter,* DEXTER.] **—dex·tral·i·ty** (děk-străl′ə-tē) *n.* **—dex·tral·ly** *adv.*

dex·tran (děk′strən) *n.* Any of various heavy long-chain polymers of glucose that are used, depending on molecular weight, as a blood-plasma substitute, in confections, lacquers, and food additives. [DEXTR(O)- + -AN (chemistry).]

dex·trin (děk′strĭn) *n.* Also **dex·trine** (děk′strĭn, -strēn′). A white or yellow powder formed by the hydrolysis of starch, having colloidal properties, and used mainly as an adhesive and thickening agent. [DEXTR(O)- + -IN.]

dex·tro (děk′strō) *adj. Chemistry.* Dextrorotatory.

dextro-, dextr- *prefix. Abbr.* **d** Indicates on or toward the right-hand side; for example, **dextrorotatory, dextran.** [Latin, from *dexter,* on the right side.]

dex·tro·am·phet·a·mine (děk′strō-ăm-fět′ə-mēn′, -mĭn) *n.* A drug, $(C_9H_{13}N)$, that is the dextrorotatory form of amphetamine, acting as a stimulant on the central nervous system. It is commonly used as a sulfate or phosphate salt.

dex·tro·glu·cose (děk′strə-glōō′kōs′, -kōz′) *n.* **Dextrose** *(see).*

dex·tro·gy·rate (děk′strə-jī′rāt) *adj.* Dextrorotatory.

dex·tro·ro·ta·tion (děk′strə-rō-tā′shən) *n. Optics.* A turning to the right. Said especially of the plane of polarization of light.

dex·tro·ro·ta·to·ry (děk′strə-rō′tə-tôr′ē, -tōr′ē) *adj.* Also **dex·tro·ro·ta·ry** (-rō′tə-rē). **1.** *Optics.* Turning or rotating the plane of polariza-

tion of light to the right or clockwise: *dextrorotatory crystals.* **2.** *Chemistry.* Of, pertaining to, or designating a solution that rotates the plane of polarized light to the right or clockwise; dextrogyrate. Compare **levorotatory.**

dex·trorse (děk′strôrs′) *adj.* Growing upward in a spiral that turns from left to right: *a dextrorse vine.* Compare **sinistrorse.** [New Latin *dextrorsus,* from Latin, turned toward the right side : DEXTRO- + *versus,* past participle of *vertere,* to turn.] **—dex·trorse·ly** *adv.*

dex·trose (děk′strōs′, -strōz′) *n.* A dextrorotatory sugar, $C_6H_{12}O_6 \cdot H_2O$, found in animal and plant tissue and derived synthetically from starch. Also called "corn sugar," "dextroglucose," "grape sugar." [DEXTR(O)- + -OSE.]

dey (dā) *n.* **1.** The title of the governor of Algiers before the French conquest in 1830. **2.** Formerly, a title held by a ruler of Tunis or Tripoli. [French, from Turkish *dayı,* maternal uncle.]

DF direction finder.

DFC, D.F.C. Distinguished Flying Cross.

DFM, D.F.M. Distinguished Flying Medal.

dg decigram.

D.G. director-general.

DH designated hitter.

D.H. Doctor of Humanities.

dhak (däk, dôk) *n.* A tree, *Butea frondosa,* of tropical Asia that yields a red resin used as an astringent. [Hindi *ḍhāk†.*]

Dhaka. See **Dacca.**

dhal, dal (däl) *n.* **1.** A tropical shrub of the genus *Cajanus,* cultivated for its pealike seeds. Also called "pigeon pea." **2.** The edible seed of this shrub. **3.** An Indian dish made from dhal or other pulses, onions, and various spices. [Hindi *dāl,* (split) pulse, from Sanskrit *dal,* to split.]

dhar·ma (där′mə, dûr′-) *n. Hinduism & Buddhism.* **1.** The ultimate law of all things. **2.** Individual right conduct in conformity to this law. [Sanskrit, law.]

Dhílos. See **Delos.**

Dhi·mo·ti·ki (thē-mô′tē-kē) *n.* The colloquial form of Modern Greek. Also called "Demotic." Compare **Katharevusa.** [Greek, "demotic."]

D.H.L. Doctor of Hebrew Letters; Doctor of Hebrew Literature.

dho·bi (dō′bē) *n.* In India, a man who washes clothes. [Hindi, from *dhōb,* washing.]

dho·bi's itch (dō′bēz) *n.* Also **dhobi itch.** A fungal skin disease, *Tinea cruris.* [The disease being common in the tropics, and supposedly contracted from other people's dirty clothes.]

Dhodhekánisos. See **Dodecanese.**

dhole (dōl) *n.* A doglike, carnivorous mammal, *Cuon alpinus,* of Asia, having brownish fur, and often hunting in packs. [Of Anglo-Indian origin, akin to Kanarese *tōla,* wolf.]

dho·ti (dō′tē) *n., pl.* **-tis.** A long cloth worn round the waist and lower half of the body by Hindu men in India. [Hindi *dhōtī†.*]

dhow (dou) *n.* A lateen-rigged Arabian vessel. [Arabic *dāw†.*]

Dhul-Hij·ja, Dul-heg·gia (dül′hĭj′ä). The 12th month of the Muslim year. Dhul-Hijja has 29 days. See feature at **calendar.** [Arabic *dhū'l-ḥijja,* "the one of the pilgrimage."]

Dhul-Qa·dah, Dul-kaa·da (dül′kăd′ä) *n.* The 11th month of the Muslim year. Dhul-Qadah has 30 days. See feature at **calendar.** [Arabic *dhū'l-ga'dah,* "the one of the sitting."]

di- *prefix.* Indicates: **1.** Twice, double, or two; for example, **dicotyledon. 2.** *Chemistry.* Having two atoms, molecules, or radicals; for example, **diacetylmorphine.** [Greek *di-,* two, twice.]

Di The symbol for didymium.

dia. diameter.

dia-, di- *prefix.* Indicates: **1.** Through or throughout; for example, **diachronic. 2.** Across or by transmission; for example, **diapophysis, diactinic. 3.** *Botany.* Over, across, or at right angles; for example, **diatropism. 4.** In opposite or different directions; for example, **diamagnetic.** [In borrowed Greek compounds, *dia-* indicates: 1. Through, throughout, as in **diapason.** 2. Across, as in **diagonal.** 3. Between, as in **diapause.** 4. Apart, as in **dialysis.** 5. From one to another, mutually, as in **dialogue.** 6. In different directions, as in **diathesis.** 7. Completely, as in **diaphragm.** 8. Made of, as in **diatessaron.** Greek *dia-* is the preverbal form of the preposition *dia†,* through.]

di·a·base (dī′ə-bās′) *n.* **1.** Dark-gray to black, fine-textured igneous rock, composed mainly of feldspar and pyroxene, and used for monuments and as crushed stone. **2.** *Chiefly British.* Dolerite in which the pyroxene has been altered to amphibole. [French, from Greek *diabasis,* a crossing over, from *diabainein,* to cross over : *dia-,* across + *bainein,* to go.]

di·a·be·tes (dī′ə-bē′tĭs, -tēz) *n.* Any of several metabolic disorders marked by excessive discharge of urine and persistent thirst, especially diabetes mellitus. [Middle English *diabete,* from Medieval Latin *diabētēs,* from Greek *diabētēs,* "a crossing over or passing through" (from the symptomatic excessive urination), from *diabainein,* to cross over : *dia-,* across + *bainein,* to go.]

diabetes in·sip·i·dus (ĭn-sĭp′ə-dəs) *n.* A disease characterized by intense thirst and excessive urination, caused by a deficiency of the pituitary hormone vasopressin. [New Latin, "insipid diabetes."]

diabetes mel·li·tus (mə-lī′təs) *n.* A chronic disease of pancreatic origin, characterized by insulin deficiency, subsequent inability to utilize carbohydrates, excess sugar in the blood and urine, excessive thirst, hunger, and urination, weakness, emaciation, imperfect combustion of fats resulting in acidosis, and, without injection of insulin, eventual coma and death. [New Latin, "honey-sweet diabetes."]

Dexter *The smallest of British cattle, Dexters were bred in the mountains of western Ireland. Rarely found now, the breed is kept both for milk and beef.*

di·a·bet·ic (dī′ə-bĕt′ĭk) *adj.* **1.** Of, pertaining to, or having diabetes. **2.** For the use of diabetics.
∼n. One afflicted with diabetes mellitus.

di·a·ble·rie (dē-ä′blə-rē; *French* dyä-blə-rē′) *n.* **1.** Dealings with demons or the devil; sorcery; witchcraft. **2. a.** The representation of devils or demons, as in paintings or fiction. **b.** Devil lore; demonology. **3.** Devilish conduct; deviltry. [French, from *diable,* devil, from Late Latin *diabolus,* DEVIL.]

di·a·bol·ic (dī′ə-bŏl′ĭk) *adj.* Also **di·a·bol·i·cal** (-ĭ-kəl). **1.** Of, concerning, or characteristic of the devil; satanic; hellish. **2.** Appropriate to a devil; extremely wicked; fiendishly cruel. [Middle English *deabolik,* from Old French *diabolique,* from Late Latin *diabolicus,* from *diabolus,* DEVIL.] **—di·a·bol·i·cal·ly** *adv.* **—di·a·bol·i·cal·ness** *n.*

di·ab·o·lism (dī-ăb′ə-lĭz′əm) *n.* **1.** Dealings with or worship of the devil or demons; sorcery; witchcraft. **2.** Devilish conduct or character. **—di·ab·o·list** *n.*

di·ab·o·lize (dī-ăb′ə-līz′) *tr.v.* **-lized, -lizing, -lizes. 1.** To cause to be diabolic or devilish. **2.** To bring under the influence of the devil. **3.** To represent as diabolic.

di·ab·o·lo (dē-ăb′ə-lō) *n., pl.* **-los. 1.** A game in which an hourglass-shaped top is spun and caught on a string held at each end by a stick. **2.** The top used in this game. [Italian, devil (the name of the top).]

di·a·caus·tic (dī′ə-kôs′tĭk) *n. Optics.* A caustic curve or surface formed by refracted rather than reflected light. Compare **catacaustic. —di·a·caus·tic** *adj.*

di·ac·e·tyl·mor·phine (dī-ăs′ə-təl-môr′fēn′) *n.* A drug, **heroin** *(see).*

di·a·chron·ic (dī′ə-krŏn′ĭk) *adj.* **1.** Considering phenomena as they occur or develop through time. **2.** *Linguistics.* Pertaining to or designating an approach to the study of language and linguistic phenomena from a historical perspective. Compare **synchronic.** [DIA- (through) + Greek *khronos,* time.]

di·ac·id (dī-ăs′ĭd) *adj.* Possessing two hydrogen atoms replaceable by metal atoms. Said of a salt.
∼n. An acid possessing two readily replaceable hydrogen atoms.

di·a·cid·ic (dī-ə-sĭd′ĭk) *adj.* Designating a base, such as calcium hydroxide, that is able to neutralize two protons. See **dibasic.**

di·ac·o·nal (dī-ăk′ə-nəl) *adj.* Of or concerning a deacon or the diaconate. [Late Latin *diācōnālis,* from *diāconus,* DEACON.]

di·ac·o·nate (dī-ăk′ə-nĭt) *n.* **1.** The rank or office of a deacon. **2.** A body of deacons. [Late Latin *diāconātus,* from *diāconus,* DEACON.]

di·a·crit·ic (dī′ə-krĭt′ĭk) *adj.* **1.** Diacritical. **2.** *Medicine.* Diagnostic or distinctive.
∼n. A diacritical mark.

di·a·crit·i·cal (dī′ə-krĭt′ĭ-kəl) *adj.* Marking a distinction; distinguishing. [Greek *diakritikos,* distinguishing, from *diakrinein,* to distinguish : *dia-,* apart + *krinein,* to separate.] **—di·a·crit·i·cal·ly** *adv.*

diacritical mark *n.* A mark added to a letter to indicate a special phonetic value; for example, in French *façade,* the cedilla indicates that the *c* does not have its regular prevocalic value (k), but a sibilant value (s).

di·ac·tin·ic (dī′ăk-tĭn′ĭk) *adj.* Capable of transmitting chemically active, or actinic, radiation. Said of a lens filter, for example. [DI(A)- (across) + ACTINIC.] **—di·ac·tin·ism** (dī-ăk′tə-nĭz′əm) *n.*

di·a·del·phous (dī′ə-dĕl′fəs) *adj. Botany.* Having stamens in two bundles owing to the fusion of filaments. Compare **monadelphous.** [DI- (two) + -ADELPHOUS.]

di·a·dem (dī′ə-dĕm′) *n.* **1.** A crown or cloth headband, worn as a sign of royalty. **2.** Royal power or dignity. [Middle English *diademe,* from Old French, from Latin *diadēma,* from Greek *diadēma,* from *diadein,* to bind on either side : *dia-,* across + *dein,* to bind.] **—di·a·demed** *adj.*

diaeresis. Variant of **dieresis.**

diag. 1. diagonal. **2.** diagram.

di·a·gen·e·sis (dī′ə-jĕn′ĭ-sĭs) *n.* The changes that occur in sediments by which they become consolidated into rock, excluding weathering and metamorphism. **—di·a·ge·net·ic** (dī′ə-jə-nĕt′ĭk) *adj.* [DIA- (through) + -GENESIS.]

di·a·ge·ot·ro·pism (dī′ə-jē-ŏt′rə-pĭz′əm) *n. Botany.* The tendency of certain parts, such as rhizomes, to become oriented at right angles to the direction of gravitational force. [DIA- (over across) + GEOTROPISM.] **—di·a·ge·o·trop·ic** (dī′ə-jē′ə-trŏp′ĭk, -trō′pĭk) *adj.*

Di·agh·i·lev (dē-äg′ə-lĕf′), **Sergei Pavlovich** (1872–1929). Russian director and ballet impresario. He started his own company, Les Ballets Russes, in 1909 and influenced the evolution of the ballet as an art form. Among his collaborators were the artists Bakst, Picasso, and Cocteau and the musicians Stravinsky, Satie, and Milhaud.

di·ag·nose (dī′əg-nōs′, -nōz′) *v.* **-nosed, -nosing, -noses.** *—tr.* To distinguish or identify (a disease, for example) by diagnosis. *—intr.* To make a diagnosis. [Back-formation from DIAGNOSIS.] **—di·ag·nos·a·ble** *adj.*

di·ag·no·sis (dī′əg-nō′sĭs) *n., pl.* **-ses** (-sēz). **1.** *Medicine.* **a.** The act or process of identifying or determining the nature of a disease or injury through examination. **b.** The opinion derived from such an examination. **2. a.** The process of investigating and determining the nature of a condition or problem; especially, the identification and analysis of faults in a machine: *a computer diagnosis of faults in a car's electrical system.* **b.** The conclusion reached by such an investigation. **3.** *Biology.* A precise and detailed description of the characteristics of an organism for taxonomic classification. [New Latin, from Greek *diagnōsis,* discernment, from *diagignōskein,* to distinguish, discern : *dia-,* apart + *gignōskein,* to perceive.]

di·ag·nos·tic (dī′əg-nŏs′tĭk) *adj.* **1.** Of, pertaining to, or used in a diagnosis. **2.** Serving to identify a particular disease; characteristic.
∼n. **1.** *Often* **diagnostics.** The art or practice of medical diagnosis. **2.** A symptom serving as supporting evidence in a diagnosis. [Greek *diagnōstikos,* from *diagnōstos,* to be distinguished, from *diagignōskein,* to distinguish. See **diagnosis.**] **—di·ag·nos·ti·cal·ly** *adv.*

di·ag·nos·ti·cian (dī′əg-nŏ-stĭsh′ən) *n.* A person who diagnoses; especially, a medical practitioner specializing in medical diagnoses.

di·ag·nos·tics (dī′əg-nŏs′tĭks) *n. Used with a singular verb.* The science or practice of making medical diagnoses.

di·ag·o·nal (dī-ăg′ə-nəl) *adj. Abbr.* **diag. 1.** *Geometry.* **a.** Joining two nonadjacent vertices of a polygon. **b.** Joining two vertices of a polyhedron not in the same face. **2.** Having a slanted or oblique direction. **3.** Having oblique lines or markings.
∼n. Abbr. **diag. 1.** A diagonal line or plane. **2. a.** Anything arranged obliquely, such as a row, course, pattern, or part. **b.** A diagonal direction. **3.** A fabric woven with diagonal lines. [Latin *diagōnālis,* from Greek *diagōnios,* from angle to angle : *dia-,* across + *gōnia,* angle.] **—di·ag·o·nal·ly** *adv.*

di·ag·o·nal·ize (dī-ăg′ə-nə-līz′) *tr.v.* **-ized, -izing, -izes.** To order a matrix so that all the nonzero elements occur on the diagonal from upper left to lower right. **—di·ag·o·nal·iz·a·ble** *adj.* **—di·ag·o·nal·i·za·tion** *n.*

diagonal matrix *n.* A matrix that has been diagonalized.

di·a·gram (dī′ə-grăm′) *n. Abbr.* **diag. 1.** A plan, sketch, drawing, or outline, not necessarily representational, designed to demonstrate, describe, or explain something or clarify the relationship existing between the parts of a whole. **2.** A graphic representation of an algebraic or geometric relationship. **3.** A chart or graph.
∼tr.v. **diagrammed** or **diagramed, -gramming** or **-graming, -grams.** To indicate or represent by or as if by a diagram. [Latin *diagramma,* from Greek, from *diagraphein,* to mark out : *dia-,* apart + *graphein,* to write.] **—di·a·gram·ma·ble** *adj.* **—di·a·gram·mat·ic, di·a·gram·mat·i·cal** *adj.* **—di·a·gram·mat·i·cal·ly** *adv.*

di·a·graph (dī′ə-grăf′) *n.* **1.** An instrument used to draw copies of other drawings, such as maps, according to a desired scale. **2.** A protractor and scale combined. [French *diagraphe,* from Greek *diagraphein,* to mark out (in lines). See **diagram.**]

di·a·ki·ne·sis (dī′ə-kə-nē′sĭs) *n., pl.* **-ses** (-sēz). *Genetics.* The final stage of the prophase in meiosis, characterized by the separation of homologous chromosomes after chiasmata formation and the disappearance of the nucleoli and nuclear membrane. [DIA- (across) + -KINESIS (division).] **—di·a·ki·ne·tic** *adj.*

di·al (dī′əl, dīl) *n.* **1.** Any graduated, usually circular face or disk on which some measurement, as of speed, pressure, or temperature, is indicated by a moving needle or pointer. **2. a.** The face of a clock. **b.** A **sundial** *(see).* **3. a.** The panel or face on a radio or television receiver on which the frequencies or channels are indicated. **b.** The control on a radio or television receiver used to change the frequency or channel. **4.** A rotatable disk on a telephone with numbers and sometimes letters used to make connections. **5.** A miner's compass with sights, a spirit level, and a vernier, used for underground surveying.
∼v. **dialed** or **-alled, -aling** or **alling, -als.** *—tr.* **1.** To measure or survey with or as with a dial. **2.** To point to, indicate, or register by means of a dial. **3.** To telephone (the number of another telephone) by means of a dial. **4.** To select (a station or program) on a radio or television receiver by means of a dial. *—intr.* To use a dial, as on a telephone. [Middle English *diall,* sundial, from Medieval Latin *diāle,* clock dial, from *diālis,* daily, from Latin *diēs,* day.] **—di·al·er, di·al·ler** *n.*

dial. dialect; dialectal.

di·a·lect (dī′ə-lĕkt′) *n. Abbr.* **dial. 1.** A regional variety of a language, distinguished from other varieties by pronunciation, grammar, or vocabulary, especially: **a.** A variety of speech differing from the standard literary language or speech pattern of the culture in which it exists. Also used adjectivally: *a dialect word.* **b.** A variety of language that, with other varieties, constitutes a single language of which no single variety is standard: *the dialects of Ancient Greek.* **2.** The spoken language peculiar to the members of an occupational or professional group, an immigrant or minority group, or a particular social class. **3.** A manner or style of expressing oneself; idiom. **4.** A language considered as part of a larger family of languages or a linguistic branch: *Spanish and French are Romance dialects.* [Old French *dialecte,* from Latin *dialectus,* from Greek *dialektos,* speech, language, dialect, from *dialegesthai,* to converse : *dia-,* one with another + *legesthai,* middle voice of *legein,* to tell.]

di·a·lec·tal (dī′ə-lĕk′təl) *adj. Abbr.* **dial.** Pertaining to, characteristic of, or of the nature of a dialect. **—di·a·lec·tal·ly** *adv.*

di·a·lec·tic (dī′ə-lĕk′tĭk) *n.* **1.** The art of arriving at the truth by exposing the contradictions in an opponent's argument or beliefs and overcoming them; especially, the Socratic method of question and answer to elicit the truth. **2. a.** The process, formulated by Hegel, of reaching the truth or the absolute through change, whereby a proposition or idea (thesis) is transformed into its opposite (antithesis) and preserved and fulfilled by it, the combination of the two being resolved in a higher form of truth (synthesis), the ultimate synthesis being for Hegel the mind or thought. **b.** Hegel's critical method for the investigation of this process. **3.** The contradiction between two conflicting forces viewed as the determining factor in their continuing interaction. [Middle English *dialetik,* from Old French *dialetique,* from Latin *dialectica,* from Greek *dia-*

PRONUNCIATION KEY

ă, pat; ā, pay; âr, care;
ä, father, are; b, bib;
ch, church; d, deed; ĕ, pet;
ē, be; f, fife; g, gag; h, hat;
hw, which; ĭ, pit; ī, pie;
îr, pier; j, judge; k, kick;
l, lid, needle; m, mum;
n, no, sudden; ng, thing;
ŏ, pot; ō, toe; ô, paw, for;
oi, noise; ou, out; ŏŏ, book;
ōō, boot; p, pop; r, roar;
s, sauce; sh, ship, dish;
t, tight; th, thin, path;
th, this, bathe; ŭ, cut; ûr, fur;
v, valve; w, with; y, yes;
z, zebra, size; zh, vision;
ə, about, item, edible,
gallop, circus, peaceful

IN FOREIGN WORDS:

à, *Fr.* ami; œ, *Fr.* feu, *Ger.* schön; ü, *Fr.* tu, *Ger.* über;
KH, *Ger.* ich, *Scot.* loch;
N, *Fr.* bon; y′, *Fr.* Compiègne

STRESS MARKS:

Primary stress: ′
in·cite′ (ĭn-sīt′)
Secondary stress: ′
in′sight′ (ĭn′sīt′)

lektikē (tekhnē), "(the art) of debate," from *dialektikos,* of conversation or discussion, from *dialektos,* discussion, debate, DIALECT.] **—di·a·lec·tic, di·a·lec·ti·cal** *adj.* **—di·a·lec·ti·cian** (dī′ə-lĕk-tĭsh′ən) *n.*

dialectical materialism *n.* The Marxist interpretation of reality, viewing matter as the primary subject of change and all change as the product of a constant conflict between opposites arising from the internal contradictions inherent in all things, these contradictions being resolved at higher levels and fresh contradictions arising. This theory has been applied to various areas of thought and scholarship, and especially to history. See **historical materialism.**

di·a·lec·tics (dī′ə-lĕk′tĭks) *n. Used with a singular verb.* **1.** Any method of argument or exposition that systematically weighs contradictory facts or ideas with a view to the resolution of their real or apparent contradictions. **2.** *Sometimes* **dialectic. a.** The Marxist doctrine, adopted from Hegel, of the process of change through the conflict of opposing forces, but asserting that matter, not mind, is the primary reality. **b.** The Marxist critique of this process. **3.** *Sometimes* **dialectic.** Logic, especially as used to expose invalid reasoning.

di·a·lec·tol·o·gy (dī′ə-lĕk-tŏl′ə-jē) *n.* The study of dialects. **—di·a·lec·to·log·i·cal** (dī′ə-lĕk′tə-lŏj′ĭ-kəl) *adj.* **—di·a·lec·tol·o·gist** *n.*

dial gauge *n.* A measuring instrument, the **indicator** *(see).*

di·a·log·ic (dī′ə-lŏj′ĭk) *adj.* Of, pertaining to, or written in dialogue. **—di·a·log·i·cal·ly** *adv.*

di·al·o·gism (dī-ăl′ə-jĭz′əm) *n.* **1.** *Obsolete.* A dialogue, especially an imaginary one contrived as a means of presenting divergent viewpoints. **2.** *Logic.* A form of argument having a single premise and resulting in a disjunctive conclusion.

di·al·o·gist (dī-ăl′ə-jĭst) *n.* **1.** One who writes dialogue. **2.** One who speaks in a dialogue. **—di·a·lo·gis·tic** (dī′ə-lō-jĭs′tĭk), **di·a·lo·gis·ti·cal** *adj.*

di·a·logue, di·a·log (dī′ə-lôg′, -lŏg′) *n.* **1.** A conversation between two or more people. **2.** A conversational passage in a play or narrative. **3.** The lines spoken by the characters in a play or narrative. **4.** A literary or philosophical work written in the form of a conversation: *the dialogues of Galileo.* **5.** An exchange of ideas or opinions. **6.** Diplomatic contact, negotiation, or discussion, especially between opposing nations or groups.
~*v.* **dialogued, -loguing, -logues.** Also **dialogged, -log·ging, -logs.** —*tr.* To express as or as in a dialogue. —*intr.* To converse in a dialogue. [Middle English *dialog(ue),* from Old French *dialogue,* from Latin *dialogus,* from Greek *dialogos,* from *dialegesthai,* to converse : *dia-,* one with another + *legesthai,* middle voice of *legein,* to tell, talk.] **—di·a·log·uer** *n.*

dial tone *n.* A low, steady tone in a telephone receiver indicating that a number may be dialed.

di·al·y·sis (dī-ăl′ə-sĭs) *n., pl.* **-ses** (-sēz′). The separation of smaller molecules from larger molecules, or of crystalloid particles from colloidal particles, in a solution by selective diffusion through a semipermeable membrane. **2. Renal dialysis** *(see).* [New Latin, from Greek *dialusis,* from *dialuein,* to tear apart : *dia-,* apart + *luein,* to loosen.] **—di·a·lyt·ic** (dī′ə-lĭt′ĭk) *adj.* **—di·a·lyt·i·cal·ly** *adv.*

di·a·lyze (dī′ə-līz′) *v.* **-lyzed, -lyzing, -lyzes.** —*tr.* To subject to dialysis; separate by dialysis. —*intr.* To undergo dialysis. [Back-formation from DIALYSIS.]

di·a·lyz·er (dī′ə-līz′ər) *n.* An apparatus for performing dialysis, especially a kidney machine.

diam diameter.

di·a·mag·net (dī′ə-măg′nət) *n.* A diamagnetic substance.

di·a·mag·net·ic (dī′ə-măg-nĕt′ĭk) *adj.* Pertaining to or designating substances exhibiting diamagnetism.

di·a·mag·net·ism (dī′ə-măg′nə-tĭz′əm) *n.* The type of magnetism occurring in substances with a small negative magnetic susceptibility and a relative permeability of less than unity. It is caused by changes in the orbital motion of the electrons in the atoms of the substance and sometimes masked by the much stronger paramagnetism and ferromagnetism.

di·a·man·té (dē′ə-män′tā′) *adj.* Decorated with or made from powdered glass or crystal, artificial jewels, or the like, in order to give the glittering effect of diamonds.
~*n.* **1.** Jewelry made from diamanté paste. **2.** Fabric having diamanté decoration. [French, past participle of *diamanter,* to stud with diamonds, from *diamant,* DIAMOND.]

di·a·man·tine (dī′ə-măn′tīn) *adj.* Of, pertaining to, or resembling diamonds. [French, from *diamant,* DIAMOND.]

di·am·e·ter (dī-ăm′ə-tər) *n. Abbr.* **dia., diam 1.** *Mathematics.* **a.** A straight line passing through the center of a figure, especially of a circle or sphere, and terminating at the periphery. **b.** The length of such a line. **2.** Loosely, the thickness or width of anything. [Middle English *diametre,* from Old French, from Latin *diametros,* from Greek *diametros (grammē),* "(line) which measures through" : *dia-,* through + *metron,* measure.] **—di·am·e·tral** *adj.*

di·a·met·ri·cal (dī′ə-mĕt′rĭ-kəl) *adj.* Also **di·a·met·ric** (-rĭk) (for sense 2). **1.** Of, pertaining to, or along a diameter. **2.** Exactly opposite; contrary.

di·a·met·ri·cal·ly (dī′ə-mĕt′rĭk-lē) *adv.* **1.** Along a diameter; straight across a circle or other figure. **2.** Absolutely; irreconcilably: *diametrically opposed ideologies.*

di·am·ine (dī-ăm′ēn, -ĭn, dī′ə-mēn′, -mĭn) *n.* Any of various chemical compounds containing two amino groups, especially **hydrazine** *(see).* [DI- (two) + -AMINE.]

dia·mond (dī′mənd, dī′ə-) *n.* **1.** A highly refractive, colorless crystalline allotrope of carbon, used as a gemstone and in rock drills, abrasives, and cutting tools. It is the hardest naturally occurring substance and may be colored yellow, orange, blue, brown, or black by impurities. **2.** A figure with four equal sides forming two inner obtuse angles and two inner acute angles; a rhombus or lozenge. **3. a.** The red symbol appearing on one of the four suits of playing cards, in the shape of a diamond. **b.** A card bearing this symbol. See **diamonds. 4.** *Baseball.* **a.** The infield. **b.** The whole playing field. **5.** *Printing.* A small type size, 4½-point.
~*adj.* **1.** Of, resembling, or made with diamonds. **2.** Designating a 60th, or sometimes a 75th, anniversary: *diamond jubilee.*
~*tr.v.* **diamonded, -monding, -monds.** To adorn with or as with diamonds. [Middle English *diamaunt,* from Old French *diamant,* from Late Latin *diamas* (stem *diamant-*), variant of Vulgar Latin *adimas* (unattested), variant of Latin *adamas,* from Greek. See **adamant.**]

diamond *The many facets cut in this gemstone give it its brilliance. Because of their hardness, diamonds are also used as cutting tools in industry and science.*

dia·mond·back (dī′mənd-băk′, dī′ə-) *n.* **1.** Any of several large, venomous rattlesnakes of the genus *Crotalus,* of the southern and western United States and Mexico, having diamond-shaped markings. Also called "diamondback rattlesnake." **2.** Any of several turtles of the genus *Malaclemys,* of the southern Atlantic and Gulf coasts of the United States, having edible flesh and a carapace with roughly diamond-shaped, ridged or knobbed markings. Also called "diamondback terrapin." **3.** A moth, *Plutella maculipennis,* that is highly destructive to vegetables.

diamondback *A coiled diamondback, one of the largest and most dangerous rattlesnakes, disturbed and getting ready to strike. The snake can grow to 2.5 meters (8 feet) long.*

diamond bird *n.* Any bird of the species *Pardalotus,* found in Australia and Tasmania. Also called "pardalote." [From the diamond-shaped pattern of its plumage.]

Diamond Head. A promontory, 232 meters (761 feet) high, on the southeastern coast of Oahu Island in Hawaii. It is a famous symbol of the Hawaiian Islands and is now a national landmark to protect it from commercial development along Waikiki Beach.

dia·mond·if·er·ous (dī′mən-dĭf′ər-əs, dī′ə-) *adj.* Bearing or yielding diamonds.

diamond point *n.* A diamond-tipped stylus used for engraving.

dia·monds (dī′məndz, dī′ə-) *n. Used with a singular or plural verb.* One of the four suits of playing cards, distinguished by red diamond-shaped figures printed on the face of each card.

Di·an·a[1] (dī-ăn′ə). Princess of Wales, formerly Lady Diana Spencer (1961–). She married Charles, Prince of Wales and heir to the British throne, in a highly publicized wedding (1981). She is the mother of Prince William (1982–), second heir to the throne, and Prince Henry (1984–).

Diana[2]. *Roman Mythology.* The goddess of chastity, hunting, and the moon; identified with the Greek goddess Artemis.

Diana[3] *n. Poetic.* The moon. [From DIANA (moon goddess).]

di·an·drous (dī-ăn′drəs) *adj. Botany.* Having two stamens. [DI- (two) + -ANDROUS.]

Di·a·net·ics (dī′ə-nĕt′ĭks). A trademark used by the Church of Scientology and its affiliated organizations to designate the spiritual healing, technology, and related products and services offered by the Church and affiliated organizations and based on the writings of L. Ron Hubbard. See **Scientology.**

di·a·no·et·ic (dī′ə-nō-ĕt′ĭk) *adj.* Of or pertaining to reasoning; intellectual. [Greek *dianoētikos,* from *dianoia,* thought, process of thinking : *dia-,* through + *nous,* mind.]

di·an·thus (dī-ăn′thəs) *n.* Any plant of the genus *Dianthus,* which includes carnations and pinks. [New Latin *Dianthus* : DI- (two) + Greek *anthos,* flower.]

di·a·pa·son (dī′ə-pā′sən, -zən) *n. Music.* **1.** Either of the two principal stops on a pipe organ, the *open diapason* and the *stopped diapason,* which form the tonal basis for the entire scale of the instrument. **2. a.** The full range of notes; the compass of a voice or instrument. **b.** Range; breadth; scope. **3.** A former standard indication of pitch fixed in 1859 by the French Commission at the note A. Also called "diapason normal." See **concert pitch. 4.** A swelling burst of harmonious sound. [Middle English *dyapason,* from Latin *diapāsōn,* from Greek *(hē) dia pasōn (khordōn sumphonia),* (concord) through all (the notes) : *dia-,* through + *pasōn,* feminine genitive plural of *pas,* all.]

di·a·pause (dī′ə-pôz′) *n. Biology.* A period during which growth or development is suspended, as in certain insects. [Greek *diapausis,* pause, from *diapauein,* to rest between times, pause : *dia-,* between + *pauein,* to stop, cease.]

di·a·pe·de·sis (dī′ə-pə-dē′sĭs) *n.* The passing of blood or any constituents, especially erythrocytes, through intact blood-vessel walls. [New Latin, from Greek *diapēdēsis,* "a leaping through," from *diapēdan,* to leap through, ooze : *dia-,* through + *pēdan,* to leap.] **—di·a·pe·det·ic** (dī′ə-pə-dĕt′ĭk) *adj.*

di·a·per (dī′ə-pər, dī′pər) *n.* **1.** A folded piece of cloth or other absorbent material placed between a baby's legs and pinned at the waist. Also *chiefly British* "nappy." **2.** A white cotton or linen fabric patterned with small diamond-shaped figures. **3.** A piece of such cloth, or such a pattern.
~*tr.v.* **diapered, -pering, -pers. 1.** To put a diaper on (a baby). **2.** To weave or decorate in a diamond-shaped pattern. [Middle English, from Old French *dia(s)pre,* from Medieval Latin *diasprum,* from Greek *diaspros,* ecclesiastical : DIA- (intensive) + *aspros,* white.]

di·aph·a·nous (dī-ăf′ə-nəs) *adj.* **1.** Allowing light to show through; transparent or translucent. **2.** Characterized by lightness or delicacy of form. [Medieval Latin *diaphanus,* from Greek *diaphanēs,* from *diaphanein,* to show through : *dia-,* through + *phainein,* to show.] —**di·aph·a·nous·ly** *adv.* —**di·aph·a·nous·ness** *n.*

di·aph·o·ny (dī-ăf′ə-nē) *n., pl.* **-nies.** *Music.* A simple form of polyphony; organum. [Medieval Latin *diaphonia,* from Greek *diaphōnia,* discord, dissonance, from *diaphōnos,* dissonant : *dia-,* apart + *phōnē,* sound.] —**di·a·phon·ic** (dī′ə-fŏn′ĭk) *adj.*

di·a·pho·re·sis (dī′ə-fə-rē′sĭs) *n.* Perspiration, especially when copious and medically induced. [Late Latin *diaphorēsis,* from Greek, from *diaphorein,* to disperse abroad (by perspiration) : *dia-,* in different directions + *phorein,* frequentative of *pherein,* to carry.]

di·a·pho·ret·ic (dī′ə-fə-rĕt′ĭk) *adj.* Producing perspiration. ∼*n.* A diaphoretic medicine or agent.

di·a·phragm (dī′ə-frăm′) *n.* **1.** *Anatomy.* A muscular membranous partition separating the abdominal and thoracic cavities and functioning in respiration. **2.** Any similar membranous part that divides or separates, such as a semipermeable membrane separating two solutions. **3.** A thin disk, especially in a microphone or telephone receiver, the vibrations of which convert electric to acoustic signals or acoustic to electric signals. **4.** A contraceptive consisting of a flexible cap that covers the uterine cervix. Also called "Dutch cap." **5.** A disk having a fixed or variable opening used to restrict the amount of light traversing a lens or optical system. [Middle English *diafragma,* from Late Latin *diaphragma,* from Greek, from *diaphrassein,* to barricade : *dia-,* completely + *phrassein,* to enclose.] —**di·a·phrag·mat·ic** (dī′ə-frăg-măt′ĭk) *adj.* —**di·a·phrag·mat·i·cal·ly** *adv.*

di·aph·y·sis (dī-ăf′ə-sĭs) *n., pl.* **-ses** (-sēz′). The shaft of a long bone. [New Latin, from Greek *diaphusis,* spinous process of the tibia, from *diaphuesthai,* to grow between : *dia-,* between + *phuesthai,* middle voice of *phuein,* to bring forth, beget.] —**di·a·phys·i·al** (dī′-ə-fĭz′ē-əl) *adj.*

di·a·poph·y·sis (dī′ə-pŏf′ĭ-sĭs) *n., pl.* **-ses** (-sēz). The superior or articular surface of a transverse vertebral process. —**di·ap·o·phys·i·al** (dī-ăp′ə-fĭz′ē-əl) *adj.*

di·ap·sid (dī-ăp′sĭd) *n.* In some classifications, a reptile of the subclass *Diapsidia,* having the upper and lower temporal regions of the skull distinct. [New Latin : DI- + Greek *hapsis* (stem *hapsid-*), arch.] —**di·ap·sid** *adj.*

di·ar·chy, dy·ar·chy (dī′är′kē) *n., pl.* **-chies.** Government by two joint rulers or ruling bodies. [DI- (two) + -ARCHY.] —**di·ar·chic** (dī′är′kĭk) *adj.*

di·a·rist (dī′ə-rĭst) *n.* A person who keeps a diary recording personal experiences and observations.

di·ar·rhe·a, di·ar·rhoe·a (dī′ə-rē′ə) *n.* **1.** Excessive and frequent evacuation of watery feces. **2.** Such feces themselves. **3.** Any uncontrolled, excessive outpouring: *verbal diarrhea.* [Middle English *diaria,* from Late Latin *diarrhœa,* from Greek *diarrhoia,* "a flowing through," from *diarrhein,* to flow through : *dia-,* through + *rhein,* to flow.] —**di·ar·rhe·al, di·ar·rhe·ic, di·ar·rhet·ic** *adj.*

di·ar·thro·sis (dī′är-thrō′sĭs) *n., pl.* **-ses** (-sēz′). Any of several types of bone articulation permitting free motion in a joint. [New Latin, from Greek *diarthrōsis,* from *diarthroun,* to fasten by a joint, articulate : *dia-,* between + *arthroun,* to fasten, from *arthron,* joint.] —**di·ar·thro·di·al** *adj.*

di·a·ry (dī′ə-rē) *n., pl.* **-ries.** **1.** A daily record, especially a personal record of events, experiences, and observations, or of engagements and appointments. **2.** A book for keeping such a record; a journal. [Latin *diārium,* daily allowance, journal, from *diēs,* day.]

Di·as (dē′əs), **Bartolomeu** (*c.* 1450–1500). Portuguese navigator. In 1487 he set sail for Africa, but was blown off course by gales and rounded the Cape of Good Hope without sighting it. On his return from the Indian Ocean (1488) he finally sighted the Cape, the first European to do so, and named it the Cape of Storms.

di·a·scope (dī′ə-skōp) *n.* **1.** A projector used to throw an optical image of a transparency onto a screen. Compare **epidiascope.** **2.** *Pathology.* A flat glass plate that is pressed against the skin in order to examine superficial lesions. [DIA- + -SCOPE.]

Di·as·po·ra (dī-ăs′pər-ə) *n.* **1. a.** The dispersion of the Jews after the Babylonian captivity. Also called the "Dispersion." **b.** The body of Jews living dispersed among the Gentiles after the Babylonian captivity. **2.** The aggregate of Jews living outside Israel. **3.** In the New Testament, the body of Christians living outside Palestine. **4.** *Often* **diaspora.** A dispersion, as of any originally homogeneous people. [Greek, "dispersion" (Deuteronomy 28:25), from *diaspeirein,* to disperse : *dia-,* apart + *speirein,* to scatter.]

di·a·spore (dī′ə-spôr′, -spōr′) *n.* A white, pearly hydrous aluminum oxide, $Al_2O_3·H_2O$, found with corundum and emery and in bauxite. It is used as a refractory and abrasive. [Greek *diaspora,* scattering, DIASPORA (from the strong decrepitation of the mineral before the blowpipe).]

di·a·stase (dī′ə-stās′) *n.* An amylase or a mixture of amylases that converts starch to maltose, found in certain germinating grains such as malt. [French, from Greek *diastasis,* separation, DIASTASIS.] —**di·a·sta·sic, di·a·stat·ic** (dī′ə-stăt′ĭk) *adj.*

di·as·ta·sis (dī-ăs′tə-sĭs) *n., pl.* **-ses** (-sēz). **1.** *Pathology.* Separation of certain muscles during pregnancy, or of normally adjacent, unjoined bones without fracture. **2.** *Physiology.* The last stage of diastole in the heart, occurring prior to contraction and during which little blood enters the filled ventricle. [New Latin, from Greek, separation, from *diistanai,* to set apart : *dia-,* apart + *histanai,* to cause to stand, set.] —**di·a·stat·ic** (dī′ə-stăt′ĭk) *adj.*

di·a·ste·ma (dī′ə-stē′mə) *n., pl.* **-mata** (-mə-tə). **1.** Any bodily fissure or cleft, especially if congenital. **2.** An abnormally large space between teeth. [New Latin, from Late Latin *diastēma,* from Greek, interval, aperture, from *diistanai,* to set apart. See **diastasis.**]

di·as·ter (dī′ăs-tər) *n. Biology.* **Anaphase** *(see).* Not in current technical usage. [DI- (two) + Greek *astēr,* star.] —**di·as·tral** *adj.*

di·as·to·le (dī-ăs′tə-lē) *n. Physiology.* The normal rhythmically occurring relaxation and dilatation of the heart cavities, during which the cavities are filled with blood. [Greek *diastolē,* dilatation, separation, from *diastellein,* to expand, separate : *dia-,* apart + *stellein,* to put.] —**di·a·stol·ic** (dī′ə-stŏl′ĭk) *adj.*

di·as·tro·phism (dī-ăs′trə-fĭz′əm) *n.* The process or series of processes by which the major features of the earth's crust, including continents, mountains, and ocean basins, are formed. [Greek *diastrophē,* twisting, distortion, from *diastrephein,* to twist different ways, distort : *dia-,* in different directions + *strephein,* to turn, twist.] —**di·a·stroph·ic** (dī′ə-strŏf′ĭk) *adj.*

di·a·style (dī′ə-stīl′) *adj. Architecture.* Having intervals of three to four diameters between the columns. ∼*n. Architecture.* A diastyle building or arrangement of columns. [Latin, from Greek *diastūlos,* having spaced pillars : *dia-,* apart, through + *stūlos,* column, STYLE.]

di·a·tes·sa·ron (dī′ə-tĕs′ər-ən) *n.* **1.** In Greek and medieval music, the interval of a fourth. **2.** A single narrative made by combining the four Gospels. [Middle English, from Late Latin, from Greek *dia tessarōn,* consisting of four : *dia,* made out of + *tessarōn,* genitive of *tessares,* four.]

di·a·ther·mic (dī′ə-thûr′mĭk) *adj.* **1.** Capable of transmitting heat or infrared radiation. **2.** Of or pertaining to diathermy.

di·a·ther·my (dī′ə-thûr′mē) *n.* The therapeutic generation of local heat in body tissues by high-frequency electromagnetic waves. [DIA-, across, by transmission + Greek *thermē,* heat (see **therm**).]

di·ath·e·sis (dī-ăth′ə-sĭs) *n., pl.* **-ses** (-sēz′). A familial predisposition of the body to a disease, group of diseases, or structural or metabolic abnormality. [New Latin, from Greek, disposition, bodily state, from *diatithenai,* to dispose : *dia-,* in different directions + *tithenai,* to put, set.] —**di·a·thet·ic** (dī′ə-thĕt′ĭk) *adj.*

di·a·tom (dī′ə-tŏm′, -təm) *n.* Any of various minute, unicellular or colonial algae of the class Bacillariophyceae, having siliceous cell walls consisting of two overlapping, symmetrical parts. [New Latin *diatoma,* from Greek *diatomē,* feminine of *diatomos,* cut in half, from *diatemnein,* to cut through, cut in half : *dia-,* through + *temnein,* to cut.]

di·a·to·ma·ceous (dī′ə-tə-mā′shəs) *adj.* Consisting of diatoms or their siliceous skeletons.

diatomaceous earth *n.* Diatomite.

di·a·tom·ic (dī′ə-tŏm′ĭk) *adj.* **1.** Made up of two atoms. Said of a molecule. **2.** Having two replaceable atoms or radicals.

di·at·o·mite (dī-ăt′ə-mīt′) *n.* A fine, powdered siliceous earth, composed of the skeletons of diatoms, used in industry as a filler, filtering agent, absorbent, clarifier, and insulator. Also called "diatomaceous earth," "kieselguhr."

diatom ooze *n.* A siliceous sediment composed largely of the skeletons of diatoms, found on the deep (abyssal) ocean floor and on lake beds.

di·a·ton·ic (dī′ə-tŏn′ĭk) *adj. Music.* Of or using only the eight notes of a standard major or minor scale without chromatic variations. [French *diatonique,* from Late Latin *diatonicus,* from Greek *diatonikos,* from *diatonos,* "at the interval of a tone" : *dia-,* throughout, at the interval of + *tonos,* TONE.] —**di·a·ton·i·cal·ly** *adv.* —**di·a·ton·i·cism** (dī′ə-tŏn′ə-sĭz′əm) *n.*

di·a·tribe (dī′ə-trīb′) *n.* A bitter and abusive criticism or denunciation; invective. [Latin *diatriba,* learned discourse, from Greek *diatribē,* "a wearing away," from *diatribein,* to rub hard, rub away, consume (time) : *dia-,* completely + *tribein,* to rub, wear out.]

di·at·ro·pism (dī-ăt′rə-pĭz′əm) *n.* The tendency of certain organisms or their parts to arrange themselves at right angles to the direction of a stimulus. [DIA- (over across, at right angles) + -TROPISM.] —**di·a·trop·ic** (dī′ə-trŏp′ĭk) *adj.*

Di·az (dē′äs), **Porfirio** (1830–1915). Mexican soldier and politician. He became president of Mexico in 1876 following a coup and remained in office until 1880. He served a second term as president (1884–1911) but was forced to flee and died in exile.

di·az·e·pam (dī-ăz′ə-păm′) *n.* A tranquilizer, **Valium** *(see).*

di·a·zine (dī′ə-zēn′, -zĭn, dī-ăz′ĭn) *n.* A compound containing a benzene ring in which two of the carbon atoms have been replaced by nitrogen atoms; especially, any of three compounds so structured and having the composition $C_4H_4N_2$. [DIAZ(O) + -INE.]

di·az·o (dī-ăz′ō) *adj.* Of, pertaining to, or consisting of a pair of nitrogen atoms bonded to each other and to an organic radical. [DI- (two) + A- (not) + Greek *zoē,* life.]

di·a·zole (dī-ā′zōl, -ăz′ōl) *n.* An organic chemical in which the molecules contain a five-membered ring consisting of three carbon atoms and two nitrogen atoms.

di·az·o·me·thane (dī-ā′zō-mĕth′ān, -ăz′ō-) *n.* A yellow explosive gas, CH_2:N:N, used as a methylating agent.

di·a·zo·ni·um (dī′ə-zō′nē-əm) *adj.* Of, pertaining to, or containing the univalent cation RN^2 +, where R is an aromatic hydrocarbon radical. [DIAZ(O) + (AMM)ONIUM.]

diazonium salt *n.* An organic compound with the general formula RN^2 + X-, where R is an aromatic hydrocarbon and X^- is an anion, such as the chloride ion, Cl^-.

di·az·o·tize (dī-ăz′ə-tīz′) *tr.v.* **-tized, -tizing, -tizes.** To cause (an aromatic hydrocarbon) to react with nitrous acid to produce a diazonium salt. —**di·az·o·ti·za·tion** (dī-ăz′ə-tə-zā′shən) *n.*

di·ba·sic (dī-bā′sĭk) *adj. Chemistry.* **1.** Containing two replaceable

PRONUNCIATION KEY

ă, pat; ā, pay; âr, care; ä, father, are; b, bib; ch, church; d, deed; ĕ, pet; ē, be; f, fife; g, gag; h, hat; hw, which; ĭ, pit; ī, pie; îr, pier; j, judge; k, kick; l, lid, needle; m, mum; n, no, sudden; ng, thing; ŏ, pot; ō, toe; ô, paw, for; oi, noise; ou, out; ŏŏ, book; ōō, boot; p, pop; r, roar; s, sauce; sh, ship, dish; t, tight; th, thin, path; *th*, this, bathe; ŭ, cut; ûr, fur; v, valve; w, with; y, yes; z, zebra, size; zh, vision; ə, about, item, edible, gallop, circus, peaceful

IN FOREIGN WORDS:

à, *Fr.* ami; œ, *Fr.* feu, *Ger.* schön; ü, *Fr.* tu, *Ger.* über; KH, *Ger.* ich, *Scot.* loch; N, *Fr.* bon; y′, *Fr.* Compiègne

STRESS MARKS:

Primary stress: ′ **in·cite′** (ĭn-sīt′)
Secondary stress: ′ **in′sight′** (ĭn′sīt′)

Dickens

THE MASTER STORYTELLER OF VICTORIAN ENGLAND

A gallery of immortal characters sprang to life from his pen

Charles Dickens was born in 1812 near Portsmouth—and his childhood was miserable. He had little regular schooling and, at the age of 12, after his father was jailed in London for debt, he was put to work in a shoe polish factory. The experience left him with an enduring sense of the intense harshness of industrial life in Victorian England and this provided the theme for such somber novels as *Bleak House* and *Hard Times*. He died suddenly of a stroke in June 1870, leaving unfinished his novel *The Mystery of Edwin Drood*.

AUTHOR'S DREAM *In this portrait Dickens dozes in his study, dreaming of the characters that crowd his books. Among them are Mr. Pickwick and Sam Weller, the comic heroes of his first literary success,* The Pickwick Papers *(published as a series of monthly chapters in 1836–37); Mr. Micaw-ber, the character based on Dickens's own father in the largely autobiographical novel* David Copperfield *(also published monthly in 1849–50); Fagin of* Oliver Twist *(published monthly in 1836–37); and the miser Scrooge in* A Christmas Carol *(1843).*

hydrogen atoms. **2.** Designating salts, or acids forming salts, with two atoms of a univalent metal. See **diacidic.** [DI- + BASIC.]

dib·ble¹ (dĭb'əl) *n.* Also **dib·ber** (dĭb'ər). A pointed gardening implement used to make holes in soil, especially for planting bulbs or seedlings.
~*tr.v.* **dibbled, -bling, -bles. 1.** To make holes in (soil) with a dibble. **2.** To plant by means of a dibble. [Middle English *debylle†*.]

dib·ble² *intr.v.* **-bled, -bling, -bles.** Also **dib** (dĭb), **dibbed, dibbing, dibs.** *British Regional.* In angling, to dip bait gently up and down in the water. [Probably variant of obsolete *dib*, to tap, dip, variant of DAB.]

di·bran·chi·ate (dī-brăng'kē-ĭt) *n.* Any of various two-gilled cephalopod mollusc of the former order Dibranchiata, which includes the octopuses, cuttlefish, and squids.
~*adj.* Of or belonging to the Dibranchiata. [New Latin *Dibranchiata* : DI- + BRANCHIATE.]

di·bro·mide (dī-brō'mīd', -mĭd) *n.* A binary chemical compound containing two bromine atoms per molecule.

dibs (dĭbz) *pl.n. Slang.* Money, especially in small amounts. —**dibs on something.** *Slang.* A claim on (something); rights. [Short for *dibstones*, a children's game played with knucklebones, hence knucklebones, counters used in a game, money, probably from *dib*, to tap, dip, variant of DAB.]

di·car·box·yl·ic (dī-kär'bŏk-sĭl'ĭk) *adj.* Designating an acid that contains two carboxyl groups per molecule.

di·cast (dī'kăst', dĭk'əst) *n.* In ancient Athens, one of the 6,000 citizens chosen each year to sit in the law courts, with functions resembling those of a judge and juror. [Greek *dikastēs*, judge, from *dikazein*, to judge, from *dikē*, custom, right, lawsuit.] —**di·cas·tic** *adj.*

dice (dīs) *n., pl.* **dice.** Also *singular* **die** (dī) (for sense 1). **1.** A small cube, as of ivory, bone, or plastic, marked on each side with a pattern of small dots, numbering from one to six, and used, usually in pairs, in games of chance. **2.** Any game of chance using dice. **3.** Any small cube. —**no dice.** *Slang.* **1.** Used to express a refusal. **2.** No luck or success.
~*v.* **diced, dicing, dices.** —*intr.* **1.** To play or gamble with dice.

2. To take risks: *dice with death.* —*tr.* **1.** To win or lose (money) by gambling with dice. **2.** To cut (food) into small cubes. **3.** To decorate with a pattern of squares. [Plural of DIE (cube).] —**dic·er** *n.*

di·cen·tra (dī-sĕn'trə) *n.* Any plant of the genus *Dicentra*, which includes the **bleeding-heart** and **Dutchman's-breeches** (*both of which see*). [New Latin *Dicentra*, "two-spurred" (from its dissected leaves) : di- (two) + Greek *kentron*, spur, point, center, from *kentein*, to prick.]

di·cey (dī'sē) *adj.* **-cier, -ciest.** Risky; unreliable. [From DICE (hence, risky).]

di·cha·si·um (dī-kā'zhē-əm) *n., pl.* **-sia** (-zhē-ə). *Botany.* A cyme in which two lateral branches occur at approximately the same level. Compare **monochasium.** [New Latin, from Greek *dikhasis*, division, from *dikhazein*, to divide in two, from *dikha*, in two.] —**di·cha·si·al** *adj.* —**di·cha·si·al·ly** *adv.*

di·chlo·ride (dī-klôr'īd, -ĭd, dī-klōr'-) *n.* A binary chemical compound containing two chloride atoms per molecule. Also called "bichloride."

di·chlo·ro·di·fluo·ro·me·thane (dī-klôr'ō-dī-flôr'ō-mĕth'ăn, -flōr'ō-, dī-klōr'-) *n.* A colorless nonflammable gas, CCl_2F_2, used as an aerosol propellant, fire extinguisher, and refrigerant. See **Freon.**

di·chlor·o·di·phen·yl·tri·chlor·o·eth·ane (dī-klôr'ō-dī-fĕn'-əl-trī-klôr'ō-ĕth'ăn', -klôr'ō-ĕth'ăn', dī-klôr'-) *n.* An organic compound, DDT (*see*).

dicho- *prefix.* Indicates two parts or a division into two parts; for example, **dichotomy, dichogamous.** [Late Latin, from Greek *dikho-*, from *dikha*, in two.]

di·chog·a·mous (dī-kŏg'ə-məs) *adj.* Having pistils and stamens that mature at different times, thus ensuring cross-fertilization rather than self-pollination. [DICHO- + -GAMOUS.] —**di·chog·a·my** *n.*

di·chot·o·mize (dī-kŏt'ə-mīz') *v.* **-mized, -mizing, -mizes.** —*tr.* To separate into two parts or classifications. —*intr.* To be or become divided into parts or branches; fork. —**di·chot·o·mist** *n.* —**di·chot·o·mi·za·tion** *n.*

di·chot·o·mous (dī-kŏt'ə-məs) *adj.* Also **di·cho·tom·ic** (dī'kə-tŏm'-ĭk). **1.** Divided or dividing into two parts or classifications. **2.** Characterized by dichotomy. —**di·chot·o·mous·ly** *adv.*

di·chot·o·my (dī-kŏt'ə-mē) *n., pl.* **-mies. 1. a.** Division into two usually contradictory parts or opinions; schism. **b.** Loosely, a lack of agreement or correspondence; discrepancy: *a dichotomy between their election promises and their performance.* **2.** *Logic.* The division or subdivision of a class into two mutually exclusive groups: *the dichotomy of truth and falsehood.* **3.** *Astronomy.* The phase of the moon, Mercury, or Venus when half of the disk is illuminated. **4.** *Botany.* Branching characterized by successive forking into two approximately equal divisions. [Greek *dikhotomia*, from *dikhotomos*, divided : DICHO- + *temnein*, to cut.]

di·chro·ic (dī-krō'ĭk) *adj.* Also **di·chro·it·ic** (dī'krō-ĭt'ĭk). **1.** Manifesting dichroism. **2.** Dichromatic. [Greek *dikhroos*, two-colored : DI- (two) + -CHROOUS.]

di·chro·ism (dī'krō-ĭz'əm) *n.* **1.** *Chemistry.* The property of showing different colors depending on the thickness of the medium and the relative concentration of coloring matter in it. **2.** The property possessed by some crystals of exhibiting different colors, especially two different colors, when viewed along different axes. Compare **pleochroism.** [Greek *dikhroos*, two-colored, DICHROIC.]

di·chro·ite (dī-krō'īt') *n.* A mineral, **cordierite** (*see*). [DICHRO(IC) + -ITE.]

di·chro·mate (dī-krō'māt') *n.* Any chemical compound which is a salt of the hypothetical acid, dichromic acid. A dichromate usually has a characteristic red-orange color. Also called "bichromate."

di·chro·mat·ic (dī'krō-măt'ĭk) *adj.* **1.** Possessing or exhibiting two colors. **2.** *Zoology.* Having two distinct color phases in the adult. Said of certain species of birds. **3.** *Pathology.* Capable of distinguishing only two colors. Also "dichroic," "dichromic."

di·chro·ma·tism (dī-krō'mə-tĭz'əm) *n.* The quality or condition of being dichromatic.

di·chro·mic (dī-krō'mĭk) *adj.* **1.** Dichromatic. **2.** *Chemistry.* Containing two chromium atoms per molecule.

dichromic acid *n.* An acid, $H_2Cr_2O_7$, known only in solution.

dick¹ *n. Slang.* A detective. [Shortened from DETECTIVE.]

dick² (dĭk) *n. British Slang.* A fellow. [From *Dick*, nickname for *Richard.*]

Dick (dĭk), **George Frederick** (1881-1967) and **Gladys Henry** (1881-1963). U.S. medical researchers. As a husband and wife team, they isolated the germ that causes scarlet fever and developed preventive medicine for the disease (1923). The next year they developed the Dick test, which determines a person's susceptibility to the disease.

dick·cis·sel (dĭk-sĭs'əl) *n.* A sparrowlike bird, *Spiza americana*, of central North America, of which the male has a yellow breast marked with black. [Imitative of its note.]

dick·ens (dĭk'ənz) *n.* Deuce; devil: *"I cannot tell what the dickens his name is"* (Shakespeare). [16th century : perhaps euphemistic for *(Old) Nick.*]

Dick·ens (dĭk'ənz), **Charles** (1812-70). British novelist. The son of an admiralty clerk who was imprisoned for debt, he was sent to work in a blacking factory at the age of 12. This, together with his school experiences, provided much of the material for his largely autobiographical *David Copperfield* (1849-50). After working in a solicitor's office, he became a journalist, going on to write sketches under the pen name "Boz" for the *Monthly Magazine*. The *Pickwick*

Papers, published from 1836 to 1837, established his popularity. His novels became an influential protest against the squalor and vices of Victorian society. Among his best-known books are *Oliver Twist, A Christmas Carol, Bleak House, A Tale of Two Cities, The Old Curiosity Shop, Nicholas Nickleby,* and *Great Expectations.*

Dick·en·si·an (dĭ-kĕn′zē-ən) *adj.* Of or characteristic of Charles Dickens, his novels, settings, and characters, or his literary style; especially, reminiscent of: **a.** The grim conditions of urban squalor and deprivation described in some of Dickens's novels: *the factory's Dickensian working conditions.* **b.** The cozy Victorian jollity of Dickens's sentimental family scenes.

dick·er (dĭk′ər) *v.* **-ered, -ering, -ers.** *—intr.* **1.** To bargain; barter; haggle. **2.** In politics, to make or attempt to make a deal by bargaining and barter. *—tr.* To trade or exchange.
~*n.* Barter or bargaining. [Probably from obsolete *dicker,* ten, ten hides (used as a unit of trade), Middle English *dyke,* Old English *dicor* (unattested), from West Germanic *dicura* (unattested), from Latin *dicuria,* set of ten, from *decem,* ten.]

dick·ey (dĭk′ē) *n., pl.* **-eys.** Also **dick·ie, dick·y** *pl.* **-ies. 1.** A woman's blouse front worn under a suit jacket or low-necked garment. **2.** A detachable shirt front. **3.** A collar for a shirt. **4.** A child's bib. **5.** A donkey. **6.** *Informal.* Any small bird. Also called "dickybird." **7.** Either of two seats on a carriage, the forward outside driver's seat or a rear seat for servants. [From *Dick,* nickname for *Richard.*]

Dick·ey (dĭk′ē), **James** (1923–). U.S. poet. His volumes of energetic and technically versatile poetry include *Drowning with Others* (1962), *Helmets* (1964), and *Buckdancer's Choice* (1965). He is probably best known for his novel, *Deliverance* (1969), which was made into a highly successful motion picture.

Dick·in·son (dĭk′ən-sən), **Emily Elizabeth** (1830–86). U.S. poet. She wrote over 1,700 poems, although only 7 were published in her lifetime. The first volume of her work appeared in 1890.

Dick test *n.* A skin test for susceptibility to scarlet fever. [After Gladys and George **Dick**.]

di·cli·nous (dī-klī′nəs) *adj. Botany.* **1.** Having stamens and pistils in separate flowers: *a diclinous plant.* **2.** Having pistils but not stamens, or stamens but not pistils: *diclinous flowers.* [DI- (two) + Greek *klinē,* bed.] **—di·cli·ny** (dī′klī-nē) *n.*

di·cot·y·le·don (dī′kŏt′l-ēd′n) *n.* Also **di·cot** (dī′kŏt). Any plant of the Dicotyledoneae, one of the two major divisions of angiosperms, characterized by a pair of embryonic seed leaves that appear at germination, and including many trees, shrubs, and other flowering plants. Compare **monocotyledon. —di·cot·y·le·don·ous** *adj.*

di·cro·tism (dī′krə-tĭz′əm) *n.* A pathological doubling of the pulse with each beat of the heart. [From Greek *dikrotos,* double-beating : DI- (two) + *krotein,* to strike.] **—di·crot·ic** (dī-krŏt′ĭk) *adj.*

dict. 1. dictation. **2.** dictionary.

dic·ta. Plural of **dictum.**

Dic·ta·phone (dĭk′tə-fōn′) *n.* A trademark for a recording apparatus used for office dictation.

dic·tate (dĭk′tāt′, dĭk-tāt′) *v.* **-tated, -tating, -tates.** *—tr.* **1.** To say or read aloud (something to be recorded or written by another). **2.** To prescribe expressly and with authority: *dictate a command.* **3.** To influence decisively; determine: *The choice of computer was dictated by the company's special needs.* *—intr.* **1.** To say or read aloud material to be transcribed by another. **2. a.** To issue orders or commands. **b.** To adopt an authoritarian attitude.
~*n.* (dĭk′tāt′). A directive or command: *the dictates of common sense.* [Latin *dictāre,* frequentative of *dīcere,* to say, tell.]

dic·ta·tion (dĭk-tā′shən) *n. Abbr.* **dict. 1.** The process of dictating material to another for transcription. **2.** The material dictated. **3.** *Formal.* Authoritative command or prescription; dictate.

dic·ta·tor (dĭk′tā-tər) *n.* **1.** A ruler having absolute authority and supreme jurisdiction over the government of a state; especially, one who is considered tyrannical or oppressive. **2.** One who has absolute authority or control in a particular sphere. **3.** One who dictates. **4.** In ancient Rome, a government official temporarily invested with absolute authority to deal with an immediate crisis or emergency.

dic·ta·to·ri·al (dĭk′tə-tôr′ē-əl, -tōr′ē-əl) *adj.* **1.** Tending to dictate; overbearing; domineering. **2.** Characteristic of or pertaining to a dictator; autocratic. **—dic·ta·to·ri·al·ly** *adv.* **—dic·ta·to·ri·al·ness** *n.*
Synonyms: *arbitrary, doctrinaire, dogmatic, imperious, overbearing.*

dic·ta·tor·ship (dĭk-tā′tər-shĭp′, dĭk′tā–) *n.* **1.** The office or tenure of office of a dictator. **2.** A state or government under dictatorial rule. **3.** Government by a dictator. **4.** Absolute or despotic control or power.

dic·tion (dĭk′shən) *n.* **1.** Choice and use of words in speech or writing; manner of expression. **2.** The degree of distinctness of speech; the manner of enunciation. [Latin *dictiō* (stem *dictiōn-*), from *dictus,* past participle of *dīcere,* to say.]
Synonyms: *articulation, enunciation.*

dic·tion·ar·y (dĭk′shə-nĕr′ē; *chiefly British* dĭk′shən-ə-rē) *n., pl.* **-ies.** *Abbr.* **dict. 1.** A reference book containing an explanatory alphabetical list of words, as: **a.** A book listing a comprehensive or restricted selection of the words of a language, identifying usually the pronunciation, grammatical function, and meanings of each word, often with other information on its origin and use. **b.** Such a book listing the words or other units of a particular category within a language: *a slang dictionary.* **2.** A book listing the words of a language with translations into another language. **3.** A book listing words or other linguistic items from particular fields, with special-

ized information about them: *a medical dictionary.* **4.** A reference book dealing with a particular subject: *a dictionary of modern history.* [Medieval Latin *dictiōnārium,* from Latin *dictiō,* DICTION.]

Dic·to·graph (dĭk′tə-grăf′, -gräf′) *n.* A trademark for a telephonic instrument that reproduces or records sounds from a transmitter by means of a small microphone.

dic·tum (dĭk′təm) *n., pl.* **dicta** (dĭk′tə) or **-tums. 1.** A dogmatic and authoritative pronouncement. **2.** *Law.* An **obiter dictum** *(see).* **3.** A popular saying; maxim. [Latin, from *dictus,* past participle of *dīcere,* to say.]

did. Past tense of **do.**

Did·a·che (dĭd′ə-kē) *n.* **1.** An anonymous church treatise of the 2nd century or possibly the 1st century A.D., known as the "Teaching of the Twelve Apostles." **2.** *didache. Theology.* The didactic element in early Christian teaching. Compare **kerygma.** [Greek *didakhē,* "a teaching," from *didaskein,* to teach.]

di·dact (dī′dăkt′) *n.* A person who is didactic. [Back-formation from DIDACTIC.]

di·dac·tic (dī-dăk′tĭk) *adj.* **1.** Intended to instruct; expository. **2.** Inclined to teach or moralize; pedantic. **3.** Intended to provide moral instruction, sometimes without regard for interest or style. Said especially of works of literature. [Greek *didaktikos,* skillful in teaching, from *didaktos,* taught, from *didaskein,* to teach.] **—di·dac·ti·cal** *adj.* **—di·dac·ti·cal·ly** *adv.* **—di·dac·ti·cism** (dī-dăk′tə-sĭz′əm) *n.*

di·dac·tics (dī-dăk′tĭks) *n. Used with a singular verb.* The art or science of teaching or instruction; pedagogy.

di·dap·per (dī′dăp′ər) *n.* A small grebe, such as the dabchick. [Middle English *didopper,* variant of *divedap, dovedop,* Old English *dūfedoppa,* pelican : *dūfan,* DIVE + *-doppa,* dapper.]

did·dle¹ (dĭd′l) *v.* **-dled, -dling, -dles.** Also *regional* **dad·dle** (dăd′l). *—tr. Informal.* To cheat; swindle. *—intr.* To waste time; dawdle.
~*n. Informal.* A swindle. [Probably back-formation from Jeremy *Diddler,* a dawdling, swindling character in *Raising the Wind* (1803), a farce by James Kenney, perhaps ultimately related to Old English *dydrian,* to delude, deceive.] **—did·dler** *n.*

diddle² *v.* **-dled, -dling, -dles.** *Scottish.* *—tr.* To jerk back and forth. *—intr.* To move jerkily from side to side; shake. [Perhaps variant of dialectal *didder,* to quiver, Middle English *dideren,* probably variant of *doderen,* perhaps from Middle Low German.]

Di·de·rot (dē′də-rō′), **Denis** (1713–84). French philosopher and writer who helped to create the philosophical movement known as the Enlightenment through the *Encyclopédie* that he edited. This project ran to 28 volumes from 1751 to 1765.

did·ger·i·doo (dĭj′ə-rē-dōō′, dĭj′-ə-rē-dōō′) *n.* An Australian Aboriginal wind instrument, made from a long hollow wooden tube and blown to produce a droning sound. [Imitative.]

did·n't (dĭd′ənt). Contraction of *did not.*

di·do (dī′dō) *n., pl.* **-dos** or **-does.** *Informal.* A mischievous prank or antic; caper. [19th century : origin obscure.]

Di·do (dī′dō). In Virgil's *Aeneid,* a Tyrian princess, founder and queen of Carthage, and lover of Aeneas.

Did·rik·son (dĭd′rĭk-sən), **Mildred Ella,** known as "Babe" (1914–56). U.S. athlete. One of the most talented and versatile athletes ever, she was an all-American basketball player (1930), won two Olympic track and field gold medals (1932), and then became a leading golfer, at one point winning 17 consecutive titles.

didst (dĭdst). *Archaic.* Second person singular, past tense, of **do.** Used with *thou.*

di·dy (dī′dē) *n., pl.* **-dies.** *Informal.* A baby's diaper. Typically said by or to children. [Variant of DIAPER.]

di·dym·i·um (dī-dĭm′ē-əm) *n. Symbol* **Di 1.** A metallic mixture, once considered an element, composed of neodymium and praseodymium. **2.** A mixture of rare-earth elements and oxides used chiefly in manufacturing and coloring various forms of glass. [New Latin, from Greek *didumos,* twin (so named from its association with lanthanum). See **didymous.**]

did·y·mous (dĭd′ə-məs) *adj. Botany.* Arranged or occurring in pairs; twin. [Greek *didumos,* twin.]

di·dyn·a·mous (dī-dĭn′ə-məs) *adj. Botany.* Having four stamens arranged in pairs that differ from one another, especially in length. [New Latin *Didynamia,* a former class of didynamous plants, "having two stamens stronger than the others" : DI- (two) + Greek *dunamis,* power (see **dynamic**).]

die¹ (dī) *v.* **died, dying, dies.** *—intr.* **1.** To cease living; become dead; expire. **2.** To cease existing, especially by degrees; fade or pass away: *The sunlight died in the west.* **3.** To lose vitality, activity, or force; become faint or weak. Often used with *away, out,* or *down: The storm died down.* **4.** To cease existing completely; become extinct. Often used with *off* or *out.* **5.** To cease functioning suddenly: *The engine died.* **6.** To experience the agony or suffering associated with death. **7.** To lose all attachment: *She died to the world.* **8.** *Informal.* To be completely overcome. Often used with *of: We died laughing. They were dying of thirst.* **9.** *Informal.* To desire something greatly or longingly: *dying for a drink; dying to go to the party.* **10.** *Theology.* To experience spiritual death. **11.** *Slang.* To get a very poor reception from an audience. *—tr.* To experience (a specified kind of death): *They died a peaceful death.* [Middle English *d(e)ien, deighen,* from late Old English *diegan,* from Old Norse *deyja.*]
Usage: Die, in its primary sense, it usually followed by *of* when expressing cause: *She died of a heart attack. From* is quite often used in informal speech.

Diesel engine

THE COMPRESSION-IGNITION ENGINE
The economy engine that is fired by hot air

Although the compression-ignition engine was invented in Britain in 1890, it was improved in Germany two years later by Rudolf Diesel. In this engine the fuel is not detonated by a spark as in the conventional internal-combustion engine but by the heat produced when air is compressed in a cylinder. It has several advantages over the gasoline engine. It needs no spark plugs or electric ignition system. Its fuel—diesel oil—is a heavier derivative of crude oil than gasoline and is cheaper.

At first Diesel's design was used as a stationary engine to generate electricity, and as a marine power unit in submarines and ships. Diesel engines are now used also in locomotives, trucks, taxis, buses, and many automobiles.

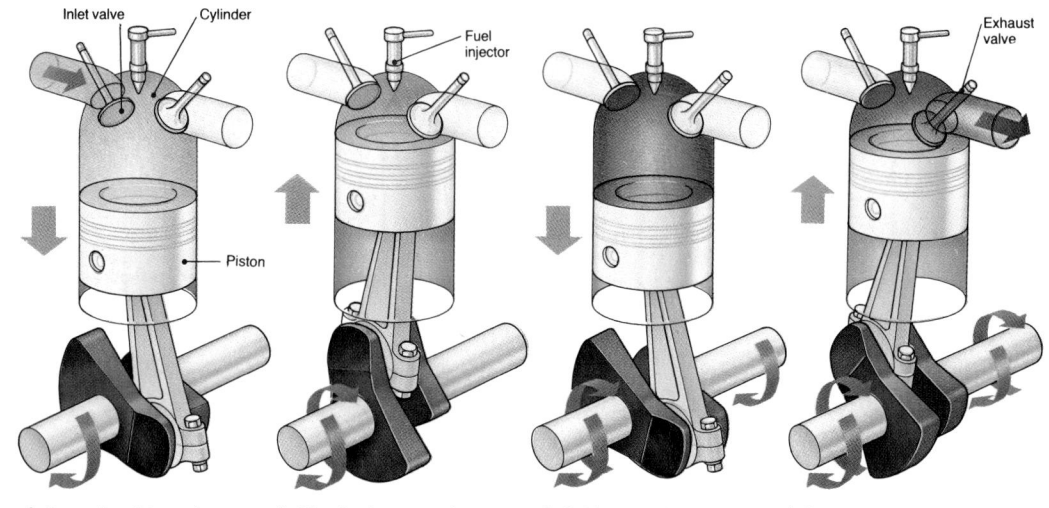

1. *Descending piston sucks air into cylinder through open inlet valve.*

2. *Inlet valve closes; ascending piston compresses and so heats air; fuel is injected.*

3. *Fuel, ignited by the heat, explodes and drives piston down.*

4. *Exhaust valve opens; ascending piston pushes burned gases out of cylinder.*

COMPRESSED POWER *In the diesel engine, the fuel is ignited by the heat developed when air is compressed in the cylinder. On the induction stroke the engine draws in a charge of air, and on the compression stroke subjects it to compression. This heats the air to a very high temperature. Fuel is injected and the temperature of the heated air is sufficient to ignite it.*

---

die² *n., pl.* **dies** (for senses 1, 2) or **dice** (dīs) (for sense 3). **1.** Any of various devices used for cutting out, forming, or stamping material, especially: **a.** An engraved metal piece used for impressing a design upon a softer metal, as in minting coins. **b.** Any of several component pieces that are fitted into a diestock to cut threads on screws or bolts. Compare **tap. c.** A part on a machine that punches shaped holes in, cuts, or forms sheet metal, cardboard, or other material. **d.** A metal block containing small conical holes through which plastic, metal, or other ductile material is extruded or drawn. **2.** *Architecture.* The dado of a pedestal, especially when cube-shaped. **3.** One of a pair of **dice** (*see*). **—the die is cast.** The decision has been made and is irrevocable.
~*tr.v.* **died, dieing, dies.** To cut, form, or stamp with or as with a die. [Middle English *dee,* from Old French *de,* from Vulgar Latin *datum* (unattested), "playing piece," from Latin, neuter past participle of *dare,* to give, "play"; idiom, translation of Latin *alea jacta est,* supposedly said by Julius Caesar upon crossing the Rubicon.]
die back *intr.v.* To be affected by dieback.
die-back (dī′băk′) *n.* A condition leading to the gradual dying of plant shoots, starting at the tips, as a result of various diseases or climatic conditions.
die-cast (dī′kăst′) *tr.v.* **-cast, -casting, -casts.** To form by pressing molten metal into a die under pressure. **—die-cast·er** *n.*
diecious. Variant of **dioecious.**
dief·fen·bach·i·a (dĕf′ən-bäk′ē-ə) *n.* Also **dif·fen·bach·i·a** (dĭf′ən-). Any of various erect evergreen plants of the genus *Dieffenbachia,* native to tropical America, often kept as house plants for their attractive spotted foliage. Also called "dumb cane." [New Latin, after J.F. *Dieffenbach* (1794–1847), German botanist.]
die-hard, die·hard (dī′härd′) *n.* One who stubbornly refuses to abandon a position or resists apparently inevitable change. **—die-hard** *adj.* **—die-hard·ism** *n.*
diel·drin (dēl′drən) *n.* A contact insecticide based on a chlorinated naphthalene derivative, $C_{12}H_8OCl_6$, that is widely used for such purposes as mothproofing furnishings. [From *Diels-Alder* reaction + -IN.]
di·e·lec·tric (dī′ə-lĕk′trĭk) *n.* A nonconductor of electricity; especially, a substance with electrical conductivity of less than a millionth (10^{-6}) of a siemens. [DI(A)- (through) + ELECTRIC.] **—di·e·lec·tric** *adj.* **—di·e·lec·tri·cal·ly** *adv.*
dielectric constant *n.* Relative permittivity. See **permittivity.**
dielectric heating *n.* The heating of electrically nonconducting materials by a rapidly varying electrostatic field, widely used in the manufacture of furniture, plastics, foam rubber, and other products.

Diels (dēlz, dēls), **Otto Paul Herman** (1876–1954). German chemist whose work with Kurt Alder (1902–58) on converting linear organic molecules into cyclic molecules earned them the 1950 Nobel Prize.
Diels-Al·der reaction (dēls′ôl′dər, -ōl′dər) *n.* A chemical reaction in which an aromatic compound is formed from a diene and a compound containing a single double bond. [After Otto DIELS and Kurt *Alder* (1902–58), German chemists.]
Di·em (dē-ĕm′, dyĕm), **Ngo Dinh** (1901–63). Vietnamese political leader. After refusing to join the Communist Party, he fled Vietnam until 1954, when he returned to head the South Vietnamese government. A Catholic, he favored members of his religion in a predominantly Buddhist country. He was assassinated by his generals during a coup d'état.
Dien Bien (dyĕn′ byĕn′). Formerly **Dien Bien Phu** (fōō′). A village in northeast Vietnam, where in 1954 a French fortress fell to Vietminh troops after two months of almost continuous fighting. The defeat led to the French withdrawal from Vietnam.
di·en·ceph·a·lon (dī′ĕn-sĕf′ə-lŏn′) *n.* The posterior part of the forebrain that connects the midbrain with the cerebral hemispheres and contains the thalamus, hypothalamus, and pituitary gland. Also called "interbrain," "thalamencephalon." [New Latin : DI(A)- (between) + ENCEPHALON.]
di·ene (dī′ēn′) *n.* An unsaturated hydrocarbon containing two double bonds. [DI- + -ENE.]
–diene *suffix. Chemistry.* Indicates a compound containing two double bonds; for example, **butadiene.** [DI- (two) + -ENE.]
Di·eppe (dē-ĕp′). Channel port and resort in Seine-Maritime department, northern France.
di·er·e·sis, di·aer·e·sis (dī-ĕr′ĭ-sĭs) *n., pl.* **-ses** (-sēz′). **1.** A mark (¨) placed over the second of two adjacent vowels, and occasionally over a vowel following a consonant, to indicate: **a.** That two separate sounds are to be pronounced; for example, Noël. **b.** That a vowel which might otherwise have been interpreted as mute is to be pronounced; for example, **Brontë.** See **umlaut. 2.** The separation of two adjacent vowels into separate syllables. **3.** In poetry, a slight pause at the end of a line that occurs when the end of a word and the end of a metric foot coincide. Compare **syneresis.** [Late Latin, from Greek *diairesis,* division, separation; from *diairein,* to separate : *dia-,* apart + *hairein,* to take.]
die·sel (dē′zəl, -səl) *n.* **1.** A diesel engine. **2.** A vehicle, especially a locomotive, using a diesel engine. **3.** Diesel fuel. [After Rudolf *Diesel* (1858–1913), German engineer.] **—die·sel** *adj.*
diesel cycle *n.* A four-stroke engine cycle in which combustion

---

takes place at constant pressure and heat is rejected at constant volume. Compare **Otto cycle.**

die·sel·e·lec·tric (dē'zəl-ĭ-lĕk'trĭk, dē'səl-) *adj.* Designating a locomotive in which a diesel engine drives an electric generator, the current from which is used to drive electric motors. —*n.* A diesel-electric locomotive.

diesel engine *n. Sometimes* **Diesel.** An internal-combustion engine that uses heat caused by high compression, rather than a spark plug, to ignite the fuel mixture. Also called "diesel motor," "diesel," "compression-ignition engine." [See **diesel.**]

diesel fuel *n.* A petroleum-based fuel used for diesel engines. Also called "diesel."

die·sel·ize (dē'zə-līz', -sə-līz') *tr.v.* **-ized, -izing, -izes.** To equip with a diesel engine or machinery using diesel engines.

Di·es I·rae (dī'ēz ī'rē; *Latin* dē'ās ē'rī) *n.* A medieval Latin hymn describing the Day of Judgment, used in some Masses for the dead. [Latin, "day of wrath."]

di·e·sis (dī'ə-sĭs) *n., pl.* **-ses** (-sēz') The **double dagger** *(see).* [Middle English, semitone, interval of a semitone (often indicated by a double dagger), from Latin, quarter tone, from Greek, "a letting through," from *diienai,* send through, discharge : *dia-,* through + *hienai,* to send.]

di·es non (dī'ēz nŏn') *n. Law.* A day on which courts may not convene nor any legal business be transacted. Also called "dies non juridicus." Compare **juridical days.** [Latin, short for *dies non juridicus,* "day without courts."]

die·stock (dī'stŏk') *n.* An apparatus for holding dies that cut threads on screws, bolts, pipes, or rods.

di·et¹ (dī'ət) *n.* **1.** The usual food and drink of a person or animal. **2.** A regulated selection of foods, especially as prescribed for gaining or losing weight or for other medical reasons: *a high-protein diet.* **3.** Anything taken or provided regularly: *her usual diet of thrillers.* —*v.* **dieted, -eting, -ets.** —*tr.* To regulate or prescribe food and drink for. —*intr.* **1.** To eat and drink according to a regulated system, especially in order to lose weight. **2.** *Archaic.* To eat or feed. [Middle English *diete,* from Old French, from Latin *diaeta,* from Greek *diaita,* mode of life, regimen, diet, from *diaitan,* to lead one's life.] —**di·et·er** *n.*

diet² *n.* **1.** *Sometimes* **Diet.** A legislative assembly in certain countries, such as Japan. **2.** *Scottish.* **a.** A single daily session of a court or local legislature. **b.** A day upon which a court convenes. **3.** **Diet.** The semiannual general assembly of the estates of the former Holy Roman Empire. [Middle English *diete, dyet,* day's journey, day for meeting, from Medieval Latin *diēta,* from Latin *diēs,* day.]

diet. dietetics.

di·e·tar·y (dī'ə-tĕr'ē) *adj.* Of or pertaining to diet. —*n., pl.* **dietaries.** **1.** A system or regimen of dieting. **2.** A regulated daily food allowance.

dietary fiber *n.* **Roughage** *(see).*

dietary laws *pl.n.* In certain religions such as Judaism or Islam, a body of regulations prescribing the kinds and combinations of food that may be eaten by the orthodox.

di·e·tet·ic (dī'ə-tĕt'ĭk) *adj.* **1.** Of or pertaining to diet or its regulation. **2.** Specially prepared or processed for restrictive diets. [Late Latin *diaetēticus,* from Greek *diaitētikos,* from *diaita,* DIET.] —**di·e·tet·i·cal·ly** *adv.*

di·e·tet·ics (dī'ə-tĕt'ĭks) *n. Used with a singular verb. Abbr.* **diet.** The study of diet and dieting as it relates to health and hygiene.

di·eth·y·lene glycol (dī-ĕth'ə-lēn') *n.* A clear, colorless, extremely hygroscopic, syrupy liquid, CH₂OHCH₂OCH₂CH₂OH, widely used as an antifreeze, solvent, softening agent, and herbicide.

di·eth·yl ether (dī'ĕth'əl) *n.* **Ether** *(see).*

di·eth·yl·stil·bes·trol (dī'ĕth'əl-stĭl-bĕs'trôl') *n. Abbr.* **DES** A synthetic estrogen, C₁₈H₂₀O₂, used as an estrogen substitute, especially in the treatment of menstrual disorders. Also called "stilbestrol."

diethyl tol·u·am·ide (tŏl'yōo-ăm'īd') *n.* **Deet** *(see).* [DIETHYL TOLU (ENE) + AMIDE.]

di·e·ti·tian, di·e·ti·cian (dī'ə-tĭsh'ən) *n.* A person specializing in dietetics.

Die·trich (dē'trĭk), **Marlene,** born Maria Magdalena von Losch (c. 1901–). German actress, singer, and film star. Her international reputation was made in 1930 with Josef von Sternberg's German film *The Blue Angel.* Her Hollywood films include *Morocco* (1930), *Shanghai Express* (1932), and *Destry Rides Again* (1939).

dif., diff. difference; different.

diffenbachia. Variant of **dieffenbachia.**

dif·fer (dĭf'ər) *intr.v.* **-fered, -fering, -fers.** **1.** To be unlike or dissimilar in nature, quality, amount, or form. Often used with *from.* **2.** To be of a different opinion; disagree; dissent. Often used with *with.* **3.** To quarrel. [Middle English *differen,* from Old French *differer,* from Latin *differre,* to carry in different directions, be different : *dis-,* apart + *ferre,* to carry.]

dif·fer·ence (dĭf'ər-əns, dĭf'rəns) *n. Abbr.* **dif., diff.** **1.** The condition or degree of being unlike, dissimilar, or diverse; disparity; variation. **2.** A specific point of disparity or unlikeness; an instance of variation. **3.** *Archaic.* A distinct mark or peculiarity. **4.** A disagreement; quarrel. **5.** A distinction or discrimination. **6. a.** A substantial change: *Do you see a difference in her these days?* **b.** A critical factor in determining an outcome: *A good pension can be the difference between hardship and comfort in old age.* **7.** *Mathematics.* **a.** The amount by which one quantity is greater or less than another. **b.** The amount that remains after one quantity is subtracted from another. Also called "remainder." **8.** *Logic.* A differentia.

9. *Heraldry.* A distinguishing mark on a coat of arms to differentiate branches of the same family. —**make a difference.** To alter matters significantly.

—*tr.v.* **differenced, -encing, -ences.** **1.** To make or cause to make a difference between or in; distinguish. **2.** *Heraldry.* To add a distinguishing mark to (a coat of arms).

Usage: difference, discrepancy, dissimilarity, distinction, divergence, unlikeness, variation. These nouns refer to lack of correspondence, agreement, or equality, as revealed by comparison. *Difference,* the most general, applies to any such condition. *Discrepancy* stresses the idea of difference, such as conflict or contradiction, that should not exist, as discrepancies in two accounts of an incident or between financial statements. *Dissimilarity* points up difference between things otherwise alike or capable of close comparison. *Distinction* usually means a slight difference in detail between like or related things, determined only by close inspection. The difference is also subjectively determined rather than palpable or factual. *Divergence* implies a gradually developing difference between things originally similar or alike. *Unlikeness* usually implies greater and more obvious difference. *Variation* is difference between things of the same class or species; often it refers to modification of something original, prescribed, or typical.

dif·fer·ent (dĭf'ə-rənt, dĭf'rənt) *adj. Abbr.* **dif., diff.** **1.** Characterized by a difference. **2.** Distinct; separate. **3.** Differing from the ordinary; special or unusual.

—*adv. Nonstandard.* Differently. [Middle English, from Old French, from Latin *differēns* (stem *different-*), present participle of *differre,* to DIFFER.] —**dif·fer·ent·ly** *adv.* —**dif·fer·ent·ness** *n.*

Usage: A long-standing usage dispute focuses on the correct choice of word to use following *different* and *differently,* in such sentences as *This book is different . . . that, She behaves differently . . . Joan. Different from* is the traditional standard form, particularly when it is followed by a single noun or pronoun or by a short phrase or clause: *This illustration is different from that. This was different from what we expected.* But *different than* has wider acceptance, as an aid to conciseness, when the passage that follows is a clause (frequently a shortened or elliptical clause): *How different things seem now than yesterday,* rather than *How different things seem now from what they were yesterday.* Here the use of *different from* becomes ponderous; consequently the alternative to *than* is to rephrase completely. *Different to,* a third form, is principally British. In an unrelated but common construction, *different* is superfluous: *Three different doctors examined him.*

dif·fer·en·ti·a (dĭf'ər-ĕn'shē-ə) *n., pl.* **-tiae** (-shē-ē', -shē-ī') *Logic.* An attribute that characterizes and distinguishes a species from others of the same genus. [Latin, difference.]

dif·fer·en·ti·a·ble (dĭf'ə-rĕn'shē-ə-bəl) *adj.* **1.** Capable of being differentiated. **2.** *Mathematics.* Possessing a derivative. —**dif·fer·en·ti·a·bil·i·ty** *n.*

dif·fer·en·tial (dĭf'ə-rĕn'shəl) *adj.* **1.** Pertaining to or showing a difference or differences. **2.** Constituting or making a difference; distinctive. **3.** Dependent on or making use of a difference or distinction. **4.** *Mathematics.* Of or pertaining to differentiation. **5.** Involving differences in speed or direction of motion: *a differential pulley.*

—*n.* **1.** A factor that constitutes or makes a difference. **2.** *Mathematics.* **a.** An infinitesimal increment in a variable. **b.** The product of the derivative of a function of one variable multiplied by the independent variable increment. **3.** A differential gear. **4.** A difference in costs, charges, or rates; especially, a difference in rates of pay, as between different types of work in the same industry or profession, or similar work done in different places or circumstances. —**dif·fer·en·tial·ly** *adv.*

differential analyzer *n.* A mechanical or electronic analog computer used to solve especially complicated differential equations.

differential calculus *n.* The mathematics of the variation of a function with respect to changes in independent variables; loosely, the study of slopes of curves, accelerations, maxima, and minima by means of derivatives and differentials.

differential coefficient *n. Mathematics.* A **derivative** *(see).*

differential diagnosis *n. Medicine.* The process or an instance of distinguishing between different diseases with similar signs or symptoms.

differential equation *n.* An equation containing derivatives or differentials of an unknown function.

differential gear *n.* An arrangement of gears in an epicyclic train permitting the rotation of two shafts at different speeds, used on the drive axle of motor vehicles to allow different rates of wheel rotation on curves.

differential operator *n. Symbol* ∇ A mathematical operator used in vector analysis.

differential windlass *n.* A hoisting device that has two drums of different sizes on the same axis. A line wound on the larger and unwound from the smaller provides extra lifting power. Also called "Chinese windlass."

dif·fer·en·ti·ate (dĭf'ə-rĕn'shē-āt') *v.* **-ated, -ating, -ates.** —*tr.* **1.** To constitute the difference in or between; serve to make a distinction between: *subspecies differentiated by the markings on their wings.* **2.** To perceive or show the difference in or between; discriminate; distinguish. **3.** To cause differences to develop in (something) by alteration or modification. Usually used in the passive. **4.** *Mathematics.* To calculate the derivative or differential of. —*intr.* **1.** To become distinct or specialized; acquire a different character. **2.** To make distinctions; discriminate. **3.** *Biology.* To develop into more specialized organs. Used especially of embryonic cells or tissues. **—dif·fer·en·ti·a·tion** *n.*

dif·fi·cult (dĭf′ĭ-kŭlt′, -kəlt) *adj.* **1.** Requiring effort or skill to do or achieve: *a difficult task.* **2.** Requiring mental effort to comprehend or solve: *a difficult puzzle.* **3.** Not easy to persuade, control, or manage; stubborn; obstinate: *a difficult child.* —See Synonyms at **hard.** [Middle English, back-formation from DIFFICULTY.] **—dif·fi·cult·ly** *adv.*

dif·fi·cul·ty (dĭf′ĭ-kŭl′tē, -kəl-tē) *n., pl.* **-ties. 1.** The condition, fact, or quality of being difficult. **2.** Something not easily done, accomplished, comprehended, or solved. **3. a.** A problem; problems; trouble: *I had difficulty catching her accent.* **b.** *Usually* **difficulties.** A troublesome or embarrassing state of affairs, especially one resulting from a shortage of money. **4.** A lack of normal ease: *Asthma can cause breathing difficulties.* **5.** A disagreement; dispute. **6.** An objection or impediment: *to make difficulties for someone.* [Middle English *difficulte,* from Latin *difficultās* (stem *difficultāt-*), from *difficilis* (earlier *difficul*), difficult : *dis-,* not + *facilis,* easy.]

dif·fi·dent (dĭf′ə-dənt, -dĕnt′) *adj.* **1.** Lacking self-confidence; timid. **2.** Not self-assertive. —See Synonyms at **shy.** [Middle English, from Latin *diffīdens* (stem *diffīdent-*), present participle of *diffīdere,* to mistrust : *dis-,* not + *fīdere, to trust.*] **—dif·fi·dence** *n.* **—dif·fi·dent·ly** *adv.*

dif·fract (dĭ-frăkt′) *tr.v.* **-fracted, -fracting, -fracts.** To cause to undergo diffraction. [Back-formation from DIFFRACTION.] **—dif·frac·tive** *adj.* **—dif·frac·tive·ly** *adv.* **—dif·frac·tive·ness** *n.*

dif·frac·tion (dĭ-frăk′shən) *n.* **1.** Modification of the intensity distribution of wave phenomena that are incident upon an object or aperture whose size is similar to that of the wavelength, resulting in dispersion and interference patterns. **2.** Any phenomenon resulting from such modification. [New Latin *diffractiō* (stem *diffractiōn-*), "a breaking up," from Latin *diffractus,* past participle of *diffringere,* to break to pieces : *dis-,* apart + *frangere,* to break.]

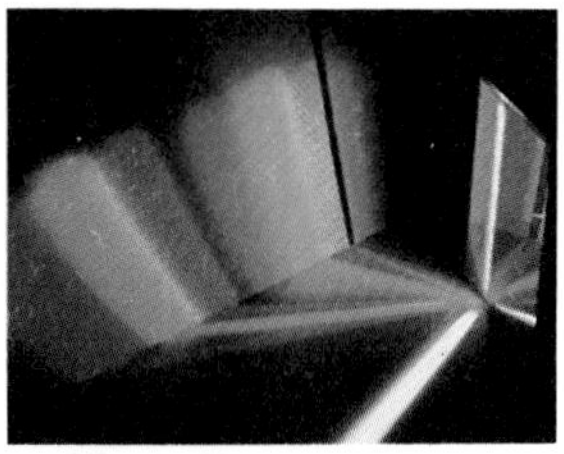

diffraction *A ray of light diffracts and breaks into the colors of the rainbow as it bounces off the finely ridged surface of a diffraction grating.*

diffraction grating *n.* A usually glass or polished metal surface having a large number of very fine parallel grooves or slits cut in the surface and used to produce optical spectra by diffraction of transmitted or reflected light. Also called "grating."

dif·fuse (dĭ-fyo͞oz′) *v.* **-fused, -fusing, -fuses.** *—tr.* **1.** To pour out and cause (a gas or liquid, for example) to spread or disperse. **2.** To spread about or scatter; disseminate. **3.** To make less brilliant; soften. *—intr.* **1.** To spread out; become widely dispersed. **2.** *Physics.* To undergo diffusion.

~adj. (dĭ-fyo͞os′). **1.** Characterized by excessive wordiness and poor organization; lacking conciseness. Said of speech or writing. **2.** Widely spread or scattered; dispersed. [Middle English, dispersed, from Old French *diffus,* from Latin *diffūsus,* past participle of *diffundere,* to pour out, spread : *dis-,* apart + *fundere,* to pour.] **—dif·fuse·ly** (dĭ-fyo͞os′lē) *adv.* **—dif·fuse·ness** (dĭ-fyo͞os′nĭs) *n.* **—dif·fus·i·ble** *adj.* **—dif·fus·i·bly** *adv.*

dif·fused junction (dĭ-fyo͞ozd′) *n.* A semiconductor junction formed by the diffusion of impurity atoms into semiconducting material to create p-type or n-type regions.

dif·fus·er, dif·fu·sor (dĭ-fyo͞o′zər) *n.* **1.** One that diffuses. **2.** A lighting fixture, such as a frosted globe or optically rough reflector, that diffuses light. **3.** A flow passage in a wind tunnel that decelerates a stream of gas or liquid from a high to a low velocity. **4.** A device, such as a cone or baffle, placed in front of a loudspeaker diaphragm to diffuse the sound waves. **5.** A medium that scatters light, used in photography to soften shadows.

dif·fu·sion (dĭ-fyo͞o′zhən) *n.* **1.** The process of diffusing or the condition of being diffused. **2.** *Physics.* The angular redistribution of radiation by a scattering, reflecting, or refracting system, ideally producing an isotropic distribution of intensity. **3.** *Physics.* The gradual mixing of the molecules of two or more substances, as a result of random thermal motion. **4. a.** Excessive wordiness; verbosity. **b.** Poor organization of material, as in a literary work, for example. **5.** *Anthropology.* The spreading of customs, skills, or the like from one group to another.

diffusion coefficient *n.* See **diffusivity** (sense 1).

dif·fu·sive (dĭ-fyo͞o′sĭv, -zĭv) *adj.* Characterized by diffusion; tending to diffuse. **—dif·fu·sive·ly** *adv.* **—dif·fu·sive·ness** *n.*

dif·fu·siv·i·ty (dĭ-fyo͞o′sĭv′ə-tē, -zĭv′-) *n. Physics.* **1.** The rate at which a substance diffuses between the opposite sides of a unit cube when there is unit concentration difference between them. Also called "diffusion coefficient." **2.** The ratio of the thermal conductivity of a substance to the product of its specific heat capacity and its density. **3.** The ability of a substance to undergo diffusion.

dig (dĭg) *v.* **dug** (dŭg) or *archaic* **digged** (dĭgd), **digging, digs.** *—tr.* **1.** To break up, turn over, or remove (earth or sand, for example) with a spade, the hands, or other tools; excavate. **2.** To make (a hole) by or as if by digging: *dig a grave.* **3.** To obtain by digging: *dig coal.* **4.** To mix with the earth when digging. Used with *in.* **5.** To learn or discover by careful research or investigation; unearth. Often used with *up* or *out.* **6. a.** To force or thrust into or against. Used with *into.* **b.** To prod or poke: *dug me in the ribs.* **7.** *Slang.* To comprehend, appreciate, or enjoy. *—intr.* **1.** To loosen or turn over the earth. **2.** To make one's way by or as if by digging. Used with *through, into,* or *under.* **3.** *Informal.* To study or work hard and diligently. **—dig in. 1.** *Military.* To dig holes or trenches. **2.** To entrench (oneself). **3.** *Informal.* To eat heartily.

~n. **1.** A poke; a thrust: *a dig in the ribs.* **2.** A sarcastic, taunting remark; a gibe. **3.** An archaeological excavation. **4. digs.** *Chiefly British Informal.* Lodgings: *student digs.* [Middle English *diggen,* from Old French *diguer,* "to make a dike or ditch," from *digue,* ditch, from Germanic.]

dig. digest (compilation).

di·gam·ma (dī-găm′ə) *n.* A letter, written *F,* occurring in certain early forms of Greek and transliterated in English as *w.* [Latin, from Greek : DI- (two) + GAMMA (from its resemblance to two capital gammas placed one above the other).]

dig·a·my (dĭg′ə-mē) *n.* Remarriage after the death or divorce of one's first wife or husband. Also called "deuterogamy." [Late Latin *digamia,* from Late Greek : DI- (two) + -GAMY.] **—dig·a·mous** *adj.*

di·gas·tric (dī-găs′trĭk) *adj.* Having two fleshy ends connected by a thinner tendinous portion. Said of certain muscles.

~n. A lower jaw muscle that assists in lowering the jaw. [New Latin *digastricus,* "having two bellies" : DI- (two) + GASTRIC.]

di·gen·e·sis (dī-jĕn′ə-sĭs) *n.* **Alternation of generations *(see).***

di·gest (dī-jĕst′, dĭ-) *v.* **-gested, -gesting, -gests.** *—tr.* **1.** To transform (food) into an assimilable condition, as by chemical and muscular action in the alimentary canal. **2.** To absorb or assimilate mentally. **3.** To organize into a systematic arrangement, usually by summarizing or classifying. **4.** *Archaic.* To endure or bear patiently. **5.** *Chemistry.* To soften or disintegrate by means of chemical action, heat, or moisture. *—intr.* **1.** To become assimilated into the body. **2.** To assimilate food substances. **3.** *Chemistry.* To undergo exposure to heat, liquids, or chemical agents.

~n. (dī′jĕst′). **1.** *Abbr.* **dig.** A systematic organization or arrangement of summarized literary, scientific, or statistical materials or data; synopsis. **2.** A periodical containing literary abridgments, brief accounts of current affairs, and the like. **3.** *Law.* A systematic arrangement of statutes or court decisions. **—the Digest.** *Roman Law.* The **Pandects *(see).*** [Middle English *digesten,* from Latin *dīgerere* (past participle *dīgestus*), to divide, distribute, digest : *di-,* apart + *gerere,* to bear, carry.]

di·gest·ant (dī-jĕs′tənt, dĭ-) *n.* A substance taken to aid digestion.

di·gest·er (dī-jĕs′tər, dĭ-) *n.* **1.** A person who makes a digest. **2.** *Chemistry.* An apparatus in which substances are softened or decomposed, usually for further processing.

di·gest·i·ble (dī-jĕs′tə-bəl, dĭ-) *adj.* Capable of being digested. **—di·gest·i·bil·i·ty, di·gest·i·ble·ness** *n.* **—di·gest·i·bly** *adv.*

di·gest·if (dĭ-zhĕs-tēf′) *n.* A drink, especially a brandy or liqueur, taken after a meal to aid digestion.

di·ges·tion (dī-jĕs′chən, dĭ-) *n.* **1.** *Physiology.* **a.** The primarily enzymatic bodily process by which foods are decomposed into simple, assimilable substances. **b.** The ability to digest food. **2.** The process of decomposing organic matter in sewage by bacteria. **3.** The assimilation of ideas or information; understanding.

di·ges·tive (dī-jĕs′tĭv, dĭ-) *adj.* **1.** Pertaining to or aiding digestion. **2.** Functioning to digest food.

~n. Any substance that aids digestion. **—di·ges·tive·ly** *adv.*

digestive gland *n.* Any of various endocrine and exocrine glands that secrete enzymes necessary for digestion.

digestive system *n.* The alimentary canal together with accessory glands including the salivary glands, liver, and pancreas, regarded as an integrated system responsible for digestion.

dig·ger (dĭg′ər) *n.* **1.** A person who digs, especially one who digs for gold. **2.** A motorized machine with an attachment for excavating earth. **3. Digger.** A member of a radical English Puritan group of the mid-17th century, advocating the communal ownership of land. **4.** *Informal.* A person, especially a soldier, from New Zealand or Australia. [Sense 4, with allusion to Australian gold miners.]

digger wasp *n.* Any of various wasps of the family Sphecidae, that burrow into the ground to build their nests.

dig·gings (dĭg′ĭngz) *pl.n.* **1.** An excavation site. **2.** Materials dug out. **3.** *Chiefly British.* Lodgings; digs. No longer in current usage.

dight (dīt) *tr.v.* **dight** or **dighted, dighting, dights.** *Archaic.* To dress; adorn. [Middle English *dighten,* Old English *dihtan,* to arrange, compose, from Latin *dictāre,* to DICTATE.]

dig·it (dĭj′ĭt) *n.* **1. a.** A finger or toe. **b.** Any of the corresponding parts of other vertebrates, the number of which may be reduced. In the horse, for example, there is a single digit on each leg. **2.** The breadth of a finger, used as a unit of measure, equal to about two centimeters (3/4 inch). **3.** Any one of the ten Arabic number symbols, 0 to 9. [Middle English, from Latin *digitus,* finger.]

dig·i·tal (dĭj′ə-təl) *adj.* **1.** Of, pertaining to, or resembling a digit, especially a finger. **2.** Done with the fingers. **3.** Having digits. **4.** Displaying measurements by means of changing numbers rather than by hands on a dial: *a digital clock.* **5.** *Computer Science.* Using digits to represent quantities. Compare **analog. 6.** Of or pertaining to digital recording.

~n. Any key played or operated with the finger, as on a piano. **—dig·i·tal·ly** *adv.*

digital computer *n.* A computer that performs operations with quantities represented electronically as digits, usually in the binary system. Compare **analog computer.**

dig·i·tal·in (dĭj′ə-tăl′ĭn) *n.* A poisonous white powder, $C_{36}H_{56}O_{14}$, used in the treatment of heart disease. [DIGITAL(IS) + -IN.]

dig·i·tal·is (dĭj′ə-tăl′ĭs) *n.* **1.** Any plant of the genus *Digitalis,* which includes the foxgloves. **2.** A drug prepared from the seeds and dried leaves of this plant, used as a cardiac stimulant. [New Latin, from Latin *digitālis,* digital (from the finger-shaped corollas of foxglove), from *digitus,* DIGIT.]

dig·i·tal·ize (dĭj′ə-tə-līz′) *tr.v.* **-ized, -izing, -izes. 1.** To treat medically with digitalis. **2.** To digitize. **—dig·i·tal·i·za·tion** *n.*

PRONUNCIATION KEY

ă, pat; ā, pay; âr, care;
ä, father, are; b, bib;
ch, church; d, deed; ĕ, pet;
ē, be; f, fife; g, gag; h, hat;
hw, which; ĭ, pit; ī, pie;
îr, pier; j, judge; k, kick;
l, lid, needle; m, mum;
n, no, sudden; ng, thing;
ŏ, pot; ō, toe; ô, paw, for;
oi, noise; ou, out; o͝o, book;
o͞o, boot; p, pop; r, roar;
s, sauce; sh, ship, dish;
t, tight; th, thin, path;
th, this, bathe; ŭ, cut; ûr, fur;
v, valve; w, with; y, yes;
z, zebra, size; zh, vision;
ə, about, item, edible, gallop, circus, peaceful

IN FOREIGN WORDS:

à, *Fr.* ami; œ, *Fr.* feu, *Ger.* schön; ü, *Fr.* tu, *Ger.* über; KH, *Ger.* ich, *Scot.* loch; N, *Fr.* bon; y′, *Fr.* Compiègne

STRESS MARKS:

Primary stress: ′
in·cite′ (ĭn-sīt′)
Secondary stress: ′
in′sight′ (ĭn′sīt′)

dig·i·tate (dĭj′ə-tāt′) *adj.* Also **dig·i·tat·ed** (-tā′tĭd) **1.** Having digits or fingerlike parts. **2.** *Botany.* Having radiating fingerlike lobes or leaflets. **—dig·i·tate·ly** *adv.*

dig·i·ta·tion (dĭj′ə-tā′shən) *n.* **1.** Division into fingerlike parts; the condition of being digitate. **2.** A fingerlike part or anatomical projection.

dig·i·ti·grade (dĭj′ə-tə-grād′) *adj.* Walking so that only the digits touch the ground, as do horses, cats, and dogs.
~*n.* A digitigrade animal. Compare **plantigrade.** [Latin *digitus,* finger, toe, DIGIT + -GRADE.]

dig·it·ize (dĭj′ə-tīz′) *tr.v.* **-ized, -izing, -izes.** To convert (continuous data) into digital form for computer processing. **—dig·it·i·za·tion** *n.*

dig·i·tox·in (dĭj′ə-tŏk′sĭn) *n.* A highly active glycoside, $C_{41}H_{64}O_{13}$, derived from digitalis. [DIGI(TALIS) + TOXIN.]

dig·i·tron (dĭj′ə-trŏn′) *n.* An electronic display tube consisting of an anode and a series of cathodes, each shaped as a number or letter, that can be separately lit by a glow discharge. Also called "Nixie tube." [DIGI(T) + -TRON.]

dig·ni·fied (dĭg′nə-fīd′) *adj.* Having or expressing dignity. **—dig·ni·fied·ly** (dĭg′nə-fīd′lē, -fī′ĭd-lē) *adv.*

dig·ni·fy (dĭg′nə-fī′) *tr.v.* **-fied, -fying, -fies. 1.** To confer dignity or honor upon. **2.** To impart a sense of dignity to. **3.** To elevate with the semblance of dignity. [Middle English *dignifien,* from Old French *dignifier,* from Late Latin *dignificāre* : Latin *dignus,* worthy + *facere,* to make, do.]

dig·ni·tar·y (dĭg′nə-tĕr′ē) *n., pl.* **-ies.** A person of high rank. [From DIGNITY.]

dig·ni·ty (dĭg′nə-tē) *n., pl.* **-ties. 1. a.** The presence of poise, self-control, and seriousness in one's deportment to a degree that inspires respect. **b.** Inherent nobility and worth: *the dignity of labor.* **c.** An imposing, formal quality; grandeur; stateliness. **2.** The respect and honor associated with an important position. **3. a.** A high office or rank. **b.** Standing or rank in relation to others. **4.** Self-esteem. **5. dignities.** The ceremonial symbols and observances attached to high office: *the dignities of office.* [Middle English *dignite,* from Old French, from Latin *dignitās* (stem *dignitāt-*), from *dignus,* worthy.]

di·graph (dī′grăf) *n.* **1.** A pair of letters that represents a single speech sound, such as the *ph* in *pheasant* or the *ea* in *beat.* **2.** Two letters run together to represent a special sound, such as Old English *æ.* [DI- + -GRAPH.] **—di·graph·ic** *adj.*

di·gress (dī-grĕs′, dĭ-) *intr.v.* **-gressed, -gressing, -gresses. 1.** To stray from the main subject in writing or speaking. **2.** To turn aside. [Latin *dīgredī* (past participle *dīgressus*), to go aside : *dis-,* apart, aside + *gradī,* to go.]

di·gres·sion (dī-grĕsh′ən, dĭ-) *n.* **1.** The act of digressing. **2.** An instance of digressing; especially, a written or spoken passage not bearing directly on the main subject. **—di·gres·sion·al** *adj.*

di·gres·sive (dī-grĕs′ĭv, dĭ-) *adj.* Characterized by digression; rambling. **—di·gres·sive·ly** *adv.* **—di·gres·sive·ness** *n.*

di·he·dral (dī-hē′drəl) *adj.* **1.** Formed by or having two plane faces; two-sided. **2.** Pertaining to, having, or forming a dihedral angle.
~*n.* **1.** A dihedral angle. **2.** The upward or downward inclination of an aircraft wing from true horizontal. [DI- + -HEDRAL.]

dihedral angle *n.* **1.** *Geometry.* The angle formed by two intersecting planes. **2.** The acute angle between an aircraft wing and true horizontal. Also called "dihedral."

di·hy·brid (dī-hī′brĭd) *n. Genetics.* **1.** A cross whose parents differ in two distinct characters. **2.** An organism that is heterozygous for two pairs of alleles.

di·hy·dric (dī-hī′drĭk) *adj.* Containing two hydroxyl radicals.

Di·jon (dē-zhôɴ′). City in east-central France, capital of Côte-d'Or department, and once the capital of Burgundy. It is a railroad junction and gastronomic and industrial center, its best-known products being mustard and cassis, a black-currant liqueur.

dik-dik (dĭk′dĭk′) *n.* Any of several very small African antelopes of the genus *Madoqua.* [Native name in East Africa, imitative of its cry.]

dike, dyke (dīk) *n.* **1.** An embankment of earth and rock, especially: **a.** A levee built to prevent floods. **b.** *British.* A low wall, often of sod, dividing or enclosing lands. **c.** A barrier blocking a passage, especially for protection. **d.** A causeway. **2.** A ditch or channel. **3.** *Geology.* A long mass of igneous rock that cuts across the structure of adjacent rock.
~*tr.v.* **diked, diking, dikes** or **dyked, dyking, dykes. 1.** To protect, enclose, or provide with a dike. **2.** To drain with dikes or ditches. [Middle English *dike,* Old English *dīc,* moat, ditch (possibly influenced in sense by Middle Low German *dīk,* ditch).] **—dik·er** *n.*

dik·kop (dĭk′ŏp) *n. South African.* A bird, the **stone curlew** *(see).* [Afrikaans : *dik,* thick + *kop,* head.]

dik·tat (dĭk-tät′) *n.* **1.** A unilaterally imposed settlement that deals harshly with a defeated party. **2.** An authoritative or dogmatic statement; command. [German, "dictation," "command," from Latin *dictātum,* neuter past participle of *dictāre,* to DICTATE.]

Di·lan·tin (dī-lăn′tĭn) *n.* A trademark for diphenylhydantoin sodium, used to treat epilepsy.

di·lap·i·date (dĭ-lăp′ə-dāt′) *v.* **-dated, -dating, -dates.** *—tr.* To bring into a state of ruin, decay, or disrepair. *—intr.* To fall into partial ruin or decay. [Latin *dīlapidāre,* to throw away, destroy : *dis-,* apart + *lapidāre,* to throw stones, from *lapis,* stone.] **—di·lap·i·da·tion** *n.*

di·lap·i·dat·ed (dĭ-lăp′ə-dā′tĭd) *adj.* Fallen into a state of disrepair; shabby; broken-down.

di·la·tan·cy (dī′lăt′n-sē, dĭ-) *n.* **1.** The increase in volume of a fixed amount of certain materials, such as wet sand, when it is subjected to a deformation that increases the interparticle distances of its constituents. **2.** Any of various related phenomena, such as increase in viscosity or solidification, resulting from such deformation.

di·la·tant (dī-lāt′ənt, dĭ-) *adj.* **1.** Tending to dilate; dilating. **2.** Exhibiting dilatancy.
~*n.* A dilator.

dil·a·ta·tion (dĭl′ə-tā′shən, dī′lə-) *n.* **1.** The act or process of dilating; expansion; dilation. **2.** The state or condition of being dilated or stretched. **3.** *Medicine.* The condition of being abnormally enlarged or dilated. **4.** Lengthy explanation or elaboration of a subject in writing or speech. **—dil·a·ta·tion·al** *adj.*

di·late (dī-lāt′, dī′lāt′, dĭ-lāt′) *v.* **-lated, -lating, -lates.** *—tr.* To make wider or larger; cause to expand. *—intr.* **1.** To become wider or larger; expand. **2.** To write or speak at length on a subject; elaborate. Used with *on* or *upon.* [Middle English *dilaten,* from Old French *dilater,* from Latin *dīlātāre,* to enlarge, extend : *dis-,* apart + *lātus,* wide.] **—di·lat·a·bil·i·ty** *n.* **—di·lat·a·ble** *adj.* **—di·la·tion** *n.* **—di·la·tive** *adj.*

di·lat·ed (dī-lā′tĭd, dī′lā′tĭd, dĭ-lā′tĭd) *adj.* **1.** Widened; expanded. **2.** Distended.

dilation and curettage *n.* A surgical operation in which the cervix is opened using a dilator and the lining of the uterus is removed with a curette, performed after an incomplete miscarriage, for example. Also called "D and C."

dil·a·tom·e·ter (dĭl′ə-tŏm′ə-tər, dī′lə-) *n.* An instrument used to measure thermal expansion in solids, liquids, and gases. [DILATE + -METER.] **—dil·a·to·met·ric** (dĭl′ə-tə-mĕt′rĭk, dī′lə-) *adj.* **—dil·a·tom·e·try** *n.*

di·la·tor, di·lat·er (dī-lā′tər, dī′lā′tər, dĭ-lā′tər) *n.* Something that dilates an object, organ, or part; especially, a drug, surgical instrument, or muscle that induces dilation.

dil·a·to·ry (dĭl′ə-tôr′ē, -tōr′ē) *adj.* **1.** Intended to cause delay. **2.** Characterized by a tendency to postpone or delay. —See Synonyms at **tardy.** [Middle English *dilatorie,* from Latin *dīlātōrius,* from *dīlātor,* delayer, from *dīlātus* (past participle of *differre,* to postpone, DEFER) : *dis-,* apart + *-lātus,* "carried."] **—dil·a·to·ri·ly** *adv.* **—dil·a·to·ri·ness** *n.*

dil·do (dĭl′dō) *n., pl.* **-dos** or **-does.** An object shaped like an erect penis, usually used for sexual penetration. [17th century : origin obscure.]

di·lem·ma (dĭ-lĕm′ə) *n.* **1.** A situation that requires one to choose between two equally balanced and often equally unpleasant alternatives. **2.** A predicament that seemingly defies a satisfactory solution. **3.** *Logic.* An argument in which a choice of two or more alternatives, each being conclusive and fatal, is presented to an antagonist. —See Synonyms at **predicament.** [Latin, from Greek *dilēmma,* ambiguous proposition : DI- (double) + *lēmma,* proposition, LEMMA.] **—dil·em·mat·ic** (dĭl′ə-măt′ĭk) *adj.*

dil·et·tante (dĭl′ə-tänt′, -tän′tē, -tănt′, -tăn′tē, dĭl′ə-tänt′) *n., pl.* **-tantes** or **-tanti** (-tän′tē, -tăn′tē). **1.** One whose interest in a subject is not serious or professional; a dabbler, especially in the arts. **2.** A lover of the fine arts; connoisseur.
~*adj.* Superficial or amateurish. [Italian *dilettante,* "amateur," from *dilettarsi,* to take pleasure in, from Latin *dēlectāre,* to DELIGHT.] **—dil·et·tan·tish** *adj.* **—dil·et·tan·tism** *n.*

dil·i·gence¹ (dĭl′ə-jəns) *n.* **1.** Earnest and persistent application to a matter in hand; steady effort; assiduity. **2.** Attentive care; heedfulness.

dil·i·gence² (dĭl′ə-jəns, dē′lē-zhäns′) *n.* In former times, a large public stagecoach. [French, from *diligence,* "speed," from *diligent,* DILIGENT.]

dil·i·gent (dĭl′ə-jənt) *adj.* **1.** Industrious; hard-working. **2.** Characterized by persevering, painstaking effort. —See Usage Note at **busy.** [Middle English, from Old French, from Latin *dīligēns* (stem *diligent-*), "loving," attentive, careful, from *dīligere,* to "single out," "choose," esteem highly, love : *dis-,* apart + *legere,* to choose, gather.] **—dil·i·gent·ly** *adv.*

dill (dĭl) *n.* **1.** An aromatic herb, *Anethum graveolens,* native to the Old World, having finely dissected leaves and small yellow flowers. **2.** The leaves or seedlike fruits of this plant, used as seasoning. Also called "dill weed." [Middle English *dile,* from Old English *dile,* from West Germanic *dilja* (unattested).]

Dil·lin·ger (dĭl′ĭn-jər), **John** (1902–34). U.S. outlaw. Named "public enemy number one" by the FBI (1933), he led a gang on a series of bank robberies, was captured and escaped from jail twice, and was involved in the deaths of three men. He was shot to death by FBI agents outside the Biograph Theater in Chicago.

dill pickle *n.* A cucumber pickled and flavored with dill.

dil·ly (dĭl′ē) *n., pl.* **-lies.** *Informal.* An excellent person or thing. [Obsolete *dilly,* delightful, from DELIGHTFUL.]

dilly bag *n. Australian.* A bag or basket, especially one made of woven rushes or bark. [From *dilli,* a native word in Queensland.]

dil·ly-dal·ly (dĭl′ē-dăl′ē) *intr.v.* **-lied, -lying, -lies.** *Informal.* **1.** To dawdle. **2.** To vacillate. [Reduplication of DALLY.]

dil·u·ent (dĭl′yo͞o-ənt) *adj.* Capable of diluting or serving to dilute.
~*n.* A substance used to dilute. [Latin *dīluēns* (stem *dīluent-*), present participle of *dīluere,* to DILUTE.]

di·lute (dī-lo͞ot′, dĭ-) *tr.v.* **-luted, -luting, -lutes. 1.** To thin or reduce the strength or concentration of by adding water or a similar fluid. **2.** To lessen the force, strength, purity, or brilliance of, especially by admixture.
~*adj.* **1.** Weakened; diluted. **2.** Designating a solution of a sub-

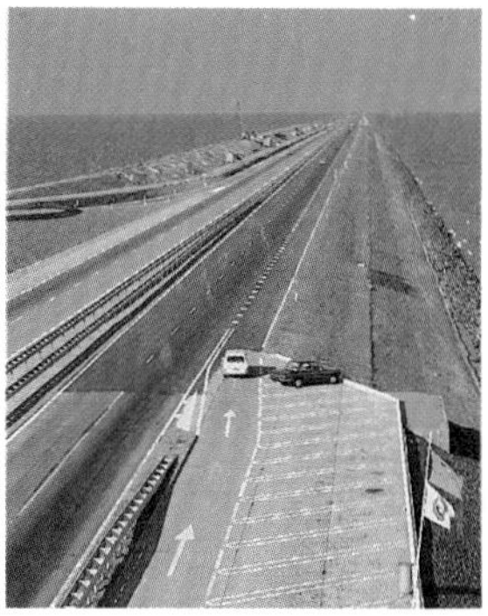

dike *This sea dike runs for 30 kilometers (19 miles) along the coast of Friesland, Holland.*

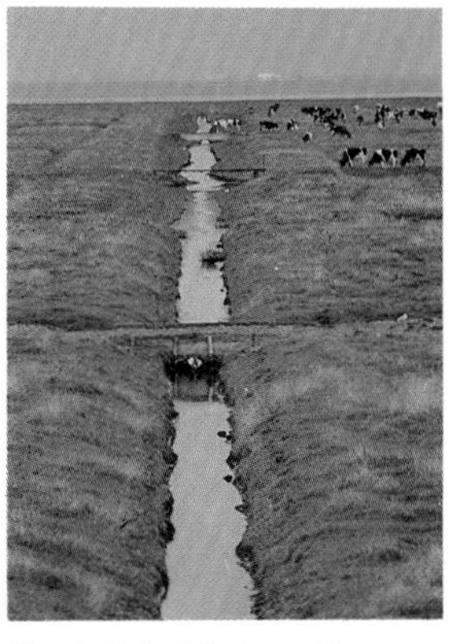

dike *An inland drainage dike in marshland near Greetsiel in northern Holland. The term is related to the Old English word* dīc, *meaning "ditch."*

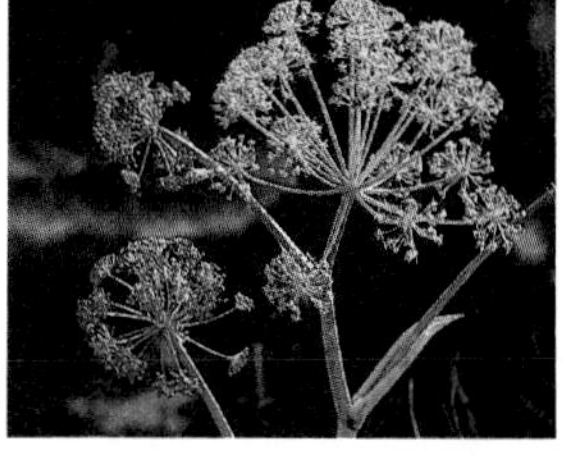

dill *An herb of the parsley family. The leaves and pungent seeds are used in cooking. The seeds are the source of dill oil, an extract used in some medicines.*

stance in which the substance is present in a low concentration. [Latin *dīluere* (past participle *dīlūtus*), to wash away, dilute : *dis-*, apart + *-luere*, from *lavere*, to wash.] —**di·lut·er** *n.*

di·lu·tion (dī-lo͞o′shən, dĭ-) *n.* **1. a.** The process of diluting or being diluted. **b.** A dilute or weakened condition. **2.** A diluted substance.

di·lu·vi·al (dĭ-lo͞o′vē-əl) *adj.* Also **di·lu·vi·an** (-ən). Of or produced by a flood, especially the Biblical Flood. [Late Latin *dīluviālis*, from Latin *dīluvium*, flood, from *dīluere*, to wash away, DILUTE.]

dim (dĭm) *adj.* **dimmer, dimmest. 1.** Faintly lit. **2.** Shedding a small amount of light; faint. **3.** Lacking brightness or luster; subdued; dull. **4.** Faintly outlined; indistinct; obscure. **5.** Lacking keenness of the senses, especially sight. **6.** *Informal.* Mentally slow; stupid. **7.** *Informal.* Negative, unfavorable, or disapproving: *She took a dim view of the plan.* —See Usage note at **dark.**
∼*v.* **dimmed, dimming, dims.** —*tr.* **1.** To make dim. **2.** To put (headlights) on low beam. —*intr.* To become dim.
∼*n.* **dims.** The parking lights on an automobile. [Middle English *dim(me)*, Old English *dimm*, from Germanic *dim-* (unattested).] —**dim·ly** *adv.* —**dim·ness** *n.*

dim. **1.** dimension. **2.** diminished. **3.** *Music.* diminuendo. **4.** diminutive.

Di Mag·gi·o (də mä′zhē-ō), **Joseph Paul** (1914–). U.S. baseball player. Called "Jolting Joe" and the "Yankee Clipper" by his fans, he was a consistently excellent all-around player for the New York Yankees for 13 seasons. He amassed a career batting average of .325 and set a major league record by hitting safely in 56 consecutive games.

Dimash. See **Damascus.**

dime (dīm) *n.* **1.** A U.S. coin worth ten cents or $^1/_{10}$ of a dollar. **2.** A similar coin in Canadian currency. See feature at **currency.** [Middle English, a tenth part, tithe, from Old French *dime, disme*, from Latin *decima (pars)*, tenth (part), tithe, from *decimus*, tenth, from *decem*, ten.]

di·men·hy·dri·nate (dī′mĕn-hī′drə-nāt′) *n.* An antihistamine, $C_{24}H_{28}ClN_5O_3$, used to treat travel sickness and allergic disorders.

dime novel *n.* A usually paperback romance or adventure novel.

di·men·sion (dĭ-mĕn′shən) *n.* *Abbr.* **dim. 1.** A measure of spatial extent, especially width, height, or length. **2.** *Often* **dimensions.** Extent; magnitude; size; scope. **3.** *Mathematics.* **a.** Any of the least number of independent coordinates required to specify a point in space uniquely. **b.** The range of any of these coordinates. **4.** *Physics.* A physical property, often mass, length, time, or some combination thereof, regarded as a fundamental measure, or as one of a set of fundamental measures, of a physical quantity: *Velocity has the dimensions of length divided by time.* **5.** An aspect of or way of regarding a whole: *This adds a whole new dimension to the problem.*
∼*tr.v.* **dimensioned, -sioning, -sions.** To cut or shape to specific dimensions. [Middle English *dimensio(u)n*, from Old French *dimension*, from Latin *dīmēnsiō* (stem *dīmēnsiōn-*), "a measuring," from *dīmētīrī* (past participle *dīmēnsus*), to measure carefully : *dis-* (intensive) + *mētīrī*, to measure.] —**di·men·sion·al** *adj.* —**di·men·sion·al·i·ty** *n.* —**di·men·sion·al·ly** *adv.*

di·mer (dī′mər) *n.* *Chemistry.* **1.** A molecule consisting of two identical simpler molecules. **2.** A chemical compound consisting of such molecules. [DI- + Greek *meros*, part.]

di·mer·cap·rol (dī′mĕr-kăp′rôl′, -rōl′) *n.* See **BAL** (liquid).

di·mer·ic (dī-mĕr′ĭk) *adj.* **1.** *Biology.* Composed of two parts or divisions. **2.** *Chemistry.* Composed of dimers.

dim·er·ous (dĭm′ər-əs) *adj.* **1.** Consisting of two parts or segments, as does the tarsus in certain insects. **2.** *Botany.* Having flower parts, such as petals, sepals, and stamens, in sets of two. Also written *2-merous.* [New Latin *dimerus* : DI- + -MEROUS.] —**dim·er·ism** *n.*

dime store *n.* A **five-and-ten** *(see).*

dim·e·ter (dĭm′ə-tər) *n.* A verse consisting of two metrical feet or of two groups of two feet. [Late Latin, (verse) of two measures or meters, from Greek *dimetros*, having two meters : DI- + *metron*, METER.]

di·meth·yl·sulf·ox·ide (dī-mĕth′əl-sŭl-fŏk′sīd′) *n.* *Abbr.* **DMSO** A colorless hygroscopic liquid, $(CH_3)_2SO$, obtained from lignin, used as a solvent and in medicine as a skin penetrant to convey medications into the tissues.

dimin. **1.** *Music.* diminuendo. **2.** diminutive.

di·min·ish (dĭ-mĭn′ĭsh) *v.* **-ished, -ishing, -ishes.** —*tr.* **1. a.** To reduce the size of; make smaller or less. **b.** To detract from the authority, rank, or prestige of. **2.** *Architecture.* To cause to taper. **3.** *Music.* To reduce (a perfect or minor interval) by a semitone. Compare **augment.** —*intr.* **1.** To become smaller or less. **2.** To become narrower; taper. —See Synonyms at **decrease.** [Middle English *deminishen*, blend of (a) *diminuen*, to reduce, lessen, from Old French *diminuer*, from Latin *dīminuere*, variant of *dēminuere* : *dē-*, from + *minuere*, to lessen; and (b) *minishen, minuisen*, to make smaller, from Old French *menuiser*, from Vulgar Latin *minūtiāre* (unattested), from Latin *minūtia*, smallness, from *minūtus*, small, from the past participle of *minuere*, to lessen.] —**di·min·ish·a·ble** *adj.* —**di·min·ish·ment** *n.*

diminishing returns *pl.n.* **1.** *Economics.* The principle that, after a certain point, further increases in a particular factor of production lead to progressively smaller increases in output. **2.** The idea that, after a certain point, more effort or investment in a project brings less reward or profit.

di·min·u·en·do (dĭ-mĭn′yo͞o-ĕn′dō) *n., pl.* **-dos** or **-does.** *Abbr.* **dim., dimin.** *Music.* A **decrescendo** *(see).* [Italian, "diminishing," from Latin *dīminuendum*, gerund of *dīminuere*, to DIMINISH.] —**di·min·u·en·do** *adj.* & *adv.*

dim·i·nu·tion (dĭm′ə-no͞o′shən, -nyo͞o′shən) *n.* **1. a.** The act or process of diminishing. **b.** The resulting reduction; decrease. **2.** *Music.* The repetition of a theme in notes of shorter duration than those of the original. Compare **augmentation.** [Middle English *diminucioun*, from Old French *diminution*, from Latin *dīminūtiō* (stem *dīminūtiōn-*), *dēminūtiō*, from *dēminuere*, to DIMINISH.]

di·min·u·tive (dĭ-mĭn′yə-tĭv) *adj.* *Abbr.* **dim., dimin. 1.** Of extremely small size; tiny. **2.** Designating certain affixes that denote smallness, youth, familiarity, affection, or contempt, such as *-let* in *booklet* or *-kin* in *lambkin.* Compare **augmentative.** —See Synonyms at **small.**
∼*n.* *Abbr.* **dim., dimin. 1.** A diminutive word or affix. **2.** *Heraldry.* A smaller form of an ordinary when repeated on a shield. [Middle English *diminutif*, from Old French, from Latin *dīminūtīvus, dēminūtīvus*, from *dēminūtus*, past participle of *dēminuere*, to DIMINISH.] —**di·min·u·tive·ly** *adv.* —**di·min·u·tive·ness** *n.*

dim·is·so·ry (dĭm′ə-sôr′ē, -sōr′ē) *adj.* **1.** Formerly, designating a letter from a bishop granting a clergyman permission to depart for another diocese. **2.** Designating a bishop's letter certifying the eligibility of the bearer for ordination. [Late Latin *dīmissōrius* (used in *dīmissōriae litterae*, "letter of dismissal," letter granting leave), from Latin *dīmittere* (past participle *dīmissus*), to send away, DISMISS.]

dim·i·ty (dĭm′ə-tē) *n., pl.* **-ties.** A sheer, crisp cotton fabric with raised woven stripes or checks, used chiefly for curtains and dresses. [Middle English *demyt*, from Medieval Latin *dimitum*, from Medieval Greek *dimitos*, double-threaded : DI- + *mitos*, thread.]

dim·mer (dĭm′ər) *n.* **1.** A rheostat or other device used to vary the electric current to a light bulb, thereby altering the intensity of illumination. **2.** Parking lights on an automobile.

di·morph (dī′môrf′) *n.* Either of two forms exhibiting dimorphism.

di·mor·phic (dī-môr′fĭk) *adj.* Also **di·mor·phous** (-fəs). Exhibiting dimorphism.

di·mor·phism (dī-môr′fĭz′əm) *n.* **1.** *Botany.* The occurrence of two distinct forms of the same parts, such as leaves, flowers, or stamens, in a single plant or in plants of the same kind. **2.** *Chemistry & Physics.* Crystallization in two distinct forms. **3.** *Zoology.* The state of having two distinct forms in the same species, especially when these forms serve to distinguish two sexes. [Greek *dimorphos*, having two forms : DI- + -MORPHOUS.]

dim-out (dĭm′out′) *n.* **1.** The restricted use or exposure of lights in wartime or as a stage effect. **2.** The semidarkness resulting from this. Compare **blackout.**

dim·ple (dĭm′pəl) *n.* **1.** A small natural indentation in the flesh on a part of the human body, especially on the chin or cheek. **2.** Any slight depression or indentation in a surface.
∼*v.* **dimpled, -pling, -ples.** —*tr.* To produce dimples in. —*intr.* To form dimples, as by smiling. [Middle English *dimple*, Old English *dympel* (unattested), pool, dimple.] —**dim·ply** *adj.*

dim sum (dĭm′so͝om′, sŭm′) *pl.n.* Light Chinese refreshments that include small steamed or fried dumplings and a variety of other delicacies. [Cantonese.]

dim·wit (dĭm′wĭt′) *n.* *Informal.* A stupid person. —**dim·wit·ted** *adj.* —**dim·wit·ted·ly** *adv.* —**dim·wit·ted·ness** *n.*

din (dĭn) *n.* A medley of resounding and discordant sounds; a continuing and unpleasant loud noise. —See Synonyms at **noise.**
∼*v.* **dinned, dinning, dins.** —*tr.* **1.** To stun or assail with deafening noise. **2.** To teach or instill by wearying repetition. Usually used with *into*: *din an idea into someone's head.* —*intr.* To make a din. [Middle English *dine, dune*, Old English *dyne.*]

DIN (dĭn) *n.* A logarithmic scale used to express the speed of a photographic emulsion, film, or the like. The speed is equal to −10 $\log_{10}E$, where *E* is the exposure of a point 0.1 density units above the fog level. [German *Deutsche Industrie-Norm*, German Industry Standard.]

din. dinar.

di·nar (dĭ-när′, dē′när′) *n.* *Abbr.* **din. 1. a.** The basic monetary unit of Bahrain, Iraq, Jordan, Kuwait, and South Yemen, equal to 1,000 fils. **b.** The basic monetary unit of Algeria, equal to 100 centimes. **c.** The basic monetary unit of Libya, equal to 1,000 dirhams. **d.** The basic monetary unit of Tunisia, equal to 1,000 millimes. **e.** The basic monetary unit of Yugoslavia, equal to 100 para. See feature at **currency. 2.** A monetary unit equal to $^1/_{100}$ of the rial of Iran. See feature at **currency. 3.** A coin or note worth one dinar. **4.** Any of several units of gold and silver currency used in the Middle East from the 8th to the 19th century. [Arabic *dīnār*, from Late Greek *dēnarion*, DENARIUS.]

Di·nar·ic Alps (dĭ-năr′ĭk ălps). *Serbo-Croatian* **Di·na·ra Pla·ni·na** (dē′nə-rä plä′nĭ-nä′). Yugoslavian mountain range, stretching 700 kilometers (435 miles) from the Julian Alps of northern Yugoslavia southeastward along the Adriatic coast to the Balkan Mts. of Albania.

dine (dīn) *v.* **dined, dining, dines.** —*intr.* **1.** To eat dinner. **2.** To eat something for dinner: *"They dined upon mince and slices of quince"* (Edward Lear). —*tr.* To entertain at dinner; give dinner to: *wined and dined the boss.* —**dine out.** To dine away from home. [Middle English *dinen*, from Old French *di(s)ner*, to dine, breakfast, from Vulgar Latin *disjējūnāre* (unattested), to break one's fast : Latin *dis-* (reversal) + Latin *jējūnus*†, fasting, hungry.]

din·er (dī′nər) *n.* **1.** A person taking dinner. **2.** A railroad dining car. **3.** A restaurant with a long counter and booths, originally shaped like a railroad car.

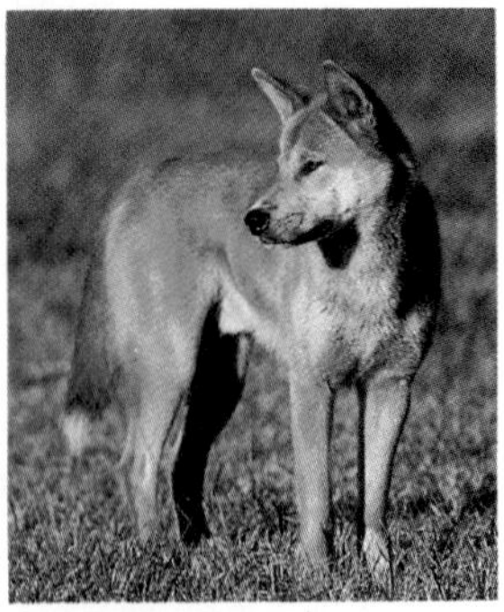

dingo The warragal, or dingo, a type of dog, is one of the few Australian mammals that are not marsupial, or pouched. It is nocturnal and chiefly solitary and is thought to have been introduced by the aborigines from Asia about 8,000 years ago.

PRONUNCIATION KEY

ă, pat; ā, pay; âr, care;
ä, father, are; b, bib;
ch, church; d, deed; ĕ, pet;
ē, be; f, fife; g, gag; h, hat;
hw, which; ĭ, pit; ī, pie;
îr, pier; j, judge; k, kick;
l, lid, needle; m, mum;
n, no, sudden; ng, thing;
ŏ, pot; ō, toe; ô, paw, for;
oi, noise; ou, out; o͝o, book;
o͞o, boot; p, pop; r, roar;
s, sauce; sh, ship, dish;
t, tight; th, thin, path;
th, this, bathe; ŭ, cut; ûr, fur;
v, valve; w, with; y, yes;
z, zebra, size; zh, vision;
ə, about, item, edible,
gallop, circus, peaceful

IN FOREIGN WORDS:

à, *Fr.* ami; œ, *Fr.* feu, *Ger.* schön; ü, *Fr.* tu, *Ger.* über; KH, *Ger.* ich, *Scot.* loch; N, *Fr.* bon; y′, *Fr.* Compiègne

STRESS MARKS:

Primary stress: ′
in·cite′ (ĭn-sīt′)
Secondary stress: ′
in′sight′ (ĭn′sīt′)

Din·e·sen (dĭn′ə-sən), **Isak,** pen name of Karen Dinesen, Baroness Blixen-Finecke (1885–1962). Danish author who lived in Kenya, East Africa, from 1914 to 1933. Among her books are *Winter's Tales* (1943), *Last Tales* (1957), *Anecdotes of Destiny* (1958), and two collections of her memoirs, *Out of Africa* (1950) and *Shadows on the Grass* (1961).

di·nette (dī-nĕt′) *n.* **1.** A nook or alcove for informal meals. **2.** The table and chairs used in a dinette. [From DINE.]

ding (dĭng) *v.* **dinged, dinging, dings.** —*intr.* **1.** To ring; clang. **2.** *Informal.* To speak persistently and repetitiously. —*tr.* **1.** To cause to clang, as by striking. **2.** *Informal.* To hammer into or at with repetitious talk.
~*n.* A ringing sound. [Probably imitative, but influenced by *ding,* to strike. See **dingbat.**]

ding-a-ling (dĭng′ə-lĭng) *n. Informal.* A silly or eccentric person.

ding·bat (dĭng′băt′) *n.* **1.** Any unspecified gadget or other article; a thingamabob. **2.** *Printing.* A typographical symbol or ornament. **3.** *Informal.* A silly or ecentric person. [Probably obsolete *ding,* to strike, Middle English *dingen,* probably from Old Norse *dengja,* to cudgel, from Germanic *ding-* (unattested) + BAT (cudgel).]

ding-dong (dĭng′dông′, -dŏng′) *n.* **1.** The peal of a bell. **2.** Any similar repeating sound.
~*intr.v.* **ding-donged, -donging, -dongs.** To ring; peal.
~*adj.* Characterized by a vigorous exchange, as of blows or insults. [Imitative.]

din·ghy (dĭng′ē) *n., pl.* **-ghies.** Also **din·gey,** *pl.* **-eys.** Any small open boat. [Hindi *ḍiṅgī, deṅgī,* diminutive of *ḍeṅgā*†, boat.]

din·gle (dĭng′gəl) *n.* A small, wooded valley; dell. [Middle English *dingle*†.]

din·go (dĭng′gō) *n., pl.* **-goes. 1.** A wild dog, *Canis dingo,* of Australia, having a yellowish-brown coat. **2.** *Australian Slang.* A cowardly or treacherous person. [From a native Australian name.]

ding·us (dĭng′əs) *n. Informal.* A gadget or other article whose name eludes one or is not known. [Dutch *dinges,* probably from German *Dinges,* genitive of *Ding,* thing, from Old High German *ding.*]

din·gy (dĭn′jē) *adj.* **-gier, -giest. 1.** Dark and dull, as from smoke, grime, or lack of daylight; dim, dirty, or discolored. **2.** Shabby; worn. [Possibly from Middle English *dinge,* rare variant of *dung, dong,* DUNG.] **—din·gi·ly** *adv.* **—din·gi·ness** *n.*

dining car *n.* A railroad car in which meals are served.

dining room *n.* A room in which meals are eaten.

di·ni·tro·ben·zene (dī-nī′trō-bĕn′zēn′, -bĕn-zēn′) *n.* Any of three isomeric compounds, $C_6H_4(NO_2)_2$, made from a mixture of nitric acid, sulfuric acid, and benzene and used in celluloid manufacture, in dyes, and in organic syntheses.

di·ni·tro·gen tetroxide (dī′nī′trə-jən, -nī′trō-) *n.* **Nitrogen tetroxide** *(see).*

Din·ka (dĭng′kä) *n., pl.* **-kas** or collectively **Dinka. 1.** A member of a group of Nilotic tribes of the southern Sudan. **2.** The East Sudanic language of this people. [Dinka *jieng,* "people."]

dink·ey (dĭng′kē) *n., pl.* **-eys.** Also **dink·y,** *pl.* **-ies.** *Informal.* A small locomotive used in a railroad yard. [From DINKY.]

din·kum (dĭng′kəm) *adj. Australian & New Zealand. Informal.* True; genuine; real. Often used interjectionally in the phrase *fair dinkum.*
~*adv. Australian & New Zealand. Informal.* Truly; honestly. [19th century : origin obscure.]

dink·y (dĭng′kē) *adj.* **-ier, -iest. 1.** *Informal.* Of small size or consequence; insignificant. **2.** *British Informal.* Small and neat; dainty. [Probably from Scottish *dink*†, trim, neat.]

din·ner (dĭn′ər) *n.* **1.** The chief meal of the day, eaten at midday or in the evening. **2.** A banquet or formal meal, especially one in honor of some person or commemorating an occasion. **3.** The food prepared for a dinner. [Middle English *diner,* from Old French *di(s)ner,* from *di(s)ner,* to DINE.]

dinner jacket *n.* See **tuxedo** (sense 1).

dinner theater *n.* A restaurant that presents a play during or after dinner.

din·ner·ware (dĭn′ər-wâr′) *n.* **1.** The tableware other than utensils used in serving a meal. **2.** A set of dishes.

di·no·flag·el·late (dī′nō-flăj′ə-lĭt, -lāt′, -flə-jĕl′ĭt) *n.* Any of numerous minute, chiefly marine organisms, characteristically having two flagella and a cellulose outer envelope, and forming one of the chief constituents of plankton. They can be classified as protozoans (group Dinoflagellata) or algae (group Dinophyceae). [New Latin *Dinoflagellata,* "ones having whirling flagella" : Greek *dinos,* whirlpool, eddy, from *dinein*†, to whirl + FLAGELLUM.]

di·no·saur (dī′nə-sôr′) *n.* **1.** Any of various extinct, often gigantic reptiles of the orders Saurischia and Ornithischia, that existed during the Mesozoic era. **2.** An outmoded person or thing. [New Latin : Greek *deinos,* fearful, monstrous + -SAUR.] **—di·no·sau·ri·an** *adj. & n.* **—di·no·sau·ric** *adj.* See feature, next page.

Dinosaur National Monument. An area of 772 square kilometers (298 square miles) in northwestern Colorado and northeastern Utah, set aside to preserve extensive remains of well-preserved animal fossils.

di·no·there (dī′nə-thîr′) *n.* Any of various extinct elephantlike mammals of the genus *Dinotherium,* that existed during the Miocene, Pliocene, and Pleistocene epochs. [New Latin *dinotherium* : Greek *deinos,* fearful, monstrous + -THERE.]

dint (dĭnt) *n.* **1.** Force or effort; power; exertion. Used in the phrase *by dint of.* **2.** A dent.
~*tr.v.* **dinted, dinting, dints.** To put a dent or dents in. [Middle English *dint, dunt,* Old English *dynt.* See **dent.**]

di·nu·cle·o·tide (dī-no͞o′klē-ə-tīd′, -nyo͞o′-) *n.* A compound consisting of two linked nucleotides, such as the coenzyme NAD.

Di·o Cas·si·us (dī′ō kăs′ē-əs) (*c.* A.D. 155–235). Roman historian. His 80 books, written in Greek, traced the history of Rome from the legendary arrival of Aeneas in Italy up to A.D. 229.

di·oc·e·san (dī-ŏs′ə-sən) *adj.* Of or pertaining to a diocese.
~*n.* **1.** A bishop of a diocese. **2.** A member of a diocese.

di·o·cese (dī′ə-sĭs, -sēs′, -sēz′) *n. Abbr.* **dioc.** The district or churches under the jurisdiction of a bishop; a bishopric. [Middle English *diocise,* from Old French, from Late Latin *diocēsis,* from Latin *dioecēsis,* jurisdiction, district, from Greek *dioikēsis,* "housekeeping," administration, from *dioikein,* to keep house, administer : *dia-,* completely + *oikein,* to inhabit, from *oikos,* house.]

Di·o·cle·tian (dī′ə-klē′shən), born Gaius Aurelius Valerius Diocletianus (A.D. 254–313). Roman emperor (284–305). In 286 he appointed Galerius (died A.D. 311) as his coemperor and divided the empire into east and west in order to govern more effectively. In 303, in a bid to revive the old religion, he instituted the last major persecution of the Christians. Two years later he and Galerius abdicated and retired to his grand palace at Salona (now Split, Yugoslavia).

di·ode (dī′ōd′) *n.* **1.** An electronic component having one semiconductor junction, used chiefly as a rectifier. **2.** A simple thermionic valve having two electrodes: a cathode and an anode. [DI- + -ODE.]

di·oe·cious, di·e·cious (dī-ē′shəs) *adj. Botany.* Having male and female flowers borne on separate plants. Compare **monoecious.** [New Latin *Dioecia* : DI- + Greek *oikia,* dwelling, from *oikos,* house.] **—di·oe·cious·ly** *adv.*

di·e·strus (dī-ĕs′trəs) *n. Biology.* A stage in the estrous cycle when the follicles and the uterus are small in size, and the epithelium layer surrounding the vagina is thin.

Di·og·e·nes (dī-ŏj′ə-nēz′), known as "the Cynic" (412–322 B.C.). Greek philosopher. Exiled with his father from Cinope in Asia Minor, he settled in Athens and founded the Cynic school of philosophy, promoting self-control, acceptance of suffering, the avoidance of physical pleasure, and a return to nature.

di·oi·cous (dī-oi′kəs) *adj. Botany.* Having antheridia and archegonia on separate plants; unisexual. Said of mosses and related plants. [New Latin *dioecus,* "having two houses" : DI- (two) + Greek *oikos,* house.]

di·ol (dī′ōl′, -ôl′) *n. Chemistry.* An alcohol that has two hydroxyl groups in its molecules; a dihydric alcohol. Also called "glycol."

Di·o·me·des (dī′ə-mē′dēz). Also **Di·o·med** (dī′ə-mĕd′), **Di·o·mede** (-mēd). *Greek Mythology.* A king of Argos and, in the Homeric poems, one of the chief heroes at Troy.

Di·o·nys·i·a (dī′ə-nĭsh′ē-ə, -nĭzh′ē-ə, -nĭs′ē-ə) *pl.n.* Any of various festivals of ancient Attica, held in honor of the god Dionysus, especially: **1.** The lesser festival, held in the autumn, in which the tragedy as a dramatic and literary form is thought to have had its origin. **2.** The great spring festival in Athens, at which competing plays were presented from the time of Pisistratus.

Di·o·nys·i·ac (dī′ə-nĭs′ē-ăk′) *adj.* **1.** Of or pertaining to Dionysus or the Dionysia. **2.** *Sometimes* **dionysiac.** Dionysian, as opposed to Apollonian. **—Di·o·ny·si·a·cal·ly** (dī′ə-nĭ-sī′ĭk-lē) *adv.*

Di·o·nys·i·an (dī′ə-nĭsh′ən, -nĭzh′ən, -nĭs′ē-ən) *adj.* **1.** Of or pertaining to any of several historical persons named Dionysius. **2.** Of or pertaining to Dionysus or the Dionysia. **3.** *Often* **dionysian. a.** Of an ecstatic, orgiastic, or irrational character. **b.** Filled with tremendous creative energy. **4.** *Sometimes* **dionysian.** In the philosophy of Nietzsche, characteristic of the spontaneous, irrational, creative, passionate qualities of human nature. Compare **Apollonian.**

Di·o·nys·i·us the Ar·e·op·a·gite (dī′ə-nĭsh′ē-əs, -nĭsh′əs, -nĭ′sē-əs; ăr′ē-ŏp′ə-jīt′, -gīt′), **Saint** (1st century A.D.). Greek martyr. A judge of the Areopagus, he was converted to Christianity by St. Paul and became the first bishop of Athens.

Di·o·ny·sus, Di·o·ny·sos (dī′ə-nī′səs). *Greek Mythology.* The god of wine and ecstasy, idol of an orgiastic religion celebrating the power and fertility of nature. Also called "Bacchus."

Di·o·phan·tine equation (dī′ə-făn′tīn, -tēn, -tən) *n. Mathematics.* An equation of two or more variables with integral coefficients, for which sets of possible integer solutions are required. [After DIOPHANTUS of Alexandria.]

Di·o·phan·tus of Alexandria (dī′ō-făn′təs) (3rd or 4th century A.D.). Greek mathematician, credited with inventing algebra. His work, preserved by Arabic mathematicians, was translated into Latin in the 16th century.

di·op·side (dī-ŏp′sīd′) *n.* A monoclinic pyroxene mineral, $CaMgSi_2O_6$, used as a gemstone and as a refractory. [French : DI- (two) + Greek *opsis* (stem *opsid-*), appearance, sight.]

di·op·ter (dī-ŏp′tər) *n. Abbr.* **D.** *Optics.* A unit, equal to a reciprocal meter, of curvature and of the power of lenses, refracting surfaces, and other optical systems. [French, from Latin, from Greek *dioptra,* an optical instrument : *dia-,* through + *opsesthai,* to see.] **—di·op·tral** *adj.*

di·op·tom·e·ter (dī′ŏp-tŏm′ə-tər) *n.* An instrument for measuring ocular refraction. [DI- + Greek *optos,* visible (see **optic**) + -METER.] **—di·op·tom·e·try** *n.*

di·op·tric (dī-ŏp′trĭk) *adj.* Also **di·op·tri·cal** (-trĭ-kəl). *Optics.* **1.** Of or pertaining to dioptrics. **2.** Pertaining to optical refraction; refractive.

di·op·trics (dī-ŏp′trĭks) *n. Used with a singular verb. Optics.* The study of the refraction of light, especially within the eye. [Greek

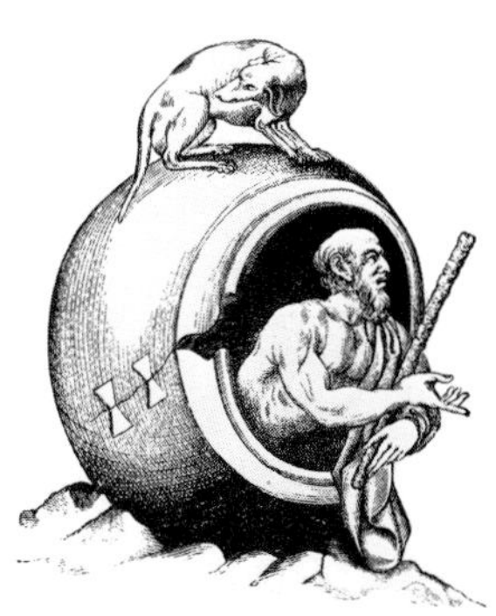

Diogenes *The Greek philosopher Diogenes rejected all luxury and is supposed to have made his home in a large earthenware barrel. His way of life earned him the name* kuon, *the Greek word for "dog"—a gibe from which is derived the word for followers of his ideas: Cynics.*

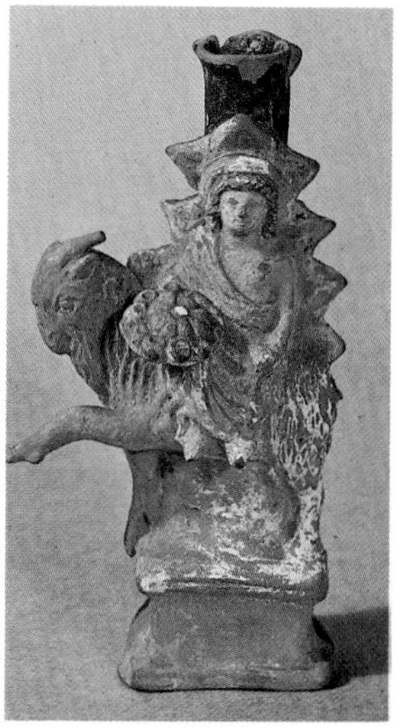

Dionysus *The Greek god of wine and revelry, here seen riding a goat on an Attic vase that was made in about 350 B.C.*

dinosaur

THE RULING REPTILES OF PREHISTORY
The variety of creatures to be found among the dinosaurs—the "monstrous lizards"

Of the reptiles that dominated life on land during the Mesozoic era, about 250 to 66 million years ago, the dinosaurs (whose Greek-derived name means "monstrous lizards") were the most successful.

There were two dinosaur orders, distinguished by differences in pelvic structure. Some of the "lizard-hipped" Saurischia, the first order to evolve, number among the most gigantic creatures ever to exist. A reconstructed skeleton of the longest, *Diplodocus,* is 26.7 meters (87 feet) long including a tail 15 meters (50 feet) long; yet it weighed relatively little. Its hollow bone structure combined strength with lightness. The heaviest dinosaur was *Brachiosaurus,* which may have weighed some 50 tons.

Many dinosaurs were bipedal—they walked on two legs. The birdlike *Coelophysis* had a modified pelvic girdle, enabling it to walk more efficiently, and well-developed arms and hands to catch prey.

Most saurischians had a full set of pointed teeth. *Tyrannosaurus,* one of the last to appear and the largest terrestrial carnivore ever known, must have used its teeth to attack its prey since its tiny forelimbs were of little use.

The "bird-hipped" Ornithischia were not as large. Most of them lacked front teeth and browsed on plants; *Camptosaurus* was typical of these. But *Hadrosaurus,* called the "duck-billed" dinosaur from the shape of its jaw, had up to 2,000 side teeth for grinding conifer needles and twigs. It was a powerful swimmer and is thought to have taken to water whenever it was startled. *Ankylosaurus,* a quadruped, was armored with a mosaic of bony plates fringed with spikes, and a tail that could be used as a club.

Stegosaurus had triangular bony plates along its neck and back, and a spiked tail. In common with many giant dinosaurs, *Stegosaurus* had an extra "brain," an enlarged area of the spinal cord located at the hip, which may have played a part in controlling the dinosaur's limbs and tail.

Climatic changes and consequent alterations in vegetation (possibly combined with a cataclysmic fire some 65 million years ago) may have been responsible for the disappearance of the dinosaurs. Yet they are aptly named Archosauria, or "ruling lizards," for they reigned for more than 100 million years.

Coelophysis
Triassic — Cretaceous
(250 – 66 million years ago)
2.4 meters (8 feet) long
23 kilograms (51 pounds)
Carnivorous

Brachiosaurus ("arm lizard")
Jurassic
(205 – 135 million years ago)
22.8 meters (75 feet) long
50 tons
Herbivorous

Diplodocus
Jurassic
(205 – 135 million
years ago)
27 meters
(87½ feet) long
10 tons
Herbivorous

Camptosaurus
Jurassic
(205 – 135 million
years ago)
1.2 – 4.5 meters
(4 – 15 feet) long
10 tons
Herbivorous

Ankylosaurus
("crooked lizard")
Early Cretaceous
(135 – 100 million years ago)
7.6 meters (25 feet) long
3 tons
Herbivorous

Hadrosaurus ("big lizard")
Cretaceous (135 – 66 million
years ago)
9 meters (30 feet) long
3 tons
Herbivorous

Stegosaurus
Jurassic (205 – 135 million years ago)
6 meters (20 feet) long
1.8 tons
Herbivorous

Tyrannosaurus
("tyrant lizard")
Late Cretaceous (100 – 66 million years ago)
14 meters (46 feet) long
7 tons Carnivorous

dioptrikos, from *dioptra,* optical instrument : *dia-,* through + *optos,* visible.]

Di·or (dē-ôr′), **Christian** (1905-57). French fashion designer noted for his "new look" for women's fashions in 1947. His styling featured fitted bodices and long, full skirts.

di·o·ram·a (dī′ə-răm′ə, -rä′mə) *n.* **1.** A three-dimensional miniature scene with painted model or wax figures or stuffed animals against a background. Dioramas are often used for museum exhibits. **2.** A scene reproduced on cloth transparencies with various lights shining through the cloths to produce changes in effect, and viewed through a small aperture. [French : DI(A)- (through) + (PAN)O-RAMA.] **—di·o·ram·ic** *adj.*

di·o·rite (dī′ə-rīt′) *n.* Any of various coarse-textured, crystalline igneous rocks rich in plagioclase and having little quartz, being intermediate between acid and basic rock. [French, from Greek *diorizein,* to distinguish : *dia-,* apart + *horizein,* to divide, from

horos, boundary.] **—di·o·rit·ic** (dī′ə-rĭt′ĭk) *adj.*

Di·o·scor·i·des Pe·dan·i·us (dī′ə-skôr′ĭ-dēz′ pə-dăn′ē-əs) (c. A.D. 40-90). Greek physician. His *De Materia Medica* catalogued and described more than 600 plants and plant principles.

Di·os·cu·ri (dī-ŏs′kyə-rī′, dī′ə-skyŏŏr′ī′). *Greek Mythology.* **Castor and Pollux** *(see).* [Greek *Dioskouroi,* "sons of Zeus" : *Dios,* genitive of ZEUS + *kouroi,* plural of *kouros,* boy, son.]

di·ox·ane (dī-ŏk′sān′) *n.* A flammable, potentially explosive, colorless liquid, $C_4H_8O_2$, used as a solvent for fats, greases, and resins and in various products including paints, lacquers, and fumigants.

di·ox·ide (dī-ŏk′sīd′) *n.* An oxide with two oxygen atoms per molecule.

di·ox·in (dī-ŏk′sĭn) *n.* An extremely toxic substance that causes chloracne and genetic mutation, formed as a by-product in the manufacture of the herbicide 2,4,5–T. Also called "TCDD."

dip (dĭp) *v.* **dipped, dipping, dips.** *—tr.* **1.** To plunge briefly in or into a liquid, usually in order to wet, coat, or saturate. **2.** To color or dye in this manner. **3.** To immerse (livestock) in a disinfectant solution. **4.** To make (a candle) by repeatedly immersing a wick in melted wax or tallow. **5.** To galvanize or plate (metal) by immersion. **6.** To scoop up by plunging the hand or a container into and out of a liquid; bail; ladle. **7.** To lower and raise (a flag) in salute. **8.** *Chiefly British.* To put (vehicle headlights) on low beam. —*intr.* **1.** To plunge into water or other liquid and come out quickly. **2.** To plunge the hand or a container into a liquid or another container, especially for the purpose of taking something up or out: *dipped into her pocket.* **3.** To drop or sink suddenly. **4.** To appear to sink. **5.** To slope downwards; decline. **6.** *Geology.* To lie at an angle to the horizontal plane, as a rock stratum may. **7.** To read here and there in a book or magazine; browse. Used with *into.* **8.** To investigate a subject superficially; dabble. **9.** To use up money, especially one's savings. Used with *into.*

∼*n.* **1.** A brief plunge or immersion; especially, a brief swim. **2.** A liquid into which something is dipped; especially, a **sheep dip** *(see).* **3.** A smooth creamed preparation into which crackers or other foods may be dipped. **4.** An amount taken up by dipping. **5.** A container for dipping. **6.** A candle made by repeated dipping in tallow or wax. **7.** A downward slope; a decline. **8.** *Geology.* The downward inclination of a rock stratum in reference to the plane of the horizontal. **9.** *Surveying.* The angular difference between eye level and the lower level of the horizon. **10. Magnetic dip** *(see).* **11.** A hollow; a depression. **12.** In gymnastics, an exercise on the parallel bars in which the body is lowered by bending the elbows until the chin reaches the level of the bars and then is raised by straightening the arms. **13.** A lowering or loss of altitude, as of an aircraft. **14.** *Slang.* A pickpocket. **15.** *Slang.* A foolish or gullible person. [Middle English *dippen,* Old English *dyppan,* from Germanic.]

di·pep·tide (dī-pĕp′tīd′) *n.* Any compound consisting of two amino acids linked by a peptide bond.

di·pet·al·ous (dī-pĕt′l-əs) *adj. Botany.* Having two petals.

di·phase (dī′fāz′) *adj.* Also **di·pha·sic** (dī-fā′zĭk). *Physics.* Having two phases.

di·phen·hy·dra·mine (dī′fĕn-hī′drə-mēn′) *n.* An antihistamine drug used to treat hay fever and other allergic conditions.

di·phen·yl (dī-fĕn′əl, -fē′nəl) *n. Chemistry.* **Biphenyl** *(see).*

di·phen·yl·a·mine (dī-fĕn-əl-ə-mēn′, -ăm′ĭn, dī-fē′nəl-) *n.* A colorless crystalline compound, $(C_6H_5)_2NH$, used as a stabilizer for plastics and in the manufacture of dyes, explosives, pesticides, and pharmaceuticals.

di·phen·yl·hy·dan·to·in sodium (dī-fĕn′əl-hī-dăn′tō-ĭn, dī-fē′nəl-) *n.* A white powder, $C_{15}H_{11}N_2O_2Na$, used as an anticonvulsant.

di·phe·ynl·ke·tone (dī-fĕn′əl-kē′tōn′, -fē′nəl-) *n.* **Benzophenone** *(see).*

di·phos·gene (dī-fŏz′jēn′) *n.* A colorless mobile liquid, $ClCOOCCl_3$, with a vapor used as a military poison gas, especially in World War I.

diph·the·ri·a (dĭf-thîr′ē-ə, dĭp-) *n.* An acute contagious disease caused by infection with the bacillus *Corynebacterium diphtheriae,* and characterized by the formation of a false membrane in the throat, causing difficulty in breathing, high fever, and weakness. [New Latin, from French *diphthérie,* from Greek *diphthera,* piece of leather (from the rough false membrane).] —**diph·the·rit·ic** (dĭf-thə-rĭt′ĭk, dĭp-), **diph·ther·ic** (dĭf-thĕr′ĭk, dĭp-), **diph·the·ri·al.** *adj.*

diph·thong (dĭf′thông′, -thŏng′, dĭp′-) *n. Phonetics.* **1.** A complex speech sound beginning with one vowel sound and moving to another vowel or semivowel position within the same syllable. For example, *oy* in the word *boy* is a diphthong. **2.** Either of the two ligatures *æ* or *œ,* originally pronounced as diphthongs in Classical Latin but in modern English rendered as single vowels. [Middle English *diptonge,* from Old French *diptongue,* from Late Latin *dipthongus,* from Greek *diphthongos* : DI- (two) + *phthongos*†, voice, sound. See also **monophthong, apothegm.**] —**diph·thon·gal** *adj.*

diph·thong·ize (dĭf′thông-īz′, dĭf′thŏng′-, dĭp′-) *v.* **-ized, -izing, -izes.** —*tr.* To pronounce as a diphthong. —*intr.* To become a diphthong. —**diph·thong·i·za·tion** *n.*

di·phy·cer·cal (dĭf′ĭ-sûr′kəl) *adj. Zoology.* Designating or having a tail fin in which the vertebral column extends to the tip, with symmetrical upper and lower parts. [Greek *diphuēs,* double, twofold + *kerkos,* tail.]

di·phy·let·ic (dī′fī-lĕt′ĭk) *adj.* Descended from two ancestral lines.

di·phyl·lous (dī-fĭl′əs) *adj. Botany.* Having two leaves. [New Latin *diphyllus* : DI- + -PHYLLOUS.]

di·phy·o·dont (dī-fī′ə-dŏnt′) *adj. Zoology.* Having two successive sets of teeth, as do humans and most other mammals. [Greek *diphuēs,* double, twofold : DI- (two) + *phuein,* to bring forth, grow + -ODONT.]

dipl. diplomat; diplomatic.

dip·la·cu·sis (dĭp′lə-ko͞o′sĭs, -kyo͞o′-) *n.* The hearing of a single sound as two sounds, due to a defect in the inner ear. [New Latin : DIPL(O)- + Greek *akousis,* hearing, from *akouein,* to hear.]

di·ple·gia (dī-plē′jə, -jē-ə) *n.* Paralysis of corresponding parts on both sides of the body. [DI- + -PLEGIA.]

di·plex (dī′plĕks′) *adj.* Capable of simultaneous transmission or reception of two messages in the same radio channel. [DI- + (DU)-PLEX.]

diplo–, dipl– *prefix.* Indicates double; for example, **diploid.** [Greek, from *diploos,* double : DI- (two) + *-ploos,* "-fold."]

dip·lo·blas·tic (dĭp′lō-blăs′tĭk) *adj.* Having two distinct cellular layers. Said of lower invertebrate animals such as sponges and coelenterates. Compare **triploblastic.** [DIPLO- + -BLASTIC.]

dip·lo·car·di·ac (dĭp′lō-kär′dē-ăk′) *adj.* Having or characterizing a heart in which the two sides are distinctly separated, as in birds and mammals. [DIPLO- + Greek *kardia,* heart.]

dip·lo·coc·cus (dĭp′lō-kŏk′əs) *n., pl.* **-cocci** (-kŏk′sī′, -kŏk′ī′). Any of various paired spherical bacteria, including those of the genus *Diplococcus,* some of which are pathogenic. [New Latin : DIPLO- + -COCCUS.] —**dip·lo·coc·cal** (dĭp′lō-kŏk′əl), **dip·lo·coc·cic** (dĭp′lō-kŏk′sĭk, -kŏk′ĭk) *adj.*

di·plod·o·cus (dĭ-plŏd′ə-kəs, dī-) *n.* A very large, extinct, long-necked, herbivorous dinosaur of the genus *Diplodocus,* that existed during the Jurassic period. [New Latin : DIPLO- + Greek *dokos,* beam.]

dip·lo·ë (dĭp′lō-ē′) *n.* The spongy, bony tissue between the outer and inner bone layers of the cranium. [New Latin, from Greek *diploē,* "doubling," "fold," from *diploos,* double. See **diplo-.**]

dip·loid (dĭp′loid′) *adj.* **1.** Double or twofold. **2.** *Genetics.* Having a homologous pair of chromosomes for each characteristic except sex, the total number of chromosomes being twice that of a gamete. Compare **haploid.**

∼*n. Genetics.* **1.** A diploid cell. **2.** An individual characterized by a diploid chromosome number. [DIPL(O)- + -OID.]

di·plo·ma (dĭ-plō′mə) *n.* **1.** A document or certificate issued by a university, college, school, or other educational institution indicating that a certain level of proficiency has been reached, examinations passed, or a particular course of study successfully completed. **2.** A certificate conferring a privilege or honor. **3.** An official document or charter. [Latin, from Greek *diplōma,* something doubled, folded paper, document, from *diploos,* double. See **diplo-.**]

di·plo·ma·cy (dĭ-plō′mə-sē) *n., pl.* **-cies. 1.** The art or practice of conducting international relations, as in negotiating alliances, treaties, and agreements. **2.** Tact or skill in dealing with people. —See Synonyms at **tact.**

dip·lo·mat (dĭp′lə-măt′) *n.* **1.** *Abbr.* **dipl.** A person appointed to represent one government in its relations with others, such as an ambassador. **2.** One who possesses skill or tact in dealing with others. [French *diplomate,* back-formation from *diplomatique,* DIPLOMATIC.]

dip·lo·mate (dĭp′lə-māt′) *n.* One who has received a diploma; especially, a physician certified as a specialist by a board of examiners.

dip·lo·mat·ic (dĭp′lə-măt′ĭk) *adj.* **1.** *Abbr.* **dipl.** Of, pertaining to, or involving diplomacy or diplomats. **2.** Characterized by tact and sensitivity in dealing with people; discreet; politic. **3. a.** Of or pertaining to diplomatics. **b.** Being an exact copy of an original: *a diplomatic edition.* —See Synonyms at **suave.** [French *diplomatique,* connected with the documents that regulate international relations, from New Latin *diplomaticus,* connected with documents or diplomatics, from Latin *diplōma,* document. See **diploma.**] —**dip·lo·mat·i·cal·ly** *adv.*

diplomatic corps *n.* The entire body of diplomatic personnel in residence at the capital of a nation.

diplomatic immunity *n.* Exemption from taxation and the ordinary processes of law afforded to diplomatic personnel in a foreign country.

dip·lo·mat·ics (dĭp′lə-măt′ĭks) *n. Used with a singular verb.* **1.** Diplomacy. **2.** The branch of paleography devoted to the study of ancient documents and the determination of their age and authenticity. [Sense 1, see **diplomatic;** sense 2, see **diploma.**]

di·plo·ma·tist (dĭ-plō′mə-tĭst) *n.* A diplomat.

dip·lont (dĭp′lŏnt′) *n. Biology.* An organism having somatic cells with diploid chromosomes. [DIPLO- + *-ont,* cell, from Greek *ōn* (stem *ont-*), present participle of *einai,* to be.]

di·plo·pi·a (dĭ-plō′pē-ə) *n. Pathology.* A disorder of vision that causes objects to appear double; double vision. [New Latin : DIPL(O)- + -OPIA.] —**di·plo·pic** (dĭ-plō′pĭk, -plĭp′ĭk) *adj.*

dip·lo·pod (dĭp′lə-pŏd′) *n.* Any of various segmented, cylindrical arthropods of the class Diplopoda, which includes the millipedes. [New Latin *Diplopoda* : DIPLO- + -POD.] —**dip·lo·pod** *adj.*

di·plo·sis (dĭ-plō′sĭs) *n.* The formation of the full (diploid) number of chromosomes found in a somatic cell by the fusion of gamete nuclei containing haploid sets in fertilization. [New Latin, from Greek *diplōsis,* a doubling, from *diploun,* to double, from *diploos,* double. See **diplo-.**]

dip·lo·tene (dĭp′lō-tēn) *n. Genetics.* A stage of the first prophase of meiosis during which crossing over occurs and the paired homologous chromosomes begin to separate. [DIPLO- + *-tene,* from Greek *tainia,* band.]

dip needle *n.* **1.** *Physics.* A magnetic needle balanced and pivoted to rotate freely in a vertical plane to indicate the local inclination of the earth's magnetic field. **2.** An instrument, the **inclinometer** *(see).*

dip·no·an (dĭp′nō-ən) *n.* Any of various fishes of the group Dipnoi, which includes the lungfishes, characterized by modified lungs that enable them to breathe atmospheric air.

∼*adj.* Of or belonging to the Dipnoi. [New Latin *Dipnoi,* from *dipnous,* having two apertures for breathing, from Greek *dipnoos* : DI- + *pnoē,* breath, from *pnein,* to breathe.]

dip·o·dy (dĭp′ə-dē) *n., pl.* **-dies.** A metrical unit in poetry consisting of two feet. [Late Latin *dipodia,* from Greek, from *dipous* (stem *dipod-*), two-footed : DI- + -POD.]

di·po·lar (dī′pō′lər) *adj.* Of or having a dipole.

di·pole (dī′pōl′) *n.* **1.** *Physics.* A pair of electric charges or magnetic poles, of equal magnitude but of opposite sign or polarity, sepa-

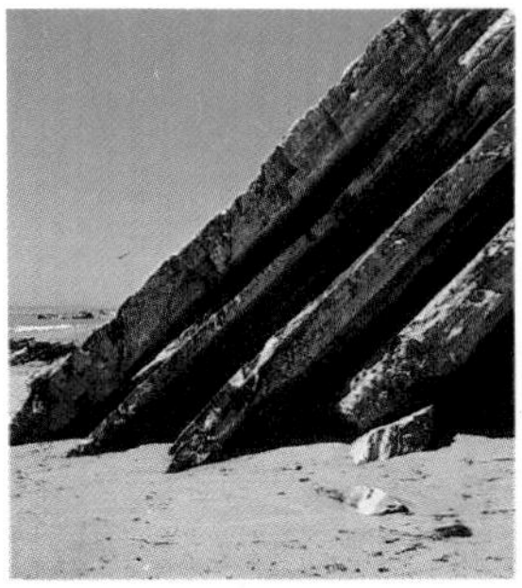

dip *In geological terms, a dip is where rock layers slope downward. The layers shown here dive into the sand at Refugio Beach, California.*

PRONUNCIATION KEY

ă, pat; ā, pay; âr, care;
ä, father, are; b, bib;
ch, church; d, deed; ĕ, pet;
ē, be; f, fife; g, gag; h, hat;
hw, which; ĭ, pit; ī, pie;
îr, pier; j, judge; k, kick;
l, lid, needle; m, mum;
n, no, sudden; ng, thing;
ŏ, pot; ō, toe; ô, paw, for;
oi, noise; ou, out; o͝o, book;
o͞o, boot; p, pop; r, roar;
s, sauce; sh, ship, dish;
t, tight; th, thin, path;
th, this, bathe; ŭ, cut; ûr, fur;
v, valve; w, with; y, yes;
z, zebra, size; zh, vision;
ə, about, item, edible,
gallop, circus, peaceful

IN FOREIGN WORDS:

à, *Fr.* ami; œ, *Fr.* feu, *Ger.* schön; ü, *Fr.* tu, *Ger.* über; KH, *Ger.* ich, *Scot.* loch; N, *Fr.* bon; y', *Fr.* Compiègne

STRESS MARKS:

Primary stress: ′
in·cite′ (ĭn-sīt′)
Secondary stress: ′
in′sight′ (ĭn′sīt′)

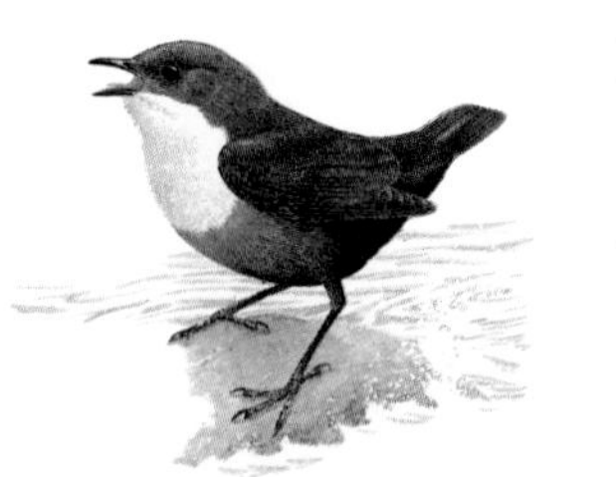

dipper *Between dives, dippers often perch on stones in the middle of streams. The birds hunt their food—insects and small fish—by plunging into the water in shallow rivers and walking along the bottom, their bodies tilted forward. This is the European dipper,* Cinclus cinclus.

rated by a small distance. **2.** *Electronics.* An antenna, usually fed from the center, consisting of two equal rods extending outward in a straight line. In this sense, also called "dipole antenna."

dipole moment *n.* **1.** The product of either charge in an electric dipole with the distance separating them. Also called "electric moment." **2.** The product of the strength of either pole in a magnetic dipole with the distance separating them. Also called "magnetic dipole moment," "magnetic moment."

dip·per (dĭp′ər) *n.* **1.** One that dips. **2.** A container used for dipping, such as a long-handled cup for taking up water. **3. Dipper.** Either of two star groups shaped like a ladle, the Big Dipper in Ursa Major or the Little Dipper in Ursa Minor. **4.** Any of several small diving birds of the genus *Cinclus.* Also called "water ouzel."

dip·py (dĭp′ē) *adj.* **-pier, -piest.** *Slang.* Foolish; not sensible. [20th century : origin obscure.]

di·pro·pel·lant (dī′prə-pĕl′ənt) *n.* A **bipropellant** *(see).*

dip·sas (dĭp′səs) *n., pl.* **-sades** (-sə-dēz′). A serpent whose bite was fabled to produce a great thirst. [Middle English, from Latin, from Greek, from *dipsa*†, thirst.]

dip slope *n.* A land surface whose degree and direction of slope corresponds roughly with the dip of the underlying rock strata.

dip·so (dĭp′sō′) *n., pl* **-sos.** *Slang.* An alcoholic; dipsomaniac.

dip·so·ma·ni·a (dĭp′sə-mā′nē-ə, -mān′yə) *n.* An insatiable, often periodic craving for alcoholic drink. [New Latin : Greek *dipsa*†, thirst + -MANIA.] **—dip·so·ma·ni·ac** *n. & adj.* **—dip·so·ma·ni·a·cal** (dĭp′sə-mə-nī′ĭ-kəl) *adj.*

dip·stick (dĭp′stĭk′) *n.* A graduated rod for measuring the depth or amount of liquid in a container, as of oil in a crankcase.

dip·ter·al (dĭp′tər-əl) *adj.* **1.** *Architecture.* Built with two rows of columns. **2.** Variant of **dipterous.**

dip·ter·an (dĭp′tər-ən) *n.* Also **dip·ter·on** (-tə-rŏn′) A dipterous insect. [New Latin *Diptera,* plural of *dipterus,* DIPTEROUS.] **—dip·ter·an** *adj.*

dip·ter·ous (dĭp′tər-əs) *adj.* Also **dipteral. 1.** Of, pertaining to, or belonging to the Diptera, a large order of insects that includes the true flies and mosquitoes, characterized by a single pair of membranous wings and a pair of club-shaped balancing organs, the halteres. **2.** *Botany.* Having two winglike parts: *the dipterous fruit of the maple.* [New Latin *dipterus,* from Greek *dipteros,* having two wings : DI- + -PTEROUS.]

dip·tych (dĭp′tĭk) *n.* **1.** An ancient writing tablet having two leaves hinged together. **2.** A pair of painted or carved panels hinged together. [Late Latin *diptycha,* from Greek *diptukha,* from *diptukhos,* double-folded : DI- + *ptukhē,* a fold, from *ptussein,* to fold.]

di·quat (dī′kwät′) *n.* A strong, nonpersistent, yellow, crystalline herbicide, $C_{12}H_{12}Br_2N_2$, used to control water weeds. [DI- + QUAT(ERNARY).]

dir. director.

dire (dīr) *adj.* **direr, direst. 1.** Having dreadful or terrible implications or consequences; calamitous. **2.** Extreme; urgent: *in dire need.* **3.** *Informal.* Hard to bear; tiresome or unpleasant. [Latin *dīrus,* fearful, ill-omened.] **—dire·ly** *adv.* **—dire·ness** *n.*

di·rect (dĭ-rĕkt′, dī-) *v.* **-rected, -recting, -rects.** *—tr.* **1.** To conduct the affairs of; manage; regulate. **2.** To take charge of with authority; control; give commands to. **3. a.** To guide (musicians, especially a small group) while playing oneself. **b.** To conduct (musicians or a choir). **4.** To move (something or someone) toward a goal; aim; point. **5.** To give instructions to (someone) for finding a place. **6.** To address (mail) to a destination. **7.** To address (a speech, remark, or the like) to a person or audience. **8. a.** To give guidance and instruction to (actors, camera technicians, or the like) in the rehearsal and performance of a play or the making of a film. **b.** To supervise the performance of actors in. **c.** To supervise the creative aspects of the making of a (film). *—intr.* **1.** To give commands or directions. **2.** To supervise a performance, rehearsal, or the making of a film. —See Synonyms at **command, conduct.**

~adj. **1.** Proceeding or lying in a straight course or line; not deviating or swerving. **2.** Straightforward; candid; frank. **3.** Without intervening persons, conditions, or agencies; immediate. **4.** By action of the voters, rather than through elected representatives or delegates. **5.** Of unbroken descent; lineal. **6.** Consisting of the exact words of the writer or speaker. **7.** Absolute; total: *direct opposites.* **8.** *Mathematics.* Varying in the same manner as another quantity; especially, increasing if another quantity increases or decreasing if it decreases. Compare **inverse. 9.** *Astronomy.* Designating a west-to-east motion of a planet or other celestial body in the same direction as the sun's movement among the stars. Compare **retrograde.**

~adv. **1.** In a direct manner; straight; directly. **2.** Without going through a telephone operator: *dial direct.* [Middle English *directen,* from Latin *dīrigere* (past participle *dīrectus*), to arrange in distinct lines, direct : *dis-,* apart + *regere,* to guide.]

direct access *n.* *Computer Science.* **Random access** *(see).*

direct action *n.* The use of strikes, demonstrations, sabotage, and similar methods to exert pressure on a government, employer, or any other established authority. **—direct actionist** *n.*

di·rect-ac·tion (dĭ-rĕkt′ăk′shən, dī-) *adj.* Operating without intermediate ingredients, components, stages, or processes.

direct current *n. Abbr.* **dc, DC, D.C.** An electric current flowing in one direction.

direct drive *n.* A mechanism in which the drive shaft is directly connected to the part to be driven.

di·rec·ted angle (dĭ-rĕk′tĭd, dī-) *n.* An angle having an indicated positive sense.

directed distance *n.* A segment of a line having an indicated positive sense.

direct evidence *n.* *Law.* Evidence that bears directly on the fact in dispute, such as that of an eyewitness. Compare **circumstantial evidence.**

di·rec·tion (dĭ-rĕk′shən, dī-) *n.* **1.** The act or function of directing. **2.** Management, supervision, or guidance of some action or operation. **3.** The art or process of film or theatrical directing. **4.** A word or phrase in a musical score indicating how a particular passage is to be played or sung. **5.** *Usually* **directions.** An instruction or series of instructions for doing something. **6.** An order or command; an authoritative indication. **7. a.** The distance-independent relationship between two points that specifies the angular position of either with respect to the other; the relationship by which the alignment or orientation of any position with respect to any other position is established. **b.** A position to which motion or another position is referred. **c.** A line leading to a place or point. **d.** The line, course, or angle along which a person or thing moves. **e.** The destination of a person or thing. **8.** The statement, in degrees, of the angle measured between due north and a given line or course on a compass. Used to indicate the course of a ship, aircraft, or the like. **9.** A course or area of development or action; a tendency toward a particular end or goal. [Middle English, arrangement, management, from Old French, from Latin *dīrectiō* (stem *dīrectiōn-*), from *dīrigere,* to DIRECT.] **—di·rec·tion·less** *adj.*

di·rec·tion·al (dĭ-rĕk′shən-əl, dī-) *adj.* **1.** Of or indicating direction: *an automobile's directional lights.* **2.** *Electronics.* Capable of receiving or sending signals in one direction only. **3.** Of or relating to guidance in effort or behavior: *directional training.*

~n. A directional signal. **—di·rec·tion·al·i·ty** *n.*

directional antenna *n.* An antenna adapted for receiving signals from or sending signals in a particular direction.

directional signal *n.* One of two flashing lights on an automotive vehicle that indicates the direction of a turn. Also called "directionals."

direction angle *n.* *Mathematics.* One of the three angles that a given line makes with the axes of a three-dimensional Cartesian coordinate system.

direction cosine *n.* *Mathematics.* The cosine of a direction angle of a given line.

direction finder *n. Abbr.* **DF** A device for determining the source of a transmitted signal, consisting mainly of a radio receiver and a coiled rotating antenna.

direction indicator *n.* A compass used in aircraft navigation to compare an intended course to the actual course.

direction ratio *n.* *Mathematics.* One of three numbers that are proportional to the direction cosines of a given line.

di·rec·tive (dĭ-rĕk′tĭv, dī-) *n.* An order or instruction, especially one issued by a central authority.

~adj. Serving to direct, indicate, or point out; directing.

di·rect·ly (dĭ-rĕkt′lē, dī-) *adv.* **1.** In a direct line or manner; straight. **2.** Without anyone or anything intervening; immediately. **3.** Exactly; totally; absolutely. **4.** At once; instantly. —See Usage note at **immediately.**

~conj. Chiefly British. As soon as: *We'll go directly she's ready.*

direct mail *n.* **1.** A method of advertising by which a business or organization approaches prospective customers or patrons directly through the mail. **2.** The advertising matter so sent.

direct method *n.* A method of teaching a foreign language using only the language being taught and introducing only a minimal amount of formal grammar.

direct object *n.* In English and some other languages, the word or words in a sentence designating the person or thing undergoing the action of a transitive verb and required to complete its syntactic function. The direct object in English is usually a noun, nominal clause or phrase, or pronoun, and generally follows the verb. In *The girl broke the dish,* the direct object is *the dish.* Compare **indirect object.**

Di·rec·toire (dē-rĕk-twȧr′) *n.* The executive body in charge of the French government from 1795 to 1799. Also called "Directory."

~adj. Of or in the ornate style characteristic of the period of the Directoire in France.

di·rec·tor (dĭ-rĕk′tər, dī-) *n. Abbr.* **dir. 1.** One who supervises, controls, or manages. **2.** A member of a board of persons that controls or governs the affairs of a business concern, institution, or the like. **3. a.** A person who supervises the creative aspects of a dramatic production and instructs the actors on stage. Compare **producer. b.** The person who supervises the creative aspects of the making of a film. **4.** The conductor of an orchestra or chorus. **5.** A surgical instrument used to control the direction and extent of an incision. **—di·rec·tor·ship** *n.*

di·rec·tor·ate (dĭ-rĕk′tər-ĭt, dī-) *n.* **1.** The office or position of a director. **2.** A board of directors.

di·rec·to·ri·al (dĭ-rĕk′tôr′ē-əl, -tōr′ē-əl) *adj.* **1.** Of or pertaining to a director or directorate. **2.** Serving to direct; directive. **—di·rec·to·ri·al·ly** *adv.*

director's chair *n.* A type of light folding chair, usually of canvas on a wooden frame, as used typically by film directors.

di·rec·to·ry (dĭ-rĕk′tə-rē, dī-) *n., pl.* **-ries. 1.** One that directs. **2.** A book listing names, addresses, and telephone numbers of: **a.** Persons living in a particular area, usually listed alphabetically. **b.** A

specific group of persons or firms, listed according to a trade or service offered. **3.** A book of rules or directions, especially for use in church worship. **4.** A directorate.
~adj. Serving to direct.

Di·rec·to·ry (dĭ-rĕk′tə-rē, dī-) *n.* The **Directoire** *(see).*

direct primary *n.* A preliminary election in which a party's candidates for public office are nominated by popular vote.

di·rec·tress (dĭ-rĕk′trĭs, dī-) *n.* A woman who is a director.

di·rec·trix (dĭ-rĕk′trĭks, dī-) *n. pl.* **-trixes** or **directrices** (dĭ′rĕk-trī′sēz). **1.** *Geometry.* **a.** The straight reference line used in generating a conic. **b.** The curve about which the generator moves in forming a cone, cylinder, or other surface. **2.** *Military.* The median line in the trajectory of fire. [New Latin, "directress," from Late Latin *dīrector,* DIRECTOR.]

direct speech *n.* Speech or writing that is reported in its exact original form. Compare **indirect speech.**

direct tax *n.* A tax, such as an income or property tax, levied directly on the taxpayer. Compare **indirect tax.**

dire·ful (dīr′fəl) *adj.* Dreadful; frightful; dire. **—dire·ful·ly** *adv.* **—dire·ful·ness** *n.*

dirge (dûrj) *n.* **1.** A funeral hymn or lament. **2.** *Ecclesiastical.* The office for the dead; a funeral service that is sung. [Middle English *dirige, derge,* from the first word in Medieval Latin *dīrige, Domine, Deus meus, in conspectu tuo viam meam,* "Direct, O Lord, my God, my way in thy sight" (an antiphon in the office of the dead, adopted from Psalms 5:9), from Latin, singular imperative of *dīrigere,* to DIRECT.] **—dirge·ful** *adj.*

dir·ham (də-răm′) *n.* **1. a.** The basic monetary unit of Morocco, divided into 100 centimes. **b.** The basic monetary unit of the United Arab Emirates, divided into 100 fils. See feature at **currency. 2. a.** A monetary unit equal to 1/20 of the dinar of Iraq. **b.** A monetary unit equal to 1/10 of the dinar of Kuwait. **c.** A monetary unit equal to 1/1000 of the dinar of Libya. **d.** A monetary unit equal to 1/100 of the riyal of Qatar. See feature at **currency. 3.** A coin of various North African and Middle Eastern countries. [Arabic *dirham,* from Greek *drakhmē,* DRACHMA.]

dir·i·gi·ble (dĭr′ə-jə-bəl, dĭ-rĭj′ə-bəl) *n.* An early steerable airship.
~adj. Able to be guided or steered. [Latin *dīrigere,* to guide, DIRECT.] **—dir·i·gi·bil·i·ty** (dĭr′ə-jə-bĭl′ə-tē) *n.*

dir·i·ment (dĭr′ə-mənt) *adj.* Rendering totally void; nullifying. Used especially in common law in the phrase *diriment impediment of marriage* to signify any sufficient cause for voiding a marriage. [Latin *dīrimēns* (stem *dīriment-*), present participle of *dīrimere,* to take apart, separate, interrupt : *dis-,* apart + *emere,* to take, buy.]

dirk (dûrk) *n.* A dagger, especially as worn by Scottish Highlanders.
~tr.v. **dirked, dirking, dirks.** To stab with a dirk. [Earlier *durk, dork,* probably related to or altered from German *Dolch,* dagger.]

dirn·dl (dûrnd′l) *n.* **1.** A full-skirted dress with a tight bodice, patterned after Tyrolean peasant wear. **2.** A gathered skirt in this style. [German, short for *Dirndlkleid* : *Dirndl,* diminutive of *Dirne,* girl, from Old High German *thiorna,* maid + *Kleid,* dress.]

dirt (dûrt) *n.* **1.** Earth or soil. **2.** A filthy or soiling substance, such as mud, dust, or excrement. **3.** Something or someone mean, contemptible, or vile. **4.** Obscene language. **5.** Malicious or scandalous gossip. **6.** Gravel, slag, or other material from which metal is extracted in mining. **7.** Earth, gravel, or the like that has been pressed down to create a road surface.
~adj. Made of dirt: *a dirt track.* [Middle English *dirt,* variant of *drit,* excrement, mud, filth, from Old Norse *drit,* from Germanic *drit-* (unattested).]

dirt bike *n.* A lightweight motorbike designed for use on rough surfaces, as dirt roads or trails.

dirt-cheap (dûrt′chēp′) *adj. Informal.* Very cheap. **—dirt-cheap** *adv.*

dirt farmer *n. Informal.* A farmer who does all his own work.

dirt·y (dûr′tē) *adj.* **-ier, -iest. 1.** Soiled, as with dirt; grimy; unclean. **2.** *Informal.* Obscene or scatological. **3.** Contemptibly contrary to honor or rules; underhand; nasty: *a dirty trick.* **4.** Of a clouded or muddy appearance. Said especially of colors. **5.** Designating a nuclear weapon that produces an excessive amount of radioactive fallout. **6.** Stormy; rough: *dirty weather.* **7.** Tending to soil or make grubby: *dirty work.* **8.** Expressing hostility or ill-will: *a dirty look.*
~v. **dirtied, -ying, -ies.** *—tr.* To make soiled; stain; tarnish. *—intr.* To become dirty. [Middle English *dritti, dirti,* from *drit,* DIRT.] **—dirt·i·ly** *adv.* **—dirt·i·ness** *n.*
Synonyms: *filthy, foul, grimy, nasty, soiled, squalid.*

dirty linen *n. Informal.* Potentially embarrassing private affairs, such as those of a married couple. Used chiefly in the phrase *wash one's dirty linen in public.*

dirty old man *n. Abbr.* **D.O.M. 1.** A man, usually middle-aged or elderly, who makes furtive and unwelcome sexual advances to women and children. **2.** Any man seen as entertaining lewd or lecherous thoughts.

dirty pool *n. Slang.* Unjust or dishonest conduct. [From POOL (gambling).]

dirty tricks *pl.n. Informal.* Underhand political activities; especially, dishonest practices used in an election campaign to discredit opponents or subvert the electoral process.

dirty word *n.* **1.** A swearword; an obscenity. **2.** Something disapproved of or regarded as objectionable.

dirty work *n. Informal.* **1.** Foul play; deceit. **2.** A difficult or distasteful chore or task, especially when delegated to a subordinate.

dis– *prefix.* Indicates: **1.** Negation, lack, invalidation, or deprivation; for example, **distrust, disuse. 2.** Reversal; for example, **disengage, disunite. 3.** Removal or rejection; for example, **discard, disbar. 4.** Intensification or completion of negative action; for example, **disrupt.** [In borrowed Latin and French compounds, Latin *dis-* (Old French *des-*) indicates: 1. Apart, asunder, aside, as in **digress, distrain.** 2. Away, abroad, in different directions, as in **dismiss, divulge, disseminate.** 3. Negation, deprivation, as in **diffident, disparage.** 4. Reversal, as in **dissimulate.** 5. Removal, as in **dismantle.** 6. Intensification or completion of divisive action, as in **disturb, dissever.** 7. Pejoration, as in **disaster.** Latin *dis-* (sometimes *di-*) is the preverbal form of *dis*†, apart, asunder.]

dis·a·bil·i·ty (dĭs′ə-bĭl′ə-tē) *n., pl.* **-ties. 1.** A disabled state or condition; incapacity. **2.** Something that disables; a handicap. **3.** A legal incapacity or disqualification.

dis·a·ble (dĭs-ā′bəl) *tr.v.* **-bled, -bling, -bles. 1.** To weaken or destroy the normal physical or mental abilities of; cripple; incapacitate. **2.** To render legally disqualified. **3. a.** To make (a machine, for example) inoperative. **b.** *Computer Science.* To suppress an interrupt feature. **—dis·a·ble·ment** *n.*

dis·a·bled (dĭs-ā′bəld) *adj.* Physically handicapped; especially, lacking full use of one's limbs.

dis·a·buse (dĭs′ə-byōōz′) *tr.v.* **-bused, -busing, -buses.** To free from a false impression or misconception; undeceive.

di·sac·cha·ride (dī-săk′ə-rīd′) *n. Chemistry.* Any of a class of carbohydrates, including lactose and sucrose, that yield two monosaccharides on hydrolysis.

dis·ac·cord (dĭs′ə-kôrd′) *n.* Lack of accord; disagreement.
~intr.v. **disaccorded, -cording, -cords.** *Rare.* To disagree.

dis·ac·cus·tom (dĭs′ə-kŭs′təm) *tr.v.* **-tomed, -toming, -toms.** To cause to become unaccustomed.

dis·ad·van·tage (dĭs′əd-văn′tĭj, -vän′tĭj) *n.* **1.** An unfavorable condition or circumstance; handicap. **2.** Detriment.
~tr.v. **disadvantaged, -taging, -tages.** To put at a disadvantage; set back.

dis·ad·van·taged (dĭs′əd-văn′tĭjd, -vän′tĭjd) *adj.* Subjected to severe economic and social disadvantage.

dis·ad·van·ta·geous (dĭs-ăd′vən-tā′jəs, dĭs′ăd-vən-) *adj.* Detrimental; unfavorable; harmful. **—dis·ad·van·ta·geous·ly** *adv.* **—dis·ad·van·ta·geous·ness** *n.*

dis·af·fect (dĭs′ə-fĕkt′) *tr.v.* **-fected, -fecting, -fects.** To cause to lose affection or loyalty; alienate.

dis·af·fect·ed (dĭs′ə-fĕk′tĭd) *adj.* No longer contented and loyal; alienated. **—dis·af·fect·ed·ly** *adv.*

dis·af·fec·tion (dĭs′ə-fĕk′shən) *n.* Absence or withdrawal of affection or loyalty.

dis·af·fil·i·ate (dĭs′ə-fĭl′ē-āt′) *v.* **-ated, -ating, -ates.** *—tr.* To disassociate (oneself or another) from an alliance. *—intr.* To sever an affiliation or association. **—dis·af·fil·i·a·tion** *n.*

dis·af·firm (dĭs′ə-fûrm′) *tr.v.* **-firmed, -firming, -firms. 1.** To deny or contradict. **2.** *Law.* **a.** To repudiate. **b.** To set aside; reverse. **—dis·af·fir·mance** (dĭs′ə-fûr′məns), **dis·af·fir·ma·tion** (dĭs′ăf-ər-mā′shən) *n.*

dis·ag·gre·gate (dĭs-ăg′rə-gĭt′, -gāt′) *intr.v.* **-gated, -gating, -gates.** To break up or break apart. **—dis·ag·gre·ga·tive** *adj.*

dis·a·gree (dĭs′ə-grē′) *intr.v.* **-greed, -greeing, -grees. 1.** To be different or inconsistent; fail to correspond. **2.** To have a different opinion; fail to agree; dissent. **3.** To dispute; quarrel. **4.** To cause adverse effects; be incompatible: *Something I ate disagreed with me.*

dis·a·gree·a·ble (dĭs′ə-grē′ə-bəl) *adj.* **1.** Unpleasant; offensive; distasteful. **2.** Quarrelsome; bad-tempered. **—dis·a·gree·a·ble·ness** *n.* **—dis·a·gree·a·bly** *adv.*

dis·a·gree·ment (dĭs′ə-grē′mənt) *n.* **1.** A failure or refusal to agree. **2.** Disparity; inconsistency. **3.** A conflict or difference of opinion.

dis·al·low (dĭs′ə-lou′) *tr.v.* **-lowed, -lowing, -lows. 1.** To refuse to allow. **2.** To reject as invalid, untrue, or improper. **—dis·al·low·a·ble** *adj.* **—dis·al·low·ance** *n.*

dis·am·big·u·ate (dĭs′ăm-bĭg′yōō-āt′) *tr.v.* **-ated, -ating, -ates.** To establish a single grammatical or semantic interpretation for (an ambiguous word or phrase). **—dis·am·big·u·a·tion** *n.*

dis·an·nul (dĭs′ə-nŭl′) *tr.v.* **-nulled, -nulling, -nuls.** To annul completely; make void; cancel. **—dis·an·nul·ment** *n.*

dis·ap·pear (dĭs′ə-pîr′) *intr.v.* **-peared, -pearing, -pears. 1. a.** To pass out of sight, either suddenly or gradually; vanish. **b.** To cease to be perceived by the senses: *the pain has disappeared.* **2.** To die out; become extinct. **3.** To become lost or absent, often in a mysterious or sinister way. **—dis·ap·pear·ance** *n.*

dis·ap·point (dĭs′ə-point′) *tr.v.* **-pointed, -pointing, -points. 1.** To fail to satisfy the hope, desire, or expectation of. **2.** To frustrate; thwart. [Middle English *disappointen,* to remove from office, dispossess, from Old French *desapointier* : *des-,* from Latin *dis-* (reversal) + *apointier,* to APPOINT.] **—dis·ap·point·er** *n.* **—dis·ap·point·ing·ly** *adv.*

dis·ap·point·ed (dĭs′ə-poin′tĭd) *adj.* Made unhappy by the failure of hopes or expectations; frustrated. **—dis·ap·point·ed·ly** *adv.*

dis·ap·point·ment (dĭs′ə-point′mənt) *n.* **1. a.** The act of disappointing. **b.** The condition or feeling of being disappointed. **c.** An instance of disappointing or being disappointed. **2.** A person, thing, or state of affairs that disappoints.

Disappointment, Cape. Projection into the Pacific Ocean on the north side of the Columbia River in southwestern Washington. It was named in 1788 by an English sea captain, John Meares, who rounded it while searching for the fabled River of the West and was "disappointed" because he could not enter the river.

PRONUNCIATION KEY

ă, pat; ā, pay; âr, care; ä, father, are; b, bib; ch, church; d, deed; ĕ, pet; ē, be; f, fife; g, gag; h, hat; hw, which; ĭ, pit; ī, pie; îr, pier; j, judge; k, kick; l, lid, needle; m, mum; n, no, sudden; ng, thing; ŏ, pot; ō, toe; ô, paw, for; oi, noise; ou, out; ŏŏ, book; ōō, boot; p, pop; r, roar; s, sauce; sh, ship, dish; t, tight; th, thin, path; *th,* this, bathe; ŭ, cut; ûr, fur; v, valve; w, with; y, yes; z, zebra, size; zh, vision; ə, about, item, edible, gallop, circus, peaceful

IN FOREIGN WORDS:

à, *Fr.* ami; œ, *Fr.* feu, *Ger.* schön; ü, *Fr.* tu, *Ger.* über; KH, *Ger.* ich, *Scot.* loch; N, *Fr.* bon; y′, *Fr.* Compiègne

STRESS MARKS:

Primary stress: ′ **in·cite′** (ĭn-sīt′)
Secondary stress: ′ **in′sight′** (ĭn′sīt′)

dis·ap·pro·ba·tion (dĭs-ăp′rə-bā′shən) *n.* Moral disapproval; condemnation.
dis·ap·prov·al (dĭs′ə-pro͞o′vəl) *n.* The act of disapproving; condemnation; censure.
dis·ap·prove (dĭs′ə-pro͞ov′) *v.* **-proved, -proving, -proves.** —*tr.* **1.** To have an unfavorable opinion of; censure; condemn. **2.** To refuse to approve. —*intr.* To regard something as wrong, especially morally wrong; have an unfavorable opinion. Used with *of.* **—dis·ap·prov·ing·ly** *adv.*
dis·arm (dĭs-ärm′) *v.* **-armed, -arming, -arms.** —*tr.* **1.** To deprive of weapons; divest of arms. **2.** To deprive of the means of attack or defense; render helpless or harmless. **3.** To overcome or allay the suspicion, hostility, or antagonism of; win the confidence of. **4.** To win the affection of; charm. —*intr.* **1.** To lay down arms. **2.** To reduce or abolish one's stock of weapons, armaments, or armed forces. **—dis·arm·er** *n.*
dis·ar·ma·ment (dĭs-är′mə-mənt) *n.* **1.** The act of laying down arms; especially, the reduction or abolition of military forces and armaments by a national government. **2.** The condition of being disarmed.
dis·arm·ing (dĭs-är′mĭng) *adj.* Tending to remove suspicion or hostility; winning; endearing. **—dis·arm·ing·ly** *adv.*
dis·ar·range (dĭs′ə-rānj′) *tr.v.* **-ranged, -ranging, -ranges.** To upset the arrangement of; disorder. **—dis·ar·range·ment** *n.*
dis·ar·ray (dĭs′ə-rā′) *n.* **1.** A state of disorder; disarrangement; confusion. **2.** Disordered or untidy dress.
~*tr.v.* **disarrayed, -raying, -rays.** To throw into confusion; upset.
dis·ar·tic·u·late (dĭs′är-tĭk′yə-lāt′) *v.* **-lated, -lating, -lates.** —*tr.* To separate at the joints; disjoint. —*intr.* To come apart at the joints; become disjointed. **—dis·ar·tic·u·la·tion** *n.* **—dis·ar·tic·u·la·tor** *n.*
dis·as·sem·ble (dĭs′ə-sĕm′bəl) *tr.v.* **-bled, -bling, -bles.** To take apart. **—dis·as·sem·bly** *n.*
dis·as·so·ci·ate (dĭs′ə-sō′shē-āt′, -sē-āt′) *tr.v.* **-ated, -ating, -ates.** To dissociate. —See Usage note at **dissociate.** **—dis·as·so·ci·a·tion** *n.*
dis·as·ter (dĭ-zăs′tər, -zäs′tər) *n.* **1. a.** An occurrence inflicting widespread destruction and distress. **b.** A grave misfortune. **2.** *Informal.* A total failure. **3.** *Obsolete.* An unfavorable influence of a celestial body. [French *désastre,* from Italian *disastro,* back-formation from *disastrato,* "ill-starred" : *dis-,* from Latin (pejorative) + *astro,* star, from Latin *astrum,* from Greek *astron.*]
Synonyms: *calamity, cataclysm, catastrophe, debacle, holocaust.*
disaster area *n.* **1.** An area where a major disaster has occurred; especially, one officially designated as such and thus eligible for government or international aid. **2.** *Informal.* An untidy or disordered place.
disaster dump *n. Computer Science.* A printout that occurs as a result of a nonrecoverable program error.
dis·as·trous (dĭ-zăs′trəs, -zäs′trəs) *adj.* Calamitous; ruinous. **—dis·as·trous·ly** *adv.* **—dis·as·trous·ness** *n.*
dis·a·vow (dĭs′ə-vou′) *tr.v.* **-vowed, -vowing, -vows.** To disclaim knowledge of, responsibility for, or association with; disown. **—dis·a·vow·al** *n.* **—dis·a·vow·er** *n.*
dis·band (dĭs-bănd′) *v.* **-banded, -banding, -bands.** —*tr.* To break up (a group or unit, such as an army); dissolve. —*intr.* To become disbanded; disperse. **—dis·band·ment** *n.*
dis·bar (dĭs-bär′) *tr.v.* **-barred, -barring, -bars.** To expel (a lawyer) from the legal profession by official action or procedure. **—dis·bar·ment** *n.*
dis·be·lief (dĭs′bĭ-lēf′) *n.* Refusal or reluctance to believe.
dis·be·lieve (dĭs′bĭ-lēv′) *v.* **-lieved, -lieving, -lieves.** —*tr.* To refuse to believe; reject. —*intr.* To withhold belief. Used with *in.* **—dis·be·liev·er** *n.* **—dis·be·liev·ing·ly** *adv.*
Usage: In standard English this verb is not a simple opposite to *believe,* but has the specific sense of resistance to or refusal of belief.
dis·branch (dĭs-brănch′, -bränch′) *tr.v.* **-branched, -branching, -branches.** **1.** To cut or break a branch or branches from (a tree). **2.** To remove (a limb or branch).
dis·bud (dĭs-bŭd′) *tr.v.* **-budded, -budding, -buds.** **1.** *Horticulture.* To remove buds from (a plant) to promote better blooms from remaining buds or to control the shape of the plant. **2.** To remove newly developing horns from (livestock).
dis·bur·den (dĭs-bûrd′n) *v.* **-dened, -dening, -dens.** —*tr.* **1.** To relieve of a burden; especially, to relieve (oneself) of a feeling of anxiety or guilt. **2.** To unload or remove (a burden). —*intr.* To remove or unload a burden. **—dis·bur·den·ment** *n.*
dis·burse (dĭs-bûrs′) *tr.v.* **-bursed, -bursing, -burses.** To pay out; expend, as from a fund. [Old French *desbourser* : *des-,* from Latin *dis-* (reversal) + *bourse,* purse, from Medieval Latin *bursa,* from Greek.] **—dis·burs·a·ble** *adj.* **—dis·burs·er** *n.*
dis·burse·ment (dĭs-bûrs′mənt) *n.* Also **dis·bur·sal** (-bûr′səl). **1.** The act of disbursing. **2.** Money paid out; expenditure.
disc (dĭsk) *n.* Also **disk.** **1.** *Informal.* A phonograph record. **2.** Variant of **disk.**
dis·calced (dĭs-kălst′) *adj.* Barefoot. Said of certain orders of monks. [Latin *discalceātus* : *dis-,* not + *calceātus,* shod, from *calceus,* shoe.]
discant. Variant of **descant.**
dis·card (dĭs-kärd′) *v.* **-carded, -carding, -cards.** —*tr.* **1.** To throw away; reject; dismiss as useless or unwanted. **2.** *Card Games.* **a.** To throw out (an undesired card or cards) from one's hand. **b.** To play (a card other than a trump and different in suit from the card led). —*intr. Card Games.* To discard a card.
~*n.* (*usually* dĭs′kärd′). **1.** The act of discarding. **2.** A person or thing that is discarded; especially, the card or cards discarded in a card game. **—dis·card·er** (dĭs-kärd′ər) *n.*
disc brake *n.* Also **disk brake.** A type of brake that works by bringing hydraulically operated friction pads into contact with a disc that is fixed to, and rotates with, the road wheel of a motor vehicle.

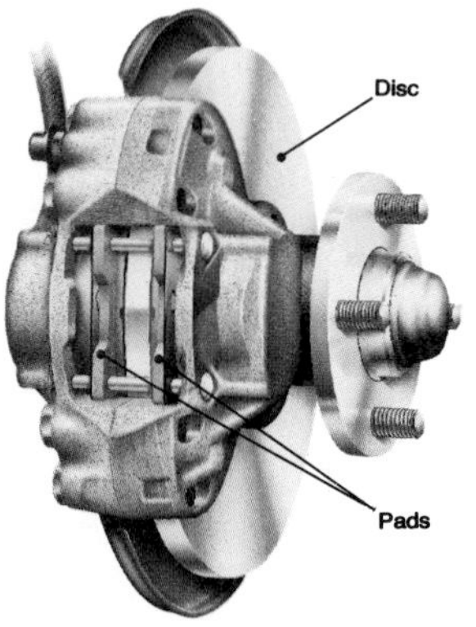

disc brake *In a car fitted with disc brakes, pressure on the brake pedal pushes the friction pads toward each other so that they rub on the disc between them. The disc is fixed to the wheel hub. The advantage of disc brakes over drum brakes is that disc brakes perform better during prolonged heavy braking. In a drum brake, the heat generated by such braking causes the drum to expand, resulting in the loss of efficiency known as "brake fade."*

dis·cern (dĭ-sûrn′, -zûrn′) *v.* **-cerned, -cerning, -cerns.** —*tr.* **1.** To perceive (something obscure or concealed); detect. **2.** To perceive as distinct; discriminate. —*intr.* To perceive differences; make distinctions. —See Synonyms at **see.** [Middle English *discernen,* from Old French *discerner,* from Latin *discernere,* to "separate by sifting," distinguish between : *dis-,* apart + *cernere,* to sift, separate, perceive.] **—dis·cern·er** *n.*
dis·cern·i·ble (dĭ-sûr′nə-bəl, dĭ-zûr′-) *adj.* Perceptible; distinguishable. —See Synonyms at **perceptible.** **—dis·cern·i·bly** *adv.*
dis·cern·ing (dĭ-sûr′nĭng, dĭ-zûr′-) *adj.* **1.** Astute; perceptive. **2.** Having or showing good taste or judgment. **—dis·cern·ing·ly** *adv.*
dis·cern·ment (dĭ-sûrn′mənt, dĭ-zûrn′-) *n.* **1.** The act or process of discerning. **2.** Keenness of discrimination; good judgment. —See Synonyms at **reason.**
dis·charge (dĭs-chärj′) *v.* **-charged, -charging, -charges.** —*tr.* **1.** To relieve of a burden or of contents; unload. **2.** To unload or empty (contents, such as ship's cargo). **3.** To release, as from confinement or hospital, or from duty. **4.** To dismiss from employment. **5.** To send or pour forth; emit. **6.** To shoot or fire (a projectile or weapon). **7.** To perform the obligations or demands of (an office, duty, or task). **8.** To acquit oneself of (a debt or promise); comply with the terms of. **9.** *Law.* **a.** To release (a defendant, for example). **b.** To set aside; dismiss; annul: *discharge a court order.* **10.** To remove (color) from cloth, as by chemical bleaching. **11.** *Electricity.* To cause electrical discharge in (a battery, for example). **12.** *Architecture.* **a.** To apportion (weight) evenly, as over a door. **b.** To relieve (a part) of excess weight by distribution of pressure. —*intr.* **1.** To get rid of a burden, load, or weight. **2.** To fire a projectile or weapon. **3.** To pour forth contents. **4.** To become blurred; run. Used of dye or dyed cloth. **5.** To undergo electrical discharge. —See Synonyms at **perform.**
~*n.* (dĭs′chärj′, dĭs-chärj′). **1.** The act of removing a load or burden; an unloading. **2.** The act of shooting or firing a projectile or weapon. **3.** A pouring forth; an emission; ejection. **4.** The amount or rate of emission or ejection. **5.** Something that is discharged, released, or emitted: *vaginal discharge.* **6.** A relieving from or elimination of an obligation, burden, or responsibility. **7.** Fulfillment or performance. **8. a.** Dismissal or release from employment, service, or confinement. **b.** A document certifying such release, especially from military service. **9.** A legal annulment or acquittal; a dismissal, as of a court order. **10.** *Electricity.* **a.** The release of stored energy in a capacitor by the flow of electric current between its terminals. **b.** The conversion of chemical energy to electric energy in a battery. **c.** A flow of electricity in a gas, especially a continuous luminous flow in a gas at low pressure. **d.** The elimination of net electric charge from any charged body. [Middle English *dischargen,* from Old French *descharger,* from Vulgar Latin *discarricāre* (unattested), to unload : *dis-* (reversal) + *carricāre* (unattested), to load, CHARGE.] **—dis·charge·a·ble** *adj.* **—dis·charg·er** *n.*
discharge lamp *n.* A lamp that generates light by means of an internal electrical discharge in a gas.
discharge tube *n.* A closed insulating tube fitted with electrodes and containing a gas in which an electrical discharge is induced by a high applied potential difference.
dis·ci. Alternative plural of **discus.**
dis·ci·ple (dĭ-sī′pəl) *n.* **1. a.** A person who subscribes to the doctrines and teachings of another, especially of a great teacher or leader. **b.** Any active adherent, as of a movement or philosophy. **2.** *Often* **Disciple.** Any of Christ's personal followers, especially, any of the 12 Apostles. **3. Disciple.** A member of the Disciples of Christ. [Middle English *disciple,* Old English *discipul,* from Latin *discipulus,* pupil, from *discere,* to learn.] **—dis·ci·ple·ship** *n.*
Disciples of Christ *n.* A Christian denomination, founded in the United States in 1809, that accepts only the Bible as the rule of Christian faith and practice.
dis·ci·pli·nar·i·an (dĭs′ə-plə-nâr′ē-ən) *n.* A person who enforces or believes in strict discipline.
dis·ci·pli·nar·y (dĭs′ə-plə-nĕr′ē) *adj.* Also **dis·ci·pli·nal** (-plə-nəl, -plĭn′əl). Promoting or used for discipline.
dis·ci·pline (dĭs′ə-plĭn) *n.* **1.** Training that is expected to produce a particular character or pattern of behavior, especially that which is expected to produce moral or mental improvement. **2.** Controlled behavior resulting from such training; self-discipline. **3.** A systematic method of obtaining obedience: *military discipline.* **4.** A state of order based upon submission to rules and authority. **5.** Punishment intended to correct or train. **6.** In some religions, the mortification of the flesh as a penance. **7.** A set of rules or methods, such as those regulating the practice of a church or monastic order. **8.** A branch of knowledge or teaching.
~*tr.v.* **disciplined, -plining, -plines.** **1.** To train by instruction and control; teach to obey rules or accept authority. **2.** To punish or penalize. **3.** To organize thoroughly; set in order: *a disciplined mind.* —See Synonyms at **teach, punish.** [Middle English, from Old French, from Latin *disciplīna,* instruction, knowledge, from *discipulus,* pupil, DISCIPLE.] **—dis·ci·plin·a·ble** *adj.* **—dis·ci·plin·er** *n.*
disc jockey *n.* Also **disk jockey.** A person who presents and com-

ments on recordings of popular music, especially on the radio. Also called "DJ."

dis·claim (dĭs-klām′) v. **-claimed, -claiming, -claims.** —tr. **1.** To deny or renounce any claim to or connection with; disown. **2.** To deny the validity of; repudiate. **3.** Law. To renounce one's right or claim to. —intr. Law. To renounce a legal right or claim.

dis·claim·er (dĭs-klā′mər) n. **1.** A repudiation or denial of a claim. **2.** A statement denying responsibility for something.

dis·cla·ma·tion (dĭs′klə-mā′shən) n. Disavowal; renunciation.

dis·cli·max (dĭs-klī′măks′) n. A normally stable ecological community that has been altered by human or other influences, as a grassland community that has been turned into desert by overgrazing.

dis·close (dĭs-klōz′) tr.v. **-closed, -closing, -closes. 1.** To expose to view, as by removing a cover; uncover. **2.** To make known; divulge (a secret, for example). —See Synonyms at **reveal.** —**dis·clos·er** n.

disclosing tablet n. A tablet used to show the presence of plaque on the teeth, reacting with it to produce a red stain.

dis·clo·sure (dĭs-klō′zhər) n. **1.** The act or process of disclosing. **2.** Something that is disclosed; a revelation.

dis·co (dĭs′kō′) n., pl. **-cos. 1.** A nightclub often having showy decor and special lighting effects and featuring live or recorded, electronically amplified music for dancing. **2. a.** Popular dance music marked by strong repetitive bass rhythms. **b.** A style of dancing done especially to disco music.
~intr.v. **-coed, -coing, -cos.** To dance to disco music. [Short for DISCOTHEQUE.]

disco- prefix. Indicates a phonograph record; for example, **discophile.** [From DISC.]

dis·cob·o·lus (dĭs-kŏb′ə-ləs) n., pl. **-li** (-lī′). A discus-thrower, or a statue of one, in ancient Greece or Rome. [Latin, from Greek diskobolos : diskos, quoit, DISK + -bolos, thrower, from ballein, to throw.]

dis·cog·ra·phy (dĭs-kŏg′rə-fē) n., pl. **-phies.** A catalogue of phonograph records; especially, a comprehensive list of the recordings made by a particular performer or of a particular composer's works. [French discographie : DISCO- + -GRAPHY.] —**dis·cog·ra·pher** n.

dis·coid (dĭs′koid′) adj. Also **dis·coi·dal** (dĭs-koid′l). **1.** Having the shape of a disk. **2.** Botany. Having disk flowers but no ray flowers. Said of the flower head of a tansy and similar composite plants.
~n. A disk or an object shaped like a disk. [Late Latin discoides, disk-shaped, from Greek diskoeidēs : diskos, DISK + -OID.]

dis·co·lor (dĭs-kŭl′ər) v. **-ored, -oring, -ors.** —tr. To alter or spoil the proper color of; stain. —intr. To become changed or spoiled in color.

dis·col·or·a·tion (dĭs-kŭl′ə-rā′shən) n. **1. a.** The act of discoloring. **b.** The condition of being discolored. **2.** A stain.

dis·com·bob·u·late (dĭs′kəm-bŏb′yə-lāt′) tr.v. **-lated, -lating, -lates.** Slang. To throw into a state of confusion; disconcert; upset. [Mock-Latin formation.]

dis·com·fit (dĭs-kŭm′fĭt) tr.v. **-fited, -fiting, -fits. 1.** To make uneasy or perplexed; disconcert; embarrass. **2.** To thwart the plans or purposes of; frustrate; foil. **3.** Archaic. To defeat in battle; rout; vanquish. [Middle English discomfiten, from Old French desconfire (past participle disconfit), to defeat, from Vulgar Latin disconficere (unattested) : Latin dis- (reversal) + conficere, to prepare, accomplish : com-, together + facere, to make.] —**dis·com·fi·ture** (dĭs-kŭm′fĭ-chŏŏr′) n.

Usage: Although discomfit was once used strictly in the sense of "to defeat or frustrate," it has also acquired the sense of "to disconcert or make uncomfortable" through confusion with the unrelated word discomfort.

dis·com·fort (dĭs-kŭm′fərt) n. **1.** The condition of being uncomfortable in body or mind; mild pain. **2.** Something that disturbs one's comfort; an annoyance.
~tr.v. **discomforted, -forting, -forts.** To make uneasy or uncomfortable. —See Usage note at **discomfit.**

dis·com·fort·a·ble (dĭs-kŭm′fʹtə-bəl, -kŭm′fər-tə-bəl) adj. Rare. Not comfortable; distressed or distressing.

dis·com·mend (dĭs′kə-mĕnd′) tr.v. **-mended, -mending, -mends.** Formal. **1.** To show or voice disapproval of. **2.** To bring into disfavor or ill regard. —**dis·com·mend·a·ble** adj.

dis·com·mode (dĭs′kə-mōd′) tr.v. **-moded, -moding, -modes.** Formal. To put to inconvenience; disturb. [French discommoder : Latin dis- (reversal) + commode, convenient (see **commode**).]

dis·com·pose (dĭs′kəm-pōz′) tr.v. **-posed, -posing, -poses. 1.** To disturb the composure or calm of; agitate; perturb. **2.** To put into a state of disorder; disarrange. —**dis·com·pos·ed·ly** (dĭs′kəm-pō′zĭd-lē) adv. —**dis·com·pos·ing·ly** adv.

dis·com·po·sure (dĭs′kəm-pō′zhər) n. Absence of composure; a state of agitation.

dis·con·cert (dĭs′kən-sûrt′) tr.v. **-certed, -certing, -certs. 1.** To upset the self-possession of; perturb; ruffle. **2.** To frustrate by throwing into disorder; upset; rout. [Obsolete French disconcerter, from Old French desconcerter : des-, from Latin dis- (reversal) + concerter, to bring into agreement, from Italian concertare (see **concert**).] —**dis·con·cert·ing·ly** adv.

dis·con·cert·ed (dĭs′kən-sûr′tĭd) adj. Deprived of one's composure; thrown into confusion or embarrassment. —**dis·con·cert·ed·ly** adv. —**dis·con·cert·ed·ness** n.

dis·con·form·i·ty (dĭs′kən-fôr′mə-tē) n., pl. **-ties.** Geology. A break in a stratigraphical sequence, caused by an interruption of sedimentation due to denudation. Compare **unconformity.**

dis·con·nect (dĭs′kə-nĕkt′) tr.v. **-nected, -necting, -nects. 1.** To break or interrupt the connection of or between. **2.** To shut off the current in (an electrical appliance) by removing its connection with the power source. **3.** Informal. To cut off a power supply to the premises of: If we don't pay the phone bill by Tuesday, we'll be disconnected. —**dis·con·nec·tion** n.

dis·con·nect·ed (dĭs′kə-nĕk′tĭd) adj. **1.** Not connected; detached. **2.** Marked by a lack of logical connections; confused; incoherent. —**dis·con·nect·ed·ly** adv. —**dis·con·nect·ed·ness** n.

dis·con·so·late (dĭs-kŏn′sə-lĭt) adj. **1.** Too unhappy to be consoled; hopelessly sad. **2.** Cheerless; gloomy; dismal. [Middle English, from Medieval Latin disconsōlātus : Latin dis- (negative) + consōlātus, past participle of consōlārī, to CONSOLE.] —**dis·con·so·late·ly** adv. —**dis·con·so·late·ness, dis·con·so·la·tion** n.

dis·con·tent (dĭs′kən-tĕnt′) n. **1.** Absence of contentment; dissatisfaction. **2.** A sense of resentment and grievance.
~adj. Discontented.
~tr.v. **discontented, -tenting, -tents.** To cause dissatisfaction in; make discontented.

dis·con·tent·ed (dĭs′kən-tĕn′tĭd) adj. Restlessly unhappy; dissatisfied. —**dis·con·tent·ed·ly** adv. —**dis·con·tent·ed·ness** n.

dis·con·tin·u·ance (dĭs′kən-tĭn′yōō-əns) n. **1.** The act of discontinuing or the condition of being discontinued; cessation. **2.** Law. The termination of an action by the plaintiff.

dis·con·tin·u·a·tion (dĭs′kən-tĭn′yōō-ā′shən) n. Discontinuance; cessation.

dis·con·tin·ue (dĭs′kən-tĭn′yōō) v. **-ued, -uing, -ues.** —tr. **1.** To cause to cease; put a stop to; terminate. **2.** To cease from; give up; abandon. **3.** Law. To terminate (an action) by discontinuance. **4.** To cease production of: a sale of discontinued merchandise. —intr. To come to an end. —**dis·con·tin·u·er** n.

dis·con·ti·nu·i·ty (dĭs′kŏn-tĭ-nōō′ə-tē, -nyōō′ə-tē) n., pl. **-ties. 1.** A lack of continuity, logical sequence, or cohesion. **2.** A break or gap. **3.** Mathematics. **a.** The property of being discontinuous. **b.** A point at which a function is defined but is not continuous. **c.** A point at which a function is undefined. **4.** Geology. A boundary across which the internal character of the earth changes abruptly, such as the Mohorovičić discontinuity. **5.** Meteorology. A front (see) or frontal zone.

dis·con·tin·u·ous (dĭs′kən-tĭn′yōō-əs) adj. **1.** Marked by breaks or interruptions; intermittent. **2.** Mathematics. Possessing one or more discontinuities. —**dis·con·tin·u·ous·ly** adv. —**dis·con·tin·u·ous·ness** n.

disc·o·phile (dĭsk′ə-fīl′) n. A collector of or specialist in phonograph records. [DISCO- + -PHILE.]

dis·cord (dĭs′kôrd) n. **1.** Lack of agreement among persons, groups, or things; dissension. **2.** A confused or harsh mingling of sounds; a din. **3.** Music. **a.** The inharmonious combination of simultaneously sounded notes; dissonance. Compare **concord. b.** Any chord exemplifying this.
~intr.v. (dĭs-kôrd′), **discorded, -cording, -cords.** To fail to agree or harmonize; clash. [Middle English, from Old French descorde, from Latin discordia, strife, from discors, disagreeing : dis-, apart + cor (stem cord-), heart.]

Synonyms: *clash, conflict, contention, dissension, strife, variance.*

dis·cor·dant (dĭs-kôr′dənt) adj. **1.** Not in accord; conflicting. **2.** Disagreeable in sound; harsh or dissonant. —See Synonyms at **inconsistent. —dis·cor·dance, dis·cor·dan·cy** n. —**dis·cor·dant·ly** adv.

dis·co·theque, dis·co·thèque n. **1.** A usually small nightclub featuring dancing to live or recorded music. **2.** See disco (sense 1). [French : DISCO- + -THÈQUE, record library, by analogy with bibliothèque, library.]

dis·count (dĭs′kount′, dĭs-kount′) v. **-counted, -counting, -counts.** —tr. **1.** To deduct or subtract (a specified sum or percentage) from a cost or price. **2. a.** To buy or sell (a promissory note such as a treasury bill) after deducting the amount of interest that will accumulate before it matures. **b.** To advance money as a loan on (a promissory note not immediately payable) after deducting the interest. **3.** To reduce in cost, quantity, or value. **4.** To leave out of account as being untrustworthy or exaggerated; disregard; ignore. **5.** To anticipate and make allowance for. —intr. To lend money after deduction of interest.
~n. (dĭs′kount). **1.** A reduction from the full or standard amount of a price or debt. **2.** The interest deducted in advance in purchasing, selling, or lending a promissory note such as a treasury bill. **3.** The rate of interest deducted in such a transaction. Also called "discount rate." **4.** The act or an instance of discounting a bill of exchange, treasury bill, or the like.
~adj. Selling at prices below those set by manufacturers. [Obsolete French descompte, descompter, from Medieval Latin discomputāre : Latin dis- (reversal) + computāre, to add, sum up, COMPUTE.] —**dis·count·a·ble** adj. —**dis·count·er** n.

dis·coun·te·nance (dĭs-koun′tə-nəns) tr.v. **-nanced, -nancing, -nances. 1.** To view or treat with disfavor. **2.** To embarrass; abash; disconcert.
~n. Disfavor; disapproval.

discount house n. A discount store.

discount store n. A store that sells merchandise, especially consumer goods, at a discount from the manufacturer's suggested retail price.

dis·cour·age (dĭs-kûr′ĭj) tr.v. **-aged, -aging, -ages. 1.** To deprive of confidence, hope, or spirit; dishearten; daunt. **2.** To hamper or hinder. **3.** To dissuade or deter. Used with from. **4.** To try to prevent by expressing disapproval or raising objections: *The report discourages smoking.* —**dis·cour·ag·er** *n.* —**dis·cour·ag·ing·ly** *adv.*

dis·cour·age·ment (dĭs-kûr′ĭj-mənt) *n.* **1. a.** The act of discouraging. **b.** The condition of being discouraged. **2.** Something that discourages; a deterrent. —See Synonyms at **despair.**

dis·course (dĭs′kôrs′, -kōrs′) *n.* **1.** Verbal expression in speech or writing. **2.** Verbal exchange; conversation. **3.** A formal and lengthy discussion of a subject, either written or spoken. **4.** *Archaic.* The process or power of reasoning.
~*v.* (dĭs-kôrs′, -kōrs′), **discoursed, -coursing, -courses.** —*intr.* **1.** To speak or write formally and at length. Used with *on* or *upon.* **2.** To engage in conversation or discussion; converse. —*tr. Archaic.* **1.** To narrate or discuss. **2.** To give forth (musical sounds); perform. —See Synonyms at **speak.** [Middle English *discours,* from Late Latin *discursus,* conversation, from Latin, "a running back and forth," from the past participle of *discurrere,* to run back and forth, speak at length : *dis-,* in different directions + *currere,* to run.] —**dis·cours·er** *n.*

dis·cour·te·ous (dĭs-kûr′tē-əs) *adj.* Lacking courtesy; impolite; rude. —**dis·cour·te·ous·ly** *adv.* —**dis·cour·te·ous·ness** *n.*

dis·cour·te·sy (dĭs-kûr′-tə-sē) *n., pl.* **-sies. 1.** Lack of courtesy; rudeness. **2.** A discourteous act or statement.

dis·cov·er (dĭs-kŭv′ər) *tr.v.* **-ered, -ering, -ers. 1.** To obtain knowledge of; arrive at through search or study. **2.** To be the first to find, learn of, or observe. **3.** To learn of or experience for the first time: *discover the pleasures of music.* **4.** *Informal.* To find that (a previously unknown person) has marketable talents. **5.** *Archaic.* To reveal; expose. —**dis·cov·er·a·ble** *adj.* —**dis·cov·er·er** *n.*

dis·cov·ert (dĭs-kŭv′ərt) *adj. Law.* Having no husband, and therefore not subject to coverture. —**dis·cov·er·ture** *n.*

dis·cov·er·y (dĭs-kŭv′ə-rē) *n., pl.* **-ies. 1.** The act or an instance of discovering. **2. a.** Something that has been discovered. **b.** A person recently found to have a special talent. **3.** *Law.* The process whereby parties in an action are obliged to disclose any documents relevant to the case.

dis·cred·it (dĭs-krĕd′ĭt) *tr.v.* **-ited, -iting, -its. 1.** To damage in reputation; disgrace; dishonor. **2.** To cast doubt on; cause to be distrusted. **3.** To give no credence to; disbelieve. —See Synonyms at **degrade.**
~*n.* **1.** Loss of or damage to one's reputation; dishonor; disgrace. **2.** Lack or loss of trust or belief; doubt. **3.** Anything damaging to one's reputation or stature. —See Synonyms at **disgrace.**

dis·cred·it·a·ble (dĭs-krĕd′ĭ-tə-bəl) *adj.* Deserving of or resulting in discredit; blameworthy. —**dis·cred·it·a·bly** *adv.*

dis·creet (dĭs-krēt′) *adj.* **1.** Showing a judicious reserve in one's speech or behavior; especially, able to keep other people's secrets. **2.** Lacking ostentation or pretension; unobtrusive; modest. [Middle English, from Old French *discret,* from Medieval Latin *discrētus,* "showing good judgment," from Latin, past participle of *discernere,* to separate, DISCERN.] —**dis·creet·ly** *adv.* —**dis·creet·ness** *n.*

dis·crep·an·cy (dĭs-krĕp′ən-sē) *n., pl.* **-cies.** Also **dis·crep·ance** (-əns). **1.** Divergence or disagreement, as between facts or claims; inconsistency. **2.** An instance of such disagreement. —See Usage note at **difference.**

dis·crep·ant (dĭs-krĕp′ənt) *adj.* Marked by discrepancy; not consistent or matching; disagreeing. [Middle English *discrepaunt,* from Latin *discrepāns* (stem *discrepant-*), present participle of *discrepāre,* to sound different, vary : *dis-,* apart + *crepāre,* to rattle, sound.] —**dis·crep·ant·ly** *adv.*

dis·crete (dĭs-krēt′) *adj.* **1.** Constituting a separate thing; individual; distinct. **2.** Consisting of unconnected distinct parts. [Middle English, from Latin *discrētus,* separate. See **discreet.**] —**dis·crete·ly** *adv.* —**dis·crete·ness** *n.*

discrete variable *n.* A mathematical variable that assumes only whole numbers.

dis·cre·tion (dĭs-krĕsh′ən) *n.* **1.** The quality of being discreet; prudent or cautious reserve. **2.** Freedom to act or judge on one's own; latitude of choice and action: *the age of discretion.* —**at someone's discretion.** In accordance with the wishes or judgment of.

dis·cre·tion·ar·y (dĭs-krĕsh′ə-nĕr′ē) *adj.* Also **dis·cre·tion·al** (dĭs-krĕsh′ən-əl). **1.** Left to or regulated by one's own discretion or judgment. **2.** Based on consideration of a particular case, not on a general regulation: *a discretionary grant.* —**dis·cre·tion·ar·i·ly** *adv.*

dis·cri·mi·nant (dĭs-krĭm′ə-nənt) *n. Mathematics.* A value or function related to a polynomial equation, giving information about the nature of the roots of the equation. It is the product of the squares of all the differences of the roots taken in pairs; for a quadratic equation $ax^2 + bx + c = 0$, the discriminant is $b^2 - 4ac$. [Latin *discrīmināns* (stem *discrīmināt-*), present participle of *discrīmināre,* to DISCRIMINATE.]

dis·crim·i·nate (dĭs-krĭm′ə-nāt′) *v.* **-nated, -nating, -nates.** —*intr.* **1.** To make a clear distinction; differentiate. Often used with *between.* **2.** To act on the basis of prejudice. —*tr.* **1.** To perceive the distinguishing features of; recognize as distinct. **2.** To serve to mark; differentiate: *The ability to reason discriminates humans from animals.*
~*adj.* (dĭs-krĭm′ə-nĭt). Discriminating. [Latin *discrīmināre,* to divide, distinguish, from *discrīmen,* distinction.] —**dis·crim·i·nate·ly** *adv.*

dis·crim·i·nat·ing (dĭs-krĭm′ə-nā′tĭng) *adj.* **1.** Able or tending to draw fine distinctions; discerning. **2.** Fastidiously selective. **3.** Serving to differentiate; distinctive. **4.** Showing favoritism or

prejudice; differential, as a tariff may be. —**dis·crim·i·nat·ing·ly** *adv.*

dis·crim·i·na·tion (dĭs-krĭm′ə-nā′shən) *n.* **1.** The act of discriminating. **2.** The ability or power to see or make fine distinctions; discernment. **3.** Attitude, behavior, or treatment based on prejudice. **4.** *Electronics.* The use of a circuit to pass signals of one characteristic while rejecting others. See **discriminator.**

dis·crim·i·na·tive (dĭs-krĭm′ə-nā′tĭv, -ə-nə-tĭv) *adj.* **1.** Drawing distinctions; discriminating. **2.** Discriminatory. —**dis·crim·i·na·tive·ly** *adv.*

dis·crim·i·na·tor (dĭs-krĭm′ə-nā′tər) *n.* **1.** One that discriminates. **2.** *Electronics.* A device that converts a property of a signal, such as frequency or phase, into an amplitude variation.

dis·crim·i·na·to·ry (dĭs-krĭm′ə-nə-tôr′ē, -tōr′ē) *adj.* **1.** Marked by or showing prejudice; biased. **2.** Discriminating. —**dis·crim·i·na·to·ri·ly** *adv.*

dis·crown (dĭs-kroun′) *tr.v.* **-crowned, -crowning, -crowns.** To deprive of a crown; dethrone; depose.

dis·cur·sive (dĭs-kûr′sĭv) *adj.* **1.** Covering a wide field of subjects; rambling; digressive. **2.** Proceeding to a conclusion through reason rather than intuition. [Medieval Latin *discursīvus,* from Latin *discursus,* "a running back and forth." See **discourse.**] —**dis·cur·sive·ly** *adv.* —**dis·cur·sive·ness** *n.*

dis·cus (dĭs′kəs) *n., pl.* **-cuses** or **disci** (dĭs′ī). **1.** A disk, usually wooden with a metal rim and weighing about 4½ pounds, thrown for distance in athletic competitions. **2.** The field event in which this disk is thrown. **3.** A small, brilliantly colored South American freshwater fish, *Symphysodon discus,* that has a disk-shaped body and is popular in home aquariums. [Latin, DISK.]

dis·cuss (dĭs-kŭs′) *tr.v.* **-cussed, -cussing, -cusses. 1.** To discourse about in speech or writing; treat of. **2.** To consider (a matter) by speaking together about it; debate. **3.** To consume (food or drink) with relish. Used humorously. [Middle English *discussen,* from Late Latin *discutere* (past participle *discussus*), to investigate, discuss, from Latin, to break up, scatter : *dis-,* apart + *quatere,* to shake.] —**dis·cuss·er** *n.* —**dis·cuss·i·ble** *adj.*
Synonyms: *argue, contend, debate, dispute.*

dis·cuss·ant (dĭs-kŭs′ənt) *n.* One who takes part in a discussion.

dis·cus·sion (dĭs-kŭsh′ən) *n.* **1.** The consideration of a subject by a group; an earnest conversation. **2.** A discourse by one person upon a topic; an exposition.

dis·dain (dĭs-dān′) *tr.v.* **-dained, -daining, -dains. 1.** To regard or treat with haughty contempt; despise. **2.** To consider unworthy of oneself; refuse with scorn.
~*n.* A feeling, attitude, or show of scornful superiority; aloof contempt: *a cold stare of disdain.* [Middle English *desdeynen,* from Old French *desdeignier,* from Vulgar Latin *disdignāre* (unattested), variant of Latin *dēdignārī,* to scorn : *dē-* (reversal) + *dignāre,* to deem worthy, from *dignus,* worthy.]

dis·dain·ful (dĭs-dān′fəl) *adj.* Feeling or showing disdain; scornful and haughty. —See Synonyms at **proud.** —**dis·dain·ful·ly** *adv.* —**dis·dain·ful·ness** *n.*

dis·ease (dĭ-zēz′) *n.* **1.** An abnormal condition of an organism or part, especially as a consequence of infection, inherent weakness, or environmental stress, that impairs normal physiological functioning. **2.** A condition or tendency, as of society, regarded as abnormal and pernicious. **3.** *Obsolete.* Lack of ease.

dis·eased (dĭ-zēzd′) *adj.* **1.** Affected with disease. **2.** Unhealthy; unsound; disordered.

dis·em·bark (dĭs′ĭm-bärk′) *v.* **-barked, -barking, -barks.** —*intr.* To go ashore from a ship. —*tr.* To put or cause to go ashore from a ship. —**dis·em·bar·ka·tion** *n.*

dis·em·bar·rass (dĭs′ĭm-bâr′əs) *tr.v.* **-rassed, -rassing, -rasses.** To free from something embarrassing, bothersome, or encumbering; relieve. —**dis·em·bar·rass·ment** *n.*

dis·em·bod·ied (dĭs′ĭm-bŏd′ēd) *adj.* **1.** No longer connected with the body; ghostly. **2.** Unrelated to the real world.

dis·em·bod·y (dĭs′ĭm-bŏd′ē) *tr.v.* **-ied, -ying, -ies. 1.** To free (the soul or spirit) from the body. **2.** To divest of reality. —**dis·em·bod·i·ment** *n.*

dis·em·bogue (dĭs′ĭm-bōg′) *v.* **-bogued, -boguing, -bogues.** —*intr.* To empty at the mouth. Used of a river. —*tr.* To discharge (waters) at the mouth. Used of a river. [Alteration of Spanish *desembocar : des-,* from Latin *dis-* (reversal) + *embocar,* to put into the mouth : *em-,* from Latin *in-,* in + *boca,* mouth, from Latin *bucca,* cheek.] —**dis·em·bogue·ment** *n.*

dis·em·bow·el (dĭs′ĭm-bou′əl) *tr.v.* **-eled, -eling, -els.** Also *chiefly British* **-elled, -elling.** To remove the bowels from. —**dis·em·bow·el·ment** *n.*

dis·em·broil (dĭs′ĭm-broil′) *tr.v.* **-broiled, -broiling, -broils.** To free from a condition of complexity or confusion; disentangle.

dis·en·chant (dĭs′ĭn-chănt′, -chänt′) *tr.v.* **-chanted, -chanting, -chants.** To free from enchantment or illusion; undeceive. —**dis·en·chant·er** *n.* —**dis·en·chant·ment** *n.*

dis·en·chant·ed (dĭs′ĭn-chănt′əd, -chänt′-) *adj.* Disappointed; disillusioned. Used with *with.*

dis·en·cum·ber (dĭs′ĭn-kŭm′bər) *tr.v.* **-bered, -bering, -bers.** To relieve of encumbrances. —**dis·en·cum·ber·ment** *n.*

dis·en·dow (dĭs′ĭn-dou′) *tr.v.* **-dowed, -dowing, -dows.** To deprive of endowments.

dis·en·fran·chise (dĭs′ĭn-frăn′chīz′) *tr.v.* **-ised, -ising, -ises.** Also **dis·fran·chise** (dĭs′frăn′chīz′). **1.** To deprive (an individual) of a right to citizenship, especially of the right to vote. **2.** To deprive (a company, for example) of a privilege or franchise. —**dis·en·fran-**

chise·ment, dis·fran·chise·ment *n.* —dis·en·fran·chis·er, dis·fran·chis·er *n.*

dis·en·gage (dĭs'ĭn-gāj') *v.* -gaged, -gaging, -gages. —*tr.* **1.** To release from something that holds fast, connects, or entangles, especially in a mechanical device. **2.** To unfasten; detach. **3.** *Archaic.* To release from an engagement, pledge, or obligation. —*intr.* To become disengaged; get loose.

dis·en·gage·ment (dĭs'ĭn-gāj'mənt) *n.* **1. a.** The act of disengaging. **b.** The condition of being disengaged. **2.** *Military.* Withdrawal of forces from a particular military theater. **3.** Freedom from obligation; ease of manner.

dis·en·tail (dĭs'ĭn-tāl') *tr.v.* -tailed, -tailing, -tails. *Law.* To release (an estate) from entail. —dis·en·tail·ment *n.*

dis·en·tan·gle (dĭs'ĭn-tăng'gəl) *v.* -gled, -gling, -gles. —*tr.* **1.** To extricate from entanglement or involvement; free. **2.** To clear up or resolve (a mystery, for example). —*intr.* To become disentangled. —dis·en·tan·gle·ment *n.*

dis·en·tomb (dĭs'ĭn-tōōm') *tr.v.* -tombed, -tombing, -tombs. To remove from or as if from a tomb. —dis·en·tomb·ment *n.*

dis·en·twine (dĭs'ĭn-twīn') *v.* -twined, -twining, -twines. —*tr.* To disentangle; untwine. —*intr.* To become untwined.

dis·e·qui·lib·ri·um (dĭs'ē-kwə-lĭb'rē-əm) *n.* Loss or lack of equilibrium or stability.

dis·es·tab·lish (dĭs'ĭ-stăb'lĭsh) *tr.v.* -lished, -lishing, -lishes. **1.** To alter the status of (something established by authority or general acceptance). **2.** To deprive (a church) of the status of an **established church** (see). —dis·es·tab·lish·ment *n.*

dis·es·teem (dĭs'ĭ-stēm') *tr.v.* -teemed, -teeming, -teems. To have little regard for; hold in disfavor. ~*n.* Lack of esteem.

dis·fa·vor (dĭs-fā'vər) *n.* **1.** Unfavorable opinion or regard; disapproval. **2.** The condition of being regarded with disapproval. **3.** A disservice. ~*tr.v.* disfavored, -voring, -vors. **1.** To view or treat with dislike or disapproval. **2.** To withhold favor from.

dis·fea·ture (dĭs-fē'chər) *tr.v.* -tured, -turing, -tures. To spoil the features of; disfigure. —dis·fea·ture·ment *n.*

dis·fig·ure (dĭs-fĭg'yər) *tr.v.* -ured, -uring, -ures. To blemish or spoil the appearance or shape of. —dis·fig·ur·er *n.*

dis·fig·ure·ment (dĭs-fĭg'yər-mənt) *n.* Also **dis·fig·u·ra·tion** (-fĭg'yə-rā'shən). **1. a.** The act of disfiguring. **b.** The condition of being disfigured. **2.** A deformity; flaw.

disfranchise. Variant of **disenfranchise.**

dis·frock (dĭs-frŏk') *tr.v.* -frocked, -frocking, -frocks. To unfrock.

dis·gorge (dĭs-gôrj') *v.* -gorged, -gorging, -gorges. —*tr.* **1.** To bring up and expel from the throat or stomach; vomit. **2.** To discharge in a violent or confused manner; spew out. **3.** To yield up reluctantly. —*intr.* To discharge or pour forth contents. —dis·gorge·ment *n.*

dis·grace (dĭs-grās') *n.* **1.** Loss of honor, respect, or reputation; shame. **2.** The condition of being out of favor or badly thought of. **3.** Something that brings shame, dishonor, or disfavor. **4.** *Informal.* Something that is shocking in its poor quality or appearance. ~*tr.v.* disgraced, -gracing, -graces. **1.** To bring shame or dishonor upon. **2.** To cause (someone) to lose favor or reputation. —dis·grac·er *n.*

Synonyms: *degradation, discredit, dishonor, disrepute, ignominy, infamy, obloquy, odium, opprobrium, scandal, shame.*

dis·grace·ful (dĭs-grās'fəl) *adj.* Bringing or deserving disgrace; shameful. —dis·grace·ful·ly *adv.* —dis·grace·ful·ness *n.*

dis·grun·tle (dĭs-grŭnt'l) *tr.v.* -tled, -tling, -tles. To make discontented or cross; put in a disagreeable mood. [DIS- (intensive) + dialectal *gruntle*, to grumble, Middle English *gruntlen*, frequentative of *grunten*, to GRUNT.] —dis·grun·tled *adj.* —dis·grun·tle·ment *n.*

dis·guise (dĭs-gīz') *tr.v.* -guised, -guising, -guises. **1.** To modify the appearance or manner of in order to prevent recognition. **2.** To conceal or obscure by false pretenses; misrepresent. ~*n.* **1. a.** The act of disguising. **b.** The condition of being disguised. **2.** Something that serves to disguise, such as a mask, costume, or pretense. [Middle English *disg(u)isen*, from Old French *desguisier* : *des-*, from Latin *dis-* (reversal) + *guise*, manner, GUISE.] —dis·guis·er *n.*

dis·gust (dĭs-gŭst') *tr.v.* -gusted, -gusting, -gusts. **1.** To be so unpleasant as to excite nausea in; sicken. **2.** To offend the taste or moral sense of; repel. ~*n.* A strong feeling of distaste excited by something physically revolting or offensive to one's moral or aesthetic values. [Old French *desgouster* : *des-*, from Latin *dis-* (negative) + *goust*, taste, from Latin *gustus*.]

dis·gust·ed (dĭs-gŭs'tĭd) *adj.* Filled with disgust or irritated impatience. —dis·gust·ed·ly *adv.*

Usage: Three prepositions are used after *disgusted* in standard English. One is *disgusted at* someone's action or behavior, especially when one is giving an immediate reaction; one is *disgusted with* a person or his action, especially when one's attitude is being maintained over a period of time; and one may also be *disgusted by* someone or something.

dis·gust·ful (dĭs-gŭst'fəl) *adj.* **1.** Causing disgust; repugnant. **2.** Full of or marked by disgust. —dis·gust·ful·ly *adv.*

dis·gust·ing (dĭs-gŭs'tĭng) *adj.* Deeply offensive to one's taste or moral values; acutely repugnant. —dis·gust·ing·ly *adv.*

dish (dĭsh) *n.* **1. a.** An open container, generally shallow and concave, for holding or serving food. **b.** Loosely, any container on

which food is placed or served, such as a plate or bowl. **c.** The portion a dish holds. **2.** A particular variety, preparation, or article of food. **3. a.** A concavity or depression like that in a dish. **b.** The degree of such a concavity. **4.** A large dish-shaped aerial, as in a radio telescope or radar apparatus. **5.** *Slang.* A good-looking person, especially a woman. ~*tr.v.* dished, dishing, dishes. **1.** To serve (food) in or from a dish, cooking pot, pan, or the like. Usually used with *up* or *out*. **2.** To hollow out; make concave. **3.** *British Slang.* To foil; ruin. **4.** *Informal.* To give out; dispense; distribute. Used with *out.* —dish it out. *Slang.* To hand out abuse or punishment. —dish up. **1.** To serve food or a meal. **2.** *Informal.* To present (a proposal, for example) in an attractive manner. [Middle English *dish*, Old English *disc*, plate, bowl, platter, from West Germanic *diskaz* (unattested), from Latin *discus*, quoit, DISK.]

dis·ha·bille (dĭs'ə-bēl', -bē') *n.* Also **des·ha·bille** (dĕs'-). The state of being partially or very casually dressed; a state of undress. [French *déshabillé*, from the past participle of *déshabiller*, to undress : *dés-*, from Latin *dis-* (reversal) + *habiller*, to dress.] —dis·ha·bille *adj.*

dis·har·mo·ny (dĭs-här'mə-nē) *n., pl.* -nies. Lack of harmony; discord. —dis·har·mo·ni·ous (dĭs'här-mō'nē-əs) *adj.*

dish·cloth (dĭsh'klôth', -klŏth') *n.* A cloth used for washing dishes or wiping surfaces. Also called "dishrag."

dishcloth gourd *n.* **1.** Any of several tropical vines of the genus *Luffa*; especially, *L. cylindrica*, cultivated for its cucumberlike fruits. **2.** The fruit of any of these plants, the fibrous skeleton of which is used as a **loofah** (see).

dis·heart·en (dĭs-härt'n) *tr.v.* -ened, -ening, -ens. To shake or destroy the courage or resolution of; dispirit. —dis·heart·en·ing·ly *adv.* —dis·heart·en·ment *n.*

dished (dĭsht) *adj.* **1.** Slanting toward one another at the bottom. Said of a pair of wheels. **2.** Dish-shaped; concave.

di·shev·el (dĭ-shĕv'əl) *tr.v.* -eled, -eling, -els. Also *chiefly British* -elled, -elling. **1.** To loosen and let fall (hair or clothing) in disarray. **2.** To disarrange the hair or clothing of (a person). [Back-formation from DISHEVELED.] —di·shev·el·ment *n.*

di·shev·eled (dĭ-shĕv'əld) *adj.* **1.** In a state of disarray; unkempt; untidy. [Middle English *discheveled*, from Old French *deschevele*, past participle of *descheveler*, to disarrange the hair : *des-*, from Latin *dis-*, apart + *chevel*, hair, from Latin *capillus*.]

dis·hon·est (dĭs-ŏn'ĭst) *adj.* **1.** Disposed to lie, cheat, or deceive. **2.** Involving deception or untruthfulness. **3.** Obtained illegally or unfairly. —dis·hon·est·ly *adv.*

Synonyms: *deceitful, lying, mendacious, shady, tricky, underhand, untruthful.*

dis·hon·es·ty (dĭs-ŏn'ĭ-stē) *n., pl.* -ties. **1.** Lack of honesty; inclination to deceive or cheat. **2.** A dishonest act or statement.

dis·hon·or (dĭs-ŏn'ər) *n.* **1.** Loss of honor, respect, or reputation; disgrace; shame. **2.** Something that causes loss of honor. **3.** An offense or insult. **4.** Failure to pay a note or bill of exchange or to meet a commercial obligation. —See Synonyms at **disgrace.** ~*tr.v.* dishonored, -oring, -ors. **1.** To deprive of honor; disgrace. **2.** To offend the dignity of; slight. **3.** To violate the chastity of. **4.** To fail to pay (a note, for example). —dis·hon·or·er *n.*

dis·hon·or·a·ble (dĭs-ŏn'ər-ə-bəl) *adj.* **1.** Characterized by or causing dishonor or discredit. **2.** Lacking integrity; unprincipled. —dis·hon·or·a·ble·ness *n.* —dis·hon·or·a·bly *adv.*

dish·pan (dĭsh'păn') *n.* A flat-bottomed pan or basin for washing dishes.

dish·rag (dĭsh'răg') *n.* A **dishcloth** (see).

dish·tow·el (dĭsh'tou'əl) *n.* A towel for drying dishes. Also *chiefly British* "tea towel."

dish·ware (dĭsh'wâr') *n.* Dishes, as of china, used in serving food.

dish·wash·er (dĭsh'wŏsh'ər, -wô'shər) *n.* **1.** An electric machine that washes dishes, cutlery, and utensils automatically. **2.** A person who washes dishes; specifically, one employed to do this in a restaurant.

dish·wa·ter (dĭsh'wô'tər, -wŏt'ər) *n.* **1.** Water in which dishes are being or have been washed. **2.** *Informal.* An unpleasantly weak-tasting drink.

dish·y (dĭsh'ē) *adj.* -ier, -iest. *Chiefly British Slang.* Very attractive. [From DISH (attractive person).]

dis·il·lu·sion (dĭs'ĭ-lōō'zhən) *tr.v.* -sioned, -sioning, -sions. **1.** To free or deprive of illusions or misconceptions. **2.** To undermine or destroy the ideals of; disenchant. ~*n.* **1.** The act of disillusioning. **2.** The condition or fact of being disillusioned. —dis·il·lu·sion·ment *n.* —dis·il·lu·sive *adj.*

dis·il·lu·sioned (dĭs'ĭ-lōō'zhənd) *adj.* **1.** No longer contented or satisfied. **2.** No longer idealistic; cynical.

dis·in·cen·tive (dĭs'ĭn-sĕn'tĭv) *n.* Something that discourages or dissuades; a deterrent. —dis·in·cen·tive *adj.*

dis·in·cli·na·tion (dĭs'ĭn'klə-nā'shən) *n.* Lack of willingness or disposition; reluctance; aversion.

dis·in·cline (dĭs'ĭn-klīn') *v.* -clined, -clining, -clines. —*tr.* To make reluctant or unwilling. —*intr.* To be reluctant or unwilling.

dis·in·clined (dĭs'ĭn-klīnd') *adj.* Unwilling; reluctant.

dis·in·fect (dĭs'ĭn-fĕkt') *tr.v.* -fected, -fecting, -fects. To cleanse of disease-carrying microorganisms. —dis·in·fec·tion *n.*

dis·in·fec·tant (dĭs'ĭn-fĕk'tənt) *n.* An agent that disinfects by destroying, neutralizing, or inhibiting the growth of disease-carrying microorganisms. ~*adj.* Serving to disinfect.

dis·in·fest (dĭs'ĭn-fĕst') *tr.v.* -fested, -festing, -fests. To rid of vermin. —dis·in·fes·ta·tion *n.*

dis·in·fla·tion (dĭs′ĭn-flā′shən) *n.* The downward movement of inflated prices to a more normal level, without necessarily entailing a reduction in the level of economic activity.

dis·in·form (dĭs′ĭn-fôrm′, -fôrm′) *tr.v.* **-formed, -forming, -forms.** To supply with disinformation.

dis·in·for·ma·tion (dĭs-ĭn′fər-mā′shən) *n.* False or misleading information deliberately spread by a propaganda agency.

dis·in·gen·u·ous (dĭs′ĭn-jĕn′yōō-əs) *adj.* Not straightforward or candid; insincere; crafty. **—dis·in·gen·u·ous·ly** *adv.* **—dis·in·gen·u·ous·ness** *n.*

dis·in·her·it (dĭs′ĭn-hĕr′ĭt) *tr.v.* **-ited, -iting, -its.** To deprive of inheritance or the right to inherit, especially by excluding members of one's family. **—dis·in·her·i·tance** *n.*

dis·in·te·grate (dĭs-ĭn′tə-grāt′) *v.* **-grated, -grating, -grates.** —*intr.* **1.** To separate into components or fragments, especially after a physical shock. **2.** To weaken or collapse, especially in the face of difficulties. —*tr.* To cause (a body) to separate into components; destroy. —See Synonyms at **decay.** **—dis·in·te·gra·tor** *n.*

dis·in·te·gra·tion (dĭs-ĭn′tə-grā′shən) *n.* **1.** The process of disintegrating or the state of being disintegrated. **2.** *Physics.* The break-up of an atomic nucleus or an unstable elementary particle into smaller fragments, either spontaneously or as a result of bombardment with radiation. See **decay.**

dis·in·ter (dĭs′ĭn-tûr′) *tr.v.* **-terred, -terring, -ters.** **1.** To dig up or remove, as from a grave or tomb; exhume. **2.** To remove from obscurity; expose. **—dis·in·ter·ment** *n.*

dis·in·ter·est (dĭs-ĭn′trĭst, -ĭn′tər-ĭst) *n.* **1.** Freedom from selfish bias or self-interest; impartiality. **2.** *Nonstandard.* Lack of interest.

dis·in·ter·est·ed (dĭs-ĭn′trĭ-stĭd, -ĭn′tə-rĕs′tĭd) *adj.* **1.** Not influenced by self-interest; impartial: *disinterested praise.* **2.** *Nonstandard.* Uninterested; indifferent. **—dis·in·ter·est·ed·ly** *adv.* **—dis·in·ter·est·ed·ness** *n.*

> *Usage:* Standard English attempts to maintain a clear distinction between *disinterested* meaning "impartial," "unbiased" and *uninterested* meaning "indifferent." The former implies a lack of self-interest, whereas the latter indicates a lack of any interest. In fact, the use of *disinterested* to mean "uninterested" came earlier than its sense of "impartial"; and conversely, the early use of *uninterested* was in the sense of "impartial." Both of these were recorded in the early 17th century.

dis·in·ter·me·di·a·tion (dĭs-ĭn′tər-me′dē-ā′shən) *n.* The process whereby savers bypass banks and savings and loan associations, lending their money directly to borrowers, such as the government, industry, and the like.

dis·in·tox·i·cate (dĭs′ĭn-tŏk′sĭ-kāt′) *tr.v.* **-cated, -cating, -cates.** To free from the effects of intoxication or from dependence on intoxicating agents. **—dis·in·tox·i·ca·tion** *n.*

dis·in·vest·ment (dĭs′ĭn-vĕst′mənt) *n. Economics.* A reduction of investment, especially through a failure to replace capital stock such as machinery.

dis·ject (dĭs-jĕkt′) *tr.v.* **-jected, -jecting, -jects.** To split or disperse with force; scatter. [Latin *disicere* (past participle *disjectus*) : *dis-,* apart + *jacere,* to throw.]

dis·join (dĭs-join′) *v.* **-joined, -joining, -joins.** —*tr.* To undo the joining of; separate. —*intr.* To become disconnected. [Middle English, from Old French *desjoindre,* from Latin *disjungere* : DIS- + *jungere,* to JOIN.]

dis·joint (dĭs-joint′) *v.* **-jointed, -jointing, -joints.** —*tr.* **1.** To put out of joint; dislocate. **2.** To take apart at the joints; separate. **3.** To destroy the coherence or connections of. —*intr.* **1.** To come apart at the joints. **2.** To become dislocated.
~*adj. Mathematics.* Having no elements in common. Said especially of sets. [Middle English *disjointen,* from Old French *desjoindre* (past participle *desjoint*), to DISJOIN.]

dis·joint·ed (dĭs-join′tĭd) *adj.* **1.** Separated at the joints. **2.** Out of joint; dislocated. **3.** Lacking order or coherence; disconnected. **—dis·joint·ed·ly** *adv.* **—dis·joint·ed·ness** *n.*

dis·junct (dĭs-jŭngkt′) *adj.* **1.** Separated; disconnected. **2.** *Music.* Pertaining to progression by intervals larger than major seconds. **3.** *Zoology.* Having the head, thorax, and abdomen separated by deep constrictions. Said of insects.
~*n. Logic.* Any of the propositions in a disjunction. [Middle English *disjuncte,* from Latin *disjunctus,* past participle of *disjungere,* to DISJOIN.]

dis·junc·tion (dĭs-jŭngk′shən) *n.* Also **dis·junc·ture** (-chər) (for sense 1). **1.** The act of disjoining or the condition of being disjointed. **2.** *Logic.* A compound proposition that presents two or more alternative terms, with the assertion that only one is true. **3.** *Genetics.* Separation of homologous pairs of chromosomes during meiosis.

dis·junc·tive (dĭs-jŭngk′tĭv) *adj.* **1.** Serving to separate or divide. **2.** *Grammar.* **a.** Serving to establish a relationship of contrast or opposition. The conjunction *but* in the phrase *beautiful but smelly* is disjunctive. **b.** Able to stand in isolation; syntactically independent; for example, the word *honestly* in *Honestly, I don't know,* is disjunctive. **3.** *Logic.* **a.** Presenting two or more alternative propositions. Said of a compound proposition. **b.** Containing a disjunction as one premise. Said of a syllogism.
~*n.* **1.** *Grammar.* A disjunctive word. **2.** *Logic.* A disjunction. **—dis·junc·tive·ly** *adv.*

disk (dĭsk) *n.* Also **disc.** **1.** A thin, flat, circular plate. **2.** Something resembling a disk, such as an astronomical body or an anatomical structure. **3.** *Botany.* The enlarged receptacle containing numerous tiny flowers in the flower head of many composite plants, such as the daisy and the coneflower. **4.** Variant of **disc** (sense 1). **5.** *Computer Science.* A round flat plate coated with a magnetic substance on which data may be stored. See **floppy disk, magnetic disk. 6.** A circular grid in a phototype setting machine.
~*tr.v.* **disked, disking, disks.** Also **disced, discing, discs.** To work (soil) with a disk harrow. [Latin *discus,* quoit < Greek *diskos* < *dikein,* to throw.]

disk crash *n. Computer Science.* A **crash** *(see)* involving a disk.

disk drive *n. Computer Science.* A device with read/write heads used for retrieving information from or storing information on a magnetic disk or tape.

dis·kette (dĭ-skĕt′) *n.* A **floppy disk** *(see).*

disk flower *n.* Any of the tiny tubular flowers forming the center of the flower head of certain composite plants, such as the daisy. Compare **ray flower.**

disk harrow *n.* A harrow equipped with a series of disks set on edge or at an angle on one or more axles.

disk jockey *n.* Variant of **disc jockey.**

disk pack *n. Computer Science.* A computer storage device consisting of several magnetic disks that can be used and stored as a unit.

dis·like (dĭs-līk′) *tr.v.* **-liked, -liking, -likes.** To regard with distaste or aversion; find unpleasant.
~*n.* An attitude or feeling of distaste or aversion.

dis·lo·cate (dĭs′lō-kāt′, dĭs-lō′kāt′) *tr.v.* **-cated, -cating, -cates.** **1.** To put out from the usual or proper relationship with contiguous parts; displace; shift. **2.** *Pathology.* To displace (a limb or organ) from the normal position; especially, to displace (a bone) from its joint. **3.** To throw into confusion or disorder; upset.

dis·lo·ca·tion (dĭs′lō-kā′shən) *n.* **1.** The act of dislocating or the state or condition of being dislocated. **2.** *Geology.* A **fault** *(see).* **3.** *Crystallography.* A line or plane in a crystal in which there is a deviation from the regular repeating order of the crystal lattice. An *edge dislocation* is a straight line marking the edge of an incomplete plane of atoms. A *screw dislocation* is a line about which atoms are arranged in helices.

dis·lodge (dĭs-lŏj′) *v.* **-lodged, -lodging, -lodges.** —*tr.* To remove or force out from a previously occupied position. —*intr.* To move or go from a dwelling or former position. **—dis·lodg·ment, dis·lodge·ment** *n.*

dis·loy·al (dĭs-loi′əl) *adj.* Lacking in loyalty. —See Synonyms at **faithless. —dis·loy·al·ly** *adv.*

dis·loy·al·ty (dĭs-loi′əl-tē) *n., pl.* **-ties.** **1.** The quality of being disloyal; faithlessness. **2.** A disloyal act.

dis·mal (dĭz′məl) *adj.* **1.** Causing dismay or depression; dreary; drab. **2.** Causing dread or dismay; ghastly. **3.** *Informal.* Incompetent; inadequate: *a dismal effort.*
~*n.* **1.** **dismals.** *Rare.* Low spirits: *in the dismals.* **2.** *Southern U.S.* An area of swampland. [Middle English, unlucky days (two days in each month that were considered unpropitious), from Medieval Latin *diēs malī* : Latin *diēs,* plural of *diēs,* day + *malī,* plural of *malus,* evil.] **—dis·mal·ly** *adv.* **—dis·mal·ness** *n.*

Dis·mal Swamp (dĭz′məl). Swampy area in southeastern Virginia and northeastern North Carolina. Thought to have once covered *c.* 5,700 square kilometers (2,200 square miles), the heavily forested swamp has been reduced to less than 1,554 square kilometers (600 square miles) by drainage, The swamp was surveyed (1763) by George Washington, a member of the company formed to drain it.

dis·man·tle (dĭs-măn′tl) *tr.v.* **-tled, -tling, -tles.** **1.** To strip (a house, for example) of furnishings or equipment. **2.** To take apart; disassemble. **3.** To tear down; destroy. **4.** To strip of clothing or covering. **—dis·man·tle·ment** *n.*

dis·mast (dĭs-măst′, -mäst′) *tr.v.* **-masted, -masting, -masts.** *Nautical.* To remove or break off the mast or masts of.

dis·may (dĭs-mā′) *tr.v.* **-mayed, -maying, -mays.** **1.** To fill with dread or apprehension; make anxious or afraid. **2.** To discourage or trouble greatly; dishearten.
~*n.* **1.** A feeling of discouragement or disappointment. **2.** A loss of courage or confidence in the face of trouble or danger; consternation. [Middle English *dismayen,* from Old French *desmayer* (attested only in past participle *dismaye*) : *des-,* from Latin *dis-* (intensive) + *esmayer,* to frighten, be frightened, from Vulgar Latin *exmagāre* (unattested), to deprive of power, from Germanic.]

dis·mem·ber (dĭs-mĕm′bər) *tr.v.* **-bered, -bering, -bers.** **1.** To cut, tear, or pull off the limbs of. **2.** To divide into pieces. **—dis·mem·ber·er** *n.* **—dis·mem·ber·ment** *n.*

dis·miss (dĭs-mĭs′) *tr.v.* **-missed, -missing, -misses.** **1.** To discharge, as from employment. **2.** To direct or allow to leave: *dismiss troops.* **3.** To rid one's mind of; dispel. **4.** To reject; repudiate: *dismiss an allegation.* **5.** To refuse to consider seriously: *They dismissed her great invention as a toy.* **6.** *Law.* To put (a claim or action) out of court without further hearing. [Middle English *dismissen,* from Medieval Latin *dismittere* (past participle *dismissus*), variant of Latin *dīmittere* : *dīs-,* away + *mittere,* to send.] **—dis·miss·i·ble** *adj.* **—dis·mis·sive** *adj.*

dis·miss·al (dĭs-mĭs′əl) *n.* Also **dis·mis·sion** (-mĭsh′ən). **1. a.** The act of dismissing. **b.** The condition of being dismissed. **2.** An order or notice of discharge.

dis·mount (dĭs-mount′) *v.* **-mounted, -mounting, -mounts.** —*intr.* To get off or down, as from a horse or bicycle; alight. —*tr.* **1.** To remove (a thing) from its support, setting, or mounting. **2.** To unseat, as from a horse. **3.** To take apart (a mechanism).
~*n.* The act of dismounting.

Dis·ney (dĭz′nē), **Walter Elias,** known as "Walt" (1901–66). U.S. film producer and animator. He founded a film empire in the 1920's and 1930's with his creation of the cartoon characters Mickey Mouse and Donald Duck. He produced feature-length cartoon films, nature documentaries, and adventure films. In 1955 he opened Disneyland, a vast amusement park with attractions based on the characters and settings of his films, in Anaheim, California. His films include *Snow White and the Seven Dwarfs* (1938), *Fantasia* (1940), and *Mary Poppins* (1964).

dis·o·be·di·ence (dĭs′ə-bē′dē-əns) *n.* The condition or fact of not obeying; deliberate failure to obey; insubordination. —**dis·o·be·di·ent** *adj.* —**dis·o·be·di·ent·ly** *adv.*

dis·o·bey (dĭs′ə-bā′) *v.* **-beyed, -beying, -beys.** —*intr.* To refuse or fail to follow an order or rule. —*tr.* To refuse or fail to obey. —**dis·o·bey·er** *n.*

dis·o·blige (dĭs′ə-blīj′) *tr.v.* **-bliged, -bliging, -bliges.** 1. To refuse or neglect to act in accord with the wishes of. 2. *Regional.* To inconvenience. —**dis·o·blig·ing·ly** *adv.*

di·so·di·um phosphate (dī′sō′dē-əm) *n.* A sodium phosphate, Na₂HPO₄.

dis·or·der (dĭs-ôr′dər) *n.* 1. A lack of order or regular arrangement; confusion. 2. A breach of civic order or peace; public disturbance. 3. Imperfect functioning of part of the body or mind. 4. A breakdown, as in a system.
~*tr.v.* **disordered, -dering, -ders.** 1. To throw into disorder; muddle. 2. To disturb the normal physical or mental health of; derange.

dis·or·dered (dĭs-ôr′dərd) *adj.* 1. In a condition of disorder; disarranged. 2. Physically or mentally ill; deranged.

dis·or·der·ly (dĭs-ôr′dər-lē) *adj.* 1. Lacking regular or logical order or arrangement; irregular; unsystematic. 2. Undisciplined; unruly; riotous. 3. *Law.* Disturbing the public peace or decorum: *drunk and disorderly.* —**dis·or·der·li·ness** *n.*

disorderly conduct *n. Law.* Any of various petty offenses of a kind likely to cause a breach of the peace.

disorderly house *n. Law.* Any house, such as a house of prostitution, whose inmates regularly violate the public order or decency.

dis·or·gan·ize (dĭs-ôr′gə-nīz′) *tr.v.* **-ized, -izing, -izes.** To destroy the organization, systematic arrangement, or unity of; throw into confusion. —**dis·or·gan·i·za·tion** *n.* —**dis·or·gan·iz·er** *n.*

dis·o·ri·ent (dĭs-ôr′ē-ĕnt′, dĭs-ōr′-) *tr.v.* **-ented, -enting, -ents.** 1. a. To cause to lose one's sense of direction or location, as by removing from a familiar environment. b. *Psychology.* To cause to lose one's awareness of time, place, or self in relation to one's environment. 2. To confuse; perplex. —**dis·o·ri·en·ta·tion** *n.*

dis·o·ri·en·tate (dĭs-ôr′ē-ĕn-tāt′, dĭs-ōr′-) *tr.v.* **-tated, -tating, -tates.** To disorient.

dis·own (dĭs-ōn′) *tr.v.* **-owned, -owning, -owns.** 1. To refuse to acknowledge or accept as one's own. 2. To renounce; repudiate.

dis·par·age (dĭs-păr′ĭj) *tr.v.* **-aged, -aging, -ages.** 1. To speak of slightingly; belittle. 2. To reduce in esteem; discredit. —See Synonyms at **decry.** [Middle English *disparagen,* to degrade, disgrace, humble, from Old French *desparager,* "to deprive someone of his rank" : *des-,* from Latin *dis-* (privative) + *parage,* rank, from *per,* PEER.] —**dis·par·ag·er** *n.* —**dis·par·ag·ing·ly** *adv.*

dis·par·age·ment (dĭs-păr′ĭj-mənt) *n.* 1. The act of disparaging; detraction. 2. A lowering of dignity or esteem; discredit. 3. Something that lowers dignity or esteem.

dis·pa·rate (dĭs′pər-ĭt, dĭs-păr′ĭt) *adj.* Completely distinct or different in kind; entirely dissimilar. [Latin *disparātus,* past participle of *disparāre,* to separate : *dis-,* apart + *parāre,* to prepare.] —**dis·pa·rate·ly** *adv.* —**dis·pa·rate·ness** *n.*

dis·par·i·ty (dĭs-păr′ĭ-tē) *n., pl.* **-ties.** 1. The condition or fact of being unequal in age, rank, degree, or other measure; difference. 2. Unlikeness; incongruity; dissimilarity.

dis·pas·sion (dĭs-păsh′ən) *n.* Freedom from passion, bias, or emotion; objectivity.

dis·pas·sion·ate (dĭs-păsh′ən-ĭt) *adj.* Devoid of or unaffected by passion, emotion, or bias; impartial; calm: *dispassionate judgment.* —See Synonyms at **fair.** —**dis·pas·sion·ate·ly** *adv.* —**dis·pas·sion·ate·ness** *n.*

dis·patch, des·patch (dĭs-păch′) *tr.v.* **-patched, -patching, -patches.** 1. To send off to a specific destination or on specific business. 2. To complete or dispose of promptly. 3. To put to death summarily.
~*n.* 1. The act of dispatching or sending off. 2. A putting to death. 3. Efficient speed or promptness; expeditious performance. 4. An official communication sent with speed; especially, a report of military operations. 5. A news item sent to a newspaper, as by a correspondent. [Spanish *despachar* or Italian *dispacciare,* perhaps from Old French *despeechier,* to set free, unshackle : *des-,* from Latin *dis-* (reversal) + *(em)peechier,* to hinder, from Late Latin *impedicāre,* to entangle : Latin *in-* + *pedica,* shackle.]

dis·patch·er (dĭs-păch′ər) *n.* 1. One that dispatches. 2. A person who sends out trains, buses, trucks, or cars according to a schedule. 3. *Computer Science.* A routine that controls the order in which input and output devices obtain access to the processing system.

dis·pel (dĭs-pĕl′) *tr.v.* **-pelled, -pelling, -pels.** To rid of by or as if by driving away or scattering; dispense with: *"the effect of his tone was to dispel her shyness"* (Henry James). [Middle English *dispellen,* from Latin *dispellere* : *dis-,* away + *pellere,* to push, drive, strike.] —**dis·pel·ler** *n.*

dis·pen·sa·ble (dĭs-pĕn′sə-bəl) *adj.* 1. Capable of being dispensed with; unimportant. 2. Able to be dispensed, administered, or dis-

tributed. 3. Subject to exemption in particular cases, as a sin may be; condonable. —**dis·pen·sa·bil·i·ty, dis·pen·sa·ble·ness** *n.*

dis·pen·sa·ry (dĭs-pĕn′sə-rē) *n., pl.* **-ries.** 1. An office in a hospital or other institution from which medical supplies and preparations are dispensed. 2. A public institution where medical aid is dispensed.

dis·pen·sa·tion (dĭs′pən-sā′shən, dĭs′pĕn-) *n.* 1. The act of dispensing or giving out; distribution; apportionment. 2. Something that is dispensed or given out. 3. A specific arrangement or system by which something is dispensed or administered. 4. Any exemption or release from an obligation or rule, granted by or as if by an authority. 5. a. An exemption from a church law, a vow, or other similar obligation granted in a particular case by an ecclesiastical authority. b. The document containing this exemption. 6. *Theology.* a. The divine ordering of worldly affairs. b. A religious system or code of commands considered to have been divinely revealed or appointed: *the Muslim dispensation.* —**dis·pen·sa·tion·al** *adj.*

dis·pen·sa·to·ry (dĭs-pĕn′sə-tôr′ē, -tōr′ē) *adj.* Of, pertaining to, or granted by dispensation.
~*n., pl.* **dispensatories.** 1. A book in which the preparation, uses, and contents of medicines are described; a pharmacopoeia. 2. *Archaic.* A dispensary.

dis·pense (dĭs-pĕns′) *v.* **-pensed, -pensing, -penses.** —*tr.* 1. To deal out or distribute in parts or portions. 2. To prepare and give out (medicines) according to a doctor's prescription. 3. To administer (justice, for example). 4. To exempt, as from a duty or religious obligation. —*intr.* To grant dispensation or exemption. —**dispense with.** 1. To manage without; forgo. 2. To do away with; make unnecessary. —See Usage note at **distribute.** [Middle English *dispensen,* from Medieval Latin *dispensāre,* to grant dispensation to, exempt, condone, from Latin, to pay out, distribute, frequentative of *dispendere,* to weigh out : *dis-,* away + *pendere,* to weigh.]

dis·pens·er (dĭs-pĕn′sər) *n.* One that dispenses or gives out; specifically: 1. A device that dispenses goods in measured amounts or single units: *a paper-cup dispenser.* 2. A person who dispenses medicines.

dis·per·sal (dĭs-pûr′səl) *n.* The act or process of dispersing or the condition of being dispersed; distribution.

dis·per·sant (dĭs-pûr′sənt) *n.* A liquid or gas in which something is dispersed, such as the liquid used as a propellant in an aerosol can.

dis·perse (dĭs-pûrs′) *v.* **-persed, -persing, -perses.** —*tr.* 1. To scatter in various directions; distribute widely. 2. To cause to vanish or evaporate; dispel. 3. To disseminate (knowledge, for example). 4. To separate (light or other radiation) into components with different wavelengths. —*intr.* To move or scatter in different directions. [Middle English *dispersen,* from Old French *disperser,* from Latin *dispergere* (past participle *dispersus*), to scatter on all sides : *dis-,* in different directions + *spargere,* to strew, scatter.] —**dis·pers·ed·ly** (dĭs-pûr′sĭd-lē) *adv.* —**dis·pers·er** *n.* —**dis·pers·i·ble** *adj.*

disperse system *n.* Any continuous medium containing dispersed entities of any size or state.

dis·per·sion (dĭs-pûr′zhən, -shən) *n.* 1. a. The state of being dispersed. b. The act or process of dispersing. 2. *Statistics.* The degree of scatter of data, usually about some mean or median value. 3. *Physics.* The separation of a complex wave into component parts according to some characteristic, such as frequency or wavelength; for example, separation of visible light into its color components by refraction or diffraction. 4. *Chemistry.* A suspension, such as smog or homogenized milk, of solid, liquid, or gaseous particles, of colloidal size or larger, in a liquid, solid, or gaseous medium. 5. **Dispersion. The Diaspora** *n.*

dis·per·sive (dĭs-pûr′sĭv, -zĭv) *adj.* 1. Tending to become dispersed. 2. Tending to produce dispersion.

dis·per·soid (dĭs-pûr′soid′) *n. Chemistry.* A colloid in which one substance is dispersed in another. Also used adjectivally: *a dispersoid sol.*

dis·pir·it (dĭs-pîr′ĭt) *tr.v.* **-ited, -iting, -its.** To lower in spirit; dishearten. [DI(s)- (negative) + SPIRIT.]

dis·pir·it·ed (dĭs-pîr′ĭt-ĭd) *adj.* Characterized by low spirits; disheartened; dejected. —**dis·pir·it·ed·ly** *adv.* —**dis·pir·it·ed·ness** *n.*

dis·place (dĭs-plās′) *tr.v.* **-placed, -placing, -places.** 1. To change the place or position of; move from the usual place. 2. To take the place of; supplant. 3. To discharge from an office or position. 4. To cause a displacement of (a body, for example). —See Synonyms at **replace.** —**dis·place·a·ble** *adj.* —**dis·plac·er** *n.*

displaced person *n. Abbr.* **DP, D.P.** A person living in a foreign country who has been driven from his or her homeland, especially by war or political unrest.

dis·place·ment (dĭs-plās′mənt) *n.* 1. a. The act of displacing. b. The condition of being displaced. 2. *Chemistry.* A reaction in which one kind of atom or group is removed from a molecule and replaced by another. 3. *Physics.* a. The weight or volume of a fluid displaced by a floating body, used especially as a measurement of the weight or bulk of ships. b. A vector, or the magnitude of a vector, from the initial position to a subsequent position assumed by a body. 4. *Psychology.* a. The shifting of a feeling, such as anger, from an appropriate to an inappropriate object. b. Engagement in inappropriate or irrelevant behavior during situations of extreme emotion or conflict. Often used adjectivally: *displacement activity.*

displacement ton *n. Nautical.* A unit for measuring the displacement of a ship afloat, equivalent to one long ton or about 35 cubic feet of salt water.

dis·play (dĭs-plā′) *tr.v.* **-played, -playing, -plays.** 1. To hold up to view; make visible; expose; exhibit. 2. To make manifest or noticeable; show evidence of. 3. To exhibit ostentatiously; show off; flaunt. 4. To spread out; unfurl: *a peacock displaying its tail.* 5. *Printing.* To give prominence to (printed letters or words, for example), as by using large type. —See Synonyms at **show.** ~*n.* 1. The act of displaying; exhibition. 2. Anything that is exhibited or displayed. 3. Vulgar ostentation. 4. *Printing.* **a.** An arrangement or style of type designed to give prominence to printed matter. **b.** Printed matter that is set off prominently. **c.** An advertisement designed to catch the eye, as distinguished from a classified advertisement. Also used adjectivally: *display advertisements.* 5. *Zoology.* A type of behavior characterized by gestures that act as specific signals in courtship and aggression, shown particularly by birds and fishes. 6. **a.** An electronic device for representing text, numbers, or diagrams visually. **b.** The material represented on such a device. [Middle English *displayen,* to unfold, unfurl, exhibit, from Old French *despleier,* from Medieval Latin *displicāre,* from Latin, to scatter : *dis-* (reversal) + *plicāre,* to fold.]

dis·played (dĭs-plād′) *adj. Heraldry.* Standing erect with wings extended.

dis·please (dĭs-plēz′) *v.* **-pleased, -pleasing, -pleases.** —*tr.* To cause annoyance or vexation to; offend. —*intr.* To cause annoyance or offense. —**dis·pleas·ing·ly** *adv.*

dis·pleas·ure (dĭs-plĕzh′ər) *n.* 1. The condition or fact of being displeased or dissatisfied; annoyance; anger. 2. *Archaic.* Discomfort; uneasiness. 3. *Archaic.* An annoying or injurious offense. ~*tr.v.* **displeasured, -uring, -ures.** *Archaic.* To displease.

dis·port (dĭs-pôrt′, -pōrt′) *v.* **-ported, -porting, -ports.** —*intr.* To play; frolic. —*tr.* To occupy (oneself) with diversion or amusement. ~*n.* Diversion; play; sport. [Middle English *disporten,* from Old French *desporter,* "to carry away," divert : *des-,* from Latin *dis-,* apart + *porter,* to carry, PORT.]

dis·pos·a·ble (dĭs-pō′zə-bəl) *adj.* 1. Designed to be disposed of after use. 2. Available for use. ~*n.* Something intended to be disposed of after use. —**dis·pos·a·bil·i·ty** *n.*

disposable income *n.* The residue of one's income that is available for use after all direct taxes have been paid.

dis·pos·al (dĭs-pō′zəl) *n.* 1. A particular order, distribution, or arrangement. 2. A particular method of attending to or settling matters. 3. The transference of something by gift or sale. 4. A throwing out or away. 5. An apparatus or device for disposing of something, such as household waste. Also used adjectivally: *a disposal unit.* 6. The liberty or power to dispose of or use someone or something: *funds at our disposal.*

dis·pose (dĭs-pōz′) *v.* **-posed, -posing, -poses.** —*tr.* 1. To place in a particular order; arrange. 2. To put (business affairs, for example) into correct, definitive, or conclusive form. 3. To make willing or receptive; incline. Often used in the passive. —*intr.* To settle or decide a matter. —**dispose of.** 1. To attend to; arrange; settle. 2. To transfer or part with, as by giving or selling. 3. To get rid of; throw away. 4. To eat or drink (food or liquid). ~*n. Obsolete.* 1. Disposal. 2. Disposition; demeanor. [Middle English *disposen,* from Old French *disposer,* reshaped (after *poser,* to POSE), from Latin *dispōnere,* to place here and there, arrange : *dis-,* in different directions + *pōnere,* to put.] —**dis·pos·er** *n.*

dis·po·si·tion (dĭs′pə-zĭsh′ən) *n.* 1. One's customary manner of emotional response; temperament: *"She had a lively, playful disposition, which delighted in anything ridiculous"* (Jane Austen). 2. A tendency or inclination, especially when habitual: *a disposition to heavy drinking.* 3. **a.** The act or manner of disposing. **b.** The condition or fact of being disposed. 4. The power or liberty to control, direct, or dispose. *Synonyms: character, nature, personality, temperament.*

dis·pos·sess (dĭs′pə-zĕs′) *tr.v.* **-sessed, -sessing, -sesses.** To deprive (someone) of the possession of something, especially property. —**dis·pos·ses·sion** *n.* —**dis·pos·ses·sor** *n.* —**dis·pos·ses·so·ry** *adj.*

dis·po·sure (dĭs-pō′zhər) *n. Rare.* Disposal.

dis·praise (dĭs-prāz′) *tr.v.* **-praised, -praising, -praises.** To express disapproval of; disparage; censure. ~*n.* Reproach; censure. [Middle English *dispreisen,* from Old French *despreiser,* from Vulgar Latin *dispretiāre* (unattested), variant of Latin *dēpretiāre,* to DEPRECIATE.] —**dis·prais·er** *n.* —**dis·prais·ing·ly** *adv.*

Dis·prin (dĭs′prĭn) *n.* A trademark for a preparation of aspirin, calcium carbonate, and anhydrous citric acid, taken, in the form of water-soluble tablets, for the relief of pain.

dis·prize (dĭs-prīz′) *tr.v.* **-prized, -prizing, -prizes.** *Archaic.* To hold in low esteem. [Middle English *disprisen, dispreisen,* to DISPRAISE.]

dis·proof (dĭs-prōōf′) *n.* 1. The act of disproving or refuting. 2. Evidence that disproves or refutes.

dis·pro·por·tion (dĭs′prə-pôr′shən, -pōr′shən) *n.* 1. The absence of due proportion; disparity. 2. An instance of a disproportionate relation, as in size. ~*tr.v.* **disproportioned, -tioning, -tions.** To make disproportionate.

dis·pro·por·tion·ate (dĭs′prə-pôr′shən-ĭt, -pōr′shən-ĭt) *adj.* Also **dis·pro·por·tion·al** (dĭs′prə-pôr′shən-əl, -pōr′shən-əl). Not proportionate; out of proportion, as in relative size, shape, or amount.

~*intr.v.* **-ated, -ating, -ates.** *Chemistry.* To undergo disproportionation. —**dis·pro·por·tion·ate·ly** *adv.* —**dis·pro·por·tion·ate·ness** *n.*

dis·pro·por·tion·a·tion (dĭs′prə-pôr′shə-nā′shən, -pōr′shə-) *n. Chemistry.* A type of chemical reaction in which one molecule of reactant is reduced and another is oxidized.

dis·prove (dĭs-prōōv′) *tr.v.* **-proved, -proving, -proves.** To prove to be false, invalid, or in error; refute. —**dis·prov·a·ble** *adj.* —**dis·prov·al** *n.*

dis·put·a·ble (dĭs-pyōō′tə-bəl, dĭs-pyōō-) *adj.* Capable of being disputed or challenged; debatable. —**dis·put·a·bil·i·ty** *n.* —**dis·put·a·bly** *adv.*

dis·pu·tant (dĭs-pyōō′tənt, dĭs′pyōō-tənt) *adj.* Engaged in argument or dispute. ~*n.* A person who disputes; debater.

dis·pu·ta·tion (dĭs′pyōō-tā′shən) *n.* 1. The act of disputing; a debate. 2. A formal academic debate or an oral defense of a thesis.

dis·pu·ta·tious (dĭs′pyōō-tā′shəs) *adj.* Argumentative; contentious. —**dis·pu·ta·tious·ly** *adv.* —**dis·pu·ta·tious·ness** *n.*

dis·pute (dĭs-pyōōt′) *v.* **-puted, -puting, -putes.** —*tr.* 1. To argue about; debate. 2. To question the truth or validity of; doubt. 3. To strive to win (a prize, for example); contend for. 4. To strive against; oppose; resist. —*intr.* 1. To argue; discuss; debate. 2. To quarrel vehemently. —See Synonyms at **discuss.** ~*n.* (also dĭs′pyōōt′). 1. A verbal controversy; an argument; a debate. 2. A quarrel. —See Synonyms at **argument.** [Middle English *disputen,* from Old French *desputer,* from Late Latin *disputāre,* from Latin, to reckon, discuss : *dis-,* separately + *putāre,* to clean, prune, settle an account, hence to reckon, think.] —**dis·put·er** *n.*

Usage: Traditionally, the stress is on the second syllable, for both the verb and the noun. In recent years, however, many people have begun to put the stress on the first syllable in the case of the noun, but there is a great deal of inconsistency; for example, the phrase *in dispute′* usually retains the stress on the second syllable, even in the speech of people who often say *dĭs′pute.*

dis·qual·i·fi·ca·tion (dĭs-kwŏl′ə-fĭ-kā′shən) *n.* 1. The act of disqualifying or the condition of being disqualified. 2. Something that disqualifies.

dis·qual·i·fy (dĭs-kwŏl′ə-fī′) *tr.v.* **-fied, -fying, -fies.** 1. To render unfit or unqualified; disable. 2. To declare ineligible or unqualified. 3. To deprive of a legal right, power, or privilege: *disqualified from driving for 12 months.* 4. To debar from a sports event, as for misconduct.

dis·qui·et (dĭs-kwī′ĭt) *tr.v.* **-eted, -eting, -ets.** To deprive of peace or rest; trouble. ~*n.* The absence of mental peace or rest; restlessness; anxiety. —**dis·qui·et·ing** *adj.* —**dis·qui·et·ing·ly** *adv.*

dis·qui·e·tude (dĭs-kwī′ə-tōōd′, -tyōōd′) *n.* A state of worry or uneasiness; anxiety.

dis·qui·si·tion (dĭs′kwə-zĭsh′ən) *n.* A formal discourse or treatise, often in writing; dissertation. [Latin *disquīsītiō* (stem *disquīsītiōn-*), enquiry, from *disquīrere,* to enquire diligently : *dis-* (intensive) + *quaerere,* to search for.]

Dis·rae·li (dĭz-rā′lē), **Benjamin,** 1st Earl of Beaconsfield, known as "Dizzy" (1804–81). British statesman. The grandson of a Venetian Jew, he became a Christian in 1817. In 1837 he entered Parliament and from 1842 led the Young England group of Conservatives. He was three times Chancellor of the Exchequer and in 1867 was responsible for the Reform Bill that gave household suffrage in the boroughs and extended the county franchise. Disraeli became prime minister in 1868 but lost office in the autumn to Gladstone and the Liberals. He returned to power in 1874. He bought Britain a major share in the Suez Canal, proclaimed Queen Victoria Empress of India (1876), and annexed Cyprus. He established the Conservative Party as a political force upholding the monarchy, the Anglican Church, and the empire.

dis·rate (dĭs-rāt′) *tr.v.* **-rated, -rating, -rates.** To reduce in rating or rank.

dis·re·gard (dĭs′rĭ-gärd′) *tr.v.* **-garded, -garding, -gards.** 1. To pay no attention or heed to; fail to consider; ignore. 2. To treat without proper respect or attentiveness. ~*n.* Lack of thoughtful attention or due regard, especially when willful. —**dis·re·gard·er** *n.* —**dis·re·gard·ful** *adj.*

dis·rel·ish (dĭs-rĕl′ĭsh) *tr.v.* **-ished, -ishing, -ishes.** To have distaste for; dislike. ~*n.* Distaste; aversion.

dis·re·mem·ber (dĭs′rĭ-mĕm′bər) *v.* **-bered, -bering, -bers.** *Regional.* —*tr.* To fail to remember. —*intr.* To forget.

dis·re·pair (dĭs′rĭ-pâr′) *n.* The condition of being in need of repairs; a state of neglect; dilapidation: *a house in disrepair.*

dis·rep·u·ta·ble (dĭs-rĕp′yə-tə-bəl) *adj.* 1. Lacking a good reputation; not esteemed. 2. Not respectable in character or appearance. 3. Disgraceful; discreditable. —**dis·rep·u·ta·bil·i·ty, dis·rep·u·ta·ble·ness** *n.* —**dis·rep·u·ta·bly** *adv.*

dis·re·pute (dĭs′rĭ-pyōōt′) *n.* Also *archaic* **dis·rep·u·ta·tion** (dĭs-rĕp′yə-tā′shən). The absence or loss of reputation; discredit; disgrace. —See Synonyms at **disgrace.**

dis·re·spect (dĭs′rĭ-spĕkt′) *n.* Lack of respect, esteem, or courteous regard; rudeness. ~*tr.v.* **disrespected, -specting, -spects.** To show a lack of respect for.

dis·re·spect·a·ble (dĭs′rĭ-spĕk′tə-bəl) *adj.* Lacking respectability; not worthy of respect. —**dis·re·spect·a·bil·i·ty** *n.*

dis·re·spect·ful (dĭs′rĭ-spĕkt′fəl) *adj.* Having or demonstrating a lack of respect; rude; discourteous. **—dis·re·spect·ful·ly** *adv.* **—dis·re·spect·ful·ness** *n.*

dis·robe (dĭs-rōb′) *v.* **-robed, -robing, -robes.** *—tr.* To remove the clothing from. *—intr.* To undress oneself. **—dis·robe·ment** *n.* **—dis·rob·er** *n.*

dis·rupt (dĭs-rŭpt′) *tr.v.* **-rupted, -rupting, -rupts. 1.** To upset the order of; throw into confusion or disorder. **2.** To interrupt or impede the progress, movement, or procedure of. **3.** To break or burst; rupture. [Latin *disrumpere* (past participle *disruptus*), to break asunder : *dis-*, asunder + *rumpere,* to break.] **—dis·rupt·er, dis·rup·tor** *n.*

dis·rup·tion (dĭs-rŭp′shən) *n.* **1.** The act of disrupting or the state of being disrupted. **2. Disruption.** The breaking away of the Free Church from the Established Church of Scotland in 1934.

dis·rup·tive (dĭs-rŭp′tĭv) *adj.* Pertaining to, causing, or produced by disruption. **—dis·rup·tive·ly** *adv.* **—dis·rup·tive·ness** *n.*

dis·sat·is·fac·tion (dĭs-săt′ĭs-făk′shən) *n.* **1.** The condition or feeling of being displeased or not satisfied; discontent. **2.** Anything that causes discontent.

dis·sat·is·fac·to·ry (dĭs-săt′ĭs-făk′tə-rē) *adj.* Unsatisfactory.

dis·sat·is·fied (dĭs-săt′ĭs-fīd′) *adj.* Affected by a sense of inadequacy, discontent, or displeasure, or by an insufficiency of something; not content. **—dis·sat·is·fied·ly** *adv.*

dis·sat·is·fy (dĭs-săt′ĭs-fī′) *tr.v.* **-fied, -fying, -fies.** To fail to meet the expectations or fulfill the desires of; disappoint.

dis·seat (dĭs-sēt′) *tr.v.* **-seated, -seating, -seats.** *Archaic.* To unseat.

dis·sect (dĭ-sĕkt, dī′sĕkt′) *tr.v.* **-sected, -secting, -sects. 1.** To cut open or apart (plant or animal tissue), especially for scientific study or in surgery. **2.** To examine, analyze, or criticize in minute detail: *dissected her motives.* **3.** *Geology.* To carve up (a land form, especially a plateau) by erosion. Used of a river. [Latin *dissecāre* (past participle *dissectus*), to cut apart : *dis-*, apart + *secāre,* to cut.] **—dis·sec·ti·ble** *adj.* **—dis·sec·tor** *n.*

dis·sect·ed (dĭ-sĕk′tĭd, dī-) *adj. Botany.* Divided into numerous narrow segments or lobes: *dissected leaves.*

dis·sec·tion (dĭ-sĕk′shən, dī-) *n.* **1.** The act or process of dissecting. **2.** Something that has been dissected, such as tissue under study. **3.** A detailed examination or analysis.

dis·seize (dĭs-sēz′) *tr.v.* **-seized, -seizing, -seizes.** Also **dis·seise.** *Law.* To dispossess (a person) of property unlawfully. [Middle English *disseisen,* from Norman French *disseisir,* variant of Old French *dessaisir* : *des-*, from Latin *dis-* (reversal) + *saisir,* to SEIZE.] **—dis·sei·zor** (dĭs-sē′zər, -zôr′) *n.*

dis·sei·zee (dĭs′sē-zē′, dĭs-sē′zē′) *n.* Also **dis·seisee.** *Law.* A person who is disseized.

dis·sei·zin (dĭs-sē′zĭn) *n.* Also **dis·sei·sin, dis·sei·sure, dis·sei·zure** (dĭs-sē′zhər). *Law.* Wrongful usurpation of the powers and privileges of ownership; ejection of the lawful holder of a freehold. [Middle English *dysseysyne,* from Norman French *disseisine,* variant of Old French *dessaisine* : *des-*, from Latin *dis-* (reversal) + SEIZIN.]

dis·sem·blance (dĭ-sĕm′bləns) *n.* **1.** The act of dissembling or disguising; dissimulation. **2.** *Archaic.* Absence of resemblance; dissimilarity.

dis·sem·ble (dĭ-sĕm′bəl) *v.* **-bled, -bling, -bles.** *—tr.* **1.** To disguise the real nature of; hide with a false appearance or semblance: *dissemble one's fears with laughter.* **2.** To make a false show of; feign. *—intr.* To conceal one's real motives, nature, or feelings under a pretense. —See Synonyms at **pretend.** [Middle English *dissemblen,* from Old French *dessembler,* to be different (influenced by *dissimuler,* to pretend, dissimulate) : *des-*, from Latin *dis-* (reversal) + *sembler,* to be like, appear, seem.] **—dis·sem·bler** *n.* **—dis·sem·bling·ly** *adv.*

dis·sem·i·nate (dĭ-sĕm′ə-nāt′) *v.* **-nated, -nating, -nates.** *—tr.* **1.** To scatter widely, as in sowing seed; distribute; disperse. **2.** To spread abroad (information, for example); promulgate widely. *—intr. Rare.* To become diffused; spread. [Latin *dissēmināre* : *dis-*, in different directions + *sēmināre,* to sow, from *sēmen,* seed.] **—dis·sem·i·na·tion** *n.* **—dis·sem·i·na·tive** *adj.* **—dis·sem·i·na·tor** *n.*

dis·sem·i·nule (dĭ-sĕm′ə-nyo͞ol′) *n.* A plant part, such as a seed, fruit, or spore, that propagates and spreads the species. [DISSEMIN(ATE) + -ULE.]

dis·sen·sion (dĭ-sĕn′shən) *n.* Disagreement or quarreling caused by a difference of opinion. —See Synonyms at **discord.** [Middle English *dissencioun,* from Old French *dissension,* from Latin *dissensiō* (stem *dissensiōn-*), from *dissentīre,* to DISSENT.]

dis·sent (dĭ-sĕnt′) *intr.v.* **-sented,-senting, -sents. 1.** To think or feel differently; disagree; differ. **2.** To refuse to conform to the authority or doctrine of an established church. **3.** To withhold assent or approval. —See Synonyms at **object** (verb).

~n. **1.** Difference of opinion or feeling; disagreement. **2.** The refusal to conform to the authority or doctrine of an established church; nonconformity. [Middle English *dissenten,* from Latin *dissentīre* : *dis-*, apart + *sentīre,* to feel.] **—dis·sent·ing·ly** *adv.*

dis·sent·er (dĭ-sĕn′tər) *n.* **1.** One who dissents. **2.** *Often* **Dissenter.** One who refuses to accept the doctrines or usages of an established or national church; especially, a Protestant who dissents from the Church of England. Compare **conformist.**

dis·sen·ti·ent (dĭ-sĕn′shənt) *adj.* Dissenting, especially from the view or policies of a majority.

~n. One who dissents. **—dis·sen·tience** *n.*

dis·sen·tious (dĭ-sĕn′shəs) *adj.* Given to dissension.

dis·sep·i·ment (dĭ-sĕp′ə-mənt) *n.* A membranous or calcareous partition between organs or parts; septum. [Latin *dissaepīmentum,* partition, from *dissaepīre,* to separate, divide : *dis-*, apart + *saepīre,* to fence in, enclose, from *saepes,* fence, hedge.] **—dis·sep·i·men·tal** *adj.* **—dis·sep·i·men·tal·ly** *adv.*

dis·ser·tate (dĭs′ər-tāt′) *intr.v.* **-tated, -tating, -tates.** Also **dis·sert** (dĭ-sûrt′), **-serted, -serting, -serts.** *Rare.* To discourse formally, learnedly, or at some length. [Latin *dissertāre,* frequentative of *disserere,* to discuss (translation of Greek *dialegesthai,* to discuss, converse, "pick out," "separate"; see **dialogue**) : *dis-*, apart + *serere,* to connect, join (in speech), discuss.] **—dis·ser·ta·tor** *n.*

dis·ser·ta·tion (dĭs′ər-tā′shən) *n.* A lengthy and formal treatise or discourse, especially one written by a candidate for a higher university degree; thesis.

dis·serve (dĭs-sûrv′) *tr.v.* **-served, -serving, -serves.** To treat badly; do a disservice to; harm.

dis·ser·vice (dĭs-sûr′vĭs) *n.* A harmful action; an ill turn.

dis·sev·er (dĭ-sĕv′ər) *v.* **-ered, -ering, -ers.** *—tr.* **1.** To separate; sever. **2.** To divide into parts; break up. *—intr.* To become separated or disunited. [Middle English *dis(s)everen,* from Old French *des(s)evrer,* from Late Latin *dissēparāre* : Latin *dis-* (intensive) + *sēparāre,* to SEPARATE.] **—dis·sev·er·ance, dis·sev·er·ment** *n.*

dis·si·dence (dĭs′ə-dəns) *n.* Disagreement, as of opinion or belief; difference; dissent.

dis·si·dent (dĭs′ə-dənt) *adj.* Disagreeing, as in opinion or belief; differing; dissenting.

~n. One who disagrees; especially, a citizen of a one-party state who is in fundamental disagreement with the prevailing politics or ideology. [Latin *dissidēns* (stem *dissident-*), present participle of *dissidēre,* "to sit apart," dissent : *dis-*, apart + *sedēre,* to sit.]

dis·sil·i·ent (dĭ-sĭl′ē-ənt) *adj.* Bursting apart, as some seed pods do when ripe. [Latin *dissiliens, dissilient,* present participle of *dissilire,* to burst apart : *dis-*, apart + *salire,* to leap.]

dis·sim·i·lar (dĭ-sĭm′ə-lər) *adj.* Distinct; unlike; different. **—dis·sim·i·lar·ly** *adv.*

dis·sim·i·lar·i·ty (dĭ-sĭm′ə-lăr′ə-tē) *n., pl.* **-ties. 1.** The quality of being distinct or unlike; difference. **2.** A point of distinction or difference. —See Usage note at **difference.**

dis·sim·i·late (dĭ-sĭm′ə-lāt′) *v.* **-lated, -lating, -lates.** *—tr.* **1.** To make dissimilar or unlike. **2.** *Linguistics.* To cause to undergo dissimilation. *—intr.* **1.** To become dissimilar. **2.** *Linguistics.* To undergo dissimilation. [DIS- + (AS)SIMILATE.]

dis·sim·i·la·tion (dĭ-sĭm′ə-lā′shən) *n.* **1.** The act or process of making or becoming dissimilar. **2.** *Linguistics.* The process by which one of two similar phonemes is displaced or changed by the other, as in the English form *marble* from French *marbre.*

dis·si·mil·i·tude (dĭs′ĭ-mĭl′ə-to͞od′, -tyo͞od′) *n.* **1.** Lack of resemblance; difference. **2.** A point of difference; a dissimilarity. [Middle English, from Latin *dissimilitūdō,* from *dissimilis,* different : *dis-*, not + *similis,* like, SIMILAR.]

dis·sim·u·late (dĭ-sĭm′yə-lāt′) *v.* **-lated, -lating, -lates.** *—tr.* To disguise (one's intentions, for example) under a feigned appearance. *—intr.* To conceal one's true feelings or intentions. **—dis·sim·u·la·tion** *n.* **—dis·sim·u·la·tive** *adj.* **—dis·sim·u·la·tor** *n.*

dis·si·pate (dĭs′ə-pāt′) *v.* **-pated, -pating, -pates.** *—tr.* **1.** To drive away or dispel by or as if by dispersing; rout; scatter. **2.** To spend or use up; waste; squander. *—intr.* **1.** To vanish by dispersion; scatter. **2.** *Physics.* To lose (energy) through conversion into another form, especially into heat. **3.** To indulge excessively in the pursuit of pleasure or debauchery. [Middle English *dissipaten,* from Latin *dissipāre,* to disperse, squander.] **—dis·si·pat·er, dis·si·pa·tor** *n.* **—dis·si·pa·tive** *adj.*

dis·si·pat·ed (dĭs′ə-pā′tĭd) *adj.* **1.** Unrestrained in the pursuit of pleasure; dissolute. **2.** Wasted; squandered. **—dis·si·pat·ed·ly** *adv.* **—dis·si·pat·ed·ness** *n.*

dis·si·pa·tion (dĭs′ə-pā′shən) *n.* **1. a.** The act of dissipating. **b.** The condition of being dissipated; dispersion. **2.** Wasteful consumption or expenditure. **3.** Dissolute indulgence in pleasure; intemperance. **4.** Amusement; diversion.

dis·so·cia·ble (dĭ-sō′shə-bəl, -shē-ə-bəl) *adj.* Capable of being dissociated; separable. **—dis·so·cia·bil·i·ty, dis·so·cia·ble·ness** *n.* **—dis·so·cia·bly** *adv.*

dis·so·ci·ate (dĭ-sō′shē-āt′, -sē-āt′) *v.* **-ated, -ating, -ates.** *—tr.* **1.** To remove from association; separate: *"Marx never dissociated man from his social environment"* (Sidney Hook). **2.** *Chemistry.* To cause to undergo dissociation. **3.** *Psychology.* To cause to undergo dissociation. *—intr.* **1.** To cease associating; part. **2.** *Chemistry.* To undergo dissociation. **3.** *Psychology.* To undergo dissociation. [Latin *dissociāre* : *dis-* (reversal) + *sociāre,* to join, associate, from *socius,* companion.] **—dis·so·ci·a·tive** *adj.*

Usage: *Dissociate* is traditionally used as the opposite of *associate,* but *disassociate* is increasing in use. Less commonly, *disassociation* is used for *dissociation.*

dis·so·ci·a·tion (dĭ-sō′sē-ā′shən, -shē-ā′shən) *n.* **1. a.** The act of dissociating. **b.** The condition of being dissociated; separation. —See Usage note at **dissociate. 2.** *Chemistry.* The chemical process, especially a reversible process, by means of which a change in physical condition, as in pressure, temperature, or the action of a solvent, causes a molecule to split into simpler groups of atoms, single atoms, or ions. **3.** *Psychology.* The separation of a belief or attitude, or a group of related psychological activities, from the rest of the personality so that they function independently, as in cases of multiple ("split") personalities. —See Usage note at **dissociate.**

dis·sol·u·ble (dĭ-sŏl′yə-bəl) *adj.* Capable of being dissolved; solu-

PRONUNCIATION KEY

ă, pat; ā, pay; âr, care;
ä, father, are; b, bib;
ch, church; d, deed; ĕ, pet;
ē, be; f, fife; g, gag; h, hat;
hw, which; ĭ, pit; ī, pie;
îr, pier; j, judge; k, kick;
l, lid, needle; m, mum;
n, no, sudden; ng, thing;
ŏ, pot; ō, toe; ô, paw, for;
oi, noise; ou, out; o͝o, book;
o͞o, boot; p, pop; r, roar;
s, sauce; sh, ship, dish;
t, tight; th, thin, path;
th, this, bathe; ŭ, cut; ûr, fur;
v, valve; w, with; y, yes;
z, zebra, size; zh, vision;
ə, about, item, edible,
gallop, circus, peaceful

IN FOREIGN WORDS:

à, *Fr.* ami; œ, *Fr.* feu, *Ger.* schön; ü, *Fr.* tu, *Ger.* über;
KH, *Ger.* ich, *Scot.* loch;
N, *Fr.* bon; y′, *Fr.* Compiègne

STRESS MARKS:

Primary stress: ′
in·cite′ (ĭn-sīt′)
Secondary stress: ′
in′sight′ (ĭn′sīt′)

ble. [Latin *dissolūbilis,* from *dissolvere,* to DISSOLVE.] **—dis·sol·u·bil·i·ty, dis·sol·u·ble·ness** *n.*

dis·so·lute (dĭs′ə-lo͞ot′) *adj.* Lacking in moral restraint; debauched. [Middle English, from Latin *dissolūtus,* loose, licentious, past participle of *dissolvere,* to DISSOLVE.] **—dis·so·lute·ly** *adv.* **—dis·so·lute·ness** *n.*

dis·so·lu·tion (dĭs′ə-lo͞o′shən) *n.* **1.** Decomposition into fragments or constituent parts; disintegration. **2.** Termination or extinction by deconcentration or dispersion. **3.** Extinction of life; death. **4.** Annulment or termination of a formal or legal bond, tie, or contract. **5.** Formal dismissal of an assembly or legislature. **6.** Reduction to a liquid form; liquefaction. **—dis·so·lu·tive** *adj.*

dis·solve (dĭ-zŏlv′) *v.* **-solved, -solving, -solves.** *—tr.* **1.** To cause to pass into solution. **2.** To reduce to liquid form; melt. **3.** To break into component parts; cause to disintegrate or disappear. **4.** To bring to an end by or as if by breaking up; terminate. **5.** To dismiss (a meeting or parliament, for example). **6.** To cause to give way emotionally or psychologically; upset. **7.** To cause to lose definition; blur; confuse. **8.** *Law.* To render null; abrogate; annul. *—intr.* **1.** To pass into solution; be mixed or dispersed in another substance. **2.** To become liquid; melt. **3.** To break up or disperse. **4.** To disintegrate or disappear. **5.** To collapse emotionally or psychologically. **6.** To lose clarity or definition; fade away. **7.** To change scenes in a film or television program by having one scene fade out while the next appears behind it and grows clearer as the first dims. —See Synonyms at **melt.**

~n. A scene transition in a film or on television, made by dissolving. [Middle English *dissolven,* from Latin *dissolvere* : *dis-,* apart + *solvere,* to loosen, untie.] **—dis·solv·a·ble** *adj.* **—dis·solv·er** *n.*

dis·sol·vent (dĭ-zŏl′vənt) *adj.* Capable of dissolving.

~n. A solvent.

dis·so·nance (dĭs′ə-nəns) *n.* **1.** A harsh or disagreeable combination of sounds; discord. **2.** An absence of agreement or consistency; disparity. **3.** *Music.* A combination of notes conventionally considered to suggest unrelieved tension and to require resolution. Compare **consonance. 4.** *Psychology.* An aversive state that arises when an individual is aware of inconsistency or conflict within himself.

dis·so·nant (dĭs′ə-nənt) *adj.* **1.** Harsh or inharmonious in sound; discordant. **2.** Disagreeing or at variance: *"Jerome's new presumption, so dissonant from his former meekness"* (Horace Walpole). **3.** *Music.* Constituting or producing a dissonance. [Middle English, from Old French *dissonant,* from Latin *dissonāns* (stem *dissonant-*), present participle of *dissonāre,* to disagree in sound, be inharmonious : *dis-,* apart + *sonāre,* to sound.] **—dis·so·nant·ly** *adv.*

dis·suade (dĭ-swād′) *tr.v.* **-suaded, -suading, -suades.** To discourage or deter (a person) from a purpose or course of action by persuasion or exhortation. Used with *from.* [Latin *dissuādēre* : *dis-* (reversal) + *suādēre,* to advise, persuade.] **—dis·suad·er** *n.*

dis·sua·sion (dĭ-swā′zhən) *n.* The act or an instance of dissuading; exhortation against a course of action. [Latin *dissuāsiō* (stem *dissuāsiōn-*), from *dissuādēre,* to DISSUADE.] **—dis·sua·sive** *adj.* **—dis·sua·sive·ly** *adv.* **—dis·sua·sive·ness** *n.*

dis·syl·la·ble (dĭs′sĭl′ə-bəl, dĭ-sĭl′-, dĭ′sĭl′-) *n.* Also **di·syl·la·ble** (dī′-sĭl′-ə-bəl, dĭ-sĭl′-) A word with two syllables. **—dis·syl·lab·ic** (dĭs′-ĭ-lăb′ĭk, dĭ′sĭ-) *adj.*

dis·sym·me·try (dĭs-sĭm′ə-trē) *n., pl.* **-tries. 1.** Lack or absence of symmetry. **2.** Mirror-image symmetry, as of a left hand and a right hand. **—dis·sym·met·ric** (dĭ′sĭ-mĕt′rĭk), **dis·sym·met·ri·cal** *adj.* **—dis·sym·met·ri·cal·ly** *adv.*

dist. 1. distance; distant. **2.** distinguished. **3.** district.

dis·taff (dĭs′tăf′, -täf′) *n., pl.* **-taffs** or *rare* **-taves** (-tăvz′). **1.** A rod or stick with a cleft end in which is held the unspun flax, wool, or tow from which thread is drawn in spinning. **2.** A woman's work and concerns. **3.** Women in general. [Middle English *distaf,* Old English *distæf,* "flax staff" : *dis-,* bunch of flax, akin to Middle Low German *dise* (see **dizen**) + STAFF.]

distaff side *n.* The female line or maternal branch of a family. Also called "spindle side." Compare **spear side.**

dis·tal (dĭs′təl) *adj. Anatomy.* Located far from the origin, point of attachment, or median line of the body: *The fingers are at the distal end of the arm.* Compare **proximal.** [DIST(ANT) + -AL.] **—dis·tal·ly** *adv.*

dis·tance (dĭs′təns) *n. Abbr.* **dist. 1.** The fact or condition of being apart in space or time. **2.** *Geometry.* **a.** A nonnegative number designating the magnitude of a path along a straight line or curve. **b.** The length of a line segment joining two points. **c.** The length of the perpendicular from a given point to a given line or plane. **3. a.** The space between any two locations or points. **b.** The interval separating any two specified instants in time. **4. a.** The degree of deviation or difference that separates two things in relationship. **b.** The extent to which difference has arisen between two points in a trend or course: *The campaign moved some distance from its original objectives.* **5.** A stretch of linear space without designation of limit. **6. a.** A point removed in space or time. **b.** A position of being uninvolved or apart: *always kept himself at a distance.* **7.** Chilliness of manner; aloofness. **8.** The scheduled duration of a race, boxing match, or other sporting contest. Used chiefly in the phrases *go the distance* and *last the distance.* **—keep one's distance.** To remain reserved or aloof.

~tr.v. **distanced, -tancing, -tances. 1.** To place or keep at a distance. **2.** To cause to appear at a distance. **3.** To leave behind, as in a race; outrun; outstrip. [Middle English *distaunce,* from Old French *destance,* from Latin *distantia,* from *distāns,* DISTANT.]

dis·tant (dĭs′tənt) *adj. Abbr.* **dist. 1.** Separate or apart in space or time. **2.** Far removed in space or time. **3.** Located at, coming from, or going to a distance. **4.** Far apart in relationship; remote: *a distant cousin.* **5.** Far removed from the present situation: *distant thoughts.* **6.** Aloof or chilly in manner; reserved. [Middle English *distaunt,* from Old French, from Latin *distāns* (stem *distant-*), present participle of *distāre,* to be remote : *dis-,* apart + *stāre,* to stand.] **—dis·tant·ly** *adv.*

Usage: *distant, far, far-off, faraway, remote, removed.* These adjectives mean to be widely apart in space or, less often, in time. *Distant* can be used (with a figure) to indicate a specific separation, or it can indicate an indefinite but sizeable interval. *Far* implies a wide but indefinite interval, principally in space. *Far-off* and *faraway* imply a wider interval in either time or space. *Remote* not only means faraway but suggests isolation from the speaker's locality or point in time. *Removed* implies distinct separation in place, time, kind, or character with respect to the speaker.

dis·taste (dĭs-tāst′) *n.* Dislike or aversion. Often used with *for.*

~tr.v. **distasted, -tasting, -tastes.** *Archaic.* **1.** To feel repugnance for; dislike. **2.** To offend; displease.

dis·taste·ful (dĭs-tāst′fəl) *adj.* Unpleasant; disagreeable. **—dis·taste·ful·ly** *adv.* **—dis·taste·ful·ness** *n.*

dis·tem·per[1] (dĭs-tĕm′pər) *n.* **1. a.** An infectious virus disease occurring in certain mammals, especially dogs, characterized by loss of appetite, a catarrhal discharge from the eyes and nose, and often partial paralysis and death. **b.** Any of various similar mammalian diseases. **2.** Any illness or disease of the body or mind; an ailment. **3.** Ill humor; testiness. **4.** Disorder or disturbance, especially of a social or political nature.

~tr.v. **distempered, -pering, -pers.** *Archaic.* To upset or disturb; disorder. [Middle English *distemperen,* to upset the proper balance of the humors, vex, be ill, from Old French *destemprer,* from Medieval Latin *distemperāre* : Latin *dis-* (reversal) + *temperāre,* to mingle in due proportion, TEMPER.]

distemper[2] *n.* **1.** A process of painting in which pigments are mixed with water and a glue-size or casein binder, used for flat wall decoration or for scenic and poster painting. **2. a.** The paint used in this process. **b.** Any of various heavily pigmented matt paints, such as whitewash, that can be thinned with water. **3.** A painting done in distemper. **4.** *British.* **Calcimine** *(see).*

~tr.v. **distempered, -pering, -pers. 1.** To mix (powdered pigments or colors) with water and size. **2.** To paint using distemper. [Middle English *distemperen,* to dilute, mix, from Medieval Latin *distemperāre* : *dis-* (intensive) + *temperāre,* to mingle, TEMPER.]

dis·tend (dĭs-tĕnd′) *v.* **-tended, -tending, -tends.** *—intr.* To become bloated and swollen from or as if from internal pressure; swell out. *—tr.* **1.** To cause to expand by or as if by internal pressure; dilate. **2.** To stretch out; extend in all directions. [Middle English *distenden,* from Latin *distendere* : *dis-,* apart + *tendere,* to stretch.]

dis·ten·si·ble (dĭs-tĕn′sə-bəl) *adj.* Capable of being distended. **—dis·ten·si·bil·i·ty** *n.*

dis·ten·tion (dĭs-tĕn′shən) *n.* Also **dis·ten·sion.** The act of distending or the condition of being distended. [Middle English *distensioun,* from Latin *distentiō* (stem *distensiōn-*), from *distendere* (past participle *distentus*), to DISTEND.]

dis·tich (dĭs′tĭk) *n., pl.* **-tichs.** In poetry, a couplet, especially one used in a Latin or Greek elegy. [Latin *distichon,* from Greek *distikhon,* neuter of *distikhos,* having two rows or verses : DI- + *stikhos,* row, line, verse.]

dis·ti·chous (dĭs′tĭ-kəs) *adj. Botany.* Arranged in two vertical rows or ranks on opposite sides of an axis. Said of leaves. [Late Latin *distichus,* with two rows, from Greek *distikhos.* See **distich.**] **—dis·ti·chous·ly** *adv.*

dis·till (dĭ-stĭl′) *v.* **-tilled, -tilling, -tills.** Also *chiefly British* **dis·til, -tilled, -tilling, -tils.** *—tr.* **1.** To subject (a substance) to distillation. **2.** To extract (a distillate) by distillation. **3.** To purify or refine by or as if by distillation. **4.** To separate or extract (an essential idea or characteristic, for example) from its context, as if by distillation. **5.** To exude or give off (a substance) in drops or small quantities. *—intr.* **1.** To undergo or be produced by distillation. **2.** To fall or exude in drops or small quantities. [Middle English *distillen,* to trickle, drip, distill, from Old French *distiller,* from Latin *dēstīllāre, dīstīllāre* : *dē-,* down + *stīllāre,* to drip, from *stīlla*†, drop.] **—dis·till·a·ble** *adj.*

dis·til·late (dĭs′tə-lāt′, -lĭt, dĭ-stĭl′ĭt) *n.* **1.** The liquid condensed from vapor in distillation. **2.** Anything regarded as an essence or purified form. Also called "distillation."

dis·til·la·tion (dĭs′tə-lā′shən) *n.* **1.** Any of various heat-dependent processes used to purify or separate a fraction of a mixture; especially, the vaporization of a liquid mixture with subsequent collection of components by differential cooling to condensation. **2.** A distillate.

distillation column *n.* A tall cylindrical metal shell fitted inside with perforated horizontal plates used to promote separation of miscible liquids ascending in the shell as vapor.

dis·till·er (dĭ-stĭl′ər) *n.* **1.** One that distills, as a condenser. **2.** A producer or maker of alcoholic drinks by the process of distillation.

dis·till·er·y (dĭ-stĭl′ə-rē) *n., pl.* **-ies.** An establishment or plant for distilling, especially alcoholic liquors, such as whiskey or gin.

dis·tinct (dĭ-stĭngkt′) *adj.* **1.** Not identical; individual; discrete. **2.** Not similar; different; unlike. **3.** Easily perceived by the senses or intellect; clear. **4.** Well-defined; unmistakable; unquestionable:

PRONUNCIATION KEY

ă, pat; ā, pay; âr, care; ä, father, are; b, bib; ch, church; d, deed; ĕ, pet; ē, be; f, fife; g, gag; h, hat; hw, which; ĭ, pit; ī, pie; îr, pier; j, judge; k, kick; l, lid, needle; m, mum; n, no, sudden; ng, thing; ŏ, pot; ō, toe; ô, paw, for; oi, noise; ou, out; o͝o, book; o͞o, boot; p, pop; r, roar; s, sauce; sh, ship, dish; t, tight; th, thin, path; *th,* this, bathe; ŭ, cut; ûr, fur; v, valve; w, with; y, yes; z, zebra, size; zh, vision; ə, about, item, edible, gallop, circus, peaceful

IN FOREIGN WORDS:

à, *Fr.* ami; œ, *Fr.* feu, *Ger.* schön; ü, *Fr.* tu, *Ger.* über; KH, *Ger.* ich, *Scot.* loch; N, *Fr.* bon; y′, *Fr.* Compiègne

STRESS MARKS:

Primary stress: ′ in·cite′ (ĭn-sīt′)
Secondary stress: ′ in′sight′ (ĭn′sīt′)

a distinct improvement. —See Synonyms at **evident.** [Middle English, separated, different, from Old French, from Latin *distinctus,* past participle of *distinguere,* to DISTINGUISH.] **—dis·tinct·ly** *adv.* **—dis·tinct·ness** *n.*

Usage: *Distinct* and *distinctive* are seldom interchangeable. *Distinct* has the meaning "unmistakable" or "clear" in most of its uses; *distinctive* has the meaning "distinguishing," "setting something apart from others." The contrast can be seen in such phrases as *a distinct smell,* where the smell is pronounced, compared with a *distinctive smell,* where the smell is uniquely identifiable.

dis·tinc·tion (dĭ-stĭngk′shən) *n.* **1.** The action of distinguishing; differentiation. **2.** The condition or fact of being dissimilar or distinct; a difference. **3.** A distinguishing factor, attribute, or characteristic. **4.** Excellence or eminence, as of performance, character, or reputation: *a man of distinction.* **5. a.** Recognition of achievement or superiority: *She graduated with distinction.* **b.** An honor conferred in recognition of achievement or superiority. —See Usage note at **difference.**

dis·tinc·tive (dĭ-stingk′tĭv) *adj.* **1.** Serving to identify; distinguishing: *distinctive tribal tattoos.* **2.** Characteristic: *distinctive habits.* **3.** *Linguistics.* Serving to distinguish meaning. Said of a phonological feature. —See Synonyms at **characteristic.** —See Usage note at **distinct.** **—dis·tinc·tive·ly** *adv.* **—dis·tinc·tive·ness** *n.*

dis·tin·gué (dēs′tăng-gā′, dĭs′-, dĭ-stăng′gā) *adj.* Distinguished in appearance, manner, or bearing. [French, "distinguished."]

dis·tin·guish (dĭ-stĭng′gwĭsh) *v.* **-guished, -guishing, -guishes.** *—tr.* **1.** To recognize as being different or distinct. **2.** To perceive distinctly; discern; make out. **3.** To detect or recognize; pick out. **4.** To make noticeable or different; set apart; characterize. **5.** To cause to be eminent or recognized. Usually used reflexively: *He distinguished himself in the exam.* *—intr.* To perceive or indicate differences; discriminate. Usually used with *among* or *between.* [Middle English *distinguen,* from Old French *distinguer* (present stem *distinguiss-*), from Latin *distinguere,* to separate, distinguish.] **—dis·tin·guish·a·ble** *adj.* **—dis·tin·guish·a·bly** *adv.*

dis·tin·guished (dĭ-stĭng′gwĭsht) *adj. Abbr.* **dist. 1.** Characterized by excellence or distinction; eminent; renowned. **2.** Having an air of distinction and dignity in conduct or appearance.

Distinguished Conduct Medal *n. Abbr.* **D.C.M.** A British military decoration for distinguished conduct in the field.

Distinguished Flying Cross *n. Abbr.* **DFC, D.F.C. 1.** A U.S. military decoration awarded for heroism or extraordinary achievement in aerial combat. **2.** A similar British decoration awarded to officers of the Royal Air Force.

Distinguished Service Cross *n. Abbr.* **DSC, D.S.C. 1.** A U.S Army decoration awarded for exceptional heroism in combat. **2.** A British decoration awarded to officers of the Royal Navy for gallantry in action.

Distinguished Service Medal *n. Abbr.* **DSM, D.S.M. 1.** A U.S. military decoration awarded for distinguished performance in a duty of great responsibility. **2.** A British decoration awarded to noncommissioned officers and men in the Royal Navy and Royal Marines for distinguished conduct in war.

Distinguished Service Order *n. Abbr.* **D.S.O.** A British military decoration for gallantry in action.

dis·tort (dĭ-stôrt′) *tr.v.* **-torted, -torting, -torts. 1.** To twist out of a proper or natural relation of parts; misshape; contort. **2.** To cast false light on; alter misleadingly; misrepresent. **3.** To cause to work in a twisted or disordered manner; pervert. **4.** To alter the original or ideal form of (an electronic signal, sound wave, or the like). [Latin *distorquēre* (past participle *distortus*) : *dis-,* apart, aside + *torquēre,* to twist.] **—dis·tort·er** *n.*

Usage: *distort, twist, deform, contort, warp, gnarl.* These verbs mean to change the form or character of something, usually to its disadvantage. *Distort* applies to physical change in shape, as by bending, wrenching, or exaggerating certain features; to verbal or pictorial misrepresentation; and to alteration or perversion of meaning of something spoken or written. *Twist* has similar application but intensifies the idea of marked and deliberate change. *Deform* refers only to physical change that disfigures and usually deprives the object of attractiveness or capacity for normal functioning. *Contort* implies violent physical change that produces unnatural or grotesque effects. *Warp* can refer to physical turning or twisting out of shape, or, figuratively, to turning something, such as the human mind or judgment, from a true course. *Gnarl* usually refers to making twisted or knotty in a physical sense.

dis·tor·tion (dĭ-stôr′shən) *n.* **1. a.** The act or an instance of distorting. **b.** A product of distorting; a distorted feature: *The newspaper article was full of distortions.* **2.** The condition of being distorted. **3.** *Optics.* A distorted image resulting from imperfections in an optical system, such as a lens. **4. a.** An undesired change in the waveform of an electronic signal, sound wave, or the like. **b.** Any consequence of such a change; especially, diminished clarity in reception or reproduction. **5.** *Psychoanalysis.* The modification of unconscious impulses into acceptable forms by conscious or dreaming perception. **—dis·tor·tion·al** *adj.*

distr. distributor.

dis·tract (dĭ-străkt′) *tr.v.* **-tracted, -tracting, -tracts. 1.** To cause to turn away from the original focus of attention or interest; sidetrack; divert. **2.** To pull in conflicting emotional directions; unsettle; bewilder. [Middle English *distracten,* from Latin *distrahere* (past participle *distractus*), to pull apart, draw away, perplex : *dis-,* apart, aside + *trahere,* to draw.] **—dis·tract·ing·ly** **—dis·trac·tive·ly** *adv.* **—dis·trac·tive** *adj.*

dis·tract·ed (dĭ-străk′tĭd) *adj.* **1.** Having the attention diverted or not paying attention. **2.** Suffering conflicting emotions; confused. **3.** Distraught; made mad; *distracted by grief.* —See Synonyms at **forgetful.** **—dis·tract·ed·ly** *adv.*

dis·tract·er, dis·trac·tor (dĭ-străk′tər) *n.* One of the incorrect answers presented as a choice in a multiple-choice test.

dis·trac·tion (dĭ-străk′shən) *n.* **1.** The act of distracting or the condition of being distracted; a diversion from an original focus. **2.** Anything that compels attention or distracts; especially, an amusement. **3.** Extreme mental or emotional disturbance; obsession: *"I loved Dora Spenlow to distraction!"* (Charles Dickens).

dis·train (dĭ-strān′) *v.* **-trained, -training, -trains.** *Law. —tr.* To seize and hold (property) to compel payment or reparation, as of debts. *—intr.* To seize a person's goods in order to compel payment of his debts to the distrainer; levy a distress. Often used with *upon.* [Middle English *distreinen,* to seize, compel, detain, from Old French *destreindre* (present stem *destreign-*), from Medieval Latin *distringere,* to seize, compel, from Latin, to draw apart, detain, hinder : *dis-,* apart + *stringere,* to draw tight.] **—dis·train·a·ble** *adj.* **—dis·train·ment** *n.* **—dis·trai·nor, dis·train·er** *n.*

dis·train·ee (dĭs′trā-nē′) *n. Law.* One whose property has been distrained.

dis·traint (dĭ-strānt′) *n. Law.* The act or process of distraining; a distress. [From DISTRAIN (by analogy with *restraint, restrain*).]

dis·trait (dĭ-strāt′) *adj.* **1.** Inattentive; distracted. **2.** Agitated; worried. [Middle English, from Old French *destrait,* past participle of *destraire,* to DISTRACT.]

dis·traught (dĭ-strôt′) *adj.* **1.** Extremely anxious or agitated; harried; frantic with worry. **2.** Crazed; mad. [Middle English, alteration of *distract,* distracted, from Latin *distractus,* past participle of *distrahere,* to perplex, DISTRACT.]

dis·tress (dĭ-strĕs′) *tr.v.* **-tressed, -tressing, -tresses. 1.** To cause anxiety or suffering to; worry or upset. **2.** To bring into difficult circumstances, especially difficult financial circumstances. **3.** *Archaic.* To constrain by harassment; force. **4.** *Law.* To hold the property of (a person) against the payment of debts; distrain upon.
~n. **1.** Anxiety or suffering; sorrow; unhappiness. **2.** Severe strain resulting from exhaustion, accident, or the like. **3.** The condition of being in need of immediate assistance: *a person in distress; a ship in distress.* Also used adjectivally: *a distress signal.* **4.** *Law.* **a.** The seizing of goods belonging to a debtor, as security or in reparation; the act of distraining. **b.** The goods thus seized. [Middle English *distressen, destressen,* from Old French *destresser,* from *destresse,* "narrow passage," strait, constraint, from Vulgar Latin *districtia* (unattested), narrowness, from Latin *districtus,* past participle of *distringere,* to "draw tight," detain, hinder. See **distrain.**] **—dis·tress·ing·ly** *adv.*

dis·tressed (dĭ-strĕst′) *adj.* **1.** Upset or worried; made anxious; made to suffer. **2.** Impoverished; poor in comparison to one's former circumstances. **3.** Deliberately treated to give an impression of age and wear. Said of furniture and leather.

dis·tress·ful (dĭ-strĕs′fəl) *adj.* **1.** Causing distress. **2.** Experiencing distress. **—dis·tress·ful·ly** *adv.* **—dis·tress·ful·ness** *n.*

dis·trib·u·tar·y (dĭ-strĭb′yə-tĕr′ē) *n., pl.* **-ies.** A branch of a river that flows away from the main stream and does not return to it; especially, such a branch in the delta of a large river. Compare **tributary.**

dis·trib·ute (dĭ-strĭb′yo͞ot) *tr.v.* **-uted, -uting, -utes. 1.** To divide and dispense in portions; parcel out. **2.** To deliver or pass out: *distribute leaflets.* **3.** To spread or diffuse over an area. Often used in the passive: *a widely distributed species.* **4.** To separate into groups or categories; arrange or classify. **5.** *Logic.* To use (a term) so as to include all individuals or entities of a given class. **6.** *Printing.* To separate (type) and replace in the proper boxes. [Middle English *distributen,* from Latin *distribuere* : *dis-,* apart + *tribuere,* to allot, grant (see **tribute**).]

Usage: *distribute, divide, dispense, dole, deal, ration.* These verbs mean to give something as a portion or share. *Distribute* is the least specific. *Divide* implies giving out portions determined by plan and purpose, often equal parts or portions based on what is due or deserved. *Dispense* stresses even more the sense of careful determination of portions according to what is considered due or proper. *Dole* (usually followed by *out*) implies careful and scant measurement of portions; often it applies to distribution of charity or something given reluctantly. *Deal* suggests orderly and equitable distribution, piece by piece. *Ration* refers to equitable division of scarce items, often necessities, by a system that limits individual portions.

dis·trib·ut·ed (dĭ-strĭb′yə-tĭd) *adj.* Characterized by a particular statistical distribution.

dis·tri·bu·tion (dĭs′trə-byo͞o′shən) *n.* **1.** The act of distributing or the condition of being distributed; an apportionment. **2.** Something distributed; an allotment. **3.** The act of dispersing or the condition of being dispersed; a diffusion. **4.** The geographical occurrence or range of an organism. **5.** Division into categories; classification. **6.** *Law.* The division of an estate or property among rightful heirs. **7.** *Commerce.* The process of getting goods from the manufacturer to the consumer, including marketing, handling of orders, and transport of goods. **8.** Any spatial or temporal array of objects or events: *the distribution of theaters on Broadway.* **9.** *Symbol* + *Statistics* The particular way in which numbers representing a given characteristic are distributed among the members of a group, usually

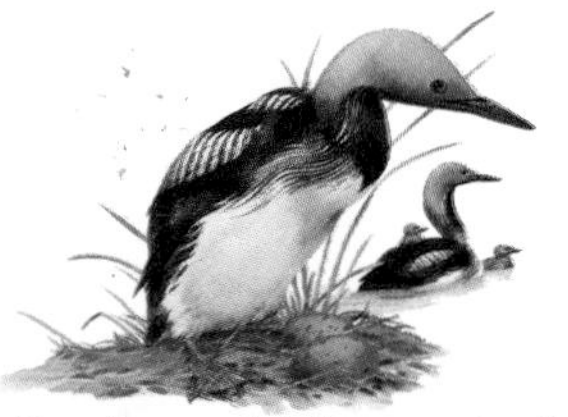

diver *Because their legs are set well back on their bodies, divers are clumsy on land. But the same feature helps to make them powerful underwater swimmers. They spend most of their time in the water, coming ashore only to nest. This is the black-throated diver of Europe,* Gavia arctica.

arranged according to frequency. See **frequency distribution.** **—dis·tri·bu·tion·al** *adj.*

dis·trib·u·tive (dĭ-strĭb′yə-tĭv) *adj.* **1.** Of or pertaining to distribution. **2.** Serving to distribute. **3.** *Grammar.* Referring to each individual or entity of a group separately rather than collectively; for example, *every* in the sentence *Every employee attended the meeting.* **4.** *Mathematics.* Of, pertaining to, or designating an operation having the same effect whether performed before or after another operation; for example, multiplication is *distributive* with respect to addition; that is, $a \times (b + c) = (a \times b) + (a \times c)$.
~*n.* A distributive word or term. **—dis·trib·u·tive·ly** *adv.* **—dis·trib·u·tive·ness** *n.*

distributive education *n.* An educational program in which students receive both classroom instruction and on-the-job training.

dis·trib·u·tor, dis·trib·ut·er (dĭ-strĭb′yə-tər) *n. Abbr.* **distr. 1.** One that distributes: *film distributors.* **2.** One that markets or sells a commodity; especially, a wholesaler. **3.** In the ignition system of an internal-combustion engine, a device for applying electric current in proper sequence to the spark plugs. **4.** *Computer Science.* The electronic circuitry that acts as an intermediate link between a computer's accumulator and drum storage.

dis·trict (dĭs′trĭkt) *n. Abbr.* **dist.** A division of an area or geographical unit either created arbitrarily, as for administrative purposes, or existing as a division by virtue of a characteristic: *an electoral district; a residential district; the District of Columbia.* —See Synonyms at **area.**
~*tr.v.* **districted, -tricting, -tricts.** To mark off or divide into districts. [French, from Medieval Latin *districtus,* (area of) jurisdiction, distraint, from Latin, past participle of *distringere,* to detain, hinder. See **distrain.**]

district attorney *n. Abbr.* **D.A.** The state's prosecuting officer in a given judicial district.

district court *n.* **1.** A U.S. Federal trial court serving a judicial district. **2.** In some states, a state court of general jurisdiction.

District of Co·lum·bi·a (kə-lŭm′bē-ə). *Abbr.* **D.C.** Federal area in the eastern United States, whose area is coextensive with Washington, the nation's capital. It is on the Potomac River.

dis·trust (dĭs-trŭst′) *n.* Lack of trust; doubtfulness or misgiving; suspicion.
~*tr.v.* **distrusted, -trusting, -trusts.** To lack confidence in; doubt or suspect.

dis·trust·ful (dĭs-trŭst′fəl) *adj.* Doubting; suspicious. **—dis·trust·ful·ly** *adv.* **—dis·trust·ful·ness** *n.*

dis·turb (dĭ-stûrb′) *tr.v.* **-turbed, -turbing, -turbs. 1.** To break up or destroy the tranquillity or settled state of. **2.** To trouble emotionally or mentally; upset or alarm. **3.** To intrude upon; interrupt: *disturb one's sleep.* **4.** To disarrange; put out of order. **5.** To put (oneself) out; inconvenience (oneself): *She need not have disturbed herself on my account.* [Middle English *destourben,* from Old French *destorber,* from Latin *disturbāre* : *dis-* (intensive) + *turbāre,* to throw into disorder, disturb, from *turba,* confusion, probably from Greek *turbē,* disorder.] **—dis·turb·er** *n.* **—dis·turb·ing·ly** *adv.*

dis·tur·bance (dĭ-stûr′bəns) *n.* **1.** The act of disturbing or the condition of being disturbed. **2.** Something that disturbs; an interruption; intrusion. **3.** A commotion, brawl, or riot; especially, a public breach of the peace. **4.** Unbalance or disorder, as of the mind. **5.** A variation in a normal course or condition. **6.** *Law.* The infringement of or interference with another's incorporeal property interests, such as easements, tenancies, franchises, or the like. **7.** *Meteorology.* A **depression** *(see),* usually one of low intensity.

dis·turbed (dĭ-stûrbd′) *adj.* Mentally unbalanced; emotionally unstable.

di·sul·fide (dī-sŭl′fīd′) *n.* A chemical compound containing two sulfur atoms combined with other elements or radicals. Also called "bisulfide."

di·sul·fi·ram (dī-sŭl′fə-răm′) *n.* A drug used in the treatment of chronic alcoholism. It acts by producing unpleasant effects, such as nausea and vomiting, when taken with alcohol. [From tetraethyl-tri*uram disulf*ide.]

dis·un·ion (dĭs-yo͞on′yən) *n.* **1.** The state of being disunited; separation. **2.** Lack of unity; discord. **—dis·un·ion·ist** *n. & adj.*

dis·u·nite (dĭs′yo͞o-nīt′) *v.* **-nited, -niting, -nites.** —*tr.* **1.** To disrupt the union of; separate. **2.** To estrange; put at odds. —*intr.* To become separate.

dis·u·ni·ty (dĭs-yo͞o′nə-tē) *n., pl.* **-ties.** Lack of unity; dissension.

dis·use (dĭs-yo͞os′) *n.* The state of not being used or of being no longer in use; desuetude. **—dis·used** *adj.*

dis·u·til·i·ty (dĭs′yo͞o-tĭl′ə-tē) *n.* The negative or harmful aspects of something; disadvantage.

disyllable. Variant of **dissyllable.**

dit (dĭt) *n.* The oral representation of the dot in radio and telegraphic codes, as in Morse code. Compare **dah.** [Imitative.]

ditch (dĭch) *n.* A long narrow trench or furrow dug in the ground, as for irrigation or drainage, or as a boundary line.
~*v.* **ditched, ditching, ditches.** —*intr.* **1.** To make or repair ditches. **2.** To make a forced landing on water. —*tr.* **1.** To dig or make a ditch in. **2.** To surround with a ditch. **3. a.** To drive (a vehicle) into a ditch. **b.** To derail (a train). **c.** To bring (an aircraft) down on water in an emergency. **4.** *Slang.* To throw aside; discard; desert. [Middle English *dich,* Old English *dīc*†, moat, ditch.] **—ditch·er** *n.*

ditch·water (dĭch′wô′tər, -wŏt′ər) *n.* Foul, stagnant water, such as that found in ditches.

di·the·ism (dī-thē′ĭz-əm) *n.* **1.** A belief in two supreme gods. **2.** The belief that good and evil govern the world as two supreme principles.

dith·er (dĭth′ər) *n.* **1.** *Chiefly British.* A state of nervous indecision or uncertainty. **2.** A state of agitation, excitement, or confusion.
~*intr.v.* **dithered, -ering, -ers. 1.** To be in a dither. **2.** To quiver or tremble, as with excitement. [Earlier *didder,* Middle English *didderen,* to DODDER.] **—dith·er·er** *n.* **—dith·er·ing, dith·er·y** *adj.*

dith·y·ramb (dĭth′ĭ-răm′, -rămb′) *n.* **1.** A frenzied and impassioned choric hymn and dance of ancient Greece, in honor of Dionysus. **2.** An irregular poetic expression suggestive of the ancient Greek dithyramb. **3.** Any piece of writing or speech in a frenzied and impassioned style. [Latin *dīthyrambus,* from Greek *dithurambos,* of non-Indo-European origin; akin to *thriambos,* TRIUMPH, and *iambos,* IAMB.] **—dith·y·ramb·ic** *adj.*

dit·ta·ny (dĭt′n-ē) *n., pl.* **-nies. 1.** An aromatic Cretan plant, *Origanum dictamnus,* with pink flowers, formerly believed to have magical powers. **2.** The **gas plant** *(see).* [Middle English *ditane, diteyne,* from Old French *ditan, ditain,* from Medieval Latin *di(p)tamnus,* variant of Latin *dictamnus,* from Greek *diktamnon,* perhaps after *Diktē,* mountain in Crete.]

dit·to (dĭt′ō) *n., pl.* **-tos.** *Abbr.* **do. 1.** The aforesaid; the above; the same as before. Used to avoid repetition and indicated by a pair of small *ditto marks* (″) placed under the word that would otherwise be repeated. **2.** A duplicate or copy.
~*adv.* As before; likewise.
~*tr.v.* **dittoed, -toing, -tos.** To duplicate or repeat.
~*interj.* Used to express agreement. [Italian dialectal (Tuscan) *ditto,* "said," from Latin *dictus,* past participle of *dīcere,* to say.]

dit·ty (dĭt′ē) *n., pl.* **-ties.** A simple song. [Middle English *dite, ditti,* from Old French *ditie,* "composition," from Latin *dictātum,* "thing dictated," from *dictāre,* to dictate, compose, frequentative of *dīcere,* to say.]

ditty bag *n.* A bag used by sailors to carry small items such as sewing implements. [Possibly from obsolete *dutty,* coarse calico, from Hindi *dhotī,* loincloth, DHOTI.]

ditty box *n.* A box used like a ditty bag.

Di·u (dē′o͞o). Island and seaport, now part of the Indian territory of Goa, Daman, and Diu.

di·u·re·sis (dī′yo͞o-rē′sĭs) *n.* Excessive discharge of urine. [New Latin, from Late Latin *diūrēticus,* DIURETIC.]

di·u·ret·ic (dī′yo͞o-rĕt′ĭk) *adj.* Tending to increase the production and discharge of urine.
~*n.* A diuretic drug. [Middle English *diuretik,* from Late Latin *diūrēticus,* from Greek *diourētikos,* from *diourein,* to pass urine : *dia-,* through + *ourein,* to urinate, from *ouron,* urine.]

di·ur·nal (dī-ûr′nəl) *adj.* **1.** Pertaining to or occurring in a day or each day; daily. **2.** Occurring or active during the daytime rather than at night. Said especially of animals. Compare **nocturnal. 3.** Opening during daylight hours and closing at night. Said of flowers. [Middle English, from Latin *diurnālis,* from *diurnus,* of a day, daily : *diēs,* day + *-urnus,* adjective suffix.] **—di·ur·nal·ly** *adv.*

diurnal parallax *n. Astronomy.* **Parallax** *(see)* caused by the earth's daily rotation, defined by the angle subtended at a celestial body by the radius of the earth. Also called "geocentric parallax."

diurnal rhythm *n.* A **circadian rhythm** *(see).*

div. 1. *Mathematics.* divergence. **2.** divided; division; divisor. **3.** dividend. **4.** divorced.

di·va (dē′və) *n., pl.* **-vas** or *Italian* **-ve** (-vā). An operatic prima donna. [Italian, "goddess," from Latin, feminine of *dīvus,* god.]

di·va·gate (dī′və-gāt′, dĭv′ə-) *intr.v.* **-gated, -gating, -gates. 1.** To wander or drift about. **2.** To ramble; digress. [Late Latin *dīvagārī* : Latin *dis-,* apart + *vagārī,* to wander, from *vagus,* wandering, VAGUE.] **—di·va·ga·tion** *n.*

di·va·lent (dī-vā′lənt) *adj.* Having a valence of two; bivalent.

di·van (dĭ-văn′, dī′văn′ *for sense 1;* dĭ-văn′, -vän′, dī-văn′ *for senses 2, 3, 4, 5) n.* Also **di·wan** (dĭ-wän′) (for senses 2, 5). **1. a.** A long backless couch, especially one against a wall with pillows. **b.** A low bed without a headboard or footboard. **2.** In Muslim countries: **a.** A council that constitutes or is a part of the government. **b.** A room where such a council is held; a court of justice; a council chamber. **3.** Any council. **4.** Formerly, a coffee house or smoking room furnished with divans. **5.** In the Middle East, a book of poems by one author. [French, from Turkish *dīvān,* from Persian *dīvān*†, register, account, hence office of accounts, council of state.]

di·var·i·cate (dī-văr′ə-kāt′, dĭ-) *intr.v.* **-cated, -cating, -cates.** To diverge at a wide angle; branch off; spread apart. Used especially of branches.
~*adj.* (dī-văr′ə-kĭt, -kāt′, dĭ-). *Biology.* Branching or spreading widely from a point or axis; diverging. [Latin *dīvāricāre,* to spread apart : *dis-,* apart + *vāricāre,* to straddle, from *vāricus,* with the feet spread apart, from *vārus,* bent, knock-kneed.] **—di·var·i·cate·ly** *adv.*

di·var·i·ca·tion (dī-văr′ə-kā′shən, dĭ-) *n.* **1.** The act of divaricating; a branching off. **2.** A divergence of opinion. **3.** The point at which branching occurs.

di·var·i·ca·tor (dī-văr′ə-kāt′ər, dĭ-) *n.* **1.** A muscle that effects the opening and closing of the shell in brachiopods. **2.** A surgical instrument used to divide tissue into two separate parts.

dive (dīv) *v.* **dived** or **dove** (dōv), **dived, diving, dives.** —*intr.* **1. a.** To plunge headfirst into water, often as a sport. **b.** To go toward the bottom of a body of water: *dive for pearls.* **c.** To submerge under power. Used of a submarine. **d.** To fall head down through the air. **e.** To descend nose down at an acceleration usually

exceeding that of free fall. Used of an airplane. **f.** To engage in the sport of skydiving. **g.** To drop sharply and rapidly; plummet. **2. a.** To rush headlong, usually downward or out of sight: *dived into an alley.* **b.** To plunge one's hand into something: *dived into my handbag for a coin.* **3.** To lunge; throw oneself. Used with *at* or *for*: *We dived for the best seats.* **4.** To plunge or rush with great enthusiasm or vigor. Used with *in* or *into*: *The children all dived in and helped themselves to the food.* —*tr.* To cause (an aircraft or a submarine, for example) to dive.
∼*n.* **1. a.** A headlong plunge into water, especially one executed deliberately. **b.** A nearly vertical descent at an accelerated speed through water, air, or space. **c.** A quick, pronounced drop. **2.** *Slang.* A disreputable or run-down bar or nightclub. **3.** *Slang.* A knockout feigned by prearrangement between boxers. Used chiefly in the phrase *to take a dive.* [Middle English *diven, duven,* to dive, to submerge, Old English *dȳfan* (transitive), to dip, immerse, and *dūfan* (intransitive), to sink, dive.]

dive-bomb (dīv′bŏm′) *tr.v.* **-bombed, -bombing, -bombs.** *Aviation.* To release a bomb at the end of a steep dive toward the target. **—dive-bomber** *n.*

div·er (dī′vər) *n.* **1.** One that dives. **2.** One who dives for something or goes underwater for work or pleasure, especially one equipped with breathing apparatus and weighted clothing. **3. a.** Any of several aquatic birds of the family Gaviidae, having black-and-white plumage and small, pointed wings and noted for their ability to dive deeply under water in search of prey. **b.** Any of various other diving birds, especially the loon.

di·verge (dĭ-vûrj′, dī-) *v.* **-verged, -verging, -verges.** —*intr.* **1.** To tend in different directions from a common point. **2.** To differ in opinion or manner. **3.** To depart from a set course or norm; deviate. **4.** *Mathematics.* To fail to approach a limit. Compare **converge.** —*tr.* To cause to diverge; deflect. —See Synonyms at **separate.** [Late Latin *dīvergere,* to turn aside : Latin *dis-,* apart + *vergere,* to bend, turn.]

di·ver·gence (dĭ-vûr′jəns, dī-) *n.* Also **di·ver·gen·cy** (-jən-sē), *pl.* **-cies.** *Abbr.* **div.** **1. a.** The act of diverging. **b.** The state of being divergent. **c.** The degree by which things diverge. **2.** Departure from a norm; deviation. **3.** Difference, as of opinion. **4.** *Mathematics.* **a.** The property or manner of diverging; failure to approach a limit. **b.** The scalar product of the del operator and a vector function. In this sense, compare **curl.** **5.** *Meteorology.* A condition characterized by a net horizontal outflow of air from a region, often compensated for by a descending air current, usually accompanied by fine dry weather. —See Usage note at **difference.**

di·ver·gent (dĭ-vûr′jənt, dī-) *adj.* **1. a.** Drawing apart from a common point; diverging. **b.** Causing divergence of radiation. **2.** Departing from convention; deviant. **3.** Differing from each other: *divergent opinions.* **4.** *Mathematics.* Failing to approach a limit; not convergent. **—di·ver·gent·ly** *adv.*

divergent thinking *n.* *Psychology.* A type of thinking characterized by breadth of vision and the use of imagination to arrive at a variety of possible solutions to a problem. Compare **convergent thinking.**

di·vers (dī′vərz) *adj.* Various; several; sundry. [Middle English *divers(e).* See **diverse.**]

di·verse (dĭ-vûrs′, dī-, dī′vûrs) *adj.* **1.** Distinct in kind; disparate; unlike. **2.** Having variety in form; diversified; multiform. [Middle English *divers(e),* from Old French *divers,* from Latin *dīversus,* contrary, diverse, from the past participle of *dīvertere,* to turn aside, DIVERT.] **—di·verse·ly** *adv.* **—di·verse·ness** *n.*

di·ver·si·form (dĭ-vûr′sə-fôrm′, dī-) *adj.* Having a variety of forms; variform. [DIVERSE + -FORM.]

di·ver·si·fy (dĭ-vûr′sə-fī′, dī-) *v.* **-fied, -fying, -fies.** —*tr.* **1.** To make diverse; give variety to; vary. **2. a.** To extend (activities) into various different disparate fields in order to increase profits, spread the risk of loss, or the like. Used of a business enterprise. **b.** To distribute (investments) among several companies in order to reduce the risk of loss. —*intr.* To engage in a wide range of activities. Used especially of a business enterprise. [Middle English *diversifien,* from Old French *diversifier,* from Medieval Latin *dīversificāre* : Latin *dīversus,* DIVERSE + *facere,* to make.] **—di·ver·si·fi·a·ble** *adj.* **—di·ver·si·fi·ca·tion** *n.*

di·ver·sion (dĭ-vûr′zhən, -shən, dī-) *n.* **1.** An act or instance of diverting; a turning aside. **2.** Something that distracts the mind and relaxes or entertains. **3.** In military strategy, a maneuver that draws the attention of the enemy away from the planned point of attack. **4.** A detour created for traffic. **—di·ver·sion·ar·y** *adj.*

di·ver·sion·ist (dĭ-vûr′zhə-nĭst, -shə-nĭst, dī-) *n.* *Politics.* One engaged in diversionary, disruptive, or subversive activities, especially from within and against a Communist state. **—di·ver·sion·ist** *adj.*

di·ver·si·ty (dĭ-vûr′sə-tē, dī-) *n., pl.* **-ties.** **1. a.** The fact or quality of being diverse; difference. **b.** A point or respect in which things differ. **2.** Variety; multiformity: *a healthy diversity in one's diet.*

di·vert (dĭ-vûrt′, dī-) *v.* **-verted, -verting, -verts.** —*tr.* **1.** To turn aside from a usual course or direction; deflect. **2.** To distract. **3.** To amuse or entertain. —*intr.* To turn aside. [Middle English *diverten,* to turn aside, digress, escape, from Old French *divertir,* from Latin *dīvertere,* to turn aside : *dis-,* aside + *vertere,* to turn.] **—di·vert·er** *n.* **—di·vert·ing·ly** *adv.*

diverticular disease *n.* A condition in which diverticula in the colon are associated with lower abdominal pain.

di·ver·tic·u·li·tis (dī′vûr-tĭk′yə-lī′tĭs) *n.* *Pathology.* Inflammation of a diverticulum.

di·ver·tic·u·lo·sis (dī′vûr-tĭk′yə-lō′sĭs) *n.* A condition characterized by the presence of numerous diverticula in the colon. [DIVERTICUL(UM) + -OSIS.]

di·ver·tic·u·lum (dī′vûr-tĭk′yə-ləm) *n., pl.* **-la** (-lə). A pouch or sac branching out from a hollow organ or structure, especially the intestine. Diverticula may occur as abnormal structures formed at weak points in the intestinal wall. [New Latin, from Latin *dēverticulum,* bypath, from *dēvertere,* to turn aside : *dē-,* away + *vertere,* to turn.] **—di·ver·tic·u·lar** *adj.*

di·ver·ti·men·to (dĭ-vĕr′tĭ-mĕn′tō) *n., pl.* **-ti** (-tē). *Music.* A chiefly 18th-century form of instrumental chamber music having several short movements. [Italian, "diversion," "amusement," from *divertire,* to DIVERT.]

di·ver·tisse·ment (dē-vĕr-tēs-mäN′) *n.* **1.** A short ballet or other performance given as an interlude in the opera or theater. **2. a.** *Music.* A divertimento. **b.** A fantasia composed using well-known melodies. **3.** A diversion; an amusement. [French, from *divertir,* to DIVERT.]

Di·ves (dī′vēz) *n.* A man of wealth. [Middle English, from Latin *Dīvēs,* the rich man in the parable of Lazarus, Luke 16:19–31, from *dīvēs,* rich, costly.]

di·vest (dĭ-vĕst′, dī-) *tr.v.* **-vested, -vesting, -vests.** **1.** To strip, as of clothes. **2.** To deprive, as of rights or property; dispossess. **3.** *Law.* To devest. —See Synonyms at **strip.** [Alteration of DEVEST.]

di·vide (dĭ-vīd′) *v.* **-vided, -viding, -vides.** —*tr.* **1. a.** To separate into parts, sections, groups, or branches. **b.** To sector into units of measurement; graduate. **c.** To separate and group according to kind; classify. **2. a.** To separate into opposing factions; disunite: *The issue of unemployment divided the party.* **b.** *British.* To cause (Members of Parliament) to vote by separating into groups for and against a motion. **3.** To separate from; cut off; serve as a boundary between. **4.** To apportion among a number; share out. **5.** *Mathematics.* **a.** To subject to the process of division. **b.** To be an exact divisor of. —*intr.* **1. a.** To become separated into parts. **b.** To branch out. Used of a river, for example. **c.** To form into factions; take sides. **d.** *British.* To vote by being divided. **2.** To perform the mathematical operation of division. —See Synonyms at **separate.** —See Usage note at **distribute.**
∼*n.* **1.** A dividing point or line. **2.** A ridge of land forming a watershed. **3.** See **Great Divide.** [Middle English *dividen,* from Latin *dīvidere.*] **—di·vid·a·ble** *adj.*

di·vid·ed (dĭ-vī′dĭd) *adj.* *Abbr.* **div.** **1.** Separated into parts or pieces. **2.** In disagreement; disunited. **3.** Pulled by conflicting interests or activities. **4.** Having the lanes for opposing traffic separated. Said of a highway. **5.** *Botany.* Having indentations extending to the midrib or base and forming distinct divisions: *divided leaves.*

div·i·dend (dĭv′ə-dĕnd′) *n.* *Abbr.* **div.** **1.** *Mathematics.* A quantity to be divided. **2. a.** A pro rata share of net profits distributed to a shareholder in a company. **b.** A share of profits received by a member of a cooperative society or by a policyholder in a mutual insurance society. **c.** A pro rata payment to a creditor of a person adjudged bankrupt. **3.** A benefit; bonus: *Our decision to buy a computer paid handsome dividends.* —See Synonyms at **bonus.** [French, from Latin *dīvidendum,* "thing to be divided," neuter gerundive of *dīvidere,* to DIVIDE.]

di·vid·er (dĭ-vī′dər) *n.* **1. a.** One that divides. **b.** A screen or other partition. **2. dividers.** A device resembling a compass with two points, used for dividing lines and transferring measurements.

div·i·div·i (dĭv′ē-dĭv′ē) *n., pl.* **-is.** **1.** A tropical American tree, *Caesalpina coriaria,* having compound leaves and long pods. **2.** The dried pods of this tree, yielding an extract used in tanning leather. [Spanish *dividivi,* from Cariban.]

div·i·na·tion (dĭv′ə-nā′shən) *n.* **1.** The art or act of foretelling events or revealing occult knowledge by means of augury or alleged supernatural agency. **2.** Inspired insight; intuition. **3.** That which has been divined; a prophecy. **—di·vin·a·to·ry** (dĭ-vĭn′ə-tôr′ē, -tōr′ē) *adj.*

di·vine¹ (dĭ-vīn′) *adj.* **-viner, -vinest.** **1. a.** Being or having the nature of a deity. **b.** Of, pertaining to, emanating from, or being the expression of a deity. **c.** In the service or worship of a deity or god; sacred; holy. **2.** Superhuman; godlike. **3.** Supremely good; magnificent. **4.** *Informal.* Heavenly; perfect.
∼*n.* A clergyman, religious, or priest, especially one knowledgeable in theology. [Middle English, from Old French *devin,* from Latin *dīvīnus,* from *dīvus,* divine, god.] **—di·vine·ly** *adv.* **—di·vine·ness** *n.*

divine² *v.* **-vined, -vining, -vines.** —*tr.* **1.** To know, foresee, predict, or come to conjecture, as by inspiration, intuition, or reflection. **2.** To locate (water, minerals, or the like) with a divining rod or pendulum.
∼*intr.* **1.** To practice divination. **2.** To guess. —See Synonyms at **foretell.** [Middle English *divinen,* from Old French *deviner,* from Latin *dīvīnāre,* from *dīvīnus,* soothsayer, "(one) inspired by the gods," DIVINE (adjective).] **—di·vin·er** *n.*

Divine Liturgy *n.* The Eastern Orthodox Eucharistic ceremony.

Divine Office *n.* *Roman Catholic Church.* The prayers and readings for the daily canonical hours; the offices and prayers in the breviary.

divine right *n.* **1.** The right of a monarch to rule, supposed to have come directly from God and to be independent of the will or consent of his subjects. Also called "divine right of kings." **2.** *Informal.* Any right or claim regarded by its holder as incontestable.

Divine Service *n.* A public service in a Christian church for the worship of God.

PRONUNCIATION KEY
ă, pat; ā, pay; âr, care;
ä, father, are; b, bib;
ch, church; d, deed; ĕ, pet;
ē, be; f, fife; g, gag; h, hat;
hw, which; ĭ, pit; ī, pie;
îr, pier; j, judge; k, kick;
l, lid, needle; m, mum;
n, no, sudden; ng, thing;
ŏ, pot; ō, toe; ô, paw, for;
oi, noise; ou, out; o͝o, book;
o͞o, boot; p, pop; r, roar;
s, sauce; sh, ship, dish;
t, tight; th, thin, path;
th, this, bathe; ŭ, cut; ûr, fur;
v, valve; w, with; y, yes;
z, zebra, size; zh, vision;
ə, about, item, edible,
gallop, circus, peaceful

IN FOREIGN WORDS:
ȧ, *Fr.* ami; œ, *Fr.* feu, *Ger.* schön; ü, *Fr.* tu, *Ger.* über; KH, *Ger.* ich, *Scot.* loch; N, *Fr.* bon; y′, *Fr.* Compiègne

STRESS MARKS:
Primary stress: ′
in·cite′ (ĭn-sīt′)
Secondary stress: ′
in′sight′ (ĭn′sīt′)

diving beetle *n.* Any of various predatory aquatic beetles of the family Dytiscidae, having streamlined bodies and flattened hind legs.

diving bell *n.* A large vessel for underwater work, open on the bottom and supplied with air under pressure.

diving board *n.* A flexible board or platform from which a dive may be executed, secured at one end and projecting over water at the other. Also called "springboard."

diving duck *n.* Any duck that dives to the bottom of a river or lake to feed. Diving ducks include the pochard, scaup, and goldeneye. Compare **dabbler.**

diving suit *n.* A heavy waterproof suit with a large detachable helmet supplied with air, used for underwater work.

divining rod *n.* A forked branch or stick that allegedly indicates subterranean water or minerals by bending downward when held over a source. Also called "dowsing rod."

di·vin·i·ty (dĭ-vĭn′ə-tē) *n., pl.* **-ties. 1.** The state or quality of being divine; especially, the state of being a deity. **2. a. Divinity.** God; the godhead. **b.** A god or goddess; a deity. **3.** Theology.

di·vis·i·ble (dĭ-vĭz′ə-bəl) *adj.* Capable of being divided, especially of being divided evenly with no remainder. **—di·vis·i·bil·i·ty** *n.* **—di·vis·i·bly** *adv.*

di·vi·sion (dĭ-vĭzh′ən) *n. Abbr.* **div. 1. a.** The act or process of dividing. **b.** The state of being divided. **2.** The act or process of sharing out; distribution. **3.** Something that serves to divide or keep separate, such as a boundary or partition. **4.** One of the parts, sections, or groups into which something is divided. **5. a.** An area of governmental, judicial, or business activity organized as an administrative or functional unit. **b.** A territorial section marked off, as for political, governmental, or policing purposes. **6.** *Military.* **a.** The major autonomous administrative and tactical unit of an army that is larger than a regiment but smaller than a corps. It is the smallest self-contained unit of an army that can engage independently in prolonged combat. **b.** A corresponding unit in any of the other armed forces. **7.** *Botany.* A major taxonomic category corresponding approximately to a phylum. **8. a.** Variance of opinion; disagreement. **b.** A splitting into factions; disunion. **9.** *British.* The physical separation of members of Parliament into groups according to their stand on an issue put to vote. Also used adjectivally: *the division bell.* **10.** *Mathematics.* The operation of determining how many times one quantity is contained in another. Compare **multiplication. 11.** A type of plant propagation in which a part separated from the parent grows into a new plant. **12.** *Sports.* Any of various competitive categories in a particular sport, organized according to age, ability, sex, or the like. [Middle English *divisioun,* from Old French *division,* from Latin *dīvīsiō* (stem *dīvīsiōn-*), from *dīvidere* (past participle *dīvīsus*), to DIVIDE.] **—di·vi·sion·al** *adj.*

di·vi·sion·ism (də-vĭzh′ə-nĭz′əm) *n.* A branch of neo-impressionism in which colors are divided into their primary components and arranged in dabs so that the eye organizes the shape. Compare **pointillism. —di·vi·sion·ist** *n. & adj.*

division lobby *n. Chiefly British.* See **lobby** (sense 3).

division sign *n.* The symbol (÷) placed between two quantities to indicate the division of the first by the second.

di·vi·sive (dĭ-vī′sĭv) *adj.* Creating discord or dissension. **—di·vi·sive·ly** *adv.* **—di·vi·sive·ness** *n.*

di·vi·sor (dĭ-vī′zər) *n. Abbr.* **div. 1.** The quantity by which another quantity, the dividend, is to be divided. **2.** A number that divides another number exactly; a factor.

di·vorce (dĭ-vôrs′, -vōrs′) *n.* **1. a.** The dissolution of a marriage by the legal judgment of a court, or in some societies, by established custom. **b.** The legal declaration of such a dissolution. **2.** A complete or radical separation of things formerly closely connected. ~*v.* **divorced, -vorcing, -vorces.** *—tr.* **1.** To dissolve the marriage bond between. **2.** To end one's marriage to (one's spouse) by legal divorce. **3.** To separate or detach; disunite. *—intr.* To become divorced. *—See Synonyms at* **separate.** [Middle English, from Old French, from Latin *dīvortium,* separation, divorce, fork in a road, from *dīvortere, dīvertere,* to turn aside, separate, DIVERT.]

di·vor·cé (dĭ-vôr-sā′, -sē′, -vōr-, -vôr′sā, -sē′, -vōr′-) *n.* A divorced man. [French, masculine past participle of *divorcer,* to divorce, from Old French.]

di·vor·cée (dĭ-vôr-sā′, -sē′, -vōr-, -vôr′sā′, -sē′, -vōr′-) *n.* A divorced woman. [French, "divorced."]

di·vorce·ment (dĭ-vôrs′mənt, -vōrs′-) *n.* A complete separation of things.

div·ot (dĭv′ət) *n.* **1.** A piece of turf torn up by a golf club in striking a ball, or by a horse's hoof. **2.** *Scottish.* A thin square of turf or sod, used especially for roofing. [Scottish *deva(i)t, dewot, duvat*†.]

di·vulge (dĭ-vŭlj′) *tr.v.* **-vulged, -vulging, -vulges. 1.** To disclose (something previously kept secret); reveal; make known. **2.** *Archaic.* To proclaim publicly. *—See Synonyms at* **reveal.** [Middle English *divulgen,* from Latin *dīvulgāre,* to spread abroad among the people : *dis-,* abroad + *vulgāre,* to make common, publish, from *vulgus,* multitude, public. See **vulgar.**] **—di·vul·gence, di·vulge·ment** *n.* **—di·vulg·er** *n.*

di·vul·sion (dĭ-vŭl′shən) *n.* A tearing apart; a violent separation. [Latin *divulsiō* (stem *divulsiōn-*), from *dīvellere* (past participle *dīvulsus*), to tear apart : *dis-,* apart + *vellere,* to tear, pluck.] **—di·vul·sive** *adj.*

div·vy (dĭv′ē) *n., pl.* **-vies.** *Informal.* A share or portion. ~*tr.v.* **divvied, -vying, -vies.** *Informal.* To divide. Usually used with **up.** [Short for DIVIDEND.]

---

diwan. 1. Variant of **dewan. 2.** Variant of **divan.**

Dix (dĭks), **Dorothea Lynde** (1802–87). U.S. social reformer. She was a pioneer in the movement for specialized treatment for the insane. Her work in Massachusetts and elsewhere led to the founding of government hospitals for the insane in many states.

Dix·ie (dĭk′sē). The Southern states of the United States that joined the Confederacy during the Civil War. Also called "Dixie Land." [Perhaps from *dixie,* a 10-dollar bill issued by a New Orleans bank prior to the Civil War, with a large *Dix* printed on each side, from French *dix,* ten.]

Dix·ie·land (dĭk′sē-lănd′) *n.* A style of instrumental jazz based on the traditional New Orleans style of jazz with a relatively fast, strongly accented two-beat rhythm and group improvisation, but having a more regular melodic structure.

di·zen (dī′zən, dĭz′ən) *tr.v.* **-ened, -ening, -ens.** *Archaic.* To deck out, especially vulgarly, in fine clothes or adornments; bedizen. [Earlier *disen,* to dress a distaff with flax, perhaps from Low German *dise*†, bunch of flax on a distaff.] **—di·zen·ment** *n.*

di·zy·got·ic (dī′zī-gŏt′ĭk) *adj.* Derived from two separate and separately fertilized ova. Said especially of fraternal twins.

diz·zy (dĭz′ē) *adj.* **-zier, -ziest. 1.** Having a sensation of whirling or feeling a tendency to fall; giddy. **2.** Bewildered or confused. **3. a.** Producing or tending to produce giddiness or a whirling sensation: *the dizzy heights of success.* **b.** Characterized by giddiness; reeling: *a dizzy spell.* **4.** *Informal.* Scatterbrained; silly; foolish. ~*tr.v.* **dizzied, -zying, -zies.** To make dizzy; confuse; bewilder. [Middle English *dusie,* foolish, giddy, from Old English *dysig,* foolish, stupid.] **—diz·zi·ly** *adv.* **—diz·zi·ness** *n.*

DJ *n., pl.* **DJ's** or **DJs.** A disc jockey *(see).*

Djakarta. See **Jakarta.**

djellaba. Variant of **jellaba.**

Dji·bou·ti or **Ji·bu·ti** (jĭ-bōō′tē). Formerly (1967–77) **French Territory of the A·fars and Is·sas** (ə-färs′; ĭ′səs). Small, arid country on the northeast coast of Africa, on the Gulf of Aden. The population, mostly Muslim, is concentrated in the port of Djibouti, which was developed by the French when the area became the colony of French Somaliland in 1888. It became independent in 1977. Area, 22,000 square kilometers (8,492 square miles). Population, 400,000. Capital, Djibouti. See map at **Ethiopia.**

Dji·las (jĭl′əs), **Milovan** (1911–). Yugoslav politician and writer. He was a member of Tito's resistance group in World War II and served in the postwar Communist government, but was demoted for criticizing the regime. His writings include *The New Class* (1957), *Land Without Justice* (1958), and *Conversations with Stalin* (1962).

djinni, djinny. Variants of **jinni.**

Djokjakarta. See **Jogjakarta.**

dk. 1. dark. **2.** deck. **3.** dock.

dl deciliter.

D/L demand loan.

D layer *n. Meteorology.* The weakly ionized layer of the ionosphere, approximately 50 to 90 kilometers (30 to 55 miles) above the earth. Also called "D region."

D line *n. Physics.* One of two closely spaced lines in the yellow region of the spectrum of sodium, used as a standard for optical measurement. The lines occur at wavelengths of 589.6 and 589.0 nanometers.

D.Lit., D.Litt. Doctor of Letters; Doctor of Literature. [Latin *Doctor Lit(t)erarum.*]

dm decimeter.

DM 1. *Chemistry.* adamsite. **2.** Deutsche mark.

DMA *Computer Science.* direct memory access.

DMSO dimethylsulfoxide.

D. Mus. Doctor of Music.

DMZ demilitarized zone.

dn. down.

DNA *n.* Deoxyribonucleic acid, a nucleic acid that is the chief constituent of chromosomes, can replicate itself, and is responsible for transmitting genetic information, in the form of genes, from parents to offspring. It consists of a double helix of two long chains of linked **nucleotides** *(see),* connected to each other by hydrogen bonds between the bases adenine and thymine or cytosine and guanine.

DNB Dictionary of National Biography.

Dnie·per (nē′pər). *Russian* **Dne·pr** (dnyĕ′pər). River in the west of the U.S.S.R., flowing from the Valdai Hills 2,286 kilometers (1,420 miles) to the Black Sea. It is the third-longest river entirely within Europe. Kiev is the biggest city on its banks. The river is an important source of hydroelectric power.

Dnie·ster (nēs′tər). River in the southwest of the U.S.S.R. It flows 1,411 kilometers (877 miles) from the Carpathian Mts. to the Black Sea near Odessa.

do¹ (dōō) *v.* **did** (dĭd), **done** (dŭn), **doing, does** (dŭz). Present tense, first person, **do;** second person, **do** or (for singular) *archaic* **doest** (dōō′əst), **dost** (dŭst); third person singular, **does** or *archaic* **doeth** (dōō′əth), **doth** (dŭth); third person plural, **do.** Used as an auxiliary in the past or present tense followed by the infinitive without *to,* or, in reply to a question or suggestion, with this infinitive understood. Its function can be: **1.** To indicate the tense of the infinitive in questions, negative statements, and inverted phrases: *Do you understand? I did not sleep well. Little did she suspect.* **2.** To intensify or emphasize: *Do be still!* **3.** To represent an antecedent verb and thus avoid its repetition: *She tries as hard as they do. Jane arrived late, and so did I.* **4.** To serve as an extra word, in verse or poetic prose,

---

which improves the sound but does not change the sense of a line, or to express certain nuances of irony or humor: *Well, I do declare.* —*tr.* **1.** To perform or execute (an action, procedure, or piece of work): *She did the driving. Have you done your homework?* **2.** To carry out; fulfill what is involved in: *We did all that was necessary.* **3.** To produce or make (a piece or amount of work): *did a portrait.* In this sense, often used in place of verbs such as *write, paint,* or *compose.* **4. a.** To bring about; achieve: *It won't do any good.* **b.** To effect (an improvement): *That hat doesn't do anything for her.* **5.** To attend to, deal with, or treat in an appropriate way: *do the dinner dishes; I must get the car done.* In this sense, often used in place of a wide variety of common verbs. **6.** To render or give: *do justice to her abilities.* **7.** To work at as an occupation or study. **8.** To work out the details of; solve: *do a crossword puzzle.* **9.** To present (a play or dramatic reading, for example); perform; stage. **10.** To have the role of; play. **11. a.** To travel over (a specified distance): *do a mile in four minutes; do 40 miles to the gallon.* **b.** To travel at or be capable of attaining (a specified speed). **12.** To travel about; visit; tour: *do Europe in five weeks.* **13.** To meet the needs of sufficiently; be suitable or convenient for; suffice: *This room will do us very nicely.* **14.** To groom or beautify (the hair, for example). **15.** To translate: *Homer's Iliad, done into English verse.* **16.** *Informal.* To serve (a term of imprisonment). **17.** *Informal.* **a.** To imitate; mimic. **b.** To behave in a manner that is characteristic of: *did a Houdini and escaped through the bars.* **18.** *Slang.* To cheat or swindle: *do someone out of an inheritance.* —*intr.* **1.** To behave or conduct oneself; act: *Do as you are told. You would do well to leave.* **2.** To act effectively or energetically; strive: *Do or die.* **3.** To get along; fare: *doing well at school.* **4.** To be suitable; serve the purpose: *This coat will do for another season.* **5.** To be sufficient or appropriate in a given situation: *That will do!* **6.** *Informal.* To happen; take place: *Was there anything doing in town yesterday?* —**do away with. 1.** To dispose of; eliminate. **2.** To destroy; kill. —**do by.** To behave with respect to; deal with. —**do for.** *Informal.* To care or provide for; take care of. —**do in.** *Slang.* **1.** To tire completely; exhaust. **2.** To kill. —**do over.** *Informal.* To redecorate. —**do up. 1.** *Informal.* To groom or adorn lavishly. **2.** To wrap and tie (a package). **3.** To tie up or arrange (the hair) so that it is off the neck. **4.** To fasten; button or zip up. —**do with.** To be glad to have; need or want: *I could do with a drink.* —**do without.** To manage easily without; be able to dispense with. —**have to do with. 1.** To have a relation to or relationship with. **2.** To be concerned with; have as subject matter: *a book having to do with religion.* —**make do.** To manage with whatever one has or whatever is available.
—*n., pl.* **do's** or **dos** (do͞oz). **1.** *Informal.* An entertainment; a party. **2.** *Informal.* A hoax or swindle; a cheat. **3.** A statement of what should be done: *do's and don'ts.* **4.** *Archaic.* Duty. Used chiefly in the phrase *to do one's do.* [Do, did, done, dost, does (or doth), didst; Middle English don, did(d)e, idon, dost, does (regularly *doth*), diddest, Old English dōn, dyde, gedōn, dēst, dēth (plural dōth), dydest, from Germanic; akin to Greek *tithēnai,* to place, Sanskrit *dádhāmi,* to put.]

Usage: The use of *don't* (*She just don't care*) for *doesn't* is nonstandard in both American and British English, but it is an extremely widespread form in regional dialects.

do² (dō) *n. Music.* The first tone of the diatonic scale in solfeggio. [Italian, variant of *du,* perhaps inverted variant of *ut.* See **gamut.**]

do. ditto.

D.O. 1. Doctor of Optometry. **2.** Doctor of Osteopathy.

D.O.A. *Medicine.* dead on arrival.

do·a·ble (do͞o′ə-bəl) *adj.* Able to be done.

doat. Variant of **dote.**

dob·bin (dŏb′ĭn) *n.* A horse, especially a workhorse. [From *Dobbin,* alteration of *Robin,* pet form for the name *Robert.*]

Do·bell's solution (dō-bĕlz′) *n.* An aqueous solution of sodium borate, sodium bicarbonate, glycerol, and phenol, used as an antibacterial agent for the mucous membranes of the nose and throat. [After Horace B. *Dobell* (1828–1917), British doctor.]

Do·ber·man pin·scher (dō′bər-mən pĭn′shər) *n.* A fairly large dog of a breed originating in Germany, having a smooth, short, usually black coat with rust-red markings and often used for guard or police work. [German *Dobermann,* after Ludwig *Dobermann,* 19th-century German dog breeder + *Pinscher,* terrier, probably from English PINCH (in allusion to its cropped ears and docked tail).]

do·bra (dō′brə) *n.* The basic monetary unit of São Tomé and Principe, equal to 100 centimos. See feature at **currency.** [Portuguese, ultimately from Latin *duplus,* double.]

dob·son (dŏb′sən) *n.* The larva of the dobson fly. Usually called "hellgrammite." [Probably from the family name *Dobson.*]

dobson fly *n.* An insect, *Corydalus cornutus,* having four large, many-veined wings and long, pincerlike mandibles. See **hellgrammite.**

doc (dŏk) *n. Informal.* A doctor.

doc. document.

do·cent (dō′sənt, dō-sĕnt′) *n.* A teacher or lecturer at certain universities who is not a full faculty member. [Obsolete German *Docent,* from Latin *docēns* (stem *docent-*), present participle of *docēre,* to teach.]

Do·ce·tism (dō-sē′tĭz′əm, dō′sə-tĭz′əm) *n.* The doctrine, espoused by a sect considered heretical in the early Christian Church, that Christ had no human body and only appeared to suffer and die on the cross. [Late Latin *Docētae,* the sect advocating this doctrine, from Late Greek *Dokētai,* from Greek *dokein,* to seem, appear.] —**Do·ce·tic** *adj.* —**Do·ce·tist** *n. & adj.*

do·cile (dŏs′əl, -sīl′) *adj.* **1.** Submissive to another's will; easily handled. **2.** Yielding to handling or treatment; easily shaped or formed: *"Metal is so docile that it will submit to any formal conception a sculptor may have"* (Herbert Read). **3.** Capable of being taught; ready and willing to learn. —See Synonyms at **obedient.** [Latin *docilis,* from *docēre,* to teach.] —**doc·ile·ly** *adv.* —**do·cil·i·ty** (dŏ-sĭl′ə-tē, dō-) *n.*

dock¹ (dŏk) *n. Abbr.* **dk. 1.** The area of water between two piers or alongside a pier that receives a ship for loading, unloading, or repairs. **2.** A pier or wharf. **3.** *Often* **docks.** A group of piers, often enclosed, on a protected basin or other waterway serving as a general landing area for ships or boats. **4.** A platform at which trucks or trains discharge or pick up freight.
—*v.* **docked, docking, docks.** —*tr.* **1.** To maneuver (a vessel) into or next to a dock. **2.** *Aerospace.* To couple (two or more spacecraft, for example) in space. —*intr.* **1.** To move or come into a dock. **2.** To join with another spacecraft while in space. [Middle Low German and Middle Dutch *docke,* probably from Vulgar Latin *ductia* (unattested), conduit, aqueduct, from Latin *dūcere,* to lead.]

dock² *n.* **1.** The solid or bony part of an animal's tail. **2.** The tail of an animal after it has been cut short.
—*tr.v.* **docked, docking, docks. 1.** To cut short or cut off (an animal's tail, for example). **2.** To deduct a part from (someone's salary or wages). **3.** To withhold or cut an amount, as of wages or salary, from. [Middle English *dok,* trimmed hair (of a tail), perhaps from Old English *docca* (attested only in *fingerdocca,* finger muscle), from Germanic *dukk-* (unattested), bundle. See also **doxy.**]

dock³ *n.* An enclosed place where the defendant stands or sits in a criminal court. —**in the dock.** On trial or under intense scrutiny. [Flemish *docke, dok†,* cage, pen.]

dock⁴ *n.* Any of various weedy plants of the genus *Rumex,* having large leaves and clusters of small greenish or reddish flowers. [Middle English *dock, docke,* Old English *docce.*]

dock·age (dŏk′ĭj) *n.* **1.** A charge for docking vessels. **2.** Facilities for docking vessels. **3.** The docking of ships.

dock·er¹ (dŏk′ər) *n.* One that docks something, as the tail of an animal.

docker² *n.* A worker at a dock who loads and unloads ships; a longshoreman.

dock·et (dŏk′ĭt) *n.* **1.** A label on or ticket affixed to a package listing the contents or directions for assembling or operating. **2.** *Law.* **a.** A brief record of the proceedings in a court of justice. **b.** The book containing such records. **3. a.** A list of the cases awaiting action in a court. **b.** Any list of things to be done; an agenda. **4.** *Archaic.* A summary or other brief statement of the contents of a document; an abstract.
—*tr.v.* **docketed, -eting, -ets. 1.** To provide with a brief identifying statement. **2.** To enter in a docket. **3.** To label or ticket (a parcel). [Middle English *doggette†.*]

dock·hand (dŏk′hănd′) *n.* A dockworker; a longshoreman.

dock·land (dŏk′lănd) *n. British. Often* **docklands.** The district surrounding a city's docks.

dock·work·er (dŏk′wûr′kər) *n.* A longshoreman.

dock·yard (dŏk′yärd′) *n.* **1.** An area with facilities for building, repairing, or dry-docking ships. **2.** *British.* A government shipyard; a navy yard.

doc·tor (dŏk′tər) *n.* **1.** *Abbr.* **D.** A person who holds the highest academic degree awarded by a college or university in any specified discipline: *a Doctor of Music.* **2.** *Abbr.* **Dr.** A person qualified to practice medicine; especially, a physician, surgeon, a dentist, or veterinarian. **3.** *Abbr.* **Dr.** The title used in addressing a person who holds the degree of doctor. **4. a.** A Doctor of the Church. **b.** *Obsolete.* Any learned person; a teacher. **5.** A person who repairs things or remedies an undesirable situation. **6.** Any device designed to repair a defect or do a special task. **7.** Any of several brightly colored artificial flies used in fly fishing: *a silver doctor.* —**the Doctor.** Any of several local winds in different parts of the world that mitigate extreme, unhealthy weather conditions, as the harmattan of West Africa.
—*v.* **doctored, -toring, -tors.** *Informal.* —*tr.* **1.** To give medical treatment to. **2.** To repair, especially in a makeshift manner. **3.** To change or falsify (evidence or data) so as to make it favorable to oneself or one's cause. **4.** To add ingredients to (food) either to improve its taste or to make it poisonous. —*intr.* To practice medicine. [Middle English, Church Father, theologian, canonist, medical doctor, scholar, from Old French *docteur,* from Medieval Latin *doctor,* from Latin, teacher, from *docēre,* to teach.]

doc·tor·al (dŏk′tər-əl) *adj.* Of, belonging, or pertaining to an academic doctor: *doctoral robes; a doctoral thesis.*

doc·tor·ate (dŏk′tər-ĭt) *n.* The degree or status of a doctor as conferred by a university.

Doctor of Philosophy *n. Abbr.* **Ph.D., D.Ph., D.Phil.** The highest academic degree granted in most arts and sciences. Compare **Bachelor of Arts, Master of Arts.**

Doctor of the Church *n.* One of the saints recognized by the Church as being especially important in the development of Christian doctrine, traditionally any of the four Doctors of the Western Church, St. Ambrose, St. Augustine, St. Jerome, and St. Gregory, or the four Doctors of the Eastern Church, St. Athanasius, St. Basil, St. Gregory of Nyssa, and St. John Chrysostom.

doc·tri·naire (dŏk′trə-nâr′) *adj.* Having or showing an inflexible

dog

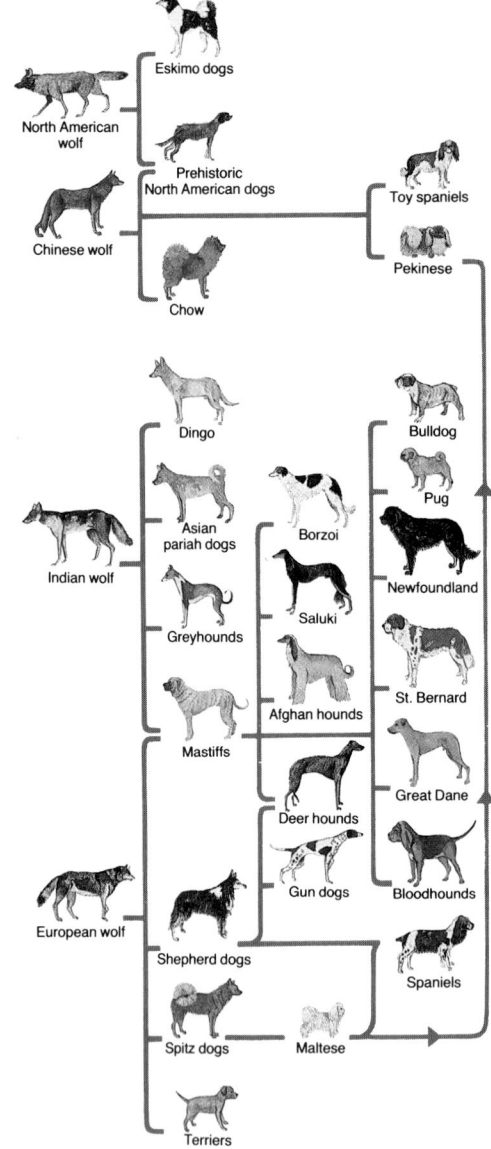

DESCENDANTS OF THE WOLF
Bred for work, looks, and company

The 400 or so breeds of domestic dog are each probably descended from the wolf, which was domesticated about 10,000 years ago by the first Neolithic settlers. The dog displayed a propensity for dependence on man and it was this quality, its intelligence, and its sociability that made it suitable for selective breeding. The combinations of characteristics obtained by breeding are valued for sport, work, companionship, or merely decoration.

Eskimo dogs

North American wolf

Prehistoric North American dogs

Toy spaniels

Chinese wolf

Pekinese

Chow

Dingo

Bulldog

Pug

Asian pariah dogs

Borzoi

Newfoundland

Indian wolf

Saluki

Greyhounds

St. Bernard

Afghan hounds

Mastiffs

Great Dane

Deer hounds

Gun dogs

Bloodhounds

European wolf

Shepherd dogs

Spaniels

Spitz dogs

Maltese

Terriers

FAMILY TREE *This is only a rough guide to the descent of modern breeds—a great deal of random crossbreeding took place before distinct breeds were established. The dingo may be the only purebred dog in the world today, that is, the only dog directly descended from a single race of wolf. Early man took it from Asia to Australia, where it reverted to the wild.*

commitment to a particular theory or principle, and seeking to apply it without regard to practicality or individual circumstances; excessively and impractically dogmatic. —See Synonyms at **dictatorial.**
~*n.* One who adopts a doctrinaire approach; an impractical, dogmatic theorist. —**doc·tri·nair·ism** *n.* —**doc·tri·nar·i·an** *n.*
doc·tri·nal (dŏk′trə-nəl; *British* dŏk-trī′nəl) *adj.* Belonging to, characterized by, or concerning doctrine. —**doc·tri·nal·ly** *adv.*
doc·trine (dŏk′trĭn) *n.* **1.** Something that is taught; a principle or

body of principles taught or advocated in instruction. **2.** A principle or system of principles presented for acceptance or belief, as by a religious, political, scientific, or philosophic group; dogma; received theory. [Middle English, from Old French, from Latin *doctrīna,* teaching, learning, from *doctor,* teacher, DOCTOR.]
doc·u·dra·ma (dŏk′yə-drä′mə, -drăm′ə) *n.* A television or film presentation of political, social, or historical events or circumstances made like a documentary but recreating events in a fictionalized way, as by using actors to portray the protagonists.
doc·u·ment (dŏk′yə-mənt) *n.* **1.** *Abbr.* **doc.** A paper, such as a deed, letter, or report, that gives evidence or information, especially of an official or legal nature. **2.** A record; historical or sociological evidence: *The archaeologists' discoveries are a fascinating document of Viking civilization.* **3.** Anything serving as evidence or proof, as a material substance bearing a revealing symbol or mark.
~*tr.v.* **documented, -menting, -ments. 1.** To furnish with a document or documents. **2.** To support (an assertion or claim, for example) with documentary evidence or decisive information. **3.** To support (statements in a book, for example) with written references or citations; annotate. **4.** To record or provide evidence of. [Middle English, precept, instruction, from Old French, from Latin *documentum,* lesson, example, warning, from *docēre,* to teach.]
doc·u·men·tal·ist (dŏk′yə-mĕn′tl-ĭst′) *n.* A specialist who conserves and studies documents.
doc·u·men·ta·ry (dŏk′yə-mĕn′tə-rē) *adj.* Also **doc·u·men·tal** (-mĕnt′l). **1.** Consisting of, concerning, or based upon documents. **2.** Presenting facts objectively without inserting fictional matter, as in a book, newspaper account, or film.
~*n., pl.* **documentaries.** A television or film presentation of political, social, or historical events or circumstances, often consisting of news film accompanied by narration.
doc·u·men·ta·tion (dŏk′yə-mĕn-tā′shən) *n.* **1.** The supplying of documents or supporting references or records. **2.** The documents or references supplied. **3.** The process or science of gathering, classifying, and storing information.
dod·der¹ (dŏd′ər) *intr.v.* **-dered, -dering, -ders. 1.** To shake or tremble, as from old age; totter. **2.** To progress in a feeble, unsteady manner. [17th century : variant of obsolete *dadder,* Middle English *dadiren,* perhaps from Scandinavian; akin to Norwegian *dudra,* to quiver.]
dod·der² *n.* Any of various parasitic vines of the genus *Cuscuta,* having slender, twining yellow or reddish stems with a few minute, scalelike leaves, and small whitish flowers. [Middle English *doder,* perhaps from Low German; akin to Middle Low German *dod(d)er.*]
dod·dered (dŏd′ərd) *adj.* Lacking the top branches as a result of age or decay. [Alteration of *doddard : dod,* to lop off, Middle English *doden†* + -ARD.]
dod·der·ing (dŏd′ər-ĭng) *adj.* Also **dod·der·y** (dŏd′ər-ē). Feeble-minded or unsteady from age; senile.
do·dec·a·gon (dō-dĕk′ə-gŏn′) *n.* A polygon having 12 sides and 12 angles. [Greek *dōdekagōnon : dōdeka, duōdeka,* twelve : *duo,* two + *deka,* ten + -GON.] —**do·de·cag·o·nal** (dō′dĕ-kăg′ə-nəl) *adj.*
do·dec·a·he·dron (dō′dĕk-ə-hē′drən) *n., pl.* **-drons** or **-dra** (-drə). A polyhedron with 12 plane surfaces. A *regular dodecahedron* has faces that are equal regular pentagons. [Greek *dōdekaedron : dōdeka,* twelve (see **dodecagon**) + -HEDRON.] —**do·dec·a·he·dral** *adj.*
Do·dec·a·nese (dō-dĕk′ə-nēs′, -nēz′). *Greek* **Dho·dhe·ká·ni·sos** (thŏ′thə-kä′nē-sôs′). Group of Greek islands in the southeast Aegean, forming part of the southern Sporades. The name means "12 islands," and there are 12 main ones, including Cos and Rhodes, and several islets. The city of Rhodes is the administrative center, and the islands are noted for tourism and sponge-diving.
do·dec·a·no·ic acid (dō′dĕk-ə-nō′ĭk) *n.* **Lauric acid** (see).
do·dec·a·phon·ic (dō′dĕk-ə-fŏn′ĭk) *adj.* Pertaining to, composed in, or consisting of 12-tone music. [Greek *dōdeka,* twelve (see **dodecagon**) + PHONIC.] —**do·dec·a·phon·ist** *n.* —**do·dec·a·phon·ism, do·dec·a·phon·y** (dō-dĕk′ə-fō′nē, dō′də-kăf′ə-nē) *n.*
do·dec·a·syl·la·ble (dō-dĕk′ə-sĭl′ə-bəl) *n.* A metrical line of 12 syllables.
dodge (dŏj) *v.* **dodged, dodging, dodges.** —*tr.* **1.** To avoid (a blow, for example) by moving or shifting quickly aside. **2.** To evade (an obligation or issue, for example) by cunning, trickery, or deceit. —*intr.* **1.** To move aside quickly, as to avoid a blow; shift or twist suddenly. **2.** To practice trickery or cunning; prevaricate.
~*n.* **1.** An act of dodging; a quick move or shift. **2.** A clever or evasive plan or device; stratagem. **3.** An ingenious method of doing something; shortcut. —See Synonyms at **artifice.** [16th century : origin obscure.]
Dodge (dŏj), **Mary Elizabeth Mapes** (1831–1905). U.S. author and editor. She is best known for her book *Hans Brinker, or the Silver Skates* (1865). As editor of *St. Nicholas Magazine* (1873–1905), she was an important influence on children's literature.
Dodge City. City of southwestern Kansas, on the Arkansas River. Laid out in 1872 on the old Santa Fe Trail, it soon became a wild and rowdy cow town. Wyatt Earp and Bat Masterson were among its famous residents. Boot Hill, an early cowboy burial ground, is a popular tourist attraction.
dodge ball *n.* A game in which the players stand in a circle and try to hit another player or players inside the circle with a large ball.
dodg·er (dŏj′ər) *n.* **1.** A person who dodges or evades. **2.** A shifty or dishonest person; a cheat; trickster. **3.** A shelter on the bridge of a ship providing protection against rain and sea-spray. **4.** *British Re-*

gional. Food. **5.** A small printed handbill. **6.** *Southern U.S.* A corndodger.

Dodg·son (dŏj′sən), **Charles Lutwidge,** known as "Lewis Carroll" (1832–98). English author of *Alice's Adventures in Wonderland* (1865) and *Through the Looking-Glass and What Alice Found There* (1872). A leading mathematician, he was ordained a deacon in the Church of England (1861) and was a pioneering portrait photographer. The Alice stories were written to amuse Alice Liddell, the daughter of the dean of Christ Church, Oxford. His other works include the nonsense poem *The Hunting of the Snark* (1876).

dodg·y (dŏj′ē) *adj.* **-ier, -iest.** *Chiefly British Informal.* **1.** Risky or dangerous. **2.** Unreliable; deceitful. **3.** Not in good health or condition; likely to give way under stress.

do·do (dō′dō) *n., pl.* **-does** or **-dos. 1.** A large flightless bird, *Raphus cucullatus,* of the island of Mauritius in the Indian Ocean, that has been extinct since the late 17th century. **2.** *Informal.* One whose ideas, dress, or manner of living are hopelessly out-of-date. [Portuguese *doudo,* from *doudo*†, stupid (from its clumsy appearance).]

Do·do·ma (dō-dō′mä). Capital of Tanzania since 1975. It is in the center of the country, and transfer of the government secretariat from the old capital, Dar es Salaam, was completed in 1983.

doe (dō) *n., pl.* **does** or **doe. 1.** The female of a deer or related animal. **2.** The female of certain other animals, such as the hare or kangaroo. [Middle English *do,* Old English *dā*†.]

Doenitz, Karl. See **Dönitz.**

do·er (do͞o′ər) *n.* **1.** A person who does something. **2.** A particularly active and energetic person who is able to achieve things.

does. Present tense, third person singular of **do.**

doe·skin (dō′skĭn′) *n.* **1.** The skin of a doe, deer, or goat. **2.** Leather made from this. **3.** A fine, soft, smooth woolen fabric.

does·n't (dŭz′ənt). Contraction of *does not.* —See Usage note at **do.**

do·est. *Archaic.* Second person singular, present tense of **do.** Used with *thou.*

do·eth. *Archaic.* Third person singular, present tense of **do.**

doff (dôf, dŏf) *tr.v.* **doffed, doffing, doffs. 1.** To remove or take off: *doff one's clothes.* **2.** To lift or remove (one's hat) in salutation. **3.** To throw out or away; discard. [Middle English *doffen,* from *don off* : *don,* to DO + OFF.]

dog (dôg, dŏg) *n.* **1.** A domesticated carnivorous mammal, *Canis familiaris,* developed in a wide variety of breeds and probably originally derived from several wild species. **2.** Any of various other animals of the family Canidae, such as the dingo. **3.** A male canine animal, especially of a domesticated breed or of the fox. **4.** Any of various other animals, such as the prairie dog. **5. a.** *Informal.* A fellow: *you lucky dog.* **b.** A contemptible, worthless fellow. **c.** *Informal.* A dashing fellow; a playboy. **6.** *Slang.* **a.** An uninteresting or unattractive person. **b.** A hopelessly inferior product or creation. **7. dogs.** *Informal.* Greyhound races. Preceded by *the.* **8. dogs.** *Slang.* The feet. **9.** A firedog; an andiron. **10. a.** Any of various hooked or U-shaped mechanical devices used for gripping or holding heavy objects. **b.** A pawl or other device engaging a gear or ratchet wheel. **11.** *Astronomy.* A **sun dog** *(see).* **—go to the dogs.** *Informal.* To go to ruin; degenerate. **—put on the dog.** *Informal.* To make an ostentatious display of elegance, wealth, or culture; feign refinement.
~*adj.* Inferior; not genuine: *dog Latin.*
~*adv.* Totally; completely. Used in combination: *dog-tired.*
~*tr.v.* **dogged, dogging, dogs. 1. a.** To follow after like a dog; pursue relentlessly. **b.** To trouble persistently; hound. **2.** To hold or fasten with a mechanical dog. [Middle English *dog, dogge,* Old English *docga*†.]

dog·bane (dôg′bān′, dŏg′-) *n.* Any of several plants of the genus *Apocynum,* mostly of tropical or subtropical regions, having bell-shaped white or pink flowers. [Said to be poisonous to dogs.]

dog·ber·ry (dôg′bĕr′ē, dŏg′-) *n., pl.* **-ries. 1.** A wild gooseberry, *Ribes cynosbati,* of eastern North America, bearing large, prickly berries. **2.** Any of several other plants or shrubs bearing berrylike fruit. **3.** The fruit of any of these plants.

dog·cart (dôg′kärt′, dŏg′-) *n.* **1.** A vehicle drawn by one horse and accommodating two persons seated back to back. **2.** A small cart pulled by dogs.

dog·catch·er (dôg′kăch′ər, dŏg′-) *n.* One appointed or elected to impound stray dogs.

dog collar *n.* **1.** A collar for a dog. **2.** *Informal.* A clerical collar. **3.** See **choker** (sense 2a).

dog days *pl.n.* **1.** In the Northern Hemisphere, the hot, sultry period between mid-July and September. **2.** A period of inactivity. [Translation of Late Latin *diēs caniculārēs,* "Dog Star days" (so called because Sirius rises and sets with the sun during this time).]

doge (dōj) *n.* The elected chief magistrate of the former republics of Venice and Genoa. [French, from Italian (Venetian dialect), from Latin *dux,* leader, from *dūcere,* to lead.]

dog-ear (dôg′îr′, dŏg′-) *n.* Also **dog's-ear** (dôgz′îr′, dŏgz′-). A turned-down corner of the page of a book. **—dog-ear** *tr.v.*

dog-eared (dôg′îrd′, dŏg′-) *adj.* **1.** Having pages with the corners turned down. Said of a book. **2.** Worn from overuse.

dog-eat-dog (dôg′ēt-dôg′, dŏg′ēt-dŏg′) *adj.* Ruthlessly competitive or acquisitive: *a dog-eat-dog society.*

dog·face (dôg′fās′, dŏg′-) *n.* *Slang.* An infantryman in the U.S. Army in World War II.

dog fennel *n.* **1.** Any of various strong-smelling plants of the genus *Anthemis,* such as the **stinking mayweed** *(see).* **2.** A weedy plant, *Eupatorium capillifolium,* of the southeastern United States, having divided leaves and long clusters of greenish flowers.

dog·fight (dôg′fīt′, dŏg′-) *n.* **1.** A violent fight between or as if between dogs; a brawl. **2.** An aerial battle, especially between fighter planes.

dog·fish (dôg′fĭsh′, dŏg′-) *n., pl.* **-fishes** or collectively **dogfish. 1.** Any of various small sharks, chiefly of the families Scyliorhinidae (*spotted dogfish*), Squalidae (*spiny dogfish*), and Triakidae (*smooth dogfish,* or *smooth hounds*). **2.** The **bowfin** *(see).*

dog·ged (dô′gĭd, dŏg′ĭd) *adj.* Not yielding readily; tenacious; stubborn and persistent: *dogged self-assertion.* See Synonyms at **obstinate. —dog·ged·ly** *adv.* **—dog·ged·ness** *n.*

dog·ger·el (dô′gər-əl, dŏg′ər-) *n.* Verse of a loose, irregular rhythm or of a trivial nature and poor quality. **—dog·ger·el** *adj.* [Middle English *dogerel,* poor, worthless, perhaps from *dogge,* DOG.]

dog·ger·y (dô′gə-rē, dŏg′ə-) *n., pl.* **-ies. 1.** Surly behavior; meanness. **2.** Undesirable elements; riffraff. **3.** A cheap bar or saloon.

dog·gish (dô′gĭsh, dŏg′ĭsh) *adj.* **1.** Pertaining to or suggestive of a dog. **2.** Surly. **3.** *Informal.* Showily stylish. **—dog·gish·ly** *adv.*

dog·go (dô′gō, dŏg′ō) *adv.* *Slang.* Quiet and out of sight. Used chiefly in the phrase *lie doggo.* [Probably from DOG.]

dog·gone (dôg′gŏn′, -gôn′, dŏg′-) *adj.* Damn. Used euphemistically. [Euphemistic for *God damn (it).*] **—dog·gone** *interj.*

dog·gy, dog·gie (dô′gē, dŏg′ē) *n., pl.* **-gies.** A dog, especially a small one.
~*adj.* **doggier, -giest. 1.** Of or like a dog. **2.** Liking and caring for dogs.

doggy bag, doggie bag *n.* *Informal.* A bag for leftover food that a diner in a restaurant may take home. [As if saving it for a pet.]

dog·house (dôg′hous′, dŏg′-) *n.* A small house or shelter for a dog. **—in the doghouse.** *Slang.* In disfavor; in trouble.

do·gie (dō′gē) *n.* Also **do·gy,** *pl.* **-gies.** *Western U.S.* A motherless or stray calf. [19th century : origin obscure.]

dog in the manger *n.* One who prevents others from enjoying what he himself has no use for. [From a fable of Aesop.]

dog·leg (dôg′lĕg′, dŏg′-) *n.* Something that has a sharp bend; especially, a golf hole in which the fairway is abruptly angled.
~*intr.v.* **-legged, -legging, -legs.** To move along a dogleg course: *The fairway doglegs to the left.* **—dog·leg·ged** (dôg′lĕg′ĭd, -lĕgd′, dŏg′-) *adj.*

dog·ma (dôg′mə, dŏg′-) *n., pl.* **-mas** or **-mata** (-mə-tə). **1.** *Theology.* A doctrine or system of doctrines proclaimed true by a religious sect: *Christian dogma.* **2.** A principle, belief, or statement of an idea or opinion, especially one that is authoritatively, sometimes arrogantly, asserted as absolute truth: *party dogma.* **3.** A system of such principles or beliefs. [Latin, from Greek, opinion, belief, public decree, from *dokein,* to seem, think.]

dog·mat·ic (dôg-măt′ĭk, dŏg-) *adj.* Also **dog·mat·i·cal** (-ĭ-kəl). **1.** Pertaining to or characteristic of dogma. **2.** Characterized by an authoritative, arrogant assertion of unproved or unprovable principles. —See Synonyms at **dictatorial.** [Late Latin *dogmaticus,* from Greek *dogmatikos,* from *dogma* (stem *dogmat-*), DOGMA.] **—dog·mat·i·cal·ly** *adv.*

dog·mat·ics (dôg-măt′ĭks, dŏg-) *n.* *Used with a singular verb.* The study of religious dogmas, especially those of the Christian church. Also called "dogmatic theology."

dog·ma·tism (dôg′mə-tĭz′əm, dŏg′-) *n.* Dogmatic assertion of opinion or belief.

dog·ma·tist (dôg′mə-tĭst, dŏg′-) *n.* **1.** An arrogantly assertive person. **2.** One who expresses or sets forth dogma.

dog·ma·tize (dôg′mə-tīz′, dŏg′-) *v.* **-tized, -tizing, -tizes.** —*intr.* To express oneself dogmatically in writing or speech. —*tr.* To proclaim as dogma. **—dog·ma·ti·za·tion** *n.*

dog·nap (dôg′năp′, dŏg′-) *tr.v.* **-napped, -napping, -naps** or **-naped, -naping, -naps.** To steal (a dog), especially in order to sell it to a research laboratory. [DOG + KID(NAP).] **—dog·nap·per** *n.*

do-good·er (do͞o′go͝od′ər) *n.* *Informal.* A person who does charitable work or supports good causes, often considered as naively idealistic or unrealistic. **—do-good·ism** *n.*

dog paddle, doggy paddle *n.* A stroke in which the swimmer's arms are bent in front of him and paddle (as a dog's forepaws do in swimming), while the legs kick vigorously in alternation.

dog rose *n.* A prickly wild rose, *Rosa canina,* native to Europe and Asia, having scentless pink or white flowers.

dog's age *n.* *Informal.* A long time.

dogs·bod·y (dôgz′bŏd′ē, dŏgz′-) *n., pl.* **-ies.** *Chiefly British Slang.* A person who is required to perform dreary tasks that others consider beneath them: *a general dogsbody.* [Originally naval slang, midshipman, from *dog's body,* slang for *pease pudding.*]

dog's-ear. Variant of **dog-ear.**

dog·sled (dôg′slĕd′, dŏg′-) *n.* A sled pulled by dogs.

dog's life *n.* *Informal.* An unhappy, slavish existence.

dog's mercury *n.* An ill-smelling Eurasian weed, *Mercurialis perennis,* having small greenish flowers and creeping rhizomes.

dog's-tail (dôgz′tāl′, dŏgz′-) *n.* Any grass of the genus *Cynosurus,* native to Europe; especially, *C. cristatus,* having spikelets in a densely crowded, narrow cluster.

Dog Star *n.* **1.** The star **Sirius** *(see).* **2.** The star **Procyon** *(see).*

dog's tongue (dôgz′tŭng′, dŏgz′-) *n.* A plant, **hound's-tongue** *(see).*

dog tag *n.* **1.** A metal identification disk attached to a dog's collar. **2.** An identification tag worn by soldiers in duplicate on a chain around the neck.

dog-tired (dôg′tīrd′, dŏg′-) *adj.* Extremely tired; exhausted.

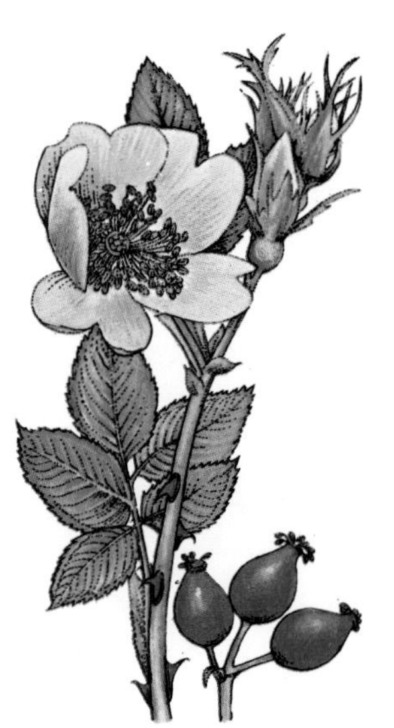

dog rose *This wild ancestor of the garden rose was the symbol of Tudor kings of England. But it is thought to get its name from an ancient Greek belief that it would cure a person who had been bitten by a mad dog.*

PRONUNCIATION KEY

ă, pat; ā, pay; âr, care; ä, father, are; b, bib; ch, church; d, deed; ĕ, pet; ē, be; f, fife; g, gag; h, hat; hw, which; ĭ, pit; ī, pie; îr, pier; j, judge; k, kick; l, lid, needle; m, mum; n, no, sudden; ng, thing; ŏ, pot; ō, toe; ô, paw, for; oi, noise; ou, out; o͝o, book; o͞o, boot; p, pop; r, roar; s, sauce; sh, ship, dish; t, tight; th, thin, path; *th*, this, bathe; ŭ, cut; ûr, fur; v, valve; w, with; y, yes; z, zebra, size; zh, vision; ə, about, item, edible, gallop, circus, peaceful

IN FOREIGN WORDS:

à, *Fr.* **ami; œ,** *Fr.* **feu,** *Ger.* **schön; ü,** *Fr.* **tu,** *Ger.* **über; KH,** *Ger.* **ich,** *Scot.* **loch; N,** *Fr.* **bon; y′,** *Fr.* **Compiègne**

STRESS MARKS:

Primary stress: ′ **in·cite′** (ĭn-sīt′)
Secondary stress: ′ **in′sight′** (ĭn′sīt′)

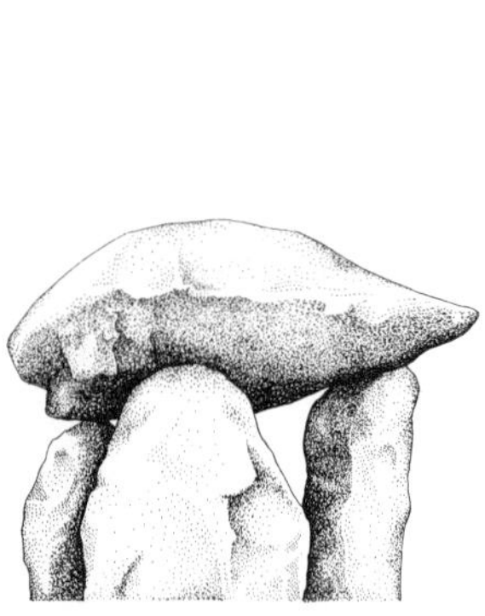

dolmen *Originally, these Neolithic burial chambers—formed by a ring of upright stones, topped by a capstone—were covered with earth. But many have been bared by erosion.*

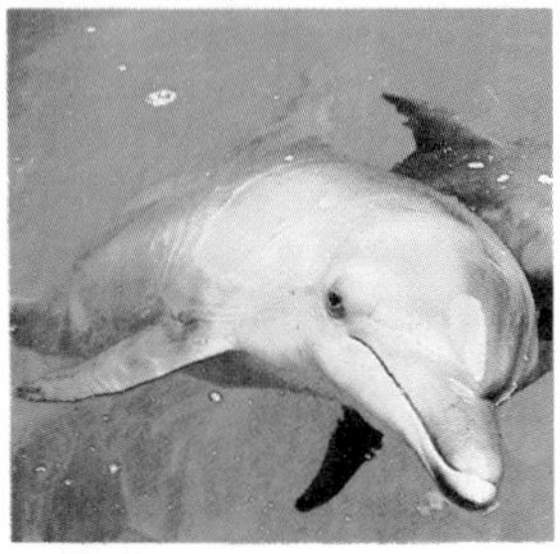

dolphin *A small whale with a beaklike snout, the dolphin has the largest brain relative to its size of any animal after man. The common dolphin,* Delphinus delphis *(above), lives in temperate and tropical seas and can swim at nearly 50 kilometers (30 miles) per hour.*

PRONUNCIATION KEY

ă, pat; ā, pay; âr, care; ä, father, are; b, bib; ch, church; d, deed; ĕ, pet; ē, be; f, fife; g, gag; h, hat; hw, which; ĭ, pit; ī, pie; îr, pier; j, judge; k, kick; l, lid, needle; m, mum; n, no, sudden; ng, thing; ŏ, pot; ō, toe; ô, paw, for; oi, noise; ou, out; o͝o, book; o͞o, boot; p, pop; r, roar; s, sauce; sh, ship, dish; t, tight; th, thin, path; *th*, this, bathe; ŭ, cut; ûr, fur; v, valve; w, with; y, yes; z, zebra, size; zh, vision; ə, about, item, edible, gallop, circus, peaceful

IN FOREIGN WORDS:

à, *Fr.* ami; œ, *Fr.* feu, *Ger.* schön; ü, *Fr.* tu, *Ger.* über; KH, *Ger.* ich, *Scot.* loch; N, *Fr.* bon; y', *Fr.* Compiègne

STRESS MARKS:

Primary stress: ′ **in·cite′** (ĭn-sīt′)
Secondary stress: ′ **in′sight′** (ĭn′sīt′)

dog·tooth (dôg′to͞oth′, dŏg′-) *n., pl.* **teeth** (-tēth). Also **dog tooth** (for sense 1). **1.** A canine tooth; an eyetooth. **2.** *Architecture.* A medieval architectural ornament consisting of four leaflike projections radiating from a raised center.

dogtooth check, dog's-tooth check *n.* **Hound's-tooth check** *(see).*

dogtooth violet *n.* Any of several plants of the genus *Erythronium,* especially *E. americanum,* of North America, having leaves with reddish blotches and nodding, lilylike yellow or purple flowers and sometimes grown as garden ornamentals. Also called "adder's-tongue," "trout lily."

dog·trot (dôg′trŏt′, dŏg′-) *n.* A steady trot like that of a dog.

dog violet *n.* A Eurasian violet, *Viola canina,* having blue-and-yellow flowers.

dog·watch (dôg′wăch′, dŏg′-) *n. Nautical.* Either of two short periods of watch duty, from 4 to 6 p.m. or from 6 to 8 p.m.

dog·wood (dôg′wo͝od′, dŏg′-) *n.* **1.** A tree, *Cornus florida,* of eastern North America, having small greenish flowers surrounded by showy white or sometimes pink bracts that resemble petals. Also called "flowering dogwood." **2.** Any of various shrubs of the genus *Cornus,* such as the European dogwood, *C. sanguinea,* which has red stems, white flowers, and black berries.

Do·ha (dō′hə, -hä). Capital of Qatar. Since 1949 oil revenues have converted it from a tiny fishing village to a large city.

doi·ly, doy·ly (doi′lē) *n., pl.* **-lies.** Also **doy·ley,** *pl.* **-leys.** A small ornamental mat made of lace, linen, paper, or other material and used on plates or to protect or adorn furniture. [After *Doyly* or *Doily,* a London draper, *c.* 1712.]

do·ing (do͞o′ĭng) *n.* **1.** The act of performing something: *a job not worth the doing.* **2.** Events or activities, especially of a social nature.

do-it-your·self (do͞o′ĭt-yər-sĕlf′) *adj. Informal.* Of, relating to, or designed to be done by an amateur or as a hobby: *do-it-yourself home repairs; a do-it-yourself stereo kit.* **—do-it-your·self·er** *n.*

do·jo (dō′jō) *n.* A school for training in Japanese arts of self-defense, such as judo and karate. [Japanese : *do,* art + *-jo,* ground.]

dol (dōl) *n.* A unit used to measure pain, or by inference analgesia, based on application of heat to the skin. See **dolorimetry.** [Latin *dolor,* pain, DOLOR.]

dol. **1.** *Music.* dolce. **2.** dollar.

do·lab·ri·form (dō′lăb′rə-fôrm′) *adj.* Also **do·lab·rate** (-rāt′). *Biology.* Having the shape of the head of an ax. [Latin *dolābra,* pickax, from *dolāre,* to hew + -FORM.]

Dol·by (dōl′bē) *adj.* Of or designating circuitry that reduces noise inherent in the tape recording process. During quiet passages the level of the incoming signal is increased; the compensating decrease during playback reduces noise (tape hiss) to below audibility. [The Dolby System (trademark) invented *c.* 1966 by R.M. *Dolby* (1933–), U.S. electronic engineer.]

dol·ce (dōl′chā′) *adv. Abbr.* **dol.** *Music.* Gently and sweetly. Used as a direction. [Italian, "sweet," from Latin *dulcis.*] **—dol·ce** *adj.*

dol·ce far nien·te (dōl′chā fär nyĕn′tā) *n. Italian.* Delicious inactivity. [Literally, "sweet doing nothing."]

Dol·ce lat·te (dl′chā lä′tā) *n.* A trademark for a smooth, blue-veined Italian cheese. [Italian, "sweet milk."]

dol·ce vi·ta (dōl′chā vē′tä) *n.* A life of comfort or luxury. [Italian, "sweet life."]

dol·drums (dōl′drəmz′, dôl′-, dŏl′-) *n. Used with a singular verb.* **1. a.** Ocean regions near the equator, characterized by calms or light winds. **b.** The calms characteristic of these areas. **2.** A period of inactivity, listlessness, or depression. **3.** A condition of stagnation or recession: *The automotive industry is in the doldrums.* In all three senses, usually preceded by *the.* [Dialect, perhaps ultimately from Old English *dol,* dull (probably influenced in form by TANTRUM).]

dole¹ (dōl) *n.* **1.** The distribution or dispensing of goods, especially of money, food, or clothing as charity. **2.** A gift or share of money, food, or clothing distributed as charity. **3.** *Chiefly British.* The distribution by the government of relief payments to the unemployed. **4.** *Archaic.* One's fate. **—on the dole.** *Chiefly British.* Receiving regular relief payments from the government.
~*tr.v.* **doled, doling, doles.** To distribute, especially in small portions. Usually used with *out*: *doled out the rations.* —See Usage note at **distribute.** [Middle English *dol(e),* part, division, Old English *dāl,* share, portion.]

dole² *n. Archaic.* Grief; sorrow; dolor. [Middle English *dol,* from Old French *dol, duel,* from Late Latin *dolus,* pain, grief, from Latin *dolēre,* to feel pain, grieve for.]

dole·ful (dōl′fəl) *adj.* Filled with grief; mournful; melancholy. —See Synonyms at **sad.** **—dole·ful·ly** *adv.* **—dole·ful·ness** *n.*

dol·er·ite (dŏl′ə-rīt′) *n.* A basic, medium-grained, intrusive igneous rock, mainly composed of feldspar, pyroxene, and sometimes olivine. Also called "diabase." [Greek *doleros,* deceitful, from *dolos,* bait, trick (so named from the difficulty in analyzing it) + -ITE.]

dol·i·cho·ce·phal·ic (dŏl′ə-kō-sə-făl′ĭk) *adj.* Also **dol·i·cho·ceph·a·lous** (-sĕf′ə-ləs). Having a relatively long head; designating a skull that is longer than it is broad, with a cephalic index of 75 or less. Compare **brachycephalic, mesocephalic.** [New Latin *dolichocephalus* : Greek *dolikhos,* long + -CEPHALOUS.] **—dol·i·cho·ceph·a·lism** (dŏl′ə-kō-sĕf′ə-lĭz′əm), **dol·i·cho·ceph·a·ly** (dŏl′ə-kō-sĕf′ə-lē) *n.*

dol·i·cho·cran·i·al (dŏl′ə-kō-krā′nē-əl) Also **dol·i·cho·cran·ic** (-nĭk) *adj.* Dolichocephalic. **—dol·i·cho·cran·y** *n.*

do·li·ne, do·li·na (də-lē′nə, dō-) *n.* A saucer-shaped or shallow funnel-shaped hollow in the ground, large enough to be cultivable, formed by dissolution of limestone. [Slavonic *dolina,* valley.]

doll (dŏl) *n.* **1. a.** A child's toy representing a baby or other human being. **b.** A dummy used by a ventriloquist. **2.** A pretty child. **3.** *Slang.* An attractive woman. **4.** *Informal.* Any person regarded with fond familiarity. **5.** *Slang.* A pep pill, sleeping pill, or other drug in capsule or tablet form.
~*v.* **dolled, dolling, dolls.** *Informal.* —*intr.* To dress up or adorn oneself smartly, as for a special occasion. Used with *up.* —*tr.* To dress up smartly, especially for ostentation. Used with *up.* [From *Doll,* pet name for *Dorothy.*]

dol·lar (dŏl′ər) *n. Abbr.* **dol.** *Symbol* **$** **1. a.** The basic monetary unit of the United States, equal to 100 cents. **b.** The basic monetary unit, equal to 100 cents, of numerous countries, including Australia, Canada, Ethiopia, Guyana, Hong Kong, Liberia, Malaysia, New Zealand, Singapore, Trinidad and Tobago, Western Samoa, and Zimbabwe. **2.** A coin or note worth one dollar. See feature at **currency.** [Low German *daler,* from German *Taler,* taler, short for *Joachimstaler,* a coin made with metal from *Joachimsthal,* Jachymov, town in the Erzgebirge Mountains, Czechoslovakia.]

dol·lar-a-year (dŏl′ər-ə-yîr′) *adj.* Designating U.S. Federal employees who receive token payment for patriotic service: *a dollar-a-year government consultant.*

dol·lar·bird (dŏl′ər-bûrd′) *n.* A bird, *Eurystomus orientalis,* of southeast Asia and Australia, having a round white spot on each wing.

dollar cost averaging *n.* The periodic investment of a fixed dollar amount in the stock market regardless of prevailing prices.

dollar diplomacy *n.* **1.** A foreign policy aimed at furthering the commercial interests and political influence of the United States by encouraging the investment of U.S. capital in foreign countries. **2.** A policy designed to safeguard such investments.

dol·lar·fish (dŏl′ər-fĭsh′) *n., pl.* **-fishes** or collectively **dollarfish.** Any of several rounded silvery fishes, such as the **moonfish** *(see).*

dollar sign *n.* The symbol ($) for a dollar or dollars when placed before a numeral. Also called "dollar mark."

dol·lop (dŏl′əp) *n. Informal.* **1.** A large lump or portion, as of mashed potatoes or ice cream. **2.** A small quantity of liquid, as of whiskey. **3.** A small amount: *not a dollop of truth to the story.* [19th century (earlier sense, tuft) : perhaps from Scandinavian.]

doll·house (dŏl′hous′) *n.* A small-scale model of a house, used as a child's toy.

dol·ly (dŏl′ē) *n., pl.* **-lies.** **1.** A doll. Used by or to children. **2.** A low mobile platform that rolls on casters, used for moving heavy loads. **3.** A similar wheeled apparatus used to move a motion-picture or television camera about a set. **4.** A small locomotive for use in a railroad yard, building site, or the like. **5.** A tool used to hold one end of a rivet while the opposite end is being hammered to form a head. **6.** A small piece of wood or metal placed on the head of a pile to prevent damage while the pile is being driven.
~*intr.v.* **dollied, -lying, -lies.** To move the dolly on which a motion-picture or television camera is mounted toward or away from the scene of action. Often used with *back, in,* or *out.* [From DOLL.]

dolly bird *n. Chiefly British Informal.* A pretty, flashily dressed young woman.

Dol·ly Var·den (dŏl′ē värd′n) *n.* **1.** A woman's large hat, trimmed with flowers. **2.** A colorfully spotted trout, *Salvelinus malma,* of northwestern North America. [After *Dolly Varden,* a character who wore such a hat in Charles Dickens's *Barnaby Rudge.*]

dol·ma (dôl′mə, -mä) *n.* Also **dol·ma·des** (dôl-mä′dēz′). A dish of Turkish origin, consisting of vine leaves stuffed with various mixtures. [Turkish, from *dolaman,* wrapping.]

dol·man (dŏl′mən) *n.* **1.** A long Turkish outer robe. **2.** A woman's cloak or coat with capelike arm pieces. **3.** A jacket, usually elaborately decorated, often worn like a cape as part of a hussar's uniform. [French, from German *Dolman,* from Turkish *dolaman,* wrapping, from *dolamak,* to wind.]

dolman sleeve *n.* A full sleeve that is very wide at the armhole and narrow at the wrist. [See **dolman.**]

dol·men (dŏl′mən) *n.* Any prehistoric megalithic structure consisting of two or more vertical stones supporting a horizontal one, typically forming a chamber. Also called "cromlech." Compare **menhir.** [French, probably coined from Breton *tol,* table, from Old Breton, from Latin *tabula,* TABLE + *men,* stone, from Celtic *magino-* (unattested); compare **menhir.**]

dol·o·mite (dŏl′ə-mīt′) *n.* **1.** A light-tinted, especially yellowish, brownish, or white mineral, essentially $CaMg(CO_3)_2$, used as a furnace refractory, construction, and ceramic material, and in fertilizers. **2.** A type of limestone consisting largely of the mineral dolomite. Also called "dolomitic limestone," "magnesian limestone." [French, after Déodat de *Dolomieu* (1750–1801), French geologist.] **—dol·o·mit·ic** (dŏl′ə-mĭt′ĭk) *adj.*

Dol·o·mites (dŏl′ə-mīts). *Italian* **Do·lo·mi·ti** (dō′lə-mē′tē). Dolomitic limestone mountain range in the Alps of northeast Italy, rising to 3,342 meters (10,965 feet) at Marmolada. Cortina d'Ampezzo is its principal tourist resort.

do·lor (dō′lər) *n.* Also *British* **do·lour.** *Poetic.* Sorrow; grief. [Middle English *dolour,* pain, suffering, grief, from Old French, from Latin *dolor,* from *dolēre,* to feel pain, grieve.]

dol·or·im·e·try (dŏl′ə-rĭm′ə-trē) *n.* A technique for measuring the intensity of pain perception ranging from unpleasant to unbearable, by applying heat to the skin. [DOLOR + -METRY.]

do·lo·ro·so (dō′lə-rō′sō) *adj. Music.* Mournful; plaintive.
~*adv. Music.* With a mournful or plaintive tempo or quality. Used as a direction. [Italian, from Latin *dolōrōsus,* DOLOROUS.]

do·lor·ous (dō′lə-rəs, dŏl′-) *adj.* **1.** Sorrowful; sad. **2.** Painful; distressing. [Middle English, from Late Latin *dolōrōsus,* from Latin *dolor,* DOLOR.] **—do·lor·ous·ly** *adv.* **—do·lor·ous·ness** *n.*

dol·phin (dŏl′fĭn, dôl′-) *n.* **1.** Any of various marine mammals, chiefly of the family Delphinidae, related to the whales but generally smaller and having a beaklike snout; especially, the common, widely distributed species *Delphinus delphis.* Sometimes called "porpoise." **2.** Either of two marine fishes, *Coryphaena hippurus* or *C. equisetis,* having iridescent coloring. **3.** A post, bollard, or the like, for mooring a boat. [Middle English *dolphin, dalphin,* from Old French *daufin, dalfin,* from Vulgar Latin *dalfīnus* (unattested), from Latin *delphīnus,* from Greek *delphis* (stem *delphin-*).]

dolt (dōlt) *n.* A stupid person; a blockhead. [Perhaps from obsolete *dol,* a variant of DULL.] **—dolt·ish** *adj.* **—dolt·ish·ly** *adv.* **—dolt·ish·ness** *n.*

Dom (dŏm; *Portuguese* dōN) *n.* **1.** A title formerly bestowed in Portugal and Brazil on a man of high rank. Compare **don. 2.** *Roman Catholic Church.* A title used before the names of monks of certain orders, especially Benedictines. [Portuguese, from Latin *dominus,* lord.]

Dom. Dominican.

–dom *suffix.* Indicates: **1.** The condition of being; for example, **boredom. 2.** The domain, position, or rank of; for example, **dukedom. 3.** The people who comprise a group, or their general character; for example, **officialdom.** [Middle English *-dom,* Old English *-dōm.*]

do·main (dō-mān′) *n.* **1.** A territory or range of rule or control; realm. **2.** A sphere of interest, special knowledge, or action; field: *the domain of history.* **3.** *Physics.* Any of numerous contiguous regions in a ferromagnetic material in which the direction of spontaneous magnetization is uniform and different from that in neighboring regions. Also called "magnetic domain." **4.** *Law.* **a.** The ownership and right of disposal of property. **b.** The right of **eminent domain** (see). **5.** *Mathematics.* **a.** The set of possible values of an independent variable of a function. Also called "region." Compare **range. b.** Any open connected set that contains at least one point. [French *domaine,* from Old French *demaine,* from Latin *dominium,* property, ownership rights, from *dominus,* lord.]

do·maine (də-mān′, dō-, dō-mĕn′) *n.* A vineyard: *domaine-bottled wine.* [French, "domain."]

dome (dōm) *n.* **1.** A generally hemispherical roof or vault. **2. a.** Any object or structure resembling the shape of this, such as a **geodesic dome** (see). **b.** A natural formation resembling a dome: *the dome of the sky.* **3.** *Poetic.* A large, stately building. **4.** *Slang.* The head. **5.** *Crystallography.* A form of crystal in which two similarly inclined faces intersect in a line parallel to the horizontal axis. **6.** *Geology.* **a.** A **pericline** (see). **b.** A **salt dome** (see). *—v.* **domed, doming, domes.** *—tr.* **1.** To cover with or as if with a dome. **2.** To shape like a dome. *—intr.* To assume the shape of a dome. [French *dôme,* from Italian *duomo,* (domed) cathedral, from Latin *domus,* house.] See feature, next page.

dome car *n.* A railroad passenger car with an elevated glassed-in section for scenic viewing.

domesday. Variant of **doomsday.**

Domes·day Book (dōmz′dā′, dŏmz′-) *n.* Also **Dooms·day Book.** The written record of a census and survey of English landowners and their property, made by order of William the Conqueror in 1085–86.

do·mes·tic (də-mĕs′tĭk) *adj.* **1.** Of or pertaining to the family or household: *domestic chores.* **2.** Fond of home life and competent in household management. **3.** Tame; domesticated. Said of animals. **4.** Of or pertaining to a country's internal affairs: *domestic politics.* **5.** Produced in or indigenous to a particular country: *domestic wine.* *—n.* **1.** A household servant. **2. domestics.** Household linens. [French *domestique,* from Latin *domesticus,* from *domus,* house.] **—do·mes·ti·cal·ly** *adv.*

do·mes·ti·cate (də-mĕs′tĭ-kāt′) *v.* **-cated, -cating, -cates.** Also **do·mes·ti·cize** (də-mĕs′tə-sīz′) **-cized, -cizing, -cizes.** *—tr.* **1.** To train to live with and be of use to man; tame. **2.** To bring into cultivation. **3.** To cause to feel comfortable at home; make domestic. **4.** To accommodate to an environment. *—intr.* To become domestic. [DOMESTIC + -ATE.] **—do·mes·ti·ca·tion** *n.*

do·mes·tic·i·ty (dō′mə-stĭs′ə-tē) *n., pl.* **-ties. 1.** The quality or condition of being domestic. **2.** Home life or devotion to it. **3. domesticities.** Household affairs.

domestic science *n.* The study of skills pertaining to cookery, dressmaking, and household management; home economics.

do·mi·cal (dō′mĭ-kəl, dŏm′ĭ-) *adj.* Also **do·mic** (dō′mĭk, dŏm′ĭk). Pertaining to, having, or shaped like a dome. **—do·mi·cal·ly** *adv.*

dom·i·cile (dŏm′ə-sīl′, -səl, dō′mə-) *n.* Also **dom·i·cil** (-səl). **1.** A residence; home. **2.** One's legal residence. *—v.* **domiciled, -ciling, -ciles.** Also **dom·i·cil·i·ate** (dŏm′ə-sĭl′ē-āt′, dō′mə-) **-ated, -ating, -ates.** *—tr.* To establish (a person or oneself) in a residence. *—intr.* To reside or dwell. [Middle English, from Old French, from Latin *domicilium,* habitation, abode.] **—dom·i·cil·i·ar·y** (dŏm′ə-sĭl′ē-ĕr′ē) *adj.*

dom·i·nance (dŏm′ə-nəns) *n.* Also **dom·i·nan·cy** (-nən-sē). The condition or fact of being dominant; ascendancy.

dom·i·nant (dŏm′ə-nənt) *adj.* **1. a.** Exercising the most influence or control. **b.** Seeking or tending to exert control or occupy a pre-eminent position. **2.** Providing a view from above; in a commanding position. **3.** Most noticeable or prevalent. **4.** *Genetics.* Producing the same phenotypic effect whether paired with an identical or a dissimilar gene. Compare **recessive. 5.** *Ecology.* Designating or pertaining to the species that is most abundant in a habitat and that

may determine the presence and type of other species. **6.** *Music.* Pertaining to or based upon the fifth note of a diatonic scale. *—n.* **1.** *Genetics.* A dominant gene or characteristic. **2.** *Ecology.* A dominant species. **3.** *Music.* The fifth note of a diatonic scale. [Old French, from Latin *domināns* (stem *dominant-*), present participle of *dominārī,* to DOMINATE.] **—dom·i·nant·ly** *adv.*

Synonyms: paramount, predominant, pre-eminent, preponderant.

dominant wavelength *n.* The wavelength of the light that, when combined in specific proportions with an achromatic standard light, matches a given color.

dom·i·nate (dŏm′ə-nāt′) *v.* **-nated, -nating, -nates.** *—tr.* **1.** To control, govern, or exert influence over by superior authority or power. **2.** To occupy the pre-eminent or most noticeable position in or over: *A large painting dominated the room.* **3.** To overlook from a height. *—intr.* To be dominant in position or authority. [Latin *dominārī,* to be lord and master, from *dominus,* master, lord.] **—dom·i·na·tive** *adj.* **—dom·i·na·tor** *n.*

dom·i·na·tion (dŏm′ə-nā′shən) *n.* **1.** The act of dominating or the condition of being dominated; rule; control. **2. dominations.** In medieval angelology, the fourth of the nine orders of angels. Also called "dominions." See **angel.**

dom·i·neer (dŏm′ə-nîr′) *v.* **-neered, -neering, -neers.** *—tr.* To rule over arbitrarily or arrogantly; tyrannize. *—intr.* To exercise control tyrannically. [Dutch *domineren,* from French *dominer,* from Latin *dominārī,* to DOMINATE.]

dom·i·neer·ing (dŏm′ə-nîr′ĭng) *adj.* Tending to domineer; overbearing. **—dom·i·neer·ing·ly** *adv.*

Do·min·go (dō-mǐng′gō, də-), **Placido** (1941–). Spanish tenor. He emigrated to Mexico as a child and made his debut at the Metropolitan Opera, New York, in 1968. He is one of the world's leading operatic tenors.

Dom·i·nic (dŏm′ə-nĭk), **Saint** (c. 1170–1221). Spanish churchman and founder of the Dominican order. He became prior at Osma Cathedral in Castile and backed the crusade of Simon IV de Montfort (c. 1160–1218) against the heretical Albigenses in southern France. He founded his order in 1216, and his zeal earned him a reputation as "the burner and slayer of heretics." His pursuit of them was ruthlessly followed by the Dominican-dominated Spanish Inquisition.

Dom·i·ni·ca (dŏm′ə-nē′kə, də-mǐn′ĭ-kə). Island country of the West Indies. The largest of the Windward Islands, it was discovered by Columbus, who named it after the day of its discovery, *Dies Dominica,* Sunday, November 3, 1493. After alternating between British and French rule, it became British in 1783. In 1978 it became an independent Commonwealth republic. Following devastating hurricanes in 1979 and 1980, government development of tourism and light industry is taking place to reduce dependence on the export of bananas. Area, 751 square kilometers (290 square miles). Population, 75,000. Capital, Roseau. See map at **Latin America.**

do·min·i·cal (də-mǐn′ĭ-kəl) *adj.* **1.** Of or associated with the Lord (Christ). **2.** Pertaining to Sunday as the Lord's day. [Medieval Latin *dominicālis,* from Latin *dominicus,* of a lord, from *dominus,* lord.]

dominical letter *n.* One of the first seven letters of the alphabet applied to Sundays in order to determine the ecclesiastical calendar for a given year, the letter being the one that corresponds with the first Sunday in January when the first seven days of the month are lettered in order; for example, if the first Sunday is January 2, *B* will be the dominical letter for the year.

Do·min·i·can (də-mǐn′ĭ-kən) *adj.* **1.** *Abbr.* **Dom.** Of, pertaining to, or designating the order of preaching friars established in 1216 by St. Dominic. **2.** Of or pertaining to the Dominican Republic. **3.** Of or pertaining to Dominica. *—n.* **1.** *Abbr.* **Dom.** A friar of the order of Saint Dominic. **2.** A native or inhabitant of the Dominican Republic. **3.** A native or inhabitant of Dominica.

Do·min·i·can Republic (də-mǐn′ĭ-kən). Mountainous country on

DOMINICAN REPUBLIC

the eastern section of the West Indian island of Hispaniola, discovered by Columbus in 1492. The present republic was established in 1844. This has been prone to economic and political instability and civil strife, and U.S. forces have intervened twice (1916–24, 1965–66). The dictator General Rafael Trujillo came to power in 1930. He was assassinated (1961) and succeeded by Joaquin Balaguer. A year later the leftist Juan Bosch was elected president—only to be deposed by a military coup (1963). A leftist revolt was put down with U.S. help in 1965. Sugar is the main industry and supplies 33 percent of the country's exports. However, after hurricane damage in 1979, tourism and mining are being developed rapidly. Gold, silver, and bauxite are also exported. Area, 48,734 square kilometers (18,811 square miles). Population, 5,400,000. Capital, Santo Domingo.

dom·i·nie (dŏm'ə-nē', dō'mə-) *n.* **1.** *Chiefly Scottish.* A schoolmaster. **2.** A clergyman of the Dutch Reformed Church. **3.** *Informal.* Any minister. [From obsolete *domine,* form of address to ministers and schoolmasters, from Latin *dominē,* vocative of *dominus,* lord, master.]

do·min·ion (də-mĭn'yən) *n.* **1.** Control or the exercise of control; rule; sovereignty. **2.** A territory or sphere of influence or control; realm; domain. **3.** *Often* **Dominion.** A term formerly applied to any of the larger self-governing nations within the British Commonwealth, such as Canada or Australia. **4.** *Law.* Dominium. **5.** **dominions.** An order of angels, dominations. [Middle English *dominioun,* from Old French *dominion,* from Medieval Latin *dominiō* (stem *dominiōn-*), from Latin *dominium,* property, ownership rights, lordship, from *dominus,* lord, master.]

Dominion Day *n.* July 1, a national holiday in Canada, the anniversary of the Dominion's formation in 1867.

do·min·i·um (də-mĭn'ē-əm) *n. Law.* Ownership of property, especially of land, and the right to its disposition. Also called "dominion." [Latin, property, DOMINION.]

---

dome

THE DOME, ARCHITECTURE'S CROWNING GLORY
How Roman builders enclosed space and height

A dome is a rounded roof, hemispherical in shape or nearly so, that adds lofty grandeur and spaciousness to the interior of a building. Its base may be a circle, an ellipse, or a polygon. It was developed by Roman builders from the barrel vault, a tunnel formed by extending an arch. Stout walls and flying buttresses were used to support the great weight of the Roman domes. One outstanding example remains, surmounting the Pantheon, Rome's only building to survive from the time of the empire with its main structure intact. The stepped dome, 43 meters (142 feet) across and more than 22 meters (71 feet) high, has a substructure built with relieving arches to distribute the massive weight. The Emperor Hadrian had the elaborate brick Pantheon with its concrete dome built (A.D. 120–124) as a temple.

It was the Byzantines who found the secret of raising a dome without huge supporting walls. In Constantinople, now Istanbul, the dome of Santa Sophia (completed in 557) is on four pendentives (below right). These are built like a dome with the top cut off, leaving a circular base on which to build the dome itself.

Filippo Brunelleschi's pointed dome on Florence Cathedral, built 1420–46, takes the dome to its culmination. It rests on an octagonal drum, on which the buttresses are only small. Reinforcing the bottom of the dome, at its spread point, is a timber and chain link hoop.

FLORENCE CATHEDRAL *Brunelleschi's triumphant octagonal dome, rising above a masonry drum and culminating in a graceful cupola, towers over the city. It is a lasting monument to the brilliance of Renaissance builders.*

THE PANTHEON *The dome of the Pantheon in Rome climbs to an oculus, or opening, 8 meters (27 feet) across, which throws light onto the Corinthian columns and marble-veneered walls. The interior is not the original; it was renewed in 1747.*

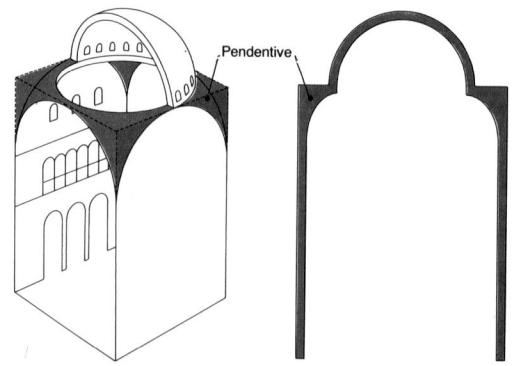

SANTA SOPHIA *At the church of Santa Sophia, now a mosque, Byzantine builders raised the spectacular dome on four pendentives. These are borne on four colossal corner pillars and constructed like a dome but with the topmost part missing, leaving a circular base on which to build the dome itself. The brick dome is 32 meters (107 feet) in diameter. It is shallower than a hemisphere and built with 40 ribs with 40 windows between them. Inside the mosque, the light pouring through this ring of windows creates the uncanny illusion that the dome is floating on air. Two huge arches between the pendentives increase the feeling of height and space.*

dom·i·no[1] (dŏm'ə-nō') *n., pl.* **-noes** or **-nos. 1. a.** A hooded robe worn with an eye mask at a masquerade. **b.** The mask itself, worn with such a robe. **2.** A person wearing such a robe or mask. [French, probably from Latin *dominus,* lord, but the reason for the name is unknown.]

domino[2] *n., pl.* **-noes. 1.** A small, rectangular block, the face of which is divided into halves, used in games of dominoes. Each half is marked by one to six dots or is blank. **2. dominoes.** *Used with a singular verb.* Any of several games played with a set of usually 28 dominoes. [French, obscurely from DOMINO (hooded robe).]

Dom·i·no (dŏm'ə-nō'), **Fats,** born Antoine Domino (1928–). U.S. singer, pianist, and songwriter. His songs, popular especially in the 1950's, include *Ain't That A Shame, I'm In Love Again,* and *Blue Monday.*

domino effect *n.* A cumulative effect produced when one event sets off a chain of similar events.

domino theory *n.* A theory that one event, if allowed to happen, will inevitably lead to a succession of similar events, as a row of upright dominoes will fall if the first one is knocked down; especially, the theory that if one vulnerable nation, as in Southeast Asia, were to come under Communist domination, the neighboring nations would naturally follow.

Do·mi·nus (dō'mĭ-no͝os', dŏm'ə-nəs) *n. Abbr.* **D.** *Latin.* The Lord. Used with reference to God or Christ.

Do·mi·tian (də-mĭsh'ən), full name **Titus Flavius Domitianus Augustus** (A.D. 51–96). Roman emperor. He succeeded his brother Titus in 81 and completed the conquest of Britain. After 89 his government became dictatorial, and with the senate firmly in his control, he instigated a reign of terror. He was murdered in his bedchamber by a freedman with the connivance of his wife.

don[1] (dŏn) *n.* **1. Don.** *Abbr.* **D.** Sir. A title formerly placed before the Christian name of a Spaniard of high rank, now used generally as a courtesy title. **2.** A Spanish gentleman. **3.** *British.* **a.** A head, tutor, or fellow of a college at Oxford or Cambridge. **b.** Any university lecturer. [Spanish, from Latin *dominus,* lord, master.]

don[2] *tr.v.* **donned, donning, dons.** To put on; dress in. [Contraction of *do on.*]

Don (dŏn). River in the southwest U.S.S.R. It flows 1,930 kilometers (1,224 miles) south to the Sea of Azov.

do·ña (dō'nyä) *n.* **1.** A Spanish gentlewoman. **2. Doña.** A title of courtesy placed before a woman's Christian name in Spanish-speaking countries. [Spanish, "lady," from Latin *domina.* See **dame.**]

do·nate (dō'nāt', dō-nāt') *tr.v.* **-nated, -nating, -nates.** To present as a gift, especially to a fund or cause; contribute. [Back-formation from DONATION.] **—do·na·tor** *n.*

Do·na·tel·lo (dŏn'ə-tĕl'ō), born Donato di Niccolò di Betto Bardi (1386–1466). Florentine sculptor who was a pioneer of the Renaissance style, breaking all traditions with his natural, lifelike figures, such as the marble sculptures of *St. Mark* and *St. George.* Michelangelo is reputed to have been so impressed with *St. Mark* that he asked the statue why it did not speak to him.

do·na·tion (dō-nā'shən) *n.* **1.** The act of making a gift, especially to a fund or cause. **2.** A gift or grant; contribution. [Middle English *donacioun,* from Old French, from Latin *dōnātiō* (stem *dōnātiōn-*), from *dōnātus,* past participle of *dōnāre,* to give, from *dōnum,* gift.]

Do·na·tist (dŏn'ə-tĭst, dō'nə-) *n.* A member of a schismatic Christian sect that arose in North Africa in the 4th century A.D. [Medieval Latin *Dōnātista,* from *Dōnātus,* probably the bishop of Carthage in the fourth century.] **—Do·na·tism** *n.* **—Do·na·tist** *adj.*

do·na·tive (dō'nə-tĭv, dŏn'ə-) *n.* **1.** A gift or donation. **2.** A benefice that can be bestowed by its founder or patron without reference to the diocesan authorities.
~adj. Constituting such a benefice. [Latin *dōnātīvum,* neuter of *dōnātīvus,* of a donation, from *dōnātus.* See **donation.**]

Donau. See **Danube.**

Don·bas (dŏn'bäs). Also **Do·nets Basin** (də-nĕts'). Major industrial region of the U.S.S.R. in the lower Dnieper, Donets, and Don valleys, eastern Ukraine. It produces more than a third of the nation's coal and has extensive chemical industries based on local salt deposits. Donetsk and Rostov are the main centers.

done (dŭn). Past participle of **do.**
~adj. **1.** Finished. **2.** Cooked adequately. **3.** Socially acceptable: *not done in polite society.* **—done for. 1.** Doomed. **2.** Dead or dying. **3.** Exhausted.
~interj. Used to express agreement when concluding a deal.

do·nee (dō-nē') *n.* **1.** A recipient of a gift. **2.** *Medicine.* The recipient of an organ transplanted from a donor. [DON(OR) + -EE.]

Don·e·gal (dŏn'ĭ-gôl', dŭn'-). Mountainous county on the northwest Atlantic coast of the Republic of Ireland. Its chief occupations are sheep and cattle rearing and potato farming. Donegal tweed and linen are also produced. Its county town is Lifford.

do·ner kebab (dō'nər) *n.* A kebab made from meat, mostly mutton, sliced from a large compressed loaf that turns on an upright spit.

Do·nets (də-nĕts'). River, *c.* 1,045 kilometers (650 miles) long, of the U.S.S.R., mainly in the Ukraine. It flows generally southeast to join the lower Don River near Rostov.

Do·netsk (də-nĕtsk'). Industrial city in southeast Ukraine, U.S.S.R., founded in the 1870's.

dong (dŏng) *n.* Symbol **D 1.** The basic monetary unit of Vietnam, equal to 100 sau. **2.** A coin or note worth one dong. See feature at **currency.** [Vietnamese.]

Dö·nitz or **Doe·nitz** (dœ'nĭts), **Karl** (1891–1981). German admiral. He developed the highly effective "pack" system of U-boat attacks in World War II. In 1943 he became grand admiral and commander in chief of the navy. Hitler nominated Dönitz as his successor, and he was briefly chancellor on Hitler's death. At the Nuremberg trials in 1946 he was sentenced to 10 years' imprisonment.

Do·ni·zet·ti (dŏn'ə-zĕt'ē), **Gaetano** (1797–1848). Italian composer of some 75 operas. His best-known work is *Lucia di Lammermoor* (1835).

don·jon (dŏn'jən, dŭn'-) *n.* The fortified main tower of a castle; a keep. Also called "dungeon." [Variant of DUNGEON.]

Don Ju·an (dŏn' wän') *n.* **1.** A man obsessed with seducing women. **2.** A libertine; profligate. [After *Don Juan,* legendary Spanish nobleman and libertine.]

don·key (dŏng'kē, dŭng'-, dông'-) *n., pl.* **-keys. 1.** The domesticated ass, probably descended from the wild ass *Equus asinus.* **2.** An obstinate, sluggish, or stupid person. [Perhaps from DUN (dark) + diminutive suffix *-ey* (influenced by MONKEY).]

donkey engine *n.* A small auxiliary steam engine used for hoisting or pumping, especially aboard ship.

donkey jacket *n.* A workman's thick jacket, usually with a piece of plastic or leather over each shoulder. [Alluding to the donkey as an animal associated with drudgery.]

donkey's years *n. British Informal.* A very long time. [Perhaps alteration of *donkey's ears,* hence, very long.]

don·key·work (dŏng'kē-wûrk', dŭng'-, dông'-) *n.* **1.** The laborious, uninteresting part of an operation. **2.** Monotonous work; drudgery.

Don·lea·vy (dŏn-lē'vē), **James Patrick** (1926–). Irish-American novelist. Born in New York City, he later settled in Ireland. *The Ginger Man* (1955) won acclaim for his comic and irreverent style. Other works include *The Beastly Beatitudes of Balthazar B* (1968).

don·na (dŏn'ə; *Italian* dôn'nä) *n.* **1.** An Italian gentlewoman or lady. **2. Donna.** A title of courtesy placed before a woman's Christian name in Italian-speaking countries. [Italian, "lady," from Latin *domina.* See **dame.**]

Donne (dŭn), **John** (*c.* 1572–1631). English poet and divine, one of the great metaphysical poets. In 1601 he married a 16-year-old girl without her father's consent and was briefly imprisoned. He joined the Anglican Church and took holy orders (1615), becoming chaplain to King James before being appointed dean of St. Paul's (1621). Among his poems are *The Ecstasie, Hymn to God the Father,* and *La Corona.*

don·nish (dŏn'ĭsh) *adj.* Resembling or characteristic of a university don; bookish; pedantically erudite.

don·ny·brook (dŏn'ē-bro͝ok') *n.* A brawl or uproar; a free-for-all. [After *Donnybrook* fair, held yearly at *Donnybrook,* near Dublin, at which such uproars were common.]

do·nor (dō'nər) *n.* **1.** One who contributes something, such as money to a cause or fund. **2. a.** One who donates blood, tissue, or an organ for use in a transfusion or transplant. **b.** One that provides semen for artificial insemination. **3.** *Chemistry.* The atom in a coordinate bond that supplies both electrons. Compare **acceptor. 4.** *Physics.* An impurity atom added to a semiconductor to increase the n-type conductivity. Compare **acceptor.** [Middle English, from Anglo-French *donour,* from Old French *doneur,* from Latin *dōnātor,* from *dōnātus.* See **donation.**]

do-no·thing (do͞o'nŭth'ĭng) *adj.* Offering no initiative for change, especially in politics.
~n. A person who is idle or lazy. **—do-no·thing·ism** *n.*

Don Qui·xo·te (dŏn'kē-hō'tē, kwĭk'sət) *n.* An impractical idealist bent on righting incorrigible wrongs. [After *Don Quixote,* hero of a satirical chivalric romance by Cervantes, published 1605–15.]

don't (dōnt). Contraction of *do not.* —See Usage note at **do.**

don't know *n.* One who has not yet arrived at a definite viewpoint, as in replying to an opinion poll, questionnaire, or the like.

donut. Variant of **doughnut.**

doo·dad (do͞o'dăd') *n. Informal.* **1.** An unnamed gadget or trinket. **2.** Any article whose name one has forgotten or does not know. [20th century : origin obscure.]

doo·dle (do͞od'l) *v.* **-dled, -dling, -dles.** *Informal.* *—intr.* To scribble mechanically or absent-mindedly. *—tr.* To draw (figures) while preoccupied.
~n. Informal. A figure, design, or scribble drawn or written absent-mindedly. [17th century (originally, simpleton) : perhaps from Low German; current sense perhaps related to dialect *doodle*†, to fritter away time.]

doo·dle·bug (do͞od'l-bŭg') *n.* **1. a.** An insect, the **ant lion** *(see),* in its larval stage. **b.** Loosely, any of various other similar insect larvae. **3.** A divining rod. **3.** A small vehicle. [Perhaps English dialect *doodle,* to waste time (see **doodle**) + BUG.]

doo·hick·ey (do͞o'hĭk'ē) *n., pl.* **-eys.** *Informal.* A doodad. [Perhaps DOO(DAD) + HICKEY.]

Doo·lit·tle (do͞o'lĭt'əl), **Hilda,** pen name "H.D." (1886–1961). U.S. poet, who lived in Europe after 1911. Friendships with Ezra Pound, Marianne Moore, and William Carlos Williams launched her career as an imagist poet.

Doolittle, James Harold, known as "Jimmy" (1896–). U.S. army officer and aviator. He first became involved in the development of military aviation in World War I and later set many speed records resulting from his work on technological improvements in aircraft and design. In World War II he led a daring bombing raid on Tokyo and other Japanese cities (1942).

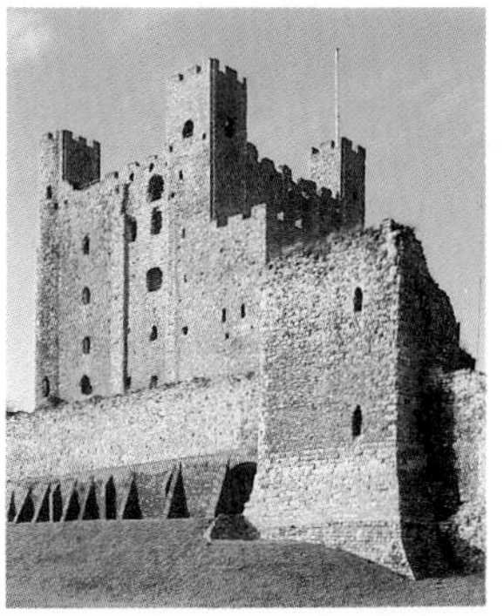

donjon *The principal tower, or donjon, of Rochester Castle in Kent, England. The castle was built in 1130.*

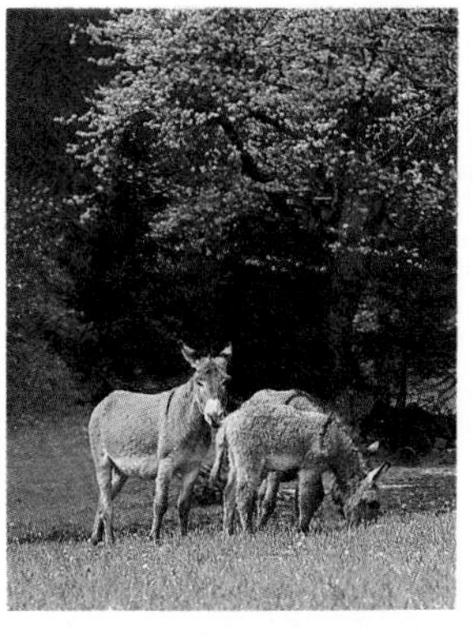

donkey *The donkey is descended from the African wild ass, which man domesticated more than 5,000 years ago as the first pack animal. Sure-footed and hardy, it can walk for long periods in hot and difficult conditions with a minimum of food and water.*

PRONUNCIATION KEY

ă, pat; ā, pay; âr, care; ä, father, are; b, bib; ch, church; d, deed; ĕ, pet; ē, be; f, fife; g, gag; h, hat; hw, which; ĭ, pit; ī, pie; îr, pier; j, judge; k, kick; l, lid, needle; m, mum; n, no, sudden; ng, thing; ŏ, pot; ō, toe; ô, paw, for; oi, noise; ou, out; o͝o, book; o͞o, boot; p, pop; r, roar; s, sauce; sh, ship, dish; t, tight; th, thin, path; *th,* this, bathe; ŭ, cut; ûr, fur; v, valve; w, with; y, yes; z, zebra, size; zh, vision; ə, about, item, edible, gallop, circus, peaceful

IN FOREIGN WORDS:

à, *Fr.* ami; œ, *Fr.* feu, *Ger.* schön; ü, *Fr.* tu, *Ger.* über; KH, *Ger.* ich, *Scot.* loch; N, *Fr.* bon; y', *Fr.* Compiègne

STRESS MARKS:

Primary stress: '
in·cite' (ĭn-sīt')
Secondary stress: '
in'sight' (ĭn'sīt')

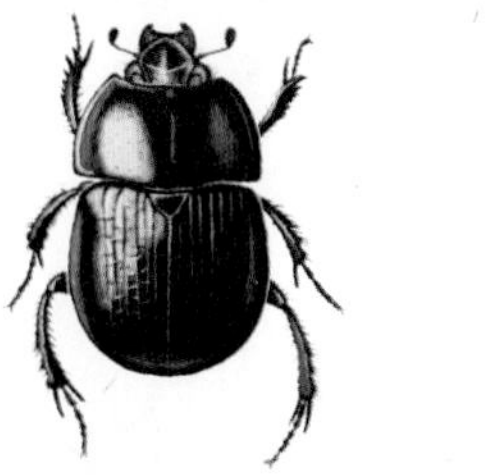

dorbeetle *A ground-living beetle that buries manure in holes beneath a patch of dung, as food for its larvae, and thus disperses the manure into the soil. The common dor (above) is one of a worldwide group of insects known as dung beetles.*

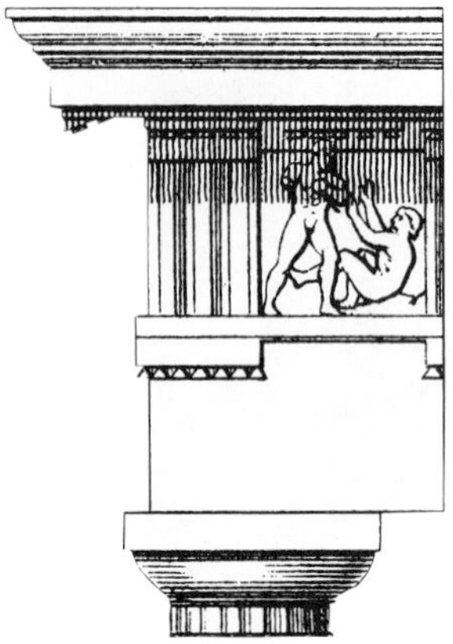

Doric order *The design of the Greek Doric order has its origins in early timber buildings. The grooved panels in the frieze (triglyphs) resemble in stylized form the ends of wooden roof beams.*

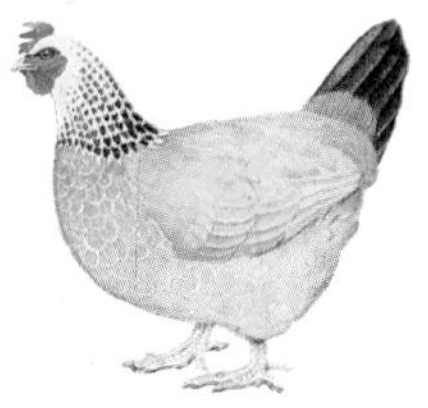

Dorking chicken *Unlike most birds, which have four toes, the Dorking chicken has five. Dorkings are good table birds, and young roosters can weigh up to about 6.4 kilograms (14 pounds).*

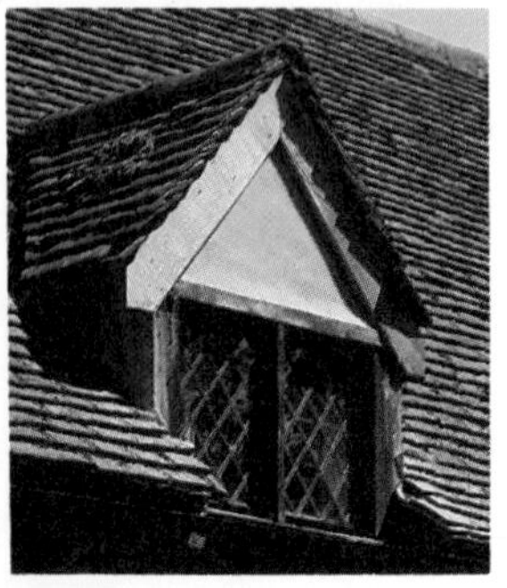

dormer *A dormer window projecting from a roof at Lavenham, Suffolk, in England.*

doom (do͞om) *n.* **1.** A predestined end in ruin or tragedy; a terrible fate. **2.** Disaster; ruin; extinction. **3.** The Last Judgment. **4.** *Archaic.* Condemnation to a severe penalty.
~*tr.v.* **doomed, dooming, dooms.** To condemn or destine to ruination or death. [Middle English *doom,* Old English *dōm.*]

doom palm. Variant of **doum palm.**

dooms·day (do͞omz′dā′) *n.* Also **domes·day** (do͞omz′dā′, dōmz′-). **1.** The day of the Last Judgment. **2.** Any dreaded day of judgment or reckoning. [Middle English *domesday,* Old English *dōmes dæg* : *dōmes,* genitive of *dōm,* DOOM + *dæg,* DAY.]

Doomsday Book. Variant of **Domesday Book.**

doom·watch (do͞om′wŏch′) *n.* A state of watching for and warning of impending disaster; especially, vigilance to protect the environment from possible destruction. **—doom·watch·er** *n.*

door (dôr, dōr) *n.* **1.** Any movable structure used to close off the entrance to a room, building, vehicle, cupboard, or the like, typically consisting of a panel of wood, glass, or metal that swings on hinges. **2.** The entranceway to a room, building, or passage. **3.** Any means of approach or access. **4.** The room or building to which a door belongs: *three doors down the hall.* **—at one's door** (or **doorstep**). Within one's sphere of responsibility: *They laid the blame at our door.* [Middle English *dor,* Old English *dor, duru,* gate, door.]

door·bell (dôr′bĕl′, dōr′-) *n.* A buzzer or bell outside a door, used as a signal for admission.

door·jamb (dôr′jăm′, dōr′-) *n.* Either of the two vertical pieces framing a doorway and supporting the lintel. Also called "doorpost."

door·keep·er (dôr′kē′pər, dōr′-) *n.* **1.** A person employed to guard an entrance or gateway. **2.** *Roman Catholic Church.* One of the **minor orders** *(see).*

door·knob (dôr′nŏb′, dōr′-) *n.* A knob-shaped handle for opening and closing a door.

door·man (dôr′măn′, -mən, dōr′-) *n., pl.* **-men** (-mĕn′, -mĭn). A man employed to stand watch at the entrance of a hotel, apartment house, or other large building.

door·mat (dôr′măt′, dōr′-) *n.* **1.** A mat placed before a doorway for wiping the shoes. **2.** *Informal.* A person who unprotestingly allows himself to be mistreated by others.

door·nail (dôr′nāl′, dōr′-) *n.* A large-headed nail formerly used as a stud on doors. **—dead as a doornail.** Undoubtedly dead.

door prize *n.* A prize awarded by lottery to the holder of a ticket purchased at or before a function.

door·sill (dôr′sĭl′, dōr′-) *n.* The threshold of a doorway.

door·step (dôr′stĕp′, dōr′-) *n.* A step leading to a door.

door·stop (dôr′stŏp′, dōr′-) *n.* **1.** A wedge inserted beneath a door to hold it open at a desired position. **2.** A weight or spring that prevents a door from slamming. **3.** A rubber-tipped projection attached to a wall to protect it from the impact of an opening door.

door-to-door (dôr′tə-dôr′, dōr′tə-dōr′) *adj.* **1.** Calling at every dwelling in a particular area. **2.** Moving directly from one place to another, especially from a place of collection or purchase to a specific address for delivery. **—door-to-door** *adv.*

door·way (dôr′wā′, dōr′-) *n.* The entrance to a room or building.

door·yard (dôr′yärd′, dōr′-) *n.* A yard in front of the door of a house.

do·pa (dō′pə) *n.* An intermediate compound in the synthesis of catecholamines from the amino acid tyrosine. It is needed for certain brain functions and the form L-dopa is used to treat Parkinson's disease. [From German, from *dioxyphenylalanine.*]

do·pa·mine (dō′pə-mēn′) *n.* A catecholamine that is an intermediate in the synthesis of noradrenalin and possibly acts as a neurotransmitter. [DOPA + AMINE.]

dop·ant (dō′pənt) *n.* A small quantity of a substance, such as phosphorus, added to another substance, such as a semiconductor, to alter the latter's properties. [DOP(E) + -ANT.]

dope (dōp) *n.* **1.** Any viscid substance or liquid; especially: **a.** A lubricant, such as axle grease. **b.** An absorbent material used in manufacturing dynamite. **c.** Any of various preparations resembling varnish formerly used to protect, waterproof, and tauten the cloth surfaces of airplane wings. **2.** *Informal.* **a.** A drug, especially a narcotic. **b.** Any illegal drug, such as marijuana. **3.** *Slang.* A very stupid person. **4.** *Slang.* Factual information, especially of a confidential nature.
~*tr.v.* **doped, doping, dopes. 1.** To add or apply dope to. **2.** *Informal.* To administer a narcotic to; drug. **3.** *Electronics.* To add an impurity to (a semiconductor). **4.** *Informal.* To work out (an outcome or puzzle) by calculation and guesswork. Often used with *out.* [Dutch *doop,* sauce, from *doopen,* to dip, mix, from Middle Dutch *dōpen.*]

dope sheet *n. Slang.* A publication giving information on the horses running in the day's races.

dope·ster (dōp′stər) *n.* One who analyzes and forecasts future events, as in sports or politics.

do·pey, do·py (dō′pē) *adj.* **-ier, -iest.** *Slang.* **1.** Dazed or lethargic, as if drugged. **2.** Stupid; silly.

dop·pel·gäng·er, dop·pel·gang·er (dŏp′əl-găng′ər, dŏp′əl-gĕng′ər) *n.* **1.** A ghostly double of a living person, especially one that haunts its own fleshly counterpart. **2.** Loosely, a double of a person. [German, "double-goer."]

Dop·pler effect (dŏp′lər) *n.* An apparent change in the frequency of sound or electromagnetic waves occurring when the source and observer are in motion relative to one another, the frequency increasing when the source and observer approach one another and decreasing when they move apart. Also called "Doppler shift." See **red shift.** [After Christian *Doppler* (1803–53), Austrian physicist, who discovered the effect for sound waves.]

Doppler radar *n.* A radar system that uses the Doppler effect to measure velocity.

dor (dôr) *n.* Any of various insects that fly with a droning sound, such as a dorbeetle. [Middle English *dorre, dore,* Old English *dora,* bumblebee (probably imitative).]

Dor. Dorian; Doric.

do·ra·do (də-rä′dō) *n., pl.* **-dos.** A large marine fish, *Coryphaena hippurus.* See **dolphin.**

Do·ra·do (də-rä′dō) *n.* A constellation of the Southern Hemisphere near Reticulum and Pictor, containing a portion of the larger **Magellanic Cloud** *(see).*

dor·bee·tle (dôr′bēt′l) *n.* An Old World dung beetle, *Geotrupes stercorarius,* that flies with a droning sound.

Dor·cas society (dôr′kəs) *n.* A women's auxiliary group, often sponsored by a church, that provides clothes for the poor. [After *Dorcas,* a Christian woman of the 1st or 2nd century A.D.]

Dor·ches·ter (dôr′chĭs-tər, -chĕs′-). Market town in the south of England, the administrative center of Dorset. Thomas Hardy, born nearby, made it the model for Casterbridge in his *Wessex Tales.*

Dor·dogne (dôr-dōn′). River in southwest France. It flows 467 kilometers (290 miles) from the Auvergne Mts. to form the Gironde estuary with the Garonne River, crossing Dordogne department on the way. Its lower banks are lined with vineyards.

Do·ré (dô-rā′), **(Paul) Gustave** (1833–83). French engraver and lithographer who illustrated Dante, La Fontaine, Balzac, and scenes of London poverty. His drawings of eerie fantasy inspired a vogue for illustrated books. He illustrated Balzac's *Droll Stories,* La Fontaine's *Fables,* and Dante's *Divine Comedy.*

Do·ri·an (dôr′ē-ən, dōr′) *n. Abbr.* **Dor.** A member of a Hellenic people that invaded Greece around 1100 B.C. and remained culturally and linguistically distinct within the Greek world, especially in Sparta, Corinth, and Argos.
~*adj.* **1.** Of or pertaining to the Dorians. **2.** *Music.* Of or designating a mode represented by the white notes of the scale D to D on the piano keyboard.

Dor·ic (dôr′ĭk, dōr′-) *n. Abbr.* **Dor. 1.** One of the four main dialects of Ancient Greece spoken chiefly in the Peloponnese, in various Aegean islands, and in Magna Graecia. Compare **Aeolic, Arcado-Cyprian, Attic-Ionic. 2.** Any broad dialect of English; especially, the dialect of northeast Scotland.
~*adj. Abbr.* **Dor. 1.** Belonging to, characteristic of, or designating the Doric dialect. **2.** In the style of or designating the Doric order. **3.** Rustic. Said of a dialect. [Latin *Dōricus,* from Greek *Dōrikos,* from *Dōris,* area of Ancient Greece, the traditional home of the Dorians.]

Doric order *n.* The oldest and simplest of the three orders of classical Greek architecture, characterized by heavy, fluted columns having plain, saucer-shaped capitals, no base, and a bold, simple cornice. Compare **Corinthian order, Ionic order.**

Dor·king (dôr′kĭng) *n.* A domestic fowl of a breed having a heavy body and raised chiefly for table use. [After *Dorking,* Surrey, England, where it was bred.]

dorm (dôrm) *n. Informal.* A dormitory in a school or college.

dor·mant (dôr′mənt) *adj.* **1.** Asleep or lying as if asleep; not awake or active. **2. a.** Latent but capable of being activated. **b.** Temporarily inactive. **3.** Designating a volcano that has not erupted within recorded history but is thought not to be extinct. **4.** *Biology.* In a relatively inactive or resting condition in which some processes are slowed down or suspended. **5.** *Heraldry.* Lying in a sleeping position, with head on paws: *a lion dormant.* —See Synonyms at **inactive, latent.** [Middle English *dormaunt,* from Old French *dormant,* from the present participle of *dormir,* to sleep, from Latin *dormīre.*] **—dor·man·cy** *n.*

dor·mer (dôr′mər) *n.* **1.** A window set vertically in a small gable projecting from a sloping roof. Also called "dormer window." **2.** The gable holding such a window. [Old French *dormeor,* "bedroom window," from *dormir,* to sleep. See **dormant.**]

dor·mi·to·ry (dôr′mə-tôr′ē, -tōr′ē) *n., pl.* **-ries. 1.** A room providing sleeping quarters for a number of persons. **2.** A hall of residence in a college or university. **3.** A suburb or small town, many of whose inhabitants commute to work in a nearby urban center. Also used adjectivally: *a dormitory town.* [Latin *dormītōrium,* from *dormītōrius,* of sleep, from *dormītus,* past participle of *dormīre,* to sleep.]

dor·mouse (dôr′mous′) *n., pl.* **-mice** (-mīs′). **Any of various small Old World rodents of the family Gliridae, especially** *Glis glis,* of Europe and Asia Minor. [Middle English *dormowse*†.]

dor·my, dor·mie (dôr′mē) *adj. Golf.* Ahead of an opponent by as many holes as remain to be played. [19th century : origin obscure.]

dor·nick[1] (dôr′nĭk) *n.* A coarse damask cloth. [Middle English *dornewick,* first manufactured in *Doornik* (French *Tournai*), city in Belgium.]

dornick[2] *n. Regional.* A small chunk of rock; a stone. [Origin obscure.]

dorp (dôrp) *n. South African.* A small township; village. [Dutch; akin to THORP.]

Dorpat. See **Tartu.**

dor·sad (dôr′săd′) *adv. Anatomy.* In the direction of the back. [DORS(O)- + -AD (toward).]

dor·sal (dôr′səl) *adj.* **1.** *Anatomy.* Of, toward, on, in, or near the back. **2.** *Botany.* Of or on the surface of an organ directed away from the main axis. [Late Latin *dorsālis,* from Latin *dorsuālis,* from *dorsum,* back.] **—dor·sal·ly** *adv.*

dorsal fin *n.* The main unpaired fin on the dorsal surface of fishes or certain marine mammals.

Dor·set (dôr′sĭt). Also **Dor·set·shire** (-shîr′, -shər). A county in southwest England. Agriculture is the main occupation, with sheep rearing on the downs and dairy cattle and crops in the lowlands. Tourism flourishes on the coast. Thomas Hardy portrayed the area in his *Wessex Tales.* Its administrative center is Dorchester.

Dorset Down *n.* A domestic sheep of a hornless breed with a brown face and legs, and fine-textured wool.

Dorset Horn *n.* A domestic sheep of a breed having large horns and fine-textured wool.

dor·si·ven·tral (dôr′sĭ-vĕn′trəl) *adj.* **1.** Having distinct upper and lower surfaces, as most leaves do. **2.** Dorsoventral.

dorso–, dorsi–, dors– *prefix.* Indicates the dorsal area; for example, **dorsoventral, dorsiventral, dorsad.** [Latin *dorsum,* back.]

dor·so·ven·tral (dôr′sō-vĕn′trəl) *adj.* Extending from a dorsal to a ventral surface. [DORSO- + VENTRAL.]

dor·sum (dôr′səm) *n., pl.* **-sa** (-sə). *Anatomy.* **1.** The back. **2.** Any part of an organ analogous to the back: *the dorsum of the hand.* [Latin, back.]

Dort·mund (dôrt′mənd). Industrial city and port at the end of the Dortmund-Ems Canal, in the Ruhr, West Germany. Other canals connect it to the Weser and Elbe rivers. Dortmund became part of the Hanseatic League in the 13th century and was ceded to Prussia in 1815.

Dort·mund-Ems Canal (dôrt′mənd-ĕmz′). An important industrial waterway in West Germany. It is some 270 kilometers (168 miles) long and links the Ruhr with the Ems River and the North Sea.

dor·ty (dôr′tē) *adj.* **-tier, -tiest.** *Scottish.* Sullen; bad-tempered. [From Scottish *dort,* sullenness.]

do·ry[1] (dôr′ē, dōr′ē) *n., pl.* **-ries.** A small, narrow, flat-bottomed fishing boat with high sides and a sharp prow. [18th century : origin obscure.]

dory[2] *n., pl.* **-ries.** **1.** Any of various marine fishes of the family Zeidae; especially, the **John Dory** *(see).* **2.** A fish, the **walleye** *(see).* [Middle English *dorre,* from Old French *doree,* gilded (from its metallic shine), from the feminine past participle of *dorer,* to gild, from Late Latin *dēaurāre* : Latin *dē-,* thoroughly + *aurum,* gold.]

dos-à-dos (dō-zä-dō′) *n., pl.* **dos-à-dos** (-dōz′; *French* -dō′). Also **do-si-do** (dō′sē-dō′) (for sense 2), *pl.* **-dos.** **1.** A sofa or carriage that accommodates two people seated back to back. **2. a.** A movement in square dancing in which two dancers approach each other and circle back to back, then return to their original positions. **b.** The call given for such a movement.
~adj. Bound together back to back with one central board. Said of two books. [French, "back to back."]

dos·age (dō′sĭj) *n.* **1.** The administration of a therapeutic agent in prescribed amounts. **2.** The amount administered. **3.** A dose of ionizing radiation. **4.** A dose added to wine.

dose (dōs) *n.* **1.** *Abbr.* **d., D.** A prescribed quantity of a therapeutic agent prescribed to be taken at one time or at stated intervals. **2.** *Informal.* An amount, especially of something unpleasant, to which one is subjected: *You need a dose of hard work.* **3.** An ingredient added to wine to impart flavor or strength. Also called "dosage." **4.** *Physics.* The energy imparted to a unit mass of matter by ionizing radiation. Also called "absorbed dose." **5.** The recommended upper limit of absorbed dose that a person should receive in a particular period. Also called "maximum permissible dose." **6.** *Slang.* A venereal infection.
~tr.v. **dosed, dosing, doses.** **1.** To give (someone) a dose, as of medicine. **2.** To give or prescribe (medicine) in doses. **3.** To treat (wine) with an ingredient, such as syrup, during bottling. [French, from Late Latin *dosis,* from Greek, a giving, dose, from *didonai,* to give.] **—dos·er** *n.*

do·sim·e·ter (dō-sĭm′ə-tər) *n.* A device that measures and indicates the amount of x-rays or other radiation absorbed by matter, or the intensity of a radioactive source. [DOS(E) + -METER.]

do·sim·e·try (dō-sĭm′ə-trē) *n. Medicine.* The accurate measurement of doses, especially of radiation for cancer treatment. [DOS(E) + -METRY.]

Dos Pas·sos (dəs păs′əs), **John Roderigo** (1896–1970). U.S. novelist. His writing combines narrative, stream-of-consciousness passages, and newspaper quotations. His best-known work is the trilogy called collectively *U.S.A.* (1930–36).

doss (dŏs) *n. British Slang.* **1.** A makeshift or crude bed. **2.** A sleep.
~intr.v. **dossed, dossing, dosses.** *British Slang.* To bed down; sleep. Often used with *down.* [Variant of earlier *dorse,* from Latin *dorsum,* back.]

dos·sal, dos·sel (dŏs′əl) *n.* **1.** An ornamental hanging of rich fabric, as behind an altar or at the sides of a chancel. **2.** An ornamental covering for the back of a chair or throne. In this sense, also called "dosser." [Medieval Latin *dossāle,* neuter of *dossālis,* of the back, from Late Latin *dorsālis,* DORSAL.]

dos·ser[1] (dŏs′ər) *n.* **1.** A large pack basket; pannier. **2.** A dossal. [Middle English *doser,* from Old French *dossier,* from Medieval Latin *dorsārium,* from Latin *dorsum,* back.]

dosser[2] *n. British Slang.* **1.** A vagrant. **2.** An idle person. [From DOSS.]

dos·si·er (dŏs′ē-ā′, dôs′yā′) *n.* A collection of papers or documents pertaining to a particular person or subject; a file. [French, from Old French, bundle of papers having a label on the back, from *dos,* back, from Latin *dorsum.*]

dost. *Archaic.* Second person singular present tense of **do.** Used with *thou.*

Dos·to·yev·sky (dŏs′tə-yĕf′skē), **Fyodor Mikhailovich** (1821–81). Russian novelist, whose works combine religious mysticism with profound psychological and social insight; he is often considered a forerunner of the existentialists. In 1849 he was found guilty of revolutionary activities and sent to a penal colony in Siberia for four years. The experience produced *Notes from The House of the Dead* (1862). His four great novels are *Crime and Punishment* (1866), *The Idiot* (1868), *The Possessed* (1871–72), and *The Brothers Karamazov* (1879–80).

dot[1] (dŏt) *n.* **1. a.** A tiny round mark made by or as if by a pointed instrument; a spot; a point. **b.** Such a mark used in orthography, such as the dot above an *i.* **2.** A tiny amount; speck. **3.** In Morse and similar codes, a short sound or signal used in combination with the dash and written as a dot to represent letters, numbers, or punctuation. Compare **dit.** **4.** *Mathematics.* **a.** A decimal point. **b.** A symbol of multiplication. **5.** *Music.* **a.** A dot after a note or rest indicating an increase in time value by half. **b.** A dot above or below a note indicating that it should be played or sung staccato. **—on the dot.** *Informal.* Absolutely punctual; on time.
~v. **dotted, dotting, dots.** *—tr.* **1.** To mark with a dot or dots. **2.** To form or make with dots. **3.** To cover at intervals with or as if with dots. *—intr.* To make a dot or dots. [16th century : perhaps from Old English *dott,* head of a boil, perhaps akin to Old English *titt,* teat, TIT.] **—dot·ter** *n.* **—dot·ted** *adj.*

dot[2] (dŏt; *French* dō) *n.* A woman's marriage portion; dowry. [French, from Latin *dōs* (stem *dōt-*), dowry.] **—do·tal** (dōt′l) *adj.*

do·tage (dō′tĭj) *n.* **1. a.** Senility. **b.** Feeble-mindedness. **2.** Foolish or excessive fondness. [Middle English, from *doten,* to DOTE.]

do·tard (dō′tərd) *n.* A senile person. [Middle English, from *doten,* to DOTE.]

dote, doat (dōt) *intr.v.* **doted** or **doated, doting** or **doating, dotes** or **doats.** **1.** To lavish excessive love or fondness. Used with *on* or *upon.* **2.** To be foolish or feeble-minded, especially as a result of senility. [Middle English *doten,* from Middle Dutch, to be silly.] **—dot·er** *n.*

doth. *Archaic.* Third person singular present tense of **do.**

dot product *n. Mathematics.* The **scalar product** *(see).* [So called because it is written **x·y.**]

dot-se·quen·tial (dŏt′sĭ-kwĕn′shəl) *adj.* Pertaining to or designating a color-television system in which the primary colors red, green, and blue are transmitted as dots in sequence and exhibited in the same sequence to produce a complete color image.

dot·ted line (dŏt′əd) *n.* A line of dots, on a legal document for example, where a signature is placed to indicate formal agreement or ratification.

dotted swiss *n.* A crisp cotton fabric, embellished with woven, flocked, or embroidered dots.

dot·ter·el (dŏt′ər-əl) *n.* Also **dot·trel** (dŏt′rəl). A small Eurasian plover, *Eudromias morinellus,* having a gray breast and a chestnut-brown belly. [Middle English, dotard, plover (apparently referring to its supposed stupidity) : DOTE + suffix *-rel,* as in *wastrel.*]

dot·tle, dot·tel (dŏt′l) *n.* The plug of tobacco left in the bowl of a pipe after it has been smoked. [From DOT (in the obsolete sense "lump").]

dot·ty (dŏt′ē) *adj.* **-tier, -tiest.** *Informal.* **1.** Daft; crazy; eccentric. **2.** Infatuated. Used with *about.* [Variant of Scottish *dottle,* silly, from Middle English *doten,* to DOTE.] **—dot·ti·ness** *n.*

Dou·ai (do͞o-ā′). *Formerly* **Dou·ay.** Industrial town in Nord department, France. A college for English Catholics was established here in 1568, where the Old Testament of the **Douay Bible** *(see)* was published in 1610.

Dou·a·la, Du·a·la (do͞o-ä′lə). Chief seaport and largest town of Cameroon. It is one of West Africa's major industrial centers, with brewing, flour-milling, textile, food-processing, and timber industries.

Dou·ay Bible, Dou·ai Bible (do͞o′ā). *Abbr.* **D.Bib., D.V.** An English translation of the Latin Vulgate Bible by Roman Catholic scholars. Also called "Douay Version."

dou·ble (dŭb′əl) *adj. Abbr.* **dbl.** **1.** Of a size, strength, number, or amount that is exactly or roughly twice as great as is usual: *a double dose.* **2.** Composed of two like parts; in a pair: *double doors.* **3.** Composed of two unlike parts; combining two; dual: *a double meaning.* **4.** Accommodating or designed for two: *a double sleeping bag.* **5. a.** Acting two parts: *a double agent.* **b.** Characterized by duplicity; deceitful: *speak with a double tongue.* **6.** *Botany.* Having many more than the usual number of petals, usually in a crowded or overlapping arrangement: *a double chrysanthemum.* **7.** *Music.* Producing pitches one octave lower than the notes written on the score: *a double bass.*
~n. Abbr. **dbl.** **1.** Something increased twofold; a double quantity or amount. **2. a.** An exact likeness or copy of a thing or person. **b.** An apparition; wraith. **3.** An actor's understudy. **4. a.** A sharp turn in running, as of a hunted animal or a river; reversal. **b.** An evasive reversal or shift in argument. **5. a.** In darts, the space between the two outer rings on a dartboard. **b.** A score made from a dart that lands in this space. **6.** A bet on two horses in different races, any winnings from the first being placed on the second.

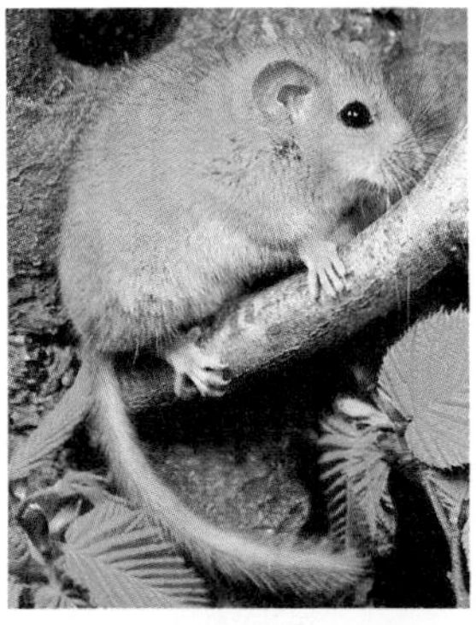

dormouse *A largely tree-dwelling European rodent that may get its name from its habit of becoming "dormant" and sleeping through the winter in a nest below ground.*

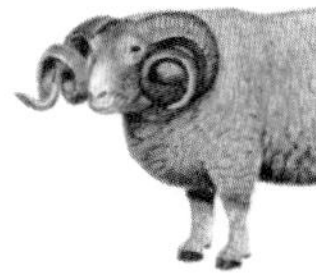

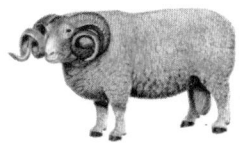

Dorset Horn *Breeding in any season, the Dorset Horn is a fast-growing sheep that can lamb three times in two years.*

PRONUNCIATION KEY

ă, pat; ā, pay; âr, care;
ä, father, are; b, bib;
ch, church; d, deed; ĕ, pet;
ē, be; f, fife; g, gag; h, hat;
hw, which; ĭ, pit; ī, pie;
îr, pier; j, judge; k, kick;
l, lid, needle; m, mum;
n, no, sudden; ng, thing;
ŏ, pot; ō, toe; ô, paw, for;
oi, noise; ou, out; o͝o, book;
o͞o, boot; p, pop; r, roar;
s, sauce; sh, ship, dish;
t, tight; th, thin, path;
th, this, bathe; ŭ, cut; ûr, fur;
v, valve; w, with; y, yes;
z, zebra, size; zh, vision;
ə, about, item, edible, gallop, circus, peaceful

IN FOREIGN WORDS:

à, *Fr.* ami; œ, *Fr.* feu, *Ger.* schön; ü, *Fr.* tu, *Ger.* über;
KH, *Ger.* ich, *Scot.* loch;
N, *Fr.* bon; y′, *Fr.* Compiègne

STRESS MARKS:

Primary stress: ′
in·cite′ (ĭn-sīt′)
Secondary stress: ′
in′sight′ (ĭn′sīt′)

7. *Bridge.* **a.** A bid indicating strength to one's partner; a request for a bid. **b.** A bid doubling one's opponent's bid, thus increasing the penalty for failure to fulfill the contract. **c.** A hand justifying such a bid. —**at** (or **on**) **the double. 1.** *Military.* In double time. **2.** *Informal.* Immediately. ~*v.* **doubled, -bling, -bles.** —*tr.* **1.** To make twice as great. **2.** To be twice as much as. **3.** To fold in two. **4.** *Bridge.* To challenge (an opponent's bid) with a double. **5.** *Music.* To duplicate (another part or voice) an octave higher or lower or in unison. **6.** *Nautical.* To sail around: *double a cape.* —*intr.* **1.** To be increased twofold. **2.** To turn sharply backward; reverse one's direction. Often used with *back: double back on one's trail.* **3.** To serve in an additional capacity: *The firefighter doubled as a carpenter in her spare time.* **4.** To replace an actor in the execution of a given action or in the actor's absence: *doubled for the star in the chase scene.* **5.** *Bridge.* To announce a double. —**double up. 1.** To bend in two: *doubled up with laughter.* **2.** To share the same living or sleeping accommodations. **3.** To cause to double up. **4.** To stake (the winnings from one horse race) on a second race. ~*adv.* **1. a.** To twice the extent; doubly. **b.** To twice the amount: *win double your money back.* **2.** Two together: *sleeping double.* **3.** In two: *bent double; fold the paper double.* —**see double.** To see two images of a single object, usually as a result of visual aberration. [Middle English, from Old French, from Latin *duplus,* twofold, double.] —**dou·ble·ness** *n.* —**dou·bler** *n.*

doub·le-act·ing (dŭb′əl-ăk′tĭng) *adj.* Designating a steam engine in which the pistons are pressurized at either end of the cylinders. Compare **single-acting.**

double agent *n.* A spy working overtly for one country or organization while secretly working for a rival country or organization.

double bar *n.* A double vertical or heavy black line drawn through a staff to indicate the end of any of the main sections of a musical composition.

dou·ble-bar·reled (dŭb′əl-băr′əld) *adj.* **1.** Having two barrels mounted side by side: *a double-barreled shotgun.* **2.** Serving two purposes; twofold; ambiguous.

double bass *n.* The largest member of the violin family, shaped like a cello, played with a bow or, especially in jazz, plucked, and having a deep range of about three octaves. Also called "bass," "bass fiddle," "contrabass," "string bass."

double bassoon *n.* The **contrabassoon** (see).

double bed *n.* A bed wide enough to accommodate two people.

double bill *n.* A bill, as at the movies or a concert, in which there are two main features.

double bind *n.* **1.** *Psychology.* A sense of impasse caused by contradictory injunctions, especially when these are uttered by the same authority. A child hearing "*You're a bad girl!*" and "*Be a good girl!*" is in a double bind, because the first statement may function subconsciously as an order. **2.** A situation that cannot be resolved; a dilemma.

double-blind (dŭb′əl-blīnd′) *adj.* Of, designating, or pertaining to an experiment in which neither the experimenter nor the subjects know, at the time of testing, which are the items or substances being tested and which are the controls. Compare **single-blind.** See **control experiment.**

double boiler *n.* A cooking utensil consisting of an upper removable pan that fits into a lower pan. Water simmering in the lower pan gently cooks the contents of the upper pan.

double bond *n.* A chemical bond that characterizes unsaturated organic molecules in which two atoms are linked by two covalent bonds.

dou·ble-breast·ed (dŭb′əl-brĕs′tĭd) *adj.* **1.** Fastened by lapping one half over the other, and usually having a double row of buttons with a single row of buttonholes: *a double-breasted jacket.* **2.** Having a jacket of this type: *a double-breasted suit.*

double check *n.* A careful reinspection or re-examination to ensure accuracy or efficiency; verification.

dou·ble-check (dŭb′əl-chĕk′) *v.* **-checked, -checking, -checks.** —*tr.* To inspect or examine again; verify. —*intr.* To make a double check.

double chin *n.* A fold of fatty flesh beneath the chin.

dou·ble-coat·ed (dŭb′əl-kō′tĭd) *adj.* Designating a mammal such as a rat or dog having two layers of hair, one longer than the other, which may give a two-tone color effect.

double coconut *n.* **1.** A tall palm tree, *Lodoicea maldivica* (or *L. seychellarum*), of the Seychelles Islands, having broad, fanlike foliage and large fruit. **2.** The two-lobed fruit of this tree, containing one enormous seed, the largest of any plant, sometimes weighing 22 kilograms (48 pounds) each. Also called "coco-de-mer."

double concerto *n. Music.* A concerto composed for two solo instruments.

double cream *n.* Thick cream with a high fat content.

dou·ble-cross (dŭb′əl-krôs′, -krŏs′) *tr.v.* **-crossed, -crossing, -crosses.** To deceive or betray by acting in contradiction to an agreed course of action. —See Synonyms at **deceive.** ~*n.* An instance of such betrayal; treachery. —**dou·ble-cross·er** *n.* —**dou·ble-cross·ing** *adj.*

double dagger *n.* In writing and printing, a reference mark (‡). Also called "dagger," "diesis."

double date *n.* A date in which two couples participate. —**dou·ble-date** *v.*

Dou·ble·day (dŭb′əl-dā′), **Abner** (1819–93). U.S. army officer and reputed inventor of baseball. As a young man in Cooperstown, New York, he was known as a team sports organizer, and in the late 1800's he was presumed to be the originator of baseball, although later investigations indicate that a game very similar to baseball predates him. A West Point graduate (1842), he had a distinguished military career, which included commanding a division at Gettysburg.

dou·ble-deal·ing (dŭb′əl-dē′lĭng) *adj.* Characterized by duplicity; deceitful; treacherous. ~*n.* An act of treachery or duplicity. —**dou·ble-deal·er** *n.*

dou·ble-deck·er (dŭb′əl-dĕk′ər) *n.* **1.** A bus with two decks or tiers for passengers. **2.** *Informal.* A sandwich having three slices of bread and two layers of filling.

double decomposition *n.* A chemical reaction between two compounds in which the first and second parts of one reactant are united, respectively, with the second and first parts of the other reactant. Also called "metathesis."

dou·ble-dig·it (dŭb′əl-dĭj′ĭt) *adj.* Relating to percentage rates between 10 and 99 percent: *double-digit inflation.*

dou·ble-dot·ted (dŭb′əl-dŏt′ĭd) *adj. Music.* Having two dots added so as to increase the time value by three quarters. Said of a note.

double dribble *n. Basketball.* An illegal dribble in which a player uses both hands simultaneously to dribble the ball or begins to dribble the ball a second time after having come to a complete stop.

double Dutch *n. Sometimes* **double dutch.** Language that cannot be understood; gibberish.

dou·ble-edged (dŭb′əl-ĕjd′) *adj.* **1.** Having two cutting edges: *a double-edged sword.* **2.** Capable of being effective or interpreted in two ways: *double-edged praise.*

dou·ble en·ten·dre (dŭb′əl än-tän′drə; *French* dōō-blän-tän′dr′) *n.* **1.** A word or phrase having a double meaning, especially when the second meaning is risqué. **2.** The use of such expressions. [From obsolete French, "double meaning."]

double entry *n.* A method of bookkeeping in which a transaction is entered both as a debit to one account and a credit to another account, so that the totals of debits and credits are equal. Compare **single entry.**

dou·ble-faced (dŭb′əl-fāst′) *adj.* **1.** Having two faces, aspects, or sides. **2.** Characterized by duplicity; hypocritical. **3.** Finished on both sides. Said of fabric.

double fault *n.* In tennis, the serving of two faults in succession, resulting in the loss of a point.

double feature *n.* A motion-picture program consisting of two full-length films.

double glazing *n.* Glazing consisting of two panes of glass separated by an air space, used to provide protection against heat loss and noise. —**dou·ble-glaze** *v.*

Double Gloucester *n.* A type of mild, orange-colored cheese.

dou·ble-head·er (dŭb′əl-hĕd′ər) *n.* **1.** Two games or events held in succession on the same program, especially in baseball. **2.** A train pulled by two locomotives.

double helix *n. Biochemistry.* The structure of a DNA molecule, consisting of two spiral chains of polynucleotides coiled around the same axis.

double indemnity *n.* A clause in an insurance policy that provides for payment of double the face value of the contract in case of accidental death.

double integration *n. Mathematics.* Two separate integrations performed on an integrand containing two independent variables. In each integration one of the independent variables is kept constant.

dou·ble-joint·ed (dŭb′əl-join′tĭd) *adj.* Having unusually flexible joints permitting connected parts, such as limbs or fingers, to be bent at unusual angles.

double knit *n.* A jerseylike fabric knitted on a machine equipped with two sets of needles so that a double thickness of fabric is produced in which the two sides of the fabric are interlocked.

dou·ble-knit (dŭb′əl-nĭt′) *adj.* Of or made of double knit.

double negative *n.* **1.** A syntactic construction that employs two negatives, especially to express a single negation. **2.** A similar construction in which the repetition of negation produces an affirmative.

Usage: There are several constructions in English in which two negative forms are used together in the same clause to express a single "positive" or "negative" meaning. The most commonly used type, illustrated by *He never said nothing* (to mean "He said nothing"), is not an acceptable standard form. However, its use is widespread in regional dialects as an emphatic expression of negation and it has considerable literary precedent in earlier periods of English. Within standard English, certain types of double negative are acceptable: when the negatives do "cancel out," or "make a positive," as in *I can't not go* (that is, I have to go); to express understatement, as in *He's a not unattractive man*; between main and subordinate clauses of certain kinds, as in *I shouldn't be surprised if he doesn't go*; and as a means of reinforcement later in the sentence, as in *He wouldn't surrender, not even after several appeals.*

dou·ble-park (dŭb′əl-pärk′) *v.* **-parked, -parking, -parks.** —*tr.* To park (a vehicle) alongside another vehicle already parked parallel to the curb. —*intr.* To park a vehicle in such a manner.

double pneumonia *n.* Pneumonia afflicting both lungs.

dou·ble-quick (dŭb′əl-kwĭk′) *adj.* Very quick; rapid. ~*n.* A marching cadence, **double time** (see). ~*intr.v.* **double-quicked, -quicking, -quicks.** To double-time. —**dou·ble-quick** *adv.*

dou·ble-reed (dŭb′əl-rēd′) *adj.* Pertaining to or designating any of a

Douglas fir *One of the world's best timber trees, the Douglas fir is also known as the Oregon fir; it grows to 100 meters (330 feet) in height. It is named after David Douglas, the plant collector who introduced its seeds into Britain in 1827.*

group of wind instruments, such as the oboe, that have a mouthpiece formed of two joined reeds that vibrate against each other.

double refraction *n. Optics.* **Birefringence** *(see).*

dou·bles (dŭb′əlz) *n. Used with a singular verb.* A game, especially of tennis, having two players on each side.

double salt *n. Chemistry.* A salt consisting, or regarded as consisting, of a molecular combination of two simple salts.

dou·ble-space (dŭb′əl-spās′) *v.* **-spaced, -spacing, -spaces.** —*intr.* To type so that there is a full line space between lines. —*tr.* To type (copy) in this way.

dou·ble-speak (dŭb′əl-spēk′) *n.* Complicated and ambiguous language, often meaning the opposite of what is said; double talk.

double standard *n.* **1.** A set of inconsistent ethical principles in which something regarded as reprehensible in one person or in some circumstances may be condoned or approved in others. **2.** A set of principles permitting greater opportunity or liberty to one than to another, especially the granting of greater sexual freedom to men than to women.

double star *n.* A binary star *(see).*

dou·blet (dŭb′lĭt) *n.* **1.** A close-fitting jacket, with or without sleeves, worn by men between the 15th and 17th centuries: *doublet and hose.* **2.** A counterfeit gem made of a piece of colored glass covered with crystal or with a thin face of real gemstone. **3. a.** A pair of similar things. **b.** One of a pair. **c.** *Physics.* A multiplet with two members. **4.** *Linguistics.* One of two words derived from the same source by different routes of transmission, such as *fragile* and *frail.* **5.** **doublets.** A throw of two dice in which the same number of dots appears on the upper face of each. [Middle English, from Old French, from *double,* DOUBLE.]

double take *n.* A delayed reaction to an unusual remark or circumstance, often used in an exaggerated form as a comic device.

double talk *n.* **1.** Meaningless speech that consists of nonsense syllables mixed with intelligible words; gibberish. **2.** Ambiguous or evasive language.

dou·ble-team (dŭb′əl-tēm′) *tr.v.* **-teamed, -teaming, -teams.** *Sports.* To guard or cover an offensive player with two defensive players simultaneously.

dou·ble-think (dŭb′əl-thĭngk′) *n.* The belief in two contradictory ideas or points of view at the same time, usually leading to a double standard.

double time *n.* **Abbr. d.t. 1.** A marching pace of 180 three-foot steps per minute. Also called "double-quick." **2.** *Music.* Duple time. **3.** *Military.* A regulation running pace.

dou·ble-time (dŭb′əl-tīm′) *v.* **-timed, -timing, -times.** —*tr.* To march (troops) in double time. —*intr.* **1.** To march in double time. **2.** To jog or run.

dou·ble-tongu·ing (dŭb′əl-tŭng′ĭng) *n.* The playing of a series of notes on a wind instrument by rapidly covering and uncovering the air passage with the tongue. Compare **single-tonguing, triple-tonguing.** —**double-tongue** *v.*

dou·ble-tree (dŭb′əl-trē) *n.* A crossbar on a wagon or coach to which two whiffletrees are attached for harnessing two animals abreast.

dou·ble-u (dŭb′əl-yōō′) *n.* The letter *w.*

double vision *n.* The simultaneous perception of two images of the same object as a result of poor coordination of the muscles that move the eyeball.

double wedding *n.* A wedding of two couples at the same time.

dou·bloon (dŭ-blōōn′) *n.* An obsolete Spanish gold coin. [Spanish *doblón,* augmentative of *dobla,* Spanish coin, from Latin *dupla,* feminine of *duplus,* DOUBLE.]

dou·blure (dōō-blōōr′) *n.* An ornamental lining, as of vellum or leather, on the inside face of a book cover. [French, lining, from Old French, from *doubler,* to double, line, from Latin *duplāre,* to double, from *duplus,* DOUBLE.]

dou·bly (dŭb′lē) *adv.* **1.** To a double degree; twice. **2.** In a twofold manner.

doubt (dout) *v.* **doubted, doubting, doubts.** —*tr.* **1.** To be uncertain or skeptical about; be undecided about. **2.** To tend to disbelieve; distrust. **3.** *Archaic.* To suspect; fear: *I doubt that Thackeray did not write the Latin epitaph"* (A. Trollope). —*intr.* To be undecided, unconvinced, or skeptical. —*n.* **1. a.** *Often* **doubts.** A lack of conviction or certainty. **b.** An instance of this; a point about which one is uncertain or skeptical. **2.** An uncertain condition or state of affairs: *an outcome still in doubt.* —See Synonyms at **uncertainty.** —**beyond doubt.** Unquestionably; definitely. —**no doubt. 1.** Certainly. **2.** Probably. —**without doubt.** Certainly. —See Usage note at **doubtless.** [Middle English *d(o)uten,* from Old French *douter,* from Latin *dubitāre,* to waver, vibrate.] —**doubt·er** *n.*

Usage: Doubt (and *doubtful*) may be followed by *whether, that,* or *if.* In positive statements intended to convey real uncertainty, *whether* is the usual choice, especially in formal contexts (*I doubt whether they can win*). *If* is acceptable but is less formal. The use of *that* in such contexts has been criticized as being "weak" in meaning, but it is quite widely used informally. In negative or interrogative constructions, where there is clear denial of doubt, *that* is appropriate (*Do you doubt that he will come?; I don't doubt that you're right*). See also Usage note at **but.**

doubt·ful (dout′fəl) *adj.* **1.** Subject to or tending to give rise to doubt; uncertain; unclear. **2.** Experiencing doubt. **3.** Of uncertain outcome; undecided. **4.** Questionable; suspect: *a governor with a*

doubtful past. —See Usage note at **doubt.** —**doubt·ful·ly** *adv.* —**doubt·ful·ness** *n.*

Synonyms: *arguable, debatable, dubious, questionable.*

doubting Thomas *n.* One who habitually expresses or feels doubts and requires concrete proof. [After St. Thomas, the apostle who doubted Christ's resurrection until he had proof.]

doubt·less (dout′lĭs) *adj.* Certain; assured: *doubtless of ultimate victory.* ~*adv.* **1.** Certainly. **2.** Presumably; probably. —**doubt·less·ly** *adv.*

Usage: Doubtless and *no doubt* are relatively weak in expressing certainty, because they can also indicate mere presumption or probability (*He's doubtless been caught in the traffic*) or concession (*No doubt you're right*). In contrast, *undoubtedly* and *without doubt* express only certainty and conviction (*You are undoubtedly/without doubt correct*).

douce (dōōs) *adj. British Regional.* Sedate; sober; gentle. [Middle English, sweet, pleasant, from Old French, from Latin *dulcis,* sweet.]

dou·ceur (dōō-sûr′) *n.* Money given as a tip, gratuity, or bribe. [French, "sweetness," from Late Latin *dulcor,* from Latin *dulcis,* sweet.]

douche (dōōsh) *n.* **1.** A stream of water or air applied to a part or cavity of the body for cleansing or medicinal purposes. **2.** The application of a douche. **3.** A syringe or other instrument for applying a douche. ~*v.* **douched, douching, douches.** —*tr.* To cleanse or treat by means of a douche. —*intr.* To be cleansed or treated by a douche. [French, douche, shower, from Italian *doccia,* conduit pipe, douche, probably from *doccione,* tube, from Latin *ductiō* (stem *ductiōn-),* a leading away, from *ductus,* past participle of *dūcere,* to lead.]

dough (dō) *n.* **1.** A soft, thick mixture of flour or meal, liquids, and various dry ingredients that is baked as bread, pastry, or the like. **2.** Any similar pasty mass. **3.** *Slang.* Money. [Middle English *dogh,* Old English *dāg;* from Germanic.]

dough·boy (dō′boi′) *n.* **1.** Bread dough that is rolled thin and cut into various shapes, then fried in deep fat, or that is made into a dumpling and boiled. **2.** *Informal.* An infantryman in World War I. [Sense 2, origin obscure.]

dough·nut, do·nut (dō′nŭt′, -nət) *n.* **1.** A small, ring-shaped or round cake made of rich, light dough that is fried in deep fat. **2.** Anything shaped like a ring; especially, a **torus** *(see).*

dough·ty (dou′tē) *adj.* **-tier, -tiest.** Characterized by courage; stouthearted; valiant. —See Synonyms at **brave.** [Middle English *doughty,* Old English *dohtig, dyhtig,* from Germanic.] —**dough·ti·ly** *adv.* —**dough·ti·ness** *n.*

dough·y (dō′ē) *adj.* **-ier, -iest.** Having the consistency or appearance of dough.

Doug·las (dŭg′ləs). Capital of the Isle of Man. Its buildings include the House of Keys (the parliament) and the Manx Museum. Douglas was the first seaport in the British Isles to be fitted with radar (1948).

Doug·las (dŭg′ləs), **Stephen Arnold** (1813–61). U.S. legislator. A congressman (1843–47) and senator (1847–61), he drafted the Kansas-Nebraska Act (1854), which gave settlers the right to determine whether their territory would be free or slaveholding. His short, thickset stature and political skills earned him the nickname "the Little Giant." Douglas's senatorial campaign of 1858 featured a famous series of debates with Abraham Lincoln. He ran unsuccessfully for president in 1860.

Douglas fir *n.* A tall evergreen timber tree, *Pseudotsuga menziesii,* of northwestern North America, having short needles and egg-shaped cones. Also called "Oregon fir." [After David *Douglas* (1798–1834), Scottish botanist.]

Doug·las-Home (dŭg′ləs-hyōōm′), **Alexander Frederick, Baron Home of the Hirsel** (1903–). British politician. He was elected as a Conservative M.P. in 1931. He lost his seat at the 1945 elections but was returned again in 1950. In 1951 he succeeded his father as the 14th Earl of Home. In 1963 he renounced his hereditary peerage in order to become prime minister and returned to the Commons as Sir Alec Douglas-Home. He was foreign secretary from 1970 to 1974, when he returned to the House of Lords as a life peer.

Douma. Variant of **Duma.**

doum palm, doom palm (dōōm) *n.* An African palm tree, *Hyphaene thebaica,* having a trunk that branches into two, fanlike foliage, and fruit that tastes like gingerbread. Also called "gingerbread palm." [From Arabic *dawm.*]

dour (dōōr, dour) *adj.* **1.** Silently ill-humored; gloomy. **2.** Marked by intractable sternness or harshness; forbidding. —See Synonyms at **glum.** [Middle English, perhaps from Latin *dūrus,* hard.]

doura, dourah. Variants of **durra.**

dou·rine (dōō-rēn′) *n.* A contagious disease of horses, asses, and mules, caused by the microorganism *Trypanosoma equiperdum,* which is transmitted during copulation. [French, from Arabic *darina,* to be dirty.]

Dou·ro (dō′rōō). *Spanish* **Due·ro** (dwā′rō). River in Portugal and Spain. It flows 722 kilometers (480 miles) from the Sierra de Cebollera, forming part of the Spanish and Portuguese border.

dou·rou·cou·li (dōō′rōō-kōō′lē) *n., pl.* **-lis.** Also **dou·ro·cou·li** (dōō′rō-). Any of various nocturnal monkeys of the genus *Aotus,* of Central and South America, having very large, round eyes. [Native South American name.]

douse¹, dowse (dous) *v.* **doused** or **dowsed, dousing** or **dowsing, douses** or **dowses.** —*tr.* **1.** To plunge into liquid; immerse. **2.** To

douroucouli *This large-eyed Central and South American primate is the only species of monkey to be active at night rather than day.*

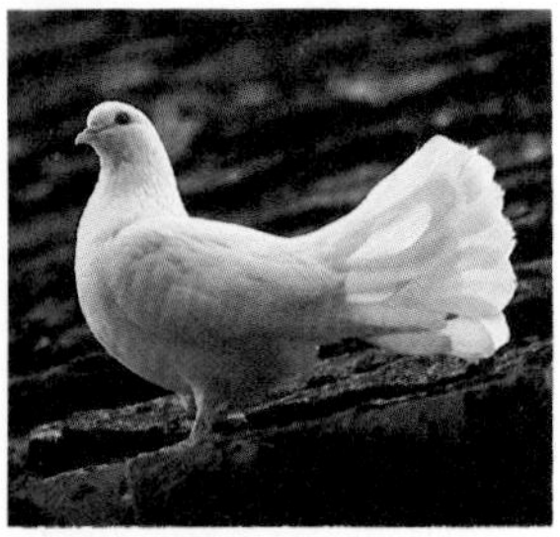

dove *Doves pair for life, and both sexes help to rear the young—a habit that may explain their use as a symbol of peace. This is a white fantail dove.*

wet thoroughly; drench. *—intr.* To become thoroughly wet; soak. *~n.* A drenching. [16th century : *douse*†, to strike, smite.] **—dous·er** *n.*

douse[2] *tr.v.* **doused, dousing, douses.** To put out (a light or fire); extinguish. [Perhaps from earlier sense (to strike, smite) of DOUSE (immerse).]

douse[3] *tr.v.* **doused, dousing, douses.** *Nautical.* **1.** To lower (a sail). **2.** To close (a porthole). [Perhaps from Low German; akin to Middle Dutch *dossen,* to beat, strike.]

douse[4] (douz). Variant of **dowse** (to use a divining rod).

DOVAP (dō′văp′) *n. Electronics.* A system for determining the velocity and position of a long-range missile using the **Doppler effect** *(see).* [*Do*ppler *v*elocity *a*nd *p*osition.]

dove[1] (dŭv) *n.* **1.** Any of various birds of the family Columbidae, which also includes the pigeons; especially, an undomesticated species, such as the **mourning dove** *(see).* **2.** A gentle or innocent child or woman. Used especially as a term of endearment. **3.** A messenger of peace or deliverance from care by allusion to the dove of Genesis 8:8–12. **4.** One advocating a policy of conciliation or moderation. **5.** *Sometimes* **Dove.** The Holy Spirit. **6.** A warm pale gray or grayish-brown color. **7. Dove.** The constellation **Columba** *(see).* [Middle English *do(u)ve,* Old English *dūfe* (unattested), from Germanic.] **—dove** *adj.*

dove[2] (dōv). Alternate past tense of **dive.**

dove·cote (dŭv′kōt′, -kŏt′) *n.* Also **dove·cot** (-kŏt′). A roost for domesticated pigeons.

dove·kie (dŭv′kē) *n.* Also **dove·key,** *pl.* **-keys.** A sea bird, the **little auk** *(see).* [Diminutive of DOVE.]

Do·ver[1] (dō′vər). Port in Kent, southeast England, the only one of the Cinque Ports that still has a major dock. It is the United Kingdom's principal ferry and hovercraft terminus for the continent, with Calais only 35 kilometers (22 miles) away. The Norman castle that overlooks the town has in its precincts a Roman lighthouse that was used to guide the legions across the Channel.

Dover[2]. The capital (since 1777) of Delaware, in the central part of the state. It was founded in 1683 on William Penn's orders and laid out in 1717. Nearby Dover Air Force Base is important to the city's economy.

Dover, Strait of. A stretch of water between England and France, connecting the English Channel with the North Sea. Its narrowest point, 34 kilometers (21 miles) between Dover and Cap Gris Nez, is the route taken by Channel swimmers. The first successful such crossing was made in 1875.

Dover sole *n.* A European sole, *Solea solea,* valued as a food fish.

Do·ver's powder (dō′vərz) *n.* A powdered drug, made essentially of ipecac and opium, formerly used to relieve pain and induce perspiration. [After Thomas *Dover* (1660–1742), English physician.]

dove·tail (dŭv′tāl′) *n.* **1.** In carpentry, a fan-shaped tenon that forms a tight interlocking joint when fitted into a corresponding mortise. **2.** A joint formed by interlocking one or more such tenons and mortises. In this sense, also called "dovetail joint."
~v. **dovetailed, -tailing, -tails.** *—tr.* **1.** To cut into or join by means of dovetails. **2.** To connect or combine precisely or harmoniously. *—intr.* To combine or interlock into a unified whole. [From its supposed resemblance to a dove's tail.]

dow·a·ger (dou′ə-jər) *n.* **1.** A widow who holds a title or property derived from her dead husband. Often used in combination with the title. **2.** An elderly woman of means or status. [Old French *douagiere,* from *douage,* dower, from *douer,* to portion, endow, from Latin *dōtāre,* from *dōs* (stem *dōt-*), dowry.]

dow·dy (dou′dē) *adj.* **-dier, -diest.** Lacking in stylishness or neatness; shabby; old-fashioned: *dowdy clothes.*
~n., pl. **dowdies.** A dowdy woman; frump. [From Middle English *doude*†, slut.] **—dow·di·ly** *adv.* **—dow·di·ness** *n.*

dow·el (dou′əl) *n.* **1.** A usually round pin that fits tightly into a corresponding hole to fasten or align two adjacent pieces of wood or stone. **2.** A round stick or rod from which dowels are cut. In this sense, also called "doweling." **3.** A piece of wood driven into a wall to act as an anchor for nails.
~tr.v. **doweled** or **-elled, doweling** or **-elling, -els. 1.** To fasten or align with dowels. **2.** To equip with dowels. [Middle English *dowle,* from Middle Low German *dovel,* peg, block, nail.]

dow·er (dou′ər) *n.* **1.** The part or interest of a deceased man's real estate allotted by law to his widow for her lifetime. Also *archaic* "dowry." **2.** A marriage portion, **dowry** *(see).* **3.** A natural endowment or gift.
~tr.v. **dowered, -ering, -ers.** To assign a dower to; endow. [Middle English *dowere,* from Old French *douaire,* from Medieval Latin *dōtārium,* from Latin *dōs* (stem *dōt-*), dowry.]

dower house *n.* A smaller house, often near a manor house, intended for occupation by a dowager.

dow·itch·er (dou′ĭ-chər) *n.* Either of two shore birds, *Limnodromus griseus* or *L. scolopaeus,* of northern regions, having brownish plumage and a long, straight bill. [Of Iroquoian origin.]

Dow-Jones Averages (dou′jōnz′) *n.* A trademark used for an index of the relative price of selected industrial, transportation, and utility stocks based on a formula developed and periodically revised by Dow Jones & Company, Inc. [After C.H. *Dow* (1851–1902) and E.D. *Jones* (1856–1920), U.S. economists.]

Dow·land (dou′lənd), **John** (1562–1626). Anglo-Irish composer, born in Dublin. He was the most celebrated lute player of his time and served the king of Denmark and Charles I of England. His *Songs or Ayres* (1597–1603) were known throughout Europe.

down[1] (doun) *adv. Abbr.* **dn. 1. a.** From a higher to a lower place or position. **b.** Downstairs. **c.** Toward, to, or on the ground, floor, or bottom. **d.** Toward a point further away. **e.** So as to be no longer erected or displayed: *took the decorations down.* **f.** So as to remain in the stomach: *can't keep her food down.* **2. a.** Into a lower posture. **b.** In or into a prostrate position. **3.** Out of one's grasp. **4.** Toward or in the south or in a southerly direction. **5. a.** Away from somewhere considered central or as a center of activity, such as a capital city. **b.** Away from a town: *down in the country; down on the farm.* **6.** To the source: *tracking a rumor down.* **7. a.** Toward or at a low or lower point on a scale. **b.** Lower in price, standing, or the like. **8.** To or in a quiescent or subdued state. **9. a.** To or in a low status, as of subjection or disgrace. **b.** Reduced to a specified condition: *down to begging from passers-by.* **c.** Progressing through all relevant stages toward the lowest stage: *down through the ranks.* **10.** *Sports.* Being a specified number of points behind a competitor: *went two goals down in the second half.* **11.** Seriously; vigorously: *get down to work.* **12.** From earlier times or people. **13 a.** To a reduced, lessened, or diluted form: *worn down; watered down.* **b.** To a reduced but more concentrated or finer consistency: *boiling down a sauce.* **14.** In writing; on paper: *taking a statement down.* **15.** In partial payment at the time of purchase: *twenty dollars down.* **16.** Into a state of silence or inaudibility: *shouted her down.* **17.** In a condition of inaction or malfunction: *The computer is down.* **18.** *Nautical.* Having the rudder to windward. **—down with.** Used to express disapproval or urge the removal of someone or something.
~adj. **1. a.** Moving or directed downward: *a down escalator.* **b.** In a low position; not up. **c.** At a reduced level. **2. a.** Ill; sick: *He's down with the flu.* **b.** Low in spirit; depressed: *feel down.* **3.** Being a deposit: *a down payment.* **4.** *Physics.* Designating a type of quark with minus one-third electronic charge, a baryon number of one-third, and no strangeness or charm. **—down on.** *Informal.* Hostile or negative toward; out of patience with.
~prep. **1.** In a descending direction along, upon, into, or through. **2.** Along the course of. **3.** Toward the mouth of a river.
~n. **1.** A downward movement; descent. **2.** A period of ill fortune or depression; *She had her ups and downs.*
~v. **downed, downing, downs.** *—tr.* **1.** To bring, put, strike, or throw down. **2.** To swallow hastily; gulp. *—intr.* To go or come down; descend. [Middle English *doun,* Old English *dūne,* short for *adūne,* reduced form of *ofdūne,* "from the hill" : *of,* OFF + *dūne,* dative of *dūn,* hill.]
Usage: As a general rule, *down* is used for travel in a southerly direction, and *up* for travel to the north.

down[2] *n.* **1.** Fine, soft, fluffy feathers forming the first plumage of a young bird and underlying the contour feathers in certain adult birds. **2.** *Botany.* A covering of soft, short fibers, as on some leaves. **3.** Any soft, silky, or feathery substance, such as the first growth of human beard. [Middle English *doun, downe,* from Old Norse *dūnn.*]

down[3] *n.* **1.** *Usually* **downs. a.** An expanse of rolling, grassy upland, especially in southern England. **b.** The temperate grasslands of New Zealand and Australia. **2.** *Often* **Down.** Any of several breeds of sheep having short wool, developed in the downs of England. [Middle English *doun, dun,* hill, Old English *dūn.*]

Down (doun). County in Northern Ireland, stretching from the Mourne Mts. to the Irish Sea. Downpatrick is the county town.

down-and-out (doun′ən-out′) *n.* **1.** A destitute person. **2.** A person who is incapacitated. **—down-and-out** *adj.*

down·beat (doun′bēt′) *n. Music.* **1.** The downward stroke made by a conductor to indicate the first beat of a measure. Compare **upbeat. 2.** The first beat of a bar.
~adj. Informal. **1.** Depressed; pessimistic. **2.** Casual; relaxed and unconcerned.

down-bow (doun′bō′) *n. Music.* A stroke made by drawing a bow from handle to tip across the strings of a violin or other bowed instrument. Compare **up-bow.**

down·cast (doun′kăst′, -käst′) *adj.* **1.** Depressed; dejected; sad. **2.** Directed downward.
~n. **1.** A ventilation shaft in a mine. **2.** A **downthrow** *(see).* **—**See Synonyms at **sad.**

down·court (doun-kôrt′, -kōrt′) *adv. & adj. Sports.* To, into, or in the far end of the court, especially in basketball.

Down East or **down East** *n.* New England, especially Maine.

Down Easter or **down-East·er** (doun-ē′stər) *n.* A native of New England, especially Maine.

down·er (dou′nər) *n. Slang.* **1.** A depressant or sedative drug, such as a barbiturate or tranquilizer. Compare **upper. 2.** A depressing experience.

down·fall (doun′fôl′) *n.* **1. a.** A sudden loss of wealth, rank, reputation, or happiness; ruin. **b.** Something causing this. **2.** A fall of rain or snow, especially a heavy or unexpected one.

down·fall·en (doun′fô′lən) *adj.* Fallen, as from prominence; ruined.

down·field (doun-fēld′) *adv. & adj. Sports.* To, into, or in the defensive team's end of the field.

down·grade (doun′grād′) *n.* A descending slope in a road. **—on the downgrade.** Declining, as in influence, reputation, or wealth; losing status.
~tr.v. **downgraded, -grading, -grades. 1.** To lower the status and salary of. **2.** To lower or minimize the importance or reputation of.

down·haul (doun′hôl′) *n. Nautical.* A rope or set of ropes for hauling down or securing a sail or spar.

down·heart·ed (doun′här′tĭd) *adj.* Low in spirit; depressed; discouraged. **—down·heart·ed·ly** *adv.* **—down·heart·ed·ness** *n.*

PRONUNCIATION KEY

ă, pat; ā, pay; âr, care; ä, father, are; b, bib; ch, church; d, deed; ĕ, pet; ē, be; f, fife; g, gag; h, hat; hw, which; ĭ, pit; ī, pie; îr, pier; j, judge; k, kick; l, lid, needle; m, mum; n, no, sudden; ng, thing; ŏ, pot; ō, toe; ô, paw, for; oi, noise; ou, out; o͝o, book; o͞o, boot; p, pop; r, roar; s, sauce; sh, ship, dish; t, tight; th, thin, path; *th,* this, bathe; ŭ, cut; ûr, fur; v, valve; w, with; y, yes; z, zebra, size; zh, vision; ə, about, item, edible, gallop, circus, peaceful

IN FOREIGN WORDS:

à, *Fr.* ami; œ, *Fr.* feu, *Ger.* schön; ü, *Fr.* tu, *Ger.* über; KH, *Ger.* ich, *Scot.* loch; N, *Fr.* bon; y′, *Fr.* Compiègne

STRESS MARKS:

Primary stress: ′ **in·cite′** (ĭn-sīt′)
Secondary stress: ′ **in′sight′** (ĭn′sīt′)

down·hill (doun′hĭl′) *adv.* Down the slope of a hill; in a downward direction. **—go downhill.** To decline, as in quality or performance. ~*adj.* (doun′hĭl′). **1.** Sloping downward; descending. **2.** Designating a skiing race run downhill. **3.** Placed lower on a slope. Said of a ski, skier's foot, or the like. **4.** Leading to failure or deterioration. **5.** Progressively easier. ~*n.* **1.** A downward slope. **2.** A skiing event in which competitors race one at a time down a slope against the clock.

down·home (doun′hōm′) *adj.* Of, relating to, or characteristic of the rural southern United States or its people, as in simplicity, informality, or earthiness.

Down·ing Street (dou′nĭng) *n.* The British prime minister or government. [From the location of the prime minister's residence at No. 10 Downing Street, off Whitehall, in Westminster, London.]

down·load (doun′lōd′) *tr.v.* **-loaded, -loading, -loads.** *Computer Science.* To transmit (programs or data) from a main computer to a smaller computer or terminal. [*downline* + *load.*]

down·play (doun′plā′) *tr.v.* **-played, -playing, -plays.** To play down; minimize the importance or significance of.

down·pour (doun′pôr′, -pōr′) *n.* A heavy fall of rain.

down·range (doun′rānj′) *adv.* In a direction away from the launch site and along the flight line of a missile test range. ~*adj.* (doun′rānj′). Designating the area and airspace along the flight line of a missile test range.

down·right (doun′rīt′) *adj.* **1.** Thoroughgoing; unequivocal. **2.** Forthright; candid. ~*adv.* Thoroughly; absolutely.

down·shift (doun′shĭft′) *intr.v.* **-shifted, -shifting, -shifts.** To shift a motor vehicle to a lower gear. **—down·shift** *n.*

Downs, North and South (dounz). Two roughly parallel ranges of chalk hills in southeast England. The North Downs run through Surrey and Kent to the white cliffs of Dover; the South Downs through Sussex to Beachy Head. Both are sheep-rearing areas.

down·spout (doun′spout′) *n.* A pipe that carries water from a roof or gutter down to a drain or into the ground.

Down's syndrome (dounz) *n.* A type of mental retardation caused by a chromosome abnormality, giving rise to certain characteristic physical features, notably an oblique slant of the eyes. In nontechnical usage also called "mongolism." —See usage note at **mongolism.** [After John Langdon-*Down* (died 1896), English physician who classified it.]

down·stage (doun′stāj′) *adv.* Toward or at the front of a stage. ~*adj.* (doun′stāj′). Pertaining to the front part of a stage. ~*n.* (doun′stāj′). The front half of a stage.

down·stairs (doun′stârz′) *adv.* **1.** Down the stairs. **2.** To or on a lower floor. ~*adj.* (doun′stârz′). Located on a lower or main floor. ~*n.* (doun′stârz′). *Used with a singular verb.* The lower or main floor.

down·stream (doun′strēm′) *adj.* **1.** In the direction of a river's or stream's current. **2.** *Finance.* Closer to the point of sale than to the point of production or manufacture. Compare **upstream.** ~*adv.* (doun′strēm′). Down a stream.

down·swing (doun′swĭng′) *n.* **1.** A swing downward, especially in golf. **2.** A declining trend, as in popularity or prosperity.

down·throw (doun′thrō′) *n.* *Geology.* The net downward movement of rocks on one side of a fault plane. Also used adjectively: *the downthrow side.* Also called "downcast."

down·tick (doun′tĭk′) *n.* A transaction in a stock market security below the price of the previous transaction.

down·time (doun′tīm′) *n.* **1.** The period of time when a factory or its machinery is inactive. **2.** Time during which a computer is inoperative because of a technical malfunction.

down-to-earth (doun′tə-ûrth′) *adj.* Realistic; sensible.

down·town (doun′toun′) *adv.* To, toward, or in the lower part or the business center of a city or town. ~*adj.* (doun′toun′). Of, pertaining to, or located in such an area. ~*n.* (doun′toun′). The business center or lower part of a city or town. Compare **uptown.**

down·trod·den (doun′trŏd′n) *adj.* **1.** Oppressed; tyrannized. **2.** Trampled down.

down·turn (doun′tûrn′) *n.* A tendency downward, especially in business or economic activity.

down under *n. Informal.* Australia or New Zealand. ~*adv.* In or to Australia or New Zealand.

down·ward (doun′wərd) *adv.* Also **down·wards** (-wərdz), **down·ward·ly** (-wərd-lē). **1.** From a higher to a lower place, point, level, or condition. **2.** From an earlier to a more recent time. ~*adj.* **1.** Descending from a higher to a lower place, point, level, or condition. **2.** Descending from a source or origin.

downward mobility *n.* The movement of an individual or group to a lower social status.

down·warp (doun′wôrp′) *n.* *Geology.* A small-scale downward movement of the earth's crust, producing no folding or faulting. **—down·warp·ing** *n.*

down·wind (doun′wĭnd′) *adv.* In the direction in which the wind is blowing; leeward. **—down·wind** *adj.*

down·y (dou′nē) *adj.* **-ier, -iest. 1.** Made of, filled with, or covered with down. **2. a.** Resembling down. **b.** Covered with something resembling down. **3.** Quietly soft; soothing.

downy mildew *n.* A disease of plants caused by fungi of the order Peronosporales and characterized by gray, velvety patches of spores on the lower surfaces of leaves.

dow·ry (dour′ē) *n., pl.* **-ries. 1.** Money or property brought by a bride to her husband at marriage. Also called "dower." **2.** *Archaic.* A widow's inheritance, formerly a **dower** *(see).* **3.** A sum of money formerly required of a postulant when entering certain orders of nuns. **4.** A natural endowment or gift. [Variant of DOWER.]

dowse[1] (douz) *intr.v.* **dowsed, dowsing, dowses.** Also **douse, doused, dousing, douses. 1.** To use a divining rod or pendulum to find underground water or minerals. **2.** To use apparently paranormal powers to make discoveries. [17th century : origin obscure.] **—dows·er** *n.*

dowse[2] (dous). Variant of **douse** (to drench).

dowsing rod *n.* A divining rod *(see).*

Dowson (dou′sən), **Ernest Christopher** (1867–1900). English poet. Alcoholic and debt-ridden, Dowson died of tuberculosis at 32. His poems include *Non Sum Qualis.*

Dow theory (dou) *n.* A theory of stock market forecasting based on the activity of the market itself. [After Charles H. *Dow* (1851–1902), U.S. economist.]

dox·as·tic (dŏk-săs′tĭk) *adj.* *Logic.* Of or pertaining to belief. [Greek *doxastikos,* having an opinion or belief, from *doxa,* belief.]

dox·ol·o·gy (dŏk-sŏl′ə-jē) *n., pl.* **-gies.** A liturgical formula of praise to God. See **Gloria in excelsis Deo, Gloria Patri.** [Medieval Latin *doxologia,* from Greek, laudation : *doxa,* opinion, judgment + -LOGY.] **—dox·o·log·i·cal** (dŏk′sə-lŏj′ə-kəl) *adj.* **—dox·o·log·i·cal·ly** *adv.*

dox·y (dŏk′sē) *n., pl.* **-ies.** *Slang.* **1.** A prostitute. **2.** A paramour. [16th century : (cant) origin obscure.]

dox·y·cy·cline (dŏk-sī-sī′klēn′) *n.* A broad-spectrum antibiotic, $C_{22}H_{24}N_2O_8$, derived from tetracycline. [D(E)- + OX(Y)- + (TETRA)-CYCLINE.]

doy·en (doi-ĕn′, doi′ən; *French* dwȧ-yăN′) *n.* The eldest or senior member of a group, as of a diplomatic corps or literary circle. [French, from Late Latin *decānus,* chief of ten, a kind of officer, from Greek *dekanos,* from *deka,* ten.]

doy·enne (doi-ĕn′; *French* dwȧ-yĕn′) *n.* A woman who is a doyen.

Doyle (doil), **Sir Arthur Conan** (1859–1930). British writer, the creator of Sherlock Holmes. He trained as a doctor but gave up medicine in 1890 after his first Sherlock Holmes book, *A Study in Scarlet.* He was knighted in 1902, the year he published his most celebrated piece of detective fiction, *The Hound of the Baskervilles.*

doyley, doyly. Variants of **doily.**

D'Oy·ly Carte (doi′lē kärt′), **Richard** (1844–1901). English theater impresario. He presented Gilbert and Sullivan's operettas and built the Savoy Theatre (1881) for the performance of their works.

doz. dozen.

doze (dōz) *intr.v.* **dozed, dozing, dozes.** To sleep lightly and intermittently; nod sleepily; nap. **—doze off.** To fall into a light sleep. ~*n.* A short, light sleep; nap. [Originally transitive, to make dull, drowse, probably of Scandinavian origin; akin to Danish *døse.*] **—doz·er** *n.*

doz·en (dŭz′ən) *n., pl.* **dozen** (for sense 1) or **-ens** (for sense 2). *Abbr.* **doz., dz. 1.** A set of 12. **2.** dozens. *Informal.* An indefinite number; a great many. **—daily dozen.** Physical exercises performed regularly in the morning. ~*adj.* Twelve. [Middle English *dozeine,* from Old French, from *doze,* twelve, from Latin *duodecim : duo,* two + *decem,* ten.] **—doz·enth** *adj.*

do·zy (dō′zē) *adj.* **-zier, -ziest.** Drowsy; half asleep. **—doz·i·ly** *adv.* **—do·zi·ness** *n.*

DP, D.P. displaced person.

D.Ph., D.Phil. Doctor of Philosophy.

dpt. 1. department. **2.** deponent.

dr dram.

dr. 1. debit. **2.** debtor. **3.** drachm. **4.** drachma. **5.** drawer.

Dr. 1. doctor. **2.** Drive (in street names).

drab[1] (drăb) *adj.* **drabber, drabbest. 1.** Faded and dull in appearance. **2.** Of a commonplace character; dreary. **3. a.** Of a dull light brown. **b.** Of a light olive brown or khaki color. ~*n.* **1.** Cloth of a light dull brown, grayish brown, or unbleached natural color; especially, a heavy woolen or cotton fabric. **2.** Moderate to grayish or light grayish yellowish brown or light olive brown. **3.** Monotony. [Variant of obsolete *drap,* cloth, from Old French. See *drape.*] **—drab·ly** *adv.* **—drab·ness** *n.*

drab[2] *n.* **1.** A slovenly woman. **2.** A prostitute. ~*intr.v.* **drabbed, drabbing, drabs.** To consort with prostitutes. [Perhaps from Low German; compare Dutch *drab,* dregs.]

drab·bet (drăb′ət) *n. British.* A yellowish-brown twilled linen. [From DRAB (cloth).]

drab·ble (drăb′əl) *v.* **-bled, -bling, -bles.** —*intr.* To draggle; become wet and muddy. —*tr.* To bedraggle. [Middle English *drabelen,* of Low German origin, akin to Low German *drabbelen,* to paddle in water or mire.]

dra·cae·na (drə-sē′nə) *n.* Any of several tropical plants of the genera *Dracaena* and *Cordyline,* some species of which are cultivated as house plants for their decorative foliage. [New Latin *Dracaena,* from Late Latin, from Greek *drakaina,* feminine of *drakōn,* serpent, DRAGON.]

drachm (drăm) *n. British. Abbr.* **dr. 1.** A dram. **2.** A drachma. [Middle English, from Old French, from Late Latin *dragma,* from Greek *drakhmē,* DRACHMA.]

drach·ma (drăk′mə) *n., pl.* **-mas** or **-mae** (-mē). *Abbr.* **d., D. dr. 1. a.** The basic monetary unit of Greece, equal to 100 lepta. **b.** A coin worth one drachma. See feature at **currency. 2.** A silver coin

Downing Street *The front door of 10 Downing Street, official residence of the British Prime Minister.*

dragon

THE UNIVERSAL MONSTER

Different roles for the dragon in myths from east and west

Every civilization creates its own legendary heroes. But most have had at least one beast in common: the dragon. Curiously, dragons are described remarkably consistently all over the world, as giant snakelike creatures with claws. Some are winged as well—like the red dragon of Wales—and some breathe fire. Christianity associated the monsters with the devil, and in Babylonian, Egyptian, and ancient Jewish legends, dragons symbolized chaos. But in Japan, the imperial family once traced its descent from a sea god called the Dragon King; and China and Scandinavia often saw dragons as guardians of treasure.

ST. GEORGE AND THE DRAGON *England's patron saint, St. George, saves a terrified maiden from death in a painting done by a 19th-century Czech artist, Josef Manes. The legend of the chivalrous Christian hero depicts the dragon as the embodiment of all evil, the devil incarnate.*

MARK OF THE BEAST *A fearsome but benevolent guardian dragon glares from a Chinese robe made during the Ch'ing dynasty (1644–1912). The beast's five-clawed limbs mark it as an exclusively imperial protector; commoners were restricted, on pain of death, to four-clawed designs.*

of ancient Greece. **3.** A unit of weight of ancient Greece. [Latin, from Greek *drakhmē.*]

Dra·co (drā′kō) *n.* A constellation in the polar region of the Northern Hemisphere near Cepheus and Ursa Major. Also called "Dragon." [Latin *dracō,* DRAGON.]

dra·co·ni·an (drā-kō′nē-ən) *adj.* Also **dra·con·ic** (drā-kŏn′ĭk). **1.** *Often* **Draconian.** Designating an ancient Athenian law or code reputed to be of extreme severity. **2.** Harsh; rigorous: *draconian measures; a draconian penalty.* [After *Draco,* Athenian statesman and lawgiver, whose code (621 B.C.) punished even the most trivial offenses by death.] —**dra·con·i·cal·ly** *adv.*

dra·con·ic[1] (drā-kŏn′ĭk) *adj.* Of or pertaining to a dragon. [Latin *dracō* (stem *dracōn-*), DRAGON.]

draconic[2]. Variant of **draconian.**

draff (drăf) *n.* Also *chiefly British* **draught.** Refuse from brewing or distilling; dregs; lees of malt. [Middle English *draf,* Old English *dræf* (unattested).]

draft (drăft, dräft) *n.* **1. a.** A current of air in an enclosed area. **b.** A current of air induced by artificial means. **c.** A device in a flue controlling the circulation of air. **2. a.** A pull or traction of a load. **b.** That which is pulled or drawn. **c.** *British.* The traction power or duty of a locomotive. **3.** The depth of a vessel's keel below the water line. **4. a.** A gulp, swallow, or inhalation. **b.** The amount taken in by a single act of drinking or inhaling. **c.** A measured portion, dose. **5.** The drawing of a liquid, as from a cask or keg. **6. a.** The drawing in of a fishnet. **b.** The catch. **7. a.** A preliminary version of a plan, document, picture, or the like. **b.** A representation of something to be constructed. **8.** A documentary instruction to transfer money. **9.** A demand, as on resources or a person's goodwill. **10. a.** The transfer of soldiers from one unit to another or to a special duty. **b.** The soldiers transferred. **11. a.** Conscription for military service. **b.** Those conscripted for military service. **12.** *Masonry.* A narrow line chiseled on a stone to guide the stone-cutter in leveling its surface. **13.** *Metallurgy.* A slight taper given a die to facilitate the removal of a casting. **14.** *Commerce.* An allowance made for loss of weight in merchandise. —**on draft.** Tapped from the keg; not bottled.

~*tr.v.* **drafted, drafting, drafts.** Also *chiefly British* **draught. 1. a.** To draw up a preliminary version of or plan for. **b.** To compose. **2.** *Military.* **a.** To attach or assign to a different unit. **b.** To conscript. **3.** To enlist the services of (a person) for a special purpose. Often used with *in.* **4.** To chisel a line on (a stone) to guide the cutter.

~*adj.* Also *chiefly British* **draught. 1.** Suited for or used for drawing heavy loads. **2.** Drawn from a cask or tap. [Middle English *draught,* a pulling, a drawing, perhaps from Old Norse *drāttr.*] —**draft·er** *n.*

draft board *n.* A local board of civilians in charge of the selection of men for compulsory military service.

draft·ee (drăf-tē′, dräf-) *n.* One conscripted for military service.

draft·ing (drăf′tĭng, dräf′-) *n.* The systematic representation and dimensional specification of mechanical and architectural structures. Also called "mechanical drawing."

drafts·man (drăfts′mən, dräfts′-) *n., pl.* **-men** (-mĭn). **1.** One who draws plans or designs. **2.** One who draws up documents. **3.** One who excels in drawing. [Drafts, genitive of DRAFT + MAN.] —**drafts·man·ship** *n.*

draft·y (drăf′tē, dräf′-) *adj.* **-ier, iest.** Having or exposed to drafts of air. —**draft·i·ly** *adv.* —**draft·i·ness** *n.*

drag (drăg) *v.* **dragged, dragging, drags.** —*tr.* **1. a.** To pull or draw along the ground by force; haul. **b.** To cause to trail along the ground. **2. a.** To search or sweep the bottom of (a body of water), as with a grappling hook or dragnet. **b.** To bring up or catch by such means. **3. a.** To take forcibly away from, to, or into. **b.** To take (a reluctant person) somewhere. **4.** To move with great reluctance, weariness, or difficulty. **5.** To break (land) with a harrow. **6.** To prolong unnecessarily or tediously. Used with *out.* **7.** To introduce gratuitously into a discussion. Used with *in.* **8.** To extract (a confession, for example) from a stubbornly reticent person. **9.** To follow (an animal or a trail). Used of hunting hounds. —*intr.* **1.** To trail along the ground. **2.** To move slowly or with effort. **3.** To lag behind. **4.** To pass or proceed slowly, tediously, or laboriously. **5.** To search or dredge the bottom of a body of water. **6.** *Slang.* To draw on a cigarette.

~*n.* **1.** The act of dragging. **2.** Something that is dragged along the ground, such as a harrow or an implement for spreading manure. **3.** A device for dragging under water, such as a grappling hook, dredge, or dragnet. **4.** A heavy sledge or cart for conveying loads. **5.** A large four-horse coach with seats inside and on top. **6.** Something that retards motion, such as a sea anchor. **7. a.** A person or thing that holds one back or hinders progress; drawback. **b.** *Slang.* Something or someone that is obnoxiously tiresome or boring: *What a drag!* **8.** The degree of resistance involved in dragging or hauling. **9.** *Aviation.* The retarding force exerted on a moving body by a fluid medium. **10.** *Billiards.* A backspin given to the cue ball to prevent it from continuing onward after hitting another ball. **11.** A

dragonfly *One of the fastest-moving insects, it can swoop across fields at up to 55 kilometers (35 miles) per hour.*

slow, laborious motion or movement. **12.** *Hunting.* Something that provides an artificial scent. Also used adjectivally: *drag hounds.* **13.** *Slang.* A puff on a cigarette, pipe, or cigar. **14.** *Slang.* **a.** A **dragster** *(see).* **b.** A race for dragsters. **15.** *Slang.* Women's clothing worn by a man. Sometimes used adjectivally: *a drag show.* [Middle English *draggen,* from Old English *dragan* or Old Norse *draga.*]

drag anchor *n. Nautical.* A **sea anchor** *(see).*

dra·gée (dra-zhā′) *n.* **1.** A tiny round, hard sweet used for decorating cakes. **2.** A small, often medicated, sweet. **3.** A sweet made of fruit and nuts and coated in hard icing. [French, "sweetmeat," from Old French *drageet.*]

drag·gle (drăg′əl) *v.* **-gled, -gling, -gles.** —*tr.* To make wet and dirty by dragging in mud. —*intr.* **1.** To become muddy by being trailed. **2.** To follow slowly; lag; straggle. [Frequentative of DRAG.]

drag·gle·tail (drăg′əl-tāl′) *n. Archaic.* A bedraggled or slatternly woman.

drag·gle·tailed (drăg′əl-tāld′) *adj.* Bedraggled.

drag·gy (drăg′ē) *adj.* **-gier, -giest. 1.** Dull and listless. **2.** *Slang.* Obnoxiously tiresome.

drag·line (drăg′līn′) *n.* **1.** A line used for dragging. **2.** A kind of dredging machine.

drag link *n.* A link for transmitting rotary motion between cranks on two parallel but slightly offset shafts, such as the rod connecting the lever of the steering gear to the steering arm in an automobile.

drag·net (drăg′nĕt′) *n.* **1. a.** A net for dragging the bottom of lakes or rivers in the search for an object. **b.** A net for catching small game. **2.** The system of interrelated police procedures used in the apprehension of criminal suspects.

drag·o·man (drăg′ə-mən) *n., pl.* **-mans** or **-men** (-mĭn). Formerly, an interpreter or guide in countries where Arabic, Turkish, or Persian was spoken. [Middle English *drogman,* from Old French *drugeman,* from Medieval Latin *dragumannus,* from Middle Greek *dragoumanos,* from Arabic *targumān,* from Aramaic *tūrgemānā,* from Akkadian *targumānu,* "interpreter," from *ragāmu,* to call, akin to Mishnaic Hebrew *targūm,* TARGUM.]

drag·on (drăg′ən) *n.* **1. a.** A fabulous monster, represented usually as a gigantic reptile breathing fire and having a lion's claws, the tail of a serpent, wings, and a scaly skin. **b.** A figure or other representation of this creature. **2.** *Archaic.* A large snake or serpent. **3.** A fiercely vigilant or intractable older woman. **4.** Any of various lizards, such as one of the genus *Draco,* or the **Komodo dragon** *(see).* **5.** A plant, the **green dragon** *(see).* **6. Dragon.** The constellation **Draco** *(see).* Preceded by *the.* **7. Dragon.** Satan; the Devil. Preceded by *the old.* [Middle English *drago(u)n,* from Old French *dragon,* from Latin *dracō* (stem *dracōn-*), dragon, serpent, from Greek *drakōn,* serpent.]

drag·on·et (drăg′ə-nĭt) *n.* Any of various small, often brightly colored marine fishes of the family Callionymidae, having a slender body and a flattened head. [Middle English, from DRAGON.]

drag·on·fly (drăg′ən-flī′) *n., pl.* **-flies.** Any of various large insects of the order Odonata, having two pairs of narrow, iridescent, net-veined wings and a long, slender body. Sometimes called "darning needle," "devil's darning needle."

drag·on·head (drăg′ən-hĕd′) *n.* Any of several plants of the genera *Dracocephalum* or *Physostegia,* having terminal spikes of rose-pink or purplish flowers.

drag·on·nade (drăg′ə-nād′) *n.* **1.** *History.* An act of persecution of the Huguenots in France in the reign of Louis XIV, consisting of the quartering of dragoons on their property. **2.** Any subjection by military force.
~*tr.v.* To subject to military persecution. [French, from *dragon,* DRAGOON.]

drag·on·root (drăg′ən-rōōt′, -rŏŏt′) *n.* A plant, the **green dragon** *(see).*

dragon's blood *n.* **1.** A red, resinous substance obtained from the fruit of certain palm trees, such as *Daemonorops draco,* and from the stems of various species of *Dracaena,* formerly used in the manufacture of varnishes and lacquers. **2.** Any of several similar resins.

dragon's teeth *pl.n. Informal.* Obstacles, such as pointed concrete stakes, placed in the ground to hinder the progress of tanks and other military vehicles.

dragon tree *n.* A tree, *Dracaena draco,* of the Canary Islands, having a thick trunk, clusters of sword-shaped leaves, and orange fruit. [Its resin was once thought to be the same substance as the blood in a dragon's veins.]

dra·goon (dra-gōōn′, dră-) *n.* **1.** A heavily armed trooper in some European armies of the 17th and 18th centuries. **2.** A type of domestic fancy pigeon.
~*tr.v.* **dragooned, -gooning, -goons. 1.** To persecute by the use of troops. **2.** To coerce; harass. [French *dragon,* carbine, "fire-breather," from Old French, DRAGON.]

drag race *n.* A race between specially modified cars to determine which can accelerate faster from a standstill.

drag rope *n.* **1.** A rope used for dragging military equipment. **2.** The rope that trails from a hot-air balloon and is used for braking or mooring.

drag·ster (drăg′stər) *n.* A car specially modified for drag races.

drail (drāl) *n.* A fishhook weighted with lead and dragged through the water. [Probably a variant of TRAIL.]

drain (drān) *v.* **drained, draining, drains.** —*tr.* **1.** To draw off (a liquid) by a gradual process. **2.** To cause liquid substance to go out from; empty; dry. **3.** To drink all the contents of. **4. a.** To consume totally; exhaust. **b.** To deplete. **c.** To fatigue or spend emotionally

or physically. —*intr.* **1.** To flow off or go out of. **2.** To become empty or dry by the drawing off of liquid. **3.** To discharge surface waters in a given tract of land or region, through natural drainage channels. —See Usage note at **deplete.**
~*n.* **1.** A pipe or channel by which liquid is drawn off, especially one carrying off rainwater, sewage, and the like. **2.** *Surgery.* A device, such as a tube, inserted into the opening of a wound or cavity to facilitate discharge of fluid. **3.** The action or process or an instance of depletion or exhaustion. **4.** *Electronics.* The electrode in a field-effect transistor into which the majority carriers flow from the interelectrode space. —**down the drain.** *Informal.* Wasted; lost. [Middle English *dreinen,* Old English *drēahnian,* from Germanic.] —**drain·a·ble** *adj.*

drain·age (drā′nĭj) *n.* **1.** The action or a given method of draining. **2.** A natural or artificial system of drains. **3.** That which is drained off. **4.** *Medicine.* The draining of fluids from wounds or body cavities.

drainage basin *n.* The area drained by a river system.

drain·er (drā′nər) *n.* One that drains, especially a device to hold objects being drained; specifically, a rack to hold tableware for drying.

drain·pipe (drān′pīp′) *n.* A pipe for carrying off rainwater or sewage.

drake¹ (drāk) *n.* A male duck. [Middle English, perhaps from Low German, from West Germanic *drako* (unattested), male.]

drake² *n.* **1.** A mayfly used as fishing bait. Also called "drake fly." **2.** *History.* A type of small cannon. [Middle English *drake,* dragon, drake fly, Old English *draca,* from West Germanic *drako* (unattested), from Latin *dracō,* DRAGON.]

Drake (drāk), **Sir Francis** (*c.* 1540–1596). English admiral and navigator, the first Englishman to circumnavigate the world (1580). In 1587, when war with Spain loomed, Drake attacked Cádiz, destroying about 30 Spanish ships. He was vice admiral of the fleet that destroyed the Spanish Armada (1588).

Dra·kens·berg Mountains (drä′kənz-bûrg′). The principal mountain range in southern Africa, extending from Cape Province through the Transvaal and Natal.

Drake Strait or **Passage.** Strait in Antarctica, extending *c.* 805 kilometers (500 miles) between the South Pacific Ocean and the South Atlantic Ocean south of Cape Horn.

dram (drăm) *n.* **1.** *Abbr.* **dr a.** A unit of weight in the U.S. Customary System, an avoirdupois unit equal to 27.344 grains or 0.0625 ounce. **b.** A unit of apothecary weight, equal to 60 grains. **2. a.** A small draft: *a dram of whiskey.* **b.** A bit: *not a dram of sympathy.* [Middle English *dragme, drame,* dram, drachma, from Old French, from Medieval Latin *dragma,* from Latin *drachma,* DRACHMA.]

dram. dramatic.

dra·ma (drä′mə, drăm′ə) *n.* **1.** A prose or verse composition written for or as if for performance by actors; a play. **2.** The dramatic art or a particular dramatic repertory: *Elizabethan drama.* **3. a.** A situation or succession of events in real life having the dramatic progression or emotional content characteristic of a play. **b.** A histrionic scene. **4.** The quality or condition of being dramatic. [Late Latin *drāma,* from Greek *drama,* deed, action on the stage, drama, from *dran,* to do.]

Dram·a·mine (drăm′ə-mēn′) *n.* A trademark for dimenhydrinate, used to treat travel sickness.

dra·mat·ic (drə-măt′ĭk) *adj. rare* **dra·mat·i·cal** (-ĭ-kəl). *Abbr.* **dram. 1.** Of or pertaining to drama or the theater. **2.** Resembling a drama in emotional content or progression. **3.** Striking in appearance or forcefully effective. [Late Latin *drāmaticus,* from Greek *dramatikos,* from *drama* (stem *dramat-*), DRAMA.] —**dra·mat·i·cal·ly** *adv.*

dramatic irony *n.* Irony occurring as in a drama, when the implications of words uttered are understood by the audience but not by the characters in the play. Also called "irony."

dramatic monologue *n.* A literary work, especially in verse, in which a figure reveals his or her character in a monologue addressed directly to the reader or to another person.

dra·mat·ics (drə-măt′ĭks) *n. Used with a singular or plural verb.* **1.** The art of acting. **2.** The study or art of staging plays. **3.** Dramatic or histrionic behavior.

dram·a·tis per·so·nae (drăm′ə-tĭs pər-sō′nē, drä′mə-tĭs) *pl.n.* **1.** *Used with a plural verb.* The characters in a play or story. **2.** *Used with a singular verb.* A list of these characters, printed at the beginning of the text. [New Latin, "characters of the drama."]

dram·a·tist (drăm′ə-tĭst, drä′mə-) *n.* A playwright.

dram·a·ti·za·tion (drăm′ə-tə-zā′shən, drä′mə-) *n.* **1.** The act of dramatizing, especially of transforming a novel or similar work into a play or drama. **2.** A dramatic version of something.

dram·a·tize (drăm′ə-tīz′, drä′mə-) *v.* **-tized, -tizing, -tizes.** —*tr.* **1.** To adapt for presentation as a drama. **2.** To present or view in a dramatic or melodramatic way; exaggerate. **3.** To bring home strikingly; emphasize. —*intr.* **1.** To be adaptable to dramatic form. **2.** To indulge in dramatic or melodramatic behavior.

dram·a·turge (drăm′ə-tûrj′, drä′mə-) *n.* A playwright. [French, from Greek *dramatourgos,* contriver, dramatist : *drama* (stem *dramat-*), DRAMA + *ergon,* work, deed.]

dram·a·tur·gy (drăm′ə-tûr′jē, drä′mə-) *n.* The art of the theater. —**dram·a·tur·gic, dram·a·tur·gi·cal** *adj.*

drank. Past tense of **drink.**

dr ap apothecaries' dram.

drape (drāp) *v.* **draped, draping, drapes.** —*tr.* **1.** To dress or hang with or as if with cloth in loose folds. **2.** To arrange or let fall in

dragon tree *An ornamental tree of the Canary Islands that can grow 18 meters (60 feet) tall and 6 meters (20 feet) across. It yields an orange fruit and a red gum once used in medicine.*

loose folds. **3.** To hang or rest limply: *I draped my legs over the chair.* —*intr.* To fall or hang in loose folds.

~*n.* **1.** A drapery. **2.** A curtain. **3.** The way in which cloth falls or hangs. [Middle English *drapen,* to weave, from Old French *draper,* from *drap,* cloth, from Late Latin *drappus,* from Celtic.]

drap·er (drā′pər) *n. British.* A dealer in cloth or clothing and haberdashery. [Middle English, from Norman French, from Old French *drap,* DRAPE.]

drap·er·y (drā′pə-rē) *n., pl.* **-ies. 1.** Cloth or clothing arranged in loose folds; especially, clothing draped on figures in sculpture and painting. **2.** *Often* **draperies.** Curtains, usually of heavy fabric, that drape. **3.** Cloth; fabric. **4.** *British.* The business or premises of a draper.

dras·tic (drăs′tĭk) *adj.* **1.** Violently effective. **2.** Especially severe; extreme. [Greek *drastikos,* active, efficient, from *drān,* to do.] —**dras·ti·cal·ly** *adv.*

drat (drăt) *tr.v.* **dratted, dratting, drats.** *Informal.* To damn. Used interjectionally to express annoyance. [Short for earlier *'od rot,* euphemism for *God rot.*]

Drau. See **Drava.**

draught. *Chiefly British.* Variant of **draft.**

draughts (drăfts, dräfts) *n. Chiefly British. Used with a singular verb.* The game of **checkers** *(see).* [Middle English *draughtes,* plural of DRAUGHT, in obsolete sense, a chess move.]

Dra·va, Dra·ve (drä′və). *German* **Drau** (drou). River in east-central Europe. It flows 724 kilometers (450 miles) from the Carnic Alps in northern Italy to join the Danube near Osijek, Yugoslavia.

dr avdp avoirdupois dram.

drave. *Archaic.* Past tense of **drive.**

Dra·vid·i·an (drə-vĭd′ē-ən) *n.* **1.** A large family of languages spoken mainly in southern India and northern Sri Lanka, and including Tamil, Telegu, Malayalam, and Kanarese. **2.** A member of any of the peoples that speak one of the Dravidian languages; especially, a member of the aboriginal population of southern India.

~*adj.* Also **Dra·vid·ic** (-vĭd′ĭk). Of or pertaining to Dravidian or the Dravidians. [Sanskrit *Drāviḍaḥ,* a Dravidian. See also **Tamil.**]

draw (drô) *v.* **drew** (drōō), **drawn, drawing, draws.** —*tr.* **1.** To pull (something) toward or after one. **2.** To pull or move (something) in a given direction or to a given position. **3. a.** To remove or take out: *draw a book from the shelf.* **b.** To extract (a tooth). **c.** To take or pull out, as from a scabbard or holster. **4.** To cause to flow forth: *a pump drawing water.* **5.** To suck or take in (air or liquid). **6.** To displace (a specified depth of water) in floating: *a boat drawing 18 inches.* **7.** To cause to move, as by leading. **8.** To induce to act. **9.** To attract. **10. a.** To extract from evidence at hand; formulate: *draw conclusions.* **b.** To bring (a fact, for example) to someone's attention. **c.** To take from a source; derive. **11. a.** To earn; bring in: *draw interest.* **b.** To withdraw (money). **c.** To use (a check, for example) when paying. **12.** To evoke; elicit. **13.** To force (a card) to be played. **14.** To take or accept as a chance: *draw lots.* **15.** To get or receive by chance. **16.** To end (a game) in a draw. **17.** To distort; contract. **18. a.** To stretch taut. **b.** To bend (a bow) by pulling back the string. **19.** To shape (wire or candles, for example). **20.** To eviscerate. **21. a.** To describe (a line or figure) with a pencil or similar instrument. **b.** To draft or sketch (a picture). **22.** To portray by lines, words, or imitative actions. **23.** To compose or write up (a will or contract, for example) in proper form. **24.** To close or open (a curtain). **25.** In billiards, to cause (a ball) to spin backward after impact with another ball. —*intr.* **1.** To proceed; move. **2.** To describe forms and figures; sketch. **3.** To be an attraction. **4.** To take in a draft of air: *The flue isn't drawing.* **5.** To use or call upon part of a fund or store. Used with *on* or *upon.* **6.** To cause suppuration. **7.** To steep in the manner of tea. **8.** To pull out a weapon for use. —**draw a blank. 1.** To be unsuccessful; lose. **2. a.** To fail to find something. **b.** To forget something completely. —**draw and quarter. 1.** To execute (a prisoner) by tying each limb to a horse and driving the horses in different directions. **2.** To disembowel and dismember after hanging. —**draw away.** To move ahead (as of a competitor in a race). —**draw back. 1.** To step backward. **2.** To hesitate to carry something out; withdraw from something. —**draw down.** To deplete by consuming or spending: *drew down our oil reserves.* —**draw in. 1.** To entice or involve. **2. a.** To become shorter. Used of days. **b.** To become longer. Used of nights. —**draw on. 1.** To approach; move along. **2.** To bring on; cause. **3.** To use as a source of supply. —**draw oneself up.** To straighten oneself up, as when provoked or annoyed. —**draw out. 1.** To cause to converse easily. **2.** To cause to behave in a relaxed or natural way. **3.** To prolong; drag out. —**draw straws.** To decide by a lottery with straws of uneven length. —**draw the line.** To set a limit, as of acceptable behavior. —**draw up. 1.** To write up in set form; draft; compose. **2.** To pull up to a halt.

~*n.* **1.** An act of drawing. **2. a.** A raffle or lottery. **b.** The random choosing of tickets, numbers, contestants, or the like in a raffle, lottery, or sporting competition. **c.** Something chosen in or as if in a lottery. **3.** A special advantage; edge: *She had the draw on her opponent.* **4.** A contest ending in a tie. **5.** *Informal.* A person, event, or other spectacle that attracts large numbers of people. **6.** A natural drainage basin; gully. [Draw, drew, drawn; Middle English *drawen, drowen, drawen,* Old English *dragan, drōh, dragen,* to drag, draw, from Germanic.]

draw·back (drô′băk′) *n.* **1.** A disadvantage or inconvenience. **2.** A refund or remittance, such as a discount on duties or taxes for

goods destined for re-export or for the manufacture of goods that are to be exported.

draw·bar (drô′bär′) *n.* **1.** A bar across the rear of a tractor to which machinery may be attached. **2.** A railroad coupler.

draw·bore (drô′bôr′, -bōr′) *n.* A hole bored in a tenon such that a pin driven into the hole will tighten the joint.

draw·bridge (drô′brĭj′) *n.* A bridge that can be raised or drawn aside either to prevent access or to permit passage beneath it.

draw·down (drô′doun′) *n.* **1.** A lowering of the water level in a reservoir. **2.** The act, process, or result of depleting.

draw·ee (drô′ē′) *n.* A person or organization, such as a bank, on whom an order for the payment of money is drawn.

draw·er (drô′ər; drôr *for sense 2;* drôrz *for sense 3) n.* **1.** One who draws, specifically: **a.** A draftsman. **b.** *Abbr.* **dr.** A person who draws an order for the payment of money. **2.** A boxlike compartment in furniture that can be drawn out on slides. **3. drawers.** Underpants.

draw·ing (drô′ĭng) *n.* **1.** The act or an instance of drawing. **2.** The art of depicting forms or figures on a surface by means of lines. **3.** A portrayal of a form or figure in lines on a surface.

drawing account *n.* An account recording cash payments to a partner or employee to cover expenses or as advances on commissions.

drawing board *n.* **1.** A flat rectangular board to which paper or canvas may be affixed for making drawings. **2.** *Informal.* The basic planning stages. Used chiefly in the phrase *back to the drawing board.*

drawing pin *n. British.* A thumbtack *(see).*

drawing room *n.* **1.** A formal reception room. **2.** Formerly, a ceremonial reception. **3.** A private room on a railroad sleeping car. [Originally, a room to which one retired for rest, short for *withdrawing room.*]

draw·knife (drô′nīf′) *n., pl.* **-knives** (-nīvz′). A woodcutting knife with a handle at each end of the blade, used to shave a surface with a drawing motion. Also called "drawshave," "spokeshave."

drawl (drôl) *v.* **drawled, drawling, drawls.** —*intr.* **1.** In the speech of certain dialects, for example, to lengthen or add vowels or to make diphthongs of vowels. **2.** To speak in a slow and lazy manner. —*tr.* To utter with a drawl.

~*n.* The speech or manner of speaking of one who drawls: *a Southern drawl.* [16th century : probably cant, from Low German.] —**drawl·er** *n.*

drawn. Past participle of **draw.**

~*adj.* **1.** Pulled out of a sheath. Said of a sword. **2.** Haggard, as from fatigue or ill health. **3.** Eviscerated, as is an oven-ready chicken. **4.** Resulting in a draw. Said of a game.

drawn butter *n.* The clarified butter that separates from the salt and curds after melting, often used with herbs as a sauce.

drawn work *n.* A type of needlework done by drawing out threads from the fabric, usually linen, which is being worked, and adding other embroidery. Also called "drawn thread work."

draw·plate (drô′plāt′) *n.* A die with conical holes through which wire is drawn to regulate its thickness.

draw poker *n.* A kind of poker in which each player is dealt five cards face down and may then discard and get replacements for a specified number of cards after the first round of betting.

draw sheet *n.* A bed sheet that can be removed easily from under an invalid.

draw·string (drô′strĭng′) *n.* A cord or ribbon run through a hem or casing and pulled to tighten or close an opening. Also used adjectivally: *a drawstring purse.*

draw·tube (drô′tōōb′, -tyōōb′) *n.* A tube that slides within another tube to form a telescopic unit.

dray (drā) *n.* A low, heavy cart, typically without sides, used especially by brewers for haulage. [Middle English *draye,* probably Old English *dræge,* dragnet, from *dragan,* to DRAW.]

dray·age (drā′ĭj) *n.* **1.** Transport by dray. **2.** A charge for transport by dray.

dray horse *n.* A horse for hauling heavy loads; a draft horse.

dray·man (drā′mən) *n., pl.* **-men** (-mĭn). A driver of a dray.

dread[1] (drĕd) *v.* **dreaded, dreading, dreads.** —*tr.* **1.** To be in terror of; fear greatly. **2.** To anticipate with alarm, anxiety, or reluctance. **3.** To hold in awe or reverence. —*intr.* To be very afraid.

~*n.* **1.** Profound fear; terror. **2.** Anxious or fearful anticipation. **3.** Awe; reverence. **4.** The object of fear, awe, or reverence. —See Synonyms at **fear.**

~*adj.* **1.** Terrifying; fearsome; dreadful. **2.** Awesome; revered. [Middle English *drēden,* Old English *drǣdan†.*]

dread[2] *n.* A man who wears dreadlocks; a Rastafarian. —**dread** *adj.*

dread·ful (drĕd′fəl) *adj.* **1.** Extremely unpleasant; distasteful or shocking. **2.** *Informal.* Used as an intensive: *a dreadful rush.* **3.** Inspiring dread; terrible. —**dread·ful·ly** *adv.* —**dread·ful·ness** *n.*

dread·locks (drĕd′lŏks′) *pl.n.* A matted, manelike hairstyle consisting of numerous twisted and waxed strands, characteristically worn by Rastafarian men. —**dread·lock** *adj.*

dread·nought (drĕd′nôt′) *n.* A heavily armed battleship.

dream (drēm) *n.* **1.** A series of images, ideas, and emotions occurring involuntarily to the mind in certain stages of sleep. **2.** A daydream; reverie. **3.** A state of abstraction; a trance. **4.** A wild fancy or hope. **5.** An aspiration; an ambition. **6.** Anything extremely beautiful, fine, or pleasant. —**like a dream.** Smoothly; successfully.

~*v.* **dreamed** or **dreamt** (drĕmt), **dreaming, dreams.** —*intr.* **1.** To experience a dream or dreams in sleep. **2.** To daydream. **3.** To have a deep aspiration; hope for something. Used with *of.* **4.** To consider something feasible or practical; conceive even remotely. Used in the negative with *of*: *I wouldn't dream of stopping you.* —*tr.* **1.** To experience an image sequence of in sleep. **2.** To conceive of; imagine. **3.** To pass idly or in reverie. Used with *away.* —**dream up.** To invent; concoct. [Middle English *drem, dreem,* Old English *drēam,* joy, gladness, music, from Germanic.]

dream·boat (drēm′bōt′) *n. Informal.* A person who is one's romantic ideal.

dream·er (drē′mər) *n.* **1.** One who dreams. **2.** A person who daydreams; an escapist. **3.** A person habitually inclined to interpret experience imaginatively without strict regard to practical concerns; a visionary.

dream·land (drēm′lănd′) *n.* An ideal or imaginary land.

dream·scape (drēm′skāp′) *n.* A dreamlike scene or illustration having surreal qualities. [*dream* + land*scape.*]

dream·y (drē′mē) *adj.* **-i·er, -i·est. 1.** Resembling a dream; vague. **2.** Given to daydreams or reverie. **3.** Soothing; quiet; serene. **4.** *Informal.* Inspiring delight; wonderful. —**dream·i·ly** *adv.* —**dream·i·ness** *n.*

drear·y (drîr′ē) *adj.* **-i·er, -i·est.** Also *poetic* **drear** (drîr). **1.** Gloomy; dismal. **2.** Boring; dull. **3.** Discouraging; depressing. —See Synonyms at **boring.** [Middle English *dreri,* Old English *drēorig,* bloody, grievous, sad, from *drēor,* blood.] —**drear·i·ly** *adv.* —**drear·i·ness** *n.*

dreck, drek (drĕk) *n. Slang.* Trash, especially inferior merchandise made to cheat the buyer. [Yiddish *drek* or German *Dreck,* from Middle High German *drëc.*]

dredge¹ (drĕj) *n.* **1.** Any of various machines equipped with scooping or suction devices used in deepening or clearing harbors and waterways and in underwater mining. **2.** A boat or barge equipped with such a machine. **3.** An implement consisting of a net on a frame, used for gathering shellfish. —*v.* **dredged, dredging, dredges.** —*tr.* **1.** To clean, deepen, or widen with a dredge. **2.** To bring up with a dredge. Used with *up.* —*intr.* To use a dredge. —**dredge up.** To come up with; unearth. [15th century (Scottish); perhaps from Low German.]

dredge² *tr.v.* **dredged, dredging, dredges.** To coat (food, for example) by sprinkling with a powder, such as flour or sugar. [From obsolete *dredge,* sweetmeat, from Old French *dragie†,* DRAGÉE.]

dredg·er¹ (drĕj′ər) *n.* A barge or boat equipped with a dredge.

dredger² *n.* A container with a perforated lid used for coating food with a powder, such as flour.

dree (drē) *tr.v.* **dreed, dreeing, drees.** *Scottish & Archaic.* To endure. [Revived (by Sir Walter Scott) from Old English *drēogan.*]

D region *n. Meteorology.* The **D layer** (see).

dregs (drĕgz) *pl.n.* **1.** The sediment of a liquid; lees. **2.** The basest or least desirable portion. **3.** *dreg.* A small amount; residue. —**the dregs.** *Informal.* A contemptible individual or group. [Middle English *dreg* (singular), from Old Norse *dregg.*] —**dreg·gy** (drĕg′ē) *adj.*

Drei·bund (drī′bŏŏnt′) *n.* An alliance of three powers, especially the Triple Alliance of Germany, Austria-Hungary, and Italy formed in 1882. [German, "triple bund."]

dreich (drēкн) *adj. Scottish.* Dreary; bleak. [Middle English *dreig,* enduring, Old English *drēog* (unattested), from *drēogan,* to endure.]

drei·del, drei·dl (drād′l) *n.* **1.** A toy similar to a top with four sides marked by Hebrew letters. **2.** A game of chance played by children at Hanukah. [Yiddish *dreydl,* from *dreyen,* to turn, from Middle High German *dræjen,* from Old High German *drāen.*]

Drei·ser (drī′sər, -zər), **Theodore** (1871–1945). U.S. novelist. His exposure of the seamier side of American life earned him charges of immorality, especially for his first novel, *Sister Carrie* (1900). He wrote *An American Tragedy* (1925), filmed as *A Place in the Sun.*

drench (drĕnch) *tr.v.* **drenched, drenching, drenches. 1.** To wet throughly; saturate. **2.** To administer a dose of liquid medicine to (an animal). —*n.* **1.** The act of drenching. **2.** A large dose of liquid medicine. [Middle English *drenchen,* to drown, from Old English *drencan,* to give to drink, soak.] —**drench·er** *n.*

Dres·den (drĕz′dən). City on the Elbe River in East Germany. It was once the capital of Saxony and in the 17th and 18th centuries was a center for the arts. It was badly damaged in 1760 during the Seven Years' War and was almost completely destroyed by Allied bombing in 1945. The famous Dresden china industry was moved to Meissen in 1710. The city now manufactures machine tools, electronics, and chemicals.

Dresden china *n.* **Meissen ware** (see). [From DRESDEN.]

dress (drĕs) *v.* **dressed, dressing, dresses.** —*tr.* **1.** To put clothes on; clothe. **2.** To trim; adorn. Sometimes used with *up.* **3.** To arrange a display in: *dress a shop window.* **4.** To arrange (troops) in ranks; align. **5.** To apply bandages or other therapeutic materials to (a wound). **6.** To arrange (the hair or a hairpiece); comb and set in a style. **7.** To groom (an animal); curry. **8.** To improve (land) by adding fertilizer, lime, or the like. **9.** To protect (seeds) with a fungicide. **10.** To clean (fish or fowl) for cooking or sale. **11.** To put a finish on (stone, fabric, or other material). **12.** To prepare (hides) in leather-making. —*intr.* **1.** To put on clothes. **2.** To wear clothes. **3.** To wear formal clothes. **4.** To get into proper alignment. —**dress down. 1.** To scold; reprimand. **2.** To wear more casual clothes than usual. —**dressed to kill.** *Informal.* Dressed with conspicuous elegance. —**dress up. 1.** To wear formal clothes, or cloth-

ing more formal than usual, as for a special occasion. **2.** To wear fancy dress. **3.** To arrange in ranks. —*n.* **1.** Clothing; apparel. **2.** A one-piece, skirted outer garment for women and children. **3.** An outer covering or appearance. **4.** *Obsolete.* A setting right; redress. —*adj.* **1.** For or pertaining to a dress. **2. a.** Suitable for a formal occasion: *a dress coat; dress uniform.* **b.** Requiring formal clothing: *a dress dinner.* [Middle English *dressen,* to place, put, prepare, from Old French *drecier, dresser,* from Vulgar Latin *dīrectiāre* (unattested), from Latin *dīrigere* (past participle *dīrectus*), to DIRECT.]

dres·sage (drə-säzh′, drē-) *n.* **1.** The guiding of a horse through a series of complex maneuvers by slight movements of the hands, legs, and body weight. **2.** The training of a horse in deportment and obedience. **3.** A part of an equestrian competition in which such skills are tested. [French, preparation, from *dresser,* to DRESS.]

dress circle *n.* A section of seats in a theater or opera house, usually the first tier above the stalls or ground floor. [Originally reserved for persons in formal dress.]

dress code *n.* A set of rules, as in a school, indicating the approved manner of dress.

dress·er¹ (drĕs′ər) *n.* **1.** One that dresses. **2.** A wardrobe assistant, as for an actor; valet. **3.** One who dresses well or in some specified way. **4.** A tool used for dressing stone, leather, or other materials.

dresser² *n.* **1.** A chest of drawers with a mirror. **2.** A cupboard or set of shelves for the open display of dishes or kitchen utensils. [Middle English *dressour,* kitchen sideboard on which food was prepared, from Old French *dreceur,* from *drecier,* to prepare, DRESS.]

dress·ing (drĕs′ĭng) *n.* **1.** The act of one that dresses. **2.** A therapeutic material applied to a wound. **3.** A sauce for certain dishes, such as salads. **4.** Manure, lime, or the like, used to dress soil. **5.** Stiffening used in the finishing of fabrics. **6.** The various processes collectively by which hides are turned into leather. **7.** Stuffing for poultry, fish, or the like. **8.** Fungicide used to coat seeds.

dress·ing-down (drĕs′ĭng-doun′) *n.* A severe scolding.

dressing gown *n.* A light coatlike garment, usually worn for lounging or before dressing.

dressing room *n.* A room in a theater or home in which one may change clothes or apply make-up.

dressing table *n.* A piece of bedroom furniture, usually consisting of a low chest of drawers with a mirror.

dress·mak·er (drĕs′mā′kər) *n.* One who makes women's clothes and household articles, such as curtains, made of fabric. —*adj.* Having soft rather than tailored lines. Said of women's clothing. —**dress·mak·ing** *n.*

dress parade *n.* A military parade in dress uniform.

dress rehearsal *n.* A final, uninterrupted run-through, as of a play complete with costumes and stage properties.

dress shield *n.* A piece of waterproof material worn under the armpit to prevent perspiration from staining the clothing.

dress shirt *n.* A man's shirt that is suitable for wear with a necktie.

dress suit *n.* A man's formal suit.

dress·y *adj.* **-i·er, -i·est. 1.** Having a penchant for smart clothing. **2.** Smart; stylish. **3.** Suitable for more formal occasions: *too dressy to wear to the office.* —**dress·i·ly** *adv.* —**dress·i·ness** *n.*

drew. Past tense of **draw.**

Drew (drōō), **John** (1827–62). U.S. actor, born in Ireland. Noted for his performances in Shakespearean comedies and society dramas, he organized a famous stock company in Philadelphia with his wife, **Louisa Lane Drew** (1820–97). Their eldest son, **John Drew** (1853–1927), was a romantic actor noted for his versatility in comedy.

drey (drā) *n.* A squirrel's nest. [17th century : origin obscure.]

Drey·fus (drā′fəs, drī′-), **Alfred** (1859–1935). Jewish captain in the French army. He was convicted of treason (that is, of passing secrets to the Germans) by a secret court martial (1894) and sentenced to solitary confinement for life on Devil's Island. Émile Zola and other friends of Dreyfus who suspected that anti-Semites had victimized him campaigned on his behalf, and in 1898 it was disclosed that the evidence against him had been forged. In 1906 Dreyfus was officially cleared, reinstated as a major, and awarded the Legion of Honor.

drib·ble (drĭb′əl) *v.* **-bled, -bling, -bles.** —*intr.* **1.** To flow or fall in drops or an unsteady stream; trickle. **2.** To drool; slobber. **3.** *Sports.* To dribble a ball. —*tr.* **1.** To let flow or fall in drops or an unsteady stream. **2.** *Sports.* To move (a ball) by repeated light hits or kicks, as in basketball or soccer. —*n.* **1.** A trickle; a drip. **2.** A small quantity; a bit. **3.** *Sports.* The act of moving a ball by dribbling. [Frequentative of obsolete *drib,* variant of DRIP.] —**drib·bler** *n.*

drib·let (drĭb′lĭt) *n.* **1.** A tiny falling drop of liquid. **2.** A small amount or portion. [From obsolete *drib,* drop, from *drib,* to dribble, variant of DRIP.]

dribs and drabs (drĭbz′n drăbz′) *pl.n.* Small and sporadic amounts. [From obsolete *drib,* a drop (see **driblet**) + *drab,* reduplication of *drib.*]

dri·er¹ (drī′ər) *n.* Also **dry·er. 1.** One that dries. **2.** A substance added to paint, varnish, or ink to speed drying.

drier². Alternate comparative of **dry.**

driest. Alternate superlative of **dry.**

drift (drĭft) *v.* **drifted, drifting, drifts.** —*intr.* **1.** To be carried along by or as if by currents of air or water. **2.** To proceed without resistance; move unhurriedly and smoothly. **3. a.** To move through life

with no particular goal. **b.** To progress without a set aim. **4. a.** To wander from a set course or point of attention; stray. **b.** To vary from or oscillate randomly about a fixed setting, position, or mode of operation. **5.** To be piled up in banks or heaps by the force of a current of wind or water. Used especially of snow. **6.** To continue in motion for a while after a switching off of power. *—tr.* **1.** To carry along by or as if by a current; cause to drift. **2.** *Western U.S.* To drive (livestock) slowly or far afield, especially for grazing.
∼n. **1.** The act or condition of drifting. **2.** Something moving along on a current of air or water. **3. a.** A bank or pile, as of sand or snow, heaped up by currents of air or water. **b.** Any bank or mass, as of flowers. **4.** *Geology.* **a.** Rock debris transported and deposited by or from ice, especially by or from a glacier or ice sheet. **b.** *British.* Any superficial, unconsolidated deposit above a solid rock layer. **5. a.** A trend or general bearing; direction. **b.** General meaning or purport; tenor. **6. a.** Lateral displacement or deviation of a ship, aircraft, projectile, or the like from a planned course, especially as a result of wind, ocean current, or other disturbance in the medium of travel. **b.** Variation or random oscillation about a fixed setting, position, or mode of behavior. **7.** The rate of flow of a water current. **8. a.** A tool for ramming or driving something down. **b.** A tapered steel pin for enlarging and aligning holes. **9.** *Mining.* **a.** A horizontal or nearly horizontal passageway running through or parallel to a vein. **b.** A secondary passageway between two main shafts or tunnels. **10.** A drove or herd, especially of swine. **11.** *Linguistics.* Gradual change in a language or group of languages. —See Synonyms at **tendency**. [Middle English, a driving, snowdrift, a drove, both from Old Norse *drift,* snowdrift, and from Middle Dutch *drift,* herd, course.] **—drift·y** *adj.*

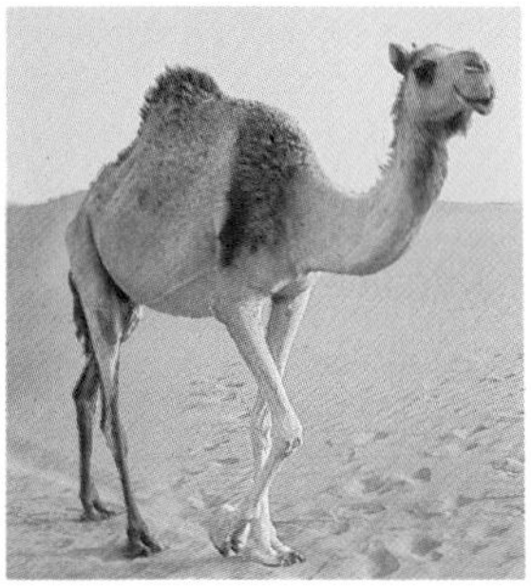

dromedary *The dromedary—an Arabian camel often bred for racing—has only one hump to the Bactrian camel's two. The hump stores fat and acts as the camel's food reserve.*

drift·age (drĭf′tĭj) *n.* **1.** Deviation from a set course caused by drifting. **2.** Anything that has been carried along or deposited by air or water currents.
drift anchor *n.* A **sea anchor** *(see).*
drift·er (drĭf′tər) *n.* **1.** One that drifts, especially: **a.** One who moves from place to place or from job to job. **b.** A vagabond. **c.** One who is passive and makes no attempt to control the course of his life. **2.** A fishing boat with a net that drifts with the current. **3.** A large sail on a ship used when there is little wind.
drift ice *n.* Loose pieces of ice floating on the sea that drift with the current or wind and so cause no danger to passing ships.
drift net *n.* A type of large fishing net with weights at the bottom and floats at the top that drifts with the tide.
drift transistor *n.* A transistor with a good high-frequency response in which the impurity concentration in the base region varies smoothly from a high level at the emitter-base junction to a low level at the base-collector junction.
drift tube *n.* *Physics.* A hollow tube formerly used as an electrode in a linear accelerator, inside which electrons, accelerated between electrodes by a radio-frequency field, drift (move at a constant velocity) toward the next electrode.
drift velocity *n.* *Physics.* The average velocity of a carrier moving in an applied electric field, especially in a semiconductor.
drift·wood (drĭft′wo͝od′) *n.* **1.** Wood floating in or washed up by a tide. **2.** A collection of worthless or trivial elements.
drill¹ (drĭl) *n.* **1. a.** An implement with cutting edges or a pointed end for boring holes in hard materials, usually by a rotating abrasion or by repeated blows. Also called "drill bit." **b.** A hand-held tool, electrically or manually powered, for rotating such an implement. **c.** A **drill press** *(see).* **2.** Disciplined, repetitious exercise as a means of teaching and perfecting a skill or procedure, especially as part of military training. **3.** A specific task or exercise designed to develop a skill or familiarity with a procedure. **4.** *Informal.* An appropriate procedure. **5.** Any of several marine gastropod mollusks of the genera *Urosalpinx, Ocenebra,* and related genera, that drill holes into the shells of bivalve mollusks; especially, *U. cinerea,* a species destructive to oysters.
∼v. **drilled, drilling, drills.** *—tr.* **1.** To make a hole in (a hard material) with a drill. **2. a.** To instruct thoroughly and by repetition in a skill or procedure. **b.** To infuse knowledge of or skill in by repetitious instruction. **3.** *Slang.* To riddle with bullets. *—intr.* **1.** To make a hole with a drill. **2.** To sink a shaft, as when searching for oil. **3.** To perform an exercise; complete a drill. —See Synonyms at **teach.** [Probably Dutch *dril* (noun), from Middle Dutch, from *drillen*† (verb).]
drill² *n.* **1.** A trench or furrow in which seeds are planted. **2.** A row of planted seeds. **3.** A machine or implement for planting seeds in holes or furrows.
∼tr.v. **drilled, drilling, drills.** **1.** To sow (seeds) in rows. **2.** To plant (a field) in drills. [18th century : perhaps special use of obsolete *drill*†, rivulet.]
drill³ *n.* Strong cotton or linen twill of varying weights, generally used for work clothes. Also called "drilling." [Shortening of *drilling,* variant of German *drillich,* from Old High German *drilīch,* from Latin *trilīx,* triple-twilled : *tri-,* three + *līcium,* thread (see **trellis**).]
drill⁴ *n.* A monkey, *Mandrillus leucophaeus,* of western Africa, related to and resembling the mandrill. [West African name.]
drill bit *n.* A boring tool, a **drill** *(see).*
drill instructor *n.* A noncommissioned officer who instructs recruits in military drill and discipline.
drill·mas·ter (drĭl′măs′tər, -mäs′tər) *n.* **1.** A military drill instructor. **2.** An instructor given to severely rigorous training.
drill press *n.* A powered vertical drilling machine, used mainly on metals, in which the drill is pressed to the metal by a hand lever or automatically. Also called "drill."
drill·ship (drĭl′shĭp′) *n.* A ship equipped for ocean floor drilling.
drill·stock (drĭl′stŏk′) *n.* The part of a drilling tool or machine that holds the shank of a drill or bit.
drink (drĭngk) *v.* **drank** (drăngk) or *archaic* **drunk** (drŭngk), **drunk** or *obsolete* **drunken** (drŭng′kən), **drinking, drinks.** *—tr.* **1. a.** To take into the mouth and swallow (a liquid). **b.** To swallow the liquid contents of (a vessel). **2.** To soak up (liquid or moisture); absorb; imbibe. **3.** To take in eagerly through the senses or intellect; receive with pleasure. Often used with *in.* **4.** To bring to a specified state by drinking alcoholic liquors: *drank himself into a stupor.* **5.** To drink something in response to (a toast) or in honor of (someone's health). *—intr.* **1.** To swallow liquid. **2.** To imbibe alcoholic liquids, especially excessively or habitually. **3.** To salute a person or occasion with a toast. Used with *to.* **—drink off.** To swallow in a single draft. **—drink up.** To finish off the contents of one's glass.
∼n. **1.** Any liquid that is fit for drinking; a beverage. **2.** An alcoholic beverage, such as a cocktail. **3. a.** An amount of liquid swallowed, such as a cupful or glassful. **b.** A liquid that is absorbed, as for example, by a plant. **4.** Alcoholic drinks collectively. **5.** Excessive or habitual indulgence in alcoholic drink. **6.** *Slang.* A body of water; the sea. Preceded by *the.* [Drink, drank or drunk, drunk or drunken; Middle English *drinken, drank* or *dronk, drunke* or *drunken,* Old English *drincan, dranc* or *druncon* (plural), *druncen,* from Germanic.]
Usage: Standard English recognizes only *drank* for the past tense form of this verb, and *drunk* for the past participle. Sentences such as *I drunk it* are common in some dialects, but are nonstandard. The adjectival form *drunk* is generally used after a verb *(I was drunk),* whereas *drunken* is generally used before a noun *(a drunken driver). Drunk* is sometimes heard before a noun, but it is generally avoided in writing.
drink·a·ble (drĭng′kə-bəl) *adj.* Suitable for drinking; potable.
∼n. A beverage. Usually used in the plural.
drink·er (drĭng′kər) *n.* **1.** One who drinks. **2.** One who enjoys alcoholic drinks; especially, one who drinks to excess: *a hard drinker.*
drinking fountain *n.* A device equipped with a nozzle that provides a stream of drinking water for public use.
dri·og·ra·phy (drī-ŏg′rə-fē) *n.* A lithographic printing process using special inks that eliminate the need for water on nonprinting areas of the plate. [DRY + -GRAPHY.] **—dri·o·graph·ic** (drī′ə-grăf′ĭk) *adj.*
drip (drĭp) *v.* **dripped** or *rare* **dript** (drĭpt), **dripping, drips.** *—intr.* **1.** To fall in drops. **2.** To shed drops. *—tr.* To let fall in or as if in drops.
∼n. **1.** The process of forming and falling in drops; trickling. **2.** Liquid or moisture that falls in drops. **3.** The sound made by dripping liquid. **4.** A projection on a cornice or sill that protects the area below from rainwater. **5.** *Slang.* An insipid or tiresomely dull person. **6.** A drip feed. [Middle English *drippen,* perhaps from Middle Danish *drippe,* from Germanic.]
drip-dry (drĭp′drī′) *adj.* Made of a fabric that, when wet, will dry to a smooth finish without having to be ironed, merely by hanging.
∼intr.v. **drip-dried, -drying, -dried.** To dry without excessive wrinkling.
drip feed *n.* *Medicine.* **1.** The administration of blood, plasma, saline, or sugar solutions, usually intravenously, a drop at a time. **2. a.** The machine or tubes by which these substances are administered. **b.** The substance administered. Also called "drip." **—drip-feed** (drĭp′fēd′) *tr.v.*
drip irrigation *n.* A form of irrigation in which water is applied to plants in small amounts at regular intervals.
drip pan *n.* Also **dripping pan.** A pan for catching the drippings from roasting meat.
drip·ping (drĭp′ĭng) *n.* **1.** The act or sound of something that drips. **2.** *Usually* **drippings.** The fat and juice exuded from roasting meat.
∼adj. Very wet.
∼adv. Completely; thoroughly. Used in the phrase *dripping wet.*
drip·py (drĭp′ē) *adj.* **-pier, -piest.** **1.** *Slang.* Mawkishly sentimental; insipid. **2.** Tending to drip.
drip·stone (drĭp′stōn′) *n.* **1.** A drip made of stone, as on a cornice over a door or window. Also called "hood mold." **2.** Calcium carbonate in the form of stalactites or stalagmites.
drive (drīv) *v.* **drove** (drōv) or *archaic* **drave** (drāv), **driven** (drĭv′ən), **driving, drives.** *—tr.* **1.** To push, propel, or press onward forcibly; urge forward. **2.** To force to work, usually excessively; overwork. **3.** To force or thrust into or from a particular act or state. **4.** *Sports.* To throw, strike, or cast (a ball, for example) hard or rapidly. **5.** To force to go through or penetrate. **6.** To create or produce (a hole) by penetrating forcibly. **7. a.** To guide, control, or direct (a vehicle). **b.** To lead or control (a draft animal, for example). **8.** To convey or transport in a vehicle. **9.** To supply the motive force to and cause to function. **10.** To carry through vigorously to a conclusion. **11. a.** To chase (game or an enemy) into the open or into a trap. **b.** To search (an area) for game or an enemy in this manner. **12.** To excavate (a mine or tunnel) horizontally. *—intr.* **1.** To move along or advance quickly as if pushed by an impelling force. **2.** To rush, dash, or advance violently against an obstruction. **3.** To hit, throw, or impel a ball or other missile forcibly. **4. a.** To operate a motor vehicle. **b.** To be able or licensed to drive a motor vehicle. **5.** To go or be transported in a car or other vehicle. **6.** To make an effort to reach or achieve a particular objective; aim. **—drive at.** To mean to do or say; imply. **—drive home.** **1.** To force in completely.

2. To cause to be evident or obvious through force or emphasis. ~*n.* **1.** The act of driving. **2. a.** *Abbr.* **Dr.** A road, usually short and residential. **b.** A private road connecting a house, garage, or other building with the street. Also called "driveway." **3.** A trip or journey in a vehicle. **4. a.** The means or apparatus for transmitting motion to a machine or machine part. **b.** The means by which power in a motor vehicle is used to propel it: *four-wheel drive.* **c.** The means or apparatus for controlling and directing a motor vehicle: *right-hand drive.* **5.** An organized effort to accomplish some purpose, such as raising money; a campaign. **6.** Energy; push; aggressiveness; initiative. **7.** *Psychology.* A strong motivating tendency or instinct, especially of sexual or aggressive origin, that prompts activity toward a particular end. **8.** A massive and sustained military offensive. **9.** *Sports.* **a.** The hitting, knocking, or thrusting of a ball very swiftly. **b.** A stroke or thrust by which a ball is driven. **10. a.** A rounding-up and driving of cattle to new pastures or to market. **b.** A similar gathering and driving of logs down a river. **c.** The cattle or logs thus driven. **11.** A device for reading and writing on magnetic tape or disks. [Drive, drove or drave, driven; Middle English *driven, drof* or *draf, driven,* Old English *drīfan, drāf, drifon,* from Germanic.] **—driv·a·ble** *adj.* **—driv·a·bil·i·ty** *n.*

drive-in (drīv′ĭn′) *n.* A retail establishment, such as a restaurant or motion-picture theater, designed to permit customers to remain in their cars. Also used adjectivally: *a drive-in bank.*

driv·el (drĭv′əl) *v.* **-eled** or **-elled, -eling** or **-elling, -els.** *—intr.* **1.** To slobber; drool. **2.** To flow like spittle or saliva. **3.** To talk stupidly or childishly. *—tr.* **1.** To allow to flow from the mouth. **2.** To say (something) stupidly.
~*n.* **1.** Stupid, childish, or senseless talk; twaddle. **2.** Saliva flowing from the mouth; slaver. [Middle English *drivelen, drevelen,* Old English *dreflian.*] **—driv·el·er** *n.*

drive·line (drīv′līn′) *n.* The components of an automotive vehicle that connect the transmission with the driving axles and include the universal joint and drive shaft.

driv·en (drĭv′ən) *adj.* **1.** Motivated by or as if by some inner compulsion. **2.** Carried along and piled into drifts by the wind.

drive-on (drīv′ôn′ *adj.* Designating a ship, ferry, or the like onto which motor vehicles can be driven.

driv·er (drī′vər) *n.* **1.** One who drives, especially: **a.** A chauffeur. **b.** A coachman. **c.** *British.* The operator of a train or bus. **d.** A drover on a cattle drive. **2.** An employer who demands hard work of subordinates. **3.** A tool or device used for driving, such as a hammer or mallet. **4.** Any machine part that transmits motion or force to another part. **5.** A wooden-headed golf club with a long shaft, used for making long shots from the tee. **6.** *Nautical.* A **spanker** *(see).* **—driv·er·less** *adj.*

driver ant *n.* Any of various rapacious tropical Old World ants of the subfamily Dorylinae, that move about in huge groups.

driver's license *n.* An official document that authorizes the holder to drive a motor vehicle on public roads.

driver's seat *n.* **1.** The seat occupied by the driver of a vehicle. **2.** *Informal.* Any position of control, authority, or superiority.

drive shaft *n.* A rotating shaft that transmits mechanical power to a point or region of application.

drive·way (drīv′wā′) *n.* A private road connecting a house, garage, or other building with the street.

driv·ing (drī′vĭng) *adj.* **1. a.** Violent, intense, or forceful. **b.** Rhythmic: *a driving beat.* **2.** Capable of eliciting work or participation from others; energetic; dynamic: *a driving force.*

driving test *n.* A practical and theoretical test of competence that all drivers of motor vehicles must pass before being allowed to drive unaccompanied on public roads.

driving wheel *n.* **1.** A wheel, especially a gear wheel, that communicates motive power in machinery. **2.** The large wheel in a steam locomotive.

driz·zle (drĭz′əl) *v.* **-zled, -zling, -zles.** *—intr.* To rain gently in fine, mistlike drops. *—tr.* **1.** To let fall in fine drops or particles. **2.** To moisten with fine drops.
~*n.* A fine, gentle, continuous rain. [Perhaps a frequentative of Middle English *dresen,* to fall, Old English *drēosan.*] **—driz·zly** *adj.*

drogue (drōg) *n.* **1.** A **sea anchor** *(see).* **2.** A drogue parachute. **3.** A funnel- or cone-shaped device towed behind an aircraft as a target. **4.** A funnel-shaped device at the end of the hose of a tanker aircraft, used as a stabilizer and receptacle for the probe of a receiving aircraft. **5.** A device for indicating wind direction, a **windsock** *(see).* [18th century : origin obscure.]

drogue parachute *n.* **1.** A parachute used in decelerating a fast-moving object, especially a small parachute used to slow down a re-entering spacecraft or satellite prior to deployment of the main parachute. **2.** A small parachute used to pull a main parachute from its storage pack.

droit (droit; *French* drwå) *n.* **1.** A legal right. **2.** That to which one has legal right. [Old French, from Late Latin *dīrectum,* from *dīrectus,* right, correct, from Latin, past participle of *dīregere,* to DIRECT.]

droit de sei·gneur (drwå′də sān-yœr′) *n., pl.* **droits de seigneur** *(pronounced as singular).* Also **droit du seigneur** (dü). **1.** The supposed right of a feudal lord to have sexual intercourse with the bride of a vassal on her wedding night. **2.** Any excessive proprietary claim. [French, "right of the lord."]

droll (drōl) *adj.* Amusingly odd; whimsically comical.
~*n.* *Archaic.* A buffoon. [French *drôle,* from noun, buffoon, from Middle Dutch *drolt,* "little man."] **—drol·ly** *adv.* **—droll·ness** *n.*

droll·er·y (drō′lə-rē) *n., pl.* **-ies.** **1.** A droll quality; quaint comedy. **2.** A droll way of acting, talking, or behaving. **3. a.** The act of joking; clowning. **b.** Something droll, such as a story.

-drome *suffix.* Indicates: **1.** A racecourse or a place for running; for example, **velodrome. 2.** A large field or arena; for example, **airdrome.** [Old French, from Latin *-dromos,* from Greek *dromos,* race, course.]

drom·e·dar·y (drŏm′ə-dĕr′ē, drŭm′-) *n., pl.* **-ies.** The one-humped domesticated camel, *Camelus dromedarius,* widely used as a beast of burden in northern Africa and western Asia. Also called "Arabian camel." Compare **Bactrian camel.** [Middle English *dromedarie,* from Old French *dromedaire,* from Late Latin *dromedārius,* from Greek *dromas* (stem *dromad-*), dromedary, runner.]

drom·ond (drŏm′ənd, drŭm′-) *n.* Also **drom·on** (-ən). A large medieval sailing galley. [Middle English *dromon(d),* from Old French *dromon,* from Late Latin *dromō* (stem *dromōn-*), a kind of fast ship, from Late Greek *dromōn,* from *dromos,* a running, race, course.]

-dromous *suffix.* Indicates running or moving; for example, **catadromous.** [New Latin *-dromus,* from Greek *-dromos,* from *dromos,* a running, race, course.]

drone[1] (drōn) *n.* **1.** A male bee, especially a honeybee, characteristically stingless, performing no work, and producing no honey. Its only function is to mate with the queen bee. **2.** An idle person who lives off the efforts of others; a sponger or parasite. **3.** A pilotless aircraft operated by remote control. [Middle English *drane, drone,* Old English *drān, drǣn.*]

drone[2] *v.* **droned, droning, drones.** *—intr.* **1.** To make a continuous low, dull, humming sound. **2.** To speak in a monotonous tone. *—tr.* To utter in a monotonous low tone: *"the mosquitoes droned their angry chant"* (Somerset Maugham). **—drone on.** To talk boringly and at length.
~*n.* **1.** A continuous low humming or buzzing sound. **2.** Any of the pipes of a bagpipe tuned to produce a single note. Also called "drone pipe." **3.** *Music.* A single sustained note. [From DRONE (bee), imitative.]

dron·go (drŏng′gō) *n., pl.* **-gos** or **goes.** **1.** Any of various tropical Old World birds of the family Dicruridae, characteristically having glossy black plumage and a forked tail. **2.** *Australian & New Zealand Informal.* A dull-witted person. [Malagasy.]

drool (dro͞ol) *v.* **drooled, drooling, drools.** *—intr.* **1.** To let saliva run from the mouth; dribble. **2.** *Informal.* To make an extravagant show of appreciation. **3.** *Informal.* To talk nonsense. *—tr.* To let run from the mouth.
~*n.* **1.** Saliva; drivel. **2.** *Informal.* Silly talk; nonsense. [Variant of DRIVEL.]

droop (dro͞op) *v.* **drooped, drooping, droops.** *—intr.* **1.** To bend or hang downward; sag. **2.** To sag in dejection, exhaustion, or lifelessness. *—tr.* To let bend or hang down.
~*n.* The act or condition of drooping. [Middle English *droupen,* from Old Norse *drūpa,* from Germanic.] **—droop·i·ly, droop·ing·ly** *adv.* **—droop·y** *adj.*

droop nose *n.* An aircraft nose that can be inclined downward to increase runway visibility on takeoff and landing. Also called "droop snoot."

drop (drŏp) *n.* **1.** The smallest quantity of liquid heavy enough to fall in a spherical or pear-shaped mass; a globule. **2.** A minute quantity of any substance. **3. drops.** Liquid medicine administered in such quantity. **4.** A trace or hint of something abstract. **5. a.** Anything shaped or hanging like a drop. **b.** A small globular candy. **6. a.** An act of dropping or allowing to fall. **b.** An act of falling or being dropped; a rapid descent. **7.** A swift decline or decrease, as in quality, quantity, or intensity. **8. a.** The vertical distance from a higher to a lower level. **b.** The distance through which something falls or drops. **9.** A sheer incline, such as the face of a cliff; a steep slope. **10. a.** A delivery of goods, as by a carrier or parachute. **b.** A parachute jump. **11.** Something arranged to fall or be lowered, specifically: **a.** An unframed curtain that forms part of the scenery on a stage. **b.** A theater curtain that can be lowered or raised. Also called "drop curtain." **c.** A trapdoor on a gallows. **12.** A slot through which something is deposited in a receptacle. **13.** *Electronics.* A connection made available for a terminal unit on a transmission line. **14.** A place where secret letters, illicit goods, or the like are deposited for someone else to collect. **—a drop in the bucket** (or **ocean**). A tiny amount in relation to what is available or required. **—at the drop of a hat.** Immediately and willingly. **—get** (or **have**) **the drop on.** To get or have a distinct advantage over.
~*v.* **dropped** or *archaic* **dropt, dropping, drops.** *—intr.* **1.** To fall in drops. **2.** To fall from a higher to a lower place or position. **3.** To become less in number, intensity, volume, or other measure; decrease; decline. **4.** To descend from one level to another. **5.** To fall or sink into a state of exhaustion or death. **6.** To pass or slip into some specified state or condition. **7.** To cease; come to an end. **8.** To crouch. Used of a hunting dog. *—tr.* **1.** To let fall by releasing hold of. **2.** To let fall in drops. **3.** To cause to become less; decrease; reduce. **4.** To cause to fall, as by hitting or shooting. **5.** To give birth to. Used of animals. **6.** To say or offer casually. **7.** To write and send off (a note, for example) at leisure. **8.** To cease consideration or treatment of; have done with. **9.** To terminate an association or relationship with. **10. a.** To leave out (a letter, for example) in speaking or writing. **b.** In knitting, to let (a stitch) fall accidentally from the needle before it has been worked. **11.** To leave out of a team. **12.** To leave or set down at a particular place. Often used with *off.* **13.** To parachute. **14.** To lower the level of

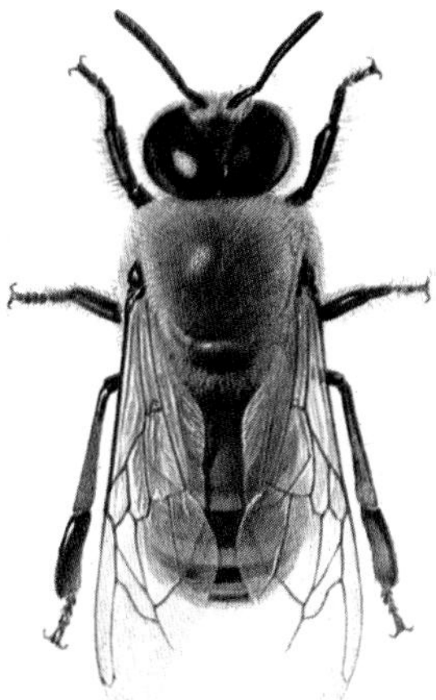

drone *Male bees, or drones, hatch from unfertilized eggs; their only function is to fertilize the queen bee, so that she can lay fertilized eggs that produce female worker bees. The workers feed all the bees in the hive, allowing the drones to starve to death when their usefulness is over.*

PRONUNCIATION KEY
ă, pat; ā, pay; âr, care;
ä, father, are; b, **bib**;
ch, **church**; d, **deed**; ĕ, **pet**;
ē, be; f, **fife**; g, **gag**; h, **hat**;
hw, **which**; ĭ, **pit**; ī, **pie**;
îr, **pier**; j, **judge**; k, **kick**;
l, lid, **needle**; m, **mum**;
n, **no**, **sudden**; ng, **thing**;
ŏ, pot; ō, **toe**; ô, **paw**, **for**;
oi, **noise**; ou, **out**; o͝o, **book**;
o͞o, **boot**; p, **pop**; r, **roar**;
s, **sauce**; sh, **ship**, **dish**;
t, **tight**; th, **thin**, **path**;
th, **this**, **bathe**; ŭ, **cut**; ûr, **fur**;
v, **valve**; w, **with**; y, **yes**;
z, **zebra**, **size**; zh, **vision**;
ə, **about**, **item**, **edible**,
gallop, **circus**, **peaceful**

IN FOREIGN WORDS:
å, *Fr.* **ami**; œ, *Fr.* **feu**, *Ger.* **schön**; ü, *Fr.* **tu**, *Ger.* **über**;
KH, *Ger.* **ich**, *Scot.* **loch**;
N, *Fr.* **bon**; y′, *Fr.* **Compiègne**

STRESS MARKS:
Primary stress: ′
in·cite′ (ĭn-sīt′)
Secondary stress: ′
in′sight′ (ĭn′sīt′)

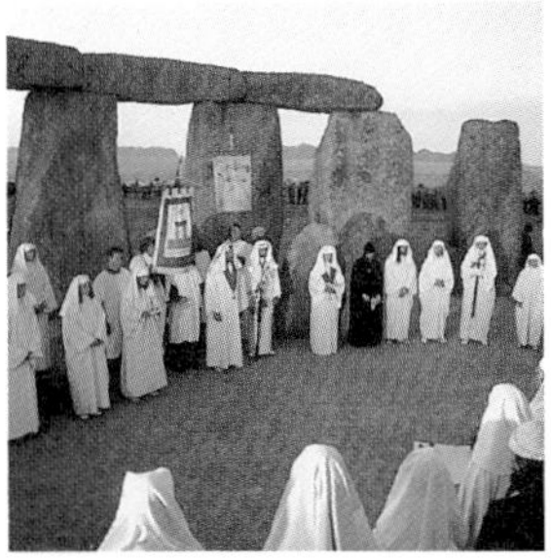

***druids** A modern convocation of druids—priests of an ancient Celtic religion—celebrates the summer solstice at Stonehenge, in England.*

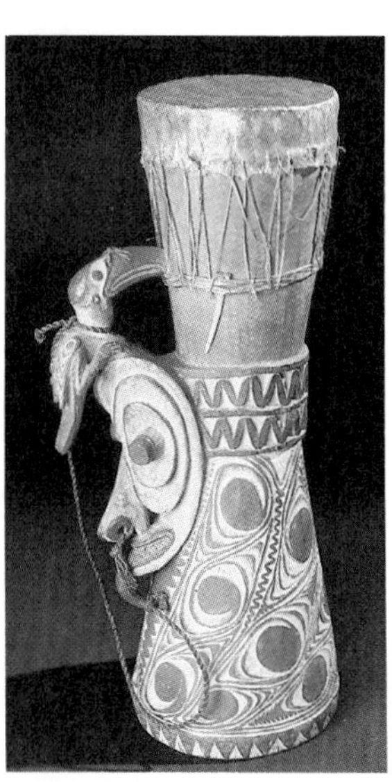

***drum** A percussion instrument, usually consisting of a hollow cylinder closed off by a resonating surface at one or both ends. This native drum from New Guinea is made of skin stretched over a wooden frame.*

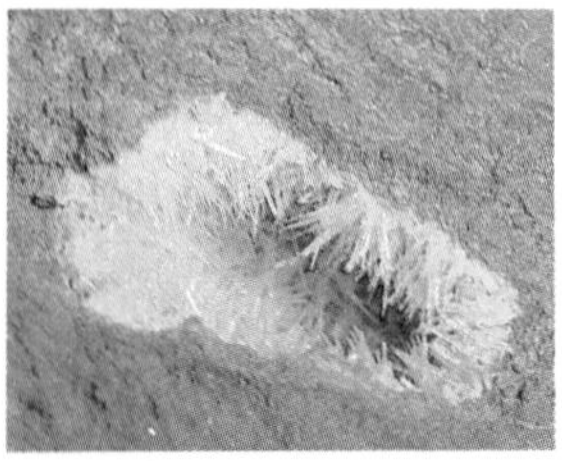

***druse** The crystals in this druse, or cavity, are formed of limestone, the same mineral as the surrounding rock.*

(the voice). **15.** To lose (a game or contest, for example). **16.** To lower (the hem of a garment). **17.** *Slang.* To take orally (a drug, such as LSD). **—drop behind.** To fall behind or back. **—drop by** (or **in**). To stop in for a short visit. [Middle English *drop(e),* Old English *dropa,* from Germanic.]

drop cloth *n.* A sheet, as of cloth or plastic, for protection against spills or dripping, used especially by painters.

drop curtain *n.* **1.** An unframed curtain that forms part of the scenery on a stage. **2.** A theater curtain that can be lowered or raised.

drop·forge (drŏp′fôrj′, -fōrj′) *tr.v.* **-forged, -forging, -forges.** To forge (a metal) between dies by the force of a drop hammer.

drop hammer *n.* A machine used to forge or stamp metal, consisting of an anvil or base aligned with a hammer that is forced down upon the molten metal. Also called "drop forge," "drop press."

drop-head (drŏp′hĕd′) *n. British.* The canvas roof of a car, which can be folded back.

drop kick *n. Football.* A kick made by dropping the ball to the ground and kicking it just as it starts to rebound. **—drop-kick** (drŏp′kĭk′) *v.*

drop leaf *n.* A wing on a table, hinged for folding down when not in use. **—drop-leaf** (drŏp′lēf) *adj.*

drop·let (drŏp′lĭt) *n.* A tiny drop.

drop letter *n.* A letter mailed and picked up at or delivered from the same post office.

drop·light (drŏp′līt′) *n.* A hanging lamp that can be lowered and raised on its cord.

drop off *intr. v.* **1.** To decrease; lessen in quantity, volume, or the like. **2.** *Informal.* To fall asleep.

drop-off (drŏp′ôf′, -ŏf′) *n.* **1.** A very steep slope. **2.** A noticeable decrease.

drop out *intr. v.* **1.** To withdraw from participation in a group or organization, such as a game, club, or school. **2.** To refuse to participate in conventional society, by deliberately avoiding employment, for example.

drop·out (drŏp′out′) *n.* **1.** A person who quits school. **2. a.** A person who drops out of a given social group, environment, or from established society. **b.** A person who abandons something attempted: *a contact-lens dropout.* **3.** *Computer Science.* A segment of magnetic tape on which expected information is absent.

drop·per (drŏp′ər) *n.* **1.** One that drops. **2.** A small tube with a suction bulb at one end for drawing in a liquid and releasing it in drops. In this sense, also called "eyedropper."

drop·ping (drŏp′ĭng) *n.* **1.** That which has fallen in drops. **2. droppings.** The dung of certain animals, such as sheep or mice.

drop shipment *n.* Goods shipped by a manufacturer or seller directly to a retailer or customer but invoiced to the wholesaler.

drop shot *n.* **1.** In racquet games such as tennis or badminton, a shot that causes the ball to drop immediately after clearing the net or hitting the front wall. **2.** Shot made by percolating molten metal through a sieve and then dropping it in water.

drop·sonde (drŏp′sŏnd′) *n.* A **radiosonde** *(see)* that is dropped by parachute.

drop·sy (drŏp′sē) *n.* Pathological accumulation of diluted lymph in body tissues and cavities. [Middle English, shortened from *hydropsy,* from earlier *ydropesie,* from Old French, from Latin *hydrōpisis,* from Greek *hudrōpisis,* from *hudrōps,* from *hudōr,* water.] **—drop·si·cal** *adj.* **—drop·si·cal·ly** *adv.*

dropt. *Archaic.* Past tense and past participle of **drop.**

drop tank *n.* A fuel tank, carried externally by an aircraft, that can be jettisoned in flight.

drop·wort (drŏp′wûrt′) *n.* **1.** A plant, *Filipendula vulgaris* (or *F. hexapetala*), native to Eurasia, having finely divided leaflets and clusters of small white flowers. **2.** Any of various water plants of the genus *Oenanthe,* having white flowers borne in an umbel.

drosh·ky (drŏsh′kē) *n., pl.* **-kies.** Also **dros·ky** (drŏs′kē). An open, four-wheeled, horse-drawn carriage formerly common in Russia. [Russian *drozhki,* diminutive of *drogi,* wagon, plural formation from *droga,* beam of the wagon.]

dro·soph·i·la (drō-sŏf′ə-lə) *n., pl.* **-las** or **-lae** (-lē). A small fly of the genus *Drosophila*; especially, the fruit fly *D. melanogaster,* used extensively in genetic studies. [New Latin : Greek *drosos*†, dew + *-philos,* loving, -PHILOUS.]

dross (drôs, drŏs) *n.* **1.** Waste product or impurities formed on the surface of molten metal during smelting. **2. a.** Worthless or waste material. **b.** Stultifying rubbish: *reading the dross in the tabloids.* [Middle English *dros,* Old English *drōs,* dregs.] **—dross·i·ness** *n.* **—dross·y** *adj.*

drought (drout) *n.* Also **drouth** (drouth). **1.** A long period with no rain, especially during a planting season. **2.** A dearth of anything; scarcity. [Middle English *drought,* Old English *drūgath,* from *drȳge,* DRY.] **—drought·y** *adj.*

drove¹. Past tense of **drive.**

drove² (drōv) *n.* **1.** A flock or herd being driven in a body. **2.** A large mass of people moving or acting as a body. **3.** A stonemason's broad-edged chisel used for rough-hewing. Also called "drove chisel." **4.** A stone surface dressed with a drove.

~*tr.v.* **droved, droving, droves. 1.** *British.* To herd (animals). **2.** To dress (stone) with a drove. [Middle English *drove,* Old English *drāf,* from *drīfan,* to DRIVE.]

drov·er (drō′vər) *n.* A driver of cattle or sheep.

drown (droun) *v.* **drowned, drowning, drowns.** —*intr.* To die by suffocating in water or other liquid. —*tr.* **1.** To kill by submerging and suffocating in water or other liquid. **2.** To drench thoroughly or cover with a liquid. **3.** To deaden one's awareness of, as by immersion: *drowned her troubles in drink.* **4.** To overwhelm and blur (a sound) by a louder sound. Often used with *out.* [Middle English *dr(o)unen,* perhaps from Scandinavian; akin to Old Norse *drukna,* to be drowned.]

drown-proof·ing (droun′pro͞of′ĭng) *n.* A technique for staying afloat for a long period by making use of controlled breathing and one's natural buoyancy.

drowse (drouz) *v.* **drowsed, drowsing, drowses.** —*intr.* To be half-asleep; doze. —*tr.* **1.** To make drowsy: *"on a half-reaped furrow sound asleep, / drowsed with the fume of poppies"* (John Keats). **2.** To pass (time) drowsing. Used with *away.*

~*n.* A sleepy condition. [Back-formation from DROWSY.]

drow·sy (drou′zē) *adj.* **-sier, -siest. 1.** Dull with sleepiness. **2.** Produced or characterized by sleepiness. **3.** Inducing sleepiness; soporific. **4.** Lethargic; lazy. [Perhaps akin to Old English *drūsian,* to be sluggish, and *drēosan,* to fall.] **—drow·si·ly** *adv.* **—drow·si·ness** *n.*

drub (drŭb) *v.* **drubbed, drubbing, drubs.** —*tr.* **1.** To thrash with a stick. **2.** To force or drive (an idea, for example). Used with *into* or *out of.* **3.** To defeat emphatically. **4.** To stamp (the feet). —*intr.* **1.** To beat the ground; stamp. **2.** To pound; throb.

~*n.* A blow with a stick. [Arabic *ḍáraba,* to beat.] **—drub·ber** *n.*

drub·bing (drŭb′ĭng) *n.* **1.** A severe thrashing. **2.** A total defeat.

drudge (drŭj) *n.* Also **drudg·er** (drŭj′ər). A person who does tedious, menial, or unpleasant work.

~*intr.v.* **drudged, drudging, drudges.** To do the work of a drudge. [Perhaps akin to DRAG.] **—drudg·ing·ly** *adv.*

drudg·er·y (drŭj′ə-rē) *n., pl.* **-ies.** Tedious, menial, or unpleasant work. —See Synonyms at **work.**

drug (drŭg) *n.* **1.** A substance used as medicine in the treatment of disease. **2.** A narcotic, especially one that is addictive. **3.** *Obsolete.* A chemical or dye. **—drug on the market.** A commodity for which there is no demand.

~*tr.v.* **drugged, drugging, drugs. 1.** To administer a drug to. **2.** To poison or mix (food or drink, for example) with drugs. **3.** To stupefy or dull with or as if with a drug. [Middle English *drogge,* from Old French *drogue*†, chemical material.]

drug addict *n.* A person addicted to a narcotic drug such as heroin.

drug·get (drŭg′ĭt) *n.* **1.** A heavy felted fabric of wool or wool and cotton, having characteristic colored designs, used for floor covering. **2.** A coarse rug made of this fabric, made in India. **3.** A fabric woven wholly or partly of wool, formerly used for clothing. [16th century : from French *droguett.*]

drug·gist (drŭg′ĭst) *n.* **1.** A pharmacist. **2.** One who owns or operates a drugstore.

drug·store (drŭg′stôr′, -stōr′) *n.* A shop where prescriptions are made up and toiletries and other articles, such as confectionery, are sold.

dru·id (dro͞o′ĭd) *n. Often* **Druid. 1.** A member of an order of priests in ancient Britain and Gaul, who appear in Welsh and Irish legend as prophets and mystics. **2.** A member of any of several modern mystical movements believing in one universal source of wisdom emanating from the sun. [Latin *druides,* druids, from Gaulish, perhaps "soothsayers," from Celtic *derwos* (unattested), true, or from Celtic *dru-* (unattested), tree (their rites being associated with the oak).] **—dru·id·ic, dru·id·i·cal** *adj.* **—dru·id·ism** *n.*

drum¹ (drŭm) *n.* **1.** A percussion instrument consisting of a hollow cylinder or hemisphere with a membrane stretched tightly over one or both ends, played by beating with the hands or sticks. **2.** A sound produced by such an instrument. **3.** Something resembling a drum in shape or structure, especially: **a.** A metal cylinder or spool, wound with cable, wire, or heavy rope. **b.** A cylindrical or barrel-like metal container. **4.** A cylindrical device in a computer on which data is stored. Also called "magnetic drum." **5.** *Anatomy.* The **eardrum** *(see).* **6.** *Architecture.* **a.** A cylindrical block or section forming the shaft of a stone pillar. **b.** A circular or polygonal wall or other structure, such as that supporting a dome. **7.** Any of various marine and freshwater fishes of the family Sciaenidae, which make a drumming sound. Also called "drumfish." **8.** A drumlin.

~*v.* **drummed, drumming, drums.** —*intr.* **1.** To play the drum. **2.** To thump or tap rhythmically or continually. **3.** To produce a booming, reverberating sound as certain birds do, by beating the wings. —*tr.* **1.** To perform (a piece or tune) on or as if on a drum. **2.** To summon by or as if by beating a drum. **3.** To force (knowledge, information, or instructions) upon a person by constant repetition. Used with *into.* **—drum out.** To expel or dismiss in disgrace, originally to the beat of a drum. **—drum up.** To obtain, create, or work up (business or support, for example) by canvassing, soliciting, or advertising. [Shortened from obsolete *dromslade,* drum, drummer, from Low German *trommelslag,* drumbeat : *trommel,* drum (akin to TRUMP) + *slag,* beat (akin to SLAY).]

drum² *n. Scottish & Irish.* A long, narrow ridge or hill.

drum·beat (drŭm′bēt′) *n.* The sound produced by beating a drum.

drum·beat·er (drŭm′bē′tər) *n.* One who supports a cause, especially vehemently. **—drum·beat·ing** *n.*

drum brake *n.* A type of brake consisting of two shoes that are forced against the inside of the brake drum of a vehicle when the brake is applied.

drum·fire (drŭm′fīr′) *n.* **1.** Heavy, continuous gunfire. **2.** A sound suggestive of this.

drum·fish (drŭm′fĭsh′) *n.* A fish, the **drum** *(see).*

drum·head (drŭm′hĕd′) *n.* **1.** The membrane stretched over the open end of a drum. **2.** *Nautical.* The circular top part of a capstan, used to hold bars for turning.

drumhead court-martial *n.* A court-martial held for the summary trial of an offense committed during military operations. [So called because it was sometimes held around a drumhead.]

drum·lin (drŭm′lĭn) *n.* A streamlined hill or ridge composed of glacial drift. Also called "drum." [Irish Gaelic *druim,* ridge, from Old Irish *druim*† + -LIN(G).]

drum major *n.* A person who leads a marching band or a corps of drums, often twirling a baton.

drum majorette *n.* **1.** A young woman who leads a marching band. **2.** A young woman who twirls a baton at the head of a marching band.

drum·mer (drŭm′ər) *n.* **1.** One who plays a drum, as in a band. **2.** A travelling salesman.

drum·roll (drŭm′rōl′) *n.* **1.** A roll on a drum. **2.** The sound of a drumroll.

drum·stick (drŭm′stĭk′) *n.* **1.** A stick for beating a drum. **2.** The lower part of the leg of a cooked fowl.

drunk (drŭngk). Past participle and *archaic* past tense of **drink.** ~*adj.* **1.** Intoxicated with alcoholic drink to the point of impairment of physical and mental faculties; inebriated. **2.** Overcome by strong feeling: *drunk with power.* —See Usage note at **drink.** ~*n.* **1.** A drunken person; especially, a drunkard. **2.** A bout of drinking; spree; binge.

drunk·ard (drŭng′kərd) *n.* One who is habitually drunk.

drunk·en (drŭng′kən) *Obsolete.* Alternate past participle of **drink.** ~*adj.* **1.** Delirious with or as with strong drink; intoxicated. **2.** Habitually intoxicated; chronically drunk: *a drunken wastrel.* **3.** Pertaining to or occurring during intoxication: *drunken driving.* —See Usage note at **drink.** —**drunk·en·ly** *adv.* —**drunk·en·ness** *n.*

drunk·o·me·ter (drŭng′kə-mē′tər, drŭng-kŏm′ə-tər) *n.* A device for determining the alcoholic content of the blood by analysis of the breath.

dru·pa·ceous (drōō-pā′shəs) *adj. Botany.* **1.** Pertaining to or consisting of a drupe: *drupaceous fruit.* **2.** Producing drupes: *a drupaceous tree.*

drupe (drōōp) *n. Botany.* A fleshy fruit, such as the peach, plum, or cherry, having a single hard stone that encloses a seed. Also called "stone fruit." [New Latin *drupa,* from Latin *drūpa, druppa,* overripe olive, from Greek *druppa,* from *drupepēs,* "ripened on a tree," overripe : *drus,* tree + *peptein,* to cook, to ripen.]

dru·pel (drōōp′əl) *n.* A collection of small drupes forming an aggregate fruit in plants such as the raspberry.

drupe·let (drōōp′lĭt) *n. Botany.* A small drupe, such as one of the many subdivisions of the raspberry or the blackberry.

druse (drōōz) *n.* A small rock cavity lined with tiny, perfectly formed crystals of the minerals making up the rock. Compare **geode.** [German *Druse,* "weathered ore," from Old High German *druos*†, bump, gland.] —**drus·y** *adj.*

Druse, Druze (drōōz) *n.* A member of a sect in Syria, Israel, and Lebanon, whose primarily Muslim religion contains some elements of Christianity. [Arabic *Durūz,* plural of *darazi,* a Druse, after Ismail al-*Darazi* (died 1019), Muslim religious leader.] —**Druse, Dru·si·an, Dru·se·an** *adj.*

dry (drī) *adj.* **drier** or **dryer, driest** or **dryest. 1.** Free from liquid or moisture; not wet, damp, or moistened. **2.** Having or characterized by little or no rain: *a dry climate.* **3.** Marked by the absence of natural or normal moisture: *a dry month.* **4.** Not under water: *dry land.* **5.** Having all or almost all the water or liquid drained away, evaporated, or exhausted: *a dry river.* **6.** No longer yielding liquid, especially milk: *a dry cow.* **7.** Lacking a mucous or watery discharge: *a dry cough.* **8.** Needing or desiring drink; thirsty. **9. a.** Of or pertaining to solid rather than liquid substances or commodities. **b.** Not requiring water for use: *dry shampoo.* **c.** Eaten without butter or other accompaniment: *dry toast.* **10.** Not sweet, as a result of the decomposition of sugar during fermentation. Said of wines. **11.** Having a large proportion of spirits to other ingredients. Said of a cocktail, such as a martini. **12. a.** Plain; bare; bald; unadorned. **b.** Lacking interest or stimulation: *a dry book.* **13.** Matter-of-fact; cold. **14.** Humorous or sarcastic in a shrewd, impersonal way: *dry wit.* **15.** *Informal.* **a.** Prohibiting or opposed to the sale or consumption of alcoholic beverages. **b.** *British.* Prohibiting the sale of alcoholic drinks on Sunday: *a dry county.* **16.** *British Informal.* Uncompromisingly conservative. ~*v.* **dried, drying, dries.** —*tr.* **1.** To make dry; free from moisture. **2.** To preserve (meat or other foods, for example) by extracting the moisture. —*intr.* To become dry or lose moisture. —**dry out. 1.** To dry completely. **2.** *Informal.* To treat for alcoholism or drug addiction. **3.** To undergo such treatment. —**dry up. 1. a.** To become intellectually unproductive. **b.** To forget one's lines in a dramatic performance. **2.** *Slang.* To stop talking; shut up. Often used in the imperative. ~*n., pl.* **drys, dries. 1.** *Informal.* A prohibitionist. **2.** *British Informal.* An uncompromisingly conservative person. [Middle English *dry, drye,* Old English *drȳge.*] —**dri·ly, dry·ly** *adv.* —**dry·ness** *n.*

dry·ad (drī′ad, -ăd′) *n., pl.* **-ads.** Sometimes **Dryad.** *Greek Mythology.* A nature divinity inhabiting or presiding over forests and trees; a wood nymph. [Latin *dryas* (stem *dryad-*), from Greek *druas,* from *drus,* tree.] —**dry·ad·ic** *adj.*

dryad's saddle *n.* A large, edible bracket fungus, *Polyporus squamosus,* that has a yellowish upper surface covered in brown scales, found growing on deciduous trees.

dry·as·dust (drī′əz-dŭst′) *n.* A dull, pedantic speaker or writer. [After Dr. Jonas *Dryasdust,* a fictitious character to whom Sir Walter Scott dedicated some of his novels.] —**dry·as·dust** *adj.*

dry battery *n.* An electric battery consisting of two or more dry cells.

dry-bone ore (drī-bōn′) *n. Mining.* **Smithsonite** *(see).*

dry-bulb thermometer (drī′bŭlb′) *n.* An ordinary thermometer used with a wet-bulb thermometer in a psychrometer to measure the relative humidity of the atmosphere.

dry cell *n.* A primary cell having an electrolyte in the form of moist paste. Compare **wet cell.** [Its contents are not spillable.]

dry-clean (drī′klēn′) *tr.v.* **-cleaned, -cleaning, -cleans.** To clean (clothing or fabrics) with chemical solvents such as trichlorethylene. —**dry-clean·er** *n.* —**dry-clean·ing** *n.*

dry-cure (drī′kyoor′) *tr.v.* **-cured, -curing, -cures.** To preserve (meat) by salting and drying.

Dry·den (drīd′n), **John** (1631–1700). English poet, dramatist, and critic, and the first poet laureate (1668). He commemorated Oliver Cromwell in *Heroic Stanzas* (1659), then on the restoration of Charles II in 1660 hailed the return of the monarchy in *Astraea Redux.* In the 1680's he wrote satirical and didactic poems on which his reputation rests, the most notable being *Absalom and Achitophel* (1681). Dryden was converted to Roman Catholicism (1686) and refused to take the oaths when William and Mary took the throne; as a result the poet laureateship was taken away from him.

dry distillation *n.* **Destructive distillation** *(see).*

dry dock *n.* A large floating or stationary dock in the form of a basin from which the water can be emptied, used for maintaining, repairing, and altering a ship below the water line.

dry-dock (drī′dŏk′) *v.* **-docked, -docking, -docks.** —*tr.* To place in a dry dock. —*intr.* To go into a dry dock. Used of a ship.

dry·er[1] (drī′ər) *n.* **1.** Any apparatus that removes moisture by heating or another process: *a grain dryer; a hair dryer; a clothes dryer.* **2.** Variant of **drier** (one that dries).

dryer[2]. Alternate comparative of **dry.**

dryest. Alternate superlative of **dry.**

dry-eyed (drī′īd′) *adj.* Not weeping: *dry-eyed mourners.*

dry farming *n.* A type of farming practiced in arid areas without irrigation by maintaining a fine surface tilth or mulch that protects the natural moisture of the soil from evaporation. —**dry farm** *n.* —**dry-farm** *v.* —**dry farmer** *n.*

dry fly *n.* An artificial fly used in fishing that floats on the water's surface when cast. Compare **wet fly.**

dry gangrene *n.* Gangrene that develops as a result of arterial obstruction and is characterized by mummification of the dead tissue and asepsis.

dry goods *pl.n.* **1.** Goods not containing liquid, such as flour, grain, or the like. **2.** Textiles, clothing, and related articles of trade. Also called "soft goods."

dry ice *n.* Solid carbon dioxide, which evaporates directly to gas at −78.5°C (−110°F) at normal atmospheric pressure and is used primarily as a refrigerant.

drying oil *n.* Any of various oily organic liquids, such as linseed oil, soyabean oil, or dehydrated castor oil, that form a tough plastic layer on exposure to air in thin films and are used as binders in paints and varnishes.

dry kiln *n.* A heated chamber in which cut timber is dried and seasoned.

dry law *n.* A law prohibiting the sale of alcoholic beverages.

dry measure *n.* A system of units for measuring dry quantities such as grains, fruits, and vegetables.

dry nurse *n.* A nurse employed to care for an infant without breast-feeding it. —**dry-nurse** *v.*

dry·o·pith·e·cine (drī′ō-pĭth′ə-sēn′) *n.* An extinct ape of the genus *Dryopithecus,* known from Old World fossil remains of the Miocene and Pliocene epochs, and believed to be an ancestor of the chimpanzees, gorillas, and man. [From New Latin *Dryopithecus* : Greek *drus,* tree + *pithēkos,* ape.] —**dry·o·pith·e·cine** *adj.*

dry point *n.* **1.** A technique of intaglio engraving in which a hard steel needle is used to incise lines in the metal plate, with the burr at the side of the furrows retained. **2.** An engraving or print made with this technique.

dry rot *n.* **1.** A fungous disease of timber that causes it to become brittle and crumble into powder. **2.** Any plant disease in which the plant tissue remains relatively dry while fungi invade and ultimately decay bulbs, fruit, or woody tissue. Compare **soft rot. 3.** A basidiomycete fungus *Serpula* (or *Merulius*) *lacrymans* that causes dry rot. **4.** Any deterioration that has gone undetected.

dry run *n.* **1.** *Military.* A test exercise in bombing, attacking, or other combat skills without the use of live ammunition. **2.** A trial run; rehearsal.

dry-salt (drī′sôlt′) *tr.v.* **-salted, -salting, -salts.** To preserve (meat or hides, for example) by salting and drying. —**dry-salt·er** *n.*

dry-shod (drī′shŏd′) *adv.* Without wetting the shoes or feet. —**dry-shod** *adj.*

dry socket *n.* A painful inflamed condition of a tooth socket after the tooth has been extracted.

dry steam *n.* Steam that does not contain drops of water.

dry-stone (drī′stōn′) *adj.* Made with stones piled on top of each other without mortar: *a dry-stone wall.*

dry wall *n.* A wall or section of a wall constructed of a prefabricated material, such as wallboard.

dry dock *A cargo ship being repaired at the dry dock in Avonmouth near Bristol, England. When repairs are completed, the dock is flooded and the ship towed out through gates at one end.*

d.s. 1. *Music.* dal segno. 2. *Commerce.* days after sight. 3. document signed.

D.S. *Music.* dal segno.

DSC, D.S.C. Distinguished Service Cross.

D.Sc. Doctor of Science.

DSM, D.S.M. Distinguished Service Medal.

D.S.O. Distinguished Service Order.

d.s.p. died without issue. [Latin *decessit sine prole.*]

DST, D.S.T. daylight-saving time.

d.t. double time.

DTL *Electronics.* diode transistor logic.

D.T.'s (dē′tēz′) *pl.n. Informal.* **Delirium tremens** *(see).*

Du. 1. duke (title). 2. Dutch.

du·ad (dōō′ăd′, dyōō′-) *n. Rare.* A unit of two objects; pair. [Greek *duas* (stem *duad*-), the number two, a pair, from *duo,* two.]

du·al (dōō′əl, dyōō′-) *adj.* 1. Composed of two parts; double; twofold: *dual controls on a car.* 2. Pertaining or relating to two. 3. *Grammar.* Designating or pertaining to a number category that indicates two persons or things, as in Greek, Sanskrit, or Old English. Compare **plural.** ~*n. Grammar.* 1. The dual number. 2. A word or expression in the dual number. [Latin *duālis,* from *duo,* two.] —**du·al·ly** *adv.*

Duala. See **Douala.**

dual-control *adj.* Having an auxiliary set of foot-operated controls. Said of a motor vehicle.

du·al·ism (dōō′ə-lĭz′əm, dyōō′-) *n.* 1. The condition of being twofold; duality. 2. *Philosophy.* The view that the world consists of or is explicable as two fundamental types of substance, such as mind and matter. Compare **monism, pluralism.** 3. *Psychology.* The view that there is a phenomenal distinction between mental and physical processes. 4. *Theology.* **a.** The concept that the world is ruled by the antagonistic forces of good and evil. **b.** The concept that humankind has two basic natures, the physical and the spiritual. **c.** The concept that there are two personalities in Christ, the human and the divine. —**du·al·ist** *n.*

du·al·is·tic (dōō′ə-lĭs′tĭk, dyōō′-) *adj.* 1. Pertaining to or having the nature of dualism. 2. Dual. —**du·al·is·ti·cal·ly** *adv.*

du·al·i·ty (dōō-ăl′ə-tē, dyōō-) *n.* The quality or character of being twofold; dichotomy.

du·al-pur·pose (dōō′əl-pûr′pəs, dyōō′-) *adj.* Having two functions or designed to serve two purposes.

dub¹ (dŭb) *tr.v.* **dubbed, dubbing, dubs.** 1. To tap lightly on the shoulder with a sword by way of conferring knighthood. 2. To honor with a new title or description; style. 3. To name facetiously or playfully; nickname. 4. To strike, cut, or rub (timber or leather, for example) so as to make even or smooth. 5. To dress (a fowl). 6. *Slang.* To execute (a golf stroke, for example) poorly; bungle. ~*n. Slang.* An awkward person or player. [Late Old English *dubbian* (unattested), from Norman French *(a)duber†,* provide with armor, equip, arrange.]

dub² *v.* **dubbed, dubbing, dubs.** —*tr.* 1. To thrust at; poke. 2. To beat (a drum). —*intr.* 1. To make a thrust. 2. To beat on a drum. ~*n.* 1. The act of dubbing. 2. A drumbeat. 3. *Music.* **a.** The basic Jamaican reggae backing rhythm, as played on bass and drums, with little or no melodic line. **b.** The purest form of instrumental reggae based on this, relying on studio effects over a heavy drum and bass. [Perhaps from Low German *dubben,* to hit, strike.]

dub³ *tr.v.* **dubbed, dubbing, dubs.** 1. To make a new recording from the original of (a record or tape) in order to make changes, cuts, or additions. 2. To insert a new sound track, often a synchronized translation of the original dialogue, into (a film). 3. To insert (sound) into a film or tape. Often used with *in.* ~*n.* The new sounds so added. [Short for DOUBLE.]

dub⁴ *n. British Regional.* A muddy, stagnant pool; a puddle. [Middle English (Scottish and northern) : perhaps from Scandinavian.]

Du·bai (dōō-bī′). *Arabic* **Du·bayy**). The second largest of the United Arab Emirates. Its capital, Dubai, containing most of the population, is on the Persian Gulf, and its Port Rashid is the chief seaport of the Emirates. The traditional occupations of smuggling and fishing have declined since the discovery of oil both onshore and offshore in the 1960's. Oil is now the major export.

du Bar·ry (dōō băr′ē, dū bä-rē′), **Marie Jeanne Bécu, Comtesse** (1743–93). Mistress of Louis XV of France. She made a marriage of convenience with the Comte du Barry in 1769. She remained Louis's lover until his death (1774).

dub·bin (dŭb′ĭn) *n.* Also **dub·bing** (-ĭng). An application of tallow and oil for dressing leather. [From DUB (to dress, trim).]

Dub·ček (dōōb′chĕk), **Alexander** (1921–). Czech politician and first secretary of the Czechoslovak Communist Party in 1968. He introduced liberal reforms, relaxing censorship and pursuing an independent foreign policy. He called his policy "socialism with a human face." Soviet authorities sent tanks into Prague (August 1968) and arrested Dubček, who was forced to resign.

du Bellay, Joachim. See **Bellay.**

du·bi·e·ty (dōō-bī′ə-tē, dyōō-) *n., pl.* **-ties.** Also **du·bi·os·i·ty** (dōō′bē-ŏs′ə-tē, dyōō′-). 1. The quality of being dubious. 2. A matter of doubt; an uncertainty. —See Synonyms at **uncertainty.** [Late Latin *dubietās* (stem *dubietat*-), from Latin *dubius,* DUBIOUS.]

du·bi·ous (dōō′bē-əs, dyōō′-) *adj.* 1. Fraught with uncertainty or doubt; not yet determined; undecided. 2. Arousing doubt as to validity, quality, or propriety; questionable: *a remark in dubious taste.* 3. Reluctant to concur; skeptical; doubtful. —See Synonyms at **doubtful.** [Latin *dubius,* dubious, fluctuating, moving in two di-

duck *The Aylesbury duck (above) is a farmyard breed reared for the table. Aylesbury ducklings gain weight fast, but the breed lays poorly.*

rections, from *duo,* two.] —**du·bi·ous·ly** *adv.* —**du·bi·ous·ness** *n.*

du·bi·ta·ble (dōō′bə-tə-bəl, dyōō′-) *adj.* Subject to doubt or question; uncertain. [Latin *dubitābilis,* from *dubitāre,* to DOUBT.] —**du·bi·ta·bly** *adv.*

du·bi·ta·tion (dōō′bə-tā′shən, dyōō′-) *n. Archaic.* Doubt.

du·bi·ta·tive (dōō′bə-tā′tĭv, dyōō′-) *adj.* Feeling or expressing doubt or hesitancy; doubting. —**du·bi·ta·tive·ly** *adv.*

Dub·lin¹ (dŭb′lĭn). *Irish* **Baile Átha Cliath** (blä′klē′ə). Seaport and capital city of the Republic of Ireland, on the Liffey River. Danes settled here in the 9th century. They were driven out by the Anglo-Normans in 1170, and a year later Henry II established English rule, which was to last for more than 700 years. Dublin prospered in the 18th century as the second-largest city of the British Empire. Violence and disorder in the 19th century led in 1905 to the formation of the Sinn Fein movement, which urged home rule. Despite the failure of the Easter Rising of 1916, the first Sinn Fein parliament was convened in 1919 under the presidency of Eamon De Valera. St. Patrick's, the principal cathedral of the Church of Ireland, was founded in 1190. Jonathan Swift was dean from 1713 to 1745 and is buried here. The city's industries include engineering, flour milling, glassmaking, and brewing. —**Dub·lin·er** *n.*

Dublin². A county in Leinster, Republic of Ireland. More than 70 percent of the population is concentrated in the city of Dublin, the county town and commercial center.

Du Bois (dōō bois′), **William Edward Burghardt** (1868–1963). U.S. sociologist, educator, and author. A founder of the NAACP, he edited several journals, including *Crisis* (1909–32), and wrote many books, such as *The Negro* (1915) and *Color and Democracy* (1945), which promoted the cause of blacks in America and African colonies.

Du·bon·net (dōō′bə-nā′; *French* dü-bô-nĕ′) *n.* A trademark for a fortified French sweet wine, often used as an apéritif.

Du·bos (dōō-bôs′, -bō′), **René Jules** (1901–82). U.S. bacteriologist, born in France. He conducted pioneer research on natural antibiotics and later studied tuberculosis and environmental factors in disease. He wrote many influential books, including his Pulitzer Prize winner *So Human an Animal* (1963).

Du·brov·nik (dōō-brôv′nĭk). *Italian* **Ra·gu·sa** (rə-gōō′zə). A seaport on the Dalmatian coast of Yugoslavia, in Croatia, founded in the 7th century by Greek refugees. Later settled by Slavs, it flourished as a virtually independent trading republic. It was ceded to Austria in 1815 and passed to Yugoslavia in 1918. It is now a tourist center.

Du·buf·fet (dōō-bə-fā′), **Jean Philippe Arthur** (1901–85). French artist. A painter, sculptor, and printmaker, he developed *art brut,* "raw art," to express the vitality and immediacy absent from some academic art. Many of his paintings consist of characters etched into a rough surface made of gravel, ashes, or sand bound with glue.

Du·buque (də-byōōk′). A city of eastern Iowa, on the Mississippi River. The town developed first as a mining town, then as a lumbering and milling center. Today it is a trade, industrial, and rail center and a river port for an agricultural and dairy area.

du·cal (dōō′kəl, dyōō′-) *adj.* Of or pertaining to a duke, duchy, or dukedom. [French, from Late Latin *ducālis,* from Latin *dux* (stem *duc*-), leader, DUKE.] —**du·cal·ly** *adv.*

duc·at (dŭk′ət) *n.* 1. Any of various gold coins formerly used in European countries. 2. *Slang.* An admission ticket. [Middle English, from Old French, from Old Italian *ducato,* from Medieval Latin *ducātus,* DUCHY (word used on one of the early ducats).]

du·ce (dōō′chā) *n. Italian.* 1. A leader or commander; chief. 2. **Duce.** The title of Benito Mussolini as the leader of Fascist Italy.

Du·champ (dōō-shäN′), **Marcel** (1887–1968). French painter. He became a leader of the Dada movement in New York and was the first to exhibit "ready-made" objects, such as a urinal (entitled *Fountain*) to show that all things were art, or that all art is junk. His major work was *The Bride Stripped Bare by Her Bachelors, Even* (1923), a painting and construction on glass.

duch·ess (dŭch′ĭs) *n. Abbr.* **D.** 1. The wife or widow of a duke. 2. A woman holding title to a duchy in her own right. [Middle English *duchesse,* from Old French, from Medieval Latin *ducissa,* from Latin *dux* (stem *duc*-), leader, DUKE.]

duch·y (dŭch′ē) *n., pl.* **-ies.** A territory formerly ruled by a duke or duchess; a dukedom. [Middle English *duchie,* from Old French *duche,* from Medieval Latin *ducātus,* from Latin *dux* (stem *duc*-), leader, DUKE.]

duck¹ (dŭk) *n., pl.* **ducks** or collectively **duck.** 1. Any of various wild or domesticated aquatic birds of the family Anatidae, characteristically having a broad, flat bill, short legs, and webbed feet. 2. The female of one of these birds, as distinguished from a drake. 3. The flesh of this bird used as food. 4. *Slang.* A person, especially a peculiar one. 5. *British Informal.* Dear. Used as a familiar term of address. In this sense, also "ducks," "ducky." [Middle English *doke,* Old English *dūce,* from *dūcan* (unattested), to dive, DUCK.]

duck² *v.* **ducked, ducking, ducks.** —*tr.* 1. To lower quickly, especially so as to avoid something: *He ducked his head as he went below deck.* 2. To evade; dodge. 3. To push suddenly under water. —*intr.* 1. To lower the head or body. 2. To move swiftly, especially so as to escape being seen. 3. To submerge the head or body briefly in water. 4. In bridge, to lose a trick deliberately. ~*n.* A quick lowering of the head or body. 2. A plunge into water; a dip. [Middle English *douken,* Old English *dūcan* (unattested), to dive, from West Germanic *dukjan* (unattested).] —**duck·er** *n.*

duck³ *n.* 1. A very durable, closely woven heavy cotton or linen fabric. **2. ducks.** Clothing made of this fabric; especially, white trousers. [Dutch *doek,* from Middle Dutch *doek, doec,* akin to Old Norse *dūkr*†.]

duck⁴ *n.* An amphibious military vehicle used during World War II. [Variant of *DUKW,* its code designation.]

duck·billed platypus (dŭk′bĭld′) *n.* An aquatic, egg-laying mammal, *Ornithorhynchus anatinus,* native to Tasmania and southeastern Australia, that has webbed feet and a large, ducklike bill. Also called "duckbill," "platypus," "ornithorhyncus," and in Australia "water mole."

duck blind *n.* A structure of wood or canvas, often camouflaged with reeds and grasses, behind which a duck hunter can hide and shelter from winds while awaiting a flight of ducks.

duck·board (dŭk′bôrd′, -bōrd′) *n.* A board or set of wooden slats laid across wet or muddy ground or flooring.

duck hawk *n.* The **peregrine falcon** *(see).*

ducking stool *n.* A device formerly used in Europe and New England for punishment, consisting of a chair on which an offender was tied and ducked into water. Compare **cucking stool.**

duck·ling (dŭk′lĭng) *n.* A young duck.

duck·pin (dŭk′pĭn′) *n.* **1.** A bowling pin, shorter and squatter than a tenpin. **2. duckpins.** *Used with a singular verb.* A bowling game played with duckpins and small balls. [From its squat appearance.]

ducks and drakes *n.* The game of skimming flat stones along the surface of water so they bounce. —**make ducks and drakes of** or **play ducks and drakes with.** To squander; waste.

duck soup *n. Slang.* Something easy to accomplish.

duck·tail (dŭk′tāl′) *n.* A hairstyle in which the hair is swept back at the sides turning up at the back like a duck's tail. Also called "D.A."

duck·weed (dŭk′wēd′) *n.* Any of various small, free-floating, stemless aquatic plants of the genera *Lemna* or *Wolffia,* having a rounded, lanceolate, or oval thallus that may be a modified leaf or stem.

duck·y (dŭk′ē) *adj.* **-ier, -iest. 1.** *Slang.* Excellent; fine. Often used ironically. **2.** *Informal.* Sweet; adorable. —*n., pl.* **duckies.** Dear. Used as a familiar term of address. [From DUCK (darling).]

duct (dŭkt) *n.* **1.** Any tubular passage through which a substance, especially a fluid, is conveyed. **2.** A bodily passage, especially one for secretion. **3.** A passage in plants into which substances such as resins are secreted. **4.** Any channel through which pipes or cables pass. —*tr.v.* **ducted, ducting, ducts.** To convey through a duct. [Latin *ductus,* a leading, a conducting, from the past participle of *dūcere,* to lead.]

duc·tile (dŭk′tĭl) *adj.* **1.** Capable of being drawn into wire or hammered thin. Said of metal. **2.** Capable of being easily molded or shaped; plastic. **3.** Readily persuaded or influenced; tractable. —See Synonyms at **flexible.** [Middle English, from Old French, from Latin *ductilis,* from *ductus,* DUCT.] —**duc·til·i·ty** *n.*

duct·less gland (dŭkt′lĭs) *n.* An endocrine gland *(see).*

duct·ule (dŭk′tōōl′, -tyōōl′) *n.* A small duct.

dud (dŭd) *n. Informal.* **1.** A bomb, shell, or cartridge that fails to explode when it should. **2.** Someone or something disappointingly ineffective or unsuccessful. **3. duds. a.** Clothes; clothing. **b.** Personal belongings. —*adj.* Useless; worthless. [Middle English *dudde*†, article of clothing, thing.]

dude (dōōd, dyōōd) *n.* **1.** *Informal.* A city-dweller, especially an Easterner who vacations on a Western ranch. **2.** *Informal.* A conspicuously overdressed man; a dandy. **3.** *Slang.* A fellow; chap. [19th century : probably from dialect German *Dude,* fool.]

du·deen, du·dheen (dōō-dēn′) *n. Irish.* A short-stemmed clay pipe. [Irish *dúidín,* diminutive of *dúd,* pipe.]

dude ranch *n.* A resort modeled on a Western ranch, featuring camping, horseback riding, and other outdoor activities.

dudg·eon¹ (dŭj′ən) *n.* A sullen, angry, or indignant mood: *"Slamming the door in Meg's face, Aunt March drove off in high dudgeon"* (Louisa May Alcott). [16th century : origin obscure.]

dudgeon² *n.* **1.** *Obsolete.* A kind of wood used in making knife handles. **2.** *Archaic.* **a.** A dagger having a hilt made from this wood. **b.** The hilt of a dagger. [Middle English *dogeon,* from Norman French *digeon*†.]

due (dōō, dyōō) *adj.* **1.** Payable immediately or on demand. **2.** Owed as a debt; owing: *the sum still due.* **3.** Owed by right, convention, or courtesy; fitting or appropriate: *due esteem.* **4.** Meeting special requirements; sufficient; adequate: *due cause to honor him.* **5.** Expected or scheduled; especially, appointed to arrive. —**due to. 1.** Attributable to; caused by. **2.** Because of. —*n.* **1.** Something that is owed or deserved. **2. dues.** A charge or fee, as for membership in a club or organization. —*adv.* **1.** Straight; directly; due west. **2.** *Archaic.* Duly. [Middle English, from Old French *deu,* from Vulgar Latin *dēbūtus* (unattested), "owed," from Latin *dēbitus,* past participle of *dēbēre,* to owe.]

Usage: The traditional view is that, since *due* is an adjective, it can be used only after a linking verb *(His hesitation was due to fear)* or after a noun when the construction is used adjectively *(His hesitation, due to fear, made him late).* Criticism focuses on the use of *due to* to introduce an adverbial phrase in sentences where *owing to, because of, on account of,* or *through* are more appropriate: *He hesitated due to fear; Due to his bad leg, he didn't come downstairs.*

Stylists have attacked this usage as illiterate for over 100 years. Nevertheless, it is widely employed in informal speech and writing and is increasingly to be encountered in formal contexts (as in *Due to circumstances beyond our control*).

due bill *n.* A written acknowledgment of indebtedness to a particular party, but not payable to his order or transferable by endorsement.

du·el (dōō′əl, dyōō′-) *n.* **1.** A prearranged combat between two persons, fought according to formal procedure with deadly weapons, typically to settle a point of honor. **2.** Any struggle for ascendancy between two contending persons, animals, groups, or ideas. —*intr. v.* **dueled** or **-elled, -eling** or **-elling, -els.** To fight a duel. [Medieval Latin *duellum,* from Latin, archaic form of *bellum,* war.] —**du·el·er, du·el·ist** *n.*

du·el·lo (dōō-ĕl′ō, dyōō-) *n.* **1.** The art of the duel. **2.** The code of rules by which duels were fought. [Italian, from Latin *duellum,* war. See **duel.**]

du·en·de (dōō-ĕn′dā′) *n. Spanish.* **1.** Powerful or magical attraction; magnetism. **2.** A demon or ghost.

du·en·na (dōō-ĕn′ə, dyōō-) *n.* **1.** An elderly woman retained by a Spanish or Portuguese family to act as governess and companion to the daughters. **2.** Any chaperone. [Spanish *dueña,* from Latin *domina,* lady, feminine of *dominus,* lord, master.]

due process *n.* An established course for judicial proceedings or other governmental activities designed to safeguard the legal rights of the individual.

Duero. See **Douro.**

du·et (dōō-ĕt′, dyōō-) *n.* **1.** A musical composition written for two voices or two instruments. **2.** The two performers presenting such a composition. **3.** Any verbal exchange between two people. **4.** Any closely related pair of individuals. [Italian *duetto,* diminutive of *duo,* duet, from Latin, two.] —**du·et·tist** *n.*

duff¹ (dŭf) *n.* A pudding, usually containing dried fruit, boiled in a cloth bag or steamed: *plum duff.* [Northern English dialectal variant of DOUGH.]

duff² *n.* **1.** Decaying leaves and branches covering a forest floor. **2.** Fine coal; coal dust; slack. [Perhaps from DUFF (dough).]

duff³ *n. Slang.* The buttocks. [Perhaps from DUFF (pudding).]

duf·fel, duf·fle (dŭf′əl) *n.* **1.** A blanket fabric made of low-grade woolen cloth with a nap on both sides. **2.** Clothing and other personal gear carried by a camper. [Dutch, from *Duffel,* town near Antwerp, Belgium.]

duffel bag *n.* A large cloth bag of canvas or duck for carrying personal belongings, originally used by soldiers and sailors.

duf·fer (dŭf′ər) *n.* **1.** *Informal.* An incompetent or slow-witted person. **2.** *Slang.* A peddler of cheap merchandise. **3.** Something worthless or useless. [Probably from Scottish *Duffart, doofart,* stupid fellow, worthless person.]

duffle coat *n.* Also **duffel coat.** A short, heavy woolen coat, usually having a hood and fastened with toggles.

Du·fy (dü-fē′), **Raoul** (1877–1953). French painter and textile designer. He produced many brightly colored racing and seaside scenes and the vast panel *La Fée Electricité* for the Paris Exhibition of 1938.

dug¹ (dŭg) *n.* An udder, breast, or teat of a female mammal. [16th century : origin obscure.]

dug². Past tense and past participle of **dig.**

du·gong (dōō′gŏng′) *n.* A herbivorous marine mammal, *Dugong dugon,* of tropical coastal waters of the Old World, having flipperlike forelimbs and a deeply notched tail fin. [Variant of Malay *dūyong.*]

dug·out (dŭg′out′) *n.* **1.** A boat or canoe made by hollowing out a log. **2.** *Military.* A pit dug into the ground or on a hillside and used as a shelter. **3.** A long sunken shelter at the side of a baseball field where the players stay while not on the field.

Du·ha·mel (dōō′ə-mĕl′, dyōō′-), **Georges** (1884–1966). French novelist and dramatist. From his experience as a surgeon in World War I he wrote *Civilisation* (1918), which won the Goncourt Prize. His most successful play was *In the Shadow of Statues* (1914).

dui. Alternate plural of **duo.**

dui·ker, duy·ker (dī′kər) *n.* **1.** Any of various small African antelopes, chiefly of the genus *Cephalophus,* having short, backward-pointing horns. Also called "duikerbok." **2.** *South African.* Any of several cormorants of the genus *Phalacrocorax.* [Afrikaans, "diver," from Dutch *duiken,* to dive, from Middle Dutch *dūken,* from West Germanic *dukjan* (unattested), to DUCK.]

Duis·burg (dōōs′bûrg′). A river port in North Rhine-Westphalia, West Germany. It is at the junction of the Rhine and the Ruhr.

dū jūn. Variant of **tuchun.**

Du·kas (dōō-kä′, dü′kä′), **Paul** (1865–1935). French composer. Before he died he burned many of his compositions, leaving little work. He is best remembered for the symphonic scherzo *The Sorcerer's Apprentice* (1897).

duke (dōōk, dyōōk) *n. Abbr.* **D., Du. 1.** A nobleman with the highest hereditary rank; especially, in Britain, a man of the highest grade of the peerage. **2.** A prince who rules an independent duchy. **3.** A type of cherry intermediate between a sweet and a sour cherry. [Middle English, from Old French *duc,* from Latin *dux* (stem *duc-*), leader, from *dūcere,* to lead.]

duke·dom (dōōk′dəm, dyōōk′-) *n.* **1.** The state or territory ruled by a duke; a duchy. **2.** The office, rank, or title of a duke.

dukes (dōōks, dyōōks) *pl.n. Slang.* The fists: *Put up your dukes!* [From *Duke of Yorks,* rhyming slang for *forks* (fingers).]

duiker *There are ten species of this African antelope that gets its name from the way it dives for cover into the undergrowth—duiker is the Afrikaans word for diver. Duikers feed at night, mainly on plants, but occasionally on carrion. The stripes of the forest-dwelling zebra duiker (above) help it to blend with the shadows cast by forest foliage.*

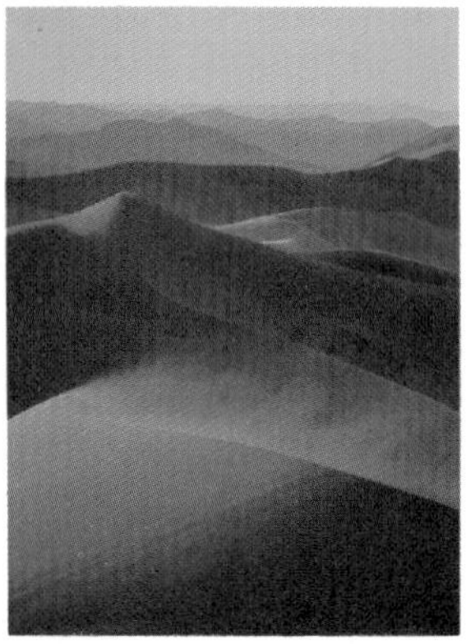

dune *A crescent-shaped sand dune, called a barchan, rises out of the wasteland of the Namib Desert in Namibia. Barchans, formed by wind action like all dunes, can move up to 30 meters (100 feet) in a year.*

Du·kho·bors, Dou·kho·bors (do͞o′kə-bôrz′) *pl.n.* The members of a Christian religious sect of Russia, many of whom migrated to Canada in the 1890's to escape persecution. [Russian *dukhoborets,* "spirit-wrestlers" : *dukh,* spirit + *borets,* wrestler, from *borot′,* to struggle.]

dul·cet (dŭl′sĭt) *adj.* **1.** Pleasing to the ear; gently melodious; soothing. **2.** *Archaic.* Sweet to the taste.
~*n.* An organ stop pitched an octave higher than the dulciana. [Learned respelling of Middle English *doucet,* from Old French, from *doux* (feminine *douce*), sweet, from Latin *dulcis.*]

dul·ci·an·a (dŭl′sē-ăn′ə) *n.* An organ stop with a sweet, somewhat thin tone suggestive of a stringed instrument. [New Latin, from Medieval Latin, bassoon, perhaps from Latin *dulcis,* sweet.]

dul·ci·fy (dŭl′sĭ-fī′) *tr.v.* **-fied, -fying, -fies.** *Rare.* **1.** To make agreeable or gentle; mollify. **2.** To sweeten. [Late Latin *dulcificāre,* to sweeten : Latin *dulcis,* sweet. + *facere,* to do.] **—dul·ci·fi·ca·tion** *n.*

dul·ci·mer (dŭl′sə-mər) *n.* **1.** A musical instrument with wire strings of graduated lengths stretched over a sound box, played with two padded hammers or by plucking. **2.** An instrument used in folk music consisting of a long, fretted fingerboard and three strings. It is usually laid across the knees and plucked. [Middle English *dowcemere,* from Old French *doulcemer, doulcemele* : probably Latin *dulcis,* sweet + *melos,* song, from Greek.]

Dul·ci·ne·a (dŭl′sĭ-nē′ə, dŭl-sĭn′ē-ə) *n. Sometimes* **dulcinea. 1.** An idealized woman. **2.** A female sweetheart. [After *Dulcinea del Toboso,* Don Quixote's idealized sweetheart in Cervantes' *Don Quixote.*]

Dulheggia. Variant of **Dhul-Hijja.**

du·li·a (do͞o′lē-ə, dyo͞o′-) *n. Theology.* Special reverence accorded to saints in the Roman Catholic and Eastern Orthodox Churches. Compare **hyperdulia, latria.**

Dulkaada. Variant of **Dhul-Qadah.**

dull (dŭl) *adj.* **duller, dullest. 1.** Lacking mental agility; slow to learn; stupid. **2.** Lacking responsiveness or alertness; insensitive. **3.** Dispirited; depressed. **4.** Not brisk or rapid; sluggish. **5.** Not sharp or keen; blunt. **6.** Not intensely or keenly felt: *a dull ache.* **7.** Arousing no interest or curiosity; unexciting; boring. **8.** Not bright or vivid; dim: *a dull brown.* **9.** Cloudy; gloomy. **10.** Muffled; indistinct. —See Synonyms at **stupid.**
~*v.* **dulled, dulling, dulls.** —*tr.* **1.** To make less sharp; blunt. **2.** To make less bright or distinct. **3.** To make (the senses, for example) less keen or receptive. —*intr.* To become dull. [Middle English *dul, dulle,* from Middle Low German *dul.*] **—dull·ish** *adj.* **—dull·ness, dul·ness** *n.* **—dul·ly** *adv.*

dull·ard (dŭl′ərd) *n.* A mentally dull person; dolt.

Dul·les (dŭl′əs), **John Foster** (1888–1959). U.S. politician. In 1953 he became secretary of state under President Eisenhower and pursued a policy of active opposition to the U.S.S.R.

dull-wit·ted (dŭl′wĭt′əd) *adj.* Slow to comprehend; stupid. **—dull-wit·ted·ness** *n.*

du·lo·sis (do͞o-lō′sĭs, dyo͞o-) *n.* A practice of certain ants in which members of one species make those of another species perform the work of the colony. Also called "helotism." **—du·lot·ic** (do͞o-lŏt′ĭk, dyo͞o-) *adj.*

dulse (dŭls) *n.* A coarse, reddish-brown seaweed, *Rhodymenia palmata,* sometimes eaten as a vegetable. [Irish Gaelic *duileasg,* from Old Irish *duilesc,* "seaweed."]

Du·luth (də-lo͞oth′). A city of northeastern Minnesota, at the western end of Lake Superior. Huge amounts of grain, iron ore, and bulk cargo are shipped on lake freighters and, since the opening of the St. Lawrence Seaway (1959), on oceangoing vessels.

du·ly (do͞o′lē, dyo͞o′-) *adv.* **1.** In a proper manner; rightfully; fittingly: *duly consecrate a church.* **2.** At the expected time; punctually. [Middle English, from DUE.]

Du·ma, Dou·ma (do͞o′mə) *n.* A Russian national parliament, convened and dissolved four times between 1905 and 1917. [Russian *duma,* thought, council, from Gothic *dōms,* judgment.]

Du·mas (do͞o-mä′, dyo͞o-), **Alexandre,** also called "Dumas père" (1802–70). French novelist and dramatist, father of Alexandre, Dumas fils. Among his most famous works are *The Three Musketeers* (1844) and *The Count of Monte Cristo* (1845).

Dumas, Alexandre, also called "Dumas fils" (1824–95). French novelist and dramatist. His first play, *La Dame aux Camélias* (1852), a frank treatment of the love affair of a courtesan, caused a sensation. Verdi used the story for *La Traviata.*

du Mau·ri·er (do͞o môr′ē-ā′), **Dame Daphne** (1907–). British novelist. Her works include *Jamaica Inn* (1936) and *Rebecca* (1938), which were both made into successful films.

du Maurier, George Louis Palmella Busson (1834–86). British novelist and illustrator, born in France of a French father and English mother. He was an illustrator for *Punch* magazine and wrote the novel *Trilby* (1894).

dumb (dŭm) *adj.* **dumber, dumbest. 1.** Lacking the power or faculty of speech; mute. **2.** Temporarily speechless with shock or fear. **3.** Unwilling to speak. **4.** Not producing or accompanied by speech or sound. **5.** Inarticulate; unable to express opinions. **6.** *Informal.* Ignorant or stupid. **7.** *Nautical.* Not self-propelling. [Middle English *dumb,* Old English *dumb*†.] **—dumb·ly** *adv.* **—dumb·ness** *n.*
Synonyms: *mute, speechless, voiceless.*

dumb·bell (dŭm′bĕl′) *n.* **1.** A weight lifted for muscular exercise, consisting of a short bar with a metal ball at each end. **2.** *Slang.* A dull, stupid person; dolt. [Sense 1 : originally the weight resembled the device used for ringing a church bell, but without the bell.]

dumb cane *n.* A tropical plant, *Dieffenbachia,* with an acrid juice that temporarily inhibits speech when a part of the plant is chewed.

dumb·found, dum·found (dŭm′found′) *tr.v.* **-founded, -founding, -founds.** To strike dumb with astonishment or amazement; stun; nonplus. —See Synonyms at **surprise.** [DUMB + (CON)FOUND.]

dumb show *n.* **1.** A part of a dramatic performance unaccompanied by speech; a pantomime. **2.** Communication by means of gestures.

dumb·struck (dŭm′strŭk′) *adj.* Temporarily unable to speak through shock or surprise.

dumb·wait·er (dŭm′wā′tər) *n.* **1.** A small elevator used to convey food or other goods from one floor to another. **2.** A portable serving table. **3.** *Chiefly British.* A revolving tray in the middle of the table.

dum·dum bullet (dŭm′dŭm′) *n.* A small-arms bullet with a soft nose designed to expand upon contact, inflicting a gaping wound. Also called "spread-on-impact bullet." [After *Dum Dum,* military arsenal near Calcutta, where it was first made (*c.* 1897).]

Dum·fries (dŭm-frēs′). A market town in Dumfries and Galloway Region, Scotland. It was the county town of the former county of Dumfriesshire (or Dumfries).

Dumfries and Gal·lo·way (găl′ə-wā′). An administrative region bordering the Solway Firth, southwest Scotland. It is chiefly agricultural, the main crops being cereals and root vegetables.

dum·my (dŭm′ē) *n., pl.* **-mies. 1.** An imitation of a real or original object, intended to be used as a practical substitute. **2.** A figure imitating the human form, especially: **a.** A model used in designing and displaying clothes. **b.** A stuffed or pasteboard figure used as a target. **c.** A figure of a person or animal manipulated by a ventriloquist. **3.** *Military.* A blank round. **4.** *Informal.* **a.** A mute person. Usually considered offensive. **b.** A blockhead; dolt. **5.** *Informal.* Someone who does not take part or contribute actively. **6.** A person or agency secretly in the service of another; a front. **7.** *Printing.* **a.** A model of a work being published, indicating its general appearance and dimensions. **b.** A model page with text and illustrations pasted into place to direct the printer; a layout. **8. a.** In the game of bridge, the partner who exposes his hand to be played by the declarer. **b.** The hand thus exposed. **c.** In the game of whist, an imaginary fourth hand. **9.** In football, a feigned pass or swerve to defeat an opponent.
~*adj.* **1.** Simulating something but lacking its function; artificial: *a dummy pocket.* **2.** Silent; mute. **3.** Secretly serving another. **4.** Played with a dummy. Said of a card game.
~*tr.v.* **dummied, -mying, -mies.** *Printing.* To make a dummy of (a publication or page). Often used with *up.* [Earlier *dummie, dumbie,* dumb person, from DUMB.]

dummy variable *n.* A mathematical variable that can be arbitrarily replaced by another.

du·mor·ti·er·ite (do͞o-môr′tē-ə-rīt′, dyo͞o-) *n.* A greenish-blue aluminum borosilicate mineral, used in spark-plug porcelain and in special refractories. [French, after Eugène *Dumortier,* 19th-century French paleontologist who discovered it.]

dump (dŭmp) *v.* **dumped, dumping, dumps.** —*tr.* **1.** To release or throw down in a large mass; drop heavily. **2.** To empty (material) out of a container or vehicle. **3.** To empty out (a container or vehicle), as by overturning or tilting. **4.** To get rid of (rubbish, for example); dispose of. **5.** To discard or reject (a burden or a problem, for example) unceremoniously. **6.** To place (goods) on the market, especially in a foreign country, in large quantities and at a lower price than in the country of origin, especially below cost price. **7.** To reproduce (data stored internally in a computer) onto an external storage medium, such as a printout. **8.** To put into temporary storage. —*intr.* **1.** To fall or drop abruptly, especially in a mass. **2.** To discharge cargo or contents; unload.
~*n.* **1.** A place where refuse is dumped. **2.** A storage place for goods or supplies; depot. **3.** An unordered accumulation; pile. **4.** An instance or the result of dumping data stored in a computer. **5.** *Slang.* A poorly maintained or disreputable place. [Middle English *dompen, dumpen,* to drop, fall, plunge, probably of Scandinavian origin; akin to Norwegian *dumpa,* to fall suddenly.] **—dump·er** *n.*

dump bin *n.* A freestanding container in a retail store, used to display goods that are being specially promoted.

dump·ling (dŭmp′lĭng) *n.* **1.** A small ball of dough cooked with stew or soup. **2.** Sweetened dough wrapped around an apple or other fruit, baked and served as a dessert. **3.** *Informal.* A short, chubby person. [16th century : origin obscure.]

dumps (dŭmps) *pl.n. Informal.* A gloomy, melancholy state of mind: *down in the dumps.* [Dutch *domp,* haze, exhalation, "hazy or gloomy state of mind," from Middle Dutch *domp, damp.* See **damp.**]

dump truck *n.* A heavy-duty truck having a bed that tilts backward to dump loose material.

dump·y[1] (dŭm′pē) *adj.* **-ier, -iest.** Short and stout; squat. [From archaic *dump,* a shapeless mass, lump, perhaps a back-formation from DUMPLING.] **—dump·i·ly** *adv.* **—dump·i·ness** *n.*

dumpy[2] *adj.* **-ier, -iest.** *Rare.* Depressed or discontented.

dumpy level *n.* A surveyor's instrument having a short telescope fixed rigidly to a horizontally rotating table.

dun[1] (dŭn) *tr.v.* **dunned, dunning, duns.** To importune (a debtor) persistently for payment.
~*n.* **1.** One who importunes debtors for payment; a debt collector. **2.** An importunate demand for payment. [Shortened from obsolete *dunkirk,* privateer, originally, ship from DUNKIRK, France.]

dun[2] *n.* **1.** A color ranging from almost neutral brownish gray to dull grayish brown. **2.** A dun-colored fishing fly. **3.** A dun-colored horse. **4.** The dun-colored subimaginal stages of a mayfly. ~*adj.* **dunner, dunnest. 1.** Dull; gloomy. **2.** Grayish brown. [Middle English *dun,* Old English *dunn.*]

Duna, Dunaj, Dunărea, Dunav. See **Danube.**

Dun·bar (dŭn-bär′), **William** (*c.* 1460–*c.* 1520). Scottish poet. He was probably a Franciscan who became attached to the court of James IV of Scotland. Most of his poems were allegories, such as *The Thistle and the Rose* (1503) and *The Dance of the Seven Deadly Sins* (*c.* 1508).

Dun·bar·ton (dŭn-bär′tən). Also **Dun·bar·ton·shire** (-shîr′, -shər). Former county in western Scotland, now part of Strathclyde Region.

Dun·can I (dŭng′kən) (died 1040). King of Scotland (1034–40). He succeeded his grandfather, Malcolm II Mackenneth. According to the legend used by Shakespeare in *Macbeth,* Duncan was slain by Macbeth at Pitvagenny, near Elgin, on August 14, 1040.

Duncan, Isadora (1878–1927). U.S. dancer. She met the choreographer Michel Fokine in Russia in 1905 and abandoned the traditional ballet costume for bare feet and Greek draperies. She danced to symphonic music not composed for dance, such as that of Wagner, Schubert, and Beethoven. Her championship of free movement made her a forerunner of modern dance. She was killed when her long scarf caught in the wheel of her car and strangled her.

dunce (dŭns) *n.* A dull-witted or stupid person. [Originally *Duns men,* a contemptuous reference to the disciples of John DUNS SCOTUS, used by their philosophical opponents.]

dunce cap *n.* Also **dunce's cap.** A cone-shaped paper cap, formerly placed upon the head of a slow or lazy pupil.

Dun·dalk (dŭn-dôk′, -dôlk′). County town of County Louth, Republic of Ireland. It was here, in 1315, that Edward Bruce declared himself king of Ireland. He was killed nearby three years later. Its port exports beef, cattle, and grain.

Dun·dee (dŭn-dē′). A city on the Firth of Tay, Scotland. It has been a royal burgh since 1190 and is linked with the south by rail over the Tay Bridge, rebuilt in 1888, and by a road bridge opened in 1966. Dundee manufactures linen, canvas, jute, and confectionery and serves the North Sea oilfields.

Dundee cake *n.* A rich fruit cake decorated with almonds.

dun·der·head (dŭn′dər-hĕd′) *n.* A numskull; dunce. [Perhaps "one stunned by a thunderstroke" : Dutch *donder,* thunder, from Middle Dutch + HEAD.] **—dun·der·head·ed** *adj.*

dun diver *n* A young male or female goosander.

dun·drear·ies (dŭn-drîr′ēz) *pl.n.* Long side whiskers with a clean-shaven chin. Also called "Dundreary whiskers." [After Lord *Dundreary,* a character in the play *Our American Cousin* (1855) by Tom Taylor (1817–80), British dramatist.]

dune (dōōn, dyōōn) *n.* A hill or ridge of wind-blown sand, especially one barren of vegetation. Also called "sand dune." [French, from Old French, from Middle Dutch *dūne.*]

dune buggy *n.* A small, light motor vehicle, generally having a rear-engine chassis and a molded fiber-glass frame without doors and roof, and usually equipped with a modified engine and oversize tires for driving on sand dunes.

Dunes State Park. See **Indiana Dunes National Lakeshore.**

dung (dŭng) *n.* **1.** The excrement of animals. **2.** Manure. **3.** Anything foul or abhorrent. ~*tr.v.* **dunged, dunging, dungs.** To fertilize with manure. [Middle English *d(o)ung,* from Old English *dung,* akin to Old Norse *dyngja,* heap, from Germanic *dung-* (unattested).] **—dung·y** *adj.*

dun·ga·ree (dŭng′gə-rē′) *n.* **1.** A sturdy, usually blue denim fabric. **2. dungarees.** Overalls or trousers made from this fabric. [Hindi *dungrī,* from *Dungrī,* name of a district of Bombay where it originated.]

dung beetle *n.* Any of various beetles of the family Scarabaeidae, that form balls of dung on which they feed and in which they lay their eggs.

dun·geon (dŭn′jən) *n.* **1.** A dark, often underground chamber or cell used to confine prisoners. **2.** A donjon *(see).* [Middle English *donjon,* from Old French, "keep of the lord's castle," from Medieval Latin *dominiō,* lordship, from Latin *dominus,* lord, master.]

dung fly *n.* Any of various flies of the genus *Scatophaga* whose larvae feed in dung.

dung·hill (dŭng′hĭl′) *n.* **1.** A heap of animal excrement or manure. **2.** A foul, degraded place or condition.

dun·ite (dōō′nīt′, dŭn′īt′) *n.* An igneous rock consisting mainly of olivine.

dunk (dŭngk) *v.* **dunked, dunking, dunks.** —*tr.* **1.** To plunge into liquid; immerse. **2.** To dip (a doughnut, for example) into coffee or other liquid before eating it. **3.** *Basketball.* To slam (a ball) through the basket from above. —*intr.* **1.** To go under water; submerge oneself briefly. **2.** *Basketball.* To dunk a basketball. ~*n.* **1.** The act or an instance of dunking. **2.** *Basketball.* A shot made by jumping and slamming the ball down through the basket. [Pennsylvania Dutch *dunke,* from Middle High German *dunken, tunken,* from Old High German *dunkōn.*] **—dunk·er** *n.*

Dun·ker (dŭng′kər) *n.* Also **Dun·kard** (-kərd). A member of the German Baptist Brethren, a sect of German-American Baptists opposed to military service and the taking of legal oaths. [Pennsylvania Dutch *dunke,* DUNK (referring to their baptismal rite by triple immersion).]

Dun·kirk (dŭn′kûrk′). *French* **Dun·kerque** (dœN-kĕrk′). Port in Nord department, France. It grew around a 7th-century church

built on the Dunes of St. Eloi giving it its name—"Church in the Dunes." It was ceded to Cromwell in 1658 and sold to Louis XIV by Charles II in 1662. In 1940, during World War II 330,000 Allied troops were evacuated from the town's beaches in the face of enemy fire. Industries include oil refining, shipbuilding, and sugar refining.

dunk shot *n.* See **dunk** (sense 2).

dun·lin (dŭn′lĭn) *n., pl.* **-lins** or collectively **dunlin.** A brown and white sandpiper, *Erolia* (or *Calidris*) *alpina,* of northern regions. Also formerly called "stint." [DUN (color) + -LIN(G), diminutive suffix.]

Dun·lop (dŭn′lŏp′, dŭn-lŏp′) *n.* A Scottish cheese, similar in flavor to Cheddar but paler in color.

Dunlop, John Boyd (1840–1921). Scottish inventor of the pneumatic rubber tire. He settled in Belfast as a veterinary surgeon and made the first pneumatic tire for his son's tricycle in 1887. The Dunlop Company began commercial production in 1890.

dun·nage (dŭn′ĭj) *n.* **1.** Loose packing material protecting a ship's cargo from damage during transport. **2.** *Informal.* Personal belongings or baggage. [Middle English *dennage, donage,* perhaps from Middle Low German *dünne,* thin, hence "loose, light stuff."]

Dunne (dŭn), **Finley Peter** (1867–1936). U.S. humorist. He is best known for his series of books featuring Mr. Dooley, an Irish saloonkeeper who comments satirically on current events, political leaders, and all aspects of the contemporary scene in a thick Irish brogue.

dun·nock (dŭn′ək) *n.* The **hedge sparrow** *(see).*

Duns Sco·tus (dŭnz skō′təs), **Joannes,** also known as "the Subtle Doctor" (*c.* 1265–*c.* 1308). Scottish Franciscan monk and theologian, who wrote *On the First Principle.* He disputed Aquinas's harmony of faith and reason and formed a school of scholasticism, known as Scotism.

Dun·stan (dŭn′stən), **Saint** (*c.* 910–988). English monk and archbishop of Canterbury (960–88). He was born near Glastonbury and became abbot of the monastery there in 943. He was exiled to Flanders by King Edwy, but King Eadgar recalled him as bishop of Winchester in 957 and two years later made him archbishop of Canterbury.

du·o (dōō′ō, dyōō′ō) *n., pl.* **-os** (-ōz) or **dui** (dōō′ē, dyōō′ē) (for senses 1, 2). **1.** *Music.* A duet. **2.** *Music.* Two performers singing or playing together. **3.** Two people in close association; a pair. —See Synonyms at **couple.** [Italian, "two," from Latin.]

duo– *prefix.* Indicates two; for example, **duologue.** [Latin, from *duo,* two.]

du·o·dec·i·mal (dōō′ō-dĕs′ə-məl, dyōō′-) *adj.* **1.** Of, pertaining to, or based on the number 12: *the duodecimal system.* **2.** Of or pertaining to twelfths. ~*n.* A twelfth. [From Latin *duodecimus,* twelfth, from *duodecim,* twelve : DUO- + *decem,* ten.] **—du·o·dec·i·mal·ly** *adv.*

du·o·dec·i·mo (dōō′ō-dĕs′ə-mō′, dyōō′-) *n., pl.* **-mos. 1.** The page size of a book, formed by folding a single printer's sheet into 12 leaves. **2.** A book composed of pages of this size. Also called "twelvemo." Also written *12mo., 12°.* ~*adj.* Having pages of this size. [Latin, ablative of *duodecimus,* twelfth, from *duodecim,* twelve. See **duodecimal.**]

du·o·den·a·ry (dōō′ō-dĕn′ə-rē, dyōō′-) *adj.* Of or pertaining to the number 12; duodecimal.

du·o·de·ni·tis (dōō′ə-də-nī′tĭs, dyōō′-) *n.* Inflammation of the duodenum. [New Latin : DUODEN(UM) + -ITIS.]

du·o·de·num (dōō′ə-dē′nəm, dyōō′-, dōō-ŏd′n-əm, dyōō-) *n., pl.* **-odena** (-ŏd′n-ə) or **-nums.** The portion of the small intestine starting at the lower end of the stomach and extending to the jejunum. [Middle English, from Medieval Latin, short for *intestinum duodenum digitōrum,* "intestine of twelve digits" (translation of the Greek *dodekadaktulon,* "twelve fingers long," the duodenum), from Latin *duodēni,* twelve each, from *duodecim,* twelve. See **duodecimal.**] **—du·o·de·nal** (dōō′ə-dē′nəl, dyōō′-, dōō-ŏd′n-əl, dyōō-) *adj.*

du·o·logue, du·o·log (dōō′ə-lôg′, dyōō′-) *n.* A play, or part of a play, in which only two actors have speaking roles.

du·op·so·ny (dōō-ŏp′sə-nē, dyōō′-) *n., pl.* **-nies.** *Economics.* A stockmarket condition wherein two rival buyers exert a controlling influence on numerous sellers. [DUO- + Greek *opsōnia,* purchasing of victuals, catering, from *opsōnēs,* victualer, caterer : *opson,* food, relish, delicacy (see **opsonin**) + *ōnē,* buying.]

du·o·tone (dōō′ō-tōn′, dyōō′-) *n.* *Printing.* **1.** A process for printing halftone illustrations in two tones of the same color or black and one color. **2.** A picture in duotone. ~*adj. Printing.* Having a two-toned effect or appearance.

dup. duplicate.

du·pat·ta (dōō′pŭt′ə) *n.* A long scarf worn by Indian women. [Hindi.]

dupe (dōōp, dyōōp) *n.* **1.** A person who is easily deceived or used. **2.** A person who mainly acts as the tool of another person or a power: *a dupe of Communism.* ~*tr.v.* **duped, duping, dupes.** To deceive easily; fool. —See Synonyms at **deceive.** [French, from dialect French *dupe,* dupe, probably jocular use of *dupe,* hoopoe (from the supposed stupid appearance of the bird), contraction of *de huppe* : *de,* of + *huppe,* HOOPOE.] **—dup·a·bil·i·ty** *n.* **—dup·a·ble** *adj.*

dup·er·y (dōō′pə-rē, dyōō′-) *n., pl.* **-ies. 1.** The action of duping. **2.** The state of being duped: *"we must think so as to avoid dupery"* (William James). [French *duperie,* from *dupe,* DUPE.]

du·ple (dōō′pəl, dyōō′-) *adj.* **1.** Double; consisting of two. **2.** *Music.* Having two beats in a bar. [Latin *duplus,* twofold, double.]

Dürer

MESSENGER OF THE RENAISSANCE
Dürer carried the Italian artistic revolution to northern Europe

Albrecht Dürer, son of a German goldsmith, introduced the Renaissance art of Italy to northern Europe. He was born in Nuremberg in 1471 and was apprenticed to a painter and engraver in 1486. He twice visited Italy—with profound consequences for him and for northern art.

Emulating the Renaissance artists' skillful use of perspective and search for truth in nature, Dürer embarked on two series of woodcuts, *The Apocalypse* (1498) and the *Great Passion* (1510). He was artist, printer, and publisher of *The Apocalypse*. From 1500, he produced brilliant engravings on copper, including *The Dream, Adam and Eve* (1504), and *St. Jerome in his Study* (1514). His major painting, an altarpiece,

is *The Feast of the Rose Garlands* (1506).

Dürer was a true Renaissance man and a recognized master of the age, with striking achievements in many spheres—woodcut designs, paintings, engravings, drawings, and theoretical books on geometry and perspective, fortification, and human proportions. His art exudes power and energy and shows a wealth of detail that is dramatic, elaborate, and inventive, but never overpowers the strong and accurate outlines of the individual subjects.

On a journey to the Netherlands in 1520-1, Dürer caught a fever in swamps where he had gone to draw a dead whale. He never recovered his health fully and died in 1528.

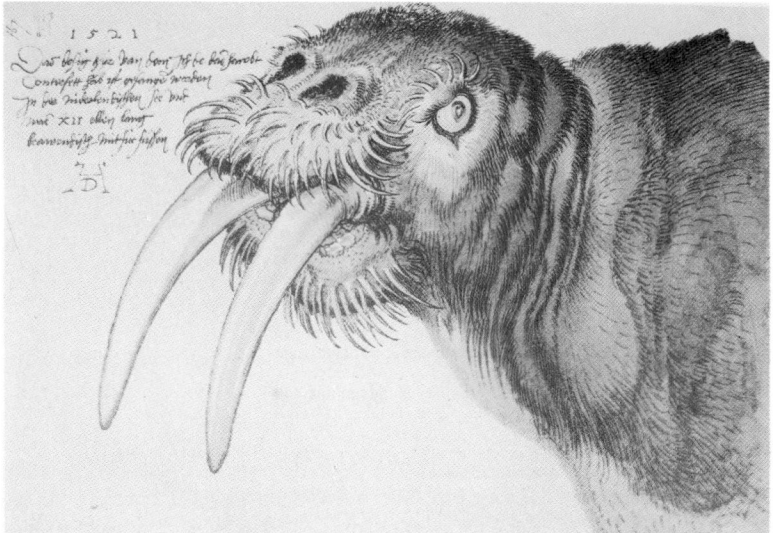

MIRROR OF NATURE *Dürer's search for truth in nature was inspired by the Italian painters. He did this brilliantly detailed head of a walrus in 1521. Two other similar watercolors are among his most famous works:* A Hare, *and* Great Piece of Turf *(both 1502).*

du·plet (dōo′plət, dyōo′-) *n.* **1.** *Music.* A pair of notes having equal time value, played in the time of three. **2.** *Electronics.* A pair of electrons shared by two atoms, forming a valence bond.

du·plex (dōo′plĕks′, dyōo′-) *adj.* **1.** Twofold. **2.** *Engineering.* Having two identical units operating in a single frame, each capable of operating independently. **3.** *Electronics.* Able to transmit two messages simultaneously in the same or opposite directions over a single wire. Compare **multiplex, simplex.**
   ~*n.* **1.** A duplex apartment or house. **2.** A DNA or RNA molecule having a double strand. [Latin, twofold, double.] —**du·plex·i·ty** *n.*

duplex apartment *n.* An apartment having rooms on two adjoining floors connected by an inner staircase.

duplex house *n.* A house divided into two living units.

du·pli·cate (dōo′plĭ-kĭt, dyōo′-) *adj. Abbr.* **dup. 1.** Identically copied from an original. **2.** Existing or growing in two corresponding parts; double. **3.** *Card Games.* Designating a manner of play in which all partnerships play the same hands and compare scores at the end.
   ~*n. Abbr.* **dup. 1.** An identical copy; facsimile. **2.** Anything that corresponds exactly to something else, especially an original; a double. **3.** A duplicate card game.
   ~*tr.v.* (dōo′plĭ-kāt′, dyōo′-) **duplicated, -cating, -cates. 1.** To make an identical copy of; reproduce; imitate. **2.** To double; make twofold. **3.** To do or effect again or similarly, possibly without real need: *duplicating the process.* [Middle English, from Latin *duplicātus,* past participle of *duplicāre,* to make twofold, from *duplex,* twofold, DUPLEX.] —**du·pli·cate·ly** *adv.*

du·pli·ca·tion (dōo′plĭ-kā′shən, dyōo′-) *n.* **1. a.** The act or procedure of duplicating. **b.** The condition of being duplicated. **2.** A duplicate; replica. —**du·pli·ca·tive** *adj.*

du·pli·ca·tor (dōo′plĭ-kā′tər, dyōo′-) *n.* A machine that reproduces printed or written material, especially one designed for large-quantity reproduction using ink and a master plate or stencil.

du·plic·i·ty (dōo-plĭs′ə-tē, dyōo-) *n., pl.* **-ties.** Deliberate deceptiveness in behavior or speech; double-dealing. [Middle English *duplicite,* from Old French, from Late Latin *duplicitās* (stem *duplicitat-*),

from Latin *duplex* (stem *duplic-*), twofold, DUPLEX.]

Du Pont (dōo pŏnt′, dyōo), **Eleuthère Irénée** (1771-1834). U.S. manufacturer, born in France. Trained in the royal gunpowder works, he came to the United States in 1800 and in 1802 began manufacturing improved gunpowder at his works near Wilmington, Delaware. Within a few years he established an extensive business for his company, which exists to this day.

Dur. Durham.

du·ra·ble (dŏor′ə-bəl, dyŏor′-) *adj.* Able to withstand the effects of time, especially wear and tear or decay; lasting.
   ~*n.* A manufactured product that does not require frequent replacing, such as a domestic appliance or item of furniture: *consumer durables.* [Middle English, from Old French, from Latin *dūrābilis,* from *dūrāre,* to last, endure.] —**du·ra·bil·i·ty, du·ra·ble·ness** *n.*

durable goods *pl.n.* Durables.

durable press *n.* **1.** A chemical process in which fabrics are permanently shaped and treated for wrinkle resistance. **2.** A fabric treated by durable press.

du·ral (dŏor′əl, dyŏor′-) *adj.* Pertaining to the dura mater.

Du·ral·u·min (dŏo-răl′yə-mĭn, dyŏo-) *n.* A trademark for an alloy of aluminum containing copper, manganese, magnesium, iron, and silicon. It is resistant to corrosion by acids and sea water.

du·ra ma·ter (dŏor′ə mā′tər, dyŏor′-) *n.* A tough fibrous membrane that covers the brain and the spinal cord. [Middle English, from Medieval Latin *dūra mater (cerebrī),* "hard mother (of the brain)" (translation from Arabic *umm al-dimāgh aṣ-ṣafīqah*) : Latin *dūra,* feminine of *dūrus,* hard + *mater,* mother.]

du·ra·men (dŏo-rā′mən, dyŏo-) *n. Botany.* **Heartwood** *(see).* [New Latin, from Latin, hardness, from *dūrāre,* to harden, from *dūrus,* hard.]

dur·ance (dŏor′əns, dyŏor′-) *n.* Forced confinement; imprisonment. [Middle English *duraunce,* duration, "prison term," from Old French *durance,* from *durer,* to last, from Latin *dūrāre.*]

Dur·and (dyŏo-rănd′), **Asher Brown** (1796-1886). U.S. artist. He was a founder of the Hudson River School, which specialized in romantic depictions of the American landscape. In his famous paintings of the Hudson River and the Catskill Mts. Durand adopted the then unusual practice of painting directly from nature.

Du·ran·go (dŏo-răng′gō) *n.* A city in north-central Mexico, the capital of Durango state. It is in a mining, agricultural, and commercial area. Durango was founded *c.* 1563 and was an important political and religious center in the early history of Mexico.

Du·ran·te (də-răn′tē), **Jimmy** (1893-1980). U.S. comedian and entertainer. Often remembered for his hoarse voice, ample nose, and time-worn hat, he was successful in nightclubs, Broadway shows such as *Red Hot and Blue* (1936), motion pictures, including *Music for Millions* (1944), and television.

du·ra·tion (dŏo-rā′shən, dyŏo-) *n.* **1.** Continuance or persistence in time. **2.** The period of time during which something exists or persists. —**for the duration.** For an indefinite period. [Medieval Latin *dūrātiō* (stem *dūrātiōn-*), from Latin *dūrāre,* to last.]

du·ra·tive (dŏor′ə-tĭv, dyŏor′-) *adj. Grammar.* Designating a verb aspect that expresses continuing action, as in Russian.

Durazzo. See **Durrës.**

Dur·ban (dûr′bən). The largest city and main seaport of Natal, South Africa. Its harbor handles more foreign trade than Cape Town, exporting coal, manganese and chrome ores, sugar, oranges, pineapple, and maize and importing machinery for the Rand goldfields. Durban is also a major resort.

dur·bar (dûr′bär′) *n.* **1. a.** A state reception, often accompanied by a military display, given formerly by an Indian prince or by a British governor in India. **b.** The reception hall. **2.** The court of an Indian prince or ruler. [Hindi *darbār,* from Persian, "court" : *dar,* door + *bār,* admission, audience, time.]

Dü·rer (dŏor′ər, dyŏor′-), **Albrecht** (1471-1528). German painter and engraver. He began as an apprentice to his goldsmith father in Nuremberg. He carried the classicism of the Italian Renaissance into northern European painting.

du·ress (dŏo-rĕs′, dyŏo-, dŏor′ĭs, dyŏor′-) *n.* **1.** Constraint by threat; coercion: *confessed under duress.* **2.** *Law.* **a.** Coercion illegally applied. **b.** Forcible confinement. [Middle English *duresse,* hardness, restraint, confinement, from Old French *dure(s)ce,* hardness, from Latin *dūritia,* from *dūrus,* hard.]

Dur·ga (dŏor′gə) *n. Hinduism.* The goddess Devi considered as a fierce though benevolent protectress of heroes and an upholder of virtue.

Dur·ham¹ (dûr′əm). *Abbr.* **Dur.** County in northeast England stretching from the Pennines to the North Sea. Coal mining, though in decline, dominates the coastal plain. Other industries include light engineering and chemicals.

Durham². Principal city and administrative center of Durham, England. The city is dominated by its magnificent Norman cathedral; its castle, founded by William the Conqueror in 1072, is now part of the University of Durham, established in 1832.

Durham³. City in north-central North Carolina. It is in the heart of a tobacco-growing region.

Durham⁴ *n.* Any of a breed of beef cattle, a **shorthorn** *(see).* [Originally bred in DURHAM (county).]

du·ri·an (dŏor′ē-ən) *n.* **1.** A tree, *Durio zibethinus,* of southeastern Asia, bearing edible fruit. **2.** The fruit of this tree, having a hard, prickly rind and soft pulp with an offensive odor but a pleasant taste. [Malay.]

dur·ing (dŏor′ĭng, dyŏor′-) *prep.* **1.** Throughout the course or duration of. **2.** Within the time of; at some time in. [Middle English (after Old French *durant,* "lasting"), from *duren,* to last, from Old French *durer,* from Latin *durāre.*]

Durk·heim (dûr′kĕm′), **Emile** (1858–1917). French social scientist, a founder of modern sociology. He applied anthropological information and statistics to the study of society.

dur·mast (dûr′măst′, -mäst′) *n.* A European oak, *Quercus petrea,* having tough, elastic wood and sessile acorns. Also called "sessile oak." [Probably alteration of *dun mast* : DUN (grayish brown) + MAST (nut, acorn).]

du·ro (dŏŏ′rō) *n., pl.* **-ros.** The silver dollar of Spain and Spanish America. [Spanish *(peso) duro,* "hard (peso)," from Latin *dūrus,* hard.]

du·roc, Du·roc (dŏŏ-rŏk′, dyŏŏ-) *n.* A large red pig of a breed developed during the 19th century in the United States. [After *Duroc,* a horse owned by the developer of the breed.]

dur·ra, dou·ra, dou·rah (dŏŏr′ə) *n.* A cereal grain, *Sorghum vulgare durra,* of Asia and northern Africa, much cultivated in dry regions. Also called "Guinea corn," "Indian millett." [Arabic *dhurah,* grain.]

Dur·rell (dûr′əl), **Gerald** (1925–). British naturalist and writer, born in India, the brother of Lawrence. In 1958 he founded the Jersey Wildlife Preservation Fund, which runs a zoo on the island for endangered species. His stories include *The Overloaded Ark* (1953) and *My Family and Other Animals* (1956).

Durrell, Lawrence George (1912–). British writer, born in India of Irish parents. His best-known work is the Alexandria Quartet: *Justine* (1957), *Balthazar* (1958), *Mountolive* (1958), and *Clea* (1960).

Dür·ren·matt (dŏŏr′ən-mät′), **Friedrich** (1921–). Swiss novelist and dramatist. His plays include *The Visit* (1956), *Romulus* (1949), and *The Physicists* (1962). His novels include *The Judge and his Hangman* (1952) and *The Quarry* (1953).

Dur·rës (dŏŏr′əs). Italian **Du·raz·zo** (dŏŏ-rät′sō). Chief seaport of Albania and its capital. A Greek city of the 7th century B.C. and important Roman port and bishopric (449), it was later held by Normans, Byzantines, Sicilians, Greeks, Serbs, and Turks until Albanian independence in 1913. A tourist center, Durrës also produces foodstuffs, tobacco, clothing, and ships.

durst. *Archaic.* Past tense of **dare.**

du·rum (dŏŏr′əm, dyŏŏr-) *n.* A hardy wheat, *Triticum durum,* grown mainly in the Mediterranean region and used chiefly in making macaroni, spaghetti, and similar products. Also called "durum wheat." [New Latin, from Latin, neuter of *dūrus,* hard.]

dur·zi (dûr′zē) *n.* An Indian tailor. [Hindi, from Persian *darzi,* from *darz,* sewing.]

Duse (dŏŏ′zā), **Eleonora** (1858–1924). Italian actress. The greatest interpretative actress of her day, she was most highly acclaimed as the heroine in the plays of her contemporaries Gabriele D'Annunzio and Henrik Ibsen. She fascinated critics and audiences around the world with her penetrating, insightful performances.

dusk (dŭsk) *n.* The darker stage of evening twilight.
~*adj.* Tending to darkness.
~*v.* **dusked, dusking, dusks.** *Poetic.* —*intr.* To become dark or dusky. —*tr.* To darken. [Middle English *dosc, dusk,* dusky, from Old English *dox,* dark, dusky.]

dusk·y (dŭs′kē) *adj.* **-ier, -iest. 1.** Dark; shadowy. **2.** Rather dark in color, especially in skin color. **3.** Gloomy. —See Usage note at **dark.** —**dusk·i·ly** *adv.* —**dusk·i·ness** *n.*

dusky grouse *n.* A bird, the **blue grouse** *(see).*

Düs·sel·dorf (dŏŏs′əl-dôrf′). City in North Rhine-Westphalia, West Germany. It is a port on the Rhine River serving the Ruhr and Wupper industrial areas. Its industries include iron, steel, car assembly, and chemicals.

dust (dŭst) *n.* **1. a.** Matter composed of fine particles, such as earth or pollen. **b.** Small particles of matter that are fine enough to be carried by the wind. **2. a.** Clouds of such matter. **b.** A state of confusion. Used in such phrases as *let the dust settle.* **3.** Such matter regarded as the result of disintegration. **4. a.** Earth, especially when regarded as the substance of the grave: *"Dust thou art, and shalt to dust return"* (Milton). **b.** The remains of a dead person. **5.** The surface of the ground. Preceded by *the.* **6.** A debased or despised condition. Used especially in the phrase *in the dust.* **7.** Something of no worth. **8.** *British.* Ashes, household dirt, or rubbish. **9.** Disturbance; fuss. **10.** *Informal.* A lung condition caused by dust, **pneumoconiosis** *(see).* —**bite the dust. 1.** To fail or be defeated. **2.** To fall dead.
~*v.* **dusted, dusting, dusts.** —*tr.* **1.** To remove dust from by wiping, brushing, or beating. **2.** To sprinkle with a powdery substance. **3.** To strew like dust: *Freckles dusted her nose.* **4.** To remove as dust: *dusted the crumbs off.* **5.** To restore to use. Used with *off.* **6.** *Archaic.* To cover with dust. —*intr.* **1.** To clean by removing dust. **2.** To cover itself with dust. Used of a bird. [Middle English *dust, doust,* Old English *dūst.*]

dust-bath (dŭst′băth′, -bäth′) *n.* The action of a bird working dust into its feathers so as to clean them or possibly help rid itself of parasites.

dust·bin (dŭst′bĭn′) *n. British.* A large cylindrical container for household rubbish.

dust bowl *n.* In semiarid regions, a barren area produced by excessive wind erosion of the soil, especially after the removal of vegetation by overgrazing or badly managed cultivation. The topsoil is removed, and the area swept by severe dust storms. —**the Dust Bowl.** Such an area that developed in the 1930's in the south-central

United States, stretching through west Kansas, Oklahoma, Texas, Colorado, and into New Mexico.

dust cover *n.* **1.** A removable or hinged plastic cover used to protect a turntable. **2.** See **dust jacket** (sense 1).

dust devil *n.* A small transient whirlwind that swirls dust, debris, and sand up into the air.

dust·er (dŭs′tər) *n.* **1.** One that dusts. **2.** A cloth used to remove dust. **3.** A device for sifting or scattering a powdered substance. **4.** A smock worn to protect one's clothing from dust. **5.** A woman's loose housecoat.

dust·ing powder (dŭs′tĭng) *n* A fine powder, such as talcum powder, used on the skin.

dust jacket *n. Abbr.* **dj 1.** A removable paper cover used to protect the binding of a book. Also called "book jacket," "dust cover," "jacket." **2.** A cardboard sleeve in which a phonograph record is packaged.

dust·man (dŭst′mən) *n., pl.* **-men** (-mĭn). *British.* A man employed to remove trash.

dust·pan (dŭst′păn′) *n.* A short-handled, shovellike pan into which dust is swept.

dust shot *n.* The smallest-sized firing shot.

dust storm *n.* In a semiarid or arid region, a severe windstorm that sweeps clouds of dust across an extensive area.

dust·up (dŭst′ŭp′) *n. Informal.* An argument, especially one involving violence; a scuffle.

dust·y (dŭs′tē) *adj.* **-ier, -iest. 1.** Covered or filled with dust. **2.** Consisting of or resembling dust; powdery. **3.** Tinged with gray; subdued; dull. **4.** Dry; uninteresting. **5.** *British.* Not satisfactory or helpful: *a dusty answer.* —**dust·i·ly** *adv.* —**dust·i·ness** *n.*

dusty miller *n.* Any of various plants having leaves and stems covered with dustlike down, such as the **beach wormwood** and the **rose campion** *(both of which see).*

Dutch (dŭch) *adj. Abbr.* **D., Du. 1.** Of or pertaining to the Netherlands, its inhabitants, or their language. **2.** *Archaic.* German.
~*n. Abbr.* **D., Du. 1.** *Used with a plural verb.* **a.** The people of the Netherlands. Preceded by *the.* **b.** *Archaic.* The Germans. **2. a.** The West Germanic language of the Netherlands. Sometimes called "Low Dutch." **b.** The German language. Now used only in the term *High Dutch.* **3.** Pennsylvania Dutch *(see).* —**in Dutch.** *Informal.* In trouble; in disfavor.
~*adv.* So that each person pays his own way: *go Dutch for lunch.*

Dutch auction *n. Informal.* An auction in which the auctioneer opens with a high price and lowers it until a buyer is found.

Dutch bargain *n. Informal.* A transaction settled while both parties are drinking.

Dutch barn *n.* A barn with open sides and a curved roof.

Dutch cap *n.* **1.** A woman's lace cap with turned-back triangular flaps on each side. **2.** A type of contraceptive, a **diaphragm** *(see).*

Dutch cheese *n.* **Cottage cheese** *(see).*

Dutch clover *n.* The **white clover** *(see).*

Dutch courage *n. Informal.* Courage from drinking liquor.

Dutch doll *n.* A jointed wooden doll.

Dutch door *n.* A door divided in half horizontally so that either part may be left open or closed.

Dutch East Indies. See **Indonesia.**

Dutch elm disease *n.* A disease of elm trees caused by a fungus, *Ceratocystis ulmi,* and resulting in eventual death of the tree due to the water-conducting vessels becoming clogged with gums produced by the fungus.

Dutch Guiana. See **Surinam.**

Dutch hoe *n.* A hoe having a crosspiece attached to two prongs, used with a pushing motion.

dutch·man (dŭch′mən) *n., pl.* **-men** (-mĭn). Something used to conceal faulty construction. [Playful use of DUTCHMAN.]

Dutch·man (dŭch′mən) *n., pl.* **-men** (-mĭn). **1.** A native or inhabitant of the Netherlands. **2.** A person of Dutch descent. **3.** *Archaic.* A German.

Dutch·man's-breech·es (dŭch′mənz-brĭch′ĭz) *n. Used with a singular or plural verb.* A woodland plant, *Dicentra cucullaria,* of eastern North America, having finely divided leaves and yellowish-white flowers with two spurs. [From its breeches-shaped blossoms.]

Dutch metal *n.* An alloy of copper and zinc used in thin sheets as a cheap imitation of gold leaf. Also called "Dutch foil," "Dutch gold," "Dutch leaf." [Originally imported from Holland.]

Dutch oven *n.* **1.** A large, heavy pot or kettle, usually of cast iron and with a tight lid, used for slow cooking. **2.** A metal utensil open on one side and equipped with shelves, that is placed before an open fire for baking or roasting food. **3.** A wall oven in which food is baked by means of preheated brick walls.

Dutch rush *n.* A horsetail, *Equisetum hyemale,* with unbranched overwintering stems.

Dutch treat *n. Informal.* An outing, as for dinner or a film, for which each person pays his own expenses.

Dutch uncle *n. Informal.* A stern and candid critic or adviser.

Dutch West Indies. See **Netherlands Antilles.**

du·te·ous (dŏŏ′tē-əs, dyŏŏ′-) *adj. Formal.* Obedient; dutiful. [From DUTY.] —**du·te·ous·ly** *adv.* —**du·te·ous·ness** *n.*

du·ti·a·ble (dŏŏ′tē-ə-bəl, dyŏŏ′-) *adj.* Subject to import tax.

du·ti·ful (dŏŏ′tĭ-fəl, dyŏŏ′-) *adj.* **1.** Filled with or motivated by a sense of duty. **2.** Showing or proceeding from a sense of duty. —See Synonyms at **obedient.** —**du·ti·ful·ly** *adv.* —**du·ti·ful·ness** *n.*

du·ty (dŏŏ′tē, dyŏŏ′-) *n., pl.* **-ties. 1.** An act or a course of action that is exacted of one by law or social custom, or by one's position or

Dutchman's-breeches *A woodland plant of North America, so called because its flowers resemble the traditional Dutch garment.*

religion. **2. a.** Moral obligation. **b.** The compulsion felt to meet such obligation. **3. a.** A service assigned to or demanded of one, especially in the armed forces. **b.** A function; an allocated task. **4.** A tax charged by a government, on imports, transactions, transference of estates, or the like. **5.** *Engineering.* **a.** The work capability of a machine under specified conditions. **b.** A measure of efficiency expressed as work per unit energy input. **6.** *Agriculture.* The amount of water required to irrigate a given area for the cultivation of some crop. **—off duty.** Not engaged in one's assigned work; not at work. **—on duty.** At one's post or work; engaged in one's work. [Middle English *duete,* from Norman French, from Old French *deu,* DUE.]

duty-bound (dōō'tē-bound', dyōō'-) *adj.* Obliged by a moral, legal, or other duty.

du·ty-free (dōō'tē-frē', dyōō'-) *adj.* Exempt from customs duties. **~n.** *Informal.* A duty-free item of merchandise. **—du·ty-free** *adv.*

duty-free shop *n.* A shop, especially one at an airport or port, that sells duty-free goods such as tobacco, spirits, or perfume.

du·um·vir (dōō-ŭm'vər, dyōō-) *n., pl.* **-virs** or **-viri** (-və-rē'). A member of a duumvirate. [Latin, variant of *duovir* : *duo,* two + *vir,* man.]

du·um·vi·rate (dōō-ŭm'vər-ĭt, dyōō-) *n.* **1.** Any of various two-man governments in the Roman Republic. **2.** Any government or authority consisting of two men.

Du·va·lier (dōō'väl-yā'), **François,** also known as "Papa Doc" (1907–71). Haitian dictator. He was elected president of Haiti in 1957, and in 1964 he declared himself president for life. Duvalier executed opponents without trial and deprived the population of civil rights and education. His practice of voodooism led some uneducated Haitians to believe that he possessed supernatural powers.

Duvalier, Jean-Claude, also known as "Baby Doc" (1951–). Dictator of Haiti, son of François. He succeeded his father as president for life in 1971 but fled the country in 1986 after widespread civil unrest.

du·vet (dōō-vā', dyōō-) *n.* A soft, light quilt filled with down, feathers, or a similar synthetic material and used in place of a sheet and blankets. [French, down, from Old French *duvet,* alteration of *dumet,* diminutive of *dum,* alteration (probably influenced by PLUME) of *dun,* from Old Norse *dūnn.*]

du·ve·tyn, du·ve·tine, du·ve·tyne (dōō'və-tēn', dyōō'-, dōō'və-tēn', dyōō'-) *n.* A soft, napped fabric with a twill weave, made of wool, cotton, rayon, or silk. [French *duvetine,* from DUVET.]

duyker. Variant of **duiker.**

D.V. **1.** Deo volente. **2.** Douay Version (of the Bible).

dvan·dva (dvän'dvä') *n.* A compound expression consisting of two elements typically belonging to the same part of speech and being of equal importance in determining the meaning of the compound; for example, a **fighter-bomber** is both a fighter and a bomber. Compare **bahuvrihi.** [Sanskrit, repeated nominative (exemplifying this compound) of *dva,* couple, pair.]

Dvi·na, Northern (dvē'nə). *Russian* **Se·ver·na·ya Dvina** (sā'vər-nə-yə). River in the northwest U.S.S.R. It flows 750 kilometers (466 miles) northwest to Dvina Bay on the White Sea.

Dvina, Western. *Russian* **Za·pad·na·ya Dvina** (zä'pəd-nə-yə). A river in western U.S.S.R. It flows 1,030 kilometers (640 miles) from the Valdai Hills into the Gulf of Riga.

D.V.M. Doctor of Veterinary Medicine.

Dvo·řák (dvôr'zhäk), **Antonín** or **Anton** (1841-1904). Czech composer. He incorporated folk tunes into his music, especially in the *Slavonic Dances.* His last symphony, the Ninth, "From the New World" (1893), was composed in the United States where he was director of the National Conservatory in New York (1892-95).

D/W dock warrant.

dwarf (dwôrf) *n., pl.* **dwarfs** or **dwarves** (dwôrvz). **1. a.** A very small person, specifically, a person afflicted with dwarfism. Compare **midget.** **b.** An atypically small animal or plant. **2.** A diminutive, often ugly, manlike creature of fairy tales and legend. **3.** A dwarf star. **~v.** **dwarfed, dwarfing, dwarfs.** **—tr.** **1.** To check the natural growth or development of; stunt: *"the oaks were dwarfed from lack of moisture"* (John Steinbeck). **2.** To cause to appear small by comparison: *an old church dwarfed by the new office buildings.* **—intr.** To become stunted or grow smaller. **~adj.** **1.** Diminutive; undersized; stunted. **2.** *Biology.* Much smaller than the usual or typical kind: *dwarf gourami; dwarf zinnias.* [Middle English *dwerf, dwergh,* Old English *dweorg, dweorh,* from Germanic *dwerg-* (unattested).]

dwarf bean *n.* A variety of **string bean** (see).

dwarf cornel *n.* A woody plant, *Cornus canadensis,* of northern North America, having inconspicuous greenish flowers surrounded by white, petallike bracts, and scarlet fruit.

dwarf·ism (dwôr'fĭz'əm) *n.* A condition of arrested growth having various causes; especially: **1. Achondroplasia** (see). **2.** A deficiency of or failure to respond to growth hormone.

dwarf star *n.* A main-sequence star having relatively high density, small mass, and average or below average luminosity. Also called "dwarf." Compare **giant star.** See **white dwarf.**

dwell (dwĕl) *intr.v.* **dwelt** (dwĕlt) or **dwelled, dwelling, dwells.** **1.** *Formal.* To live as a resident; reside. **2.** To exist in some place or state. **3. a.** To fasten one's attention; reflect at length or in detail, especially in speech or writing. Used with *on* or *upon.* **b.** To emphasize or stress something: *dwelt on the importance of health care.* **c.** *Music.* To hold or sustain a note or phrase: *dwell on high C.*

~n. **1.** A short regular pause in the motion of a mechanical part of the constant-radius portion of a cam that causes it. **2.** *Computer Science.* A programmed time delay of variable duration. [Middle English *dwellen,* to delay, linger, remain, reside, Old English *dwellan,* deceive, hinder, delay (meaning influenced by Old Norse *dvelja,* "sojourn," "dwell").]

dwell·er (dwĕl'ər) *n.* A person or animal that lives in a specified place. Used in combination: *cave-dweller, city-dweller.*

dwell·ing (dwĕl'ĭng) *n.* *Formal.* A place of residence; a house; an abode.

dwelling house *n.* A building intended for occupation; a residence.

dwel·ling-place (dwĕl'ĭng-plās') *n.* A dwelling.

dwin·dle (dwĭnd'l) *v.* **-dled, -dling, -dles.** **—intr.** To become gradually less until little remains; waste away; diminish. **—tr.** To make smaller or less; cause to shrink. **—See Synonyms at decrease.** [Frequentative of obsolete *dwine,* to waste away, diminish, languish, Middle English *dwinen,* Old English *dwīnan.*]

d.w.t. deadweight tonnage.

Dy The symbol for the element dysprosium.

dy·ad (dī'ăd') *n.* **1.** Two units regarded as a pair. **2.** *Biology.* One pair of chromosomes separated from a tetrad in meiosis. **3.** *Chemistry.* A divalent atom or radical. **4.** A mathematical operator represented as a pair of vectors juxtaposed without multiplication. **~adj.** Made up of two units. [From Greek *duas* (stem *duad-*), pair, from *duo,* two.]

dy·ad·ic (dī-ăd'ĭk) *adj.* **1.** Twofold. **2.** Of or relating to a dyad. **~n.** *Mathematics.* The direct product *(B·C) AD* of two dyads *AB* and *CD.*

Dy·ak, Day·ak (dī'ăk') *n.* **1.** A member of any of various Indonesian peoples of Borneo and the Sulu Sea islands **2.** The language of the Dyaks. [Malay *Dayak,* "upcountry," from *darat,* land.]

dyarchy. Variant of **diarchy.**

dyb·buk (dĭb'ək) *n.* In Jewish folklore, a malevolent spirit that enters the body of a person and controls his actions. [Yiddish, devil, from Hebrew *dibbūg,* from *dābhaq,* to cling.]

dye (dī) *n.* **1. a.** Any substance used to color materials. **b.** A liquid containing such a substance: *a vat of dye.* **2.** A color imparted by or as if by dyeing. **~v.** **dyed, dyeing, dyes.** **—tr.** **1.** To color (a material) with or as if with a dye, especially by soaking in a coloring solution. **2.** To add (color) with a dye. **—intr.** To take on or impart color. [Middle English *deie,* Old English *dēah, dēag†,* hue, tinge.] **—dy·er** *n.*

dyed-in-the-wool (dīd'ĭn-*th*ə-wŏŏl') *adj.* **1.** Dyed before being woven into cloth. **2.** Inflexible, especially in opinions, views, or the like; out-and-out.

Dy·er (dī'ər), **Mary** (died 1660). Quaker martyr in Massachusetts, born in England. She first came to America *c.* 1635. While on a visit to England in the 1650's she became a Quaker, and after her return to Boston in 1657, she was arrested and banished, returning twice (1659, 1660) to aid imprisoned Quakers. She was ultimately condemned for sedition and hanged.

dyer's greenweed *n.* A small broomlike shrub, *Genista tinctoria,* native to Eurasia, having clusters of yellow flowers. Also called "dyer's broom," "woadwaxen," "woodwaxen." [So called because it yields a green dye.]

dyer's rocket *n.* A plant, *Reseda luteola,* native to Europe, having long spikes of small, yellowish-green flowers and yielding a yellow dye. Also called "weld."

dy·er's-weed (dī'ərz-wēd') *n.* Any of various plants yielding coloring matter used as dye.

dye·stuff (dī'stŭf') *n.* Any substance used as or yielding a dye. [Probably translation of German *Farbstoff.*]

dye·wood (dī'wŏŏd') *n.* Any wood from which dyestuffs are obtained.

Dy·fed (dĭv'ĕd). County in southwest Wales, the largest of the Welsh counties, bordering the Irish Sea. Agriculture and stock rearing are widespread. Its administrative center is Carmarthen.

dy·ing (dī'ĭng) *adj.* **1.** About to die. **2.** Drawing to an end; declining. **3.** Done or uttered just before death. **4.** Of or pertaining to death: *one's dying day.*

dyke. Variant of **dike.**

Dyl·an (dĭl'ən), **Bob,** born Robert Allen Zimmerman (1941–). U.S. singer and songwriter. His protest songs with their plaintive surrealism made him a notable figure in popular music in the 1960's.

dy·nam·ic (dī-năm'ĭk) *adj.* Also **dy·nam·i·cal** (-ĭ-kəl). **1.** Of or pertaining to energy, force, or motion in relation to force. **2.** Characterized by or tending to produce continuous change or advance. **3.** Energetic and enterprising; forceful. **4.** Of or pertaining to variation of intensity or volume, as in musical sound. **5.** Designating a computer memory that needs periodic updates. **—See Synonyms at active.** **~n.** A social or psychological system or drive that underlies any relationship between individuals: *the parent-child dynamic.* [French *dynamique,* from Greek *dunamikos,* powerful, from *dunamis,* power, from *dunasthai,* to be able.] **—dy·nam·i·cal·ly** *adv.*

dynamical geology *n.* Geodynamics (see).

dynamic psychology *n.* A method in psychology that emphasizes the fluidity and energy of mental life and the motives of the individual that condition it.

dy·nam·ics (dī-năm'ĭks) *n.* **1.** Used with a singular verb. *Physics.* A branch of mechanics comprising the study of the relationship between motion and the forces affecting the motion of physical systems. Also called "kinetics." Compare **kinematics, statics.** **2.** Used *with a plural verb.* The forces that produce motion and change in any field or system. **3.** *Used with a plural verb.* Variation in volume, force, or intensity, especially in musical sound. **4.** *Psychology.* **a.** *Used with a singular verb.* The action, fluidity, and energy of mental life. **b.** *Used with a plural verb.* The motives, needs, and drives of an individual or group.

dy·na·mism (dī′nə-mĭz′əm) *n.* **1.** Any of various theories or philosophical systems that explain the universe in terms of an immanent force or in terms of natural forces and their interplay. **2.** A process or mechanism responsible for the development or motion of a system. **3.** The quality of being dynamic. [French *dynamisme* : DY-NAM(O)- + -ISM.] —**dy·na·mist** *n.* —**dy·na·mis·tic** *adj.*

dy·na·mite (dī′nə-mīt′) *n.* **1.** A powerful explosive composed of nitroglycerin or ammonium nitrate dispersed in an absorbent material such as wood pulp and an antacid such as calcium carbonate. **2.** *Informal.* **a.** Someone or something that is potentially dangerous or violent. **b.** Someone or something outstandingly fine. **3.** *Slang.* Heroin.
~*tr.v.* **dynamited, -miting, -mites. 1.** To blow up, shatter, or destroy with or as if with dynamite. **2.** To charge with dynamite. [Swedish *dynamit* : DYNAM(O)- + -ITE.] —**dy·na·mit·er** *n.*

dy·na·mo (dī′nə-mō′) *n., pl.* **-mos. 1.** A generator, especially one for producing direct current. **2.** *Informal.* An extremely energetic and forceful person. [Short for *dynamo(electric) machine,* translation of German *dynamoelektrische Maschine.*]

dynamo– *prefix.* Indicates power; for example, **dynamoelectric.** [Greek *dunamo-,* from *dunamis,* power, from *dunasthai,* to be able.]

dy·na·mo·e·lec·tric (dī′nə-mō′ə-lĕk′trĭk) *adj.* Also **dy·na·mo·e·lec·tri·cal** (-trĭ-kəl). Relating to the conversion of mechanical energy into electrical energy, or vice versa.

dy·na·mom·e·ter (dī′nə-mŏm′ə-tər) *n.* Any of several instruments used to measure force or power. [French *dynamomètre* : DYNAMO- + -METER.]

dy·na·mom·e·try (dī′nə-mŏm′ə-trē) *n.* Measurement by means of a dynamometer. —**dy·na·mo·met·ric** (dī′-nə-mō-mĕt′rĭk), **dy·na·mo·met·ri·cal** *adj.*

dy·na·mo·tor (dī′nə-mō′tər) *n.* A rotating electric machine with two armatures, used to convert alternating to direct current. [DYNA(MO)- + MOTOR.]

dy·nast (dī′năst′, -nəst) *n.* A lord or ruler; especially, a hereditary ruler. [Latin *dynastēs,* from Greek *dunastēs,* lord, master, from *dunasthai,* to be able.]

dy·nas·ty (dī′nə-stē) *n., pl.* **-ties. 1.** A succession of rulers from the same family or line. **2.** A family or group that maintains power or supremacy in a particular field for a considerable length of time. [French *dynastie,* from Latin *dynasteia,* domination, lordship, from *dunastēs,* ruler, DYNAST.] —**dy·nas·tic** (dī-năs′tĭk) *adj.* —**dy·nas·ti·cal·ly** *adv.*

dy·na·tron (dī′nə-trŏn′) *n. Electronics.* A tetrode with grid and anode potentials so arranged that anode current decreases when the anode potential increases. [DYNA(MO)- + -TRON.]

dyne (dīn) *n. Physics.* A centimeter-gram-second unit of force, equal to the force required to impart an acceleration of one centimeter per second per second to a mass of one gram. [French, from Greek *dunamis,* power. See **dynamic.**]

Dy·nel (dī′nĕl′) *A* trademark for a copolymer of vinyl chloride and acrylonitrile, used to make fire-resistant, insect-resistant, and easily dyed textile fiber.

dy·node (dī′nōd′) *n.* An electrode used in certain electron tubes to provide secondary emission. [DYN(AMO)- + -ODE.]

dys– *prefix.* Indicates diseased, painful, difficult, faulty, or bad; for example, **dysentery, dyslexia.** [Middle English *dis-,* from Old French, from Latin *dus-,* from Greek *dus-.*]

dys·cra·si·a (dĭs-krā′zhē-ə, -zhə) *n. Rare.* Loosely, a morbid state or condition resulting from the presence of abnormal material in the blood. [New Latin, from Medieval Latin, disease, distemper, "disproportionate mixture of the humors," from Greek *duskrasia* : DYS- + *krasis,* mixing.]

dys·en·ter·y (dĭs′ən-tĕr′ē) *n.* An infection of the lower intestinal tract producing pain, fever, and severe diarrhea, often with blood and mucus. [Middle English *dissenterie,* from Latin *dysenteria,* from Greek *dusenteria* : DYS- + *enteron,* intestine.] —**dys·en·ter·ic** *adj.*

dys·func·tion (dĭs-fŭngk′shən) *n.* Disordered or impaired functioning, as of a bodily system or organ.

dys·gen·ic (dĭs-jĕn′ĭk) *adj.* Pertaining to or causing the deterioration of hereditary qualities. [DYS- + -GENIC.]

dys·gen·ics (dĭs-jĕn′ĭks) *n. Used with a singular verb.* The biological study of the factors producing racial degeneration. Also called "cacogenics."

dys·graph·i·a (dĭs-grăf′ē-ə) *n.* Impairment of the ability to write. [New Latin : DYS- + *-graphia,* -graphy.]

dys·lex·i·a (dĭs-lĕk′sē-ə) *n.* A learning disorder causing impairment of the ability to read; incomplete alexia. Also called "word blindness." [New Latin : DYS- + Greek *lexis,* speech, from *legein,* to speak.] —**dys·lec·tic** (dĭs-lĕk′tĭk) *adj. & n.* —**dys·lex·ic** *adj. & n.*

dys·lo·gis·tic (dĭs′lō-jĭs′tĭk) *adj.* Conveying censure; disapproving. [DYS- + (EU)LOGISTIC.] —**dys·lo·gis·ti·cal·ly** *adv.*

dys·men·or·rhe·a, dys·men·or·rhoe·a (dĭs-mĕn′ə-rē′ə) *n.* Difficult or painful menstruation. [New Latin : DYS- + Greek *mēn* (stem *mēno-*), month + -RRHEA.]

dys·pa·reu·ni·a (dĭs′pə-rōō′nē-ə) *n.* Pain or difficulty experienced during sexual intercourse.

dys·pep·si·a (dĭs-pĕp′shə, -sē-ə) *n.* Disturbed digestion; indigestion. [Latin, from Greek *duspepsia* : DYS- + *-pepsia,* digestion.]

dys·pep·tic (dĭs-pĕp′tĭk) *adj.* Also **dys·pep·ti·cal** (-tĭ-kəl). **1.** Pertaining to or having dyspepsia. **2.** Morose; gloomy.
~*n.* One who suffers from dyspepsia. —**dys·pep·ti·cal·ly** *adv.*

dys·pha·gi·a (dĭs-fā′jē-ə) *n.* Difficulty in swallowing. [New Latin : DYS- + -PHAGIA.] —**dys·phag·ic** (dĭs-fāj′ĭk) *adj.*

dys·pha·sia (dĭs-fā′zhə, -zhē-ə) *n.* Impairment of speech and verbal comprehension, especially when associated with brain injury. [New Latin : DYS- + -PHASIA.] —**dys·pha·sic** (dĭs-fā′zĭk) *adj.*

dys·phe·mism (dĭs′fə-mĭz′əm) *n.* **1.** The substitution of an unpleasant or derogatory term for an inoffensive one. **2.** The term thus substituted. [DYS- + EUPHEMISM.]

dys·pho·ni·a (dĭs-fō′nē-ə) *n.* Difficulty in speaking, usually resulting in hoarseness. [New Latin : DYS- + Greek *-phōnia,* -PHONY.] —**dys·phon·ic** (dĭs-fŏn′ĭk) *adj.*

dys·pho·ri·a (dĭs-fôr′ē-ə, -fōr′ē-ə) *n.* An emotional state characterized by anxiety, depression, and restlessness. [New Latin, from Greek *dusphoria,* distress, from *dusphoros,* hard to bear : DYS- + -PHOROUS.] —**dys·phor·ic** (dĭs-fôr′ĭk, -fōr′ĭk) *adj.*

dys·pla·sia (dĭs-plā′zhə, -zē-ə) *n.* Abnormal development of tissues, organs, or cells. [New Latin : DYS- + Greek *plasis,* formation, from *plassein,* to mold.] —**dys·plas·tic** (dĭs-plăs′tĭk) *adj.*

dysp·ne·a (dĭsp-nē′ə) *n.* A sense of difficulty in breathing, often associated with lung or heart disease. [New Latin, from Greek *duspnoia,* from *duspnoos,* short of breath : DYS- + *-pnoos,* from *pnoē,* breathing, from *pnein,* to breathe.] —**dysp·ne·ic** *adj.*

dys·pro·si·um (dĭs-prō′zē-əm) *n. Symbol* **Dy** A soft, silvery rare-earth metal used in nuclear research. Atomic number 66, atomic weight 162.50, melting point 1,407°C, boiling point 2,335°C, specific gravity 8.536, valence 3. [New Latin, from Greek *dusprositos,* difficult to approach : DYS- + *prositos,* approachable, from *prosienai,* to approach : *pros-,* toward + *ienai,* to go.]

dys·tel·e·ol·o·gy (dĭs′tĕl-ē-ŏl′ə-jē, dĭs′tē-lē-) *n.* **1.** The doctrine of purposelessness in nature. Compare **teleology. 2.** Purposelessness in natural structures, as manifested by the existence of vestigial or nonfunctional organs or parts. [German *Dysteleologie* : DYS- + New Latin *teleologia,* TELEOLOGY.] —**dys·tel·e·o·log·i·cal** *adj.* —**dys·tel·e·ol·o·gist** *n.*

dys·thy·mi·a (dĭs-thī′mē-ə) *n. Psychiatry.* **1.** A form of neurosis characterized by depression, anxiety, obsessions, and compulsive behavior. **2.** Any condition caused by malfunction of the thymus during childhood. [New Latin, from Greek: DYS- + *thumos,* mind.]

dys·toc·ia (dĭs-tōk′yə) *n.* Difficult birth. [New Latin : DYS- + *-tocia,* from Greek *tokos,* offspring.]

dys·to·pi·a (dĭs-tō′pē-ə) *n.* An imaginary place where everything is as bad as it could possibly be. Compare **utopia.** [DYS- + (U)TOPIA) (coined by J.S. Mill).]

dys·tro·phy (dĭs′trə-fē) *n.* Also **dys·tro·phi·a** (dĭs-trō′fē-ə). **1.** Defective nutrition characterized by wasting of the tissues. **2.** Any disorder caused by defective nutrition. See **muscular dystrophy.** [New Latin *dystrophia* : DYS- + -TROPHY.] —**dys·troph·ic** *adj.*

dys·u·ri·a (dĭs-yŏŏr′ē-ə) *n.* Painful or difficult urination. [New Latin, from Greek *dusouria* : DYS- + -URIA.] —**dys·u·ric** *adj.*

dz. dozen.

dzo (zō) *n., pl.* **dzos** or collectively **dzo.** Also **zo** (zō), *pl.* **zos** or collectively **zo.** A cross between a Tibetan yak and a cow, or between a bull and a female yak. [Tibetan.]

Dzun·gar·i·a (zŭn-gâr′ē-ə, dzŭn-). A vast arid region of northwestern China. Wheat, barley, oats, and sugar beets are grown, and cattle, sheep, and horses raised. There are deposits of coal, iron, gold, and oil.

E

eagle *Found in the wilder parts of much of the Northern Hemisphere, the golden eagle hunts for birds, small animals, and carrion over a territory of up to 250 square kilometers (100 square miles). With its powerful wings, up to 2 meters (6¹/₂ feet) across, the eagle can carry off prey as heavy as a fox.*

e, E (ē) *n., pl.* **e's** or *rare* **es, E's** or **Es. 1.** The fifth letter of the modern English alphabet. See feature at **alphabet. 2.** Any of the speech sounds represented by this letter. **3. E.** *Music.* **a.** The third tone in the scale of C major. **b.** The key or a scale in which E is the tonic. **c.** A written or printed note representing E. **d.** A string, key, or pipe tuned to the pitch of E. **4.** The fifth in a series.

e, E, e., E. *Note:* As an abbreviation or symbol, *e* may be a small or a capital letter, with or without a period. Established forms or those generally preferred precede the definition. When no form is given, all four forms are in general use in that sense. **1. E.** earl. **2. E** earth. **3.** east; eastern. **4. e** electron. **5. E** energy. **6. e., E.** engineer; engineering. **7. E, E.** English. **8. E** excellent. **9. E** illumination. **10. E** irradiance; irradiant. **11. e** *Mathematics.* The base of the natural system of logarithms, having a numerical value of approximately 2.718... .

each (ēch) *adj. Abbr.* **ea.** Every single person or thing considered individually: *Each man cast a vote.*
~*pron.* Every one of a group of objects, persons, or things considered individually; each one. Usually regarded as singular: *Each presented his gift.*
~*adv.* For or to each one; apiece: *ten dollars each.* [Middle English *ech, ælc,* Old English *ǣlc;* akin to Old High German *eogilīh,* from West Germanic *aiwō galikaz* (unattested), "ever alike."]
Usage: When the subject of a sentence begins with *each,* it is traditionally held to be grammatically singular, and the verb and following pronouns must be singular as well: *Each of the pitchers has* (not *have*) *his* (not *their*) *good curve ball.* When *each* follows a plural subject, however, the verb and following pronouns generally remain in the plural: *The boys each have their jobs to do.* The expression *each and every* is likewise followed by a singular verb and singular pronouns in formal style: *Each and every driver knows what his or her job is supposed to be.* —See also Usage note at **everyone.**

each other *pron.* **1.** Each the other. Used as a compound reciprocal pronoun: *They met each other* (each met the other). **2.** One another.
Usage: According to some traditional grammarians, *each other* is used of two, *one another* of more than two. This distinction has been ignored by many of the best writers, however, and many traditionalists find these examples acceptable: *The four partners regarded each other with suspicion. A husband and wife should confide in one another.* When speaking of an ordered series of events or stages, only *one another* can be used: *The Caesars exceeded one another* (not *each other*) *in cruelty* means that each Caesar was crueler than the last. • *Each other* cannot be used as the subject of a clause in formal writing. Instead of *We know what each other are thinking,* one should write *Each of us knows what the other is thinking.* Instead of *The men know that each other are coming,* write *Each of the men knows that the other is coming.* Instead of *We are all each other has,* write *Each of us is all the other has.* • The possessive forms of *each other* and *one another* are written *each other's* and *one another's: The boys wore each other's* (not *each others'*) *coats. They had forgotten one another's* (not *one anothers'*) *names.*

Eadger. See **Edgar.**

Eads (ēdz), **John Buchanan** (1820–87). U.S. engineer. He built the triple-arch steel bridge (opened 1874) that spans the Mississippi River at St. Louis.

ea·ger¹ (ē′gər) *adj.* **-gerer, -gerest. 1.** Intensely desirous of something; impatiently expectant. **2.** Showing intense desire or impatient expectancy: *an eager search for a familiar face in the crowd.* **3.** Very willing. [Middle English *egre,* sharp, keen, eager, from Old French *aigre,* from Latin *ācer* (stem *acr-*), keen, sharp.] —**ea·ger·ly** *adv.* —**ea·ger·ness** *n.*
Synonyms: anxious, avid, earnest, fervid, keen, zealous.

eager². Variant of **eagre.**

eager beaver *n. Informal.* An industrious, overzealous person.

ea·gle (ē′gəl) *n.* **1.** Any of various large birds of prey of the family Accipitridae, including members of the genera *Aquila, Haliaeetus,* and other genera, characterized by a powerful hooked bill, long, broad wings, and strong, soaring flight. See **golden eagle. 2.** A representation of an eagle used as an emblem, insignia, seal, or the like. **3.** A former gold coin of the United States having a face value of ten dollars. **4.** A score in golf of two below par on a hole. [Middle English *egle,* from Old French *egle, aigle,* from Latin *aquila†.*]

ea·gle-eyed (ē′gəl-īd′) *adj.* **1.** Having keen eyesight. **2.** Highly observant.

eagle owl *n.* A large Eurasian owl, *Bubo bubo,* having brownish plumage and prominent ear tufts.

ea·glet (ē′glĭt) *n.* A young eagle.

ea·gle·wood (ē′gəl-wŏŏd′) *n.* See **aloes** (sense 2).

ea·gre, ea·ger (ē′gər, ā′gər) *n.* A tidal flood, a **bore** *(see).* [Perhaps ultimately from Old English *ēagor,* flood tide.]

Ea·kins (ā′kĭns), **Thomas** (1844–1916). U.S. artist. His portraits and starkly realistic paintings have contributed to his reputation as one of the foremost U.S. painters of all time, although he won little recognition in his own day. He used his knowledge of anatomy in his masterpiece, *The Surgical Clinic of Professor Gross* (1875), which scandalized the public when it was first exhibited.

eal·dor·man (ôl′dər-mən) *n., pl.* **-men** (-mĭn). The chief official or governor of a shire in Anglo-Saxon England. [Old English *ealdormann,* prince. See **alderman.**]

Eames (ēmz), **Charles** (1907–78). U.S. designer. He designed an innovative series of chairs that were featured in the Museum of Modern Art's first one-designer furniture exhibit (1946). Originally using molded plywood and aluminum tubing, he later incorporated plastics and coated wire meshes into his popular chairs.

-ean. Variant of **-ian.**

ear¹ (îr) *n.* **1.** *Anatomy.* **a.** The vertebrate organ of hearing, responsible, in general, for maintaining equilibrium as well as sensing sound, and divided in humans into the **external ear,** the **middle ear,** and the **internal ear** *(all of which see).* **b.** The part of this organ that is externally visible. **2.** An analogous organ in some invertebrates, such as insects. **3.** The sense of hearing. **4.** Aural sensitivity, as to differences in musical pitch or to speech sounds: *a good ear for foreign languages.* **5.** Attention; especially, favorable attention; heed: *"I shall beg your patient ear a little longer"* (Izaak Walton). **6.** Anything resembling or suggestive of the shape or position of the external ear, such as a tuft of feathers on the head of some owls or a projecting handle on a vase. **7.** A small box appearing in either of the upper corners of the front page of a newspaper, often containing an advertisement. —**all ears.** Acutely attentive: *If you want to tell your story, we're all ears.* —**by the ears.** Involved in a quarrel; at odds. —**fall on deaf ears.** To be ignored: *His advice fell on deaf ears.* —**have** (or **keep**) **an ear to the ground.** To give attention to or watch the trend of events and opinions. —**have the ear of.** To have one's advice or requests heeded by; be able to influence. —**in one ear and out the other.** Heard but without influence or effect. —**play by ear.** To perform music without reference to or memorization of a score. —**play it by ear.** *Informal.* To act without plan; improvise. —**turn a deaf ear.** To be unwilling to listen or pay heed. —**up to one's** (or **the**) **ears.** Deeply involved or committed: *up to one's ears in debt.* —**wet behind the ears.** Inexperienced or immature. [Middle English *ere,* Old English *ēare,* from Germanic; akin to Latin *auris,* Greek *ous.*] —**ear·less** *adj.*

ear² *n.* The seed-bearing spike of a cereal plant such as wheat.
~*intr.v.* **eared, earing, ears.** To form or grow ears. Used of cereal plants. [Middle English *ere, er,* Old English *ēar,* from Germanic.]

ear·ache (îr′āk′) *n.* Pain in the ear.

ear·bash (îr′băsh′) *v.* **-bashed, -bashing, -bashes.** *Australian Slang.* —*tr.* To talk incessantly to. —*intr.* To talk incessantly.

ear·drop (îr′drŏp′) *n.* **1.** A pendent earring. **2.** **eardrops.** Medicinal drops for inserting in the ear.

ear·drum (îr′drŭm′) *n. Anatomy.* The **tympanic membrane** *(see).*

eared (îrd) *adj.* **1.** Having ears or earlike projections. **2.** Having a specified kind or number of ears. Often used in combination: *a crop-eared puppy.*

eared seal *n.* Any of various seals of the family Otariidae, which includes the sea lions and fur seals, characterized by external ears, oarlike front flippers, and hind flippers that can be turned forward for walking on land. Compare **earless seal.**

ear·flap (îr′flăp′) *n.* Either of two cloth or fur appendages to a cap that may be turned down over the ears. Also called "earlap."

ear·ful (îr′fŏŏl′) *n. Informal.* **1.** A quantity of information or gossip. **2.** A severe reprimand.

Ear·hart (âr′härt′) **Amelia** (1898–1937). U.S. aviator. In May 1932 she became the first woman to fly solo across the Atlantic and in January 1935 the first to make a solo flight from Hawaii to California. Two years later she tried to fly around the world, but the plane crashed in the Pacific, and she and her navigator were never found.

ear·ing (îr′ĭng) *n. Nautical.* A short line attaching an upper corner of a sail to the yard. [Perhaps from EAR (part of body).]

earl (ûrl) *n. Abbr.* **E.** A British peer next in rank above a viscount and below a marquis. [Middle English *erl,* Old English *eorl,* warrior, chief, nobleman; akin to Old Saxon *erl,* Old Norse *jarl*†.]

ear·lap (îr′lăp′) *n.* An earflap.

earl·dom (ûrl′dəm) *n.* **1.** The rank or title of an earl. **2.** The territory under the jurisdiction of an earl.

earless seal *n.* Any of various seals of the family Phocidae, which includes the typical seals, having rudimentary hind limbs and no external ears. Compare **eared seal.**

ear lobe *n.* The soft, fleshy tissue at the lowest portion of the external ear.

ear·ly (ûr′lē) *adj.* **-lier, -liest. 1.** Near the beginning of a given series, period of time, or course of events: *in the early evening.* **2.** In or belonging to a distant or remote period or stage of development; primitive: *Early man discovered fire.* **3.** Occurring, developing, or appearing before the expected or usual time. **4.** Occurring in the near future: *Experts are hoping for an early settlement of the dispute.* ~*adv.* **1.** Near the beginning of a given series, period of time, or course of events. **2.** Before the expected or arranged time: *They left early.* —**early on.** Near the beginning of a given period or course of events. [Middle English *erly, erliche,* Old English *ǣrlīce,* from *ǣr,* ERE.] —**ear·li·ness** *n.*
   Usage: The phrase *earlier on* is criticized on the grounds that the *on* is neither necessary nor compatible in meaning with *earlier* (which is backward in time, not onward).

early bird *n.* A person who habitually arises early or arrives before others.

Early Bird *n.* Any of a number of communication satellites that provide telephone channels between Europe and the United States. The first was launched into stationary orbit in 1965.

ear·ly-clos·ing day (ûr′lē-klō′zĭng) *n. British.* A day, usually Wednesday or Thursday, on which many shops close after lunchtime to satisfy legal requirements.

Early English *n.* A style of architecture prevalent in England from the late 12th to the late 13th centuries, characterized by pointed arches, lancet windows, and simple tracery.

ear·ly-warn·ing system (ûr′lē-wôr′nĭng) *n.* A system designed to give warning of some forthcoming danger, such as an enemy attack or an earthquake.

ear·mark (îr′märk′) *n.* **1.** An identifying mark on the ear of a domestic animal. **2.** Any identifying feature or characteristic. ~*tr.v.* **-marked, -marking, -marks. 1.** To mark the ear of (a domestic animal) for identification. **2.** To place an identifying or distinctive mark on. **3.** To reserve or set aside for some purpose: *earmark goods for special customers.*

ear·muff (îr′mŭf′) *n.* Either of a pair of fur or warm cloth ear coverings often attached to an adjustable headband and worn to protect the ears against cold.

earn[1] (ûrn) *tr.v.* **earned, earning, earns. 1.** To gain or deserve (a salary, wages, or other reward) for one's service, labor, or performance. **2. a.** To acquire or deserve as a result of one's behavior: *He has earned the disapproval of his peers.* **b.** To make liable to: *His incompetence earned him a severe scolding.* **3.** To produce (interest or return) as profit. [Middle English *ernen,* Old English *earnian,* to earn, merit; akin to *esne,* laborer.] —**earn·er** *n.*

earn[2] *intr.v.* **earned, earning, earns.** *Obsolete.* To yearn. [Variant of YEARN.]

ear·nest[1] (ûr′nĭst) *adj.* **1.** Seriously determined; eager; zealous: *an earnest attempt.* **2.** Showing deep sincerity or feeling; serious: *an earnest gesture of good will.* **3.** Of an important or vital nature; not trivial or petty: *an earnest conference affecting world peace.* —See Synonyms at **eager, serious.** —**in earnest.** With a purposeful or serious intent. [Middle English *ernest,* Old English *eornost,* zeal, seriousness.] —**ear·nest·ly** *adv.* —**ear·nest·ness** *n.*

earnest[2] *n.* **1.** Money paid in advance as part payment to bind a contract or bargain. Also called "earnest money." **2.** A token of something to come; a promise or assurance. [Middle English *ernest, ernes,* from Old French *erres,* plural of *erre,* pledge, earnest money, from Latin *arra, arrha,* short for *arrabō, arrhabō,* pledge, from Greek *arrabōn,* from Hebrew 'ērābhōn, security, pledge, from 'ārabh, he pledged.]

earn·ings (ûr′nĭngz) *pl.n.* Something earned, especially: **1.** The salary or wages of a person. **2.** The profits of a business enterprise. **3.** Gains from investment.

Earp (ûrp) **Wyatt Berry Stapp** (1848–1929). U.S. frontier figure, buffalo hunter, and gambler. In Tombstone, Arizona, he came into conflict with Ike Clanton and his gang, which led to the gunfight at the O.K. Corral on October 26, 1881.

ear·phone (îr′fōn′) *n.* A device that converts electric signals, as from a telephone or radio receiver, to audible sound and that is worn or held in contact with the ear.

ear·piece (îr′pēs′) *n.* **1.** The part of something, as a telephone hand-

set, that is held next to the ear. **2.** One of the two parts of the frame that supports eyeglasses by passing around the ears.

ear·pierc·ing (îr′pîr′sĭng) *adj.* Loud and shrill enough to hurt the ears; deafening.

ear·plug (îr′plŭg′) *n.* A small wad, as of cotton or wax, placed in the ear to exclude noise or water.

ear·ring (îr′rĭng, îr′ĭng) *n.* An ornament or jewel worn on or hanging from the ear lobe.

ear shell *n.* The shell of the abalone.

ear·shot (îr′shŏt′) *n.* The range within which sound can be heard; hearing distance.

ear·split·ting (îr′splĭt′ĭng) *adj.* Loud and shrill enough to hurt the ears; deafening.

earth (ûrth) *n.* **1. a.** *Abbr.* **E** Often **Earth.** The third planet from the

---

ear

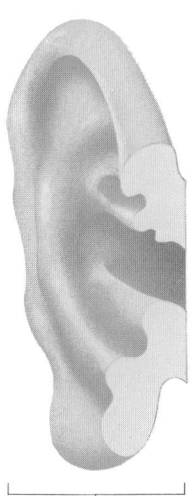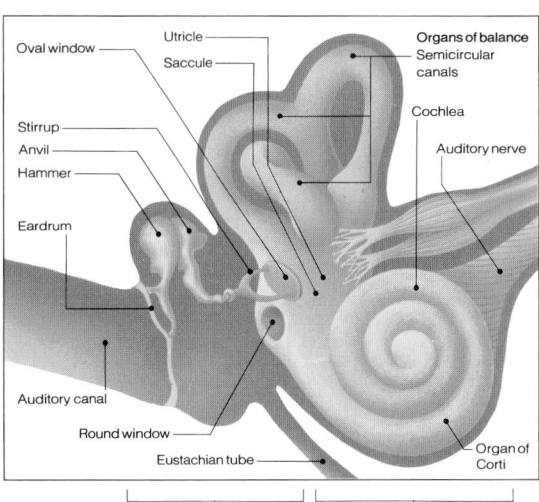

AN ORGAN WITH TWO FUNCTIONS: HEARING AND BALANCE
How the human ear transmits sound and motion to the brain

EXTERNAL EAR   MIDDLE EAR   INNER EAR

The ear is designed to convert sounds into electrical impulses and transmit them to the brain for interpretation. Sounds are waves of vibration that spread in all directions from the source, a vibrating object. People with normal hearing can detect sounds at frequencies from 20 to 20,000 Hz (hertz, that is, cycles per second), but some can hear sounds as low as 15 Hz, or higher than 20,000 Hz. The external ear is shaped to receive sound waves and direct them into the auditory canal, a tube about 25 millimeters (1 inch) long. It is lined with hairs, and glands that secrete waxy cerumen, to trap dust and dirt.

The auditory canal acts as a resonance chamber, that is, it increases the amplitude, or loudness, of sound waves directed into it, funneling them toward the eardrum. This is a thin membrane that, as long as the pressure on either side of it is equal, vibrates like a drum skin in sympathy with the frequency of the sound waves striking it. Sudden changes in pressure in aircraft during takeoff and landing briefly cause deafness and pain; swallowing opens the Eustachian tube that links the middle ear with the throat, and equalizes the pressure.

Fixed to the center of the eardrum is the hammer, the first of three tiny bones called the ossicles, which bridge the middle ear. The other ossicles are the anvil and the stirrup. They convert the large but weak sound waves from the eardrum into smaller, but more powerful, waves that are transmitted through the footplates of the stirrup to the oval window. This membrane, which separates the middle from the inner ear, is similar to, but smaller than, the eardrum and vibrates in sympathy with it.

The sound vibrations from the oval window vibrate the fluid within the cochlea, a shell-like spiral tube, about 30 millimeters (1½ inches) long, in the inner ear. The round window, a membrane at the end of the cochlea, bulges out when the oval window bulges in, and vice versa. The vibrations passing along the cochlea stimulate the basilar membrane that winds around within it. The membrane in turn stimulates the hairlike receptor cells of the organ of Corti that lies upon it. Groups of receptor cells lying on different parts of the membrane respond to different frequencies: low-pitched sounds are detected by the cells at the membrane's upper end; high-pitched sounds are detected by cells at the lower end.

The organ of Corti when stimulated acts like a microphone, converting sound vibrations into electrical impulses whose voltage is higher the lower the note. Nerve fibers from each of its receptor cells communicate with the brain by way of the auditory nerve, enabling the brain's auditory centers to interpret the differences in frequency and amplitude as differences in pitch and loudness.

The inner ear also contains the organs of balance. The three semicircular canals, each lying at right angles to the others, sense rotary motion and changes in speed. As the head moves, corresponding movement of the fluid in the canals stimulates their receptor cells, which send corresponding impulses along the nerve pathways to the reflex centers of the brain.

Each end of each canal meets the utricle, which, together with the adjoining saccule, senses the position of the head in space. Both contain hairlike receptor cells responsive to gravity. Those of the utricle point upward when the head is upright and are increasingly stimulated as the body turns upside-down. Those of the saccule point sideways and are increasingly stimulated as the head tilts to one side. As the head moves, the stimulated receptor cells trigger the transmission of impulses to the brain.

sun, having a sidereal period of revolution about the sun of 365.26 days at a mean distance of 92.96 million miles, an axial rotation period of 23 hours 56.07 minutes, an average radius of 3,963 miles, and a mass of 13.17×10^{24} pounds. **b.** The land surface of the world as distinguished from the oceans and air. **2.** The softer, friable part of land; soil, especially productive soil. **3.** The dwelling place of mortal men as distinguished from heaven and hell; the temporal world. **4.** All of the human inhabitants of the world: *The earth received the news with joy.* **5.** Worldly affairs; temporal matters as distinguished from spiritual concerns: *the temptations of the earth.* **6.** The material body of the human being considered as made of dust or clay. **7.** In ancient thought, one of the four **elements** *(see).* **8.** The lair of a burrowing animal. **9.** *Chiefly British Informal.* A large or excessive amount of money: *charged us the earth.* **10.** *Chiefly British. Electricity.* The ground of an electrical circuit. **11.** *Chemistry.* Any of several metallic oxides that are difficult to reduce, such as alumina or zirconia, formerly regarded as elements. **12.** *Geology.* A loose, fine-grained amorphous deposit such as fuller's earth or diatomaceous earth. See **alkaline earth, rare earth.** —**down to earth.** Without sentimentality or frills; sensible and realistic. —**on earth.** Used as an intensive: *Where on earth have you been all this time?* —**run to earth. 1.** To pursue (a fox, for example) to its lair; hunt down. **2.** *Informal.* To find; track down. ~*v.* **earthed, earthing, earths.** —*tr.* **1.** To cover or heap up (plants) with soil for protection. **2.** To chase into an underground lair. **3.** *Chiefly British.* To ground (an electrical device or circuit). —*intr.* To burrow or hide in the ground, as a hunted fox does. [Middle English *erthe,* Old English *eorthe,* from Germanic.]

earth·born (ûrth′bôrn′) *adj.* **1.** Springing from or born on the earth. **2.** Human; mortal.

earth·bound, earth-bound (ûrth′bound′) *adj.* **1. a.** Attached or confined to or by the earth and earthly interests. **b.** Unimaginative; ordinary. **2.** Heading for the earth: *an earthbound meteor.*

earth closet *Chiefly British. n.* An outhouse in which excreted matter is covered with earth.

earth·en (ûr′thən, -thən) *adj.* **1.** Made of dirt, soil, or earth: *an earthen fortification.* **2.** Made of baked clay: *an earthen vase.*

earth·en·ware (ûr′thən-wâr′, ûr′thən-) *n.* **1.** A variety of coarse, porous baked clay. **2.** Ware made from clay, such as dishes, pots, and tableware. ~*adj.* Made of earthenware.

earth·light (ûrth′līt′) *n.* **Earthshine** *(see).*

earth·ling (ûrth′lĭng) *n.* **1.** One who inhabits the earth; a human being, especially as opposed to an extraterrestrial being. **2.** A person devoted to worldly things.

earth·ly (ûrth′lē) *adj.* **1.** Of the earth, specifically: **a.** Not heavenly or divine; secular. **b.** Terrestrial. **2.** Conceivable; feasible; possible: *no earthly meaning whatever.* —**earth·li·ness** *n.*

Usage: earthly, terrestrial, worldly, mundane, earthy. These adjectives all indicate relationship to the earth but are not always interchangeable. *Earthly* is used principally in opposition or contrast to *heavenly. Terrestrial* is in opposition to *celestial* or specifies earth distinguished from other planets or land distinguished from water. *Worldly,* in opposition to spiritual, describes the actions and

---

Earth

THE LAYERS OF THE EARTH

Earthquakes reveal the mystery of the earth's core

Although the earth's interior cannot be studied directly, the measurement of earthquake waves as they bend through it has revealed three major layers.

The outermost layer of the planet is the crust (upper layer) beneath which lies the mantle (middle layer) and the core (lower layer). The place of contact between the crust and mantle is called the Mohorovičić discontinuity (Moho for short). As earth-

quake waves cross from the crust to the mantle, they increase in speed by 15 percent.

The crust is divided into two types, the oceanic and continental, and the mantle is divided into upper and lower regions with a transition zone between. Around the solid inner core there is a fluid outer core, in which the circulation of electrical currents causes the earth's magnetic field.

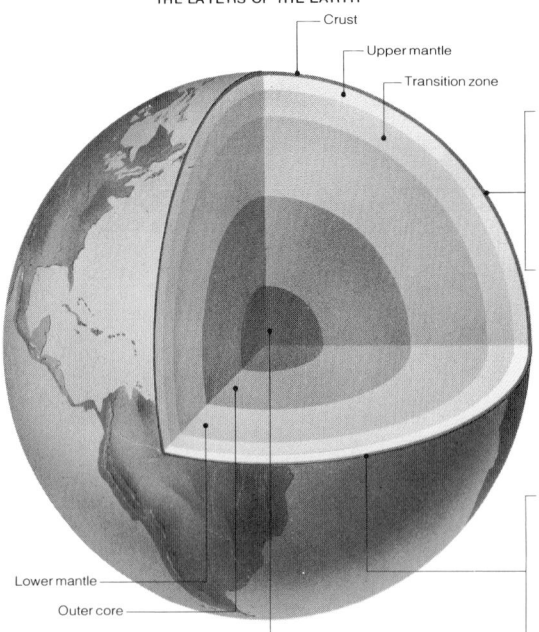

THE LAYERS OF THE EARTH

- Crust
- Upper mantle
- Transition zone
- Lower mantle
- Outer core
- Inner core

The earth's crust was once part of the mantle, but it separated over many millions of years. It is less dense than the mantle. The mantle, less dense than the core, is mainly silicates of iron and magnesium. The core is probably iron and iron sulfide.

DIVISIONS OF THE CRUST

Sea level — Oceanic ridge — Continental crust — Continent — Sea level — Oceanic crust — Moho discontinuity — **UPPER MANTLE**

Continental crust is much thicker than oceanic crust and is thickest beneath mountain ranges. The depth of the Moho varies—from 5 kilometers (3 miles) beneath the seabed to 70 kilometers (45 miles) beneath high mountains.

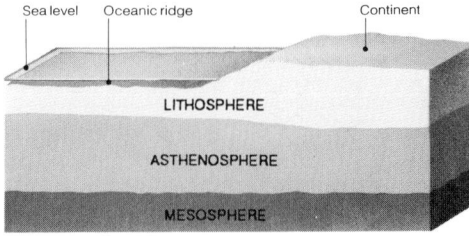

SOLID AND SEMIFLUID LAYERS

Sea level — Oceanic ridge — Continent — **LITHOSPHERE** — **ASTHENOSPHERE** — **MESOSPHERE**

An alternative division of the earth, based on its physical rather than its chemical properties, shows the solid lithosphere, which comprises the crust and upper mantle, lying above the semifluid asthenosphere and the solid mesosphere.

Planet location guide

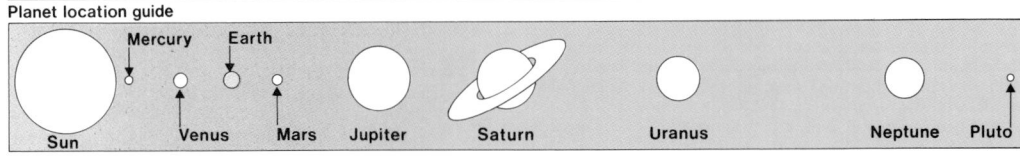

Sun — Mercury — Venus — Earth — Mars — Jupiter — Saturn — Uranus — Neptune — Pluto

---

earthquake

VIOLENT SHIFTS IN THE EARTH'S CRUST
Clashes between the earth's plates can cause devastation

Every year there are about one million earthquakes around the world. Some of these tremors are so slight that they can be detected only by the most sensitive seismographs; others can unleash the destructive energy of a nuclear bomb.

Earthquakes are caused by movement of the plates that form the earth's crust. Where the plates meet there are fractures in the earth's surface. Pushed by slow convection currents from within the earth's molten interior, the plates grind against each other, building up tension and producing sudden violent shocks. Along the lines where these plates are pushing into one another the risk of severe shocks is greater, but where they are moving apart, which usually occurs on the ocean floor, molten rock pours up through the widening fracture.

Earthquakes coincide most often with plate margins along three main belts. One of these encircles the Pacific and is called the Ring of Fire. It is bordered roughly by the west coast of the American continent, Asia, Indonesia, New Zealand, and the Antarctic. It is joined by the second belt, which stretches west through China along the Himalayas and across Iran to the north and south of the Mediterranean.

The third of these danger zones lies under the oceans. When earthquakes are generated on the seabed, they can set up the monstrous waves that are misnamed tidal waves but should correctly be known by their Japanese name of tsunami.

EARTHQUAKES OF THE TWENTIETH CENTURY			
Date	Place	Magnitude	Deaths
1906	San Francisco	8.3	700
1908	Italy	7.5	83,000
1920	China	8.6	180,000
1923	Japan	8.3	99,000
1927	China	8.3	200,000
1931	New Zealand	7.9	255
1935	Pakistan	7.5	20,000–60,000
1952	California	7.7	11
1962	Chile	8.5	4,000–5,000
1963	Yugoslavia	6.0	1,000
1964	Alaska	8.5	178
1968	Iran	7.4	12,000
1970	Peru	7.7	50,000–70,000
1976	China	8.0	655,000
1976	China	7.8	240,000
1977	Iran	8.0	189
1978	Iran	7.7	15,000
1979	Ecuador	7.9	600
1980	Algeria	7.7	3,500
1980	Italy	7.2	3,000
1986	Mexico	7.8	5,550

By measuring the size of an earthquake's shock waves, scientists can determine its magnitude—the amount of energy released at its focus. This is measured on the Richter scale devised by Californian scientist Charles Richter in 1935. Some of the most powerful shocks have occurred in sparsely populated areas and so caused less loss of life than other earthquakes of smaller magnitude.

DAMAGE TO BUILDINGS *Ground movement in an earthquake is usually slight. It is the sudden vibration that causes damage, and buildings are very vulnerable—as a photograph taken after the 1964 Alaskan earthquake shows (left). Unless they are protected by special foundations, modern concrete buildings do not survive the shock any better than timber structures.*

concerns of people, especially as they pertain to this life (distinguished from afterlife); the term is associated with the pursuit of pleasure, wealth, or success. *Mundane* likewise refers to what is secular rather than spiritual or eternal and especially to the more ordinary, routine aspects of life on the earth. *Earthy,* in opposition to spiritual, suggests what is down to earth, especially the satisfaction of material wants and the more primitive human instincts.

earth·man (ûrth′măn′) *n., pl.* **-men** (-měn′). An inhabitant of the earth; an earthling. Used chiefly in science fiction.

earth mother *n.* **1.** A mother goddess considered as the giver of life. **2.** A woman combining maternal and sensual qualities.

earth·mov·er (ûrth′mōō′vər) *n.* A piece of heavy machinery, as a bulldozer, for excavating or moving large amounts of soil, dirt, or earth.

earth·nut (ûrth′nŭt′) *n.* **1. a.** An Old World plant, *Conopodium denudatum,* having edible, nutlike tubers. **b.** The tuber of this plant. Also called "pignut." **2.** Any of various other plants having similar edible tubers or underground parts.

earth·quake (ûrth′kwāk′) *n.* A series of shock waves in the earth's crust or upper mantle, caused by sudden release of strains accumulated along geologic faults and by volcanic action, and resulting in movements in the earth's surface. Also called "seism."

earth·rise (ûrth′rīz′) *n.* The rise of the earth above the moon's horizon, as seen from the lunar surface or from a satellite.

earth satellite *n.* A satellite that orbits the earth.

earth science *n.* Any of several essentially geologic sciences concerned with the origin, structure, and physical phenomena of the earth.

earth·shak·ing (ûrth′shā′kĭng) *adj.* Of enormous consequence or fundamental importance.

earth·shat·ter·ing (ûrth′shăt′ər-ĭng) *adj.* Earthshaking.

earth·shine (ûrth′shīn′) *n.* The sunlight reflected from the earth's surface that illuminates the part of the moon not directly lit by the sun. Also called "earthlight."

earth·star (ûrth′stär′) *n.* A fungus of the genus *Geastrum,* related to the puffballs and having an outer covering that splits open in a starlike form.

earth station *n.* An on-ground terminal linked to a spacecraft or satellite by an antenna and associated electronic equipment for the purpose of transmitting or receiving messages, tracking, or control.

earth·ward (ûrth′wərd) *adj.* Heading toward the earth; earthbound. ~*adv.* Toward the earth. **—earth·wards** *adv.*

earth wax *n.* **Ozocerite** (see).

earth·work (ûrth′wûrk′) *n.* **1.** Often **earthworks.** An earthen embankment, especially when used as a military fortification. **2.** *Engineering.* Excavation and embankment of earth, as in the building of a railroad. **—See Synonyms at bulwark.**

earth·worm (ûrth′wûrm′) *n.* Any of various terrestrial annelid worms of the class Oligochaeta, and especially of the family Lumbricidae, that burrow into and help aerate and enrich soil.

earth·y (ûr′thē) *adj.* **-ier, -iest. 1.** Consisting of or resembling earth or soil. **2.** Pertaining to or characteristic of this world; worldly. **3.** Crude or coarse; unrefined: *earthy humor.* **4.** Uninhibited; hearty. **—See Usage note at earthly. —earth·i·ness** *n.*

ear trumpet *n.* A horn-shaped instrument formerly used to direct sound into the ear of a partially deaf person.

ear·wax (îr′wăks′) *n.* The waxlike secretion of certain glands lining the canal of the outer ear; cerumen.

ear·wig (îr′wĭg′) *n.* Any of various insects of the order Dermaptera, such as the European species *Forficula auricularia,* having pincerlike appendages protruding from the rear of the abdomen. ~*tr.v.* **earwigged, -wigging, -wigs.** To attempt to influence by insinuation or subterfuge. [Middle English *erwigge,* Old English *ēarwicga,* "ear insect" (thought to be able to penetrate a person's head

earthstar *An inedible fungus with an outer skin that splits and folds back into a starlike shape a few days after it breaks through the soil. This species is* Geastrum triplex, *which grows in beech woods during summer and autumn.*

earwig *A nocturnal and widely distributed insect easily identified by the pincerlike claws at the end of its body. The claws are thought to be defensive, but it is not known whether they inflict damage on the insect's enemies. Earwigs feed on carrion, leaves, and roots and often hide by day in small crevices—the origin, perhaps, of the mistaken belief for which they were named: that they like to crawl into the ears of humans.*

Easter egg *Painted and beribboned eggs are a traditional Easter gift in central Europe.*

Easter Island *These long-faced statues dominate the landscape of Easter Island, named because its first European explorers, the Dutch, landed on Easter Day 1722. Some of the statues are more than 9 meters (30 feet) tall and weigh up to 90 tons. All are made from the island's volcanic rock and the earliest date from about* A.D. *1100.*

through the ear) : EAR + *wicga,* insect.]

ease (ēz) *n.* **1.** The condition of being without discomfort; freedom from pain, worry, or agitation. **2.** Freedom from constraint, embarrassment, or awkwardness; poise; naturalness: *the ease of his approach to a stranger.* **3. a.** Freedom from difficulty, hard work, or great effort: *He could take his ease only after he had met the deadline.* **b.** Readiness in performance; facility: *play tennis with ease.* **4.** A state of rest or relaxation. **5.** Freedom from financial difficulty; affluence. **—at ease.** *Military.* In a position of rest, with the feet apart. —See Synonyms at **rest.**
~*v.* **eased, easing, eases.** —*tr.* **1.** To free from pain, worry, agitation, or trouble; soothe; comfort: *The good news eased her mind considerably.* **2.** To alleviate or lighten (discomfort); mitigate; lessen: *took aspirin to ease his headache.* **3.** To slacken the strain, pressure, tension, or stress of; loosen. Often used with *away, down, up,* or *off: ease off a cable.* **4.** To reduce the difficulty of. **5.** To move or fit into place or position slowly and carefully: *ease the patient onto the stretcher.* —*intr.* To lessen in discomfort, effort, difficulty, pressure, or the like. Often used with *up* or *off.* [Middle English *ese,* from Old French *aise,* comfort, convenience, from Latin *adjacēns,* nearby, adjacent, from *adjacēre,* to lie near : *ad-,* near to + *jacēre,* to lie, from *jacere,* to throw.]

ease·ful (ēz'fəl) *adj.* Affording or characterized by comfort and peace; restful. **—ease·ful·ly** *adv.* **—ease·ful·ness** *n.*

ea·sel (ē'zəl) *n.* A frame, usually in the form of an upright tripod, upon which something may be displayed or which may support an artist's canvas. [Dutch *ezel,* "as," from Middle Dutch *esel,* from Common Germanic *asiluz* (unattested), from Latin *asinus.*]

ease·ment (ēz'mənt) *n.* **1.** The act of easing or the condition of being eased. **2.** Something that affords ease or comfort. **3.** *Law.* A right afforded a person to make limited use of another's land, as a right of way.

eas·i·ly (ē'zə-lē) *adv.* **1.** Without difficulty or stress: *a problem easily solved.* **2.** Without doubt or question; certainly: *easily the best play this season.* **3.** In all likelihood; well: *That might easily have been a mistake.*

eas·i·ness (ē'zē-nĭs) *n.* **1.** The condition or quality of being easy to accomplish, acquire, or the like. **2.** Ease of manner; nonchalance; poise.

east (ēst) *n. Abbr.* **e, E, e., E. 1. a.** The direction of the earth's axial rotation. **b.** The cardinal point on the mariner's compass 90° clockwise from north and directly opposite west. **2.** An area or region lying in the east. **3. a.** One of the four positions occupied by players in a game of bridge. **b.** The player occupying this position. **—the East. 1.** The eastern part of the earth, especially Asia and its neighboring islands; the Orient. **2.** The region of the United States east of the Alleghenies and north of the Mason-Dixon line. **3.** The Communist countries of Eastern Europe.
~*adj.* **1.** To, toward, of, facing, or in the east. **2.** Coming from or originating in the east, as a wind. **3. East.** Officially or conventionally designating the eastern part of a country, continent, or other geographic area: *East Germany.*
~*adv.* In, from, or toward the east. [Middle English *e(a)st,* Old English *ēast,* from Germanic.]

East An·gli·a (ăng'glē-ə). Region in the east of England consisting of Norfolk, Suffolk, and parts of Cambridgeshire and Essex. It was once an Anglo-Saxon kingdom. Its main crops are wheat, barley, and sugar beets, and some of the best agricultural land in England is found in the low, flat land. In the Middle Ages wool made it an area of great wealth. **—East An·gli·an** *n. & adj.*

East Asia. See **Far East, the.**

East Berlin. See **Berlin.**

east·bound (ēst'bound') *adj.* Going toward the east.

east by north *n.* The direction or point on the mariner's compass halfway between due east and east-northeast. It is 78° 45′ east of due north.

east by south *n.* The direction or point on the mariner's compass halfway between due east and east-southeast. It is 101° 15′ east of due north.

East Caribbean dollar *n.* The basic monetary unit of Dominica, Grenada, St. Lucia, and St. Vincent & the Grenadines.

East China Sea. Shallow section of the western Pacific Ocean. Bounded by China, South Korea, Taiwan, and the Ryukyu and Kyushu islands, it is a rich fishing ground.

East End. A densely populated working-class and immigrant area of London containing industrial and dock areas. **—East End·er** *n.*

Eas·ter (ē'stər) *n.* **1.** A festival in the Christian Church commemorating the Resurrection of Christ, celebrated on the first Sunday following the full moon that occurs on or just after March 21. **2.** The Sunday on which the festival of Easter is held. Also called "Easter Day," "Easter Sunday." [Middle English *ester, estre,* Old English *ēastre* (usually in plural *ēastron*); probably from *Eostre,* Germanic goddess whose festival occurred in the spring.]

Easter egg *n.* A chocolate egg, decorated hen's egg, or egg-shaped ornament offered as a gift at Easter.

Easter Island. Volcanic island in the South Pacific Ocean, 3,700 kilometers (2,300 miles) west of Chile, of which it is a part, discovered on Easter Day, 1722, by the Dutch navigator Jakob Roggeven. It is famous for its colossal heads (up to 9 meters or 30 feet high) carved from tufa from the Rano Roraku volcano and its wooden tablets with their ideographic scripts, which may be the work of the ancestors of the island's Polynesian inhabitants.

Easter lily *n.* Any of various white-flowered lilies that bloom around Easter, especially *Lilium longiflorum.* This species is also called "Bermuda lily."

east·er·ly (ē'stər-lē) *adj.* **1.** Situated in or toward the east. **2.** From the east. Said of wind.
~*n., pl.* **easterlies.** A storm or wind from the east. **—east·er·ly** *adv.*

Easter Monday *n.* The Monday following Easter Sunday.

east·ern (ē'stərn) *adj. Abbr.* **e, E, e., E. 1.** Situated toward, in, or facing the east. **2.** Coming from the east. Said of wind. **3.** Native to or growing in the east. **4.** *Often* **Eastern.** Of, pertaining to, or characteristic of eastern regions or the East. **5. Eastern.** Of, pertaining to, or characteristic of the eastern part of the earth, especially Asia and its neighboring islands; Oriental: *Eastern philosophy.* **6. Eastern.** Of or pertaining to the Eastern Churches, especially the Eastern Orthodox Church as distinguished from the Roman Catholic Church. [Middle English *esterne,* Old English *ēasterne.*]

Eastern Bloc. The countries associated under the **Warsaw Pact** *(see).*

Eastern Church *n.* **1.** The Church of the Roman Empire in the east, as distinguished from the Western Church, and including the patriarchates of Constantinople, Antioch, Alexandria, and Jerusalem. Also called "Greek Church." **2.** Any of the churches that have developed from this, especially: **a.** The Eastern Orthodox Church. **b.** Any of the Uniat Churches following the rites of the Eastern Orthodox Church.

Eastern Empire. See **Byzantine Empire.**

east·ern·er (ē'stər-nər) *n. Often* **Easterner.** A native or inhabitant of the east, especially of the eastern United States.

Eastern Europe. Political region of Europe comprising Albania, Bulgaria, Czechoslovakia, East Germany, Hungary, Poland, Romania, Yugoslavia, and the U.S.S.R. west of the Ural Mts. After World War II Communist regimes friendly to the U.S.S.R. were set up in the eight other countries. The U.S.S.R. refused Marshall Plan aid, forced its satellites to do the same, and founded Comecon (1949) to coordinate economic planning for the region. The U.S.S.R. also set up the Warsaw Pact (signed 1955). Eastern Europe is a transitional area between the temperate Atlantic lands and the central Eurasian landmass with its climatic extremes. Northeastward, winters are progressively harsh, and only the Adriatic and Black Sea coasts are above the freezing point in January. Apart from some southern mountains, Eastern Europe generally has less than 750 millimeters (30 inches) of rain a year. Some 45 percent of Eastern Europe is cultivated, and a further 20 percent is grazing land. Potatoes, sugar beets, rye, oats, wheat, and corn are grown on the best land. Bohemia is noted for hops, the Balkan basins for cotton and tobacco, and the Adriatic coast for citrus fruits and olives, while parts of the south produce grapes and wines. Eastern Europe outside the U.S.S.R. has few natural resources and relies on Soviet raw materials. Czechoslovakia, East Germany, Poland, and, to a lesser extent, Hungary are the most industrialized countries of the region.

Eastern European Mutual Assistance Treaty *n.* The **Warsaw Pact** *(see).*

Eastern Ghats. See **Ghats.**

Eastern Hemisphere. The part of the earth, approximately half, that is east of the Greenwich meridian and includes the continents of Europe, Africa, Asia, and Australia.

east·ern·most (e'stərn-mōst') *adj.* Farthest east.

Eastern Orthodox Church *n.* The body of modern churches, including the Greek and Russian Orthodox, derived from the church of the Byzantine Empire and acknowledging the primacy of the patriarch of Constantinople. Also called "Eastern Church," "Greek Church," "Orthodox Church."

Eastern Roman Empire. See **Byzantine Empire.**

Eastern Samoa. See **American Samoa.**

Eastern Standard Time *n. Abbr.* **EST, E.S.T.** One of the four standard time zones of North America, based on the local time at the 75th meridian west of Greenwich, England, five hours behind Greenwich Mean Time.

Eas·ter·tide (ē'stər-tīd') *n.* **1.** The Easter season, extending in different churches from Easter to Ascension Day, Whitsunday, or Trinity Sunday. **2.** The week following Easter Sunday.

East Frisians. See **Frisian Islands.**

East Germanic *n.* A subdivision of the Germanic languages, represented only by Gothic.

East Germany. Official name German Democratic Republic. People's republic in Eastern Europe. Formed from the Soviet-occupied zone of Germany following World War II, it became an independent Communist state. Economic austerity, curbs on civil liberties, and the Sovietization of industry and agriculture led to riots and discontent (crushed by Soviet forces in 1953) and mass migration to West Germany. The Berlin Wall, erected in 1961 by the East German government, effectively put a stop to the migration. Its industries, planned in close cooperation with the U.S.S.R., include shipbuilding, machinery, chemicals, textiles, optical and precision instruments, and printing. Lignite is the country's chief mineral and supplies 70 percent of the energy. A member of Comecon, East Germany conducts nearly half of its foreign trade with the U.S.S.R. and over three quarters within the Communist bloc. It became a member of the United Nations in 1973. Area, 108,178 square kilometers (41,757 square miles). Population, 16,700,000. Capital, East Berlin. See also **Germany.** **—East German** *n. & adj.*

East Greek *n.* A principal dialectal division of Ancient Greek, comprising Mycenaean Greek, Arcado-Cyprian, Attic-Ionic, and Aeolic.

East India Company *n.* Any of several European companies organized in the 17th and 18th centuries to trade with the East Indies; especially, the company chartered to do so by the British government in 1600.

East In·di·a·man (ĭn′dē-ə-mən) *n., pl.* **East In·di·a·men** (-mĭn). A large, full-rigged merchant ship that was formerly used in trade with the East Indies.

East In·dies (ĭn′dēz). *Abbr.* **E.I.** Name formerly applied to India, the Malay Peninsula, and the Malay Archipelago. Subsequently it included only the Malay Archipelago or the Dutch East Indies (the islands of the Malay Archipelago that became Indonesia after World War II).

east·ing (ē′stĭng) *n.* **1.** *Nautical.* **a.** The distance sailed by a ship on an easterly course. **b.** The longitudinal distance from a given meridian on an easterly course. **2.** An easterly direction.

East Lo·thi·an (lō′thē-ən). Former county, now part of Lothian Region, southeastern Scotland.

East·man (ēst′mən), **George** (1854–1932). U.S. businessman and inventor. He invented a dry-plate process of film development, the roll of film, the Kodak camera, and a process for color photography. In 1892 he founded the Eastman Kodak Company in Rochester, New York.

east-north-east (ēst′nôrth-ēst′; *Nautical* -nôr-ēst′) *n. Abbr.* **ENE** The direction or point on the mariner's compass halfway between due east and northeast. It is 67° 30′ east of due north.

~*adj.* Situated toward, facing, or in this direction.

~*adv.* In, from, or toward this direction.

East Pakistan. See **Bangladesh.**

East River. Narrow tidal strait, 26 kilometers (16 miles) long and 183 to 1,200 meters (600 to 4,000 feet) wide, connecting Upper New York Bay and Long Island Sound. It separates the boroughs of Manhattan and the Bronx from Brooklyn and Queens.

East Slavic *n.* The eastern division of the Slavic languages, consisting of Russian, Ukrainian, and Byelorussian.

east-south-east (ēst′south-ēst′) *n. Abbr.* **ESE** The direction or point on the mariner's compass halfway between due east and southeast. It is 112° 30′ east of due north.

~*adj.* Situated toward, facing, or in this direction.

~*adv.* In, from, or toward this direction.

East St. Lou·is (sānt lōō′ĭs). City in southwestern Illinois, on the Mississippi River opposite St. Louis. It is an important manufacturing and railway center; its industries include a large aluminum works, and meat-packing and oil-refining plants.

East Sus·sex (sŭs′ĭks). County in southeastern England consisting of the eastern parts of the former county of Sussex and bordering on the English Channel.

east·ward (ēst′wərd) *adj.* Toward, facing, or in the east.

~*n.* An eastward direction, point, or region.

~*adv.* Toward the east. —**east·ward·ly** *adv.* —**east·wards** *adv.*

eas·y (ē′zē) *adj.* **-i·er, -i·est. 1.** Capable of being accomplished or ac-

EASTERN EUROPE

quired with ease; posing no difficulty: *"How easy is success to those who will only be true to themselves"* (Anthony Trollope). **2.** Free from worry, anxiety, trouble, or pain: *"Now as I was young and easy under the apple boughs"* (Dylan Thomas). **3.** Conducive to rest or comfort; pleasant and relaxing. **4.** Relaxed; easygoing; informal: *an easy, sociable manner.* **5.** Not strict or severe; lenient: *an easy teacher.* **6. a.** Readily persuaded or influenced; compliant. **b.** Not hard to trick or victimize: *an easy target for swindlers.* **7.** Not strained, hurried, or forced; moderate: *walked at an easy pace.* **8.** *Economics.* **a.** Less in demand and therefore readily obtainable: *Commodities are easier.* **b.** Plentiful and therefore obtainable at low interest rates: *easy credit.* **9.** *Informal.* Easily, often dishonestly obtained: *easy money.* —*adv.* **1.** In a relaxed manner: *breathe easy.* **2.** In an easy manner; easily: *Success came too easy to them.* **3.** In a cautious manner; carefully: *Go easy on this icy road.* **4.** Without being harshly penalized: *If he wasn't put in jail, he got off easy.* **—go easy on.** *Informal.* To exercise moderation in one's approach to: *Go easy on the new recruits.* **—take it easy.** *Informal.* **1.** To refrain from exertion; relax. **2.** To refrain from anger or violence; stay calm. [Middle English *esy,* from Old French *aisie,* past participle of *aisier,* to put at ease, from *aise,* EASE.]

    Usage: Easy is used in standard English as an adverb in only a few idiomatic or informal constructions, such as *easy come easy go, easier said than done,* and *take things easy.* The usual adverbial form is *easily,* as in *The handle turns easily.*

easy chair *n.* A large, comfortable, well-upholstered chair.
eas·y·go·ing, eas·y-go·ing (ē'zē-gō'ĭng) *adj.* **1. a.** Living without intense worry; placid. **b.** Lazy and careless. **c.** Lax in moral attitudes. **2.** Undemanding: *an easygoing life.* **3.** Having or moving at an even gait. Said of a horse.
easy mark *n.* A person who is easily persuaded or taken advantage of.
easy street *n. Slang.* A condition of financial security or independence: *A substantial inheritance put them on easy street.*
eat (ēt) *v.* **ate** (āt; *British & Regional* ĕt), **eaten** (ēt'n), **eating, eats.** —*tr.* **1. a.** To take into the mouth, chew, and swallow (food). **b.** To consume the edible parts of: *eat a chop.* **c.** To take regularly as food. **2.** To consume, ravage, or destroy by or as if by eating. Usually used with *away* or *up.* **3.** To erode or corrode. **4.** *Slang.* To bother or annoy: *What's eating him?* —*intr.* **1.** To consume food; have or take a meal or meals. **2.** To exercise a gradual consuming or eroding effect. Used with *into: eating into our resources.* **—eat crow.** *Informal.* To be forced to accept a humiliating defeat. **—eat one's heart out.** To feel bitter, hopeless anguish or longing. **—eat one's words.** To retract something that one has said. **—eat out.** To eat in a restaurant or public place. **—eat out of someone's hand.** To be manipulated or dominated by another. **—eat up.** *Slang.* To absorb enthusiastically or avidly: *He eats up old movies.* [Eat, ate, eaten; Middle English *eten, et, eten,* Old English *etan, ǣt, eten.*]
eat·a·ble (ē'tə-bəl) *adj.* Fit to be eaten; edible. —*n. Usually* **eatables.** Something fit to be eaten; food.

    Usage: Eatable and *edible* are sometimes interchangeable in the sense of "fit to be eaten," but usually there is a difference. *Eatable* refers to the extent to which food has been well prepared and is palatable. *Edible* refers to the extent to which it is possible to treat a substance as food. Food that is edible may on occasion be uneatable because of its condition. The colloquial use of *inedible* as a synonym for *uneatable* in such contexts is often heard.

eat·er (ē'tər) *n.* One that eats: *She's a light eater.*
eat·er·y (ē'tə-rē) *n., pl.* **-ies.** *Informal.* A place for eating, such as a cafeteria.
eat·ing (ē'tĭng) *n.* Food with respect to its flavor or quality: *The peaches were not only beautiful, they were good eating.* —*adj.* Suitable for eating raw: *eating apples.*
eats (ēts) *pl.n. Slang.* Food.
eau de co·logne (ō' də kə-lōn') *n., pl.* **eaux de cologne** (ō', ōz'). A toilet water, **cologne** (see).
eau de nile (ō' də nēl', nīl') *n., pl.* **eaux de nile** (ō', ōz'). A pale green. [French, "water of (the) Nile."]
eau de vie (ō' də vē') *n., pl.* **eaux de vie** (ō', ōz'). Brandy. [French, "water of life."]
eaves (ēvz) *pl.n.* The projecting overhang at the lower edge of a roof. [Middle English *eves,* Old English *yfes, efes,* eaves, edge, border; probably akin to OVER.]
eaves·drop (ēvz'drŏp') *intr.v.* **-dropped, -dropping, -drops.** To listen secretly to the private conversation of others. Used with *on.* [Back-formation from *eavesdropper,* Middle English *evesdropper,* from *evesdrop,* water from the eaves, probably from Old English *yfesdrype.*] **—eaves·drop·per** *n.*
E_B The symbol for binding energy.
ebb (ĕb) *n.* **1. a.** The drawing back of the tide from the shore. **b.** An ebb tide. **2.** A fading away or diminishing; a decline: *"insistence upon rules of conduct marks the ebb of religious fervor"* (A.N. Whitehead). —*intr.v.* **ebbed, ebbing, ebbs. 1.** To draw back from the shore. Used of a tide. **2.** To fade or diminish. Often used with *away.* [Middle English *ebban* (verb), *ebba* (noun), from West Germanic *abhigo* (unattested); akin to Gothic *ibuks,* moving backward.]
ebb tide *n.* **1.** The receding tide between high water and a succeeding low water. Also called "ebb." **2.** The period during which the tide is receding. Compare **flood tide.**
EBCDIC (ĕb'sĭ-dĭk') *n.* A code for representing alphanumeric infor-

mation. [E(XTENDED) + B(INARY) + C(ODED) + D(ECIMAL) + I(NTERCHANGE) + C(ODE).]
Eb·lis (ĕb'lĭs). The principal evil spirit or devil of Islamic mythology. [Arabic *Iblīs,* from Greek *diabolos,* slanderer. See **devil.**]
E-boat (ē'bōt') *n.* A German torpedo boat in World War II. [From enemy *boat.*]
eb·on (ĕb'ən) *adj. Poetic.* **1.** Made of ebony. **2.** Black. [Middle English *eban, ebenus,* from Old French, from Medieval Latin *ebanus,* from Greek *ebenos* (the tree), from Semitic.]
eb·on·ite (ĕb'ə-nīt') *n.* Hard rubber *(see),* especially when it is colored black. [EBON + -ITE.]
eb·on·ize (ĕb'ə-nīz') *tr.v.* **-ized, -izing, -izes.** To finish with an ebony stain. **—eb·on·i·za·tion** *n.*
eb·on·y (ĕb'ə-nē) *n., pl.* **-ies. 1.** Any of several chiefly tropical trees of the genus *Diospyros;* especially, *D. ebenum,* of southern Asia, having hard, dark-colored heartwood. **2.** The wood of such a tree, used in cabinetmaking and for piano keys. **3.** Black. —*adj.* **1.** Made of or suggesting ebony. **2.** Black. [Middle English, from Late Latin *ebeninus,* (made) of ebony, from Greek *ebeninos,* from *ebenos,* ebony tree, EBON.]
e·brac·te·ate (ē-brăk'tē-āt') *adj. Botany.* Without bracts. [New Latin *ebracteatus* : EX- (out, without) + BRACTEATE.]
E·bro (ē'brō). Longest river completely in Spain. It rises in the Cantabrian Mts. in Santander province and flows 925 kilometers (575 miles) southeast to the Mediterranean. It is navigable by seagoing vessels as far as Tortosa, 32 kilometers (20 miles) inland.
e·bul·lient (ĭ-bŏol'yənt, ĭ-bŭl'-) *adj.* **1.** Overflowing with excitement, enthusiasm, or exuberance. **2.** Boiling. Said of a liquid. [Latin *ēbulliēns* (stem *ēbullient-*), present participle of *ēbullīre,* to boil over : *ex-,* completely + *bullīre,* to boil.] **—e·bul·lience** (ĭ-bŏol'yəns, ĭ-bŭl'-), **e·bul·lien·cy** (-yən-sē) *n.* **—e·bul·lient·ly** *adv.*
e·bul·li·os·co·py (ĭ-bŏol'ē-ŏs'kə-pē, ĭ-bŭl'-) *n.* A method of determining the molecular weight of a substance, based on measurements of the extent to which the boiling point of a solvent is altered by its presence in solution. [Latin *ēbullīre,* to boil over (see **ebullient**) + -SCOPY.] **—e·bul·li·o·scop·ic** (ĭ-bŏol'ē-ə-skŏp'ĭk, ĭ-bŭl'-) *adj.*
eb·ul·li·tion (ĕb'ə-lĭsh'ən) *n.* **1.** The bubbling or effervescence of a liquid; a boiling. **2.** A sudden, violent outpouring, as of emotion or unrest: *"did not . . . give way to any ebullitions of private grief"* (W.M. Thackeray). [Late Latin *ēbullītiō* (stem *ēbullītiōn-*), from Latin *ēbullīre,* to boil over. See **ebullient.**]
eb·ur·na·tion (ĕb'ər-nā'shən, ē'bər-) *n. Pathology.* The degeneration of bone into a hard, ivorylike mass, such as occurs at the articulating surfaces of bones in osteoarthritis. [Latin *eburnus,* (made) of ivory, from *ebur,* IVORY.]
E.C. Established Church.
e·cad (ē'kăd', ĕk'ăd') *n. Biology.* An organism or group of organisms that differs from other members of its species as a result of environmental conditions. [EC(OLOGY) + -AD.]
é·car·té (ā'kär-tā') *n.* **1.** A card game for two players. **2.** In ballet, a position with an arm and a leg extended on the same side of the body. [French, past participle of *écarter,* to discard.]
ec·bol·ic (ĕk-bŏl'ĭk) *adj.* Stimulating childbirth or abortion. —*n.* A drug or other agent that stimulates childbirth or abortion. [Greek *ekbolē,* a throwing out, ejection, from *ekballein* : *ek-,* out + *ballein,* to throw.]
ec·ce ho·mo (ĕk'sē hō'mō, ĕk'ē) *n.* A picture depicting Christ wearing the crown of thorns. [Latin, "Behold the Man," words used by Pontius Pilate to present Christ crowned with thorns to his accusers. John 19:5.]
ec·cen·tric (ĕk-sĕn'trĭk, ĭk-) *adj.* **1.** Departing or deviating from the conventional norm, especially in an odd or amusing way: *an eccentric recluse.* **2.** Deviating from a circular form, as in an elliptical orbit. **3.** Not situated at or in the center. **4.** Not having the same center. Said of figures such as circles, cylinders, and spheres. Compare **concentric.** —See Synonyms at **strange.** —*n.* **1.** One that deviates markedly from a normal, conventional, or expected course or pattern; an odd or erratic person or thing. **2.** *Machinery.* A disk or wheel having its axis of revolution displaced from its center so that it is capable of imparting reciprocating motion. [Middle English *excentryke,* not having the same center (said of planets), from Late Latin *eccentricus,* from Greek *ekkentros* : *ex-,* out + *kentron,* point, center, from *kentein,* to prick.] **—ec·cen·tri·cal·ly** *adv.*
ec·cen·tric·i·ty (ĕk'sĕn-trĭs'ə-tē) *n., pl.* **-ties. 1. a.** Deviation from the normal, conventional, or expected. **b.** An instance of such deviation: *Storing old newspapers in the attic was one of his eccentricities.* **2. a.** The quality of being eccentric. **b.** The degree of being off-center or not concentric. **3.** *Machinery.* The distance between the center of an eccentric and its axis; the throw. **4.** *Mathematics.* The ratio of the distance of any point on a conic section from a focus to its distance from the corresponding directrix.

    Synonyms: idiosyncrasy, quirk.

ec·chy·mo·sis (ĕk'ĭ-mō'sĭs) *n.* **1.** The passage of blood from ruptured blood vessels into subcutaneous tissue as a result of bruising, marked by a purple discoloration of the skin. **2.** The resultant skin discoloration. [New Latin, from Greek *ekkhumōsis,* from *ekkhumousthai,* to pour out : *ex-,* out of + *khumos,* juice, from *khein,* to pour.] **—ec·chy·mot·ic** (ĕk'ĭ-mŏt'ĭk) *adj.*
Ec·cles (ĕk'əlz). Town in Greater Manchester, England, on the Irwell River and the Manchester Ship Canal. Its industries include textiles, machinery, and chemicals.

Eccles cake *n. British.* A round or oval cake with a case of sugared flaky pastry and a currant filling. [After ECCLES in Greater Manchester, England.]

ec·cle·si·a (ĭ-klē′zhē-ə, -zē-ə, -zhə) *n., pl.* **-siae** (-zhē-ē′, -zē-ē′). 1. The political assembly of citizens of an ancient Greek state. 2. A church or congregation. [Latin *ecclēsia,* from Greek *ekklēsia,* duly summoned assembly, from *ekkalein,* to call out, summon : *ex-,* out + *kalein,* to call.] **—ec·cle·si·al** *adj.*

Ec·cle·si·as·tes (ĭ-klē′zē-ăs′tēz′) *n. Abbr.* **Eccles.** A book of the Old Testament traditionally attributed to Solomon. [Latin *Ecclēsiastēs,* from Greek *ekklēsiastēs,* member of the assembly of citizens, from *ekklēsia,* ECCLESIA.]

ec·cle·si·as·tic (ĭ-klē′zē-ăs′tĭk) *adj.* Ecclesiastical.
~*n.* A clergyman; a priest.

ec·cle·si·as·ti·cal (ĭ-klē′zē-ăs′tĭ-kəl) *adj. Abbr.* **eccles.** Of or pertaining to a church, especially as an organized institution; clerical. **—ec·cle·si·as·ti·cal·ly** *adv.*

ecclesiastical calendar *n.* The calendar of feasts celebrated by the Christian Church, in which the year begins on the first Sunday of Advent.

ec·cle·si·as·ti·cism (ĭ-klē′zē-ăs′tə-sĭz′əm) *n.* 1. Ecclesiastical principles, practices, and activities. 2. Excessive adherence to ecclesiastical principles and forms.

Ec·cle·si·as·ti·cus (ĭ-klē′zē-ăs′tĭ-kəs) *n.* A book of the Apocrypha. Also called "Wisdom of Jesus, the Son of Sirach."

ec·cle·si·ol·a·try (ĭ-klē′zē-ŏl′ə-trē) *n.* Worship of the church, especially extreme devotion to its principles or traditions. [From ECCLESI(A) + -LATRY.] **—ec·cle·si·ol·a·ter** (ĭ-klē′zē-ŏl′ə-tər) *n.*

ec·cle·si·ol·o·gy (ĭ-klē′zē-ŏl′ə-jē) *n.* 1. The study of the Christian Church as an institution. 2. The study of ecclesiastical art, especially in relation to the architecture and decoration of churches. **—ec·cle·si·o·log·i·cal** (ĭ-klē′zē-ə-lŏj′ĭ-kəl) *adj.* **—ec·cle·si·ol·o·gist** (ĭ-klē′zē-ŏl′ə-jĭst) *n.*

ec·crine (ĕk′rĭn, -rīn′, -rēn′) *adj.* 1. Secreting externally; especially, pertaining to an eccrine gland or its secretion. 2. Exocrine *(see).* [From Greek *ekkrinein,* to secrete : *ex-,* out + *krinein,* to separate.]

eccrine gland *n.* Any of the small sweat glands distributed over the body's surface.

ec·crin·ol·o·gy (ĕk′rə-nŏl′ə-jē) *n.* The study of eccrine secretions and secretory organs. [ECCRINE + -LOGY.]

ec·dem·ic (ĕk-dĕm′ĭk, ĭk-) *adj.* Designating diseases that do not normally occur in a given population but that have been brought in, as by immigrants or travelers; not endemic. [Greek *ek-,* out, outside + *dēmos,* people (by analogy with *epidemic*).]

ec·dys·i·ast (ĕk-dĭz′ē-ăst′, -əst) *n.* A striptease artist. Used humorously. [From ECDYSIS; coined by H.L. MENCKEN.]

ec·dy·sis (ĕk′də-sĭs) *n., pl.* **-ses** (-sēz′). The shedding of an outer integument or layer of skin, as by insects, crustaceans, and snakes. [New Latin, from Greek *ekdusis,* a stripping, from *ekduein,* to take off : *ex-* (reversal) + *duein,* to put on, put on, enter.]

ec·dy·sone (ĕk′dĭ-sōn′) *n.* A hormone secreted by insects and crustaceans that stimulates growth and molting. [ECDYS(IS) + -ONE.]

e·ce·sis (ĭ-sē′sĭs, ĭ-kē′-) *n.* The successful establishment of an organism in a new environment. [Greek *oikēsis,* habitation, from *oikein,* to dwell, from *oikos,* house.]

ECG electrocardiogram; electrocardiograph.

ec·hard (ĕk′härd′) *n. Ecology.* Soil water not available for absorption by plants. [Greek *ekhein,* to hold, hold back + *ardein†,* to water, irrigate.]

ech·e·lon (ĕsh′ə-lŏn′) *n.* 1. a. A formation of troops in which parallel units are arranged to the left or right of the rear unit in a steplike fashion. b. A similar formation of groups, units, or individuals. c. A similar formation or arrangement of vessels or aircraft. 2. A subdivision of a military or naval force: *command echelon.* 3. A level of responsibility or authority in a hierarchy. 4. *Optics.* A specialized form of diffraction grating consisting of parallel glass plates of successively varying sizes, used to determine wavelengths, especially of extremely fine structures.
~*v.* **echeloned, -loning, -lons.** *—tr.* To arrange in an echelon. *—intr.* To form, march, or move in an echelon. [French *échelon,* "rung of a ladder," from Old French *eschelon,* from *eschile,* ladder, from Latin *scālae,* ladder, stairs.]

ech·e·ve·ri·a (ĕch′ə-və-rē′ə) *n.* Any of various tropical American plants of the genus *Echeveria,* having thick, succulent leaves often clustered in a rosette and commonly cultivated as house plants. [New Latin *Echeveria,* after M. *Echeveri,* 19th-century Mexican botanical illustrator.]

e·chid·na (ĭ-kĭd′nə) *n., pl.* **-nas** or **-nae** (-nē′). Any of several burrowing, egg-laying mammals of the genera *Tachyglossus* and *Zaglossus,* of Australia, Tasmania, and New Guinea, having a spiny coat, a slender snout, and a sticky tongue used for catching ants and termites. Also called "spiny anteater." [New Latin, from Latin, viper, from Greek *ekhidna.*]

ech·i·nate (ĕk′ə-nāt′) *adj. Biology.* Bearing or covered with spines; prickly; spiny. [Latin *echinātus,* from *echinus,* hedgehog. See **echino-**.]

echino-, echin- *prefix.* Indicates prickly or covered with spines; for example, echinoderm, echinoid. [New Latin, from Latin *echinus,* hedgehog, sea urchin, from Greek *ekhinos.*]

e·chi·no·coc·co·sis (ĭ-kī′nə-kə-kō′sĭs) *n., pl.* **-ses** (-sēz′). Also **e·chi·no·coc·ci·a·sis** (-kə-kī′ə-sĭs) *pl.* **-ses** (-sēz′). Infestation with echinococci; especially, **hydatid disease** *(see).* [ECHINOCC(US) + -OSIS.]

e·chi·no·coc·cus (ĭ-kī′nə-kŏk′əs) *n., pl.* **-cocci** (-kŏk′sī′, -kŏk′ī′).

Any of several parasitic tapeworms of the genus *Echinococcus,* the larvae of which infect mammals and form large, spherical cysts, causing serious or fatal disease. [New Latin *Echinococcus* : ECHINO- + COCCUS.]

e·chi·no·derm (ĭ-kī′nə-dûrm′) *n.* Any of numerous radially symmetrical marine invertebrates of the phylum Echinodermata, which includes the starfishes, sea urchins, and sea cucumbers, having a calcareous skeleton just beneath the skin that is often covered with spines. [ECHINO- + -DERM.] **—e·chi·no·der·mal** (ĭ-kī′nə-dûr′məl), **e·chi·no·der·ma·tous** (-dûr′mə-təs) *adj.*

e·chi·noid (ĭ-kī′noid′) *n.* Any echinoderm of the class Echinoidea, which includes the sand dollars and sea urchins. [ECHIN(O)- + -OID.]

e·chi·nus (ĭ-kī′nəs) *n., pl.* **-ni** (-nī′). *Architecture.* A curved molding just below the abacus of a Doric capital. [Latin, "hedgehog," "sea urchin" (from the shape). See **echino-**.]

ech·o (ĕk′ō) *n., pl.* **-oes.** 1. a. Repetition of a sound by reflection of sound waves from a surface. b. The sound produced in this manner. c. An electronic sound effect repeating a recorded sound. 2. Any repetition or imitation of something, as of the opinions, speech, or dress of another: *The dress is an echo of Edwardian fashion.* 3. One who imitates another, as in opinions, speech, or dress. 4. A sympathetic response. 5. A consequence or repercussion: *Her assassination had political echoes.* 6. The repetition of certain sounds or syllables in poetry. 7. *Music.* The soft repetition of a note or phrase. 8. A signal to a partner at bridge or whist that the same suit is to be continued. 9. *Electronics.* A reflected wave received by a radio or radar.
~*v.* **echoed, -oing, -oes.** *—tr.* 1. To repeat by or as if by an echo; send back the sound of: *The canyon echoed her cry.* 2. To repeat or imitate: *followers echoing the thoughts of the leader.* 3. To be reminiscent of; resemble: *events echoing those of a century ago. —intr.* 1. To be repeated by or as if by an echo. 2. To resound with or emit an echo; reverberate: *woods echoing with hunting cries.* [Middle English *ecco, ecko,* from Old French *echo,* from Latin *ēchō,* from Greek *ēkhō.*] **—ech·o·er** *n.* **—ech·o·ey** *adj.*

Ech·o (ĕk′ō). *Greek Mythology.* A nymph whose unrequited love for Narcissus caused her to pine away until only her voice remained.

ech·o·car·di·og·ra·phy (ĕk′ō-kär′dē-ŏg′rə-fē) *n. Medicine.* A diagnostic technique that uses ultrasound waves to investigate the action of the beating heart and to depict this on a screen. **—ech·o·car·di·o·graph** (ĕk′ō-kär′dē-ə-grăf′) *n.* **—ech·o·car·di·o·graph·ic** (ĕk′ō-kär′dē-ə-grăf′ĭk) *adj.*

echo chamber *n.* A room fitted with wall panels that reflect sound, used for making acoustic measurements and recordings requiring echo effects.

echo check *n.* An error-control technique in which the receiving terminal or computer returns the original message to verify its correct reception.

ech·og·ra·phy (ĕk-ŏg′rə-fē) *n.* Investigation of the internal organs of the body using ultrasound waves, which are reflected from the tissues.

e·cho·ic (ĭ-kō′ĭk) *adj.* 1. Being or resembling an echo. 2. Imitative of sounds; onomatopoeic. **—e·cho·i·cal·ly** *adv.*

ech·o·ism (ĕk′ō-ĭz′əm) *n.* The formation of words in imitation of sounds; onomatopoeia.

ech·o·la·li·a (ĕk′ō-lā′lē-ə) *n. Psychology.* Involuntary repetition of words or phrases just spoken by others, occurring in some mental and language disorders. [ECHO + Greek *lalia,* talk, from *lalos,* talkative.] **—ech·o·lal·ic** (-lā′lĭk) *adj.*

ech·o·lo·ca·tion (ĕk′ō-lō-kā′shən) *n.* 1. The ability of an animal that emits high-frequency sounds, such as a bat or dolphin, to orient itself by means of the reflected sound waves. 2. *Electronics.* Ranging by acoustical echo analysis.

ech·o·prax·i·a (ĕk′ō-prăk′sē-ə) *n. Psychology.* Pathological imitation of the actions of another person, occurring as a symptom of certain mental disorders. **—ech·o·prac·tic** (ĕk′ō-prăk′tĭk) *adj.*

echo sounder *n.* A device for measuring the depth of water by sending a high-frequency pulse to the bottom and measuring the time taken for the echo to return. **—echo sounding** *n.* See feaure, next page.

ech·o·vi·rus (ĕk′ō-vī′rəs) *n.* Any virus of a group originally isolated from the intestinal tract and thought to cause nonspecific meningitis, many illnesses causing symptoms of the common cold, and various gastrointestinal and respiratory-tract infections. [*E*nteric *C*ytopathic *H*uman *O*rphan + VIRUS.]

echt (ĕkt, ĕкнt) *adj.* Genuine or typical. [German.]

Eck (ĕk), **Johann Maier von** (1486–1543). German theologian. When Luther published his 95 theses in 1517, Eck became his principal opponent and went to Rome to bring back the papal bull condemning him in 1520.

Eck·hart (ĕk′härt′), **Johannes,** also known as "Meister Eckhart" (*c.* 1260–*c.* 1328). German theologian and mystic. He was considered the most accomplished scholar and preacher of his day but in 1326 was accused of heresy.

é·clair (ā-klâr′, ā′klâr′) *n.* A tube-shaped cream puff that is filled with whipped cream or custard and usually iced with chocolate. [French, "lightning," from Old French *esclair,* from *esclairier,* to light, flash, from Vulgar Latin *exclāriāre* (unattested), variant of Latin *exclārāre* : *ex-,* completely + *clārāre,* to brighten, clarify, from *clārus,* bright, clear.]

e·clamp·si·a (ĭ-klămp′sē-ə) *n. Pathology.* Coma and convulsions arising from any of several conditions during or immediately after

echidna *A primitive egg-laying mammal, the echidna feeds on ants that it digs from the ground with its powerful claws. Echidnas are native to Australia and New Guinea.*

echo sounder

TRACING THE HAZARDS AND TREASURES OF THE OCEANS
Pictures of fish, rocks, and wrecks beneath the sea are drawn from echoes

Dramatic losses of shipping, caused by the iceberg that sank the *Titanic* in 1912 and by the German U-boats in World War I, intensified work on devices to locate underwater dangers. By 1918 Allied warships were using echo-sounding equipment. It sent a pulse of sound down through the water and measured the time that passed before its echo bounced back from the seabed or from an obstacle. Such depth detectors were widely used in the 1930's. During World War II, sideways scanning was developed to locate objects near the surface. Since 1940 the system's American name "sonar" has replaced the British name "asdic."

Today, pinpointing of direction and distance has become precise, and fine detail of an object is re-vealed. Detection is possible over a range of 10 kilometers (6 miles); beyond that the returning signal cannot be distinguished from the background noise of the sea itself. Sonar equipment is used in military vessels and also to aid navigation in deep-sea vessels, to locate shoals of fish, to survey oil pipeline routes, and to search for wrecks of archeological interest.

HYDROSEARCH SYSTEM *The display screen of a hydro-search echo-sounding device shows a submarine resting on the ocean floor. Such devices are capable of a high degree of detail: the submarine's conning tower and peri-scope are visible in close-up in the panel on the right of the display screen.*

A transducer, set in a ship's hull, sends out and receives sound waves. It translates the returning waves into electrical pulses that form the patterns on the display screen

The sonar beam spreads out in stages until it detects the submarine

The submarine's presence is reflected back to the ship

Shoal of fish

Weed-covered rock

CHROMOSCOPE SYSTEM *Shoals of fish are located using the chromoscope, a Japanese echo-sounding device. The pattern on the screen (below) is made up of dots whose colors—from white, through deepening shades of yellow, to red—indicate the density of the ob-ject being scanned: the deeper the shade, the denser the object located. The dense red and yellow areas indi-cate objects covered with seaweed, and the small white area to the right represents a shoal of fish. Areas of the picture can be enlarged. Such sound-ers may be so accurate that they can be used to detect and identify individual fish.*

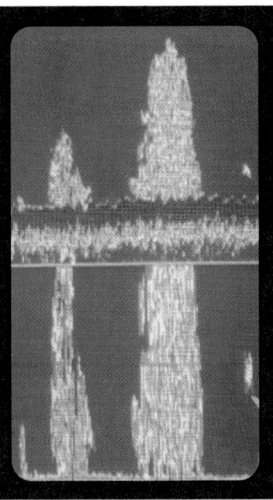

SCANNING THE DEPTHS *An echo sounder works by means of a transducer, a device that converts electricity into sound waves. It transmits pulses that travel at about 1,460 meters (4,800 feet) per second until they hit the seabed or an obstacle. This reflects them as echoes to the transducer. The time that elapses between transmitting a pulse and receiving its echo is recorded by an electrical circuit, displayed on a screen or on electrically sensitive paper, and measured to find the range.*

pregnancy. [New Latin, from Greek *eklampsis,* a shining forth, brightness, from *eklampein,* to shine forth : *ex-,* out + *lampein,* to shine.] —**e·clamp·tic** (ĭ-klămp′tĭk) *adj.*

é·clat (ā-klä′, ā′klä′) *n.* **1.** Great brilliance, as of performance or achievement. **2.** Conspicuous success or acclaim. [French, explo-sion, from *éclater,* to burst, explode, from Old French *esclater,* from Germanic *slītan* (unattested), to tear, SLIT.]

e·clec·tic (ĭ-klĕk′tĭk) *adj.* **1.** Choosing what appears to be the best from diverse sources, systems, or styles. **2.** Consisting of compo-nents selected from diverse sources.
—*n.* One who follows an eclectic method. [Greek *eklektikos,* from *eklektos,* selected, from *eklegein,* to single out : *ex-,* out + *legein,* to choose.] —**e·clec·ti·cal·ly** *adv.*

e·clec·ti·cism (ĭ-klĕk′tə-sĭz′əm) *n.* **1.** An eclectic system or method. **2.** Free selection, as of ideas, from diverse sources.

e·clipse (ĭ-klĭps′) *n.* **1. a.** The partial or complete obscuring, relative to a designated observer, of one celestial body by another. **b.** The period of time during which such an obscuring occurs. **2.** Any tem-porary or permanent dimming or cutting off of light. **3.** Any falling into obscurity; an overshadowing or decline.
—*tr.v.* **eclipsed, eclipsing, eclipses. 1.** To cause an eclipse or ob-scuring of; darken. **2.** To obscure or overshadow the importance, fame, or reputation of; reduce in importance by comparison. [Mid-dle English *eclipse,* from Old French, from Latin *eclīpsis,* from Greek *ekleipsis,* cessation, abandonment, from *ekleipein,* to leave out, abandon : *ek-, ex-,* out + *leipein,* to leave.]

eclipsing binary *n. Astronomy.* A binary star one component of which is regularly eclipsed by the other because its orbital plane lies in or near the line of sight. Also called "eclipsing variable."

e·clip·tic (ĭ-klĭp′tĭk) *n. Astronomy.* **1.** The apparent path of the sun relative to the stars; the intersection plane of the earth's solar orbit with the celestial sphere. **2.** A great circle on a terrestrial globe inclined at an approximate angle of 23° 27′ to the equator. [Middle English *ecliptik,* from Late Latin *eclīpticus,* from Latin, of an eclipse, from Greek *ekleiptikos,* from *ekleipein,* to abandon. See **eclipse.**] —**e·clip·tic** *adj.*

ec·lo·gite (ĕk′lə-jīt′) *n.* A coarse-grained basic rock consisting of a greenish mixture of pyroxene, quartz, and feldspar with large red garnet inclusions. [Greek *eklogē,* selection (see **eclectic**) + -ITE.]

ec·logue (ĕk′lôg′, -lŏg′) *n.* A bucolic poem, typically a pastoral dia-logue. [French *églogue,* from Old French *eglogue,* from Latin *ecloga,* "selection," from Greek *eklogē,* from *eklegein,* to single out. See **eclectic.**]

e·clo·sion (ĭ-klō′zhən) *n.* The emergence of an adult insect from a pupal case or of an insect larva from an egg. [French *éclosion,* from *éclore,* to open, be hatched, from Vulgar Latin *exclaudere* (unat-tested), variant of Latin *exclūdere,* to shut out : EX- + *claudere,* to shut, close.]

eco– *prefix.* Indicates ecology; for example, **ecosystem.** [From ECOLOGY.]

ec·o·cide (ĕk′ō-sīd′, ē′kō-) *n.* Deliberate or avoidable destruction of the natural environment, as by pollutants. [ECO- + -CIDE.]

e·col·o·gy (ĭ-kŏl′ə-jē) *n. Abbr.* **ecol. 1. a.** The science of the relationships between organisms and their environments. Also called "bionomics." **b.** The relationship between organisms and their environment. **2. a.** The study of the relationships between people and their environment. **b.** The relationship between a human group and its environment. In this sense, also called "human ecology." [German *Ökologie* : Greek *oikos,* house + -LOGY.] —**ec·o·log·i·cal** (ĕk′ə-lŏj′ĭ-kəl, ē′kə-), **ec·o·log·ic** (-lŏj′ĭk) *adj.* —**ec·o·log·i·cal·ly** *adv.* —**e·col·o·gist** (ĭ-kŏl′ə-jĭst) *n.*

e·con·o·met·rics (ĭ-kŏn′ə-mĕt′rĭks) *n. Used with a singular verb.* The application of statistical techniques to economics in the study of problems, the analysis of data, and the development of theory. [ECONO(MICS) + -METRIC.] —**e·con·o·met·ric, e·con·o·met·ri·cal** *adj.*—**e·con·o·me·tri·cian** (ĭ-kŏn′ə-mə-trĭsh′ən), **e·con·o·met·rist** (-mĕt′rĭst) *n.*

ec·o·nom·ic (ĕk′ə-nŏm′ĭk, ē′kə-) *adj.* **1.** Of or pertaining to the production, development, and management of material wealth, as of a country, household, or business enterprise. **2.** Of or pertaining to economics. **3.** Of or pertaining to matters of finance. **4.** *Chiefly British.* Financially self-sustaining or self-justifying. **5.** Economical. **6.** Of or pertaining to the necessities of life; utilitarian. —See Usage note at **economical.**

ec·o·nom·i·cal (ĕk′ə-nŏm′ĭ-kəl, ē′kə-) *adj.* **1.** Not wasteful or extravagant; prudent in management of resources. **2.** Operating or designed in a way that avoids waste or excessive costs. —See Synonyms at **sparing.** —**ec·o·nom·i·cal·ly** *adv.*

Usage: Economical can only be used in the context of "saving," "not being wasteful": *an economical way of life. Economic* is the only form to use when referring to the field of economics (*economic issues; economic growth*). On the other hand, *economic* is also sometimes found as an alternative to *economical* in the sense of "saving" (as in *It's not economic to have a home freezer unless you buy in bulk*). In such pairs as *economic prices* and *economical prices,* the former is the more likely to mean "prices that do not lose money" (for the producer), while the latter is the more likely to mean "prices that save money" (for the consumer).

economic geography *n.* The study of the distribution and use of economic resources throughout the world.

ec·o·nom·ics (ĕk′ə-nŏm′ĭks, ē′kə-) *n. Abbr.* **econ. 1.** *Used with a singular verb.* The social science that deals with the production, distribution, and consumption of commodities and the theory and operation of financial systems. **2.** *Used with a plural verb.* **a.** An economic basis. **b.** Relevant financial considerations.

e·con·o·mist (ĭ-kŏn′ə-mĭst) *n. Abbr.* **econ.** A specialist in economics.

e·con·o·mize (ĭ-kŏn′ə-mīz′) *v.* **-mized, -mizing, -mizes.** —*intr.* To be frugal; reduce expenses. —*tr.* To use or manage in an economical way; save. —**e·con·o·mi·za·tion** *n.*

e·con·o·miz·er (ĭ-kŏn′ə-mī′zər) *n.* **1.** One that economizes. **2.** A device, as in power stations or steam engines, that uses some of the waste heat from a boiler flue to preheat the feed water.

e·con·o·my (ĭ-kŏn′ə-mē) *n., pl.* **-mies.** *Abbr.* **econ. 1.** The careful or thrifty use or management of resources, as of income, materials, or labor. **2.** An example of this; a saving. **3. a.** The management of the resources of a country, community, or business. **b.** A system for the management and development of such resources: *an agricultural economy.* **4.** The economic system of a country or area: *Floods disrupted the economy of the region.* **5.** Artistic restraint or avoidance of ornamentation. **6.** The functional arrangement of elements within a structure or system: *the economy of an organism.* **7.** *Theology.* The divine plan or system for the government of the world or for a specific period or nation. **8.** Economy class. ~*adj.* Allowing a saving to be made, as through bulk purchase: *economy size; an economy car.* [Old French *economie,* management of a household, from Latin *oeconomia,* from Greek *oikonomia,* from *oikonomos,* manager of a household : *oikos,* house + *-nomos,* managing (see **-nomy**).]

economy class *n.* The least expensive and least luxurious category of airline seating and service.

é·cor·ché (ā′kôr-shā′) *n.* A picture of the body or part of the body with the skin removed so as to show the appearance of the muscles. [French, "skinned."]

ec·o·spe·cies (ĕk′ō-spē′shēz, -sēz, ē′kō-) *n.* A taxonomic species considered in terms of its ecological characteristics and usually including several ecotypes. [ECO- + SPECIES.]

ec·o·sphere (ĕk′ō-sfîr′, ē′kō-) *n.* The regions of the universe, particularly on the earth, that are capable of supporting life.

é·cos·saise (ā′kô-sāz′) *n. Music.* **1.** A piece of music with a dance-like rhythm in ²/₄ time. **2.** A lively dance to an écossaise. [French, "Scottish (dance)."]

ec·o·sys·tem (ĕk′ō-sĭs′təm, ē′kō-) *n.* An ecological community together with its physical environment, considered as a unit. [ECO- + SYSTEM.]

ec·o·tone (ĕk′ə-tōn′, ē′kə-) *n.* An ecological community of mixed vegetation formed by the overlapping of adjoining communities. [ECO- + Greek *tonos,* tension, TONE.]

ec·o·type (ĕk′ō-tīp′, ē′kō-) *n.* The smallest taxonomic subdivision of an ecospecies, consisting of subspecies or varieties adapted to a particular set of environmental conditions. [ECO- + TYPE.]

ec·ru (ĕk′rōō, ā′krōō) *n.* A grayish to pale yellow or light grayish yellowish brown. [French *écru* : *é-* (intensive) + *cru,* crude, raw.] —**ec·ru** *adj.*

E.C.S.C. European Coal and Steel Community.

ec·sta·sy (ĕk′stə-sē) *n., pl.* **-sies. 1.** A state of exalted delight. **2.** A state of any emotion experienced very intensely: *an ecstasy of anger.* **3. a.** The trance, frenzy, or rapture associated with mystic or prophetic exaltation. **b.** *Psychology.* An emotional state, associated with religious or sexual experience or with drug taking, characterized by exuberant behavior and loss of self-control. [Middle English *extasie,* from Old French, from Late Latin *extasis, ecstasis,* from Greek *ekstasis,* from *existanai,* to displace, drive out of one's senses : *ex-,* out + *histanai,* to place.]

Synonyms: bliss, delight, euphoria, exaltation, rapture, transport.

ec·stat·ic (ĕk-stăt′ĭk, ĭk-) *adj.* **1.** Of, relating to, induced by, or inducing ecstasy. **2.** In a state of ecstasy; enraptured. ~*n.* One subject to ecstasies. —**ec·stat·i·cal·ly** *adv.*

ECT, E.C.T. electroconvulsive therapy.

ec·thy·ma (ĕk-thī′mə) *n.* An inflammatory skin disease characterized by ulcerating pustules that penetrate to the lower layer of the skin and cause scarring when they heal. [New Latin, from Greek *ekthuma,* pustule, from *ekthuein,* to break out : *ek-,* out + *thuein,* to seethe.]

ecto- *prefix.* Indicates outside or external part or surface; for example, **ectoderm, ectoplasm.** [Greek *ekto-,* from *ektos,* outside (after *entos,* inside), from *ek, ex,* out.]

ec·to·derm (ĕk′tə-dûrm′) *n.* The outermost of the three primary germ layers of an embryo, developing into the epidermis, nervous tissue, and, in vertebrates, sense organs. Also called "exoderm."

eclosion *A lesser vine hawk moth emerges from its pupa case. The process is known as eclosion.*

---

eclipse

BLOTTING OUT THE SUN AND MOON

When earth and moon cast their shadows on each other

Eclipses are of two kinds—solar and lunar. Although the sun and moon appear almost the same size in the sky, the sun has 400 times the moon's diameter—but it is also nearly 400 times farther away. So when the moon passes between sun and earth, it blots out some or all of the sun, producing a partial or total solar eclipse. At a total eclipse, the solar atmosphere flashes into view, and the spectacle is magnificent. When the three bodies line up exactly but the moon is at its farthest from the earth, the moon appears too small to hide the sun, and a ring (annulus) of sun is seen around the dark body of the moon; this is an annular eclipse.

Because the moon's shadow is only just long enough to reach the earth, it can blot out the sun completely for only a short time. At any one point on the earth's surface a total eclipse can never last for more than 7 minutes 40 seconds, and then only near the equator; farther to the north or south the duration of the eclipse will be shorter.

A lunar eclipse occurs when the earth passes between the sun and the moon; the moon then passes through the cone of shadow cast by the earth. Direct sunlight is no longer reaching the moon, which turns a dim, coppery color until it emerges from the shadow. Usually the moon does not vanish completely, since some sunlight is bent or refracted onto its surface by the ring of atmosphere around the earth. A total lunar eclipse may last for 1 hour 40 minutes. A lunar eclipse can be seen from any point on the earth where the moon is above the horizon.

If the plane of the moon's orbit coincided exactly with the earth's there would be a solar and lunar eclipse every month. But, as the moon's orbit is offset by about 5 degrees, the three bodies align only occasionally—at most seven times a year.

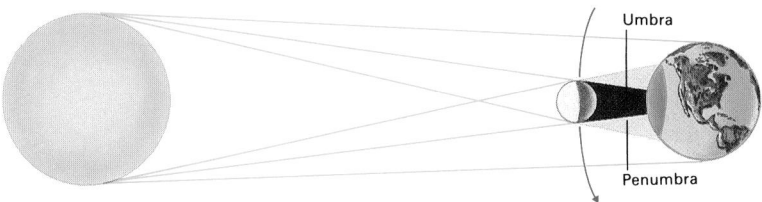

Umbra

Penumbra

ECLIPSE OF THE SUN *During a total eclipse of the sun, the main cone of the shadow that falls on the earth is the umbra. Only there will the eclipse be total. The shadow of the partial eclipse to either side is the penumbra.*

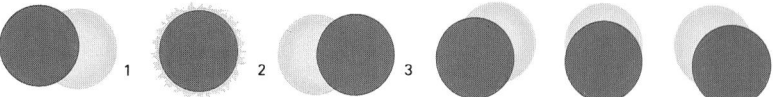

1   2   3

TOTAL ECLIPSE *The moon and sun approach totality (1), arrive at totality (2), and leave totality (3) in a matter of minutes.*

PARTIAL ECLIPSE *When the sun, earth, and moon are almost, but not exactly, in line, the eclipse is only partial anywhere on earth.*

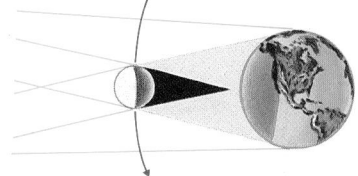

ANNULAR ECLIPSE *An eclipse is called annular (above and right) when the moon throws its shadow on the earth from the farthest part of its orbit. From earth, a circle of sun is visible around the moon (above and right).*

Compare **endoderm, mesoderm.** [ECTO- + -DERM.]

ec·tog·e·nous (ĕk-tŏj′ə-nəs) *adj.* Also **ec·to·gen·ic** (ĕk′tə-jĕn′ĭk). Able to live and develop outside a host. Said of certain pathogenic microorganisms. [ECTO- + -GENOUS.]

ec·to·mere (ĕk′tə-mîr′) *n. Biology.* A blastomere that develops into ectoderm. [ECTO- + -MERE.]

ec·to·morph (ĕk′tə-môrf′) *n.* A lean, slightly muscular human build with a large surface area of skin in relation to body weight. Compare **endomorph, mesomorph.** [ECTO- + -MORPH.] —**ec·to·mor·phic** (ĕk′tə-môr′fĭk) *adj.* —**ec·to·mor·phy** (ĕk′tə-môr′fē) *n.*

-ectomy *suffix.* Indicates removal of a part by surgery; for example, **tonsillectomy.** [New Latin *-ectomia* : Greek *ek-, ex-,* out + -TOMY.]

ec·to·par·a·site (ĕk′tə-păr′ə-sīt′) *n.* A parasite, such as a flea, that lives on the exterior of another organism.

ec·to·pi·a (ĕk-tō′pē-ə) *n. Pathology.* **1.** Misplacement of an organ or part, which may be congenital or due to injury. **2.** The occurrence of something in an unusual position. [New Latin, from Greek *ektopos,* away from a place : *ex-,* out of + *topos,* place (see **topic**).] —**ec·top·ic** (ĕk-tŏp′ĭk) *adj.*

ectopic beat *n. Pathology.* An **extrasystole** *(see).*

ectopic pregnancy *n. Pathology.* Gestation outside the uterus, often in a Fallopian tube.

ec·to·plasm (ĕk′tə-plăz′əm) *n.* **1.** *Biology.* A portion of the cytoplasm distinguishable in some cells as a relatively rigidly gelled outer layer just beneath the cell membrane. Compare **endoplasm.** **2.** The specter or emanation allegedly conjured up by a spiritualistic medium. [ECTO- + -PLASM.] —**ec·to·plas·mic** (ĕk′tə-plăz′mĭk) *adj.*

ec·to·sarc (ĕk′tə-särk′) *n.* The relatively clear outermost layer of protoplasm of certain protozoans, such as the amoeba. [ECTO- + Greek *sarx* (stem *sark-*), flesh.]

E·CU (ā-kōō′) *n., pl.* **ECU's.** A notional unit used for pricing goods within the European Economic Community in the currencies of individual member countries. [From *European Currency Unit.*]

é·cu (ā-kyōō′) *n., pl.* **écus** *(pronounced as singular).* Any of various old French gold or silver coins. [French, from Old French *escu,* from Latin *scūtum,* shield (from the shield stamped on the coin).]

Ec·ua·dor (ĕk′wə-dôr′). *Abbr.* **Ecua.** Country in northwestern South America. The Spanish occupied Quito, part of the Inca empire, in 1534, and the region became part of the viceroyalty of Peru and later of New Granada. By 1830 Ecuador had become an independent republic. Ecuador consists of a coastal plain in the west separated from Oriente in the Amazon Basin by the Andes. The Galapagos Islands, 1,000 kilometers (600 miles) offshore in the Pacific, belong to Ecuador. The country is South America's second largest oil producer, an important member of OPEC, and the world's largest producer of balsa. Area, 283,561 square kilometers (109,483 square miles). Population, 8,400,000. Capital, Quito. —**E·cua·do·ri·an, E·cua·do·re·an** (ĕk′wə-dôr′ē-ən) *n. & adj.*

ec·u·men·i·cal (ĕk′yə-mĕn′ĭ-kəl) *adj.* Also **ec·u·men·ic** (-mĕn′ĭk). **1.** Universal; worldwide. **2.** Of or pertaining to the worldwide Christian church. **3.** Concerned with promoting unity among the churches. [Late Latin *oecumenicus,* from Greek *oikoumenikos,* of the whole world, from *oikoumenē,* the inhabited world, from *oikein,* to inhabit, from *oikos,* house.] —**ec·u·men·i·cal·ism** *n.* —**ec·u·men·i·cal·ly** *adv.*

ecumenical council *n.* **1.** Any of several councils of the early Christian church. **2.** *Roman Catholic Church.* A general council of bishops.

ecumenical patriarch *n.* A **patriarch** *(see)* of the Eastern Orthodox Church.

ec·u·me·nism (ĕk′yə-mə-nĭz′əm, ĭ-kyōō′mə-, ĕk′yə-mĕn′ĭz′-) *n.* **1.** A movement or doctrine promoting unity among the Christian churches. **2.** A movement or doctrine promoting worldwide unity among religions through greater cooperation and improved understanding.

ec·ze·ma (ĕk′sə-mə, ĕg′zə-, ĭg-zē′-) *n.* A noncontagious inflammation of the skin, marked mainly by redness, itching, and the outbreak of lesions that discharge serous matter and become encrusted and scaly. [New Latin, from Greek *ekzema,* eruption : *ex-,* out + *zema,* fermentation, boiling, from *zeein,* to boil.] —**ec·zem·a·tous** (ĕg-zĕm′ə-təs, -zē′mə-təs, ĭg-) *adj.*

-ed¹ *suffix.* Used to form the past tense of most verbs; for example, **removed.** [Middle English *-ede,* Old English *-ode, -ede, -ade.*]

-ed² *suffix.* Used to form the past participle of most verbs; for example, **hoped.** [Middle English *-ed,* Old English *-od, -ed, -ad.*]

-ed³ *suffix.* Indicates possessing, characterized by, or provided with; for example, **forked, gray-haired.** [Middle English *-ede, -de,* Old English *-ede.*]

ed. **1.** edited; edited by; edition; editor. **2.** education.

e·da·cious (ĭ-dā′shəs) *adj.* Gluttonous; voracious. [Latin *edax* (stem *edāc-*), gluttonous, from *edere,* to eat.] —**e·dac·i·ty** (ĭ-dăs′ə-tē), **e·da·cious·ness** *n.*

E·dam (ē′dəm, ē′dăm′) *n.* A mild yellow Dutch cheese pressed into balls and usually covered with red wax. [After *Edam,* northwestern Netherlands, town in which it is made.]

e·daph·ic (ĭ-dăf′ĭk) *adj.* Of or pertaining to soil, especially as it affects living organisms. [Greek *edaphos,* ground, foundation, floor.] —**e·daph·i·cal·ly** *adv.*

E.D.C. European Defense Community.

Ed·da (ĕd′ə) *n.* **1.** A collection of Old Norse poems called the *Elder* or *Poetic Edda,* assembled in the 12th or early 13th century. **2.** A manual of Icelandic poetry called the *Younger* or *Prose Edda,* compiled a generation later. [Old Norse *edda;* perhaps from *óthr,* poetry.]

Ed·ding·ton (ĕd′ĭng-tən), **Sir Arthur Stanley** (1882–1944). British astronomer and physicist. He was one of the earliest exponents of the theory of relativity (his *Mathematical Theory of Relativity* appeared in 1923).

ed·do (ĕd′ō) *n., pl.* **-does.** A plant, **taro** *(see).* [From an African word akin to Twi *ode,* yam.]

ed·dy (ĕd′ē) *n., pl.* **-dies. 1.** A current, as of water or air, moving contrary to the direction of the main current, especially in a circular motion. **2.** A current that runs contrary to the main current or tradition, as of life, art, or philosophy; a byway.
~*v.* **eddied, -dying, -dies.** —*intr.* To move against the main current, as in an eddy. —*tr.* To cause to move against the main current, as in an eddy. —See Synonyms at **turn.** [Middle English *ydy,* probably from Old English *ed-,* back, again; akin to Old Norse *idha,* "that which flows back," whirlpool, from *idh-,* again.]

Ed·dy (ĕd′ē), **Mary Baker** (1821–1910). U.S. religious leader. She founded the Church of Christ, Scientist.

eddy current *n. Electricity.* An induced electric current in the iron core of an electromagnet, transformer, or the like, causing a loss of energy. Also called "Foucault current."

Ed·dy·stone Rocks (ĕd′ē-stōn′). Group of rocks dangerous to shipping, in the English Channel, 23 kilometers (14 miles) southwest of Plymouth. It has been the site of a lighthouse since 1698.

e·del·weiss (ā′dəl-vīs′, -wīs′) *n.* A plant, *Leontopodium alpinum,* of mountainous regions, especially Alpine regions, having leaves covered with whitish down and small flowers surrounded by conspicuous whitish bracts. [German *Edelweiss,* "noble white."]

e·de·ma, oe·de·ma (ĭ-dē′mə) *n., pl.* **-mas** or **-mata** (-mə-tə). **1.** *Pathology.* An excessive accumulation of serous fluid in the tissues. **2.** *Botany.* Extended swellings in plant organs caused primarily by an excessive accumulation of water. [New Latin, from Greek *oidēma,* tumor, swelling, from *oidein,* to swell.] —**e·dem·a·tous** (ĭ-dĕm′ə-təs) *adj.*

E·den (ēd′n) *n.* **1.** In the Bible, the first home of Adam and Eve; the earthly Paradise. Also called "Garden of Eden." **2.** Any delightful place or dwelling; a paradise. **3.** A state of bliss or ultimate happiness. [Middle English, from Late Latin *Ēden,* from Greek *Ēdēn,* from Hebrew *'ēdhen,* "(the place of) delight."]

E·den (ēd′n), **Robert Anthony, Earl of Avon** (1897–1977). British Conservative politician; foreign secretary 1935–38, 1940–45, and 1951–55, prime minister 1955–57. He entered Parliament in 1923 and in the 1930's was a determined opponent of Hitler and Mussolini. Convinced that Egypt's leader, Gamal Nasser, was a threat to world peace, he supported the 1956 Anglo-French invasion of Egypt in collusion with Israel; but international hostility to this policy forced a cease-fire. Domestic criticism and ill health caused his resignation.

e·den·tate (ē-dĕn′tāt′) *adj. Biology.* **1.** Lacking teeth. **2.** Of or belonging to the order Edentata, which includes mammals, such as anteaters, armadillos, and sloths, having few or no teeth.
~*n.* A member of the Edentata. [Latin *edentātus,* toothless, from the past participle of *edentāre,* to take out the teeth : *ex-,* out + *dēns* (stem *dent-*), tooth.]

e·den·tu·lous (ē-dĕn′chə-ləs) *adj.* Lacking teeth. [See **edentate, -ulous.**]

edelweiss *Although the edelweiss is Switzerland's national flower, it is native to South America as well as Europe. Its distinctive stars are formed by petallike white woolly bracts surrounding small yellow flowers.*

ECUADOR 80° W

COLOMBIA

PACIFIC OCEAN

Ibarra

Otavalo

Equator

QUITO
PICHINCHA
Latacunga ▲Cotopaxi 5896m

E C U A D O R

▲Chimborazo 6310m

Riobamba

Guayaquil
Playas
G. de Guayaquil

Cuenca

Loja

P E R U

A N D E S

Km 0   200   400

Miles 0   100   200

E·der·le (ā′dər-lē), **Gertrude Caroline** (1906–). U.S. swimmer. On August 26, 1926, she became the first woman to swim the English Channel, setting a new record of 14 hours and 31 minutes.

E·des·sa (ĭ-dĕs′ə). *Modern Greek* **E·dhes·sa** (ə-*th*ä′sə). Town in Macedonia, northern Greece. In ancient times it was Macedonia's capital, known as Aegea. It is a commercial and industrial center also serving as a market town for the wine, fruit, and tobacco grown in the district.

Ed·gar (ĕd′gər) or **Ead·gar** (ĕd′gär′), known as "the Peaceful" (*c.* 943–75). King of the English, son of Edmund I. After a revolt against his brother, Edwy, king of the English, he became king of the Mercians and Northumbrians and king of the English when Edwy died in 959.

Edgar the Aeth·e·ling (ăth′ə-lĭng) (*c.* 1050–*c.* 1130). English prince, grandson of Edmund Ironside. He was chosen king of the English when Harold was slain in the Battle of Hastings (1066) but submitted to the rule of William the Conqueror. After unsuccessful attempts to regain his kingdom, he led the English expedition that deposed Donald III of Scotland and placed his nephew, also called Edgar, on the Scottish throne.

edge (ĕj) *n.* **1. a.** The usually thin, sharpened side of the blade of a cutting instrument, weapon, or tool. **b.** The degree of sharpness of a cutting blade. **c.** A penetrating or incisive quality: *"His simplicity sets off the satire, and gives it a finer edge"* (William Hazlitt). **2.** Keenness, as of desire or enjoyment; zest. **3.** A rim, brink, or crest, as of a cliff or ridge of hills. **4. a.** The line at the outside of a surface. **b.** The part of a surface nearest this line: *lying at the edge of the road.* **c.** A point close to an action or state: *on the edge of divorce.* **5.** The line of intersection of two surfaces of a solid: *the edge of a cube.* **6.** A margin of superiority; an advantage: *a slight edge over the opposition.* —See Synonyms at **border.** **—on edge. 1.** Highly tense or nervous; irritable. **2.** Eagerly anticipatory; impatient. **—set one's teeth on edge.** *Informal.* **1.** To give one an unpleasant nervous reaction or sensation, as of tingling. **2.** To provoke strong feelings of irritation or annoyance. **—take the edge off.** To soften or dull the pleasure, excitement, pain, or force of: *ate an apple to take the edge off her appetite.* **~v. edged, edging, edges.** *—tr.* **1.** To give an edge to; sharpen. **2.** To put a border or edging on. **3.** To advance or push gradually: *The dog edged the ball toward the child with its nose.* **4. a.** To be the edge of. **b.** To be at the edge of. **5.** To cut the edge of (a lawn, for example). **6.** To dig the edge of (a ski) into the snow surface. *—intr.* To move gradually or hesitantly: *She edged toward the door.* [Middle English *egge*, Old English *ecg*, edge, point, sword; akin to Latin *acer*, sharp.]

edg·er (ĕj′ər) *n.* A tool for trimming the edge of a lawn.

edge tool *n.* A tool, such as a chisel, having a cutting edge.

edge·wise (ĕj′wīz′) *adv.* Also **edge·ways** (-wāz′). **1.** With the edge foremost. **2.** On, by, with, or toward the edge. **—get a word in edgewise.** To manage to interrupt a talkative speaker.

Edge·worth (ĕj′wûrth′), **Maria** (1767–1849). Irish writer, born in England. Her most famous novel, *Castle Rackrent* (1800), a tale of ordinary Irish life, broke away from the romantic tradition of the 18th-century Gothic novel and helped to establish a realist tradition in English literature.

edg·ing (ĕj′ĭng) *n.* Something that forms or serves as an edge; a trimming; a border.

edg·y (ĕj′ē) *adj.* **-i·er, -i·est. 1.** On edge; tense; nervous. **2.** With a sharp edge. **—edg·i·ly** *adv.* **—edg·i·ness** *n.*

edh, eth (ĕth) *n.* **1.** A letter (ð) appearing in Old and Middle English, Old Saxon, Old Norse, and modern Icelandic. In the Scandinavian languages it represents the interdental voiced fricative (transliterated as *dh* in the etymologies) and is distinguished from the voiceless thorn. In Old English the distinction between edh and thorn (both transliterated as *th*) was not observed. **2.** The letter in the International Phonetic Alphabet representing the interdental voiced fricative, as in *the, other.*

Edhessa. See **Edessa.**

ed·i·ble (ĕd′ə-bəl) *adj.* **1. a.** Capable of being eaten. **b.** Fit to eat; nonpoisonous. **2.** Ready to be eaten. —See Usage note at **eatable.** *~n. Often* **edibles.** Something fit to be eaten; food. —See Usage note at **eatable.** [Late Latin *edibilis*, from Latin *edere*, to eat.] **—ed·i·bil·i·ty, ed·i·ble·ness** *n.*

e·dict (ē′dĭkt′) *n.* **1.** An official decree or proclamation issued by an authority. **2.** A formal command or decree. [Latin *ēdictum*, from *ēdīcere*, to speak out, proclaim : *ex-*, out + *dīcere*, to speak.]

ed·i·fi·ca·tion (ĕd′ə-fĭ-kā′shən) *n.* Intellectual, moral, or spiritual improvement; enlightenment: *"I am now writing this book for the edification of the world"* (Laurence Sterne).

ed·i·fice (ĕd′ə-fĭs) *n.* **1.** A building, especially one of imposing appearance or size. **2.** Something with an elaborate structure: *an edifice of regulations.* [Middle English, from Old French, from Latin *aedificium*, from *aedificāre*, to build : *aedēs*, building, house + *fa-c(e)re*, to make.]

ed·i·fy (ĕd′ə-fī′) *tr.v.* **-fied, -fying, -fies.** To instruct or enlighten so as to encourage moral or spiritual improvement. [Middle English *edifien*, from Old French *edifier*, from Latin *aedificāre*, to build, instruct. See **edifice.**] **—ed·i·fi·ca·to·ry** (ĭ-dĭf′ə-kə-tôr′ē, -tōr′ē) *adj.* **—ed·i·fi·er** *n.*

Ed·in·burgh (ĕd′n-bûr′ə) Capital of Scotland and the administrative center of the Lothian region. The city, once known as Auld Reekie because of the cloud of smoke that hung over low-lying areas, includes printing, publishing, brewing, whiskey distilling, confectionery, and chemicals among its industries. Edinburgh is the home of an international festival of the arts, held annually. It takes its name from Edwin, king of Northumbria in the 7th century.

Edinburgh, Duke of. See Prince **Philip.**

E·dir·ne (e-dĭr′ne). Formerly **A·dri·a·no·ple** (ā′drē-ə-nō′pəl). Capital of Edirne province in European Turkey. It was expanded in the 2nd century A.D. by the Roman emperor Hadrian and was taken by the Goths in 378 and later by the Bulgarians before becoming the residence of the Turkish sultans from 1365 to 1453. Ceded to Greece after World War I, it was returned to Turkey once more in 1923.

Ed·i·son (ĕd′ə-sən), **Thomas Alva** (1847–1931). U.S. inventor. He held more than 1,300 U.S. and foreign patents for his inventions, most of them concerned with electricity. Among his first inventions were the carbon telephone transmitter (1877), the phonograph (1878), and the incandescent lamp with a carbon filament (1879). In New York he installed (1880) an experimental electric railway and (1881–82) the first central electric power plant in the world.

ed·it (ĕd′ĭt) *tr.v.* **-ited, -iting, -its. 1. a.** To make (written material) suitable for publication or presentation. **b.** To prepare an edition of for publication: *edit a collection of short stories.* **2.** To supervise the publication of (a newspaper or magazine, for example). **3.** To omit or eliminate; delete. Usually used with *out.* **4.** To integrate the component parts of (a film, electronic tape, or sound track) by cutting, combining, and splicing. *~n.* An instance of editing: *I gave his article a preliminary edit.* [Back-formation from **editor.**]

e·di·tion (ĭ-dĭsh′ən) *n. Abbr.* **ed., edit. 1.** *Printing.* **a.** The entire number of copies of a publication printed from a single typesetting or other form of reproduction. Compare **printing.** **b.** A single copy from this group. **c.** A version of an earlier publication having substantial changes or additions. **2. a.** Any of the various forms in which something is issued or produced, as publications, music, or stamps. **b.** Any of the forms in which a publication is produced: *a leather-bound edition.* **c.** One closely similar to an original; a version: *The boy was a smaller edition of his father.* **3.** An issue of a work identified by its editor or publisher: *the Oxford edition of Shakespeare.* **4.** All the copies of a single print run of a newspaper: *the morning edition.* [Old French, from Latin *ēditiō* (stem *ēditiōn-*), a bringing forth, publication, from *ēdere* (past participle *ēdictus*), to bring forth, publish : *ex-*, out + *dāre*, to give.]

e·di·ti·o prin·ceps (ĭ-dĭsh′ē-ō prĭn′sĕps′) *n., pl.* **editiones principes** (ĭ-dĭsh′ē-ō′nēz prĭn′sə-pēz′). A first printed edition of a work. [Latin, "first edition."]

ed·i·tor (ĕd′ə-tər) *n. Abbr.* **ed., edit. 1.** A person who edits a written work or musical composition for publication or public presentation. **2.** A person who supervises the policies or production of a publication or broadcast. **3.** A person in charge of a department of a publication: *a sports editor.* **4.** One who writes editorials. **5. a.** A person responsible for the editing of a film, sound track, or the like. **b.** A device for editing film, consisting basically of a splicer and viewer. **6.** *Computer Science.* A routine that performs editing functions. [Late Latin, publisher, from Latin *ēdere*, to bring forth, publish. See **edition.**] **—ed·i·tor·ship** *n.*

ed·i·to·ri·al (ĕd′ə-tôr′ē-əl, -tōr′ē-əl) *n.* **1.** An article in a newspaper or magazine expressing the opinion of its editors or publishers. **2.** A commentary on radio or television expressing the opinion of the station or network. *~adj.* **1.** Of, concerning, or prepared by an editor or editors. **2.** Having the nature of an editorial in expressing opinion: *editorial comments.* **—ed·i·to·ri·al·ly** *adv.*

ed·i·to·ri·al·ize (ĕd′ə-tôr′ē-ə-līz′, -tōr′ē-ə-līz′) *intr.v.* **-ized, -izing, -izes. 1.** To express an opinion in or as if in an editorial. **2.** To present a supposedly objective report in a way intended to implant an opinion. **—ed·i·to·ri·al·i·za·tion** *n.* **—ed·i·to·ri·al·iz·er** *n.*

editor in chief *n., pl.* **editors in chief.** The editor having final responsibility for the operations and policies of a publication.

Ed·mon·ton (ĕd′mən-tən). Capital of Alberta, western Canada, on the North Saskatchewan River. It is an industrial center in an agricultural and oil- coal-, and gas-producing region.

Ed·mund I (ĕd′mənd) (*c.* 921–46). King of the English. He succeeded his half brother, Athelstan, in 939. He expelled the Danish rulers Olaf and Ragnald from Northumbria in 944 and in the following year received the homage of the king of Scotland in return for Cumbria.

Edmund I·ron·side (ī′ərn-sīd′) (*c.* 981–1016). King of the English, succeeding his father, Ethelred the Unready (1016). He led the resistance against Canute's invasion (1015), but when he became king most of the nobles supported Canute and he was forced to partition the country.

Edmund, Saint (*c.* 840–70). King of East Anglia. He was born in Germany and adopted by Offa, king of East Anglia, as his heir. He was killed, either during a battle with the Danes at Hoxne or shortly afterward. He is buried at the town named after him, Bury St. Edmunds.

Edo. See **Tokyo.**

E·dom (ē′dəm). Ancient country between the Dead Sea and the Gulf of Aqaba, now forming parts of Jordan and Israel. According to the Old Testament, the original inhabitants, the Edomites, were descended from Esau. **—E·dom·ite** *n.*

EDP electronic data processing.

EDTA (ē′dē′tē′ā′) *n. Chemistry.* A colorless crystalline compound, [(HOOCCH₂)₂NCH₂]₂, used as a chelating agent in inorganic chemistry and biochemistry and as an antidote to metal poisoning. [From ethylene *d*iamine*t*etra-*a*cetic acid.]

ed·u·ca·ble (ĕj′ə-kə-bəl) *adj.* Capable of being educated. [EDUC(ATE) + -ABLE.]

ed·u·cate (ĕj′ə-kāt′) *v.* **-cated, -cating, -cates.** —*tr.* **1.** To provide with knowledge or training, especially through formal schooling; teach. **2.** To provide with specialized training for a particular purpose: *educated him for the priesthood.* **3.** To provide with information; inform. **4.** To stimulate or develop the mental or moral growth of; enlighten. **5.** To discipline, train, or develop (a taste or skill, for example). —*intr.* To teach or instruct a person or group: *Their purpose is to educate through the use of visual aids.* —See Synonyms at **teach.** [Middle English *educaten,* from Latin *ēducāre,* to bring up, educate. See **educe.**]

ed·u·cat·ed (ĕj′ə-kā′tĭd) *adj.* **1.** Having an education, especially one above the average. **2.** Showing evidence of having been taught or instructed; cultivated; cultured. **3.** Based primarily on experience and some factual knowledge: *an educated guess.*

ed·u·ca·tion (ĕj′ə-kā′shən) *n. Abbr.* **ed., educ. 1.** The act or process of imparting knowledge or skill; systematic instruction; teaching. **2.** The obtaining of knowledge or skill through such a process; learning. **3. a.** The knowledge or skill obtained or developed by such a process. **b.** A program of instruction of a specified kind or level: *a classical education.* **4.** The field of study that is concerned with teaching and learning; the theory of teaching; pedagogy. **5.** An enlightening experience: *His visit to India was an education.*

ed·u·ca·tion·al (ĕj′ə-kā′shə-nəl) *adj. Abbr.* **educ. 1.** Of or pertaining to education: *educational psychology.* **2.** Serving to educate; instructive: *an educational film.* —**ed·u·ca·tion·al·ly** *adv.*

ed·u·ca·tion·al·ist (ĕj′ə-kā′shə-nə-lĭst) *n.* Also **ed·u·ca·tion·ist** (-shə-nĭst). An educational theorist.

educational television *n.* **1. Public television** *(see).* **2.** A video system that provides instructional material.

ed·u·ca·tive (ĕj′ə-kā′tĭv) *adj.* Serving to educate or instruct.

ed·u·ca·tor (ĕj′ə-kā′tər) *n.* **1.** One trained in teaching; a teacher. **2.** A specialist in the theory and practice of education.

e·duce (ĭ-dōōs′, ĭ-dyōōs′) *tr.v.* **educed, educing, educes. 1.** To draw or bring out; elicit; evoke. **2.** To infer or work out from given facts; deduce. [Latin *ēdūcere* : *ex-,* out + *dūcere,* to lead.] —**e·duc·i·ble** *adj.*

e·duct (ē′dŭkt′) *n.* A substance that has been separated from another substance without chemical change. Compare **product.** [Latin *ēductus,* "drawn out," past participle of *ēducere.* See **educe.**]

e·duc·tion (ĭ-dŭk′shən) *n.* **1.** An act or the process of educing. **2.** The result of educing; an inference. **3.** The exhaust phase of an internal-combustion engine. [Middle English *educcion,* from Late Latin *ēductiō,* from Latin *ēdūcere,* to EDUCE.]

Ed·ward I (1239–1307). King of England (1272–1307). Son of Henry III. His reign was marked by successful military campaigns against Wales and victory against the Scots at Falkirk (1298). His Model Parliament of 1295 is sometimes looked upon as the first full English parliament.

Edward II (1284–1327). King of England (1307–27). Son of Edward I. The Scots defeated Edward's army at Bannockburn (1314). In 1326 the rebellion of the Earl of March led to Edward's capture and deposition (1327). He was imprisoned in Berkeley Castle and almost certainly murdered there.

Edward III (1312–77). King of England (1327–77). Son of Edward II. During the Hundred Years' War with France his armies won victories at Crécy (1346) and Poitiers (1356).

Edward IV (1442–83). King of England (1461–70, 1471–83). Son of Richard, Duke of York. As leader of the Yorkist faction in the Wars of the Roses, Edward defeated the Lancastrians at Mortimer's Cross (1461) and was proclaimed king. In 1470 the Earl of Warwick raised a rebellion against him and Edward fled to France. Henry VI, whom he had deposed, was restored to the throne, but a year later Edward returned, defeated the Lancastrians at Tewkesbury, and regained the throne. Henry VI was put to death, possibly on Edward's orders.

Edward V (1470–83). King of England (1483). Son of Edward IV. On Edward's accession to the throne at the age of 13, he was confined to the Tower of London with his younger brother Richard, Duke of York. There they were murdered, possibly on the orders of their uncle the Duke of Gloucester (later Richard III) or possibly by Henry Stafford or by Henry VII. Skeletons of boys aged about 13 and 10 were unearthed in the Tower in 1674.

Edward VI (1537–53). King of England (1547–53). Son of Henry VIII and Jane Seymour. He came to the throne at the age of 9 and died of tuberculosis at the age of 15.

Edward VII (1841–1910). King of Great Britain and Ireland (1901–10). Son of Queen Victoria, he became a popular figure as Prince of Wales. His personal popularity in France helped create the conditions for the Entente Cordiale (1904).

Edward VIII (1894–1972). King of Great Britain and Ireland (1936). Son of George V. On succeeding to the throne he precipitated a constitutional crisis by his determination to marry Mrs. Wallis Warfield Simpson, an American divorcée. Opposition from Church and government caused him to abdicate after a reign of 325 days. Thereafter, as the Duke of Windsor, he lived with his wife in France, except for the years 1940 to 1945, when he was the governor of the Bahamas. He died in Paris but was buried in Windsor, in England.

Edward, Prince of Wales (1330–76). Eldest son of Edward III, he played a valiant part in the Hundred Years' War, especially at Crécy (1346) and Poitiers (1356), where he led the English forces that captured John II of France. He was named the Black Prince by the French, presumably because of his black armor.

Ed·ward·i·an (ĕd-wôr′dē-ən, ĕd-wär′-) *adj.* **1.** Of, pertaining to, or characteristic of the reign or person of any of several kings of England named Edward. **2.** Of, pertaining to, or characteristic of the reign or person of King Edward VII, especially with respect to the lighthearted elegance considered typical of his reign. —*n.* A person living during the reign of one of these kings.

Edward the Confessor (died 1066). King of the English (1042–66). Son of Ethelred the Unready, and later stepson of Canute. Edward devoted much of his time to religious work, including the rebuilding of Westminster Abbey. He was canonized in the 12th century.

Edward the Elder (died 924). King of Wessex (899–924). Son of Alfred the Great. He fought the Danes and the Viking invaders and by 918 ruled all of England south of the Humber.

-ee¹ *suffix.* Indicates: **1.** The recipient or object of a specified action; for example, **addressee, endorsee. 2.** One who is in a specified condition; for example, **refugee. 3.** One who is carrying out or has carried out a specified act; for example, **escapee.** [Middle English *-e,* from Old French *-e,* from the past participial ending *-e,* from Latin *-ātus,* -ATE.]

Usage: The suffix *-ee* has generally been used to indicate a person to whom something has been done or upon whom some right has been conferred: *appointee; grantee.* It has come to be used also with reference to a person in a specified condition (*absentee; refugee; amputee*) or even a person performing a particular action (*escapee; standee*).

-ee² *suffix.* Indicates: **1.** A particular type of, especially when small; for example, **bootee. 2.** Something resembling or suggestive of; for example, **goatee.** [Originally *-ie,* variant of -Y.]

e.e. errors excepted.

E.E. electrical engineer; electrical engineering.

E.E. & M.P. Envoy Extraordinary and Minister Plenipotentiary.

EEC *n.* The **European Economic Community** *(see).*

EEG electroencephalogram; electroencephalograph.

eel (ēl) *n., pl.* **eels** or collectively **eel. 1.** Any of various long, snakelike marine or freshwater fishes of the order Anguilliformes (or Apodes); especially, *Anguilla rostrata,* of eastern North America, or *A. anguilla,* of Europe, characteristically migrating from fresh water to the Sargasso Sea to spawn. **2.** Any of several similar or related fishes. [Middle English *ele,* Old English *ǣl,* from Common Germanic *ǣlaz†* (unattested).]

eel·grass (ēl′grăs′, -gräs′) *n.* **1.** Any of several submerged aquatic plants of the genus *Zostera,* of coastal areas, having narrow, grasslike leaves and growing in dense masses. **2.** Any of several similar or related plants, such as **tape grass** *(see).*

eel·pout (ēl′pout′) *n., pl.* **-pouts** or collectively **eelpout.** Any of various marine fishes of the family Zoarcidae, having an elongated body and a large head. The European species *Zoarces viviparus* produces live young. [Middle English *elepout* (unattested), Old English *ǣlepūte* : EEL + POUT (fish).]

eel·worm (ēl′wûrm′) *n.* Any of various often parasitic nematode worms, such as the **vinegar eel** *(see).*

e'en¹ (ēn) *n. Poetic.* Evening.

e'en² *adv. Poetic.* Even.

-eer *suffix.* Indicates: **1.** One who works with or is concerned with; for example, **auctioneer, volunteer, profiteer, racketeer. 2.** One who makes or composes; for example, **balladeer.** [Old French *-ier,* from Latin *-ārius,* -ARY.]

e'er (âr) *adv. Poetic.* Ever.

ee·rie, ee·ry (ir′ē) *adj.* **-rier, -riest. 1.** Inspiring fear or dread without being openly threatening; peculiarly unsettling: *heard an eerie noise in the attic.* **2.** Supernatural in aspect or character; uncanny; mysterious. —See Synonyms at **weird.** [Middle English *eri,* fearful, cowardly, Old English *earg,* cowardly, timid, from Common Germanic *arg-* (unattested).] —**ee·ri·ness** *n.*

EEZ Economic Exclusion Zone.

ef-. Variant of **ex-¹.**

eff. efficiency.

ef·fa·ble (ĕf′ə-bəl) *adj. Archaic.* Capable of being expressed in words. [Latin *effābilis,* from *effārī,* to speak out : *ex-,* out + *fārī,* to speak.]

ef·face (ĭ-fās′) *tr.v.* **-faced, -facing, -faces. 1.** To rub or wipe out; obliterate; erase. **2.** To make faded or indistinct as if by rubbing out. **3.** To conduct (oneself) inconspicuously or humbly: *"When the two women went out together, Anna deliberately effaced herself and played to the dramatic Molly"* (Doris Lessing). —See Synonyms at **erase.** [Old French *effacer,* "to remove the face" : *ef-,* out, from Latin *ex-* + *face,* FACE.] —**ef·face·a·ble** *adj.* —**ef·face·ment** *n.* —**ef·fac·er** *n.*

ef·fect (ĭ-fĕkt′) *n.* **1.** Something brought about by a cause or agent; a result: *"Fortunately in England, at any rate, education produces no effect whatsoever"* (Oscar Wilde). **2.** The way in which something acts upon or influences an object: *the effect of a drug on the nervous system.* **3.** The final or comprehensive result; an outcome. **4.** The power or capacity to achieve the desired result; efficacy; influence. **5.** The condition of being in full force or execution; being; realization: *The law will come into effect tomorrow.* **6.** An impression produced by an artifice or manner of presentation: *an effect of spaciousness.* **7.** The basic meaning or tendency of something said or written; purport: *He said he approved, or something to that effect.*

EEC (European Economic Community)

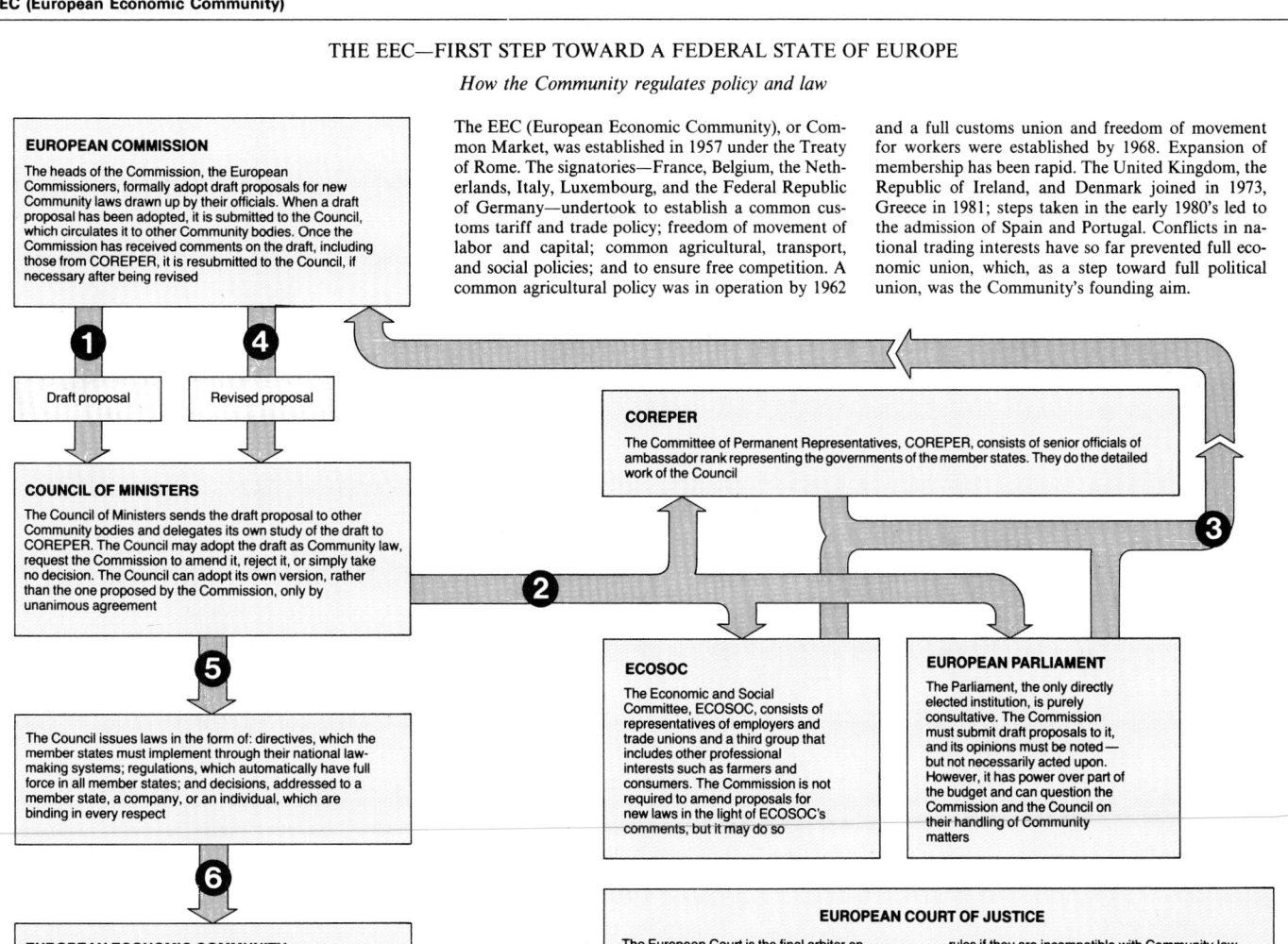

THE EEC—FIRST STEP TOWARD A FEDERAL STATE OF EUROPE

How the Community regulates policy and law

The EEC (European Economic Community), or Common Market, was established in 1957 under the Treaty of Rome. The signatories—France, Belgium, the Netherlands, Italy, Luxembourg, and the Federal Republic of Germany—undertook to establish a common customs tariff and trade policy; freedom of movement of labor and capital; common agricultural, transport, and social policies; and to ensure free competition. A common agricultural policy was in operation by 1962 and a full customs union and freedom of movement for workers were established by 1968. Expansion of membership has been rapid. The United Kingdom, the Republic of Ireland, and Denmark joined in 1973, Greece in 1981; steps taken in the early 1980's led to the admission of Spain and Portugal. Conflicts in national trading interests have so far prevented full economic union, which, as a step toward full political union, was the Community's founding aim.

EUROPEAN COMMISSION

The heads of the Commission, the European Commissioners, formally adopt draft proposals for new Community laws drawn up by their officials. When a draft proposal has been adopted, it is submitted to the Council, which circulates it to other Community bodies. Once the Commission has received comments on the draft, including those from COREPER, it is resubmitted to the Council, if necessary after being revised

Draft proposal | Revised proposal

COUNCIL OF MINISTERS

The Council of Ministers sends the draft proposal to other Community bodies and delegates its own study of the draft to COREPER. The Council may adopt the draft as Community law, request the Commission to amend it, reject it, or simply take no decision. The Council can adopt its own version, rather than the one proposed by the Commission, only by unanimous agreement

COREPER

The Committee of Permanent Representatives, COREPER, consists of senior officials of ambassador rank representing the governments of the member states. They do the detailed work of the Council

The Council issues laws in the form of: directives, which the member states must implement through their national law-making systems; regulations, which automatically have full force in all member states; and decisions, addressed to a member state, a company, or an individual, which are binding in every respect

ECOSOC

The Economic and Social Committee, ECOSOC, consists of representatives of employers and trade unions and a third group that includes other professional interests such as farmers and consumers. The Commission is not required to amend proposals for new laws in the light of ECOSOC's comments, but it may do so

EUROPEAN PARLIAMENT

The Parliament, the only directly elected institution, is purely consultative. The Commission must submit draft proposals to it, and its opinions must be noted — but not necessarily acted upon. However, it has power over part of the budget and can question the Commission and the Council on their handling of Community matters

EUROPEAN ECONOMIC COMMUNITY

Most Community laws are applied to people living in the twelve member states, through their national legal system, in the same way as national laws. Community laws take precedence over national laws

EUROPEAN COURT OF JUSTICE

The European Court is the final arbiter on Community law, but it is not an appeal court that can overrule a national court. It may, if requested by a national court, give an interpretation of Community law that the national court is then bound to apply. The Court may amend Community rules if they are incompatible with Community law. It can hear cases brought by member states or individuals against the Community institutions and by the institutions against the member states. It cannot impose fines or prison sentences to enforce its decision

---

8. A scientific law, hypothesis, or phenomenon: *the Faraday effect; photovoltaic effect.* **9. effects.** Physical belongings; goods. **10. effects. a. Sound effects** *(see).* **b. Special effects** *(see).* —See Synonyms at **assets.** —**for effect.** In order to impress or influence. —**in effect. 1.** In fact; actually. **2.** In essence; virtually. —**take effect.** To become operative; gain active force. ~*tr.v.* **effected, -fecting, -fects. 1.** To produce as a result. **2.** To cause to occur; bring about. —See Synonyms at **perform.** —See Usage note at **affect¹.** [Middle English, from Old French, from Latin *effectus,* past participle of *efficere,* to accomplish, perform, work out : *ex-,* out + *facere,* to do.] —**ef·fect·er** *n.* —**ef·fect·i·ble** *adj.*

   Synonyms: *consequence, outcome, result, sequel, upshot.*

ef·fec·tive (ĭ-fĕk′tĭv) *adj.* **1.** Having the intended or expected effect; serving the purpose. **2.** Producing or adapted to produce the desired impression or response; striking: *an effective speech.* **3.** Operative; in effect: *The law is effective immediately.* **4.** Real and actual rather than supposed. **5.** Prepared for use or action in warfare: *We have eight effective troop divisions.* **6.** *Electricity.* Designating an alternating quantity, such as current, having a value equal to the square root of the mean of the squares of the instantaneous values over one cycle.

~*n.* **1.** A member of a military force or a piece of equipment that is ready for action. **2.** The total number of men prepared and available for military action. —**ef·fec·tive·ness** *n.*

   Usage: The adjectives *effective, efficacious, effectual,* and *efficient* overlap in meaning but should be distinguished: *effective* and *effectual* may imply proven capacity for doing the job in question, and *efficacious* may suggest having the potential to do it. *Efficient* implies proven capability based on productiveness in operation and especially stresses ability to perform well and economically.

ef·fec·tive·ly (ĭ-fĕk′tĭv-lē) *adv.* **1.** In an effective way. **2.** In effect; for all practical purposes.

ef·fec·tor (ĭ-fĕk′tər) *n.* **1.** A nerve ending that activates either gland secretion or muscular contraction. **2.** A cell or organ, such as a muscle or gland, specialized to respond to nervous stimulation.

ef·fec·tu·al (ĭ-fĕk′chōō-əl) *adj.* **1.** Producing or sufficient to produce a desired effect; fully adequate. **2.** Valid or legally binding. —See Usage note at **effective.** —**ef·fec·tu·al·i·ty** (ĭ-fĕk′chōō-ăl′ə-tē), **ef·fec·tu·al·ness** *n.* —**ef·fec·tu·al·ly** *adv.*

ef·fec·tu·ate (ĭ-fĕk′chōō-āt′) *tr.v.* **-ated, -ating, -ates.** To cause; bring about; effect. [Medieval Latin *effectuāre,* from Latin *efficere,* to accomplish, EFFECT.] —**ef·fec·tu·a·tion** *n.*

ef·fem·i·nate (ĭ-fĕm′ə-nĭt) *adj.* **1.** Having qualities associated with women rather than those regarded as befitting a man; unmanly. Said of a man. **2.** Characterized by weakness or lack of force; not dynamic or vigorous. [Middle English *effeminat,* from Latin *effēminātus,* past participle of *effēmināre,* "to make a woman out of," to make effeminate : *ex-,* out of + *fēmina,* woman.] —**ef·fem·i·na·cy** (ĭ-fĕm′ə-nə-sē) *n.* —**ef·fem·i·nate·ly** *adv.* —**ef·fem·i·nate·ness** *n.*

ef·fen·di (ĭ-fĕn′dē) *n.* **1.** Used in Turkey and the Middle East as a term of respectful address, equivalent to *Sir.* **2.** An educated or respected man in the Ottoman Empire. [Turkish *efendi,* "master," from Medieval Greek *aphentē,* vocative of *aphentēs,* lord, master, from Greek *authentēs.* See **authentic.**]

ef·fer·ent (ĕf′ər-ənt) *adj.* Directed or conducting away from an organ or section; especially, designating nerves that carry impulses from the central nervous system to an effector. Compare **afferent.** ~*n.* An efferent organ or part. [French *efférent,* from Latin *efferēns* (stem *efferent-*), present participle of *efferre,* to carry away : *ex-,* away from + *ferre,* to carry.]

ef·fer·vesce (ĕf′ər-vĕs′) *intr.v.* **-vesced, -vescing, -vesces. 1.** To emit small bubbles of gas, as a carbonated or fermenting liquid does. **2.** To appear and come out of a liquid in bubbles; bubble forth. **3.** To show high spirits; be lively or vivacious. [Latin *effervēscere,* to boil over : *ex-* (intensive) + *fervēscere,* to start to boil, from *fervēre,* to be hot, boil.]

ef·fer·ves·cent (ĕf′ər-vĕs′ənt) *adj.* **1.** Emitting a profusion of small

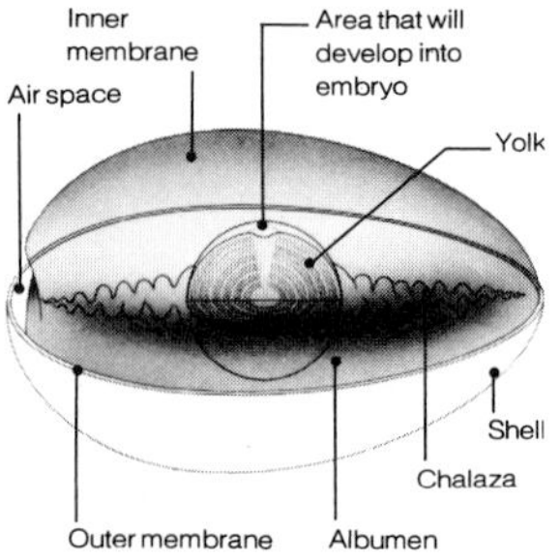
Inner membrane
Area that will develop into embryo
Air space
Yolk
Shell
Chalaza
Outer membrane
Albumen

egg *The embryo inside a bird's egg develops from a tiny disk of cytoplasm on top of the yolk. The watery albumen (the white of the egg) and the yolk are its main sources of nourishment; the twisted strands of albumen, the chalazae, keep the embryo disk upright.*

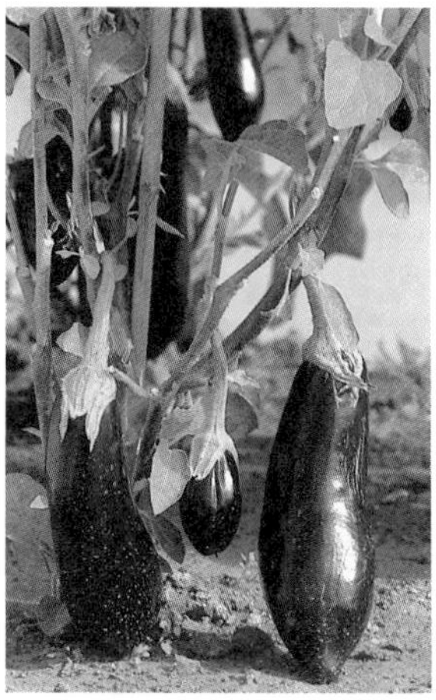

eggplant *The fruit of this tender annual plant, which is native to tropical Asia, is eaten as a vegetable. The variety shown here is "Long Purple."*

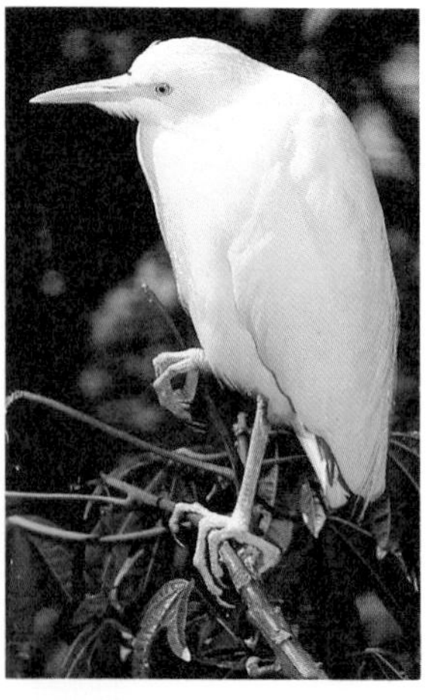

egret *A type of heron that is found worldwide. The great white egret produces feathers that were once used to decorate hats. The smaller cattle egret (above) feeds on insects disturbed by the hoofs of grazing animals.*

bubbles of gas; bubbling. **2.** Produced by bubbles of gas: *an effervescent hiss.* **3.** High-spirited; vivacious. **—ef·fer·ves·cence** *n.*

ef·fete (ĭ-fēt′) *adj.* **1.** Exhausted of vitality, force, or effectiveness; depleted of vigor: *effete romanticism.* **2.** Characterized by unproductive self-indulgence, self-absorption, or decadence: *effete manners.* **3.** Unable to produce further offspring or fruit; barren. Said of animals or plants. [Latin *effētus,* worn out by childbearing : *ex-,* out + *fētus,* childbearing, offspring.] **—ef·fete·ly** *adv.* **—ef·fete·ness** *n.*

ef·fi·ca·cious (ĕf′ĭ-kā′shəs) *adj.* Capable of producing the desired effect. —See Usage note at **effective.** [Latin *efficāx* (stem *efficāc-*), effective, from *efficere,* to EFFECT.] **—ef·fi·ca·cious·ly** *adv.* **—ef·fi·ca·cious·ness** *n.*

ef·fi·ca·cy (ĕf′ĭ-kə-sē) *n.* Power or capacity to produce a desired effect; effectiveness. [Latin *efficācia,* from *efficāx,* EFFICACIOUS.]

ef·fi·cien·cy (ĭ-fĭsh′ən-sē) *n., pl.* **-cies. 1. a.** The quality or property of being efficient. **b.** The degree to which this quality is exercised. **2.** *Abbr.* **eff.** The ratio of the effective or useful output to the total input in any system; especially, the ratio of the energy delivered by a machine to the energy supplied for its operation, often expressed as a percentage. **3.** *Informal.* An efficiency apartment.

efficiency apartment *n.* A small, usually furnished apartment with a kitchenette and a private bathroom.

ef·fi·cient (ĭ-fĭsh′ənt) *adj.* **1.** Having a direct effect; causative. **2. a.** Acting or producing effectively with a minimum of waste, expense, or unnecessary effort. **b.** Exhibiting a high ratio of output to input. —See Usage note at **effective.** [Middle English, from Old French, from Latin *efficiēns* (stem *efficient-*), present participle of *efficere,* to EFFECT.] **—ef·fi·cient·ly** *adv.*

efficient cause *n.* That which renders a thing what it is; that which causes an effect. [Translation of Latin *causa efficiens.*]

ef·fi·gy (ĕf′ə-jē) *n., pl.* **-gies. 1.** A painted or sculptured representation of a person, as on a stone wall or monument. **2.** A crude image or dummy fashioned in the likeness of a person, often as an expression of mockery or hatred. **—hang** (or **burn**) **in effigy.** To hang (or burn) the effigy of a hated person in public. [Middle English *effigie,* from Latin *effigiēs,* likeness, image, from *effingere,* to form, portray : *ex-,* out of + *fingere,* to fashion, shape.]

ef·flo·resce (ĕf′lə-rĕs′) *intr.v.* **-resced, -rescing, -resces. 1.** To blossom; flower; bloom. **2.** *Chemistry.* **a.** To become a powder by losing water of crystallization. **b.** To become covered with a powdery deposit, as by evaporation. [Latin *efflōrēscere,* to blossom out : *ex-,* out + *flōrēscere,* inceptive of *flōrēre,* to blossom, from *flōs* (stem *flōr-*), flower.]

ef·flo·res·cence (ĕf′lə-rĕs′əns) *n.* **1.** A state or time of flowering. **2. a.** A gradual process of developing; blossoming. **b.** The highest point; culmination. **3.** *Chemistry.* **a.** The process of efflorescing. **b.** The deposit that results from this process. **c.** A growth of salt crystals on surfaces, such as those of wells, due to evaporation of salt-laden water. **—ef·flo·res·cent** *adj.*

ef·flu·ence (ĕf′lo͞o-əns) *n.* **1.** The act or an instance of flowing out. **2.** Something that flows out or forth; an emanation.

ef·flu·ent (ĕf′lo͞o-ənt) *adj.* Flowing out or forth.
∼*n.* **1.** Something that flows out or forth. **2.** A stream flowing out of a lake or other body of water. **3.** An outflow of a sewer, storage tank, irrigation canal, or other channel. **4.** Liquid waste resulting from an industrial process. **5.** Radioactive waste from a nuclear power station. [Middle English, from Latin *effluēns* (stem *effluent-*), present participle of *effluere,* to flow out : *ex-,* out + *fluere,* to flow.]

ef·flu·vi·um (ĭ-flo͞o′vē-əm) *n., pl.* **-via** (-vē-ə) or **-ums. 1.** An outflow or rising vapor of invisible or barely visible gas or particles. **2.** Foul-smelling vapor or fumes emanating from decaying matter. **3.** An imaginary outflow of imponderable radiation or invisible vapor; an aura. [Latin, from *effluere,* to flow out. See **effluent.**] **—ef·flu·vi·al** *adj.*

ef·flux (ĕf′lŭks′) *n.* Also **ef·flux·ion** (ĭ-flŭk′shən). **1.** An outward flowing; an emanating. **2.** Something that flows out or forth; an emanation. [Latin *efflūxus,* past participle of *effluere,* to flow out. See **effluent.**]

ef·fort (ĕf′ərt) *n.* **1.** The use of physical or mental energy to do something; exertion. **2.** A difficult or tiring exertion of the strength or will: *It was an effort to get up.* **3.** An attempt; especially, an earnest attempt: *Please make an effort to arrive on time.* **4.** Something done or produced through exertion; an achievement or creation: *His most recent symphony is his finest effort so far.* **5.** *Physics.* Force applied against inertia. [Old French *effort, esfort,* from *esforcier,* to force (reflexive *s'esforcier,* to exert oneself), from Vulgar Latin *exfortiāre* (unattested), to show strength : Latin *ex-,* out + *fortis,* strong.] **—ef·fort·ful** *adj.*
Synonyms: *endeavor, exertion, strain.*

ef·fort·less (ĕf′ərt-lĭs) *adj.* Calling for, requiring, or showing little or no effort. **—ef·fort·less·ly** *adv.* **—ef·fort·less·ness** *n.*

ef·front·er·y (ĭ-frŭn′tə-rē) *n., pl.* **-ies.** Impudent and insulting boldness; presumptuous self-assertion; audacity. —See Synonyms at **temerity.** [French *effronterie,* from *effronté,* shameless, from Vulgar Latin *exfrontātus* (unattested), from Late Latin *effrōns* (stem *effront-*), shameless, "barefaced" : *ex-,* out of + *frōns,* forehead (see **front**).]

ef·ful·gent (ĭ-fo͝ol′jənt, ĭ-fŭl′-) *adj.* Shining forth brilliantly; resplendent. [Latin *effulgēns* (stem *effulgent-*), present participle of *effulgēre,* to shine out : *ex-,* out + *fulgēre,* to shine.] **—ef·ful·gence** *n.*

ef·fuse (ĭ-fyo͞os′) *adj. Botany.* Spreading out loosely on a surface. Said especially of flower inflorescences.
∼*v.* (ĭ-fyo͞oz′) **effused, -fusing, -fuses.** —*tr.* To pour or spread out; disseminate. —*intr.* **1.** To spread out. **2.** To exude. **3.** To flow out. [Latin *effūsus,* past participle of *effundere,* to pour out : *ex-,* out + *fundere,* to pour.]

ef·fu·si·om·e·ter (ĭ-fyo͞o′zē-ŏm′ĭ-tər) *n.* An apparatus for determining molecular weights by measuring the rate of effusion of gases.

ef·fu·sion (ĭ-fyo͞o′zhən) *n.* **1. a.** The act or an instance of pouring forth. **b.** Something that is poured forth. **2.** An unrestrained outpouring of feeling, as in speech or writing: *"The devout effusions of sacred eloquence"* (Edmund Burke). **3.** *Pathology.* **a.** The seeping of serous, purulent, or bloody fluid into a body cavity. **b.** The effused fluid. **4.** *Physics.* The flow of gas through an aperture under pressure in circumstances in which the diameter of the aperture is small compared to the mean distance between the gas molecules.

ef·fu·sive (ĭ-fyo͞o′sĭv) *adj.* **1.** Irrepressibly demonstrative. **2.** Unrestrained in emotional expression; gushing. **3.** *Geology.* Poured out in a molten state and then solidified. Said of igneous rock. —See Synonyms at **talkative. —ef·fu·sive·ly** *adv.* **—ef·fu·sive·ness** *n.*

Ef·ik (ĕf′ĭk) *n., pl.* **-iks** or collectively **Efik. 1.** A member of a people of southeastern Nigeria. **2.** The Ibibio language of this people. **—Ef·ik** *adj.*

eft (ĕft) *n.* A newt; especially, the reddish-orange immature terrestrial form of a North American species, *Diemictylus viridescens.* [Middle English *evete,* Old English *efeta*†, lizard.]

E.F.T.A. European Free Trade Association.

eft·soons (ĕft-so͞onz′) *adv.* Also **eft·soon** (-so͞on′). *Archaic.* **1.** Soon afterward. **2.** Once again. [Middle English *eftsōne,* Old English *eftsōna* : *eft,* again + *sōna,* SOON.]

e.g. for example. —See Usage note at **i.e.** [Latin *exempli gratia.*]

Eg. Egypt; Egyptian.

e·gad (ĭ-găd′) *interj.* Used as a mild oath expressing surprise or enthusiasm. [Euphemism for *oh God* or *ah God.*]

e·gal·i·tar·i·an (ĭ-găl′ə-târ′ē-ən) *adj.* **1.** Advocating the doctrine of equal political, economic, and legal rights for all citizens. **2.** Pertaining to or arising from this doctrine.
∼*n.* One who holds or advances egalitarian opinions. [French *égalitaire,* from *égalité,* equality, from Latin *aequālitās,* from *aequālis,* EQUAL.] **—e·gal·i·tar·i·an·ism** *n.*

e·gest (ē-jĕst′) *tr.v.* **egested, egesting, egests.** To discharge or excrete from the body. [Latin *ēgerere* (past participle *ēgestus*), to carry out, expel : *ex-,* out + *gerere,* to carry.] **—e·ges·tion** *n.* **—e·ges·tive** *adj.*

e·ges·ta (ē-jĕs′tə) *pl.n.* Egested matter, especially excrement. [Latin *ēgesta,* neuter plural of Latin *ēgestus.* See **egest.**]

egg[1] (ĕg) *n.* **1.** Any of the female reproductive cells of various animals, consisting usually of an embryo surrounded by nutrient material with a protective covering, and often deposited externally. **2.** A female gamete; ovum. **3.** The oval, thin-shelled ovum of a bird, especially a domestic fowl, used as food. **4.** Something having the characteristic shape of a hen's egg. **5.** *Slang.* A fellow; a person: *a good egg.* **—have egg on one's face.** To be humiliated or embarrassed. **—put** (or **have**) **all one's eggs in one basket.** To risk everything on a single venture, method, or act.
∼*tr.v.* **egged, egging, eggs.** To mix or cover with beaten egg, as in cooking. [Middle English *egge,* from Old Norse *egg.*]

egg[2] *tr.v.* **egged, egging, eggs.** To encourage or incite with taunts, dares, or similar verbal appeals; urge; spur. Used with *on.* [Middle English *eggen,* Old English *eggian,* from Old Norse *eggja.*]

egg-and-dart (ĕg′ən-därt′) *n.* A decorative molding common in classical architecture and in cabinetwork that consists of a series of egg-shaped figures alternating with dart-, anchor-, or tongue-shaped figures.

egg-and-spoon race (ĕg′ən-spo͞on′) *n.* A running race in which competitors must carry an egg in a spoon without dropping it.

egg·beat·er (ĕg′bē′tər) *n.* A kitchen utensil with rotating blades for beating eggs, whipping cream, or mixing cooking ingredients.

egg·cup (ĕg′kŭp′) *n.* A small cup-shaped holder for a boiled egg.

eg·ger, eg·gar (ĕg′ər) *n.* Any of various moths of the family Lasiocampidae, of which the larvae often construct tentlike webs. [From EGG, from its egg-shaped cocoon.]

egg·head (ĕg′hĕd′) *n. Slang.* An intellectual; highbrow: *a lecture that attracted every egghead in town.* [Said to be originally applied to an intellectual who supported (1952) the U.S. Presidential candidate Adlai Stevenson, with reference to Stevenson's baldness.]

egg·nog (ĕg′nŏg′) *n.* A drink consisting of milk and beaten eggs, commonly mixed with rum, brandy, or wine. Also called "nog." [EGG + NOG (original sense "ale").]

egg·plant (ĕg′plănt′, -plänt′) *n.* **1. a.** A tropical Old World plant, *Solanum melongena,* cultivated for its edible fruit. **b.** The glossy, ovoid fruit of the eggplant. Also called "aubergine." **2.** A blackish purple.

egg roll *n.* A cylindrical case of egg dough filled with minced vegetables and often seafood or meat and fried.

egg·shell (ĕg′shĕl′) *n.* **1.** The thin, brittle exterior covering of a bird's egg. **2.** A pale yellow to yellowish white.
∼*adj.* **1.** Of or being a paint surface that has a mat rather than a glossy sheen. **2.** Very brittle and thin, as certain china. **3.** Pale yellow to yellowish white.

egg timer *n.* A small device, usually in the shape of an hourglass, for timing the boiling of an egg.

egg tooth *n.* A structure in embryo birds and reptiles that is used to pierce the eggshell. In birds it is a projection on the beak and in reptiles a temporary tooth.

egg white *n.* The albumen of an egg.

egis. Variant of **aegis.**

eg·lan·tine (ĕg'lən-tīn', -tēn') *n.* A rose, the **sweetbrier** *(see).* [Middle English *eglentyn,* from Old French *aiglantine,* from *aiglent,* from Vulgar Latin *aquilentum* (unattested), "prickly," irregularly from Latin *aculeus,* diminutive of *acus,* needle.]

Eg·mont (ĕg'mŏnt'), **Lamoral, Count van** (1522–68). Flemish general and statesman who served in the army of Philip II of Spain. He is the Egmont of Goethe's tragedy of the same name and also of Beethoven's *Egmont* overture.

e·go (ē'gō, ĕg'ō) *n.* **1.** The conscious subject, as designated by the first person singular pronoun; the self. **2.** *Psychoanalysis.* The personality component that is conscious, most immediately controls behavior, and is most in touch with external reality. See **id, super-ego. 3.** *Informal.* **a.** A sense of self-esteem. **b.** Conceit; egotism. [New Latin, from Latin, I.]

e·go·cen·tric (ē'gō-sĕn'trĭk, ĕg'ō-) *adj.* **1.** Thinking or acting with the view that one's self is the center, object, and norm of all experience. **2.** Self-centered; selfish. **3.** *Philosophy.* Real or valid only as perceived or conceived by the individual mind.

~*n.* An egocentric person. —**e·go·cen·tric·i·ty** (ē'gō-sĕn-trĭs'ə-tē, ĕg'ō-) *n.*

ego ideal *n.* **1.** *Psychoanalysis.* An individual's conception of the person he would wish to be, based on identification with persons admired during his development. **2.** Self-idealization.

e·go·ism (ē'gō-ĭz'əm, ĕg'ō-) *n.* **1.** The quality of thinking or acting with only oneself and one's own interests in mind; preoccupation with one's own welfare and advancement. **2.** *Ethics.* **a.** The doctrine that morality has its foundations in self-interest. **b.** The belief that self-interest is the just and proper motive for all human conduct. **3.** Conceit; egotism.

e·go·ist (ē'gō-ĭst, ĕg'ō-) *n.* **1.** One devoted to his own interests and advancement; an egocentric person. **2.** *Ethics.* An adherent of egoism. **3.** An egotist. [French *égoiste,* from EGO.] —**e·go·is·tic** (ē'gō-ĭs'tĭk, ĕg'ō-), **e·go·is·ti·cal** (-tĭ-kəl) *adj.* —**e·go·is·ti·cal·ly** *adv.*

e·go·ma·ni·a (ē'gō-mā'nē-ə, -mān'yə, ĕg'ō-) *n.* Obsessive or pathological preoccupation with the self; extreme egotism. [New Latin : EGO + -MANIA.] —**e·go·ma·ni·ac** (ē'gō-mā'nē-ăk', ĕg'ō-) *n.* —**e·go·ma·ni·a·cal** (ē'gō-mə-nī'ə-kəl, ĕg'ō-) *adj.*

e·go·tism (ē'gə-tĭz'əm, ĕg'ə-) *n.* **1.** An inordinately large sense of self-importance; egoism. **2.** The tendency to speak or write of oneself excessively and boastfully. [EGO + -ISM (by analogy with nouns such as NEPOTISM).]

e·go·tist (ē'gə-tĭst, ĕg'ə-) *n.* **1.** A conceited, boastful person. **2.** A person who acts selfishly; an egoist. —**e·go·tis·tic** (ē'gə-tĭs'tĭk, ĕg'ə-), **e·go·tis·ti·cal** (-tĭ-kəl) *adj.* —**e·go·tis·ti·cal·ly** *adv.*

ego trip *n. Slang.* **1.** An experience that boosts or gratifies the ego. **2.** An act of self-aggrandizement or self-indulgence.

e·go-trip (ē'gō-trĭp', ĕg'ō-) *intr.v.* **-tripped, -tripping, trips.** *Slang.* To seek personal gratification, as by self-aggrandizement or self-indulgence.

e·gre·gious (ĭ-grē'jəs, -jē-əs) *adj.* Outstandingly bad; blatant; outrageous. [Latin *ēgregius,* "standing out from the herd" : *ex-,* out of + *grex* (stem *greg-*), herd, flock.] —**e·gre·gious·ly** *adv.* —**e·gre·gious·ness** *n.*

e·gress (ē'grĕs') *n.* **1.** The act of going out; emergence. **2.** The path or opening by means of which one goes out; an exit. **3.** The right of going out: *deny egress.* **4.** *Astronomy.* The emergence of a celestial body from eclipse or occultation. Also called "emersion." [Latin *ēgressus,* from the past participle of *ēgredī,* to go out : *ex-,* out + *gradī,* to go, step.]

e·gret (ē'grĭt, ĕg'rĭt) *n.* Any of several usually white wading birds of the genera *Bubulcus, Casmerodius, Leucophoyx,* and related genera, characteristically having long, showy, drooping plumes during the breeding season. [Middle English *egrete,* from Old French *aigrette,* from Old Provençal *aigreta,* from *aigron,* heron, from Germanic.]

E·gypt (ē'jĭpt). *Abbr.* **Eg.** A country of northeastern Africa, bordering the Mediterranean. It is mainly desert and includes the Sinai peninsula, the upland Eastern desert, and the low-lying Western Desert, with its population concentrated along the fertile Nile Valley. Early Egyptian history is generally divided into 31 dynasties. The Old Kingdom, the third to the sixth dynasties, from *c.* 2700 to *c.* 2200 B.C., reached its peak when the pyramids of Giza were built. Under a succession of vigorous rulers of the early New Kingdom (*c.* 1570–*c.* 1200 B.C.), notably Thutmosis I and Thutmosis II, the kingdom extended its frontiers into Syria and Mesopotamia. The temples of Luxor and Karnak and the famous tomb of Tutankhamun were built during that period. By the end of the 20th dynasty, decline had set in and the Egyptian empire was conquered by the Assyrians in the 7th century B.C. and twice by the Persians. Liberated from Persian rule by Alexander the Great, the kingdom passed at his death to his general Ptolemy, whose descendants ruled until the suicide of Cleopatra VII in 30 B.C. After Egypt was conquered by the Romans, communications were improved and irrigation of the land gave the country a century of renewed wealth. In A.D. 642 it fell to the Arabs and was absorbed into the Islamic world. Other conquerers included the Fatimids (968), who founded Cairo, and Saladin, who restored Egypt to Baghdad in 1171. It was ruled by the Mamelukes from 1250 and was under Turkish rule from 1517 until 1798, when Napoleon made it a French protectorate (until 1801). By the mid-19th century British and French interests in Egypt had intensified, and the opening of the Suez Canal in 1869 gave Egypt international prominence. Britain dominated Egyptian

Egypt

"THE GIFT OF THE NILE"

On rich floodplains, Egyptians created a civilization lasting nearly 3,000 years

The Greek historian Herodotus said that Egypt was given to the Egyptians by the Nile. Along the river's narrow fertile strip, they built one of the world's earliest and greatest civilizations.

It emerged about 3000 B.C. Hieroglyphics, the early Egyptian system of writing, date from about the same time. Until the conquest of Egypt by Alexander the Great in 332 B.C., the country was ruled by a succession of more than 200 kings in 31 dynasties. The kings were regarded as gods.

The Egyptians believed in an afterlife and, to preserve their dead for it, developed mummification. They buried the dead with possessions needed for the afterlife.

The most remarkable Egyptian achievements were in architecture. Using ramps, levers, rollers, and huge numbers of men, they constructed pyramids, tombs, and temples that remain among the wonders of the world.

The Great Pyramid at Giza, just outside Cairo, built as a tomb for Cheops (or Khufu) in about 2650 B.C., contains over two million 2.5-ton blocks and covers 13 acres.

MODEL HOUSE *Complete with pots and food, the house above was made in about 1900 B.C. to be buried with its owner. The style—one or two rooms set in a courtyard—was standard for the wealthier Egyptians. A stairway leads to the roof, which was used for sleeping, baking, and storing food.*

NOBLE AND HIS WIFE *This statue (left), made about 1450 B.C., portrays a couple in conventionally stiff poses clad in wigs and linen skirts. The detailed features suggest that the faces are lifelike, if idealized, portraits.*

HOW THEY FARMED *A carving shows a farmer's plow of about 2000 B.C.—a wooden share, perhaps tipped with metal, a long shaft, and a yoke set on the necks of the two draft animals. Farmers plowed after the annual retreat of the Nile's floodwaters, which left a new, rich layer of silt for growing wheat and barley.*

A RIVER OUTING *A nobleman, Sennufer, and his wife are rowed on the Nile, while a slave serves food and drink. The scene—in traditional style, with heads in profile and shoulders squared to the* front—*is a mural in Sennufer's tomb, one of hundreds of noblemen's tombs in the ancient capital of Thebes (now Luxor). Above it there is an inscription in hieroglyphics.*

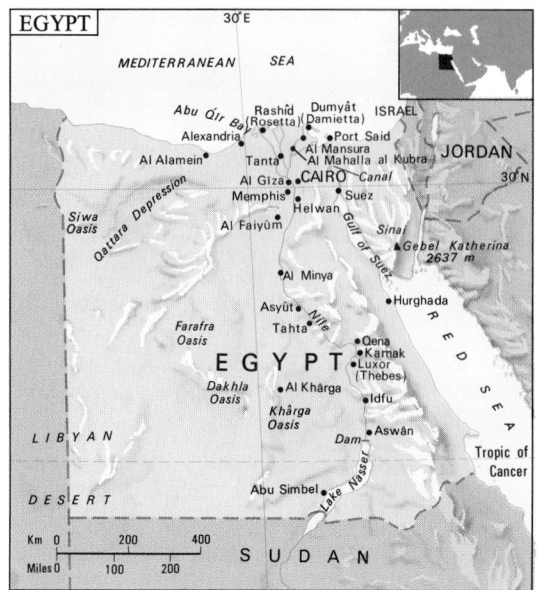

EGYPT

eider *The soft down plucked from the breast of the female eider is used to stuff pillows and quilts. Eiders breed in colonies in northern regions. The males are distinguished from the females by their distinctive black and white plumage.*

politics, despite nominal Ottoman sovereignty, and made Egypt a protectorate at the outbreak of World War I. It became a sovereign state in 1922. Corruption brought an end to its monarchy with the military coup and the abdication of King Farouk in 1952. Egypt became a republic in 1953. Under Col. Gamal Nasser the Suez Canal was nationalized in 1956, precipitating the Suez crisis and invasion by Israeli and Anglo-French forces, who later withdrew on orders from the United Nations. From 1958 to 1961 Egypt combined with Syria as the United Arab Republic. In 1967 Egypt fought the Six-Day War against Israel and lost the Sinai peninsula. Under President Anwar el-Sadat the country fought another Arab-Israeli war (1973) and signed the Camp David peace treaty with Israel (1979). Sadat was assassinated by Muslim fanatics (1981), and Vice President Hosni Mubarak succeeded him. Despite the lack of water, the Aswan High Dam and other modern irrigation systems have greatly increased the production of cotton (the chief cash crop), rice, millet, corn, sugar cane, fruit, and vegetables. Since the 1950's heavy industries (iron, steel, and engineering) have been introduced and are now supplied with power from the Aswan High Dam. Area, 1,001,449 square kilometers (386,559 square miles). Population, 41,600,000. Capital, Cairo.

E·gyp·tian (ĭ-jĭp'shən) *adj. Abbr.* **Eg.** **1.** Of or pertaining to Egypt, its people, or its culture. **2.** *Obsolete.* Of or pertaining to Gypsies. —*n.* **1.** A native or citizen of Egypt. **2.** The extinct Hamitic language spoken by the ancient Egyptians. **3.** *Obsolete.* A Gypsy.

Egyptian clover *n.* A plant, **berseem** (*see*).

Egyptian cotton *n.* A long-staple, fine cotton grown chiefly in northern Africa.

E·gyp·tol·o·gy (ē'jĭp-tŏl'ə-jē) *n.* The study of the language, culture, and artefacts of the ancient Egyptian civilization. —**E·gyp·to·log·i·cal** (ĭ-jĭp'tə-lŏj'ĭ-kəl) *adj.* —**E·gyp·tol·o·gist** *n.*

eh (ā, ĕ) *interj.* **1.** Used interrogatively: *Eh? What was that?* **2.** Used in asking for confirmation: *He is a shrewd one, eh?*

EHF extremely high frequency.

Eh·ren·burg (âr'ən-bŏŏrg'), **Ilya Gregorievich** (1891-1967). Russian writer who was awarded the Stalin Prize twice, for *The Fall of Paris* (1941) and *The Storm* (1948). In the West he is best known for his novel *The Thaw* (1954), which described repression under Stalin's regime.

Ehr·lich (âr'lĭKH), **Paul** (1854-1915). German bacteriologist who discovered arsenic compounds that were used to treat syphilis before the discovery of antibiotics. He shared the Nobel Prize in physiology and medicine with Ilya Metchnikoff (1845-1916) in 1908.

EHV extra high voltage.

E.I. East Indian; East Indies.

Eich·mann (īKH'män'), **Adolf** (1906-62). German official of the Nazi S.S. As head of the Gestapo's Jewish section after 1939, he was chiefly responsible for the murder of millions of Jews in occupied Europe. Arrested by the Allies in 1945, he escaped and fled to South America. He was captured by the Israeli secret service in Argentina (1960), taken to Jerusalem, tried, and executed (1962).

ei·der (ī'dər) *n.* Any of several sea ducks of the genus *Somateria* and related genera, especially *S. mollissima*, of northern regions, the females of which are the source of eiderdown. The males have predominantly black and white plumage. [Icelandic *ædhur* (genitive *ædhar*), from Old Norse *ædhr*.]

ei·der-down (ī'dər-doun') *n.* **1.** The downy breast feathers of the female eider duck, used as stuffing for quilts and pillows. **2.** A quilt stuffed with eiderdown. **3.** A warm, napped fabric. [Probably from German *Eiderdaune*, from Icelandic *ædhardúnn* : *ædhar*, genitive of *ædhur*, EIDER + *dúnn*, DOWN.]

ei·det·ic (ī-dĕt'ĭk) *adj.* **1.** Especially vivid but unreal. Said of images experienced especially in childhood. **2.** Of or pertaining to vivid mental images: *an eidetic memory.* —*n.* One who experiences vivid mental images. [German *eidetisch*, from Greek *eidētikos*, relating to images or knowledge, from *eidēsis*, knowledge, from *eidos*, form, shape.] —**ei·det·i·cal·ly** *adv.*

ei·do·lon (ī-dō'lən) *n., pl.* **-lons** or **-la** (-lə). **1.** A phantom; an apparition. **2.** An image of an ideal. [Greek *eidōlon*, from *eidos*, form, shape.]

Eif·fel Tower (ī'fəl, ĕ-fĕl') *n.* An iron tower on the left bank of the Seine in Paris, now standing 300 meters (984 feet) high, designed by the French engineer Alexandre Gustave Eiffel (1823-1923) and originally erected for the Paris Exhibition of 1889.

eigen- *prefix.* Indicates proper or characteristic; for example, **eigenvalue.** [German, "own."]

ei·gen·func·tion (ī'gən-fŭngk'shən) *n. Physics.* An allowed function for a system as determined by wave mechanics, enabling a meaningful solution to be obtained from the Schrödinger wave equation.

ei·gen·val·ue (ī'gən-văl'yōō) *n. Physics.* Any of a set of allowed energies of a particle in a system as determined by wave mechanics.

Ei·ger (ī'gər). Mountain (3,970 meters; 13,025 feet) in the Bernese Oberland, central Switzerland. Its steep north face was not conquered until 1938.

eight (āt) *n.* **1. a.** The cardinal number that is one more than seven. **b.** A symbol representing this, such as 8, VIII, or viii. **2.** A set made up of eight persons or things. **3. a.** The eighth in a series. **b.** A playing card marked with eight pips. **4.** Eight parts: *cut in eight.* **5.** A size, as in clothing, designated as eight. **6. a.** An eight-oared racing shell. **b.** A rowing crew of eight people. **7.** Eight hours after midnight or midday; eight o'clock. **8.** A figure eight (*see*). [Middle English *eighte, eihte,* Old English *eahta.*] —**eight** *adj.* —**eight·fold** (āt'fōld') *adj. & adv.*

eight ball *n.* A black pool ball bearing the number eight that may place a player at a disadvantage. —**behind the eight ball.** *Slang.* In an unfavorable, disadvantageous, or uncomfortable position.

eight·een (ā-tēn') *n.* **1. a.** The cardinal number that is one more than 17. **b.** A symbol representing this, such as 18, XVIII, or xviii. **2.** A set made up of 18 persons or things. **3.** The eighteenth in a series. **4.** A size, as in clothing, designated as eighteen. [Middle English *eightetene, eihtene,* Old English *eahtatīene* : EIGHT + -TEEN.] —**eight·een** *adj.*

eight·een·mo (ā-tēn'mō') *n., pl.* **-mos.** A size of a page or a book, **octodecimo** (*see*). [EIGHTEEN + -MO.] —**eight·een·mo** *adj.*

eight·eenth (ā-tēnth') *n.* **1.** The ordinal number 18 in a series. **2.** One of 18 equal parts. —**eight·eenth** *adj. & adv.*

eighth (ātth, āth) *n.* **1.** The ordinal number eight in a series. **2.** One of eight equal parts. —**eighth** *adj. & adv.*

eighth note *n. Music.* A note having one eighth the time value of a whole note.

eight·i·eth (ā'tē-ĭth) *n.* **1.** The ordinal number 80 in a series. **2.** One of 80 equal parts. —**eight·i·eth** *adj. & adv.*

eight·some reel (āt'səm) *n.* A Scottish dance in which eight people take part.

eight·vo (āt'vō') *n., pl.* **-vos.** A size of a page or a book, **octavo** (*see*). [EIGHT + (OCTA)VO.] —**eight·vo** *adj.*

eight·y (ā'tē) *n., pl.* **-ies. 1. a.** The cardinal number that is ten more than seventy. **b.** A symbol representing this, such as 80 or LXXX. **2.** The eightieth in a series. **3.** A set made up of 80 persons or things. **4.** A size, as in clothing, designated as 80. **5. eighties. a.** The range of numbers from 80 to 89, considered as a range of age, price, temperature, or the like. **b.** The years numbered 80-89 in a century. Also used adjectively: *an eighties fashion.* [Middle English *eigh(te)ty,* Old English *eahtatig* : *eahta,* EIGHT + -*tig,* -TY (ten).] —**eight·y** *adj.*

Eijk·man (īk'män'), **Christiaan** (1858-1930). Dutch physician. He was awarded the Nobel Prize in physiology and medicine with F.G. Hopkins (1929) for his work on the causes of beriberi.

eikon. Variant of **icon.**

Eilat. See **Elat.**

-ein. Variant of **-in.**

Eind·ho·ven (īnt'hō'vən). Industrial town of North Brabant province in the Netherlands. It manufactures electrical goods, motor vehicles, textiles, plastics, and cigars.

ein·korn (īn'kôrn') *n.* A one-seeded wheat, *Triticum monococcum,* grown in arid regions. [German *Einkorn* : *ein,* one, from Old High German *ein* + *Korn,* grain, from Old High German *korn.*]

Ein·stein (īn'stīn'), **Albert** (1879-1955). U.S. physicist, born in Germany. His special and general theories of relativity revolutionized man's thinking about the nature of space and time. Einstein showed that the mass of a body is a measure of its energy content. He expressed his findings in the equation known as Einstein's law. Einstein was awarded the Nobel Prize in physics (1921) for his work in explaining the photoelectric effect.

ein·stein·i·um (īn-stī'nē-əm) *n. Symbol* **Es** A synthetic transuranic element first produced by neutron irradiation of uranium in a thermonuclear explosion. It has 12 known isotopes with half-lives ranging between 1.2 minutes and 270 days and mass numbers from 245 to 256. Atomic number 99. [New Latin, after Albert EINSTEIN.]

Einstein shift *n. Astronomy.* A small displacement toward the red in a star's spectrum, predicted by Einstein's general theory of relativity and caused by the interaction between the radiation and a gravitational field.

Einstein's law *n.* **1.** The law that $E = mc^2$, where E is the energy associated with a mass *m* and *c* is the speed of light. Also called "Einstein's equation." **2.** The law that the energy of an electron emitted in the photoelectric effect is $h\nu-\Phi$, where ν is the frequency of the incident radiation, Φ is the work function of the electron emitter, and *h* is the Planck constant.

Eire. See **Ireland.** [Irish Gaelic *Éire,* from Old Irish *Ēriu.* See **Erin.**]

eirenic, eirenical. Variants of **irenic.**

ei·ren·i·con, i·ren·i·con (ī-rĕn′ĭ-kŏn′, -kən) *n.* A proposal that attempts to create harmony between conflicting viewpoints. [Greek, from *eirēnikos,* relating to peace, from *eirēnē,* peace.]

ei·se·ge·sis (ī′sə-jē′sĭs) *n., pl.* **-ses** (-sēz′). An explanation or analysis, especially of a Biblical text, using one's own ideas. Compare **exegesis.** [19th century : from Greek *eis,* into + *-egesis,* as in EXEGESIS (with which the term was coined to contrast).]

Ei·sen·how·er (ī′zən-hou′ər), **Dwight David** (1890-1969). U.S. general and 34th President of the United States (1953–61). In 1943 he was made supreme commander of the Allied Expeditionary Forces, and he launched the D-Day invasion of Europe in 1944. In 1950 he was made supreme commander of NATO but resigned when he won the Republican Presidential nomination in 1952.

Ei·sen·stein (ī′zən-stīn′), **Sergei Mikhailovich** (1898–1948). Russian film director whose work included *Strike* (1924), *Battleship Potemkin* (1925), and *October* (1927), a film about the Bolshevik revolution. His first sound film was *Alexander Nevsky* (1938). His last film, *Ivan the Terrible,* was intended to be a trilogy, but he died after completing only the first two parts.

ei·stedd·fod (ī-stĕ*th*′vôd′, ā-stĕ*th*′-) *n., pl.* **-fods** or **-fodau** (ī-stĕ*th*′vô′-dī′). Any of various annual assemblies of or competitions between Welsh poets and musicians. [Welsh, "session," "a sitting" : *eistedd,* to sit, from *sedd,* seat + *-fod,* from *bod,* to be.]

ei·ther (ē′*th*ər, ī′*th*ər) *pron.* One or the other: *Choose either.*
~*conj.* Used before the first of two or more stated alternatives, the following alternatives being signaled by *or*: *Either we go now, or we remain here forever.*
~*adj.* **1.** One or the other; any one of two: *Wear either coat.* **2.** One and the other; each: *She wore rings on either hand.*
~*adv.* Likewise; any more so; also. Used as an intensive following negative statements: *If you don't order a dessert, I won't either.* [Middle English *aither, either,* Old English *ǣgther, ǣghwæther.*]

Usage: *Either* is normally used to mean "one of two," although it is sometimes used of three or more: *either corner of the triangle.* When referring to more than two, *any* or *any one* is preferred. • *Either* takes a singular verb: *Either plant grows in the shade.* Sometimes it is used informally with a plural verb, especially when followed by *of* and a plural: *I doubt whether either of them are available.* But such use is usually considered unacceptable in formal writing. • In *either . . . or* constructions, the two conjunctions should be followed by parallel elements. The following is held to be incorrect: *You may either have the ring or the bracelet* (properly, *You may have either the ring or the bracelet*). The following is also incorrect: *He can take either the examination offered to all applicants or ask for a personal interview* (properly, *He can either take . . .*). • When all the elements in an *either . . . or* construction are singular, the verb is singular: *Either Mary's father or Tom's mother is coming.* When one element is singular and the other plural, it is sometimes suggested that the verb should agree with whichever element is closest to it: *Either Kim or the boys are going* but *Either the boys or Kim is going.* Some traditionalists, however, insist that such constructions should be avoided entirely and that substitutes such as *Either Kim is going, or the boys are* must be found for them. There is no generally accepted rule in these cases. See also Usage notes at **everyone** and **neither.**

ei·ther–or (ē′*th*ər-ôr′, ī′*th*ər-) *adj.* Requiring a choice between two exclusive alternatives: *an either-or situation.*

e·jac·u·late (ĭ-jăk′yə-lāt′) *v.* **-lated, -lating, -lates.** —*tr.* **1.** To eject or discharge abruptly; especially, to discharge (semen) in orgasm. **2.** To utter suddenly and passionately; exclaim. —*intr.* To discharge semen.
~*n.* (-lĭt). Semen ejaculated in orgasm. [Latin *ējaculārī* (past participle *ējaculātus*) : *ex-,* out + *jaculārī,* to throw, shoot, from *jaculum,* dart, from *jacere,* to throw.] **—e·jac·u·la·tor** *n.*

e·jac·u·la·tion (ĭ-jăk′yə-lā′shən) *n.* **1.** The act of ejaculating. **2.** An abrupt discharge of fluid; especially, an emission of seminal fluid. **3. a.** A sudden, emphatic utterance; an exclamation. **b.** A brief, pious utterance or prayer.

e·jac·u·la·to·ry (ĭ-jăk′yə-lə-tôr′ē, -tōr′ē) *adj.* Also **e·jac·u·la·tive** (-lā′-tĭv, -lə-tĭv). **1.** Of or pertaining to ejaculation. **2.** Pertaining to or constituting a sudden, brief utterance; exclamatory.

e·ject (ĭ-jĕkt′) *v.* **ejected, ejecting, ejects.** —*tr.* **1.** To throw out forcefully; expel. **2.** To compel to leave; evict. **3.** To emit. —*intr.* To make an emergency exit by ejection capsule or seat. [Middle English *ejecten,* from Latin *ēicere* (past participle *ējectus*) : *ex-,* out + *jacere,* to throw.]

Synonyms: *evict, expel, throw out.*

e·jec·ta (ĭ-jĕk′tə) *pl.n.* Ejected matter, as that from an erupting volcano. [New Latin, from Latin *ējectus,* ejected. See **eject.**]

e·jec·tion (ĭ-jĕk′shən) *n.* **1.** The act of ejecting or the condition of being ejected. **2.** Ejected matter.

ejection seat *n.* Also **ejector seat.** A seat designed to eject an occupant, as the pilot, clear of an aircraft and enable him to parachute to the ground in an emergency.

e·ject·ment (ĭ-jĕkt′mənt) *n.* **1.** The act of ejecting; eviction; dispossession. **2.** *Law.* An action to regain possession of real estate held by another.

e·jec·tor (ĭ-jĕk′tər) *n.* **1.** A person or thing that ejects. **2.** A device in a gun that ejects the empty shell after each firing.

Ekaterinburg. See **Sverdlovsk.**

eke¹ (ēk) *tr.v.* **eked, eking, ekes.** **1.** To supplement with great effort; strain to fill out: *He eked out his income by working at night.* **2.** To earn with great effort or strain. Used with *out*: *eke out a living.* **3.** To cause (a limited resource) to last longer by careful management: *They eked out their emergency rations for a whole week.* [Middle English *eken,* Old English *ēacan,* to increase.]

eke² *adv. Archaic.* Also. [Middle English *ec, eke,* Old English *ēac.*]

EKG electrocardiogram; electrocardiograph.

e·kis·tics (ĭ-kĭs′tĭks) *n. Used with a singular verb.* The science of human settlements, including town or community planning and design. [Greek *oikistikē,* feminine of *oikistikos,* of settlements, from *oikizein,* to settle, from *oikos,* house. See **ecumenical.**] **—e·kis·tic, e·kis·ti·cal** *adj.* **—ek·is·ti·cian** (ĕk′ĭ-stĭsh′ən) *n.*

e·kue·le (ā-kwā′lā) *n., pl.* **ekuele.** The basic monetary unit of Equatorial Guinea, equal to 100 centimos. See feature at **currency.** [Native word in Equatorial Guinea.]

el¹ (ĕl) *n.* The letter *l.*

el² *n. Informal.* An elevated railway.

el. elevation.

e·lab·o·rate (ĭ-lăb′ər-ĭt) *adj.* **1.** Planned or executed with painstaking attention to numerous parts or details. **2.** Rich in detail; complicated; ornate.
~*v.* (-ə-rāt′) **elaborated, -rating, -rates.** —*tr.* **1.** To work out with care and detail; develop thoroughly. **2.** To produce by effort; create. **3.** To add more detail to; make more complex; enrich. **4.** *Physiology.* To convert (food, for example) into a more complex chemical state for use by the body. —*intr.* To express oneself at greater length or in greater detail; provide further information. Often used with *on* or *upon.* [Latin *ēlabōrātus,* past participle of *ēlabōrāre,* "to work out" : *ex-,* out + *labōrāre,* to work, from *labor,* work.] **—e·lab·o·rate·ly** *adv.* **—e·lab·o·rate·ness** *n.* **—e·lab·o·ra·tion** (ĭ-lăb′ə-rā′shən) *n.* **—e·lab·o·ra·tor** *n.*

Elagabalus. See **Heliogabalus.**

E·laine (ĭ-lān). One of two women in Arthurian legend who loved Lancelot: **a.** One who died of unrequited love for him. **b.** One who was the mother of Galahad by Lancelot.

El A·la·mein (ĕl ăl′ə-mān′). Railway junction on the coast road of northern Egypt. It gave its name to a decisive battle of World War II when the British Eighth Army defeated the German Afrika Corps.

E·lam (ē′ləm). Also **Su·si·a·na** (so͞o′zē-ă′nə, -ā′nə). Ancient country now in Iran. It was established east of the Tigris *c.* 3000 B.C., and Susa, its capital, later became a capital of the Persian Achaemenid Empire. The Elamites were thought to be descended from Shem, the son of Noah.

E·lam·ite (ē′lə-mīt′) *n.* Also **E·lam·it·ic** (ē′lə-mĭt′ĭk) (for sense 2). **1.** A native or inhabitant of Elam. **2.** An unclassified language spoken by the ancient Elamites. In this sense, also called "Susian." **—E·lam·ite, E·lam·it·ic** *adj.*

é·lan (ā-läN, ā-län′) *n.* **1.** Enthusiastic vigor and liveliness. **2.** Style; flair: *played the violin with élan.* [French *élan,* from Old French *eslan,* a rush, dash, from *eslancer,* to throw out : *es-,* out, from Latin *ex-* + *lancer,* to throw, from Late Latin *lanceāre,* to throw a lance, from Latin *lancea,* LANCE.]

e·land (ē′lənd) *n.* Either of two large African antelopes, *Taurotragus oryx* or *T. derbianus,* having a light-brown or grayish coat, a shoulder hump, and spirally twisted horns. [Afrikaans, from Dutch *eland,* elk, from late Middle Dutch *elen, elant,* from (obsolete) German *elen, elend,* from (Old) Lithuanian *ellenis,* stag.]

eland *The largest antelope in the world, the giant eland,* Taurotragus derbianus, *stands up to 1.8 meters (6 feet) tall at the shoulder and can weigh nearly a ton. It was once common in central and southern Africa, but its numbers have been reduced by hunting.*

élan vi·tal (vē-täl′) *n.* The vital force hypothesized by Henri Bergson as a source of causation and evolution in nature. See **Bergsonism.** [French, "vital ardor."]

el·a·pid (ĕl′ə-pĭd) *n.* Any of various venomous snakes of the family Elapidae, which includes the cobras and coral snakes.
~*adj.* Of or belonging to the Elapidae. [New Latin *Elapidae,* from Medieval Greek *elaps* (stem *elapid-*), variant of Greek *elops,* a fish.]

e·lapse (ĭ-lăps′) *intr.v.* **elapsed, elapsing, elapses.** To pass; slip by. Used of time.
~*n.* Passage of time: *returned to school after an elapse of 10 years.* [Latin *ēlābī* (past participle *ēlapsus*) : *ex-,* away + *lābī,* to slip, glide.]

elapsed time *n.* The measured duration of an event; especially, the actual time spent in transit, as in flight, by a moving body.

e·las·mo·branch (ĭ-lăz′mə-brăngk′) *n.* Any of numerous fishes of the subclass Elasmobranchii within the class Chondricthyes, characterized by a cartilaginous skeleton and including the sharks, rays, and skates. [New Latin *Elasmobranchii,* "plate-gilled ones" : Greek *elasmos,* metal plate, from *elaunein,* to drive, beat + -BRANCH.] **—e·las·mo·branch** *adj.*

e·las·mo·saur (ĭ-lăz′mə-sôr′, -sōr′) *n.* Also **e·las·mo·sau·rus** (ĭ-lăz′-mə-sôr′əs, -sōr′əs) An extinct marine reptile that had a very long neck. [New Latin *elasmosaurus,* from Greek *elasmos,* metal plate (see **elasmobranch**) + *sauros,* lizard.]

e·las·tance (ĭ-lăs′təns) *n. Electricity.* The reciprocal of capacitance, measured in reciprocal farads (darafs).

e·las·tic (ĭ-lăs′tĭk) *adj.* **1.** *Physics.* **a.** Returning or capable of returning to an initial form or state after deformation. **b.** Conserving total kinetic energy of translation. Said of certain collisions. **2.** Capable

of adapting to change or a variety of circumstances; flexible: *an elastic schedule.* **3.** Quick to recover, as from disappointment, depression, or adversity; resilient: *an elastic spirit.* **4.** Springy; firm. **5.** Made of or containing elastic: *elastic thread.*
~*n.* **1. a.** A flexible stretchable fabric made with interwoven strands of rubber or an imitative synthetic fiber. **b.** Something, as a garter, made of this fabric. **2.** A **rubber band** *(see).* [New Latin *elasticus,* from Late Greek *elastikos,* from Greek *elastos, elatos,* beaten, from *elaunein,* to drive.] —**e·las·ti·cal·ly** *adv.*

elastic band *n.* A **rubber band** *(see).*

elastic collision *n.* A collision of particles in which the total kinetic energy of translation is conserved.

e·las·tic·i·ty (ĭ-lăs'tĭs'ə-tē, ē'lăs-) *n., pl.* **-ties. 1.** The condition or property of being elastic; resilience; flexibility. **2.** *Physics.* **a.** The property of returning to an initial form or state following deformation. **b.** The degree to which this property is exhibited.

e·las·ti·cized (ĭ-lăs'tə-sīzd') *adj.* Made with elastic thread.

e·las·ti·ciz·er (ĭ-lăs'tə-sī'zər) *n.* An additive that increases the elasticity of a solid propellant to prevent cracking of the propellant grain in the combustion chamber.

elastic limit *n.* The maximum stress that can be applied to a body or substance without causing a permanent deformation.

e·las·tin (ĭ-lăs'tĭn) *n. Biochemistry.* A protein that is the principal component of *elastic tissue,* found in the walls of arteries, the dermis of the skin, and other elastic structures. [ELAST(IC) + -IN.]

e·las·to·mer (ĭ-lăs'tə-mər) *n.* Any of various polymers having the elastic properties of natural rubber. [Greek *elastos,* ELASTIC + -MER(E).]

E·las·to·plast (ĭ-lăs'tə-plăst') *n.* A trademark for an adhesive surgical dressing.

E·lat, Ei·lat (ā-lät'). Israeli port on the Gulf of Aqaba, the country's only outlet to the Red Sea.

e·late (ĭ-lāt') *tr.v.* **elated, elating, elates.** To raise the spirits of; excite feelings of pride or optimism in; encourage.
~*adj.* Elated; joyful; lively. [Latin *ēlātus* (past participle of *efferre,* to carry out, lift up) : *ex-,* out + *-lātus,* "carried."]

e·lat·ed (ĭ-lā'tĭd) *adj.* In high spirits; lively and joyful. —**e·lat·ed·ly** *adv.* —**e·lat·ed·ness** *n.*

el·a·ter (ĕl'ə-tər) *n.* **1.** An elaterid beetle. **2.** *Botany.* An elongated, often spirally thickened filament occurring in the spore-bearing structures of liverworts and other bryophytes, thought to aid spore dispersal. [New Latin, from Greek *elatēr,* driver, from *elaunein,* to drive.]

e·lat·er·id (ĭ-lăt'ər-ĭd) *n.* Any of numerous beetles of the family Elateridae, which includes the click beetles. [New Latin *Elateridae,* from *elater,* elongated filament, ELATER.] —**e·lat·er·id** *adj.*

el·a·te·ri·um (ĕl'ə-tîr'ē-əm) *n.* A sediment produced from the squirting cucumber and containing a crystalline substance used as a purgative. [Latin, from Greek *elatērion,* squirting cucumber, from *elatērios,* purgative, from *elaunein,* to drive.]

e·la·tion (ĭ-lā'shən) *n.* An exalted feeling arising typically from a sense of triumph, achievement, or relief.

E layer *n.* A region, or any of various layers in the region, of the ionosphere, occurring between about 90 kilometers (55 miles) and 150 kilometers (95 miles) above the earth and influencing long-distance communications by strongly reflecting radio waves in the range from one to three megahertz. Also called "E region," "Heaviside layer," "Kennelly-Heaviside layer." [*E* (arbitrary designation) + LAYER.]

El·ba (ĕl'bə). Largest island (223 square kilometers; 86 square miles) in the Tuscan Archipelago, part of Italy's Livorno province. Napoleon I spent a year in exile on Elba (1814–15).

El·be (ĕl'bə, ĕlb). *Czech* **La·be** (lä'bĕ). River in central Europe. It rises on the south side of the Riesengebirge in northeastern Bohemia, Czechoslovakia, flows 1,167 kilometers (725 miles) into East Germany, passes Dresden and Magdeburg, enters West Germany, and flows through Hamburg and into the North Sea at Cuxhaven.

el·bow (ĕl'bō') *n.* **1. a.** The joint or bend of the arm between the forearm and the upper arm. **b.** The bony outer projection of this joint. **c.** The part of a garment that covers this joint. **2.** A joint, as of a bird or quadruped, corresponding to the human elbow. **3.** Something having a bend or angle similar to an elbow, especially: **a.** A length of pipe with a sharp bend in it. **b.** A sharp bend in a river or a road. —**at one's elbow.** Close at hand; nearby. —**bend** (or **lift**) **an elbow.** *Informal.* To drink alcohol; especially, to drink too much. —**up to the elbows in** (or **with**). Busily occupied with; engrossed in.
~*v.* **elbowed, -bowing, -bows.** —*tr.* **1. a.** To push, jostle, or shove with or as if with the elbows. **b.** To make (one's way) by such pushing, jostling, or shoving. **2.** To knock or hit with one's elbow. —*intr.* To push, jostle, or shove one's way. [Middle English *elbowe,* Old English *elnboga,* "bow of the forearm" : ELL + BOW.]

elbow grease *n. Informal.* The vigorous exertion of energy, especially in strenuous physical effort.

el·bow·room (ĕl'bō-rōom', -rŏom') *n.* **1.** Room enough to move around or function in. **2.** Adequate scope or leeway.

El·brus or **El·bruz, Mount** (ĕl-brōōz'). Highest mountain in Europe, lying in the Caucasus of the U.S.S.R. It consists of two extinct volcanic peaks, one to the west rising to 5,633 meters (18,481 feet).

el Cid (ĕl sĭd'), born Rodrigo (or Ruy) Díaz de Vivar (c. 1060–99). Spanish soldier and national hero. He fought against the Moors in the service of Ferdinand I and Sancho II of Castile, but was banished from Castile in 1081 by Alfonso VI, who feared him as a rival.

He then fought for the Moorish rulers of Saragossa against Christians and Moors and in 1094 conquered the kingdom of Valencia, which he ruled until his death. His exploits were recounted in the anonymous 12th-century epic *The Song of the Cid.*

eld·er¹ (ĕl'dər) *n.* **1.** An older person. **2.** An ancestor; a predecessor; a forefather. **3.** An older, influential man of a family, tribe, or community. **4. a.** One of the governing officers of a church. **b.** A member of the higher order of priesthood in the Mormon Church.
~*adj.* Born before; older; especially, being the older of two members of a family. [Middle English *eldre,* Old English *ieldra, eldra.*] —**el·der·ship** *n.*
Usage: *Elder* and *eldest* refer only to people; *older* and *oldest* apply also to things. There is also a difference in construction: *elder* is not followed by *than,* and neither *elder* nor *eldest* can be used without *the* when following a verb, as in *John is the elder* (but *John is older/John is older than Mary*).

eld·er² *n.* **1.** Any of various shrubs or small trees of the genus *Sambucus,* having clusters of small white flowers and red or blackish berrylike fruits. Also called "elderberry." **2.** Any of several similar trees or shrubs. [Middle English *eller, eldre,* Old English *ellaern, ellen.*]

el·der·ber·ry (ĕl'dər-bĕr'ē) *n., pl.* **-ries. 1.** The small, edible fruit of an elder, used to make wine or preserves. **2.** A shrub or tree producing such fruit; an elder.

eld·er·ly (ĕl'dər-lē) *adj.* Rather old. —See Synonyms at **old.** —**el·der·li·ness** *n.*

elder statesman *n.* An elderly person, usually a retired statesman, who acts as an unofficial adviser on national problems.

eld·est (ĕl'dĭst) *adj.* Oldest. Said of a person. —See Usage note at **elder.** [Middle English *eldest,* Old English *ieldesta, eldesta.*]

El Do·ra·do (ĕl' də-rä'dō) *n.* **1.** A legendary kingdom or city in Spanish America rich in precious metals and jewels, sought after by 16th-century explorers. **2.** Any place of fabulous wealth or opportunity. [Spanish, "the gilded (one)" : *el,* the, from Latin *ille,* that + *dorado,* past participle of *dorar,* to gild, from Latin *dēaurāre* : *de-,* thoroughly + *aurum,* gold.]

E·le·a (ē-lē'ə). Ancient Greek colony in southern Italy, site of the founding of the Eleatic school of philosophy.

El·ea·nor of Aq·ui·taine (ĕl'ə-nər, -nôr'; ăk'wə-tān') (c. 1122–1204). Queen consort of Louis VII of France and subsequently of Henry II of England. Her marriage to Louis VII was annulled in 1152. She then married Henry, adding to his lands of Normandy and Anjou her vast possessions in Aquitaine. She bore him three daughters and five sons, including the future English kings Richard I and John.

Eleanor of Cas·tile (kă-stēl') (died 1290). Queen consort of Edward I of England, daughter of Ferdinand III of Castile. She died in 1290, and in her memory Edward had crosses erected at 12 stages of her funeral procession from Nottinghamshire to London.

El·e·at·ic (ĕl'ē-ăt'ĭk) *adj.* Of or characteristic of Elea or the school of philosophy founded there in the 6th and 5th centuries B.C. by Xenophanes and Parmenides.
~*n.* An adherent of the Eleatic school, which held immutable being to be the only knowable reality and change and sensory perceptions to be illusory. —**El·e·at·i·cism** (ĕl'ē-ăt'ĭ-sĭz'əm) *n.*

elec. electric; electrical; electrician; electricity.

el·e·cam·pane (ĕl'ĭ-kăm-pān') *n.* A tall, coarse plant, *Inula helenium,* native to Eurasia, having rayed yellow flowers. [Middle English *elycampane,* from Old French *enule campane,* from Medieval Latin *enula campāna* : *enula,* from Latin *inula,* elecampane, from Greek *helenion* + *campāna,* variant of Latin *campānea,* feminine of *campāneus,* of the field, from *campus,* field (see **camp**).]

e·lect (ĭ-lĕkt') *v.* **elected, electing, elects.** —*tr.* **1. a.** To select by vote for an office, usually by a majority or plurality over other candidates. **b.** To select by vote for membership. **2.** To choose; decide in favor of: *elect to pursue an arts course.* **3.** *Theology.* To predestine for salvation. Used in the passive. —*intr.* To make a choice, especially with deliberation; decide. —See Synonyms at **choose.**
~*adj.* **1.** Chosen deliberately; singled out. **2.** Elected but not yet installed in office. Used in combination: *the governor-elect.* **3.** *Theology.* Selected by the divine will for salvation.
~*n.* **1.** A person who is chosen or selected. **2.** *Theology.* Those selected by the divine will for salvation. Preceded by *the.* **3.** *Used with a plural verb.* An exclusive group. [Middle English *electen,* from Latin *ēligere* (past participle *ēlectus*), to pick out, select : *ex-,* out + *legere,* to gather, choose.]

elect. electric; electrical; electrician; electricity.

e·lec·tion (ĭ-lĕk'shən) *n.* **1.** The act or power of choosing. **2. a.** The act or process of choosing by vote among candidates to fill an office or position, especially a political one. **b.** The fact of being so chosen. **3.** *Theology.* Predestined salvation.

e·lec·tion·eer (ĭ-lĕk'shə-nîr') *intr.v.* **-eered, -eering, -eers.** To work actively for a particular candidate or political party, as by canvassing.
~*n.* One who electioneers. —**e·lec·tion·eer·ing** *n. & adj.*

e·lec·tive (ĭ-lĕk'tĭv) *adj.* **1.** Of or pertaining to a selection by vote. **2.** Filled or obtained by election: *elective office.* **3.** Having the power or authority to elect; electoral. **4.** Permitting or involving a choice; optional: *Cosmetic surgery is usually elective.*
~*n.* An academic course or subject that is optional rather than obligatory. —**e·lec·tive·ly** *adv.*

e·lec·tor (ĭ-lĕk'tər) *n.* **1.** A person who elects; a qualified voter. **2.** A member of the Electoral College of the United States. **3.** *Usually*

Elector. Any of the German princes in the Holy Roman Empire who were entitled to elect the emperor.

e·lec·tor·al (ĭ-lĕk′tər-əl) *adj.* **1.** Of, pertaining to, or composed of electors. **2.** Of or pertaining to election.

Electoral College *n.* A popularly elected body of electors chosen to elect the President and Vice President of the United States.

e·lec·tor·ate (ĭ-lĕk′tər-ĭt) *n.* **1.** A body of qualified voters. **2.** In certain countries, a district or division of voters. **3.** The dignity or territory of an elector of the Holy Roman Empire.

E·lec·tra¹, E·lek·tra (ĭ-lĕk′trə). In Greek legend, the daughter of Clytemnestra and Agamemnon. She avenged the murder of Agamemnon with the help of her brother Orestes, who killed their mother and her lover, Aegisthus.

Electra² *n.* A star in the constellation Pleiades. [After *Electra,* daughter of Atlas.]

Electra complex *n. Psychoanalysis.* Unconscious sexual desire of a daughter for her father, generally manifesting itself first between the ages of three and five. Compare **Oedipus complex.**

e·lec·tret (ĭ-lĕk′trĭt) *n.* A solid dielectric that exhibits persistent dielectric polarization. [ELECTR(ICITY) + (MAGN)ET.]

e·lec·tric (ĭ-lĕk′trĭk) *adj.* Also **e·lec·tri·cal** (-trĭ-kəl). *Abbr.* **elec., elect. 1.** Of, pertaining to, producing, derived from, produced by, powered by, or operated by electricity. **2. a.** Emotionally exciting; thrilling. **b.** Exceptionally tense; charged with emotion. ~*n.* **electric.** An electrically powered machine, especially a vehicle. [New Latin *electricus,* "like amber," because amber produces sparks when rubbed, from Latin *ēlectrum,* amber, from Greek *ēlektron†.*] —**e·lec·tri·cal·ly** *adv.*

Usage: *Electric* is used of anything producing or powered by electricity: *electric light, electric chair. Electrical* has a looser connection with the physical power of electricity, being mainly used to characterize general concepts associated with the subject or the people and activities involved in its study: *electrical engineer; electrical design.*

electrical engineering *n. Abbr.* **E.E.** The study of the design and application of circuitry and equipment for power generation and distribution, machine control, and communications. —**electrical engineer** *n.*

electric blanket *n.* A blanket heated by means of internal electric wiring.

electric blue *n.* A metallic blue.

electric chair *n.* **1.** A chair used to restrain and electrocute a person sentenced to death. **2.** The punishment of death by electrocution. **3.** Execution by means of electrocution.

electric charge *n. Electricity.* **Charge** *(see).*

electric constant *n. Symbol* **ε₀** The permittivity of free space, having the value 8.854×10^{-12} farad per meter. Also called "absolute permittivity."

electric current *n. Electricity.* **Current** *(see).*

electric displacement *n.* The product of the electric field strength and the absolute permittivity. Also called "electric flux density."

electric eel *n.* A long, eellike freshwater fish, *Electrophorus electricus,* of northern South America, having organs capable of producing a powerful electric discharge.

electric eye *n.* A **photoelectric cell** *(see),* especially when used as a sensor for an automatic switch.

electric fence *n.* A fence, usually consisting of a single strand of wire, that is charged with electricity.

electric field *n.* A region of space characterized by the existence of a force that is experienced by a stationary charged particle placed at any point within it.

electric field strength *n.* The strength of an electric field equal to the force experienced by a stationary charge within the field divided by the charge. It is measured in volts per meter.

electric flux *n.* The integral over a designated surface of the component of electric displacement normal to the surface.

electric flux density *n.* Electric displacement.

electric furnace *n.* An industrial or laboratory furnace heated by an electric arc, electric induction, or electric resistance.

electric guitar *n.* A guitar that transmits sounds to an amplifier by means of an electronic pickup placed under the strings.

e·lec·tri·cian (ĭ-lĕk′trĭsh′ən, ē′lĕk-) *n. Abbr.* **elec., elect.** A person whose occupation is the installation, maintenance, repair, or operation of electrical equipment and circuitry.

e·lec·tric·i·ty (ĭ-lĕk′trĭs′ə-tē, ē′lĕk-) *n. Abbr.* **elec., elect. 1.** The class of physical phenomena arising from the existence and interactions of positively and negatively charged particles. **2.** The physical science of such phenomena. **3.** Electric current used or regarded as a source of power. **4.** Intense emotional excitement.

electric lamp *n.* A lamp that uses electricity to produce light.

electric light *n.* **1.** An electric lamp. **2.** Light that is produced electrically.

electric moment *n.* The **dipole moment** *(see)* of an electric dipole.

electric motor *n.* A device for converting electrical energy directly

---

electric motor

THE PRINCIPLE OF THE ELECTRIC MOTOR

How magnets and electric current produce continuous rotary motion

An electric motor utilizes the basic principle of magnetism—that like poles repel, whereas unlike poles attract: two north magnetic poles or two south poles will repel each other; a north pole and a south pole will attract each other. In a motor, current is passed through a coil of wire, which sets up a magnetic field. This field is made to interact with another magnetic field producing rotary motion as the magnetic poles attract or repel each other. Thus in a simple electric motor (below) at least two coils are wound around the poles of an armature that is mounted on an axle between the poles of a stationary magnet. When a direct current is supplied to the coils, they effectively become magnets and the armature turns on its axle to align its north pole with the stationary magnet's south pole. A commutator then changes the polarity of the armature, which turns further to align its new north pole with the stationary magnet's south pole.

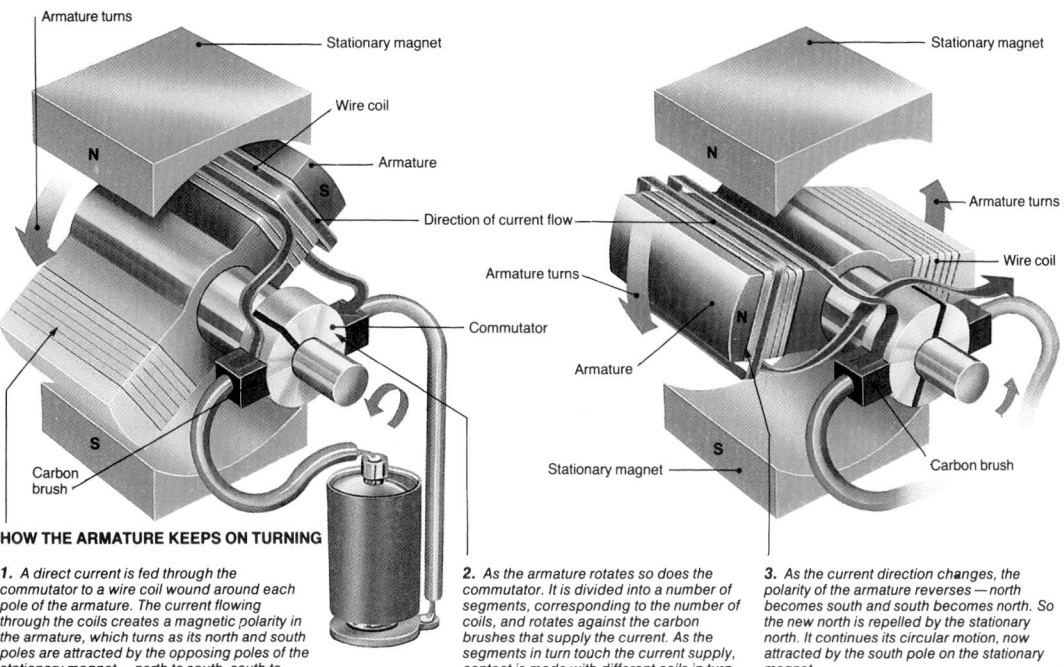

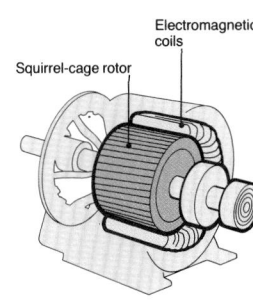

INDUCTION MOTOR *The rotary induction motor (above) works on the principle of electromagnetic conduction: whenever a conductor moves through a magnetic field, a current is induced in it. The rotor of the motor is a cylinder of metal bars that is known as a squirrel cage. Surrounding the cage are the coils of an electromagnet. When alternating current is fed to the coils, a rotating magnetic field is set up. It induces a second magnetic field, in the squirrel cage, which then 'chases" the rotating field.*

HOW THE ARMATURE KEEPS ON TURNING

1. A direct current is fed through the commutator to a wire coil wound around each pole of the armature. The current flowing through the coils creates a magnetic polarity in the armature, which turns as its north and south poles are attracted by the opposing poles of the stationary magnet—north to south, south to north

2. As the armature rotates so does the commutator. It is divided into a number of segments, corresponding to the number of coils, and rotates against the carbon brushes that supply the current. As the segments in turn touch the current supply, contact is made with different coils in turn and the current changes direction

3. As the current direction changes, the polarity of the armature reverses—north becomes south and south becomes north. So the new north is repelled by the stationary north. It continues its circular motion, now attracted by the south pole on the stationary magnet

into mechanical energy by electromagnetic induction, having a fixed part (the stator), which produces a magnetic field, and a rotating coil or conductor (the rotor), which moves under the influence of an induced force. See **induction motor, synchronous motor, linear motor.**

electric needle *n.* A cutting instrument used in surgery and powered by a high-frequency current.

electric organ *n.* **1.** *Music.* An organ operated by electricity. **2.** A group of cells in some fishes, such as the electric eel and electric ray, that generate electricity.

electric ray *n.* Any of various fishes of the family Torpedinidae, having a rounded body and a pair of electric organs capable of producing a fairly strong electric discharge. Also called "numbfish."

e·lec·tri·fy (ĭ-lĕk′trə-fī′) *tr.v.* **-fied, -fying, -fies.** **1.** To produce electric charge on or in (a conductor). **2. a.** To wire or otherwise equip (a building, for example) for the use of electric power. **b.** To convert (a railway system, for example) to enable it to operate by electricity. **c.** To provide with electric power. **3.** To thrill, startle greatly, or shock. [ELECTRI(C) + -FY.] —**e·lec·tri·fi·a·ble** *adj.* —**e·lec·tri·fi·ca·tion** *n.* —**e·lec·tri·fi·er** *n.*

e·lec·tro (ĭ-lĕk′trō) *n., pl.* **-tros.** **1. Electroplate** (see). **2. Electrotype** (see).

electro-, electr– *prefix.* Indicates: **1.** Electric; for example, **electromagnet, electrode.** **2.** Electrically; for example, **electrocute, electrograph.** **3.** Electrolysis; for example, **electrolyte.** [New Latin, from Latin *ēlectrum,* amber, from Greek *ēlektron.* See **electric.**]

e·lec·tro·a·cous·tics (ĭ-lĕk′trō-ə-kōō′stĭks) *n. Used with a singular verb.* The science of the interaction or interconversion of electric and acoustic phenomena. —**e·lec·tro·a·cous·tic** *adj.* —**e·lec·tro·a·cous·ti·cal·ly** *adv.*

e·lec·tro·a·nal·y·sis (ĭ-lĕk′trō-ə-năl′ə-sĭs) *n., pl.* **-ses** (-sēz′). Chemical analysis using electrolytic techniques. —**e·lec·tro·an·a·lyt·ic** (ĭ-lĕk′trō-ăn′ə-lĭt′ĭk), **e·lec·tro·an·a·lyt·i·cal** (-ĭ-kəl) *adj.*

e·lec·tro·car·di·o·gram (ĭ-lĕk′trō-kär′dē-ə-grăm′) *n. Abbr.* **ECG, EKG.** The curve traced by an electrocardiograph, used to diagnose heart disease.

e·lec·tro·car·di·o·graph (ĭ-lĕk′trō-kär′dē-ə-grăf′, -grăf′) *n. Abbr.* **ECG, EKG.** An instrument used to record electric potentials associated with the electric currents that initiate the heartbeat. —**e·lec·tro·car·di·o·graph·ic** (ĭ-lĕk′trō-kär′dē-ə-grăf′ĭk) *adj.* —**e·lec·tro·car·di·og·ra·phy** (ĭ-lĕk′trō-kär′dē-ŏg′rə-fē) *n.*

e·lec·tro·chem·i·cal series (ĭ-lĕk′trō-kĕm′ĭ-kəl) *n.* The **electromotive series** (see).

e·lec·tro·chem·is·try (ĭ-lĕk′trō-kĕm′ĭ-strē) *n.* The science of the interaction or interconversion of electric and chemical phenomena. —**e·lec·tro·chem·i·cal** *adj.* —**e·lec·tro·chem·i·cal·ly** *adv.* —**e·lec·tro·chem·ist** *n.*

e·lec·tro·co·ag·u·la·tion (ĭ-lĕk′trō-kō-ăg′yə-lā′shən) *n. Medicine.* The use of a high-frequency electric current to coagulate tissue so that bloodless incisions can be made during operations.

e·lec·tro·con·vul·sive therapy (ĭ-lĕk′trō-kən-vŭl′sĭv) *n. Abbr.* **ECT, E.C.T.** Treatment of certain mental disorders by passing an electric current through the brain to cause a convulsion.

e·lec·tro·cute (ĭ-lĕk′trə-kyōōt′) *tr.v.* **-cuted, -cuting, -cutes.** To kill with electricity; especially, to execute (a condemned criminal) by means of a high-voltage electric current. [ELECTRO- + (EXE)CUTE.] —**e·lec·tro·cu·tion** *n.*

e·lec·trode (ĭ-lĕk′trōd′) *n.* **1.** A solid electric conductor through which an electric current enters or leaves a medium such as an electrolyte, a nonmetallic solid, a molten metal, a gas, or a vacuum. **2.** A collector or emitter of electric charge or electric-charge carriers, as in a semiconducting device. [ELECTR(O)- + -ODE.]

e·lec·tro·de·pos·it (ĭ-lĕk′trō-dĭ-pŏz′ĭt) *tr.v.* **-ited, -iting, -its.** To deposit (a dissolved or suspended substance) on an electrode by electrolysis. ~*n.* The substance so deposited. —**e·lec·tro·dep·o·si·tion** (ĭ-lĕk′trō-dĕp′ə-zĭsh′ən, -dē′pə-zĭsh′ən) *n.*

e·lec·tro·di·al·y·sis (ĭ-lĕk′trō-dī-ăl′ə-sĭs) *n., pl.* **-ses** (-sēz′). Dialysis at a rate speeded by the application of an electric potential across the dialysis membrane, used especially to remove electrolytes from a colloidal suspension.

e·lec·tro·dy·nam·ics (ĭ-lĕk′trō-dī-năm′ĭks) *n. Used with a singular verb.* The physics of the relationship between electric, magnetic, and mechanical phenomena. —**e·lec·tro·dy·nam·ic** *adj.*

e·lec·tro·dy·na·mom·e·ter (ĭ-lĕk′trō-dī′nə-mŏm′ə-tər) *n.* An instrument that uses the interaction of the magnetic fields of fixed and moving sets of coils to measure current, voltage, or power.

e·lec·tro·en·ceph·a·lo·gram (ĭ-lĕk′trō-ĕn-sĕf′ə-lə-grăm′) *n. Abbr.* **EEG** A graphic record of the electrical activity of the brain as recorded by an electroencephalograph. Also called "encephalogram."

e·lec·tro·en·ceph·a·lo·graph (ĭ-lĕk′trō-ĕn-sĕf′ə-lə-grăf′, -grăf′) *n. Abbr.* **EEG** An instrument that records the electrical activity of the brain. —**e·lec·tro·en·ceph·a·lo·graph·ic** (ĭ-lĕk′trō-ĕn-sĕf′ə-lə-grăf′ĭk) *adj.* —**e·lec·tro·en·ceph·a·log·ra·phy** (ĭ-lĕk′trō-ĕn-sĕf′ə-lŏg′rə-fē) *n.*

e·lec·tro·form (ĭ-lĕk′trə-fôrm′) *tr.v.* **-formed, -forming, -forms.** To produce or reproduce by electrodeposition in a mold. [ELECTRO- + -FORM.]

e·lec·tro·gen·e·sis (ĭ-lĕk′trō-jĕn′ə-sĭs) *n.* The production of electrical activity, especially that produced in living tissue. —**e·lec·tro·gen·ic** (ĭ-lĕk′trō-jĕn′ĭk) *adj.*

e·lec·tro·graph (ĭ-lĕk′trə-grăf′, -grăf′) *n.* **1.** Any electrically pro-

duced graph or tracing. **2.** Equipment used to produce such graphs or tracings in facsimile transmission. **3.** A visual record of the composition of a metal surface obtained by placing the surface on a paper soaked in an electrolyte and passing a current from the surface through the paper to an electrode placed on the other side of the paper. [ELECTRO- + -GRAPH.]

e·lec·tro·ki·net·ics (ĭ-lĕk′trō-kĭ-nĕt′ĭks) *n. Used with a singular verb.* The electrodynamics of heating effects and of current distribution in electric networks. —**e·lec·tro·ki·net·ic** *adj.*

e·lec·tro·lu·mi·nes·cence (ĭ-lĕk′trō-lōō′mə-nĕs′əns) *n.* **1.** The direct conversion of electric energy to light by a solid phosphor subjected to an alternating electric field. **2.** The emission of light caused by electric discharge in a gas. —**e·lec·tro·lu·mi·nes·cent** *adj.*

e·lec·trol·y·sis (ĭ-lĕk′trŏl′ə-sĭs, ē′lĕk-) *n.* **1.** Chemical change, especially decomposition, produced in an electrolyte by an electric current. **2.** Destruction of living tissue, as of hair roots, by an electric current. [ELECTRO- + -LYSIS.]

e·lec·tro·lyte (ĭ-lĕk′trə-līt′) *n.* A substance that dissociates into ions in solution or when fused, thereby becoming electrically conducting. [ELECTRO- + -LYTE.]

e·lec·tro·lyt·ic (ĭ-lĕk′trə-lĭt′ĭk) *adj.* **1. a.** Of or pertaining to electrolysis. **b.** Produced by electrolysis. **2.** Of or pertaining to an electrolyte.

electrolytic cell *n.* **1.** A cell containing an electrolyte through which an externally generated electric current is passed by a system of electrodes in order to produce an electrochemical reaction. **2.** A cell containing an electrolyte in which an electrochemical reaction produces an electromotive force.

electrolytic gas *n.* A gas formed by the electrolysis of water, consisting of two parts of hydrogen and one part of water.

e·lec·tro·lyze (ĭ-lĕk′trō-līz′) *tr.v.* **-lyzed, -lyzing, -lyzes.** To decompose by electrolysis. [Back-formation from ELECTROLYSIS.]

e·lec·tro·mag·net (ĭ-lĕk′trō-măg′nĭt) *n.* A magnet consisting essentially of a soft-iron core wound with a current-carrying coil of insulated wire, the current in which produces the magnetization of the core.

e·lec·tro·mag·net·ic (ĭ-lĕk′trō-măg-nĕt′ĭk) *adj.* Of or exhibiting electromagnetism. —**e·lec·tro·mag·net·i·cal·ly** *adv.*

electromagnetic field *n.* The field of force associated with an accelerating electric charge, having both electric and magnetic components and containing a definite amount of electromagnetic energy.

electromagnetic interaction *n.* A form of interaction between particles that are charged as a result of their electric or magnetic fields or the exchange of virtual photons between them. Compare **strong interaction, weak interaction, gravitational interaction.**

electromagnetic pump *n.* A pump for moving liquid metals in which the pipe containing the liquid metal is placed between the poles of an electromagnet and a current is passed through the liquid metal.

electromagnetic radiation *n.* Radiation consisting of an electric field and a magnetic field perpendicular to each other and to the direction of propagation. The speed of propagation in a vacuum is 2.9979 x 10⁸ meters per second.

electromagnetic spectrum *n.* The entire range of radiation extending in frequency approximately from 10^{21} hertz to 0 hertz (or, in corresponding wavelengths, from 10^{-13} meter to infinity) and including, in order of decreasing frequency, gamma rays, x-rays, ultraviolet radiation, visible light, infrared radiation, microwaves, and radio waves.

electromagnetic unit *n.* Any of a system of units for electricity and magnetism based on a system of equations in which the magnetic constant is taken as unity and by means of which the abampere is defined as the fundamental unit of current.

electromagnetic wave *n.* A wave propagating as a periodic disturbance of the electromagnetic field and having a frequency in the electromagnetic spectrum.

e·lec·tro·mag·net·ism (ĭ-lĕk′trō-măg′nə-tĭz′əm) *n.* **1.** Magnetism arising from an accelerating electric charge. **2.** The physics of electricity and magnetism.

e·lec·tro·me·chan·i·cal (ĭ-lĕk′trō-mĭ-kăn′ĭ-kəl) *adj.* Of or designating a mechanical device that is operated by electricity. —**e·lec·tro·me·chan·i·cal·ly** *adv.*

e·lec·trom·er·ism (ĭ-lĕk′trŏm′ə-rĭz′əm, ē′lĕk-) *n. Chemistry.* A form of tautomerism in which the isomers differ in the way in which electric charge is distributed in their molecules. [ELECTRO- + (ISO)MERISM.]

e·lec·tro·met·al·lur·gy (ĭ-lĕk′trō-mĕt′ə-lûr′jē) *n.* The use of electricity to purify metals or to reduce metallic compounds to metals. —**e·lec·tro·met·al·lur·gi·cal** (ĭ-lĕk′trō-mĕt′ə-lûr′jĭ-kəl) *adj.*

e·lec·trom·e·ter (ĭ-lĕk′trŏm′ə-tər, ē′lĕk-) *n.* An instrument for detecting or measuring potential differences, electric charge, or, indirectly, electric current by means of mechanical forces exerted between electrically charged bodies. [ELECTRO- + -METER.]

e·lec·tro·mo·tive (ĭ-lĕk′trō-mō′tĭv) *adj.* Of, pertaining to, or producing electric current.

electromotive force *n. Abbr.* **emf, EMF** The energy per unit charge that is converted reversibly from chemical, mechanical, or other forms of energy into electrical energy in a conversion device such as a battery or dynamo. It is measured in volts.

electromotive series *n.* A series of metals, with hydrogen included, arranged in order of their electrode potentials. The series represents the order in which metals replace one another from their salts, those high in the series replacing those lower down. The series of the commoner metals is Na, Mg, Al, Zn, Fe, Co, Ni, Sn, Pb, H, Cu, Hg, Ag, Au. Also called "electrochemical series."

e·lec·tro·my·o·gram (ĭ-lĕk′trō-mī′ə-grăm′) *n.* A record of the electrical activity of a muscle obtained using an electromyograph.

e·lec·tro·my·o·graph (ĭ-lĕk′trō-mī′ə-grăf′, -gräf′) *n.* An instrument that records the electrical activity of a muscle by means of electrodes inserted into the muscle fiber. **—e·lec·tro·my·og·ra·phy** (ĭ-lĕk′trō-mī-ŏg′rə-fē) *n.*

e·lec·tron (ĭ-lĕk′trŏn′) *n. Abbr.* **e** A subatomic particle in the lepton family having a rest mass of 9.1096 $\times$ 10^{-28} gram and a unit negative electric charge of approximately 1.602 $\times$ 10^{-19} coulomb. [ELECTR(O)- + -ON.]

electron camera *n.* A device forming part of a television camera in which an optical image is converted into an electrical signal.

e·lec·tro·neg·a·tive (ĭ-lĕk′trō-nĕg′ə-tĭv) *adj.* **1.** Having a negative electric charge. **2.** Tending to attract electrons to form a chemical bond. **—e·lec·tro·neg·a·tiv·i·ty** (ĭ-lĕk′trō-nĕg′ə-tĭv′ə-tē) *n.*

electron gun *n.* An electron-emitting electrode and associated elements, especially in a cathode-ray tube, that produce a beam of accelerated electrons.

e·lec·tron·ic (ĭ-lĕk′trŏn′ĭk, ē′lĕk-) *adj.* **1.** Of or pertaining to electrons. **2.** Of, pertaining to, based on, operated by, or otherwise involving the controlled conduction of electrons or other charge carriers, especially in a vacuum, gas, or semiconducting material. **3.** Of or pertaining to electronics. **—e·lec·tron·i·cal·ly** *adv.*

electronic data processing *n. Abbr.* **EDP** Data processing in which electronic computers are used to manipulate the information.

electronic music *n.* **1.** Music produced entirely or in part by manipulating natural or artificial sounds with tape recorders or other electronic devices. **2.** Music consisting of sounds produced by oscillating electronic signals.

e·lec·tron·ics (ĭ-lĕk′trŏn′ĭks, ē′lĕk-) *n. Used with a singular verb.* **1.** The science and technology of electronic phenomena. **2.** The commercial industry of electronic devices and systems.

electron lens *n.* Any of various devices that use an electric or a magnetic field to focus a beam of electrons.

electron micrograph *n.* A micrograph made by an electron microscope.

electron microscope *n.* Any of a class of microscopes that use a beam of electrons rather than visible light to produce magnified images, especially of objects having dimensions smaller than the wavelengths of visible light, with linear magnification up to or exceeding a million (10^6). See **scanning electron microscope.**

electron multiplier *n.* A vacuum tube in which a single electron produces a large number of secondary electrons by collision with an anode, the process generally being repeated through a number of stages to achieve great amplification.

electron optics *n. Used with a singular verb.* The science of the control of electron motion by electron lenses in systems or under conditions analogous to those involving or affecting visible light.

electron pair *n.* **1.** Any two electrons functioning or regarded as functioning in concert; especially, two electrons shared by two atoms joined by a covalent chemical bond. **2.** The combination of an electron and a positron as produced by a high-energy photon. Also called "pair." See **pair production.**

electron probe microanalysis *n. Chemistry.* A method of analyzing tiny quantities (as little as 10^{-13} gram) of material by bombarding the specimen with a finely focused beam of electrons and examining the resulting x-ray emission spectrum.

electron spin resonance *n. Abbr.* **ESR** *Chemistry.* A method of examining the molecular structure of paramagnetic substances by subjecting them to high-frequency radiation in a strong magnetic field. Changes in the spin of unpaired electrons in the molecules cause radiation to be absorbed at certain characteristic frequencies.

electron telescope *n.* An astronomical telescope that converts infrared radiation emitted by the planets into an optical image.

electron tube *n.* A sealed enclosure, either highly evacuated or containing a controlled quantity of gas, in which electrons can be made sufficiently mobile to act as the principal carriers of current between at least one pair of electrodes, often under the control of one or more additional electrodes.

electron volt *n. Abbr.* **eV** A unit of energy equal to the energy acquired by an electron falling through a potential difference of one volt, approximately 1.602 $\times$ 10^{-19} joule.

e·lec·tro·phil·ic (ĭ-lĕk′trō-fĭl′ĭk) *n. Chemistry.* Designating an atom, molecule, or ion that behaves as an electron acceptor. [ELECTRO- + -PHIL(E) + -IC.]

e·lec·tro·pho·re·sis (ĭ-lĕk′trō-fə-rē′sĭs) *n.* The motion of charged particles, especially colloidal particles, through a relatively stationary liquid under the influence of an applied electric field provided, in general, by immersed electrodes. Also called "cataphoresis." [ELECTRO- + -PHORESIS.]

e·lec·troph·o·rus (ĭ-lĕk′trŏf′ər-əs, ē′lĕk-) *n., pl.* **-ori** (-ə-rī′). An apparatus for generating static electricity, consisting of a disk that is given a negative charge by friction and a metal plate that is charged by induction when in contact with the disk. [ELECTRO- + -PHOROUS.]

e·lec·tro·plate (ĭ-lĕk′trə-plāt′) *tr.v.* **-plated, -plating, -plates.** To coat or cover with a thin layer of metal by electrodeposition.
∼n. **1.** An article that has been electroplated. **2.** Electroplated articles collectively. Also called "electro."

e·lec·tro·pos·i·tive (ĭ-lĕk′trō-pŏz′ə-tĭv) *adj.* **1.** Having a positive electric charge. **2.** Tending to release electrons to form a chemical bond.

e·lec·tro·scope (ĭ-lĕk′trə-skōp′) *n.* An instrument used to detect the presence, the sign, and in some configurations the magnitude of an electric charge by the mutual attraction or repulsion of metal foils. [ELECTRO- + -SCOPE.]

e·lec·tro·stat·ic (ĭ-lĕk′trō-stăt′ĭk) *adj.* **1. a.** Of or pertaining to stationary electric charges. **b.** Produced or caused by such charges. **2.** Of or pertaining to electrostatics. **—e·lec·tro·stat·i·cal·ly** *adv.*

electrostatic generator *n.* Any of various devices, including the electrophorus, the Wimshurst machine, and especially the **Van de Graaff generator** *(see),* that generate high voltages by accumulating large quantities of electric charge.

electrostatic precipitation *n.* The removal of particles suspended in a gas by electrostatic charging and subsequent precipitation onto a collector in a strong electric field.

e·lec·tro·stat·ics (ĭ-lĕk′trō-stăt′ĭks) *n. Used with a singular verb.* The branch of physics dealing with electrostatic phenomena.

electrostatic unit *n. Abbr.* **esu** Any of a system of units for electricity and magnetism based on a system of equations in which the electric constant is defined as unity and by means of which a fundamental unit of charge is defined.

e·lec·tro·stric·tion (ĭ-lĕk′trō-strĭk′shən) *n.* A change in the dimensions of a dielectric as the result of an applied electric field.

e·lec·tro·sur·ger·y (ĭ-lĕk′trō-sûr′jə-rē) *n.* Surgery using electrical methods, as in cauterization.

e·lec·tro·ther·a·peu·tics (ĭ-lĕk′trō-thĕr′ə-pyōō′tĭks) *n. Used with a singular verb.* The branch of medicine concerned with the use of electrotherapy. **—e·lec·tro·ther·a·peu·tic** *adj.*

e·lec·tro·ther·a·py (ĭ-lĕk′trō-thĕr′ə-pē) *n.* Medical therapy using electric currents, especially for stimulating muscles and nerves. **—e·lec·tro·ther·a·pist** *n.*

e·lec·tro·ther·mal (ĭ-lĕk′trō-thûr′məl) *adj.* Of or involving both electricity and heat; especially, producing heat electrically.

e·lec·trot·o·nus (ĭ-lĕk′trŏt′ə-nəs, ē′lĕk-) *n. Physiology.* The alteration in excitability and conductivity of a nerve caused by the passage of an electric current. [ELECTRO- + TONUS.] **—e·lec·tro·ton·ic** (ĭ-lĕk′trō-tŏn′ĭk) *adj.*

e·lec·tro·type (ĭ-lĕk′trə-tīp′) *n.* **1.** A duplicate metal plate used in letterpress printing, made by electroplating a lead or plastic mold of the original plate. Also called "electro." **2.** The process of making such a plate.
∼tr.v. **electrotyped, -typing, -types.** To make an electrotype of. **—e·lec·tro·typ·er** *n.* **—e·lec·tro·typ·ic** (ĭ-lĕk′trə-tĭp′ĭk) *adj.*

e·lec·tro·va·lence (ĭ-lĕk′trō-vā′ləns) *n.* Also **e·lec·tro·va·len·cy** (-lən-sē). **1.** Valence characterized by the transfer of electrons from atoms of one element to atoms of another. **2.** The number of electric charges lost or gained by an atom in such a transfer. **—e·lec·tro·va·lent** *adj.*

electrovalent bond *n. Chemistry.* An **ionic bond** *(see).*

e·lec·trum (ĭ-lĕk′trəm) *n.* An alloy of varying proportions of silver and gold, especially one used in ancient metallurgy. [Middle English *electrum,* from Latin *ēlectrum,* amber, from Greek.]

e·lec·tu·ar·y (ĭ-lĕk′chōō-ĕr′ē) *n., pl.* **-ies.** A drug mixed with sugar and water or honey into a pasty mass suitable for oral administration. [Middle English *electuarie,* from Late Latin *ēlectuārium,* something that melts in the mouth.]

el·ee·mos·y·nar·y (ĕl′ə-mŏs′ə-nĕr′ē, ĕl′ē-ə-) *adj.* **1.** Of or pertaining to alms or the giving of alms; charitable. **2.** Dependent upon or supported by alms. **3.** Contributed as alms or charity. [Medieval Latin *eleēmosynārius,* from Late Latin *eleēmosyna,* ALMS.]

el·e·gance (ĕl′ə-gəns) *n.* **1. a.** Refinement and grace in movement, appearance, or manners. **b.** Tasteful opulence in form, decoration, or presentation. **2.** Something that is elegant.

el·e·gant (ĕl′ə-gənt) *adj.* **1.** Characterized by or exhibiting elegance; refined; graceful. **2.** Scientifically exact and simple: *an elegant mathematical proof.* [Old French, from Latin *ēlegāns* (stem *ēlegant-*), choice, fine, from *ēligere,* to choose out, select : *ex-,* out + *legere,* to choose.] **—el·e·gant·ly** *adv.*

el·e·gi·ac (ĕl′ə-jī′ăk′, ĭ-lē′jē-ăk′) *adj.* **1. a.** Pertaining to an elegy. **b.** Expressing sorrow; mournful. **2.** Composed in classical distichs, having the first line a dactylic hexameter and the second a pentameter: *an elegiac couplet.* [French *élégiaque,* from Late Latin *elegīacus,* from Greek *elegeiakos,* from *elegeia,* ELEGY.]

el·e·gist (ĕl′ə-jĭst) *n.* The composer of an elegy or elegies.

e·le·git (ĭ-lē′jĭt) *n. Law.* A writ of execution against a debtor by which the plaintiff may enter the debtor's land until the debtor can settle his debt. [Latin *ēlēgit,* "he has chosen" (the first word in a phrase often used in such writs), from *ēligere,* to choose out. See **elegant.**]

el·e·gize (ĕl′ə-jīz′) *v.* **-gized, -gizing, -gizes.** *—intr.* To compose an elegy. *—tr.* To compose an elegy upon or for.

el·e·gy (ĕl′ə-jē) *n., pl.* **-gies.** **1.** A poem composed in elegiac distichs. **2.** A mournful poem; especially, a poem composed to lament one who is dead. **3.** A mournful musical composition. [French *élégie,* from Latin *elegīa,* from Greek *elegeia,* from *elegos,* lament, probably from Phrygian.]

Elektra. Variant of **Electra** (daughter of Agamemnon).

el·e·ment (ĕl′ə-mənt) *n. Abbr.* **elem.** **1. a.** A fundamental, essential, or irreducible constituent of a composite entity. **b.** A part of a larger unit, especially one with special characteristics, such as a military or social grouping. **c.** A factor affecting a decision, condition, or the like: *a stubborn element in his personality.* **2. a.** A basic

electrostatic generator *When the handle is turned on this 18th-century electrostatic generator, the silk cloth rubs against the glass cylinder, producing static electricity by friction.*

elephant *A lone African bull elephant by a watering hole in Manyara National Park, Tanzania. Its larger ears and humped back differentiate it from the Indian species.*

elephant seal *Bull elephant seals like this one may be up to 6 meters (20 feet) long and weigh nearly 4 tons. They fight one another in the breeding season to win a harem of cow seals. The elephant seal's name comes not just from its size but also from the short trunk that hangs over the bull's mouth.*

assumption or proposition. **b. elements.** The first principles of a subject: *elements of geometry.* **3.** *Mathematics.* **a.** A member of a set. **b.** A point, line, or plane. **c.** A part of a geometric configuration, such as an angle in a triangle. **d.** The generatrix of a geometric figure. **e.** Any of the terms in the rectangular array of terms that constitute a matrix or determinant. **4.** *Chemistry & Physics.* A substance composed of atoms having an identical number of protons in each nucleus. **5.** *Astronomy.* A numerical quantity used in describing the orbit of a planet or satellite. **6.** Earth, air, fire, or water regarded as a fundamental constituent of the universe in ancient and medieval cosmologies. **7. elements.** The forces that collectively constitute the weather; especially, cold, wind, rain, or other harsh conditions. **8.** An environment naturally occupied, preferred, or regarded as being preferred by an individual. **9.** A very small amount; a hint: *an element of doubt as to his success.* **10.** The resistance wire in an electrical appliance such as a stove or heater. **11. elements.** The bread and wine of the Eucharist. [Middle English, from Old French, from Latin *elementum,* rudiment, first principle, perhaps from Etruscan.]

el·e·men·tal (ĕl′ə-mĕnt′l) *adj.* **1.** Of, pertaining to, or being an element. **2.** Fundamental or essential; basic. **3.** Resembling a force of nature in power or effect. **—el·e·men·tal·ly** *adv.*

el·e·men·ta·ry (ĕl′ə-mĕn′tə-rē, -trē) *adj. Abbr.* **elem. 1.** Fundamental, essential, or irreducible. **2. a.** Rudimentary; simple. **b.** Of, involving, or introducing the fundamental or simplest aspects of a subject: *an elementary text.* **—el·e·men·tar·i·ly** (ĕl′ə-mĕn-târ′ə-lē) *adv.* **—el·e·men·ta·ri·ness** *n.*

elementary particle *n.* **1.** Any of the four stable particles, the photon, the electron, the neutrino, and the proton, regarded as indivisible. **2.** Any member of the lepton, meson, or baryon family that may decay into a stable particle or particles. Also called "fundamental particle."

elementary school *n.* A school attended for the first six to eight years of a child's school career. Also called "grade school," "grammar school."

el·e·mi (ĕl′ə-mē) *n., pl.* **-mis.** Any of various oily resins derived from certain tropical trees, especially *Canarium luzonicum,* of the Philippines, used in making varnishes and inks. [Spanish *elemí,* from Arabic *elemī,* dialectal variant of *al-lāmi,* the elemi.]

e·len·chus (ĭ-lĕng′kəs) *n., pl.* **-chi** (-kī′, -kē′). **1.** *Logic.* A refutation that disproves an opponent's conclusion or establishes a proposition contrary to his. **2.** A syllogistic refutation. [Latin, from Greek *elenkhos,* refutation, from *elenkhein,* to refute.]

e·lenc·tic (ĭ-lĕngk′tĭk) *adj. Logic.* Refuting by proving the opposite. Compare **deictic.** [Greek *elenktikos,* from *elenkhein,* to refute. See **elenchus.**]

el·e·phant (ĕl′ə-fənt) *n.* **1.** Either of two very large herbivorous mammals, *Elephas maximus,* of south-central Asia, or *Loxodonta africana,* of Africa, having thick, almost hairless skin, a long, flexible prehensile trunk, upper incisors forming long, curved tusks, and, in the African species, large, fan-shaped ears. **2.** Any of several animals related to the elephant, including some species now extinct. [Middle English *elifaunt, elephan,* from Old French *olifant, elifant,* from Vulgar Latin *olifantus* (unattested), from Latin *elephantus,* from Greek *elephas* (stem *elephant-*), ivory, elephant, probably of non-Indo-European origin.]

elephant bird *n.* A large, extinct, flightless bird of the genus *Aepyornis,* remains of which have been found in Madagascar.

Elephant Butte Dam. A dam across the Rio Grande in southwestern New Mexico, 1,674 feet long and over 300 feet high, forming Elephant Butte Reservoir.

el·e·phant-ear (ĕl′ə-fənt-îr′) *n.* Also **el·e·phant's-ear** (ĕl′ə-fənts-). **1.** A plant, *Colocasia antiquorum,* native to the East Indies, having edible tubers and large leaves resembling an elephant's ears. **2.** A similar or related plant, such as the taro.

el·e·phan·ti·a·sis (ĕl′ə-fən-tī′ə-sĭs) *n.* A chronic, often extreme enlargement and hardening of the cutaneous and subcutaneous tissue, especially of the legs and the scrotum, resulting from lymphatic obstruction, and usually caused by a nematode worm, *Wuchereria bancrofti.* See **filariasis.** [Latin *elephantiāsis* : Greek *elephas,* ELEPHANT (so called because the affected skin resembles an elephant's hide) + -IASIS.]

el·e·phan·tine (ĕl′ə-făn′tēn′, -tīn′, ĕl′ə-fən-) *adj.* **1.** Of or pertaining to an elephant. **2.** Oversized and unwieldy.

elephant seal *n.* Either of two large seals, *Mirounga angustirostris* or *M. leonina,* of Pacific coastal waters of North and South America, having a trunklike proboscis. Also called "sea elephant."

elephant shrew *n.* Any insectivorous African mammal of the family Macroscelididae, having a long pointed nose and large ears.

El·eu·sin·i·an mysteries (ĕl′yo͞o-sĭn′ē-ən) *pl.n.* The ancient religious rites of spring celebrated at Eleusis in Greece in honor of the goddess Demeter.

E·leu·sis (ĭ-lo͞o′sĭs). A town in east-central Greece 16 kilometers (10 miles) east of Athens, site of the Eleusinian mysteries and the birthplace of Aeschylus.

el·e·vate (ĕl′ə-vāt′) *tr.v.* **-vated, -vating, -vates. 1.** To raise to a higher place or position; lift up. **2.** To increase the amplitude, intensity, or volume of. **3.** To promote to a higher rank. **4.** To raise to a higher moral, cultural, or intellectual level. **5.** To lift the spirits of; elate. **6.** *Roman Catholic Church.* To raise (the host or chalice) after the consecration at Mass. —See Synonyms at **lift.** [Middle English *elevaten,* from Latin *ēlevāre* : *ex-,* up + *levāre,* to lighten, raise.] **—el·e·va·to·ry** (el′ə-və-tôr′ē, -tōr′ē) *adj.*

el·e·vat·ed (ĕl′ə-vā′tĭd) *adj.* **1.** Raised above a given level. **2.** Exalted; high; lofty: *an elevated tone.* —See Synonyms at **high.**

elevated railway *n.* A railway that operates on a raised structure in order to permit passage of vehicles or pedestrians beneath it.

el·e·va·tion (ĕl′ə-vā′shən) *n. Abbr.* **el., elev. 1.** The act of elevating or the condition of being elevated. **2.** An elevated place or position. **3.** The height to which something is elevated above a reference point, especially above the ground. **4.** Loftiness of thought or feeling. **5.** A scale drawing of the side, front, or rear of a given structure. **6.** *Geography & Astronomy.* **Altitude** *(see).* **7.** *Surveying.* The angular distance between the plane through a point and an object above it. **8. a.** A leap, as by a dancer, in which the performer appears to be suspended in midair. **b.** The ability of a performer to execute an elevation.

el·e·va·tor (ĕl′ə-vā′tər) *n.* **1. a.** A platform or enclosure raised and lowered in a vertical shaft to transport freight or passengers. **b.** The platform or enclosure with its operating equipment, motor, cables, and accessories. **2.** A mechanism, used for hoisting material, that usually consists of buckets or scoops attached to a conveyor. **3.** A granary equipped with devices for hoisting and discharging grain. **4.** A movable control surface, usually attached to the horizontal stabilizer of an aircraft, used to produce up or down motion.

e·lev·en (ĭ-lĕv′ən) *n.* **1. a.** The cardinal number that is one more than ten. **b.** A symbol representing this, such as 11, XI, or xi. **2.** A set made up of eleven persons or things. **3.** The eleventh in a series. **4.** A size, as in clothing, designated as eleven. **5.** Eleven hours after midnight or midday; eleven o'clock. **6.** In sports, especially soccer, cricket, and hockey, a team of eleven players. [Middle English *ellevene, enlevene,* Old English *endleofan,* from Germanic : *aninaz* (unattested), ONE + *-lif* (unattested), probably "left" (that is, one left over after ten).] **—e·lev·en** *adj.*

e·lev·en-plus (ĭ-lĕv′ən-plŭs′) *n.* Formerly, an examination taken by children around the age of 11 in British state schools for admission to grammar school.

e·lev·ens·es (ĭ-lĕv′ən-zĭz) *pl.n. Used with a singular verb. British.* A snack, often accompanied by coffee or tea, taken at about 11 o'clock in the morning.

e·lev·enth (ĭ-lĕv′ənth) *n.* **1.** The ordinal number 11 in a series. **2.** One of 11 equal parts. **—e·lev·enth** *adj. & adv.*

eleventh hour *n.* The latest possible time. [By allusion to the parable (Matthew 20:1–16) in which the workers hired at the eleventh hour received the same wages as those hired earlier.]

el·e·von (ĕl′ə-vŏn′) *n.* An airplane control surface combining the functions of an elevator and an aileron. [*Elev*ator + aileron.]

elf (ĕlf) *n., pl.* **elves** (ĕlvz). **1.** In folklore, a small, manlike creature, usually represented as mischievous and having magical powers. **2.** A mischievous child. **3.** A dwarf. [Middle English *elf,* Old English *ælf,* from Germanic.]

elf·in (ĕl′fĭn) *adj.* **1.** Pertaining to or of the nature of an elf; elfish. **2.** Having physical characteristics associated with elves, especially smallness, delicacy, and slightly pointed features. [Probably from Middle English *elvene,* genitive plural of ELF.]

elf·ish (ĕl′fĭsh) *adj.* Also **elv·ish** (ĕl′vĭsh). **1.** Of or pertaining to elves; elfin. **2.** Supernatural; weird. **3.** Mischievous. **—elf·ish·ly** *adv.* **—elf·ish·ness** *n.*

elf·lock (ĕlf′lŏk′) *n.* A tangled lock of hair.

El·gar (ĕl′gär′), **Sir Edward William** (1857–1934). English composer. His works include the *Enigma Variations* (1899), two symphonies (1908, 1911), a violin concerto (1910), and a cello concerto (1919). The song *Land of Hope and Glory* is set to the first of his five *Pomp and Circumstance* marches, written between 1901 and 1930.

El·gin Marbles (ĕl′gĭn) *pl.n.* Ancient Greek sculptures from the frieze of the Parthenon and other buildings on the Acropolis in Athens, taken to England by the 7th Earl of Elgin and now in the British Museum.

El Gre·co (ĕl grĕk′ō), born Domenicos Theotocopoulos and called in Spanish "the Greek" (*c.* 1541–1614). Spanish painter born in Greece. He excelled chiefly at religious subjects, such as the masterpieces *Christ Stripped of his Garments* (1579) and the *Assumption* (1613).

e·lic·it (ĭ-lĭs′ĭt) *tr.v.* **-ited, -iting, -its. 1.** To bring or draw out (something latent). **2.** To evoke; call forth. [Latin *ēlicere* (past participle *ēlicitus*) : *ex-,* out + *lacere,* to allure, deceive (see **delight**).] **—e·lic·i·ta·tion** *n.* **—e·lic·i·tor** *n.*

e·lide (ĭ-līd′) *v.* **elided, eliding, elides.** *—tr.* **1.** To omit or slur over (a vowel or syllable) in pronunciation. **2.** To run together; confuse; blur. *—intr.* To be omitted or slurred over. [Latin *ēlīdere,* to strike out : *ex-,* out + *laedere,* to strike, hurt (see **lesion**).]

el·i·gi·ble (ĕl′ĭ-jə-bəl) *adj.* **1.** Qualified for an office, position, or other function. **2.** Worthy of choice, acceptance, adoption, or the like. **3.** Qualified and desirable, especially for marriage: *an eligible bachelor.* [Middle English, from Old French, from Late Latin *ēligibilis,* from Latin *ēligere,* to choose, ELECT.] **—el·i·gi·bil·i·ty** *n.* **—el·i·gi·ble** *n.* **—el·i·gi·bly** *adv.*

E·li·jah (ĭ-lī′jə). Also **E·li·as** (ĭ-lī′əs). Hebrew prophet of the 9th century B.C.

e·lim·i·nate (ĭ-lĭm′ə-nāt′) *tr.v.* **-nated, -nating, -nates. 1.** To get rid of; remove. **2. a.** To leave out or omit from consideration; reject. **b.** To exclude from a contest by defeating; knock out. **3.** *Mathematics.* To remove (an unknown quantity) by combining equations. **4.** *Physiology.* To excrete (waste products). **5.** To murder. Used euphemistically. [Latin *ēlīmināre,* "to drive outside the threshold" : *ex-,* out + *līmen* (stem *līmin-*), threshold (see **limen**).] **—e·lim·i·na·**

tion *n.* —**e·lim·i·na·tive** (ĭ-lĭm'ə-nā'tĭv), **e·lim·i·na·to·ry** (-nə-tôr'ē, -tōr'ē) *adj.* —**e·lim·i·na·tor** *n.*

El·i·ot (ĕl'ē-ət), **George,** pen name of Mary Ann Evans (1819–80). English novelist of the 19th-century realist tradition. Her writings include *Adam Bede* (1859), *The Mill on the Floss* (1860), *Silas Marner* (1861), and *Romola* (1862–63). Most critics consider *Middlemarch* (1871–72) to be her masterpiece.

Eliot, Thomas Stearns, known as "T.S. Eliot" (1888–1965). English poet, playwright, and critic, born in the United States. He went to London in 1914 and became a British citizen in 1927. His early poems, *Prufrock and Other Observations* (1917) and *The Waste Land* (1922), depicted the spiritual desolation of the postwar world. In 1927 he was converted to Anglo-Catholicism, and his new faith found expression in his later poetry, notably *Ash Wednesday* (1930) and *The Four Quartets* (1935–42). His most famous verse dramas are *Murder in the Cathedral* (1935), *The Family Reunion* (1939), and *The Cocktail Party* (1950). He won the Nobel Prize for literature in 1948.

Elisabethville. See **Lubumbashi.**

e·li·sion (ĭ-lĭzh'ən) *n.* **1.** The action of eliding. **2.** The omission of an unstressed vowel or syllable, as in scanning a line of verse. **3.** An omission. [Latin *ēlīsiō* (stem *ēlīsiōn-*), from *ēlīdere* (past participle *ēlīsus*), to ELIDE.]

e·lite, é·lite (ĭ-lēt', ā-lēt') *n.* **1. a.** The best, most skilled, or most privileged members of a given social group. **b.** A narrow and powerful clique. **2.** A size of type on a typewriter, allowing 12 characters to an inch. [French *élite,* from Old French *eslite,* feminine past participle of *eslire,* to choose, from Vulgar Latin *exlegere* (unattested), variant of Latin *ēligere,* to ELECT.] —**e·lite** *adj.*

e·lit·ism, é·lit·ism (ĭ-lē'tĭz'əm, ā-lē'-) *n.* **1. a.** Belief in the right to power of an elite. **b.** Rule or domination by an elite. **2.** A sense of being part of a superior or privileged group: *intellectual elitism.* —**e·lit·ist** *adj.* & *n.*

e·lix·ir (ĭ-lĭk'sər) *n.* **1.** A sweetened aromatic preparation of alcohol and water, serving as a vehicle for medicine. **2.** A medicinal potion thought to have generalized curative or restorative powers. **3.** *Alchemy.* **a.** A substance believed to have the power to transmute base metals to gold. Also called "philosopher's stone." **b.** A substance believed to have the power to cure all human disorders. Also called "panacea." **c.** A substance believed to maintain life indefinitely. Also called "elixir of life." The three substances were often regarded as one. **4.** The quintessence or underlying principle of something. [Middle English *elixir,* from Medieval Latin, from Arabic *al-iksīr,* "the elixir" : *al-,* the + *iksīr,* probably from Greek *xērion,* dry powder medicine, from *xēros,* dry.]

E·liz·a·beth[1] (ĭ-lĭz'ə-bəth). The mother of John the Baptist and wife of Zacharias, and a kinswoman of Mary. Luke 1.

Elizabeth[2], born Elizabeth Bowes-Lyon, now the Queen Mother (1900–). Queen consort of King George VI and the mother of Elizabeth II. She was the daughter of the 14th Earl of Strathmore and Kinghorne and is sometimes called Elizabeth of Glamis. She married the future king in April, 1923, when he was George, Duke of York.

Elizabeth I (1533–1603). Queen of England (1558–1603), daughter of Henry VIII and Anne Boleyn. In 1558 she succeeded the Catholic Mary I on the throne and re-established the Protestant religion in England. She survived several plots to murder her and place the Catholic Mary, Queen of Scots, on the throne. Elizabeth, who never married, kept Mary imprisoned from 1568 until her execution in 1587. In 1588 Philip of Spain began a Catholic crusade against Protestant England. The defeat of the Spanish Armada in that year was a mark of England's rising status.

Elizabeth II (1926–). Queen of Great Britain and Northern Ireland (1952–), daughter of George VI. In 1947 she married Philip Mountbatten, Duke of Edinburgh. While she was in Kenya, on a Commonwealth tour, George VI died, on February 6, 1952. Her coronation took place on June 2, 1953. National celebrations marked her silver jubilee in 1977.

E·liz·a·be·than (ĭ-lĭz'ə-bē'thən, -bĕth'ən) *adj.* Of, pertaining to, or characteristic of the reign of Elizabeth I of England.
~*n.* One living during the reign of Elizabeth I.

Elizabethan sonnet *n.* A **Shakespearean sonnet** *(see).*

elk (ĕlk) *n., pl.* **elks** or collectively **elk. 1.** A large deer, *Alces alces,* of northern regions, having large, palmate antlers, and called "moose" in North America. **2.** A North American deer, the **wapiti** *(see).* **3.** A light, pliant leather of horsehide or calfskin, tanned and finished to resemble elk hide. [Middle English *elke,* from Old Norse *elgr.*]

elk·hound (ĕlk'hound') *n.* A hunting dog of a breed developed in Scandinavia, having a grayish coat and a tail curled up over the back. Also called "Norwegian elkhound."

ell[1] (ĕl) *n.* **1.** A wing of a building at right angles to the main structure. **2.** A pipe or tube with a right-angle bend. [From its resemblance to the shape of the capital letter *L.*]

ell[2] *n.* An English linear measure equal to 45 inches, or 114 centimeters, formerly used in measuring cloth. [Middle English *elle, eln,* Old English *eln,* forearm, ell (originally about the length from the elbow to tip of the middle finger).]

el·lag·ic acid (ĭ-lăj'ĭk) *n.* A yellow crystalline compound, $C_{14}H_6O_8$, that is obtained from tannins. [French *ellagique,* from *ellag,* backward spelling of *galle,* plant gall, from Latin *galla.*]

Ellas. See **Greece.**

Elles·mere Island (ĕlz'mîr'). Most northerly part of Canada. An island in Northwest Territories, it is separated from Greenland by a narrow passage. Ellesmere Island has a small Eskimo population and a number of scientific stations.

Ellice Islands. See **Tuvalu.**

El·ling·ton (ĕl'ĭng-tən), **Edward Kennedy,** known as "Duke" (1899–1974). U.S. jazz musician and composer. He began his career in Washington, D.C., as a jazz pianist and in 1918 formed his own dance band. His best-loved compositions include *Mood Indigo* (1930), *Sophisticated Lady* (1933), and *Don't Get Around Much Anymore* (1942). He also wrote a number of longer suites for concert performances, among them *Black, Brown, and Beige* (1943) and *Liberian Suite* (1947).

el·lipse (ĭ-lĭps') *n.* **1.** A plane curve formed by: **a.** A conic section taken neither parallel to an element nor parallel to the axis of the intersected cone. **b.** The locus of points the sum of the distances of each of which from two fixed points is the same constant. **2.** Ellipsis. [Back-formation from ELLIPSIS; when an ellipse is formed from a conic section the angle made by the base of the cone and the intersecting plane is less than, or "falls short of," the angle made by the intersecting plane, which forms a parabola.]

el·lip·sis (ĭ-lĭp'sĭs) *n., pl.* **-ses** (-sēz'). **1.** *Grammar.* The omission of a word or phrase necessary for a complete syntactic construction but not necessary for understanding, as *Coming!* for *I am coming.* **2.** The use of ellipsis, especially as a literary device. **3.** A mark or series of marks (. . . or ***) used in writing or printing to indicate an omission, especially of letters or words. [Latin *ellīpsis,* from Greek *elleipsis,* a falling short, defect, from *elleipein,* to leave in or behind, leave out : *en-,* in + *leipein,* to leave.]

el·lip·soid (ĭ-lĭp'soid') *n.* A geometric surface whose plane sections are all either ellipses or circles. [ELLIPS(E) + -OID.] —**el·lip·soid, el·lip·soid·al** (ĭ-lĭp'soid'l, ĕl'ĭp-) *adj.*

el·lip·tic (ĭ-lĭp'tĭk) *adj.* Also **el·lip·ti·cal** (-tĭ-kəl). **1. a.** Of, pertaining to, or having the shape of an ellipse. **b.** Resembling or having the shape of a flattened circle. **2.** *Grammar.* Containing or characterized by ellipsis; having a word or words omitted. **3.** Expressing ideas in a compressed way that leaves much to be supplied by the understanding of the reader or hearer: *an elliptical style.* [Greek *elleiptikos,* defective, from *elleipein,* to fall short. See **ellipsis.**] —**el·lip·ti·cal·ly** *adv.*

elliptical polarization *n. Physics.* A type of polarization in which the radiation is composed of two plane-polarized waves at right angles, having different amplitudes, and having a phase difference of 90°. The end of the electric or magnetic vector describes an ellipse as the wave progresses.

elliptic geometry *n.* A form of non-Euclidean geometry, **Riemannian geometry** *(see).*

el·lip·tic·i·ty (ĭ-lĭp'tĭs'ə-tē, ĕ'lĭp-) *n.* **1.** Deviation from perfect circular or spherical form toward elliptic or ellipsoidal form. **2.** The degree of such deviation, expressed as the ratio of the length of the major axis to that of the minor axis.

El·lis (ĕl'ĭs), **(Henry) Havelock** (1859–1939). English writer and psychologist. His monumental *Studies in the Psychology of Sex* was published in seven volumes (1897–1928).

Ellis Island. Small island in Upper New York Bay, the reception center for immigrants to the United States from 1892 to 1943.

Ells·worth Land (ĕlz'wûrth'). Situated at the base of the Antarctic Peninsula, it contains the Ellsworth Mts., with Vinson Massif, at 5,140 meters (16,864 feet), the highest peak in the continent.

Ellul. Variant of **Elul.**

elm (ĕlm) *n.* **1.** Any of various deciduous trees of the genus *Ulmus,* widely planted as shade trees and characteristically having coarsely toothed leaves with one side longer than the other. **2.** The wood of an elm. [Middle English *elm,* Old English *elm.*]

el·o·cu·tion (ĕl'ə-kyōō'shən) *n.* **1.** The art of public speaking, emphasizing gesture and vocal production and delivery. **2.** Style or manner of speaking, especially in public. [Middle English *elocucion,* from Latin *ēlocūtiō* (stem *ēlocūtiōn-*), from *ēloquī* (past participle *ēlocūtus*), to speak out : *ex-,* out + *loquī,* to speak.] —**el·o·cu·tion·ar·y** (ĕl'ə-kyōō'shə-nĕr'ē) *adj.* —**el·o·cu·tion·ist** *n.*

E·lo·him (ĕ-lō'hĭm, ĕl'ō-hēm'). The Hebrew name for God most frequently encountered in the Old Testament. Compare **Yahweh.** [Hebrew *'Elōhim,* plural of *'Elōah,* God, perhaps enlarged from *'Ēl,* God.]

E·lo·hist (ĕ-lō'hĭst, ĕl'ō-hĭst) *n.* The author of the passages of the Hexateuch in which the name *Elohim* is used to designate God rather than the name *Yahweh.* —**El·o·his·tic** (ĕl'ō-hĭs'tĭk) *adj.*

e·lon·gate (ĭ-lông'gāt', ĭ-lŏng'-) *v.* **-gated, -gating, -gates.** —*tr.* To lengthen or extend. —*intr.* To grow in length.
~*adj.* **1.** Lengthened; extended. **2.** Slender; tapered. [Late Latin *ēlongāre* : Latin *ex-,* out + *longus,* long.]

e·lon·ga·tion (ĭ-lông'gā'shən, ĭ-lŏng'-, ē'lông-, ē'lŏng-) *n.* **1.** The act of elongating or the condition of being elongated. **2.** Something that elongates; an extension. **3.** *Physics.* The amount of elongation, usually expressed as a percentage of original length. **4.** *Astronomy.* The difference in celestial longitude between the sun and the moon or a planet.

e·lope (ĭ-lōp') *intr.v.* **eloped, eloping, elopes. 1.** To run away with a lover, especially with the intention of getting married, usually without parental consent. **2.** To run away; abscond. [Norman French *aloper,* legal term applied to a wife who ran away with her lover, from Middle English *alopen* (unattested), past participle of *alepen* (unattested), to run away : *a-* (away) + *lepen,* to run, leap, Old English *hlēopan.*] —**e·lope·ment** *n.* —**e·lop·er** *n.*

el·o·quence (ĕl'ə-kwəns) *n.* **1.** Persuasive and fluent discourse.

elm *The English elm (above)—once common in America and Britian—has had its ranks severely reduced by Dutch elm disease. The species' botanical name is* Ulmus procera.

PRONUNCIATION KEY

ă, pat; ā, pay; âr, care;
ä, father, are; b, bib;
ch, church; d, deed; ĕ, pet;
ē, be; f, fife; g, gag; h, hat;
hw, which; ĭ, pit; ī, pie;
îr, pier; j, judge; k, kick;
l, lid, needle; m, mum;
n, no, sudden; ng, thing;
ŏ, pot; ō, toe; ô, paw, for;
oi, noise; ou, out; ŏŏ, book;
ōō, boot; p, pop; r, roar;
s, sauce; sh, ship, dish;
t, tight; th, thin, path;
th, this, bathe; ŭ, cut; ûr, fur;
v, valve; w, with; y, yes;
z, zebra, size; zh, vision;
ə, about, item, edible, gallop, circus, peaceful

IN FOREIGN WORDS:

à, *Fr.* ami; œ, *Fr.* feu, *Ger.* schön; ü, *Fr.* tu, *Ger.* über; KH, *Ger.* ich, *Scot.* loch; N, *Fr.* bon; y', *Fr.* Compiègne

STRESS MARKS:

Primary stress: ' **in·cite'** (ĭn-sīt')
Secondary stress: ' **in'sight'** (ĭn'sīt')

2. The ability or power to persuade with discourse.

el·o·quent (ĕl′ə-kwənt) *adj.* **1.** Persuasive, fluent, and graceful in speech or writing. **2.** Vividly or movingly expressive, as of an emotion: *"Each face eloquent of polite misgiving"* (Evelyn Waugh). [Middle English, from Old French, from Latin *ēloquēns* (stem *ēloquent-*), present participle of *ēloquī,* to speak out. See **elocution.**] **—el·o·quent·ly** *adv.* **—el·o·quent·ness** *n.*

El Pas·o (ĕl păs′ō). A city of western Texas, on the Rio Grande just across the Mexican border.

El Sal·va·dor (ĕl săl′və-dôr′). The smallest and most densely populated state in mainland Latin America. Its early colonizers, the Aztecs, were conquered by Spain in *c.* 1526. Since 1979 there has been civil war between left-wing guerrillas and the government. The country is chiefly agricultural, producing coffee, cotton, and hardwoods. The predominantly Roman Catholic population is of mixed European and Indian descent. Area, 21,041 square kilometers (8,122 square miles). Population, 4,800,000. Capital, San Salvador. See map at **Central America.**

else (ĕls) *adj.* **1.** Other; different: *somebody else.* **2.** In addition; additional; more: *Would you like anything else?*
~adv. **1.** In a different time, place, or manner; differently: *How else could it be done?* **2.** If not; otherwise: *Be careful, or else you will make a mistake.* **—or else.** Or there will be unpleasant consequences. Used as a threat: *Behave yourself or else!* [Middle English *elles,* Old English *elles,* otherwise, else; akin to Latin *alius,* Greek *allos.*]
Usage: The possessive forms of constructions using this word are written *anyone else's, someone else's,* and so on. *Who else's,* whether used singly or in combination with a noun *(Who else's car was stolen?),* is felt to be an awkward construction, and stylists try to avoid it by using some phrase such as *Who else had a car stolen? Whose else* is often heard, especially governed by the verb *be*: *Whose else should it have been?* The use of *else* as a coordinating conjunction is common in informal speech *(Run, else you'll be late!),* but *or else* is recommended as the general rule.

else·where (ĕls′hwâr′) *adv.* To or in a different or other place: *The book isn't on the desk; you'll have to look elsewhere.*

ELT English language teaching.

El·ton (ĕl′tən), **Charles Sutherland** (1900–). British biologist, a founder of the modern science of ecology. His most important writings include *Animal Ecology* (1927) and *The Pattern of Animal Communities* (1966).

el·u·ant, el·u·ent (ĕl′yo͞o-ənt) *n. Chemistry.* A substance used as a solvent in the process of elution. [Latin *ēluere,* to wash out : *ē-, ex-,* out + *luere,* to wash.]

e·lu·ci·date (ĭ-lo͞o′sə-dāt′) *v.* **-dated, -dating, -dates.** *—tr.* To make clear or plain; clarify. *—intr.* To clarify something. —See Synonyms at **explain.** [Late Latin *ēlūcidāre* : Latin *ex-,* completely + *lūcidus,* bright, clear, from *lūcēre,* to shine.] **—e·lu·ci·da·tion** *n.* **—e·lu·ci·da·tive** (ĭ-lo͞o′sə-dā′tĭv) *adj.* **—e·lu·ci·da·tor** *n.*

e·lude (ĭ-lo͞od′) *tr.v.* **eluded, eluding, eludes. 1.** To avoid or escape from, as by cunning, daring, or artifice; evade: *elude capture.* **2.** To escape understanding or detection by; baffle: *The meaning of her glance eluded him.* —See Synonyms at **escape.** [Latin *ēlūdere,* "to take away from (someone) at play," to cheat, deceive : *ex-,* away + *lūdere,* to play, from *lūdus,* play.] **—e·lu·sion** (ĭ-lo͞o′zhən) *n.*

E·lul, El·lul (ĕ-lo͞ol′, ĕl′o͞ol) *n.* The 12th month of the year in the Hebrew calendar. See feature at **alphabet.** [Hebrew *'Elūl,* from Akkadian *ulūlu, elūlu,* "(time when the harvest is) brought in."]

e·lu·sive (ĭ-lo͞o′sĭv) *adj.* **1.** Tending to elude grasp, perception, or comprehension: *an elusive goal.* **2.** Difficult to define or describe: *an elusive charm.* **—e·lu·sive·ly** *adv.* **—e·lu·sive·ness** *n.*

e·lute (ē-lo͞ot′) *tr.v.* **eluted, eluting, elutes.** *Chemistry.* To remove (a mixture or a component from a mixture) by means of a solvent. [Latin *ēluere* (past participle *ēlutus*), to wash out. See **eluant.**] **—e·lu·tion** *n.*

e·lu·tri·ate (ĭ-lo͞o′trē-āt′) *tr.v.* **-ated, -ating, -ates.** To purify, separate, or remove (ore, for example) by washing, settling, and decanting. [Latin *ēlūtriāre,* from *ēluere,* to wash out. See **eluvium.**] **—e·lu·tri·a·tion** *n.*

e·lu·vi·al (ĭ-lo͞o′vē-əl) *adj.* Of, pertaining to, or consisting of eluvium.

e·lu·vi·a·tion (ĭ-lo͞o′vē-ā′shən) *n.* Internal movement of substances in solution or in suspension from the upper and middle layers of soil by water percolating downward or horizontally. Leaching is a form of eluviation. [ELUVI(UM) + -ATION.]

e·lu·vi·um (ĭ-lo͞o′vē-əm) *n.* Residual deposits of soil, dust, and rock particles produced by the action of the wind. [New Latin, from Latin *ēluere,* to wash out : *ex-,* out + *luere,* to wash.]

el·ver (ĕl′vər) *n.* A young or immature eel. [Variant of *eelfare,* originally "the passage of young eels up a river" : EEL + FARE.]

elves. Plural of **elf.**

elvish. Variant of **elfish.**

E·ly (ē′lē). A city on the Ouse River, in Cambridgeshire, England. The city is dominated by its cathedral, dating back to the 11th century and housing many Saxon relics.

Ely *Once a beacon for travelers through the surrounding fens, the tower of Ely Cathedral still commands the landscape for miles around as it has done for more than 800 years.*

Ely, Isle of. Region of Cambridgeshire in east-central England. The region has extensive fens, now drained and devoted to the cultivation of sugar beets and vegetables. The name *Isle* comes from the high ground amid the fens; the name *Ely* supposedly refers to the eels formerly found in the fens.

E·ly·sée (ā′lē-zā′) *n.* The residence of the president of France, in Paris on the Champs Elysées.

E·ly·sian (ĭ-lĭzh′ən) *adj.* **1.** Pertaining to or suggestive of Elysium. **2.** Blissful; delightful.

E·ly·si·um (ĭ-lĭz′ē-əm, ĭ-lĭzh′əm) *n.* **1.** *Greek Mythology.* The abode of the blessed after death. Also called "Elysian Fields." **2.** A place or condition of ideal happiness. [Latin *Ēlysium,* from Greek *Ēlusion*† *(pedion),* Elysian (fields).]

E·ly·tis (ĭ-lē′tĭs), **Odysseus,** born Odysseus Alepoudelis (1911–). Greek poet educated in Athens and Paris. His works include *Axion Esti* (1959), *Orientations* (1940), *The Light Tree* (1971), and *Maria Nefeli* (1978). In 1979 he received the Nobel Prize for literature.

el·y·tron (ĕl′ə-trŏn′) *n., pl.* **-tra** (-trə). Either of the leathery or chitinous forewings of a beetle or related insect, serving to encase the thin, membranous hind wings used in flight. [New Latin, from Greek *elutron,* covering, sheath.] **—el·y·troid** (ĕl′ə-troid′) *adj.*

em (ĕm) *n.* **1.** The letter *m.* **2.** *Printing. Abbr.* **m, M** The square of the body size of any type, used as a unit of measure; especially, that of a pica M. Originally, an em was equivalent to the space occupied by the letter M in any given font.
~adj. Printing. Designating a dash or space equal to the width of an em.

'em (əm) *pron. Informal.* Them. [Originally from Middle English *hem,* Old English *him, heom,* dative and accusative plural of *hē,* HE; but now felt as a shortened form of *them.*]

em–¹. Variant of **en-** (put into).

em–². Variant of **en-** (into).

e·ma·ci·ate (ĭ-mā′shē-āt′) *tr.v.* **-ated, -ating, -ates.** To make abnormally thin, as by starvation or illness. [Latin *ēmaciāre* : *ex-,* completely + *maciāre,* to make thin, from *macer,* thin.] **—e·ma·ci·a·tion** *n.*

em·a·lan·ge·ni. Plural of **lilangeni.**

em·a·nate (ĕm′ə-nāt′) *v.* **-nated, -nating, -nates.** *—intr.* To come forth or proceed, as from a source or origin; issue; originate. *—tr.* To send forth; emit. [Latin *ēmānāre,* to flow out : *ex-,* out + *mānāre,* to flow.] **—em·a·na·tive** *adj.*

em·a·na·tion (ĕm′ə-nā′shən) *n.* **1.** An act or instance of emanating; a coming or flowing forth. **2. a.** Something that emanates or issues from a source; an effluence. **b.** *Chemistry.* A gaseous product of radioactive disintegration.

e·man·ci·pate (ĭ-măn′sə-pāt′) *tr.v.* **-pated, -pating, -pates. 1.** To free from oppression, bondage, or restraint; liberate. **2.** To free from constraints imposed by social or moral conventions. Often used in the passive. **3.** In Roman law, to release (a child) from the control of his parents. [Latin *ēmancipāre,* "to release from slavery or tutelage" : *e-,* out of, EX- + *mancipium,* ownership, purchase, from *manceps* (stem *mancip-*), purchaser.] **—e·man·ci·pa·tive** *adj.* **—e·man·ci·pa·tor** *n.*

e·man·ci·pat·ed (ĭ-măn′sə-pā′tĭd) *adj.* **1.** No longer subject to official authority or control. **2.** No longer subscribing to accepted moral and social conventions: *an emancipated woman.*

e·man·ci·pa·tion (ĭ-măn′sə-pā′shən) *n.* **1.** The act of emancipating. **2.** The condition of being emancipated; freedom; liberation.

e·mar·gi·nate (ĭ-mär′jə-nĭt, -nāt′) *adj.* Having a notched tip. Said of a leaf or petal. [Latin *ēmarginātus,* past participle of *ēmargināre,* to take the edge away : *ex-,* away + *margō* (stem *margin-*), MARGIN.]

e·mas·cu·late (ĭ-măs′kyə-lāt′) *tr.v.* **-lated, -lating, -lates. 1.** To remove the male organs of; castrate. **2.** To deprive of vigor or character; make weak or ineffectual.
~adj. (-lĭt, -lāt′). **1.** Emasculated. **2.** Weak; ineffectual. [Latin *ēmasculāre* : *ex-* (removal) + *masculus,* male, manly.] **—e·mas·cu·la·tion** *n.* **—e·mas·cu·la·tive, e·mas·cu·la·to·ry** (ĭ-măs′kyə-lə-tôr′ē, -tōr′ē) *adj.* **—e·mas·cu·la·tor** *n.*

em·balm (ĕm-bäm′, ĭm-) *tr.v.* **-balmed, -balming, -balms. 1.** To prevent the decay of (a corpse) by treatment with preservatives. **2.** To save from oblivion; preserve the memory of. [Middle English *embaumen, embalmen,* from Old French *embaumer, embasmer* : *en-,* to put on + *basme,* BALM.] **—em·balm·er** *n.* **—em·balm·ment** *n.*

em·bank (ĕm-băngk′, ĭm-) *tr.v.* **-banked, -banking, -banks.** To confine, support, or protect with a bank or embankment.

em·bank·ment (ĕm-băngk′mənt, ĭm-) *n.* **1.** The act of embanking. **2.** A mound of earth or stone built to hold back water or to support a road or railway.

em·bar·go (ĕm-bär′gō, ĭm-) *n., pl.* **-goes. 1.** An order by a government prohibiting the movement of merchant ships into or out of its ports. **2.** A governmental suspension of foreign trade or of foreign trade in a particular commodity. **3.** An injunction forbidding the acceptance of particular freight for shipment. **4.** Any prohibition.
~tr.v. **embargoed, -going, -goes. 1.** To impose an embargo upon. **2.** To commandeer for state use. [Spanish, from *embargar,* to impede, restrain, from Vulgar Latin *imbarricāre* (unattested), "to place behind bars" : Latin *in-,* in + *barra* (unattested), BAR.]

em·bark (ĕm-bärk′, ĭm-) *v.* **-barked, -barking, -barks.** *—tr.* **1.** To cause to board a vessel or aircraft. **2.** To enlist (a person) or invest (money) in an enterprise. *—intr.* **1.** To go aboard a vessel or aircraft, especially at the start of a journey. **2.** To set out on a venture; commence. Used with *on* or *upon.* [Old French *embarquer,* from Late Latin *imbarcāre* : *in-,* in + *barca,* BARK.] **—em·bar·ka·tion** (ĕm′bär-kā′shən), **em·bark·ment** *n.*

em·bar·ras de ri·chesses (äɴ′bä-rä′ də-rē-shĕs′) *n.* An abundance of possible choices so great as to perplex. [French, "embarrassment of riches."]

em·bar·rass (ĕm-băr′əs, ĭm-) *tr.v.* **-rassed, -rassing, -rasses. 1.** To cause to feel self-conscious or ill at ease; disconcert. **2.** To involve in or hamper with financial difficulties. Usually used in the passive.

3. To beset with difficulties; impede. **4.** To complicate. [French *embarrasser*, from Spanish *embarazar*, from Italian *imbarazzare*, from *imbarrare*, "to put in bars," impede : *in-*, in, from Latin + *barra* (unattested), BAR.] —**em·bar·rass·ed·ly** (ĕm-băr'əst-lē, ĭm-) *adv.* —**em·bar·rass·ing·ly** *adv.*

em·bar·rass·ment (ĕm-băr'əs-mənt, ĭm-) *n.* **1.** The state of being embarrassed. **2.** Something that embarrasses. **3.** A state of financial difficulty. **4.** An overabundance. Used chiefly in the phrase *an embarrassment of riches.*

em·bas·sy (ĕm'bə-sē) *n., pl.* **-sies. 1.** The position, function, or duties of an ambassador. **2.** A mission to a foreign government headed by an ambassador. **3.** An ambassador and his staff. **4.** The official headquarters of an ambassador and his staff. [Middle English, from Old French *ambassee*, from Old Italian *ambasciata*, from Old Provençal *ambaissada*, from *ambaissa* (unattested), service, from Medieval Latin *ambactia*. See **ambassador.**]

em·bat·tle¹ (ĕm-băt'l, ĭm-) *tr.v.* **-tled, -tling, -tles. 1.** To prepare or array for battle. **2.** To prepare to struggle or resist. **3.** To fortify. [Middle English *embatailen*, from Old French *embataillier* : *en-*, in + *batailler*, to battle, from *bataille*, BATTLE.]

embattle² *tr.v.* **-tled, -tling, -tles.** To furnish with battlements for defense. [Middle English *embatailen* : *en-*, in + *batailen*, to build, fortify, from Old French *bataillier*, from *bataille*, battlement, BATTLE.]

em·bat·tled (ĕm-băt'əld, ĭm-) *adj.* Involved in an argument, contest, or struggle.

em·bay (ĕm-bā', ĭm-) *tr.v.* **-bayed, -baying, -bays. 1.** To put or force (a vessel) into a bay; shelter or detain in a bay. **2.** To enclose in or as if in a bay. **3.** To form into a bay.

em·bay·ment (ĕm-bā'mənt, ĭm-) *n.* **1.** A bay or baylike indentation in a coastline. **2.** The formation of a bay.

em·bed (ĕm-bĕd', ĭm-) *v.* **-bedded, -bedding, -beds.** Also **im·bed** (ĭm-). —*tr.* **1.** To fix firmly in a surrounding mass. **2.** To enclose snugly or firmly. **3.** To fix in the memory. **4.** To include (a subordinate clause, for example) in a sentence. —*intr.* To become embedded.

em·bel·lish (ĕm-bĕl'ĭsh, ĭm-) *tr.v.* **-lished, -lishing, -lishes. 1.** To make more beautiful, as by ornamentation; adorn. **2.** To add fanciful or fictitious details to (a statement or narrative). **3.** To provide with a musical embellishment. [Middle English *embelisshen*, from Old French *embellir* (present stem *embelliss-*) : *en-* (causative) + *bel*, beautiful, from Latin *bellus*.]

em·bel·lish·ment (ĕm-bĕl'ĭsh-mənt, ĭm-) *n.* **1.** The act of embellishing. **2.** The state of being embellished. **3.** Something that serves to embellish; ornamentation. **4.** *Music.* A note or group of notes, as a trill, that embellishes a melody.

em·ber (ĕm'bər) *n.* **1.** A small piece of live coal or wood, as in a dying fire. **2. embers.** The smoldering coal or ash of a dying fire. **3. embers.** What is left of a past, more intense feeling. [Middle English *embre, emere*, Old English *ǣmerge*, embers, ashes.]

Ember day *n.* Any of three days out of each calendar season observed by special prayer and formerly by fasting in some Christian churches, falling on the Wednesday, Friday, and Saturday after the first Sunday of Lent, after Whitsunday, after September 14, and after December 13. [Middle English *Ymber Daye*, Old English *Ymbrendǣg*, "recurring day" : *ymbryne*, "a running around," circuit : *ymbe*, around + *ryne*, a running + *dǣg*, DAY.]

Ember week *n.* A week in which Ember days fall.

em·bez·zle (ĕm-bĕz'əl, ĭm-) *v.* **-zled, -zling, -zles.** —*tr.* To take (money or property) for one's own use in violation of a trust. —*intr.* To embezzle money or property. [Middle English *embesilen*, from Norman French *enbesiler* : Old French *en-* (intensive) + *besillert*, to do away with, destroy.] —**em·bez·zle·ment** *n.* —**em·bez·zler** *n.*

em·bit·ter (ĕm-bĭt'ər, ĭm-) *tr.v.* **-tered, -tering, -ters. 1.** To arouse bitter feelings in; make resentful or hostile. **2.** To make (a trouble or quarrel, for example) more distressing; aggravate. —**em·bit·ter·ment** *n.*

em·blaze (ĕm-blāz', ĭm-) *tr.v.* **-blazed, -blazing, -blazes. 1.** To set on fire. **2.** To cause to glow or glitter.

em·bla·zon (ĕm-blā'zən, ĭm-) *tr.v.* **-zoned, -zoning, -zons. 1.** To ornament with heraldic devices or armorial bearings. **2.** To depict according to heraldic convention. **3.** To make resplendent with brilliant colors or other ornamentation. **4.** To proclaim or display conspicuously; celebrate. [EM- + BLAZON.] —**em·bla·zon·er** *n.* —**em·bla·zon·ment** *n.*

em·bla·zon·ry (ĕm-blā'zən-rē, ĭm-) *n.* **1.** The art of emblazoning according to heraldic convention. **2.** Heraldic devices collectively.

em·blem (ĕm'bləm) *n.* **1.** An object or a depiction of an object that comes to represent something else, usually by suggesting its nature or history; a pictorial symbol. **2.** A distinctive badge, design, or device. **3.** A typical representation or embodiment; a personification. [Middle English *emblem*, from Latin *emblēma*, inlaid work, from Greek, insertion, from *emballein*, to throw in, insert : *en-*, in + *ballein*, to throw.]

em·blem·at·ic (ĕm'blə-măt'ĭk) *adj.* Also **em·blem·at·i·cal** (-ĭ-kəl). **1.** Of, pertaining to, or serving as an emblem. **2.** Symbolic. —**em·blem·at·i·cal·ly** *adv.*

em·blem·a·tize (ĕm-blĕm'ə-tīz') *tr.v.* **-tized, -tizing, -tizes.** Also **em·blem·ize** (ĕm'blə-mīz') **-ized, -izing, -izes.** To represent with or as if by an emblem; symbolize.

em·ble·ments (ĕm'blə-mənts) *pl.n. Law.* The annual crops or profits of land cultivated by a tenant farmer. [Middle English *emblay-*

ment, from Old French *emblaement*, land sown with wheat, from *blé*, wheat, corn.]

em·bod·i·ment (ĕm-bŏd'ĭ-mənt, ĭm-) *n.* **1.** The act of embodying or the condition of being embodied. **2.** One that embodies something: *"The flag is the embodiment, not of sentiment, but of history"* (Woodrow Wilson).

em·bod·y (ĕm-bŏd'ē, ĭm-) *tr.v.* **-bodied, -bodying, -bodies. 1.** To invest with or as if with bodily form; make corporeal; incarnate. **2.** To express (a feeling or concept, for example) in tangible or concrete form: *The painting embodies the artist's horror of war.* **3.** To be a typical and concrete example or manifestation of; personify: *dedicated men who embodied the tradition of public service.* **4.** To include in a larger whole; incorporate.

em·bold·en (ĕm-bōl'dən, ĭm-) *tr.v.* **-ened, -ening, -ens.** To foster boldness in; encourage.

em·bo·lec·to·my (ĕm'bə-lĕk'tə-mē) *n., pl.* **-mies.** The surgical removal of an embolus. [EMBOL(US) + -ECTOMY.]

em·bol·ic (ĕm-bŏl'ĭk) *adj. Pathology.* Of or pertaining to an embolus or an embolism.

em·bo·lism (ĕm'bə-lĭz'əm) *n.* **1.** Obstruction or occlusion of a blood vessel by an embolus. **2.** The insertion of a period of time into a calendar; intercalation. [Middle English *embolisme*, from Medieval Latin *embolismus*, from Late Latin, insertion, from Greek *embolismos*, from *emballein*, "to throw in," insert. See **emblem.**] —**em·bo·lis·mic** (ĕm'bə-lĭz'mĭk) *adj.*

em·bo·lus (ĕm'bə-ləs) *n., pl.* **-li** (-lī'). An air bubble, detached clot, mass of bacteria, or other foreign body that obstructs a blood vessel. [New Latin, from Latin, piston, from Greek *embolos*, "something inserted," stopper, from *emballein*, to throw in, insert. See **emblem.**]

em·bo·ly (ĕm'bə-lē) *n. Embryology.* The development of a gastrula from a blastula by invagination. [Greek *embolē*, insertion, entrance, from *emballein*, to insert. See **emblem.**]

em·bon·point (än'bôn-pwăn') *n.* A well-fed appearance; plumpness. [French, from Old French, from *en bon point,* in good condition.]

em·bos·om (ĕm-bo͝oz'əm, -bo͞o'zəm, ĭm-) *tr.v.* **-omed, -oming, -oms. 1.** *Archaic.* To clasp to or hold in the bosom; embrace. **2.** To envelop or enclose protectively; shelter.

em·boss (ĕm-bôs', -bŏs', ĭm-) *tr.v.* **-bossed, -bossing, -bosses. 1.** To represent, mold, or carve (a design) in relief. **2.** To raise (an inscription, for example) in relief on paper, metal, or the like. **3.** To cover with or as if with bosses: *"The whole buoy was embossed with barnacles"* (Herman Melville). **4.** To ornament lavishly; adorn. [Middle English *embosen*, from Old French *embocer* (unattested), "to put a knob in" : *en-*, in + *boce*, BOSS (knob).] —**em·boss·ment** *n.*

em·bou·chure (ŏm'bo͝o-sho͝or') *n.* **1. a.** The mouth of a river. **b.** The opening out of a valley into a plain. **2. a.** The mouthpiece of a wind instrument. **b.** The manner in which the lips and tongue are applied to such a mouthpiece. [French, from Old French *emboucher*, "to put in one's mouth" : *en-*, in + *bouche*, mouth, from Latin *bucca*, puffed-out cheek.]

em·bowed (ĕm-bōd', ĭm-) *adj.* **1.** Bent or curved like a bow. **2.** *Architecture.* **a.** Arched. **b.** Protruding in an outward curve so as to form a recess.

em·bow·el (ĕm-bou'əl, ĭm-) *tr.v.* **-eled, -eling, -els** or *chiefly British* **-elled, -elling, -els.** To disembowel.

em·bow·er (ĕm-bou'ər, ĭm-) *tr.v.* **-ered, -ering, -ers.** To enclose in or as if in a bower; surround, as with sheltering foliage.

em·brace¹ (ĕm-brās', ĭm-) *v.* **-braced, -bracing, -braces.** —*tr.* **1.** To clasp or hold to one with the arms, usually as a display of affection. **2. a.** To encircle or surround. **b.** To twine around. **3.** To include, comprise, or contain; encompass. **4.** To take up (a cause or doctrine, for example); adopt. **5.** To avail oneself of; accept eagerly: *embrace an opportunity.* **6.** To take in with the eyes or mind. **7.** To submit to with dignity or fortitude: *embrace misfortune.* —*intr.* To join in an embrace; hug affectionately: *They embraced, then said good-by.* —See Synonyms at **include.**
~*n.* **1.** An act of embracing; an affectionate hug. **2.** An enclosure or encirclement. **3.** Eager acceptance. [Middle English *embracen*, from Old French *embracer*, from Vulgar Latin *imbracchiāre* (unattested) : Latin *in-* + *bracchium*, arm, from Greek *brakhīōn*.] —**em·brace·a·ble** *adj.* —**em·brace·ment** *n.* —**em·brac·er** *n.*

embrace² *tr.v.* **-braced, -bracing, -braces.** *Law.* To try to influence (a judge or jury) by corrupt means. [Back-formation from EMBRACER.] —**em·brac·er·y** (ĕm-brā'sə-rē, ĭm-) *n.*

em·brac·er, em·brace·or (ĕm-brā'sər, ĭm-) *n. Law.* One guilty of attempting to influence a court illegally. [Middle English *embraceor*, from Old French *embraseor*, instigator, from *embraser*, "to set on fire," instigate : *en-*, in + *brese*, embers.]

em·branch·ment (ĕm-brănch'mənt, ĕm-brănch'-, ĭm-) *n.* **1.** A branching out or off, as of a mountain range or river. **2.** A subdivision; a ramification.

em·bra·sure (ĕm-brā'zhər, ĭm-) *n.* **1.** *Architecture.* An opening in a wall for a door or window, slanted so that its interior dimensions are larger than those of its exterior. **2.** An opening for a gun in a wall or parapet. [French, from *embraser*, to set on fire, fire a gun. See **embracer.**]

em·bro·cate (ĕm'brə-kāt') *tr.v.* **-cated, -cating, -cates.** To moisten and rub (a painful part of the body) with a liniment or lotion. [Medieval Latin *embrocāre*, from Late Latin *embrocha*, lotion, from

embrasure *Light from a window brightens a recess, or embrasure, inside a 13th-century tower in Pembroke Castle, Wales.*

Greek *embrokhē,* from *embrekhein,* to moisten with a lotion : *en-,* in + *brekhein,* to wet.]

em·bro·ca·tion (ĕm′brə-kā′shən) *n.* A liniment.

em·broi·der (ĕm-broi′dər, ĭm-) *v.* **-dered, -dering, -ders.** *—tr.* **1.** To ornament (fabric) with needlework. **2.** To work (a design) into fabric with a needle and thread. **3.** To embellish (a narrative, for example) with fictitious details or exaggerations. *—intr.* To make embroidery. [Middle English *embroderen,* from Norman French *enbrouder* : Old French *en-,* in + *brouder, brosder,* to embroider, from (unattested) Frankish *brusdan.*] **—em·broi·der·er** *n.*

em·broi·der·y (ĕm-broi′də-rē, ĭm-) *n., pl.* **-ies. 1.** The art, act, or practice of embroidering. **2.** Ornamentation on fabric done in needlework. **3.** A piece of embroidered fabric. **4.** Fictitious or exaggerated detail added, as to a narrative.

em·broil (ĕm-broil′, ĭm-) *tr.v.* **-broiled, -broiling, -broils. 1.** To involve in argument, conflict, or difficulties: *embroiled in a diplomatic scandal.* **2.** To throw (a situation, for example) into confusion or disorder; entangle. [French *embrouiller* : Old French *en-,* in + *brouiller,* to mix, confuse, probably from *breu,* broth, from Germanic.] **—em·broil·ment** *n.*

em·brown (ĕm-broun′, ĭm-) *tr.v.* **-browned, -browning, -browns.** To make brown or dusky; darken.

embrue. Variant of **imbrue.**

em·bry·ec·to·my (ĕm′brē-ĕk′tə-mē) *n., pl.* **-mies.** The surgical removal of an extrauterine embryo. [EMBRY(O) + -ECTOMY.]

em·bry·o (ĕm′brē-ō′) *n., pl.* **-os. 1.** *Biology.* **a.** An organism in its early stages of development, especially before it has reached a distinctively recognizable form. **b.** Such an organism at any time before full development, birth, or hatching. **2. a.** The fertilized egg of a vertebrate animal following cleavage. **b.** In man, the prefetal product of conception up to the beginning of the third month of pregnancy. **3.** *Botany.* The minute, rudimentary plant contained within a seed or archegonium. **4. a.** A rudimentary or initial stage. **b.** Something at a rudimentary or undeveloped stage: *the embryo of an idea.* ~*adj.* Incipient; rudimentary. [Medieval Latin *embryo* (stem *embryon-*), from Greek *embruon,* "something that grows in the body" : *en-,* in + *bruein,* to grow.]

em·bry·o·gen·e·sis (ĕm′brē-ō-jĕn′ə-sĭs) *n.* Also **em·bry·og·e·ny** (-ŏj′ə-nē). The development and growth of an embryo. **—em·bry·o·gen·ic** (-ō-jĕn′ĭk) or **em·bry·o·ge·net·ic** (-jə-nĕt′ĭk) *adj.*

em·bry·ol·o·gy (ĕm′brē-ŏl′ə-jē) *n.* **1.** The science dealing with the formation, early growth, and development of living organisms. **2.** The embryonic structure and development of a particular organism. **—em·bry·o·log·ic** (-ə-lŏj′ĭk), **em·bry·o·log·i·cal** (-ĭ-kəl) *adj.* **—em·bry·o·log·i·cal·ly** *adv.* **—em·bry·ol·o·gist** *n.*

em·bry·on·ic (ĕm′brē-ŏn′ĭk) *adj.* Also **em·bry·on·al** (ĕm′brē-ə-nəl) (for sense 1). **1.** Of, pertaining to, or in the state of being an embryo. **2.** Still at an early stage of development; rudimentary.

embryo sac *n.* The large oval cell in which the embryo develops in seed plants.

em·bus (ĕm-bŭs′, ĭm-) *v.* **-bused** or **-bussed, -busing** or **-bussing, -buses** or **-busses.** *—tr.* To transport (troops, for example) by bus. *—intr.* To board a bus.

em·cee (ĕm′sē′) *n. Informal.* A master of ceremonies *(see).* ~*v.* **emceed, -ceeing, -cees.** *Informal.* *—tr.* To serve as master of ceremonies of. *—intr.* To act as master of ceremonies. [From *master of ceremonies.*]

-eme *suffix.* Indicates an irreducible unit of linguistic structure; for example, **morpheme, phoneme.** [French *-ème,* abstracted from *phonème,* PHONEME.]

emeer. Variant of **emir.**

e·mend (ĭ-mĕnd′) *tr.v.* **emended, emending, emends. 1.** To correct and improve (a text) by critical editing. **2.** *Archaic.* To free from faults. *—See* Usage note at **amend.** [Middle English *emenden,* from Latin *ēmendāre* : *ex-* (removal) + *mendum,* fault.]

e·men·date (ē′mĕn-dāt′, ĭ-mĕn′-) *tr.v.* **-dated, -dating, -dates.** To emend (a text). **—e·men·da·tor** *n.*

e·men·da·tion (ĭ-mĕn′dā′shən, ē′mĕn-) *n.* **1.** The act of emending. **2.** An alteration that improves something; especially, a textual correction, as in a literary work. **—e·men·da·to·ry** (ĭ-mĕn′də-tôr′ē, -tōr′ē) *adj.*

em·er·ald (ĕm′ər-əld, ĕm′rəld) *n.* **1.** A brilliant, transparent green beryl used as a gemstone. **2.** A brilliant green color. ~*adj.* **1.** Of, pertaining to, or similar to an emerald. **2.** Of a brilliant green color. [Middle English *emeraude,* from Old French *esmeraude,* from Vulgar Latin *smaralda* (unattested), variant of Latin *smaragdus,* SMARAGDITE.]

Emerald Isle. The island of Ireland.

e·merge (ĭ-mûrj′) *intr.v.* **emerged, emerging, emerges. 1.** To rise up or come forth from or as if from immersion. **2.** To become evident or known. **3.** To issue, as from obscurity or difficulties: *They emerged from the war changed men.* **4.** To come into existence. [Latin *ēmergere* : *ex-,* out of + *mergere,* to dip, immerse.]

e·mer·gence (ĭ-mûr′jəns) *n.* **1.** The act or process of emerging. **2.** *Botany.* A superficial outgrowth of plant tissue, such as a thorn, containing no conducting tissues. **3.** *Philosophy.* The unpredicted appearance of new characteristics or phenomena in the course of biological or social evolution.

e·mer·gen·cy (ĭ-mûr′jən-sē) *n., pl.* **-cies. 1.** An unexpected situation or sudden occurrence of a serious and urgent nature that demands immediate action. **2.** A pressing need, as after a flood, for relief or help: *a state of emergency.*

e·mer·gent (ĭ-mûr′jənt) *adj.* **1.** Coming into existence, view, or attention; issuing forth. **2.** Newly independent. Said of a state. ~*n. Botany.* An emersed plant.

emergent evolution *n.* A theory holding that completely new types of organisms, modes of behavior, and consciousness appear at certain stages of the evolutionary process, usually as a result of an unpredictable rearrangement of the pre-existing elements.

e·mer·i·tus (ĭ-mĕr′ə-təs) *adj.* Retired but retaining an honorary title corresponding to that held immediately before retirement: *a professor emeritus.* ~*n., pl.* **emeriti** (-tī′). One who is emeritus. [Latin *ēmeritus,* past participle of *ēmerērī,* to earn by service : *ex-,* out of + *merērī, merēre,* to earn, deserve.]

e·mersed (ĭ-mûrst′) *adj. Botany.* Rising above the surface of the water. Said of the leaves or stems of aquatic plants.

e·mer·sion (ĭ-mûr′zhən, -shən) *n.* **1.** The act of emerging; emergence. **2.** *Astronomy.* Egress *(see).* [Latin *ēmergere* (past participle *ēmersus*), to EMERGE.]

Em·er·son (ĕm′ər-sən), **Ralph Waldo** (1803–82). U.S. poet and essayist. A Unitarian pastor from 1829 to 1832, he subsequently became a writer and lecturer. *Nature* (1836) was an early manifesto of transcendentalist belief in the mystical unity of nature. His essays are regarded as landmarks in the development of American thought and literary expression. **—Em·er·son·i·an** (ĕm′ər-sō′nē-ən) *n. & adj.*

em·er·y (ĕm′ə-rē, ĕm′rē) *n.* A fine-grained impure form of corundum used for grinding and polishing. [Middle English *emery,* from Old French *emeri, esmeril,* from Vulgar Latin *smericulum* (unattested), from Medieval Greek *smēri,* variant of Greek *smuris†,* emery powder.]

emery board *n.* A small, flat strip of cardboard or thin wood coated with powdered emery, used to file the nails.

emery paper *n.* Paper coated with powdered emery, used as a fine abrasive.

emery wheel *n.* An abrasive wheel containing emery powder in a resinous binder, rotated by a motor, and used for smoothing or grinding.

em·e·sis (ĕm′ə-sĭs) *n.* Vomiting. [New Latin, from Greek, from *emein,* to vomit.]

e·met·ic (ĭ-mĕt′ĭk) *adj.* Causing vomiting. ~*n.* An emetic agent or medicine. [Latin *emeticus,* from Greek *emetikos,* inclined to vomit, from *emetos,* vomiting, from *emein,* to vomit.] **—e·met·i·cal·ly** *adv.*

em·e·tine (ĕm′ə-tēn′) *n.* A bitter-tasting, crystalline alkaloid, $C_{29}H_{40}O_4N_2$, derived from ipecac root, and used as an emetic. [French *émétine : émétique,* causing vomiting, from Latin *emeticus* (see **emetic**) + -INE.]

emf, EMF electromotive force.

-emia, -aemia, -hemia *suffix.* Indicates blood; for example, **leukemia.** [New Latin, from Greek *-aimiā,* from *haima,* blood.]

em·i·grant (ĕm′ĭ-grənt) *n.* One who emigrates. **—em·i·grant** *adj.*

em·i·grate (ĕm′ĭ-grāt′) *intr.v.* **-grated, -grating, -grates.** To leave one country or region, especially one's native country or region, to settle in another. *—See* Usage note at **migrate.** [Latin *ēmigrāre,* to move away from : *ex-,* away + *migrāre,* to move.] **—em·i·gra·tion** *n.*

é·mi·gré (ĕm′ĭ-grā′) *n.* An emigrant, especially one who has fled his country during a political upheaval. [French, past participle of *émigrer,* to emigrate, from Latin *ēmigrāre.* See **emigrate.**]

E·mil·ia-Ro·ma·gna (ā-mēl′yä-rō-män′yä). Formerly **Emilia.** Region in northern Italy comprising the fertile lowlands of the Po River and part of the Apennines in the south.

em·i·nence (ĕm′ə-nəns) *n.* Also **em·i·nen·cy** (-nən-sē) *pl.* **-cies. 1.** A position of great distinction or superiority in achievement, rank, or character. **2.** A rise of ground; a hill. **3. Eminence.** A title of or form of address for a cardinal of the Roman Catholic Church. Used with *His* or *Your.* *—See* Synonyms at **fame.**

é·mi·nence grise (ā′mē-näns′ grēz′) *n., pl.* **éminences grises** (pronounced as singular). A person who exercises power behind the scenes through his influence with prominent people. Also called "gray eminence." [French, "gray eminence" (that is, cardinal), after the French monk Père Joseph (François Le Clerc du Tremblay, 1577–1638), who served as Cardinal Richelieu's secretary.]

em·i·nent (ĕm′ə-nənt) *adj.* **1. a.** Outstanding in performance or character; distinguished: *an eminent historian.* **b.** Of high rank or station. **2.** Towering or standing out above others; prominent. **3.** Remarkable or noteworthy: *a man esteemed for his eminent achievements.* [Middle English, from Old French, from Latin *ēminēns* (stem *ēminent-*), present participle of *ēminēre,* to stand out : *ex-,* out + *minēre,* to stand, project.]

Usage: Similarity in sound often leads to a confusion in spelling between *eminent* and *imminent,* but there is no overlap of meaning. *Eminent* means "prominent, outstanding"; *imminent* means "impending, about to occur."

eminent domain *n. Law.* The right of a government to appropriate private property for public use, usually with compensation to the owner.

em·i·nent·ly (ĕm′ə-nənt-lē) *adv.* Extremely; especially. Used as an intensive: *eminently suitable.*

e·mir, e·meer, a·mir, a·meer (ĭ-mîr′, ä-mîr′) *n.* **1.** A prince, chieftain, or governor, especially in the Middle East. **2.** An honorary title given to the descendants of Muhammad. [French *émir,* from Spanish *emir,* from Arabic *'amīr,* commander, from *amara,* he commanded.]

e·mir·ate (ĭ-mîr′ĭt, ä-mîr′-, -āt′) *n.* **1.** The office or jurisdiction of an

embroidery *An embroidered sampler by Hannah Taylor, made in 1774 in Newport, Rhode Island. Before printed embroidery patterns became available, samplers included a variety of stitches as demonstrations, or samples, of their creator's skill.*

emir. **2.** A country ruled over by an emir.

em·is·sar·y (ĕm′ə-sĕr′ē) *n., pl.* **-ies. 1.** A messenger or agent sent to represent or advance the interests of a person or state. **2.** An agent with a secret mission. [Latin *ēmissārius,* from *ēmittere* (past participle *ēmissus*), to send out, EMIT.]

e·mis·sion (ĭ-mĭsh′ən) *n.* **1.** The action of emitting. **2.** Something that is emitted, such as the exhaust from an automobile engine. **3. a.** *Physics.* A discharge, as of electrons or radiation. **b.** The amount or rate of this discharge. **4.** An issue, as of paper money or shares. [Latin *ēmittere* (past participle *ēmissus*), to EMIT.]

emission nebula *n.* A nebula that absorbs ultraviolet radiation from stars and re-emits it as visible light.

emission spectrum *n.* The spectrum of bright lines, bands, or continuous radiation characteristic of and determined by a specific emitting substance subjected to a specific kind of excitation. Compare **absorption spectrum.**

e·mis·sive (ĭ-mĭs′ĭv) *adj.* **1.** Sending forth; emitting. **2.** Sent forth; emitted.

em·is·siv·i·ty (ĕm′ə-sĭv′ə-tē) *n.* The ratio of the radiation intensity emitted from a surface to the radiation intensity at the same wavelength emitted from a blackbody at the same temperature.

e·mit (ĭ-mĭt′) *tr.v.* **emitted, emitting, emits. 1.** To give off or send out (liquid, gas, or radiation, for example). **2.** To utter: *"she emitted her small strange laugh"* (Edith Wharton). **3.** To issue with authority; especially, to put (paper currency or shares in a company, for example) into circulation. [Latin *ēmittere,* to send out : *ex-,* out + *mittere,* to send.]

e·mit·ter (ĭ-mĭt′ər) *n.* **1.** An object that emits something. **2.** *Electronics.* The region in a transistor from which charge carriers flow into the base.

Emmanuel. Variant of **Immanuel.**

em·men·a·gogue (ĭ-mĕn′ə-gôg′, -gŏg′) *n.* A medicine that induces or hastens the menstrual flow. [Greek *emmēna,* the menses, from *emmēnos,* monthly : *en-,* in + *mēnē, mēn,* month + -AGOGUE.]

Em·men·thal[1], **Em·men·tal** (ĕm′ən-täl′). Valley of the upper Emme River in Bern canton, Switzerland, famous for its cheese. —**Em·men·thal·er** *n. & adj.*

Emmenthal[2], **Emmental** *n.* A hard cheese with holes. It is made in Emmenthal.

em·mer (ĕm′ər) *n.* A slender-eared Eurasian wheat, *Triticum dicoccum,* cultivated as a cereal grain and livestock feed. [German *Emmer,* from Old High German *amaro.* See **yellowhammer.**]

em·met (ĕm′ĭt) *n. Archaic.* An ant. [Middle English *emete,* from Old English *ǣmete.*]

Em·met (ĕm′ĭt), **Robert** (1778–1803). Irish revolutionary nationalist who in July, 1803, took part in a bungled uprising against British rule. A few weeks later he was captured in Dublin and hanged.

em·me·tro·pi·a (ĕm′ə-trō′pē-ə) *n.* The condition of the normal eye when parallel rays are focused exactly on the retina and vision is perfect. [New Latin : Greek *emmetros,* in measure : *en-,* in + *metron,* measure + -OPIA.] —**em·me·trop·ic** (ĕm′ə-trŏp′ĭk) *adj.*

Em·my (ĕm′ē) *n., pl.* **-mys** or **-mies.** One of the statuettes presented annually by the Academy of Television Arts and Sciences for outstanding television performances and productions. [Alteration of *Immy,* nickname for *image orthicon tube.*]

e·mol·lient (ĭ-mŏl′yənt) *adj.* Having softening and soothing qualities, especially for the skin.
~*n.* **1.** An agent that softens or soothes the skin. **2.** Anything that assuages or mollifies. [Latin *ēmolliēns* (stem *ēmollient-*), present participle of *ēmollīre,* to soften, soothe : *ex-,* completely + *mollīre,* to soften, from *mollis,* soft.]

e·mol·u·ment (ĭ-mŏl′yə-mənt) *n.* Profit derived from one's office or employment; payment for services rendered. [Middle English, from Latin *ēmolumentum,* originally "miller's fee for grinding grain," from *ēmolere,* to grind out : *ex-,* out + *molere,* to grind.]

e·mote (ĭ-mōt′) *intr.v.* **emoted, emoting, emotes.** *Informal.* To express emotion or sentiment, especially in an effusive and theatrical manner. [Back-formation from EMOTION.] —**e·mot·er** *n.*

e·mo·tion (ĭ-mō′shən) *n.* **1. a.** A complex and usually strong subjective response, as love or fear. **b.** Such a response involving physiological changes as a preparation for action. **2.** A state of agitation or disturbance: *controlled her emotions with effort.* **3.** The part of the consciousness that involves feeling or sensibility: *a choice determined by emotion rather than reason.* —See Synonyms at **feeling.** [French *émotion,* earlier *esmocion,* from Old French *esmovoir,* to excite, from Vulgar Latin *exmovēre* (unattested), variant of Latin *ēmovēre,* to move out, stir up, excite : *ex-,* out + *movēre,* to move.]

e·mo·tion·al (ĭ-mō′shə-nəl) *adj.* **1.** Of or pertaining to emotion. **2.** Readily affected with or stirred by emotion. **3.** Capable of stirring the emotions; emotional appeal. **4.** Revealing emotion; agitated. —**e·mo·tion·al·i·ty** (ĭ-mō′shə-năl′ə-tē) *n.* —**e·mo·tion·al·ly** *adv.*

e·mo·tion·al·ism (ĭ-mō′shə-nə-lĭz′əm) *n.* **1.** An inclination to encourage or yield to emotion: *the emotionalism of adolescents.* **2.** Undue display of emotion. **3.** An ethical or aesthetic attitude basing conduct or value on emotion. —**e·mo·tion·al·ist** *n.* —**e·mo·tion·al·is·tic** (ĭ-mō′shə-nə-lĭs′tĭk) *adj.*

e·mo·tion·al·ize (ĭ-mō′shə-nə-līz′) *tr.v.* **-ized, -izing, -izes.** To impart an emotional character to.

e·mo·tion·less (ĭ-mō′shən-lĭs) *adj.* Devoid of apparent emotion.

e·mo·tive (ĭ-mō′tĭv) *adj.* Pertaining to, expressing, or tending to excite emotion; especially, likely to arouse an ill-considered or irra-

tional response. —**e·mo·tive·ly** *adv.* —**e·mo·tive·ness, e·mo·tiv·i·**
ty (ē′mō-tĭv′ə-tē) *n.*

e·mo·tiv·ism (ĭ-mō′tĭv-ĭz′əm) *n. Philosophy.* The doctrine that cal propositions are neither true nor false statements, but sions of emotion. Compare **descriptivism, prescr** —**e·mo·tiv·ist** *n. & adj.*

Emp. 1. emperor; empress. **2.** empire.

empale. Variant of **impale.**

empanel. Variant of **impanel.**

em·path·ic (ĕm-păth′ĭk, ĭm-) *adj.* Also **em·pa·thet·ic** (ĕm′pə-thĕt′ĭk). Of, pertaining to, or characterized by empathy. —**em·path·i·cal·ly, em·pa·thet·i·cal·ly** *adv.*

em·pa·thize (ĕm′pə-thīz′) *intr.v.* **-thized, -thizing, -thizes.** To feel or experience empathy. Often used with *with.*

em·pa·thy (ĕm′pə-thē) *n.* **1.** Understanding so intimate that the feelings, thoughts, and motives of one person are readily comprehended by another. **2.** The attribution of feelings aroused by an object in nature or art to the object itself, as when one speaks of a painting full of love. [EN- (in) + -PATHY (translation of German *Einfühlung,* "a feeling in"), after Greek *empatheia,* passion.]

Em·ped·o·cles (ĕm-pĕd′ə-klēz′) (*fl.* 5th century B.C.). Greek philosopher, poet, physician, and statesman, born in Sicily. He taught that all matter is composed of particles of fire, water, earth, and air. More important for the future of physics was his belief that all change is caused by motion.

em·pen·nage (ĕm′pə-nĭj, ŏm′pə-näzh′) *n. Aeronautics.* The **tail** (see). [French, originally "the feathers on an arrow," from *empenner,* to put feathers on an arrow : *en-,* in + *penne,* feather, from Latin *pinna.*]

em·per·or (ĕm′pər-ər) *n.* **1.** *Abbr.* **Emp.** The male ruler of an empire, having power either absolute or subject to constitutional restrictions. **2. a.** Any of several brightly colored butterflies of the family Nymphalidae, such as *Asterocampa clyton,* having orange-tawny wings with dark markings. Also called "emperor butterfly." **b.** Any of several moths of the family Saturniidae; especially, an Old World species, *Saturnia pavonia,* having distinctively patterned wings. Also called "emperor moth." [Middle English *emperour,* from Old French *empereor,* from Latin *imperātor,* emperor, commander, from *imperāre* (past participle *imperātus*), "to prepare against (an occasion)," hence to command : *in-,* against + *parāre,* to prepare.] —**em·per·or·ship** *n.*

emperor penguin *n.* A large penguin, *Aptenodytes forsteri,* of Antarctic regions, having yellow-orange patches on the neck.

em·per·y (ĕm′pə-rē) *n., pl.* **-ies. 1.** Absolute dominion or jurisdiction; sovereignty. **2.** *Archaic.* The domain of an emperor. [Middle English *emperie,* from Old French, EMPIRE.]

em·pha·sis (ĕm′fə-sĭs) *n., pl.* **-ses** (-sēz′). **1.** Special importance or significance placed upon or imparted to something: *put too much emphasis on being neat.* **2.** Stress applied to a syllable, word, or passage by the use of vocal expression, gesture, italics, or other indication. **3.** Force or intensity of expression, feeling, or action. **4.** Sharpness or vividness of outline; prominence. [Latin, from Greek, reflection, meaning, significance, from *emphainein,* to exhibit, indicate : *en-,* in + *phainein,* to show.]

em·pha·size (ĕm′fə-sīz′) *tr.v.* **-sized, -sizing, -sizes.** To impart emphasis to; stress.

em·phat·ic (ĕm-făt′ĭk) *adj.* **1.** Expressed or performed with emphasis. **2.** Bold and definite in expression or action; positive. **3.** Standing out in a striking and clearly defined way; definite: *an emphatic victory.* **4.** Designating an English verb form using the auxiliary verb *do* to make a strong assertion. **5.** *Phonetics.* Having a hard constrictive velarized quality, as certain Arabic consonants do. [Late Latin *emphaticus,* from Greek *emphatikos,* exhibited, hence emphatic, from *emphainein,* to exhibit. See **emphasis.**] —**em·phat·i·cal·ly** *adv.*

em·phy·se·ma (ĕm′fə-sē′mə) *n.* **1.** An abnormal condition of the lungs marked by dilation of the air sacs resulting in labored breathing. **2.** A distention of connective tissues due to retention of air. [New Latin, from Greek *emphusēma,* swelling, inflation, from *emphusan,* to blow in : *en-,* in + *phusan,* to blow, from *phusai,* bellows.] —**em·phy·sem·a·tous** (ĕm′fə-sĕm′ə-təs) *adj.*

em·pire (ĕm′pīr′) *n. Abbr.* **Emp. 1.** A political unit, usually larger than a kingdom and often comprising a number of territories or nations, ruled by a single supreme authority. **2.** The territory included in such a unit. **3. a.** Imperial dominion. **b.** The period during which such dominion exists. **4.** An extensive enterprise under a unified authority: *a publishing empire.* [Middle English *empire,* from Old French *empire, emperie,* from Latin *imperium,* dominion, empire, from *imperāre,* to command. See **emperor.**]

Em·pire (ŏm-pîr′, ĕm′pîr′) *adj.* Of, pertaining to, or characteristic of a neoclassic style, as in clothing or the decorative arts, prevalent in France during the first part of the 19th century. [After the 1st *Empire* of France (1804-15).]

empire builder *n.* A person who seeks to increase his influence, power, or control by constantly acquiring new operations or staff. —**empire building** *n.*

em·pir·ic (ĕm-pîr′ĭk, ĭm-) *n.* One who believes that practical experience is the sole source of knowledge. [Latin *empiricus,* from Greek *empeirikos,* from *empeirā,* experience, from *empeiros,* experienced in : *en-,* in + *peira,* experiment, trial.]

em·pir·i·cal (ĕm-pîr′ĭ-kəl, ĭm-) *adj.* **1.** Relying upon or derived from observation or experiment: *empirical methods; an empirical conclu-*

emperor moth *The feathery antennae of the male emperor moth—varieties of which are found all over Europe and Asia—can detect the scent of a female from more than half a mile away. The cocoon of the moth's caterpillar has a ring of spines at its exit, like a lobster pot in reverse, preventing predators from entering.*

emu *Standing up to 1.8 meters (6 feet) tall and weighing more than 45 kilograms (100 pounds), the emu is a flightless bird of the Australian grasslands. It can run up to 50 kilometers (30 miles) per hour.*

enamel *Blue and red areas of glasslike enamel decorate a 19th-century thimble from Russia.*

sion. **2.** Guided by practical experience and not theory, especially in medicine. **—em·pir·i·cal·ly** *adv.*
empirical formula *n.* A type of chemical formula that indicates the ratio of the elements rather than the total number of atoms in a molecule. Compare **molecular formula, structural formula.**
em·pir·i·cism (ĕm-pîr′ə-sĭz′əm, ĭm-) *n.* **1. a.** The view that experience, especially of the senses, is the only source of knowledge. **b.** *Philosophy.* The doctrine based on this view. Compare **rationalism. 2. a.** The employment of empirical methods, as in an art or science. **b.** An empirical conclusion. **3.** The practice of medicine that is based upon practical experience rather than scientific theory. **—em·pir·i·cist** *n.*
em·place (ĕm-plās′, ĭm-) *tr.v.* **-placed, -placing, -places.** To put in place or position.
em·place·ment (ĕm-plās′mənt, ĭm-) *n.* **1.** A prepared position, such as a mounting or platform, for military equipment and guns. **2.** The act of setting in position; placement. **3.** Position; location. [French, place, situation, from (obsolete) *emplacer,* to place in (a position) : *em-,* in + *placer,* to PLACE.]
emplane. Variant of **enplane.**
em·ploy (ĕm-ploi′, ĭm-) *tr.v.* **-ployed, -ploying, -ploys. 1.** To use in some process or effort; put to service. **2.** To devote or apply (one's time or energies, for example) to some activity. **3. a.** To engage the services of; put to work. **b.** To provide with a job and livelihood.
∼n. **1.** The state of being employed. **2.** *Archaic.* Occupation. [Middle English *emploien,* from Old French *employer, emplier,* from Latin *implicāre,* to infold, involve : *in-,* in + *plicāre,* to fold.] **—em·ploy·a·bil·i·ty** *n.* **—em·ploy·a·ble** *adj.*
em·ploy·ee (ĕm-ploi′ē, ĭm-, ĕm′ploi-ē′) *n.* A person who works for another in return for financial or other compensation.
em·ploy·er (ĕm-ploi′ər, ĭm-) *n.* A person or concern that employs persons for wages or a salary.
em·ploy·ment (ĕm-ploi′mənt, ĭm-) *n.* **1. a.** The act of employing; a putting to use. **b.** The state of being employed. **2.** The work in which one is engaged; business or profession. **3.** The purpose for which something is used. **4.** An activity to which one devotes time.
em·po·ri·um (ĕm-pôr′ē-əm, -pōr′ē-əm, ĭm-) *n., pl.* **-riums** or **-poria** (-pôr′ē-ə, -pōr′ē-ə). **1.** A large retail shop, such as a department store, carrying a wide variety of merchandise. **2.** A place, town, or city that is an important trade center; a marketplace. [Latin, from Greek *emporion,* market, from *emporos,* merchant, traveler : *en-,* in + *poros,* path, journey.]
em·pow·er (ĕm-pou′ər, ĭm-) *tr.v.* **-ered, -ering, -ers. 1.** To invest with legal power; authorize. **2.** To enable or permit. **—em·pow·er·ment** *n.*
em·press (ĕm′prĭs) *n. Abbr.* **Emp. 1.** A female sovereign of an empire. **2.** The wife or widow of an emperor. [Middle English *emperesse,* from Old French, feminine of *empereor,* EMPEROR.]
em·prise, em·prize (ĕm-prīz′) *n.* **1.** Chivalrous daring or prowess. **2.** An undertaking, especially one of a chivalrous or adventurous nature. [Middle English *emprise,* from Old French, from the feminine past participle of *emprendre,* to undertake, from Vulgar Latin *imprendere* (unattested) : Latin *in-,* in + *prendere, prehendere,* to take, seize.]
emp·ty (ĕmp′tē) *adj.* **-tier, -tiest. 1.** Void of content; containing nothing: *an empty bottle.* **2.** Having no occupants or inhabitants; vacant: *an empty chair.* **3.** Having no load or cargo: *an empty truck.* **4.** Lacking force or power: *an empty threat.* **5.** Lacking purpose or substance; meaningless: *an empty life.* **6.** Idle: *empty hours.* **7.** Vacuous; inane: *an empty mind.* **8.** Needing nourishment; hungry. **9.** Devoid; destitute. Used with *of*: *empty of pity.*
∼v. **emptied, -tying, -ties.** *—tr.* **1.** To remove the contents of; make empty: *empty one's pockets.* **2.** To transfer or pour off: *empty the ashes into a pail.* **3.** To unburden; relieve. Used with *of*: *empty oneself of doubt.* *—intr.* **1.** To become empty. **2.** To discharge or flow. Used with *into*: *The river empties into a bay.*
∼n., pl. **empties.** An empty container: *returned the empties to the store.* [Middle English *empty, emptie,* Old English *ǣmettig, ǣmtig,* empty, unoccupied, from *ǣmetta,* rest, leisure.] **—emp·ti·ly** *adv.* **—emp·ti·ness** *n.*
Synonyms: *bare, barren, blank, vacant, vacuous, void.*
emp·ty-hand·ed (ĕmp′tē-hăn′dĭd) *adj.* **1.** Bearing no gift, possessions, or the like: *They arrived empty-handed.* **2.** Having received or gained nothing.
emp·ty-head·ed (ĕmp′tē-hĕd′ĭd) *adj.* Lacking sense or discretion; foolish; scatterbrained.
Empty Quarter. See **Rub al Khali.**
empty set *n. Mathematics.* A set that has no members. Also called "null set."
em·pur·ple (ĕm-pûr′pəl, ĭm-) *tr.v.* **-pled, -pling, -ples.** To color or tinge with purple.
em·py·e·ma (ĕm′pī-ē′mə) *n., pl.* **-mata** (-mə-tə). Pus in a body cavity, especially the pleural cavity. [Medieval Latin, from Greek *empuēma,* from *empuein,* to suppurate.] **—em·py·e·mic** *adj.*
em·py·re·al (ĕm′pī-rē′əl, ĕm-pîr′ē-əl, ĭm-) *adj.* **1.** Empyrean. **2.** Of or pertaining to the sky; celestial. **3.** Formed of pure fire or light; fiery. **4.** Heavenly; sublime. [Middle English *imperyale,* from Late Latin *empyrius, empyreus,* from Greek *empurios, empuros,* fiery : *en-,* in + *pur,* fire.]
em·py·re·an (ĕm′pī-rē′ən, ĕm-pîr′ē-ən, ĭm-) *n.* **1.** The highest reaches of heaven, believed by the ancients to be a realm of pure fire and by early Christians to be the abode of God and the angels. **2.** The sky; space.
∼adj. Of or pertaining to the empyrean of ancient belief. [Late Latin *empyreus,* EMPYREAL.]
EMS European Monetary System.
e·mu (ē′myōō) *n., pl.* **emus.** A large, flightless Australian bird, *Dromaius novaehollandiae,* related to and resembling the cassowary. [Portuguese *ema,* perhaps from Moluccan *eme.*]
emu electromagnetic unit.
em·u·late (ĕm′yə-lāt′) *tr.v.* **-lated, -lating, -lates. 1.** To strive to equal or excel, especially through imitation. **2.** To compete with or rival successfully: *Korea emulates Japan in its single-minded productivity.* **3.** *Computer Science.* To imitate one system with another so that both accept the same data, execute the same programs, and achieve the same results. —See Synonyms at **rival.** [Latin *aemulārī,* from *aemulus,* EMULOUS.] **—em·u·la·tive** *adj.* **—em·u·la·tive·ly** *adv.* **—em·u·la·tor** *n.*
em·u·la·tion (ĕm′yə-lā′shən) *n.* **1.** Effort or ambition to equal or surpass another. **2.** Imitation of another.
em·u·lous (ĕm′yə-ləs) *adj.* **1.** Eager or ambitious to equal or surpass another. **2.** Characterized or prompted by a spirit of rivalry. [Latin *aemulus,* imitating, probably related to *imitārī,* to IMITATE.] **—em·u·lous·ly** *adv.* **—em·u·lous·ness** *n.*
e·mul·si·fy (ĭ-mŭl′sə-fī′) *tr.v.* **-fied, -fying, -fies.** To make into an emulsion. [EMULSI(ON) + -FY.] **—e·mul·si·fi·ca·tion** *n.* **—e·mul·si·fi·er** *n.*
e·mul·sion (ĭ-mŭl′shən) *n.* **1. a.** A suspension of small globules of one liquid in a second liquid with which the first will not mix, such as milk fats in milk. **b.** Any milklike liquid. **2.** A light-sensitive coating, usually of silver halide grains in a thin gelatin layer, on photographic film, paper, or glass. **3.** Emulsion paint. [New Latin, from Latin *ēmulgēre* (past participle *ēmulsus*), to drain out, milk out : *ex-,* out + *mulgēre,* to milk.] **—e·mul·sive** *adj.*
emulsion paint *n.* A type of paint in which the pigment is dispersed in an oil that forms an emulsion with water.
e·mul·soid (ĭ-mŭl′soid′) *n. Chemistry.* A type of colloid in which small droplets of a liquid are dispersed throughout a solid continuous phase. [*Emul*sion + col*loid.*]
e·munc·to·ry (ĭ-mŭngk′tə-rē) *adj.* Serving to carry waste matter out of the body; excretory.
∼n., pl. **emunctories.** An emunctory organ or passage. [Middle English *emunctorie,* from Medieval Latin *ēmunctōrius,* from Latin *ēmungere* (past participle *ēmunctus*), to blow the nose : *ex-,* completely + *mungere,* to blow the nose.]
en (ĕn) *n.* **1.** The letter *n.* **2.** *Printing. Abbr.* **n, N** A space equal to half the width of an **em** *(see).*
∼adj. Printing. Designating a dash or space that is equal to the width of an en.
en-¹ *prefix.* Also **em-** before *b, p,* and sometimes *m.* Indicates: **1.** To put into or on; for example, **encompass, enthrone. 2.** To go into or on; for example, **entrain. 3.** To cover, surround, or imbue with; for example, **enrobe, empurple. 4.** To provide with; for example, **empower. 5.** To cause to be in a specified state or condition; for example, **endanger, enslave.** [Middle English, from Old French, from Latin *in-, im-.*]
en-² *prefix.* Also **em-** before *b, m, p,* or *ph.* Indicates in, into, or within; for example, **enzootic, empathy.** [Middle English *en-,* from Latin, from Greek. In borrowed Greek compounds, *en-* also becomes *el-* before *l,* as in **ellipsis.**]
-en¹ *suffix.* Indicates: **1.** To be, become, or cause to be; for example, **cheapen, redden. 2.** To cause to have or gain; for example, **lengthen, hearten.** [Middle English *-nen, -nien,* Old English *-nian.*]
-en² *suffix.* Indicates made of, composed of, or resembling; for example, **wooden, earthen, ashen.** [Middle English *-en,* Old English *-en.*]
en·a·ble (ĕn-ā′bəl) *tr.v.* **-bled, -bling, -bles. 1. a.** To supply with the means, knowledge, or opportunity to be or do something. **b.** To make feasible or possible. **2.** To give legal power, capacity, or sanction to; permit.
enabling act *n. British.* A law passed to give certain powers to a person or organization, as a governmental department.
en·act (ĕn-ăkt′) *tr.v.* **-acted, -acting, -acts. 1.** To give effect to (legislation); decree by legislative process; pass. **2.** To act out, as on a stage; represent. **—en·act·a·ble** *adj.* **—en·ac·tor** *n.*
en·ac·tive (ĕn-ăk′tĭv) *adj.* Having the capacity or force to enact.
en·act·ment (ĕn-ăkt′mənt) *n.* **1.** The act of enacting. **2.** The state of being enacted. **3.** A law or statute.
en·am·el (ĭ-năm′əl) *n.* **1.** A smooth, glassy, usually opaque protective or decorative coating baked on metal, glass, or ceramic ware. **2.** An object with an enameled surface, as a piece of cloisonné. **3.** A paint that dries to a hard, glossy surface. **4.** A glossy, hard coating resembling enamel: *nail enamel.* **5.** *Anatomy.* The hard, calcium-containing substance covering the exposed portion of a tooth.
∼tr.v. **enameled** or **-elled, -eling** or **-elling, -els. 1.** To coat, inlay, or decorate with enamel. **2.** To give a glossy or brilliant surface to. **3.** To adorn with or as if with bright colors. [Middle English *enamelen,* from Norman French *enameller, enamailler* : *en-,* in + *amail,* enamel, from Old French *esmail,* from Germanic.] **—en·am·el·er, en·am·el·ist** *n.*
en·am·el·ing (ĭ-năm′ə-lĭng) *n.* **1.** The art, craft, or occupation of a person who enamels. **2.** A coating or decoration of enamel.
en·am·el·ware (ĭ-năm′əl-wâr′) *n.* Articles coated with enamel.
en·am·or (ĭ-năm′ər) *tr.v.* **-ored, -oring, -ors.** Also *chiefly British* **en·am·our, -oured, -ouring, -ours.** To inspire with love; charm; captivate: *enamored of his surroundings.* [Middle English *enamouren,*

from Old French *enamourer* : *en-*, in + *amour*, love, from Latin *amor*, from *amāre*, to love.]

en·an·ti·o·mer (ĕn-ăn′tē-ə-mər) *n.* An enantiomorph. [Greek *enantios*, opposite (see **enantiomorph**) + -MER.] —**en·an·ti·o·mer·ic** (ĕn-ăn′tē-ə-mĕr′ĭk) *adj.*

en·an·ti·o·morph (ĕn-ăn′tē-ə-môrf′) *n. Chemistry.* Either of a pair of crystals that are similar in form but cannot be superimposed, one crystal being the mirror image of the other. [Greek *enantios*, opposite : *en-*, in + *antios*, opposite, from *anti*, over against + -MORPH.] —**en·an·ti·o·morph·ism** (ĕn-ăn′tē-ə-môr′fĭz′əm) *n.* —**en·an·ti·o·mor·phous** (-môr′fəs), **en·an·ti·o·mor·phic** (-môr′fĭk) *adj.*

en·ar·thro·sis (ĕn′är-thrō′sĭs) *n., pl.* **-ses** (-sēz′). *Anatomy.* A ball-and-socket joint. [New Latin, from Greek *enarthrōsis*, from *enarthros*, jointed : *en-*, in + *arthron*, joint.]

e·nate (ē′nāt′, ĭ-nāt′) *adj.* Also **e·nat·ic** (ĭ-năt′ĭk) (for sense 2). **1.** Growing outward. **2.** Related on the mother's side. ~*n.* A relative on one's mother's side. [Latin *ēnātus*, past participle of *ēnāscī*, to be born from : *ex-*, out of + *nāscī*, to be born.]

en bloc (än blŏk′) *adv.* All together; collectively; as a whole or single unit. [French, "in (a) block."]

en bro·chette (äN′ brô-shĕt′) *adj.* Broiled or roasted on a skewer. [French, "on (a) skewer."]

en brosse (äN brôs′) *adj.* Standing stiffly upright as a result of being cut very short. Said of hair. [French, "in (a) brush."]

enc. enclosed; enclosure.

en·cae·nia (ĕn-sēn′yə, -sē′nē-ə, ĭn-) *n.* An annual commemoration held at universities, especially in England, honoring founders and benefactors. [Latin, feast of dedication, from Greek *enkainia* (plural) : *en-*, in + *kainos*, new.]

en·cage (ĕn-kāj′, ĭn-) *tr.v.* **-caged, -caging, -cages.** To confine in or as if in a cage.

en·camp (ĕn-kămp′, ĭn-) *v.* **-camped, -camping, -camps.** —*intr.* To set up or live in a camp. —*tr.* To provide quarters for in a camp.

en·camp·ment (ĕn-kămp′mənt, ĭn-) *n.* **1.** The act of setting up a camp. **2.** A camp or campsite.

en·cap·su·late (ĕn-kăp′sə-lāt′, ĭn-) *v.* **-lated, -lating, -lates.** Also **in·cap·su·late** (ĭn-). —*tr.* **1.** To encase in or as if in a capsule. **2.** To summarize very concisely. —*intr.* To become encapsulated. —**en·cap·su·la·tion** (ĕn-) *n.*

en·case (ĕn-kās′, ĭn-) *tr.v.* **-cased, -casing, -cases.** Also **in·case** (ĭn-). To enclose in or as if in a case. —**en·case·ment** *n.*

en·cash (ĕn-kăsh′, ĭn-) *tr.v.* **-cashed, -cashing, -cashes.** *British.* To cash (a check). —**en·cash·a·ble** *adj.* —**en·cash·ment** *n.*

en·caus·tic (ĕn-kô′stĭk, ĭn-) *adj.* Pertaining to a painting process in which colored beeswax is applied and fixed with heat. ~*n.* **1.** The art of painting in this way. **2.** An encaustic painting. [Latin *encausticus*, from Greek *enkaustikos*, from *enkaiein*, to burn in : *en-*, in + *kaiein*, to burn.]

–ence, –ency *suffix.* Indicates action, state, quality, or condition; for example, **competence, patience.** [Middle English *-ence*, from Old French, from Latin *-entia*, from *-ēns*, present participial suffix.]

en·ceinte[1] (äN-săNt′) *adj.* Being with child; pregnant. [French, from Old French, from Vulgar Latin *incienta* (unattested), from Latin *inciens*.]

enceinte[2] **1.** An encircling fortification around a fort, castle, or town. **2.** The structures or area protected by such a fortification. [French, from Latin *incincta*, feminine past participle of *incingere*, to gird in : *in-*, in + *cingere*, to gird.]

en·ce·phal·ic (ĕn′sə-făl′ĭk) *adj.* **1.** Of or pertaining to the brain. **2.** Located within the cranial cavity.

en·ceph·a·li·tis (ĕn-sĕf′ə-lī′tĭs) *n.* Inflammation of the brain. Also called "brain fever," "phrenitis." —**en·ceph·a·lit·ic** (ĕn-sĕf′ə-lĭt′ĭk) *adj.*

encephalitis le·thar·gi·ca (lə-thär′jĭ-kə) *n.* A viral epidemic encephalitis often held to be associated with some forms of influenza and marked by apathy, double vision, and extreme muscular weakness. Also called "lethargic encephalitis," "sleeping sickness." [New Latin, "lethargic encephalitis."]

encephalo–, encephal– *comb. form.* Indicates the brain; for example, **encephalogram, encephalitis.** [New Latin, from Greek *(muelos) enkephalos*, "(marrow) in the head," the brain : *en-*, in + *kephalē*, head.]

en·ceph·a·lo·gram (ĕn-sĕf′ə-lə-grăm′) *n.* **1.** An x-ray picture of the brain taken by encephalography. **2.** An **electroencephalogram** *(see).*

en·ceph·a·log·ra·phy (ĕn-sĕf′ə-lŏg′rə-fē) *n.* A technique for recording the structure of the brain by tracing electrical activity, detecting ultrasonic pulses, or introducing air to provide a contrast medium for x-rays. —**en·ceph·a·lo·graph** (ĕn-sĕf′ə-lə-grăf′) *n.* —**en·ceph·a·lo·graph·ic** (ĕn-sĕf′ə-lə-grăf′ĭk) *adj.*

en·ceph·a·lo·ma (ĕn-sĕf′ə-lō′mə) *n., pl.* **-mas** or **-mata** (-mə-tə). A tumor of the brain. [ENCEPHAL(O)- + -OMA.]

en·ceph·a·lo·my·e·li·tis (ĕn-sĕf′ə-lō-mī′ə-lī′tĭs) *n.* Acute inflammation of the brain and the spinal cord.

en·ceph·a·lon (ĕn-sĕf′ə-lŏn′) *n., pl.* **-la** (-lə). The brain of a vertebrate. [New Latin, from Greek *enkephalon, enkephalos.* See **encephalo-.**] —**en·ceph·a·lous** *adj.*

en·ceph·a·lop·a·thy (ĕn-sĕf′ə-lŏp′ə-thē) *n., pl.* **-thies.** Any of various diseases that affect the brain. [ENCEPHALO- + -PATHY.] —**en·ceph·a·lo·path·ic** (ĕn-sĕf′ə-lō-păth′ĭk) *adj.*

en·chain (ĕn-chān′, ĭn-) *tr.v.* **-chained, -chaining, -chains. 1.** To bind with or as if with chains; fetter: *Superstition enchains the mind.* **2.** To hold fast; rivet (the attention, for example). [Middle English

encheynen, from Old French *enchaeiner* : *en-*, in + *chaeine*, CHAIN.] —**en·chain·ment** *n.*

en·chant (ĕn-chănt′, -chänt′, ĭn-) *tr.v.* **-chanted, -chanting, -chants. 1.** To cast under a spell; bewitch. **2.** To delight completely; charm; enrapture. [Middle English *enchanten*, Old French *enchanter*, from Latin *incantāre*, to chant (magic words) : *in-* (intensive) + *cantāre*, frequentative of *canere*, to sing.]

en·chant·er (ĕn-chăn′tər, -chän′tər, ĭn-) *n.* One that enchants; especially, a sorcerer or magician.

enchanter's nightshade *n.* Any of several plants of the genus *Circaea*, especially *C. lutetiana*, having small white flowers and bristly, clinging fruit.

en·chant·ing (ĕn-chăn′tĭng, -chän′tĭng, ĭn-) *adj.* Having the power to enchant; delightful: *a children's book with enchanting illustrations.* —**en·chant·ing·ly** *adv.*

en·chant·ment (ĕn-chănt′mənt, -chänt′mənt, ĭn-) *n.* **1. a.** An act of enchanting. **b.** The state of being enchanted. **2.** Something that enchants; an irresistible charm or allure. **3.** A magic spell.

en·chant·ress (ĕn-chăn′trĭs, -chän′trĭs, ĭn-) *n.* **1.** A woman of unusual allure or fascination. **2.** A sorceress.

en·chase (ĕn-chās′, ĭn-) *tr.v.* **-chased, -chasing, -chases. 1.** To set (a gem, for example) in some material. **2.** To set with or as if with gems. **3.** To decorate or ornament (a surface) by inlaying, engraving, or chasing. [Middle English *enchasen*, from Old French *enchasser* : *en-*, in + *chasse*, case, from Latin *capsa*, box.]

en·chi·la·da (ĕn′chə-lä′də) *n.* A dish consisting of a tortilla rolled and stuffed usually with a mixture containing meat or cheese and served with a sauce spiced with chili. [American Spanish, feminine past participle of *enchilar*, to put chili in : *en-*, in, from Latin *in-* + *chile*, CHILI.]

en·chi·rid·i·on (ĕn′kī-rĭd′ē-ən) *n., pl.* **-ons** or **-ridia** (-rĭd′ē-ə). A handbook; a manual. [Late Latin, from Greek *enkheiridion* : *en-*, in + *-kheiridion*, diminutive of *kheir*, hand.]

en·chon·dro·ma (ĕn′kŏn-drō′mə) *n., pl.* **-mas** or **-mata** (-mə-tə). A benign cartilaginous tumor that occurs at the growing zone of a bone, between the end and the shaft. [EN- + CHONDR(O)- + -OMA.]

en·cho·ri·al (ĕn-kôr′ē-əl, -kōr′ē-əl, ĭn-) *adj.* Also **en·chor·ic** (-kôr′ĭk, -kōr′ĭk). Belonging or native to a particular region or people. Said especially of demotic writing. [Greek *enkhōrios*, indigenous, native : *en-*, in + *khōra*, country, place.]

–enchyma *suffix.* Indicates cellular tissue; for example, **collenchyma.** [New Latin, from (PAR)ENCHYMA.]

en·ci·pher (ĕn-sī′fər, ĭn-) *tr.v.* **-phered, -phering, -phers.** To put (a message) into cipher. —**en·ci·pher·er** *n.* —**en·ci·pher·ment** *n.*

en·cir·cle (ĕn-sûr′kəl, ĭn-) *tr.v.* **-cled, -cling, -cles. 1.** To form a circle around; surround. **2.** To move or go around; make a circuit of. —**en·cir·cle·ment** *n.*

En·cke's comet (ĕng′kēz) *n.* A comet with a period of 3.3 years, decreasing by 2½ hours each revolution. First observed in 1786, it is the most studied of all comets. [After Johann *Encke* (1791–1865), German astronomer.]

encl. enclosed; enclosure.

en clair (äN klâr′) *adj.* In ordinary uncoded language. [French, "in (the) clear."] —**en clair** *adv.*

en·clasp (ĕn-klăsp′, -kläsp′, ĭn-) *tr.v.* **-clasped, -clasping, -clasps.** To hold in or as if in a clasp; embrace.

en·clave (ĕn′klāv′, ŏn′-) *n.* **1.** A country or part of a country lying wholly within the boundaries of another. Compare **exclave. 2.** A distinctly bounded area enclosed within a larger area. **3.** An area, as of a city, in which a particular group of people lives or works: *an enclave of artists.* [French, from Old French *enclaver*, to enclose, from Vulgar Latin *inclāvāre* (unattested), to lock in with a key : Latin *in-*, in + *clāvis*, key.]

en·clit·ic (ĕn-klĭt′ĭk, ĭn-) *adj. Linguistics.* Having no independent accent in a sentence and forming an accentual and sometimes also graphemic unit with the preceding word. Used of a word or particle; for example, *'em* in informal English *Give 'em the works* or *-que* in Latin *Senatus populusque Romanus* ("The senate and people of Rome"). Compare **proclitic.** ~*n.* An enclitic word or particle. [Late Latin *encliticus*, from Greek *enklitikos*, "leaning (on the preceding word for accent)," from *enklinein*, to lean on : *en-*, in + *klinein*, to lean.]

en·close (ĕn-klōz′, ĭn-) *tr.v.* **-closed, -closing, -closes.** Also **in·close** (ĭn-). **1.** To surround on all sides; fence in; close in. **2. a.** To place within a container. **b.** To insert in the same envelope or package with the main letter. **3.** To contain, especially so as to shelter or hide: *"every one of those darkly clustered houses encloses its own secret"* (Charles Dickens). —See Usage note at **inclose.** [Middle English *enclosen*, from Old French *enclore* (past participle *enclose*), from Vulgar Latin *inclaudere* (unattested), variant of Latin *inclūdere*, to INCLUDE.]

en·clo·sure (ĕn-klō′zhər, ĭn-) *n. Abbr.* **enc., encl. 1.** The act of enclosing. **2.** The state of being enclosed or shut up: *The house smelled stale from prolonged enclosure.* **3.** An area that is enclosed. **4.** Something that encloses, such as a wall or fence. **5.** Something, as a letter, that is enclosed in an envelope or package: *The note from his little daughter was a welcome and unexpected enclosure.*

en·code (ĕn-kōd′, ĭn-) *tr.v.* **-coded, -coding, -codes. 1.** To put (a message) into code. **2.** *Computer Science.* To convert (a character) into an equivalent combination of bits. —**en·cod·er** *n.*

en·co·mi·ast (ĕn-kō′mē-ăst′) *n.* A person who delivers or writes encomiums; a eulogist. [Greek *enkōmiastēs*, from *enkōmiazein*, to praise, from *enkōmion*, ENCOMIUM.]

en·co·mi·as·tic (ĕn-kō′mē-ăs′tĭk) *adj.* Also **en·co·mi·as·ti·cal** (-tĭ-kəl). Pertaining to, containing, or being an encomium. **—en·co·mi·as·ti·cal·ly** *adv.*

en·co·mi·um (ĕn-kō′mē-əm) *n., pl.* **-ums** or **-mia** (-mē-ə). 1. Warm or glowing praise. 2. A formal expression of praise; a tribute. [Latin *encomium,* from Greek *enkōmion (epos),* "(speech) in praise of a conqueror," from *enkōmios,* belonging to revels : *en-,* in + *kōmos,* celebration, revel (see **comedy**).]

en·com·pass (ĕn-kŭm′pəs, ĭn-) *tr.v.* **-passed, -passing, -passes.** 1. To form a circle or ring about; surround. 2. To enclose; envelop. 3. To comprise; include. 4. To succeed in completing or perfecting; accomplish: *an assignment that only the most skilled could encompass.* **—en·com·pass·ment** *n.*

en·core (ŏn′kôr′, -kōr′) *n.* 1. A demand by an audience for an additional performance. 2. An additional performance in response to such a demand.
~*tr.v.* **encored, -coring, -cores.** 1. To demand an encore of (a performer). 2. To demand as an encore.
~*interj.* Used to demand an additional performance. [French, still, yet, again, probably from Latin *hinc ad hōram,* from that to this hour : *hinc,* from here, from *hic,* this + *ad,* to + *hōram,* accusative of *hōra,* hour, from Greek *hōra.*]

en·coun·ter (ĕn-koun′tər, ĭn-) *n.* 1. A meeting, especially when casual and unplanned. 2. A hostile confrontation; clash.
~*v.* **encountered, -tering, -ters.** *—tr.* 1. To meet or come upon, especially casually or unexpectedly. 2. To confront in battle or contention. 3. To come up against; be faced with or exposed to: *encounter numerous obstacles.* *—intr.* To meet, especially in conflict. [Middle English *encountre,* from Old French *encontre,* from *encontrer,* to meet, from Vulgar Latin *incontrāre* (unattested) : Latin *in-,* in + *contrā,* opposite, against.]

encounter group *n.* A typically unstructured therapy group in which individuals seek to increase their sensitivity and responsiveness, reveal their feelings, and relate to others openly and intimately, as by verbalizing freely.

en·cour·age (ĕn-kûr′ĭj, ĭn-) *tr.v.* **-aged, -aging, -ages.** 1. To inspire to continue on a chosen course; impart courage or confidence to; embolden; hearten. 2. To give support to; foster. **—See Synonyms at urge.** [Middle English *encoragen,* from Old French *encorager* : *en-* (causative) + *corage,* COURAGE.] **—en·cour·age·ment** *n.*

en·cour·ag·ing (ĕn-kûr′ə-jĭng, ĭn-) *adj.* Permitting one to be confident or hopeful. **—en·cour·ag·ing·ly** *adv.*

en·croach (ĕn-krōch′, ĭn-) *intr.v.* **-croached, -croaching, -croaches.** 1. To intrude gradually or insidiously upon the domain, possessions, or rights of another; trespass. Used with *on* or *upon.* 2. To advance beyond proper or prescribed limits. [Middle English *encroachen,* from Old French *encrochier,* "to catch in a hook," seize : *en-,* in + *croc,* hook, from (unattested) Frankish *krōk.*]

en·croach·ment (ĕn-krōch′mənt, ĭn-) *n.* The act or an instance of encroaching. **—See Synonyms at breach.**

en·crust (ĕn-krŭst′, ĭn-) *tr.v.* **-crusted, -crusting, -crusts.** Also **in·crust** (ĭn-). 1. To cover or surmount with a crust or crustlike layer. 2. To adorn, as with jewels. [Probably from French *incruster,* from Latin *incrustāre* : *in-* (causative) + *crusta,* CRUST.] **—en·crust·a·tion** (ĕn′krŭ-stā′shən) *n.*

en·cryp·tion (ĕn-krĭp′shən, ĭn-) *n.* A process for scrambling access codes to computer programs to prevent illicit entry into and control of the system.

en·cum·ber (ĕn-kŭm′bər, ĭn-) *tr.v.* **-bered, -bering, -bers.** 1. To weigh down unduly; lay too much upon. 2. To hinder, impede, or clutter, as with useless articles or unwanted additions. 3. To handicap or burden, as with obligations or legal claims. **—See Synonyms at hinder.** [Middle English *encombren,* from Old French *encombrer,* to block up : *en-,* in + *combre,* hindrance, from Gaulish *comboros*† (unattested).]

en·cum·brance (ĕn-kŭm′brəns, ĭn-) *n.* 1. One that encumbers; a burden, impediment, or obstacle. 2. *Law.* A lien or claim upon property, such as a mortgage. **—See Synonyms at obstacle.**

en·cum·branc·er (ĕn-kŭm′brən-sər, ĭn-) *n. Law.* A person who holds an encumbrance, as on another's property.

ency., encyc., encycl. encyclopedia.

-ency. Variant of **-ence.**

en·cyc·li·cal (ĕn-sĭk′lĭ-kəl, ĭn-) *adj.* Intended for general or wide circulation. Said of letters.
~*n. Roman Catholic Church.* A papal letter on a specific subject addressed officially to the clergy or to the hierarchy of a particular country. [Late Latin *encyclicus,* from Greek *enkuklios,* in a circle, circular : *en-,* in + *kuklos,* circle.]

en·cy·clo·pe·di·a, en·cy·clo·pae·di·a (ĕn-sī′klə-pē′dē-ə, ĭn-) *n. Abbr.* **ency., encyc., encycl.** A comprehensive, often multivolume reference work containing articles on a wide range of subjects or on numerous aspects of a particular field, usually arranged alphabetically. [Medieval Latin *encyclopaedia,* general education course, from Greek *enkuklopaideiā,* a mistaken transcription of *enkuklios paideia,* general education : *enkuklios,* circular, general (see **encyclical**) + *paideia,* education, training, from *pais* (stem *paid-*), child.]

en·cy·clo·pe·dic, en·cy·clo·pae·dic (ĕn-sī′klə-pē′dĭk, ĭn-) *adj.* 1. Of, pertaining to, or characteristic of an encyclopedia. 2. Embracing many subjects; comprehensive. **—en·cy·clo·pe·di·cal·ly** *adv.*

en·cy·clo·pe·dism, en·cy·clo·pae·dism (ĕn-sī′klə-pē′dĭz′əm, ĭn-) *n.* Encyclopedic learning.

en·cy·clo·pe·dist, en·cy·clo·pae·dist (ĕn-sī′klə-pē′dĭst, ĭn-) *n.* 1. A person who writes for or compiles an encyclopedia. 2. **Encyclopedist.** Any of the writers of the French *Encyclopédie* (1751-72), including its editors, Diderot and d'Alembert.

en·cyst (ĕn-sĭst′, ĭn-) *v.* **-cysted, -cysting, -cysts.** *—tr.* To enclose in a cyst. *—intr.* To take the form of or become enclosed in a cyst. **—en·cyst·ment, en·cys·ta·tion** (ĕn′sĭ-stā′shən) *n.*

end (ĕnd) *n.* 1. The outer extremity of something that has length. 2. The outside or extreme edge or limit of a space, form, or area; a boundary. 3. The point in time at which an action, event, or phenomenon ceases or is completed; a conclusion: *the end of a day.* 4. A result; an outcome: *The end of the negotiations was agreement.* 5. The termination of life or existence; death. 6. An ultimate extent; limit: *soon reached the end of her patience.* 7. a. That toward which one strives; a goal: *"The end of Poetry is to produce excitement in coexistence with an overbalance of pleasure"* (William Wordsworth). b. The reason or object by virtue of which something exists or takes place. 8. *Often* **ends.** A remainder, leftover, scrap, or remnant: *My desk is littered with odds and ends.* 9. a. A share of a responsibility or obligation; part: *Try to keep up your end of the bargain.* b. A particular area or phase of an enterprise or undertaking: *He is involved with the packaging end of the business.* 10. *Football.* a. Either of the players in the outermost position at the line of scrimmage. b. The position played by an end. **—See Synonyms at boundary, intention. —at a loose ends.** Aimless; unoccupied. **—make (both) ends meet.** To manage to live within one's means. **—no end.** *Informal.* A great deal: *no end of stories to tell.* **—the end.** *Informal.* An extremely exasperating person or situation.
~*v.* **ended, ending, ends.** *—tr.* 1. To bring to an end; finish; conclude. 2. To form the end or concluding part of. 3. To bring about the extinction of; destroy. 4. To be the finest of (a kind); surpass: *a prize to end all prizes.* *—intr.* 1. To come to an end; cease. 2. To die. **—See Synonyms at complete. —end it all.** *Informal.* To commit suicide. **—end up.** 1. To conclude. 2. To find or put oneself in a specified state, position, or the like: *We ended up laughing.*
~*adj.* At a position on the end; final; concluding: *end man; end point.* [Middle English *ende,* Old English *ende,* from Germanic.]

end-. Variant of **endo-.**

endamoeba. Variant of **entamoeba.**

en·dan·ger (ĕn-dān′jər, ĭn-) *tr.v.* **-gered, -gering, -gers.** To expose to danger or harm; imperil. **—en·dan·ger·ment** *n.*

endangered species *n.* A species in danger of extinction.

end·ar·ter·ec·to·my (ĕnd′är-tə-rĕk′tə-mē) *n., pl.* **-mies.** *Medicine.* The surgical excision of the lining of an artery that has become clogged with atherosclerotic buildup. [END(O)- + ARTER(Y) + -ECTOMY.]

end·brain (ĕnd′brān′) *n. Anatomy.* The **telencephalon** (see).

en·dear (ĕn-dîr′, ĭn-) *tr.v.* **-deared, -dearing, -dears.** To cause to inspire affection or warm sympathy. **—en·dear·ing·ly** *adv.*

en·dear·ment (ĕn-dîr′mənt, ĭn-) *n.* 1. The act of endearing. 2. An expression of affection; a loving word or caress.

en·deav·or (ĕn-dĕv′ər, ĭn-) *n.* Also *chiefly British* **en·deav·our.** 1. A conscientious or concerted effort toward a given end; an earnest attempt. 2. *Often* **endeavors.** Earnest striving. **—See Synonyms at effort.**
~*intr.v.* **endeavored, -oring, -ors.** Also *chiefly British* **endeavour -oured, -ouring, -ours.** To make an earnest attempt; strive. Usually used with an infinitive: *endeavor to stay solvent.* [Middle English *endevour,* from *endeveren,* to exert oneself, from the phrase *putten in dever,* to put in duty, make it one's duty : IN + *dever,* duty, from Old French *devoir,* DEVOIR.] **—en·deav·or·er** *n.*

en·dem·ic (ĕn-dĕm′ĭk, ĭn-) *adj.* Also **en·de·mi·al** (-dē′mē-əl), **en·dem·i·cal** (-dĕm′ĭ-kəl). 1. Prevalent in or peculiar to a particular group or locality: *"Disorder in some sense appears to be endemic in all societies"* (Crane Brinton). 2. *Ecology.* Native or confined to a certain region; having a characteristically restricted distribution. 3. *Medicine.* Peculiar to and recurring in a particular locality. Said of a disease.
~*n. Ecology.* An endemic plant or animal. [French *endémique,* from Greek *endēmios, endēmos,* dwelling in a place, indigenous : *en-,* in + *dēmos,* people.] **—en·dem·i·cal·ly** *adv.* **—en·dem·ism** (ĕn-dĕm′ĭz′əm, ĭn-) *n.*

En·der·by Land (ĕn′dər-bē). Area in Antarctica, on the Indian Ocean. Discovered in 1831, it is claimed by Australia.

en·der·mic (ĕn-dûr′mĭk, ĭn-) *adj. Medicine.* Acting by absorption through the skin. Said of lotions and similar preparations. [EN- + -DERM + -IC.]

end·game (ĕnd′gām′) *n.* The final stage of a game; especially, the final stage of chess, when only a few pieces survive.

end·ing (ĕn′dĭng) *n.* 1. A conclusion or termination. 2. The concluding part, especially of a book, play, or film; a finale: *a happy ending.* 3. The letter, letters, sound, or sounds added to a word or word part, especially to make a derivative or inflectional form.

en·dive (ĕn′dīv′, ŏn′dēv′) *n.* 1. A plant, *Cichorium endivia,* cultivated for its crown of crisp, succulent leaves, used in salads. 2. A variety of the common chicory, *Cichorium intybus,* cultivated to produce a narrow, pointed cluster of whitish leaves used in salads. [Middle English, from Old French, from Medieval Latin *endiva,* variant of Latin *entubus, entibus,* chicory, from Greek *entubioi,* perhaps from Egyptian *tybi,* January, because the plant grows in this month.]

end leaf *n.* An **endpaper** (see).

end·less (ĕnd′lĭs) *adj.* 1. Being or seeming to be without an end; infinite; boundless. 2. Incessant; interminable: *an endless conversa-*

endocrine gland

CHEMICAL ORDERS TO THE BODY

How hormones travel to where they are needed

Bodily changes such as growth, digestion, and cell reproduction are controlled by the brain just as much as is the voluntary decision to stand up or sit down. Such changes are responses to messages sent by the brain—not sent along the nerve pathways, however, but delivered by chemicals known as hormones.

Various organs and tissues secrete hormones in response to chemical instructions from the brain, but the chief producers are the endocrine glands. They are called ductless glands because unlike most glands, for example the sweat glands, whose secretions are carried through ducts opening on the skin surface, endocrine glands pump their hormones directly into the bloodstream. The blood carries them to the places—target tissues—they are intended to affect.

Hormones released by the six main sets of glands in the endocrine system control the inner rhythms of the body. The pituitary, at the base of the brain, is the master gland. It produces hormones that act purely as messengers to stimulate hormone production in other endocrine glands. It also secretes a hormone that controls body growth.

Hormones produced by the thyroid gland control heat and energy production. The parathyroid glands secrete a hormone that maintains calcium levels; the thymus gives infants a defense against infection. Adrenalin, from the adrenals, boosts energy production during stress, and insulin, produced by the islets of Langerhans in the pancreas, is essential for the efficient utilization of sugar. The sex glands, or gonads, produce sex hormones, for example the estrogens responsible for the menstrual cycle in women.

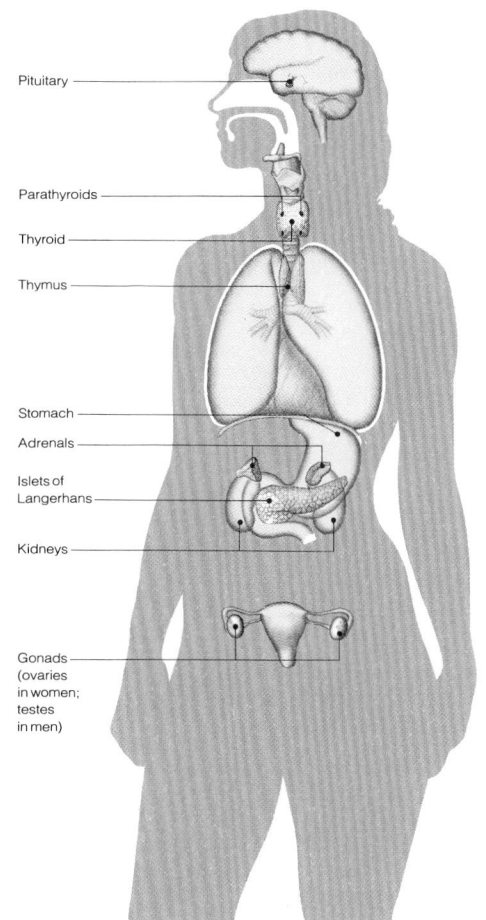

ENDOCRINE GLANDS AND TISSUES *As well as the six main endocrine glands, various tissues secrete hormones. Secretions in the stomach regulate digestion, and secretions in the kidneys control the production of red blood cells.*

tion. **3.** Formed with the ends joined; continuous: *an endless chain.* —**end·less·ly** *adv.* —**end·less·ness** *n.*

end man *n.* A man in a minstrel show who sits at one end of the company and banters with the interlocutor.

end matter *n.* Material, often including an index, appendix, bibliography, or notes, that follows the main part of a book. Also called "back matter." Compare **front matter.**

end·most (ĕnd′mōst′) *adj.* Being at or closest to the end; last.

endo–, end– *prefix.* Indicates inside or within; for example, **endocarp, endomorph.** [Greek, from *endon,* within.]

en·do·blast (ĕn′də-blăst′, -blăst′) *n.* Also **en·to·blast** (ĕn′tə-). In embryology, the inner layer of the blastoderm that becomes the endoderm at gastrulation. Also called "hypoblast." [ENDO- + -BLAST.] —**en·do·blas·tic** (ĕn′də-blăs′tĭk) *adj.*

en·do·car·di·tis (ĕn′dō-kär-dī′tĭs) *n.* Inflammation of the endocardium. [ENDOCARD(IUM) + -ITIS.] —**en·do·car·dit·ic** (ĕn′dō-kär-dĭt′ĭk) *adj.*

en·do·car·di·um (ĕn′dō-kär′dē-əm) *n., pl.* **-di·a** (-dē-ə). The thin, endothelial, serous membrane that lines the interior of the heart. [New Latin : ENDO- + Greek *kardia,* heart.] —**en·do·car·di·al** *adj.*

en·do·carp (ĕn′də-kärp′) *n. Botany.* The often hard or leathery inner layer of the pericarp of many fruits. [ENDO- + -CARP.]

en·do·cen·tric (ĕn′dō-sĕn′trĭk) *adj. Grammar.* Designating a construction with the same grammatical function in combination as at least one of its constituents; for example, *five gold rings* is an endocentric construction, since the entire noun phrase functions grammatically in the same way as its head noun, *rings.* Compare **exocentric.** [ENDO- + -CENTRIC.]

en·do·cra·ni·um (ĕn′dō-krā′nē-əm) *n., pl.* **-ni·a** (-nē-ə). The outermost layer of the dura mater.

en·do·crine (ĕn′də-krĭn, -krēn′, -krīn′) *adj.* Also **en·do·cri·nal** (ĕn′də-krī′nəl, -krē′nəl), **en·do·crin·ic** (ĕn′də-krĭn′ĭk), **en·doc·ri·nous** (ĕn-dŏk′rə-nəs). **1.** Secreting internally. **2.** Of or pertaining to any of the ductless or endocrine glands. ~*n.* An endocrine gland. [ENDO- + Greek *krīnein,* to separate, "secrete."]

endocrine gland *n.* Any of the ductless glands, such as the thyroid or adrenal, the secretions of which pass directly into the bloodstream from the cells of the gland. Also called "ductless gland." See **hormone.**

en·do·cri·nol·o·gy (ĕn′də-krə-nŏl′ə-jē) *n.* The study of the endocrine glands, their secretions, and their diseases. —**en·do·cri·no·log·ic** (ĕn′də-krĭn′ə-lŏj′ĭk), **en·do·cri·no·log·i·cal** (-ĭ-kəl) *adj.* —**en·do·cri·nol·o·gist** (ĕn′də-krə-nŏl′ə-jĭst) *n.*

en·do·derm (ĕn′də-dûrm′) *n.* Also **en·to·derm** (ĕn′tə-). The innermost of the three primary germ layers of an embryo, developing into the lining of the intestinal tract and its derivatives. [ENDO- + -DERM.] —**en·do·der·mal** (ĕn′də-dûr′məl) *adj.*

en·do·der·mis (ĕn′də-dûr′mĭs) *n. Botany.* The innermost layer of the cortex, found in all roots and in the stems of certain plants, which controls the passage of water. [ENDO- + Greek *derma,* skin, DERMA.]

en·do·don·tics (ĕn′də-dŏn′tĭks) *n.* Also **en·do·don·tia** (-shə, -shē-ə). *(Used with a singular verb).* The branch of dentistry dealing with diseases of the tooth pulp. [ENDO- + -ODONT + -ICS.] —**en·do·don·tic** *adj.* —**en·do·don·tist** *n.*

en·do·en·zyme (ĕn′dō-ĕn′zīm′) *n.* **1.** An enzyme that acts upon inner chemical bonds in a chain molecule. **2.** An enzyme that acts inside the cell that produces it.

en·do·er·gic (ĕn′dō-ûr′jĭk) *adj. Physics.* Of or involving absorption of energy. Said of nuclear reactions. [ENDO- + *-ergic,* from Greek *ergon,* work.]

en·dog·a·my (ĕn-dŏg′ə-mē) *n.* **1.** *Anthropology.* Marriage within a particular group, caste, class, or tribe in accordance with set custom or law. Compare **exogamy. 2.** *Biology.* **a.** The fusion of gametes from closely related parents. **b.** Pollination between two flowers of the same plant. [ENDO- + -GAMY.] —**en·dog·a·mous** *adj.*

en·dog·e·nous (ĕn-dŏj′ə-nəs) *adj.* **1.** Produced from within. **2.** *Biology.* Originating within an organ or part. [ENDO- + -GENOUS.] —**en·dog·e·nous·ly** *adv.* —**en·dog·e·ny** *n.*

en·do·lymph (ĕn′də-lĭmf′) *n.* The fluid in the cochlear duct of the labyrinth of the ear.

en·do·me·tri·o·sis (ĕn′dō-mē′trē-ō′sĭs) *n.* The presence of endometrium, which is normally confined to the uterus, in other parts of the pelvic cavity, such as the ovaries, resulting in localized monthly pain.

en·do·me·tri·um (ĕn′dō-mē′trē-əm) *n., pl.* **-tria** (-trē-ə). The mucous membrane lining the uterus. [ENDO- + METR(O)- (uterus) + -IUM.] —**en·do·me·tri·al** *adj.*

en·do·morph (ĕn′də-môrf′) *n.* **1.** *Mineralogy.* A mineral found as an inclusion in another, as rutile or tourmaline may be found in quartz. Compare **perimorph. 2.** *Physiology.* A person of a type having a relatively fat body with prominent abdominal parts and weak muscular and skeletal development. Compare **ectomorph, mesomorph.** [ENDO- + -MORPH.]

en·do·mor·phic (ĕn′də-môr′fĭk) *adj.* **1.** *Mineralogy.* **a.** Of or pertaining to an endomorph. **b.** Created through endomorphism. **2.** *Physiology.* Of, pertaining to, or characteristic of an endomorphic individual. —**en·do·mor·phy** *n.*

en·do·mor·phism (ĕn′də-môr′fĭz′əm) *n. Geology.* The metamorphism of igneous rock as it cools, resulting from contact with and assimilation of the wall rock.

en·do·par·a·site (ĕn′dō-păr′ə-sīt′) *n.* An organism, such as a tape-

endomorph *One mineral enclosed within another: in this case, crystals of lead set in rock from the German Dolomites.*

worm, that lives parasitically within another organism. **—en·do·par·a·sit·ic** (ĕn'dō-păr'ə-sĭt'ĭk) *adj.*

en·do·phyte (ĕn'də-fīt') *n.* A plant, such as any of certain fungi, growing within another plant. [ENDO- + -PHYTE.] **—en·do·phyt·ic** (ĕn'də-fĭt'ĭk) *adj.*

en·do·plasm (ĕn'də-plăz'əm) *n.* The inner, less viscous portion of the cytoplasm distinguishable within some cells. Compare **ectoplasm**. [ENDO- + -PLASM.] **—en·do·plas·mic** (ĕn'də-plăz'mĭk) *adj.*

endoplasmic reticulum *n. Abbr.* **ER** A system of membrane-bounded sacs in the cytoplasm of cells that functions in intracellular transport.

en·do·ra·di·o·sonde (ĕn'dō-rā'dē-ō-sŏnd') *n.* A microelectronic device that is introduced into the body by swallowing to record physiological data.

end organ *n. Anatomy.* The expanded functional termination of a sensory or motor nerve.

en·dor·phin (ĕn-dôr'fĭn, ĭn-) *n.* Any of a group of hormonelike substances with pain-killing and tranquilizing properties that are secreted by the brain. [ENDO- + -orphin, as in morphine.]

en·dorse (ĕn-dôrs', ĭn-) *tr.v.* **-dorsed, -dorsing, -dorses.** Also **indorse** (ĭn-). **1.** To write one's signature on the back of (a check or money order, for example) as evidence of the legal transfer of its ownership, especially in return for the cash or credit indicated on its face. **2. a.** To place (one's signature) on a contract or other document to indicate approval of its contents or terms. **b.** To allow one's name and reputation to be used to publicize (a product) in return for payment. **3.** To acknowledge (receipt of payment) by signing a bill, draft, or other document. **4.** To give approval of or support to; sanction. —See Synonyms at **approve**. —See Usage note at **indorse**. [Middle English *endosen,* from Old French *endosser,* "to put on the back of": *en-,* to put on + *dos,* back, from Latin *dorsum.*] **—en·dors·a·ble** *adj.* **—en·dors·er, en·dor·sor** *n.*

en·dor·see (ĕn-dôr'sē', ĭn-, ĕn'dôr-sē') *n.* One to whom ownership of a negotiable document is transferred by endorsement.

en·dorse·ment (ĕn-dôrs'mənt, ĭn-) *n.* **1.** An act of endorsing. **2.** Something that endorses or validates, such as a signature or voucher. **3.** Approbation; sanction; support. **4.** An amendment to a contract, such as an insurance policy, permitting a change in the original terms.

endorsement in blank *n.* A blank endorsement (see).

en·do·scope (ĕn'də-skōp') *n.* An instrument for examining the interior of a bodily canal or hollow organ. [ENDO- + -SCOPE.] **—en·do·scop·ic** (ĕn'də-skŏp'ĭk) *adj.* **—en·do·scop·i·cal·ly** *adv.* **—en·dos·co·pist** (ĕn-dŏs'kə-pĭst) *n.* **—en·dos·co·py** (-pē) *n.*

en·do·skel·e·ton (ĕn'dō-skĕl'ə-tən) *n.* An internal supporting skeleton characteristic of vertebrates. Compare **exoskeleton**. **—en·do·skel·e·tal** *adj.*

en·dos·mo·sis (ĕn'dŏz-mō'sĭs, ĕn'dŏs-) *n.* The flow of a solvent through a semipermeable membrane from a surrounding fluid; especially, the flow of water through a cell membrane into a cell or organism. Compare **exosmosis**. [END(O)- + OSMOSIS.] **—en·dos·mot·ic** (ĕn'dŏz-mŏt'ĭk, ĕn'dŏs-) *adj.* **—en·dos·mot·i·cal·ly** *adv.*

en·do·some (ĕn'də-sōm') *n.* A discrete darker area within a nucleus, especially the nucleolus.

en·do·sperm (ĕn'də-spûrm') *n. Botany.* The nutritive tissue surrounding and absorbed by the embryo in flowering plants. [ENDO- + -SPERM.] **—en·do·sper·mic** (ĕn'də-spûr'mĭk) *adj.*

en·do·spore (ĕn'də-spôr', -spōr') *n.* An asexual spore formed within the cells of certain bacteria and acting as a resting stage.

en·do·spo·ri·um (ĕn'də-spôr'ē-əm, -spōr'ē-əm) *n.* The **intine** (see). [New Latin, from ENDO- + SPORE.]

en·dos·te·um (ĕn-dŏs'tē-əm) *n., pl.* **-tea** (-tē-ə). The membrane that lines the marrow cavity of a long bone. [New Latin : END(O)- + Greek *osteon,* bone.] **—en·dos·te·al** *adj.*

en·do·the·ci·um (ĕn'dō-thē'sē-əm, -shē-əm) *n., pl.* **-cia** (-sē-ə, -shē-ə). *Botany.* The inner tissue of an anther or a moss capsule. [New Latin : ENDO- + Greek *thēkion,* diminutive of *thēkē,* chest.] **—en·do·the·ci·al** *adj.*

en·do·the·li·o·ma (ĕn'dō-thē'lē-ō'mə) *n., pl.* **-mas** or **-mata** (-mə-tə). Any of various tumors derived from endothelial tissue. [ENDOTHELI(UM) + -OMA.]

en·do·the·li·um (ĕn'dō-thē'lē-əm) *n., pl.* **-lia** (-lē-ə). A thin layer of flat cells that lines serous cavities, lymph vessels, and blood vessels. [New Latin : ENDO- + Greek *thēlē,* nipple.] **—en·do·the·li·al** (ĕn'dō-thē'lē-əl), **en·do·the·li·oid** (-lē-oid') *adj.*

en·do·ther·mic (ĕn'dō-thûr'mĭk) *adj.* Also **en·do·ther·mal** (-məl). Characterized by or causing the absorption of heat. Said especially of chemical reactions. Compare **exothermic**. [ENDO- + THERM + -IC.] **—en·do·ther·mi·cal·ly** *adv.*

en·do·tox·in (ĕn'dō-tŏk'sĭn) *n.* A toxin produced within a microorganism and released upon destruction of the cell in which it is produced. [ENDO- + TOXIN.] **—en·do·tox·ic** *adj.*

en·do·tra·che·al (ĕn'də-trā'kē-əl) *adj.* Within the trachea.

en·dow (ĕn-dou', ĭn-) *tr.v.* **-dowed, -dowing, -dows. 1.** To provide with property, income, or a source of income. **2.** To invest with specified qualities or characteristics. Used with *with.* [Middle English *endowen,* from Norman French *endouer* : Old French *en-* (intensive) + *douer,* to provide with a dowry, from Latin *dōtāre,* from *dōs* (stem *dōt-*), dowry.]

en·dow·ment (ĕn-dou'mənt, ĭn-) *n.* **1.** An act of endowing. **2.** Funds or property donated to an institution, individual, or group as a source of income. **3.** A natural gift or quality; an attribute, such as beauty or talent.

~*adj.* Designating or involving a form of life insurance in which the policy matures within a specific period after issuance and becomes a claim payable to the insured at that time, or to his beneficiary upon the death of the insured before that time.

end·pa·per (ĕnd'pā'pər) *n.* Either of two folded sheets of heavy paper having one half pasted to the inside front or back cover of a book and the other half pasted to the base of the first or last page to form a flyleaf. Also called "end leaf."

end·plate (ĕnd'plāt') *n. Physiology.* A flattened motor nerve terminal that transmits nerve impulses to muscle.

end·play (ĕnd'plā') *tr.v.* **-played, -playing, -plays.** In bridge, to force (an opponent) to play a particular card during a late trick. **—end·play** *n.*

end·point (ĕnd'point') *n.* **1.** *Chemistry.* The point at which a titration is complete, with neither reactant in excess. **2.** Either of two points marking the end of a line segment. **3.** Any completion point.

end product *n.* The final conclusion of a series or process; specifically, the finished product of a manufacturing or similar process.

end·stopped (ĕnd'stŏpt') *adj.* Having a punctuation mark or distinct pause at the end of a line. Said of verse.

en·due (ĕn-dōō', -dyōō', ĭn-) *tr.v.* **-dued, -duing, -dues.** Also **in·due** (ĭn-). **1.** To provide with some specified quality or trait. Used with *with.* **2. a.** To put on; dress in. **b.** To clothe. [Sense 1, Middle English *enduen, endeuen,* from Old French *enduire,* to lead in, induct (meaning influenced by Middle English *endowen,* to endow), from Latin *indūcere,* to INDUCE. Sense 2, Middle English *induen,* from Latin *induere,* to don.]

en·dur·ance (ĕn-dōōr'əns, -dyōōr'əns, ĭn-) *n.* **1.** The act, quality, or power of withstanding hardship or stress. **2.** The state or fact of persevering. **3.** Continuing existence; survival.

en·dure (ĕn-dōōr', -dyōōr', ĭn-) *v.* **-dured, -during, -dures.** *—tr.* **1.** To carry on through despite hardships; undergo: *endure an Arctic winter.* **2.** To bear with tolerance; put up with: *endure insults.* *—intr.* **1.** To continue in existence; remain; last: *buildings that endure for centuries.* **2.** To suffer patiently without yielding; persevere; hold out. —See Synonyms at **bear**. [Middle English *enduren,* from Old French *endurer,* from Late Latin *indūrāre,* "to harden one's heart against," bear, from Latin, to harden : *in-* (intensive) + *dūrāre,* to harden, from *dūrus,* hard.] **—en·dur·a·bil·i·ty** *n.* **—en·dur·a·ble** *adj.* **—en·dur·a·bly** *adv.*

en·dur·ing (ĕn-dōōr'ĭng, -dyōōr'ĭng, ĭn-) *adj.* **1.** Lasting; durable. **2.** Chronic; unresolved: *an enduring problem.* **3.** Long-suffering. **—en·dur·ing·ly** *adv.* **—en·dur·ing·ness** *n.*

end·wise (ĕnd'wīz') *adv.* Also **end·ways** (-wāz'). **1.** On end. **2.** With the end foremost. **3.** Lengthwise. **4.** End to end. **—end·wise** *adj.*

En·dym·i·on (ĕn-dĭm'ē-ən) *Greek Mythology.* A handsome young man who was loved by the moon goddess Selene and whose youth was preserved by eternal sleep. [Latin, from Greek *Endumiōn,* "diver" (so called perhaps because Endymion was originally a sun god), from *enduein,* to dive into : *en-,* into + *duein†,* to dive, sink, set (as the sun).]

ENE east-northeast.

-ene *suffix. Chemistry.* Indicates unsaturation of an organic compound, especially one having a double bond; for example, **ethylene**. [Greek *-ēnē,* feminine patronymic suffix.]

en·e·ma (ĕn'ə-mə) *n., pl.* **-mas** or **enemata** (ĕn'ə-mä'tə). **1.** The injection of liquid into the rectum for cleansing, laxative, or other therapeutic purposes. **2.** The fluid injected as an enema. [Late Latin, from Greek, from *enienai,* to throw in, inject : *en-,* in + *hienai,* to send, throw.]

en·e·my (ĕn'ə-mē) *n., pl.* **-mies. 1. a.** One who shows malice or hostility toward another; a foe. **b.** One who opposes the purposes or interests of another; an opponent. **2. a.** A hostile, usually armed power or force, such as a nation. **b.** A member or unit of such a force. **3.** Something destructive or injurious in its effects: *Fear is our chief enemy.*

~*adj.* Of or pertaining to a hostile power or force. [Middle English *enemi,* from Old French, from Latin *inimīcus* : *in-,* not + *amīcus,* friend.]

en·er·get·ic (ĕn'ər-jĕt'ĭk) *adj.* Possessing, exerting, or displaying energy; vigorous. —See Synonyms at **active**. [Greek *energētikos,* active, from *energein,* to be active, from *energos,* active. See **energy**.] **—en·er·get·i·cal·ly** *adv.*

en·er·get·ics (ĕn'ər-jĕt'ĭks) *n.* **1.** *Used with a plural verb.* The energy changes in a particular physical system: *the energetics of a chemical reaction.* **2.** *Used with a singular verb.* The physics of energy and of transformations of energy.

en·er·gid (ĕn'ər-jĭd) *n. Biology.* A unit that consists of a nucleus surrounded by cytoplasm but that does not constitute a cell. [ENERG(Y) + -ID.]

en·er·gize (ĕn'ər-jīz') *v.* **-gized, -gizing, -gizes.** *—tr.* **1.** To give energy to; charge. **2.** To power (a device, such as the winding of an electric motor) with electricity. *—intr.* To release or put out energy. **—en·er·giz·er** *n.*

en·er·gu·men (ĕn'ər-gyōō'mən) *n.* **1.** One believed to be possessed by an evil spirit; a demoniac. **2.** A zealot; a fanatic. [Late Latin *energūmenus,* from Greek *energoumenos,* worked on, "possessed," from *energein,* to be active, effect, from *energos,* active. See **energy**.]

en·er·gy (ĕn'ər-jē) *n., pl.* **-gies. 1. a.** Vigor or power as shown in action, exertion, or performance. **b.** Vitality and intensity of expression. **2.** The capacity for action or accomplishment: *lacked energy to finish the job.* **3.** Often **energies**. Power exercised with vigor and determination: *devote one's energies to a worthy cause.*

4. a. *Physics.* **Abbr. E** The work that a physical system is capable of doing in changing from its actual state to a specific reference state, the total including, in general, contributions of **potential energy**, **kinetic energy**, and **rest energy** *(all of which see).* **b.** The capacity to activate systems, as machines, or to generate light and heat: *solar energy.* **c.** Energy-generating fuels or sources collectively. Also used adjectivally: *the energy crisis.* —See Synonyms at **strength.** [Late Latin *energīa,* from Greek *energeia,* coined by Aristotle from *energēs, energos,* active, at work : *en-,* at + *ergon,* work.]

energy band *n. Physics.* A range of allowed energies of electrons in a solid.

energy density *n.* The energy per unit area or volume of a surface or region of space.

energy gap *n.* The discrepancy between the amount of fuel needed to satisfy current levels of energy consumption and the actual quantities likely to be available in the future.

energy level *n. Physics.* **1.** The energy characteristic of a stationary state of a quantum mechanical system. **2.** The stationary state of a quantum mechanical system.

en·er·vate (ĕn′ər-vāt′) *tr.v.* **-vated, -vating, -vates.** To deprive of strength or vitality; weaken. —See Usage note at **deplete.**
~*adj.* (ĭ-nûr′vĭt). Deprived of strength or vitality; devitalized. [Latin *ēnervāre,* "to remove the sinews from" : *ex-* (removal) + *nervus,* sinew, nerve.] —**en·er·va·tion** (ĕn′ər-vā′shən) *n.* —**en·er·va·tor** (ĕn′ər-vā′tər) *n.*

en·face (ĕn-fās′, ĭn-) *tr.v.* **-faced, -facing, -faces.** To write, stamp, or print on the face of (a check or other document). —**en·face·ment** *n.*

en fa·mille (äN′ fȧ-mē′) *adv.* In or with the family; at home and without ceremony. [French, "in (the) family."]

en·fant ter·ri·ble (äN-fäN′ tĕ-rē′bl′) *n., pl.* **enfants terribles** *(pronounced as singular).* **1.** A child who habitually causes embarrassment by his conduct or remarks. **2.** A person whose startlingly unconventional behavior and ideas are a source of consternation or dismay to a cause, group, or profession. [French, "terrible child."]

en·fee·ble (ĕn-fē′bəl, ĭn-) *tr.v.* **-bled, -bling, -bles.** To make feeble; deprive of strength. [Middle English *enfeblen,* from Old French *enfebler* : *en-* (causative) + *feble,* FEEBLE.] —**en·fee·ble·ment** *n.* —**en·fee·bler** *n.*

en·fet·ter (ĕn-fĕt′ər, ĭn-) *tr.v.* **-tered, -tering, -ters.** To bind in fetters; enchain; enslave.

En·field rifle (ĕn′fēld′) *n.* Any of several rifles of varying calibers used formerly by British and American troops, especially the .30 or .303 bolt-action breechloading model. Also called "Enfield." [After *Enfield,* England, where it was first made.]

en·fi·lade (ĕn′fə-lād′, -läd′) *n.* **1.** The firing of a gun or guns so as to sweep the length of a target such as a column of troops. **2.** A position or emplacement under enfilade.
~*tr.v.* **enfiladed, -lading, -lades.** To rake with gunfire. [French, "series," from *enfiler,* to thread, from Old French : *en-,* in + *fil,* thread, from Latin *fīlum.*]

en·fleu·rage (ŏn′flə-räzh′, -räj′) *n.* A process used in the making of perfume to extract essential oils from plant material, such as leaves or petals, by placing the material in contact with an odorless fat that absorbs the essential oil. The essential oil is subsequently extracted from the fat by a solvent. [French, from *enfleurer,* to cause to take in the fragrance of flowers : Old French *en-,* in + *fleur, flor,* flower, from Latin *flōs* (stem *flōr-*).]

en·flu·rane (ĕn-floor′ān′, ĭn-) *n.* A nonexplosive anesthetic, C₃H₂ClF₃O. [EN- + FLU(O)- + (ETH)ANE.]

en·fold (ĕn-fōld′, ĭn-) *tr.v.* **-folded, -folding, -folds.** Also **in·fold** (ĭn-). **1.** To cover with or as if with folds; wrap up: *The fog seemed to enfold the whole village.* **2.** To hold within limits; enclose. **3.** To embrace. **4.** To form or shape into folds. —**en·fold·er** *n.*

en·force (ĕn-fôrs′, -fōrs′, ĭn-) *tr.v.* **-forced, -forcing, -forces. 1.** To compel observance of or obedience to: *enforce a regulation.* **2.** To impose (specified action or behavior); compel. **3.** To give force to; stress; underline; reinforce. [Middle English *enforcen,* from Old French *enforcier,* from Vulgar Latin *infortiāre* (unattested), to make strong : Latin *in-* (causative) + *fortis,* strong.] —**en·force·a·ble** *adj.* —**en·force·ment** *n.* —**en·forc·er** *n.*

en·fran·chise (ĕn-frăn′chīz′, ĭn-) *tr.v.* **-chised, -chising, -chises. 1.** To endow with the rights of citizenship, especially the right to vote. **2.** To give (a town, for example) the right to political representation. **3.** To bestow a franchise upon. **4.** To free, as from slavery. [Middle English *enfraunchisen,* from Old French *enfranchir* (present stem *enfranchiss-*) : *en-* (causative) + *franche, franc,* free (see **franchise**).]

eng (ĕng) *n.* A phonetic symbol (ŋ) representing in some pronunciation alphabets the velar nasal consonantal sound of *ng,* as in *bring* or *long,* or of *n,* as in *link.* Also called "agma."

eng. 1. engine. **2.** engineer; engineering.

Eng. England; English.

En·ga·dine (ĕng′gə-dēn′). Swiss part of the upper Inn Valley, in Grisons (or Graubünden) canton. It has several winter sports centers, including St. Moritz.

en·gage (ĕn-gāj′, ĭn-) *v.* **-gaged, -gaging, -gages.** —*tr.* **1.** To obtain or contract for the services of; employ: *engage a carpenter.* **2.** To contract for the use of; reserve: *engage a room.* **3.** To obtain and hold the attention of; engross: *The project engaged her interest for months.* **4.** To require the use of; occupy: *Studying engages most of a student's time.* **5.** To pledge; especially, to promise to marry; betroth. Usually used in the passive: *She is engaged to Harry.* **6.** To meet in or bring into conflict: *We have engaged the enemy.* **7.** To

cause to interlock or mesh. **8.** To please or attract; win. **9.** To occupy or involve. Often used with *in: engage someone in idle chatter.* **10.** *Archaic.* To give or take as security; attach. —*intr.* **1.** To involve oneself or become occupied; participate. Usually used with *in: engage in conversation.* **2.** To assume an obligation; pledge; agree. **3.** To enter into conflict or battle. **4.** To become meshed or interlocked. [Middle English *engagen,* from Old French *engager,* from Vulgar Latin *inwadiāre* : *in-,* in + *wadiāre* (unattested), to pledge, GAGE.] —**en·gag·er** *n.*

en·ga·gé (äN′gä-zhä′) *adj.* Actively committed, as to a political cause. [French, "committed."]

en·gaged (ĕn-gājd′, ĭn-) *adj.* **1. a.** Employed, occupied, or busy. **b.** *British.* In use. Said of a telephone line. **2.** Contracted for; pledged. **3.** Bound by a promise to marry; betrothed: *an engaged couple.* **4.** *Architecture.* Partly sunk, built into, or attached to another part, as columns on a wall.

en·gage·ment (ĕn-gāj′mənt, ĭn-) *n.* **1.** An act of engaging or the state or period of being engaged. **2.** A promise of marriage; betrothal. **3.** A person or thing that engages. **4.** A promise, pledge, or obligation; especially, a commitment to appear at a certain time, as for business or social activity; an appointment. **5. a.** Employment, especially for a specific time. **b.** The period of employment. **6.** A battle or encounter. **7.** The condition of being in gear.

en·gag·ing (ĕn-gā′jĭng, ĭn-) *adj.* Tending to attract; charming; pleasing. —**en·gag·ing·ly** *adv.*

en garde (äN gärd′) *interj.* Used to warn a fencer to assume the first position preparatory to a match. [French, "on guard."]

En·gels (ĕng′əlz, ĕng′gəlz), **Friedrich** (1820–95). German political theorist and socialist revolutionary. He met Karl Marx in Paris in 1844 and published *The Condition of the Working Classes in England. The Communist Manifesto* was published in 1848. Engels settled in England in 1850 and played an important part in the founding of the First and Second Internationals. *Anti-Dühring* (1878) and *The Origin of the Family, Private Property, and the State* (1884) were major contributions to the development of Communist theory.

en·gen·der (ĕn-jĕn′dər, ĭn-) *v.* **-dered, -dering, -ders.** —*tr.* **1.** To bring into existence; give rise to; produce. **2.** To procreate; propagate. —*intr.* To come into existence; be born; be produced. [Middle English *engenderen,* from Old French *engenderer,* from Latin *ingenerāre* : *in-,* in + *generāre,* to GENERATE.]

engin. engineering.

en·gine (ĕn′jĭn) *n.* **Abbr. eng. 1. a.** A machine that converts some form of energy into mechanical motion. **b.** Such a machine distinguished from an electric, spring-driven, or hydraulic motor by its consumption of a fuel. **c.** Any mechanical appliance, instrument, or tool. **2.** A locomotive. **3.** *Archaic.* An agent, instrument, or means of accomplishment. [Middle English *engin,* from Old French, skill, invention, from Latin *ingenium,* inborn talent, skill.]

engine block *n.* The metal block containing the cylinders of an internal-combustion engine. Also called "block."

engine driver *n. Chiefly British.* A person who drives a locomotive; engineer.

en·gi·neer (ĕn′jə-nîr′) *n.* **Abbr. e., E., eng. 1.** A person trained in, skilled at, or professionally engaged in a branch of engineering: *a mining engineer.* **2.** A person who skillfully or shrewdly manages an enterprise: *He was the engineer of the treaty that ended the war.* **3.** A person who operates an engine, especially a railroad locomotive. **4.** A person who oversees, services, or repairs engines or systems or appliances run by engines: *a central-heating engineer.* **5.** A soldier employed or trained in engineering as applied to military purposes.
~*tr.v.* **engineered, -neering, -neers. 1.** To plan, construct, and manage as an engineer; act as engineer of or for. **2.** To plan, manage, and put through by skillful acts or contrivance; maneuver: *"Claudius's murder was engineered by his wife Agrippina"* (Robert Graves). [Middle English *enginer,* from Old French *enginneor,* from Medieval Latin *ingeniātor,* contriver, from *ingeniāre,* to contrive, from Latin *ingenium,* talent. See **engine.**]

en·gi·neer·ing (ĕn′jə-nîr′ĭng) *n.* **Abbr. e., E., eng., engin. 1.** The application of scientific principles to such practical ends as the design, construction, and operation of efficient and economical structures, equipment, and systems. **2.** The profession of or the work performed by an engineer. **3.** Skillful management; maneuvering or contrivance.

en·gine·ry (ĕn′jĭn-rē) *n.* **1.** Machines and tools; machinery. **2.** Engines or instruments of war.

en·gird (ĕn-gûrd′, ĭn-) *tr.v.* **-girt** (-gûrt′) or **-girded, -girding, -girds.** Also **en·gir·dle** (-gûrd′l) **-dled, -dling, -dles.** To surround with or as if with a girdle; encircle.

en·gla·cial (ĕn-glā′shəl, ĭn-) *adj.* Located or occurring within a glacier: *an englacial stream.* —**en·gla·cial·ly** *adv.*

Eng·land (ĭng′glənd). Largest political division of the United Kingdom, settled by the Celts, subsequently conquered by the Romans, Angles, Saxons, Jutes, Danes, and finally the Normans. A major trading nation, its main ports are London, Liverpool, and Southampton. Though heavily agricultural, England became a leading manufacturing nation after the Industrial Revolution of the mid-18th century. Foreign competition and the loss of cheap imports from its former empire have contributed to a decline in the 20th century. England's chief industries today include shipbuilding, coal mining, motor vehicle production, iron and steel, electronics, aircraft building, petroleum, chemicals, and tourism. Area, 130,357 square kilometers (50,331 square miles). Capital, London. See also **Great Britain.**

Eng·lish (ĭng′glĭsh) *adj.* **1. a.** Of, pertaining to, or characteristic of England and its inhabitants. **b.** Of a type or style predominant in England: *English breakfast.* **2.** Of, belonging to, or spoken or written in the English language. **3.** Loosely, British. ~*n. Abbr.* **E., E., Eng. 1.** *Used with a plural verb.* **a.** The people of England collectively. **b.** Loosely, the British. **2.** The West Germanic language of the English, divided historically into Old English, Middle English, and Modern English and now spoken in the British Isles, the United States, and numerous other countries. **3.** The English language as spoken or written at a specified time, in a specified region, or by a specified person or group of people: *Australian English; Shakespeare's English.* **4.** A translation into or an equivalent in the English language. **5.** A course or individual class in the study of English literature, language, or composition. **6.** *Printing.* A size of type, 14-point. **7.** *Often* **english.** The spin given to a ball by striking it on one side or releasing it with a sharp twist.

English bond *n.* A common masonry bond consisting of alternate rows of headers and stretchers.

English Channel. *French* **La Manche** (lä mäNsh′). One of the world's busiest shipping lanes, lying between England and France. It is 560 kilometers (350 miles) long, 160 kilometers (100 miles) wide at the west end between Ushant and the Scilly Isles, and 34 kilometers (21 miles) wide at the Strait of Dover at the east end.

English Civil War *n.* In England, the war between Charles I and Parliament. Hostilities commenced in 1642 and Charles finally surrendered at Newark (1646). A Royalist uprising in 1648 prompted the second part of the Civil War and led to the execution of the king

in 1649. A commonwealth was established and the Civil War was concluded by the subjection of Ireland (1649–50) and the defeat of Charles's heir at Dunbar in 1650. Also called the "Great Rebellion."

English daisy *n.* See **daisy** (sense 2).

English finish *n.* A smooth, nonglossy finish for paper.

English flute *n.* A musical instrument, the **recorder** *(see).*

English horn *n.* A double-reed woodwind instrument similar to but larger than the oboe and pitched lower by a fifth. Also called "cor anglais."

Eng·lish·man (ĭng′glĭsh-mən) *n., pl.* **-men** (-mĭn). **1.** A native or inhabitant of England. **2.** Loosely, a British man.

Englishman's tie *n. Nautical.* A **fisherman's knot** *(see).* Also called "Englishman's knot."

English muffin *n.* A flat round of yeast dough that has been baked on a griddle and is usually split and toasted before eating.

English setter *n.* A dog of a breed developed in England, having a silky white coat usually with black or brownish markings.

English sheepdog *n.* The **Old English sheepdog** *(see).*

English sonnet *n.* A **Shakespearean sonnet** *(see).*

English sparrow *n.* The **house sparrow** *(see).*

English walnut *n.* **1.** A Eurasian tree, *Juglans regia,* cultivated in southern Europe and California. **2.** The large edible nut of the English walnut tree.

Eng·lish·wom·an (ĭng′glĭsh-wŏŏm′ən) *n., pl.* **-women** (-wĭm′ĭn). **1.** A woman who is a native or inhabitant of England. **2.** Loosely, a British woman.

en·glut (ĕn-glŭt′, ĭn-) *tr.v.* **-glutted, -glutting, -gluts.** To gulp down; swallow greedily. [EN- + GLUT.]

en·gorge (ĕn-gôrj′, ĭn-) *tr.v.* **-gorged, -gorging, -gorges. 1.** To devour greedily. **2.** To gorge; glut. **3.** To congest or fill to excess, as with blood or other fluid. Usually used in the passive. [French *engorger* : *en-,* in + *gorge,* throat, GORGE.] **—en·gorge·ment** *n.*

en·graft (ĕn-grăft′, -gräft′, ĭn-) *tr.v.* **-grafted, -grafting, -grafts.** Also **in·graft** (ĭn-). **1.** To graft (a shoot or bud) onto or into another plant. **2.** To implant firmly; incorporate. **—en·graft·ment** *n.*

en·grail (ĕn-grāl′, ĭn-) *tr.v.* **-grailed, -grailing, -grails. 1.** To indent (the edge of something) with small curves. **2.** To decorate the edge of by adding a series of curved indentations. [Middle English *engrelen,* from Old French *engresler* : *en-,* in + *gresle,* hail (the indentations were imagined to resemble hailstones).]

en·grain (ĕn-grān′, ĭn-) *tr.v.* **-grained, -graining, -grains. 1.** To treat, dye, or color so as to suggest the grain of wood. **2.** Variant of **ingrain.** [Middle English *engreinen,* from Old French *engrainer,* to dye in grain, from *en graine,* in grain : *en-,* in + *graine,* cochineal dye, kermes, from Latin *grāna,* plural of *grānum,* GRAIN.]

en·gram, en·gramme (ĕn′grăm′) *n.* A persistent protoplasmic alteration hypothesized to occur on stimulation of living neural tissue and to account for memory. Also called "memory engram," "neurogram." [EN- + -GRAM.] **—en·gram·mat·ic** (ĕn′grə-măt′ĭk), **en·gram·mic** (ĕn-grăm′ĭk) *adj.*

en·grave (ĕn-grāv′, ĭn-) *tr.v.* **-graved, -graving, -graves. 1.** To carve, cut, or etch (a design or letters) into a material. **2. a.** To carve, cut, or etch (a design or letters) into a block or surface used for printing. **b.** To carve a design on (a printing block or plate). **c.** To print from a block or plate made by such a process. **3.** To impress deeply; fix permanently. [EN- + GRAVE (to carve).] **—en·grav·er** *n.*

en·grav·ing (ĕn-grā′vĭng, ĭn-) *n.* **1.** The art or technique of one that engraves. **2.** An engraved surface for printing. **3.** A print made from an engraved plate or block. See feature page 562.

en·gross (ĕn-grōs′, ĭn-) *tr.v.* **-grossed, -grossing, -grosses. 1.** To occupy the complete attention of; absorb wholly. **2.** To acquire most or all of (a commodity); monopolize (a market). Compare **forestall. 3. a.** To write or transcribe in a large, clear hand. **b.** To prepare the text of (an official document) by an officially prescribed process, such as handwriting or printing. [Senses 1 and 2, Middle English *engrossen,* from Norman French *engrosser,* from *en gros,* in large quantity, wholesale. Sense 3, Middle English, from Norman French *engrosser,* from *en grosse,* in large handwriting.] **—en·gross·er** *n.*

en·grossed (ĕn-grōst′, ĭn-) *adj.* Having one's attention completely occupied; totally absorbed.

en·gross·ing (ĕn-grō′sĭng, ĭn-) *adj.* Occupying one's complete attention; wholly absorbing. **—en·gross·ing·ly** *adv.*

en·gross·ment (ĕn-grōs′mənt, ĭn-) *n.* **1.** The state of being completely absorbed, occupied, or monopolized. **2.** A document, such as a deed or will, that has been engrossed.

en·gulf (ĕn-gŭlf′, ĭn-) *tr.v.* **-gulfed, -gulfing, -gulfs.** Also **in·gulf** (ĭn-). **1.** To surround completely. **2.** To swallow up or overwhelm by or as if by flowing over and enclosing: *engulfed by bad luck.* **—en·gulf·ment** *n.*

en·hance (ĕn-hăns′, -häns′, ĭn-) *tr.v.* **-hanced, -hancing, -hances. 1.** To increase or make greater, as in value, cost, beauty, or reputation; augment. **2.** To increase the clarity of (a photograph, especially one taken from space or the air), by using a computer to improve contrast. **—See Synonyms at improve.** [Middle English *enhauncen,* from Norman French *enhauncer,* variant of Old French *enhaucer,* from Vulgar Latin *inaltiāre* (unattested), to raise : Latin *in-* (intensive) + *altus,* high.] **—en·hance·ment** *n.* **—en·hanc·er** *n.* **—en·hanc·ive** *adj.*

enhanced radiation *n.* Radiation released by certain nuclear devices in the form of neutrons and gamma rays, able to destroy life

---

English Civil War

THE KING WHO LOST HIS HEAD

The English Civil War broke the monarch's power

The first English Civil War (1642–46) broke the power of the throne and established the parliamentary rule that exists today. Growing confidence among the merchant classes steeled Parliament to challenge Charles I's unshakable belief in the divine right of kings. Charles needed Parliament only to raise taxes, and for 11 years, from 1629–40, he ruled without it.

In 1639, the Archbishop of Canterbury, William Laud, tried to force the Reformed prayer book on Scotland. The Scots rebelled. Charles called Parliament to raise money to fight them. The House agreed—on condition that he approved the Grand Remonstrance, a document denying his right to dismiss Parliament and rule without it. The king refused. His bid to arrest the Parliamentary leaders failed and he prepared

for war, raising his standard in November 1642.

After initial successes by the Royalist troops, called Cavaliers, parliamentary troops—the Roundheads—led by Oliver Cromwell, were the victors at Marston Moor (1644) and at Naseby (1645). Finally in May 1646, Charles surrendered to the Scots. No settlement was reached despite negotiations and further fighting (the second Civil War). Cromwell's army was again victorious. Charles was tried by Parliament, found guilty of murder and treason, and executed on January 30, 1649.

For nine years, Cromwell ruled as dictator. But after his death, the monarchy was restored. Charles I's son became King Charles II in 1660, but he had to accept that Parliament was the supreme arm of government.

EXECUTION OF A KING *On January 30, 1649, Charles I placed his head on the block in Whitehall, London. He died still believing that he had a divine right to rule England as he wished. That night, Oliver Cromwell looked at the royal corpse in St. James's Palace and muttered: "Cruel necessity."*

but having a reduced nuclear blast and thus causing limited damage to the nonliving environment.

enhanced radiation bomb *n.* A neutron bomb *(see).*

en·har·mon·ic (ĕn′här-mŏn′ĭk) *adj. Music.* **1.** Of, pertaining to, or being an ancient Greek scale consisting of quartertones. **2.** Of, pertaining to, or being a note of the same pitch but different written representation, as C and D♭, on all instruments such as pianos that are tuned to the tempered scale. [Late Latin *enharmonicus,* from Greek *enarmonikos,* "in harmony" : *en-,* in + *harmonia,* HARMONY.] —**en·har·mon·i·cal·ly** *adv.*

e·nig·ma (ĭ-nĭg′mə) *n.* **1.** An obscure riddle. **2.** An obscure piece of speech or writing. **3.** Someone or something that is puzzling, ambiguous, or inexplicable. [Latin *aenigma,* from Greek *ainigma,* from *ainissesthai,* to speak in riddles, hint, from *ainos,* tale, story.]

en·ig·mat·ic (ĕn′ĭg-măt′ĭk) *adj.* Also **en·ig·mat·i·cal** (-ĭ-kəl). Of or resembling an enigma; puzzling: *an enigmatic smile.* —**en·ig·mat·i·cal·ly** *adv.*

en·isle (ĕn-īl′, ĭn-) *tr.v.* **-isled, -isling, -isles. 1.** To make into an island. **2.** To set apart from others; isolate.

E·ni·we·tok (ĕn′ə-wē′tŏk′). An uninhabited coral atoll in the Ralik Chain of the Marshall Islands, west-central Pacific Ocean. Atomic tests were conducted here from 1948 to 1954.

en·jamb·ment, en·jambe·ment (ĕn-jăm′mənt, -jămb′mənt, ĭn-, äN′-zhäNb-mäN′) *n.* The continuation of a sentence or idea from one line or couplet of a poem to the next. [French, from Old French *enjamber,* to straddle : *en-,* in + *jambe,* leg (see **jamb**).] —**en·jambed** (ĕn-jämd′, ĭn-) *adj.*

en·join (ĕn-join′, ĭn-) *tr.v.* **-joined, -joining, -joins. 1.** To require or direct with authority and emphasis; command; impose. **2.** To urge or order (a person) to do something. **3.** To prohibit or forbid, especially by legal action: *The court enjoined him from visiting his children.* —See Synonyms at **command.** [Middle English *enjoinen,* from Old French *enjoindre,* from Latin *injungere,* to join to, impose : *in-,* in, to + *jungere,* to join.] —**en·join·er** *n.* —**en·join·ment** *n.*

en·joy (ĕn-joi′, ĭn-) *tr.v.* **-joyed, -joying, -joys. 1.** To experience joy in or receive pleasure from; relish: *They enjoy good food and the companionship of friends.* **2.** To have the use of or benefit from: *She enjoyed a generous allowance.* **3.** To have as one's lot; experience: *His parents enjoy excellent health.* **4.** To have sexual intercourse with. —See Synonyms at **like.** —**enjoy oneself.** To have a pleasant time. [Middle English *enjoien,* from Old French *enjoir* : *en-,* in + *joir,* to rejoice, from Latin *gaudēre.*] —**en·joy·er** *n.*

en·joy·a·ble (ĕn-joi′ə-bəl, ĭn-) *adj.* Giving or capable of giving enjoyment; pleasurable; agreeable. —**en·joy·a·ble·ness** *n.* —**en·joy·a·bly** *adv.*

en·joy·ment (ĕn-joi′mənt, ĭn-) *n.* **1.** The act or state of experiencing joy or pleasure in something. **2.** The use or possession of something, as: **a.** Something beneficial or pleasurable. **b.** A legal right: *enjoyment of the right to vote.* **3.** Something that is enjoyed. **4.** Pleasure; joy. —See Synonyms at **pleasure.**

en·keph·a·lin (ĕn-kĕf′ə-lĭn) *n.* A chemical occurring naturally in the brain and having effects similar to those of morphine. [ENCEPHALO- + -IN.]

en·kin·dle (ĕn-kĭnd′l, ĭn-) *tr.v.* **-dled, -dling, -dles. 1.** To set on fire; light; kindle. **2.** To incite; arouse. **3.** To make luminous and glowing. —**en·kin·dler** *n.*

enl. 1. enlarged. **2.** enlisted.

en·lace (ĕn-lās′, ĭn-) *tr.v.* **-laced, -lacing, -laces.** Also **in·lace** (ĭn-). **1.** To wrap or wind about with or as if with a lace or laces; encircle. **2.** To interlace; entangle; entwine. —**en·lace·ment** *n.*

en·large (ĕn-lärj′, ĭn-) *v.* **-larged, -larging, -larges.** —*tr.* **1. a.** To make larger; add to: *We enlarged the kitchen.* **b.** To make (a photographic print) larger than the original print or larger than the standard size. **2.** To give greater scope to; expand: *Travel enlarged the child's experience.* **3.** To set free; liberate. —*intr.* **1.** To become larger; grow. **2.** To speak or write at greater length or in greater detail: *He enlarged on his plans.* —See Synonyms at **increase.** [Middle English *enlargen,* from Old French *enlargier* : *en-,* in + *large,* LARGE.]

en·large·ment (ĕn-lärj′mənt, ĭn-) *n.* **1.** An act of enlarging or the state of being enlarged. **2.** Something, such as an addition, expansion, or increase, that enlarges something else. **3.** A reproduction or copy larger than the original; especially, an optically magnified print of a photographic negative.

en·larg·er (ĕn-lär′jər, ĭn-) *n.* An optical instrument for producing enlarged photographic prints by projecting an image of the negative onto sensitive paper.

en·light·en (ĕn-līt′n, ĭn-) *tr.v.* **-ened, -ening, -ens. 1. a.** To give knowledge or truth to. **b.** To endow with spiritual understanding. **2.** To acquaint (someone) with information; inform. **3.** To free (someone) from prejudice or false belief. —**en·light·en·er** *n.*

en·light·en·ment (ĕn-līt′n-mənt, ĭn-) *n.* **1.** An act or means of enlightening. **2.** The state of being enlightened. **3.** *Buddhism.* A state marked by spiritual insight and freedom from illusory appearances. **4. Enlightenment.** A philosophical movement of the 18th century, concerned with the critical examination of previously accepted doctrines and institutions from the point of view of rationalism. —See Synonyms at **knowledge.**

en·list (ĕn-lĭst′, ĭn-) *v.* **-listed, -listing, -lists.** —*tr.* **1.** To persuade to enter the armed forces. **2.** To engage the assistance or cooperation of; secure on one's behalf. —*intr.* **1.** To enter the armed forces voluntarily. **2.** To participate actively in some cause or enterprise. [EN- + LIST (roster).] —**en·list·ment** *n.*

enlisted man *n.* A man or woman who has enlisted in the armed forces without an officer's commission or warrant.

en·liv·en (ĕn-lī′vən, ĭn-) *tr.v.* **-ened, -ening, -ens. 1.** To make lively or spirited; animate; invigorate. **2.** To brighten; cheer. [EN- + LIVE (adjective).] —**en·liv·en·er** *n.* —**en·liv·en·ment** *n.*

en masse (ŏn măs′, äN mäs′) *adv.* In one group or body; all together. [French : *en,* in + *masse,* MASS (body).]

en·mesh (ĕn-mĕsh′, ĭn-) *tr.v.* **-meshed, -meshing, -meshes.** Also **in·mesh** (ĭn-), **im·mesh** (ĭ-mĕsh′). **1.** To entangle, involve, or catch in or as if in a net. **2.** To cover with net or mesh.

en·mi·ty (ĕn′mə-tē) *n., pl.* **-ties.** Deep-seated hatred, as between rivals or opponents; antagonism. [Middle English *enemite,* from Old French *enemiste,* from Vulgar Latin *inimīcītās* (unattested), from Latin *inimīcus,* ENEMY.]

Synonyms: animosity, animus, antagonism, antipathy, rancor.

en·ne·ad (ĕn′ē-ăd′) *n.* Any group or set of nine. [Greek *enneas* (stem *ennead-*), from *ennea,* nine.]

en·ne·a·he·dron (ĕn′ē-ə-hē′drən) *n., pl.* **-drons** or **-dra** (-drə). *Mathematics.* A solid that has nine faces. [Greek *ennea,* nine + -HEDRON.]

en·no·ble (ĕn-nō′bəl, ĭn-) *tr.v.* **-bled, -bling, -bles. 1.** To invest with nobility; bring honor or glory to. **2.** To raise to the rank of nobleman; confer nobility upon. [Middle English *ennoblen,* from Old French *ennoblir* : *en-,* in + NOBLE.] —**en·no·ble·ment** *n.*

en·nui (ŏn-wē′, ŏn′wē) *n.* Listlessness and dissatisfaction resulting from lack of interest; boredom: *gossiping to relieve their ennui.* [French, from Old French *enui,* from Latin *in odiō,* "in hate," odious : *in,* in + *odium,* hate.]

E·noch[1] (ē′nək, ē′nŏk′). The eldest son of Cain. Genesis 4:17. [Late Latin, from Greek *Enōkh,* from Hebrew *Ḥanōkh,* "consecrated," "initiated," from *hānakh,* he initiated.]

Enoch[2]. The father of Methuselah. Genesis 5:21.

e·nol (ē′nôl′, ē′nōl′) *n.* An organic compound containing a hydroxyl group bonded to a carbon atom that in turn is doubly bonded to another carbon atom. See **keto-enol tautomerism.** [-ENE + -OL.] —**e·nol·ic** (ē-nŏl′ĭk) *adj.*

e·no·lase (ē′nə-lās′, -lāz′) *n.* An enzyme present in muscle tissue that acts in carbohydrate metabolism. [ENOL + -ASE.]

enology. Variant of **oenology.**

e·nor·mi·ty (ĭ-nôr′mə-tē) *n., pl.* **-ties. 1.** The quality of passing all moral bounds; excessive wickedness; outrageousness. **2.** A monstrous offense or evil; an outrage.

e·nor·mous (ĭ-nôr′məs) *adj.* **1.** Very great in size, extent, number, or degree; immense: *swam in an enormous pool.* **2.** *Archaic.* Very wicked; heinous. [Middle English *enormous,* from Latin *ēnormis,* unusual, immense : *ex-,* out of + *norma,* pattern, rule.] —**e·nor·mous·ly** *adv.* —**e·nor·mous·ness** *n.*

Synonyms: colossal, gargantuan, gigantic, huge, immense, mammoth, tremendous, vast.

E·nos (ē′nəs, ē′nŏs′). A son of Seth. Genesis 4:26. [Greek *Enōs,* from Hebrew *Enōsh,* "man."]

e·nough (ĭ-nŭf′) *adj.* **1.** Sufficient to meet a need or satisfy a desire; adequate: *enough food for two.* **2.** Used in requests to stop: *That's enough, now!* ~*pron.* An adequate quantity or number: *He ate enough for two.* ~*adv.* **1.** To a satisfactory amount or degree; sufficiently. **2.** Very; fully; quite: *We were glad enough to leave.* **3.** Tolerably; rather: *She sang well enough, but the show was a failure.* **4.** Used as an intensive following certain adverbs: *funnily enough; sure enough; oddly enough.* [Middle English *ynough, inough,* Old English *genōg,* from Germanic.]

e·nounce (ĭ-nouns′) *tr.v.* **enounced, enouncing, enounces. 1.** To declare publicly or formally; state; announce. **2.** To pronounce; enunciate. [French *énoncer,* from Latin *ēnuntiāre,* to ENUNCIATE.] —**e·nounce·ment** *n.*

e·now (ĭ-nou′) *adj. Archaic.* Enough. —**e·now** *adv.*

en pas·sant (äN′ pä-säN′) *adv.)* In passing; by the way. ~*n.* The capture of a chess pawn after an initial move of two squares by an enemy pawn in a position to make a capture on the first of the two squares so crossed. [French.]

en·phy·tot·ic (ĕn′fĭ-tŏt′ĭk) *adj.* Designating or characterizing a plant disease that causes a relatively constant amount of damage each year. [EN- + -PHYT(E) + -OTIC.]

en·plane (ĕn-plān′, ĭn-) *intr.v.* **-planed, -planing, -planes.** Also **em·plane** (ĕm-, ĭm-). To board an airplane.

enquire. Variant of **inquire.**

enquiry. Variant of **inquiry.**

en·rage (ĕn-rāj′, ĭn-) *tr.v.* **-raged, -raging, -rages.** To put in a rage; infuriate; anger.

en·rapt (ĕn-răpt′, ĭn-) *adj.* **1.** Enraptured. **2.** Enthralled.

en·rap·ture (ĕn-răp′chər, ĭn-) *tr.v.* **-tured, -turing, -tures.** To move to rapture; overwhelm with delight.

en·rich (ĕn-rĭch′, ĭn-) *tr.v.* **-riched, -riching, -riches. 1.** To make rich or richer. **2. a.** To add to in quality or quantity; improve. **b.** To make fuller, more meaningful, or more rewarding: *Reading enriches the vocabulary.* **3.** To add fertilizer to (soil) to increase productivity. **4.** To add nutrients to (foodstuffs) during processing. **5.** To add to the beauty or character of; embellish or adorn: *The carved moldings enriched the walls.* **6.** *Physics.* To increase the ratio of radioactive isotopes in (a sample); especially, to increase the ratio of amount of fissionable uranium 235 in (natural uranium) so that it can be used as a nuclear fuel. **7.** *Chemistry.* To increase the amount of a particular substance in (a mixture or solution). [Middle English *enrichen,* from Old French *enricher* : *en-* (causative) + *riche*, RICH.] —**en·rich·er** *n.*

en·rich·ment (ĕn-rĭch′mənt, ĭn-) *n.* **1. a.** The act of enriching. **b.** The state of being enriched. **2.** Something that enriches: *added butter to the sauce as an enrichment.*

en·robe (ĕn-rōb′, ĭn-) *tr.v.* **-robed, -robing, -robes. 1.** To put a robe on. **2.** To dress richly as if in a robe.

en·roll, en·rol (ĕn-rōl′, ĭn-) *v.* **-rolled, -rolling, -rolls** or **-rols.** —*tr.* **1.** To enter the name of in a register, record, or roll. **2.** To put on record; record. **3.** To roll or wrap up. **4.** To cause (a person) to become a member. —*intr.* **1.** To place one's name on a roll or register. **2.** To become a member. [Middle English *enrollen,* from Old French *enroller* : *en-,* in + *rolle,* ROLL.]

en·roll·ment, en·rol·ment (ĕn-rōl′mənt, ĭn-) *n.* **1. a.** The action of enrolling. **b.** The state or process of being enrolled. **c.** The number enrolled. **2.** A record or entry.

en·root (ĕn-rōōt′, -rŏŏt′, ĭn-) *tr.v.* **-rooted, -rooting, -roots.** To establish firmly by or as if by roots; implant.

en route (ŏn rōōt′, ĕn, än) *adv.* On the route; on or along the way. [French.]

ens (ĕnz) *n., pl.* **entia** (ĕn′shē-ə, -shə). *Philosophy.* **1.** Existence or being as an abstract concept. **2.** An entity as opposed to an attribute. [Medieval Latin, from Latin, irregular present participle of *esse,* to be.]

Ens. ensign.

en·san·guine (ĕn-săng′gwĭn, ĭn-) *tr.v.* **-guined, -guining, -guines. 1.** To cover or stain with or as if with blood. **2.** To color or stain a crimson red.

en·sconce (ĕn-skŏns′, ĭn-) *tr.v.* **-sconced, -sconcing, -sconces. 1.** To settle (oneself) securely or comfortably: *ensconced in an armchair.* **2.** To place, fix, or conceal in a secure place. [EN- + SCONCE (fortification), originally meaning to take shelter, as behind a fortification.]

en·sem·ble (ŏn-sŏm′bəl) *n.* **1.** A unit or group of complementary parts that contribute to a single effect. **2.** A coordinated outfit or costume. **3.** A set, as of furniture. **4.** A group of musicians, singers, dancers, or actors who perform together. **5. a.** Music for two or more vocalists or instrumentalists. **b.** The musicians who perform in an ensemble. **c.** The quality of performance of a musical ensemble, especially as judged in regard to unity and balance of style and technique: *The individual players were all virtuosos, but the ensemble was poor.* Also used adjectivally: *ensemble playing.* **6.** *Physics.* A large collection of atoms, or a collection of assemblies of atoms, used in statistical mechanics to calculate the thermodynamic properties of a system. [French, "together," from Vulgar Latin *insemul* (unattested), from Latin *insimul,* at the same time : *in-,* in + *simul, semul,* at the same time.]

en·shrine (ĕn-shrīn′, ĭn-) *tr.v.* **-shrined, -shrining, -shrines.** Also **in·shrine** (ĭn-). **1.** To enclose in or as if in a shrine: *a book enshrining their ideals.* **2.** To cherish as sacred. —**en·shrine·ment** *n.*

en·shroud (ĕn-shroud′, ĭn-) *tr.v.* **-shrouded, -shrouding, -shrouds.** To shroud or cover; veil or conceal.

en·si·form (ĕn′sə-fôrm′) *adj.* Sword-shaped, as the leaf of an iris or gladiolus. [French *ensiforme,* from Latin *ēnsis,* sword + -FORM.]

en·sign (ĕn′sən; also ĕn′sīn′ *for senses 1, 2, 3, 5*) *n.* **1. a.** A national flag displayed on ships and aircraft, often with the special insignia of a branch or unit of the armed forces: *the naval ensign.* **b.** *British.* A flag, usually on a ship, incorporating the Union Jack in the top left-hand corner. **2.** A standard or banner, as of a military unit. **3.** *Archaic.* A standard-bearer. **4. a.** *Abbr.* **Ens.** A commissioned officer of the lowest rank in the U.S. Navy or Coast Guard. **b.** Formerly, a commissioned officer of the lowest rank in the British infantry. **5. a.** A badge; emblem. **b.** A sign; token. [Middle English *ensigne,* from Old French *enseigne,* from Latin *insignia,* INSIGNIA.]

en·si·lage (ĕn′sə-lĭj) *n.* **1.** The process of storing and fermenting green fodder in a silo. **2.** Fodder thus preserved; silage. ~*tr.v.* **ensilaged, -laging, -lages.** To ensile.

en·sile (ĕn-sīl′, ĭn-) *tr.v.* **-siled, -siling, -siles. 1.** To store (fodder) in a silo for preservation. **2.** To convert (green fodder) into silage.

en·slave (ĕn-slāv′, ĭn-) *tr.v.* **-slaved, -slaving, -slaves.** To make a slave of; reduce to slavery, bondage, or dependence. —**en·slave·ment** *n.* —**en·slav·er** *n.*

en·snare (ĕn-snâr′, ĭn-) *tr.v.* **-snared, -snaring, -snares.** Also **in·snare** (ĭn-). To catch in or as if in a snare; trap. —**en·snare·ment** *n.*

en·soul (ĕn-sōl′, ĭn-) *tr.v.* **-souled, -souling, -souls. 1.** To endow with a soul. **2.** To unite with the soul.

en·sphere (ĕn-sfîr′, ĭn-) *tr.v.* **-sphered, -sphering, -spheres.** Also **in·sphere** (ĭn-). **1.** To enclose in or as if in a sphere. **2.** To give spherical form to.

en·sta·tite (ĕn′stə-tīt′) *n.* A variety of orthorhombic pyroxene having a magnesium silicate base, mainly $Mg_2Si_2O_6$, usually found embedded in igneous rocks. [German *Enstatit* : Greek *enstatēs,* adversary (from its refractory nature) : *en-,* in, at, near + -*statēs,* standing + -ITE.]

en·sue (ĕn-sōō′, ĭn-) *intr.v.* **-sued, -suing, -sues. 1.** To follow immediately afterward; take place subsequently. **2.** To follow as a consequence; result. —See Synonyms at **follow.** [Middle English *ensuen,* from Old French *ensuivre* (stem *ensu-*), from Vulgar Latin *insequere* (unattested), variant of Latin *insequī,* to follow after or on : *in-,* in, onward + *sequī,* to follow.]

en suite (än swēt′) *adv.* As part of a unit or set: *a master bedroom en suite with bathroom.* [French, "in sequence."]

en·sure (ĕn-shŏŏr′, ĭn-) *tr.v.* **-sured, -suring, -sures.** To make sure or certain; make secure; guarantee.

–ent *suffix.* **1.** Indicates performing, promoting, or causing a specified action; for example, **effervescent, absorbent. 2.** Indicates one that performs, promotes, or causes a specified action; for example, **referent.** [Middle English *-ent,* from Old French, from Latin *-ens* (stem *-ent-*). Compare **-ant.**]

E.N.T. *Medicine.* ear, nose, and throat.

en·tab·la·ture (ĕn-tăb′lə-chŏŏr′, -chər, ĭn-) *n. Architecture.* **1.** The upper section of a classical order, resting on the capital and including the architrave, frieze, and cornice. **2.** Any raised, horizontal architectural feature. [Obsolete French, from Italian *intavolatura,* from *intavolare,* to put on the table : *in-,* in, from Latin + *tavola,* table, from Latin *tabula,* board, TABLE.]

en·ta·ble·ment (ĕn-tā′bəl-mənt, ĭn-) *n.* The platform supporting a statue, above the base and the dado. [French, from Old French : *en-,* in + TABLE.]

en·tail (ĕn-tāl′, ĭn-) *tr.v.* **-tailed, -tailing, -tails. 1.** To have as a necessary accompaniment or consequence. **2.** To limit the inheritance of (property) to a specific, unalterable succession of heirs.

---

engraving

ENGRAVING: PRINTING PICTURES FROM A METAL PLATE

An art form that was also used to mass-produce original works of art

In Europe, engraving pictures on metal plates began in the 15th century, probably in the Rhineland. Until the advent of photography four centuries later it was used to mass-produce original drawings and paintings and to illustrate books. Great artists—including Dürer, Rembrandt, Goya, and Picasso—have used the technique to produce original works of art.

In line engraving, the artist draws on a plate of metal, usually copper, using a sharp tool. The plate is then inked and wiped clean, leaving ink in the engraved furrows. A damp piece of paper is laid on the plate, and both are rolled through a heavy press. The paper is forced into the furrows, picking up the ink; on the finished print the engraved lines stand up in relief.

In drypoint, the burr at the side of the furrow is left, rather than being scraped off, and is used together with the line itself to add character to the drawing. This produces a broad soft line rather than a thin clean one.

Etching is done on a plate coated with an acid-resistant ground. The artist's needle exposes the copper, and the plate is then put in an acid bath, which eats away the exposed parts.

Aquatint is a form of etching in which dots give gradations of light and dark. It uses a porous ground that the acid penetrates to form tiny dots. Tone is controlled by the length of time different areas are exposed to the acid.

Mezzotint is a process that was widely used to reproduce paintings in the 18th century. The plate surface is covered with innumerable minute pits by a tool called a rocker, and so prints as a uniform velvety black. Whites and grays are achieved by burnishing the metal surface.

DÜRER *An engraving by Albrecht Dürer of a peasant couple dancing, dated 1514. In his lifetime (1471–1528), Dürer's works of art included 250 woodcuts and more than 100 engravings. He drew the sketches for his woodcuts, but they were cut into the woodblock by skilled artisans. The engravings, however, are entirely Dürer's own work, and he created them as individual works of art. A number of his engravings are portraits of peasants who were regular marketgoers to his local market square at Nuremberg, in Germany, and the fairs at Frankfurt.*

~*n.* (ĕn'tāl', ĕn-tāl', ĭn-). **1. a.** The act of entailing, especially property. **b.** The state of being entailed. **2.** An entailed estate. **3.** A predetermined order of succession, as to an estate or to an office. **4.** Something transmitted as if by unalterable inheritance. [Middle English *entaillen, entailen* : EN- + *taille,* TAIL (limitation).] —**en·tail·ment** *n.*

en·ta·moe·ba (ĕn'tə-mē'bə) *n., pl.* **-bas** or **-bae** (-bē). Also **en·da·moe·ba** (ĕn'də-). Any of several parasitic amoebas of the genus *Entamoeba;* especially, *E. histolytica,* causing dysentery and ulceration of the colon and liver. [New Latin *Entamoeba* : ENT(O)- + AMOEBA.]

en·tan·gle (ĕn-tăng'gəl, ĭn-) *tr.v.* **-gled, -gling, -gles. 1.** To twist together so that disengagement is difficult; make tangled; snarl. **2.** To complicate; confuse. **3.** To involve inextricably, as in complications or difficulties. —**en·tan·gler** *n.*

en·tan·gle·ment (ĕn-tăng'gəl-mənt, ĭn-) *n.* **1. a.** The act of entangling. **b.** The state of being entangled. **2.** Something that entangles, as a dangerous or compromising relationship, especially a sexual one. **3.** A military barrier of barbed wire.

en·ta·sis (ĕn'tə-sĭs) *n., pl.* **-ses** (-sēz'). *Architecture.* A slight bulge in a column, introduced to avoid the illusion of concavity that a straight column would give. [New Latin, from Greek, from *enteinein,* to stretch tight : *en-* (intensive) + *teinein,* to stretch.]

En·teb·be (ĕn-tĕb'ē). Town in Uganda, situated on Lake Victoria, south of Kampala. At its airport in 1976 an Israeli airborne commando force rescued all but 3 of 110 hostages after the hijacking of an Air France plane by Palestinian guerrillas.

en·tel·e·chy (ĕn-tĕl'ə-kē, ĭn-) *n., pl.* **-chies. 1.** In the philosophy of Aristotle, the condition of a thing whose essence is fully realized; actuality as distinguished from potentiality. **2.** In various philosophical systems, a vital force urging an organism toward self-fulfillment: *"Courage is the affirmation of one's essential nature, one's inner aim or entelechy"* (Paul Tillich). [Late Latin *entelechia,* from Greek *entelekheia,* complete reality : *entelēs,* complete, full : *en-,* in + *telos,* perfection, end + *ekhein,* to have.]

en·tente (ŏn-tŏnt', äN-täNt') *n.* **1.** An agreement, usually unformalized, between two or more governments or powers for cooperative action or policy. **2.** The coalition resulting from an entente. [French, "understanding," from Old French *entendre,* to understand, INTEND.]

en·ter (ĕn'tər) *v.* **-tered, -tering, -ters.** —*tr.* **1.** To come or go into. **2.** To penetrate; pierce. **3.** To introduce; insert. **4.** To become an element in or a part of. **5.** To begin (an age or phase); embark upon: *He was entering a period of crisis.* **6. a.** To obtain admission to (a school, for example). **b.** To secure the admission of. **c.** To enroll. **7. a.** To submit or register as an entry in an exhibition or competition: *enter dahlias in a flower show.* **b.** To become a participant or a contestant in. **8.** To take up (a profession or career); embrace: *Their son entered the priesthood.* **9.** *Law.* **a.** To place formally before a court or upon the records: *enter a plea.* **b.** To go upon or into (real property) as a trespasser or with felonious intent. See **breaking and entering. c.** To go upon in order to take possession of (real property, especially land). **10.** To record, as in a register or on a list. **11.** To make known; register: *enter a protest.* —*intr.* **1.** To come or go in; make an entry. **2.** To gain entry; penetrate. **3.** To become a member of a group. **4.** To come on-stage in a theater: *Enter stage left.* —**enter into. 1.** To participate in; take an active interest in. **2.** To be a component of; form a part of. **3.** To consider; delve into. **4.** To become party to (a contract). **5.** To empathize with; be in sympathy with. —**enter on** (or **upon**). **1.** To set out upon; embark upon. **2.** To take legal possession of (real property, especially land). **3.** To begin to consider or deal with (a subject). [Middle English *entren,* from Old French *entrer,* from Latin *intrāre,* from *intrā,* within.]

en·ter·ic (ĕn-tĕr'ĭk, ĭn-) *adj.* Also **en·ter·al** (ĕn'tər-əl). Of, pertaining to, or affecting the intestine. [Greek *enterikos,* from *enteron,* ENTERON.]

enteric fever *n. Pathology.* **Typhoid fever** *(see).*

en·ter·i·tis (ĕn'tə-rī'tĭs) *n.* Inflammation of the intestinal tract. [New Latin : ENTER(O)- + -ITIS.]

entero–, enter– *prefix.* Indicates the intestine; for example, **enterostomy, enteritis.** [New Latin, from Greek *enteron,* intestine.]

en·ter·o·bi·a·sis (ĕn'tə-rō-bī'ə-sĭs) *n.* Infestation of the intestine with pinworms. Also called "oxyuriasis." [New Latin *enterobius (vermicularis),* pinworm (see **entero-**) + -IASIS.]

en·ter·o·gas·trone (ĕn'tə-rō-găs'trōn') *n.* A hormone liberated by the small intestine (duodenum) that inhibits secretion of gastric juice by the stomach. [ENTERO- + GASTR(O)- + (HORM)ONE.]

en·ter·o·ki·nase (ĕn'tə-rō-kī'nās', -nāz') *n.* An enzyme found in intestinal juice that converts trypsinogen to trypsin. [ENTERO- + KINASE.]

en·ter·on (ĕn'tə-rŏn') *n.* The intestine, especially that of an embryo or coelenterate. [New Latin, from Greek, intestine, entrails.]

en·ter·os·to·my (ĕn'tə-rŏs'tə-mē) *n., pl.* **-mies.** Surgical formation of an opening into the intestine through the abdominal wall. [ENTERO- + -STOMY.] —**en·ter·os·to·mal** *adj.*

en·ter·ot·o·my (ĕn'tə-rŏt'ə-mē) *n., pl.* **-mies.** Surgical incision into the intestine. [ENTERO- + -TOMY.]

en·ter·o·vir·us (ĕn'tə-rō-vī'rəs) *n.* Any virus, such as the polio virus, that enters the body through and multiplies in the gastrointestinal tract, and then usually invades the central nervous system.

en·ter·prise (ĕn'tər-prīz') *n.* **1.** An undertaking, especially of some scope, complication, and risk. **2. a.** Commercial or economic activity; business: *private enterprise.* **b.** A business or company. **3.** Industrious effort, especially when directed toward making money. **4.** Readiness to venture; boldness; initiative. [Middle English, from Old French *entreprise,* from the feminine past participle of *entreprendre,* to undertake : *entre-,* between, from Latin *inter-* + *prendre,* to take, from Latin *prendere, prehendere.*] —**en·ter·pris·er** *n.*

en·ter·pris·ing (ĕn'tər-prī'zĭng) *adj.* Showing imagination, initiative, and readiness to undertake new ventures. —**en·ter·pris·ing·ly** *adv.*

en·ter·tain (ĕn'tər-tān') *v.* **-tained, -taining, -tains.** —*tr.* **1.** To hold the attention of; especially, to perform for the pleasure of; amuse. **2.** To extend hospitality toward: *entertain friends for dinner.* **3. a.** To mull over; contemplate: *entertain an idea.* **b.** To hold in mind; harbor: *entertain illusions.* **4.** *Sports.* To play at home against (an opposing team, for example). —*intr.* **1.** To have guests, as for dinner or a party. **2.** To provide entertainment. [Middle English *entertinen,* to maintain, from Old French *entretenir,* from Vulgar Latin *intertenēre* (unattested), "to hold between" : Latin *inter-,* between + *tenēre,* to hold.]

en·ter·tain·er (ĕn'tər-tā'nər) *n.* **1.** A person who performs, as by singing or dancing, as a profession. **2.** Someone who entertains.

en·ter·tain·ing (ĕn'tər-tā'nĭng) *adj.* Serving to entertain; agreeably diverting; amusing. —**en·ter·tain·ing·ly** *adv.*

en·ter·tain·ment (ĕn'tər-tān'mənt) *n.* **1.** The act of entertaining. **2.** The art, profession, or field of entertaining. **3.** Something that entertains; especially, a performance or show designed to amuse or divert. **4.** The pleasure afforded by being entertained; amusement. **5.** Hospitality extended toward guests.

en·thal·py (ĕn'thăl'pē, ĕn-thăl'-) *n.* A thermodynamic function of a system, equivalent to the internal energy plus the product of the pressure and the volume. Also called "heat content." [Greek *enthalpein,* to heat in : *en-,* in + *thalpein*†, to warm, heat.]

en·thrall, en·thral (ĕn-thrôl', ĭn-) *tr.v.* **-thralled, -thralling, -thralls** or **-thrals. 1.** To hold spellbound; captivate; charm. **2.** To reduce to thralldom; enslave. [Middle English *enthrallen* : EN- + THRALL.] —**en·thrall·ment** *n.*

en·throne (ĕn-thrōn', ĭn-) *tr.v.* **-throned, -throning, -thrones. 1.** To seat on a throne. **2.** To invest with sovereign power or with the authority of high office. **3.** To raise to a lofty position; revere; exalt. —**en·throne·ment** *n.*

en·thuse (ĕn-tho͞oz', ĭn-) *v.* **-thused, -thusing, -thuses.** *Informal.* —*tr.* To stimulate enthusiasm in. —*intr.* To show enthusiasm. [Back-formation from ENTHUSIASM.]

en·thu·si·asm (ĕn-tho͞o'zē-ăz'əm, ĭn-) *n.* **1. a.** Keen interest or excitement. **b.** Eagerness; zeal. **c.** Ardent fondness. **2.** A subject or activity that inspires a lively interest. **3.** *Archaic.* **a.** Ecstasy arising from supposed possession by a god. **b.** Fanatical religious ardor. —See Synonyms at **passion.** [Late Latin *enthūsiasmus,* from Greek *enthousiasmos,* inspiration, from *enthousiazein,* to be inspired by a god, from *enthous, entheos,* possessed, inspired : *en-,* in + *theos,* god.]

en·thu·si·ast (ĕn-tho͞o'zē-ăst', ĭn-) *n.* **1.** A person filled with enthusiasm; especially, one ardently preoccupied with a particular subject: *a baseball enthusiast.* **2.** *Archaic.* A religious zealot, fanatic, or visionary. —See Synonyms at **fanatic.** —**en·thu·si·as·tic** (ĕn-tho͞o'zē-ăs'tĭk, ĭn-) *adj.* —**en·thu·si·as·ti·cal·ly** *adv.*

en·thy·meme (ĕn'thə-mēm') *n. Logic.* A syllogism with one of the premises implicit or unexpressed because it is thought to be self-evident. [Latin *enthȳmēma,* from Greek *enthumēma,* from *enthumeisthai,* "to have in mind," consider : *en-,* in + *thūmos,* mind.]

en·ti·a. Plural of **ens.**

en·tice (ĕn-tīs', ĭn-) *tr.v.* **-ticed, -ticing, -tices.** To attract by arousing hope or desire; lure. —See Synonyms at **lure.** [Middle English *enticen,* from Old French *enticier,* from Vulgar Latin *intītiāre* (unattested), to set on fire : Latin *in-,* in + *tītiō*†, firebrand.] —**en·tice·ment** *n.* —**en·tic·er** *n.* —**en·tic·ing·ly** *adv.*

en·tire (ĕn-tīr', ĭn-) *adj.* **1.** Having no part missing or excepted; whole: *an entire set of the encyclopedia; the entire country.* **2.** Without reservation or limitation; total; complete: *entire freedom; my entire approval; his entire attention.* **3.** All in one piece; unbroken; intact: *The ship was still entire after the typhoon.* **4.** Of one piece; continuous. **5.** Not castrated. **6.** *Botany.* Not indented or toothed, as the margin of a leaf.

~*n.* **1.** The whole of something; entirety. **2.** An uncastrated horse. [Middle English *entier,* from Old French, from Latin *integrum,* accusative of *integer,* intact.] —**en·tire·ness** *n.*

en·tire·ly (ĕn-tīr'lē, ĭn-) *adv.* **1.** Wholly; completely. **2.** Solely or exclusively.

en·tire·ty (ĕn-tī'rə-tē, -tīr'tē, ĭn-) *n., pl.* **-ties. 1.** The state or condition of being entire or complete; completeness. **2.** Something that is entire; a whole. **3.** The entire amount or extent; the sum total.

en·ti·tle (ĕn-tīt'l, ĭn-) *tr.v.* **-tled, -tling, -tles. 1.** To give a name or title to; designate: *a novel entitled "Summer."* **2. a.** To give (a person) the right to do or have something; qualify. **b.** To give to or prove a legal right to or claim on something. [Middle English *entitlen,* from Old French *entiteler,* from Late Latin *intitulāre* : *in-,* in + *titulus,* TITLE.] —**en·ti·tle·ment** *n.*

en·ti·ty (ĕn'tə-tē) *n., pl.* **-ties. 1.** The fact of existence; being. **2.** Something that exists independently and apart from other things. **3.** A particular and discrete unit: *Persons and corporations are equivalent entities under the law.* [Medieval Latin *entitās,* from Latin *ēns* (stem *ent-*), irregular present participle of *esse,* to be.]

ento– *prefix.* Indicates within, inside; for example, **entozoa.** [New Latin, from Greek *entos,* within.]

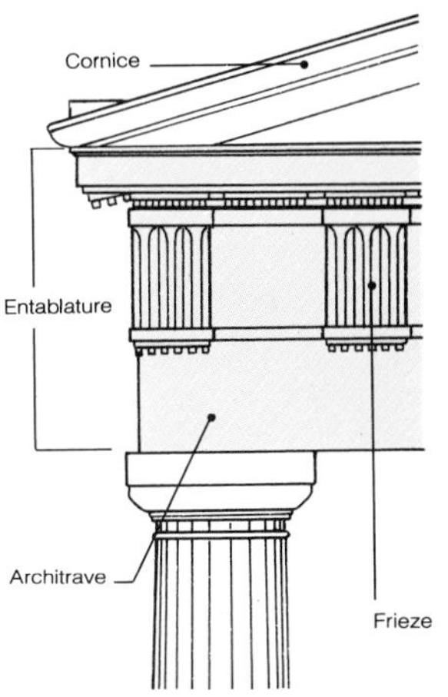

entablature *In classical architecture, the entablature is the collective name for the horizontal parts of a building above the supporting columns. It consists of three elements: the architrave; the frieze; and the cornice.*

PRONUNCIATION KEY

ă, pat; ā, pay; âr, care;
ä, father, are; b, bib;
ch, church; d, deed; ĕ, pet;
ē, be; f, fife; g, gag; h, hat;
hw, which; ĭ, pit; ī, pie;
îr, pier; j, judge; k, kick;
l, lid, needle; m, mum;
n, no, sudden; ng, thing;
ŏ, pot; ō, toe; ô, paw, for;
oi, noise; ou, out; o͝o, book;
o͞o, boot; p, pop; r, roar;
s, sauce; sh, ship, dish;
t, tight; th, thin, path;
th, this, bathe; ŭ, cut; ûr, fur;
v, valve; w, with; y, yes;
z, zebra, size; zh, vision;
ə, about, item, edible,
gallop, circus, peaceful

IN FOREIGN WORDS:

à, *Fr.* ami; œ, *Fr.* feu, *Ger.* schön; ü, *Fr.* tu, *Ger.* über; KH, *Ger.* ich, *Scot.* loch; N, *Fr.* bon; y', *Fr.* Compiègne

STRESS MARKS:

Primary stress: '
in·cite' (ĭn-sīt')
Secondary stress: '
in'sight' (ĭn'sīt')

entoblast. Variant of **endoblast.**

entoderm. Variant of **endoderm.**

entom. entomological; entomology.

en·tomb (ĕn-to͞om′, ĭn-) *tr.v.* **-tombed, -tombing, -tombs. 1.** To place in or as if in a tomb or grave; bury. **2.** To serve as a tomb for. [Middle English *entoumben,* from Old French *entomber* : *en-,* in + *tombe,* tomb, from Late Latin *tumba,* TOMB.] **—en·tomb·ment** *n.*

entomo– *prefix.* Indicates insect; for example, **entomology, entomophagous.** [French, from Greek *entomon,* insect, "one whose body is cut into segments," from *entomos,* cut up, from *entemnein,* to cut in, cut up : *en-,* in + *temnein,* to cut.]

entomol. entomology.

en·to·mol·o·gize (ĕn′tə-mŏl′ə-jīz′) *intr.v.* **-gized, -gizing, -gizes.** To study or collect insects.

en·to·mol·o·gy (ĕn′tə-mŏl′ə-jē) *n. Abbr.* **entom., entomol.** The scientific study of insects. [ENTOMO- + -LOGY.] **—en·to·mo·log·i·cal** (ĕn′tə-mə-lŏj′ĭ-kəl) *adj.* **—en·to·mo·log·i·cal·ly** *adv.* **—en·to·mol·o·gist** (-mŏl′ə-jĭst) *n.*

en·to·moph·a·gous (ĕn′tə-mŏf′ə-gəs) *adj.* Feeding on insects; insectivorous. [ENTOMO- + -PHAGOUS.]

en·to·moph·i·lous (ĕn′tə-mŏf′ə-ləs) *adj.* Pollinated by insects. [ENTOMO- + -PHILOUS.] **—en·to·moph·i·ly** *n.*

en·tou·rage (ŏn′to͞o-räzh′) *n.* **1.** A group of attendants, followers, or associates. **2.** One's environment or surroundings. [French, from *entourer,* to surround, from Old French *entour,* surroundings : *en-,* in + *tour,* circuit, TOUR.]

en·to·zo·a (ĕn′tə-zō′ə) *pl.n. Singular* **-zoan** (-zō′ən) or **-zoon** (-zō′ŏn′). Various animals, such as tapeworms, that live within other animals, usually as parasites. [New Latin : ENTO- + -ZOA.] **—en·to·zo·ic** *adj.*

en·tr'acte (ŏn′träkt′, äɴ-träkt′) *n.* **1.** The interval between two successive acts of a theatrical performance. **2.** An entertainment, especially a piece of music, provided during this interval. [French, "between act."]

en·trails (ĕn′trālz′, -trəlz) *pl.n.* **1.** The internal organs, especially the intestines; viscera. **2.** The inner parts of something. [Middle English *entrailles,* from Old French, from Medieval Latin *intrālia,* variant of Latin *interānea,* from the neuter plural of *interāneus,* internal, from *inter,* within.]

en·train¹ (ĕn-trān′, ĭn-) *tr.v.* **-trained, -training, -trains.** To pull or draw along after itself. [Old French *entrainer* : *en-,* in + *trainer,* to draw (see **train**).]

entrain² *v.* **-trained, -training, -trains.** *—tr.* To put on a train. *—intr.* To board a train. **—en·train·ment** *n.*

en·trance¹ (ĕn′trəns) *n.* **1.** The act or an instance of entering; especially, the entry of an actor into the performing area. **2.** Any passage, opening, doorway, or the like where one can enter. **3.** The permission, power, or liberty to enter; admission. Also used adjectivally: *entrance money.* **4.** The point in a script or musical score at which a performer is to begin. [Middle English *entraunce,* from Old French *entrance,* from *entrer,* to ENTER.]

en·trance² (ĕn-trăns′, -träns′, ĭn-) *tr.v.* **-tranced, -trancing, -trances. 1.** To put into a trance. **2.** To fill with great pleasure, wonder, or enchantment; fascinate: *a child entranced by his own reflection.* **—en·trance·ment** *n.* **—en·tranc·ing·ly** *adv.*

en·trant (ĕn′trənt) *n.* **1.** One who enters; especially, one who enters a competition: *There were ten entrants in the beauty contest.* **2.** A new member, as of a profession, organization, university, or the like. [French, from the present participle of *entrer,* to ENTER.]

en·trap (ĕn-trăp′, ĭn-) *tr.v.* **-trapped, -trapping, -traps. 1.** To catch in or as if in a trap. **2.** To lure into danger, difficulty, or self-incrimination. [Old French *entraper* : *en-,* in + *trape,* trap.] **—en·trap·ment** *n.*

en·treat (ĕn-trēt′, ĭn-) *v.* **-treated, -treating, -treats.** Also **in·treat** (ĭn-). *—tr.* **1.** To ask (someone) earnestly; beseech; implore; beg. **2.** To ask for (something) earnestly; petition for. *—intr.* To make an earnest request or petition; plead. —See Synonyms at **beg.** [Middle English *entreten,* to deal with, plead with, from Old French *entraitier* : *en-,* in + *traitier, traiter,* to TREAT.] **—en·treat·ing·ly** *adv.* **—en·treat·ment** *n.*

en·treat·y (ĕn-trē′tē, ĭn-) *n., pl.* **-ies.** An earnest request; a plea.

en·tre·chat (ŏn′trə-shä′, äɴ′trə-shä′) *n.* A leap in ballet during which the dancer crosses his feet a number of times, often beating them together. [French, earlier *entrecha(se),* by folk etymology (influenced by *chasse,* chase) from Italian *(capriola) intrecciata,* "interlaced (caper)," from the feminine past participle of *intrecciare,* to interlace, entwine : *in-,* in, from Latin + *treccia,* tress, akin to Old French *tresse,* TRESS.]

en·tre·côte (ŏn′trə-kōt′) *n.* A cut of steak taken from between the ribs. [French, "between the ribs."]

en·trée, en·tree (ŏn′trā′, ŏn-trā′) *n.* **1. a.** The power, permission, or liberty to enter; admittance. **b.** Access by special privilege to a place normally inaccessible. **2. a.** A dish served between the fish course and the main meat course, or immediately before the main course, especially in an elaborate or formal dinner. **b.** The main course, especially in an ordinary or simple meal. [French, ENTRY.]

en·tre·mets (ŏn′trə-mā′, äɴ′-) *n., pl.* **entremets** (-māz′, -mā′). A side dish or dishes; especially, a dish served between principal courses or as a dessert. [French, earlier *entremes* : Old French *entre-,* between + *mes,* dish, MESS.]

en·trench (ĕn-trĕnch′, ĭn-) *v.* **-trenched, -trenching, -trenches.** Also **in·trench** (ĭn-). *—tr.* **1.** *Military.* **a.** To provide with a trench or trenches for the purpose of draining, fortifying, defending, or supporting. **b.** To set up (a base, for example) in a defensible position. **2.** To establish firmly or securely: *entrenched prejudices.* *—intr.* **1.** To dig a trench or trenches. **2.** To adopt a safe or strongly defended position. **3.** To encroach or trespass.

en·trench·ment (ĕn-trĕnch′mənt, ĭn-) *n.* Also **in·trench·ment** (ĭn-). **1.** The act of entrenching or the condition of being entrenched. **2.** A fortification; especially, a series of banked trenches.

en·tre nous (ŏn′trə no͞o′, äɴ′trə) *adv.* Between ourselves; confidentially. [French.]

en·tre·pôt (ŏn′trə-pō′, äɴ′-) *n.* **1.** A place where goods are stored or deposited and from which they are distributed. **2.** A trading or market center. [French, from *entreposer,* to put in, to store : Old French *entre-,* in, between, from Latin *inter-* + *poser,* to put, POSE.]

en·tre·pre·neur (ŏn′trə-prə-nûr′, -no͝or′, -nyo͝or′) *n.* A person who organizes, operates, and assumes the risk for business ventures. [French, from Old French, from *entreprendre,* to undertake. See **enterprise.**] **—en·tre·pre·neur·i·al** *adj.*

en·tre·sol (ŏn′trə-sŏl′, -sôl′, äɴ′-) *n.* A floor just above the ground floor; mezzanine. [French, "between floors."]

en·tro·py (ĕn′trə-pē) *n., pl.* **-pies. 1.** A measure of the capacity of a system to undergo spontaneous change, thermodynamically specified by the relationship $dS = dQ/T$, where dS is an infinitesimal change in the measure for a system absorbing an infinitesimal quantity of heat dQ at thermodynamic temperature T. **2.** The tendency of the energy of a closed system, including that of the universe itself, to become less available to do work with the passage of time. **3.** A measure of the randomness, disorder, or chaos in a system specified in statistical mechanics by the relationship $S = k\ln P + c$, where S is the value of the measure for a system in a given state, P is the probability of occurrence of that state, k is the Boltzmann constant, and c is an arbitrary constant. [German *Entropie* : Greek *en-,* in + *tropē,* a turning, change.]

en·trust (ĕn-trŭst′, ĭn-) *tr.v.* **-trusted, -trusting, -trusts.** Also **in·trust** (ĭn-). **1.** To give over to another for care, protection, or performance: *entrusted the task to his aides.* **2.** To commit something trustfully to; place a trust upon: *entrusted his aides with the task.* —See Synonyms at **commit.**

en·try (ĕn′trē) *n., pl.* **-tries. 1.** The act or an instance of entering. **2.** The right to enter: *It was difficult to gain entry to the club.* **3. a.** The inclusion or insertion of an item in a diary, register, list, or other record. **b.** An item thus entered: *I made no entries in the journal for a week.* **4.** An item in a reference book, such as an article in an encyclopedia or a word, term, or phrase defined or identified in a dictionary, together with the text related to it. **5. a.** One registered as a participant in a competition. **b.** All such participants collectively. **6.** The entrance on-stage or manner of entering of an actor. **7.** *Law.* The act of taking possession of land or property by entering. **8.** A passage or opening where one can enter. [Middle English *entre,* from Old French *entree,* from Vulgar Latin *intrāta* (unattested), from the feminine past participle of Latin *intrāre,* to ENTER.]

en·try·way (ĕn′trē-wā′) *n.* A passage or opening serving as an entrance.

en·twine (ĕn-twīn′, ĭn-) *v.* **-twined, -twining, -twines.** Also **in·twine** (ĭn-). *—tr.* To twine or twist around or about: *Ivy entwined the pillar.* *—intr.* To twine or twist together.

en·twist (ĕn-twĭst′, ĭn-) *tr.v.* **-twisted, -twisting, -twists.** Also **in·twist** (ĭn-). To twist together; entwine.

e·nu·cle·ate (ĭ-no͞o′klē-āt′, ĭ-nyo͞o′-) *tr.v.* **-ated, -ating, -ates. 1.** In surgery, to remove (a tumor or eyeball, for example) from its enveloping cover or sac. **2.** *Biology.* To remove the nucleus of (a cell). **3.** *Archaic.* To explain or elucidate.
~*adj.* (-ĭt, -āt′). Lacking a nucleus. [Latin *ēnucleāre,* to take out the kernel : *ex-,* out + *nucleus,* kernel, NUCLEUS.] **—e·nu·cle·a·tion** *n.* **—e·nu·cle·a·tor** *n.*

e·nu·mer·ate (ĭ-no͞o′mə-rāt′, ĭ-nyo͞o′-) *tr.v.* **-ated, -ating, -ates. 1.** To count off or name one by one; list: *Let me enumerate all the good reasons for going.* **2.** To determine the number of; count. [Latin *ēnumerāre,* to count out : *ex-,* out + *numerus,* number.] **—e·nu·mer·a·tive** (ĭ-no͞o′mə-rā′tĭv, -mər-ə-tĭv, ĭ-nyo͞o′-) *adj.*

e·nu·mer·a·tion (ĭ-no͞o′mə-rā′shən, ĭ-nyo͞o′-) *n.* **1.** The act of enumerating. **2.** A detailed list of items.

e·nu·mer·a·tor (ĭ-no͞o′mə-rā′tər, ĭ-nyo͞o′-) *n.* **1.** One that enumerates. **2.** *British.* A person involved in the distribution and collection of census forms.

e·nun·ci·ate (ĭ-nŭn′sē-āt′) *v.* **-ated, -ating, -ates.** *—tr.* **1.** To pronounce or articulate (speech sounds); especially, to pronounce with clarity or in another specified manner. **2.** To state or set forth precisely or systematically: *enunciate a doctrine.* **3.** To announce; proclaim. *—intr.* To pronounce words, especially distinctly. [Latin *ēnuntiāre, ēnunciāre* : *ex-,* out + *nuntiāre,* to announce, from *nuncius, nuntius,* message, messenger.] **—e·nun·ci·a·ble** (ĭ-nŭn′sē-ə-bəl), **e·nun·ci·a·tive** (-ā′tĭv, -ə-tĭv), **e·nun·ci·a·to·ry** (-tôr′ē, -tōr′ē) *adj.* **—e·nun·ci·a·tive·ly** *adv.* **—e·nun·ci·a·tor** *n.*

e·nun·ci·a·tion (ĭ-nŭn′sē-ā′shən) *n.* **1.** The act or manner of enunciating; especially, the manner in which a speaker articulates words or speech sounds. **2.** An announcement, declaration, or similar official statement. —See Synonyms at **diction.**

enure. Variant of **inure.**

en·u·re·sis (ĕn′yə-rē′sĭs) *n.* Involuntary urination. [New Latin, from Greek *enourein,* to urinate in : *en-,* in + *ourein,* to urinate, from *ouron,* urine.] **—en·u·ret·ic** (ĕn′yə-rĕt′ĭk) *n. & adj.*

env. envelope.

PRONUNCIATION KEY

ă, pat; ā, pay; âr, care; ä, father, are; b, bib; ch, church; d, deed; ĕ, pet; ē, be; f, fife; g, gag; h, hat; hw, which; ĭ, pit; ī, pie; îr, pier; j, judge; k, kick; l, lid, needle; m, mum; n, no, sudden; ng, thing; ŏ, pot; ō, toe; ô, paw, for; oi, noise; ou, out; o͝o, book; o͞o, boot; p, pop; r, roar; s, sauce; sh, ship, dish; t, tight; th, thin, path; *th,* this, bathe; ŭ, cut; ûr, fur; v, valve; w, with; y, yes; z, zebra, size; zh, vision; ə, about, item, edible, gallop, circus, peaceful

IN FOREIGN WORDS:

à, *Fr.* ami; œ, *Fr.* feu, *Ger.* schön; ü, *Fr.* tu, *Ger.* über; KH, *Ger.* ich, *Scot.* loch; ɴ, *Fr.* bon; y′, *Fr.* Compiègne

STRESS MARKS:

Primary stress: ′ **in·cite′** (ĭn-sīt′)
Secondary stress: ′ **in′sight′** (ĭn′sīt′)

en·vel·op (ĕn-vĕl′əp, ĭn-) *tr.v.* **-oped, -oping, -ops.** **1.** To enclose, cover, or obscure with or as if with a covering or wrapping. **2.** To serve as a covering or wrapping for. **3.** To surround or enfold: *enveloped in the cheerful atmosphere.* **4.** To attack (an enemy's flank). [Middle English *enveloupen,* from Old French *enveloper* : *en-,* in + *veloper,* to wrap up (see **develop**).] **—en·vel·op·er** *n.* **—en·vel·op·ment** *n.*

en·ve·lope (ĕn′və-lōp′, ŏn′-) *n. Abbr.* **env. 1.** Something that envelops; an enclosing or surrounding cover, coat, or wrapping. **2.** A flat, folded paper container for a letter or similar object, usually rectangular and having a gummed sealing flap. **3.** *Biology.* Any enclosing covering, membrane, or structure. **4.** The bag containing the gas in a balloon. **5.** *Mathematics.* **a.** A curve that is a tangent to all the curves of a family of curves. **b.** A surface that is a tangent to a family of surfaces. **6.** The glass or metal casing of an electronic valve or similar device. [French *enveloppe,* from Old French *envelope,* from *enveloper,* to **ENVELOP**.]

en·ven·om (ĕn-vĕn′əm, ĭn-) *tr.v.* **-omed, -oming, -oms. 1.** To put venom into or on; make poisonous or noxious. **2.** To fill with malice; embitter. [Middle English *envenimen,* from Old French *envenimer* : **IN** + **VENOM**.]

en·vi·a·ble (ĕn′vē-ə-bəl) *adj.* **1.** Arousing strong envy. **2.** Highly desirable but rare: *"the enviable English quality of being able to be mute without unrest"* (Henry James). **—en·vi·a·bly** *adv.*

en·vi·ous (ĕn′vē-əs) *adj.* **1.** Feeling, expressing, or characterized by envy. **2.** *Obsolete.* Eager to emulate; emulous. **—en·vi·ous·ly** *adv.* **—en·vi·ous·ness** *n.*

en·vi·ron (ĕn-vī′rən, ĭn-) *tr.v.* **-roned, -roning, -rons.** To encircle; surround. [Middle English *environen,* from Old French *environer,* from *environ,* around : *en-,* in + *viron,* circle, from *virer,* to turn, **VEER**.]

en·vi·ron·ment (ĕn-vī′rən-mənt, ĭn-) *n.* **1.** Something that surrounds; surroundings. **2.** The aggregate of circumstances surrounding an organism or group of organisms, specifically: **a.** The combination of external or extrinsic physical conditions that affect and influence the growth and development of organisms. **b.** The complex of social and cultural conditions affecting the nature of an individual or community. Compare **heredity. —en·vi·ron·men·tal** (ĕn-vī′rən-mĕnt′l) *adj.* **—en·vi·ron·men·tal·ly** *adv.*

en·vi·ron·men·tal·ism (ĕn-vī′rən-mĕn′tə-lĭz′əm, ĭn-) *n.* **1.** The theory that environment rather than heredity is the primary influence on intellectual growth and cultural development. **2.** Belief that the natural environment should be protected.

en·vi·ron·men·tal·ist (ĕn-vī′rən-mĕn′tə-lĭst, ĭn-) *n.* **1.** A person who seeks to protect the natural environment. **2.** An adherent of the theory of environmentalism.

en·vi·rons (ĕn-vī′rənz, ĭn-) *pl.n.* **1.** The surrounding area, especially of a city; the suburbs; the outskirts. **2.** Surroundings; environment.

en·vis·age (ĕn-vĭz′ĭj, ĭn-) *tr.v.* **-aged, -aging, -ages.** To conceive of, especially as a future possibility. [French *envisager* : **IN** + **VISAGE**.]

en·vi·sion (ĕn-vĭzh′ən, ĭn-) *tr.v.* **-sioned, -sioning, -sions.** To picture in the mind; foresee.

en·voi (ĕn′voi, ŏn′-) *n.* A short concluding stanza of certain French verse forms, such as the ballade, originally serving as a postscript dedicating the poem to a patron and later as a pithy summation of the poem. [Middle English *envoie,* from Old French *envoy,* "a sending away," conclusion, from *envoier,* to send. See **envoy** (messenger).]

en·voy¹ (ĕn′voi, ŏn′-) *n.* **1.** A messenger or other agent sent on a mission. **2.** A representative of a government or faction sent on a special diplomatic mission. [French *envoyé,* one who is sent, from the past participle of *envoyer,* to send, from Old French *envoier, enveier,* from Late Latin *inviāre,* to put on the way : Latin *in-,* in + *via,* way.]

envoy². Variant of **envoi.**

en·vy (ĕn′vē) *n., pl.* **-vies. 1. a.** A feeling of discontent and resentment aroused by contemplation of another's possessions, qualities, or achievements, with a strong wish that they were one's own. **b.** A more moderate feeling aroused by admiration rather than resentment. **2. a.** A possession of another that is strongly desired. **b.** One who possesses what another strongly desires: *She was the envy of her friends.* **3.** *Obsolete.* Malevolence. *~v.* **envied, -vying, -vies.** *—tr.* To feel envy for; regard with envy. *—intr.* To be filled with envy. [Middle English *envie,* from Old French, from Latin *invidia,* from *invidēre,* to look at with malice : *in-,* in, upon + *vidēre,* to see.] **—en·vi·er** *n.* **—en·vy·ing·ly** *adv.*

en·wind (ĕn-wīnd′, ĭn-) *tr.v.* **-wound** (-wound′), **-winding, -winds.** To wind around or about; encircle.

en·wrap (ĕn-răp′, ĭn-) *tr.v.* **-wrapped, -wrapping, -wraps. 1.** To wrap up; enclose; enfold. **2.** To engross.

En·zed (ĕn-zĕd′) *n. Australian & New Zealand Informal.* **1.** New Zealand. **2.** A New Zealander. [From the initials *N.Z.*]

en·zo·ot·ic (ĕn′zō-ŏt′ĭk) *adj.* Affecting or peculiar to animals of a specific area or limited district. Said of diseases. *~n.* An enzootic disease. [**EN-** (within) + **ZO(O)-** + **-OTIC**.]

en·zyme (ĕn′zīm′) *n.* Any of numerous proteins or conjugated proteins produced by living organisms and functioning as biochemical catalysts. [German *Enzym,* from Medieval Greek *enzumos,* leavened : Greek *en-,* in + *zumē,* leaven.] **—en·zy·mat·ic** (ĕn′zī-măt′ĭk) *adj.* **—en·zy·mic** (ĕn-zī′mĭk) *adj.*

en·zy·mol·o·gy (ĕn′zī-mŏl′ə-jē) *n.* The biochemistry of enzymes. **—en·zy·mol·o·gist** *n.*

eo- *prefix.* Indicates: **1.** An early period of time; for example, **Eo-**

cene. **2.** An early form or representative; for example, **eohippus.** [Greek *ēo-,* from *ēōs,* dawn.]

e.o. ex officio.

E·o·cene (ē′ə-sēn′) *adj.* Of, pertaining to, or designating the geologic time, rock system, and fossils of the second oldest of the five epochs of the Tertiary period of the Cenozoic era, extending from the end of the Paleocene to the beginning of the Oligocene and characterized by the rise of mammals. *~n.* The Eocene epoch. Preceded by *the.* [**EO-** + **-CENE.**]

e·o·hip·pus (ē′ō-hĭp′əs) *n.* An extinct, small, herbivorous mammal of the genus *Hyracotherium* (or *Eohippus*), of the Eocene epoch, having four-toed front feet and three-toed hind feet, and related ancestrally to the horse. [New Latin : **EO-** + Greek *hippos,* horse.]

EOKA. See **Cyprus, Republic of.**

e·o·lith (ē′ə-lĭth′) *n. Archaeology.* Any of the stone artefacts allegedly characterizing the Eolithic period. [**EO-** + **-LITH.**]

E·o·lith·ic (ē′ə-lĭth′ĭk) *adj. Archaeology.* Of or pertaining to the postulated earliest period of human culture preceding the Lower Paleolithic. *~n.* The Eolithic period. Preceded by *the.* [**EO-** + **-LITHIC.**]

e.o.m. end of month.

e·on, ae·on (ē′ŏn′, ē′ən) *n.* **1.** An indefinitely long period of time; age. **2.** *Geology.* The longest division of geologic time, containing two or more eras. [Late Latin *aeōn,* age, from Greek *aiōn.*]

e·on·ism (ē′ə-nĭz′əm) *n. Transvestism* (see) when practiced by a man. [After Charles *Éon* de Beaumont (1728–1810), French transvestite.]

E·os (ē′ŏs′). *Greek Mythology.* The goddess of the dawn, identified with the Roman goddess Aurora. [Greek *Ēōs,* from *ēōs,* dawn.]

e·o·sin (ē′ə-sĭn) *n.* Also **e·o·sine** (-sĭn, -sēn′). A red crystalline powder, $C_{20}H_8Br_4O_5$, used in textile dyeing, histology, and the manufacture of inks. [Greek *ēōs,* dawn + **-IN.**]

e·o·sin·o·phil (ē′ə-sĭn′ə-fĭl) *n.* Also **e·o·sin·o·phile** (-fīl′). *Physiology.* A type of leukocyte with a lobed nucleus that stains with an eosin dye. **—e·o·sin·o·phil·ic** (ē′ə-sĭn′ə-fĭl′ĭk), **e·o·si·noph·i·lous** (ē′ə-sə-nŏf′ə-ləs) *adj.*

-eous *suffix.* Having the nature of or akin to; for example, **gaseous, beauteous.** [Latin *-eus.*]

e·pact (ē′păkt′, ĕp′ăkt′) *n.* **1.** The excess of time, about 11 days, of the solar year over the lunar year. **2.** The age of the moon at the beginning of the calendar year. **3.** The excess of time of a calendar month over a lunar month. [Old French *epacte,* from Late Latin *epacta,* from Greek *epaktai (hēmerai),* "(days) brought in," from *epaktos,* brought in from abroad, from *epagein,* to lead on, bring in : *epi-,* on + *agein,* to lead.]

ep·arch (ĕp′ärk′) *n.* **1.** The chief administrator of an eparchy. **2.** *Greek Orthodox Church.* A bishop or metropolitan. [Greek *eparkhos,* commander, governor : *epi-,* on, over + **-ARCH.**] **—e·par·chi·al** (ĭ-pär′kē-əl) *adj.*

ep·ar·chy (ĕp′är′kē) *n., pl.* **-chies. 1.** An administrative subdivision of modern Greece. **2.** *Greek Orthodox Church.* An ecclesiastical district; a diocese.

ep·au·let, ep·au·lette (ĕp′ə-lĕt′, ĕp′ə-lĕt′) *n.* A shoulder ornament; especially, either of two fringed straps on certain military uniforms. [French *épaulette,* diminutive of *épaule,* shoulder, from Old French *espaule,* from Latin *spatula.* See **spatula.**]

é·pée, e·pee (ā-pā′, ĕp′ā′) *n.* **1.** A fencing sword with a bowl-shaped guard and a long, narrow, fluted blade that has no cutting edge and tapers to a blunted point. **2.** The art of fencing with the épée. [French, from Latin *spatha,* sword, blade. See **spatula.**] **—é·pée·ist** *n.*

ep·ei·rog·e·ny (ĕp′ī-rŏj′ə-nē) *n.* Also **ep·ei·ro·gen·e·sis** (ə-pī′rō-jĕn′ə-sĭs). The deformation of the crust of the earth by which continents and oceanic basins, or parts of these, are formed. [Greek *ēpeiros,* continent + **-GENY.**] **—e·pei·ro·gen·ic** (ĭ-pī′rō-jĕn′ĭk) *adj.*

ep·en·the·sis (ĭ-pĕn′thə-sĭs) *n., pl.* **-ses** (-sēz′). *Linguistics.* The insertion of an extra sound into the pronunciation of a word, especially before an *l* or *r* sound, either as a process of phonetic development or as a feature of nonstandard speech; for example, the nonstandard pronunciation of *umbrella* as (ŭm′bə-rĕl′ə). [Late Latin, from Greek, from *epentithenai,* to insert : *epi-,* in addition to + *entithenai,* to put in : *en-,* in + *tithenai,* to place.] **—ep·en·thet·ic** (ĕp′ən-thĕt′ĭk) *adj.*

e·pergne (ĭ-pûrn′, ā-pârn′) *n.* A large silver or glass centerpiece for a table consisting of a frame with extended arms or branches supporting holders, as for flowers, fruit, or candies. [Probably from French *épargne,* saving, from *épargner,* to save, from Old French *espargnier,* from Germanic *sparōjan* (unattested), to **SPARE.**]

É·per·nay (ā′pĕr-nā′). Town in northeastern France, on the Marne River. After Rheims it is the most important center for the production of champagne.

ep·ex·e·ge·sis (ĕp′ĕk′sə-jē′sĭs) *n., pl.* **-ses** (-sēz′). **1.** The addition of explanatory material to clarify something immediately preceding it. **2.** The additional material itself. [Greek *epexegēsis,* from *epexegeisthai,* to explain in detail : *epi-,* in addition to + *exēgeisthai,* to explain (see **exegesis**).] **—ep·ex·e·get·ic** (ĕp′ĕk′sə-jĕt′ĭk), **ep·ex·e·get·i·cal** (-ĭ-kəl) *adj.*

Eph. Ephesians (New Testament).

e·phah, e·pha (ē′fə, ĕf′ə) *n.* A unit of dry measure equal to slightly more than a bushel, used by the ancient Hebrews. [Hebrew *'ephāh,* probably from Egyptian *'pt.*]

e·phebe (ĕf′ēb′, ĭ-fēb′) *n.* In ancient Greece, a youth in military training who is between eighteen and twenty years of age. [Latin *ephēbus,* from Greek *ephēbos* : *epi-,* at + *hēbē,* youth.] —**e·phe·bic** (ĭ-fē′bĭk) *adj.*

e·phed·ra (ĭ-fĕd′rə, ĕf′ĭ-drə) *n.* Any gymnosperm shrub of the genus *Ephedra,* found in Eurasia and the United States. [New Latin, from Greek, from *ephedros,* "a sitting upon" : *ep-,* EPI- + *hedra,* seat.]

e·phed·rine (ĭ-fĕd′rĭn, ĕf′ə-drēn′) *n.* A white, odorless, powdered or crystalline alkaloid, $C_{10}H_{15}NO$, isolated from shrubs of the genus *Ephedra* or made synthetically, used to treat allergies and asthma and as a vasoconstrictor. [New Latin *Ephedra,* genus name of mahuang, from Latin *ephedra,* horsetail, from Greek *ephedros,* sitting upon : *epi-,* upon + *hedra,* seat + -INE.]

e·phem·er·a (ĭ-fĕm′ər-ə) *n., pl.* **-as** or **-erae** (-ə-rē′) or **ephemera** (for sense 2). **1.** Something short-lived or transitory. **2.** ephemera. Printed matter of passing interest, as periodicals, handbills, and topical pamphlets. [From the plural of EPHEMERON.]

e·phem·er·al (ĭ-fĕm′ər-əl) *adj.* **1.** Lasting for a brief time; short-lived; transitory. **2.** Living or lasting only one day, as certain flowers or adult insects do. —See Synonyms at **transient.**
~*n.* An ephemeral thing or organism. [Greek *ephēmeros* : *epi-,* on + *hēmera,* day.] —**e·phem·er·al·i·ty** (ĭ-fĕm′ə-răl′ə-tē) *n.* —**e·phem·er·al·ly** *adv.*

e·phem·er·id (ĭ-fĕm′ər-ĭd) *n.* An insect of the order Ephemeroptera, which comprises the mayflies. [New Latin *Ephemeridae,* former name of the order, from Greek *ephemeros,* EPHEMERAL.]

e·phem·er·is (ĭ-fĕm′ər-ĭs) *n., pl.* **ephemerides** (ĕf′ə-mĕr′ə-dēz′). **1.** A table giving the coordinates of one or a number of celestial bodies at a number of specific times during a given period. **2.** A publication that presents a collection of such tables; an astronomical almanac. [Late Latin *ephēmeris,* diary, from Greek, from *ephēmeros,* EPHEMERAL.]

ephemeris time *n.* A highly accurate astronomical system for the measurement of time based on the period of the earth's orbit, but in practice relying on lunar observations and an accurate lunar ephemeris to calculate corrections to be applied to clocks. The unit is the ephemeris second, equal to 1/31,556,925.9747 of the tropical year for epoch 1900 January 0.

e·phem·er·on (ĭ-fĕm′ə-rŏn′) *n., pl.* **-era** (-ər-ə) or **-ons.** A short-lived thing or organism. [New Latin, from Greek *ephēmeron,* mayfly, from the neuter of *ephēmeros,* EPHEMERAL.]

E·phe·sian (ĭ-fē′zhən) *adj.* Of or pertaining to Ephesus or its people.
~*n.* A native or inhabitant of Ephesus.

E·phe·sians (ĭ-fē′zhənz) *n. Used with a singular verb. Abbr.* **Eph.** A book of the New Testament consisting of the Apostle Paul's epistle to the Christians of Ephesus.

Eph·e·sus (ĕf′ə-səs). Ancient Greek city of Asia Minor, in what is now western Turkey, near the mouth of the Kücük Menderes. Its great Temple of Artemis, one of the Seven Wonders of the World, was destroyed by the Goths (A.D. 262).

eph·od (ĕf′ŏd′, ē′fŏd) *n.* An embroidered vestment worn by ancient Hebrew priests. [Hebrew *ēphōdh.*]

eph·or (ĕf′ôr, -ər) *n., pl.* **-ors** or **-ori** (-ə-rī′). Any of a body of five elected officials exercising a supervisory power over the kings of ancient Sparta. [Latin *ephorus,* from Greek *ephoros,* from *ephoran,* to oversee : *epi-,* over + *horan,* to see.]

E·phra·im[1] (ē′frē-əm, ē′frəm) *n.* The younger son of Joseph. Genesis 41:52. [Hebrew, perhaps "meadows."]

Ephraim[2] *n.* A tribe of Israel descended from the younger son of Joseph.

E·phra·im·ite (ē′frē-ə-mīt′, ē′frə-) *n.* A member of the tribe of Ephraim. —**E·phra·im·ite** *adj.*

epi- *prefix.* Indicates: **1.** On, upon; for example, **epiphyte. 2.** Over, above; for example, **epicenter. 3.** Around, covering; for example, **epicardium. 4.** To, toward, close to, next to; for example, **epicalyx. 5.** Besides, in addition; for example, **epiphenomenon. 6.** After; for example, **epigenesis. 7.** Among; for example, **epizootic.** [Greek *epi-* (before a vowel *ep-*), from *epi,* upon, near, at, after.]

ep·i·blast (ĕp′ə-blăst′, -bläst′) *n.* The outer layer of a gastrula. —**ep·i·blas·tic** (ĕp′ə-blăs′tĭk) *adj.*

e·pib·o·ly (ĭ-pĭb′ə-lē) *n. Zoology.* A process in the development of the embryo in which the part of the blastula that was nearest the nucleus of the ovum grows over and encloses the part farthest from the nucleus and eventually forms the ectoderm. [Greek *epibolē,* a throwing on, from *epiballein,* to throw on : *epi-,* on + *ballein,* to throw.] —**ep·i·bol·ic** (ĕp′ə-bŏl′ĭk) *adj.*

ep·ic (ĕp′ĭk) *n.* **1.** An extended narrative poem, such as *Beowulf* or the *Iliad,* celebrating episodes of a people's heroic tradition, typically developed by oral composition within a standard formulaic diction and set of metrical and narrative conventions, a final version being transcribed after the introduction of writing. **2.** The genre represented by such poems; epos. **3.** A formal poem, such as the *Aeneid,* composed in literary imitation of these conventions. **4.** A story, film, or the like thought to embody the qualities characteristic of epic poetry. **5.** An event or series of events regarded as a fit subject for an epic: *the epic of man's first journey to the moon.*
~*adj.* **1.** Of or designating an epic: *an epic poem.* **2.** Occurring in or characteristic of epics: *an epic simile.* **3. a.** Suitable for or typical of an epic. **b.** Large-scale in grandeur, scope, or theme; heroic. [Latin *epicus,* from Greek *epikos,* from *epos,* song, word.]

ep·i·ca·lyx (ĕp′ĭ-kā′lĭks, -kăl′ĭks) *n., pl.* **-calyxes** or **-calyces** (-kā′lə-sēz′, -kăl′ə-sēz′). *Botany.* A set of bracts close to and resembling a calyx. Also called "calycle."

ep·i·can·thic fold (ĕp′ĭ-kăn′thĭk) *n.* A fold of skin of the upper eyelid that tends to cover the inner corner of the eye, characteristic of many Mongolian peoples and found in certain congenital conditions, such as Down's syndrome. Also called "epicanthus."

ep·i·car·di·um (ĕp′ĭ-kär′dē-əm) *n., pl.* **-dia** (-dē-ə). The inner layer of the pericardium that is in actual contact with the heart. [New Latin : EPI- + Greek *kardia,* heart.]

ep·i·carp (ĕp′ĭ-kärp′) *n. Botany.* An exocarp (*see*). [French *épicarpe* : EPI- + -CARP.]

ep·i·ce·di·um (ĕp′ə-sē′dē-əm) *n., pl.* **-dia** (-dē-ə). A funeral hymn or dirge. [Latin *epicēdium,* from Greek *epikēdeion,* from the neuter of *epikēdeios,* of a funeral : *epi-,* at + *kēdos,* sorrow, grief.]

ep·i·cene (ĕp′ə-sēn) *adj.* **1. a.** Belonging to or having the characteristics of both the male and the female: *an epicene statue; an epicene angel.* **b.** Effeminate; effete. **c.** Sexless; neuter. **2.** *Linguistics.* Designating a noun that may be applied to both the male and the female without a change in form, as Greek *pais,* child (*ho pais,* the boy; *hē pais,* the girl).
~*n.* **1.** *Linguistics.* An epicene noun. **2.** An epicene person or object. [Middle English *epicene,* from Latin *epicoenus,* from Greek *epikoinos,* common to many, promiscuous : *epi-,* to + *koinos,* common.]

ep·i·cen·ter (ĕp′ə-sĕn′tər) *n.* **1.** The part of the earth's surface directly above the focus of an earthquake. **2.** A focal point. [New Latin *epicentrum* : EPI- + Latin *centrum,* CENTER.]

ep·i·cle·sis (ĕp′ĭ-klē′sĭs) *n., pl.* **-ses** (-sēz′). A prayer in the Mass calling on the Holy Spirit to turn the bread and wine into the body and blood of Christ. [Greek, invocation : *epi-,* EPI- + *klēsis,* prayer, from *kalein,* to call.]

ep·i·cot·yl (ĕp′ĭ-kŏt′l) *n. Botany.* The part of the stem of a seedling or embryonic plant that is above the cotyledons and below the first true leaves. [EPI- + COTYL(EDON).]

ep·i·cri·sis (ĕp′ĭ-krī′sĭs) *n., pl.* **-ses** (-sēz′). *Pathology.* A crisis that occurs after the primary crisis of a disease.

ep·i·crit·ic (ĕp′ĭ-krĭt′ĭk) *adj.* Pertaining to or designating sensory nerve fibers that make possible acute sensitivity to temperature and touch. Compare **protopathic.** [Greek *epikritikos,* decisive, from *epikritos,* decided on, from *epikrinein,* to decide.]

ep·i·cure (ĕp′ĭ-kyoor′) *n.* **1.** A person with refined taste in food and wine. **2.** *Archaic.* A person devoted to sensuous pleasure and luxurious living. [After EPICURUS, who supposedly advocated sensuous pleasure as the highest good.]

Ep·i·cu·re·an (ĕp′ĭ-kyoo-rē′ən) *adj.* **1.** Of or associated with the philosophy of Epicurus. **2. epicurean.** Devoted to the pursuit of pleasure; fond of good food, comfort, and ease; hedonistic. **3. epicurean.** Suited to the tastes of an epicure: *an epicurean repast.* —See Synonyms at **sensuous.**
~*n.* **1.** A follower of Epicurus. **2. epicurean.** An epicure.

Ep·i·cu·re·an·ism (ĕp′ĭ-kyoo-rē′ə-nĭz′əm) *n.* Also **Ep·i·cur·ism** (ĕp′ĭ-kyoo-rĭz′əm). **1.** The philosophy advanced by Epicurus. **2. epicureanism.** The beliefs, tastes, or way of life of an epicure.

E·pi·cu·rus (ĕp′ĭ-kyoor′əs) (*c.* 341-270 B.C.). Greek philosopher, born at Samos. From his philosophy the word "Epicurean" was derived to describe a life of indulgent pleasure seeking, but his hedonism exalted the avoidance of pain rather than the satisfying of desires and was governed by a strict code of social behavior.

ep·i·cy·cle (ĕp′ĭ-sī′kəl) *n.* **1.** In Ptolemaic cosmology, a small circle, the center of which moves on the circumference of a larger circle at whose center is the earth and the circumference of which describes the orbit of a planet around the earth. **2.** A small circle that moves around the circumference of a larger circle, either on the inside or outside. [Middle English, from Old French or Late Latin, from Greek : *epi-,* EPI- + *kuklos,* circle.] —**ep·i·cy·clic** (ĕp′ə-sī′klĭk, -sĭk′lĭk) *adj.*

epicyclic train *n.* A system of gears in which at least one wheel axis revolves about another. It usually consists of a large annulus wheel with internal teeth, a small coaxial wheel with external teeth, and one or more planetary gears engaging with both of them.

ep·i·cy·cloid (ĕp′ĭ-sī′kloid′) *n.* The curve described by a point fixed on the circumference of a circle as it rolls on the outside of the circumference of a fixed coplanar circle. [EPICYCL(E) + -OID.] —**ep·i·cy·cloid·al** (ĕp′ə-sī-kloid′l) *adj.*

epicycloidal wheel *n.* A planetary wheel in an epicyclic train.

Ep·i·dau·rus (ĕp′ĭ-dôr′əs). Ancient town of Greece, near the eastern shore of the Peloponnese; the site of the best-preserved ancient Greek theater.

ep·i·deic·tic (ĕp′ə-dīk′tĭk) *adj.* Intended for rhetorical effect or display. [Greek, from *epideiknunai,* to display, show off : *epi-,* EPI- + *deiknunai,* to show.]

ep·i·dem·ic (ĕp′ə-dĕm′ĭk) *adj.* **1.** Spreading rapidly and extensively among many individuals in an area. Said especially of contagious diseases. **2.** Resembling or characteristic of a rapidly spreading disease: *Street crime has reached epidemic proportions.*
~*n.* **1.** An outbreak of a contagious disease that spreads rapidly and widely. **2.** A temporary, widespread popularity, as of a fashion or a fad. **3.** A rapid spread, growth, or development. [French *épidémique,* from *épidémie,* from Old French *espydymie,* from Late Latin *epidēmia,* from Greek *epidēmia (nosos),* "(illness) prevalent among people," from *epidēmos,* prevalent, common : *epi-,* among + *dēmos,* people.] —**ep·i·dem·i·cal·ly** *adv.*

ep·i·de·mi·ol·o·gy (ĕp′ə-dē′mē-ŏl′ə-jē, -dĕm′ē-ŏl′ə-jē) *n.* The study of epidemics and the causes and distribution of epidemic diseases. [Late Latin *epidēmia,* an EPIDEM(IC) + -LOGY.] —**ep·i·de·mi·o·log·**

i·cal (ĕp′ə-dē′mē-ə-lŏj′ĭ-kəl, ĕp′ə-dĕm′ē-), **ep·i·de·me·o·log·ic** (-ĭk) *adj.* **—ep·i·de·mi·ol·o·gist** *n.*

ep·i·der·mis (ĕp′ə-dûr′mĭs) *n.* **1.** *Zoology.* **a.** The outer, protective layer of the skin in vertebrates. **b.** A single outer layer of cells in invertebrates. **2.** *Botany.* The outermost layer of cells or protective covering of a plant or plant part. [Late Latin, from Greek : *epi-*, over + *derma*, skin.] **—ep·i·der·mal** (ĕp′ə-dûr′məl), **ep·i·der·mic** (-mĭk), **ep·i·der·moid** (-moid′) *adj.*

ep·i·di·a·scope (ĕp′ə-dī′ə-skōp′) *n.* An optical device for projecting onto a screen the images of opaque objects or transparencies. Compare **diascope, episcope.** [EPI- + DIA- + -SCOPE.]

ep·i·did·y·mis (ĕp′ə-dĭd′ə-mĭs) *n., pl.* **-mides** (-mə-dēz′). A long, narrow, flattened convoluted tube that is part of the spermatic duct system, connecting the testicle to the vas deferens. [New Latin, from Greek : *epi-*, at, near + *didumos*, testicle.] **—ep·i·did·y·mal** *adj.*

ep·i·dote (ĕp′ə-dōt′) *n.* A natural yellow, green, or black mineral consisting mainly of a silicate of calcium, aluminum, and iron, commonly found in metamorphic rock. [French *épidote*, from Greek *epididonai*, to give additionally, increase (so called because two sides of the mineral's base are longer than the other two) : *epi-*, in addition + *didonai*, to give.] **—ep·i·dot·ic** (ĕp′ə-dŏt′ĭk) *adj.*

ep·i·du·ral (ĕp′ə-dŏŏr′əl, -dyŏŏr′əl) *adj.* On or administered outside the dura mater.
~*n.* **1.** An injection of anesthetic into the outer lining of the spinal cord. **2.** Anesthesia resulting from such an injection. Also called "epidural anesthesia." [EPI- + DURA (MATER) + -AL.]

ep·i·fo·cal (ĕp′ə-fō′kəl) *adj. Geology.* Of, occurring at, or pertaining to an epicenter.

ep·i·gas·tri·um (ĕp′ĭ-găs′trē-əm) *n., pl.* **-tria** (-trē-ə). The upper middle region of the abdomen. [New Latin, from Greek *epigastrion* : *epi-*, above + *gastrium*, diminutive of *gastēr*, stomach.] **—ep·i·gas·tric** (ĕp′ĭ-găs′trĭk) *adj.*

ep·i·ge·al (ĕp′ə-jē′əl) *adj.* Also **ep·i·ge·an** (-ən), **ep·i·ge·ous** (-əs). **1.** *Botany.* Characterized by germination in which the cotyledons appear above the surface of the ground. Compare **hypogeal. 2.** *Biology.* Living or occurring on or near the surface of the ground. [Greek *epigaios*, on the earth : *epi-*, on + *gaia, gē*, earth.]

ep·i·gene (ĕp′ə-jēn′) *adj.* **1.** Formed, originating, or occurring on or just below the surface of the earth. **2.** Foreign; not natural to the material in which found. Said of crystals. [French *épigène*, from Greek *epigenēs*, arising after, from *epigignesthai*, to be born after : *epi-*, after + *gignesthai*, to be born.]

ep·i·gen·e·sis (ĕp′ə-jĕn′ə-sĭs) *n.* **1.** *Biology.* The generally accepted theory that the individual is developed by structural elaboration of the unstructured egg rather than by a simple enlarging of a preformed entity. Compare **preformation. 2.** *Geology.* Change in the mineral characteristics of a rock due to outside influence. [EPI- + GENESIS.] **—ep·i·ge·net·ic** (ĕp′ə-jə-nĕt′ĭk) *adj.*

e·pig·e·nous (ĭ-pĭj′ə-nəs) *adj. Botany.* Developing or growing on an upper surface, as fungi on leaves. [EPI- + -GENOUS.]

ep·i·glot·tis (ĕp′ĭ-glŏt′ĭs) *n., pl.* **-tises** or **-glottides** (-glŏt′ə-dēz′). An elastic cartilage, located at the root of the tongue, that folds over the glottis to prevent food from entering the windpipe during the act of swallowing. [New Latin, from Greek *epiglōttis* : *epi-*, over + *glōttis*, GLOTTIS.]

ep·i·gone (ĕp′ĭ-gōn′) *n.* Also **ep·i·gon** (-gŏn′). A second-rate imitator or follower, as of an artist or philosopher. [From Greek *Epigonoi*, sons of the Seven against Thebes who imitated their fathers by attacking Thebes, from the plural of *epigonos*, born after : EPI- + *gonos*, child.] **—ep·i·gon·ic** (ĕp′ĭ-gŏn′ĭk) *adj.*

ep·i·gram (ĕp′ĭ-grăm′) *n.* **1.** A short poem expressing a single thought or observation with terseness and wit. **2.** A concisely and cleverly worded statement making a pointed observation and often concluding with a satirical twist. **3.** Discourse or expression by means of such statements. —See Synonyms at **saying.** [Old French *epigramme*, from Latin *epigramma*, from Greek, inscription, from *epigraphein*, to write on : *epi-*, on + *graphein*, to write.]

ep·i·gram·mat·ic (ĕp′ĭ-grə-măt′ĭk) *adj.* **1.** Of or having the nature of an epigram. **2.** Full of or given to the use of epigrams. —See Synonyms at **concise. —ep·i·gram·mat·i·cal·ly** *adv.*

ep·i·gram·ma·tize (ĕp′ĭ-grăm′ə-tīz′) *v.* **-tized, -tizing, -tizes.** —*tr.* To express (a thought or sentiment) in an epigram or epigrams. —*intr.* To speak or write in epigrams. **—ep·i·gram·ma·tist** (ĕp′ĭ-grăm′ə-tĭst) *n.*

ep·i·graph (ĕp′ĭ-grăf′, -gräf′) *n.* **1.** An inscription, as on a statue or building. **2.** A motto or quotation, as at the beginning of a book or chapter, usually intended to give an idea of its theme. [Greek *epigraphē*, from *epigraphos*, written on, from *epigraphein*, to write on. See **epigram.**] **—ep·i·graph·ic** (ĕp′ĭ-grăf′ĭk), **ep·i·graph·i·cal** *adj.* **—ep·i·graph·i·cal·ly** *adv.*

e·pig·ra·phy (ĭ-pĭg′rə-fē) *n.* **1.** Inscriptions collectively. **2. a.** The study of inscriptions. **b.** The interpretation of ancient inscriptions. Compare **paleography. —e·pig·ra·pher, e·pig·ra·phist** *n.*

e·pig·y·ny (ĭ-pĭj′ə-nē) *n. Botany.* A condition in which the petals, sepals, and male organs of flowers are above the female organs so that the ovary is enclosed by and fused with the tip of the flower stalk. [EPI- + -GYNY.] **—e·pig·y·nous** *adj.*

ep·i·lep·sy (ĕp′ə-lĕp′sē) *n.* Any of various disorders characterized by sudden recurring attacks of motor, sensory, or psychic malfunction with or without unconsciousness or convulsive movements. See **grand mal, petit mal.** [Old French *epilepsie*, from Late Latin *epilēpsia*, from Greek, from *epilambanein* (stem *epilab-*), to seize upon : *epi-*, upon + *lambanein*, to take hold of.] **—ep·i·lep·tic** (ĕp′ə-lĕp′tĭk) *n.* & *adj.*

ep·i·lep·toid (ĕp′ə-lĕp′toid′) *adj.* Resembling epilepsy or any of its symptoms. [EPILEPT(IC) + -OID.]

ep·i·logue, ep·i·log (ĕp′ə-lôg′, -lŏg′) *n.* **1. a.** A short poem or speech spoken directly to the audience following the conclusion of a play. **b.** The performer or performers who speak this. **2.** A short addition or concluding section at the end of a literary work, often dealing with the future of its characters. **3.** *British.* A short religious program at the end of a day's broadcasting. [Middle English *epiloge*, from Old French *epilogue*, from Latin *epilogus*, from Greek *epilogos*, from *epilegein*, to say more, to add : *epi-*, in addition + *legein*, to say.]

e·pim·er·ism (ĭ-pĭm′ə-rĭz′əm) *n. Chemistry.* A form of optical isomerism in which isomers can form about asymmetric atoms. [EPI- + (ISO)MERISM.] **—ep·i·mer·ic** (ĕp′ə-mĕr′ĭk) *adj.*

ep·i·mys·i·um (ĕp′ə-mĭz′ē-əm, -mĭzh′ē-əm) *n., pl.* **-mysia** (-mĭz′ē-ə, -mĭzh′ē-ə). The fibrous sheath enclosing a muscle. [New Latin : EPI- + Greek *mus*, muscle.]

ep·i·nas·ty (ĕp′ə-năs′tē) *n., pl.* **-ties.** A downward bending of leaves or other plant parts, resulting from greater growth of the upper side than of the lower side. [EPI- + -NASTY.] **—ep·i·nas·tic** (ĕp′ə-năs′tĭk) *adj.*

ep·i·neph·rine, ep·i·neph·rin (ĕp′ə-nĕf′rĭn) *n.* **1.** An adrenal hormone that stimulates autonomic nerve action. **2.** A white to brownish crystalline compound, $C_9H_{13}NO_3$, isolated from the adrenal glands of certain mammals or synthesized and used as a heart stimulant, vasoconstrictor, and in the treatment of asthma. Also called "adrenalin." [EPI- + NEPHR(O)- + -INE.]

ep·i·neu·ri·um (ĕp′ə-nŏŏr′ē-əm, -nyŏŏr′ē-əm) *n., pl.* **-neuria** (-nŏŏr′ē-ə, -nyŏŏr′ē-ə). The connective tissue sheath surrounding the bundles of fibers that make up a nerve. [EPI- + NEUR(O)- + -IUM.] **—ep·i·neu·ri·al** *adj.*

e·piph·a·ny (ĭ-pĭf′ə-nē) *n., pl.* **-nies. 1.** A revelatory manifestation of a divine being. **2.** A spiritual event in which the essential nature of something appears to the subject, as in a sudden flash of recognition. **3.** A revelation or experience of insight. [Greek *epiphaneia*, manifestation, appearance, from *epiphanēs*, appearing, manifest, from *epiphainein*, to manifest : *epi-*, to + *phainein*, to show.]

E·piph·a·ny (ĭ-pĭf′ə-nē) *n.* A Christian festival held on January 6 in celebration of the manifestation of the divine nature of Christ to the Gentiles as represented by the Magi.

ep·i·phe·nom·e·nal·ism (ĕp′ə-fĭ-nŏm′ə-nə-lĭz′əm) *n. Philosophy.* The doctrine that mental activities are simply epiphenomena of the neural processes of the brain and have no causal influence.

ep·i·phe·nom·e·non (ĕp′ə-fĭ-nŏm′ə-nŏn′) *n., pl.* **-na** (-nə). **1.** A secondary phenomenon accompanying and resulting from another. **2.** *Pathology.* An unusual additional condition in the course of a disease, not necessarily connected with the disease. **—ep·i·phe·nom·e·nal** (ĕp′ə-fĭ-nŏm′ə-nəl) *adj.*

e·piph·y·sis (ĭ-pĭf′ə-sĭs) *n., pl.* **-ses** (-sēz′). *Anatomy.* **1.** A part of a bone that is separated from the shaft by cartilage until growth is complete. **2.** The **pineal body** *(see).* [New Latin, from Greek *epiphusis*, a growth upon : *epi-*, upon + *phusis*, growth, from *phuein*, to grow.] **—ep·i·phys·i·al, ep·i·phys·e·al** (ĕp′ə-fĭz′ē-əl) *adj.*

ep·i·phyte (ĕp′ə-fīt′) *n.* A plant, such as any of certain orchids or ferns, that grows on another plant or object upon which it depends for mechanical support but not as a source of nutrients. Also called "air plant," "aerophyte." [EPI- + -PHYTE.] **—ep·i·phyt·ic** (ĕp′ə-fĭt′ĭk), **ep·i·phyt·i·cal** *adj.*

ep·i·phy·tot·ic (ĕp′ə-fī-tŏt′ĭk) *adj.* Of, pertaining to, or designating a sudden or abnormally destructive outbreak of a plant disease, usually over an extended geographic area.
~*n.* An outbreak of such a disease. [EPI- + PHYT(O)- + -OTIC.]

Epis. 1. Episcopal; Episcopalian. **2.** Epistle.

Episc. Episcopal; Episcopalian.

e·pis·co·pa·cy (ĭ-pĭs′kə-pə-sē) *n., pl.* **-cies. 1.** An episcopate. **2.** The system of church government in which bishops are the chief ministers. [From EPISCOPATE.]

e·pis·co·pal (ĭ-pĭs′kə-pəl) *adj.* **1.** Of or pertaining to a bishop. **2.** Of, having, or advocating church government by bishops. **3. Episcopal.** *Abbr.* **Epis., Episc.** Of, pertaining to, or belonging to the Protestant Episcopal Church. [Middle English, from Old French, from Late Latin *episcopālis*, from *episcopus*, bishop, from Greek *episkopos*, overseer : *epi-*, over + *skopos*, watcher, seer.]

Episcopal Church *n.* **1.** The **Protestant Episcopal Church** *(see).* **2.** Any of the branches of the Anglican Communion outside England, especially that in Scotland.

e·pis·co·pa·li·an (ĭ-pĭs′kə-pā′lē-ən, -pāl′yən) *adj.* **1.** Of or advocating church government by bishops. **2. Episcopalian.** *Abbr.* **Epis., Episc.** Of, pertaining to, or belonging to the Protestant Episcopal Church. **—e·pis·co·pa·li·an** *n.*

e·pis·co·pal·ism (ĭ-pĭs′kə-pə-lĭz′əm) *n.* The belief that the power to govern the church should rest with bishops.

e·pis·co·pate (ĭ-pĭs′kə-pĭt, -pāt′) *n.* **1.** The position or term of office of a bishop. **2.** The area of jurisdiction of a bishop; a diocese. **3.** Bishops collectively. [Late Latin *episcopātus*, from *episcopus*, bishop. See **episcopal.**]

ep·i·scope (ĕp′ə-skōp′) *n.* An optical device for projecting onto a screen an enlarged image of an opaque object. Compare **epidiascope.** [EPI- + -SCOPE.]

e·pi·si·ot·o·my (ĭ-pē′zē-ŏt′ə-mē) *n., pl.* **-mies.** A surgical incision into the tissues around the vagina during childbirth to enlarge the

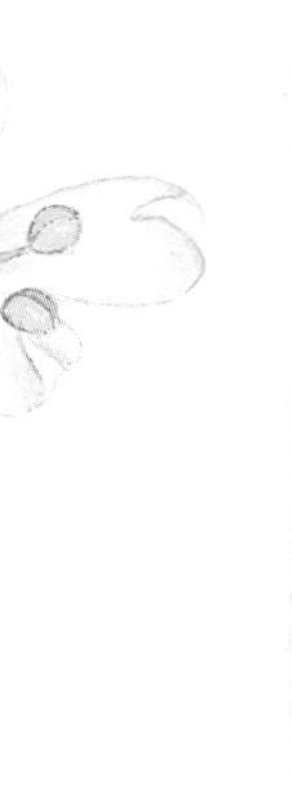

epigyny *In most flowers, the ovary of the plant is set above the base of the petals. In the flower head (above) of* Scandix pecten-veneris, *or shepherd's needle, however, the ovary is contained in the oval hairy bulge below the petals. Botanists describe plants with this rarer structure as epigynous.*

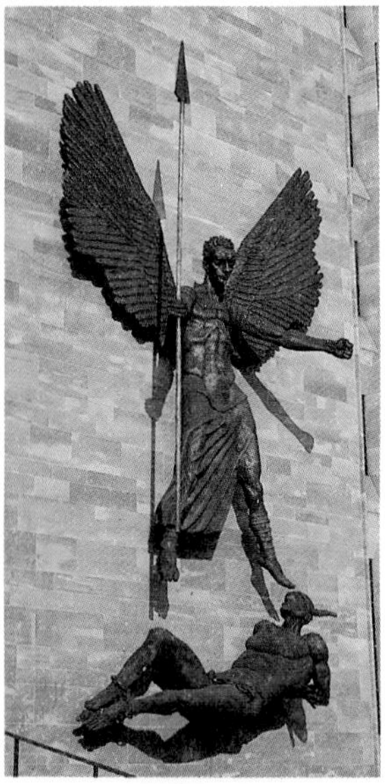

Epstein sculpture Saint Michael and the Devil, *on the east front of Coventry Cathedral, England.*

opening and make delivery easier. [Greek *epision,* pubic area + -TOMY.]

ep·i·sode (ĕp′ə-sōd′) *n.* **1.** An incident or series of related events in the course of a continuous experience: *an episode from her childhood.* **2.** A portion of a narrative that relates an event or series of connected events and forms a coherent story in itself; an incident: *an episode of a picaresque novel.* **3.** A separately presented portion of a serialized novel, play, radio or television drama, or the like; an installment. **4.** A section of a classical Greek tragedy that occurs between two choric songs. **5.** *Music.* A passage between statements of a main subject or theme, as in a rondo or fugue. —See Synonyms at **occurrence.** [Greek *epeisodion,* "addition," from *epeisodios,* coming in besides : *epi-,* besides + *eisodios,* coming in : *eis,* into + *hodos,* way, road.]

ep·i·sod·ic (ĕp′ə-sŏd′ĭk) *adj.* Also **ep·i·sod·i·cal** (-ĭ-kəl). **1.** Of, pertaining to, or resembling an episode. **2.** Composed of a series of episodes: *an episodic narrative.* **3.** Not in a continuous sequence; disjointed. **4.** Occasional, sporadic, or unpredictable: *Their efforts were episodic.* —**ep·i·sod·i·cal·ly** *adv.*

ep·i·spas·tic (ĕp′ə-spăs′tĭk) *adj.* Causing blisters.
~*n.* A blistering agent; a vesicatory. [Greek *epispastikos,* drawing after (because blisters were thought to be humors drawn toward the skin), from *epispatos,* drawn, from *epispan,* to draw after one, attract : *epi-,* after + *span,* to draw (see **spasm**).]

Epist. Epistle.

e·pis·ta·sis (ĭ-pĭs′tə-sĭs) *n., pl.* **-ses** (-sēz′). **1.** *Genetics.* A nonreciprocal interaction between nonalternative forms of genes in which one gene suppresses the expression of another affecting the same part of an organism. **2.** *Medicine.* Matter that rises to the surface of a bodily discharge. [New Latin, from Greek, stoppage, stopping, from *ephistanai,* to place upon, stop : *epi-,* upon + *histanai,* to place, set.] —**ep·i·stat·ic** (ĕp′ə-stăt′ĭk) *adj.*

ep·i·stax·is (ĕp′ə-stăk′sĭs) *n., pl.* **-ses** (-sēz′). *Pathology.* A nosebleed. [New Latin, from Greek, "dropping," from *epistazein,* to let fall in drops upon : *epi-,* upon + *stazein,* to drip.]

e·pis·te·mol·o·gy (ĭ-pĭs′tə-mŏl′ə-jē) *n., pl.* **-gies. 1.** The division of philosophy that investigates the nature and origin of knowledge. **2.** A theory of the nature of knowledge. [Greek *epistēmē,* knowledge, understanding, from *epistanai,* "to stand upon," understand : *epi-,* upon + *histanai,* to stand, place + -LOGY.] —**e·pis·te·mo·log·i·cal** (ĭ-pĭs′tə-mə-lŏj′ĭ-kəl) *adj.* —**e·pis·te·mo·log·i·cal·ly** *adv.* —**e·pis·te·mol·o·gist** (-mŏl′ə-jĭst) *n.*

e·pis·tle (ĭ-pĭs′əl) *n.* **1.** A letter, especially a formal one. **2.** *Usually* **Epistle.** *Abbr.* **Epis., Epist. a.** Any of the letters written by any of various Apostles or their helpers to early Christians and included in the New Testament. **b.** An excerpt from any of these letters, read as part of a religious service. **3.** A verse letter of the genre invented by Horace and imitated by poets of the 17th and 18th centuries. **4.** A prefatory dedication in the form of a letter. [Middle English, from Old French, from Latin *epistola,* from Greek *epistolē,* from *epistellein,* to send to : *epi-,* to + *stellein,* to send.]

e·pis·tler (ĭ-pĭs′lər) *n.* Also **e·pis·to·ler** (ĭ-pĭs′tə-lər). **1.** A writer of epistles. **2.** *Usually* **Epistler.** The person who reads the Epistle in a religious service.

e·pis·to·lar·y (ĭ-pĭs′tə-lĕr′ē) *adj.* **1.** Of or associated with letters or letter writing. **2.** In the form of a letter or series of letters. Said of a literary work. **3.** Carried on by or made up of letters: *an epistolary friendship.* [Latin *epistolāris,* from *epistola,* EPISTLE.]

ep·i·style (ĕp′ə-stīl′) *n. Architecture.* An **architrave** *(see).* [Latin *epistylium,* from Greek *epistulion* : *epi-,* upon + *stulos,* pillar.]

ep·i·taph (ĕp′ə-tăf′, -täf′) *n.* **1.** An inscription on a tombstone or monument in memory of the one or ones buried there. **2.** A brief literary piece summarizing or epitomizing a deceased person. **3.** A final view, opinion, or judgment on someone or something past: *an epitaph on her ex-husband.* [Middle English *epitaphe,* from Old French, from Latin *epitaphium,* funeral oration, from Greek *epitaphion,* neuter of *epitaphios,* "over a tomb" : *epi-,* over + *taphos,* tomb.] —**ep·i·taph·ic** (ĕp′ə-tăf′ĭk) *adj.*

e·pit·a·sis (ĭ-pĭt′ə-sĭs) *n., pl.* **-ses** (-sēz′). The part of a play, especially in classical Greek drama, in which the plot develops toward its dénouement. [Greek, a stretching over, intensification, from *epiteinein,* to stretch over : *epi-,* over + *teinein,* to stretch.]

ep·i·tax·i·al (ĕp′ə-tăk′sē-əl) *adj.* **1.** Designating a thin layer on the surface of a crystal, especially one that has the same structure as the underlying crystal. **2.** Designating a transistor made by depositing such a layer of semiconductor on a crystal support. [EPI- + -TAXY + -AL.] —**ep·i·tax·y** (ĕp′ə-tăk′sē) *n.*

ep·i·tha·la·mi·um (ĕp-ə-thə-lā′mē-əm) *n., pl.* **-ums** or **-mia** (-mē-ə). A lyric ode in honor of a marriage. [Latin, from Greek *epithalamion,* from the neuter of *epithalamios,* belonging to a wedding : *epi-,* at + *thalamos,* bridal chamber (see **thalamus**).]

ep·i·the·li·o·ma (ĕp′ə-thē′lē-ō′mə) *n., pl.* **-mata** (-mə-tə) or **-mas.** A benign or malignant tumor derived from the epithelium. [New Latin : EPITHEL(IUM) + -OMA.] —**ep·i·the·li·om·a·tous** (ĕp′ə-thē′lē-ŏm′ə-təs) *adj.*

ep·i·the·li·um (ĕp′ə-thē′lē-əm) *n., pl.* **-ums** or **-lia** (-lē-ə). Membranous tissue, usually in a single layer, composed of closely arranged cells separated by very little intercellular substance and forming the covering of most internal surfaces and organs and the outer surface of an animal body. [New Latin : EPI- + Greek *thēlē,* nipple.] —**ep·i·the·li·al** *adj.*

ep·i·thet (ĕp′ə-thĕt′) *n.* **1.** A term used to characterize the nature of a person or thing: *"Moderate" is a much misused epithet in politics.* **2.** An adjective or descriptive phrase that comes to form part of or to substitute for a person's name or title: *"The Lion-Hearted" is an epithet for Richard I.* **3.** An abusive or contemptuous word or phrase used to describe a person: *Her sarcastic smile made "Your Honor" an epithet.* [Latin *epitheton,* from Greek, "an addition," from *epitithenai,* to put on, add : *epi-,* on + *tithenai,* to place, put.] —**ep·i·thet·ic** (ĕp′ə-thĕt′ĭk), **ep·i·thet·i·cal** (-ĭ-kəl) *adj.*

e·pit·o·me (ĭ-pĭt′ə-mē) *n.* **1.** A summary of a book, article, event, or the like; an abridgment; an abstract. **2.** One that is perfectly and strikingly representative or expressive of an entire class or type; an embodiment: *Keats was the epitome of the Romantic poet.* [Latin *epitomē,* from Greek, from *epitemnein,* to cut upon the surface, cut short : *epi-,* upon + *temnein,* to cut.]

e·pit·o·mize (ĭ-pĭt′ə-mīz′) *tr.v.* **-mized, -mizing, -mizes. 1.** To make an epitome of; sum up. **2.** To typify (an entire class, type, or quality); represent or express the essence of: *A baby epitomizes innocence.*

ep·i·zo·ic (ĕp′ə-zō′ĭk) *adj.* Living or growing on the exterior of a living animal: *epizoic fungi.* [EPI- + -ZOIC.]

ep·i·zo·ot·ic (ĕp′ə-zō-ŏt′ĭk) *adj.* **1.** Attacking a large number of animals within a short time. Said of a disease. **2.** Prevalent among a group of animals. Said of a disease.
~*n.* An epizootic disease. [EPI- + ZO(O)- + -OTIC.]

e plu·ri·bus u·num (ē′ plo͝or′ə-bəs yo͞o′nəm, o͞o′nəm) *n.* One out of many. The motto of the United States. [Latin.]

E.P.N.S. electroplated nickel silver.

ep·och (ĕp′ək, ē′pŏk′) *n.* **1.** A period of history; especially, one characterized by remarkable events or by the predominance of a particular person, group, or state of affairs; an era. **2.** A point in time or progress that marks the beginning of such a period; a milestone; a breakthrough: *The addition of sound marked an epoch in film history.* **3.** *Geology.* A unit of geologic time that is a division of a period. **4.** *Astronomy.* An instant in time that is arbitrarily selected as a reference point. [New Latin *epocha,* from Greek *epokhē,* pause.]

ep·och·al (ĕp′ə-kəl, -ŏk′əl) *adj.* **1.** Of, pertaining to, or characteristic of an epoch. **2.** Epoch-making.

ep·och-mak·ing (ĕp′ək-mā′kĭng, ē′pək-) *adj.* Highly significant or important; momentous.

ep·ode (ĕp′ōd′) *n.* **1.** The last strophe of the triad (strophe, antistrophe, and epode) that forms the basic compositional unit of the lyric ode. **2.** A lyric composition of a type invented by Archilochus and used by Horace, characterized by couplets of a long line followed by a shorter one. [Latin *epōdos,* from Greek *epōidos,* "a singing after," from *epaidein,* to sing after : *epi-,* after + *aidein,* to sing.]

ep·o·nym (ĕp′ə-nĭm′) *n.* A real or mythical person whose name is or is thought to be the source of the name of a city, country, era, institution, or the like: *"Romulus" is the eponym of Rome.* [Greek *epōnumos,* EPONYMOUS.] —**ep·o·nym·ic** (ĕp′ə-nĭm′ĭk) *adj.*

e·pon·y·mous (ĭ-pŏn′ə-məs) *adj.* Of, pertaining to, or designating a person after whom something, such as a city, era, book, or play, is named or thought to be named: *In the movie "Ben Hur" the eponymous hero was played by a famous actor.* [Greek *epōnumos* : *epi-,* to + *onoma,* name.]

e·pon·y·my (ĭ-pŏn′ə-mē) *n.* The derivation of the name of a city, country, era, institution, or the like, from that of a person.

ep·o·pee (ĕp′ə-pē′) *n.* **1.** Epic poetry, especially as a literary genre. **2.** An epic poem. [French *épopée,* from Greek *epopoiia,* from *epopoios,* epic poet : *epos,* word, EPIC + *poiein,* to make (see **poet**).]

ep·os (ĕp′ŏs′) *n.* **1.** Oral epic poetry. **2.** An epic poem. [Latin, from Greek, word, poem.]

ep·ox·y (ĕp′ŏk′sē, ĭ-pŏk′-) *adj.* Of, composed of, or containing a substance with a molecular structure in which an oxygen atom is joined to two different groups that are themselves joined to other groups.
~*n., pl.* **-ies.** Any of various usually thermosetting resins characterized by toughness, strong adhesion, and high corrosion and chemical resistance, used especially in surface coatings and adhesives. Also called "epoxy resin." [EP(I)- + OXY-.]

Ep·ping (ĕp′ĭng). Town in Essex, now virtually a northeast suburb of London. It is famous for Epping Forest (2,270 hectares; 5,600 acres), formerly a royal hunting park.

ep·si·lon (ĕp′sə-lŏn′, -lən) *n.* The fifth letter in the Greek alphabet, written Ε, ε. Transliterated in English as *E, e.* See feature at **alphabet.** [Greek *e psilon,* "simple *e,*" from *psilos,* mere, simple.]

Ep·som (ĕp′səm). Town in Surrey, England, now part of the municipal borough of Epsom and Ewell. The Derby is run annually at Epsom Downs, a racecourse here.

Epsom salts *pl.n.* Hydrated **magnesium sulfate** *(see)* used especially as a cathartic and to reduce swellings. [After EPSOM, where it was originally obtained from a mineral spring.]

Ep·stein (ĕp′stīn′), **Sir Jacob** (1880–1959). British sculptor, born in New York of Russian-Polish parents. He studied in Paris with Rodin before settling in England (1905). He became famous for his massive subjects in bronze and stone, among them the marble *Venus* (1917), a bronze *Christ* (1919), and the alabaster *Adam* (1939).

Ep·stein-Barr virus (ĕp′stīn-bär′) *n.* The virus that is believed to cause infectious mononucleosis. [After M.A. *Epstein* (1921–) and Y.M. *Barr* (1932–), British pathologists who discovered it.]

eq. 1. equal. **2.** equation. **3.** equivalent.

eq·ua·ble (ĕk′wə-bəl, ē′kwə-) *adj.* **1.** Unvarying; uniform: *an equable climate.* **2.** Not easily disturbed; serene: *an equable temperament.* —See Synonyms at **steady.** [Latin *aequābilis,* from *aequāre,*

PRONUNCIATION KEY

ă, pat; ā, pay; âr, care;
ä, father, are; b, bib;
ch, church; d, deed; ĕ, pet;
ē, be; f, fife; g, gag; h, hat;
hw, which; ĭ, pit; ī, pie;
îr, pier; j, judge; k, kick;
l, lid, needle; m, mum;
n, no, sudden; ng, thing;
ŏ, pot; ō, toe; ô, paw, for;
oi, noise; ou, out; o͝o, book;
o͞o, boot; p, pop; r, roar;
s, sauce; sh, ship, dish;
t, tight; th, thin, path;
th, this, bathe; ŭ, cut; ûr, fur;
v, valve; w, with; y, yes;
z, zebra, size; zh, vision;
ə, about, item, edible,
gallop, circus, peaceful

IN FOREIGN WORDS:

à, *Fr.* ami; œ, *Fr.* feu, *Ger.* schön; ü, *Fr.* tu, *Ger.* über; KH, *Ger.* ich, *Scot.* loch; N, *Fr.* bon; y′, *Fr.* Compiègne

STRESS MARKS:

Primary stress: ′
in·cite′ (ĭn-sīt′)
Secondary stress: ′
in′sight′ (ĭn′sīt′)

to make even, from *aequus,* level, even, EQUAL.] **—eq·ua·bil·i·ty** (ĕk′wə-bĭl′ə-tē), **eq·ua·ble·ness** *n.* **—eq·ua·bly** *adv.*

e·qual (ē′kwəl) *adj. Abbr.* **eq. 1.** Having the same capability, quantity, or effect as another: *equal strength.* **2.** *Mathematics.* Related by a reflexive, symmetrical, and transitive relationship; broadly, alike or in agreement in a specific sense with respect to specific properties. **3.** Having the same privileges, status, or rights: *equal before the law.* **4.** Fairly and evenly available or granted: *equal rights.* **5.** Fairly and evenly balanced: *an equal contest.* **6. a.** Having the requisite qualities, as strength, ability, or determination, to accomplish a task or cope with a situation: *"Elizabeth found herself quite equal to the scene"* (Jane Austen). **b.** Adequate in extent, amount, or degree: *money equal to their needs.* **7.** *Archaic.* Impartial; just; equitable: *equal laws.* **8.** *Archaic.* Tranquil; equable. —See Synonyms at **same.**

~n. A person or thing that is equal to another, especially: **1.** One who is equal in rank or status. **2.** A worthy substitute or rival: *I am his equal in every respect.*

~tr.v. **equaled** or **equalled, equaling** or **equalling, equals. 1.** To be equal to, especially in amount or value. **2.** To do, make, or produce something equal to: *He equaled the world record for the mile.* **—equal out.** To reach a point of equilibrium; become equal. [Latin *aequālis,* from *aequus*†, even, level.]

Usage: The main problem is whether *equal* can be used along with *more* and *most.* Purists point out that if two things are equal, then one cannot be more equal than the other. But a sentence such as *There is a more equal distribution of wealth* is possible, with *equal* having the sense "more equitable" or "more nearly equal." *Most* is less often encountered but is still possible in such sentences as *That's the most equal division of opinion I have ever seen.* • *Equally* gives rise to two problems. It is often used with *as: Equally as interesting is his new book* would be reduced in careful usage to either *Equally interesting . . .* or *As interesting. . . .* It is usual to use *as* when a comparison is explicit, and *equally* when it is not: *His new book is equally interesting, His new book is as interesting as his earlier books,* but not *His new book is equally interesting as his earlier books.* When comparisons are made like those in the sentence *The device is equally useful inside and outside the house, equally . . . and* demonstrates more respect for careful usage than the informal *equally . . . or.*

e·qual-ar·e·a projection (ē′kwəl-âr′ē-ə) *n.* A map projection reproducing the same area ratios as exist on the earth's surface. Also called "homolographic projection."

e·qual·i·ty (ĭ-kwŏl′ə-tē) *n. pl.* **-ties. 1.** The state or an instance of being equal; especially, the state of enjoying equal rights in political, economic, and social affairs. **2.** A mathematical statement, usually an equation, that one thing equals another. [Middle English *equalite,* from Old French, from Latin *aequālitās,* from *aequālis,* EQUAL.]

e·qual·ize (ē′kwə-līz′) *v.* **-ized, -izing, -izes.** *—tr.* **1.** To make equal. **2.** To make uniform. *—intr.* To constitute or induce equality, equilibrium, or balance.

e·qual·iz·er (ē′kwə-lī′zər) *n.* **1.** One that equalizes. **2.** A device for equalizing pressure or strain. **3.** *Electronics.* A tone control system for frequency distortion in audio systems. **4.** *Slang.* A weapon, especially a revolver.

e·qual·ly (ē′kwə-lē) *adv.* **1.** In an equal or even manner. **2.** To an equal degree: *applies equally to children and adults.* **3.** In the same manner or way; likewise: *I taught and equally learned from my students.* —See Usage note at **equal.**

Equal Rights Amendment *n. Abbr.* **ERA** A proposed amendment to the U.S. Constitution to guarantee equal rights under the law to both sexes.

equal sign *n.* Also **equals sign.** The symbol (=) used, especially in an equation, to indicate that one thing is logically or mathematically equal to another.

equal temperament *n. Music.* The tuning of keyboard instruments, as pianos, to produce octaves of 12 equal semitones. Also called "temperament."

e·qua·nim·i·ty (ē′kwə-nĭm′ə-tē, ĕk′wə-) *n.* The quality or characteristic of being calm and even-tempered; composure. [Latin *aequanimitās,* from *aequanimis,* even-tempered : *aequus,* even, EQUAL + *animus,* mind.] **—e·quan·i·mous** (ĭ-kwŏn′ə-məs) *adj.*

Synonyms: *composure, sang-froid, serenity.*

e·quate (ĭ-kwāt′) *v.* **equated, equating, equates.** *—tr.* **1.** To make, treat, or regard as equal or equivalent: *Many people equate wisdom with old age.* **2.** To reduce to a standard or average; equalize or stabilize; balance: *equate profit and loss.* **3.** To show or state the equality of; express in or as if in an equation. *—intr.* To be or seem to be equal; correspond; accord: *She equates easily with our conception of classic beauty.* [Middle English *equaten,* from Latin *aequāre,* from *aequus,* EQUAL.]

e·qua·tion (ĭ-kwā′zhən, -shən) *n. Abbr.* **eq. 1.** The process or act of equating or state of being equated. **2.** The state of being equal; a balanced state. **3.** *Mathematics.* A linear array of mathematical symbols separated into left and right sides that are designated at least conditionally equal by an equal sign. **4.** Broadly, a concept of equivalence or balance between a variety of factors: *Salaries have risen dramatically, but on the other side of the equation there has been a comparable rise in output.* **5.** *Chemistry.* A symbolic representation of a chemical reaction as a linear array of symbols for the reacting atomic and molecular species, separated into left and right sides by an equal sign, arrow, or opposing arrows. **6.** A complex of variable factors or considerations that must be taken into account, especially a **personal equation** *(see).* **—e·qua·tion·al** *adj.* **—e·qua·tion·al·ly** *adv.*

e·qua·tor (ĭ-kwā′tər) *n.* **1. a.** *Often* **Equator.** The great circle circumscribing the earth's surface, the reckoning datum of latitudes and the dividing boundary of Northern and Southern hemispheres, formed by the intersection of a plane passing through the earth's center perpendicular to its axis of rotation. **b.** A similar great circle drawn on the surface of a celestial body at right angles to the axis of rotation. **2.** The **magnetic equator** *(see).* **3.** *Astronomy.* The **celestial equator** *(see).* [Middle English, from Medieval Latin *(circulus) aequator (diei et noctis),* (circle) equalizing (day and night), from Latin *aequāre,* to EQUATE.]

e·qua·to·ri·al (ē′kwə-tôr′ē-əl, -tōr′ē-əl, ĕk′wə-) *adj.* **1.** Of or pertaining to the equator. **2.** Characteristic of or existing at or near the earth's equator: *equatorial climate; equatorial rain forests.* **3.** Lying in the same plane on the equator: *an equatorial orbit.* **4.** Having a support with two perpendicular axes, one of which is parallel to the earth's rotational axis. Said of a telescope.

~n. Astronomy. An equatorial telescope. **—e·qua·to·ri·al·ly** *adv.*

Equatorial Gui·nea (gĭn′ē). Formerly **Span·ish Guinea** (spăn′ĭsh). Country of West Africa. Most of the people are subsistence farmers, but cocoa, coffee, and hardwoods are exported. The country gained independence from Spain in 1968 but relies on Spanish, Soviet, and Chinese aid. Area, 28,051 square kilometers (10,828 square miles). Population, 250,000. Capital, Malabo.

eq·uer·ry (ĕk′wə-rē) *n., pl.* **-ries. 1.** An attendant to the British royal household. **2.** An officer charged with supervision of the horses belonging to a royal or noble household. [Earlier *escurie,* from obsolete French *escuirie*†, stable, mistakenly associated with Latin *equus,* horse.]

e·ques·tri·an (ĭ-kwĕs′trē-ən) *adj.* **1.** Of or pertaining to horsemanship or horseback riding. **2.** Depicted or represented on horseback: *an equestrian statue of an emperor.* **3.** Of, pertaining to, or composed of knights, horsemen, or cavalry: *equestrian troops.*

~n. One who rides a horse or performs on horseback. [Latin *equester,* from *equus,* horse.]

e·ques·tri·enne (ĭ-kwĕs′trē-ĕn′) *n.* A female equestrian.

equi- *prefix.* Indicates equality; for example, **equiangular.** [Middle English *equi-,* from Latin *aequi-,* from *aequus,* EQUAL.]

e·qui·an·gu·lar (ē′kwē-ăng′gyə-lər, ĕk′wē-) *adj.* Having all angles equal.

e·qui·dis·tant (ē′kwə-dĭs′tənt, ĕk′wə-) *adj.* Equally distant. **—e·qui·dis·tance** *n.* **—e·qui·dis·tant·ly** *adv.*

e·qui·lat·er·al (ē′kwə-lăt′ər-əl, ĕk′wə-) *adj.* Having all sides or faces equal.

~n. **1.** A side exactly equal to others. **2.** A geometric figure having equal sides. **—e·qui·lat·er·al·ly** *adv.*

e·quil·i·brant (ĭ-kwĭl′ə-brənt) *n.* A force capable of balancing a system of forces to produce equilibrium. [EQUILIBR(ATE) + -ANT.]

e·quil·i·brate (ĭ-kwĭl′ə-brāt′) *v.* **-brated, -brating, -brates.** *—intr.* To be in or bring about equilibrium. *—tr.* To maintain in or bring into equilibrium. [Latin *aequilibrāre,* to balance, from *aequilībris,* in perfect balance, from *aequilibrium,* EQUILIBRIUM.] **—e·quil·i·bra·tion** *n.*

e·quil·i·bra·tor (ĭ-kwĭl′ə-brā′tər) *n.* A device that brings about and helps maintain equilibrium.

e·quil·i·brist (ĭ-kwĭl′ə-brĭst) *n.* A person who performs feats of balance, such as tightrope walking. [French *équilibriste,* from Latin *aequilībrium,* EQUILIBRIUM.]

e·qui·lib·ri·um (ē′kwə-lĭb′rē-əm, ĕk′wə-) *n.* **1.** A condition in which all acting influences are cancelled by others, resulting in a stable, balanced, or unchanging state. **2.** *Physics.* The condition of a system in which the resultant of all acting forces is zero and the sum of all torques about any axis is zero. **3.** *Chemistry.* The state of a reaction in which its forward and reverse reactions occur at equal rates so that the concentration of the reactants does not change with time. **4.** Mental or emotional balance; psychological stability. [Latin *aequilībrium,* even balance : EQUI- + *libra,* balance.]

e·qui·mo·lec·u·lar (ē′kwə-mə-lĕk′yə-lər, ĕk′wə-) *adj.* Designating solutions, substances, or the like that contain equal numbers of molecules.

e·quine (ē′kwīn′, ĕk′wīn′) *adj.* **1.** Of, pertaining to, or characteristic of a horse. **2.** Of or belonging to the family Equidae, which includes the horses, asses, and zebras.

~n. A member of the Equidae. [Latin *equīnus,* from *equus,* horse.]

e·qui·noc·tial (ē′kwə-nŏk′shəl, ĕk′wə-) *adj.* **1.** Pertaining to or occurring at an equinox. **2.** Pertaining to the celestial equator. **3.** *Botany.* Having or characterizing flowers that open and close at specific times.

~n. **1.** *Meteorology.* A violent storm of wind and rain reputed to occur at or near the time of the equinox. **2.** The equinoctial circle. [Middle English *equinoxial,* from Old French, from Latin *aequinoctiālis,* from *aequinoctium,* EQUINOX.]

equinoctial circle *n.* The **celestial equator** *(see).* Also called "equinoctial," "equinoctial line."

e·qui·nox (ē′kwə-nŏks′, ĕk′wə-) *n.* **1.** Either of two points on the celestial sphere at which the ecliptic intersects the celestial equator. **2.** Either of the two times during a year when the sun crosses the celestial equator and when the length of day and night are approximately equal: the **vernal equinox** and the **autumnal equinox** *(both of which see).* [Middle English *equinox,* from Old French, from Medieval Latin *aequinoxium,* variant of Latin *aequinoctium* : EQUI- + *nox* (stem *noct-*), night.]

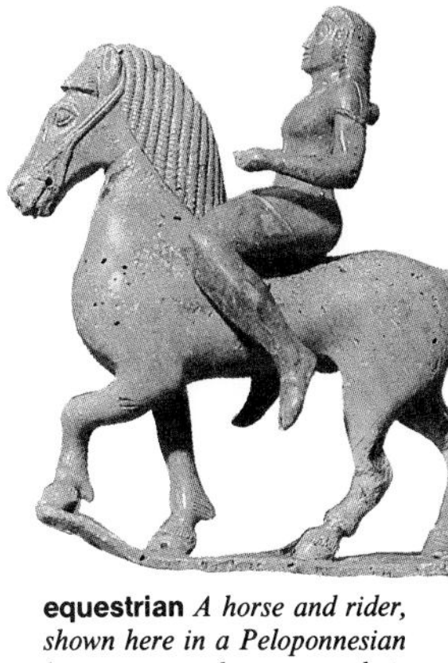

equestrian *A horse and rider, shown here in a Peloponnesian bronze statue that was made in about 550 B.C.*

e·quip (ĭ-kwĭp′) *tr.v.* **equipped, equipping, equips. 1.** To supply with material necessities such as tools, gear, provisions, or furnishings. **2.** To prepare in an intellectual, emotional, or spiritual way: *His training equipped him for such problems.* **3.** To dress or array. [Old French *eschiper, e(s)quiper,* to put to sea, embark, from Germanic.]

eq·ui·page (ĕk′wə-pĭj) *n.* **1.** Equipment or furnishings, especially of a military unit or ship; accouterments. **2. a.** A carriage that is elegantly equipped, as with caparisoned horses and liveried footmen. **b.** Any carriage. **3.** *Archaic.* A retinue, as of a person of royalty or nobility. **4.** *Archaic.* A set of articles, such as a dinner service or collection of jewelery.

e·quip·ment (ĭ-kwĭp′mənt) *n.* **1.** The act of equipping or the state of being equipped. **2.** Something material with which a person, organization, or thing is equipped; especially, the tools, apparatus, or the like required for a particular job or purpose: *camping equipment.* **3.** A person's intellectual or emotional resources.

e·qui·poise (ē′kwə-poiz′, ĕk′wə-) *n.* **1.** Equality in distribution, as of weight, relationship, or emotional forces; balance; equilibrium. **2.** A counterpoise; a counterbalance.
~*tr.v.* **equipoised, -poising, -poises.** To counterbalance.

e·qui·pol·lence (ē′kwə-pŏl′əns, ĕk′wə-) *n.* Also **e·qui·pol·len·cy** (-ən-sē). Equality, as in effectiveness or validity; equivalence.

e·qui·pol·lent (ē′kwə-pŏl′ənt, ĕk′wə-) *adj.* **1.** Equal in power, effectiveness, significance, or the like. **2.** *Logic.* Expressing the same thing; validly derived from each other. Said of two propositions. **3.** Equivalent.
~*n.* An equivalent. [Middle English *equipollent,* from Old French, from Latin *aequipollēns* (stem *aequipollent-*) : EQUI- + *pollēns,* present participle of *pollēre*†, to be powerful.]

e·qui·pon·der·ate (ē′kwə-pŏn′də-rāt′, ĕk′wə-) *tr.v.* **-ated, -ating, -ates. 1.** To counterbalance. **2.** To give equal balance or weight to. [Medieval Latin *aequiponderāre* : EQUI- + Latin *ponderāre,* to weigh.]

e·qui·po·ten·tial (ē′kwə-pə-tĕn′shəl, ĕk′wə-) *adj.* **1.** Having equal potential. **2.** *Physics.* Having the same potential at every point: *an equipotential surface.*

eq·ui·se·tum (ĕk′wə-sē′təm) *n.* Any of the flowerless, seedless plants of the genus *Equisetum,* which includes the horsetails. [New Latin, from Latin *equisaetum,* the horsetail : *equus,* horse + *saeta,* bristle, SETA.]

eq·ui·ta·ble (ĕk′wə-tə-bəl) *adj.* **1.** Exhibiting or characterized by equity; impartial or reasonable in judgment or treatment; fair; just. **2.** *Law.* Concerned with or valid in equity as distinguished from statute and common law. —See Synonyms at **fair.** [French *équitable,* from Old French, from *equite,* EQUITY.] —**eq·ui·ta·ble·ness** *n.* —**eq·ui·ta·bly** *adv.*

eq·ui·tant (ĕk′wə-tənt) *adj.* *Botany.* Overlapping at the base to form a flat, fanlike arrangement, as the leaves of some irises do. [Latin *equitāns* (stem *equitant-*), present participle of *equitāre,* to ride, from *eques* (stem *equit-*), horseman, from *equus,* horse.]

eq·ui·ta·tion (ĕk′wə-tā′shən) *n.* The art or practice of riding a horse; horsemanship. [Old French, from Latin *equitātiō* (stem *equitātiōn-*), riding, from *equitāre,* to ride. See **equitant.**]

eq·ui·ty (ĕk′wə-tē) *n., pl.* **-ties. 1.** The state, ideal, or quality of being just, impartial, and fair. **2.** Something that is just, impartial, and fair. **3.** The residual value of a business or property beyond any mortgage thereon and liability therein. **4.** *Law.* **a.** An organized body of legal rules based ultimately on principles of natural justice and applied either to cover cases not foreseen by common or statute law or to modify the rigor of common or statute law. **b.** An equitable right or claim. **5.** *Law.* Equity of redemption. **6. Equity.** *British.* The actors' trade union. [Middle English *equite,* from Old French, from Latin *aequitās* (stem *aequitāt-*), from *aequus,* EQUAL.]

equity of redemption *n. Law.* The right of one who has mortgaged his property to redeem that property upon payment of the sum due within a reasonable amount of time after the due date. Also called "equity."

equity stock *n.* **Common stock** (see).

equiv. equivalent.

e·quiv·a·lence (ĭ-kwĭv′ə-ləns) *n.* Also **e·quiv·a·len·cy** (-lən-sē) *pl.* **-cies. 1.** The state or condition of being equivalent; equality. **2.** *Mathematics.* A reflexive, symmetric, and transitive relation between elements of a set that establishes any two elements in the set as equivalent or nonequivalent. In this sense, also called "equivalence relationship." **3.** *Logic.* **a.** The relationship between two propositions having the same truth-value. **b.** The relationship between two propositions such that for one to be true and the other false gives rise to a contradiction. Compare **biconditional.**

e·quiv·a·lent (ĭ-kwĭv′ə-lənt; ē′kwə-vā′lənt, ĕk′wə- *for sense 4 only*) *adj. Abbr.* **eq., equiv. 1. a.** Equal in substance, degree, value, force, or meaning. **b.** Having similar or identical effects. **2.** Virtually the same; tantamount. Used with *to: This request was equivalent to an order.* **3.** *Mathematics.* **a.** Capable of being put into a one-to-one relationship. Said of two sets. **b.** Broadly, having identical corresponding parts. **c.** Equal. **4.** *Chemistry.* Having the same ability to combine. **5.** *Logic.* Exhibiting equivalence. Said of propositions. —See Synonyms at **same.**
~*n. Abbr.* **eq., equiv. 1.** Something that is equivalent. **2.** *Chemistry.* Equivalent weight. [Middle English, from Old French, from Late Latin *aequivalēns* (stem *aequivalent-*), present participle of *aequivalēre,* to be equal in value : EQUI- + *valēre,* to be strong, be worth.] —**e·quiv·a·lent·ly** *adv.*

equivalent weight *n.* The number of parts by weight of any element combining with or replacing the equivalent of half the atomic weight of oxygen or one atomic weight of hydrogen. Also called "combining weight," "equivalent."

e·quiv·o·cal (ĭ-kwĭv′ə-kəl) *adj.* **1.** Capable of two interpretations; ambiguous: *an equivocal statement.* **2.** Of uncertain nature; indeterminate: *an equivocal result.* **3.** Misleading; evasive. **4.** Of questionable integrity: *an equivocal sort of man.* [Late Latin *aequivocus* : EQUI- + Latin *vōx* (stem *vōc-*), voice.] —**e·quiv·o·cal·ly** *adv.* —**e·quiv·o·cal·ness** *n.*

e·quiv·o·cate (ĭ-kwĭv′ə-kāt′) *intr.v.* **-cated, -cating, -cates.** To use equivocal language intentionally; hedge. [Middle English *equivocaten,* from Medieval Latin *aequivocāre,* from Late Latin *aequivocus,* EQUIVOCAL.] —**e·quiv·o·ca·tion** *n.*

eq·ui·voque, eq·ui·voke (ĕk′wə-vōk′, ē′kwə-) *n.* **1.** A play on words; a pun. **2.** A double meaning. [French *équivoque,* from adjective, EQUIVOCAL.]

E·quu·le·us (ĭ-kwōō′lē-əs) *n.* A constellation in the equatorial region of the Northern Hemisphere near Delphinus and Pegasus. [Latin, diminutive of *equus,* horse.]

Er The symbol for the element erbium.

ER endoplasmic reticulum.

–er¹ *suffix.* **1.** Indicates: **a.** Someone who or something that performs the specified action; for example, **helper, blender. b.** Someone performing or involved with a specified occupation or function; for example, **photographer, bookkeeper. c.** Geographic origin or residence; for example, **Vermonter, northerner. d.** Nature or appearance; for example, **two-seater. 2.** Used to form informal versions of certain words; for example, **homer** instead of **home run.** [Middle English *-ere, -er,* Old English *-ere,* from Common Germanic *-ārjaz* (unattested), from Latin *-ārius.* See **-ary.**]

–er², –r *suffix.* Used to form the comparative degree of adjectives and adverbs; for example, **whiter, slower.** [Middle English *-ere, -re,* Old English *-re, -ra.*]

e·ra (îr′ə, ĕr′ə) *n.* **1.** A period of time that utilizes a specific point in history as the basis of its chronology: *After 1492 a new era in the history of mankind began.* **2.** A period of time that is distinctive or notable because of its new or different aspects, events, or personages: *the era of the computer.* **3.** The beginning or onset of such a period of time; a turning point or milestone; an epoch. **4.** *Geology.* The longest division of geologic time comprising one or more periods. [Late Latin *aera,* era, from Latin, "counters for calculating," a number as a basis for calculating, an era from which time is reckoned, from *aes* (stem *aer-*), brass, copper, money.]

ERA Equal Rights Amendment.

e·ra·di·ate (ĭ-rā′dē-āt′) *v.* **-ated, -ating, -ates.** —*tr.* To send out (radiation); radiate. —*intr.* To emanate. [EX- + RADIATE.] —**e·ra·di·a·tion** *n.*

e·rad·i·cate (ĭ-răd′ĭ-kāt′) *tr.v.* **-cated, -cating, -cates. 1.** To get rid of completely; remove totally: *The goal was to eradicate corruption.* **2.** To pull or tear up by or as if by the roots; uproot. —See Synonyms at **abolish.** [Latin *ērādicāre,* to pluck up by the roots, to root out : *ē-,* out, from *ex-* + *rādix* (stem *rādic-*), root.] —**e·rad·i·ca·ble** *adj.* —**e·rad·i·ca·tion** *n.* —**e·rad·i·ca·tive** (ĭ-răd′ĭ-kā′tĭv, -kə-tĭv) *adj.* —**e·rad·i·ca·tor** *n.*

e·rase (ĭ-rās′) *tr.v.* **erased, erasing, erases. 1.** To remove; rub, wipe, scrape, or blot out; efface. **2. a.** To remove (a sound recording) from magnetic tape. **b.** To remove a sound recording from (magnetic tape). **3.** To remove (information) from a computer memory. **4.** To destroy all traces of: *a civilization erased by time.* [Latin *ērādere* (past participle *ērāsus*), to scrape out, scrape off : *ex-,* out + *rādere,* to scrape.] —**e·ras·a·ble** *adj.*
Synonyms: blot, cancel, delete, efface, expunge.

e·ras·er (ĭ-rā′sər) *n.* Something used for erasing writing, especially a piece of rubber.

e·ra·sion (ĭ-rā′zhən, -shən) *n.* **1.** An act of erasing. **2.** *Surgery.* The removal of diseased tissue, especially bone, by scraping.

Er·a·sis·tra·tus of Ce·os (ĕr′ə-sĭs′trə-təs; sē′ŏs′) (*fl.* 3rd century B.C.). Greek physician who described with great accuracy (derived from surgery and post-mortem examinations) many vital organs, especially the heart and liver. He also correctly distinguished between motor and sensory nerves.

E·ras·mus (ĭ-răz′məs), **Desiderius** (*c.*1466–1536). Dutch scholar and humanist who worked to revive classical texts from antiquity and to restore simple Christian faith by the study of the Scriptures. His books *In Praise of Folly* (1509) and *The Handbook of a Christian Knight* (1503) exposed the worldliness of the medieval church.

E·ras·tian·ism (ĭ-răs′chə-nĭz′əm, ĭ-răs′tē-ə-) *n.* A doctrine attributed to the Swiss theologian Thomas Erastus (1524–83) advocating the submission of the church to civil authority in all matters. —**E·ras·tian** *adj. & n.*

e·ra·sure (ĭ-rā′shər) *n.* **1.** An act of erasing. **2.** Something that has been erased; a deletion.

Er·a·to (ĕr′ə-tō′). *Greek Mythology.* The Muse of lyric poetry. [Latin *Eratō,* from Greek, from *eratos,* loved, from *eran,* to love, akin to *erōs*†, love.]

Er·a·tos·the·nes of Cy·re·ne (ĕr′ə-tŏs′thə-nēz′; sī-rē′nē). (*c.* 276–*c.* 194 B.C.). Greek astronomer. He was the first man known to have measured the circumference of the earth, by measuring the sun's position at the summer solstice at different places.

er·bi·um (ûr′bē-əm) *n. Symbol* **Er** A soft, malleable, silvery rare-earth element, used in metallurgy, nuclear research, and to color glass and porcelain. Atomic number 68, atomic weight 167.26, melting point 1,497° C, boiling point 2,900° C, specific gravity 9.051, valence 3. [New Latin, after *Ytterby,* Sweden, where it was discovered.]

ere (âr) *prep. Archaic.* Previous to; before.
~*conj. Archaic.* **1.** Before. **2.** Sooner than; rather than. [Middle English *ar, er,* Old English *ær,* before.]

Er·e·bus (ĕr′ə-bəs). *Greek Mythology.* The dark region beneath the earth through which the dead must pass before they reach Hades. [Latin, from Greek *Erebos.*]

Erebus, Mount. Volcanic mountain (3,794 meters; 12,447 feet) on Ross Island, in the Ross Sea, eastern Antarctica. It was discovered in 1841 by the British explorer James C. Ross.

e·rect (ĭ-rĕkt′) *adj.* **1.** Directed or pointing upward; standing upright; vertical: *erect posture.* **2.** Being in a stiff, rigid condition: *every hair erect.* **3.** *Physiology.* In erection. Said of parts of the body. **4.** *Archaic.* Wide-awake; alert.
~*v.* **erected, erecting, erects.** —*tr.* **1.** To raise (a building, for example); construct: *erect a skyscraper.* **2.** To raise upright; set on end; lift up: *erect a Christmas tree for decorating.* **3.** To put together; fashion; assemble: *erect a child's model airport; erect a theory.* **4.** To set up; establish: *erect a dynasty.* **5.** To transform and exalt: *He erected the editorial into an art form.* **6.** *Geometry.* To construct (an altitude, for example) from or upon a given base. —*intr. Physiology.* To become rigid and upright by filling with blood. [Middle English, from Latin *ērectus,* past participle of *ērigere,* to raise up, set up, erect : *ē-,* out, up, from *ex-* + *regere,* to direct, to set.] —**e·rect′ly** *adv.* —**e·rect′ness** *n.*

e·rec·tile (ĭ-rĕk′təl, -tīl′) *adj.* **1.** Capable of being erected or raised upright. **2.** *Physiology.* Of or pertaining to vascular tissue, such as that of the penis and the clitoris, that is capable of filling with blood and becoming rigid. —**e·rec·til·i·ty** (ĭ-rĕk-tĭl′ə-tē) *n.*

e·rec·tion (ĭ-rĕk′shən) *n.* **1.** The act of erecting. **2.** The state of being erected. **3.** Something erected; especially, a construction or edifice. **4.** *Physiology.* **a.** The firm and enlarged condition of erectile tissue when filled with blood. **b.** The process of filling with blood. **c.** An erect penis.

e·rec·tor, e·rect·er (ĭ-rĕk′tər) *n.* **1.** One that erects. **2.** *Anatomy.* A muscle that causes or maintains the erection of a body part.

E region *n.* A layer of the ionosphere, the **E layer** (*see*).

er·e·mite (ĕr′ə-mīt′) *n.* A person who isolates himself from society, especially as a religious recluse. [Middle English *(h)ermite,* HERMIT.] —**er·e·mit·ic** (ĕr′ə-mĭt′ĭk), **er·e·mit·i·cal** (-ĭ-kəl) *adj.*

e·rep·sin (ĭ-rĕp′sĭn) *n.* A mixture of peptidases in the small intestine that breaks down proteins into amino acids. [Probably Latin *ēr(i)-pere,* to snatch away : *ē-,* away, from *ex-* + *rapere,* to snatch.]

er·e·thism (ĕr′ə-thĭz′əm) *n.* Abnormal irritability and sensibility to stimulation in any part of the body. [French *éréthisme,* from Greek *erethismos,* irritation, annoyance, from *erethizein, erethein†,* to irritate, stir.] —**er·e·this·mic** (ĕr′ə-thĭz′mĭk) *adj.*

erg¹ (ûrg) *n.* A centimeter-gram-second unit of energy or work equal to the work done by a force of one dyne acting over a distance of one centimeter. [Greek *ergon,* work.]

erg² (ârg, ûrg) *n.* An area of shifting sand dunes in the Sahara desert. [Arabic *'irj.*]

er·go (ûr′gō, âr′-) *conj.* Consequently; therefore.
~*adv.* Consequently; hence. [Latin *ergō,* therefore.]

er·go·cal·cif·er·ol (ûr′gō-kăl-sĭf′ə-rôl′, -rŏl′) *n.* vitamin D₂ (*see*). [ERGO(T) + CALCIFEROL.]

er·go·graph (ûr′gə-grăf′, -grăf′) *n.* A device for determining the work capacity and rate of fatigue of a muscle or group of muscles by measuring the extent of movement. [Greek *ergon,* work (see **erg**) + -GRAPH.]

er·gom·e·ter (ûr-gŏm′ə-tər) *n.* An apparatus for measuring the amount of work done by a group of muscles under control conditions. [Greek *ergon,* work (see **erg**) + -METER.] —**er·go·met·ric** (ûr′gə-mĕt′rĭk) *adj.*

er·go·nom·ics (ûr′gə-nŏm′ĭks) *n.* The study of the application of biology and engineering to the relationship between workers and their environment. Also called "biotechnology."

er·gos·ter·ol (ûr-gŏs′tə-rôl′, -rŏl′) *n.* A plant sterol, C₂₈H₄₄O, converted by ultraviolet radiation to vitamin D₂. [ERGO(T) + STEROL.]

er·got (ûr′gət, -gŏt′) *n.* **1.** Any fungus of the genus *Claviceps,* especially *C. purpurea,* infecting various cereal plants, and forming black sclerotia, or compact masses of branching filaments, that replace many of the seeds of the host plant. **2.** The disease caused by such a fungus. **3.** The dried sclerotia of such a fungus, usually obtained from rye seed, and used as a source of several medicinally important alkaloids and as the basic source of lysergic acid. [French, "cock's spur," which the fungus resembles, from Old French *argor, argot†.*]

er·got·ism (ûr′gə-tĭz′əm) *n.* Poisoning by ergot-infected grain, notably rye, characterized by gangrene of the extremities and in some cases convulsions and mental disturbance.

Er·hard (ĕr′härt′) **Ludwig** (1897-1977). Chancellor of West Germany (1963-66). As minister for economic affairs (1949-63), he was the chief architect of the so-called German economic miracle.

er·i·ca (ĕr′ĭ-kə) *n.* Any shrub of the genus *Erica,* which includes the heathers and heaths. [Latin, from Greek *ereikē,* heath.]

Er·ic·son or **Er·ic·sson** (ĕr′ĭk-sən), **Leif** (*fl.* 1000). Norse navigator. According to Norse sagas, on his return from Greenland in 1000 he was blown off course to an unknown land, called Vinland after the vines supposedly growing there. It is thought to lie somewhere between Newfoundland and Virginia.

Er·ic the Red (ĕr′ĭk) (*fl.* 10th century). Norse chieftain who in *c.* 982 sailed west and discovered Greenland. Four years later he established a small colony of about 500 people there.

E·rid·a·nus (ĭ-rĭd′n-əs) *n.* A constellation located in the Southern Hemisphere near Orion and Fornax and containing the star Achernar. [Greek *Ēridanos,* a mythical river associated with the myth of Phaethon.]

E·rie (îr′ē). The fourth-largest of the Great Lakes, between central Canada and the United States.

Erie Canal. An artificial waterway, 580 kilometers (360 miles) long, extending across central New York State from Albany to Buffalo and connecting the Hudson River with Lake Erie. The canal was opened in 1825, but shipping volume declined in the 1860's with the rise of the railroads for long-distance hauling. Much of the canal is now part of the New York State Barge Canal System.

Er·in (ĕr′ĭn). *Poetic.* Ireland. [Middle English *Erin,* from Old Irish *Ērinn,* dative of *Ēriu,* Ireland.]

E·rin·y·es (ĭ-rĭn′ē-ēz′) *pl.n. Greek Mythology.* The Furies. [Latin *Erīnyes,* from Greek *Erinues,* plural of *Erinus†,* a Fury.]

e·ris·tic (ĭ-rĭs′tĭk) *adj.* **1.** Of or relating to argument, controversy, or discord. **2.** Given to argument or dispute, especially when specious; disputatious.
~*n.* **1.** One given to or expert in argument or dispute. **2.** The art or practice of debate. [Greek *eristikos,* eager for strife, from *erizein,* to strive, wrangle, from *eris,* strife, discord.]

Er·i·tre·a (ĕr′ĭ-trē′ə). Province of Ethiopia, mainly desert, bordering the Red Sea. In 1890 it was proclaimed an Italian colony and was used as the stepping-off point for Italy's conquest of Ethiopia in 1935-36. After World War II it was administered by Britain, was federated with Ethiopia in 1952, and by 1962 had become an integral part of Ethiopia. Since then Eritrean rebels have been fighting to win back their independence. —**Er·i·tre·an** *n. & adj.*

erk (ûrk) *n. British Slang.* **1.** A rating in the navy or an aircraftman in the Royal Air Force. **2.** A person one dislikes. [20th century : perhaps a corruption of *A.C.* (aircraftman).]

Er·len·mey·er flask (ûr′lən-mī′ər, âr′-) *n.* A conical laboratory flask with a narrow neck and flat, broad bottom. [Originated by Emil *Erlenmeyer* (1825-1909), German chemist.]

erl·king (ûrl′kĭng′, ârl′-) *n.* An evil spirit of Germanic mythology and folklore, typically represented as abducting children to the land of death. [Partial translation of German *Erlkönig,* "king of alders," coined by Herder in a misunderstanding of Danish *ellerkonge,* variant of *elverkonge,* elf-king : *elver,* elf + *konge,* king.]

er·mine (ûr′mĭn) *n.* **1.** A weasel, *Mustela erminea,* of northern regions, having brownish fur that in winter turns to white with a black tail tip. **2.** The valuable white fur of the ermine, used for ornament, as on the robes of peers or judges. **3.** A stylized representation of ermine fur in heraldry. [Middle English *ermin,* from Old French *ermin,* from Medieval Latin *(mūs) Armenius,* "Armenian (mouse)."]

erne, ern (ûrn) *n.* Any of several sea eagles, especially *Haliaeetus albicella,* of the Old World. [Middle English *ern,* eagle, Old English *earn.*]

Ernst (ĕrnst), **Max** (1891-1976). German painter and sculptor. In 1922 he moved to Paris and became a leading figure in the surrealist movement and an exponent of collage and photomontage.

e·rode (ĭ-rōd′) *v.* **eroded, eroding, erodes.** —*tr.* **1.** To wear down or wear away by or as if by the action of water, ice, wind, or the like. **2.** To destroy gradually; undermine: *His status has been eroded.* **3.** To eat away; corrode. **4.** To make or form by wearing away. —*intr.* To become eroded or worn. [Latin *ērōdere,* to gnaw off, eat away : *ē-,* off, from *ex-* + *rōdere,* to gnaw.]

e·rog·e·nous (ĭ-rŏj′ə-nəs) *adj.* Also **er·o·gen·ic** (ĕr′ə-jĕn′ĭk). Arousing sexual desire; especially, indicating or pertaining to parts of the body sensitive to sexual stimulation: *erogenous zones.* [Greek *erōs†,* desire, sexual love + -GENOUS.]

Er·os¹ (ĕr′ŏs′, îr′-). *Greek Mythology.* The god of love, son of Aphrodite. [Latin *Erōs,* from Greek *erōs†,* love, desire.]

Eros² *n. Psychoanalysis.* **1.** The sum of all self-preservative, as contrasted with self-destructive, instincts. **2.** Sexual drive; libido. [From EROS.]

e·rose (ĭ-rōs′) *adj.* Irregularly notched, toothed, or indented, as if gnawed; jagged: *erose leaves.* [Latin *ērōsus,* past participle of *ērōdere,* to ERODE.]

e·ro·sion (ĭ-rō′zhən) *n.* **1.** The state of being eroded or the process of eroding. **2.** *Geology.* The group of natural processes, including weathering, dissolution, abrasion, and corrosion, all involving transport of material, by which earthy or rocky material is removed from the earth's surface.

e·ro·sive (ĭ-rō′sĭv) *adj.* Causing erosion.

e·rot·ic (ĭ-rŏt′ĭk) *adj.* **1.** Of, concerning, or tending to arouse sexual love or desire: *erotic literature.* **2.** Dominated by sexual love or desire. **3.** Of or caused by love, from *erōs†* (stem *erōt-*), love, desire.] —**e·rot·i·cal·ly** *adv.*

e·rot·i·ca (ĭ-rŏt′ĭ-kə) *pl.n.* Literature or art concerning sex or intended to arouse sexual desire. [New Latin, from Greek *erōtika,* plural of *erōtikos,* EROTIC.]

e·rot·i·cism (ĭ-rŏt′ĭ-sĭz′əm) *n.* Also **er·o·tism** (ĕr′ə-tĭz′əm). **1.** Erotic quality or character. **2. a.** Sexual excitement. **b.** Abnormally persistent sexual excitement. **3.** The use of erotic themes in literature and art, especially to a degree that amounts to preoccupation.

er·o·tol·o·gy (ĕr′ə-tŏl′ə-jē) *n.* **1.** The study of sexual phenomena. **2.** Erotic art and literature; erotica.

ermine The fur of the stoat—a member of the weasel family native to the cooler regions of the Northern Hemisphere—changes from brown to white in winter. The fur, and the animal, are then known as ermine.

e·ro·to·ma·ni·a (ĭ-rō'tə-mā'nē-ə, -măn'yə, ĭ-rŏt'ə-) n. Abnormally strong sexual desire. [New Latin : Greek erōs† (stem erōt-), love + -MANIA.]

err (ûr, ĕr) intr.v. **erred, erring, errs. 1.** To make an error or mistake; be incorrect: We erred on the side of caution. **2.** To violate accepted moral standards; sin. **3.** Archaic. To go astray. [Middle English erren, to wander about, from Old French errer, from Latin errāre.] —**err·ing·ly** adv.

er·ran·cy (ĕr'ən-sē) n., pl. **-cies.** A state or instance of erring; especially, the condition of being in doctrinal error.

er·rand (ĕr'ənd) n. **1.** A short trip taken to convey a message or perform a particular task. **2.** The purpose or object of such a trip: His errand was to mail a letter. [Middle English erend, business, message, from Old English āerende, message, from Germanic arundjam (unattested).]

er·rant (ĕr'ənt) adj. **1.** Roving, especially in search of adventure: knights errant. **2.** Straying from the proper course or standards; erring. [Middle English erraunt, from Old French errant, present participle of both errer, to travel, to look for an adventure, from Vulgar Latin iterāre (unattested), from Late Latin itinerārī, to ITINERATE, and errer, to ERR.] —**er·rant·ly** adv.

er·rant·ry (ĕr'ən-trē) n. The condition of being errant; especially, the conduct or attitudes characteristic of a knight errant.

er·rat·ic (ĭ-răt'ĭk) adj. **1.** Without a fixed or regular course; straying; wandering: an erratic route to the capital. **2.** Deviating from the customary course in conduct or opinion; unconventional; eccentric: erratic behavior. **3.** Lacking consistency, regularity, or uniformity. ~n. Geology. A piece of rock differing from surrounding rocks, having been moved from its original position, especially by glacial action. [Middle English erratik, from Old French erratique, from Latin errāticus, wandering, from errāre, to wander.] —**er·rat·i·cal·ly** adv.

er·ra·tum (ĭ-rä'təm, ĭ-rā'-) n., pl. **-ta** (-tə). An error in printing or writing, especially such an error noted in a list of corrections appended to a book. [Latin errātum, neuter past participle of errāre, to wander, ERR.]

   Usage: The use of errata as if it were singular (an errata . . . the errata is . . . .) is considered unacceptable in standard English. This rule applies even when errata is being used in the collective sense of "a list of errors."

er·rhine (ĕr'īn') adj. Promoting nasal discharge. ~n. An errhine medicine. [Greek errhinos : en-, in + rhis (stem rhin-), nose.]

er·ro·ne·ous (ĭ-rō'nē-əs) adj. Containing or derived from error; mistaken; false. [Middle English, from Old French erroneus or Latin errōneus, wandering, from errāre, to wander, ERR.] —**er·ro·ne·ous·ly** adv. —**er·ro·ne·ous·ness** n.

er·ror (ĕr'ər) n. **1.** An act, assertion, or belief that unintentionally deviates from what is correct, right, or true. **2.** The condition of having mistaken beliefs or false knowledge. **3.** The act or an instance of deviation from an accepted code of behavior. **4.** A mistake: a clerical error. **5.** The difference between a computed or measured value and a correct value. **6. a.** In tennis, a failure to return the ball during play. **b.** In baseball, a defensive fielding or throwing misplay by a player when a play should have resulted in an out or prevented an advance by a base runner. [Middle English errour, from Old French, from Latin error, from errāre, to ERR.]

   Synonyms: blunder, mistake, oversight, slip.

er·satz (ĕr'zäts', ĕr-zäts') adj. **1.** Substitute; artificial: ersatz mink. **2.** Being an inferior imitator or imitation of a specified person or thing: an ersatz Dickens. —See Synonyms at **artificial.** ~n. A substitute; especially, an inferior imitation. [German, from Ersatz, compensation, replacement, from ersetzen, to replace, from Old High German irsezzen : ir- (perfective prefix) + sezzen, to set.]

Erse (ûrs) n. The Gaelic language; **Irish Gaelic** or **Scottish Gaelic** (both of which see). ~adj. Of or pertaining to the Scottish or Irish Celts or their language. [Middle English (Scottish) Erisch, variant of IRISH.]

erst·while (ûrst'hwīl') adj. Former. ~adv. Archaic. Formerly.

er·u·bes·cence (ĕr'ə-bĕs'əns, ĕr'yə-) n. A reddening of the skin; a blush. [Latin ērubēscentia, from ērubēscēns (stem ērubēscent-), present participle of ērubēscere, to blush, to grow red : ē-, out, "completely," from ex- + rubēscere, to grow red, from rubēre, to be red.] —**er·u·bes·cent** adj.

e·ruct (ĭ-rŭkt') v. **eructed, eructing, eructs.** —intr. To belch. —tr. **1.** To belch (gas from the stomach). **2.** To emit (fumes) violently. Used of a volcano. [Latin ēructāre : ē-, out, from ex- + ructāre, to belch.]

e·ruc·ta·tion (ĭ-rŭk'tā'shən, ē'rŭk-) n. **1.** The act or an instance of eructing or belching. **2.** Matter belched forth.

er·u·dite (ĕr'yə-dīt', ĕr'ə-) adj. **1.** Deeply learned. **2.** Characterized by erudition. [Middle English erudit, from Latin ērudītus, past participle of ērudīre, "to take the roughness out of," polish, teach : ē-, out of, from ex- + rudis, rough, RUDE.] —**er·u·dite·ly** adv. —**er·u·dite·ness** n.

er·u·di·tion (ĕr'yə-dĭsh'ən, ĕr'ə-) n. Deep and extensive knowledge, especially when derived from books; profound learning. —See Synonyms at **knowledge.**

e·rum·pent (ĭ-rŭm'pənt) adj. Bursting through or as if through a surface or covering. [Latin ērumpens (stem ērumpent-), present participle of ērumpere, to ERUPT.]

e·rupt (ĭ-rŭpt') v. **erupted, erupting, erupts.** —intr. **1.** To emerge violently from limits or restraint; explode. **2.** To become violently active and discharge lava. Used of a volcano. **3.** To force out or suddenly release something enclosed or pent up: The geyser erupts periodically. **4.** To give sudden and forceful expression to an emotion: The crowd erupted in fury. **5. a.** To pierce the gum. Used of a tooth. **b.** To appear on the skin. Used of a skin blemish. —tr. To eject (steam or lava, for example) violently. [Latin ērumpere (past participle ēruptus), to erupt, to break out, to burst : ē-, out, from ex- + rumpere, to break.] —**e·rup·tive** adj. —**e·rup·tive·ly** adv.

e·rup·tion (ĭ-rŭp'shən) n. **1.** An act, process, or instance of erupting; especially, the discharge of lava from a volcano, or of water or mud from a geyser. **2.** A sudden, often violent outburst. **3. a.** A rash or blemish on the skin. **b.** The passage of a tooth through the gum.

-ery, –ry suffix. Used to form nouns from verbs or other nouns to indicate: **1.** A place for a specified business or activity; for example, **bakery, hatchery. 2.** A specified class of persons; for example, **Jewry. 3.** A collection or class of objects of a specified type; for example, **jewelry, cutlery. 4.** A specified craft, study, or practice; for example, **cookery, husbandry. 5. a.** Certain specified characteristics; for example, **snobbery. b.** A specified kind of behavior; for example, **knavery. 6.** A specified condition or status; for example, **slavery.** [Middle English -erie, from Old French : -er, -ier, from Latin -ārius (see -ary) + -ie, from Latin -ia (see -ia).]

e·ryn·go (ĭ-rĭng'gō) n., pl. **-goes.** Any of several plants of the genus Eryngium, such as the sea holly, having spiny leaves and dense clusters of small bluish flowers. [Latin ēryngion, from Greek ērungion, diminutive of ērungos, eryngo, sea holly, possibly from ēr, ear, spring, in the sense "spring flower."]

er·y·sip·e·las (ĕr'ə-sĭp'ə-ləs, îr'-) n. An acute disease of the skin and subcutaneous tissue caused by a streptococcus and marked by spreading inflammation. Also called "St. Anthony's fire." [Middle English erisipila, herisipila, from Latin erysipelas, from Greek erusipelas, "red skin" : eruthros, red + -pelas, skin.] —**er·y·si·pel·a·tous** (ĕr'ə-sĭ-pĕl'ə-təs, îr'-) adj.

er·y·sip·e·loid (ĕr'ə-sĭp'ə-loid', îr'-) n. An infectious disease of the hands characterized by red lesions and caused by the bacterium Erysipelothrix rhusiopathiae, found in infected meat or fish. [ERYSIPEL(AS) + -OID.]

er·y·the·ma (ĕr'ə-thē'mə) n. A redness of the skin, due to dilation of the blood capillaries, that may be caused by toxins in the blood, heat, infection, or injury. [New Latin, from Greek eruthēma, from eruthainein, to be red, from eruthros, red.] —**er·y·them·a·tous** (ĕr'ə-thĕm'ə-təs, -thē'mə-təs), **er·y·the·mat·ic** (-thī-măt'ĭk), **er·y·the·mic** (-thē'mĭk) adj.

e·ryth·rism (ĭ-rĭth'rĭz'əm) n. Unusual redness of pigmentation, as of hair or plumage. [ERYTHR(O)- + -ISM.] —**er·y·thris·mal** (ĕr'ə-thrĭz'məl) adj.

e·ryth·rite (ĭ-rĭth'rīt') n. A reddish mineral, the hydrated arsenate of cobalt, used in coloring glass. [ERYTHR(O)- + -ITE.]

erythro-, erythr– prefix. Indicates red; for example, **erythrocyte, erythrite.** [From Greek eruthros, red.]

e·ryth·ro·blast (ĭ-rĭth'rə-blăst', -blăst') n. Any of the nucleated cells in bone marrow that develop into erythrocytes. [ERYTHRO- + -BLAST.] —**e·ryth·ro·blas·tic** (ĭ-rĭth'rə-blăs'tĭk) adj.

e·ryth·ro·cyte (ĭ-rĭth'rə-sīt') n. The nonnucleated, disk-shaped blood cell containing the red pigment hemoglobin, which transports oxygen and carbon dioxide around the body. It is responsible for the color of the blood. Also called "red blood cell." [ERYTHRO- -CYTE.] —**e·ryth·ro·cyt·ic** (ĭ-rĭth'rə-sĭt'ĭk) adj.

e·ryth·ro·cy·tom·e·ter (ĭ-rĭth'rə-sī-tŏm'ə-tər) n. An apparatus for counting the number of erythrocytes in a blood sample. [ERYTHROCYT(E) + -METER.]

e·ryth·ro·my·cin (ĭ-rĭth'rə-mī'sĭn) n. An antibiotic agent from cultures of the bacterium Streptomyces erythreus, effective especially against Gram-positive bacteria. [ERYTHRO- + -MYCIN.]

Erz·ge·bir·ge (ĕrts'gə-bîr'gə). A mountain range on the border between Czechoslovakia and East Germany. It is rich in mineral resources, including uranium, lead, zinc, tin, copper, and wolframite. The highest point is Klínovec (1,245 meters; 4,800 feet), in Czechoslovakia.

Es The symbol for the element einsteinium.

-es¹ suffix. Indicates the plural form, for which it is used in nouns ending in a sibilant or an affricate and in some nouns ending in a vowel or a postconsonantal y; for example, **trusses, switches, cargoes, ladies.** Compare **-s** (in nouns). [Middle English -es, -s, -s (plural).]

-es² suffix. Indicates the third person singular form of the present indicative, for which it is used in most verbs ending in a sibilant, an affricate, a vowel, or a postconsonantal y; for example, **guesses, rushes, does, defies.** Compare **-s** (in verbs). [Middle English -es, -s, -s (third person singular indicative suffix).]

E·sa·ki diode (ĭ-sä'kē) n. Electronics. A **tunnel diode** (see).

E·sau (ē'sô'). The son of Isaac and Rebecca, who sold his birthright to his brother Jacob. Genesis 25:25. [Late Latin Ēsau, from Greek, from Hebrew 'Ēsāw, "hairy."]

ESCA (ĕ'ĕs'sē'ä') n. A technique for analyzing or investigating chemical compounds by irradiating them with x-rays and monitoring the characteristic energy spectrum of electrons emitted. [Electron spectroscopy for chemical analysis.]

es·ca·lade (ĕs'kə-lād', -läd') n. The act of scaling a fortified wall or rampart, especially during an assault. [French, from Italian scalata, from scalare, to climb, from scala, ladder, from Late Latin scāla, from Latin scālae, steps.] —**es·ca·lade** v.

es·ca·late (ĕs′kə-lāt′) v. **-lated, -lating, -lates.** —*tr.* To increase, enlarge, or intensify; especially, to increase the scale or intensity of (a conflict). —*intr.* To increase in intensity or extent. [Back-formation from ESCALATOR.] —**es·ca·la·tion** n.

es·ca·la·tor (ĕs′kə-lā′tər) n. **1.** A moving stairway consisting of steps attached to a continuously circulating belt, for moving passengers up and down between floors. Also called "moving staircase." **2.** An escalator clause. [Originally a trademark : perhaps *escala*de + elevator.]

escalator clause n. A provision in a contract stipulating an increase or decrease, as in wages, benefits, or prices, under certain conditions, such as changes in the cost of living or in production costs. Also called "escalator."

es·cal·lo·ni·a (ĕs′kə-lō′nē-ə) n. Any evergreen shrub of the South American genus *Escallonia*, cultivated for its red or white flowers. [After *Escallon*, 18th-century Spanish traveler who discovered it.]

escallop. Variant of **scallop.**

es·ca·pade (ĕs′kə-pād′) n. **1. a.** An act of breaking loose from restraint. **b.** A flight from confining rules. **2.** A carefree or reckless adventure; a fling or a caper. [French, from Old French, from Old Italian *scappata,* from the feminine past participle of *scappare,* to escape, from Vulgar Latin *excappāre* (unattested), to ESCAPE.]

es·cape (ĭ-skāp′) v. **-caped, -caping, -capes.** Also *archaic* **scape** (skāp), **scaped, scap·ing, scapes.** —*intr.* **1.** To break loose from confinement; get free: *The prisoner escaped.* **2.** To issue from confinement or an enclosure; leak or seep out. **3.** To succeed in avoiding capture, danger, or harm. **4.** To grow beyond a cultivated area or a condition of cultivation. Used of plants. —*tr.* **1. a.** To break loose from; get free of. **b.** To succeed in avoiding (capture, danger, or harm). **2. a.** To elude the comprehension of: *The meaning of this cryptic note escapes me.* **b.** To elude the attention, memory, or detection of: *The mistake escaped my notice.* **3.** To issue involuntarily from: *A regretful sigh escaped her lips.*
~n. **1.** The act or an instance of escaping. **2.** A means of escaping. **3. a.** Temporary freedom from worry, care, or unpleasantness. **b.** A means of obtaining this: *Television is his escape from worry.* **4.** A gradual and accidental pouring out or leaking from an enclosure, as a container; leakage: *an escape of gas.* **5.** A cultivated plant that has become established away from cultivation.
~adj. **1.** Affording a means of escape, especially in an emergency: *an escape hatch.* **2.** Providing a legal basis for avoiding liability or responsibility: *an escape clause.* [Middle English *escapen,* from Old North French *escaper,* "to take off one's cloak," to emerge from restraint, escape, from Vulgar Latin *excappāre* (unattested) : *ex-,* out, off + Late Latin *cappa,* cloak, hood (see **cape**).] —**es·cap·a·ble** adj. —**es·cap·er** n.
Synonyms: avoid, elude, eschew, evade, shun.

es·cap·ee (ĭ-skā′pē′, ĕs′kā-) n. One that has escaped; especially, an escaped prisoner.

es·cape·ment (ĭ-skāp′mənt) n. **1.** A mechanism consisting in general of an escape wheel and anchor, used especially in timepieces to control the wheel movement and to provide periodic energy impulses to a pendulum or balance. **2.** The mechanism in a typewriter that controls the lateral movement of the carriage. **3.** An escape. **4.** A means of escape.

escape velocity n. The minimum velocity that a body, such as a space rocket, must attain to overcome the gravitational attraction of another body, such as the earth.

escape wheel n. The rotating notched wheel periodically engaged and disengaged by the anchor in the escapement of a timepiece.

es·cap·ism (ĭ-skā′pĭz′əm) n. The habit or tendency of seeking escape from unpleasant realities in self-deceiving fantasy or entertainment. —**es·cap·ist** adj. & n.

es·cap·ol·o·gist (ĕs′kā-pŏl′ə-jĭst, ĭ-skā′-) n. A person who escapes from confinement, usually as a form of public entertainment. —**es·cap·ol·o·gy** n.

es·car·got (ĕs′kär-gō′) n., pl. **-gots** (-gō′). An edible snail, especially when cooked. [French, a snail, from Old French, from Old Provençal *escaragol†.*]

es·carp (ĭ-skärp′) n. **1.** A steep slope or cliff; an escarpment. **2.** The inner wall of a ditch or trench dug around a fortification.
~tr.v. **escarped, -carping, -carps.** To cut or erode so as to form a steep slope. [French *escarpe,* from Old French, from Italian *scarpa,* SCARP.]

es·carp·ment (ĭ-skärp′mənt) n. **1.** A steep slope or long cliff resulting from erosion or faulting and separating two relatively level areas of differing elevations. **2.** The steeper slope of an asymmetrical ridge, especially one formed when gently dipping rock strata are denuded differentially. **3.** A steep slope in front of a fortification.

Escaut. See **Scheldt.**

-escence suffix. Indicates a beginning or continuing state; for example, *opalescence, luminescence.* [Old French, from Latin *-ēscentia,* from *-ēscēns* (stem *-ēscent-*), -ESCENT.]

-escent suffix. Indicates beginning to be or exhibit; for example, *luminescent, phosphorescent.* [Old French, from Latin *-ēscēns* (stem *-ēscent-*), present participial suffix of *-ēscere,* chiefly inceptives of verbs in *-ēre.* See **-ent.**]

esch·a·lot (ĕsh′ə-lŏt′) n. A shallot. [French *eschalote,* from obsolete French *eschalotte,* SHALLOT.]

es·char (ĕs′kär′) n. A dry scab or slough formed on the skin as a result of a burn or by the action of a corrosive or caustic substance. [Middle English *escare,* scab, SCAR.]

es·cha·rot·ic (ĕs′kə-rŏt′ĭk) adj. Producing or capable of producing an eschar.
~n. An escharotic substance or drug.

es·cha·tol·o·gy (ĕs′kə-tŏl′ə-jē) n. The branch of theology that is concerned with the ultimate or last things, such as death, judgment, heaven, and hell. [Greek *eskhatos,* last, extreme + -LOGY.] —**es·chat·o·log·i·cal** (ĭ-skăt′l-ŏj′ĭ-kəl, ĕs′kə-tə-lŏj′-) adj. —**es·cha·tol·o·gist** n.

es·cheat (ĭs-chēt′) n. **1.** The reversion of land held under feudal tenure to the manor in the absence of legal heirs or claimants. **2.** The reversion of property to the state in the absence of legal heirs or claimants. **3.** Land or property that has reverted in the absence of legal heirs or claimants.
~v. **escheated, -cheating, -cheats.** —*intr.* To revert to the state by escheat. —*tr.* To cause (property) to revert to the state by escheat. [Middle English *eschete,* from Old French *eschete, escheoite,* from *escheoit,* past participle of *escheoir,* to fall out, from Vulgar Latin *excadēre* (unattested) : Latin *ex-,* out + *cadere,* to fall.] —**es·cheat·a·ble** adj.

es·cheat·age (ĭs-chē′tĭj) n. The right of the state to acquire property by escheat.

es·chew (ĭs-chōō′) tr.v. **-chewed, -chewing, -chews. 1.** To take care to avoid; shun. **2.** To abstain from. —See Synonyms at **escape.** [Middle English *escheuen, eschiuen,* from Old French *eschiver, eschiuver,* to shun, to avoid, from Vulgar Latin *scivāre* (unattested), from Germanic *skiuhwan* (unattested), from *skiuhwaz* (unattested), SHY.] —**es·chew·al** n.

Es·cof·fier (ĕs′kô-fyā′), **Auguste** (c. 1846–1935). French chef. His reputation as "the king of chefs and the chef of kings" was made chiefly in England.

es·co·lar (ĕs′kə-lär′) n., pl. **-lars** or collectively **escolar.** Any of several slender carnivorous fishes of the family Gempylidae, of warm marine waters. Also called "snake mackerel." [Spanish, "scholar" (from the spectaclelike rings around its eyes), from Late Latin *scholāris,* SCHOLAR.]

Es·co·ri·al, El (ĕ-skôr′ē-əl). Granite palace and monastery near Madrid in Spain, one of the world's great architectural monuments. It was begun by Juan Bautista de Toledo in 1563 and completed by Juan de Herrera (1530–97) in 1584.

es·cort (ĕs′kôrt′) n. **1.** One or more persons accompanying another to give guidance or protection or as a mark of honor. **2.** One or more guards, often armed, traveling with important persons or goods. **3.** A man who is the companion of a woman, especially on a social occasion. **4. a.** One or more vehicles accompanying another vehicle to guide, protect, or honor its passengers. **b.** A warship or plane or a group of warships or planes used to defend or protect other craft from enemy attack. **5.** The state of being accompanied by an escort.
~tr.v. (ĭ-skôrt′, ĕ-skôrt′, ĕs′kôrt′) **escorted, -corting, -corts.** To accompany as an escort. —See Synonyms at **accompany.** [French *escorte,* from Old French *(e)scorte,* from Old Italian *scorta,* guide, an escorting, from the feminine past participle of *scorgere,* to show, to guide, from Vulgar Latin *excorrigere* (unattested), to conduct, guide, escort : Latin *ex-,* out + *corrigere,* to set right, CORRECT.]

escort agency n. An agency that provides male or female partners for social outings.

e·scribe (ĭ-skrīb′) tr.v. **escribed, escribing, escribes.** To draw (a circle or other curve) touching one side of a triangle or other plane figure and the extensions of the two adjacent sides. [EX- (out) + Latin *scribere,* to write.]

es·cri·toire (ĕs′krĭ-twär′) n. A writing desk, especially one consisting of a stand or chest of drawers surmounted by smaller drawers or compartments that are concealed by a hinged lid that when opened provides a writing surface. [French, from Old French *escriptoire,* a study, from Medieval Latin *scriptorium,* SCRIPTORIUM.]

es·crow (ĕs′krō′, ĕ-skrō′) n. **1. a.** A written agreement, such as a deed or bond, put into the custody of a third party and not in effect until certain conditions are fulfilled by the grantee. **b.** Money or property held in this way. **2.** The condition of being ineffective until certain conditions are fulfilled: *a deed held in escrow.* [Old French *escroe,* strip of parchment, scroll, from Frankish *scrōda* (unattested), piece.]

es·cu·do (ĭ-skōō′dō) n., pl. **-dos. 1. a.** The basic monetary unit of Portugal, equal to 100 centavos. **b.** The basic monetary unit of Cape Verde, equal to 100 centavos. **2.** A coin worth one escudo. See feature at **currency.** [Portuguese and Spanish, "shield," from Latin *scūtum,* shield.]

es·cu·lent (ĕs′kyə-lənt) adj. Suitable for eating; edible.
~n. Something edible, as a vegetable. [Latin *esculentus,* from *esca,* food, from *edere,* to eat.]

es·cutch·eon (ĭ-skŭch′ən) n. Also **scutch·eon** (skŭch′ən). **1.** A shield or shield-shaped emblem bearing a coat of arms. **2.** An ornamental or protective shield-shaped object, as a movable plate covering a keyhole or a plate on which a door knocker is mounted. **3.** *Nautical.* The ornamented plate in the middle of a ship's stern inscribed with the ship's name and home port. [Middle English *escochon,* from Old French *escuchon, escusson,* from Vulgar Latin *scūtiō* (stem *scūtiōn-*) (unattested), from Latin *scūtum,* shield.] —**es·cutch·eoned** adj.

Es·dra·e·lon (ĕz′drə-ē′lən). One of the most fertile plains in Israel. It stretches about 40 kilometers (25 miles) from the coastal lowland near Mt. Carmel to the Jordan River valley.

Es·dras (ĕz′drəs) n. Abbr. **Esd. 1.** Either of the first two books of the

escapement *A facsimile of Galileo's escapement, the mechanism that regulates the action of a traditional clock or watch.*

Apocrypha, I Esdras and II Esdras, called in the Douay Bible III Esdras and IV Esdras. **2.** Either of two books of the Douay Bible Old Testament, I Esdras and II Esdras, corresponding to the books Ezra and Nehemiah in the King James Bible and other versions.

ESE east-southeast.

-ese *suffix.* Indicates: **1.** A native or inhabitant; for example, **Sudanese. 2.** A language or dialect; for example, **Japanese. 3.** A literary style or diction; for example, **journalese.** In this sense, usually used derogatorily. [Old French *-eis* and Italian *-ese,* from Latin *-ēnsis,* "originating in."]

es·er·ine (ĕs'ə-rēn') *n.* Biochemistry. **Physostigmine** (see). [*Eser-,* native African name + -INE.]

es·ker (ĕs'kər) *n.* Also **es·kar** (ĕs'kär', -kər). A long, narrow ridge of sand and gravel deposited by a stream flowing between a valley glacier and the valley wall, or in a tunnel under a retreating glacial ice sheet. Also called "os." [Irish *eiscir,* ridge, from Old Irish *escir†.*]

Es·ki·mo (ĕs'kə-mō') *n., pl.* **-mos** or collectively **Eskimo.** Also **Es·qui·mau** *pl.* **-maux** (-mōz'). *Abbr.* **Esk. 1.** A member of a people native to the Arctic coastal regions of North America and to parts of Greenland and northeastern Siberia. **2.** The language spoken by this people.
~ *adj.* Also **Esquimau.** *Abbr.* **Esk.** Of, pertaining to, or concerning the Eskimos or their language. [Earlier *Esquimawes,* perhaps from Micmac *eskameege,* to eat raw fish : Proto-Algonquian *ašk-* (unattested), "raw" + *-amekw-* (unattested), "fish."]

Es·ki·mo-Al·e·ut (ĕs'kə-mō-ăl'ē-ōōt') *n.* A family of languages spoken chiefly among peoples native to the Arctic coastal regions of North America, Greenland, the Aleutian Islands, and the northeastern tip of Siberia.

Eskimo dog *n.* A large dog of a breed used in Arctic regions as a sled dog, having a thick coat and a plumed tail.

e·soph·a·gus, oe·soph·a·gus (ĭ-sŏf'ə-gəs) *n., pl.* **-gi** (-jī'). A muscular, membranous tube for the passage of food from the pharynx to the stomach. [Middle English *ysophagus,* from Greek *oisophagos,* gullet.] **—e·soph·a·ge·al** (ĭ-sŏf'ə-jē'əl) *adj.*

es·o·ter·ic (ĕs'ə-tĕr'ĭk) *adj.* **1.** Intended for, limited to, or understood by only a small group. Compare **exoteric.** *an esoteric cult.* **2.** Difficult to understand; abstruse: *The theory remained esoteric despite efforts to popularize it.* **3.** Not publicly disclosed; confidential. [Late Latin *esōtericus,* from Greek *esōterikos,* from *esōterō,* comparative of *esō,* within.] **—es·o·ter·i·cal·ly** *adv.*

ESP (ē'ĕs-pē') *n.* Extrasensory perception.

esp. especially.

es·pa·drille (ĕs'pə-drĭl') *n.* A light shoe having a rope or fiber sole and a canvas upper part. [French, variant of *espardille,* from Provençal *espardilho,* diminutive of *espart,* esparto, from Latin *spartum,* ESPARTO.]

es·pal·ier (ĭ-spăl'yər, -yā') *n.* **1.** A tree or shrub that is trained to grow flat against a wall, often in a symmetrical pattern. **2.** A framework, as a trellis, on which an espalier is grown.
~ *tr.v.* **espaliered, -iering, -iers.** To train (a plant) on an espalier. [French, from Italian *spalliera,* applied to shoulder supports, hence stakes of that height, from *spalla,* shoulder, from Latin *spatula,* broad piece, flat piece. See **spatula.**]

es·par·to (ĭ-spär'tō) *n., pl.* **-tos.** A tough, wiry grass, *Stipa tenacissima,* of Spain and northern Africa, yielding a fiber used in making paper and as cordage. [Spanish, from Latin *spartum,* from Greek *sparton,* rope, cable, esparto.]

es·pe·cial (ĭ-spĕsh'əl) *adj.* **1.** Outstanding; exceptional: *of especial value.* **2.** Pertaining uniquely to one person, group, or thing; particular: *her own especial quality.* **—See Usage note at special.** [Middle English, from Old French, from Latin *speciālis,* from *speciēs,* a view, appearance.]

es·pe·cial·ly (ĭ-spĕsh'ə-lē) *adv.* *Abbr.* **esp.** To an extent or degree deserving of special emphasis; particularly.

Es·pe·ran·to (ĕs'pə-rän'tō, -rän'tō) *n.* An artificial international language, invented in 1887, characterized by a vocabulary based on word roots common to many European languages, a single, unvarying ending for each principal part of speech, and a regularized system of conjugation and inflection. [After Dr. *Esperanto* ("one who hopes"), pen name of Lazarus Ludwig Zamenhof (1859-1917), Polish philologist.]

es·pi·al (ĭ-spī'əl) *n.* **1.** The act of catching sight of something. **2.** The act of watching, especially in secret. **3.** The fact of being seen or noticed. [Middle English *espiaille,* from Old French, from *espier,* to watch; to spy.]

es·pi·o·nage (ĕs'pē-ə-näzh', -näj', -nĭj) *n.* The practice of spying or using spies to obtain secret information about the activities and plans of another government or rival group. [French *espionnage,* from Old French, from *espionner,* to spy, from *espion,* spy, from Old Italian *spione,* from *spia,* spy, from Germanic.]

es·pla·nade (ĕs'plə-näd', -nād') *n.* **1.** A flat, open, often paved stretch of ground used as a promenade; especially, such a promenade along the shore. **2.** A level area in front of a fortification. [French, from Italian *spianala,* from *spianare,* to level, from *explānāre,* to flatten, EXPLAIN.]

es·pou·sal (ĭ-spou'zəl) *n.* **1.** An espousing or adoption, as of an idea or cause. **2. a.** A betrothal. **b.** A wedding.

es·pouse (ĭ-spouz') *tr.v.* **-poused, -pousing, -pouses. 1.** To take in marriage; marry. **2.** To give (a woman) in marriage. **3.** To adopt and support (a cause, belief, or the like). [Middle English *espousen,* from Old French *espouser,* from Late Latin *spōnsāre,* from Latin

spondēre (past participle *spōnsus*), to promise solemnly.]

es·pres·so (ĭ-sprĕs'ō) *n., pl.* **-sos.** A strong coffee brewed by forcing steam or hot water under pressure through long-roasted, powdered beans. [Italian (*caffè*) *espresso,* "pressed out (coffee)," from the past participle of *esprimere,* to press out, express, from Latin *exprimere* : *ex-,* out + *premere,* to PRESS.]

es·prit (ĕ-sprē') *n.* **1.** Spirit. **2.** Liveliness of mind and expression; wit. [French, from Latin *spīritus,* SPIRIT.]

esprit de corps (də kôr', kōr') *n.* A spirit of devotion and enthusiasm among members of a group for one another, their group, and its purposes. [French, "spirit of (the) body."]

esprit d'es·cal·ier (dĕs'kăl-yā') *n.* A witty retort that occurs to one too late. [French, "spirit of (the) stairs."]

es·py (ĭ-spī') *tr.v.* **-pied, -pying, -pies.** To catch sight of; glimpse (something distant or partly obscured): *"Through one of the rents of his gown, you espied a fat capon hung round the monk's waist"* (Henry James). **—See Synonyms at see.** [Middle English *(e)spien,* from Old French *espier,* from SPY.]

Esq. Esquire (title).

-esque *suffix.* Indicates possession of a specified manner or quality; for example, **statuesque, Kafkaesque.** [French, from Italian *-esco,* from Germanic *-iskaz* (unattested). See also **-ish.**]

Es·qui·line (ĕs'kwə-līn'). One of the seven hills of Rome.

Esquimau. Variant of **Eskimo.**

es·quire (ĕs'kwīr', ĭ-skwīr') *n.* **1.** A candidate for knighthood in medieval times, serving a knight as attendant and shield-bearer; a squire. **2.** Formerly, a member of the English gentry ranking just below a knight. **3.** *Esquire. Abbr.* **Esq.** Used as a title of courtesy after a man's full name: *Martin Chuzzlewit, Esq.* [Middle English *esquier, esquire,* from Old French *esquier, escuier,* squire, "shield-carrier," from Late Latin *scūtārius,* from Latin *scūtum,* shield.]
Usage: The term *Esquire,* and its abbreviation *Esq.,* traditionally reserved for men, is now sometimes used in correspondence addressed to women, especially female attorneys: *Jane Roe, Esq.*

ESR electron spin resonance.

ess (ĕs) *n.* The letter *s.*

-ess *suffix.* Indicates a female; for example, **heiress, lioness.** [Middle English *-esse,* from Old French *-esse,* from Late Latin *-issa,* from Greek.]
Usage: The use of this suffix is changing in the wake of changing attitudes to feminine roles in society. Originally the suffix simply indicated female gender and had no additional overtones; a *poetess* was simply a female poet. These days several *-ess* forms are considered pejorative. Strongly disliked are *Negress* and *Jewess;* less pejorative are *authoress, poetess, sculptress,* and the like. Several words, such as *waitress, actress,* and *heiress,* remain relatively unaffected, but even these can become a focus of contention on occasion. See also Usage note at **person.**

Ess. Essex.

es·say (ĕ-sā', ĕs'ā') *tr.v.* **-sayed, -saying, -says. 1.** To make an attempt at; try, especially in a tentative manner. **2.** To subject to a test; try out.
~ *n.* (ĕs'ā', ĕ-sā' *for senses 1, 3;* ĕs'ā' *for sense 2*). **1.** An attempt; an endeavor. **2. a.** A short literary composition on a single subject, usually presenting the personal views of the author. **b.** An academic composition by a student on a set subject. **3.** A testing or trial. [Middle English, from Old French *essaier, assaier,* from *essai, assai,* a trial, from Vulgar Latin *exagiāre* (unattested), to weigh out, from Late Latin *exagium,* a weighing, from Latin *exigere,* to weigh out, examine. See **exact.**] **—es·say·er** *n.*

es·say·ist (ĕs'ā'ĭst) *n.* A writer of essays.

Es·sen (ĕs'ən). Industrial city on the Ruhr River, North Rhine-Westphalia, West Germany. In the second half of the 19th century it became one of Germany's leading manufacturing towns.

es·sence (ĕs'əns) *n.* **1.** The quality or qualities of a thing that give it its identity; the intrinsic or indispensable properties of a thing: *"Government and Law, in their very essence, consist of restrictions on freedom"* (Bertrand Russell). **2.** The most important ingredient; the crucial element. **3.** *Philosophy.* The inherent, unchanging nature of a thing or class of things, as distinguished from its attributes or its existence. **4. a.** An extract of a substance that retains its fundamental or most desirable properties in concentrated form. **b.** Such an extract in a solution of alcohol. **c.** A perfume or scent. **d.** A flavoring. **5.** An embodiment or personification: *the essence of kindness.* **6.** A spiritual or incorporeal entity. **—of the essence.** Of supreme importance: *Speed is of the essence if we are to finish the job on time.* [Middle English *essence, essencia,* from Old French *essence,* from Latin *essentia,* from *esse,* to be.]

Es·sene (ĕs'ēn', ĭ-sēn') *n.* A member of an ascetic Jewish sect that existed in ancient Palestine from the 2nd century B.C. to the 3rd century A.D. **—Es·se·ni·an** (ĕ-sē'nē-ən), **Es·sen·ic** (ĕ-sĕn'ĭk) *adj.*

es·sen·tial (ĭ-sĕn'shəl) *adj.* **1.** Constituting or part of the essence of something: *the essential simplicity of the idea.* **2.** Of basic importance; indispensable: *essential ingredients.* **3.** Constituting or containing an essence of a plant, liquid, or other substance. **—See Synonyms at necessary.**
~ *n.* A fundamental, necessary, or indispensable part, item, or principle. [Middle English, from Late Latin *essentiālis.* See **essence, -ial.**] **—es·sen·ti·al·i·ty** (ĭ-sĕn'shē-ăl'ə-tē), **es·sen·tial·ness** *n.* **—es·sen·tial·ly** *adv.*

essential amino acid *n.* Any of eight amino acids that must be included in the human diet, since they cannot be synthesized by the body.

essential oil *n.* A volatile oil, usually having the characteristic odor or flavor of the plant from which it is obtained, used to make perfumes and flavorings.

Es·sex (ĕs'ĭks). *Abbr.* **Ess.** Originally an early kingdom of Anglo-Saxon England, it was settled by Saxons, probably early in the 6th century. It is now a county in southeastern England; its administrative center is Chelmsford.

Essex, Robert Devereux, 2nd Earl of (1566–1601). English courtier and man of arms. He was a favorite at the court of Elizabeth I but imperiled his position by marrying Sir Philip Sidney's widow in 1590 and scheming to overthrow the queen's principal adviser, Lord Burghley. His part in a rising of the people of London led to his arrest and execution for treason.

es·so·nite (ĕs'ə-nīt') *n.* Also **hes·son·ite** (hĕs'-). A reddish-brown variety of garnet. Also called "cinnamon stone." [French, from Greek *hēssōn,* inferior to, less than (it is less hard than true hyacinth), from *hēka,* a little, slightly.]

EST, E.S.T. Eastern Standard Time.

est. **1.** established. **2.** *Law.* estate. **3.** estimate; estimated.

–est¹ *suffix.* Indicates the superlative degree of adjectives and adverbs; for example, **greatest, earliest.** [Middle English *-est,* Old English *-est, -ost,* from Common Germanic *-istaz* (unattested).]

–est², –st *suffix.* Indicates the archaic second person singular form of the present and past indicative tenses, with the pronoun *thou;* for example, **comest, didst.** [Middle English *-est,* Old English *-est, -ast.*]

es·tab·lish (ĭ-stăb'lĭsh) *tr.v.* **-lished, -lishing, -lishes.** Also *archaic* **stab·lish** (stăb'lĭsh). **1.** To settle (a person) permanently or securely in a position or condition; install. **2.** To found or set up on a lasting basis: *establish a business.* **3.** To bring about; create: *establish order.* **4.** To introduce or institute (laws, for example). **5.** To turn (a church or religion) into a national institution. **6. a.** To gain recognition for or acceptance of: *The book established his reputation.* **b.** To make familiar to a reader or audience: *establish a character.* **7.** To prove the validity or truth of: *establish the facts.* **8.** *Card Games.* To gain control of (a suit) so that all remaining tricks can be won. —See Synonyms at **confirm.** [Middle English *establissen,* from Old French *establir* (stem *establiss-*), from Latin *stabilīre,* to make firm, from *stabilis,* firm.] **—es·tab·lish·er** *n.*

established church *n.* A church that is officially recognized and given support as a national institution by a government.

es·tab·lish·ment (ĭ-stăb'lĭsh-mənt) *n.* **1.** The act of establishing. **2.** The condition or fact of being established. **3. a.** An institution, such as a business, club, or hotel. **b.** The premises of such an institution. **c.** The permanent staff of such an institution. **d.** An organized group, such as a government, political party, or military force. **4. a.** A place of residence. **b.** Those living and working in it. **5.** An established church. **6. Establishment. a.** The people and institutions, such as prominent politicians, financiers, the armed forces, and the civil service, that collectively constitute the power structure of a given society and are regarded as exerting a strongly conservative influence. **b.** A powerful group that tacitly controls a specified field of activity, usually in a conservative manner: *the literary Establishment.*

es·tab·lish·men·tar·i·an (ĭ-stăb'lĭsh-mĕn-târ'ē-ən) *adj.* **1.** Of or pertaining to an established church. **2.** Advocating the introduction or continuance of an established church. **—es·tab·lish·men·tar·i·an** *n.* **—es·tab·lish·men·tar·i·an·ism** *n.*

es·ta·mi·net (ĕ-stä'mē-nā') *n.* A small café. [French.]

es·tan·cia (ĕ-stäns'yä) *n.* A large estate or cattle ranch in Latin America. [American Spanish, from Spanish, room, enclosure, from Vulgar Latin *stantia* (unattested), a standing (thing), from Latin *stāns* (stem *stant-*), present participle of *stāre,* to stand.]

es·tate (ĭ-stāt') *n.* **1. a.** A sizable piece of rural land, usually with a large house. **b.** Such a piece of land used for the cultivation of crops such as tobacco or rubber; plantation. **2.** *British.* An area developed for a specific use, such as housing or factories: *an industrial estate.* **3.** The whole of one's possessions; especially, all of the property and debts left by a deceased or bankrupt person. **4.** *Law. Abbr.* **est.** The nature and extent of an owner's rights with respect to his property and its use. **5.** A stage in one's development or maturation: *"When that I reached a man's estate"* (Shakespeare). **6. a.** A condition of life, wealth, or status; rank. **b.** High rank or status: *gentlemen of estate.* **7.** A class of citizens, as the nobility, that formerly possessed distinct political rights. Often called Estates of the Realm. [Middle English *estat,* state, condition, from Old French, STATE.]

estate agent *n. British.* One who handles the advertising and sale of buildings and land.

estate car *n. British.* A station wagon *(see).*

Es·tates-Gen·er·al (ĭ-stāts' jĕn'ər-əl) *n.* The **States-General** *(see).* [Translation of French *états généraux.*]

Es·te (ĕs'tā). Distinguished Italian family, celebrated as patrons of art. The line was founded by Oberto, who was invested with the fief of Este by the emperor Otto I. His descendants were the rulers of Ferrara (1240-1597) and Modena (1288-1796).

es·teem (ĭ-stēm') *tr.v.* **-teemed, -teeming, -teems. 1.** To regard as of a high order; think of with respect; prize: *Oysters were much esteemed as a delicacy.* **2.** To judge to be; regard as; consider. —See Synonyms at **appreciate.**
~*n.* **1.** Favorable regard; respect: *He is held in high esteem.* **2.** *Archaic.* Judgment; opinion. —See Synonyms at **regard.** [Middle

English *estemen,* from Old French *estimer,* from Latin *aestimāre,* to ESTIMATE.]

es·ter (ĕs'tər) *n.* Any of a class of organic compounds derived from an acid by the replacement of hydrogen by an alkyl radical. Esters, which are analogous to inorganic salts, are formed by reaction of acids with alcohols. [German *Ester,* short for *Essigäther,* "vinegar ether" : *Essig,* vinegar, from Middle High German *ezzich,* from Old High German *ezzīh,* from Latin *acētum* + *Äther,* from Latin *aethēr,* ETHER.]

es·ter·ase (ĕs'tə-rās', -rāz') *n.* An enzyme that catalyzes the hydrolysis of an ester.

Es·ter·há·zy (ĕs'tər-hä'zē), **Nikolaus Joseph, Prince Esterházy von Galantha** (1714–90). Member of a princely Hungarian family, famous for his association with Haydn, whom he appointed musical director at the Esterházy seat of Eisenstadt in 1766.

es·ter·i·fy (ĕ-stĕr'ə-fī') *v.* **-fied, -fying, -fies.** *Chemistry.* —*intr.* To change to an ester. —*tr.* To change (a compound) into an ester.

Es·ther (ĕs'tər) *n.* A book of the Old Testament recounting the story of Esther, the Jewish queen of Persia who saved her people from massacre.

es·the·sia (ĕs-thē'zhə, -zhē-ə) *n.* The ability to receive sense impressions. [Back-formation from ANESTHESIA.]

esthete. Variant of **aesthete.**

esthetic. Variant of **aesthetic.**

esthetician. Variant of **aesthetician.**

estheticism. Variant of **aestheticism.**

esthetics. Variant of **aesthetics.**

es·ti·ma·ble (ĕs'tə-mə-bəl) *adj.* **1.** Capable of being estimated or evaluated; calculable. **2.** Deserving of esteem; admirable. **—es·ti·ma·ble·ness** *n.* **—es·ti·ma·bly** *adv.*

es·ti·mate (ĕs'tə-māt') *tr.v.* **-mated, -mating, -mates. 1.** To calculate approximately the cost, quantity, or extent of. **2.** To form a tentative opinion about; evaluate: *"While an author is yet living we estimate his powers by his worst performance"* (Samuel Johnson). —See Synonyms at **calculate.**
~*n.* (-mĭt). *Abbr.* **est. 1.** A tentative evaluation or rough calculation. **2. a.** A preliminary calculation of the cost of work to be undertaken. **b.** The statement of such a calculation. **3.** A judgment based upon one's impressions; an opinion. [From Latin *aestimāre†.*] **—es·ti·ma·tive** (ĕs'tə-mā'tĭv, -mə-tĭv) *adj.* **—es·ti·ma·tor** *n.*
Synonyms: *appraise, assay, assess, evaluate, rate.*

es·ti·ma·tion (ĕs'tə-mā'shən) *n.* **1.** The act or an instance of estimating. **2.** An opinion reached by estimating; a judgment. **3.** Favorable regard; esteem.

estival. Variant of **aestival.**

estivate. Variant of **aestivate.**

estivation. Variant of **aestivation.**

Es·to·ni·a, Es·tho·ni·a (ĕ-stō'nē-ə). Republic of the U.S.S.R., lying on the Baltic Sea. After World War I it gained independence from Russia but was taken over by the U.S.S.R. in 1940. About 75 percent of the population is Estonian, with the rest mainly Russian. Its capital is Tallinn.

Es·to·ni·an, Es·tho·ni·an (ĕ-stō'nē-ən) *n.* **1.** A native or inhabitant of Estonia. **2.** The Finno-Ugric language of Estonia. **—Es·to·ni·an, Es·tho·ni·an** *adj.*

es·top (ĕ-stŏp') *tr.v.* **-topped, -topping, -tops. 1.** *Law.* To prohibit, preclude, or impede by estoppel. **2.** *Archaic.* To stop up. [Middle English *estoppen,* from Old French *estoper, estouper,* from Late Latin *stuppāre,* to stop up. See stop.] **—es·top·page** (ĕ-stŏp'ĭj) *n.*

es·top·pel (ĕ-stŏp'əl) *n. Law.* A restraint on a person to prevent him from contradicting his own previous assertion. Also called "conclusion." [Old French *estoupail, estouppail,* from *estouper,* to ESTOP.]

estr–, estro–, oestr–, oestro– *prefix.* Indicates estrus; for example, **estrogen.**

es·tra·di·ol, oes·tra·di·ol (ĕs'trə-dī'ôl', -ōl') *n.* An estrogenic hormone, $C_{18}H_{24}O_2$, used in treating estrogen deficiency. [ESTR(US) + -OL.]

es·trange (ĭ-strānj') *tr.v.* **-tranged, -tranging, -tranges. 1.** To remove from an accustomed place or relation. **2.** To alienate the affections of; make hostile or unsympathetic. [Old French *estranger, estrangier,* from Medieval Latin *extrāneāre,* from Latin *extrāneus,* STRANGE.] **—es·trange·ment** *n.* **—es·trang·er** *n.*

es·tray (ĭ-strā') *n.* **1.** *Law.* A stray domestic animal. **2.** *Archaic.* A stray person, animal, or thing.
~*intr.v.* **estrayed, -traying, -trays.** *Archaic.* To stray. [Norman French *estray,* from Old French *estraie,* stray, wandering, from *estraier,* to STRAY.]

Es·tre·ma·du·ra¹ (ĕs'trə-mə-dŏŏr'ə). Former province of central Portugal, comprising the lower Tagus River valley, one of the country's richest farming areas. Lisbon, the national capital, is the chief town. **—Es·tre·ma·du·ran** *n. & adj.*

Estremadura². See Extremadura.

es·tri·ol, oes·tri·ol (ĕs'trī-ôl', -ōl', ĕ-strī'-) *n.* An estrogenic hormone, $C_{18}H_{24}O_3$, that is obtained commercially from the urine of pregnant animals and used in treating estrogen deficiency. [ES(TRUS) + TRI- + -OL.]

es·tro·gen, oes·tro·gen (ĕs'trə-jən) *n.* Any of several steroid hormones produced chiefly by the ovary and responsible for promoting estrus and the development and maintenance of female secondary sex characteristics. [ESTR(US) + -GEN.] **—es·tro·gen·ic** (ĕs'trə-jĕn'ĭk) *adj.*

es·trone, oes·trone (ĕs'trōn') *n.* An estrogenic hormone, $C_{18}H_{22}O_2$, isolated from the urine of pregnant females for use in treating estrogen deficiency. [ESTR(US) + -ONE.]

es·trous, oes·trus (ĕs′trəs) *adj.* **1.** Of or pertaining to estrus. **2.** Being in heat.

estrous cycle, oestrus cycle *n.* The series of chemical and physiological changes in female mammals from the onset of one period of estrus to the onset of the next.

es·trus, oes·trus (ĕs′trəs) *n.* A regularly recurring period of ovulation and sexual excitement in female mammals other than humans; heat. [New Latin, from Latin *oestrus*, frenzy, from Greek *oistros*.]

es·tu·a·rine (ĕs′chŏŏ-ə-rīn′, -rēn′) *adj.* Of, pertaining to, or found in an estuary.

es·tu·ar·y (ĕs′chŏŏ-ĕr′ē) *n., pl.* **-ies. 1.** The part of the wide lower course of a river where its current is met by the tides. **2.** An arm of the sea that extends inland to meet the mouth of a river. [Latin *aestuārium*, estuary, tidal channel, from *aestus*, heat, swell, surge, tide.] **—es·tu·ar·i·al** (ĕs′chŏŏ-âr′ē-əl) *adj.*

esu electrostatic unit.

e·su·ri·ent (ĭ-sŏŏr′ē-ənt, ĭ-zŏŏr′-) *adj.* Hungry; greedy. [Latin *ēsuriēns* (stem *ēsurient-*), present participle of *ēsurīre*, to want food, to be hungry, desiderative of *edere* (past participle *ēsus*), to eat.] **—e·su·ri·ence** (ĕ-sŏŏr′ē-əns, ĭ-zŏŏr′-), **e·su·ri·en·cy** (-ən-sē) *n.*

-et *suffix.* Indicates smallness or lesser status; for example, **baronet, pullet.** [Middle English *-et*, from Old French *-et*, from Common Romance *-itta, -ētto* (both unattested).]

e·ta (ā′tə, ē′tə) *n.* The seventh letter in the Greek alphabet, written H, η. Transliterated in English as *e*. See feature at **alphabet.** [Late Latin *ēta*, from Greek, from a Phoenician source, akin to Hebrew *hēth,* HETH.]

e.t.a. estimated time of arrival.

é·ta·gère, e·ta·gere (ā′tä-zhâr′) *n.* A piece of furniture with open shelves for ornaments or bric-a-brac. [French, from Old French *estagiere, estage,* floor of a building, position. See **stage.**]

et al. and others [Latin *et alii.*]

etc. et cetera.

et cet·er·a, et·cet·er·a (ĕt-sĕt′ər-ə, -sĕt′rə) *adv. Abbr.* **etc.** And further unspecified things of the same class; and so forth. [Latin, "and other (things)" : *et,* and + *cētera,* the rest, from the neuter plural of *cēterus,* remaining.]

Usage: The use of *et cetera* and its abbreviation *etc.* is principally appropriate to informal writing or to special areas such as technical reporting or business correspondence. It is not appropriate to formal writing in general.

et·cet·er·as (ĕt-sĕt′ər-əz, -sĕt′rəz) *pl.n.* Other incidental items not mentioned individually.

etch (ĕch) *v.* **etched, etching, etches.** *—tr.* **1.** To wear away (metal or glass, for example) with or as if with acid. **2.** To make (a pattern) on a metal plate or other surface with acid. **3.** To cut or engrave. **4.** To impress or imprint (an event, for example) clearly in the mind. *—intr.* To practice etching. [Dutch *etsen,* from German *ätzen,* to etch, to bite, to feed, from Old High German *ezzen,* to feed.] **—etch′er** *n.*

etch·ing (ĕch′ĭng) *n.* **1.** The art of preparing etched plates from which designs and pictures are printed. **2.** A design etched on a plate. **3.** An impression made from an etched plate.

e.t.d. estimated time of departure.

e·ter·nal (ĭ-tûr′nəl) *adj.* **1.** Without beginning or end; existing outside time: *eternal God.* **2.** Having a beginning but without interruption or end: *an eternal flame.* **3.** Unaffected by time; timeless: *eternal truths.* **4.** Seemingly endless; interminable: *tired of your eternal complaining.* **5.** Of or relating to existence after death: *went to their eternal rest.* **—See Synonyms at continual, infinite.** *—n.* **1.** Something eternal. **2. Eternal.** God. [Middle English, from Old French, from Late Latin *aeternālis,* from Latin *aeternus,* eternal.] **—e·ter·nal·i·ty** (ē′tûr-năl′ə-tē), **e·ter·nal·ness** *n.* **—e·ter·nal·ly** *adv.*

e·ter·nal·ize (ĭ-tûr′nə-līz′) *tr.v.* **-ized, -izing, -izes.** To eternize.

e·terne (ĭ-tûrn′) *adj. Archaic.* Eternal. [Middle English, from Old French, from Latin *aeternus,* ETERNAL.]

e·ter·ni·ty (ĭ-tûr′nə-tē) *n., pl.* **-ties. 1.** The totality of time without beginning or end; infinite time. **2.** The state or quality of being eternal; everlastingness. **3. a.** The endless period of time following death. **b.** The afterlife; immortality. **4.** *Informal.* A very long or seemingly very long time. [Middle English *eternite,* from Old French, from Latin *aeternitās* (stem *aeternitāt-*), from *aeternus,* ETERNAL.]

e·ter·nize (ĭ-tûr′nīz′) *tr.v.* **-nized, -nizing, -nizes. 1.** To make eternal. **2.** To make perpetually famous; immortalize. [Old French *eterniser,* from ETERNE.]

e·te·sian (ĭ-tē′zhən) *adj.* Recurring annually. Said of prevailing northerly summer winds of the Mediterranean. [Latin *etēsius,* from Greek *etēsios,* from *etos,* year.]

eth. Variant of **edh.**

eth-, etho- *suffix.* Indicates the presence of an ethyl group or derivation from ethane; for example, **ethoxide.**

-eth[1]**, -th** *suffix.* Indicates the archaic third person singular form of the present indicative tense; for example, *leadeth, praiseth.* [Middle English *-eth,* Old English *-eth, -th.*]

-eth[2]. Variant of **-th** (in ordinal numbers).

eth·an·am·ide (ĕth-ăn′ə-mīd′) *n.* **Acetamide** *(see).*

eth·ane (ĕth′ān′) *n.* A colorless, odorless gas, C_2H_6, occurring as a constituent of natural gas and used as a fuel and refrigerant. [ETH(YL) + -ANE.]

eth·ane·di·o·ic acid (ĕth′ān-dī-ō′ĭk) *n.* An organic acid, **oxalic acid** *(see).*

eth·ane·di·ol (ĕth′ān-dī′ôl′, -ōl′) *n.* An alcohol, **ethylene glycol** *(see).*

eth·a·no·ic acid (ĕth′ə-nō′ĭk) *n.* **Acetic acid** *(see).*

Eth·el·red or **Aeth·el·red** (ĕth′əl-rĕd′), known as "the Unready" (*c.* 968–1016). King of the English (978–1016). Most of his reign was spent unsuccessfully resisting Danish invasions. He was driven from London (1013) and fled to Normandy, but he returned a year later to be restored to the throne.

eth·ene (ĕth′ēn′) *n. Chemistry.* **Ethylene** *(see).* [ETH(YL) + -ENE.]

e·ther (ē′thər) *n.* Also **ae·ther** (for sense 3). **1.** Any of a class of organic compounds in which two hydrocarbon groups are linked by an oxygen atom. **2.** A volatile, highly flammable liquid, $C_4H_{10}O$, derived from the distillation of ethanol with sulfuric acid and widely used in industry and as an anesthetic. Also called "diethyl ether," "ethyl ether," "ethoxyethane." **3.** The regions of space beyond the earth's atmosphere; the heavens. **4.** *Physics.* An all-pervading, infinitely elastic, massless medium formerly postulated as the medium of propagation of electromagnetic waves. [Middle English, from Latin *aethēr,* the upper or bright air, ether, from Greek *aithēr.*] **—e·ther·ic** (ĭ-thĕr′ĭk, ĭ-thîr′-) *adj.*

e·the·re·al, ae·the·re·al (ĭ-thîr′ē-əl) *adj.* **1.** Marked by lightness and insubstantiality; intangible. **2.** Highly refined; delicate. **3. a.** Of the celestial spheres; heavenly: *"Him the almighty power/ Hurl'd headlong flaming from th' Ethereal Sky"* (Milton). **b.** Unearthly; spiritual. **4.** *Chemistry.* Of, pertaining to, or dissolved in ether. [Latin *aetherius,* ethereal, from Greek *aitherios,* from *aithēr,* ETHER.] **—e·the·re·al·i·ty** (ĭ-thîr′ē-ăl′ə-tē), **e·the·re·al·ness** *n.* **—e·the·re·al·ly** *adv.*

e·the·re·al·ize (ĭ-thîr′ē-ə-līz′) *v.* **-ized, -izing, -izes.** *—tr.* To make or treat as being ethereal; spiritualize. *—intr.* To become ethereal. **—e·the·re·al·i·za·tion** *n.*

e·ther·i·fy (ĭ-thĕr′ə-fī′) *tr.v.* **-fied, -fying, -fies.** To convert (an alcohol) into an ether. **—e·ther·i·fi·ca·tion** *n.*

e·ther·ize (ē′thə-rīz′) *tr.v.* **-ized, -izing, -izes. 1.** To subject to the fumes of ether; anesthetize. **2.** *Chemistry.* To etherify. **—e·ther·i·za·tion** *n.*

eth·ic (ĕth′ĭk) *n.* **1.** A principle of right or good conduct. **2.** A body of such principles: *the work ethic.* [Middle English *et(h)ik,* the science of ethics, from Old French *ethique,* from Late Latin *ēthica* and Latin *ēthicē,* from Greek *ēthikē,* from *ēthikos,* ethical, from *ēthos,* moral custom.]

eth·i·cal (ĕth′ĭ-kəl) *adj.* **1.** Of, pertaining to, or dealing with ethics: *an ethical dilemma.* **2.** In accordance with the accepted principles of right and wrong governing the conduct of a profession. **3.** Designating a medicinal preparation dispensed solely on a doctor's prescription. **—See Synonyms at moral. —eth·i·cal·ly** *adv.* **—eth·i·cal·ness, eth·i·cal·i·ty** (ĕth′ĭ-kăl′ə-tē) *n.*

eth·ics (ĕth′ĭks) *pl.n.* **1.** *Used with a singular verb.* **a.** The study of the general nature of morals and of the specific moral choices to be made by the individual in his relationship with others. Also called "moral philosophy." **b.** The moral sciences as a whole, including moral philosophy and customary, civil, and religious law. **2.** The rules or standards governing the conduct of the members of a profession: *medical ethics.* **3.** The moral quality of a course of action; propriety: *I question the ethics of his decision.*

E·thi·op (ē′thē-ŏp′) *n.* Also **E·thi·ope** (-ōp′). *Archaic.* An Ethiopian. [Latin *Aethiops,* from Greek *Aithiops,* "burnt face" : *aithein,* to burn + *ōps,* face.]

E·thi·o·pi·a (ē′thē-ō′pē-ə). Formerly **Ab·ys·sin·i·a** (ăb′ə-sĭn′ē-ə). A poor, largely mountainous country in northeastern Africa. An ancient Christian kingdom, Ethiopia was taken over by a Communist military junta in 1974 following widespread famine. Already, in the 1960's, secessionist wars had begun in Muslim Eritrea and the Somali-peopled Ogaden. Area, 1,221,900 square kilometers (471,653 square miles). Population, 31,000,000. Capital, Addis Ababa.

E·thi·o·pi·an (ē′thē-ō′pē-ən) *adj.* **1.** Of or pertaining to Ethiopia, its languages, or its people. **2.** *Ecology.* Of or designating the zoogeographic region that includes Africa south of the Sahara and most of Arabia. Also called "Ethiopian region." **3.** *Archaic.* Black African. *—n.* **1.** A native or inhabitant of Ethiopia. **2.** *Archaic.* A member of the ancient Greek classification of dark-skinned Africans from the lands beyond Egypt; a Negro.

E·thi·op·ic (ē′thē-ŏp′ĭk, -ō′pĭk) *n.* The Semitic language of ancient Ethiopia that is still used as a liturgical language in the Christian church in Ethiopia. Also called "Geez." **—E·thi·op·ic** *adj.*

eth·moid (ĕth′moid′) *adj.* Also **eth·moid·al** (ĕth-moid′l). Of or designating a light spongy bone located between the eye sockets that forms part of the walls of the superior nasal cavity. *—n.* The ethmoid bone. [French *ethmoïde,* from Old French, from Greek *ēthmoeidēs,* perforated (the bone contains many perforations) : *ēthmos,* strainer, from *ēthein,* to strain, to sift + -OID.]

eth·narch (ĕth′närk′) *n.* The ruler of a province or a people. [Greek *ethnarkhēs,* ruler of the people : ETHN(O)- + *arkhos,* -ARCH.] **—eth·nar·chy** *n.*

eth·nic (ĕth′nĭk) *adj.* Also **eth·ni·cal** (-nĭ-kəl). **1. a.** Of, pertaining to, or designating a social group within a cultural and social system that claims or is accorded special status on the basis of complex, often variable traits including religious, linguistic, ancestral, or physical characteristics. **b.** Pertaining to the study and classification of such groups. **2. a.** Broadly, characteristic of a religious, ra-

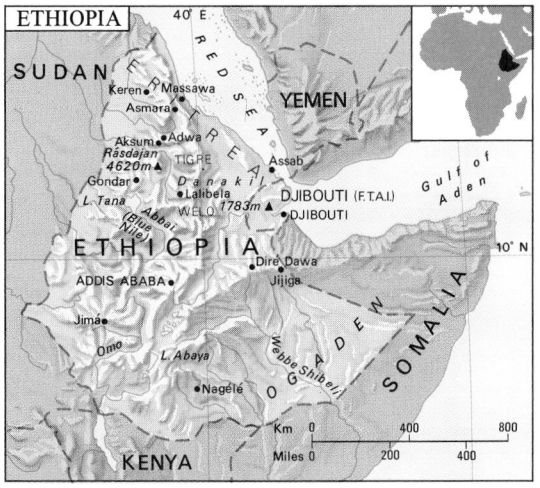

ETHIOPIA

SUDAN
YEMEN
Keren • Massawa
Asmara
Aksum • Adwa
Räsdajan
4620m ▲ TIGRE
Gondar • Danakil
L. Tana • Lalibela
WELO 1783m ▲ DJIBOUTI (F.T.A.I.)
DJIBOUTI
ETHIOPIA
• Dire Dawa
ADDIS ABABA
Jijiga
Jima •
Omo
L. Abaya
SOMALIA
• Nagélé
Webbe Shibeli
KENYA
Km 0   400   800
Miles 0   200   400

cial, national, or cultural group. **b.** Characteristic of traditional folk styles of food, dress, or other customs. **c.** *Informal.* Quaint; picturesque. **3.** Of or pertaining to a people not Christian or Jewish; heathen.
~*n.* **ethnic.** *Informal.* A member of a particular ethnic group. [Late Latin *ethnicus,* heathen, foreign, from Greek *ethnikos,* of a national group, foreign, from *ethnos,* people, nation.] —**eth·ni·cal·ly** *adv.*

eth·nic·i·ty (ĕth-nĭs′ə-tē) *n.* **1.** The condition of belonging to a particular ethnic group. **2.** Ethnic pride.

ethnic minority *n.* An ethnic group living in a society where members of a different race or culture predominate.

ethno–, ethn– *prefix.* Indicates race, culture, or people; for example, **ethnocentrism.** [French, from Late Greek, from Greek *ethnos,* people.]

eth·no·bot·a·ny (ĕth′nō-bŏt′n-ē) *n.* The branch of botany relating to the use of plants in religion, folk medicine, and the like. —**eth·no·bot·a·nist** *n.*

eth·no·cen·trism (ĕth′nō-sĕn′trĭz′əm) *n.* **1.** Belief in the superiority of one's own ethnic group. **2.** Overriding concern with race. [ETHNO- + CENTR(O)- + -ISM.] —**eth·no·cen·tric** *adj.*

eth·nog·ra·phy (ĕth-nŏg′rə-fē) *n., pl.* **-phies. 1.** The descriptive anthropology of ethnic groups, especially technologically primitive societies. **2.** Ethnology. [French *ethnographie* : ETHNO- + -GRAPHY.] —**eth·nog·ra·pher** *n.* —**eth·no·graph·ic** (ĕth′nə-grăf′ĭk), **eth·no·graph·i·cal** (-ĭ-kəl) *adj.* —**eth·no·graph·i·cal·ly** *adv.*

eth·nol·o·gy (ĕth-nŏl′ə-jē) *n.* The anthropological study of socioeconomic systems and cultural heritage, especially of cultural origins and of factors influencing cultural growth and change, usually in technologically primitive societies. [ETHNO- + -LOGY.] —**eth·no·log·ic** (ĕth′nə-lŏj′ĭk), **eth·no·log·i·cal** (-ĭ-kəl) *adj.* —**eth·no·log·i·cal·ly** *adv.* —**eth·nol·o·gist** *n.*

eth·no·mu·si·col·o·gy (ĕth′nō-myōō′zĭ-kŏl′ə-jē) *n.* The study of the music and musical traditions of ethnic groups. —**eth·no·mu·si·col·o·gist** *n.*

etho–. Variant of eth-.

e·thol·o·gy (ĭ-thŏl′ə-jē, ē-thŏl′-) *n.* The scientific study of animal behavior in the natural environment. [Latin *ēthologia,* the art of depicting character, from Greek *ēthologia* : *ēthos,* ETHOS + -LOGY.] —**eth·o·log·i·cal** (ĕth′ə-lŏj′ĭ-kəl, ē′thə-) *adj.* —**e·thol·o·gist** *n.*

e·thos (ē′thŏs′) *n.* **1.** The disposition, character, or attitude peculiar to a specific people, culture, or group that distinguishes it from other peoples or groups; fundamental values or spirit; mores. **2.** The essential character of a period, movement, work of art, mode of expression, or the like: *the revolutionary ethos.* [New Latin, from Greek *ēthos,* custom, usage, trait.]

eth·ox·ide (ĭ-thŏk′sīd′) *n. Chemistry.* A salt formed by the reaction of a metal with alcohol, HOC₂H₅. Also called "ethylate."

eth·ox·y·eth·ane (ĕth′ŏk′sē-ĕth′ān′) *n.* An organic compound, **ether** (see).

eth·yl (ĕth′əl) *n.* A univalent organic radical, C₂H₅. [ETH(ER) + -YL.] —**eth·yl·ic** (ĕ-thĭl′ĭk) *adj.*

ethyl acetate *n.* A colorless, volatile, flammable liquid, CH₃COOC₂H₅, used in perfumes, flavorings, lacquers, pharmaceuticals, and rayon, and as a general solvent.

ethyl alcohol *n.* **Alcohol** (see).

eth·yl·a·mine (ĕth′ə-lə-mēn′) *n.* A colorless, volatile liquid, C₂H₅NH₂, used in petroleum refining, detergents, and organic synthesis.

eth·yl·ate (ĕth′ə-lāt′) *tr.v.* **-ated, -ating, -ates.** *Chemistry.* To introduce the ethyl group into (a compound).
~*n.* An ethoxide. [ETHYL + -ATE.] —**eth·yl·a·tion** *n.*

ethyl carbamate *n.* A chemical compound, **urethane** (see).

ethyl chloride *n.* A chemical compound, C₂H₅Cl, a gas at ordinary temperatures and a colorless, volatile, flammable liquid when compressed, used as a solvent, refrigerant, and in the manufacture of tetraethyl lead.

eth·yl·ene (ĕth′ə-lēn′) *n.* **1.** A colorless, flammable gas, C₂H₄, de-

rived from natural gas and petroleum and used as a source of many organic compounds, in welding and cutting metals, to color citrus fruits, and as an anesthetic. **2.** The bivalent organic radical C₂H₄. Also called "ethene." [ETHYL + -ENE.]

ethylene glycol *n.* A colorless, syrupy alcohol, C₂H₆O₂, used as an antifreeze in cooling and heating systems. Also called "ethanediol."

ethyl ether *n. Chemistry.* **Ether** (see).

ethyl mercaptan *n. Chemistry.* See **mercaptan.**

eth·yne (ē′thīn′, ĕth′īn′) *n.* A gaseous hydrocarbon, **acetylene** (see).

e·ti·o·late (ē′tē-ə-lāt′) *v.* **-lated, -lating, -lates.** —*tr.* **1.** To cause (a plant) to develop without normal green coloring by preventing exposure to sunlight; blanch; whiten. **2.** To cause (a person) to lose healthy coloring and become weak. **3.** To cause to lose vigor, body, force, or the like. —*intr.* **1.** To become blanched or whitened and abnormally elongated, as when grown without sunlight. **2.** To lose healthy coloring and become weak. [French *étioler,* from *eteule,* a stalk, from Old French *estuble,* from Latin *stipula,* stalk, straw, stubble.] —**e·ti·o·la·tion** *n.*

e·ti·ol·o·gy, ae·ti·ol·o·gy (ē′tē-ŏl′ə-jē) *n.* **1.** The study of causes or origins. **2.** The branch of medicine that deals with the causes of disease. **3. a.** The assignment of a cause, origin, or reason for something. **b.** The cause of a disease or disorder as determined by medical diagnosis. [Late Latin *aetiologia,* from Greek *aitiologia,* a giving the cause of : *aita,* responsibility, cause + -LOGY.] —**e·ti·o·log·ic** (ē′tē-ə-lŏj′ĭk), **e·ti·o·log·i·cal** (-ĭ-kəl) *adj.* —**e·ti·o·log·i·cal·ly** *adv.* —**e·ti·ol·o·gist** *n.*

et·i·quette (ĕt′ĭ-kĕt′, -kĭt) *n.* A code of behavior prescribed or conventionally accepted as correct or polite, as at court, among a profession, or in society at large. [French *etiquette,* prescribed routine, label, ticket, from Old French *estiqu(i)er,* to attach, from Middle Dutch *steken.*]

Synonyms: *decorum, propriety, protocol.*

Et·na (ĕt′nə). Europe's highest active volcano (3,340 meters; 10,958 feet), near the east coast of Sicily. It is first known to have erupted in 475 B.C.

E·ton (ēt′n). Town in Buckinghamshire on the Thames River. It is the home of Britain's most famous public school, Eton College, founded by King Henry VI in 1440.

Eton collar *n.* A broad, stiff white collar worn overlapping the lapels of a jacket.

Eton jacket *n.* A waist-length jacket that has wide lapels and is cut square at the hips.

E·to·sha Game Park (ē-tō′shə). Largest game reserve in southern Africa. Lying in northwest Namibia, it covers 22,270 square kilometers (8,600 square miles) and includes Etosha Pan, a dried-up salt lake.

é·tri·er (ā′trē-ā′) *n.* A short rope ladder used in mountaineering. [French, "stirrup."]

E·tru·ri·a (ĭ-trŏŏr′ē-ə). Ancient country in Italy, now Tuscany and part of Umbria. It was the center of the civilization of the Etruscans, but by the end of the 5th century B.C. it succumbed to Rome.

E·tru·ri·an (ĭ-trŏŏr′ē-ən) *n.* Etruscan. —**E·tru·ri·an** *adj.*

E·trus·can (ĭ-trŭs′kən) *adj.* Of, pertaining to, or characteristic of Etruria, its inhabitants, or their language or culture.
~*n.* **1.** A person who lived in ancient Etruria. **2.** The pre-Roman, now extinct language of the Etruscans, of undetermined linguistic affiliation. See feature, next page.

et seq. and the following. [Latin *et sequens, et sequentia.*]

-ette *suffix.* Indicates: **1.** Small or diminutive; for example, **kitchenette. 2.** An imitation of or a substitute for; for example, **leatherette. 3.** Female or feminine; for example, **usherette.** [Middle English *-ette,* from Old French, feminine of -ET.]

e·tude (ā′tōōd′, ā′tyōōd′, ā-tüd′) *n.* **1.** A piece of music composed as an exercise for the development of a given point of technique. **2.** A composition embodying some point of technique but intended for performance. [French *étude,* study, from Old French *estudie,* STUDY.]

é·tui (ā-twē′) *n., pl.* **étuis** (ā-twēz′). A case for holding small articles, such as needles or toiletries. [French, from Old French *estui,* container, prison, from *estuier,* to shut up, guard, probably from Vulgar Latin *estudiāre* (unattested), to take care of, from Latin *studium,* STUDY.]

et·y·mo·log·i·cal (ĕt′ə-mə-lŏj′ĭ-kəl) *adj.* Also **et·y·mo·log·ic** (-lŏj′ĭk). *Abbr.* **etym., etymol.** Of or pertaining to etymology, or based upon the principles of etymology. —**et·y·mo·log·i·cal·ly** *adv.*

et·y·mol·o·gist (ĕt′ə-mŏl′ə-jĭst) *n.* A specialist in the principles of etymology and their application.

et·y·mol·o·gize (ĕt′ə-mŏl′ə-jīz′) *v.* **-gized, -gizing, -gizes.** —*tr.* To trace and state the etymology of (a word or words). —*intr.* To give or suggest the etymology of a word or words.

et·y·mol·o·gy (ĕt′ə-mŏl′ə-jē) *n., pl.* **-gies.** *Abbr.* **etym., etymol. 1.** The origin and historical development of a word or word part, as evidenced by study of its basic elements, earliest known use, and changes in form and meaning; semantic derivation and evolution. **2.** An account of the history of a specific word. **3.** The branch of linguistics that studies the derivation of words. [Learned respelling of Middle English *ethimologie,* from Old French, from Medieval Latin *ethimologia,* from Latin *etymologia,* from Greek *etumologiā* : *etumon,* ETYMON + -LOGY.]

et·y·mon (ĕt′ə-mŏn′) *n., pl.* **-mons** or **-ma** (-mə). **1.** The earlier form of a word or word part in the same language or in an ancestor language. **2.** A word or morpheme from which compounds and derivatives are formed. **3.** A foreign word from which a particular

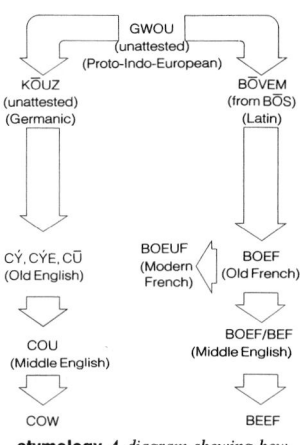

GWOU
(unattested)
(Proto-Indo-European)
KŌUZ
(unattested)
(Germanic)
BŌVEM
(from BŌS)
(Latin)

CŸ, CŸE, CŪ
(Old English)
BOEUF
(Modern French)
BOEF
(Old French)

COU
(Middle English)
BOEF/BEF
(Middle English)

COW
BEEF

etymology *A diagram showing how the words "cow" and "beef" developed from a common origin. Major changes only are shown; a full etymological account would include how the words were used and how the meanings changed in the various languages.*

loan word is derived. [Latin, origin of a word, from Greek *etumon*, true sense of a word, etymology, from *etumos*, true, real.]

Eu The symbol for the element europium.

eu– *prefix.* Indicates: **1.** Well, pleasant, or beneficial; for example, **euphony. 2.** Derivative of a specified substance; for example, **eu-caine. 3.** True; truly so; for example, **eubacteria.** [Middle English *eu-*, from Latin, from Greek, from *eus*, good.]

Etruscan

THE BURIED TREASURE OF THE ETRUSCANS

The civilization that flourished in Italy before the Romans

The Etruscans, who dominated central Italy from the 8th to the 5th century B.C., are known from archaeological remains and the writings of Roman historians. More than 8,000 inscriptions exist in the Etruscan language. Most are personal names and not all have been fully deciphered, but the alphabet is of Greek derivation.

It was trade with Greece as well as their own industry, in metalware for example, that made the Etruscans wealthy and powerful. Their navy was one of the strongest in the Mediterranean.

The Etruscan state (Etruria) was not close-knit but a loose association of city settlements. The people lived in brick houses with stone foundations, and they built extensive underground tombs whose walls bore colorful paintings. Oriental motifs in the paintings may have come from Greece. The tombs contained fine gray pottery (called Bucchero) and metalwork. Etruscan metalwork was widely exported.

The Etruscans' power declined from the 4th century B.C. as the Romans overcame them.

POWER BASE *The core of Etruria was central Italy (blue on the map), but at their peak, about 600 B.C., the Etruscans dominated most of the peninsula.*

BRONZE AMAZON *The lid of an Etruscan burial chest (left) made about 500 B.C. bears a bronze statuette of a mounted Amazon—one of the race of women warriors from Asia Minor whose deeds are legendary.*

FUNERAL WRESTLING *A wall painting found in a tomb at Tarquinia shows professional wrestlers about to fight for a prize of gold and silver bowls during funeral games. These were held after prominent Etruscans had died. The combatants are naked, in the style of Greek wrestlers.*

---

eu·bac·te·ri·a (yōō′băk-tîr′ē-ə) *pl.n.* A large and diverse group of bacteria characterized by rigid cell walls; true bacteria.

Eu·boe·a (yōō-bē′ə). *Modern Greek* **Év·voia** (ĕv′yä). Island in the Aegean Sea. The largest of the Greek islands after Crete, it produces sheep, goats, cattle, grapes, olives, and wheat.

eu·caine (yōō′kān′) *n.* A crystalline substance, $C_{15}H_{21}NO_2$, formerly used as a local anesthetic. [EU- + -CAINE.]

eu·ca·lyp·tol (yōō′kə-lĭp′tôl′, -tŏl′) *n.* Also **eu·ca·lyp·tole** (-tōl′). A colorless oily liquid, $C_{10}H_{18}O$, derived from eucalyptus oil and used in pharmaceuticals, flavoring, and perfumery. Also called "cineol." [EUCALYPT(US) + -OL.]

eu·ca·lyp·tus (yōō′kə-lĭp′təs) *n.,* pl. **-tuses** or **-ti** (-tī′). Any of numerous tall trees of the genus *Eucalyptus,* mostly native to Australia, cultivated for their aromatic leaves that yield eucalyptus oil, for their wood valued as timber, and for ornament. [New Latin : EU- + Greek *kaluptos,* covered (from the flower, which is covered before it opens), from *kaluptein,* to cover, hide.]

eucalyptus oil *n.* An oil derived from the leaves of the eucalyptus, used as a flavoring and as an expectorant and antiseptic.

eu·car·y·ote, eu·kar·y·ote (yōō-kăr′ē-ōt′, -ət) *n. Biology.* An organism in which the genetic material is enclosed by a membrane to form a nucleus. Eucaryotes include all organisms except bacteria, blue-green algae, and viruses. Compare **procaryote.** [EU- + -*karyote,* irregularly from Greek *karuon,* kernel, nucleus. See KARYO-.] —**eu·car·y·ot·ic** (yōō-kăr′ē-ŏt′ĭk) *adj.*

Eu·cha·rist (yōō′kər-ĭst) *n.* **1. a.** The Christian sacrament instituted at the Last Supper in which bread and wine are consecrated and then eaten and drunk as a memorial of Christ's death. Also called "Communion," "Holy Communion." **b.** The consecrated elements of bread and wine used in this sacrament. **2.** *Christian Science.* Spiritual communion with God. [Middle English *eukarist,* from Old French *eucariste,* from Late Latin *eucharistia,* from Greek *eukharistia,* gratitude, from *eukharistos,* grateful : *eu-,* well, good + *kharizesthai,* to show favor, from *kharis,* favor, grace.] —**Eu·cha·ris·tic** (yōō′kə-rĭs′tĭk), **Eu·cha·ris·ti·cal** (-tĭ-kəl) *adj.*

eu·chre (yōō′kər) *n.* **1.** A card game in which each player is dealt five cards and the player making the trump is required to take at least three tricks to win. **2.** The action of euchring an opponent. ~*tr.v.* **euchred, -chring, -chres. 1.** To prevent (an opponent) from taking three tricks in euchre. **2.** *Informal.* To deceive by sly or underhand means; cheat: *euchred them out of their savings.* [Origin unknown.]

eu·chro·ma·tin (yōō-krō′mə-tĭn) *n.* The chromosome material that stains most deeply with basic dyes when the cell is dividing and represents the major genes involved in protein synthesis. Compare **heterochromatin.**

Eu·clid (yōō′klĭd) (*fl.* 300 B.C.). Greek mathematician. His most important contribution to mathematics was the use of the deductive principles of logic as the basis of his geometry, deriving statements from clearly defined axioms.

Eu·clid·e·an, Eu·clid·i·an (yōō-klĭd′ē-ən) *adj.* Of or pertaining to Euclid's geometric principles.

Euclidean algorithm *n.* A method of finding the greatest common divisor of two numbers by dividing one by the other, the second by the remainder, the remainder by the second remainder, and so on until an exact division is reached, when the last divisor is the greatest common divisor of the two numbers.

Euclidean geometry *n.* Geometry based on the postulates of Euclid; especially, the parallel postulate that for a point outside a line only one other line can be drawn through the point parallel to the first line.

eu·de·mon, eu·dae·mon (yōō-dē′mən) *n.* A benevolent spirit.

eu·de·mo·ni·a, eu·dae·mo·ni·a (yōō′də-mō′nē-ə, -mōn′yə) *n.* **1.** Happiness or well-being. **2.** In Aristotelian philosophy, an active, rational life. [Greek *eudaimonia,* from *eudaimōn,* lucky, with a good spirit : *eu-,* good + *daimōn,* spirit.]

eu·de·mon·ism, eu·dae·mon·ism (yōō-dē′mə-nĭz′əm) *n.* A system of ethics that evaluates the morality of actions in terms of their capacity to produce happiness. —**eu·de·mon·ist** *n.* —**eu·de·mon·is·tic** (yōō-dē′mə-nĭs′tĭk), **eu·de·mon·is·ti·cal** *adj.*

eu·di·om·e·ter (yōō′dē-ŏm′ə-tər) *n. Chemistry.* A graduated glass apparatus used to study gas reactions by volume changes. [From Greek *eudios,* "clear-skied" : EU- + *dios,* genitive of *Zeus,* god of the heavens + METER; the apparatus was originally used to measure the amount of oxygen present in the air, believed to be greater in clear weather.] —**eu·di·o·met·ric** (yōō′dē-ə-mĕt′rĭk), **eu·di·o·met·ri·cal** *adj.* —**eu·di·om·e·try** *n.*

eu·gen·ic (yōō-jĕn′ĭk) *adj.* **1.** Of or pertaining to eugenics. **2.** Pertaining or adapted to the production of good offspring. —**eu·gen·i·cal·ly** *adv.*

eu·gen·i·cist (yōō-jĕn′ə-sĭst) *n.* Also **eu·gen·ist** (yōō-jĕ′nĭst, yōō′jə-nĭst). An advocate of or specialist in eugenics.

eu·gen·ics (yōō-jĕn′ĭks) *n. Used with a singular verb.* The study of the hereditary improvement of the human race by controlled selective breeding. Compare **euthenics.** [Greek *eugenēs,* well-born : EU- + -GEN.]

Eu·gé·nie (yōō′zhä-nē′) (1826-1920). French empress, born in Spain and the consort of Napoleon III from her marriage to him in 1853 until his overthrow in 1870. She acted as regent during Napoleon's absences from France and is believed to have had much influence on events that led to the Franco-Prussian War of 1870. She fled to England after Napoleon's capture at Sedan in September, 1870.

eu·ge·nol (yōō'jə-nôl', -nŏl') *n.* A colorless aromatic oil, $C_{10}H_{12}O_2$, the chief constituent of oil of cloves. [New Latin *Eugenia*, genus of the clove, after *Eugene*, Prince of Savoy (1633–1736) + -OL.]

eu·gle·na (yōō-glē'nə) *n.* Any of various minute unicellular freshwater organisms of the genus *Euglena*, characterized by the presence of chlorophyll, a reddish eyespot, and a single anterior flagellum. [New Latin : EU- + Greek *glēnē,* eyeball.]

eu·glob·u·lin (yōō-glŏb'yə-lĭn) *n.* A globulin that is soluble in dilute salt solutions and insoluble in distilled water.

eu·he·mer·ism (yōō-hē'mə-rĭz'əm, -hĕm'ə-rĭz'əm) *n.* 1. A theory attributing the origin of the gods to the deification of historical heroes. 2. A theory linking mythology or folklore with real persons or events. [After *Euhemerus* (c. 300 B.C.), Greek philosopher.] —**eu·he·mer·ist** *n.* —**eu·he·mer·is·tic** (yōō-hē'mə-rĭs'tĭk, yōō-hĕm'ə-) *adj.* —**eu·he·mer·is·ti·cal·ly** *adv.*

eu·he·mer·ize (yōō-hē'mə-rīz', -hĕm'ə-rīz') *tr.v.* -ized, -izing, -izes. To explain or interpret (myths) euhemeristically.

eu·la·chon (yōō'lə-kŏn') *n., pl.* -chons or collectively **eulachon.** The **candlefish** *(see).* [Chinook *ulâkân.*]

Eu·ler (oi'lər), **Leonhard** (1707–83). Swiss mathematician. His fame rests mainly on his pioneering development of the methods of calculus and on the differential equation named after him.

Euler's formula *n. Mathematics.* 1. The formula $v + f - e = 2$ relating the numbers of vertices *(v)*, faces *(f)*, and edges *(e)* of a polyhedron. 2. The formula $e^{i\theta} = cos\theta + i\,sin\theta$ for complex numbers.

eu·lo·gi·a (yōō-lō'jē-ə, -jə) *n.* Blessed bread distributed to the congregation after the liturgy in the Greek Orthodox Church. [Greek, "blessing."]

eu·lo·gize (yōō'lə-jīz') *tr.v.* -gized, -gizing, -gizes. 1. To write or deliver a eulogy about or for. 2. To praise highly; extol. —**eu·lo·gist, eu·lo·giz·er** *n.*

eu·lo·gy (yōō'lə-jē) *n., pl.* -gies. 1. A public speech or written tribute extolling the virtues of a person or thing; especially, an oration honoring one recently deceased. 2. Great praise or commendation. [Middle English *euloge,* from Medieval Latin *eulogium,* probably variant of *eulogia,* from Greek, praise, eulogy : EU- + -LOGY.] —**eu·lo·gis·tic** (yōō'lə-jĭs'tĭk) *adj.*

Eu·men·i·des (yōō-mĕn'ə-dēz') *pl.n. Greek Mythology.* The **Furies** *(see).* [Latin, from Greek, "well-minded (ones)," euphemism for the Furies, from *eumenēs,* kindly, well-disposed : *eu-,* well + *menos,* spirit.]

eu·nuch (yōō'nək) *n.* 1. A castrated man; especially, one of those who were employed as harem attendants or functionaries in certain Oriental courts and under the Roman emperors. 2. An ineffectual or powerless man: *an artistic eunuch.* [Middle English *eunuke,* from Latin *eunūchus,* from Greek *eunoukhos,* "bed-watcher," eunuch : *eunē†,* bed + *ekhein,* to have, to hold.]

eu·on·y·mus (yōō-ŏn'ə-məs) *n.* Any of various trees, shrubs, or vines of the genus *Euonymus,* many of which are cultivated for their decorative foliage or fruits. [New Latin, from Latin *euōnymus,* spindle, tree, from Greek *euōnumos,* of good name : *eu-,* good + *onoma,* name.]

eu·pat·rid (yōō-păt'rĭd, -pā'trĭd) *n., pl.* -ridae (-păt'rĭ-dē', -pā'trĭ-dē') or -rids. A member of the hereditary aristocracy of ancient Athens. [Greek *eupatridēs,* of noble family : *eu-,* well + *patēr* (stem *patr-*), father + -*idēs,* patronymic suffix.] —**eu·pat·rid** *adj.*

eu·pep·si·a (yōō-pĕp'sē-ə, -shə) *n.* Good digestion. [New Latin, from Greek, from *eupeptos,* EUPEPTIC.]

eu·pep·tic (yōō-pĕp'tĭk) *adj.* 1. Pertaining to or having good digestion. 2. Conducive to digestion. 3. Cheerful. [Greek *eupeptos,* having good digestion : *eu-,* well + *peptein,* to digest, cook.] —**eu·pep·ti·cal·ly** *adv.*

eu·phau·si·id (yōō-fô'zē-ĭd) *n.* Any small, shrimplike crustacean of the order Euphausiacea. See **krill.**

eu·phe·mism (yōō'fə-mĭz'əm) *n.* 1. The substitution of an inoffensive term for one considered offensively explicit. 2. The term thus substituted: *"Euphemisms such as 'slumber room'... abound in the funeral business"* (Jessica Mitford). [Greek *euphēmismos,* from *euphēmizein,* to speak with good words, from *euphēmia,* use of good words : *eu-,* good + *phēmē,* speech, saying.] —**eu·phe·mist** *n.* —**eu·phe·mis·tic** (yōō'fə-mĭs'tĭk) *adj.* —**eu·phe·mis·ti·cal·ly** *adv.*

eu·phe·mize (yōō'fə-mīz') *v.* -mized, -mizing, -mizes. —*tr.* To speak of or refer to euphemistically. —*intr.* To speak with euphemisms.

eu·pho·ni·ous (yōō-fō'nē-əs) *adj.* Characterized by euphony; agreeable to the ear. —**eu·pho·ni·ous·ly** *adv.*

eu·pho·ni·um (yōō-fō'nē-əm) *n.* A brass wind instrument similar to the tuba but having a somewhat higher pitch and a mellower sound. [Greek *euphōnos,* sweet-voiced. See **euphony.**]

eu·pho·nize (yōō'fə-nīz') *tr.v.* -nized, -nizing, -nizes. To make euphonious. —**eu·pho·ni·za·tion** *n.*

eu·pho·ny (yōō'fə-nē) *n., pl.* -nies. 1. Agreeable sound, especially in the phonetic quality of words. 2. *Phonetics.* The tendency to change speech sounds for the sake of easier pronunciation. [French *euphonie,* from Late Latin *euphōnia,* from Greek, from *euphōnos,* sweet-voiced, euphonious : *eu-,* good + *phōnē,* sound.] —**eu·phon·ic** (yōō-fŏn'ĭk) *adj.*

eu·phor·bi·a (yōō-fôr'bē-ə) *n.* A plant of the genus *Euphorbia,* which includes the spurges and poinsettia. [New Latin, from *euphorbea,* from *Euphorbus,* Greek physician of the 1st century A.D.]

eu·pho·ri·a (yōō-fôr'ē-ə, -fōr'ē-ə) *n.* 1. A feeling of great happiness or well-being; bliss. 2. *Psychiatry.* An exaggerated sense of well-

being in pathological cases involving sympathetic delusions. —See Synonyms at **ecstasy.** [New Latin, from Greek, from *euphoros,* easy to bear, well-borne : *eu-,* well + *pherein,* to bear.] —**eu·phor·ic** (yōō-fôr'ĭk, -fōr'ĭk) *adj.*

eu·pho·ri·ant (yōō-fôr'ē-ənt, -fōr'ē-ənt) *adj.* Tending to produce euphoria. —*n.* An agent that produces euphoria.

eu·phot·ic (yōō-fōt'ĭk, -fō'tĭk) *adj.* Pertaining to, designating, or characterizing the uppermost layer of a body of water that receives sufficient light for photosynthesis and the growth of green plants. [EU- + PHOTIC.]

eu·phra·sy (yōō'frə-sē) *n. Archaic.* A plant of the genus *Euphrasia;* eyebright. [Middle English *eufrasie,* from Medieval Latin *eufrasia,* from Greek *euphrasia,* good cheer, from *euphrainein,* to cheer, gladden : *eu-,* good + *phrēn,* mind.]

Eu·phra·tes (yōō-frā'tēz). River in southwestern Asia, formed by the confluence of the Murad and Kara rivers and flowing for 2,740 kilometers (1,700 miles) from central Turkey through Syria into Iraq, where it joins with the Tigris River to form the Shatt al Arab. The Euphrates is too shallow for heavy craft.

eu·phroe (yōō'frō') *n.* 1. *Nautical.* A perforated batten through which the lines of a crowfoot are passed to suspend an awning. 2. A piece of wood having holes through which a tent rope, for example, is passed, and by means of which tension on the rope can be adjusted. [Dutch *juffrouw,* maiden, euphroe, from Middle Dutch *joncfrouwe.*]

Eu·phros·y·ne (yōō-frŏz'ə-nē). *Greek Mythology.* One of the three **Graces** *(see.)* [Latin *Euphrosynē,* from Greek *Euphrosunē,* "mirth," from *euphrōn,* of good mind, cheerful : *eu-,* good + *phrēn,* mind.]

eu·phu·ism (yōō'fyōō-ĭz'əm) *n.* 1. An affectedly elegant style of speech or writing used by imitators of John Lyly in the late 16th and early 17th centuries, characterized by elaborate alliteration, antitheses, and similes. 2. Broadly, affected elegance of language: *"Among his contemporaries, Willie's euphuisms only raised a laugh"* (Aldous Huxley). [After *Euphues,* a character in two works by John Lyly, from Greek *euphuēs,* shapely, well-grown : *eu-,* well + *phuein,* to grow, to bring forth.] —**eu·phu·ist** *n.* —**eu·phu·is·tic** (yōō'fyōō-ĭs'tĭk) *adj.* —**eu·phu·is·ti·cal·ly** *adv.*

eu·plas·tic (yōō-plăs'tĭk) *adj.* Healing readily.

eu·ploid (yōō'ploid') *n.* An organism or cell whose chromosome number is an exact multiple of the haploid number characteristic of the species. [EU- + (HA)PLOID.] —**eu·ploid** *adj.* —**eu·ploi·dy** *n.*

eup·ne·a, eup·noe·a (yōōp-nē'ə) *n.* Normal, unlabored breathing. [New Latin, from Greek *eupnoia,* from *eupnoos,* breathing well : *eu-,* good + *pnoē, pnoiē,* a breathing, from *pnein,* to breathe.]

Eur. Europe; European.

Eu·rail·pass (yōō-rāl'păs', -päs') *n.* A season ticket, sold only outside Europe, allowing extended rail travel in most countries of continental western Europe.

Eur·a·sia (yōō-rā'zhə). The landmass that comprises the continents of Europe and Asia.

Eur·a·sian (yōō-rā'zhən, -shən) *adj.* 1. Of, pertaining to, or originating in Eurasia. 2. Of mixed European and Asian ancestry. —*n.* A person of mixed European and Asian ancestry.

Eur·at·om, EUR·AT·OM (yōō-răt'əm) *n.* The European Atomic Energy Commission.

eu·re·ka (yōō-rē'kə) *interj.* Used to express triumph upon finding or discovering something. [Greek *heurēka,* "I have found (it)" (see **Archimedes**), perfect indicative of *heuriskein,* to find.]

eurhythmic. Variant of **eurythmic.**

eurhythmics. Variant of **eurythmics.**

eurhythmy. Variant of **eurythmy.**

Eu·rip·i·des (yōō-rĭp'ĭ-dēz') (c. 480–406 B.C.). Greek dramatist who ranks with Sophocles and Aeschylus as one of the great writers of classical tragedy. He wrote over 90 plays; among those that survive are *Alcestis, Hippolytus, The Trojan Women, Electra, Medea,* and *Iphigenia in Tauris.*

eu·ri·pus (yōō-rī'pəs) *n., pl.* -pi (-pī') A sea channel characterized by turbulent and unpredictable currents in either direction. [Latin, from Greek *euripos,* strait, place where the current is violent : *eu-,* well (euphemistic) + *ripē,* rush, force, from *rīptein,* to throw.]

eu·ro (yōōr'ō) *n., pl.* -ros. A kangaroo, the **wallaroo** *(see).* [Native word in Australia.]

Euro- *prefix.* Indicates: 1. Europe, especially Western Europe, or European; for example, **Eurodollar.** 2. The European Economic Community; for example, **Eurocrat.**

Eu·ro·bond (yōōr'ō-bŏnd') *n.* A bond of a United States corporation issued in Europe. [EURO- + BOND.]

Eu·ro·com·mu·nism (yōōr'ō-kŏm'yə-nĭz'əm) *n.* The variety of Communist theory and practice favored by most of the Communist parties in Western Europe, characterized by a more liberal outlook than and nonalignment with the Communist parties of Eastern Europe and Asia. —**Eu·ro·com·mu·nist** *n. & adj.*

Eu·ro·crat (yōōr'ə-krăt', yōōr'ō-) *n. Informal.* A senior official in the administration of the European Economic Community. Sometimes used derogatorily. [EURO- + (BUREAU)CRAT.]

Eu·ro·cur·ren·cy (yōōr'ō-kûr'ən-sē) *n., pl.* -cies. Any of various national currencies used for trade and exchange dealings in Europe and elsewhere.

Eu·ro·dol·lar (yōōr'ō-dŏl'ər) *n.* A United States dollar on deposit with a bank abroad, especially in Europe.

Eu·ro·mar·ket (yōōr'ō-mär'kĭt) *n.* Also **Eu·ro·mart** (-märt'). The European Economic Community.

eucalyptus *An evergreen tree native to Australia. There are over 500 species of eucalyptus, some of which produce an oil used in cough medicines. The cider gum tree, Eucalyptus gunnii (above), can grow to 30 meters (100 feet).*

Eu·ro·pa (yŏŏ-rō′pə). *Greek Mythology.* A Phoenician princess abducted to Crete by Zeus, in the guise of a white bull.

Eu·rope (yŏŏr′əp). *Abbr.* **Eur.** The world's second-smallest major land area, after Oceania. It has only 7 percent of the globe's land, but with 15 percent of the world's people it is the second most populous continent after Asia. Europe includes part of the world's largest country, the U.S.S.R., and also its smallest sovereign state, the Vatican City. Since World War II, the U.S.S.R. has dominated Eastern Europe, also known as the Eastern or Communist Bloc, where the countries have centrally planned economies. The nations of Western Europe, with capitalist or mixed economies, have largely looked to the United States for military alliance. Area, 10,498,000 square kilometers (4,053,000 square miles), including the U.S.S.R. west of the Ural Mts.

Eu·ro·pe·an (yŏŏr′ə-pē′ən) *adj. Abbr.* **Eur. 1.** Of, pertaining to, or derived from the continent of Europe, its peoples, cultures, or languages. **2.** Indigenous to or native to Europe. **3.** Of or pertaining to the European Economic Community.
~*n.* **1.** A native or inhabitant of Europe. **2.** One of European ancestry. **3.** A citizen of a country belonging to the European Economic Community, especially with reference to the extent of the person's support for the Community: *good Europeans.* **4.** *South African.* A white native of South Africa.

European Communities *pl.n.* A union of three communities that share a common administrative organization: the European Coal and Steel Community, the European Economic Community, and the European Atomic Energy Commission (Euratom).

European Court of Justice *n.* A court in Luxembourg that deals with cases involving the laws of the European Economic Community.

European Economic Community *n. Abbr.* **EEC** An association of ten member countries (Belgium, France, West Germany, Luxembourg, the Netherlands, and Italy, founder members; subsequently joined by the United Kingdom, the Republic of Ireland, Denmark, and Greece), founded by the Treaty of Rome (1957) as a customs union and to promote economic and political cooperation between the member countries. Also called "European Community," "Common Market." See feature page 539.

Eu·ro·pe·an·ism (yŏŏr′ə-pē′ə-nĭz′əm) *n.* **1.** A political movement promoting a policy of unity among European countries, especially the European Economic Community. **2.** Support for such a policy; a favorable attitude toward the European Economic Community. —**Eu·ro·pe·an·ist** *n.*

Eu·ro·pe·an·ize (yŏŏr′ə-pē′ə-nīz′) *tr.v.* **-ized, -izing, -izes. 1.** To make European in culture, political institutions, or customs. **2.** To introduce the institutions and regulations of the European Economic Community into (a country). —**Eu·ro·pe·an·i·za·tion** (yŏŏr′-ə-pē′ə-nə-zā′shən) *n.*

European Parliament *n.* The legislative assembly of the European Economic Community.

European plan *n.* A system of hotel tariffs in which a guest pays for his room and services separately from his payment for meals. Compare **American plan.**

European Recovery Program *n.* An American program to provide economic aid to European nations following World War II that was initiated by General George C. Marshall.

eu·ro·pi·um (yŏŏ-rō′pē-əm) *n. Symbol* **Eu** A silvery-white, soft rare-earth element occurring in monazite and bastnaesite. It is used as a laser dopant, phosphor, and in research to absorb neutrons. Atomic number 63, atomic weight 151.96, melting point 826°C, boiling point 1,439°C, specific gravity 5.259, valences 2, 3. [New Latin, from EUROPE.]

Eu·ro·vi·sion (yŏŏr′ə-vĭzh′ən) *n.* The television network of the European Broadcasting Union, through which news and programs are exchanged or relayed.

Eu·rus (yŏŏr′əs). *Greek Mythology.* The god of the east or southeast wind. [Latin, from Greek *Euros,* possibly from *heuein,* to burn, to singe.]

eury- *prefix.* Indicates wide or broad; for example, **eurypterid.** [New Latin, from Greek *euru-,* from *eurus,* wide.]

Eu·ry·a·le (yŏŏ-rī′ə-lē). *Greek Mythology.* One of the three Gorgons.

Eu·ryd·i·ce (yŏŏ-rĭd′ə-sē). *Greek Mythology.* The wife of Orpheus, who was permitted by Pluto to follow her husband out of Hades provided that he refrain from looking back at her; Orpheus did look back, and Eurydice was doomed to return to the dead. [Latin, from Greek *Eurudikē,* "wide justice" : *euru-,* EURY- + *dikē,* justice, custom, law.]

eu·ry·ha·line (yŏŏr′ə-hā′lĭn′, -hăl′ĭn′) *adj.* Able to tolerate wide variations in salt concentration. Said of aquatic animals such as eels. Compare **stenohaline.**

eu·ryp·ter·id (yŏŏ-rĭp′tər-ĭd) *n.* Any of various large, extinct aquatic arthropods of the order Eurypterida, existing from the Ordovician to the Permian period. [New Latin *Eurypterida,* from *Eurypterus* (genus) : EURY- + -PTEROUS.]

eu·ry·ther·mal (yŏŏr′ə-thûr′məl) *adj.* Also **eu·ry·ther·mic** (-mĭk), **eu·ry·ther·mous** (-məs). Adaptable to a wide range of temperatures. Said of an organism.

eu·ryth·mic, eu·rhyth·mic (yŏŏ-rĭth′mĭk) *adj.* **1.** Harmonious in rhythm or proportions. **2.** Of or pertaining to eurythmics.

eu·ryth·mics, eu·rhyth·mics (yŏŏ-rĭth′mĭks) *n. Used with a singular verb.* The choreographic art of interpreting music through rhythmical, free-style, graceful movement of the body.

eu·ryth·my, eu·rhyth·my (yŏŏ-rĭth′mē) *n.* **1.** Harmony of proportions in architecture. **2.** Rhythmical or graceful movements. **3.** A system of rhythmical body movements in harmony with the rhythm of the spoken word, used in a form of dance training.

eu·ry·top·ic (yŏŏr′ə-tŏp′ĭk) *adj.* Capable of existing in a wide range of environmental conditions. Said of plant and animal species.

eu·spo·ran·gi·ate (yŏŏ′spə-răn′jē-ĭt, -āt′) *adj.* Of or designating ferns in which the sporangium develops from a group of cells. Compare **leptosporangiate.**

Eu·sta·chian tube (yŏŏ-stā′shən, -shē-ən, -stā′kē-ən) *n.* A bony and cartilaginous tube that connects the tympanic cavity with the nasal part of the pharynx and equalizes pressure on either side of the eardrum. [After Bartolommeo *Eustachio* (c. 1524–74), Italian anatomist.]

eu·stat·ic (yŏŏ-stăt′ĭk) *adj.* Of or pertaining to overall changes in sea level, as produced by large-scale geologic changes such as movement of the ocean floor or melting of ice caps.

eu·tec·tic (yŏŏ-tĕk′tĭk) *adj.* **1.** Of, pertaining to, or formed at the lowest possible temperature of solidification for any mixture of specific constituents. Said especially of alloys. **2.** Exhibiting the constitution or properties of a solid so formed.
~*n.* **1.** A eutectic mixture, solution, or alloy. **2.** The temperature at which a eutectic forms. [Greek *eutēktos,* easily melted : *eu-,* well + *tēktos,* melted, from *tēkein,* to melt.]

Eu·ter·pe (yŏŏ-tûr′pē). *Greek Mythology.* The Muse of lyric poetry and music.

eu·tha·na·sia (yŏŏ′thə-nā′zhə, -zhē-ə) *n.* The action of inducing the painless death of a person from motives of compassion. Also called "mercy killing." [Greek : *eu-,* good + *thanatos,* death.]

eu·then·ics (yŏŏ-thĕn′ĭks) *n. Used with a singular verb.* The study of the improvement of human functioning and well-being by adjustment of environment. Compare **eugenics.** [Greek *euthenein,* to flourish, thrive.]

eu·the·ri·an (yŏŏ-thîr′ē-ən) *adj.* Of, pertaining to, or designating mammals of the subclass Eutheria, characterized by the formation of a placenta and including all mammals except the monotremes and marsupials. [New Latin *Eutheria* : Greek *eu-,* well + *thēria,* plural of *thērion,* beast.] —**eu·the·ri·an** *n.*

eu·troph·ic (yŏŏ-trŏf′ĭk, -trō′fĭk) *adj.* Designating a body of water in which the increase of mineral and organic nutrients has reduced the dissolved oxygen, producing an environment that favors plant life over animal life. [Probably from German *Eutroph,* from Greek *eutrophos,* well-nourished, from *eutrophein,* to thrive : *eu-,* well + *trephein,* to nourish.] —**eu·troph·i·ca·tion** (yŏŏ-trŏf′ĭ-kā′shən, yŏŏ-trō′fĭ-) *n.*

eux·e·nite (yŏŏk′sə-nīt′) *n.* A lustrous blackish-brown mineral consisting of cerium, erbium, niobium, titanium, uranium, and yttrium. [German *Euxenit,* from Greek *euxenos,* kind to strangers (it contains many rare or "strange" elements) : *eu-,* good + *xenos,* stranger.]

eV electron volt.

EVA extravehicular activity.

e·vac·u·ant (ĭ-văk′yŏŏ-ənt) *adj.* Causing evacuation of an organ, especially of the bowels.
~*n.* An evacuant medicine or agent; a purgative or emetic.

e·vac·u·ate (ĭ-văk′yŏŏ-āt′) *v.* **-ated, -ating, -ates.** —*tr.* **1. a.** To cause to be empty by removing the contents. **b.** To create a vacuum in. **2.** To excrete or discharge (waste matter), especially from the bowels. **3.** *Military.* **a.** To relinquish possession or occupation of (a town, fortress, or encampment, for example). **b.** To withdraw or send away (troops or inhabitants) from a threatened area. **4.** To withdraw or depart from; vacate. —*intr.* **1.** To withdraw from or vacate any place or area, especially a threatened area. **2.** To discharge waste matter from the body. [Latin *ēvacuāre,* to empty out, to evacuate : *ē-,* out, from *ex-* + *vacuus,* empty.] —**e·vac·u·a·tion** *n.* —**e·vac·u·a·tor** *n.*

e·vac·u·ee (ĭ-văk′yŏŏ-ē′) *n.* A person withdrawn or sent away from a threatened or dangerous area.

e·vade (ĭ-vād′) *v.* **evaded, evading, evades.** —*tr.* **1.** To escape or avoid by cleverness or deceit: *evade arrest.* **2.** To avoid fulfilling, answering, or performing: *evade responsibility.* **3.** To baffle or elude: *The accident evades explanation.* —*intr.* To use cleverness or deceit in avoiding or escaping. —See Synonyms at **escape.** [Old French *evader,* from Latin *ēvādere,* to evade, go out, escape : *ē-,* out, from *ex-* + *vādere,* to go.] —**e·vad·a·ble** *adj.* —**e·vad·er** *n.*

e·vag·i·nate (ĭ-văj′ə-nāt′) *tr.v.* **-nated, -nating, -nates.** *Medicine.* To cause (a body part) to turn inside out by eversion of an inner surface. [Latin *ēvāgināre,* to unsheath : *ē-* (indicating removal), from *ex-* + *vāgīna,* sheath.] —**e·vag·i·na·tion** *n.*

e·val·u·ate (ĭ-văl′yŏŏ-āt′) *tr.v.* **-ated, -ating, -ates. 1.** To ascertain or fix the value or worth of. **2.** To examine and judge; appraise; estimate. **3.** *Mathematics.* To calculate or set down the numerical value of; express numerically. —See Synonyms at **estimate.** [Back-formation from *evaluation,* from French *évaluation,* from Old French, from *evaluer,* to evaluate : *e-,* out, from Latin *ex-* + VALUE.] —**e·val·u·a·tion** *n.*

ev·a·nesce (ĕv′ə-nĕs′) *intr.v.* **-nesced, -nescing, -nesces.** To dissipate like vapor; disappear gradually; fade away; vanish. [Latin *ēvānēscere,* to vanish : *ē-,* completely, from *ex-* + *vānēscere,* to vanish, from *vānus,* empty, vain.] —**ev·a·nes·cence** *n.*

ev·a·nes·cent (ĕv′ə-nĕs′ənt) *adj.* Vanishing or likely to vanish; transitory; fleeting: *"Seeking permanence in the midst of what was only perpetually evanescent"* (Malcolm Lowry). —See Synonyms at **transient.** —**ev·a·nes·cent·ly** *adv.*

e·van·gel (ĭ-văn′jəl) n. **1.** *Usually* **Evangel.** The Christian gospel; especially, any of the four Gospels of the New Testament. **2.** Glad tidings. **3.** An evangelist. [Middle English *evangile,* from Old French *evangile,* from Late Latin *evangelium,* from Greek *euangelion,* good news, reward for bringing good news, from *euangelos,* bringing good news : *eu-,* good + *angelos,* messenger.]

e·van·gel·i·cal (ē′văn-jĕl′ĭ-kəl, ĕv′ən-) adj. Also **e·van·gel·ic** (-jĕl′ĭk). **1.** Of, pertaining to, or in accordance with the Christian gospel, especially the four Gospels of the New Testament. **2.** *Often* **Evangelical.** Protestant. **3.** Of, pertaining to, or being a Protestant group emphasizing the authority of the gospel and the importance of personal conversion and faith in Christ as one's own savior. **4. Evangelical.** Pertaining or belonging to the Evangelical Church in Germany. **5.** Pertaining or belonging to the Low Church party in the Church of England. **6.** Characterized by evangelism; zealous. —n. A member of an evangelical church or party. **—e·van·gel·i·cal·ly** adv.

e·van·gel·i·cal·ism (ē′văn-jĕl′ĭ-kə-līz′əm, ĕv′ən-) n. **1.** Evangelical beliefs or doctrines. **2.** Adherence to a church or party professing such beliefs or doctrines.

e·van·gel·ism (ĭ-văn′jə-līz′əm) n. **1.** The zealous preaching and dissemination of the gospel, as through missionary work. **2.** Militant zeal for any cause.

e·van·gel·ist (ĭ-văn′jə-līst) n. **1.** *Usually* **Evangelist.** Any of the authors of the four New Testament Gospels: Matthew, Mark, Luke, or John. **2.** One who practices evangelism; especially, a Protestant preacher or missionary. **3.** In the Mormon Church, a **patriarch** *(see).* **—e·van·gel·is·tic** (ĭ-văn′jə-līs′tĭk) adj. **—e·van·gel·is·ti·cal·ly** adv.

e·van·gel·ize (ĭ-văn′jə-līz′) v. **-ized, -izing, -izes.** —tr. **1.** To preach the gospel to. **2.** To convert to Christianity. —intr. To preach the gospel; be an evangelist. **—e·van·gel·i·za·tion** n. **—e·van·gel·iz·er** n.

Ev·ans (ĕv′ənz), **Sir Arthur John** (1851–1941). British archaeologist. His excavations in Crete, mostly at Knossos, unearthed a Bronze Age civilization that he named Minoan, after the legendary King Minos.

Evans, Dame Edith (1888–1976). English actress. After winning acclaim for her performance as Cressida in 1912, she joined the Old Vic and thereafter played a wide variety of roles, of which her most famous was Lady Bracknell in *The Importance of Being Earnest.* Her films include *Look Back in Anger* (1959).

Evans, Mary Ann. See George **Eliot.**

Evans, Walker (1903–75). U.S. photographer. His best-known works are studies of Victorian architecture and photographs of the rural South during the Depression. He collaborated with James Agee on the book *Let Us Now Praise Famous Men* (1941).

Ev·ans·ton (ĕv′ən-stən). A city in northeastern Illinois, on Lake Michigan. It is mainly residential with some industries, including publishing and food processing. Northwestern University is here.

Ev·ans·ville (ĕv′ənz-vĭl′). A city of extreme southwestern Indiana, on the Ohio River. It is the shipping and commercial center for a coal, oil, and farm region. Its manufactures include heavy machinery and pharmaceuticals.

e·vap·o·ra·ble (ĭ-văp′ər-ə-bəl) adj. Capable of being evaporated. **—e·vap·o·ra·bil·i·ty** n.

e·vap·o·rate (ĭ-văp′ə-rāt′) v. **-rated, -rating, -rates.** —tr. **1. a.** To convert or change into a vapor, especially at a temperature below the boiling point. **b.** To draw off in the form of vapor. **2.** To draw moisture from, leaving only the dry solid portion. **3.** To deposit (a metal) on a substrate by vacuum sublimation. —intr. **1. a.** To change into vapor. **b.** To pass off in or as vapor. **2.** To produce vapor. **3.** To disappear; vanish: *His fears evaporated.* [Middle English *evaporaten,* from Latin *ēvaporāre* (past participle *ēvaporātus*), "to go out in vapor," evaporate : *ē-,* out of, from *ex-* + *vapor,* steam, vapor.] **—e·vap·o·ra·tion** n. **—e·vap·o·ra·tive** (ĭ-văp′ə-rā′tĭv, -ər-ə-tĭv) adj. **—e·vap·o·ra·tor** n.

evaporated milk n. Concentrated, unsweetened milk processed by evaporating some of the water from whole milk. Compare **condensed milk.**

e·vap·o·rite (ĭ-văp′ə-rīt′) n. A sedimentary rock or mineral, such as rock salt or gypsum, that has been formed by evaporation of salt water.

e·va·sion (ĭ-vā′zhən) n. **1.** The act of avoiding, evading, or escaping. **2.** A means of evading; a subterfuge. **3.** An excuse or equivocal answer. [Middle English *evasioun,* from Old French *evasion,* from Late Latin *ēvāsiō* (stem *ēvāsiōn-*), from Latin *ēvāsus,* past participle of *ēvādere,* to EVADE.]

e·va·sive (ĭ-vā′sĭv, -zĭv) adj. **1.** Characterized by or exhibiting evasion. **2.** Intentionally vague or ambiguous; equivocal: *an evasive statement.* **—e·va·sive·ly** adv. **—e·va·sive·ness** n.

eve (ēv) n. **1.** *Often* **Eve.** The evening or day preceding a special day, such as a saint's day or holiday: *Saint Agnes' Eve; New Year's Eve.* **2.** The period immediately preceding a certain event: *the eve of war.* **3.** *Poetic.* Evening. [Middle English *eve,* variant of EVEN (evening).]

Eve (ēv). In the Bible, the first woman and wife of Adam. Genesis 3:20.

e·vec·tion (ĭ-vĕk′shən) n. *Astronomy.* Solar perturbation of the lunar orbit. [Latin *ēvectiō* (stem *ēvectiōn-*), a going up, from *ēvectus,* past participle of *ēvehere,* to carry out : *ē-,* out, upward, from *ex-* + *vehere,* to carry.] **—e·vec·tion·al** adj.

Eve·lyn (ĕv′lĭn, ēv′-), **John** (1620–1706). English writer and one of the founders of the Royal Society. He is best known for his *Diary,* which covers most of his life and is rich in information about 17th-century England.

e·ven[1] (ē′vən) adj. **1. a.** Having a horizontal surface; flat: *an even floor.* **b.** Having no irregularities, roughness, or indentations; smooth. **2.** Having the same plane or line; at the same height or depth; parallel; level: *The picture is even with the window.* **3.** Having no variations or fluctuations; uniform; steady; regular: *an even rate of speed.* **4.** Of uniform thickness; uniformly distributed: *an even application of varnish.* **5.** Tranquil; calm; placid: *an even temper.* **6.** Equally matched or balanced: *an even contest.* **7.** Equal or identical in degree, extent, or amount: *even amounts of wine and water.* **8.** Having equal probability. Said of alternatives, possibilities, or events: *an even chance of winning or losing.* **9. a.** Having an equal score: *The teams are even.* **b.** Being equal for each opponent. Said of a score. **10.** Neither owing nor being owed; having nothing due: *Give him five dollars, and you will be even.* **11.** Having exacted full revenge. **12. a.** *Mathematics.* Exactly divisible by 2. **b.** Characterized or indicated by a number exactly divisible by 2. Compare **odd. 13. a.** Having an even number in a series. **b.** Having an even number of members. **14.** Having an exact amount, extent, or number: *an even pound.* —See Synonyms at **level, steady.**
—adv. **1.** Used to stress something that might not be expected: *He even drove us home.* **2.** At the same time as; just: *Even as we watched, the building collapsed.* **3.** In spite of; notwithstanding: *Even with his head start, I soon overtook him.* **4. a.** To a higher degree or extent; yet; still. Used as an intensive: *an even worse condition.* **b.** Indeed; in fact; moreover. Used as an intensive: *unhappy, even weeping.* **5.** To a degree that extends as specified: *loyal even unto death.* **6.** *Archaic.* The same as; identical with: *It is I, even I.* **—break even.** *Informal.* To have neither losses nor gains. **—get even.** To exact one's full measure of revenge.
—v. **evened, evening, evens.** —tr. **1.** To make even, smooth, or level. **2.** To settle or balance (accounts, debts, or the like); square. Often used with *off* or *up.* —intr. To become even or smooth. Used with *off, out,* or *up.* [Middle English *even,* Old English *ef(e)n,* even, level, from Common Germanic *ibnaz* (unattested).] **—e·ven·ly** adv. **—e·ven·ness** n.

even[2] n. *Archaic.* Evening. [Middle English *eve, even,* Old English *ǣfen.*]

e·ven·fall (ē′vən-fôl′) n. *Poetic.* The beginning of evening; twilight.

e·ven·hand·ed (ē′vən-hăn′dĭd) adj. Dealing equitably with all; impartial. **—e·ven·hand·ed·ly** adv. **—e·ven·hand·ed·ness** n.

eve·ning (ēv′nĭng) n. *Abbr.* **evg. 1.** The period of decreasing daylight during the decline and setting of the sun between afternoon and night. **2. a.** The period between the termination of one's daily activities and bedtime. **b.** This period occupied in a given manner: *an evening at home.* **3.** Any latter period or time of decline: *in the evening of his life.* [Middle English *evening,* Old English *ǣfnung,* evening, from *ǣfnian,* to become evening, from *ǣfen,* evening.]

evening dress n. **1.** Clothing, especially formal clothing, such as a man's dinner jacket, worn for evening social events. **2.** A woman's formal dress, usually long, that is worn especially in the evening. In this sense, also called "evening gown."

Evening Prayer n. An evening prayer service that is read or sung; especially, evensong in the Anglican Church or vespers in the Roman Catholic Church.

evening primrose n. Any of various North American plants of the genus *Oenothera,* characteristically having four-petaled yellow flowers that open in the evening and containing an oil with a high concentration of essential fatty acids.

eve·nings (ēv′nĭngs) adv. Regularly or habitually in the evening: *They read evenings.*

evening star n. A planet that crosses the local meridian before midnight, especially Mercury or Venus when either is prominent in the west shortly after sunset. Also, especially referring to Venus, formerly called "Vesper."

evening stock n. A plant, *Mathiola bicornis,* native to Eurasia, having fragrant purple flowers that bloom at night. Also called "night-scented stock."

e·vens (ē′vənz) adj. *British.* **1.** Standing to win exactly the sum staked. Said of a bet. **2.** Being offered at these odds. Said of a horse or other racing animal. **—e·vens** adv.

e·ven·song (ē′vən-sông′, -sŏng′) n. **1.** The service of Evening Prayer in the Anglican Church, often a choral service. **2.** A vesper service. **3.** A song sung in the evening. **4.** *Archaic.* Evening.

e·vent (ĭ-vĕnt′) n. **1.** An occurrence, incident, or experience, especially one of some significance. **2.** The actual outcome or final result. **3.** One of the items in a calendar or program of sports. **4.** An important social occasion. **5.** *Physics.* A coincidence of two or more points at a particular position in space at a particular instant of time, regarded as the fundamental observational entity in relativity theory. —See Synonyms at **occurrence. —at all events** or **in any event.** In any case; whatever the circumstances. **—in the event.** **1.** If it should happen; in case: *what to do in the event of an accident.* **2.** *Chiefly British.* As it turned out; as things happened: *In the event I'd had nothing to fear after all.* [Latin *ēventus,* a coming out, event, from the past participle of *ēvenīre,* to come out, happen : *ē-,* out, from *ex-* + *venīre,* to come.]

e·ven·tem·pered (ē′vən-tĕm′pərd) adj. Not easily disturbed; equable.

e·vent·ful (ĭ-vĕnt′fəl) adj. **1.** Full of or rich in events: *an eventful week.* **2.** Important; momentous: *an eventful decision.* **—e·vent·ful·ly** adv. **—e·vent·ful·ness** n.

event horizon *n. Astronomy.* The spherical surface marking the boundary of a black hole, being the place at which the escape velocity is equal to the speed of light, so that no electromagnetic radiation or information can leave the black hole.

e·ven·tide (ē′vən-tīd′) *n. Poetic.* Evening. [Middle English *eventide,* Old English *ǣfentīd* : *ǣfen,* EVEN (evening) + *tīd,* time, season.]

e·ven·tu·al (ĭ-vĕn′cho͞o-əl) *adj.* **1.** Occurring at an unspecified time in the future; ultimate: *his eventual death.* **2.** Occurring or having occurred after some time has elapsed. **3.** *Archaic.* Dependent on circumstance; possible; contingent. —See Synonyms at **last.** [From EVENT.]

e·ven·tu·al·i·ty (ĭ-vĕn′cho͞o-ăl′ə-tē) *n., pl.* **-ties.** Something that may occur; a contingency; a possibility.

e·ven·tu·al·ly (ĭ-vĕn′cho͞o-ə-lē) *adv.* **1.** Finally; as the last step in a process. **2.** After a long delay.

e·ven·tu·ate (ĭ-vĕn′cho͞o-āt′) *intr.v.* **-ated, -ating, -ates.** To result ultimately: *Their debate eventuated in peaceable agreement.* —**e·ven·tu·a·tion** *n.*

Evert Lloyd, Chris *Born in Florida in December 1954, Chris Evert Lloyd won the women's singles championship at Wimbledon in 1974, 1976, and 1981. She married British tennis player John Lloyd in 1979.*

ev·er (ĕv′ər) *adv.* **1. a.** At all times; always; constantly. Sometimes used in combination: *his ever-patient sister.* **b.** Repeatedly: *ever complaining.* **2.** At any time: *Have you ever seen a circus?* **3.** Used to add emphasis, especially in questions: *How could you ever treat him so?* **4.** *Chiefly British Informal.* To a great degree; very much. Used as an intensive: *I'm ever so relieved.* **5.** *Informal.* Certainly; without doubt: *Happy? Is she ever!* —**for ever and a day.** Always; forever. [Middle English *ever,* Old English *ǣfre.*]

Ev·er·est (ĕv′ər-ĭst, ĕv′rĭst) *n.* The ultimate or highest point of achievement or ambition: *The marathon is a runner's Everest.*

Everest, Mount. The world's highest mountain (8,848 meters; 29,028 feet) in the central Himalayas, on the border of Nepal and Tibet. In Tibet it is called Chomolungma ("Mother Goddess of the World"); it takes its English name from the surveyor general of India, Sir George Everest (1790–1866). The summit was first reached by Sir Edmund Hillary and Tenzing Norgay on May 28, 1953.

ev·er·glade (ĕv′ər-glād′) *n.* A tract of marshland, usually under water and covered in places with tall grass; a swamp. [Perhaps EVER ("interminable") + GLADE (open space).]

Ev·er·glades (ĕv′ər-glādz′). Swampy region of 13,000 square kilometers (5,000 square miles) at the southern tip of Florida. It is abundant in crocodiles, alligators, egrets, and bald eagles. Its national park is the third largest in the United States.

ev·er·green (ĕv′ər-grēn′) *adj.* **1. a.** Having foliage that persists and remains green throughout the year: *evergreen trees.* **b.** Persisting and remaining green throughout the year: *evergreen foliage.* Compare **deciduous. 2.** Retaining freshness and popularity over a long period: *an evergreen musical.*
∼*n.* **1.** An evergreen tree or shrub. **2.** Something that retains freshness and popularity over a long period.

ev·er·last·ing (ĕv′ər-lăs′tĭng, -lä′stĭng) *adj.* **1.** Lasting forever; eternal. **2.** Continuing indefinitely or for a long period of time; perpetual. **3.** Lasting too long; tedious: *his everlasting complaints.* **4.** Retaining color and form for a long time when cut or dried, as certain plants do.
∼*n.* **1. Everlasting.** God. Preceded by *the.* **2.** Eternal duration; eternity. **3.** Any of various everlasting plants, such as *Helichrysum bracteatum.*

ev·er·more (ĕv′ə-môr′, -mōr′) *adv.* **1.** Forever. Obsolete except in the phrase *for evermore.* **2.** Constantly; always.

e·vert (ĭ-vûrt′) *tr.v.* **everted, everting, everts.** To turn (the cervix, intestines, or other part of the body) inside out or outward. [Latin *ēvertere,* to turn out, overturn : *ē-,* out, from *ex-* + *vertere,* to turn.] —**e·ver·sion** (ĭ-vûr′zhən, -shən) *n.* —**e·ver·si·ble** (ĭ-vûr′sə-bəl) *adj.*

Ev·ert Lloyd (ĕv′ərt loid′), **Christine,** known as "Chris" (1954–). U.S. tennis player. She was U.S. women's singles champion (1975–78, 1980, 1982) and won the Wimbledon title in 1974, 1976, and 1981.

e·ver·tor (ĭ-vûr′tər) *n.* A muscle that acts to turn a part outward or inside out.

eve·ry (ĕv′rē) *adj.* **1.** Each and all single members of an aggregate; each without exception: *every student in the class.* **2.** Each particular member of a series. Used where a qualification is involved: *every third seat; every two hours.* **3.** Each thing or all possible things without exception; no matter which or when: *arrive late at every party.* **4.** The utmost, most earnest, or most extensive: *gave him every care.* ∼*adv.* More or less; periodically. Used as an intensive with idioms indicating indefinite or occasional recurrence: *every once in a while.* —**every bit.** *Informal.* In all ways; quite; equally: *He is every bit as mean as she is.* —**every other. 1.** Each alternate; each second: *Leave every other door unmarked.* **2.** *Informal.* Almost each: *Every other cup is chipped.* —**every so often.** From time to time; occasionally: *They met on the street every so often.* —**every which way. 1.** *Informal.* In complete disorder; chaotic. **2.** In every sequence or direction. [Middle English *every, everich, everulch,* Old English *ǣfre ǣlc,* "ever each," every, each one : *ǣfre,* EVER + *ǣlc,* EACH.]

Usage: *Every* takes a singular verb: *Every person has to get what he wants.* There is rarely a problem over agreement with the verb, but there is some variability over agreement with a pronoun later in the sentence, especially when the speaker does not wish to select a pronoun such as *he* or *she. Every person knows what they have to do* may therefore be heard, alongside the more careful (but also more awkward) *Every person knows what he or she has to do* and the simpler (but, to some, sexist) use of *he,* as above. • The phrase *each and every* has attracted occasional criticism as a redundant expression, *each and every day* being felt to be equivalent to *each day* or *every day.* But the extra emphasis conveyed by this phrase seems sufficient to explain its continued use in both formal and informal styles. —See also Usage note at **each** and **everyone.**

eve·ry·bod·y (ĕv′rē-bŏd′ē) *pron.* Every person; everyone. —See Usage note at **everyone.**

eve·ry·day (ĕv′rē-dā′) *adj.* **1.** Suitable for ordinary days or routine occasions: *an everyday suit.* **2.** Commonplace; usual; ordinary: *everyday worries.*

Usage: This is written as a single word only when it is used as an adjective, as in *an everyday happening.* In other circumstances, it is written as two words: *I go there every day.* In speech, the stress pattern is usually different, with *day* being more strongly stressed in the latter sense.

eve·ry·man (ĕv′rē-măn′) *n. Often* **Everyman.** The common, typical, or ordinary man, with all his weaknesses and failings. [After the central character in the medieval morality play *Everyman.*]

eve·ry·one (ĕv′rē-wŭn′) *pron.* Every person; everybody.

Usage: There are a large number of words and expressions in English that are singular in form but felt to be plural in sense, so that speakers are uncertain as to whether to use a singular or plural pronoun in referring back to them. For example, strict grammarians have long insisted that it is correct to say *everyone took his coat,* not *their coat* or *their coats,* and that we must say *no one is happy when he is abandoned,* and not *when they are abandoned.* Yet speakers persist in using the plural pronouns, and the most thoughtful grammarians, like Fowler, have recognized that there is no entirely happy solution to the problem. • The constructions affected fall into three classes. First, there are words formed with the word elements *-one* and *-body,* such as *anyone, somebody, everyone, nobody,* together with the two-word form *no one.* Second, there are the words *either, each, none,* and *any,* either used alone, as in *each found his seat,* or together with a noun, as in *each of the boys has his notebook* and *none of the books has its cover intact.* Finally, there are the words *whoever, whatever,* and *whichever,* either used as indefinite pronouns, as in *whoever talks out of turn will have his name sent to the office,* or together with a noun, as in *whichever nation is attacked first will find itself at a disadvantage.* • The traditional rule is that only a singular pronoun can be used in referring back to these constructions, as in the preceding examples of correct usage. But the rule as stated creates grammatical complications. For one thing, a pronoun outside the sentence containing the element it refers to *cannot* be in the singular. Thus, it is simply not English to say: *Everybody left in a hurry. He took his coat with him.* Nor can one say: *No one could be seen. He must have been hiding behind a rock.* Constructions with *whoever* are exceptions. One says: *Whoever is elected will take office in January. I am sure he will do a good job.* Writers who do not want to risk a violation of the traditional rule will have to find other ways of expressing the meaning. One may rephrase so as to get the pronoun into the same sentence as its antecedent, saying, for example, *Everybody left carrying his raincoat with him.* One may also substitute other words, for example the plural *all,* as in *All the guests left. They took their coats with them.* • *Each* presents some special problems. When it precedes the noun, a following pronoun is correctly singular: *Each of the actors has learned his* (not *their*) *part.* When *each* follows the noun, however, the pronoun is generally plural: *The actors have each learned their parts* (not *his part*). It should also be noted that *none* has for centuries been used by the best writers as if it were a plural form, taking both plural verb and plural pronouns: *None of them have learned their parts* must be considered an entirely acceptable variant of *None of them has learned his part.* Only the mixture of singular verb and plural pronoun would be considered incorrect, as in *None of them has learned their parts.* • The traditional rule may also be politically offensive to many speakers. When referring back to a group consisting of both men and women, strict grammarians have insisted that the masculine singular *him* or *his* be used as a "neutral" form; one is thus required to say *Every one of the actors and actresses has learned his part.* Since the last century, however, feminists and their allies have objected to this presumption. The writer who finds the singular *he* and *his* distasteful in these cases has the choice of flying in the face of traditional grammar and using *they* and *their* or of using the somewhat clumsier variants *his and her* (or *her and his*); attempts to introduce new pronouns like *s/he* appear unlikely to win general acceptance. The entire matter is properly outside the scope of grammar. In the end, as Fowler put it, "everyone must decide for himself (or for himself and herself, or for themselves)." —See also Usage note at **each** and **neither.**

eve·ry·place (ĕv′rē-plās′) *adv. Informal.* Everywhere.

Usage: *Everyplace* and *every place* used adverbially for *everywhere* are appropriate principally to informal writing or speech: *Everyplace* (or *every place*) *I go, I see her* (in formal writing, preferably *everywhere I go*). *Every place,* as a combination of adjective and noun, is, of course, standard English: *I searched in every place he suggested.*

eve·ry·thing (ĕv′rē-thĭng′) *pron.* **1.** All things or factors that exist or pertain to a given instance; the entirety or totality: *everything in this room.* **2.** All relevant items or factors: *Tell him everything.* **3.** The most important fact or consideration, especially for success or happiness; the principal concern: *Her children mean everything to her.* **4.** All aspects of something; life in general: *Everything went wrong.*

PRONUNCIATION KEY

ă, pat; ā, pay; âr, care;
ä, father, are; b, bib;
ch, church; d, deed; ĕ, pet;
ē, be; f, fife; g, gag; h, hat;
hw, which; ĭ, pit; ī, pie;
îr, pier; j, judge; k, kick;
l, lid, needle; m, mum;
n, no, sudden; ng, thing;
ŏ, pot; ō, toe; ô, paw, for;
oi, noise; ou, out; o͝o, book;
o͞o, boot; p, pop; r, roar;
s, sauce; sh, ship, dish;
t, tight; th, thin, path;
th, this, bathe; ŭ, cut; ûr, fur;
v, valve; w, with; y, yes;
z, zebra, size; zh, vision;
ə, about, item, edible,
gallop, circus, peaceful

IN FOREIGN WORDS:

à, *Fr.* ami; œ, *Fr.* feu, *Ger.* schön; ü, *Fr.* tu, *Ger.* über;
KH, *Ger.* ich, *Scot.* loch;
N, *Fr.* bon; y′, *Fr.* Compiègne

STRESS MARKS:

Primary stress: ′
in·cite′ (ĭn-sīt′)
Secondary stress: ′
in′sight′ (ĭn′sīt′)

5. Every desirable or necessary quality or possession: *The paintings in his collection are everything to him.*
eve·ry·where (ĕv′rē-hwâr′) *adv.* In or to any or every place; in all places.
∼*n.* Any or every place; all places: *Music lovers came from everywhere to hear the concert.*
Usage: The only acceptable word is *everywhere* (not *everywheres*). The use of *that* with *everywhere* (*everywhere that I go*) is superfluous. —See also Usage note at **everyplace.**
evg. evening.
e·vict (ĭ-vĭkt′) *tr.v.* **evicted, evicting, evicts. 1.** To expel (a tenant, for example) by legal process; put out. **2.** To force out; eject; dispossess: *"We have allowed the Communists to evict us from our rightful estate"* (John F. Kennedy). **3.** To recover (property, for example) by a superior claim or legal process. —See Synonyms at **eject.** [Middle English *evicten,* from Latin *ēvincere* (past participle *ēvictus*), to conquer, overcome : *ē-,* completely, from *ex-* + *vincere,* to conquer.] **—e·vic·tion** *n.* **—e·vic·tor** *n.*
ev·i·dence (ĕv′ə-dəns) *n.* **1.** The data on which a judgment or conclusion may be based or by which proof or probability may be established: *fossilized evidence of climatic change.* **2.** Something that serves to indicate or suggest: *His reaction was evidence of guilt.* **3.** *Law.* The documentary or verbal statements and the material objects admissible as testimony in a court of law. **—in evidence. 1.** Present and plainly visible; conspicuous: *He was very much in evidence at the convention.* **2.** As legal evidence: *The lawyer handed the clerk the documents in evidence.*
∼*tr.v.* **evidenced, -dencing, -dences. 1.** To indicate clearly; exemplify or prove. **2.** To support by testimony; attest. [Middle English, from Old French, from Late Latin *ēvidentia,* from Latin *ēvidēns,* EVIDENT.]
ev·i·dent (ĕv′ə-dənt) *adj.* Easily recognized or understood; clear and obvious. [Middle English, from Old French, from Latin *ēvidēns* (stem *ēvident-*), evident, clear : *ē-,* completely, from *ex-* + *vidēns,* present participle of *vidēre,* to see.]
Synonyms: *apparent, distinct, manifest, obvious, plain.*
ev·i·den·tial (ĕv′ə-dĕn′shəl) *adj.* Pertaining to, providing, or having the nature of evidence. **—ev·i·den·tial·ly** *adv.*
ev·i·dent·ly (ĕv′ə-dənt-lē, -dĕnt′lē) *adv.* **1.** Obviously; perceptibly; clearly: *He was quite evidently dead.* **2.** Apparently or seemingly; probably: *She's evidently going to be late.*
e·vil (ē′vəl) *adj.* **1.** Morally bad or wrong; wicked and malevolent: *an evil tyrant.* **2.** Causing an undesirable condition, such as ruin, injury, or pain; harmful or injurious: *an evil suggestion.* **3.** Characterized by or boding misfortune; foreboding; ominous: *evil omens.* **4.** Actually or purportedly bad or blameworthy; infamous: *an evil reputation.* **5.** Characterized by anger or spite; malicious: *an evil temper.* **6.** Very unpleasant; objectionable: *an evil smell.*
∼*n.* **1.** Something that is destructive, corruptive, or injurious, whether from natural circumstances or by human ignorance, error, or design: *"The evil that men do lives after them"* (Shakespeare). **2. a.** Something that is morally bad or wrong; wickedness; sin: *was eulogized as a person who had done no evil to those around him.* **b.** Something that causes or constitutes misfortune, suffering, injury, or difficulty: *The use of addictive drugs is one of the greatest evils of our times.* **3.** Something that is undesirable because of its injurious nature or effect: *the evils of war; the lesser of two evils.* **4.** *Archaic.* A disease.
∼*adv. Archaic.* In an evil manner. [Middle English *evel, ivel,* Old English *yfel.*] **—e·vil·ly** *adv.* **—e·vil·ness** *n.*
e·vil·do·er (ē′vəl-dōō′ər) *n.* A person who does evil; a perpetrator of evil. **—e·vil·do·ing** *n.*
evil eye *n.* **1. a.** A look or a stare superstitiously believed to cause injury or misfortune to others. **b.** The power supposedly possessed by certain people to bring misfortune to others with such looks. **2.** The power of evil personified as an all-watching eye and warded off since ancient times by symbols, amulets, and beads themselves representing an eye.
e·vil-mind·ed (ē′vəl-mīn′dĭd) *adj.* Having evil thoughts, opinions, or intentions. **—e·vil-mind·ed·ly** *adv.* **—e·vil-mind·ed·ness** *n.*
Evil One *n.* The Devil. Preceded by *the.*
e·vince (ĭ-vĭns′) *tr.v.* **evinced, evincing, evinces.** To show or demonstrate clearly or convincingly; manifest; exhibit: *evince surprise.* [Latin *ēvincere,* to conquer, to prove. See **evict.**] **—e·vinc·i·ble** *adj.*
e·vis·cer·ate (ĭ-vĭs′ə-rāt′) *v.* **-ated, -ating, -ates.** —*tr.* **1.** To remove the entrails of; disembowel: *The cook eviscerated the chicken.* **2.** To take away a vital or essential part of. **3.** *Medicine.* **a.** To remove the contents of (an eyeball). **b.** To remove an organ, such as an eye, from (a patient). —*intr. Medicine.* To protrude through an incision after an operation.
∼*adj.* (-ər-ĭt, -ə-rāt′). Disemboweled. [Latin *ēviscerāre,* "to remove the viscera from," to disembowel : *ē-,* indicating removal, from *ex-* + VISCERA.] **—e·vis·cer·a·tion** *n.*
ev·i·ta·ble (ĕv′ə-tə-bəl) *adj.* Avoidable. [Latin *ēvītabilis,* from *ēvītāre,* to avoid : *ē-,* away, from *ex-* + *vītāre*†, to shun.]
ev·o·ca·tion (ĕv′ə-kā′shən, ē′və-) *n.* The act of calling forth or conjuring up: *an evocation of childhood memories.*
e·voc·a·tive (ĭ-vŏk′ə-tĭv) *adj.* Tending or having the power to evoke. **—e·voc·a·tive·ly** *adv.*
ev·o·ca·tor (ĕv′ə-kā′tər, ē′və-) *n.* **1.** One that evokes. **2.** A naturally occurring substance that induces undifferentiated embryonic tissue to develop in a particular way.
e·voc·a·to·ry (ĭ-vŏk′ə-tôr′ē, -tōr′ē) *adj.* Evocative.
e·voke (ĭ-vōk′) *tr.v.* **evoked, evoking, evokes. 1.** To summon or call forth (memories, for example); reawaken; inspire. **2.** To produce or elicit (a reaction, emotion, or response): *evoke curiosity.* **3.** To cause (a spirit, for example) to appear; call up; conjure up. [Latin *ēvocāre,* to call forth, to call out, summon : *ē-,* out, from *ex-* + *vocāre,* to call.] **—ev·o·ca·ble** (ĕv′ə-kə-bəl, ĭ-vō′kə-) *adj.*
ev·o·lute (ĕv′ə-lōōt′, ē′və-) *n.* The locus of the centers of curvature of a given curve. [Back-formation from EVOLUTION.]
ev·o·lu·tion (ĕv′ə-lōō′shən, ē′və-) *n.* **1.** A gradual process in which something changes into a significantly different and usually more complex or more sophisticated form. **2.** *Biology.* **a.** The theory that groups of organisms may change with the passage of time so that new species differing morphologically and physiologically from their ancestors are formed. See **natural selection. b.** The historical development of a related group of organisms; phylogeny. **3.** The gradual process of the development or growth of something, as of a social institution, geographic division, or system of thought. **4.** *Often* **evolutions.** A turning movement that is part of a larger pattern, as: **a.** A wheeling motion in a dance. **b.** A tactical or parade-ground maneuver. **5.** A yielding or throwing off of gas, vapor, or heat. **6.** *Mathematics.* The extraction of a root of a quantity. In this sense, compare **involution.** [Latin *ēvolūtiō,* an opening, an unrolling, from *ēvolūtus,* past participle of *ēvolvere,* to roll out, to open, EVOLVE.] See feature, next page.
ev·o·lu·tion·al (ĕv′ə-lōō′shə-nəl, ē′və-) *adj.* Evolutionary.
ev·o·lu·tion·ar·y (ĕv′ə-lōō′shə-nĕr′ē, ē′və-) *adj.* **1.** Of, pertaining to, or resulting from evolution: *a continuous evolutionary process.* **2.** In accord with the theory of biological evolution. **3.** Developing or evolving as a slow or historical process; gradually changing or progressing.
ev·o·lu·tion·ism (ĕv′ə-lōō′shə-nĭz′əm, ē′və-) *n.* **1.** A theory of biological evolution, especially that formulated by Charles Darwin. Compare **creationism. 2.** Advocacy of or belief in an evolutionary process. **—ev·o·lu·tion·ist** *n.*
e·volve (ĭ-vŏlv′) *v.* **evolved, evolving, evolves.** —*tr.* **1.** To develop or achieve gradually; devise or formulate. **2.** *Biology.* To develop by evolutionary processes. **3.** To yield, give, or throw off (gas, vapor, or heat, for example); set free. —*intr.* **1.** To be part of or subject to the process of natural, temporal, or biological evolution, as in an organism or rock stratum. **2.** To be developed, disclosed, or unfolded: *The plot evolves in many subtle ways.* **3.** To undergo change or transformation; develop. [Latin *ēvolvere,* to roll out, unfold : *ē-,* out, from *ex-* + *volvere,* to roll.] **—e·volv·a·ble** *adj.* **—e·volve·ment** *n.*
e·vul·sion (ĭ-vŭl′shən) *n.* A pulling out; a forcible extraction. [Latin *ēvulsiō* (stem *ēvulsiōn-*), a pulling out, from *ēvulsus,* past participle of *ēvellere,* to pull out : *ē-,* out, from *ex-* + *vellere,* to pull.]
Évvoia. See **Euboea.**
ev·zone (ĕv′zōn′) *n.* An infantryman of a special corps of the Greek army. [Modern Greek *euzōnos,* from Greek, well-girdled, active : *eu-,* well + *zōnē,* girdle.]
ewe (yōō) *n.* A female sheep, especially when full-grown. [Middle English *ewe,* Old English *ēowu.*]
E·we (ā′wā′, ā′vā′) *n.* **1.** A member of a Negroid people of Togo, Ghana, and parts of Benin. **2.** The language of this people, belonging to the Niger-Congo family of languages.
ewe-neck (yōō′nĕk′) *n.* A defect in a horse or dog in which the neck is thin and has a concave arch. **—ewe-necked** *adj.*
ew·er (yōō′ər) *n.* A large, wide-mouthed pitcher or jug. [Middle English, from Norman French, from Old North French *eviere,* from Vulgar Latin *aquāria* (unattested), from Latin *āquārius,* relating to water, from *aqua,* water.]
ex[1] (ĕks) *prep. Abbr.* **x. 1.** *Finance.* Not including or participating in; without: *ex dividend; ex rights.* **2.** *Commerce.* Free of charge to the purchaser until removed from a particular place or thing. [Latin *ex,* out of, from.]
ex[2] *n. Informal.* A former wife, husband, or lover.
ex-[1], **ef-** *prefix.* Indicates: **1.** Removal out of or from; for example, **explant. 2.** Former; for example, *ex-president.* [Middle English, from Old French, from Latin. In borrowed Latin compounds *ex-* indicates: 1. out or out of, as in **expire.** 2. away from or removed away from, as in **expropriate.** 3. up, as in **elevate.** 4. completely or intensively, as in **execute.** 5. opposing, as in **execrate.** *Ex-* becomes *ef-* before *f.* [Latin *ex-,* from *ex,* out, out of.]
ex-[2] *prefix.* Indicates out of; for example, **exergue.** [In borrowed Greek compounds *ex-* indicates: 1. out of, as in **exegesis.** 2. away from, as in **exorcise.** Greek *ex-,* from *ex,* out of.]
ex. 1. examination. **2.** example. **3.** except; excepted; exception. **4.** exchange. **5.** executive. **6.** express. **7.** extra.
Ex. Exodus (Old Testament).
ex·ac·er·bate (ĭg-zăs′ər-bāt′, ĭk-săs′-) *tr.v.* **-bated, -bating, -bates. 1.** To increase the severity of (a pain, emotion, disease, problem, or the like). **2.** To embitter or irritate (a person). [Latin *exacerbāre,* to aggravate, make harsh : *ex-,* completely + *acerbus,* bitter, harsh.] **—ex·ac·er·ba·tion** *n.*
ex·act (ĭg-zăkt′) *adj.* **1. a.** Accurate in every respect: *an exact copy.* **b.** Specific in every detail: *exact instructions.* **2.** Precise in quantity, weight, or the like, as opposed to approximate: *the exact amount.* **3.** Precise in technique or movement: *an exact measuring device.* **4.** Designating a science based on verifiable facts. **5.** Identical; very same: *the exact place.* **6.** Meticulously observing or adhering to a standard.
∼*tr.v.* **exacted, -acting, -acts. 1.** To demand and enforce (payment

ewer A jug used to bring water to a washbasin for washing the hands before faucets became common. This ewer was made in 1828 at the Tucker factory in Philadelphia.

THE AMAZING VARIETY OF LIFE ON EARTH

A fan of life forms developed in the course of 2.5 billion years

Single-celled life forms probably appeared in earth's oceans more than 2.5 billion years ago. They gradually evolved into organisms made up, like sponges, of groups of semi-independent cells, which evolved in turn into multicellular animals such as jellyfish and worms. Creatures with external skeletons, the ancestors of lobsters, crabs, and snails, flourished during the Cambrian period, but by the start of the Ordovician period shell-skinned fish, jawless like lampreys, had developed a notochord, a primitive spine. Their vertebrate descendants dominated the Devonian, the period when the lobefins first moved from water to land, using their fleshy fins as legs. Their relatives, the first amphibians, found shores dense with fernlike psilophytes, descendants of seaweeds evolved during the pre-Cambrian period. The Carboniferous saw the emergence of seed-bearing plants and the reptiles, the first true land animals. Tortoises and turtles are the descendants of the first reptiles, the anapsids. Mammals evolved from the synapsids, also descended from the reptiles. Catastrophic geological and climatic changes at the end of the Permian may have caused many fish and amphibians to become extinct. Archeopteryx, the first-known bird, was descended from the diapsids, which were also the ancestors of the dinosaurs. Dinosaurs were successful until the end of the Cretaceous period, during which flowering plants developed. Then, changes in geology and climate may have affected evolution again. The Cenozoic era saw an explosion of species. Mammals branched into egg-layers, marsupials that carry their young in pouches, and placental mammals whose young grow to an advanced stage in the maternal uterus. The primates, a forest group of placental mammals, became adept coordinators of hand and eye. It was from a primate that man evolved.

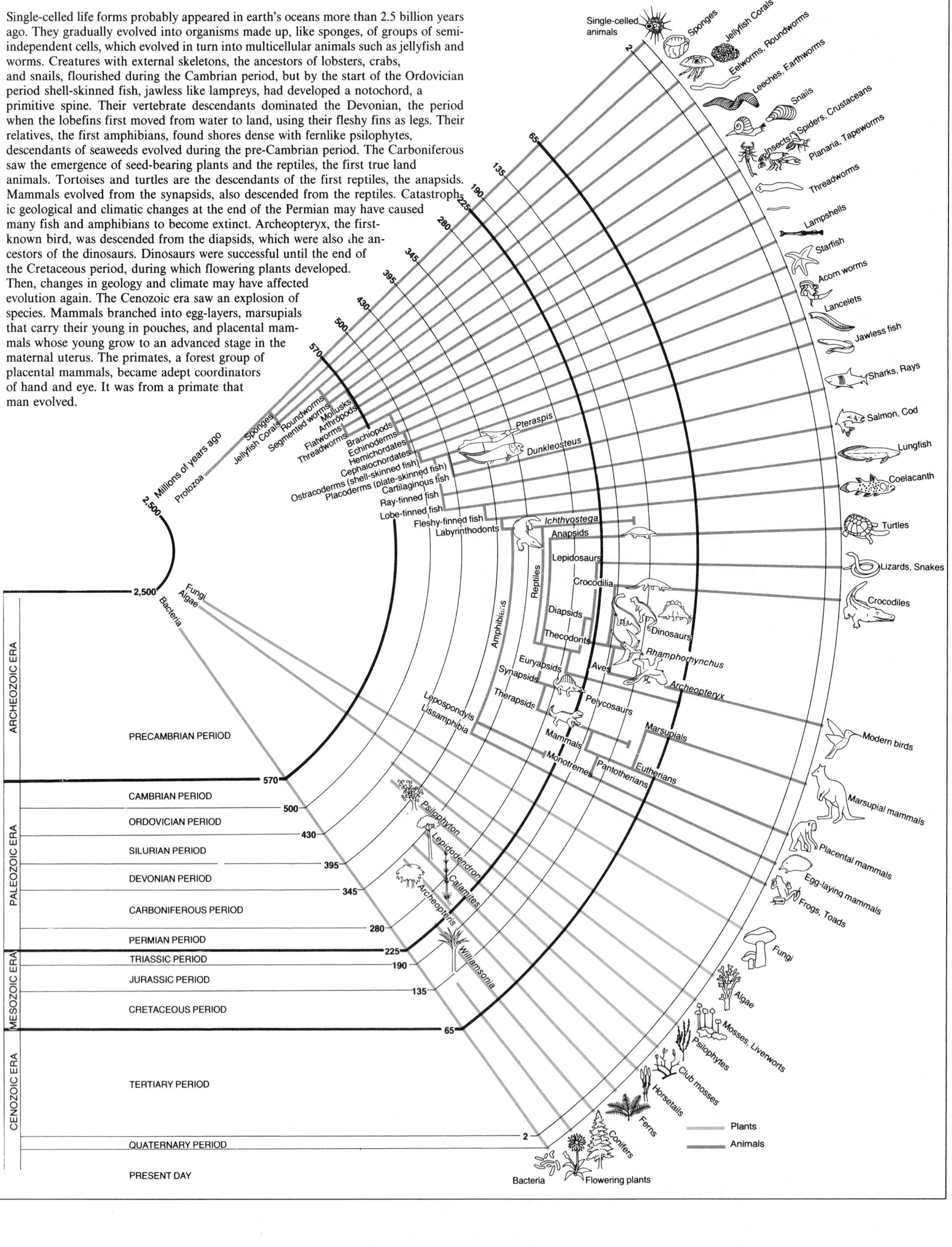

ARCHEOZOIC ERA

PRECAMBRIAN PERIOD

570

CAMBRIAN PERIOD — 500

ORDOVICIAN PERIOD — 430

SILURIAN PERIOD — 395

DEVONIAN PERIOD — 345

CARBONIFEROUS PERIOD — 280

PERMIAN PERIOD — 225

TRIASSIC PERIOD — 190

JURASSIC PERIOD — 135

CRETACEOUS PERIOD — 65

TERTIARY PERIOD

QUATERNARY PERIOD — 2

PRESENT DAY

PALEOZOIC ERA

MESOZOIC ERA

CENOZOIC ERA

Plants
Animals

or performance of something, for example); extort. **2.** To call for; require. [Latin *exactus,* past participle of *exigere,* "to drive out," require, examine : *ex-*, out + *agere,* to lead, drive.] **—ex·act·a·ble** *adj.* **—ex·act·ness** *n.* **—ex·ac·tor, ex·act·er** *n.*

ex·act·a (ĭg-zăk'tə) *n.* A method of betting, as on a horse race, in which the bettor must pick those finishing in first and second place in exactly that sequence. [American Spanish *quiniela exacta,* exact quinella.]

ex·act·ing (ĭg-zăk'tĭng) *adj.* **1.** Making severe or unremitting demands: *an exacting taskmaster.* **2.** Requiring great care, effort, or attention: *an exacting task.* —See Synonyms at **burdensome, severe.** **—ex·act·ing·ly** *adv.* **—ex·act·ing·ness** *n.*

ex·ac·tion (ĭg-zăk'shən) *n.* **1.** The act of exacting. **2.** Something that is exacted, such as a sum of money or act of obedience.

ex·act·i·tude (ĭg-zăk'tə-to͞od', -tyo͞od') *n.* The state or quality of being exact.

ex·act·ly (ĭg-zăkt'lē) *adv.* **1.** In an exact manner; accurately. **2.** In all respects; just: *Do exactly as you please.*
~interj. Used to express agreement.

ex·ag·ger·ate (ĭg-zăj'ə-rāt') *v.* **-ated, -ating, -ates.** *—tr.* **1.** To enlarge (something) disproportionately; increase to an abnormal degree. **2.** To make (something) appear greater than is actually the case; magnify beyond the truth. *—intr.* To distort through overstatement. [Latin *exaggerāre,* to pile up, exaggerate : *ex-*, completely + *aggerāre,* to pile up, from *agger*†, pile, heap.] **—ex·ag·ger·a·tive** (ĭg-zăj'ə-rā'tĭv, -ər-ə-tĭv), **ex·ag·ger·a·to·ry** (-rə-tôr'ē, -tōr'ē) *adj.* **—ex·ag·ger·a·tor** *n.*

ex·ag·ger·at·ed (ĭg-zăj'ə-rā'tĭd) *adj.* **1.** Unduly emphasized or magnified; going beyond truth, fact, or reality. **2.** Physically enlarged; abnormally or disproportionately developed. **—ex·ag·ger·at·ed·ly** *adv.*

ex·ag·ger·a·tion (ĭg-zăj'ə-rā'shən) *n.* **1.** The act of exaggerating. **2.** An instance of exaggerating; an overstatement.

ex·alt (ĭg-zôlt') *tr.v.* **-alted, -alting, -alts.** **1.** To raise in position, character, or status; elevate: *"Do away with masters, exalt the will of the people"* (D.H. Lawrence). **2.** To glorify, praise, or honor. **3.** To increase the effect or intensity of; heighten. [Middle English *exalten,* from Old French *exalter,* from Latin *exaltāre,* to lift up, exalt : *ex-*, up + *altus,* high.] **—ex·alt·er** *n.*

ex·al·ta·tion (ĕg'zôl-tā'shən) *n.* **1.** The act of exalting. **2.** The state of being exalted; elevation. **3.** A state or feeling of intense, often excessive exhilaration and well-being; elation. —See Synonyms at **ecstasy.**

ex·alt·ed (ĭg-zôl'tĭd) *adj.* **1.** Elevated in rank, character, or status. **2.** Lofty; noble: *"That provision should be made for continuing the race of . . . so exalted . . . a Being as man — I am far from denying"* (Laurence Sterne). **3.** Exaggeratedly favorable: *had an exalted view of their own importance.* **—ex·alt·ed·ly** *adv.* **—ex·alt·ed·ness** *n.*

ex·am (ĭg-zăm') *n. Informal.* An examination.

ex·a·men (ĭg-zā'mən) *n. Roman Catholic Church.* A usually daily examination of one's conscience. [Latin *exāmen,* consideration, examination, from *exigere,* to EXAMINE.]

ex·am·i·nant (ĭg-zăm'ə-nənt) *n.* **1.** One who examines. **2.** One who is examined; examinee.

ex·am·i·na·tion (ĭg-zăm'ə-nā'shən) *n. Abbr.* **ex., exam.** **1.** The act of examining or the state or result of being examined. **2.** An instance of examining; a thorough inspection or scrutiny. **3.** A set of questions or exercises testing knowledge or skills; a written, practical, or oral test. **4.** Formal interrogation; official inquiry. **—ex·am·i·na·tion·al** *adj.*

ex·am·ine (ĭg-zăm'ĭn) *tr.v.* **-ined, -ining, -ines.** **1.** To inspect or scrutinize (a person, thing, or situation) in detail; observe or analyze carefully. **2.** To test the state of health of. **3.** To test the qualifications, aptitude, or knowledge of (a candidate) by means of an examination. **4.** To interrogate or question formally to elicit facts, information, or the like. **5.** To consider or test introspectively; reflect upon: *"The time has come, God knows, for us to examine ourselves"* (James Baldwin). —See Synonyms at **ask.** [Middle English *examinen,* from Old French *examiner,* from Latin *exāmināre,* to weigh accurately, examine, from *exāmen,* a weighing, consideration, from *exigere,* to examine, to lead out : *ex-*, out + *agere,* to lead.] **—ex·am·in·a·ble** *adj.* **—ex·am·in·er** *n.*

ex·am·in·ee (ĭg-zăm'ə-nē') *n.* One who is examined.

ex·am·ple (ĭg-zăm'pəl, -zäm'pəl) *n. Abbr.* **ex.** **1.** One that is representative of a group as a whole; a sample; a specimen. **2.** Someone or something that serves as a model or pattern for imitation or duplication; an exemplar. **3.** A previous case or situation that is the same as or similar to one at hand; a precedent. **4.** One that serves as a warning, such as a punishment or a punished person. **5.** An illustrative problem or exercise with its solution. **—for example.** Serving as an illustration, a model, or an instance. [Middle English *examuple,* from Old French *example, essample,* from Latin *exemplum,* "(something) taken out," example, sample, from *eximere,* to take out : *ex-*, out + *emere,* to take.]
Synonyms: *case, illustration, instance, sample, specimen.*

ex·an·i·mate (ĭg-zăn'ə-mĭt) *adj.* Lifeless; dead.

ex·an·the·ma (ĕg'zăn-thē'mə) *n., pl.* **-mata** (-mə-tə) or **-mas.** Also **ex·an·them** (ĭg-zăn'thəm). **1.** A skin eruption accompanying a disease or fever. **2.** A disease, such as measles or scarlet fever, accompanied by a skin eruption. [New Latin, from Late Latin *exanthēma,* from Greek, "a blooming out," eruption, from *exanthein,* to bloom out, burst forth : *ex-*, out + *anthein,* to bloom, from *anthos,* flower.] **—ex·an·the·mat·ic** (ĭg-zăn'thə-măt'ĭk), **ex·an·them·a·tous** (ĕg'-zăn-thĕm'ə-təs) *adj.*

ex·a·rate (ĕk'sə-rāt') *adj. Zoology.* Designating pupae whose wings and legs are free and able to make limited movements. [Latin *exarātus,* "plowed up" (apparently referring to the pupa's method of shedding its larval skin), past participle of *exarāre* : EX- + *arāre,* to plow.]

ex·arch[1] (ĕk'särk') *n.* **1.** The ruler of a province in the Byzantine Empire. **2.** *Eastern Orthodox Church.* **a.** The deputy of a patriarch. **b.** A bishop ranking immediately below a patriarch. **c.** The head of certain independent churches. [Late Latin *exarchus,* from Greek *exarkhos,* leader, from *exarkhein,* to initiate, lead out : *ex-*, out + *arkhein,* to rule, lead.] **—ex·arch·al** (ĭk-sär'kəl) *adj.*

exarch[2] *adj. Botany.* Having vascular tissue in which the first-formed xylem is external to that formed later. [EX- (outside) + Greek *arkhē,* beginning, origin.]

ex·ar·chate (ĕk'sär'kĭt) *n.* Also **ex·ar·chy** (-kē) *pl.* **-chies.** The office, rank, jurisdiction, or province of an exarch.

ex·as·per·ate (ĭg-zăs'pə-rāt') *tr.v.* **-ated, -ating, -ates.** **1.** To make very angry or irritated; tax the patience of; provoke; irk. **2.** To increase the gravity or intensity of (a passion or pain, for example). [Latin *exasperāre,* to exasperate, irritate, make rough : *ex-*, entirely + *asperāre,* to make rough, from *asper,* rough.] **—ex·as·per·at·ed·ly** *adv.* **—ex·as·per·at·ing·ly** *adv.*

ex·as·per·a·tion (ĭg-zăs'pə-rā'shən) *n.* **1.** An act or instance of exasperating. **2.** The state of being exasperated; extreme annoyance or irritation.

exc. **1.** excellent. **2.** except; excepted; exception.

Exc. Excellency.

Ex·cal·i·bur (ĭk-skăl'ə-bər) *n.* King Arthur's sword. [Middle English *Excalibur,* from Old French *Escalibor,* from Medieval Latin *Caliburnus,* from Welsh *Caledvwlch,* from Celtic *kaleto-* (unattested), hard.]

ex ca·the·dra (ĕks' kə-thē'drə) *adj. & adv.* With the authority derived from one's office or position. Said especially of official or papal pronouncements. [Latin : *ex,* from + CATHEDRA.]

ex·cau·date (ĕk-skô'dāt') *adj. Zoology.* Tailless; without a tail.

ex·ca·vate (ĕk'skə-vāt') *v.* **-vated, -vating, -vates.** *—tr.* **1.** To make a cavity or hole in; dig out; hollow out. **2.** To form (a tunnel, for example) by such hollowing out; dig. **3.** To remove (soil) by digging or scooping out. **4.** To expose or uncover by digging, especially in search of historical or archaeological information. *—intr.* To engage in digging, hollowing out, or removing. [Latin *excavāre,* to hollow out : *ex-*, out + *cavāre,* to hollow, from *cavus,* hollow.]

ex·ca·va·tion (ĕk'skə-vā'shən) *n.* **1.** The act or process of excavating. **2.** A cavity formed by excavating. —See Synonyms at **hole.** **—ex·ca·va·tion·al** *adj.*

ex·ca·va·tor (ĕk'skə-vā'tər) *n.* **1.** One that excavates. **2.** A power-operated digging machine; especially, a tractor with endless chain treads and digging attachments.

ex·ceed (ĭk-sēd') *tr.v.* **-ceeded, -ceeding, -ceeds.** **1.** To be greater than; surpass. **2.** To go beyond the prior or proper limits of. —See Synonyms at **excel.** [Middle English *exceden,* from Old French *exceder,* from Latin *excēdere,* to depart, to go out, surpass : *ex-*, out + *cēdere,* to go.]

ex·ceed·ing (ĭk-sē'dĭng) *adj.* Extreme; extraordinary.
~adv. Archaic. Exceedingly.

ex·ceed·ing·ly (ĭk-sē'dĭng-lē) *adv.* To an advanced or unusual degree; extremely.

ex·cel (ĭk-sĕl') *v.* **-celled, -celling, -cels.** *—tr.* To be or do better than; surpass: *excels the rest of the class in English.* *—intr.* To be better or do better than others; be superior to others: *a musician who excels in the performance of the classics.* [Middle English *excellen,* from Latin *excellere,* to excel, raise up.]
Synonyms: *exceed, outdo, outstrip, surpass, transcend.*

ex·cel·lence (ĕk'sə-ləns) *n.* **1.** The state, quality, or condition of excelling; superiority. **2.** Something in which a person or thing excels. **3. Excellence.** Excellency. [From EXCEL.]

Ex·cel·len·cy (ĕk'sə-lən-sē) *n., pl.* **-cies.** *Abbr.* **Exc.** A title of or form of address for certain high officials, such as ambassadors, bishops, or governors. Usually used with *His, Her,* or *Your.*

ex·cel·lent (ĕk'sə-lənt) *adj.* **1.** *Abbr.* **E, exc.** Being of the highest or finest quality; exceptionally good of its kind: *We had an excellent dinner.* **2.** *Archaic.* Surpassing; superior. [Middle English, from Old French, from Latin *excellēns* (stem *excellent-*), present participle of *excellere,* to EXCEL.] **—ex·cel·lent·ly** *adv.*

ex·cel·si·or (ĭk-sĕl'sē-ər) *n.* Slender, curved wood shavings used for packing, stuffing, or the like. [Latin, comparative of *excelsus,* high, from the past participle of *excellere,* to EXCEL.]

ex·cept (ĭk-sĕpt') *prep. Abbr.* **ex., exc.** With the exclusion of; but: *After the party all the guests left except for one. All the eggs except one broke.*
~conj. **1.** If it were not for the fact that; only: *He would buy the suit except that it costs too much.* **2.** Otherwise than; with any purpose or manner other than. Usually used with an adverb, a clause, or a phrase: *He would not open his mouth except to yell.* **3.** *Archaic.* Unless.
~v. **excepted, -cepting, -cepts.** *—tr.* To leave out; exclude or excuse. *—intr.* To object. Usually used with *to* or *against.* [Middle English, from Latin *exceptus,* past participle of *excipere,* to take out, except : *ex-*, out + *capere,* to take.]
Usage: *Except,* in the sense of *with the exclusion of, other than,* or *but,* is usually construed as a preposition (as it is defined above)

excavator *This giant electrically powered excavator is used to mine coal near Erfstadt in West Germany. Each tooth on the wheel is a claw-edged bucket.*

PRONUNCIATION KEY

ă, pat; ā, pay; âr, care; ä, father, are; b, bib; ch, church; d, deed; ĕ, pet; ē, be; f, fife; g, gag; h, hat; hw, which; ĭ, pit; ī, pie; îr, pier; j, judge; k, kick; l, lid, needle; m, mum; n, no, sudden; ng, thing; ŏ, pot; ō, toe; ô, paw, for; oi, noise; ou, out; o͝o, book; o͞o, boot; p, pop; r, roar; s, sauce; sh, ship, dish; t, tight; th, thin, path; *th,* this, bathe; ŭ, cut; ûr, fur; v, valve; w, with; y, yes; z, zebra, size; zh, vision; ə, about, item, edible, gallop, circus, peaceful

IN FOREIGN WORDS:

à, *Fr.* ami; œ, *Fr.* feu, *Ger.* schön; ü, *Fr.* tu, *Ger.* über; KH, *Ger.* ich, *Scot.* loch; N, *Fr.* bon; y', *Fr.* Compiègne

STRESS MARKS:

Primary stress: '
in·cite' (ĭn-sīt')
Secondary stress: '
in'sight' (ĭn'sīt')

rather than as a conjunction. When a pronoun follows *except* in this sense, therefore, it is in the objective case: *No one except me knew it. Every member of the original cast was signed except her.* In this sense *except* is much more common than *excepting*, in modern usage. *Excepting* appears principally in negative constructions: *All money received, not excepting bonuses, must be reported.*

ex·cept·ing (ĭk-sĕp′tĭng) *prep.* Excluding; except. —See Usage note at **except.**
~*conj. Archaic.* Except; unless.

ex·cep·tion (ĭk-sĕp′shən) *n. Abbr.* **ex., exc. 1.** The act of excepting or state of being excepted; exclusion. **2.** One that is excepted; a case that does not conform to normal rules or general principles: *We all want to be liked—and I am no exception.* **3.** An objection or criticism; opposition: *open to exception.* **4.** *Law.* **a.** A formal objection taken in the course of an action or proceeding. **b.** A restricting clause or provision in a contract or similar document. —**take exception.** To object or take offense; take issue. Usually used with *to*: *I take exception to your remarks.*

ex·cep·tion·a·ble (ĭk-sĕp′shə-nə-bəl) *adj.* Open or liable to objection or exception. —See Usage note at **exceptional.** —**ex·cep·tion·a·bly** *adv.*

ex·cep·tion·al (ĭk-sĕp′shə-nəl) *adj.* **1.** Being an exception; uncommon or extraordinary. **2.** Unusually skillful, accomplished, or intelligent; gifted. —**ex·cep·tion·al·ly** *adv.*

    Usage: Exceptional and *exceptionable* are not interchangeable. *Exceptionable* has the meaning of "objectionable" or "debatable" — something to which exception can be taken. *Exceptional* has the meaning of "uncommon" or "extraordinary."

ex·cep·tive (ĭk-sĕp′tĭv) *adj.* **1.** Of, being, or containing an exception. **2.** *Archaic.* Tending to object or criticize; captious.

ex·cerpt (ĕk′sûrpt′, ĕg′zûrpt′) *n.* A passage or scene selected from a speech, book, film, or play; an extract.
~*tr.v.* (ĭk-sûrpt′, ĭg-zûrpt′) **excerpted, -cerpting, -cerpts.** To select, quote, or take out (a passage or scene) from a book, speech, play, film, or the like. [Latin *excerptum,* "something picked out," excerpt, from the neuter past participle of *excerpere,* to pick out, excerpt : *ex-,* out + *carpere,* to pick, pluck.]

ex·cess (ĭk-sĕs′, ĕk′sĕs′) *n.* **1.** The state of exceeding what is normal or sufficient. **2.** An amount or quantity beyond what is requisite; a superfluity. **3.** The amount or degree by which one quantity exceeds another; a remainder. **4.** Lack of moderation and self-restraint; overindulgence: *youthful excess.* **5.** *Chemistry.* An amount of a reagent that is present in a greater quantity than that necessary to complete a given reaction. —**in excess of.** Greater than; more than. —**to excess.** To an extreme degree or extent; too much.
~*tr.v.* **excessed, -cessing, -cesses.** To eliminate the job or position of.
~*adj.* **1.** Being more than is required, usual, or permitted. **2.** Due; not having previously been paid in full: *excess postage.* [Middle English, from Old French *exces,* from Latin *excessus,* past participle of *excēdere,* to EXCEED.]

excess baggage *n.* **1.** Baggage, as on airplanes, in excess of the amount carried free, for which the passenger pays an extra charge. **2.** Something that is useless or hampers.

ex·ces·sive (ĭk-sĕs′ĭv) *adj.* Exceeding a reasonable degree of propriety, necessity, or the like; extreme; inordinate: *excessive charges.* —**ex·ces·sive·ly** *adv.*
    Synonyms: *exorbitant, extravagant, extreme, immoderate, inordinate, unreasonable.*

exch. 1. exchange. **2.** exchequer.

ex·change (ĭks-chānj′) *v.* **-changed, -changing, -changes.** —*tr.* **1.** To give and receive in a reciprocal manner; interchange: *exchange ideas.* **2.** To relinquish (one thing) for another; give over. **3.** To replace (something unsatisfactory) with something else: *exchange defective goods.* **4.** To provide or transfer (goods or services, for example) in return for something of equal value. **5.** In chess, to capture (an opponent's piece) immediately after sacrificing a piece, usually of similar value. —*intr.* To transfer something and receive something equivalent in return; reciprocate; swap.
~*n. Abbr.* **ex., exch. 1.** An act or instance of exchanging. **2.** One that is exchanged. **3.** A usually short and often lively or caustic conversation: *a noisy exchange.* **4.** A **telephone exchange** (see). **5.** A place where things are exchanged; especially, a center where securities and commodities are bought and sold: *a stock exchange.* **6.** A system of payments using instruments such as negotiable drafts instead of money. **7.** The fee or percentage charged for participating in such a system of payment. **8.** **Rate of exchange** (see). **9.** The amount of difference in the actual value of two or more currencies, or between values of the same currency at two or more places. **10.** *Usually* **exchanges.** The instruments, as checks or drafts, presented to a clearing house for settlement or exchange. **11.** In chess, the capture in successive moves of pieces, usually equivalent in value, by each of the two players. **12.** *Physics.* The transfer of a real or virtual particle between two other particles, as the transfer of a meson between two nucleons. [Middle English *eschaungen,* from Norman French *eschaunge,* from Old French *eschangier,* from Vulgar Latin *excambiāre* (unattested) : Late Latin *ex-,* showing change + *cambiāre,* to exchange.] —**ex·chang·er** *n.*

ex·change·a·ble (ĭks-chān′jə-bəl) *adj.* Able to be exchanged; remittable. —**ex·change·a·bil·i·ty** *n.*

exchange force *n. Physics.* **1.** A force between two elementary particles, such as nucleons, caused by an exchange of real or virtual

particles between them. **2.** A force that aligns the magnetic dipole moments of atoms in a ferromagnetic material.

exchange rate *n.* **Rate of exchange** (see).

ex·cheq·uer (ĕks′chĕk′ər, ĭks-chĕk′-) *n.* **1. Exchequer.** The department of the British and some other governments in charge of the collection and care of the national revenue. **2.** *Abbr.* **exch.** A treasury, as of a nation or an organization. **3.** *Informal.* The total of one's financial resources; funds. [Middle English *escheker,* from Norman French, from Old French *eschequier,* chessboard, a counting table usually covered with a checkered cloth, from *eschec,* CHECK (at chess).]

ex·ci·mer (ĕk′sə-mər, ĭk-sī′mər) *n. Chemistry.* A dimer formed by the association of excited and unexcited molecules, which in the ground state would remain dissociated. [*Excited* di*mer.*]

ex·cip·i·ent (ĭk-sĭp′ē-ənt) *n.* An inert substance used as a diluent or vehicle for a drug. [Latin *excipiēns* (stem *excipient-*), present participle of *excipere,* to EXCEPT.]

ex·cis·a·ble (ĭk-sī′zə-bəl) *adj.* Subject to excise.

ex·cise¹ (ĕk′sīz′) *n.* **1.** An indirect tax levied on the production, sale, or consumption of certain commodities, such as tobacco or alcohol, within a country. Also called "excise tax." **2.** A license fee paid to allow a person to pursue certain types of employment or amusement, such as operating a gambling casino. **3.** In Britain, the branch of the civil service that is responsible for the collection of excise tax.
~*tr.v.* **-cised, -cising, -cises.** To levy an excise on. [Obsolete Dutch *excijs,* from Middle Dutch, probably from Old French *acceis,* from Vulgar Latin *accēnsum* (unattested) : Latin *ad-,* against, to + *cēnsus,* tax, CENSUS.]

ex·cise² (ĭk-sīz′) *tr.v.* **-cised, -cising, -cises. 1.** To delete (a passage of text). **2.** To remove by or as if by cutting; especially, to remove (an organ or part) surgically. [Latin *excīdere* (past participle *excīsus*), to cut out : *ex-,* out + *caedere,* to cut.] —**ex·ci·sion** (ĭk-sĭzh′ən) *n.*

ex·cise·man (ĕk′sīz′mən, ĭk-sīz′-) *n., pl.* **-men** (-mĭn). *British.* An officer who collects excise taxes or enforces excise laws.

ex·cit·a·ble (ĭk-sī′tə-bəl) *adj.* **1. a.** Capable of being excited. **b.** Easily excited; sensitive or volatile. **2.** Capable of responding to stimuli. Said especially of nerves. —**ex·cit·a·bil·i·ty, ex·cit·a·ble·ness** *n.* —**ex·cit·a·bly** *adv.*

ex·ci·tant (ĭk-sī′tənt) *adj.* Also **ex·ci·ta·tive** (-sī′tə-tĭv), **ex·ci·ta·to·ry** (-tə-tôr′ē, -tōr′ē). Capable of exciting or stimulating. —**ex·ci·tant** *n.*

ex·ci·ta·tion (ĕk′sī-tā′shən) *n.* **1.** The act or process of exciting something. **2.** An agent or means used to excite or stimulate. **3.** The state or condition of being excited. **4.** The stimulus-induced response of an organ or tissue, especially that of a nerve cell. **5.** The electric current producing a magnetic field in an electromagnetic device, as in a motor, generator, or transformer.

ex·cite (ĭk-sīt′) *tr.v.* **-cited, -citing, -cites. 1.** To stir to activity; put into motion. **2.** To elicit (a reaction or emotion, for example); induce: *excite a response.* **3. a.** To affect with a feeling of agitated elation. **b.** To arouse strong feeling in; provoke: *She excited him to anger.* **c.** To stir the sexual passions of; arouse. **4.** *Biology.* To produce increased activity in (an organism or part); stimulate. **5.** *Physics.* **a.** To increase the energy of. **b.** To raise (an atom, molecule, nucleus, or electron) to a higher energy level than the ground state. **c.** To supply current to (the coils of a motor or generator) to create a magnetic field. **d.** To supply a signal to (a transistor circuit). —See Synonyms at **provoke.** [Middle English *exciten,* from Old French *exciter,* from Latin *excitāre,* to excite, arouse, frequentative of *exciēre* (past participle *excitus*), to call or bring out : *ex-,* out + *ciēre, cīre,* to call, put in motion.]

ex·cit·ed (ĭk-sī′tĭd) *adj.* **1.** In a state of agitated elation or sexual arousal. **2.** Caused by or characterized by excitement: *an excited hush.* **3.** *Physics.* At an energy level higher than the ground state. —**ex·cit·ed·ly** *adv.*

ex·cite·ment (ĭk-sīt′mənt) *n.* **1.** The state or condition of being excited; agitation. **2.** Something that excites.

ex·cit·er (ĭk-sī′tər) *n.* **1.** One that excites. **2.** An auxiliary generator used to provide field current for a larger generator or alternator. **3.** *Electronics.* An oscillator for generating the carrier frequency of a transmitter.

ex·cit·ing (ĭk-sī′tĭng) *adj.* Creating excitement or agitation; rousing. —**ex·cit·ing·ly** *adv.*

ex·ci·ton (ĕk′sī-tŏn′, ĕk′sī′-) *n.* An electrically neutral excited state of a crystal, often regarded as a bound state of an electron and a hole. [EXCIT(ATION) + -ON.]

ex·ci·tor (ĭk-sī′tər) *n.* Any nervous or chemical agent that induces activity in an organism.

excl. excluding; exclusive.

ex·claim (ĭk-sklām′) *v.* **-claimed, -claiming, -claims.** —*intr.* To cry out or speak suddenly or vehemently, as from surprise or emotion. —*tr.* To cry out or utter suddenly or vehemently. [Old French *exclamer,* from Latin *exclāmāre,* to call out, exclaim : *ex-,* out + *clāmāre,* to call.] —**ex·claim·er** *n.*

ex·cla·ma·tion (ĕk′sklə-mā′shən) *n.* **1.** An abrupt, forceful utterance. **2.** An outcry.

exclamation point *n.* **1.** A punctuation mark (!) used after an exclamation. **2.** An exclamation point used as a symbol, as in mathematics or logic.

ex·clam·a·to·ry (ĭk-sklăm′ə-tôr′ē, -tōr′ē) *adj.* Constituting, containing, relating to, or using exclamation.

ex·claus·tra·tion (ĕk′sklô-trā′shən) *n.* The release from vows and return to the outside world of a monk or nun. [Medieval Latin *exclaustrātiō* (stem *exclaustrātiōn-*), a putting outside the cloister. See **ex-**, **cloister.**]

ex·clave (ĕk′sklāv′) *n.* A portion of a country that is isolated from the main part and that exists as an enclave in alien territory: *Cabinda, in Zaire, is an exclave of Angola.* Compare **enclave.** [EX- + (EN)CLAVE.]

ex·clo·sure (ĭk-sklō′zhər) *n.* An area, as in a forest, fenced off to prevent intrusion.

ex·clude (ĭk-sklōōd′) *tr.v.* **-cluded, -cluding, -cludes. 1.** To prevent or keep from entering a place, group, or the like; bar; reject. **2.** To avoid noticing or considering; leave out; disregard. **3.** To eject; expel. [Middle English *excluden,* from Latin *exclūdere* : *ex-,* out + *claudere,* to shut.] **—ex·clud·a·bil·i·ty** *n.* **—ex·clud·a·ble, ex·clud·i·ble** *adj.* **—ex·clud·er** *n.*

ex·clu·sion (ĭk-sklōō′zhən) *n.* **1.** The act of excluding; rejection. **2.** The state of being excluded. [Latin *exclūsiō* (stem *exclūsiōn-*), from *exclūsus,* past participle of *exclūdere,* to EXCLUDE.] **—ex·clu·sion·ar·y** (ĭk-sklōō′zhə-nĕr′ē) *adj.*

ex·clu·sion·ist (ĭk-sklōō′zhə-nĭst) *n.* One who favors or practices excluding others from rights or privileges. **—ex·clu·sion·ism** *n.* **—ex·clu·sion·ist** *adj.*

exclusion principle *n.* The principle that no two particles of a given type, such as electrons, protons, or neutrons, can occupy a particular quantum state. Also called "Pauli exclusion principle."

ex·clu·sive (ĭk-sklōō′sĭv) *adj. Abbr.* **excl. 1.** Pertaining to, characterized by, or requiring exclusion. **2. a.** Not divided or shared with others: *exclusive publishing rights.* **b.** Available through only one retail outlet. **3.** Single or independent; sole: *your exclusive function.* **4.** Regarded as unrelated or autonomous; separate; incompatible: *mutually exclusive roles in life.* **5.** Concentrated on the matter at hand; undivided; undistracted. **6.** Not including the specified limits or items: *paragraphs 8 to 17 exclusive.* **7. a.** Admitting only certain people to membership, participation, or the like; select. **b.** Catering to a wealthy clientele; expensive; chic: *exclusive shops.* **8.** *Logic.* Designating a disjunction that is valid if one but not both of its elements is true. **—exclusive of.** Not including or considering: *exclusive of other factors.*
~n. **1.** A news item granted to or obtained by only one person or source. **2.** An exclusive right or privilege, as to market a product. **—ex·clu·siv·i·ty** (ĕk′sklōō-sĭv′ə-tē) *n.* **—ex·clu·sive·ly** *adv.* **—ex·clu·sive·ness** *n.*

ex·cog·i·tate (ĭk-skŏj′ə-tāt′) *tr.v.* **-tated, -tating, -tates. 1.** To think out in great detail. **2.** To devise; contrive. [Latin *excōgitāre,* to find out by thinking : *ex-,* out + *cōgitāre,* to COGITATE.] **—ex·cog·i·ta·tion** *n.* **—ex·cog·i·ta·tive** (ĭk-skŏj′ə-tā′tĭv, -tə-tĭv) *adj.*

ex·com·mu·ni·ca·ble (ĕks′kə-myōō′nĭ-kə-bəl) *adj.* Liable to, meriting, or punishable by excommunication.

ex·com·mu·ni·cate (ĕks′kə-myōō′nĭ-kāt′) *tr.v.* **-cated, -cating, -cates. 1.** To cut off from the rites, privileges, or fellowship of a church by ecclesiastical authority; exclude from religious membership. **2.** To exclude from membership or participation in a group.
~n. (-kĭt). A person who has been excommunicated.
~adj. (-kĭt, -kāt′). Excommunicated. [Middle English *excommunicaten,* from Late Latin *excommūnicāre* (past participle *excommūnicātus*), to put out of the (church) community : Latin *ex-,* out + *commūnicāre,* to COMMUNICATE.] **—ex·com·mu·ni·ca·tive** (ĕks′kə-myōō′nĭ-kā′tĭv, -kə-tĭv), **ex·com·mu·ni·ca·to·ry** (-kə-tôr′ē, -tōr′ē) *adj.* **—ex·com·mu·ni·ca·tor** *n.*

ex·com·mu·ni·ca·tion (ĕks′kə-myōō′nĭ-kā′shən) *n.* **1.** The act of excommunicating. **2.** The state of being excommunicated; exclusion. **3.** The formal ecclesiastical censure or motion by which one is excommunicated.

ex·co·ri·ate (ĭk-skôr′ē-āt′, ĭk-skōr′-) *tr.v.* **-ated, -ating, -ates. 1.** To censure strongly; denounce severely; upbraid. **2.** To tear or wear off the skin of; abrade; chafe. [Middle English *excoriaten,* from Latin *excoriāre* (past participle *excoriātus*), to strip of its skin : *ex-,* removal from + *corium,* skin, hide, leather.]

ex·co·ri·a·tion (ĭk-skôr′ē-ā′shən, ĭk-skōr′-) *n.* **1. a.** The act of excoriating. **b.** The state of being excoriated. **2.** The raw skin surface resulting from abrasion or scraping; a sore.

ex·cre·ment (ĕk′skrə-mənt) *n.* Waste material expelled from the body; especially, fecal matter. [Latin *excrēmentum,* from *excrētus,* past participle of *excernere,* to sift out : *ex-,* out + *cernere,* to sift.] **—ex·cre·men·tal** (ĕk′skrə-mĕn′təl) *adj.*

ex·cres·cence (ĭk-skrĕs′əns) *n.* **1.** An abnormal, disfiguring outgrowth or enlargement: *"a weird horny excrescence that had detached itself from the ceremonious big toe"* (John Cowper Powys). **2.** A normal outgrowth or appendage, such as a beard or toenail. [Middle English, from Latin *excrēscentia,* from *excrēscēns,* present participle of *excrēscere,* to grow out : *ex-,* out + *crēscere,* to grow.]

ex·cres·cen·cy (ĭk-skrĕs′ən-sē) *n., pl.* **-cies. 1.** The state of being excrescent. **2.** An excrescence.

ex·cres·cent (ĭk-skrĕs′ənt) *adj.* **1.** Growing out abnormally, excessively, or superfluously. **2.** *Linguistics.* Designating a speech sound added without any grammatical or etymological basis; epenthetic. **—ex·cres·cent·ly** *adv.*

ex·cre·ta (ĭk-skrē′tə) *pl.n.* Waste matter, such as sweat, urine, or feces, excreted from the body. [New Latin, from Latin *excrēta,* from the neuter plural past participle of *excernere,* to sift out. See **excrement.**] **—ex·cre·tal** *adj.*

ex·crete (ĭk-skrēt′) *tr.v.* **-creted, -creting, -cretes.** To eliminate (waste matter) from the blood, tissues, or organs. [Latin *excernere* (past participle *excrētus*), to sift out. See **excrement.**]

ex·cre·tion (ĭk-skrē′shən) *n.* **1.** The process or act of excreting undigested food residues or metabolic wastes. **2.** The matter so excreted.

ex·cre·to·ry (ĕk′skrə-tôr′ē) *adj.* Also **ex·cre·tive** (ĭk-skrē′tĭv). **1.** Of or pertaining to excretion. **2.** Having the function of excreting: *excretory organs.*

ex·cru·ci·ate (ĭk-skrōō′shē-āt′) *tr.v.* **-ated, -ating, -ates. 1.** To inflict severe pain on; torture. **2.** To inflict great mental pain on; torment. [Latin *excruciāre,* to torment : *ex-,* completely + *cruciāre,* to torment, crucify, from *crux* (stem *cruc-*), CROSS.] **—ex·cru·ci·a·tion** *n.*

ex·cru·ci·at·ing (ĭk-skrōō′shē-ā′tĭng) *adj.* **1.** Intensely painful; agonizing: *an excruciating headache.* **2.** Marked by great intensity. **—ex·cru·ci·at·ing·ly** *adv.*

ex·cul·pate (ĕk′skəl-pāt′, ĭk-skŭl′-) *tr.v.* **-pated, -pating, -pates.** To clear of a charge; prove guiltless or blameless; exonerate. [Medieval Latin *exculpāre* : Latin *ex-* (removal away from) + *culpa,* guilt, blame (see **culpa**).] **—ex·cul·pa·ble** *adj.* **—ex·cul·pa·tion** (ĕk′skəl-pā′shən) *n.*

ex·cul·pa·to·ry (ĭk-skŭl′pə-tôr′ē, -tōr′ē) *adj.* Proving or tending to prove guiltless; exculpating.

ex·cur·rent (ĭk-skûr′ənt) *adj.* **1. a.** Running or flowing in an outward direction. **b.** Having an outward flow. Said of a duct, tube, or anatomical passage. **2.** *Botany.* **a.** Having a single, undivided trunk with lateral branches, as do many coniferous trees. **b.** Extending beyond the apex of a leaf, as a midrib or vein does. [Latin *excurrens* (stem *excurrent-*), present participle of *excurrere,* to run out. See **excursion.**]

ex·cur·sion (ĭk-skûr′zhən) *n.* **1.** A usually short journey made with the intention of returning to the starting point; an outing. **2. a.** A pleasure tour, as in a bus or train, especially one of limited duration and at a special low fare. **b.** The people on such a tour. **3.** A rambling from the main topic; a digression. **4.** *Obsolete.* A military raid; a sortie. **5. a.** A movement from a mean position or axis in an oscillating or alternating motion. **b.** The distance traversed in such a movement. **6.** An explosion of fissionable material in a nuclear reactor, caused by an uncontrollable chain reaction of neutrons. [Latin *excursiō* (stem *excursiōn*), from *excursus,* past participle of *excurrere,* to run out : *ex-,* out + *currere,* to run.]

ex·cur·sion·ist (ĭk-skûr′zhə-nĭst) *n.* A person who goes on an excursion.

ex·cur·sive (ĭk-skûr′sĭv) *adj.* **1.** Given to digression; rambling: *an excursive lecturer.* **2.** Unmethodical; desultory: *excursive reading habits.* [From Latin *excursus.* See **excursion.**] **—ex·cur·sive·ly** *adv.* **—ex·cur·sive·ness** *n.*

ex·cur·sus (ĭk-skûr′səs) *n., pl.* **-suses** or **excursus. 1.** A lengthy, appended exposition of a topic or point, as in a text. **2.** A digression. [Latin, from the past participle of *excurrere,* to run out. See **excursion.**]

ex·cus·a·to·ry (ĭk-skyōō′zə-tôr′ē, -tōr′ē) *adj.* Tending or serving to excuse; apologetic.

ex·cuse (ĭk-skyōōz′) *tr.v.* **-cused, -cusing, -cuses. 1.** To grant pardon to; forgive: *She excused him for his clumsiness.* **2.** To make allowance for (a shortcoming); overlook: *I hope you'll excuse my mistake.* **3.** To serve as justification for; vindicate: *Her brilliance does not excuse her rudeness.* **4.** To free, as from an obligation or duty; exempt: *The sick child was excused from basketball practice.* **5.** To give (someone) permission to leave; dismiss or release. **6.** To refrain from exacting; remit: *excuse taxes.* —See Synonyms at **forgive. —excuse me. 1.** Used, sometimes ironically, as an apology. **2.** Used to request someone to move out of the way. **3.** Used to request someone to repeat what he has just said. **—excuse oneself. 1.** To request forgiveness; seek indulgence or apologize. **2.** To request exemption, as from an obligation or duty. **3.** To request permission to leave.
~n. (ĭk-skyōōs′) **1.** A plea or explanation offered to elicit pardon. **2.** The reason or ground for excusing. **3.** An act of excusing; forgiveness or indulgence. **4.** A note explaining an absence. **5.** *Informal.* One that falls short of certain standards or expectations: *He is a poor excuse for a poet.* [Middle English *excusen,* from Old French *excuser,* from Latin *excūsāre* : *ex-,* removal from + *causa,* accusation, CAUSE.] **—ex·cus·a·ble** *adj.* **—ex·cus·a·ble·ness** *n.* **—ex·cus·a·bly** *adv.* **—ex·cus·er** *n.*
Usage: The expression *excuse away* has no meaning beyond that of *excuse* (unlike *explain away,* which has a different meaning from *explain*): *His behavior cannot be excused* (not *excused away*).

ex-di·rec·to·ry (ĕks′dĭ-rĕk′tə-rē, ĕks′dī-) *adj. British.* Unlisted in the telephone directory and not procurable by inquiry.

ex dividend *adj. Abbr.* **ex div.** *Finance.* Without claim on the current dividend.

ex·e·at (ĕk′sē-ăt′) *n. British.* **1.** Official permission to be absent from classes or from residence in an institution. **2.** Official permission from a bishop for a clergyman to leave the diocese. [Latin, "let him go out."]

ex·e·cra·ble (ĕk′sĭ-krə-bəl) *adj.* **1.** Detestable; abominable; abhorrent. **2.** Extremely inferior; very bad. [Middle English, from Old French, from Latin *ex(s)ecrābilis,* from *ex(s)ecrārī,* to EXECRATE.] **—ex·e·cra·bly** *adv.*

ex·e·crate (ĕk′sĭ-krāt′) *tr.v.* **-crated, -crating, -crates. 1.** To inveigh against; denounce. **2.** To abominate; abhor. **3.** *Archaic.* To invoke a curse upon; curse. [Latin *ex(s)ecrārī,* to curse, execrate : *ex-,* opposing + *sacrāre,* to be sacred, from *sacer,* sacred.] **—ex·e·cra·tive**

adj. **—ex·e·cra·tor** *n.* **—ex·e·cra·to·ry** (ĕk′sĭ-krə-tôr′ē, -tōr′ē) *adj.*
ex·e·cra·tion (ĕk′sĭ-krā′shən) *n.* **1.** The act of execrating. **2.** A curse. **3.** Detestation; abhorrence. **4.** That which is execrated; something that is loathed.
ex·ec·u·tant (ĭg-zĕk′yə-tənt) *n.* One who performs or carries out; especially, a musical performer.
ex·e·cute (ĕk′sĭ-kyōōt′) *tr.v.* **-cuted, -cuting, -cutes. 1.** To carry out; put into effect: *execute a law.* **2.** To perform; do. **3.** To produce (a work of art, for example) in accordance with a prescribed design. **4.** To make valid, as by signing and sealing; legalize: *execute a deed.* **5.** To perform or carry out what is required by: *execute a will.* **6.** To subject to capital punishment. —See Synonyms at **perform.** [Middle English *executen,* from Old French *executer,* from Medieval Latin *executāre,* from Latin *ex(s)equī* (past participle *ex(s)ecūtus*), to execute, follow to the end : *ex-,* completely + *sequī,* to follow.] **—ex·e·cut·a·ble** *adj.* **—ex·e·cut·er** *n.*
ex·e·cu·tion (ĕk′sĭ-kyōō′shən) *n.* **1.** The act of executing. **2.** The state of being executed. **3.** The manner, style, or result of performance. **4.** A putting or being put to death as a legal penalty. **5.** *Law.* **a.** The carrying into effect of a court judgment. **b.** A writ empowering an officer to enforce a judgment. **6.** *Law.* The validating of a legal document by the performance of certain formalities, such as signing or sealing. **7.** Effective, punitive, or destructive action.
ex·e·cu·tion·er (ĕk′sĭ-kyōō′shə-nər) *n.* **1.** One who administers capital punishment. **2.** One who puts another to death.
ex·ec·u·tive (ĭg-zĕk′yə-tĭv) *n. Abbr.* **ex., exec. 1.** A person or group having administrative or managerial authority in an organization. **2.** The branch of government charged with putting into effect a country's laws and with the administration of its functions. **3.** The chief officer of a government, state, or political division.
∼*adj. Abbr.* **ex., exec. 1.** Of, pertaining to, capable of, or suited for carrying out plans, duties, or the like. **2.** Of or pertaining to the branch of government charged with the execution and administration of a nation's laws. Compare **legislative, judicial. 3.** Of, pertaining to, or suitable for an executive: *an executive suite.*
executive officer *n.* **1.** A person holding executive power in an organization. **2.** The officer second in command of a military unit smaller than a division. **3.** The officer second in command of a naval unit.
executive routine *n. Computer Science.* A set of coded instructions given to a computer in order to use it to develop or control other routines.
executive secretary *n.* A secretary having administrative duties and responsibilities.
executive session *n.* A legislative session, usually one closed to the public.
ex·ec·u·tor (ĭg-zĕk′yə-tər; *also* ĕk′sĭ-kyōō′tər *for sense 1*) *n.* **1.** A person who carries out or performs something. **2.** *Law.* A person who is appointed by a testator to execute his will. **—ex·ec·u·to·ri·al** (ĭg-zĕk′yə-tôr′ē-əl, -tōr′ē-əl) *adj.* **—ex·ec·u·tor·ship** *n.*
ex·ec·u·to·ry (ĭg-zĕk′yə-tôr′ē, -tōr′ē) *adj.* **1.** Administrative. **2.** Operative; in effect. **3.** *Law.* Intended to go into effect, or having the potential of becoming effective at some future time; contingent.
ex·ec·u·trix (ĭg-zĕk′yə-trĭks) *n., pl.* **-trixes** or **executrices** (ĭg-zĕk′yə-trī′sēz′). *Law.* A woman who is appointed by a testator to execute his will.
ex·e·dra (ĕk′sĭ-drə, ĭk-sē′-) *n., pl.* **-drae** (-drē′). **1.** In classical architecture, a portico with a curved continuous bench where discussions were held. **2.** A usually curved outdoor bench of masonry with a high back. [Latin, from Greek *exedra,* out(door) seat, bench : *ex-,* out + *hedra,* seat.]
ex·e·ge·sis (ĕk′sə-jē′sĭs) *n., pl.* **-ses** (-sēz′). Critical explanation or analysis; especially, interpretation of the Scriptures. Compare **eisegesis.** [New Latin, from Greek *exēgēsis,* from *exēgeisthai,* to show the way, expound : *ex-,* out of + *hēgeisthai,* to lead.]
ex·e·gete (ĕk′sə-jēt′) *n.* Also **ex·e·get·ist** (ĕk′sə-jĕt′ĭst). A person skilled in exegesis. [Greek *exēgētes,* from *exēgeisthai,* to expound. See **exegesis.**]
ex·e·get·ic (ĕk′sə-jĕt′ĭk) *adj.* Also **ex·e·get·i·cal** (-ĭ-kəl). Of or pertaining to exegesis; analytic. **—ex·e·get·i·cal·ly** *adv.*
ex·e·get·ics (ĕk′sə-jĕt′ĭks) *n. Used with a singular verb.* The science of exegesis. Compare **hermeneutics.**
ex·em·plar (ĭg-zĕm′plär′, -plər) *n.* **1.** One that is worthy of being copied; a model. **2.** One considered typical or representative; an example; a specimen. **3.** An original, whether real or ideal; an archetype. **4.** A copy, as of a book, especially one that provided the basis for other copies. —See Synonyms at **ideal.** [Middle English, from Old French *exemplaire,* from Late Latin *exemplārium,* from Latin *exemplum,* EXAMPLE.]
ex·em·pla·ry (ĭg-zĕm′plə-rē) *adj.* **1.** Worthy of being imitated; commendable: *exemplary behavior.* **2.** Serving as a model or archetype. **3.** Serving as an illustration; typical. **4.** Serving as a warning: *exemplary punishment.* **—ex·em·plar·i·ly** (ĕg′zĕm-plâr′ə-lē) *adv.* **—ex·em·pla·ri·ness** *n.*
exemplary damages *pl.n.* **Punitive damages** *(see).*
ex·em·pli·fi·ca·tion (ĭg-zĕm′plə-fĭ-kā′shən) *n.* **1.** The act of exemplifying. **2.** One that exemplifies; an example. **3.** *Law.* An official and certified copy of a document from public records.
ex·em·pli·fi·ca·tive (ĭg-zĕm′plə-fĭ-kā′tĭv) *adj.* Serving to exemplify; providing an example.
ex·em·pli·fy (ĭg-zĕm′plə-fī′) *tr.v.* **-fied, -fying, -fies. 1. a.** To illustrate by example. **b.** To serve as an example of. **2.** *Law.* To make a certified copy of (a document from public records). [Middle English *exemplifien,* from Old French *exemplifier,* from Medieval Latin *exemplificāre* : Latin *exemplum,* EXAMPLE + *facere,* to make.] **—ex·em·pli·fi·a·ble** *adj.* **—ex·em·pli·fi·er** *n.*
ex·em·pli gra·ti·a (ĭg-zĕm′plē grä′tē-ä′, grā′shē-ə, -shə) *adv. Abbr.* **e.g.** For the sake of example; for example. [Latin.]
ex·em·plum (ĭg-zĕm′pləm) *n., pl.* **-pla** (-plə). **1.** A short moral story or fable used to illustrate an argument, especially in medieval sermons. **2.** Any illustrative example. [Latin, example.]
ex·empt (ĭg-zĕmpt′) *tr.v.* **-empted, -empting, -empts.** To free from an obligation or duty required of others.
∼*adj.* Freed from or not liable to something to which others are subject: *Nobody is exempt from blame.* Often used in combination: *a tax-exempt benefit.*
∼*n.* One who is exempted from an obligation. [Middle English *exempten,* from Latin *eximere* (past participle *exemptus*), to take out, exempt. See **example.**] **—ex·empt·i·ble** *adj.*
ex·emp·tion (ĭg-zĕmp′shən) *n.* **1. a.** An act of exempting. **b.** The state of being exempt; immunity. **2. a.** Something that exempts. **b.** Something that is exempted, especially from taxable income.
ex·en·ter·ate (ĭg-zĕn′tə-rāt′) *tr.v.* **-ated, -ating, -ates. 1.** To disembowel; eviscerate. **2.** *Surgery.* To remove the contents of (an organ). [Latin *exenterāre* (past participle *exenterātus*), to disembowel : *ex,* from, out of + Greek *enteron,* insides, intestines.] **—ex·en·ter·a·tion** *n.*
ex·e·qua·tur (ĕk′sĭ-kwā′tər, -kwä′tər) *n.* **1.** An official document recognizing a consul or commercial agent, granted by the country to which he is assigned. **2.** Authorization by a secular authority for the publication of ecclesiastical documents or for the performance by a bishop of his duties. [Latin, "let him perform," third person singular present subjunctive of *exequī,* to EXECUTE.]
ex·e·quies (ĕk′sĭ-kwēz) *pl.n.* Funeral rites. [Middle English *exequies,* from Old French, from Latin *exsequiae,* funeral ceremonies, from *ex(s)equī,* to follow, EXECUTE.]
ex·er·cise (ĕk′sər-sīz′) *n.* **1.** An act of employing or putting into play; use: *"the demand for orthodoxy is stifling to any free exercise of intellect"* (Bertrand Russell). **2.** The discharge of a duty, function, or office. **3.** Activity that requires physical or mental exertion, especially when performed to develop or maintain fitness. **4. a.** A lesson, composition, problem, or the like, designed to increase one's skill, discipline, or fitness in some capacity: *a piano exercise.* **b.** A written task assigned to school pupils. **5.** *Military.* A program of practice maneuvers undertaken as part of military training. **6.** Any of the various events in gymnastics. **7. exercises.** A ceremony, either religious or secular, including speeches, awards, and other traditional rites: *graduation exercises.*
∼*v.* **exercised, -cising, -cises.** *—tr.* **1.** To put into play or operation; employ. **2.** To bring to bear; exert: *"the desire to be re-elected exercises a strong brake on independent courage"* (John F. Kennedy). **3.** To subject to forms of practice or exertion in order to train, strengthen, or condition; put through exercises: *exercise the memory; exercise a platoon.* **4.** To carry out the functions of; execute; perform: *exercise the role of disciplinarian.* **5.** To absorb the attentions of; especially, to worry, upset, or make anxious: *He was greatly exercised by his wife's illness.* *—intr.* To take exercise or do exercises. [Middle English, from Old French *exercice,* from Latin *exercitium,* exercise, from *exercitus,* past participle of *exercēre,* to drive on, drill, practice : *ex-,* out of, from + *arcēre,* to enclose, restrain.] **—ex·er·cis·a·ble** *adj.*
ex·er·cis·er (ĕk′sər-sī′zər) *n.* **1.** A person who exercises or performs exercises. **2.** A device for exercising the body.
ex·er·ci·ta·tion (ĭg-zûr′sə-tā′shən) *n.* **1.** Exercise, as of a particular faculty or power: *intellectual exercitation.* **2.** Practice, as of an art, with a view to improvement: *rhetorical exercitation.* **3.** A display of oratorical skill: *the exercitations of Demosthenes.* [Middle English *exercitacioun,* from Latin *exercitātiō* (stem *exercitātiōn-*), from *exercitāre,* to exercise often, frequentative of *exercēre* (past participle *exercitus*), to EXERCISE.]
ex·er·gon·ic (ĕk′sər-gŏn′ĭk) *adj. Physics.* Designating a reaction, especially a nuclear reaction, that releases energy. [EX- (out) + Greek *ergon,* energy, work + -IC.]
ex·ergue (ĕk′sûrg′, ĕg′zûrg′) *n.* **1.** The space on the reverse of a coin or medal, usually below the central design. **2.** The inscription in an exergue, often showing the date and place of engraving. [French, from New Latin *exergum* : Greek *ex-,* out of + *ergon,* work.] **—ex·ergu·al** (ĕk-sûr′gəl) *adj.*
ex·ert (ĭg-zûrt′) *tr.v.* **-erted, -erting, -erts. 1.** To put forth (strength or effort, for example). **2.** To bring to bear; exercise: *exert influence.* **3.** To cause (oneself) to make strenuous efforts. **4.** To make use of; employ: *took every opportunity to exert their authority.* [Latin *ex(s)erere* (past participle *ex(s)ertus*), to stretch out : *ex-,* out + *serere,* to join, put in a row, unite.]
ex·er·tion (ĭg-zûr′shən) *n.* An act or instance of exerting, especially a strenuous effort. —See Synonyms at **effort.**
Ex·e·ter (ĕk′sə-tər). County town of Devon, in southwestern England on the Exe River. It was a Roman fortress town, Isca Damnoniorum. Exeter's cathedral is a fine example of Gothic architecture.
ex·e·unt (ĕk′sē-ənt, -ōōnt′). Used as a stage direction to indicate that two or more actors leave the stage. [Latin, "they go out."]
exeunt om·nes (ŏm′nēz′). Used as a stage direction to indicate that all actors leave the stage. [Latin, "they all go out."]
ex·fo·li·ate (ĕks-fō′lē-āt′) *v.* **-ated, -ating, -ates.** *—tr.* **1.** To remove (skin or bark, for example) in flakes or scales; peel. **2.** To cast off in scales, flakes, or the like. *—intr.* To come off or separate in scales,

PRONUNCIATION KEY

ă, pat; ā, pay; âr, care;
ä, father, are; b, bib;
ch, church; d, deed; ĕ, pet;
ē, be; f, fife; g, gag; h, hat;
hw, which; ĭ, pit; ī, pie;
îr, pier; j, judge; k, kick;
l, lid, needle; m, mum;
n, no, sudden; ng, thing;
ŏ, pot; ō, toe; ô, paw, for;
oi, noise; ou, out; ŏŏ, book;
ōō, boot; p, pop; r, roar;
s, sauce; sh, ship, dish;
t, tight; th, thin, path;
th, this, bathe; ŭ, cut; ûr, fur;
v, valve; w, with; y, yes;
z, zebra, size; zh, vision;
ə, about, item, edible,
gallop, circus, peaceful

IN FOREIGN WORDS:

à, *Fr.* ami; œ, *Fr.* feu, *Ger.* schön; ü, *Fr.* tu, *Ger.* über; KH, *Ger.* ich, *Scot.* loch; N, *Fr.* bon; y′, *Fr.* Compiègne

STRESS MARKS:

Primary stress: ′
in·cite′ (ĭn-sīt′)
Secondary stress: ′
in′sight′ (ĭn′sīt′)

flakes, sheets, or layers. [Latin *exfoliāre,* to strip of leaves : *ex-,* removal from + *folium,* leaf.] **—ex·fo·li·a·tion** *n.* **—ex·fo·li·a·tive** (ĕks-fō′lē-ā′tĭv, -ə-tĭv) *adj.*

ex gra·ti·a (ĕks grā′shē-ə, -shə) *adj.* Given without legal obligation; given as a favor: *an ex gratia payment.* [Latin, "from favor."]

ex·ha·lant (ĕks-hā′lənt, ĕk-sā′-) *adj.* Performing or functioning in exhalation.

ex·ha·la·tion (ĕks′hə-lā′shən, ĕk′sə-) *n.* **1.** An act of exhaling. **2.** Something that is exhaled, as air or vapor.

ex·hale (ĕks-hāl′, ĕk-sāl′) *v.* **-haled, -haling, -hales.** *—intr.* **1. a.** To breathe out. **b.** To emit air or vapor. **2.** To be given off or emitted. *—tr.* **1.** To blow forth or breathe out (vapor, smoke, or the like). **2.** To give off; emit. **3.** To draw out or off; evaporate. [Middle English *exalen,* from Old French *exhaler,* from Latin *exhālāre,* to breathe out : *ex-,* out + *hālāre,* to breathe.] **—ex·hal·a·ble** *adj.*

ex·haust (ĭg-zôst′) *v.* **-hausted, -hausting, -hausts.** *—tr.* **1.** To let out or draw off (air or fumes). **2. a.** To draw out the contents of; drain. **b.** To draw off; drain: *exhaust the oil from a storage tank.* **3.** To create a vacuum or partial vacuum in (a container). **4.** To use up; consume: *exhaust one's money.* **5.** To wear out completely; tire. **6.** To drain of resources or properties; deplete: *cotton crops that exhausted the soil.* **7.** To study or deal with comprehensively: *exhaust a topic.* *—intr.* To escape or pass out, as steam. —See Usage note at **deplete.**
∼n. **1. a.** The escape or release of gas or vapor, as from an engine. **b.** The fumes or gases released. **2.** A device or part, such as a pipe, through which waste material is emitted. **3.** An apparatus for drawing out noxious air or waste material by means of a partial vacuum.
∼adj. **1.** Designating a part of an engine through which expanded steam or the products of combustion pass: *exhaust valve; exhaust manifold.* **2.** Of, pertaining to, or designating the expanded steam or products of combustion of an engine or any phase of the engine's cycle relating to their extraction: *exhaust gas; exhaust stroke.* [Latin *exhaurīre* (past participle *exhaustus*), to draw out, exhaust : *ex-,* out + *haurīre,* to draw up.] **—ex·haust·er** *n.* **—ex·haust·i·bil·i·ty** *n.* **—ex·haust·i·ble** *adj.* **—ex·haust·ing·ly** *adv.*

ex·haus·tion (ĭg-zôs′chən) *n.* **1.** The act or an instance of exhausting. **2.** The state of being exhausted. **3.** A state of great weariness; extreme fatigue.

ex·haus·tive (ĭg-zô′stĭv) *adj.* **1.** Dealing with or taking account of all aspects; comprehensive; thorough. **2.** Tending to exhaust. **—ex·haus·tive·ly** *adv.* **—ex·haus·tive·ness** *n.*

ex·haust·less (ĭg-zôst′lĭs) *adj.* Impossible to exhaust; inexhaustible. **—ex·haust·less·ness** *n.*

ex·hib·it (ĭg-zĭb′ĭt) *v.* **-ited, -iting, -its.** *—tr.* **1.** To show; display. **2. a.** To present for the public to view. **b.** To enter or show in an exhibition or contest. **3.** To give an instance or evidence of; demonstrate: *The specimen exhibits a cancerous condition.* **4.** *Law.* To submit (objects or documents) as evidence in a court; introduce officially. *—intr.* To put something on display; have an exhibition. —See Synonyms at **show.**
∼n. **1.** An act of exhibiting. **2.** Something that is exhibited. **3.** *Law.* Something, such as a document, formally introduced as evidence in court. [Middle English *exhibiten,* from Latin *exhibēre* (past participle *exhibitus*), to hold forth, exhibit : *ex-,* out + *habēre,* to hold.] **—ex·hib·i·tive** *adj.* **—ex·hib·i·tive·ly** *adv.*

ex·hi·bi·tion (ĕk′sə-bĭsh′ən) *n.* **1.** An act of exhibiting: *Don't make an exhibition of yourself.* **2.** Something exhibited. **3.** A display for the public, as of art objects, industrial achievements, or agricultural products. **4.** *British.* A scholarship given to a student by a public school or university.

ex·hi·bi·tion·er (ĕk′sə-bĭsh′ə-nər) *n.* *British.* A student who has received an exhibition.

ex·hi·bi·tion·ism (ĕk′sə-bĭsh′ə-nĭz′əm) *n.* **1.** The act or practice of behaving in an ostentatious way in order to attract attention. **2.** *Psychology.* Compulsive exposure of the sexual organs in public. **—ex·hi·bi·tion·ist** *n.* & *adj.* **—ex·hi·bi·tion·is·tic** *adj.*

ex·hib·i·tor (ĭg-zĭb′ə-tər) *n.* One that exhibits; especially, a person or group exhibiting articles in a show.

ex·hil·a·rant (ĭg-zĭl′ər-ənt) *adj.* Exhilarating.
∼n. A stimulant or euphoriant.

ex·hil·a·rate (ĭg-zĭl′ə-rāt′) *tr.v.* **-rated, -rating, -rates.** **1.** To make cheerful; elate. **2.** To invigorate; stimulate. [Latin *exhilarāre* : *ex-,* completely + *hilarāre,* to make happy, from *hilaris,* cheerful, happy, from Greek *hilaros.*] **—ex·hil·a·ra·tion** *n.* **—ex·hil·a·ra·tive** *adj.* **—ex·hil·a·ra·tor** *n.*

ex·hil·a·rat·ing (ĭg-zĭl′ə-rā′tĭng) *adj.* **1.** Cheering; gladdening. **2.** Invigorating; stimulating. **—ex·hil·a·rat·ing·ly** *adv.*

ex·hort (ĭg-zôrt′) *v.* **-horted, -horting, -horts.** *—tr.* To urge or incite by strong argument, advice, or appeal; admonish earnestly. *—intr.* To make urgent appeal. —See Synonyms at **urge.** [Middle English *exhorten,* from Old French *exhorter,* from Latin *exhortārī* : *ex-,* completely + *hortārī,* to encourage.] **—ex·hor·ta·tive** (ĭg-zôr′tə-tĭv), **ex·hor·ta·to·ry** (-tôr′ē, -tōr′ē) *adj.* **—ex·hort·er** *n.*

ex·hor·ta·tion (ĕg′zôr-tā′shən, ĕk′sôr-) *n.* **1.** An act of exhorting. **2.** The practice of exhorting. **3.** A speech or discourse intended to advise, incite, or encourage.

ex·hume (ĭg-zo͞om′, -zyo͞om′, ĭk-so͞om′, -syo͞om′) *tr.v.* **-humed, -huming, -humes.** **1.** To remove (a dead body) from a grave; disinter. **2.** To bring to light; uncover: *exhume ancient superstitions.* [French *exhumer,* from Medieval Latin *exhumāre* : Latin *ex-,* out of + *humus,* earth.] **—ex·hu·ma·tion** (ĕg′zo͞o-mā′shən, ĕg′zyo͞o-, ĕk′so͞o-, ĕk′syo͞o-) *n.* **—ex·hum·er** *n.*

ex hy·poth·e·si (ĕks′ hī-pŏth′ə-sī′) *adv.* Following from the premise of the argument; in accordance with the stated hypothesis. [New Latin, "according to the hypothesis."]

ex·i·gen·cy (ĕk′sə-jən-sē) *n., pl.* **-cies.** Also **ex·i·gence** (-jəns). **1.** The state or quality of being exigent. **2.** A situation demanding swift attention; emergency. **3.** *Often* **exigencies.** Urgent requirement; pressing need.

ex·i·gent (ĕk′sə-jənt) *adj.* **1.** Requiring immediate attention or remedy; urgent. **2.** Excessively demanding; exacting. [Latin *exigēns* (stem *exigent-*), present participle of *exigere,* to demand.] **—ex·i·gent·ly** *adv.*

ex·i·gi·ble (ĕk′sə-jə-bəl) *adj.* Able to be exacted; demandable; requirable. [French, from *exiger,* to demand, from Latin *exigere.*]

ex·ig·u·ous (ĭg-zĭg′yo͞o-əs, ĭk-sĭg′-) *adj.* Scanty; meager. [Latin *exiguus,* from *exigere,* to weigh exactly, demand. See **exact.**] **—ex·i·gu·i·ty** (ĕk′sə-gyo͞o′ə-tē), **ex·ig·u·ous·ness** *n.* **—ex·ig·u·ous·ly** *adv.*

ex·ile (ĕg′zīl′, ĕk′sīl′) *n.* **1. a.** Enforced removal from one's native country by authoritative decree; banishment. **b.** Self-imposed separation from one's country. **2. a.** The state or circumstance of being in exile. **b.** The period of time in exile. **3.** One who is separated or has been banished from his country.
∼tr.v. **exiled, -iling, -iles.** To send (a person) into exile. —See Synonyms at **banish.** [Middle English *exil,* from Old French, from Latin *exilium,* from *exul,* one who is exiled.] **—ex·il·ic** (ĕg-zĭl′ĭk, ĕk-sĭl′-), **ex·il·ian** (ĕg-zĭl′yən, -zĭl′ē-ən, ĭk-sĭl′yən, -sĭl′ē-ən) *adj.*

ex in. *Finance.* Without interest. [Latin *ex,* without + *in*terest.]

ex·ine (ĕk′sēn′, -sĭn′) *n.* The outer wall of a spore or pollen grain. Also called "exosporium." [Latin *ex(timus),* outermost + -INE.]

ex·ist (ĭg-zĭst′) *intr.v.* **-isted, -isting, -ists.** **1.** To have being or actuality; be. **2. a.** To have life; live. **b.** To continue to live; survive, especially in difficult or reduced circumstances. **3.** To be present under certain circumstances or in a specified place; occur: *Tapeworms exist in human intestines.* [Latin *ex(s)istere,* to exist, come forth : *ex-,* out + *sistere,* to take a position, stand firm.]

ex·is·tence (ĭg-zĭs′təns) *n.* **1.** The fact or state of existing; being. **2.** The fact or state of continued being; life; survival. **3. a.** All that exists. **b.** A thing that exists; an entity. **4.** A mode or manner of existing: *a meager existence.* **5.** Occurrence; specific presence: *the existence of life on other planets.*

ex·is·tent (ĭg-zĭs′tənt) *adj.* **1.** Having life or being; existing. **2.** Occurring or present at the moment; current. —See Synonyms at **real.**
∼n. One that exists.

ex·is·ten·tial (ĕg′zĭ-stĕn′shəl, ĕk′sĭ-) *adj.* **1.** Of, pertaining to, or dealing with existence. **2.** Based on experience; empirical. **3.** Of or pertaining to existentialism. **4.** *Logic.* Of, pertaining to, or designating a proposition that implies or specifies the existence of at least one of its elements. **—ex·is·ten·tial·ly** *adv.*

ex·is·ten·tial·ism (ĕg′zĭ-stĕn′shə-lĭz′əm, ĕk′sĭ-) *n.* A body of ethical thought, current in the 20th century, centering on the uniqueness and isolation of individual experience in a universe indifferent or even hostile to man, regarding human existence as unexplainable, and emphasizing man's freedom of choice and responsibility for the consequences of his acts. **—ex·is·ten·tial·ist** *adj.* & *n.*

ex·it[1] (ĕg′zĭt, ĕk′sĭt). Used as a stage direction for a specified actor to leave the stage. [Latin, "He (or she) goes out."]

exit[2] *n.* **1.** The departure of a performer from the stage. **2. a.** The act of going away or out. **b.** Death; demise. **3.** A way out; a door or passage through which one can leave.
∼intr.v. **exited, -iting, -its.** To go away or out. [Latin *exitus,* exit, departure, from the past participle of *exīre,* to go out : *ex-,* out + *īre,* to go.]

ex·i·tance (ĕk′sə-təns) *n.* A measure of the ability of a surface to emit radiation. See **luminous exitance, radiant exitance.** [Latin *exitus,* departure, emission + -ANCE.]

exit permit *n.* In South Africa, a permit to emigrate without the right to return.

ex li·bris (ĕks lī′brĭs, lē′-) *n., pl.* **ex libris.** *Abbr.* **ex lib.** A bookplate. [Latin, "from the books."]

ex·li·brist (ĕks-lī′brĭst, -lē′brĭst) *n.* One who collects bookplates. **—ex·li·brism** *n.*

Ex·moor (ĕks′mo͝or′). A thinly populated moorland in southwestern England, forming much of Exmoor National Park. The moor contains a number of prehistoric earthworks.

Exmoor pony *n.* A pony of a hardy, sure-footed breed that originated in the Exmoor region of England and has short ears, large eyes, and a bay, brown, or dun coat.

Exmoor pony *One of nine breeds of pony that roam the mountains and moors of the British Isles. It stands about 12 hands high at the shoulder (a hand is about 10 centimeters, or 4 inches) and is distinguished from its close relative, the Dartmoor pony, by its longer and larger head.*

ex ni·hi·lo (ĕks nē′ə-lō′, nī′ə-lō′) *adj.* & *adv.* Out of nothing. [Latin.]

exo– *prefix.* Indicates outside, external, or beyond; for example, **exocarp, exoskeleton.** [Greek *exō,* outside, from *ex,* out of.]

ex·o·bi·ol·o·gy (ĕk′sō-bī-ŏl′ə-jē) *n.* **1.** A branch of biology that deals with the search for and study of extraterrestrial living organisms. Also called "astrobiology." **2.** A branch of biology that deals with the effects of extraterrestrial space on living organisms. In this sense, also called "space biology."

ex·o·carp (ĕk′sō-kärp′) *n.* *Botany.* The outermost layer of the pericarp of fruit. Also called "epicarp." [EXO- + -CARP.]

ex·o·cen·tric (ĕk′sō-sĕn′trĭk) *adj.* *Grammar.* Designating a construction that serves a grammatical function different from that of any of its constituents; for example, *toward the icy summit* is an exocentric construction, since while it functions adverbially, none of its constituent words does. Compare **endocentric.**

Ex·o·cet (ĕk′sō-sĕt′) *n.* A trademark for a versatile guided missile steered by a preset guidance system until it is near the target, after

which it is guided by radar signals. [French, from New Latin *exo-coeta (volans)*, the (flying) fish, from Greek *exōkoitos*, name of a fish believed to sleep out of the water at night : *exō*, out of + *koitos*, bed.]

ex·o·crine (ĕk'sə-krĭn, -krēn', -krīn') *adj.* **1.** Having or secreting through a duct. Said of a gland. **2.** Of or pertaining to the secretion of a gland having a duct. [EXO- + Greek *krinein*, to separate.]

Exod. Exodus (Old Testament).

ex·o·derm (ĕk'sō-dûrm') *n.* An embryonic germ layer, the **ectoderm** *(see).* [EXO- + -DERM.]

ex·o·der·mis (ĕk'sō-dûr'mĭs) *n. Botany.* A layer of protective cells in roots, lying just beneath the epidermis.

ex·o·don·tia (ĕk'sə-dŏn'shə, -shē-ə) *n.* Dentistry involving the extraction of teeth. [New Latin : EX- + *-odontia*, from -ODONT.] —**ex·o·don·tist** *n.*

ex·o·dus (ĕk'sə-dəs) *n.* **1.** A movement away; a departure, usually of a large number of people. **2. Exodus.** The departure of the Israelites from Egypt. Preceded by *the.* [Late Latin, from Greek *exo-dos*, a going out, a way out : *ex-*, out + *hodos*, way.]

Exodus *n. Abbr.* **Ex., Exod.** The second book of the Old Testament, which recounts the Exodus of the Israelites.

ex·o·en·zyme (ĕk'sō-ĕn'zīm') *n.* **1.** An enzyme that acts on the terminal chemical bonds in a chain molecule. **2.** An enzyme, such as a digestive enzyme, that functions outside a cell.

ex·o·er·gic (ĕk'sō-ûr'jĭk) *adj. Physics.* Exergonic.

ex of·fi·ci·o (ĕks' ə-fĭsh'ē-ō') *adj. Abbr.* **e.o., ex off.** By virtue of office or position. [Latin.] —**ex officio** *adv.*

ex·og·a·my (ĕk-sŏg'ə-mē) *n.* **1.** The custom of marrying outside the tribe, family, clan, or other social unit. Compare **endogamy. 2.** *Biology.* Reproduction by the fusion of gametes that are not closely related. [EXO- + -GAMY.] —**ex·o·gam·ic** (ĕk-sə-găm'ĭk), **ex·og·a·mous** (ĕk-sŏg'ə-məs) *adj.*

ex·og·e·nous (ĕk-sŏj'ə-nəs) *adj.* **1.** *Biology.* Derived or developed from outside the body, as substances derived from diet rather than metabolism are. **2.** *Botany.* Characterized by the addition of layers of woody tissue. **3.** Having a cause external to the body. Said of diseases. **4.** Having an outside origin: *exogenous political unrest.* [French *exogène*, having additional layers : EXO- + -GEN.] —**ex·o·gen·ic** (ĕk'sə-jĕn'ĭk) *adj.* —**ex·og·e·nous·ly** *adv.*

ex·o·in·tine (ĕk'sō-ĭn'tĭn, -tēn', -tīn') *n.* The middle layer of a spore or pollen grain, between the intine and the exine. Also called "mesosporium."

ex·on·er·ate (ĭg-zŏn'ə-rāt') *tr.v.* **-at·ed, -at·ing, -ates. 1.** To free from a charge; declare blameless; exculpate. **2.** To free from a responsibility, obligation, or task; exempt. [Middle English *exoneraten*, from Latin *exonerāre* (past participle *exonerātus*), to free from a burden : *ex-*, removal from + *onus* (stem *oner-*), load, burden.] —**ex·on·er·a·tion** *n.*

ex·o·nu·mi·a (ĕk'sō-nōō'mē-ə, -nyōō'mē-ə) *n.* The study and collection of small items, such as tickets or labels, that are not traditionally classified as numismatic objects. [EXO- (outside, beyond) + *-numia*, from Latin *nummus*, coin.]

ex·o·nym (ĕk'sə-nĭm') *n.* Any of the names of a city, river, or the like, in a language other than the language of the region or country in which that place or geographic feature is located; for example, *Londres* is an exonym of *London.* [EX(O)- + -ONYM.]

ex·oph·thal·mic goiter (ĕk'sŏf-thăl'mĭk) *n.* A disease caused by the excessive production of thyroid hormone and characterized by an enlarged thyroid gland, protrusion of the eyeballs, a rapid heartbeat, weight loss, and nervous excitability. Also called "Graves' disease." [From EXOPHTHALMOS.]

ex·oph·thal·mos (ĕk'sŏf-thăl'məs) *n.* Also **ex·oph·thal·mi·a** (-mē-ə), **ex·oph·thal·mus** (-məs). Abnormal protrusion of the eyeballs. [New Latin, from Greek, with prominent eyes : *ex-*, out of + *oph-thalmos*, eye.]

ex·or·bi·tant (ĭg-zôr'bə-tənt) *adj.* Beyond reasonable limits or bounds; immoderate. —See Synonyms at **excessive.** [Middle English, from Old French, from Late Latin *exorbitāns*, present participle of *exorbitāre*, to deviate : Latin *ex-*, out + *orbita*, route, ORBIT.] —**ex·or·bi·tance** *n.* —**ex·or·bi·tant·ly** *adv.*

ex·or·cise, ex·or·cize (ĕk'sôr-sīz', ĕk'sər-) *tr.v.* **-cised, -cis·ing, -cis·es** or **-cized, -ciz·ing, -ciz·es. 1.** To expel (an evil spirit) by or as if by incantation or prayer. **2.** To free from evil spirits. [Middle English *exorcisen*, from Old French *exorciser*, from Late Latin *exor-cīzāre*, from Greek *exorkizein*, to exorcise (an evil spirit) with an oath : *ex-*, away + *horkos†*, oath.] —**ex·or·cis·er** *n.*

ex·or·cism (ĕk'sôr-sĭz'əm, ĕk'sər-) *n.* **1.** The act of exorcising. **2.** A formula used in exorcising. —**ex·or·cist** *n.*

ex·or·di·um (ĭg-zôr'dē-əm, ĭk-sôr'-) *n., pl.* **-ums** or **-di·a** (-dē-ə). An introductory part, especially of a speech or treatise. [Latin, from *exōrdīrī*, to begin : *ex-*, completely + *ōrdīrī*, to begin.] —**ex·or·di·al** *adj.*

ex·o·skel·e·ton (ĕk'sō-skĕl'ə-tən) *n.* The external protective or supporting structure of many invertebrates, such as insects and crustaceans. Compare **endoskeleton.**

ex·os·mo·sis (ĕk'sŏz-mō'sĭs) *n.* The flow of a solvent through a semipermeable membrane into a surrounding fluid; especially, the flow of water through a cell membrane into the external medium. Compare **endosmosis.** [EX(O)- + OSMOSIS.] —**ex·os·mot·ic** (ĕk'-sŏz-mŏt'ĭk) *adj.*

ex·o·sphere (ĕk'sō-sfîr') *n.* The outermost portion of the atmosphere, estimated to begin 300 to 600 miles above the earth and characterized by the ability of constituent molecules with appropri-

ate velocities to escape from the earth without colliding with other molecules. [EXO- + -SPHERE.]

ex·o·spore (ĕk'sō-spôr', -spōr') *n. Botany.* The outermost layer of a spore in some algae and fungi. [EXO- + SPORE.]

ex·o·spo·ri·um (ĕk'sō-spôr'ē-əm, -spōr'ē-əm) *n.* **Exine** (see).

ex·os·to·sis (ĕk'sŏ-stō'sĭs) *n., pl.* **-ses** (-sēz'). A bony tumor on the surface of a bone. [New Latin, from Greek *exostōsis* : *ex-*, out of + *osteon*, bone.]

ex·o·ter·ic (ĕk'sə-tĕr'ĭk) *adj.* **1.** Not confined to an inner circle of disciples or initiates. **2.** Comprehensible to or suited to the general public; popular. Compare **esoteric. 3.** Pertaining to the outside; external. [Latin *exōtericus*, external, from Greek *exōterikos*, from *exōterō*, comparative of *exō*, outside, from *ex*, out.]

ex·o·ther·mic (ĕk'sō-thûr'mĭk) *adj.* Also **ex·o·ther·mal** (-məl). Characterized by or causing the release of heat. Compare **endothermic.** [EXO- + THERM(O)- + -IC.]

ex·ot·ic (ĭg-zŏt'ĭk) *adj.* **1.** From another part of the world; not indigenous; foreign. **2.** Having the charm of the unfamiliar; strikingly and intriguingly unusual, different, or beautiful. —See Synonyms at **fantastic.**
~*n.* Something that is exotic, such as an alien plant, animal, or disease. [Latin *exōticus*, from Greek *exōtikos*, from *exō*, outside, from *ex*, out.] —**ex·ot·i·cal·ly** *adv.* —**ex·ot·i·cism** (ĭg-zŏt'ĭ-sĭz'əm), **ex·ot·ic·ness** *n.*

ex·ot·i·ca (ĭg-zŏt'ĭ-kə) *pl.n.* Exotic things, as in a collection. [Latin, neuter plural of *exōticus*, EXOTIC.]

ex·o·tox·in (ĕk'sō-tŏk'sĭn) *n.* A toxin excreted by a microorganism into a surrounding medium and recoverable from a culture without destruction of the producing agent. See **toxin.**

exp exponential.

ex·pand (ĭk-spănd') *v.* **-pand·ed, -pand·ing, -pands.** —*tr.* **1.** To open up or out; spread out; unfold. **2.** To increase the dimensions of; cause to swell; distend. **3.** To increase the scope of; extend; develop. **4.** *Mathematics.* To write (a quantity) as a sum of terms, as a continued product, or as another extended form. —*intr.* **1.** To open up; unfold. **2.** To become larger or wider. **3.** To speak or write at length; expatiate. **4.** To become expansive. —See Synonyms at **increase.** [Middle English *expanden*, from Latin *expandere* : *ex-*, out + *pandere*, to spread.] —**ex·pand·a·ble** *adj.*

ex·pand·ed (ĭk-spăn'dĭd) *adj.* **1.** *Printing.* Wider than normal in proportion to its height; extended. Said of type. Compare **condensed. 2.** Puffed into a foamlike texture by the addition of gas during solidification. Said of a plastic or similar material used in packaging or insulating.

expanded metal *n.* An open metal mesh used for reinforcing brittle materials and in fencing.

ex·pand·er, ex·pan·dor (ĭk-spăn'dər) *n.* **1.** *Electronics.* A device for expanding the range of output voltages for a given range of input voltages according to a specific law. **2.** A device for exercising and developing body muscles: *a chest expander.*

expanding universe theory *n.* **1.** A theory that interprets the shifts of the lines in the spectra of galaxies as resulting from a Doppler effect, with the result that all galaxies are assumed to be retreating from each other at speeds proportional to the distance separating them and that the universe is expanding. **2.** The cosmological theory in which violent eruption from a point source leads to the formation of elementary particles, the subsequent formation of hydrogen and helium, and the dispersion of the galaxies that develop from this matter. Compare **steady-state theory.** See **big-bang theory.**

ex·panse (ĭk-spăns') *n.* **1.** A wide and open extent, as of land, sky, or water. **2.** Expansion. [Latin *expansum*, from the neuter participle of *expandere*, to EXPAND.]

ex·pan·si·ble (ĭk-spăn'sə-bəl) *adj.* Capable of expanding or of being expanded. —**ex·pan·si·bil·i·ty** *n.*

ex·pan·sile (ĭk-spăn'səl, -sīl') *adj.* Of, pertaining to, or adapted for expansion.

ex·pan·sion (ĭk-spăn'shən) *n.* **1.** The act or process of expanding. **2.** The state of being expanded. **3.** A part or form produced by expanding. **4.** The extent or amount by which something has expanded. **5.** An enlargement, increase, or extension, as of business, currency, or territory. **6.** Increase in the dimensions of a body. **7.** *Mathematics.* **a.** A quantity written in an extended form, such as a series. **b.** The process of obtaining this form. **8.** An expanse. —**ex·pan·sion·ar·y** (ĭk-spăn'shə-nĕr'ē) *adj.*

expansion bolt *n.* A bolt having an attachment that expands as the bolt is driven into a surface.

ex·pan·sion·ism (ĭk-spăn'shə-nĭz'əm) *n.* The practice or policy of territorial or economic expansion, as by a nation. —**ex·pan·sion·ist** *n. & adj.* —**ex·pan·sion·is·tic** (ĭk-spăn'shə-nĭs'tĭk) *adj.*

ex·pan·sive (ĭk-spăn'sĭv) *adj.* **1.** Capable of expanding or tending to expand. **2.** Wide; sweeping; comprehensive. **3.** Disposed to be open and outgoing. **4.** *Psychology.* Marked by euphoria and delusions of grandeur. **5.** Grand in scale: *expansive living.* —**ex·pan·sive·ly** *adv.* —**ex·pan·sive·ness** *n.*

ex par·te (ĕks pär'tē) *adj. & adv.* **1.** *Law.* From or on one side only. **2.** One-sided; partisan. [Latin.]

ex·pa·ti·ate (ĭk-spā'shē-āt') *intr.v.* **-at·ed, -at·ing, -ates. 1.** To speak or write at length on a subject; dilate. Often used with *on* or *upon.* **2.** *Archaic.* To wander freely. [Latin *ex(s)patiārī*, to spread out, digress, expatiate : *ex-*, out + *spatiārī*, to walk, to spread, from *spa-tium*, SPACE.] —**ex·pa·ti·a·tion** *n.* —**ex·pa·tia·to·ry** (ĭk-spā'shə-tôr'ē, -tōr'ē) *adj.*

ex·pa·tri·ate (ĕks-pā'trē-āt') v. **-ated, -ating, -ates.** —*tr.* **1.** To banish (a person) from his native land; exile. **2.** To banish (oneself) from one's native land. —*intr.* To leave one's homeland, and often renounce one's citizenship, to reside in another country. —See Synonyms at **banish.**
~*n.* (-ĭt, -āt'). An expatriated person; an exile.
~*adj.* (-āt', -ĭt). Expatriated. [Medieval Latin *expatriāre* : Latin *ex-,* out of + *patria,* native land, from *pater* (stem *patr-*), father.] —**ex·pa·tri·a·tion** *n.*

ex·pect (ĭk-spĕkt') *tr.v.* **-pected, -pecting, -pects. 1.** To look forward to the probable occurrence or appearance of. **2.** To consider likely or certain. **3.** To consider reasonable or due: *I expect an apology.* **4.** To consider obligatory; require. **5.** *Informal.* To presume; suppose. —See Usage note at **anticipate.** [Latin *ex(s)pectāre,* to look out (for), expect : *ex-,* out + *spectāre,* to look at, frequentative of *specere,* to see, look at.]
  Synonyms: anticipate, await, foresee, hope.

ex·pec·tan·cy (ĭk-spĕk'tən-sē) *n., pl.* **-cies.** Also **ex·pec·tance** (-təns). **1.** The act or state of expecting; expectation. **2.** The state of being expected. **3. a.** Something expected. **b.** An expected amount calculated on the basis of statistical probability: *a life expectancy of seventy years.*

ex·pec·tant (ĭk-spĕk'tənt) *adj.* **1.** Having or marked by expectation: *an expectant pause.* **2.** Awaiting the birth of a child: *an expectant mother.* **3.** Waiting in confident expectation. Used with *of: expectant of praise.*
~*n.* A person who is expecting something. —**ex·pec·tant·ly** *adv.*

ex·pec·ta·tion (ĕk'spĕk-tā'shən) *n.* **1. a.** The act or state of expecting. **b.** Eager anticipation: *The child's eyes were bright with expectation.* **2.** The state of being expected. **3. expectations.** Prospects, especially of inheritance. **4.** Something expected or hoped for. **5.** The expected value of a random variable, especially the **mean** *(see).* —See Usage note at **prospect.**

ex·pec·ta·tive (ĭk-spĕk'tə-tĭv) *adj.* Of, pertaining to, or characterized by expectation.

ex·pect·ing (ĭk-spĕk'tĭng) *adj. Informal.* Awaiting the birth of a child; pregnant.

ex·pec·to·rant (ĭk-spĕk'tər-ənt) *adj.* Promoting or facilitating the secretion or expulsion of phlegm or other matter from the mucous membrane of the air passages.
~*n.* An expectorant medicine.

ex·pec·to·rate (ĭk-spĕk'tə-rāt') v. **-rated, -rating, -rates.** —*tr.* **1.** To eject from the mouth; spit. **2.** To cough up and eject by spitting. —*intr.* **1.** To spit. **2.** To clear out the chest and lungs by coughing up and spitting out matter. [Latin *expectorāre,* to drive from the breast : *ex-,* from, out of + *pectus* (stem *pector-*), breast.] —**ex·pec·to·ra·tion** *n.*

ex·pe·di·en·cy (ĭk-spē'dē-ən-sē) *n., pl.* **-cies.** Also **ex·pe·di·ence** (-dē-əns). **1.** Appropriateness to the purpose at hand. **2.** Adherence to what is personally advantageous; self-interest. **3.** An expedient.

ex·pe·di·ent (ĭk-spē'dē-ənt) *adj.* **1.** Appropriate to the purpose at hand. **2.** Serving to promote one's own interests; politic though perhaps unprincipled.
~*n.* **1.** Something that answers an immediate purpose; a means to an end. **2.** A contrivance adopted to meet an urgent need. [Middle English, from Old French, from Latin *expediēns* (stem *expedient-*), present participle of *expedīre,* to free, make ready. See **expedite.**] —**ex·pe·di·ent·ly** *adv.*

ex·pe·di·en·tial (ĭk-spē'dē-ĕn'shəl) *adj.* Of, pertaining to, or concerned with what is expedient. —**ex·pe·di·en·tial·ly** *adv.*

ex·pe·dite (ĕk'spə-dīt') *tr.v.* **-dited, -diting, -dites. 1.** To speed up the progress of; help along; assist; facilitate. **2.** To perform quickly and efficiently. **3.** To issue officially; dispatch. —See Synonyms at **speed.** [Latin *expedīre* (past participle *expedītus*), to free the feet, to extricate.] —**ex·pe·dit·er, ex·pe·di·tor** *n.*

ex·pe·di·tion (ĕk'spə-dĭsh'ən) *n.* **1. a.** A journey undertaken by an organized group of people with a definite objective, such as exploration. **b.** The people on such a journey. **2. a.** A long march or voyage made by military forces to a scene of battle. **b.** The force sent out, with vehicles and equipment. **3.** Speed in performance; promptness. [Middle English *expedicioun,* from Old French *expedition,* from Latin *expedītiō* (stem *expedītiōn-*), from *expedītus,* past participle of *expedīre,* to extricate. See **expedite.**]

ex·pe·di·tion·ar·y (ĕk'spə-dĭsh'ə-nĕr'ē) *adj.* Of, pertaining to, or being an expedition, especially a military expedition.

ex·pe·di·tious (ĕk'spə-dĭsh'əs) *adj.* Acting or done with speed and efficiency. —See Synonyms at **fast.** —**ex·pe·di·tious·ly** *adv.* —**ex·pe·di·tious·ness** *n.*

ex·pel (ĭk-spĕl') *tr.v.* **-pelled, -pelling, -pels. 1.** To force or drive out; eject forcefully. **2.** To discharge, as from the body or a receptacle: *expelled a huge sigh of relief.* **3.** To dismiss, as from a school, by official decision; turn out. —See Synonyms at **eject.** [Middle English *expellen,* from Latin *expellere* : *ex-,* out + *pellere,* to drive.] —**ex·pel·la·ble** *adj.* —**ex·pel·ler** *n.*

ex·pel·lant, ex·pel·lent (ĭk-spĕl'ənt) *adj.* Expelling or tending to expel; expulsive.
~*n.* A medicine used to expel substances or organisms from the body, especially worms from the intestines.

ex·pend (ĭk-spĕnd') *tr.v.* **-pended, -pending, -pends. 1.** To put out or lay out; spend. **2.** To use up; consume. [Middle English *expenden,* from Latin *expendere,* to pay out : *ex,* out + *pendere,* to weigh, pay.]

ex·pend·a·ble (ĭk-spĕn'də-bəl) *adj.* **1.** Subject to use or consump-

tion. **2.** Liable to being sacrificed in the interests of gaining an objective, especially a military one.
~*n.* Something that is expendable.

ex·pen·di·ture (ĭk-spĕn'də-chər, -chŏor') *n.* **1.** The act or process of expending; outlay. **2. a.** The amount expended. **b.** An expense. —See Synonyms at **price.**

ex·pense (ĭk-spĕns') *n.* **1. a.** Cost; charge. **b.** Outlay of money: *He was put to considerable expense.* **c.** A sacrifice; a price: *"Every attempt at a system is made at the expense of facts"* (Bernard Berenson). **2. expenses. a.** Charges incurred while performing one's job. **b.** *Informal.* Money allotted for payment of such charges. **3.** Something requiring the expenditure of money: *Educating his children was an enormous expense.* **4.** *Archaic.* An act of expending; expenditure. —See Synonyms at **price.**
~*tr.v.* **-pensed, -pensing, -penses. 1.** To charge with expenses. **2.** To write off as an expense. [Middle English, from Old French *espense,* from Late Latin *expensa,* from the feminine past participle of Latin *expendere,* to EXPEND.]

expense account *n.* An account of expenses for travel, entertainment, or the like, incurred by an employee in the course of his work and repaid by his employer.

ex·pen·sive (ĭk-spĕn'sĭv) *adj.* **1.** Involving a large expenditure; high-priced; costly. **2.** Involving considerable loss or sacrifice: *an expensive mistake.* —See Synonyms at **costly.** —**ex·pen·sive·ly** *adv.* —**ex·pen·sive·ness** *n.*

ex·pe·ri·ence (ĭk-spîr'ē-əns) *n.* **1.** The apprehension of an object, thought, or emotion through the senses or mind: *the experience of art.* **2.** Active participation in events or activities, leading to the accumulation of knowledge or skill. **3.** The knowledge or skill so derived. **4.** An event or series of events participated in or lived through, especially one that makes a powerful impression on the mind or senses. **5.** The totality of such events in the past of an individual or group.
~*tr.v.* **experienced, -encing, -ences.** To participate in or partake of personally; undergo: *experience a feeling of loneliness.* [Middle English, from Old French, from Latin *experientia,* from *experiēns,* present participle of *experīrī,* to try, test.]

ex·pe·ri·enced (ĭk-spîr'ē-ənst) *adj.* **1.** Skilled through frequent use or practice. **2.** Knowledgeable from long or wide experience: *an experienced teacher.*

experience table *n.* A table compiled from life-insurance statistics to indicate life expectancy.

ex·pe·ri·en·tial (ĭk-spîr'ē-ĕn'shəl) *adj.* Pertaining to or derived from experience. —**ex·pe·ri·en·tial·ly** *adv.*

ex·pe·ri·en·tial·ism (ĭk-spîr'ē-ĕn'shə-lĭz'əm) *n. Philosophy.* The doctrine that knowledge is derived only from experience.

ex·per·i·ment (ĭk-spĕr'ə-mənt) *n.* **1.** A test made to demonstrate a known truth, to examine the validity of a hypothesis, or to determine the efficacy of something previously untried: *a laboratory experiment.* **2.** The process of conducting an experiment. **3.** An act or approach that is original or unusual: *Presenting a classical opera with the singers in modern dress was an experiment.*
~*intr.v.* (-mĕnt') **experimented, -menting, -ments.** To conduct an experiment or experiments; try or test. [Middle English, from Old French, from Latin *experīmentum,* from *experīrī,* to try, test. See **experience.**] —**ex·per·i·ment·er** *n.* —**ex·per·i·men·ta·tion** (ĭk-spĕr'-ə-mĕn-tā'shən) *n.*

ex·per·i·men·tal (ĭk-spĕr'ə-mĕnt'l) *adj.* **1. a.** Pertaining to or based upon experiment. **b.** Given to experimenting. **2.** Provisional; tentative. **3.** Founded upon experience; empirical. —**ex·per·i·men·tal·ly** *adv.*

ex·per·i·men·tal·ism (ĭk-spĕr'ə-mĕnt'l-īz'əm) *n.* The use of empirical or experimental methods in determining the validity of an idea. —**ex·per·i·men·tal·ist** *n.*

ex·pert (ĕk'spûrt') *n.* A person with a high degree of skill in or knowledge of a certain subject.
~*adj.* (ĕk'spûrt', ĭk-spûrt'). Having or demonstrating impressive skill, dexterity, or knowledge. [Middle English, from Old French, from Latin *expertus,* past participle of *experīrī,* to try.] —**ex·pert·ly** *adv.* —**ex·pert·ness** *n.*

ex·per·tise (ĕk'spər-tēz', -tēs') *n.* **1.** Expert advice or opinion. **2.** Specialized knowledge; expertness. [French, survey, evaluation, from Old French, expertness, from EXPERT.]

ex·pi·a·ble (ĕk'spē-ə-bəl) *adj.* Capable of being expiated.

ex·pi·ate (ĕk'spē-āt') v. **-ated, -ating, -ates.** —*tr.* To make atonement for; redress. —*intr.* To make expiation. [Latin *expiāre* : *ex-,* completely + *piāre,* to appease, atone, from *pius,* devout.] —**ex·pi·a·tor** *n.*

ex·pi·a·tion (ĕk'spē-ā'shən) *n.* **1.** The act of expiating; atonement. **2.** The means of redress or atonement; amends. —**ex·pi·a·to·ry** (ĕk'-spē-ə-tôr'ē, -tōr'ē) *adj.*

ex·pi·ra·tion (ĕk'spə-rā'shən) *n.* **1.** A coming to a close; a termination; an ending. **2.** The act or sound of breathing out.

ex·pi·ra·to·ry (ĭk-spîr'ə-tôr'ē, -tōr'ē) *adj.* Of, pertaining to, or involving the expiration of air from the lungs.

ex·pire (ĭk-spîr') v. **-pired, -piring, -pires.** —*intr.* **1.** To come to an end; terminate: *His membership expired.* **2.** To breathe one's last breath; die. **3.** To breathe out; exhale. —*tr.* **1.** To breathe out. **2.** *Archaic.* To give off (moisture, for example); exude. [Middle English *expiren,* from Old French *exspirer,* from Latin *ex(s)pīrāre,* to breathe out, to expire : *ex-,* out + *spīrāre,* to breathe.]

ex·pir·ee (ĕk'spī-rē', ĭk-spī'-) *n.* Formerly, a British convict who had been transported to Australia and whose sentence had expired.

ex·pi·ry (ĭk-spīr′ē) *n., pl.* **-ries.** An expiration, especially of a contract or agreement. [From EXPIRE.]

ex·plain (ĭk-splān′) *v.* **-plained, -plaining, -plains.** —*tr.* **1.** To make plain or comprehensible; remove obscurity from; elucidate: *explain a puzzle.* **2.** To define; explicate; expound: *He explained his plan.* **3.** To offer reasons for or a cause of; answer for; justify: *explain an error.* —*intr.* To give an explanation. —**explain away.** To minimize, excuse, or nullify by explanation. —**explain oneself.** To clarify the meaning of what one has said or the motives for one's actions. [Middle English *explanen,* from Latin *explānāre,* to explain, to spread out : *ex-,* completely + *plānus,* plain, flat.] —**ex·plain·a·ble** *adj.*

Synonyms: *elucidate, explicate, expound, interpret.*

ex·pla·na·tion (ĕk′splə-nā′shən) *n.* **1.** The act or process of making plain or comprehensible; elucidation; clarification: *His plan requires explanation.* **2.** That which serves to explain or to account for something: *He always has a ready explanation.* **3.** A mutual clarification of misunderstandings; a reconciliation.

ex·plan·a·tive (ĭk-splăn′ə-tĭv) *adj.* Explanatory.

ex·plan·a·to·ry (ĭk-splăn′ə-tôr′ē, -tōr′ē) *adj.* Serving or intended to explain. —**ex·plan·a·to·ri·ly** *adv.*

ex·plant (ĕks-plănt′, -plänt′) *tr.v.* **-planted, -planting, -plants.** To take (living tissue) from the natural site of growth and place in a medium or culture.
~*n.* (ĕks′plănt′, -plänt′). Material explanted. —**ex·plan·ta·tion** (ĕks′plăn-tā′shən) *n.*

ex·ple·tive (ĕk′splə-tĭv) *n.* **1.** An exclamation or oath, especially one that is profane or obscene. **2. a.** A word or phrase added to a line of verse or a sentence in order to ease syntax or rhythm but not to add any meaning. **b.** A word that stands in place of and anticipates a following word or phrase; for example, the word *it* is an expletive in the sentence *It is nice to see you.*
~*adj.* Also **ex·ple·to·ry** (ĕk′splə-tôr′ē, -tōr′ē). Added or inserted in order to fill out something, such as a metrical line or a sentence. [Late Latin *explētīvus,* from Latin *explētus,* past participle of *explēre,* to fill out : *ex-,* out + *plēre,* to fill.]

ex·pli·ca·ble (ĕk′splĭ-kə-bəl, ĭk-splĭk′ə-) *adj.* Capable of being explained; explainable.

ex·pli·cate (ĕk′splĭ-kāt′) *tr.v.* **-cated, -cating, -cates.** **1.** To make clear the meaning of; explain. **2.** To devise or elaborate (a theory). —See Synonyms at **explain.** [Latin *explicāre,* to unfold, explicate : *ex-* (reversal) + *plicāre,* to fold.] —**ex·pli·ca·tor** *n.*

ex·pli·ca·tion (ĕk′splĭ-kā′shən) *n.* **1.** An explanation. **2.** Exhaustive exposition and elucidation. **3.** Critical exposition and interpretation, as of literary texts.

ex·pli·ca·tive (ĕk′splĭ-kā′tĭv, ĭk-splĭk′ə-) *adj.* Also **ex·pli·ca·to·ry** (ĕk′splĭ-kə-tôr′ē, -tōr′ē, ĭk-splĭk′ə-). Serving to explain; explanatory.

ex·plic·it[1] (ĭk-splĭs′ĭt) *adj.* **1.** Expressed fully and with precision; clearly defined; specific. **2. a.** Forthright and unreserved in expression; outspoken: *They were explicit in their criticism.* **b.** Describing sexual acts in detail. Used euphemistically. **3.** Designating a function having an equation $y = f(x)$, in which y can be expressed directly in terms of x. Compare **implicit.** [French *explicite,* from Latin *explicitus,* past participle of *explicāre,* to EXPLICATE.] —**ex·plic·it·ly** *adv.* —**ex·plic·it·ness** *n.*

ex·pli·cit[2] (ĕk′splĭ-kĭt, -sĭt) *n.* A word formerly used to indicate the close of a manuscript or book. [Late Latin, short for *explicitus (est liber),* "(the book is) unrolled," from Latin *explicitus,* EXPLICIT.]

ex·plode (ĭk-splōd′) *v.* **-ploded, -ploding, -plodes.** —*intr.* **1.** To release mechanical, chemical, or nuclear energy in an explosion. **2.** To burst and be destroyed by explosion. **3.** To burst forth or break out suddenly: *explode into action.* **4.** To fly into a sudden rage. **5.** To increase suddenly, sharply, and without control. —*tr.* **1.** To cause to explode or burst violently and noisily; detonate. **2.** To expose as false, unreliable, or irrelevant; confute: *explode a hypothesis.* [Latin *explōdere,* to drive out by clapping : *ex-,* out + *plaudere*†, to clap.] —**ex·plod·er** *n.*

exploded view *n.* An illustration or diagram of a construction that shows its parts separately but in positions that indicate their proper relationships to the whole.

ex·ploit (ĕk′sploit′, ĭk-sploit′) *n.* An act or deed, especially a brilliant or heroic feat.
~*tr.v.* (ĭk-sploit′, ĕk′sploit′) **exploited, -ploiting, -ploits.** **1. a.** To employ to the greatest possible advantage; utilize: *exploit an advantage.* **b.** To turn to maximum commercial advantage. **2.** To make use of selfishly or unethically; take advantage of: *exploit peasant labor.* [Middle English *esploit, expleit,* from Old French *exploit, esplait,* achievement, from Gallo-Romance *explictum* (unattested), from Latin *explicitus,* EXPLICIT.] —**ex·ploit·a·ble** *adj.* —**ex·ploit·a·tive** (ĭk-sploi′tə-tĭv), **ex·ploit·ive** (-sploi′tĭv) *adj.* —**ex·ploit·er** *n.*

ex·ploi·ta·tion (ĕk′sploi-tā′shən) *n.* **1.** The act of exploiting. **2.** The utilization of another person for selfish purposes.

ex·plo·ra·tion (ĕk′splə-rā′shən) *n.* The act or an instance of exploring; an investigation or search.

ex·plore (ĭk-splôr′, -splōr′) *v.* **-plored, -ploring, -plores.** —*tr.* **1.** To investigate systematically; examine: *explore every possibility.* **2.** To search into or range over (a country) for the purpose of discovery. **3.** *Medicine.* To examine for diagnostic purposes. —*intr.* **1.** To make an examination; study. **2.** To travel through an unfamiliar region with a view to learning about it. [Latin *explōrāre,* to search out, explore : *ex-,* out + *plōrāre,* to cry aloud (see **deplore**).] —**ex·plor·a·to·ry** (ĭk-splôr′ə-tôr′ē, -splōr′ə-tōr′ē) *adj.*

ex·plor·er (ĭk-splôr′ər, -splōr′ər) *n.* **1.** One who explores; especially, one who explores a geographic area. **2.** An implement or tool used for exploring; a probe. **3. Explorer.** Any of a series of early U.S. satellites, the first of which confirmed the existence of the Van Allen belts, others being used for scientific study, as of the atmosphere, the earth's magnetic field, solar radiation, and x-rays from space.

ex·plo·sion (ĭk-splō′zhən) *n.* **1.** A sudden rapid violent release of mechanical, chemical, or nuclear energy from a confined region; especially, such a release that generates a radially propagating shock wave accompanied by a loud, sharp report, flying debris, heat, light, and fire. **2.** The loud, sharp sound accompanying such a release. **3.** Anything regarded as having the characteristics or destructive potential of such a release. **4.** A sudden and often vehement outburst, as of emotion: *an abrupt explosion of rage.* **5.** A sudden and great increase: *the population explosion.* **6.** *Phonetics.* **Plosion** *(see).* [Latin *explōsiō* (stem *explōsiōn-*), from *explōsus,* past participle of *explōdere,* to EXPLODE.]

ex·plo·sive (ĭk-splō′sĭv, -zĭv) *adj.* **1.** Pertaining to or involving an explosion. **2.** Tending or liable to explode. **3.** Liable to give rise to conflict or argument: *an explosive topic.* **4.** *Phonetics.* Pertaining to plosion; plosive.
~*n.* **1.** A substance, especially a prepared chemical, that explodes or causes explosion. **2.** *Phonetics.* A **plosive** *(see).* [Old French *explosif,* from Latin *explōsus.* See **explosion.**] —**ex·plo·sive·ly** *adv.* —**ex·plo·sive·ness** *n.*

ex·po (ĕk′spō) *n., pl.* **-pos.** *Informal.* An exhibition, as of industrial products. [Short for EXPOSITION.]

ex·po·nent (ĭk-spō′nənt, ĕk′spō′-) *n.* **1.** One that defines, expounds, or interprets. **2.** One that speaks for, represents, or advocates: *an exponent of international cooperation.* **3.** An interpretive artist, especially one highly skilled in a particular musical instrument. **4.** *Mathematics.* A number or symbol, as *3* in $(x+y)^3$, placed to the right of and above another number, symbol, or expression, denoting the number of times the number, symbol, or expression is to be multiplied by itself. In this sense, also called "power."
~*adj.* Giving an explanation or analysis; explanatory. [Latin *expōnēns* (stem *expōnent-*), present participle of *expōnere,* to EXPOUND.]

ex·po·nen·tial (ĕk′spə-nĕn′shəl) *adj.* **1.** *Mathematics.* **a.** Containing, involving, or expressed as an exponent. **b.** *Abbr.* **exp** Expressed in terms of a designated exponent of *e,* the base of natural logarithms. **2.** Of or pertaining to an exponent.
~*n.* An exponential function. —**ex·po·nen·tial·ly** *adv.*

exponential growth *n. Ecology.* Optimal growth of numbers in a population, where the rate of increase is proportional to the number of individuals and thus becomes increasingly fast until some factor, such as lack of food, limits further increase.

exponential series *n. Mathematics.* The series $e^x = 1 + x + x^2/2! + x^3/3! \ldots + x^n/n!$ When $x = 1$, $e = 2.718$.

ex·po·ni·ble (ĭk-spō′nə-bəl) *adj.* Requiring or admitting of explanation. Said especially of an obscure logical proposition. [Medieval Latin *expōnibilis,* from Latin *expōnere,* to EXPOUND.]

ex·port (ĭk-spôrt′, -spōrt′, ĕk′spôrt′, -spōrt′) *v.* **-ported, -porting, -ports.** —*tr.* **1. a.** To sell (goods or services) to a foreign country. **b.** To send or carry (goods) abroad, especially for sale or trade. Compare **import.** **2.** To encourage or propagate (an idea, for example) abroad: *export revolution.* —*intr.* To send or carry goods abroad, especially for sale or trade.
~*n.* (ĕk′spôrt′, -spōrt′). **1.** The act of exporting: *the export of heavy machinery.* **2.** Something that is exported. [Latin *exportāre,* to carry out or away : *ex-,* out + *portāre,* to carry.] —**ex·port** (ĕk′spôrt′, -spōrt′) *adj.* —**ex·port·a·bil·i·ty** *n.* —**ex·port·a·ble** *adj.* —**ex·port·er** *n.*

ex·por·ta·tion (ĕk′spôr-tā′shən, ĕk′spōr-) *n.* **1.** The act, process, or business of exporting. **2.** Something that is exported.

ex·pose (ĭk-spōz′) *tr.v.* **-posed, -posing, -poses.** **1. a.** To lay open to something undesirable or injurious; make vulnerable: *expose a child to an unnecessary risk.* **b.** To lay open or introduce to something beneficial or positive: *She was exposed to music before she had even learned to talk.* **2.** To subject (a photographic film or plate) to the action of light. **3.** To make visible or known; make manifest: *Cleaning exposed the grain of the wood.* **4.** To disclose or unmask (a crime or criminal, for example); lay bare; make known. **5.** *Roman Catholic Church.* To leave (the Host) displayed on the altar for veneration. **6.** To abandon (an infant, for example) without food or shelter. —See Synonyms at **reveal, show.** —**expose oneself.** To engage in exhibitionism. [Middle English *exposen,* from Old French *exposer,* from Latin *expōnere,* to expose, EXPOUND.] —**ex·pos·er** *n.*

ex·po·sé (ĕk′spō-zā′) *n.* **1.** An exposure or revelation of something discreditable or scandalous. **2.** Something, as a book, that contains an exposé. **3.** A detailed account or statement of the facts; an exposition. [French, from the past participle of *exposer,* to EXPOSE.]

ex·posed (ĭk-spōzd′) *adj.* **1.** Open to view; not hidden. **2.** Unsheltered or uncovered: *an exposed layer of rock.* **3.** Open to attack, criticism, or danger; vulnerable; susceptible.

ex·po·si·tion (ĕk′spə-zĭsh′ən) *n.* **1.** A setting forth of meaning or intent. **2.** A precise statement or definition; an explication; an elucidation. **3.** *Music.* The first part of a sonata or fugue that introduces the themes. **4.** The part of a play or story that introduces the theme and chief characters. **5.** The act of exposing or the condition of being exposed. **6.** A public exhibition or show, as of artistic or industrial products. **7.** *Roman Catholic Church.* The displaying of

PRONUNCIATION KEY

ă, pat; ā, pay; âr, care;
ä, father, are; b, bib;
ch, church; d, deed; ĕ, pet;
ē, be; f, fife; g, gag; h, hat;
hw, which; ĭ, pit; ī, pie;
îr, pier; j, judge; k, kick;
l, lid, needle; m, mum;
n, no, sudden; ng, thing;
ŏ, pot; ō, toe; ô, paw, for;
oi, noise; ou, out; ŏŏ, book;
ōō, boot; p, pop; r, roar;
s, sauce; sh, ship, dish;
t, tight; th, thin, path;
th, this, bathe; ŭ, cut; ûr, fur;
v, valve; w, with; y, yes;
z, zebra, size; zh, vision;
ə, about, item, edible,
gallop, circus, peaceful

IN FOREIGN WORDS:

à, *Fr.* ami; œ, *Fr.* feu, *Ger.* schön; ü, *Fr.* tu, *Ger.* über; KH, *Ger.* ich, *Scot.* loch; N, *Fr.* bon; y′, *Fr.* Compiègne

STRESS MARKS:

Primary stress: ′
in·cite′ (ĭn-sīt′)
Secondary stress: ′
in′sight′ (ĭn′sīt′)

the Host on the altar for public veneration. **8.** *Archaic.* Exposure. [Middle English *exposicioun,* from Old French *exposition,* from Latin *expositiō* (stem *expositiōn-*), from *expositus,* past participle of *expōnere,* to EXPOUND.] **—ex·pos·i·tive** (ĭk-spŏz′ə-tĭv), **ex·pos·i·to·ry** (-tôr′ē, -tōr′ē) *adj.* **—ex·pos·i·tor** *n.*

ex post fac·to (ĕks′ pōst′ făk′tō) *adj.* Formulated, enacted, or operating retroactively. Said especially of a law. [Medieval Latin *ex postfacto,* "from what is done afterward."]

ex·pos·tu·late (ĭk-spŏs′chə-lāt′) *intr.v.* **-lated, -lating, -lates.** To reason earnestly with someone in an effort to dissuade or correct; remonstrate. —See Synonyms at **object.** [Latin *expostulāre,* to demand strongly : *ex-,* entirely + *postulāre,* to demand.] **—ex·pos·tu·la·tor** *n.* **—ex·pos·tu·la·to·ry** (ĭk-spŏs′chə-lə-tôr′ē, -tōr′ē), **ex·pos·tu·la·tive** (-lā′tĭv, -lə-tĭv) *adj.*

ex·pos·tu·la·tion (ĭk-spŏs′chə-lā′shən) *n.* The act or an instance of expostulating; remonstrance.

ex·po·sure (ĭk-spō′zhər) *n.* **1.** The act or an instance of exposing. **2. a.** The condition of being exposed, as to influences or danger: *The exposure of children to drugs is a matter of grave concern.* **b.** Lack of protection from harsh weather conditions, especially cold: *die of exposure.* **3.** The fact or state of being presented to public view, as before an audience: *The candidates for election sought maximum television exposure.* **4.** A position in relation to climatic or weather conditions or points of the compass: *a room with a southern exposure.* **5. a.** The act of exposing sensitized photographic film or plate. **b.** A film or plate so exposed. **c.** The amount of radiant energy needed to expose a photographic film. **d.** A part of a film for individual pictures: *A 35-millimeter film often has 36 exposures.* **e.** The time, shutter speed, or aperture, or a combination of two or all three, that is used in exposing film.

exposure meter *n.* A photoelectric instrument that measures light intensity in a given area and in photographic use indicates the proper exposure for a particular shutter speed and type of film. Also called "light meter."

ex·pound (ĭk-spound′) *v.* **-pounded, -pounding, -pounds.** *—tr.* **1.** To give a detailed statement of; set forth. **2.** To elucidate or explain; interpret. *—intr.* To make a detailed statement; explain a point of view: *He was expounding on his favorite sport.* —See Synonyms at **explain.** [Middle English *expoun(d)en,* from Old French *espondre,* from Latin *expōnere,* to put forth, expose : *ex-,* out + *pōnere,* to place, put.] **—ex·pound·er** *n.*

ex·press (ĭk-sprĕs′) *tr.v.* **-pressed, -pressing, -presses. 1.** To make known or set forth in words; state; utter: *express one's wishes.* **2.** To manifest or communicate, as by a gesture; show; exhibit: *His posture expressed his exhaustion.* **3.** To make (one's opinions, for example) known: *expressed his feelings forcefully.* **4.** To convey or represent through words or other artistic means: *His poems express a sense of wonder.* **5.** To represent by a sign or symbol; symbolize: *The ∞ sign expresses infinity.* **6.** To squeeze or press out (juice from a fruit, for example). **7.** To send by special courier or rapid transport. —See Synonyms at **vent. —express oneself.** To communicate one's thoughts or feelings through words, gestures, or artistic activity.

∼adj. Abbr. **ex., exp. 1.** Definitely and unmistakably stated; explicit: *an express wish.* **2.** Particular; specific: *an express purpose.* **3. a.** Sent out with or moving at high speed. **b.** Direct, rapid, and usually nonstop: *express mail.* **c.** Of, pertaining to, or appropriate for rapid travel.

∼adv. By express delivery or transport.

∼n. Abbr. **ex., exp. 1. a.** A means of transport, as a train, that travels rapidly and makes few or no stops. **b.** A company that deals in such transport. **2. a.** A special courier. **b.** A message delivered by special courier. **3. a.** A rapid, efficient system for the delivery of goods and mail. **b.** Goods and mail conveyed by such a system. **4.** An express rifle. [Middle English *expressen,* from Old French *expresser,* from Vulgar Latin *expressāre* (unattested), to press out, express : Latin *ex-,* out + *pressāre,* to press, from *premere* (past participle *pressus*), to press.] **—ex·press·er** *n.* **—ex·press·i·ble** *adj.*

ex·press·age (ĭk-sprĕs′ĭj) *n.* **1.** The conveyance of goods by express. **2.** The amount charged for such conveyance.

ex·pres·sion (ĭk-sprĕsh′ən) *n.* **1.** The act of expressing, conveying, or representing in words, art, music, or movement; a manifestation: *the expression of an idea.* **2.** That which communicates, indicates, embodies, or symbolizes something; a symbol; a sign; a token. **3.** *Mathematics.* Any symbolic mathematical form, such as an equation. **4. a.** The means by which something is expressed: *expression through music.* **b.** The quality of expressing feelings, attitudes, or the like through means such as tone or gesture: *His playing lacked expression.* **5.** The manner in which one expresses oneself, especially in speaking, depicting, or performing. **6.** A particular word or phrase: *a slang expression.* **7.** The outward manifestation of an inner mood or disposition: *Her tears were an expression of her grief.* **8.** A facial aspect or look that conveys a special feeling: *an expression of scorn in his eyes.* **9.** *Genetics.* **Penetrance** *(see).* **10.** The act of removing a liquid from a solid by squeezing.

ex·pres·sion·ism (ĭk-sprĕsh′ə-nĭz′əm) *n.* A movement in the fine arts during the first half of the 20th century that originated in Europe and tried to convey the quality of emotional experience rather than representing the physical world. In painting, this was achieved by the use of exaggeration and distortion, strong colors, and simplified outlines. **—ex·pres·sion·ist** *n.* & *adj.* **—ex·pres·sion·is·tic** (ĭk-sprĕsh′ə-nĭs′tĭk) *adj.*

ex·pres·sion·less (ĭk-sprĕsh′ən-lĭs) *adj.* **1.** Lacking expression. **2.** Having a fixed facial expression that shows or reveals no emotion. **—ex·pres·sion·less·ly** *adv.*

ex·pres·sive (ĭk-sprĕs′ĭv) *adj.* **1.** Pertaining to, related to, or characterized by expression: *expressive hands.* **2.** Serving to express or indicate: *His actions are expressive of frustration.* **3.** Full of expression; significant: *an expressive glance.* **—ex·pres·sive·ly** *adv.* **—ex·pres·sive·ness** *n.*

ex·pres·siv·i·ty (ĕk′sprĕ-sĭv′ə-tē) *n.* **1.** The quality of being expressive. **2.** *Genetics.* The degree to which a particular gene can affect the phenotype of an organism.

ex·press·ly (ĭk-sprĕs′lē) *adv.* **1.** In an express or definite manner; explicitly: *I expressly order you to leave.* **2.** Especially; particularly: *These chocolates are expressly for you.*

express rifle *n.* A hunting rifle having low trajectory, high velocity, and a long point-blank range.

express train *n.* A passenger or freight train that travels at high speed and makes a minimum of stops.

ex·press·way (ĭk-sprĕs′wā′) *n.* A major divided highway designed for fast travel.

ex·pro·pri·ate (ĕks-prō′prē-āt′) *tr.v.* **-ated, -ating, -ates. 1.** To deprive (a person) of ownership or property. **2.** To take away or transfer (ownership or property, for example) from an owner; especially, to acquire for public use. [Medieval Latin *expropriāre* : Latin *ex-* (removal away from) + *proprius,* one's own.] **—ex·pro·pri·a·tion** *n.* **—ex·pro·pri·a·tor** *n.* **—ex·pro·pri·a·to·ry** (ĕks-prō′prē-ə-tôr′ē, -tōr′ē) *adj.*

ex·pugn·a·ble (ĭk-spyo͞o′nə-bəl) *adj.* Capable of being defeated or taken by force. [Latin *expugnabilis* : *expugnāre,* to take by storm + *abilis,* -ABLE.]

ex·pul·sion (ĭk-spŭl′shən) *n.* The act of expelling or the state of being expelled. **—ex·pul·sive** (ĭk-spŭl′sĭv) *adj.*

ex·punc·tion (ĭk-spŭngk′shən, -spŭng′shən) *n.* The act of expunging or the condition of being expunged; deletion. [Latin *expunctus,* past participle of *expungere,* to EXPUNGE + -ION.]

ex·punge (ĭk-spŭnj′) *tr.v.* **-punged, -punging, -punges. 1.** To omit, erase, strike out, or obliterate (a word or sentence, for example). **2.** To eliminate physically; annihilate. —See Synonyms at **erase.** [Latin *expungere,* to prick out, erase : *ex-,* out + *pungere,* to prick.] **—ex·pung·er** *n.*

ex·pur·gate (ĕk′spər-gāt′) *tr.v.* **-gated, -gating, -gates. 1.** To amend (a text) by removing obscene or objectionable passages, especially prior to publication. **2.** To cleanse; purge. [Latin *expurgāre,* to purge out, purify : *ex-,* out + *purgāre,* to purge.] **—ex·pur·ga·tion** *n.* **—ex·pur·ga·tor** *n.* **—ex·pur·ga·to·ry** (ĭk-spûr′gə-tôr′ē, -tōr′ē), **ex·pur·ga·to·ri·al** (ĭk-spûr′gə-tôr′ē-əl, -tōr′ē-əl) *adj.*

ex·qui·site (ĕk′skwĭ-zĭt, ĭk-skwĭz′ĭt) *adj.* **1.** Beautifully made or designed: *an exquisite chalice.* **2.** Of such beauty or delicacy as to arouse delight: *an exquisite sunset.* **3.** Acutely perceptive or discriminating: *an exquisite sense of color.* **4.** Intense; keen: *an exquisite pain.*

∼n. One who is excessively sensitive and fastidious in dress, manners, or taste; a dandy; a fop. [Middle English *exquisit,* from Latin *exquīsītus,* chosen, exquisite, from the past participle of *exquīrere,* to search out : *ex-,* out + *quaerere,* to seek.] **—ex·qui·site·ly** *adv.* **—ex·qui·site·ness** *n.*

ex·san·gui·nate (ĕks-săng′gwə-nāt′) *tr.v.* **-nated, -nating, -nates.** To drain of blood. [From Latin *exsanguinātus,* bloodless : *ex-,* without + *sanguis* (stem *sanguin-*), blood (see **sanguine**).] **—ex·san·gui·na·tion** *n.*

ex·san·guine (ĕks-săng′gwĭn) *adj.* Also **ex·san·gui·nous** (-gwĭ-nəs). Lacking blood; anemic. [Latin *exsanguis,* deprived of blood : *ex-,* without + *sanguis* (stem *sanguin-*), blood (see **sanguine**).]

ex·scind (ĭk-sĭnd′) *tr.v.* **-scinded, -scinding, -scinds.** To excise or cut out; extirpate. [Latin *exscindere* : *ex-,* out + *scindere,* to cut.]

ex·sect (ĭk-sĕkt′) *tr.v.* **-sected, -secting, -sects.** To cut out. [Latin *exsecāre* (past participle *exsectus*) : *ex-,* out + *secāre,* to cut.] **—ex·sec·tion** *n.*

ex·sert (ĭk-sûrt′) *tr.v.* **-serted, -serting, -serts.** To thrust out or forth; cause to protrude.

∼adj. Also **ex·sert·ed** (-sûr′tĭd). *Biology.* Thrust outward or protruding, as stamens protruding beyond the petals. [Latin *ex(s)erere* (past participle *ex(s)ertus*), to EXERT.] **—ex·ser·tion** *n.*

ex-ser·vice (ĕks′sûr′vĭs) *adj.* **1.** Having formerly served in the armed forces. **2.** Formerly belonging to the armed forces.

ex-ser·vice·man (ĕks′sûr′vĭs-măn′) *n., pl.* **-men** (-mĕn′). One who has formerly served in the armed forces.

ex·sic·cate (ĕk′sĭ-kāt′) *v.* **-cated, -cating, -cates.** *—tr.* To make dry; remove the moisture from; dehydrate. *—intr.* To dry up. [Latin *exsiccāre,* to dry out : *ex-,* out + *siccāre,* to dry, from *siccus,* dry.] **—ex·sic·ca·tion** *n.* **—ex·sic·ca·tive** (ĕk′sĭ-kā′tĭv) *adj.* **—ex·sic·ca·tor** *n.*

ex·stip·u·late (ĕks-stĭp′yə-lĭt, -lāt′) *adj. Botany.* Having no stipules. [From EX- + STIPULE.]

ext. **1.** extension. **2.** exterior. **3.** external. **4.** extra.

ex·tant (ĕk′stənt, ĕk-stănt′) *adj.* Still in existence; not destroyed, lost, or extinct: *extant manuscripts; extant species of mammals.* —See Synonyms at **living.** [Latin *ex(s)tāns* (stem *ex(s)tant-*), present participle of *ex(s)tāre,* to stand out, exist, be prominent : *ex-,* out + *stāre,* to stand.]

ex·tem·po·ra·ne·ous (ĭk-stĕm′pə-rā′nē-əs) *adj.* **1.** Done, made, spoken, or otherwise performed with little or no preparation or practice; impromptu: *an extemporaneous recital.* **2.** Delivered without notes or text: *an extemporaneous sermon.* **3.** Provided, made, or

Expression in repose

"Grin face"

"Play face"

Pout

expression *Chimpanzees, like humans, can convey a wide range of emotions through their faces. The "grin face," with bared upper teeth, is a reaction to a threat and may express a mixture of anger, fear, and surprise; the "play face," with upper teeth hidden, is a friendly invitation to play; and the pout is an expression of interest or curiosity.*

adapted as an expedient; improvised; makeshift. [Late Latin *extemporāneus,* from Latin *ex tempore,* EXTEMPORE.] **—ex·tem·po·ra·ne·ous·ly** *adv.* **—ex·tem·po·ra·ne·ous·ness** *n.*

Synonyms: *ad lib, impromptu, improvised, unpremeditated, unrehearsed.*

ex·tem·po·rar·y (ĭk-stĕm′pə-rĕr′ē) *adj.* Extemporaneous. [Latin *ex tempore,* EXTEMPORE.] **—ex·tem·po·rar·i·ly** (ĭk-stĕm′pə-râr′ə-lē) *adv.*

ex·tem·po·re (ĭk-stĕm′pə-rē) *adv.* **1.** Without preparation; impromptu. **2.** Without notes or text: *speak extempore.* **3.** By improvising. [Latin *ex tempore* : *ex-,* out of + *tempore,* ablative of *tempus,* time (see **temporal**).] **—ex·tem·po·re** *adj.*

ex·tem·po·rize (ĭk-stĕm′pə-rīz′) *v.* **-rized, -rizing, -rizes.** *—tr.* To perform, utter, or do (something) extempore. *—intr.* To perform, utter, or do something extempore; improvise. **—ex·tem·po·ri·za·tion** *n.* **—ex·tem·po·riz·er** *n.*

ex·tend (ĭk-stĕnd′) *v.* **-tended, -tending, -tends.** *—tr.* **1.** To open or straighten out to full length; unbend: *extend the leg.* Compare **flex. 2.** To stretch out or spread to fullest length: *The ladder was fully extended.* **3. a.** To exert (oneself) vigorously or to full capacity. **b.** To cause (a horse, for example) to move at full gallop. **4. a.** To enlarge the area or scope of; expand: *extend our boundaries.* **b.** To expand the influence, range, or meaning of; make more comprehensive or inclusive: *extend his responsibilities.* **5.** To offer to give or grant; afford: *extend one's greetings.* **6.** *Finance.* To cause to be longer; especially, to prolong the time of payment of (a debt, for example). **7. a.** To increase in quantity or bulk by adding a cheaper substance. **b.** To adulterate. *—intr.* **1.** To be or become extended. **2.** To stretch or reach, as in a certain direction or for a certain time: *His influence extended to other continents.* —See Synonyms at **increase.** —See Usage note at **prolong.** [Middle English *extenden,* from Latin *extendere* : *ex-,* out + *tendere,* to stretch.] **—ex·tend·i·bil·i·ty** *n.* **—ex·tend·i·ble** *adj.*

ex·tend·ed (ĭk-stĕn′dĭd) *adj.* **1.** Stretched or pulled out. **2.** Continued for a long period of time. **3.** Enlarged or extensive; widespread: *extended television coverage.* **—ex·tend·ed·ly** *adv.*

extended family *n.* A family unit consisting of parents, children, and other close relatives, such as grandparents or aunts and uncles, who live together. Compare **nuclear family.**

ex·tend·er (ĭk-stĕn′dər) *n.* A substance added to another substance to modify, dilute, or adulterate.

ex·ten·si·ble (ĭk-stĕn′sə-bəl) *adj.* **1.** Capable of being extended or protruded. **2.** Extensile. [Latin *extensus,* past participle of *extendere,* to EXTEND.] **—ex·ten·si·bil·i·ty** *n.*

ex·ten·sile (ĭk-stĕn′səl, -sīl′) *adj.* Capable of being stretched out or protruded, especially without breaking; extensible.

ex·ten·sion (ĭk-stĕn′shən) *n. Abbr.* **ext. 1. a.** The act of extending or the condition of being extended. **b.** That which is extended. **2.** The amount, degree, or range to which something extends or can extend; compass. **3. a.** The act of straightening or extending a limb. **b.** The position assumed by an extended limb. **4.** *Medicine.* The application of traction to a fractured or dislocated limb to restore the normal position. **5.** A part added to or extended from a main structure to form an addition: *an extension to a hospital.* **6.** An additional telephone connected to the main line. **7. a.** A granting of extra time, especially for the repayment of a debt or compliance with a legal formality. **b.** The period of this extra time. **8.** The property of an object by which it occupies space; spatial magnitude. **9.** *Logic.* The class of objects designated by a specific term or concept; denotation. Compare **intension. 10.** A program of instruction offered, as by a university or college, to outside or part-time students. **11.** *Mathematics.* A set that includes a given and similar set as a subset. [Middle English *extensioun,* from Old French *extension,* from Late Latin *extensiō* (stem *extensiōn-*), from Latin *extensus,* past participle of *extendere,* to EXTEND.]

ex·ten·si·ty (ĭk-stĕn′sə-tē) *n.* **1.** The attribute of sensation that enables one to perceive space or size. **2.** The quality of having extension or being extensive.

ex·ten·sive (ĭk-stĕn′sĭv) *adj.* **1.** Having a great extent; vast; broad: *an extensive meadow.* **2.** Having a wide range; inclusive; comprehensive: *an extensive library.* **3.** Considerable in amount: *Extensive capital was invested.* **4.** Pertaining to or characterized by extension. **5.** Designating or pertaining to the agricultural cultivation of vast areas of land with a minimum of labor or expense. Compare **intensive. 6.** *Physics.* **a.** Having a value that is the sum of the values for subdivisions of a thermodynamic system. Said of volume, for example. **b.** Designating a property or measurement that is dependent on mass. In this sense, compare **intensive.** **—ex·ten·sive·ly** *adv.* **—ex·ten·sive·ness** *n.*

ex·ten·som·e·ter (ĕk′stĕn-sŏm′ə-tər) *n.* An instrument used to measure minute deformations in a test specimen of a material. [EXTENS(ION) + -O- + -METER.]

ex·ten·sor (ĭk-stĕn′sər) *n.* A muscle that extends or stretches a limb. Compare **flexor.** [New Latin, from Latin *extensus,* past participle of *extendere,* to EXTEND.]

ex·tent (ĭk-stĕnt′) *n.* **1.** The range over which something extends; scope; comprehensiveness. **2. a.** The dimensions to which something is extended; magnitude; spread. **b.** The distance over which a thing extends or the space it occupies. **3.** Any extensive space or area: *an extent of desert.* **4.** A certain degree, usually specified: *to a great extent; to some extent.* [Middle English *extente,* from Norman French, from Medieval Latin *extenta,* from Latin, feminine past participle of *extendere,* to EXTEND.]

ex·ten·u·ate (ĭk-stĕn′yo͞o-āt′) *tr.v.* **-ated, -ating, -ates. 1.** To lessen or attempt to lessen the magnitude of (guilt or an offense) by providing partial excuses. **2.** To cause to appear less serious or blameworthy: *circumstances extenuating the error.* [Latin *extenuāre,* to thin out, lessen : *ex-,* out + *tenuāre,* to make thin, from *tenuis,* thin.] **—ex·ten·u·a·tive** (ĭk-stĕn′yo͞o-ā′tĭv) *adj.* & *n.* **—ex·ten·u·a·to·ry** (-ə-tôr′ē, -tōr′ē) *adj.*

ex·ten·u·at·ing (ĭk-stĕn′yo͞o-ā′tĭng) *adj.* Serving to lessen, excuse, or qualify guilt or blame: *extenuating circumstances.*

ex·ten·u·a·tion (ĭk-stĕn′yo͞o-ā′shən) *n.* **1.** The act of extenuating or the condition of being extenuated; partial justification. **2.** That which serves to extenuate; a partial excuse.

ex·te·ri·or (ĭk-stîr′ē-ər) *adj. Abbr.* **ext. 1.** Outer; external. **2.** Originating or acting from the outside. **3.** Suitable for use outside: *an exterior paint.* **4.** Not situated or placed inside a building; outdoor. **5.** Outwardly apparent: *an exterior affability.*

~n. Abbr. **ext. 1.** A part or surface that is outside. **2.** An external or outward appearance; an aspect: *a friendly exterior.* **3.** A representation, as a picture or photograph, of an outdoor scene. [Latin, comparative of *exterus,* outward, outside.] **—ex·te·ri·or·i·ty** (ĭk-stîr′ē-ôr′ə-tē, -ōr′ə-tē) *n.* **—ex·te·ri·or·ly** *adv.*

exterior angle *n.* **1.** The angle between any side of a polygon and an extended adjacent side. **2.** Any of the four angles that do not include a region of the space between two lines intersected by a transversal.

ex·te·ri·or·ize (ĭk-stîr′ē-ə-rīz′) *tr.v.* **-ized, -izing, -izes. 1.** To externalize. **2.** *Surgery.* To bring (an organ or part) out of the abdominal cavity. **—ex·te·ri·or·i·za·tion** *n.*

ex·ter·mi·nate (ĭk-stûr′mə-nāt′) *tr.v.* **-nated, -nating, -nates.** To get rid of by destroying completely; extirpate: *a spray to exterminate insects.* [Latin *extermināre,* to drive out : *ex-,* out of + *termināre,* to limit, end.] **—ex·ter·mi·na·tion** *n.* **—ex·ter·mi·na·tive** (ĭk-stûr′mə-nā′tĭv, -nə-tĭv), **ex·ter·mi·na·to·ry** (-nə-tôr′ē, -tōr′ē) *adj.*

extermination camp *n.* In World War II, a Nazi concentration camp in which large numbers of people, especially Jews, were executed. Also called "death camp."

ex·ter·mi·na·tor (ĭk-stûr′mə-nā′tər) *n.* One that exterminates; especially, one whose occupation is the extermination of vermin.

ex·tern, ex·terne (ĕk′stûrn′) *n.* A person associated with but not officially residing in an institution, especially a nonresident doctor on a hospital staff. [Old French *externe,* from Latin *externus,* EXTERNAL.]

ex·ter·nal (ĭk-stûr′nəl) *adj. Abbr.* **ext. 1. a.** Pertaining to, existing or visible on, or connected with the outside or an outer part; exterior. **b.** Pertaining to the outside of the body: *for external use only.* **2.** Affecting or capable of affecting the outside: *an external application.* **3.** *Philosophy.* Existing independently of the mind; objective; phenomenal: *external objects.* **4.** Acting or coming from the outside: *external pressures.* **5.** Of or pertaining to the outward appearance; superficial. **6.** Of or pertaining to foreign affairs or foreign countries; international.

~n. Abbr. **ext. 1.** An exterior part or surface. **2. externals.** External circumstances; appearances. [Middle English, from Latin *externus,* from *exterus,* outward.] **—ex·ter·nal·ly** *adv.*

ex·ter·nal-com·bus·tion engine (ĭk-stûr′nəl-kəm-bŭs′chən) *n.* An engine, such as a steam engine, in which the fuel is burned outside the engine cylinder.

external ear *n.* The portion of the ear including the auricle (or pinna) and the passage leading to the eardrum.

ex·ter·nal·ism (ĭk-stûr′nə-lĭz′əm) *n.* **1.** *Philosophy.* The doctrine that only objects perceived by the senses are capable of being judged real; phenomenalism. **2.** Devotion to externals or to matters of form or procedure, as in religion. **—ex·ter·nal·ist** *n.*

ex·ter·nal·i·ty (ĕk′stər-năl′ə-tē) *n., pl.* **-ties. 1.** The condition or quality of being external or externalized. **2.** *Philosophy.* The quality of being external to the perceiving subject.

ex·ter·nal·ize (ĭk-stûr′nə-līz′) *tr.v.* **-ized, -izing, -izes. 1.** To make external. **2.** To project (a feeling or opinion) onto others or one's environment; rationalize: *tending to externalize his insecurity.* **3.** To express (personal feelings or problems, for example) freely, especially in words. **—ex·ter·nal·i·za·tion** *n.*

ex·ter·o·cep·tor (ĕk′stə-rō-sĕp′tər) *n.* A sense organ receiving and responding to external stimuli. [New Latin : Latin *exter, exterus,* EXTER(IOR) + -O- + (RE)CEPTOR.] **—ex·ter·o·cep·tive** (ĕk′stə-rō-sĕp′tĭv) *adj.*

ex·ter·ri·to·ri·al (ĕks′tĕr′ə-tôr′ē-əl, -tōr′ē-əl) *adj.* Beyond the territorial limits; extraterritorial. **—ex·ter·ri·to·ri·al·i·ty** (ĕks′tĕr′ə-tôr′ē-ăl′ə-tē, -tōr′ē-ăl′ə-tē) *n.* **—ex·ter·ri·to·ri·al·ly** *adv.*

ex·tinct (ĭk-stĭngkt′) *adj.* **1.** Extinguished or inactive, as a fire or volcano might be. **2.** No longer existing in living form; having died out: *extinct birds such as the dodo and moa.* **3.** Lacking a claimant; void: *an extinct title.* **4.** No longer in use; superseded: *an extinct custom.* —See Usage note at **dead.** [Middle English, from Latin *ex(s)tinctus,* past participle of *ex(s)tinguere,* to EXTINGUISH.]

ex·tinc·tion (ĭk-stĭngk′shən) *n.* **1.** The act of extinguishing or making extinct. **2.** The fact or condition of being extinguished or extinct. **3.** *Physics.* A reduction in the intensity of light or other radiation passing through a medium, caused by absorption or scattering. **4.** The absorption of light from a planet or star by the earth's atmosphere. **5.** Complete destruction; annihilation. **—ex·tinc·tive** (ĭk-stĭngk′tĭv) *adj.*

ex·tin·guish (ĭk-stĭng′gwĭsh) *tr.v.* **-guished, -guishing, -guishes. 1.** To put out (a fire or light); quench. **2.** To put an end to (hope, for example); destroy. **3.** *Law.* **a.** To settle or discharge (a debt).

PRONUNCIATION KEY

ă, pat; ā, pay; âr, care;
ä, father, are; b, bib;
ch, church; d, deed; ĕ, pet;
ē, be; f, fife; g, gag; h, hat;
hw, which; ĭ, pit; ī, pie;
îr, pier; j, judge; k, kick;
l, lid, needle; m, mum;
n, no, sudden; ng, thing;
ŏ, pot; ō, toe; ô, paw, for;
oi, noise; ou, out; o͝o, book;
o͞o, boot; p, pop; r, roar;
s, sauce; sh, ship, dish;
t, tight; th, thin, path;
th, this, bathe; ŭ, cut; ûr, fur;
v, valve; w, with; y, yes;
z, zebra, size; zh, vision;
ə, about, item, edible,
gallop, circus, peaceful

IN FOREIGN WORDS:

à, *Fr.* ami; œ, *Fr.* feu, *Ger.* schön; ü, *Fr.* tu, *Ger.* über;
KH, *Ger.* ich, *Scot.* loch;
N, *Fr.* bon; y′, *Fr.* Compiègne

STRESS MARKS:

Primary stress: ′
in·cite′ (ĭn-sīt′)
Secondary stress: ′
in′sight′ (ĭn′sīt′)

b. To nullify. [Latin *ex(s)tinguere* : *ex-*, out + *stinguere*, to quench.] **—ex·tin·guish·a·ble** *adj.* **—ex·tin·guish·ment** *n.*

ex·tin·guish·er (ĭk-stĭng′gwĭ-shər) *n.* One that extinguishes, especially: **a.** A small metal cone on a long handle that is used for snuffing out candles. **b.** A fire extinguisher (*see*).

ex·tir·pate (ĕk′stər-pāt′) *tr.v.* **-pated, -pating, -pates. 1.** To pull up by or as if by the roots; root out. **2.** To destroy wholly; exterminate. **3.** To remove by surgery. **—See** Synonyms at **abolish.** [Latin *ex(s)tirpāre*, to pluck up by the roots : *ex-*, out + *stirps*, root, stem (see **stirps**).] **—ex·tir·pa·tion** *n.* **—ex·tir·pa·tive** *adj.* **—ex·tir·pa·tor** *n.*

ex·tol, ex·toll (ĭk-stōl′) *tr.v.* **-tolled, -tolling, -tols** or **-tolls.** To praise lavishly; laud or eulogize. **—See** Synonyms at **praise.** [Middle English *extollen*, to lift up, praise, from Latin *extollere* : *ex-*, up + *tollere*, to lift, raise.] **—ex·tol·ler** *n.* **—ex·tol·ment** *n.*

ex·tort (ĭk-stôrt′) *tr.v.* **-torted, -torting, -torts. 1.** To obtain (money or information, for example) from another by coercion, intimidation, or the wrong use of an official position. **2.** To exact; wring. [Latin *extorquēre* (past participle *extortus*), to twist out : *ex-*, out + *torquēre*, to twist.] **—ex·tort·er** *n.* **—ex·tor·tive** *adj.*

ex·tor·tion (ĭk-stôr′shən) *n.* **1.** The act or an instance of extorting. **2.** The criminal offense of using one's official position or power to obtain property, funds, or patronage to which one is not entitled. **3.** An exorbitant price. **4.** Something extorted. **—ex·tor·tion·ar·y** (ĭk-stôr′shə-nĕr′ē) *adj.* **—ex·tor·tion·ist, ex·tor·tion·er** *n.*

ex·tor·tion·ate (ĭk-stôr′shə-nĭt) *adj.* **1.** Exorbitant; excessive. **2.** Characterized by extortion. **—ex·tor·tion·ate·ly** *adv.*

ex·tra (ĕk′strə) *adj. Abbr.* **ex., ext. 1.** More or beyond what is usual, normal, expected, or necessary; additional: *extra pay.* **2.** Better than ordinary; superior: *extra fineness.* **3.** Liable to an additional charge: *Salad is extra.*
~*n.* **1.** Something more than what is usual or necessary: *I put out a second blanket as an extra.* **2.** Something, such as an accessory on a car, for which an additional charge is made. **3.** A special edition of a newspaper. **4.** An additional or alternate worker. **5.** An actor hired to play a minor part, as in a crowd scene. **6.** Something of exceptional quality.
~*adv.* Exceptionally; unusually: *extra dry.* [Probably short for EXTRAORDINARY, by analogy with similar French and German shortenings.]

extra– *prefix.* Indicates outside a boundary or scope; for example, **extragalactic. Note:** Many compounds other than those entered here may be formed with *extra-*. In forming compounds, *extra-* is often joined with the following element without a space or hyphen: *extracurricular.* However, if the second element begins with a capital letter or with the letter *a*, it is separated with a hyphen: *extra-Biblical, extra-alimentary.* [Middle English, from Latin *extrā*, outside, above, beyond, without, short for *extera*, ablative feminine of *exterus*, outward.]

ex·tra-base hit (ĕk′strə-bās′) *n. Baseball.* A double, a triple, or a home run.

ex·tra·ca·non·i·cal (ĕk′strə-kə-nŏn′ĭ-kəl) *adj.* Not included in any ecclesiastical canon of Scripture; noncanonical.

ex·tra·cel·lu·lar (ĕk′strə-sĕl′yə-lər) *adj.* Located or occurring outside a cell. **—ex·tra·cel·lu·lar·ly** *adv.*

ex·tract (ĭk-străkt′) *tr.v.* **-tracted, -tracting, -tracts. 1.** To draw out or forth forcibly; pull out: *extract a tooth.* **2.** To obtain despite resistance, as by contrivance or extortion: *extract a promise.* **3.** To obtain from a substance by chemical or mechanical action, as by pressure, distillation, or evaporation: *extract juice from an orange.* **4. a.** To remove (a literary passage, for example) for separate consideration or publication. **b.** To remove and separate. **5.** *Mathematics.* To determine or calculate (the root of a number). **6.** To derive.
~*n.* (ĕk′străkt′). **1.** Something drawn or pulled out. **2.** A passage from a literary work; an excerpt. **3.** A concentrated preparation of the essential constituents of a food, flavoring, or other substance: *vanilla extract.* [Middle English *extracten*, from Latin *extrahere* (past participle *extractus*), to draw out : *ex-*, out + *trahere*, to draw.] **—ex·tract·a·ble, ex·tract·i·ble** *adj.*

ex·trac·tion (ĭk-străk′shən) *n.* **1.** The act of extracting or the condition of being extracted. **2.** Something obtained by extracting; an extract. **3.** Origin; descent; lineage: *of Asian extraction; of noble extraction.*

ex·trac·tive (ĭk-străk′tĭv) *adj.* **1.** Used in or obtained by extraction. **2.** Capable of being extracted.
~*n.* **1.** Something that may be extracted. **2.** The insoluble portion of an extract.

ex·trac·tor (ĭk-străk′tər) *n.* One that extracts, especially a device such as a forceps used for extracting teeth or for delivering a baby.

ex·tra·cur·ric·u·lar (ĕk′strə-kə-rĭk′yə-lər) *adj.* **1.** Carried on outside the curriculum or regular course of study in school or college life. **2.** Outside the usual duties of a job or profession.

ex·tra·dit·a·ble (ĕk′strə-dī′tə-bəl) *adj.* Subject to or making one liable to extradition: *an extraditable crime.*

ex·tra·dite (ĕk′strə-dīt′) *tr.v.* **-dited, -diting, -dites. 1.** To surrender (an alleged criminal) to another authority, such as the government of a foreign country, for trial. **2.** To obtain (an alleged criminal held by another authority) for trial. **—See** Synonyms at **banish.** [Back-formation from EXTRADITION.]

ex·tra·di·tion (ĕk′strə-dĭsh′ən) *n.* The legal surrender of an alleged criminal to the jurisdiction of another state, country, or government

for trial. [French : Latin *ex-*, out + *trāditiō* (stem *trāditiōn-*), a surrendering (see **tradition**).]

ex·tra·dos (ĕk′strə-dŏs′, -dō′, ĕk-strā′dŏs′) *n., pl.* **extrados** (-dōz′, -dŏs′) or **-doses.** *Architecture.* The upper or exterior curve of an arch. [French : Latin *extrā*, outside (see **extra-**) + French *dos*, back, from Latin *dorsum.*]

ex·tra·ga·lac·tic (ĕk′strə-gə-lăk′tĭk) *adj.* Located or originating beyond the galaxy.

ex·tra·ju·di·cial (ĕk′strə-jōō-dĭsh′əl) *adj.* **1.** Outside the authority of a court. **2.** Outside usual judicial proceedings. **—ex·tra·ju·di·cial·ly** *adv.*

ex·tra·mar·i·tal (ĕk′strə-măr′ə-təl) *adj.* Of or pertaining to a spouse's relationships, usually sexual, outside marriage; adulterous.

ex·tra·mun·dane (ĕk′strə-mŭn-dān′, -mŭn′dān′) *adj.* Occurring or existing outside the physical world or universe.

ex·tra·mu·ral (ĕk′strə-myŏŏr′əl) *adj.* **1.** Occurring or situated outside the walls or boundaries, as of a fortress or city: *extramural skirmishes.* **2.** Connected with a university or college but taking place outside. Said especially of nonresident students or their studies.

ex·tra·ne·ous (ĭk-strā′nē-əs) *adj.* **1.** Coming from outside; foreign: *extraneous interference.* **2.** Present but not essential or vital; accidental. **3.** Irrelevant. **—See** Synonyms at **extrinsic.** [Latin *extrāneus*, strange, from *extrā*, outward.] **—ex·tra·ne·ous·ly** *adv.* **—ex·tra·ne·ous·ness** *n.*

ex·tra·nu·cle·ar (ĕk′strə-nōō′klē-ər, -nyōō′klē-ər) *adj. Biology.* Located or occurring outside the nucleus.

ex·traor·di·nar·y (ĭk-strôr′də-nĕr′ē, ĕk′strə-ôr′-) *adj.* **1.** Beyond what is ordinary, usual, or commonplace: *extraordinary authority.* **2.** Exceeding the ordinary degree, amount, or extent; exceptional; remarkable: *an extraordinary feat.* **3.** Used, held, or appointed for a special service or occasion: *an extraordinary general meeting; an ambassador extraordinary.* **—ex·traor·di·nar·i·ly** (ĭk-strôr′də-nâr′ə-lē, ĕk′strə-ôr′də-) *adv.*

extraordinary ray *n.* The plane-polarized ray of light that is produced by a doubly refracting crystal and does not obey the laws of refraction. Compare **ordinary ray.**

ex·trap·o·late (ĭk-străp′ə-lāt′) *v.* **-lated, -lating, -lates.** *—tr.* **1.** *Mathematics.* To estimate (a value or values of a function) for values of the argument not used in the process of estimation; broadly, to infer (a value or values) from known values. **2.** To infer or estimate (unknown information) from known information. *—intr.* To engage in the process of extrapolating. [EXTRA- + (INTER)POLATE.] **—ex·trap·o·la·tion** *n.* **—ex·trap·o·la·tive** (ĭk-străp′ə-lā′tĭv, -lə-tĭv) *adj.*

ex·tra·sen·so·ry (ĕk′strə-sĕn′sə-rē) *adj.* **1.** Outside the normal range or bounds of the senses. **2.** Perceptible by supernatural means. **3.** Supernatural.

extrasensory perception *n. Abbr.* **ESP** Powers of perception of occurrences or objects that are not perceptible by the ordinary senses.

ex·tra·sys·to·le (ĕk′strə-sĭs′tə-lē) *n. Medicine.* A generally premature heartbeat caused by a heart impulse generated outside the sinoatrial node.

ex·tra·ter·res·tri·al (ĕk′strə-tə-rĕs′trē-əl) *adj.* Originating, located, or occurring outside the earth or its atmosphere.

ex·tra·ter·ri·to·ri·al (ĕk′strə-tĕr′ə-tôr′ē-əl, -tōr′ē-əl) *adj.* **1.** Located outside territorial boundaries. **2.** Of or pertaining to persons exempt from the legal jurisdiction of the country in which they reside. **—ex·tra·ter·ri·to·ri·al·ly** *adv.*

ex·tra·ter·ri·to·ri·al·i·ty (ĕk′strə-tĕr′ə-tôr′ē-ăl′ə-tē, -tôr′ē-ăl′ə-tē) *n.* **1.** Exemption from local legal jurisdiction, such as is granted to foreign diplomats. **2.** The jurisdiction of a country over its nationals abroad.

ex·tra·u·ter·ine (ĕk′strə-yōō′tər-ĭn, -tə-rīn′) *adj.* Located or occurring outside the uterus: *extrauterine pregnancy.*

ex·trav·a·gance (ĭk-străv′ə-gəns) *n.* Also **ex·trav·a·gan·cy** (-gən-sē) *pl.* **-cies. 1.** The quality of being extravagant; immoderation, especially in expenditure. **2.** An immoderate expense or display. **3.** Something costly and self-indulgent. **4.** An instance of excess, as in behavior.

ex·trav·a·gant (ĭk-străv′ə-gənt) *adj.* **1.** Given to lavish or imprudent expenditure; prodigal. **2.** Exceeding reasonable bounds; excessive: *extravagant demands.* **3.** Extremely abundant; profuse: *extravagant vegetation.* **4.** Unreasonably high; exorbitant: *That boutique charges extravagant prices.* **—See** Synonyms at **excessive.** [Middle English *extravagaunt*, from Old French *extravagant*, from Medieval Latin *extrāvagāns* (stem *extrāvagant-*), present participle of *extrāvagārī*, to wander beyond : Latin *extrā*, beyond + *vagārī*, to wander, akin to *vagus*, VAGUE.] **—ex·trav·a·gant·ly** *adv.* **—ex·trav·a·gant·ness** *n.*

ex·trav·a·gan·za (ĭk-străv′ə-găn′zə) *n.* **1.** A light orchestral composition marked by freedom and diversity of form, often with burlesque elements. **2.** An elaborate, spectacular entertainment. **3.** An instance of extravagant behavior or activity. [Italian *(e)stravaganza*, from *(e)stravagant*, extravagant, from Medieval Latin *extrāvagāns*, EXTRAVAGANT.]

ex·trav·a·sate (ĭk-străv′ə-sāt′) *v.* **-sated, -sating, -sates.** *—tr. Pathology.* To force the flow of (blood or lymph) out into surrounding tissue. *—intr. Pathology.* To exude into the surrounding tissues. Used of blood or lymph. [EXTRA- + VAS + -ATE.] **—ex·trav·a·sa·tion** *n.*

ex·tra·vas·cu·lar (ĕk′strə-văs′kyə-lər) *adj.* Located or occurring outside a blood vessel or the vascular system.

ex·tra·ve·hic·u·lar activity (ĕk'strə-vē-hĭk'yə-lər) *n.* *Abbr.* **EVA** Activity or maneuvers performed by an astronaut outside a spacecraft in space.

extraversion. Variant of **extroversion.**

extravert. Variant of **extrovert.**

Ex·tre·ma·du·ra or **Es·tre·ma·du·ra** (ĕs'trə-mə-dōōr'ə). Region of west-central Spain comprising Badajoz and Cáceres provinces. Long a generally poor farming area, it is being developed with irrigation, and is also noted for its cork-oak forests and pigs. —**Ex·tre·ma·du·ran** *n. & adj.*

ex·treme (ĭk-strēm') *adj.* **1.** Outermost or farthest; most remote in any direction: *the extreme edge of the field.* **2.** Final; last. **3.** Being in or attaining the greatest or highest degree; very intense: *extreme pleasure; extreme degradation.* **4.** Extending far beyond the norm; radical: *an extreme conservative.* **5.** Of the greatest severity; drastic: *extreme measures.* —See Synonyms at **excessive.** ~*n.* **1.** The greatest or utmost degree or point: *eager in the extreme.* **2.** Either of the two ends of a state or condition considered as a measurable or approximately measurable continuum: *the extremes of boiling and freezing; the extremes of wealth and poverty.* **3.** An extreme condition. **4.** A drastic or immoderate expedient: *driven to extremes.* **5.** *Mathematics.* The first or last term of a ratio or series. **6.** *Logic.* The major or minor term of a syllogism. [Middle English, from Old French, from Latin *extrēmus.*] —**ex·treme·ly** *adv.* —**ex·treme·ness** *n.*

extremely high frequency *n.* *Abbr.* **EHF** A radio-frequency band with a range of 30,000 to 300,000 megahertz.

extreme unction *n. Roman Catholic Church.* The sacrament in which a priest anoints and prays for one in danger of death.

ex·trem·ist (ĭk-strē'mĭst) *n.* A person who advocates or resorts to extreme measures, especially in politics; a radical. —See Synonyms at **fanatic.** ~*adj.* Belonging or pertaining to extremists. —**ex·trem·ism** *n.*

ex·trem·i·ty (ĭk-strĕm'ə-tē) *n., pl.* **-ties. 1.** The outermost or farthest point or portion; an end; an edge. **2.** The greatest or utmost degree: *the extremity of despair.* **3.** Grave danger, necessity, or distress. **4.** The moment at which the end, as of life, is imminent. **5.** A bodily limb or appendage. **6.** A hand or foot.

ex·tri·cate (ĕk'strĭ-kāt') *tr.v.* **-cated, -cating, -cates. 1.** To release from an entanglement or difficulty; disengage. **2.** To cause to be liberated or emitted: *extricate gas from a solution.* [Latin *extrīcāre* : *ex-*, out + *trīcae†,* perplexities.] —**ex·tri·ca·ble** *adj.* —**ex·tri·ca·tion** *n.*

ex·trin·sic (ĭk-strĭn'sĭk, -zĭk) *adj.* **1.** Not forming an essential part of a thing; extraneous; inessential. **2.** Not inherent; accessory; accidental. **3.** Originating from the outside; external. [Late Latin *extrinsecus,* outer, from Latin, outwardly : *exterus,* EXTERIOR + *secus,* alongside.] —**ex·trin·si·cal·ly** *adv.*
   Synonyms: alien, extraneous, foreign.

ex·trorse (ĕk-strôrs') *adj. Botany.* Facing outward; turned away from the axis. Said especially of anthers. [Late Latin *extrōrsus,* outward : *extrā,* outside + *introrsus,* INTRORSE.]

ex·tro·ver·sion, ex·tra·ver·sion (ĕk'strə-vûr'zhən, -shən) *n.* **1. a.** Interest in and aptitude for dealing with the external world and other people as opposed to or to the neglect of oneself or one's inner feelings. **b.** A disposition toward extroversion. Compare **introversion. 2.** A turning inside out, as of an organ or part. [From *extro-,* variant of EXTRA- + Latin *versus,* past participle of *vertere,* to turn.] —**ex·tro·ver·sive** (ĕk'strə-vûr'sĭv, -zĭv) *adj.* —**ex·tro·ver·sive·ly** *adv.*

ex·tro·vert, ex·tra·vert (ĕk'strə-vûrt') *n.* **1.** A person whose behavior is characterized by extroversion. **2.** An outgoing, gregarious, lively person. Compare **introvert.** [From *extro-,* variant of EXTRA- + Latin *vertere,* to turn.] —**ex·tro·vert·ed** (ĕk'strə-vûr'tĭd) *adj.*

ex·trude (ĭk-strōōd') *v.* **-truded, -truding, -trudes.** —*tr.* **1.** To push or thrust out. **2.** To shape (metal or plastic, for example) by forcing through a die. —*intr.* To protrude or project. [Latin *extrūdere,* to thrust out : *ex-,* out + *trūdere,* to thrust.]

ex·tru·sion (ĭk-strōō'zhən) *n.* **1.** The act or process of extruding. **2.** Material that has been extruded. **3.** *Geology.* **a.** The movement of magma through volcanic craters and fissures in the earth's crust, forming igneous rocks. **b.** The igneous rocks so formed. [Medieval Latin *extrūsiō* (stem *extrūsiōn-*), from Latin *extrūsus,* past participle of *extrūdere,* to EXTRUDE.]

ex·tru·sive (ĭk-strōō'sĭv, -zĭv) *adj.* **1.** Tending to extrude. **2.** *Geology.* Derived from magma that has cooled and solidified on the earth's surface. Said of rock.

ex·u·ber·ant (ĭg-zōō'bər-ənt) *adj.* **1.** Full of unrestrained high spirits; abandonedly joyous. **2.** Lavish; effusive; overflowing. **3.** Growing or producing abundantly; luxuriant. [Middle English, from Old French, from Latin *exūberāns* (stem *exūberant-*), present participle of *exūberāre,* to EXUBERATE.] —**ex·u·ber·ance** (ĭg-zōō'bər-əns) *n.* —**ex·u·ber·ant·ly** *adv.*

ex·u·ber·ate (ĭg-zōō'bə-rāt') *intr.v.* **-ated, -ating, -ates. 1.** To be exuberant. **2.** *Archaic.* To abound or overflow. [Latin *exūberāre* : *ex-,* completely + *ūberāre,* to be fruitful, from *ūber,* fertile.]

ex·u·date (ĕks'yōō-dāt') *n.* An exuded substance; an exudation. [From EXUDE.]

ex·u·da·tion (ĕks'yōō-dā'shən) *n.* **1.** The act or an instance of exuding. **2.** Something that is exuded; exudate: *an exudation of sweat.* —**ex·u·da·tive** (ĕks'yōō-dā'tĭv) *adj.*

ex·ude (ĭg-zōōd', ĭk-sōōd') *v.* **-uded, -uding, -udes.** —*intr.* To ooze forth; come gradually through an opening: *Sap exudes from the pine.* —*tr.* **1.** To discharge or emit gradually. **2.** To give off copiously; make (a quality) felt: *"he exuded about as much menace as boiled haddock"* (S.J. Perelman). [Latin *ex(s)ūdāre,* to sweat out, exude : *ex-,* out + *sūdāre,* to sweat, ooze.]

ex·ult (ĭg-zŭlt') *intr.v.* **-ulted, -ulting, -ults.** To rejoice greatly; be jubilant or triumphant: *exulted in their victory.* [Latin *ex(s)ultāre,* frequentative of *exsilīre,* to leap up, rejoice : *ex-,* up + *salīre,* to leap.] —**ex·ul·ta·tion** (ĕk'səl-tā'shən, ĕg'zəl-), **ex·ul·tan·cy** (ĭg-zŭl'tən-sē) *n.* —**ex·ult·ing·ly** *adv.*

ex·ul·tant (ĭg-zŭl'tənt) *adj.* Joyful; jubilant; triumphant. —**ex·ul·tant·ly** *adv.*

ex·ur·ban·ite (ĕk-sûr'bə-nīt', ĕg-zûr'-) *n.* A person living in a community, usually a well-to-do town, beyond the suburbs of a major city. [EX- + (SUB)URBANITE.]

ex·ur·bi·a (ĕk-sûr'bē-ə, ĕg-zûr'-) *n.* A semirural residential area situated beyond the suburbs of a city and inhabited principally by well-to-do people. [EX- + (SUB)URBIA.]

ex·u·vi·ae (ĭg-zōō'vē-ē') *pl.n.* The cast-off skins or coverings of various animals, especially of the larvae and nymphs of insects. [Latin, stripped-off clothing, spoils, from *exuere,* to take off.] —**ex·u·vi·al** *adj.*

ex·u·vi·ate (ĭg-zōō'vē-āt') *v.* **-ated, -ating, -ates.** —*tr.* To shed (a covering, such as a skin). —*intr.* To shed or cast off exuviae. [From EXUVIAE.] —**ex·u·vi·a·tion** *n.*

-ey¹. Variant of **-y** (existence or possession).

-ey². Variant of **-y** (smallness).

ey·as (ī'əs) *n.* A nestling hawk or falcon, especially one to be trained for falconry. [Middle English, variant (by incorrect division of *an ias* for *a nias*) of *niyas,* from Old French *niais,* bird taken from the nest, from Vulgar Latin *nidax* (unattested), from Latin *nīdus,* nest.]

eye (ī) *n.* **1.** An organ of vision or of light sensitivity. **2. a.** The vertebrate organ of vision; either of a pair of hollow structures located in fixed bony sockets of the skull, functioning together or independently, each having a lens capable of focusing incident light

---

eye

THE MIRACLE OF SIGHT

How the eyes and brain work together

Much of the knowledge we absorb is gathered by the eyes—two small spheres each 25 millimeters (1 inch) across. In common with those animals that rely on their eyes for hunting and collecting food, man has binocular vision. Both eyes can focus on one target, a help in judging distance.

In contrast, animals such as cows and rabbits have eyes that function independently on each side of the head, so that they can keep an all-around watch for danger.

The human eye depends on the brain. For example, the eye does not take in a scene or an object at one glance but sees it as a rapid series of images.

It is the brain that, in effect, blends the successive frames of a film into a continuous vision. And it is the brain that stores, organizes, and assesses visual impressions and compares them with past experiences.

Most people receive positive evidence of the brain's role in sight only when they dream. For they "see" pictures with their eyes closed. Those people who have been born blind dream in terms of other sensory stimuli: touch, sound, and even smell.

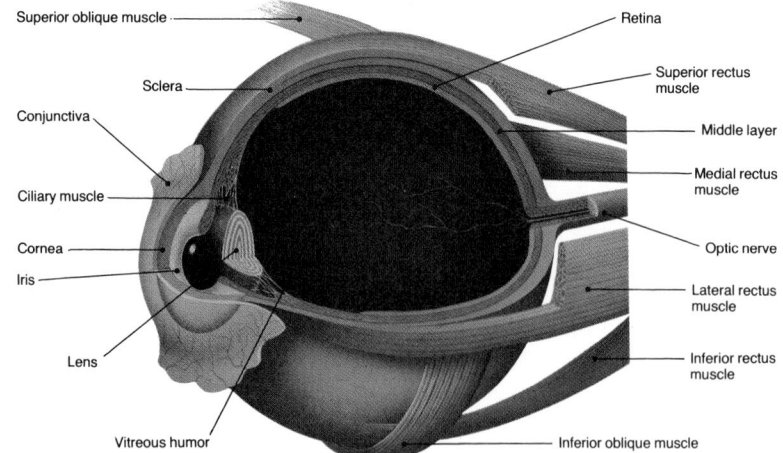

Superior oblique muscle — Retina — Sclera — Superior rectus muscle — Conjunctiva — Middle layer — Ciliary muscle — Medial rectus muscle — Cornea — Iris — Optic nerve — Lens — Lateral rectus muscle — Inferior rectus muscle — Vitreous humor — Inferior oblique muscle

STRUCTURE OF THE EYE *The eye functions much as a camera, with a lens at the front and a light-sensitive screen, the retina, at the rear. The intervening space contains a transparent jelly, the vitreous humor, which together with the outer layer, or sclera, helps the eyeball to hold its shape.*

Light enters through the cornea, a transparent domed window at the front of the eyeball. The size of the pupil, an aperture in the center of the iris, controls the amount of light that is then focused by the lens onto the retina as an upside-down image.

Contractions of the ciliary muscle control the shape and power of the lens. The retina, which is nourished by the blood vessels of the middle layer, contains more than 130 million light-receptor cells. These convert light into nerve impulses that are transmitted right side up by the optic nerve to the brain, where they are interpreted.

The conjunctiva, a transparent membrane, lines the eyelids and partly covers the eyeball. Muscles attached to the eye control its movements—sideways, up and down, and rotating.

on an internal photosensitive retina from which nerve impulses are sent to the brain. **b.** The external, visible portion of this organ together with its associated structures, such as the eyelids, eyelashes, and eyebrows. **c.** The pigmented iris of this organ. **3.** The faculty of seeing; vision. **4.** The ability to discriminate or appreciate; discernment: *a good eye for fashion.* **5. a.** A look; gaze. **b.** A way of regarding something; a point of view: *You're wrong, at least in my eyes.* **6.** Something suggestive of an eye in appearance, such as an opening in a needle, a marking on a peacock feather, or a hole in cheese. **7.** A loop, such as one for attaching a hook. **8.** *Botany.* **a.** A bud on a twig or tuber: *the eye of a potato.* **b.** The often differently colored center of the corolla of some flowers. **9.** *Meteorology.* The circular area of relative calm at the center of a cyclone. **10.** Something construed as a center or focal point: *Corruption is the eye of the problem.* **11.** Keen observation; attention: *Keep an eye on the baby while I'm out.* **12.** A photosensitive device, such as a photoelectric cell. **13.** *Informal.* A detective. **—all eyes.** Alert; observant. **—an eye for an eye.** Punishment requiring that the offender suffer what he has caused another to suffer. [A Biblical phrase: ". . . life shall go for life, eye for eye, tooth for tooth, hand for hand, foot for foot" (Deuteronomy 19:21; also Exodus 21:2).] **—catch someone's eye.** *Informal.* To attract someone's attention. **—give someone the eye.** *Informal.* To look at admiringly or invitingly. **—have an eye to. 1.** To be on the lookout for. **2.** To have as an aim. **—have eyes only for.** To be attentive solely to; be interested exclusively in: *She has eyes only for you.* **—in one's mind's eye.** Pictured, remembered, or clearly imagined in the mind. **—in the eye of the wind.** *Nautical.* In the direction opposite to that of the wind; close to the wind. **—keep one's eyes peeled (or skinned).** To be constantly vigilant and observant. **—make eyes at.** To glance or gaze at flirtatiously. **—my eye.** *Slang.* In no way; not at all. **—see eye to eye.** To be in complete agreement. **—turn a blind eye to.** To ignore deliberately (a prohibited action that one witnesses, for example). **—up to one's eyes.** Fully occupied; overwhelmed, as with work. **—with an eye to.** With a view to: *saving money with an eye to future need.*
~*tr.v.* **eyed, eyeing** or **eying, eyes. 1.** To concentrate the eyes on; stare at. **2.** To watch attentively: *The hungry child eyed my sandwich.* [Middle English *eie, eighe,* Old English *ēage.*]
eye·ball (ī′bôl′) *n.* **1.** The ball-shaped portion of the eye enclosed by the socket and eyelids. **2.** The eye. **—eyeball to eyeball.** *Informal.* Face to face.
~*tr.v.* **eyeballed, -balling, -balls.** *Informal.* **1.** To stare steadily at, especially in a menacing way. **2.** To confront (a rival, for example) in an uncompromising way.
eye bank *n.* A place at which corneas taken from human bodies immediately after death are stored and preserved for subsequent transplantation to individuals with corneal defects.
eye bath *n.* An eyecup.
eye·bolt (ī′bōlt′) *n.* A bolt having a looped head designed to receive a hook or rope.
eye·bright (ī′brīt′) *n.* Any of several plants of the genus *Euphrasia;* especially, *E. officinalis,* native to the Old World, having small white and purplish flowers and formerly used in the preparation of eye lotions.
eye·brow (ī′brou′) *n.* **1.** The bony ridge extending over the eye. **2.** The arch of short hairs covering this ridge.
eyebrow pencil *n.* A cosmetic in pencil form used for extending, redrawing, or darkening the eyebrows.
eye·catch·ing (ī′kăch′ĭng) *adj.* Attracting the eye; striking.
eye contact *n.* Direct visual contact with the eyes of another person.
eye·cup (ī′kŭp′) *n.* A small cup with a rim contoured to fit the outside of the eye, used for applying a liquid medicine or wash to the eye.
eyed (īd) *adj.* **1.** Having an eye or eyes, as a sail might. **2.** Having eyes of a specified number or kind. Used in combination: *one-eyed; blue-eyed.* **3.** Having markings that resemble eyes.
eye dialect *n.* The use of misspellings, such as *wimmin* for *women,* to represent dialectal or nonstandard speech.
eye·drop·per (ī′drŏp′ər) *n.* A dropper for applying liquid eye medicines.
eye·ful (ī′fool′) *n.* **1.** An amount of something that covers the eye: *an eyeful of salt water.* **2.** *Informal.* All that the eye can encompass at one time; a good look. **3.** *Informal.* A sight to please the eyes; especially, a good-looking person.
eye·glass (ī′glăs′, ī′gläs′) *n.* **1. a. eyeglasses.** A pair of lenses used to correct faulty vision; glasses. **b.** A monocle. **2.** An eyepiece. **3.** An eyecup.
eye·hole (ī′hōl′) *n.* **1.** The socket of the eye. **2.** A peephole. **3.** An eye for the insertion of a rope, pin, hook, or the like.

eye·hook (ī′hook′) *n.* A hook attached to a ring at the end of a rope or chain.
eye·lash (ī′lăsh′) *n.* **1.** Any of a row of short hairs fringing the edge of the eyelid. **2.** A row of these hairs.
eye·let (ī′lĭt′) *n.* **1. a.** A small hole or perforation, usually rimmed with metal, cord, fabric, or leather, used for fastening with a cord or hook. **b.** A metal ring designed to reinforce such a hole; a grommet. **2. a.** A small hole edged with fine embroidered stitches as part of a design. **b.** A piece of embroidery so worked. Also called "eyelet embroidery." **c.** Cloth that is ornamented with machine-produced eyelet embroidery. **d.** A small hole created in knitted or crocheted material and lace by combining and separating different stitches. **3.** An aperture or peephole. **4.** A small eye.
~*tr.v.* **eyeletted, -letting, -lets.** To make eyelets in. [Middle English *oilet,* from Old French *oillet,* diminutive of *oil,* eye, from Latin *oculus,* eye.]
eye·let·eer (ī′lə-tîr′) *n.* A pointed instrument for piercing eyelets in cloth; a bodkin; a stiletto.
eye·lid (ī′lĭd′) *n.* Either of two folds of skin and muscle that can be closed over the exposed portion of the eyeball.
eye·lin·er (ī′lī′nər) *n.* A cosmetic preparation that is applied close to the eyelashes to accentuate the eyes.
eye·o·pen·er (ī′ō′pə-nər) *n.* **1.** A revelation, usually a startling or shocking one. **2.** A drink of liquor taken especially when one wakes up.
eye·piece (ī′pēs′) *n.* The lens or lens group closest to the eye in a microscope, telescope, or other optical instrument; an ocular.
eye rhyme *n.* A false rhyme consisting of words, as *lint* and *pint,* with similar spellings but different sounds.
eye·shade (ī′shād′) *n.* A visor made of tinted plastic or a similar opaque material, used to protect the eyes from glare.
eye shadow *n.* A cosmetic available in various colors or tints and applied to the eyelids to enhance the eyes.
eye·shot (ī′shŏt′) *n.* The range of vision; view; sight.
eye·sight (ī′sīt′) *n.* **1.** The faculty of sight; vision. **2.** The range of vision; view.
eyes·on·ly (īz′ōn′lē) *adj.* Of, pertaining to, or being top-secret: *an eyes-only memorandum.*
eye·sore (ī′sôr′, ī′sōr′) *n.* Something ugly or offensive to look at.
eye splice *n.* *Nautical.* A loop formed at the end of a rope by turning it back and splicing in the end strands.
eye·spot (ī′spŏt′) *n.* **1.** A light-sensitive, pigmented area in certain algae, protozoans, and other primitive animals. **2.** A rounded, eye-like marking, as on the tail of a peacock.
eye·stalk (ī′stôk′) *n.* A movable, stalklike structure bearing at its tip one of the eyes of a crab, shrimp, or similar crustacean.
eye·strain (ī′strān′) *n.* Aching and fatigue of the eyes, often accompanied by headache, resulting from prolonged close work, uncorrected errors of vision, or an imbalance of the eye muscles.
eye·tooth (ī′tooth′) *n., pl.* **eyeteeth** (ī′tēth′). A canine *(see)* of the upper jaw. **—give one's eyeteeth for.** To be willing to give up a great deal to acquire something much desired. [So called because it lies immediately under the eye.]
eye·wash (ī′wŏsh′, ī′wôsh′) *n.* **1.** A medicated solution applied as a wash for the eyes. **2.** Misleading, evasive, or meaningless speech or writing.
eye·wink (ī′wĭngk′) *n.* **1.** A wink of the eye. **2.** An instant. **3.** *Obsolete.* A glance.
eye·wit·ness (ī′wĭt′nəs) *n.* A person who has seen a particular event or act and can describe it, as in court.
eyot (āt, ā′ŏt) *n.* Also **ait** (āt). *British.* A small island, especially in a river. [Middle English *eigt, eyt, eit,* Old English *iggath, ȳgett,* from *īeg, ȳg,* ISLAND + *-ett, -ath,* diminutive suffix.]
Eyre, Lake (âr). Largest lake in Australia, lying in central South Australia. It is salty and shallow and in the hot, arid summers of the Australian interior can dry up. At 16 meters (52 feet) below sea level, it is Australia's lowest point.
eyrie. Variant of **aerie.**
ey·rir (ā′rîr′) *n., pl.* **aurar** (ou′rär′, œ′rär′). A coin equal to 1/100 of the krona of Iceland. See feature at **currency.** [Icelandic, from Old Norse, an ounce, probably from Latin *aureus,* gold coin, from *aurum,* gold.]
Ezek. Ezekiel (Old Testament).
E·ze·ki·el¹ (ĭ-zē′kē-əl). A major Hebrew prophet of the 6th century B.C., author of the Old Testament Book of Ezekiel. [Greek *Iezekiēl,* from Hebrew *Y'hezkēl,* "may God strengthen."]
Ezekiel² *n. Abbr.* **Ezek.** The Old Testament book bearing the name of the prophet Ezekiel.
Ez·ra¹ (ĕz′rə). A Hebrew high priest of the 5th century B.C. [Hebrew, "help."]
Ezra² *n.* A book of the Old Testament bearing the name of the priest Ezra. Also called "Esdras" in the Douay Bible.

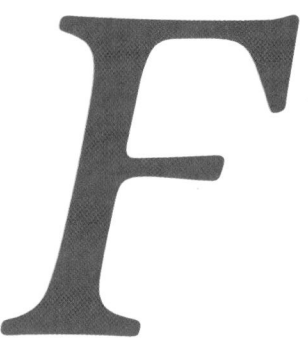

Fabergé egg *This golden egg set with enamel and diamonds was made by the Russian jeweler and goldsmith in 1897 in honor of the coronation of the czar, Nicholas II. Standing only 12.5 centimeters (5 inches) high, it contains a minute replica of the imperial coach used at the coronation.*

f, F (ĕf) *n., pl.* **f's** or **F's. 1.** The sixth letter of the modern English alphabet. **2.** Any of the speech sounds represented by this letter. **3. F. a.** The fourth tone in the scale of C major. **b.** The key or a scale in which F is the tonic. **c.** A written or printed note representing F. **d.** A string, key, or pipe tuned to the pitch of F. **4.** Something shaped like the letter F. **5.** The sixth in a series.

f, F, f., F. *Note:* As an abbreviation or symbol, *f* may be a small or a capital letter, with or without a period. Established forms or those generally preferred precede the definition. When no form is given, all four forms are in general use in that sense. **1.** F Fahrenheit. **2.** F farad. **3.** f. farthing. **4.** F. February. **5.** F, F. fellow (of a university or other institution). **6.** female. **7.** f., F. *Grammar.* feminine. **8.** f *Physics.* femto-. **9.** f., F. *Metallurgy.* fine. **10.** F The symbol for the element fluorine. **11.** f., F. folio. **12.** f. following. **13.** F *Physics.* force. **14.** f, F *Music.* forte. **15.** f. *Sports.* foul. **16.** f. franc. **17.** F. French. **18.** F. Friday. **19.** F A failing grade in academic work. **20.** *Genetics.* A filial generation, F_1 being the first generation resulting from a given cross, F_2 the second generation resulting from crossing within the F_1 generation, and so on.

fa (fä) *n. Music.* The fourth tone of the diatonic scale in solmization. [Middle English, from Medieval Latin, short for *famuli,* servants, word sung to this note in a hymn to St. John the Baptist (see **gamut**), plural of Latin *famulus,* servant. See **family.**]

FA 1. field artillery. **2.** fine art. **3.** football association.

F.A. 1. fine art. **2.** football association.

F.A.A. Federal Aviation Administration.

Fab·er·gé (făb′ər-zhā′), **Peter Carl** (1846–1920). Russian goldsmith who made ornate decorative objects for European royalty. He was famous for his jeweled eggs containing surprise gifts.

Fa·bi·an (fā′bē-ən) *adj.* **1.** Using or characterized by a cautious strategy of gradual social progress and avoidance of direct confrontation with the state. **2.** Of or relating to the Fabian Society. ~*n.* A member or supporter of the Fabian Society. [Latin *Fabiānus,* after Quintus *Fabius* Maximus (died 203 B.C.), known as *Cunctator* ("Delayer"), Roman general who defeated Hannibal by avoiding direct conflict.] —**Fa·bi·an·ism** *n.* —**Fa·bi·an·ist** *n. & adj.*

Fabian Society *n.* An organization founded in Great Britain in 1883 to promote the gradual spread of democratic socialism.

fa·ble (fā′bəl) *n.* **1.** A concise narrative making an edifying, moral, or cautionary point and often employing as characters animals that speak and act like human beings. **2. a.** A story or myth about legendary persons and exploits. **b.** Such stories and myths collectively. **c.** A literary genre consisting of such stories. **3.** A falsehood; a lie. ~*v.* **fabled, -bling, -bles.** —*tr.* To recount as if true. —*intr. Archaic.* To compose fables. [Middle English, from Old French, from Latin *fābula,* narration, account, story, from *fārī,* to speak.] —**fa·bler** *n.*

fa·bled (fā′bəld) *adj.* **1.** Made known or famous by fable; legendary. **2.** Existing only in fable; fictitious.

fab·li·au (făb′lē-ō′) *n., pl.* **-liaux** (-lē-ō′, -ōz′). A medieval verse tale that is characterized by comic and ribald treatment of themes drawn from life, such as Chaucer's "Miller's Tale." [French, from Old French (Picardy dialect) *fabliaux,* plural of *fablel,* diminutive of *fable,* FABLE.]

Fa·bre (fä′brə), **Jean Henri** (1823–1915). French entomologist and man of letters. He conducted important research on bees and wasps, grasshoppers and crickets, and beetles, describing the importance of instincts to insect behavior. He also wrote many popular books on science.

fab·ric (făb′rĭk) *n.* **1.** Any material structure consisting of connected parts; a framework. **2.** A structure consisting of human relations or of relations between ideas, expressions, emotions, or the like: *"the pattern of her mind, the whole fabric of her nature"* (James Thurber). **3.** A method or style of construction. **4. a.** Any cloth produced by joining fibers, as by knitting, weaving, or felting. **b.** The texture or quality of such cloth. **5.** The walls, roof, and floor of a building. [Middle English, from Old French *fabrique,* from Latin *fabrica,* workshop, a trade, from *faber,* workman, artisan.]

fab·ri·cate (făb′rĭ-kāt′) *tr.v.* **-cated, -cating, -cates. 1.** To prepare, make, or fashion. **2.** To construct by putting together finished parts; assemble. **3.** To invent (a story); devise (a deception). [Middle English *fabricaten,* from Latin *fabricārī* (past participle *fabricātus*), to fabricate, build, from *fabrica,* workshop. See **fabric.**] —**fab·ri·ca·tor** *n.*

fab·ri·ca·tion (făb′rĭ-kā′shən) *n.* **1. a.** Something, such as a deliberately false statement, that is made up or fabricated. **b.** The action of inventing a false statement or of forging a document. **2.** The process of fabricating; manufacture.

fab·u·list (făb′yə-lĭst) *n.* **1.** A composer of fables, especially of moral tales. **2.** An inventor or teller of falsehoods. [French *fabuliste,* from Latin *fābula,* FABLE.]

fab·u·lous (făb′yə-ləs) *adj.* **1.** Of the nature of a fable or myth; legendary. **2.** Told of or celebrated in fables or legends. **3.** Barely credible; astonishing: *fabulous riches.* **4.** *Informal.* Extremely pleasing or successful: *We had a fabulous time at the carnival.* [Middle English, from Latin *fābulōsus,* from *fābula,* FABLE.] —**fab·u·lous·ly** *adv.* —**fab·u·lous·ness** *n.*

fac. facsimile.

fa·çade, fa·cade (fə-säd′) *n.* **1.** *Architecture.* A face of a building; especially, a front face that is given distinguishing treatment. **2.** The face or front part of anything; especially, an artificial or false appearance or aspect. [French, from Italian *facciata,* from *faccia,* face, from Vulgar Latin *facia* (unattested), FACE.]

face (fās) *n.* **1.** The surface of the front of the head from the top of the forehead to the base of the chin and from ear to ear. Also used adjectivally: *face cream.* **2.** The arrangement or expression of the features of this part of the head; the countenance. **3.** An exaggerated facial expression; a grimace. **4. a.** The outward appearance, aspect, or look: *The face of the city has changed.* **b.** An assumed bearing; a front: *We must put a good face on things.* **5.** Value or standing in the eyes of others; dignity; prestige: *The country feared it would lose face.* **6.** *Informal.* Effrontery; impudence. **7.** The most significant or prominent surface of any object, especially: **a.** The surface presented to view; the front: *the face of a building.* **b.** The outer surface: *the face of the earth.* **c.** A steep side of a hill or mountain. **d.** The upper or marked side; the most meaningful surface: *the face of a clock.* **e.** The side of an instrument or device that is applied or makes contact: *the face of a golf club.* **f.** Either side of a coin; especially, a side bearing the representation of a head. **8.** *Geometry.* A planar surface bounding a solid. **9.** Any of the surfaces of a rock or crystal. **10.** *Military.* Any of the sides of a formation of men or of a fortified position. **11.** The appearance and geologic surface features of an area of land; topography. **12.** The exposed working surface of an ore, as coal, in a mine. **13.** A type-face *(see).* —**face to face. 1.** In each other's presence; in direct communication: *We finally spoke face to face.* **2.** Directly confronting. Used with *with: His illness brought him face to face with death.* —**fly in the face of.** To defy openly. —**in the face of. 1.** Despite the opposition of; notwithstanding. **2.** Considering the fact of; in view of. —**laugh in someone's face.** To be openly disrespectful or contemptuous toward someone. —**on the face of it.** From its appearance alone; apparently. —**put one's face on.** *Informal.* To put on make-up. —**set one's face against.** To oppose resolutely. —**show one's face.** To make an appearance. —**to someone's face.** In someone's physical presence; directly, boldly, and frankly: *She accused the offender to his face.* ~*v.* **faced, facing, faces.** —*tr.* **1.** To turn or be turned or situated in the direction of. **2.** To be opposite; have the front directly opposite to; front: *a window facing the south.* **3. a.** To realize; be cognizant of: *facing facts.* **b.** To confront or deal with boldly or bravely: *"What this generation must do is face its problems"* (John F. Kennedy). **4.** To be certain to encounter; have in store: *The unskilled youth faces a difficult life.* **5.** To cause (a soldier or formation of troops) to change direction sharply by giving a command. **6.** To turn (a playing card) so that the face is up. **7.** To furnish with a surface or cover of a different material: *bronze faced with gold foil.* **8.** To provide the edge or edges of (a cloth or garment) with finishing or trimming. **9.** To treat or dress the surface of (a material);

smooth. —*intr.* **1.** To be turned or placed with the front toward a specified direction. **2.** To turn the face in a specified direction. —**face down.** To overcome or prevail over by a stare or a resolute manner. —**face out.** To endure to the end. —**face up to. 1.** To recognize the existence or importance of. **2.** To confront bravely. [Middle English, from Old French, from Vulgar Latin *facia* (unattested), from Latin *faciēs*, form, shape, face, from *facere*, to make, form.] —**face·a·ble** *adj.*

face-ache (fās′āk′) *n. British.* Neuralgia of a cranial nerve; specifically, trigeminal neuralgia.

face card *n.* A playing card bearing a jack, queen, or king. Also called "court card."

face-cen·tered (fās′sĕn′tərd) *adj.* Designating a crystal or crystal lattice in which there is a lattice point at the center of each face of each unit cell. Compare **body-centered.**

face-cloth (fās′klôth′, -klŏth′) *n.* A washcloth.

faced (fāst) *adj.* **1.** Having a face or faces. **2.** Having a specified number or kind of faces. Used in combination: *two-faced; red-faced.*

face-hard·en (fās′här′dn) *tr.v.* **-ened, -ening, -ens.** To harden the surface of (a metal).

face·less (fās′lĭs) *adj.* **1.** Without a face. **2.** Anonymous; hard to identify: *faceless bureaucrats.*

face lifting *n.* Also **face-lift** (fās′lĭft′) **1.** A cosmetic plastic-surgery operation for tightening facial tissues and improving the appearance of facial skin. **2.** A restyling or modernizing of an outward appearance.

face off *intr.v.* To start play in hockey, lacrosse, and other games by releasing the puck or ball between two opposing players.

face-off (fās′ôf′, -ŏf′) *n.* **1.** A method of starting play in hockey, lacrosse, and other games in which an official drops the puck or ball between two opposing players who contend for its control. **2.** A confrontation.

face pack *n.* A cosmetic preparation used for cleansing and toning the complexion, usually consisting of a thick paste that is washed or peeled off when dry. Also called "face mask," "pack."

face-plate (fās′plāt′) *n.* **1.** A disk that is attached to the headstock of a lathe to hold flat or irregularly shaped work. **2.** A **planometer** *(see).*

fac·er (fā′sər) *n.* **1.** A person or thing that faces; especially, a device used in smoothing or dressing metal, stone, or other material. **2.** *Chiefly British.* An unexpected blow or defeat.

face-sav·ing (fās′sā′vĭng) *adj.* Preserving prestige or respect in the face of potential embarrassment or humiliation. —**face-sav·er** (fās′sā′vər) *n.*

fac·et (fās′ĭt) *n.* **1.** Any of the flat polished surfaces cut on a gemstone. **2.** A small planar or rounded smooth surface on a bone or tooth. **3.** Any of the lenslike divisions of a compound eye, as of an insect. **4.** An aspect or phase: *The four principal characters are facets of the author's personality.* —*tr.v.* **faceted** or **facetted, -eting** or **-etting, -ets.** To cut facets in (a gemstone). [French *facette*, diminutive of FACE.]

fa·ce·ti·ae (fə-sē′shē-ē′) *pl.n.* Witty or coarsely humorous writings and sayings; pleasantries. [Latin *facētiae*, plural of *facētia*, a jest, from *facētus*, FACETIOUS.]

fa·ce·tious (fə-sē′shəs) *adj.* Playfully and often unsuitably jocular; flippant: *a facetious remark.* [Old French *facetieux*, from *facetie*, a jest, from Latin *facētia*, from *facētus†*, elegant, fine, facetious.] —**fa·ce·tious·ly** *adv.* —**fa·ce·tious·ness** *n.*

face value *n.* **1.** The value printed or written on a bill, bond, coin, or the like. **2.** The apparent value or significance: *He accepted their professed loyalty at face value.*

facia. Variant of **fascia.**

fa·cial (fā′shəl) *adj.* Of or concerning the face. —*n.* A treatment for the face, usually consisting of a massage and the application of cosmetic creams. [Medieval Latin *faciālis.* See **face, -al.**] —**fa·cial·ly** *adv.*

facial nerve *n.* The seventh cranial nerve, which supplies motor fibers to the muscles of the face and carries sensory fibers from the tastebuds and salivary glands.

-facient *suffix.* Indicates a bringing about or causing to become; for example, **absorbefacient, abortifacient.** [Latin *faciēns* (stem *facient-*), present participle of *facere*, to do.]

fa·ci·es (fā′shē-ēz′) *n., pl.* **facies. 1.** The general aspect or outward appearance, as of a given growth of flora. **2.** *Medicine.* A patient's facial expression, especially when typical of a certain disorder or disease. **3.** *Geology.* The total characteristics of a rock, including appearance, composition, and fossil content, as used to distinguish rocks of the same age, according to the lateral differences. [New Latin, from Latin *faciēs*, shape, form, FACE.]

fac·ile (fās′əl) *adj.* **1.** Done or achieved with little effort or difficulty; easy. **2.** Working, acting, or speaking effortlessly; fluent: *a facile speaker.* **3.** Arrived at without due care, effort, or examination; superficial; glib. **4.** Easy and relaxed in manner. **5.** *Archaic.* Yielding; compliant. [French, from Latin *facilis*, from *facere*, to do.] —**fac·ile·ly** *adv.* —**fac·ile·ness** *n.*

fa·cil·i·tate (fə-sĭl′ə-tāt′) *tr.v.* **-tated, -tating, -tates.** To free from difficulties or obstacles; make easier; aid; assist. [French *faciliter*, from Italian *facilitare*, from *facile*, easy, from Latin *facilis*, FACILE.] —**fa·cil·i·ta·tion** (fə-sĭl′ə-tā′shən) *n.*

fa·cil·i·ty (fə-sĭl′ə-tē) *n., pl.* **-ties. 1.** Ease in moving, acting, or doing; aptitude. **2.** Ready skill derived from practice or familiarity: *"the workman's quick facility with his hands"* (Sherwood Anderson). **3.** *Often* **facilities.** The means or equipment to facilitate an action or process; provision: *the facilities of a library; sports facilities.* **4.** *Archaic.* An agreeable, pliable disposition. **5. facilities.** *Informal.* The available toilet arrangements. [French *facilité.* See **facile, -ity.**]

fac·ing (fā′sĭng) *n.* **1. a.** A piece of material sewn to the edge of a dress, coat, or other garment as lining or decoration. **b.** Fabric used for this. **c. facings.** Fabric of contrasting color used to trim the collar, cuffs, or similar parts of the jacket of a military uniform. **2.** An outer layer or coating of different material applied to a surface for protection or decoration: *a stone wall with wood facing.*

fac·sim·i·le (făk-sĭm′ə-lē) *n. Abbr.* **fac., facsim. 1.** An exact copy or reproduction, as of a document. **2. a.** A method of transmitting images by converting the information into an electronic signal for transmission by cable or radio. **b.** An image so transmitted. —*adj.* **1.** Of or used to produce facsimiles. **2.** Exactly reproduced; duplicate. —*tr.v.* **facsimiled, -leing** (-lē-ĭng), **-les.** To make a facsimile of. [Latin *fac simile*, make (it) similar : *fac*, imperative of *facere*, to make, do + *simile*, neuter of *similis*, SIMILAR.]

fact (făkt) *n.* **1.** Something known with certainty. **2.** Something asserted as certain. **3.** Something that has been objectively verified. **4.** Something having real, demonstrable existence. **5.** *Law.* **a.** An act considered with regard to its legality. Used chiefly in the phrases *before* or *after the fact.* **b.** The aspect of a case at law comprising events determined by evidence as distinguished from interpretation of law: *The jury made a finding of fact.* —**as a matter of fact.** Actually; interestingly enough. —**in (point of) fact.** In reality; in truth; actually. [Latin *factum*, a deed, from *factus*, past participle of *facere*, to do.]

fact-find·ing (făkt′fīn′dĭng) *n.* The discovery or determination of facts or accurate information. —*adj.* Engaged in or designed to ascertain facts: *a fact-finding committee.* —**fact-find·er** *n.*

fac·tion (făk′shən) *n.* **1.** A group of persons forming a cohesive, usually contentious minority within a larger group. **2.** Internal dissension; conflict within an organization or nation: *"And whereas our own beloved country . . . is now afflicted with faction and civil war"* (Lincoln). [Old French, from Latin *factiō* (stem *factiōn-*), an acting (together), a making, from *factus*, past participle of *facere*, to do, make.]

fac·tion·al (făk′shə-nəl) *adj.* Of, characterized by, or causing a contentious faction or factions; partisan. —**fac·tion·al·ism** *n.*

fac·tious (făk′shəs) *adj.* **1.** Produced or characterized by contentious faction. **2.** Creating or promoting faction; divisive: *"The . . . injustice with which a factious spirit has tainted our public administration"* (James Madison). —See Usage note at **insubordinate.** —**fac·tious·ly** *adv.* —**fac·tious·ness** *n.*

fac·ti·tious (făk-tĭsh′əs) *adj.* **1.** Produced artificially rather than by natural process; contrived: *speculators responsible for the factitious value of some stocks.* **2.** Lacking authenticity or genuineness; sham: *a factitious smile.* [Latin *factīcius*, made by art, from *facere*, to make, do.] —**fac·ti·tious·ly** *adv.* —**fac·ti·tious·ness** *n.*

fac·ti·tive (făk′tə-tĭv′) *adj. Grammar.* Of or constituting a transitive verb that in some constructions takes an objective complement to modify its direct object. For example, the verb *elect* is factitive in *They elected him chairman.* [New Latin *factitivus*, from Latin *factus*, done. See **fact.**] —**fac·ti·tive·ly** *adv.*

fact of life *n.* **1.** A fact or situation that must be faced in a realistic manner. **2. facts of life.** The facts about human reproduction and sexuality.

fac·tor (făk′tər) *n.* **1. a.** One who acts for someone else; especially, one who buys and sells on commission; an agent. **b.** *Scottish.* An estate manager; a steward. **c.** A person or company that accepts trade debts as security for short-term loans. **2.** An element that actively contributes to an accomplishment, result, or process: *Cloudy weather was a factor in our decision to stay home.* **3.** *Mathematics.* One of two or more quantities having a designated product: *2 and 3 are factors of 6.* **4.** A gene. No longer in technical usage. —*v.* **factored, -toring, -tors.** —*tr.* To separate into factors or components. —*intr.* To act as a factor; do business as a factor. [Middle English *factour*, from Old French *facteur*, from Latin *factor*, maker, doer, from *factus*, FACT.] —**fac·tor·ship** *n.*

fac·tor·a·ble (făk′tər-ə-bəl) *adj.* Capable of being expressed as a product of factors. Said especially of mathematical expressions.

fac·tor·age (făk′tər-ĭj) *n.* **1.** The business of a factor. **2.** The commission or fee paid to a factor.

fac·to·ri·al (făk-tôr′ē-əl, -tōr′ē-əl) *n.* The product of all the positive integers from 1 to a given number. For example, 4 factorial, usually written 4!, is the product $1 \cdot 2 \cdot 3 \cdot 4 = 24$. —*adj.* Of or relating to a factor or factorial.

fac·tor·ize (făk′tə-rīz′) *tr.v.* **-ized, -izing, -izes.** To resolve (a mathematical expression) into factors. —**fac·tor·i·za·tion** (făk′tə-rə-zā′shən) *n.*

factor of safety *n.* The ratio of the stress required to break a material, part, or structure to the calculated maximum working stress to which it will be subjected in use. Also called "safety factor."

fac·to·ry (făk′tə-rē) *n., pl.* **-ries.** A building or group of buildings in which goods are manufactured; a plant. [Medieval Latin *factōria*, establishment for factors, from Latin *factor*, FACTOR.]

factory farming *n.* A method of farming employing industrial methods, such as the automated feeding of livestock, to increase production and reduce labor costs. —**factory farm** *n.*

factory ship *n.* A whaling or fishing vessel that has equipment for processing its catch on board.

faience *This faience plaque from ancient Egypt depicts the hippopotamus goddess Thoueris. Egyptian faience usually consisted of a ground-quartz or rock-crystal base under a glasslike glaze. The plaque's vivid color was obtained by adding a copper compound to the glaze.*

fac·to·tum (făk-tō′təm) *n., pl.* **-tums.** An employee or assistant who serves in a wide range of capacities. [Medieval Latin *factōtum,* from Latin *fac tōtum,* do everything : *fac,* imperative of *facere,* to do + *tōtum,* everything, the whole, from *tōtus,* all.]

fac·tu·al (făk′cho͞o-əl) *adj.* **1.** Of the nature of fact; actual; real. **2.** Of or containing facts. **—fac·tu·al·ly** *adv.*

fac·tu·al·ism (făk′cho͞o-ə-lĭz′əm) *n.* Devotion or adherence to fact. **—fac·tu·al·ist** *n.*

fac·ture (făk′chər) *n.* **1.** The process or manner of making something. **2.** That which is made.

fac·u·la (făk′yə-lə) *n., pl.* **-lae** (-lē′). Any of various large bright spots or streaks on the sun's photosphere, most conspicuous at the solar edge or near sunspots. [Latin, diminutive of *fax*† (stem *fac-*), flame, torch.]

fac·ul·ta·tive (făk′əl-tā′tĭv) *adj.* **1.** Of or associated with a mental faculty or faculties. **2.** Capable of occurring or not occurring; contingent. **3.** Granting permission or authority. **4.** Not obligatory; optional. **5.** *Biology.* Capable of existing in very different environmental conditions, as certain microorganisms that can live with or without oxygen. Compare **obligate.** **—fac·ul·ta·tive·ly** *adv.*

fac·ul·ty (făk′əl-tē) *n., pl.* **-ties.** **1.** An inherent power or ability: *"Her strength lay in her extraordinary faculty for . . . observation"* (J.B. Priestly). **2.** Any of the powers or capacities possessed by the human mind: *The blow deprived him of his faculties.* **3.** The ability to perform well in a given activity; skill. **4.** *Archaic.* An occupation; a trade. **5. a.** Any of the divisions or comprehensive branches of learning at a college or university: *the faculty of law.* **b.** The teachers within such a division. **c.** The teachers of a school, college, or university. **6.** All of the members of a learned profession: *the medical faculty.* **7.** Authorization granted by authority; conferred power. [Middle English *facultе,* from Old French, from Latin *facultās* (stem *facultāt-*), power, capability, from Old Latin *facul,* easy.]

fad (făd) *n.* **1.** A fashion in dress, behavior, or speech that enjoys brief popularity. **2.** The object of this fashion. [19th century : originally dialect, perhaps from *fidfad,* shortening of FIDDLE-FADDLE.] **—fad·dist** *n.*

FAD (ĕf′ā-dē′) *n. Biochemistry.* A derivative of riboflavin that is a coenzyme in many oxidation-reduction reactions. [*F*lavin *a*denine *d*inucleotide.]

fad·dish (făd′ĭsh) *adj.* **1.** Of the nature of a fad: *a faddish fondness for the latest hats.* **2.** Given to fads. **—fad·dish·ly** *adv.* **—fad·dish·ness** *n.*

fade (fād) *v.* **faded, fading, fades.** *—intr.* **1.** To lose brightness, loudness, or brilliance gradually; dim. **2.** To lose freshness; wither. **3.** To lose strength or vitality; decline in energy; wane. **4.** To disappear slowly or gradually; die out; vanish. Often used with *out* or *away: All hope of reaching the camp by nightfall soon faded away.* **5.** To lose power gradually. Used of brakes. **6.** To move back from the scrimmage line. Used of a football quarterback. *—tr.* **1.** To cause to fade. **2.** *Slang.* To meet the bet of (an opposing player) in a dice game.
~n. **1.** An act or instance of fading. **2.** A dissolve in motion pictures or television. [Middle English *faden,* from Old French *fader,* from *fade,* faded, vapid, from Vulgar Latin *fatidus* (unattested), probably a blend of Latin *fatuus,* insipid, foolish, FATUOUS, and *vapidus,* VAPID.] **—fade·less** *adj.* **—fade·less·ly** *adv.*

fade in *intr.v.* To appear gradually. Used of a motion-picture or television image or of a sound. *—tr.* To make (an image or sound) appear gradually.

fade-in (fād′ĭn′) *n.* **1.** The gradual coming or bringing into full visibility of an image in motion pictures or television. **2.** The gradual coming or bringing into audibility of a sound, as in broadcasting.

fade out *intr.v.* To disappear gradually. Used of a motion-picture or television image or of a sound. *—tr.v.* To make (an image or sound) disappear gradually.

fade-out (fād′out′) *n.* **1.** The gradual disappearance of a motion-picture or television image or of a sound. **2.** A reduction in strength in or temporary loss of a radio or television signal. **3.** A gradual decline or disappearance.

fad·ing (fā′dĭng) *n.* **1.** A waning; a decline: *the gradual fading of imperial power.* **2.** Fluctuation in the strength of received radio signals because of variations in the transmission medium.

fa·do (fä′do͞o) *n., pl.* **-dos.** A plaintive, usually sentimental Portuguese folk song. [Portuguese, fado, "fate," from Latin *fātum,* FATE.]

faecal. Variant of **fecal.**

faeces. Variant of **feces.**

Fa·en·za (fä-ĕn′zə). Town in the Emilia-Romagna district of northern Italy, on the Lamone River. Since the 12th century the pottery faience has been made here.

fa·er·ie (fā′ə-rē, fâr′ē) *n.* Also **fa·er·y** *pl.* **-ies.** *Archaic.* **1.** A fairy. **2.** The land or realm of the fairies.
~adj. Also **fa·er·y.** **1.** *Archaic.* Of or like a fairy or fairies. **2.** Enchanted; visionary; fanciful. [Variant (in Spenser's *The Faerie Queen,* 1590–96) of FAIRY.]

Faer·oe or **Far·oe Islands** (fâr′ō). *Danish* **Fær·ø·er·ne** (fâr′û′ər-nə). Group of 22 volcanic islands belonging to Denmark, lying in the North Atlantic Ocean between Iceland and the Shetland Islands. Seventeen are inhabited; on the largest of them, Streymoy, is the islands' capital, Tórshavn. The economy is based on fish and wool. See map at **Western Europe.**

Faeroese. Variant of **Faroese.**

Faf·nir (fäv′nər, -nîr′). The dragon in Norse mythology that guarded the treasure of the Nibelungs and was slain by Sigurd. [Old Norse *Fafnir.*]

fag[1] (făg) *n.* **1.** *Informal.* **a.** Fatiguing or tedious work; drudgery. **b.** A drudge. **2.** *British.* A schoolboy at some English public schools who is required to perform menial tasks for a pupil in a higher class.
~v. **fagged, fagging, fags.** *—intr.* **1.** *Informal.* To work to exhaustion; become weary from toil. **2.** *British.* To serve as the fag of another pupil. *—tr.* **1.** *Informal.* To exhaust from long work or vigorous activity; weary; fatigue. Often used with *out: was fagged out at the end of three hours on the tennis court.* **2.** *British.* To use (a boy) as a fag. [16th century (to droop, hang down, flag) : origin obscure.]

fag[2] *n. Slang.* A cigarette. [Short for FAG END.]

fag[3] *n. Slang.* A male homosexual. Usually used derogatorily. [Short for FAGGOT.] **—fag·gy** *adj.*

fag end *n.* **1.** The frayed end of a length of cloth or rope. **2.** An inferior remnant or last part of anything; that which remains of something exhausted of its quality or utility. **3.** *Slang.* A cigarette stub. [Middle English *fagge*†.]

Fa·gin (fā′gən) *n.* A man who trains children to steal. [After *Fagin,* an old man in Dickens's *Oliver Twist* who trains children to be pickpockets.]

fag·ot, fag·got (făg′ət) *n.* **1.** A bundle of twigs, sticks, or branches bound together. **2.** A bundle of pieces of iron or steel to be welded or hammered into bars. **3.** A ball or cube of chopped meat, usually pig's offal, bread, and herbs, served baked or fried. **4.** *Slang.* A male homosexual. Usually used derogatorily.
~tr.v. **fagoted, -oting, -ots.** Also **faggot.** **1.** To collect or bind into a fagot or fagots; bundle. **2.** To decorate with fagoting. [Middle English, from Old French, from Italian *fagotto,* from Vulgar Latin *facus* (unattested), back-formation from Greek *phakelos*†. Sense 4, from earlier derogatory sense applied abusively to women (compare **baggage**).]

fag·ot·ing, fag·got·ing (făg′ə-tĭng) *n.* **1.** A method of decorating cloth by pulling out horizontal threads and tying the remaining vertical threads into hourglass-shaped bunches. **2.** A method of joining hemmed edges by crisscrossing thread over an open seam.

fah-fee, fa-fi (fä′fē′) *n.* In South Africa, an illegal gambling game popular among black city-dwellers. It is a form of roulette in which a bet is placed on any number from 1 to 36, often chosen on the basis of dreams. [20th century : origin obscure.]

Fahr. Fahrenheit.

Fahr·en·heit (făr′ən-hīt′) *adj. Abbr.* **F, Fahr.** Of or pertaining to a temperature scale that registers the freezing point of water as 32° and the boiling point as 212° under standard atmospheric pressure. Fahrenheit temperatures are related to Celsius temperatures by the equation $F = 1.8C + 32$. [After Gabriel FAHRENHEIT.]

Fahrenheit, Gabriel Daniel (1686–1736). German physicist resident in Holland. He developed the use of mercury in thermometry and devised the temperature scale that bears his name.

fa·ience (fī-äns′, fā-, fä-yäNs′) *n.* A kind of fine glazed pottery, usually decorated with colorful glazes. [French, short for *(vaisselle de) Faïence,* "(vessel of) Faenza."]

fail (fāl) *v.* **failed, failing, fails.** *—intr.* **1.** To prove deficient or lacking; perform ineffectively or inadequately. **2.** To be unsuccessful in attempting to do or become something. **3. a.** To receive a mark or grade, usually an academic grade, below the acceptable minimum. **b.** To fall below an acceptable standard. **4.** To prove insufficient in quantity or duration; give out. **5.** To decline in strength or effectiveness; wane; fade away. **6.** To cease functioning properly. **7.** To become bankrupt or insolvent. *—tr.* **1.** To disappoint or prove undependable to: *Our sentries failed us.* **2.** To abandon; forsake: *His strength failed him.* **3.** To omit or neglect. Used with an infinitive: *The defendant failed to appear in court.* **4. a.** To receive a mark or grade below the acceptable minimum in (a course, examination, or the like). **b.** To fall below an acceptable standard in (a test, for example). **5. a.** To give a mark or grade of failure to (a student). **b.** To decide that (a candidate or student) has not reached an acceptable standard.
~n. A failure to reach an acceptable standard. **—without fail.** Certainly; definitely. [Middle English *failen, faillen,* from Old French *faillir,* from Vulgar Latin *fallīre* (unattested), from Latin *fallere*†, to deceive, disappoint, fail.]

fail·ing (fā′lĭng) *n.* **1.** The act of a person or thing that fails; a failure. **2.** A minor fault or weakness; a shortcoming; a defect. **—See Synonyms at fault.**
~prep. In the absence of; unless there is: *Failing a rainstorm, the game will be played this afternoon.*

faille (fāl, fīl) *n.* A slightly ribbed, woven fabric of silk, cotton, or rayon. [French, from Old French *faille*†.]

fail-safe (fāl′sāf′) *adj.* **1.** Capable of compensating automatically for a failure. Said of a mechanical device. **2.** Capable of returning to a safe condition in the event of a malfunction. **3.** Acting to stop a military attack on the occurrence of any of a variety of predetermined conditions.
~n. A fail-safe mechanism.

fail·ure (fāl′yər) *n.* **1.** The condition or fact of not achieving the desired end or ends: *the failure of an experiment.* **2. a.** One that fails. **b.** *Informal.* An unsuccessful or generally ineffectual person. **3.** The condition or fact of being insufficient or lacking; a falling short: *the failure of the sugar-cane harvest.* **4.** A cessation of proper functioning or performance: *an electric power failure.* **5.** Nonperformance of what is requested or expected; omission: *failure to re-*

port a change of address. **6.** The act or fact of failing to pass a course, examination, or test, or to reach an acceptable standard. **7.** A decline in strength or effectiveness; a weakening. **8.** The act or fact of becoming bankrupt or insolvent. [Variant of earlier *failer,* from Norman French *failer,* from Old French *faillir,* to FAIL.]

fain (fān) *adv. Archaic.* Preferably; gladly.
~*adj. Archaic.* **1.** Ready; willing. **2.** Obliged or required. [Middle English, from *fain,* joyful, happy, Old English *fægen.*]

fai·né·ant (fā'nā-äN') *adj.* Given to doing nothing; idle; lazy.
~*n.* An irresponsible idler. [French, folk etymological variant (influenced by *fait,* does + *néant,* nothing) of Old French *faignant,* idler, present participle of *faindre,* to be idle, FEIGN.]

faint (fānt) *adj.* **fainter, faintest. 1.** Lacking strength or vigor; feeble. **2.** Lacking conviction, boldness, or courage; timid. **3.** Barely perceptible; indistinct; dim. **4.** Ready to fall into a faint; suddenly dizzy and weak.
~*n.* An abrupt, usually brief loss of consciousness, generally associated with failure of normal blood circulation.
~*intr.v.* **fainted, fainting, faints. 1.** To fall into a faint; swoon. **2.** *Archaic.* To weaken in purpose or spirit; languish. [Middle English *feint, faint,* faint, feigned, from Old French, past participle of *faindre,* to FEIGN.] **—faint·er** *n.* **—faint·ly** *adv.* **—faint·ness** *n.*

faint·est (fān'tĭst) *n. Informal.* The least idea: *I haven't the faintest.*

faint·heart (fānt'härt') *n.* A faint-hearted person; a coward. [Back-formation from FAINT-HEARTED.]

faint-heart·ed (fānt'här'tĭd) *adj.* Deficient in conviction or courage; cowardly; timid. **—faint-heart·ed·ly** *adv.* **—faint-heart·ed·ness** *n.*

faints, feints (fānts) *pl.n.* The impure spirits produced in the first and last stages of the distillation of liquors. [From FAINT.]

fair[1] (fâr) *adj.* **fairer, fairest. 1.** Visually beautiful or admirable; lovely: *a fair maiden.* **2.** Of light color, as: **a.** Blond: *fair hair.* **b.** Pale or white; not ruddy: *fair skin.* **3.** Clear and sunny; free of clouds or storms: *fair skies.* **4.** Free of blemishes; unstained; clean: *one's fair name.* **5.** Regular and even: *a fair edge.* **6.** Free of obstacles; open: *fair sailing.* **7.** Promising; likely; propitious: *in a fair way to succeed.* **8.** Free of favoritism or bias; impartial: *a fair judge.* **9.** Just to all parties; equitable: *a fair compromise.* **10.** Consistent with rules, standards, logic, or ethics: *a fair tactic.* **11.** Moderately good; mildly satisfying: *a fair job of redecorating.* **12.** Courteous; agreeable: *fair manners.* **13.** Superficially true or good; specious: *They coaxed us with fair words.* **14.** Favorable: *a fair wind for sailing.* **15.** *Informal.* Considerable: *a fair distance.* **16.** *Baseball.* Designating or falling into the area of the playing field bounded by the foul lines. —See Synonyms at **average, beautiful.**
~*adv.* **1.** In a fair manner; correctly; properly: *playing fair.* **2.** Directly; squarely; straight: *a blow caught fair in the stomach.* **—fair and square.** Justly and honestly. **—look fair to.** To be likely to.
~*n. Archaic.* **1.** Loveliness; beauty. **2.** A person or thing that is fair; especially, a beautiful or beloved woman.
~*v.* **faired, fairing, fairs.** —*tr.* To make (timber, a surface, or a joint) smooth, even, or regular. —*intr. Regional.* To become cloudless or mild: *The weather should fair by morning.* [Middle English *fair, fager,* Old English *fæger,* from Germanic.] **—fair·ness** *n.*
Synonyms: *dispassionate, equitable, impartial, just, objective, straightforward, unbiased, unprejudiced.*

fair[2] *n.* **1.** A gathering held at a specified time and place for the buying and selling of goods; a market. **2.** A regional event, usually held annually, with displays of farm and home products and various competitions and entertainments: *a state fair.* **3. a.** An exhibition presented by representatives of a particular trade in order to facilitate business. **b.** A large exhibition presented jointly by a number of nations, each of which maintains a public building containing educational, artistic, and trade exhibits: *world's fair.* **4.** An event, usually for the benefit of a charity or public institution, including entertainment and the sale of goods; a bazaar: *a church fair.* **5.** *Chiefly British.* An amusement park. [Middle English *feire,* from Old French, from Late Latin *fēria,* from Latin *fēriæ,* holiday.]

fair ball *n. Baseball.* A batted ball that first strikes the ground or leaves the playing field beyond first or third base within the foul lines or that is within the foul lines as it bounces past first or third base or that comes to rest or is touched by a fielder in front of first or third base within the foul lines.

Fair·banks (fâr'băngks'). Town in central Alaska, on the Chena River. Although it was the scene of a gold rush in 1902, its mining now has little commercial value.

Fairbanks, Douglas Elton, born Douglas Ulman (1883–1939). U.S. silent screen actor famed for swashbuckling heroics in romantic adventures. His better-known films include *The Mark of Zorro* (1920), *The Three Musketeers* (1921), and *Robin Hood* (1922). His son, **Douglas Elton Fairbanks, Jr.** (1909–), was also a swashbuckling film adventurer, adding a debonair quality to the Fairbanks tradition. He starred in *The Prisoner of Zenda* (1937) and *Sinbad the Sailor* (1947).

fair copy *n.* A copy of a document made after all corrections and revisions have been completed.

fair game *n.* **1.** Game, such as deer or pheasant, that it is lawful to pursue and kill. **2.** Something deserving criticism or ridicule; something that it is legitimate to attack.

fair·ground (fâr'ground') *n.* An open space where fairs are held.

fair·ing[1] (fâr'ĭng) *n.* An auxiliary structure or the external surface of an aircraft, car, or vessel serving to reduce drag. [From FAIR (to make smooth).]

fairing[2] *n. British.* A gift, especially one bought or given at a fair.

fair·ish (fâr'ĭsh) *adj.* **1.** Moderately fair. **2.** Of moderately good size or quality.

fair isle *n.* **1.** A knitting technique of working yarns of many different colors in stocking stitch to produce geometric designs such as those that originated in Fair Isle in the Shetlands. **2. a.** The multicolored pattern formed by this technique. **b.** Material or garments worked in fair isle. **—fair-isle** (fâr'īl') *adj.*

Fair Isle. The southernmost of the Shetland Islands, Scotland. It is known for its knitted woolen garments with distinctive colored patterns and for its bird sanctuary.

fair-lead (fâr'lēd') *n.* Also **fair-lead·er** (-lē'dər). *Nautical.* A device such as a ring or block of wood with a hole in it through which rigging is passed to hold it in place or prevent it from snagging or chafing.

fair·ly (fâr'lē) *adv.* **1. a.** In a fair or just manner; equitably. **b.** Legitimately; suitably. **2.** Actually; completely; fully: *The walls fairly shook with his bellowing.* **3.** Moderately; rather: *a fairly good dinner.* **4.** Clearly; distinctly.

fair-mind·ed (fâr'mīn'dĭd) *adj.* Just and impartial in judgment; unprejudiced. **—fair-mind·ed·ness** *n.*

fair play *n.* Conformance to the established rules or ethics of a sport, business, or other activity.

fair sex *n.* Women collectively. Preceded by *the.*

fair-spo·ken (fâr'spō'kən) *adj.* Civil, courteous, and gentle in speech.

fair trade *n.* Trade that conforms to a fair-trade agreement.

fair-trade (fâr'trād') *tr.v.* **-trad·ed, -trad·ing, -trades.** To sell (a commodity) at a price consistent with a fair-trade agreement.

fair-trade agreement *n.* A commercial agreement under which distributors sell products of a given kind at no less than a minimum price set by the manufacturer.

fair·way (fâr'wā') *n.* **1.** A stretch of ground free of obstacles to movement. **2.** The part of a golf course covered with short grass and extending from the tee to the putting green. **3.** *Nautical.* **a.** A navigable deep-water channel in a river harbor or along a coastline. **b.** The usual course taken by vessels through a harbor or coastal waters.

fair-weath·er (fâr'wĕth'ər) *adj.* **1.** Suitable or used only during fair weather. **2.** Only engaging in an activity during good weather. Used derogatorily : *fair-weather cyclists.* **3.** Present and dependable only in good times; failing in times of trouble: *fair-weather friends.*

fair·y (fâr'ē) *n., pl.* **-ies. 1.** A tiny supernatural being in human form, typically female and depicted as clever, mischievous, and capable of assisting or harassing humans. **2.** *Slang.* A male homosexual. **—away with the fairies.** *Chiefly Scottish.* Abstracted or eccentric in behavior.
~*adj.* **1.** Of or associated with fairies. **2.** Resembling a fairy; fanciful, graceful, or delicate. [Middle English *fairie,* from Old French *faerie, faierie,* enchantment, from *fae,* fairy, from Latin *fāta,* the Fates, plural of *fātum,* FATE.]

fairy godmother *n.* A benefactress or sometimes a benefactor; especially, one who appears unexpectedly to help in a crisis. [After similar characters in such well-known tales as *Cinderella.*]

fairy gold *n.* **1.** In fairy tales, a gift or theft of gold from fairyland, which turns to dust before the eyes or overnight. **2.** Anything likened to this in elusiveness; a disappointing illusion.

fair·y·land (fâr'ē-lănd') *n.* **1.** The imaginary land of the fairies. **2.** Any charming, enchanting place; a wonderland.

fairy lights *pl.n. Chiefly British.* Small colored lights used for decoration, as on Christmas trees or in window displays.

fairy ring *n.* A circle of darker luxuriant grass corresponding to an area of underground mycelial growth, the periphery of which is seasonally marked by an overground growth of mushrooms. [The circle is superstitiously believed to be produced by dancing fairies.]

fairy shrimp *n.* Any of various transparent freshwater crustaceans of the order Anostraca that characteristically swim on their backs.

fairy tale *n.* **1.** A story about fairies. **2.** A fanciful tale of legendary deeds and romance, usually intended to please children. **3.** A fictitious, highly fanciful story or explanation.

fair·y-tale (fâr'ē-tāl') *adj.* Suitable for or like a fairy tale; especially, so delightful as to be like a fantasy: *a fairy-tale wedding.*

Fai·sal (fī'səl), **Ibn Abdul Aziz al-Saud** (1905–75). King of Saudi Arabia. He succeeded to the throne on the abdication of his brother King Saud in 1964. During his reign, government oil profits were used to increase industrialization, education, and health in Saudi Arabia. He was assassinated by his nephew.

fait ac·com·pli (fā'tä-kôN-plē', fĕt'ä-) *n., pl.* **faits accomplis** (*pronounced as singular*). An accomplished and presumably irreversible deed or fact. [French, "accomplished fact."]

faith (fāth) *n.* **1. a.** A confident belief in the truth, value, or trustworthiness of a person, idea, or thing. **b.** Reliance; trust. **2.** Belief that does not rest on logical proof or material evidence: *faith in miracles.* **3.** Loyalty to a person or thing; allegiance: *keeping faith with one's supporters.* **4.** Belief and trust in God and in the doctrines expressed in the Scriptures or other sacred works; religious conviction. **5.** A system of religious beliefs: *the Muslim faith.* **6.** Any set of principles or beliefs: *"Realism had been his literary faith from his earliest days"* (Alfred Kazin). —See Synonyms at **trust.** [Middle English *feith, feth,* from Old French *feid, feit,* from Latin *fidēs.*]

faith cure *n.* A cure of an ailment held to be accomplished through religious faith.

faith·ful (fāth'fəl) *adj.* **1.** Adhering strictly to the person, cause, or idea to which one is bound; dutiful and loyal. **2.** Worthy of trust or

PRONUNCIATION KEY

ă, pat; ā, pay; âr, care;
ä, father, are; b, bib;
ch, church; d, deed; ĕ, pet;
ē, be; f, fife; g, gag; h, hat;
hw, which; ĭ, pit; ī, pie;
îr, pier; j, judge; k, kick;
l, lid, needle; m, mum;
n, no, sudden; ng, thing;
ŏ, pot; ō, toe; ô, paw, for;
oi, noise; ou, out; ŏŏ, book;
ōō, boot; p, pop; r, roar;
s, sauce; sh, ship, dish;
t, tight; th, thin, path;
th, this, bathe; ŭ, cut; ûr, fur;
v, valve; w, with; y, yes;
z, zebra, size; zh, vision;
ə, about, item, edible, gallop, circus, peaceful

IN FOREIGN WORDS:

à, *Fr.* ami; œ, *Fr.* feu, *Ger.* schön; ü, *Fr.* tu, *Ger.* über;
KH, *Ger.* ich, *Scot.* loch;
N, *Fr.* bon; y', *Fr.* Compiègne

STRESS MARKS:

Primary stress: '
in·cite' (ĭn-sīt')
Secondary stress: '
in'sight' (ĭn'sīt')

credence; consistently reliable: *a faithful guide.* **3.** Consistent with truth or actuality; accurate; exact: *a faithful reproduction.* **4.** Not having sexual relations with anyone other than one's spouse or lover. **—the faithful. 1.** The practicing members of a religious faith, especially of Christianity or Islam. **2.** The steadfast adherents of any faith or cause. **—faith·ful·ly** *adv.* **—faith·ful·ness** *n.*

Synonyms: *constant, dependable, devoted, loyal, steadfast, true.*

faith healer *n.* One who attempts to effect faith cures; one who tries to heal by prayer and religious faith.

faith·less (fāth′lĭs) *adj.* **1.** Untrue to duty or obligation; breaking faith; disloyal. **2.** Lacking confidence or trust in a given person or cause. **3. a.** Without religious faith. **b.** Without faith in Christianity; heathen. **4.** Unworthy of faith or trust; unreliable. **—faith·less·ly** *adv.* **—faith·less·ness** *n.*

Synonyms: *disloyal, false, fickle, inconstant, perfidious, traitorous, undependable, unfaithful.*

fake¹ (fāk) *adj.* **1.** Having a false or misleading appearance; fraudulent. **2.** Counterfeit: *a fake Rubens.*

~n. **1.** A person, act, or thing that is not genuine or authentic; a sham; a counterfeit. **2.** *Sports.* A feint or aborted change of direction intended to mislead one's opponents.

~v. **faked, faking, fakes.** *—tr.* **1.** To contrive and present as genuine; counterfeit. **2.** To simulate; pretend; feign. *—intr.* **1.** To engage in faking. **2.** *Sports.* To perform a fake. —See Synonyms at **pretend.** [19th century (thieves' slang) : from obsolete *feak,* to beat, from German *fezen,* to polish, beat, rebuke.]

fake² *n. Nautical.* One loop of a coiled rope or cable.

~tr.v. **faked, faking, fakes.** *Nautical.* To coil (a rope or cable). [Middle English *faken*†.]

fak·er (fā′kər) *n.* **1.** A person who fakes or who produces fakes. **2.** One who practices fraud; a swindler. **—fak·er·y** *n.*

fa·kir (fə-kîr′, fā′kər) *n.* Also **fa·keer** (fə-kîr′). **1.** A Muslim religious mendicant. **2.** A Hindu ascetic or religious mendicant; especially, one who performs feats of magic or endurance. [Arabic *faqīr,* from *faqura,* he was poor.]

fa·la·fel, fe·la·fel (fə-lä′fəl) *n.* **1.** Ground, spiced chickpeas or fava beans shaped into balls and fried. **2.** A sandwich filled with falafel. [Arabic.]

falconry *A jessed peregrine—one fitted with a short strap to its leg for tethering—being launched from a falconer's gauntlet to hunt grouse in Scotland.*

Fa·laise (fə-lāz′). Market town in Normandy, northern France, and birthplace of William the Conqueror. In the Normandy campaign of 1944 the British captured Falaise, thus opening the way for the Allied armies to liberate northern France.

Fa·lange (fā′lănj′, fə-lănj′) *n.* A fascist organization constituting the official ruling party of Spain under General Franco. [Spanish, from *falange,* phalanx, from Latin *phalanx* (stem *phalang-*), PHALANX.] **—Fa·lan·gist** (fə-lan′jĭst, fā′lăn′-) *n.*

fal·ba·la (făl′bə-lə) *n.* A flounce, frill, or ruffle. [18th century : French, from dialectal *ferbelà*†, akin to FURBELOW.]

fal·cate (făl′kāt′) *adj.* Also **fal·cat·ed** (făl′kā′tĭd). *Biology.* Curved and tapering to a point at either end; sickle-shaped. [Latin *falcātus,* from *falx*† (stem *falc-*), sickle.]

fal·chion (fôl′chən, -shən) *n.* **1.** A short, broad sword with a convex cutting edge and a sharp point, used in medieval times. **2.** *Archaic.* Any sword. [Middle English *fauchoun,* from Old French *fauchon,* from Vulgar Latin *falciō* (stem *falciōn-*) (unattested), from Latin *falx* (stem *falc-*), sickle.]

fal·ci·form (făl′sə-fôrm′) *adj.* Curved or sickle-shaped; falcate. [Latin *falx* (stem *falc-*), sickle (see **falcate**) + -FORM.]

fal·con (făl′kən, fôl′-, fô′-) *n.* **1. a.** Any of various birds of prey of the family Falconidae, and especially of the genus *Falco,* having long, pointed, powerful wings adapted for swift flight. **b.** Any of several species of these birds or related birds such as hawks, trained to hunt small game. **c.** In falconry, a female bird of this type. **2.** A small cannon of the 15th to 17th century. [Middle English *faucoun,* from Old French *faucon,* from Late Latin *falcō* (stem *falcōn-*).]

fal·con·er (făl′kə-nər, fôl′-, fô′-) *n.* **1.** A person who breeds and trains falcons. **2.** One who hunts with falcons.

fal·co·net (făl′kə-nĕt′, fôl′-, fô′-) *n.* **1.** A small or young falcon. **2.** Any of several small falcons of the genus *Microhierax,* chiefly of tropical Asia.

fal·con-gen·tle (făl′kən-jĕn′təl, fôl′-, fô′-) *n.* A female falcon, especially a peregrine falcon. [Middle English *faucoun gentil,* from Old French *faucon gentil,* "noble falcon" : *faucon,* FALCON + *gentil,* noble (see **gentle**).]

fal·con·ry (făl′kən-rē, fôl′-, fô′-) *n.* **1.** The sport of hunting with falcons. **2.** The art of training falcons for hunting.

falderal, falderol. Variants of **folderol.**

fald·stool (fôld′sto͞ol′) *n.* **1.** A small, usually cushioned stool at which worshipers kneel to pray; especially, one on which the British sovereign kneels at the coronation. **2.** A portable, backless chair or stool used by a bishop when not occupying his throne or when presiding away from his own cathedral. **3.** *Anglican Church.* A desk at which the litany is recited. [Partial translation of Medieval Latin *faldistolium,* folding stool, from Germanic.]

Falk·land Islands (fôk′lənd). *Spanish* **Is·las Mal·vi·nas** (ēz′läz mäl-vē′nəs). Group of 202 small islands *c.* 480 kilometers (300 miles) east of the Strait of Magellan in the South Atlantic Ocean. The two largest islands are East Falkland and West Falkland. The capital is Port Stanley (also called Stanley). The islands have been a British crown colony since 1833 but are claimed by Argentina. In 1982 Argentine forces seized the islands and were expelled by a British military expedition. The colony includes the dependencies of South Georgia, 1,290 kilometers (800 miles) southeast of East Falkland, and the South Sandwich Islands, 760 kilometers (470 miles) southeast of South Georgia. See map at **Argentina.**

fall (fôl) *v.* **fell** (fĕl), **fallen** (fô′lən), **falling, falls.** *—intr.* **1.** To move under the influence of gravity; especially, to drop without restraint. **2.** To drop oneself from an erect to a less erect position: *He stumbled and fell.* **3.** To be severely wounded or to be killed in battle. **4.** To collapse from lack of structural support: *Several buildings fell during the earthquake.* **5.** To come to rest; strike bottom; land: *The aircraft fell in an uninhabited region.* **6.** To hang down: *Her hair fell in ringlets.* **7.** To be cast down; be averted: *Her eyes fell.* **8.** To assume an expression of disappointment: *Her face fell when she heard the report.* **9.** To be conquered or seized: *The city fell after a long siege.* **10.** To lose power; be defeated or overthrown: *During periods of crisis, governments may fall.* **11.** To follow a downward direction; slope: *The plain falls gently toward the coast.* **12.** To undergo a reduction in amount, degree, or value; diminish: *The air pressure is falling.* **13.** To diminish in pitch or volume: *His voice fell to a whisper.* **14.** To decline in rank, status, or importance. **15.** To yield to temptation; err or sin. **16.** To pass into a specified condition: *The crowd fell silent.* **17.** To arrive and pervade: *A hush fell on the crowd.* **18.** To occur at a specified time: *Christmas falls on a Tuesday this year.* **19.** To occur at a specified place: *The stress falls on the last syllable.* **20.** To come or be allotted by chance or distribution: *The greatest task fell to him.* **21.** To be given by right or stipulation: *The estate fell to the eldest surviving son.* **22.** To divide naturally. Used with *into: The specimens fall into three categories.* **23.** To be directed; come to rest: *His gaze fell on a small book in the corner.* **24.** To be uttered as if involuntarily; slip out: *A murmur of impatience fell from his lips.* **25.** To be born. Used chiefly of lambs. *—tr.* To cut down (a tree); fell. **—fall among.** To come casually into the company of. **—fall away. 1.** To decline; languish; weaken. **2.** To withdraw friendship or support; part company. **3.** To slope downward. **—fall back. 1.** To give ground; recede; retreat. **2.** To move backward. **—fall back on** (or **upon**). **1.** To retreat to. **2.** To resort to. **—fall behind. 1.** To lag behind; fail to keep up with. **2.** To be in arrears. **3.** To move behind. **—fall down.** *Informal.* To prove unsuccessful; fail or lag in performance. **—fall flat.** *Informal.* To fail completely to achieve the intended effect. **—fall for.** *Informal.* **1.** To become infatuated with; fall suddenly in love with. **2.** To be tricked or deceived by. **—fall foul** (or **afoul**). *Nautical.* **1.** To collide. Used of vessels. **2.** To become entangled. Used of rigging. **—fall foul of.** To incur the displeasure of; come into conflict with. **—fall in.** *Military.* To take one's place in a formation; form ranks. **—fall in with. 1.** To agree. **2.** To meet by chance; join. **—fall on** (or **upon**). To attack suddenly; ambush. **—fall short. 1.** To fail to attain a specified amount, level, or degree. **2.** To prove inadequate or lacking. **—fall through. 1.** To fail; collapse; miscarry. **2.** To fail to occur. **—fall to. 1.** To begin an activity energetically. **2.** To shut or move into place unaided. **—fall under. 1.** To occur in the class of; be listed or located within. **2.** To succumb to; come under the influence or power of.

~n. **1.** The act or an instance of falling; a dropping down; a free descent. **2.** A sudden drop from a relatively erect to a less erect position: *He had a bad fall.* **3.** That which has fallen: *The field was covered with a fall of hail.* **4. a.** The amount of what has fallen: *a fall of two inches of rain.* **b.** The distance that something falls: *a fall of three stories.* **5.** *Often* **Fall.** Autumn. **6.** *Often* **falls.** A waterfall; a cascade. **7.** A downward movement or slope: *the fall of a river toward its mouth.* **8.** Any of several hanging articles of dress, especially: **a.** A veil hung from a woman's hat and down her back. **b.** An ornamental cascade of lace or trimming attached to a dress, usually at the collar. **c.** A woman's hairpiece with long, free-hanging hair. **9.** A capture, overthrow, or collapse: *the fall of a government.* **10.** A reduction in value, amount, or degree. **11.** A decline in status, rank, or importance. **12.** A loss of virtue or moral innocence; a yielding to sin. **13.** *Usually* **Fall.** *Theology.* Adam's sin of disobeying God by eating the forbidden fruit in the Garden of Eden and the consequent loss of innocence and grace of all his descendants. Preceded by *the.* **14.** In wrestling: **a.** The act of throwing or forcing an opponent down on his back. **b.** Any of various maneuvers used for this. **15.** *Nautical.* A break or rise in the level of a deck. **16. falls.** *Nautical.* The apparatus used to hoist and transfer cargo or lifeboats. **17.** The end of a cable, rope, or chain that is pulled by the power source in hoisting. **18. a.** The birth of an animal; especially, the birth of a lamb. **b.** All of the animals born at one birth; a litter. **—ride for a fall.** To court danger or disaster. [Fall, fell, fallen; Middle English *fallen, fell, fallen,* Old English *feallan, fēol, feallan,* from Germanic *fallan* (unattested).]

Fal·la (fä′yə), **Manuel de** (1876–1946). Spanish composer and pianist. He was influenced by Debussy and Ravel and blended elements of their music with his own ebullient style, as in *Nights in the Gardens of Spain* (1916). His music later became starker, as in the ballet for Diaghilev, *The Three-Cornered Hat* (1919).

fal·la·cious (fə-lā′shəs) *adj.* **1.** Containing or based on a fallacy: *a fallacious syllogism.* **2.** Deceptive in appearance or meaning; misleading: *fallacious evidence.* **3.** Not real or sound; delusive: *fallacious signs of a change in the weather.* **—fal·la·cious·ly** *adv.* **—fal·la·cious·ness** *n.*

fal·la·cy (făl′ə-sē) *n., pl.* **-cies. 1.** An idea or opinion founded on mistaken logic or perception; a false notion. **2.** An argument or thesis that is inconsistent with logic or fact and thus renders the conclusion invalid. **3.** The quality of being in error; incorrectness of reasoning or belief. **4.** The quality of being deceptive. [Latin *fallā-*

PRONUNCIATION KEY

ă, pat; ā, pay; âr, care;
ä, father, are; b, bib;
ch, church; d, deed; ĕ, pet;
ē, be; f, fife; g, gag; h, hat;
hw, which; ĭ, pit; ī, pie;
îr, pier; j, judge; k, kick;
l, lid, needle; m, mum;
n, no, sudden; ng, thing;
ŏ, pot; ō, toe; ô, paw, for;
oi, noise; ou, out; o͝o, book;
o͞o, boot; p, pop; r, roar;
s, sauce; sh, ship, dish;
t, tight; th, thin, path;
th, this, bathe; ŭ, cut; ûr, fur;
v, valve; w, with; y, yes;
z, zebra, size; zh, vision;
ə, about, item, edible,
gallop, circus, peaceful

IN FOREIGN WORDS:

à, *Fr.* ami; œ, *Fr.* feu, *Ger.* schön; ü, *Fr.* tu, *Ger.* über;
KH, *Ger.* ich, *Scot.* loch;
N, *Fr.* bon; y′, *Fr.* Compiègne

STRESS MARKS:

Primary stress: ′
in·cite′ (ĭn-sīt′)
Secondary stress: ′
in′sight′ (ĭn′sīt′)

cia, deceit, trick, from *fallāx* (stem *fallāc-*), deceitful, from *fallere,* to deceive. See **fail.**]

fal·lal (fă-lăl′, făl′ăl′) *n.* A trifling, showy article of dress; a piece of finery; frippery.
~*adj. Archaic.* Affected; foppish. [18th century : perhaps akin to FALBALA.]

fallen arch *n.* A collapse of the normally arch-shaped instep of the foot that results in a flat foot.

fall guy *n. Slang.* **1.** One who takes the responsibility or blame, as for another's dereliction or delinquency; a scapegoat. **2.** An easy victim, as of a confidence trick.

fal·li·ble (făl′ə-bəl) *adj.* **1.** Capable of erring. **2.** Tending or likely to err. [Middle English, from Medieval Latin *fallibilis,* from Latin *fallere,* to deceive. See **fail.**] —**fal·li·bil·i·ty** (făl′ə-bĭl′ə-tē), **fal·li·ble·ness** *n.* —**fal·li·bly** *adv.*

falling band *n.* A wide collar of linen or lace turned down over the shoulders, worn during the 17th century.

fall·ing-out (fô′lĭng-out′) *n., pl.* **fallings-out** or **falling-outs.** A personal disagreement that has resulted in a broken or more distant relationship; an estrangement; a breach.

falling sickness *n.* Epilepsy. Not in technical usage.

falling star *n.* Any object, such as a meteoroid, rendered visible as a bright streak in the sky by falling and being ignited by atmospheric friction.

fall line *n.* **1.** *Geography.* An imaginary line marking a drop in land level or height, formulated by connecting the waterfalls of nearly parallel rivers. **2. Fall Line.** The line between the Piedmont Plateau and the Atlantic coastal plain where the Appalachians slope sharply. **3.** *Skiing.* The natural line of descent between two points on a slope.

fall off *intr.v.* **1.** To lessen in intensity, volume, number, or the like: *Ticket sales are falling off.* **2.** *Nautical.* To change course to leeward.

fall-off (fôl′ôf′, -ŏf′) *n.* A decline or decrease: *a falloff in sales.*

Fal·lo·pi·an tube (fə-lō′pē-ən) *n.* Either of a pair of slender ducts along which eggs pass from the ovaries to the womb in the female reproductive system of humans and other mammals. [After Gabriel FALLOPIUS.]

Fal·lo·pi·us (fə-lō′pē-əs), **Fal·lo·pi·o** (-pē-ō′), **Gabriel** (1523–62). Italian anatomist who discovered the Fallopian tubes, which connect the ovaries with the uterus in females.

fall out *intr.v.* **1.** *Military.* To leave ranks; withdraw from formation. **2.** To quarrel; become estranged. **3.** To happen; occur.

fall-out (fôl′out′) *n.* **1. a.** The slow descent of minute particles of radioactive debris in the atmosphere following a nuclear explosion in which radioactive material escapes into the atmosphere. **b.** The particles so descending. **c.** Such particles collectively. **2.** An incidental result or side effect: *the technological fallout of the space program; political fallout.*

fal·low (făl′ō) *adj.* **1. a.** Plowed and tilled but left unseeded during a growing season: *a fallow field.* **b.** Uncultivated. Said of land. **2. a.** Not pregnant: *a fallow mare.* **b.** Marked by the absence of pregnancy. —**lie fallow.** To go unexercised or unrealized.
~*n.* **1.** Land that has been plowed but left unseeded during a growing season. **2.** The process of leaving plowed land unseeded during a growing season.
~*tr.v.* **fallowed, -lowing, -lows.** **1.** To make (land) fallow by plowing. **2.** To plow (land) by way of preparing it for sowing. [Middle English *falow, falwe,* Old English *fealh†,* arable land.] —**fal·low·ness** *n.*

fallow crop *n.* A crop that tends to nourish soil and is rotated with a more demanding crop to maintain productivity of the soil.

fallow deer *n.* Either of two Eurasian deer, *Dama dama* or *D. mesopotamica,* having a yellowish-red coat spotted with white in summer, and broad, flattened antlers in the male. [From obsolete *fallow,* reddish-yellow, from Middle English *falwe,* sallow, Old English *fealu.*]

Fall River (fôl). An industrial city in southeastern Massachusetts, at the mouth of the Taunton River. It was once the foremost U.S. cotton textile center. Lizzie Borden lived in Fall River and was tried here (1892) for the murder of her father and stepmother.

Fal·mouth (făl′məth). A resort town on Cape Cod, in southeastern Massachusetts. It was settled *c.* 1660 and was once a whaling and shipbuilding center. The town includes Woods Hole, site of a major oceanographic institute.

false (fôls) *adj.* **falser, falsest.** **1.** Contrary to fact or truth; without grounds; incorrect. **2.** Fallacious; specious: *false logic.* **3.** Untruthful. **4. a.** Without meaning or sincerity; deceiving; sham: *false promises.* **b.** Misplaced and unjustified: *false modesty.* **c.** Deceptive; belying appearances: *a false start.* **5.** Not keeping faith; treacherous: *a false lover.* **6.** Not real or natural; artificial; synthetic: *false fur.* **7.** Resembling but not accurately or properly designated as such. Often used in plant names: *false hellebore.* **8.** *Music.* Of incorrect pitch. —See Synonyms at **faithless.** —**play someone false.** To betray. [Middle English *fals,* from Old French, from Latin *falsus,* past participle of *fallere,* to deceive. See **fail.**] —**false·ly** *adv.* —**false·ness** *n.*

false alarm *n.* An emergency alarm set off unnecessarily, whether by accident or intentionally; especially, a fire alarm where no fire exists. **2.** *Informal.* Any seeming crisis, signal, or warning that is groundless or abortive.

false arrest *n. Law.* An unlawful or unjustifiable arrest.

false bottom *n.* **1.** A partition that seems to be the bottom of a trunk, case, chest, or other receptacle but under which is another compartment. **2.** A base, as of a glass or bowl, that by its shape gives a false idea of the capacity of the vessel.

false brome *n.* Either of two grasses, *Brachypodium sylvaticum* or *B. pinnatum,* having long awns like the true brome grasses.

false colors *pl.n.* **1.** The flag or symbol of another country when used for deception, as by pirates on the high seas. **2.** Misleading representation; pretense.

false dawn *n.* **1.** Faint light observed low in the sky before dawn, caused by **zodiacal light** (*see*). **2.** An apparent arrival or advent that turns out to be short-lived and premature.

false friend *n.* A word in another language that is identical or almost identical to a word in one's own but that has a quite different meaning, as the French word *éventuel,* meaning "possible," and the German *Gift,* "poison."

false fruit *n.* A **pseudocarp** (*see*).

false-heart·ed (fôls′här′tĭd) *adj.* Having a deceitful nature; disloyal; treacherous.

false hellebore *n.* A species of **hellebore** (*see*).

false·hood (fôls′hŏŏd′) *n.* **1.** Contradiction to or disparity with truth or fact; that which is groundless or specious; an inaccuracy. **2.** The act of deceiving; lying. **3.** An untrue statement; a deception; a lie.

false imprisonment *n. Law.* Unlawful arrest or detention of a person, such as that enforced without a warrant or with an illegal one.

false indigo *n.* **1.** A shrub, *Amorpha fruticosa,* of eastern North America, having compound leaves with numerous leaflets and long clusters of purplish flowers. **2.** A plant, *Baptista australis,* of the southeastern United States, having compound leaves and purplish flowers.

false keel *n.* A protective strip fixed below a ship's main keel.

false position *n.* **1.** A situation in which a person's actions or motives, however good or well-intentioned, will be misconstrued or seen as wrong. **2.** A situation in which a person will be forced to act against his principles.

false pretenses *pl.n.* Misrepresentations of fact for an ulterior motive.

false rib *n.* In human beings, any of the ten lower ribs that do not unite directly with the sternum.

false step *n.* **1.** A slip; a stumble. **2.** A social blunder; a faux pas.

false teeth *pl.n.* Removable artificial teeth for one or both jaws.

fal·set·to (fôl-sĕt′ō) *n., pl.* **-tos.** A singing voice, typically male, marked by artificially produced notes in an upper register beyond its normal range.
~*adj.* Having the quality of falsetto: *a falsetto tone.*
~*adv.* In falsetto. [Italian, diminutive of *falso,* false, from Latin *falsus,* FALSE.]

false·work (fôls′wûrk′) *n.* A temporary supporting framework for a structure during construction or demolition.

fals·ies (fôl′sēz) *pl.n. Informal.* Pads or padding worn inside, or as part of, a brassiere to exaggerate the dimensions of the breasts.

fal·si·fy (fôl′sə-fī′) *v.* **-fied, -fying, -fies.** —*tr.* **1.** To state untruthfully; misrepresent. **2.** To alter (a document) in order to deceive. **3.** To counterfeit; forge. **4.** *Philosophy.* To show to be false. —*intr.* To make untrue statements; lie. [Middle English *falsifien,* from Old French *falsifier,* from Medieval Latin *falsificāre* : Latin *falsus,* FALSE + *facere,* to make.] —**fal·si·fi·a·bil·i·ty** (fôl′sə-fī′ə-bĭl′ə-tē) *n.* —**fal·si·fi·a·ble** (fôl′sə-fī′ə-bəl) *adj.* —**fal·si·fi·ca·tion** (fôl′sə-fĭ-kā′shən) *n.* —**fal·si·fi·er** *n.*

fal·si·ty (fôl′sə-tē) *n., pl.* **-ties.** **1.** The condition of being false. **2.** Something false; an untruth; a lie or falsehood.

Fal·staff·i·an (fôl-stăf′ē-ən) *adj.* Resembling or characteristic of Falstaff, a fat, merry, ribald, and boastful knight in Shakespeare's *Henry IV: Parts I and II* and *The Merry Wives of Windsor.*

falt·boat (fält′bōt′) *n.* A small boat consisting of canvas stretched over a collapsible frame and resembling a kayak. Also called "fold-boat." [Partial translation of German *Faltboot,* folding boat, from *falten,* to fold, from Old High German *falden.*]

fal·ter (fôl′tər) *intr.v.* **-tered, -tering, -ters.** **1.** To waver in confidence; hesitate. **2.** To speak hesitatingly; stammer. **3. a.** To move ineptly or haltingly; stumble; stagger. **b.** To operate unsteadily or ineffectively. —See Synonyms at **hesitate.**
~*n.* **1.** An unsteadiness in speech or action. **2.** A faltering sound. [Middle English *falteren†.*] —**fal·ter·ing·ly** *adv.*

fam. **1.** familiar. **2.** family.

F.A.M. Free and Accepted Masons.

Fa·ma·gu·sta (fä′mə-gōō′stə). Port on Famagusta Bay, an inlet of the Mediterranean, in eastern Cyprus. It is an ancient fishing and trading town, with remains of medieval walls.

fame (fām) *n.* **1.** Great reputation and recognition, usually favorable; public esteem; renown. **2.** Reputation. **3.** *Archaic.* Rumor.
~*tr.v.* **famed, faming, fames.** *Archaic.* To make famous by talking of. [Middle English, from Old French, from Latin *fāma,* talk, reputation.]
Synonyms: *eminence, glory, notoriety, renown, repute.*

famed (fāmd) *adj.* Having great fame; publicly acclaimed; celebrated; famous.

fa·mil·ial (fə-mĭl′yəl) *adj.* **1.** Of or pertaining to a family. **2.** *Genetics.* Passed on in a family; hereditary: *a familial trait.*

fa·mil·iar (fə-mĭl′yər) *adj. Abbr.* **fam.** **1.** Of frequent instance or occurrence; often encountered; common: *a familiar sight.* **2.** Having fair knowledge of something; acquainted. Used with *with: familiar with those roads.* **3.** Of established friendship; close; intimate: *be on familiar terms.* **4.** Natural and unstudied; informal: *He lectured in a*

fallow deer *The antlers of a young fallow deer buck (above) have a soft covering, called velvet, which is shed in the autumn as the breeding season approaches.*

familiar style. **5.** Presuming upon acquaintance; taking liberties. **6.** *Archaic.* Familial. —See Synonyms at **common.** —*n.* **1.** A close friend or associate. **2.** A spirit, often taking animal form, thought to attend a witch or wizard. **3.** *Roman Catholic Church.* One who performs domestic service in the household of a bishop. [Middle English, familial, from Old French *familier,* from Latin *familiāris,* from *familia,* FAMILY.] —**fa·mil·iar·ly** *adv.*
Synonyms: *chummy, close, fraternal, intimate.*
fa·mil·iar·i·ty (fə-mĭl′yăr′ə-tē, -ē-ăr′ə-tē) *n., pl.* -**ties.** **1.** Substantial or reasonable acquaintance with something; moderate understanding; knowledge. Used with *with.* **2.** Established friendship; candor; intimacy. **3.** Presumption; undue liberty; boldness. **4.** *Often* **familiarities.** Actions or behavior presuming intimacy, especially sexual advances; liberties.
fa·mil·iar·ize (fə-mĭl′yə-rīz′) *tr.v.* -**ized, -izing, -izes. 1.** To make generally known, recognized, or familiar; popularize. **2.** To make (oneself or another) acquainted. —**fa·mil·iar·i·za·tion** (fə-mĭl′-yər-ĭ-zā′shən) *n.* —**fa·mil·iar·iz·er** *n.*

fam·i·ly (făm′ə-lē, făm′lē) *n., pl.* -**lies.** *Abbr.* **fam. 1. a.** The fundamental social or mating group among human beings and animals. **b.** Two or more adults and the children living with them. **2. a.** One's spouse and children. **b.** One's children. **c.** One's parents and siblings. **3.** Persons related by blood or marriage; relatives; kin. **4.** Lineage; especially, upper-class lineage. **5.** All the members of a household; those who share a home. **6. a.** A group of like things; a class. **b.** A special or particular world of something; a kingdom; a fellowship: *the family of man.* **7.** *Biology.* A taxonomic category ranking below an order and above a genus. **8.** *Linguistics.* A language group derived from the same parent language. **9.** A locally independent unit of the Mafia. **10.** A set of related curves or surfaces that are given by different values of a constant in a single equation. For example, different values of *r* in the equation $x^2 + y^2 = r^2$ generate a family of concentric circles.
—*adj.* **1.** Of or pertaining to a family: *a family reunion.* **2.** Suitable or intended for children and their parents: *a family show.* —**in the family way.** *Informal.* Pregnant. [Middle English *familie,* from

---

family tree

CHARTING A FAMILY'S HISTORY

Two billion ancestors in 30 generations

In each generation the number of any person's direct ancestors—their parents, grandparents, great-grandparents, and so on—doubles. So, theoretically, over 30 generations everyone has, amazingly, more than 2 billion ancestors.

A family tree can be necessary to establish the transmission of property or title from one generation to another. Some cultures use a matrilineal line, which traces descent through the mother. Most, however, use

patrilineage, which traces descent through the father. Since Roman times it has been customary in the West to trace descent through the male line.

The legally enforced registration of births, marriages, and deaths, introduced in many countries during the 19th century, has made it reasonably simple to trace ancestors back over the last three or four generations. Research is also made easier by census returns, wills, parish registers, and records of service in the

armed forces. The British royal family can trace its ancestors back through 53 generations and 1,500 years to Cerdic, a Saxon invader who became king of the West Saxons; he died in 534.

The largest family tree known to exist was compiled by Nellaray Holt of Union Gap in Washington State, over a period of 16 years. It is the record of a family called Borton, which contains 6,820 names and goes back to 1562.

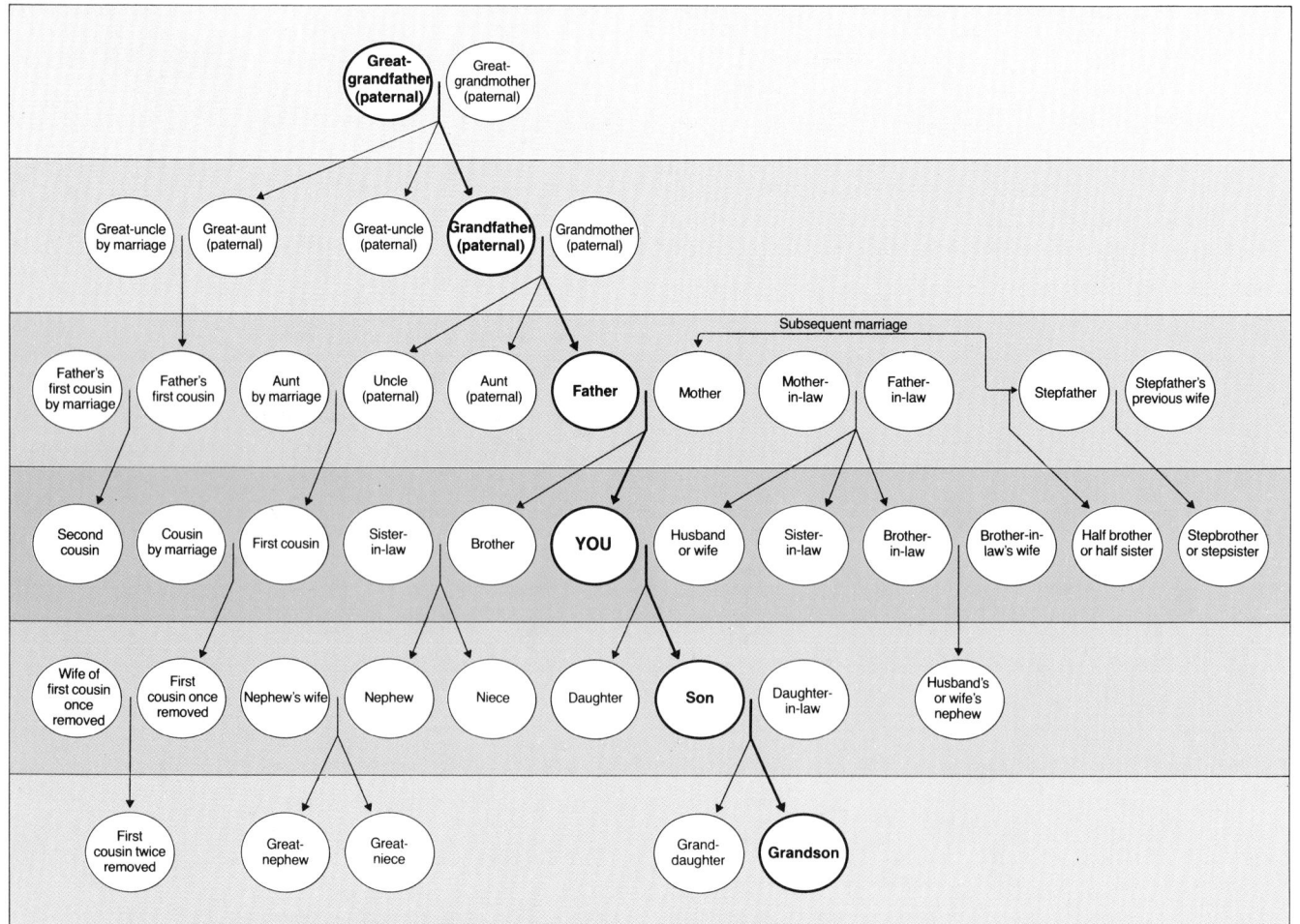

HOW YOU ARE RELATED TO THE REST OF YOUR FAMILY *In large families, relationships can become complicated—particularly if some members have remarried and had a second family of children. This chart gives the terms used to refer to relatives. For simplicity, it follows the male side of the family only. The terms used for the female side are the same except that great-grandparents, grandparents, uncles, and aunts are referred to as ma-* *ternal rather than paternal. Terms most often confused are second cousin and first cousin once removed. Your second cousin is the child of the first cousin of one of your parents. He is the same generation as yourself. A first cousin once removed is the child of your own first cousin; he is a generation later than you. "Once removed" means removed by one generation.*

Latin *familia,* family, household, servants of a household, from *famulus*†, servant.]

family Bible *n.* A Bible with special pages to record a family's births, deaths, and marriages.

family circle *n.* A section of less expensive theater seats.

family doctor *n.* A **general practitioner** *(see).*

family man *n.* **1.** A man who is devoted to his family, especially his wife and children, and who enjoys domestic life. **2.** A man who has a wife and children.

family name *n.* **1. a.** A surname. **b.** A surname considered as standing for the whole family and its honor. **2.** A first or middle name, often a former surname, given to many members of a family.

family planning *n.* **1.** The regulation of the number of children conceived and the intervals between them by some means of contraception. **2.** Contraception.

family tree *n.* **1.** A genealogical diagram of a family. **2.** The ancestors and descendants collectively of a family.

fam•ine (făm′ĭn) *n.* **1.** A drastic and wide-reaching shortage of food. **2.** A drastic shortage of anything; a dearth. **3.** *Archaic.* Severe hunger; starvation. **4.** Extreme appetite, as of a starving person. [Middle English *famine,* from Old French, from Vulgar Latin *famina* (unattested), from Latin *fames*†, hunger.]

fam•ish (făm′ĭsh) *v.* **-ished, -ishing, -ishes.** *Archaic.* —*tr.* **1.** To cause to endure severe hunger; starve. **2.** To cause to die from hunger; starve to death. —*intr.* **1.** To endure severe hunger; starve. **2.** To die from hunger; starve to death. [Middle English *famishen,* extended form of *famen,* from Old French *afamer,* from Vulgar Latin *affamāre* (unattested) : Latin *ad-,* toward + *fames*†, hunger.] **—fam•ish•ment** *n.*

fam•ished (făm′ĭsht) *adj.* Extremely hungry; starving.

fa•mous (fā′məs) *adj.* **1.** Generally recorded in history or currently renowned; publicly acclaimed; celebrated. **2.** *Informal.* First-rate; excellent. **3.** *Archaic.* Infamous; notorious. [Middle English, from Old French *fameus,* from Latin *famōsus,* from *fāma,* FAME.] **—fa•mous•ly** *adv.* **—fa•mous•ness** *n.*

fam•u•lus (făm′yə-ləs) *n., pl.* **-li** (-lī′). An attendant or servant, especially of a medieval magician or scholar. [German *Famulus,* from Latin *famulus*†, servant.]

fan¹ (făn) *n.* **1.** A hand-waved implement for creating a current of air or a breeze; especially, one in the form of a flat, fixed or collapsible device, usually round or approximately semicircular, and made of a light material such as silk, paper, or fine ivory. **2.** Anything resembling a fan, especially in being shaped like a semicircle or segment of a circle, such as an arrangement of seats in an auditorium. **3.** Any device for creating air movement, such as: **a.** An array of thin, rigid blades attached to a central hub. **b.** A machine that rotates one or more such arrays on electrically powered shafts in order to move air, as for cooling or to exhaust an enclosure. **4.** A machine that throws grain and chaff into the air so that the latter will be blown away. **5.** A small rudderlike vane that keeps the sails of a windmill at right angles to the wind.
~*v.* **fanned, fanning, fans.** —*tr.* **1.** To cause a current of or move (air) with or as if with a fan. **2.** To direct a current of air or a breeze upon, especially in order to cool: *fan one's face.* **3.** To stir up; activate: *fan resentment.* **4.** To open out (a hand of cards, for example) to a fan shape. **5. a.** To fire (an automatic gun) in a continuous sweep while keeping one's finger on the trigger. **b.** To fire (a nonautomatic gun) rapidly by chopping the hammer with the palm. **6.** To winnow; separate (grain) from chaff by air or wind. **7.** *Baseball.* To strike out (a batter). —*intr.* **1.** To spread like a fan. Used with *out.* **2.** *Baseball.* To strike out. [Middle English *fan(ne),* Old English *fann,* from Latin *vannus.*]

fan² *n. Informal.* An ardent devotee or admirer, as of a sport, athletic team, or famous person. [Short for FANATIC.]

Fan•a•ga•lo (făn′ə-gə-lō′) *n.* Also **Fan•a•ka•lo** (-kə-lō′). A pidgin language spoken in southern Africa, containing elements of Zulu, English, and Afrikaans. [From *fana ga lo,* "like this" (a common phrase in the language) : Zulu *fana,* be like + *ka,* "of" (possessive prefix) + *lo,* this.]

fa•nat•ic (fə-năt′ĭk) *n.* A person possessed by an excessive and irrational zeal, especially for a religious or political cause. Sometimes used humorously: *an opera fanatic.*
~*adj.* Variant of **fanatical.** [Latin *fānāticus,* of a temple, inspired by a god, mad, from *fānum,* temple.]
Synonyms: *enthusiast, extremist, zealot.*

fa•nat•i•cal (fə-năt′ĭ-kəl) *adj.* Also **fa•nat•ic** (-năt′ĭk). **1.** Possessed or driven by excessive or irrational zeal. **2.** Pertaining to or characteristic of a fanatic. **—fa•nat•i•cal•ly** *adv.*

fa•nat•i•cism (fə-năt′ə-sĭz′əm) *n.* Excessive, irrational zeal; extreme or unscrupulous dedication; monomania.

fan belt *n.* A belt that transfers torque from the crankshaft of an internal-combustion engine to the shaft of the cooling fan and the dynamo or alternator.

fan•cied (fan′sēd) *adj.* **1.** Produced by the fancy; imaginary; unreal. **2.** Supposed: *this fancied insult.* **3.** Expected to do well or to win.

fan•ci•er (făn′sē-ər) *n.* **1.** A person who has a special enthusiasm for something and who makes a hobby of his interest: *a fancier of antiques.* **2.** A person who breeds plants or animals: *a pigeon fancier.* **3.** A person given to reverie or whimsy; a dreamer.

fan•ci•ful (făn′sĭ-fəl) *adj.* **1.** Created in the fancy; unreal; wishful; dubious: *a fanciful story.* **2.** Showing invention or whimsy in design; imaginative; curious: *a fanciful pattern.* **3.** Indulging in imagination and fancy: *a fanciful novelist.* —See Synonyms at **fantastic.** **—fan•ci•ful•ly** *adv.* **—fan•ci•ful•ness** *n.*

fan•cy (făn′sē) *n., pl.* **-cies. 1. a.** The light invention or play of the mind through which whims, visions, fantasies, or the like are summoned up; imagination, especially in a conscious or direct sense; caprice. **b.** In the literary theory of Coleridge, an aspect of the faculty of memory that merely combines images, in contrast with true creative imagination. **2.** An associative image; fantastical invention. **3.** A notion not derived from evidence; an unfounded opinion; a delusion. **4.** A capricious idea; a whim; an impulse. **5.** *Informal.* A capricious or sudden liking; a frivolous inclination. **6.** Taste or preference; critical sensibility. **7.** The art, hobby, or profession of breeding fancy animals. —See Synonyms at **caprice.** **—the fancy. 1.** *Archaic.* **a.** The sport of boxing. **b.** The followers and patrons of this sport. **2. a.** Any sport or hobby. **b.** The followers and patrons of a sport or hobby.
~*adj.* **fancier, -ciest. 1.** Decorative and ornamental rather than plain: *fancy socks.* **2.** Fanciful; illusory or vain. **3.** Characterized by skill or some other quality that is felt to be more ostentatious than worthwhile: *fancy speeches.* Used derogatorily. **4.** Out of the ordinary; superior; fine. **5.** Excessive or exorbitant; inordinate: *a fancy bid.* **6.** Bred for unusual qualities or special points. Said of birds and other animals.
~*tr.v.* **fancied, -cying, -cies. 1.** To visualize; imagine; picture: *"And she tried to fancy what the flame of a candle looks like after the candle is blown out"* (Lewis Carroll). **2.** To suppose; surmise. **3.** To take to or like; be fond of. **4.** *Informal.* **a.** To desire; want. **b.** To desire sexually; be physically attracted to. **5.** *Informal.* To have an unduly good or inflated opinion of (oneself): *He fancies himself as a musician.* **6.** To consider (a racehorse, for example) as likely to win or be successful. **7.** To breed (pigeons or rabbits, for example) for unusual qualities or special points. —See Synonyms at **like.**
~*interj.* Used to express surprise. Often used with *that.* [Middle English *fantsy,* short for *fantasie,* fancy, FANTASY.] **—fan•ci•ly** *adv.* **—fan•ci•ness** *n.*

fancy dress *n.* Special clothes, such as a uniform or a masquerade costume, worn for a party or similar entertainment. **—fan•cy-dress** (făn′sē-drĕs′) *adj.*

fan•cy-free (făn′sē-frē′) *adj.* Carefree; without commitment or restriction; unattached.

fancy goods *pl.n.* Ornamental items; small decorative goods.

fancy man *n.* **1.** A boyfriend; a lover. **2.** A pimp. In both senses, used derogatorily.

fan•cy•work (făn′sē-wûrk′) *n.* Any decorative needlework, such as crochet, embroidery, or needlepoint.

fan•dan•gle (făn-dăng′gəl) *n.* **1.** Elaborate ornamentation. **2.** Nonsense; foolishness. [Perhaps alteration (influenced by *newfangle*) of FANDANGO.]

fan•dan•go (făn-dăng′gō) *n., pl.* **-gos. 1.** An animated Spanish or Latin-American dance in triple time. **2.** A piece of music for such a dance. [Spanish *fandango*†.]

fan•fare (făn′fâr′) *n.* **1.** A loud flourish or ceremonial sounding of trumpets or other brass instruments. **2.** *Informal.* A clamorous or spectacular public display, ceremony, or reaction; a stir. [French (imitative).]

fan•fa•ron•ade (făn′fər-ə-nād′) *n.* **1.** Any vaunting or blustering manner or behavior. **2.** A fanfare. [French *fanfaronnade,* from Spanish *fanfarronada,* from *fanfarrón* (imitative).]

fang (făng) *n.* **1.** A long, pointed tooth, especially: **a.** Any of the hollow, grooved teeth with which a venomous snake injects its venom. **b.** Any of the teeth of a carnivorous animal with which it seizes and tears its prey. **c.** Either of the sharp upper incisors of the true vampire bats. **2.** A similar structure, such as a chelicera of a venomous spider. **3. fangs.** *Informal.* The teeth. [Middle English *fang,* prey, spoils, Old English *fang,* plunder, from Germanic *fang-* (unattested), to catch.] **—fanged** *adj.*

fan heater *n.* A **convector heater** *(see)* in which a fan blowing air over heated wires causes heat to be transferred by forced convection.

fan-in (făn′ĭn′) *n. Computer Science.* The number of inputs available to a given function or logic stage.

fan•kle (făng′kəl) *tr.v.* **fan•kled, -kling, -kles.** *Scottish.* To entangle.
~*n. Scottish.* A muddle. [From *fank,* coil of rope, variant of *fang,* obsolete variant of VANG.]

fan•light (făn′līt′) *n.* **1.** *Architecture.* A half-circle window, often with sash bars arranged like the ribs of a fan. Also called "fan window." **2.** *British.* A transom.

fan mail *n.* Letters, usually of praise, to a public figure from his devotees or admirers.

fan•ny (făn′ē) *n., pl.* **-nies.** *Slang.* The buttocks. [20th century : origin obscure.]

fan•on (făn′ən) *n. Ecclesiastical.* **1.** A capelike garment formerly worn only by a pope when celebrating Solemn High Mass. **2.** Formerly, any of various embroidered cloths, such as a maniple, a piece of silk attached to a bishop's crosier, or a cover for the offerings brought by worshipers. [Middle English *fanoun,* from Old French *fanon,* from Frankish *fanon* (unattested).]

fan-out (făn′out′) *n. Computer Science.* The number of circuits fed input signals from an output terminal.

fan palm *n.* Any palm tree having leaves with a short axis and consequently fanlike. Compare **feather palm.**

fan•tail (făn′tāl′) *n.* **1.** Any of a breed of domestic pigeons having a rounded, fan-shaped tail. **2.** Any of several birds of the genus *Rhi-*

fan *This fan would have been used by a French lady of the mid-18th century. It is now in the Victoria and Albert Museum, London.*

fanlight *Named after their resemblance to fans, fanlights were often installed over doorways to improve the lighting in hallways and corridors.*

fantail *Many varieties of the fantail have been bred from the wild rock dove, mostly for show or to grace ornamental dovecotes. There are 175 species worldwide.*

fan vaulting *One of the marvels of English Perpendicular architecture, fan vaulting is so called because its intricately carved beams resemble a lady's fan. This 14th-century ceiling is in the cloister of Gloucester Cathedral, England.*

pidura, of eastern Asia and Australia, having a long, fan-shaped tail. **3.** A goldfish of a breed having a wide, fanlike double tail fin. **4.** A tail, end, or part having a fanlike shape. **5.** The stern overhang of a ship. **6.** Something shaped like a fantail, as a flat jet of flame in certain types of burners. **—fan·tailed** *adj.*

fan-tan (făn′tăn′) *n.* **1.** A Chinese betting game in which the players lay wagers on the number of beans, coins, or other counters that will remain when a hidden pile of them has been divided by four. **2.** A card game in which sevens and their equivalent are played in sequence and the first to discard all his cards is the winner. [Cantonese *fan t'an,* "repeated division" : *fan,* times, division + *t'an,* distribution, division.]

fan·ta·sia (făn-tā′zhə, -zhē-ə, făn′tə-zē′ə) *n.* **1.** An improvised musical composition structured according to the composer's fancy. **2.** A medley of familiar musical themes with variations and interludes. **3.** A poem or other work that is highly imaginative or fanciful. [Italian, fantasy, from Latin *phantasia,* FANTASY.]

fan·ta·sist (făn′tə-sĭst) *n.* Someone, especially an author or artist, who creates fantasies or fantasias.

fan·ta·size (făn′tə-sīz′) *v.* **-sized, -sizing, -sizes.** *—tr.* To portray in the mind; imagine; picture; fancy. *—intr.* To indulge in fantasies.

fan·tast (făn′tăst′) *n.* A visionary; a dreamer. [German *Fantast, Phantast,* from Medieval Latin *phantasta,* from Greek *phantastēs,* a boaster, one who is ostentatious, from *phantazein,* to make visible. See **fantasy.**]

fan·tas·tic (făn-tăs′tĭk) *adj.* Also **fan·tas·ti·cal** (-tĭ-kəl) (for senses 1, 2, 3, 4). **1.** Bizarre in form, conception, or appearance; strange; wondrous; fanciful. **2. a.** Unbelievable; preposterous. **b.** Existing in the fancy; unreal; illusory. **3.** Unrestrainedly fanciful; extravagant: *fantastic hopes.* **4.** Capricious or fitful: *in a fantastic mood.* **5.** *Informal.* **a.** Wonderful or remarkable. **b.** Very large; great.
~n. **fantastic.** *Archaic.* A person who is unrestrainedly fanciful or eccentric in behavior or appearance. [Middle English *fantastik,* from Old French *fantastique,* from Medieval Latin *fantasticus,* from Late Latin *phantasticus,* imaginary, from Greek *phantastikos,* able to produce the appearance of, from *phantazein,* to make visible. See **fantasy.**] **—fan·tas·ti·cal·i·ty** (făn-tăs′tĭ-kăl′ə-tē), **fan·tas·ti·cal·ness** *n.* **—fan·tas·ti·cal·ly** *adv.*
Synonyms: bizarre, exotic, fanciful, grotesque.

fan·ta·sy, phan·ta·sy (făn′tə-sē, -zē) *n., pl.* **-sies. 1.** The realm of vivid imagination, reverie, depiction, illusion, and the like; the natural conjurings of mental invention and association; the visionary world; make-believe. **2.** A mental image, especially a disordered and weird image; an illusion; a phantasm. **3.** A capricious or whimsical idea or notion; a conceit. **4. a.** Literary or dramatic fiction characterized by highly fanciful or supernatural elements. **b.** An example of such fiction. **5.** *Psychology.* An imagined event or condition fulfilling a wish. Also used adjectivally: *a fantasy world.* **6.** *Music.* A fantasia. **7.** A coin, such as a commemorative coin, that is not intended for use as legal tender.
~tr.v. **fantasied, -sying, -sies.** To imagine; visualize. [Middle English *fantasie,* fancy, fantasy, from Old French, from Latin *phantasia,* from Greek, appearance, perception, faculty of imagination, from *phantazein,* to make visible, from *phainein,* to show.]

Fan·tin-La·tour (fäN-täN′ lə-to͝or′), **Ignace Henri Joseph Théodore** (1836–1904). French painter noted for his meticulous still-life paintings of flowers and portrait groups.

fan·toc·ci·ni (făn′tə-chē′nē) *pl.n.* **1.** Puppets animated by moving wires; marionettes. **2.** Plays with marionettes; puppet shows. [Italian, plural of *fantoccino,* diminutive of *fantoccio,* puppet, doll, augmentative of *fante,* child, servant, short for *infante,* from Latin *infāns* (stem *infant-*), INFANT.]

fan·tod (făn′tŏd′) *n.* **1.** Irritable behavior. **2. fantods.** A state of restlessness. [19th century : origin obscure.]

fan vaulting *n. Architecture.* An intricate style of traceried vaulting, common in late English Gothic, in which ribs arch out like a fan from a single point such as a capital or corbel.

fan window *n. Architecture.* A **fanlight** *(see).*

fan worm *n.* Any bristle worm of the family Sarbellidae, living in tubes of mud on the seashore and having fans of feathery tentacles that protrude from the tube when it is covered by the tide.

fan·zine (făn-zēn′) *n.* A magazine for fans of a particular person, hobby, or interest, such as science fiction. [*fan* + maga*zine.*]

FAO Food and Agriculture Organization.

FAQ fair average quality.

far (fär) *adv.* **farther** (fär′*th*ər) or **further** (fûr′*th*ər), **farthest** (fär′*th*ĭst) or **furthest** (fûr′*th*ĭst). **1.** To, from, or at considerable distance, time, degree, or position. **2.** To or at a specific distance, time, degree, or position: *Just how far are you taking this argument?* **3.** To a considerable degree; much. Used chiefly in comparisons: *"It is a far, far better thing I do"* (Charles Dickens). **—as far as.** To the distance, extent, or degree that: *as far as I know.* **—by far.** To a considerable or evident degree. **—far and away.** By a considerable margin: *He's far and away the better skier.* **—far and wide.** All over; everywhere. **—far be it from me.** May I never; I neither hope nor dare: *Far be it from me to insult you.* **—far from.** Not at all; by no means: *Far from being annoyed about it, she was very glad.* **—far gone. 1.** In a very poor state; much deteriorated. **2.** So advanced as to be irreversible. **3.** Drunk. Used humorously. **—from far.** From a great distance. **—go far. 1.** To be successful; accomplish a great deal: *That boy will go far.* **2.** To provide for much or many; last a long time. **—so far. 1.** Up to the present moment. **2.** To a limited extent: *You can only go so far on two dollars.* **—so far as.** To the extent that: *so far as I can tell.* **—so far so good.** Used to express satisfaction with current progress while anticipating further difficulties.
~adj. **farther** or **further, farthest** or **furthest. 1.** At a considerable distance: *a far country.* **2.** More distant; opposite: *the far corner.* **3.** Extensive or lengthy: *a far trek.* **4.** Politically extreme: *the far right.* —See Synonyms at **distant.** [Middle English *fer,* Old English *feor(r),* far, distant, remote.]

far·ad (făr′əd, -ăd′) *n. Abbr.* **F** A unit of capacitance equal to the capacitance of a capacitor having a charge of 1 coulomb on each plate and a potential difference of 1 volt between the plates. [After Michael FARADAY.]

far·a·day (făr′ə-dā′) *n.* The quantity of electricity that is capable of depositing or dissolving 1 gram equivalent weight of a substance in electrolysis, approximately 9.6494×10^4 coulombs. [After Michael FARADAY.]

Far·a·day (făr′ə-dā′), **Michael** (1791–1867). British chemist and physicist, discoverer of electromagnetism. In 1831 he discovered the connection between electricity and magnetism, producing an electric current by rotating a copper disk between the poles of a magnet. He also investigated the process of electrolysis.

fa·rad·ic (fə-răd′ĭk) *adj.* Also **far·a·da·ic** (făr′ə-dā′ĭk). Of, pertaining to, or using an intermittent asymmetric alternating electric current produced by an induction coil. [After Michael FARADAY.]

far·a·di·za·tion (făr′ə-də-zā′shən) *n.* Also **far·a·dism** (făr′ə-dĭz′əm). Medical therapy by application of faradic currents to stimulate nerve and muscle activity.

far·a·dize (făr′ə-dīz′) *tr.v.* **-dized, -dizing, -dizes.** *Medicine.* To treat (an organ or part) with faradic currents.

far·an·dole (făr′ən-dōl′) *n.* **1.** A spirited circle dance of Provençal derivation. **2.** The music for this dance. [French, from Provençal *farandoulo*†.]

far·a·way (fär′ə-wā′) *adj.* **1.** Very distant; beyond immediate contact; remote: *faraway lands.* **2.** Bemused or abstracted; dreamy: *a faraway smile.* —See Synonyms at **distant.**

farce (färs) *n.* **1.** A theatrical composition in which broad improbabilities of plot and characterization are used for humorous effect. **2.** Something ludicrous; an empty show; a mockery: *"childish family portraits, with their farce of sentiment and smiling lies"* (Thackeray).
~tr.v. **farced, farcing, farces. 1.** To intersperse or fill out (one's speech or a play) with jokes or witticisms. **2.** *Obsolete.* To stuff (a bird, for example) for roasting. [Middle English *farse,* stuffing, from Old French *farce,* stuffing, farce, from *farcir,* from Latin *farcīre,* to stuff, hence to pad out with interludes.]

far·ceur (fär-sœr′) *n.* Also **farc·er** (fär′sər). **1.** An actor in a farce. **2.** A writer of farces. **3.** A comic; a joker. [French, from Old French, author or actor of farce, from *farce,* FARCE.]

far·ci (fär-sē′) *adj.* Stuffed. Said of food. [French, past participle of *farcir.*]

far·ci·cal (fär′sĭ-kəl) *adj.* **1.** Pertaining to farce. **2.** Resembling farce; ludicrous; absurd. **—far·ci·cal·i·ty** (fär′sĭ-kăl′ə-tē), **far·ci·cal·ness** *n.* **—far·ci·cal·ly** *adv.*

far·cy (fär′sē) *n. Veterinary Medicine.* Chronic cutaneous **glanders** *(see).* [Middle English *farsi(n),* from Old French *farcin,* from Late Latin *farcīmen,* farcy, from Latin, sausage, from *farcīre,* to stuff. See **farce.**]

farcy bud *n. Veterinary Medicine.* A craterlike ulcer characteristic of farcy.

fard·ed (fär′dĭd) *adj.* Painted with cosmetics. [Past participle of obsolete *fard,* from Old French *farder,* to paint (the face) with cosmetics, from Germanic.]

far·del (fär′dəl) *n. Archaic.* A pack; a load; a burden. [Middle English, from Old French, diminutive of *farde,* package, from Vulgar Latin *fardum* (unattested), from Arabic *fardah, farde,* load.]

fare (fâr) *intr.v.* **fared, faring, fares. 1.** To get along: *How did he fare with his project?* **2.** To turn out; go. Used impersonally: *How does it fare with you?* **3.** *Rare.* To be entertained with food and drink. **4.** *Archaic.* To travel; wander.
~n. **1.** A transportation charge, as for a bus or taxi. **2.** A passenger transported for a fee. **3.** Food and drink: *modest fare.* **4.** *Archaic.* The condition of things. [Middle English *faren,* to travel, go, fare, Old English *faran,* from Germanic.] **—far·er** *n.*

Far East. Also **East Asia.** The countries of China, Japan, North and South Korea, and Mongolia and, sometimes, Indochina, Malaysia, and Indonesia. **—Far-East·ern** *adj.*

fare·well (fâr-wĕl′) *interj.* May you fare well; Godspeed; good-by.
~n. **1.** An acknowledgment at parting; a good-by. **2.** A leave-taking; a departure.
~adj. (fâr′wĕl′). Pertaining to parting or leave-taking: *a farewell party.* [Middle English *fare wel!* : *fare,* go, fare, imperative of *faren,* to FARE + WELL.]

far-fetched (fär′fĕcht′) *adj.* Strained or improbable in nature or relevance: *a far-fetched alibi.*

far-flung (fär′flŭng′) *adj.* **1.** Widely distributed; wide-ranging: *far-flung reporters.* **2.** Remote; distant.

fa·ri·na (fə-rē′nə) *n.* **1.** Fine meal prepared from cereal grain and various other plant products and often used as a cooked cereal or in puddings. **2.** Starch, especially that prepared from potato flour. [Latin *farīna,* ground corn, meal, from *far,* a kind of grain.]

far·i·na·ceous (făr′ə-nā′shəs) *adj.* **1.** Made from, rich in, or consisting of starch. **2.** Having a mealy or powdery texture. **3.** Made from or with pasta. [Late Latin *farīnāceus*, mealy : Latin *farīna*, FARINA + -ACEOUS.]

far·i·nose (făr′ə-nōs′) *adj.* **1.** Similar to or yielding farina. **2.** *Biology.* Covered with short hairs resembling mealy dust or powder. [Late Latin *farīnōsus*, mealy, from Latin *farīna*, FARINA.]

far·kle·ber·ry (fär′kəl-běr′ē) *n., pl.* **-ries.** A shrub or small tree, *Vaccinium arboreum*, of the southeastern United States, having leathery leaves and hard black berries. [*Farkle-*† + BERRY.]

farm (färm) *n.* **1.** A tract of agricultural land on which livestock or crops are raised. **2.** Any land or water area devoted to the raising, breeding, or production of a specified type of animal or vegetable life: *a trout farm.* **3.** A minor-league baseball club affiliated with a major-league club for the training of recruits and the maintenance of temporarily unneeded players. **4.** A country rest home for alcoholics or psychiatric patients. **5.** *Obsolete.* **a.** The system of leasing out the rights of collecting and retaining taxes in a certain district. **b.** A district so leased.
~*v.* **farmed, farming, farms.** —*tr.* **1. a.** To cultivate or produce a crop or raise livestock on (land). **b.** To cultivate or produce (a crop). **c.** To breed (livestock). **2.** To have the right to operate or supervise and retain profits from (a business or tax district, for example). **3.** To let to a concessionaire the rights to operate or supervise and retain profits from (a business or tax district, for example). Used with *out.* **4.** To offer the services of (a worker) for a fee or rent. **5.** To send (work) from a central point to be done elsewhere. Used with *out: farm out typing.* **6.** To assign (a baseball player) to a minor-league team. Used with *out.* —*intr.* To engage in farming; be a farmer. [Middle English *ferme*, lease, rent, from Old French, from Medieval Latin *firma*, fixed payment, from Latin *firmāre*, to fortify, fix, confirm, from *firmus*, firm.]

farm·er (fär′mər) *n.* **1.** One who owns, operates, or works on a farm. **2.** *Archaic.* One who is paid for and holds a concession on the rights of collecting and retaining taxes.

Far·mer (fär′mər), **Fannie Merritt** (1857–1915). U.S. cookery expert. Prevented from attending college by a paralytic stroke, she turned to studying cooking, first at home and then at the Boston Cooking School, which she directed from 1891 until 1902, when she opened her own school. She edited the *Boston Cooking School Cook Book* (1896), which has been revised many times over the years as *The Fannie Farmer Cookbook.*

farmer's lung *n.* An occupational lung disease characterized by chronic breathlessness and caused by an allergic reaction to fungal spores in hay that has not been properly dried.

farm hand *n.* A farm laborer.

farm·house (färm′hous′) *n., pl.* **-houses** (-hou′zĭz). **1.** The farmer's dwelling on a farm. **2.** A type of large loaf of white bread.

farm·stead (färm′stěd′) *n.* **1.** A farm, including its land and buildings. **2.** That part of a farm including and surrounding the farmhouse.

farm·yard (färm′yärd′) *n.* An area surrounded by or adjacent to farm buildings.

Farne Islands (färn). Group of islets of dolerite rock in the North Sea off Northumberland. The islands are a bird sanctuary.

Far·ne·se (fär-nā′zē), **Alessandro, Duke of Parma** (1545–92). Italian general, nephew of King Philip II of Spain. He fought the Turks at the Battle of Lepanto (1571) in which the Holy League under John of Austria destroyed the Ottoman navy.

far·ne·sol (fär′nə-sôl′, -sōl′) *n.* A compound, $C_{15}H_{26}O$, extracted from the flowers and essential oils of various plants, and used in perfumery. [New Latin *farnesiana*, from *Acacia farnesiana* (a plant whose flowers yield the compound), after Odoardo *Farnese*, 17th-century Italian cardinal + -OL.]

Farns·worth (färnz′wûrth′), **Philo Taylor** (1906–71). U.S. engineer and inventor. As early as 1927 he was demonstrating his working model of a television set. His "dissector tube" separated an image into electronic particles that could be transmitted over a distance, then re-formed to produce a replica of the original.

far·o (fâr′ō) *n.* A card game in which the players lay bets on the top card of the dealer's pack. [Variant of PHARAOH; perhaps the name originally applied to the king of hearts.]

Fa·ro (fä′rōō). Atlantic port and southernmost town of Portugal, capital of the Algarve.

Faroe. See **Faeroe Islands.**

Far·o·ese, Faer·o·ese (fâr′ō-ēz′, -ēs′) *n., pl.* **Faroese** or **Faeroese.** **1.** A member of a Germanic people inhabiting the Faeroe Islands. **2.** The North Germanic language spoken by the inhabitants of the Faeroe Islands.
~*adj.* Of or pertaining to the Faeroe Islands, the Faroese people, or their language.

far-off (fär′ôf′, -ŏf′) *adj.* Remote in space or time; distant; faraway. —See Synonyms at **distant.**

fa·rouche (fə-rōōsh′) *adj.* **1.** Sullenly shy. **2.** Wild. [Old French *faroche*, from Medieval Latin *forasticus*, from Latin *foras*, out of doors.]

Fa·rouk I (fə-rōōk′) (1920–65). The last king of Egypt (1936–52). The defeat of the Egyptian army in the first Arab-Israeli war (1948–49) and Farouk's extravagant lifestyle alienated the people. In July 1952 his administration was overthrown by the Free Officers led by Gen. Muhammad Naguib and a junior officer, Gamal Abdul Nasser. Farouk was forced to abdicate.

far-out (fär′out′) *adj. Slang.* **1.** Extremely unconventional. **2.** Excellent; marvelous.

far point *n.* The farthest point at which an object can be seen distinctly by the eye at rest.

far·ra·go (fə-rā′gō, -rä′gō) *n., pl.* **-gos.** A medley; a conglomeration; a mixture: *"This is a farrago of absurdity"* (Virginia Woolf). [Latin *farrāgo*, mixed fodder for cattle, from *far* (stem *farr-*), a grain.] —**far·rag·i·nous** (fə-răj′ə-nəs) *adj.*

Far·ra·gut (făr′ə-gət), **David Glasgow** (1801–70). U.S. naval officer. During the Civil War, he commanded Union ships on daring, pivotal missions, including the capture of New Orleans (1862) and the taking of Mobile Bay (1864), during which he uttered his famous rallying cry, "Damn the torpedoes—full speed ahead!"

far-reach·ing (fär′rē′chĭng) *adj.* Having a wide range, influence, or effect; extending far.

Far·rell (făr′əl), **Eileen** (1920–). U.S. soprano. Gifted with a voice of enormous power and clarity of tone, she began her career in radio and debuted in New York at Carnegie Hall (1950). Her first appearance with the Metropolitan Opera was in 1960.

Farrell, James Thomas (1904–79). U.S. novelist. His naturalistic works often decried the economic and social conditions that produced emotional and material poverty. He is best known for his trilogy (1932–35) about Studs Lonigan, a poor Irish Catholic from the South Side of Chicago.

far·ri·er (făr′ē-ər) *n. Chiefly British.* One who shoes horses or treats them medically. [Old French *ferrier*, blacksmith, from Latin *ferrārius*, from *ferrum*, iron.]

far·row¹ (făr′ō) *n.* **1.** A litter of pigs. **2.** The act of giving birth to a litter of pigs.
~*v.* **farrowed, -rowing, -rows.** —*tr.* To give birth to (a litter of pigs). —*intr.* To produce a farrow. [Perhaps Middle English *faren* (plural), Old English *fearh*, little pig.]

farrow² *adj.* Not pregnant; barren. Said of a cow. [Middle English (Scottish dialect) *fer(r)ow*, from Middle Dutch *verwe-* (unattested), cow past the age of bearing.]

far-see·ing (fär′sē′ĭng) *adj.* **1.** Prudent; foresighted. **2.** Able to see far; keen-sighted.

far-sight·ed (fär′sī′tĭd) *adj.* **1. a.** Able to see objects better from a distance than from short range. **b.** Hyperopic. See **hyperopia.** **2.** Planning prudently for the future; foresighted. —**far-sight·ed·ly** *adv.* —**far-sight·ed·ness** *n.*

far·ther (fär′thər) *adv.* **1.** To or at a more distant or more remote point in space or time. **2.** In addition.
~*adj.* **1.** Remoter; more distant. **2.** Additional. [Middle English *ferther*, variant of *further*, FURTHER.]

> *Usage:* According to many traditional grammarians, the etymological distinction between *farther* ("more far") and *further* ("more to the fore") should be preserved. In that case *farther* should be used only for physical distance, as in *They went farther down the road. Further* should be used in most other senses, especially when referring to degree, quantity, or time: *further in debt; further steps must be taken; a further reason.* In some cases either word is acceptable; one may say either *further from the truth* or *farther from the truth.* It should be noted that writers since Shakespeare have often ignored the distinction between the two words.

far·ther·most (fär′thər-mōst′) *adj.* Farthest.

far·thest (fär′thĭst) *adj.* Most remote or distant.
~*adv.* To or at the most distant or remote point in space or time. —See Usage note at **farther.** [Middle English *ferthest*, from *ferther*, FARTHER.]

far·thing (fär′thĭng) *n. Abbr.* **f. 1.** A former British bronze coin worth one quarter of an old penny. It was abolished as legal tender in 1961. **2.** The sum of one quarter of an old penny. **3.** Something of little value. [Middle English *ferthing*, Old English *fēorthing* : *fēortha*, FOURTH + -ING.]

far·thin·gale (fär′thĭng-gāl′) *n.* **1.** A hoop or series of hoops extending horizontally from the waist, worn beneath a woman's skirts in the 16th and 17th centuries. **2.** The skirt worn over this device. [Variant of Old French *verdugale, vertugalle*, from Spanish *verdugado*, from *verdugo*, rod, stick, shoot of a tree, from *verde*, green, from Latin *virdis*, from *virēre*, to be green.]

farthingale chair *n.* A type of chair, used in the 16th and 17th centuries in England, having no arms, a straight, low back, and a high seat.

Fas. See **Fès.**

f.a.s., F.A.S. free alongside ship.

fasc. fascicle.

fas·ces (făs′ēz′) *pl.n.* **1.** A bundle of rods bound together around an ax with the blade projecting, carried before magistrates of ancient Rome as an emblem of authority. **2.** This emblem used as a symbol of the Fascists in modern Italy. [Latin, plural of *fascis*, bundle.]

fas·ci·a (făsh′ē-ə, fā′shē-ə; fā′shə *for sense 5*) *n., pl.* **-ciae** (făsh′ē-ē′, fā′shē-ē′). Also **fa·ci·a** (for sense 4). **1.** *Anatomy.* A sheet of fibrous tissue beneath the surface of the skin, enveloping the body, enclosing muscles or muscular groups, and separating muscular layers. **2.** A broad and distinct band of color, especially that on an insect or plant. **3.** *Architecture.* A flat horizontal band or member between moldings; especially, such a member in a classical entablature. **4.** The board above a shop or other business on which the name or nature of the business is displayed. **5.** *Chiefly British.* A dashboard, as of an automobile. [New Latin, from Latin, band, bandage, fillet.] —**fas·ci·al** *adj.*

fas·ci·ate (făsh′ē-āt′) *adj.* Also **fas·ci·at·ed** (-ā′tĭd). **1.** *Botany.* Abnormally flattened or compressed, as certain stems are. **2.** *Zoology.*

Marked by broad bands of color, as certain insects. [New Latin *fasciatus* : FASCI(A) + -ATE.]

fas·ci·a·tion (făsh'ē-ā'shən) *n.* **1.** The act of binding up or fastening, as with bandages or bands. **2.** The manner in which something is bound up or fastened. **3.** *Botany.* An abnormal flattening or compression of stems or leaf stalks.

fas·ci·cle (făs'ĭ-kəl) *n.* Also **fas·ci·cule** (-kyo͞ol') (for sense 2). *Abbr.* **fasc. 1.** A small bundle. **2.** One of the separately published parts or installments of a book. **3.** *Botany.* A bundlelike cluster, especially of leaves, branches, roots, or fibers. **4.** *Anatomy.* A fasciculus. [Latin *fasciculus,* diminutive of *fascis,* a bundle.] **—fas·ci·cled** *adj.*

fas·cic·u·late (fə-sĭk'yə-lĭt, -lāt') *adj.* Also **fas·cic·u·lar** (-lər), **fas·cic·u·lat·ed** (-lā'tĭd). Of, pertaining to, or resembling a fascicle. **—fas·cic·u·late·ly** *adv.* **—fas·cic·u·la·tion** (fə-sĭk'yə-lā'shən) *n.*

fas·cic·u·lus (fə-sĭk'yə-ləs) *n., pl.* **-li** (-lī'). A bundle of anatomical fibers; especially, a bundle of nerve fibers having common functions and connections. [New Latin, from Latin, FASCICLE.]

fas·ci·nate (făs'ə-nāt') *tr.v.* **-nated, -nating, -nates. 1.** To be an object of intense interest to; attract irresistibly. **2.** To hold motionless; spellbind or mesmerize. **3.** *Obsolete.* To bewitch; cast under a spell. [Latin *fascināre,* to enchant, bewitch, from *fascinus,* a bewitching amulet in the shape of a phallus.]

fas·ci·nat·ing (făs'ə-nā'tĭng) *adj.* Arousing unflagging interest, as by charm or beauty; captivating. **—fas·ci·nat·ing·ly** *adv.*

fas·ci·na·tion (făs'ə-nā'shən) *n.* **1.** The power of fascinating. **2.** The condition of being fascinated. **3.** A fascinating quality.

fas·ci·na·tor (făs'ə-nā'tər) *n.* **1.** One that fascinates. **2.** A woman's head scarf made of net or lace.

fas·cine (fă-sēn', fə-) *n.* A bundle of sticks bound together and used for various engineering purposes, especially the construction of fortresses, earthworks, or reinforced trenches. [French, from Latin *fascīna,* from *fascis,* bundle.]

fas·ci·o·li·a·sis (fə-sē'ə-lī'ə-sĭs, fə-sī'-) *n.* Infestation with parasitic flukes of the family Fasciolidae; especially, infestation of the liver and bile ducts with the liver fluke *Fasciola hepatica.* [New Latin *Fasciolidae* (family name), from Latin *fasciola,* augmentative of *fascia,* band, fillet (see **fascia**) + -IASIS.]

fas·cism (făsh'ĭz'əm) *n.* **1.** A philosophy or system of government that advocates or exercises a dictatorship of the extreme right, typically through the merging of state and business leadership, together with an ideology of belligerent nationalism. **2. Fascism.** The governmental system of Italy under Benito Mussolini from 1922 to 1943. [Italian *fascismo,* from *fascio,* bundle, group, assemblage, from Latin *fascis,* bundle.]

fas·cist (făsh'ĭst) *n.* **1.** A person who advocates or practices fascism. **2.** *Often* **Fascist.** A person who belongs to a party or organization that promotes fascism. **3.** *Informal.* Any right-wing or authoritarian person. [Italian *fascista,* from *fascio,* bundle, group. See **fascism.**] **—fas·cist, fa·scis·tic** (fə-shĭs'tĭk) *adj.*

Fa·scis·ti (fə-shĭs'tē; *Italian* fä-shē'stē) *pl.n.* The members of the Italian political organization led by Benito Mussolini. [Italian, plural of *fascista,* FASCIST.]

fash (făsh) *n. Scottish.* Trouble; worry; inconvenience.
~*tr.v.* **fashed, fashing, fashes.** *Scottish.* To trouble; annoy. [Obsolete French *fascher,* to annoy, from Vulgar Latin *fastidicare* (unattested), from Latin *fastidium,* aversion, disdain, from *fastus,* disdain.]

fash·ion (făsh'ən) *n.* **1.** The current style or custom, as in dress or behavior; the mode for the present: *out of fashion.* **2.** Something that is in the current mode. **3.** Fashionable or style-conscious people in general; the social elite. **4.** The way in which something is formed; a configuration; an aspect: *"as he prayed, the fashion of his countenance was altered"* (Luke 9:29). **5.** A kind or variety; a sort. **6.** A manner of performing; a way: *Do it in this fashion.* —See Synonyms at **habit. —after** (or **in**) **a fashion.** In some way or other; to some extent: *She sings after a fashion.*
~*tr.v.* **fashioned, -ioning, -ions. 1. a.** To make into a particular shape or form: *"And wilt thou have me fashion into speech/The love I bear thee"* (Elizabeth Barrett Browning). **b.** To train or influence into a particular state or character. **2.** To make suitable; adapt, as to a purpose or occasion. **3.** *Obsolete.* To contrive. [Middle English *facioun,* from Old French *facon,* from Latin *factiō* (stem *factiōn-*), "a making," from *factus,* past participle of *facere,* to make, do.]
Synonyms: *mode, style, vogue.*

fash·ion·a·ble (făsh'ə-nə-bəl) *adj.* **1.** Conforming to the current style; in fashion. **2.** Frequented by or associated with persons of fashion. **—fash·ion·a·ble·ness** *n.* **—fash·ion·a·bly** *adv.*

fash·ion·mon·ger (făsh'ən-mŭng'gər, -mŏng'gər) *n.* A person much concerned with following, setting, or spreading fashions.

fashion plate *n.* **1.** An illustration of current styles in dress. **2.** A person who consistently wears the latest fashions.

Fass·bin·der (fäs'bĭn'dər), **Rainer Werner** (1946–82). German film director. His films, both realistic and despairing, include *Fear Eats the Soul* (1974), *Fox* (1975), *Despair* (1978), and *Lola* (1982).

fast[1] (făst, fäst) *adj.* **faster, fastest. 1.** Acting, moving, or capable of moving quickly; swift; rapid. **2.** Accomplished in relatively little time: *a fast visit.* **3.** Indicating a time somewhat ahead of the actual time: *My wrist watch is fast.* **4. a.** Adapted to or suitable for rapid movement: *a fast road.* **b.** Showing rapidity of movement: *a fast game.* **5.** Disposed to flout conventional or moral standards; especially, sexually active: *a fast life.* **6.** Resistant. Often used in combination: *acid-fast.* **7.** Firmly fixed or fastened; not readily moved, removed, or loosened. **8.** Fixed firmly in place; secure: *"O that I past changing were/Fast in thy paradise"* (George Herbert). **9.** Loyal; constant; firm. **10.** Permanent; resisting fading: *fast dyes.* **11.** Deep; sound: *a fast sleep.* **12.** *Photography.* **a.** Compatible with a high shutter speed: *a fast lens.* **b.** Designed for short exposure; highly sensitive: *fast film.*
~*adv.* **1.** Firmly; securely; tightly. **2.** Deeply; soundly: *fast asleep.* **3.** Quickly; rapidly. **4.** In a dissipated, immoderate way: *living fast.* **5.** *Archaic.* Close by; near. **—play fast and loose.** To behave without integrity or consideration. [Middle English *fast,* Old English *fæst,* from Germanic.]
Synonyms: *accelerated, expeditious, fleet, hasty, quick, rapid, speedy, swift.*

fast[2] *intr.v.* **fasted, fasting, fasts.** To abstain from eating all or certain foods, especially as a religious discipline or as a means of protest.
~*n.* The act or a period of fasting. [Middle English *fasten,* Old English *fæstan,* to hold fast, to observe, to abstain from food, from Germanic.]

fast·back (făst'băk', fäst'-) *n.* A car having a straight or slightly curved sloping back.

fast·ball (făst'bôl', fäst'-) *n. Baseball.* A pitch that is thrown at the pitcher's maximum speed.

fast-breed·er reactor (făst'brē'dər, fäst'-) *n.* A fast nuclear reactor that produces more fissionable material than it consumes.

fast buck *n. Informal.* Money easily made: *earn a fast buck.*

fast day *n.* A day reserved for fasting; especially, a day thus reserved by ecclesiastical authority.

fas·ten (făs'ən, fä'sən) *v.* **-tened, -tening, -tens.** —*tr.* **1.** To attach; join; connect: *fasten the button to the skirt.* **2. a.** To make fast or secure. **b.** To close, as by shutting or fixing firmly in place. **3.** To fix or direct (the gaze, attention, or the like) steadily: *"My eyes fastened themselves upon the old scarlet letter"* (Hawthorne). **4.** To place; attribute: *Don't fasten the blame on him.* —*intr.* **1.** To become attached, fixed, or joined. **2.** To take firm hold; cling fast. Usually used with *on* or *upon.* [Middle English *fastnen,* Old English *fæstnian,* to settle, establish, make fast.] **—fas·ten·er** *n.*

fas·ten·ing (făs'ə-nĭng, fä'sə-) *n.* **1.** The act or a method of making something fast. **2.** Something used to fasten, as a lock or hook.

fast-food (făst'fo͞od', fäst'-) *adj.* Specializing in foods prepared and served quickly: *a fast-food restaurant.*

fas·tid·i·ous (fă-stĭd'ē-əs, fə-) *adj.* **1.** Careful in all details; exacting; meticulous. **2.** Difficult to please; overcritical. **3.** Easily disgusted; squeamish. —See Synonyms at **meticulous.** [Middle English, disdainful, distasteful, loathsome, from Latin *fastīdiōsus,* from *fastīdium,* a loathing, from *fastus,* disdain.] **—fas·tid·i·ous·ly** *adv.* **—fas·tid·i·ous·ness** *n.*

fas·tig·i·ate (fă-stĭj'ē-ĭt, -āt', fə-) *adj.* Also **fas·tig·i·at·ed** (-ā'tĭd). **1.** Tapering to a point; forming a cone or similar shape. **2.** *Botany.* Erect and almost parallel, as certain branches are. [Medieval Latin *fastīgiātus,* high, lofty, from Latin *fastīgium,* top, summit, height.]

fas·tig·i·um (fă-stĭj'ē-əm) *n.* The period of maximum development of a disease. [New Latin, from Latin, extremity.]

fast·ness (făst'nĭs, fäst'-) *n.* **1. a.** A fortified place; a stronghold or fortress. **b.** A remote and secret place. **2.** The condition or quality of being fast, especially: **a.** Firmness; security. **b.** Rapidity; swiftness. **c.** Colorfastness.

fast neutron *n.* A neutron produced during nuclear fission that has kinetic energy in excess of 0.1 MeV, having lost little energy in collisions.

fast one *n. Slang.* A deceptive or unfair action done to gain an advantage. Used chiefly in the phrase *pull a fast one.*

fast reactor *n.* A nuclear reactor that uses little or no moderator, the fission resulting from fast neutrons.

fast talk *n. Informal.* Rapid deceptive patter, as that aimed at persuading someone to buy something not really wanted. **—fast-talk** (făst'tôk', fäst'-) *v.* **—fast-talk·er** *n.*

fat (făt) *n.* **1. a.** The glyceride ester of a **fatty acid** *(see).* **b.** Any of various soft solid or semisolid organic compounds comprising the glyceride esters of fatty acids and associated phosphatides, sterols, alcohols, hydrocarbons, ketones, and related compounds. **c.** A mixture of such compounds occurring widely in organic tissue, especially in the subcutaneous connective tissue of animals and in the seeds, nuts, and fruits of plants. **d.** Loosely, organic tissue containing such substances. **e.** A solidified animal or vegetable oil. See **oil. 2.** Plumpness; obesity. **3.** The best or most desirable part of something. **—chew the fat.** *Slang.* To have a leisurely conversation.
~*adj.* **fatter, fattest. 1.** Having much or too much fat or flesh; plump or obese. **2.** Full of fat or oil; oily; greasy. **3.** Abounding in desirable elements: *Fat pine yields much resin.* **4.** Fertile or productive; rich: *"It was a fine, green, fat landscape"* (R.L. Stevenson). **5.** Having an abundance or amplitude; well-stocked: *a fat larder.* **6.** Yielding profit or plenty; lucrative: *a fat promotion.* **7.** Thick; broad; large: *a fat plank.* **8.** *Slang.* Small; meager: *a fat chance.*
~*v.* **fatted, fatting, fats.** —*tr.* To make fat. —*intr.* To become fat. [Middle English, Old English *fǣtt,* from Germanic.] **—fat·ly** *adv.* **—fat·ness** *n.*
Synonyms: *chubby, corpulent, fleshy, obese, plump, portly, pudgy, rotund, stout.*

Fa·tah (fä-tä') *n.* Also **Al Fa·tah** (äl' fä-tä') A Palestinian nationalist organization, founded in 1956, the largest grouping in the PLO. [Arabic, "opening."]

fa·tal (fāt'l) *adj.* **1.** Causing or capable of causing death; mortal. **2.** Causing ruin or destruction; disastrous: *"Such doctrines, if true,*

PRONUNCIATION KEY

ă, pat; ā, pay; âr, care;
ä, father, are; b, bib;
ch, church; d, deed; ĕ, pet;
ē, be; f, fife; g, gag; h, hat;
hw, which; ĭ, pit; ī, pie;
îr, pier; j, judge; k, kick;
l, lid, needle; m, mum;
n, no, sudden; ng, thing;
ŏ, pot; ō, toe; ô, paw, for;
oi, noise; ou, out; o͝o, book;
o͞o, boot; p, pop; r, roar;
s, sauce; sh, ship, dish;
t, tight; th, thin, path;
th, this, bathe; ŭ, cut; ûr, fur;
v, valve; w, with; y, yes;
z, zebra, size; zh, vision;
ə, about, item, edible, gallop, circus, peaceful

IN FOREIGN WORDS:

à, *Fr.* ami; œ, *Fr.* feu, *Ger.* schön; ü, *Fr.* tu, *Ger.* über; KH, *Ger.* ich, *Scot.* loch; N, *Fr.* bon; y', *Fr.* Compiègne

STRESS MARKS:

Primary stress: '
in·cite' (ĭn-sīt')
Secondary stress: '
in'sight' (ĭn'sīt')

would be absolutely fatal to my theory" (Charles Darwin). **3.** Of decisive importance; fateful. **4.** Controlling destiny. **5.** *Obsolete.* Destined; inevitable. [Middle English, fated, fatal, from Old French, from Latin *fātālis,* from *fātum,* FATE.]
Synonyms: deadly, lethal, mortal.
fa·tal·ism (fāt′l-ĭz′əm) *n.* **1.** The doctrine that all events are predetermined by fate and therefore unalterable by man. **2.** The acceptance of this doctrine; submission to fate. —**fa·tal·ist** *n.* —**fa·tal·is·tic** (fāt′l-ĭs′tĭk) *adj.* —**fa·tal·is·ti·cal·ly** *adv.*
fa·tal·i·ty (fā-tăl′ə-tē, fə-) *n., pl.* **-ties. 1. a.** A death that results from an unexpected occurrence: *fatalities from road accidents.* **b.** One who is killed as a result of such an occurrence. **c.** An occurrence or accident that results in a death. **2.** The ability to cause death or disaster; a lethal quality. **3.** The condition or quality of being governed or determined by fate. **4.** A dictate or determination by fate. **5.** A liability to disaster: *the fatality of his decision.*
fatality rate *n.* **Death rate** *(see).*
fa·tal·ly (fāt′l-ē) *adv.* **1.** So as to cause death, ruin, or disaster; mortally. **2.** According to the decree of fate; inevitably.
Fatal Sisters *pl.n.* The Fates. Preceded by *the.*
fa·ta mor·ga·na (fä′tə môr-gä′nə) *n.* A **mirage** *(see).* [Italian, Morgan le Fay (the mirage was attributed to her witchcraft).]
fat·back (fāt′băk′) *n.* The strip of fat taken from the upper part of a side of pork and usually dried and salt-cured.
fat cat *n. Slang.* A wealthy and highly privileged person; especially, a heavy contributor to a political party.
fate (fāt) *n.* **1.** The supposed force, principle, or power that predetermines events. **2.** The inevitable event or events predestined by this force. **3.** A final result or consequence; an outcome. **4.** An unfavorable destiny; doom. [Middle English, from Old French, from Latin *fātum,* from the neuter past participle of *fārī,* to speak.]
fat·ed (fā′tĭd) *adj.* **1.** Governed by fate; predetermined: *his fated lot.* **2.** Condemned to death or destruction; doomed.
fate·ful (fāt′fəl) *adj.* **1.** Affecting one's destiny or future; crucially important: *the fateful final examination.* **2.** Controlled by or as if by fate; predetermined. **3.** Bringing death or disaster; fatal. **4.** Portentous; ominous: *a fateful sign.* —**fate·ful·ly** *adv.* —**fate·ful·ness** *n.*
Fa·teh·pur Si·kri (fä′tə-pŏŏr′ sē′krə). City in the state of Uttar Pradesh in northern India. It was the capital of the Mogul Empire, under Akbar, from its foundation in 1569 until 1584, but in the 17th century it was deserted because of an inadequate water supply. It is now carefully preserved as a virtually unaltered Mogul city.
Fates (fāts). *Greek & Roman Mythology.* The three goddesses who govern human destiny. Preceded by *the.* See **Atropos, Clotho,** and **Lachesis.** Also called the "Fatal Sisters," "Moirae," "Parcae."
fath, fath. fathom.
fat·head (fāt′hĕd′) *n. Slang.* A stupid person; a dolt.
fat hen *n. Chiefly British.* A plant, **pigweed** (sense 2) *(see).*
fa·ther (fä′thər) *n.* **1.** A male parent. **2.** A male who functions in a paternal capacity with regard to another; especially, a man who adopts a child. **3.** Any male ancestor; especially, the founder of a line of descent; a forefather. **4.** A man who creates, founds, or originates something: *Chaucer is considered by many to be the father of English poetry.* **5. Father. a.** God. **b.** The first member of the Trinity. **6.** Any elderly or venerable man. Used as a title of respect. **7.** A member of the senate in ancient Rome. **8.** *Sometimes* **Father.** Any of the authoritative early writers in the Christian Church who formulated doctrines and codified religious observances. **9.** *Often* **Father.** *Abbr.* **Fr.** A priest or other clergyman or dignitary in the Roman Catholic or Anglican churches. Often used as a title of respect with or without the clergyman's name. **10.** *British.* The member holding the longest tenure in a profession, society, or similar organization. **11.** A leader of a council, branch of a union, or similar organization: *the city fathers; father of the chapel.*
~*tr.v.* **fathered, -thering, -thers. 1.** To beget. **2.** To act or serve as a father to. **3.** To create, found, or originate. **4.** To acknowledge as one's work; accept responsibility for. **5. a.** To attribute the paternity, creation, or origin of. Used with *on* or *upon.* **b.** To assign falsely or unjustly; foist. Used with *on* or *upon: You father undue significance upon my words.* [Middle English *fader,* Old French *fæder,* from Germanic *fadēr* (unattested).]
Father Christmas *n. Chiefly British.* **Santa Claus** *(see).*
father confessor *n.* **1.** A priest who hears confessions. **2.** Any person in whom one confides.
father figure *n.* An older person who acts in a fatherly way or is looked up to as being stable and dependable.
fa·ther·hood (fä′thər-hŏŏd′) *n.* The condition of being a father; paternity.
fa·ther-in-law (fä′thər-ĭn-lô′) *n., pl.* **fathers-in-law.** The father of one's husband or wife.
fa·ther·land (fä′thər-lănd′) *n.* **1.** A person's native country. **2.** The land of one's forebears.
fa·ther·ly (fä′thər-lē) *adj.* **1.** Pertaining to, characteristic of, or appropriate to a father. **2.** Showing the affection of a father.
~*adv.* In a fatherly manner. —**fa·ther·li·ness** *n.*
Father's Day *n.* An annual day of honoring fathers and fatherhood, observed on the third Sunday in June.
Father Time *n.* Time personified as an old man with a long beard carrying a scythe and an hourglass.
fath·om (fāth′əm) *n., pl.* **fathoms** or **fathom.** *Abbr.* **fath, fath., fm. 1.** A unit of length equal to 6 feet (1.829 meters), and used principally in the measurement and specification of marine depths. **2.** A unit of volume equal to 6 cubic feet (0.17 cubic meters).

~*tr.v.* **fathomed, -oming, -oms. 1.** To determine the depth of; sound. **2.** To get to the bottom of; penetrate to the meaning of: *"Her simplicity fathomed what clever people falsified"* (Virginia Woolf). [Middle English *fadme,* Old English *fæthm,* a measure of length equal to two arms; akin to Old Norse *fathmr,* embrace.] —**fath·om·a·ble** *adj.*
Fa·thom·e·ter (fă-thŏm′ə-tər) *n.* A trademark for a sonic depth finder.
fath·om·less (fāth′əm-lĭs) *adj.* **1.** Too deep to be fathomed or measured; unfathomable. **2.** Too abstruse or complicated to be understood.
fa·tid·ic (fə-tĭd′ĭk) *adj.* Also **fa·tid·i·cal** (-ĭ-kəl). Pertaining to or characterized by prophecy; prophetic. [Latin *fātidicus : fātum,* FATE + *dīcere,* to say.]
fat·i·ga·ble (fāt′ĭ-gə-bəl) *adj.* Subject to weariness; easily tired. [Late Latin *fatigābilis,* from Latin *fatigāre,* to FATIGUE.]
fa·tigue (fə-tēg′) *n.* **1.** Physical or mental weariness or exhaustion resulting from exertion. **2.** Tiring effort or activity; labor. **3.** *Physiology.* The decreased capacity or complete inability of an organism, organ, or part to function normally because of excessive stimulation or prolonged exertion. **4.** Weakness in metal, wood, or other material resulting from prolonged stress. **5.** Manual or menial labor, such as barracks cleaning, assigned to soldiers, often as a punishment: *a weekend on fatigue.* Also called "fatigue duty." **6. fatigues.** Clothing designated or permitted for work and field duty.
~*v.* **fatigued, -tiguing, -tigues.** —*tr.* **1.** To tire out; exhaust. **2.** To weaken (a metal, for example) by prolonged stress. —*intr.* **1.** To be or become exhausted or tired out. **2.** To become weakened as a result of stress. Used of metals and other materials. [French, from Old French, from *fatiguer,* to fatigue, from Latin *fatigāre†.*]
fa·tigued (fə-tēgd′) *adj.* Exhausted. —See Synonyms at **tired.**
Fa·ti·ha, Fa·ti·hah (fä-tē-hä′) *n. Islam.* The first sura of the Koran, used as a prayer. [From Arabic, "opening."]
Fat·i·ma or **Fat·i·mah** (făt′ə-mə) (died A.D. 632). The daughter of the prophet Muhammad, she married Ali, one of the first to embrace Islam. She is considered by Muslims to be one of the Four Perfect Women.
Fát·i·ma (făt′ə-mə). Small hamlet in west-central Portugal and site of the national shrine for Our Lady of the Rosary of Fátima. Apparitions of the Virgin Mary were reputedly seen here in 1917.
Fat·i·mid[1] (făt′ə-mĭd) *n.* A member of a Muslim dynasty that ruled over parts of northern Africa and Egypt between A.D. 909 and 1171. —**Fat·i·mid, Fat·i·mite** (făt′ə-mīt′) *adj.*
Fatimid[2] *n.* A person descended from Fatima, the daughter of Muhammad. —**Fat·i·mid, Fat·i·mite** *adj.*
fat·ling (făt′lĭng) *n.* A young animal, such as a lamb or calf, fattened for slaughter.
fat mouse *n.* Any of various African mice of the genus *Steatomys,* eaten as a delicacy in Africa because of their high content of fat.
fat·so (făt′sō) *n., pl.* **-soes.** *Slang.* A fat person. [FAT + -s (plural suffix) + -o.]
fat·sol·u·ble (făt′sŏl′yə-bəl) *adj.* Soluble in fats or fat solvents, such as ether; lipid-soluble. Said of certain vitamins.
fat·stock (făt′stŏk′) *n. Used with a singular or plural verb.* Livestock that have been fattened up for market.
fat·ten (făt′n) *v.* **-tened, -tening, -tens.** —*tr.* **1.** To make plump or fat. Often used with *up.* **2.** To fertilize (land). **3.** To increase the amount or substance of; swell. —*intr.* To grow fat or fatter. —**fat·ten·er** *n.*
fat·tish (făt′ĭsh) *adj.* Somewhat fat; chubby. —**fat·tish·ness** *n.*
fat·ty (făt′ē) *adj.* **-tier, -tiest. 1. a.** Containing fat. **b.** Containing excessive amounts of fat. **2.** Characteristic of fat; especially, greasy. **3.** Derived from or chemically related to fat.
~*n., pl.* **-ties.** *Informal.* A fat person. Often used in direct address. —**fat·ti·ly** *adv.* —**fat·ti·ness** *n.*
fatty acid *n.* Any of a large group of monobasic acids having the general formula $C_nH_{2n+1}COOH$; especially, any of a commercially important subgroup obtained from animals and plants, characteristically saturated or unsaturated aliphatic compounds with an even number of carbon atoms, the most abundant of which contain 16 or 18 carbon atoms and include palmitic, stearic, and oleic acids.
fatty degeneration *n.* Deterioration in the functioning of a tissue or organ, such as the liver or heart, due to the abnormal deposition within it of large amounts of fat.
fa·tu·i·ty (fə-tōō′ə-tē, -tyōō′ə-tē) *n., pl.* **-ties. 1.** Stupidity accompanied by an air of pride or self-satisfaction. **2.** A fatuous act, remark, or sentiment. **3.** Futility; vanity. [Old French *fatuite,* from Latin *fatuitās* (stem *fatuitāt-*), from *fatuus,* FATUOUS.]
fat·u·ous (făch′ōō-əs) *adj.* **1.** Complacently or unconsciously stupid; asinine; inane. **2.** Delusive; self-deceiving: *fatuous hopes.* —See Synonyms at **foolish.** [Latin *fatuus†,* silly, fatuous, absurd.] —**fat·u·ous·ly** *adv.* —**fat·u·ous·ness** *n.*
fau·bourg (fō′bŏŏrg′, fō-bōōr′) *n.* A suburb, district, or quarter of a town, especially in a French-speaking country. [Middle English *fabour,* from Old French *faubourg,* variant (influenced by *faux,* false) of *forsbo(u)rc,* "(something) outside the city" : *fors,* outside of, from Latin *forīs,* out, outside + *borc,* fortified town, from Late Latin *burgus,* from Germanic.]
fau·cal (fô′kəl) *adj.* Also **fau·cial** (-shəl). **1.** *Anatomy.* Of or relating to the fauces. **2.** *Phonetics.* Produced in or near the fauces. Said of a sound.
fau·ces (fô′sēz′) *pl.n. Anatomy.* The space between the mouth and

pharynx bounded by the soft palate, the base of the tongue, and the palatine arches. [Latin *faucēs†,* throat.]

fau·cet (fô′sĭt) *n.* A device for drawing a flow of a liquid from a pipe, drum, or other reservoir; tap. [Middle English *faucet,* from Old French *fausset,* plug, from *fausser,* to break into, from Late Latin *falsāre,* to falsify, from Latin *falsus,* FALSE.]

faugh (fô) *interj.* Used to express contempt, disgust, or dismissal. [Imitative.]

fauld (fôld) *n.* A skirt-shaped piece of armor protecting the area between the waist and the top of the thighs. [Variant of FOLD.]

Faulk·ner (fôk′nər), **William,** originally spelled Falkner (1897–1962). U.S. novelist. Raised in Oxford, Mississippi, he drew on the history, legends, and social problems of his native South. His early work includes *Sartoris, The Sound and the Fury* (both 1929), and *As I Lay Dying* (1930). He consolidated his reputation with *Sanctuary* (1931) and *Absalom, Absalom!* (1936). In 1949 he was awarded the Nobel Prize.

fault (fôlt) *n.* **1.** Something that prevents perfection, as: **a.** A flaw, blemish, or defect. **b.** A mistake; an error. **c.** An offense, transgression, or minor vice. **2.** Responsibility for such a mistake or offense; culpability. **3.** *Geology.* A break in the continuity of a rock formation, caused by a shifting or dislodging of the earth's crust, in which adjacent surfaces are differentially displaced parallel to the plane of fracture. Also called "dislocation." **4.** *Electricity.* A defect in a circuit or wiring caused by imperfect connections, poor insulation or grounding, or shorting. **5.** *Sports.* **a.** A bad service, as in tennis. **b.** A penalty incurred in show jumping when a horse hits or refuses to jump a fence. **6.** In hunting, the loss of the scent by a dog or dogs. **7.** *Obsolete.* A lack or deficiency. —See Synonyms at **blemish.** —**at fault. 1.** Deserving of blame; guilty. **2.** Confused and puzzled. **3.** In hunting, unable to recapture the scent of the game. —**find fault.** To seek, find, and complain about faults; carp. —**to a fault.** Excessively.

~*v.* **faulted, faulting, faults.** —*tr.* **1.** To find a fault in; criticize or blame. **2.** *Geology.* To produce a fault in; fracture. —*intr.* **1.** To commit a fault or error. **2.** *Geology.* To shift so as to produce a fault. [Middle English *faute,* from Old French, from Vulgar Latin *fallita* (unattested), feminine past participle of Latin *fallere,* to fail, deceive. See **fail.**]

  Synonyms: *foible, frailty, vice, weakness.*

fault·find·er (fôlt′fīn′dər) *n.* One who seeks out faults; a chronic complainer.

fault·find·ing (fôlt′fīn′dĭng) *n.* Petty criticism; carping. —*adj.* Disposed to find trivial faults; captious.

fault·less (fôlt′lĭs) *adj.* **1.** Without fault; blameless. **2.** Without a fault; flawless. —**fault·less·ly** *adv.* —**fault·less·ness** *n.*

fault plane *n. Geology.* The plane along which the break or shear of a geologic fault occurs.

fault·y (fôl′tē) *adj.* **-ier, -iest. 1.** Containing a fault or faults; imperfect or defective. **2.** *Obsolete.* Deserving of blame; guilty. —**fault·i·ly** *adv.* —**fault·i·ness** *n.*

faun (fôn) *n. Roman Mythology.* Any of a group of rural deities represented as having the body of a man and the horns, ears, tail, and sometimes legs of a goat. [Middle English *faun,* from Latin *Faunus,* FAUNUS.]

fau·na (fô′nə) *n., pl.* **-nas** or **-nae** (-nē′). **1.** Animals collectively; especially, the animals of a particular region or time. **2.** A descriptive list of animals. [New Latin, from Latin *Fauna,* sister of FAUNUS.]

Fau·nus (fô′nəs). *Roman Mythology.* A god of nature and fertility, worshiped by shepherds and farmers, and identified with the Greek Pan. [Latin *Faunus†.*]

Fau·ré (fô-rā′), **Gabriel Urbain** (1845–1924). French composer and organist. His compositions include *Requiem* (1888), the song cycle *La Bonne Chanson* (1891–92), and the opera *Pénélope* (1913).

Faust (foust). Also **Faust·us** (fou′stəs, fô′-). A magician and alchemist, hero of several poetic and dramatic works, who sells his soul to the devil in exchange for power and knowledge. [German, after Johann *Faust,* 16th-century magician and astrologer.] —**Faust·i·an** (fou′stē-ən) *adj.*

faute de mieux (fōt′ də myœ′) *adv.* For want of anything better: *wanted to go to Europe but visited home faute de mieux.* —*adj.* Accepted or undertaken for want of anything better. [French.]

fau·teuil (fō′tĭl; *French* fō-tœ′ē) *n.* **1.** *British.* A stall in a theater. **2.** An armchair. [French, from Old French *faudestuel, faldestoel,* folding stool, from Germanic.]

fauv·ism (fō′vĭz′əm) *n. Often* **Fauvism.** An art movement originating in Paris in 1905 as a revolt against impressionism, characterized by simplified form and the use of vivid colors. Its members included Dufy, Matisse, and Rouault. [From French *fauve,* wild beast (term applied to Matisse, Vlaminck, and other members of the group because of their use of violent colors).] —**fauve** (fōv) *n. & adj.* —**fauv·ist** *n. & adj.*

faux-na·ïf (fō′nä-ēf′) *adj.* Seeming or pretending to be ingenuous and unsophisticated. —*n.* One who pretends to be ingenuous and unsophisticated. [French, "false naïve."]

faux pas (fō pä′) *n., pl.* **faux pas** (fō päz′). A social blunder; a breach of etiquette. [French, "false step."]

fa·va bean (fä′və) *n.* A **broad bean** *(see).* [Italian *fava,* from Latin *faba,* bean + BEAN.]

---

fault

THE EARTH'S FAULTY SURFACE
How rocks are distorted by underground movement

A fault is a fracture in the earth's crust where two blocks of rock are moving against each other. The fracture is caused by stresses arising from movements in the earth's crust. There are three main types of fault—normal dip-slip and reverse dip-slip (characterized by vertical movement), and strike-slip (characterized by horizontal movement).

  Movement of the two blocks of fractured rock is slow; they pass each other at about 10 millimeters (²⁄₅ inch) or less a year. But occasionally two blocks get stuck, movement ceases, and tension builds up. Eventually a sudden movement makes up for lost time. These sudden displacements along faults are the most frequent causes of earthquakes.

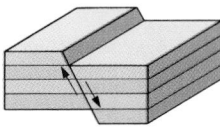

NORMAL FAULT *One side is displaced downward along a fault plane (inclined) at an angle of more than 45°, as in the Utah–Nevada region of the United States. It is also called a gravity fault.*

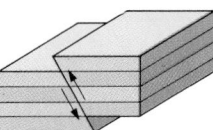

REVERSE FAULT *Produced by shortening or compression within the crust. One block is forced over another along a fault plane, as in the Highland Boundary Fault in Scotland.*

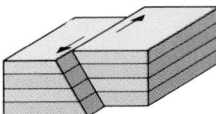

STRIKE-SLIP FAULT *The movement of rock blocks is horizontal, as in the San Andreas Fault in California.*

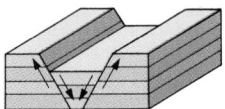

RIFT VALLEY *This occurs when the rocks between two faults drop, as in the Great Rift Valley of East Africa.*

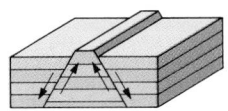

HORST *The opposite of a rift valley, a horst is created when land on either side of a central block sinks. This is how the Vosges Mountains in France were formed.*

---

fa·ve·o·late (fə-vē′ə-lāt′) *adj.* Pitted with cavities or cells; honeycombed. [New Latin *faveolus,* diminutive of Latin *favus†,* honeycomb.]

fa·vo·ni·an (fə-vō′nē-ən) *adj.* **1.** Of the west wind. **2.** Mild; benign. [Latin *Favōniānus,* from *Favōnius†,* west wind.]

fa·vor (fā′vər) *n.* Also *chiefly British* **fa·vour. 1. a.** A gracious, kind, or friendly attitude. **b.** An act that reveals such an attitude; an act of kindness: *Will you do me a favor?* **c.** *Often* **favors.** An act requiring sacrifice or special generosity. **2. a.** Friendly regard shown by a group or a superior. **b.** The state of being held in such regard. **3.** Approval or support; sanction. **4.** Partiality; favoritism. **5.** *Usually* **favors.** Sexual privileges, as granted by a woman. **6. a.** Something given as a token of love, loyalty, affection, or remembrance. **b.** A small, decorative gift given to each guest at a party or ball. **7.** Advantage; benefit: *a balance in our favor.* **8.** *Obsolete.* A communication, especially a letter. **9.** *Obsolete.* **a.** The aspect or appearance. **b.** A countenance; a visage; a face. **c.** Any part of the face; a feature. —**in favor of. 1.** In support of; approving. **2.** To the advantage of. **3.** Inscribed or made out to, as a check. **4.** Preferring: *She turned down my suggestion in favor of yours.* —*tr.v.* **favored, -voring, -vors.** Also *chiefly British* **fa·vour, -voured, -vouring, -vours. 1.** To perform a kindness for; oblige. **2.** To regard with approval; like. **3.** To be partial to; indulge a liking for: *He favors garish ties.* **4.** To be or tend to be in support of. **5.** To make easier or more possible; facilitate. **6.** To resemble in appearance: *"Annie May favors her Father and his people who were small and lightly built"* (James Agee). **7.** To treat with care; be gentle with: *The soldier favored his wounded leg.* [Middle English *favour,* from Old French, from Latin *favor,* from *favēre,* to favor, be favorable.] —**fa·vor·er** *n.* —**fa·vor·ing·ly** *adv.*

fa·vor·a·ble (fā′vər-ə-bəl, fāv′rə-) *adj.* **1.** Advantageous; helpful. **2.** Propitious; encouraging. **3.** Manifesting approval; commendatory. **4.** Embodying or conceding that which was desired or re-

quested: *a favorable reply.* **5.** Indulgent or partial. —**fa·vor·a·ble·ness** *n.* —**fa·vor·a·bly** *adv.*
   Synonyms: *auspicious, benign, conducive, propitious.*

fa·vored (fā′vərd) *adj.* **1.** Treated or thought of with kindness or liking; indulged; privileged. **2.** Having special talents, gifts, or beauty. **3.** Having a physical appearance of a specified kind. Used chiefly in the combinations *well-favored* and *ill-favored.*

fa·vor·ite (fā′vər-ĭt, fāv′rĭt) *n.* **1. a.** A person or thing liked or preferred above all others. **b.** A person especially indulged by a superior. **2.** *Sports.* A competitor regarded as most likely to win. ~*adj.* Liked or preferred above all others; regarded with special favor. [Obsolete French *favorit,* from Italian *favorito,* past participle of *favorire,* to favor, from *favore,* favor, from Latin *favor,* FAVOR.]

favorite son *n.* A man nominated as a presidential candidate, often merely as an honorary gesture, by the delegates from his own constituency at a national political convention.

fa·vor·it·ism (fā′vər-ə-tĭz′əm, fāv′rə-) *n.* **1.** A display of privileged treatment or partiality, especially when unjust, toward a favored person or group. **2.** The state of being held in special favor.

fav·rile glass (făv-rēl′) *n.* **Tiffany glass** *(see).* [Former trademark (1894) for Tiffany glass, based on *fabrile,* "of a craftsman," from Old French, from Latin *fabrīlis,* from *faber,* artificer.]

fa·vus (fā′vəs) *n.* A chronic fungous infection of the scalp and nails. [New Latin, from Latin, honeycomb. See **faveolate.**]

Fawkes (fôks), **Guy** (1570–1606). English conspirator in the Gunpowder Plot. Fawkes, a Roman Catholic, took part in a plot to blow up King James I and the English Parliament on November 5, 1605, to avenge the persecution of Roman Catholics in England. He was found in a cellar with the gunpowder, was tortured, and disclosed his accomplices. He was hanged in 1606. Guy Fawkes Day is widely celebrated each November 5 by burning effigies of Fawkes on bonfires.

fawn¹ (fôn) *intr.v.* **fawned, fawning, fawns. 1.** To attempt to please or exhibit affection, as in the manner of a dog wagging its tail and whining. Used with *on* or *upon.* **2.** To seek favor or attention by flattery and obsequious behavior. Often used with *on* or *upon.* [Middle English *faunen,* Old English *fagnian, fægnian,* to rejoice, from *fægen,* FAIN.] —**fawn·er** *n.* —**fawn·ing·ly** *adv.*

fawn² *n.* **1.** A young deer, especially one less than a year old. **2.** Light yellowish brown to light grayish brown. [Middle English *foun, fawn,* from Old French *foun, feon,* offspring of an animal, from Vulgar Latin *fētō,* from Latin *fētus,* offspring, a giving birth.] —**fawn** *adj.*

fawn lily *n.* Any of several North American plants of the genus *Erythronium,* especially *E. grandiflorum,* of western North America, having nodding yellow flowers.

fax (făks) *n.* A facsimile.

fay¹ (fā) *v.* **fayed, faying, fays.** —*tr.* To join (beams, for example) closely or tightly. —*intr.* To be fitted or joined tightly. [Middle English *feien,* Old English *fēgan.*]

fay² *n.* A fairy, sprite, or elf. ~*adj.* Pertaining to or resembling a fairy or elf. [Middle English *faie,* one possessing magical powers, from Old French *faie, fae,* from Latin *fāta,* the Fates, plural of *fātum,* FATE.]

fay³ *Obsolete.* Faith. Used in oaths: *"sirrah, by my fay, it waxes late"* (Shakespeare). [Middle English *fai, fei,* FAITH.]

fay·al·ite (fā′ə-līt′) *n.* A yellowish to black mineral, mostly Fe₂SiO₄, of the olivine group. [German *Fayalit : Fayal,* German form for *Faial* (island in the Azores where it was first found) + -ITE.]

faze (fāz) *tr.v.* **fazed, fazing, fazes.** To disrupt the composure of; bother; disconcert. [Variant of FEEZE.]

fa·zen·da (fə-zĕn′də) *n., pl.* **-das.** In Brazil, a hacienda, estate, or plantation, especially a coffee plantation. [Portuguese, from Latin *facienda,* things to be done, neuter plural gerundive of *facere,* to do.]

fb, f.b. fullback.

F.B.A. Fellow of the British Academy.

FBI, F.B.I. Federal Bureau of Investigation.

fc foot-candle.

f.c. *Printing.* follow copy.

fcap., fcp. foolscap.

FCC Federal Communications Commission.

F clef *n. Music.* A **bass clef** *(see).*

F.D. **1.** Fidei Defensor. **2.** fire department.

FDA Food and Drug Administration.

FDIC Federal Deposit Insurance Corporation.

FDR Franklin Delano Roosevelt.

Fe The symbol for the element iron [Latin *ferrum*].

fe·al·ty (fē′əl-tē) *n., pl.* **-ties. 1.** The obligation of loyalty owed by a vassal to his feudal lord. **2.** Faithfulness; allegiance. —See Synonyms at **fidelity.** [Middle English *fealtye, feute,* from Old French *fealte, feau(l)te,* from Latin *fidēlitās* (stem *fidēlitāt-*), faithfulness, from *fidēlis,* faithful, from *fidēs,* faith.]

fear (fîr) *n.* **1.** A feeling of alarm or disquiet caused by the expectation of danger, pain, disaster, or the like; terror; dread; apprehension. **2.** An instance or manifestation of such a feeling. **3.** A state or condition of alarm or dread: *The prisoners spent the night in fear.* **4.** Extreme reverence or awe, as toward a supreme power. **5.** A ground for dread or apprehension; a possibility of danger. —**for fear of.** So as to prevent or avoid: *She tiptoed for fear of waking the children.* —**for fear that.** Lest; in case: *He hurried home for fear that he might miss his guests.* —**no fear of.** No chance or possibility of: *There's no fear of that happening.* —**without fear or favor.** Impartially; without bias.

~*v.* **feared, fearing, fears.** —*tr.* **1.** To be afraid or frightened of. **2.** To be anxious or apprehensive about. **3.** To be in awe of; revere. **4. a.** To suspect: *I fear you are wrong.* **b.** To be sorry: *I fear I have some bad news for you.* —*intr.* **1.** To be afraid, frightened, or terrified. **2.** To feel anxious or apprehensive. Used with *for.* [Middle English *fer,* Old English *fǣr,* danger, sudden calamity, from Germanic.] —**fear·er** *n.*
   Synonyms: *alarm, dread, fright, panic, terror, trepidation.*

fear·ful (fîr′fəl) *adj.* **1.** Causing or capable of causing fear; frightening; terrifying. **2.** Experiencing fear; frightened. **3.** Feeling anxious or apprehensive. **4.** Feeling reverence, dread, or awe. **5.** *Informal.* Very bad; dreadful: *a fearful blunder.* —**fear·ful·ness** *n.*

fear·ful·ly (fîr′fə-lē) *adv.* **1.** In a fearful manner. **2.** *Informal.* Extremely; very: *I'm fearfully sorry.*

fear·less (fîr′lĭs) *adj.* Having no fear; unafraid; brave. —See Synonyms at **brave.** —**fear·less·ly** *adv.* —**fear·less·ness** *n.*

fear·nought, fear·naught (fîr′nôt′) *n.* **1.** A heavy, thick, often rough woolen material used in making overcoats. **2.** A garment made of this cloth.

fear·some (fîr′səm) *adj.* **1.** Causing or capable of causing fear; frightening; awesome. **2.** Afraid; frightened; fearful; timid. —**fear·some·ly** *adv.* —**fear·some·ness** *n.*

fea·sance (fē′zəns) *n. Law.* The execution of an obligation or duty. [Norman French *fesance,* from *faire,* to do, from Latin *facere.*]

fea·si·ble (fē′zə-bəl) *adj.* **1.** Capable of being accomplished or brought about; practicable; possible: *a feasible outline for the project.* **2.** Capable of being utilized or dealt with successfully; suitable. **3.** Logical; likely: *He gave a feasible excuse for his absence.* —See Synonyms at **possible.** [Middle English *faisible, fesable,* from Old French *faisible,* from *faire* (present stem *fais-*), to do, from Latin *facere.*] —**fea·si·bil·i·ty** (fē′zə-bĭl′ə-tē), **fea·si·ble·ness** *n.* —**fea·si·bly** *adv.*

feast (fēst) *n.* **1. a.** A large, elaborately prepared meal, usually for many persons and often with entertainment; a banquet. **b.** Any large, sumptuous, or delicious meal. **2.** A periodic religious festival in commemoration of an event or in honor of a god or saint. **3.** Something giving great pleasure or satisfaction: *a feast for the mind.*

~*v.* **feasted, feasting, feasts.** —*tr.* **1.** To give a feast for; entertain or feed sumptuously. **2.** To provide with pleasure; delight; gratify: *"Augustus too feasted his eyes on the same plate of fruit"* (Virginia Woolf). —*intr.* **1.** To partake of a feast. **2.** To eat with great enjoyment. Used with *on: The boys feasted on the fish they caught.* **3.** To experience something with gratification or delight. [Middle English

---

Fauvism

THE WILD BEASTS

An exuberant use of color that outraged the critics

Fauvism was a brief, vigorous reaction by French artists in the early 20th century against the conservatism of the artistic establishment. Its main proponent was Matisse, its main weapon was color. To Matisse, color transmitted intensity of feeling. The style got its name when a group of painters, which included Maurice Vlaminck and André Derain, had embraced Matisse's approach and exhibited works at the Salon d'Automne in Paris in 1905.

   One critic, seeing a Renaissance-style sculpture among them, remarked: "Donatello among the wild beasts *(les fauves)!*" The name stuck. But the group had no real coherence or direction. It broke up by 1908, having left its mark on German expressionism and cubism.

LONDON BRIDGE, *1906 Derain displays the bold slabs of strong color that typified the work of Fauvists. They aimed to portray the world with all the immediacy of primitive or untutored artists.*

feste, from Old French, from Latin *fēsta,* neuter plural (taken as feminine singular) of *fēstus,* joyous, festal.] **—feast·er** *n.*

Feast of Dedication *n.* A Jewish holiday, **Chanukah** *(see).*

Feast of Lanterns *n.* **1.** A Chinese festival, held at the first full moon of the new year, at which colored lanterns are displayed. **2.** A Japanese festival, **Bon** *(see).* **3.** A Hindu festival in October or November, lasting five days and dedicated to the goddess of wealth.

Feast of Lights *n.* A Jewish holiday, **Chanukah** *(see).*

Feast of Tabernacles *n.* A Jewish holiday, **Succoth** *(see).*

Feast of Weeks *n.* A Jewish holiday, **Shavuot** *(see).*

feat¹ (fēt) *n.* **1.** Any act or deed; especially, an act of courage. **2.** Any act or product of skill, endurance, imagination, or strength; an achievement. [Middle English *fete,* from Old French *fait, fet,* from Latin *factum,* something done, from the neuter past participle of *facere,* to do.]

feat² *adj.* **feater, featest.** *Archaic.* **1.** Adroit; dexterous; skillful. **2.** Neat; trim. [Middle English *fete,* adroit, skillful, from Old French *fait,* from Latin *factum,* deed. See **feat¹**.] **—feat·ly** *adv.*

feather *One of the jay's wing coverts: the interlocking feathers that give the bird's wings their smooth, aerodynamic surface. They cover the bases of the main flight feathers (remiges), which give the bird lift and propel it through the air. Fossil evidence suggests that birds evolved feathers millions of years before they developed flight—their original function was simply to provide warmth.*

feath·er (fĕth′ər) *n.* **1.** Any of the light, flat structures constituting the plumage of birds, consisting of numerous slender, closely arranged parallel barbs forming a vane on either side of a tapering hollow shaft. **2. feathers.** Plumage. **3. feathers.** *Informal.* Clothing; attire. **4.** A tuft or fringe of hair resembling a feather, as on the legs or tail of some dogs. **5.** Character, kind, or nature: *Birds of a feather flock together.* **6.** Something small, trivial, or inconsequential. **7. a.** A strip, wedge, or flange used as a strengthening part. **b.** A wedge or key that fits into a groove to make a joint. **8.** The vane of an arrow, made of real or imitation feathers. **9.** A feather-shaped flaw, as in a gem or precious stone. **10.** The wake made by a submarine periscope. **11.** The act of feathering the blade of an oar in rowing. **—a feather in one's cap.** A distinctive achievement; an act or deed to one's credit. **—in fine** (or **good**) **feather.** In excellent form, health, or humor. **—in full feather. 1.** Having plenty of money. **2.** Elaborately dressed or equipped.
~v. **feathered, -ering, -ers.** *—tr.* **1.** To cover, dress, or decorate with or as if with feathers. **2.** To fit (an arrow) with a feather; fletch. **3. a.** To thin, reduce, or fringe the edge of by cutting, shaving, or wearing away. **b.** To shorten and taper (hair) by cutting and thinning. **4.** To connect with a tongue-and-groove joint. **5.** To turn (an oar blade) horizontal to the surface of the water between strokes. **6.** *Aeronautics.* To alter the pitch of (a propeller) so that the blade chords are parallel with the line of flight. *—intr.* **1.** To grow feathers or become feathered. **2.** To move, spread, or grow in a manner suggestive of feathers. **3.** To feather an oar. **4.** *Aeronautics.* To feather a propeller. **5.** To quiver through the whole body. Used of a hound when hunting. **—feather one's nest.** To grow wealthy by making use of property or funds left in one's trust. [Old English *fether.*] **—feath·er·less** *adj.*

feather bed *n.* A mattress stuffed with feathers or down.

feath·er·bed (fĕth′ər-bĕd′) *v.* **-bedded, -bedding, -beds.** *—intr.* **1.** To employ more workers than are actually needed for a given purpose. **2.** To be so employed. *—tr.* To pamper or spoil.

feath·er·brain (fĕth′ər-brān′) *n. Informal.* A silly, flighty, or empty-headed person. Also called "featherhead," "featherpate." **—feath·er·brained** *adj.*

feather duster *n.* A brush consisting of a bunch of feathers fastened to the end of a stick, used for dusting delicate objects or clearing away cobwebs.

feath·ered (fĕth′ərd) *adj.* **1.** Having feathers; covered or adorned with feathers. **2.** *Aeronautics.* Having the propeller blade chords parallel to the line of flight.

feath·er·edge (fĕth′ər-ĕj′) *n.* **1.** A thin fragile edge; especially, a tapering edge of a board. **2.** A **deckle edge** *(see).* **—feath·er·edged** *adj.*

feather grass *n.* Any of various grasses of the genus *Stipa,* having clusters of featherlike spikelets.

feath·er·ing (fĕth′ər-ĭng) *n.* **1.** Plumage. **2.** The feathers fitted to an arrow. **3.** A fringe of long hair on an animal's coat, especially that on a dog's leg. **4.** *Architecture.* The cusps in Gothic tracery.

feather palm *n.* Any palm tree having pinnate leaves forming featherlike fronds. Compare **fan palm.**

feather palm *The feather palm gets its name from its feathery leaves, seen here on a group of the palms near a Tunisian oasis.*

feather star *n.* Any of numerous crinoids of the genus *Antedon* and related genera, having a free-moving, stalkless adult stage with branched, feathery arms.

feath·er·stitch (fĕth′ər-stĭch′) *n.* An embroidery stitch that produces a decorative zigzag line. **—feath·er·stitch** *v.*

feath·er-veined (fĕth′ər-vānd′) *adj.* Having veins branching from either side of a midrib. Said of leaves.

feath·er·weight (fĕth′ər-wāt′) *n.* **1.** A boxer or wrestler weighing between 119 and 126 pounds or 54 and 57 kilograms. **2.** A person or thing of little weight or size. **3.** An insignificant person or thing.
~adj. **1.** Of or pertaining to featherweights: *a featherweight match.* **2.** Unimportant; trivial; superficial.

feath·er·y (fĕth′ə-rē) *adj.* **1.** Covered with or consisting of feathers. **2.** Resembling or suggestive of a feather or feathers, as in form or lightness. **—feath·er·i·ness** *n.*

fea·ture (fē′chər) *n.* **1. features.** The make-up or appearance of the face or its parts. **2.** Any of the distinct parts of the face, such as the nose, mouth, or eyes. **3.** Any prominent or distinctive aspect, quality, or characteristic: *Indecision was a strong feature of his character.* **4. a.** The main presentation at a motion-picture theater. **b.** A full-length fictional motion picture, especially as opposed to a documentary. **5.** A prominent or extra article or story in a newspaper or periodical. **6.** Anything advertised as especially attractive or as an inducement, such as an item on sale at a discount in a department store. **7.** *Archaic.* Form; shape; appearance.
~v. **featured, -turing, -tures.** *—tr.* **1.** To give special attention to; make prominent, display, or publicize. **2.** To have or include as a prominent part or characteristic: *The film featured many well-known actors.* **3.** To draw or otherwise portray the features of. **4.** *Informal.* To picture mentally; imagine. *—intr.* **1.** To be a feature. **2.** To be a prominent or distinct part or characteristic. [Middle English *feture,* from Old French *feture, faiture,* form, from Latin *factūra,* a making, formation, from *factus,* past participle of *facere,* to do, make.]

fea·tured (fē′chərd) *adj.* **1.** Given special attention or publicity; made prominent: *a featured role in a movie.* **2.** Having a specified kind of facial features. Often used in combination: *small-featured; sharp-featured.*

fea·ture-length (fē′chər-lĕngkth′, -lĕngth′) *adj.* Of normal or full length: *a feature-length film.*

fea·ture·less (fē′chər-lĭs) *adj.* With no distinguishing characteristics; unremarkable.

Feb. February.

febri– *prefix.* Indicates fever; for example, **febrifuge.** [Latin *febris,* FEVER.]

fe·bric·i·ty (fĭ-brĭs′ə-tē) *n.* The condition of having a fever. [Medieval Latin *febricitās* (stem *febricitāt-*), from Latin *febris,* FEVER.]

feb·ri·fa·cient (fĕb′rə-fā′shənt) *n.* A substance that causes a fever.
~adj. Causing fever. [Latin *febris,* FEVER + -FACIENT.]

fe·brif·ic (fĭ-brĭf′ĭk) *adj.* **1.** Causing fever. **2.** Having a fever; feverish. [Latin *febris,* FEVER + -FIC.]

feb·ri·fuge (fĕb′rə-fyo͞oj′) *n.* Any agent that reduces a fever.
~adj. Fever-reducing. [French *fébrifuge,* from New Latin *febrifugus* : Latin *febris,* FEVER + *fugāre,* to drive away, from *fugere,* to flee.]

feb·rile (fĕb′rəl, fē′brəl; *British* fē′brīl′) *adj.* Of or pertaining to fever; feverish. [French *fébrile,* from Latin *febris,* FEVER.]

Feb·ru·ar·y (fĕb′ro͞o-ĕr′ē, fĕb′yo͞o-) *n., pl.* **-ies** or **-ys.** *Abbr.* **Feb.** The second month of the year according to the Gregorian calendar. February has 28 days, 29 in leap years. See feature at **calendar.** [Middle English *feveryer,* from Old French *feverier,* from Late Latin *febrārius,* from Latin *februārius,* from *februa,* festival of purification held on February 15, of Sabine origin.]

fe·cal, fae·cal (fē′kəl) *adj.* Of, pertaining to, or constituting feces.

fe·ces, fae·ces (fē′sēz) *pl.n.* Waste excreted from the bowels; excrement. [Middle English, from Latin, plural of *faex* (stem *faec-*), dregs.]

fe·cit (fā′kĭt, fē′sĭt) *n. Abbr.* **fec.** *Latin.* He (or she) made (or did) it. Used before or after an artist's name on a work of art.

feck·less (fĕk′lĭs) *adj.* **1.** Lacking purpose or vitality; feeble; ineffective. **2.** Careless; irresponsible. [Scottish *feck,* efficacy, short for EFFECT + -LESS.] **—feck·less·ly** *adv.* **—feck·less·ness** *n.*

fec·u·lent (fĕk′yə-lənt) *adj.* Full of foul matter, dregs, or sediment; foul; fetid. [Middle English *feculent,* from Latin *faeculentus,* from *faex* (stem *faec-*), FECES.] **—fec·u·lence** *n.*

fe·cund (fē′kənd, fĕk′ənd) *adj.* **1.** Capable of producing offspring or vegetation; fertile; productive; fruitful. **2.** Marked by intellectual productivity. [Middle English *fecound,* from Old French *fecond,* from Latin *fēcundus,* perhaps akin to *fēlix,* happy.]

fe·cun·date (fē′kən-dāt′, fĕk′ən-) *tr.v.* **-dated, -dating, -dates. 1.** To make fecund or fruitful. **2.** To impregnate; fertilize. [Latin *fēcundāre,* from *fēcundus,* FECUND.]

fe·cun·di·ty (fĭ-kŭn′də-tē) *n.* **1.** The quality or power of producing abundantly; fertility. **2.** The capacity for or power of producing young, especially in abundance; productiveness. **3.** Productive or creative power: *the fecundity of his mind.*

fed. Past tense and past participle of **feed.**

Fed (fĕd) *n. Informal.* **1.** An agent or representative of the federal government. **2.** The Federal Reserve Board.

Fed., fed. federal; federated; federation.

Fe·da·yee (fĕ-dä′yē′) *n., pl.* **-yeen** (-yēn′). An Arab commando, especially one operating against Israel. [Arabic *fedā'yūn,* commandos, from *fidā'ī,* one who sacrifices himself for his country, from *fidā',* redemption.]

fed·er·al (fĕd′ər-əl) *adj. Abbr.* **Fed., fed. 1.** Of, pertaining to, or designating a form of government in which states, provinces, or other political units recognize the sovereignty of a central authority while retaining certain residual powers of government. **2.** Of or pertaining to the central government of a federation, as distinct from the governments of its constituent political units. **3.** Of, pertaining to, or formed by a treaty or compact between constituent political units: *"Our connection had been federal only, and was now dissolved by the commencement of hostilities"* (Thomas Jefferson). **4.** *Often* **Federal. a.** Of, pertaining to, or designating the central government of the United States or Canada. **b.** Of, pertaining to, or characterizing the U.S. Federalist Party or Federalism. **c.** Of, pertaining to, or supporting the Federal government during the Civil War; pro-Union. **5. Federal.** Pertaining to or characteristic of a style of architecture, furniture, and decoration produced in the United States (1783–1815) and characterized by adaptations of classical forms often combined with typically American motifs.
~n. **1.** A supporter of federation or federal government. **2. Federal. a.** A Federalist. **b.** A supporter of the Union during the U.S. Civil War; especially, a Union soldier. [Latin *foedus* (stem *foeder-*), league, treaty, compact.] **—fed·er·al·ly** *adv.*

Federal Bureau of Investigation *n. Abbr.* **FBI, F.B.I.** An agency of the U.S. Justice Department responsible for investigating violations of federal law.

Federal Capital Territory. See **Australian Capital Territory.**

Federal Communications Commission *n. Abbr.* **FCC** A U.S. government agency responsible for the supervision and regulation of wire, radio, and television communication.

Federal Deposit Insurance Corporation *n. Abbr.* **FDIC** An independent U.S. government agency primarily responsible for insuring bank depositors against loss.

Federal District *n.* An area in certain federal countries that is reserved as the site of the national capital, such as the District of Columbia. Also called "Federal Territory."

fed·er·al·ism (fĕd′ər-ə-lĭz′əm) *n.* **1. a.** The doctrine or system of federal government. **b.** The advocacy of such a government. **2. Federalism.** The doctrine of the Federalist Party.

fed·er·al·ist (fĕd′ər-ə-lĭst) *n.* **1.** An advocate of federalism. **2. Federalist.** A member or supporter of the Federalist Party. **—fed·er·al·ist, fed·er·al·is·tic** (fĕd′ər-ə-lĭs′tĭk) *adj.*

Federalist Party *n.* Also **Federal Party.** A U.S. political party founded in 1787 that favored a strong central government.

fed·er·al·ize (fĕd′ər-ə-līz′) *tr.v.* **-ized, -izing, -izes. 1.** To unite in a federal union. **2.** To subject to the authority of a federal government; put under federal control. **—fed·er·al·i·za·tion** *n.*

Federal Republic of Germany. See **Germany, West Germany.**

Federal Reserve System *n. Abbr.* **FRS** A U.S. banking system consisting of 12 Federal Reserve banks, each serving member banks in a Federal Reserve District and supervised by the Federal Reserve Board, appointed by the President.

fed·er·ate (fĕd′ə-rāt′) *v.* **-ated, -ating, -ates.** *—tr.* To join or bring together in a league, federal union, or similar association. *—intr.* To unite in a federal union.
~adj. (fĕd′ər-ĭt). United under a central government; federated. [Latin *foederāre,* from *foedus* (stem *foeder-*), league, treaty.] **—fed·er·a·tive** (fĕd′ə-rā′tĭv, fĕd′ər-ə-) *adj.*

fed·er·a·tion (fĕd′ə-rā′shən) *n. Abbr.* **fed. 1.** The act of federating; especially, a joining together of states in a league or federal union. **2.** A league or association formed by federating, especially a political unit or country so formed, in which the central government is relatively powerful. Compare **confederation.**

fe·do·ra (fĭ-dôr′ə, -dōr′ə) *n.* A soft felt hat with a brim that can be turned up or down and a fairly low crown creased lengthwise. [From *Fédora* (1882), play by Victorien Sardou (1831–1908), French playwright.]

fed up *adj.* **1.** Out of patience; irritated: *I'm fed up with your nagging.* **2.** Bored; having had too much.

fee (fē) *n.* **1. a.** A charge fixed by an institution or by law: *tuition fees; the fee for a fishing license.* **b.** Any fixed charge. **2.** A payment for professional or special service: *a tax consultant's fee.* **3.** A tip; a gratuity. **4.** *Law.* An inherited or heritable estate in land. See **fee simple, fee tail. 5. a.** In feudal law, an estate in land granted by a lord to his vassal on condition of homage and service. In this sense, also called "feoff," "feud," "feudality," "fief." **b.** The land so held. —See Synonyms at **price. —hold in fee.** To have absolute and legal possession of.
~tr.v. **feed, feeing, fees.** To give a fee to. [Middle English *fe,* inherited estate, payment, from Old French *fe, fief,* from Frankish *fehu-ōd* (unattested), cattle, property; akin to FIEF, FEUD (estate).]

fee·ble (fē′bəl) *adj.* **-bler, -blest. 1. a.** Lacking strength; weak; especially, frail or infirm: *a feeble old woman.* **b.** Indicating weakness: *a feeble walk.* **2.** Lacking vigor or force; inadequate; ineffective: *a feeble attempt.* **3.** Barely discernible; faint; slight: *a feeble cry.* —See Synonyms at **weak.** [Middle English *feble,* from Old French *feble, fieble, fleible,* from Latin *flēbilis,* to be wept over, lamentable, from *flēre,* to weep.] **—fee·ble·ness** *n.* **—fee·bly** *adv.*

fee·ble-mind·ed (fē′bəl-mīn′dĭd) *adj.* **1.** Mentally deficient; subnormal in intelligence. **2.** Dull-witted; stupid; foolish. **3.** Irresolute; indecisive. **—fee·ble-mind·ed·ly** *adv.* **—fee·ble-mind·ed·ness** *n.*

feed (fēd) *v.* **fed** (fĕd), **feeding, feeds.** *—tr.* **1. a.** To give food to; supply with nourishment: *feed the children.* **b.** To provide as food or nourishment: *feed fish to a cat.* **2. a.** To serve as food for: *The turkey is large enough to feed a dozen.* **b.** To produce food for: *The valley feeds an entire county.* **3. a.** To supply or maintain a flow of (a material to be consumed, utilized, or worked upon): *feed ammunition to a gun crew.* **b.** To supply with fuel: *Leaking oil fed the flames.* **4. a.** To minister to; gratify: *The story fed their appetite for the morbid.* **b.** To support or promote: *feed suspicions.* **5.** *Sports.* To pass the ball or puck to (a teammate), especially in order to score. *—intr.* To eat. Used chiefly of animals. **—feed on** (or **upon**). **1.** To consume as food. **2.** To draw support or satisfaction from: *His ego feeds on flattery.*
~n. **1.** An act or instance of feeding. **2. a.** Food for animals or birds; fodder. **b.** The allowance of fodder given at one time. **3.** *Informal.* A meal. **4. a.** Material or an amount of material supplied to a machine. **b.** The act of supplying this material. **5. a.** The apparatus that supplies material to a machine. **b.** The aperture through which such material enters a machine. **—off one's feed.** *Slang.* Temporarily without appetite. [Feed, fed, fed; Middle English *feden, fed, fedde,* Old English *fēdan, fēdde, fēd,* from Germanic.]

feed back *tr.v.* To return by feedback. *—intr.v.* To return as feedback.

feed·back (fēd′băk′) *n.* **1. a.** The return of a portion of the output of any process or system to the input, especially when used to maintain the output within predetermined limits. See **positive feedback, negative feedback. b.** The portion of the output so returned. **c.** Control of a system or process by such means: *"When feedback is possible and stable, its advantage . . . is to make performance less dependent on the load"* (Norbert Wiener). **d.** The high-pitched whistle produced in a public-address system that occurs when sound from the loudspeaker is picked up by the microphone. **2.** Any information about the result of a process; a response: *The magazine likes to get feedback from its readers.*

feedback inhibition *n.* A biological control mechanism that causes excessive accumulation of the end product of a biochemical pathway to inhibit the action of an enzyme near the beginning of the pathway.

feed·bag (fēd′băg′) *n.* A bag that fits over a horse's muzzle and holds feed. Also called "nosebag."

feed·er (fē′dər) *n.* **1. a.** One that supplies food. **b.** One that is fed, especially an animal that is being fattened. **2.** One that feeds materials into a machine for further processing. **3.** Something that contributes to the operation, maintenance, or supply of something else, as: **a.** A tributary. **b.** A secondary bus, road, airway, or railroad line linking a small community with a main bus, road, airway, or railroad line. **4.** *Electricity.* Any of the medium-voltage lines used to distribute electric power from a substation to consumers or smaller substations.
~adj. Being or functioning as a feeder: *a feeder airline.*

feed·lot (fēd′lŏt′) *n.* An area where animals are fattened up for market.

feed·pipe (fēd′pīp′) *n.* A pipe through which water or some other fluid is introduced into a system, such as the pipe through which feedwater is fed into a boiler.

feed·stock (fēd′stŏk) *n.* Raw materials fed into a machine or chemical plant for processing.

feed·wa·ter (fēd′wô′tər, -wŏt′ər) *n.* The clean, air-free water that is fed into a boiler or some other equipment or system.

feel (fēl) *v.* **felt** (fĕlt), **feeling, feels.** *—tr.* **1. a.** To perceive through the sense of touch. **b.** To perceive as a localized physical sensation: *feel a sharp pain.* **c.** To perceive as a nonlocalized physical sensation: *feel the cold.* **2. a.** To touch. **b.** To examine by touching. **c.** To test carefully; explore with caution: *feel one's way in a new job.* **3. a.** To experience (an emotion): *I felt great shame.* **b.** To be aware of; sense: *She felt his annoyance.* **c.** To suffer from; experience the impact of: *feel the loss of someone.* **d.** To be emotionally convinced of: *feel it in one's bones.* **4.** To believe or consider: *His answer was felt to be evasive.* *—intr.* **1.** To experience sensations of touch. **2.** To give or produce sensation or feeling, especially through the sense of touch: *The sheets felt smooth.* **3. a.** To perceive oneself to be: *I feel so stupid.* **b.** To have or experience a specified physical or emotional sensation: *I feel tired. He felt very sad.* **4.** To search or be guided by or as if by the sense of touch: *feeling for the light switch in the dark.* **5.** To have compassion or sympathy. Used with *with* or *for*: *I feel for him in his troubles.* **6. a.** To be emotionally moved: *feel strongly about the election.* **b.** To be guided by sentiment or emotion: *"We all do no end of feeling and we mistake it for thinking"* (Mark Twain). **—feel like.** *Informal.* To be in the mood for; have a desire for. **—feel (like) oneself.** To sense oneself as being in a normal state of health or spirits: *I don't feel quite myself today.* **—feel out.** To try cautiously or indirectly to ascertain the viewpoint of (a person) or the nature of (a situation). **—feel up to.** To feel capable of or ready for.
~n. **1. a.** The sensation experienced by touching or feeling: *the feel of a rose petal.* **b.** The act or an instance of touching or feeling: *have a feel under the chair for the pen.* **2.** The sense of touch: *rough to the feel.* **3.** The nature, condition, or quality of something perceived physically or emotionally: *the feel of a sports car; get the feel of one's audience.* [Feel, felt, felt; Middle English *felen, felde, feld,* Old English *fēlan, fēlde, fēld,* from West Germanic.]

Usage: *Feel* (verb) is followed by an adjective when the sense relates to a person's perception of his condition of being: *I was sick last week but now I feel different; today I feel strong.* The adjectives *different* and *strong* describe the subject in such examples. In other senses of *feel* an adverb is possible in the position following the verb, as, for example, when *feel* means to have an opinion, conviction, or the like: *She feels strongly about equal rights for women. He used to agree with her position, but he feels differently now.* Here *strongly* and *differently* modify the verb with respect to degree and condition.

feel·er (fē′lər) *n.* **1.** One that feels. **2.** A remark, hint, question, or the like, designed to elicit the attitude or intention of others. **3.** A sensory or tactile organ, such as an antenna, tentacle, or barbel.

feel·ing (fē′lĭng) *n.* **1. a.** The sensation involving perception by touch. **b.** A sensation perceived by touch. **c.** Any physical sensation. **2.** Any affective state of consciousness, such as that resulting from emotions, sentiments, or desires: *a feeling of excitement.* **3.** An awareness; an impression: *a feeling that one is being followed.* **4. a.** An emotional state or disposition; emotion: *expressed deep feeling.* **b.** A tender emotion; love; fondness. **5. a.** Refined sensibility, often approaching sentimentality: *a man of feeling.* **b. feelings.** Emotional responses; tendency to feel wounded, moved, offended, or the like: *hurt one's feelings.* **6.** Opinion based on emotional reaction rather than on reason. **7.** An impression produced by a person, place, thing, or event. **8. a.** An appreciative regard and understanding. Used with *for*: *a feeling for propriety.* **b.** A bent; an aptitude. Used with *for*: *a feeling for carpentry.* —See Synonyms at **opinion.**
~adj. **1. a.** Having the ability to react or feel emotionally; sentient;

PRONUNCIATION KEY

ă, pat; ā, pay; âr, care;
ä, father, are; b, bib;
ch, church; d, deed; ĕ, pet;
ē, be; f, fife; g, gag; h, hat;
hw, which; ĭ, pit; ī, pie;
îr, pier; j, judge; k, kick;
l, lid, needle; m, mum;
n, no, sudden; ng, thing;
ŏ, pot; ō, toe; ô, paw, for;
oi, noise; ou, out; ŏŏ, book;
ōō, boot; p, pop; r, roar;
s, sauce; sh, ship, dish;
t, tight; th, thin, path;
th, this, bathe; ŭ, cut; ûr, fur;
v, valve; w, with; y, yes;
z, zebra, size; zh, vision;
ə, about, item, edible, gallop, circus, peaceful

IN FOREIGN WORDS:

à, *Fr.* ami; œ, *Fr.* feu, *Ger.* schön; ü, *Fr.* tu, *Ger.* über; KH, *Ger.* ich, *Scot.* loch; N, *Fr.* bon; y′, *Fr.* Compiègne

STRESS MARKS:

Primary stress: ′
in·cite′ (ĭn-sīt′)
Secondary stress: ′
in′sight′ (ĭn′sīt′)

sensitive. **b.** Easily moved emotionally. **2.** Having sensibility; sympathetic. **3.** Expressive of sensibility; indicating emotion: *a feeling glance.* **—feel·ing·ly** *adv.*

Synonyms: *emotion, passion.*

fee simple *n., pl.* **fees simple.** *Law.* An estate in land of which the inheritor has unqualified ownership and power of disposition.

feet. Plural of **foot.** **—feet of clay.** A weakness or flaw in someone who is apparently faultless. [Biblical allusion to the "great image" described in Daniel (2:31–34): "a stone . . . smote the image upon his feet that were iron and clay, and brake them to pieces."] **—find one's feet.** To become settled or accustomed, as in a new environment. **—have** (or **keep**) **both feet on the ground.** To be or remain practical and down-to-earth. **—land on one's feet.** To recover quickly from a setback or mishap. **—on one's feet. 1.** Well after an illness. **2.** Progressing or thriving. Said of a project, business, or the like. **—run** (or **rushed**) **off one's feet.** Very busy; frantic. **—stand on one's own (two) feet.** To be or become independent. **—sweep one off one's feet. 1.** To fill with enthusiasm. **2.** To cause to fall in love; enchant; enrapture. **—vote with one's feet.** To express one's disapproval of a regime, employer, policy, or the like by resigning, physically distancing oneself, or emigrating.

fee tail *n., pl.* **fees tail.** *Law.* An estate in land limited in inheritance to a specified individual, group, or class of heirs.

feeze (fēz, fāz) *n. Regional.* **1.** A heavy impact. **2.** A state of vexation.

~*tr.v.* **feezed, feezing, feezes.** *Regional.* **1.** To drive off; put to flight. **2.** To faze; disconcert. [Middle English *fese,* from *fesen,* to drive off, Old English *fēsian*†.]

Feif·fer (fī'fər), **Jules** (1927–). U.S. cartoonist. Since 1956 he has been producing his satiric strips that feature the struggles between the individual and the state, between the races, and between the sexes. He has also written plays and screenplays.

feign (fān) *v.* **feigned, feigning, feigns.** —*tr.* **1. a.** To give a false appearance of; pretend; sham: *jump into bed and feign sleep.* **b.** To represent falsely; pretend to: *feign authorship of a novel.* **2.** To invent; make up; fabricate: *feign an experience.* **3.** To imitate: *feign another's handwriting.* —*intr.* To pretend; dissemble. —See Synonyms at **pretend.** [Middle English *feinen,* from Old French *faindre, feindre* (present stem *fei(g)n-*), from Latin *fingere,* to form, shape, alter.]

feigned (fānd) *adj.* **1.** Not real; simulated: *"those who, with a feigned modesty, condemn as useless what they write"* (John Locke). **2.** Made-up; fictitious. **—feign·ed·ly** (fā'nĭd-lē) *adv.*

Fei·ning·er (fī'nĭng-ər), **Lyonel** (1871–1956). U.S. painter and illustrator. After studying in Berlin, Hamburg, and Paris, he spent many years in Europe, returning to the United States in 1937. His delicately geometric works often feature sailboats or skyscrapers.

feint[1] (fānt) *n.* **1.** A misleading movement or feigned attack designed to draw defensive action away from an intended target or objective. **2.** A pretense intended to mislead; a stratagem. —See Synonyms at **artifice.**

~*intr.v.* **feinted, feinting, feints.** To make a feint. [French *feinte,* from Old French, from the past participle of *feindre,* to FEIGN.]

feint[2] *n. Printing.* The finest line used in the printing of ruled paper. [Variant of FAINT.]

feints. Variant of **faints.**

feist (fīst) *n.* Also **fice** (fīs). *Regional.* A small dog of mixed ancestry; mongrel. [Shortening and variation of obsolete *fisting (dog),* from obsolete *fist,* to break wind, from Middle English *fisten,* Old English *fistān* (unattested).]

feis·ty (fī'stē) *adj.* **-tier, -tiest. 1.** *Regional.* Touchy; excitable; quarrelsome. **2.** Spirited, tough, or frisky. [From FEIST.]

felafel. Variant of **falafel.**

feld·spar (fĕld'spär', fĕl'-) *n.* Also **fel·spar** (fĕl'-). Any of a group of abundant rock-forming minerals occurring in most igneous and many sedimentary and metamorphic rocks and consisting of a silicate of aluminum with one or two of the following metals: potassium, sodium, calcium, and rarely barium. [Partial translation of obsolete German *Feldspath,* "field spar" : *Feld,* field + *Spath,* spar.]

feld·spath·ic (fĕld-spăth'ĭk, fĕl-) *adj.* Of, relating to, or containing feldspar. [From obsolete German *Feldspath,* feldspar: *Feld,* field (see **feldspar**) + *Spath,* spar, from Middle High German *spat.*]

fe·li·cif·ic (fē'lə-sĭf'ĭk) *adj.* Producing or bringing about happiness. [Latin *fēlīx* (stem *fēlīc-*), favorable, fertile + -FIC.]

fe·lic·i·tate (fĭ-lĭs'ə-tāt') *tr.v.* **-tated, -tating, -tates. 1.** To wish happiness to; congratulate. **2.** *Archaic.* To make happy.

~*adj. Obsolete.* Made happy. [Latin *fēlīcitāre,* to make happy, from *fēlīx* (stem *fēlīc-*), happy, FELICIFIC.] **—fe·lic·i·ta·tor** *n.*

fe·lic·i·ta·tion (fĭ-lĭs'ə-tā'shən) *n. Usually* **felicitations.** Congratulations.

fe·lic·i·tous (fĭ-lĭs'ə-təs) *adj.* **1. a.** Well-chosen; apt; appropriate: *a felicitous comparison.* **b.** Having an appropriate and agreeable manner or style: *a felicitous writer.* **2.** Marked by well-being or good fortune: *a felicitous life.* —See Synonyms at **fit.** **—fe·lic·i·tous·ly** *adv.* **—fe·lic·i·tous·ness** *n.*

fe·lic·i·ty (fĭ-lĭs'ə-tē) *n., pl.* **-ties. 1. a.** Great happiness; bliss. **b.** An instance of this. **2.** Something that causes or produces happiness. **3. a.** An appropriate and pleasing manner or style: *felicity of speech.* **b.** An instance of this. [Middle English *felicite,* from Old French, from Latin *fēlīcitās* (stem *fēlīcitāt-*), from *fēlix* (stem *fēlīc-*), happy, FELICIFIC.]

fe·lid (fē'lĭd) *n.* A feline. **—fe·lid** *adj.*

fe·line (fē'līn') *adj.* **1.** Of or belonging to the family Felidae, which includes the lions, tigers, jaguars, and wild and domestic cats. **2.** Resembling or suggestive of a cat, as in suppleness, slyness, or stealthiness.

~*n.* A feline animal. [Latin *fēlīnus,* from *fēlēs*†, cat.] **—fe·line·ly** *adv.* **—fe·line·ness, fe·lin·i·ty** (fĭ-lĭn'ə-tē) *n.*

fell[1] (fĕl) *tr.v.* **felled, felling, fells. 1.** To cause to fall; cut or knock down: *fell a tree; fell an opponent.* **2.** To sew or finish (a seam) with the raw edges flattened, turned under, and stitched down.

~*n.* **1.** The timber cut down in one season. **2.** A felled seam. [Middle English *fellen,* Old English *fellan, fyllan,* to strike down, fell.] **—fell·a·ble** *adj.*

fell[2] *adj.* **1.** Of an inhumanly cruel nature; fierce; unsparing: *fell hordes.* **2.** Able to destroy; lethal: *a fell blow.* **3.** Dire; sinister: *by some fell chance.* **4.** *Scottish.* Sharp and biting: *a fell word.* **—at one fell swoop.** All at once. [Middle English *fel,* from Old French, from Medieval Latin *fellō,* wicked person, FELON.] **—fell·ness** *n.*

fell[3] *n.* The hide of an animal; a skin; a pelt. [Middle English *fel,* Old English *fell.*]

fell[4] *n. British Regional.* **1.** An upland stretch of open country; a moor. **2.** The highest point of a fell. [Middle English, from Old Norse *fjall,* hill; probably akin to Old Saxon *felis,* rock.]

fell[5]. Past tense of **fall.**

fel·la (fĕl'ə) *n.* Also **fel·ler** (fĕl'ər). *Informal.* **1.** A man or boy. **2.** A boyfriend or lover. **3.** A husband.

fel·lah (fĕl'ə, fə-lä') *n., pl.* **fellahin** or **fellaheen** (fĕl'ə-hēn', fə-lä'hēn'). A peasant or agricultural laborer in an Arab country, as Syria. [Arabic *fellāḥ,* dialectal variant of *fallāḥ,* from *falaḥa,* to cultivate, till.]

fell·er[1] (fĕl'ər) *n.* **1.** One that fells. **2.** A sewing machine attachment for felling seams.

feller[2]. Variant of **fella.**

Fel·li·ni (fə-lē'nē), **Federico** (1920–). Italian film director. His films combine social satire with elements of fantasy. His successes include *La Dolce Vita (The Sweet Life)* (1960) and *Satyricon* (1969). *Amarcord* (1974) won an Academy Award in 1975.

fell·mon·ger (fĕl'mŭng'gər, -mŏng'gər) *n. British.* One who sells hides or prepares hides for making leather. **—fell·mon·ger·ing, fell·mon·ger·y** *n.*

fel·low (fĕl'ō) *n.* **1. a.** A man or boy. **b.** *Informal.* A boyfriend or lover. **c.** *Informal.* A husband. **2. a.** Anybody in general; any human being. **b.** A person considered to be worthless or unimportant. **3.** A companion; a comrade; an associate. **4. a.** A person similar to oneself in rank, position, or background; an equal; a peer. **b.** Either of a pair; a counterpart; a mate. **5.** *Abbr.* **F, F.** A member of a learned society or similar association. **6.** *Abbr.* **F, F.** A graduate student appointed to a position granting financial aid for a period of research. **7.** *British.* **a.** An incorporated senior member of certain colleges and universities. **b.** A member of the governing body of certain colleges and universities.

~*adj.* Being of the same kind, group, occupation, society, or locality; having in common certain characteristics or interests: *fellow workers.* [Middle English *felawe,* Old English *fēolaga,* from Old Norse *fēlagi,* partner, fellow, one who lays down money : *fē,* cattle, money + *lag,* a laying down.]

fellow creature *n.* A kindred creature; especially, another member of the human race.

fellow feeling *n.* **1.** Sympathetic awareness of others; rapport. **2.** Common interests or opinions.

fellow man *n., pl.* **fellow men.** Also **fel·low·man** (fĕl'ō-măn') *pl.* **-men** (-mĕn'). **1.** All humanity regarded as united in shared experience. **2.** Any person regarded as related to one through the general human experience.

fellow servant *n. Law.* Any of a group of employees working together under such circumstances that the employer cannot be expected to protect against or be liable for harm to one employee caused by the negligence of another.

fel·low·ship (fĕl'ō-shĭp') *n.* **1. a.** The condition of being together or of sharing similar interests or experiences, as do members of a profession, religion, or nationality; companionship. **b.** The companionship of individuals in a congenial atmosphere and on equal terms. **2. a.** A union of friends or equals sharing similar interests; a club; a brotherhood. **b.** A church association. **3. a.** Friendship; comradeship. **b.** Mutual concern and trust among Christians. **4. a.** A scholarship or grant awarded to a graduate student in a college or university. **b.** The state of having been awarded such a scholarship or grant. **c.** A foundation established for the awarding of such a scholarship or grant.

fellow traveler *n.* One who sympathizes with the tenets and program of an organized group without actually joining it; especially, a supporter of the Communist Party.

fel·ly (fĕl'ē) *n., pl.* **-lies.** Also **fel·loe** (fĕl'ō). **1.** The rim of a wheel supported by spokes. **2.** A section of such a rim. [Middle English *fely,* Old English *felg,* from West Germanic *felgam* (unattested).]

fe·lo-de-se (fĕl'ō-də-sā', -sē') *n., pl.* **fe·lo·nes-de-se** (fə-lō'nēz-) or **fe·los-de-se** (fĕl'ōz-). *Law.* **1.** The act of suicide. **2.** One who commits suicide. [Medieval Latin, "felon of himself" : *felō, fellō,* FELON + *dē,* of + *sē,* ablative of *suī,* himself, oneself, from Latin.]

fel·on[1] (fĕl'ən) *n.* **1.** *Law.* A person who has committed a felony. **2.** *Archaic.* An evil person.

~*adj. Archaic.* Evil; cruel. [Middle English *feloun,* from Old French *felon,* from Medieval Latin *fellō* (stem *fellōn-*), from Vulgar Latin *fellō*† (unattested).]

felon[2] *n.* A purulent infection at the end of a finger near or around

PRONUNCIATION KEY

ă, pat; ā, pay; âr, care;
ä, father, are; b, bib;
ch, church; d, deed; ĕ, pet;
ē, be; f, fife; g, gag; h, hat;
hw, which; ĭ, pit; ī, pie;
îr, pier; j, judge; k, kick;
l, lid, needle; m, mum;
n, no, sudden; ng, thing;
ŏ, pot; ō, toe; ô, paw, for;
oi, noise; ou, out; o͝o, book;
o͞o, boot; p, pop; r, roar;
s, sauce; sh, ship, dish;
t, tight; th, thin, path;
th, this, bathe; ŭ, cut; ûr, fur;
v, valve; w, with; y, yes;
z, zebra, size; zh, vision;
ə, about, item, edible,
gallop, circus, peaceful

IN FOREIGN WORDS:

à, *Fr.* ami; œ, *Fr.* feu, *Ger.* schön; ü, *Fr.* tu, *Ger.* über; KH, *Ger.* ich, *Scot.* loch; N, *Fr.* bon; y', *Fr.* Compiègne

STRESS MARKS:

Primary stress: '
in·cite' (ĭn-sīt')
Secondary stress: '
in'sight' (ĭn'sīt')

the nail or the bone. [Middle English *feloun,* from Old French, possibly from Latin *fel,* bile, venom.]

fe·lo·ni·ous (fə-lō′nē-əs) *adj.* **1.** *Law.* **a.** Of or pertaining to a felony. **b.** Characterized by or of the nature of a felony: *felonious intent.* **2.** *Archaic.* Evil; wicked. **—fe·lo·ni·ous·ly** *adv.* **—fe·lo·ni·ous·ness** *n.*

fel·on·ry (fĕl′ən-rē) *n.* **1.** Felons collectively. **2.** *Australian.* Formerly, the convict population of a penal settlement.

fel·o·ny (fĕl′ə-nē) *n., pl.* **-nies.** *Law.* **1.** Any of several crimes, such as murder, rape, or burglary, considered more serious than a misdemeanor and punishable by a more stringent sentence. Compare **misdemeanor. 2.** Any of several crimes in early English law that were punishable by forfeiture of land or goods and by possible loss of life or a bodily part.

fel·site (fĕl′sīt′) *n.* A fine-grained igneous rock, chiefly feldspar and quartz. [FELS(PAR) + -ITE.] **—fel·sit·ic** (fĕl-sĭt′ĭk) *adj.*

felspar. Variant of **feldspar.**

felt[1] (fĕlt) *n.* **1.** A fabric of matted, compressed animal fibers, such as wool or fur, sometimes mixed with vegetable or synthetic fibers. **2.** Any fabric or material resembling this. **3.** Something made of felt or a similar material.
~*adj.* **1.** Made of felt. **2.** Pertaining or similar to felt.
~*v.* **felted, felting, felts.** —*tr.* **1.** To make into felt. **2.** To cover with felt. —*intr.* To become like felt; mat together. [Middle English *felt,* Old English *felt,* from West Germanic.]

felt[2]**.** Past tense and past participle of **feel.**

felt·ing (fĕl′tĭng) *n.* **1.** The practice or process of making felt. **2.** The materials from which felt is made. **3.** Felted fabric.

fe·luc·ca (fə-lo͞o′kə, -lŭk′ə) *n.* A narrow, swift vessel, chiefly of the Mediterranean, propelled by lateen sails or oars or both. [Italian *feluc(c)a,* from obsolete Spanish *faluca,* from Arabic *fulk,* ship.]

fel·wort (fĕl′wûrt′, -wôrt′) *n.* Any of several plants of the genera *Gentianella* or *Swertia;* especially, *G. amarella,* having small, purplish flowers. [Middle English *feldwort,* Old English *feldwyrt* : *feld,* FIELD + *wyrt,* WORT.]

fem. **1.** female. **2.** feminine.

FEM field-emission microscope; field-emission microscopy.

fe·male (fē′māl′) *adj. Abbr.* **f, F, f., F., fem. 1.** Of, pertaining to, or designating the sex that produces ova. **2.** Characteristic of or appropriate to this sex; feminine. **3.** Consisting of members of this sex. **4.** *Botany.* **a.** Pertaining to or designating an organ, such as a pistil or ovary, that functions in producing seeds or spores after fertilization. **b.** Bearing pistils but not stamens: *female flowers.* **5.** Designating or having a part, such as a slot or receptacle, designed to receive a complementary male part, such as a plug or prongs.
~*n. Abbr.* **f, F, f., F., fem. 1.** A member of the sex that produces ova. **2.** Anything or anyone female. **3.** A woman or girl, as distinguished from a man or boy. **4.** *Botany.* A plant having only pistillate flowers. [Middle English, variant (influenced by *male*) of *femelle,* from Old French, from Latin *fēmella,* diminutive of *fēmina,* woman, female.] **—fe·male·ness** *n.*

female impersonator *n.* A male entertainer who dresses up as a woman.

feme (fĕm, fēm) *n.* **1.** *Law.* A wife. **2.** *Obsolete.* A woman. [Norman French, from Latin *fēmina,* woman, FEMALE.]

feme cov·ert (fĕm′ kŭv′ərt, fēm′) *n. Law.* A married woman.

feme sole (fĕm′ sōl′, fēm′) *n. Law.* A single woman, whether divorced, widowed, or never married.

fem·i·ne·i·ty (fĕm′ə-nē′ə-tē) *n.* Womanliness; femininity.

fem·i·nie (fĕm′ə-nē) *n. Archaic.* Women collectively; womankind. [Middle English, from Old French, from Latin *fēmina,* FEMALE.]

fem·i·nine (fĕm′ə-nĭn) *adj. Abbr.* **f., F., fem. 1.** Of or belonging to the female sex. Said especially of members of the human species. **2.** Characterized by or possessing qualities generally attributed to or considered appropriate to a woman; womanly: *"an artist of feminine and receptive temperament"* (Havelock Ellis). **3.** Effeminate; womanish. **4.** *Grammar.* Indicating or belonging to the gender that includes words and grammatical forms associated chiefly with femaleness: *the feminine pronoun "she"; a feminine noun.* Compare **masculine, neuter.**
~*n. Abbr.* **f., F., fem.** *Grammar.* **1.** The feminine gender. **2.** A word or form belonging to that gender. [Middle English, from Old French, from Latin *fēminīnus,* from *fēmina,* FEMALE.] **—fem·i·nine·ly** *adv.* **—fem·i·nine·ness** *n.*

feminine ending *n.* **1.** The termination of a line or verse in an unaccented syllable. **2.** *Grammar.* A final syllable or ending that marks or forms words in the feminine gender; for example, the ending *-ess* added to *lion* to form *lioness.*

feminine rhyme *n.* **1.** A rhyme of two syllables in which the second syllable is unstressed; for example, *follow* and *hollow; brightly* and *nightly.* **2.** A rhyme of three syllables in which only the first syllable is stressed; for example, *edible* and *incredible.* Compare **masculine rhyme.**

fem·i·nin·i·ty (fĕm′ə-nĭn′ə-tē) *n., pl.* **-ties. 1.** The quality or condition of being feminine; womanhood; womanliness. **2.** Women collectively.

fem·i·nism (fĕm′ə-nĭz′əm) *n.* **1.** A social movement that seeks to change the traditional role and image of women, to eliminate sexism, and to heighten appreciation of the experiences and qualities unique to the female sex. See **Women's Liberation Movement. 2.** The doctrine of this movement. **—fem·i·nist** *n. & adj.*

fem·i·nize (fĕm′ə-nīz′) *v.* **-nized, -nizing, -nizes.** —*tr.* To make feminine. —*intr.* To become feminine. **—fem·i·ni·za·tion** (fĕm′ə-nĭ-zā′shən) *n.*

femme (fĕm) *n.* A woman who plays the female role in a lesbian relationship.

femme fa·tale (fĕm′ fə-tăl′, -täl′, făm′) *n., pl.* **femmes fatales** (*pronounced as singular*). A woman whose sexual attractiveness leads a man into compromising or dangerous situations. [French.]

fem·o·ral (fĕm′ər-əl) *adj.* Of or pertaining to the thigh or the femur: *femoral artery.* [Latin *femur* (stem *femor-*), FEMUR.]

femto- *prefix. Symbol* **f** Indicates one quadrillionth (10^{-15}); for example, **femtometer.** [Danish or Norwegian *femten,* fifteen, from Old Norse *fimmtān.*]

fem·to·joule (fĕm′tə-jo͞ol′, -joul′) *n. Abbr.* **fJ** 10^{-15} joule.

fem·tom·e·ter (fĕm-tŏm′ə-tər) *n. Abbr.* **fm** 10^{-15} meter.

fe·mur (fē′mər) *n., pl.* **-murs** or **femora** (fĕm′ər-ə). **1. a.** The proximal bone of the lower or hind limb in vertebrates, situated between the pelvis and knee in humans. Also called "thighbone." **b.** The thigh. **2.** The usually stout third segment of an insect's leg. [Latin *femur*†, thigh.]

fen[1] (fĕn) *n.* Low, flat, swampy land; a bog; a marsh. [Middle English *fen,* Old English *fenn,* from Germanic.] **—fen·ny** *adj.*

fen[2] *n., pl.* **fen.** A coin that is equal to 1/100 of the yuan of China. Also called "jiao." See feature at **currency.** [Mandarin Chinese *fĕn,* division, part.]

fence (fĕns) *n.* **1.** A structure serving as an enclosure, barrier, or boundary, usually made of posts or stakes joined together by boards, wire, or rails. **2.** *Archaic.* Something intended as a means of defense; a protection. **3.** The art or practice of swordplay; fencing. **4. a.** One who receives and sells stolen goods. **b.** A place where such goods are received and sold. **5.** An attachment on a machine or tool that directs, regulates, and limits its action. **—on the fence.** *Informal.* Undecided as to which of two sides to support, especially in order to protect one's own interests; neutral. **—mend one's fences.** To restore good relations.
~*v.* **fenced, fencing, fences.** —*tr.* **1.** To surround or close in by means of a fence. **2.** To separate or close off by means of a fence. **3.** *Archaic.* To defend or ward off. **4.** To sell (stolen goods) to a fence. —*intr.* **1.** To practice or demonstrate the art of fencing. **2.** To engage in the art of skillful conversation or debate. **3.** To avoid giving direct answers; be evasive. **4.** To act as a fence for stolen goods. [Middle English *fens,* short for *defens,* DEFENSE.]

fenc·er (fĕn′sər) *n.* **1.** A person who fences, as with a foil; a swordsman. **2.** A person who erects or repairs fences.

fence·row (fĕns′rō′) *n.* The uncultivated land alongside a fence.

fen·ci·ble (fĕn′sə-bəl) *n.* Formerly, a soldier enlisted for home service only. [Middle English, aphetic variant of DEFENSIBLE.]

fenc·ing (fĕn′sĭng) *n.* **1.** The art, practice, or sport of using a foil, épée, or saber; swordplay. **2.** The art or practice of skillful conversation or debate; repartee. **3.** Evasiveness in answering questions or giving information. **4. a.** Material, such as wire, stakes, rails, and the like, used in the construction of fences. **b.** Fences collectively. **c.** The work, skill, or business of erecting or repairing fences.

fend (fĕnd) *v.* **fended, fending, fends.** —*tr. Archaic.* To defend. —*intr.* To resist. **—fend for oneself.** To provide for oneself; survive without help; manage alone. **—fend off.** To turn aside; deflect; parry. [Middle English *fenden,* shortening of *defenden,* to DEFEND.]

fend·er (fĕn′dər) *n.* **1.** One that fends or wards off. **2.** A shaped metal structure or a portion of the automotive body over each wheel of an automotive vehicle. **3.** A usually metal structure over the top of a bicycle or motorcycle wheel, placed so as to block thrown-up water and mud; mudguard. **4.** A device at the front end of a streetcar or locomotive designed to push aside obstructions. **5.** A metal device placed in front of a fireplace to keep hot coals and debris from falling out; a fireguard. **6.** *Nautical.* A device, such as a bundle of rope, a piece of timber, or an automobile tire, used on the side of a vessel or dock to absorb impact or friction.

fen·es·tel·la (fĕn′ə-stĕl′ə) *n., pl.* **-tellae** (-stĕl′ē). **1.** A small niche in the wall of a church containing the piscina. **2.** *Architecture.* A small window. [Latin, diminutive of *fenestra,* window.]

fe·nes·tra (fĭ-nĕs′trə) *n., pl.* **-trae** (-trē′). **1.** *Anatomy.* A small opening; especially, either of two apertures in the medial wall of the middle ear. **2.** A windowlike opening. **3.** *Biology.* A transparent spot or marking, as on the wing of an insect. [New Latin, from Latin *fenestra*†, opening in the wall, window.]

fen·es·trat·ed (fĕn′ə-strā′tĭd) *adj.* Also **fen·es·trate** (fĕn′ə-strāt′, fĭ-nĕs′trāt′) (especially for sense 2). **1.** Having windows or windowlike openings. **2.** *Biology.* Having fenestrae. [Latin *fenestrātus,* past participle of *fenestrāre,* to provide with windows or openings, from *fenestra,* window, FENESTRA.]

fen·es·tra·tion (fĕn′ə-strā′shən) *n.* **1.** *Architecture.* The design and placement of windows in a building. **2.** An opening in a structure. **3.** In surgery, the cutting of an opening from the external auditory canal to the labyrinth of the internal ear to restore hearing.

Fe·ni·an (fē′nē-ən) *n.* **1. a. Fenians.** A legendary group of heroic Irish warriors of the 2nd and 3rd centuries A.D. Also called "Fianna." **b.** A member of this group. **2.** A member of a secret organization in the United States and Ireland in the mid-19th century, whose goal was the overthrow of British rule in Ireland. **3.** *Sometimes* **fenian.** Loosely, a supporter of the republican cause in Northern Ireland. [Sense 2 : from Old Irish *féne,* an ancient Irish people, confused with *fíann,* legendary group of warriors, after *Fíann,* legendary hero.] **—Fe·ni·an** *adj.* **—Fe·ni·an·ism** *n.*

felucca *Swift lateen-rigged feluccas still ply parts of the Mediterranean. This one was photographed on the Nile near Luxor in Egypt.*

fencing *Two fencers in combat, one lunging to strike the chest of his opponent with his foil.*

fen·nec (fĕn′ĭk) *n.* A nocturnal small fox, *Fennecus ƶerda,* of desert regions of northern Africa, having fawn-colored fur and large, pointed ears. [Arabic *fanak, fenek,* fox, small furry animal.]

fen·nel (fĕn′əl) *n.* **1. a.** A plant, *Foeniculum vulgare,* native to Eurasia, having finely dissected leaves, clusters of small yellow flowers, and aromatic seeds. **b.** The seeds or leaves of this plant, used for flavoring. **2.** A variety of this plant, **finochio** *(see).* **3.** Any of several similar or related plants. [Middle English *fenel,* Old English *fenol, finugle,* from Vulgar Latin *fēnoclum* (unattested), from Latin *fēniculum,* diminutive of *fēnum, faenum,* hay.]

fen·u·greek (fĕn′yŏŏ-grēk′) *n.* **1.** A cloverlike Eurasian plant, *Trigonella foenum-graecum,* having white flowers and pungent, aromatic seeds used as flavoring. **2.** The seeds of this plant. [Middle English *fenigrek,* from Old French *fenugrec,* from Latin *fēnugraecum,* from *fēnum graecum,* "Greek hay" (from the use of the dried plant as fodder).]

fen·u·ron (fĕn′yə-rŏn′) *n.* A white compound, $C_9H_{12}N_2O$, used as a herbicide. [*fen-,* alteration of PHEN- + U(REA) + -ON.]

feoff (fĕf, fēf) *tr.v.* **feoffed, feoffing, feoffs.** To grant a feudal estate or fee to; enfeoff.
~*n.* A feudal estate, a **fee** *(see).* [Middle English *feoffen, feffen,* from Norman French *feoffer,* from Old French *fieffer,* from *fief,* FIEF.]

feoff·ee (fĕ-fē′, fē-fē′) *n.* A person to whom a feoffment is granted.

feoff·er, feof·for (fĕf′ər, fē′fər) *n.* A person who grants a feoffment.

feoff·ment (fĕf′mənt, fēf′-) *n.* A grant of lands as a fee.

-fer *suffix.* Indicates agency, bearing, or production; for example, **aquifer, conifer.** [Latin, from *ferre,* to carry, bear.]

fe·ral (fîr′əl, fĕr′-) *adj.* **1.** Existing in a wild or untamed state; especially, having reverted to such a state from domestication. **2.** Of or characteristic of a wild animal; savage. [Latin *fera,* wild animal, from *ferus,* wild.]

fer·bam (fûr′băm′) *n.* A black iron compound, $C_9H_{18}FeN_3S_6$, used as an agricultural fungicide. [*Fer*ric dimethyl-dithiocar*bam*ate.]

Fer·ber (fûr′bər), **Edna** (1887–1968). U.S. author. She wrote several best-selling novels, including her Pulitzer Prize winner *So Big* (1924), a number of plays, such as *Dinner at Eight* (1932), and many magazine articles that examined and exalted the American spirit. Many of her works were made into successful motion pictures.

fer-de-lance (fĕr′də-läns′, -läns′) *n.* A venomous tropical American snake, *Bothrops atrox,* having brown and grayish markings. [French, iron (head) of a lance.]

Fer·di·nand II (fûrd′n-ănd′) (1578–1637). King of Bohemia (1617–37) and Hungary (1618–37) and Holy Roman Emperor (1619–37).

Ferdinand V, II, and III, also known as "Ferdinand the Catholic" (1452–1516). King of Castile as Ferdinand V (1474–1504), king of Aragon as Ferdinand II (1479–1516), and king of Naples as Ferdinand III (1504–16), joint ruler with his wife, Isabella I of Castile. He and Isabella sent Columbus to America in 1492.

fere (fîr) *n. Archaic.* **1.** A companion. **2.** A spouse. [Middle English *fere,* Old English *gefēra.*]

fer·e·to·ry (fĕr′ə-tôr′ē, -tōr′ē) *n., pl.* **-ries. 1.** A shrine to hold the relics of saints. **2.** An area of a church in which such shrines are kept. [Middle English *fertre, feretory,* from Old French *fiertre,* from Latin *feretrum,* bier, from Greek *pheretron,* from *pherein,* to bear, carry.]

fe·ri·a (fîr′ē-ə, fĕr′-) *n., pl.* **-as** or **feriae** (fîr′ē-ē′, fĕr′-). *Ecclesiastical.* A day of the week on which no feast is observed. [From Medieval Latin *fēria,* from Late Latin *fēria,* day of the week, from Latin *fēriae,* days of rest, holidays, festivals.] —**fe·ri·al** (fîr′ē-əl, fĕr′-) *adj.*

fe·rine (fîr′īn′) *adj.* Untamed; feral. [Latin *ferīnus,* from *fera,* wild animal. See **feral.**]

fer·i·ty (fĕr′ə-tē) *n.* **1.** The condition of being feral; existence in a wild state. **2.** The condition of being savage; ferocity. [Latin *feritās* (stem *feritāt-*), from *ferus,* wild. See **feral.**]

Fer·lin·ghet·ti (fûr′lĭng-gĕt′ē), **Lawrence** (1920–). U.S. poet. He was a leader of the 1950's beat movement that opposed social, moral, and literary conventions. His collections include *Pictures of the Gone World* (1955) and *Tyrannus Nix?* (1969).

Fer·mat (fĕr-mä′), **Pierre de** (1601–65). French mathematician. He formulated Fermat's theorem and the least-time law, Fermat's principle, to explain the diffraction of light.

fer·ma·ta (fĕr-mä′tə) *n. Music.* **1.** The holding or sustaining of a tone, chord, or rest beyond its indicated time value. **2.** The sign that indicates such a prolongation. [Italian, pause, stop, from the feminine past participle of *fermare,* to pause, stop, from Latin *firmāre,* to make firm, from *firmus,* firm.]

Fermat's principle *n. Physics.* The principle that the path taken by a ray of light through any system is always the one that takes the shortest possible time.

Fermat's theorem *n.* The theorem, postulated by Pierre de Fermat but never proven, that the equation $x^n + y^n = z^n,$ where n is an integer, has no integral solutions for $x, y,$ and z for any value of n greater than 2. Also called "Fermat's last theorem."

fer·ment (fûr′mĕnt) *n.* **1.** Anything that causes fermentation, such as a yeast, bacterium, mold, or enzyme. **2.** Fermentation. **3.** A state of agitation; unrest; turbulence.
~*v.* (fər-mĕnt′) **fermented, -menting, -ments.** —*tr.* **1.** To produce by or as if by fermentation. **2.** To cause to undergo fermentation. **3.** To generate or stir up (trouble, for example). —*intr.* **1.** To undergo fermentation. **2.** To be turbulent; seethe. [Middle English, leaven, yeast, from Old French, from Latin *fermentum.*] —**fer·**

ment·a·bil·i·ty (fər-mĕn′tə-bĭl′ə-tē) *n.* —**fer·ment·a·ble** (fər-mĕn′tə-bəl) *adj.* —**fer·ment·er** *n.*

fer·men·ta·tion (fûr′mĕn-tā′shən) *n.* **1.** Any of a group of chemical reactions induced by living or nonliving ferments that split complex organic compounds into relatively simple substances; especially, the anaerobic conversion of sugar to carbon dioxide and alcohol by yeast, as in the making of alcoholic beverages. **2.** Unrest; commotion; agitation.

fer·men·ta·tive (fər-mĕn′tə-tĭv) *adj.* **1. a.** Causing fermentation. **b.** Capable of causing or undergoing fermentation. **2.** Pertaining to or of the nature of fermentation.

fer·mi (fĕr′mē, fûr′-) *n.* A unit of length equal to one femtometer (10^{-15} meter), used in nuclear physics. [After Enrico FERMI.]

Fer·mi (fĕr′mē), **Enrico** (1901–54). Italian-born physicist. He left Italy in 1938 to settle in the United States. That same year he was awarded a Nobel Prize for his work on artificial radioactivity caused by neutron bombardment. In 1942 Fermi produced the first controlled nuclear chain reaction in a squash court at the University of Chicago. He also helped develop the first atomic bomb.

Fer·mi-Dir·ac statistics (fĕr′mē-dĭ-răk′) *n. Physics.* A type of quantum statistics used for elementary particles that obey the exclusion principle (only two particles can occupy a given energy level). Compare **Bose-Einstein statistics.** [After Enrico FERMI and Paul DIRAC.]

fer·mi·on (fĕr′mē-ŏn′, fûr′-) *n.* A particle, such as an electron, proton, or neutron, having half-integral spin and obeying statistical rules requiring that not more than one in a set of identical particles may occupy a particular quantum state. Compare **boson.** [After Enrico FERMI.]

fer·mi·um (fĕr′mē-əm, fûr′-) *n.* **Symbol Fm** A synthetic transuranic metallic element having 10 isotopes with mass numbers ranging from 248 to 257 and corresponding half-lives ranging from 0.6 minute to approximately 100 days. Atomic number 100. [New Latin, after Enrico FERMI.]

fern (fûrn) *n.* Any of numerous flowerless, seedless pteridophytic plants of the class Filicinae, characteristically having fronds with divided leaflets, and reproducing by means of spores produced on the undersurface of the fronds. [Middle English *fern,* Old English *fearn.*]

Fer·nan·del (fâr′näN-dĕl′), born Fernand Joseph Désiré Contandin (1903–71). French comedian with a toothy grin. He starred in the 1950's *Don Camillo* film series. Other films include *Fric Frac* (1939), *The Red Inn* (1951), and *The Sheep Has Five Legs* (1954).

fern·er·y (fûr′nə-rē) *n., pl.* **-ies. 1.** A place or container in which ferns are grown. **2.** A bed or collection of ferns.

fern seed *pl.n.* The minute spores of ferns, formerly believed to be seeds, and supposed to have the power of making one invisible.

fern·y (fûr′nē) *adj.* **-ier, -iest. 1.** Abounding in ferns. **2.** Of, pertaining to, or characteristic of ferns.

fe·ro·cious (fə-rō′shəs) *adj.* **1.** Extremely savage; fierce. **2.** Extreme; intense: *a ferocious blizzard.* —See Synonyms at **cruel.** [Latin *ferōx* (stem *ferōc-*), wild, fierce.] —**fe·ro·cious·ly** *adv.* —**fe·ro·cious·ness** *n.*

fe·roc·i·ty (fə-rŏs′ə-tē) *n., pl.* **-ties.** The condition or quality of being ferocious.

-ferous *suffix.* Indicates bearing, producing, or containing; for example, **crystalliferous, umbelliferous.** [Middle English : -FER + -OUS.]

Fer·ra·ra (fə-rär′ə). Capital city of the province of the same name in the Emilia-Romagna region of northern Italy.

fer·rate (fĕr′āt′) *n.* A ferrite *(see).* [FERR(O)- + -ATE.]

fer·re·dox·in (fĕr′ĭ-dŏk′sĭn) *n.* Any of a group of red-brown iron-containing proteins that are strong reducing agents and function in electron transport in many organisms, as in photosynthetic plants. [Latin *ferrum,* iron + REDOX + -IN.]

fer·ret¹ (fĕr′ĭt) *n.* **1.** A domesticated, usually albino form of the Old World polecat, often trained to hunt rats or rabbits. **2.** A black-footed ferret *(see).*
~*v.* **ferreted, -reting, -rets.** —*tr.* **1.** To hunt (rats, for example) with a ferret. **2.** To drive out; expel: *ferret the troublemakers from the team.* **3.** To uncover and bring to light by intensive investigation. Used with *out: "piqued by the failure of all his endeavors to ferret out the assassins"* (Edgar Allan Poe). —*intr.* **1.** To hunt with a ferret or ferrets. **2.** To search about; rummage. [Middle English *feret, firette,* from Old French *fuiret, furet,* from Vulgar Latin *fūrittus* (unattested), little thief, from Latin *fūr,* thief. See **furtive.**] —**fer·ret·er** *n.* —**fer·ret·y** *adj.*

ferret² Also **fer·ret·ing** (fĕr′ĭ-tĭng). A narrow piece of tape used to bind or edge fabric. [Probably from Italian *fioretti,* floss silk, plural of *fioretto,* diminutive of *fiore,* flower, from Latin *flōs* (stem *flōr-*), flower.]

ferri- *prefix. Chemistry.* Indicates iron, especially with a valence of 3; for example, **ferricyanide.** [Latin *ferrum,* iron.]

fer·ri·age (fĕr′ē-ĭj) *n.* **1.** The act or business of ferrying. **2.** The toll charged for ferrying.

fer·ric (fĕr′ĭk) *adj.* Of, pertaining to, or containing iron; especially, containing iron with a valence of 3 or with a valence higher than in a corresponding ferrous compound. [FERR(O)- + -IC.]

ferric oxide *n.* A dark compound, Fe_2O_3, occurring naturally as hematite ore and rust, and used in pigments, metallurgy, polishing compounds, and magnetic tapes.

fer·ri·cy·an·ic acid (fĕr′ĭ-sī-ăn′ĭk, fĕr′ĭ-) *n.* A reddish-brown solid compound, $H_3[Fe(CN)_6]$.

fer·ri·cy·a·nide (fĕr′ĭ-sī′ə-nīd′, fĕr′ĭ-) *n.* Any of various salts derived from ferricyanic acid and used in making blue pigments.

fer·rif·er·ous (fə-rĭf′ər-əs, fĕ-) *adj.* Containing or yielding iron: *ferriferous rock.* [FERRI- +-FEROUS.]

fer·ri·mag·net·ic (fĕr′ĭ-măg-nĕt′ĭk, fĕr′ĭ-) *adj.* Pertaining to or characteristic of substances, such as certain ferrites and garnets, that have magnetic properties similar to ferromagnetic materials. Ferrimagnetic substances have weaker magnetism than ferromagnetic substances; their properties arise because the different types of atom in the crystal have unequal antiparallel magnetic moments. **—fer·ri·mag·net·ism** (fĕr′ĭ-măg′nə-tĭz′əm, fĕr′ĭ-) *n.*

Fer·ris wheel (fĕr′ĭs) *n. Often* **ferris wheel.** A large, upright, rotating wheel having suspended cars in which passengers ride for amusement. [Designed for the Chicago World's Fair in 1893 by George W.G. *Ferris* (1859–96), U.S. engineer.]

fer·rite (fĕr′īt′) *n.* **1.** Any of a group of nonmetallic, ceramiclike, usually ferromagnetic compounds of ferric oxide with other oxides; especially, such a compound with spinel crystalline structure, characterized by extremely high electrical resistivity and used in computer memory elements, permanent magnets, and various solid-state devices. Also called "ferrate." **2.** Iron having a body-centered cubic crystalline form, occurring commonly in steel, cast iron, and pig iron below 910°C. [FERR(O)- + -ITE.]

fer·ri·tin (fĕr′ĭ-tĭn) *n.* An iron-containing protein complex that is one of the forms in which iron is stored in the tissues. [FERRITE + -IN.]

ferro–, ferr– *prefix.* Indicates: **1.** Iron; for example, **ferromagnetic, ferrite. 2.** Iron in alloy; for example, **ferromanganese. 3.** Iron in its ferrous valence; for example, **ferrocyanide.** [Latin *ferrum*, iron.]

fer·ro·al·loy (fĕr′ō-ăl′oi′, -ə-loi′) *n.* Any of various alloys of iron and one or more other elements, such as manganese or silicon, used in the production of steel.

fer·ro·cene (fĕr′ō-sēn′, fĕr′ə-) *n.* A reddish crystalline compound, Fe(C_5H_5), the first known sandwich compound.

fer·ro·chro·mi·um (fĕr′ō-krō′mē-əm) *n.* An alloy of iron and chromium (50–70%) used in making chromium alloy steels.

fer·ro·con·crete (fĕr′ō-kŏn′krēt′, -kŏn-krēt′) *n.* **Reinforced concrete** *(see).*

fer·ro·cy·an·ic acid (fĕr′ō-sī-ăn′ĭk) *n.* A solid, white compound, $H_4Fe(CN)_6$.

fer·ro·cy·a·nide (fĕr′ō-sī′ə-nīd′) *n.* A salt derived from ferrocyanic acid, the sodium and potassium salts being used in making blue pigments, blueprint paper, and ferricyanide.

fer·ro·e·lec·tric (fĕr′ō-ĭ-lĕk′trĭk) *adj.* Of or pertaining to a crystalline dielectric that can be given a permanent electric polarization by application of an electric field. **~***n.* A ferroelectric substance. **—fer·ro·e·lec·tric·i·ty** (fĕr′ō-ĭ-lĕk′trĭs′ə-tē, fĕr′ō-ē′lĕk-) *n.*

fer·ro·mag·ne·sian (fĕr′ō-măg-nē′zhən, -shən) *adj.* Containing iron and magnesium. Said especially of certain minerals.

fer·ro·mag·net (fĕr′ō-măg′nĭt) *n.* **1.** A ferromagnetic substance; broadly, a substance with magnetic properties resembling those of iron. **2.** A permanent magnet *(see).*

fer·ro·mag·net·ism (fĕr′ō-măg′nə-tĭz′əm) *n.* A type of magnetism occurring in substances, such as iron, nickel, and cobalt, that exhibit extremely high magnetic permeability, the ability to acquire high magnetization and saturation in relatively weak magnetic fields, a large positive magnetic susceptibility, and magnetic hysteresis. **—fer·ro·mag·net·ic** (fĕr′ō-măg-nĕt′ĭk) *n.*

fer·ro·man·ga·nese (fĕr′ō-măng′gə-nēz′, -nēs′) *n.* An alloy of iron and manganese (70–80%).

fer·ro·sil·i·con (fĕr′ō-sĭl′ĭ-kən, -kŏn′) *n.* An alloy of iron and silicon (up to 15%) used in making alloy steels.

fer·ro·type (fĕr′ə-tīp′) *n.* **1.** A positive photograph made directly on an iron plate varnished with a sensitized film. Also called "tintype." **2.** The process by which such photographs are made.

fer·rous (fĕr′əs) *adj.* Of, pertaining to, or containing iron, especially with a valence of 2. [New Latin *ferrosus* : Latin *ferrum*, iron + -OUS.]

ferrous oxide *n.* A black powdery compound, FeO, used in the manufacture of steel, green heat-absorbing glass, and enamels.

ferrous sulfate *n.* A greenish crystalline compound, $FeSO_4 \cdot 7H_2O$, used as a pigment, fertilizer, feed additive, and in the medical treatment of iron-deficiency anemia. Also called "green vitriol."

ferrous sulfide *n.* A black to brown sulfide of iron, FeS, used in making hydrogen sulfide.

fer·ru·gi·nous (fə-rōō′jə-nəs, fĕ-) *adj.* **1.** Of, containing, or similar to iron. **2.** Having the color of iron rust. [Latin *ferrūginus*, from *ferrūgō* (stem *ferrūgin-*), iron rust, from *ferrum*, iron.]

fer·rule, fer·ule (fĕr′əl, -ōōl′) *n.* **1.** A metal ring or cap attached to or near the end of a pole, cane, wooden handle, or the like, for reinforcement or to prevent splitting. **2.** A bushing used to secure a pipe joint. **~***tr.v.* **ferruled, -ruling, -rules.** To furnish with a ferrule. [Variant (influenced by Latin *ferrum*, iron) of earlier *verrel, virl*, from Middle English *verelle, virol*, from Old French *virelle, virole*, from Latin *viriola*, little bracelet, diminutive of *viriae*, bracelets.]

fer·ry (fĕr′ē) *n., pl.* **-ries. 1.** A commercial service for transporting people, vehicles, goods, or the like, across a body of water. **2.** A boat used in such transportation. **3.** The place of embarkation of a ferryboat. **4.** A franchise or legal right to operate such a service for a fee. **5.** The transporting of a vehicle, especially an aircraft, under its own power to its eventual user. **6.** A module for transporting astronauts from a spacecraft to the surface of a planet. **~***v.* **ferried, -rying, -ries.** *—tr.* **1.** To transport (a person or thing) across a body of water. **2.** To cross (a body of water) on or as if on a ferry. **3.** To deliver (a vehicle, especially an aircraft) under its own power to its eventual user. **4.** To transport (people or goods), especially to and fro over short distances. *—intr.* To cross a body of water on or as if on a ferry. [Middle English *fery, ferie,* probably from Old Norse *ferja.*]

fer·ry·boat (fĕr′ē-bōt′) *n.* A boat used to ferry passengers or goods.

fer·ry·man (fĕr′ē-mən) *n., pl.* **-men** (-mĭn). A person who owns, administers, or operates a ferry.

fer·tile (fûr′tl) *adj.* **1.** *Biology.* **a.** Capable of reproducing. **b.** Capable of growing and developing; able to mature: *fertile seeds.* **2.** *Botany.* Capable of producing spores, pollen, seeds, or fruit. **3.** Rich in material needed to sustain plant growth: *fertile soil.* **4.** Producing many offspring. **5.** Highly or continuously productive; prolific: *a fertile imagination.* **6.** *Physics.* Capable of being converted into fissionable material. [Middle English, from Old French, from Latin *fertilis*, from *ferre*, to bear, carry, produce.] **—fer·tile·ly** *adv.* **—fer·tile·ness** *n.*

---

fern

THE DOUBLE LIFE OF A FERN
Survivors from 370 million years ago

Ferns were among the first plants on earth to grow big aerial leaves that could photosynthesize sunlight in the way most plants do today. Fossil evidence shows that they appeared, along with the primitive club mosses and horsetails, during the Devonian period about 370 million years ago. Descendants of early ferns survive today, some as high as 15 meters (49 feet) in tropical rain forests. Their slender trunks produce new fronds only at the crowns.

There are at least 10,000—possibly 15,000 —species of fern. They grow best in a hot, damp climate but have spread to most regions of the earth. A fern's life cycle has two distinct stages: the main plant, which produces spores, not flowers; and a very small plant, which is the sexual stage and produces new main plants.

ADAPTABLE *Ferns have adapted to most climates. These plants flourish on a rugged Welsh hillside.*

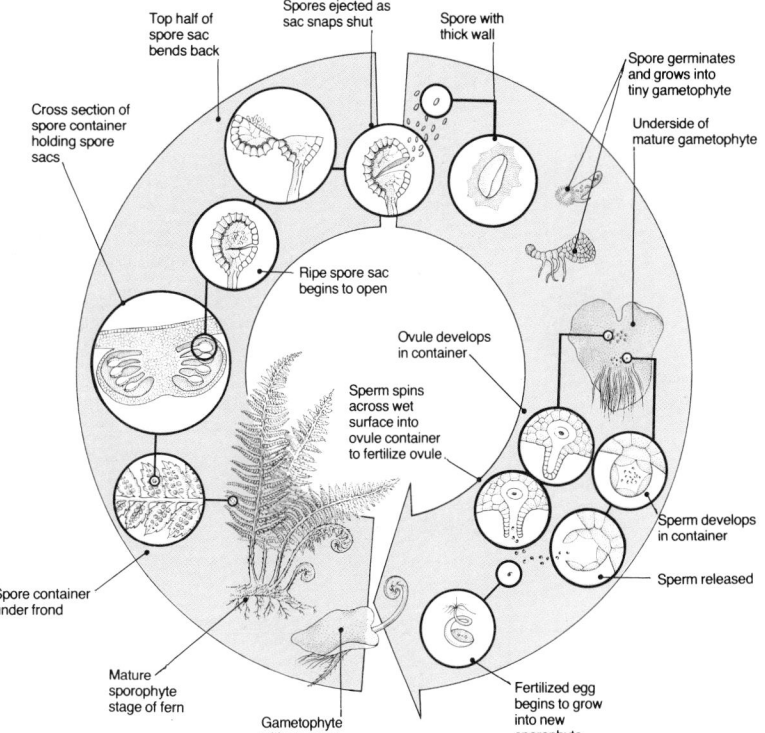

Top half of spore sac bends back

Spores ejected as sac snaps shut

Spore with thick wall

Spore germinates and grows into tiny gametophyte

Underside of mature gametophyte

Cross section of spore container holding spore sacs

Ripe spore sac begins to open

Ovule develops in container

Sperm spins across wet surface into ovule container to fertilize ovule

Sperm develops in container

Sperm released

Spore container under frond

Mature sporophyte stage of fern

Gametophyte withers away

Fertilized egg begins to grow into new sporophyte

LIFE CYCLE *The fern exists in two stages, one tiny, the other large. The large stage, the sporophyte, produces spores in containers under its leaves. Each spore is ejected, lands in the soil, and forms the fern's tiny stage—a little heart-shaped plant called a gametophyte. The gametophyte stage is sexual: each gametophyte forms ovules and sperm cells. The sperm cells fertilize the ovules and give rise to a new generation of the large sporophyte plants.*

Fertile Crescent. The crescent-shaped area of relatively fertile land in the Middle East in ancient times. The area extended from Mesopotamia to Assyria, then westward to the Mediterranean and south through Palestine to the Nile Valley.

fer·til·i·ty (fər-tĭl′ə-tē) *n.* The state or quality of being fertile.

fertility cult *n.* The celebration of various ceremonies or magical rites, usually in primitive agricultural communities, with the aim of increasing crops, bringing rain, or the like.

fertility drug *n.* Any of various drugs, such as a **gonadotropin** *(see)*, taken by infertile women to stimulate the release of an egg cell from the ovary and therefore increase the chances of pregnancy.

fertility rate *n.* The number of live births that occur in a year per thousand women of childbearing age.

fer·til·i·za·tion (fûrt′l-ə-zā′shən) *n.* **1.** The act or process of initiating biological reproduction. **2.** The process in which two gametes unite to form a zygote. **3.** The act or process of rendering fertile, especially by use of fertilizer.

fer·til·ize (fûrt′l-īz′) *v.* **-ized, -izing, -izes.** —*tr.* **1.** To cause fertilization of (an ovum, animal, or plant) by providing with sperm or pollen. **2.** To render fertile, especially by spreading fertilizer. —*intr.* To spread fertilizer. —**fer·til·iz·a·ble** *adj.*

fer·til·iz·er (fûrt′l-ī′zər) *n.* **1.** A person or agent that causes fertilization of an animal or plant. **2.** Any of a large number of natural and synthetic materials, including manure and nitrogen, phosphorus, and potassium compounds, spread on or worked into soil to increase its fertility.

fer·u·la (fĕr′yə-lə, fĕr′ə-) *n., pl.* **-las** or **-lae** (-lē′). **1.** A flat piece of wood, such as a stick; a ferule. **2.** Any plant of the genus *Ferula,* of Mediterranean regions, containing resins for which it is cultivated. [New Latin, from Latin, giant fennel. See **ferule.**]

fer·ule¹ (fĕr′əl, -ōōl′) *n.* A baton, cane, strap, or stick used in punishing children.

—*tr.v.* **feruled, -uling, -ules.** To punish or discipline with a ferule. [Latin *ferula†,* giant fennel, rod used to punish.]

ferule². Variant of **ferrule.**

fer·ven·cy (fûr′vən-sē) *n., pl.* **-cies.** The condition or quality of being fervent.

fer·vent (fûr′vənt) *adj.* **1.** Having or showing great emotion or warmth; passionate; ardent. **2.** Extremely hot; glowing. [Middle English, from Old French, from Latin *fervēns* (stem *fervent-*), present participle of *fervēre,* to boil, glow.] —**fer·vent·ly** *adv.* —**fer·vent·ness** *n.*

fer·vid (fûr′vĭd) *adj.* **1.** Intensely fervent or zealous; impassioned. **2.** Extremely hot; burning. —See Synonyms at **eager.** [Latin *fervidus,* glowing, from *fervēre,* to glow, boil.] —**fer·vid·ly** *adv.* —**fer·vid·ness** *n.*

fer·vor (fûr′vər) *n.* Also *chiefly British* **fer·vour.** **1.** Intensity of emotion; fervency; zeal. **2.** Intense heat. —See Synonyms at **passion.** [Middle English *fervour,* from Old French, from Latin *fervor,* a boiling, from *fervēre,* to boil.]

Fès (fĕs). Also **Fez** (fĕz). *Arabic* **Fas** (fäs). City in northern Morocco, consisting of the old city (A.D. 808) and the new city (1276).

fes·cen·nine (fĕs′ə-nīn′, -nēn′) *adj.* Licentious; obscene. [Latin *Fescennīnus,* of the town *Fescennia* in Etruria, noted for licentious festivals and verses.]

fes·cue (fĕs′kyōō) *n.* **1.** Any of various grasses of the genus *Festuca,* often cultivated as pasturage and for lawns. **2.** A stick used as a pointer. [Middle English *festu,* from Old French, from Vulgar Latin *festūcum* (unattested), from Latin *festūca†,* stalk, stem.]

fess, fesse (fĕs) *n. Heraldry.* A wide horizontal band forming the middle section of an escutcheon. [Middle English *fesse,* from Old French, from Latin *fascia,* band, fillet.]

fess point *n. Heraldry.* The center point of an escutcheon.

-fest *suffix.* Indicates a gathering or occasion characterized by a specified activity; for example, **slugfest.** [From German *Fest,* feast, festival, from Middle High German *vest,* from Latin *fēstum,* neuter of *fēstus,* festival.]

fes·tal (fĕs′təl) *adj.* Of, pertaining to, or of the nature of a feast or festival; festive; joyous. [Old French, from Latin *fēsta,* FEAST.] —**fes·tal·ly** *adv.*

fes·ter (fĕs′tər) *v.* **-tered, -tering, -ters.** —*intr.* **1.** To generate pus; suppurate. **2.** To form an ulcer. **3.** To decay; rot. **4.** To be or become a source of irritation; rankle. —*tr.* To infect, inflame, or corrupt.

—*n.* A small, festering sore or ulcer. [Middle English *festre,* from Old French, from Latin *fistula,* FISTULA.]

fes·ti·na len·te (fĕ-stē′nä lĕn′tä). *Latin.* Make haste slowly.

fes·ti·val (fĕs′tə-vəl) *n.* **1.** An occasion for feasting or celebration; especially, a day or time of religious significance that recurs at regular intervals: *a harvest festival; the festival of Chanukah.* **2.** A series of related performances, exhibitions, competitions, or the like: *a film festival.* **3.** Conviviality; revelry.

—*adj.* Festive. [Middle English, from Old French, from Medieval Latin *fēstivālis,* from *fēstīvus,* FESTIVE.]

fes·tive (fĕs′tĭv) *adj.* **1.** Of, pertaining to, or appropriate to a feast or festival. **2.** Merry; joyous: *a festive occasion.* [Latin *fēstīvus,* from *fēstus,* joyous.] —**fes·tive·ly** *adv.* —**fes·tive·ness** *n.*

fes·tiv·i·ty (fĕ-stĭv′ə-tē) *n., pl.* **-ties.** **1.** A joyous feast, holiday, or celebration; a festival. **2.** The pleasure, joy, and gaiety of a festival or celebration. **3.** **festivities.** The proceedings or events of a festival or celebration; festive activity.

fes·toon (fĕ-stōōn′) *n.* **1.** A string or garland of leaves, flowers, ribbon, or the like, suspended in a loop or curve between two points.

2. A representation of this, as in sculpture or architecture.

—*tr.v.* **festooned, -tooning, -toons.** **1.** To decorate with or as if with a festoon or festoons. **2.** To form or make into a festoon or festoons. **3.** To join together by festoons. [French *feston,* from Italian *festone,* festal ornament, from *fēsta,* feast, festival, from Latin, plural of *fēstus,* joyous, festal.]

fes·toon·er·y (fĕ-stōō′nə-rē) *n., pl.* **-ies.** **1.** An arrangement of or into festoons. **2.** Festoons collectively.

fest·schrift (fĕst′shrĭft′) *n., pl.* **-schriften** (-shrĭf′tən) or **-schrifts.** A volume of learned essays or articles contributed by colleagues and admirers as a tribute to a scholar. [German, "festival writing."]

fet·a, fet·ta (fĕt′ə) *n.* A white, crumbly Greek cheese made usually of goat's or ewe's milk and preserved in brine. [Modern Greek, short for *turi pheta,* "cheese slice" : *turi,* cheese + *pheta,* from Italian *fetta,* slice.]

FET field-effect transistor.

fe·tal, foe·tal (fēt′l) *adj.* Of, pertaining to, or having the nature of a fetus.

fetal alcohol syndrome *n.* A group of birth defects including retarded growth and cardiac abnormalities, occurring in infants born to alcoholic mothers.

fetal position *n.* A position of the body at rest in which the spine is curved, the head is bowed forward, and the arms and legs are drawn in toward the chest. [From its resemblance to the position of the fetus in the womb.]

fe·ta·tion, foe·ta·tion (fē-tā′shən) *n.* The development of a fetus; pregnancy. [FET(US) + -ATION.]

fetch¹ (fĕch) *v.* **fetched, fetching, fetches.** —*tr.* **1.** To go after and return with; get; bring. **2.** To cause to come or be drawn forth: *A bell fetched the receptionist.* **3. a.** To draw in (breath); inhale. **b.** To bring forth (a sigh, for example). **4.** *Informal.* To bring in (a price); sell for. **5.** To interest; attract: *How does this idea fetch you?* **6.** *Archaic.* To perform or make (a movement, step, or the like). **7.** *Informal.* To strike or deal (a blow, punch, or the like). **8.** *Nautical.* To arrive at; come to; reach. —*intr.* **1.** To go after and return with things. **2.** In hunting, to retrieve game. Often used as a command to a dog. **3.** *Nautical.* **a.** To hold a course. **b.** To turn about; veer. —**fetch and carry.** To do minor tasks. —**fetch up.** To reach a place and halt there; end up.

—*n.* **1.** An act or instance of fetching. **2.** A stratagem or trick. [Middle English *fecchen,* Old English *feccan, fetian.*] —**fetch·er** *n.*

fetch² *n.* An apparition of a living person; a doppelgänger. [18th century : origin obscure.]

fetch·ing (fĕch′ĭng) *adj. Informal.* Very attractive; charming; captivating. —**fetch·ing·ly** *adv.*

fete, fête (fāt, fĕt) *n.* **1.** A festival or elaborate feast. **2.** A bazaar or fair, usually held outdoors, to raise money for charity. **3.** Especially in Roman Catholic countries, the feast day of a saint, observed as a festival by those bearing the name of the saint.

—*tr.v.* **feted, feting, fetes.** Also **fête.** **1.** To celebrate with a festival or party. **2.** To pay honor to, especially by entertaining. [French *fête,* from Old French *feste,* FEAST.]

fête cham·pê·tre (fĕt′ shän-pĕt′rə) *n., pl.* **fêtes champêtres** *(pronounced as singular).* An outdoor dinner, party, or similar entertainment. [French.]

fet·e·ri·ta (fĕt′ə-rē′tə) *n.* A variety of sorghum, *Sorghum vulgare caudatum,* grown in warm regions for its grain and as forage. [Arabic (Sudanese dialect).]

fet·id, foe·tid (fĕt′ĭd, fē′tĭd) *adj.* Having an offensive odor; foul-smelling; stinking: *fetid air swarming with mosquitoes.* [Middle English, from Latin *fētidus, foetidus,* from *fētēre, foetēre†,* to stink.] —**fet·id·ly** *adv.* —**fet·id·ness** *n.*

fet·ish, fet·ich (fĕt′ĭsh, fē′tĭsh) *n.* **1. a.** A material object believed among primitive cultures to have magical power. **b.** Belief in the power of such objects. **2.** An object, principle, activity, or the like that receives unreasonably excessive attention or reverence. **3.** *Psychology.* **a.** An abnormal sexual attraction to some object or part of the body not normally considered erogenous: *a foot fetish.* **b.** The object of this attraction. [French *fétiche,* from Portuguese *feitiço,* charm, sorcery, from Latin *factītius,* made by art, from *facere,* to make, do.]

fet·ish·ism (fĕt′ĭ-shĭz′əm, fē′tĭ-) *n.* **1.** The worship of or belief in fetishes. **2.** Excessive attention to or attachment for something. **3.** *Psychology.* A condition involving a fetish. —**fet·ish·ist** *n.* —**fet·ish·is·tic** (fĕt′ĭ-shĭs′tĭk, fē′tĭ-) *adj.*

fet·lock (fĕt′lŏk′) *n.* **1. a.** A projection on the lower part of the leg of a horse or related animal, above and behind the hoof. **b.** A tuft of hair on such a projection. **2.** The joint marked by this projection. In this sense, also called "fetlock joint." [Middle English *fitlok,* from Germanic; akin to Middle High German *vizzelach.*]

fe·tor, foe·tor (fē′tər, fē′tôr′) *n.* An exceptionally offensive odor; a strong stench. [Middle English *fetour,* from Latin *fētor, foetor,* from *fētēre, foetēre†,* to stink.]

fetta. Variant of **feta.**

fet·ter (fĕt′ər) *n.* **1.** A chain or shackle attached to the ankle to restrain movement. **2. fetters.** Anything that serves to restrict; a restraint.

—*tr.v.* **fettered, -tering, -ters.** **1.** To put fetters on; shackle. **2.** To restrict the freedom of action or thought of; confine; impede. [Middle English *feter,* Old English *feter, fetor,* from Germanic.]

fet·tle (fĕt′l) *tr.v.* **-tled, -tling, -tles.** *Metallurgy.* To line (the hearth of a reverberatory furnace) with loose sand or ore preparatory to pouring molten metal.

~*n.* **1.** The material used to line a furnace in fettling. **2.** Proper or sound condition; good spirits: *in fine fettle.* [Middle English *fetlen*, to shape, make ready, probably from Old English *fetel*, girdle, belt, from Germanic.]

fet·tling (fĕt′lĭng) *n.* The material, such as loose ore and sand, used to line a reverberatory furnace.

fet·tuc·ci·ne, fet·tu·ci·ni (fĕt′ə-chē′nē) *n.* Used with a singular or plural verb. Italian pasta in the form of narrow strips. [Italian *fettucine* (plural), diminutive of *fetta*, slice.]

fe·tus, foe·tus (fē′təs) *n., pl.* **–tuses.** The unborn young of a viviparous vertebrate; in human beings, the young from the end of the eighth week to the moment of birth, as distinguished from the earlier embryo. [Middle English, from Latin *fētus*, pregnancy, offspring.]

Feucht·wang·er (foiKHt′väng′ər), **Lion** (1884–1958). German novelist and dramatist. He wrote *The Ugly Duchess* (1923) and *Jud Süss* (1925). He was exiled in 1933 and settled in California in 1940.

feud¹ (fyōōd) *n.* **1.** A bitter, prolonged state of hostility between two families, individuals, or clans; vendetta. **2.** An often prolonged quarrel.

~*intr.v.* **feuded, feuding, feuds.** To carry on a feud. [Middle English *fede, feide*, from Old French, from Old High German *fēhida*; akin to Old English *fǣhthu*, enmity (see FOE, -TH).]

feud² *n.* A feudal estate, a fee *(see).* [Medieval Latin *feudum*, probably from Germanic.]

feu·dal (fyōōd′l) *adj.* **1.** Of, pertaining to, or characteristic of feudalism. **2.** Of or pertaining to lands held in fee or to the holding of such lands. [Medieval Latin *feudālis*, from *feudum*, FEUD (estate).] —**feu·dal·ly** *adv.*

feu·dal·ism (fyōōd′l-ĭz′əm) *n.* A political and economic system of medieval Europe, based on the relation of lord to vassal, in which land was held on condition of homage and service. —**feu·dal·ist** *n.* —**feu·dal·is·tic** (fyōōd′l-ĭs′tĭk) *adj.*

feu·dal·i·ty (fyōō-dăl′ə-tē) *n., pl.* **-ties. 1.** The state or quality of being feudal. **2.** A feudal estate, a fee *(see).*

feu·dal·ize (fyōōd′l-īz′) *tr.v.* **-ized, -izing, -izes.** To organize into a feudal system; make feudal. —**feu·dal·i·za·tion** *n.*

feu·da·to·ry (fyōō′də-tôr′ē, -tōr′ē) *n., pl.* **-ries. 1.** A person who holds a feudal fee; a vassal. **2.** A feudal fee.

~*adj.* **1.** Of, pertaining to, or characteristic of the feudal relationship between vassal and lord. **2.** Owing feudal homage or allegiance. [Medieval Latin *feudātōrius*, from *feudātus*, past participle of *feudāre*, to enfeoff, from *feudum*, FEUD (estate).]

feud·ist (fyōō′dĭst) *n.* A person who feuds with another.

Feu·er·bach (foi′ər-bäKH′), **Ludwig Andreas** (1804–72). German philosopher. He explained history in materialistic terms, claiming that "Man is what he eats." In *The Essence of Christianity* (1841) he argued that God was a projection of man's inner self.

feuil·le·ton (fœ′yə-tôN′) *n.* **1.** The part of a French or other European newspaper devoted to light fiction, reviews, and similar articles. **2.** An article appearing in a feuilleton, such as an installment of a serialized novel. [French, from *feuillet*, diminutive of *feuille*, leaf, from Old French *fueille, foille*, from Latin *folia*, plural of *folium*, leaf.] —**feuil·le·ton·ism** (fœ′yə-tŏ′nĭz′əm, -tôN′nĭz-əm) *n.* —**feuil·le·ton·ist** (-nĭst) *n.*

Feul·gen reaction (foil′gən) *n.* A staining reaction in which the presence of DNA is demonstrated by the appearance of purple color upon contact with a reagent containing fuchsin and sulfuric acid. [After R.J. *Feulgen* (1884–1955), German biochemist.]

fe·ver (fē′vər) *n.* **1.** Abnormally high body temperature, usually associated with shivering and a fast pulse. **2.** Any disease characterized by abnormally high body temperatures. **3.** A condition of heightened activity or excitement; a ferment; agitation: *a fever of anticipation.* **4.** A contagious, usually short-lived enthusiasm or eagerness.

~*tr.v.* **fevered, -vering, -vers.** To put into a fever. [Middle English *fever*, Old English *fēfor, fēfer*, from Latin *febris†.*]

fever blister *n.* A cold sore *(see).*

fe·ver·few (fē′vər-fyōō′) *n.* An aromatic plant, *Chrysanthemum parthenium*, native to Eurasia, having clusters of buttonlike, white-rayed flowers. [Middle English *feverfu*, from Norman French *fevrefue* (unattested), from Latin *febrifugia* : *febris*, FEVER + *fugāre*, to drive away, from *fugere*, to run away.]

fe·ver·ish (fē′vər-ĭsh) *adj.* Also **fe·ver·ous** (-əs) (for sense 1). **1. a.** Having a fever, especially a slight fever. **b.** Of, pertaining to, or resembling a fever. **c.** Causing or tending to cause fever. **2.** In an agitated or restless state; intensely emotional or active. —**fe·ver·ish·ly** *adv.* —**fe·ver·ish·ness** *n.*

fever pitch *n.* An intense degree of excitement or agitation.

fever therapy *n.* Treatment of disease by means of artificially induced fever.

fever tree *n.* Any of several trees, such as certain species of eucalyptus or *Pinckneya pubens*, of the southeastern United States, having leaves or bark capable of reducing fever.

fe·ver·wort (fē′vər-wûrt′, -wôrt′) *n.* Any of several plants considered to have medicinal properties, such as the **horse gentian** and **bone·set** *(both of which see).*

few (fyōō) *adj.* **fewer, fewest.** Amounting to or consisting of a small number. —**few and far between.** Scarce; in short supply.

~*n.* Used with a plural verb. **1.** An indefinitely small number of persons or things; not many: *Bring me a few of your books.* **2.** A limited number of people; the select. Usually preceded by *the: the discerning few.* —**a good few.** Several or many. —**have a few too**

many. *Informal.* To consume too many alcoholic drinks. —**quite a few.** A lot; many.

~*pron.* Used with a plural verb. A small number of persons or things: *"many are called, but few are chosen"* (Matthew 22:14). [Middle English *fewe*, Old English *fēa, fēawe.*] —**few·ness** *n.*

Usage: *Fewer* and *less* sometimes overlap in usage. *Fewer* is the preferred word when the reference is to numbers or to entities considered as individuals that can be counted or listed. *Less* is preferred when the reference is to collective quantity or to something abstract. Contrast *fewer workers, less production,* and *fewer opportunities, less opportunity.* Informally there is a tendency for *less* to be used in place of *fewer,* especially when there is an implicit contrast with *more: No less than 15 people telephoned. There are 15 less trains on the line now than there were last year.* Here formal English prefers *fewer.* However, even formal English will accept *less* when the contrast is explicit, as in *We want a few more cars and a few less buses* (where *a few fewer* would be unacceptable); or in expressions of measurement, since the sense is collective: *less than 60 years old; less than 50 feet; less than $4,000.*

fey (fā) *adj.* **1.** *Scottish.* **a.** Fated to die soon. **b.** Full of the sense of approaching death. **2.** Having visionary power; clairvoyant. **3.** Appearing as if under a spell; enchanted; touched. **4.** Whimsical or fanciful. [Middle English *feie*, Old English *fǣge.*]

Fey·deau (fā′dō, fā-dō′), **Georges** (1862–1921). French playwright. He wrote many farcical comedies, including *The Lady From Maxim's* (1899) and *A Flea in Her Ear* (1907).

Feyn·man (fīn′mən), **Richard Phillips** (1918–). U.S. physicist. He is best known for his work in quantum electrodynamics, especially the Feynman diagrams, which illustrate interactions between charged particles as an exchange of virtual photons. He shared the Nobel Prize in 1965.

fez (fĕz) *n., pl.* **fezzes.** A man's felt cap in the shape of a truncated cone, usually red with a black tassel hanging from the crown, worn chiefly in the eastern Mediterranean region. [French, from Turkish, perhaps after Fès.]

Fez. See **Fès.**

ff *Music.* fortissimo.

ff. **1.** folios. **2.** following.

Ffestiniog. See **Meirionydd.**

FFV Order of the First Families of Virginia.

FG fine grain.

f.g. *Sports.* field goal; field goals.

FH fire hydrant.

FHA Federal Housing Administration.

FHLBB Federal Home Loan Bank Board.

f.h.p. friction horsepower.

fi·a·cre (fē-ä′krə) *n.* A small hackney coach. [French, after the Hôtel de St. *Fiacre*, Paris.]

fi·an·cé (fē′än-sā′, fē-än′sā′) *n.* A man engaged to be married. [French, past participle of *fiancer*, to betroth, from Old French *fiancier*, from *fier*, to trust, from Vulgar Latin *fidāre* (unattested), from Latin *fīdere.*]

fi·an·cée (fē′än-sā′, fē-än′sā′) *n.* A woman engaged to be married. [French, feminine of FIANCÉ.]

Fi·an·na (fē′ə-nə) *n.* **Fenian** *(see).*

Fi·an·na Fáil (fē′ə-nə foil′) *n.* A major Irish political party founded in 1926 by Eamon De Valera with the aim of removing all British influence from Ireland. [Irish, "Fenians of the land" : *Fianna* (see **Fenian**) + *Fáil*, from *fál*, earth, sod.]

fi·as·co (fē-ăs′kō, -ä′skō) *n., pl.* **-coes** or **-cos.** A complete failure, especially a very embarrassing one. [French, from Italian *(far) fiasco*, "(to make) a bottle," an unexplained allusion, perhaps from Late Latin *flascō*, FLASK.]

fi·at (fē′ăt′, fī′ăt′, -ət) *n.* **1.** An arbitrary order or decree. **2.** Authorization; sanction. [Latin *fīat*, "let it be done," third person singular present subjunctive of *fierī*, to become, representing the passive of *facere*, to do.]

fiat money *n.* Paper money decreed legal tender, not backed by gold or silver, and not necessarily redeemable in coin.

fib (fĭb) *n.* An inconsequential lie.

~*intr.v.* **fibbed, fibbing, fibs.** To tell a fib. [17th century : perhaps shortened from obsolete *fible-fable*, nonsense, reduplication of FABLE.] —**fib·ber** *n.*

fi·ber (fī′bər) *n.* Also *chiefly British* **fi·bre. 1.** A slender, elongated structure; thread or strand. **2.** Any of the elongated, thick-walled cells that give strength and support to plant tissue. **3.** Any of the filaments constituting the intracellular matrix of connective tissue. **4.** *Anatomy.* Any of various threadlike structures; especially, a **muscle fiber** or a **nerve fiber** *(both of which see).* **5. a.** A natural or synthetic thread, as of cotton or nylon, capable of being spun into yarn. **b.** Material made of such filaments. **6.** The essential substance: *"stirred the deeper fibers of my nature"* (Oscar Wilde). **7.** Internal strength; character: *lacking in moral fiber.* [Middle English, from Old French *fibre*, from Latin *fibra†.*]

fi·ber·board (fī′bər-bôrd′, -bōrd′) *n.* **1.** A building material composed of wood or other plant fibers bonded together and pressed into rigid sheets. **2.** A sheet of this material.

Fi·ber·fill (fī′bər-fĭl′) *n.* A trademark for a synthetic resin used as quilt filling.

Fi·ber·glas (fī′bər-glăs′, -gläs′) *n.* A trademark for a type of fiber glass.

fiber glass *n.* Spun filaments of glass made into yarn and textiles

feverfew *A pungently aromatic plant, feverfew grows wild in Europe and Asia. Now considered only a weed, it was so named because it was once thought to be effective in driving away fevers.*

or, when hardened with resin, used as a strong, lightweight construction material.

fiber optics *n. Used with a singular verb.* The optics of light transmission through very fine, flexible glass fibers by internal reflection. **—fi·ber-op·tic** (fī′bər-ŏp′tĭk) *adj.*

fi·ber·scope (fī′bər-skōp′) *n.* A flexible fiber-optic instrument used to view objects that would otherwise be inaccessible, especially tissues and organs in inaccessible parts of the body.

Fi·bo·nac·ci (fē′bə-nä′chē), **Leonardo** (*c.* 1170–*c.* 1240). Italian mathematician. In North Africa he learned the decimal system of numerals, which he published in his *Liber Abaci* (1202).

Fibonacci sequence *n.* A sequence of numbers (Fibonacci numbers), each of which is the sum of the two preceding numbers: 1, 1,

2, 3, 5, 8, 13, 21 . . . . . . [After Leonardo FIBONACCI.]

fi·bri·form (fī′brə-fôrm′) *adj.* Similar in form or structure to a fiber.

fi·bril (fī′brəl, fĭb′rəl) *n.* Also **fi·bril·la** (fī-brĭl′ə) *pl.* **-brillae** (-brĭl′ē). A small, slender fiber, such as a root hair or a constituent thread of a muscle fiber. [New Latin *fibrilla,* diminutive of Latin *fibra,* FIBER.] **—fi·bril·lar** (fī′brə-lər, fĭb′rə-), **fi·bril·lar·y** (-lĕr′ē) *adj.*

fib·ril·la·tion (fĭb′rə-lā′shən, fī′brə-) *n.* **1.** The forming of fibers. **2.** Uncoordinated twitching of individual muscle fibers with little or no movement of the muscle as a whole. **3.** *Pathology.* Fine, rapid fibrillar movements that replace the normal contraction of the heart muscle. [New Latin *fibrilla,* FIBRIL.]

fi·bril·li·form (fī-brĭl′ə-fôrm′, fī-brĭl′-) *adj.* Having the form of a fibril.

fi·bril·lose (fī′brə-lōs′, fĭb′rə-) *adj.* Having or consisting of fibrils.

fi·brin (fī′brĭn) *n.* An elastic, insoluble protein derived from the interaction of fibrinogen with thrombin and forming a fibrous network in the coagulation of blood. [FIBR(O)- + -IN.]

fi·brin·o·gen (fī-brĭn′ə-jən) *n.* A protein in the blood plasma that is converted to fibrin by the action of thrombin in the presence of ionized calcium. [FIBRIN + -O-GEN.]

fi·bri·nol·y·sin (fī′brə-nŏl′ə-sĭn) *n.* An enzyme, **plasmin** (*see*). [FIBRIN + -O- + LYSIN.]

fi·bri·nol·y·sis (fī′brə-nŏl′ə-sĭs) *n.* The breakdown of blood clots, which involves the dissolution of fibrin by the enzyme plasmin. [FIBRIN + -O-LYSIS.]

fi·brin·ous (fī′brə-nəs) *adj.* Of, pertaining to, or having the nature of fibrin.

fibro–, fibr– *prefix.* Indicates: **1.** Fibrous tissue; for example, **fibrovascular, fibrosis. 2.** Fiber; for example, **fibrocement.** [Latin *fibra,* FIBER.]

fi·bro·blast (fī′brə-blăst′, -bläst′) *n.* A cell in connective tissue that is responsible for producing fibers. [FIBRO- + -BLAST.]

fi·bro·car·ti·lage (fī′brō-kär′tə-lĭj) *n.* A type of cartilage containing many fibers, as found in the intervertebral disks.

fi·bro·ce·ment (fī′brō-sĭ-ment′) *n.* A building material made out of cement and asbestos mixed together and formed into sheets.

fi·broid (fī′broid′) *adj.* Resembling or composed of fibrous tissue. ~*n.* A benign tumor of smooth muscle, especially in the uterine wall. [FIBR(O)- + -OID.]

fi·bro·in (fī′brō-ĭn) *n.* A white protein that is the essential component of raw silk and spider-web filaments. [French *fibroïne* : FIBRO- + -IN.]

fi·bro·ma (fī-brō′mə) *n., pl.* **-mas** or **-mata** (-mə-tə). Any benign tumor derived from fibrous tissue, such as a fibroid. [New Latin : FIBR(O)- + -OMA.] **—fi·brom·a·tous** (fī-brŏm′ə-təs, fī-brō′mə-) *adj.*

fi·bro·sis (fī-brō′sĭs) *n.* The formation of excess fibrous tissue in an organ, such as the lung, usually as a result of inflammation or injury. See **cystic fibrosis.** [New Latin : FIBR(O)- + -OSIS.]

fi·bro·si·tis (fī′brə-sī′tĭs, fĭb′rə-) *n.* Inflammation of fibrous connective tissue, especially in the muscles and muscle sheaths of the back. [New Latin *fibrosus,* FIBROUS + -ITIS.]

fi·brous (fī′brəs) *adj.* Having, consisting of, or resembling fibers.

fi·bro·vas·cu·lar (fī′brō-văs′kyə-lər) *adj. Botany.* Having fibrous tissue and vascular tissue. Said of the vascular bundles in woody tissue.

fib·u·la (fĭb′yə-lə) *n., pl.* **-lae** (-lē′) or **-las. 1.** The outer and smaller of two bones of the human leg or the hind leg of an animal, in humans between the knee and ankle. **2.** A broochlike clasp used in the ancient world. [Latin *fibula,* perhaps from the root of *figere,* to fix.] **—fib·u·lar** *adj.*

–fic *suffix.* Indicates making, causing, or creating; for example, **morbific.** [New Latin *-ficus,* from Latin, from *facere,* to do, make.]

FICA Federal Insurance Contributions Act.

fice. Variant of **feist.**

fiche (fēsh) *n.* A **microfiche** (*see*).

Fich·te (fĭKH′tə), **Johann Gottlieb** (1762–1814). German philosopher. He argued that moral reason is the base of all reason, knowledge, and humanity. His philosophical works include *The Vocation of Man.* Fichte is considered one of the most important transcendental idealists.

fi·chu (fĭsh′oo, fē-shoo′) *n.* A woman's triangular scarf of lightweight fabric, worn over the shoulders and crossed or tied in a loose knot at the breast. [French, from the past participle of *ficher,* to fix, attach, from Vulgar Latin *figicāre* (unattested), from Latin *figere,* to FIX.]

fick·le (fĭk′əl) *adj.* Changeable, especially with regard to affections or attachments; inconstant; capricious. —See Synonyms at **faithless.** [Middle English *fikel,* false, treacherous, Old English *ficol.*] **—fick·le·ness** *n.*

fic·tile (fĭk′təl, -tīl′) *adj.* **1.** Able to be molded; plastic. **2.** Formed of a moldable substance, such as clay or earth. **3.** Of or pertaining to earthenware or pottery. [Latin *fictilis,* from *fictus,* past participle of *fingere,* to touch, form, mold, shape.]

fic·tion (fĭk′shən) *n.* **1.** An event, statement, or occurrence that has been invented or feigned rather than having actually taken place. **2.** The act of producing such inventions; a feigning. **3.** A lie. **4. a.** A literary work whose content is produced by the imagination and is not necessarily based on fact. **b.** The category of literature comprising works of this kind, including novels and short stories. **5.** Something accepted as true without any real justification, but merely for the sake of convenience: *a legal fiction.* [Middle English *ficcioun,* invention, from Old French *fiction,* from Latin *fictiō* (stem *fictiōn-*), a making, fashioning, from *fictus,* past participle of *fingere,*

---

fiber optics

MAKING LIGHT THE SERVANT OF SCIENCE

See and be seen (and heard) along a glass thread

Fiber optics is a branch of engineering concerned with the transmission of light along flexible glass fibers and plays an increasing role in medicine and telecommunications.

The basic element in fiber optics is a glass thread less than a millimeter thick, along which light will travel by bouncing from side to side, however curved the fiber. The first use of fiber optics came in 1955. The technique has since been used to improve ways of seeing inside the body; light is shone in through the fibers and they return a clear image. In the 1960's, it was seen that fiber-optic cables could be used to carry telecommunications signals in much greater quantity and for longer distances than copper wires. In fiber-optic systems information is transmitted by means of coded laser beams.

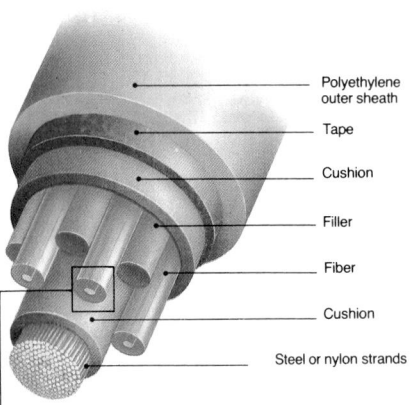

Polyethylene outer sheath
Tape
Cushion
Filler
Fiber
Cushion
Steel or nylon strands

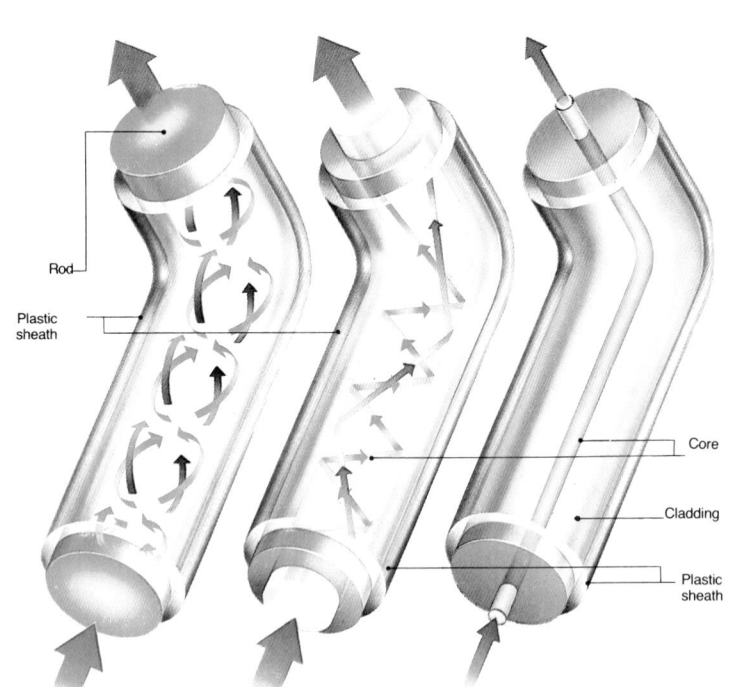

Rod
Plastic sheath
Core
Cladding
Plastic sheath

FIBER-OPTIC CABLE *The cable contains bundles of fine glass fibers in a protective sheath and with strengthening strands of steel or nylon at the center. A fiber may be a "graded-index" rod (left) that bends light by decreasing amounts from its center outward; or it may be a "stepped-index" rod (center and right) consisting of two types of glass, one outside the other, that bend light by different amounts.*

Light signals may be sent in quantity or singly. In multiple transmissions (left and center) a thick fiber carries up to 10,000 signals, but with some loss of quality. Single signals are transmitted along a minute stepped-index fiber (right) that is hard to make—it is only eight times wider than the wavelength of the infrared light used—but the signal is remarkably true.

to touch, form, mold.] **—fic·tion·al** *adj.* **—fic·tion·al·ly** *adv.*

fic·tion·al·ize (fĭk′shə-nə-līz′) *tr.v.* **-ized, -izing, -izes.** To treat as or make into fiction by changing details such as names and locations. **—fic·tion·al·i·za·tion** (fĭk′shə-nə-lĭ-zā′shən) *n.*

fic·ti·tious (fĭk-tĭsh′əs) *adj.* **1.** Of, pertaining to, or characterized by fiction; nonexistent; imaginary; unreal: *a fictitious event.* **2.** Purposefully deceptive; false; untrue: *a fictitious name.* **—fic·ti·tious·ly** *adv.* **—fic·ti·tious·ness** *n.*

fictitious force *n. Physics.* A force, such as centrifugal or Coriolis force, that arises because of the frame of reference of the observer and disappears on transformation to a more suitable frame.

fic·tive (fĭk′tĭv) *adj.* **1.** Of or pertaining to the creation of fiction. **2.** Pertaining to or characterized by fiction; fictitious; imaginary. **3.** Feigned; sham. **—fic·tive·ly** *adv.*

fid (fĭd) *n. Nautical.* **1.** A square bar used as a support for a topmast. **2.** A large, tapering pin used to open the strands of a rope prior to splicing. [17th century : origin obscure.]

fid. fidelity.

-fid *suffix.* Indicates a division or separation into parts or lobes; for example, **pinnatifid.** [Latin *-fidus,* from *findere,* to split.]

Fid. Def. Fidei Defensor.

fid·dle (fĭd′l) *n.* **1. a.** *Informal.* A **violin** *(see).* **b.** Any member of the violin family, including similarly designed medieval and Oriental instruments. **2.** *Nautical.* A guard rail used on a table during rough weather to prevent things from slipping off. **3.** *Informal.* Nonsensical trifling; stupidity. **4.** *British Informal.* An illegal or underhand practice or act: *a tax fiddle.* **—fit as a fiddle.** Very healthy. **—play second fiddle.** *Informal.* To be subordinate.

~v. **fiddled, -dling, -dles.** *—intr.* **1. a.** To move one's fingers or hands in a restless fashion; fidget. **b.** To putter or tamper with something: *Don't fiddle with my belongings.* **2.** To waste time. Usually used with *around* or *about.* **3.** *Informal.* To play a violin. *—tr. Informal.* **1.** To arrange or contrive, especially by slightly underhand methods. **2.** To waste or squander: *fiddled away the day.* **3.** To cheat or swindle. **4.** To play (a tune) on a violin. [Middle English *fithele, fidle,* Old English *fithele,* from West Germanic *fithula* (unattested), from Medieval Latin *vītula,* from Latin *vītulārī,* to celebrate a victory, from *Vītula,* goddess of joy and victory, probably of Sabine origin.]

fid·dle·back (fĭd′l-băk′) *adj.* Shaped like the body of a violin: *a fiddleback chair.*

fid·dle-de-dee (fĭd′l-dē-dē′) *interj.* Used to express mild annoyance or impatience. [Nonsensical formation from FIDDLE.]

fid·dle-fad·dle (fĭd′l-făd′l) *interj.* Used to express mild annoyance or impatience.

~n. Nonsense or petty matters.

~intr.v. **fiddle-faddled, -dling, -dles.** To fritter away one's time; dally. [Reduplication of FIDDLE.] **—fid·dle-fad·dler** *n.*

fid·dle·head (fĭd′l-hĕd′) *n.* A curved, scroll-like ornamentation at the top of a ship's bow that resembles the neck of a violin.

fid·dler (fĭd′lər) *n. Informal.* A person who plays the violin.

fiddler crab *n.* Any of various burrowing crabs of the genus *Uca,* having one of the anterior claws much enlarged in the male. [So called from its large claw that it seems to hold like a fiddle.]

fid·dle·sticks (fĭd′l-stĭks′) *interj.* Used to express mild annoyance or impatience.

fid·dling (fĭd′lĭng) *adj.* Unimportant; trifling; silly.

fid·dly (fĭd′lē) *adj.* **-dlier, -dliest.** Awkward or difficult to do, use, or handle, as because of smallness of size or extreme detail.

F.I.D.E. (fē′dā′) *n.* The World Chess Federation. [*F*édération *I*nternationale *d*es *É*checs.]

Fi·de·i De·fen·sor (fĭ′dē-ī′ dĭ-fĕn′sôr′, fē′dā-ē′ dā-fĕn′sōr′) *n. Abbr.* **F.D., Fid. Def.** *Latin.* Defender of the Faith. Used as one of the titles of the British sovereign.

fi·de·ism (fē′dā-ĭz′əm) *n.* The belief or doctrine that knowledge of religious matters can be obtained only through revelation or faith and cannot be established by rational means. [Latin *fidēs,* faith + -ISM.]

fi·del·i·ty (fĭ-dĕl′ə-tē, fī-) *n., pl.* **-ties. 1.** Faithfulness to obligations, duties, or observances; loyalty. **2.** Faithfulness or loyalty, as to a friend or cause; specifically, faithfulness to a spouse or lover. **3.** Correspondence with fact or a given quality, condition, or event; verity; truthfulness; accuracy. **4.** *Abbr.* **fid.** The degree to which an electronic system, such as a radio or record player, accurately reproduces at its output the essential characteristics of its input signal. [Middle English *fidelite,* from Old French, from Latin *fidēlitās* (stem *fidēlitāt-*), from *fidēlis,* faithful, from *fidēs,* faith.]

Synonyms: *allegiance, devotion, fealty, loyalty.*

fidg·et (fĭj′ĭt) *v.* **-eted, -eting, -ets.** *—intr.* **1.** To keep some part of one's body in continuous motion, as by shifting one's hands or feet; move nervously or restlessly. **2.** To play with or finger something nervously. Used with *with*: *The lecturer fidgeted with his notes. —tr.* To cause (someone) to fidget; make restless or nervous.

~n. **1. fidgets.** A condition of restlessness. **2.** One who fidgets. [Frequentative of obsolete *fidge,* variant of *fitch, fike,* from Middle English *fiken,* probably from Old Norse *fīkjast,* akin to Old English *fāciant,* to try to obtain.]

fidg·et·y (fĭj′ĭ-tē) *adj.* **1.** Habitually fidgeting; nervous; restless. **2.** Unnecessarily fussy. **—fidg·et·i·ness** *n.*

fi·du·cial (fĭ-dōō′shəl, -dyōō′shəl, fī-) *adj.* **1.** Based on or pertaining to faith or trust. **2.** Pertaining to a legal trust; fiduciary. **3.** Regarded or employed as a standard of reference, as in measurement. [Late Latin *fīdūciālis,* from Latin *fīdūcia,* trust, from *fīdere,* to trust.] **—fi·du·cial·ly** *adv.*

fi·du·ci·ar·y (fĭ-dōō′shē-ĕr′ē, fĭ-dyōō′-, fī-) *adj.* **1.** Of, pertaining to, or involving one who holds something in trust for another: *a fiduciary heir; a fiduciary contract.* **2. a.** Of, pertaining to, or designating a trustee or trusteeship. **b.** Held in trust. **3.** Of, pertaining to, or consisting of paper currency that is issued without being backed by gold.

~n., pl. **fiduciaries.** A person who stands in a special relation of trust, confidence, or responsibility in his obligations to others, such as a company director or an agent of a principal. [Latin *fīdūciārius,* from *fīdūcia,* trust. See **fiducial.**]

fie (fī) *interj.* **1.** Used to express distaste or shock. **2.** Used humorously to express pretended shock. [Middle English *fi,* from Old French, from Latin *fī,* expression of disgust at a bad smell.]

Fied·ler (fēd′lər), **Arthur** (1894–1979). U.S. conductor. He studied music in Berlin, then returned to his birthplace, Boston, to join the Boston Symphony Orchestra. In 1929 he founded the popular summer Esplanade Concerts and in 1930 became conductor of the Boston Pops, an institution famous for its performances on radio and public television.

fief (fēf) *n.* **1.** A feudal estate, a **fee** *(see).* **2.** A sphere of authority or influence. [French, from Old French *fie(f),* FEE.]

fief·dom (fēf′dəm) *n.* **1.** A fief. **2.** A person's sphere of influence or control.

field (fēld) *n. Abbr.* **fld. 1.** A broad, level, open expanse of land; a meadow: *a field of buttercups.* **2.** An expanse of land, usually enclosed grassland, used for pasturage. **3.** A cultivated expanse of land, especially one devoted to a particular crop. **4.** A portion of land or a geologic formation containing a specified natural resource: *an oil field.* **5.** A large, flat surface used by aircraft for landing and taking off; an airfield. **6.** A background area, as on a flag, painting, or coin: *a blue insignia on a field of red.* **7.** *Heraldry.* The background area of a shield, or one of the divisions of the background. **8.** *Sports.* **a.** A delineated area on which a sports event, such as a baseball or football game, takes place. **b.** The portion of a playing field having specific dimensions on which the action of a game takes place: *The spectators were ordered to stay off the field.* **c.** All the contestants or participants in an event. **d.** All the contestants except those specified: *Her horse led the field in the stretch.* **e.** The body of horsemen following a pack of hounds. **9.** A group of rival candidates for selection: *chosen from a talented field of applicants.* **10. a.** An area of human activity or interest: *a field of endeavor.* **b.** A topic, subject, or area of academic interest or specialization. **c.** Profession, employment, or business: *Data processing is definitely not his field.* **11.** An area or setting of practical activity or application, especially as distinguished from one of academic study or theoretical research: *out in the field selling encyclopedias.* **12. a.** The scene of a battle. **b.** A battle while it is in progress. **c.** The land, especially when considered topographically, where a battle has been fought; a battlefield. **13.** *Mathematics.* A set with two binary operations, *addition* and *multiplication,* satisfying the conditions that the set is a commutative group with respect to addition, that the set with the zero omitted is a commutative group with respect to multiplication, and that multiplication is distributive over addition for all elements in the set. **14.** *Physics.* A region of space characterized by a physical property, such as gravitational or electromagnetic force or fluid pressure, having a determinable value at every point in the region. **15.** *Optics.* The usually circular area in which the image is rendered by the lens system of an optical instrument. **16.** *Computer Science.* **a.** A group of characters treated as a unit of information. **b.** The characters recorded in a vertical column on a punched card. **—keep** (or **hold**) **the field.** To continue in one's position in the face of adversity. **—leave the field.** *Informal.* To concede one's interest to another or others. **—play the field.** *Informal.* To maintain a broad range of options in personal or business matters, rather than making a specific commitment. **—take the field.** To begin or resume activity, as in military operations or in a sport.

~v. **fielded, fielding, fields.** *—tr.* **1.** *Sports.* **a.** To retrieve, catch, or stop (a ball): *The shortstop fielded the ground ball and threw the batter out.* **b.** To place (a team or player) in playing position. **c.** To be able to put (a team, for example) into a contest: *The coach fielded a strong team.* **2.** To handle adequately and be able to return in kind; cope with: *The mayor fielded the question very clumsily. —intr. Sports.* **1.** To retrieve, catch, or stop a ball. **2.** To play or take a turn as a fielder.

~adj. **1.** Of, pertaining or appropriate to, or carried out in a field or fields: *field work.* **2.** Growing or living in a field or fields: *field crops.* [Middle English *feld, field,* Old English *feld,* from West Germanic.]

Field (fēld), **Cyrus West** (1819–92). U.S. financier. In 1854 he conceived the idea of a transatlantic telegraph cable and was persistent in accomplishing his goal (1866) despite numerous setbacks. Later he was instrumental in organizing the elevated rapid-transit system of New York City.

Field, Marshall (1834–1906). U.S. merchant. Starting as a clerk in a Chicago dry-goods store, he eventually organized Marshall Field and Company, the largest wholesale and retail dry-goods establishment in the world from 1881 to 1906. He is especially noted for his philanthropy, giving land and money to such institutions as the Art Institute of Chicago and the University of Chicago.

field artillery *n. Abbr.* **FA** Artillery, with the exception of antiair-

fiddler crab *This crab, found on tidal mud flats in temperate and tropical parts of the world, takes its name from the way it moves its bright-red claw to and fro, in the manner of a violinist, to warn off attackers.*

PRONUNCIATION KEY

ă, pat; ā, pay; âr, care;
ä, father, are; b, bib;
ch, church; d, deed; ĕ, pet;
ē, be; f, fife; g, gag; h, hat;
hw, which; ĭ, pit; ī, pie;
îr, pier; j, judge; k, kick;
l, lid, needle; m, mum;
n, no, sudden; ng, thing;
ŏ, pot; ō, toe; ô, paw, for;
oi, noise; ou, out; ŏŏ, book;
ōō, boot; p, pop; r, roar;
s, sauce; sh, ship, dish;
t, tight; th, thin, path;
th, this, bathe; ŭ, cut; ûr, fur;
v, valve; w, with; y, yes;
z, zebra, size; zh, vision;
ə, about, item, edible,
gallop, circus, peaceful

IN FOREIGN WORDS:

à, *Fr.* ami; œ, *Fr.* feu, *Ger.* schön; ü, *Fr.* tu, *Ger.* über; KH, *Ger.* ich, *Scot.* loch; N, *Fr.* bon; y′, *Fr.* Compiègne

STRESS MARKS:

Primary stress: ′
in·cite′ (ĭn-sīt′)
Secondary stress: ′
in′sight′ (ĭn′sīt′)

craft artillery, light enough to be mounted for use in the field.

field battery *n.* A tactical artillery unit usually consisting of four or six field guns.

field coil *n.* An electric coil used to generate a magnetic field, as in a motor or direct-current generator.

field day *n.* 1. A day spent outdoors engaged in a planned activity such as an athletic competition or nature study. 2. A festive day, such as one on which a fair is held. 3. *Informal.* An opportunity for expressing or asserting oneself with the fullest pleasure or triumph.

field-ef·fect transistor (fēld'ĭ-fĕkt') *n. Abbr.* **FET** A transistor device in which a current flowing in a narrow channel between two regions (the source and the drain) is controlled by an electric field applied to a third region (the gate).

field emission *n.* The emission of electrons from the surface of a conductor, caused by a strong electric field at the surface distorting the potential barrier.

field·e·mis·sion microscope (fēld'ĭ-mĭsh'ən) *n. Abbr.* **FEM** An instrument for investigating metal surfaces, consisting of a sharply pointed piece of metal to which a high electric field is applied in a vacuum, so that electrons escaping by field emission are accelerated to a fluorescent screen where they produce a highly magnified image of the tip of the sample. —**field·e·mis·sion microscopy** *n.*

field·er (fēl'dər) *n. Sports.* 1. A person who fields a ball. 2. A person who plays a field position, especially in baseball or cricket.

fielder's choice *n.* A baseball play in which the batter reaches first base while a fielder is attempting to put out an advancing base runner.

field event *n.* A throwing or jumping event of a track meet as distinguished from a running event.

field·fare (fēld'fâr') *n.* A European thrush, *Turdus pilaris,* having gray and brown plumage. [Middle English *feldefare,* probably late Old English *feldefare,* "field-goer" : FIELD + *faran,* to go.]

field glass *n. Often* **field glasses.** A portable binocular instrument used for magnifying and viewing distant objects.

field goal *n. Abbr.* **f.g.** 1. *Football.* A score counting three points made on an ordinary down by place-kicking or drop-kicking the ball over the crossbar and between the goal posts. 2. *Basketball.* A score counting two points made by throwing the ball through the basket in regulation play.

field gun *n.* A mobile piece of field artillery.

field hand *n.* A hired laborer or worker on a farm.

field hockey *n.* A form of **hockey** *(see)* played on a turf field.

field hospital *n.* A hospital set up on a temporary basis for soldiers serving in a remote area.

Field·ing (fēl'dĭng), **Henry** (1707-54). English novelist and dramatist. He wrote numerous plays and novels, many of them satirical, and topical comedies. His most successful novel was *Tom Jones* (1749); his other works include *Joseph Andrews* (1742).

field intensity *n.* The effectiveness of a field of force at any point as measured by the force exerted on a unit entity, as a unit charge or unit magnetic pole, subjected to the field at that point. Also called "field strength."

field·i·on microscope (fēld'ī'ən, -ŏn') *n. Abbr.* **FIM** An instrument for investigating metal surfaces, consisting of a sharply pointed piece of metal to which a high electric field is applied in a low pressure of helium gas. Helium ions formed at the surface by field ionization are accelerated to a fluorescent screen, where they produce a highly magnified image of the tip of the sample. —**field·i·on microscopy** *n.*

field lens *n.* The lens that is farthest from the eye in a compound eyepiece.

field magnet *n.* A magnet used to provide a magnetic field in an electrical device such as a generator or motor.

field marshal *n. Abbr.* **F.M.** 1. The highest-ranking officer in the British and Australian armies. 2. An officer in some European armies usually ranking just below the commander in chief.

field mouse *n.* Any of various small, nocturnal, long-tailed mice of the genus *Apodemus,* inhabiting meadows and fields and often causing damage to crops. Also called "meadow mouse."

field mushroom *n.* A common edible fungus, *Agaricus campestris,* having a white cap and pink or brown gills. Also called "meadow mushroom."

field officer *n. Abbr.* **F.O.** *Military.* An officer, such as a major, lieutenant colonel, or colonel, ranking above a captain and below a brigadier general.

field of force *n.* A region of space throughout which the force produced by a single agent, such as an electric current, is operative. Also called "force field."

field of honor *n.* 1. The scene of a duel involving a matter of personal honor. 2. A battlefield.

field·piece (fēld'pēs') *n.* A field gun.

Fields (fēldz), **Gracie,** born Grace Stansfield (1898-1979). British singer and comedienne. Her Lancashire humor and inimitable voice won her great popularity, especially during the Depression of the 1930's. Her most notable films include *Sally in Our Alley* (1931) and *Sing as We Go* (1934).

Fields, W.C., born William Claude Dukenfield (1880-1946). U.S. screen actor and comedian. He began making films in the early 1920's and quickly found fame as an offbeat misogynist, a screen character he based on his own genuine eccentricity.

fields·man (fēldz'mən) *n., pl.* **-men** (-mĭn). *Cricket.* A fielder.

field·stone (fēld'stōn') *n.* A stone naturally occurring in fields, often used as a building material.

field strength *n.* Field intensity *(see).*

field-strip (fēld'strĭp') *tr.v.* **-stripped, -stripping, -strips.** To disassemble (a weapon) for cleaning, repair, and inspection.

field theory *n.* The theory concerned with algebraic fields.

field trial *n.* 1. A test for young, untried hunting dogs to determine their competence in pointing and retrieving. 2. **field trials.** Tests to observe efficiency, durability, or performance, as of a special vehicle or invention or of a new product or plant variety.

field trip *n.* A group excursion or expedition for the purpose of firsthand observation, as to a museum, woods, or historical site.

field winding *n.* The electrically conducting winding of a field magnet that produces electrical excitation, especially of a motor or generator.

field·work (fēld'wûrk') *n.* 1. *Military.* A temporary fortification erected in the field. 2. Work done or observations made in the field, as at a site of archaeological or geologic study, rather than in a library, laboratory, or other place of academic study. —**field·work·er** *n.*

fiend (fēnd) *n.* 1. An evil spirit; a demon. 2. **Fiend.** Satan; the Devil. 3. A diabolically evil or wicked person. 4. *Informal.* **a.** One who is addicted to a specified vice: *a dope fiend.* **b.** A person completely absorbed in or obsessed with a specified job or pastime: *a crossword-puzzle fiend.* [Middle English *fe(o)nd,* enemy, devil, fiend, Old English *fēond, fīond.*]

fiend·ish (fēn'dĭsh) *adj.* 1. Pertaining to, similar to, or suggestive of a fiend; diabolical. 2. **a.** Extremely difficult or grueling. **b.** Extremely clever but devious: *a fiendish maneuver.* —**fiend·ish·ly** *adv.* —**fiend·ish·ness** *n.*

fierce (fîrs) *adj.* **fiercer, fiercest.** 1. Having a savage and violent nature; ferocious. 2. Extremely severe or violent; terrible: *fierce thunder.* 3. Intense or ardent; extreme: *fierce loyalty.* 4. Very difficult or unpleasant. [Middle English *f(i)ers,* from Old French, from Latin *ferus,* wild.] —**fierce·ly** *adv.* —**fierce·ness** *n.*

fi·e·ri fa·ci·as (fī'ə-rī' fā'shē-əs, fē'ə-rē' fä'kē-äs') *n. Law.* A writ of execution commanding a sheriff to lay a claim to and seize the goods and chattels of a debtor to fulfill a judgment against him. [Latin, "cause (it) to be done" (words used in such a writ).]

fier·y (fîr'ē, fī'ə-rē) *adj.* **-ier, -iest.** 1. Consisting of or containing fire: *a fiery furnace.* 2. Of, pertaining to, or resembling a fire: *a fiery sunset.* 3. Torridly hot: *a fiery gust of the sirocco.* 4. Flammable; liable to explode. Said of gas, a mine, or the like. 5. Causing a hot, burning sensation; strong or highly spiced. Said of food or drink: *a fiery curry.* 6. Emitting or appearing to emit sparks; glowing. 7. **a.** Easily excited or emotionally volatile; tempestuous: *a fiery temper.* **b.** Showing passion or strong feeling: *a fiery outburst.* 8. Inflamed. Said of the skin. [Middle English *fiery, firi,* from FIRE.] —**fier·i·ly** *adv.* —**fier·i·ness** *n.*

fiery cross *n.* 1. Formerly, a wooden cross with charred or bloody ends used by the Scottish clans to summon forth men into battle. 2. A burning cross used by the Ku Klux Klan as a symbol or emblem.

Fi·e·so·le (fē-ā'zə-lĕ', -lä') Ancient town founded by the Etruscans, near present-day Florence in Tuscany, Italy. It is a tourist spot because of its Etruscan and Roman museum.

fi·es·ta (fē-ĕs'tə) *n.* 1. A religious feast or holiday; especially, a saint's day celebrated in Spanish-speaking countries. 2. A celebration or festival. [Spanish, from Latin *fēsta,* neuter plural of *fēstus,* joyous, festive.]

FI·FA (fē'fə) *n.* The international governing body of soccer. [*Fédération Internationale de Football Association.*]

fife (fīf) *n.* A musical instrument similar to a flute but higher in range, used primarily to accompany drums in military music. —*v.* **fifed, fifing, fifes.** —*tr.* To play (a tune) on a fife. —*intr.* To play a fife. [German *Pfeife,* from Old High German *pfīffa,* from West Germanic *pīpa* (unattested), from Vulgar Latin *pīpa* (unattested), from Latin *pīpāre,* to chirp.]

fife rail *n.* A rail around the lower part of a ship's mast to which the belaying pins for the rigging are secured.

Fife Region (fīf). Unit of local administration in east-central Scotland, formerly the county of Fife. It borders on the North Sea between the Firth of Tay and the Firth of Forth. Fishing, arable farming, and coal mining make it one of the most prosperous regions in Scotland.

fif·teen (fĭf-tēn') *n.* 1. **a.** The cardinal number that is one more than fourteen. **b.** A symbol representing this, such as 15 or XV. 2. A set made up of fifteen persons or things. 3. The fifteenth in a series. 4. A size, as in clothing, designated as fifteen. [Middle English *fiftene,* Old English *fīftȳne, fīftēne.*] —**fif·teen** *adj. & pron.*

Fifteen *n.* In British history, the **Jacobite Rebellion** *(see)* of 1715. Preceded by *the.*

fif·teenth (fĭf-tēnth') *n.* 1. The ordinal number 15 in a series. 2. One of 15 equal parts. 3. *Music.* **a.** An interval of two octaves. **b.** An organ stop pitched two octaves above the normal pitch. —**fif·teenth** *adj. & adv.*

fifth (fĭfth) *n.* 1. The ordinal number five in a series. 2. Any of five equal parts. 3. **a.** A musical interval encompassing five diatonic tones, such as C, D, E, F, and G. **b.** The combination of the two tones constituting the extremities of such an interval. **c.** The dominant of a tonality. 4. **a.** One fifth of a gallon of liquor. **b.** A bottle containing a fifth of liquor. [Middle English *fifthe, fifte,* Old English *fīfta.*] —**fifth** *adj. & adv.* —**fifth·ly** *adv.*

Fifth Amendment *n.* An amendment to the Constitution of the United States, ratified in 1791, that deals with the rights of accused

criminals by providing for due process of law, forbidding double jeopardy, and stating that no person may be forced to testify as a witness against himself.

fifth column *n.* **1.** A clandestine subversive organization working within a given country to further an invading enemy's military and political aims. **2.** Any subversive element working within an organization or institution. [First applied in 1936 to the Franco supporters in Madrid by Gen. Emilio Mola, who was leading four rebel columns of troops against that city.] **—fifth columnist** *n.*

fifth wheel *n.* **1.** A wheel or portion of a wheel placed horizontally over the forward axle of a carriage to provide support and stability during turns. **2.** An additional wheel carried on a four-wheeled vehicle as a spare. **3.** Any extra and unnecessary person or thing.

fif·ti·eth (fĭf′tē-ĭth) *n.* **1.** The ordinal number 50 in a series. **2.** Any of 50 equal parts. **—fif·ti·eth** *adj. & adv.*

fif·ty (fĭf′tē) *n.* **1. a.** The cardinal number that is ten more than forty. **b.** A symbol representing this, such as 50 or L. **2.** A set made up of fifty persons or things. **3.** The fiftieth in a series. **4.** A size, as in clothing, designated as fifty. **5.** A bill or coin having a denomination of fifty: *I'll take the money in fifties.* **6. fifties. a.** The numbers from 50 to 59, considered as a range of age, price, temperature, or the like. **b.** The years numbered 50 to 59 in a century. [Middle English *fifti,* Old English *fīftig.*] **—fif·ty** *adj. & pron.*

fif·ty-fif·ty (fĭf′tē-fĭf′tē) *adj. Informal.* **1.** Divided or shared in two equal portions: *a fifty-fifty split of the profits.* **2.** Even: *a fifty-fifty chance.* **—fif·ty-fif·ty** *adv.*

fig¹ (fĭg) *n.* **1.** Any of several trees or shrubs of the genus *Ficus;* especially, *F. carica,* native to the Mediterranean region and widely cultivated for its edible fruit. Also called "fig tree." **2.** The sweet, pear-shaped, many-seeded fruit of this tree. **3. a.** Any of several plants bearing similar edible fruit, such as the Hottentot fig, *Mesembryanthemum edule,* of southern Africa. See **fig marigold. b.** The fruit of such a plant. **4.** A trivial or contemptible amount; a jot; a whit: *"None of them . . . would have cared a fig the more for me"* (Hawthorne). [Middle English *fig(e),* from Old French *figue,* from Old Provençal *figa,* from Vulgar Latin *fīca* (unattested), from Latin *fīcus,* from the same Mediterranean source as Greek *sukon.* See also **syconium.**]

fig² *tr.v.* **figged, figging, figs.** *Informal.* **1.** To dress or furnish; array; furbish. Used with *out: all figged out.* **2.** To make (a horse) appear lively, usually by means of drugs. Used with *up* or *out.*
~n. Informal. **1.** Dress; array: *in full fig.* **2.** Physical condition; shape: *in poor fig.* [Variant of obsolete *feague,* from German *fegen,* to polish, furbish. See **fake.**]

fig³ *n.* An obscene gesture of contempt made by brandishing a fist with the thumb held between the first and second fingers. [French *(faire la) figue,* to make this gesture, from Italian *fica,* vulva, fig, from Vulgar Latin *fīca* (unattested), FIG (tree).]

fig. **1.** figurative; figuratively. **2.** figure.

fig-bird (fĭg′bûrd′) *n.* An Australian oriole of the genus *Sphecotheres* that feeds on figs and other fruits.

fight (fīt) *v.* **fought** (fôt), **fighting, fights.** *—intr.* **1.** To participate in combat or battle. **2.** To make a strenuous effort; struggle: *fight against oppression.* **3.** To quarrel; argue. **4.** To participate in boxing or wrestling: *He fights professionally.* *—tr.* **1.** To contend with physically or in battle. **2.** To box or wrestle against in a ring. **3.** To contend with or struggle against: *fight prejudice.* **4.** To strive to prevent or undo the development or occurrence of: *fight a fire; fought temptation; fought back her tears.* **5. a.** To wage (a battle or war, for example). **b.** To engage in (a lawsuit, election, or other contest) against another. **6.** To do battle for; contend for: *"I now resolved that Calais should be fought to the death"* (Winston Churchill). **7.** To make (one's way) as if by fighting: *He fought his way to the top of his profession.* **8.** To set in combat with another: *fighting cocks.* **—fight off.** To defend against or drive back (a hostile force). **—fight it out.** To fight until something is settled or until one side is clearly the victor: *fight it out in public.* **—fight shy of.** To be reluctant to confront; avoid.
~n. **1.** A battle waged between opposing groups; combat. **2.** A struggle, quarrel, or conflict. **3. a.** A physical conflict between two or more individuals; a brawl. **b.** A boxing or wrestling match; a bout. **4.** The power or inclination to fight; pugnacity. **5.** A struggle to achieve an objective. **—put up a fight.** To make a determined show of resistance. —See Synonyms at **conflict.** [Fight, fought, fought; Middle English *fighten, fa(u)ght, fo(u)ghten,* Old English *feohtan, feaht, fohten,* from Germanic.]

fight·er (fī′tər) *n.* **1.** One engaged in fighting. **2.** One employed to fight; a boxer. **3.** A pugnacious, unyielding, or determined person. **4.** *Military.* A fast, maneuverable combat aircraft used to engage enemy aircraft and to escort and defend bombers.

fight·er-bomb·er (fī′tər-bŏm′ər) *n.* An airplane capable of functioning both as a fighter and bomber.

fight·ing (fī′tĭng) *adj.* **1.** Ready to fight; equipped, prepared, or inclined to oppose. **2.** Liable to provoke conflict: *fighting words.* **—fighting fit.** Very fit; in peak condition.

fighting chance *n.* A slight chance to win, following a struggle.

fighting cock *n.* **1.** A cock bred for fighting. **2.** *Informal.* A quarrelsome person.

fighting fish *n.* Any of various small freshwater fishes of the genus *Betta,* of tropical Asia; especially, the **Siamese fighting fish** *(see).*

fighting fund *n. Chiefly British.* A fund set up to finance a campaign.

fig leaf *n.* **1.** A stylized representation of the leaf of a fig, used especially to conceal the genitalia on statues. **2.** A device intended to conceal something offensive or discreditable.

fig marigold *n.* Any of various plants of the genus *Mesembryanthemum,* native to southern Africa, having thick, fleshy leaves and variously colored flowers.

fig·ment (fĭg′mənt) *n.* **1.** Something imaginary; a fabrication. **2.** An arbitrary notion. [Middle English, from Latin *figmentum,* a formation, from *fingere,* to mold, fashion.]

fig tree *n.* A tree, the **fig** *(see).*

fig·ur·al (fĭg′yər-əl) *adj.* Consisting of or forming a pictorial composition or design of human or animal figures.

fig·u·rant (fĭg′yə-ränt′, -rănt′, -räN′) *n.* **1.** A member of a corps de ballet who does not perform solos. **2.** A stage performer without a speaking part. [French, from the present participle of *figurer,* to figure, represent, from Old French, from Latin *figūrāre,* to form, from *figūra,* FIGURE.]

fig·u·rate (fĭg′yər-ĭt, -yə-rāt′) *adj.* **1.** Having a definite or particular shape or form; figured. **2.** *Music.* Characterized by figuration; ornamented. [Latin *figūrātus,* past participle of *figūrāre,* to shape, from *figūra,* form, FIGURE.]

fig·u·ra·tion (fĭg′yə-rā′shən) *n.* **1.** The act of forming something into a particular shape. **2.** A shape, form, or outline. **3.** The act of representing with figures. **4.** A figurative representation, often symbolic or emblematic. **5.** *Music.* **a.** The continuous repetition of a pattern of notes or musical figures for decorative purposes. **b.** Ornamentation. **6.** The ornamentation of something with small designs.

fig·u·ra·tive (fĭg′yər-ə-tĭv) *adj. Abbr.* **fig. 1. a.** Based on or making use of figures of speech, especially metaphor; not literal; metaphorical: *figurative language.* **b.** Containing many figures of speech; ornate. **2.** Represented by a figure or figures; symbolic or emblematic. **3.** *Art.* **a.** Of or relating to representation by means of animal or human figures; figural. **b.** Representational rather than abstract. **c.** Designating a style of painting in which the subjects are recognizable but not conventionally depicted. **—fig·u·ra·tive·ly** *adv.* **—fig·u·ra·tive·ness** *n.*

fig·ure (fĭg′yər) *n. Abbr.* **fig. 1.** A written symbol representing anything other than a letter; especially, a number. **2. figures.** Mathematical calculation involving the use of such symbols: *She is good at figures.* **3. a.** An amount represented in numbers: *a large figure.* **b.** An estimate: *Can you give me a figure?* **4.** The outline, form, or silhouette of a thing. **5. a.** The shape or form of a human body, especially as regards weight and proportion: *a pear-shaped figure.* **b.** A slim, attractive body: *still hasn't lost her figure at 52.* **6.** An individual, especially a well-known personage. **7.** The impression an individual makes through behavior or appearance: *He cuts a dashing figure.* **8.** A person, animal, or object that symbolizes something: *She'll always be a mother figure to me.* **9.** A pictorial or sculptural representation, especially of the human body. **10. a.** A diagram. **b.** A design or pattern. **11.** An illustration printed from an engraved plate or block. **12.** A configuration or distinct group of steps in skating or a dance. **13.** *Music.* A brief melodic or harmonic unit often constituting the base for a larger musical phrase or structure. **14.** *Logic.* Any one of the forms that a syllogism can take, depending on the position of the middle term. **15.** A **figure of speech** *(see).* **16.** *Mathematics.* A geometric shape formed by lines, curves, or surfaces, either a *plane figure* in two dimensions or a *solid figure* in three. —See Synonyms at **form.**
~v. **figured, -uring, -ures.** *—tr.* **1.** To calculate with numbers; tally or work out mathematically. **2. a.** To make a likeness of; depict. **b.** To symbolize; represent. **3.** To adorn with a design or figures. **4.** *Music.* To indicate the chordal structure of (a bass line of single notes) with a sequence of conventionalized numbers. **5.** *Informal.* To conclude, believe, or predict: *What do you figure will happen?* *—intr.* **1.** To calculate; compute. **2.** To be an element; be involved: *Your name didn't even figure in the conversation.* **3.** *Informal.* To make sense; add up: *That figures!* **—figure on** (or **upon**). *Informal.* **1.** To count on. **2.** To take into consideration; expect. **—figure out.** *Informal.* To solve; comprehend; work out. [Middle English, from Old French, from Latin *figūra,* form, shape, figure.]

fig·ured (fĭg′yərd) *adj.* **1.** Decorated with a design; patterned: *"My dress is richly figured"* (Amy Lowell). **2.** Represented, as in graphic art or sculpture; depicted.

figured bass *n. Music.* A **continuo** *(see).*

figure eight *n.* **1.** *Aeronautics.* A maneuver in which an aircraft flies a path tracing the outline of the number 8. **2.** A skating figure or dance pattern shaped like the number 8. **3.** Any of various forms having the shape of the number 8, such as a knot.

fig·ure-ground (fĭg′yər-ground′) *n. Psychology.* The organization of visual perception into a unified object standing out from a background. The organization of a visual field can change depending on the individual and the familiarity or regularity of parts of the field, or those parts of the field being attended to, and is used as the basis for many types of optical illusion.

fig·ure·head (fĭg′yər-hĕd′) *n.* **1.** A person given a position of nominal leadership but having no actual authority or responsibility. **2.** *Nautical.* A carved, decorative figure placed on the prow of a ship.

figure of speech *n.* An expression in which words are used, not in their literal sense, but to create a more forceful or dramatic image, as **metaphor, simile,** or **hyperbole** *(all of which see).*

fig·u·rine (fĭg′yə-rēn′) *n.* A small ornamental figure, as one carved or formed from wood, porcelain, glass, or metal; a statuette.

fig-bird *Figs are only part of the diet of the southern fig-bird,* Sphecotheres vieilloti, *which also feeds on other fruit and on berries.*

figurine *A porcelain figurine of the Chinese goddess of mercy, Guanyin. The crayfish on which she stands is an emblem of wealth and harmony.*

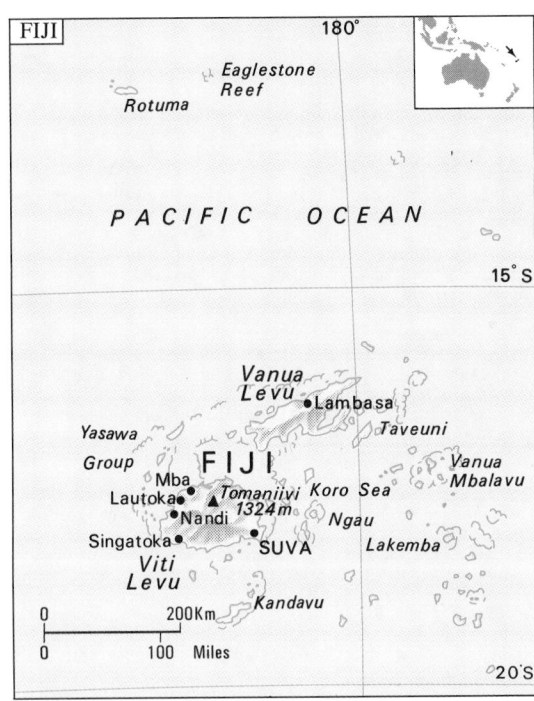

[French, from Italian *figurina*, diminutive of *figura*, figure, from Latin *figūra*, FIGURE.]

fig wasp *n.* A small wasp of the genus *Blastophaga*, which is the agent for caprification in figs.

fig·wort (fĭg′wûrt′, -wôrt′) *n.* Any of various plants of the genus *Scrophularia*, having loose, branching clusters of small greenish or purple flowers. [From FIG, alluding to swellings, as in scrofula, for which the plant was believed to be a remedy.]

Fi·ji[1] (fē′jē). Independent republic within the British Commonwealth, consisting of more than 330 islands and islets in the South Pacific Ocean. Some 106 of the larger islands are inhabited. The capital, Suva, is on the largest island, Viti Levu. The islands were discovered by the Dutch explorer Abel Tasman in 1643 and explored by Capt. William Bligh after he was set adrift by the *Bounty* mutineers (1789). Annexed by Great Britain in 1874, they remained a crown colony until 1970. Sugar is the most important crop. Population, 600,000.

Fi·ji[2] *n.* 1. A Fijian. 2. The language of the Fijians.

Fi·ji·an (fē′jē-ən) *adj.* Of Fiji or the Fiji Islands, or the people or language of these places.
~*n.* 1. A native of Fiji or the Fiji Islands, being of predominantly Melanesian stock with an admixture of Polynesian. 2. The Oceanic language of Fiji or the Fiji Islands.

fi·la. Plural of **filum.**

filagree. Variant of **filigree.**

fil·a·ment (fĭl′ə-mənt) *n.* 1. A fine or thinly spun thread, fiber, wire, or the like. 2. *Biology.* A slender, threadlike appendage, part, or structure, especially: **a.** The slender stalk of a stamen on which the anther is borne. **b.** A chainlike series of cells, as in some algae and bacteria. **c.** The free barb of a down feather. 3. **a.** *Electricity.* A fine wire heated electrically to incandescence in an electric lamp. **b.** *Electronics.* A high-resistance wire or ribbon forming the cathode in some thermionic valves. [Old French, from Medieval Latin *fīlamentum*, from Late Latin *fīlāre*, to wind threads, spin, from Latin *fīlum*, thread.] —**fil·a·men·tous** (fĭl′ə-mĕn′təs), **fil·a·men·ta·ry** (fĭl′ə-mĕn′tə-rē) *adj.*

fi·lar (fī′lər) *adj.* 1. Of or pertaining to a thread or threads. 2. Having fine threads across the field of view for measuring small distances, as in a microscope or telescope eyepiece. [Latin *fīlum*, thread.]

fil·a·ree (fĭl′ə-rē′) *n.* A plant, the **alfilaria** (*see*). [Variant of American Spanish *alfilerillo*, ALFILARIA.]

fi·lar·i·a (fĭ-lâr′ē-ə) *n., pl.* -**iae** (-ē-ē′). Any of various parasitic nematode worms of the superfamily Filarioidea that infest man and other vertebrates. [New Latin *Filaria* (former genus name), "threadworm," from Latin *fīlum*, thread.] —**fi·lar·i·al, fi·lar·i·an** *adj.*

fil·a·ri·a·sis (fĭl′ə-rī′ə-sĭs) *n.* Infestation of the lymph glands with the filaria *Wuchereria bancrofti* or *Brugia malayi*, resulting in inflammation and **elephantiasis** (*see*). [New Latin : FILAR(IA) + -IASIS.]

fil·a·ture (fĭl′ə-chŏŏr′, -chər) *n.* 1. The act or process of spinning, drawing, or twisting into threads. 2. The reeling of raw silk from cocoons. 3. A reel used in this process. 4. An establishment where this process is performed. [French, from Late Latin *fīlātus*, past participle of *fīlāre*, to draw out thread, spin. See **filament.**]

fil·bert (fĭl′bərt) *n.* 1. A Eurasian shrub or tree, *Corylus maxima*, a species of hazel, cultivated for its edible nuts. 2. The rounded, smooth-shelled nut of this shrub. 3. Any hazelnut. [Middle English

filefish *Filefish, which are found in warm seas all over the world, get their name from their sandpapery skin that is covered with tiny close-set spikes. This is the fringed filefish, a Caribbean species.*

filigree *Silver wire twisted into the delicate lacelike pattern known as filigree decorates these 19th-century thimble holders that contain miniature sewing kits.*

filbert, philliberd, from Norman French (*noix de*) *filbert,* "nut of St. *Philbert*" (died A.D. 684), Frankish abbot whose feast day on August 22 marks the ripening season of the nut.]

filch (fĭlch) *tr.v.* **filched, filching, filches.** To steal (something) in a furtive manner; pilfer. —See Synonyms at **rob.** [Middle English *filchen*†.] —**filch·er** *n.*

file[1] (fīl) *n.* 1. A receptacle, such as a folder or box, that keeps loose objects, such as papers, cards, or any collection of small items, in useful order. 2. A collection of objects kept thus; especially, a set of documents related to one subject, such as a particular client or case. 3. **a.** A line of persons, animals, or things positioned one behind another. **b.** *Military.* A line of soldiers or vehicles so positioned. 4. Any of the rows of squares that run vertically on a chessboard. 5. A set of data with an identifying label held in a computer storage device. —**on file.** Catalogued or recorded in a file.
~*v.* **filed, filing, files.** —*tr.* 1. To put or keep (papers or cards, for example) in useful order; catalogue. 2. **a.** To enter (a legal document, for example) on public record or official record. **b.** To submit (a complaint or legal petition, for example) to a relevant authority. 3. To send or submit (copy) to a newspaper or other news agency. —*intr.* 1. To march or walk in a line or lines. 2. To submit a formal application, as for divorce. [Noun, sense 1: Old French *fil*, "thread," wire or string on which documents are strung, from Latin *fīlum*, thread. Noun, sense 3: Old French *file*, from *filer*, "to draw out thread," march in a line, from Late Latin *fīlāre*, to spin, from Latin *fīlum*, thread.] —**fil·er** *n.*

file[2] *n.* 1. Any of several steel tools with hardened ridged surfaces, used in smoothing, polishing, grinding down, or boring. 2. *Archaic British Slang.* A deceitful, cunning person.
~*tr.v.* **filed, filing, files.** To smooth, polish, grind, bore, or remove with or as if with a file. [Middle English *file, fyle*, Old English *fēol, fīl.*] —**fil·er** *n.*

file clerk *n.* A person employed to maintain the files and records of an office.

file·fish (fīl′fĭsh′) *n., pl.* -**fishes** or collectively **filefish.** Any of various chiefly tropical marine fishes of the family Balistidae, related to and resembling the triggerfishes. [Referring to the rough scales of some species.]

fi·let (fĭ-lā′, fĭl′ā′) *n.* A net or lace with a simple pattern of squares. [French, from Old French *filé*, from Old Provençal *filat*, "made of threads," from *fil*, thread, from Latin *fīlum.*]

filet[2]. Variant of **fillet.**

fi·let mi·gnon (fĭ-lā′ mĭn-yŏn′, fĭl′ā mēn-yôN′) *n.* A small, round, very choice cut of beef from the center of the fillet. [French, "dainty fillet."]

fil·i·al (fĭl′ē-əl) *adj.* Of, pertaining to, or befitting a son or daughter. [Middle English, from Late Latin *fīliālis*, from Latin *fīlius*, son.] —**fil·i·al·ly** *adv.* —**fil·i·al·ness** *n.*

filial generation *n.* A set of offspring from a specific mating that follows the parental generation.

fil·i·ate (fĭl′ē-āt′) *tr.v.* -**ated, -ating, -ates.** 1. *Rare.* To affiliate. 2. *Law.* To assign paternity to (an illegitimate child, for example). [Medieval Latin *fīliāre*, to acknowledge as a son, from Latin *fīlius*, son.]

fil·i·a·tion (fĭl′ē-ā′shən) *n.* 1. The condition or fact of being the child of a certain parent. 2. A line of descent; derivation; lineage. 3. **a.** The act or fact of forming a new branch, as of a society or language group; expansion or division. **b.** The branch thus formed; an offshoot. 4. *Law.* Affiliation.

fil·i·beg (fĭl′ə-bĕg′) *n.* A kilt. [Scottish Gaelic *féileadhbeag* : *féileadh*†, fold, kilt + *beag*, small, little, akin to Old Irish *becc*, small, from Common Celtic *biggo-* (unattested).]

fil·i·bus·ter (fĭl′ə-bŭs′tər) *n.* 1. **a.** The use of obstructionist tactics, such as the making of prolonged speeches or the introduction of irrelevant material, for the purpose of delaying legislative action. **b.** An instance of the use of such tactics in a legislative body. **c.** A user of such tactics. 2. An adventurer who engages in a private military action in a foreign country.
~*v.* **filibustered, -tering, -ters.** —*intr.* 1. To use obstructionist tactics, especially prolonged speeches, in a legislative body. 2. To engage in a private military action in a foreign country. —*tr.* To use obstructionist tactics against (legislation, for example). [Originally "freebooter," from Spanish *filibustero*, from French *flibustier*, from Dutch *vrijbuiter*, pirate, "one who plunders freely" : *vrij*, free + *-buiter*, plunderer, from *buit*, BOOTY.] —**fil·i·bus·ter·er** *n.*

fil·i·cide (fĭl′ə-sīd′) *n. Rare.* 1. The act of killing one's child. 2. One who kills his child. [Latin *fīlius*, son, or its derivative *fīlia*, daughter + -CIDE.] —**fil·i·cid·al** (fĭl′ə-sīd′l) *adj.*

fil·i·form (fĭl′ə-fôrm′) *adj. Biology.* Resembling or having the form of a thread; threadlike. [Latin *fīlum*, thread + -FORM.]

fil·i·gree, fil·a·gree, fil·la·gree (fĭl′ə-grē′) *n.* 1. Delicate and intricate ornamental work made from gold, silver, or other fine twisted wire. 2. Any intricate, delicate, or fanciful ornamentation.
~*adj.* Resembling or made of filigree.
~*tr.v.* **filigreed, -greeing, -grees.** To decorate with or as if with filigree. [Earlier *filigreen*, from French *filigrane*, from Italian *filigrana* : *fili-*, from Latin *fīlum*, thread + *grana*, grain, from Latin *grānum.*]

fil·ing (fī′lĭng) *n.* 1. The act of using a file. 2. A particle or shaving removed by a file.

filing cabinet *n.* A cabinet with drawers used for holding documents, files, or the like.

filing clerk *n.* A file clerk.

Fil·i·pi·no (fĭl′ə-pē′nō) *n., pl.* **-nos.** A native, citizen, or inhabitant of the Philippines.
~*adj.* Of or pertaining to the Philippines or Filipinos. [Spanish, from *(Islas) Filipinas,* the PHILIPPINE(S).]

fill (fĭl) *v.* **filled, filling, fills.** —*tr.* **1.** To put into as much as can be held; load completely; make full. **2.** To close or plug up (an opening, for example). **3.** To stop up a cavity in (a tooth). **4.** To produce a sensation of fullness in (the stomach, for example). **5.** To supply (an empty space) with material, such as writing, an inscription, or an illustration. **6.** To put someone into or elect to (an office or position); furnish with a holder or occupant. **7.** To occupy or hold (an office or position). **8. a.** To occupy the whole of: *fill one's time.* **b.** To pervade: *Cries filled the air.* **9.** To affect profoundly (the mind or thoughts, for example): *The prospect filled him with dread.* **10.** To add an inferior substance or substances to (a product) to increase bulk. **11. a.** To cause (a sail) to swell. **b.** To adjust (a yard) so that wind will cause a sail to swell. —*intr.* To become full. **—fill out. 1.** To make or become fuller, rounder, broader, or shapelier. **2.** To complete (a form, for example) by adding the necessary information. **—fill someone's shoes.** To assume someone's duties or position. **—fill the bill.** *Informal.* To serve a given purpose.
~*n.* **1.** That which is needed to make full, complete, or satisfied: *eat one's fill.* **2. a.** A built-up piece of land; an embankment. **b.** The material, such as earth, gravel, or sand, used for this. **—have one's fill.** To be thoroughly sated or weary. [Middle English *fillen,* Old English *fyllan.*]

fille de joie (fē′ də zhwä′) *n., pl.* **filles de joie** *(pronounced as singular).* A prostitute. [French, "daughter of joy."]

filled gold *n.* A base metal such as brass with a surface layer of bonded gold, used especially in jewelry.

fill·er (fĭl′ər) *n.* **1.** One who fills. **2.** Something added in order to augment weight or size or to fill space. **3.** A composition, especially a semisolid that hardens on drying, used to fill pores, cracks, or holes in a wood, plaster, or other construction surface prior to finishing. **4.** Tobacco used in a plug or to form the body of a cigar. **5.** A short item used to fill space in a newspaper, magazine, or other publication. **6.** Something, such as a news item or piece of music, used to fill time in a radio, television, or theatrical presentation. **7.** A device, such as a funnel, used to fill something. **8.** *Architecture.* Any element, such as a plate, used to fill the space between two supporting members.

fil·lér (fĭl′âr′) *n., pl.* **-lérs** or collectively **fillér.** A coin equal to 1/100 of the forint of Hungary. See feature at **currency.** [Hungarian.]

fil·let (fĭl′ĭt; *usually* fĭ-lā′, fĭl′ā′ *for sense 2*) *n.* Also **fi·let** (for sense 2). **1.** A narrow strip of ribbon or similar material or a thin band of metal, often worn in the hair or around the head. **2. a.** A strip or compact piece of boneless meat or fish. **b.** A cut of beef taken from the underside of the loin. **c.** A cut of pork, veal, or lamb taken from the top of the hind leg. **3.** *Architecture.* **a.** A thin, flat molding used as separation between or ornamentation for larger moldings. **b.** A ridge between the indentations of a fluted column. **4. a.** A narrow decorative line impressed upon the cover of a book. **b.** A hand tool or wheel used in making such a line. **5.** *Heraldry.* A narrow horizontal band placed in the lower fourth area of the chief. **6.** *Anatomy.* A loop-shaped band of fibers, such as the lemniscus. **7.** A raised band or rim on a surface. **8.** A structure added to round off an angle; a fairing.
~*tr.v.* **filleted** (fĭl′ĭ-tĭd; *usually* fĭ-lād′, fĭl′ād′ *for sense 2*), **-leting** (fĭl′ĭ-tĭng; *usually* fĭ-lā′ĭng, fĭl′ā′ĭng *for sense 2*), **-lets** (fĭl′ĭts; *usually* fĭ-lāz′, fĭl′āz′ *for sense 2*). Also **fi·let** (for sense 2). **1.** To bind or decorate with or as if with a fillet. **2.** To slice, bone, or make into a fillet or fillets. [Middle English *filet,* from Old French, diminutive of *fil,* thread, from Latin *fīlum.*]

fill in *tr.v.* **1.** To place material in (a hole or space, for example) so as to occupy completely. **2.** To complete (a form, for example) by adding the necessary information. **3.** To occupy (time). **4.** To set down (information), as on a form: *Fill in your name and address.* **5.** *Informal.* To inform. Used with *on*: *Fill me in on what's happening.* —*intr.v.* To act as a substitute.

fill-in (fĭl′ĭn′) *n. Informal.* **1.** One that fills a vacancy, gap, or temporary need. **2.** A summary of necessary or important information; a briefing.

fill·ing (fĭl′ĭng) *n.* **1.** Something used to fill a space or container. **2.** Any of various substances, such as amalgam or cement, used to fill a cavity in a tooth. **3.** An edible mixture used to fill sandwiches, cakes, and pastries. **4.** The horizontal threads that cross the warp in weaving; weft.
~*adj.* Tending to fill; especially, tending to cause a sensation of fullness in the stomach.

filling station *n.* A retail establishment at which vehicles are serviced, especially with gasoline, oil, water, and air. Also called "gas station, "service station."

fil·lip (fĭl′əp) *n.* **1.** A light blow or flick made by pressing a fingertip against the thumb and suddenly releasing it. **2.** A slight goad or incentive; a stimulus.
~*v.* **filliped, -liping, -lips.** —*tr.* **1.** To strike or propel with a fillip. **2.** To excite, arouse, or stimulate. —*intr.* To make a fillip. [15th century : imitative.]

Fill·more (fĭl′môr′, -mōr′), **Millard** (1800–74). 13th U.S. President (1850–53). Assuming the Presidency on the death of Zachary Taylor (July 9, 1850), he struggled to keep the nation intact, signing the Compromise of 1850 and the Fugitive Slave Law. The latter act cost him the Whig Party renomination in 1852. Fillmore later campaigned unsuccessfully as a candidate for the Know-Nothing Party (1856).

fill up *tr.v.* **1. a.** To fill completely. **b.** To fill (the gas tank of a motor vehicle). **2.** To fill in (a form, for example). —*intr.v.* To become full.

fill-up (fĭl′ŭp′) *n.* An act or instance of filling up.

fil·ly (fĭl′ē) *n., pl.* **-lies. 1.** A young female horse; a young mare. **2.** *Informal.* A lively and high-spirited girl. [Middle English *filli,* from Old Norse *fylja,* from Germanic *ful-* (unattested), FOAL.]

film (fĭlm) *n.* **1. a.** A thin covering or coating. **b.** A thin, generally flexible transparent sheet, as of plastic or rubber, used in wrapping or packaging. **2.** A thin skin or membranous coating. **3.** An abnormal, thin, opaque coating on the cornea in certain eye diseases. **4.** A thin sheet or strip of flexible cellulose material coated with a photosensitive emulsion, used to make photographic negatives or transparencies. **5. a.** A motion picture. **b.** Motion pictures collectively; the cinema. **6.** A haze or mist.
~*v.* **filmed, filming, films.** —*tr.* **1.** To cover with or as if with a film. **2.** To photograph (an event, scene, or person, for example) in the making of a motion picture. **3.** To turn (a novel, for example) into a motion picture. —*intr.* **1.** To become coated or obscured with or as if with a film. **2.** To make a motion picture. **3.** To be reproduced in a motion picture. [Middle English *film,* Old English *filmen,* from Germanic.]

film·go·er (fĭlm′gō′ər) *n.* One who regularly goes to see motion pictures.

film·ic (fĭl′mĭk) *adj.* Of, pertaining to, or resembling motion pictures. **—film·i·cal·ly** *adv.*

film·mak·ing (fĭlm′mā′kĭng) *n.* The production of motion pictures. **—film·mak·er** *n.*

fil·mog·ra·phy (fĭl-mŏg′rə-fē) *n., pl.* **-phies.** A list of the motion pictures that a given actor or director, for example, has made, or that have a similar subject.

film pack *n.* A pack of photographic sheet films that can be exposed in succession and withdrawn from the exposure position for storage at the rear of the pack.

film·set (fĭlm′sĕt′) *tr.v.* **-set, -setting, sets.** *Printing.* To set (type matter) by means of photocomposition; photocompose. **—film·set·ter** *n.*

film·set·ting (fĭlm′sĕt′ĭng) *n.* **Photocomposition** *(see).*

film·strip (fĭlm′strĭp′) *n.* A length of film containing photographs, diagrams, or other graphic matter prepared for still projection.

film·y (fĭl′mē) *adj.* **-ier, -iest. 1.** Resembling or consisting of film; transparent; gauzy. **2.** Covered by or as if by a film; blurred; hazy. **—film·i·ly** *adv.* **—film·i·ness** *n.*

filmy fern *n.* Any fern having fronds only one cell thick and consequently usually limited to very humid or shady habitats.

fil·o·plume (fĭl′ə-plo͞om′, fī′lə-) *n.* A hairlike feather having few or no barbs, occurring between the contour feathers. [Latin *fīlum,* thread + PLUME.]

fi·lose (fī′lōs′) *adj. Biology.* **1.** Threadlike. **2.** Having or ending in a threadlike part. [Latin *fīlum,* thread.]

fils[1] (fĭls) or **fil** (fĭl) *n., pl.* **fils.** A monetary unit equal to 1/1000 of the dinar of Bahrain, Iraq, Jordan, Kuwait, and South Yemen, 1/100 of the dirham of the United Arab Emirates, or 1/100 of the rial of Yemen. See feature at **currency.** [Arabic.]

fils[2] (fēs). *French.* Son. Used after a proper name to distinguish a son from a father with the same name. Compare **père.**

fil·ter (fĭl′tər) *n.* **1.** Any porous substance through which a liquid or gas is passed in order to remove suspended matter. **2. a.** A device containing or consisting of such a substance, especially when used to extract impurities from air, water, or the like. **b.** A filter tip. **3.** Any of various electric, electronic, acoustic, or optical devices used to reject signals, vibrations, or radiations of certain frequencies while passing others.
~*v.* **filtered, -tering, -ters.** —*tr.* **1.** To pass (a liquid or gas) through a filter. **2.** To remove by passing through a filter. —*intr.* **1.** To pass through or as if through a filter: *"The chapel was flooded by the dull scarlet of light that filtered through the lower blinds"* (James Joyce). **2.** To emerge gradually. Used of news, facts, or other information. **3.** To flow or proceed gradually: *People filtered into the room.* [Middle English *filtre,* a piece of felt (used to strain liquid), from Old French, from Medieval Latin *filtrum,* from Frankish *filtir* (unattested).] **—fil·ter·er** *n.*

fil·ter·a·ble (fĭl′tər-ə-bəl, fĭl′trə-) *adj.* Also **fil·tra·ble** (fĭl′trə-bəl). **1.** Capable of being filtered; especially, capable of being removed by filtering. **2.** Sufficiently minute to pass through a fine filter, thereby maintaining the infectivity of the filtrate. Said of certain viruses. **—fil·ter·a·bil·i·ty** (fĭl′tər-ə-bĭl′ə-tē, fĭl′trə-) *n.*

filter bed *n.* A layer of sand or gravel on the bottom of a reservoir or tank used to filter water or sewage.

filter feeder *n.* Any aquatic animal that uses a filtering mechanism to ingest minute food particles from the water.

filter paper *n.* Porous paper suitable for use as a filter.

filter pump *n.* A simple vacuum pump by which air is removed from a system by carrying it away in a narrow, fast jet of water.

filter tip *n.* **1.** A small tube of porous material attached to the end of a cigarette to remove part of the harmful substances from the smoke. **2.** A cigarette with such an attachment.

filth (fĭlth) *n.* **1. a.** Foul or dirty matter. **b.** Refuse. **2.** A dirty or corrupt condition; foulness. **3.** Material or language considered obscene, prurient, or immoral. [Middle English *filth, fulth,* Old English *fȳlth,* putrid matter.]

PRONUNCIATION KEY
ă, pat; ā, pay; âr, care;
ä, father, are; b, bib;
ch, church; d, deed; ĕ, pet;
ē, be; f, fife; g, gag; h, hat;
hw, which; ĭ, pit; ī, pie;
îr, pier; j, judge; k, kick;
l, lid, needle; m, mum;
n, no, sudden; ng, thing;
ŏ, pot; ō, toe; ô, paw, for;
oi, noise; ou, out; o͝o, book;
o͞o, boot; p, pop; r, roar;
s, sauce; sh, ship, dish;
t, tight; th, thin, path;
th, this, bathe; ŭ, cut; ûr, fur;
v, valve; w, with; y, yes;
z, zebra, size; zh, vision;
ə, about, item, edible,
gallop, circus, peaceful

IN FOREIGN WORDS:
à, *Fr.* ami; œ, *Fr.* feu, *Ger.* schön; ü, *Fr.* tu, *Ger.* über;
KH, *Ger.* ich, *Scot.* loch;
N, *Fr.* bon; y′, *Fr.* Compiègne

STRESS MARKS:
Primary stress: ′
in·cite′ (ĭn-sīt′)
Secondary stress: ′
in′sight′ (ĭn′sīt′)

filth·y (fĭl′thē) *adj.* **-ier, -iest. 1.** Heavily soiled; very dirty. **2.** Obscene; scatological. **3.** Highly objectionable; vile; nasty. **4.** *Informal.* Very bad; unpleasant: *filthy weather.* —See Synonyms at **dirty.** —**filth·i·ly** *adv.* —**filth·i·ness** *n.*

fil·trate (fĭl′trāt′) *v.* **-trated, -trating, -trates.** —*tr.* To put through a filter. —*intr.* To go through a filter.
~*n.* The portion of filtered material that passes through the filter. [Medieval Latin *filtrāre,* from *filtrum,* FILTER.]

fil·tra·tion (fĭl-trā′shən) *n.* The act or process of filtering.

fi·lum (fī′ləm) *n., pl.* **-la** (-lə). Any threadlike anatomical structure; a filament. [Latin *fīlum,* thread.]

FIM field-ion microscope; field-ion microscopy.

fim·bri·a (fĭm′brē-ə) *n., pl.* **-briae** (-brē-ē′). A fringelike structure, as at the opening of the Fallopian tube in mammals. [Late Latin, fiber, fringe, from Latin *fimbriae*†, fibers, threads. See also **fringe.**]

fim·bri·ate (fĭm′brē-ĭt, -āt′) *adj.* Also **fim·bri·at·ed** (-ā′tĭd). Fringed, as the edge of a petal or the opening of a duct may be. [Late Latin *fimbriātus,* fringed, from FIMBRIA.] —**fim·bri·a·tion** *n.*

fin[1] (fĭn) *n.* **1.** A membranous appendage extending from the body of a fish or other aquatic animal, used for propelling, steering, or maintaining balance. **2.** Something resembling a fin in shape or function, such as a diver's flipper. **3.** A fixed or movable vane or airfoil used to stabilize an aircraft or missile in flight. **4.** An appendage on a boat, such as a submarine; especially, a **fin keel** *(see).* **5.** A projecting vane used for cooling, as on a radiator or engine cylinder. **6.** An ornamental projection, as on the rear wing of a car.
~*v.* **finned, finning, fins.** —*tr.* **1.** To equip with fins. **2.** To cut the fins from. —*intr.* To emerge with the fins above water. [Middle English *finne,* Old English *finn,* akin to Middle Low German *finne*†.]

fin[2] *n. Slang.* A five-dollar bill [Yiddish *finf,* five, from Middle High German *vimf,* from Old High German *funf, finf.*]

fin. 1. finance; financial. **2.** finish.

Fin. Finland; Finnish.

fin·a·ble, fine·a·ble (fī′nə-bəl) *adj.* Liable to a fine or fines.

fi·na·gle (fĭ-nā′gəl) *v.* **-gled, -gling, -gles.** *Informal.* —*tr.* **1.** To achieve by dubious or crafty methods; wangle. **2.** To trick or delude; deceive. —*intr.* To use crafty, deceitful methods. [Probably from dialectal *fainaigue*†, to cheat.] —**fi·na·gler** *n.*

fi·nal (fī′nəl) *adj.* **1. a.** Forming or occurring at the end; concluding; last. **b.** *Phonetics.* Occurring at the end of a word or syllable. **2.** Pertaining to or constituting the end result of a process or procedure; ultimate: *the final purpose.* **3.** Decisive; conclusive; unalterable: *The judges' decision is final.* **4.** *Grammar.* Indicating purpose: *a final clause.* —See Synonyms at **last.**
~*n.* Something that comes at or forms the end, especially: **1.** The last or one of the last of a series of sports contests or other competitions. **2.** The last examination of an academic course. **3.** The edition of a newspaper published last in the day. [Middle English, from Old French, from Latin *fīnālis,* from *fīnis*†, end.]

final cause *n. Philosophy.* The ultimate purpose of something.

fi·na·le (fĭ-năl′ē, -nä′lē) *n.* The concluding part of an entertainment or work, especially a musical composition. [Italian, "final," from Latin *fīnālis,* FINAL.]

fi·nal·ist (fī′nə-lĭst) *n.* A contestant in the final session of a competition.

fi·nal·i·ty (fī-năl′ə-tē, fĭ-) *n., pl.* **-ties. 1.** The condition or fact of being final; conclusiveness. **2.** A final, conclusive, or decisive act or utterance.

fi·nal·ize (fī′nə-līz′) *tr.v.* **-ized, -izing, -izes. 1.** To put into final form. **2.** To complete arrangements for. —**fi·nal·i·za·tion** (fī′-nə-lĭ-zā′shən) *n.*
Usage: *Finalize* is widely used in official communications. Because of its bureaucratic associations, many people avoid using it, preferring *complete, conclude, make final,* or *put in final form.*

fi·nal·ly (fī′nə-lē) *adv.* **1.** At the final point; at the end; last. **2.** Decisively; irrevocably. **3.** After a considerable delay; eventually; at last. **4.** Ultimately; in the end. **5.** Used to introduce a concluding point of discussion: *Finally, we must consider . . .*

Final Solution *n.* **1.** The Nazi plan in World War II for the mass killing of European Jews. **2. final solution.** Any attempt at mass destruction of a people.

fi·nance (fĭ-năns′, fī-, fī′năns′) *n.* **1.** *Abbr.* **fin. a.** The science of the management of money and other assets. **b.** The disposition of public revenues by a government. **2. finances. a.** Monetary resources or funds, especially of a government or corporate body. **b.** The monetary affairs or arrangements of a person, company, or the like. **3.** The obtainment of funds; financing.
~*v.* **financed, -nancing, -nances.** —*tr.* To supply or raise the funds or capital for. —*intr.* **1.** To raise or supply funds. **2.** To manage finances. [Middle English *finaunce,* end, settlement, payment, from Old French *finance,* from *finer,* to end, settle, from *fin,* end, from Latin *fīnis*†.]

finance bill *n.* A legislative act designed to raise public revenues.

finance company *n.* A company offering loans to individuals, as for the purchase of goods or property.

fi·nan·cial (fĭ-năn′shəl, fī-) *adj. Abbr.* **fin.** Of or pertaining to finances or those who deal with finances. —**fi·nan·cial·ly** *adv.*
Synonyms: *fiscal, monetary, pecuniary.*

financial year *n.* A **fiscal year** *(see).*

fin·an·cier (fĭn′ən-sîr′, fĭ-năn′-, fī′năn-) *n.* One who is occupied with or expert in large-scale financial affairs. [French, from FINANCE.]

fin·back (fĭn′băk′) *n.* A whale, the **rorqual** *(see).*

finch (fĭnch) *n.* Any of various relatively small birds of the family Fringillidae, such as a goldfinch, cardinal, or canary, having a short, stout bill adapted for cracking seeds. [Middle English *finch,* Old English *finc,* from Germanic.]

find (fīnd) *v.* **found** (found), **finding, finds.** —*tr.* **1.** To come upon by accident; discover by chance. **2.** To come upon after a search: *find the cause of the trouble.* **3.** To come upon through experience or effort; obtain knowledge of; attain: *found contentment at last.* **4.** To succeed in reaching; arrive at: *The dart found the mark.* **5. a.** To learn by inquiry or research; determine; ascertain: *found the solution to the problem.* **b.** To learn accidentally. **6.** To consider; regard: *I find her charm irresistible.* **7.** To recover (something lost). **8.** To recover the use of; regain: *found his voice and responded.* **9.** To manage to obtain: *find money for food.* **10.** To declare as a verdict or conclusion. **11.** To furnish; supply. —*intr.* To come to a legal decision or verdict: *The jury found for the defendant.* —**find oneself. 1.** To discover what one truly wishes to be and do in life. **2.** To become aware of being in a condition or place. —**find out. 1.** To learn by accident or through inquiry. **2.** To discover the dishonesty, bad reputation, or deceit of (a person).
~*n.* **1.** An act of finding. **2.** That which is found; especially, a rare or valuable discovery. [Find, found, found; Middle English *finden, found, founden,* Old English *findan, fand* (plural *fundon*), *funden,* from Germanic.]

find·er (fīn′dər) *n.* **1.** One that finds. **2.** A **viewfinder** *(see).* **3.** *Astronomy.* A small telescope attached to the body of a larger one for locating an object to be observed with the larger telescope.

fin-de-siè·cle (făN′də-sē-ĕk′lə) *adj.* Of or characteristic of the last part of the 19th century, especially with reference to its artistic climate of effete sophistication. [French, "end of (the) century."]

find·ing (fīn′dĭng) *n.* **1.** Something that has been found. **2.** The result of a trial or legal inquiry: *a finding of accidental death.* **3.** *Usually* **findings.** A conclusion reached after examination or investigation. **4. findings.** Small tools and materials used by an artisan, as a jeweler.

fine[1] (fīn) *adj.* **finer, finest. 1.** Of superior quality, skill, or appearance; admirable. **2.** Most enjoyable; pleasant. **3.** Free from impurities: *fine copper.* **4.** *Abbr.* **f., F.** Containing pure metal in a specified proportion or amount: *gold 21 carats fine.* **5.** Cut or honed to great sharpness: *a blade with a fine edge.* **6. a.** Thin; slender. **b.** Not coarse in texture: *fine hair.* **7.** Showing workmanship of great care and delicacy: *fine china.* **8.** Consisting of extremely small particles; not coarse: *fine dust.* **9.** Subtle or precise: *a fine shade of meaning.* **10.** Able to make or detect subtle or precise effects; sensitive: *a fine eye for color.* **11.** Trained to the highest degree of physical efficiency; superbly conditioned: *a fine racehorse.* **12.** Of refined manners; elegant. **13.** Grand or elevated in a somewhat pompous way: *fine speeches.* **14.** Awful; terrible. Used ironically: *That's a fine position to be in.* **15.** Satisfactory or acceptable: *A cup of tea would be fine.* **16.** Having no clouds; clear; sunny: *a fine day.* **17.** *Informal.* Quite well; in satisfactory health: *I'm fine, and you?*
~*adv.* **1.** Finely. **2.** *Informal.* Very well: *doing fine.*
~*v.* **fined, fining, fines.** —*tr.* **1.** To make finer; refine. **2.** To taper or make smaller or thinner. **3.** To clarify (wine, for example). —*intr.* To become finer, purer, or cleaner. —**fine up.** *Australian.* To become fine. Said of weather. [Middle English *fin,* from Old French, from Latin *fīnis*†, the end (as in *fīnis honorum,* the height of honor).]

fine[2] *n.* **1.** A sum of money imposed as a penalty for an offense. **2.** *Law.* Formerly, a fee paid to a feudal lord by his tenant. **3.** *Obsolete.* Finish; end; termination. —**in fine. 1.** In conclusion; finally. **2.** In summation; in brief.
~*tr.v.* **fined, fining, fines.** To require the payment of a fine from; impose a fine on. [Middle English *fin,* a fine, a payment for completion, an end, from Old French, from Latin *fīnis*†, limit, end.]

fi·ne[3] (fē′nā) *n. Music.* The end. Used to indicate the end of a passage that has been repeated. [Italian, from Latin *fīnis*†, end.]

fine[4] (fēn) *n.* A cognac, **fine champagne** *(see).*

fineable. Variant of **finable.**

fine art *n.* **1.** Art produced or intended primarily for beauty alone rather than utility. **2.** *Often* **fine arts.** Any of the forms such art takes, including sculpture, painting, drawing, and often architecture, literature, drama, music, and the dance. **3.** An activity requiring or demonstrating considerable skill: *the fine art of freeway driving.* [Translation of French *beaux arts* (plural).]

fine cham·pagne (fēn′ shäN-pän′yə) *n. French.* A cognac made from grapes from the Grande Champagne and Petite Champagne districts in southwestern France. Also called "fine." [Contraction of *eau-de-vie de la Champagne,* "fine brandy from Champagne."]

fine-cut (fīn′kŭt′) *adj.* Finely and evenly shredded, as tobacco.

fine-draw (fīn′drô′) *tr.v.* **-drew** (-dro͞o′), **-drawn** (-drôn′), **-drawing, -draws. 1.** To mend or sew (a seam or tear) in such a way that the joint is invisible. **2.** To draw out (wire, for example) to a slender, threadlike state.

fine-drawn (fīn′drôn′) *adj.* **1.** Drawn out to a slender, threadlike state, as wire may be. **2.** Subtly or precisely fashioned, as an argument or theory may be. **3.** Delicately formed; suggestive of refinement: *fine-drawn features.*

fine-grained (fīn′grānd′) *adj.* Having a fine, smooth, even grain, as leather or wood.

fine·ly (fīn′lē) *adv.* **1.** In a fine manner; excellently; splendidly. **2.** To a fine point; discriminatingly. **3.** Delicately or subtly. **4.** In small pieces or parts: *finely chopped nuts.*

PRONUNCIATION KEY

ă, pat; ā, pay; âr, care;
ä, father, are; b, bib;
ch, church; d, deed; ĕ, pet;
ē, be; f, fife; g, gag; h, hat;
hw, which; ĭ, pit; ī, pie;
îr, pier; j, judge; k, kick;
l, lid, needle; m, mum;
n, no, sudden; ng, thing;
ŏ, pot; ō, toe; ô, paw, for;
oi, noise; ou, out; o͝o, book;
o͞o, boot; p, pop; r, roar;
s, sauce; sh, ship, dish;
t, tight; th, thin, path;
th, this, bathe; ŭ, cut; ûr, fur;
v, valve; w, with; y, yes;
z, zebra, size; zh, vision;
ə, about, item, edible,
gallop, circus, peaceful

IN FOREIGN WORDS:

à, *Fr.* ami; œ, *Fr.* feu, *Ger.* schön; ü, *Fr.* tu, *Ger.* über; KH, *Ger.* ich, *Scot.* loch; N, *Fr.* bon; y′, *Fr.* Compiègne

STRESS MARKS:

Primary stress: ′
in·cite′ (ĭn-sīt′)
Secondary stress: ′
in′sight′ (ĭn′sīt′)

fine·ness (fīn′nĭs) *n.* **1.** The condition or quality of being fine. **2.** The proportion of pure metal, such as gold, in an alloy.
fine print *n.* Matter printed with small type; especially, parts of a contract or other agreement printed inconspicuously and often containing provisions or conditions that might easily be overlooked. Also called "small print."
fin·er·y[1] (fī′nə-rē) *n.* Elaborate adornment; fine clothing and accessories. [From FINE (excellent).]
finery[2] *n., pl.* **-ies.** A furnace or hearth where cast iron is made malleable. [French *finerie,* from *finer,* to REFINE.]
fines herbes (fēn′ ûrbz′, fēn′ zĕrb′) *pl.n.* Finely chopped herbs, such as parsley, chives, tarragon, and thyme, used as a seasoning. [French.]
fine-spun (fīn′spŭn′) *adj.* **1.** Spun or drawn out to extreme fineness or subtlety; elaborate and delicate. **2.** Developed to excessive fineness; oversubtle.
fi·nesse (fĭ-nĕs′) *n.* **1.** Restraint and delicacy of performance or behavior. **2.** Subtlety or tact in maneuvering; craftiness. **3.** In bridge and whist, the playing of a card in a suit in which one holds a nonsequential higher card, either to induce an opponent to play an intermediate card that one's partner can then top, or to win the trick economically. **4.** Any stratagem in which one appears to decline an advantage. —See Synonyms at **artifice, tact.**
∼*v.* **finessed, -nessing, -nesses.** —*tr.* **1.** To accomplish with finesse. **2.** To handle with a deceptive or evasive strategy. **3.** To play (a card) as a finesse. —*intr.* **1.** To employ finesse. **2.** To make a finesse in a card game. [Old French, delicacy, fineness, from *fin,* FINE.]
fine structure *n.* **1.** *Physics.* Structure in spectral lines caused by the magnetic moments of orbiting electrons. Under high resolution certain lines can be resolved into two or more closely spaced lines. See **hyperfine structure. 2.** *Biology.* **Ultrastructure** *(see).*
fine-toothed comb (fīn′tōōtht′, -tōōthd′) *n.* A comb with thin, closely spaced teeth. **—go over with a fine-toothed comb.** To examine in exhaustive detail.
fine-tune (fīn′tōōn′, -tyōōn′) *tr.v.* **-tuned, -tuning, -tunes. 1.** To make small adjustments to the tuning of (a radio receiver, car engine, or the like) to obtain efficient or improved operation. **2.** To make small adjustments or changes to. **—fine-tun·er** *n.*
fin·foot (fĭn′fŏŏt′) *n., pl.* **-foots** or collectively **finfoot.** Any of various aquatic, tropical, or subtropical cranelike birds of the family Heliornithidae, having lobed toes and pale brown plumage. Also called "sungrebe."
fin·ger (fĭng′gər) *n.* **1.** Any of the five digits of the hand; especially, any one other than the thumb. **2.** The part of a glove designed to cover such a digit. **3.** Something resembling a finger, such as a peninsula. **4.** The length or width of a finger. **5.** *Informal.* A measure of spirits, a quantity approximately one fingerbreadth deep in a glass. **6.** *Machinery.* Any small projecting machine part. **—burn one's fingers.** To suffer as a result of meddlesome, inquisitive, or incautious behavior. **—have a finger in the pie.** To be involved, especially in a meddlesome way, in a matter. **—put one's finger on.** To identify or point out with precision. **—put the finger on.** *Slang.* **1.** To inform on. **2.** To designate, especially as an intended victim. **—snap one's fingers at. 1.** To treat contemptuously. **2.** To disobey or ignore defiantly. **—twist** (or **wrap**) **around one's little finger.** *Informal.* To dominate utterly and effortlessly.
∼*v.* **fingered, -gering, -gers.** —*tr.* **1.** To touch with the fingers; handle. **2.** *Music.* To mark (a score) with indications of which fingers are to play the notes. **3.** *Music.* To play (an instrument) by using the fingers in a particular order or way. **4.** *Slang.* **a.** To inform on. **b.** To designate as an intended victim. —*intr.* **1.** To handle something with the fingers. **2.** To use the fingers, especially in playing an instrument. **3.** To be played by using the fingers in a specified way: *His clarinet fingers like yours.* [Middle English *finger,* Old English *finger,* from Germanic.] **—fin·ger·er** *n.*
fin·ger·board (fĭng′gər-bôrd′, -bōrd′) *n.* A strip of wood on the neck of a stringed instrument against which the strings are pressed in playing.
finger bowl *n.* A small bowl or basin to hold water for rinsing the fingers at the table.
fin·ger·breadth (fĭng′gər-brĕdth′, -brĕtth′) *n.* Also **finger's breadth.** The breadth of one finger; approximately 3/4 of an inch.
fin·gered (fĭng′gərd) *adj.* **1.** Having a finger or fingers. **2.** Having a specified number or kind of fingers. Used in combination: *four-fingered; rosy-fingered.*
fin·ger·ing[1] (fĭng′gər-ĭng) *n.* **1.** The technique used in playing a musical instrument with the fingers. **2.** The indication on a score of which fingers are to be used in playing.
fingering[2] *n.* Fine knitting wool. [From obsolete *fingram,* probably from French *fin grain,* fine grain.]
finger lake *n.* A long, narrow lake formed when glacial debris impedes drainage of a U-shaped glaciated valley.
Finger Lakes. A group of 11 long, narrow glacial lakes in west-central New York. Cayuga and Seneca are the longest and deepest lakes. The region is a grape- and truck-farming area, with many resorts and state parks.
fin·ger·ling (fĭng′gər-lĭng) *n.* **1.** A young or small fish; especially, a young salmon or trout. **2.** Any small object or creature.
fin·ger·mark (fĭng′gər-märk′) *n.* A mark left on a surface by a dirty or greasy finger.
fin·ger·nail (fĭng′gər-nāl′) *n.* A thin, horny, transparent plate covering the upper surface of the tip of each finger.
fin·ger-paint (fĭng′gər-pānt′) *v.* **-painted, -painting, -paints.** —*intr.* To engage in finger painting. —*tr.* To make by finger painting.
finger painting *n.* **1.** The technique of painting by applying colors to moistened paper with the fingers. **2.** A painting so made.
fin·ger·plate (fĭng′gər-plāt′) *n.* A plate of metal, plastic, or the like fixed to a door near the handle to protect it from fingermarks.
finger post *n.* A guidepost resembling a pointing finger.
fin·ger·print (fĭng′gər-prĭnt′) *n.* An impression of the curves formed by the system of ridges on the skin surface of the end of a finger; especially, such an impression made in ink for purposes of identification.
∼*tr.v.* **fingerprinted, -printing, -prints.** To take an ink impression of a fingerprint or the fingerprints of.
fin·ger·stall (fĭng′gər-stôl′) *n.* A protective covering worn on an injured finger. Also called "stall."
finger tip, fin·ger·tip (fĭng′gər-tĭp′) *n.* The extreme end or tip of a finger. **—have at one's finger tips. 1.** To have readily or instantly available. **2.** To have a thorough knowledge of.
finger wave *n.* A wave set into damp hair using only the fingers.
fin·i·al (fĭn′ē-əl) *n.* **1.** *Architecture.* An ornament fixed to the peak of a gable, arched structure, or the like. **2.** Any ornamental terminating part, such as the screw on top of a piece of furniture. [Middle English *finial,* from adjective, "final," variant of FINAL.]
fin·i·cal (fĭn′ĭ-kəl) *adj.* Fastidious; finicky. [Probably originally university slang, irregularly from FINE (delicate).] **—fin·i·cal·i·ty** (fĭn′-ĭ-kăl′ə-tē), **fin·i·cal·ness** *n.* **—fin·i·cal·ly** *adv.*
fin·ick·y (fĭn′ĭ-kē) *adj.* Also **fin·ick·ing** (fĭn′ĭ-kĭng). Highly fastidious in tastes or standards; hard to please; fussy. [From FINICAL.]
fin·ing (fī′nĭng) *n.* **1.** The process of clarifying wines or other liquids. **2. finings.** A substance, such as isinglass, used in this process.
fi·nis (fĭn′ĭs, fī′nĭs) *n.* The end. Formerly used to indicate the end of a book or film. [Middle English, from Latin *fīnis.*]
fin·ish (fĭn′ĭsh) *v.* **-ished, -ishing, -ishes.** —*tr.* **1.** To arrive at or attain the end of: *finish a race.* **2.** To bring to an end; terminate; accomplish: *finish a task.* **3.** To consume all of; use up: *finish a pie.* **4.** To put the final touches to; bring to a desired or required state; perfect: *finish a painting.* **5.** To give (wood or cloth, for example) a desired surface texture. **6.** To complete the education of, especially with training in artistic tastes and social graces. **7.** To vanquish; destroy; kill: *finish an enemy.* **8.** To bring about the ruin of; overcome: *The stock-market crash finished him.* —*intr.* **1.** To come to a conclusion; end; stop. **2.** To reach the end of a task, course, or relationship. **—finish off. 1.** To bring to a final conclusion. **2.** To kill (a wounded person, for example). **3.** To ruin completely (a failing venture, for example). **—finish up.** To end. Often used with *by* or a participle: *I finished up paying the whole bill.* **—finish with. 1.** To have no further use for. **2.** To end a relationship with (someone). —See Synonyms at **complete.**
∼*n. Abbr.* **fin. 1. a.** The final part or conclusion of something; end: *a close finish in the race.* **b.** The reason for one's ruin; downfall. **2.** Something that completes, concludes, or perfects. **3. a.** The last treatment or coating of a surface. **b.** The surface texture thus produced. **4.** The material used in surfacing or finishing something: *a wax finish.* **5.** Completeness, thoroughness, or smoothness of execution; perfection. **6.** Polish or refinement in speech, manners, and the like. **7.** High-grade lumber used to finish the interior of a building. **8.** *Sports.* The ability to perform well at the end of a contest. [Middle English *finishen,* from Old French *fenir, finir* (stems *feniss-, finiss-*), from Latin *fīnīre,* to limit, complete, from *fīnis,* end.] **—fin·ish·er** *n.*
fin·ished (fĭn′ĭsht) *adj.* **1.** Skilled; accomplished; perfected. **2.** Smooth and polished, as wood. **3.** Having all hopes destroyed; undone; ruined.
finishing school *n.* A private school that trains girls in the social graces for life in society.
finishing touch *n.* A final act or decorative addition that achieves a desired total effect.
Fin·is·tère (fĭn′ə-stâr′). A department in Brittany, occupying the most westerly tip of France.
Fin·is·terre, Cape (fĭn′ə-stâr′). Rugged, steep promontory at the tip of an Atlantic peninsula forming the westernmost point of Spain. It takes its name from the Latin phrase *finis terrae,* "land's end."
fi·nite (fī′nīt′) *adj.* **1. a.** Having boundaries; limited. **b.** Capable of being bounded, enclosed, or encompassed. **2.** Being neither infinite nor infinitesimal. **3.** *Mathematics.* **a.** Bounded in an interval. Said of a quantity defined in an interval. **b.** Incapable of being put into one-to-one correspondence with a part of itself. Said of a set. **c.** Real or complex, as distinguished from ideal. Said of a number. **4.** Existing, persisting, or enduring for a limited time only; impermanent; transient. **5.** *Grammar.* Limited by person, number, tense, and mood; not an infinitive, gerund, or participle. Said of verbs.
∼*n.* Finite entities collectively. Preceded by *the.* [Middle English *finit,* from Latin *fīnītus,* past participle of *fīnīre,* to limit, FINISH.] **—fi·nite·ly** *adv.* **—fi·nite·ness** *n.*
fin·i·tude (fĭn′ə-tōōd′, -tyōōd′, fī′nə-) *n.* The quality or condition of being finite.
fink (fĭngk) *n. Slang.* **1.** A hired strikebreaker. **2.** A person who informs against another. **3.** A person who is despised or regarded with contempt.
∼*intr.v.* **finked, finking, finks.** *Slang.* **1.** To inform. Used with *on.* **2.** To withhold support or participation. Used with *out: He promised to help, but finked out.* [20th century : origin obscure.]

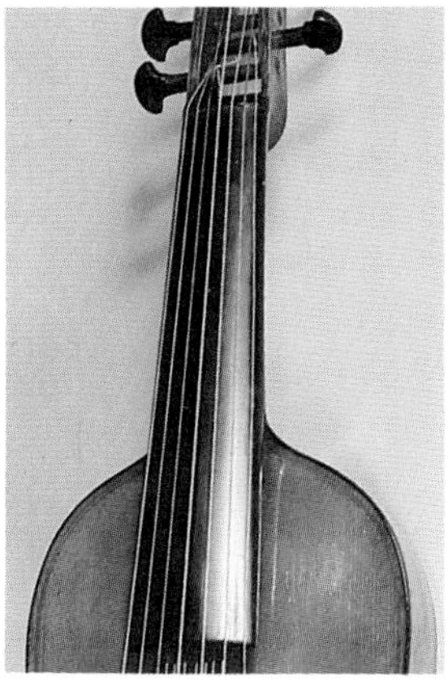

fingerboard *Board at the neck of a stringed instrument such as a violin or guitar, where the musician stops the strings with his fingers to raise the pitch of notes. This is the board of a viola d'amore, made by the Parisian instrument maker Jean Nicolas Lambert in 1772.*

FINLAND

fin keel *n.* A short keel usually made of metal, with ballast on the lower edge, used chiefly on racing yachts.

Fin·land (fĭn′lənd). *Abbr.* **Fin.** *Finnish* **Suo·mi** (swô′mē). Republic of northern Europe. It has been independent since 1919, when it gained its freedom from the U.S.S.R., having been a grand duchy of Russia since the early 19th century. After World War II Finland was forced to cede part of the Karelian Isthmus and other land totaling 12 percent of its area to the U.S.S.R. Finland is largely a barren, ice-scoured "shield," covered by more than 70,000 lakes and vast forests. Its forest-based industries account for more than half its exports. The chief port and capital is Helsinki. Area, 337,009 square kilometers (130,085 square miles). Population, 4,800,000.

Finland, Gulf of. Eastern arm of the Baltic Sea. About 460 kilometers (285 miles) long, with a maximum width of 120 kilometers (75 miles), it separates Finland's southern coast from the U.S.S.R. It is an important shipping lane, whose chief ports are Leningrad and Helsinki, but it is frozen from December to March.

Fin·land·i·za·tion (fĭn′lən-dĭ-zā′shən, -dī-zā′shən) *n.* The adoption of a neutral or conciliatory policy in relations with a powerful neighboring country as practiced by Finland with respect to the U.S.S.R.

Finn (fĭn) *n.* **1.** A native or inhabitant of Finland. Also called "Finlander." **2.** One who speaks Finnish or a Finnic language. [Swedish *Finne* (superseding Old English *Finnas,* Finns), from Germanic *Finnar* (unattested).]

fin·nan had·die (fĭn′ən hăd′ē) *n.* Also **fin·nan haddock.** Smoked haddock. [Earlier *findon haddock,* from earlier *findhorn haddock,* after the river *Findhorn* in Scotland.]

finned (fĭnd) *adj.* Having a fin, fins, or finlike parts.

Fin·ney (fĭn′ē), **Albert** (1936-). British actor. Following his early successes in the theater, he made a number of films, including *Saturday Night and Sunday Morning* (1960), *Tom Jones* (1963), and *Charlie Bubbles* (1968).

Finn·ic (fĭn′ĭk) *adj.* Of or pertaining to Finland or the Finns.
~*n.* A branch of Finno-Ugric that includes Finnish, Estonian, and Lapp.

Finn·ish (fĭn′ĭsh) *adj. Abbr.* **Fin.** Of or pertaining to Finland, its language, or its people.
~*n.* The Finno-Ugric language of the Finns.

Fin·no-U·gric (fĭn′ō-ōō′grĭk, -yōō′grĭk) *n.* Also **Fin·no-U·gri·an** (-ōō′grē-ən, -yōō′grē-ən). A subfamily of the Uralic language group including Finnish and Hungarian.
~*adj.* **1.** Pertaining to the Finns and the Ugrians. **2.** Pertaining to the languages of the Finns and the Ugrians.

fin·ny (fĭn′ē) *adj.* **-nier, -niest. 1.** Having a fin or fins. **2.** Resembling a fin; finlike. **3.** Of, pertaining to, or full of fish.

fi·no (fē′nō) *n., pl.* **-nos.** The driest variety of sherry. [Spanish, "fine."]

fi·no·chi·o, fi·noc·chi·o (fĭ-nō′kē-ō′) *n.* A variety of fennel, *Foeniculum vulgare dulce,* whose thickened leafstalks are eaten as a vegeta-

ble. Also called "Florence fennel," "sweet fennel." [Italian *finocchio,* from Vulgar Latin *fēnuculum* (unattested), fennel, from Latin *fēniculum,* diminutive of *fēnum,* hay.]

fin rot *n.* A bacterial disease of fish marked by the progressive deterioration of the fin tissue.

fiord. Variant of **fjord.**

fip·ple (fĭp′əl) *n.* **1.** A wooden block that forms a flue at the mouth end of certain musical wind instruments. **2.** A similar object in an organ pipe. [17th century : origin obscure.]

fipple flute *n.* A flute with a fipple, such as a recorder.

fir (fûr) *n.* **1.** Any of various evergreen coniferous trees of the genus *Abies,* having flat needles and erect cones. **2.** Any of several similar or related trees, such as the **Douglas fir** *(see).* **3.** The wood of any of these trees. [Middle English *fir(re),* Old English *furh,* probably from Old Norse *fyri-,* from Germanic.] —**fir·ry** *adj.*

Fir·bank (fûr′băngk′), **(Arthur Annesley) Ronald** (1886–1926). British novelist. His work, set in the Edwardian period, reflects his eccentricity and has a witty and impressionistic style. It includes the novels *Caprice* (1916) and *Valmouth* (1919).

fire (fīr) *n.* **1.** A rapid, persistent chemical reaction that releases heat and light; especially, the exothermic combination of a combustible substance with oxygen. **2. a.** A quantity of combustible material, such as wood or coal, undergoing this reaction and used for heating, cooking, or the like. **b.** *Chiefly British.* Combustible material intended to undergo this reaction; kindling: *lay a fire.* **c.** A destroying or consuming of an object by fire. **3.** A heating appliance powered by gas or electricity. **4. a.** Intensity, as of feeling; ardor, especially in love or rage. **b.** Enthusiasm or energy. **5.** Luminosity or brilliance, as of a cut and polished gemstone. **6.** The result of inspiration; vividness; brilliance: *the fire of his verse.* **7.** A sensation of heat or burning, such as that produced by fever or by drinking alcoholic liquor. **8.** A torment, trial, or tribulation. **9. a.** The discharge of firearms; firing. **b.** The bullets, shells, or similar projectiles discharged. **10.** A rapid succession of questions, criticisms, or the like. **11.** In ancient thought, one of the four elements. —**between two fires.** Being attacked from two sources or sides simultaneously. —**catch** (or **take**) **fire. 1.** To become ignited. **2.** To become excited or enthusiastic. —**hang fire. 1.** To fail to fire or be slow in firing, as a gun. **2.** To be delayed, as an event or decision. —**on fire. 1.** Ignited; burning; ablaze. **2.** Filled with enthusiasm or excitement. —**open fire. 1.** To commence shooting. **2.** To commence asking questions or making criticisms. —**play with fire.** To take part in a dangerous or risky activity; be foolhardy. —**set fire to** or **set on fire. 1.** To ignite. **2.** To make excited; inflame. —**under fire. 1.** Exposed or subjected to armed attack. **2.** Exposed or subjected to criticism or censure.
~*v.* **fired, firing, fires.** —*tr.* **1.** To cause to burn; ignite. **2. a.** To add fuel to (something burning). **b.** To maintain or intensify a fire in (a boiler, for example). **c.** To be the fuel for (a central heating system, for example). **3.** To bake in a kiln: *fire a flowerpot.* **4.** To dry or cure by heat: *fire tobacco.* **5. a.** To arouse the emotions of; make enthusiastic or ardent: *He was fired by patriotism.* **b.** To stimulate (enthusiasm, for example). **6.** To cause to glow. **7.** To detonate or discharge (a firearm, explosives, or a projectile): *fire a rifle; fire a rocket.* **8.** To cauterize (an animal's wound). **9.** *Informal.* To project or hurl suddenly and forcefully: *fire a ball at a batter; fire questions at a witness.* **10.** *Informal.* To discharge from a position; dismiss: *fire an employee.* —*intr.* **1. a.** To become ignited; flame up. **b.** To allow internal combustion to occur. Said of the cylinders in an engine. **2.** To become excited or ardent; feel deeply. **3.** To tend a fire. **4.** To have a specified reaction to being fired in a kiln: *This bowl will fire beautifully.* **5.** To become yellowed, brown, or blotchy before reaching maturity: *The drought caused the grain to fire.* **6.** To discharge; go off: *The mortar fired toward the enemy.* **7.** To detonate or shoot a weapon: *He fired at the enemy.* **8.** *Informal.* To project or hurl a missile. —**fire away.** To bombard someone, as with projectiles or questions. —**fire up. 1.** To inspire with enthusiasm. **2.** To become excited or emotional. [Middle English *fir, fur, feir, fire,* Old English *fȳr,* from West Germanic *fūir* (unattested).]

fire alarm *n.* **1.** A warning of the outbreak of a fire. **2.** A device, such as a bell or siren, used in announcing the outbreak of a fire.

fire-and-brim·stone (fīr′ən-brĭm′stōn′) *adj.* **1.** Characteristic or suggestive of hellfire. **2.** Extremely zealous in warning of divine punishment awaiting sinners. [From the Biblical *fire and brimstone,* which God often used to destroy sinners. Revelation 20:10.]

fire ant *n.* Any of several ants of the genus *Solenopsis;* especially, *S. geminata* or *S. saevissima,* of the southern United States and tropical America, that can inflict a painful bite.

fire·arm (fīr′ärm′) *n.* Any weapon capable of firing a missile; especially, a pistol or rifle using an explosive charge as a propellant.

fire·back (fīr′băk′) *n.* **1.** An iron plate, usually ornamental, at the back of a fireplace. **2.** A pheasant of the genus *Lophura,* of southeastern Asia.

fire·ball (fīr′bôl′) *n.* **1.** Any brilliantly burning sphere; especially, a flash of **ball lightning** *(see).* **2.** An exceptionally bright meteor. **3.** A highly luminous, intensely hot, spherical cloud of dust, gas, and vapor generated by a nuclear explosion. **4.** *Slang.* A highly energetic person.

fire beetle *n.* Any of various tropical American click beetles of the genus *Pyrophorus,* especially *P. noctilucus,* having brightly luminous spots.

fire·bird (fīr′bûrd′) *n.* Any of various birds, as the Baltimore oriole, having bright scarlet or orange plumage.

fire blight *n.* A destructive disease of apples, pears, and related plants, caused by a bacterium, *Erwinia amylovora.*

fire bomb *n.* An **incendiary bomb** (see). —**fire-bomb** (fīr′bŏm′) *v.*

fire·box (fīr′bŏks′) *n.* A chamber in which fuel is burned; especially, the furnace of a steam locomotive.

fire·brand (fīr′brănd′) *n.* 1. A piece of burning wood. 2. A person who stirs up trouble or kindles a revolt.

fire·brat (fīr′brăt′) *n.* A small, wingless insect, *Thermobia domestica,* frequenting warm areas of buildings.

fire·break (fīr′brāk′) *n.* A strip of cleared or plowed land used to stop the spread of a fire. Also called "fireguard," "fire line."

fire·brick (fīr′brĭk′) *n.* A refractory brick, especially of fire clay, used for lining furnaces, fireboxes, chimneys, or fireplaces.

fire brigade *n.* 1. An organized body of firefighters. 2. A body of reinforcements or helpers called in to help in an emergency.

fire bug *n.* The **harlequin bug** (see).

fire·bug (fīr′bŭg′) *n. Informal.* A person who deliberately sets fire to property; a pyromaniac.

fire clay *n.* A type of heat-resistant clay used to make firebricks, crucibles, and other objects exposed to high temperatures.

fire company *n.* 1. An organized body of firefighters. 2. A business firm that sells fire insurance.

fire control *n. Abbr.* **FC** The control of the delivery of gunfire on military targets.

fire·crack·er (fīr′krăk′ər) *n.* A small explosive charge in a cylinder of heavy paper, used to make noise.

fire·crest (fīr′krĕst′) *n.* A small European warbler, *Regulus ignicapillus,* having a crown with yellow, black, and white stripes.

fire·cure (fīr′kyōor′) *tr.v.* **-cured, -curing, -cures.** To cure (tobacco, for example) by exposing it to the heat and smoke of a wood fire.

fire·damp (fīr′dămp′) *n.* 1. A combustible gas, chiefly methane, occurring naturally in coal mines and forming explosive mixtures with air. 2. The explosive mixture itself. Compare **damp.**

fire department *n. Abbr.* **F.D.** A department, especially of a municipal government, whose purpose is to prevent and put out fires and to conduct emergency evacuations and resuscitations.

fire·dog (fīr′dôg′, -dŏg′) *n.* An andiron (see).

fire door *n.* An internal door in a building with a strong spring that makes it self-closing, designed to stop the spread of fire by eliminating through drafts.

fire·drake (fīr′drāk′) *n.* A fiery dragon of Germanic mythology. [Middle English *firdrake,* Old English *fȳr-draca* : *fȳr,* FIRE + *draca,* dragon, DRAKE.]

fire drill *n.* A practice exercise in the use of firefighting equipment or the exit procedure to be followed in case of a fire.

fire·eat·er (fīr′ē′tər) *n.* 1. A performer who pretends to swallow fire. 2. A vigorous or pugnacious person.

fire engine *n.* Any of various large motor vehicles that carry firefighters and equipment to a fire and that support extinguishing operations, as by pumping water or raising ladders.

fire escape *n.* Any structure or device, as a metal ladder or an outside stairway attached to a building, erected for emergency exit in the event of fire.

fire extinguisher *n.* A portable apparatus containing water or chemicals that can be discharged in a jet to extinguish a small fire.

fire·fight·er (fīr′fī′tər) *n.* A person employed by a fire department to fight fires. —**fire·fight·ing** *adj. & n.*

fire·fly (fīr′flī′) *n., pl.* **-flies.** Any of various nocturnal beetles of the family Lampyridae, characteristically having luminous abdominal organs that produce a flashing light.

fire·guard (fīr′gärd′) *n.* 1. A metal screen placed in front of an open fireplace to catch sparks. Also called "fire screen." 2. A **firebreak** (see).

fire hall *n. Chiefly Canadian.* A fire station.

fire·house (fīr′hous′) *n.* A **fire station** (see).

fire hydrant *n.* A hydrant (see).

fire insurance *n.* Insurance against the damage or loss of property as a result of fire or lightning.

fire irons *pl.n.* The equipment used to tend a fireplace, including tongs, a shovel, and a poker.

Fire Island. A narrow barrier island, 52 kilometers (32 miles) long, off the southern coast of Long Island, southeastern New York. It has many resort communities, a state park, and the Fire Island National Seashore, which includes the Sunken Forest with its unusual plant and animal life.

fire·less cooker (fīr′lĭs) *n.* An insulated container that when preheated retains sufficient heat to cook food.

fire·light (fīr′līt′) *n.* The light from a fire, as in a fireplace or at a campsite.

fire line *n.* A strip of cleared land, a **firebreak** (see).

fire·lock (fīr′lŏk′) *n.* A flintlock (see).

fire·man (fīr′mən) *n., pl.* **-men** (-mĭn). 1. A firefighter. 2. A man who tends a boiler or furnace; a stoker. 3. **a.** A man who tends the boiler of a steam locomotive. **b.** A locomotive engineer's assistant. 4. An enlisted man in the U.S. Navy engaged in the operation of the engineering machinery. 5. *Baseball.* A relief pitcher.

Firenze. See Florence.

fire opal *n.* An opal with brilliant flamelike yellow, orange, and red colors. Also called "girasol."

fire·pan (fīr′păn′) *n.* A metal grate or brazier for holding fire.

fire·place (fīr′plās′) *n.* 1. An open recess for holding a fire at the base of a chimney; a hearth. 2. A structure, usually of stone or brick, for holding an outdoor fire.

fire·plug (fīr′plŭg′) *n.* A hydrant (see).

fire·pow·er (fīr′pou′ər) *n.* The capacity, as of a weapon, military unit, or ship, for discharging ammunition.

fire·proof (fīr′prōōf′) *adj.* Capable of withstanding or resisting damage by fire.
~*tr.v.* **fireproofed, -proofing, -proofs.** To make fireproof.

fir·er (fīr′ər) *n.* 1. One that kindles, builds, or tends a fire. 2. A firearm considered with respect to the speed or technique of its firing. Often used in combination: *rapid-firer.*

fire-rais·er (fīr′rā′zər) *n. British.* An arsonist. —**fire-rais·ing** *n.*

fire sale *n.* A sale of commodities damaged by fire.

fire screen *n.* 1. An ornamental screen placed in front of a fireplace that is not in use. 2. A **fireguard** (see).

fire ship *n.* A vessel loaded with explosives and combustible material and set adrift among enemy ships to destroy them.

fire·side (fīr′sīd′) *n.* 1. The area immediately surrounding a fireplace or hearth. 2. Home.

fire station *n.* A building for firefighting equipment and firefighters. Also called "firehouse."

fire·stone (fīr′stōn′) *n.* 1. A flint or other stone used to strike a spark of fire. 2. A fire-resistant stone, as certain sandstones, used as a construction material.

fire·storm (fīr′stôrm′) *n.* A violent storm caused by hot air rising from an area that is on fire, typically following a heavy bombing attack, characterized by very high winds rushing in to replace the rising air.

fire·thorn (fīr′thôrn′) *n.* Any of various thorny shrubs of the genus *Pyracantha,* native to Asia, and often cultivated for their evergreen foliage and showy reddish or orange berries.

fire·trap (fīr′trăp′) *n.* A building susceptible to catching fire easily or difficult to escape from in the event of fire.

fire wall *n.* A fireproof wall used to prevent the spread of a fire.

fire warden *n.* An official responsible for the prevention or putting out of fires, especially in forested areas.

fire·watch·er (fīr′wŏch′ər) *n. British.* One who keeps a lookout for fires started by bombs. —**fire·watch·ing** *n.*

fire·wa·ter (fīr′wô′tər, -wŏt′ər) *n. Slang.* Strong liquor, especially when of poor quality. [Translation of an Algonquian term such as Ojibwa *iškotēwābō.*]

fire·weed (fīr′wēd′) *n.* 1. A species of willow herb, *Epilobium angustifolium,* having terminal clusters of pinkish-purple flowers. 2. A weedy North American plant, *Erechtites hieracifolia,* having small white or greenish flowers. 3. Any of various other plants often appearing as the first vegetation in burned-over areas.

fire·wood (fīr′wood′) *n.* Wood used as fuel.

fire·work (fīr′wûrk′) *n.* 1. Any of various devices using combinations of explosives and combustibles to generate colored lights, smoke, and noise for amusement. 2. A display of such devices. 3. **fireworks.** An exciting or spectacular display, as of musical or literary virtuosity. 4. **fireworks.** A temperamental outburst.

fir·ing (fīr′ĭng) *n.* 1. Fuel for fires. 2. The application of fire or heat, as in the hardening or glazing of ceramics.

firing line *n.* 1. The line of positions from which fire is directed against a target. 2. A position in which one is exposed to criticism or attack.

firing party *n. British.* A detachment of soldiers chosen to fire a salute at a military funeral. Also called "firing squad."

firing pin *n.* The part of the bolt or breech of a firearm that strikes the primer and explodes the charge of the projectile.

firing squad *n.* 1. A detachment assigned to shoot persons condemned to death. 2. A firing party.

fir·kin (fûr′kĭn) *n.* 1. A small wooden barrel or keg, used especially for storing butter, cheese, or lard. 2. Any of several British units of capacity, usually equal to about 9 gallons (41 liters). [Middle English *ferdekin, ferken,* a cask, one-fourth of a barrel, probably from Middle Dutch *vierdelkijn* (unattested), "little quarter," diminutive of *vierdel,* fourth part.]

firm¹ (fûrm) *adj.* **firmer, firmest.** 1. Unyielding to pressure; rigid or solid to the touch. 2. Not easily moved or detached; securely fixed in place. 3. Showing determination or resolution; unshakable. 4. Constant; steadfast: *a firm ally.* 5. Fixed formally; definite; final: *a firm offer.* 6. Unfluctuating; steady. Said of prices. 7. Strong and sure: *a firm handshake.*
~*v.* **firmed, firming, firms.** —*tr.* To make firm. —*intr.* 1. To become firm. 2. To begin to rise again after a decline. Used of prices.
~*adv.* Resolutely; unwaveringly: *stand firm; hold firm.* [Middle English *ferm,* from Old French *ferme,* from Latin *firmus.*] —**firm·ly** *adv.* —**firm·ness** *n.*

firm² (fûrm) *n.* 1. A commercial partnership of two or more people. 2. The name or designation under which a firm transacts business. [Italian *firma,* signature, name of a business establishment or partnership, from *firmare,* to sign, "confirm by signature," from Late Latin *firmāre,* to confirm, from Latin, to strengthen, from *firmus,* FIRM.]

fir·ma·ment (fûr′mə-mənt) *n.* The vault or expanse of the heavens; the sky. [Middle English, from Old French, from Late Latin *firmāmentum* (translation of Greek *stereōma,* heavenly vault, translation of Hebrew *rāqī'a*), from Latin, a strengthening, support, from *firmāre,* to make firm, from *firmus,* FIRM.] —**fir·ma·men·tal** (fûr′-mə-mĕnt′l) *adj.*

fir·mer chisel (fûr′mər) *n.* A chisel or gouge with a thin blade, used to shape and finish wood. Also called "firmer." [French *fermoir,*

fireworks *The Chinese invented these gunpowder-based devices in about the tenth century A.D. Modern fireworks are even more spectacular because of new ingredients such as magnesium, first used in the nineteenth century.*

variant (influenced by *fermer*, to make firm) of Old French *formoir*, from *former*, to form, shape, from Latin *formāre*, from *forma*, FORM.]

firm·ware (fûrm'wâr') *n.* **1.** A computer program that is stored in a read-only memory so that it cannot be accidentally overwritten or erased. **2.** An electronic device incorporating such programs. Compare **software, hardware.**

firn (fîrn) *n.* Snow that has been partially consolidated by thawing and freezing but not yet converted to glacial ice. [German *Firn*, "last year's (snow)," from (Swiss dialect) *firn*, of last year, from Old High German *firni*, old.]

first (fûrst) *adj.* **1.** Coming, counted, or located before all others. **2.** Occurring or acting prior to all others; earliest. **3.** Ranking above all others; foremost in position, quality, or importance: *the king's first secretary; matters of the first importance.* **4.** *Music.* Highest in pitch or foremost in carrying melody: *first soprano; first trumpet.* **5.** Of or pertaining to the transmission gear, or corresponding gear ratio, used to produce the range of lowest drive speeds in a motor vehicle.
~*adv.* **1.** Before anything else. **2.** Before or above all others in time or rank. **3.** For the first time: *since you first came.* **4.** Preferably; rather: *I'd die first.*
~*n.* **1.** The ordinal number one in a series. **2.** The one coming, counted, occurring, or ranking before or above all others. **3.** The beginning; the outset: *from the first; at first.* **4.** *Music.* The voice or instrument highest in pitch or foremost in carrying melody. **5.** The transmission gear or corresponding gear ratio used to produce the range of lowest drive speeds in a motor vehicle. **6.** The winner or winning position in a contest. **7.** An innovation or breakthrough: *a first for the human race.* **8. firsts.** The best grade or quality of merchandise. [Middle English *first*, Old English *fyrst*, from Germanic *furistaz* (unattested), superlative of *fur-, for-* (unattested).]

INHABITANTS OF A WATERY PLANET

Species that have adapted to almost every ecological niche

Fish are the most numerous vertebrates. The 20,000 or so species range from the 8-millimeter (5/16-inch) dwarf pygmy goby to the whale shark, which has been known to reach a length of 18 meters (59 feet). Seventy percent of the earth's surface is covered by water and most of the water, whether salt or fresh, is inhabited by fish. Although cold-blooded, fish live in temperatures from 38°C (100°F) down to freezing.

There are three classes of fish: the primitive, jawless agnatha, of which lampreys and hagfish are the only survivors; the sharklike fish with cartilaginous skeletons; and the bony fish, which include almost all fish species. Despite their differences, fish share several features. They are streamlined and slimy to allow them to slip through the water easily; they have gills and fins; and they almost all lay eggs.

BONY FISH

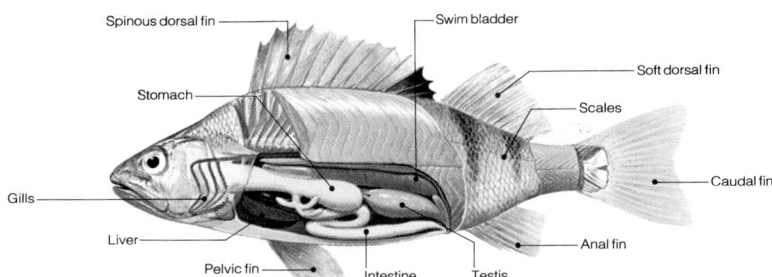

The bony fish (Osteichthyes) are divided into fleshy-finned and ray-finned fish, the latter including 95 percent of all fish species. Early bony fish evolved lungs. These remain in some archaic spe- *cies, such as the lungfish, but in most the lung has become a swim bladder that buoys up the body. Bony fish have scales, and fertilization of the eggs takes place outside the body.*

CARTILAGINOUS FISH

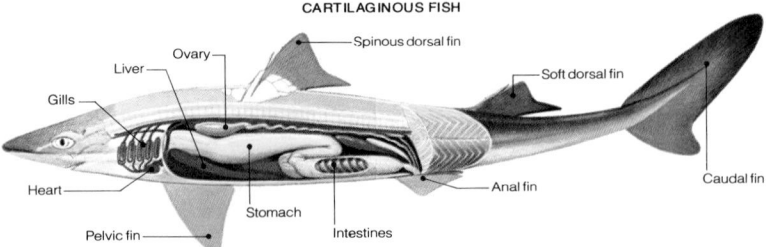

Cartilaginous fish (Chondrichthyes)—sharks, rays, and chimaeras—are survivors of an earlier stage of evolution. They have skeletons of tough gristle instead of bone. They have no swim bladders and most move constantly to prevent themselves from sinking. The skin consists of rough *denticles that are modified in the mouth to form sawlike teeth set in rows that move forward continuously to replace worn sets. Fertilization takes place inside the female. The male has copulatory organs—claspers—on the inside of the pelvic fin. Many species bear live young.*

Usage: *First* and *last* usually precede a numeral in expressions such as *the first two chapters* and *the last four chapters,* with reference to a single book or the like. An alternative and older form, illustrated by *the two first chapters* and *the four last pages,* is used only where low numerals or numbers are involved.

first aid *n.* Emergency treatment administered to injured or sick persons before professional medical care is available.

first base *n.* **1.** *Baseball.* **a.** The first of the bases in the infield, counterclockwise from home plate. **b.** The fielding position played by the first baseman. **2.** *Informal.* The first step toward achievement or success: *The reform bill never got to first base.*

first baseman *n. Baseball.* The infielder stationed at or near first base.

first-born (fûrst'bôrn') *adj.* First in order of birth; born first. ~*n.* A first-born child.

first class *n.* **1.** The first, highest, or best group of a particular category. **2.** The most luxurious and most expensive class of accommodation on a train or other means of transport. **3.** A class of mail given priority for handling and delivery.

first-class (fûrst'klăs', -kläs') *adj.* **1.** Indicating the first, highest, or best group of a particular category. **2.** Of the foremost excellence or highest quality; first-rate: *a first-class mind.* ~*adv.* **1.** In first-class accommodations. **2.** By first-class mail.

first cousin *n.* See **cousin.**

first-day cover (fûrst'dā') *n.* An envelope bearing stamps postmarked on their day of issue.

first-de·gree burn (fûrst'dĭ-grē') *n.* A mild burn that produces redness of the skin but no blistering.

first floor *n.* **1.** The ground floor of a building. **2.** *British.* The floor immediately above the ground floor.

first-foot (fûrst'fŏŏt') *n. British.* The first person to enter a house at New Year.
~*intr.v.* **first-footed, -footing, -foots.** *British.* To be the first person to enter a house at New Year.

first fruit *n.* Also **first fruits. 1.** The first product of a season's harvest. **2.** The first result or profit of an undertaking.

first-gen·er·a·tion (fûrst'jĕn'ə-rā'shən) *adj.* Of, pertaining to, or being the offspring of immigrant parents: *a first-generation American.*

first·hand (fûrst'hănd') *adj.* Received from the original source: *firsthand information.*
~*adv.* From the original source; directly. [Originally, *at (the) first hand.*]

First International *n.* See **International** (sense 1a).

first lady *n.* **1.** *Sometimes* **First Lady.** The wife or hostess of the chief executive of a country, state, or city. **2.** The foremost woman of a specified profession or art: *the first lady of the ballet.*

first lieutenant *n.* A commissioned officer in the U.S. Army, Air Force, or Marine Corps ranking above a second lieutenant and below a captain.

first·ling (fûrst'lĭng) *n.* **1.** The first of a kind or category. **2.** The first-born offspring.

first·ly (fûrst'lē) *adv.* **1.** Before anything else. **2.** Before all others. **3.** In the first place; to begin with.
Usage: *Firstly* may be used in a sequence: *firstly, secondly, thirdly,* and so on. However, it has fallen into disuse among many writers, who prefer this sequence: *first, secondly, thirdly.* Another alternative, since all these ordinals can be used adverbially, is *first, second, third.*

first mate *n.* A ship's officer ranking immediately below the captain. Also called "first officer."

first name *n.* A person's given, personal, or Christian name. —**on first-name terms.** Friendly enough to use first names.

first night *n.* The official opening performance of a play, opera, or the like.

first-night·er (fûrst'nī'tər) *n.* One attending a first night.

first offender *n.* One found guilty of an offense who has no previous convictions.

first papers *pl.n.* The documents first filed by a person applying for U.S. citizenship.

first person *n.* **1.** A category of linguistic forms, such as verbs and pronouns, designating the speaker or writer of the sentence in which they appear. **2.** Any of these forms as *I* or *we.* **3.** A discourse or literary style in which the narrator recounts his or her own experiences and impressions using such forms: *a novel written in the first person.*

first principles *pl.n.* The basic premises from which any intellectual argument proceeds.

first-rate (fûrst'rāt') *adj.* Foremost in quality or rank.

first refusal *n.* The right to be the first to be offered something.

first sergeant *n.* In the U.S. Army, the highest-ranking noncommissioned officer of a company or other military unit.

first strike *n.* An aggressive rather than retaliatory attack with nuclear weapons, intended to reduce or destroy an enemy's ability to strike back. Also used adjectively: *first-strike missiles.*

first-string (fûrst'strĭng') *adj.* **1.** Being a regular team member rather than a reserve or substitute: *the first-string quarterback.* **2.** First-rate; of high importance or quality.

first thing *adv.* At the earliest possible moment.

first water *n.* **1.** The highest degree of quality or value in gems or pearls. **2.** The foremost rank or quality: *a pianist of the first water.*

First World *n.* The industrialized nations of the world, including Western Europe, North America, Australia and New Zealand, and Japan, and sometimes thought to include the Soviet bloc.

First World War *n.* **World War I** *(see).*

firth (fûrth) *n.* In Scotland, a long, narrow inlet of the sea; a fjord. [Middle English *ford, furth,* from Old Norse *fjörthr,* FIORD.]

fisc (fĭsk) *n.* The treasury of a kingdom or country. [Old French, from Latin *fiscus†,* woven basket, money basket used by tax collectors, treasury.]

fis·cal (fĭs′kəl) *adj.* **1.** Of or pertaining to the treasury or finances of a nation or branch of government; especially, of or pertaining to matters of taxation. **2.** Of or pertaining to finances in general: *a fiscal agent.* —See Synonyms at **financial.** ~*n.* A procurator fiscal *(see).* [Old French, from Latin *fiscālis,* from *fiscus†,* treasury, basket.] —**fis·cal·ly** *adv.*

fiscal drag *n.* The limitation of economic growth caused by taxation affecting a higher proportion of taxpayers as inflation reduces the real value of money.

fiscal year *n. Abbr.* **FY** A 12-month period for which an organization plans the use of its funds. The fiscal year of the U.S. government begins October 1. Also called "financial year."

Fisch·er (fĭsh′ər), **Bobby,** born Robert James Fischer (1943–). U.S. chess player. He was world champion (1972–74).

fish¹ (fĭsh) *n., pl.* **fishes** or collectively **fish. 1.** Any of numerous cold-blooded aquatic vertebrates of the superclass Pisces, characteristically having fins, gills, and a streamlined body, and including: **a.** Any of the class Osteichthyes, having a bony skeleton. **b.** Any of the class Chondrichthyes, having a cartilaginous skeleton, and including the sharks, rays, and skates. **c.** The flesh of such animals for use in cooking. **2.** Any aquatic vertebrate of the class Agnatha, lacking jaws, and including the lampreys and hagfishes. **3.** Loosely, any of various unrelated aquatic animals, such as a jellyfish, cuttlefish, or crayfish. **4.** *Informal.* A person likened to a fish for lacking some human attribute or advantage: *a cold fish.* **5. Fish.** The constellation and sign of the Zodiac **Pisces** *(see).* ~*v.* **fished, fishing, fishes.** —*intr.* **1.** To catch or try to catch fish. **2.** To search or hunt for something in or under water: *fish for sponges.* **3.** To look for something by feeling around: *fished for the map in the glove compartment.* **4.** To seek to elicit information, compliments, or the like. —*tr.* **1.** To catch or try to catch fish in: *fish a lake.* **2.** To pull out or up in the manner of one who fishes. Used with *out* or *from: fished the keys out of her purse.* [Middle English *fish, fisk,* Old English *fisc,* from Germanic.]

Usage: This word has two plural forms: *fish* and *fishes. Fish* is the more widely used, referring to fish viewed collectively (*the fish in the sea). Fishes* is used to refer to individual species or members of a group: *The fishes pass through the hole one at a time.*

fish² *n., pl.* **fishes.** A piece of wood or an iron plate used to join or strengthen a beam, bar, or the like. ~*tr.v.* **fished, fishing, fishes.** To join, reinforce, or mend with a fish. [French *ficher,* to fix, from Vulgar Latin *figicare* (unattested), from Latin *figere.*]

fish and chips *pl.n.* Fried fillets of fish and French-fried potatoes.

fish-bolt (fĭsh′bōlt′) *n.* A bolt used in a fish joint.

fish-bowl (fĭsh′bōl′) *n.* **1.** A transparent bowl in which live fish are kept. **2.** A location or situation that is lacking in privacy.

fish cake *n.* A fried cake, patty, or ball of chopped fish, often mixed with potato or rice.

fish crow *n.* A crow, *Corvus ossifragus,* of the coast and rivers of the eastern United States.

fish eagle *n.* The osprey *(see).*

fish·er (fĭsh′ər) *n.* **1. a.** One that fishes. **b.** A fisherman. **2. a.** A carnivorous mammal, *Martes pennanti,* of northern North America, having thick, dark brown fur. Also called "pekan." **b.** The fur of this animal.

fish·er·man (fĭsh′ər-mən) *n., pl.* **-men** (-mĭn). **1.** One who fishes as an occupation or sport. **2.** A commercial fishing vessel.

fisherman's bend *n.* A knot used to secure the end of a line to a ring or spar, made by two turns with the end passing back under both.

fisherman's knot *n.* A knot used to join two lines, made by securing either end to the opposite standing part by an overhand knot. Also called "Englishman's tie."

fish·er·y (fĭsh′ə-rē) *n., pl.* **-ies. 1. a.** The industry or occupation of catching, processing, or selling fish and fish products. **b.** A place where fish are processed and sold. **2.** An area where commercial fishing is carried on; a fishing ground. **3.** A hatchery for fish. **4.** The legal right to fish in specific waters or areas.

Fish·es (fĭsh′ĭz) *pl.n.* The constellation and sign of the zodiac **Pisces** *(see).*

fish-eye lens (fĭsh′ī′) *n. Photography.* A lens with a large curvature used to take pictures over a very wide field of view but producing a somewhat distorted image of the sides.

fish farm *n.* A place in which food fish are bred commercially in tanks or ponds.

fish-gig (fĭsh′gĭg) *n.* Also **fiz-gig** (fĭz′-). A pronged instrument for spearing fish. Also called "gig." [Variant (influenced by FISH) of earlier *fisgig,* from Spanish *fisga†.*]

fish hawk *n.* The osprey *(see).*

fish-hook (fĭsh′hŏŏk′) *n.* A barbed metal hook used for catching fish.

fish·ing (fĭsh′ĭng) *n.* The sport or occupation of catching fish.

fishing rod *n.* A rod of wood, steel, or fiber glass used with a line for catching fish.

fish joint *n.* A joint formed by bolting fishplates to either side of two rails or beams.

fish kettle *n.* A long, oval-shaped saucepan with a lid and usually a detachable grid that fits inside, for poaching or steaming whole fish.

fish ladder *n.* A set of pools one above the other that enables fish to pass over a dam or similar obstacle when swimming upstream.

fish louse *n.* Any of various small, rounded parasitic crustaceans of the subclass Branchiura that live attached to fish.

fish·meal (fĭsh′mēl′) *n.* A nutritive mealy substance produced from fish and used as animal feed and fertilizer.

fish·mon·ger (fĭsh′mŭng′gər, -mŏng′gər) *n. Chiefly British.* One who sells fish.

fish·net (fĭsh′nĕt′) *n.* **1.** A meshed openwork fabric. **2.** A net for catching fish, often fitted with floats or a supporting frame. ~*adj.* Meshed or woven together like a fish net: *fishnet tights.*

fish·plate (fĭsh′plāt′) *n.* Any of the connecting metal plates bolted along the side of two rails or beams placed end to end, used especially in the laying of railroad track.

fish·pond (fĭsh′pŏnd′) *n.* A small body of water stocked with fish.

Fish River Canyon. A spectacular canyon formed by the Fish River in southern Namibia, second in size only to the Grand Canyon of the Colorado River in Arizona. Its maximum depth is approximately 600 meters (2,000 feet).

fish·tail (fĭsh′tāl′) *adj.* Resembling or suggestive of the tail of a fish in shape or movement. ~*intr.v.* **fishtailed, -tailing, -tails.** To swing the rear end of a motor vehicle or aircraft from side to side while moving forward. ~*n.* **1.** A fishtailing maneuver. **2.** An attachment for a Bunsen burner that produces a thin, broad flame.

fish·wife (fĭsh′wīf′) *n., pl.* **-wives** (-wīvz′). **1.** A woman who sells fish. **2.** A coarse, abusive woman.

fish·y (fĭsh′ē) *adj.* **-ier, -iest. 1.** Resembling or suggestive of fish, as in taste or smell. **2.** Cold or expressionless: *a fishy stare.* **3.** *Informal.* **a.** Unlikely; questionable. **b.** Giving rise to suspicion; dubious. —**fish·i·ly** *adv.* —**fish·i·ness** *n.*

fissi– *prefix.* Indicates a split or cleft shape; for example, **fissipalmate.** [Latin *fissus,* past participle of *findere,* to cleave, split.]

fis·sile (fĭs′əl, -īl′) *adj.* **1.** Capable of being split. **2.** *Physics.* Fissionable, especially by neutrons of all energies. [Latin *fissilis,* from *fissus,* split. See **fissi–.**] —**fis·sil·i·ty** (fĭ-sĭl′ə-tē) *n.*

fis·sion (fĭsh′ən) *n.* **1.** The act or process of splitting into parts. **2.** *Physics.* A nuclear reaction in which any of certain heavy atomic nuclei split into fragments, usually two fragments of comparable mass, releasing a large amount of energy. Also called "nuclear fission." Compare **fusion. 3.** *Biology.* An asexual reproductive process in which a unicellular organism splits into two or more independently maturing daughter cells. [Latin *fissiō* (stem *fissiōn-*), from *fissus,* past participle of *findere,* to split.]

fis·sion·a·ble (fĭsh′ə-nə-bəl) *adj.* Capable of undergoing fission; especially, capable of being induced to undergo nuclear fission by slow neutrons. Said of isotopes.

fission bomb *n.* A bomb in which the explosion is produced by nuclear fission; an atomic bomb.

fission reactor *n.* A nuclear reactor that produces energy by controlled nuclear fission of a radioactive fuel.

fis·si·pal·mate (fĭs′ə-păl′māt′) *adj.* Having lobed or partially webbed separated toes, as the feet of certain birds.

fis·sip·a·rous (fĭ-sĭp′ər-əs) *adj.* Reproducing by biological fission. [FISSI– + -PAROUS.]

fis·si·ped (fĭs′ə-pĕd′) *adj.* Having the toes separated from one another, as certain carnivorous mammals. ~*n.* A carnivorous mammal having such toes, such as a dog or cat. [Late Latin *fissipēs* : FISSI– + -PED.]

fis·sure (fĭsh′ər) *n.* **1.** A narrow crack or cleft, as in a rock face. **2.** A schism; a split. **3.** *Anatomy.* A groove or furrow, as in the liver or brain, that divides an organ into lobes or separates it into areas. **4.** *Pathology.* A cleft in the skin or mucous membrane resulting from disease. **5.** A crack in the surface of a tooth. ~*v.* **fissured, -suring, -sures.** —*tr.* To cause a fissure in; split. —*intr.* To form fissures; become cleft; crack. [Middle English, fracture, opening, from Old French, from Latin *fissūra,* from *fissus.* See **fission.**]

fist (fĭst) *n.* **1.** The hand closed tightly with the fingers bent against the palm. **2.** *Informal.* A grasping hand; a clutch: *Don't let him get his fists on this.* **3.** A printer's mark, an **index** *(see).* ~*tr.v.* **fisted, fisting, fists. 1.** To hit with the fist. **2.** *Nautical.* To grasp or handle: *fisting a slippery anchor chain.* [Middle English *fist, fust,* Old English *fȳst,* from Germanic.]

fist-fight (fĭst′fīt′) *n.* A fight with the fists.

fist-ful (fĭst′fŏŏl′) *n., pl.* **-fuls.** A handful.

fist·ic (fĭs′tĭk) *adj.* Of or pertaining to fighting with the fists; pugilistic.

fist·i·cuffs (fĭs′tĭ-kŭfs′) *pl.n.* **1.** A fistfight. **2.** Boxing. [Earlier *fisty cuff* : *fisty,* from FIST + CUFF (a blow).] —**fist·i·cuff·er** *n.*

fis·tu·la (fĭs′chŏŏ-lə) *n., pl.* **-las** or **-lae** (-lē′). An abnormal duct or passage from an abscess, cavity, or hollow organ to the body surface or to another hollow organ. [Middle English, from Latin *fistula†,* pipe, tube, fistula.]

fis·tu·lous (fĭs′chŏŏ-ləs) *adj.* **1.** Of or resembling a fistula. **2.** Tubular and hollow; reedlike. **3.** Made of or containing tubular parts.

fit¹ (fĭt) *v.* **fitted** or **fit, fitted, fitting, fits.** —*tr.* **1.** To be the proper size and shape for. **2.** To be appropriate or suitable to; be in keeping with. **3.** To modify or adapt so as to be of the desired size or

fisherman's bend *This knot is used for securing a hauling rope to an anchor ring. The double turn on the rope reduces the risk from chafing.*

type. **4.** To be in conformity with; correspond to; suit: *Let the punishment fit the crime.* **5.** To render competent or qualified; prepare. **6.** To equip or furnish. Used with *up* or *out.* **7.** To provide a place or time for. Used with *in* or *into.* **8.** To insert so as to be properly in place; install: *fit a new gearbox.* —*intr.* **1.** To conform as to size and shape. **2.** To be appropriate or suitable. **3.** To correspond or agree, as with the circumstances of a given situation. Often used with *in* or *into.*
~*adj.* **fitter, fittest. 1.** Suited, adapted, or adequate to a given circumstance, end, or design. **2.** Appropriate; proper; fitting. **3.** Rightly deserving or entitled: *not fit to live.* **4.** Ready; disposed: *fit to drop from exhaustion.* **5.** Physically sound, especially as a result of regular exercise.
~*n.* **1.** Adjustment or alteration to a given pattern or standard. **2.** The manner in which clothing fits. **3.** The degree of precision with which surfaces or parts are adjusted or adapted to each other at a joint or edge. **4.** *Slang.* The needle and other equipment of a narcotics user.
~*adv. Informal.* In a manner likely to lead to a specified outcome: *They were laughing fit to burst.* [Middle English, probably from the past participle of *fitten*†, to marshal troops, (hence) to arrange.] **—fit·ly** *adv.* **—fit·ness** *n.*

Synonyms: *appropriate, apt, felicitous, fitting, happy, proper, suitable.*

Usage: When *fit* is used to mean "to cause to fit," only *fitted* is used as the past tense: *The tailor fitted* (not *fit*) *the suit in a few minutes.* In other uses either *fitted* or *fit* is correct as the past tense of *fit: The suit fitted* (or *fit*) *me well the last time I tried it on.*

fit[2] *n.* **1.** *Medicine.* **a.** A seizure or convulsion, especially one due to epilepsy. **b.** A sudden attack, as of coughing. **2.** A sudden outburst or display of some specified emotion: *a fit of jealousy.* **3.** A sudden period of vigorous activity. **—by** (or **in**) **fits and starts.** With irregular intervals of action and inaction; intermittently; spasmodically. [Middle English *fit,* hardship, painful experience, Old English *fitt*†, conflict.]

fit[3] *n. Archaic.* A section of a poem or ballad; a canto. [Middle English *fit,* Old English *fit(t)*†.]

fitch (fĭch) *n.* The Old World polecat or its fur. [Middle Dutch *fisse*†.]

fit·ful (fĭt′fəl) *adj.* Occurring in or characterized by intermittent bursts of activity; irregular. —See Synonyms at **periodic. —fit·ful·ly** *adv.* **—fit·ful·ness** *n.*

fit·ted (fĭt′ĭd) *adj.* **1.** Cut for a close fit: *a fitted shirt.* **2.** Cut and laid so as to fit a floor area exactly: *a fitted carpet.* **3.** Forming a fixed, integral part of a structure: *fitted wardrobes.*

fit·ter (fĭt′ər) *n.* **1.** One who alters or adjusts garments. **2.** One who installs or adjusts parts of machines or other equipment.

fit·ting (fĭt′ĭng) *adj.* Suitable; appropriate: *The host offered a few fitting expressions of welcome.* —See Synonyms at **fit.**
~*n.* **1.** The act of trying on clothes whose fit is being adjusted. **2.** A small, detachable part for a machine or an apparatus. **3.** *British.* **fittings.** Movable furnishings or accessories. Compare **fixture. 4.** The work of a fitter. **—fit·ting·ly** *adv.* **—fit·ting·ness** *n.*

Fitz·Ger·ald (fĭts-jĕr′əld), **Edward** (1809–83). British poet and translator. His English version of the *Rubáiyát of Omar Khayyám* (1859) is by far the best known.

Fitzgerald, Ella (1918–). U.S. jazz singer. Her first worldwide hit came in 1938 with "A-tisket, A-tasket." Often called the First Lady of Jazz, she is considered the greatest of all female jazz singers.

Fitzgerald, Francis Scott Key, known as F. Scott Fitzgerald (1896–1940). U.S. novelist and short-story writer. After the success of his first novel, the autobiographical *This Side of Paradise* (1920), he married Zelda Sayre (1900–47). In the 1920's he lived on the French Riviera, where he wrote his best-known novel, *The Great Gatsby* (1925).

Fiume. See **Rijeka.**

five (fīv) *n.* **1. a.** The cardinal number that is one more than four. **b.** A symbol representing this, such as 5, V, or v. **2.** A set made up of five persons or things. **3. a.** The fifth in a series. **b.** A playing card marked with five pips. **4.** Five parts: *cut in five.* **5.** A size, as in clothing, designated as five. **6.** A bill or coin having a denomination of five. **7.** Five hours after midnight or midday. [Middle English *fif, five,* Old English *fīf.*] **—five** *adj. & pron.*

five-and-ten-cent store (fīv′ən-tĕn′sĕnt′) *n.* A large variety store selling inexpensive merchandise such as household items and toys. Also called "dime store," "five-and-dime."

five-fin·ger (fīv′fĭng′gər) *n.* Any of several plants having compound leaves with five leaflets, such as the **cinquefoil** *(see).*

five-finger exercise *n.* **1.** A piano exercise to develop fingering technique. **2.** A simple task.

five·fold (fīv′fōld′) *adj.* **1.** Consisting of five parts. **2.** Five times as many or as much. **—five·fold** *adv.*

Five Nations *n.* See **Iroquois.**

five-o'clock shadow (fīv′ə-klŏk′) *n.* The beard stubble visible on the face of a clean-shaven man by early evening.

five·pins (fīv′pĭnz′) *n. Used with a singular verb.* An indoor bowling game common in Canada, using five pins. Also called "fivepin bowling."

fiv·er (fī′vər) *n. Informal.* **1.** A five-dollar bill. **2.** *British.* A five-pound note.

fives (fīvz) *n. Used with a singular verb.* A British form of handball, often played doubles and on a four-walled court. [17th century : plural of FIVE (perhaps originally played by two teams of five each).]

Five-Year Plan (fīv′yîr′) *n.* A program for national economic development over a five-year period, administered by a socialist government. [Translation of Russian *pyatilyetnii plan, pyatilyetka.*]

fix (fĭks) *v.* **fixed, fixing, fixes.** —*tr.* **1. a.** To place or fasten securely; attach: *fix the notice to the wall.* **b.** To set or implant permanently: *fix something in one's memory.* **2.** To put into a stable or unalterable form, as: **a.** *Chemistry.* To make (a substance) nonvolatile or solid. **b.** *Biology.* To convert (nitrogen) into stable, biologically assimilable compounds. **c.** To kill, harden, and preserve (a specimen) for microscopic study. **d.** To prevent discoloration of (a photographic image) by washing or coating with a chemical preservative. **3.** To set (one's jaw, for example) firmly. **4.** To immobilize; rivet: *fixed to the spot.* **5. a.** To direct (the gaze, for example) steadily; concentrate. **b.** To give (a person, for example) a penetrating look. **6.** To establish definitely; specify: *fix a time.* **7.** To ascribe; allot: *fixing the blame.* **8.** To restore to proper condition or functioning; set right; repair. **9.** To arrange; adjust: *Just let me fix my hair.* **10.** *Informal.* To make ready (a meal, for example); put together; prepare. **11.** To spay or castrate (an animal). **12.** *Informal.* **a.** To take revenge upon; get even with. **b.** To deal with (a troublesome person). **c.** To put a stop to (something troublesome). **13.** To determine (a location, for example) with precision. **14.** *Informal.* To influence or arrange the outcome of (a contest, for example) by unlawful means. —*intr.* **1.** To become fixed, firm, or secure. **2.** *Regional.* To make plans or preparations; get ready: *We're fixing to leave town.* **—be fixed for.** *Informal.* To be in a specified position with regard to: *How are we fixed for time?* **—fix on** (or **upon**). To decide or agree on. **—fix up.** *Informal.* **1.** To set right; repair. **2.** To provide; equip. **3.** To assemble or prepare. **4.** To arrange: *The travel agent fixed up a tour for us.*
~*n.* **1.** A difficult or embarrassing position; a predicament. **2.** The position, as of a ship or aircraft, as determined by observations or radio. **3.** *Informal.* A contest whose outcome has been fraudulently predetermined. **4.** *Slang.* An intravenous injection of heroin or a similar drug. [Middle English *fixen,* partly from Medieval Latin *fīxāre,* to fix, from Latin *fīgere* (past participle *fīxus*), to fasten, partly from Old French *fix,* fixed, from Latin *fīxus,* past participle of *fīgere.*] **—fix·a·ble** *adj.*

fix·ate (fĭk′sāt′) *v.* **-ated, -ating, -ates.** —*tr.* **1.** To make fixed, stable, or stationary. **2.** To focus one's eyes or concentrate one's attention on. **3.** *Psychology.* **a.** To cause (the libido) to be arrested at an immature stage of psychosexual development. **b.** To cause (a person) to become attached to someone or something in an immature or neurotic fashion. —*intr.* **1.** To focus or concentrate one's attention. **2.** *Psychology.* To become fixated; form a fixation.

fix·a·tion (fĭk-sā′shən) *n.* **1.** The act or process of fixing or fixating. **2.** *Psychology.* A strong attachment to a person or thing; especially, such an attachment formed in childhood or infancy and persisting in immature or neurotic behavior.

fix·a·tive (fĭk′sə-tĭv) *adj.* Acting to fix; tending to make permanent.
~*n.* Something that fixes, protects, or preserves, especially: **1.** A liquid preservative applied to works of art, such as water-color paintings or charcoal drawings. **2.** A fluid, such as alcohol, used to preserve and harden fresh tissue for microscopic examination. **3.** A substance mixed with perfume to prevent rapid evaporation.

fixed (fĭkst) *adj.* **1.** Firmly in position; stationary; unmovable. **2.** *Chemistry.* **a.** Nonvolatile: *fixed oils.* **b.** In a stable combined form: *fixed nitrogen.* **3.** Not subject to change or variation; constant: *a fixed routine.* **4.** Officially established; unchangeable: *fixed prices.* **5.** No longer developing: *The language became fixed in the 17th century.* **6.** Firmly, often dogmatically held to: *a fixed notion.* **7.** *Informal.* Illegally prearranged as to outcome. **—fix·ed·ly** (fĭk′sĭd-lē) *adv.* **—fix·ed·ness** *n.*

fixed assets *pl.n.* The capital assets of a commercial enterprise, as equipment or a factory.

fixed head *n.* A fixed device for reading or imprinting information on a single track of magnetic tape, as in a tape recorder.

fixed idea *n.* An idea, especially an incorrect idea, held persistently despite contrary evidence or rational refutation; an idée fixe.

fixed oil *n.* A nonvolatile oil; especially, a fatty oil from a plant as distinguished from an essential oil.

fixed point *n.* **1.** *Physics.* A reference temperature used in defining a practical temperature scale at standard pressure, usually a boiling, melting, or triple point of some pure substance, such as water, helium, or gold. **2.** *Mathematics.* A point that is not changed by a given transformation.

fixed-point (fĭkst′point′) *adj. Mathematics.* Designating or pertaining to a system of representing numbers by a single string of digits, with the position of a digit in the string determining the power of the base of the number system. Compare **floating-point.**

fixed-point theorem *n. Mathematics.* The principle that for all points within a closed cell, as a circle, polygon, sphere, or polyhedron, any transformation that takes all points of the set into points of the same set will leave at least one point fixed.

fixed star *n.* A star so distant from the earth that its movements can be measured only over long periods of time. The term was used originally to distinguish such stars from wandering stars (planets).

fix·er (fĭk′sər) *n.* **1.** A fixative agent used in developing photographic prints. **2.** *Informal.* One who arranges; especially, one who makes fraudulent arrangements in an attempt to change the normal outcome of a contest, political process, or the like.

fix·ings (fĭk′sĭngz) *pl.n. Informal.* Accessories; trimmings.

fix·i·ty (fĭk′sə-tē) *n., pl.* **-ties. 1.** The quality or condition of being fixed; immutability; stability. **2.** Something that is fixed.

fix·ture (fĭks′chər) *n.* **1.** Something securely fixed in place. **2.** Something attached as a permanent appendage, apparatus, or appliance: *plumbing fixtures.* **3.** *Law.* A chattel considered to belong to or be part of a property. **4.** A person or thing long associated with, established in, or restricted to a position or function. [Variant of obsolete *fixure* (influenced by MIXTURE), Late Latin *fixūra,* from Latin *fīxus.* See **fix.**]

fiz·gig^1 (fĭz′gĭg′) *n.* **1.** *Archaic.* A frivolous, giddy woman. **2.** A firework that produces a hissing or sputtering sound. [Earlier *fisgigg* : probably obsolete *fise,* breaking wind, fart, probably from Scandinavian + GIG (carriage, original sense, "frivolous woman").]

fizgig^2. Variant of **fishgig.**

fizz (fĭz) *intr.v.* **fizzed, fizzing, fizzes. 1.** To make a hissing or bubbling sound. **2.** To effervesce. Used of drinks.
∼*n.* **1.** A hissing or bubbling sound. **2.** Effervescence. **3.** An effervescent drink, especially lemonade or champagne. [Imitative.]

fiz·zle (fĭz′əl) *intr.v.* **-zled, -zling, -zles. 1.** To make a hissing or sputtering sound. **2.** *Informal.* To fail or die out, especially after a hopeful beginning. Usually used with *out.*
∼*n.* **1.** A fizzling sound. **2.** *Informal.* A failure; a fiasco. [Probably frequentative of obsolete *fist,* to break wind. See **feist.**]

fjeld (fyĕld) *n.* A high, barren plateau in the Scandinavian countries. [Danish, from Old Norse *fjall,* mountain.]

fjord, fiord (fyôrd, fyōrd) *n.* A long, narrow, deep inlet of the sea bordered by steep slopes. Fjords are submerged U-shaped glaciated valleys found especially along the coasts of Norway and Alaska. [Norwegian, from Old Norse *fjörthr,* from Germanic; akin to FIRTH, FORD.]

fl fluid.

fL foot-lambert.

FL Florida (used with a Zip Code).

fl. 1. floor. **2.** *Latin.* floruit (flourished). **3.** fluid.

Fla. Florida.

flab (flăb) *n.* Loose, unwanted fatty tissue on the body. [Back-formation from FLABBY.]

flab·ber·gast (flăb′ər-găst′, -gäst′) *tr.v.* **-gasted, -gasting, -gasts.** To confound or overwhelm with astonishment; astound. —See Synonyms at **surprise.** [18th century (slang) : perhaps humorous blend of FLABBY + AGHAST.]

flab·by (flăb′ē) *adj.* **-bier, -biest. 1.** Lacking firmness; loose and yielding to the touch; flaccid: *flabby skin.* **2.** Obese. **3.** Lacking force or vitality; feeble; ineffectual. [Variant of *flappy,* from FLAP.] **—flab·bi·ly** *adv.* **—flab·bi·ness** *n.*

fla·bel·late (flə-bĕl′ĭt, -āt′) *adj.* Also **fla·bel·li·form** (flə-bĕl′ə-fôrm′). *Biology.* Fan-shaped. [Latin *flābellum,* fan. See **flabellum.**]

fla·bel·lum (flə-bĕl′əm) *n., pl.* **-bella** (-bĕl′ə). **1.** A fan-shaped biological structure. **2.** A fan used in certain religious ceremonies. [Latin *flābellum,* small fan, diminutive of *flābrum* (usually in plural *flābra*), gust of wind, from *flāre,* to blow.]

flac·cid (flăk′sĭd, flăs′ĭd) *adj.* Lacking firmness; soft and limp; flabby: *"His mouth, pink and flaccid, trembled sometimes like the underlip of a cow"* (H.E. Bates). [French *flaccide,* from Latin *flaccidus,* from *flaccus*†, hanging, flabby.] **—flac·cid·i·ty** (flăk-sĭd′ə-tē, flə-sĭd′-), **flac·cid·ness** *n.* **—flac·cid·ly** *adv.*

flack. Variant of **flak.**

flac·on (flăk′ən, -ŏn′) *n.* A small stoppered bottle, as for perfume. [French, from Old French *fla(s)con,* FLAGON.]

flag^1 (flăg) *n.* **1.** A piece of cloth or bunting varying in size, color, and design, used as a symbol, standard, signal, and especially as a national emblem. **2.** *Chiefly British.* A small paper badge given to contributors to a charity. **3.** A ship carrying the flag of an admiral; a flagship. **4.** The masthead of a newspaper. **5.** A distinctively shaped or marked tail, as of a dog or deer. **6.** In musical notation, a cross stroke added to a note that is less than a quarter note in value. **—fly the flag.** *Informal.* To represent one's country in a particular field or activity with exuberance and pride.
∼*tr.v.* **flagged, flagging, flags. 1.** To decorate with a flag or flags. **2.** To signal or communicate (a message) with or as if with a flag. **3.** To mark with a symbol for purposes of identification. **—flag down.** To signal (a vehicle) to stop. [16th century : perhaps from obsolete *flag*†, hanging limp, drooping.] **—flag·ger** *n.* See feature, pages 634–637.

flag^2 *n.* Any of various plants having long bladelike leaves, especially the sweet flag (*Acorus calamus*). [Middle English *flagge*†, rush, reed.]

flag^3 *intr.v.* **flagged, flagging, flags. 1.** To hang limply; droop. **2.** To become tired; decline in vigor. **3.** To decline in interest; grow dull. [16th century : akin to obsolete *flag*†, drooping.]

flag^4 *n.* **1.** A slab of flagstone used for paving. **2.** *Geology.* **Flagstone** *(see).*
∼*tr.v.* **flagged, flagging, flags.** To pave with flags. [Middle English *flagge,* piece of turf, sod, probably from Old Norse *flaga,* slab of stone.]

flag captain *n.* The captain of a flagship.

Flag Day *n.* An annual holiday on June 14 celebrating the adoption in 1777 of the official U.S. flag.

flag·el·lant (flăj′ə-lənt, flə-jĕl′ənt) *n.* One who whips; especially, one who scourges himself by way of religious discipline or for sexual stimulation. [Latin *flagellāns* (stem *flagellant-*), present participle of *flagellāre,* to FLAGELLATE.] **—flag·el·lant** *adj.*

flag·el·late (flăj′ə-lāt′) *tr.v.* **-lated, -lating, -lates.** To whip or flog; scourge.
∼*adj.* (-lĭt, -lāt′, flə-jĕl′ĭt). **1.** Having a flagellum or flagella, as do unicellular animals of the class Flagellata (or Mastigophora). **2.** Resembling or having the form of a flagellum; whiplike.
∼*n.* (-lĭt, -lāt′, flə-jĕl′ĭt). A flagellate organism. [Latin *flagellāre,* to whip, scourge, from *flagellum,* diminutive of *flagrum,* whip.] **—flag·el·la·tion** (flăj′ə-lā′shən) *n.*

fla·gel·li·form (flə-jĕl′ə-fôrm′) *adj.* Long, thin, and tapering; whipshaped: *flagelliform appendages.* [Latin *flagellum,* small whip (see **flagellate**) + -FORM.]

fla·gel·lin (flə-jĕl′ĭn) *n.* A protein that is a constituent of flagella. [FLAGELL(A) + -IN.]

fla·gel·lum (flə-jĕl′əm) *n., pl.* **-gella** (-jĕl′ə). *Biology.* A long, threadlike appendage; especially, one of the whiplike extensions of certain cells or unicellular organisms, usually functioning in locomotion. [New Latin, from Latin, small whip. See **flagellate.**] **—fla·gel·lar** *adj.*

flag·eo·let (flăj′ə-lĕt′, -lā′) *n.* **1.** A small flutelike instrument having a cylindrical mouthpiece, four fingerholes, and two thumbholes. **2.** A haricot bean. [French, diminutive of Old French *flajol,* from Vulgar Latin *flabeolum* (unattested), flute, from Latin *flāre,* to blow.]

Flagg (flăg), **James Montgomery** (1877–1960). U.S. painter, illustrator, and author. After studying in England and France, he returned to his native New York and began a highly successful career as an artist. He is best known for his series of World War I recruitment posters.

flag·ging^1 (flăg′ĭng) *adj.* **1.** Drooping; languid. **2.** Declining; weakening. **—flag·ging·ly** *adv.*

flagging^2 *n.* A pavement laid with flagstones.

fla·gi·tious (flə-jĭsh′əs) *adj.* **1.** Guilty of or addicted to extremely brutal or cruel crimes; vicious. **2.** Shockingly evil; infamous; scandalous; heinous. [Middle English *flagicious,* from Latin *flāgitiōsus,* from *flāgitium,* noisy protest against one's conduct, scandal, shameful act, from *flāgitāre,* to demand fiercely.] **—fla·gi·tious·ly** *adv.* **—fla·gi·tious·ness** *n.*

flag·man (flăg′mən) *n., pl.* **-men** (-mĭn). One who signals with or carries a flag.

flag of convenience *n.* A flag of a country that offers ship owners financial and in some cases legal advantages to register their ships in that country.

flag officer *n.* A naval or coast guard officer holding the rank of rear admiral, vice admiral, or admiral.

flag of truce *n.* A white flag brought or displayed to an enemy as an invitation to a conference or a signal of surrender.

flag·on (flăg′ən) *n.* **1.** A vessel for holding liquor, as wine, usually made of metal or pottery and having a handle and spout and often a lid. **2.** The quantity of liquid contained in a flagon. [Middle English *flagon, flakon,* from Old French *fla(s)con,* from Late Latin *flascō* (stem *flascōn-*), bottle, FLASK.]

flag·pole (flăg′pōl′) *n.* A pole on which a flag is hoisted; a flagstaff.

flag rank *n.* The rank of a flag officer.

fla·grant (flā′grənt) *adj.* **1.** Outstanding or conspicuous in being wrong or evil; notorious; shocking: *a flagrant miscarriage of justice.* **2.** *Obsolete.* Flaming; blazing. —See Usage note at **blatant.** [Latin *flagrāns* (stem *flagrant-*), present participle of *flagrāre,* to burn, blaze.] **—fla·gran·cy, fla·grance** *n.* **—fla·grant·ly** *adv.*
Synonyms: *glaring, gross, rank.*

flag·ship (flăg′shĭp′) *n.* **1.** A ship bearing the flag of a fleet or squadron commander. **2.** The best or largest ship operated by a passenger line. **3.** The leading member of a group or chain.

Flag·stad (flăg′städ′), **Kirsten** (1895–1962). Norwegian soprano, celebrated for her performances of Wagner's heroines, such as Brünnhilde in *Der Ring des Nibelungen* and Kundry in *Parsifal.*

flag·staff (flăg′stăf′, -stäf′) *n., pl.* **-staffs** or **-staves** (-stāvz′). A flagpole.

Flag·staff (flăg′stăf′, -stäf′). A city of northern Arizona, near the San Francisco Peaks. It is a tourist center for a region containing ruined Indian pueblos, state parks, lakes, and pine forests.

flag·stone (flăg′stōn′) *n.* **1.** A flat, natural or artificial stone used in paving. **2.** *Geology.* Hard, fine-grained sedimentary rock easily split into layers or large slabs, usually a sandstone or sandy limestone. In both senses, also called "flag." [FLAG (stone) + STONE.]

flag-wav·ing (flăg′wā′vĭng) *n.* A display of patriotic fervor.

Fla·her·ty (flä′ər-tē, flâ′-), **Robert Joseph** (1884–1951). U.S. film director and explorer. His films, including *Nanook of the North* (1921) and *Moana* (1926), were the first major documentaries. They greatly influenced documentary filmmaking.

flail (flāl) *n.* A manual threshing device consisting of a long wooden handle or staff with a shorter free-swinging stick attached to its end.
∼*v.* **flailed, flailing, flails.** —*tr.* **1.** To thresh using a flail. **2.** To beat, thrash, or strike with or as if with a flail. —*intr.* To move about erratically; thrash about: *arms flailing.* [Middle English *fleil, flail,* from Old English *flegil* (unattested) and Old French *flaiel,* both from Latin *flagellum,* diminutive of *flagrum,* whip.]

flair (flâr) *n.* **1.** A natural talent or aptitude; a bent; a knack: *a flair for interior decorating.* **2.** Instinctive discernment; keenness: *"Boswell, with his usual flair, arrived in Florence at a most exciting time"* (Frederick A. Pottle). **3.** A natural and exuberant sense of style. [French, "sense of smell," from Old French, from *flairer,* to scent, smell, from Vulgar Latin *flāgrāre* (unattested), from Latin *frāgrāre,* to emit a smell.]

fjord *A glacial valley invaded by the sea. This one is in Norway. Fjords are usually deep—sometimes more than 1,200 meters (4,000 feet) in places—but often have a shallow mouth.*

PRONUNCIATION KEY

ă, pat; ā, pay; âr, care;
ä, father, are; b, bib;
ch, church; d, deed; ĕ, pet;
ē, be; f, fife; g, gag; h, hat;
hw, which; ĭ, pit; ī, pie;
îr, pier; j, judge; k, kick;
l, lid, needle; m, mum;
n, no, sudden; ng, thing;
ŏ, pot; ō, toe; ô, paw, for;
oi, noise; ou, out; o͝o, book;
o͞o, boot; p, pop; r, roar;
s, sauce; sh, ship, dish;
t, tight; th, thin, path;
th, this, bathe; ŭ, cut; ûr, fur;
v, valve; w, with; y, yes;
z, zebra, size; zh, vision;
ə, about, item, edible,
gallop, circus, peaceful

IN FOREIGN WORDS:

à, *Fr.* ami; œ, *Fr.* feu, *Ger.* schön; ü, *Fr.* tu, *Ger.* über; KH, *Ger.* ich, *Scot.* loch; N, *Fr.* bon; y′, *Fr.* Compiègne

STRESS MARKS:

Primary stress: ′
in·cite′ (ĭn-sīt′)
Secondary stress: ′
in′sight′ (ĭn′sīt′)

flak, flack (flăk) *n.* **1.** Antiaircraft artillery. **2.** The bursting shells fired from such artillery. **3.** *Slang.* Excessive criticism; abuse. [German *Flak,* short for *Fl(ieger)a(bwehr)k(anone),* "aircraft defense gun."]

flake¹ (flăk) *n.* **1.** A flat, thin piece or layer; a chip. **2.** A small piece of something that has been peeled, rubbed, or sliced off: *flakes of fish.* **3.** A small, crystalline particle of snow. **4.** *Slang.* An eccentric or oddly humorous person; oddball. ~*v.* **flaked, flaking, flakes.** —*tr.* **1.** To break flakes from; take off in flakes; chip. **2.** To cover, mark, or overlay with or as if with flakes; fleck. **3.** To form into flakes: *Flake the almonds with a sharp knife.* —*intr.* To come off in flakes; chip off. —**flake out.** *Slang.* To fall asleep or collapse from fatigue or exhaustion. [Middle English, from Scandinavian, akin to Norwegian *flak.*] —**flak·er** *n.*

flake² *n.* **1.** A frame or platform for drying fish or produce. **2.** A scaffold lowered over the side of a ship to support workmen. [Middle English *fleke,* from Old Norse *fleki, flaki.*]

flake white *n.* A pigment made of flakes of white lead.

flak jacket *n.* A bulletproof jacket or vest.

flak·y (flā'kē) *adj.* **-ier, -iest. 1.** Made of or resembling flakes. **2.** Forming or tending to form flakes or thin, crisp fragments. **3.** *Slang.* Eccentric; crazy. —**flak·i·ly** *adv.* —**flak·i·ness** *n.*

flaky pastry *n.* A type of pastry resembling puff pastry but less rich and firm in texture.

flam¹ (flăm) *n. Informal.* **1.** A lie or hoax; a deception. **2.** Nonsense; drivel. [Short for FLIMFLAM.]

flam² *n.* A drumbeat produced by two almost simultaneous strokes. [Perhaps imitative.]

flam·bé (flăm-bā', fläN-bā') *adj.* Served flaming in ignited liquor, as brandy. Said of food. ~*tr.v.* **flambéd, -béing, -bés.** To drench with a liquor, as brandy,

and ignite. [From French, past participle of *flamber,* to flame, from Old French *flambe,* flame.]

flam·beau (flăm'bō') *n., pl.* **-beaux** (-bōz') or **-beau. 1.** A flaming torch. **2.** A large ornamental candlestick. [French, from Old French, from *flambe, flamble,* "small flame," from Latin *flammula,* diminutive of *flamma,* FLAME.]

flam·boy·ant (flăm-boi'ənt) *adj.* **1.** Given to or characterized by elaborate ostentation; showy: *a flamboyant dresser.* **2.** Richly colored; vivid; resplendent. **3.** *Architecture.* Pertaining to or designating a style of 15th- and 16th-century French Gothic architecture characterized by waving lines and flamelike forms. —See Synonyms at **ornate.** ~*n.* A tree, the **royal poinciana** (*see*). [French, from Old French, present participle of *flamboyer, flambeiier,* to blaze, from *flambe, flamble,* small flame. See **flambeau.**] —**flam·boy·ance, flam·boy·an·cy** *n.* —**flam·boy·ant·ly** *adv.*

flame (flām) *n.* **1. a.** The zone of burning gases and fine suspended matter associated with the combustion of a substance. **b.** Broadly, a hot, luminous mass of burning gas or vapor, typically tongue-shaped and flickering. **2.** *Often* **flames.** The condition of active, blazing combustion: *burst into flames.* **3.** Something flamelike in motion, brilliance, intensity, or shape. **4.** A violent or intense passion; a burning emotion. **5.** A reddish orange. **6.** *Informal.* A sweetheart: *an old flame.* —See Synonyms at **blaze.** ~*v.* **flamed, flaming, flames.** —*intr.* **1.** To burn brightly; give off flames or a flame; blaze. Often used with *up.* **2.** To color or glow suddenly. **3. a.** To display a violent or intense emotion: *flaming with indignation.* **b.** To burst out with violent and intense expression: *The people's anger flamed up.* —*tr.* **1.** To burn, ignite, or scorch. **2.** *Obsolete.* To inflame. [Middle English *flaume, flam(m)e,* from Old French *flam(m)e,* from Latin *flamma.*] —**flam·y** *adj.*

FLAGS OF THE WORLD

Since the days of ancient China flags have expressed national pride

The flying of flags—as a rallying sign or distinguishing mark—has been practiced since the days of ancient China. The Emperor Chou, founder of the Chou (Zhou) dynasty in the 10th century B.C., had a white flag carried before him on horseback to announce his presence. In the West, symbolic objects raised on staffs were used as a group's badge, but the first flags were the *vexilla*—the emblem-bearing cloths borne by

Roman soldiers, who used them to distinguish one legion from another.

The first recorded use of flags in England is in the Bayeux Tapestry, which depicts the dragon banner of King Harold, who was slain in the Battle of Hastings in 1066.

With the growth of nationalism, the flags of individual countries have become potent patriotic symbols.

Each new independent state devises for itself a unique flag. As of 1985, there were 177 countries with their own flags.

The current interest in vexillology—the study of flags and their meanings—has given rise throughout the world to some 200 flag-study societies. In 1967 the societies came together under the International Federation of Vexillological Associations.

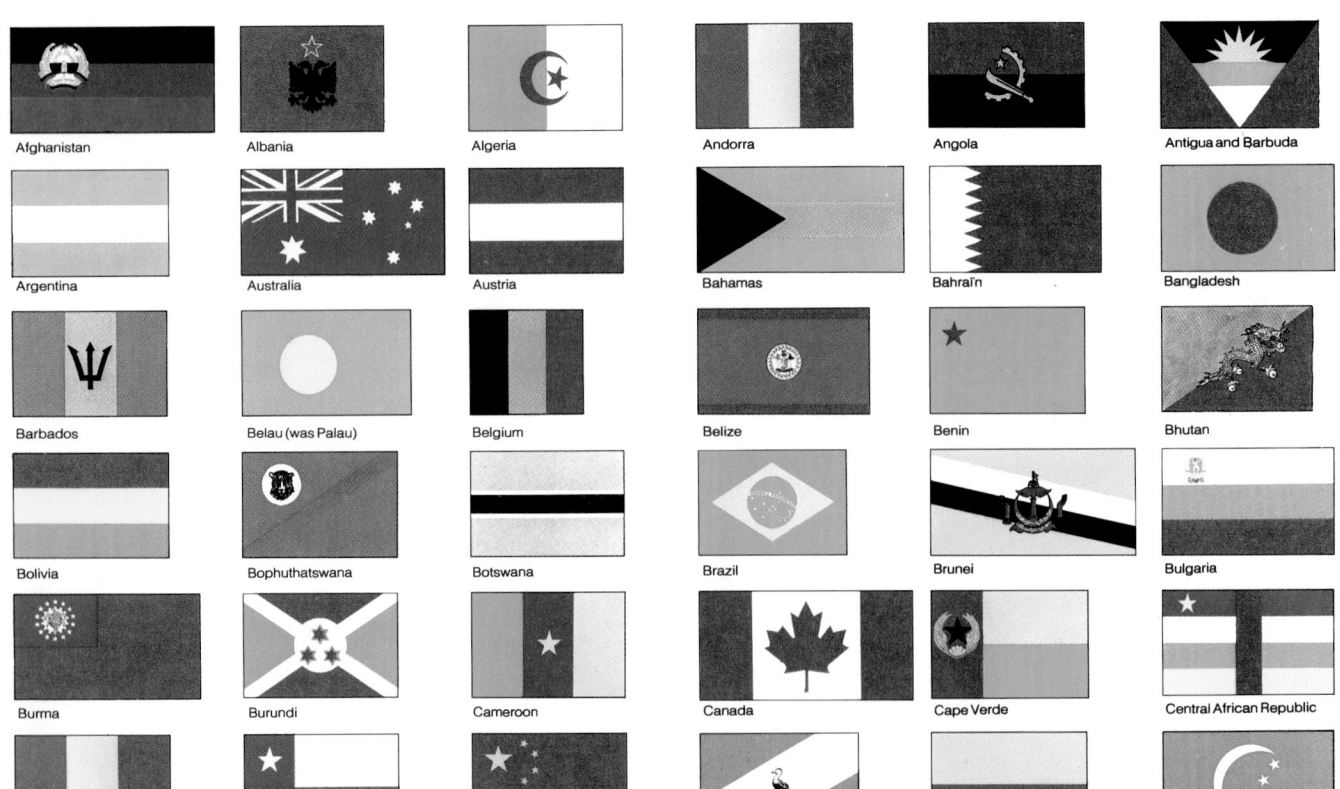

Afghanistan   Albania   Algeria   Andorra   Angola   Antigua and Barbuda

Argentina   Australia   Austria   Bahamas   Bahraïn   Bangladesh

Barbados   Belau (was Palau)   Belgium   Belize   Benin   Bhutan

Bolivia   Bophuthatswana   Botswana   Brazil   Brunei   Bulgaria

Burma   Burundi   Cameroon   Canada   Cape Verde   Central African Republic

Chad   Chile   China, People's Republic of   Ciskei   Colombia   Comoros

flame cell *n.* A hollow cell in flatworms and certain other invertebrates that contains cilia and functions as an organ of excretion.

flame gun *n.* A portable gas or oil burner used to destroy weeds.

fla·men (flā′mən) *n., pl.* **-mens** or **flamines** (flăm′ə-nēz′). A priest or servant of a Roman deity. [Middle English *flamin,* from Latin *flāmen;* akin to Sanskrit *Brahmán,* BRAHMA.]

fla·men·co (flə-mĕng′kō) *n., pl.* **-cos. 1.** A dance style of the Andalusian Gypsies characterized by forceful, often improvised rhythms. **2.** The guitar music that usually accompanies this dance style. ~*adj.* Of or pertaining to such dancing or music: *a flamenco guitar.* [Spanish *flamenco,* Gypsy living in Andalusia, resembling a Gypsy, Flemish, from Middle Dutch *Vlāming,* FLEMING.]

flame-out (flām′out′) *n.* Failure of a jet aircraft engine in flight.

flame-proof (flām′prōōf′) *adj.* **1.** Able to withstand direct contact with flame; specifically, able to be used over a gas flame. Compare **ovenproof. 2.** Insulated to prevent sparks from igniting any surrounding gas. Said of electrical apparatus. —**flame-proof** *v.*

flame-re·tard·ant (flām′rĭ-tär′dənt) *adj.* Resistant to catching fire. —**flame-re·tard·ant** *n.*

flame test *n. Chemistry.* A simple qualitative test for the presence of certain metals by in which the sample is held in a flame and the characteristic colors produced are observed. A blue flame, for example, indicates the presence of copper.

flame-throw·er (flām′thrō′ər) *n.* A weapon that projects ignited incendiary fuel, such as napalm, in a steady stream.

flame tree *n.* Any of several trees with red or orange flowers, such as *Butea frondosa,* of India and Burma, or *Brachychiton acerifolium,* of Australia.

flam·ing (flā′mĭng) *adj.* **1.** On fire; in flames; ablaze. **2.** Brilliant; splendid; flamelike. **3.** Intense; passionate: *a flaming accusation.* **4.** Arrant; flagrant. —**flam·ing·ly** *adv.*

fla·min·go (flə-mĭng′gō) *n., pl.* **-gos** or **-goes. 1.** Any of several large, gregarious wading birds of the family Phoenicopteridae, of tropical regions, having reddish or pinkish plumage, long legs, a long, flexible neck, and a bill turned downward at the tip. **2.** Moderate pinkish orange. [Perhaps Portuguese *flamengo,* from Provençal *flamenc,* probably "fire bird" (from its bright plumage) : *flama,* flame, from Latin *flamma,* FLAME + *-enc,* from Germanic *-ing,* suffix denoting "belonging to."]

Fla·min·i·an Way (flə-mĭn′ē-ən). Great Roman road, the chief transport route between Rome and the Adriatic. Construction was begun by Gaius Flaminius in *c.* 220 B.C. and the original road ran to Ariminum (Rimini), a distance of *c.* 208 miles (335 kilometers).

flam·ma·ble (flăm′ə-bəl) *adj.* Easily ignitable and capable of burning with rapidity; inflammable. [Latin *flammāre,* to blaze, from *flamma,* FLAME.] —**flam·ma·bil·i·ty** (flăm′ə-bĭl′ə-tē) *n.* —**flam·ma·ble** *n.*

Usage: Flammable and *inflammable* have the same meaning, "highly combustible." The prefix *in-* is an intensive here, and not an expression of negation, so that *inflammable* really means *inflame + -able.* Something that cannot be burned is *nonflammable.* Because of the widespread use of the prefix *in-* with a negative meaning, however (*invisible, incapacity*), *inflammable* is sometimes mistakenly interpreted as "noncombustible." For this reason *flammable* is the preferred term in technical writing and in contexts where people are being warned. In figurative usage only *inflammable* is used: *an inflammable nature* or *temper.*

flan (flăn, flän) *n.* **1.** An open tart with a sweet or savory filling, often containing eggs, cheese, or cream. **2.** A metal disk to be stamped as a coin; a blank. [French, from Old French *fla(o)n,* from Germanic.]

flanch¹ (flănch) *n.* Also **flaunch** (flônch). A slope of cement or simi-

continued

Congo	Costa Rica	Cuba	Cyprus	Czechoslovakia	Denmark
Djibouti	Dominica	Dominican Republic	Ecuador	Egypt	El Salvador
Equatorial Guinea	Ethiopia	Fiji	Finland	France	Gabon
Gambia	East Germany (GDR)	West Germany (FRG)	Ghana	Greece	Grenada
Guatemala	Guinea	Guinea-Bissau	Guyana	Haiti	Honduras
Hungary	Iceland	India	Indonesia	Iran	Iraq
Ireland, Republic of	Israel	Italy	Ivory Coast	Jamaica	Japan
Jordan	Kampuchea	Kenya	Kiribati	North Korea	South Korea

lar material surrounding a structure such as a chimney top to drain off rainwater.
~*v.* **flanched, flanching, flanches.** Also **flaunch, flaunched, flaunching, flaunches.** —*tr.* To provide with a flanch. —*intr.* To have a flanch. [Variant of FLANGE.]

flanch² *n.* Either of two inward-curving segments at each side of a heraldic field. [18th century : perhaps from Old French *flanchir,* from *flanche,* variant of *flanc,* FLANK.]

Flan·ders (flăn′dərz). Former county of the Low Countries, west of the Scheldt River. It included the present East and West Flanders provinces of Belgium, the Nord and Pas-de-Calais departments of France (where it is known as French Flanders), and a small part of Zeeland province in the Netherlands. During the Middle Ages the county was the center of the rich Flemish cloth industry. The area saw heavy fighting in both World Wars.

Flanders poppy *n.* The **corn poppy** (see).

flâ·ne·rie (flän-rē′, flä′nə-rē′) *n.* Aimless idling; dawdling. [French.]

flâ·neur (flä-nœr′) *n.* An aimless idler. [French.]

flange (flănj) *n.* A protruding rim, edge, rib, or collar, as on a wheel or a pipe shaft, used to strengthen an object, hold it in place, or attach it to another object.
~*tr.v.* **flanged, flanging, flanges.** To furnish with a flange. [17th century : perhaps from obsolete *flange,* to widen, from Old French *flangir,* variant of *flanchir.* See **flanch, flank.**]

flank (flăngk) *n.* **1. a.** The section of flesh between the last rib and the hip; a side. **b.** A cut of meat from this section of an animal. **2.** The side of the thigh. **3.** A side or lateral part: *the flank of a mountain.* **4. a.** The right or left side of a military formation: *attack on both flanks.* **b.** The right or left side of a bastion.
~*tr.v.* **flanked, flanking, flanks. 1.** To protect or guard the flank of. **2.** To menace, attack, or maneuver around the flank of. **3.** To be placed or situated at the flank or side of. **4.** To put something on each side of. [Middle English *fla(u)nke,* from Old French *flanc,* from Frankish *hlanca* (unattested), side.]

flank·er (flăng′kər) *n.* **1.** One that flanks. **2.** A division of soldiers guarding the flank of a marching column. **3.** A fortification attached to the side or flank of another part. **4.** *Informal.* An unscrupulous trick. **5.** *Football.* A flankerback.

flank·er·back (flăng′kər-băk′) *n.* *Football.* An offensive back stationed wide of his team's formation and just behind the line of scrimmage. Also called "flanker."

flan·nel (flăn′əl) *n.* **1.** A soft woven cloth of wool or of a blend of wool and cotton or synthetics. **2.** Flannelette. **3. flannels.** Clothing, especially trousers, made of flannel.
~*tr.v.* **flanneled** or **-nelled, -neling** or **-nelling, -nels. 1.** To wash, clean, or rub with flannel. **2.** To wrap in flannel. [Middle English, probably from *flanen,* sackcloth, from Welsh *gwlanen,* "woolen cloth," from *gwlân,* wool.] —**flan·nel·ly** *adj.*

flan·nel·board (flăn′əl-bôrd′, -bōrd′) *n.* A piece of board covered in flannel or similar material to which paper or cloth cutouts may be attached, as in making a collage or as a visual aid in teaching.

flannel bush *n.* A shrub or small tree, *Fremontia californica,* of California and northern Mexico, having downy, lobed leaves and showy yellow flowers.

flan·nel·ette (flăn′ə-lĕt′) *n.* A cotton cloth processed to resemble flannel.

Flan·ner (flăn′ər), **Janet** (1892–1978). U.S. journalist. Raised in Indianapolis, she traveled extensively after 1918 and spent most of her life abroad. She is best known for her "Letters from Paris," which she wrote for the *New Yorker* and signed with the pen name Genêt.

flap (flăp) *v.* **flapped, flapping, flaps.** —*tr.* **1.** To wave (wings or

flags *continued*

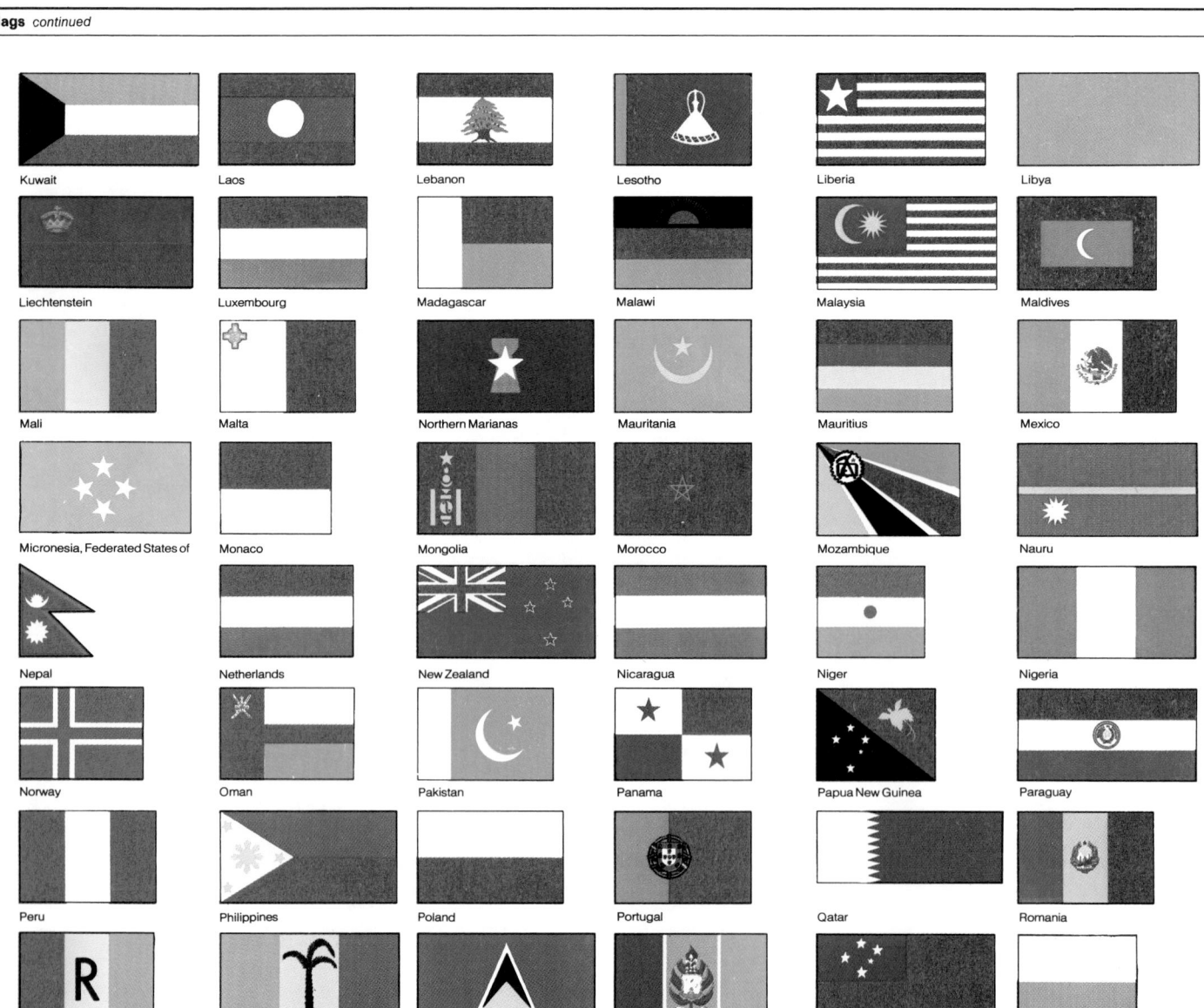

Kuwait   Laos   Lebanon   Lesotho   Liberia   Libya

Liechtenstein   Luxembourg   Madagascar   Malawi   Malaysia   Maldives

Mali   Malta   Northern Marianas   Mauritania   Mauritius   Mexico

Micronesia, Federated States of   Monaco   Mongolia   Morocco   Mozambique   Nauru

Nepal   Netherlands   New Zealand   Nicaragua   Niger   Nigeria

Norway   Oman   Pakistan   Panama   Papua New Guinea   Paraguay

Peru   Philippines   Poland   Portugal   Qatar   Romania

Rwanda   St. Kitts-Nevis   St. Lucia   St. Vincent and the Grenadines   Western Samoa   San Marino

arms, for example) up and down; beat. **2.** To cause to wave or undulate; agitate. **3.** To hit with something broad and flat; slap. **4.** *Phonetics.* To produce (an r sound) while bringing the tongue rapidly in contact with the alveolar ridge. —*intr.* **1.** To wave about while fixed at one edge or corner to something stationary; flutter. **2.** To wave arms or wings up and down; beat the air. **3.** To fly by beating the air with the wings. **4.** *Informal.* To become agitated or nervous.
~*n.* **1.** A flat covering piece usually intended to double over and protect or seal something, as on an envelope, pocket, or hat. **2.** The action of waving or fluttering; flapping. **3.** The sound of flapping. **4.** A blow given with something flat; a slap. **5.** *Aeronautics.* A variable control surface on the trailing edge of an aircraft wing, used primarily to increase lift or drag. **6.** *Surgery.* Tissue that has been partially detached and used in plastic surgery to fill an adjacent defect or to cover the cut end of a bone after amputation. **7.** *Phonetics.* A flapped (r) sound. **8.** *Informal.* A condition of agitated distress. [Middle English *flappe,* slap, from *flappen,* to beat.]
flap·doo·dle (flăp′dōōd′l) *n. Slang.* Foolish talk; nonsense. [Origin obscure.]
flap·jack (flăp′jăk′) *n.* A pancake. [FLAP (to toss) + *Jack* (name).]
flap·pa·ble (flăp′ə-bəl) *adj. Slang.* Easily excited or upset.
flap·per (flăp′ər) *n.* **1.** One that flaps, such as a device for swatting flies. **2.** A flipper or similar broad, flexible part. **3.** *Informal.* A young woman, especially one in the 1920's who flaunted her disdain for conventional dress and behavior.
flare (flâr) *v.* **flared, flaring, flares.** —*intr.* **1.** To flame up with a bright, wavering light; blaze unsteadily. **2.** To burst into intense, short-lived flame. Often used with *up.* **3.** To widen gradually, as a skirt or vase might. **4.** *Metallurgy.* To give off burning gas. Used of a molten metal. —*tr.* **1.** To cause (something) to flare. **2.** To signal

with flares. **3.** To burn off (gas given off at a wellhead). Used with *off.*
~*n.* **1.** A brief, wavering blaze of light. **2.** A device that can be fired into the sky to produce a bright light for signaling, illumination, or identification. **3.** An outbreak, as of emotion or activity. **4.** A gradual widening: *trousers with a slight flare.* **5.** *Photography.* A lens reflection or the resultant film fogging. **6.** Reddening of the skin due to infection, irritation, or an allergic reaction. **7.** *Astronomy.* A localized outburst of radiation from the surface of the sun. —See Synonyms at **blaze.** [Origin unknown.]
flare-back (flâr′băk′) *n.* A flame produced in the breech of a gun by ignition of residual gases.
flare star *n. Astronomy.* A star that shows sudden, short-lived increases in brightness. Flares can increase the luminosity of a star by several magnitudes for a few minutes.
flare up *intr.v.* **1.** To display sudden intense emotion or passion. **2. a.** To break out suddenly or undergo a sudden increase in intensity. Used of wars, quarrels, or the like. **b.** To become active suddenly, causing reddening of the skin: *Her rash has flared up again.*
flare-up (flâr′ŭp′) *n.* **1.** A sudden outbreak of flame or light. **2.** An outburst or eruption: *a flare-up of anger.* **3.** An intensification of something hitherto mild or dormant: *a flare-up of old antagonisms.*
flash (flăsh) *v.* **flashed, flashing, flashes.** —*intr.* **1.** To appear or emerge suddenly in or as if in bright flame. **2.** To appear or be perceived for an instant only. **3.** To be lighted intermittently; sparkle; scintillate. **4.** To move rapidly. **5.** To be suddenly perceived by the mind or sight. **6.** To flow rapidly; rush. Used of water. **7.** *Informal.* To expose oneself indecently. —*tr.* **1. a.** To cause (light) to appear suddenly or in intermittent bursts. **b.** To cause to shine or reflect light briefly: *flashed his light at the intruders.* **c.** To cause to burst into flame. **d.** To reflect (light). **e.** To reflect light from (a

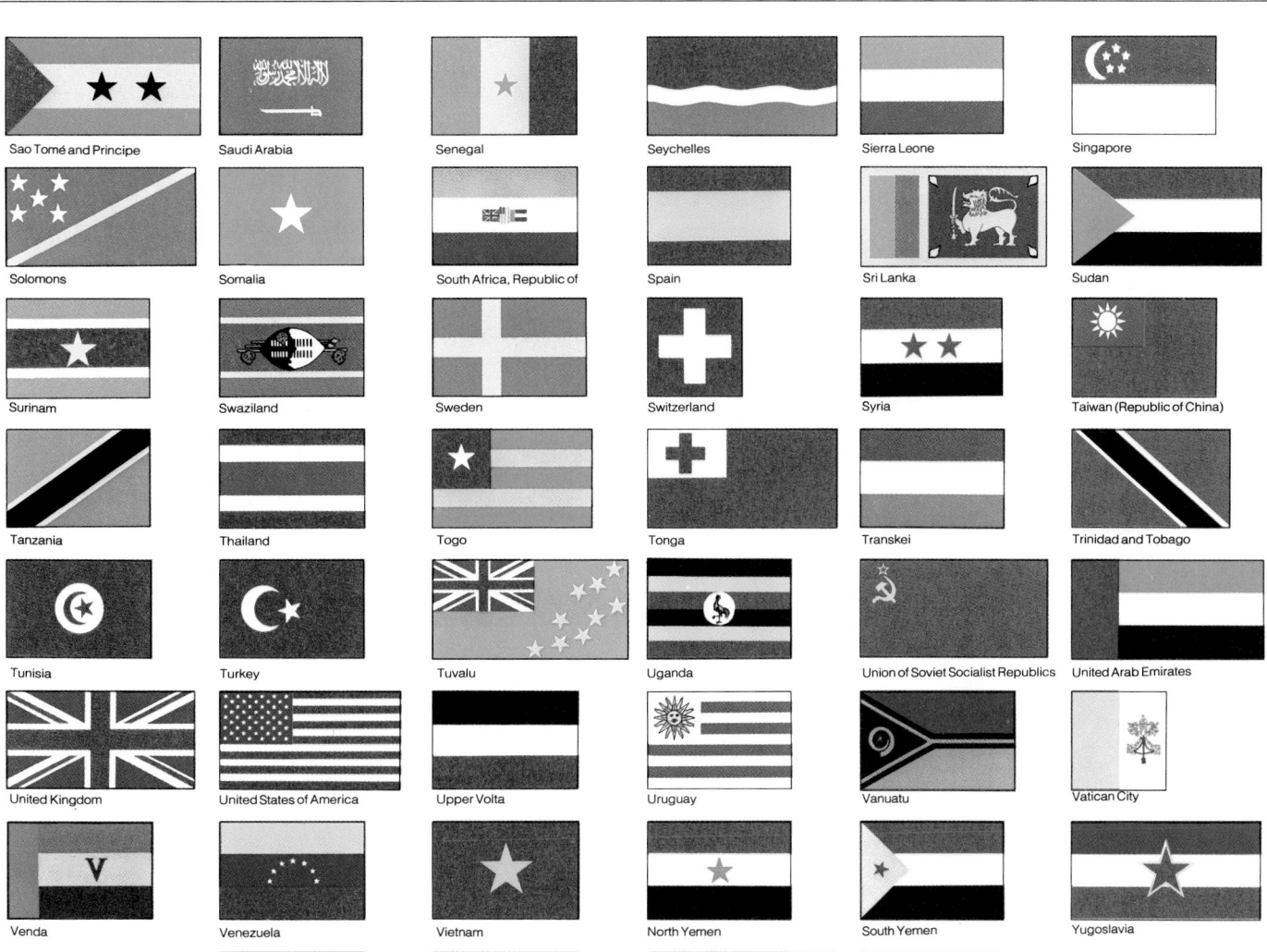

Sao Tomé and Principe · Saudi Arabia · Senegal · Seychelles · Sierra Leone · Singapore · Solomons · Somalia · South Africa, Republic of · Spain · Sri Lanka · Sudan · Surinam · Swaziland · Sweden · Switzerland · Syria · Taiwan (Republic of China) · Tanzania · Thailand · Togo · Tonga · Transkei · Trinidad and Tobago · Tunisia · Turkey · Tuvalu · Uganda · Union of Soviet Socialist Republics · United Arab Emirates · United Kingdom · United States of America · Upper Volta · Uruguay · Vanuatu · Vatican City · Venda · Venezuela · Vietnam · North Yemen · South Yemen · Yugoslavia · Zaire · Zambia · Zimbabwe · United Nations Organisation

surface). **2. a.** To expose to a flash or flashes of light. **b.** To expose to a flash of radiation. **3.** To display as if by a flash of light: *Her eyes flashed hatred at me.* **4. a.** To send (a message) with light signals. **b.** To signal to (another driver) with a flash of one's car headlights. **5. a.** To communicate (information) at great speed. **b.** To display (a picture, for example) rapidly on a screen. **6.** To reveal (something concealed) briefly: *The police officer flashed her badge.* **7.** *Informal.* To display ostentatiously; flaunt. **8. a.** To fill suddenly with a rush of water. **b.** To sweep away (a boat, for example) on a rush of water. **9.** To cover (glass) with a thin layer of metal or different-colored glass, for example. **10.** To cause (a liquid) to boil and evaporate through direct contact with a hot surface. **11.** To provide (a roof, for example) with flashing.

~*n.* **1.** A sudden, brief, intense display of light. **2.** A sudden manifestation of a quality, such as insight or wit. **3.** A split second; an instant: *in a flash.* **4.** A brief, important news dispatch or transmission. Also called "newsflash." **5. a.** Instantaneous illumination for photography. **b.** Any equipment or device, such as a flash bulb, flash gun, or flash lamp, used to produce such illumination. **6.** In a motion picture, a brief display of a scene. **7.** *Informal.* A sudden brief display: *He gave me a flash of his wallet.* **8.** *Chiefly British.* A patch of colored cloth on a military uniform for identification. **9.** A patch of coloring on an animal's coat. **10.** *Archaic.* A sudden heavy onrush of water deliberately released to take a boat over a shallow stretch of water. —See Synonyms at **blaze, moment.** —**flash in the pan. 1.** An explosion of the gunpowder in the pan of a flintlock rifle that does not set off the charge. **2.** Someone or something that has merely transitory interest, success, or appeal.

~*adj.* **1.** Happening suddenly or very quickly: *flash freezing.* **2.** *Informal.* Ostentatious or showy: *a flash car.* **3.** Counterfeit; bogus. **4.** Of or pertaining to gamblers and followers of racing and boxing. **5.** Of or pertaining to thieves, confidence men, and underworld figures. [Middle English *flashen,* to splash, burst into flame (imitative).]

Usage: *flash, gleam, glance, glint, sparkle, glitter, glisten, shimmer, glimmer, twinkle, spark, scintillate.* These verbs mean to send forth or reflect light. *Flash* refers to a sudden and brilliant but short-lived outburst of light. *Gleam* implies light of moderate brightness, either transient or constant and often appearing against a dark background. *Glance* refers most often to light reflected obliquely. *Glint* refers to emitted or reflected light in flashes. *Sparkle* suggests a rapid succession of flashes of high brilliance, and *glitter* a similar succession of even greater intensity. *Glisten* usually refers to lustrous, reflected light, and *shimmer* to the reflection of soft, undulating light. *Glimmer* is applied to emission or reflection of subdued, fleeting light. *Twinkle* refers to the intermittent emission of soft, wavering light, and *spark* to the production of brief flashes of light or fire. *Scintillate* is applied to what flashes as if throwing off sparks in a continuous stream.

flash back *intr.v.* To interrupt a story in order to portray or recount an incident or scene from the past; cut back.

flash·back (flăsh′băk′) *n.* In a novel, motion picture, or other narrative, a depiction of events belonging to an earlier part of the story or a reversion to previously depicted events.

flash·board (flăsh′bôrd′, -bōrd′) *n.* Boarding that extends above a dam to increase the depth of water held.

flash bulb *n.* A glass bulb filled with finely shredded aluminum or magnesium foil that is ignited by electricity to produce a short-duration, high-intensity light flash for taking photographs. Also called "photoflash."

flash burn *n.* A burn resulting from brief exposure to intense radiation.

flash card *n.* Any of a set or integrated series of cards used for brief, usually successive display; especially, such a card used by a teacher as a visual aid in spelling or other exercises.

flash·cube (flăsh′kyo͞ob′) *n.* A small cube that contains four flash bulbs and that rotates automatically when a picture is taken with a camera to which it is attached.

flash·er (flăsh′ər) *n.* **1.** One that flashes. **2.** A device that automatically switches an electric lamp off and on, such as a car's direction indicator. **3.** *Informal.* A person who exposes himself indecently.

flash flood *n.* A sudden, violent flood after a heavy rain.

flash gun *n.* A photographic apparatus that holds and electrically triggers a flash bulb.

flash·ing (flăsh′ĭng) *n.* Sheet metal or weather stripping used to reinforce and weatherproof the joints and angles of a roof.

flash lamp *n.* An electric lamp for producing a high-intensity light of very short duration for use in photography.

flash·light (flăsh′līt′) *n.* **1.** A small, portable lamp usually powered by batteries and encased in a metal or plastic cylinder. **2.** A brief, brilliant flood of light from a photographic lamp. **3.** A bright, flashing beam or light, as of a beacon or signal lamp.

flash·o·ver (flăsh′ō′vər) *n.* An unintended electric arc, as between two pieces of apparatus.

flash photolysis *n.* A technique for studying the spectra and reactions of short-lived free radicals by subjecting a sample, usually a gas in a glass or quartz tube, to a brief intense pulse of light and recording an absorption spectrum using a separate continuous light source.

flash point *n.* **1.** The lowest temperature at which the vapor of a combustible liquid can be made to ignite momentarily in air. **2.** The point at which a situation or person erupts or may erupt, as into violence.

flash tube *n.* A gas discharge tube used in an electronic flash to produce a brief, intense pulse of light.

flash unit *n.* **1.** An electronic flash system containing both power supply and flash tube in a single compact unit. **2. a.** A flash gun. **b.** A flash gun and reflector.

flash·y (flăsh′ē) *adj.* **-ier, -iest. 1.** Giving a momentary or superficial impression of brilliance. **2.** Cheap-looking and showy; tastelessly ostentatious. —**flash·i·ly** *adv.* —**flash·i·ness** *n.*

flask (flăsk, fläsk) *n.* **1.** A small bottle or other container with a narrow neck and usually a cap, especially: **a.** A pocket-sized, flat-shaped container for holding liquor. **b.** A container or case for carrying gunpowder or shot. **c.** A vial or round long-necked bottle for laboratory use. **2.** A frame for holding a sand mold in a foundry. [Old French *flasque, flaske,* from Late Latin *flascō, flasca,* probably from Germanic *flaska-* (unattested).]

flask·et (flăs′kĭt, flä′skĭt) *n.* **1.** A long, shallow basket. **2.** A small flask. [Old North French *flasquet,* diminutive of Old French *flasque,* FLASK.]

flat¹ (flăt) *adj.* **flatter, flattest. 1.** Having no curves; of zero curvature. **2.** Extending or lying completely in a plane, especially a horizontal plane; planar. **3. a.** Having a smooth, even, level surface. **b.** Not hilly; generally level: *a flat landscape.* **c.** Lying closely against another surface: *clasped it flat against his chest.* **d.** Extended or leveled after being rolled up, folded, or the like. **4.** Not deep or high; shallow; low: *a flat box.* **5.** Lying prone; prostrate. **6.** Unequivocal; unqualified; absolute: *a flat refusal.* **7.** Fixed; unvarying: *a flat rate.* **8.** Neither more nor less; to the exact measure: *ten minutes flat.* **9.** Uninteresting; dull: *The party was rather flat.* **10. a.** Lacking zest or animation. **b.** Having lost a characteristic effervescence; dead; stale. Said of beverages. **11. a.** Deflated. Said of a tire. **b.** Electrically discharged. Said of a battery or accumulator. **12.** Commercially inactive; sluggish: *a flat market.* **13.** Unmodulated; monotonous: *a flat voice.* **14. a.** Executed with an even thickness of paint; lacking relief. **b.** Lacking contrast in tint or shading; uniform. Said of a painting or photograph. **15.** Mat; not glossy. Said of a paint. **16.** *Music.* **a.** Below the intended pitch. **b.** Designating a key with one or more flats in the signature. **c.** Being half a step lower than the corresponding natural key: *the key of B flat.* Compare **sharp. 17.** Designating the vowel *a* as pronounced in *bad* or *cat.* **18.** With low heels. Said of shoes. **19.** Having little or no arch. Said of a foot. **20.** *Chiefly British.* Designating horse races run over level ground without obstacles. —See Synonyms at **level.**

~*adv.* **1. a.** Horizontally; level with the ground. **b.** Prostrate. **2.** So as to be flat. **3.** Directly; completely: *He went flat against the rules.* **4.** *Music.* Below the intended pitch: *sing flat.* —**fall flat.** To fail: *Our plans fell flat.* —**flat out.** *Informal.* **1.** With the utmost effort or vigor. **2.** In a direct manner; bluntly. **3.** At top speed.

~*n.* **1.** A flat surface or part. **2. a.** *Often* **flats.** A stretch of level ground: *the salt flats.* **b.** Low-lying, partly flooded ground such as tideland. **c.** A shallow; a shoal. **3.** Stage scenery on a movable wooden frame. **4.** The inner side of the extended hand. **5.** A shallow frame or box for seeds or seedlings. **6.** A shoe with a flat heel. **7.** A flatcar. **8.** A deflated tire. **9.** *Music.* **a.** A sign (♭) affixed to a note to indicate that it is to be lowered by half a tone below its natural pitch. **b.** A note that is lowered in this way: *B flat.* In this sense, compare **sharp.**

~*tr.v.* **flatted, flatting, flats. 1.** To make flat; flatten. **2.** *Music.* To lower (a note) by a semitone. [Middle English, from Old Norse *flatr,* from Germanic.] —**flat·ly** *adv.* —**flat·ness** *n.*

flat² *n.* **1.** *Chiefly British.* An apartment on one floor of a building. **2.** *Archaic.* A story in a house.

~*tr.v.* **flatted, flatting, flats.** *Chiefly British.* To divide (a building) into separate flats. [Variant (influenced by the adjective) of obsolete *flet,* interior of a house, Middle English *flet,* Old English *flett,* floor, ground, hall.]

flat-bed press (flăt′bĕd′) *n.* A printing press in which the type is supported by a flat surface (bed) and the paper is applied to the type either by a flat platen (in older models) or by a cylinder against which the bed moves.

flat·boat (flăt′bōt′) *n.* A boat with a flat bottom and square ends, used for transporting goods on inland waterways.

flat·car (flăt′kär′) *n.* A railroad freight car without sides or roof.

flat·fish (flăt′fĭsh′) *n., pl.* **-fishes** or collectively **flatfish.** Any of numerous chiefly marine fishes of the order Pleuronectiformes (or Heterosomata), which includes the sole, halibut, and turbot.

flat·foot (flăt′fo͝ot′) *n., pl.* **-feet** (-fēt′) (for sense 1) or **-foots** (for sense 2). **1.** A condition in which the arch of the foot is flattened so that the entire sole makes contact with the ground. **2. a.** *Informal.* A person with flat feet. **b.** *Slang.* A police officer.

flat-foot·ed (flăt′fo͝ot′ĭd) *adj.* **1.** Of or suffering from flatfoot. **2.** *Informal.* Without reservation; forthright; uncompromising: *a flat-footed denial.* **3.** *Informal.* Clumsy; graceless. **4.** *Informal.* Uninspired; tedious. **5.** *Informal.* Unprepared; unable to react quickly: *caught him flat-footed.* —**flat-foot·ed·ly** *adv.* —**flat-foot·ed·ness** *n.*

flat·head (flăt′hĕd′) *n.* A food fish of the family Platycephalidae, of Pacific waters, having a tapering body and a large, flat head covered with spines and ridges.

flat·i·ron (flăt′ī′ərn) *n.* An externally heated iron for pressing clothes.

flat knot *n.* A **reef knot** *(see).*

flat·let (flăt′lĭt) *n.* *Chiefly British.* A small apartment.

PRONUNCIATION KEY

ă, pat; ā, pay; âr, care;
ä, father, are; b, bib;
ch, church; d, deed; ĕ, pet;
ē, be; f, fife; g, gag; h, hat;
hw, which; ĭ, pit; ī, pie;
îr, pier; j, judge; k, kick;
l, lid, needle; m, mum;
n, no, sudden; ng, thing;
ŏ, pot; ō, toe; ô, paw, for;
oi, noise; ou, out; o͝o, book;
o͞o, boot; p, pop; r, roar;
s, sauce; sh, ship, dish;
t, tight; th, thin, path;
th, this, bathe; ŭ, cut; ûr, fur;
v, valve; w, with; y, yes;
z, zebra, size; zh, vision;
ə, about, item, edible, gallop, circus, peaceful

IN FOREIGN WORDS:

à, *Fr.* ami; œ, *Fr.* feu, *Ger.* schön; ü, *Fr.* tu, *Ger.* über; KH, *Ger.* ich, *Scot.* loch; N, *Fr.* bon; y′, *Fr.* Compiègne

STRESS MARKS:

Primary stress: ′
in·cite′ (ĭn-sīt′)
Secondary stress: ′
in′sight′ (ĭn′sīt′)

flat spin *n.* **1.** *Aeronautics.* A spin around a nearly horizontal axis. **2.** *Slang.* A state of great agitation.
flat·ten (flăt′n) *v.* **-tened, -tening, -tens.** —*tr.* **1.** To make flat or flatter. **2.** To knock down; lay low. **3.** *Informal.* To humiliate or subdue. —*intr.* **1.** To become flat or more nearly flat. **2.** To become flat, horizontal, or prostrate. Used with *out.* **3.** *Aeronautics.* To bring an aircraft into a horizontal position. Used with *out.* **—flat·ten·er** *n.*
flat·ter¹ (flăt′ər) *v.* **-tered, -tering, -ters.** —*tr.* **1.** To compliment excessively and often insincerely, especially in order to win favor; court; blandish. **2.** To please or gratify; feed the vanity of: *"What really flatters a man is that you think him worth flattering"* (G.B. Shaw). **3. a.** To portray favorably. **b.** To show off becomingly or advantageously. **4.** To persuade (oneself) that something one wants to believe is the case: *"many flattered themselves that I had turned out a failure"* (John Stuart Mill). —*intr.* To practice flattery. [Middle English *flateren,* from Old French *flat(t)er,* "to caress with the hand," smooth, flatter, from Frankish *flat* (unattested), flat, flat part of a person's hand.] **—flat·ter·er** *n.* **—flat·ter·ing·ly** *adv.*
flatter² *n.* **1.** A flat-faced swage or hammer used by blacksmiths. **2.** A die plate for flattening metal into strips, as in the manufacture of watch springs.
flat·ter·y (flăt′ə-rē) *n., pl.* **-ies. 1.** The act or practice of flattering. **2.** Excessive, false, or sycophantic praise.
Flattery, Cape. A headland in northwestern Washington, at the entrance to Juan de Fuca Strait. It was discovered in 1778 by Capt. James Cook.
flat·ting (flăt′ĭng) *n.* The process of rolling sheet metal.
flat·tish (flăt′ĭsh) *adj.* Somewhat flat.
flat·top (flăt′tŏp′) *n. Informal.* **1.** A U.S. aircraft carrier. **2.** A man's short haircut with a flat, brushlike crown.
flat·u·lence (flăch′o͝o-ləns) *n.* Also **flat·u·len·cy** (-lən-sē). **1.** The presence of excessive gas in the digestive tract. **2.** Windy, high-flown speech; pomposity.
flat·u·lent (flăch′o͝o-lənt) *adj.* **1. a.** Of, suffering from, or caused by flatulence. **b.** Inducing flatulence. **2.** Inflated with self-importance; pompous and pretentious: *flatulent oratory.* [French, from New Latin *flatulentus,* from Latin *flātus,* a breaking wind. See **flatus.**] **—flat·u·lent·ly** *adv.*
fla·tus (flā′təs) *n.* Gas generated in the stomach or intestines. [Latin *flātus,* a breaking wind, a blowing, from the past participle of *flāre,* to blow.]
flat·ware (flăt′wâr′) *n.* **1.** Tableware that is fairly flat and fashioned usually of a single piece, such as plates and saucers. **2.** Table utensils such as knives, forks, and spoons. Compare **hollowware.**
flat·wise (flăt′wīz′) *adv.* Also **flat·ways** (-wāz′). With the flat side down or in contact with a surface.
flat·worm (flăt′wûrm′) *n.* Any wormlike animal of the phylum Platyhelminthes; a **platyhelminth** *(see).*
Flau·bert (flō-bâr′), **Gustave** (1821–80). French novelist. His novels include *Madame Bovary* (1856), *Salammbô* (1862), and *La Tentation de Saint Antoine* (1874). *Trois Contes* (1877) established him as a master of the short story. **—Flau·bert·i·an** (flō-bâr′tē-ən) *adj.*
flaunch. Variant of **flanch.**
flaunt (flônt) *v.* **flaunted, flaunting, flaunts.** —*tr.* **1.** To exhibit ostentatiously; show off: *She flaunted her engagement ring.* **2.** *Nonstandard.* To flout. —*intr.* **1.** To parade oneself ostentatiously or pertly; show oneself off. **2.** To be gaudily in evidence. **3.** To wave proudly, as a flag does. —See Synonyms at **show.** [16th century : origin obscure.] **—flaunt·er** *n.* **—flaunt·ing·ly** *adv.*
Usage: Although they are similar in form, *flaunt* and *flout* have distinctly different senses. *Flaunt* means "to show off," while *flout* means "to treat with contempt." Thus a soldier who *flaunts* his new uniform is proud of it and is not likely to *flout* the regulations ordering him to wear it. The substitution of *flaunt* for *flout,* though frequent in modern usage, is not generally considered acceptable in formal contexts.
flau·tist (flô′tĭst, flou′-) *n.* A **flutist** *(see).* [Italian *flautista,* from *flauto,* FLUTE.]
fla·ves·cent (flə-vĕs′ənt) *adj.* Turning yellow; yellowish. [Latin *flāvēscens,* present participle of *flāvēscere,* to turn yellow, inceptive of *flāvēre,* to be yellow, from *flāvus,* yellow.]
fla·vin (flā′vĭn) *n.* Also **fla·vine** (flā′vēn′). **1.** Any of various water-soluble yellow pigments derived from riboflavin, including **FAD** and **FMN** *(both of which see),* found in plant and animal tissue as prosthetic groups of flavoprotein. **2.** A compound, $C_{10}H_6N_4O_2$, that is the nucleus of various natural yellow pigments. [Latin *flāvus,* yellow + -IN.]
flavin adenine dinucleotide *n.* **FAD** *(see).*
fla·vine (flā′vēn′) *n.* **1.** A brownish-red crystalline powder, $C_{14}H_{15}N_3Cl_2$, used as an antiseptic. **2.** Variant of **flavin.**
flavin mononucleotide *n.* **FMN** *(see).*
fla·vone (flā′vōn′) *n.* A crystalline compound, $C_{15}H_{10}O_2$, the parent substance of a number of important yellow pigments. [Latin *flāvus,* yellow + -ONE.]
fla·von·oid (flā′və-noid′) *n.* Any of a large group of plant pigments, including the anthocyanins. [FLAVON(E) + -OID.]
fla·vo·pro·tein (flā′vō-prō′tēn′, -tē-ĭn) *n.* Any of a class of enzymes containing flavin bound to protein and acting as dehydrogenation catalysts in biological reactions. [Latin *flāvus,* yellow + PROTEIN.]
fla·vor (flā′vər) *n.* Also *chiefly British* **fla·vour. 1.** Distinctive taste; savor: *a flavor of smoke in bacon.* **2.** An ineffable quality felt to be characteristic of a specified thing: *the flavor of the Orient.* **3.** A seasoning; a flavoring. **4.** *Archaic.* Aroma. **5.** *Physics.* Any of various types of quark. Symmetry between quarks and leptons requires at least six flavors, these quarks being designated as up, down, charmed, strange, top, and bottom.
~*tr.v.* **flavored, -voring, -vors.** Also *chiefly British* **fla·vour, -voured, -vouring, -vours.** To give flavor to. [Middle English *flavour,* aroma, variant (influenced by *savour*) of Old French *flaor,* from Vulgar Latin *flātor* (unattested), from Latin *flātus,* blowing, breeze, from the past participle of *flāre,* to blow.] **—fla·vor·er** *n.* **—fla·vor·ous, fla·vor·some** *adj.* **—fla·vor·less** *adj.*
fla·vor·ful (flā′vər-fəl) *adj.* Full of flavor; savory; tasty. **—fla·vor·ful·ly** *adv.*
fla·vor·ing (flā′vər-ĭng) *n.* A substance that imparts flavor, such as an extract or spice.
flaw¹ (flô) *n.* **1.** An imperfection; a blemish or defect. **2.** *Law.* A defect in a legal document, proceeding, or piece of evidence that renders it invalid. **3.** A small fissure; a crack. —See Synonyms at **blemish.**
~*v.* **flawed, flawing, flaws.** —*tr.* To make defective; mar. —*intr.* To become defective. [Middle English *flawe, flai,* flake, fragment, from Old Norse *flaga,* slab or layer of stone.] **—flaw·less** *adj.* **—flaw·less·ly** *adv.* **—flaw·less·ness** *n.*
flaw² *n.* **1.** A brief gust or blast of wind; a squall. **2.** A brief spell of stormy weather. [Probably from Middle Low German *vlāge* or Middle Dutch *vlāghe,* a push, attack, storm.] **—flaw·y** *adj.*
flax (flăks) *n.* **1.** Any of several plants of the genus *Linum;* especially, a widely cultivated species, *L. usitatissimum,* having blue flowers, seeds that yield linseed oil, and slender stems from which a fine, light-colored textile fiber is obtained. **2.** The textile fiber obtained from this plant, from which linen is made. **3.** Any of several plants resembling flax. **4.** Grayish yellow. [Middle English *flax, flex,* Old English *fleax, flæx.*] **—flax·y** *adj.*
flax·en (flăk′sən) *adj.* **1.** Made of or resembling flax. **2.** Having the color of flax fiber; pale yellow.
Flax·man (flăks′mən), **John Henry** (1755–1826). British sculptor and book illustrator. A designer of friezes and portrait medallions for Wedgwood, he also established a reputation as a neoclassical artist with illustrations for the *Odyssey* and *Iliad* (1792).
flax·seed (flăks′sēd′) *n.* The seed of flax, the source of linseed oil and of emollient medicinal preparations.
flay (flā) *tr.v.* **flayed, flaying, flays. 1. a.** To skin (an animal). **b.** To strip off the skin of (a person), as by whipping. **2.** To strip of money or goods, especially by fraud; fleece. **3.** To assail with stinging criticism. [Middle English *flen,* Old English *flēan.*] **—flay·er** *n.*
F layer *n.* **1.** The highest zone of the ionosphere, extending continuously at night from approximately 120 to 250 miles (195 to 400 kilometers). **2.** Either of two layers into which this zone is divided during the day, especially in summer, usually designated F_1 and F_2, and extending respectively from 90 to 150 miles (145 to 240 kilometers) and from 150 miles (240 kilometers) upward. Also called "F region," "Appleton layer." [*F* (arbitrary designation) + LAYER.]
fld. field.
flea (flē) *n.* **1.** Any of various small, wingless, bloodsucking insects of the order Siphonaptera that have legs adapted for jumping and are parasitic on warm-blooded animals. **2.** Any of various small crustaceans that resemble or move like fleas, such as the **water flea** *(see).* **—a flea in one's ear.** A sharp, stinging rebuke or pointed, annoying hint. [Middle English *fle,* Old English *flēa(h),* from Germanic.]
flea·bag (flē′băg′) *n.* **1.** A bed or sleeping bag. **2.** A cheap, disreputable hotel or lodging place.
flea·bane (flē′bān′) *n.* Any of various plants of the genus *Erigeron,* having variously colored, daisylike flowers, such as the **horseweed** *(see).* [From its supposed ability to drive away fleas.]
flea beetle *n.* Any of various small beetles of the family Chrysomelidae that have hind legs enlarged for jumping.
flea·bite (flē′bīt′) *n.* **1. a.** The bite of a flea. **b.** The little red mark caused by a flea's bite. **2.** A trifling loss or inconvenience.
flea-bit·ten (flē′bĭt′n) *adj.* **1.** Covered with fleas or fleabites. **2.** *Informal.* Shabby; mean; wretched. **3.** Having a pale coat with reddish-brown flecks. Said of horses.
flea collar *n.* A collar containing an insecticide, worn by dogs and cats to kill fleas and ticks.
flea market *n.* A shop or open market selling antiques, used household goods, curios, and the like.
flea·pit (flē′pĭt′) *n. British Slang.* A cheap or squalid theater.
flea·wort (flē′wûrt′) *n.* Any of various plants reputed to repel fleas, such as *Senecio integrifolius,* which has yellow, daisylike flowers, and a species of plantain, *Plantago psyllium.*
flèche (flĕsh) *n.* **1.** *Architecture.* A slender spire, especially one on a church above the intersection of the nave and transepts. Also called "spirelet." **2.** *Architecture.* An outward-pointing parapet on a fortified wall. **3.** Any of the points on a backgammon board. **4.** In fencing, a lunging attack. [French, "arrow," from Old French, from Frankish *fliugika* (unattested).]
flé·chette (flā-shĕt′) *n.* A steel missile or dart dropped from an aircraft, as used in World War I. [French, from FLÈCHE.]
fleck (flĕk) *n.* **1.** A tiny mark or spot, such as a freckle. **2.** A small bit or flake. **3.** A small patch of color or light.
~*tr.v.* **flecked, flecking, flecks.** To spot or streak. [Probably from Middle English *flecked,* spotted, dappled, from Old Norse *flekkōttr,* from *flekkr,* spot, stain.]
flec·tion (flĕk′shən) *n.* Also *chiefly British* **flex·ion. 1.** The act or

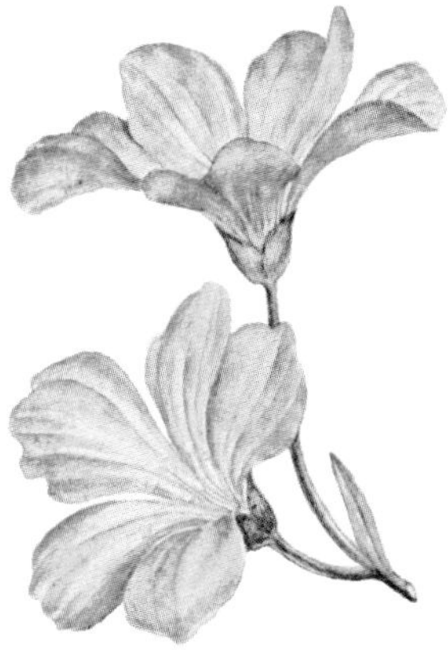

flax *Pale-blue flowers of the flax plant,* Linun usitatissimum. *Flax flowers through the summer and its stems, soaked and combed, once provided the fiber for linen. The word linen comes from* lin, *the Old English name for flax.*

process of bending or flexing. **2.** A bent part; a curve; a bend. **3.** *Grammar.* Inflection. [Latin *flexiō* (stem *flexiōn-*), a bending, from *flexus,* past participle of *flectere,* to bend, FLEX.] **—flec·tion·al** *adj.*

fled. Past tense and past participle of **flee.**

fledge (flĕj) *v.* **fledged, fledging, fledges.** *—tr.* **1.** To take care of (a young bird) until it is ready to fly. **2.** To cover with or as if with feathers. **3.** To provide (an arrow) with feathers; feather; fletch. *—intr.* To grow the plumage necessary for flight. [Probably from obsolete *fledge,* feathered, from Middle English *flegge,* Old English *flycge.*]

fledg·ling, fledge·ling (flĕj′lĭng) *n.* **1.** A young bird that has recently acquired its flight feathers. **2.** One that is young and inexperienced. Also used adjectivally: *a fledgling republic.*

fledg·y (flĕj′ē) *adj.* **-ier, -iest.** Covered with feathers; feathery. **—fledg·i·ness** *n.*

flee (flē) *v.* **fled** (flĕd), **fleeing, flees.** *—intr.* **1.** To run away, as from trouble or danger. **2.** To withdraw abruptly; rush off: *She fled to her bedroom.* **3.** To pass swiftly away; vanish: *time fleeing.* *—tr.* To run away from; shun: *The child forgot her lines and fled the auditorium in embarrassment.* [Middle English *flen, fleon,* Old English *flēon,* from Germanic. (The past tense *fled* and past participle *fled* are from Middle English *fledde* and *fledd,* which superseded the strong forms inherited from Old English.)] **—fle·er** *n.*

fleece (flēs) *n.* **1.** The coat of wool of a sheep or similar animal. **2.** The yield of wool shorn from a sheep at one time. **3.** A soft, woolly covering or mass. **4.** Fabric with a soft, deep pile.
∼tr.v. **fleeced, fleecing, fleeces. 1.** To shear the fleece from. **2.** To defraud of money or property; swindle. **3.** To cover with or as if with fleece. [Middle English *flees, fles,* Old English *flēos,* from Germanic.] **—fleec·er** *n.*

fleec·y (flē′sē) *adj.* **-ier, -iest.** Of, like, or covered with fleece: *"a thick fleecy sky threatened snow"* (Edith Wharton). **—fleec·i·ly** *adv.* **—fleec·i·ness** *n.*

fleer (flîr) *v.* **fleered, fleering, fleers.** *—tr.* To sneer at; scoff; scorn. *—intr.* To smirk or laugh in contempt or derision.
∼n. A scoffing or taunting look or gibe. [Middle English *flerien,* to laugh mockingly, jeer, from Scandinavian; akin to Norwegian and Swedish dialectal *flira,* to laugh, Danish dialectal *flire,* to giggle. See **flimflam.**] **—fleer·ing·ly** *adv.*

fleet¹ (flēt) *n.* **1. a.** A number of warships operating together under one command. **b.** The entire navy of a state. **2.** Any group of craft or vehicles, such as taxis or fishing boats, owned or operated as a unit. [Middle English *flete,* Old English *flēot,* from *flēotan,* to float.]

fleet² *adj.* **fleeter, fleetest. 1.** Moving swiftly; rapid or nimble. **2.** *Archaic.* Fleeting. —See Synonyms at **fast.**
∼v. **fleeted, fleeting, fleets.** *—intr.* **1.** To move or pass swiftly. **2.** To glide away; fade; vanish. *—tr.* **1.** To pass (time) quickly. **2.** *Nautical.* To alter the position of (tackle, rope, or the like). [Probably from Middle English *fleten,* to flow, glide swiftly, Old English *flēotan,* to float, drift.] **—fleet·ly** *adv.* **—fleet·ness** *n.*

fleet³ *n. British Regional.* A small inlet or creek. [Middle English *flete,* Old English *flēot.*]

Fleet Admiral *n.* The officer having the highest rank in the U.S. and some other navies. See **Admiral of the Fleet.**

fleet-foot·ed (flēt′fo͝ot′ĭd) *adj.* Capable of running fast.

fleet·ing (flē′tĭng) *adj.* Passing quickly; very brief. —See Synonyms at **transient. —fleet·ing·ly** *adv.* **—fleet·ing·ness** *n.*

Fleet Street *n.* **1.** A thoroughfare of central London along which many British newspaper publishers are located. **2.** British journalism.

Flem·ing (flĕm′ĭng) *n.* **1.** A native of Flanders. **2.** A Belgian who speaks Flemish. Compare **Walloon.** [Middle English, from Old Norse *Flæmingi,* from Middle Dutch *Vlāming,* from *Vlām-,* FLANDERS.]

Fleming, Sir Alexander (1881–1955). British bacteriologist, discoverer of penicillin. Fleming was unable to isolate or identify the antibiotic, but this was later achieved by H.W. Florey and E.B. Chain, with whom Fleming shared the Nobel Prize in medicine in 1945.

Fleming, Ian Lancaster (1908–64). British writer. His most famous character, the superspy James Bond, first appeared in 1953.

Fleming, Sir John Ambrose (1849–1945). British electrical engineer. He was a pioneer in the development of electric lighting, the telephone, and wireless telegraphy in England. In 1904 he devised the first electron tube, which he called a "thermionic valve."

Flem·ish (flĕm′ĭsh) *adj. Abbr.* **Flem.** Of or pertaining to Flanders, the Flemings, or their language.
∼n. Abbr. **Flem. 1.** The West Germanic language, very similar to Dutch, that is one of Belgium's two official languages. **2.** *Used with a plural verb.* The Flemings. Preceded by *the.* [Middle English, from Old Norse *Flæmskr,* from Middle Dutch *Vlāmish,* from *Vlām-,* FLANDERS.]

Flemish bond *n.* In masonry, a bond consisting of alternate headers and stretchers in each course.

flench. Variant of **flense.**

flense (flĕns) *tr.v.* **flensed, flensing, flenses.** Also **flench** (flĕnch), **flenched, flenching, flenches.** To strip the blubber or skin from (a whale, for example). [Danish *flense.*] **—flens·er** *n.*

flesh (flĕsh) *n.* **1.** The soft tissue of the body; especially, skeletal muscle as opposed to bone and viscera. **2.** The meat of animals as distinguished from the edible tissue of fish or sometimes poultry. **3.** The pulpy, usually edible part of a fruit or vegetable. **4.** Excess tissue; fat; plumpness. **5.** The surface or skin of the human body. **6. a.** The body as distinguished from the mind or soul. **b.** Man's physical or carnal nature. **c.** Sensual appetites. **7. a.** Mankind: *"The glory of the Lord shall be revealed, and all flesh shall see it together"* (Isaiah 40:3). **b.** All living animals. **8.** One's family; kin. **9.** Yellowish pink to pale grayish brown. **—in the flesh. 1.** Alive. **2.** In person; present.
∼v. **fleshed, fleshing, fleshes.** *—tr.* **1.** To encourage (a hunting dog or falcon) to participate in the chase by feeding it flesh from a kill; blood. **2.** To inure to battle or bloodshed. **3.** To fill out or give substance to (a framework or plan, for example). Used with *out.* **4.** To plunge or thrust (a weapon) into flesh. **5.** To clean (a hide) of adhering flesh. *—intr.* To gain weight; become plump or fleshy. Usually used with *out.* [Middle English *flesh, fleish,* Old English *flǣsc,* from Germanic.]

flesh and blood *n.* **1.** Human nature or physical existence, together with its weaknesses. **2.** One's blood relatives; kin.

flesh·er (flĕsh′ər) *n.* **1.** A person who fleshes hides. **2.** An instrument for fleshing hides. **3.** *Scottish.* A butcher.

flesh fly *n.* Any of various flies of the genus *Sarcophaga,* the larvae of which are parasitic in animal tissue or feed on carrion.

flesh·ings (flĕsh′ĭngz) *pl.n.* **1.** Flesh-colored tights, as those worn by actors. **2.** Bits of flesh removed from a hide in cleaning.

flesh·ly (flĕsh′lē) *adj.* **-lier, -liest. 1.** Of or pertaining to the body; corporeal. **2.** Inclined to or concerned with carnality; sensual. **3.** Not spiritual; worldly. **4.** Tending to plumpness; fleshy. **—flesh·li·ness** *n.*

flesh·pot (flĕsh′pŏt′) *n.* **1.** *Archaic.* A pot for cooking meat. **2. fleshpots. a.** Sensual gratification; self-indulgence. **b.** A place in which such gratification is obtained.

flesh wound *n.* A wound that penetrates the flesh but does not damage bones or vital organs.

flesh·y (flĕsh′ē) *adj.* **-ier, -iest. 1.** Pertaining to, consisting of, or resembling flesh. **2.** Having much flesh; corpulent; plump. **3.** Not fibrous; firm and pulpy. Said of fruit, leaves, or the like. —See Synonyms at **fat. —flesh·i·ness** *n.*

fleshy fruit *n.* A fruit, such as a drupe or berry, whose pericarp is soft and pulpy as opposed to hard and dry.

fletch (flĕch) *tr.v.* **fletched, fletching, fletches.** To feather (an arrow); fledge. [Perhaps from FLETCHER.]

fletch·er (flĕch′ər) *n.* One who makes arrows. [Middle English *flecher,* from Old French *flech(i)er,* from *fleche,* arrow, from Frankish *fliugika* (unattested).]

Fletch·er (flĕch′ər), **John** (1579–1625). English dramatist and poet. With Francis Beaumont he wrote a number of romantic tragicomedies, including *Philaster* (1610) and *The Maid's Tragedy* (1611).

flet·ton (flĕt′n) *n.* A common type of brick made by compressing ground clay, mixed with a minimum of water, in a steel mold before firing. [After *Fletton,* Cambridgeshire, England, near the source of the clay originally used for this brick.]

fleur de coin (flœr′ də kwăN′) *adj.* In mint condition. Said of a coin. [French, "flower of the minting die."]

fleur-de-lis, fleur-de-lys (flûr′də-lē′, flo͝or′-) *n., pl.* **fleurs-de-lis, fleurs-de-lys** (flûr′də-lēz′, flo͝or′-). Also *archaic* **flow·er-de-luce** (flou′ər-də-lo͞os′), *pl.* **flowers-de-luce. 1.** *Heraldry.* A device consisting of a stylized three-petaled iris flower, used as the armorial emblem of the kings of France. **2.** An iris; especially, a white-flowered form of *Iris germanica.* [Middle English, from Old French *flor de lis,* lily flower : *flo(u)r,* FLOWER + *de,* of + *lis,* LILY.]

fleur·on (flûr′ŏn′, flo͝or′-) *n.* A crescent-shaped piece of puff pastry used as a garnish in cooking. [French, from Old French *floron,* from *flor, flour, flur,* FLOWER.]

flew¹. Past tense of **fly** (to move through the air).

flew². Variant of **flue** (fishing net).

flews (flo͞oz) *pl.n.* The pendulous corners of the upper lip of certain dogs, such as the bloodhound. [16th century : origin obscure.]

flex (flĕks) *v.* **flexed, flexing, flexes.** *—tr.* **1. a.** To bend (something pliant or elastic). **b.** To bend (a joint). **c.** To bend (a joint) repeatedly. **2.** To contract (a muscle). Compare **extend.** *—intr.* To bend: *"His hands flexed nervously as he spoke"* (Mary McCarthy).
∼n. British. Flexible insulated electric wire. [Latin *flectere*† (past participle *flexus*), to bend.]

flex·a·gon (flĕk′sə-gŏn′) *n.* A folded paper construction capable of being flexed along its folds to reveal different combinations of faces. [FLEX + -GON.]

flex·i·ble (flĕk′sə-bəl) *adj.* Also **flex·ile** (flĕk′səl, -sĭl′). **1.** Capable of being bent or flexed; pliable. **2.** Susceptible to influence or persuasion; tractable. **3.** Responsive to change; adaptable. **4.** Capable of variation or modification. **—flex·i·bil·i·ty** (flĕk′sə-bĭl′ə-tē), **flex·i·ble·ness** *n.* **—flex·i·bly** *adv.*
Synonyms: *adaptable, ductile, plastic, pliable, pliant, supple.*

flexible sandstone *n.* **Itacolumite** *(see).*

flex·ion (flĕk′shən) *n.* **1.** *Anatomy.* **a.** The act of bending a limb or joint. **b.** The condition of being bent. **2.** A part that is bent. **3.** *Chiefly British.* Variant of **flection.** [Variant of FLECTION.] **—flex·ion·al** *adj.* **—flex·ion·less** *adj.*

flex·og·ra·phy (flĕk-sŏg′rə-fē) *n. Printing.* **1.** A system of rotary printing used especially for printing on metal or plastic sheets. **2.** Anything printed by this method. [From Latin *flexus,* past participle of *flectere,* to bend + -GRAPHY.] **—flex·o·graph·ic** (flĕk′sə-grăf′ĭk) *adj.* **—flex·o·graph·i·cal·ly** *adv.*

flex·or (flĕk′sər) *n.* A muscle that acts to bend a joint. Compare

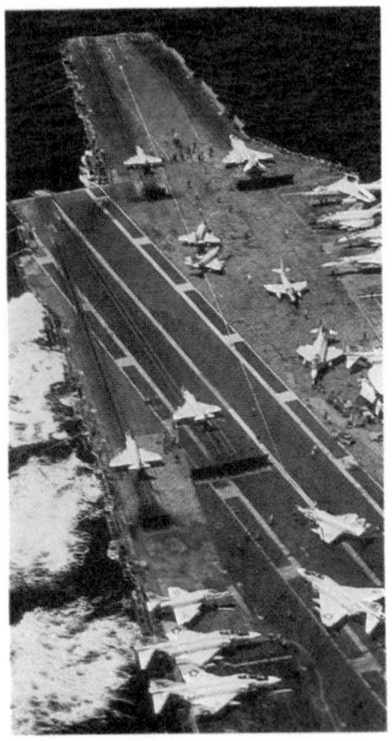

flight deck *Modern aircraft carriers have an angled flight deck. This British invention allows aircraft to be parked on each side while others are taking off or landing. The deck shown here is on the U.S.S.* Enterprise.

PRONUNCIATION KEY

ă, pat; ā, pay; âr, care;
ä, father, are; b, bib;
ch, church; d, deed; ĕ, pet;
ē, be; f, fife; g, gag; h, hat;
hw, which; ĭ, pit; ī, pie;
îr, pier; j, judge; k, kick;
l, lid, needle; m, mum;
n, no, sudden; ng, thing;
ŏ, pot; ō, toe; ô, paw, for;
oi, noise; ou, out; o͝o, book;
o͞o, boot; p, pop; r, roar;
s, sauce; sh, ship, dish;
t, tight; th, thin, path;
th, this, bathe; ŭ, cut; ûr, fur;
v, valve; w, with; y, yes;
z, zebra, size; zh, vision;
ə, about, item, edible,
gallop, circus, peaceful

IN FOREIGN WORDS:

à, *Fr.* ami; œ, *Fr.* feu, *Ger.* schön; ü, *Fr.* tu, *Ger.* über; KH, *Ger.* ich, *Scot.* loch; N, *Fr.* bon; y′, *Fr.* Compiègne

STRESS MARKS:

Primary stress: ′
in·cite′ (ĭn-sīt′)
Secondary stress: ′
in′sight′ (ĭn′sīt′)

extensor. [New Latin, from Latin *flexus,* past participle of *flectere,* to FLEX.]
flex·time (flĕks′tīm′) *n.* An arrangement by which employees may vary their own starting and finishing hours within agreed limits while maintaining a fixed average number of hours per working day. [FLEX(IBLE) + TIME.]
flex·u·ous (flĕk′sho͞o-əs) *adj.* Also **flex·u·ose** (-ōs′). Bending or winding alternately from side to side; sinuous. [Latin *flexuōsus,* from *flexus.* See **flex**.] —**flex·u·ous·ly** *adv.*
flex·ure (flĕk′shər) *n.* **1.** A bend, curve, or turn, such as a bend in a tubular organ: *the hepatic flexure of the colon.* **2.** A bending or flexing; flexion. —**flex·ur·al** *adj.*
fley (flā) *v.* **fleyed, fleying, fleys.** *Chiefly Scottish.* —*tr.v.* **1.** To frighten. **2.** To cause to run away in fright; scare off. —*intr.* To be frightened; take fright. [Middle English *flayen, fleien,* to put to flight, frighten, Old English *flȳgan.*]
flib·ber·ti·gib·bet (flĭb′ər-tē-jĭb′ĭt) *n.* A silly, scatterbrained, or garrulous person, especially a young girl. [Earlier *flibbergib, fliper-gebet*† (imitative of foolish talk).]
flick¹ (flĭk) *n.* **1.** A light, quick blow, jerk, or touch, as with a whip or fingernail. **2.** The sound accompanying such a movement; a snap. **3.** A light splash, dash, or streak.
∼*v.* **flicked, flicking, flicks.** —*tr.* **1.** To touch or hit with a light, quick movement. **2.** To cause to move with a light movement, usually of the hand or finger; snap. **3.** To remove with a light, quick movement. —*intr.* **1.** To look through reading matter inattentively or very quickly. Used with *through.* **2.** To twitch or flutter. [Middle English (imitative).]
flick² *n. Slang.* A motion picture. [Back-formation from FLICKER.]
flick·book (flĭk′bo͝ok′) *n.* A booklet consisting of a series of images that give the illusion of continuous movement when the edges of the pages are observed quickly. Also called "flipbook."
flick·er¹ (flĭk′ər) *v.* **-ered, -ering, -ers.** —*intr.* **1.** To give off inconstant, fitful light; burn unsteadily. **2.** To shine or blaze momentarily, as lightning does. **3.** To move waveringly; flutter. —*tr.* To cause to flicker.
∼*n.* **1.** An inconstant or wavering light: *"a flicker like green fire in his eyes"* (J.R.R. Tolkien). **2.** A brief or slight sensation, as of an emotion: *a flicker of hope.* **3.** A tremor or flutter. [Middle English *flikeren, flekeren,* to flutter, flicker, Old English *flicorian*†, to flutter, hover.]
flicker² *n.* Any of several large North American woodpeckers of the genus *Colaptes,* especially *C. auratus,* the common flicker, having a brown back and a white rump. [Imitative of its call.]
flick knife *n. British.* A **switchblade** *(see).*
flied. Past tense and past participle of **fly** (to hit a fly ball).
fli·er, fly·er (flī′ər) *n.* **1. a.** One that flies. **b.** An aircraft pilot; an aviator. **2.** A step in a straight as opposed to winding staircase. Compare **winder. 3.** *Informal.* A daring financial venture. **4.** An advertising pamphlet or circular.
flight¹ (flīt) *n.* **1. a.** The motion of an object in or through a medium, especially through the earth's atmosphere or through space, that is characterized by lack of contact with any other object, especially with the earth. **b.** An instance of such motion: *the flight of a spacecraft.* **c.** The duration of or distance covered in a flight. **2. a.** The act or process of flying; locomotion through the air by means of wings. **b.** The ability to engage in such motion. **3.** Any swift passage or movement. **4. a.** A journey in an aircraft, especially a scheduled airline trip. **b.** The aircraft making such a trip: *Your flight leaves in 15 minutes.* **5.** A group, especially of birds or aircraft, flying together. **6.** A number of military aircraft forming a subdivision of a squadron. **7.** An effort that transcends the usual restraints; a soaring: *a flight of fancy.* **8.** A flight feather. **9.** A series of stairs rising from one landing to another. **10.** A series or line of hurdles, gates, canal locks, or the like. **11.** The flared tail of an arrow or dart, usually made of feathers or plastic, that is designed to give stability. **12.** In archery, a thin, light arrow designed for long-range shooting. Also called "flight arrow." **13.** In angling, a device that whirls the bait rapidly in trolling.
∼*v.* **flighted, flighting, flights.** —*intr.* To migrate or fly in flocks. —*tr. Sports.* To cause (a ball or dart, for example) to float in an unpredictable trajectory: *a flighted delivery.* [Middle English *flight,* Old English *flyht;* akin to FLY (verb).]
flight² *n.* A running away; an escape. —**put to flight.** To drive or frighten away; repel; rout. —**take (to) flight.** To run or fly away; withdraw rapidly; flee. [Middle English *flight,* Old English *flyht* (unattested); akin to FLEE.]
flight attendant *n.* An attendant who assists passengers in an airplane.
flight bag *n.* A lightweight, flexible piece of luggage with zippered outside pockets.
flight check *n.* A proficiency check in an airborne aircraft of the pilot, crew members, or a piece of equipment.
flight deck *n.* **1.** The upper deck of an aircraft carrier, used as a runway. **2.** The forward compartment in a large aircraft, used by the pilot, copilot, and flight engineer.
flight engineer *n.* The crew member responsible for the mechanical performance of an aircraft flight.
flight feather *n.* Any of the comparatively large, stiff feathers of a bird's wing or tail that are necessary for flight. Also called "flight."
flight·less (flīt′lĭs) *adj.* Incapable of flying. Said of certain birds and insects.
flight lieutenant *n.* An officer in the British and certain other air forces ranking between a squadron leader and a flying officer and equivalent in rank to a captain in the army.
flight path *n.* The precise route taken or due to be taken through the air by an aircraft or spacecraft.
flight plan *n.* A detailed statement of an aircraft's expected departure time, route, and so on.
flight recorder *n.* An electronic device that records details of an aircraft's performance during flight. Also called "black box."
flight surgeon *n.* An air force medical officer who specializes in aviation medicine.
flight·y (flī′tē) *adj.* **-ier, -iest. 1.** Given to capricious behavior; fickle or unstable. **2.** Given to flirting. **3.** Easily excited; skittish. Said of a horse. [Originally "swift," from FLIGHT.] —**flight·i·ly** *adv.* —**flight·i·ness** *n.*
flim·flam (flĭm′flăm′) *n. Informal.* **1.** Nonsense; humbug. **2.** A deception; a swindle.
∼*tr.v.* **flimflammed, -flamming, -flams.** *Informal.* To swindle or dupe. [Reduplication (imitative) of an unknown Scandinavian word akin to Old Norse *flīm,* mockery, Danish dialectal *flire,* to giggle, from Germanic *fli-* (unattested).] —**flim·flam·mer** *n.* —**flim·flam·mer·y** *n.*
flim·sy (flĭm′zē) *adj.* **-sier, -siest. 1.** Light, thin, and insubstantial. **2.** Lacking solidity or strength: *a flimsy building.* **3.** Lacking plausibility; unconvincing: *a flimsy theory.*
∼*n., pl.* **flimsies. 1.** Thin paper usually used to make multiple copies. **2.** Something written on such paper. [17th century : origin obscure.] —**flim·si·ly** *adv.* —**flim·si·ness** *n.*
flinch (flĭnch) *intr.v.* **flinched, flinching, flinches. 1.** To betray fear, pain, or surprise with an involuntary gesture such as a start; wince. **2.** To draw away; retreat. —See Synonyms at **recoil.**
∼*n.* An act or instance of flinching. [Old French *flenchir, flainchir,* from Germanic.] —**flinch·er** *n.* —**flinch·ing·ly** *adv.*
flin·ders (flĭn′dərz) *pl.n.* Bits; fragments; splinters. [Middle English *flenderis,* from Scandinavian; akin to Norwegian *flindra,* splinter.]
Flin·ders (flĭn′dərz). River in northern Queensland, Australia. It rises in the Eastern Highlands and flows 837 kilometers (520 miles) northwest to the Gulf of Carpentaria.
Flinders, Matthew (1774–1814). British navigator and hydrographer. In 1795 he sailed to New South Wales and subsequently made a thorough study of the Australian coast. Among his scientific works is *A Voyage to Terra Australis* (1814).
Flinders Ranges. Mountain chain between Lake Torrens and Lake Frome, in South Australia. About 420 kilometers (260 miles) long, it has valuable deposits of uranium and copper.
fling (flĭng) *v.* **flung** (flŭng), **flinging, flings.** —*tr.* **1.** To throw violently or carelessly; hurl. **2.** To put or send suddenly or unexpectedly: *The army was flung into battle.* **3.** To throw (oneself) into some activity with abandon and energy. **4.** To throw (an opponent or rider, for example) to the ground. **5.** To toss aside; discard: *fling propriety away.* **6.** To speak or shout (words) in a passionate way. —*intr.* To move quickly, violently, or impulsively: *She flung out of the room in a rage.* —See Synonyms at **throw.**
∼*n.* **1.** An act of flinging or hurling; a throw. **2.** A brief period of indulging one's impulses; a spree. **3.** A dance in which the arms and legs are flung about; especially, the **Highland fling** *(see).* **4.** *Informal.* A brief attempt: *Have a fling at it.* [Fling, flung, flung; Middle English *flingen, flung* (more often *flang*), *flungen,* from Scandinavian; akin to Old Norse *flengja,* to flog.]
flink·ite (flĭng′kīt′) *n.* A brownish-green mineral form of magnesium arsenate. [German *Flinkit,* after Gustav *Flink* (1849–1931), Swedish mineralogist.]
flint (flĭnt) *n.* **1.** A very hard, fine-grained quartz that sparks when struck with steel. **2.** A piece of flint fashioned into a tool by human beings of the Stone Age. **3. a.** A piece of flint used to produce a spark. **b.** A small solid cylinder of a spark-producing alloy, used in lighters to ignite the fuel. **4.** Anything likened to flint in hardness: *a jaw of flint.* [Middle English *flint,* Old English *flint,* from Germanic.]
Flint (flĭnt). A city in southern Michigan, on the Flint River. A fur-trading post was established here in 1819. Since 1902 the city has been a major automobile-manufacturing center.
flint glass *n.* A soft, fusible, lustrous, brilliant lead-oxide optical glass with high refraction and low dispersion. Also called "lead glass." Compare **crown glass.**
flint·lock (flĭnt′lŏk′) *n.* **1.** An obsolete gunlock in which a flint embedded in the hammer produces a spark that ignites the charge. **2.** A firearm having such a gunlock. Also called "firelock."
Flint·shire (flĭnt′shîr′, -shər). A former county in Wales, in the northeast on the Dee estuary. Since 1974 it has been part of the county of Clwyd.
flint·y (flĭn′tē) *adj.* **-ier, -iest. 1.** Containing or composed of flint. **2.** Unyielding or unfeeling; stony. —**flint·i·ly** *adv.* —**flint·i·ness** *n.*
flip (flĭp) *v.* **flipped, flipping, flips.** —*tr.* **1.** To throw or flick with a brisk motion, especially of the finger and thumb; toss. **2.** To toss (a coin, for example) in the air, imparting a spin. **3.** To reverse or turn over quickly and effortlessly. —*intr.* **1.** To strike at something quickly or lightly, as with a fillip. **2.** To move suddenly or jerkily. **3.** *Slang.* **a.** To be overwhelmed by excitement or enthusiasm: *They flipped when they saw the new car.* **b.** To fly into a rage. **c.** To lose one's mind; go mad. Often used with *out.* **4.** To look through or read something, such as a book, very quickly or inattentively. Used with *through.*
∼*n.* **1.** An act of flipping, especially: **a.** A fillip or tap. **b.** A quick,

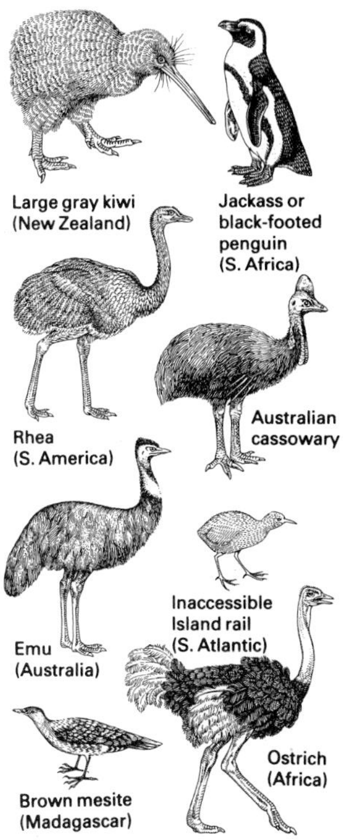

Large gray kiwi (New Zealand)
Jackass or black-footed penguin (S. Africa)
Rhea (S. America)
Australian cassowary
Inaccessible Island rail (S. Atlantic)
Emu (Australia)
Ostrich (Africa)
Brown mesite (Madagascar)

flightless birds *Some birds have lost the ability to fly, simply because they live in regions where flight is of no advantage to them — on islands where there are no predators, for example. They all have vestigial wings, though the kiwi's are so small that the bird appears to be wingless. Some flightless birds have developed to great size, such as the ostrich, which stands about 2.5 meters (8 feet) tall and is the largest living bird.*

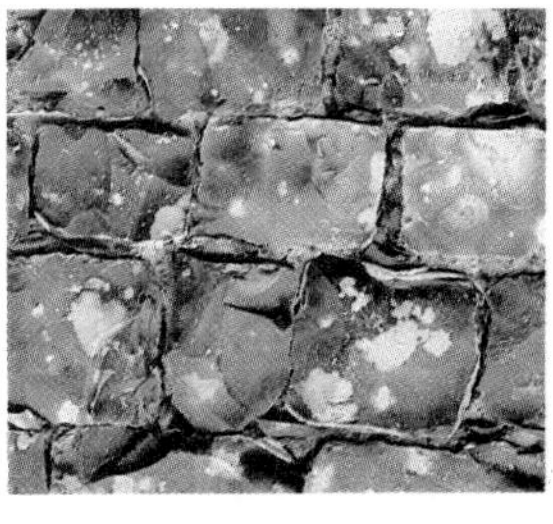
flint *Widely used as a building material, flint is often chipped, to form a regular surface, as in this picture. The stone is split to reveal a dark, shiny face.*

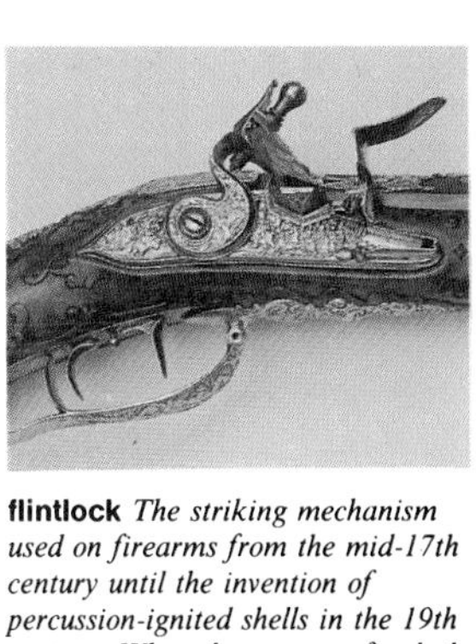
flintlock *The striking mechanism used on firearms from the mid-17th century until the invention of percussion-ignited shells in the 19th century. When the gun was fired, the flint clamped in the hammer struck a spark from a steel plate to ignite the charge.*

jerky movement. **c.** A somersault. **2.** A mixed drink made with any of various alcoholic beverages, usually including beaten eggs.
~*adj. Informal.* Disrespectful; impertinent: *a flip attitude.* [Perhaps from FILLIP.]

flip·book (flĭp′bo͝ok′) *n.* A **flickbook** *(see).*

flip-flop (flĭp′flŏp′) *n.* **1.** The movement or sound of repeated flapping: *the flip-flop of sandals on a tile floor.* **2.** A simple sandal, a **thong** *(see).* **3.** *Electronics.* An electronic circuit having two stable states, either of which can be assumed depending on the input signal. Flip-flops are used in computers to store a single bit of information. **4.** A backward somersault or handspring. **5.** *Informal.* A reversal, as of opinion: *The senator did a complete flip-flop on arms reduction.* [Reduplication of FLIP.] **—flip-flop** *v. & adv.*

flip·pant (flĭp′ənt) *adj.* **1. a.** Marked by disrespectful and insensitive levity; pert. **b.** Clever in a shallow or superficial way. **2.** *Archaic.* Talkative; voluble. [Probably FLIP + -ANT.] **—flip·pan·cy** *n.* **—flip·pant·ly** *adv.*

flip·per (flĭp′ər) *n.* **1.** One that flips. **2.** A wide, flat limb, as of a seal, whale, or other aquatic animal, adapted especially for swimming. **3.** A rubber foot covering with a flat, flexible portion that widens as it extends forward from the toes to increase propulsion in swimming. **4.** *Slang.* A hand.

flip side *n.* The reverse side, as of a phonograph record.

flirt (flûrt) *v.* **flirted, flirting, flirts.** *—intr.* **1.** To amuse oneself in playful amorousness; play lightly or teasingly at courtship. **2.** To deal with something playfully, triflingly, or coyly; toy: *The bullfighter flirted with death. We flirted with the idea of buying a new car.* **3.** To move abruptly or jerkily. *—tr.* **1.** To toss or flip suddenly; flick. **2.** To move quickly; jerk or wave briskly: *The dancer flirted her fan.*
~*n.* **1.** One given to flirting. **2.** An abrupt, jerking movement. [16th century ("sudden pull or twist," brisk movement, as of a bird's tail, flighty woman, hence current senses) : imitative.]

flir·ta·tion (flûr-tā′shən) *n.* **1.** The practice of flirting; coquetry. **2.** A casual, playful romance. **3.** Any brief involvement.

flir·ta·tious (flûr-tā′shəs) *adj.* **1.** Given to flirting. **2.** Full of playful allure: *a flirtatious glance.* **—flir·ta·tious·ly** *adv.* **—flir·ta·tious·ness** *n.*

flit (flĭt) *intr.v.* **flitted, flitting, flits.** **1.** To move about rapidly and nimbly. **2.** To move quickly from one situation or location to another. **3.** *British Informal.* To move house; relocate.
~*n.* **1.** A fluttering or darting movement. **2.** *British Informal.* A hasty escape or departure, as to avoid payment of rent. Used especially in the phrase *do a moonlight flit.* [Middle English *flitten,* to transport, convey, from Old Norse *flytja,* to convey.] **—flit·ter** *n.*

flitch (flĭch) *n.* **1.** A salted and cured side of bacon. **2.** A longitudinal cut from the trunk of a tree. **3.** Any of several planks secured together to form a single beam. [Middle English *fliche,* side of animal salted and cured, Old English *flicce,* from Germanic.]

flit·ter (flĭt′ər) *intr.v.* **-tered, -tering, -ters.** To flit about; flutter. [Frequentative of FLIT.]

flit·ter·mouse (flĭt′ər-mous′) *n., pl.* **-mice** (-mīs′). A **bat** *(see).* [Translation of German *Fledermaus.*]

fliv·ver (flĭv′ər) *n.* An old or cheap car. [Origin unknown.]

float (flōt) *v.* **floated, floating, floats.** *—intr.* **1. a.** To remain suspended within or on the surface of a fluid without sinking. **b.** To be suspended unsupported in space without falling. **2.** To move from position to position, especially at random; drift. **3.** To move easily and lightly as if suspended: *"Miss Golightly . . . floated round in their arms light as a scarf"* (Truman Capote). **4.** *Finance.* To find a level in relation to other currencies solely in response to the law of supply and demand: *The dollar should be allowed to float.* *—tr.* **1.** To cause to remain suspended without sinking or falling. **2.** To flood (land), as for irrigation. **3. a.** To launch or establish (a business enterprise, for example). **b.** To set (an idea, rumor, or the like) in circulation. **4.** To offer (shares, bonds, or the like) for sale. **5.** To make the surface of (plaster, for example) level or smooth. **6.** To seek support for (a scheme or idea). **7.** *Finance.* To allow (the exchange value of a currency) to find its real level freely in relation to other currencies.
~*n.* **1.** Something that floats, as: **a.** A raft. **b.** A buoy. **c.** A life belt. **d.** A cork or other floating object on a fishing line. **e.** A pontoon for amphibious aircraft. **f.** A hollow ball attached to a lever to regulate the water level in a tank. **g.** An air-filled or gas-filled organ or sac that enables an organism to remain suspended in water. **2. a.** An exhibit carried through the streets in a parade. **b.** A large, flat vehicle bearing such an exhibit. **3.** A tool for smoothing the surface of plaster or cement. **4.** A soft drink with ice cream floating in it. **5.** Any of the blades on a paddle wheel. **6.** *Finance.* The amount of money representing debts still outstanding. **7. floats.** Footlights in a theater. [Middle English *floten,* Old English *flotian.*] **—float·a·ble** *adj.* **—float·y** *adj.*

floatage. Variant of **flotage.**

floatation. Variant of **flotation.**

float·er (flō′tər) *n.* **1.** One that floats. **2.** One who wanders from place to place or job to job; drifter. **3.** An employee who is reassigned from job to job or shift to shift within an operation. **4.** One who votes illegally in a number of polling places. **5.** An insurance policy that protects movable property such as jewelry or artwork.

float glass *n.* Flat plate glass made by floating molten glass on molten lead or some other liquid and allowing the glass to harden.

float·ing (flō′tĭng) *adj.* **1.** Buoyed on or suspended in or as if in a fluid. **2.** Not secured in place; unattached. **3.** Inclined to move about; drifting; errant. **4.** *Finance.* **a.** Available for use; in circulation. Said of capital. **b.** Short-term and usually unfunded. Said of a debt. **c.** Freed to rise and fall in value in relation to other currencies. Said of a currency.

floating dock *n.* A structure that can be submerged to permit the entry and docking of a ship and then raised to lift the ship from the water for repairs. Also called "floating dry dock."

floating island *n.* **1.** A solid mass of soil and vegetation floating in water. **2.** A dessert of soft custard with beaten egg whites or whipped cream floating on its surface.

floating kidney *n. Medicine.* **1.** An abnormal condition in which one or both kidneys are mobile and descend into the pelvis. **2.** Such a kidney.

float·ing-point (flō′tĭng-point′) *adj. Mathematics.* Designating or pertaining to a system of expressing numbers by two separate numbers, one giving the value of the digits and the other the power of the number base. For example, 2,3 is 2×10^3 (or 2,000) in base 10. Compare **fixed-point.**

floating rib *n.* Any of the four lower ribs of man that, unlike the other ribs, are not attached at the front to the breastbone.

floc (flŏk) *n.* A flocculent mass as formed in certain serological precipitin tests. [Latin *floccus,* tuft of wool.]

floc·cu·late (flŏk′yə-lāt′) *v.* **-lated, -lating, -lates.** *—tr.* **1.** To cause (soil or chemical precipitates, for example) to form lumps or masses. **2.** To cause (clouds) to form fluffy masses. *—intr.* To turn into lumpy or fluffy masses. [From FLOCCULE.] **—floc·cu·la·tion** *n.*

floc·cule (flŏk′yo͞ol) *n.* Any small, loosely held mass or aggregate of fine particles suspended in or precipitated from a solution. [From FLOCCULUS.]

floc·cu·lent (flŏk′yə-lənt) *adj.* **1.** Having a fluffy or woolly appearance. **2.** *Chemistry.* Made up of or containing woolly masses. **3.** *Biology.* Flaky, waxy, and woollike, as is the secretion covering some insects. [Latin *floccus,* tuft + -ULENT.] **—floc·cu·lence** *n.* **—floc·cu·lent·ly** *adv.*

floc·cu·lus (flŏk′yə-ləs) *n., pl.* **-li** (-lī′). **1.** A small, fluffy mass. **2.** *Anatomy.* Either of two small lobes on the lower posterior border of each lobe of the cerebellum. **3.** *Astronomy.* Any of various masses of gases appearing as bright or dark patches on the sun's surface. Also called "plage." [New Latin, diminutive of Latin *floccus,* tuft of wool.]

floc·cus (flŏk′əs) *n., pl.* **flocci** (flŏk′ī′, flŏk′sī′). **1.** The downy or woolly covering of the young of certain birds. **2.** A woolly tuft of hairs or filaments. [Latin, FLOCK.]

flock[1] (flŏk) *n.* **1.** A group of animals, such as birds or sheep, that live, travel, or feed together. **2.** A group of people under the leadership of one person; especially, the members of a church or congregation. **3.** A large crowd or number.
~*intr.v.* **flocked, flocking, flocks.** To congregate or travel in a flock or crowd: *flock to the January sales.* [Middle English *flok,* Old English *flocc,* from Germanic *flugnaz* (unattested).]

flock[2] *n.* **1.** A tuft, as of fiber or hair. **2.** Waste wool or cotton used for stuffing furniture and mattresses. **3.** An inferior grade of wool added to cloth for extra weight. **4.** Pulverized wool applied to paper, cloth, or metal to produce a texture or pattern. **5.** A floccule.
~*tr.v.* **flocked, flocking, flocks.** **1.** To stuff with flock. **2.** To texture or pattern with flock. [Middle English *flok,* probably from Old French *floc,* from Latin *floccus.*]

Flod·den (flŏd′n). Hillside in Northumberland, England, where on September 9, 1513, the English routed the Scots. James IV and more than 10,000 men were slain.

floe (flō) *n.* **1.** A large, flat mass of ice formed on the surface of a body of water. **2.** A segment separated from such an ice mass. [Probably from Norwegian *flo,* layer, slab, from Old Norse *flō,* stratum, coating.]

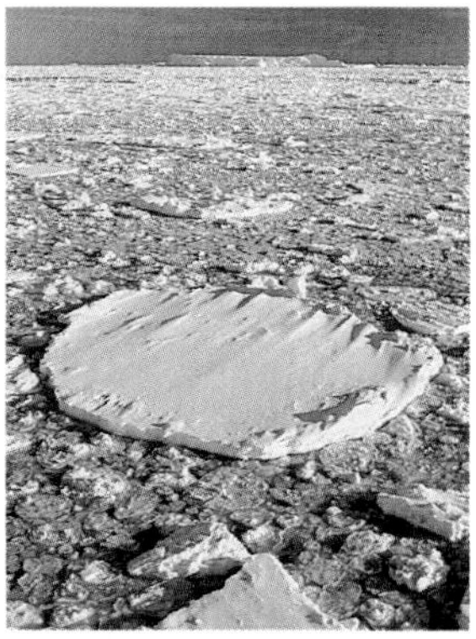

floe *Open pack ice in the sea off Antarctica, with larger floes known as "pancake ice."*

flog (flŏg, flôg) *tr.v.* **flogged, flogging, flogs.** **1.** To beat severely with a whip or rod. **2.** *Slang.* To exert (oneself) strenuously. **3.** *Chiefly British Slang.* To sell. **4.** To criticize severely. [Perhaps shortened from Latin *flagellāre,* to whip, from *flagellum,* diminutive of *flagrum,* whip.] **—flog·ger** *n.*

flong (flŏng, flông) *n. Printing.* Papier-mâché or a paperlike substance used in making a stereotype mold. [From French *flan,* FLAN.]

flood (flŭd) *n.* **1.** An overflowing of water onto land that is normally dry; a deluge. **2.** Flood tide. **3.** Any abundant flow or outpouring: *choke back a flood of tears.* **4.** *Archaic.* A sea. **5.** *Informal.* A floodlight. **—in flood.** At an abnormally high level. Said of a river. **—the Flood.** The universal deluge recorded in the Bible as having occurred during the life of Noah. Genesis 7.
~*v.* **flooded, flooding, floods.** *—tr.* **1.** To cover or submerge with a flood; inundate. **2.** To fill with an abundance or an excess. **3.** To hinder the operation of (a carburetor) by supplying too much fuel: *I flooded the engine.* *—intr.* **1.** To become inundated or submerged. **2.** To pour or flow in or as if in a flood: *Applications flooded in.* [Middle English *flod, flud,* Old English *flōd,* from Germanic.]

flood·gate (flŭd′gāt′) *n.* **1.** A gate used to control the flow of a body of water. Also called "water gate." **2.** *Often* **floodgates.** Anything that restrains a flood or onrush.

flood·light (flŭd′līt′) *n.* **1.** Artificial light in an intensely bright and broad beam, as that used to illuminate a sports field. **2.** A lamp or lighting unit that produces such a beam.
~*tr.v.* **floodlighted** or **-lit** (-lĭt′), **-lighting, -lights.** To illuminate with a floodlight.

flood plain *n.* A plain bordering a river subject to flooding.

flood tide *n.* The incoming or rising tide. Compare **ebb tide.**

floor (flôr, flōr) *n. Abbr.* **fl.** **1.** The surface of a room on which one stands. **2.** The lower or supporting surface of any structure. **3.** A minimum or base; a lower limit, especially of wages or prices. **4.** The ground or lowermost surface, together with accumulated layers of detritus, as of a forest or ocean. **5.** A level area on which a specified activity takes place: *a dance floor; a factory floor; a threshing floor.* **6.** The lower part of a room, such as a legislative chamber or stock exchange, where business is conducted. **7. a.** The right to address an assembly, as granted under parliamentary procedure: *be given the floor.* **b.** The body of assembly members: *a motion from the floor.* **8. a.** A story or level of a building. **b.** The occupants of such a story or level.
~*tr.v.* **floored, flooring, floors. 1.** To provide with a floor. **2.** To knock or press to the floor or ground: *The wrestler floored his opponent.* **3.** *Informal.* To stun; overwhelm. **4.** To press (the accelerator of a motor vehicle) to the floor. [Middle English *flor,* Old English *flōr,* from Germanic.] **—floor·er** *n.*

floor·age (flôr′ĭj, flōr′-) *n.* A stretch of floor; floor space.

floor·board (flôr′bôrd′, flōr′bōrd′) *n.* Any of the boards forming a floor.

floor exercise *n. Sports.* An event in competitive gymnastics that consists of various tumbling maneuvers performed on a mat.

floor·ing (flôr′ĭng, flōr′-) *n.* **1. a.** Floors collectively. **b.** A floor. **2.** Material, such as wood or tiles, used in making floors.

flooring saw *n.* A saw with a curved toothed edge used for cutting through floorboards.

floor manager *n.* A person who supervises or directs something, as at a political convention, from the floor.

floor plan *n.* A scale diagram of a room or building drawn as if seen from above.

floor show *n.* A series of entertainments presented in a nightclub, hotel, or the like.

floor·walk·er (flôr′wô′kər, flōr′-) *n.* An employee of a department store who supervises sales personnel and assists customers in a designated area of the store.

floo·zy, floo·zie (flo͞o′zē) *n., pl.* **-zies.** *Slang.* A slovenly or vulgar woman; especially, a cheap prostitute. [Origin unknown.]

flop (flŏp) *v.* **flopped, flopping, flops.** —*intr.* **1.** To move or fall heavily and clumsily. **2.** To swing or move about in a loose, noisy way; flap. **3.** *Informal.* To fail. **4.** *Slang.* To go to bed. Often used with *out.* —*tr.* To cause to fall down suddenly and noisily.
~*n.* **1.** The action of flopping. **2.** The sound of flopping; a dull thud. **3.** *Informal.* An utter failure. [Variant of FLAP.] **—flop·per** *n.*

flop·house (flŏp′hous′) *n., pl.* **-houses** (-hou′zĭz). A cheap hotel for indigent transients.

flop·py (flŏp′ē) *adj.* **-pier, -piest.** Tending to flop; loose and flexible.
~*n. Computer Science.* A floppy disk. **—flop·pi·ness** *n.*

floppy disk *n. Computer Science.* A thin flexible plastic disk with a magnetic coating used to store computer data. Also called "magnetic disk," "floppy," "diskette."

flo·ra (flôr′ə, flōr′ə) *n., pl.* **-ras** or **florae** (flôr′ē′, flōr′ē′). **1.** Plants collectively; especially, the plants of a particular region or time. **2.** A systematic compilation describing plants. **3. intestinal flora** *(see).* [From FLORA.]

Flo·ra (flôr′ə, flōr′ə). *Roman Mythology.* The goddess of flowers. [Latin *Flōra,* from *flōs* (stem *flōr-*), flower.]

flo·ral (flôr′əl, flōr′-) *adj.* Of, pertaining to, consisting of, or suggestive of a flower or flowers. **—flo·ral·ly** *adv.*

floral envelope *n.* The perianth of a flower, which surrounds the stamens and pistil; the sepals and petals collectively.

Flor·ence (flôr′əns, flŏr′-). *Italian* **Fi·ren·ze** (fē-rĕnt′sä). City in the Tuscany region of north-central Italy, on the Arno River at the foot of the Apeninnes. Originally an Etruscan settlement, then a Roman town on the Cassian way, Florence was one of the most powerful and artistically brilliant city-states of the Italian Renaissance, when it was under the rule of the Medici family. Giotto, Michelangelo, Leonardo, Raphael, Dante, and Donatello were all active in the city.

Florence fennel *n.* A variety of fennel, **finochio** *(see).*

Flor·en·tine (flôr′ən-tēn′, -tīn′, flŏr′-) *adj.* **1.** Of or pertaining to the city of Florence. **2.** Of or pertaining to the style of art and architecture that flourished in Renaissance Florence. **3.** *Often* **florentine.** Cooked or served with spinach. Said of eggs and other dishes.
~*n.* **1.** A native or inhabitant of Florence. **2.** *Often* **florentine.** A large rich pastry containing nuts and preserved fruit and coated with chocolate on one side. [Latin *Flōrentīnus,* from *Flōrentia,* FLORENCE.]

flo·res·cence (flô-rĕs′əns, flō-, flə-) *n.* The condition, time, or period of blossoming. [New Latin *florescentia,* from Latin *flōrēscens,* present participle of *flōrēscere,* to begin to bloom, inceptive of *flōrēre,* to bloom, from *flōs* (stem *flōr-*), FLOWER.] **—flo·res·cent** *adj.*

flo·ret (flôr′ĭt, flōr′-) *n.* A small flower, usually part of a dense cluster; especially, one of the disk or ray flowers of a composite plant, such as a daisy. [Middle English *flouret,* from Old French *florete,* diminutive of *flo(u)r,* FLOWER.]

Flo·rey (flôr′ē, flōr′ē), **Howard Walter, Baron** (1898–1968). Australian pathologist. Working with Sir Ernest Chain, he isolated and purified the antibiotic penicillin, discovered by Sir Alexander Fleming in 1928. Florey, Chain, and Fleming shared the Nobel Prize in medicine in 1945.

flo·ri·at·ed, flo·re·at·ed (flôr′ē-ā′tĭd, flōr′-) *adj.* Decorated with floral designs; flowery or flowerlike. [Latin *flōs* (stem *flōr-*), flower.]

flo·ri·bun·da (flôr′ə-bŭn′də, flōr′-) *n.* Any of several hybrid roses bearing numerous single or double flowers. [New Latin, feminine of *floribundus,* blossoming freely, from Latin *flōs* (stem *flōr-*), FLOWER.]

flo·ri·cul·ture (flôr′ĭ-kŭl′chər, flōr′-) *n.* The cultivation of flowering plants. [Latin *flōs* (stem *flōr-*), flower + CULTURE.] **—flo·ri·cul·tur·al** (flôr′ĭ-kŭl′chər-əl, flōr′-) *adj.* **—flo·ri·cul·tur·ist** *n.*

flor·id (flôr′ĭd, flŏr′-) *adj.* **1.** Flushed with rosy color; ruddy. **2.** Heavily adorned or embellished; flowery: *"their style is clear, masculine, and smooth, but not florid"* (Jonathan Swift). **3.** *Archaic.* Healthy; blooming. —See Synonyms at **ornate.** [French *floride,* from Latin *flōridus,* from *flōrēre,* to bloom, from *flōs* (stem *flōr-*), FLOWER.] **—flo·rid·i·ty** (flə-rĭd′ə-tē), **flor·id·ness** *n.* **—flor·id·ly** *adv.*

Flor·i·da (flôr′ə-də, flŏr′-). *Abbr.* **Fla.** State of the United States occupying a long peninsula between the Atlantic Ocean and the Gulf of Mexico. It was admitted to the Union in 1845. Florida's wide, sandy beaches and hot climate make it one of the country's leading tourist regions. Its southern swamps form the Everglades National Park. Florida is the leading producer of citrus fruits in the United States. Tallahassee is the capital. **—Flo·rid·i·an** (flə-rĭd′ē-ən), **Flor·i·dan** (flôr′ə-dən, flŏr′-) *adj. & n.*

Florida, Straits of. Sea passage, *c.* 145 kilometers (90 miles) wide, between the Florida Keys and Cuba. It connects the Atlantic Ocean with the Gulf of Mexico.

Florida Keys. Chain of small, sandy coral and limestone islands and reefs *c.* 240 kilometers (150 miles) off southern Florida, from south of Miami Beach to Key West. The subtropical keys are popular tourist resorts. The world's longest overwater highway links the islands with 42 bridges.

flo·rif·er·ous (flô-rĭf′ər-əs, flō-) *adj.* Bearing flowers; especially, flowering abundantly. [Latin *flōrifer* : *flōs* (stem *flōr-*), FLOWER + -FEROUS.]

flo·ri·gen (flôr′ə-jən, flōr′-) *n.* A hypothetical plant hormone thought to be produced in the leaves and transmitted to the growing points where it causes the initiation of flower buds. [Latin *flōs* (stem *flōr-*), flower + -GEN.]

flor·in (flôr′ĭn, flŏr′-) *n. Abbr.* **fl.** **1. a.** A former British coin worth two shillings (ten pence). **b.** The sum of two shillings (ten pence). **2.** A monetary unit, the **guilder** *(see).* See feature at **currency.** **3. a.** A gold coin first issued in Florence in 1252. **b.** Any of several obsolete European gold coins similar to the Florentine florin. [Middle English *flore(i)n,* from Old French *florin,* from Italian *fiorino,* from *fiore,* flower, from Latin *flōs* (stem *flōr-*), FLOWER.]

flo·rist (flôr′ĭst, flōr′-, flŏr′-) *n.* A person whose business is the growing or selling of flowers and ornamental plants. [Latin *flōs* (stem *flōr-*), FLOWER + -IST.]

flo·ris·tic (flô-rĭs′tĭk, flō-) *adj.* Of or pertaining to flowers, flora, or floristics. [Back-formation from FLORISTICS.] **—flo·ris·ti·cal·ly** *adv.*

flo·ris·tics (flô-rĭs′tĭks, flō-) *n. Used with a singular verb.* The study of the types and numerical distribution of the plant species in a particular area. [FLOR(A) + (STAT)ISTICS.]

-florous *suffix.* Indicates number or kind of flowers; for example, **tubuliflorous.** [Late Latin *-flōrus,* from Latin *flōs* (stem *flōr-*), FLOWER.]

flo·ru·it (flôr′o͞o-ĭt, -yo͞o-ĭt, flōr′-) *n. Abbr.* **fl.** The period during which a person, or sometimes a group, movement, or the like, was most active or flourishing. [Latin, he (or she) flourished, from *flōrēre,* to bloom, FLOURISH.]

floss (flôs, flŏs) *n.* **1. a.** Short fibers or waste silk from the cocoon of a silkworm. **b.** The fluffy mass of fibers from cotton or similar plants. **2.** A soft, loosely twisted thread used in embroidery. **3.** A soft, silky, fibrous substance, such as the styles and stigmas of corn. **4. Dental floss** *(see).*
~*v.* **flossed, flossing, flosses.** —*tr.* To clean between (teeth) with dental floss. —*intr.* To use dental floss. [Possibly from French *floche,* from Old French *flosche*†, down.]

floss·y (flô′sē, flŏs′ē) *adj.* **-ier, -iest.** **1.** Made of or resembling floss; downy; silky. **2.** *Slang.* Ostentatiously stylish; flashy.

flo·tage, float·age (flō′tĭj) *n.* **1.** Flotation. **2.** Floating objects or material.

flo·ta·tion, float·a·tion (flō-tā′shən) *n.* **1.** The act, process, or condition of floating or launching. **2.** *Finance.* **a.** An act or instance of launching or financing a business venture by selling an issue of shares or bonds. **b.** The raising of a loan by such an issue. **3.** Any of several processes in which different materials, notably minerals, are separated by agitation of a pulverized mixture of the material with water, oil, and chemicals that cause differential wetting of the suspended particles, the unwetted particles being carried by air bubbles to the surface for collection. [Alteration of earlier *floatation* (FLOAT + -ATION), after *rotation.*]

flo·til·la (flō-tĭl′ə) *n.* **1. a.** A fleet of small ships. **b.** A small fleet of ships. **2.** Any group resembling a small fleet: *a flotilla of taxis.* [Spanish, diminutive of *flota,* fleet, from Old French *flote,* from Old Norse *floti,* raft, fleet.]

flot·sam (flŏt′səm) *n.* **1.** Any wreckage or cargo that remains afloat after a ship has sunk. Compare **jetsam.** **2.** Any discarded odds and ends. **3.** Unemployed and vagrant people; drifters. **4.** Miscellaneous articles. [Earlier *flotsen, flotson,* from Norman French *floteson,* from *floter,* to float, from Vulgar Latin *flottāre* (unattested), from Germanic.]

flounce[1] (flouns) *n.* A strip of gathered or pleated material secured on its upper edge to another surface, as on a garment or curtain.
~*tr.v.* **flounced, flouncing, flounces.** To trim with a flounce or

PRONUNCIATION KEY

ă, pat; ā, pay; âr, care;
ä, father, are; b, bib;
ch, church; d, deed; ĕ, pet;
ē, be; f, fife; g, gag; h, hat;
hw, which; ĭ, pit; ī, pie;
îr, pier; j, judge; k, kick;
l, lid, needle; m, mum;
n, no, sudden; ng, thing;
ŏ, pot; ō, toe; ô, paw, for;
oi, noise; ou, out; o͝o, book;
o͞o, boot; p, pop; r, roar;
s, sauce; sh, ship, dish;
t, tight; th, thin, path;
th, this, bathe; ŭ, cut; ûr, fur;
v, valve; w, with; y, yes;
z, zebra, size; zh, vision;
ə, about, item, edible,
gallop, circus, peaceful

IN FOREIGN WORDS:

à, *Fr.* ami; œ, *Fr.* feu, *Ger.* schön; ü, *Fr.* tu, *Ger.* über;
KH, *Ger.* ich, *Scot.* loch;
N, *Fr.* bon; y′, *Fr.* Compiègne

STRESS MARKS:

Primary stress: ′
in·cite′ (ĭn-sīt′)
Secondary stress: ′
in′sight′ (ĭn′sīt′)

flounces. [Variant of obsolete *frounce,* Middle English *frounce,* a wrinkle, crease, from Old French *fronce,* from *froncir,* to wrinkle, from Frankish *hrunkjan* (unattested).]

flounce² *intr.v.* **flounced, flouncing, flounces.** To move with exaggerated motions expressive of displeasure or impatience.   ~*n.* The act of flouncing. [Possibly of Scandinavian origin.]

floun·der¹ (floun′dər) *intr.v.* **-dered, -dering, -ders. 1.** To move clumsily and with difficulty, as if trying to regain balance. **2.** To proceed clumsily and in confusion.   ~*n.* The act of floundering. [Probably blend of FOUNDER and BLUNDER (and influenced by FLOUNCE, to move jerkily).]

floun·der² *n., pl.* **-ders** or collectively **flounder. 1.** A European flatfish, *Platichthys flesus,* that has a grayish-brown mottled body and is an important food fish. **2.** Any other flatfish of the families Bothidae and Pleuronectidae. [Middle English, from Norman French *floundre,* probably from Scandinavian.]

flour (flour) *n.* **1.** A soft, fine, powdery substance obtained by grinding and sifting the meal of a grain, especially wheat. **2.** Any similar soft, fine powder.   ~*tr.v.* **floured, flouring, flours. 1.** To cover or coat with flour. **2.** To make into flour. [Middle English *flour, flur,* finer meal, farina, FLOWER.] **—flour·y** *adj.*

flour·ish (flûr′ĭsh) *v.* **-ished, -ishing, -ishes.** —*intr.* **1.** To grow well or luxuriantly: *Most flowers flourish in full sunlight.* **2.** To fare well; thrive; prosper. **3.** To be active; especially, to be at the peak of one's activity, fame, or the like. See **floruit. 4.** To make bold, sweeping movements; wave vigorously: *The flag flourished in the wind.* —*tr.* To wield, wave, or exhibit dramatically: *flourish a baton.*   ~*n.* **1.** An act or instance of ostentatiously waving or brandishing: *The swordsman made a flourish.* **2.** An embellishment or ornamentation, as in handwriting or literary composition. **3.** A dramatic action or gesture. **4.** A musical fanfare or similar passage. **5.** *Obsolete.* A period or state of thriving or of being in flower. [Middle

English *florishen,* from Old French *florir* (stem *floriss-*), to bloom, from Vulgar Latin *flōrīre* (unattested), from Latin *flōrēre,* from *flōs* (stem *flōr-*), flower.] **—flour·ish·er** *n.*

flout (flout) *v.* **flouted, flouting, flouts.** —*tr.* To show contempt for, especially in one's actions; scorn: *flout convention.* —*intr.* To be scornful; jeer. —See Usage note at **flaunt.**   ~*n.* A contemptuous action or remark; an insult. [Probably extended use of Middle English *flouten,* to play the flute, from Old French *flauter,* from *flaute,* FLUTE.] **—flout·er** *n.* **—flout·ing·ly** *adv.*

flow (flō) *v.* **flowed, flowing, flows.** —*intr.* **1.** To move or run freely in the manner characteristic of a fluid. **2.** To circulate, as the blood in the body does. **3.** To discharge in a stream; pour forth. **4.** To move or proceed smoothly and steadily as if in an uninterrupted stream: *The traffic flowed across the bridge.* **5.** To proceed with ease: *The conversation flowed.* **6.** To appear smooth, harmonious, or graceful: *the building's flowing lines.* **7.** To rise. Used of the tide. **8.** To arise; derive: *Several conclusions flow from this hypothesis.* **9.** To abound or be plentiful. **10.** To hang loosely and gracefully: *The cape flowed from his shoulders.* **11.** To undergo plastic deformation without cleavage or breaking, as slate might. —*tr.* **1.** To release as a flow. **2.** To cause to flow. **3.** To flood.   ~*n.* **1. a.** The smooth motion characteristic of fluids. **b.** The act of flowing. **2.** A stream. **3. a.** A continuous output or outpouring; a flood: *a flow of ideas.* **b.** A continuous movement or circulation: *the flow of traffic.* **4.** The amount that flows in a given period of time. **5.** The incoming or rise of the tide. **6.** Continuity and smoothness of appearance. **7.** Menstrual discharge. [Middle English *flouen,* Old English *flōwan,* from Germanic.] **—flow·ing·ly** *adv.*

flow·age (flō′ĭj) *n.* **1.** The act of flowing or overflowing. **2.** The state of being flooded. **3.** A liquid that flows or overflows. **4.** The gradual plastic deformation of a solid body, as by stress.

flow chart *n.* A schematic representation of a sequence of operations, as in a manufacturing process or a computer program. Also called "flow diagram," "flow sheet."

flow·er (flou′ər) *n.* **1. a.** The reproductive structure of an angiosperm plant, characteristically having specialized male and female organs (stamens and a pistil) enclosed in an outer envelope of petals and sepals, all borne on a receptacle. **b.** Any such structure having showy or colorful parts; a blossom. **2.** Any similar reproductive organ of other plants, as gymnosperms and mosses. **3. a.** A plant cultivated or conspicuous for its blossoms. **b.** The condition of being in blossom: *in flower.* **4.** That which is produced by any natural process; an outgrowth: *"His attitude was simply a flower of his general good-nature"* (Henry James). **5.** The period of highest development; peak. **6.** The highest or brightest example; the best representative of something: *the flower of our generation.* **7.** An embellishment. **8.** *Usually* **flowers.** *Chemistry.* A fine powder produced by condensation or sublimation.   ~*v.* **flowered, -ering, -ers.** —*intr.* **1.** To produce a flower or flowers; blossom; bloom. **2.** To develop fully; reach a peak. —*tr.* To decorate with flowers or with a floral pattern. [Middle English *flo(u)r,* from Old French *flo(u)r,* from Latin *flōs* (stem *flōr-*).] **—flow·er·less** *adj.*

flow·er·age (flou′ər-ĭj) *n.* **1.** Flowers collectively. **2.** The process or state of flowering.

flow·er·bed (flou′ər-bĕd′) *n.* A plot of earth, as in a garden or park, in which flowers are grown.

flower-de-luce. *Archaic.* Variant of **fleur-de-lis.**

flow·ered (flou′ərd) *adj.* **1.** Having flowers. **2.** Decorated with flowers or a floral pattern: *flowered wallpaper.*

flow·er·er (flou′ər-ər) *n.* A plant that flowers in a specified way or at a specified time: *a late flowerer.*

flow·er·et (flou′ər-ĭt) *n.* A small flower. [Middle English *flourette,* from Old French *flo(u)rete,* diminutive of *flo(u)r,* FLOWER.]

flower girl *n.* **1.** A girl or woman who sells flowers in the street. **2.** A little girl who carries flowers in a wedding procession.

flower head *n.* A dense cluster of very small flowers at the tip of the plant stem.

flow·er·ing (flou′ər-ĭng) *adj.* Capable of producing decorative flowers. Said of plants, especially trees.

flowering currant *n.* An ornamental shrub, *Ribes sanguineum,* native to North America but widely cultivated for its drooping clusters of small pink flowers, which appear before the leaves.

flowering dogwood *n.* See **dogwood.**

flowering maple *n.* Any of several tropical shrubs of the genus *Abutilon;* especially, *A. hybridum,* having lobed leaves resembling those of the maple and variously colored flowers.

flowering plant *n.* An angiosperm (see).

flowering quince *n.* See **japonica** (sense 1).

flow·er·peck·er (flou′ər-pĕk′ər) *n.* Any small bird of the family Dicaeidae, of Australia and southeast Asia.

flow·er·pot (flou′ər-pŏt′) *n.* A pot in which plants are grown.

flower power *n. Informal.* **1.** The goal or ethos of a youth cult prevalent in the 1960's, advocating peace and love. A flower was used to symbolize the ideals of the *flower children* or *flower people* involved. **2.** The cult itself.

flow·er·y (flou′ə-rē) *adj.* **-ier, -iest. 1.** Abounding in or bedecked with flowers. **2.** Suggestive of flowers: *a flowery perfume.* **3.** Having a floral pattern. **4.** Full of figurative and ornate expressions; highly embellished. **—flow·er·i·ness** *n.*

flow meter *n.* An apparatus for monitoring, measuring, or recording fluid flow, especially of a gaseous fuel.

flown. Past participle of **fly** (to move through the air).

---

flower

THE REPRODUCTIVE PROCESSES OF FLOWERS

How flowers are fertilized by pollen grains

Flowers are the reproductive parts of seed-bearing plants (angiosperms). The central part of the flower consists of the sexual organs—the male pollen-producing stamen and the female pistil, which contains the ovules. Pollen is generally transmitted by wind or insects to other flowers; self-pollination occurs in some species, but in most it is prevented because the stamen and pistil mature at different times.

In insect-pollinated plants the flower is surrounded by the perianth—the sepals, which protect the flower in bud, and the petals, which are colored and scented to attract insects. Most wind-pollinated flowers have no perianths.

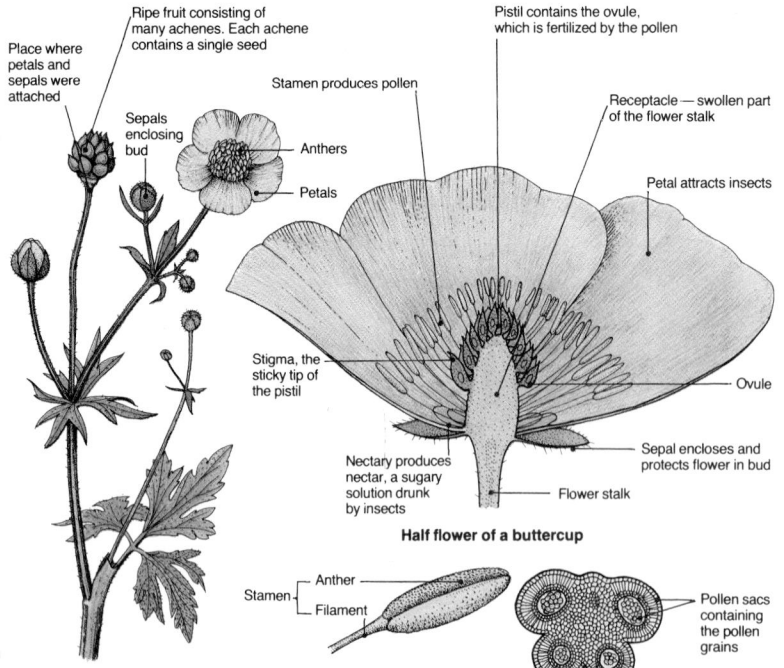

Ripe fruit consisting of many achenes. Each achene contains a single seed

Place where petals and sepals were attached

Sepals enclosing bud

Stamen produces pollen

Anthers

Petals

Pistil contains the ovule, which is fertilized by the pollen

Receptacle — swollen part of the flower stalk

Petal attracts insects

Stigma, the sticky tip of the pistil

Ovule

Nectary produces nectar, a sugary solution drunk by insects

Sepal encloses and protects flower in bud

Flower stalk

Half flower of a buttercup

Stamen — Anther — Filament

Pollen sacs containing the pollen grains

Meadow buttercup

Close-up of stamen and cross section of anther containing pollen

MEADOW BUTTERCUP *The reproductive processes of the buttercup are typical of all flowers, except that some are pollinated by the wind instead of by insects. Sacs in the anther burst to release pollen grains. These stick first to the anther and then to an insect when it settles on the flower. When the insect lands on another flower, pollen grains stick to the stigmas at the tip of the pistils. A tube grows from the grain to the ovule and fertilizes it, initiating its change into a seed.*

flow sheet *n.* A **flow chart** *(see).*

fl. oz. fluid ounce.

flu (flōō) *n. Informal.* Influenza.

fluc·tu·ant (flŭk′chōō-ənt) *adj.* Varying; fluctuating; unstable. [Latin *fluctuāns* (stem *fluctuant-*), present participle of *fluctuāre*, to FLUCTUATE.]

fluc·tu·ate (flŭk′chōō-āt′) *v.* **-ated, -ating, -ates.** —*intr.* **1.** To vary irregularly. **2.** To waver; vacillate. **3.** To rise and fall like waves; undulate. —*tr.* To cause to fluctuate. —See Synonyms at **swing.** [Latin *fluctuāre*, from *fluctus*, a flowing, from the past participle of *fluere*, to flow.] —**fluc·tu·a·tion** *n.*

flue¹ (flōō) *n.* **1.** A pipe, tube, or channel through which hot air, gas, steam, or smoke may pass, as in a furnace or to a chimney. **2. a.** A flue pipe. **b.** The air passage in such a pipe. [Origin unknown.]

flue² *n.* Fluffy waste, as from a textile. [Flemish *vluwe*, from French *velu*, velvety, from Old French, shaggy. See **velvet.**]

flue³, **flew** *n.* Any of several kinds of fishing net. [Middle English *flue*, from Middle Dutch *vluwe.*]

flu·ent (flōō′ənt) *adj.* **1. a.** Expressing oneself readily and effortlessly: *a fluent speaker.* **b.** Effortless; flowing; polished: *speak fluent French.* **2.** Flowing smoothly and easily; graceful: *fluent curves.* **3.** Flowing or capable of flowing; fluid; liquid. [Latin *fluēns* (stem *fluent-*), present participle of *fluere*, to flow.] —**flu·en·cy** *n.* —**flu·ent·ly** *adv.*

flue pipe *n.* An organ pipe sounded by means of a current of air striking a lip in the side of the pipe and causing the air within to vibrate. Also called "flue." Compare **reed pipe.**

flue stop *n.* An organ stop controlling a set of flue pipes. Compare **reed stop.**

fluff (flŭf) *n.* **1.** Light, feathery down or nap. **2.** Something having a light, soft, or frothy consistency or appearance. **3.** Something of little consequence; a trifle. **4.** *Informal.* An error or lapse of memory in the reading, recitation, or delivery of lines, as by an actor or announcer. —*v.* **fluffed, fluffing, fluffs.** —*tr.* **1.** To make light and puffy by shaking or patting into a soft, loose mass: *fluff a pillow.* **2.** *Informal.* To misread or forget (one's lines). **3.** *Informal.* To mar or ruin by making a mistake or blunder. —*intr.* **1.** To become soft and puffy or feathery. **2.** *Informal.* To make an error; especially, to forget or botch one's lines. [Probably variant of FLUE (down).]

fluff·y (flŭf′ē) *adj.* **-ier, -iest.** **1.** Of, like, or covered with fluff or down. **2.** Light and airy; soft: *fluffy curls.* —**fluff·i·ly** *adv.* —**fluff·i·ness** *n.*

flü·gel·horn (flōō′gəl-hôrn′, flü′-) *n.* A bugle with valves, similar to the cornet but having a wider bore. [German : *Flügel*, wing, flank (from its use to summon flanks during a battle), from Middle High German *vlügel* + *Horn*, horn.]

flu·id (flōō′ĭd) *n.* A substance that has a low resistance to flow and the tendency to assume the shape of its container; a liquid or a gas. —*adj. Abbr.* **fl, fl. 1.** Characteristic of a fluid; especially, flowing easily. **2.** Used in the measurement of fluids. **3.** Readily reshaped; pliable. **4.** Smooth and effortless; flowing. **5.** Likely or tending to change; not stable: *The political situation remains fluid and uncertain.* **6.** Convertible into cash: *fluid assets.* [Middle English, from Old French *fluide*, from Latin *fluidus*, from *fluere*, to flow.] —**flu·id·i·ty** (flōō-ĭd′ə-tē), **flu·id·ness** *n.* —**flu·id·ly** *adv.*

fluid dram *n.* One-eighth of a fluid ounce *(see).*

flu·id·ex·tract (flōō′ĭd-ĕk′străkt′) *n.* A concentrated alcohol solution of a vegetable drug containing the equivalent of one gram in powdered form of the active principle in each milliliter.

flu·id·ic (flōō-ĭd′ĭk) *adj.* Of, pertaining to, or operated by fluids.

flu·id·ics (flōō-ĭd′ĭks) *n. Used with a singular verb.* The technology of fluids used as nonmoving, nonelectrical components of control and sensing systems.

flu·id·ize (flōō′ĭ-dīz′) *tr.v.* **-ized, -izing, -izes.** To convert (a solid) into a fine, flowing powder that can be conveyed in a stream of gas. —**flu·id·i·za·tion** *n.*

fluid mechanics *n. Used with a singular verb.* The branch of engineering concerned with the study and applications of fluid flow. Also called "hydraulics."

fluid ounce *n. Abbr.* **fl. oz. 1.** A unit of volume or capacity in the U.S. Customary System, used in liquid measure, equal to 29.6 cubic centimeters (1.804 cubic inches). **2.** A unit of volume or capacity in the British Imperial System, used in liquid and dry measure, equal to 28.41 cubic centimeters (1.734 cubic inches).

fluke¹ (flōōk) *n., pl.* **fluke** (for sense 2) or **flukes. 1.** A flatworm, a **trematode** *(see);* especially, any of various parasitic species. See **liver fluke. 2.** Any of various flatfishes; especially, a **flounder** *(see).* [Middle English *fluke, flok*, Old English *flōc*, from Germanic.]

fluke² *n.* **1.** The triangular blade at the end of either arm of an anchor, designed to catch in the ground. **2.** A barb or barbed head, as on an arrow or harpoon. **3.** Either of the two horizontally flattened divisions of the tail of a whale or related animal. [Probably from FLUKE (fish or worm, from its shape).]

fluke³ *n.* **1.** A stroke of good luck. **2.** A chance occurrence. **3.** An accidentally good or successful stroke in billiards or pool. —*v.* **fluked, fluking, flukes.** —*tr.* To get, make, or do by chance. —*intr.* To produce a fluke. [19th century : origin obscure.]

fluk·y, fluk·ey (flōō′kē) *adj.* **-ier, -iest.** *Informal.* **1.** Resulting from mere chance. **2.** Constantly shifting; uncertain; variable: *a fluky wind.* [From FLUKE (chance shot).]

flume (flōōm) *n.* **1.** A narrow defile or gorge, usually with a stream

flowing through it. **2.** An artificial channel or chute for a stream of water, as for furnishing power or conveying logs. —*tr.v.* **flumed, fluming, flumes. 1.** To divert (water) by means of a flume. **2.** To transport (logs, for example) by the use of a flume. [Earlier, "river," from Middle English *flum*, from Old French, from Latin *flūmen*, from *fluere*, to flow.]

flum·mer·y (flŭm′ə-rē) *n., pl.* **-ies. 1. a.** Any of several soft, light, bland foods, such as a custard or blancmange. **b.** Originally, a soft gelatinous food made by straining boiled oatmeal, to which fruit, honey, or the like, could be added. **2.** Meaningless flattery; mere nonsense; humbug. [Welsh *llymru*†.]

flum·mox (flŭm′əks) *tr.v.* **-moxed, -moxing, -moxes.** *Slang.* To confuse; perplex. [Origin unknown.]

flung. Past tense and past participle of **fling.**

flunk (flŭngk) *v.* **flunked, flunking, flunks.** *Informal.* —*intr.* To fail an examination or course of study. —*tr.* **1.** To fail (an examination or course). **2.** To give (someone) a failing mark. —**flunk out.** To be expelled from an educational institution or course because of failure to meet required standards. [19th century : origin obscure.]

flun·ky (flŭng′kē) *n., pl.* **-kies.** Also **flun·key,** *pl.* **-keys. 1.** A liveried manservant or valet; a lackey. **2.** An obsequious or fawning person; a toady. **3.** A person who does menial or trivial work. [Originally Scottish (dialectal) *flunky*†.] —**flun·ky·ism** *n.*

flu·or (flōō′ôr′, flōō′ôr) *n.* Fluorite. [New Latin, from Latin, a flowing, fluid (from its use as a flux in smelting), from *fluere*, to flow.]

flu·o·resce (flōō′ə-rĕs′, flōō-rĕs′) *v.* **-resced, -rescing, -resces.** —*intr.* To undergo, produce, or show fluorescence. —*tr.* To cause to produce fluorescence. [Back-formation from FLUORESCENCE.]

flu·o·res·ce·in (flōō′ə-rĕs′ē-ĭn, flōō-rĕs′-) *n.* An orange-red compound, $C_{20}H_{12}O_5$, that exhibits intense fluorescence in alkaline solution. It is used to dye sea water for spotting or tracing operations and as a chemical indicator.

flu·o·res·cence (flōō′ə-rĕs′əns, flōō-rĕs′-) *n.* **1.** The emission of electromagnetic radiation, especially of light, resulting from irradiation with other electromagnetic radiation or with particles, and persisting only as long as the stimulating radiation is continued. **2.** The radiation so emitted. Compare **bioluminescence, phosphorescence.** [FLUOR- -ESCENCE.]

flu·o·res·cent (flōō′ə-rĕs′ənt, flōō-rĕs′-) *adj.* Exhibiting or capable of exhibiting fluorescence.

fluorescent lamp *n.* A lamp that produces light by fluorescence; especially, a glass tube the inner wall of which is coated with a material that fluoresces when bombarded by a gaseous discharge within the tube. See feature, next page.

flu·o·ri·date (flōō′ôr′ə-dāt′, flôr′-, flōr′-) *tr.v.* **-dated, -dating, -dates.** To add a fluorine compound to (a water supply, for example) for the purpose of preventing tooth decay. [Back-formation from *fluoridation* : FLUORID(E) + -ATION.] —**flu·o·ri·da·tion** *n.*

flu·o·ride (flōō′ə-rīd′, flōōr′īd′) *n.* Any binary compound of fluorine with another element. [FLUOR(O)- + -IDE.]

flu·o·rine (flōō′ə-rēn′, -rĭn, flōōr′ēn′, -ĭn) *n. Symbol* **F** A pale yellow, highly corrosive, highly poisonous, gaseous halogen element, the most electronegative and most reactive of all the elements. It is used in a wide variety of industrially important compounds. Atomic number 9, atomic weight 18.9984, freezing point –219.62°C, boiling point –188.14°C, specific gravity of liquid 1.108, valence 1. [French, from New Latin *fluor*, generic name for a group of minerals used as fluxes, FLUOR.] —**flu·o·ri·nate** (flōō′ə-rə-nāt′, flōōr′ə-) *v.* —**flu·o·ri·na·tion** *n.*

flu·o·rite (flōō′ə-rīt′, flōōr′īt′) *n.* A white or colorless mineral, CaF_2, often tinged green, blue, violet, yellow, or brown by impurities. The colored varieties are fluorescent in ultraviolet radiation. Also called "fluorspar."

fluoro-, fluor– *prefix.* Indicates: **1.** *Chemistry.* Fluorine in compound; for example, **fluorosis. 2.** Fluorescence; for example, **fluoroscope.** [From FLUORINE and FLUORESCENCE.]

flu·o·ro·car·bon (flōō′ə-rō-kär′bən, flōōr′ō-) *n.* Any of various inert organic compounds derived from hydrocarbons with fluorine replacing all or part of the hydrogen, used as aerosol propellants, refrigerants, solvents, lubricants, and in making plastics and resins.

flu·o·rom·e·ter (flōō′ə-rŏm′ə-tər, flōō-rŏm′-) *n.* Any instrument for detecting and measuring fluorescence. [FLUORO- + -METER.] —**flu·o·rom·e·try** *n.*

flu·o·ro·scope (flōōr′ə-skōp′, flōō′ər-ə-) *n.* A suitably mounted fluorescent screen on which the contents or internal structure of an object, the human body, or the like, may be continuously viewed as shadows formed by differential transmission of x-rays through the object. Also called "radioscope." —*tr.v.* **fluoroscoped, -scoping, -scopes.** To examine the interior of (an object) with a fluoroscope. [FLUORO- + -SCOPE.] —**flu·o·ro·scop·ic** (flōōr′ə-skŏp′ĭk, flōō′ər-ə-) *adj.* —**flu·o·ro·scop·i·cal·ly** *adv.*

flu·o·ros·co·py (flōō′ə-rŏs′kə-pē, flōō-rŏs′-) *n.* Examination with the use of a fluoroscope.

flu·o·ro·sis (flōō′ə-rō′sĭs, flōō-rō′-) *n.* An abnormal condition caused by excessive intake of fluorides, as in drinking water, characterized chiefly by mottling of the teeth. [New Latin : FLUOR(O)- + -OSIS.]

flu·o·ro·u·ra·cil (flōō′ə-rō-yŏŏr′ə-sĭl, flōōr′ō-) *n.* A drug, $C_4H_3FN_2O_2$, used in the treatment of cancer of the breast and digestive system.

flu·or·spar (flōō′ôr-spär′, flōōr′-) *n.* Fluorite. [FLUOR(O)- + SPAR.]

flur·ry (flûr′ē) *n., pl.* **-ries. 1.** A sudden gust of wind. **2.** A sudden

fluorescent lamp

COMBINING GAS AND ELECTRICITY TO PRODUCE LIGHT
An economical lamp that gives a bright light

A fluorescent lamp contains, at low pressure, a gas—typically neon, sodium vapor, or mercury vapor—that produces light (though not always visible light) when excited by an electric current. In a domestic fluores-cent lamp, a tube is filled with mercury vapor, which emits ultraviolet light when bombarded by electrons. The ultraviolet light is converted into visible light by a coating of phosphors (fluorescent chemicals) on the inside of the tube. The fluorescent lamp is much more efficient than the ordinary tungsten-filament electric light bulb: it gives about four times as much light for the same amount of electricity.

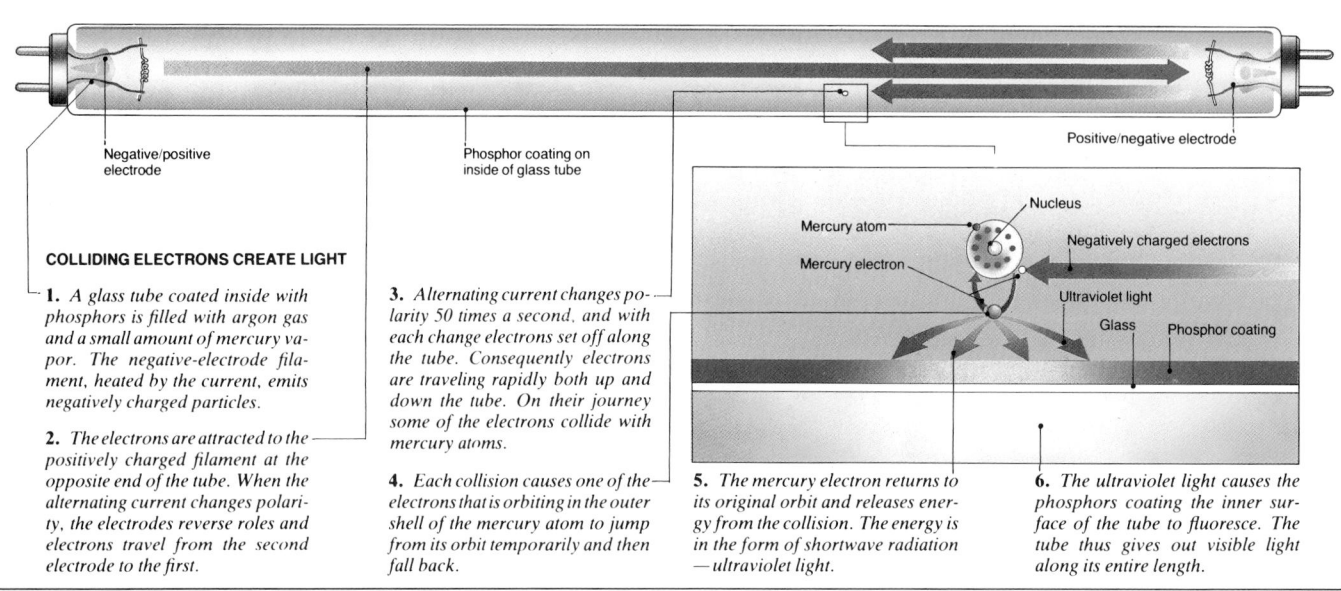

Negative/positive electrode

Phosphor coating on inside of glass tube

Positive/negative electrode

Nucleus

Mercury atom

Negatively charged electrons

Mercury electron

Ultraviolet light

Glass

Phosphor coating

COLLIDING ELECTRONS CREATE LIGHT

1. *A glass tube coated inside with phosphors is filled with argon gas and a small amount of mercury vapor. The negative-electrode filament, heated by the current, emits negatively charged particles.*

2. *The electrons are attracted to the positively charged filament at the opposite end of the tube. When the alternating current changes polarity, the electrodes reverse roles and electrons travel from the second electrode to the first.*

3. *Alternating current changes polarity 50 times a second, and with each change electrons set off along the tube. Consequently electrons are traveling rapidly both up and down the tube. On their journey some of the electrons collide with mercury atoms.*

4. *Each collision causes one of the electrons that is orbiting in the outer shell of the mercury atom to jump from its orbit temporarily and then fall back.*

5. *The mercury electron returns to its original orbit and releases energy from the collision. The energy is in the form of shortwave radiation —ultraviolet light.*

6. *The ultraviolet light causes the phosphors coating the inner surface of the tube to fluoresce. The tube thus gives out visible light along its entire length.*

fluting *Rounded grooves carved in architectural columns, as here at the Temple of Zeus, in Athens, Greece.*

fly *A large and worldwide group of two-winged insects. The larvae of many species of fly feed on decaying plant and animal matter. The adults of some—such as mosquitoes and tsetse flies—are bloodsuckers and can transmit diseases to humans.*

---

burst of confusion, excitement, or bustling activity; a stir. **3.** A light shower of snow or rain.
~*v.* **flurried, -rying, -ries.** —*tr.* To agitate, confuse, or make nervous; fluster. —*intr.* To become agitated or confused. [From obsolete *flurr,* to whirl up, scatter, probably an expressive formation on analogy with HURRY.]
flush¹ (flŭsh) *v.* **flushed, flushing, flushes.** —*intr.* **1.** To turn red in the face from fever, embarrassment, or strong emotion; color; blush. **2.** To flow suddenly and abundantly; spread out quickly; flood. **3.** To glow, especially with a reddish color. **4. a.** To be cleaned by a rapid, brief gush of water. **b.** To function by means of a flushing mechanism. Used of a toilet. —*tr.* **1.** To cause to redden or glow. **2.** To excite or elate, as with a feeling of pride or accomplishment. Usually used in the passive: *flushed with victory.* **3. a.** To wash, empty, or purify with a sudden, rapid flow of water or other liquid. **b.** To remove or dispose of by flushing.
~*n.* **1.** A blush or glow: *a flush of red on a cloud.* **2.** A brief but copious flow or gushing, as of water. **3.** Redness of the skin, as with fever. **4.** A feeling of animation or exhilaration; a rush of emotion. **5.** A freshness, development, or growth.
~*adj.* **flusher, flushest. 1. a.** Having surfaces in the same plane; even; level. **b.** Arranged with adjacent sides, surfaces, or edges touching. **2.** Abundant; plentiful. **3.** *Informal.* Having an abundant supply of money; prosperous; affluent. **4.** Lively; vigorous; lusty. **5.** Having a healthy reddish color; blushing; glowing. **6.** *Printing.* Having the copy lined up evenly at the margins with no indentations. —See Synonyms at **level.**
~*adv.* **1.** So as to be even, in one plane, or aligned with a margin. **2.** Squarely; solidly: *The ball hit him flush on the face.* [Probably from FLUSH (to take flight, dart out).] —**flush·ness** *n.*
flush² *n.* In poker or similar games, a hand in which all the cards are of the same suit, rated above a straight and below a full house. See **royal flush, straight flush.** [Probably from Old French *flus, flux,* from Latin *fluxus,* a flow, FLUX.]
flush³ *v.* **flushed, flushing, flushes.** —*tr.* **1.** To frighten (a game bird, for example) from cover. **2.** To cause to leave a place of concealment. Used with *out: used tear gas to flush out the terrorists.* —*intr.* To dart out or fly from cover; take flight. [Middle English *flusshen,* perhaps from (unattested) Old English *flyscan* (imitative).]
Flush·ing (flŭsh′ĭng) Former village of eastern Long Island, part of Queens, New York City. Flushing Meadow was the site of two world's fairs (1939–40 and 1964–65) and temporary headquarters of the United Nations (1946–49). The U.S. Open tennis tournament has been held here since 1978.
flus·ter (flŭs′tər) *v.* **-tered, -tering, -ters.** —*tr.* To make nervous, confused, or agitated. —*intr.* To become nervous or excited, as from confusion or bewilderment.
~*n.* A state of agitation, confusion, or excitement; flurry; flap. [Middle English *flostren,* possibly from Scandinavian, akin to Icelandic *flaustra,* to bustle.]

flute (flōōt) *n. Abbr.* **fl. 1.** A high-pitched instrument of the woodwind family, tubular in shape and with fingerholes and keys on the side and a reedless mouthpiece either at the end, as in the recorder, or on the side, as in the transverse flute. **2.** An organ stop whose flue pipe produces a flutelike tone. **3.** *Architecture.* Any of the long parallel grooves, usually with rounded inner surfaces, incised on the shaft of a column as a decorative motif. **4.** A groove similar to a flute, as on the leg of a chair.
~*v.* **fluted, fluting, flutes.** —*tr.* **1.** To play (a tune) on a flute. **2.** To sing, whistle, or otherwise produce (a flutelike sound). **3.** To make flutes in (a column or piece of cloth, for example). —*intr.* **1.** To play a flute. **2.** To sing, whistle, or utter with a flutelike sound. [Middle English *floute, floite,* from Old French *flaute, fleute* (probably imitative); the initial consonant cluster was probably influenced by FLAGEOLET and Latin *flāre,* to blow.] —**flut·y** *adj.*
flut·ed (flōō′tĭd) *adj.* **1.** Decorated with parallel grooves, as a column or ruffle. **2.** Having a sound like that of a flute; high-pitched and clear.
flut·er (flōō′tər) *n.* **1. a.** One who makes flutings. **b.** A device used in making flutings. **2.** A flutist.
flut·ing (flōō′tĭng) *n.* **1.** A decorative motif consisting of a series of long, rounded, parallel grooves, such as those incised in the surface of a column. **2.** The grooves formed by narrow pleats in cloth, as in a ruffle.
flut·ist (flōō′tĭst) *n.* One who plays a flute.
flut·ter (flŭt′ər) *v.* **-tered, -tering, -ters.** —*intr.* **1.** To wave or flap lightly and rapidly in an irregular manner: *The curtains fluttered in the breeze.* **2. a.** To fly by a quick, light flapping of the wings. **b.** To flap the wings without flying. **3.** To move or fall in a manner suggestive of tremulous flight: *"Her arms rose, fell, and fluttered with the rhythm of the song"* (Evelyn Waugh). **4.** To vibrate or beat rapidly or erratically: *His heart fluttered wildly.* **5.** To move quickly in a nervous, restless, or excited fashion; flit. **6.** To be excited, flustered, or nervous. —*tr.* **1.** To cause to flutter; wave; flap: *fluttering her eyelashes.* **2.** To make excited or nervous; confuse; fluster.
~*n.* **1.** An act of fluttering; a quick flapping. **2.** A condition of nervous excitement or agitation. **3.** A brief state of excitement, surprise, or bewilderment; commotion; flurry. **4.** *Medicine.* Abnormally rapid beating of the heart. **5.** *Electronics.* A distortion in reproduced sound due to frequency deviations created by faulty recording or reproduction techniques. **6.** *British Informal.* A small bet. [Middle English *floteren,* to flutter, be tossed by waves, Old English *floterian.*] —**flut·ter·er** *n.* —**flut·ter·y** *adj.*
flutter kick *n.* A swimming kick in which the legs are held horizontally and alternately moved up and down in rapid strokes without bending the knees.
flutter tonguing *n.* The technique of vibrating the tongue rapidly to produce a trill-like sound on a wind instrument.
flu·vi·al (flōō′vē-əl) *adj.* **1.** Of, pertaining to, or inhabiting a river or stream. **2.** Formed or produced by the action of flowing water.

[Middle English, from Latin *fluviālis,* from *fluvius,* river, from *fluere,* to flow.]

flu·vi·o·ma·rine (flo͞o′vē-ō-mə-rēn′) *adj. Geology.* Pertaining to deposits formed by the joint action of the sea and a river. [Latin *fluvius,* river, from *fluere,* to flow + MARINE.]

flux (flŭks) *n.* **1. a.** A flow or flowing. **b.** A continued flow or flood. **2.** *Physics.* **a.** The rate of flow across a unit area of a fluid, electromagnetic energy, or particles such as neutrons. **b.** Flux density. **3.** *Medicine.* The discharge of large quantities of fluid material from the body, such as watery feces in diarrhea. **4.** Continuous change: *a state of flux.* **5.** *Chemistry & Metallurgy.* A substance that aids, induces, or otherwise actively participates in a flowing, as: **a.** A mineral added to a furnace charge to promote fusing of metals or to prevent the formation of oxides. **b.** A substance applied in soldering and brazing to portions of a surface to be joined, acting on application of heat to prevent oxide formation and to facilitate the flowing of solder. **c.** Any readily fusible glass or enamel used as a base in ceramic work.
~*v.* **fluxed, fluxing, fluxes.** —*tr.* **1.** To melt; fuse. **2.** To apply a flux to. —*intr.* **1.** To become fluid. **2.** To flow; stream. [Middle English, from Old French, from Latin *fluxus,* from the past participle of *fluere,* to flow.]

flux density *n. Physics.* The strength of a magnetic or electric field or the like per unit area.

flux·ion (flŭk′shən) *n.* **1.** Continual change. **2.** Something that flows; a discharge or issue. **3.** *Mathematics. Archaic.* **a.** A derivative. **b. fluxions.** Differential calculus. [Old French, from Latin *fluxiō* (stem *fluxiōn-*), from *fluxus,* FLUX.] **—flux·ion·al, flux·ion·ar·y** (flŭk′shə-nĕr′ē) *adj.* **—flux·ion·al·ly** *adv.*

fly[1] (flī) *v.* **flew** (flo͞o), **flown** (flōn), **flying, flies.** —*intr.* **1.** To engage in flight, especially: **a.** To move through the air with the aid of wings. **b.** To travel by air. **c.** To pilot an aircraft. **2.** To glide through the air sustained by winglike parts. **3. a.** To rise in the air or be carried through the air by the wind. **b.** To float or flutter in the air. **4.** To be sent or driven through the air with great speed or force. **5. a.** To rush; run. **b.** To flee; escape or try to escape. **c.** To hasten; spring: *He flew to my defense.* **6.** To pass by swiftly, as time or youth might. **7.** To be dissipated rapidly; vanish unaccountably, as money might. **8.** *Past tense and past participle* **flied.** *Baseball.* To hit a fly ball. **9.** To react explosively; burst: *He flew into a rage.* **10.** To shoot forth: *Sparks flew in all directions from the torch.* —*tr.* **1. a.** To cause to fly, hover, or float in the air. **b.** To keep (a flag) aloft. **2. a.** To pilot (an aircraft). **b.** To transport or dispatch in an aircraft. **c.** To pass over in an aircraft: *fly the ocean.* **d.** To travel by air using (a particular airline). **3.** To shun; run away from; flee from. **—fly at.** To attack suddenly, either physically or verbally. **—fly blind.** To fly an aircraft relying wholly on instruments, as in bad visibility. **—fly high. 1.** To be in the clouds; be elated. **2.** To prosper; be successful. **—fly in the face** (or **teeth**) **of.** To resist or defy openly. **—fly off the handle.** To lose control of one's temper. **—fly the coop.** To get away; escape. **—let fly. 1.** To emit, send forth, or direct with force or violence. **2.** To release pent-up feelings of anger. Used with *at.* **—make the fur** (or **feathers**) **fly.** To cause a commotion or upset with an insult or by provoking a fight.
~*n., pl.* **flies. 1.** An overlapping fold of cloth that hides a zipper, buttons, or other fastening, as in a pair of trousers. **2.** A cloth flap that covers an entrance or forms a roof extension for a tent or wagon. **3.** A flyleaf. **4.** A fly ball. **5.** The length of a flag from the staff to the outer edge. **6.** The outer edge of a flag. **7.** A flywheel or similar mechanism. **8.** *Printing.* A person or device that carries the printed sheets from the press and places them in a flat pile. **9. flies.** The area directly over the stage of a theater and behind the proscenium, containing the overhead lights, drop curtains, and equipment for raising and lowering sets. **10.** *British.* A one-horse carriage, formerly hired out. **—on the fly.** In flight; on the run; in a hurry. [Fly, flew, flown; Middle English *flien, flew, flowen,* Old English *flēogan, flēah* (plural *flugon*), *flogen,* from Germanic.]

fly[2] *n., pl.* **flies. 1.** Any of numerous two-winged insects of the order Diptera; especially, any of the family Muscidae, which includes the **housefly** *(see).* **2.** Any of various other flying insects, such as the caddis fly. **3.** A fishing lure simulating a fly. **—fly in the ointment.** *Informal.* Something that detracts from the pleasure, value, or effectiveness of something; a jarring or negative factor. [Biblical allusion: "Dead flies cause the ointment of the apothecary to send forth a stinking savor. . ." (Ecclesiastes 10:1).] **—fly on the wall.** One who is in a position to observe others while not being seen himself. [Middle English *flie,* Old English *flēoge,* from Germanic.]

fly[3] *adj. British Informal.* Alert; clever; sharp. [Probably from FLY (to go swiftly).]

fly agaric *n.* A poisonous mushroom, *Amanita muscaria,* usually having a red or orange cap with white patches. Also called "fly amanita." [From its use as a fly poison.]

fly ash *n.* Fine ash carried into the air during combustion.

fly·a·way (flī′ə-wā′) *adj.* **1.** Blown or appearing to be blown by the wind; fluttering or streaming. **2.** Flighty; frivolous; giddy.
~*n.* One that is restless, flighty, or elusive.

fly ball *n. Baseball.* A ball that is batted in a high arc, usually to the outfield.

fly·blow (flī′blō′) *n.* The egg or larva of a blowfly, usually deposited on food.
~*tr.v.* **flyblew** (-blo͞o′), **-blown** (-blōn′), **-blowing, -blows. 1.** To deposit (the eggs of a blowfly) in. **2.** To taint; contaminate.

fly·blown (flī′blōn′) *adj.* **1.** Contaminated with flyblows. **2. a.** Spoiled; tainted; corrupt. **b.** Seedy; shabby.

fly book *n.* A case in which artificial flies for fishing are carried.

fly·boy (flī′boi′) *n. Slang.* An air force pilot.

fly·by (flī′bī′) *n., pl.* **-bys.** A flight passing close to a specific target or position; especially, a maneuver in which a spacecraft passes sufficiently close to a planet to make relatively detailed observations without landing.

fly-by-night (flī′bī-nīt′) *adj. Informal.* **1.** Unreliable with regard to business dealings; shady. **2.** Dubious and temporary.
~*n.* **1.** One who cheats his creditors, as by absconding in the night. **2.** Something of a dubiously transitory nature.

fly·catch·er (flī′kăch′ər) *n.* **1.** Any of various birds of the Old World family Muscicapidae that feed on insects, usually catching them in flight. **2.** Any similar bird of the American family Tyrannidae. In this sense, also called "tyrant flycatcher."

fly-drive (flī′drīv′) *n.* An organized vacation providing air travel to a destination and a rented car on arrival. **—fly-drive** *adj. & adv.*

flyer. Variant of **flier.**

fly-fishing (flī′fĭsh′ĭng) *n.* Angling using artificial flies for bait. **—fly-fish** *v.* **—fly-fish·er** *n.* **—fly-fish·er·man** *n.*

fly front *n.* A garment front that has a fly concealing the fastenings.

fly·ing (flī′ĭng) *adj.* **1.** Moving through the air with or as if with wings. **2.** Brief; hurried: *a flying visit.* **3.** Concerned with or used in aviation: *a flying jacket.* **4.** *Nautical.* Not secured by spars or stays. Said of sails.
~*n.* **1.** Flight in an aircraft. **2.** The piloting of an aircraft.

flying boat *n.* A large seaplane that is kept afloat by its hull rather than by pontoons.

flying bomb *n.* A **robot bomb** *(see).*

flying buttress *n. Architecture.* An arched masonry prop that springs from a pier or other support and abuts against another part of the structure to receive thrust. Also called "arc-boutant."

flying circus *n.* **1.** A squadron of fighter planes in World War I. **2.** An exhibition of stunt flying; an aerobatics display. **3.** The aircraft and team of men involved in such an exhibition.

flying colors *pl.n..* Triumph; outstanding success: *pass an exam with flying colors.*

flying dragon *n.* The flying lizard.

Flying Dutchman *n.* **1.** A legendary mariner condemned to sail the seas against the wind until Judgment Day. **2.** His spectral ship, said to appear in storms near the Cape of Good Hope.

flying field *n.* An airfield.

flying fish *n.* Any of various marine fishes of the family Exocoetidae, having enlarged pectoral or pelvic fins capable of sustaining them in brief, gliding flight over the water.

flying fox *n.* **1.** Any of various fruit bats of the genus *Pteropus,* chiefly of tropical Africa, Asia, and Australia, having a foxlike muzzle and ears. **2.** Any of several similar or related mammals.

flying frog *n.* A tree-dwelling frog, *Rhacophorus reinwardtii,* of southeastern Asia, having toes connected by broad webbing and capable of gliding considerable distances.

flying gurnard *n.* Any of various chiefly tropical marine fishes of the family Dactylopteridae, having winglike, much enlarged pectoral fins, and capable of gliding flight over the water.

flying jib *n. Nautical.* A light sail that extends beyond the jib and is attached to an extension of the jib boom.

flying lemur *n.* Either of two mammals, *Cynocephalus volans* or *C. variegatus,* of tropical Asia, that are sustained in gliding leaps by a wide, fur-covered membrane extending from each side of the body. Also called "gliding lemur," "colugo."

flying lizard *n.* Any of various small tropical Asian lizards of the genus *Draco,* capable of gliding by spreading the winglike membranes on each side of the body. Also called "flying dragon."

flying machine *n.* A machine designed for flight; especially, any of the early experimental types of aircraft.

flying mare *n.* In wrestling, a throw in which one grabs the opponent's wrist or head, turns around quickly, and flips him over one's shoulder onto the ground.

flying officer *n. Abbr.* **F.O.** An officer in the British and certain other air forces ranking between a flight lieutenant and a pilot officer and equivalent in rank to a lieutenant in the army and a sublieutenant in the navy.

flying phalanger *n.* Any of several small marsupials of the family Phalangeridae, especially one of the genus *Petaurus,* of Australia, New Guinea, and Tasmania, capable of gliding through the air sustained by large folds of skin between the forelegs and hind legs. Also called "gliding possum."

flying saucer *n.* Any of various unidentified flying objects typically described as luminous disks and alleged to have come from outer space.

flying snake *n.* A tree-dwelling snake of the genus *Chrysopelea,* of southern Asia and the East Indies, that can glide for short distances by flattening its belly scales.

flying squad *n. Chiefly British.* A small mobile group, especially of policemen equipped with motor vehicles, capable of moving very swiftly into action when summoned or alerted.

flying squirrel *n.* Any of various nocturnal squirrels of the genera *Pteromys, Glaucomys,* and related genera, having membranes between the forelegs and hind legs that enable them to glide.

flying start *n.* **1.** The crossing of the starting line of a race at full speed. **2.** Any quick or promising start. **3.** An advantage over one's rivals at the outset.

flying wing *n.* **1.** An aircraft in which a single large streamlined

fly agaric *This poisonous Northern Hemisphere fungus, with its white-speckled red cap, is found in damp woods from August to November.*

flycatcher *The spotted flycatcher,* Muscicapa striata *(above), breeds in summer mostly in Europe and parts of Asia, but it spends the northern winter in tropical and southern Africa. It feeds almost exclusively on insects, especially flies, which it catches on the wing.*

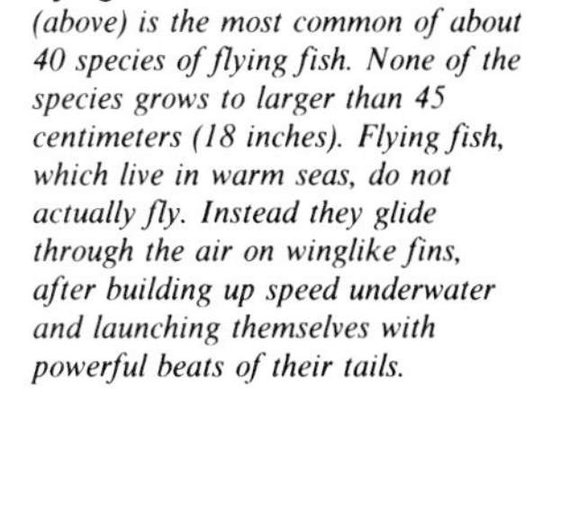

flying fish Exocoetus volitans *(above) is the most common of about 40 species of flying fish. None of the species grows to larger than 45 centimeters (18 inches). Flying fish, which live in warm seas, do not actually fly. Instead they glide through the air on winglike fins, after building up speed underwater and launching themselves with powerful beats of their tails.*

fly-tying

MAKING AN IMITATION TO DECEIVE A FISH
To many fishermen fly-tying is part of the art of fishing

Fly-fishermen use artificial flies to imitate any one of thousands of insects that might tempt a trout to feed. Lacy-winged flies, of which the mayfly is one of the best known, and caddis (or sedge) flies are the insects most usually imitated.

As any insect grows to maturity through various stages, and male and female often vary, the number of possible imitations runs to hundreds of thousands. In addition, the factors that tempt fish to feed change with place and time of year.

Imitation flies are made from fur, feathers, tinsel, raffia, and any other material that will help them to resemble natural flies. Many fishermen consider tying their own flies successfully to be part of the art of fishing. In dry-fly fishing the fly rests on the water to tempt, for example, feeding trout. The wet fly is made to imitate an insect in its subaquatic stage and is allowed to sink.

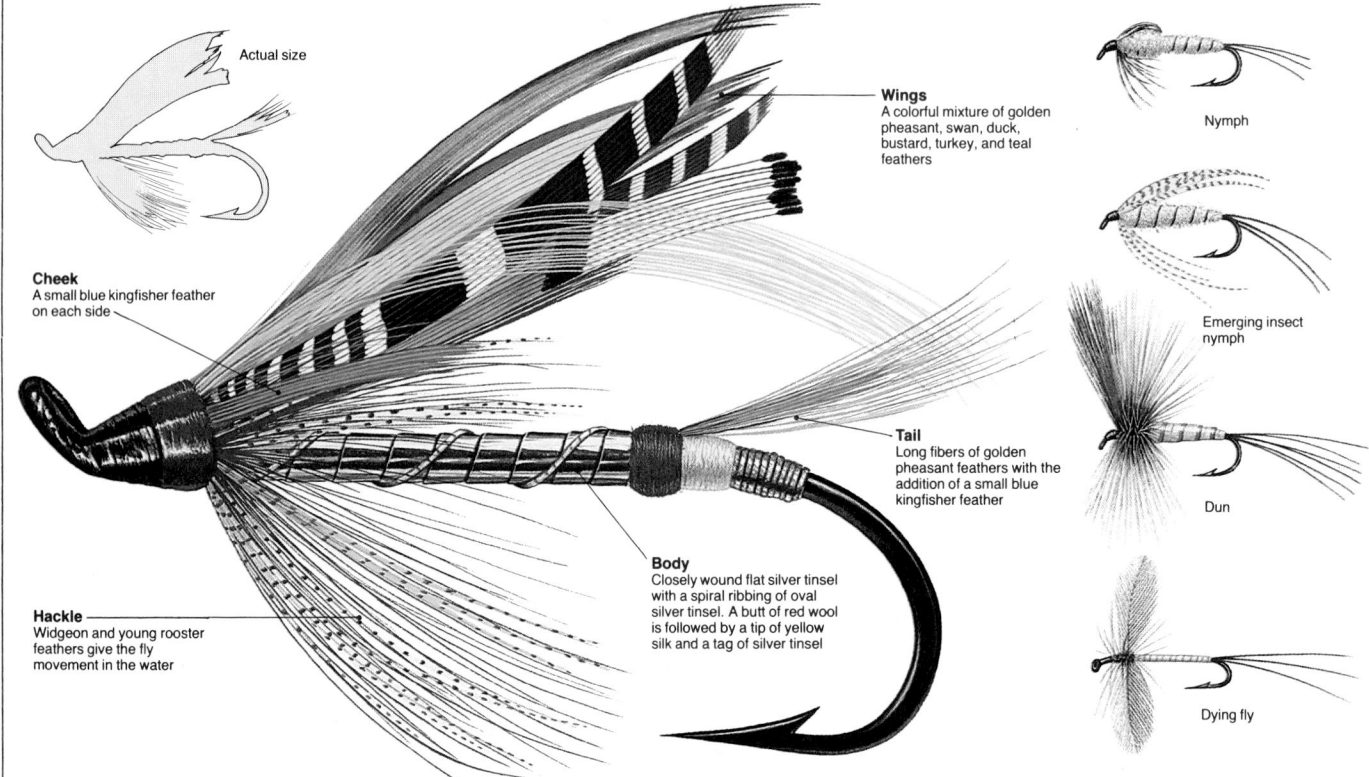

Actual size

Wings A colorful mixture of golden pheasant, swan, duck, bustard, turkey, and teal feathers

Cheek A small blue kingfisher feather on each side

Tail Long fibers of golden pheasant feathers with the addition of a small blue kingfisher feather

Body Closely wound flat silver tinsel with a spiral ribbing of oval silver tinsel is followed by a tip of yellow silk and a tag of silver tinsel

Hackle Widgeon and young rooster feathers give the fly movement in the water

Nymph

Emerging insect nymph

Dun

Dying fly

SALMON FLY *The Silver Wilkinson is a popular salmon fly that bears no resemblance to any real insect. Because salmon do not feed on their way upriver to spawn, salmon flies are made to excite the fishes' attention and provoke them to attack. Trout flies are intended to be realistic imitations.*

LIFE CYCLE *The mayfly egg, laid on the surface, sinks to the bed and becomes a larva (nymph). The nymph surfaces for the winged dun to emerge.*

wing incorporating the fuselage constitutes the principal portion of the airframe. **2.** In Canadian football, a backfield man who moves to various positions behind the line of scrimmage.

fly·leaf (flī′lēf′) *n., pl.* **-leaves** (-lēvz′). A blank leaf at the beginning or end of a book, between the lining paper and the first or last signature. See **endpaper.**

fly net *n.* A net covering used to keep flies off or out.

Flynn (flĭn), **Errol** (1909–59). Australian-born actor, noted for his swashbuckling roles in such films as *Captain Blood* (1935), *The Adventures of Robin Hood* (1938), and *Too Much Too Soon* (1958).

fly·o·ver (flī′ō′vər) *n.* **1.** A flight of aircraft at low altitude over a particular area, usually as a military or ceremonial display. **2.** *British.* An overpass on a highway.

fly·pa·per (flī′pā′pər) *n.* A ribbon of paper coated with a sticky, sometimes poisonous substance used to catch flies.

fly·past (flī′pǎst′, -päst′) *n. British.* A flyover (sense 1).

fly·poi·son (flī′poi′zən) *n.* A poisonous plant, *Amianthium muscaetoxicum,* of the southeastern United States, having narrow basal leaves and a terminal cluster of small white or greenish leaves.

fly·speck (flī′spěk′) *n.* **1.** A small, dark speck or stain made by the excrement of a fly. **2.** A minute spot. —*tr.v.* **flyspecked, -specking, -specks.** To mark or befoul with flyspecks.

fly swatter *n.* A swatter used to kill flies or other insects.

fly·trap (flī′trǎp′) *n.* **1.** A trap for catching flies. **2.** A plant, as the Venus's-flytrap, that traps insects.

fly·ty·ing (flī′tī′ĭng) *n.* The art or hobby of making artificial fishing flies out of materials such as colored feathers or tinsel.

fly·weight (flī′wāt′) *n.* **1.** In professional boxing, a boxer of the lightest weight class, weighing 112 pounds (51 kilograms) or less. **2.** In amateur boxing, a boxer weighing 48 to 51 kilograms (106 to 112 pounds).

fly·wheel (flī′hwēl′) *n.* A heavy rotating wheel used to minimize speed variation in a machine subject to fluctuation in drive and load.

fm, FM frequency modulation.

Fm The symbol for the element fermium.

fm. fathom.

F.M. field marshal.

FMN (ěf′ěm-ěn′) *n.* A derivative of riboflavin that functions, as FAD does, as a coenzyme in many oxidation-reduction reactions. [*F*lavin *m*ono*n*ucleotide.]

fn. footnote.

f-num·ber (ěf′nŭm′bər) *n.* The ratio of focal length to the effective aperture diameter in a lens or lens system. Also called "f-stop." [*F*, symbol for *focal length.*]

F.O. 1. field officer. **2.** flying officer. **3.** Foreign Office.

foal (fōl) *n.* The young offspring of a horse or other equine animal, especially when under a year old. —*v.* **foaled, foaling, foals.** —*tr.* To give birth to (a foal). —*intr.* To give birth to a foal. [Middle English *fole,* Old English *fola,* from Germanic.]

foam (fōm) *n.* **1.** A mass of gas bubbles; especially, a light, bubbly gas and liquid mass formed by agitating a liquid containing certain soaps or detergents. **2. a.** Frothy saliva from the mouth. **b.** The frothy sweat of a horse or other equine animal. **3.** *Poetic.* The sea. **4.** Any of various light, bulky materials used as thermal or mechanical insulators in packaging, furniture, and the like, made by injecting a gas into a material such as latex or polystyrene. Also used adjectively: *foam plastic.* **5.** Any of various chemical substances used in fire extinguishers. —*v.* **foamed, foaming, foams.** —*intr.* **1.** To produce or come forth in foam; froth. **2.** *Informal.* To be extremely angry. —*tr.* To cause to foam. [Middle English *fom,* saliva, foam, Old English *fām.*] —**foam·ing·ly** *adv.*

foam rubber *n.* A light, firm, spongy rubber made by beating air into latex with subsequent curing and used as an upholstery material and insulating medium.

foam·y (fō′mē) *adj.* **-ier, -iest. 1.** Pertaining to or resembling foam. **2.** Consisting of or covered with foam. —**foam·i·ly** *adv.* —**foam·i·ness** *n.*

fob¹ (fŏb) *n.* **1.** A small pocket at the front waistline of a man's trousers or in the front of a vest, used to hold a watch or coins. **2.** A short chain or ribbon attached to a pocket watch and worn hanging in front of the vest or waist. **3.** An ornament or seal attached to a watch chain. [17th century (originally cant): probably akin to German (dialectal) *Fuppe*†, pocket.]

fob[2] *tr.v.* **fobbed, fobbing, fobs. 1.** To put off or appease by deceitful or evasive means. Used with *off.* **2.** To dispose of (goods) by fraud or deception; palm off. Used with *off.* **3.** *Archaic.* To deceive; cheat. [Middle English *fobben*†.]

f.o.b., F.O.B. free on board.

fo·cal (fō'kəl) *adj.* **1.** Of or pertaining to a focus. **2.** Placed at or measured from the focus. **—fo·cal·ly** *adv.*

focal infection *n.* An infection localized in a specific part of the body.

fo·cal·ize (fō'kə-līz') *v.* **-ized, -izing, -izes.** *—tr.* To adjust or bring to a focus. *—intr.* To come or be brought to a focus. **—fo·cal·i·za·tion** *n.*

focal length *n. Physics.* The distance of the focal point from the surface of a mirror or from the center of a lens. Also called "focal distance," "focus."

focal plane *n.* A plane in which the image from a lens, mirror, or optical instrument is in focus.

focal point *n.* **1.** A point on the axis of symmetry of an optical system, as of a mirror or lens, to which parallel incident rays converge or from which they appear to diverge after reflection or transmission. Also called "principal focus." **2.** A center of activity or interest; a focus.

Foch (fôsh, fŏsh), **Ferdinand** (1851–1929). French marshal who in World War I was largely responsible for halting the German advance at the Marne (1914) and for the Allied victory at Ypres (1915). In 1918, as Allied commander, he launched the July advance that pushed the Germans back to the Rhine and ended the war.

fo'c's'le. Variant of **forecastle.**

fo·cus (fō'kəs) *n., pl.* **-cuses** or **-ci** (-sī'). **1.** A point at which something converges or from which something diverges. **2.** *Physics.* **a.** A point in an optical system to which rays converge or from which they appear to diverge; a focal point. **b.** Focal length. **c.** The distinctness or clarity with which an optical system renders an image. **d.** Adjustment for distinctness or clarity. **3.** Something, as a place, person, or issue, on which attention converges or around which activity centers. **4.** A condition in which something can be clearly perceived: *couldn't get the problem into focus.* **5.** *Pathology.* The region of a localized bodily infection. **6.** *Geology.* The point of origin of an earthquake. **7.** *Geometry.* A point that together with a directrix determines a conic section. **—in focus.** Sharply or clearly defined; distinct. **—out of focus.** Not distinct; blurred or cloudy.
~*v.* **focused** or **focussed, -cusing** or **-cussing, -cuses** or **-cusses.** *—tr.* **1. a.** To produce a clear image of (photographed material, for example) by adjustment of a projection lens or other optical equipment. **b.** To adjust the setting of (a lens, for example) to produce a clear image. **2.** To direct (attention or effort, for example) toward a particular point or purpose. *—intr.* **1.** To converge at a point of focus; be focused. **2.** To bring objects into focus. [Latin *focus,* fireplace, hearth (the center of the home).]

fod·der (fŏd'ər) *n.* **1.** Feed for livestock, especially hay, straw, and other plants. **2.** Raw material, as for artistic creation. **3.** People viewed as raw material for the achievement of a specified commercial, political, or military end: *cannon fodder.*
~*tr.v.* **foddered, -dering, -ders.** To feed (animals) with fodder. [Middle English *fodder,* Old English *fōdor,* from Germanic.]

foe (fō) *n.* **1.** A personal enemy: *tried to win over his political foes.* **2.** An enemy in war. **3.** An adversary; opponent: *My representative in Congress is a foe of tax reform.* **4.** Something that serves to oppose, injure, or impede. [Middle English *fo,* Old English *gefā,* from *gefāh,* at feud with, hostile, from Germanic.]

foehn. Variant of **föhn.**

foe·man (fō'mən) *n., pl.* **-men** (-mĭn). A foe in battle; enemy.

foetal. Variant of **fetal.**

foetid. Variant of **fetid.**

foetor. Variant of **fetor.**

foetus. Variant of **fetus.**

fog[1] (fôg, fŏg) *n.* **1.** Condensed water vapor droplets with particles of dust and smoke in suspension, occurring in cloudlike masses close to the ground and limiting visibility to less than one kilometer (0.6 mile). **2.** Any mass of floating material, such as dust or smoke, that forms an obscuring haze. **3.** A state of bewilderment. **4.** In photography, a dark blur on a developed negative.
~*v.* **fogged, fogging, fogs.** *—tr.* **1.** To cover or envelop with fog. **2.** To cause to be clouded or obscured; blur. **3.** To make uncertain or unclear; bewilder. **4.** In photography, to obscure or dim (a negative) with a dark blur. *—intr.* **1.** To be covered or enveloped with fog. Often used with *up* or *over.* **2.** To be blurred or obscured. **3.** In photography, to be dimmed or obscured with a dark blur. Used of a print or negative. [Perhaps a back-formation from earlier *foggy,* murky, moist, boggy, from FOG (rank grass).]

fog[2] *n.* **1.** A second growth of grass on a field that has been mowed or grazed. **2.** Tall, thick grass left standing after cutting or grazing. [Middle English *fogge, fog,* perhaps from Scandinavian.]

fog bank *n.* An opaque mass of fog sharply defined in contrast to surrounding, clearer air; especially, such a fog occurring at sea.

fog·bound (fôg'bound', fŏg'-) *adj.* **1.** Immobilized by heavy fog. **2.** Clouded or obscured by fog.

fog·bow (fôg'bō', fŏg'-) *n.* A faint white or yellowish arc-shaped light, similar to a rainbow, often seen opposite the sun in a fog bank. Also called "seadog."

fog·dog (fôg'dôg', fŏg'dŏg') *n.* A bright spot in a fog bank.

fog·gy (fô'gē, fŏg'ē) *adj.* **-gier, -giest. 1.** Full of, surrounded by, or suggestive of fog. **2.** Clouded, obscured, or blurred by or as if by fog. **3.** In photography, obscured or dimmed by a fog or dark blur. **—fog·gi·ly** *adv.* **—fog·gi·ness** *n.*

fog·horn (fôg'hôrn', fŏg'-) *n.* **1.** A horn used by ships and coastal installations to sound warning signals, typically of long, deep tones, in fog or darkness. **2.** A loud, booming voice.

fo·gy (fō'gē) *n., pl.* **-gies.** Also **fo·gey** *pl.* **-geys.** A person of old-fashioned habits and outmoded attitudes: *an old fogy.* [Origin obscure.] **—fo·gy·ish** *adj.*

föhn, foehn (fœn, fān) *n.* A warm dry wind coming off the leeward side of a mountain range, especially off the northern slopes of the Alps. [German, from Old High German *phōnno,* from Latin *Favōnius*†, the west wind. See **favonian.**]

foi·ble (foi'bəl) *n.* **1.** A minor weakness or failing of character; a small personal fault. **2.** The weaker section of a sword blade, from the middle to the tip. In this sense, compare **forte.** —See Synonyms at **fault.** [Obsolete French, variant of *faible,* weak, FEEBLE.]

foie gras (fwä' grä') *n.* **Pâté de foie gras** *(see).*

foil[1] (foil) *tr.v.* **foiled, foiling, foils. 1.** To prevent from being successful; thwart. **2.** To obscure or confuse (a trail or scent) so as to evade pursuers. —See Synonyms at **frustrate.**
~*n.* **1.** *Archaic.* A foiling; a repulse; setback. **2.** The trail or scent of a hunted animal, especially one that confuses its pursuer. [Originally to trample, tread upon, Middle English *foilen,* perhaps from Norman French *fuler* (unattested), variant of Old French *fouler,* to FULL (cloth).]

foil[2] *n.* **1.** A thin, flexible leaf or sheet of a metal. **2.** A thin layer of bright metal placed under a displayed gem or piece of jewelry to lend it brilliance. **3.** A person or thing that by strong contrast underlines or enhances the distinctive characteristics of another. **4.** The metal coating applied to the back of a plate of glass to form a mirror. **5.** *Architecture.* A leaflike design or space worked in stone or glass, found especially in Gothic window tracery. **6.** An **airfoil** *(see).* **7.** A **hydrofoil** *(see).* **8. Aluminum foil** *(see).*
~*tr.v.* **foiled, foiling, foils. 1.** To back or cover with a thin, pliant sheet of metal. **2.** To serve as a foil to; set off by contrast. **3.** *Architecture.* To ornament (windows or walls) with foils. [Middle English *foil(le), foile,* thin sheet of metal, leaf, from Old French, from Latin *folium.*]

foil[3] *n.* **1.** A fencing sword with a flat guard for the hand and a thin blade with a blunt point to prevent injury. **2.** *Often* **foils.** The art or act of fencing with foils. [Origin unknown.]

foils·man (foilz'mən) *n., pl.* **-men** (-mĭn). One who fences with a foil; fencer.

foin (foin) *intr.v.* **foined, foining, foins.** *Archaic.* To thrust with a pointed weapon.
~*n.* *Archaic.* A lunge or thrust with a pointed weapon. [Middle English *foinen,* from *foin,* a thrust, a three-pronged fork for spearing fish, from Old French *foin, foisne,* from Latin *fuscina*†, trident.]

Fo·ism (fō'ĭz'əm) *n.* Chinese Buddhism. [Mandarin Chinese *fó,* Buddha, from Sanskrit *Buddha,* BUDDHA.] **—Fo·ist** *n. & adj.*

foi·son (foi'zən) *n. Archaic.* **1.** A plentiful harvest; a good crop. **2.** Abundance; plenty. [Middle English *foisoun,* from Old French *foison,* power, abundance, from Vulgar Latin *fusiō* (unattested), from Latin *fūsiō* (stem *fūsiōn-*), an outpouring, effusion, from *fūsus,* past participle of *fundere,* to pour.]

foist (foist) *tr.v.* **foisted, foisting, foists. 1.** To pass off as genuine, valuable, or worthy; palm off. **2.** To impose (someone or something unwanted) upon another by coercion or trickery. **3.** To insert fraudulently or deceitfully. [Original sense, to introduce a palmed dice surreptitiously, from Dutch (dialectal) *vuisten,* from *vuist,* fist.]

Fo·kine (fō-kēn'), **Michel** (1880–1942). Russian dancer and choreographer. Working with Diaghilev's Ballets Russes in Paris from 1909, he was partly responsible for revitalizing the ballet through his choreography for such revolutionary works as Stravinsky's *Firebird* (1910) and *Petruskha* (1912). After 1923 he worked in the United States.

Fok·ker (fŏk'ər), **Anthony Hermann Gerard** (1890–1939). Dutch aircraft engineer. In 1912 he opened an aircraft factory in Germany that supplied the Germans with some of the most advanced planes of World War I. He revolutionized aerial warfare in 1915 by synchronizing a machine gun to fire through the propeller of a plane.

fol. folio.

fo·late (fō'lāt') *n.* **Folic acid** *(see).* [FOL(IC ACID) + -ATE.]

fold[1] (fōld) *v.* **folded, folding, folds.** *—tr.* **1.** To bend over or double up so that one part lies on another part: *fold a newspaper.* **2.** To make compact by successively bending over parts. Sometimes used with *up.* **3.** To bring from an extended to a closed position: *On alighting, the hawk folded its wings.* **4.** To place together and intertwine: *fold one's arms.* **5.** To bend, clasp, or entwine. **6.** To surround with the arms; enfold; embrace. **7.** To wrap; envelop. **8.** In cooking, to mix in (an ingredient) by slowly and gently turning one part over another. **9.** *Geology.* To form (rock) into folds. *—intr.* **1.** To become folded or be capable of being folded: *a folding bed.* **2.** *Informal.* To close for lack of funds; fail financially. **3.** *Informal.* To weaken or collapse, as from exertion or laughter. Usually used with *up.* **4.** *Geology.* To form folds. Used of stratified rocks.
~*n.* **1.** The act or an instance of folding. **2.** A part or section that has been folded over another. **3.** The space or hollow at the junc-

PRONUNCIATION KEY

ă, pat; ā, pay; âr, care;
ä, father, are; b, bib;
ch, church; d, deed; ĕ, pet;
ē, be; f, fife; g, gag; h, hat;
hw, which; ĭ, pit; ī, pie;
îr, pier; j, judge; k, kick;
l, lid, needle; m, mum;
n, no, sudden; ng, thing;
ŏ, pot; ō, toe; ô, paw, for;
oi, noise; ou, out; o͝o, book;
o͞o, boot; p, pop; r, roar;
s, sauce; sh, ship, dish;
t, tight; th, thin, path;
th, this, bathe; ŭ, cut; ûr, fur;
v, valve; w, with; y, yes;
z, zebra, size; zh, vision;
ə, about, item, edible,
gallop, circus, peaceful

IN FOREIGN WORDS:

à, *Fr.* ami; œ, *Fr.* feu, *Ger.* schön; ü, *Fr.* tu, *Ger.* über;
KH, *Ger.* ich, *Scot.* loch;
N, *Fr.* bon; y', *Fr.* Compiègne

STRESS MARKS:

Primary stress: '
in·cite' (ĭn-sīt')
Secondary stress: '
in'sight' (ĭn'sīt')

tion of two folded parts. **4.** A hollow or dale in hilly country. **5.** *Geology.* A bend in rock strata. **6.** A coil, as of rope or a snake. **7.** *Anatomy.* A crease apparently formed by folding, as of a membrane; a plica. [Middle English *folden, falden,* Old English *faldan, fealdan,* from Germanic.]

fold² *n.* **1.** A fenced enclosure for domestic animals, especially sheep. **2.** The sheep enclosed in such a pen. **3.** A flock of sheep. **4.** Any group of people bound together by common beliefs and aims, or by mutual loyalty; especially, the members of a church. ~*tr.v.* **folded, folding, folds.** To place or keep (sheep) in a fold. [Middle English *fold,* Old English *fald, falod,* akin to Middle Low German *valt*†.]

-fold *suffix.* Indicates: **1.** Division into a specified number of parts; for example, *fivefold.* **2.** Multiplication by a specified number; for example, *fiftyfold.* [Middle English, from Old English *-f(e)ald.*]

fold·a·way (fōld'ə-wā') *adj.* Designating a piece of furniture, especially a bed, that can be folded up when not in use.

fold·boat (fōld'bōt') *n.* A **faltboat** *(see).* [Translation of German *Faltboot.*]

fold·er (fōl'dər) *n.* **1.** One that folds. **2.** A sheet of cardboard or thick paper folded in the center and used as a holder for loose paper. **3.** A folded sheet of printed matter.

fol·de·rol (fŏl'də-rŏl') *n.* Also **fal·de·ral** (făl'də-răl'), **fal·de·rol** (făl'də-rŏl'). **1.** Foolish talk or procedure; nonsense. **2.** A worthless trifle; gewgaw. [From *fol-de-rol* and *fal-deral,* a meaningless refrain in some old songs.]

fold-out (fōld'out') *n. Printing.* A **gatefold** *(see).*

fo·li·a. Plural of **folium.**

fo·li·a·ceous (fō'lē-ā'shəs) *adj.* **1.** Of, relating to, or resembling the leaf of a plant. **2.** Having leaves or leaflike structures. **3.** Consisting of thin laminated layers, as do certain rocks. [Latin *foliāceus,* from *folium,* leaf, FOLIUM.]

fo·li·age (fō'lē-ĭj) *n.* **1.** The leaves of growing plants; plant leaves collectively. **2.** An ornamental representation of leaves, branches, or flowers. [Middle English *foilage,* from Old French *feuillage, foillage,* from *feuille, foille,* leaf, from Latin *folium.*] —**fo·li·aged** *adj.*

foliage plant *n.* A plant cultivated chiefly for its ornamental leaves.

fo·li·ar (fō'lē-ər) *adj.* Of or pertaining to a leaf or leaves. [French *foliaire,* from Latin *folium,* leaf, FOLIUM.]

fo·li·ate (fō'lē-ĭt, -āt') *adj.* **1.** Of or pertaining to leaves. **2.** Shaped like a leaf. **3.** Having a specified number or kind of leaves or layers. Used in combination: *trifoliate; perfoliate.*
~*v.* (fō'lē-āt') **foliated, -ating, -ates.** —*tr.* **1.** To hammer or cut (metal) into thin plates, leaf, or foil. **2. a.** To coat (glass) with metal foil. **b.** To furnish or adorn with metal foil. **3.** *Architecture.* To decorate (an arch, for example) with foils. **4.** To number the leaves of (a book). In this sense, compare **paginate.** —*intr.* **1.** To produce foliage; put forth leaves. **2.** To become split into thin layers. [Latin *foliātus,* bearing leaves, from *folium,* leaf, FOLIUM.]

fo·li·a·tion (fō'lē-ā'shən) *n.* **1.** *Botany.* The state of being in leaf or putting forth leaves. **2.** Decoration with foliage. **3.** *Architecture.* The decoration of an archway, window, or other opening with cusps and foils, as in Gothic tracery. **4. a.** The act or process of foliating metal. **b.** The foliating of glass. **5.** The process of numbering consecutively the leaves of a book. [Latin *folium,* leaf, FOLIUM.]

fo·lic acid (fō'lĭk) *n.* A yellowish-orange compound, $C_{19}H_{19}N_7O_6$, a member of the vitamin B complex, occurring in green plants, fresh fruit, liver, and yeast, and used medicinally to treat pernicious anemia. Also called "folate," "vitamin B_c." [Latin *fol(ium),* leaf, FOLIUM + -IC.]

fo·lie à deux (fō-lē' ä dœ', fŏl'ē) *n.* The simultaneous presence of symptoms of mental illness in two closely attached people, usually a married couple or siblings. [French, "madness of two."]

fo·li·ic·o·lous (fō'lē-ĭk'ə-ləs) *adj.* Thriving on or parasitic to leaves. [Latin *folium,* leaf + -COLOUS.]

fo li·o (fō'lē-ō') *n., pl.* **-os.** *Abbr.* **f., F., fol. 1.** A large sheet of paper folded once in the middle, making two leaves or four pages of a book or manuscript. **2. a.** The largest common size of book or manuscript, usually about 38 centimeters (15 inches) in height and made up of such folded sheets. **b.** A book or manuscript of this size. **3.** A leaf of a book numbered only on the front side. **4.** A page number in a book; especially, one assigned to a page during the printing process. **5.** *Accounting.* A page in a ledger or two facing pages assigned a single number. **6.** *Law.* A specific number of words used as a unit for measuring the length of the text of a document.
~*adj.* **1.** Of or pertaining to a folio: *folio pages.* **2.** Presented in the form of a folio: *a folio edition.*
~*tr.v.* **folioed, -oing, -os.** To number consecutively the pages of (a book). [Medieval Latin, ablative (used for page references, "at leaf *x*") of Latin *folium,* leaf, FOLIUM.]

fo·li·o·late (fō'lē-ə-lāt') *adj. Botany.* Having or consisting of leaflets. Usually used in combination: *bifoliolate.* [From earlier *foliole,* leaflet, from French, from New Latin *foliolum,* diminutive of Latin *folium,* leaf, FOLIUM.]

fo·li·ose (fō'lē-ōs') *adj.* **1.** *Botany.* Bearing numerous leaves or leaflets; leafy. **2.** Of, pertaining to, or resembling a leaf or leaves. [Latin *foliōsus,* from *folium,* leaf, FOLIUM.]

fo·li·ot (fō'lē-ət) *n.* A clock escapement of the earliest type, consisting of a bar adjusted by weights placed along its length. [French, from Old French, probably from *folier,* to play the fool, from *fol,* foolish. See **fool.**]

fo·li·um (fō'lē-əm) *n., pl.* **-lia** (-lē-ə). **1.** *Geology.* A thin layer or stratum occurring especially in metamorphic rock. **2.** *Geometry.* A plane cubic curve having a single loop, a node, and two ends asymptotic to the same line. In this sense, also called "folium of Descartes." [New Latin, from Latin, leaf.]

folk (fōk) *n., pl.* **folk** or **folks. 1.** *Often* **folks.** People of a specified group or kind: *city folk.* **2. folks.** *Informal.* **a.** The members of one's family or childhood household; one's relatives. **b.** One's parents. **3. folks.** *Informal.* People in general: *Folks will talk.* **4.** An ethnic group; a people or race. **5.** *Informal.* Folk music.
~*adj.* Of, occurring in, or originating among the common people; especially, untutored or unrefined: *folk painting.* [Middle English *folk,* Old English *folc,* the people, nation, tribe, from Germanic *folkam* (unattested).]

folk dance *n.* **1.** A traditional dance originating among the rural areas of a nation or region. **2.** The music accompanying such a dance. **3.** A social gathering at which such dances are performed. —**folk dancing** *n.*

Folke·stone (fōk'stən). Residential town and resort in Kent, southeastern England. Its harbor is a leading departure point for cross-Channel ferry services to France.

Fol·ke·ting, Fol·ke·thing (fōl'kə-tĭng) *n.* The parliament of Denmark, consisting of a single chamber. [Danish : *folk,* the people, FOLK + *ting,* assembly, from Old Norse *thing.*]

folk etymology *n.* **1.** A change in form of a word or phrase resulting from an incorrect popular notion of the origin or meaning of the term or from the influence of a more familiar term mistakenly taken to be analogous. **2.** A word or phrase that is a product of this modification, as *sparrowgrass* from *asparagus.* **3.** A popular but mistaken view of the origin of a word, as if *hybrid* were to be taken to derive from *high-bred.* —**folk-et·y·mo·log·i·cal** (fōk'ĕt'ə-mə-lŏj'ĭ-kəl) *adj.*

folk·lore (fōk'lôr', -lōr') *n.* **1.** The traditional orally transmitted beliefs, practices, and tales of a people. **2.** The comparative study of folk knowledge and culture. **3.** A body of widely accepted but specious notions about a place, group, or institution: *the folklore of Hollywood.* —**folk·lor·ic** *adj.* —**folk·lor·ist** *n.*

folk mass *n.* A mass in which folk music is used instead of liturgical music for part of the service.

folk medicine *n.* Medicine as practiced among primitive peoples, usually involving the use of natural remedies, as herbs.

folk·moot (fōk'mo͞ot') *n.* Also **folk·mote** (-mōt'). A general assembly of the people of a town, district, or shire in medieval England. [Old English *folcmōt* : *folc,* FOLK + *mōt,* meeting, assembly.]

folk music *n.* **1.** Music and song originating among the common people of a nation or region and characterized by a tradition of oral transmission and usually anonymous authorship. **2.** Contemporary music and song using elements of the style of traditional folk music.

folk rock *n.* A variety of popular music that combines elements of rock 'n' roll and folk music.

folk singer *n.* A singer of folk songs. —**folk singing** *n.*

folk song *n.* **1.** A song belonging to the folk music of a people or area, characterized chiefly by directness and simplicity of expression and often sung or performed in several versions. **2.** A song of known authorship composed in imitation of such songs.

folk·sy (fōk'sē) *adj.* **-sier, -siest.** *Informal.* **1.** Simple and unpretentious in social behavior. **2.** Affectedly rustic or simple. **3.** Characterized by congeniality and affability. —**folk·si·ness** *n.*

folk tale *n.* A story or legend forming part of an oral tradition and passed on from generation to generation.

folk·way (fōk'wā') *n.* A way of thinking or acting practiced by the members of a group as part of their shared culture.

folk weave *n.* A type of cloth with a loose or rough weave.

fol·li·cle (fŏl'ĭ-kəl) *n.* **1.** *Anatomy.* An approximately spherical group of cells containing a cavity, such as a sac from which a hair grows or any of the cavities in the ovary containing ova. **2.** *Botany.* A single-chambered fruit, such as that of larkspur, that splits along only one seam to release its seeds. [Latin *folliculus,* little bag, diminutive of *follis,* bellows.] —**fol·lic·u·lar** (fə-lĭk'yə-lər), **fol·lic·u·late** (fə-lĭk'yə-lĭt), **fol·lic·u·lat·ed** (fə-lĭk'yə-lā'tĭd) *adj.*

fol·li·cle-stim·u·lat·ing hormone (fŏl'ĭ-kəl-stĭm'yə-lā'tĭng) *n. Abbr.* **FSH** A gonadotropic hormone of the anterior pituitary gland that stimulates the growth of follicles in the ovary and induces the formation of sperm in the testis.

fol·li·cu·li·tis (fə-lĭk'yə-lī'tĭs) *n.* Inflammation of a follicle, especially of a hair follicle. [Latin *folliculus,* FOLLICLE + -ITIS.]

fol·lies (fŏl'ēz) *n. Used with a singular verb.* An elaborate, richly costumed theatrical revue consisting of a series of musical or dance skits. [Plural of FOLLY.]

fol·low (fŏl'ō) *v.* **-lowed, -lowing, -lows.** —*tr.* **1.** To come or go after; move behind and in the same direction as. **2.** To go after with or as if with the intention of overtaking; pursue. **3.** To come or go with; accompany; attend. **4.** To move along the course of; take (a course or direction): *We followed a path to the shore.* **5.** To accept the guidance or leadership of; have as a model; emulate. **6.** To adhere to the cause or principles of; advocate: *follow outdated doctrines.* **7.** To be governed by; obey; comply with: *We follow the rules.* **8. a.** To occur after (a specified event) in a temporal sequence. **b.** To occupy a position that occurs after (a specified position) in a hierarchy, list, or other ordering: *Captain follows major in rank.* **9.** To succeed to the place or position of: *Elizabeth II followed George VI.* **10.** To engage in; work at (a trade or occupation). **11.** To occur or be evident as a consequence of: *Your conclusion does not follow your premise.* **12.** To be attentive to; listen to or

PRONUNCIATION KEY

ă, pat; ā, pay; âr, care;
ä, father, are; b, bib;
ch, church; d, deed; ĕ, pet;
ē, be; f, fife; g, gag; h, hat;
hw, which; ĭ, pit; ī, pie;
îr, pier; j, judge; k, kick;
l, lid, needle; m, mum;
n, no, sudden; ng, thing;
ŏ, pot; ō, toe; ô, paw, for;
oi, noise; ou, out; o͝o, book;
o͞o, boot; p, pop; r, roar;
s, sauce; sh, ship, dish;
t, tight; th, thin, path;
th, this, bathe; ŭ, cut; ûr, fur;
v, valve; w, with; y, yes;
z, zebra, size; zh, vision;
ə, about, item, edible,
gallop, circus, peaceful

IN FOREIGN WORDS:

à, *Fr.* ami; œ, *Fr.* feu, *Ger.* schön; ü, *Fr.* tu, *Ger.* über; KH, *Ger.* ich, *Scot.* loch; N, *Fr.* bon; y', *Fr.* Compiègne

STRESS MARKS:

Primary stress: '
in·cite' (ĭn-sīt')
Secondary stress: '
in'sight' (ĭn'sīt')

watch closely: *I was too sleepy to follow the sermon.* **13.** To grasp the meaning or logic of; keep up with the reasoning of: *Do you follow my argument?* **14.** To inform oneself of the course or progress of: *follow the stock market.* **15.** To be a keen and knowledgeable fan of (a sport, team, or the like). *—intr.* **1.** To come, move, or take place after some other person or thing in order or time. **2.** To occur or be evident as a consequence; result; ensue: *If you ignore your diet, trouble will follow.* **3.** To grasp the meaning or reasoning of what is said; understand. **—as follows.** As is now to be given or explained; as listed or explained below. **—follow out.** To comply with fully; carry out. **—follow suit.** **1.** *Card Games.* To play a card of the same suit as the one led. **2.** To act after another's example. *∼n.* A billiards shot in which the cue ball is struck in such a way that it follows the path of the object ball after impact. [Middle English *fol(o)wen,* Old English *folgian* and *fylgan,* from Germanic *fulg-* (unattested).]

Synonyms: *ensue, result, succeed, supervene.*

Usage: *As follows* is a fixed phrase in standard English and does not change along with the number of the noun that precedes it. *His reply was as follows* is found alongside *His replies were as follows. As follow* in this last example would be unacceptable.

fol·low·er (fŏl′ō-ər) *n.* **1.** One that comes or occurs after another. **2.** One who is keenly interested in a sport, team, fashion, or the like; devotee. **3.** An attendant, servant, or subordinate. **4.** One who subscribes to the teachings or methods of another; adherent. **5.** A machine element moved by another machine element. **6.** *Archaic.* A male admirer of a woman.

fol·low·ing (fŏl′ō-ĭng) *adj. Abbr.* **f., ff., foll.** **1.** Coming next in time or order: *in the following chapter.* **2.** Now to be enumerated: *The following men will report for duty.* **3.** Blowing in the same direction as the course of a ship or aircraft. Said of a wind.
∼n. A group or gathering of admirers, adherents, or disciples: *a lecturer with a large following.* **—the following.** **1.** What is to be mentioned or listed next: *Please buy the following.* **2.** What is now to be said or specified: *Listen closely to the following.*

follow through *intr.v.* **1.** *Sports.* To continue a stroke or shot to natural completion after hitting the ball. **2.** To carry an act, project, or train of thought to completion; pursue fully.

fol·low-through (fŏl′ō-thro͞o′) *n.* **1.** The carrying of a stroke to natural completion after the ball has been hit, as in tennis, golf, or baseball. **2.** The concluding part of a stroke, after the ball has been hit. **3.** The completion of a sequence of acts or processes.

follow up *tr.v.* **1.** To carry to completion; follow through. **2.** To increase the effectiveness of by further action. *—intr.v.* To take further action: *I followed up on your comment by working harder.*

fol·low-up (fŏl′ō-ŭp′) *n.* **1.** The act or an instance of repeating or adding to previous action so as to increase effectiveness. **2.** The means, such as a letter, procedure, or visit, used to increase or reinforce the effectiveness of previous action. Also used adjectivally: *a follow-up letter.* **3.** A newspaper article giving further information on a previously published item of news.

fol·ly (fŏl′ē) *n., pl.* **-lies.** **1.** The condition or quality of being foolish; a lack of good sense, understanding, or foresight. **2. a.** Any act or instance of foolishness. **b.** A costly undertaking having an absurd or ruinous outcome. **3.** *Archaic.* Action or behavior considered immoral or criminal. **4.** An ornamental building or structure built purely for decoration. **5.** *Obsolete.* Evil; wickedness. [Middle English *folie,* from Old French, from *fol,* foolish, from Latin *follis,* bellows. See **fool.**]

Fol·som (fōl′səm) *adj.* Of or relating to an early North American culture of the Pleistocene period flourishing east of the Rocky Mountains and notable chiefly for the use of leaf-shaped flint implements. [After *Folsom,* New Mexico.]

Fo·mal·haut (fō′məl-hôt′) *n.* The brightest star in the constellation Piscis Austrinus, 24 light-years from earth. [Arabic *fum'l-ḥūt,* "mouth of the fish."]

fo·ment (fō-mĕnt′) *tr.v.* **-mented, -menting, -ments.** **1.** To promote the growth or arousal of (discontent or strife); stir up; instigate. **2.** To treat (the skin) by fomentation. [Middle English *fomenten,* from Old French *fomenter,* from Late Latin *fōmentāre,* from Latin *fōmentum,* warm application, short for *fovementum* (unattested), from *fovēre,* to warm, cherish.] **—fo·ment·er** *n.*

fo·men·ta·tion (fō′mən-tā′shən) *n.* **1.** The act or an instance of promoting discontent, rebellion, or strife; instigation. **2. a.** A warm, moist medicinal compress; poultice. **b.** The therapeutic application of warmth and moisture.

fo·mite (fō′mīt′) *n.* An inanimate object or substance that serves to transfer infectious organisms from one individual to another. Also called "fomes." [Back-formation from New Latin *fomites,* plural of Latin *fomes,* tinder.]

fond[1] (fŏnd) *adj.* **fonder, fondest.** **1.** Affectionate; tender: *a fond embrace.* **2.** Having a tender interest or affection or great liking. Used with *of*: *"He was fond of the fine arts, fond of long words, and fond of me"* (Mary McCarthy). **3.** Immoderately or irrationally affectionate; infatuated; doting. **4.** Cherished; dear: *my fondest hopes.* **5.** *Archaic.* Naively credulous; foolish. [Middle English *fonned,* foolish, probably from *fon*†, a fool.] **—fond·ly** *adv.*

fond[2] *n.* **1.** A foundation; basis. **2.** The background of a design in lace. [French, from Latin *fundus,* bottom.]

Fon·da (fŏn′də), **Henry** (1905–82). U.S. actor. He made his film debut in *The Farmer Takes a Wife* (1935). He went on to become a Hollywood star with such films as *Young Mr. Lincoln* (1939), *The Grapes of Wrath* (1940), and *Twelve Angry Men* (1957). He received an Academy Award in 1982 for his part in *On Golden Pond.* His daughter **Jane** (1937–) made her first major film appearance in *Barbarella* (1968). Later films included *Klute* (1971) and *Coming Home* (1978). Her brother **Peter** (1939–) starred in *Easy Rider* (1969).

fon·dant (fŏn′dənt; *French* fôN-däN′) *n.* **1.** A sweet, creamy sugar paste eaten as a candy or used in icings or as a filling for other candies. **2.** A candy made of or containing fondant. [French, from the present participle of *fondre,* to melt (it melts quickly in the mouth), from Latin *fundere,* to pour, melt.]

fon·dle (fŏnd′l) *v.* **-dled, -dling, -dles.** *—tr.* To handle or stroke with affection; caress lovingly with the hands. *—intr.* To show fondness or affection by caressing. [Frequentative of obsolete *fond,* to show fondness for.]

fond·ness (fŏnd′nĭs) *n.* **1.** Warm affection; tender liking. **2.** Strong preference; inclination; relish. **3.** *Archaic.* Naive trustfulness; credulity. —See Synonyms at **love.**

fon·due, fon·du (fŏn-do͞o′, -dyo͞o′) *n.* **1.** A hot dish made of melted cheese and wine into which pieces of bread or meat are dipped. **2. a.** A dish made with pieces of beef that are cooked individually on skewers in hot oil at table and eaten with a variety of sauces. **b.** A similar dish made with pieces of fruit or vegetable dipped in a hot sauce and eaten. [French, feminine past participle of *fondre,* to melt. See **fondant.**]

font[1] (fŏnt) *n.* **1.** A basin, usually mounted on a stone pedestal, holding baptismal water in a church. **2.** A receptacle for holy water; stoup. **3.** The oil reservoir in an oil-burning lamp. **4.** *Archaic.* A fountain or spring. **5.** Any source of abundance; fount: *a font of knowledge.* [Middle English, Old English *font, fant,* from Latin *fōns* (stem *font-*), spring, fountain.] **—font·al** *adj.*

font[2] *n.* *Printing.* A complete set of type of one size and face. [Old French, casting, from *fondre,* to melt, cast. See **fondant.**]

Fon·taine·bleau (fŏn′tən-blō′). Town in France, 59 kilometers (37 miles) southeast of Paris. From the 10th century it was a residence of the French kings, chiefly because of the good hunting ground offered by the Forest of Fontainebleau. Its magnificent palace, an outstanding example of French Renaissance architecture, was built by Francis I in the 16th century and decorated by Il Rosso, Francesco Primaticcio, and other members of the so-called Fontainebleau School.

fon·ta·nel, fon·ta·nelle (fŏn′tə-nĕl′) *n.* Any of the soft membranous gaps between the incompletely formed cranial bones of fetuses and infants. Also called "soft spot." [Middle English *fontinel,* a hollow, from Old French *fontenele,* diminutive of *fontaine,* FOUNTAIN.]

Fon·tanne (fŏn-tăn′), **Lynn** (1887–1983). U.S. actress; born in England. After making her acting debut in London (1905), she moved to the United States (1910), where she won fame as the lead in *Dulcy* (1921). The next year she married Alfred Lunt, creating one of America's premier husband-and-wife acting teams.

Fon·teyn (fŏn-tān′), **Dame Margot,** born Margaret Hookham (1919–). British ballerina. She joined the Sadler's Wells Company (subsequently the Royal Ballet Company) in 1934. The beauty of her line, her musicality, and her dramatic interpretation of roles made her famous, especially in partnership with Rudolph Nureyev.

Foochow. See **Fuzhou.**

food (fo͞od) *n.* **1.** Any material, usually of plant or animal origin, containing or consisting of essential nutrients, such as carbohydrates, fats, proteins, vitamins, or minerals, that is taken in and assimilated by an organism to maintain life and growth. **2.** A specified kind of nourishment: *breakfast food; plant food.* **3.** Nourishment eaten in solid form, as distinguished from liquid nourishment: *good food and wine.* **4.** Anything that nourishes or sustains in a way suggestive of physical nourishment: *food for thought.* [Middle English *fode,* Old English *fōda,* from Germanic.]

food chain *n.* A succession of organisms in an ecological community, each of which feeds on a lower member and is in turn eaten by a higher member. See feature, next page.

food fish *n.* Any edible fish, such as a cod, flounder, or herring, that is used commercially as a source of human food.

food poisoning *n.* **1.** Poisoning caused by eating food contaminated by bacteria, especially bacteria of the genus *Salmonella,* and characterized, with varying severity, by vomiting, diarrhea, prostration, and sometimes shock. See **salmonellosis.** **2.** Poisoning caused by eating foods containing natural toxins.

food processor *n.* An appliance consisting of a container with interchangeable blades that processes food, as by mincing, shredding, slicing, or mixing, at very high speed.

food stamp *n.* A stamp or coupon issued by the government and sold or given to low-income persons to be redeemed for food.

food·stuff (fo͞od′stŭf′) *n.* **1.** Any substance suitable for food; especially, a crude product suitable for food after processing. **2.** Any substance, such as protein or fat, that forms part of a variety of foods.

food web *n.* A group of organisms in an ecological community that forms a complex of interconnected food chains.

fool[1] (fo͞ol) *n.* **1.** One who shows himself, by words or actions, to be deficient in judgment, sense, or understanding; a stupid or thoughtless person. **2.** One who acts unwisely on a given occasion: *I was a fool to have refused the job.* **3.** Formerly, a member of a royal or noble household who entertained the court with jests, mimicry, and the like; jester; buffoon. **4.** One who has been or can be easily deceived or imposed upon; dupe: *They made a fool of me.* **5.** *Obso-*

font *A medieval Gothic font from Fosdyke in Lincolnshire, England.*

food chain

NATURE'S COMPLEX CHAIN OF REGENERATION
The intricate pattern of life on a forest floor

All living things in a particular environment are part of a food chain. A typical community of organisms, such as that found on the floor of a deciduous forest, includes producers, consumers, and decomposers.

The producers are green plants, which use light to make food from carbon dioxide and water. The plants are then eaten by herbivorous animals (primary consumers), which in turn are eaten by carnivores (secondary consumers). Finally, decomposers and scavengers break down the remains of the dead organisms and waste materials, releasing substances that enrich the soil and are used by the producers.

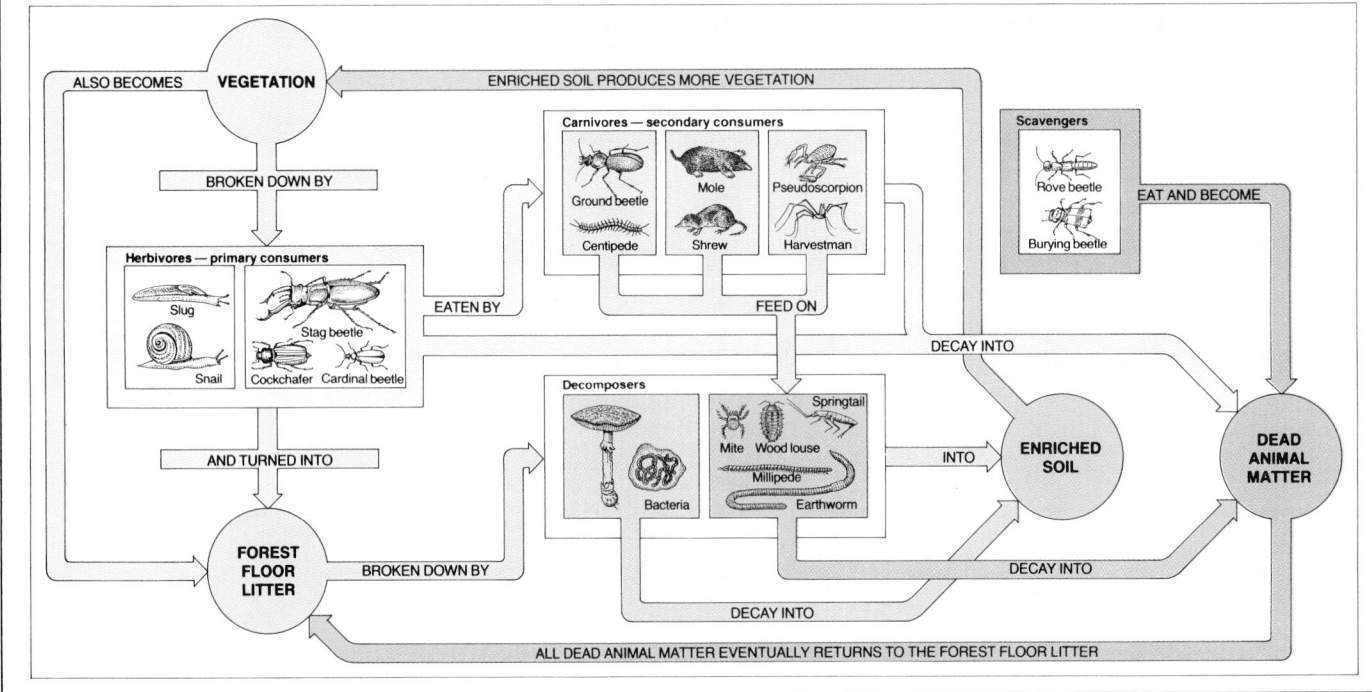

lete. A feeble-minded person; an idiot. **6.** *Informal.* A person with extreme fondness or enthusiasm for a specified activity or person: *a fool for weightlifting.* —**no** (or **nobody's**) **fool.** A shrewd or wise person. —**play** (or **act**) **the fool. 1.** To act in an irresponsible or foolish manner. **2.** To behave in a playful or comical manner. ~*v.* **fooled, fooling, fools.** —*tr.* To deceive or misinform, especially for amusement or to gain an advantage; trick; dupe. —See Synonyms at **deceive.** —*intr.* **1.** To act or speak in jest; play; joke; be amusing. **2.** To act, speak, argue, or contend without but as if with serious or harmful intent: *They thought he might shoot, but he was only fooling.* —**fool around** (or **about**). *Informal.* **1.** To engage in or amuse oneself with useless or trifling activity. **2.** To trifle; not treat seriously. Used with *with.* **3.** To behave irresponsibly. —**fool with.** To toy or tamper aimlessly with; meddle with. [Middle English *fol(e),* a fool, foolish, from Old French *fol,* from Latin *follis,* bellows, windbag.]

fool² *n. Chiefly British.* A dessert made of crushed, stewed, or puréed fruit mixed with cream or custard and served cold. [Perhaps a specialized use of FOOL.]

fool·er·y (fōō′lə-rē) *n., pl.* **-ies. 1.** Foolish behavior or speech; playfulness or facetiousness. **2.** An instance of this; a jest or trick.

fool·har·dy (fōōl′här′dē) *adj.* **-dier, -diest.** Unwisely bold or adventurous; rash. —See Synonyms at **reckless.** [Middle English *folhardi,* from Old French *folhardi : fol,* foolish (see **fool**) + *hardi,* HARDY.] —**fool·har·di·ly** *adv.* —**fool·har·di·ness** *n.*

fool·ish (fōō′lĭsh) *adj.* **1.** Lacking good sense or judgment; silly: *foolish remarks.* **2.** Resulting from stupidity or misinformation; ill-advised; unwise: *a foolish decision.* **3.** Ridiculous; inane: *a foolish grin.* **4.** Abashed; embarrassed: *I feel foolish telling you this.* **5.** *Archaic.* Insignificant; worthless: *"We have a trifling foolish banquet"* (Shakespeare). —**fool·ish·ly** *adv.* —**fool·ish·ness** *n.*

    Synonyms: *absurd, fatuous, inane, ludicrous, preposterous, ridiculous, silly.*

fool·proof (fōōl′prōōf′) *adj.* **1.** Designed so as to be proof against or resistant to human incompetence, error, or misuse: *a foolproof detonator.* **2.** Always effective; infallible: *a foolproof scheme.*

fools·cap (fōōlz′kăp′) *n. Abbr.* **fcp., fcap.** A sheet of writing or printing paper approximately 34x34 centimeters (13½x17 inches). [From the watermark of a fool's cap with bells originally marking this type of paper.]

fool's errand *n.* A fruitless errand or undertaking.

fool's gold *n.* A mineral, such as pyrite, found in gold-colored veins or nuggets and sometimes mistaken for gold.

fool's paradise *n.* A state of delusive contentment or false hope.

fool's-pars·ley (fōōlz′pär′slē) *n.* A poisonous plant, *Aethusa cynapium,* native to Eurasia, having finely divided leaves, clusters of small white flowers, and an unpleasant smell.

foot (fŏot) *n., pl.* **feet** (fēt) or **foot** (for sense 8). **1.** The lower extremity of the vertebrate leg that is in direct contact with the ground in standing or walking. **2.** A structure used for locomotion or attachment in an invertebrate animal, such as the muscular organ extending from the ventral side of a mollusk. **3.** *Botany.* The lower part of some plants or plant structures. **4.** Something resembling or suggestive of a foot in position or function, especially: **a.** The bottom or lowest part of anything standing vertically or considered in its vertical dimension: *the foot of a mountain; the foot of a page.* **b.** The termination of the leg on a table or chair. **c.** The end or final section of an order or series; rear: *the foot of a parade.* **d.** The inferior part or rank: *the foot of the class.* **5.** The lower end of an object or the end opposite the head, as of a bed or table. **6.** The part of a stocking, sock, boot, or the like that encloses the foot. **7.** A manner of moving; a step: *He walks with a light foot.* **8.** Foot soldiers; infantry. **9.** The attachment on a sewing machine that clamps down and guides the cloth. **10.** *Prosody.* A metric unit consisting of a stressed or unstressed syllable or syllables. **11.** *Symbol* ′ *Abbr.* **ft** A unit of length in the U.S. Customary and British Imperial systems equal to ⅓ yard, or 12 inches, and equivalent to 0.3048 meter. —**have one foot in the grave.** To be very old or very ill and so be unlikely to live for much longer. —**my foot.** Used to express contemptuous disbelief. —**on foot.** Walking or standing; not riding or traveling in a vehicle. —**put one's best foot forward.** *Informal.* To make a good beginning or favorable first impression. —**put one's foot down.** *Informal.* To assert one's will emphatically. —**put one's foot in one's mouth.** *Informal.* To make an embarrassing or tactless blunder. —**under foot. 1.** At one's feet; on the ground or floor. **2.** Obstructing free movement; in the way.

~*v.* **footed, footing, foots.** —*intr.* **1.** To go on foot; walk. Often used with *it.* **2.** To dance. Often used with *it.* —*tr.* **1.** To go by foot on or through; pace; tread. **2.** To provide (a stocking, for example) with a foot. **3.** To add (a column of numbers) and write the total at the bottom; total. Used with *up: Foot up the bill.* **4.** *Informal.* To pay: *Can you foot the bill?* [Foot, feet; Middle English *fot, fet,* Old English *fōt, fēt,* from Germanic.]

    Usage: Foot and *feet,* as units of measure, are employed typically in the following: *a four-foot plank; a plank four feet long* (or *four feet in length); a man six feet tall; a ledge two feet below.*

foot·age (fŏot′ĭj) *n.* **1.** The length or extent of something as expressed in feet. **2.** A portion of cinematic film; especially, an amount of film depicting a specified event or kind of action: *news footage.* **3.** *Mining.* **a.** Payment calculated on the number of feet mined. **b.** The amount of payment thus calculated.

foot-and-mouth disease (foŏot′n-mouth′) *n.* An acute, highly contagious, usually nonfatal viral disease of cattle and other cloven-hoofed animals such as pigs, sheep, and goats, characterized by fever and the eruption of vesicles around the mouth and hoofs.

foot·ball (foŏot′bôl′) *n.* **1. a.** A game played by two teams of 11 players each on a rectangular, 100-yard-long field with goal lines and posts at either end, the object being to gain possession of the ball and advance it in running or passing plays across the opponent's goal line. **b.** The inflated oval ball used in this game. **2.** *Chiefly British.* **a.** Soccer (see). Also used adjectivally: *football supporter; Football League.* **b.** Rugby football (see). **c.** The ball used in such games. **3.** Any problem or issue that is passed about among groups or persons without being settled: *Unemployment has become a political football.* —**foot·ball·er** *n.*

foot·bath (foŏot′băth′, -bäth′) *n., pl.* -**baths.** **1.** A small bath used for washing or disinfecting the feet. **2.** An act of washing the feet.

foot·board (foŏot′bôrd′, -bōrd′) *n.* **1.** A board or small raised platform on which to support or rest the feet, as in a carriage. **2.** An upright board across the foot of a bedstead.

foot·boy (foŏot′boi′) *n.* A youth employed as a servant or page.

foot brake *n.* A brake operated by pressure of the foot on a pedal, as in a car.

foot·bridge (foŏot′brĭj′) *n.* A narrow bridge designed to carry only pedestrians.

foot·can·dle (foŏot′kănd′l) *n. Abbr.* **fc** *Physics.* The illumination of a surface one foot distant from a source of one candela, equal to one lumen per square foot. Also called "candle-foot."

foot·ed (foŏot′ĭd) *adj.* **1.** Having a foot or feet. **2.** Having a specified kind or number of feet. Used in combination: *web-footed.*

foot·er (foŏot′ər) *n.* A person or thing measuring a specified number of feet in height or length. Used in combination: *a six-footer.*

foot·fall (foŏot′fôl′) *n.* **1.** A footstep. **2.** The sound of a footstep.

foot fault *n.* A fault against the server, as in tennis, called for failure to keep both feet behind the base line when serving. —**foot-fault** (foŏot′fôlt′) *v.*

foot·gear (foŏot′gîr′) *n.* Sturdy footwear, such as shoes or boots.

foot·hill (foŏot′hĭl′) *n.* A low hill near the base of a mountain or mountain range.

foot·hold (foŏot′hōld′) *n.* **1.** A place affording support for the foot in climbing or standing. **2.** A firm or secure position enabling one to proceed with confidence.

foot·ing (foŏot′ĭng) *n.* **1.** A secure placement of the feet in standing or moving. **2.** A place on which one can stand or move securely. **3.** A surface or the condition of a surface with respect to the ease with which one may walk or run on it: *poor footing on the track.* **4.** *Architecture.* The supporting base or groundwork of a structure, as for a monument or wall. **5.** A basis; foundation: *a business on a good footing.* **6.** A social or business relationship; standing. **7.** The sum of a column of figures.

foot-lam·bert (foŏot′lăm′bərt) *n. Abbr.* **fL** *Physics.* A unit of luminance equal to 1/π candela per square foot.

foot·le (foŏot′l) *intr.v.* -**led,** -**ling,** -**les.** *Informal.* **1.** To waste time; trifle. Used with *around* or *about.* **2.** To talk nonsense. —*n. Informal.* Foolishness; nonsense. [Probably a variant of dialectal *footer,* probably from French *foutre,* to copulate with, from Old French, from Latin *futuere.*]

foot·less (foŏot′lĭs) *adj.* **1.** Without feet. **2.** Without basis; groundless. **3.** Without skill; inept. —**foot·less·ly** *adv.*

foot·lights (foŏot′līts′) *pl.n.* **1.** Lights placed in a row along the front of a stage floor. **2.** The theater as a profession; the stage.

foot·ling (foŏot′lĭng) *adj. Informal.* **1.** Foolish; trifling; insignificant. **2.** Stupid; inept. [Present participle of FOOTLE.]

foot·lock·er (foŏot′lŏk′ər) *n.* A small trunk for storing personal belongings and small items, especially one kept at the foot of the bed.

foot·loose (foŏot′loŏos′) *adj.* Having no attachments or ties; free to do as one pleases.

foot·man (foŏot′mən) *n., pl.* -**men** (-mĭn). **1.** A male servant employed in the house to wait at table, attend to the door, and run various errands. **2.** A metal stand or trivet used in a fireplace for keeping things hot. **3.** *Archaic.* A foot soldier; infantryman.

foot·mark (foŏot′märk′) *n.* A footprint.

foot·note (foŏot′nōt′) *n. Abbr.* **fn.** A note placed at the bottom of a page of a book or manuscript or at the end of a chapter that comments on or cites a reference for a designated part of the text. **2.** Something said or done after the more important work has been completed; an afterthought. —*tr.v.* **footnoted,** -**noting,** -**notes.** To furnish with footnotes.

foot·pace (foŏot′pās′) *n.* **1.** A walking pace. **2.** A raised platform in a room, as for a lecturer's dais.

foot·pad (foŏot′păd′) *n. Archaic.* A highwayman or street robber who goes about on foot. [FOOT + earlier *pad,* path, probably from Middle Dutch, path.]

foot·path (foŏot′păth′, -päth′) *n., pl.* -**paths** (-păthz′, -päthz′, -păths′, -päths′). A narrow path for persons on foot; especially, one along the side of a road.

foot-pound (foŏot′pound′) *n. Abbr.* **ft-lb** A unit of work equal to the work done by a force of one pound weight acting through a distance of one foot in the direction of the force.

foot-pound·al (foŏot′pound′l) *n.* A unit of work equal to the work

done by a force of one poundal acting through a distance of one foot in the direction of the force.

foot-pound-sec·ond (foŏot′pound′sĕk′ənd) *adj. Abbr.* **fps** Of, designating, or characteristic of a system of units based on the foot, the pound, and the second as the fundamental units of length, mass, and time.

foot·print (foŏot′prĭnt′) *n.* **1.** An outline or indentation left by a foot on a surface. **2.** In telecommunications, the area of the earth's surface where adequate reception of a signal from a communications satellite in a geostationary orbit may be obtained. Also called "groundprint."

foot·rest (foŏot′rĕst′) *n.* A low stool, metal bar, or other support on which to rest the feet.

foot·rope (foŏot′rōp′) *n. Nautical.* **1.** A rope attached to the lower border of a sail. **2.** A rope, rigged beneath a yard, for men to stand on during the reefing or furling of sail.

foot-rot (foŏot′rŏt′) *n.* **1.** An inflammatory infection of the feet in certain hoofed animals, especially cattle or sheep, often resulting in loss of the hoof. **2.** Any of various plant diseases caused by fungi that attack the base of the stem or trunk and bring about the eventual death of the plant. **3.** *Informal.* Athlete's foot (see).

foot rule *n.* A rigid measure one foot (304 millimeters) long.

foots (foŏots) *pl.n.* The sediment that forms during the refining of oils and other liquids; dregs. [A plural of FOOT.]

foot·sie, **foot·sy** (foŏot′sē) *n. Informal.* A flirting game in which a couple touch feet or legs, usually in secret, as under a table. Used especially in the phrase *play footsie.* [From FOOT.]

foot·slog (foŏot′slŏg′) *intr.v.* -**slogged,** -**slogging,** -**slogs.** *Informal.* To walk, tramp, or march, especially over a long distance. —**foot·slog·ger** *n.* —**foot·slog·ging** *n.*

foot soldier *n.* A soldier who fights on foot; infantryman.

foot·sore (foŏot′sôr′, -sōr′) *adj.* Having sore or tired feet from much walking. —**foot·sore·ness** *n.*

foot·stalk (foŏot′stôk′) *n. Biology.* A supporting stalk, such as a peduncle or pedicel.

foot·stall (foŏot′stôl′) *n.* **1.** The pedestal or plinth of a pillar. **2.** The stirrup on a sidesaddle.

foot·step (foŏot′stĕp′) *n.* **1.** A step with the foot. **2.** The distance covered by one step: *a footstep away.* **3.** The sound of a foot stepping. **4.** A footprint. **5.** A step up or down: *the footsteps of a stairway.* —**follow in someone's footsteps.** To carry on the work or tradition of a predecessor.

foot·stone (foŏot′stōn′) *n.* A marking stone placed at the foot of a grave.

foot·stool (foŏot′stoŏol′) *n.* A low stool for supporting the feet.

foot·wall (foŏot′wôl′) *n.* The mass of rock underlying the mineral deposit in a mine.

foot·way (foŏot′wā′) *n.* A walk or path for pedestrians.

foot·wear (foŏot′wâr′) *n.* Covering for the feet, as shoes, boots, or slippers.

foot·work (foŏot′wûrk′) *n.* **1.** The manner in which the feet are employed, as in dancing, boxing, fencing, or tennis. **2.** Skillful maneuvering to attain one's ends: *fancy footwork.*

foot·worn (foŏot′wôrn′, -wōrn′) *adj.* **1.** Footsore. **2.** Having been worn down by feet, as a path or carpet.

foo yong (foŏo′ yŭng′) *n.* In Chinese cooking, an omelet made with green peppers, bean sprouts, and onion. [Cantonese *foo yong (dan),* Mandarin *fú róng (dàn),* hibiscus (egg) (from the fancied resemblance between the omelet and the large showy flower).]

fop (fŏp) *n.* A vain, affected man who is preoccupied with his clothes and manners; a dandy. [Middle English *fop, foppe,* a fool, perhaps akin to *fobben,* to cheat, FOB.]

fop·per·y (fŏp′ə-rē) *n., pl.* -**ies.** The dress or manner of a fop.

fop·pish (fŏp′ĭsh) *adj.* Of, pertaining to, or characteristic of a fop; dandified. —**fop·pish·ly** *adv.* —**fop·pish·ness** *n.*

for (fôr; *unstressed* fər) *prep.* **1.** Directed or sent to: *a letter for me.* **2.** Directed or inclined toward: *an eye for pretty girls.* **3.** As a result of; out of: *crying for joy.* **4.** To the extent of: *The road is paved for one mile.* **5.** Through the length or duration of: *sit still for an hour.* **6.** In order to go to: *leave for Scotland.* **7.** With an aim or view to: *We swim for fun.* **8.** In order to have or find: *look for a bargain.* **9.** In order to serve in or as: *train for the ministry.* **10.** In or to the amount of: *a bill for fifty dollars.* **11.** At the price of: *buy a dog for ten dollars.* **12.** In response to; as requital of: *good for bad.* **13.** Considering the nature or usual character of: *very warm for April.* **14.** Appropriate or suitable to: *a time for rejoicing.* **15.** At or on an appointed time or occasion: *an appointment for three o'clock.* **16.** Notwithstanding; despite: *For all his experience, he is inefficient.* **17.** Intended to be received: *Books are for reading.* **18.** With a desire or longing toward: *The puppy whimpered for his supper.* **19.** So as to obtain: *work for a salary.* **20.** In honor of: *a dinner for the ambassador.* **21.** In place of: *use artificial flowers for real ones.* **22.** In its effect on: *Fresh air is good for you.* **23.** In favor, defense, or support of: *vote for the candidate of one's choice.* **24.** Accompanying; paired with: *one rotten apple for every good one.* **25.** As against; as measured or compared with: *pound for pound.* **26.** As being: *We mistook her for the waitress.* **27.** In order to retain, conserve, or save: *Run for your life!* **28.** As the duty or task of; up to: *It is for the judge to rule.* **29. a.** To the advantage of: *I built up the business for my daughter.* **b.** In order to help or remedy: *took pills for his headache.* **30.** Conducive to or resulting in: *motives for action.* **31.** Because of the fact or existence of; on account of: *If it weren't for the rain, we*

could go. **32.** Allocated to: *one for you, two for me.* **—for to.** *Archaic & Regional.* In order to.
~conj. Because; since. [Middle English *for,* Old English *for* (the conjunction develops from Old English phrases such as *for thon the,* "for the (reason) that").]

for– *prefix.* Indicates: **1.** Completely; to exhaustion; excessively; for example, **forspent, forlorn. 2.** Prohibition; abstention; for example, **forswear, forbid.** [Old English *for-, fær-*; akin to Latin *per-,* Greek *peri-.*]

fo•ra. Alternate plural of **forum.**

for•age (fôr′ĭj, fŏr′-) *n.* **1.** Food for domestic animals, such as horses, cows, and sheep; fodder. Also used adjectivally: *forage crop.* **2.** The act of looking or searching for such food. **3.** The act of looking or searching for supplies of any kind.
~v. **foraged, -aging, -ages.** *—intr.* **1.** To search for food or provisions. **2.** To make a raid, as for food, supplies, or anything needed or desired. **3.** To hunt or search about. *—tr.* **1.** To wander or rummage through, especially in search of provisions. **2.** To raid; plunder. **3.** To provide with fodder; feed. **4.** To secure by searching about. [Middle English, from Old French *fo(ur)rage,* from *feurre,* fodder, from Germanic.] **—for•ag•er** *n.*

forage cap *n.* A brimless, close-fitting military cap with a central dent running lengthwise.

fo•ra•men (fə-rā′mən) *n., pl.* **-ramina** (-răm′ə-nə) or **-mens.** An opening or perforation in a bone or through a membranous anatomical structure. [New Latin, from Latin *forāmen,* an opening, from *forāre,* to bore.] **—fo•ram•i•nal** (fə-răm′ə-nəl) *adj.*

foramen mag•num (măg′nəm) *n.* The large orifice in the base of the skull through which the spinal cord passes and becomes continuous with the medulla oblongata. [New Latin, "large orifice."]

foramen o•val•e (ō-văl′ē, -vā′lē, -vä′lē) *n.* An opening in the septum between the right and left atria in the heart of a fetus. [New Latin, oval opening.]

for•a•min•i•fer•an (fôr′ə-mĭn′ə-fər-ən, fŏr′-) *n.* Also **for•am** (fôr′əm, fŏr′-), **for•a•min•i•fer** (fôr′ə-mĭn′ə-fər, fŏr′-). Any of the unicellular microorganisms of the order Foraminifera, characteristically having a calcareous shell with perforations through which numerous pseudopodia protrude. [New Latin *Foraminifera* : *forāmen,* opening, FORAMEN + -FER.] **—fo•ram•i•nif•er•ous** (fə-răm′ə-nĭf′ər-əs), **fo•ram•i•nif•er•al** *adj.*

for•as•much as (fôr′əz-mŭch′ əz) *conj.* Inasmuch as; since.

for•ay (fôr′ā′, fŏr′ā′) *n.* **1.** A sudden raid or military advance. **2.** A venture or initial attempt in some field. **3.** *Chiefly British.* An outing or expedition with the object of finding certain animals or plants in their natural surroundings: *a fungus foray.*
~v. **forayed, -aying, -ays.** *—intr.* To make a raid. *—tr.* To make a raid against; plunder. [Middle English *forrai,* from *forraien,* to foray, back-formation from *forreour,* raider, plunderer, from Old French *forrier,* from Vulgar Latin *fodrārius* (unattested), from Germanic.]

forb (fôrb) *n.* Any herbaceous plant other than a grass, especially one growing in a field or meadow. [Greek *phorbē,* fodder, from *pherbein*†, to feed, graze.]

for•bear[1] (fôr-bâr′) *v.* **-bore** (-bôr′, -bōr′), **-borne** (-bôrn′, -bōrn′), **-bearing, -bears.** *—tr.* **1.** To refrain from; keep oneself from: *forbear replying.* **2.** To desist from; cease. **3.** *Archaic.* To endure; tolerate. *—intr.* **1.** To hold back; refrain. **2.** To be tolerant or patient. [Middle English *forberen,* Old English *forberan,* to bear, endure, from Germanic.] **—for•bear•er** *n.*

forbear[2]**.** Variant of **forebear.**

for•bear•ance (fôr-bâr′əns) *n.* **1.** The act of refraining from something; abstinence. **2.** Tolerance and restraint in the face of provocation; patience. **3.** *Law.* The act of a creditor who refrains from enforcing a debt when it falls due. —See Synonyms at **mercy, patience.**

for•bear•ing (fôr-bâr′ĭng) *adj.* Tolerant; patient.

for•bid (fər-bĭd′, fôr-) *tr.v.* **-bade** (-băd′, -bād′) or **-bad** (-băd′), **-bidden** (-bĭd′n) or **-bid, -bidding, -bids. 1.** To command (someone) not to do something: *I forbid you to go.* **2.** To prohibit; interdict: *Smoking is forbidden.* **3.** To have the effect of preventing; preclude. **—God forbid.** Let it not happen; I do not wish it to happen. [Middle English *forbidden, forbeden,* Old English *forbēodan,* from Germanic.] **—for•bid•dance** *n.* **—for•bid•der** *n.*
Usage: The standard English constructions with this verb are the infinitive (*I forbid you to go*) and the *-ing* form of the verb (*I forbid your going*), which is a little more formal. The use of *from* with *forbid* (*I forbid you from going*) is not standard. See also **prevent, prohibit.**

for•bid•den (fər-bĭd′n, fôr-) *adj. Physics.* Of or pertaining to secondary quantum effects: *forbidden spectral lines.*

Forbidden City. Name given to the ancient imperial residence and seat of central government within the Inner or Tatar City, Beijing (Peking), China. Now a vast museum, it comprises two sets of three imperial palaces and some smaller palaces, laid out within a walled enclosure.

forbidden fruit *n.* Anything desirable but forbidden; especially, illicit sexual pleasure. [Alluding to the fruit forbidden to Adam in the garden of Eden (Genesis 2:17).]

for•bid•ding (fər-bĭd′ĭng, fôr-) *adj.* **1.** Tending or threatening to impede progress. **2.** Unfriendly; disagreeable. **3.** Grim; ominous.

for•bye, for•by (fôr-bī′) *prep. Scottish.* Besides.
~adv. In addition. [Middle English : FOR- + BY.]

force (fôrs, fōrs) *n.* **1.** Capacity to do work or cause physical change; strength; power. **2.** Power made operative against resistance; exertion: *use force in driving a nail.* **3.** Violence or the threat of violence used against a person or thing. **4.** Intellectual power or vigor, as of a statement. **5.** A capacity for influencing the mind or behavior; efficacy. **6.** Anything or anyone possessing such capacity: *forces of evil.* **7.** A body of persons or other resources organized or available for a specified purpose: *a work force.* **8. a.** A group organized for military, police, or hostile purposes: *an armed force.* **b. forces.** The armed forces of a country; the navy, army, and air force. **9.** *Law.* Legal validity; efficacy. **10.** *Symbol* **F** *Physics.* A vector quantity that tends to produce an acceleration of a body in the direction of its application. —See Synonyms at **strength. —in force. 1.** In full strength. **2.** In effect; operative: *a rule no longer in force.* **—join forces.** To unite; combine efforts.
~tr.v. **forced, forcing, forces. 1.** To compel to perform an action; coerce. **2.** To obtain by the use of force or coercion: *force a confession.* **3.** To produce by effort: *force a tear from one's eye.* **4.** To move (something) against resistance; push: *force open the barricaded door.* **5.** To move, open, or clear by force: *force one's way through a crowd.* **6.** To break down or open by force: *force a lock.* **7.** To rape. **8.** To inflict or impose: *force one's will on someone.* **9.** To place undue strain upon; push beyond normal capacity or use: *force one's voice.* **10.** To cause to grow or mature by artificially accelerating the normal processes: *force flowers in a greenhouse.* **11.** *Baseball.* **a.** To put (a runner) out by tagging the base to which he must advance. **b.** To allow (a run) to be scored by walking a batter when the bases are loaded. [Middle English, from Old French, from Vulgar Latin *fortia* (unattested), from Latin *fortis,* strong.] **—force•a•ble** *adj.* **—forc•er** *n.*
Synonyms: *coerce, compel, constrain, necessitate, oblige.*

forced (fôrst, fōrst) *adj.* **1.** Enforced; compulsory; involuntary: *forced labor.* **2.** Produced under strain; not spontaneous: *forced laughter.* **3.** Effected in an emergency: *a forced landing.* **—forc•ed•ly** (fôr′sĭd-lē, fōr′-) *adv.* **—forc•ed•ness** *n.*

forced march *n.* A long march made at a rigorously fast pace over a longer distance than normal.

force feed *n.* A system that supplies lubricants under pressure, as to a car engine.

force-feed (fôrs′fēd′, fōrs′-) *tr.v.* **-fed** (-fĕd′), **-feeding, -feeds. 1.** To force to ingest food; feed forcibly. **2.** To force to assimilate ideas, information, or the like. **—force-feed•ing** *n.*

force field *n.* A **field of force** *(see).*

force•ful (fôrs′fəl, fōrs′-) *adj.* Characterized by or full of force; effective; persuasive. **—force•ful•ly** *adv.* **—force•ful•ness** *n.*

force ma•jeure (fôrs′ mä-zhûr′, fōrs′) *n.* An unexpected or uncontrollable event that upsets one's plans or releases one from obligations, especially legal obligations. [French, "superior force."]

force•meat (fôrs′mēt′, fōrs′-) *n.* Finely chopped spiced meat or poultry, used in stuffing or as a garnish. [From *force,* variant of FARCE (to stuff).]

force of habit *n.* Automatic behavior, as from long practice or frequent repetition.

force-out (fôrs′out′, fōrs′-) *n. Baseball.* An out made by tagging a base to which a runner must advance.

for•ceps (fôr′səps) *n., pl.* **forceps. 1.** An instrument resembling a pair of pincers or tongs, used for grasping, manipulating, or extracting; especially, such an instrument used by surgeons or dentists. **2.** A pincerlike clasping organ at the posterior end of the abdomen in certain insects, such as earwigs. [Latin *forceps,* fire tongs, pincers.]

force pump *n.* A pump with a solid piston and valves used to raise a liquid or expel it under pressure.

for•ci•ble (fôr′sə-bəl, fōr′-) *adj.* **1.** Effected through the use of force: *a forcible entry.* **2.** Characterized by force; forceful; persuasive. **—for•ci•ble•ness** *n.* **—for•ci•bly** *adv.*

for•ci•pate (fôr′sə-pāt′) *adj.* Shaped like a forceps. [Latin *forceps, forcip-,* pincers + -ATE.]

ford (fôrd, fōrd) *n.* A shallow place in a body of water, such as a river, where a crossing can be made on foot or in a vehicle.
~tr.v. **forded, fording, fords.** To cross (a body of water) at a ford. [Middle English *ford,* Old English *ford.*] **—ford•a•ble** *adj.*

Ford (fôrd, fōrd), **Ford Madox** (1873–1939). British novelist and editor. He collaborated with Joseph Conrad on *The Inheritors* (1901) and *Romance* (1903) and wrote novels, verse, and criticism. He founded the *English Review* (1908) and the *Transatlantic Review* (1924).

Ford, Gerald Rudolph, born Leslie Lynch King, Jr. (1913–). 38th president of the United States. He was elected to the House of Representatives in 1949. In 1973 he became vice president to Richard Nixon, and a year later, after Nixon's resignation over the Watergate scandal, he became president. He was defeated by Jimmy Carter (1976).

Ford, Henry (1863–1947). U.S. automobile manufacturer. He founded the Ford Motor Company in 1903 and produced the first of the legendary Model T's in 1908. With assembly-line production he was turning out two million cars a year by 1924, at prices that made them accessible to the general public. His son **Henry, Jr.** (1917–) became president of the company in 1945.

Ford, John[1] (*c.* 1586–*c.* 1640). English dramatist. He collaborated with other dramatists, notably Dekker and Webster, and wrote works of his own, including *'Tis Pity She's a Whore* (1633) and *Perkin Warbeck* (1634).

Ford, John[2]**,** born Sean O'Feeney (1895–1973). U.S. director of 125

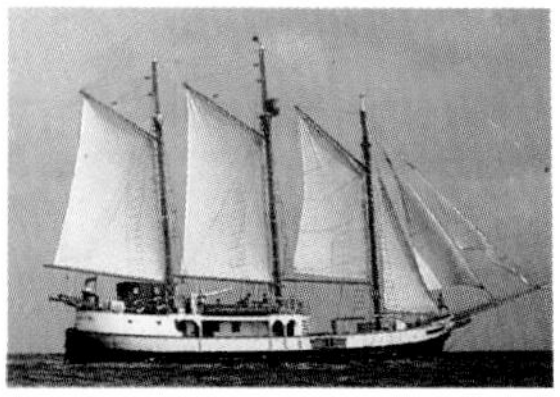

fore-and-aft rig *The sails in a fore-and-aft rig lie along the length of a ship, not across it, enabling the vessel to sail closer to the wind. Fore-and-aft sails, which are typically quadrilateral and triangular, were probably first used on Arab ships in the Mediterranean in the ninth century* A.D.

feature films. His best-known films, starring John Wayne, include *Stagecoach* (1939) and *The Man Who Shot Liberty Valance* (1962). Other films include *The Informer* (1935), *The Grapes of Wrath* (1940), *How Green Was My Valley* (1941), and *The Quiet Man* (1952), all of which won Academy Awards.

for·do, fore·do (fôr-do͞o′, fōr-) *tr.v.* **-did** (-dĭd′), **-done** (-dŭn′), **-doing, -does** (-dŭz′). *Archaic.* **1.** To kill. **2.** To bring to ruin. **3.** To exhaust utterly. [Middle English *fordon,* Old English *fordōn* : FOR- (indicating destruction) + *dōn,* to DO.]

fore (fôr, fōr) *adj.* Located at or toward the front; anterior. *~n.* **1.** Something at or toward the front. **2.** The front part. **3.** The bow of a ship. **—to the fore.** In, into, or toward a position of prominence. *~adv.* Toward or at the bow of a ship; forward. *~prep.* Also **'fore.** *Archaic.* Before. Frequently used in oaths: *Fore God, Sir, you are mistaken!* *~interj. Golf.* Used to warn those ahead that a ball is about to be driven in their direction. [Middle English *fore,* probably from adverb, "beforehand," Old English *for(e).*]

fore– *prefix.* Indicates: **1.** Before in time; for example, **forebode, foresight. 2.** The front or first part; for example, **foredeck, foreskin.** [Middle English *for-, fore-,* Old English *fore-,* from *fore* (adverb), in front, beforehand.]

fore and aft *adv.* **1.** From the bow to the stern of a ship; lengthwise of a ship. **2.** In, at, or toward both ends of a ship.

fore-and-aft (fôr′ən-ăft′, -äft′, fōr′-) *adj.* Parallel with the keel of a ship.

fore-and-aft·er (fôr′ən-ăf′tər, -äf′tər, fōr′-) *n.* A sailing ship, such as a ketch or schooner, carrying a fore-and-aft rig.

fore-and-aft rig *n.* A ship rig with quadrilateral and triangular fore-and-aft sails. Compare **square rig. —fore-and-aft-rigged** *adj.*

fore-and-aft sail *n.* A sail set parallel with the keel of a vessel as opposed to being hung from a horizontal bar (yard) across the mast as in a **square rig** (*see*).

fore·arm¹ (fôr-ärm′, fōr-) *tr.v.* **-armed, -arming, -arms.** To prepare or arm in advance of some confrontation.

fore·arm² (fôr′ärm′, fōr′-) *n.* The part of the arm between the wrist and elbow.

fore·bear, for·bear (fôr′bâr′, fōr′-) *n.* A forefather; ancestor. [Middle English (Scottish dialect) *forebear* : FORE- + *bear,* "be-er," from *been,* to BE.]

fore·bode (fôr-bōd′, fōr-) *tr.v.* **-boded, -boding, -bodes. 1.** To indicate the threatening likelihood of; give warning of; portend. **2.** To have a premonition of (a future misfortune). **—See Synonyms at foretell.**

fore·bod·ing (fôr-bō′dĭng, fōr-) *n.* **1.** A dark sense of impending evil; premonition. **2.** An evil omen; portent. **—See Synonyms at apprehension.** *~adj.* Ominous. **—fore·bod·ing·ly** *adv.*

fore·brain (fôr′brān′, fōr′-) *n.* **1.** The anterior region of the embryonic brain from which the telencephalon and diencephalon develop. Also called "prosencephalon." **2.** The segment of the adult brain that develops from the embryonic forebrain and includes the cerebrum, thalamus, and hypothalamus.

fore·cast (fôr′kăst′, -käst′, fōr′-) *v.* **-cast** or **-casted, -casting, -casts.** *—tr.* **1.** To estimate or calculate in advance, especially: **a.** To predict (weather conditions) by analysis of meteorological data. **b.** To predict (the behavior of the economy, financial markets, or the like) by the analysis of economic and financial data. **2.** To serve as an advance indication of; foreshadow. *—intr.* To make an estimation in advance. **—See Synonyms at foretell.** *~n.* **1.** A prediction, as of the weather. **2.** A conjecture concerning the future. [Middle English *forecasten,* to devise beforehand : FORE- + CAST.] **—fore·cast·er** *n.*

fore·cas·tle (fōk′səl, fôr′kăs′əl, -kä′səl, fōr′-) *n.* Also **fo'c's'le** (fōk′səl). **1.** The section of the upper deck of a ship located at the bow, in front of the foremast. **2.** A raised deck at the bow of a merchant ship where the crew is housed.

fore·close (fôr-klōz′, fōr-) *v.* **-closed, -closing, -closes.** *—tr.* **1.** *Law.* **a.** To deprive (a mortgagor) of the right to redeem mortgaged property, as when he has failed in his payments; repossess the mortgaged property of. **b.** To bar the right to redeem (a mortgage). **2.** To shut out; bar. **3.** To settle or resolve beforehand. **4.** To hinder; deter; thwart. *—intr.* To foreclose a mortgage. Often used with *on.* [Middle English *forclosen,* to shut out, preclude, from Old French *forclore* (past participle *forclos*) : *fors-,* outside, from Latin *forīs* + *clore,* from Latin *claudere,* to CLOSE.] **—fore·clos·a·ble** *adj.*

fore·clo·sure (fôr-klō′zhər, fōr′-) *n.* The act of foreclosing; especially, a legal proceeding by which a mortgage is foreclosed.

fore·course (fôr′kôrs′, fōr′kōrs′) *n.* A foresail.

fore·court (fôr′kôrt′, fōr′kōrt′) *n.* **1.** A courtyard in front of a building. **2.** The part of a playing court nearest the net or wall, as in tennis and handball.

fore·date (fôr-dāt′, fōr′-) *tr.v.* **-dated, -dating, -dates.** To antedate.

fore·deck (fôr′dĕk′, fōr′-) *n.* The forward part of a deck, usually the main deck.

foredo. Variant of **fordo.**

fore·doom (fôr-do͞om′, fōr′-) *tr.v.* **-doomed, -dooming, -dooms.** To doom or condemn beforehand. **—fore·doom** (fôr′do͞om′, fōr′-) *n.* An ancestor.

forefend. Variant of **forfend.**

fore·fa·ther (fôr′fä′thər, fōr′-) *n.* An ancestor.

fore·fin·ger (fôr′fĭng′gər, fōr′-) *n.* The **index finger** (*see*).

fore·foot (fôr′fo͝ot′, fōr′-) *n., pl.* **-feet** (-fēt′). **1.** Either of the front feet of a quadruped. **2.** *Nautical.* The part of a ship at which the prow joins the keel.

fore·front (fôr′frŭnt′, fōr′-) *n.* **1.** The foremost part or area of something. **2.** The position of most importance, prominence, or responsibility.

foregather. Variant of **forgather.**

fore·go¹ (fôr-gō′, fōr-) *tr.v.* **-went** (-wĕnt′), **-gone** (-gôn′, -gŏn′), **-going, -goes** (-gōz′). To precede or go before, as in time or place. **—fore·go·er** *n.*

forego². Variant of **forgo.**

fore·go·ing (fôr-gō′ĭng, fōr-, fôr′gō′ĭng, fōr′-) *adj.* Just past; preceding; previously said or written.

fore·gone (fôr-gôn′, -gŏn′, fōr′-) *adj.* Having gone or been completed previously; departed; past. [Past participle of FOREGO.]

foregone conclusion *n.* An end or result regarded as inevitable.

fore·ground (fôr′ground′, fōr′-) *n.* **1.** The part of a view or sight that is nearest to the viewer. **2.** The part of a picture, as in a painting or photograph, that is represented as nearest to the viewer. **3.** The most important or prominent position.

fore·gut (fôr′gŭt′, fōr′-) *n.* The anterior part of the digestive tract, which in vertebrates extends from the buccal cavity to the bile duct and in arthropods comprises the buccal cavity, esophagus, crop, and gizzard.

fore·hand (fôr′hănd′, fōr′-) *adj.* **1. a.** Made with the hand moving palm forward: *a forehand tennis stroke.* **b.** Pertaining to the side of the body on which a forehand stroke is played. **2.** Foremost; leading. **3.** *Archaic.* Taking place beforehand; prior. *~n.* **1. a.** A forehand stroke, as in tennis. **b.** The side of the body on which a forehand stroke is played. **2.** The part of a horse in front of the rider. **—fore·hand** *adv.*

fore·hand·ed (fôr-hăn′dĭd, fōr′-) *adj.* **1.** Forehand, as in tennis. **2.** Looking or planning ahead. **3.** Having ample financial resources; well-off. **—fore·hand·ed·ness** *n.*

fore·head (fôr′ĭd, fōr′-, fôr′hĕd′, fōr′-) *n.* The part of the head or face between the eyebrows, the normal hairline, and the temples.

for·eign (fôr′ĭn, fōr′-) *adj.* **1.** Located away from one's native country: *a foreign city.* **2.** Of, characteristic of, or from a country other than one's own: *a foreign custom.* **3.** Conducted or involved with other nations or governments; not domestic: *foreign trade.* **4.** Situated in an abnormal or improper place: *a foreign body in one's eye.* **5.** Outside of a scope, range, or essential nature; alien: *Lying is quite foreign to her nature.* **6.** Not to the point; extraneous; irrelevant. **7.** *Law.* Subject to the jurisdiction of another political unit. **—See Synonyms at extrinsic.** [Middle English *forein, forain,* from Old French *forein, forain,* from Late Latin *forānus,* from Latin *forās,* out of doors, abroad.] **—for·eign·ness** *n.*

foreign affairs *pl.n.* **1.** A country's relationships and dealings with other countries. **2.** Events that take place in another country.

foreign aid *n.* Financial and practical assistance given by one country to another, especially by a technologically advanced country to a less developed one. Also called "aid."

foreign bill *n.* A draft for a sum of money to be paid in another country. Also called "foreign bill of exchange," "foreign draft."

foreign correspondent *n.* A journalist or reporter who sends news reports or commentary from a foreign country for publication or broadcasting.

for·eign·er (fôr′ə-nər, fōr′-) *n.* A person from a foreign country.

foreign exchange *n.* **1.** The transaction of international monetary business, as between governments or businessmen of different countries. **2.** Negotiable bills drawn in one country to be paid in another country.

Foreign Legion *n.* A French military unit composed of volunteers of any nationality.

foreign minister, Foreign Minister *n.* The government minister in charge of dealings between his own government and those of foreign countries.

foreign mission *n.* **1.** A group sent to a foreign country for missionary service, as in religion or medicine. **2.** A group sent to a foreign country for diplomatic service.

Foreign Office *n. Abbr.* **F.O.** The official government department in several countries that is in charge of foreign affairs.

foreign policy *n.* The diplomatic policy of a nation in its interactions with other nations.

fore·judge, for·judge (fôr-jŭj′, fōr-) *v.* **-judged, -judging, -judges.** *—tr.* To judge beforehand; prejudge. *—intr.* To judge something or someone beforehand.

fore·knowl·edge (fôr-nŏl′ĭj, fōr-) *n.* Knowledge or awareness of something prior to its existence or occurrence; prescience.

fore·la·dy (fôr′lā′dē, fōr′-) *n., pl.* **-dies.** A forewoman.

fore·land (fôr′lənd, -lănd′, fōr′-) *n.* **1.** A projecting land mass; promontory; cape. **2.** Land or territory lying to the fore, as borderland or land at the edge of a body of water.

fore·leg (fôr′lĕg′, fōr′-) *n.* Either of the front legs of a quadruped.

fore·limb (fôr′lĭm′, fōr′-) *n.* An anterior appendage, such as a leg, wing, or flipper in a vertebrate.

fore·lock¹ (fôr′lŏk′, fōr′-) *n.* A lock of hair that grows or falls on the forehead; especially, the part of a horse's mane that falls forward between the ears.

forelock² *n.* A cotter pin; linchpin.

fore·man (fôr′mən, fōr′-) *n., pl.* **-men** (-mĭn). **1.** A man who has charge of a group of workers, as at a factory. **2.** The chairman and spokesman for a jury. **—fore·man·ship** *n.*

fore·mast (fôr′məst, -măst′, -mäst′, fōr′-) *n.* The forward mast on any sailing vessel with two or more masts, with the exception of the ketch and the yawl.

fore·milk (fôr′mĭlk′, fōr′-) *n.* **Colostrum** *(see).*

fore·most (fôr′mōst′, fōr′-) *adj.* Ahead of all others, especially in position or rank; paramount. —See Synonyms at **chief.**
~*adv.* In the front or first position. [Variant (influenced by FORE-) of Middle English *formest, formost,* Old English *formest,* superlative of *forma,* first.]

fore·name (fôr′nām′, fōr′-) *n.* A first name.

fore·named (fôr′nāmd′, fōr′-) *adj.* Named earlier; aforesaid.

fore·noon (fôr′nōōn′, fōr′-, fôr-nōōn′, fōr-) *n.* **1.** The period of time between sunrise and noon; daylight morning hours. **2.** The latter part of the morning.

fo·ren·sic (fə-rĕn′sĭk, -zĭk) *adj.* **1.** Pertaining to or employed in legal proceedings or argumentation. **2.** Pertaining to a forensic science, such as pathology: *a forensic laboratory.* **3.** Of or employed in debate or argument; rhetorical. [Latin *forēnsis,* of a market or forum, public, from *forum,* forum.] —**fo·ren·si·cal·ly** *adv.*

forensic medicine *n.* The application of medical science to interpret or establish the facts in civil or criminal law cases. Also called "medical jurisprudence."

fo·ren·sics (fə-rĕn′sĭks, -zĭks) *n. Used with a singular verb.* The study or practice of formal debate; argumentation.

fore·or·dain (fôr′ôr-dān′, fōr′-) *tr.v.* **-dained, -daining, -dains.** To appoint, determine, or ordain beforehand; predestine. —**fore·or·dain·ment** *n.* —**fore·or·di·na·tion** (fôr-ôr′də-nā′shən, fōr-) *n.*

fore·part (fôr′pärt′, fōr′-) *n.* The first or foremost part.

fore·paw (fôr′pô′, fōr′-) *n.* Either of the front feet of a land mammal that does not have hoofs.

fore·peak (fôr′pēk′, fōr′-) *n.* The section of the hold of a ship that is within the angle made by the bow.

fore·per·son (fôr′pûr′sən, fōr′-) *n.* A foreman or forewoman.

fore·play (fôr′plā′, fōr′-) *n.* Sexual stimulation that precedes sexual intercourse.

fore·quar·ter (fôr′kwôr′tər, fōr′-) *n.* **1.** The front section of a side of meat. **2. forequarters.** The forelegs, shoulders, and adjacent parts of an animal, especially a horse.

fore·reach (fôr-rēch′, fōr′-) *v.* **-reached, -reaching, -reaches.** —*tr.* **1.** To get ahead of; pass, especially in a sailing vessel. **2.** To get the advantage over; excel. —*intr.* To move up; gain ground, especially upon a sailing vessel.

fore·run (fôr-rŭn′, fōr′-) *tr.v.* **-ran** (-răn′), **-run, -running, -runs. 1.** To run in advance or in front of. **2.** To be the precursor of; foreshadow. **3.** To forestall; prevent.

fore·run·ner (fôr′rŭn′ər, fōr′-) *n.* **1.** Someone who or something that precedes, as in time; predecessor. **2.** An ancestor; forebear. **3.** Someone who or something that provides advance notice of the coming of others; harbinger; precursor.

fore·said (fôr′sĕd′, fōr′-) *adj.* Previously named or said; aforesaid.

fore·sail (fôr′səl, -sāl′, fōr′-) *n. Nautical.* **1.** The principal square sail hung to the foremast of a square-rigged vessel. Also called "forecourse." **2.** The principal triangular sail hung to the mast of a fore-and-aft-rigged vessel. **3.** The triangular sail hung to the forestay of a cutter or sloop. **4. foresails.** The sails on the foremast or before the mast.

fore·see (fôr-sē′, fōr-) *tr.v.* **-saw** (-sô′), **-seen** (-sēn′), **-seeing, -sees.** To see or know beforehand; anticipate; envision: *"many families, foreseeing the approach of the distemper, laid up stores of provisions"* (Defoe). —See Synonyms at **expect.** —**fore·see·a·ble** *adj.* —**fore·se·er** *n.*

fore·shad·ow (fôr-shăd′ō, fōr-) *tr.v.* **-owed, -owing, -ows.** To present an often ominous indication or suggestion of beforehand; portend.

fore·sheet (fôr′shēt′, fōr′-) *n.* **1.** A rope used in trimming a foresail. **2. foresheets.** The space near the bow of an open boat.

fore·shock (fôr′shŏk′, fōr′-) *n.* A minor tremor that precedes an earthquake.

fore·shore (fôr′shôr′, fōr′shōr′) *n.* **1.** The part of a shore covered at high tide. **2.** The part of a shore between the water and occupied or cultivated land.

fore·short·en (fôr-shôrt′n, fōr-) *tr.v.* **-ened, -ening, -ens. 1.** In drawing or painting, to represent the long axis of (an object or form) by contracting its lines so as to produce an illusion of depth or distance. **2.** To shorten beforehand; curtail.

fore·show (fôr-shō′, fōr-) *tr.v.* **-showed, -shown** (-shōn′) or **-showed, -showing, -shows.** To show in advance; prognosticate.

fore·side (fôr′sīd′, fōr′-) *n.* The front or upper side.

fore·sight (fôr′sīt′, fōr′-) *n.* **1.** The ability to foresee. **2.** The act of looking forward. **3.** Concern or prudence with respect to the future. —**fore·sight·ed** *adj.* —**fore·sight·ed·ly** *adv.* —**fore·sight·ed·ness** *n.*

fore·skin (fôr′skĭn′, fōr′-) *n.* The loose fold of skin that covers the glans of the penis. Also called "prepuce."

fore·speak (fôr-spēk′, fōr-) *tr.v.* **-spoken** (-spō′kən), **-speaking, -speaks. 1.** To speak of in advance; predict. **2.** To arrange for or engage in advance.

forespent. Variant of **forspent.**

for·est (fôr′ĭst, fōr′-) *n.* **1. a.** A large area covered by a dense growth of trees, together with other plants. **b.** The trees themselves. **2.** Something that resembles a forest in density, quantity, or profusion: *a forest of skyscrapers.* **3.** *Law.* A defined area of land formerly set aside in England as a royal hunting ground.
~*tr.v.* **forested, -esting, -ests.** To plant trees on; transform into a forest. [Middle English, from Old French, from the Late Latin expression *forestis (silva),* outside (forest), referring originally to the royal forest or game preserve of Charlemagne, probably from Latin *forīs,* outside, outdoors.] —**for·est·al, fo·res·tial** (fə-rĕs′chəl) *adj.* —**for·es·ta·tion** (fôr′ə-stā′shən, fōr′-) *n.*

fore·stall (fôr-stôl′, fōr′-) *tr.v.* **-stalled, -stalling, -stalls. 1.** To prevent, delay, or take precautionary measures against beforehand. **2.** To deal with or think of beforehand; anticipate. **3.** To prevent or hinder normal sales of by buying up merchandise, discouraging others from bringing their goods to market, or encouraging an increase in prices of goods already on the market. Compare **engross.** —See Synonyms at **prevent.** [Middle English *forestallen,* to forestall, obstruct, from *forestal,* the crime of waylaying or ambushing on the highway, Old English *foresteall,* waylaying, interception : *fore-,* in front of + *steall,* position, place.] —**fore·stall·er** *n.* —**fore·stall·ment** *n.*

fore·stay (fôr′stā′, fōr′-) *n.* A stay extending from the head of the foremast to the bowsprit of a ship.

fore·stay·sail (fôr′stā′səl, -sāl′, fōr′-) *n.* A triangular sail set on the forestay.

for·est·er (fôr′ĭ-stər, fōr′-) *n.* **1.** A person trained in forestry. **2.** One that inhabits a forest. **3.** Any of various chiefly tropical moths of the genus *Ino,* many of which are a brilliant green.

For·est·er (fôr′ĭ-stər, fōr′-), **Cecil Scott** (1899-1966). British novelist. He is best known for his *Captain Horatio Hornblower* series, sea adventures set in Napoleonic times. His other books include *Payment Deferred* (1926) and *The African Queen* (1935).

Forest Hills. Residential section of central Queens borough in New York City. Until 1978 the U.S. Open Championship tennis matches were held at the West Side Tennis Club here.

for·est·land (fôr′ĭst-lănd′, fōr′-) *n.* A section of land covered with forest.

forest ranger *n.* An officer in charge of protecting or managing a public forest or section of a public forest.

for·est·ry (fôr′ĭ-strē, fōr′-) *n.* **1.** The science and art of cultivating, maintaining, and developing forests. **2.** The management of forestland. **3.** Forestland.

foreswear. Variant of **forswear.**

fore·taste (fôr′tāst′, fōr′-) *n.* An advance taste, experience, or realization: *a foretaste of doom.*
~*tr.v.* (fôr-tāst′, fōr-, fôr′tāst′, fōr′-) **foretasted, -tasting, -tastes.** To have an advance realization of; anticipate.

fore·tell (fôr-tĕl′, fōr-) *tr.v.* **-told** (-tōld′), **-telling, -tells.** —*tr.* To tell of or indicate beforehand; prophesy; predict. —*intr.* To tell beforehand. Often used with *of: foretell of disaster.* —**fore·tell·er** *n.*
Synonyms: *augur, bode, divine, forebode, forecast, portend, predict, presage, prophesy.*

fore·thought (fôr′thôt′, fōr′-) *n.* **1.** Deliberation, consideration, or planning beforehand. **2.** Preparation or thought for the future; prudent anticipation. —**fore·thought·ful** *adj.* —**fore·thought·ful·ly** *adv.* —**fore·thought·ful·ness** *n.*

fore·time (fôr′tīm′, fōr′-) *n. Archaic.* Former time; the past.

fore·to·ken (fôr-tō′kən, fōr-) *tr.v.* **-kened, -kening, -kens.** To foreshadow; presage.
~*n.* (fôr′tō′kən, fōr′-). An advance warning.

fore·top (fôr′tŏp′, -təp, fōr′-) *n.* **1.** A platform at the top of a ship's foremast. **2.** A forelock, especially of a horse.

fore·top·gal·lant (fôr′tŏp′găl′ənt, fōr′-, fôr′tə-, fōr′tə-) *adj. Nautical.* Of or relating to the mast directly above the foremast.

fore·top·gal·lant·mast (fôr′tŏp-găl′ənt-măst′, -mäst′, fôr′tə-, fōr′tə-) *n.* The mast above the fore-topmast.

fore·top·mast (fôr′tŏp′məst, fōr′-, fôr′təp-măst′, -mäst′, fōr′təp-) *n.* The mast that is above the foretop.

fore·top·sail (fôr′tŏp′səl, fōr′-, fôr′təp-, fōr′təp-) *n.* The sail hung from the fore-topmast.

for·ev·er (fôr-ĕv′ər, fər-) *adv.* **1.** For everlasting time; eternally. **2.** At all times; incessantly.

for·ev·er·more (fôr-ĕv′ər-môr′, -mōr′, fər-) *adv.* Forever.

fore·warn (fôr-wôrn′, fōr-) *tr.v.* **-warned, -warning, -warns.** To warn clearly in advance. —See Synonyms at **warn.**

fore·went. Past tense of **forego** (to go before).

fore·wing (fôr′wĭng′, fōr′-) *n.* Either of a pair of anterior wings, as in certain insects.

fore·wom·an (fôr′wŏŏm′ən, fōr′-) *n., pl.* **-women** (-wĭm′ĭn). **1.** A woman who has charge of a group of workers, as at a factory. **2.** The chairwoman and spokeswoman for a jury.

fore·word (fôr′wûrd′, -wərd, fōr′-) *n.* A preface or introductory note, especially at the beginning of a book. [Translation of German *Vorwort.*]

foreworn. Variant of **forworn.**

fore·yard (fôr′yärd′, fōr′-) *n. Nautical.* The lowest yard on a foremast.

for·feit (fôr′fĭt) *n.* **1.** Something surrendered as punishment for a crime, offense, error, or breach of contract; a penalty or fine. **2.** Something given up or surrendered for a breach of rules or a mistake in a game. **3.** A forfeiture. **4.** *Often* **forfeits.** A game in which forfeits are required.
~*adj.* Surrendered or alienated for a crime, offense, error, or breach of contract.
~*tr.v.* **forfeited, -feiting, -feits. 1.** To surrender or be forced to surrender as a forfeit. **2.** To subject to forfeiture. [Middle English *forfet,* forfeit, transgression, from Old French *forfet,* from *for(s)faire,* to commit a crime : *fors-,* beyond (here, beyond what is permitted),

forge *A blacksmith's workshop and the furnace or hearth where the metal is heated are both known as forges. In front of the hearth in this picture is the quenching trough, which contains water to cool the metal being worked or the smith's tools.*

from Latin *forīs,* outside + *faire,* to do, act, from Latin *facere.*] **—for·feit·a·ble** *adj.* **—for·feit·er** *n.*

for·fei·ture (fôr′fĭ-cho͝or′, -chər) *n.* **1.** The act of surrendering something as a forfeit. **2.** Something that is forfeited.

for·fend, fore·fend (fôr-fĕnd′, fōr-) *tr.v.* **-fended, -fending, -fends. 1.** To keep or ward off; avert. **2.** *Archaic.* To forbid. **3.** To defend or protect. [Middle English *forfenden,* to forbid, prevent : FOR- (prohibition) + FEND.]

for·fi·cate (fôr′fĭ-kĭt, -kāt′) *adj.* Deeply forked, as is the tail of certain birds. [Latin *forfex* (stem *forfic-*), a pair of scissors + -ATE.]

for·gath·er, fore·gath·er (fôr-găth′ər, fōr-) *intr.v.* **-ered, -ering, -ers. 1.** To gather together; assemble. **2.** To have a chance encounter; meet by accident. **3.** To keep company or consort. Used with *with.* [Originally Scottish : FOR- + GATHER.]

for·gave. Past tense of **forgive.**

forge[1] (fôrj, fōrj) *n.* **1.** A furnace or hearth where metals are heated or wrought; smithy. **2.** A workshop where pig iron is transformed into wrought iron.
∼*v.* **forged, forging, forges.** —*tr.* **1.** To form (metal) by heating in a forge and beating or hammering into shape. **2.** To give form or shape to; bring about, especially by dint of effort or application: *forge a friendship.* **3.** To fashion or reproduce for fraudulent purposes; fake; counterfeit. —*intr.* **1.** To work at a forge or smithy. **2.** To make a forgery or counterfeit. [Middle English, from Old French, from Vulgar Latin *faurga* (unattested), from Latin *fabrica,* smithy, artisan's workshop, from *faber,* smith.] **—forg·er** *n.*

forge[2] *intr.v.* **forged, forging, forges. 1.** To advance gradually but steadily. Often used with *ahead.* **2.** To advance with an abrupt increase of speed. Often used with *ahead.* [Perhaps a variant of FORCE, which has been used in the same senses.]

for·ger·y (fôr′jə-rē, fōr′-) *n., pl.* **-ies. 1.** The crime of producing something counterfeit or forged. **2.** Something counterfeit, forged, or fraudulent.

for·get (fər-gĕt′, fôr-) *v.* **-got** (-gŏt′), **-gotten** (-gŏt′n) or **-got, -getting, -gets.** —*tr.* **1.** To be unable to remember or call to mind. **2.** To lack concern for; treat with inattention; neglect: *forget one's family.* **3.** To leave behind unintentionally. **4.** To fail to mention; pass over. **5.** To banish from one's thoughts: *forget a disgrace.* —*intr.* **1.** To cease remembering. **2.** To fail or neglect to become aware at the proper moment: *forget about paying one's taxes.* **—forget oneself.** To lose one's proper sense of decorum or self-restraint. [Middle English *forgeten,* Old English *forgietan,* from Germanic.] **—for·get·ta·ble** *adj.* **—for·get·ter** *n.*

for·get·ful (fər-gĕt′fəl, fôr-) *adj.* **1.** Tending or likely to forget. **2.** Neglectful; thoughtless; careless: *forgetful of one's duties.* **—for·get·ful·ly** *adv.* **—for·get·ful·ness** *n.*
Synonyms: *absent-minded, abstracted, distracted, heedless, oblivious, unmindful.*

for·get-me-not (fər-gĕt′mē-nŏt′, fôr-) *n.* **1.** Any of various plants of the genus *Myosotis,* having small blue flowers. Also called "scorpion grass." **2.** Any of several similar or related plants. [Translation of Old French *ne m'oubliez mie.*]

forg·ing (fôr′jĭng, fōr′-) *n.* Something that is forged.

for·give (fər-gĭv′, fôr-) *v.* **-gave** (-gāv′), **-given** (-gĭv′ən), **-giving, -gives.** —*tr.* **1.** To excuse for a fault or offense; pardon. **2.** To renounce anger or resentment against; cease to blame. **3.** To absolve from payment of. —*intr.* To grant forgiveness. [Middle English *foryeven, forgiven,* Old English *forgiefan* (translation of Medieval Latin *perdōnāre,* to pardon).] **—for·giv·a·ble** *adj.* **—for·giv·er** *n.*
Synonyms: *condone, excuse, pardon.*

for·give·ness (fər-gĭv′nĭs, fôr-) *n.* **1.** The act of forgiving. **2.** The willingness to forgive. **3.** Pardon.

for·go, fore·go (fôr-gō′, fōr-) *tr.v.* **-went** (-wĕnt′), **-gone** (-gôn′, -gŏn′), **-going, -goes. 1.** To relinquish; give up; forsake. **2.** To abstain from; do without. —See Synonyms at **relinquish.** [Middle English *forgon, forgan,* Old English *forgān,* originally to pass on, pass away : FOR- (exclusion) + *gān,* to go.] **—for·go·er** *n.*

for·got. Past tense and alternate past participle of **forget.**

for·got·ten. Past participle of **forget.**

for·int (fôr′ĭnt′) *n.* **1.** The basic monetary unit of Hungary, equal to 100 fillér. **2.** A coin worth one forint. See feature at **currency.** [Hungarian, from Italian *fiorino,* FLORIN.]

forjudge. Variant of **forejudge.**

fork (fôrk) *n.* **1.** An implement or piece of equipment with two or more prongs used for raising, carrying, piercing, or digging. **2.** A utensil with prongs for serving or eating food. **3.** Any device, piece of machinery, or the like with two or more prongs. **4. a.** A bifurcation or separation into two or more branches or parts. **b.** The point at which such a bifurcation or separation occurs: *a fork in a road.* **c.** Either of the branches of such a bifurcation or separation: *take the right fork.* **5.** A simultaneous attack on two chessmen by one.
∼*v.* **forked, forking, forks.** —*tr.* **1.** To raise, carry, pitch, or pierce with a fork. **2.** To give the shape of a fork to. **3.** To launch an attack on (two chessmen) with one chessman. —*intr.* **1.** To make a fork; divide into two or more branches. **2.** To take one branch at a fork in a road, river, or the like. **3.** *Informal.* To hand over; pay. Used with *out, over,* or *up*: *forked over their savings to buy a TV.* [Middle English *forke,* Old English *force, forca,* fork (for digging), from Latin *furca*†, two-pronged fork, fork-shaped prop.]

forked (fôrkt, fôr′kĭd) *adj.* **1.** Containing or characterized by a fork: *a forked river.* **2.** Shaped like or similar to a fork: *forked lightning; a forked tail.* **3.** Ambiguous; equivocal; deceitful: *a forked tongue.*

fork·ful (fôrk′fo͝ol′) *n., pl.* **forkfuls** or **forksful.** As much as a fork will hold or lift.

fork lift *n.* A small industrial vehicle with a power-operated pronged platform that can be raised and lowered for insertion under a load to be lifted and carried.

for·lorn (fôr-lôrn′, fər-) *adj.* **1.** Wretched or pitiful in appearance or condition. **2.** Suffering extreme want; destitute. **3.** Deserted; abandoned. **4.** Nearly hopeless; desperate. **5.** Very unhappy; miserable. **6.** Bereft: *forlorn of hope.* [Middle English *forloren,* past participle of *forlēsen,* to forfeit, lose, abandon, Old English *forlēosan.*] **—for·lorn·ly** *adv.* **—for·lorn·ness** *n.*

forlorn hope *n.* **1.** A hopeless or arduous undertaking. **2.** A misguided or vain hope. **3.** An advance guard of men sent on a hazardous mission. [Variant by folk etymology of Dutch *verloren hoop,* "lost troop" : *verloren,* past participle of *verliezen,* to lose + *hoop,* "heap," band, troop.]

form (fôrm) *n.* **1. a.** Shape or outward appearance. **b.** The contour, structure, or pattern of something as distinguished from its substance or content. **2.** The body or outward appearance of a person or animal, especially considered separately from the face or head. **3.** *Philosophy.* The essence of something as distinguished from its matter. **4. a.** The way or mode in which a thing exists, acts, or manifests itself: *Help appeared in the form of a lifeboat.* **b.** Kind; type; variety: *Ice is a form of water.* **c.** A group of organisms that differ in color, size, or some other aspect from other members of the same species. **5.** Procedure as determined or governed by regulation or custom: *know the form.* **6.** Manners as governed by etiquette, decorum, or custom: *good form.* **7. a.** Performance or condition considered with regard to acknowledged criteria: *true to form.* **b.** Mental or physical state, especially when good. **8. a.** Fitness, as of an athlete or animal, with regard to health or training. **b.** The record, as of a racehorse or greyhound, of training and races run; details of previous performances. **9.** A fixed order of words or procedures, as used in a ceremony or other regulated social situation. Also used adjectivally: *a form letter.* **10.** A document with blanks for the insertion of details or information: *an entry form.* **11.** Style or manner of presenting ideas or concepts in literary or musical composition or in organized discourse. **12.** The design, structure, or pattern of a work of art. **13.** A model for making a mold. **14.** A copy of the human figure used for modeling clothes. **15.** Linotype that has been assembled and locked up in a chase for printing. **16.** In Britain and some other countries, a class or all the children in the same year in a school: *sixth form.* **17. a.** A **linguistic form** *(see).* **b.** The external aspect of words with regard to their inflections, pronunciation, or spelling: *verb forms.* **18.** *Chiefly British.* A backless bench. **19.** The resting place of a hare.
∼*v.* **formed, forming, forms.** —*tr.* **1.** To give form to; shape; mold. **2. a.** To shape or mold into a particular form. **b.** To make; bring into being. **3.** To fashion, train, or develop by instruction or precept: *form the mind.* **4.** To come to have; develop; acquire: *form a habit.* **5.** To constitute or compose an element, part, or characteristic of. **6.** To develop in the mind; conceive: *form an opinion.* **7.** To produce (a tense, for example) by assuming an inflection: *form the pluperfect.* **8.** To make (a word) by derivation or composition. **9.** To put in order; draw up; arrange. —*intr.* **1.** To become formed or shaped. **2.** To be created; come into being; arise. **3.** To assume a specified form, shape, or pattern. Often used with *up.* [Middle English *forme, fourme,* from Old French, from Latin *fōrma,* form, contour, shape.]
Synonyms: *contour, figure, outline, profile, shape.*

-form *suffix.* Indicates having the form of; for example, **cuneiform, cruciform.** [New Latin *-formis,* from Latin *-fōrmis,* from *fōrma,* FORM.]

for·mal (fôr′məl) *adj.* **1. a.** Pertaining to the external, extrinsic aspect of something as distinguished from its substance or material. **b.** Pertaining to structure rather than content: *formal logic.* **2.** *Philosophy.* Being or pertaining to the essential form or constitution of something. **3.** Following or adhering to accepted forms, conventions, or regulations: *a formal requirement.* **4.** Done in proper, regular, or official form: *a formal reprimand.* **5.** Characterized by strict or meticulous observation of forms; ceremonial; proper. **6.** Stiff or cold; ceremonious: *a formal manner.* **7.** Done for the sake of form only; having the outward appearance but wanting in substance: *a purely formal greeting.*
∼*n.* **1.** An occasion or ceremony requiring formal attire. **2.** Formal attire. [Middle English, from Old French, from Latin *fōrmālis,* of or for form, from *fōrma,* FORM.] **—for·mal·ly** *adv.*

for·mal·de·hyde (fôr-măl′də-hīd′) *n.* A colorless, gaseous compound, HCHO, used to manufacture melamine and phenolic resins, fertilizers, dyes, and, in aqueous solution, as a preservative and disinfectant. [German *Formaldehyd* : FORM(IC ACID) + ALDEHYDE.]

For·ma·lin (fôr′mə-lĭn) *n.* A trademark for a 37 percent by weight solution of formaldehyde in water with some methanol, used especially for preserving biological specimens.

for·mal·ism (fôr′mə-lĭz′əm) *n.* **1.** Rigorous or excessive adherence to recognized forms, especially as opposed to content. **2.** The mathematical or logical structure of a scientific argument, especially as distinguished from its content. **3.** In the philosophy of mathematics, the doctrine that mathematics has no subject matter or content and is purely the study of symbols and their rule-governed configurations and manipulation. **—for·mal·ist** *n.* **—for·mal·is·tic** (fôr′mə-lĭs′tĭk) *adj.*

for·mal·i·ty (fôr-măl′ə-tē) *n., pl.* **-ties. 1.** The quality or condition of

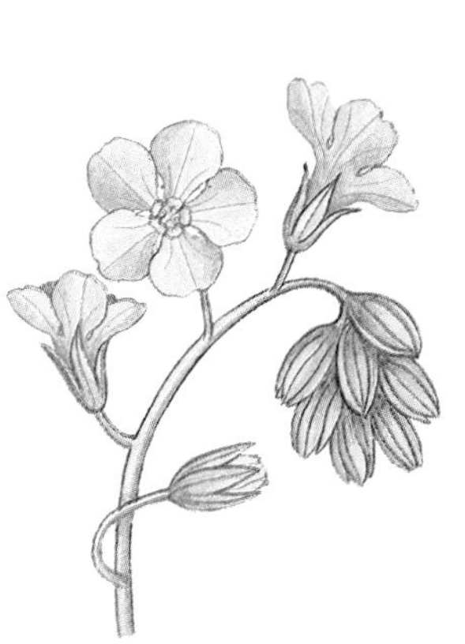

forget-me-not *The 19th-century poet Samuel Taylor Coleridge gave this Eurasian and North American wildflower its common English name. In his poem* The Keepsake, *published in 1802, he described it as "That blue and bright-eyed flowerlet of the brook, Hope's gentle gem, the sweet forget-me-not." This is the common forget-me-not,* Myosotis arvensis.

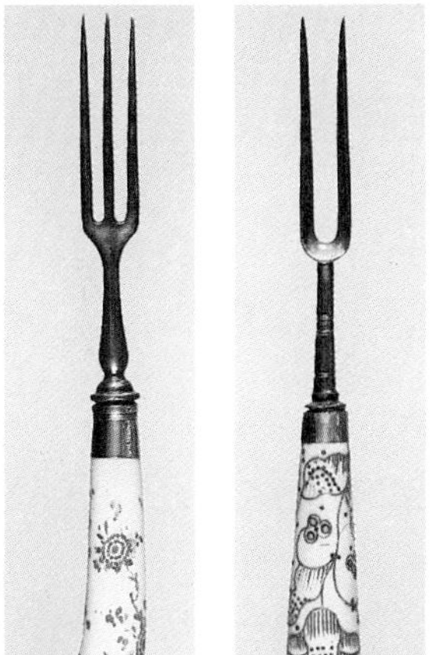

fork *Knives and spoons are very ancient eating utensils. But forks are much more recent; in Britain, for example, they were not in common use until about 1700. Early forks were two-pronged, like the ivory-handled one shown here on the right, which dates from 1685. The three-pronged porcelain-handled fork on the left was made between 1750 and 1775.*

being formal. **2.** Rigorous or ceremonious adherence to established forms, rules, or customs. **3.** An established form, rule, or custom. **4.** Something done for the sake of form, custom, or decorum.

for·mal·ize (fôr′mə-līz′) *tr.v.* **-ized, -izing, -izes. 1.** To give a definite form or shape to. **2. a.** To render formal. **b.** *Logic.* To translate into logical symbolism. **3.** To give formal endorsement to. **—for·mal·i·za·tion** *n.*

formal logic *n.* The study of the properties of propositions by abstraction and analysis of their form rather than their content, especially by the use of rules and symbols. See **symbolic logic.**

form·am·id·ase (fôr-măm′ĭ-dās′, -dāz′) *n.* An enzyme that participates in the catabolism of the amino acid tryptophan. [FORM(IC ACID) + AMID(E) + -ASE.]

For·man (fôr′mən), **Miloš** (1932–). Czech film director, known for his use of comedy and disturbing realism. His films include *A Blonde in Love* (1965) and *One Flew Over the Cuckoo's Nest* (1975).

for·mant (fôr′mənt) *n.* Any of several frequency regions of relatively great intensity in a sound spectrum, which together determine the characteristic quality of a vowel sound, musical instrument, or other sound source. [German *Formant,* from Latin *fōrmāns* (stem *fōrmant-*), present participle of *fōrmāre,* to form, from *fōrma,* FORM.]

for·mat (fôr′măt′) *n.* **1.** A plan for the organization and arrangement of a production, such as a television program. **2.** The material form or layout of a publication. **3.** The way in which data are arranged in a computer storage device.
~*tr.v.* **-matted, -matting, -mats.** To put into a particular format; especially, to arrange (data) in a suitable format for use in a computer. [French, from German *Format,* from Latin *fōrmātus,* past participle of *fōrmāre,* to form, from *fōrma,* FORM.]

for·mate (fôr′māt′) *n.* A salt or ester of formic acid. [FORM(IC ACID) + -ATE.]

for·ma·tion (fôr-mā′shən) *n.* **1.** The process of forming or producing. **2.** Something that is formed. **3.** The manner or style in which something is formed. **4.** A specific arrangement, configuration, or deployment, as of troops, aircraft in flight, dancers, or the like. Also used adjectivally: *formation dancing.* **5.** *Geology.* The primary unit of lithostratigraphy, consisting of a succession of strata useful for mapping or description. **6.** *Ecology.* A plant community, such as a savanna, that extends over a large area. **—for·ma·tion·al** *adj.*

for·ma·tive (fôr′mə-tĭv) *adj.* **1.** Forming or capable of forming. **2.** Susceptible of transformation by growth and development. **3.** Pertaining to formation, growth, or development: *a formative stage.* **4.** Pertaining to the formation or inflection of words.
~*n.* The element of a word that is not contained in the base and that gives the word a suitable form.

form class *n.* A set of linguistic forms that share one or more morphological or syntactic features, such as a plural or past tense form.

form drag *n.* A component of the drag on a body moving through a fluid that is dependent on the shape of the body.

form·er[1] (fôr′mər) *n.* **1.** One that forms. **2.** A tool or device that gives something a particular shape or form.

for·mer[2] (fôr′mər) *adj.* **1.** Occurring earlier in time; pertaining to a period previous to the one specified. **2.** Coming before in place or order. **3.** Being the first mentioned of two.
~*n.* The first mentioned of two. Used with *the.* [Middle English, earlier, from *forme,* first, from Old English *forma.*]

Usage: *Former* is applicable only to the first of two in an enumeration. When reference to the first of three or more is intended, either *first* or *first-named* is possible, but often a repetition of the name of the person or thing involved is an aid to clarity.

for·mer·ly (fôr′mər-lē) *adv.* At a former time; previously.

form·fit·ting (fôrm′fĭt′ĭng) *adj.* Closely fitted to the body.

for·mic (fôr′mĭk) *adj.* **1.** Of or pertaining to ants. **2.** Of, derived from, or containing formic acid. [Latin *formīca,* ant.]

For·mi·ca (fôr-mī′kə) *n.* A trademark for any of various high-pressure laminated plastic sheets of melamine and phenolic materials used especially for chemical and heat-resistant surfaces.

formic acid *n.* A colorless caustic fuming liquid, HCOOH, used in dyeing and finishing textiles and paper and in the manufacture of fumigants, insecticides, and refrigerants. [From FORMIC (from its natural occurrence in ants).]

for·mi·car·y (fôr′mĭ-kĕr′ē) *n., pl.* **-ies. 1.** A nest of ants; an anthill. **2.** A glass-sided box containing a colony of ants kept for observational purposes. [Medieval Latin *formīcārium,* from Latin *formīca,* ant.]

for·mi·cate (fôr′mĭ-kāt′) *intr.v.* **-cated, -cating, -cates. 1.** To swarm with or as if with ants. **2.** To crawl like ants. [Latin *formīcāre,* to swarm like ants, from *formīca,* ant. See **formic.**]

for·mi·ca·tion (fôr′mĭ-kā′shən) *n.* A spontaneous abnormal sensation of ants or other insects running over the skin.

for·mi·civ·o·rous (fôr′mĭ-sĭv′ər-əs) *adj.* Feeding on ants. [Latin *formica,* ant + -VOROUS.]

for·mi·da·ble (fôr′mə-də-bəl) *adj.* **1.** Arousing fear, dread, or alarm. **2.** Admirable or awe-inspiring. **3.** Difficult to surmount, defeat, or undertake; awesome. [Middle English, from Old French, from Latin *formīdābilis,* from *formīdāre,* to dread, from *formīdō,* fright, fear.] **—for·mi·da·bil·i·ty, for·mi·da·ble·ness** *n.* **—for·mi·da·bly** *adv.*

form·less (fôrm′lĭs) *adj.* Having no specified form; shapeless.

form letter *n.* A usually impersonal letter in a standardized format that may be sent to different people or to large numbers of people.

Formosa. See **Taiwan.**

For·mo·sa Strait (fôr-mō′sə). Arm of the Pacific Ocean between Taiwan and the coast of Fujian province, China. It links the East China and South China seas.

for·mu·la (fôr′myə-lə) *n., pl.* **-las** or **-lae** (-lē′). **1.** An established form of words or symbols for use in a ceremony or procedure. **2.** An utterance of conventional notions or beliefs; a hackneyed expression; cliché. **3.** *Chemistry.* **a.** A symbolic representation of the composition or of the composition and structure of a chemical compound. **b.** The chemical compound so represented. **4.** A prescription of ingredients in fixed proportion; recipe. **5.** A mathematical statement, especially an equation, of a rule, principle, answer, or other logical relation. **6.** A method, procedure, or specified combination of actions tending toward an end or result: *a formula for success; a peace formula.* **7.** A category of racing car defined by its engine size, weight, and fuel capacity. **8.** A specially prepared liquid food for infants. [Latin *fōrmula,* diminutive of *fōrma,* FORM.] **—for·mu·la·ic** (fôr′myə-lā′ĭk) *adj.*

for·mu·la·rize (fôr′myə-lə-rīz′) *tr.v.* **-rized, -rizing, -rizes.** To formulate. **—for·mu·la·ri·za·tion** *n.*

for·mu·lar·y (fôr′myə-lĕr′ē) *n., pl.* **-ies. 1.** A book or other collection of formulas. **2.** A statement expressed in formulas. **3.** A formula. **4.** A book containing the names of pharmaceutical substances, their uses, and the means by which they are prepared.
~*adj.* **1.** Using or containing formulas. **2.** Pertaining to formulas.

for·mu·late (fôr′myə-lāt′) *tr.v.* **-lated, -lating, -lates. 1.** To state as a formula. **2.** To express in systematic terms or concepts. **3.** To devise; invent. **4.** To prepare according to a specific formula. **—for·mu·la·tion** *n.* **—for·mu·la·tor** *n.*

formula weight *n.* **Molecular weight** *(see).*

for·mu·lism (fôr′myə-lĭz′əm) *n.* Adherence to or dependence upon formulas. **—for·mu·lis·tic** (fôr′myə-lĭs′tĭk) *adj.*

for·mu·lize (fôr′myə-līz′) *tr.v.* **-lized, -lizing, -lizes.** To formulate. **—for·mu·li·za·tion** *n.* **—for·mu·liz·er** *n.*

form word *n.* A **function word** *(see).*

for·myl (fôr′mĭl) *n.* The univalent radical CHO. [FORM(IC ACID) + -YL.]

For·nax (fôr′năks′) *n.* A constellation in the Southern Hemisphere near Sculptor and Eridanus. [Latin *fornāx,* furnace, oven.]

for·ni·cate[1] (fôr′nĭ-kĭt, -kāt′) *adj.* Also **for·ni·cat·ed** (-kā′tĭd). *Biology.* Arched or vaulted. [Latin *fornicātus,* from *fornix* (stem *fornic-*), vault, arch.]

for·ni·cate[2] (fôr′nĭ-kāt′) *intr.v.* **-cated, -cating, -cates.** To commit fornication. [Late Latin *fornicārī,* from *fornix* (stem *fornic-*), vault, arch, in the late republican period a vaulted underground dwelling in Rome where poor people and prostitutes lived, hence (especially in early Christian writings) a brothel.] **—for·ni·ca·tor** *n.*

for·ni·ca·tion (fôr′nĭ-kā′shən) *n.* **1.** Voluntary sexual intercourse between two unmarried persons. **2.** Voluntary sexual intercourse between a married person and an unmarried person.

for·nix (fôr′nĭks) *n., pl.* **-nices** (-nə-sēz′). **1.** *Anatomy.* Any vaultlike structure; especially the *fornix cerebri,* an arched band of white matter in the brain between the hippocampus and hypothalamus. **2.** A vaulted space. [New Latin, from Latin, vault, arch.]

for·sake (fôr-săk′, fər-) *tr.v.* **-sook** (-so͝ok′), **-saken** (-sā′kən), **-saking, -sakes. 1.** To give up; renounce. **2.** To leave altogether; desert; abandon. [Forsake, forsook, forsaken; Middle English *forsaken, forsok, forsaken,* to object to, reject, from Old English *forsacan, forsōc, forsacen.*]

for·sooth (fôr-so͞oth′, fər-) *adv. Archaic.* In truth; indeed. [Middle English *for soth,* Old English *forsōth* : FOR + SOOTH.]

for·spent, fore·spent (fôr-spĕnt′, fər-) *adj. Archaic.* Worn out with exertion; exhausted.

For·ster (fôr′stər), **Edward Morgan,** known as E.M. Forster (1879–1970). British novelist and essayist. Following his first novel, *Where Angels Fear to Tread* (1905), he wrote such classics as *A Room with a View* (1908), *Howards End* (1910), and his masterpiece, *A Passage to India* (1924).

for·ster·ite (fôr′stə-rīt′) *n.* A white or yellow olivine mineral, Mg_2SiO_4. [After Johann *Forster* (1729–98), Prussian naturalist.]

for·swear, fore·swear (fôr-swâr′, fōr-) *v.* **-swore** (-swôr′, -swōr′), **-sworn** (-swôrn′, -swōrn′), **-swearing, -swears.** —*tr.* **1.** To renounce or forsake unalterably. **2.** To disavow or repudiate unalterably. **3.** To perjure (oneself). —*intr.* To swear falsely; commit perjury. [Middle English *forsweren,* from Old English *forswerian,* to swear falsely : *for-,* wrongly + *swerian,* to SWEAR.]

for·syth·i·a (fôr-sĭth′ē-ə, fər-) *n.* Any shrub of the genus *Forsythia,* native to Asia, cultivated for its early-blooming yellow flowers. [After William *Forsyth* (1737–1804), English botanist.]

fort (fôrt, fōrt) *n. Abbr.* **ft.** A fortified place or position stationed with troops; fortification; bastion. **—hold the fort.** To manage or cope, especially in a difficult situation, while acting as a substitute for someone else. [Middle English, from Old French *fort,* from *fort(e),* strong, from Latin *fortis.*]

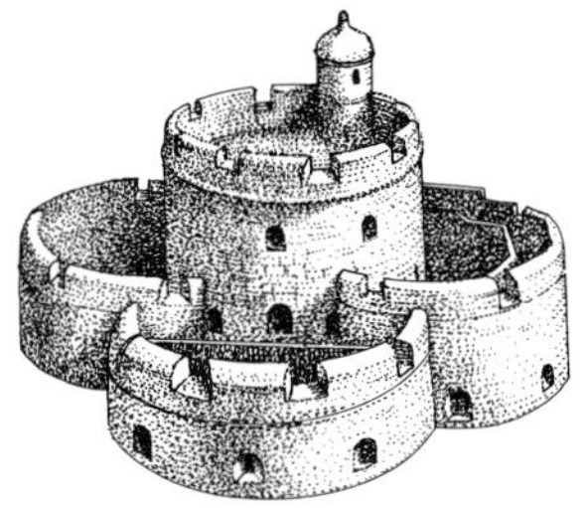

fort *The English king Henry VIII built a chain of coastal forts, like this one at St. Mawes, Cornwall. The cloverleaf design of the outer walls was intended to deflect cannon shot.*

for·ta·lice (fôr′tə-lĭs) *n.* A minor defensive structure or position; a small fort. [Middle English, from Medieval Latin *fortalitia,* from Latin *fortis,* strong.]

Fort-de-France (fôr′də-fräɴs′). Capital of Martinique. It is a tourist resort and exports sugar, bananas, and rum.

forte[1] (fôrt, fōrt, fôr′tā) *n.* **1.** Something in which a person excels; strong point. **2.** The strong part of a sword blade, between the middle and the hilt. Compare **foible.** [Old French *fort,* from adjective, "strong." See **fort.**]

for·te[2] (fôr′tā) *adv. Abbr.* **f, F** *Music.* Loudly; forcefully. Used as a direction.

~*n. Music.* A note, passage, or chord played forte.
~*adj. Music.* Loud; forceful. [Italian, "strongly," from adjective, "strong," from Latin *fortis.*]

for·te·pi·an·o (fôr'tā-pē-än'ō, -ä'nō) *adv. Music.* Loudly and then softly. Used as a direction
~*adj. Music.* Loud and then soft. [Italian : *forte,* loud + *piano,* soft.]

for·te·pi·an·o (fôr'tā-pē-än'ō) *n.* The pianoforte of the 18th and 19th centuries, as distinct from the modern piano.

Fort Fred·er·i·ca National Monument (frĕd'ə-rē'kə). Ruins of an early British fort, on St. Simon Island in southeastern Georgia.

forth (fôrth, fōrth) *adv.* **1.** Forward in time, place, or order; on; onward. **2.** Out into view, as from confinement or concealment. **3.** Away from a specified place; abroad.
~*prep. Archaic.* Out of; forth from. [Middle English *forth,* Old English *forth.*]

Forth, Firth of (fôrth, fōrth). The estuary of the Forth River, Scotland, forming an arm of the North Sea. It is *c.* 80 kilometers (50 miles) long and some 30 kilometers (18 miles) wide at its entrance. It is a major seaway with several ports, including Edinburgh's port, Leith, and the Rosyth naval base. Three bridges span the firth: the Forth Bridge (1936), the Forth Road Bridge (1964), one of the longest suspension bridges in Europe, and the Forth Railway Bridge (1890), the world's first cantilever bridge.

forth·com·ing (fôrth-kŭm'ĭng, fōrth-) *adj.* **1.** About to appear; approaching; coming: *the forthcoming elections.* **2.** Available when required or as promised. **3.** Responsive; open; informative. —**forth·com·ing·ness** *n.*

forth·right (fôrth'rīt', fōrth'-) *adj.* Straightforward; frank; candid: *a forthright appraisal.*
~*adv.* **1.** Unhesitatingly; frankly. **2.** *Archaic.* At once; directly; immediately. —**forth·right·ly** *adv.* —**forth·right·ness** *n.*

forth·with (fôrth-wĭth', -wĭth', fōrth-) *adv.* At once; immediately; without delay. —See Usage note at **immediately.**

for·ti·eth (fôr'tē-ĭth) *n.* **1.** The ordinal number 40 in a series. **2.** Any of 40 equal parts. —**for·ti·eth** *adj. & adv.*

for·ti·fi·ca·tion (fôr'tə-fĭ-kā'shən) *n. Abbr.* **ft. 1.** The act, science, or art of fortifying. **2.** Something that serves to defend, strengthen, or fortify; especially, a military defensive work.

fortified wine *n.* An alcoholic drink, such as sherry or port, made from wine to which extra alcohol, usually in the form of brandy, has been added.

for·ti·fy (fôr'tə-fī') *v.* **-fied, -fying, -fies.** —*tr.* **1.** To strengthen and secure (a position) with fortifications. **2.** To add strength to (a structure) by reinforcement; reinforce. **3.** To impart physical strength to; invigorate: *The coffee fortified her.* **4.** To give moral or mental strength to; encourage: *He fortified his troubled spirit by praying.* **5.** To corroborate; confirm; support. **6.** To strengthen or increase the content of (a substance), as by adding extra alcohol to wine or vitamins to food: *milk fortified with vitamin D.* —*intr.* To prepare defensive works; build fortifications. [Middle English *fortifien,* from Old French *fortifier,* from Late Latin *fortificāre,* from Latin *fortis,* strong.] —**for·ti·fi·a·ble** *adj.* —**for·ti·fi·er** *n.*

for·tis (fôr'tĭs) *adj. Phonetics.* Pronounced with tension and strong articulation. Said of certain consonants such as *f* and *p.* Compare **lenis.**
~*n. Phonetics.* A fortis consonant. [New Latin, from Latin *fortis,* strong.]

for·tis·si·mo (fôr-tĭs'ə-mō') *adv. Abbr.* **ff** *Music.* Very loudly. Used as a direction.
~*n., pl.* **fortissimos.** *Music.* A fortissimo note, passage, or chord. [Italian, from Latin *fortissimus,* superlative of *fortis,* strong.] —**for·tis·si·mo** *adj.*

for·ti·tude (fôr'tə-tōōd', -tyōōd') *n.* Strength of mind that allows one to endure pain or adversity with courage. —See Synonyms at **courage.** [Middle English, from Latin *fortitūdō,* from *fortis,* strong.] —**for·ti·tu·di·nous** (fôr'tə-tōōd'n-əs, -tyōōd'n-əs) *adj.*

Fort Knox (nŏks). U.S. military reservation, occupying 44,550 hectares (110,000 acres) in northern Kentucky. Most of the country's reserves of gold bullion are stored in the steel and concrete vaults of the depository built here in 1936–37.

Fort Lamy. See **N'djamena.**

Fort Lar·a·mie National Historic Site (lăr'ə-mē). Area in southwestern Wyoming, site of a trading post on the Oregon Trail.

Fort Lau·der·dale (lô'dər-dāl'). City and resort on the Atlantic coast of southeastern Florida. It is built on the site of a fort established in 1837 during the Seminole War.

Fort Leav·en·worth (lĕv'ən-wûrth'). A military post in northeastern Kansas on the Missouri River. It was established in 1827 to protect travelers on the Santa Fe Trail. The oldest U.S. military prison (1874) is here.

Fort Ma·tan·zas National Monument (mə-tăn'zəs). Site of historic Spanish ruins in St. Augustine, northeastern Florida.

Fort Mc·Hen·ry (mək-hĕn'rē). A former military post in Baltimore harbor. In the War of 1812 it was bombarded (September 13–14, 1814) by the British, but it resisted the attack, inspiring Francis Scott Key's poem "The Star-Spangled Banner." The restored fort is now a national monument.

Fort Mon·roe (mən-rō'). A fort in southeastern Virginia, at the entrance to Chesapeake Bay and Hampton Roads. The English built fortifications here in 1609 and 1727. The present six-sided fort (1819–34), surrounded by a moat, is the only one of its kind left in the United States.

fort·night (fôrt'nīt') *n.* A period of 14 days and nights; two weeks. [Middle English *fourtenight,* Old English *fēowertīene niht* : FOURTEEN + NIGHT.]

fort·night·ly (fôrt'nīt'lē) *adj.* Happening or appearing once in or every two weeks.
~*adv.* Once in two weeks; every fortnight.
~*n., pl.* **fortnightlies.** A publication issued every two weeks.

Fort Pu·las·ki National Monument (pə-lăs'kē). Site of a brick fortification on an island in southeastern Georgia, built in 1829–47 and captured by Union troops in April 1862.

FORTRAN, For·tran (fôr'trăn') *n.* A computer programming language for problems that can be expressed in algebraic terms. [*For*mula *tran*slation.]

for·tress (fôr'trĭs) *n.* A fortified place, especially a large and permanent military stronghold, often including a town; a fort.
~*tr.v.* **fortressed, -tressing, -tresses.** To strengthen or fortify with or as if with a fortress; fortify. [Middle English *forteresse,* from Old French, from Vulgar Latin *fortaritia* (unattested), from Latin *fortis,* strong.]

Fort Sum·ter (sŭm'tər). Fortification, built 1829–60, at the entrance to Charleston harbor, South Carolina. It was the site of the opening engagement of the Civil War (April 12–14, 1861). Confederate forces took the fort after a 34-hour bombardment and retained control until April 1865.

for·tu·i·tous (fôr-tōō'ə-təs, fôr-tyōō'-) *adj.* Happening by accident or chance; unplanned. [Latin *fortuitus,* from *forte,* by chance, ablative of *fors,* chance.] —**for·tu·i·tous·ly** *adv.* —**for·tu·i·tous·ness** *n.*
    Usage: Fortuitous is often confused with *fortunate.* What is *fortuitous* happens by chance or accident or without plan; *fortunate* and *lucky* are not thus restricted in meaning. What is *fortuitous* can also be *fortunate* or *lucky,* but to employ *fortuitous* in the sense of those terms, without clear indication in the context of chance or accident, is loose usage. The following example, in which there is no such indication, is considered unacceptable: *The meeting proved fortuitous; I came away with a much better idea of my role.*

for·tu·i·ty (fôr-tōō'ə-tē, fôr-tyōō'-) *n., pl.* **-ties. 1.** An accidental occurrence. **2.** The quality or condition of being fortuitous.

For·tu·na (fôr-tōō'nə, -tyōō'nə). The Roman goddess of fortune. [Latin *Fortūna,* from *fortūna,* FORTUNE.]

for·tu·nate (fôr'chə-nĭt) *adj.* **1.** Occurring by good fortune or favorable chance; bringing something good and unforeseen; auspicious. **2.** Having unusual good fortune; lucky. —**for·tu·nate·ly** *adv.*

for·tune (fôr'chən) *n.* **1.** A hypothetical, often personified force or power that favorably or unfavorably governs the events of one's life: *Fortune is on our side.* **2.** The good or bad luck that is to befall someone; destiny; fate: *It is my fortune to be a failure.* **3.** Luck, especially when good; success: *Fortune accompanied his endeavors.* **4. a.** A person's condition or standing in life determined by material possessions or money. **b.** Extensive amounts of material possessions or money. **c.** A large sum of money. **5.** Material or financial success; prosperity. [Middle English, fortune, chance, luck, from Old French, from Latin *fortūna,* chance, fate, (good or bad) luck, from *fors†,* chance, luck.]

fortune cookie *n.* A small cookie made from a thin layer of dough folded and baked around a slip of paper bearing a prediction of fortune or a maxim.

fortune hunter *n.* A person who seeks to become wealthy, especially through marriage.

for·tune-tell·er (fôr'chən-tĕl'ər) *n.* A person who, usually for a fee, will undertake to predict future events in a person's life. —**for·tune·tell·ing** *n. & adj.*

Fort Van·cou·ver National Historic Site (văn-kōō'vər). Area in southwestern Washington State, site of a Hudson's Bay Company post (1825–49) and later a U.S. Army fort.

Fort Wayne (wān). A city of northeastern Indiana. The French built a trading post here *c.* 1680. Today the city is a major railroad, shipping, distribution, and manufacturing center.

Fort Worth (wûrth). City in northern Texas. An army post was established in 1847, and the settlement became a railroad town and a center for meatpacking and later an oil refining center. Since 1945 it has been dominated by the aircraft industry.

for·ty (fôr'tē) *n., pl.* **-ties. 1. a.** The cardinal number that is ten more than thirty. **b.** A symbol representing this, such as 40 or XL. **2.** A set made up of forty persons or things. **3.** The fortieth in a series. **4.** A size, as in clothing, designated as forty. **5. forties. a.** The range of numbers from 40 to 49, considered as a range of age, price, temperature, or the like. **b.** The years numbered 40 to 49 in a century. Also used adjectively: *a forties film.* —**for·ty** *adj. & pron.*

for·ty-five (fôr'tē-fīv') *n.* **1.** A .45-caliber pistol. **2.** A phonograph record, a **single** *(see).*

Forty-Five *n.* In British history, the later **Jacobite Rebellion** *(see)* of 1745. Preceded by *the.*

for·ty-nin·er (fôr'tē-nī'nər) *n.* One who took part in the 1849 California gold rush.

forty winks *n. Informal.* Used with a singular verb. A short nap.

fo·rum (fôr'əm, fōr'-) *n., pl.* **-rums** or **fora** (fôr'ə, fōr'ə). **1.** The public square or marketplace of an ancient Roman city that was the assembly place for judicial and other public activity. **2. a.** Any public meeting place for open discussion. **b.** A meeting for open discussion. **c.** Any medium for open discussion, such as a magazine or radio or television program. **3.** A court of law; a tribunal. **4. Fo·rum.** The forum in ancient Rome. [Middle English, from Latin, forum, place out-of-doors.]

for·ward (fôr′wərd) *adj.* **1. a.** At, near, or belonging to the front; fore: *the forward part of a train.* **b.** Toward the front of a ship: *a forward cabin.* **c.** Lying ahead or in the line of motion. **2. a.** Going, tending, or moving toward a position in front: *a forward thrust of a sword; a forward fall down a flight of stairs.* **b.** *Sports.* Going, tending, or moving toward an opponent's goal. **3. a.** Ardently inclined; eager; anxious. **b.** Presumptuous; impudent; bold: *a forward manner.* **4.** Progressive, especially technologically, politically, or economically: *a forward new nation; a forward concept.* **5.** Mentally, physically, socially, or biologically advanced; precocious: *a forward child.* **6.** Prompt; eager. **7.** For the future; completed or made in advance: *My broker does not intend to bid on forward contracts for corn.* —See Synonyms at **shameless.**
~*adv.* Also **for·wards** (for sense 1). **1.** Toward or tending to the front; frontward: *step forward.* **2.** In or toward the future; at a future time; onward: *I look forward to seeing you.* **3.** Into view or prominence; forth; out: *Neighbors came forward to help.*
~*n. Abbr.* **fwd.** *Sports.* **1.** A player in certain games, such as basketball or soccer, who is part of the front line and usually plays in an attacking position. **2.** The position itself.
~*tr.v.* **forwarded, -warding, -wards. 1.** To send on (letters, for example) to a subsequent destination or address. **2.** To advance; promote; advocate. **3.** To prepare (a book) for the finisher by supplying with a paper cover. [Middle English *for(e)ward*, Old English *foreweard* : FORE- + -WARD.]
for·ward·er (fôr′wər-dər) *n.* One that forwards; especially, a forwarding agent.
forwarding agent *n.* An agent, agency, or other business that facilitates and assures the passage of received goods to their destination; a forwarder of goods.
for·ward-look·ing (fôr′wərd-lŏŏk′ĭng) *adj.* **1.** Having advanced and enlightened views; progressive. **2.** Careful of and concerned with the future.
for·ward·ly (fôr′wərd-lē) *adv.* **1.** At or toward the front; forward. **2.** In a bold or forward manner; presumptuously. **3.** With dispatch or eagerness; promptly.
for·ward·ness (fôr′wərd-nĭs) *n.* **1.** The condition or state of being forward; readiness; zeal; eagerness. **2.** An advanced state of development or progress; precocity. **3.** Overeagerness to promote oneself; audacity; boldness.
forward pass *n. Football. Abbr.* **fp** A pass thrown in the direction of the opponent's goal.
for·wards (fôr′wərdz) *adv.* Forward (sense 1).
for·went. Past tense of **forgo.**
for·why (fôr-hwī′) *adv. Obsolete.* For what reason; why.
~*conj. Obsolete.* Because; since. [Middle English *forwhy*, Old English *for hwȳ* : FOR + *hwȳ*, instrumental of *hwæt*, WHAT.]
for·worn, fore·worn (fôr-wôrn′, -wōrn′) *adj. Archaic.* Worn-out. [Past participle of obsolete *forwear*, from Middle English *forweren*, to hollow out : FOR- (destruction) + WEAR.]
forzando. Variant of **sforzando.**
Fos·bur·y flop (fŏz′bĕr′ē flŏp′) *n.* A technique in modern high-jumping whereby the jumper goes over the bar headfirst with the back toward the ground and the face up. [After Richard *Fosbury*, U.S. Olympic champion (Mexico, 1968).]
fos·sa¹ (fŏs′ə) *n., pl.* **fossae** (fŏs′ē′). *Anatomy.* A hollow or depression, as in a bone. [Latin, ditch, trench, from the feminine past participle of *fodere*, to dig.]
fossa² *n.* **1.** A carnivorous Madagascan mammal, *Cryptoprocta ferox*, of the family Viverridae, having a long tail, short legs, and a pointed snout. **2.** Any animal of the genus *Fossa*, which includes the Madagascan civets. [Malagasy.]
fosse, foss (fŏs) *n.* A ditch; especially, a moat around a fortification. [Middle English, from Old French, from Latin *fossa*.]
fos·sick (fŏs′ĭk) *v.* **-sicked, -sicking, -sicks.** *Chiefly Australian.* —*intr.* **1.** To search for gold, especially by reworking washings or waste piles. **2.** To rummage or search, especially for a possible profit. —*tr.* To search for by or as if by rummaging. [Perhaps variant of dialectal *fussick*, to bustle about, from FUSS.] —**fos·sick·er** *n.*
fos·sil (fŏs′əl) *n.* **1.** A remnant or trace of an organism of a past geologic age, as a skeleton, footprint, or leaf imprint, embedded in the earth's crust. **2.** One that is outdated or antiquated; especially, a person with outmoded ideas. **3.** An obsolete word or word element used only in an idiom, as *fro* in *to and fro.*
~*adj.* **1.** Of or pertaining to a fossil or fossils. **2.** Derived from fossils: *Coal is a fossil fuel.* [Latin *fossilis*, dug up, from *fossus*, past participle of *fodere*, to dig.]
fossil fuel *n.* A carbon or hydrocarbon fuel, such as coal, petroleum, or natural gas, derived from the decomposition of organisms of an earlier geologic period.
fos·sil·if·er·ous (fŏs′ə-lĭf′ər-əs) *adj.* Containing fossils. [FOSSIL + -FEROUS.]
fos·sil·ize (fŏs′ə-līz′) *v.* **-ized, -izing, -izes.** —*tr.* **1.** To convert into a fossil. **2.** To make outmoded, rigid, or fixed; antiquate. —*intr.* **1.** To become a fossil. **2.** To become outmoded, rigid, or fixed. —**fos·sil·i·za·tion** *n.*
fos·so·ri·al (fŏ-sôr′ē-əl, -sōr′ē-əl) *adj. Zoology.* Adapted for or used in burrowing or digging. [Medieval Latin *fossorius*, from *fossus*, past participle of *fodere*, to dig.]
fos·ter (fŏs′tər, fôs′tər) *tr.v.* **-tered, -tering, -ters. 1.** To bring up, rear, or nurture; especially, to bring up (a child that is not one's own or one's adopted child). **2.** To promote the development or growth of; encourage; cultivate: *fostered his love of music.* **3.** To nurse; cherish: *foster a secret hope.* **4.** *Chiefly British.* To place (a child) in a foster home.
~*adj.* Receiving, sharing, or affording parental care and nurture although not related through legal or blood ties: *a foster child; a foster home.* [Middle English *fostren*, Old English *fōstrian*, to provide with food, nourish, from *fōstor*, food.] —**fos·ter·age** *n.*
Fos·ter (fŏ′stər, fôs′tər), **Stephen Collins** (1826–64). U.S. songwriter. Among the popular quasi-folk songs he composed are "The Old Folks at Home," "My Old Kentucky Home," and "Swanee River."
fos·ter·ling (fŏ′stər-lĭng, fôs′tər-) *n.* A foster child.
Foth·er·ing·hay (fŏth′ər-ĭng-gā′, fŏth′rĭng-). Small village in Northamptonshire in central England, on the Nene River. Its 12th-century castle, now marked only by a mound and a few railings, was the birthplace of Richard III and the scene of the imprisonment and execution in 1587 of Mary, Queen of Scots.
Fou·cault (fōō-kō′), **Jean Bernard Léon** (1819–68). French physicist. In 1851 he demonstrated the rotation of the earth with the Foucault pendulum. He also measured the velocity of light and showed that it travels more slowly in water. He is credited with inventing the gyroscope in 1852.
Foucault current *n.* An **eddy current** (see). [After J.B.L. FOUCAULT.]
Foucault pendulum *n.* A simple pendulum suspended so that the plane of motion is not fixed, set into motion along a meridian, and appearing to turn clockwise in the Northern Hemisphere or counterclockwise in the Southern Hemisphere, demonstrating the axial rotation of the earth. [Demonstrated by J.B.L. FOUCAULT.]
fou·droy·ant (fōō-droi′ənt, fōō′drwä-yäN′) *adj.* **1.** Dazzling; stunning. **2.** Designating a disease occurring suddenly and with great severity. [French, present participle of *foudroyer*, to strike (as with lightning), from Old French *foudroier*, from *foudre*, lightning, from Latin *fulgur*, from *fulgēre*, to shine.]
fought. Past tense and past participle of **fight.**
foul (foul) *adj.* **fouler, foulest. 1.** Offensive to the senses; disgusting; revolting. **2.** Having an offensive odor; fetid; rank; smelly. **3.** Spoiled; rotten; putrid. Said especially of food. **4.** Full of dirt or mud; dirty; filthy. **5.** Immoral; wicked; detestable. **6.** Vulgar; obscene; profane: *foul language.* **7.** *Archaic.* Ugly; unattractive. **8.** *Informal.* Terrible; disagreeable; displeasing: *a foul party.* **9.** Unpleasant; bad; unfavorable. Often said of weather: *a foul day.* **10.** Not according to accepted standards or rules; unfair; dishonorable: *win by foul means.* **11.** *Sports.* Contrary to the rules of a game or sport. **12.** Covered with barnacles, weed, or the like. Said of a ship's bottom. **13.** Entangled; twisted: *a foul anchor.* **14.** Clogged or obstructed by something; blocked: *a foul ventilator shaft.* —See Synonyms at **dirty.**
~*n.* **1.** Anything that is dirty or foul. **2.** *Sports.* An infraction or violation of the rules of play. **3.** An entanglement or collision. **4.** A clogging or obstructing.
~*adv.* In a foul manner.
~*v.* **fouled, fouling, fouls.** —*tr.* **1.** To make dirty or foul; soil; pollute; sully. **2.** To bring into dishonor; disgrace; besmirch. **3.** To clog or obstruct; block. **4.** To entangle or catch. Used of a rope. **5.** To encrust (a ship's hull) with foreign matter, such as barnacles. **6.** *Sports.* To commit a foul against. **7.** To deposit excrement on. —*intr.* **1.** To become foul. **2.** *Sports.* To commit a foul. **3.** To become entangled or twisted: *The anchor fouled on a rock.* **4.** To become clogged or obstructed. —**foul out. 1.** *Baseball.* To make an out by hitting a foul ball that is caught before it touches the ground. **2.** *Sports.* To be put out of play by exceeding the number of permissible fouls. [Middle English *foul*, Old English *fūl*, from Germanic.] —**foul·ly** *adv.*
fou·lard (fōō-lärd′) *n.* **1.** A lightweight twill or plain-woven fabric of silk or silk and cotton, usually having a small printed design. **2.** An article, especially a handkerchief or scarf, made of this fabric. [French *foulard†*.]
foul ball *n. Baseball.* A batted ball that touches the ground outside of fair territory.
foul line *n.* **1.** *Baseball.* Either of two straight lines extending from the rear of home plate to the boundary of the playing field to indicate the area in which a fair ball can be hit. **2.** *Basketball.* A line from which a player makes a foul shot. **3.** *Sports.* Any boundary limiting the playing area, especially in bowling and tennis.
foul-mouthed (foul′mouthd′, -moutht′) *adj.* Using obscene or scurrilous language.
foul·ness (foul′nĭs) *n.* **1.** The state or condition of being foul. **2.** Foul matter; filth; trash; waste. **3.** Obscenity; vulgarity; wickedness.
foul play *n.* **1.** Malicious or treacherous action, especially when involving violence. **2.** Conduct that is unsportsmanlike.
foul shot *n. Basketball.* An unguarded throw to the basket from the foul line awarded to a fouled player and scored as one point if successful.
foul tip *n. Baseball.* A pitched ball that is slightly deflected off the bat into the foul zone.
foul up *tr.v.* **1.** To make dirty; contaminate. **2.** To entangle, choke, or obstruct. **3.** To cause to go wrong because of mistakes, poor judgment, or unforeseen difficulties.
foul-up (foul′ŭp′) *n. Informal.* **1.** A condition of confusion caused by poor judgment, mistakes, or unforeseen difficulties. **2.** Mechanical trouble.

Fosbury flop *The modern high-jumping technique, named after American Olympic champion Richard Fosbury, who first popularized it.*

found¹ (found) *v.* **founded, founding, founds.** —*tr.* **1.** To originate or establish (a business or college, for example); create; set up. **2.** To establish the foundation of (a building); lay a base for. **3.** To base (an argument or story, for example). Used with *on* or *upon.* —*intr.* To have a foundation or base. Used with *on* or *upon.* [Middle English *founden,* from Old French *fonder,* from Latin *fundāre,* to lay the foundation for, from *fundus,* bottom.]

found² *tr.v.* **founded, founding, founds. 1.** To melt (a material such as metal) and pour into a mold. **2.** To make (objects) in this fashion; cast. [Middle English *founden,* from Old French *fondre,* from Latin *fundere,* to pour, melt.]

found³. Past tense and past participle of **find.**

foun·da·tion (foun-dā'shən) *n.* **1.** The act of founding or state of being founded; especially, the establishment of an institution with provision for future maintenance. **2. a.** The basis on which a thing stands, is founded, or is supported; an underlying support. **b.** Often **foundations.** The part of a building or other structure that is below the ground and on which it rests or is supported. **c.** The grounds or basis for a claim, argument, story, or the like. **3.** Funds for the perpetual support of an institution, such as a school; an endowment. **4.** An institution supported by such a fund; an endowed institution. **5.** A foundation garment. **6.** A cosmetic used as a base for facial make-up. —See Synonyms at **base.** —**foun·da·tion·al** *adj.*

foundation garment *n.* A woman's supporting undergarment, such as a corset or girdle.

foundation stone *n.* A stone, usually bearing a commemorative inscription, normally laid at a ceremony marking the beginning of a building's construction.

found·er¹ (foun'dər) *n.* **1.** One who founds an institution, business, movement, or the like; one who initiates or lays the basis. **2.** One who casts metal: *a bell founder.*

foun·der² (foun'dər) *v.* **-dered, -dering, -ders.** —*intr.* **1.** To stumble; especially, to stumble and as a consequence go lame. Used of horses. **2.** To fail utterly; collapse or break down; give way. **3.** *Nautical.* To sink below the water. **4.** To cave in; fall in; sink. Used of ground or buildings. **5.** *Veterinary Medicine.* To be afflicted with founder. Used of horses. **6.** To become ill from overeating. Used of livestock. —*tr.* To cause to founder. —*n. Veterinary Medicine.* A disease of horses, **laminitis** *(see).* [Middle English *foundren,* to fall to the ground, from Old French *fondrer,* to submerge, from Vulgar Latin *fundorāre* (unattested), from Latin *fundus,* bottom.]

founders' shares *pl.n.* Shares issued to the founders or original subscribers of a company and often carrying special privileges.

found·ing father (foun'dĭng) *n.* **1. Founding Father.** A member of the American Constitutional Convention of 1787. **2.** One considered as having an important role as an innovator or originator: *one of the founding fathers of socialism.*

found·ling (found'lĭng) *n.* A child deserted by parents whose identity is not known. [Middle English, probably from *founden,* past participle of *finden,* to **find.**]

foun·dry (foun'drē) *n., pl.* **-dries. 1.** An establishment in which metal castings are made. **2. a.** The art or operation of casting metals. **b.** The castings made in a foundry.

foundry proof *n.* A proof taken from composed type for a final check before plates are made.

fount¹ (fount) *n.* **1.** A fountain. **2.** Any source. Used especially in the phrase *a fount of wisdom.* **3.** A reservoir for liquids; especially, one for ink in a fountain pen. [Probably a back-formation from **FOUNTAIN.**]

fount² *n. Chiefly British.* A type font.

foun·tain (foun'tən) *n.* **1.** A spring; especially, the source of a stream. **2.** A source; point of origin. **3. a.** An artificially created jet or stream of water. **b.** A device that produces and contains such a jet or stream: *a drinking fountain.* **4.** A reservoir, tank, or chamber containing a supply of something, such as ink or oil, that can be siphoned off as needed. **5.** A soda fountain *(see).* [Middle English *fountaine,* spring, from Old French *fontaine,* from Late Latin *fontāna,* from *fontānus,* of a spring, from *fons* (stem *font-*), spring.]

foun·tain·head (foun'tən-hĕd') *n.* **1.** A spring that is the source or head of a stream. **2.** A principal source or origin.

Fountain of Youth *n.* A legendary spring believed to have the power of rejuvenation, sought by Ponce de León and other explorers in Florida and the West Indies.

fountain pen *n.* A pen filled from an external source and containing an ink reservoir that automatically feeds the nib.

four (fôr, fōr) *n.* **1. a.** The cardinal number that is one more than three. **b.** A symbol representing this, such as 4, IV, or iv. **2.** A set made up of four persons or things. **3.** The fourth in a series. **4.** Four parts: *cut in four.* **5.** A size, as in clothing, designated as four. **6.** Four hours after midnight or midday. **7. a.** A racing boat for four oarsmen. **b.** Its crew. [Middle English, from Old English *fēower;* akin to German *vier,* Latin *quattuor,* Greek *tettares,* and Sanskrit *catur.*] —**four** *adj. & pron.*

four-ball (fôr'bôl', fōr'-) *n.* A golf match between two pairs of players with only the score of the better-playing partner of each pair being counted at the end of the game.

four-chette (foor-shĕt') *n.* **1.** A narrow, forked strip of material joining the front and back sections of the fingers of gloves. **2.** *Anatomy.* The fold of skin forming the posterior margin of the vulva. **3.** *Anatomy.* A **furcula** *(see).* [French, "fork," from Old French *forchete,* diminutive of *forche,* fork, pitchfork, from Latin *furca,* (two-pronged) **FORK.**]

four-col·or (fôr'kŭl'ər) *adj.* Designating a color printing or photographic process in which three primary colors and black (used in combination) are transferred by four different plates or filters to a surface, reproducing the colors of the subject matter.

four-di·men·sion·al (fôr'dĭ-mĕn'shən-əl, fōr'-) *adj.* Exhibiting or being specified by four dimensions, especially the three spatial dimensions and single temporal dimension of relativity theory.

Four·drin·i·er (foor-drĭn'ē-ər) *adj.* Designating a papermaking machine used to produce paper in a continuous roll or web. [After Henry (1766–1854) and Sealy (died 1847) *Fourdrinier,* English papermakers.]

four-eyed fish (fôr'īd', fōr'-). Either of two freshwater fishes, *Anableps anableps* or *A. microlepis,* of tropical America, having bulging eyes divided longitudinally, with the upper part adapted for aerial vision, the lower part for underwater vision.

four flush *n.* In poker, a five-card hand having four cards in the same suit.

four-flush (fôr'flŭsh', fōr'-) *intr.v.* **-flushed, -flushing, -flushes. 1.** To bluff in poker with a four-flush hand. **2.** *Slang.* To bluff.

four-flush·er (fôr'flŭsh'ər, fōr'-) *n. Slang.* A person who cannot or does not substantiate his pretensions; bluffer; faker.

four-fold (fôr'fōld', fōr'-) *adj.* **1.** Having four units or aspects; quadruple. **2.** Being four times as much or as many as some understood figure. —*adv.* (fôr'fōld', fōr'-). In quadrupled measure.

four-foot·ed (fôr'foot'ĭd, fōr'-) *adj.* Having four feet.

Four Freedoms *pl.n.* Four basic human freedoms, freedom of speech and religion and freedom from want and fear. Preceded by *the.*

four·gon (foor-gôn') *n., pl.* **-gons** (-gôn', -gônz'). A wagon used mainly for carrying baggage. [French.]

four·hand·ed (fôr'hăn'dĭd, fōr'-) *adj.* **1.** Involving or requiring four players, as some games do. **2.** Designed to be played by four hands, as a piano duet: *a four-handed waltz.* **3.** Having four extremities functioning like hands; quadrumanous.

Four-H Club (fôr'āch', fōr'-) *n.* A youth organization sponsored by the Department of Agriculture and offering instruction in agriculture and home economics. [From its four goals to improve head, heart, hands, and health.] —**Four-H'er** (fôr'ā'chər, fōr'-) *n.*

four hundred *n.* Often **Four Hundred.** The wealthiest and most exclusive social set. Preceded by *the.* [Term introduced (1892) by Ward McAllister (1827–95), New York socialite, to describe members of "true" New York society.]

Fou·ri·er (foor'ē-ā'), **François Marie Charles** (1772–1837). French utopian socialist philosopher. He believed that social harmony could be achieved through "phalanxes," small self-sustaining communal groups of people who would live in communal "phalansteries." Work would be shared according to each person's natural abilities and preferences. —**Fou·ri·er·ism** (foor'ē-ə-rĭz'əm) *n.* —**Fou·ri·er·ist, Fou·ri·er·ite** (foor'ē-ə-rīt') *n. & adj.*

Fourier, Jean Baptiste Joseph, Baron (1768–1830). French mathematician and physicist. He made valuable contributions to scientific knowledge, especially in the field of heat theory.

Fourier analysis *n. Mathematics.* A method of analyzing a periodic function into its harmonic components, the sum of which form a Fourier series. [After J.B.J. **FOURIER.**]

Fourier series *n.* An infinite series of sine and cosine functions, capable if uniformly convergent of approximating a wide variety of mathematical functions. [Devised by J.B.J. **FOURIER.**]

four-in-hand (fôr'ĭn-hănd', fōr'-) *n.* **1.** A vehicle drawn by four horses and driven by one person. **2.** A team of four horses. **3.** A tie tied in a slipknot with the ends left hanging and overlapping. —*adj.* Designating or pertaining to a four-in-hand.

four-leaf clover (fôr'lēf', fōr'-) *n.* Also **four-leaved clover** (-lēvd'). A clover leaf having four leaflets instead of the normal three, considered to be an omen of good luck.

four-let·ter word (fôr'lĕt'ər, fōr'-) *n.* Any of several short English words generally regarded as vulgar or obscene.

four-mast·ed (fôr'măs'tĭd, -mä'stĭd, fōr'-) *adj. Nautical.* Having four masts. —**four-mast·er** *n.*

four-o'clock (fôr'ə-klŏk', fōr'-) *n.* Any of several plants of the genus *Mirabilis;* especially, *M. jalapa,* native to tropical America, and widely cultivated for its tubular, variously colored flowers that open in the late afternoon. Also called "marvel-of-Peru."

four·pence (fôr'pəns, fōr'-) *n. British.* **1.** A sum of money equal to four pence or four old pennies. Used chiefly before the decimalization of British currency. **2.** Formerly, a small silver coin of this value.

four-post·er (fôr'pō'stər, fōr'-) *n.* A bed having tall corner posts to support curtains or a canopy. Also called "four-poster bed."

four·ra·gère (foor'ə-zhâr') *n.* **1.** An ornamental braided cord usually looped around the left shoulder. **2.** Such a cord awarded to an entire military unit. [French, from the feminine of *fourrager,* of forage, from *fourrage,* forage, from Old French *forage,* **FORAGE.**]

four·score (fôr'skôr', fōr'skōr') *adj.* Eighty; four times twenty.

four·some (fôr'səm, fōr'-) *n.* **1.** Any group of four persons; especially, two couples. **2. a.** A game, such as a golf match, played by four persons, two on each side. **b.** The players in such a game. —*adj.* Consisting of or involving a group of four. [Middle English *four-sum,* from Old English *fēowra sum,* one of four : *fēowra,* genitive of *fēower,* **FOUR** + *sum,* one, **SOME.**]

four-poster *This large square bedstead with its canopy on four upright posts is at Crathes Castle, Scotland.*

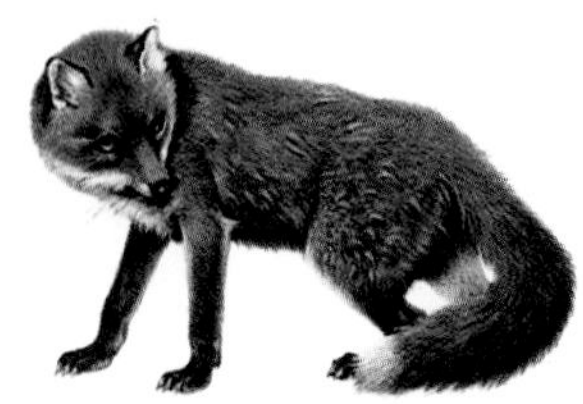

fox *The red fox of Eurasia,* Vulpes vulpes, *breeds once a year, usually in January. Its cubs are born in late March or early April.*

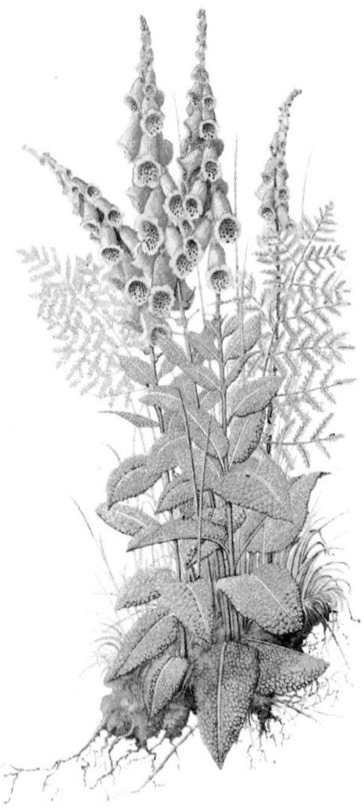

foxglove *This perennial herb,* Digitalis purpurea, *grows wild throughout Europe and Asia on banks and hillsides. Digitalin, a drug extracted from its leaves, is used by doctors as a heart stimulant.*

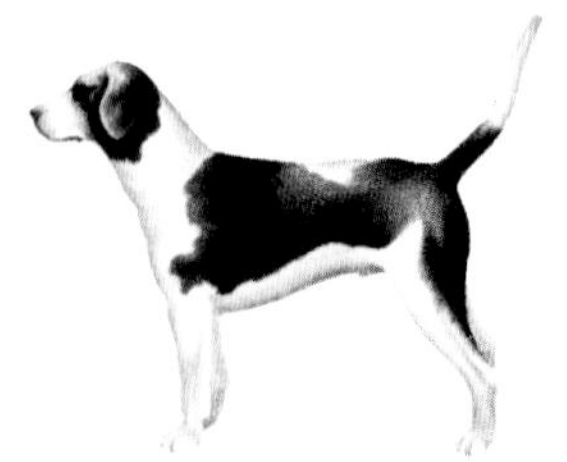

foxhound *Packs of foxhounds, bred for stamina and their acute sense of smell, are used as hunting dogs to find and chase foxes. They are rarely kept as pets. There are two breeds: the English foxhound (above) and the lighter American foxhound, developed from English dogs first taken across the North Atlantic in 1650.*

four·square (fôr′skwâr′, fōr′-) *adj.* **1.** Unyielding; firm. **2.** Forthright; honest; frank.
~adv. Squarely; forthrightly.

four-stroke (fôr′strōk′, fōr′-) *adj.* Designating an internal-combustion engine in which the pistons make four strokes for each explosion. Compare **two-stroke.**

four·teen (fôr-tēn′, fōr-) *n.* **1. a.** The cardinal number that is one more than 13. **b.** A symbol representing this, such as 14 or XIV. **2.** A set made up of 14 persons or things. **3.** The 14th in a series. **4.** A size, as in clothing, designated as 14. [Middle English *fourtene,* from Old English *fēowertīene.*] **—four·teen** *adj. & pron.*

four·teenth (fôr-tēnth′, fōr-) *n.* **1.** The ordinal number 14 in a series. **2.** One of 14 equal parts. **—four·teenth** *adj. & adv.*

fourth (fôrth, fōrth) *n.* **1.** The ordinal number four in a series. **2.** Any of four equal parts. **3.** *Music.* **a.** In a diatonic scale, a tone four degrees above or below any given tone. **b.** The interval between two such tones. **c.** The harmonic combination of these tones. **d.** In a scale, the subdominant. **4.** The fourth forward gear of a motor vehicle. **5. Fourth.** The Fourth of July. [Middle English *fourthe,* earlier *ferthe, furthe,* Old English *fēortha, fēowertha.*] **—fourth** *adj. & adv.* **—fourth·ly** *adv.*

fourth-class (fôrth′klăs′, -kläs′, fōrth′-) *adj.* Designating a class of mail consisting of merchandise or certain printed matter weighing over eight ounces and not sealed against inspection.
~adv. As or by fourth-class mail.

fourth dimension *n.* Time regarded as a dimension, that together with the three spatial dimensions is required to specify completely the location of any event in a space-time continuum.

fourth estate *n. Sometimes* **Fourth Estate.** The public press; journalism or journalists generally. [Formerly used jocularly to refer to something outside the (three) Estates of the Realm.]

Fourth International *n.* See **International.**

Fourth of July *n.* Independence Day.

four-wheel drive (fôr′hwēl′, fōr′-) *n. Abbr.* **f.w.d.** An automotive drive mechanism in which all four wheels are connected to the source of driving power.

fo·ve·a (fō′vē-ə) *n., pl.* **-veae** (-vē-ē′). **1.** A shallow cuplike depression or pit in a bone or other organ. **2.** The fovea centralis. [New Latin, from Latin *fovea,* small pit, possibly from Etruscan.] **—fo·ve·al, fo·ve·ate** *adj.*

fovea cen·tra·lis (sĕn-trā′lĭs) *n.* A small depression in the retina of the eye, constituting the area of most distinct vision. Also called "fovea."

fowl (foul) *n., pl.* **fowls** or collectively **fowl. 1.** Any of various birds of the order Galliformes; especially, the common, widely domesticated chicken, *Gallus gallus.* **2.** Any bird used as food or hunted as game. **3.** The edible flesh of such a bird. **4.** *Archaic.* Any bird.
~intr.v. **fowled, fowling, fowls.** To hunt, trap, or shoot wild fowl. [Middle English *foul,* Old English *fugol.*] **—fowl·er** *n.*

fowl cholera *n.* An acute, infectious, often fatal intestinal disease of domestic poultry and wild birds, caused by a bacterium, *Pasteurella multocida,* and characterized by enteritis, submucous hemorrhage, and vascular congestion.

Fow·ler (fou′lər), **Henry Watson** (1858–1933). British lexicographer. He collaborated with his brother, **Francis Fowler** (1870–1918), on a number of English dictionaries and edited the *Concise Oxford Dictionary* (1911). His best-known work is *Modern English Usage* (1926; revised 1965).

Fowles (foulz), **John** (1926–). British novelist. Though *The Magus* (1966) was his first novel, it was not published until after *The Collector* (1963). His other works include *The French Lieutenant's Woman* (1969), *Daniel Martin* (1977), and *Mantissa* (1982).

fowl·ing (fou′lĭng) *n.* The hunting of wild fowl.

fowling piece *n.* A light shotgun for shooting birds and small animals.

fowl pox *n.* A viral infection of poultry and other birds, characterized by wartlike nodules on the skin and cankers in the digestive and upper respiratory tracts.

fox (fŏks) *n.* **1.** Any of various carnivorous mammals of the genus *Vulpes* and related genera, related to the dogs and wolves, and characteristically having upright ears, a pointed snout, and a long, bushy tail. **2.** The fur of a fox. **3.** A crafty, sly, or clever person. **4.** *Archaic.* A sword. **5.** *Nautical.* Small cordage made by twisting together two or more strands of tarred yarn.
~v. **foxed, foxing, foxes.** *—tr.* **1. a.** To trick or fool by ingenuity or cunning; outwit. **b.** To baffle or confuse. **2.** *Archaic.* To make drunk; intoxicate. **3.** To make (beer) sour by fermenting. **4.** To repair (a shoe) by adding a new upper. *—intr.* **1.** To act deceitfully or craftily; pretend. **2.** To turn sour in fermenting. Used of beer. [Middle English, from Old English.]

Fox (fŏks), **Charles James** (1749-1806). English Whig statesman. He entered parliament in 1768 and in 1782 was appointed Britain's first foreign secretary. An ardent promoter of liberal causes, he supported American independence, parliamentary reform, and the French Revolution, but he was dismissed from the Privy Council in 1798 for opposing war with France.

Fox, George (1624–91). Founder of the Society of Friends (Quakers). Originally a shoemaker's apprentice, he became a traveling preacher in 1647. His stand against the established church won him many supporters, but he was frequently imprisoned for his beliefs.

foxed (fŏkst) *adj.* Discolored with yellowish-brown stains, as an old book or print may be. [From the resemblance of the stain to the color of a fox.]

fox·fire (fŏks′fīr′) *n.* A phosphorescent glow, especially that produced by certain fungi found on rotting wood. [Middle English, perhaps from the silvery quality of some fox fur.]

fox·glove (fŏks′glŭv′) *n.* **1.** Any of several plants of the genus *Digitalis;* especially, *D. purpurea,* native to Europe, having a long cluster of large, tubular, pinkish-purple flowers, and leaves that are the source of the medicinal drug digitalis. **2.** Any of several similar or related plants. [Middle English *foxes-glove,* Old English *foxes glōfa,* "fox's glove" (the reason for association with the fox is not known).]

fox·hole (fŏks′hōl′) *n.* A shallow pit dug by a soldier for immediate individual refuge against enemy fire.

fox·hound (fŏks′hound′) *n.* A dog developed for fox hunting; especially, a short-haired hound of either of two breeds, the *English foxhound* and the *American foxhound.*

fox hunt *n.* The hunting of a fox with hounds.

fox-hunt·ing (fŏks′hŭn′tĭng) *n.* The sport of hunting a fox with hounds, usually by people on horseback.

fox·ing (fŏk′sĭng) *n.* A brownish discoloration of paper or a book, caused by damp.

fox squirrel *n.* A squirrel, *Sciurus niger,* of the United States, having rusty or grayish fur.

fox·tail (fŏks′tāl′) *n.* **1.** Any of several grasses of the genus *Alopecurus,* having dense, silky or bristly flowering spikes. **2.** Any of several similar or related plants.

fox terrier *n.* A small dog having a white coat with dark markings, bred in both wire-haired and smooth-coated varieties.

fox·trot (fŏks′trŏt′) *n.* **1.** A ballroom dance in 2/4 or 4/4 time, composed of a variety of slow and fast steps. **2.** The music or a piece of music for this dance.
~intr.v. **fox·trotted, -trotting, -trots.** To dance a foxtrot. [From the short steps attributed to the comparatively short-legged fox.]

fox·y (fŏk′sē) *adj.* **-ier, -iest. 1.** Suggestive of a fox; sly; cunning; clever. **2.** Having a reddish-brown color. **3.** Discolored, as by decay; stained; foxed. **4.** Having the distinctive sharp flavor of some American grapes. Said of wine. **5.** *Informal.* Sexually attractive: *a foxy lady.* —See Synonyms at **sly. —fox·i·ly** *adv.* **—fox·i·ness** *n.*

foy (foi) *n. Chiefly Scottish.* A farewell entertainment, feast, drink, or gift, as at the end of a harvest or on the eve of a wedding. [Dialectal Dutch *fooi,* feast given for farm laborers after harvest, from Middle Dutch *foye, voye,* "voyage," feast given at parting, from Old French *voie,* way, journey, from Latin *via.*]

foy·er (foi′ər, foi′ā′, fwä′yā′) *n.* **1.** The entrance hall, lobby, or anteroom of a public building, such as a theater, hotel, or concert hall. **2.** The entrance hall or vestibule of a private dwelling. [French, hearth, home, foyer, from Medieval Latin *focārius,* from Latin *focus,* hearth, fireplace.]

Foyle, Lough (foil). Sea lough on the western border of Northern Ireland with the Republic of Ireland.

fp 1. forward pass. **2.** freezing point.

fpm, f.p.m. feet per minute.

FPO fleet post office.

fps foot-pound-second.

f.p.s. 1. feet per second. **2.** frames per second. **3.** foot-pound-second.

Fr The symbol for the element francium.

fr. 1. franc. **2.** from.

Fr. 1. father (clergyman). **2.** France; French. **3.** frater. **4.** Frau. **5.** friar.

Fra (frä) *n.* Brother. Used as a title for an Italian monk or friar. [Italian, short for *frate,* "brother," from Latin *frāter.*]

frab·jous (frăb′jəs) *adj. Informal.* Delightful; wonderful. [Coined by Lewis Carroll, perhaps based on *fair* and *joyous.*]

fra·cas (frā′kəs, frăk′əs; *British* frăk′ä′) *n., pl.* **fracas.** A disorderly uproar; a noisy quarrel; brawl. [French, from Italian *fracasso,* from *fracassare,* probably a blend of Latin *frangere,* to break, and *quassāre,* to shatter.]

frac·tion (frăk′shən) *n.* **1.** A small part of something; a scant portion: *a fraction of the populace.* **2.** A disconnected piece of something; a fragment; scrap; bit. **3.** *Mathematics.* An indicated quotient of two quantities. **4.** *Chemistry.* A component separated by a fractional process; a product of fractionation. **5.** The breaking of the host in the Eucharist. [Middle English *fraccioun,* from Late Latin *fractiō* (stem *fractiōn-*), act of breaking (especially bread), from Latin *fractus,* past participle of *frangere,* to break.]

frac·tion·al (frăk′shə-nəl) *adj.* **1.** Of, pertaining to, or constituting a fraction or fractions. **2.** Very small; insignificant; infinitesimal. **3.** Being in fractions or pieces; broken; fragmentary. **4.** Designating a chemical process in which components of a mixture are separated on the basis of differences in their physical properties: *fractional crystallization.* **—frac·tion·al·ly** *adv.*

fractional currency *n.* Any currency in a denomination less than the standard monetary unit.

fractional distillation *n.* **1.** Distillation in which the purity of the product is increased by bringing the vapor into contact with the condensed liquid in a countercurrent system. **2.** Distillation in which the product is collected in a series of separate fractions.

frac·tion·ate (frăk′shə-nāt′) *tr.v.* **-ated, -ating, -ates.** To separate (a chemical compound) into components by a fractional process, as by distillation or crystallization. **—frac·tion·a·tion** *n.* **—frac·tion·a·tor** *n.*

frac·tion·ize (frăk′shə-nīz′) *v.* **-ized, -izing, -izes.** *—tr.* To divide into fractions. *—intr.* To divide something into fractions. **—frac·tion·i·za·tion** *n.*

frac·tious (frăk′shəs) *adj.* **1.** Inclined to make trouble; unruly: *He was very fractious when drunk.* **2.** Having a peevish nature; irritable. [From FRACTION, in the sense of "breaking."] **—frac·tious·ly** *adv.* **—frac·tious·ness** *n.*

frac·to·cu·mu·lus cloud (frăk′tō-kyo͞om′yə-ləs) *n.* A low, ragged cumulus cloud. [Latin *fractus,* broken (past participle of *frangere*) + CUMULUS.]

frac·to·stra·tus cloud (frăk′tō-strā′təs, -străt′əs) *n.* A low, ragged stratus cloud. [Latin *fractus,* broken (see **fractocumulus cloud**) + STRATUS.]

frac·ture (frăk′chər) *n.* **1. a.** The act or process of breaking. **b.** The condition of being broken. **2.** A break, rupture, tear, or crack, as in bone or cartilage, as: a *comminuted fracture,* a fracture in which the bone is broken into several pieces; a *compound* or *open fracture,* a fracture with an open wound, often with the broken bone exposed; an *impacted fracture,* a fracture in which the broken ends have been forced into each other; a *simple* or *closed fracture,* a fracture with no break in the skin. **3.** *Mineralogy.* **a.** The characteristic manner in which a mineral breaks. **b.** The characteristic appearance of a broken mineral.
∼*v.* **fractured, -turing, -tures.** —*tr.* To break; crack. —*intr.* To undergo a fracture. —See Synonyms at **break.** [Middle English, from Old French, from Latin *fractūra,* from *fractus,* broken. See **fraction.**]

frae (frā) *prep. Scottish.* From. [Middle English *fra,* from Old Norse *frā.*]

fraenulum. Variant of **frenulum.**

fraenum. Variant of **frenum.**

frag·ile (frăj′əl, -īl′) *adj.* **1.** Easily broken or damaged; brittle. **2.** Physically weak; frail. **3.** Suggesting fragility; delicate. **4.** Tenuous; flimsy: *a fragile claim to fame.* [Old French, from Latin *fragilis,* from *frangere,* to break.] **—frag·ile·ly** *adv.* **—fra·gil·i·ty** (frə-jĭl′ə-tē), **frag·ile·ness** *n.*
Synonyms: *breakable, brittle, delicate, frail.*

frag·ment (frăg′mənt) *n.* **1.** A part broken off or detached from a whole. **2.** Something incomplete or unconnected; an odd bit or piece: *a fragment of conversation.* **3.** An extant part of an unfinished or lost text.
∼*v.* (frăg′mĕnt′) **fragmented, -menting, -ments.** —*tr.* To break or separate (something) into fragments. —*intr.* To break into pieces. [Middle English, from Latin *fragmentum,* from *frangere,* to break.]

frag·men·tal (frăg-mĕnt′l) *adj.* **1.** Fragmentary. **2.** *Geology.* Consisting of broken material moved from its place of origin.

frag·men·tar·y (frăg′mən-tĕr′ē) *adj.* Consisting of fragments or disconnected parts; broken. **—frag·men·tar·i·ly** (frăg′mən-târ′ə-lē) *adv.* **—frag·men·tar·i·ness** *n.*

frag·men·ta·tion (frăg′mən-tā′shən, frăg′mĕn-) *n.* **1.** The act or process of breaking into fragments. **2.** The scattering of the fragments of an exploding grenade, bomb, or shell; dispersion.
∼*adj.* Exploding into lethal high-velocity fragments of metal: *a fragmentation grenade.*

fragmentation bomb *n.* An aerial antipersonnel bomb that scatters shrapnel over a wide area.

frag·ment·ed (frăg′mĕn′tĭd) *adj.* Broken into fragments.

frag·ment·ize (frăg′mən-tīz′) *v.* **-ized, -izing, -izes.** —*tr.* To break (something) into fragments. —*intr.* To fragment.

Fra·go·nard (frăg′ə-när′), **Jean Honoré** (1732-1806). French painter and engraver. He is best known for his rococo paintings depicting lovers in exotic settings, cupids, nymphs, and other romantic figures.

fra·grance (frā′grəns) *n.* **1.** The state or quality of being fragrant. **2.** A sweet or pleasant odor; perfume. —See Synonyms at **smell.**

fra·grant (frā′grənt) *adj.* Having a pleasant odor; sweet-smelling; perfumed. [Middle English, from Old French, from Latin *fragrāns* (stem *fragrant-*), present participle of *fragrāre,* to emit an odor (good or bad), to reek.]

frail[1] (frāl) *adj.* **frailer, frailest. 1.** Having a delicate constitution; physically weak; not robust. **2.** Slight; weak; not strong or substantial. **3.** Easily broken or destroyed; vulnerable; fragile; uncertain. **4.** Morally weak; easily led astray or into evil. —See Synonyms at **fragile, weak.** [Middle English *frele, frail,* from Old French *frele, fraile,* from Latin *fragilis,* FRAGILE.] **—frail·ly** *adv.* **—frail·ness** *n.*

frail[2] *n.* **1.** A rush basket for holding fruit, especially dried fruit. **2.** The quantity of fruit, such as raisins or figs, contained in a frail, usually from 23 to 34 kilograms (50 to 75 pounds). [Middle English *fraiel,* from Old French *fraiel*†.]

frail·ty (frāl′tē) *n., pl.* **-ties. 1.** The condition or quality of being frail; weakness, especially of resolution. **2.** A fault arising from weakness; a failing: *human frailties.* —See Synonyms at **fault.**

fraise (frāz) *n.* **1.** A barrier or defense of pointed, inclined stakes or of barbed wire. **2.** A ruff for the neck, worn in the 16th century. **3.** A tool for enlarging a small circular hole. **4.** A tool for cutting teeth on a wheel, especially on a watch wheel. [French, "mesentery of a calf or lamb," originally "outer covering," "casing," from Old French *fraiser,* to remove the outer covering (used especially of beans), from Vulgar Latin *frēsāre* (unattested), from Latin *(faba) frēsa,* ground (bean), from *frēsus,* past participle of *frendere,* to grind with the teeth.]

frak·tur (fräk-to͝or′) *n.* A style of letter formerly used in German manuscripts and printing. [German *Fraktur,* from Latin *fractūra,* a breaking (from the curlicues that appear to break up the word), FRACTURE.]

fram·be·sia (frăm-bē′zhə) *n. Pathology.* **Yaws** *(see).* [New Latin, from French *framboise,* raspberry (from the appearance of the excrescences), from Old French, variant (influenced by *fraise,* strawberry) of Frankish *brām-besi* (unattested), "brambleberry."]

fram·boise (fräN-bwäz′) *n.* A clear French brandy distilled from raspberries. [French, "raspberry." See **frambesia.**]

frame (frām) *v.* **framed, framing, frames.** —*tr.* **1.** To construct by putting together the various parts of; build. **2.** To formulate or conceive; fashion; design; draw up. **3.** To arrange or adjust for a purpose; compose. **4. a.** To put into words; phrase: *frame a reply.* **b.** To form (words) silently with the lips. **5.** To provide with or as if with a surrounding or bordering frame; enclose or encircle. **6.** *Slang.* **a.** To rig evidence or events so as to incriminate (a person) falsely. **b.** To fix (a contest, for example) so as to ensure a desired fraudulent outcome: *frame a prizefight.* —*intr.* **1.** *Archaic.* To resort; proceed. **2.** *Obsolete.* To manage or contrive to do something.
∼*n.* **1.** Something composed of parts fitted and joined together; a structure, as: **a.** A basic or skeletal structure designed to give shape or support: *the frame of a house.* **b.** An open structure or rim for encasing, holding, or bordering something: *a window frame; a picture frame; glasses frames.* **c.** The human body. **d.** A **cold frame** *(see).* **e.** A climbing apparatus as used in a gymnasium or children's playground. **2.** A machine built upon or utilizing a frame. **3.** The general structure of something; system; order: *the frame of government.* **4. a.** Any of the transverse ribs of a ship's hull from the gunwale to the keel or the bilge, consisting of either a *square frame,* perpendicular to the keel's vertical plane, or a *cant frame,* at an oblique angle to it. **b.** A transverse stiffening rib in the fuselage of an aircraft. **5. a.** In billiards, a rigid triangular device for arranging the balls at the beginning of a game; a rack. **b.** The balls so arranged. **6. a.** A round or period of play in some games, such as bowling or billiards. **b.** *Baseball.* An inning. **7. a.** A single exposure on a roll of motion-picture film. **b.** A single scene in a cartoon strip. **8.** The total area of a television picture formed by a single traverse of the scanning spot. **9.** In electronics, computer science, and telecommunications, a cycle of regularly recurring pulses in a train of pulses. **10.** A slat or slats, serving as a base for building honeycombs, that is part of the structure of a man-made beehive. **11.** *Slang.* A frame-up. **12.** *Obsolete.* Shape; form. [Middle English *framen, framien,* to be advantageous, benefit, form, construct, Old English *framian,* to benefit, avail.] **—fram·er** *n.*

frame aerial *n.* A **loop aerial** *(see).*

frame house *n.* A house constructed with a wooden framework and usually covered with wooden boards.

frame of mind *n.* Mental state or attitude; mood.

frame of reference *n.* **1.** *Physics.* A set of coordinate axes in terms of which position or movement may be specified, or with reference to which physical laws may be mathematically stated. **2.** A set or system of ideas, as of philosophical or religious doctrine, in terms of which other ideas are interpreted or assigned meaning.

frame-up (frām′ŭp′) *n. Informal.* **1.** A prearranged or fraudulent scheme; a fix. **2.** A conspiracy to throw guilt on an innocent person; a scheme involving falsified charges or evidence.

frame·work (frām′wûrk′) *n.* **1.** A structure for supporting, defining, or enclosing something; especially, skeletal erections and supports used as the basis for something being constructed. **2.** Any outlying erection or work platform that allows access to something being constructed or worked on in some way; a rig; scaffolding. **3.** A basic arrangement, form, or system; a design.

fram·ing (frā′mĭng) *n.* A frame, framework, or system of frames.

franc (frăngk) *n. Abbr.* **f., fr. 1.** The basic monetary unit of France, Belgium, Switzerland, and numerous other countries, especially former French colonies. It is equal to 100 centimes. **2.** A coin worth one franc. See feature at **currency.** [Middle English *frank,* from Old French *franc,* from the Latin legend *Francorum rex,* "king of the Franks," on gold coins struck during the reign of Jean le Bon (1350–64).]

France (frăns, fräns). *Abbr.* **Fr.** Republic on the western seaboard of Europe. It is the continent's oldest state and largest country excluding the U.S.S.R. It was settled by the Franks, a Germanic people from across the Rhine, after the retreat of the Romans, who had conquered the Celtic Gauls in 57–51 B.C. The country enjoys all three European climates—maritime, continental, and Mediterranean. Its richest resource is its soil; 90 percent of the land is productive, either as arable land, permanent pasture, or forest. France is the world's second-largest producer of wine, after Italy, and is self-sufficient in meat and cereals. It is also heavily industrialized, and tourism is a major industry. Area, 547,026 square kilometers (211,208 square miles). Population, 53,800,000. Capital, Paris. [Middle English *Fraunce,* from Old French *France,* from Late Latin *Francia,* country of the Franks, from *Francus,* a FRANK.] See map, next page.

France (frăns, fräns, fräNs), **Anatole,** born Jacques Anatole France Thibault (1844–1924). French novelist. He was a great short-story writer and literary satirist. His works include *Thaïs* (1890), *L'Ile des Pingouins* (1908), and *La Révolte des Anges* (1914). He won the Nobel Prize in 1921.

Francesca, Piero della. See **Piero della Francesca.**

Fran·ces·ca de Ri·mi·ni (frăn-chĕs′kə də rĭm′ĭ-nē) (died *c.* 1285). Italian noblewoman. Unhappy in her arranged marriage to an Italian nobleman, she fell in love with her husband's brother, Paolo Malatesta. When her husband discovered the affair, he murdered both Francesca and her lover. This tragic love story is recounted in Dante's *Inferno* and several plays and operas.

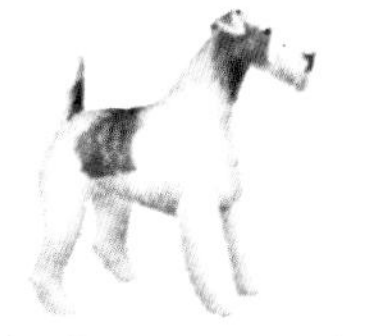

fox terrier *Fox terriers were bred as short-legged sporting dogs, small enough to get into a fox's earth or lair and drive it out into the open. This is a wire-haired fox terrier.*

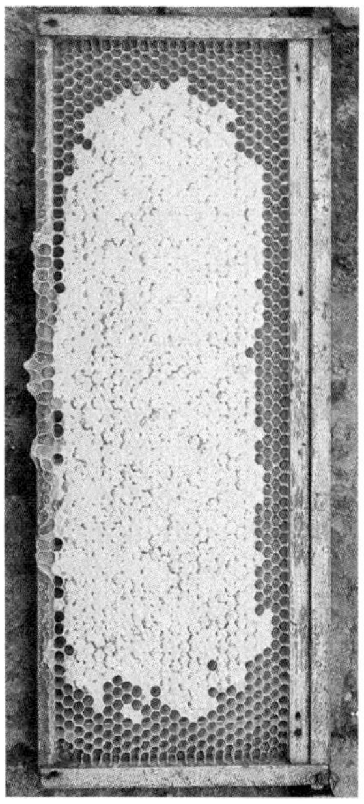

frame *A manmade honeycomb frame.*

PRONUNCIATION KEY

ă, pat; ā, pay; âr, care;
ä, father, are; b, bib;
ch, church; d, deed; ĕ, pet;
ē, be; f, fife; g, gag; h, hat;
hw, which; ĭ, pit; ī, pie;
îr, pier; j, judge; k, kick;
l, lid, needle; m, mum;
n, no, sudden; ng, thing;
ŏ, pot; ō, toe; ô, paw, for;
oi, noise; ou, out; o͝o, book;
o͞o, boot; p, pop; r, roar;
s, sauce; sh, ship, dish;
t, tight; th, thin, path;
th, this, bathe; ŭ, cut; ûr, fur;
v, valve; w, with; y, yes;
z, zebra, size; zh, vision;
ə, about, item, edible,
gallop, circus, peaceful

IN FOREIGN WORDS:

à, *Fr.* ami; œ, *Fr.* feu, *Ger.* schön; ü, *Fr.* tu, *Ger.* über; KH, *Ger.* ich, *Scot.* loch; N, *Fr.* bon; y′, *Fr.* Compiègne

STRESS MARKS:

Primary stress: ′
in·cite′ (ĭn-sīt′)
Secondary stress: ′
in′sight′ (ĭn′sīt′)

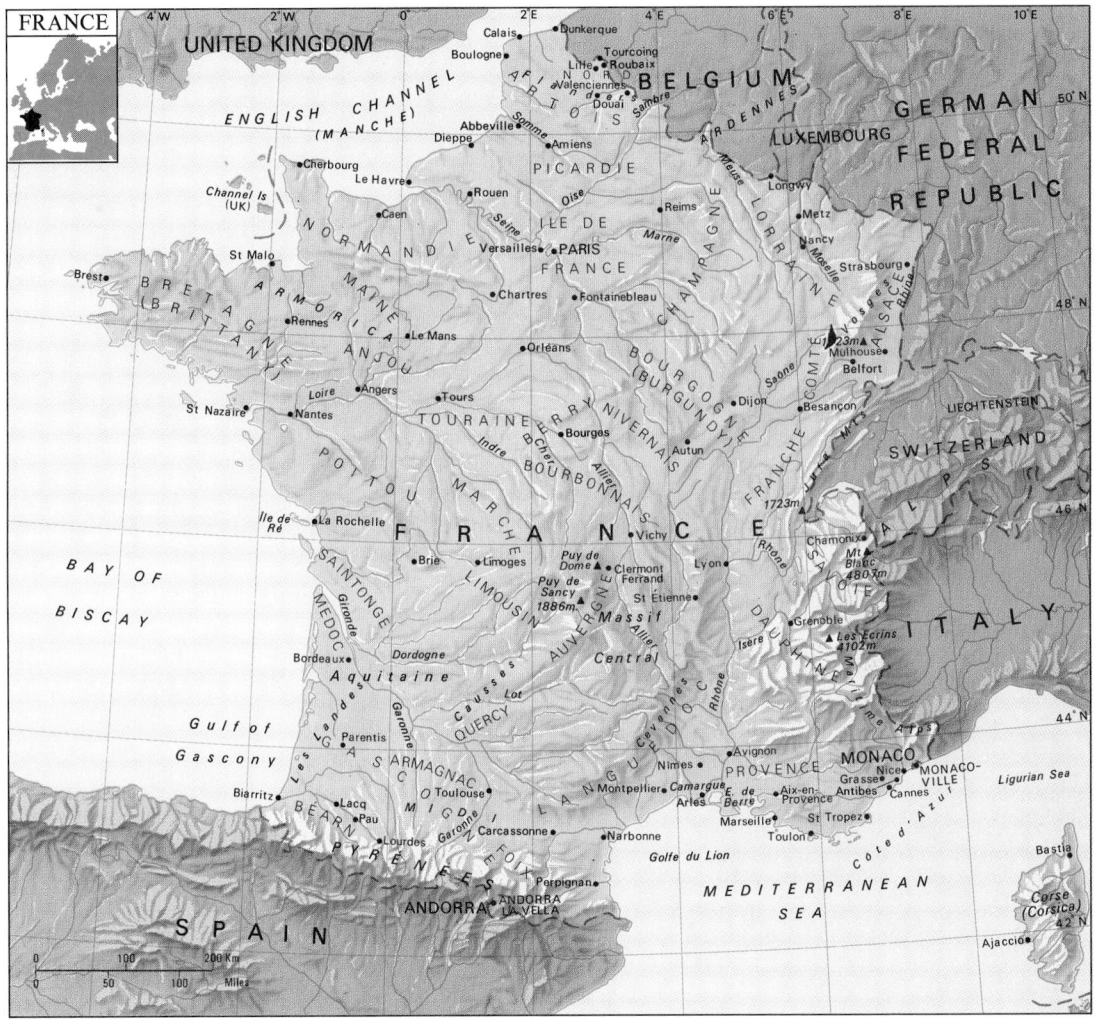

fran·chise (frăn'chīz') n. **1.** A privilege or right granted a person or a group by a government, state, or sovereign, especially: **a.** The constitutional or statutory right to vote; suffrage. **b.** Formerly, legal immunity from certain burdens, servitude, or other restrictions. **2.** Authorization granted by a manufacturer to a distributor or dealer to sell his products. **3.** The territory or limits within which some privilege, right, or immunity may be exercised. —See Synonyms at **right**.
~*tr.v.* **franchised, -chising, -chises.** To endow with a franchise. [Middle English *fraunchise,* freedom, privilege, from Old French *franchise,* from *franc* (feminine *franche*), free, FRANK.]

Fran·cis·can (frăn-sĭs'kən) n. A member of a religious mendicant order founded by St. Francis of Assisi in 1209 and now divided into three independent branches. Often called "Gray Friar." ~*adj.* Of or pertaining to St. Francis of Assisi or to the order founded by him.

Fran·cis Jo·seph (frăn'sĭs, frän'-; jō'zəf, -səf) (1830–1916). *German* **Franz Jo·sef** (fränts' yō'zĕf'). Austrian emperor. His reign (1848–1916) began at the height of the 1848 Revolution and was marked by a succession of crises. To ease tensions within his empire, he created the Dual Monarchy (1867) with Austria and Hungary. He was defeated by the Prussians (1866) but later allied with the German Empire (1879) and with Italy (1882) to form the Triple Alliance. Following the assassination (1914) of his nephew, Archduke Francis Ferdinand, by a Serbian nationalist, he issued an ultimatum to Serbia that was to lead to World War I.

Francis of As·si·si (ə-sē'zē, -sē) **Saint** (c. 1182–1226). Founder of the Franciscan order. He served for a time as soldier, but in 1206 devoted himself to a life of poverty. In 1210 he received papal permission to found his holy order, and he and his followers took Christ's teaching as far as North Africa and the Holy Land. His *Canticle to the Sun* (1225–26) testifies to his love of nature. He was canonized in 1228 and in 1980 was declared patron saint of ecology.

Francis of Sales (sălz, säl), **Saint** (1567–1622). French ecclesiastic. In his many spiritual works, including *Introduction to a Devout Life* (1609), he maintained that spiritual perfection is possible not just for religious contemplatives but also for people involved in secular pursuits. He is the patron saint of writers.

Francis Xa·vi·er (ză'vē-ər, zăv'ē-). **Saint** (1506–52). Spanish Jesuit missionary. He was cofounder, with St. Ignatius Loyola, of the Jesuit order. Known as the Apostle of the Indies, he established

missions in the East Indies, Japan, and Ceylon.

fran·ci·um (frăn'sē-əm) n. *Symbol* **Fr** An extremely unstable radioactive metallic element, having 20 known isotopes, the most stable of which is Fr 223 with a half-life of 21 minutes. Atomic number 87, valence 1. [New Latin, from FRANCE.]

Franck (frängk, fräNk), **César Auguste** (1822–90). Belgian composer and organist. He traveled to Paris in 1834 and became one of the most influential musical figures in mid-19th-century France. Though he composed mainly for the organ, his works also include an orchestral symphony and some oratorios.

Fran·co (fräng'kō, fräng'-), **Francisco** (1892–1975). Spanish dictator. As military governor of the Canary Islands, he helped direct the uprising of July 1936 and later that year became head of the Nationalist government and rebel armed forces. Following the defeat of the Republicans in the Spanish Civil War (1939), he ruled Spain until his death, when he was succeeded by a restored Bourbon monarchy.

Franco– *prefix.* Indicates France or French; for example, **Francophile, Francophobe.** [Medieval Latin *Francus,* a Frenchman, from Late Latin, a FRANK.]

fran·co·lin (fräng'kə-lĭn) n. **1.** Any of various Old World birds of the genus *Francolinus,* related to and resembling the quails and partridges. **2.** Any of various related birds, such as the Chinese francolin, *Excalfactoria.* [French, from Italian *francolino†.*]

Fran·co·phile (fräng'kə-fīl') n. Also **Fran·co·phil** (-fĭl'). An admirer of France, its people, and its customs. [FRANCO- + -PHILE.] —**Fran·co·phile** *adj.*

Fran·co·phobe (fräng'kə-fōb') n. One who fears or dislikes France, its people, or its customs. [FRANCO- + -PHOBE.] —**Fran·co·phobe** *adj.*

Fran·co·phone (fräng'kə-fōn') *adj.* French-speaking. ~*n.* A French-speaking person. [FRANCO- + -PHONE.]

Fran·co-Prus·sian War (fräng'kō-prŭsh'ən) n. The war of 1870–71 between Prussia and France.

franc ti·reur (frän' tē-rœr') n., pl. **francs tireurs** (*pronounced as singular*). A soldier or guerrilla who is not a member of a regular military force. [French, literally "free shooter."]

fran·gi·ble (frăn'jə-bəl) *adj.* Easily broken; breakable. [Middle English, from Old French, from Medieval Latin *frangibilis,* from Latin *frangere,* to break.] —**fran·gi·bil·i·ty, fran·gi·ble·ness** n.

fran·gi·pan·i (frăn'jə-păn'ē, -pä'nē) n. Also **fran·gi·pane** (frăn'-

jə-pān′) (for senses 2, 3). **1.** Any of various tropical American shrubs of the genus *Plumeria,* having milky juice and showy, fragrant, variously colored flowers. **2.** A perfume derived from or similar in scent to these flowers. **3.** A creamy pastry filling flavored with almonds. [French *frangipane,* from *(gants de) frangipane,* (gloves with) frangipani, after the Marquis *Frangipani* of Rome, who invented a perfume for scenting gloves in the 16th century.]

Fran·glais (frăn-glā′) *n.* French as used with numerous English words, word endings, and other borrowings from English. [Blend of French *Français,* French, and *Anglais,* English.]

frank (frăngk) *adj.* **franker, frankest. 1.** Open and sincere in expression; straightforward. **2.** Clearly manifest; undisguised; evident: *frank enjoyment.* **3.** *Rare.* Liberal in giving; generous. **4.** *Obsolete.* Free; open.
~*tr.v.* **franked, franking, franks. 1. a.** To put an official mark on (a letter, for example) to ensure free delivery through special official privilege. **b.** To send (mail) free of charge. **2.** To place a stamp or mark on (a letter or parcel) to show the payment of postage. **3.** To place a postmark on. **4.** To enable (a person) to come and go easily; especially, to allow to go free of charge.
~*n.* **1.** A mark or signature placed on a letter or parcel to indicate the right to send it free of postage. **2.** A franked letter or parcel. [Middle English, free, generous, from Old French *franc,* free, from Medieval Latin *francus,* from Late Latin *Francus,* FRANK (in Frankish Gaul full freedom was the right only of the conquering people or those under their protection).] —**frank·ly** *adv.* —**frank·ness** *n.*
   Synonyms: candid, ingenuous, open, outspoken.

Frank (frăngk) *n.* A member of one of the Germanic tribes of the Rhine region in the early Christian era; especially, one of the Salian Franks who conquered Gaul about 500 A.D. and established an extensive empire that reached its greatest power in the 9th century. [Middle English *Franc,* from Old English *Franca* and Old French *Franc,* from Late Latin *Francus,* from Germanic.]

Frank (frăngk, frăngk), **Anne** (1929–45). A Jewish girl who fled Germany with her family in 1933 to escape Nazi persecution, she was trapped in Amsterdam by the German invasion (1941). The family hid in a sealed room from 1942 until her arrest in 1944. She died in Bergen-Belsen concentration camp. The diary of her years in hiding was published in 1947; the house in Amsterdam is preserved as a museum.

Frank·en·stein monster (frăng′kən-stīn′) *n.* Also **Frank·en·stein's monster** (-stīnz′). **1.** Any agency or creation that slips from the control of and ultimately destroys its creator. **2.** A monster having the appearance of a man; specifically, the monster created by the protagonist of Mary Shelley's novel *Frankenstein* (1818), which brought about the ruin of its creator. Also called "Frankenstein."

Frank·en·thal·er (frăng′kən-thô′lər, -thôl′ər), **Helen** (1928–). U.S. artist. An abstract expressionist painter, she has used brilliant colors and innovative techniques to create graceful, stirring works, including *Mountains and Sea* (1952), *Arcadia* (1962), and *The Human Edge* (1967).

Frank·fort (frăngk′fərt). The capital of Kentucky, on the Kentucky River in the north-central part of the state. In the heart of the Bluegrass Country, Frankfort has diversified manufactures and is a trade and shipping center for an area yielding tobacco, livestock, and limestone.

Frank·furt am Main (frăngk′fərt äm mīn′, frăngk′foŏrt). Industrial city, financial center, and river port in Hesse, central West Germany. From 1816 to 1866, the city was the virtual capital of Germany and the seat of the Federal Diet (parliament).

Frankfurt an der O·der (än′ dĕr ō′dər). Town in eastern East Germany, on the Oder River, at the Polish border. It is an industrial center and agricultural market.

frank·furt·er, frank·fort·er (frăngk′fər-tər) *n.* Also **frank·furt, frank·fort** (frăngk′fərt). A smoked sausage of pork, beef, or beef and pork made in long, reddish links. [From FRANKFURT (AM MAIN), where it was originally made.]

Frank·furt·er (frăngk′fər-tər), **Felix** (1882–1965). U.S. jurist; Supreme Court Justice (1939–62); born in Austria. A founder of the American Civil Liberties Union (1920), he was appointed to the U.S. Supreme Court (1939) and, despite his liberal background, maintained that overliberal interpretations of the Constitution, particularly the First Amendment, could be detrimental to society.

frank·in·cense (frăng′kĭn-sĕns′) *n.* An aromatic gum resin obtained from African and Asian trees of the genus *Boswellia* and used chiefly as incense. Also called "olibanum." [Middle English *frank encens,* from Old French *franc encens : franc,* free, superior, FRANK + *encens,* INCENSE.]

Frank·ish (frăng′kĭsh) *adj.* Of or pertaining to the Franks or their language.
~*n.* The West Germanic language of the Franks.

frank·lin (frăng′klĭn) *n.* In England during the late medieval period, a freeholder not of noble birth but with extensive property; a country gentleman. [Middle English *frankelein,* from Medieval Latin *francālānus,* from *francālis,* (feudal estate) held without dues, from *francus,* free, FRANK.]

Frank·lin (frăng′klĭn). District within the Northwest Territories, Canada. It comprises the islands of the Canadian Arctic Archipelago and the Boothia and Melville peninsulas. It was named after the British Arctic explorer Sir John Franklin (1786–1847).

Franklin, Benjamin (1706–90). U.S. statesman, philosopher, physicist, and journalist. Following the success of his *Poor Richard's Almanac,* he entered politics and played a major part in the American Revolution. He negotiated French support for the colonists, promoted the Declaration of Independence (1776), and signed the Treaty of Paris (1783). He is remembered for his work on the drafting of the Constitution and his development of the lightning rod.

frank·lin·ite (frăng′klə-nīt′) *n.* A blackish, slightly magnetic mineral of zinc, iron, and manganese that is a valuable source of zinc. [After *Franklin,* New Jersey, where it is mined.]

frank·pledge (frăngk′plĕj′) *n.* **1.** In old English law, a system in which units or tithings composed of ten households were formed, in each of which members were held responsible for one another's conduct. **2.** A member of such a group, bound in pledge for his neighbors. **3.** The tithing itself. [Middle English *fraunkiplegge,* from Norman French *frauncplege : Old French *franc,* free, FRANK + Old French *plege,* PLEDGE.]

fran·tic (frăn′tĭk) *adj.* **1.** Emotionally distraught, as from fear, pain, worry, or passion; desperate; overwrought. **2.** Uncontrolled; wildly excited; frenzied. **3.** *Archaic.* Mad; insane. [Middle English *frantik, frenetik,* FRENETIC.] —**fran·ti·cal·ly, fran·tic·ly** *adv.* —**fran·tic·ness** *n.*

Franz Josef. See **Francis Joseph.**

Franz Jo·sef Land (fränts′ jō′səf, fränts′ yō′zĕf′). Also **Fridt·jof Nan·sen Land** (frĭt′yôf nän′sən). Arctic archipelago north of Novaya Zemlya. It was claimed by the U.S.S.R. in 1926 and is its most northerly territory. The 87 islands are mostly ice-covered all year and are inhabited mainly by polar bears, arctic foxes, walrus, and seals. The only human inhabitants are scientists at Soviet weather stations. The group was first explored by an Austrian expedition in 1873 and was named after the Austrian emperor. The group's alternate name, Fridtjof Nansen Land, comes from the Norwegian explorer who led an expedition to the archipelago (1895–99).

frap (frăp) *tr.v.* **trapped, trapping, traps.** *Nautical.* **1.** To make secure by lashing: *frap a sail.* **2.** To tighten; take up the slack of. [Middle English *frapen,* to strike, from Old French *fraper,* possibly from Frankish *hrappan*† (unattested).]

frap·pé (fră-pā′, frăp) *n., pl.* **frappés. 1.** A frozen, fruit-flavored mixture similar to sherbet and served as a dessert or appetizer. **2.** A beverage, usually a liqueur, poured over crushed ice. **3.** A milk shake containing ice cream. [French, from the past participle of *frapper,* "to strike," chill, from Old French *fraper,* to strike. See **trap.**] —**frap·pé** *adj.*

Fras·ca·ti (frä-skä′tē). Town in southern Italy *c.* 16 kilometers (10 miles) east of Rome. It is the site of the ruins of Cicero's villa and is also known for its dry white wine.

Fra·ser (frā′zər, -zhər). Chief river of British Columbia, Canada. It rises in the Rocky Mts. near the border with Alberta and flows *c.* 1,370 kilometers (850 miles) northwest and then south and west to the Strait of Georgia at Vancouver. The river is a major salmon-spawning ground, and its delta is a fertile agricultural region. Logging is important along its upper course.

Fraser, Simon (1776–1862). Canadian fur trader and explorer. He worked for the North West Company and explored the river named after him in British Columbia.

frat (frăt) *n. Informal.* A college fraternity.

fra·ter[1] (frā′tər) *n. Abbr.* **Fr.** A brother, as in a religious order or a fraternity. [Medieval Latin *frāter,* from Latin.]

frater[2] *n.* A refectory in a medieval monastery. [Middle English, from Old French *fraitur,* aphetic variant of *refreitor,* from Medieval Latin *refectorium,* REFECTORY.]

fra·ter·nal (frə-tûr′nəl) *adj.* **1. a.** Of or pertaining to brothers. **b.** Brotherly. **2.** Pertaining to or constituting a fraternity. **3.** *Biology.* Of, pertaining to, or being a twin or twins developed from separately fertilized ova. —See Synonyms at **familiar.** [Middle English, from Medieval Latin *frāternālis,* from Latin *frāternus,* from FRATER (brother).] —**fra·ter·nal·ism** *n.* —**fra·ter·nal·ly** *adv.*

fra·ter·ni·ty (frə-tûr′nə-tē) *n., pl.* **-ties. 1.** A body of men, such as a religious order or a guild, associated for some common purpose or interest. **2.** A group of men linked together by similar backgrounds, predilections, or occupations: *the fraternity of birdwatchers.* **3.** A chiefly social organization of male college students, usually designated by Greek letters. Compare **sorority. 4.** The relationship of a brother or brothers; brotherhood. **5.** Brotherliness. [Middle English *fraternite,* from Old French, from Latin *frāternitās* (stem *frāternitāt-*), from *frāternus,* FRATERNAL.]

frat·er·nize (frăt′ər-nīz′) *intr.v.* **-nized, -nizing, -nizes. 1.** To associate with others in a brotherly or congenial way. **2.** To mix intimately with the people of an enemy or conquered country, often in violation of military law. [French *fraterniser,* from Medieval Latin *frāternizāre,* from Latin *frāternus,* FRATERNAL.] —**frat·er·ni·za·tion** *n.* —**frat·er·niz·er** *n.*

frat·ri·cide (frăt′rə-sīd′) *n.* **1.** The killing of one's brother or sister. **2.** One who has killed his brother or sister. [Middle English (sense 2 only), from Old French (both senses), from Latin *frātricīda* (the person) and *frātricīdium* (the act) : *frāter,* FRATER + -CIDE.] —**frat·ri·cid·al** (frăt′rə-sīd′l) *adj.*

Frau (frou) *n., pl.* **Frauen** (frou′ən). *Abbr.* **Fr. 1.** A married woman in a German-speaking country or district. Used as a title corresponding to *Mrs.* **2.** *Informal.* A German woman. [German *Frau,* from Middle High German *vrouwe,* from Old High German *frouwa.*]

fraud (frôd) *n.* **1.** A deception deliberately practiced in order to secure unfair or unlawful gain. **2.** A piece of trickery; a swindle. **3. a.** One that defrauds; a cheat. **b.** One who assumes a false pose; an impostor. **c.** Something that is not what it appears or is claimed to be; a sham. [Middle English *fraude,* from Old French, from Latin *fraus†* (stem *fraud-*).]

fraud·u·lent (frô′jə-lənt) *adj.* **1.** Engaging in fraud; deceitful. **2.** Characterized by, constituting, or gained by fraud: *a fraudulent contract.* [Middle English, from Old French, from Latin *fraudulentus,* from *fraus,* FRAUD.] —**fraud·u·lence** *n.* —**fraud·u·lent·ly** *adv.*

fraught (frôt) *adj.* **1.** Filled or attended; charged. Used with *with: an occasion fraught with peril.* **2.** *Informal.* **a.** Causing anxiety or difficulty. **b.** Anxious or harassed. **3.** *Archaic.* Laden; freighted. [Middle English, past participle of *fraughten,* to load a ship, from Middle Dutch *vrachten,* from *vracht,* freight.]

Fräu·lein (froi′līn′, frou′-) *n., pl.* **Fräulein.** *Abbr.* **Frl. 1.** An unmarried girl or woman in a German-speaking country or district. Used as a title corresponding to *Miss.* **2.** *Chiefly British.* A German governess. [German, from Middle High German *vrouwelīn,* diminutive of *vrouwe,* wife, FRAU.]

Fraun·ho·fer (froun′hō′fər), **Joseph von** (1787–1826). German physicist. His development of optical lenses led to important discoveries in spectroscopy.

Fraunhofer lines *pl.n.* A set of several hundred dark lines appearing against the bright background of the continuous solar spectrum, produced by the absorption of light by cooler gases in the sun's outer atmosphere at frequencies corresponding to the atomic transition frequencies of these gases. [After J. von FRAUNHOFER.]

frax·i·nel·la (frăk′sə-nĕl′ə) *n.* The **gas plant** *(see).* [New Latin, diminutive of Latin *fraxinus,* ash tree (from the resemblance of its leaves to those of the ash).]

fray¹ (frā) *n.* **1.** A scuffle or brawl. **2.** A heated dispute or contest. [Middle English, fright, commotion, conflict, from *fraien,* to frighten, short for *afraien, affraien,* from Old French *affreer,* to AFFRAY.]

fray² *v.* **frayed, fraying, frays.** —*tr.* **1.** To unravel, wear away, or tatter (the edges of fabric, for example) by rubbing. **2.** To strain; chafe: *nerves frayed by noise.* —*intr.* To become tattered, unraveled, or threadbare along the edges.
~*n.* A frayed or threadbare spot, as on fabric. [Middle English *fraien,* from Old French *fraier,* from Latin *fricāre,* to rub.]

Fray Ben·tos (frā bĕn′təs). River port in southwestern Uruguay, on the Uruguay River. It was founded in 1859 and has long been an important meat-packing center, noted for corned beef.

Fra·zer (frā′zər), **Sir James George** (1854–1941). British anthropologist and writer. His most famous work, *The Golden Bough* (1890), examined the development of human thought with reference to magic, religion, and science.

Fra·zier (frā′zhər), **Joe** (1944–). U.S. boxer. He was Olympic heavyweight champion (1964) and later won the world professional heavyweight title (1970), but lost it to George Foreman (1973).

fra·zil (frā′zəl, frăz′əl) *n.* Ice fragments, often sharp and pointed, that occur in turbulent water in which sheets of ice cannot form. [Canadian French *frasil;* akin to French *fraisil,* cinders.]

fraz·zle (frăz′əl) *v.* **-zled, -zling, -zles.** *Informal.* —*tr.* **1.** To fray; chafe. **2.** To wear out the nerves or strength of. —*intr.* To become frazzled or worn out.
~*n.* **1.** A frayed or tattered condition. **2.** A condition of nervous exhaustion: *The racket the children made wore me to a frazzle.* [Probably a blend of FRAY (wear) and dialectal *fazzle,* to fray, from Middle English *faselen,* from *fasel,* fringe, frayed edge, diminutive of *fas,* fringe, Old English *fæs,* from Germanic *fas-* (unattested).]

F.R.B. Federal Reserve Board.

F.R.C.P. Fellow of the Royal College of Physicians.

F.R.C.S. Fellow of the Royal College of Surgeons.

freak¹ (frēk) *n.* **1.** A thing or occurrence that is very unusual or irregular: *A freak of nature produced the midsummer snowstorm.* Also used adjectivally: *a freak wind; a freak accident.* **2.** An abnormally formed organism; especially, a person or animal regarded as a curiosity or monstrosity. **3.** A sudden capricious turn of the mind; whim. **4.** *Slang.* **a.** A drug user or addict: *a speed freak.* **b.** A person with a great enthusiasm or liking for a particular subject, interest, or activity: *a baseball freak.* **5.** *Slang.* An unconventional or intentionally bizarre person.
~*v.* **freaked, freaking, freaks.** *Slang.* —*intr.* **1.** To become highly excited and emotional about something. **2.** To become emotionally or mentally unstable or outlandishly uninhibited in behavior. Often used with *out.* **3.** To undergo a hallucinatory experience, especially as a result of taking drugs. Often used with *out.* —*tr.* To cause to freak or freak out. [16th century : of dialect origin.] —**freak′i·ly** *adv.* —**freak′i·ness** *n.* —**freak′y** *adj.*

freak² *n.* A fleck or streak of color.
~*tr.v.* **freaked, freaking, freaks.** To speckle or streak with color. [Originally *freaked,* probably formed by Milton, probably variant (influenced by STREAK) of obsolete *freckt,* from FRECKLE.]

freak·ish (frē′kĭsh) *adj.* **1.** Unusual; outlandish; abnormal. **2.** Pertaining to or characteristic of a freak. **3.** Capricious. —**freak′ish·ly** *adv.* —**freak′ish·ness** *n.*

freck·le (frĕk′əl) *n.* A small brown mark or precipitation of pigment in the skin, often brought out by the sun.
~*v.* **freckled, -ling, -les.** —*tr.* To dot with freckles or spots of color. —*intr.* To become dotted with freckles. [Middle English *frakles* (plural), variant of *fraknes,* from Old Norse *freknur* (plural).] —**freck′ly** *adj.*

Fred·er·ick I (frĕd′ər-ĭk), known as "Barbarossa" (Redbeard) (c. 1123–90). Holy Roman Emperor (1155–90). On his accession he asserted imperial power against the papacy in an at-

tempt to enforce his feudal rights in Italy, but was crushingly defeated at Legnano (1176). He drowned while leading the Third Crusade.

Frederick II, known as "the Great" (1712–86). King of Prussia (1740–86). In a brilliant military career he elevated Prussia to a position of great power in Germany. He pursued a policy of enlightened despotism, laying the foundations of the Prussian military state.

Fred·er·icks·burg (frĕd′rĭks-bûrg′). City of northern Virginia, midway between Washington, D.C., and Richmond. Noted for its fine old houses, it was the site of a Civil War battle (1862) in which Gen. Robert E. Lee's Confederate forces routed the Union troops of Gen. Ambrose E. Burnside.

Fred·er·ic·ton (frĕd′ər-ĭk-tən, frĕd′rĭk-). Capital of New Brunswick, eastern Canada, in the south-central part of the province on the St. John River. The city was founded by Loyalists in 1783. Shoes and wood products are manufactured here.

free (frē) *adj.* **freer, freest. 1.** At liberty; not bound or constrained. **2.** Discharged from arrest or detention. **3.** Not under obligation or necessity. **4. a.** Politically independent. Said of a country or nation. **b.** Governed by consent and possessing civil liberties: *a free society.* **c.** Immune to arbitrary interference by government or others: *a free press.* **5. a.** Not affected or restricted by a given condition or circumstance. Used with *from* or *of: free from need.* Often used in combination: *trouble-free.* **b.** Not subject to a given condition; exempt. Often used in combination: *duty-free.* **c.** Not containing; without. Often used in combination: *fat-free; sugar-free.* **6. a.** Not subject to external constraint: *free criticism.* **b.** Not subject to external physical restraint: *free fall.* **c.** Graceful; easy: *free gestures.* **d.** Not fixed, attached, or tied: *the free end of a rope.* **7. a.** Not strict or literal: *a free translation.* **b.** Not following formal rules or conventions: *free verse.* **c.** Not subject to any melodic or rhythmic patterns; completely improvised: *free jazz.* **8. a.** Costing nothing; gratuitous: *a free ticket.* **b.** Public; open to all: *free education.* **c.** Not paying the usual fee: *a free patient.* **9. a.** Unoccupied; available for use: *a free shelf.* **b.** Not busy; available: *a free afternoon; free to see you now.* **c.** Unobstructed; clear: *a free lane.* **10.** Guileless; frank: *"The Moor is of a free and open nature"* (Shakespeare). **11.** Taking undue liberties; forward. **12.** Liberal or lavish: *free with his money.* **13.** Uninhibited; racy: *much free talking and flirting at the party.* **14.** Uncommitted; independent: *a free woman.* **15.** *Chemistry & Physics.* **a.** Unconstrained; unconfined: *free expansion.* **b.** Not fixed in position; capable of relatively unrestricted motion: *a free electron.* **c.** Not chemically bound; uncombined: *free oxygen.* **d.** Involving no collisions or interactions: *a free path.* **16.** *Nautical.* Favorable. Said of a wind. **17.** *Phonetics.* Designating a vowel in an open syllable unchecked by a consonant; for example, *o* in *go* is a free vowel. **18.** *Botany.* Not joined to one another or to other organs. Said especially of flower parts, as petals.
~*adv.* **1.** In a free manner; freely. **2.** Without charge. —**make free with.** To take liberties with. —**run free.** *Nautical.* To sail with the wind aft.
~*tr.v.* **freed, freeing, frees. 1.** To set at liberty; release. **2.** To rid or release. Used with *of* or *from: a people freed from fear.* **3.** To disengage; untangle: *free a rope.* [Middle English *fre(e),* Old English *frēo,* from Germanic *frijaz* (unattested).] —**free′ly** *adv.* —**free′ness** *n.*

Usage: In its sense "unaffected or unrestricted by a given condition," *free* takes both *from* and *of.* *Of* is found in the context of finance (*free of charge; free of tax*) and where the general sense is one of removing a problem or restriction: *The room has been disinfected and is now free of germs.* *From* tends to be used where the general sense is one of actively preventing a problem from developing: *kept the garden free from weeds.*

free agent *n.* A person unconstrained by ties of emotion, contract, or other commitments; especially, a professional athlete who is free to sign a contract with any sports team.

free alongside ship *adj. Abbr.* **f.a.s., F.A.S.** Delivered to the pier or dock at no extra charge. Said of cargo going by sea.

free-and-eas·y (frē′ən-ē′zē) *adj.* Also **free and easy.** Informal in manner and unconcerned with strict niceties.

free-as·so·ci·ate (frē′ə-sō′shē-āt′, -sē-āt′) *intr.v.* **-ated, -ating, -ates.** To engage in free association.

free association *n.* **1.** A spontaneous, logically unconstrained association of ideas and feelings. **2.** A psychoanalytic technique in which a patient's articulation of such associations is encouraged in order to elicit repressed thoughts and emotions.

free·bie, free·bee (frē′bē) *n. Slang.* A free gift; something provided without payment. [From FREE.]

free·board (frē′bôrd′, -bōrd′) *n.* **1.** *Nautical.* The distance between the water line and the uppermost full deck. **2.** The distance between the ground and the undercarriage of an automobile.

freeboard deck *n.* The uppermost deck that is officially considered completely watertight.

free·boot (frē′bōōt′) *intr.v.* **-booted, -booting, -boots.** To act as a freebooter; plunder. [Back-formation from FREEBOOTER.]

free·boot·er (frē′bōō′tər) *n.* A person who pillages and plunders; especially, a pirate; buccaneer. [Partial cognate translation of Dutch *vrijbuiter,* from *vrijbuit,* free booty : *vrij,* FREE + *buit,* BOOTY.]

free·born (frē′bôrn′) *adj.* **1.** Born as a free person. **2.** Pertaining to or befitting a person born free.

free capital *n.* **1.** Capital available for investment. **2.** Capital not earmarked for a specific use.

Free Church *n. Chiefly British.* **1.** Any non-Anglican Protestant Church; a Nonconformist church. **2.** Any church that is not the established church of a state or that is free of state control. —**Free-Church** (frē'chûrch') *adj.*

free city *n.* **1.** A sovereign city-state, such as those established in Germany and Italy in the Middle Ages. **2.** A city governed as an autonomous political unit under international auspices.

free companion *n.* A mercenary of the Middle Ages.

free company *n.* A company of free companions.

freed·man (frēd'mən) *n., pl.* **-men** (mĭn). A man who has been freed from bondage; an emancipated slave.

free·dom (frē'dəm) *n.* **1.** The condition of being free of restraints. **2.** The condition of not being subject to slavery, oppression, or imprisonment. **3. a.** Political independence. **b.** Possession of civil rights; immunity from the arbitrary exercise of authority. **4.** Exemption from unpleasant or onerous conditions. Used with *from: freedom from fear and want.* **5.** The capacity to exercise choice; free will. **6.** Facility or ease, as of movement. **7.** Originality of style or conception. **8.** Frankness. **9. a.** Boldness; impertinence. **b.** An instance of improper boldness; a liberty. **10.** Unrestricted use or access. **11.** The right of enjoying all of the privileges of membership or citizenship: *the freedom of the city.* [Middle English *fredom,* Old English *frēodōm : frēo,* FREE + -DOM.]

freedom fighter *n.* One who takes militant action against an established government, usually one of an authoritarian nature.

freedom of the seas *n. International Law.* **1.** The doctrine that ships of any nation may travel through international waters unhampered. **2.** The right of neutral shipping in wartime to trade at will except where blockades are established.

freed·wom·an (frēd'wŏom'ən) *n., pl.* **-women** (-wĭm'ĭn). A woman freed from bondage.

free electron *n.* An electron that is not bound to an atom, such as an electron in a conductor that is available to move in a current.

free energy *n.* **1.** A thermodynamic quantity that is the difference between the internal energy and the product of the thermodynamic temperature and entropy of a system. Also called "Helmholtz free energy." **2.** A thermodynamic quantity that is the difference between the enthalpy and the product of the thermodynamic temperature and entropy of a system. In this sense, also called "Gibbs free energy."

free enterprise *n.* The freedom of private businesses to operate competitively for profit, with minimal government regulation.

free fall *n.* **1.** The fall of a body within the atmosphere without a drag-producing device such as a parachute. **2.** The unconstrained motion of a body in a gravitational field.

free flight *n.* Flight, as of an aircraft or spacecraft, after termination of powered flight.

free·float·ing (frē'flō'tĭng) *adj.* **1.** Not attached or fixed to any specific base or source. **2.** Not committed to any particular viewpoint or course of action; independent.

free-for-all (frē'fər-ôl') *n.* A brawl, argument, or competition in which everyone present takes part.

free form *n. Linguistics.* A morpheme capable of standing alone and retaining meaning. Compare **bound form.**

free·form (frē'fôrm') *adj.* Designating a form in music, art, literature, or the like that is free of stylistic conventions.

free gift *n.* An object given away with or accompanying without extra charge a purchased object. Often used as an inducement to purchase, especially in mail-order selling.

free hand *n.* Full liberty to do as one sees fit.

free·hand (frē'hănd') *adj.* Drawn by hand without the aid of tracing or guiding instruments: *a freehand sketch.*
～*adv.* By hand without mechanical aids.

free·hand·ed (frē'hăn'dĭd) *adj.* Openhanded; generous; unstinting. —**free·hand·ed·ly** *adv.* —**free·hand·ed·ness** *n.*

free·heart·ed (frē'här'tĭd) *adj.* Unreserved; open; generous; liberal. —**free·heart·ed·ly** *adv.* —**free·heart·ed·ness** *n.*

free·hold (frē'hōld') *n.* **1.** *Law.* **a.** An estate held in fee simple, fee tail, or for life. **b.** The tenure by which such an estate is held. Compare **leasehold.** **2.** Loosely, outright ownership of land. **3.** A tenure of an office or a dignity for life. [Middle English *frehold* (translation of Norman French *fraunc tenement,* "free or frank holding") : FREE + HOLD.] —**free·hold** *adj.* —**free·hold·er** *n.*

free kick *n.* In various types of football, an unhindered kick awarded to a team for an infringement of the rules by the opposing team.

free·lance (frē'lăns', -läns') *n.* Also **free·lanc·er** (frē'lăn'sər, -län'sər). **1.** A person, especially a writer or an artist, who sells his services to employers without a long-term commitment to any one of them. **2.** One who remains uncommitted to a party and proceeds as an independent. **3.** A medieval mercenary; a free companion.
～*v.* **freelanced, -lancing, -lances.** —*intr.* To work as a freelance. —*tr.* To produce and sell as a freelance.
～*adj.* Pertaining to or produced by a freelance.
～*adv.* On a freelance basis.

free-liv·ing (frē'lĭv'ĭng) *adj.* **1.** Given to self-indulgence. **2.** *Biology.* Living or moving independently; not part of a parasitic or symbiotic relationship.

free·load (frē'lōd') *intr.v.* **-loaded, -loading, -loads.** *Slang.* To act as a freeloader; sponge.

free·load·er (frē'lō'dər) *n. Slang.* One who takes advantage of the generosity or hospitality of others; a sponger.

free love *n.* The practice of sexual relations without marriage and without formal or legal obligations.

free·man (frē'mən) *n., pl.* **-men** (-mĭn). **1.** A person not in slavery or serfdom. **2.** One who possesses the rights or privileges of a citizen.

free·mar·tin (frē'märt'n) *n.* A sterile or otherwise sexually deficient female calf born as the twin of a bull calf. [17th century : origin obscure.]

free·ma·son (frē'mā'sən) *n.* **1.** A member of a guild of skilled itinerant masons of the Middle Ages. **2. Freemason.** A member of the Free and Accepted Masons, an international secret society. In this sense, also called "Mason." [Originally, perhaps a mason not subject to guild control and so free to work anywhere.]

free·ma·son·ry (frē'mā'sən-rē) *n.* **1.** Tacit fellowship and sympathy among a number of people. **2. Freemasonry. a.** The institutions, precepts, and rites of the Freemasons. **b.** The Freemasons. In this sense, also called "Masonry."

free on board *adj. Abbr.* **f.o.b., F.O.B. 1.** In international commerce, designating goods delivered and insured at the seller's expense until arriving at the port of shipment named by the buyer. **2.** Delivered on board or into a carrier without charge.

free port *n.* **1.** A port open on equal terms to all commercial vessels. **2.** An area in which imported goods can be held or processed before re-export, free of customs duties.

fre·er¹ (frē'ər) *n.* One who frees.

fre·er². Comparative of **free.**

free radical *n.* An atom or group of atoms containing at least one unpaired electron and having a short lifetime before reacting to form a stable molecule.

free·si·a (frē'zhē-ə, -zhə, -zē-ə) *n.* Any of several widely cultivated plants of the genus *Freesia,* native to southern Africa, having one-sided clusters of fragrant, variously colored flowers. [New Latin, after Friedrich H.T. *Freese* (died 1876), German physician.]

free silver *n.* The free coinage of silver, especially at a fixed ratio to gold.

free soil *n.* U.S. territory in which slavery was prohibited before the Civil War.

free-soil (frē'soil') *adj.* **1.** Prohibiting slavery: *free-soil states.* **2.** Opposing the extension of slavery prior to the Civil War. **3. Free-Soil.** Pertaining to or designating a U.S. political party founded in 1848 to oppose the extension of slavery into U.S. Territories and the admission of slave states into the Union.

free speech *n.* The right to express any opinion in public.

free·spo·ken (frē'spō'kən) *adj.* Candid in expression; outspoken; frank. —**free·spo·ken·ness** *n.*

fre·est. Superlative of **free.**

free·stand·ing (frē'stăn'dĭng) *adj.* Standing independently; free of support or attachment.

Free State. A U.S. state prohibiting slavery prior to the Civil War.

free·stone (frē'stōn') *n.* **1.** A stone, such as some sandstones or limestones, fine-grained and even-textured enough to be cut easily in any direction without shattering or splitting. **2.** A fruit, especially a peach, having a stone that does not adhere to the pulp. In this sense, compare **clingstone.**
～*adj.* Having a stone that does not adhere to the pulp.

free·style (frē'stīl') *n.* **1.** In swimming, a race in which any stroke may be used. The **crawl** *(see)* is usually chosen because of the speed achieved with this stroke. **2.** In various sports, a contest or style of performing in which any movements are allowed. Also used adjectivally: *freestyle wrestling.* —**free·style** *adv.*

free·swim·ming (frē'swĭm'ĭng) *adj. Zoology.* Able to swim freely; not sessile or attached: *the free-swimming larva of the oyster.* —**free·swim·mer** *n.*

free·think·er (frē'thĭng'kər) *n.* One who has rejected authority and dogma, especially in his religious thinking, in favor of rational inquiry and speculation. —**free·think·ing** *adj. & n.*

free thought *n.* Freethinking; unorthodox thought.

free throw *n. Basketball.* A foul shot *(see).*

free-throw line (frē'thrō') *n. Basketball.* The **foul line** *(see).*

Free·town (frē'toun'). Capital of Sierra Leone. Situated on the Sierra Leone peninsula, with an exceptional natural harbor, it is also one of West Africa's chief ports. The town was founded by freed slaves sent from North America in 1787 by the Sierra Leone Company.

free trade *n.* Trade between nations or states without protective customs tariffs or other restrictions.

free verse *n.* Verse that does not follow a conventional metrical or stanzaic pattern and has either an irregular rhyme or no rhyme. [Translation of French *vers libre.*]

free·way (frē'wā') *n.* **1.** A highway with several lanes and no intersections or stoplights; expressway. **2.** A highway without tolls.

free·wheel (frē'hwēl') *n.* **1.** A transmission device in a motor vehicle that allows the drive shaft to continue turning when its speed is greater than that of the engine shaft. **2.** A device in the rear-wheel hub of a bicycle that permits the wheel to turn without pedal action. Also used adjectivally: *a freewheel bicycle.*
～*intr.v.* **freewheeled, -wheeling, -wheels.** To live or move freely, aimlessly, or irresponsibly.

free·wheel·ing (frē'hwē'lĭng) *adj.* **1.** Pertaining to or equipped with a freewheel. **2.** *Informal.* **a.** Free of restraints or rules in organization, methods, or procedure. **b.** Heedless; carefree.

free will *n.* **1.** The power or discretion to choose; free choice. **2.** The belief that man's choices ultimately are or can be voluntary, and are not determined by external causes. Compare **determinism.** [Translation of Late Latin *liberum arbitrium.*]

free world *n. Sometimes* **Free World.** The portion of the world marked by democratic and capitalistic or socialistic systems rather than by Communist or totalitarian systems.

freeze (frēz) *v.* **froze** (frōz), **frozen** (frō′zən), **freezing, freezes.** —*intr.* **1. a.** To pass from the liquid to the solid state by loss of heat. **b.** To acquire a surface of ice from cold. Often used with *over.* **2.** To become inoperative owing to frost or the formation of ice: *The pipes froze.* **3.** To become hard from cold, as laundry or the ground. **4.** To undergo freezing and thawing successfully: *Raspberries don't freeze well.* **5. a.** To be at that degree of temperature at which ice forms. Used impersonally: *It may freeze tonight.* **b.** To be uncomfortably cold. Used impersonally: *It's freezing in here.* **6.** To be harmed, ruined, or killed by cold or frost: *The crops froze.* **7.** To feel the cold acutely: *I'm freezing.* **8.** To become fixed, stuck, or attached by or as if by frost: *The bolt had frozen in place.* **9.** To become motionless, as from fear, horror, or shyness. **10.** To become icily silent in manner. Often used with *up: She froze up at the rebuke.* —*tr.* **1. a.** To convert into ice. **b.** To cause ice to form upon. **c.** To cause to become solid, congeal, or stiffen from extreme cold. **2.** To preserve by subjecting to freezing temperatures. **3.** To damage, kill, or make inoperative by cold or by the formation of ice. **4. a.** To make very cold; chill. **b.** To chill with an icy or formal manner. **5.** To make rigid and inflexible. **6.** To fix (prices or wages) at a given or current level. **7.** To prohibit further manufacture or use of. **8.** To prevent or restrict the exchange, liquidation, or granting of by law: *The banks have agreed to freeze investment loans.* **9. a.** *Surgery.* To anesthetize by freezing. **b.** Loosely, to apply a local anesthetic to. **10. a.** To stop (a moving film) at a particular frame. **b.** To repeat a frame in (a moving film) to give the impression of arrested movement. **11.** To stop (a process or action) at a particular point in development. —**freeze in one's tracks.** To stop short and remain motionless, as with fear. —**freeze out.** *Informal.* To shut out or bar, as from a business or a social group, by boycotting, snubbing, or cold treatment.
~*n.* **1. a.** An act of freezing. **b.** The state of being frozen. **2.** A spell of cold weather; a frost. [Freeze, froze, frozen; Middle English *fresen, frose, frosen,* variant (influenced by present tense) of *froren,* from Old English *frēosan, frēas, froren,* from Germanic.]

freeze-dry (frēz′drī′) *tr.v.* **-dried, -drying, -dries.** To preserve by freeze-drying.

freeze-dry·ing (frēz′drī′ĭng) *n.* Preservation, as of foodstuffs or histological specimens, by rapid freezing and drying in a high vacuum.

freeze-etch·ing (frēz′ĕch′ĭng) *n.* A method of preparing a specimen for examination under an electron microscope whereby the specimen is frozen and then fractured with a knife so that a shadowed replica of the surface can be made.

freeze-frame (frēz′frām′) *n.* The capacity in film projection systems to stop a moving film at a particular frame. Also used adjectivally: *freeze-frame capacity.*

freez·er (frē′zər) *n.* **1.** One that freezes. **2.** A thermally insulated cabinet, compartment, or room that maintains a subfreezing temperature for the rapid freezing and storing of perishable food. Also called "deepfreeze."

freeze-up (frēz′ŭp′) *n. Informal.* **1.** A period of intensely cold weather. **2.** The freezing over of lakes and rivers.

freez·ing (frē′zĭng) *adj.* Extremely cold.
~*adv.* Used as an intensive: *freezing cold.*

freezing mixture *n.* A mixture of two substances, usually ice and salt, that gives a temperature of less than 0°C.

freezing point *n. Abbr.* **fp 1.** The temperature at which a liquid solidifies. **2.** The temperature at which the liquid and solid phases of a substance are in equilibrium at atmospheric pressure.

free zone *n.* An area at a port or city where goods may be received and held without the payment of duty.

F region *n.* A region of the ionosphere, the **F layer** *(see).*

Freiburg. See **Fribourg.**

Frei·burg im Breis·gau (frī′bûrg ĭm brīs′gou′, frī′boŏrk′). City in Baden-Württemberg in West Germany, on the western edge of the Black Forest. The city, seat of a university (founded 1457), is a tourist center, with some light manufacturing, notably of textiles, paper and musical and optical instruments.

freight (frāt) *n. Abbr.* **frt. 1. a.** Goods carried by a vessel or aircraft; lading. **b.** Goods transported as cargo by a commercial carrier, as distinguished from luggage and mail. **2.** A charge or burden. **3.** The commercial transportation of goods. **4.** The charge for transporting goods by cargo carrier. **5.** *Chiefly British.* The cargo of a ship or airplane.
~*tr.v.* **freighted, freighting, freights. 1.** To convey commercially as cargo. **2.** To load with goods to be transported. **3.** To load; charge. [Middle English *fraught, freight,* from Middle Dutch *vrecht, vracht,* cargo, fee for a transport vessel.]

freight·age (frā′tĭj) *n.* **1.** The commercial transportation of goods. **2.** The charge for such transportation. **3.** Cargo.

freight car *n.* A railroad car designed for carrying freight.

freight·er (frā′tər) *n.* **1.** A ship or aircraft for carrying freight. **2.** A shipper of cargo.

freight train *n.* A railroad train made up of freight cars.

Fre·man·tle (frē′mănt′l). Chief port of Western Australia, now part of the city of Perth. It is one of the oldest European settlements in Australia.

frem·i·tus (frĕm′ə-təs) *n., pl.* **fremitus.** *Pathology.* A palpable vibra-

tion, as felt by the hand placed on the chest during coughing or speaking. [Latin, noise, roar, from the past participle of *fremere,* to roar.]

Fré·mont (frē′mŏnt′), **John Charles** (1813-90). U.S. explorer, soldier, and politician. He explored the West and Northwest, mapping much of the region and earning himself wide repute as an adventurer. During the Mexican War he twice captured Los Angeles (1847). After a stint as a U.S. senator (1850-51) and a bid for the Presidency (1856), he resumed his volatile military career.

fre·na. Alternate plural of **frenum.**

french (frĕnch) *tr.v.* **frenched, frenching, frenches. 1.** To cut into thin strips before cooking. **2.** To trim fat or bone from (a chop, for example).

French (frĕnch) *adj. Abbr.* **F., Fr.** Of, pertaining to, or characteristic of France or its people, language, or culture.
~*n. Abbr.* **F., Fr. 1.** The Romance language spoken by the people of France, western Switzerland, and southern Belgium, and in various former French possessions. **2.** *Used with a plural verb.* The people of France. Preceded by *the.* [Middle English *french,* Old English *frencisc,* FRANKISH.]

French, Daniel Chester (1850-1931). U.S. sculptor. Largely self-taught, he created notable works of sculpture such as *The Minute Man* (1875). His best-known work, the seated marble figure of Abraham Lincoln at the Lincoln Memorial in Washington, D.C., has inspired countless visitors since its dedication in 1922.

French, John Denton Pinkstone, 1st Earl of Ypres (1852-1925). British field marshal. He led the British Expeditionary Force to Europe at the outbreak of World War 1, but following its near annihilation in the first two battles of Ypres he resigned his command (1915).

French and Indian War. A war (1754-63) that was fought in North America between England and France, who had the support of Indian allies.

French bread *n.* Bread made with water, flour, and yeast and baked in long, crusty loaves.

French bulldog *n.* A small compact dog of a breed developed in France from toy English bulldogs and native breeds.

French Canada. The region of Canada dominated by French-Canadians; especially, Quebec.

French-Ca·na·di·an (frĕnch′kə-nā′dē-ən) *n.* Also **French Canadian. 1.** A Canadian of French descent. **2.** The French language as spoken in Canada. —**French-Ca·na·di·an** *adj.*

French chalk *n.* Chalk made of a soft, white variety of talc, used by tailors for marking fabrics, and by dry cleaners for removing grease.

French chop *n.* A rib chop with the meat and fat trimmed from the end of the rib.

French Community. Association of France and its territories and some former colonies, established in 1958 by the constitution of the Fifth Republic. It is made up of the French Republic, comprising metropolitan France (mainland France and Corsica) and the overseas departments and territories, and several independent African republics. It is a loose association, designed to promote members' cooperation in military, economic, and cultural affairs.

French cuff *n.* A wide cuff that is folded back to make a double cuff and fastened with a cufflink.

French curve *n.* A flat instrument with curved edges and scroll-shaped cutouts, used by draftsmen for drawing irregular curves and as a guide in connecting a set of individual points with a smooth curve.

French door *n.* A door of light construction with glass panes often extending the full length, and usually hung in pairs.

French dressing *n.* A seasoned oil-and-vinegar salad dressing.

French Equatorial Africa. A former French territory in west-central Africa, known before 1910 as the French Congo. It consisted of Gabon, Middle Congo (now Congo), Chad, and Ubangi-Shari (now the Central African Republic); its capital was Brazzaville. When each constituent voted to become independent in 1958, the territory broke up, and in 1960 the four new republics became members of the French Community.

French fries *pl.n.* Also **french fries.** Thin strips of potatoes fried in deep fat.

French-fry (frĕnch′frī′) *tr.v.* **-fried, -frying, -fries.** To fry (potato strips, for example) in deep fat.

French Gui·an·a (gē-ăn′ə, -ä′nə). French overseas department on the Atlantic coast of northeastern South America. It became a permanent French colony in 1817 and in 1946 was given the status of an overseas department. Devil's Island, just off the coast, was formerly the site of a penal colony. The capital is Cayenne. See map at **Guyana.**

French Guinea. See **Guinea.**

French harp *n. Informal.* A mouth organ; harmonica.

French heel *n.* A curved moderately high heel on a woman's shoe.

French horn *n.* A valved brass wind instrument with a circular shape, tapering from a narrow mouthpiece to a flaring bell at the other end, and producing a mellow tone.

French ice cream *n.* An ice cream rich in egg yolks and cream.

French·i·fy (frĕn′chə-fī′) *v.* **-fied, -fying, -fies.** —*tr.* To give a French character or quality to. —*intr.* To assume French ways or characteristics.

French India. A former overseas territory of France in India, including the settlements of Chandernagore, Pondicherry (the capital), and Yanaon on the east coast and Mahé on the west, with a combined area of 500 square kilometers (193 square miles). The territory was returned to India (1949–54).

French Indochina. Part of Southeast Asia formerly controlled by France, mostly until 1954. Set up in 1887, it included Cochin China, Annam and Tonkin (which now make up Vietnam), and Cambodia (now Kampuchea). Laos was added in 1893.

French kiss *n. Slang.* A kiss in which the tongue enters the partner's mouth. **—French-kiss** (frĕnch'kĭs') *v.*

French knitting *n.* A technique of braiding yarn around pins attached to the top of a cotton reel. The finished work is pulled through the center of the reel as a knitted tube, which is then rolled up and sewn into mats.

French knot *n.* A decorative stitch made by looping the thread two or more times around the needle, which is then inserted into the fabric.

French leave *n.* An unauthorized or unannounced departure or absence. [From an 18th-century French custom of leaving without bidding good-by to the host or hostess.]

French·man (frĕnch'mən) *n., pl.* **-men** (-mĭn). **1.** A native or citizen of France. **2.** A French ship.

French marigold *n.* A widely cultivated plant, *Tagetes patula*, native to Mexico, having divided leaves and yellow flowers with reddish markings.

French Morocco. A former French protectorate established over most of the area of present-day Morocco in 1912, and now part of the kingdom of Morocco.

French mulberry *n.* A species of **beautyberry** *(see).*

French navy *n.* Lightish navy blue.

French North Africa. A term formerly used to designate Algeria, French Morocco, and Tunisia collectively.

French pastry *n.* Any of a wide variety of rich and elaborate pastries prepared in individual portions.

French polish *n.* **1.** A wood varnish consisting of a solution of shellac dissolved in methanol. **2.** The finish produced on a piece of furniture by this varnish.

French-pol·ish (frĕnch'pŏl'ĭsh) *tr.v.* **-polished, -polishing, -polishes.** To apply French polish to (a surface).

French Polynesia. A French overseas territory consisting of c. 130 tropical islands scattered over some 4 million square kilometers (1.5 million square miles) of the eastern Pacific Ocean. The capital, Papeete, is on Tahiti. The island groups became a French colony in 1880 and in 1958 opted to become an overseas territory within the French Community. Tourism and copra export are the mainstays of the economy. See map at **Pacific Ocean.**

French provincial *n.* A style of architecture or furniture characteristic of the provinces in 17th- and 18th-century France.

French Revolution *n.* A revolt in France against the monarchy and aristocracy lasting from 1789 to 1799, when Napoleon gained control.

French roll *n.* A woman's hairstyle with the hair pulled back from the face and worn in a vertical cylindrical roll at the back of the head. Also called "French pleat."

French roof *n. Architecture.* A curb roof resembling the mansard and having nearly perpendicular slopes.

French seam *n.* A seam stitched first on the right side and then turned in and stitched on the wrong side so that the raw edges are enclosed in the seam.

French Somaliland. See **Djibouti.**

French Southern and Antarctic Territories. An overseas territory of France comprising Adélie Land in Antarctica and several islands south of 38° S. The islands are the Kerguelen and Crozet groups and Amsterdam (formerly Nouvelle Amsterdam) and Saint-Paul islands. The only population of the territory, administered from Paris, is the staff of the hospital and office on Amsterdam and scientific and meteorological research workers scattered over the territory.

French Sudan. See **Mali.**

French toast *n.* Sliced bread soaked in a milk and egg batter and lightly fried.

French To·go·land (tō'gō-lănd') A former United Nations Trust Territory in western Africa, administered by France (1946–60). See **Togo.**

French vermouth *n.* A dry vermouth.

French West Africa. Former federation of French colonies in Africa. Established in 1895, it included Senegal, French Guinea, the Ivory Coast, and French Sudan (Mali) and was administered as one colony from Dakar. Later Dahomey, Upper Senegal-Niger, Mauritania, and Upper Volta were incorporated. The federation was dissolved in 1958 and the territories, with the exception of French Guinea, became independent republics within the French Community.

French West Indies. Unofficially, the French overseas departments of Guadeloupe and Martinique, in the Caribbean.

French window *n.* A door with one large or several small glass panes, or a casement window extending to floor level, usually hung in pairs and often giving access to a garden or balcony.

French·wom·an (frĕnch'woom'ən) *n., pl.* **-women** (-wĭm'ĭn). A woman who is a native or citizen of France.

French·y (frĕn'chē) *adj.* **-ier, -iest.** *Informal.* Displaying French characteristics.

~n., pl. **Frenchies.** *Slang.* A French person.

Fre·neau (frĭ-nō') **Philip Morin** (1752–1832). U.S. author and sailor. Before the American Revolution he penned several satirical

---

French Revolution

VIOLENT CLIMAX OF AN AGE OF UNREST
Liberty, Equality, and Fraternity at the cost of Terror

The French Revolution of 1789–99 was part of an age of social uprising involving America and Europe from about 1770 to the 1840's. Its roots lay in the strain of long wars and heavy taxation imposed by the autocratic Louis XIV (died 1715). An absolute monarchy and an entrenched nobility and clergy formed too rigid a system to allow the changes needed by a rising middle class, a burgeoning population, and a peasantry restless under feudal obligations.

The immediate cause of violence was to try to eradicate the national debt by increasing taxes. When the States General, the national assembly, met in May 1789 to resolve the crisis, it was bombarded with demands for more basic changes. In response, the commons, the middle-class majority in the Third Estate of the national assembly, claimed supremacy, declared itself to be the National Assembly, and prepared to draft France's first constitution. The king, Louis XVI, grudgingly agreed.

On July 14, Parisian mobs supporting the commons stormed the Bastille, a prison that symbolized absolutism. Riots spread among the peasants across the nation. The Assembly proclaimed a new era of liberty and equality. Louis withheld agreement, and both he and his wife, Marie Antoinette, were seized. The royal couple managed to flee, only to be caught and forced to accede in June 1791.

In 1792 the Assembly sought to spread revolution by war and attacked Austria and Prussia. Soon most of Europe was involved in the revolutionary wars, and there was much bloodshed in France. Fearing betrayal, revolutionaries imprisoned the king and ordered elections for a National Convention. In September hundreds of royalists were murdered.

The Convention established a republic and on January 21, 1793, the king was executed. War was declared against Holland, Spain, and Britain. Then to protect its reforms, the Convention, dominated by Maximilian Robespierre, initiated a Reign of Terror in which 300,000 were arrested and 17,000 executed by the guillotine. Eventually, the Convention, fearful for their own lives, turned against Robespierre himself and executed him.

The Convention proceeded to draw up a new constitution and established a five-man Directory in October 1795 to govern France. The Directory was split by corruption, intrigue, and a fatal dependence on the army to maintain order. This internal conflict led to a coup d'état, in September 1797, directed against those who wished to restore constitutional monarchy. However, in 1799 Napoleon Bonaparte returned from fighting in Egypt and overthrew the Directory. He established the Consulate and thereby ended the Revolution.

DEATH OF THE KING *Louis XVI, as much a victim of his time as he was a poor ruler, was unable to stem the flow of revolutionary violence. In 1793 the Republicans executed him by the guillotine.*

---

pamphlets and his most critically acclaimed poems. During the war he served in the navy and was captured by the British, an experience recounted in *The British Prison Ship: A Poem* (1781).

fre·net·ic (frə-nĕt'ĭk) *adj.* Frantic; frenzied. [Middle English *frenetik*, frenzied, insane, from Old French *frenetique*, from Latin *phrenēticus*, from Greek *phrenitikos*, from *phrenitis*, brain disease, insanity, from *phrēn*, mind.] **—fre·net·i·cal·ly** *adv.*

fren·u·lum, fraen·u·lum (frĕn'yə-ləm) *n., pl.* **-la** (-lə). **1.** A bristly structure on the hind wing of certain moths and other insects that holds the forewing and hind wing together during flight. **2.** A small **frenum** *(see).* [New Latin, diminutive of FRENUM.]

fre·num, frae·num (frē'nəm) *n., pl.* **-nums** or **-na** (-nə). A membranous fold that supports or restricts the movement of a part, such as the fold under the tongue. [Latin, "bridle."]

fren·zied (frĕn'zēd) *adj.* Characterized by, affected with, or filled with frenzy; frantic. **—fren·zied·ly** *adv.*

fren·zy (frĕn'zē) *n., pl.* **-zies.** **1.** A seizure of violent agitation or wild excitement, often accompanied by manic activity. **2.** Temporary madness or delirium: *"I struggled with the frenzy, though I felt it must tear me in pieces"* (Mary Renault). **3.** An extravagant idea;

fresco *A detail from* The Annunciation of the Virgin *by Pontormo (1494–1557). In fresco painting, mineral and earth colors are applied quickly on fresh plaster or mortar before it dries.*

friarbird *Also called the leatherhead, the friarbird is native to Australia, using its long bill to suck nectar from flowers. It gets its name from a bald patch on its head that resembles a friar's tonsure.*

mania; craze. Used with *for*: *"man had a frenzy for getting away from any control"* (D.H. Lawrence).
~*tr.v.* **frenzied, -zying, -zies.** To drive into a frenzy. [Middle English *frenesie,* from Old French, from Medieval Latin *phrenēsia,* from Latin *phrenēsis,* from *phrēn,* mind, from Greek.]

Fre·on (frē'ŏn') *n.* A trademark for any of various nonflammable gaseous or liquid fluorocarbons that are used mainly as working fluids in refrigeration and air conditioning and as aerosol propellants.

freq. 1. frequentative. **2.** frequently.

fre·quence (frē'kwəns) *n.* Frequency. [Middle English, multitude, from Latin *frequentia,* from *frequens,* crowded.]

fre·quen·cy (frē'kwən-sē) *n., pl.* **-cies. 1.** *Mathematics & Physics.* The number of times a specified phenomenon occurs within a specified interval, as: **a.** The number of repetitions of a complete sequence of values of a periodic function per unit variation of an independent variable. **b.** The number of complete cycles of a periodic process occurring per unit time. **c.** The number of repetitions per unit time of a complete waveform, as of an electric current. **2.** *Statistics.* **a.** The number of measurements in an interval of a frequency distribution. **b.** The ratio of the number of times an event occurs in a series of trials of a chance experiment to the number of trials of the experiment performed. **3.** The property or condition of occurring repeatedly at short intervals. **4.** The number of times that something regularly recurs. [Latin *frequentia,* crowd, from *frequēns,* FREQUENT.]

frequency band *n.* A band of frequencies. See **band.**

frequency curve *n. Statistics.* A graphic representation of a frequency distribution obtained by plotting the variable property along the x-axis divided into intervals and the numbers of members along the y-axis. If there is a finite number of intervals of significant size and if the points are joined by straight lines, the resulting diagram is a frequency polygon.

frequency distribution *n. Statistics.* The way in which some property is distributed among members of a set, according to the numbers of members having particular values of the property. It is obtained by dividing the variable (property) into intervals and specifying the number of members of the set having a value of the property lying within each interval.

frequency modulation *n. Abbr.* **fm, FM** *Electronics.* The encoding of a carrier wave by variation of its frequency in accordance with an input signal. Compare **amplitude modulation.**

frequency polygon *n.* A graphic representation of a frequency distribution consisting of a set of points each obtained by plotting class frequency as ordinate and class mark as abscissa, together with line segments joining points of adjacent classes.

fre·quent (frē'kwənt) *adj.* Occurring or appearing quite often or at close intervals.
~*tr.v.* (frē-kwĕnt', fre'kwənt) **frequented, -quenting, -quents.** To pay frequent visits to; be often in, at, or in the company of. [Middle English, profuse, ample, from Old French, from Latin *frequēns* (stem *frequent-*), full, frequent.] **—fre·quent·er** (frē-kwĕn'tər) *n.* **—fre·quent·ly** *adv.* **—fre·quent·ness** *n.*

fre·quen·ta·tion (frē'kwĕn-tā'shən, frē'kwən-) *n.* The act or practice of frequenting a place.

fre·quen·ta·tive (frē-kwĕn'tə-tĭv) *adj. Abbr.* **freq.** *Grammar.* Expressing or denoting repeated action.
~*n. Abbr.* **freq.** A frequentative verb or verb form.

fres·co (frĕs'kō) *n., pl.* **-coes** or **-cos. 1.** The art of painting by applying pure pigments dissolved in water onto fresh lime plaster. **2.** A painting executed on plaster.
~*tr.v.* **frescoed, -coing, -coes.** To paint on fresh plaster. [Italian, from phrases such as *(in) fresco,* (on the) fresh (plaster), from West Germanic *friskaz* (unattested), FRESH.] **—fres·co·er, fres·co·ist** *n.*

fresh (frĕsh) *adj.* **fresher, freshest. 1.** New to one's experience; not encountered before. **2.** Novel; different; original: *a fresh slant.* **3.** Recently made, produced, or harvested; not stale, spoiled, or withered: *fresh bread.* **4.** Not preserved, as by canning, smoking, drying, or freezing: *fresh vegetables.* **5.** Not saline or salty: *fresh water.* **6.** Not yet used or soiled; clean: *a fresh sheet of paper.* **7.** Additional; new: *a fresh start.* **8.** Bright and clear; not dull or faded: *a fresh color; a fresh memory.* **9.** Having the glowing, unspoiled appearance of youth or health: *a fresh complexion.* **10.** Untried; inexperienced: *fresh recruits.* **11.** Having just arrived; straight: *fresh from Paris.* **12. a.** Revived or reinvigorated; refreshed: *got up fresh as a daisy after her afternoon nap.* **b.** Charged with energy; frisky. **13.** Revivifying; cool and invigorating: *fresh morning air.* **14.** Fairly strong; brisk: *a fresh wind.* **15.** Having recently calved and therefore with milk. Said of a cow. **16.** *Informal.* Bold and saucy; impudent: *scolded for such a fresh answer.*
~*adv.* Recently; newly. Usually used in combination: *fresh-baked bread.*
~*n.* **1.** The early and fresh part: *the fresh of the day.* **2.** A freshet. [Middle English, from Old French *freis* (feminine *fresche*), from West Germanic *friskaz* (unattested).] **—fresh·ly** *adv.* **—fresh·ness** *n.*

fresh breeze *n.* A wind whose speed is approximately 31 to 39 kilometers or 19 to 24 miles per hour, force 5 on the Beaufort scale.

fresh·en (frĕsh'ən) *v.* **-ened, -ening, -ens.** —*intr.* **1.** To become fresh. Often used with *up.* **2.** To make oneself clean and fresh. Used with *up*: *freshen up after a day's work.* **3.** To become brisk; increase in strength. Used of a wind. **4.** To lose saltiness. Used of water. **5.** To calve and therefore produce milk. —*tr.* To impart a fresh quality to; make fresh. **—fresh·en·er** *n.*

fresh·et (frĕsh'ĭt) *n.* **1.** A sudden surge of water down a small stream resulting from a heavy rainstorm or a thaw. **2.** A stream of fresh water that empties into a body of salt water. [FRESH + -ET.]

fresh gale *n.* A wind whose speed is approximately 63 to 74 kilometers or 39 to 46 miles per hour, force 8 on the Beaufort scale.

fresh·man (frĕsh'mən) *n., pl.* **-men** (-mĭn). **1.** A first-year student, as in high school or college. **2.** A beginner; novice.

fresh·wa·ter (frĕsh'wô'tər, -wŏt'ər) *adj.* **1.** Pertaining to, living in, or consisting of fresh water. **2.** Unaccustomed to the seas: *a freshwater sailor.* **3.** Located away from the sea; inland.

fres·nel (frā-nĕl') *n.* A unit of frequency equal to 10^{12} hertz. [After A.J. *Fresnel* (1788–1827), French physicist.]

Fres·nel lens (frā-nĕl') *n.* An optical lens made up of a number of smaller lenses arranged to give a short focal length. [After A.J. *Fresnel* (see **fresnel**).]

fret[1] (frĕt) *v.* **fretted, fretting, frets.** —*tr.* **1.** To cause to be uneasy; distress; vex. **2. a.** To gnaw or wear away. **b.** To produce a hole or worn spot in; chafe; corrode. **3.** To form (a passage or channel) by erosion. **4.** To disturb the surface of (water or a stream); agitate. —*intr.* **1.** To be vexed or troubled; worry. **2.** To be worn or eaten away; become corroded. **3.** To move agitatedly; be ruffled.
~*n.* **1.** An act or instance of fretting. **2.** A hole, worn spot, or path made by abrasion or erosion. **3.** A state of irritation, annoyance, or worry. [Middle English *freten,* to devour, irritate, Old English *fretan,* from Germanic *fra-*†, FOR- + *etan*†, to EAT.]

fret[2] *n.* Any of several guide ridges, usually of metal, set across the fingerboard of a guitar or other stringed instrument.
~*tr.v.* **fretted, fretting, frets.** To provide with frets. [15th century : origin obscure.]

fret[3] *n.* **1.** An ornamental design contained within a band or border, consisting of repeated, symmetrical, and often geometric figures. **2.** Such an ornamental design made in relief, often with numerous small openings.
~*tr.v.* **fretted, fretting, frets.** To provide with a fret or frets. [Middle English, from Old French *frete*†, trellis, embossed work.]

fret·ful (frĕt'fəl) *adj.* Inclined to fret; peevish; plaintive. **—fret·ful·ly** *adv.* **—fret·ful·ness** *n.*

fret·saw (frĕt'sô') *n.* A narrow-bladed saw having fine teeth, used in producing ornamental work in thin wood or metal.

fret·work (frĕt'wûrk') *n.* **1.** Ornamental work consisting of three-dimensional frets; geometric openwork. **2.** Such ornamental work represented graphically in monochrome or contrasting colors.

Freud (froid), **Sigmund** (1856–1939). Austrian psychiatrist. After long experience working with hysterical and neurologically disturbed patients, he developed the theory of psychoanalysis. When first publicized in the 1880's, his ideas attracted hostility, but by 1910 they had gained general recognition, and works such as *The Interpretation of Dreams* (1899) and *The Ego and the Id* (1923) have had a profound influence on 20th-century thought. He fled to London (1938) to escape Nazi persecution.

Freud·i·an (froi'dē-ən) *adj.* **1.** Pertaining to or in accordance with the psychoanalytic theories of Sigmund Freud. **2.** *Informal.* Psychologically telling or revealing.
~*n.* **1.** One who actively applies the psychoanalytic methods or theories of Freud in conducting psychotherapy. **2.** One who studies or applies the psychoanalytic theories of Freud for interpretation or explanation, as in historical or literary criticism.

Freudian slip *n.* A slip of the tongue or pen, or some other unintentional act, that seems to reveal an individual's real state of mind.

Frey (frā). Also **Freyr** (frâr). *Norse Mythology.* The god who dispenses peace, good weather, prosperity, and bountiful crops.

Frey·a, Frey·ja (frā'ə). *Norse Mythology.* The sister of Frey and the goddess of love and beauty.

Fri. Friday.

fri·a·ble (frī'ə-bəl) *adj.* Readily crumbled. [French, from Latin *friābilis,* crumbling, from *friāre,* to crumble.] **—fri·a·bil·i·ty, fri·a·ble·ness** *n.*

fri·ar (frī'ər) *n. Abbr.* **Fr.** A member of a Roman Catholic order, such as the Dominicans or Franciscans, that was originally mendicant. [Middle English *frere,* from Old French, from Latin *frāter* (stem *frātr-*), brother.]

fri·ar·bird (frī'ər-bûrd') *n.* Any of various birds of the genus *Philemon,* of Australia and adjacent regions, having a partly naked head. Also called "leatherhead." [From its bare head, likened to a friar's tonsure.]

friar's lantern *n.* **ignis fatuus** *(see).*

fri·ar·y (frī'ə-rē) *n., pl.* **-ies.** A monastery of friars.

frib·ble (frĭb'əl) *v.* **-bled, -bling, -bles.** —*tr.* To waste (time, for example). —*intr.* To waste time; trifle.
~*n.* **1.** A frivolity; trifle. **2.** A frivolous person. [17th century (imitative).] **—frib·bler** *n.*

Fri·bourg (frē-bo͝or', frī'bûrg'). *German* **Frei·burg** (frī'bo͝ork'). Mainly French-speaking canton of northern Switzerland. It occupies the west of the Swiss plateau and is a rich agricultural region noted for its cheeses, including Gruyère.

fric·an·deau (frĭk'ən-dō') *n., pl.* **-deaux** (-dōz'). A cut of veal, usually rump or shoulder, that has been larded and braised or roasted with vegetables. [French, from *fricasser,* to FRICASSEE.]

fric·as·see (frĭk'ə-sē') *n.* Poultry or meat cut into pieces and stewed in a thick gravy.
~*tr.v.* **fricasseed, -seeing, -sees.** To prepare as a fricassee.

[French *fricassée*, feminine past participle of *fricasser†*, to fry.]

fric·a·tive (frĭk′ə-tĭv) *adj. Phonetics.* Produced by the forcing of breath through a constricted passage, as are such consonantal sounds as (f) and (v), (s) and (z), (sh) and (zh), (th) and (*th*). —*n. Phonetics.* A fricative consonant. Also called "spirant." [New Latin *fricativus*, from *fricāre*, to rub.]

Frick (frĭk), **Henry Clay** (1849–1919). U.S. industrialist. He made his fortune primarily in the steel business and worked closely with Andrew Carnegie until 1899. His mansion in New York City, together with his art collection and an endowment of 15 million dollars, was willed to the public and is now a museum.

fric·tion (frĭk′shən) *n.* **1.** The rubbing of one object or surface against another. **2.** Conflict, as of dissimilar ideas, persons, or interests obliged to coexist; clashing. **3.** *Physics.* A force tangential to the common boundary of two bodies in contact that resists the motion or tendency to motion of one relative to the other. **4.** A massage of the body or scalp for therapeutic purposes. [French, from Latin *frictiō* (stem *frictiōn-*), from *frictus*, past participle of *fricāre*, to rub.] —**fric·tion·al** *adj.* —**fric·tion·al·ly** *adv.*

friction clutch *n.* A clutch in which axial pressure with resultant friction between the clutch faces, rather than the interlocking of mated parts, transmits torque.

friction drive *n.* A transmission system in which motion is transmitted from one part to another by the surface friction of rolling contact rather than by toothed gears.

friction match *n.* A match that ignites when struck on an abrasive surface.

friction tape *n.* A sturdy moisture-resistant adhesive tape used chiefly to insulate electrical conductors.

Fri·day (frī′dē, -dā′) *n. Abbr.* **Fri.** The day of the week following Thursday; the fifth day of the working week. [Middle English *fridai*, Old English *frīgedæg*, "day of *Frīg* (wife of Odin)," a translation of Late Latin *Veneris dies*, day of (the planet) Venus, based on Greek *Aphroditēs hēmera*, Aphrodite's day. See **Frigg.**]

fridge (frĭj) *n. Informal.* A refrigerator.

Fridtjof Nansen Land. See **Franz Josef Land.**

Frie·dan (frĭ-dăn′), **Betty Naomi** (1921–). U.S. social reformer and feminist. In 1963 she published *The Feminine Mystique*, debunking the popular notion that women could find fulfillment only in homemaking and raising children. She founded the National Organization for Women (NOW) in 1966.

Fried·man (frēd′mən), **Milton** (1912–). U.S. economist. He set out his philosophy of monetary control and government nonintervention in *Capitalism and Freedom* (1962). Several Western governments have pursued his policies after the stagnation and inflation of the mid-1970's. He was awarded a Nobel Prize (1976).

fried cake *n.* A small pastry, such as a doughnut, fried in deep fat.

Frie·drich (frē′drĭкн), **Caspar David** (1774–1840). German painter. His mysterious landscapes are characteristic of the romantic movement. His later works symbolize man's insignificance in relation to the elements, as in *Wreck of the Hope* (1822).

friend (frĕnd) *n.* **1.** A person whom one knows, likes, and trusts. **2.** Any associate or acquaintance. Often used as a form of address: *my honorable friend.* **3.** A favored companion: *Man's best friend is his dog.* **4.** One with whom one is allied in a struggle or cause; a comrade. **5.** One who supports, sympathizes with, or patronizes a group, cause, or movement. **6. Friend.** A member of the Society of Friends; a Quaker. Also used by Quakers as a term of address. —**be friends with.** To be a friend of. —**make friends with.** To enter into friendship with. —*tr.v.* **friended, friending, friends.** *Archaic.* To befriend. [Middle English *frend*, Old English *frēond*, from Germanic.]

friend at court *n.* An influential person whom one knows and who will be able to advance one's interests.

friend·less (frĕnd′lĭs) *adj.* Without friends.

friend·ly (frĕnd′lē) *adj.* **-li·er, -li·est.** **1.** Of, pertaining to, or befitting a friend. **2.** Favorably disposed; not antagonistic; amicable. **3.** Warm; welcoming. —*adv.* Also **friend·li·ly** (frĕnd′lə-lē). In the manner of a friend; amicably. —*n., pl.* **friendlies.** One that is friendly; especially, one fighting on or favorable to one's own side. —**friend·li·ness** *n.*

Friendly Islands. See **Tonga.**

friend·ship (frĕnd′shĭp′) *n.* **1.** The condition or relation of being friends. **2.** Friendly feeling toward another; friendliness.

frier. Variant of **fryer.**

Frie·sian¹ (frē′zhən) *n. Chiefly British.* A **Holstein** (*see*).

Friesian². Variant of **Frisian.**

Fries·land (frēz′lənd, -lănd′) *Dutch* **Vries·land** (vrēz′-). Province in the northern Netherlands. It includes the West Frisian Islands and land reclaimed from the Ijsselmeer. The district is chiefly a beef-producing and dairying area, and the Friesian breed of cow that originated here is highly prized worldwide.

frieze¹ (frēz) *n. Architecture.* **1.** A plain or decorated horizontal part of an entablature between the architrave and cornice. **2.** Any decorative horizontal band, as along the upper part of a wall in a room. [French *frise*, from Old French, from Medieval Latin *frisium*, *frigium*, fringe, embroidered cloth, from Latin *Phrygium*, of Phrygia, a place noted for its embroidery.]

frieze² *n.* A coarse woolen cloth with an uncut nap. Also called "frisé." [Middle English *frise*, from Old French, from Middle Dutch *vriese*, perhaps from *Vriese*, **Frisian**.]

frig·ate (frĭg′ĭt) *n.* **1.** A high-speed, medium-sized sailing war vessel

of the 17th, 18th, and 19th centuries. **2.** A British warship intermediate between a corvette and a destroyer. **3.** A U.S. warship intermediate between a cruiser and a destroyer. **4.** *Archaic.* Any fast, light vessel. [French *frégate*, from Italian *fregata†.*]

frigate bird *n.* Any of various large, tropical sea birds of the genus *Fregata*, which characteristically snatch food from other birds in flight. Also called "man-o'-war bird."

Frigg (frĭg). Also **Frig·ga** (frĭg′ə). *Norse Mythology.* The consort of Odin and goddess of married lore and the hearth. [Old Norse, from Germanic *frijaz* (unattested), noble, **FREE**.]

fright (frīt) *n.* **1.** Sudden, intense fear, as of something immediately threatening; alarm. **2.** *Informal.* Something extremely unsightly, alarming, or strange. —See Synonyms at **fear.** —**take fright.** To become frightened. —*tr.v.* **frighted, frighting, frights.** *Archaic.* To frighten. [Middle English *fright*, Old English *fryhto, fyrhto*, from Germanic *furht-* (unattested), afraid.]

fright·en (frīt′n) *tr.v.* **-ened, -ening, -ens.** **1.** To make suddenly afraid; alarm or startle. **2.** To drive or force by arousing fear. Used with *away, into, off,* or *out: He was frightened into confessing.* [From **FRIGHT.**] —**fright·en·er** *n.*

Synonyms: alarm, panic, scare, terrify, terrorize.

fright·ened (frīt′ənd) *adj.* **1.** Afraid. **2.** Timid.

fright·en·ing (frīt′nĭng) *adj.* Causing fright or sudden alarm. —**fright·en·ing·ly** *adv.*

fright·ful (frīt′fəl) *adj.* **1.** Causing disgust or shock; horrifying. **2.** Causing fright; terrifying. **3.** *Informal.* **a.** Excessive; extreme: *a frightful liar.* **b.** Disagreeable; distressing: *frightful weather.* —**fright·ful·ly** *adv.* —**fright·ful·ness** *n.*

frig·id (frĭj′ĭd) *adj.* **1.** Extremely cold. **2.** Lacking warmth of feeling; stiff and formal in manner: *a frigid refusal to a request.* **3. a.** Disliking sexual intercourse. Usually said of women. **b.** Unable to experience orgasm in sexual intercourse. Used of females. [Latin *frīgidus*, from *frīgēre*, to be cold, from *frīgus*, cold.] —**fri·gid·i·ty** (frĭ-jĭd′ə-tē), **frig·id·ness.** —**frig·id·ly** *adv.*

Frigid Zone *n.* The area within the Arctic Circle or that within the Antarctic Circle.

frig·o·rif·ic (frĭg′ə-rĭf′ĭk) *adj.* Causing coldness; chilling. [Latin *frīgorificus* : *frīgus* (stem *frīgor-*), **FRIGID** + **-FIC.**]

fri·jol (frē-hōl′, frē′hōl′) *n., pl.* **frijoles** (frē-hō′lēz). Also **fri·jo·le** (frē-hō′lē). A bean cultivated and used for food, especially in Mexico and in the southwestern United States. [Spanish, variant of *fresol*, from Latin *phaseolus*, diminutive of *phasēlus*, kidney bean, from Greek *phasēlos†.*]

frill (frĭl) *n.* **1. a.** A ruffled, gathered, or pleated border or projection, such as a fabric edge used to trim clothing. **b.** A similar curled paper strip used, for example, for decorating the bone of a piece of meat. **2.** *Zoology.* A ruff of hair or feathers or a similar membranous projection about the neck of an animal or bird. **3.** *Photography.* A wrinkling of the edge of a film. **4.** *Usually* **frills.** *Informal.* Something superfluous; an embellishment: *plain home cooking and no frills; cheap, no-frills flights to London.* —*v.* **frilled, frilling, frills.** —*tr.* **1.** To make into a ruffle or frill. **2.** To add a ruffle or frill to. —*intr. Photography.* To become wrinkled along the edge. [16th century : origin obscure.]

frilled lizard *n.* An Australian lizard, *Chlamydosaurus kingi*, having a broad membrane extending from the neck and throat that can be extended like a ruff when the mouth is opened.

frill·y (frĭl′ē) *adj.* **-i·er, -i·est.** **1.** Decorated with or having a frill or frills. **2.** Similar to or suggesting a frill or frills. **3.** *Informal.* Superfluously ornamental.

Friml (frĭm′əl), **(Charles) Rudolf** (1879–1972). U.S. composer, born in Czechoslovakia. He wrote some 33 light operas, including *The Firefly* (1912), *Rose Marie* (1924), and *The Vagabond King* (1925).

fringe (frĭnj) *n.* **1.** A decorative border or edging of hanging threads, cords, or strips, often attached to a separate band. **2.** Hair combed over the forehead and cut near eyebrow level. **3.** Anything placed or growing along an edge. **4.** A marginal or peripheral part; an edge: *the fringes of the crowd.* **5.** Artistic activities that are considered to lie outside the mainstream or that are deliberately unconventional or uncommercial. Also used adjectivally: *fringe theater.* **6.** Those members of a group or political party holding extreme views. **7.** *Optics.* Any of the light or dark bands produced by the diffraction or interference of light. —*tr.v.* **fringed, fringing, fringes.** **1.** To decorate with a fringe. **2.** To grow or occur along the edge of; border: *"deep and sullen pools fringed with tall rushes"* (H. Rider Haggard). [Middle English *frenge*, from Old French, from Vulgar Latin *frimbia* (unattested), from Late Latin *fimbria*. See **fimbria.**] —**fring·y** *adj.*

fringe benefit *n.* An employment benefit given in addition to one's wages or salary.

fringed orchis *n.* Any of various orchids of the genus *Habenaria*, having variously colored flowers with a fringed lip.

frin·gil·lid (frĭn-jĭl′ĭd) *adj.* Of or belonging to the family Fringillidae, which includes relatively small birds, such as the finches, sparrows, and buntings. —*n.* A member of the Fringillidae. [New Latin *Fringillidae* : *Fringilla* (type genus), from Latin *fringilla†*, finch + **-ID.**]

fringing reef *n.* A coral reef along a coast.

frip·per·y (frĭp′ə-rē) *n., pl.* **-ies.** **1.** Pretentious finery; excessively ornamented dress. **2.** Pretentious elegance; ostentation. **3.** Trivia. —*adj.* Pretentious and trivial. [French *friperie*, from Old French

fritillary *The fritillary butterflies are named after their resemblance to the checkered flowers of the* Fritillaria *genus, native to the Northern Hemisphere. The high brown fritillary, shown here, lives mostly on the edges of woodlands. Its caterpillars feed only on violets.*

frog *Unlike the toad, whose skin is dry to the touch, the common frog has a soft, moist skin. The frog's skin can become darker or lighter in color to match its surroundings.*

freperie, from *frepe, felpe,* frill, from Medieval Latin *faluppa*†, fiber.]

Fris. Frisian.

Fris·bee (frĭz′bē) *n.* A trademark for a concave disk made of light plastic that is thrown in the air with a spinning motion as a game.

Frisch (frĭsh), **Karl von** (1886–1982). Austrian zoologist. He is best known for his discovery of the "dance" of the bees, by which the location of flowers is communicated. In 1973 he shared the Nobel Prize for physiology and medicine with Konrad Lorenz (1903–) and Nikolaas Tinbergen (1907–).

Frisch, Max Rudolf (1911–). Swiss writer. In his plays and novels, including *I'm not Stiller* (1954), *Homo Faber* (1957), and *Andorra* (1961), he explores the existential plight of the modern, complicated individual in a society that stereotypes its members and defeats those who attempt to change it.

fri·sé (frē-zā′) *n.* A fabric, **frieze** *(see).* [French, from the past participle of *friser,* to curl, FRIZZ.]

frisette. Variant of **frizette.**

Fris·i·a (frĭz′ē-ə). Ancient country of the Frisians. In the 8th century it included what is now northern Belgium, the Netherlands, and West Germany west of the Weser River.

Fri·sian (frĭzh′ən, frē′zhən) *adj.* Also **Frie·sian** (frē′zhən). *Abbr.* **Fris., Frs.** Of the Frisian Islands, Friesland, or Frisia.
~*n.* Also **Frie·sian.** *Abbr.* **Fris., Frs. 1.** A native or inhabitant of the Frisian Islands or Friesland. **2.** The Germanic language spoken by the Frisian people.

Frisian Islands. Group of *c.* 30 low, sandy islands in the North Sea off northwestern Europe. The West Frisians belong to the Netherlands, the East Frisians to West Germany, and the North Frisians are divided between West Germany and Denmark. There are few permanent inhabitants, although there are numerous summer homes. See also **Friesland.**

frisk (frĭsk) *v.* **frisked, frisking, frisks.** —*intr.* To move about briskly and playfully, as a puppy does; gambol; frolic. —*tr.* To search (a person) for something concealed, especially weapons, by passing the hands quickly over clothes or through pockets.
~*n.* **1.** An energetic, playful movement; a gambol; caper. **2.** An act of frisking, as for concealed weapons. [From obsolete *frisk,* lively, from Old French *frisque,* from Common Germanic *friskaz* (unattested), FRESH.] —**frisk·er** *n.*

fris·ket (frĭs′kĭt) *n.* A light frame with a windowed sheet of parchment that protects areas of the paper not to be printed in a hand printing press. [French *frisquette*†.]

frisk·y (frĭs′kē) *adj.* **-ier, -iest.** Energetic, lively, and playful. [From obsolete *frisk,* lively. See **frisk.**] —**frisk·i·ly** *adv.* —**frisk·i·ness** *n.*

fris·son (frē-sôɴ′) *n.* A pleasurable shiver caused by excitement or thrilling danger. [French, shiver.]

frit (frĭt) *n.* **1.** The fused or partially fused materials used in making glass. **2.** A vitreous substance used in making porcelain or glazes.
~*tr.v.* **fritted, fritting, frits.** To make into frit. [Italian *fritta,* from the feminine past participle of *friggere,* to fry, from Latin *frīgere,* to FRY.]

frit fly *n.* Any of several small flies of the family Chloropidae; especially, *Oscinella frit,* having larvae that are destructive to cereal plants, particularly oats. [19th century : origin obscure.]

frith (frĭth) *n. Scottish.* An estuary. [Variant of FIRTH.]

frit·il·lar·y (frĭt′l-ĕr′ē) *n., pl.* **-ies. 1.** Any of various bulbous plants of the genus *Fritillaria,* having nodding, variously colored, often spotted or checkered bell-shaped flowers. In this sense, also called "snakeshead." **2.** Any of various butterflies of the family Nymphalidae, having brownish wings marked with black or silvery spots. [New Latin *Fritillaria,* from Latin *fritillus*†, dice box, a reference to the checkered markings.]

frit·ter¹ (frĭt′ər) *tr.v.* **-tered, -tering, -ters. 1.** To reduce wastefully or squander little by little. Usually used with *away*: *He frittered his money away on expensive cars.* **2.** To break, tear, or cut into bits; shred. [Probably from obsolete *fritter,* to break in pieces, perhaps related to Middle High German *vetze,* rags.]

fritter² *n.* A small cake made of batter, often containing fruit, vegetables, meat, or fish, sautéed or fried in deep fat. [Middle English *friture,* from Old French, from Vulgar Latin *frīctūra* (unattested), from Latin *frīctus,* past participle of *frīgere,* to FRY.]

Fri·u·li (frē-ōō′lē). A historic region and former duchy of northeastern Italy, part of which now extends into Yugoslavia.

Fri·u·li·an (frē-ōō′lē-ən) *n.* **1.** A member of a people inhabiting Friuli in northeastern Italy. **2.** The Rhaeto-Romanic dialect spoken by these people.

friv·ol (frĭv′əl) *v.* **-oled** or **-olled, -oling** or **-olling, -ols.** *Informal.* —*tr.* To squander. Used with *away.* —*intr.* To behave frivolously. [Back-formation from FRIVOLOUS.] —**friv·ol·er** *n.*

fri·vol·i·ty (frĭ-vŏl′ə-tē) *n., pl.* **-ties. 1.** The condition or quality of being frivolous. **2.** A frivolous act or thing.

friv·o·lous (frĭv′ə-ləs) *adj.* **1.** Unworthy of serious attention; insignificant; trivial. **2.** Marked by flippancy; silly. —See Synonyms at **playful.** [Middle English, from Latin *frīvolus*†.] —**friv·o·lous·ly** *adv.* —**friv·o·lous·ness** *n.*

fri·zette, fri·sette (frĭ-zĕt′) *n.* A curled fringe of hair, usually worn on the forehead by a woman. [French *frisette,* "little curl," from *friser,* to curl, FRIZZ.]

frizz¹, friz (frĭz) *v.* **frizzed, frizzing, frizzes.** —*tr.* To form (nap or hair, for example) into small, tight curls or tufts. —*intr.* To be formed into small, tight curls or tufts.
~*n.* **1.** The condition of being frizzed. **2.** A tight curl or tight curls of hair or fabric. **3.** A hairstyle consisting of small, tight curls. [French *friser,* to curl, to shrivel up (as when fried), perhaps from *frire* (stem *fris-*), to FRY.] —**frizz·er** *n.*

frizz², friz *v.* **frizzed, frizzing, frizzes.** —*tr.* To fry or burn with a sizzling noise. —*intr.* To be fried or burned with a sizzling noise. [Perhaps from FRIZZLE (to fry).]

friz·zle¹ (frĭz′əl) *v.* **-zled, -zling, -zles.** —*tr.* **1.** To fry until crisp and curled: *frizzled the bacon.* **2.** To scorch or sear with heat. —*intr.* **1.** To fry or sear with a sizzling noise. **2.** To scorch. [Perhaps blend of FRY and SIZZLE.]

frizzle² *v.* **-zled, -zling, -zles.** —*tr.* To frizz (hair). —*intr.* To form tight curls.
~*n.* A small, tight curl. [16th century : origin uncertain, earlier than FRIZZ (to form curls).]

friz·zly (frĭz′lē) *adj.* **-zlier, -zliest.** Tightly curled.

friz·zy (frĭz′ē) *adj.* **-zier, -ziest.** Tightly curled; frizzly. —**friz·zi·ly** *adv.* —**friz·zi·ness** *n.*

Frl. Fräulein.

fro (frō) *adv.* Away; back again. Used in the phrase *to and fro.*
~*prep. Scottish.* From. [Middle English *fra, fro,* adverb and preposition, from Old Norse *frā.*]

Fro·bi·sher (frō′bĭ-shər), **Sir Martin** (*c.* 1535–94). English explorer. He made three voyages to the Canadian Arctic in 1576, 1577, and 1578, seeking the Northwest Passage.

Frobisher Bay. Arm of the North Atlantic Ocean, cutting deeply into Baffin Island, Canada. It is *c.* 240 kilometers (150 miles) long and 65 kilometers (40 miles) at its widest.

frock (frŏk) *n.* **1.** A long, loose outer garment, such as that worn by artists and craftsmen; a smock. **2.** A woolen garment formerly worn by sailors; jersey. **3.** A frock coat. **4.** A robe worn by monks, friars, and other clerics; habit. **5.** The state of being a priest or clergyman. **6.** A woman's or girl's dress.
~*tr.v.* **frocked, frocking, frocks. 1.** To clothe in a frock. **2.** To invest with clerical office. [Middle English *frok,* from Old French *froc,* from Germanic *hrok-* (unattested).]

frock coat *n.* A man's dress overcoat with knee-length skirts, worn chiefly in the 19th century.

froe, frow (frō) *n.* A cleaving tool having a heavy blade set at right angles to the handle. [Origin uncertain.]

Froe·bel (frœ′bəl), **Friedrich Wilhelm August** (1782–1852). German educator who believed that school should be happy. His book *Education of Man* (1826) was profoundly influential. In 1837 he opened the first kindergarten, at Blankenburg.

frog¹ (frôg, frŏg) *n.* **1.** Any of numerous tailless, chiefly aquatic amphibians of the order Anura, and especially of the family Ranidae, characteristically having a smooth, moist skin, webbed feet, and long hind legs adapted for leaping. **2.** A spiked or perforated object placed in a container and used to support stems in a decorative floral arrangement. **3.** A recess or groove in one side or on opposite sides of a brick. **4.** *Informal.* Hoarseness in the throat. [Middle English *frogge,* Old English *frogga,* a pet form of *forse, frosc,* from Germanic.]

frog² *n.* A grooved iron or steel plate that guides the wheels of a train over an intersection in the track. [Origin obscure.]

frog³ *n.* **1.** A loop fastened to a belt to hold a tool or weapon. **2.** An ornamental looped braid or cord with a button or knot for fastening the front of a garment. [18th century : origin obscure.]

frog⁴ *n.* A wedge-shaped, horny prominence in the sole of a horse's hoof. [17th century : perhaps from FROG (animal), influenced by French *fourchette* and Italian *forchetta* (diminutives of *fourche, forca,* FORK, referring to the shape of the prominence).]

frog·eye (frôg′ī′, frŏg′ī′) *n.* A plant disease caused by fungi and characterized by rounded spots on the leaves.

frog·fish (frôg′fĭsh′, frŏg′-) *n., pl.* **-fishes** or collectively **frogfish.** Any of various anglerfishes of the family Antennariidae, of tropical and temperate seas, characteristically covered with fleshy or filamentous processes.

frogged (frôgd, frŏgd) *adj.* Decorated with ornamental frogs. Said of a garment, as a coat or uniform.

frog·ging (frô′gĭng, frŏg′ĭng) *n.* The ornamental loops of braid or cord on a garment; decorative frogs collectively.

frog·gy (frô′gē, frŏg′ē) *adj.* **-gier, -giest. 1.** Of, resembling, or characteristic of a frog. **2.** Full of frogs.

frog·hop·per (frôg′hŏp′ər, frŏg′-) *n.* Any of various jumping insects of the family Ceropidae, the nymphs of which secrete a protective spittlelike substance (cuckoo spit) around themselves. Also called "spittle insect," "spittlebug."

frog kick *n.* A swimming kick in which the legs are drawn up close beneath one, then thrust outward and together vigorously.

frog·man (frôg′măn′, -mən, frŏg′-) *n., pl.* **-men** (-mĕn′, -mĭn). A swimmer provided with breathing apparatus and other equipment, such as a rubber suit and flippers, to execute underwater maneuvers, especially military maneuvers.

frog·mouth (frôg′mouth′, frŏg′-) *n.* Any of various brown or gray nocturnal insectivorous birds of the genera *Podargus* and *Batrachostomus,* of southeastern Asia and Australia, having a wide mouth and a hooked bill.

frog·spawn (frôg′spôn′, frŏg′-) *n.* A transparent gelatinous mass interspersed with black dots, comprising many fertilized frogs' eggs or developing tadpoles, each surrounded by nutrient jelly.

frog spit *n.* Also **frog spittle. 1.** An insect secretion, **cuckoo spit** *(see).* **2.** A foamlike aggregation of small aquatic plants, such as green algae, on the surface of a pond.

frol·ic (frŏl′ĭk) *n.* **1.** Gaiety; merriment. **2.** A gay, carefree time. **3.** A prank, trick, or antic.
∼*intr.v.* **frolicked, -icking, -ics. 1.** To behave playfully and uninhibitedly; romp. **2.** To engage in merrymaking, joking, or teasing.
∼*adj. Archaic.* Merry; frisky; prankish. [Dutch *vrolijk,* from Middle Dutch *vrolijc* : *vro,* gay, happy + *-lijc,* -ly.] **—frol·ick·er** *n.*

frol·ic·some (frŏl′ĭk-səm) *adj.* Full of high-spirited fun; frisky.

from (frŭm, frŏm) *prep. Abbr.* **fr. 1.** Beginning at a specified place or time: *walked home from the station; from six o'clock on.* **2. a.** With a specified time or point as the first of two limits: *from age four to age eight.* **b.** With a specified lowest limit: *real leather shoes from $20.* **3.** With a person, place, or thing as the source, cause, or instrument: *a note from the teacher.* **4.** Out of: *take a book from the shelf.* **5.** Out of the jurisdiction, control, restraint, or possession of: *escaped from jail; free from pain.* **6.** So as not to be engaged in: *keep someone from making a mistake.* **7.** Measured by or with reference to: *far away from home.* **8.** As opposed to: *know right from wrong.* **9.** Because of: *faint from hunger; crying from desperation.* **10.** Beginning with or in a specified state: *from rags to riches; from annoyance to fury.* **11.** Belonging to: *memories from childhood.* **12.** On the basis of: *judging from appearances.* [Middle English *from, fram,* Old English *from, fram.*]

fromenty. Variant of **frumenty.**

Fromm (frŏm, frôm), **Erich** (1900–80). German-born American psychoanalyst.

frond (frŏnd) *n.* **1.** The usually compound leaf of a fern. **2.** A large compound leaf of certain other plants, such as a palm. **3.** A leaflike thallus, as of a seaweed or lichen. [Latin *frōns*† (stem *frond-*), branch, leaf.] **—frond·ed** *adj.*

Fronde (frônd, frŏnd; *French* frôɴd) *n.* The French political movement that opposed Cardinal Mazarin and the court during the minority of Louis XIV in the mid-17th century.

fron·des·cent (frŏn-dĕs′ənt) *adj.* Bearing, resembling, or having a profusion of leaves or fronds; leafy. [Latin *frondescens* (stem *frondescent-*), present participle of *frondescere,* to become leafy, from *frondēre,* to put forth leaves, from *frōns* (stem *frond-*), leaf, FROND.] **—fron·des·cence** *n.*

fron·dose (frŏn′dōs′) *adj.* **1.** Bearing fronds. **2.** Resembling a frond or fronds; frondlike. [Latin *frondōsus* : *frōns* (stem *frond-*), FROND + -OSE.] **—fron·dose·ly** *adv.*

front (frŭnt) *n.* **1.** The forward part or surface, as of a building. **2.** The area, location, or position directly before or ahead. **3.** The position of leadership or superiority; forefront. **4.** The first part; beginning; opening. **5.** The forehead, especially of an animal or bird. **6.** *Archaic.* The entire face; countenance. **7.** Demeanor or bearing when faced with a particular situation: *maintain a brave front.* **8.** An outward or feigned aspect; a false appearance or manner. **9.** Land bordering a lake, river, or street: *a house on the lake front.* **10.** A promenade along a beach. **11.** The top forward part of a garment: *spilled gravy down his front.* **12.** A detachable part of a man's dress shirt covering the chest; a dickey. **13.** *Military.* **a.** The most forward line of a military combat force. **b.** An area of contact between opposing combat forces. **14.** *Meteorology.* The interface between air masses at different temperatures. Also called "discontinuity." **15.** A group or movement uniting various individuals or organizations for the achievement of a common purpose; coalition. **16.** An apparently respectable person, group, or business under whose cover secret or illegal activities are carried on. **17.** A field of activity: *the economic front.*
∼*adj.* **1.** Of, pertaining to, aimed at, or located in the front. **2.** *Phonetics.* Produced with the front of the tongue in a forward position. Said of vowel sounds.
∼*v.* **fronted, fronting, fronts.** —*tr.* **1.** To look out upon; face. **2.** To meet in opposition; confront. **3.** To provide a front for. **4.** To serve as a front for; head. —*intr.* **1.** To have a front; face. Usually used with *on: Her property fronts on the main road.* **2.** To act as a front. Used with *for.* [Middle English, from Old French, from Latin *frōns*† (stem *front-*), front, forehead.]

front. frontispiece.

front·age (frŭn′tĭj) *n.* **1.** The front part of a piece of property, such as a lot or building. **2.** The length of such a part. **3.** The land between a building and the street. **4.** The direction in which something faces. **5.** Land adjacent to something such as a street or body of water.

fron·tal¹ (frŭnt′l) *adj.* **1.** Of, pertaining to, directed toward, or situated at the front. **2.** Of or pertaining to a meteorological front. **3.** Of or pertaining to the forehead. **—fron·tal·ly** *adv.*

frontal² *n.* **1.** An ornamental drapery covering the front of an altar. **2.** The façade of a building. [Middle English *frontel,* from Medieval Latin *frontellum,* from Latin *frōns* (stem *front-*), FRONT.]

frontal bone *n.* A cranial bone consisting of a vertical portion corresponding to the forehead and a horizontal portion that forms the roofs of the orbital and nasal cavities.

frontal lobe *n.* The anterior portion of each cerebral hemisphere, extending back to the central sulcus.

frontal plane *n. Anatomy.* A plane parallel to the long axis of the body that is perpendicular to the sagittal plane.

front bench *n.* The front row of seats on either side of the House of Commons or a similar legislative body, traditionally reserved for government ministers and leading members of the opposition. **—front-bench** (frŭnt′bĕnch′) *adj.* **—front-bench·er** *n.*

front·court (frŭnt′kôrt′, -kōrt′) *n.* The offensive half of the court used by a team in basketball.

Fron·te·nac (frŏn′tə-năk′), **Louis de Buade, Comte de Palluau et de** (1620–98). French soldier and governor of New France (1672–82 and 1689–98). He held Quebec against the English in the early part of the French and Indian War.

front end *n. Computer Science.* A piece of software designed to make another piece of software easier to operate or understand.

front-end (frŭnt′ĕnd′) *adj.* **1.** Of or pertaining to the initial phase of a project. **2.** *Computer Science.* Designating or pertaining to a computer that is attached to another computer to relieve it of some of its basic tasks.

front-end load *n.* The amount deducted from early payments made to a mutual fund purchase plan that covers expenses such as sales commissions.

fron·ten·is (frŭn-tĕn′ĭs, frŏn-) *n.* A Latin-American tennis game played on a three-walled court. [American Spanish, blend of Spanish *fronton,* gable, jai alai court (from *frenta,* forehead, from Latin *frons*) and *tenis,* tennis (from English TENNIS).]

fron·tier (frŭn-tîr′) *n.* **1.** An international border, or the area along it. **2.** A region just beyond or at the edge of a settled area. **3.** The limit of what is known in a science or other branch of knowledge. —See Synonyms at **boundary.**
∼*adj.* Of, pertaining to, or situated at a frontier. [Middle English *frountier,* from Old French *frontiere,* from *front,* FRONT.]

fron·tiers·man (frŭn-tîrz′mən) *n., pl.* **-men** (-mĭn). A man who lives on the frontier.

fron·tis·piece (frŭn′tĭs-pēs′) *n.* **1.** *Abbr.* **front.** An illustration that faces or immediately precedes the title page of a book, book section, or magazine. **2.** *Architecture.* A façade; especially, an ornamental façade. **3.** *Architecture.* A small ornamental pediment, as on top of a door or window. [Variant (influenced by PIECE) of earlier *frontispice,* from Old French, from Late Latin *frontispicium,* "examination of the front," building exterior : Latin *frōns* (stem *front-*), FRONT + *specere,* to look at.]

front·let (frŭnt′lĭt) *n.* **1.** An ornament or band worn on the forehead. **2.** The forehead of an animal or bird, especially when distinctively marked. **3.** *Ecclesiastical.* The ornamental border of a frontal. [Middle English, from Old French *frontelet,* diminutive of *frontel,* from Latin *frontāle,* from *frōns* (stem *front-*), FRONT.]

front-line (frŭnt′līn′) *adj.* **1.** Located or used at a military front. **2.** Of or relating to the most important or advanced position or activity in a field or undertaking.

front man *n.* **1.** A person who serves as nominal leader but lacks real authority. **2.** A person who acts as a front for groups or organizations carrying on secret or illegal activities.

front matter *n.* The material, such as the preface, frontispiece, and title page, preceding the text in a book. Compare **end matter.**

front office *n.* The policy-making members of an organization.

fron·to·gen·e·sis (frŭn′tō-jĕn′ə-sĭs) *n.* Development or intensification of a meteorological front. [New Latin : FRONT + -GENESIS.]

fron·tol·y·sis (frŭn-tŏl′ə-sĭs) *n.* The disintegration of a meteorological front. [New Latin : FRONT + -LYSIS.]

front-page (frŭnt′pāj′) *adj.* Receiving or worthy of coverage on the front page of a newspaper.

Front Range. Line of mountains running *c.* 480 kilometers (300 miles) through Wyoming and Colorado. It is the loftiest part of the U.S. Rocky Mts.; its highest elevation is Mt. Elbert (4,399 meters; 14,432 feet).

front-run·ner (frŭnt′rŭn′ər) *n.* A leading contender in a contest, election, or the like.

front·ward (frŭnt′wərd) *adv.* Also **front·wards** (-wərdz). At or toward the front.

front-wheel drive (frŭnt′hwēl) *n. Abbr.* **f.w.d.** An automotive drive mechanism in which the drive is applied only to the front wheels.

frosh (frŏsh) *n., pl.* **frosh.** *Informal.* A freshman. [Shortening and alteration of FRESHMAN.]

frost (frôst, frŏst) *n.* **1.** A deposit or covering of minute ice crystals formed from frozen water vapor. **2.** The atmospheric conditions when the temperature is at or below the freezing point of water. **3.** The process of freezing. **4.** A cold or icy manner; aloofness. **5.** *Informal.* Something given a cold reception; fiasco; failure.
∼*v.* **frosted, frosting, frosts.** —*tr.* **1.** To cover with frost. **2.** To damage or kill by frost. **3.** To cover (glass or metal) with a roughened or speckled decorative surface. **4.** To cover or decorate (a cake) with icing. —*intr.* To become covered with or as if with frost. [Middle English *frost,* Old English *frost, forst,* from Germanic.]

Frost (frôst, frŏst), **Robert Lee** (1874–1963). U.S. poet. From the age of 10 he spent much of his life in rural New England, and his work frequently uses aspects of this experience to explore man's relationship with nature. His collections include *A Boy's Will* (1913) and *In the Clearing* (1962).

frost·bite (frôst′bīt′, frŏst′-) *n.* Tissue destruction resulting from ice forming in the tissues, especially of the nose, fingers, toes, and ears.
∼*tr.v.* **frostbit** (-bĭt′), **-bitten** (-bĭt′n), **-biting, -bites.** To injure or damage by freezing.

frost·bit·ten (frôst′bĭt′n, frŏst′-) *adj.* Affected by frostbite.

frost·ed (frô′stĭd, frŏs′tĭd) *adj.* **1.** Covered by frost. **2.** Covered or decorated with icing. **3.** Decorated with frosting, as glass. **4.** Subjected to frosting. Said of hair.

frost heave *n.* An uplifting of soil, a pavement, or a similar surface as a result of freezing below the surface.

frost·ing (frô′stĭng, frŏs′tĭng) *n.* **1.** Icing. **2.** A roughened surface imparted to glass or metal. **3.** The use of bleach to lighten strands of hair over the entire head and create a two-tone appearance.

frost *Ice crystals, formed when the dew freezes, produce hoarfrost that gives plants a hoary, aged look.*

PRONUNCIATION KEY

ă, pat; ā, pay; âr, care;
ä, father, are; b, bib;
ch, church; d, deed; ĕ, pet;
ē, be; f, fife; g, gag; h, hat;
hw, which; ĭ, pit; ī, pie;
îr, pier; j, judge; k, kick;
l, lid, needle; m, mum;
n, no, sudden; ng, thing;
ŏ, pot; ō, toe; ô, paw, for;
oi, noise; ou, out; ŏŏ, book;
ōō, boot; p, pop; r, roar;
s, sauce; sh, ship, dish;
t, tight; th, thin, path;
th, this, bathe; ŭ, cut; ûr, fur;
v, valve; w, with; y, yes;
z, zebra, size; zh, vision;
ə, about, item, edible,
gallop, circus, peaceful

IN FOREIGN WORDS:

à, *Fr.* ami; œ, *Fr.* feu, *Ger.* schön; ü, *Fr.* tu, *Ger.* über; KH, *Ger.* ich, *Scot.* loch; N, *Fr.* bon; y′, *Fr.* Compiègne

STRESS MARKS:

Primary stress: ′
in·cite′ (ĭn-sīt′)
Secondary stress: ′
in′sight′ (ĭn′sīt′)

fruit bat *Sometimes known as flying foxes, fruit bats—which feed chiefly on fruit—are found in tropical and subtropical regions of Asia. Most species have good eyesight, unlike the smaller insect-eating bats that find their way by echolocation. This is a Malaysian fruit bat.*

fruit fly *Fruit flies—members of a large and widely distributed family of insects—breed on fruit trees during the growing season, causing considerable damage to fruit harvests.*

frost line *n.* The limit to which frost penetrates the earth.
frost·re·sis·tant (frôst′rĭ-zĭs′tənt, frŏst′-) *adj.* Designating plants that are able to survive the period of winter frost.
frost·work (frôst′wûrk′, frŏst′-) *n.* **1.** The intricate patterns produced by frost, as on a windowpane. **2.** Similar ornamental patterns produced artificially, as on metal or glass.
frost·y (frô′stē, frŏs′tē) *adj.* **-ier, -iest. 1.** Producing or characterized by frost; freezing. **2.** Covered with or as if with frost. **3.** Silvery white; hoary. **4.** Cold in manner; haughty; distant. **—frost·i·ly** *adv.* **—frost·i·ness** *n.*
froth (frôth, frŏth) *n.* **1.** A mass of bubbles in or on a liquid; foam. **2.** A salivary foam released as a result of disease or exhaustion. **3.** Anything unsubstantial or trivial.
∼*v.* **frothed, frothing, froths.** —*tr.* **1.** To exude or expel in the form of foam. **2.** To cover with foam. **3.** To cause to foam. —*intr.* To exude or expel froth; foam. [Middle English, from Old Norse *frodha,* from Germanic *frudh-* (unattested).]
froth·y (frô′thē, frŏth′ē) *adj.* **-ier, -iest. 1.** Made of, covered with, or resembling froth; foamy. **2.** Playfully frivolous in character or content. **—froth·i·ly** *adv.* **—froth·i·ness** *n.*
frot·tage (frô-täzh′) *n.* **1.** A method of making a design by placing a piece of paper on top of an object and then rubbing over it, as with charcoal or a pencil. **2.** A design made by frottage. [French, rubbing, from *frotter,* to rub.]
frou-frou (frōō′frōō) *n.* **1.** A rustling sound, as of silk. **2.** Fussy or showy dress or ornamentation. [French (imitative).]
frow. Variant of **froe.**
fro·ward (frō′wərd, frō′ərd) *adj.* Stubbornly contrary and disobedient; obstinate. [Middle English *froward* : FRO + -WARD.] **—fro·ward·ly** *adv.* **—fro·ward·ness** *n.*
frown (froun) *v.* **frowned, frowning, frowns.** —*intr.* **1.** To wrinkle the brow, as in thought, worry, or displeasure. **2.** To regard with disapproval or distaste. Used with *on* or *upon*: *"The English frown on the use of tea bags"* (Craig Claiborne). —*tr.* **1.** To express (disapproval or distaste, for example) by wrinkling the brow. **2.** To wrinkle the brow so as to dismiss (a person or statement, for example): *frown objections away.*
∼*n.* A wrinkling of the brow in thought, worry, or displeasure. [Middle English *frounen,* from Old French *froigner,* from Celtic, akin to Welsh *ffroen*†, nose.] **—frown·er** *n.* **—frown·ing·ly** *adv.*
frowst (froust) *n. Chiefly British.* A hot and stuffy atmosphere.
∼*intr.v.* **frowsted, frowsting, frowsts.** To lounge in a hot and stuffy atmosphere. [Back-formation from FROWSTY.] **—frowst·er** *n.*
frowst·y (frou′stē) *adj.* **-ier, -iest.** *Chiefly British.* Having a hot and stuffy atmosphere. [Perhaps a variant of FROWZY.]
frow·zy, frow·sy (frou′zē) *adj.* **-zier, -ziest** or **-sier, -siest. 1.** Unkempt in appearance; slovenly; shabby. **2.** Having an unpleasant smell; musty. —See Synonyms at **sloppy.** [17th century : origin obscure.] **—frow·zi·ly** *adv.* **—frow·zi·ness** *n.*
froze. Past tense of **freeze.**
fro·zen (frō′zən). Past participle of **freeze.**
∼*adj.* **1.** Made into, covered with, or surrounded by ice. **2.** Affected or killed by extreme cold. **3.** Preserved by freezing. **4.** Rendered immobile. **5.** Expressive of cold unfriendliness or disdain: *a frozen stare.* **6. a.** Fixed at an arbitrary level. Said of wages, profits, or the like. **b.** Incapable of being withdrawn, sold, or liquidated. Said of investments, assets, or the like. **—fro·zen·ness** *n.*
frozen food *n.* Food that has undergone quick freezing and that is intended to remain frozen until used.
FRS Federal Reserve System.
Frs. Frisian.
F.R.S. Fellow of the Royal Society.
frt. freight.
fruc·tif·er·ous (frŭk-tĭf′ər-əs, frōōk-) *adj.* Bearing fruit. [Latin *frūctifer* : *frūctus,* FRUIT + -FEROUS.]
fruc·ti·fi·ca·tion (frŭk′tə-fĭ-kā′shən, frōōk′-) *n.* **1.** The producing of fruit. **2.** The fruit of a seed-bearing plant. **3.** A spore-bearing structure.
fruc·ti·fy (frŭk′tə-fī′, frōōk′-) *v.* **-fied, -fying, -fies.** —*tr.* To cause to produce fruit; make fruitful or productive. —*intr.* To bear fruit. [Middle English *fructifien,* from Old French *fructifier,* from Latin *frūctificāre* : *frūctus,* FRUIT + *facere,* to make, do.]
fruc·tose (frŭk′tōs′, frōōk′-) *n.* A very sweet sugar, $C_6H_{12}O_6$, occurring in many fruits and honey and used as a preservative for foodstuffs and as an intravenous nutrient. Also called "fruit sugar," "levulose." [Latin *frūctus,* FRUIT + -OSE.]
fruc·tu·ous (frŭk′chōō-əs, frōōk′-) *adj.* Fruitful; productive. [Middle English, from Old French, from Latin *frūctuōsus,* from *frūctus,* FRUIT.]
fru·gal (frōō′gəl) *adj.* **1.** Avoiding unnecessary expenditure of money; thrifty. **2.** Not plentiful and costing little: *a frugal lunch.* —See Synonyms at **sparing.** [Latin *frūgālis,* back-formation from *frūgālior,* comparative of *frūgī,* useful, worthy, dative of *frūx* (stem *frūg-*), fruit.] **—fru·gal·i·ty** (frōō-găl′ə-tē), **fru·gal·ness** *n.* **—fru·gal·ly** *adv.*
fru·giv·o·rous (frōō-jĭv′ər-əs) *adj.* Feeding on fruit; fruit-eating. [Latin *frūx* (stem *frūg-*), fruit + -VOROUS.]
fruit (frōōt) *n., pl.* **fruit** or **fruits. 1. a.** The ripened ovary or ovaries of a seed-bearing plant, containing the seeds and occurring in a wide variety of forms. **b.** Any other edible fleshy part of a plant that contains seeds but consists of other tissue, such as the receptacle, in addition to the ripened ovary; a pseudocarp or false fruit. **2. a.** Such parts collectively, considered as a type of food. **b.** A vegetable fruit, such as rhubarb. **c.** A part or amount of such a plant product, served as food. **3.** The spore-bearing structure of a plant that does not bear seeds. **4.** A plant crop or product. **5.** Result; issue; outcome: *the fruits of their labor.* **6.** Offspring; progeny. **7.** *Slang.* A male homosexual.
∼*v.* **fruited, fruiting, fruits.** —*intr.* To produce fruit. —*tr.* To cause to produce fruit. [Middle English, from Old French, from Latin *frūctus,* enjoyment, use, produce, fruit, from the past participle of *fruī,* to enjoy, to eat fruit.]
fruit·age (frōō′tĭj) *n.* **1.** The process, time, or condition of bearing fruit. **2.** Fruit collectively. **3.** A result or effect.
fruit·ar·i·an (frōō-târ′ē-ən) *n.* One who lives entirely on fruit. [Formed by analogy with *vegetarian.*] **—fruit·ar·i·an** *adj.* **—fruit·ar·i·an·ism** *n.*
fruit bat *n.* Any of various fruit-eating bats of the family Pteropodidae, of tropical and subtropical regions of the Old World.
fruit·cake (frōōt′kāk′) *n.* **1.** A heavy spiced cake containing citron, nuts, raisins, and preserved fruits. **2.** *Informal.* A person whose behavior is considered strange or eccentric.
fruit cocktail *n.* A fruit cup.
fruit cup *n.* A mixture of fresh or preserved fruits cut into pieces and served as an appetizer or dessert.
fruit·er (frōō′tər) *n.* **1.** A tree that produces fruit. **2.** One who grows fruit. **3.** A ship that transports fruit.
fruit·er·er (frōō′tər-ər) *n. Chiefly British.* A fruit grower or retailer. [Middle English, from FRUITER (grower).]
fruit fly *n.* **1.** Any of various small flies of the family Drosophilidae, having larvae that feed on ripening or fermenting fruit; especially, a common species, *Drosophila melanogaster.* **2.** Any of various flies of the family Trypetidae (or Tephritidae), having larvae that hatch in and damage plant tissue.
fruit·ful (frōōt′fəl) *adj.* **1.** Producing fruit. **2.** Producing fruit or offspring in abundance; prolific. **3.** Conducive to productivity; leading to abundant crops: *a fruitful climate.* **4.** Producing results; profitable. **—fruit·ful·ly** *adv.* **—fruit·ful·ness** *n.*
fruiting body *n.* A specialized spore-producing structure, especially of a fungus.
fru·i·tion (frōō-ĭsh′ən) *n.* **1.** Enjoyment derived from use or possession; pleasure. **2.** The achievement of something desired or worked for; accomplishment; realization. **3.** The condition of bearing fruit. [Middle English *fruicioun,* from Old French *fruition,* from Late Latin *fruitiō* (stem *fruitiōn-*), from *fruī,* to enjoy, eat fruit.]
fruit·less (frōōt′lĭs) *adj.* **1.** Producing no fruit. **2.** Having negligible or no results; unproductive: *"In these fruitless searches he spent ten months"* (Samuel Johnson). **—fruit·less·ly** *adv.* **—fruit·less·ness** *n.*
fruit salad *n.* **1.** A salad containing fruit. **2.** *Slang.* Ribbons and decorations worn on the breast of a military uniform.
fruit salts *pl.n.* Mineral salts.
fruit sugar *n.* **Fructose** *(see).*
fruit tree *n.* Any tree that produces fruit.
fruit·y (frōō′tē) *adj.* **-ier, -iest. 1.** Of, containing, or relating to fruit. **2. a.** Tasting and smelling richly of fruit. **b.** Tasting of the grape. Said of a wine. **3.** Mellow; rich: *a fruity voice.* **4.** Exuding sentiment or unctuousness. **5.** *Slang.* **a.** Homosexual. **b.** Crazy; odd. **—fruit·i·ness** *n.*
fru·men·ta·ceous (frōō′mən-tā′shəs, frōō′mĕn-) *adj.* Resembling or consisting of grain, especially wheat. [Late Latin *frūmentāceus* : Latin *frūmentum,* grain, perhaps from *fruī,* to enjoy + -ACEOUS.]
fru·men·ty (frōō′mən-tē) *n.* Also **fur·men·ty** (fûr′-), **fro·men·ty** (frō′-). *British.* Hulled wheat boiled in milk and flavored with sugar and spices. [Middle English *frumente,* from Old French *frumentee,* from *frument,* grain, from Latin *frūmentum.* See **frumentaceous.**]
frump (frŭmp) *n.* A dull, plain, unfashionably dressed girl or woman. [Perhaps short for dialectal *frumple,* to wrinkle, from Middle English *fromplen,* from Middle Dutch *verrompelen* : *ver-,* for- + *rompelen,* to RUMPLE.] **—frump·ish, frump·y** *adj.* **—frump·ish·ly, frump·i·ly** *adv.* **—frump·ish·ness, frump·i·ness** *n.*
frus·trate (frŭs′trāt′) *tr.v.* **-trated, -trating, -trates. 1. a.** To prevent from accomplishing a purpose or fulfilling a desire; thwart. **b.** To cause feelings of discouragement or dissatisfaction in. **c.** To hinder from finding an outlet for sexual desire. **2.** To prevent the accomplishment or development of; nullify.
∼*adj. Archaic.* Baffled or thwarted. [Middle English *frustraten,* from Latin *frūstrāre* (past participle *frūstrātus*), to disappoint, frustrate, from *frūstrā*†, in error, uselessly.] **—frus·trat·er** *n.* **—frus·trat·ing·ly** *adv.*
Synonyms: *balk, foil, thwart.*
frus·trat·ed (frŭs′trā′tĭd) *adj.* **1.** Suffering from feelings of annoyance or dissatisfaction through the frustration of one's aims or desires. **2.** Unsuccessful in some activity; unfulfilled.
frus·tra·tion (frŭ-strā′shən) *n.* **1.** The condition or an instance of being frustrated. **2.** One that frustrates. **3.** *Psychology.* **a.** Feelings of dissatisfaction caused by an inability to achieve personal or sexual fulfillment. **b.** Something that gives rise to such feelings.
frus·tule (frŭs′chōōl, -tyōōl) *n.* The hard, siliceous shell of a diatom. [French, from Latin *frustulum,* diminutive of *frustum,* piece.]
frus·tum (frŭs′təm) *n., pl.* **-tums** or **-ta** (-tə). A part of a solid, such as a cone or pyramid, between two parallel planes cutting the solid, especially the section between the base and a plane parallel to it. [Latin, piece, piece cut off.]
fru·tes·cent (frōō-tĕs′ənt) *adj.* Pertaining to, resembling, or assuming the form of a shrub; shrubby. [Latin *frutex,* bush (see **fruticose**) + -ESCENT.] **—fru·tes·cence** *n.*

fru·ti·cose (fro͞o′tĭ-kōs′) *adj.* Shrublike, especially in form. [Latin *fruticōsus,* from *frutex*† (stem *frutic-*), shrub, bush.]

fry¹ (frī) *v.* **fried, frying, fries.** —*tr.* To cook over direct heat in hot oil or fat. —*intr.* **1.** To undergo frying. **2.** *Informal.* To swelter. **3.** *Slang.* To undergo execution in the electric chair.
∼*n., pl.* **fries. 1.** A dish of any fried food. **2.** A social gathering featuring fried food: *a fish fry.* [Middle English *frien,* from Old French *frire,* from Latin *frīgere.*]

fry² *n., pl.* **fry. 1.** A small fish; especially, a recently hatched fish. **2.** The similar young of certain other animals. **3.** Individuals; people: *invited the young fry to a party.* See **small fry.** [Middle English, young offspring, perhaps from Norman French *frie,* from Old French *freier,* to spawn, rub, from Latin *fricāre,* to rub.]

Fry (frī), **Christopher,** born Christopher Harris (1907–). British playwright. He became a major figure in postwar drama with his verse plays, especially *A Phoenix Too Frequent* (1946) and *The Lady's Not for Burning* (1948).

Fry, Roger Eliot (1866–1934). British painter and critic. His exhibitions (1910–12) did much to promote recognition of the postimpressionist movement in Britain. His works include studies of Paul Cézanne (1927) and Henri Matisse (1930), *Vision and Design* (1920), and *Reflections on British Paintings* (1934).

Frye (frī), **H(erman) Northrop** (1912–). Canadian literary critic. He wrote *Fearful Symmetry* (1947), a study of William Blake, and *Anatomy of Criticism* (1957).

fry·er, fri·er (frī′ər) *n.* **1.** One that fries, especially a deep pan or vessel that is suitable for frying food. **2.** A small, young chicken that is suitable for frying.

frying pan *n.* A shallow, long-handled pan used for frying food.

FSH follicle-stimulating hormone.

f-stop (ĕf′stŏp′) *n.* **1.** A camera lens aperture setting calibrated to a corresponding f-number. **2.** An **f-number** *(see).* [*F*ocal length *stop.*]

f-sys·tem (ĕf′sĭs′təm) *n.* A method of indicating the relative aperture of a camera lens based on the f-number.

ft foot.

ft. fort; fortification.

F.T.A. Future Teachers of America.

FTC Federal Trade Commission.

ft-c foot-candle.

FT Index (ĕf′tē′) *n.* The daily index of prices on the London stock exchange based on the average price of 30 selected shares. Called in full "Financial Times Industrial Ordinary Share Index." Compare **Dow-Jones average.**

ft-lb foot-pound.

fub·sy (fŭb′zē) *adj.* **-sier, -siest.** *British Regional.* Somewhat fat and squat. [From obsolete *fubs*†, a chubby person.]

Fu-chien. See **Fujian.**

Fu-chou. See **Fuzhou.**

Fuchs (fo͝oks), **Klaus Emil Julian** (1911–). German-born physicist. He worked on atomic research in Britain during and after World War II and was imprisoned (1950–59) for passing secret information to the Soviet government.

fuch·sia (fyo͞o′shə) *n.* **1.** Any of various chiefly tropical shrubs of the genus *Fuchsia,* widely cultivated for their showy, drooping purplish, reddish, pink, or white flowers. **2.** The hardy or common fuchsia, *F. magellanica,* having flowers with scarlet sepals and purple-blue petals forming a bell. **3.** Strong, vivid purplish red. [New Latin, after Leonhard *Fuchs* (1501–1566), German botanist.]

fuch·sin, fuch·sine (fyo͞ok′sĭn, -sēn′) *n.* A dark-green synthetic aniline dyestuff, the hydrochloride of rosaniline, used to make a purple-red dye used to color textiles and leather and as a bacterial stain. Also called "magenta." [FUCHS(IA) + -IN.]

fu·coid (fyo͞o′koid′) *adj.* Of or belonging to the order Fucales, which includes brown algae such as wracks, kelps, and similar seaweeds.
∼*n.* **1.** A member of the Fucales. **2.** A fossilized cast or impression of a seaweed. [Perhaps FUC(US) + -OID.]

fu·cose (fyo͞o′kōs′) *n.* An aldose, $C_6H_{12}O_5$, present in the polysaccharides associated with several blood groups. [FUC(US) + -OSE.]

fu·co·xan·thin (fyo͞o′kō-zăn′thĭn) *n.* A brown carotenoid pigment, $C_{40}H_{60}O_6$, found in brown algae. [FUC(US) + XANTH(O)- + -IN.]

fu·cus (fyo͞o′kəs) *n.* Any of various brown algae of the genus *Fucus,* which includes many of the larger seaweeds found between high and low tide mark. [New Latin *Fucus,* from Latin *fūcus,* red dye, orchil, from Greek *phukos.* See **phyco-.**]

fud·dle (fŭd′l) *v.* **-dled, -dling, -dles.** —*tr.* To muddle with or as if with strong drink; intoxicate. —*intr.* To drink; tipple.
∼*n.* A state of intoxication or confusion. [16th century : origin obscure.]

fud·dy-dud·dy (fŭd′ē-dŭd′ē) *n., pl.* **-dies.** One who is old-fashioned and fussy. [20th century : origin obscure.] **—fud·dy-dud·dy** *adj.*

fudge (fŭj) *n.* **1.** A soft, rich candy made of sugar, butter, milk, and flavoring. **2.** Nonsense; humbug. **3.** A small section of a newspaper page in which last-minute copy may be inserted after the plate or type is on the printing press. **4.** The news item so inserted.
∼*interj.* Used to express disbelief, disappointment, or annoyance.
∼*v.* **fudged, fudging, fudges.** —*tr.* **1.** To make or repair in a clumsy way; botch. **2.** To evade (an issue, for example); dodge. **3.** To fake or falsify. —*intr.* **1.** To act or talk in an evasive or indecisive manner. **2.** To act dishonestly; cheat. [Perhaps from obsolete *fadge*†, to adjust, fit, fake, deceive.]

Fue·gi·an (fwā′jē-ən) *adj.* Of or relating to Tierra del Fuego, its inhabitants, or its culture.
∼*n.* An inhabitant of Tierra del Fuego.

fuehrer. Variant of **führer.**

fu·el (fyo͞o′əl) *n.* **1.** Anything consumed to produce energy, especially: **a.** A material such as coal, gas, or oil burned to produce heat. **b.** Fissionable material used in a nuclear reactor. **c.** Nutritive material metabolized by a living organism. **2.** Anything that maintains or heightens an activity or an emotion.
∼*v.* **fueled** or **-elled, -eling** or **-elling, -els.** —*tr.* **1.** To provide with fuel. **2.** To stimulate: *His insolence fueled her anger.* —*intr.* To take in fuel. [Middle English *feuel,* from Old French *fouaille,* from Vulgar Latin *focālia* (unattested), from Latin *focus*†, fire, hearth.] **—fu·el·er** *n.*

fuel cell *n.* An electrochemical cell in which the energy of a reaction between a fuel such as liquid hydrogen and an oxidant such as liquid oxygen is converted directly and continuously into the energy of direct electric current.

fuel element *n.* A can that contains the nuclear fuel in a nuclear reactor.

fuel injection *n.* Any of several methods or mechanical systems by which a fuel is vaporized and sprayed into the cylinders of an internal-combustion engine without the use of a carburetor.

fuel oil *n.* Any liquid or liquefiable petroleum product that ignites spontaneously at a temperature above 100°F, used to generate heat or power.

fug (fŭg) *n.* A hot, stuffy, and usually smoke-laden atmosphere. [19th century : origin obscure.] **—fug·gy** *adj.*

fu·ga·cious (fyo͞o-gā′shəs) *adj.* **1.** Passing away quickly; evanescent. **2.** *Botany.* Withering or dropping off early: *fugacious petals.* [Latin *fugāx* (stem *fugāc-*), swift, fleeting, from *fugere,* to flee.] **—fu·ga·cious·ly** *adv.* **—fu·ga·cious·ness** *n.*

fu·gac·i·ty (fyo͞o-găs′ĭ-tē) *n.* **1.** The state or quality of being fugacious. **2.** A property of a gas that is a measure of its ability to escape or expand, given by $d(\log_e f) = d\mu/RT$, where μ is the chemical potential, R is the gas constant, and T is the thermodynamic temperature.

Fu·gard (fo͞o′gärd′), **Athol** (1932–). South African playwright and actor. His plays, including *The Blood Knot* (1962), *Boesman and Lena* (1973), and *A Lesson from Aloes* (1981), examine the treatment of society's misfits and outcasts.

-fuge *suffix.* Indicates an expulsion or driving away; for example, **vermifuge.** [Latin *fugāre,* to put to flight, expel, from *fuga,* flight.]

fu·gi·tive (fyo͞o′jə-tĭv) *adj.* **1.** Running or having run away; fleeing, as from justice or the law. **2. a.** Passing quickly; fleeting: *fugitive hours.* **b.** Difficult to comprehend or retain; elusive. **c.** Given to change or disappearance; perishable. **3.** Having to do with topics of temporary interest; ephemeral. —See Synonyms at **transient.**
∼*n.* **1.** One who flees; a runaway; refugee. **2.** Anything fleeting or ephemeral. [Middle English *fugitif,* from Old French, from Latin *fugitīvus,* from adjective, "fleeing," from *fugitus,* past participle of *fugere,* to flee.] **—fu·gi·tive·ly** *adv.* **—fu·gi·tive·ness** *n.*

fu·gle (fyo͞o′gəl) *intr.v.* **-gled, -gling, -gles.** *Archaic.* To act as a fugleman. [Back-formation from FUGLEMAN.]

fu·gle·man (fyo͞o′gəl-mən) *n., pl.* **-men** (-mĭn). **1.** *Archaic.* A soldier who serves as a guide and model for his company. **2.** A leader; especially, a political leader. [German *Flügelmann,* soldier, "man on the wing" : *Flügel,* wing + *Mann,* man.]

fugue (fyo͞og) *n.* **1.** A polyphonic musical form or composition in which a theme or themes stated successively by a number of voices in imitation are developed contrapuntally. **2.** A pathological amnesiac condition during which the patient is apparently conscious of his actions but on return to normal has no recollection of them. [French *fugue* or Italian *fuga,* flight, from Latin, flight.] **—fu·gal** *adj.* **—fu·gal·ly** *adv.*

füh·rer, fueh·rer (fyo͝or′ər; *German* fü′rər) *n.* **1.** A leader; especially, one exercising the powers of a dictator. **2. Führer.** The title of Adolf Hitler as the leader of the German Nazis. [German *Führer,* from Middle High German *vüerer,* bearer, from *vüeren,* to lead, bear, from Old High German *fuoren,* to lead.]

Fu·jian or **Fu-chien** (fo͞o′jĕn′). Also **Fu·kien** (-kyĕn′). Province in southeastern China. It has some of Asia's finest scenery, with wooded mountains such as the Wuyi Shan, terraced rice paddies, orchards, and tea gardens. [Chinese, "happy establishment."]

Fu·ji·ya·ma (fo͞o′jē-yä′mə). Also **Fu·ji·san** (fo͞o′jē-sän′) or **Mount Fu·ji** (fo͞o′jē). Active volcano on the island of Honshu and the highest mountain (3,776 meters; 12,388 feet) in Japan. Its summit is a place of pilgrimage, and its snow-capped, strikingly symmetrical cone has long been a favorite subject of Japanese painters. The last major eruption took place in 1707.

-ful *suffix.* Indicates: **1.** Having the characteristics of; for example, **masterful. 2.** Tendency or ability; for example, **useful. 3.** The amount or number that will fill; for example, **armful.** [Middle English *-ful,* Old English *-ful, -full,* from *full,* FULL.]

Fu·la, Fu·lah (fo͞o′lə) *n., pl.* **-las** or **-lahs** or collectively **Fula** or **Fulah.** A mostly Muslim people of the western Sudan region of Africa, of mixed Hamitic and Negroid stock.

Fu·la·ni (fo͞o′lä′nē, fo͞o-lä′nē) *n., pl.* **-nis** or collectively **Fulani. 1.** A member of the Fula. **2.** The language of the Fula.

ful·crum (fo͝ol′krəm, fŭl′-) *n., pl.* **-crums** or **-cra** (-krə). **1.** The point or support on which a lever turns. **2.** A factor critically affecting an outcome, reaction, or the like: *Cost was the fulcrum of their decision.* [Latin, bedpost, support, from *fulcīre,* to prop up, support.]

ful·fill, ful·fil (fo͝ol-fĭl′) *tr.v.* **-filled, -filling, -fills** or **-fils. 1.** To realize (expectations or promise, for example); achieve. **2.** To carry out (an order or duty, for example). **3.** To measure up to; satisfy. **4.** To go

fuchsia *There are more than 100 species of fuchsia, most of which are native to Central and South America and New Zealand. They have brightly colored pendant flowers and are often grown in hanging baskets.*

PRONUNCIATION KEY

ă, pat; ā, pay; âr, care;
ä, father, are; b, bib;
ch, church; d, deed; ĕ, pet;
ē, be; f, fife; g, gag; h, hat;
hw, which; ĭ, pit; ī, pie;
îr, pier; j, judge; k, kick;
l, lid, needle; m, mum;
n, no, sudden; ng, thing;
ŏ, pot; ō, toe; ô, paw, for;
oi, noise; ou, out; o͝o, book;
o͞o, boot; p, pop; r, roar;
s, sauce; sh, ship, dish;
t, tight; th, thin, path;
th, this, bathe; ŭ, cut; ûr, fur;
v, valve; w, with; y, yes;
z, zebra, size; zh, vision;
ə, about, item, edible,
gallop, circus, peaceful

IN FOREIGN WORDS:

à, *Fr.* ami; œ, *Fr.* feu, *Ger.* schön; ü, *Fr.* tu, *Ger.* über; KH, *Ger.* ich, *Scot.* loch; N, *Fr.* bon; y′, *Fr.* Compiègne

STRESS MARKS:

Primary stress: ′
in·cite′ (ĭn-sīt′)
Secondary stress: ′
in′sight′ (ĭn′sīt′)

to the end of (a period of time); finish or complete. —See Synonyms at **perform.** —**fulfill oneself.** To achieve personal fulfillment. [Middle English *fulfillen,* Old English *fullfyllan,* to fill full : *ful,* FULL + *fyllan,* to FILL.] —**ful·fill·er** *n.*

ful·fill·ment, ful·fil·ment (fo͝ol-fĭl′mənt) *n.* **1.** The act or process of fulfilling. **2.** The state or quality of being fulfilled; completion. **3.** Satisfaction gained from fully realizing one's personal aims or potential. **4.** The processing of orders in a direct mail operation, as for magazine subscriptions.

ful·gent (fŭl′jənt, fo͝ol′-) *adj.* Shining brilliantly. [Middle English, from Latin *fulgēns* (stem *fulgent-*), present participle of *fulgēre,* to flash, shine.] —**ful·gent·ly** *adv.*

ful·gu·rant (fŭl′gyər-ənt, fo͝ol′-) *adj.* **1.** Flashing like lightning. **2.** *Medicine.* Fulminant. [Latin *fulgurāns* (stem *fulgurant-*), present participle of *fulgurāre,* to FULGURATE.]

ful·gu·rate (fŭl′gyə-rāt′, fo͝ol′-) *v.* **-rated, -rating, -rates.** —*intr.* To give off or seem to give off flashes of lightning. —*tr. Medicine.* To destroy (tissue) by fulguration. [Latin *fulgurāre,* to flash, glow like lightning, from *fulgur,* lightning, from *fulgēre,* to flash, shine.]

ful·gu·ra·tion (fŭl′gyə-rā′shən, fo͝ol′-) *n.* **1.** The act of flashing like lightning or flashing with light. **2.** The destruction of unwanted tissue, such as warts, with electric current.

ful·gu·rite (fŭl′gyə-rīt′, fo͝ol′-) *n.* A tubular body of glassy rock produced by lightning striking loose unconsolidated sand or more solid rock. [Latin *fulgur,* lightning (see **fulgurate**) + -ITE.]

ful·gu·rous (fŭl′gyər-əs, fo͝ol′-) *adj.* **1.** Emitting flashes of lightning. **2.** Appearing or acting like lightning.

fu·lig·i·nous (fyo͞o-lĭj′ə-nəs) *adj.* **1.** Sooty. **2.** Colored by or as if by soot. [Late Latin *fūlīginōsus,* from Latin *fūlīgō* (stem *fūlīgin-*), soot.] —**fu·lig·i·nous·ly** *adv.*

fulmar *The northern fulmar defends itself by squirting stinking oil—produced from its stomach—over an intruder. It nests on cliffs around the Arctic Circle and western Europe.*

full[1] (fo͝ol) *adj.* **fuller, fullest. 1.** Containing all that is normal or possible; filled: *a full bottle.* **2. a.** Not deficient or partial: *a full view of the stage.* **b.** Complete; no less than: *a full half hour.* **c.** Maximum: *its full length.* **d.** Whole; entire: *He realized the full implications of his act.* **e.** At the highest degree or at the greatest extent: *at full speed; in full color.* **3. a.** Having a great deal or many of. Used with *of: a room full of people.* **b.** Abounding in. Used with *of: full of enthusiasm.* **4. a.** Profoundly affected by an emotion. **b.** Deeply engrossed or preoccupied by; talking and thinking of nothing else. Used with *of: They were all full of the idea.* **5. a.** Very busy: *a full day.* **b.** Satisfying; fulfilling: *a full life.* **6. a.** Having all appropriate rights and responsibilities: *a full member.* **b.** Designating a relation or relationship based on descent from the same parents: *full brothers.* **7. a.** Rounded in shape; plump: *a full figure.* **b.** Of ample cut or generous proportions; wide: *full draperies.* **8.** Satiated, especially with food or drink; abundantly fed. **9. a.** Having depth and body; rich: *a full color.* **b.** Resonant: *the full tone of the cellos.* **10.** Full-bodied. Said of wines. **11.** Thoroughly documented and presented; detailed: *a full report.* **12.** Having the observable surface completely illuminated. Said of the moon. **13.** At the flood; high. Said of the tide. **14.** Extended by the wind. Said of sails.
~*adv.* **1.** To a complete extent; entirely. Often used in combination: *full-grown.* **2.** Exactly; directly: *full in the path of the ball.* **3.** Quite; equally: *full as wicked as I am.* —**full well.** Very well: *I know full well how you feel.*
~*v.* **fulled, fulling, fulls.** —*tr.* To make (a garment) full, as by pleating or gathering. —*intr.* To become full. Used of the moon.
~*n.* The maximum or complete size, amount, or development. —**at the full.** At the state or period of fullness. —**in full. 1.** To, for, or with the entire amount. **2.** With nothing left out; completely. —**to the full.** To the utmost extent; completely. [Middle English *ful(l),* Old English *full.*]

full[2] *v.* **fulled, fulling, fulls.** —*tr.* To clean and increase the weight and bulk of (cloth) by washing, shrinking, and beating or pressing. —*intr.* To become heavier and more compact. Used of cloth. [Middle English *fullen,* from Old French *fouler,* from Vulgar Latin *fullāre* (unattested), from Latin *fullō*†, a fuller.]

full·back (fo͝ol′băk′) *n. Abbr.* **fb, f.b. 1. a.** *Football.* A backfield player whose position is behind the quarterback and halfbacks and who performs offensive blocking and line plunges and defensive linebacking. **b.** A similar player in field hockey, soccer, and rugby. **2.** The position played by a fullback.

full blood *n.* **1.** Relationship established through having the same parents. **2.** A person or animal of unmixed race or breed; a purebred.

full-blood·ed (fo͝ol′blŭd′ĭd) *adj.* Also **full-blood** (fo͝ol′blŭd′) (for sense 1). **1. a.** Of unmixed ancestry; purebred. **b.** Related through having the same parents. **2.** Vigorous; forceful. **3.** Thoroughgoing: *a full-blooded communist.*

full-blown (fo͝ol′blōn′) *adj.* **1.** In full blossom; fully open: *a full-blown tulip.* **2.** Fully developed or matured: *a full-blown beauty.*

full-bod·ied (fo͝ol′bŏd′ēd) *adj.* Having richness and intensity of flavor. Said of wines.

full brother *n.* See **brother.**

full cousin *n.* See **cousin.**

full-cream (fo͝ol′krēm′) *adj.* Designating or made with milk that has had none of the cream skimmed off.

full dress *n.* The attire appropriate for formal or ceremonial events.

full-dress (fo͝ol′drĕs′) *adj.* **1.** Requiring or consisting of full dress; formal: *a full-dress banquet.* **2.** Full-scale: *a full-dress investigation.*

full·er[1] (fo͝ol′ər) *n.* A person who fulls cloth. [Middle English *fullere,* Old English *fullere,* from Latin *fullō.* See **full** (to clean).]

full·er[2] *n.* **1.** A hammer used by a blacksmith for grooving or spreading iron. **2.** A groove made with this tool.
~*tr.v.* **fullered, -ering, -ers.** To make (a groove) with a fuller. [Perhaps from the name *Fuller.*]

Ful·ler (fo͝ol′ər), **(Richard) Buckminster** (1895–1983). U.S. designer and architect. His high-efficiency, low-pollution prefabricated geodesic domes were very popular, and his book *Operating Manual for Spaceship Earth* (1969) was influential in the environmentalist movement of the 1970's.

Fuller, (Sarah) Margaret (1810–50). U.S. author, critic, and reformer. An editor of the transcendentalist periodical *Dial* (1840) and the literary critic for the *New York Tribune* (1844–45), she was regarded as one of America's premier critics. On a European tour (1845–50), she married an Italian marquis, joined the ill-fated Roman Revolution, and wrote a history of that rebellion. While en route to the United States, she perished in a shipwreck.

fuller's earth *n.* A highly absorbent clay used in fulling woolen cloth, in talcum powders, as a filter, and as a catalyst.

fuller's teasel *n.* A European plant, *Dipsacus fullonum,* having bristly flower heads used by fullers to raise the nap on cloth. See **teasel.**

full face *adv.* Face on to an observer or a specified object.

full-fash·ioned (fo͝ol′făsh′ənd) *adj.* Knitted in a shape that conforms closely to body lines.

full-fledged (fo͝ol′flĕjd′) *adj.* **1.** Having fully developed adult plumage. **2.** Having reached full development; mature. **3.** Having full status or rank: *a full-fledged lawyer.*

full gainer *n.* A forward dive in which one executes a full back somersault before entering the water.

full house *n.* **1.** In poker, a hand containing three of a kind and a pair. **2.** A movie theater, concert hall, or the like in which every seat for a performance is taken. **3.** A winning set of numbers at bingo.

full-length (fo͝ol′lĕngkth′, -lĕngth′) *adj.* **1.** Showing, covering, or fitted to the entire length of someone or something: *a full-length mirror.* **2.** Of a normal or standard length; unabridged: *a full-length novel.*

full moon *n.* **1.** The phase of the moon when it is visible as a fully illuminated disk. **2.** The period of the month when this occurs. **3.** The fully illuminated moon.

full-mouthed (fo͝ol′mouthd′, -moutht′) *adj.* **1.** Having a complete set of teeth. Said of cattle and other livestock. **2.** Uttered loudly or noisily: *a full-mouthed oath.*

full nelson *n.* A wrestling hold in which both hands are first thrust under the opponent's arms from behind and then pressed against the back of his neck. Compare **half nelson.**

full·ness, ful·ness (fo͝ol′nĭs) *n.* The quality or state of being full. —**in the fullness of time.** At the proper, appointed time.

full-out (fo͝ol′out′) *adj.* **1.** Total; complete. **2.** *Printing.* Not indented; aligned with the margin. —**full-out** *adv.*

full-rigged (fo͝ol′rĭgd′) *adj.* Having three or more masts all square-rigged.

full rhyme *n.* A **perfect rhyme** *(see).*

full-scale (fo͝ol′skāl′) *adj.* **1.** Of the actual or full size; not reduced: *a full-scale model.* **2.** Carried out in a thoroughgoing manner and with a total commitment of effort: *a full-scale campaign.* **3.** Occurring on a large scale: *a full-scale disaster.*

full sister *n.* See **sister.**

full stop *n. Chiefly British.* A dot indicating the end of a sentence or an abbreviation; period.

full tilt *adv.* At high or top speed: *ran full tilt into the tree.*

full-time (fo͝ol′tīm′) *adj.* **1.** Of, pertaining to, or designating work requiring attendance throughout the working week. Compare **part-time. 2.** Performing an activity or job for the normal or required amount of time: *a full-time student.* **3.** Of or pertaining to an activity that requires a person's full attention. —**full-time** *adv.*

ful·ly (fo͝ol′ē) *adv.* **1.** Totally or completely. **2.** Adequately; sufficiently. **3.** At a conservative estimate; at least.

ful·mar (fo͝ol′mər, -mär′) *n.* **1.** A gull-like bird, *Fulmarus glacialis,* of Arctic regions, having smoky gray plumage. Also called "fulmar petrel." **2.** Any of several similar related birds. [Perhaps from Old Norse *fúlmār,* "foul gull" (probably referring to its smell) : *fúll,* foul + *mār,* gull, from Germanic *maiwa-* (unattested), gull, MEW.]

ful·mi·nant (fŭl′mə-nənt, fo͝ol′-) *adj.* **1.** Fulminating. **2.** *Pathology.* Occurring suddenly, rapidly, and with great intensity. Said of symptoms, especially of pain. [Latin *fulmināns* (stem *fulminant-*), present participle of *fulmināre,* to strike with lightning, FULMINATE.]

ful·mi·nate (fŭl′mə-nāt′, fo͝ol′-) *v.* **-nated, -nating, -nates.** —*intr.* **1.** To issue a thunderous verbal attack or denunciation; inveigh: *fulminate against political chicanery.* **2.** To explode or detonate with sudden violence. —*tr.* **1.** To thunder out or issue (a decree or denunciation, for example). **2.** To cause to explode.
~*n.* An explosive salt or ester of fulminic acid; especially, fulminate of mercury. [Middle English *fulminaten,* from Medieval Latin *fulmināre* (past participle *fulminātus*), to censure (in ecclesiastical decrees), from Latin, to strike with lightning, from *fulmen* (stem *fulmin-*), lightning.] —**ful·mi·na·tor** *n.* —**ful·mi·na·to·ry** (fŭl′mə-nə-tôr′ē, -tōr′ē, fo͝ol′-) *adj.*

fulminate of mercury *n.* A gray crystalline powder, $Hg(CNO)_2$, that explodes on impact when dry and is used as a high explosive.

fulminating powder *n.* An explosive powder that can be detonated by impact.

ful·mi·na·tion (fŭl′mə-nā′shən, fo͝ol′-) *n.* **1.** The act of fulminating. **2.** A thunderous denunciation or censure. **3.** A violent explosion.

ful·min·ic acid (fŭl-mĭn′ĭk, fo͝ol-) *n.* An unstable acid, HONC, that forms highly explosive salts and esters. [Latin *fulmen* (stem *fulmin-*), lightning. See **fulminate.**]

ful·some (fo͝ol'səm) *adj.* **1.** Offensively excessive, flattering, or insincere: *fulsome praise.* **2.** Offensive to the taste or sensibilities; loathsome; disgusting. **3.** *Archaic.* Copious or abundant in supply. [Middle English *fulsom,* abundant : *ful,* FULL + -SOME.] **—ful·some·ly** *adv.* **—ful·some·ness** *n.*

Usage: *Fulsome* is often misused, especially in the phrase *fulsome praise,* by those who think that the term is equivalent merely to *full* and *abundant.* In modern usage *full* and *abundant* are obsolete as senses of *fulsome,* which now combines the idea of fullness or abundance with that of excess or insincerity.

Ful·ton (fo͝ol'tən), **Robert** (1765–1815). U.S. engineer. He developed the first practical submarine and torpedo (1800) and is most famous as the inventor of the steamship. His first steamboat, the *Clermont,* made the round trip from New York City to Albany on the Hudson River in 62 hours (1806).

ful·vous (fo͝ol'vəs, fŭl'-) *adj.* Tawny yellowish-brown. [Latin *fulvus;* akin to *fulgēre,* to shine.]

fu·mar·ic acid (fyo͞o-măr'ĭk) *n.* An acid, $C_4H_4O_4$, found in various plants and produced synthetically, used mainly in resins, paints, and varnishes. [New Latin *Fumaria,* genus of fumitory, from Late Latin *fūmāria,* fumitory, from Latin *fūmus,* smoke.]

fu·ma·role (fyo͞o'mə-rōl') *n.* A vent or small hole in a volcanic area from which hot smoke and gases arise. [Italian *fumarola,* from Late Latin *fūmāriolum,* smoke hole, from Latin *fūmārium,* smoke chamber, from *fūmus,* smoke.]

fu·ma·to·ri·um (fyo͞o'mə-tôr'ē-əm, -tōr'ē-əm) *n., pl.* **-ums** or **-toria** (-tôr'ē-ə, -tōr'ē-ə). An airtight fumigation chamber in which chemical vapors are used to destroy insects and fungi on plants. [New Latin, from Latin *fūmātus,* past participle of *fūmāre,* to smoke, from *fūmus,* smoke.]

fu·ma·to·ry (fyo͞o'mə-tôr'ē, -tōr'ē) *adj.* Of or pertaining to smoke or fumigating.
∼*n., pl.* **fumatories.** A fumatorium. [New Latin *fumatorius,* from FUMATORIUM.]

fum·ble (fŭm'bəl) *v.* **-bled, -bling, -bles.** *—intr.* **1.** To touch or handle nervously or idly: *fumble with a necktie.* **2.** To grope awkwardly to find or to accomplish: *fumble for a key.* **3.** To proceed awkwardly and uncertainly; blunder: *fumble through a speech.* **4. a.** *Baseball.* To mishandle a ground ball. **b.** *Football.* To drop a ball that is in play. *—tr.* **1.** To catch, touch, or handle clumsily or idly. **2. a.** To feel or make (one's way) awkwardly. **b.** To make a botch of; bungle. **3. a.** *Baseball.* To mishandle (a ground ball). **b.** *Football.* To drop (a ball that is in play).
∼*n.* **1.** The act of fumbling. **2.** An instance of fumbling. **3.** *Sports.* A ball that has been fumbled. [Low German *fummeln*†.] **—fum·bler** *n.*

fume (fyo͞om) *n.* **1.** *Often* **fumes.** An exhalation of smoke, vapor, or gas; especially, an irritating or disagreeable exhalation. **2.** A strong or acrid odor. **3.** A state of irritation or anger.
∼*v.* **fumed, fuming, fumes.** *—tr.* **1.** To subject to or treat with fumes. **2.** To give off in or as if in fumes. *—intr.* **1.** To emit fumes. **2.** To rise or dissipate in vapor. **3.** To feel or show anger. [Middle English, from Old French *fum,* from Latin *fūmus,* smoke, steam.]

fume cupboard *n. British.* A cupboard or glass chamber in a laboratory within which operations involving chemicals that emit harmful vapors are performed or where such chemicals are stored.

fu·mi·gate (fyo͞o'mĭ-gāt') *tr.v.* **-gated, -gating, -gates.** To subject to smoke or fumes, usually in order to exterminate vermin or insects. [Latin *fūmigāre* : *fūmus,* smoke, FUME + *agere,* to make, do.] **—fu·mi·gant** *n.* **—fu·mi·ga·tion** *n.* **—fu·mi·ga·tor** *n.*

fuming sulfuric acid *n.* A mixture of sulfuric acids made by dissolving sulfur trioxide in concentrated sulfuric acid. It is principally pyrosulfuric acid, $H_2S_2O_7$. Also called "oleum," "Nordhausen acid."

fu·mi·to·ry (fyo͞o'mə-tôr'ē, -tōr'ē) *n., pl.* **-ries.** **1.** A climbing annual plant, *Fumaria officinalis,* native to Europe, having finely divided leaves and spurred purplish flowers. **2.** Any other plants of the genus *Fumaria.* [Middle English *fumetere,* from Old French *fumeterre,* from Medieval Latin *fūmus terrae,* "smoke of the earth" (its growth resembles a cloud of smoke over the ground) : Latin *fūmus,* smoke, FUME + *terrae,* genitive of *terra,* earth.]

fun (fŭn) *n.* **1.** A source of enjoyment or pleasure; amusing diversion: *Clowns are fun.* **2.** Enjoyment; pleasure; amusement: *have fun at the beach.* **3.** Excited, playful activity or altercation. **—for** (or **in**) **fun.** As a joke; playfully. **—like fun.** *Slang.* Absolutely not; of course not. **—make fun of.** To ridicule.
∼*intr.v.* **funned, funning, funs.** To behave playfully; joke.
∼*adj. Informal.* Providing fun; amusing: *a fun group of people.* [Perhaps from obsolete *fun,* to trick, from Middle English *fonnen,* to make fun of, from *fon, fonne,* a fool. See **fond.**]

fu·nam·bu·list (fyo͞o-năm'byə-lĭst) *n.* One who performs on a tightrope or a slack rope. [Probably from Latin *fūnambulus,* rope dancer : *fūnis*†, rope + *ambulāre,* to walk around.] **—fu·nam·bu·lism** *n.*

Fun·chal (fo͞on-shäl'). Popular winter resort city on Madeira island and capital of the Funchal overseas district of Portugal, comprising the Madeira archipelago.

func·tion (fŭngk'shən) *n.* **1.** The natural or proper action for which a person, office, thing, or organ is fitted or employed. **2. a.** Assigned duty or activity: *His functions include maintaining office records.* **b.** Specific occupation or role: *in her function as mayor.* **3.** An official ceremony or elaborate social occasion. **4.** Something closely related to another thing and dependent upon it for its existence, value, or significance. **5.** *Grammar.* The role or position of a linguistic element in a construction. **6.** *Mathematics.* **a.** A variable so related to another that for each value assumed by one there is a value determined for the other. **b.** A rule of correspondence between two sets such that there is a unique element in one set assigned to each element in the other.
∼*intr.v.* **functioned, -tioning, -tions.** To have or perform a function; serve. [Latin *functiō* (stem *functiōn-*), activity, performance, from *functus,* past participle of *fungī,* to perform.]

func·tion·al (fŭngk'shə-nəl) *adj.* **1.** Of or pertaining to a function or functions. **2. a.** Designed for or adapted to a particular practical need or activity: *functional clothing for infants.* **b.** Stressing practical usefulness and function other than extraneous embellishment: *functional architecture.* **3.** Capable of performing; operative. **4.** *Pathology.* Pertaining to a disease having no apparent physiological or structural cause. **5.** *Mathematics.* Of, relating to, or indicating a function or functions. **—func·tion·al·ly** *adv.*

functional disease *n.* Any disease having no apparent physiological or structural cause. Compare **organic disease.**

functional group *n. Chemistry.* The group of atoms in a molecule that determines its chemical behavior; for example, -CHO is the functional group in aldehydes.

func·tion·al·ism (fŭngk'shə-nə-lĭz'əm) *n.* **1.** The doctrine or the application of the doctrine that the function of an object should determine its design and materials. **2.** Any doctrine or its application stressing purpose, practicality, and utility.

functional shift *n. Linguistics.* A shift in the syntactic function of a word without a change in its form, as when a noun serves as a verb.

func·tion·ar·y (fŭngk'shə-nĕr'ē) *n., pl.* **-ies.** A person who holds an office or a trust; an official.

function word *n. Linguistics.* A word that chiefly indicates a grammatical relationship in a sentence or phrase, as a preposition, conjunction, or auxiliary verb. Also called "form word."

fund (fŭnd) *n.* **1.** A source of supply; a stock: *a fund of good will.* **2. a.** A sum of money or other resources set aside for a specific purpose. **b. funds.** Available money; finances. **3. funds.** *British.* The permanent national debt, considered as securities. Preceded by *the.* **4.** An organization established to administer a fund.
∼*tr.v.* **funded, funding, funds.** **1.** To provide money for paying off the interest or principal of (a debt). **2.** To convert (a debt) into a long-term or floating debt with fixed interest payments. **3.** To place or accumulate in a fund. **4.** To furnish a fund or financing for: *fund cancer research.* [Blend of French *fond,* bottom, and *fonds,* stock, both from Latin *fundus,* bottom, landed property.]

fun·da·ment (fŭn'də-mənt) *n.* **1. a.** The buttocks. **b.** The anus. **2.** The natural features of a land surface unaltered by human beings. **3.** A foundation. **4.** A theoretical basis; an underlying principle. [Middle English *foundement,* foundation, lower part, from Old French *fondement,* from Latin *fundāmentum,* from *fundāre,* to lay the bottom for, from *fundus,* bottom.]

fun·da·men·tal (fŭn'də-mĕnt'l) *adj.* **1. a.** Having to do with the foundation; elemental; basic. **b.** Critical or central: *of fundamental importance.* **2.** Having to do with the origin; generative; primary: *fundamental research.* **3.** *Physics.* **a.** Of or pertaining to the component of lowest frequency of a periodic wave or quantity. **b.** Of or pertaining to the lowest possible frequency at which a system or element will vibrate naturally.
∼*n.* **1.** Something that is an elemental part of a system, such as a principle or law; an essential. **2.** *Physics.* The lowest frequency of a periodically varying quantity or of a vibrating system. **3.** *Music.* The lowest or bass note of a chord, considered as the root of the chord. **—fun·da·men·tal·ly** *adv.*

fundamental constant *n. Physics.* The value of a physical quantity, such as the speed of light in a vacuum or the electronic charge, that is regarded as basic and constant under all circumstances. Also called "universal constant."

fun·da·men·tal·ism (fŭn'də-mĕnt'l-ĭz'əm) *n.* **1.** Belief in the Bible as factual historical record and incontrovertible prophecy, including such doctrines as the Creation, the Virgin Birth, and the Second Coming. **2. a.** *Often* **Fundamentalism.** A movement among Protestants based upon this belief. **b.** Adherence to this belief. **3.** Unswerving belief in a set of basic and unalterable principles of a religious or philosophical nature. **—fun·da·men·tal·ist** *n. & adj.* **—fun·da·men·tal·is·tic** (fŭn'də-mĕnt'l-ĭs'tĭk) *adj.*

fundamental particle *n. Physics.* An **elementary particle** *(see).*

fundamental unit *n.* Any of a set of unrelated units used to measure different quantities, such as length, mass, and time, that form the basis of a system of units.

fun·di (fo͞on'dē) *n.* **1.** *East African.* A maintenance man or mechanic; a mechanical expert. **2.** *South African.* An expert or authority in any field; a pundit. [Swahili.]

fun·dus (fŭn'dəs) *n., pl.* **-di** (-dī'). *Anatomy.* The inner basal surface of an organ farthest away from the opening, as in the eye or uterus. [New Latin, from Latin, bottom.]

Fun·dy, Bay of (fŭn'dē). Arm of the Atlantic Ocean between the provinces of Nova Scotia and New Brunswick in eastern Canada. It is *c.* 270 kilometers (168 miles) long, with a maximum width of 80 kilometers (50 miles). The bay's tidal range, which can be as much as 21 meters (68 feet), is the greatest in the world.

fu·ner·al (fyo͞o'nər-əl) *n.* **1.** The ceremonies held in connection with the burial or cremation of the dead. **2.** A party accompanying a body to the grave; a funeral procession. **3.** *Informal.* A problem; a

PRONUNCIATION KEY

ă, pat; ā, pay; âr, care;
ä, father, are; b, bib;
ch, church; d, deed; ĕ, pet;
ē, be; f, fife; g, gag; h, hat;
hw, which; ĭ, pit; ī, pie;
îr, pier; j, judge; k, kick;
l, lid, needle; m, mum;
n, no, sudden; ng, thing;
ŏ, pot; ō, toe; ô, paw, for;
oi, noise; ou, out; o͝o, book;
o͞o, boot; p, pop; r, roar;
s, sauce; sh, ship, dish;
t, tight; th, thin, path;
th, this, bathe; ŭ, cut; ûr, fur;
v, valve; w, with; y, yes;
z, zebra, size; zh, vision;
ə, about, item, edible,
gallop, circus, peaceful

IN FOREIGN WORDS:

à, *Fr.* ami; œ, *Fr.* feu, *Ger.* schön; ü, *Fr.* tu, *Ger.* über; KH, *Ger.* ich, *Scot.* loch; N, *Fr.* bon; y', *Fr.* Compiègne

STRESS MARKS:

Primary stress: '
in·cite' (ĭn-sīt')
Secondary stress: '
in'sight' (ĭn'sīt')

fungus

SIMPLE AND ANCIENT PLANTS

Different species give us food, diseases, and cures

Fungi are nonflowering plants that lack chlorophyll—the pigment that enables green plants to synthesize food from sunlight. For sustenance fungi rely instead on other plants and animals. Some 50,000 species are known, and there may be that many, or even more, still unidentified. Dating back some 500 million years, fungi include some of the simplest and most ancient plants.

Although some scientists consider slime molds to be fungi, their status is disputed and true fungi are divided into three groups:
- sac fungi (Ascomycetes), which include truffles, yeasts, powdery mildew, Dutch elm disease fungus, and blue-green molds (such as those that tint blue cheeses and form penicillin);
- club fungi (Basidiomycetes), which include mushrooms, puffballs, and various crop rusts;
- algal fungi (Phycomycetes), which include the white and gray molds such as those that grow on old bread and cause athlete's foot.

Fungi multiply by releasing spores, not seeds. When a spore germinates, it produces fine threads—hyphae—that form a microscopic branched system—a mycelium—to penetrate the food source. The hyphae secrete enzymes that digest the tissues of dead or living organisms. Hyphae may combine and coalesce to form large bodies such as the mushroom. In some species the hyphae spread in a circle underground and break the surface at the edges to make "fairy rings." Mature fungi grow spores by the billion. A mushroom 100 millimeters (4 inches) wide may produce 16 billion spores. In 28 grams (1 ounce) of soil there may be 2,500,000 fungal spores.

The best-known fungi are mushrooms, a term that technically includes toadstools, which is the popular name for inedible mushrooms. The only way to tell edible from inedible species is to identify each one individually.

HOW A MUSHROOM IS FORMED

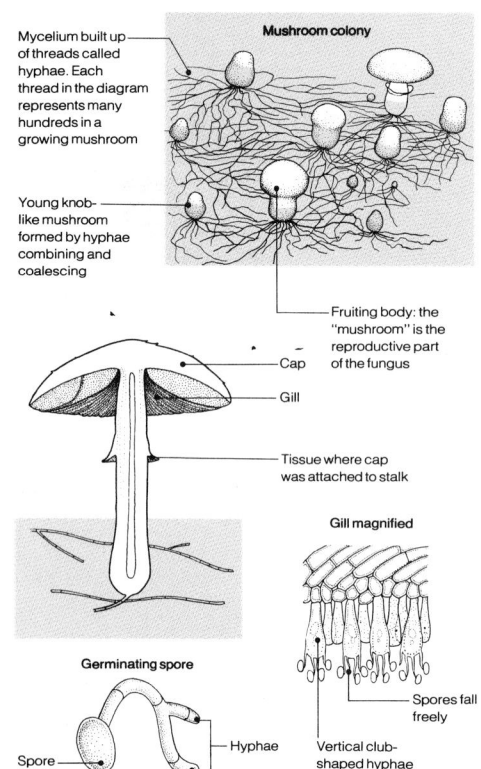

Mycelium built up of threads called hyphae. Each thread in the diagram represents many hundreds in a growing mushroom

Mushroom colony

Young knob-like mushroom formed by hyphae combining and coalescing

Fruiting body: the "mushroom" is the reproductive part of the fungus

Cap

Gill

Tissue where cap was attached to stalk

Gill magnified

Germinating spore

Spore

Hyphae

Spores fall freely

Vertical club-shaped hyphae

Like all fungi, mushrooms are formed of hyphae that grow from spores in the soil. The familiar stalk and cap are devices to ensure the spread of new spores. Hyphae combine to form the stalk, then radiate out into the cap. Beneath the cap grow thin, bladelike gills that produce and release the spores.

source of trouble or worry: *If he runs out of money, that's his funeral.* —*adj.* Of or relating to a funeral. [Middle English *funerelles*, rites for a dead person, from Old French *funerailles*, from Medieval Latin *fūnerālia*, from Late Latin, neuter plural of *fūnerālis*, funereal, from Latin *fūnus*† (stem *fūner-*), funeral, death.]

funeral director *n.* An undertaker.

funeral home *n.* Also **funeral parlor.** An establishment in which the dead are prepared for burial or cremation and in which wakes and funerals may be held.

fu·ner·ar·y (fyōō′nə-rĕr′ē) *adj.* Of or suitable for a funeral or burial. [Latin *fūnerārius,* from *fūnus* (stem *fūner-*), FUNERAL.]

fu·ne·re·al (fyōō-nîr′ē-əl) *adj.* **1.** Of or suitable for a funeral: *a funereal wreath.* **2.** Suggesting gloom; mournful. [From Latin *fūnereus,* from *fūnus* (stem *fūner-*), FUNERAL.] —**fu·ne·re·al·ly** *adv.*

fun·gal (fŭng′gəl) *adj.* Of, pertaining to, or caused by a fungus; fungous.

fun·gi. Plural of **fungus.**

fun·gi·ble (fŭn′jə-bəl) *adj. Law.* Being of such a nature or kind that one unit or part may be exchanged or substituted for another equivalent unit or part in the discharging of an obligation. —*n.* Something fungible, such as money or grain. [Medieval Latin *fungibilis,* serving a function, from *fungī,* to perform.]

fun·gi·cide (fŭn′jə-sīd′, fŭng′gə-) *n.* A substance that destroys or inhibits the growth of fungi. [FUNG(US) + -CIDE.] —**fun·gi·cid·al** (fŭn′jə-sīd′l, fŭng′gə-) *adj.*

fun·gi·form (fŭn′jə-fôrm′, fŭng′gə-) *adj.* Shaped like a mushroom. [FUNG(US) + -FORM.]

fun·gi·stat (fŭn′jə-stăt′, fŭng′gə-) *n.* A substance that stops or is capable of stopping the growth of fungi.

fun·go (fŭng′gō) *n., pl.* **-goes.** *Baseball.* A practice fly ball hit to a fielder with a specially designed bat. [Origin unknown.]

fun·goid (fŭng′goid′) *adj.* Resembling a fungus.

fun·gous (fŭng′gəs) *adj.* **1.** Of, pertaining to, resembling, or characteristic of a fungus; fungal. **2.** Caused by a fungus. [Middle English, from Latin *fungōsus,* from *fungus,* FUNGUS.]

fun·gus (fŭng′gəs) *n., pl.* **fungi** (fŭn′jī′) or **-guses.** Any of numerous organisms of the divisions Eumycophyta (true fungi) or Myxomycophyta (slime fungi), which lack chlorophyll and are generally parasitic or saprophytic. They range from single cells to masses of filamentous hyphae that often produce specialized fruiting bodies and include the yeasts, molds, mildews, and toadstools. [Latin, probably from Greek *sp(h)ongos,* SPONGE.]

fu·ni·cle (fyōō′nĭ-kəl) *n. Botany.* The stalk connecting the ovule with the placenta in angiosperm ovaries. [Latin *fūniculus,* diminutive of *fūnis,* rope.]

fu·nic·u·lar (fyōō-nĭk′yə-lər, fə-) *adj.* **1.** Of, pertaining to, or resembling a rope or cord. **2.** Operated or moved by a cable. **3.** Of, pertaining to, or constituting a funiculus. —*n.* A cable railway on a steep incline; especially, such a railway with simultaneously ascending and descending cars counterbalancing one another. Also called "funicular railway."

fu·nic·u·lus (fyōō-nĭk′yə-ləs, fə-) *n., pl.* **-li** (-lī′). **1.** *Anatomy.* A slender cordlike strand or band, especially: **a.** A bundle of nerve fibers in the nerve trunk; a fasciculus. **b.** One of the three major columns of white matter in each lateral half of the spinal cord. **c.** The umbilical cord. **2.** *Botany.* A funicle (see). [New Latin, from Latin *fūniculus,* diminutive of *fūnis,* rope.]

funk¹ (fŭngk) *n. Informal.* **1. a.** A state of cowardly fright; panic. **b.** A state of extreme depression. **2.** A cowardly, fearful person. —*v.* **funked, funking, funks.** *Informal.* —*tr.* **1.** To try to avoid out of fright; shrink from. **2.** To frighten. —*intr.* To shrink in fright; cower. [Probably from obsolete Flemish *fonck.*]

funk² *n. Slang.* Funky music. [Back-formation from FUNKY.]

funk·y¹ (fŭng′kē) *adj.* **-ier, -iest.** Frightened; panicky.

funky² *adj.* **-ier, -iest.** *Slang.* **1.** Designating a type of popular music combining elements from jazz and blues and characterized by a slow, syncopated rhythm and a heavily repetitive bass line. **2.** Characterized by self-expression, originality, and modishness; trendy and unconventional: *funky clothes.* [Originally "smelly," from obsolete *funk,* tobacco smoke.] —**funk·i·ness** *n.*

fun·nel (fŭn′əl) *n.* **1.** A conical utensil with a small hole or narrow tube at the apex used to channel a substance into a small-mouthed container or to support a filter paper in filtration. **2.** Something having such a conical form. **3.** A shaft, flue, or chimney for the passage of smoke or fumes; especially, the smokestack of a ship or locomotive. —*v.* **funneled, -neling, -nels.** Also *chiefly British* **-nelled, -nelling.** —*intr.* **1.** To assume the shape of a funnel. **2.** To move through or as if through a funnel: *Tourists funnel slowly through customs.* —*tr.* To cause to funnel. [Middle English *fonel,* from Provencal *fonilh,* from Latin *infundibulum,* from *infundere,* to pour in : *in-,* in + *fundere,* to pour.]

fun·nel-web spider (fŭn′əl-wĕb′) *n.* Any large, black, poisonous spider of the family Agelemidae, constructing funnel-shaped webs.

fun·ny (fŭn′ē) *adj.* **-nier, -niest.** **1.** Causing laughter or amusement; humorous or witty. **2.** Strangely or suspiciously odd; curious. **3.** Tricky or deceitful. **4.** Dizzy or unwell. —*n., pl.* **funnies.** *Informal.* **1.** A joke or witticism. **2. funnies.** Comic strips. [From FUN.] —**fun·ni·ly** *adv.* —**fun·ni·ness** *n.*

funny bone *n. Informal.* **1.** The point near the elbow where the ulnar nerve runs close to the surface and if accidentally knocked against the bone produces a tingling sensation; the **olecranon** (see). Also called "crazy bone." **2.** A sense of humor.

funny book *n.* A comic book.
funny farm *n. Slang.* A mental hospital.
funny paper *n.* A newspaper section or supplement containing comic strips.
fur (fûr) *n.* **1.** The thick coat of hair covering the body of any of various animals, such as a fox, beaver, or cat. **2. a.** A dressed animal pelt, or part of one, used in the making of garments, trimmings, or decoration. **b.** Such pelts collectively. **c.** A synthetic fabric resembling dressed animal pelts. **3.** Any garment made of or lined with such pelts. **4.** Any coating of furlike material. **5.** A coating of whitish cellular debris on the tongue caused by stomach upset or smoking, for example. **6.** A grayish deposit, consisting mainly of calcium carbonate, deposited from hard water onto the internal surfaces of pipes, boilers, kettles, and the like. **—make the fur fly.** *Slang.* To cause or engage in a dispute or brawl.
~adj. Made of or lined with fur.
~v. **furred, furring, furs.** *—tr.* **1.** To cover or line with fur. **2.** To provide fur garments for. **3.** To cover with a furlike deposit: *intestinal disorders that fur the tongue.* **4.** To line (a wall or floor) with furring. *—intr.* To become coated with or as if with fur. [Middle English *furre,* from *furren,* to line with fur, from Old French *forrer,* from *forre,* lining, from Germanic.]
fur. furlong.
fu·ran (fyo͝or′ăn′, fyo͞o-răn′) *n.* Also **fur·fu·ran** (fûr′fə-răn′, fûr′fyə-). A colorless, volatile, liquid heterocyclic compound, C_4H_4O, that is derived from the dehydration of certain carbohydrates and is used in the synthesis of organic compounds, especially nylon. [FUR(FURAL) + -AN.]
fur·be·low (fûr′bə-lō′) *n.* **1.** A ruffle or flounce on a garment. **2.** Any small piece of showy ornamentation.
~tr.v. **furbelowed, -lowing, -lows.** To decorate with furbelows. [Alteration of FALBALA.]
fur·bish (fûr′bĭsh) *tr.v.* **-bished, -bishing, -bishes. 1.** To brighten by cleaning or rubbing; burnish. **2.** To restore to attractive or serviceable condition; renovate. [Middle English *furbishen,* from Old French *fo(u)rbir* (stem *fo(u)rbiss-*), from Germanic.] **—fur·bish·er** *n.*
fur·cate (fûr′kāt′) *intr.v.* **-cated, -cating, -cates.** To divide into branches; fork.
~adj. Forked. [Late Latin *furcātus,* from Latin *furca,* FORK.] **—fur·ca·tion** *n.*
fur·cu·la (fûr′kyə-lə) *n., pl.* **-lae** (-lē′). Also **fur·cu·lum** (fûr′kyə-ləm) *pl.* **-la** (-lə). A forked part or bone; especially, the wishbone of a bird. [New Latin, from Latin, diminutive of *furca,* FORK.]
fur·fur (fûr′fər) *n., pl.* **-fures** (-fyə-rēz′). *Sometimes* **furfures.** A skin scale, as in dandruff. [Latin *furfur*†, bran, scales.]
fur·fur·a·ceous (fûr′fyə-rā′shəs) *adj.* **1.** Made of or covered with scaly particles, such as dandruff. **2.** Pertaining to or resembling bran. [Late Latin *furfurāceus* : FURFUR + -ACEOUS.]
fur·fur·al (fûr′fə-răl′, fûr′fyə-) *n.* A colorless mobile liquid, C_4H_3OCHO, used as a solvent for cellulose nitrate and in the manufacture of dyes and plastics. Also called "furfuraldehyde." [*furfur* + *al*dehyde.]
Fu·ries (fyo͝or′ēz). *Greek & Roman Mythology.* The three terrible, winged goddesses with serpents for hair, Alecto, Megaera, and Tisiphone, who pursue doers of unavenged crimes. Also called "Erinyes," "Eumenides." [Latin *Furiae,* plural of *furia,* FURY.]
fu·ri·o·so (fyo͝or′ē-ō′sō, -zō) *adv. Music.* In a tempestuous and headlong manner. Used as a direction. [Italian, from Latin *furiōsus,* FURIOUS.] **—fu·ri·o·so** *adj.*
fu·ri·ous (fyo͝or′ē-əs) *adj.* **1.** Full of or characterized by extreme anger; raging. **2.** Wild or frenetic in action or appearance: *the furious sea.* [Middle English, from Old French *furieus,* from Latin *furiōsus,* from *furia,* FURY.] **—fu·ri·ous·ly** *adv.* **—fu·ri·ous·ness** *n.*
furl (fûrl) *v.* **furled, furling, furls.** *—tr.* **1.** To take in and secure (a sail) to a yard or mast. **2.** To roll up (an umbrella, flag, or the like). *—intr.* **1.** To be rolled up. **2.** To disappear as if furled.
~n. **1.** The act of furling. **2.** A single roll or rolled section of something furled. [Old French *ferler, ferlier* : *fer(m),* firm, from Latin *firmus,* FIRM + *lier,* to bind, from Latin *ligāre.*]
fur·long (fûr′lông′, -lŏng′) *n. Abbr.* **fur.** A unit for measuring distance, equal to 201 meters, ⅛ mile, or 220 yards. [Middle English, from Old English *furlang* : *furh,* FURROW + *lang,* LONG. Originally the length of the furrow made on a square field of 10 acres.]
fur·lough (fûr′lō) *n.* **1.** A leave of absence; especially, a leave of absence from duty granted to enlisted personnel of the armed services. **2.** The papers authorizing a furlough.
~tr.v. **furloughed, -loughing, -loughs.** To grant a furlough to. [Dutch *verlof,* leave, permission, from Middle Dutch.]
furmenty. Variant of **frumenty.**
furn. furnished.
fur·nace (fûr′nĭs) *n.* **1.** An enclosure in which energy in a nonthermal form is converted to heat; especially, such an enclosure in which heat is generated by the combustion of a suitable fuel. **2.** Any intensely hot, enclosed place. **—tried in the furnace.** Severely tested. [Middle English *furna(i)s,* from Old French *fornais,* from Latin *fornāx* (stem *fornāc-*), oven.]
fur·nish (fûr′nĭsh) *tr.v.* **-nished, -nishing, -nishes. 1.** To equip with what is needed. **2.** To provide furniture and other accessories for. **3.** To provide; supply: *The dictionary furnished an apt quotation.* [Middle English *furnisshen,* from Old French *furnir* (stem *furniss-*), *fornir,* from Common Romance *fornir* (unattested), to supply, from Germanic.] **—fur·nish·er** *n.*
fur·nish·ings (fûr′nĭ-shĭngz) *pl.n.* **1.** The furniture, curtains, carpets, and similar articles used to decorate and furnish a home or office. **2.** Wearing apparel and accessories.
fur·ni·ture (fûr′nə-chər) *n.* **1.** The movable articles in a room or establishment that make it fit for living or working in. **2.** The necessary equipment for a factory, ship, or the like. **3.** *Printing.* Blank strips of wood or metal placed between and around type on a page to hold it in place. [Old French *fourniture,* from *fournir, furnir,* to FURNISH.]
fu·ror (fyo͝or′ôr′, -ōr′) *n.* Also *chiefly British* **fu·rore. 1.** Violent anger; frenzy. **2.** A general commotion; public disorder or uproar. **3.** A fashion adopted enthusiastically by the public; fad. [Latin, from *furere,* to rage. See **fury.**]
fu·ro·se·mide (fyo͞o-rō′sə-mīd′) *n.* A compound, $C_{12}H_{11}ClN_2O_5S$, used as a diuretic. [FUR(FURAL) + S(ULF)- + *emide,* alteration of AMIDE.]
furred (fûrd) *adj.* **1.** Bearing fur. **2.** Made, covered, or trimmed with fur. **3.** Wearing fur garments. **4.** Covered with a furlike deposit. **5.** Provided with furring, as a wall, ceiling, or floor.
fur·ri·er (fûr′ē-ər) *n.* One whose occupation is the dressing, designing, selling, or repairing of furs. [Middle English *furrer,* from Old French *forreor,* from *forrer,* to line with fur. See **fur.**]
fur·ri·er·y (fûr′ē-ə-rē) *n., pl.* **-ies. 1.** Fur garments and trimmings collectively. **2.** The business of a furrier.
fur·ring (fûr′ĭng) *n.* **1. a.** A trimming or lining made of fur. **b.** Fur trimmings and linings collectively. **2.** A furlike coating, as on the tongue or in a pipe. **3. a.** The act of preparing a wall, ceiling, or floor with strips of wood or metal to provide a level surface for the fixing of floorboards, plasterboard, or the like. **b.** Strips of material used for this. Also used adjectivally: *a furring strip.*
fur·row (fûr′ō) *n.* **1.** A long, narrow, shallow trench made in the ground by a plow or other implement. **2.** Any rut, groove, or narrow depression similar to this. **3.** A deep wrinkle in the skin, as on the forehead. **—plow a lonely furrow.** To pursue one's objectives alone and unaided.
~v. **furrowed, -rowing, -rows.** *—tr.* **1.** To make furrows in; plow. **2.** To form deep wrinkles in. *—intr.* To become furrowed or deeply wrinkled. [Middle English *for(o)we, furgh,* Old English *furh.*]
fur·ry (fûr′ē) *adj.* **-rier, -riest. 1.** Consisting of or decorated with fur. **2.** Covered with fur or a furlike coating. **3.** Resembling fur in thickness or softness. **—fur·ri·ness** *n.*
fur seal *n.* Any of several eared seals of the genera *Callorhinus* or *Arctocephalus,* having thick, soft underfur that is valued commercially.

fur seal *The thick underfur of fur seals distinguishes them from sea lions, which belong to the same family. The Kerguelen fur seal (above) breeds on remote islands in the seas of the Southern Hemisphere.*

fur·ther (fûr′*th*ər) *adj.* **1.** More distant in time or degree. **2.** Additional. **3.** More distant in space. —See Usage note at **farther.**
~adv. **1.** To a greater extent; more. **2.** In addition; furthermore; also. **3.** At or to a more distant point in space or time. —See Usage note at **farther.**
~tr.v. **furthered, -thering, -thers.** To help the progress of; advance. —See Synonyms at **advance.** [Middle English *further,* earlier, from Old English *furthor.*] **—fur·ther·er** *n.*
fur·ther·ance (fûr′*th*ər-əns) *n.* **1.** The act of furthering, advancing, or helping forward. **2.** One that furthers or assists.
fur·ther·more (fûr′*th*ər-môr′, -mōr′) *adv.* Moreover; in addition. —See Synonyms at **also.**
fur·ther·most (fûr′*th*ər-mōst′) *adj.* Most distant or remote.
fur·thest (fûr′*th*ĭst) *adj.* **1.** Most distant in time or degree. **2.** Most distant in space. —See Usage note at **farther.**
~adv. **1.** To the greatest extent or degree. **2.** At or to the most distant point in space or time. —See Usage note at **farther.** [Middle English, from FURTHER.]
fur·tive (fûr′tĭv) *adj.* **1.** Characterized by stealth; surreptitious. **2.** Suggesting hidden motives or purposes; shifty. —See Synonyms at **secret.** [French *furtif,* from Old French, from Latin *furtīvus,* from *furtum,* theft, from *fūr*†, thief.] **—fur·tive·ly** *adv.* **—fur·tive·ness** *n.*
Furt·wäng·ler (fo͝ort′vĕng′lər, -vĕng′glər), **Wilhelm** (1886–1954). German orchestral and operatic conductor. The conductor of the Berlin Philharmonic Orchestra from 1922 until his death except for a short interval in 1934, he was the leading interpreter of 19th-century romantic composers.
fu·run·cle (fyo͝or′ŭng′kəl) *n. Pathology.* A **boil** *(see).* [Latin *fūrunculus,* petty thief, vine knob that "steals" the sap from the main branches, boil, diminutive of *fūr,* thief.] **—fu·run·cu·lar** *adj.*
fu·run·cu·lo·sis (fyo͞o-rŭng′kyə-lō′sĭs) *n.* A skin complaint characterized by the simultaneous occurrence or continuing recurrence of furuncles. [Latin *fūrunculus,* FURUNCLE + -OSIS.]
fu·ry (fyo͝or′ē) *n., pl.* **-ries. 1.** Violent anger; rage. **2.** An outburst of violent rage. **3.** Violent, uncontrolled action; turbulence. **4.** One given to fits of violent anger. **5. Fury.** Any of the **Furies** *(see).* —See Synonyms at **anger.** [Middle English *furie,* from Old French, from Latin *furia,* from *furere*†, to rage.]
furze (fûrz) *n.* A spiny shrub, **gorse** *(see).* [Middle English *furse, firse,* Old English *fyrs.*]
fu·sain (fyo͞o-zān′, fyo͞o′zān′) *n.* **1.** Fine charcoal in stick form, made from the wood of a spindle tree. **2.** A sketch or drawing made with this. [French, from Vulgar Latin *fūsāgō* (unattested), spindle (formerly made from the wood of the spindle tree), from Latin *fūsus,* spindle. See **fuse.**]
fuse¹ (fyo͞oz) *n.* **1.** A length of readily combustible material that is lighted at one end to carry a flame to and detonate an explosive at the other. **2.** Variant of **fuze.**

PRONUNCIATION KEY

ă, pat; ā, pay; âr, care;
ä, father, are; b, bib;
ch, church; d, deed; ĕ, pet;
ē, be; f, fife; g, gag; h, hat;
hw, which; ĭ, pit; ī, pie;
îr, pier; j, judge; k, kick;
l, lid, needle; m, mum;
n, no, sudden; ng, thing;
ŏ, pot; ō, toe; ô, paw, for;
oi, noise; ou, out; o͝o, book;
o͞o, boot; p, pop; r, roar;
s, sauce; sh, ship, dish;
t, tight; th, thin, path;
th, this, bathe; ŭ, cut; ûr, fur;
v, valve; w, with; y, yes;
z, zebra, size; zh, vision;
ə, about, item, edible,
gallop, circus, peaceful

IN FOREIGN WORDS:

à, *Fr.* ami; œ, *Fr.* feu, *Ger.* schön; ü, *Fr.* tu, *Ger.* über; KH, *Ger.* ich, *Scot.* loch; N, *Fr.* bon; y', *Fr.* Compiègne

STRESS MARKS:

Primary stress: ′
in·cite′ (ĭn-sīt′)
Secondary stress: ′
in′sight′ (ĭn′sīt′)

~*tr.v.* **fused, fusing, fuses.** To provide or equip with a fuse. [Italian *fuso,* from Latin *fūsus†,* spindle.]

fuse² *v.* **fused, fusing, fuses.** —*tr.* **1.** To liquefy or reduce to a plastic state by heating; melt. **2.** To mix together by or as if by melting; blend. **3.** To fit a fuse to (an electric plug, for example). **4.** To stop (an electrical appliance, for example) from functioning by overloading the fuse. —*intr.* **1.** To become liquefied from heat. **2.** To become mixed or united by or as if by melting together: *Joy and sorrow fused into one.* **3.** To stop functioning when an electrical fuse has been overloaded.

~*n.* **1.** A device containing an element that protects an electric circuit by melting when overloaded, thereby opening the circuit. **2.** A circuit breaker fulfilling the same function. —See Synonyms at **mix.** [Latin *fundere* (past participle *fūsus*), to pour, melt.]

fuse box *n.* A box in which the fuses protecting a number of electrical circuits are housed.

fu·see, fu·zee (fyōō-zē′) *n.* **1.** A friction match with a large head capable of burning in a wind. **2.** A grooved, cone-shaped pulley in old-style clocks. **3.** A fuse for detonating explosives. [French *fusée,* spindle-shaped figure, from Old French *fusee,* from *fus,* spindle, from Latin *fūsus.* See **fuse.**]

fu·se·lage (fyōō′sə-läzh′, fyōō′zə-) *n.* The central body of an aircraft that accommodates passengers, cargo, and crew, and to which the wings and tail assembly are attached. [French, from *fuseler,* to shape like a spindle, from *fuseau,* spindle, from Old French *fusel,* spindle, diminutive of *fus,* spindle, from Latin *fūsus.* See **fuse.**]

Fu·se·li (fyōō′zə-lē) **Henry,** earlier Johann Heinrich Füssli (1741–1825). Swiss-born British artist. His works, including *The Nightmare* (1782) and illustrations of the works of Shakespeare and Milton, display a fantastic, macabre quality that was to influence the surrealists of the 1920's and 1930's.

fu·sel oil (fyōō′zəl) *n.* A clear, colorless, poisonous, liquid mixture of amyl alcohols, obtained as a by-product of the fermentation of starch-containing and sugar-containing plant materials, and used as a solvent for fats, oils, resins, and waxes, and in the manufacture of explosives and pure amyl alcohols. [German *Fusel†,* bad liquor.]

fuse wire *n.* Thin metal wire, used in electrical fuses, that melts when a current passed through it exceeds a specific safe limit.

fu·si·ble (fyōō′zə-bəl) *adj.* Capable of being fused or melted by heating. —**fu·si·bil·i·ty, fu·si·ble·ness** *n.*

fusible metal *n.* A metal alloy having a melting point below 300°F, used as solder and for safety plugs and fuses. Also called "fusible alloy."

fu·si·form (fyōō′zə-fôrm′) *adj.* Tapering at each end; spindle-

---

Futurism

THE PACE OF LIFE CAPTURED IN ART

Futurism welcomed the new machine age and denounced all links with the past

Futurism aimed to reflect in the arts the dynamism of life as it was experienced in a world dominated by machines. Its main theme was movement and the rhythm of space and time. It was inaugurated by a manifesto published in Paris in 1909 by the Italian poet and playwright Marinetti, who glorified speed, aggression, patriotism, and war.

Despite its political bias, Futurism revitalized Italian art. Carra, Boccioni, Balla, and Severini joined Marinetti and published a "Manifesto of Futurist painting" (1910). Their "new form of beauty, the beauty of speed" was exemplified in their paintings, for example in Boccioni's *States of Mind: the Farewells* (1911) and Balla's *Rhythms of the Bow* (1912). Their abusive public meetings were a vital feature of the movement's style and had a profound effect later on the Dada circle.

A Russian version of Futurism emerged in 1910 with an almanac entitled "A Trap for Judges," which appeared in St. Petersburg. In 1912 Burliuk published "A Slap in the Face of Public Taste," which rejected the recognized masters of Russian literature, including Tolstoy and Pushkin, and wanted the language of the streets to be used for literature. Burliuk was soon joined by Mayakovsky, the renowned poet, playwright, and artist. When revolution came in 1917, the Russian Futurists embraced it as their own, and almost all were ready to serve the state. The early 1920's was a golden age of Russian art, with Mayakovsky, Lissitzky, and Kandinsky seeking to merge realism with total abstraction.

The Russian Futurists were notable for their inspired multimedia approach, experimenting in architecture, typography, film, theater, and literature. In literature, for example, Zamyatin's *We* was the forerunner of *Brave New World* and *1984.* However, the exuberance of the years immediately after the revolution was constricted with the advent of Stalin, and one of the most vital art movements of the 20th century was swamped by the Soviet Socialist Realism of the official propaganda machine. Although Mayakovsky in his photomontages was occasionally able to produce messages contrary to the aims of the regime, the restrictions under which he was forced to work contributed to his suicide in 1930.

MOTION PICTURES *Balla's painting,* Rhythms of the Bow, *focuses on the action of the musician. Balla had long been interested in photographic techniques and wished to emulate the ability of a film to record motion in one image.*

shaped. [Latin *fūsus*, spindle (see **fuse**) + -FORM.]

fu·sil (fyōō′zəl) *n.* A light flintlock musket. [French, musket, from Old French *fuisil*, fusil, steel for a tinderbox, from Vulgar Latin *focīle* (unattested), from Latin *focus*, fireplace. See **fuel**.]

fu·sile (fyōō′zəl, -zīl′) *adj.* Also **fu·sil** (-zəl). 1. Formed by melting or casting. 2. Capable of being fused. [Latin *fūsilis*, from *fūsus*, past participle of *fundere*, to melt, pour.]

fu·si·lier (fyōō′zə-lîr′) *n.* Also **fu·si·leer** (for sense 2). 1. A soldier armed with a fusil. 2. **Fusilier.** A soldier belonging to certain British army regiments. [French, from FUSIL.]

fu·sil·lade (fyōō′sə-lād′, -läd′, fyōō′zə-) *n.* 1. A discharge of many firearms, simultaneously or in rapid succession. 2. Any rapid outburst or barrage: *a fusillade of insults.*
~*tr.v.* **fusilladed, -lading, -lades.** To attack or shoot down with a fusillade. [French, from *fusiller*, to shoot, from FUSIL.]

fu·sion (fyōō′zhən) *n.* 1. The act or procedure of liquefying or melting together by heat. 2. The liquid or melted state induced by heat. 3. A union resulting from fusing. 4. The merging of different elements into a union. 5. *Physics.* A nuclear reaction in which any of certain light atomic nuclei combine to form more massive nuclei with the simultaneous release of energy. In this sense, also called "nuclear fusion." Compare **fission.** [Latin *fūsiō* (stem *fūsiōn-*), from *fūsus*, past participle of *fundere*, to pour, melt.]

fusion bomb *n.* An atomic bomb that derives its energy output principally from fusion reactions among light nuclei; especially, a **hydrogen bomb** (*see*).

fu·sion·ism (fyōō′zhə-nĭz′əm) *n.* The theory, practice, or advocacy of forming coalitions of political groups or factions. —**fu·sion·ist** *n.*

fuss (fŭs) *n.* 1. Needless or useless excited activity; commotion; bustle. 2. **a.** A state of excessive and unwarranted concern over an unimportant matter. **b.** Objections; protests. 3. A quarrel.
~*v.* **fussed, fussing, fusses.** —*intr.* 1. To trouble or worry over trifles. 2. To be excessively careful or solicitous. —*tr. Informal.* To disturb or vex with unimportant matters. [18th century (Anglo-Irish) : origin obscure.] —**fuss·er** *n.*

fuss·budg·et (fŭs′bŭj′ĭt) *n.* A person who fusses over trifles.

fuss·pot (fŭs′pŏt′) *n.* A fussbudget.

fuss·y (fŭs′ē) *adj.* **-ier, -iest.** 1. Given to fussing; easily upset: *"The bridegroom, fussy as a poodle, pops his eyes"* (Kenneth Tynan). 2. Paying great attention to petty matters or details; fastidious. 3. Calling for or requiring great attention to trivial details; meticulous. 4. Full of superfluous details or trimmings; ornate. —**fuss·i·ly** *adv.* —**fuss·i·ness** *n.*

fus·ta·nel·la (fŭs′tə-nĕl′ə, fōō′stə-) *n.* A short, stiff skirt of white cloth worn by men in modern Greece. [Italian, from Modern Greek *phoustanella*, diminutive of *phoustani*, from Italian *fustagno*, coarse cloth, from Medieval Latin *fustāneus*, FUSTIAN.]

fus·tian (fŭs′chən) *n.* 1. Any of several thick, twilled cotton fabrics with a short nap. 2. Pretentious, pompous speech or writing.
~*adj.* 1. Made of fustian. 2. Pompous; ranting; bombastic. [Middle English, from Old French *fustai(g)ne*, from Medieval Latin *fustāneus*, cloth, perhaps after *Fostat*, a suburb of Cairo, Egypt.]

fus·tic (fŭs′tĭk) *n.* 1. A tropical American tree, *Chlorophora tinctoria*, having wood yielding a yellow dyestuff. 2. The wood of this tree. 3. The dyestuff obtained from such wood. 4. Any of various trees, such as sumacs, that yield a similar dye. [Middle English *fustik*, from Old French *fustoc*, from Arabic *fustuq*, from Greek *pistakē*, PISTACHIO.]

fus·ti·gate (fŭs′tə-gāt′) *tr.v.* **-gated, -gating, -gates.** To beat with a club. [Late Latin *fūstigāre* : Latin *fūstis*†, club + *agere*, to do.]

fus·ty (fŭs′tē) *adj.* **-tier, -tiest.** 1. Smelling of mildew or decay; musty; moldy. 2. Old-fashioned; antiquated. [Middle English, from Old French *fuste*, barrel, stale odor of a barrel, from *fust*, barrel, tree trunk, club, from Latin *fūstis*†, club.] —**fus·ti·ly** *adv.* —**fus·ti·ness** *n.*

fut. *Grammar.* future.

fu·thark, fu·tharc (fōō′thärk′) *n.* Also **fu·thork, fu·thorc** (-thôrk′). The runic alphabet. [From the first six letters of the alphabet: *f, u, th* (thorn), *a* or *o, r, k.*]

fu·tile (fyōōt′l, fyōō′tīl′) *adj.* 1. Having no useful result; ineffectual; useless; vain. 2. Unproductive; frivolous; idle: *futile talk.* [Latin *futtilis, fūtilis*, untrustworthy, useless.] —**fu·tile·ly** *adv.* —**fu·tile·ness** *n.*

fu·til·i·tar·i·an (fyōō-tĭl′ə-târ′ē-ən) *adj.* Holding or based on the view that human endeavor is futile.
~*n.* One who holds such a view. [Blend of FUTILE and UTILITARIAN.]

fu·til·i·ty (fyōō-tĭl′ə-tē) *n., pl.* **-ties.** 1. The quality of being futile; uselessness; ineffectiveness. 2. Lack of importance or purpose. 3. Anything that is futile.

fu·ton (fōō′tŏn) *n.* A Japanese mattress for sleeping on. [Japanese.]

fut·tock (fŭt′ək) *n. Nautical.* Any of the curved timbers that form a rib in the frame of a wooden ship. [Middle English *fottek*, perhaps variant of *fothok* (unattested) : FOOT + HOOK.]

futtock plate *n. Nautical.* Any of the iron plates attached to the top of a mast to hold the ends of the futtock shrouds.

futtock shroud *n. Nautical.* Any of the iron rods extending from the futtock plate, used to brace the base of a mast.

fu·ture (fyōō′chər) *n.* 1. The indefinite period of time yet to be; time that is to come. 2. That which will happen in time to come. 3. The prospective or foreseen condition of a person or thing: *a student's future.* 4. Prospects of advancement; chances of success: *a business with no future.* 5. **futures.** Commodities or shares bought or sold at an agreed price for delivery in time to come. 6. *Abbr.* **fut.** *Grammar.* **a.** The future tense. **b.** A verb in the future tense.
~*adj.* 1. That is to be or come in the future. 2. Of or relating to time to come. 3. That will be as specified at a later time: *a future politician.* [Middle English, from Old French *futur*, from Latin *futūrus*, future participle of *esse*, to be.] —**fu·ture·less** *adj.*

future perfect *n. Grammar.* 1. A verb tense expressing action completed by a specified time in the future. This tense is formed in English by combining *will have* or *shall have* with a past participle, as *will have counted* in *They will have counted all the votes by midnight.* 2. A verb in the future perfect tense.

future shock *n.* The disorientation suffered by people bewildered by rapid changes in the social structure or technology of modern society. [After the book *Future Shock* (1970) by Alvin Toffler (born 1928), U.S. author.]

future tense *n.* A verb tense used to express action in the future, as *will see* in *I will see you tomorrow.*

Fu·tur·ism (fyōō′chə-rĭz′əm) *n.* An artistic movement originating in Italy in about 1909 and marked by an attempt to depict vividly the energetic and dynamic quality of contemporary life as influenced by the motion and force of modern machinery. —**Fu·tur·ist** *n.*

fu·tur·is·tic (fyōō′chə-rĭs′tĭk) *adj.* 1. **Futuristic.** Of, pertaining to, or characteristic of Futurism. 2. Suggesting the future; indicating advanced thinking: *futuristic design.*

fu·tur·ist·ics (fyōō′chə-rĭs′tĭks) *n. Used with a singular verb.* Futurology. —**fu·tur·ist** *n.*

fu·tu·ri·ty (fyōō-tŏor′ə-tē, fyōō-tyŏor′-, fyōō-chŏor′-) *n., pl.* **-ties.** 1. The future. 2. The condition or quality of being in or of the future. 3. A future event or possibility. 4. A futurity race.

futurity race *n.* A race, especially a horse race, for which entries are made well in advance, as at birth.

futurity stakes *pl.n.* 1. The stakes awarded to the winner or winners in a futurity race. 2. A futurity race.

fu·tur·ol·o·gy (fyōō′chə-rŏl′ə-jē) *n.* The study or prediction of the likely future state of the world and its inhabitants. —**fu·tur·ol·o·gist** *n.*

fuze, fuse (fyōōz) *n.* A mechanical or electrical mechanism used to detonate an explosive charge or device such as a bomb or grenade. [Variant of FUSE (detonator).]

fuzee. Variant of **fusee.**

Fu·zhou, Fu-chou, Foo-chow (fōō′jō′). Capital city of the southeastern province of Fujian in China, on the estuary of the Min Jiang. It is an ancient walled city, dating from at least the 2nd century B.C., and has been the capital of Fujian province since the 10th century. Since the mid-19th century it has been one of China's major naval stations and international trading ports.

fuzz[1] (fŭz) *n.* 1. A mass of fine, light particles, fibers, or hairs; down: *the fuzz on a peach.* 2. A blur.
~*v.* **fuzzed, fuzzing, fuzzes.** —*tr.* To cover with fuzz. —*intr.* To become blurred. [Perhaps back-formation from FUZZY.]

fuzz[2] *n. Slang.* The police; policemen collectively. Preceded by *the.* [20th century : origin obscure.]

fuzz·y (fŭz′ē) *adj.* **-ier, -iest.** 1. Covered with fuzz. 2. Of or resembling fuzz. 3. Not sharply delineated or focused; indistinct; blurred. 4. Not clearly reasoned or expressed; confused. 5. Frizzy or very tightly curled. Said of hair. [Perhaps from Low German *fussig*, spongy.] —**fuzz·i·ly** *adv.* —**fuzz·i·ness** *n.*

fwd. forward.

f.w.d. 1. four-wheel drive. 2. front-wheel drive.

FY fiscal year.

-fy *suffix.* Indicates a making or forming into; for example, **reify, nitrify.** [Middle English *-fien*, from Old French *-fier*, from Latin *-ficāre*, from *-ficus*, -FIC.]

fyke (fīk) *n.* A long, bag-shaped net held open by hoops, used for catching fish. [Dutch *fuik*, from Middle Dutch *fūke*†.]

fyl·fot (fĭl′fŏt′) *n.* An ornamental figure identified with the swastika. [Middle English, device for filling the foot of a painted window : *fillen*, to FILL + FOOT.]

G

gable *A generally triangular portion of wall at the end of a pitched roof. The shaped gable above, on a house in Holland, is typical of Dutch architecture.*

g, G (jē) *n., pl.* **g's** or **G's. 1.** The seventh letter of the modern English alphabet. **2.** Any of the speech sounds represented by this letter. **3.** G *Music.* **a.** The fifth tone in the scale of C major. **b.** The key or a scale in which G is the tonic. **c.** A written or printed note representing G. **4.** Something shaped like the letter G. **5.** G *Slang.* One thousand dollars. **6.** The seventh in a series.

g, G, g., G. *Note:* As an abbreviation or symbol, *g* may be a small or a capital letter, with or without a period. Established forms or those generally preferred precede the definition. When no form is given, all four forms are in general use in that sense. **1. g** acceleration of gravity. **2. g.** gallon. **3. g., G.** gauge. **4. G** *Physics.* gauss. **5. g.** gelding. **6. g.** gender. **7. g.** genitive. **8. G.** German. **9. G** giga-. **10. g., G.** good. **11. g., G.** gourde. **12. g.** gram. **13. G** *Physics.* gravitation constant. **14. g.** guide. **15. g., G.** guilder. **16. g., G.** guinea. **17. g., G.** gulf (ocean area).

Ga The symbol for the element gallium.

GA Georgia (used with a Zip Code).

Ga. Georgia.

gab (găb) *intr.v.* **gabbed, gabbing, gabs.** *Informal.* To talk easily or excessively about trivial matters; chatter. **~***n.* *Informal.* Idle talk; chatter: *bored by the gab at the dinner table.* [Perhaps from Scottish *gab,* mouthful, lump, mouth, variant of GOB (lump).] **—gab·ber** *n.*

gab·ar·dine (găb′ər-dēn′, găb′ər-dēn′) *n.* **1.** A worsted cotton, wool, or rayon twill used in making dresses, suits, and coats. **2.** A gaberdine. [Alteration of GABERDINE.]

gab·bart (găb′ərt) *n.* Also **gab·bard** (-ərd). *Scottish.* A flat-bottomed barge used to load and unload cargo offshore or to transport goods on inland waterways. [Modification of Old French *gab(b)arre,* from Old Provençal *gabarra,* probably from Late Latin *carabus,* a small, rawhide-covered boat, from Greek *karabos†,* horned beetle, crayfish, light ship.]

gab·ble (găb′əl) *v.* **-bled, -bling, -bles. —***intr.* **1.** To speak rapidly or incoherently; jabber. **2.** To make rapid, repeated cackling noises, as a goose or duck does. **—***tr.* To utter quickly or unintelligibly. **~***n.* **1.** Rapid, incoherent, or meaningless speech. **2.** A jumble of cackling noises or meaningless utterances. [Middle Dutch *gabbelen* (imitative).]

gab·bro (găb′rō) *n., pl.* **-bros.** A coarse-grained, intrusive igneous rock composed chiefly of calcic plagioclase and pyroxene, sometimes with other minerals. Also called "norite." [Italian, from Latin *glaber,* smooth, bald.]

gab·by (găb′ē) *adj.* **-bier, -biest.** *Informal.* Tending to talk excessively.

gab·er·dine (găb′ər-dēn′, găb′ər-dēn′) *n.* **1.** A long, coarse garment, such as a cloak or frock, worn during the Middle Ages. **2.** *British.* A loose smock worn by laborers. **3.** Gabardine. [Earlier *gawbardine,* from Old French *gauvardine, gallevardine,* "pilgrim's frock," from Middle High German *wallevart,* pilgrimage : *wallen,* to roam, from Old High German *wallōn* + *vart,* journey, way, from *faran,* to go.]

gab·fest (găb′fĕst′) *n.* *Slang.* An informal gathering for the exchange of news and gossip.

Ga·bin (gă-băN′), **Jean,** born Jean Alexis Moncorgé (1904–76). French film actor. He starred in *La Grande Illusion* (1937), and in other films played Georges Simenon's detective, Inspector Maigret.

ga·bi·on (gā′bē-ən, găb′ē-) *n.* **1.** A cylindrical wicker basket filled with earth and stones, formerly used in building fortifications. **2.** A similar cylinder, often of metal, used in constructing dams, foundations, and the like. [Old French *gabion,* from Old Italian *gabbione,* augmentative of *gabbia,* cage, from Latin *cavea,* a hollow, enclosure, from *cavus,* hollow.]

ga·bi·on·ade (gā′bē-ə-nād′, -năd′, găb′ē-) *n.* A fortification or defensive embankment or wall built with gabions. [French *gabionnade,* from Old Italian *gabbionata,* from *gabbione,* GABION.]

ga·ble (gā′bəl) *n. Architecture.* **1.** The triangular wall section at the ends of a pitched roof, bounded by the two roof slopes and the ridge. **2.** An end of a building having a gable in the roof section. Also called "gable end." **3.** A triangular architectural section, usually ornamental, as over a door or window. [Middle English *gable,*

gabyl, from Old French *gable,* probably from Old Norse *gafl.*] **—ga·bled** *adj.*

Ga·ble (gā′bəl), **(William) Clark** (1901–60). U.S. actor. He became known as "the King of Hollywood" after his success in *Gone With the Wind* (1939). He died shortly after making *The Misfits* (released 1961), in which he did his own stunt work.

gable roof *n.* A pitched roof that ends in a gable.

Ga·bon (gə-bōn′). Country in Equatorial Africa. European slavers reached the area *c.* 1470. The French dominated it in the 19th century, settling freed slaves at Libreville ("free town"), and in 1910 it became part of French Equatorial Africa. Dr. Albert Schweitzer founded the region's first hospital in 1913 at Lambaréné. Gabon became independent in 1960. French remains the official language. Area, 267,667 square kilometers (103,319 square miles). Population, 550,000. Capital and chief port, Libreville. **—Gab·o·nese** (găb′ə-nēz′) *n. & adj.*

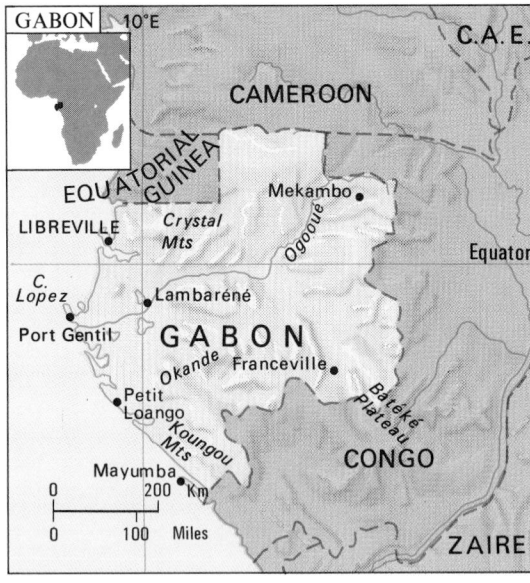

Ga·bor (gä′bôr, gə-bôr′), **Dennis** (1900–79). Hungarian-born British electrical engineer. He won the Nobel Prize in physics (1971) for his work on holography.

Ga·bo·ro·ne (găb′ə-rō′nē). Capital of Botswana, near the border with South Africa.

Ga·bri·el (gā′brē-əl). An archangel who acts as the messenger of God in the Bible.

ga·by (gā′bē) *n., pl.* **-bies.** *Archaic & British Regional.* A simpleton. [18th century : origin obscure.]

gad¹ (găd) *interj.* Used to express surprise or as a mild oath. [Euphemistic for *God.*]

gad² (găd) *intr.v.* **gadded, gadding, gads. 1.** To roam about aimlessly or restlessly. **2.** To go about in search of pleasure or entertainment. Used with *about* or *around.* **~***n.* The action of gadding. Used only in the phrase *on the gad.* [Middle English *gadden,* probably back-formation from *gadeling,* companion, (hence) wanderer, Old English *gædeling.*] **—gad·der** *n.*

gad³ *n.* **1.** *Mining.* A spike or other pointed tool for working or breaking rock or ore. **2.** A goad, as for prodding cattle to make them move. **~***tr.v.* **gadded, gadding, gads. 1.** *Mining.* To break up (rock or ore,

for example) with a gad. **2.** To goad (cattle). [Middle English *gad(de)*, from Old Norse *gaddr*, rod, goad, spike.]
Gad¹ (găd). A son of Zilpah and Jacob. Genesis 30:11. [Hebrew *Gādh*, from *gādh*, fortune.]
Gad² *n.* The tribe of Israel descended from Gad.
gad·a·bout (găd′ə-bout′) *n. Informal.* One who goes about seeking amusement or excitement.
Gad·a·rene (găd′ə-rēn′) *adj.* Involving or taking part in a headlong rush; precipitate. [Late Latin, from Greek *gadarēnos*, referring to the Gadarene swine in the Bible (Matthew 8:28-33).]
Gaddafi, Muammar. See **Qaddafi**.
gad·fly (găd′flī′) *n., pl.* -flies. **1.** Any of various flies, especially of the family Tabanidae, that bite or annoy livestock and other animals. **2.** A person who is persistently critical, irritating, or provocative. **3.** Something that acts as a provocative stimulus. [GAD (goad, sting) + FLY.]
gadg·et (găj′ĭt) *n.* **1.** A small specialized mechanical or electronic device; a contrivance. —See Synonyms at **tool**. [19th century (nautical) : origin obscure.]
gadg·et·ry (găj′ĭ-trē) *n.* **1.** Gadgets collectively. **2.** The designing or constructing of gadgets.
Gadhelic. Variant of **Goidelic**.
ga·doid (gā′doid′, găd′oid′) *adj.* Also **ga·did** (gā′dĭd) *adj.* Of or belonging to the family Gadidae, which includes fishes such as the cod and the hake.
~*n.* A member of the Gadidae. [New Latin *Gadus* (genus name), from Greek *gados†*, a kind of fish + -OID.]
gad·o·lin·ite (găd′l-ə-nīt′) *n.* A rare blackish mineral silicate of iron, beryllium, and yttrium, $2BeO·FeO·Y_2O_3·2SiO_2$. Also called "ytterbite." [After Johan *Gadolin* (1760-1852), Finnish chemist.]
gad·o·lin·i·um (găd′l-ĭn′ē-əm) *n. Symbol* **Gd** A silvery-white, malleable, ductile metallic rare-earth element obtained from monazite and bastnaesite. It has the highest neutron-absorption cross-section known and is useful in improving high-temperature characteristics of iron, chromium, and related metallic alloys. Atomic number 64, atomic weight 157.25, melting point 1,312°C, boiling point approximately 3,000°C, specific gravity 7.9, valence 3. [New Latin, after Johan *Gadolin* (1760-1852), Finnish chemist.]
ga·droon (gə-drōōn′) *n.* **1.** *Architecture.* A band of convex molding ornamentally carved with beading or reeding. **2.** An ornamental band, especially as used in silverwork, embellished with fluting, reeding, or some other pattern. [French *godron*, from Old French *goderon*, perhaps diminutive of *godet*, drinking cup, from Middle Dutch *codet†*, cylindrical piece of wood.]
Gads·den Purchase (gădz′dən). Strip of land, *c.* 77,000 square kilometers (33,000 square miles), in present-day southern New Mexico and Arizona. It was purchased (1853) from Mexico for 10 million dollars and named after James Gadsden (1788-1858), U.S. minister to Mexico who negotiated the sale.
gad·wall (găd′wôl′) *n.* A widely distributed duck, *Anas strepera*, having grayish or brown plumage. [17th century : origin obscure.]
gad·zooks (găd-zōōks′, -zōōks′) *interj. Archaic.* Used to express surprise or annoyance. [17th century : GAD (God) + *zooks†*; perhaps originally *Gad's hooks*, "God's hooks," that is, the nails of the Crucifixion.]
Gae·a (jē′ə). Also **Gai·a** (gā′ə), **Ge** (jē, gē). *Greek Mythology.* The goddess of the earth, who bore and married Uranus and became the mother of the Titans and the Cyclopes. [Greek *Gaia*, personification of *gaia*, *gē*, earth.]
Gael (gāl) *n.* **1.** A Gaelic-speaking Celt of Scotland, Ireland, or the Isle of Man. **2.** A Scottish Highlander. [Scottish Gaelic *Gaidheal*, probably from Old Irish *goidel*, a Celt, from Old Welsh *Gwyddel*, Irishman, probably from *gwydd*, wild.]
Gael·ic (gā′lĭk) *adj. Abbr.* **Gael.** Of or relating to the Gaels or their languages.
~*n. Abbr.* **Gael.** **1.** The Goidelic family of the Celtic languages. **2.** Any of the languages of the Gaels; Irish, Manx, or the language of the Scottish Highlanders. [Scottish Gaelic *Gaidhealach*, of the Gaels, and *Gaidhlig*, the Gaelic language, from *Gaidheal*, GAEL.]
Gaelic football *n.* A type of football similar to rugby that is chiefly played in Ireland.
Gael·tacht (gāl′tŭкнт′) *n.* Any region in Ireland where the vernacular speech is Irish Gaelic.
gaff¹ (găf) *n.* **1.** An iron hook attached to a pole and used to land and maneuver large fish. **2.** *Nautical.* A spar used to extend the top edge of a fore-and-aft sail. **3.** A metal spur attached to the leg of a gamecock during a cockfight. **4.** *Slang.* Harshness of treatment; abuse.
~*tr.v.* gaffed, gaffing, gaffs. **1.** To hook or land (a fish) using a gaff. **2.** *Slang.* To alter or fix (dice, for example) in order to cheat. [Middle English *gaffe*, from Old French, from Old Provençal *gaf†*.]
gaff² *n. British Slang.* A public place of entertainment; especially, a cheap or disreputable music hall or theater. [18th century : origin obscure.]
gaffe (găf) *n.* A clumsy social error; a faux pas. [French, from *gaffer*, to hook, hence in seaman's slang, to blunder, from *gaffe*, hook, GAFF.]
gaf·fer (găf′ər) *n.* **1.** *Regional.* An old man or rustic. **2.** *British Informal.* A boss or foreman. **3.** An electrician who deals with lighting on a motion-picture or television set. [Contraction of GODFATHER.]
gaff-top·sail (găf′tŏp′səl, -sāl′) *n. Nautical.* A light, triangular or quadrilateral sail set over a gaff.
gag (găg) *n.* **1.** Something forced into or put over the mouth to

prevent the utterance of sound. **2.** Any obstacle to or censoring of free expression. **3.** A device placed in the mouth to keep it open, as in dentistry or surgery. **4.** *Informal.* **a.** A practical joke; a hoax. **b.** A comic effect or remark; a joke. —See Synonyms at **joke**.
~*v.* gagged, gagging, gags. —*tr.* **1.** To prevent from uttering any sounds by using a gag. **2.** To repress or censor (free speech, the press, and the like). **3.** To keep (the mouth) open by using a gag. **4.** To block off or stop up (a pipe or valve, for example). **5.** To cause to choke or retch. —*intr.* **1.** To choke or retch from nausea. **2.** *Informal.* To make jokes or quips. [Middle English *gaggen*, to suffocate (probably imitative).]
ga·ga (gä′gä) *adj. Informal.* **1.** Senseless; crazy. **2.** Senile. [French, from *gaga*, foolish old man (imitative of stammering).]
Ga·ga·rin (gə-gä′rĭn), **Yuri Alexeevich** (1934-68). Russian cosmonaut. In 1961 he became the first man to travel in space. He died in an airplane crash.
gage¹ (gāj) *n.* **1.** Something deposited or given as security against an obligation; a pledge. **2.** Something, such as a glove, offered or thrown down as a pledge or challenge to fight. **3.** Any test or challenge.
~*tr.v.* gaged, gaging, gages. *Archaic.* **1.** To pledge as security. **2.** To offer as a stake in a bet; wager. [Middle English, from Old French, from Germanic *wadhjam* (unattested).]
gage² *n.* Any of several varieties of plum, as the greengage.
gage³. Variant of **gauge**.
gag·ger (găg′ər) *n.* **1.** One that gags. **2.** A piece of iron used to keep the core in position in a foundry mold.
gag·gle (găg′əl) *intr.v.* -gled, -gling, -gles. To make gabbling sounds, as geese do; cackle.
~*n.* **1.** A flock of geese. **2.** An often disorderly group, as of people; cluster. [Middle English *gagelen†*.]
gag·man (găg′măn′) *n., pl.* -men (-mĕn′). A person who writes jokes or comedy routines for plays, films, or performers.
gag rein *n.* A horse's rein adjusted to make the bit more powerful.
gag rule *n.* A rule, as in a legislative body, limiting discussion or debate on a given issue. Also called "gag law."
gag·ster (găg′stər) *n.* A gagman.
gahn·ite (gä′nīt′) *n.* A gray mineral, $ZnO·Al_2O_3$. Also called "zinc spinel." [German *Gahnit*, after Johan G. *Gahn* (1745-1818), Swedish chemist.]
Gaia. Variant of **Gaea**.
gai·e·ty, gay·e·ty (gā′ə-tē) *n., pl.* -ties. **1.** A state of being cheerful or merry. **2.** Activity brought about by or inspiring joyousness; festivity; merriment. **3.** Gay color or showiness, as of dress; finery. [French *gaieté*, from Old French *gai*, GAY.]
Gail·lard Cut (gĭl-yärd′). Formerly **Cu·le·bra Cut** (kyōō-lā′brə). Excavation, 13 kilometers (8 miles) long, through a hill in the Canal Zone, Panama. It forms the southeastern part of the Panama Canal. U.S. Army engineer David Du Bose Gaillard (1859-1913) was in charge of the excavation work (completed 1908).
gail·lar·di·a (gə-lär′dē-ə) *n.* Any of several plants of the genus *Gaillardia*, of western North America, having yellow or reddish rayed flowers. [New Latin *Gaillardia*, after *Gaillard* de Marentonneau, 18th-century French botanist.]
gai·ly, gay·ly (gā′lē) *adv.* **1.** In a joyful, cheerful, or happy manner; merrily. **2.** With brightness; colorfully or showily: *gaily dressed*.
gain¹ (gān) *v.* gained, gaining, gains. —*tr.* **1.** To become the owner of; obtain; get. **2.** To acquire in competition or battle; win. **3.** To achieve through one's efforts or merits, or as a natural development: *gained recognition; gained widespread support*. **4.** To secure as a profit or through labor. **5.** To build up an increase of (weight or momentum, for example). **6.** To come to; arrive at; reach. **7.** To become fast by (the specified amount of time). Used of a timepiece: *My watch gains two minutes a day*. —*intr.* **1.** To become better or greater; advance or progress. **2.** To come nearer; get closer. Used with *on* or *upon*. **3.** To increase a lead. Used with *on*, *upon*, or *over*. **4.** To run fast. Used of a timepiece. —See Synonyms at **reach**.
~*n.* **1.** Something earned, won, or otherwise acquired; a profit; an advantage; an increase. **2.** The act of acquiring something; attainment. **3.** *Electronics.* **a.** An increase in signal power. **b.** The ratio of output to input, as of output power to input power in an aerial or of output voltage to input voltage in an amplifier. [Old French *gaaignier*, *gaigner*, from Germanic *waithanjan* (unattested).]
gain² *n.* A notch or mortise cut into a board to receive another part. [17th century : origin obscure.]
gain·er (gā′nər) *n.* **1.** One that gains. **2.** A dive in which the diver leaves the board facing forward, does a backward somersault, and enters the water feet first.
gain·ful (gān′fəl) *adj.* Providing a gain; profitable. —**gain·ful·ly** *adv.* —**gain·ful·ness** *n.*
gain·ings (gā′nĭngz) *pl.n.* The amount of money earned; profits.
gain·say (gān-sā′) *tr.v.* -said (-sĕd′), -saying, -says. **1.** To declare false; deny. **2.** To be contrary to; oppose; contradict. —See Synonyms at **deny**. [Middle English *gaynsayen*, "to say against" : *gayn-*, against, Old English *gegn-* + SAY.] —**gain·say·er** *n.*
Gains·bor·ough (gānz′bûr′ō, -bər-ə), **Thomas** (1727-88). English landscape and portrait painter. His masterpieces include *The Blue Boy* (early 1770's) and *The Harvest Wagon* (1767).
'gainst, gainst (gĕnst, gănst) *prep. Poetic.* Against.
gait (gāt) *n.* **1.** A way of moving on foot; a particular fashion of walking or running. **2.** Any of the ways a horse or other four-legged animal may move by lifting the feet in different order or rhythm, as

gadwall *Found through much of the Northern Hemisphere, this duck eats roots and water plants in reed-fringed inland lakes.*

a canter, trot, or walk. [Middle English *gate, gait,* way, passage, from Old Norse *gata,* path, street.]

gait·ed (gā'tĭd) *adj.* Having a specified gait or number of gaits. Usually used in combination: *fast-gaited; a three-gaited mare.*

gai·ter (gā'tər) *n.* **1.** A leather or heavy cloth covering for the legs extending from the knee to the instep; a legging. **2.** An ankle-high shoe with elastic insets in the sides. **3.** An overshoe with a cloth top. [French *guêtre,* from Old French *guestre, guietre,* probably from Frankish *wrist* (unattested), instep.]

Gait·skell (gāt'skəl), **Hugh Todd Naylor** (1906–63). British politician. He became an M.P. (1945), Chancellor of the Exchequer (1950–51), and leader of the Labour Party (1955–63). He persuaded the party to abandon unilateral disarmament (1961).

gal (găl) *n. Informal.* A girl.

gal. gallon.

Gal. Galatians (New Testament).

---

galaxy

THE MILLIONS OF GALAXIES THAT MAKE UP THE UNIVERSE

Our galaxy is a spiral of millions of stars

Almost all the matter in the universe is collected into galaxies, of which there are a billion within range of our telescopes. The largest galaxies contain a trillion stars. Galaxies are classified according to their shape into barred or normal spirals, which form the vast majority; ellipticals, which form 20 percent; and irregulars, which form 5 percent.

Many of the spiral galaxies are disk-shaped. They have a nucleus of old stars and orbiting arms of young stars. Our own Milky Way is a typical spiral some 100,000 light-years across, containing 100 billion stars.

Galaxies form irregular groups, some with thousands of members. The Milky Way is part of the so-called Local Group of about 25, of which the Great Spiral in Andromeda, 2.2 million light-years away, is the largest. Our nearest galactic neighbors are the two irregular Magellanic clouds, 160,000 light-years away.

SPIRAL *Seen obliquely through a haze of Milky Way stars is a spiral in the constellation Sculptor.*

ELLIPTICAL *Galaxies like this satellite of the Andromeda galaxy are systems that range from a million times the size of the sun to supergiants much more extensive than the Milky Way.*

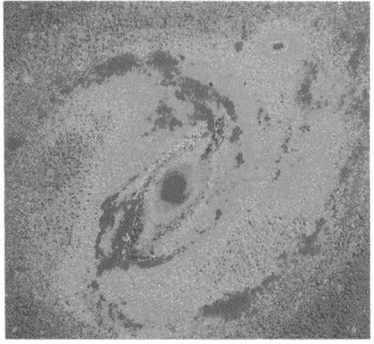

BARRED SPIRAL *The galaxy pictured here in false colors (to heighten the contrast between old and young stars) shows the flattened nucleus that gives this type of galaxy its name.*

---

ga·la (gā'lə, găl'ə, gä'lə) *n.* **1.** A festive occasion or celebration; a festival. **2.** *British.* A competitive sports meeting, especially a swimming competition.
—*adj.* Characterized by or suitable to celebration; festive. [Italian, from Spanish, from Old French *gale,* pleasure, merrymaking, from *galer,* to make merry, live a gay life, from Gallo-Roman *walare* (unattested), from Frankish *wala* (unattested), well.]

ga·lac·ta·gogue (gə-lăk'tə-gŏg', -gŏg') *n.* A substance that induces a flow of milk.
—*adj.* Inducing a flow of milk. [GALACT(O)- + -AGOGUE.]

ga·lac·tic (gə-lăk'tĭk) *adj.* **1.** Of or pertaining to a galaxy or galaxies. **2.** *Sometimes* **Galactic.** Of, pertaining to, occurring, or originating in the Milky Way. [Late Latin *galacticus,* from Greek *galaktikos,* from *gala* (stem *galakt-*), milk. See **galaxy.**]

galactic equator *n.* The great circle of the celestial sphere that lies in the plane bisecting the band of the Milky Way, inclined at an angle of approximately 62° to the celestial equator.

galactic nebula *n.* A nebula lying within the Milky Way Galaxy.

galactic noise *n.* Radio-frequency radiation originating within the Milky Way.

galactic year *n.* The **cosmic year** *(see).*

galacto–, galact– *prefix.* Indicates milk or milky; for example, **galactopoiesis, galactose.** [Greek *gala* (stem *galakt-*), milk.]

ga·lac·to·poi·e·sis (gə-lăk'tə-poi-ē'sĭs) *n.* The secretion and continued production of milk. [GALACTO- + -POIESIS.] —**ga·lac·to·poi·et·ic** (gə-lăk'tə-poi-ĕt'ĭk) *adj.*

ga·lac·tose (gə-lăk'tōs') *n.* A simple sugar, $C_6H_{12}O_6$, commonly occurring in **lactose** *(see).* [French : GALACT(O)- + -OSE.]

ga·lac·to·se·mi·a (gə-lăk'tə-sē'mē-ə) *n.* A congenital disease characterized by the inability to metabolize galactose, which consequently accumulates in the blood and if untreated causes mental retardation and stunted growth. [GALACTOSE + -EMIA.]

ga·la·go (gə-lā'gō', gə-lä'-) *n., pl.* **-gos.** A small primate, the **bush baby** *(see).* [New Latin *Galago,* perhaps from an African word *goigkh,* monkey.]

ga·lah (gə-lä') *n.* **1.** An Australian cockatoo, *Cacatua* (or *Kakatoe*) *roseicapilla,* having pale blue-gray plumage and a pink breast. **2.** *Australian Slang.* A fool; an idiot. [From a native Australian language.]

Gal·a·had (găl'ə-hăd') *n.* Any man considered to be noble, pure, or chivalrous. [After *Galahad,* a knight of King Arthur's Round Table who was known for his purity and who alone succeeded in the quest for the Holy Grail.]

ga·lan·gal (gə-lăng'gəl) *n.* **1.** A plant, *Alpinia officinarum,* of eastern Asia, having pungent, aromatic roots used medicinally and as seasoning. **2.** The dried roots of this plant. **3.** The **galingale** *(see).* [Originally a variant of GALINGALE.]

gal·an·tine (găl'ən-tēn') *n.* A dish of boned, stuffed poultry, meat, or fish cooked and served cold coated with aspic or its own jelly. [Middle English *galauntyne,* a sauce for fish and poultry, from Old French *galantine, galatine,* from Medieval Latin *galatīna, gelatīna,* probably from Latin *gelāre,* to freeze.]

ga·lan·ty show (gə-lăn'tē) *n.* A play performed by casting the shadows of miniature figures on a screen or wall. [Perhaps from Italian *galanti,* plural of *galante,* a gallant, from Old French *galant* (from the stories of gallantry portrayed in the show).]

Ga·lá·pa·gos Islands (gə-lä'pə-gəs, -lăp'ə-). *Spanish* **Ar·chi·pié·la·go de Co·lón** (är'chī-pyĕl'ə-gō de kə-lōn'). An Ecuadorian archipelago in the Pacific Ocean. The 15 large and many small volcanic islands lie *c.* 970 kilometers (600 miles) west of Ecuador. The population is concentrated on Isabela (Albemarle), the largest island, and San Cristóbal (Chatham). Most of the reptile life and over half the flora are unknown outside the islands, now a nature reserve. In 1835 Charles Darwin collected a wealth of scientific data here, which led to his theory of evolution. Giant tortoises once abounded on the islands, which take their name from the Spanish word *galpágo,* "tortoise." See map at **Pacific Ocean.**

gal·a·te·a (găl'ə-tē'ə) *n.* A durable cotton fabric, often striped, used in making clothing. [Originally used for children's sailor suits, after the *Galatea,* 19th-century British warship.]

Gal·a·te·a (găl'ə-tē'ə). *Greek Mythology.* An ivory statue of a maiden, brought to life by Aphrodite in answer to the pleas of the sculptor, Pygmalion, who had fallen in love with his creation.

Ga·la·tia (gə-lā'shə). Ancient country forming part of central Asia Minor. Chief city, Ancyra (modern Ankara, Turkey). —**Ga·la·tian** *adj. & n.*

Ga·la·tians (gə-lā'shənz) *n. Abbr.* **Gal.** A book of the New Testament consisting of an Epistle written to the Christians of Galatia by the apostle Paul in about A.D. 58. Called in full "Epistle to the Galatians."

galavant. Variant of **gallivant.**

ga·lax (gā'lăks') *n.* A plant, *Galax aphylla,* of the southeastern United States, having glossy, evergreen leaves and a cluster of small white flowers. [New Latin *Galax,* probably from Greek *galaxias,* the Milky Way, GALAXY (from its white flowers).]

gal·ax·y (găl'ək-sē) *n., pl.* **-ies.** **1.** *Astronomy.* **a.** Any of numerous large-scale aggregates of stars, gas, and dust, having one of several more or less definite overall structures, containing an average of 100 billion (10^{11}) solar masses, and ranging in diameter from 1,500 to 300,000 light-years. **b.** *Often* **Galaxy.** The galaxy of which the earth's sun is a part, the **Milky Way** *(see).* Usually preceded by *the.* **2.** An assembly of brilliant, beautiful, or distinguished persons or things. [Middle English *galaxie,* the Milky Way, from Old French, from Latin *galaxiās,* from Greek *galaxias (kuklos),* "milky (circle)," from *gala,* milk.]

gal·ba·num (găl′bə-nəm, gôl′-) *n.* A bitter, aromatic gum resin extracted from an Asiatic plant, *Ferula galbaniflua,* or any of several related plants, and used in incense and medicinally as a counterirritant. [Middle English, from Latin, from Greek *khalbanē,* from Hebrew *ḥelbənāh.*]

Gal·braith (găl′brāth′), **John Kenneth** (1908–). Canadian-born U.S. economist. His works include *The Great Crash* (1955), *The Affluent Society* (1958), and *The New Industrial State* (1967). He was U.S. ambassador to India (1961–63).

gale[1] (gāl) *n.* **1. a.** A very strong wind. **b.** *Meteorology.* A wind whose speed is between 39 and 46 miles per hour, force 8 on the Beaufort scale. **2.** *Archaic.* A breeze. **3.** A forceful outburst, as of laughter. —See Synonyms at **wind.** [Probably short for *gale wind,* "bad wind," perhaps from Norwegian *galen,* bad, probably from Old Norse *galinn,* bewitched, enchanted, from *gala,* to sing, enchant, bewitch.]

gale[2] *n.* A plant, the **sweet myrtle** *(see).* [Middle English, *gale, gayl,* Old English *gagel,* akin to Middle Dutch *gaghel†.*]

ga·le·a (gā′lē-ə) *n., pl.* **-leae** (-lē-ē′). *Biology.* A helmet-shaped part, such as the upper petal of certain plants or part of the maxilla of an insect. [Latin, leather helmet, originally "cap made of weasel skin," from Greek *galeē,* weasel.]

ga·le·ate (gā′lē-āt′) *adj.* Also **ga·le·at·ed** (-ā′tĭd). *Biology.* **1.** Having a galea. **2.** Helmet-shaped. [Latin *galeātus,* from *galea,* GALEA.]

ga·le·i·form (gā′lē-ə-fôrm′, gə-lē′-) *adj.* Helmet-shaped. [French *galéiforme* : Latin *galea,* GALEA + -FORM.]

Ga·len (gā′lən). (A.D. *c.* 130–*c.* 200). Greek physician. He compiled Greek medical knowledge into treatises that formed the basis of European medicine until the Renaissance.

ga·le·na (gə-lē′nə) *n.* A gray mineral, essentially PbS, the principal ore of lead. Also called "lead glance." [Latin *galēna†,* lead ore.]

ga·len·ic (gə-lĕn′ĭk, gā-) *adj.* Also **ga·len·i·cal** (-ĭ-kəl). Designating a drug preparation of plant or animal origin. [After GALEN.] **—ga·len·ic, ga·len·i·cal** *n.*

Ga·len·ism (gā′lə-nĭz′əm) *n.* The medical system based on Galen's surviving treatises, including the notion of the four bodily humors. **—Ga·len·ic** (gə-lĕn′ĭk, gā-), **Ga·len·i·cal** (-ĭ-kəl) *adj.* **—Ga·len·ist** *adj. & n.*

ga·lère (gə-lâr′) *n. French.* A group or coterie, especially of undesirable people. [French, "galley."]

Ga·li·bi (gə-lē′bē, găl′ə-) *n., pl.* **-bis** or collectively **Galibi. 1.** A member of the Carib people of French Guiana. **2.** The language of this people. [Carib *galibi,* "strong man," akin to Cariban *caribe,* brave, CARIB.]

Ga·li·cia[1] (gə-lĭsh′ə, -lĭsh′ē-ə). Region and former kingdom in northwest Spain, on the Atlantic Ocean south of the Bay of Biscay. Colonized by the Goths in the 6th century, it became a subject of Castile in the 11th century.

Galicia[2]. *Polish* **Ha·licz** (hä′lĭch). *Russian* **Ga·lich** (gä′lĭch) or **Ga·li·tsi·ya** (gə-lē′tsē-yə). Historic region in Central Europe. It became an independent principality in 1087 but was conquered by the Russians in the 12th century. Absorbed by Poland in the 14th century, it became Austrian four centuries later. Following World War I it was returned to Poland, but after World War II East Galicia was ceded to the U.S.S.R.

Ga·li·cian (gə-lĭsh′ən) *adj.* **1.** Of or pertaining to Spanish Galicia, its people, or their language. **2.** Of or pertaining to Polish Galicia or its people.
~n. **1.** A native or inhabitant of Spanish or Polish Galicia. **2.** The Portuguese dialect spoken in Spanish Galicia.

Gal·i·le·an[1] (găl′ə-lē′ən) *adj.* Of or pertaining to Galilee or its people.
~n. **1.** A native or inhabitant of Galilee. **2.** A Christian. **3.** Jesus.

Gal·i·le·an[2] (găl′ə-lē′ən, -lā′ən) *adj.* Of, pertaining to, or in accordance with the work of Galileo.

gal·i·lee (găl′ə-lē′) *n.* A small chapel or porch at the western end of some medieval English churches and cathedrals. Also called "galilee porch." [Middle English *galile,* from Old French *galilee,* from Medieval Latin *galilaea,* from Latin *Galilaea,* GALILEE.]

Gal·i·lee (găl′ə-lē′). A region in northern Israel. The northernmost region of Palestine and of the ancient Jewish kingdom of Israel, Galilee was the province where Jesus Christ began his ministry. It became part of the newly founded state of Israel in 1949.

Galilee, Sea of. Biblical names **Sea of Ti·be·ri·as** (tī-bîr′ē-əs) or **Lake of Gen·nes·a·ret** (gə-nĕs′ə-rĕt′) or **Sea of Chin·ne·reth** (kĭn′ə-rĕth′). Lake in northern Israel. It is 21 kilometers (13 miles) long and lies in the Great Rift Valley, its surface being 209 meters (686 feet) below sea level.

Gal·i·le·o Gal·i·le·i (găl′ə-lā′ō găl′ə-lā′ē) (1564–1642). Italian astronomer and mathematician. He developed his own telescope (1609) and discovered four satellites of Jupiter and the nature of lunar illumination. His belief that Copernicus was right to claim that the sun was the center of our universe led to his persecution by the Inquisition (1633). He recanted but is said to have muttered under his breath "But it (the earth) does move."

gal·i·ma·ti·as (găl′ə-mā′shē-əs, -shəs, -măt′ē-əs) *n.* Nonsensical talk; gibberish. [French, perhaps originally students' jargon : Latin *gallus,* "cock," student who takes part in a discussion + Greek *-mathia,* knowledge, from *manthanein,* to learn.]

gal·in·gale (găl′ən-gāl′, găl′ĭng-) *n.* Any of various sedges of the genus *Cyperus;* especially, *C. longus,* of Europe, having rough-edged leaves, reddish spikelets, and aromatic roots. Also called "galangal." [Middle English, from Old French *galingal,* from Arabic *khalanjān,* from Chinese *gāo liáng jiāng,* good ginger from Gaozhou (present-day Maoming in Guangdong Province).]

galiot. Variant of **galliot.**

gal·i·pot (găl′ə-pŏt′, -pō′) *n.* The crude turpentine resin that is obtained from various pine species, especially the cluster pine, *Pinus pinaster,* of southern Europe, and is often seen as a hardened mass on the bark. [18th century : from French, of obscure origin.]

Galitsiya. See **Galicia** (Central Europe).

gall[1] (gôl) *n.* **1. a. Bile** *(see).* **b.** The gallbladder. **2.** Bitterness of feeling; rancor. **3.** Something bitter to endure: *the gall of disappointment.* **4.** Impudence; effrontery: *He had the gall to try to borrow money.* —See Synonyms at **temerity.** [Middle English *gall(e),* Old English *gealla,* from Germanic.]

gall[2] *n.* **1.** A skin sore caused by friction and abrasion: *a saddle gall.* **2. a.** Exasperation; irritation; vexation. **b.** The cause of such vexation.
~v. **galled, galling, galls.** *—tr.* **1.** To make (the skin) sore by abrasion; chafe. **2.** To damage or break the surface of by or as if by friction or abrasion; abrade: *the bark of saplings galled by improper staking.* **3.** To exasperate; vex. *—intr.* To become irritated, chafed, or sore. [Middle English *galle,* from Middle Low German; akin to Old English *gealla,* sore place, Old Norse *galli,* fault.]

gall[3] *n.* An abnormal swelling of plant tissue, caused by insects, microorganisms, or external injury. [Middle English *galle,* from Old French, from Latin *galla†.*]

gall. gallon.

Gal·la (găl′ə) *n., pl.* **-las** or collectively **Galla. 1.** A member of a pastoral Hamitic people of southern Ethiopia and Somalia. **2.** The language of this people, belonging to the Ethiopian or Cushitic group of the Afro-Asiatic languages.
~adj. Of or pertaining to this people or their language. [Perhaps from Arabic *ghalīz,* rough.]

gal·lant (găl′ənt *for senses 1, 3, 4;* gə-lănt′, -länt′, găl′ənt *for sense 2*) *adj.* **1.** Courageous; daring; valorous: *gallant soldiers.* **2. a.** Attentive to women; chivalrous; courteous. **b.** Amorous. **3.** Stately; majestic; noble: *"On my word, master, this is a gallant trout"* (Isaak Walton). **4.** Showy and gay in appearance, dress, or bearing; dashing. —See Synonyms at **brave.**
~n. (gə-lănt′, -länt′, găl′ənt). **1.** A fashionable young man. **2. a.** A man courteously attentive to women; a ladies' man. **b.** A woman's lover; a paramour.
~v. (gə-lănt′, -länt′) **gallanted, -lanting, -lants.** *—tr.* To woo, attend, or escort (a lady); pay court to. *—intr.* To play the gallant. [Middle English *galaunt,* from Old French *galant,* gorgeous, showy, brave, from the present participle of *galer,* to rejoice, from Gallo-Roman *walāre* (unattested), from Frankish *wala* (unattested), well.] **—gal·lant·ly** *adv.*

gal·lant·ry (găl′ən-trē) *n., pl.* **-ries. 1.** Nobility of spirit or action; great courage. **2. a.** Chivalrous attention toward women; courtliness; courteousness. **b.** Amorous attentiveness to a woman. **3.** An act or instance of gallantry in speech or behavior. **4.** *Archaic.* A bold or colorful display or appearance.

Gal·la·tin Range (găl′ə-tən). Section of the Rocky Mts. in northwestern Wyoming and southwestern Montana. The highest elevation is Electric Peak, rising to 3,402 meters (11,155 feet), in the northwestern corner of Yellowstone National Park.

gall·blad·der, gall blad·der (gôl′blăd′ər) *n.* A small, pear-shaped muscular sac located under the right lobe of the liver, in which bile secreted by the liver is stored.

Galle (gäl, găl). Formerly **Point de Galle** (point′ də gäl′, găl′). Seaport and commercial center of Sri Lanka. It was the country's main port under the Arabs and Portuguese and the capital under the Dutch until 1656.

gal·le·ass, gal·li·ass (găl′ē-əs) *n.* A large, heavily armed, three-masted Mediterranean galley of the 16th and 17th centuries. [Old French *galeasse,* from Old Italian *galeaza,* augmentative of *galea,* galley, from Medieval Latin, GALLEY.]

gal·le·on (găl′ē-ən) *n.* A large, three-masted sailing ship generally having two or more decks, used during the 15th and 16th centuries by Spain and other countries as a merchantman or warship. [Spanish *galeon,* from Old French *galion,* from *galie,* GALLEY.]

gal·ler·y (găl′ə-rē, găl′rē) *n., pl.* **-ies. 1.** A roofed promenade, especially one extending along the wall of a building, with its roof supported by pillars on the outer side; a colonnade. **2.** An elevated covered platform along the outer wall of a building; a long balcony. **3. a.** An enclosed narrow passageway, such as a hall or corridor. **b.** A long room or passage resembling such a corridor and used for a specified purpose: *a shooting gallery.* **4. a.** An upper floor projecting over the main floor of a theater, and usually providing cheaper seats than those in the orchestra. **b.** The seats in such a section. **c.** The audience occupying these seats. **d.** A similar projecting upper floor in a large building, as in a church, law court, or legislative assembly. **5.** A large audience or group of spectators, as in a stadium, grandstand, or legislative assembly. **6. a.** A building or hall in which sculpture, paintings, photographs, or other works of art are exhibited. **b.** A private institution that exhibits and sells works of art. **7.** An underground tunnel or other passageway, such as one dug for military or mining purposes, or found in animal burrows, insects' nests, and so on. **8.** *Nautical.* A platform or balcony at the stern or quarters of certain early sailing ships. **9.** A decorative upright trimming or molding along the edge of a table top, tray, or

gall *These abnormal swellings on plants are caused by parasitic infections, often transmitted by insects. The gall shown here is an oak marble, caused by the larva of a tiny wasp.*

PRONUNCIATION KEY

ă, pat; ā, pay; âr, care;
ä, father, are; b, bib;
ch, church; d, deed; ĕ, pet;
ē, be; f, fife; g, gag; h, hat;
hw, which; ĭ, pit; ī, pie;
îr, pier; j, judge; k, kick;
l, lid, needle; m, mum;
n, no, sudden; ng, thing;
ŏ, pot; ō, toe; ô, paw, for;
oi, noise; ou, out; ŏŏ, book;
ōō, boot; p, pop; r, roar;
s, sauce; sh, ship, dish;
t, tight; th, thin, path;
th, this, bathe; ŭ, cut; ûr, fur;
v, valve; w, with; y, yes;
z, zebra, size; zh, vision;
ə, about, item, edible,
gallop, circus, peaceful

IN FOREIGN WORDS:

à, *Fr.* ami; œ, *Fr.* feu, *Ger.* schön; ü, *Fr.* tu, *Ger.* über;
KH, *Ger.* ich, *Scot.* loch;
N, *Fr.* bon; y′, *Fr.* Compiègne

STRESS MARKS:

Primary stress: ′
in·cite′ (ĭn-sīt′)
Secondary stress: ′
in′sight′ (ĭn′sīt′)

galley *A detail from* Battle of Lepanto, *a painting of one of the last major actions between galleys. In the battle, on October 7, 1571, the Muslim Ottoman Turks were decisively defeated by a Christian armada under Don John of Austria, losing all but 40 of their 300 war galleys.*

gallinule *This wading bird is found in most parts of the world except Australia, nesting beside freshwater ponds, lakes, and rivers. When alarmed, it can sink below the surface, leaving only its bill protruding like a snorkel. In the U.S.A. it is sometimes called marsh hen.*

Galloway *A distinctive Scottish breed of beef cattle with a shaggy coat of black, gray-brown, or silvery hair and no horns.*

shelf. **—play to the gallery.** **1.** To perform a play, scene, or role in a manner calculated to please the less sophisticated members of an audience who, in former times, were mainly congregated in the gallery. **2.** To try to gain the favor or applause of the general public, especially by crude or obvious means.
~*tr.v.* **galleried, -lerying, -leries.** To provide with a gallery. [Middle English *galerie,* from Old French, portico, from Italian *galleria,* from Medieval Latin *galeria,* perhaps variant of *galilaea,* porch of a church, GALILEE.]

gallery forest *n.* A stretch of forest bordering a river and surrounded by treeless country.

gal·ley (găl′ē) *n., pl.* **-leys.** **1.** A large medieval ship of shallow draft that had a single deck, was propelled by sails and oars, and was used as a merchantman or warship in the Mediterranean. **2.** An ancient seagoing vessel propelled by oars. **3.** A large rowboat, such as one formerly used by British customs officers. **4.** The kitchen of a ship, boat, or airliner. **5.** *Printing.* **a.** A long tray, usually of metal, used for holding composed type. **b.** A galley proof. [Middle English *galeie, galy,* from Old French *galie, galee,* from Medieval Latin *galea,* from Medieval Greek *galea*†.]

galley proof *n. Printing.* A printer's proof taken from composed type before page composition to allow for the detection and correction of errors. Also called "galley."

galley slave *n.* **1.** A slave or convict forced to man an oar of a galley. **2.** A person forced to perform tedious or menial tasks; a drudge.

galley west *adv. Informal.* Out of shape; out of commission. Used in the phrase *to knock galley west.* [Perhaps alteration of dialectal *collywest,* askew, perhaps from *Collyweston,* village in Northamptonshire, England.]

gall·fly (gôl′flī′) *n., pl.* **-flies.** Any of various small insects, such as the gall midge or gall wasp, that deposit their eggs on plant stems or in the bark of trees, causing the formation of galls in which their larvae grow.

Gallia. See **Gaul.**

gal·li·am·bic (găl′ē-ăm′bĭk) *adj.* Designating or characteristic of a verse meter formed by two iambic dimeters. [Latin *galliambus,* song of the *Gallī* (priests of Cybele); see **iamb.**]

gal·liard (găl′yərd) *adj. Archaic.* Spirited; lively; gay.
~*n.* **1.** A spirited dance popular in the 16th and 17th centuries. **2.** The music for this dance. [Middle English *galiard, gaillard,* valiant, lively, from Old French *gaillard,* from Gallo-Roman *galia* (unattested), strength, power.]

galliass. Variant of **galleass.**

gal·lic (găl′ĭk) *adj. Chemistry.* Of or pertaining to gallium. Used especially of chemical compounds that contain gallium with a valence of 3.

Gal·lic (găl′ĭk) *adj.* Of or pertaining to ancient Gaul or to modern France; French. [Latin *Gallicus,* Gaulish, from *Galli,* Gauls.]

gal·lic acid (găl′ĭk) *n.* A colorless crystalline compound, $C_7H_6O_5 \cdot H_2O$, derived from tannin and used in photography, as a tanning agent, and in ink and paper manufacture.

Gal·li·can (găl′ĭ-kən) *adj.* Pertaining to or characteristic of Gallicanism.
~*n.* A supporter of Gallicanism. [Middle English, from Old French, from Medieval Latin *Gallicānus,* French, from Latin, Gaulish, from *Gallicus,* GALLIC.]

Gal·li·can·ism (găl′ĭ-kə-nĭz′əm) *n.* A movement originating among the French Roman Catholic clergy, favoring the restriction of papal control and the achievement by each nation of individual administrative autonomy. Compare **Ultramontanism.**

Gal·li·cism (găl′ĭ-sĭz′əm) *n.* **1.** A French phrase or idiom appearing in another language. **2.** A characteristic French trait.

Gal·li·cize (găl′ĭ-sīz′) *v.* **-cized, -cizing, -cizes.** —*intr.* To become like the French, as in speech, character, or custom. —*tr.* To make like the French, as in speech, character, or custom.

gal·li·gas·kins (găl′ĭ-găs′kĭnz) *pl.n.* **1.** Full-length, loosely fitting hose or breeches worn in the 16th and 17th centuries. **2.** Loose breeches or trousers. **3.** *Regional.* Leggings. [Earlier *gallogascaine, garragascoyne,* perhaps from Old French *garguesque, greguesque,* from Old Italian *grechesca,* "Grecian breeches," from the feminine of *grechesco,* Grecian, from *greco,* Greek, from Latin *Graecus,* GREEK.]

gal·li·mau·fry (găl′ə-mô′frē) *n., pl.* **-fries.** A jumble; a hodgepodge. [French *galimafrée,* from Old French *calimafree* : probably *galer,* to live a gay life (see **gallant**) + Picard *mafrer,* to eat voraciously, from Middle Dutch *maffelen*†.]

gal·li·na·ceous (găl′ə-nā′shəs) *adj.* **1.** Of, belonging to, or characteristic of the order Galliformes, which includes the common domestic fowl as well as the pheasants, turkeys, and grouse. **2.** Relating to or resembling the domestic fowl. [Latin *gallīnāceus,* of poultry, from *gallīna,* hen, feminine of *gallus,* cock.] **—gal·li·na·cean** (găl′ə-nā′shən) *n.*

gall·ing (gô′lĭng) *adj.* Causing acute irritation, humiliation, exasperation, or discomfort. **—gall·ing·ly** *adv.*

gal·li·nip·per (găl′ə-nĭp′ər) *n.* A large mosquito or similar insect capable of inflicting a painful bite. [Origin unknown.]

gal·li·nule (găl′ə-no͞ol′, -nyo͞ol′) *n.* Any of various wading birds of the genera *Gallinula, Porphyrio,* or *Porphyrula,* frequenting swampy regions and characteristically having dark, iridescent plumage. [New Latin *Gallinula,* from Latin *gallīnula,* chicken, pullet, diminutive of *gallīna,* hen, feminine of *gallus,* cock.]

gal·li·ot, gal·i·ot (găl′ē-ət) *n.* **1.** A light, swift galley propelled by sails and oars, formerly used on the Mediterranean. **2.** A light, single-masted, flat-bottomed Dutch merchant ship or seagoing barge. [Middle English, from Old French *galiote,* from Italian *galeotta,* from Medieval Latin *galea,* GALLEY.]

Gal·lip·o·li (gə-lĭp′ə-lē). *Turkish* **Ge·li·bo·lu** (gĕl′ə-bə-lo͞o′). Seaport of European Turkey. It lies on the Gallipoli Peninsula in the Dardanelles, and in 1354 was the Ottoman Turks' first European conquest. From April 1915 to January 1916 the peninsula was the scene of unsuccessful and costly landings by Australian, New Zealand, French, and British troops in an attempt to clear the Dardanelles and thus the sea route to Russia. The devastated town was ceded to Greece in 1920 but was returned to Turkey in 1923.

gal·li·pot (găl′ə-pŏt′) *n.* A small glazed earthenware jar formerly used by pharmacists for medicaments. [Middle English *galy pott* : probably GALLEY + POT (originally imported from the Mediterranean by galleys).]

gal·li·um (găl′ē-əm) *n. Symbol* **Ga** A rare metallic element that is liquid near room temperature, expands on solidifying, and is found as a trace element in coal, bauxite, and other minerals. It is used in semiconductor technology and as a component of various low-melting alloys. Atomic number 31, atomic weight 69.72, melting point 29.78°C, boiling point 2,403°C, specific gravity 5.907 (20°C), valences 2, 3. [New Latin, from Latin *gallus,* cock (playful translation of the name of its discoverer, *Lecoq* de Boisbaudran, 1838–1912, French chemist). See **gallinaceous.**]

gallium arsenide *n.* A dark-gray crystalline compound, GaAs, used in transistors, solar cells, and semiconducting lasers.

gal·li·vant, gal·a·vant (găl′ə-vănt′) *intr.v.* **-vanted, -vanting, -vants.** **1.** To roam about aimlessly or frivolously; gad about. **2.** To consort frivolously with members of the opposite sex; flirt. [Perhaps alteration of GALLANT.]

gal·li·wasp (găl′ə-wŏsp′, -wôsp′) *n.* Any of several long-bodied lizards of the genera *Diploglossus* or *Celestus,* of Central America and the West Indies. [18th century : origin obscure.]

gall midge *n.* Any of various small, mosquitolike flies making up the family Cecidomyiidae, the larvae of which produce galls in plants.

gall mite *n.* Any of various mites of the family Eriophyidae that produce galls in plants.

gall·nut (gôl′nŭt′) *n.* A plant gall having a rounded form suggestive of a nut.

Gallo– *prefix.* Indicates Gaul or France; for example, **Gallo-Roman.** [Latin *Gallus,* a Gaul.]

galloglass. Variant of **gallowglass.**

Gal·lo·ma·ni·a (găl′ə-mā′nē-ə) *n.* A strong predilection for anything French. [French *gallomanie* : GALLO- + -MANIA.]

gal·lon (găl′ən) *n. Abbr.* **g., gal., gall.** **1.** A unit of volume or capacity in the U.S. Customary System, used in liquid measure, equal to 4 quarts, or 3.79 liters (231 cubic inches, or 0.83 of a British gallon). **2.** A unit of volume in the British Imperial system, used in liquid and dry measure, equal to 4.55 liters (277.420 cubic inches). [Middle English *gallun, gallon,* from Old North French, from Medieval Latin *gallēta,* jug, measure for wine, perhaps from Celtic.]

gal·lon·age (găl′ə-nĭj) *n.* The amount of something measured in gallons.

gal·loon (gə-lo͞on′) *n.* A narrow band or braid used as trimming, and commonly made of lace, metallic thread, or embroidery. [French *galon,* from Old French *galonner,* to decorate with ribbons, perhaps from Frankish *wōlōn,* to tie up with cord.]

gal·lop (găl′əp) *n.* **1.** The fastest gait of a horse or other quadruped, in which all four legs are off the ground at the same time. **2.** A ride taken at the gallop. **3.** A fast pace.
~*v.* **galloped, -loping, -lops.** —*tr.* **1.** To cause to gallop. **2.** To transport at or as if at a gallop. —*intr.* **1.** To go at a gallop. Used of a horse or its rider. **2.** To move or progress rapidly: *galloped through the agenda.* [Middle English *galopen,* from Old French *galoper,* variant of Old North French *waloper,* from Frankish *walahlaupan* (unattested), "to run well" : *wala* (unattested), well + *hlaupan* (unattested), to jump, run.] **—gal·lop·er** *n.*

gallopade. Variant of **galop.**

gal·lop·ing (găl′ə-pĭng) *adj.* **1.** Of or resembling a gallop, especially in rhythm or rapidity. **2. a.** Developing at an accelerated rate and leading to death. Said of certain diseases, principally in nontechnical contexts. **b.** Increasing rapidly or uncontrollably: *galloping inflation.*

Gal·lo-Ro·man (găl′ō-rō′mən) *n.* **1.** A native or inhabitant of Roman Gaul. **2.** The Vulgar Latin spoken by the Romanized inhabitants of Gaul. **—Gal·lo-Ro·man** *adj.*

Gal·lo-Ro·mance (găl′ō-rō-măns′, -rō′măns′) *n.* The language supposed by scholars to have developed from the Vulgar Latin that was spoken in Gaul after the end of Roman rule, before the development of Old French. **—Gal·lo-Ro·mance** *adj.*

Gal·lo·way¹ (găl′ə-wā′) *n. Often* **galloway.** **1.** Any of a breed of hornless black cattle. **2.** Any of a breed of small hardy horses. [After GALLOWAY in Scotland, where they were originally bred.]

Gal·lo·way² (găl′ə-wā). Area in southwest Scotland. It comprises part of Dumfries and Galloway Region and part of Strathclyde.

gal·low·glass, gal·lo·glass (găl′ō-glăs′, -gläs′) *n.* Formerly, an armed retainer or mercenary in the service of an Irish chieftain. [Irish Gaelic *galloglach,* "foreign youth" : *gall,* foreigner + *oglach,* youth : *og,* young, from Old Irish *ōac* + *-lach,* abstract suffix.]

gal·lows (găl′ōz) *n., pl.* **gallows.** **1. a.** A device usually consisting of two upright beams supporting a crossbeam from which a noose is suspended and used for execution by hanging. Also called "gallows tree." **b.** A similar structure used for supporting or suspending; especially, in Australia, a frame on which slaughtered cattle are hoisted. **2.** Execution on a gallows or by hanging. [Middle English *galwes, galawis*, plural of *galwe*, gallows, cross, from Old English *gealga*.]

gallows bird *n. Informal.* One who deserves to be hanged.

gallows humor *n.* Humorous treatment of a situation that is actually frightening or very grave.

gall·stone (gôl'stōn') *n.* A small, hard pathological concretion of cholesterol, calcium salts, and bile pigments, formed in the gallbladder or in a bile duct.

Gal·lup (găl'əp), **George Horace** (1901–). U.S. statistician. Through his techniques of polling the public, he accurately predicted the result of the 1936 presidential election. Gallup polls have been used regularly ever since.

Gal·lup poll (găl'əp) *n.* A sampling of the views of a representative section of the population on a particular issue; especially, one taken to assess the relative popularity of different political parties or to forecast the outcome of an election.

gal·lus·es (găl'ə-sĭz) *pl.n. Informal.* Suspenders for trousers. [Plural of *gallus*, variant of GALLOWS (obsolete sense "braces").]

gall wasp *n.* Any of various wasps of the family Cynipidae that produce distinctively shaped galls on oaks and other plants.

ga·loot (gə-lōōt') *n. Slang.* A clumsy, uncouth, or stupid person. [19th century (nautical slang) : origin obscure.]

gal·op (găl'əp) *n.* Also **gal·o·pade, gal·lo·pade** (găl'ə-pād', -päd'). **1.** A lively dance in duple rhythm, popular in the 19th century. **2.** The music for this dance. [French, gallop, from Old French *galoper*, to GALLOP.]

ga·lore (gə-lôr', -lōr') *adj. Informal.* In great numbers; in abundance. Used after a noun: *dresses galore; opportunities galore.* [Irish Gaelic *go leór* : *go*, to, from Old Irish *co, cu†* + *leór*, sufficiency, enough, from Old Irish *lour*.]

ga·losh (gə-lŏsh') *n.* **1.** *Usually* **galoshes.** A waterproof overshoe. **2.** *Obsolete.* A sturdy heavy-soled boot or shoe. [Middle English *galoche*, from Old French, probably from Late Latin *gallicula*, diminutive of Latin *gallica (solea)*, "Gaulish (sandal)," from the feminine of *gallicus*, Gaulish, Gaelic, from *Galli*, Gauls.]

Gals·wor·thy (gôlz'wûr'thē), **John** (1867–1933). British novelist and playwright. He wrote the *The Forsyte Saga* (1906–21) and many other *Forsyte* novels and stories, and was awarded the Nobel Prize for literature (1932).

Gal·ton (gôl'tən), **Sir Francis** (1822–1911). British biologist. He showed that mental characteristics could be inherited and developed a method of identification by fingerprints.

ga·lumph (gə-lŭmpf', -lŭmf') *intr.v.* **-lumphed, -lumphing, -lumphs.** *Informal.* To move or jump about in a clumsy way. [19th century (coined by Lewis Carroll) : probably a blend of GALLOP + TRIUMPH.]

galv. galvanized.

Gal·va·ni (găl-vä'nē), **Luigi** (1737–98). Italian physician. His experiments making frogs' legs twitch led him to believe, erroneously, that electricity was a fluid in nerve tissue. He gave his name to galvanism, electricity generated by chemical means.

gal·van·ic (găl-văn'ĭk) *adj.* **1.** Of or pertaining to direct-current electricity, especially when produced chemically. **2.** Having the effect of or produced as if by an electric shock. [French *galvanique*, from *galvanisme*, GALVANISM.] —**gal·van·i·cal·ly** *adv.*

galvanic cell *n. Electricity.* A primary cell *(see).*

galvanic couple *n. Electricity.* A voltaic couple *(see).*

galvanic pile *n. Electricity.* A voltaic pile *(see).*

gal·va·nism (găl'və-nĭz'əm) *n.* **1.** Direct-current electricity, especially when produced chemically. Also called "voltaism." **2.** A form of medical treatment using direct-current electricity. [French *galvanisme*, from Italian *galvanismo*, first described by Luigi GALVANI.]

gal·va·nize (găl'və-nīz') *tr.v.* **-nized, -nizing, -nizes.** **1.** To stimulate or shock with an electric current. **2.** To arouse to awareness or action; spur. **3.** To coat (iron or steel) with rust-resistant zinc by spraying, immersion, or electrolytic deposition. —**gal·va·ni·za·tion** *n.* —**gal·va·niz·er** *n.*

gal·va·nom·e·ter (găl'və-nŏm'ə-tər) *n.* A device for detecting or measuring small electric currents by means of mechanical effects produced by the current to be measured. [GALVAN(ISM) + -METER.] —**gal·va·no·met·ric** (găl'və-nō-mĕt'rĭk), **gal·va·no·met·ri·cal** *adj.* —**gal·va·nom·e·try** (găl'və-nŏm'ə-trē) *n.*

gal·va·no·scope (găl'văn-ə-skōp', găl'və-nə-) *n.* A galvanometer used to detect the presence and direction of electric currents by the deflection of a magnetic needle. [GALVAN(ISM) + -SCOPE.] —**gal·va·no·scop·ic** (găl'văn'ə-skŏp'ĭk, găl'və-nə-) *adj.* —**gal·va·nos·co·py** (găl'və-nŏs'kə-pē) *n.*

Gal·ves·ton (găl'və-stən). A port city in southeastern Texas, on Galveston Island, at the entrance to Galveston Bay, an inlet of the Gulf of Mexico. The Spanish explorer Cabeza de Vaca may have been shipwrecked on the island in 1528. Settlement began in the 1830's. The city was damaged by hurricanes in 1900 and 1961.

Gal·way¹ (gôl'wā). County in Connacht in the west of the Republic of Ireland. The western section is mountainous; the eastern section is a rolling plain.

Galway². Fishing port and the county town of County Galway in the Republic of Ireland. Situated at the mouth of the Corrib River, it is a well-known salmon-fishing center.

Galway, James (1939–). Irish flutist. He has been lead flutist with the London Symphony and Royal Philharmonic orchestras.

gal·yak (găl'yăk') *n.* A flat, glossy fur made from the pelt of a stillborn lamb or kid. [Russian dialectal *galyak*, perhaps from Russian *golyĭ*, bald, naked.]

gam¹ (găm) *n.* **1.** A school or herd of whales. **2.** A social meeting, especially between whalers at sea. —*v.* **gammed, gamming, gams.** —*intr.* To come together socially, especially while at sea. —*tr.* To socialize with. [Perhaps short for GAMMON (deceptive talk).]

gam² *n. Slang.* A person's leg. [Probably from obsolete *gamb*, leg of an animal, from Old North French *gambe*, Late Latin *gamba*, hook, leg, from Greek *kampē*, a bend.]

Ga·ma (găm'ə, gä'mə), **Vasco da** (*c.* 1469–1524). Portuguese navigator. He discovered the sea route from Europe to India via the Cape of Good Hope (1497–98).

gam·a grass (găm'ə, gä'mə) *n.* A perennial grass, *Tripsacum dactyloides*, of southern North America, that is grown for fodder. [*Gama*, probably alteration of Spanish *grama*, from Latin *grāmen*, grass.]

ga·may (gă-mā', găm'ā') *n.* A variety of red grape used for making red wines, especially Beaujolais. [French, after *Gamay*, a hamlet in the wine-growing area of Beaune.]

gam·ba (găm'bə, găm'-) *n.* A viola da gamba *(see).* [Italian, leg, shortened from VIOLA DA GAMBA.]

gam·ba·do¹ (găm-bā'dō) *n., pl.* **-does** or **-dos.** Also **gam·bade** (-bād', -bäd'). **1.** In dressage, a low leap of a horse in which all four feet are off the ground. **2.** A leaping or gamboling movement. [Spanish *gambada*, from Italian *gambata*, GAMBOL.]

gambado² *n., pl.* **-does** or **-dos.** **1.** Either of a pair of protective leather gaiters attached to a saddle. **2.** A rider's legging or gaiter. [Italian *gamba*, leg (perhaps influenced by BASTINADO). See **gambol.**]

gam·be·son (găm'bə-sən, -zən) *n.* A sleeveless garment of leather or quilted material worn under armor in the Middle Ages. [Middle English *gambisoun*, from Old French *gambe(i)son*, from *gambais, wambais*, probably from Frankish *wamba* (unattested), belly, from Common Germanic *wambō* (unattested), WOMB.]

Gam·bet·ta (găm-bĕt'ə), **Léon** (1838–82). French politician. After the defeat of Napoleon III at the Battle of Sedan (1870), Gambetta helped set up the Third Republic, escaping from the siege of Paris by balloon. He virtually ruled France until its defeat by Germany (1871). He was premier (1881–82).

Gam·bi·a¹ (găm'bē-ə). River in West Africa. Rising in the Fouta Djallon Plateau of Guinea, it flows 1,126 kilometers (700 miles) through Senegambia to the Atlantic Ocean, and can take oceangoing vessels almost 320 kilometers (199 miles) inland.

Gambia². Africa's smallest independent state. Lying in West Africa, it comprises the lower valley of the Gambia River. It is primarily agricultural, peanuts being the mainstay of the economy. The Portuguese reached the Gambia region in 1456, and British merchants were granted trading rights in 1588. The area became a British protectorate in 1894 and an independent republic within the Commonwealth in 1970. In 1981 Gambia joined Senegal in the Confederation of Senegambia, which involves economic integration and cooperation in foreign policy. Area, 11,295 square kilometers (4,360 square miles). Population, 600,000. Capital, Banjul (formerly Bathurst). —**Gam·bi·an** *adj. & n.*

gam·bier, gam·bir (găm'bîr') *n.* A resinous, astringent extract obtained from a woody vine, *Uncaria gambier* (or *gambir*), of south-central Asia, used medicinally and in tanning and dyeing. [Malay *gambir*.]

gam·bit (găm'bĭt) *n.* **1.** A chess opening in which one or more pawns are offered in exchange for a favorable position. **2.** An opening remark or maneuver, as in a conversation or series of negotiations. [Earlier *gamet*, from Italian *gambetto*, "a tripping up," from *gamba*, leg. See **gambol.**]

gam·ble (găm'bəl) *v.* **-bled, -bling, -bles.** —*intr.* **1. a.** To bet money on the outcome of a game, contest, or other event. **b.** To play a game of chance for money or other stakes. **2.** To take a risk in the hope of gaining an advantage; speculate: *I gambled on his willingness to help me.* —*tr.* **1.** To put up in gambling; wager. **2.** To expose to hazard; risk. **3.** To lose by gambling: *gambled away their future.*
—*n.* **1.** A bet, wager, or other gambling venture. **2.** An act or undertaking of uncertain outcome; a risk. [Probably from earlier *gamel*, from *gamner*, gambler, from *gamene*, to gamble, Middle English *gamenen*, Old English *gamenian*, to sport, play, from *gamen*, amusement. See **game.**] —**gam·bler** *n.*

gam·boge (găm-bōj', -bōōzh') *n.* **1.** A brownish or orange resin obtained from any of several trees of the genus *Garcinia*, of south-central Asia, and yielding a golden-yellow pigment. Also called "cambogia." **2.** A strong yellow. [New Latin *gambogium, cambugium*, altered from CAMBODIA.] —**gam·boge** *adj.*

gam·bol (găm'bəl) *intr.v.* **-boled** or **-bolled, -boling** or **-bolling, -bols.** To leap about playfully; frolic; skip.
—*n.* A skipping or frolicking about. [Earlier *gamba(u)de*, from Old French *gambade*, from Italian *gambata*, from Late Latin *gamba*, hoof, leg, from Greek *kampē*, bend.]

gam·brel (găm'brəl) *n.* **1.** The hock of a horse or other animal. **2.** A wooden or metal frame used by butchers for hanging carcasses by the legs. [Old North French *gamberel*, diminutive of *gambier*, gambrel, from *gambe*, leg, from Late Latin *gamba*, hoof, leg.]

gambrel roof *n.* **1.** A ridged roof with two slopes on each side, the lower slope having the steeper pitch. **2.** *British.* A hipped roof that is topped by a small gable with vertical ends.

game¹ (gām) n. **1.** A way of amusing oneself; diversion: *Until she sold her first story, she thought of writing simply as a game.* **2. a.** A sport or other competitive activity governed by specific rules: *the game of tennis.* **b.** A single instance of such an activity: *We lost the first game.* **c. games.** A series of events, especially sporting events, for which competitors gather: *the Olympic Games.* **d.** The rules governing a game: *Her grandfather taught her the game.* **3. a.** The total number of points required to win a game: *One hundred points is game in bridge.* **b.** The score accumulated at any given time in a game: *At half time, the game was 14 to 12.* **4.** The equipment needed for playing certain games: *pack the children's games in the car.* **5.** A particular style or manner of playing a game: *His bridge game is only adequate.* **6. a.** A calculated plan or action for attaining an end: *The negotiators played a stalling game.* **b.** A scheme, especially one of dubious legality: *We saw through his game.* **7. a.** Wild animals, birds, or fish hunted for food or sport. Also used adjectivally: *game birds.* **b.** The flesh of game, eaten as food. **8. a.** Something hunted or fit to be hunted; quarry. **b.** An object of ridicule, teasing, or scorn: *His arrogance makes him fair game.* **9.** *Mathematics.* A set of rules defining an abstract model of a strategic competition. See **game theory. 10.** *Informal.* A vocation or business, especially a competitive one: *the publishing game.*
~v. **gamed, gaming, games.** —*tr. Archaic.* To waste or lose by gambling. —*intr.* To play for money or other stakes.
~*adj.* **gamer, gamest. 1.** Plucky and unyielding in spirit; resolute. **2.** *Informal.* Ready and willing: *Are you game for a swim?* —See Synonyms at **brave.** [Middle English *game(n),* Old English *gamen,* amusement, sport, from Common Germanic *gam-* (unattested), to enjoy.]

game² *adj.* **gamer, gamest.** Crippled; lame: *had a game leg.* [Perhaps from French *gambi†,* crooked.]

game·cock (gām′kŏk′) n. A rooster trained for cockfighting. Also called "fighting cock."

game fowl n. **1.** A bird sought after as game. **2.** Any of several breeds of domestic fowl bred especially for cockfighting.

game·keep·er (gām′kē′pər) n. A person employed to protect and maintain game birds and animals, especially on an estate or game preserve.

gam·e·lan (găm′ə-lăn′) n. A type of orchestra common in Southeast Asia, consisting mainly of tuned metal or wooden chimes and other percussion instruments. [Javanese.]

game laws *pl.n.* Regulations for the protection of game animals, including birds and fish, that define the hunting season for each species and place restrictions on the method of capture and on the number of animals that may be taken.

game·ly (gām′lē) *adv.* With pluck; courageously.

game·ness (gām′nĭs) n. Courage; pluck.

game plan n. **1.** A strategy devised for winning a game, as in football. **2.** A strategy for reaching an objective.

game point n. A state in a game, especially tennis, in which one side or player will win after gaining the next point.

game show n. A television show in which contestants vie for prizes, usually by playing a competitive game.

games·man·ship (gāmz′mən-shĭp′) n. The art or practice of winning a game or contest by methods that may be unsportsmanlike or devious but that do not actually break the rules.

game·some (gām′səm) *adj.* Frolicsome; playful; merry. —**game·some·ly** *adv.* —**game·some·ness** n.

game·ster (gām′stər) n. A habitual gambler.

gam·e·tan·gi·um (găm′ə-tăn′jē-əm) n., *pl.* **-gia** (-jē-ə). *Botany.* An organ or cell in which gametes are produced, especially in primitive plant forms. [GAMET(O)- + Greek *angeion,* vessel.] —**gam·e·tan·gi·al** *adj.*

gam·ete (găm′ēt′, gə-mēt′) n. A germ cell possessing the haploid number of chromosomes (half the number of chromosomes possessed by the somatic or body cells); especially, a mature sperm or egg capable of participating in fertilization. See **fertilization.** [New Latin *gameta,* from Greek *gametē,* wife, and *gametēs,* husband, both from *gamos,* marriage.]

game theory n. The mathematical analysis of abstract models of situations involving a conflict of interest with the object of determining the best strategy and anticipating the reactions of opponents. It has applications in linear programming, statistical decision making, operations research, and military and economic planning. Also called "theory of games."

gameto– *prefix.* Indicates gamete; for example, **gametophyte, gametophore.** [New Latin *gameta,* GAMETE.]

ga·me·to·cyte (gə-mē′tə-sīt′) n. A cell from which gametes develop by meiotic division; a spermatocyte or an oocyte. [GAMETO- + -CYTE.]

ga·me·to·gen·e·sis (gə-mē′tə-jĕn′ĭ-sĭs) n. Also **gam·e·tog·e·ny** (găm′ə-tŏj′ə-nē). The production of gametes. Also called "maturation." [GAMETO- + -GENESIS.] —**ga·me·to·gen·ic** (gə-mē′tə-jĕn′ĭk), **gam·e·tog·e·nous** (găm′ə-tŏj′ə-nəs) *adj.*

ga·me·to·phore (gə-mē′tə-fôr′, -fōr′) n. *Botany.* A structure, as in mosses, on which gametangia are borne. [GAMETO- + -PHORE.] —**ga·me·to·phor·ic** (gə-mē′tə-fôr′ĭk) *adj.*

ga·me·to·phyte (gə-mē′tə-fīt′) n. *Botany.* The generation or form that reproduces sexually in a plant characterized by alternation of generations. Compare **sporophyte.** [GAMETO- + -PHYTE.] —**ga·me·to·phyt·ic** (gə-mē′tə-fīt′ĭk) *adj.*

game warden n. One who looks after game, especially in a preserve or park.

gamey. Variant of **gamy.**

gam·ic (găm′ĭk) *adj.* Of or requiring fertilization in reproduction; sexual. [Greek *gamos,* marriage. See **gamete.**]

gam·i·ly (gā′mə-lē) *adv.* gamely.

gam·in (găm′ĭn) n. A boy who roams about the streets; urchin. [French, perhaps from German *Gammel,* loud rejoicing, (hence) ungainly young man, good-for-nothing, from Old High German *gaman,* amusement, game, from Common Germanic *gam-* (unattested), to enjoy.]

gam·ine (gă-mēn′) n. **1.** A girl who roams about the streets; urchin. **2.** An attractively boyish girl or young woman. [French, feminine of GAMIN.]

gam·ing (gā′mĭng) n. The playing of games of chance; gambling. Also used adjectivally: *the gaming laws; a gaming house.*

gam·ma (găm′ə) n. **1.** The third letter in the Greek alphabet, written γ. Transliterated in English as *g,* or as *n* before *g, k,* or *kh.* See feature at **alphabet. 2.** A gamma ray. [Greek *gamma,* from Semitic, akin to Hebrew *gīmel,* probably "camel."]

gam·ma·di·on (gə-mā′dē-ŏn′, -măd′ē-ŏn′) n., *pl.* **-dia** (-dē-ə). A cross composed of four capital Greek gammas, especially so as to form a swastika; a fylfot. [Medieval Greek, from Greek, from GAMMA.]

gamma globulin n. Any of several globulin fractions of blood serum, most of which are immunoglobulins, used to treat infectious diseases, as measles.

gamma iron n. An allotropic form of iron that exists between 910°C and 1400°C and is nonmagnetic.

gamma ray n. **1.** Electromagnetic radiation emitted by radioactive decay and having energies in a range overlapping that of the highest energy x-rays, extending up to several hundred thousand electron volts. **2.** Electromagnetic radiation with energy greater than several hundred thousand electron volts. **3.** A high-energy photon.

gam·mer (găm′ər) n. *Regional.* An elderly woman. [Probably contraction of GODMOTHER or GRANDMOTHER.]

gam·mon¹ (găm′ən) n. A victory in backgammon occurring before the loser has removed a single man.
~*tr.v.* **gammoned, -moning, -mons.** To defeat in backgammon by scoring a gammon. [Probably from Middle English *gamen,* GAME.]

gammon² n. *British Informal.* Misleading or nonsensical talk; blather.
~v. **gammoned, -moning, -mons.** *British Informal.* —*tr.* To mislead by deceptive talk. —*intr.* To talk gammon. [Perhaps from thieves' slang expressions *to give gammon, to keep in gammon,* to talk to and divert the attention of someone while another thief is robbing him, perhaps slang use of GAMMON (backgammon term).] —**gam·mon·er** n.

gammon³ n. **1.** A ham that has been cured or smoked. **2.** The lower or bottom part of a side of bacon. [Old North French *gambon,* from *gambe,* leg, from Late Latin *gamba,* hoof, leg, from Greek *kampē,* a bend.]

gammon⁴ *tr.v.* **-moned, -moning, -mons.** *Nautical.* To fasten (a bowsprit) to the stem of a ship. [Perhaps from GAMMON (cured ham, hence "the tying up of a ham").]

gam·my (găm′ē) *adj.* **-mier, -miest.** *British Slang.* Lame; injured: *a gammy leg.* [Dialectal variant of GAME (lame).]

gamo– *prefix.* Indicates: **1.** Sexual union; for example, **gamogenesis. 2.** Union or fusion; for example, **gamopetalous.** [Greek *gamos,* marriage.]

gam·o·gen·e·sis (găm′ə-jĕn′ə-sĭs) n. Sexual reproduction. [GAMO- + -GENESIS.] —**gam·o·ge·net·ic** (găm′ə-jə-nĕt′ĭk) *adj.* —**gam·o·ge·net·i·cal·ly** *adv.*

gam·o·pet·al·ous (găm′ə-pĕt′l-əs) *adj.* *Botany.* Having or designating a corolla with the petals fused or partially fused; sympetalous. [New Latin *gamopetalus* : GAMO- + PETALOUS.]

gam·o·phyl·lous (găm′ə-fĭl′əs) *adj.* *Botany.* Having or designating united leaves or leaflike parts. [GAMO- + -PHYLLOUS.]

gam·o·sep·al·ous (găm′ə-sĕp′ə-ləs) *adj.* *Botany.* Having the sepals united or partly united; synsepalous. [GAMO- + -SEPALOUS.]

–gamous *suffix.* Indicates marriage or sexual union; for example, **bigamous, dichogamous.** [Greek *gamos,* marriage.]

gamp (gămp) n. *British Informal.* A large, baggy umbrella. Used humorously. [After Mrs. Sarah *Gamp,* nurse in Charles Dickens's *Martin Chuzzlewit* (1844), who owns such an umbrella.]

gam·ut (găm′ət) n. **1.** A complete range; extent: *a face that expresses the gamut of emotion, from rage to peaceful contentment.* **2.** The entire series of recognized musical notes. [Middle English, contracted from Medieval Latin *gamma ut* : *gamma,* one tone lower than the first note in Guido d'Arezzo's scale, from the Greek letter GAMMA + *ut* (now *do*), lowest note in Guido's scale. (The notes of the scale are named after syllables in a Latin hymn to St. John: *Ut queant laxis resonāre fibris Mira gestorum famuli tuorum, Solve polluti labii reatum, Sancte Iohannes.*)]

gam·y, gam·ey (gā′mē) *adj.* **-ier, -iest. 1.** Having the flavor or odor of game, especially of game that has been hung too long. **2.** Showing an unyielding spirit; plucky; hardy: *a gamy little mare.* **3.** Scandalous; risqué. —**gam·i·ness** n.

–gamy *suffix.* Indicates marriage or sexual union; for example, **allogamy.** [Greek *-gamia,* from *gamos,* marriage.]

gan (găn) *intr.v.* **ganned, ganning, gans.** *British Regional.* To go. [Old English *gangan;* see **gang** (group).]

Gand. See **Ghent.**

---

gan·der (găn′dər) *n.* **1.** A male goose. **2.** *Informal.* A simpleton; a halfwit. **3.** *Slang.* A quick look; a glance. [Middle English *gander*, Old English *gandra, ganra*.]

Gan·der (găn′dər). A town in northeastern Newfoundland, Canada. It has grown around Gander Airport, one of the world's largest air terminals, whose air-traffic controllers take over North America-bound aircraft from Europe in mid-Atlantic.

Gan·dhi (găn′dē, gän′-), **Indira** (1917-84). Indian politician. She followed her father, Jawaharlal Nehru, India's first prime minister, into politics and became prime minister in 1966. In 1975 she declared a state emergency following allegations of repression and corruption, and was defeated in the 1977 election. She was re-elected in 1980 but was assassinated in 1984.

Gandhi, Mohandas Karamchand, known as "Mahatma" (1869-1948). Indian politician. He went to South Africa in 1893 to defend the Asian community there and developed his policy of Satyagraha, passive resistance. He returned to India in 1914 and became leader of the home rule movement. The British frequently imprisoned him for acts of civil disobedience. Independence was achieved in 1947, and Gandhi won worldwide respect for the bloodless way his aims had been achieved. He was murdered by a fanatic for his commitment to Hindu-Muslim reconciliation. **—Gan·dhi·an** *adj.*

Gandhi, Rajiv (1945-). Indian politician, prime minister (1984-). The son of Indira Gandhi, he played no part in politics until the death of his brother Sanjay in 1981. He became general secretary of the Congress (I) Party in 1983, and after Mrs. Gandhi's assassination the following year he was sworn in as prime minister. He called for a general election, which he won by a landslide majority.

gan·dy dancer (găn′dē) *n. Slang.* **1.** A railroad worker. **2.** An itinerant laborer. [From the rhythmic movements of the railroad laborer working with tools produced by the now defunct *Gandy Manufacturing Company* in Chicago.]

ga·nef, go·nef (gä′nəf) *n.* A thief, scoundrel, or rascal. [Yiddish *ganef, gannef*, from Hebrew *gannābh*, from *gānnabh*, he stole.]

gang¹ (găng) *n.* **1.** A group of people who associate regularly on a social basis. **2.** A group of criminals, juvenile delinquents, or hoodlums who band together for mutual protection and profit. **3.** A group of laborers organized together on one job or under one foreman: *a railroad gang.* **4.** A set, especially of matched tools: *a gang of chisels.* **5. a.** A herd, especially of buffalo or elk. **b.** A pack of wolves or wild dogs.
~*v.* **ganged, ganging, gangs.** —*intr.* To band together as a group or gang. —*tr.* **1.** To group together into a gang. **2.** *Electronics.* To arrange (two or more components) so that they can be varied by a single control. **—gang up.** *Informal.* **1.** To make an attack as a group: *ganged up on him and thrashed him soundly.* **2.** To act together as a group: *Countries should gang up against terrorism.* [Originally "a going," "journey," "way," Middle English *gang*, Old English *gang*, from Germanic.]

gang² *intr.v.* **ganged, ganging, gangs.** *Scottish.* To go. [Old English *gangan*; see **gang** (group).]

gang·bust·er (găng′bŭs′tər) *n. Slang.* A law officer who fights to break up organized criminal groups. **—like gangbusters.** *Slang.* With great force or zeal.

gang·er (găng′ər) *n. Chiefly British.* A gang foreman.

Gan·ges (găn′jēz′). *Hindi* **Gan·ga** (gŭng′gä). River of India and Bangladesh. It flows 2,505 kilometers (1,557 miles) from the Himalayas to the Bay of Bengal and has the largest delta in the world. It is the Hindus' most sacred river.

gang hook *n.* A multiple fishhook consisting of two or more hooks joined shank to shank. [From GANG (set of tools).]

gang·land (găng′lănd′) *n. Informal.* The criminal underworld.

gan·gli·at·ed (găng′glē-ā′tĭd) *adj.* Also **gan·gli·ate** (-ĭt, -āt′). Having ganglia.

gan·gling (găng′glĭng) *adj.* Also **gang·ly** (-glē), **-lier, -liest.** Tall, thin, and ungraceful; rangy. [Irregularly from dialectal *gang*, to go, from, Middle English *gangen*, from Old English *gangan*.]

gan·gli·on (găng′glē-ən) *n., pl.* **-glia** (-glē-ə) or **-ons.** **1.** *Anatomy.* A group of nerve cell bodies, such as one located outside the brain or spinal cord. **2.** A center of power, activity, or energy. **3.** *Pathology.* A harmless cystic lesion resembling a tumor, occurring in a tendon sheath or joint capsule. [Greek *ganglion*, cystlike tumor, hence nerve bundle, ganglion.] **—gan·gli·on·ic** (găng′glē-ŏn′ĭk) *adj.*

gang·plank (găng′plăngk′) *n.* A board or ramp used as a removable footway between a ship and a pier. [GANG (in obsolete sense "passage") + PLANK.]

gang·plow (găng′plou′) *n.* A plow equipped with several blades that make parallel furrows. [GANG (set of tools) + PLOW.]

gan·grel (găng′grəl) *n. British Regional.* A vagabond; a drifter. [Middle English, from *gangen*, to go, Old English *gangan*.]

gan·grene (găng′grēn′, găng-grēn′) *n.* **1.** Death and decay of tissue in a part of the body, usually a limb, due to failure of blood supply, injury, or disease. Compare **necrobiosis.** **2. a.** Moral decay. **b.** Something causing or symptomatic of moral decay.
~*v.* **gangrened, -grening, -grenes.** —*tr.* To affect with gangrene. —*intr.* To become affected with gangrene. [Old French *gangrine*, from Latin *gangraena*, from Greek *gangraina*.] **—gan·gre·nous** (găng′grə-nəs) *adj.*

gang saw *n.* A saw in which a group of blades fitted in a frame make parallel simultaneous cuts.

gang·ster (găng′stər) *n.* A member of an organized group of criminals; a racketeer. [GANG + -STER.]

gangue (găng) *n.* The worthless rock or other material in which valuable minerals are found. [French, from German *Gang*, course, lode, vein, from Old High German, a going.]

gang·way (găng′wā′) *n.* **1.** *Nautical.* **a.** A passage along either side of a ship's upper deck. **b.** A gangplank. **c.** An opening in the bulwark of a ship through which passengers may board. **2.** *British.* **a.** The aisle that runs lengthwise and divides the seating sections of the House of Commons, separating the front and back benches. **b.** An aisle between seating sections, as in a theater. **3.** *Mining.* The main level of a mine.
~*interj.* Used to clear a passage through a crowd or obstructed area. [GANG (in obsolete sense "passage") + WAY.]

gan·is·ter, gan·nis·ter (găn′ə-stər) *n.* **1.** A silicon-rich sedimentary rock used for refractory furnace linings. **2.** A mixture of fire clay and ground quartz used to line furnaces. [Origin unknown.]

gan·ja (găn′jə, gän′-) *n.* A highly resinous form of marijuana, prepared by collecting only the flowering tops and leaves of carefully selected and cultivated plants. [Hindi *gānjhā*, from Sanskrit *grñja.*]

gan·net (găn′ĭt) *n.* Any of several large sea birds of the genus *Morus*; especially, *M. bassanus*, of northern coastal regions, having white plumage with black wing tips and a yellow crown. [Middle English *ganat, ganett*, Old English *ganot.*]

gan·oid (găn′oid′) *adj.* Of, pertaining to, or characteristic of certain bony fishes, such as the sturgeon and the gar, having armorlike scales consisting of bony plates covered with layers of dentine and enamel.
~*n.* A ganoid fish. [New Latin *Ganoidei* (former designation), from French *ganoïde*, having a shiny surface : Greek *ganos*, brightness, joy, from *ganusthai*, to rejoice.]

gansey. Variant of **ganzie.**

Gan·su or **Kan·su** (găn′sōō′). Province in north-central China. Much of its population is Muslim. Its capital is Lanzhou (Lanchow).

gannet *An adult gannet reaches maturity in its third year, when its plumage is all white except for black wing tips and a buff-colored head. It has a wingspan of up to 1.8 meters (6 feet).*

gant·let¹, gaunt·let (gônt′lĭt, gŏnt′-, gănt′-) *n.* A section of double railroad tracks where the two inner tracks are overlapped in order to afford passage at a narrow place without switching.
~*tr.v.* **gantleted, -leting, -lets.** To overlap (railroad tracks) to form a gantlet. [Alteration (influenced by GAUNTLET) of earlier *gant(e)-lope*, from Swedish *gatlopp*, from Old Swedish *gatulop*, "passageway" : *gata*, road, way + *lop*, course.]

gant·let². **1.** Variant of **gauntlet** (glove). **2.** Variant of **gauntlet** (ordeal).

gant·line (gănt′lĭn′, -lĭn) *n.* A rope passed through a single block at the top of a mast or stackpole and used for hoisting. [Perhaps alteration of *girtline* : GIRT (girdle) + LINE.]

gan·try (găn′trē) *n., pl.* **-tries.** **1.** A bridgelike frame over which a traveling crane moves. **2.** A similar spanning frame supporting a group of railroad signals over several tracks. **3.** *Aerospace.* A massive vertical structure used in assembling or servicing rockets. **4.** A support for a barrel lying on its side. [Probably dialectal variant of *gallon-tree.*]

Gan·y·mede¹ (găn′ə-mēd′). *Greek Mythology.* A Trojan prince of great beauty whom Zeus carried away to be cupbearer to the gods.

Ganymede² *n. Astronomy.* The third moon of Jupiter, one of the largest planetary satellites in the solar system. [After GANYMEDE.]

gan·zie, gan·sey (găn′zē) *n. Northern British.* A knitted woolen pullover. [Alteration of GUERNSEY (pullover).]

gaol. *Chiefly British.* Variant of **jail.**

gap (găp) *n.* **1.** An opening, as in a partition or wall; cleft. **2.** A break in a mountain range; a pass or gorge. **3.** A suspension of continuity; hiatus: *a gap in his report.* **4.** A conspicuous difference; disparity: *a gap between expenses and receipts.* **5.** *Electricity.* A space traversed by an electric spark; spark gap. **6.** *Computer Science.* An absence of information on a recording medium, often used to signal the end of a segment of information. **7.** *Electronics.* The distance between the head of a recording device and the surface of the recording medium.
~*v.* **gapped, gapping, gaps.** —*tr.* To make a gap in. —*intr.* To be or become open. [Middle English *gap(pe)*, from Old Norse *gap*, chasm.]

gape (gāp, găp) *intr.v.* **gaped, gaping, gapes.** **1.** To open the mouth wide; yawn. **2.** To stare wonderingly, as with the mouth open. **3.** To become widely open or separated: *The curtains gaped when the wind blew.* **—See Synonyms at gaze.**
~*n.* **1.** An act or instance of gaping. **2.** A large opening. **3.** *Zoology.* The width of the space between the open jaws or mandibles of a vertebrate. **4.** **gapes.** *Used with a singular verb.* A disease of birds, especially young domesticated poultry, caused by gapeworms and resulting in obstructed breathing. **5. gapes.** A fit of yawning. [Middle English *gapen*, Old Norse *gapa*, to open the mouth.]

gap·er (gā′pər) *n.* Any of various marine bivalve mollusks of the genera *Lutraria* and *Mya*, having oval shells that gape at both ends; especially, the **soft-shell clam** (see).

gape·worm (gāp′wûrm′, găp′-) *n.* Any of several nematode worms of the genus *Syngamus*; especially, *S. trachea*, infecting the trachea of certain birds and causing gapes.

gap·ing (gā′pĭng) *adj.* Deep and wide open; cavernous: *a gaping wound.* **—gap·ing·ly** *adv.*

gap-toothed (găp′tōōtht′, -tōōthd′) *adj.* Having wide gaps between the teeth.

gap·y (gā′pē) *adj.* Afflicted with the gapes, as a bird.

gar¹ (gär) *n.* **1.** Any of several ganoid fishes of the genus *Lepisosteus*, of fresh and brackish waters of North and Central America, having

garganey *During courtship the male garganey throws back its head in a characteristic display. Garganeys migrate 5,000 kilometers (3,000 miles) from Africa to Europe to breed. They feed as they swim, dipping their heads underwater.*

gargoyle *This grotesque figure peers down from the roof of a church at Thaxted, England.*

PRONUNCIATION KEY

ă, pat; **ā**, pay; **âr**, care;
ä, father, are; **b**, bib;
ch, church; **d**, deed; **ĕ**, pet;
ē, be; **f**, fife; **g**, gag; **h**, hat;
hw, which; **ĭ**, pit; **ī**, pie;
îr, pier; **j**, judge; **k**, kick;
l, lid, needle; **m**, mum;
n, no, sudden; **ng**, thing;
ŏ, pot; **ō**, toe; **ô**, paw, for;
oi, noise; **ou**, out; **o͝o**, book;
o͞o, boot; **p**, pop; **r**, roar;
s, sauce; **sh**, ship, dish;
t, tight; **th**, thin, path;
th, this, bathe; **ŭ**, cut; **ûr**, fur;
v, valve; **w**, with; **y**, yes;
z, zebra, size; **zh**, vision;
ə, about, item, edible, gallop, circus, peaceful

IN FOREIGN WORDS:

à, *Fr.* ami; **œ**, *Fr.* feu, *Ger.* schön; **ü**, *Fr.* tu, *Ger.* über; **KH**, *Ger.* ich, *Scot.* loch; **N**, *Fr.* bon; **y'**, *Fr.* Compiègne

STRESS MARKS:

Primary stress: ′
in·cite′ (ĭn-sīt′)
Secondary stress: ′
in′sight′ (ĭn′sīt′)

an elongated body and a long snout. **2.** A similar or related fish, such as the needlefish. Also called "garfish," "garpike." [Short for GARFISH.]

gar² *tr.v.* **garred, garring, gars.** *Chiefly Scottish.* To cause or compel. [Middle English *gere,* from Old Norse *gera,* to make, do.]

ga·rage (gə-räzh′, -räj′) *n.* **1.** A building or wing of a building, as of a house, in which to park a car or cars. **2.** A commercial establishment where cars are repaired, serviced, or parked.
—*tr.v.* **garaged, -raging, -rages.** To put or store in a garage. [French, from *garer,* to dock (ships), store in a garage, from Old French, to warn, protect, guard, from Frankish *warōn* (unattested).]

garage sale *n.* A sale of used household items or clothing held at the home of the seller. Also called "tag sale."

ga·ram ma·sa·la (gä′rəm mä-sä′lə) *n.* A mixture of spices used in Indian cooking.

garb (gärb) *n.* **1.** Clothing, especially if distinctive or unusual: *clerical garb.* **2.** An outward appearance; guise.
—*tr.v.* **garbed, garbing, garbs.** To cover with or as if with clothing; dress; array. [Obsolete French *garbe,* graceful appearance, from Italian *garbo,* grace, elegance of dress, from Germanic.]

gar·bage (gär′bĭj) *n.* **1. a.** Food wastes, as from a kitchen. **b.** Refuse. **2.** Worthless matter; trash; rubbish: *rhetorical garbage.* **3.** *Computer Science.* Unwanted or incorrect information in a device's input, output, or storage. [Middle English, probably from Norman French *garbelage,* removal of discarded matter.]

gar·ban·zo (gär-bän′zō, -băn′zō) *n., pl.* **-zos.** A plant, the **chickpea** *(see),* or its edible seed. [Spanish *garbanzo,* alteration (influenced by *garroba,* carob) of Old Spanish *arvanço,* from Germanic, akin to Old High German *araweiz,* pea, Latin *ervum,* bitter vetch, probably of Asiatic origin.]

gar·ble (gär′bəl) *tr.v.* **-bled, -bling, -bles. 1.** To unintentionally distort or confuse (an account or message) so that it becomes unintelligible. **2.** To deliberately distort (an account or message), especially by the selective omission of relevant data. **3.** *Archaic.* To sort out; cull.
—*n.* The act or an instance of garbling. [Middle English *garbelen,* to sift, select, from Italian *garbellare,* from Arabic *gharbala,* from *ghirbāl,* sieve, from Late Latin *crībellāre,* to sift, from *crībellum,* diminutive of *crībrum,* sieve.] —**gar·bler** *n.*

gar·bo (gär′bō) *n., pl.* **-bos.** *Australian Informal.* A person employed to remove trash. [From *garbage.*]

Gar·bo (gär′bō), **Greta,** born Greta Gustavson or Gustaffson (1905–). Swedish-born U.S. actress. She became a Hollywood star in 1926 but kept herself aloof and mysterious, retiring suddenly in 1941. Her films include *Queen Christina* (1933) and *Camille* (1936). She received a special Academy Award (1954).

gar·board (gär′bôrd′, -bōrd′) *n. Nautical.* The first range or strake of planks laid next to the ship's keel. [Obsolete Dutch *gaarboord* : perhaps *garen,* to gather, contraction of Middle Dutch *gaderen* + Dutch *boord,* border, ship's side, from Middle Dutch *bort,* board.]

gar·boil (gär′boil′) *n. Archaic.* Confusion; uproar. [Old French *garbouil(le),* from Old Italian *garbuglio,* reduplicative formation (with *gar-* for *bar-*) from Latin *bullīre,* to boil, bubble.]

García Lorca, Federico. See **Lorca.**

Garcia Márquez, Gabriel. See **Márquez.**

Gar·ci·la·so de la Ve·ga (gär-sē-lä′sô dā lä vā′gə) (1503–36). Spanish poet and soldier. The first and most influential major poet in the Golden Age of Spanish literature, he incorporated Italian meter into his poetry, a small but highly acclaimed body of work. At the age of 33, he was fatally wounded in battle.

gar·çon (gär-sôN′) *n., pl.* **-çons** (-sôN′). A waiter, especially in a French restaurant. [French, from old French *garçun,* servant.]

Gar·da, Lake (gär′də). Lake in northern Italy, the largest in the country. The sheltering Alps to the north and the mitigating effects of the lake give its shores an unusually temperate climate.

gar·den (gärd′n) *n.* **1.** A plot of land, often adjoining a house, used for the cultivation of grass, flowers, vegetables, or fruit. **2.** *Often* **gardens.** Grounds adorned with flowers, shrubs, and trees for public enjoyment. **3.** An open-air business establishment where refreshments are served: *a tea garden.* **4.** A fertile, well-cultivated region: *California is the garden of the United States.* —**lead someone up the garden path.** *Informal.* To mislead.
—*v.* **gardened, -dening, -dens.** —*tr.* To cultivate (a plot of ground) as a garden. —*intr.* **1.** To tend a garden. **2.** To work as a gardener.
—*adj.* **1.** Of, pertaining to, intended for, or found in a garden: *garden flowers.* **2.** Surrounded by gardens; provided with open areas and greenery: *a garden community.* **3.** Of, pertaining to, or being an apartment situated on the ground floor of a building and usually having access to a garden. [Middle English *gardyn,* from Old North French *gardin,* from Vulgar Latin *(hortus) gardīnus* (unattested), "enclosed (garden)," from *gardo* (unattested), fence, enclosure, from Frankish *gardo* (unattested).]

garden center *n.* A place where trees, plants, gardening tools, garden furniture, and similar items are sold.

garden city *n.* A town of limited size planned so as to provide a pleasant nonurban environment, with low-density housing and plenty of trees and open space.

garden cress *n.* A pungent-tasting plant, *Lepidium sativum,* that has fragrant white or pinkish flowers and is cultivated for use in salads.

gar·den·er (gärd′nər, gärd′n-ər) *n.* A person who works in or tends a garden for pleasure or profit.

garden heliotrope *n.* A widely cultivated species of valerian, *Valeriana officinalis,* having clusters of small purplish, pink, or white flowers.

gar·de·nia (gär-dēn′yə, -dē′nē-ə) *n.* **1.** Any of various shrubs and trees of the genus *Gardenia;* especially, *G. jasminoides,* native to China, having glossy, evergreen leaves and large, fragrant, usually white waxy flowers. This species is also called "Cape jasmine." **2.** The flower of this shrub. [New Latin *Gardenia,* after Dr. Alexander *Garden* (*c.* 1730–91), Scottish-born naturalist.]

gar·den·ing (gärd′nĭng, gärd′n-ĭng) *n.* The work or occupation of tending a garden or cultivating plants.

Garden of Eden *n.* **Eden** *(see).*

garden party *n.* A social gathering held on a lawn, at which refreshments are served.

garden suburb *n.* A planned, low-density residential suburb with gardens and community facilities.

garde·robe (gärd′rōb′) *n. Archaic.* **1. a.** A chamber for storing clothes; a wardrobe. **b.** The contents of a wardrobe. **2.** Any private chamber. [Middle English, from Old French : *garder, guarder,* to GUARD + *robe,* ROBE.]

Gard·ner (gärd′nər), **Erle Stanley** (1889–1970). U.S. author. While working as a lawyer in California, he began writing magazine detective stories, then full-length books. Most of them featured a wily attorney, Perry Mason, his secretary, Della Street, and adroit legal maneuvering to unmask the murderers.

Gar·field (gär′fēld′), **James Abram** (1831–81). 20th U.S. president (1881). After serving as a Civil War officer and as a U.S. congressman (1863–80), he won the controversial Republican nomination and the presidential election of 1880. On July 2, 1881, five months into his term, he was mortally wounded by Charles Guiteau (1841–82), a frustrated office seeker. Garfield died 11 weeks later.

gar·fish (gär′fĭsh′) *n., pl.* **-fishes** or collectively **garfish.** Either of two fishes, the **gar** or the **garpike** *(both of which see).* [Middle English *garfyssh,* probably "spear fish" : *gare, gore,* spear, Old English *gār* + FISH.]

gar·ga·ney (gär′gə-nē) *n., pl.* **-neys** or collectively **garganey.** An Old World duck, *Anas querquedula,* having a conspicuous white stripe over each eye and down the back of the head in the male. Also called "garganey teal." [Italian dialectal *gargenei* (imitative).]

Gar·gan·tu·a (gär-găn′cho͞o-ə). A giant king noted for his enormous physical and intellectual appetites, the hero of Rabelais' satires *Gargantua* and *Pantagruel.*

gar·gan·tu·an (gär-găn′cho͞o-ən) *adj. Often* **Gargantuan.** Of immense size or volume; gigantic; colossal; huge. —See Synonyms at **enormous.**

gar·get (gär′gĭt) *n.* Mastitis of domestic animals, especially cattle. [Perhaps specialized use of Middle English *garget, gargat,* throat; from Old French *garguette, gargate,* from Old Provençal *gargata,* probably from Latin *gurges,* throat.]

gar·gle (gär′gəl) *v.* **-gled, -gling, -gles.** —*intr.* **1.** To force exhaled air through a liquid held in the back of the mouth, with the head tilted back, in order to cleanse or medicate the mouth or throat. **2.** To produce the characteristic sound of gargling. —*tr.* **1.** To rinse or medicate (the mouth or throat) by gargling. **2.** To circulate or apply (a solution or medicine) by gargling. **3.** To utter with a gargling sound.
—*n.* **1.** A medicated solution for gargling. **2.** An act of gargling. **3.** A gargling sound. [Old French *gargouiller,* from *gargouille, garoule,* throat, GARGOYLE.]

gar·goyle (gär′goil′) *n.* **1.** A roof spout carved to represent a grotesque human or animal figure, and projecting from a gutter to carry rainwater clear of the wall. **2.** Any grotesque ornamental figure or projection. **3.** A person of grotesque appearance. [Middle English *gargoyl,* from Old French *gargouille, gargoul,* "throat," from Latin *gurguliō,* windpipe.]

gar·i·bal·di (găr′ə-bôl′dē) *n.* **1.** A loose high-necked blouse styled after the red shirts of Garibaldi and his soldiers, fashionable among women in the mid-19th century. **2.** *British.* A type of cooky containing a layer of currants.

Ga·ri·bal·di (găr′ə-bôl′dē), **Giuseppe** (1807–82). Italian soldier and nationalist leader. He and his 1,000 volunteers, the Redshirts, captured Sicily and Naples (1860) to add to the kingdom of Italy.

gar·ish (gâr′ĭsh, găr′-) *adj.* **1. a.** Marred by strident color or excessive ornamentation; gaudy; tawdry. **b.** Loud and flashy: *garish make-up.* **2.** Glaring; dazzling: *"Hide me from Day's garish eye"* (Milton). [Formerly also *gaurish,* perhaps from obsolete *gaur,* to stare, Middle English *gauren*†.] —**gar·ish·ly** *adv.* —**gar·ish·ness** *n.*

gar·land (gär′lənd) *n.* **1.** A wreath, circlet, or festoon of flowers, leaves, or other material worn as a crown or collar, or hung as an ornament. **2.** A representation of a garland in metal or other material, for ornamentation or as a heraldic device. **3.** Something resembling a garland. **4.** A mark of victory or distinction; a prize. **5.** *Nautical.* A ring or collar of rope or wire used to hoist spars or prevent rubbing or fraying. **6.** An anthology, as of ballads or poems.
—*tr.v.* **garlanded, -landing, -lands. 1.** To embellish or deck with a garland. **2.** To serve as a garland for. [Middle English *gerlond, garland,* from Old French *gerlande, garlande,* "ornament made with gold threads," from Frankish *wiara, weara* (unattested), wire, thread.]

Gar·land (gär′lənd), **(Hannibal) Hamlin** (1860–1940). U.S. author. He spent most of his life in the farming country of the Middle West and used the harsh realities of the farmers' lives as the inspiration for his stories and novels. Garland is best known for his autobiographical work *Son of the Middle Border* (1917).

Garland, Judy, born Frances Gumm (1922–69). U.S. singer and actress. She made her stage debut at five and starred in *The Wizard of Oz* (1939). In 1939 she received a special Academy Award.

gar·lic (gär′lĭk) *n.* **1.** A plant, *Allium sativum,* related to the onion, having a bulb with a strong, distinctive odor and flavor. **2.** The bulb of this plant, divisible into separate cloves and used as a flavoring. [Middle English *garlec, garly,* Old English *gārlēac,* "spear leek" (from its spear-shaped leaves) : *gār,* spear + *lēac,* leek.]

gar·lick·y (gär′lĭ-kē) *adj.* Containing, tasting of, or smelling of garlic.

garlic mustard *n.* A weedy plant, *Alliaria officinalis* (or *petiolata*), native to Europe, having small white flowers and an odor of garlic. Also called "hedge mustard."

gar·ment (gär′mənt) *n.* Any article of clothing.
~*tr.v.* **garmented, -menting, -ments.** To clothe; to dress. Usually used in the passive. [Middle English *gar(ne)ment,* from Old French *garnement,* "equipment," from *g(u)arnir,* to furnish, equip.]

garn (gärn) *interj. British Informal.* Used to express derision or disbelief. [Cockney pronunciation spelling of *go on.*]

gar·ner (gär′nər) *tr.v.* **-nered, -nering, -ners. 1.** To gather and store in or as if in a granary. **2.** To amass; acquire.
~*n.* A granary. [Middle English *gerner, garner,* granary, from Old French *gernier, grenier,* from Latin *grānārium,* from *grānum,* grain.]

gar·net[1] (gär′nĭt) *n.* **1.** Any of several widespread silicate minerals, often embedded in igneous and metamorphic rocks, colored red, brown, black, green, yellow, or white and used both as gemstones and as abrasives. **2.** A dark to very dark red. [Middle English *gernet, granate,* from Old French *grenat,* dark red, garnet, pomegranate-colored, from *pome grenate,* POMEGRANATE.]

garnet[2] *n. Nautical.* A tackle for hoisting light cargo. [Middle English *garnett,* probably from Middle Dutch *garnaat, karnaat*†.]

gar·ni·er·ite (gär′nē-ə-rīt′) *n.* A mineral, $(Ni,Mg)_6(OH)_8Si_4O_8 \cdot H_2O$, apple-green in color and an important nickel ore. [Discovered by Jules *Garnier* (died 1904), French geologist.]

gar·nish (gär′nĭsh) *tr.v.* **-nished, -nishing, -nishes. 1.** To enhance the appearance of by adding decorative touches; especially, to embellish (food) by decorating it, as with a sprig of parsley or a slice of lemon. **2.** *Law.* To garnishee.
~*n.* **1. a.** Ornamentation; embellishment. **b.** Something used to garnish food. **2.** An unwarranted fee, as one formerly extorted from a new prisoner in an English jail by a jailer. [Middle English *garnysshen,* to equip, adorn, from Old French *guarnir, garnir* (present stem *garniss-*), from Germanic.] **—gar·nish·er** *n.*

gar·nish·ee (gär′nĭ-shē′) *n. Law.* **1.** A debtor against whom a plaintiff has instituted a process of garnishment. **2.** A third party who has been warned that money or property in his control but due or belonging to the defendant has been attached.
~*tr.v.* **garnisheed, -eeing, -ees.** *Law.* **1.** To attach (a debtor's pay, for example) by garnishment. **2.** To serve with a garnishment.

gar·nish·ment (gär′nĭsh-mənt) *n.* **1.** Ornamentation; embellishment. **2.** *Law.* **a.** A legal proceeding whereby money or property due or belonging to a debtor but currently in the possession of a third party, such as a trustee, is applied to the payment of the debt to the plaintiff. **b.** A court order directing a third party who owes a defendant money or holds property belonging to him, to withhold such money or property. Also called "trustee process."

gar·ni·ture (gär′nĭ-chər) *n.* Something that garnishes or decorates; embellishment. [Old French *garniture, garneture,* from *garnir,* to GARNISH.]

Ga·ronne (gä-rôn′). River of southwest France. It rises in the Spanish Pyrenees and flows 503 kilometers (312 miles) through Toulouse and Bordeaux to the Gironde estuary. Its main tributaries are the Lot, Tarn, and Ariège.

gar·pike (gär′pīk′) *n.* **1.** A fish, the **gar** *(see).* **2.** A marine fish, *Belone belone,* of European waters, having long toothed jaws and green bones. Also called "garfish."

gar·ret (găr′ĭt) *n.* A room on the top floor of a house, typically immediately under a pitched roof; an attic. [Middle English *garet(te),* turret, watchtower, from Old French *garite,* from *g(u)arir,* to defend, protect, from Germanic.]

gar·ret·eer (găr′ə-tîr′) *n.* A person who lives in a garret, especially a struggling artist.

Gar·rick (găr′ĭk), **David** (1717–79). English actor and theater manager. He was considered the foremost Shakespearean actor of his time.

gar·ri·son (găr′ĭ-sən) *n.* **1.** A military post, especially one permanently established. **2.** The troops stationed at such a post.
~*tr.v.* **garrisoned, -soning, -sons. 1.** To assign (troops) to a military post. **2.** To supply (a post) with troops. **3.** To occupy as or convert into a garrison. [Middle English *gariso(u)n,* protection, fortress, from Old French *garison,* from *g(u)arir,* to protect, from Germanic.]

Gar·ri·son (găr′ĭ-sən), **William Lloyd** (1805–79). U.S. abolitionist. On January 1, 1831, he published the first issue of his militant weekly *The Liberator,* which he continued publishing until the passage of the Thirteenth Amendment in 1865. Garrison was best known for his fiery polemics and his demand, "I will be heard."

garrison cap *n.* A soft cloth cap without a visor, worn as a dress headgear chiefly by Army and Air Force personnel. Also called "overseas cap."

gar·rote, gar·rotte (gə-rŏt′, -rōt′) *n.* **1. a.** A former Spanish method of execution by strangulation or by breaking the neck with an iron collar screwed tight with a knoblike device. **b.** A collar used for this. **2.** Strangulation, especially in order to rob.
~*tr.v.* **garroted** or **garrotted, -roting** or **-rotting, -rotes** or **rottes. 1.** To execute by garrote. **2.** To strangle or throttle, especially in order to rob. [Spanish, cudgel, probably from Old French *garrot,* earlier *guaroc,* club turning rod, from *garokier*†, to bend down, strangle.] **—gar·rot·er** *n.*

gar·ru·li·ty (gə-rōō′lə-tē) *n.* Talkativeness; chattiness: *"Its style is relaxed to the point of garrulity"* (Dwight Macdonald).

gar·ru·lous (găr′ə-ləs, găr′yə-) *adj.* **1.** Habitually talkative; loquacious. **2.** Wordy; prolix. —See Synonyms at **talkative.** [Latin *garrulus,* from *garrīre,* to chatter.] **—gar·ru·lous·ly** *adv.* **—gar·ru·lous·ness** *n.*

gar·ry·a (găr′ē-ə) *n.* Any evergreen shrub of the American genus *Garrya,* some species of which have long catkins and are grown for ornament. [New Latin, after Nicholas *Garry,* 19th-century English official of the Hudson's Bay Company.]

gar·ter (gär′tər) *n.* **1. a.** An elasticized band worn around the leg to support a sock or stocking. **b.** A suspender strap with a fastener attached to a girdle or belt for supporting hose. **c.** An elasticized band worn around the arm to keep the sleeve pushed up. **2. Garter. a.** The **Order of the Garter** *(see).* **b.** The badge of this order. **c.** Membership in this order.
~*tr.v.* **gartered, -tering, -ters. 1.** To fasten and hold with a garter. **2.** To put a garter upon. [Middle English *garter, garder,* from Old North French *gartier,* from *garet,* bend of the knee, from Gaulish *garr-* (unattested), leg.]

garter belt *n.* An undergarment for women consisting of an adjustable belt with garters for the support of hose. Also *British* "suspender belt."

garter snake *n.* **1.** Any of various nonvenomous North American snakes of the genus *Thamnophis,* having longitudinal stripes. **2.** Any of several African snakes of the genus *Elaps,* marked with black and white bands.

garter stitch *n.* **1.** A knitting stitch formed by working each row in plain stitch only. **2. a.** The raised pattern formed by this technique. **b.** Material worked in garter stitch.

garth (gärth) *n.* **1.** A grassy quadrangle surrounded by cloisters. **2.** *Archaic.* A yard, garden, or paddock. [Middle English, from Old Norse *garthr,* yard.]

Gar·vey (gär′vē), **Marcus (Moziah) Aurelius** (1887–1940). Jamaican black nationalist active in America. The founder of the Universal Negro Improvement Association (1914), he moved to New York (1916) and became a highly influential leader who called for economic independence of blacks and a large-scale resettlement of blacks in Liberia.

gas (găs) *n., pl.* **gases** or **gasses. 1. a.** The state of matter distinguished from the solid and liquid states by very low density and viscosity, relatively great expansion and contraction with changes in pressure and temperature, the ability to diffuse readily, and the spontaneous tendency to become distributed uniformly throughout any container. **b.** A substance in this state. **c.** A substance in this state at room temperature and atmospheric pressure. **2.** A gaseous fuel such as **natural gas** *(see).* **3.** *Mining.* An explosive mixture of firedamp (methane) and air. **4.** A gaseous asphyxiant, irritant, or poison. **5.** A gaseous anesthetic. **6. a.** Gasoline. **b.** The speed control of a gasoline engine: *pressed the gas to the floor.* **7.** *Slang.* Idle or boastful talk. **8.** *Slang.* Something providing great fun and excitement: *The party was a real gas.* **—step on the gas. 1.** *Informal.* To accelerate in a motor vehicle. **2.** To go faster; hurry up.
~*v.* **gassed, gassing, gases** or **gasses.** —*tr.* **1.** To supply with gas or gasoline. **2.** To treat chemically with gas. **3.** To disable or kill with gas. —*intr.* **1.** To give off gas. **2.** *Slang.* To talk excessively. **3.** *Informal.* To fill the tank of a motor vehicle with gasoline: *gassed up before leaving on our vacation.* [Dutch *gas,* an occult principle supposed to be present in all bodies, coined (by J.B. van Helmont, 1577–1644, Belgian chemist) from Greek *khaos,* CHAOS.]

gas·bag (găs′băg′) *n.* **1.** An expandable bag for holding gas. **2.** *Slang.* One given to empty chatter.

gas burner *n.* A nozzle or jet on a fitting through which combustible gas is released to burn.

gas chamber *n.* A sealed enclosure in which prisoners sentenced to death are killed by means of a poisonous gas.

gas chromatography *n.* Chromatography in which the substance to be analyzed is vaporized and diffused along with a carrier gas through a liquid or solid adsorbent for differential adsorption. See **gas-liquid chromatography.**

gas coal *n.* Coal containing a large amount of volatile hydrocarbons, suitable for converting into fuel gas.

gas·con (găs′kən) *n.* A boastful person; a braggart. [French, from Old French *gascon,* GASCON (from the traditional garrulity of the Gascons).]

Gas·con (găs′kən) *n.* **1.** A native of Gascony. **2.** The French dialect of the Gascons.
~*adj.* Of or pertaining to Gascony or the Gascons.

gas·con·ade (găs′kə-nād′) *n.* Boastfulness; bravado; swagger.
~*intr.v.* **gasconaded, -ading, -ades.** To boast or swagger.

gas constant *n.* *Symbol* **R.** The constant in the ideal gas law, equal to 8.3143 joules per kelvin per mole. Also called "universal gas constant."

Gas·co·ny (găs′kə-nē). *French* **Gas·cogne** (gȧs-kôn′yə). Ancient province in southwest France. It is bounded by the Garonne River,

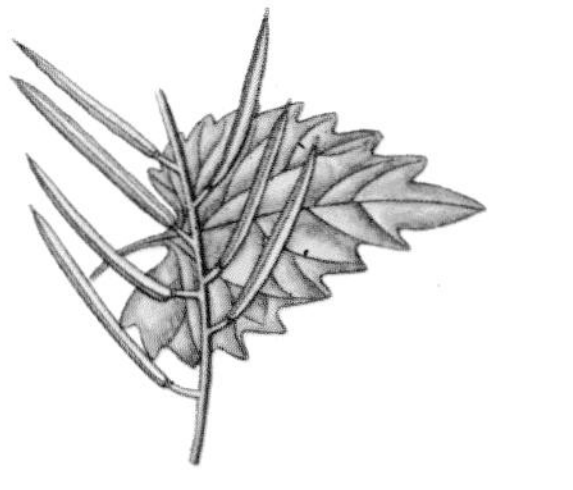

garlic mustard *Known also as hedge garlic, its leaves give off a strong smell of garlic when crushed.*

garnet *Garnet is the name given to a group of minerals that share a common crystalline structure and similar chemical composition. As jewelry, it was popular in Victorian times.*

the Pyrenees, and the Atlantic. In the 6th century it was settled by the Vascones (Basques), who later set up the duchy of Vasconia. This was united with neighboring Aquitaine in 1052.

gas-cooled reactor (găs′kōōld′) *n.* A nuclear reactor in which heat is removed from the core by a gaseous coolant, usually carbon dioxide. See **advanced gas-cooled reactor.**

gas·e·lier, gas·o·lier (găs′ə-lîr′) *n.* A chandelier having tubular branches with gas jets. [*gas* +chand*elier.*]

gas·e·ous (găs′ē-əs, găsh′əs) *adj.* **1.** Of, pertaining to, or existing as a gas. **2.** Lacking concreteness; tenuous.

gas equation *n.* An equation applying to ideal gases: $pV = nRT$, where p is the pressure, V the volume, n the amount of substance (number of moles), R the gas constant, and T the thermodynamic temperature. The equation approximately describes the behavior of real gases. Also called "ideal gas law."

gas fitter *n.* A workman who installs or repairs gas pipes, fixtures, or appliances.

gas gangrene *n.* Gangrene occurring in a wound infected with bacteria of the genus *Clostridium*, especially with *C. welchii* or *C. oedematiens*, and characterized by the presence of gas in the affected tissue and constitutional septic symptoms.

gash (găsh) *tr.v.* **gashed, gashing, gashes.** To make a long, deep cut in; slash deeply.
~*n.* **1.** A long, deep cut. **2.** A deep flesh wound. [Earlier *garsh, garse,* Middle English *garsen,* to cut, slash, from Old North French *garser,* probably from Late Latin *charaxāre,* from Greek *kharassein,* to carve, cut.]

gas·hold·er (găs′hōl′dər) *n.* A storage container for fuel gas, especially a large, telescoping, cylindrical tank. Also called "gasometer."

gas·i·form (găs′ə-fôrm′) *adj.* In the form of gas; gaseous.

gas·i·fy (găs′ə-fī) *v.* **-fied, -fying, -fies.** *—tr.* **1.** To convert into gas. **2.** To produce gas from (wood or coal, for example). *—intr.* To become gas. **—gas·i·fi·a·ble** *adj.* **—gas·i·fi·ca·tion** *n.*

gas jet *n.* **1.** A gas burner. **2.** The flame of burning gas from a gas burner.

Gas·kell (găs′kəl), **Elizabeth Cleghorn,** born Elizabeth Cleghorn Stevenson (1810–65). English novelist. She wrote *Cranford* (1853), *North and South* (1855), and a biography of her friend Charlotte Brontë (1857).

gas·ket (găs′kĭt) *n.* **1.** Any of a wide variety of seals or packings used between matched machine parts or around pipe joints to prevent the escape of a gas or fluid. **2.** *Nautical.* A cord or canvas strap used to secure a furled sail to a yard boom or gaff. **—blow a gasket.** *Slang.* To explode with anger. [Perhaps variant of obsolete *gassit,* from French *garcette,* "little girl," rope, diminutive of *garce,* girl, from *gars,* boy.]

gas·kin (găs′kĭn) *n.* **1.** The part of the hind leg of a horse or related animal between the stifle and the hock. **2.** **gaskins.** *Obsolete.* Galligaskins. [Probably shortened from GALLIGASKINS.]

gas law *n.* A law, as Boyle's law or Charles's law, relating to the pressure, volume, and temperature of gases.

gas·light (găs′līt′) *n.* **1.** Light produced by burning illuminating gas. **2.** A gas burner or lamp.

gas-liq·uid chromatography (găs′lĭk′wĭd) *n. Abbr.* **GLC** A form of gas chromatography in which the adsorbent medium is an inert solid coated with a liquid.

gas log *n.* A gas heater designed to look like a log for use in a fireplace.

gas main *n.* A major pipeline or conduit conveying gas to smaller pipes for distribution to consumers.

gas·man (găs′măn′) *n., pl.* **-men** (-mĕn′). **1.** A person employed to read gas meters for the billing of consumers. **2.** A gas fitter.

gas mantle *n.* An incandescent mantle used in a gaslight.

gas mask *n.* A respirator covering the face and having a chemical air filter to protect against poisonous gases.

gas meter *n.* A device for measuring the rate of flow of a gas; especially, a device for measuring and recording the amount of fuel gas used by a domestic consumer.

gas·o·hol (găs′ə-hôl′) *n.* A fuel consisting of a blend of ethanol and unleaded gasoline, especially a blend of 10 percent ethanol and 90 percent gasoline. [GAS(OLINE) + (ALC)OHOL.]

gas oil *n.* A mixture of hydrocarbons intermediate between paraffin and lubricating oil, obtained by distilling petroleum and used as fuel.

gasolier. Variant of **gaselier.**

gas·o·line, gas·o·lene (găs′ə-lēn′, găs′ə-lēn′) *n.* A volatile mixture of flammable liquid hydrocarbons derived chiefly from crude petroleum and used principally as a fuel for internal-combustion engines and as a solvent, illuminant, and thinner.

gas·om·e·ter (gă-sŏm′ə-tər) *n.* **1.** A gasholder (see). **2.** An apparatus for measuring the volume of gases. [French *gazomètre* : *gaz,* from GAS + -METER.]

gasp (găsp, gäsp) *v.* **gasped, gasping, gasps.** *—intr.* **1.** To draw in or catch the breath sharply, as from shock. **2.** To breathe convulsively or laboriously. **3.** *Informal.* To long; crave. Used with *for: gasping for a drink. —tr.* To utter between gasps. Often used with *out.*
~*n.* A short convulsive intake or catching of the breath. [Middle English *ga(y)spen,* from Old Norse *geispa.*]

Gaspar. See **Caspar.**

Gas·pé Peninsula (găs-pā′). A peninsula in eastern Quebec, Canada, between the mouth of the St. Lawrence River and Chaleur Bay. The peninsula has mountains, forests, and picturesque villages

along the coast and is noted for its hunting, fishing, and spectacular scenery.

gasp·er (găs′pər, gä′spər) *n.* **1.** One who gasps. **2.** *British Slang.* A cigarette.

gas plant *n.* A plant, *Dictamnus albus,* native to Eurasia, having aromatic foliage and white flowers and emitting a vapor capable of being ignited. Also called "burning bush," "dittany," "fraxinella."

gas poker *n.* A device resembling a hollow poker that is fitted with a gas jet and ignited to kindle a fire.

gas ring *n.* A device consisting of a set of gas jets arranged in a circle, as on a gas stove.

gas·ser (găs′ər) *n.* **1.** A well or drilling that yields natural gas. **2.** *Slang.* Something unusually entertaining; a gas.

gas station *n.* A filling station (*see*).

gas·sy (găs′ē) *adj.* **-sier, -siest. 1.** Containing, full of, or resembling gas. **2.** *Slang.* Bombastic; boastful.

gast (găst) *tr.v.* **gasted, gasting, gasts.** *Obsolete.* To scare. [Middle English *gasten,* Old English *gæstan.*]

gast·ar·bei·ter (gäst′är′bī′tər) *n., pl.* **gastarbeiter.** An immigrant worker; especially a worker in West Germany of Italian, Yugoslav, or Turkish origin. [German, "guest worker."]

gas thermometer *n.* An apparatus for measuring temperature by determining the volume of a gas at constant pressure (*constant-pressure gas thermometer*) or by the pressure at constant volume (*constant-volume gas thermometer*).

gas·tight (găs′tīt′) *adj.* Not permitting the escape or entry of gas.

gas·trec·to·my (gă-strĕk′tə-mē) *n., pl.* **-mies.** Surgical excision of part or all of the stomach. [GASTR(O)- + -ECTOMY.]

gas·tric (găs′trĭk) *adj.* Of, pertaining to, or near the stomach. [French *gastrique,* from New Latin *gastricus,* from Greek *gastēr,* (stem *gastr-*), belly, womb.]

gastric gland *n.* Any of various tubular glands in the mucous membrane lining the stomach that secrete gastric juice.

gastric juice *n.* The colorless, watery, acidic digestive fluid secreted by the gastric glands of the stomach and containing hydrochloric acid, pepsin, rennin, and mucin.

gastric ulcer *n.* An ulcer in the mucous membrane lining the stomach.

gas·trin (găs′trĭn) *n.* A hormone secreted by the gastric mucosa that stimulates production of gastric juice. [GASTR(O)- + -IN.]

gas·tri·tis (gă-strī′tĭs) *n.* Chronic or acute inflammation of the stomach. [New Latin : GASTR(O)- + -ITIS.]

gastro-, gastr– *prefix.* Indicates stomach; for example, **gastroscope, gastritis.** [Greek *gastēr* (stem *gastr-*), belly, womb.]

gas·troc·ne·mi·us (găs′trŏk-nē′mē-əs) *n.* The muscle that forms the major part of the calf of the leg. [New Latin, from Greek *gastroknēmē,* calf of the leg : GASTRO- (belly) + *knēmē,* shin, leg.]

gas·tro·en·ter·ic (găs′trō-ĕn-tĕr′ĭk) *adj.* Gastrointestinal.

gas·tro·en·ter·i·tis (găs′trō-ĕn′tə-rī′tĭs) *n.* Inflammation of the mucous membrane of the stomach and intestine.

gas·tro·en·ter·ol·o·gy (găs′trō-ĕn′tə-rŏl′ə-jē) *n.* The medical study of diseases of the stomach and the intestines. **—gas·tro·en·ter·o·log·i·cal** (găs′trō-ĕn′tər-ə-lŏj′ĭ-kəl) *adj.* **—gas·tro·en·ter·ol·o·gist** *n.*

gas·tro·en·ter·os·to·my (găs′trō-ĕn′tə-rŏs′tə-mē) *n., pl.* **-mies.** The surgical formation of a passage between the stomach and the small intestine.

gas·tro·in·tes·ti·nal (găs′trō-ĭn-tĕs′tə-nəl) *adj.* Of or pertaining to the stomach and intestines; gastroenteric.

gas·tro·lith (găs′trə-lĭth′) *n.* A small, pathological stony mass formed in the stomach; a gastric calculus. [GASTRO- + -LITH.]

gas·trol·o·gy (gă-strŏl′ə-jē) *n.* The medical study of the stomach and its diseases. [GASTRO- + -LOGY.] **—gas·tro·log·i·cal** (găs′trə-lŏj′ĭ-kəl) *adj.* **—gas·trol·o·gist** *n.*

gas·tro·nome (găs′trə-nōm′) *n.* Also **gas·tron·o·mer** (gă-strŏn′ə-mər). A connoisseur of good food and drink; a gourmet. [From GASTRONOMY.]

gas·tro·nom·ic (găs′trə-nŏm′ĭk) *adj.* Also **gas·tro·nom·i·cal** (-ĭ-kəl). Of or pertaining to gastronomes or gastronomy. **—gas·tro·nom·i·cal·ly** *adv.*

gas·tron·o·my (gă-strŏn′ə-mē) *n.* **1.** The art or science of good eating. **2.** Cooking, as of a particular region or country. [French *gastronomie,* from Greek *gastronomia* : GASTRO- + -NOMY.]

gas·tro·pod (găs′trə-pŏd′) *n.* A mollusk of the class Gastropoda, as a snail, slug, cowry, or limpet, characteristically having a single, usually coiled shell and a ventral muscular foot serving as an organ of locomotion.
~*adj.* Of or belonging to the Gastropoda. [New Latin *Gastropoda,* "belly-footed creatures" (from their ventral disks used as feet) : GASTRO- + -POD.] **—gas·trop·o·dan** (gă-strŏp′ə-dən), **gas·trop·o·dous** *adj.*

gas·tro·scope (găs′trə-skōp′) *n.* An instrument used for examining the interior of the stomach. [GASTRO- + -SCOPE.] **—gas·tro·scop·ic** (găs′trə-skŏp′ĭk) *adj.* **—gas·tros·co·pist** (gă-strŏs′kə-pĭst) *n.* **—gas·tros·co·py** (gă-strŏs′kə-pē) *n.*

gas·tros·to·my (gă-strŏs′tə-mē) *n., pl.* **-mies.** The surgical construction of a permanent opening from the external surface of the body into the stomach, usually for inserting a feeding tube. [GASTRO- + -STOMY.]

gas·trot·o·my (gă-strŏt′ə-mē) *n., pl.* **-mies.** A surgical incision into the stomach. [GASTRO- + -TOMY.]

gas·tro·trich (găs′trə-trĭk′) *n.* Any minute aquatic animal of the phylum Gastrotricha, having a wormlike, ciliated body. [GASTRO- + -TRICH.]

gas·tro·vas·cu·lar (găs′trō-văs′kyə-lər) *adj.* Having both a digestive and a circulatory function. Said especially of the body cavity of a coelenterate.

gas·tru·la (găs′trə-lə) *n.*, *pl.* **-las** or **-lae** (-lē′). An embryo at the stage following the blastula, consisting of a layer of cells differentiated into ectoderm, endoderm, and mesoderm and enclosing a cavity, the archenteron, which opens to the exterior by the blastopore. [New Latin, "small stomach" (from its shape), diminutive of Greek *gastēr* (stem *gastr-*), belly, womb.] —**gas·tru·lar** *adj.*

gas·tru·late (găs′trə-lāt) *intr.v.* **-lated, -lating, -lates.** To form or become a gastrula. —**gas·tru·la·tion** *n.*

gas turbine *n.* An internal-combustion engine consisting essentially of an air compressor, a combustion chamber, and a turbine wheel, used especially for propulsion rather than fixed power generation.

gas well *n.* A well that yields natural gas.

gas·works (găs′wûrks′) *n. Used with a singular verb.* An industrial plant in which gas for heating and lighting is produced.

gat¹ (găt) *n.* **1.** A narrow passage extending inland from a shore. **2.** A tidal channel between offshore islands or shoals. [Probably from Dutch *gat,* "opening," from Middle Dutch, from Germanic *gatam* (unattested). See **gate¹**.]

gat² *n. Slang.* A pistol. [Short for GAT(LING GUN).]

gat³. *Archaic.* Past tense of **get**.

gate¹ (gāt) *n.* **1.** A structure that may be swung, drawn, or lowered to block an entrance or passageway. **2. a.** An opening in a wall or fence for entrance or exit; a gateway. **b.** The structure surrounding such an opening, as the monumental or fortified entrance to a palace or walled town. **3. a.** Something that gives access: *the gate to fortune.* **b.** A place giving access to another region or country; especially, a mountain pass. **4.** A device for controlling the passage of water or gas through a dam, lock, or pipe. **5. a.** The number of spectators attending an event such as a football match: *the problem of falling gates.* **b.** The total admission receipts at such an event. In this sense, also called "gate money." **6.** Any of the numbered exits, as in an airport terminal, through which passengers proceed for embarkation. **7.** *Metallurgy.* The channel through which molten metal flows into the shaped cavity of a mold. **8.** *Electronics.* **a.** A circuit extensively used in computers that has an output dependent on some function of its input. **b.** Such a circuit having an output when any or all of a designated set of inputs are received within a given time interval. In this sense, also called "coincidence gate." **c.** A circuit designed to cut out part of a signal. **d.** The region or electrode that controls the current in a field-effect transistor. **9.** In photography, a device that holds a frame of film in place behind the lens. **10.** A slotted frame enabling the gearshift lever of a motor vehicle to be moved into different positions when engaging gears. ~*tr.v.* **gated, gating, gates. 1.** *British.* To punish (a student) by confining within the school or college gates after a certain hour or for a certain period of time. **2.** *Electronics.* To connect (one or more inputs) to a gate. [Middle English *gat, g(e)ate,* Old English *geat,* from Common Germanic *gatam* (unattested).]

gate² *n.* **1.** *Archaic & Regional.* A path or road; a way. **2.** *Regional.* A particular way of acting or doing; a manner. [Middle English, from Old Norse *gata,* path, passage.]

gâ·teau, ga·teau (gä-tō′) *n. pl.* **-teaux** (-tō′, -tōz′) or **-teaus.** A cake, especially a large, elaborate one. [French, "cake."]

gate-crash·er (gāt′krăsh′ər) *n. Informal.* A person who gains admittance, as to a party or concert, without being invited or without paying. —**gate-crash** *v.*

gate·fold (gāt′fōld′) *n.* A folded insert in a book or magazine whose full size exceeds that of the regular page. Also called "fold-out."

gate·house (gāt′hous′) *n.* **1.** A lodge at the entrance to the driveway of a country house or estate. **2.** A fortified room built over a gateway to a city or castle, formerly used as a prison. **3.** A building that houses the controls of a dam or lock.

gate·keep·er (gāt′kē′pər) *n.* A person in charge of a gate. Also called "gateman."

gate-leg table (gāt′lĕg′) *n.* A drop-leaf table with movable legs arranged in pairs.

gate·man (gāt′mən, -măn′) *n.*, *pl.* **-men** (-mĭn, -mĕn′). A gatekeeper.

gate·post (gāt′pōst′) *n.* An upright post on which a gate is hung or against which a gate is closed.

gate·way (gāt′wā′) *n.* **1.** A structure, such as an arch, framing an entrance or passage that may be closed by a gate. **2.** A place or a thing that serves as an entrance or means of access: *a gateway to success.* **3.** *Computer Science.* A link that enables information to be exchanged between one computer network and another.

gath·er (găth′ər) *v.* **-ered, -ering, -ers.** —*tr.* **1.** To cause to come together; convene. **2. a.** To accumulate gradually; amass. **b.** To harvest or pick: *gather flowers; gather in the crops.* **c.** To gain by a process of gradual increase: *The ship began to gather speed as it left the harbor.* **3. a.** To collect into one place; assemble. **b.** In bookbinding, to arrange (signatures) in sequence. **4.** To pick up and embrace. Used with *in* or *into*: *gathered the child into his arms.* **5. a.** To pull (cloth) along a thread so as to create small folds or puckers. **b.** To contract (the brow) so as to form wrinkles. **6.** To draw (a garment, for example) about or closer to something. **7.** To conclude or apprehend; infer: *I gather that a decision has not been reached.* **8. a.** To summon up; muster: *gather courage.* **b.** To collect (one's wits or powers). Often used with *together.* **9.** To attract or be a center of attraction for: *a movement that is gathering support; books gathering dust.* —*intr.* **1.** To come together or assemble. **2.** To accumulate. **3.** To grow or increase by degrees. **4.** To come to a head, as a boil does; fester. ~*n.* **1. a.** An act or instance of gathering. **b.** A quantity that is gathered. **2.** A small tuck or pucker in cloth. [Middle English *gad(e)ren,* Old English *gad(e)rian,* to put together, come together, from Germanic.] —**gath·er·er** *n.*

Synonyms: *accumulate, amass, assemble, collect, marshal, rally.*

gath·er·ing (găth′ər-ĭng) *n.* **1.** Something gathered or amassed; a collection or accumulation. **2.** An assembly of persons; a meeting: *a cultural gathering.* **3.** A gather in cloth. **4.** A suppurated swelling; a boil or abscess.

Gat·ling gun (găt′lĭng) *n.* A machine gun having a cluster of barrels, each of which is fired as the cluster is turned. [Designed by Richard J. *Gatling* (1818–1903), American inventor.]

Gat·wick (găt′wĭk). Village in West Sussex, England. Lying 43 kilometers (27 miles) south of London, it is the site of one of London's principal airports.

gauche (gōsh) *adj.* **1.** Awkward in manner; lacking social grace; tactless; clumsy. **2.** *Chemistry.* Of or designating a conformation of a chemical compound in which two groups or atoms attached to two adjacent atoms are on the same side of the bond but one is displaced rotationally with respect to the other. —See Synonyms at **awkward.** [French, "left," originally "bent," "askew," from Old French *gauchir,* to turn aside, detour, probably altered from earlier *guenchir,* from Frankish *wenkjan* (unattested).] —**gauche·ly** *adv.* —**gauche·ness** *n.*

gau·che·rie (gō′shə-rē′, gōsh-rē′) *n.* **1.** An awkward or tactless action, manner, or expression. **2.** Tactlessness; awkwardness. [French, from *gauche,* left, GAUCHE.]

Gau·cher's disease (gō-shāz′) *n.* A metabolic disease in which fatty compounds accumulate in the liver, spleen, lymph nodes, and nervous system. [After Ernest *Gaucher* (1854–1918), French physician.]

gau·cho (gou′chō) *n.*, *pl.* **-chos.** A cowboy of the South American pampas. [American Spanish, probably from Quechua *wáhcha,* poor person, vagabond.]

gaud (gôd) *n.* Something gaudy or showy. [Middle English *gaude, gawde,* jest, plaything, toy, from Old French *gaudir,* to rejoice, from Latin *gaudēre,* to delight in.]

gaud·er·y (gô′də-rē) *n.*, *pl.* **-ies.** Showy things; finery.

Gau·dí (gou′dē), **Antonio** (1852–1926). Spanish architect. He worked mainly in Barcelona, developing a startling new style that paralleled developments in art nouveau and incorporated color and odd bits of material, such as rubble, bricks, and polychrome tiles. His most famous work is the Church of the Holy Family (1882–1930).

gaud·y¹ (gô′dē) *adj.* **-ier, -iest. 1.** Characterized by tasteless or showy colors; garish. **2.** Crude and showy. —See Synonyms at **ornate.** [From GAUD.] —**gaud·i·ly** *adv.* —**gaud·i·ness** *n.*

gaudy² *n.*, *pl.* **-ies.** *British.* A feast; especially, an annual university dinner. [Latin *gaudium,* joy, from *gaudēre,* to rejoice.]

gauffer. Variant of **goffer.**

gauge, gage (gāj) *n. Abbr.* **g., G. 1. a.** A standard or scale of measurement. **b.** A standard dimension, quantity, or capacity. **2.** An instrument for measuring or testing. **3.** A means of estimating or evaluating; a test: *a gauge of character.* **4.** *Nautical.* The position of a vessel in relation to another vessel and the wind. **5. a.** The distance between the two rails of a railroad. **b.** The distance between two wheels on an axle. **6.** The diameter of a shotgun barrel as determined by the number of lead balls in a pound that exactly fit the barrel. **7.** The amount of plaster of Paris mixed with common plaster to speed its setting. **8.** Thickness or diameter, as of sheet metal or wire. **9.** The fineness of knitted cloth as determined by the number of loops per 1½ inches. **10.** The distance between nails securing tiles or slates to a roof. ~*tr.v.* **gauged, gauging, gauges** or **gaged, gaging, gages. 1.** To measure precisely. **2.** To determine the capacity, volume, or contents of. **3.** To evaluate or judge: *gauge ability.* **4.** To adapt to a specified measurement. **5.** To mix (plaster) in specific proportions. **6.** To chip or rub (bricks or stones) to size. ~*adj. Physics.* Measured above or below atmospheric pressure as the zero reference. Used after the noun: *7 bar gauge.* Compare **absolute** (pressure). [Middle English, from Old North French *gauget.*]

gaug·er (gā′jər) *n.* **1.** One that gauges. **2.** *Chiefly British.* **a.** A revenue officer who inspects bulk goods subject to duty. **b.** A collector of excise duties.

Gau·guin (gō-găN′), **(Eugène Henri) Paul** (1848–1903). French painter, regarded as a postimpressionist. In 1891 he settled in Tahiti and his paintings of the islanders show the influence of primitive art.

Gaul¹ (gôl). Latin name **Gal·li·a** (găl′ē-ə). The name given in antiquity to the region in Europe south and west of the Rhine, west of the Alps, and north of the Pyrenees, comprising approximately the territory of modern France and Belgium. [French *Gaule,* from Latin *Gallia,* from *Galli,* the Gauls.]

Gaul² *n.* **1.** A Celt of ancient Gaul. **2.** A Frenchman.

gau·lei·ter (gou′lī′tər) *n.* **1.** A governor of a district in Germany during the Nazi regime. **2.** A person similar to a gauleiter, as in point of view; petty tyrant. [German *Gau,* administrative district + *Leiter,* leader.]

Gaul·ish (gô′lĭsh) *n.* The Celtic language of ancient Gaul.

~*adj.* Of or pertaining to ancient Gaul or to its people, language, and culture.

Gaull·ism (gô'lĭz'əm, gô'-) *n.* **1.** The political movement supporting Charles de Gaulle as leader of the French government in exile during World War II. **2.** The body of political theory and practice characteristic of Charles de Gaulle and his followers. —**Gaull·ist** *adj. & n.*

gault (gôlt) *n. Geology.* **1.** *Often* **Gault.** A formation of Cretaceous origin in Britain, consisting of clay and marl and occurring between the Greensand formations. **2.** The clay and marl comprising this formation. **3.** A brick made from this type of clay. [16th century : origin obscure.]

gaul·the·ri·a (gôl-thîr'ē-ə) *n.* Any shrub of the genus *Gaultheria,* having aromatic evergreen foliage; especially, the **wintergreen** (*see*). [New Latin, after Jean-François *Gaultier,* 18th-century Canadian botanist.]

gaum (gôm) *tr.v.* **gaumed, gauming, gaums.** *Regional.* To smudge or smear. [Dialectal variant of GUM (verb).]

gaunt (gônt, gänt) *adj.* **gaunter, gauntest. 1.** Thin and bony; angular; lank. **2.** Emaciated and haggard; drawn. **3.** Bleak and desolate; barren. —See Usage note at **lean.** [Middle English *gawnt, gaunt,* lean, perhaps from Scandinavian; akin to Norwegian dialectal *gand†,* thin stick, lanky person.] —**gaunt·ly** *adv.* —**gaunt·ness** *n.*

gaunt·let¹, gant·let (gônt'lĭt, gänt'-) *n.* **1.** A protective glove worn as a part of medieval armor. **2.** A protective glove with a flaring cuff, used in manual labor, for driving, and in some sports. **3.** A challenge. Used chiefly in the phrases *fling* or *throw down the gauntlet.* [Middle English *gaunt(e)let,* from Old French *gantelet,* diminutive of *gant,* glove, from Frankish *want†* (unattested), mitten.]

gauntlet², gantlet *n.* **1.** Two lines of men facing each other and armed with sticks or other weapons with which they beat a person forced to run between them. **2.** A severe trial; ordeal: *The candidate was subjected to a gauntlet of searching questions from the journalists at the press conference.* [Earlier *gantlope.* See **gantlet** (railroad track).]

Usage: In the expression *run the gauntlet,* this spelling alternates with *gantlet. Gantlet* is the more common spelling in earlier American usage, and is still considered preferable by some authorities and mandatory by others, but *gauntlet* is acceptable in this expression to most users. *Gauntlet* is the term used in *fling* (or *throw*) *down the gauntlet,* to issue a challenge, and *take up the gauntlet,* to accept a challenge. *Run the gauntlet* (or *gantlet*) is sometimes confused with *run the gamut,* to cover an entire range.

gauntlet³. Variant of **gantlet** (railroad track).

gaur (gour, gou'ər) *n.* A large, dark-coated bovine mammal, *Bos gaurus,* of hilly areas of southeastern Asia. [Hindi *gaur,* from Sanskrit *gaura.*]

gauss (gous) *n. Abbr.* **G** The centimeter-gram-second electromagnetic unit of magnetic flux density, equal to one maxwell per square centimeter (10⁻⁴ tesla.) [After Karl Friedrich GAUSS.]

Gauss (gous), **(Johann) Karl Friedrich** (1777–1855). German mathematician. His contributions to algebra, differential geometry, probability theory, and number theory were of vital importance. He also worked in astronomy and contributed to the invention of the telegraph.

Gauss·i·an distribution (gou'sē-ən) *n.* **Normal distribution** (*see*).

gauss·me·ter (gous'mē'tər) *n. Physics.* Any of various instruments used to measure magnetic flux density. [After Karl Friedrich GAUSS.]

Gau·tier (gō-tyā') , **Théophile** (1811–72). French author. A poet, critic, journalist, novelist, and playwright, he influenced French literature during its shift from romanticism to aestheticism and naturalism. Among his many works are *Young France* (1833), *Enamels and Cameos* (1852), and *The Dead Lover, Avatar* (1857).

gauze (gôz) *n.* **1. a.** A thin, transparent fabric with a loose open weave, used for curtains or clothing. **b.** A thin, open-woven cotton surgical dressing. **c.** A thin plastic or metal woven mesh. **2.** A mist or haze. [French *gaze,* probably after GAZA, where it was supposed to be made.]

gauz·y (gô'zē) *adj.* **-ier, -iest.** Of, pertaining to, or like gauze: *I bought a gauzy silk scarf.* —**gauz·i·ly** *adv.* —**gauz·i·ness** *n.*

ga·vage (gə-väzh', gä-) *n.* The introduction of material, especially nutritive material, into the stomach by means of a tube. [French, from *gaver,* to force down the throat, stuff, from Picard, from Old Latin *gaba†* (unattested), throat.]

gave. Past tense of **give.**

gav·el¹ (găv'əl) *n.* **1.** The mallet or hammer used by a presiding officer, a judge, or an auctioneer to signal for attention or order. **2.** A maul used by masons in fitting stones. —*tr.v.* **-eled** or **-elled, -eling** or **-elling, -els.** To cause or compel by using a gavel: *The judge gaveled the courtroom into silence.* [19th century : origin obscure.]

gavel² *n.* Tribute or rent in ancient and medieval England. [Middle English *gavel,* Old English *gafol,* tribute.]

gav·el·kind (găv'əl-kīnd') *n.* An English system of tenure, prevalent especially in Kent from Anglo-Saxon times until 1926, whereby land was held in exchange for rent rather than services and could be inherited by all qualified heirs rather than by primogeniture. [Middle English *gavelkynde,* Old English *gafolgecynd* (unattested), "tenure by payment of rent" : *gafol,* GAVEL (rent) + *cynd, gecynd,* KIND.]

ga·vi·al (gā'vē-əl) *n.* A large reptile, *Gavialis gangeticus,* of southern Asia, related to and resembling the crocodiles and having a long,

slender snout. Also called "gharial." [French, from Hindi *ghariyāl†.*]

ga·votte (gə-vŏt') *n.* **1.** A French dance resembling the minuet. **2.** Music for this dance, or in a similar style, in moderately quick ⁴/₄ time. [French, from Provençal *gavoto,* from *Gavot,* "mountaineer," "rustic," inhabitant of the Alps (where the dance originated), perhaps from *gava,* crop of a bird, frill, goiter, from Old Latin *gaba†* (unattested), throat.]

Ga·wain (gə-wān', gä'wän, gou'ən). A nephew of King Arthur and a knight of the Round Table.

Gawd (gôd) *interj. Slang.* Used as an expression of annoyance, surprise, or the like. [Cockney pronunciation spelling of *God.*]

gawk (gôk) *n.* An awkward or self-conscious person. —*intr.v.* **gawked, gawking, gawks.** *Informal.* To stare like a gawk; gape stupidly. [Perhaps alteration of obsolete *gaw,* to stare, gape, Middle English *gawen,* from Old Norse *gā,* to heed.]

gawk·y (gô'kē) *adj.* **-ier, -iest.** Awkward; ill-at-ease. —**gawk·i·ly** *adv.* —**gawk·i·ness** *n.*

gawp (gôp) *intr.v.* **gawped, gawping, gawps.** To gawk; gape. [Variant of earlier *gaup, galp,* Middle English *galpen,* to yawn, YELP.]

gay (gā) *adj.* **gayer, gayest. 1.** Showing or characterized by cheerfulness and light-hearted excitement; merry. **2.** Bright or brilliant, especially in color: *a gay, sunny room.* **3. a.** Homosexual. **b.** Of, pertaining to, or for homosexuals. **4.** Full of or given to social pleasures. **5.** Dissolute; licentious. —*n.* A homosexual. [Middle English *gay, gai,* from Old French *gai,* from Old Provençal, probably from Gothic *gaheis* (unattested), akin to Old High German *gāhi†,* sudden, impetuous.] —**gay** *adv.* —**gay·ness** *n.*

Gay (gā), **John** (1685–1732). English poet and dramatist. A friend and protégé of Pope, he is best remembered for *The Beggar's Opera* (1728), a colorful satire that shocked many of his contemporaries by its candid portrayal of low life.

Ga·ya (gə-yä', gī'ə). City in central Bihar state, India. It is the capital and market center of a district that is famous for its strong Hindu and Buddhist associations and attracts many pilgrims.

ga·yal (gə-yäl') *n.* A domesticated bovine mammal, *Bos frontalis,* of India and Burma, having thick, pointed horns, a dark coat, and a tufted tail. [Bengali *gayāl,* probably from Sanskrit *gauḥ,* cow.]

gayety. Variant of **gaiety.**

Gay Gordons *n. Used with a singular verb.* A lively Scottish dance. [After the *Gordon Highlanders* (2nd Battalion, 92nd Highlanders).]

Gay-Lus·sac (gā-lü-säk'), **Joseph Louis** (1778–1850). French chemist and physicist. His experiments added considerably to knowledge of the way in which elements combine to form compounds. He discovered Gay-Lussac's law and isolated the element boron.

Gay-Lus·sac's law (gā'lü-säks') *n.* **1.** The principle that gases react in volumes that have a simple ratio to each other and to the volumes of gaseous products. **2. Charles's law** (*see*). [After J.L. GAY-LUSSAC.]

gayly. Variant of **gaily.**

Gay·nor (gā'nər), **Janet** (1906–84). U.S. actress. She started as an extra and became one of the most important movie stars of the late 1920's and early 1930's. For her performances in *Seventh Heaven, Street Angel,* and *Sunrise* she was awarded the first Academy Award as best actress (1928).

gaz. gazette; gazetteer.

Ga·za (gä'zə, gā'ə). Arabic **Ghaz·zah.** City in the Gaza Strip. Inhabited for more than 3,000 years, it was a major city of the Philistines, where Samson killed himself and his jailers by bringing down its temple (Judges 16).

ga·za·bo (gə-zā'bō) *n., pl.* **-bos** or **-boes.** *Slang.* A fellow; guy. [Origin unknown.]

ga·za·ni·a (gə-zā'nē-ə) *n.* Any South African plant of the genus *Gazania,* some species of which are grown for their ornamental yellow or orange flowers. [New Latin, irregularly from Teodoro *Gaza,* 15th-century Greek scholar.]

Gaza Strip. A territory between southwest Israel and the Mediterranean Sea. It was part of the British League of Nations mandate for Palestine (1920–48), but following the Arab-Israeli war of 1948–49 it came under Egyptian military rule. Apart from a brief Israeli occupation (November 1956–March 1957) it remained under Egyptian rule until taken in 1967 by the Israelis, who set up a military regime. The Camp David Accords of 1979 included provisions for its self-government. A scene of sporadic unrest, the strip has several huge refugee camps.

gaze (gāz) *intr.v.* **gazed, gazing, gazes.** To look or stare steadily for some length of time, often in an absorbed or abstracted way. —*n.* A steady look. [Middle English *gazen,* probably from Scandinavian, akin to Swedish dialectal *gasa†.*] —**gaz·er** *n.*

Synonyms: gape, glare, ogle, peer, stare.

ga·ze·bo (gə-zā'bō, -zē'bō) *n., pl.* **-bos** or **-boes. 1.** A free-standing, roofed, often open-sided structure providing a shady resting place. **2.** A belvedere, especially one having a view. [Probably mock Latin formation from GAZE (with Latin future suffix *-ēbō,* as in *vidēbō,* I shall see).]

gaze·hound (gāz'hound') *n.* A dog that hunts its prey by sight rather than scent.

ga·zelle (gə-zĕl') *n.* Any of various small antelopes of the genus *Gazella* and related genera, of Africa and Asia, characteristically having a slender neck, and ringed, lyrate horns. [Old French, probably from Spanish *gacela,* from Arabic *ghazāl.*]

gazelle *The common name for an antelope group of animals native to Africa and Asia. This is a Grant's gazelle, an East African species distinguished by the white stripes running from each horn to the muzzle.*

ga·zette (gə-zĕt′) *n. Abbr.* **gaz.** **1.** A newspaper. **2.** An official journal. **3.** *Chiefly British.* An announcement or report in an official journal.
~*tr.v.* **gazetted, -zetting, -zettes.** *British.* To announce or publish in a gazette. *"Sham colonels gazetted"* (W.S. Gilbert). [French, from Italian *gazzetta,* from Venetian *gazeta (de la novita),* (newspaper sold for) a small copper coin, from *gazeta,* a small copper coin, probably diminutive of *gaz(z)a,* magpie, from Latin *gaia,* from *gaius,* jay (perhaps imitative).]

gaz·et·teer (găz′ə-tîr′) *n. Abbr.* **gaz.** **1.** A geographic dictionary or index. **2.** *Archaic.* A person who writes for a gazette or newspaper; journalist.

gaz·pa·cho (gə-spä′chō, gəz-pä′-) *n., pl.* **-chos.** A Spanish soup made from salad ingredients, such as tomatoes, peppers, garlic, and olive oil, and served chilled. [Spanish.]

ga·zump (gə-zŭmp′) *v.* **-zumped, -zumping, -zumps.** *British.* —*tr.* **1.** To go back on an agreement with (a prospective purchaser of a property) by raising a previously agreed price. **2.** To swindle. —*intr.* To raise the previously agreed price of a property. [20th century : origin obscure.] —**ga·zump·er** *n.*

G.B. Great Britain.
G.B.E. Grand Cross of the British Empire (in Britain).
GC gigacycle.
GCA *Aviation.* ground control approach.
G.C.B. Grand Cross of the Bath (in Britain).
g.c.d. greatest common divisor.
GCE, G.C.E. (jē′sē-ē′) *n., pl.* **GCE's, G.C.E.'s.** In Britain, the General Certificate of Education: either of two sets of public examinations that may be taken in a variety of subjects either at *O level* or *A level.* **2.** A certificate awarded for passing such an examination.
g.c.f. greatest common factor.
GCI *Aviation.* ground control intercept.
G clef *n.* The **treble clef** *(see).*
GCM Good Conduct Medal.
Gd The symbol for the element gadolinium.
G.D. grand duchess; grand duchy; grand duke.
Gdańsk (gə-dänsk′, -dănsk′). *German* **Dan·zig** (dăn′sĭg, dän′-). Polish port and industrial center on the Baltic Sea. A rich Hanseatic town from the 13th century, it was a free city 1466–1793 (under Polish sovereignty), 1807–14, and 1919–39. Hitler's claim to Danzig in 1939 led to the German invasion of Poland and World War II. Returned to Poland in 1945, the city was rebuilt and its shipyards are among the world's largest. Riots by shipworkers in 1970 led to government changes, and in 1980 Solidarity, Communist Poland's first independent trade union, was established here.
gde. gourde.
G.D.R. German Democratic Republic (East Germany).
gds. goods.
Gdy·nia (gə-dĭn′yə). *German* **Gding·en** (gə-dĭng′ən). Polish port and rail center on the Baltic Sea, 19 kilometers (12 miles) from Gdańsk.
Ge The symbol for the element germanium.
Ge. Variant of **Gaea.**
gean (gēn) *n. Chiefly British.* A wild cherry tree, *Prunus avium,* of Eurasia and North Africa, from which cultivated trees bearing sweet cherries have been derived. See **sweet cherry, wild cherry.** [French *guine†.*]
ge·an·ti·cline (jē-ăn′tĭ-klīn′) *n.* A large upward fold of the earth's crust. [Greek *gē,* earth + ANTICLINE.] —**ge·an·ti·cli·nal** (jē-ăn′tĭ-klī′nəl) *adj.*
gear (gîr) *n.* **1. a.** A toothed wheel, cylinder, or other machine element that meshes with another toothed element to transmit motion or to change speed or direction. **b.** A complete assembly that performs a specific function in a larger machine. **c.** A transmission configuration for a specific ratio of engine to axle torque in a motor vehicle. **2. a.** Equipment or tackle required for a particular activity or purpose; paraphernalia: *a plumber's gear.* **b.** *Informal.* Clothing and accessories, especially as worn by young people following fashion. **3.** The harness for a draft animal. **4.** The rigging of a ship. **5. a.** A sailor's personal effects. **b.** *Informal.* Personal belongings: *I keep my gear in that closet.* —**in** (or **out of**) **gear. 1.** Having a gear engaged (or not engaged). **2.** Performing (or not performing) well. ~*v.* **geared, gearing, gears.** —*tr.* **1. a.** To provide with gears. **b.** To connect by gears. **c.** To put into gear. **2. a.** To adjust or adapt: *geared the speed to the conservative audience.* **b.** To prepare for action: *geared themselves up for the big game.* **3.** To provide with gear. —*intr.* **1.** To be or become in gear. **2.** To adjust so as to fit or blend. [Middle English *gere,* from Old Norse *gervi,* equipment, gear.]
gear·box (gîr′bŏks′) *n.* An automotive transmission.
gear·ing (gîr′ĭng) *n.* **1.** A system of gears and associated elements by which motion is transferred within a machine. **2.** The act or technique of providing with gears. **3.** *British.* The ratio of a company's fixed-interest debt to its equity capital.
gear·le·ver (gîr′lē′vər, -lĕv′ər) *n. British.* A gearshift.
gear·shift (gîr′shĭft′) *n.* A mechanism for changing from one gear to another in a transmission.
gear train *n.* A system of interconnected gears.
gear·wheel (gîr′hwēl′) *n.* A wheel with a toothed rim.
geck·o (gĕk′ō) *n., pl.* **-os** or **-oes.** Any of various usually small lizards of the family Gekkonidae, of warm regions, having toes with adhesive pads that enable them to climb on vertical surfaces. [Malay *ge'kok* (imitative of its cry).]
gee¹ (jē) *interj.* Gee whiz. [Euphemistic shortening of JESUS.]

gee² *n.* The gravitational acceleration at the earth's surface. [From the symbol *g* for gravitational acceleration.]
gee³ *n. Slang.* A thousand dollars. [Short for GRAND.]
gee⁴ *interj.* Used to encourage a horse or similar animal to turn to the right or go forward. Compare **haw.** ~*intr.v.* **geed, geeing, gees.** To turn to the right. [Origin obscure.]
gee⁵ *n.* The letter *g.*
gee-gee (jē′jē) *n. Informal.* A horse. [Child's word for horse, from GEE (interjection).]
geek (gēk) *n. Slang.* **1.** A carnival performer whose act consists of biting the head off a live animal, such as a chicken or snake. **2.** Broadly, any person whose behavior is considered to be eccentric or freakish. [Perhaps variant of Scottish *geck,* fool, from Middle Low German.]
Gee·long (jĭ-lông′). Port in Victoria, Australia. It was founded in 1837 on the western shore of Corio Bay, 68 kilometers (42 miles) southwest of Melbourne.
gee·pound (jē′pound′) *n.* A unit of mass, the **slug** *(see).* [GEE (gravitational acceleration) + POUND (weight).]
geese. Plural of **goose.**
gee whiz, gee whizz *interj.* Used to express mild surprise or delight.
Ge·ez (gē-ĕz′, gā-) *n.* Ethiopic *(see).*
gee·zer (gē′zər) *n. Slang.* A man; especially, an eccentric old man. [Probably dialectal pronunciation of *guiser,* one in disguise, masquerader, from GUISE.]
ge·fil·te fish, ge·füll·te fish (gə-fĭl′tə) *n.* Chopped fish mixed with crumbs, eggs, and seasonings, cooked in stock and usually served chilled in the form of balls or oval-shaped cakes. [Yiddish, "filled fish."]
ge·gen·schein (gā′gən-shīn′) *n.* A faint, glowing spot in the sky exactly opposite the position of the sun. Also called "counterglow." [German *Gegenschein,* "opposite light" : *gegen,* against, + *Schein,* light.]
Ge·hen·na (gə-hĕn′ə) *n.* **1.** A place or state of burning, torment, or suffering. **2.** Hell. [Late Latin, from Greek *Geenna,* from Hebrew *Gê' Hinnōm,* Valley of Hinnom, a ravine outside ancient Jerusalem where refuse was dumped, (hence figuratively) hell.]
Geh·rig (gĕr′ĭg), **Henry Louis,** known as "Lou" (1903–42). U.S. baseball player. As a New York Yankee first baseman, he had a lifetime batting average of .340, was the American League's most valuable player four times, and, most remarkably, never missed a game in fourteen seasons, playing in 2,130 consecutive contests.
Gei·ger (gī′gər), **Hans** (1882–1945). German physicist. He is best known for his work with Ernest Rutherford at Manchester, which resulted in the invention of the Geiger counter.
Geiger counter *n.* An instrument consisting of a Geiger tube and associated electronic equipment, used to detect, measure, and record ionizing radiation and charged particles. Also called "Geiger-Müller counter." [After Hans GEIGER.]
Geiger tube *n.* A gas-filled tube containing a fine wire electrode inside a coaxial cylindrical electrode, between which a potential difference slightly below the breakdown voltage is maintained, so that production of a pair of ions in the gas by the passage of a charged particle or by ionizing radiation causes a breakdown throughout the volume of the tube. Also called "Geiger-Müller tube." [After Hans GEIGER.]
Gei·sel (gī′zəl), **Theodor Seuss,** pen name "Dr. Seuss" (1904–). U.S. author and illustrator. He has combined light, sometimes nonsense verse and prose with imaginative artwork to produce popular and highly acclaimed children's books, including *And to Think That I Saw It on Mulberry Street* (1937), *The Cat in the Hat* (1957), and *The Butter Battle Book* (1984).
gei·sha (gā′shə, gē′-) *n., pl.* **geisha** or **-shas.** A Japanese girl trained to provide entertainment, such as singing, dancing, or amusing talk, especially for men. [Japanese, "artist" : *gei,* art + *sha,* person.]
Geis·sler tube (gī′slər) *n. Physics.* An electric discharge tube having two electrodes separated by a narrow capillary, used as a source of visible or ultraviolet radiation. [After Heinrich *Geissler* (1815–79), German mechanic.]
geist (gīst) *n.* **1.** Reason or intelligence, especially of an individual. **2.** Prevailing intellectual character. [German, "spirit."]
gel (jĕl) *n.* **1.** A colloid in which the disperse phase has combined with the continuous phase to produce a semisolid material, such as a jelly. **2.** *Informal.* A gelatin used in theatrical lighting. ~*v.* **gelled, gelling, gels.** —*intr.* To form into a gel. —*tr.* To cause (a colloid) to become a gel. [Short for GELATIN.]
gel·a·ble (jĕl′ə-bəl) *adj.* Capable of gelling.
gel·a·da (jĕl′ə-də, gĕl′-, jə-lä′də, gə-) *n.* A baboon, *Theropithecus gelada,* of Ethiopia, having a dark coat with a bare reddish area on the chest, and a mane covering the shoulders. Also called "gelada baboon." [Perhaps from Arabic *qilādah,* mane.]
ge·län·de·sprung (gə-lĕn′də-shprŏŏng′, -sprŏŏng′) *n.* A jump in skiing made from a crouching position with the use of both poles. [German : *Gelände,* level land + *Sprung,* a jump.]
gel·a·tin, gel·a·tine (jĕl′ə-tĭn) *n.* **1.** A colorless or slightly yellow, transparent, brittle protein formed by boiling the specially prepared skin, bones, and connective tissue of animals and used in foods, drugs, and photographic film. **2.** Any of various similar substances. **3.** A jelly made with gelatin, used as a dessert or salad base. **4.** A thin, transparent colored membrane used in theatrical lighting. [French *gélatine,* from Italian *gelatina,* diminutive of *gelata,* jelly,

gecko *This striped gecko is a small member of a largely tropical lizard family, the Gekkonidae, and is active mainly at night.*

gem

CRYSTALLINE DELIGHT
Earth's most precious stones

Men and women have worn colored stones for decoration and as talismans for thousands of years. Valued for their color, translucency, durability, and scarcity, gems have been polished and cut to enhance their beauty since at least early Egyptian times. Today diamond, emerald, ruby, and sapphire are the most prized gems, with flawless fine-colored rubies and emeralds the rarest and most costly.

Other valuable rarities are alexandrite with its red-green color change, green demantoid garnet, and Imperial jade. There is a profusion of colors and lusters, ranging from subtle to dazzling, in the less rare aquamarine, garnet, jade, lapis lazuli, moonstone, opal, peridot, quartz family, spinel, topaz, tourmaline, turquoise, and zircon.

FIVE WAYS IN WHICH A JEWELER CAN CUT GEMS

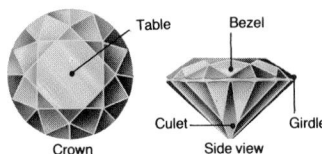
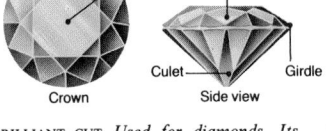
Table   Bezel   Culet   Girdle   Crown   Side view

Crown   Pavilion (underside)

Crown

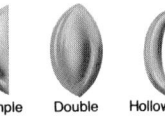
Crown

Simple   Double   Hollowed   Tallow top

BRILLIANT CUT *Used for diamonds. Its precisely angled facets and perfect proportions both reflect and split light in a play of fiery brilliance.*

TRAP CUT *Intricate shaping of the pavilion, a spider's web of angled surfaces, enhances color and emphasizes flawlessness. Used for colored stones.*

ROSE CUT *An old-fashioned cut used mainly for small diamonds.*

TABLE CUT *The simple forerunner of the brilliant and trap cuts.*

SECTIONS OF CABOCHONS *The oldest of all cuts, polished round or oval domes. Ideal for opaque gems, such as lapis lazuli, or star rubies and sapphires.*

BRILLIANCY OF THE FINISHED STONE

DIAMOND *Supremely hard and lustrous, diamond retains its brilliant polish and fire for generations.*

RUBY *Rarest of the precious stones; chromium imparts the glowing and most prized "pigeon's blood" red.*

EMERALD *Also colored by chromium, emerald's velvety green is rarely flawless. A brittle gem, it may chip.*

SAPPHIRE *The hardest gem after diamond, it varies from pure blue to purple, pink, orange, gold, green, and white.*

NATURAL STATE OF GEMSTONES

DIAMOND *The hardest natural stone, a form of carbon crystallized under enormous pressure and in great heat.*

RUBY *Rich red rubies, formed in thermally altered limestones, are quarried from the Burma gem gravels.*

EMERALD *A silicate of beryllium and aluminum. The finest emeralds are mined from veins in shales in Colombia.*

SAPPHIRE *Like ruby, it is a variety of the aluminum oxide corundum. Sri Lanka is a famous source of all colors.*

from Vulgar Latin *gelāta* (unattested), from Latin, feminine past participle of *gelāre,* to freeze, congeal.]

ge·lat·i·nize (jə-lăt′n-īz′, jĕl′ə-tə-nīz′) *v.* **-nized, -nizing, -nizes.** —*tr.* **1.** To convert to gelatin or jelly. **2.** To coat with gelatin. —*intr.* To become gelatinous. **—ge·lat·i·ni·za·tion** *n.*

ge·lat·i·nous (jə-lăt′n-əs) *adj.* **1.** Thick and viscous; resembling jelly. **2.** Of, pertaining to, containing, or similar to gelatin. **—ge·lat·i·nous·ly** *adv.* **—ge·lat·i·nous·ness** *n.*

ge·la·tion (jə-lā′shən) *n.* **1.** Solidification by cooling or freezing. **2.** The process of forming a gel. [Latin *gelātiō* (stem *gelātiōn-*), from *gelāre,* to freeze, congeal.]

geld¹ (gĕld) *tr.v.* **gelded** or **gelt** (gĕlt), **gelding, gelds. 1.** To castrate (a horse or other animal). **2.** To emasculate; weaken. [Middle English *gelden,* from Old Norse *gelda.*]

geld² *n.* A tax paid to the crown by English landholders under Anglo-Saxon and Norman kings. [Medieval Latin (Domesday Book) *geldum,* from Old English *g(i)eld,* payment, tribute.]

geld·ing (gĕl′dĭng) *n. Abbr.* **g.** A castrated animal; especially, a castrated male horse. [Middle English, from Old Norse *geldingr,* from *gelda,* GELD (to castrate).]

Gelibolu. See **Gallipoli.**

gel·id (jĕl′ĭd) *adj.* Very cold; icy. [Latin *gelidus,* from *gelū,* cold, frost.] **—ge·lid·i·ty** (jə-lĭd′ə-tē), **gel·id·ness** *n.* **—gel·id·ly** *adv.*

gel·ig·nite (jĕl′ĭg-nīt′) *n.* A high explosive made by combining nitroglycerin with wood pulp and sodium or potassium nitrate. [From GELATIN + Latin *ign(is),* fire + -ITE.]

Gell-Mann (gĕl′män′), **Murray** (1929–). U.S. physicist. In 1954 he introduced the concept of "strangeness" to explain the slow decay of certain particles and in 1961 postulated the existence of elementary particles he called "quarks." He was awarded the Nobel Prize in 1969.

gel·se·mi·um (jĕl-sē′mē-əm) *n.* **1.** Any shrub of the genus *Gelsemium,* such as *G. sempervirens,* yellow jasmine, of the southeastern United States. **2.** The powdered root of the yellow jasmine, which has sedative properties. [New Latin, from Italian *gelsomino,* JASMINE.]

gelt¹ (gĕlt) *n. Slang.* Money. [Yiddish *gelt* and German *Geld,* from Old High German *gelt,* recompense, reward.]

gelt². Alternate past tense and past participle of **geld.**

gem¹ (jĕm) *n.* **1.** A precious or semiprecious stone that has been cut and polished. **2. a.** Something that is valued for its beauty or per-

fection. **b.** A beloved or highly prized person: *a real gem.* **3.** A type of muffin.
~*tr.v.* **gemmed, gemming, gems.** To adorn with or as if with gems. [Middle English *gemme,* from Old French, from Latin *gemma,* bud, precious stone.]
gem² *adj. Chemistry.* Designating or pertaining to a chemical compound that has two identical atoms or groups attached to the same atom. Compare **vicinal.** [Shortened from GEMINATE.]
Ge·ma·ra (gə-mär′ə, -môr′ə) *n.* The second part of the Talmud, consisting chiefly of commentary on the Mishnah. [Aramaic *gemārā,* completion, from *gemar,* to complete.] —**Ge·mar′ic** (jə-mär′ĭk, -môr′ĭk) *adj.* —**Ge·ma·rist** *n.*
gem·i·nate (jĕm′ə-nāt′) *v.* **-nated, -nating, -nates.** —*tr.* To arrange in pairs or to double. —*intr.* To occur in pairs.
~*adj.* (jĕm′ə-nĭt, -nāt′) Forming a pair; doubled. [Latin *gemināre,* from *geminus,* twin.] —**gem·i·na·tion** *n.*
Gem·i·ni (jĕm′ə-nī′, -nē′) *n.* **1.** *Astronomy.* A constellation in the Northern Hemisphere containing the stars Castor and Pollux. **2. a.** The third sign of the **zodiac** (*see*). Also called the "Twins." **b.** One born under this sign. **3.** Any of a series of U.S. space probes designed to gain experience of manual flight and practice docking methods. There were 12 Gemini flights (1964–66), the first two unmanned and the others each carrying two astronauts. [Latin, plural of *geminus,* twin.] —**Gem·i·ni·an** (jĕm′ə-nī′ən) *adj. & n.*
gem·ma (jĕm′ə) *n., pl.* **gemmae** (jĕm′ē′). An asexual reproductive structure, as in liverworts and mosses, consisting of a cell or group of cells capable of developing into a new individual; a bud. [Latin, bud, precious stone.]
gem·mate (jĕm′āt′) *adj.* Having or reproducing by gemmae.
~*intr.v.* **gemmated, -mating, -mates.** To produce gemmae or reproduce by means of gemmae. [Latin *gemmāre,* to bud, from *gemma,* bud, GEMMA.] —**gem·ma·tion** *n.*
gem·mip·a·rous (jĕ-mĭp′ər-əs) *adj.* Reproducing by buds or gemmae. [New Latin *gemmiparus* : Latin *gemma,* bud, GEMMA + -PAROUS.]
gem·mu·la·tion (jĕm′yə-lā′shən) *n.* Production of or reproduction by gemmules.
gem·mule (jĕm′yool) *n.* **1.** A small gemma or similar structure; especially, a reproductive structure in some sponges that remains dormant through the winter and later develops into a new individual. **2.** A hypothetical particle of heredity postulated in the theory of **pangenesis** (*see*). [French, from Latin *gemmula,* diminutive of *gemma,* GEMMA.]
gem·my (jĕm′ē) *adj.* **1.** Full of or set with gems. **2.** Like a gem; glittering.
gem·ol·o·gy, gem·mol·o·gy (jĕ-mŏl′ə-jē) *n.* The study of gemstones. —**gem·o·log·i·cal** (jĕm′ə-lŏj′ĭ-kəl) *adj.* —**gem·o·o·gist** (jĕ-mŏl′ə-jĭst) *n.*
ge·mot, ge·mote (gə-mōt′) *n.* A public meeting or local judicial assembly in England prior to the Norman Conquest. [Old English *gemōt* : *ge-,* perfective prefix + *mōt,* assembly, council.]
gems·bok (gĕmz′bŏk′) *n.* An antelope, *Oryx gazella,* of arid regions of southern Africa, having long, sharp, straight horns and a black band along each flank. [Afrikaans, from Dutch *gemsbok,* "male chamois," from German *Gemsbock* : *Gemse,* chamois + *Bock,* he-goat, buck.]
gem·stone (jĕm′stōn′) *n.* A precious or semiprecious stone that may be used as a gem when cut and polished.
ge·müt·lich (gə-müt′lĭKH) *adj.* Having a feeling of warmth or congeniality; friendly. [German, from *gemüt,* spirit.]
ge·müt·lich·keit (gə-müt′lĭKH-kīt′) *n.* A feeling of warmth; congeniality. [German, from GEMÜTLICH.]
-gen, -gene *suffix.* Indicates: **1.** That which produces; producing; for example, *antigen.* **2.** Something produced; for example, *phosgene.* [French *-gène,* from Greek *-genēs,* born.]
gen (jĕn) *n. British Informal.* Relevant information.
~*tr.v.* **genned, genning, gens.** *British Informal.* To give (a person) relevant information on a subject. Used with *up.* [Probably from *general information.*]
gen. **1.** gender. **2.** general; generally. **3.** generator. **4.** generic. **5.** genitive. **6.** genus.
Gen. **1.** general (military rank). **2.** Genesis (Old Testament).
ge·nappe (jə-năp′, zhə-) *n.* An exceptionally smooth worsted yarn used in the manufacture of fringes and braids. [After *Genappe,* Belgium, where it was originally made.]
gen·darme (zhän′därm′, jän′-) *n.* **1.** A member of a national police organization in France and some countries formerly controlled by France, constituting a branch of the armed forces with responsibilities for internal defense, frontier and customs guard, traffic control, and general law enforcement in rural districts. **2.** A cavalryman belonging to any of various units organized under royal authority in France from the 15th century until 1789. **3.** *Informal.* A French policeman. **4.** *Slang.* A policeman. **5.** An isolated pinnacle on a mountain ridge forming an obstacle to climbers. [French, from *gens d'armes,* "men of arms."]
gen·dar·mer·ie, gen·dar·mer·y (zhän-där′mə-rē, jän-) *n.* **1.** A military police organization having general responsibility for public security and law enforcement in France and some countries formerly controlled by France. **2.** A headquarters of a body of gendarmes. **3.** A French royal cavalry corps, as variously organized at different times between the 15th century and 1789. [French, from GENDARME.]
gen·der (jĕn′dər) *n. Abbr.* **g., gen. 1.** *Grammar.* **a.** Any set of two or more categories, such as masculine, feminine, and neuter, into which words are divided according to sex, animation, psychological associations, or some other characteristic, and that determine agreement with or the selection of modifiers, referents, or grammatical forms. **b.** One category of such a set. See **common gender, grammatical gender, natural gender. c.** The classification of a word or grammatical form in such a category. **d.** The distinguishing form or forms used. **2. a.** Classification of sex. **b.** The sex of a person.
~*tr.v.* **gendered, -dering, -ders.** *Archaic.* To engender. [Middle English *gendre,* from Old French *gen(d)re,* kind, sort, from Latin *genus* (stem *gener-*), race, kind.]
gene (jēn) *n.* A hereditary unit located on a chromosome that determines a specific characteristic or function in an organism. Genes are capable of replication and recombination, exist in a number of different forms, called **alleles** (*see*), and can undergo mutation. [German *Gen,* short for *Pangen* : PAN- + -GEN.]
-gene. Variant of **-gen.**
ge·ne·al·o·gy (jē′nē-ăl′ə-jē, -ŏl′ə-jē, jĕn′ē-) *n., pl.* **-gies.** *Abbr.* **geneal. 1.** A record or table of the descent of a family, group, or person from an ancestor or ancestors; a family tree. **2.** Direct descent from an ancestor; lineage; pedigree. **3.** The study or investigation of ancestry and family histories. **4.** The study of the development of plants and animals from their earlier forms. [Middle English *genealogie,* from Old French, from Late Latin *genealogia,* from Greek : *genea,* race, generation + -LOGY.] —**ge·ne·a·log·i·cal** (jē′nē-ə-lŏj′ĭ-kəl, jĕn′ē-) *adj.* —**ge·ne·a·log·i·cal·ly** *adv.* —**ge·ne·al·o·gist** *n.*
gen·e·col·o·gy (jē′nĭ-kŏl′ə-jē, jĕn′ĭ-) *n.* The study of the genetics of populations in relation to their environment. [GENE(TICS) + ECOLOGY.] —**gen·e·col·o·gi·cal** (jē′nĭ-kə-lŏj′ĭ-kəl, jĕn′ĭ-) *adj.*
gene flow *n.* The introduction and movement of new allelic forms of genes in populations due to immigration and subsequent interbreeding.
gene frequency *n.* The frequency of occurrence of an allelic form of a gene in relation to that of other alleles of the same gene.
gene pool *n.* The total number of genes in an interbreeding population at a given time.
gen·e·ra. Plural of **genus.**
gen·er·a·ble (jĕn′ər-ə-bəl) *adj.* Capable of being generated. [Middle English *generabill,* from Latin *generābilis,* from *generāre,* to GENERATE.]
gen·er·al (jĕn′ər-əl, jĕn′rəl) *adj. Abbr.* **gen., genl. 1. a.** Relating to, concerned with, or applicable to the whole or to every member of a class or category: *a program to improve the general welfare.* **b.** *Medicine.* Pertaining to or involving the whole body. **2.** Affecting or characteristic of the majority of those involved; prevalent: *a general discontent.* **3.** Being usually the case; true or applicable in most instances but not all: *the general correctness of his decisions.* **4. a.** Not limited in scope, area, or application; not restricted: *a general rule to follow.* **b.** Not limited to or dealing with one class of things; diversified; miscellaneous: *general studies; a general store.* **5.** Involving only the main or more obvious features of something rather than details or particulars: *a general grasp of a subject.* **6.** Highest or superior in rank; chief within a particular sphere: *the general manager; secretary general.*
~*n.* **1.** *Abbr.* **Gen. a.** An officer in the U.S. Army, Air Force, or Marine Corps holding a rank above colonel; especially, an officer of the second-highest rank in the U.S. Army or Air Force and the highest rank in the Marine Corps. **b.** An officer of the British and Australian armies ranking between a field marshal and a lieutenant general and equivalent in rank to an admiral in the Navy and an air chief marshal in the Air Force. **c.** An officer of the highest rank in the Royal Marines. **2. a.** The head of certain Roman Catholic religious orders. **b.** The head of the Salvation Army. **3.** Something, such as a condition, principle, or fact, that embraces or is applicable to the whole. **4.** *Archaic.* The public: " *'twas caviare to the general* " (Shakespeare). —**in general.** Generally. [Middle English, from Old French, from Latin *generālis,* belonging to a kind or species, relating to all, from *genus* (stem *gener-*), birth, race, kind.] —**gen·er·al·ness** *n.*
general anesthetic *n.* An anesthetic that causes loss of sensation in the entire body and induces unconsciousness. Compare **local anesthetic.**
general assembly *n. Abbr.* **GA, G.A. 1. General Assembly.** The principal deliberative body of the United Nations, in which each member nation is represented and has one vote. **2.** The supreme governing body of some religious denominations, especially that of the Church of Scotland and other Presbyterian churches. **3.** Any of various legislative bodies, especially that of a U.S. state.
General Certificate of Education *n.* See **GCE.**
general confession *n.* **1.** In the services of the Anglican Church, a prayer of confession recited by the whole congregation. **2.** In the Roman Catholic Church, a confession in which the penitent considers his life in general rather than his recent past.
General Court *n.* **1.** A Colonial legislative body with judicial powers. **2.** The state legislature of Massachusetts and New Hampshire.
general court-martial *n.* A court-martial consisting of at least five officers for trying major offenses.
gen·er·al·cy (jĕn′ər-əl-sē) *n., pl.* **-cies.** The rank, appointment, authority, or tenure of a general.
general delivery *n.* **1.** A department of a post office that holds mail for addressees until it is called for. Also *chiefly British* "poste restante." **2.** Mail sent to general delivery.
general election *n.* An election at which all or most constituencies

gemsbok *Native to southern and eastern Africa, the gemsbok, a type of antelope, can survive long periods without water by eating moisture-filled tubers and roots. Once widely hunted, it is now an endangered species.*

return a representative to a legislative body.
general hospital *n.* A hospital that provides basic services for its patients without specializing in particular diseases.
gen·er·al·is·si·mo (jĕn′ər-ə-lĭs′ə-mō′) *n., pl.* **-mos.** The commander in chief of all the armed forces in certain countries, or, occasionally, of the armed forces of allied countries in a joint campaign. [Italian, superlative of *generale,* general, from Latin *generālis,* belonging to a kind, GENERAL.]
gen·er·al·ist (jĕn′ər-ə-lĭst) *n.* A person with broad general knowledge and skills in several disciplines, fields, or areas.
gen·er·al·i·ty (jĕn′ə-răl′ə-tē) *n., pl.* **-ties. 1.** The condition or quality of being general. **2.** An observation or principle having general application; a generalization. **3.** A statement or idea that is imprecise or vague. **4.** The greater portion or number; the majority.
gen·er·al·i·za·tion (jĕn′ər-ə-lə-zā′shən) *n.* **1.** An act or instance of generalizing. **2.** A general principle, statement, or idea having general application. **3.** *Psychology.* A process by which behavior prompted by a particular stimulus can also be prompted by a similar stimulus.
gen·er·al·ize (jĕn′ər-ə-līz′) *v.* **-ized, -izing, -izes.** *—tr.* **1. a.** To reduce to a general form, class, or law. **b.** To render indefinite or unspecific. **2. a.** To infer from many particulars. **b.** To draw inferences or a general conclusion from. **3. a.** To make generally or universally applicable. **b.** To popularize. *—intr.* **1. a.** To form a concept inductively. **b.** To form general notions or conclusions, especially after incomplete consideration of the facts. **2.** To speak or think in generalities; speak vaguely. **3.** *Medicine.* To spread through the body. Used of a usually localized disease.
gen·er·al·ized (jĕn′ər-ə-līzd′) *adj.* **1.** Generally prevalent. **2. a.** General; unspecific. **b.** Not well adapted to a specific environment or function; undifferentiated.
generalized order *n. Psychology.* An organized group whose group identity allows an individual to establish a personal identity by reference to it.
general knowledge *n.* Knowledge of a wide variety of facts from many fields.
gen·er·al·ly (jĕn′ər-ə-lē, jĕn′rə-) *adv. Abbr.* **gen. 1.** For the most part; widely: *generally known.* **2.** As a rule; usually; ordinarily. **3.** Viewing circumstances overall; not specifically: *generally speaking.*
general officer *n.* Any officer ranking above colonel.
general paresis *n.* A brain disease occurring as a late consequence of syphilis and characterized by mental deterioration, speech disturbances, and progressive muscular weakness. Also called "paresis."
General Post Office *n. Abbr.* **GPO 1.** Formerly in Britain, the central governmental department providing postal and telecommunications services. **2.** The main post office in a large city.
general practitioner *n. Abbr.* **G.P.** A physician in general practice who treats a variety of medical problems but sends patients requiring more specialized treatment to a hospital or a consultant. Also called "family doctor."
gen·er·al-pur·pose (jĕn′ər-əl-pûr′pəs, jĕn′rəl-) *adj.* Capable of being used or applied in many circumstances.
general relativity *n. Physics.* The later part of the theory of **relativity** *(see),* dealing with accelerated motion.
general semantics *n. Used with a singular verb.* A doctrine proposed by Alfred Korzybski (1879–1950) that presents a method of improving human behavior through a more critical use of words and symbols.
gen·er·al·ship (jĕn′ər-əl-shĭp′, jĕn′rəl-) *n.* **1.** The rank, office, or tenure of a general. **2.** Leadership or skill in the conduct of a war. **3.** Skillful management or leadership.
general staff *n. Abbr.* **GS, G.S.** *Military.* A group of officers, usually of the rank of major and above, who are charged with assisting senior officers in planning and supervising operations.
general strike *n.* A simultaneous strike by all workers of the unionized industries of a nation or area.
General Synod *n.* The governing body of the Church of England, composed of the diocesan bishops and elected clerical and lay representatives.
gen·er·ate (jĕn′ə-rāt′) *tr.v.* **-ated, -ating, -ates. 1. a.** To bring into existence; give rise to: *generate discussion.* **b.** To produce (electricity or heat, for example) as a result of a chemical or physical process. **2.** To engender (offspring); beget. **3.** To form (a geometric figure) by describing a curve or surface. **4.** *Computer Science.* To produce (a program) by instructing a computer to follow given parameters with a skeleton program. [Latin *generāre,* from *genus* (stem *gener-*), birth, race, kind.] **—gen·er·a·tive** (jĕn′ər-ə-tĭv, -ə-rā′-tĭv) *adj.*
gen·er·a·tion (jĕn′ə-rā′shən) *n.* **1.** The act or process of generating; especially, origination, production, or procreation. **2.** Offspring having a common parent or parents and constituting a single stage of descent. **3.** *Biology.* All the individuals produced during a particular phase of the life cycle that have the same method of reproduction. **4.** A class of objects derived from a preceding class: *the new generation of minicomputers.* **5. a.** A group of contemporaneous individuals. **b.** A group of individuals, usually contemporaneous, regarded as having a common cultural or social attribute: *music that inspired a whole generation of composers.* **6.** The average time interval between the birth of parents and the birth of their offspring. **7.** *Computer Science.* The technique of generating programs. **—gen·er·a·tion·al** *adj.*
generation gap *n.* The differences in outlook and attitude between people of different generations, especially between young people and their parents.
generative grammar *n. Linguistics.* An ordered set of rules intended to produce all and only the well-formed sentences of a language; specifically, **transformational-generative grammar** *(see).*
generative semantics *n. Used with a singular verb.* A theory based on the belief that syntactic and semantic structures are of the same nature and that the mind relates surface structure to meaning.
gen·er·a·tor (jĕn′ə-rā′tər) *n. Abbr.* **gen. 1.** One that generates. **2.** A machine that converts mechanical energy into electrical energy, as a dynamo in a power station. **3.** An apparatus that generates a vapor or gas. **4.** A generatrix. **5.** *Computer Science.* A routine that performs a generating function.
gen·er·a·trix (jĕn′ə-rā′trĭks) *n., pl.* **generatrices** (-rā′trə-sēz′, -ər-ə-trī′sēz′). A point, line, or plane that generates a geometric figure; especially, a straight line that generates a surface by moving in a given fashion.
ge·ner·ic (jə-nĕr′ĭk) *adj. Abbr.* **gen. 1.** Relating to or descriptive of an entire group or class; general. **2.** *Biology.* Of or relating to a genus. **3.** Not protected by trademark; nonproprietary.
~n. A generic product, especially a drug. [French *générique,* from Latin *genus* (stem *gener-*), race, species, kind.] **—ge·ner·i·cal·ly** *adv.*
gen·er·os·i·ty (jĕn′ə-rŏs′ə-tē) *n., pl.* **-ties. 1.** The quality of being generous; liberality in giving or willingness to give. **2.** Nobility of thought or behavior; magnanimity. **3.** Amplitude; abundance. **4.** A generous act.
gen·er·ous (jĕn′ər-əs) *adj.* **1.** Willing to give or share; unselfish. **2.** Lacking pettiness or meanness in thought or behavior; magnanimous. **3.** Characterized by abundance; bountiful; ample. **4.** Having a rich bouquet and flavor. Said of wine. **5.** Fertile. Said of soil. [Old French *genereux,* from Latin *generōsus,* of noble birth, excellent, magnanimous, from *genus* (stem *gener-*), birth, race, kind.] **—gen·er·ous·ly** *adv.* **—gen·er·ous·ness** *n.*
gen·e·sis (jĕn′ə-sĭs) *n., pl.* **-ses** (-sēz′). The coming into being of something; origin. [Latin, from Greek, generation, birth, origin.]
Gen·e·sis (jĕn′ə-sĭs) *n. Abbr.* **Gen.** The first book of the Old Testament, recounting the creation of the world and the establishment and early history of Israel.
-genesis *suffix.* Indicates generation; for example, **biogenesis, paragenesis.** [New Latin, from Latin *genesis,* birth, GENESIS.]
gene-splic·ing (jĕn′splī′sĭng) *n.* The process in which DNA fragments from one or more different organisms are combined and made to function within the cells of a host organism.
gen·et¹ (jĕn′ĭt, jə-nĕt′) *n.* Any of several Old World carnivorous mammals of the genus *Genetta,* having grayish or yellowish fur with dark spots and a long, ringed tail. [Middle English *genete,* from Old French, from Arabic *jarnayt.*]

genet *These stealthy woodland hunters are related to the mongoose. Several species of genet live in Africa and one species in Europe.*

genet². Variant of **jennet.**
Ge·net (zhə-nā′), **Jean** (1910–86). French novelist and playwright. After many convictions for theft and homosexuality, he was released from a life sentence when many of France's leading intellectuals, led by Jean Cocteau, petitioned the president. His early works, such as *The Miracle of the Rose* (1946) and *A Thief's Journal* (1948), draw on his prison experiences. His later works tend toward the nihilistic and the absurd.
ge·net·ic (jə-nĕt′ĭk) *adj.* Also **ge·net·i·cal** (-ĭ-kəl). **1.** Of or pertaining to the origin or development of something. **2. a.** Of or pertaining to genetics or genes. **b.** Affecting or affected by genes: *a genetic disorder.* [From GENESIS.] **—ge·net·i·cal·ly** *adv.*
genetic code *n.* The information carried by DNA, which determines the nature of all the proteins made in the cell. The code is expressed by the sequence of nitrogenous bases in the DNA molecule, three consecutive bases (a codon) coding for a particular amino acid in the protein.
genetic drift *n.* The tendency for a genetic variant to become fixed in or lost from a population by chance rather than by natural selection. It most commonly occurs in small, isolated populations. Also called "Sewall Wright effect."
genetic engineering *n.* The modification of the structure of the chromosomes of living organisms, especially bacteria and viruses, in such a way as to benefit man. It has been employed in agriculture and medicine. See **biotechnology. —genetic engineer** *n.*
ge·net·i·cist (jə-nĕt′ə-sĭst) *n.* One who specializes in genetics.
ge·net·ics (jə-nĕt′ĭks) *n.* **1.** *Used with a singular verb.* The biology of heredity; especially, the study of the mechanisms of hereditary transmission and the variation of heritable characteristics. **2.** *Used with a singular or plural verb.* The genetic constitution of an individual, group, or class.
Ge·ne·va (jə-nē′və). *French* **Ge·nève** (zhə-nĕv′). *German* **Genf** (gĕnf). A city in Switzerland, on the southwest corner of Lake Geneva. It is the country's third-largest city and capital of Geneva canton. Many international organizations, such as the Red Cross, and agencies of the United Nations, including the World Health Organization, have their headquarters here.
Geneva, Lake. *French* **Lac Lé·man** (lăk lĕ′mən, lĕm′ən, lə-măn′). *German* **Gen·fer·see** (gĕn′fər-zā). Lake of Switzerland and France. Approximately 72 kilometers (45 miles) long and 13 kilometers (8 miles) at its widest point, it lies between southwest Switzerland and the Haute-Savoie department of France. The surface is subject to changes of level caused by variations in atmospheric pressure and wind direction.
Ge·ne·va bands (jə-nē′və) *pl.n.* Two strips of white cloth hanging

from the collar of some clerical and academic robes. [Originally worn by Calvinist clergymen in Geneva.]

Geneva Convention *n.* Any of several agreements, the first of which was formulated in 1864 at an international convention held in Geneva, Switzerland, establishing rules for the wartime treatment of prisoners and the sick or wounded.

Geneva cross *n.* A red Greek or St. George's cross on a white ground, used as a symbol by the Red Cross and as a sign of neutrality.

Geneva gown *n.* A loose black academic or clerical gown with wide sleeves. [Originally worn by Calvinist clergymen in Geneva.]

Ge·ne·van (jə-nē′vən) *adj.* Also **Gen·e·vese** (jĕn′ə-vēz′, -vēs′). **1.** Of or relating to Geneva, Switzerland. **2.** Of or relating to Geneva during the time of John Calvin; Calvinist.
~ *n.* Also **Genevese. 1.** A native or inhabitant of Geneva, Switzerland. **2.** A follower of Calvin; a Calvinist.

Geneva Protocol *n.* A document drafted in 1925 that sought to ban the use of poison gas in warfare and to enforce sanctions against the aggressors in wars.

Genf. See Geneva.

Gen·ghis Khan (jĕng′gĭz kän, gĕng′-), **Chin·giz Khan** (chĭng′-), **Jen·ghiz Khan** (jĕng′-, gĕng′-), or **Jin·ghiz Khan** (jĭng′-), born Temujin (c. 1162–1227). Mongolian emperor. The son of a Mongol chieftain, he united the Mongolian tribes by conquest, and in 1206 took the title Genghis Khan (supreme ruler). By brilliant use of light cavalry, he annexed northern China, central Asia, Iran, and southern Russia. Though capable of horrific cruelty in battle, he was a far-sighted administrator and lawmaker.

gen·ial¹ (jēn′yəl) *adj.* **1.** Having a pleasant or friendly disposition or manner; cordial and kindly. **2.** Conducive to life or growth; mild. **3.** *Obsolete.* Characteristic of or relating to genius. [Latin *geniālis,* of generation or birth, nuptial, hence festive, joyous, from *genius,* deity of generation and birth.] —**gen·ial·ly** *adv.* —**ge·ni·al·i·ty** (jē′nē-ăl′ə-tē), **gen·ial·ness** *n.*

ge·ni·al² (jə-nī′əl) *n. Anatomy.* Of or pertaining to the chin. [Greek *geneion,* chin, from *genus,* jaw.]

gen·ic (jĕn′ĭk, jĕn′ĭk) *adj.* Of, relating to, produced by, or being a gene or genes; genetic.

-genic *suffix.* Indicates: **1.** Generation or production; for example, **antigenic. 2.** Suitability for; for example, **photogenic.** [From -GEN.]

ge·nic·u·late (jə-nĭk′yə-lĭt) *adj.* Also **ge·nic·u·lat·ed** (-lā′tĭd). **1.** *Biology.* Bent at an abrupt angle like that of a bent knee. **2.** Jointed so as to be capable of bending at an abrupt angle. [Latin *geniculātus,* with bent knee, curved, from *geniculum,* diminutive of *genu,* knee.] —**ge·nic·u·late·ly** *adv.* —**ge·nic·u·la·tion** *n.*

ge·nie (jē′nē) *n.* A supernatural creature who does one's bidding. [French *génie,* spirit, from Latin *genius,* guardian spirit, GENIUS.]

ge·ni·i. Alternate plural of **genius.**

gen·ip (jĕn′əp) *n.* **1.** A tropical American tree, *Melicocca bijuga,* having small greenish-white flowers and small yellow fruit. **2.** The sweet, edible fruit of the genip. **3.** The genipap. [Spanish *genipa,* a kind of palm, probably of Carib origin.]

gen·i·pap (jĕn′ə-păp′) *n.* **1.** An evergreen tree, *Genipa americana,* of the West Indies, having yellowish-white flowers and edible fruit. **2.** The reddish-brown fruit of the genipap. Also called "genip," "marmalade box." [Portuguese *genipapo,* from Tupi.]

ge·nis·ta (jə-nĭs′tə) *n.* Any shrub of the European genus *Genista,* similar and related to the broom; especially, **dyer's greenweed** *(see).* [New Latin *Genista* (genus), from Latin, broom.]

genit. genitive.

gen·i·tal (jĕn′ə-təl) *adj.* **1.** Of or relating to biological reproduction. **2.** Of or pertaining to the genitals. **3.** *Psychoanalysis.* Pertaining to or designating a stage at which a child's anal and oral impulses give way to more mature personal relationships. Compare **anal, oral.** [Middle English *genytal,* from Old French *genital,* from Latin *genitālis,* from *gignere* (past participle *genitus*), to beget, produce.]

genital herpes *n.* A recurrent viral infection of the genital region that may cause painful eruptions of the skin or be symptomless. See **herpes.**

gen·i·ta·li·a (jĕn′ə-tā′lē-ə, -tāl′yə) *pl.n.* The reproductive organs; especially, the external sex organs. [Latin *genitālia (membra),* genital (members), neuter plural of *genitālis,* GENITAL.]

gen·i·tals (jĕn′ə-təlz) *pl.n.* Genitalia.

gen·i·ti·val (jĕn′ə-tī′vəl) *adj. Grammar.* Of, pertaining to, or in the genitive case. —**gen·i·ti·val·ly** *adv.*

gen·i·tive (jĕn′ə-tĭv) *n. Abbr.* **g., gen., genit. 1.** The grammatical case in certain languages, usually expressed in English by a prepositional phrase with *of,* that denotes possession, measurement, or source. **2.** A form or construction in this case.
~ *adj. Abbr.* **g., gen., genit.** *Grammar.* Designating, pertaining to, or inflected in the genitive. [Middle English *genitif (case),* from Latin *(casus) genitīvus,* "case of production or origin" (translation of Greek *genikē ptōsis,* "case of race"), from *gignere* (past participle *genitus*), to beget, produce.]

gen·i·tor (jĕn′ə-tər) *n.* **1.** One who begets or creates. **2.** *Anthropology.* A natural father as distinguished from the socially responsible foster father in certain cultures. [Middle English *genytur,* from Latin *genitor,* from *gignere* (past participle *genitus*), to beget.]

gen·i·to·u·ri·nar·y (jĕn′ə-tō-yŏŏr′ə-nĕr′ē) *adj.* Of or pertaining to the genital and urinary organs or their functions. [GENIT(AL) + URINARY.]

gen·ius (jēn′yəs) *n., pl.* **-iuses** or **genii** (jē′nē-ī′) (for senses 4, 6).

1. a. Exceptional or transcendent intellectual and creative power. **b.** One who possesses such power. **2. a.** A natural talent or inclination. Used with *to* or *for: She has a genius for acting.* **b.** One who has such a talent or inclination: *He is a genius at diplomacy.* **3.** The prevailing spirit or character, as of a place, person, time, or group: *the genius of the Elizabethan poets.* **4.** *Roman Mythology.* **a.** A tutelary deity or guardian spirit allotted to a person from birth. **b.** Any guiding spirit of a person or place. **5.** A person who has great influence over another. **6.** In Muslim legend, a jinni or demon. [Latin *genius,* deity of generation and birth, guardian spirit.]

ge·ni·us lo·ci (jē′nē-əs lō′sī′) *n.* **1.** A guardian deity of a particular locality. **2.** The distinctive atmosphere or particular character of a place. [Latin.]

ge·ni·zah (gə-nē′zə) *n.* A room adjacent to a synagogue where discarded books and sacred relics are stored. [Hebrew, "hiding place," from *gānaz,* to hide.]

genl. general.

Gennesaret, Lake of. See Galilee, Sea of.

Gen·o·a (jĕn′ō-ə). Italian **Ge·no·va** (jĕn′ə-və). Port on the Gulf of Genoa, Italy. The capital of Liguria and of Genoa province, it is Italy's chief seaport and handles over one third of the country's shipping. —**Gen·o·ese** (jĕn′ō-ēz′) *adj. & n.*

Gen·o·a cake (jĕn′ō-ə) *n.* A rich sponge cake, sometimes made with cherries. [After GENOA, Italy.]

Genoa jib *n. Nautical.* A large jib used on a racing yacht. [After GENOA, Italy.]

gen·o·cide (jĕn′ə-sīd′) *n.* The systematic, planned annihilation of a racial, political, or cultural group. [Greek *genos,* race + -CIDE.] —**gen·o·cid·al** (jĕn′ə-sīd′l) *adj.*

ge·nome (jē′nōm′) *n.* Also **ge·nom** (-nŏm′). *Biology.* A complete haploid set of chromosomes. [German *Genom : Gen,* GENE + (CHROMOS)OME.]

gen·o·type (jĕn′ə-tīp′, jē′nə-) *n.* **1.** The genetic constitution of an organism, especially as distinguished from its physical appearance. Compare **phenotype. 2.** A group or class of organisms having the same genetic constitution. [Greek *genos,* race + TYPE.] —**gen·o·typ·ic** (jĕn′ə-tĭp′ĭk, jē′nə-), **gen·o·typ·i·cal** *adj.* —**gen·o·typ·i·cal·ly** *adv.* —**gen·o·ty·pic·i·ty** (jĕn′ə-tī-pĭs′ə-tē, jē′nə-) *n.*

-genous *suffix.* Indicates: **1.** Generating or producing; for example, **androgenous. 2.** Generated by, produced by, or arising from; for example, **endogenous.** [From -GEN.]

Genova. See Genoa.

gen·re (zhän′rə) *n.* **1.** Type; class. **2. a.** A category of artistic composition, as of music, marked by a distinctive style, form, or content, especially a style of painting concerned with depicting scenes and subjects of common everyday life. **b.** A distinctive class or category of literary composition.
~ *adj.* Of or relating to genre. [French, kind, from Old French *gen(d)re,* from Latin *genus* (stem *gener-*), race, kind.]

gen·ro (gĕn′rō′) *n., pl.* **-ros. 1.** In Japan, a group of elder statesmen, formerly advisers to the emperor. **2.** Any of these elder statesmen. [Japanese *genrō.*]

gens (jĕnz, gĕnz) *n., pl.* **gentes** (jĕn′tēz′, gĕn′tās′). **1.** The patrilineal clan forming the basic unit of the Roman tribe and having originally a common name, land, cult, and burial ground. **2.** *Anthropology.* An exogamous patrilineal clan. [Latin *gēns,* clan.]

gent (jĕnt) *n. Informal.* A gentleman; a man. [Shortened from GENTLEMAN.]

Gent. See Ghent.

gen·ta·mi·cin (jĕn′tə-mī′sĭn) *n.* An antibiotic used to treat a wide variety of infections and applied in or in the form of a cream or drops. [Variant of earlier *gentamycin : genta-* (probably irregularly formed from *gentian violet,* referring to the color of the organism from which it is derived) + *-mycin,* as in STREPTOMYCIN.]

gen·teel (jĕn-tēl′) *adj.* **1. a.** Striving to convey a manner or appearance of refinement and respectability. **b.** Marked by affected and somewhat prudish refinement. **2.** Refined in manner; well-bred; polite. **3.** Free from vulgarity or rudeness. **4.** Fashionable; elegant: *"It was a genteel old-fashioned house, very quiet and orderly"* (Charles Dickens). —See Synonyms at **polite.** [Old French *gentil,* GENTLE.] —**gen·teel·ly** *adv.* —**gen·teel·ness** *n.*

gen·teel·ism (jĕn-tē′lĭz′əm) *n.* A word or expression thought by its user to be genteel.

gen·tian (jĕn′shən) *n.* **1.** Any of numerous plants of the genus *Gentiana,* characteristically having showy blue, yellow, or red flowers. **2.** The dried rhizome and roots of a yellow-flowered European gentian, *G. lutea,* sometimes used as a tonic. [Middle English *gencian,* from Old French *genciane,* from Latin *gentiāna,* probably after *Gentius,* king of Illyria (2nd century B.C.), supposed discoverer of the medicinal properties of the plant.]

gen·tia·nel·la (jĕn′shə-nĕl′ə, jĕn′shē-ə-) *n.* **1.** An alpine plant, *Gentiana acaulis,* with ornamental blue flowers. **2.** Any of several similar and related plants. [New Latin, diminutive of GENTIAN.]

gentian violet *n.* A purple dye used chiefly as a biological stain and bactericide. Also called "crystal violet."

gen·tile (jĕn′tīl′) *adj.* **1.** Of or pertaining to the gens or to the tribal society based on it. **2.** Of or relating to Gentiles. **3.** *Grammar.* Of or pertaining to a noun or adjective designating a nation, place, or people; for example, *American* and *Italian* are gentile nouns.
~ *n.* **1.** A member of a gens. **2.** A gentile noun or adjective. [Latin *gentīlis,* from *gēns,* clan, GENS.]

Gen·tile (jĕn′tīl′) *n.* **1.** A person who is not of the Jewish faith or is of a non-Jewish nation. **2.** A Christian as distinguished from a Jew.

gentian *One of the wildflowers most favored by herbalists. Gentians have been used for curing indigestion, bites and stings, dysentery and catarrh, and as a flavoring for bitter beer. This is the marsh gentian, Gentiana pneumonanthe.*

geological time scale

HOW WE GAUGE EARTH'S AGE
The planet's story, revealed by its rocks

The eras of the earth have been well established by isotope dating in which the age of rocks is determined by the amount of radioactive-decay products they contain. Major divisions reflect changes in the positions of continents and the emergence of new forms of life.

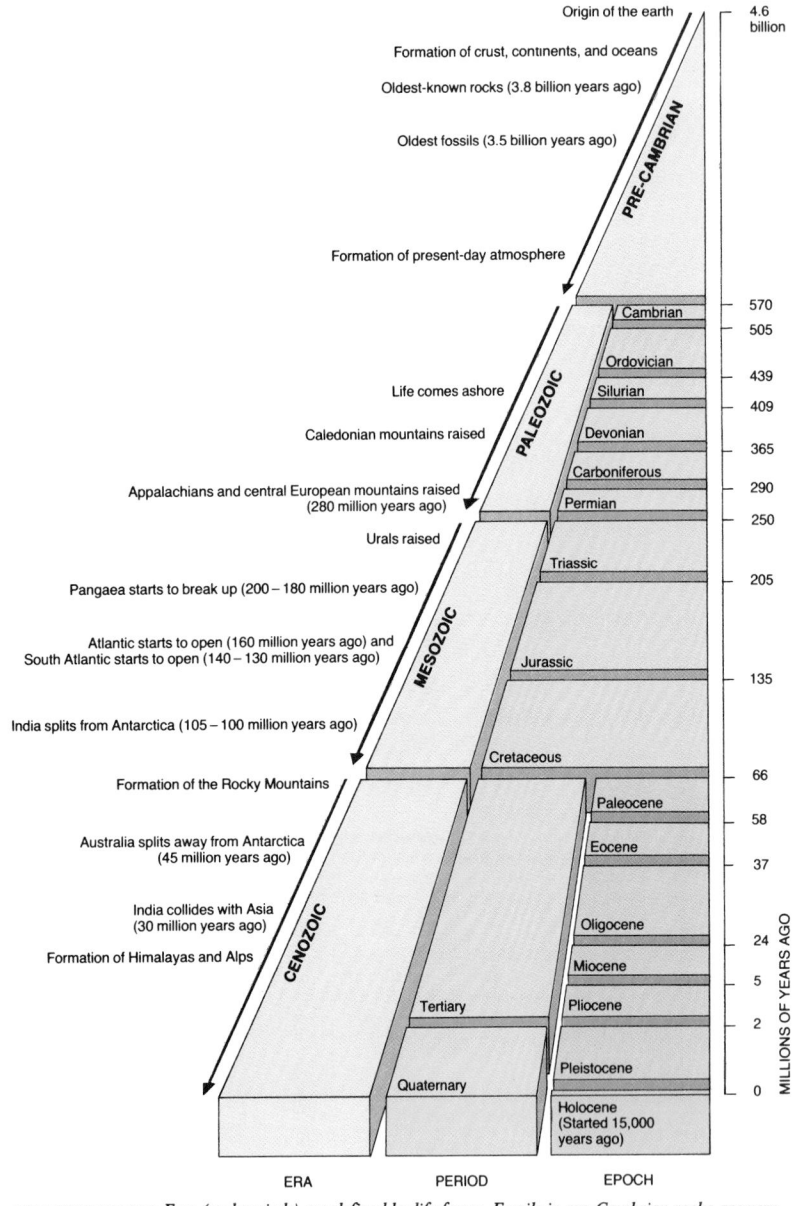

ERAS OF THE WORLD *Eras (and periods) are defined by life forms. Fossils in pre-Cambrian rocks are very rare. The Paleozoic ("old life") saw the rise of invertebrates and amphibians. The Mesozoic ("middle life") was the age of reptiles. The Cenozoic ("recent life") is the age of mammals.*

3. A pagan or heathen. **4.** Among Mormons, a person who is not a Mormon. ~*adj.* Of or pertaining to a Gentile. [Middle English *gentil, gentyle,* from Late Latin *gentīles,* pagans, heathens, from *gentīlis,* pagan, from Latin, of the same clan, from *gēns,* clan, GENS.]

gen·ti·lesse (jěn′tə-lěs′) *n. Archaic.* Refinement and courtesy resulting from good breeding. [Middle English, from Old French, from *gentil,* GENTLE.]

gen·til·i·ty (jěn-tĭl′ə-tē) *n.* **1.** The condition of being genteel. **2.** The condition of being born to the gentry. **3.** Persons of gentle birth collectively; the gentry. **4.** The attempt to convey or maintain the appearance of refinement and respectability. —See Usage note at **culture.** [Middle English *gentilete,* from Old French, from Latin *gentīlitās* (stem *gentīlitāt-*), clanship, from *gentīlis,* belonging to a clan, GENTLE.]

gen·tle (jěnt′l) *adj.* **-tler, -tlest. 1.** Considerate or kindly in disposition; tender and patient: *a gentle mother.* **2.** Not harsh, severe, or violent; mild: *a gentle scolding.* **3.** Easily managed or handled; docile; tame: *a gentle horse.* **4.** Gradual; not steep or sudden: *a gentle incline.* **5.** Moderate. **6.** Of good family; well-born. **7.** *Archaic.* Noble; chivalrous: *a gentle knight.* ~*n.* **1.** *Archaic.* One of gentle birth or station. **2.** The larva of a bluebottle. ~*tr.v.* **gentled, -tling, -tles. 1.** To make gentle; pacify; mollify. **2.** To tame (a horse, for example). [Middle English *gentil,* well-born, noble, graceful, from Old French, from Latin *gentīlis,* of the same clan, of noble birth, from *gēns,* clan.] —**gen′tly** *adv.*

gentle breeze *n.* A wind whose speed is between 12.9 and 19.3 kilometers, or 8 and 12 miles, per hour, force 3 on the Beaufort scale.

gen·tle·folk (jěnt′l-fōk′) *pl.n.* Also **gen·tle·folks** (-fōks′). Persons of good family and breeding.

gen·tle·man (jěnt′l-mən) *n., pl.* **-men** (-mĭn). **1.** A polite, gracious, or considerate man with high standards of propriety or correct behavior. **2.** A man of gentle or noble birth or superior social position. **3. a.** A man. **b. gentlemen.** A form of address for a group of men. Used both in speech and in writing. **4.** A manservant; valet. **5.** *British.* Formerly, a man higher than a yeoman in social position. **6.** A man of independent means who does not or need not work to support himself. [GENTLE + MAN (after French *gentilhomme*).] —**gen·tle·man·ly** *adj.*

   Usage: Gentleman is used instead of *man* only in restricted contexts, and usually carries a nuance: *He's no gentleman* (meaning that he does not act in a well-mannered, considerate way). The form is used neutrally in direct address: *Ladies and gentlemen; We must now turn, gentlemen, to the second point on the agenda.* It is also preferred when referring to a person in his presence: *You had better ask this gentleman to wait outside* (where *man* would sound abrupt and rude).

gen·tle·man-at-arms (jěnt′l-mən-ət-ärmz′) *n., pl.* **gen·tle·men-at-arms** (jěnt′l-mĭn-). Any of a corps of about 35 senior retired army officers who attend the British sovereign as a ceremonial guard on state occasions.

gentleman farmer *n., pl.* **gentlemen farmers.** A man who farms chiefly for pleasure rather than income or whose means permit him to be an absentee proprietor of his farming interests.

gentleman's agreement *n.* An agreement guaranteed only by the honor of the participants and not legally binding.

gentleman's gentleman *n.* A manservant; a valet.

gen·tle·ness (jěnt′l-nĭs) *n.* **1.** The quality of being gentle. **2.** *Physics.* A property or quantum number of elementary particles, similar to charm. It is conserved in strong interactions.

gentle sex *n.* Women collectively.

gen·tle·wom·an (jěnt′l-wŏom′ən) *n., pl.* **-women** (-wĭm′ĭn). **1.** A woman of gentle birth or superior social position. **2.** A polite, gracious, or considerate woman. **3.** A woman acting as a personal attendant to a lady of rank.

Gen·too (jěn′tōō) *n., pl.* **-toos.** *Archaic.* A Hindu. [Portuguese *gentio,* "a pagan," from Late Latin *gentīlis,* pagan, GENTILE.]

gen·tri·fy (jěn′trə-fī′) *tr.v.* **-fied, -fying, -fies.** To change the character of (restored property, especially in a working-class neighborhood) by an influx of middle-class or upper-class residents. [GENTRY + -FY.] —**gen·tri·fi·ca·tion** *n.*

gen·try (jěn′trē) *n., pl.* **-tries. 1.** People of gentle birth, good breeding, or high social position. **2.** In Britain, the upper middle classes. **3.** People of a particular class or group: *another commuter from the suburban gentry.* [Middle English *gentri(se),* gentle birth, from Old French *genterise, gentelise,* from *gentil,* GENTLE.]

gen·u (jěn′yōō) *n., pl.* **genua** (jěn′yōō-ə). *Anatomy.* The knee. [New Latin, from Latin.]

gen·u·flect (jěn′yə-flěkt′) *intr.v.* **-flected, -flecting, -flects. 1.** To bend the knee in a kneeling or half-kneeling position, as in reverence. **2.** To exhibit a deferential or obsequious attitude or manner. [Late Latin *genuflectere* : Latin *genu,* knee + *flectere,* to bend.]

gen·u·flec·tion (jěn′yə-flěk′shən) *n.* Also *chiefly British* **gen·u·flex·ion.** The act of kneeling briefly by bending one knee, as in reverence.

gen·u·ine (jěn′yōō-ĭn) *adj.* **1.** Actually possessing or produced by the alleged or apparent attribute, character, or source: *genuine sorrow; genuine leather.* **2.** Not spurious or counterfeit; authentic: *a genuine claim.* **3.** Free from hypocrisy or dishonesty; sincere: *genuine admiration.* **4.** Being of pure or original stock. —See Synonyms at **real.** [Latin *genuīnus,* perhaps originally "placed on the knees" (from the ancient custom that a father acknowledges a child by placing him or her on his knees), from *genu,* knee.] —**gen·u·ine·ly** *adv.* —**gen·u·ine·ness** *n.*

ge·nus (jē′nəs) *n., pl.* **genera** (jěn′ər-ə). *Abbr.* **gen. 1.** *Biology.* A taxonomic category ranking below a family and above a species, used in taxonomic nomenclature followed by a Latin adjective or epithet to form the name of a species. **2.** *Logic.* A class of objects divided into subordinate species having certain common attributes. **3.** Any class, group, or kind with common attributes. **4.** *Mathematics.* A number denoting the topological complexity of a surface. A sphere has a genus of 0; a torus has a genus of 1. [Latin *genus,* birth, race, kind.]

–geny *suffix.* Indicates manner of origin or development; for example, **ontogeny.** [Greek *-geneia,* from *-genēs,* born.]

geo– *prefix.* Indicates the earth; for example, **geotropism, geology.** [Greek *geō-*, from *gē*, earth.]

ge•o•cen•tric (jē′ō-sĕn′trĭk) *adj.* **1.** Pertaining to, measured from, or observed from the center of the earth. **2.** Having the earth as a center. **—ge•o•cen•tri•cal•ly** *adv.*

geocentric parallax *n. Astronomy.* **Diurnal parallax** *(see).*

ge•o•chem•is•try (jē′ō-kĕm′ĭ-strē) *n.* The science and study of the composition and chemical processes that take place in the earth's crust. **—ge•o•chem•i•cal** *adj.* **—ge•o•chem•ist** *n.*

ge•o•chro•nol•o•gy (jē′ō-krə-nŏl′ə-jē) *n.* The chronology of the earth's history as determined by geologic events. **—ge•o•chron•o•log•ic** (jē′ō-krŏn′ə-lŏj′ĭk), **ge•o•chron•o•log•i•cal** *adj.*

geod. **1.** geodesy. **2.** geodesic. **3.** geodetic.

ge•ode (jē′ōd′) *n.* A small, hollow, usually spheroidal nodule with crystals lining the inside wall. [Latin *geōdēs,* from Greek, earthlike : *gē,* earth + -ODE (resembling).]

ge•o•des•ic (jē′ə-dĕs′ĭk, -dēz′ĭk, -dē′sĭk, -dē′zĭk) *adj. Abbr.* **geod.** **1.** *Mathematics.* Of or pertaining to the geometry of geodesics. **2.** Geodetic.
∼*n. Mathematics.* In three-dimensional Euclidean space, a curve whose principal normal at any point is the normal to the surface on which the curve occurs; the shortest line between two points on any mathematically derived surface.

geodesic dome *n.* A domed or vaulted structure of lightweight straight elements that form interlocking polygons.

ge•od•e•sy (jē-ŏd′ə-sē) *n. Abbr.* **geod.** The branch of mathematics concerned with the size and shape of the earth, including the techniques of measuring distance on the earth's surface and of determining exact geographic location. [French *geodesie,* from New Latin *geodaesia,* from Greek *geōdaisia,* "division of the earth" : GEO- + *daiesthai,* to divide.] **—ge•od•e•sist** *n.*

ge•o•det•ic (jē′ə-dĕt′ĭk) *adj.* Also **geo•det•i•cal** (-ĭ-kəl). *Abbr.* **geod.** **1.** Of or pertaining to geodesy. **2.** Geodesic. **—ge•o•det•i•cal•ly** *adv.*

geo•duck (gōō′ē-dŭk′) *n.* A very large edible clam, *Panope generosa,* of the Pacific coast of northwestern North America. [Chinook jargon *go-duck.*]

ge•o•dy•nam•ics (jē′ō-dī-năm′ĭks) *n. Used with a singular verb.* The study of the forces acting inside the earth's crust and the way in which they affect its formation, alteration, and disturbance. **—ge•o•dy•nam•ic** *adj.* **—ge•o•dy•nam•i•cist** *n.*

Geof•frey of Mon•mouth (jĕf′rē; mŏn′məth) (*c.* 1100–54). English writer. His *History of the Kings of Britain,* tracing an almost entirely fictitious line of descent from the Trojans to King Arthur, recorded British folk history and inspired the Arthurian writers and Shakespeare's *King Lear* and *Cymbeline.*

geog. **1.** geographer. **2.** geographic. **3.** geography.

ge•og•no•sy (jē-ŏg′nə-sē) *n.* The scientific study of the organization and structure of the earth and its materials. [GEO- + Greek *-gnosia,* knowledge, -GNOSIS.]

ge•o•graph•ic (jē′ə-grăf′ĭk), **ge•o•graph•i•cal** (-ĭ-kəl) *adj. Abbr.* **geog.** **1.** Pertaining to geography. **2.** Concerning the topography of a specific region. **—ge•o•graph•i•cal•ly** *adv.*

geographic mile *n.* A nautical mile.

ge•og•ra•phy (gē-ŏg′rə-fē) *n., pl.* **-phies.** *Abbr.* **geog.** **1. a.** The study of the earth and its surface features, how they influence human distribution and activity, and how they in turn are affected by human activity. **b.** Broadly, the science of the distribution of all the components of the physical world. **2.** The geographic characteristics of an area. **3.** A book on geography. **4.** An ordered arrangement of constituent elements. [Latin *geōgraphia,* from Greek : GEO- + -GRAPHY.] **—ge•og•ra•pher** *n.*

ge•oid (jē′oid′) *n.* **1.** The hypothetical surface of the earth formed from mean sea level and its continuation through the continents. **2.** A geometric figure similar to this surface. [German *Geoid,* from Greek *geoidēs,* earthlike : GE(O)- + -OID.]

geol. **1.** geologic. **2.** geologist. **3.** geology.

geologic time *n.* The period of time covering the earth's geologic history.

geological time scale *n.* The division of geological time into chronological units. The last 570–600 million years are divided into the units **era, period, epoch,** and **age** *(all of which see).* The time before this is the **Precambrian** *(see).*

ge•ol•o•gize (jē-ŏl′ə-jīz′) *intr.v.* **-gized, -gizing, -gizes.** To study geology or make geologic investigations.

ge•ol•o•gy (jē-ŏl′ə-jē) *n., pl.* **-gies.** *Abbr.* **geol.** **1.** The scientific study of the origin, history, structure, and processes of the earth. **2.** The structure of a specific region of the earth's surface. **3.** A book on geology. **4.** The scientific study of the origin, history, and structure of the solid matter of a celestial body. [New Latin *geologia* : GEO- + -LOGY.] **—ge•o•log•ic** (jē′ə-lŏj′ĭk), **ge•o•log•i•cal** *adj.* **—ge•o•log•i•cal•ly** *adv.* **—ge•ol•o•gist, ge•ol•o•ger** *n.*

geom. **1.** geometric. **2.** geometry.

geomagnetic equator *n.* The great circle on the earth's surface formed by the intersection of a plane passing through the earth's center perpendicular to the axis connecting the north and south magnetic poles. It is the geometric rationalization of the empirically defined **magnetic equator** *(see).*

ge•o•mag•ne•tism (jē′ō-măg′nə-tĭz′əm) *n.* **1.** The magnetism of the earth. **2.** The study of the earth's magnetic field. **—ge•o•mag•net•ic** (jē′ō-măg-nĕt′ĭk) *adj.* **—ge•o•mag•net•i•cal•ly** *adv.*

ge•o•man•cy (jē′ə-măn′sē) *n.* Divination by means of dust patterns, or of lines and figures. [Middle English, from Old French *geomancie,* from Medieval Latin *geōmantia,* from Late Greek *geōmanteia,* divination from signs obtained from the earth : GEO- + -MANCY.] **—ge•o•man•cer** *n.* **—ge•o•man•tic** (jē′ə-măn′tĭk) *adj.*

ge•o•me•chan•ics (jē′ō-mə-kăn′ĭks) *n. Used with a singular verb.* The study of the mechanics of rock and soil and its application in civil engineering.

ge•om•e•ter (jē-ŏm′ə-tər) *n.* **1.** A geometrician. **2.** A geometrid moth.

ge•o•met•ric (jē′ə-mĕt′rĭk) *adj.* Also **ge•o•met•ri•cal** (-rĭ-kəl). *Abbr.* **geom.** **1.** Of or pertaining to geometry and its methods and principles. **2.** Using simple geometric forms in design and decoration. **—ge•o•met•ri•cal•ly** *adv.*

geometrical isomerism *n.* **Cis-trans isomerism** *(see).*

geometric isomer *n. Chemistry.* A type of **isomer** *(see).*

geometric mean *n.* The *n*th root, usually the positive *n*th root, of a product of *n* factors; for example, the geometric mean of 1, 3, and 9 is the cube root of 1 × 3 × 9.

geometric optics *n.* The study of reflection, refraction, and other optical phenomena using rays to represent the paths of light without reference to the wave properties of the light.

geometric progression *n.* A sequence of terms, such as 1, 3, 9, 27, 81, each of which is a constant multiple of the immediately preceding term. Also called "geometric sequence."

geometric series *n.* A sum in which the terms are members of a geometric progression.

ge•om•e•trid (jē-ŏm′ə-trĭd, jē′ə-mĕt′rĭd) *n.* Any of various moths of the family Geometridae, having caterpillars that move by looping the body in alternate contractions and expansions.
∼*adj.* Of or belonging to the Geometridae. [New Latin *Geometridae,* "land measurers" (from the movement of the caterpillars), from Latin *geōmetrēs,* geometrician, from Greek, from *geōmetrein,* to measure land. See **geometry.**]

ge•om•e•trize (jē-ŏm′ə-trīz′) *v.* **-trized, -trizing, -trizes.** *—intr.* To study geometry. *—tr.* To apply the methods of geometry to (a physical theory, for example).

ge•om•e•try (jē-ŏm′ə-trē) *n., pl.* **-tries.** *Abbr.* **geom.** **1. a.** The mathematics of the properties, measurement, and relationships of points, lines, angles, surfaces, and solids. **b.** A system of geometry: *Euclidean geometry.* **c.** A geometry restricted to a class of problems or objects: *solid geometry.* **2.** Configuration; arrangement. **3.** A surface shape. **4.** Any physical arrangement suggesting geometric forms or lines. [Middle English, from Old French *geometrie,* from Latin *geōmetria,* from Greek, from *geōmetrein,* to measure land : GEO- + *metrein,* to measure, from *metron,* measure.] **—ge•om•e•tri•cian** (jē-ŏm′ə-trĭsh′ən, jē′ə-mə-) *n.*

ge•o•mor•phic (jē′ə-môr′fĭk) *adj.* Of or like the earth, its shape, or its surface configuration. [GEO- + -MORPHIC.]

ge•o•mor•phol•o•gy (jē′ō-môr-fŏl′ə-jē) *n.* The scientific study of the configuration and evolution of land forms. **—ge•o•mor•pho•log•ic** (jē′ə-môr′fə-lŏj′ĭk), **ge•o•mor•pho•log•i•cal** *adj.* **—ge•o•mor•pho•log•i•cal•ly** *adv.*

ge•oph•a•gy (jē-ŏf′ə-jē) *n.* Also **ge•o•pha•gia** (jē′ə-fā′jə, -jē-ə). The practice of eating earthy substances, such as clay. [GEO- + -PHAGY.] **—ge•oph•a•gist** *n.*

ge•o•phys•ics (jē′ō-fĭz′ĭks) *n. Used with a singular verb.* The physics of the earth and of the processes that take place on and within it, sometimes including fields such as meteorology and climatology and also the physics of the moon and planets. **—ge•o•phys•i•cal** *adj.* **—ge•o•phys•i•cist** *n.*

ge•o•phyte (jē′ə-fīt′) *n. Botany.* A perennial plant propagated by underground buds. [GEO- + -PHYTE.]

ge•o•pol•i•tics (jē′ō-pŏl′ə-tĭks) *n. Used with a singular verb.* **1.** The study of the relationship between politics and geography. **2.** A Nazi doctrine of expansion that concentrated on the reallocation of geographic, economic, and political boundaries. **—ge•o•po•lit•i•cal** (jē′ō-pə-lĭt′ĭ-kəl) *adj.*

ge•o•pon•ic (jē′ə-pŏn′ĭk) *adj.* **1.** Of or relating to agriculture or farming. **2.** Rustic; bucolic. [Greek *geōponikos,* from *geōponia,* tillage, from *geōponein,* to till land : GEO- + *ponein,* to toil, labor.]

ge•o•pon•ics (jē′ə-pŏn′ĭks) *n. Used with a singular verb.* The study or science of agriculture.

George I (jôrj) (1660–1727). Elector of Hanover (1698–1727), and king of Great Britain and Ireland (1714–27). As a Protestant he was offered the British throne in 1714, the Roman Catholic James Stuart having been excluded by Parliament. He left the running of the country to his Whig ministers, the chief of whom, Sir Robert Walpole, is regarded as Britain's first prime minister.

George II (1683–1760). King of Great Britain and Ireland and elector of Hanover (1727–60). His victory at the Battle of Dettingen (1743) was the last time that a British monarch led his troops in the field.

George III (1738–1820). King of Great Britain and Ireland (1760–1820) and of Hanover (1815–20). His attempts to interfere in government were instrumental in the loss of the American colonies (1776).

George IV (1762–1830). King of Great Britain and Ireland (1820–30) and of Hanover. As regent during his father's 30-year long mental and physical illness, he patronized art and fashion, but scandals involving his two marriages brought the monarchy into disrepute.

George V (1865–1936). King of Great Britain and Northern Ireland and emperor of India (1910–36). He changed the name of the royal house to Windsor during World War I.

George VI (1895–1952). King of Great Britain and Northern Ire-

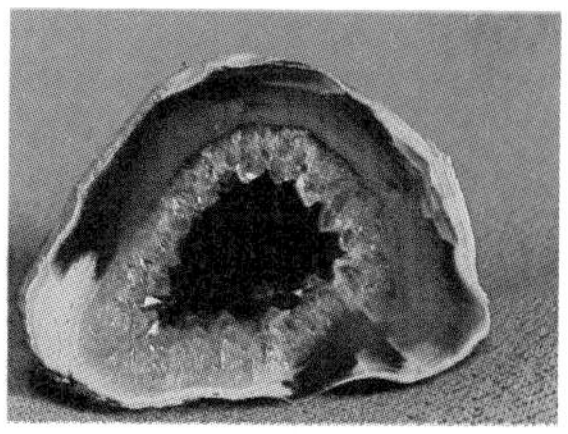

geode *A rounded nodule of stone containing a small cavity, usually lined with crystals. This geode is lined with amethyst.*

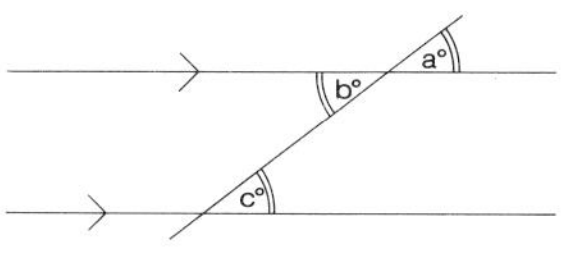

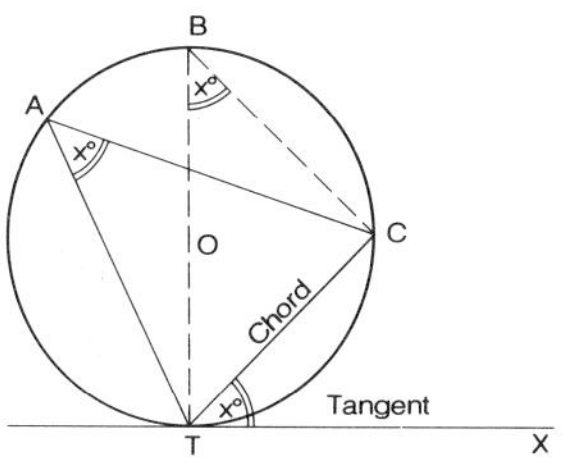

geometry *The study of the mathematical relationships between lines, angles, areas, and volumes—the discipline called geometry—is an essential tool of navigators, surveyors, engineers, and builders. The diagrams above illustrate some of the major theorems. When a straight line cuts a pair of parallel lines (upper drawing), the angles a, b, and c will be equal. In a circle (lower drawing), the angle between the chord TC and the tangent TX is equal to the angle at B, and lines drawn from the ends of the chord to any other point on the circle will contain the same angle. If the chord—like the line BT—passes through the center of the circle O, the angle between the lines (here, BC and CT) will be a right angle.*

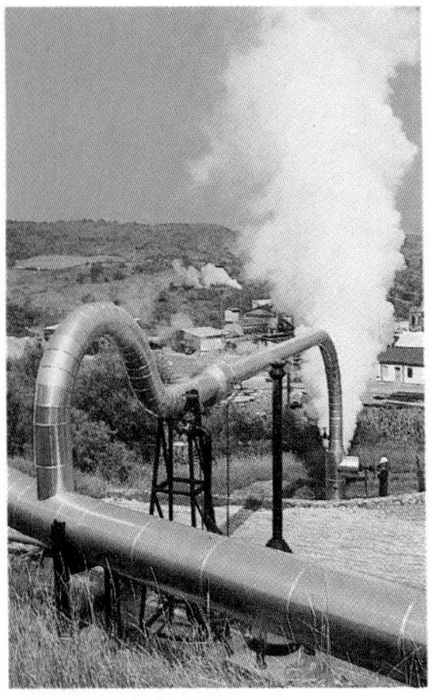

geothermal *Steam from underground springs, heated by the earth's molten interior, drives turbine generators at this geothermal power plant at Larderello, Italy.*

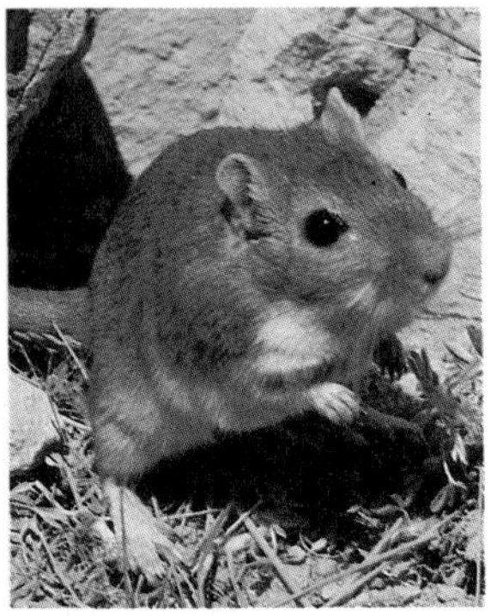

gerbil *There are about a dozen genera and almost 100 species of this burrowing rodent.*

PRONUNCIATION KEY

ă, pat; ā, pay; âr, care;
ä, father, are; b, bib;
ch, church; d, deed; ĕ, pet;
ē, be; f, fife; g, gag; h, hat;
hw, which; ĭ, pit; ī, pie;
îr, pier; j, judge; k, kick;
l, lid, needle; m, mum;
n, no, sudden; ng, thing;
ŏ, pot; ō, toe; ô, paw, for;
oi, noise; ou, out; o͝o, book;
o͞o, boot; p, pop; r, roar;
s, sauce; sh, ship, dish;
t, tight; th, thin, path;
th, this, bathe; ŭ, cut; ûr, fur;
v, valve; w, with; y, yes;
z, zebra, size; zh, vision;
ə, about, item, edible, gallop, circus, peaceful

IN FOREIGN WORDS:

à, *Fr.* ami; œ, *Fr.* feu, *Ger.* schön; ü, *Fr.* tu, *Ger.* über; KH, *Ger.* ich, *Scot.* loch; N, *Fr.* bon; y', *Fr.* Compiègne

STRESS MARKS:

Primary stress: ′
in·cite′ (ĭn-sīt′)
Secondary stress: ′
in′sight′ (ĭn′sīt′)

land (1936–52) and emperor of India (1936–48). He acceded to the throne on the abdication of his brother Edward VIII and won enormous popularity by his dedication to his duties as a constitutional monarch, especially during World War II.

George, Lake. Glacial lake in the foothills of the Adirondack Mts., northeastern New York. It was the scene of many battles in the French and Indian War and the American Revolution. Today it is the center of an extensive resort area.

George Cross *n. Abbr.* **G.C.** A British civilian award for bravery.

George Town. Also **Pe·nang** (pə-năng′). City in northwest Malaysia. The capital of Penang state, it is the country's chief port, exporting tin, rubber, and copra. It became part of the British Straits Settlements in 1867, joining the Federation of Malaya in 1948.

George·town[1] (jôrj′toun′). Capital and chief port of Guyana, in the north at the mouth of the Demerara River.

Georgetown[2]. Capital of the Cayman Islands, on Grand Cayman, in the West Indies.

Georgetown[3]. Mainly residential section of western Washington, D.C. It was settled *c.* 1665, incorporated as a town in 1789, and annexed to Washington in 1878. Its beautiful old houses and gardens attract many tourists.

geor·gette (jôr-jĕt′) *n.* A sheer, strong silk or silklike crepe fabric with a dull surface, used for dresses, blouses, or trimming. Also called "georgette crepe." [Originally a trademark, after Madame *Georgette* de la Plante, a French modiste.]

George Wash·ing·ton Birthplace National Monument (wŏsh′ĭng-tən, wôsh′-). Area in northeastern Virginia preserving the estate, called Wakefield, where the first president was born.

George Washington Car·ver National Monument (kär′vər). Site in southwestern Missouri containing the birthplace and boyhood home of the famed botanist and agricultural pioneer.

Geor·gia[1] (jôr′jə). *Abbr.* **Ga.** State of the southeast United States. Named after George II, it was founded in 1732, the last of the original 13 colonies. As a supporter of the Confederate cause, it suffered considerable damage in the Civil War. In the 20th century it has experienced many social and economic problems. Atlanta is the capital.

Georgia[2]. See **Georgian S.S.R.**

Georgia, Strait of. Channel, *c.* 240 kilometers (150 miles) long, bordered on the west by Vancouver Island, on the east and northeast by the mainland of British Columbia, and on the southeast by Washington State. It links Puget Sound to Queen Charlotte Sound and is the gateway to the Inside (Inland) Passage to Alaska.

Geor·gian (jôr′jən) *adj.* **1.** Of, pertaining to, or characteristic of any of the reigns of the four Georges who ruled Great Britain from 1714 to 1830; especially, of or pertaining to the architectural style of this period, characterized by plain, symmetrical façades including many classical features. **2.** Of, pertaining to, or characteristic of the reign of King George V of Great Britain: *Georgian poetry.* **3.** Of or pertaining to the U.S. state of Georgia or to its inhabitants. **4.** Of or pertaining to the Georgian S.S.R. or to its people or their language. ~*n.* **1.** A native or inhabitant of the state of Georgia. **2.** A native or inhabitant of the Georgian S.S.R. **3.** The Caucasian language of the Georgian S.S.R. **4.** A person belonging to or whose style is imitative of the period of any of the reigns of the Georges in Great Britain.

Georgian Bay. Large bay of Lake Huron in Ontario, Canada. Forty islands and part of the mainland comprise the Georgian Bay Islands National Park.

Georgian Soviet Socialist Republic or **Georgia.** *Russian* **Gru·zin·ska·ya S.S.R.** (gro͞o-zĭn′skĭ-ə). Constituent republic of the U.S.S.R., on the Black Sea. An independent kingdom in the Middle Ages, it was invaded by the Mongols in 1234, divided between Persia and Turkey in 1555, and annexed by Russia in the 19th century. Independent in 1918, it joined the U.S.S.R. in 1922 as a member of the Transcaucasian S.F.S.R., becoming a separate republic in 1936. Georgia is rich in minerals, especially manganese, coal, oil, and gold. Its capital is Tbilisi.

geor·gic (jôr′jĭk) *adj.* Of or pertaining to agriculture or rural life. ~*n.* **1. Georgics.** A poem by Virgil in four books, concerning agriculture and country life. **2.** A poem concerning farming or rural life. [Latin *Georgica,* from Greek *geōrgika,* cultivated lands, from neuter plural of *geōrgikos,* agricultural, from *geōrgos,* farmer, "(one) tilling the soil" : GEO- + *ergon,* work.]

ge·o·sci·ence (jē′ō-sī′əns) *n.* A science dealing with the earth, including geology, geophysics, oceanography, and applied sciences such as mining and engineering geology. Sometimes meteorology, climatology, and similar subjects are included.

ge·o·stat·ics (jē′ō-stăt′ĭks) *n. Used with a singular verb.* The study of the forces within the earth, as, for example, the pressure exerted by rock or soil. **—ge·o·stat·ic** *adj.*

ge·o·sta·tion·ar·y (jē′ō-stā′shə-nĕr′ē) *adj.* Of, pertaining to, or designating an artificial satellite that maintains a constant position above a point on the earth's equator.

ge·o·stroph·ic (jē′ə-strŏf′ĭk) *adj.* Of or pertaining to force caused by the earth's rotation: *a geostrophic wind.* [GEO- + Greek *strophē,* a turning, STROPHE.]

ge·o·syn·chro·nous (jē′ō-sĭng′krə-nəs, -sĭn′krə-nəs) *adj.* Of or pertaining to an artificial satellite that orbits the earth in the same direction as the earth's rotation and with an orbital period equal to the earth's rotation period.

ge·o·syn·cline (jē′ō-sĭn′klīn′) *n.* An extensive, usually linear depression in the earth's crust in which a succession of sedimentary strata has accumulated.

ge·o·tax·is (jē′ō-tăk′sĭs) *n. Biology.* The movement of an organism in response to the forces of gravity. **—ge·o·tac·tic** (jē′ō-tăk′tĭk) *adj.* **—ge·o·tac·ti·cal·ly** *adv.*

ge·o·tec·ton·ic (jē′ō-tĕk-tŏn′ĭk) *adj.* Of or relating to the mode of formation, shape, structure, and arrangement of the rock masses constituting the earth's crust.

ge·o·ther·mal (jē′ō-thûr′məl) *adj.* Also **ge·o·ther·mic** (-mĭk). Of or pertaining to the internal heat of the earth. **—ge·o·ther·mal·ly** *adv.*

geothermal power *n.* Heat originating in the earth's interior, as in volcanoes or geysers, and used as a source of energy.

ge·ot·ro·pism (jē-ŏt′rə-pĭz′əm) *n. Biology.* The response of a plant organ to gravity, as the downward growth of plant roots (*positive geotropism*). [GEO- + -TROPISM.] **—ge·o·tro·pic** (jē′ə-trō′pĭk, -trŏp′ĭk) *adj.* **—ge·o·tro·pi·cal·ly** *adv.*

ger. gerund.

Ger. **1.** German. **2.** Germany.

ge·rah (gîr′ə) *n.* **1.** An ancient Hebrew unit of weight equal to $^1/_{20}$ of a shekel. **2.** An ancient Hebrew coin. [Hebrew *gērāh,* "bean."]

ge·ra·ni·al (jə-rā′nē-ăl′) *n.* A perfume and flavoring ingredient, an isomer of **citral** *(see).* [GERANI(UM) + -AL (aldehyde).]

ge·ra·ni·ol (jə-rā′nē-ôl′, -ōl′) *n.* A fragrant pale yellow liquid, $C_{10}H_{18}O$, derived chiefly from the oils of geranium and citronella and used in cosmetics and flavorings. [GERANI(UM) + -OL (alcohol).]

ge·ra·ni·um (jə-rā′nē-əm) *n.* **1.** Any of various plants of the genus *Pelargonium,* native chiefly to southern Africa; especially, *P. domesticum,* widely cultivated for its rounded, often variegated leaves and showy clusters of red, pink, or white flowers. **2.** Any of various plants of the genus *Geranium,* having divided leaves and pink or purplish flowers. **3.** A strong to vivid red. [Latin, from Greek *geranion,* "small crane" (because the fruit resembles a crane's bill), from *geranos,* crane.]

ger·a·tol·o·gy (jĕr′ə-tŏl′ə-jē) *n.* The scientific study of the aging process and the problems and diseases associated with it. [Greek *gēras* (stem *gērat-*), old age + -LOGY.]

ger·bil (jûr′bəl) *n.* Any of various small, mouselike rodents of the genus *Gerbillus* and related genera, of arid regions of Africa and Asia Minor, having long hind legs and a long tail. [French *gerbille,* from New Latin *Gerbillus,* diminutive of *gerboa, jerboa,* JERBOA.]

ge·rent (jîr′ənt) *n.* A ruler or manager; an overseer. [Latin *gerēns* (stem *gerent-*), present participle of *gerere,* to carry, conduct, govern.]

ger·e·nuk (gĕr′ə-no͝ok′) *n.* An African gazelle, *Litocranius walleri,* having long legs, a long, slender neck, and backward-curving horns in the male. [Somali *garanug.*]

gerfalcon. Variant of **gyrfalcon.**

ger·i·at·ric (jĕr′ē-ăt′rĭk, jîr′-) *adj.* **1.** Of or pertaining to geriatrics. **2.** Of or pertaining to the aged or to their characteristic afflictions. ~*n.* An aged person, especially one requiring medical or social care. [Greek *gēras,* old age + -IATRIC.]

ger·i·at·rics (jĕr′ē-ăt′rĭks, jîr′-) *n. Used with a singular verb.* The branch of medicine concerned with the diagnosis and treatment of diseases of the elderly. **—ger·i·a·tri·cian** (jĕr′ē-ə-trĭsh′ən, jîr′-), **ger·i·at·rist** (jĕr′ē-ăt′rĭst, jə-rī′ə-trĭst) *n.*

Gé·ri·cault (zhā-rē-kō′), **Théodore** (1791–1824). French painter. His most famous work, *The Raft of the Medusa* (1819), portrayed an actual maritime disaster that had caused a political scandal.

germ (jûrm) *n.* **1.** A microorganism such as a bacterium or virus, especially one causing disease. **2.** *Biology.* A small organic structure or cell from which a new organism may develop. **3.** Something that may serve as the basis of further growth or development: *the germ of an idea.* [French *germe,* from Latin *germen,* offshoot, sprout, fetus.]

Usage: *Germ, microbe, bacteria, bacillus,* and *virus* are nouns denoting minute organisms or agents invisible to the unaided human eye, some of which are related to the production of disease. They are not interchangeable in careful usage except as indicated. *Germ* and *microbe* are nonscientific terms for such microorganisms; in popular usage they usually refer to disease-producing bodies. *Bacteria* (plural of *bacterium*) is the scientific term for a large group of microorganisms, only some of which produce disease. Many others are active in processes beneficial or not harmful to human, animal, and plant life. *Bacillus* is the scientific designation for a specific class of bacteria that includes some disease-producing microorganisms; only in loose popular usage is the term employed as the equivalent of any bacterium or any pathogenic bacterium. *Virus* is the technical term for any of a group of extremely small agents capable of producing certain diseases in human, animal, and plant life.

ger·man[1] (jûr′mən) *n.* **1.** An intricate dance for many couples. **2.** A party for dancing at which the german is featured. [Short for *German cotillion.*]

german[2] *adj.* **1.** Having the same parents or having the same grandparents on one side. Obsolete except as the second element in combinations: *cousin-german.* **2.** *Archaic.* Related; germane. [Middle English *germa(i)n,* from Old French *germain,* from Latin *germānus,* "from the same race," from *germen,* offshoot, fetus.]

Ger·man (jûr′mən) *adj. Abbr.* **G., Ger.** Of, pertaining to, or characteristic of Germany, its people, or their language.
~*n. Abbr.* **G., Ger.** **1. a.** A native or citizen of Germany. **b.** A person of German descent. **c.** A person whose native language is

German. **2.** The West Germanic language spoken in Germany, Austria, and part of Switzerland. [Middle English *Germanes*, Teutons, Germans, from Latin *Germānus*, German, perhaps from Celtic, akin to Old Irish *gair*†, neighbor.]

German cockroach *n.* A small cockroach, *Blatella germanica*, that is a common household pest.

German Democratic Republic. *Abbr.* **G.D.R.** See **Germany, East Germany.**

ger·man·der (jər-măn′dər) *n.* Any of various usually aromatic plants of the genus *Teucrium*, having purplish or reddish two-lipped flowers. [Middle English *germandre*, from Old French *germandree*, from Medieval Latin *germandra*, alteration of *gama(n)drea*, from Latin *chamadreos*, from Greek *khamaidrus*, "ground oak" : *khamai*, on the ground + *drus*, oak.]

ger·mane (jər-mān′) *adj.* Having a significant bearing upon a point at issue; pertinent: *The question you raised is not germane to the discussion.* —See Synonyms at **relevant.** [Middle English *germa(i)n*, having the same parents, GERMAN.]

ger·man·ic (jər-măn′ĭk) *n.* Of or pertaining to germanium. Said especially of compounds that contain germanium with a valence of 4. [GERMAN(IUM) + -IC.]

Ger·man·ic (jər-măn′ĭk) *adj.* **1. a.** Of, pertaining to, or characteristic of Germany or of the German people or their culture. **b.** Of or pertaining to Teutons. **c.** Of or pertaining to a Germanic-speaking people. **2.** Of, pertaining to, or constituting Germanic. ~*n.* **1.** A branch of the Indo-European language family divided into North Germanic, West Germanic, and East Germanic. It includes English, Dutch, German, and the Scandinavian languages. **2.** The unrecorded ancestor language of this branch, **Proto-Germanic** *(see).*

Ger·man·ism (jûr′mə-nĭz′əm) *n.* **1.** An attitude, custom, or practice that seems characteristically German. **2.** A German idiom or phrasing that appears in another language. **3.** Esteem for Germany and emulation of German ways.

ger·man·ite (jûr′mə-nīt′) *n.* A mineral consisting of a complex sulfide of copper and arsenic with small amounts of germanium, gallium, and other metals. It is an ore of germanium and gallium. [GERMAN(IUM) + -ITE.]

ger·ma·ni·um (jər-mā′nē-əm) *n. Symbol* **Ge** A brittle, crystalline, gray-white metalloid element, widely used as a semiconductor, as an alloying agent and catalyst, and in certain optical glasses. Atomic number 32, atomic weight 72.59, melting point 937.4°C, boiling point 2,830°C, specific gravity 5.323 (25°C), valences 2, 4. [New Latin, from Latin *Germānia*, Germany, from Latin *Germānus*, GERMAN.]

Ger·man·ize (jûr′mə-nīz′) *v.* **-ized, -izing, -izes.** —*tr.* **1.** To give a German quality or character to; make German. **2.** *Archaic.* To translate into German. —*intr.* To adopt German customs or attitudes. —**Ger·man·i·za·tion** *n.* —**Ger·man·iz·er** *n.*

German measles *n.* A mild, contagious, eruptive disease caused by a virus spread in droplet sprays from the nose and throat. It is capable of causing congenital defects in infants born to mothers infected during the first three months of pregnancy. Also called "rubella."

Ger·man·o·phile (jər-măn′ə-fīl′) *n.* One who loves or admires Germany, the Germans, or German ways. [Latin *Germānus*, GERMAN + -PHILE.]

Ger·man·o·phobe (jər-măn′ə-fōb′) *n.* One who hates or has an obsessive fear of Germany, the Germans, or German ways. [Latin *Germānus*, GERMAN + -PHOBE.]

ger·ma·nous (jər-mā′nəs) *n.* Of or pertaining to germanium. Said especially of compounds that contain germanium with a valence of 2.

German shepherd *n.* A large breed of dog with a thick brownish coat, often used as a guard dog, as a police dog, or as a guide dog for the blind. Also called "Alsatian."

German silver *n.* An alloy, **nickel silver** *(see).*

Ger·ma·ny (jûr′mə-nē) *Abbr.* **Ger.** *German* **Deutsch·land** (doich′länt′). *Abbr.* **Ger.** Country in central Europe, divided since 1945 into the **Federal Republic of Germany (West Germany)** and the **German Democratic Republic (East Germany).** Occupied from *c.* 500 B.C. by Germanic tribes, it had become part of the kingdom of the Franks by the time of Charlemagne. After the death of Charlemagne in 814, Germany became a loose federation of principalities. This was strengthened under the Saxon dynasty. The third in this line of rulers, Otto I, was crowned Holy Roman Emperor by Pope John XII in 962. By the 14th century Germany's frontiers extended as far east as the Vistula. The 16th and 17th centuries, however, were dominated by religious strife and dynastic feuds culminating in the "Thirty Years' War" (1618–48), which left Germany divided into a predominantly Roman Catholic south and a Protestant north. In 1806 Napoleon finally broke up the empire and united the country. From 1815 Germany was a confederation, with Prussia being the dominant state. Prussia defeated Austria in 1866 and France in 1871, and Bismarck realized his dream of a united German Empire with the Prussian king as hereditary ruler. Rapid industrialization and colonial expansion took place in the late 19th and early 20th centuries; the international aspirations were a major cause of World War I (1914–18). Following defeat in 1918, the empire was dissolved and the Weimar Republic established. By the end of the 1920's, the depressed economy facilitated Hitler's rise to power. His aggressive and expansionist foreign policy led to the outbreak of World War II in 1939, defeat at the hands of the Allies

in 1945, and the subsequent split into East and West Germany. See map, next page.

Germany, Federal Republic of. See **Germany, West Germany.**

germ cell *n.* A cell having reproduction as its principal function; especially, an egg or sperm cell.

ger·mi·cide (jûr′mə-sīd′) *n.* An agent that kills germs. [GERM + -CIDE.] —**ger·mi·cid·al** (jûr′mə-sīd′l) *adj.*

ger·mi·nal (jûr′mə-nəl) *adj.* **1.** Of, pertaining to, or having the nature of a germ cell. **2.** Of, in, or pertaining to the earliest stage of development; embryonic. [French, from Latin *germen* (stem *germin*-), offshoot, GERM.]

germinal disc *n. Biology.* A disklike region from which the embryo begins to develop in certain ova. Also called "blastodisc."

germinal epithelium *n.* The epithelium of the ovary or testis, containing cells that develop into ova or spermatozoa.

germinal vesicle *n. Biology.* The nucleus of an oocyte.

ger·mi·nant (jûr′mə-nənt) *adj.* Germinating; sprouting.

ger·mi·nate (jûr′mə-nāt′) *v.* **-nated, -nating, -nates.** —*intr.* **1.** *Biology.* To begin to grow; sprout. **2.** To come into being and develop: *His hatred germinated slowly.* —*tr.* **1.** *Biology.* To cause (seeds or spores) to sprout. **2.** To bring into being; produce. [Latin *germināre*, to sprout, from *germen* (stem *germin*-), sprout, GERM.] —**ger·mi·na·ble** (jûr′mə-nə-bəl), **ger·mi·na·tive** (jûr′mə-nā′tĭv, -nə-tĭv) *adj.* —**ger·mi·na·tion** *n.* —**ger·mi·na·tor** *n.*

Ger·mis·ton (jûr′mĭ-stən). Town in the Transvaal in South Africa. It has the world's largest gold refinery, serving the Witwatersrand mines.

germ layer *n.* Any of three cellular layers, the **ectoderm, endoderm,** or **mesoderm** *(all of which see),* into which most animal embryos differentiate.

germ plasm *n.* **1.** The protoplasm of an egg cell, especially that part containing the hereditary material. **2.** Germ cells collectively. **3.** The hereditary material postulated by Weismann and other 19th-century biologists, thought to be transmitted in the germ cells and to remain unchanged from one generation to the next.

germ theory *n.* **1.** The doctrine that infectious diseases are caused by the activity of microorganisms within the body. **2.** The theory that living organisms can only develop from other living organisms through the fusion and subsequent differentiation of germ cells.

germ warfare *n.* **Biological warfare** *(see).*

Ge·ron·i·mo (jə-rŏn′ə-mō′) (1829–1909). North American Indian chief. From 1871 to 1886 he led the Chiricahua Apaches in daring guerrilla campaigns against the U.S. and Mexican governments.

geronto–, geront– *prefix.* Indicates old people or old age; for ex-

---

germination

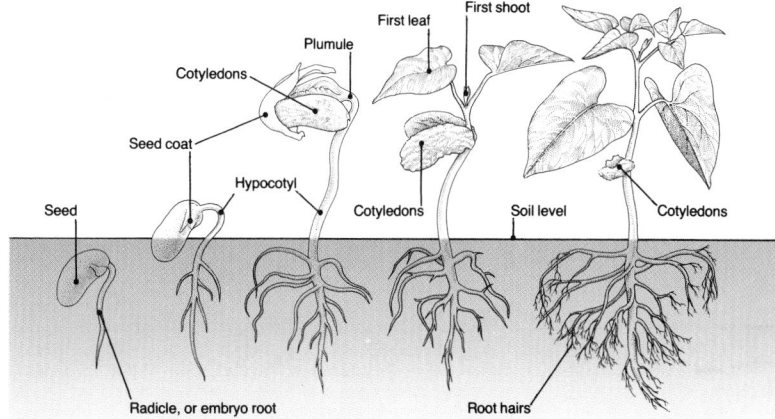

FROM DORMANT SEED TO LIVING PLANT
The varied conditions that are needed to start growth

Germination is the process by which a seed becomes a plant. Shortly before a seed is shed by its parent, it becomes dormant to await good growing conditions. Seeds remain able to sprout for some time, from a few weeks to an extreme of about 10,000 years in the case of an arctic lupine seed found frozen in the Yukon in 1966.

The conditions that revive a seed vary. Warmth, water, and oxygen are usually needed. Some seeds, such as peas, do not need water but require certain bacteria in the soil. Winter annuals respond to cold, not warmth.

THE GERMINATION OF A BEAN

Generally, germination begins when air and water enter the seed through a tiny hole (micropyle) in the coat. The seed revives and begins to feed off its one or two seed leaves (cotyledons). The radicle, or embryo root, emerges and grows downward. It is followed by the plumule, or embryo shoot, which grows upward. In some seeds the cotyledons remain below the soil, but in others they are carried above ground by a stemlike hypocotyl. The main shoot grows on above the cotyledons that wither when the food contained in them is exhausted. The plant then feeds itself.

GERMANY

NORTH SEA

DENMARK

BALTIC SEA

NETHERLANDS

BELGIUM

LUX.

FRANCE

WEST GERMANY (GERMAN FED. REP.)

EAST GERMANY (GERMAN DEM. REP.)

POLAND

CZECHOSLOVAKIA

AUSTRIA

SWITZERLAND

LIECHTENSTEIN

ITALY

ample, **gerontology**. [French *géronto-*, from Greek *gerōn* (stem *ge-ront-*), old man.]

ger·on·toc·ra·cy (jĕr′ən-tŏk′rə-sē) *n., pl.* **-cies. 1.** Government based on rule by old men. **2.** A governing group of old men. [French *gérontocratie* : GERONTO- + -CRACY.] **—ge·ron·to·crat·ic** (jə-rŏn′tə-krăt′ĭk) *adj.*

ger·on·tol·o·gy (jĕr′ən-tŏl′ə-jē) *n.* The study of the diseases and other phenomena associated with old age. [GERONTO- + -LOGY.] **—ger·on·to·log·i·cal** (jə-rŏn′tə-lŏj′ĭ-kəl) *adj.* **—ger·on·tol·o·gist** *n.*

ger·ry·man·der (jĕr′ē-măn′dər, gĕr′-) *v.* **-dered, -dering, -ders.** **—***intr.* To divide a constituency, county, or city into voting districts so as to give unfair advantage to one party in elections. **—***tr.* To divide (a voting area) so as to give unfair advantage to one party in elections.

~n. An act or product of gerrymandering. [From Elbridge *Gerry*, 18th-century U.S. politician + (SALA)MANDER, from the shape of an election district formed (1812) in Massachusetts while Gerry was governor.]

Gersh·win (gûrsh′wĭn), **George,** born Jacob Gershvin (1898–1937). U.S. composer. A master of most forms of popular music of his day, he is best known for his experiments in orchestral jazz, notably

Rhapsody in Blue (1924) and the folk opera *Porgy and Bess* (1935), with lyrics by his brother Ira (1896–1983).

ger·und (jĕr′ənd) *n. Abbr.* **ger. 1.** In Latin, a verbal form that can be used as a noun in all singular cases except the nominative while conveying the meaning of the verb; for example, in the phrase *modus vivendi* ("a manner of living"), *vivendi* is a gerund formed from the verb *vivere*, to live. **2.** In English, the verbal form ending in *-ing* when used as a noun while conveying the meaning of the verb; for example, in the sentences *Cooking is an art* and *I don't like cooking*, *cooking* is a gerund formed from the verb *cook*. **3.** An analogous grammatical form in some other languages. [Late Latin *gerundium*, from Latin *gerundum, gerendum*, acting, carrying, gerund of *gerere*, to carry, act.] **—ge·run·di·al** (jə-rŭn′dē-əl) *adj.*

Usage: When a verb form ending in *-ing* is used as a noun it raises different problems of usage from when it is used as a verb (see also **participle**). The *-ing* form used as a noun (or gerund, as it is known in traditional grammar) is illustrated in *The inspector objected to my going.* In formal English, the possessive form of the item preceding the gerund is standard, and this involves the use of the apostrophe when the item is a noun, as in *He objected to John's going.* Informal English, on the other hand, often uses the neutral form, as in *He objected to me/John going.* Even in formal English the use of the possessive is sometimes very awkward or impossible, as in *His absence prevented anything (not anything's) being accomplished.* In such cases it is usually recommended that the construction be rephrased (for example, *prevented the accomplishment of anything*). Similarly, in cases where the addition of an 's would lead to ambiguity it is generally avoided: *He objected to his son leaving the room,* where *son's* might be confused with *sons.* It is also not used when there is an irregular plural noun: *the problems of mice (not mice's) damaging the wires.*

ge·run·dive (jə-rŭn′dĭv) *n.* **1.** In Latin, a verbal adjective with the construction of a future passive participle, suggesting appropriateness, necessity, or imminence; for example, in the sentence *Legibus parendum est* ("The laws must be obeyed" or "The laws are to be obeyed"), *parendum* is a gerundive. **2.** An analogous grammatical form or construction in some other languages. —*adj.* Pertaining to or like a gerund or gerundive. [Middle English *gerundif,* from Late Latin *gerundivus,* from *gerundium,* GERUND.]

Ge·ry·on (jîr′ē-ən, gĕr′-). *Greek Mythology.* A monster with three heads and upper bodies who was robbed of his herd of cattle and slain by Hercules.

Ge·sell (gĭ-zĕl′), **Arnold Lucius** (1880–1961). U.S. psychologist and pediatrician. He conducted research of normal child development and outlined the progressive stages of a child's life in many scholarly books, such as *Studies in Child Development* (1948), and three popular works, including *Infant and Child in the Culture of Today* (1943).

ges·so (jĕs′ō) *n.* **1.** A preparation of plaster of Paris and glue used as a base for low relief sculpting or as a surface for painting. **2.** A surface of this preparation. [Italian, gypsum, chalk, from Latin *gypsum,* GYPSUM.]

gest¹, geste (jĕst) *n. Archaic.* **1.** A feat or exploit; a notable deed. **2. a.** A verse romance or tale. **b.** A prose romance. [Middle English *geste, jeste,* from Old French, from Latin *gesta,* actions, exploits, from *gestus,* past participle of *gerere,* to act, carry.]

gest², geste (jĕst) *n. Archaic.* **1.** Mien or bearing. **2.** A gesture. [Old French *geste,* from Latin *gestus.* See **gesture.**]

ge·stalt, Ge·stalt (gə-shtält′, -stält′, -shtôlt′, -stôlt′) *n., pl.* **-stalts** or **-stalten** (-shtält′n, -stält′n, -shtôlt′n, -stôlt′n). **1.** A unified physical, psychological, or symbolic configuration having properties that cannot be derived from its parts. **2.** A complicated combination, as of experiences that constitute a relationship. [German *Gestalt,* form, shape, from Middle High German *gestalt,* from *ungestalt,* deformity, from Old High German *ungistalt,* ugly : *un-,* not + *gistalt,* past participle of *stellen,* to set, place.]

Gestalt psychology *n.* A school or doctrine of psychology holding that psychological phenomena are made up of irreducible gestalts. Also called "configurationism."

Ge·sta·po (gə-stä′pō, -shtä′pō) *n.* The German internal security police as organized under the Nazi regime. [German, short for *Ge(heime) Sta(ats)po(lizei),* "secret state police."]

Ges·ta Ro·ma·no·rum (jĕs′tə rō′mə-nôr′əm, -nōr′əm) *n.* An anthology of popular tales in Latin, collected in England in the late 13th or early 14th century and used as a source by preachers and by Chaucer and Shakespeare. [Latin, "deeds of the Romans."]

ges·tate (jĕs′tāt′) *v.* **-tated, -tating, -tates.** —*tr.* **1.** To carry (unborn young) within the uterus for a period following conception. **2.** To conceive and develop (a plan or idea, for example) in the mind. —*intr.* **1.** To carry unborn young for a period following conception; be pregnant. **2.** To develop slowly in the mind, as an idea or plot might. [Back-formation from GESTATION.]

ges·ta·tion (jĕ-stä′shən) *n.* **1.** The period between conception and birth during which an embryo grows and develops in the uterus; pregnancy. **2.** The development or duration of development of a plan or idea in the mind. [Latin *gestātiō* (stem *gestātiōn-*), from *gestāre,* frequentative of *gerere* (past participle *gestus*), to carry, bear.] —**ges·ta·to·ry** (jĕs′tə-tôr′ē, -tōr′ē) *adj.*

geste. **1.** Variant of **gest** (feat). **2.** Variant of **gest** (mien).

ges·tic (jĕs′tĭk) *adj.* Pertaining to movement of the body, especially in dancing. [From GEST (mien).]

ges·tic·u·late (jĕ-stĭk′yə-lāt′) *v.* **-lated, -lating, -lates.** —*intr.* To make animated and vigorous motions or gestures, especially as an expression complementing or substituting for speech. —*tr.* To say or express by gestures. [Latin *gesticulārī,* from *gesticulus,* diminutive of *gestus,* action, GEST.] —**ges·tic·u·la·tive** (jĕ-stĭk′yə-lā′tĭv, -lə-tĭv) *adj.* —**ges·tic·u·la·tor** *n.*

ges·tic·u·la·tion (jĕ-stĭk′yə-lā′shən) *n.* **1.** The act of gesticulating. **2.** A deliberate and vigorous motion or gesture. —**ges·tic·u·la·to·ry** (jĕ-stĭk′yə-lə-tôr′ē, -tōr′ē) *adj.*

ges·ture (jĕs′chər) *n.* **1.** A motion of the limbs or body made to express or help express thought or to emphasize speech. **2.** The use of gestures as a means of expression. **3.** An act or expression made as a sign, often formal, of intention or attitude: *a gesture of friendship; a mere gesture.* —*v.* **gestured, -turing, -tures.** —*intr.* To make gestures. —*tr.* To show, express, or direct by gestures. [Medieval Latin *gestūra,* bearing, carriage, from Latin *gestus,* past participle of *gerere,* to carry, act.] —**ges·tur·er** *n.*

Ge·sund·heit (gə-zo͝ont′hīt′) *interj. German.* Used to wish good health to a person who has just sneezed.

get¹ (gĕt; gĭt *for intransitive sense 6*) *v.* **got** (gŏt) or archaic **gat** (găt), **got** or **gotten** (gŏt′n), **getting, gets.** —*tr.* **1.** To obtain or acquire. **2.** To procure; gain; secure. **3.** To go after; fetch; retrieve. **4.** To reach or make contact with by or as if by radio or telephone. **5.** To

earn; gain: *get a reward.* **6.** To receive or come into possession of: *get a present.* **7.** To buy. **8.** To incur: *get a tongue-lashing.* **9.** *Informal.* To meet with; suffer: *He got a few knocks, but he'll recover.* **10.** To catch; contract: *They all got chicken pox at once.* **11.** To have or reach by calculation: *If you add them, you'll get 1,000.* **12.** To have obtained or received and now possess. Used only in the form of the present perfect, and generally equivalent to *have: I've got a large collection of books.* **13.** To possess or gain understanding or mastery of by study: *I must get this by heart.* **14.** To understand; comprehend: *Do you get his point?* **15.** *Informal.* To register or catch, as by eye or ear: *I'm sorry, I didn't get your name.* **16.** *Informal.* To understand the meaning of a remark made by or the behavior of (a person): *I don't quite get you.* **17.** To put: *get your hat on.* **18.** To cause to become or to be in a specified condition: *He got the hook loose. Don't get your friends into trouble.* **19.** To cause to move,

gestation

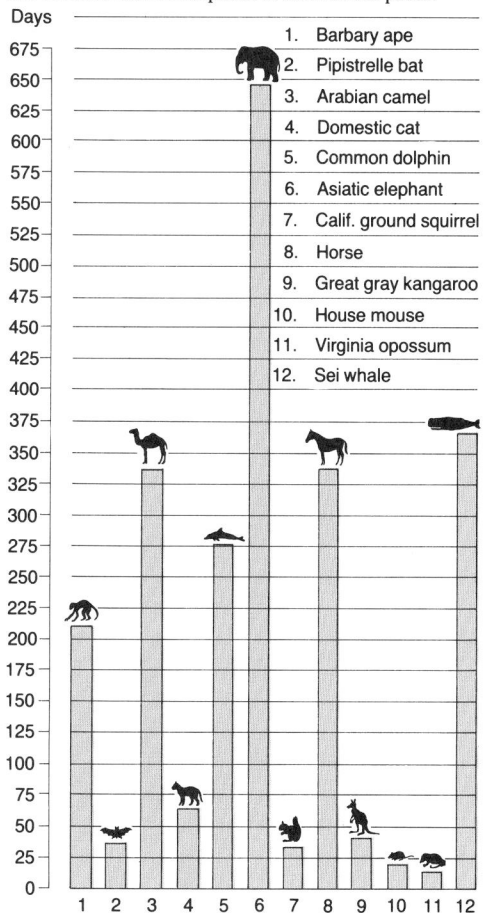

HOW LONG TO MAKE A MAMMAL?

Factors that affect the gestation period

The period from a mammal's conception to its birth varies from the Virginia opossum's 12 days to an elephant's 22 months. The reasons are many. Size is a major factor. Another is the need to bear young when food is available. This may be why in some species, weasels for example, the embryo lies dormant for months before developing.

Animals whose young are born in the open—potential prey—carry their young longer than burrowers. Rabbits, for example, have a gestation period of 31 days before their young are born in the burrow. Hares, who give birth in the open, have a gestation period of 39 days and the young are more highly developed when they are born into this less protected environment.

Marsupials have gestation periods that are short in relation to their size. The young are highly developed at birth and continue their development in the maternal pouch.

1.	Barbary ape
2.	Pipistrelle bat
3.	Arabian camel
4.	Domestic cat
5.	Common dolphin
6.	Asiatic elephant
7.	Calif. ground squirrel
8.	Horse
9.	Great gray kangaroo
10.	House mouse
11.	Virginia opossum
12.	Sei whale

GESTATION AND SIZE *There is generally a correlation between the length of a mammal's gestation period and its size. The human gestation period (average 267 days) is less than that of a horse and about the same as that of a dolphin.*

come, or go: *Get that dog out of here!* **20. a.** To bring: *I'll get him in here, and you can talk to him.* **b.** To gather: *get a few clothes together.* **21.** To induce or persuade; prevail upon: *I'll get my friend to show you his house.* **22.** To overpower; destroy: *Frost got our tomato crop.* **23.** To capture or catch: *The police got him.* **24.** *Slang.* To cause harm to; especially, to reciprocate by causing harm to: *I'll get you for that remark.* **25.** *Informal.* To strike or hit: *That blow got him on the chin.* **26. a.** In baseball, to put out: *The catcher got him sliding into home plate.* **b.** In football, to tackle; touch. **27.** *Slang.* To baffle; puzzle: *You've got me on that one!* **28.** *Slang.* To elicit a strong, usually negative reaction in: *Noisy eaters really get me.* **29.** To catch (a scheduled train or plane, for example). **30.** To have as an obligation; be constrained. Used only in the form of the present perfect and equivalent to *must*: *I have got to go.* —*intr.* **1.** To become, as by: **a.** Change: *get well again; get angry.* **b.** Movement: *get out of earshot.* **c.** Endeavor: *get to be chairman; get into Congress.* **2.** To move as specified: *get down from the ladder; get off the bus; get out.* **3.** To continue or proceed. Used with *back to, on,* or *on with*: *get back to work; get on with the job.* **4.** To arrive at or reach a particular point. Often used with *in, into,* or *to*: *The train gets in at midnight. We got to the end.* **5.** *Informal.* To start: *Get going!* **6.** *Regional & Informal.* To be off; depart: *Now get!* **7.** To work for gain or profit; make money: *He spends all his time getting and spending.* **—get about. 1.** *Informal.* To be active socially; go to many social events. **2.** To move around freely: *He no longer needs his crutches; he can get about without help.* **3.** To spread or travel. Used of a rumor or news. **—get across. 1.** To make understandable or clear: *Am I getting this across to you?* **2.** To be clear or understandable: *It's not getting across to him.* **3.** To communicate one's meaning or personality, as to an audience. **—get ahead.** To be successful; attain prosperity. **—get along. 1.** To be mutually congenial; be at harmony. **2.** To manage or fare with reasonable success: *He hasn't much money, but he gets along.* **3.** To advance, especially in years. **—get around. 1.** To avoid or circumvent (a problem, obstacle, or the like). **2.** *Informal.* To persuade or convince by wheedling or flattering. **3.** To consider or deal with after an initial delay: *I finally got around to writing the letter.* **—get at. 1.** To reach; find a way to: *It's under the desk and I can't get at it.* **2.** To lead up to or arrive at (a conclusion or meaning, for example): *Do you understand what I'm getting at?* **3.** To attack or try to attack and injure: *we went where they couldn't get at us.* **4.** *Informal.* To influence, especially by bribery. **—get away with.** *Informal.* To be successful in avoiding the discovery of (something done that deserves criticism or punishment). **—get back at.** *Informal.* To retaliate against or have revenge on: *He swears he'll get back at me.* **—get by.** To manage; survive; fare: *It will be a hard year, but we'll get by.* **—get down. 1.** To take cover; hide. **2.** To write (something) down. **3.** To depress or demoralize: *You mustn't let a small setback get you down.* **4.** To succeed in swallowing: *The pill was too big for him to get down.* **—get down to.** To begin doing; actively engage in: *They got down to some serious thinking.* **—get in. 1.** *Slang.* To gain the favor of. Used with *with*: *He wants to get in with that teacher.* **2.** To become involved in or part of. Used with *with*: *She wants to get in with a different crowd.* **3.** To be elected to office or accepted for membership. **—get into.** *Informal.* To develop an interest in or enthusiasm for: *I'm really getting into my new job.* **—get it. 1.** To comprehend; understand. **2.** *Informal.* To be punished or scolded. **—get nowhere.** To make no progress; have no success. **—get off. 1.** To send (a letter, for example). **2.** To escape, as from punishment or labor: *He got off scot-free.* **3.** To gain a release or lesser penalty for (a person). **4.** *Slang.* To get high, especially on a drug. **5.** *Slang.* To feel great pleasure or gratification. **—get off on.** *Slang.* **1.** To reach a state of euphoric consciousness through; get high on: *get off on acid.* **2.** To be stimulated or excited by; enjoy greatly: *get off on Mozart.* **—get on. 1.** To succeed; fare well. **2.** To advance. Used of time or aging: *It's getting on toward noon. He's getting on in years.* **3.** To be friendly or well disposed toward another or each other. Often used with *with.* **—get out of. 1.** To derive or draw: *He gets out of it what he can.* **2.** To avoid or get around. **—get over. 1.** To recover from (a sorrow or illness, for example). **2.** To overcome or rise above (a difficulty): *He'll soon get over his unfamiliarity with our procedures.* **3.** To complete (something, especially something unpleasant). Often used with *with*: *Let's get the shopping over with first.* **—get somewhere.** To make progress; achieve success. **—get there.** *Informal.* To attain one's goal. **—get through. 1.** To finish or complete. **2.** To undergo and survive: *I wonder if that tree will get through the winter.* **3.** To reach a destination, especially in the face of difficulties. **4.** To pass an examination. **5.** To succeed in making contact by telephone. Often used with *to.* **—get through to.** To make oneself or something understandable or apparent to. **—get to. 1.** To have the opportunity of or be able to: *I hope I get to go.* **2.** *Informal.* To happen to start; begin: *Then we got to remembering good times.* **3.** *Slang.* To impress or affect emotionally: *Her singing really gets to me.* **—get with it.** *Slang.* To become up to date.
~*n.* **1.** The act of begetting. **2.** Progeny; offspring. **3.** *Tennis.* A return on a shot that seems impossible to reach. [Get, got, got; Middle English *getten, gat, getten,* from Old Norse *geta, gat, getinn.*] **—get·a·ble, get·ta·ble** *adj.*

Usage: *Get* has a great number of uses, some of which are acceptable at all levels and some of which are generally felt to be informal (though never incorrect). Some uses better avoided in writing are: (1) The use of *get* in place of *be* or *become* in sentences as *He got arrested.* (2) The use of *get* or *get to* in place of *start* or *begin,* as in *When he gets* (or *gets to*) *reminiscing, he can't stop.* (3) The use of *have got to* in place of *must* in sentences like *I have got to go now.* • *Gotten* is a common past participle form, but it is not used when the senses involved are those of obligation or possession, as in *I've got to do it* and *I've got one in my hand. I've gotten to do it* means "I have succeeded in doing it," and *I've gotten a new car* means "I have just obtained a new car."

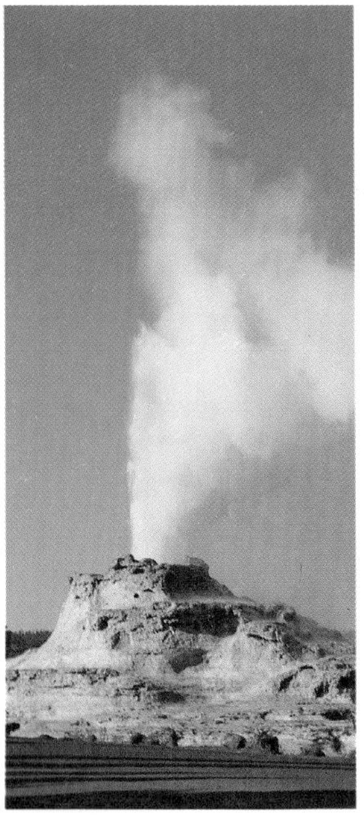

geyser *Superheated water and steam spurt into the air from Castle Geyser in Yellowstone National Park. The geyser gets its name from the ramparts around its vent, built from silica deposited by the mineral-rich water.*

get², gett *n.* A Jewish bill of divorce. [Hebrew *gēṭ.*]
get·a (gĕt′ə, gā′tə) *n., pl.* **geta** or **-as.** A wooden-soled shoe worn by the Japanese. [Japanese.]
get away *intr.v.* **1.** To escape. **2.** To leave; depart. **3.** To go away, as on a vacation. **4.** To start off in a race.
get·a·way (gĕt′ə-wā′) *n.* **1.** The act or an instance of escaping. **2.** A start, as of a race; takeoff.
~*adj.* Used for escape: *a getaway car.*
geth·sem·a·ne (gĕth-sĕm′ə-nē) *n.* Any instance or place of great suffering.
Geth·sem·a·ne (gĕth-sĕm′ə-nē). The garden outside Jerusalem that was the scene of the agony and arrest of Jesus. Matthew 26:36–56.
get out *intr.v.* **1.** To become public or known: *The news got out.* **2.** To go out or away; leave: *got out unharmed.* —*tr.v.* **1.** To publish (a newspaper, for example). **2.** To cause to go out or away. **3.** To say with an effort: *He stammered but managed to get the name out finally.*
get-out (gĕt′out′) *n. Informal.* An escape or means of avoiding difficulty: *A feigned headache was his get-out.* **—all get-out.** *Informal.* Used as a generalized superlative in comparisons: *cold as all get-out.*
get-rich-quick (gĕt′rĭch′kwĭk′) *adj.* Of, pertaining to, or being a plan or project designed to make money by rapid and often unscrupulous methods.
get·ter (gĕt′ər) *n.* **1.** One that gets. **2. a.** A material added in small amounts during a chemical or metallurgical process to absorb impurities. **b.** A substance, usually a metal, used to remove residual gas from a high-vacuum enclosure.
~*v.* **gettered, -tering, -ters.** —*tr.* **1.** To remove impurities from (a metal, for example) with a getter. **2.** To remove (gas) with a getter. —*intr.* To use a getter, as in removing impurities from a substance.
get together *intr.v.* To come together; assemble, especially socially: *Let's get together for a drink.* **—get it together.** *Slang.* **1.** To achieve personal fulfillment. **2.** To function with optimum efficiency in a particular sphere.
get-to·geth·er (gĕt′tə-gĕth′ər) *n. Informal.* **1.** A small party. **2.** A meeting or informal conference.
Get·ty (gĕt′ē), **J(ean) Paul** (1892–1976). U.S. financier and art collector. A millionaire by the age of 22, he turned his father's oil business into one of the world's largest financial empires.
Get·tys·burg (gĕt′ĭz-bûrg′). Town in southern Pennsylvania. It was here that the Union Army under Gen. George Meade defeated the Confederates under Gen. Robert E. Lee in July 1863 during the Civil War.
get up *intr.v.* **1.** To arise, as from bed or a stooping or prone position. **2.** To rise to one's feet. **3.** To increase in force or intensity: *The wind's getting up.* —*tr.v.* **1.** To study or revise. **2.** To act as the creator or organizer of: *get up a party; got up a petition against the new tax.* **3.** *Informal.* To dress or make up (oneself) elaborately. **4.** To bring into being in oneself; generate: *couldn't get up the indignation to protest.*
get-up (gĕt′ŭp′) *n.* **1.** An outfit or costume, especially one that is remarkable or bizarre. **2.** The arrangement and production style, as of a magazine or book.
get-up-and-go (gĕt′ŭp′ən-gō′) *n. Informal.* Energy and ambition; initiative and determination; drive.
ge·um (jē′əm) *n.* Any plant of the genus *Geum,* which includes **avens** and **herb bennet** *(both of which see).* [New Latin, from Latin *gaeum,* herb bennet.]
GeV *Physics.* Giga (10^9) electron volts. See **BeV.**
gew·gaw (gyōō′gô′) *n.* **1.** A decorative trinket; a bauble. **2.** Something that is decorative and showy but valueless. [Middle English : origin obscure.]
Ge·würz·tram·i·ner (gə-vōōrts′trăm′ə-nər, -trä′mə-nər) *n.* A dry white table wine with a distinctive spicy flavor produced in Alsace.
gey (gā) *adv. Scottish.* Very: *It's gey wet today.* [Variant of GAY.]
gey·ser (gī′zər *for sense 1;* gē′zər, gī′- *for sense 2*) *n.* **1.** A natural hot spring that intermittently ejects a column of water and steam into the air. **2.** *British.* A domestic, usually gas-operated hot-water heater. [Icelandic *Geysir,* "gusher," the name of a hot spring in Iceland, from *geysa,* to gush, from Old Norse.]
gey·ser·ite (gī′zə-rīt′) *n.* An opaline, usually siliceous deposit formed around natural hot springs. It is a form of sinter.
GFWC General Federation of Women's Clubs.
Gha·na (gä′nə). Country in West Africa on the Gulf of Guinea. In 1472 European trading posts were established, and the territory subsequently became a center of the slave trade and the scene of bitter rivalries between British, Danish, French, and Dutch companies. In 1874 the south was established as the British colony of the Gold Coast, and the north was added by 1901. Together with the British section of Togo, the country became independent in 1957, and in 1960 it became a republic within the Commonwealth. Agriculture is important; cocoa, of which Ghana is one of the world's principal producers, is the major export. Area, 238,305 square kilometers (92,010 square miles). Population, 11,450,000. Capital, Ac-

cra. See map at **West African States.** —**Gha·na·ian** (gä-nä′ən), **Gha·ni·an** (gä′nē-ən) *adj. & n.*

gha·ri·al (gä′rē-əl) *n.* A reptile, the **gavial** *(see).*

ghar·ry, ghar·ri (gär′ē, gär′ē) *n., pl.* **-ries.** A small horse-drawn carriage in India. [Hindi *gārī.*]

ghast·ly (gäst′lē, gäst′-) *adj.* **-lier, -liest. 1.** Terrifying; dreadful: *a ghastly accident.* **2.** Having a deathlike pallor: *"amid the dim and ghastly glare of a snowy night"* (Washington Irving). **3.** Extremely unpleasant or bad: *a ghastly little book.*
—*adv.* Dreadfully; horribly. [Middle English *gastlich,* Old English *gāstlīc,* spiritual, ghostly, ghastly, from *gāst,* soul, ghost.] —**ghast·li·ness** *n.*
Synonyms: grim, grisly, gruesome, lurid, macabre.

ghat, ghaut (gôt, gät) *n.* In India: **1.** A mountain pass. **2.** A mountain chain. **3.** A flight of steps down to the bank of a river. **4.** An area beside a river, used for bathing. [Hindi *ghāt,* from Sanskrit *ghaṭṭa,* perhaps from *ghṛṣṭa,* rubbed.]

Ghats (gôts, gäts). Two coastal mountain ranges in India, forming the edges of the Deccan plateau. The Western Ghats extend approximately 1,500 kilometers (932 miles) along the west coast and rise to 2,698 meters (8,852 feet) at Anai Mudi. The Eastern Ghats extend approximately 1,400 kilometers (880 miles) along the east coast, rising to 2,637 meters (8,651 feet) at Doda Betta.

gha·zi (gä′zē) *n., pl.* **-zies. 1.** A Muslim warrior who has fought successfully against infidels. Often used as a title of honor. **2.** A high-ranking Turkish warrior. [Arabic *ghāzi,* participle of *ghazā,* he made war.]

Ghazzah. See **Gaza.**

ghee (gē) *n.* Clarified butter from the butterfat of buffalo or other milk. It is used in cooking, especially in India and neighboring countries. [Hindi *ghī,* from Sanskrit *ghṛta,* present participle of *ghṛ†,* to sprinkle.]

Ghent (gĕnt). *Flemish* **Gent** (gĕnt); *French* **Gand** (gäɴ). A city and port in northwest-central Belgium, the capital of East Flanders.

ghe·rao (gə-rou′) *n.* In India, a coercive tactic adopted during industrial disputes whereby workers surround an employer and detain him on his own premises until he agrees to their demands. —*tr.v.* **gheraoed, -raoing, -raoes.** To coerce (an employer) by using this technique. [Bengali, to surround, from Indic *gher-* (unattested), causative of *ghir-* (unattested), "to go around," from Dravidian.]

gher·kin (gûr′kĭn) *n.* **1.** A small cucumber, especially one used for pickling. **2.** A tropical American vine, *Cucumis anguria,* bearing prickly, edible fruit. **3.** The fruit of this vine. [Dutch *agurk(je),* from Low German *agurke,* from Lithuanian *agurkas,* from Polish *ogorek, ogurek,* from Medieval Greek *angourion,* probably from Greek *agouros,* youth, "unripe," from *aōros* : *a-,* not + *ōros,* time.]

ghet·to (gĕt′ō) *n., pl.* **-tos** or **-toes. 1.** A slum section of a city occupied predominantly by members of a minority group who live there because of social or economic pressure. **2.** A section or quarter in a European city to which Jews were formerly restricted. **3.** An area occupied by a group, institution, or the like, with a distinctive, and often exclusive, specified common trait: *a cultural ghetto.* [Italian *ghetto†.*]

Ghib·el·line (gĭb′ə-lēn′, -lĭn′, -lĭn) *n.* Any of the members of the aristocratic political faction who fought during the Middle Ages for German imperial control of Italy, in opposition to the Guelphs, who favored papal control. Compare **Guelph.** [Italian *Ghibellino,* from Middle High German *Waiblingen,* name of a Hohenstaufen estate.]

Ghi·ber·ti (gē-bĕr′tē), **Lorenzo** (c.1378–1455). Italian goldsmith and sculptor. He is best known for his series of bronze panels for the doors of the baptistry of Florence Cathedral, depicting scenes from the New and Old Testaments.

ghilgai. Variant of **gilgai.**

ghil·lie (gĭl′ē) *n., pl.* **-lies. 1.** A low-cut sports shoe with fringed laces, originally worn by the Scots. **2.** Variant of **gillie.** [Scottish Gaelic *gille,* boy, servant, GILLIE.]

ghost (gōst) *n.* **1.** The spirit of a dead person, supposed to haunt living persons or former habitats; a specter; a phantom; a wraith. **2.** *Archaic.* The animus or soul as opposed to the body. **3.** A returning or haunting memory or image. **4.** A slight trace or vestige of something; a hint; a semblance: *a ghost of a smile; a ghost of a chance.* **5.** A faint, false secondary image, such as: **a.** A displaced image in a mirror caused by reflection from the front of the glass. **b.** A displaced image in a photograph caused by the optical system of the camera. **c.** A secondary image on a television or radar screen caused by reflected waves. **d.** A false spectral line caused by imperfections in the diffraction grating. **6.** *Printing.* A variation or unevenness of color intensity on a surface intended to be solidly tinted, as the result of irregular distribution of ink. **7.** *Obsolete.* The Holy Ghost. **8.** *Informal.* A ghostwriter. **9.** A nonexistent publication listed in bibliographies. In this sense, also called "ghost edition." **10.** A ghost word. —**give up the ghost.** To die.
—*v.* **ghosted, ghosting, ghosts.** —*intr. Informal.* To work as a ghostwriter. —*tr.* **1.** To haunt. **2.** *Informal.* To write (a work) as a ghostwriter. [Middle English *gost, gast,* Old English *gāst,* from Germanic.]

ghost crab *n.* Any of several light-colored burrowing crabs of the genus *Ocypoda,* frequenting the tide line along sandy shores.

ghost dance *n.* Either of two religious dances practiced chiefly by certain North American Indians of the southwestern United States and California during the latter half of the 19th century to invoke a return of their former condition.

ghost gum *n.* Any of various Australian eucalyptus trees with a smooth, whitish trunk and branches.

ghost·ly (gōst′lē) *adj.* **-lier, -liest. 1.** Pertaining to or resembling a ghost or apparition; spectral; eerie. **2.** Pertaining to the spirit or to religion; spiritual. —**ghost·li·ness** *n.*

ghost moth *n.* Any of various moths of the family Hepialidae that have large, pale wings and are active at dusk. Also called "swift moth."

ghost town *n.* A town, especially a boom town of the West, that has now been completely abandoned.

ghost word *n.* A word that has come into a language through the perpetuation of a misreading of a manuscript, a typographical error, or a misunderstanding. For example, in *Ye Olde Sweete Shoppe, Ye* is a ghost word, the *y* having been a misreading of the runic letter thorn.

ghost·write (gōst′rīt′) *v.* **-wrote** (-rōt′), **-written** (-rĭt′n), **-writing, -writes.** —*intr.* To work as a ghostwriter. —*tr.* To write (something) as a ghostwriter.

ghost·writ·er (gōst′rī′tər) *n.* A person who is hired to write for another person who then takes credit of authorship. Also informally called "ghost."

ghoul (gōōl) *n.* **1.** One who delights in what is revolting, macabre, or loathsome. **2.** A grave robber. **3. a.** A malevolent ghost. **b.** An evil spirit or demon in Muslim folklore supposed to plunder graves and feed on corpses. [Arabic *ghūl,* from *ghāla,* he took suddenly.] —**ghoul·ish** *adj.* —**ghoul·ish·ly** *adv.* —**ghoul·ish·ness** *n.*

GHQ, G.H.Q. general headquarters.

ghyll. Variant of **gill** (stream or ravine).

gi gill (liquid measure).

Gi gilbert (unit of magnetomotive force).

GI (jē′ī′) *n., pl.* **GIs** or **GI's.** A serviceman in or ex-serviceman of any of the U.S. armed forces.
—*adj.* **1.** Pertaining to or characteristic of a GI. **2.** In conformity to or accordance with U.S. military regulations or procedures. **3.** Issued by an official U.S. military supply department. [Abbreviation of *general issue* or *government issue.*]

GI 1. general issue. **2.** Government Issue.

G.I. Government Issue.

Gia·co·met·ti (jä′kō-mĕt′ə), **Alberto** (1901–66). Swiss painter and sculptor. From 1922 to 1935 he experimented with cubism but later evolved a distinctive, elongated style of representing the human figure.

gi·ant (jī′ənt) *n.* **1. a.** A person or thing of extraordinary size or strength. **b.** A person of outstanding importance or achievement: *He is a giant in his field.* **2. a.** *Greek Mythology.* Any of a race of manlike beings of enormous strength and stature who warred with the Olympians, by whom they were finally destroyed. **b.** Any similar being in folklore or myth.
—*adj.* Of immense size; gigantic; huge. [Middle English *geant,* from Old French, from Vulgar Latin *gangante* (unattested), from Latin *gigās* (stem *gigant-*), from Greek *gigas†.*]

giant anteater *n.* See **anteater.**

giant axon *n.* A giant fiber *(see).*

giant chromosome *n.* A chromosome consisting of many parallel strands of chromatids that have failed to separate after duplication. Giant chromosomes, which occur in the salivary glands of *Drosophila* and other insects, are used to study gene activity.

gi·ant·ess (jī′ən-tĭs) *n.* A female giant.

giant fiber *n. Zoology.* A nerve fiber with a very large diameter found in many invertebrate animals that is capable of rapid conduction of impulses. Also called "giant axon."

giant hogweed *n., pl.* **giant hogweeds** or collectively **giant hogweed.** A very tall plant, *Heracleum mantegazzianum,* with clusters of small white flowers, found especially on waste ground.

gi·ant·ism (jī′ən-tĭz′əm) *n.* **1.** The condition of being a giant. **2.** *Pathology.* Gigantism *(see).*

gi·ant-kill·er (jī′ənt-kĭl′ər) *n.* An individual, such as a sportsman, that defeats an apparently more powerful opponent against all expectations.

giant panda *n.* See **panda.**

giant planet *n.* A planet with a large mass of low density. The giant planets are **Jupiter, Saturn, Neptune,** and **Uranus.**

giant powder *n.* A high explosive consisting of trinitroglycerin absorbed in kieselguhr.

Giant's Causeway. Promontory on the northern coast of County Antrim, Northern Ireland on the North Channel. It consists of thousands of basaltic columns formed by a flow of lava into the sea. Legend has it that it was once a bridge for giants to cross between Ireland and Scotland.

giant sequoia *n.* A very tall evergreen tree, *Sequoia gigantea,* of mountainous regions of southern California, having a massive trunk and light-colored, reddish wood. Also called "big tree," "wellingtonia." Compare **redwood.**

giant star *n.* Any of a class of highly luminous, exceptionally massive stars having relatively low density and lying above the main sequence. Compare **dwarf star.**

giaour (jour) *n.* A nonbeliever in the Muslim faith; especially, a Christian. [Turkish *giaur,* infidel, from Persian *gaur,* variant of *gäbr†,* fire worshiper.]

gi·ar·di·a·sis (jē′är-dī′ə-sĭs) *n.* A disease caused by infestations of the small intestine with the parasitic protozoan *Giardia lamblia* and characterized by diarrhea and nausea. [New Latin *giardia,* after A.M. *Giard* (died 1908), French biologist + -IASIS.]

gib¹ (gĭb) *n.* A plain or notched, often wedge-shaped piece of wood or metal designed to hold parts of a machine or structure in place or to provide a bearing surface, usually adjusted by a screw or key. —*tr.v.* **gibbed, gibbing, gibs.** To apply a gib to. [18th century : origin obscure.]

gib² *n.* A male cat, especially one that has been castrated. [Perhaps from *Gib,* the nickname for *Gilbert.*]

Gi·ba·ra Bay (hē-bär′ə). Inlet of the Atlantic Ocean on the northeastern coast of Cuba. It is traditionally considered to be the site of Columbus's first landing in the New World (1492).

gib·ber¹ (jĭb′ər) *intr.v.* **-bered, -bering, -bers. 1.** To make rapid, chattering noises, as a monkey does. **2.** To prattle or chatter unintelligibly.
—*n.* Senseless talk or prate; gibberish. [Imitative.]

gib·ber² (jĭb′ər) *n. Australian.* A stone or rock, especially one polished by the wind. [From a native Australian language.]

gib·ber·el·lic acid (jĭb′ə-rĕl′ĭk) *n.* A substance, C₁₉H₂₂O₆, first isolated from a fungus, *Gibberella fujikuroi,* and occurring naturally in many plants, where it promotes elongation of the cells. [From GIBBERELLIN.]

gib·ber·el·lin (jĭb′ə-rĕl′ĭn) *n.* Any of a class of natural plant growth substances, such as gibberellic acid, that promote elongation of the stems and leaves. [New Latin *Gibberella,* diminutive of Latin *gibber,* hunchbacked, akin to Latin *gibbus,* hump.]

gib·ber·ish (jĭb′ər-ĭsh) *n.* Nonsensical, rapid talk; prattle.

gib·bet (jĭb′ĭt) *n.* **1.** A gallows. **2.** An upright post with a crosspiece, forming a T-shaped structure from which executed criminals were hung for public viewing.
—*tr.v.* **gibbeted** or **gibbetted, -beting** or **-betting, -bets. 1.** To execute by hanging. **2.** To hang on a gibbet for public viewing. **3.** To expose to infamy or public ridicule. [Middle English *gibet,* from Old French, diminutive of *gibe,* staff, club, possibly from Frankish *gibb*† (unattested), forked stick.]

gib·bon (gĭb′ən) *n.* Any of several apes of the genera *Hylobates* or *Symphalangus,* of tropical Asia, that live in trees and have a slender body and long arms. [French, perhaps from a native word in India.]

Gib·bon (gĭb′ən), **Edward** (1737–94). British historian. His principal work, *The History of the Decline and Fall of the Roman Empire* (1776–88), covers some 1,200 years of history and remains a monumental work of its kind.

Gib·bons (gĭb′ənz), **Grinling** (1648–1721). Dutch-born British sculptor. He excelled in the carving of fruit and flowers in wood and was commissioned by Sir Christopher Wren to work on the choir stalls and organ screen of St. Paul's Cathedral.

Gibbons, Orlando (1583–1625). English composer. Organist at the Chapel Royal from 1604, he was appointed organist of Westminster Abbey in 1623. His sacred and secular compositions include some beautiful madrigals.

gib·bos·i·ty (gĭ-bŏs′ə-tē) *n., pl.* **-ties. 1.** The condition of being gibbous. **2.** A rounded hump or protuberance; a swelling. **3.** *Pathology.* A sharply angled curvature of the spine, formerly commonly caused by tuberculosis.

gib·bous (gĭb′əs) *adj.* **1.** Rounded; convex; protuberant. **2.** More than half but less than fully illuminated. Said of the moon or a planet. **3.** Humpbacked. [Middle English, from Late Latin *gebbōsus,* humpbacked, from *gibbus,* hump (expressive).] —**gib·bous·ly** *adv.* —**gib·bous·ness** *n.*

Gibbs free energy (gĭbz) *n.* Gibbs function.

Gibbs function *n.* A measure of the thermodynamic free energy of a system, used for changes at constant pressure equal to the enthalpy minus the product of entropy and thermodynamic temperature. Also called "Gibbs free energy." [After Josiah Willard *Gibbs* (1839–1903), U.S. physicist and mathematician.]

gibbs·ite (gĭb′zīt′) *n.* Hydrated aluminum oxide, Al₂O₃·3H₂O, a constituent of bauxite. [After George *Gibbs* (1776–1833), U.S. mineralogist.]

gibe (jīb) *v.* **gibed, gibing, gibes.** Also **jibe, jibed, jibing, jibes.** —*intr.* To make heckling or mocking remarks; scoff. Usually used with *at.* —*tr.* To reproach by taunting; deride. —See Synonyms at **ridicule.**
—*n.* A derisive remark; a taunt. [Perhaps from Old French *giber*†, to handle roughly.] —**gib·er** *n.* —**gib·ing·ly** *adv.*

Gib·e·on·ite (gĭb′ē-ə-nīt′) *n.* Any of the inhabitants of Gibeon, a village of ancient Palestine, condemned by Joshua to serve as manual laborers for the Israelites. Joshua 9.

gib·lets (jĭb′lĭts) *pl.n.* The edible inside parts of a fowl, such as the heart, liver, or gizzard. [Middle English *gibelet,* from Old French, probably variant of *giberet* (unattested), diminutive of *gibier,* hunting, game, from Frankish *gabaiti* (unattested), hunting with falcons.]

Gib·ral·tar (jĭ-brôl′tər). British crown colony at the western entrance to the Mediterranean Sea. Linked by a sandy isthmus to the Spanish mainland, it rises to 427 meters (1,400 feet) at the Rock of Gibraltar. In ancient times it was the Calpe of the Greeks and the Romans, forming, with ancient Abyla on the African coast, the Pillars of Hercules, long thought to mark the western edge of the world. Successively ruled by the Moors and Castile, it was taken by Adm. George Rooke in 1704 and has remained a British possession since. In 1967 it was granted a measure of internal self-government. Following Spanish demands for decolonization (1967), a referendum was held; the population voted 12,138 to 44 in favor of the status quo. Gibraltar has few natural resources and relies chiefly on its strategic position as a port. Tourism is also important. Its name

gibbon The common or lar gibbon—one of several Southeast Asian species of this ape—lives almost entirely in the trees. It is a remarkable acrobat, swinging from branch to branch in leaps of up to 15 meters (50 feet).

is derived from Jabel-al-Tarik, after its Moorish conqueror of 711, Tarik. —**Gib·ral·tar·i·an** (jĭ′brōl-târ′ē-ən) *n. & adj.*

Gibraltar, Strait of. Channel between southern Spain and Morocco in northwest Africa. Some 58 kilometers (36 miles) long and 13 kilometers (8 miles) wide at its narrowest point, it links the Mediterranean Sea with the Atlantic Ocean.

Gib·ran (jə-brän′), **Khalil** (1883–1931). Lebanese poet. His major work in the English language, *The Prophet* (1923), expounds his philosophy with a vivid use of metaphor.

Gib·son Desert (gĭb′sən). The central section of the desert of western Australia, lying between the Great Sandy Desert and the Victoria Desert.

Gib·son girl (gĭb′sən) *n.* The ideal American girl of the 1890's as portrayed in sketches by the illustrator Charles Dana Gibson (1867–1944), typically dressed in a tailored shirtwaist with leg-of-mutton sleeves and a long skirt.

gid (gĭd) *n.* A disease of sheep caused by the presence in the brain of the larva of a tapeworm, *Taenia caenurus,* and resulting in a staggering gait. Also called "sturdy," "waterbrain." [Back-formation from GIDDY.]

gid·dy (gĭd′ē) *adj.* **-dier, -diest. 1. a.** Having a reeling, light-headed sensation; dizzy. **b.** Causing or capable of causing dizziness: *a giddy climb to the top of the tower.* **2.** Frivolous and lighthearted; flighty: *giddy young girls.*
—*v.* **giddied, -dying, -dies.** —*intr.* To become giddy. —*tr.* To make giddy. [Middle English *gidy,* mad, foolish, Old English *gydig,* possessed by a god, insane.] —**gid·di·ly** *adv.* —**gid·di·ness** *n.*

gid·dy·ap (gĭd′ē-ăp′, -ŭp′) *interj.* Also **gid·dap** (gĭ-dăp′). Used as a command to make an animal, especially a horse, move or go faster. [From *get up.*]

Gide (zhēd), **André** (1869–1951). French novelist and diarist. Much of his work examines the tensions between desire and duty, with particular reference to his own Christianity and homosexuality. His novels include *La Porte Étroite* (1909) and *Les Faux Monnayeurs* (1925). He was awarded the Nobel Prize for literature in 1947.

Gid·e·on (gĭd′ē-ən). A judge of Israel and conqueror of the Midianites. Judges 6–8. [Hebrew *Gidh'ōn,* "hewer," "feller," from *gādha,* "he cut down."]

Gideon Bible *n.* A Bible put in a public place, especially a hotel room, by a member of the Gideons, a Christian organization. [After GIDEON.]

gie (gē) *v.* **gied** or **gae** (gā), **gied** or **gien** (gēn), **gieing, gies.** *Scottish.* To give.

Giel·gud (gēl′gʊʊd′, gēl′-), **Sir (Arthur) John** (1904–). British actor and director. He won popular acclaim with his performances in and productions of Shakespeare's plays.

gift (gĭft) *n.* **1.** Something that is bestowed voluntarily and without compensation; a present. **2.** The act, right, or power of giving: *The privilege is in the gift of the bishop.* **3.** A talent, endowment, aptitude, or power: *a gift for languages.* **4.** *Informal.* Something obtained very easily or cheaply. —**(the) gift of gab.** A talent for speaking easily or well.
—*tr.v.* **gifted, gifting, gifts. 1.** To present with a gift. **2.** *Chiefly British.* To bestow as a gift. **3.** To endow with; invest. [Middle English *gift, yift,* from Old Norse *gipt, gift.*]

gift certificate *n.* A certificate given as a present that can be exchanged at the store that issued it for goods to the amount stated on it.

gift·ed (gĭf′tĭd) *adj.* **1.** Endowed with natural ability, talent, or other assets; especially, endowed with exceptional intelligence: *a gifted child.* **2.** Revealing talent: *a gifted rendition of a song.* —**gift·ed·ly** *adv.* —**gift·ed·ness** *n.*

gift horse *n.* —**look a gift horse in the mouth.** To be suspicious of or to find fault with a gift or lucky chance. [Alluding to the practice of examining a horse's teeth to determine its age.]

gift of tongues *n.* An ecstatic utterance that is partly or wholly unintelligible to hearers, especially as practiced liturgically in certain Christian congregations. Also called "glossolalia." [By allusion to the Pentecostal miracle whereby the Apostles "were all filled with the Holy Ghost, and began to speak with other tongues, as the Spirit gave them utterance." Acts 2:4.]

gift-wrap (gĭft′răp′) *tr.v.* **-wrapped, -wrapping, -wraps.** To wrap (a purchase or present) in fancy paper with elaborate trimmings.

gig¹ (gĭg) *n.* **1.** A light, two-wheeled vehicle drawn by one horse. **2. a.** A long, light ship's boat having oars, sails, or a motor and usually reserved for use by the ship's captain. **b.** A fast, light rowboat. [Middle English *gigg*†, giddy girl, something that whirls.]

gig² *n.* **1.** An arrangement of barbless hooks that is dragged through a school of fish to hook them in the bodies. **2.** A spear for fishing, a **fishgig** (see).
—*v.* **gigged, gigging, gigs.** —*tr.* **1.** To catch with a gig. **2.** *Regional.* To goad; prod. —*intr.* To fish with a gig. [Short for FISHGIG.]

gig³ *n. Slang.* **1.** A job, engagement, or booking for musicians, especially pop or jazz musicians. **2.** A performance by pop or jazz musicians, as at a club or concert.
—*intr.v.* **gigged, gigging, gigs.** *Slang.* To perform a gig, as at a club or concert. [20th century : origin obscure.]

giga– *prefix. Abbr.* **G** Indicates one thousand million (10⁹); for example, *gigavolt* (1,000,000,000 volts). [Greek *gigas,* GIANT.]

gi·gan·tic (jī-găn′tĭk) *adj.* **1.** Pertaining to or suitable for a giant. **2. a.** Exceedingly large of its kind: *a gigantic toadstool.* **b.** Very large or extensive: *a gigantic radio network.* —See Synonyms at **enor-**

mous. [Latin *gigās* (stem *gigant*-), GIANT.] —**gi·gan·ti·cal·ly** *adv.*

gi·gan·tism (jī-găn'tĭz'əm, jī'gən-) *n.* **1.** Excessive growth of the body or any of its parts as a result of oversecretion of the pituitary growth hormone during childhood. Also called "giantism." **2.** Abnormal size.

gi·gan·tom·a·chy (jī'găn-tŏm'ə-kē) *n.* Also **gi·gan·to·ma·chi·a** (jī-găn'tə-mā'kē-ə). **1.** *Greek Mythology.* The war of the giants against Zeus and the other Olympian gods. **2.** Any battle or contest on a massive scale. [Greek *gigantomakhia* : *gigas* (stem *gigant*-), GIANT + -MACHY.]

gig·gle (gĭg'əl) *intr.v.* **-gled, -gling, -gles.** To laugh with repeated short, high-pitched, convulsive sounds, as when nervous or when attempting to suppress mirth.
~*n.* A high-pitched, spasmodic laugh. [Imitative.] —**gig·gler** *n.* —**gig·gling·ly** *adv.*

gig·gly (gĭg'lē) *adj.* **-glier, -gliest.** Inclined to giggle.

gig·o·lo (jĭg'ə-lō', zhĭg'-) *n., pl.* **-los. 1.** A young man who is kept as a lover by a woman, especially an older woman. **2.** A paid male escort or dancing partner. [French, from *gigolette*, dance-hall partner, from *giguer*, to dance, from *gigue*, leg, fiddle, from Old French, from Old High German *giga*†.]

gig·ot (jĭg'ət, zhē-gō') *n.* **1.** A leg of mutton or lamb for cooking. **2.** A leg-of-mutton sleeve. Also called "gigot sleeve." [Old French, diminutive of *gigue*, leg, fiddle. See **gigolo**.]

gigue (zhēg) *n.* **1.** A dance, the **jig** (*see*). **2.** *Music.* A lively piece of music in 6/8, 9/8, or 12/8 time, often forming the final movement of the classical suite. [French, from English JIG.]

GI Joe *n. Informal.* A serviceman in the U.S. Army, especially during World War II.

Gi·jón (gē-hôn', hē-). Port in northwestern Spain, on the Bay of Biscay, in Oviedo province in Asturias. It is an important industrial center.

Gi·la (hē'lə). River rising in the mountains of western New Mexico. It flows 1,014 kilometers (630 miles) across southern Arizona to the Colorado River at Yuma, on the border with California. Ancestors of the Pima and Papago Indians used irrigation to farm the river's valley.

Gila Cliff Dwellings National Monument. A park, 65 hectares (160 acres), in southwestern New Mexico, set aside to preserve Pueblo Indian dwellings built into the side of a cliff 46 meters (150 feet) high.

Gila monster *n.* A venomous lizard, *Heloderma suspectum*, of the southwestern United States and northern Mexico, having a stout body covered with black and orange or yellowish scales. [After the GILA River.]

gil·bert (gĭl'bərt) *n. Abbr.* **Gi** The centimeter-gram-second electromagnetic unit of magnetomotive force, equal to 10/4π ampere-turn. [After William GILBERT.]

Gil·bert (gĭl'bərt), **William** (1544–1603). English physicist. His work on magnets led to his theory, broadly correct, that the earth is a magnet with its poles at the North and South poles. He also coined the term "electricity" and was a physician to Elizabeth I.

Gilbert, Sir William Schwenk (1836–1911). English librettist and humorist. He is best known for the Savoy operas he wrote with the composer Sir Arthur Sullivan.

Gilbert Islands. See Kiribati, Republic of.

gild¹ (gĭld) *tr.v.* **gilded** or **gilt** (gĭlt), **gilding, gilds. 1.** To cover with or as if with a thin layer of gold. **2.** To give an often deceptively attractive or improved appearance to; gloss or gloss over. **3.** *Archaic.* To smear with blood. —**gild the lily.** To adorn unnecessarily something that is already beautiful. [Middle English *gilden*, Old English *gyldan*.]

gild². Variant of **guild**.

gild·er¹ (gĭl'dər) *n.* A person whose work is gilding.

gilder². Variant of **guilder**.

gild·ing (gĭl'dĭng) *n.* **1.** The art or process of applying gilt to a surface. **2.** Gilt. **3.** Something used to give a superficially attractive appearance.

gi·let (zhē-lā') *n.* A waistcoat. [French.]

gil·gai, ghil·gai (gĭl'gī') *n.* In Australia, a cracked, uneven natural depression in the ground; a water hole. [From a native Australian language.]

gill¹ (gĭl) *n.* **1.** *Zoology.* The respiratory organ of fishes, larval amphibians, and numerous aquatic invertebrates, typically consisting of a membranous appendage well supplied with blood vessels for gaseous exchange. **2.** *Usually* **gills.** The wattle of a bird. **3.** *Usually* **gills.** *Informal.* The area around the chin and neck. **4.** *Botany.* Any of the thin, platelike, spore-producing structures on the underside of the cap of a mushroom or similar fungus. —**green around** (or **about**) **the gills.** Looking or feeling nauseated.
~*tr.v.* **gilled, gilling, gills. 1.** To catch (fish) in a gill net. **2.** To gut or clean (fish). [Middle English *gille*, probably from Old Norse *gil* (unattested).]

gill² (jĭl) *n. Abbr.* **gi 1.** A unit of volume or capacity in the U.S. Customary System, used in liquid measure, equal to 4 fluid ounces (¼ pint) or 23.656 milliliters. **2.** A unit of volume or capacity in the British Imperial System, used in dry and liquid measure, equal to 5 fluid ounces (¼ pint) or 28.423 milliliters. [Middle English *gille*, from Old French *gille, gelle*, from Late Latin *gillo*†, water pot.]

gill³, ghyll (gĭl) *n. British Regional.* **1.** A swift-flowing mountain stream. **2.** A ravine. [Middle English *gille*, from Old Norse *gil*.]

gill bar (gĭl) *n.* Any of a series of skeletal structures in the pharyngeal wall of fishes that supports the tissue separating the gill slits.

gill books (gĭl) *pl.n.* The respiratory organs of king crabs, consisting of layers of thin vascular plates attached to the abdominal appendages.

Gil·les·pie (gĭ-lĕs'pē), **John Birks** known as "Dizzy" (1917–). U.S. jazz trumpeter. After 1944 he began to develop the style known as "bop."

Gil·lette (jə-lĕt'), **King Camp** (1855–1932). U.S. inventor and manufacturer. He was first a traveling salesman, but in the late 1890's developed a crude model of a razor using a thin, double-edged, disposable blade. His new product, manufactured by his company, soon became greatly popular.

gill fungus (gĭl) *n.* Any fleshy fungus having a cap with gills on the underside.

gil·lie, gil·ly, ghil·lie (gĭl'ē) *n., pl.* **-lies.** *Scottish.* A professional guide and servant for sportsmen, especially in fishing and deerstalking. [Scottish Gaelic *gille*, boy, servant, akin to Irish *giolla*†.]

gil·lion (jĭl'yən) *n. British.* One thousand million. [Blend of GIGA- + MILLION.]

gill net (gĭl) *n.* A fishing net set vertically in the water so that fish swimming into it are entangled by the gills in its mesh.

gill-o·ver-the-ground (gĭl'ō-vər-thə-ground') *n.* A plant, the **ground ivy** (*see*).

gill pouch (gĭl) *n.* Any of a series of paired pouches in the pharyngeal wall of chordate embryos that become the gill slits of aquatic vertebrates.

gill slit (gĭl) *n.* Any of several narrow, paired external openings connecting with the pharynx, present in all vertebrates during embryonic development, and characteristic of adult fishes and other aquatic vertebrates.

gil·ly·flow·er, gil·li·flow·er (gĭl'ē-flou'ər) *n.* **1.** The carnation or a similar plant of the genus *Dianthus*. **2.** Any of several plants having fragrant flowers, as the stock or wallflower. [Alteration (influenced by FLOWER) of Middle English *gilofre, gelofer*, from Old French *girofre, girofle*, from Medieval Latin *caryophylum*, clove, from Greek *karuophullon* : *karuon*, nut + *phullon*, leaf.]

Gil·son·ite (gĭl'sə-nīt') *n.* A trademark for a natural black bitumen found in Utah and Colorado, used in the manufacture of acid, alkali, and waterproof coatings. Also called "uintaite." [After S.H. Gilson, of Salt Lake City, Utah.]

gilt¹ (gĭlt). Alternate past tense and past participle of **gild**.
~*adj.* **1.** Covered with gold or a substance simulating gold; gilded. **2.** Having the appearance of gold.
~*n. Abbr.* **gt. 1.** A thin layer of gold or something simulating gold that is applied in gilding. **2. a.** Shining brilliance; glitter. **b.** Superficial brilliance or gloss.

gilt² *n.* A young sow that has not yet produced a litter. [Middle English *gilt*, young sow, from Old Norse *gylta*, sow.]

gilt-edged (gĭlt'ĕjd') *adj.* Also **gilt-edge** (-ĕj'). **1.** Having gilded edges, as the pages of a book. **2. a.** Of the highest quality or value: *gilt-edged securities.* **b.** Of a high degree of reliability.

gim·bals (gĭm'bəlz, jĭm'-) *pl.n.* A device consisting of two rings mounted on axes at right angles to each other so that an object such as a ship's compass will remain suspended in a horizontal plane between them regardless of their motion. [Plural of *gimbal*, from Old French *gemel*, GIMMAL.]

gim·crack (jĭm'krăk') *n.* A cheap and showy object of little or no use; a knickknack.
~*adj.* Cheap and shoddy; flimsy. [Middle English *gibecrake*†, ornament, gimcrack.] —**gim·crack·er·y** *n.*

gim·el (gĭm'əl) *n.* The third letter of the Hebrew alphabet. See feature at **alphabet**. [Hebrew *gīmel*, "camel" (from the ancient form of the letter), akin to *gāmāl*, CAMEL.]

gim·let (gĭm'lĭt) *n.* **1.** A small hand tool for boring holes, having a spiraled shank, a screw tip, and a cross handle. **2.** A cocktail made with vodka or gin and sweetened lime juice, garnished with a slice of lime.
~*tr.v.* **gimleted, -leting, -lets.** To penetrate with or as if with a gimlet; puncture; pierce.
~*adj.* Piercing; penetrating: *gimlet eyes.* [Middle English, from Old French *guimbelet*, probably from Middle Dutch *wimmelkijn*, diminutive of *wimmel*, auger.]

gim·mal (gĭm'əl, jĭm'-) *n.* A ring made of two narrower rings interlocked. [Earlier *gemel*, from Old French, from Latin *gemellus*, diminutive of *geminus*, twin.]

gim·me (gĭm'ē). *Slang.* Contraction of **give me**.

gim·mick (gĭm'ĭk) *n.* **1.** A device employed, often illegally, to cheat, deceive, or trick, especially a mechanism for the secret control of a gambling wheel. **2.** A clever device or stratagem used to promote or publicize a project: *an advertising gimmick.* **3.** A significant feature that is obscured or misrepresented; catch. **4.** A trivial or unnecessary innovation, as a gadget, used to attract attention or interest. **5.** A small object whose name eludes one.
~*tr.v.* **gimmicked, -micking, -micks.** To add gimmicks to: *gimmicked up the dress with fringe and sequins.* [20th century (American) : origin obscure.] —**gim·mick·ry** *n.* —**gim·mick·y** *adj.*

gimp¹ (gĭmp) *n.* A narrow braid or cord of fabric, sometimes stiffened, used to trim or pipe clothes, curtains, or upholstered furniture. Also called "guimpe," "guipure."
~*tr.v.* **gimped, gimping, gimps.** To trim or edge with gimp. [Dutch *gimp*†.]

gimp² *n. Slang.* Spirit; courage. [20th century : origin obscure.]

gimp³ *n. Slang.* **1.** A limp or limping gait. **2.** A person who limps.
~*intr.v. Slang.* To limp. [Origin unknown.] —**gimp·y** *adj.*

Gila monster *This venomous lizard is found in the Arizona desert. It can survive without food or water for several months and grows to a length of almost 60 centimeters (2 feet).*

giraffe *Found in the savannah lands of Africa, the giraffe is the tallest living mammal. It can be nearly 6 meters (20 feet) tall and feeds mainly on thorn trees.*

girandole *The characteristically radiating design known as girandole is used here in a gold and emerald earring made in the 18th century in Spain or Portugal.*

gin[1] (jĭn) *n.* **1.** A strong alcoholic liquor distilled from grain, as rye or barley, and flavored with juniper berries. **2.** A liquor similar to gin but flavored with some other aromatic substance, as aniseed. [Shortened from Dutch *jenever,* from Middle Dutch *geniver, genever,* juniper, from Old French *geneivre,* from Latin *jūniperus,* JUNIPER.]

gin[2] (jĭn) *n.* **1.** Any of several machines or devices, as: **a.** A machine for hoisting or moving heavy objects. **b.** A **pile driver** *(see).* **c.** A snare or trap for game. **d.** A pump operated by a windmill. **2.** A **cotton gin** *(see).*
~*tr.v.* **ginned, ginning, gins. 1.** To remove the seeds from (cotton) with a cotton gin. **2.** To trap (game) in a gin. [Middle English *gin,* short for *engin,* ENGINE.]

gin[3] (jĭn) *n.* A card game, **gin rummy** *(see).*

gin[4] (jĭn) *n. Australian.* An aboriginal woman. [From a native Australian language.]

gin[5] (gĭn) *prep. Scottish.* If. [Probably akin to *gif,* IF.]

gin and tonic (jĭn) *n.* A drink made with gin and quinine water with a garnish of a slice or wedge of lemon or lime.

gin·ger (jĭn′jər) *n.* **1. a.** A plant, *Zingiber officinale,* of tropical Asia, having yellowish-green flowers and a pungent, aromatic rootstock. **b.** The rootstock of this plant, often dried and powdered and used as a spice. **c.** The rootstock of this plant cooked in a heavy sugar syrup until glazed, used as a candy. **2.** Any of various plants of the family Zingiberaceae, having variously colored, often fragrant flowers. **3.** The **wild ginger** *(see).* **4.** A reddish yellow or yellowish brown. **5.** *Informal.* Liveliness; vigor.
~*tr.v.* **gingered, -gering, -gers. 1.** To spice with ginger. **2.** *Informal.* To make more lively. Often used with *up*: *She gingered up the party.* [Middle English *gingivere,* from Old English *gingifer* and Old French *gingivre, gingembre,* from Medieval Latin *gingiber, gingiver,* from Latin *zinziberi,* from Greek *ziggiberis,* from Prakrit *singabēra,* from Sanskrit *śṛṅgaveram* : *śṛṅga-,* horn + *vera-*†, body (so called from its shape).]

ginger ale *n.* An effervescent soft drink, pale orange or brown in color, that is flavored with ginger.

ginger beer *n.* An effervescent soft drink, popular in England, that is cloudy gray in color and flavored with fermented ginger.

gin·ger·bread (jĭn′jər-brĕd′) *n.* **1. a.** A dark molasses cake flavored with ginger. **b.** A soft molasses and ginger cooky cut in various shapes and sometimes elaborately decorated with colored icing. **2. a.** Elaborate ornamentation. **b.** Superfluous or tasteless embellishment, especially in architecture.
~*adj.* **1.** Made of gingerbread. **2.** Tastelessly elaborate. [Middle English *gingebred,* preserved ginger, alteration (influenced by *bred,* BREAD) of Old French *gingebras,* from Medieval Latin *gingibrātum,* from *gingiber,* GINGER.]

gingerbread palm *n.* A tree, the **doum palm** *(see).*

gingerbread tree *n.* An African tree, *Parinarium macrophyllum,* having large edible fruits and useful wood. Also called "gingerbread plum."

ginger group *n. Chiefly British.* A group of people within an association or organization that represent a challenging, progressive, or radical viewpoint. [From GINGER (verb).]

gin·ger·ly (jĭn′jər-lē) *adv.* **1.** With great care or delicacy. **2.** Cautiously; carefully; timidly.
~*adj.* Cautious; careful; timid. [Earliest sense "daintily," perhaps from Old French *gensor, genzor,* comparative of *gent,* pretty, of noble birth, from Latin *genitus,* past participle of *gignere,* to bring forth.] **—gin·ger·li·ness** *n.*

gin·ger·root (jĭn′jər-ro͞ot′, -ro͝ot′) *n.* The rootstock of the ginger plant.

gin·ger·snap (jĭn′jər-snăp′) *n.* A flat, brittle cooky sweetened with molasses and spiced with ginger.

gin·ger·y (jĭn′jə-rē) *adj.* **1.** Having the spicy flavor of ginger. **2.** Sharp and pungent; biting: *a gingery remark.* **3.** Reddish yellow or yellowish brown.

ging·ham (gĭng′əm) *n.* A yarn-dyed cotton fabric woven in stripes, checks, or plaids. [Dutch *gingang,* from Malay *ginggang, gĕnggang,* "interspace."]

gin·gi·li (jĭn′jə-lē) *n.* **1.** Oil extracted from sesame seeds. Also called "gingili oil." **2.** The sesame plant. [Hindi *jingali.*]

gin·gi·va (jĭn′jə-və, jĭn-jī′-) *n., pl.* **-vae** (-vē′). *Anatomy.* The **gum** *(see).*

gin·gi·val (jĭn′jə-vəl, jĭn-jī′-) *adj.* Of or having to do with the gums. [From Latin *gingīva*†, gum.]

gin·gi·vi·tis (jĭn′jə-vī′tĭs) *n.* Inflammation of the gums. [New Latin : Latin *gingīva*†, gum + -ITIS.]

gingko. Variant of **ginkgo.**

gin·gly·mus (jĭng′glə-məs, gĭng′-) *n., pl.* **-mi** (-mī′). *Anatomy.* A hinge joint, such as the elbow or knee joint, allowing movement in one plane only. [New Latin, from Greek *ginglumos,* hinge.]

gink (gĭngk) *n. Slang.* A man or boy, especially one considered odd in some way. [19th century (American) : origin obscure.]

gink·go (gĭng′kō) *n., pl.* **-goes.** Also **ging·ko,** *pl.* **-koes.** A gymnosperm tree, *Ginkgo biloba,* native to China, having fan-shaped leaves and fleshy, yellowish fruit and often planted for ornament. Also called "maidenhair tree." [Japanese *ginkyō,* from ancient Chinese *ngien hang* (Mandarin *yín xìng*), "silver apricot" : *ngien,* silver + *hang,* apricot.]

gin mill (jĭn) *n. Slang.* A saloon.

gin rummy (jĭn) *n.* A variety of rummy for two or more persons in which a person may win by matching all his cards or may end the game by melding when his unmatched cards add up to ten points or less. Also called "gin." [GIN (alcohol) + RUMMY, suggested by a play on RUM (alcohol).]

Gins·berg (gĭnz′bərg), **Allen** (1926–). U.S. poet. He became a celebrity in the 1960's for his part in campaigns on behalf of civil rights and against the Vietnam War. His books include *Howl* (1956), *Kaddish* (1960), and *Reality Sandwiches* (1963).

gin·seng (jĭn′sĕng′) *n.* **1.** Any of several plants of the genus *Panax*; especially, *P. schinseng,* of eastern Asia, or *P. quinquefolium,* of North America, having small greenish flowers and a forked root believed to have medicinal properties, especially the power to promote long life. **2.** The root of either of these plants. [Mandarin Chinese *rén shēn* : *rén,* man (because the forked root resembles a human being with limbs) + *shēn,* ginseng.]

gin sling (jĭn) *n.* An iced, often sweetened cocktail made from gin, lime or lemon juice, and water.

Gior·gio·ne (jôr-jō′nē), **Il,** originally Giorgio Barbarelli, also known as "Giorgio da Castelfranco" (*c.*1477–1511). Italian painter of the Venetian school. He left not a single signed and dated painting. Giorgione was one of the first to paint small canvases for private collectors.

Gior·gi system (jôr′jē) *n. Physics.* A system of units based on the meter, kilogram, second, and ampere in which the magnetic constant has the value $4\pi \times 10^{-7}$ henries per meter. [After Giovanni *Giorgi* (1871–1950), Italian physicist.]

Giot·to (jô′tō, jŏt′ō), in full, Giotto di Bondone (*c.* 1266–1337). Italian Florentine painter, architect, and sculptor. Among his most famous works is the fresco cycle *Lives of the Virgin and Christ* that decorates the walls of the Arena chapel at Padua. Other great fresco cycles are at Assisi and in Santa Croce, Florence.

gip. Variant of **gyp.**

Gipsy. Variant of **Gypsy.**

gi·raffe (jə-răf′, -räf′) *n.* An African ruminant mammal, *Giraffa camelopardis,* having a very long neck and legs, a tan coat with brown blotches, and short horns. It is the tallest living mammal. [Italian *giraffa,* from Arabic *zirāfah,* probably of African origin.]

Gi·ral·dus Cam·bren·sis (jĭ-răl′dəs kăm-brĕn′sĭs), also known as Gerald de Barri (*c.*1146–*c.*1223). Welsh churchman and historian. His writings provide a vivid picture of early medieval life in Wales and Ireland, especially the *Topographia Hibernica,* the *Expugnatio Hibernica,* and the *Itinerarium Cambriae.*

gir·an·dole (jĭr′ən-dōl′) *n.* **1. a.** A composition or structure in radiating form or arrangement, as a rotating display of fireworks. **b.** A branched candleholder, sometimes backed by a mirror. **2.** A piece of jewelry, such as an earring, having a large stone surrounded by small drops. [French *girandole,* from Italian *girandola,* from *girare,* to turn, from Latin *gȳrāre,* to GYRATE.]

gir·a·sol, gir·o·sol, gir·a·sole (jĭr′ə-sôl′, -sōl′, -sŏl′) *n.* A **fire opal** *(see).* [Italian *girasole* : *girare,* to turn (see **girandole**) + *sole,* sun, from Latin *sōl.*]

Gi·rau·doux (zhē-rō-do͞o′), **Jean** (1882–1944). French novelist and playwright. His literary career began with a novel, *Suzanne et le Pacifique* (1921), but he wrote principally for the stage. *La Guerre de Troie n'aura pas lieu* (1935) was his most famous play.

gird[1] (gûrd) *v.* **girded** or **girt** (gûrt), **girding, girds.** *—tr.* **1. a.** To encircle with a belt or band. **b.** To fasten or secure with a belt, cord, or the like. **c.** To surround: *an island girded by water.* **2. a.** To supply with something needed or desired; equip: *girded with the sword of knighthood.* **b.** To endow with an attribute: *girded with righteousness.* **3.** To make (oneself) ready for action. *—intr.* To make oneself ready for action. **—gird one's loins.** To prepare for a severe test, as of courage or strength. [Middle English *girden,* Old English *gyrdan.*]

gird[2] *v.* **girded, girding, girds.** *—tr. Obsolete.* To jeer at; mock. *—intr.* To make taunting remarks; jeer.
~*n. Obsolete.* A sarcastic remark. [Middle English *girden*†, to strike, cut, charge.] **—gird·er** *n.*

gird·er (gûr′dər) *n.* A horizontal beam, as of steel or wood, used as a main support for a vertical load.

gir·dle (gûrd′l) *n.* **1. a.** A belt, sash, or the like, worn at the waist. **b.** A band or structure that encircles like a belt. **2.** An elasticized, flexible corset worn over the waist and hips. **3.** A band made around the trunk of a tree by the removal of a strip of bark. **4.** The edge of a cut gem held by the setting. **5.** *Anatomy.* The **pelvic girdle** or **pectoral girdle** *(both of which see).*
~*tr.v.* **girdled, -dling, -dles. 1.** To encircle with or as if with a belt. **2.** To put a girdle on or around. **3.** To remove a band of bark completely from the circumference of (a tree), usually to kill it. [Middle English *girdel,* Old English *gyrdel.*]

gird·ler (gûrd′lər) *n.* **1.** One that girdles. **2.** Any of various insects that chew circular bands around twigs or stems in preparing nesting sites. **3.** One who makes girdles.

girl (gûrl) *n.* **1.** A female who has not yet attained womanhood. **2.** A female child. **3.** A single young woman. **4.** *Informal.* A woman: *invited the girls over for a game of bridge.* **5.** A daughter. **6.** A girlfriend. **7. a.** A female worker or employee. **b.** A female servant. [Middle English *girle, gerle, gurle*†.]

girl Friday *n. Informal.* A female employee, especially one having a great variety of responsibilities. [By analogy with MAN FRIDAY.]

girl·friend (gûrl′frĕnd′) *n.* **1.** A favorite female friend, especially one with whom a person is sexually or romantically involved. **2.** A female friend.

Girl Guide *n. Often* **girl guide.** A member of the Girl Guides Association.

Girl Guides Association *n.* A British youth organization founded in 1910 to promote character development and practical skills.

girl·hood (gûrl′ho͝od′) *n.* The state or time of being a girl.

girl·ie, girl·y (gûr′lē) *adj. Informal.* Containing or displaying pictures of naked or almost naked women that are intended to be sexually stimulating: *girlie magazines.*

girl·ish (gûr′lĭsh) *adj.* Pertaining to, characteristic of, or suitable for a girl. **—girl·ish·ly** *adv.* **—girl·ish·ness** *n.*

Girl Scout *n.* A member of the Girl Scouts, a youth organization founded in the United States in 1912 on the plan of the Girl Guides Association.

girn (gûrn) *intr.v.* **girned, girning, girns.** *Scottish.* To complain in a whining voice. [Middle English *girnen,* variant of *grinnen,* to grimace, whimper, GRIN.]

gi·ro (jîr′ō, zhîr′ō, jī′rō) *n., pl.* **-ros.** A centrally operated system of settling debts and transferring credits between different European banks or post offices. [German, from Italian, "circulation."] **—gi·ro** *adj.*

Gi·ronde[1] (jĭ-rŏnd′). France's largest department, in the southwest on the Bay of Biscay. It contains some of the country's finest vineyards, the districts of Médoc, Graves, and Sauternes having given their names to several famous wines. Bordeaux is the capital.

Gironde[2]. Estuary in southwest France, formed by the Garonne and Dordogne rivers. Some 70 kilometers (45 miles) long, it is the seaway to the port of Bordeaux.

Gi·rond·ist (jə-rŏn′dĭst, zhĭ-) *n.* A member of a moderate republican political party of revolutionary France (1791–93). See **Jacobin.** [After GIRONDE, because the leaders of the party were deputies of that department.] **—Gi·rond·ist** *adj.*

girosol. Variant of **girasol.**

girt[1] (gûrt) *v.* **girted, girting, girts.** *—tr.* **1.** To gird; encircle or bind. **2.** To measure the girth of. *—intr.* To measure in girth. [Variant of GIRD.]

girt[2]. Alternate past tense and past participle of **gird** (to encircle).

girth (gûrth) *n.* **1.** The distance around something; the circumference. **2.** The size of something; bulk. **3.** A strap encircling the body of; an animal, as a horse, to secure a load or saddle upon its back; cinch.
~*tr.v.* **girthed, girthing, girths. 1.** To measure the circumference of. **2.** To encircle. **3.** To secure with a girth. [Middle English *gerth,* from Old Norse *györth,* girdle.]

gi·sarme (gĭ-zärm′) *n.* A halberd with a long shaft and a two-sided blade, carried by medieval foot soldiers. [Middle English, from Old French *g(u)isarme,* from Old High German *getīsarn* : *getan*†, to weed + *īsarn,* iron, from Common Germanic *īsarna-* (unattested), IRON.]

Gis·card d'Es·taing (zhĭ-skär′ dĕ-stăng′), **Valéry** (1926–). French politician. He was first elected to the National Assembly at the age of 29 and twice held office as minister of finance (1962–66 and 1969–74). He was elected president of the republic as leader of the Independent Republicans in 1974 and was defeated in his attempt to be re-elected in 1981.

Gish (gĭsh), **Lillian** (*c.* 1896–). U.S. actress. She made her film debut in 1912 and won international acclaim in 1915 for her role in *The Birth of a Nation.* Her later films included *Way Down East* (1920) and *Duel in the Sun* (1946).

gis·mo, giz·mo (gĭz′mō) *n., pl.* **-mos.** *Slang.* A mechanical device or part whose name is forgotten, unknown, or not yet designated. [20th century : origin obscure.]

Gis·sing (gĭs′ĭng), **George Robert** (1857–1903). British novelist. His best-known works are *New Grub Street* (1891) and the semiautobiographical, imaginary journal, *The Private Papers of Henry Ryecroft* (1903).

gist (jĭst) *n.* **1.** The central idea of a matter, such as an argument or a speech; the essence: *The gist of what he was saying was that he flatly refused to help.* **2.** *Law.* The grounds for action in a suit. [Old French *(cest action) gist,* (this action) lies, from *gesir,* to lie, from Latin *jacēre,* from *jacere,* to throw.]

git (gĭt) *n. British Slang.* A silly or contemptible person. [Variant of GET (offspring, fool).]

give (gĭv) *v.* **gave** (gāv), **given** (gĭv′ən), **giving, gives.** *—tr.* **1. a.** To make a present of; bestow ownership of on: *gave her flowers for her birthday.* **b.** To deliver in exchange or in recompense; pay: *He will give you five dollars for the book.* **c.** To put temporarily at the disposal of; entrust to: *give them the cottage for a week.* **d.** To place in the hands of; pass: *Give me the scissors.* **2. a.** To convey or offer for conveyance; communicate: *Give him my best wishes.* **b.** To bestow, especially officially; confer: *give authority.* **c.** To accord or tender to another; grant: *give permission.* **3.** To supply, especially in common with others; donate: *give one's time.* **4. a.** To be a source of; afford: *His remark gave offense.* **b.** To cause to have or be subject to: *She gave him the measles.* **5.** To bring forth; produce or yield: *This cow gives three gallons of milk per day.* **6.** To provide (something required or expected): *Please give your name and address.* **7. a.** To inflict as punishment: *gave the naughty child a spanking.* **b.** To mete out as a remedy; administer: *gave the patient a prescription cough syrup.* **8. a.** To grant; concede: *I'll give you that point.* **b.** To allow: *give odds of five to one.* **c.** To relinquish; yield: *give ground.* **9.** To emit or utter: *give a sigh of contentment.* **10. a.** To assign as one's portion; allot: *give her five minutes to finish.* **b.** To select and cite for a particular time or purpose; designate: *give a departure date.* **11.** To award as due: *The judges gave him first prize for the best roses.* **12.** To ascribe to a particular cause or source; attribute: *give him the blame.* **13.** To grant as a supposition; acknowledge: *Given their superiority, we can't expect to win.* **14. a.** To cause to take place, especially for entertainment: *give a dinner party.* **b.** To proffer: *give a toast.* **c.** To offer to observation or view; manifest: *give promise of brilliance.* **d.** *Informal.* To offer by way of explanation: *Don't give me that old story!* **e.** To perform for an audience: *gave a series of concerts.* **f.** To perform by moving the body or a part of the body: *give a bow.* **g.** To engage in: *give battle.* **15.** To submit for consideration or acceptance; tender: *give an opinion.* **16.** To cause or be responsible for; lead or allow: *She gave me to think she loved me.* **17.** To apply entirely to a particular activity, pursuit, cause, or person; devote: *give oneself to one's work.* **18.** To undergo the loss of; sacrifice: *give a son to the war.* **19.** To propose as a toast to: *I give you the regiment.* *—intr.* **1.** To make gifts or donations: *Please give generously.* **2.** To be unable to hold up; yield or collapse: *The roof gave under the weight of the snow.* **3.** To afford a view of or access to something: *The French doors give onto a terrace.* **4.** *Informal.* To be happening; occur: *What gives?* **—give a good account of oneself.** To behave or perform creditably. **—give as good as one gets.** To respond to an attack with equal effect or force. **—give forth. 1.** To report; circulate. **2.** To emit. **—give in. 1.** To cease opposition; concede. **2.** To hand in; submit: *She gave in her report.* **—give off.** To send forth; emit: *Chemical changes that give off energy.* **—give or take.** Adding or subtracting: *I'll be there at five, give or take ten minutes.* **—give out. 1.** To let (something) be known: *gave out the good news.* **2.** To stop functioning; fail. **3.** To become used up; run out: *Our supply of firewood gave out.* **—give over. 1.** To relinquish the care of; hand over. **2.** To make available for a particular purpose or use; devote: *a week given over to indulgence.* **3.** To surrender completely and unrestrainedly; abandon: *gave herself over to her grief.* **4.** To stop; desist. **—give rise to.** To be the cause of; occasion. **—give someone one.** *Slang.* To hit with or as if with the fists; strike. **—give someone what for.** *Slang.* To punish, especially by blows or a sharp reproof. **—give up. 1.** To surrender: *Give yourself up to the police.* **2.** To leave off; stop: *give up smoking.* **3.** To part with; relinquish: *gave up all hope.* **4.** To abandon hope for: *give her up as lost.* **5.** To admit defeat. **—give way. 1. a.** To withdraw; retreat. **b.** To make room for or wait for the passage of: *give way to an oncoming car.* **2.** To collapse from or as if from physical pressure: *The ladder gave way.* **3.** To abandon oneself: *give way to hysteria.*
~*n.* **1.** The act or process of yielding, adapting, or bending under pressure. **2.** The quality or state of being resilient; springiness: *The mattress has lots of give.* [Give, gave, given; Middle English *given, gaf, given,* Old English *giefan, geaf, giefen.*]

give and take *intr.v.* To engage in give-and-take.

give-and-take (gĭv′ən-tāk′) *n.* **1.** The practice of compromise. **2.** Lively exchange of ideas or conversation.

give away *tr.v.* **1.** To make a gift of. **2.** To observe ceremonially the transfer of (a bride) from her family to her husband. **3.** To reveal or make known, often accidentally.

give·a·way (gĭv′ə-wā′) *n. Informal.* **1.** Something that betrays or exposes, often accidentally. **2.** Something offered at a bargain price. **3.** Something given away at no charge.

giv·en (gĭv′ən) *adj.* **1. a.** Specific: *a given date.* **b.** Issued on a specific date. Said of legal documents. **2.** Accepted as a fact; acknowledged; assumed. **3.** Habitually inclined. Used with *to*: *given to shyness.* **4.** Bestowed; presented.

given name *n.* A name given to a person at birth or at baptism; a Christian name.

Gi·za, Al (gē′zə). Town in Egypt. The capital of the Giza governate, it is on the west bank of the Nile River. Nearby is the Great Pyramid of Cheops (Khufu), one of the Seven Wonders of the Ancient World.

giz·zard (gĭz′ərd) *n.* **1.** An enlargement of the alimentary canal in birds, often having dense muscular walls and containing fine grit eaten to aid in breaking up hard food. **2.** A similar digestive organ of certain invertebrates, such as the earthworm. **3.** The **proventriculus** *(see)* of insects and crustaceans. **4.** *Informal.* The stomach. [Middle English *giser,* from Old French *giser, gezier,* from Vulgar Latin *gicerium* (unattested), from Latin *gigeria,* cooked entrails of poultry, perhaps from Persian *jigar.*]

Gk. Greek.

gla·bel·la (glə-bĕl′ə) *n., pl.* **-bellae** (-bĕl′ē). *Anatomy.* The smooth area between the eyebrows just above the nose, formed by part of the frontal bone. [New Latin, from Latin *glabellus,* hairless, from *glaber,* hairless, bald, GLABROUS.]

gla·brous (glā′brəs) *adj. Biology.* Having no hairs or down; smooth. [Latin *glaber,* hairless, bald.]

gla·cé (glă-sā′) *adj.* **1.** Having a glazed, glossy surface. **2.** Coated with a sugar glaze or icing.
~*tr.v.* **glacéed, -céing, -cés.** To coat with sugar glaze or icing. [French, past participle of *glacer,* to ice, glaze, from *glace,* ice, from Latin *glaciēs.*]

gla·cial (glā′shəl) *adj.* **1.** Of, pertaining to, or derived from a glacier or ice sheet. **2.** *Often* **Glacial.** Characterized or dominated by the existence of glaciers or ice sheets. Said especially of the Pleistocene. **3.** Extremely cold; icy: *glacial waters.* **4.** Having the appearance of ice. **5.** Lacking warmth and friendliness: *a glacial stare.* [Latin *glaciālis,* icy, from *glaciēs,* ice.] **—gla·cial·ly** *adv.*

glacial acetic acid *n.* **Acetic acid** *(see)* that is almost pure.

PRONUNCIATION KEY

ă, **pat**; ā, **pay**; âr, **care**;
ä, **father**, **are**; b, **bib**;
ch, **church**; d, **deed**; ĕ, **pet**;
ē, **be**; f, **fife**; g, **gag**; h, **hat**;
hw, **which**; ĭ, **pit**; ī, **pie**;
îr, **pier**; j, **judge**; k, **kick**;
l, **lid**, **needle**; m, **mum**;
n, **no**, **sudden**; ng, **thing**;
ŏ, **pot**; ō, **toe**; ô, **paw**, **for**;
oi, **noise**; ou, **out**; o͝o, **book**;
o͞o, **boot**; p, **pop**; r, **roar**;
s, **sauce**; sh, **ship**, **dish**;
t, **tight**; th, **thin**, **path**;
th, **this**, **bathe**; ŭ, **cut**; ûr, **fur**;
v, **valve**; w, **with**; y, **yes**;
z, **zebra**, **size**; zh, **vision**;
ə, **about**, **item**, **edible**,
gallop, **circus**, **peaceful**

IN FOREIGN WORDS:

à, *Fr.* **ami**; œ, *Fr.* **feu**, *Ger.* **schön**; ü, *Fr.* **tu**, *Ger.* **über**;
KH, *Ger.* **ich**, *Scot.* **loch**;
N, *Fr.* **bon**; y′, *Fr.* **Compiègne**

STRESS MARKS:

Primary stress: ′
in·cite′ (ĭn-sīt′)
Secondary stress: ′
in′sight′ (ĭn′sīt′)

glacier *As the climate in the Himalayas of northern Nepal gradually becomes warmer, the Langtang glacier (above) is slowly shrinking. The melting ice exposes jumbled debris (moraines) eroded from the rock on the glacier's journey down the mountain.*

glacial epoch *n.* **1.** Any of several periods during the Pleistocene epoch up to 1,000,000 years ago, when much of the earth's surface was covered by glaciers. **2.** The Pleistocene epoch.

gla·ci·ate (glā'shē-āt', -sē-) *v.* **-ated, -ating, -ates.** —*tr.* **1.** To subject to the effects of glaciers. **2.** To freeze. —*intr.* To become covered with glaciers or ice sheets. [Latin *glaciāre*, to freeze, from *glaciēs*, ice. See **glacier.**]

gla·ci·a·tion (glā'shē-ā'shən, -sē-) *n. Geology.* **1.** The formation, movement, and retreat of ice sheets and glaciers. **2.** The overall effects on a landscape produced by glacial action.

gla·cier (glā'shər, -zhər) *n.* **1.** A huge mass of ice, originating from compacted snow, moving slowly in a continuous stream down a valley under its own weight. **2.** An ice sheet that has spread out from a central mass and covers a large part of a continent. [French, from *glace*, ice, from Latin *glaciēs*.]

Glacier Bay National Park. An area of 1,135,555 hectares (2,803,-840 acres) in southeastern Alaska, in the Panhandle near Juneau. The park has towering snow-covered mountains, spectacular glaciers, many of them flowing into the Pacific Ocean, and wildlife ranging from bears and mountain goats to whales and porpoises.

Glacier National Park. A park comprising 410,306 hectares (1,013,040 acres) in northwestern Montana, straddling the Continental Divide of the Rocky Mts. The primitive wilderness area includes glaciers, glacier-fed lakes, waterfalls, sheer rock precipices, extensive forests, and a wide variety of wildlife and wild flowers.

gla·ci·ol·o·gy (glā'shē-ŏl'ə-jē, -sē-) *n.* The scientific study of glaciers. [GLACIER + -LOGY.] —**gla·ci·o·log·ic** (glā'shē-ə-lŏj'ĭk, -sē-), **gla·ci·o·log·i·cal** *adj.* —**gla·ci·ol·o·gist** *n.*

gla·cis (glā-sē', glăs'ē, glā'sĭs) *n.* **1.** A gentle slope; an incline. **2.** A slope extended in front of a fortification in such a way that approaching attackers are made particularly vulnerable to the defenders' fire. [French, from Old French *glacier*, to slide, from *glace*, ice, from Latin *glaciēs*.]

Glack·ens (glăk'ənz), **William James** (1870–1938). U.S. artist. He studied at the Pennsylvania Academy of Fine Arts and in Paris, where he was influenced by the works of Manet and Renoir. Glackens is particularly known for his landscapes and genre paintings, including *Parade, Washington Square.*

glad¹ (glăd) *adj.* **gladder, gladdest.** **1.** Experiencing or exhibiting joy and pleasure. **2.** Providing joy and pleasure: *a glad occasion.* **3.** Pleased; willing: *glad to help.* **4.** *Archaic.* Of a cheerful disposition. —*tr.v.* **gladded, gladding, glads.** *Obsolete.* To gladden. [Middle English *glad*, joyful, happy, shining, Old English *glæd*, from Germanic.] —**glad·ly** *adv.* —**glad·ness** *n.*
    Synonyms: *cheerful, happy, joyful, joyous, light-hearted.*

glad² *n. Informal.* A gladiolus.

glad·den (glăd'n) *v.* **-dened, -dening, -dens.** —*tr.* To make glad. —*intr. Archaic.* To become glad.

glade (glād) *n.* An open space in a wood or forest. [16th century : origin obscure.]

glad eye *n. Slang.* A provocative look: *He gave her the glad eye.*

glad hand *n. Informal.* **1.** A hearty and friendly handshake, welcome, or greeting. **2.** A hearty, often insincere and offensively familiar welcome or greeting.

glad-hand (glăd'hănd') *v.* **-handed, -handing, -hands.** *Informal.* —*tr.* To extend a glad hand to. —*intr.* To extend a glad hand. —**glad-hand·er** *n.*

glad·i·ate (glăd'ē-āt', -ĭt, glā'dē-) *adj.* Sword-shaped, as a leaf. [New Latin *gladiatus*, from Latin *gladius*, sword.]

glad·i·a·tor (glăd'ē-ā'tər) *n.* **1.** In ancient Rome, a professional combatant, slave, captive, or condemned prisoner trained to entertain the public by engaging in combat in the arena. **2.** A contender or debater, especially one chosen to represent his faction or party in public. **3.** A prizefighter. [Middle English, from Latin *gladiātor*, from *gladius*, sword.] —**glad·i·a·to·ri·al** (glăd'ē-ə-tôr'ē-əl, -tōr'-) *adj.*

glad·i·o·lus (glăd'ē-ō'ləs) *n., pl.* **-li** (-lī', -lē') or **-luses.** Also **glad·i·o·la** (-lə) (for sense 1). **1.** Any of various plants of the genus *Gladiolus,* native to tropical regions but widely cultivated elsewhere, having sword-shaped leaves and a spike of showy, variously colored flowers. Also called "sword lily." **2.** *Anatomy.* The large middle section of the sternum. [Latin, diminutive of *gladius*, sword.]

glad rags *pl.n. Informal.* One's best or most elegant clothes.

glad·some (glăd'səm) *adj.* **1.** Glad; joyful. **2.** Causing gladness. —**glad·some·ly** *adv.* —**glad·some·ness** *n.*

Glad·stone (glăd'stōn', -stən) *n.* **1.** A light four-wheeled convertible carriage with two interior seats and places outside for a driver and footman. **2.** A Gladstone bag. [After W.E. GLADSTONE.]

Gladstone, William Ewart (1809–98). British statesman. He was Liberal prime minister four times (1868–74, 1880–85, 1886, and 1892–94). His first government passed a Land Act to protect Irish tenants, established national education in England, and introduced the secret ballot in parliamentary elections. During his second term of office the Reform Act of 1884 was passed. His third and fourth terms of office were taken up with unsuccessful attempts to gain support for a Home Rule Bill for Ireland.

Gladstone bag *n.* A piece of light hand luggage consisting of two hinged compartments. [After W.E. GLADSTONE.]

Glag·o·lit·ic (glăg'ə-lĭt'ĭk) *adj.* Also **Glag·o·lith·ic** (-lĭth'ĭk). Belonging to or written in an alphabet attributed to St. Cyril, formerly used in the writing of various Slavic languages but now limited to the Catholic liturgical books used by some communities along the Dalmatian coast. Compare **Cyrillic alphabet.** [New Latin *glagoliticus,* from Serbo-Croatian *glagolica,* the Glagolitic alphabet, from *glagól,* word; akin to Old Church Slavonic *glagolŭ,* word.]

glai·kit, glai·ket (glā'kĭt) *adj. Chiefly Scottish.* Foolish; empty-headed. [15th century : origin obscure.]

glair, glaire (glâr) *n.* **1.** Raw egg white used in sizing or glazing. **2. a.** A sizing, glaze, or adhesive made of egg white. **b.** Any similar viscous substance. —*tr.v.* **glaired, glairing, glairs.** To apply glair to. [Middle English *glaire,* from Old French, from Vulgar Latin *clāria ovi* (unattested), white of egg, from *clārus,* clear.]

glair·y (glâr'ē) *adj.* **-ier, -iest.** Also **glair·e·ous** (-ē-əs). **1.** Like glair. **2.** Coated with glair. —**glair·i·ness** *n.*

glaive (glāv) *n. Archaic & Poetic.* A sword; especially, a broadsword. [Middle English *glaive,* from Old French, from Latin *gladius,* sword.]

Gla·mor·gan (glə-môr'gən). Also **Gla·mor·gan·shire** (-shîr, -shər). A former county of southern Wales. Since the reorganization of local government in 1974, it has been fragmented to form parts of Mid Glamorgan, South Glamorgan, West Glamorgan, and Gwent.

glam·or·ize, glam·our·ize (glăm'ə-rīz') *tr.v.* **-ized, -izing, -izes.** **1.** To make glamorous or add glamour to. **2.** To treat or portray in a romantic manner; romanticize, idealize, or glorify. —**glam·or·i·za·tion** *n.* —**glam·or·iz·er** *n.*

glam·or·ous, glam·our·ous (glăm'ər-əs) *adj.* Characterized by glamour. —**glam·or·ous·ly** *adv.* —**glam·or·ous·ness** *n.*

glam·our, glam·or (glăm'ər) *n.* **1.** Compelling charm, romance, and excitement, especially when delusively alluring: *the glamour of the foreign service.* **2.** Sophisticated or fashionable attractiveness, especially when aided by the use of cosmetics. Also used adjectivally: *a glamour show.* **3.** *Archaic.* Magic; enchantment. [Scottish variant of GRAMMAR (from the association of learning with magic).]

glance¹ (glăns, glăns) *v.* **glanced, glancing, glances.** —*intr.* **1.** To strike a surface at such an angle as to be deflected: *A pebble glanced off the windshield.* **2.** To direct the gaze briefly: *glance at the menu.*

---

glaciation

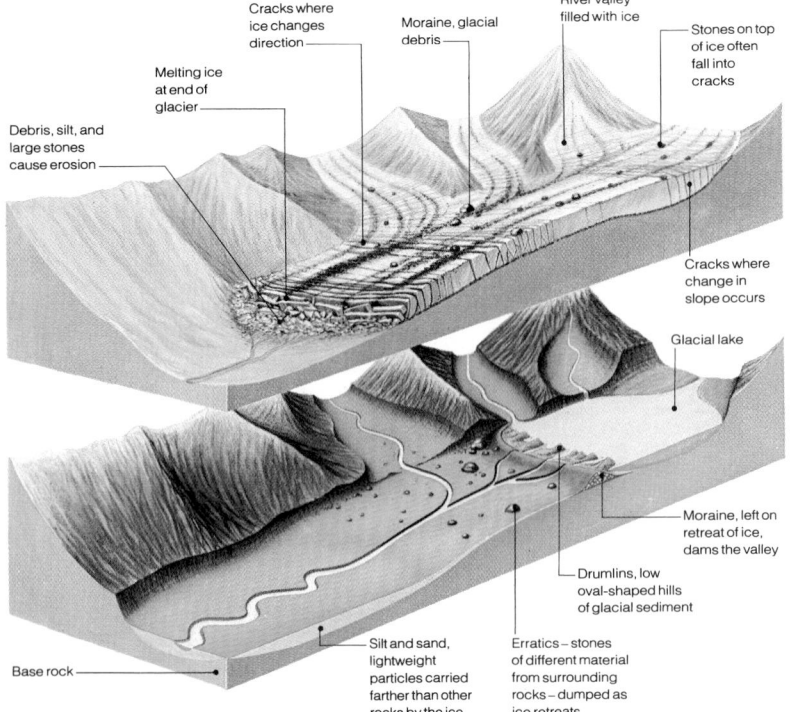

CHANGING THE SURFACE OF THE LAND
Ice that gouges and planes the earth's features

Glaciers are slow-moving rivers of ice formed by compacted snow. As they flow downhill, they alter landscapes in several ways, principally by erosion and by depositing moraines, or sediments, that remain when the glaciers melt. The effects of erosion range from the gouging of valleys (as in Scotland and Norway) to the planing of vast areas (as in Canada).

Moraines are ridge-shaped and occur at the sides and end of a glacier. They may become the dam for a lake or form islands such as Long Island, New York.

Cracks where ice changes direction

Moraine, glacial debris

River valley filled with ice

Stones on top of ice often fall into cracks

Melting ice at end of glacier

Debris, silt, and large stones cause erosion

Cracks where change in slope occurs

Glacial lake

Moraine, left on retreat of ice, dams the valley

Drumlins, low oval-shaped hills of glacial sediment

Base rock

Silt and sand, lightweight particles carried farther than other rocks by the ice

Erratics – stones of different material from surrounding rocks – dumped as ice retreats

EFFECTS IN MOUNTAINS *During the Ice Age, which ended 10,000 years ago, glaciers in mountains ground out steep valley heads known as cirques and wore V-shaped valleys into U-shapes. The moraines they deposited across valleys became dams behind which lakes formed.*

3. To shine briefly; glint. **4.** To refer to or touch upon briefly: *a survey of music history that glances at the styles of the major composers of each period.* —*tr.* **1.** To strike (a surface) at an angle; graze: *The baseball glanced the fence.* **2.** To cause to strike a surface at an angle: *glance a stone over the stream.* —See Usage note at **flash.**
∼*n.* **1.** An oblique movement following impact; a deflection. **2.** A brief or cursory look: *The defendant darted surreptitious glances at the prosecutor and the jury.* **3.** A quick flash of light; a gleam: *the glance of a mirror struck by a ray of sunlight.* **—at a glance.** Immediately; with only a brief look: *I could tell at a glance that he was upset.* [Alteration of Middle English *glacen* (influenced by *glenten,* to shine, GLINT), from Old French *glacier,* to slide, from *glace,* ice, from Latin *glaciēs.*]

glance² *n.* Any of various minerals, usually sulfides, that have a brilliant luster: *silver glance.* [German *Glanz,* from Old High German *glanz,* bright.]

gland (glănd) *n.* **1. a.** *Anatomy.* An organ that synthesizes specific substances, such as hormones, and secretes them into the bloodstream or elsewhere. See **endocrine gland, exocrine. b.** Any of various nonsecretory or excretory organs that resemble such organs, as a lymph node. **2.** *Botany.* An organ or cell that secretes a substance. **3.** *Machinery.* A part that seals a casing to prevent fluid leakage at a point where a moving shaft comes out. [French *glande,* from Old French, glandular swelling, acorn, from Latin *glāns* (stem *gland-*), acorn.]

glan·ders (glăn′dərz) *n. Used with a singular or plural verb.* A contagious, often chronic, sometimes fatal disease of horses and other animals, caused by a bacillus, *Actinobacillus mallei,* and characterized by a nasal discharge and ulcers in the lungs, respiratory tract, and skin. [Old French *glandres,* plural of *glandre,* glandular swelling, from Latin *glandula,* diminutive of *glāns* (stem *gland-*), acorn.] **—glan·der·ous** *adj.*

glan·du·lar (glăn′jə-lər) *adj.* **1.** Of, pertaining to, affecting, or resembling a gland or its secretion. **2.** Functioning as a gland. **3.** Having glands. **4.** Resulting from abnormal gland function. **5.** Possessed as an essential characteristic; inherent. [French *glandulaire,* from *glandule,* small gland, from Latin *glandula,* glandular swelling.] **—glan·du·lar·ly** *adv.*

glandular fever *n. Pathology.* **Mononucleosis** *(see).*

glan·dule (glăn′jōōl) *n.* A small gland. [From Latin *glandula,* diminutive of *glāns* (stem *gland-*), gland.]

glans (glănz) *n., pl.* **glandes** (glăn′dēz′). *Anatomy.* **1.** The glans penis. **2.** The glans clitoridis. [Latin *glāns,* "acorn" (from its shape).]

glans cli·tor·i·dis (klĭ-tôr′ə-dĭs, -tōr′-, klī-) *n.* The small mass of erectile tissue at the tip of the clitoris. Also called "glans."

glans penis *n.* The head or tip of the penis. Also called "glans."

glare¹ (glâr) *v.* **glared, glaring, glares.** —*intr.* **1.** To stare fixedly and angrily. **2.** To shine intensely and blindingly: *The spotlight glared mercilessly on the lone skater.* **3.** To be conspicuous; stand out obtrusively. —*tr.* To express (an emotion) by staring fixedly and angrily: *glared his disapproval.* —See Synonyms at **gaze.**
∼*n.* **1.** A fixed, angry stare: *The teacher gave the unruly student a glare.* **2.** An intense and blinding light: *the glare of the sun on the water.* **3.** Unwelcome attention: *The senator's wife detested the glare of publicity.* **4.** Showy brilliance; gaudiness: *the pomp and glare of rhetoric.* —See Synonyms at **blaze.** [Middle English *glaren,* probably from Middle Low German, to gleam.]

glare² *n.* A sheet or surface of slick, glassy ice. [Probably from GLARE (shine).]

glar·ing (glâr′ĭng) *adj.* **1.** Staring fixedly and angrily: *glaring eyes.* **2.** Shining intensely and blindingly: *The glaring sun.* **3.** Gaudy; garish. **4.** Painfully conspicuous; egregious: *a glaring error.* —See Synonyms at **flagrant. —glar·ing·ly** *adv.*

glar·y (glâr′ē) *adj.* **-ier, -iest.** Dazzlingly bright; glaring.

Gla·ser (glā′zər), **Donald Arthur** (1926–) U.S. physicist. He invented the bubble chamber for the study of subatomic particles, and for this he was awarded the Nobel Prize for physics in 1960. Since then he has undertaken important research into DNA.

Glas·gow (glăs′gō, -kō, gläs′-). The largest city in Scotland, a major port and the administrative center of Strathclyde Region, situated on the Clyde River in the west of the country. A cathedral city since the 12th century, Glasgow prospered in the 18th century through trade in sugar and tobacco with the Americas. A major industrial center, its traditional shipbuilding industry has suffered a decline but remains an important source of income.

glass (glăs, gläs) *n.* **1.** Any of a large class of materials with highly variable mechanical and optical properties that solidify from the molten state without crystallization and are typically based on silicon dioxide, boric oxide, aluminum oxide, or phosphorus pentoxide. They are generally transparent or translucent and are regarded physically as supercooled liquids rather than true solids. **2.** Objects made of glass collectively; glassware. **3.** Something made of glass, especially: **a.** A drinking vessel. **b.** A mirror. **c.** A barometer. **d.** A windowpane. **4. a.** A device, as a telescope, containing a lens or lenses and used as an aid to vision. **b. glasses.** A pair of lenses mounted in a light frame that passes over the nose and around the ears and that is used to correct faulty vision or to protect the eyes. Also called "spectacles," "eyeglasses." **6.** The quantity contained by a drinking vessel; a glassful: *drank a glass of grapefruit juice.* **7.** *Geology.* Hard, shiny rock that has no crystalline structure.
∼*adj.* Of, pertaining to, or made of glass.
∼*v.* **glassed, glassing, glasses.** —*tr.* **1.** To place within glass or a glass container. **2.** To provide with glass or glass parts. **3. a.** To see reflected, as in a mirror. **b.** To mirror; reflect. —*intr.* To become like glass. [Middle English *glas,* Old English *glæs,* from Germanic.]

glass blowing *n.* The art or process of shaping an object from molten glass by blowing air into it through a tube. **—glass blower** *n.*

glass cutter *n.* **1.** One who cuts or etches patterns on glass. **2.** A tool for cutting glass. **—glass cutting** *n.*

glass eel *n.* An eel in its transparent, postlarval stage.

glass electrode *n.* An instrument for measuring pH (acidity or alkalinity), consisting of a thin glass bulb containing a buffer solution with a platinum wire dipping into it. The bulb is placed in the solution to be investigated and the pH is indicated by the potential difference between the glass and the platinum.

glass eye *n.* An artificial eye made of glass.

glass·fish (glăs′fĭsh′, gläs′-) *n., pl.* **-fishes** or collectively **glassfish.** Any of various fishes of the family Centropomidae, of warm and tropical waters, having a transparent body and a cleft dorsal fin. Also called "glassperch."

glass·ful (glăs′fŏŏl′, gläs′-) *n., pl.* **-fuls.** The quantity contained in a glass.

glass harmonica *n.* An 18th-century musical instrument consisting of a set of graduated glass bowls that produce tones when a moistened finger is passed over their rims.

glass·house (glăs′hous′; gläs′-) *n.* **1.** A glassworks. **2.** *Chiefly British.* A greenhouse. **3.** *British Slang.* A military prison.

glass·ine (glă-sēn′) *n.* A nearly transparent, resilient, glazed paper resistant to the passage of air and grease.

glass jaw *n.* A jaw, specifically a boxer's jaw, that is very vulnerable to punches.

glass·mak·er (glăs′mā′kər, gläs′-) *n.* One who makes glass. **—glass·mak·ing** *n.*

glass·man (glăs′mən, -măn′, gläs′-) *n., pl.* **-men** (-mĭn, -mĕn′). **1.** One who sells glass. **2.** A glassmaker.

glass·pa·per (glăs′pā′pər, gläs′-) *n.* Strong paper in which small glass particles are embedded that is used to smooth surfaces, as of wood.
∼*tr.v.* **glasspapered, -pering, -pers.** To smooth (a surface) with glasspaper.

glass·perch (glăs′pûrch′, gläs′-) *n.* A **glassfish** *(see).*

glass snake *n.* Any of several slender, limbless, snakelike lizards of the genus *Ophisaurus,* having a tail that breaks or snaps off readily. [From the brittleness of its tail.]

glass·ware (glăs′wâr′, gläs′-) *n.* Objects, especially tableware, made of glass.

glass wool *n.* Fine-spun fibers of glass used especially for insulation, in air filters, and for synthetic composite materials.

glass·work (glăs′wûrk′, gläs′-) *n.* **1. a.** The manufacture of glassware or glass. **b.** The cutting and fitting of glass panes; glaziery. **2.** Glassware. **3. glassworks.** *Used with a singular verb.* An establishment, as a workshop or factory, where glass is made. **—glass·work·er** *n.*

glass·wort (glăs′wûrt′, -wôrt′, gläs′-) *n.* **1.** Any of various plants of the genus *Salicornia,* growing in salt marshes and having fleshy stems and rudimentary, scalelike leaves. Also called "samphire." **2.** A plant, the **saltwort** *(see).* [Formerly used in making glass.]

glass·y (glăs′ē, glä′sē) *adj.* **-ier, -iest. 1.** Made of or resembling glass. **2.** Lifeless; expressionless: *a glassy stare.* **—glass·i·ly** *adv.* **—glass·i·ness** *n.*

Glas·ton·bur·y (glăs′tən-bĕr′ē). A market town in Somerset in the southwest of England. It is the traditional site of King Arthur's Isle of Avalon. Its ruined Benedictine abbey of St. Mary (*c.* 678) is built on the site of an earlier Celtic monastery.

Glau·ber's salts, Glau·ber's salt (glou′bərz) *n.* A hydrated sodium sulfate, $Na_2SO_4 \cdot 10H_2O$, used in paper and glass manufacturing and as a laxative. [After J.R. *Glauber* (1604–68), German chemist.]

glau·co·ma (glou-kō′mə, glô-) *n.* A disease of the eye characterized by high intraocular pressure, damaged optic disk, hardening of the eyeball, and partial or complete loss of vision. [Latin *glaucōma,* cataract, from Greek *glaukōma,* from *glaukos,* GLAUCOUS.] **—glau·co·ma·tous** (glou-kō′mə-təs, glô-) *adj.*

glau·co·nite (glô′kə-nīt′) *n.* A greenish mineral consisting essentially of a hydrous silicate of potassium and iron that is found most commonly in greensand and is used as a water softener and a fertilizer. [Greek *glaukon,* neuter of *glaukos,* GLAUCOUS + -ITE.] **—glau·co·nit·ic** (glô′kə-nĭt′ĭk) *adj.*

glau·cous (glô′kəs) *adj.* **1.** Grayish green or bluish green. **2.** *Botany.* Covered with a fine, whitish, powdery coating. [Latin *glaucus,* from Greek *glaukos*†, gleaming, bluish green or gray.]

glaur (glôr) *n. Scottish.* Mire or mud. [Middle English (Scottish and northern English); perhaps akin to Old Norse *leir,* mud.] **—glaur·y** *adj.*

glaze (glāz) *n.* **1. a.** A thin, smooth, shiny coating. **b.** The substance of which this coating is made. **2.** A coating of colored, opaque, or transparent material applied to ceramics before firing to produce a glassy, waterproof surface. **3.** A substance, as syrup or gelatin, applied to food, on which it solidifies to form a thin coating. **4.** A transparent coating applied to the surface of a painting to modify the color tones. **5.** A glassy film, as over the eyes. **6.** A thin, glassy coating of ice.
∼*v.* **glazed, glazing, glazes.** —*tr.* **1.** To fit or furnish (a window, for example) with glass. **2.** To apply a glaze to: *glaze a doughnut; glaze pottery.* **3.** To give a smooth, lustrous surface to. —*intr.* **1.** To be or become glazed or glassy: *eyes glazing over from boredom.*

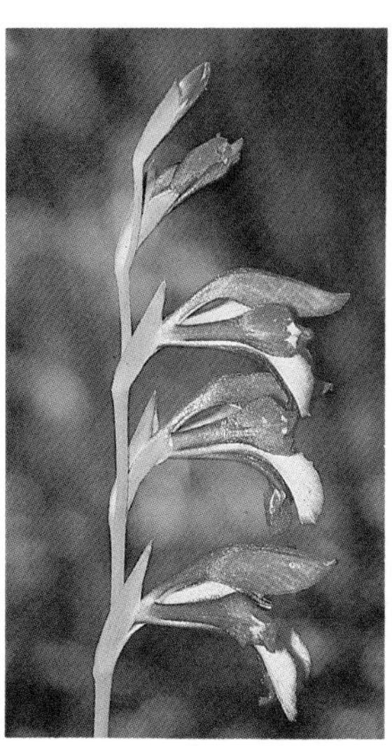

gladiolus *The many garden varieties of gladiolus originated in southern Africa but a wild gladiolus, the crimson-purple* Gladiolus illyricus *(above), does occur in scrub and open woods in Europe.*

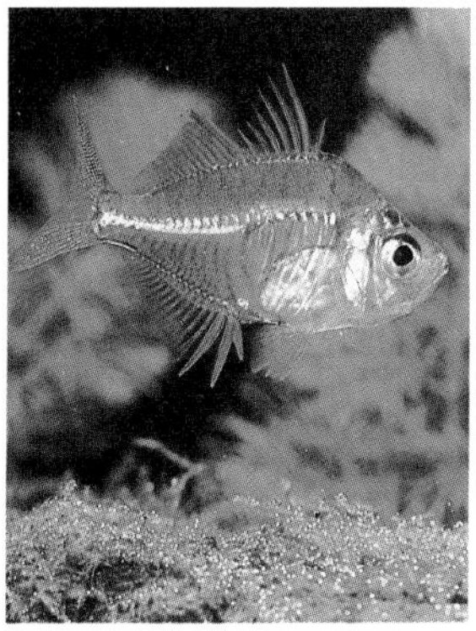

glassfish *The Siamese glassfish, or glassperch, is one of about 20 Indo-Pacific fish with transparent bodies. It reflects light in the manner of glass.*

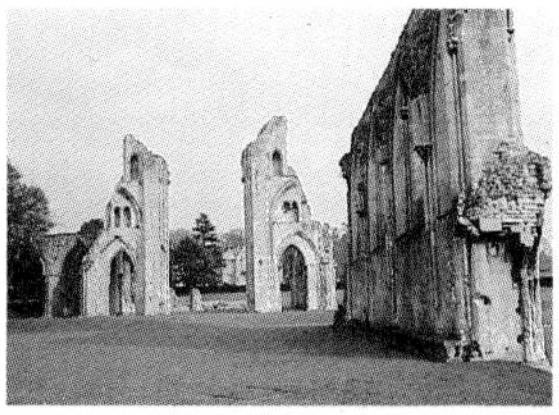

Glastonbury *This English abbey was destroyed by Henry VIII during the Dissolution of the Monasteries in 1539.*

2. To form a glaze. [Middle English *glāsen*, to provide with glass or a glassy surface, from *glas*, GLASS.] —**glaz·er** *n.*

glaze ice *n. British.* A thin, glassy coating of ice; glaze.

gla·zier (glā′zhər) *n.* One who cuts and fits window glass. [Middle English *glasier*, from *glas*, GLASS.]

gla·zier·y (glā′zhə-rē) *n.* **1.** The cutting and fitting of window glass. **2.** Glasswork.

glaz·ing (glā′zĭng) *n.* **1. a.** Glasswork. **b.** Glass set or made to be set in frames. **2. a.** A glaze. **b.** The act or process of applying a glaze.

Gla·zu·nov (glăz′ə-nôf′, -nôv′), **Alexander Konstantinovich** (1865–1936). Russian composer. He was taught by Rimsky-Korsakov, with whom he completed Borodin's opera *Prince Igor.* He wrote eight symphonies and many chamber works.

GLC gas-liquid chromatography.

gld. guilder.

gleam (glēm) *n.* **1.** A fleeting beam or flash of light: *saw gleams of daylight through the cracks.* **2.** A steady but subdued shining; a glow: *the gleam of a steel blade.* **3.** A brief or dim manifestation or indication: *a gleam of intelligence.*
~*intr.v.* **gleamed, gleaming, gleams. 1.** To emit a gleam; flash or glow: *"It shone with gold and gleamed with ivory"* (Edith Hamilton). **2.** To be manifested or indicated briefly or faintly. —See Usage note at **flash.** [Middle English *gleem, glem,* Old English *glǣm,* from Germanic.]

gleam·er (glē′mər) *n.* **1.** One that gleams. **2.** Make-up applied to the face or lips to give a glossy appearance.

glean (glēn) *v.* **gleaned, gleaning, gleans.** —*intr.* To gather grain left behind in a field after the crop has been harvested. —*tr.* **1.** To gather (grain left behind in a field after harvesting). **2.** To collect (knowledge or information, for example) bit by bit: *Historians glean their knowledge from old records and documents.* [Middle English *glenen,* from Old French *glener,* from Late Latin *glennāre,* from Celtic *glend-no-* (unattested).] —**glean·er** *n.*

glean·ings (glē′nĭngz) *pl.n.* **1.** Knowledge or information collected bit by bit. **2.** The grain left behind in a field after the crop has been harvested.

Glea·son (glē′sən), **Herbert John,** known as "Jackie" (1916–). U.S. entertainer. He first gained popularity in 1949 in the television series *The Life of Riley,* but is best known for his role as the bus driver Ralph Kramden in the weekly series *The Honeymooners,* which is still being rerun in many parts of the world.

gle·ba (glē′bə) *n., pl.* **-bae** (-bē). *Botany.* The inner, spore-bearing mass of puffballs and related fungi. [New Latin, from Latin *glēba, glǣba,* clod, GLEBE.]

glebe (glēb) *n.* **1.** *British.* A plot of land granted to a clergyman as part of his benefice during his tenure of office. **2.** *Archaic.* The soil or earth, especially when regarded as the source of vegetation; land. [Middle English, from Latin *glēba, glǣba,* clod.]

glede (glēd) *n. British Regional.* A predatory bird, the red kite, *Milvus milvus.* [Middle English *glede,* Old English *glida,* from Germanic; akin to GLIDE.]

glee (glē) *n.* **1.** Jubilant gaiety; merriment. **2.** An unaccompanied part song scored for three or more male voices that was popular in the 18th century. —See Synonyms at **mirth.** [Middle English *glē,* Old English *glēo,* merriment, play, music, from Germanic.]

glee club *n.* A group of singers who perform usually short pieces of choral music.

gleed (glēd) *n. British Regional.* A glowing coal; an ember. [Middle English *glede, gleed,* Old English *glēd.*]

glee·ful (glē′fəl) *adj.* Full of glee; merry. —**glee·ful·ly** *adv.* —**glee·ful·ness** *n.*

glee·man (glē′mən) *n., pl.* **-men** (-mĭn). *Archaic.* A medieval itinerant singer; a minstrel. [Middle English *gleeman,* Old English *glēoman* : *glēo,* GLEE + *mann,* MAN.]

gleet (glēt) *n.* **1.** Inflammation of the urethra resulting from chronic gonorrhea and characterized by mucopurulent discharge. **2.** The discharge that is characteristic of gleet. [Middle English *glet,* slime, mucus, from Old French *glete,* from Latin *glittus,* sticky.] —**gleet·y** *adj.*

gleg (glĕg) *adj. Scottish.* Alert and quick to respond. [Middle English *gleg,* clear-sighted, from Old Norse *glöggr.*]

glen (glĕn) *n.* A narrow, flat-bottomed, steep-sided valley. [Middle English *glen,* from Scottish Gaelic *gle(a)nn,* from Old Irish *glend*†.]

Glen·dow·er (glĕn′dou′ər), **Owen** (*c.* 1359–*c.* 1416). Welsh national leader. He led a revolt against the English in 1400 and by 1404 controlled most of Wales. In 1405 he summoned a Welsh parliament, but two defeats marked the end of his rebellion, and he ended his life in hiding.

glen·gar·ry (glĕn-găr′ē) *n., pl.* **-ries.** A brimless woolen cap that originated in Scotland, is creased lengthwise, and often has short ribbons at the back. Also called "glengarry bonnet." [After *Glengarry,* Scotland.]

Glenn (glĕn), **John Herschel, Jr.** (1921–). U.S. astronaut and politician. A highly decorated military aviator, he became a test pilot and was selected as one of America's first seven astronauts. On February 20, 1962, he became the first American to orbit the earth. He was elected a U.S. senator in 1976 and unsuccessfully sought the Democratic presidential nomination in 1984.

gle·noid cavity (glē′noid′) *n. Anatomy.* The cavity at the top of the scapula that forms the socket of the shoulder joint, into which the head of the humerus fits. [From Greek *glēnoeidēs,* from *glēnē,* socket of a joint, eyeball.]

gley (glā) *n.* A sticky, bluish-gray soil layer formed under the influ-

ence of excessive moisture. [Ukrainian, CLAY.]

gli·a (glē′ə, glī′ə) *n.* **Neuroglia** *(see).*

gli·a·din (glī′ə-dĭn) *n.* Any of several simple proteins derived from rye or wheat gluten. [Italian *gliadina,* from Medieval Greek *glia, gloia,* glue.]

glib (glĭb) *adj.* **glibber, glibbest. 1. a.** Performed with a natural, offhand ease: *a glib conversation.* **b.** Showing little thought, preparation, or concern: *glib replies.* **2.** Marked by a quickness or fluency that often suggests or stems from insincerity or deception: *glib politicians.* [Probably from Low German *glibbrig,* from Middle Low German *glibberich,* slippery.] —**glib·ly** *adv.* —**glib·ness** *n.*

glide (glīd) *v.* **glided, gliding, glides.** —*intr.* **1.** To move in a smooth, effortless manner. **2.** To move silently and furtively. **3.** To occur or pass imperceptibly. **4. a.** To fly a glider. **b.** *Aeronautics.* To fly without propulsion. **5.** *Music.* To blend one note into the next; slur. **6.** *Phonetics.* To articulate a glide. **7.** *Physics.* To deform so that one crystal plane slips over another. Used of solids. —*tr.* To cause to glide.
~*n.* **1.** The act or an instance of gliding. **2.** *Music.* A slur. **3.** *Phonetics.* **a.** The transitional sound produced by passing from the articulatory position of one speech sound to that of another. **b.** A **semivowel** *(see).* [Middle English *gliden,* Old English *glīdan,* from Germanic.]

glide path *n.* The path of an aircraft when descending to land as marked out by a radio beam.

glid·er (glī′dər) *n.* **1.** One that glides. **2.** A light, engineless aircraft designed to glide after being towed aloft or launched from a catapult. **3.** A swinging couch suspended from a vertical frame. **4.** A device that aids gliding.

glid·ing (glī′dĭng) *n.* The practice or sport of flying gliders.

gliding lemur *n.* The **flying lemur** *(see).*

gliding possum *n.* The **flying phalanger** *(see).*

glim (glĭm) *n. Archaic Slang.* **1.** A source of light, such as a candle. **2.** An eye. [Perhaps shortened from GLIMMER.]

glim·mer (glĭm′ər) *n.* **1.** A dim or intermittent light; a flicker. **2.** A faint manifestation or indication; a glimpse: *a glimmer of hope.*
~*intr.v.* **glimmered, -mering, -mers. 1.** To emit a dim or intermittent light. **2.** To appear or be indicated faintly. —See Usage note at **flash.** [From Middle English *glimeren,* probably from Scandinavian, akin to Swedish *glimra.*]

glimpse (glĭmps) *n.* **1.** A brief, incomplete view or look. **2.** *Archaic.* A brief flash of light.
~*v.* **glimpsed, glimpsing, glimpses.** —*tr.* To obtain a brief, incomplete view of. —*intr.* To obtain a brief, incomplete view: *glimpsed at the headlines.* [Middle English *glimsen, glymsen,* from Germanic; akin to Middle High German *glimsen,* to gleam.]

Glin·ka (glĭng′kə), **Mikhail Ivanovich** (1803–57). Russian composer, often called "the Father of Russian music." His two most famous operas, which display Russian folk influences, are *A Life for the Czar* (1836) and *Russlan and Ludmilla* (1842).

glint (glĭnt) *n.* **1.** A momentary flash of light; a sparkle. **2.** A faint or fleeting manifestation; a trace. **3.** *Archaic.* A glance.
~*v.* **glinted, glinting, glints.** —*intr.* **1.** To gleam or flash. **2.** *Archaic.* To move abruptly; dart. —*tr.* To cause to gleam or flash. —See Usage note at **flash.** [From Middle English *glinten, glenten,* to shine, move quickly, from Scandinavian; akin to Swedish dialectal *glänta, glinta,* to shine.]

gli·o·ma (glē-ō′mə, glī-) *n., pl.* **-mas** or **-mata** (-mə-tə). A tumor that consists of neuroglia cells. [New Latin : GLIA + -OMA.]

glis·sade (glĭ-säd′, -sād′) *n.* **1.** A gliding ballet step. **2.** A controlled slide in a standing or sitting position used in descending a steep icy or snowy incline.
~*intr.v.* **glissaded, -sading, -sades.** To perform a glissade. [French, from Old French, sliding motion, from *glisser,* to slide, from *glier,* to glide, from Frankish *glīdan* (unattested).]

glis·san·do (glĭ-sän′dō) *n., pl.* **-di** (-dē) or **-dos.** *Music.* A rapid slide through a series of consecutive notes in a scalelike passage. [Probably pseudo-Italian formation from GLISSADE.]

glis·ten (glĭs′ən) *intr.v.* **-tened, -tening, -tens.** To shine by reflection; reflect or be reflected lustrously. —See Usage note at **flash.**
~*n.* A shine or sparkle. [Middle English *glistnen,* Old English *glisnian.*]

glis·ter (glĭs′tər) *intr.v.* **-tered, -tering, -ters.** To shine; glisten.
~*n.* Glitter; brilliance. [Middle English *glistren,* probably from Middle Dutch *glisteren.*]

glitch (glĭch) *n.* **1.** A minor malfunction, mishap, or technical problem. **2.** *Astronomy.* A temporary change in the frequency of emission of a pulsar. **3.** *Electronics.* A false or spurious electronic signal caused by a brief unwanted surge of electric power. [Perhaps from German *Glitsche,* a slip, slide.] —**glitch·y** *adj.*

glit·ter (glĭt′ər) *n.* **1.** A sparkling light or brightness. **2. a.** Brilliant attractiveness. **b.** Showy splendor: *the glitter of show business.* **3.** Small pieces of light-reflecting decorative material.
~*intr.v.* **glittered, -tering, -ters. 1. a.** To sparkle brilliantly; glisten. **b.** To sparkle malevolently or coldly; flash: *eyes glittering at the prospect of revenge.* **2.** To be brilliantly and often deceptively attractive. —See Usage note at **flash.** [Middle English *gliteren,* from Old Norse *glitra.*] —**glit·ter·ing·ly** *adv.* —**glit·ter·y** *adj.*

glitz (glĭts) *n. Slang.* Excessive showiness; flashiness. [Yiddish, glitter.] —**glitz·y** *adj.*

gloam·ing (glō′mĭng) *n.* Also *archaic* **gloam** (glōm). Twilight; dusk. [Middle English *gloming* (Scottish dialect), Old English *glōmung,* from *glōm,* dusk; akin to GLOW.]

gloat (glōt) *intr.v.* **gloated, gloating, gloats.** To feel or express great, often malicious pleasure or self-satisfaction: *gloated over his opponent's defeat.*
∼*n.* **1.** The act of gloating. **2.** A feeling of great, often malicious pleasure or self-satisfaction. [Perhaps from Scandinavian; akin to Old Norse *glotta,* to smile scornfully.] **—gloat·ing·ly** *adv.*
glob (glŏb) *n.* **1.** A small drop; globule. **2.** A rounded, usually large lump or mass: *a glob of mashed potatoes.* [Middle English *globbe,* large mass, from Latin *globus,* GLOBE.]
glob·al (glō′bəl) *adj.* **1.** Of, pertaining to, or involving the entire earth; worldwide: *a global disarmament treaty.* **2.** Comprehensive; entire; total. **—glob·al·ly** *adv.*
glob·al·ism (glō′bə-lĭz′əm) *n.* **1.** Globalization. **2.** A policy promoting globalization. **—glob·al·ist** *n.*
glob·al·i·za·tion (glō′bə-lĭ-zā′shən) *n.* The act, process, or policy of making something worldwide in scope or application.
glob·al·ize (glō′bə-līz′) *tr.v.* **-ized, -izing, -izes.** To make global; make worldwide. **—glob·al·iz·er** *n.*
glo·bate (glō′bāt′) *adj.* Also **glo·bat·ed** (-bā′tĭd). Having the shape of a globe; globular. [Latin *globātus,* past participle of *globāre,* to form into a globe, from *globus,* GLOBE.]
globe (glōb) *n.* **1.** A body having the shape of a sphere; especially, a representation of the earth or heavens in the form of a hollow ball. **2. a.** The earth. **b.** A planet. **3.** An object resembling a globe; especially, a rounded container, as a glass sphere covering a light bulb. **4.** A sphere emblematic of sovereignty; an orb.
∼*v.* **globed, globing, globes.** —*intr.* To assume the shape of a globe. —*tr.* To form into a globe. [Middle English, from Old French, from Latin *globus.*]
globe amaranth *n.* A tropical Old World plant, *Gomphrena globosa,* cultivated for its variously colored flowers that retain their colors when dried.
globe artichoke *n.* An **artichoke** *(see).*
globe·fish (glōb′fĭsh′) *n., pl.* **-fishes** or collectively **globefish.** Any of various fishes, such as the ocean sunfish, having or capable of assuming a globular shape.
globe·flow·er (glōb′flou′ər) *n.* Any of several plants of the genus *Trollius,* having globe-shaped, usually yellow flowers.
globe thistle *n.* A tall thistle of the genus *Echinops,* native to south and central Europe and often planted in gardens for its large, spherical, usually blue flower heads.
globe·trot·ter (glōb′trŏt′ər) *n.* One who travels often and widely. **—globe·trot·ting** *n.* & *adj.*
glo·big·er·i·na (glō-bĭj′ə-rī′nə, -rē′nə) *n.* Any of the small marine protozoans of the genus *Globigerina,* having rounded spiny shells that accumulate in large numbers on the ocean floor to form a deposit. [New Latin : from Latin *globus,* GLOBE + *gerere,* to bear.]
glo·bin (glō′bĭn) *n.* A simple protein that is a constituent of hemoglobin. [Latin *globus,* GLOBE + -IN.]
glo·boid (glō′boid′) *adj.* Having a globelike shape; spheroid.
∼*n.* A globe-shaped object; a spheroid. [GLOB(E) + -OID.]
glo·bose (glō′bōs′) *adj.* Also **glo·bous** (-bəs). Spherical; globular. [Latin *globōsus,* from *globus,* GLOBE.] **—glo·bose·ly** *adv.* **—glo·bose·ness, glo·bos·i·ty** (glō-bŏs′ə-tē) *n.*
glob·u·lar (glŏb′yə-lər) *adj.* **1.** Having the shape of a globe or globule; spherical. **2.** Consisting of globules. **3.** Worldwide; global. **—glob·u·lar·ly** *adv.* **—glob·u·lar·ness** *n.*
globular cluster *n. Astronomy.* A roughly spherical cluster of stars.
glob·ule (glŏb′yo͞ol) *n.* A small, often minute spherical mass; especially, a small drop of liquid. [Latin *globulus,* diminutive of *globus,* GLOBE.]
glob·u·lif·er·ous (glŏb′yə-lĭf′ər-əs) *adj.* Composed of or producing globules. [GLOBUL(E) + -FEROUS.]
glob·u·lin (glŏb′yə-lĭn) *n.* Any of a class of simple proteins that are found extensively in blood, milk, muscle, and plant seeds and that are insoluble in pure water, soluble in dilute salt solution, and coagulable by heat. [GLOBUL(E) + -IN.]
glo·chid·i·um (glō-kĭd′ē-əm) *n., pl.* **-ia** (-ē-ə). Also **glo·chid** (glō′kĭd) (for sense 2). **1.** *Zoology.* A parasitic larva of certain freshwater mussels of the family Unionidae, having hooks for attaching to a host fish. **2.** *Botany.* Any of the barbed hairs or bristles on certain plants, such as the prickly pear and some ferns. [New Latin, from Greek *glōkhīs,* barb of an arrow.] **—glo·chid·i·ate** (glō-kĭd′ē-ĭt, -āt′) *adj.*
glock·en·spiel (glŏk′ən-spēl′, -shpēl′) *n.* A percussion instrument consisting of a series of metal bars tuned to the chromatic scale and played with two light hammers. [German *Glockenspiel,* "play of bells" : *Glocke,* bell, from Old High German *glocka* (imitative) + *Spiel,* play.]
glogg (glŏg) *n.* Also **glögg** (glœg). A hot punch, originally from Sweden, made of red wine and brandy and flavored with almonds, raisins, and orange peel.
glom·er·ate (glŏm′ər-ĭt, -ə-rāt′) *adj.* Formed into a compact, rounded mass; tightly clustered; conglomerate. [Latin *glomerātus,* past participle of *glomerāre,* to make into a ball, from *glomus* (stem *glomer-*), ball.]
glom·er·a·tion (glŏm′ə-rā′shən) *n.* A compact, rounded mass; a cluster; a conglomeration.
glom·er·ule (glŏm′ə-ro͞ol′, glŏm′yə-) *n.* **1.** *Botany.* A compact cluster of flowers borne on a single stem. **2.** *Anatomy.* A glomerulus. [New Latin *glomerulus,* from Latin *glomus* (stem *glomer-*), ball.] **—glo·mer·u·late** (glə-mĕr′yə-lĭt) *adj.*
glo·mer·u·lo·ne·phri·tis (glə-mĕr′yə-lō-nə-frī′tĭs) *n.* An inflammatory disease of the kidney affecting the glomeruli, occurring in acute and chronic forms. [New Latin : GLOMERULUS + NEPHRITIS.]
glo·mer·u·lus (glə-mĕr′yə-ləs, glō-) *n., pl.* **-li** (-lī′). *Anatomy.* **1.** A tuft of capillaries situated within the capsule at the end of a urine-secreting tubule in the vertebrate kidney. **2.** The twisted secretory portion of a sweat gland. Also called "glomerule." [New Latin, GLOMERULE.]
glo·mus (glō′məs) *n., pl.* **glomera** (glŏm′ər-ə, glō′mər-ə). *Anatomy.* A small body that forms a connection between fine arteries and veins. [New Latin, from Latin *glomus,* ball.]
gloom (glo͞om) *n.* **1.** Partial or total darkness; dimness. **2.** A partially or totally dark place, area, or location. **3. a.** An appearance or atmosphere of melancholy or depression. **b.** A state of melancholy or depression; dejection.
∼*v.* **gloomed, glooming, glooms.** —*intr.* **1.** To be or become dark, shaded, or obscure. **2.** To feel, appear, or act despondent, sad, or mournful. —*tr.* **1.** To make dark, shaded, or obscure. **2.** To make despondent; sadden. [Middle English *gloum(b)en*†, to look glum, become dark.]
gloom·y (glo͞o′mē) *adj.* **-ier, -iest.** **1.** Dismal, dark, or dreary. **2.** Showing or filled with gloom; despondent: *gloomy faces.* **3. a.** Causing or producing gloom or dejection; depressing: *gloomy news.* **b.** Marked by hopelessness; pessimistic: *gloomy predictions.* —See Synonyms at **glum.** **—gloom·i·ly** *adv.* **—gloom·i·ness** *n.*
glop (glŏp) *n. Slang.* A messy mixture, as of food. [Imitative of the sound of food being mixed.] **—glop·py** *adj.*
glo·ri·a (glôr′ē-ə, glōr′-) *n.* **1.** A halo, aureole, or nimbus. **2.** A lightweight fabric, chiefly of silk, wool, or cotton, used for umbrellas and dresses. [Late Latin *glōria,* from Latin, GLORY.]
Glo·ri·a (glôr′ē-ə, glōr′-) *n.* **1.** Any of the Christian prayers of praise beginning with the word *Gloria.* **2.** The music to which any of these is set. [Middle English, from Latin *glōria*†, glory.]
Gloria in ex·cel·sis De·o (ĭn ĭk-sĕl′sĭs dā′ō, dē′ō) *n.* A Latin doxology forming part of the Ordinary of the Mass, beginning with the words *Gloria in excelsis Deo.* Also called "greater doxology." [Late Latin, "Glory to God in the highest."]
Gloria Pa·tri (păt′rē, pä′trē) *n.* A short Latin prayer of praise to the Trinity, beginning with the words *Gloria Patri* and often sung or recited at the end of another prayer, as to conclude a psalm. Also called "lesser doxology." [Late Latin, "Glory to the Father."]
glo·ri·fi·ca·tion (glôr′ə-fĭ-kā′shən, glōr′-) *n.* **1.** The act of glorifying or the state of being glorified. **2.** *Informal.* An enhanced or exaggerated version of something.
glo·ri·fy (glôr′ə-fī′, glōr′-) *tr.v.* **-fied, -fying, -fies.** **1.** To give glory, honor, or high praise to; exalt. **2.** To cause to be or seem more glorious or excellent than is actually the case: *His description glorified the simple cottage into a mansion.* **3.** To give glory to, especially through worship. [Middle English *glorifien,* from Old French *glorifier,* from Late Latin *glōrificāre* : Latin *glōria,* GLORY + -FY.] **—glo·ri·fi·er** *n.*
glo·ri·ole (glôr′ē-ōl′, glōr′-) *n.* A halo, aureole, or nimbus; a gloria. [French, from Latin *glōriola,* diminutive of *glōria,* GLORY.]
glo·ri·ous (glôr′ē-əs, glōr′-) *adj.* **1.** Having or deserving glory; famous; illustrious. **2.** Conferring or advancing glory: *a glorious achievement.* **3.** Characterized by great beauty and splendor; magnificent: *a glorious sunset.* **4.** *Informal.* Very pleasant; delightful: *had a glorious visit.* **—glo·ri·ous·ly** *adv.* **—glo·ri·ous·ness** *n.*
Glorious Revolution. The period in British history (1688–89) during which King James II was deposed and his sister Mary and her husband William of Orange were invited to assume the throne as joint monarchs Mary II and William III. Also called "Bloodless Revolution."
glo·ry (glôr′ē, glōr′ē) *n., pl.* **-ries.** **1.** Exalted honor, praise, or distinction accorded by common consent; renown. **2.** Something that brings honor or renown: *the glory of her position as president of the corporation.* **3.** A highly praiseworthy asset: *Her hair is her crowning glory.* **4.** Adoration, praise, and thanksgiving offered in worship: *We sing Thy glory.* **5.** Majestic beauty and splendor; resplendence: *The sun set in a blaze of glory.* **6.** The splendor and bliss of heaven; a state of perfect happiness. **7.** A height of achievement, enjoyment, or prosperity: *Paris in its greatest glory.* **8.** A halo, nimbus, or aureole. —See Synonyms at **fame.**
∼*intr.v.* **gloried, -rying, -ries.** **1.** To rejoice triumphantly; exult: *petty generals who gloried in war.* [Middle English *glorie,* from Old French, from Latin *glōria*†, glory.]
glory hole *n. Informal.* A box, drawer, small space, or room in a house or on a ship where unwanted or unsorted articles are stored.
glo·ry-of-the-snow (glôr′ē-əv-*th*ə-snō′, glōr′-) *n.* A small bulbous plant, *Chionodoxa luciliae,* native to Asia Minor, cultivated for its early-blooming blue flowers.
gloss[1] (glŏs, glôs) *n.* **1.** A surface shininess or luster. Also used adjectivally: *gloss paint.* **2.** A deceptive or superficially attractive appearance. **3.** A cosmetic applied to give shine or brilliance: *lip gloss.*
∼*v.* **glossed, glossing, glosses.** —*tr.* **1.** To give a bright sheen or luster to. **2.** To apply a gloss to. **3.** To make attractive or acceptable by deception or superficial treatment: *She praised the candidate, glossing over his many weaknesses.* —*intr.* To become shiny or lustrous. [Perhaps from Scandinavian; akin to Icelandic *glossi,* spark.]
gloss[2] *n.* **1.** A brief explanatory note or translation of a difficult or technical expression, often inserted in the margin or between lines of a text or manuscript. **2.** An expanded version of such notes; a

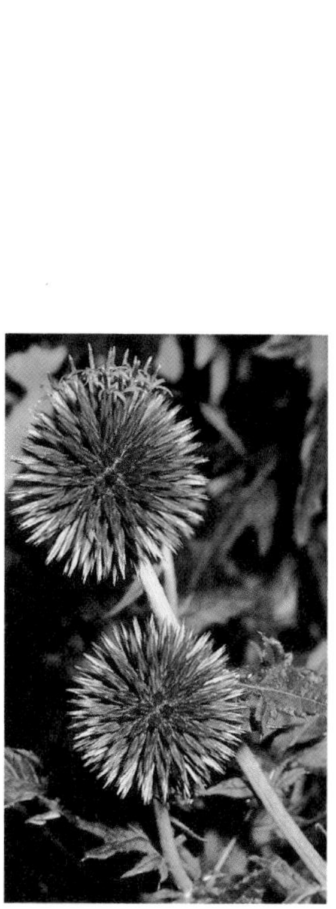

globe thistle *This hardy biennial or perennial flower is a member of the* Echinops *genus, which includes about 100 species native to Europe and Asia.*

glossary. **3.** A purposely misleading interpretation or explanation. **4.** An extensive commentary, often accompanying a text or publication.
~*v.* **glossed, glossing, glosses.** —*tr.* **1.** To provide (a word, expression, or text) with a gloss or glosses. **2.** To give a false interpretation to. —*intr.* To make a gloss or glosses. [Middle English *glose,* from Old French, from Medieval Latin *glōsa,* from Latin *glōssa,* word that needs explanation, from Greek *glōssa,* tongue, language.] —**gloss·er** *n.*

gloss. glossary.

glos·sa (glŏs′ə, glô′sə) *n., pl.* **-sae** (-sē′, -sī′) or **-sas. 1.** *Anatomy.* The tongue. **2.** *Zoology.* A tonguelike structure in the labium of an insect. [Greek *glōssa,* tongue.]

glos·sal (glŏs′əl, glô′səl) *adj.* Of or pertaining to the tongue. [Greek *glōssa,* tongue. See **gloss** (explanation).]

glos·sa·ry (glŏs′ə-rē, glô′sə-) *n., pl.* **-ries.** *Abbr.* **gloss.** A collection of glosses, as a list of specialized terms with accompanying definitions. [Latin *glossārium,* from *glōssa,* GLOSS (explanation).] —**glos·sar·i·al** (glŏ-sâr′ē-əl, glô-) *adj.* —**glos·sar·i·al·ly** *adv.* —**glos·sa·rist** (glŏs′ər-ĭst, glô′sər-) *n.*

glos·sec·to·my (glŏ-sĕk′tə-mē, glô-) *n., pl.* **-mies.** The surgical removal of the tongue. [GLOSSO- + -ECTOMY.]

glos·seme (glŏs′ēm′, glô′sēm′) *n. Linguistics.* Any of the most basic elements of meaning in a language, as a morpheme or a unit of stress. [Greek *glōssēma.* See **glosso-, -eme.**] —**glos·se·mic** (glŏ-sē′mĭk, glô-) *adj.*

glos·si·tis (glŏ-sī′tĭs, glô-) *n.* Inflammation of the tongue. [GLOSSO- + -ITIS.]

glosso-, gloss- *prefix.* Indicates the tongue or language; for example, **glossitis, glossology.** [Greek *glōssa,* tongue. See **gloss** (explanation).]

glos·sog·ra·phy (glŏ-sŏg′rə-fē, glô-) *n.* The writing and compilation of glosses or glossaries. [Greek *glōssa,* tongue, language, GLOSS (explanation) + -GRAPHY.] —**glos·sog·ra·pher** *n.*

glos·so·la·li·a (glŏs′ə-lā′lē-ə, -lāl′yə, glô′sə-) *n.* **1.** Fabricated, incoherent, or nonsensical speech, especially as associated with certain schizophrenic syndromes. **2.** The **gift of tongues** (see). [New Latin *glossolalia,* from (New Testament) Greek *glōssais lalein,* "to speak with tongues" : *glossa,* tongue + *lalein,* to talk, babble.]

glos·sol·o·gy (glŏ-sŏl′ə-jē, glô-) *n. Obsolete. Linguistics.* [Greek *glōssa,* tongue, language, GLOSS (explanation) + -LOGY.] —**glos·sol·o·gist** *n.*

glos·so·phar·yn·ge·al nerve (glŏs′ō-fär′ĭn-jē′əl, -fə-rĭn′jē-əl, glô′sō-) *n.* The ninth cranial nerve, which supplies the tongue, soft palate, pharynx, and parotid salivary gland.

gloss·y (glŏs′ē, glô′sē) *adj.* **-ier, -iest. 1.** Having a smooth, shiny, lustrous surface: *glossy satin; glossy hair.* **2.** Superficially, artificially, and speciously attractive; slick: *We listened to the salesman's glossy pitch with amusement.*
~*n., pl.* **glossies. 1.** In photography, a print on smooth, shiny paper. Also called "glossy print." **2.** *Chiefly British.* An expensively produced magazine printed on high-quality glossy paper; slick. —**gloss·i·ly** *adv.* —**gloss·i·ness** *n.*

glost (glŏst, glôst) *n.* A lead glaze used for pottery. [Variation of GLOSS (sheen).]

glot·tal (glŏt′l) *adj.* **1.** Of or relating to the glottis. **2.** *Phonetics.* Articulated in the glottis. [From GLOTTIS.]

glottal stop *n. Phonetics.* A speech sound produced by a momentary complete closure of the glottis, followed by an explosive release.

glot·tis (glŏt′ĭs) *n., pl.* **-tises** or **glottides** (-ə-dēz′). **1.** The space between the vocal cords at the upper part of the larynx. **2.** The vocal structures of the larynx. [New Latin, from Greek *glōttis,* from *glōtta, glōssa,* tongue, language.]

glot·to·chro·nol·o·gy (glŏt′ō-krə-nŏl′ə-jē) *n. Linguistics.* The investigation by means of statistics of the historical relationships between various languages, including the approximate times when related languages began to diverge from one another. —**glot·to·chron·o·log·i·cal** (glŏt′ō-krŏn′ə-lŏj′ĭ-kəl) *adj.*

Glouces·ter (glŏs′tər, glôs′-). A city in the west of England, the administrative center of Gloucestershire, on the Severn River. Known as Glevum to the Romans, it became the capital of Mercia in Anglo-Saxon times. Its cathedral (founded 1100) contains fine examples of Norman work.

Glouces·ter·shire (glŏs′tər-shîr, -shər, glŏs′-). A county in the west of England. It encompasses much of the Cotswolds to the east, the Forest of Dean to the west, and a central region formed by the valley of the Severn River. Agriculture is the main occupation. Gloucester is its administrative center.

glove (glŭv) *n.* **1. a.** A fitted covering for the hand, usually made of leather, wool, or cloth, having a separate sheath for the thumb and for each finger. **b.** A gauntlet. **2. a.** *Baseball.* An oversized padded leather covering for the hand that is used in catching balls; especially, such a glove with more finger sheaths than a catcher's or first baseman's mitt. **b.** A **boxing glove** (see). —**hand in glove.** In a close or harmonious relationship: *worked together hand in glove.* —**with gloves off.** Without moderation; mercilessly.
~*tr.v.* **gloved, gloving, gloves. 1.** To furnish with gloves. **2.** To cover with or as if with a glove. [Middle English *glove,* Old English *glōf,* from Germanic.]

glove box *n.* **1.** An enclosure with a window and two long rubber gloves sealed into the front that is used for handling toxic, corro-

glowworm *Several species of insect can glow in the dark; the female of the European firefly,* Lampyris noctiluca *(above), is perhaps the best known.*

gloxinia *A member of the* Sinningia *genus grown in temperate climates as a hothouse plant. This variety is "Pink Beauty."*

sive, or radioactive substances. **2.** *Chiefly British.* A glove compartment.

glove compartment *n.* A small storage container in the dashboard of an automobile.

glove puppet *n.* A puppet that fits over the hand and is manipulated by the fingers.

glov·er (glŭv′ər) *n.* One who makes or sells gloves.

glow (glō) *intr.v.* **glowed, glowing, glows. 1. a.** To burn or shine brightly and steadily, especially without a flame: *embers glowing in the furnace.* **b.** To shine as if with intense heat. **c.** To have a feeling of suffusing warmth: *exercised until we glowed all over.* **2.** To have a bright, warm, usually reddish color: *cheeks glowing from the cold.* **3. a.** To have a healthy, ruddy complexion. **b.** To flush; blush: *We knew he was embarrassed because his face glowed.* **4.** To be exuberant or radiant, as with pride.
~*n.* **1. a.** A light produced by a body heated to luminosity; incandescence. **b.** A bright, warm, steady light. **2.** Brilliance or warmth of color, especially redness: *"the evening glow of the city streets when the sun has gone behind the tallest houses"* (Sean O'Faolain). **3.** A sensation of physical warmth. **4.** A warm feeling of passion or emotion; ardor. **5.** A glow discharge. —See Synonyms at **blaze.** [Middle English *glowen,* Old English *glōwan,* from Germanic.]

glow discharge *n.* A continuous luminous discharge of electricity through a gas at low pressure, as in neon or fluorescent lighting. Also called "glow."

glow·er (glou′ər) *intr.v.* **-ered, -ering, -ers.** To look or stare angrily or sullenly; frown.
~*n.* An angry, sullen, or threatening stare. [Middle English *glo(u)ren,* to shine, stare, probably from Scandinavian; akin to Norwegian dialectal *glora.*] —**glow·er·ing·ly** *adv.*

glow·ing (glō′ĭng) *adj.* **1.** Incandescent; luminous. **2.** Characterized by rich, warm coloration; especially, having a ruddy, healthy complexion. **3.** Ardently enthusiastic or favorable: *glowing praise.*

glow lamp *n.* A small electric light bulb, as in a night light, in which a glow discharge occurs between two small electrodes in a medium of neon or similar gas at low pressure.

glow plug *n.* A small heating element in a diesel-engine cylinder used to facilitate starting.

glow·worm (glō′wûrm′) *n.* The luminous larva or wingless, grublike female of a firefly, especially the European species, *Lampyris noctiluca.*

glox·in·i·a (glŏk-sĭn′ē-ə) *n.* Any of several tropical South American plants of the genus *Sinningia;* especially, *S. speciosa,* cultivated as a house plant for its showy, variously colored flowers. [New Latin, after Benjamin Peter *Gloxin,* 18th-century German botanist and physician.]

gloze (glōz) *v.* **glozed, glozing, glozes.** —*tr.* **1.** To minimize or underplay; gloss. Used with *over.* **2.** *Archaic.* To explain or comment on; gloss. —*intr. Archaic.* To use flattery or cajolery. [Middle English *glosen,* to gloss, falsify, flatter, from Old French *glosser,* from *glose,* GLOSS (explanation).]

glu·ca·gon (glōō′kə-gŏn′) *n.* A hormone produced by the pancreas that stimulates an increase in the amount of sugar in the blood, thus opposing the action of insulin. [GLUC(OSE) + Greek *agōn,* leading.]

Gluck (glŏŏk), **Christoph Willibald** (1714–87). German composer. He rid opera music of baroque ornamentation of the Italian style and began to write unified lyrical tragedy in a manner that foreshadowed Wagner. His best-known operas are *Orpheus and Eurydice* (1762) and *Alceste* (1767).

gluco-, gluc- *prefix.* Indicates glucose; for example, **gluconeogenesis.**

glu·co·cor·ti·coid (glōō′kō-kôr′tĭ-koid′) *n.* Any of a group of corticosteroids that control carbohydrate, fat, and protein metabolism and have anti-inflammatory properties.

glu·co·ne·o·gen·e·sis (glōō′kō-nē′ō-jĕn′ə-sĭs) *n.* The biochemical process in which glucose is formed from noncarbohydrate sources, such as amino acids.

glu·cos·a·mine (glōō-kō′sə-mēn′, -zə-mēn′) *n.* An amino sugar, $C_6H_{13}NO_5$, that is a constituent of heparin and other polysaccharides. [GLUCOSE + AMINE.]

glu·cose (glōō′kōs′, -kōz′) *n.* **1.** A white monosaccharide sugar, $C_6H_{12}O_6$, the most abundant form of which is **dextrose** (see), a major energy source for plants and animals. **2.** A colorless to yellowish syrupy mixture of dextrose, maltose, and dextrins with about 20 percent water, used in confectionery, alcoholic fermentation, tanning, and treating tobacco. [French, from Greek *gleukos,* sweet new wine, must.]

glu·co·side (glōō′kə-sīd′) *n.* A **glycoside** (see), the sugar component of which is glucose. —**glu·co·sid·ic** (glōō′kə-sĭd′ĭk) *adj.*

glue (glōō) *n.* **1.** An adhesive substance or solution; a viscous substance used to join or bond. **2.** An adhesive obtained by boiling animal **collagen** (see) and drying the residue. In this sense, also called "animal glue."
~*tr.v.* **glued, gluing, glues. 1.** To stick or fasten together with glue: *glued the parts of the picture frame together.* **2.** To fasten on something steadily and attentively: *Our eyes were glued to the stage.* [Middle English *gleu,* glue, birdlime, gum, from Old French *glu,* from Late Latin *glūs* (stem *glūt-*), from Latin *glūten.*] —**glu·er** *n.* —**glue·y** *adj.*

glum (glŭm) *adj.* **glummer, glummest. 1.** In low spirits; dejected. **2.** Gloomy; dismal. [Middle English *glomen, gloumen,* to look sullen, GLOOM.] —**glum·ly** *adv.* —**glum·ness** *n.*
  Synonyms: dour, gloomy, morose, mournful.

glu·ma·ceous (gloō-mā′shəs) *adj.* Having or resembling a glume or glumes.

glume (gloōm) *n. Botany.* A chaffy basal bract on the spikelet of a grass. [New Latin *gluma*, from Latin *glūma*, husk.]

glu·on (gloō′ŏn′) *n. Physics.* A hypothetical elementary particle postulated to be exchanged between quarks to hold them together. There are eight types of gluon distinguished by different combinations of color and anticolor.

glut (glŭt) *v.* **glutted, glutting, gluts.** —*tr.* **1.** To fill beyond capacity; satiate. **2.** To flood (a market) with an excess of goods so that supply exceeds demand. —*intr.* To eat excessively. —See Synonyms at **satiate.** ~*n.* **1.** An oversupply. **2.** The act or process of glutting. [Middle English *glotten, glouten*, probably from Old French *gloutir*, to swallow, from Latin *gluttīre*.]

glu·ta·mate (gloō′tə-māt′) *n.* A salt of glutamic acid, especially a sodium salt, **monosodium glutamate** (*see*). [GLUTAM(IC) + -ATE.]

glu·tam·ic acid (gloō-tăm′ĭk) *n.* An amino acid, $C_5H_9NO_4$, present in all complete proteins, found widely in plant and animal tissue, and having an important role in nitrogen metabolism. [GLUT(EN) + AM(IDE) + -IC.]

glu·ta·mine (gloō′tə-mēn′) *n.* A white crystalline amino acid, $C_5H_{10}N_2O_3$, occurring in plant and animal tissue and produced commercially for use in medicine and biochemical research. [GLUT(EN) + AMINE.]

glu·ta·thi·one (gloō′tə-thī′ōn′) *n.* A peptide consisting of glutamic acid, cysteine, and glycine that functions as a coenzyme in various oxidation-reduction reactions. [GLUTA(MIC) + THI- + -ONE.]

glu·te·lin (gloō′tl-ĭn) *n.* Any of a group of simple proteins occurring in cereals and soluble only in dilute acids and bases. [Irregularly from GLUTEN + -IN.]

glu·ten (gloō′tn) *n.* A mixture of plant proteins occurring in cereal grains, chiefly wheat, and used as an adhesive and as a flour substitute. [Latin *glūten*, glue.] —**glu·ten·ous** *adj.*

gluten bread *n.* Bread made from flour with a high gluten content and low starch content.

glu·te·us (gloō′tē-əs, gloō-tē′-) *n., pl.* **glutei** (gloō′tē-ī′, gloō-tē′ī′). Any of three large muscles of the buttocks: **a.** *gluteus maximus,* which extends the thigh; **b.** *gluteus medius,* which rotates and abducts the thigh; **c.** *gluteus minimus,* which abducts the thigh. [New Latin, from Greek *gloutos,* buttock.] —**glu·te·al** *adj.*

glu·ti·nous (gloōt′n-əs) *adj.* Resembling or of the nature of glue; sticky; viscous. [Latin *glūtinōsus,* from *glūten,* glue.] —**glu·ti·nous·ly** *adv.* —**glu·ti·nous·ness, glu·ti·nos·i·ty** (gloōt′n-ŏs′ə-tē) *n.*

glut·ton[1] (glŭt′n) *n.* **1.** A person who eats or consumes immoderate amounts of food and drink. **2.** A person with an inordinate capacity to receive or withstand something: *a glutton for punishment.* [Middle English *glotoun,* from Old French *gluton, gloton,* from Latin *gluttō* (stem *gluttōn-*); akin to *gluttire,* to swallow, and *gluttus,* greedy.] —**glut·ton·ous** *adj.* —**glut·ton·ous·ly** *adv.*

glut·ton[2] *n.* A mammal, the **wolverine** (*see*). [From GLUTTON (eater), translation of German *Vielfrass,* "great eater."]

glut·ton·y (glŭt′n-ē) *n.* Excess in eating or drinking.

glyc·er·al·de·hyde (glĭs′ə-răl′də-hīd′) *n.* A sweet colorless solid, $C_3H_6O_3$, that is an intermediate compound in carbohydrate metabolism. [GLYCER(IN) + ALDEHYDE.]

gly·cer·ic acid (glĭ-sĕr′ĭk) *n.* A syrupy compound, $C_3H_6O_4$. [From GLYCERIN.]

glyc·er·ide (glĭs′ə-rīd′) *n.* An ester of glycerol and fatty acids. [GLYCER(IN) + -IDE.]

glyc·er·in, glyc·er·ine (glĭs′ər-ĭn) *n.* Glycerol. [French, from Greek *glukeros,* sweet.]

glyc·er·ol (glĭs′ə-rôl′, -rōl′, -rŏl′) *n.* A syrupy, sweet, colorless or yellowish liquid, $C_3H_8O_3$, obtained from fats and oils as a by-product of the manufacture of soaps and fatty acids. It is used as a solvent, antifreeze and antifrost fluid, plasticizer and sweetener, and in the manufacture of dynamite, cosmetics, liquid soaps, inks, and lubricants. [GLYCER(IN) + -OL.]

glyc·er·yl (glĭs′ər-əl) *n.* The trivalent radical of glycerol, CH_2CHCH_2. [GLYCER(IN) + -YL.]

gly·cin (glī′sĭn) *n.* Also **gly·cine** (-sēn′, -sĭn). A poisonous compound, $C_8H_9NO_3$, used as a photographic developer. [From GLYCINE.]

gly·cine (glī′sēn′, -sĭn) *n.* **1.** A white, very sweet crystalline amino acid, $C_2H_5NO_2$, the principal amino acid occurring in sugar cane, derived by alkaline hydrolysis of gelatin, and used in biochemical research and medicine. **2.** Variant of **glycin.** [GLYC(O)- + -INE.]

glyco-, glyc- *prefix.* Indicates: **1.** Sugar; for example, **glycine.** **2.** Glycogen; for example, **glycogenesis.** [Greek *glukus,* sweet.]

gly·co·gen (glī′kə-jən) *n.* A carbohydrate, $(C_6H_{10}O_5)_n$. It is the main form in which carbohydrate is stored in animals and occurs primarily in the liver and muscles. Also called "animal starch," "liver starch." [GLYCO- + -GEN.] —**gly·co·gen·ic** (glī′kə-jĕn′ĭk) *adj.*

gly·co·gen·e·sis (glī′kə-jĕn′ĭ-sĭs) *n.* The formation of glycogen. **2.** The formation of sugar from glycogen. [GLYCO- + -GENESIS.] —**gly·co·ge·net·ic** (glī′kə-jə-nĕt′ĭk) *adj.*

gly·col (glī′kôl′, -kŏl′, -kōl′) *n.* **1.** Ethylene glycol (*see*). **2.** An alcohol with two hydroxyl groups. [GLYC(O)- + -OL.]

gly·col·ic acid (glī-kŏl′ĭk) *n.* A colorless crystalline compound, $C_2H_4O_3$, found in sugar beets, cane sugar, and unripe grapes, and used in leather dyeing and tanning and in pharmaceuticals, pesticides, adhesives, and plasticizers.

gly·co·lip·id (glī′kō-lĭp′ĭd) *n.* Any of a group of lipids that contain one or more sugar molecules.

gly·col·y·sis (glī-kŏl′ə-sĭs) *n.* The biochemical breakdown of glucose to lactic acid, with the production of energy in the form of ATP. [GLYCO- + -LYSIS.]

gly·co·pro·tein (glī′kō-prō′tēn′, -tē-ĭn) *n.* Any of several conjugated proteins that contain carbohydrates as prosthetic groups.

gly·co·side (glī′kə-sīd′) *n.* Any of a group of organic compounds, occurring abundantly in plants, that produce sugars and related substances on hydrolysis. A medically important example is digitalis. [*Glycose,* variant of GLUCOSE + -IDE.] —**gly·co·sid·ic** (glī′kə-sĭd′ĭk) *adj.*

gly·co·su·ri·a (glī′kə-soōr′ē-ə, -shoōr′ē-ə) *n.* The excretion of excess quantities of sugar in the urine, as occurs in diabetes. [*Glycose,* variant of GLUCOSE + -URIA.] —**gly·co·su·ric** *adj.*

Glyn (glĭn), **Elinor Sutherland** (1864–1943). British author. She wrote many sensational and highly romantic novels in the early 1900's, including *Three Weeks* (1907), a steamy (for then) tale of illicit passion complete with tiger-skin rugs, and *It* (1927).

Glynde·bourne (glīnd′bôrn′, -bōrn′). An estate in East Sussex in southeast England. Since 1934 it has been the site of an annual opera festival.

gly·ox·a·line (glī-ŏk′sə-lēn′, -lĭn) *n.* A chemical compound, **imidazole** (*see*). [GLY(COL) + OXAL(IC ACID) + -INE.]

glyph (glĭf) *n.* **1.** *Architecture.* A vertical groove, especially in a Doric column or frieze. **2.** A symbolic figure, either engraved or incised; a hieroglyph. **3.** A symbol, as figures of people on a road sign, that imparts information nonverbally. [Greek *gluphē,* carving, from *gluphein,* to carve.] —**glyph·ic** *adj.*

glyp·tal (glĭp′təl) *n.* A synthetic resin used for surface coatings, made by copolymerizing dihydric alcohols and dibasic acids.

glyp·tic (glĭp′tĭk) *adj.* Of or pertaining to engraving or carving, especially on precious stones. [Greek *gluptikos,* from *gluptēs,* carver, from *gluphein,* to carve.]

glyp·tics (glĭp′tĭks) *n. Used with a singular verb.* The art of engraving or carving, especially on precious stones.

glyp·to·dont (glĭp′tə-dŏnt′) *n.* An extinct South American mammal of the genus *Glyptodon* and related genera that lived in the late Cenozoic period and resembled a giant armadillo. [New Latin : Greek *gluptos,* carved, from *gluphein,* to carve + -ODONT.]

glyp·to·graph (glĭp′tə-grăf′, -grāf′) *n.* An engraved inscription on a precious stone. [Greek *gluptos,* carved, from *gluphein,* to carve + -GRAPH.]

glyp·tog·ra·phy (glĭp-tŏg′rə-fē) *n.* The art or process of carving or engraving on precious stones. —**glyp·tog·ra·pher** *n.* —**glyp·to·graph·ic** (glĭp′tə-grăf′ĭk), **glyp·to·graph·i·cal** *adj.*

gm gram.

G.M. 1. general manager. **2.** grand master.

G-man (jē′măn′) *n., pl.* **-men** (-mĕn′). An agent of the Federal Bureau of Investigation. [G(OVERNMENT) + MAN.]

GMAT Greenwich mean astronomical time.

GM counter (jē′ĕm′) *n.* A **Geiger counter** (*see*).

GMT, G.m.t. Greenwich mean time.

GM tube *n.* A **Geiger tube** (*see*).

gnarl (närl) *n.* A protruding knot on a tree. ~*tr.v.* **gnarled, gnarling, gnarls.** To knot and cause to be deformed; twist. —See Usage note at **distort.** [Back-formation from GNARLED.]

gnarled (närld) *adj.* **1.** Having gnarls; knotty or misshapen: *gnarled branches.* **2.** Crabbed in temperament; bad-tempered. **3.** Rugged and roughened, as from old age or hard work: *The gnarled hands of a carpenter.* [Probably variant of KNURLED.]

gnash (năsh) *v.* **gnashed, gnashing, gnashes.** —*tr.* **1.** To grind or strike (the teeth, for example) together. **2.** To bite or chew by grinding the teeth. —*intr.* To grind the teeth together. ~*n.* **1.** The grinding together of the teeth. **2.** An action or sound resembling a gnash. [Middle English *gnasten, gnaisten,* probably from Scandinavian, akin to Old Norse *gnast(r)an,* gnashing (probably imitative).]

gnat (năt) *n.* Any of numerous small, biting, winged insects, especially the common gnat, *Culex pipiens,* common in swarms over stagnant water. [Middle English *gnat,* Old English *gnæt.*]

gnat·catch·er (năt′kăch′ər) *n.* Any of several small New World birds of the genus *Polioptila* and related genera, having grayish and white plumage and a long tail.

gna·thal (nā′thəl, năth′əl) *adj.* Gnathic.

gnath·ic (năth′ĭk) *adj. Anatomy.* Of or relating to the jaw. [Greek *gnathos,* jaw.]

gna·thi·on (nā′thē-ŏn′, năth′ē-) *n. Anatomy.* The lowest point of the midline of the lower jaw. [New Latin, from Greek *gnathos,* jaw.]

gna·thite (nā′thīt′, năth′īt′) *n.* A jaw or jawlike appendage of an insect or other arthropod. [Greek *gnathos,* jaw + -ITE.]

-gnathous *suffix.* Indicates the jaw; for example, **prognathous.** [New Latin *-gnathus,* from Greek *gnathos,* jaw.]

gnaw (nô) *v.* **gnawed, gnawed** or **gnawn** (nôn), **gnawing, gnaws.** —*tr.* **1.** To bite, chew on, or erode with the teeth. **2.** To produce by gnawing: *gnaw a hole.* **3.** To erode or diminish gradually as if by gnawing: *waves gnawing the rocky shore.* **4.** To afflict or trouble persistently: *fear gnawing her.* —*intr.* **1.** To bite or chew persistently: *The dog gnawed at the bone.* **2.** To cause erosion or gradual diminishment. **3.** To cause persistent trouble or distress: *What I had done gnawed at my conscience.*

glyph *A representational carving. This is a scarab, or dung beetle, a sacred symbol in ancient Egypt. Egyptian representational writing carved on monuments came to be called "hieroglyphic" (sacred carving).*

gnat *Small flying insects, the females of which are bloodsucking. The name is often used loosely for other similar insects that do not bite.*

~*n.* The action or an instance of gnawing. [Middle English *gnawen,* Old English *gnagan.*]

gnaw·ing (nô'ĭng) *adj.* Persistently troublesome or distressing: *a gnawing doubt.* —**gnaw·ing·ly** *adv.*

gneiss (nīs) *n. Geology.* A coarse-grained banded or foliated metamorphic rock in which the minerals are arranged in darker and lighter layers. [German *Gneis,* perhaps from Middle High German *gneiste,* spark, from Old High German *gneisto.*] —**gneiss·ic** (nī'sĭk), **gneiss·oid** (nī'soid'), **gneiss·ose** (nī'sōs') *adj.*

gnoc·chi (nyô'kē) *pl.n.* Dumplings made of flour, semolina, or potato starch, boiled or baked and served with grated Parmesan cheese or with various sauces. [Italian, plural of *gnocco, nocchio,* "knot (of a tree)," "lump," from Germanic.]

gnome¹ (nōm) *n.* **1.** Any of a fabled race of dwarflike creatures, often portrayed as wizened old men, who live underground and guard treasure hoards. **2.** A shriveled old man. [French, from New Latin *gnomus†* (coined by Paracelsus).] —**gnom·ish** *adj.*

gnome² *n.* A pithy saying that expresses a general truth or fundamental principle; a maxim; an aphorism. [Greek *gnōmē,* intelligence, judgment, maxim, from *gignōskein,* to know.]

gno·mic (nō'mĭk) *adj.* Of or of the nature of pithy sayings; aphoristic: *gnomic utterances.*

gno·mon (nō'mŏn', -mən) *n.* **1.** An object, such as the projecting arm of a sundial, that casts a shadow used as an indicator. **2.** *Mathematics.* The figure that remains after a parallelogram has been removed from a similar but larger parallelogram with which it has a common corner. [Latin *gnōmōn,* from Greek, one who knows, indicator, interpreter, from *gignōskein,* to know.]

gno·mon·ic projection (nō-mŏn'ĭk) *n.* A type of azimuthal or zenithal map projection in which great circles of the earth are shown as straight lines and all straight lines are great circles.

gno·sis (nō'sĭs) *n.* Intuitive apprehension of spiritual truths, an esoteric form of knowledge sought by the Gnostics. [Greek *gnōsis,* knowledge, from *gignōskein,* to know.]

-gnosis *suffix. Medicine.* Indicates knowledge or recognition; for example, **psychognosis.** [Latin, from Greek *-gnōsia,* from *gnōsis,* knowledge, GNOSIS.]

gnos·tic (nŏs'tĭk) *adj.* **1.** Of, relating to, or possessing knowledge, especially spiritual knowledge. **2. Gnostic.** Of or pertaining to Gnostics or Gnosticism. —*n.* **Gnostic.** A believer in Gnosticism.

Gnos·ti·cism (nŏs'tĭ-sĭz'əm) *n.* The doctrines of certain early Christian sects, considered heretical, that valued inquiry into spiritual truth above faith, thought salvation attainable only by the few whose faith enabled them to transcend matter, and viewed Christ as noncorporeal.

gno·to·bi·ot·ics (nō'tō-bī-ŏt'ĭks) *n. Used with a singular verb.* The study of organisms in relation to the effects of known microorganisms on them. [New Latin : Greek *gnōtos,* known, past participle of *gignōskein,* to know + *bios,* life.] —**gno·to·bi·ot·ic** *adj.* —**gno·to·bi·ot·i·cal·ly** *adv.*

GNP gross national product.

gnu (nōō, nyōō) *n.* Either of two large African antelopes, *Connochaetes gnou* or *C. taurinus,* having a drooping beard, a long, tufted tail, and curved horns in both sexes. Also called "wildebeest." [Xhosa *nqu.*]

go¹ (gō) *v.* **went** (wĕnt), **gone** (gôn, gŏn), **going, goes.** —*intr.* **1.** To move along; proceed: *going by bus; went fast.* **2.** To move to a particular place: *went to town.* **3.** To move from a place; depart: *Go before I really get mad.* **4. a.** To pursue a certain course, method, or procedure: *Instructions go from parent to child.* **b.** To resort to someone, as for aid: *went directly to the voters of her district.* **5.** To proceed to the performance of an activity: *went to eat.* **6.** Used in the form *be going* with the sense of *will* to indicate indefinite future intent or expectation: *He is going to learn to fly.* **7.** To engage in an activity. Used with a present participle: *go riding.* **8.** To function, move, or operate properly: *The car won't go.* **9.** To make a specified sound: *The glass went crack.* **10. a.** To be customarily located; belong: *The fork goes to the left of the plate.* **b.** To be capable of entering or being held: *Will the bike go into the trunk of your car?* **11.** To extend between two points or in a certain direction: *curtains going from the ceiling to the floor.* **12.** To give entry; lead: *a bulkhead going to the cellar.* **13.** To pass or be given into someone's possession: *Her jewelry went to her granddaughter.* **14.** To be allotted or awarded: *money to go for food.* **15.** To be a factor that contributes or leads: *It goes to show he was wrong.* **16. a.** To be compatible; harmonize: *The rug goes well with this room.* **b.** To match or fit. **c.** To occur with or together. **17.** To have a particular form or proceed in a particular sequence: *Is this the way the song goes?* **18.** To die. **19.** To come apart or break up. **20.** To become weak; fail: *His hearing began to go.* **21.** To be consumed or used up: *Our money is going fast.* **22.** To lose effect; disappear. **23.** To be given up or abolished: *Unnecessary expenditures must go.* **24.** To pass by; elapse: *Where did the time go?* **25.** To pass in a commercial transaction; be sold or auctioned off: *The house will go to the highest bidder.* **26.** To come to be in a specified condition; become: *go insane; go to sleep.* **27.** To be or continue to be in a specified condition: *go unchallenged.* **28.** To get along; fare: *How are things going?* **29.** To be as a general rule: *As cats go, this one is well behaved.* **30.** To carry out an action to a certain point or extent: *go too far; go to a lot of trouble.* **31.** To act, especially under guidance or on advice: *We have to go by the rules.* **32.** To pass from one person to another: *Measles went through the whole school. A rumor was going*

gnu *Also called wildebeest, the gnu—a type of antelope—is a native of the East African plains. Herds of up to 10,000 animals may gather in the dry season when grazing becomes scarce.*

around the office. **33.** To have a successful outcome: *made a huge effort to make the campaign go.* **34.** To attend regularly: *Does he go to school yet?* **35. a.** To be accepted or acceptable: *Anything goes.* **b.** To be the rule; be the only acceptable thing: *What I say goes.* **36.** To be contained: *5 goes into 25 five times.* **37.** To be known: *goes by a different name now.* **38.** *Informal.* To excrete waste from the bladder or bowels. —*tr.* **1.** To proceed along; follow: *We're not going the same way.* **2.** To make as a wager; bet: *He went $100 on the result.* **3.** To take part to the extent of: *go fifty-fifty on a deal.* **4.** To take on the responsibility of furnishing: *go bail for a client.* —**go about. 1.** To busy oneself with; undertake. **2.** To change direction in a sailing vessel; tack. —**go after.** To pursue in an effort to take; seek. —**go along.** To be in agreement; cooperate. —**go around** (or **round**). **1.** To move from one place to another. **2.** To be habitually in the company of, especially in public. Used with *with.* **3.** To be engaged in: *She goes around making a nuisance of herself.* **4.** To spread; circulate: *a rumor going around.* **5.** To satisfy a demand or requirement; be sufficient: *enough to go round.* —**go at. 1.** To attack verbally or physically. **2.** To work at diligently or energetically. —**go away.** To take a vacation away from home. —**go back.** To be established or be recorded in history; have existed in an earlier time. —**go back on.** To back down on; repudiate. —**go down. 1.** To be defeated; lose. **2.** To sink. Used of ships. **3.** To decrease in size, level, or weight: *The temperature went down.* **4.** *British.* To fall ill: *He went down with measles.* **5.** *British.* To travel away or graduate from a university. **6.** *British Slang.* To go to prison. **7.** To go below the horizon: *The sun went down.* **8.** To be renowned or remembered: *This occasion will go down in history.* **9.** *Slang.* To take place; happen: *Something big is going down.* —**go for. 1.** To try to obtain. **2.** *Informal.* To enjoy or appreciate: *goes for Chinese cooking.* **3.** To pass as; be thought of as. **4.** To make an attack on; assail. **5.** To apply to: *That goes for you too!* **6.** To find acceptable: *don't go for the plan.* —**go in. 1.** To be obscured by a cloud. Used of the sun and sometimes of the moon. **2.** To take part in a cooperative venture: *went in with the others to buy a present.* —**go in for.** *Informal.* **1.** To enjoy doing or participating in. **2.** To enter or participate in (a competition or contest). —**go into. 1.** To inquire about; investigate: *went into the reasons for our failure.* **2.** To take up or turn to as an occupation, study, or pastime. —**go it.** *Informal.* **1.** To move very fast. **2.** To participate energetically. —**go it alone.** To be independent; act by oneself. —**go off. 1.** To happen in a specified manner: *The dinner went off according to plan.* **2.** To be fired or shot; explode: *The gun went off.* **3.** To make a noise; sound: *The alarm clock went off.* **4.** To go away; leave. —**go on. 1.** To continue as before: *went on eating.* **2.** To happen; occur: *don't know what's going on.* **3.** To make one's entrance on the stage of a theater. **4.** To talk at length: *went on about his trip.* **5.** To use as evidence or a basis for further action: *You've got to give me more than that to go on.* **6.** Used as an interjection to express surprise or disbelief. —**go one better.** To surpass or outdo. —**go out. 1.** To stop burning or casting light; become extinguished. **2.** To cease to be popular; become unfashionable. **3.** To try to become a member of or a participant in: *went out for the basketball team.* **4.** In card games, to lay down all one's cards. —**go over. 1.** To check or examine. **2.** To be received in a specified manner: *a speech that went over well.* —**go through. 1.** To search or examine thoroughly. **2. a.** To suffer; undergo. **b.** To participate in; experience. **3.** To use up entirely: *went through his inheritance quickly.* **4.** To be voted for, as a plan or law; pass. —**go to one's head. 1.** To make excited or dizzy. **2.** To make vain or overconfident. —**go to pieces.** To lose one's self-control or health. —**go under. 1.** To lose consciousness. **2.** To be overwhelmed by difficulties. —**go with.** To be the regular romantic or sexual partner of.

~*n., pl.* **goes.** *Informal.* **1.** An attempt; try: *had a go at acting.* **2.** The act or an instance of going. **3.** A turn, as in a game. **4.** Energy; vitality. —**from the word go.** *Informal.* From the very beginning. —**no go.** *Informal.* Of no use; ineffective. —**on the go.** *Informal.* Perpetually busy; active.

~*adj. Informal.* Functioning correctly and ready for action: *All systems are go.* [Go, going; Middle English *gon, gōn(e),* Old English *gān, gegān.* Went; Middle English *wente,* past tense of *wenden,* to turn, WEND.]

go² *n.* A Japanese game for two played with pebblelike counters on a board divided into 361 squares. [Japanese.]

GO general order.

go·a (gō'ə) *n.* A gazelle, *Procapra picticaudata,* of eastern Asia, the male of which has backward-curving horns. [Tibetan *dgoba.*]

Go·a (gō'ə). District on the west coast of India, formerly a Portuguese possession. Annexed by India in 1961, it now forms part of the territory of Goa, Daman, and Diu. The district centers on the port of Goa, which formerly controlled the spice trade with the East.

Goa, Da·man, and Di·u (də-män', dē'ōō). Territory of India, formed from three former Portuguese possessions on the west coast. Goa lies south of Bombay, Daman to the north, while Diu is an island off Gujarat. Though separated by long stretches of coastline, they share a common cultural background and were all annexed by India in 1961. Panaji (in Goa) is the capital.

goad (gōd) *n.* **1.** A long stick with a pointed end used for prodding animals. **2.** Something that prods or urges; a stimulus or irritating incentive.

~*tr.v.* **goaded, goading, goads.** To prod with or as if with a goad;

give impetus to; incite. [Middle English *gode,* Old English *gād,* from Germanic.]

go ahead *intr.v.* To start or continue, especially after an interruption; proceed.

go·a·head (gō′ə-hĕd′) *n. Informal.* Permission to proceed: *The manager gave the clerk the go-ahead to mark the suit down.*
~*adj. Informal.* **1.** Enterprising and adventurous: *The young entrepreneur had real go-ahead spirit.* **2.** Indicating permission to proceed: *a go-ahead sign.*

goal (gōl) *n.* **1.** The purpose toward which an endeavor is directed; objective: *Her goal was to attend graduate school.* **2.** The finishing point or line of a race. **3.** *Sports.* **a.** A structure or area into or over which players endeavor to advance a ball or puck. **b.** A successful attempt at advancing a ball or puck into or over a goal. **c.** The score awarded for such an act. **—**See Synonyms at **intention.** [Middle English *gol,* boundary, limit, probably from Old English *gāl*† (unattested), obstacle.]

goal area *n.* In soccer, a rectangular area in front of the goal, 6 yards deep and 20 yards wide, in which goal kicks are taken.

goal·ie (gō′lē) *n. Informal.* A goalkeeper.

goal·keep·er (gōl′kē′pər) *n.* A player assigned to protect the goal in various sports.

goal kick *n.* In soccer, a free kick taken from the goal area, awarded to the defending team when the ball has been put out of play over the goal line by an attacking player.

goal line *n. Sports.* Either of two lines running the width of the playing area at each end of the field. In games such as soccer and hockey, the goals are located along the goal line, which also marks the boundary of the playing area; in games such as football, the ball must be carried over the goal line to score a touchdown.

goal·mouth (gōl′mouth′) *n. Sports.* The area between the goalposts just in front of the goal.

goal·post (gōl′pōst′) *n.* Either of a pair of posts joined with a crossbar and set at each end of a football or soccer field to form the goal.

goal·tend·er (gōl′tĕn′dər) *n.* A goalkeeper.

goal·tend·ing (gōl′tĕn′dĭng) *n.* **1.** The act of protecting the goal in various sports, as hockey. **2.** *Basketball.* An illegal play in which a player deflects a ball that is on the downward path to the basket or is already inside the rim of the cylinder, carrying the penalty of an automatic score for the offensive team.

go·an·na (gō-ăn′ə) *n.* Any of various monitor lizards of Australia. [Mispronunciation of IGUANA.]

Goa powder *n.* **Araroba** *(see).*

goat (gōt) *n.* **1.** Any of various horned, bearded ruminant mammals of the genus *Capra,* originally of mountainous regions of the Old World; especially, any of the domesticated forms of *C. hircus,* kept for milk, wool, and meat. **2. Goat.** *Astronomy.* The constellation and sign of the zodiac **Capricornus** *(see).* Usually preceded by *the.* **3.** A lecherous man. **4.** A silly person; a fool. **5.** A scapegoat. **—get someone's goat.** *Informal.* To make (someone) angry or annoyed. [Middle English *gote,* Old English *gāt.*]

goat antelope *n.* Any of various ruminant mammals, such as the mountain goat or the chamois, having characteristics of both goats and antelopes.

goat·ee (gō-tē′) *n.* A small chin beard trimmed to a point and resembling that of a goat. [From GOAT + -EE.]

goat·fish (gōt′fĭsh′) *n., pl.* **-fishes** or collectively **goatfish.** Any of various brightly colored fishes of the family Mullidae, of warm seas, having two sensory barbels on the chin. Also called "surmullet" or *British* "red mullet."

goat·herd (gōt′hûrd′) *n.* A person who looks after goats.

goat·ish (gō′tĭsh) *adj.* **1.** Of, pertaining to, or resembling a goat. **2.** Lecherous; lustful. **—goat·ish·ly** *adv.* **—goat·ish·ness** *n.*

goat moth *n.* A European moth, *Cossus cossus,* with large, pale brownish wings.

goats·beard, goat's-beard (gōts′bîrd′) *n.* **1.** A plant, *Tragopogon pratensis,* native to Europe, having grasslike leaves and yellow, dandelionlike flowers. **2.** A tall plant, *Aruncus dioicus,* having compound leaves and branching clusters of small white flowers.

goat·skin (gōt′skĭn′) *n.* **1.** The skin of a goat. **2.** Leather made from goatskin. **3.** A container, as for wine, made from goatskin.

goat's-rue (gōts′ro͞o′) *n.* **1.** A Eurasian plant, *Galega officinalis,* cultivated for its showy, variously colored flowers. **2.** A North American plant, *Tephrosia virginiana,* having yellow and pink flowers.

goat·suck·er (gōt′sŭk′ər) *n.* Any of various chiefly nocturnal birds of the family Caprimulgidae, which includes the nighthawk and the whippoorwill. [The bird was thought to suck goat's milk.]

go-away bird (gō′ə-wā′) *n.* Any of various touracos of the genus *Corythaixoides,* of Africa. [Imitative of its call.]

gob¹ (gŏb) *n.* **1.** A small piece or lump. **2.** A small mass or lump of spit or phlegm. **3.** *Often* **gobs.** *Informal.* A large quantity, as of money: *They have gobs of books in their library.*
~*intr.v.* **gobbed, gobbing, gobs.** *British Informal.* To spit. [Middle English *gobbe,* lump, mass, from Old French *gobe,* mouthful, lump, from *gober,* to swallow, gulp, from Gallo-Roman *gobb-* (unattested), from Celtic *gobbo-* (unattested), mouth, beak, GOB.]

gob² *n. Slang.* The mouth. [Perhaps from Scottish and Irish Gaelic *gob,* beak, mouth, from Celtic *gobbo-* (unattested).]

gob³ *n. Slang.* A sailor. [20th century : origin obscure.]

gob·bet (gŏb′ĭt) *n.* **1.** An extract from a text. **2.** A piece or chunk, especially of raw meat. [Middle English *gobet,* from Old French, diminutive of *gobe,* GOB (lump).]

gob·ble¹ (gŏb′əl) *v.* **-bled, -bling, -bles.** *—tr.* **1.** To devour in large, greedy gulps: *gobbled up his dinner.* **2.** To snatch greedily; grab: *All the remaining tickets were gobbled up within an hour.* *—intr.* To eat greedily or rapidly. [Frequentative of Middle English *gobben,* to drink greedily, probably from *gobbe,* lump, GOB.]

gobble² *intr.v.* **-bled, -bling, -bles.** To make the guttural, chortling sound of a male turkey. *—n.* The guttural, chortling sound made by a male turkey. [Imitative.]

gob·ble·de·gook, gob·ble·dy·gook (gŏb′əl-dē-go͝ok′) *n.* **1.** Unclear, often verbose language. **2.** Gobbledegook that is associated with bureaucracy: *The current tax law is gobbledegook.* [From GOBBLE (to sound like a turkey), influenced by GOOK.]

gob·bler (gŏb′lər) *n.* A male turkey.

Go·be·lin (gō′bə-lĭn, gŏb′ə-, gō-blăN′) *n.* A tapestry of a kind woven at the Gobelin works in Paris, France, noted for its rich pictorial design.

go-be·tween (gō′bĭ-twēn′) *n.* One who acts as an intermediary or messenger between two sides.

Go·bi (gō′bē). A vast desert in northern China and southern Mongolia, encompassing an area of some 1,295,000 square kilometers (500,000 square miles). It lies on a plateau roughly 1,200 meters (4,000 feet) high and consists chiefly of sand and gravel plains broken by low rocky ranges and salt pans. It is mostly dry but has some small lakes. Its fringe of sparce pastureland is inhabited by Mongolian nomads.

gob·let (gŏb′lĭt) *n.* **1.** A drinking glass or similar vessel with a stem and base. **2.** *Archaic.* A drinking bowl without handles. [Middle English *gobelet,* from Old French, diminutive of *gobel,* cup, from Gallo-Roman *gobb-* (unattested), from Celtic *gobbo-* (unattested), mouth, beak, GOB.]

goblet cell *n. Biology.* Any of the pear-shaped cells in vertebrate epithelium that secrete the chief constituents of mucus.

gob·lin (gŏb′lĭn) *n.* A grotesque, elfin creature of folklore, thought to work mischief or evil. [Middle English *gobelin,* from Old French, from Middle High German *kobolt,* goblin.]

go·bo (gō′bō) *n., pl.* **-bos** or **-boes.** **1.** A screen around a microphone to reduce extraneous sound. **2.** A screen around a camera lens to block unwanted light. [20th century : origin obscure.]

gob·stop·per (gŏb′stŏp′ər) *n. British.* **1.** A large round, hard candy with layers of different colors. **2.** Loosely, any large mouth-filling candy.

go by *intr.v.* To pass: *Three minutes went by. Four buses went by.* ~*tr.v.* **1.** To estimate; judge: *go by appearances.* **2.** To be guided by; follow: *go by the instructions.*

go-by (gō′bī′) *n., pl.* **-bys.** *Informal.* An act of intentional avoidance; run-around: *Why did you give me the go-by?*

go·by (gō′bē) *n., pl.* **-bies** or collectively **goby.** Any of numerous usually small freshwater and marine fishes of the family Gobiidae, having the pelvic fins united to form a sucking disk. [Latin *gōbius,* variant of *cōbius,* from Greek *kōbios*†, GUDGEON.]

go-cart (gō′kärt′) *n.* **1.** A small wagon for children to ride in, drive, or pull. **2.** A handcart. **3.** A stroller. **4.** A small frame on casters designed to help support a child who is learning to walk.

god (gŏd) *n.* **1.** A being of supernatural powers or attributes, believed in and worshiped by a people; especially, a male deity thought to control some part of nature or reality or to personify some force or activity. **2.** An image of a supernatural being; idol. **3.** Something that is worshiped or idealized as a god: *Money was his god.* **4. a.** A man who is godlike in aspect or power. **b.** A man of great beauty. [Middle English *god,* Old English *god.*]

God (gŏd) *n.* **1. a.** A being conceived as the perfect, omnipotent, omniscient originator and ruler of the universe, the principal object of faith and worship in monotheistic religions. **b.** The force, effect, or a manifestation or aspect of this being. **c.** *Christian Science.* "Infinite Mind; Spirit; Soul; Principle; Life; Truth; Love" (Mary Baker Eddy). **2.** The single supreme agency postulated in some philosophical systems to explain the phenomena of the world, having a nature variously conceived in such terms as prime mover, an immanent vital force, or infinity.
~*interj.* Used as an oath or to express surprise, dismay, impatience, or the like, often in phrases such as *Oh God!* and *Thank God!*

Go·dard (gō-där′), **Jean Luc** (1930–). French film director, a leading figure of the 1960's "new wave." His films, which use experimental narrative techniques and reflect his Marxist views, include *A Married Woman* (1964), *Weekend* (1968), *Tout Va Bien* (1972), and *Slow Motion* (1980).

god·aw·ful (gŏd′ô′fəl) *adj. Slang.* Extremely trying; atrocious: *a brat with godawful manners.*

god·child (gŏd′chīld′) *n., pl.* **-children** (-chĭl′drən). A person who is sponsored at baptism by an adult.

God damn *interj.* Also **god·damn** (gŏd′dăm). Used as a profane oath, once a strong one invoking God's curses.

god·damned (gŏd′dămd′) *adj. Informal.* **1.** Very bad; atrocious: *I hate this goddamned weather.* **2.** Total; complete: *He's a goddamned idiot.*
~*adv. Informal.* Very; exceptionally: *a goddamned interesting play.* ~*interj. Informal.* Used to express surprise, frustration, and sometimes delight.

God·dard (gŏd′ərd), **Robert Hutchings** (1882–1945). U.S. physicist. He made and successfully launched the first liquid-fueled rocket.

god·daugh·ter (gŏd′dô′tər) *n.* A female godchild.

God·den (gŏd′n), **Rumer** (1907–). British novelist and short-story author. She spent many years in India and Kashmir, and her novels

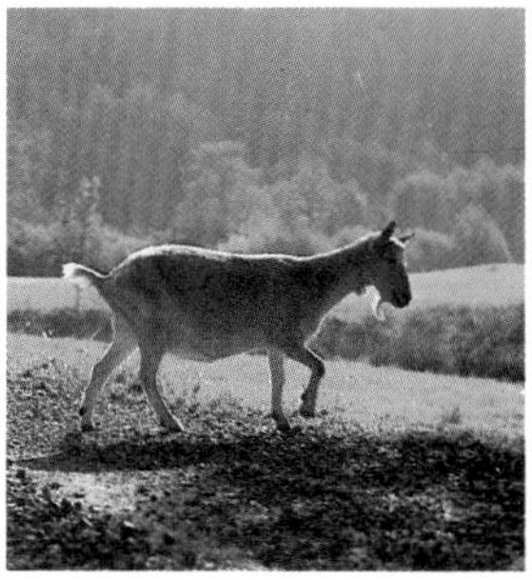

goat *Voracious eaters, goats will severely damage vegetation over a wide area if not tethered. They are widely kept as domestic animals, especially by the nomadic tribes of Africa and the Middle East.*

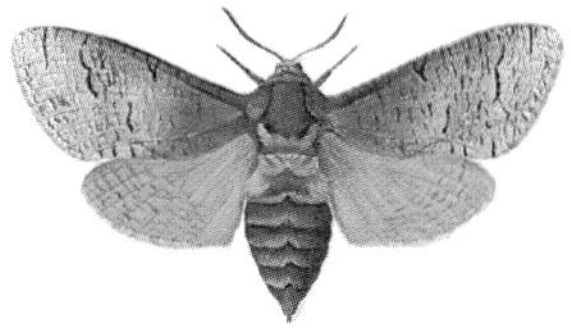

goat moth *The goat moth,* Cossus cossus*—varieties of which are found throughout Europe—is so called because the caterpillar gives off an odor similar to that of a male goat.*

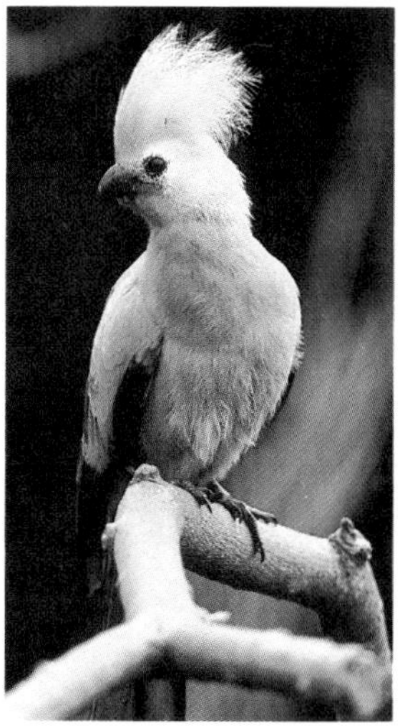

go-away bird *This African fruit eater gets its name from the call it makes when disturbed.*

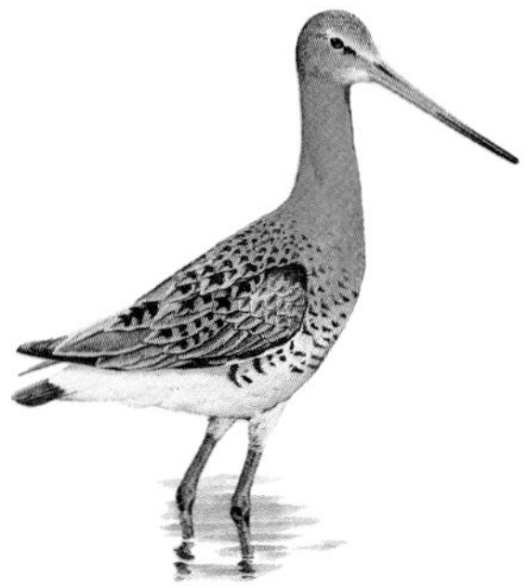

godwit *An adult black-tailed godwit,* Limosa limosa, *in its summer plumage. In winter the birds are brown-gray with pale undersides. Black-tailed godwits nest in May in grass-lined scraped hollows in the ground, and the young leave the nest only a few hours after hatching. They breed in northern Europe and Asia but migrate during the winter, some birds flying as far as Tasmania and New Zealand.*

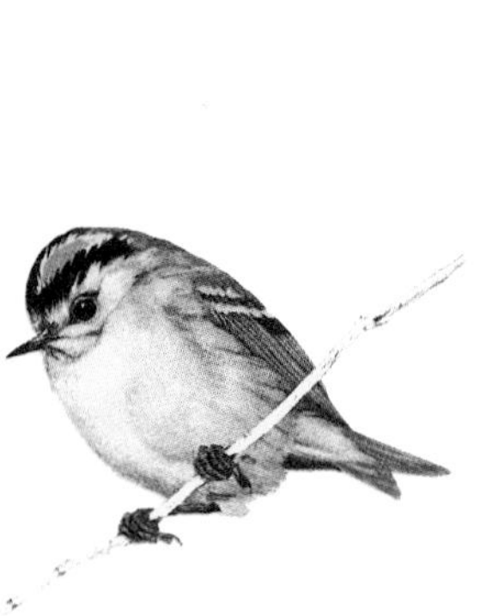

goldcrest *One of the smallest European birds, the goldcrest,* Regulus regulus, *grows to only 90 millimeters (3½ inches) in length. It usually nests in coniferous trees, laying up to ten eggs at a time, and is native to Europe and Asia.*

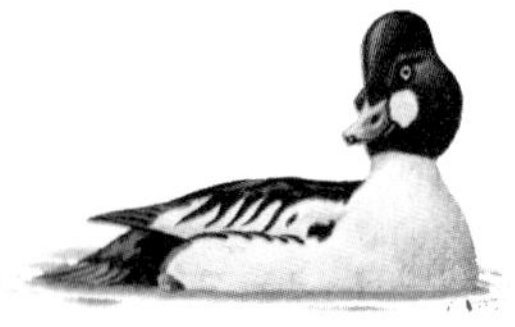

goldeneye *A winter visitor to the Gulf Coast and Florida as well as Mediterranean Europe. Goldeneye ducks form large flocks that rarely come ashore. They breed on lakes and ponds in northern regions. The male (above) can be recognized by its black-green head and white cheek patches.*

include *A Candle for St. Jude* (1948), *An Episode for Sparrows* (1955), and *The Diddakoi* (1972).

god·dess (gŏd′ĭs) *n.* **1.** A female being of supernatural powers or attributes, believed in and worshiped by a people. **2.** An image of a goddess; idol. **3.** A woman of great beauty or grace. **4.** A woman who is adored.

Gö·del (gœd′l), **Kurt** (1906–78). U.S. mathematician and logician, born in Czechoslovakia. He settled in the United States in 1940. In 1951 he was awarded the Albert Einstein award for outstanding achievement in the natural sciences.

Gödel's proof *n.* A mathematical proof that under a given consistency condition, any sufficiently strong formal axiomatic system must contain a proposition such that neither it nor its negation is provable and that any consistency proof for the system must use ideas and methods beyond those of the system itself. [After Kurt GÖDEL.]

go·de·tia (gō-dē′shə, -shē-ə) *n.* Any plant of the genus *Godetia,* some species and varieties of which are cultivated because of their showy, colorful flowers. [After C.H. *Godet* (died 1879), Swiss botanist.]

go-dev·il (gō′dĕv′əl) *n.* **1.** A jointed tool for cleaning an oil pipeline and disengaging obstructions. **2.** An iron dart dropped into an oil well to explode a charge of dynamite. **3.** A logging sled. **4.** A railroad handcar.

god·fa·ther (gŏd′fä′*th*ər) *n.* **1.** A man who sponsors a child at its baptism. **2.** *Slang. Often* **Godfather.** The head of a criminal organization, especially a Mafia family. **3.** A man who has a relationship to another that resembles the relationship of a godfather to his godchild: *The teacher had been godfather to many promising students.*

god-fear·ing (gŏd′fîr′ĭng) *adj.* Religious; devout.

god·for·sak·en (gŏd′fər-sā′kən) *adj.* **1.** Located in a dismal or remote area. **2.** Desolate; forlorn.

god·head (gŏd′hĕd′) *n.* **1.** Divinity; godhood. **2. Godhead. a.** God. **b.** The essential and divine nature of God regarded abstractly. Preceded by *the.* [Middle English *godhede* : GOD + *-hede,* variant of *-hode,* -HOOD.]

god·hood (gŏd′ho͝od′) *n.* The quality or state of being a god; divinity. [Middle English *godhode,* Old English *godhād* : GOD + -HOOD.]

Go·di·va (gə-dī′və), **Lady** (*fl.* 1040–80). English heroine, the wife of Leofric, Earl of Mercia. She was the benefactor of several monasteries, including one at Coventry in 1043. She is famous for the episode, probably legendary, in which, to secure a promise from her husband that he would reduce taxation in Coventry, she rode naked through the town on a white horse.

god·less (gŏd′lĭs) *adj.* **1.** Lacking reverence for God and God's laws; impious. **2.** Recognizing or worshiping no god. **—god·less·ly** *adv.* **—god·less·ness** *n.*

god·like (gŏd′līk′) *adj.* Resembling or of the nature of a god or God; divine.

god·ly (gŏd′lē) *adj.* **-lier, -liest. 1.** Having great reverence for God; divine. **2.** Divine. **—god·li·ness** *n.*

god·moth·er (gŏd′mŭ*th*′ər) *n.* A woman who sponsors a child at its baptism.

Go·dol·phin (gə-dŏl′fĭn), **Sidney, 1st Earl of** (1645–1712). English courtier and politician, the lifelong ally of John Churchill, 1st Duke of Marlborough. He first became an M.P. in 1668 and served in the administrations of Charles II, James II, William III, and Anne.

go·down (gō′doun′) *n.* In India and east Asia, a warehouse, especially one at a dock. [Portuguese *gudão,* from Malay *godong,* perhaps from Telugu *gidangi,* warehouse, from *kidu,* to lie.]

god·par·ent (gŏd′pâr′ənt) *n.* A godfather or godmother.

God's acre *n.* A churchyard or burial ground. [Translation of German *Gottesacker,* God's field.]

god·send (gŏd′sĕnd′) *n.* An unexpected boon or stroke of luck that comes just when it is most needed; a windfall. [Middle English *goddes sand,* God's message : GOD + *sand,* message, Old English *sand,* message, messenger.]

god·son (gŏd′sŭn′) *n.* A male godchild.

God slot *n. British Slang.* **1.** A religious program on radio or television. **2.** The period of time during which such a program is regularly broadcast.

God·speed (gŏd′spēd′) *n.* Success or good fortune. Used in the phrase *wish someone Godspeed.* [From the phrase *God speed,* may God prosper (someone).]

Godthåb. See **Nuuk.**

Go·du·nov (gō′də-nôf′, go͝od′ə-), **Boris** (*c.* 1550–1605). Russian statesman, czar of Russia (1598–1605). He was chief adviser to Ivan the Terrible, upon whose death in 1584 he became regent to Fyodor I and virtual dictator of Russia. He may have been implicated in the murder of Dimitry, Fyodor's younger brother and heir to the throne, in 1591. On Fyodor's death in 1598 he was chosen as czar.

God·win (gŏd′wĭn), **William** (1756–1836). British political theorist and novelist, husband of Mary Wollstonecraft and father-in-law of the poet Shelley. A staunch supporter of the French Revolution and an adherent of utilitarian principles in ethics, his most important work was the radical, pro-anarchist *Enquiry Concerning Political Justice* (1793).

God·win-Aus·ten, Mount (gŏd′wĭn-ô′stĭn). Also **Dap·sang** (dăp′săng′) or **K2** (kā-to͞o′). The world's second-highest mountain (after Mt. Everest), in the Karakoram Range of northern India. It rises to 8,611 meters (28,250 feet) and is also known as K2 because it was the second Karakoram peak to be measured for height.

god·wit (gŏd′wĭt′) *n.* Any of various wading birds of the genus *Limosa,* having a long, slender, slightly upturned bill. [16th century : origin obscure.]

Goeb·bels (gœb′əls), **(Paul) Joseph** (1897–1945). German politician. After a brief career as a journalist and unsuccessful novelist, he joined the Nazi Party and by 1926 was appointed district party leader in Berlin. There he founded and edited the party's propaganda organ, *Der Angriff* ("Attack"). In 1928 he was elected to the Reichstag, and when Hitler was made chancellor (1933), he was appointed minister of propaganda. His venomous attacks on the Jews, his powerful oratory, and his use of radio and mass meetings made him the second most powerful man in the party. He played an important part in the "final solution" directed against the Jews and remained loyal to Hitler until April 1945, when he and his wife killed their children and committed suicide in Hitler's bunker.

go·er (gō′ər) *n.* **1.** A person who goes to or attends something regularly. Usually used in combination: *a theatergoer.* **2.** *Informal.* One that moves very fast. **3.** *Australian & New Zealand Informal.* An idea, project, or proposal that seems likely to be successful.

Goe·ring or **Gö·ring** (gœr′ĭng), **Hermann Wilhelm** (1893–1946). German politician and high-ranking Nazi official. He joined the National Socialist Party and took part with Hitler in the Munich putsch of 1923. In 1928 he was elected to the Reichstag, and when Hitler became chancellor (1933), he was appointed air minister. During World War II he was in command of the German air offensive until he lost favor with Hitler (1943) and was stripped of authority. He committed suicide before his sentence of death at the Nuremberg trials (1946) could be carried out.

Goe·thals (gō′thəlz), **George Washington** (1858–1928). U.S. army officer. He was appointed chief engineer of the Panama Canal project in 1907. Though forced to deal with unexpected engineering difficulties and problems of climate, disease, and low morale, he managed to complete the canal in just seven years.

Goe·the (gœ′tə), **Johann Wolfgang von** (1749–1832). German writer, scientist, and a major figure in world literature. Although trained as a lawyer, he devoted his life to his poetry, novels, and dramas. He first gained notice with the historical drama *Götz von Berlichingen* (1773) and the novel *The Sorrows of Young Werther* (1774). In 1775 he was invited to the ducal court at Weimar, where he spent the remainder of his life. His two greatest works were the novel *Wilhelm Meister,* completed in 1829, and the poetic drama *Faust,* the first part of which appeared in 1808 and the second part after his death.

goe·thite (gō′thīt′, gœ′tīt′) *n.* A brown mineral, essentially a hydrated oxide of iron, $Fe_2O_3 \cdot H_2O$, used as an iron ore. [Named in honor of Johann W. von GOETHE.]

go·fer (gō′fər) *n. Slang.* An employee who runs errands in addition to regular duties. [From the phrase *go for* (i.e., fetch something).]

gof·fer, gauf·fer (gŏf′ər, gô′fər) *tr.v.* **-fered, -fering, -fers. 1.** To press ridges or narrow pleats into (a frill, for example); flute or crimp. **2.** To emboss (the edges of paper or a book) with a repeating pattern.

∼*n.* **1.** An iron used for goffering. **2. a.** Ridged or pleated ornamentation produced by goffering. **b.** An embossed pattern produced by goffering. [French *gaufrer,* to crimp lace, from Old French *gaufre,* honeycomb, waffle, from Middle Low German *wāfel.*]

Gog and Ma·gog (gŏg′; mā′gŏg′). In Biblical prophecy, the heathen nations to be led by Satan in a war against the Kingdom of God. Revelation 20:7–8.

go-get·ter (gō′gĕt′ər) *n. Informal.* An enterprising, forceful, and ambitious person.

gog·gle (gŏg′əl) *v.* **-gled, -gling, -gles.** —*intr.* **1.** To stare with wide and bulging eyes. **2.** To roll or bulge. Used of the eyes. —*tr.* To roll or bulge (the eyes).

∼*n.* **1.** A stare or leer. **2. goggles. a.** Eye coverings that look like glasses but have shielding sidepieces and are worn as a protection, as against water, snow, wind, or dust. **b.** *Slang.* A pair of spectacles; glasses. [Middle English *gog(e)len,* to roll the eyes, perhaps from *gog-,* root expressive of up and down movement.] **—gog·gly** *adj.*

gog·gle·box (gŏg′əl-bŏks′) *n. British Slang.* A television set.

gog·gle-eyed (gŏg′əl-īd′) *adj.* Having prominent, bulging, or rolling eyes.

Gogh, Vincent van. See **van Gogh.**

go-go dancer (gō′gō′) *n.* A girl who dances in a lively, titillating manner, often on a platform, in a discothèque or cabaret. **—go-go dancing** *n.*

Go·gol (gō′gəl), **Nikolay Vasilyevich** (1809–52). Russian writer, one of the founders of the Russian realist tradition. He was of Cossack descent, and his first literary success was a collection of tales of the Ukraine, *Evenings on a Farm near Dikanka* (1832). His most famous play, *The Inspector General* (1836), revealed his talent for satirizing Russian officialdom, a talent that reached its highest expression in the novel *Dead Souls* (1842).

Goi·del (goid′l) *n.* A member of a Goidelic-speaking people. [Old Irish.]

Goi·del·ic, Goi·dhel·ic (goi-dĕl′ĭk) *n.* Also **Ga·dhel·ic** (gə-dĕl′ĭk, gă-). A group of Celtic languages comprising Irish Gaelic, Scottish Gaelic, and Manx.

∼*adj.* Also **Gadhelic. 1.** Of or pertaining to the Gaels. **2.** Of, pertaining to, or characteristic of Goidelic. [Old Irish *Goidel,* Gael, Celt, from Old Welsh *gwyddel,* from *gwydd,* wild.]

go·ing (gō′ĭng) *n.* **1. a.** Departure: *comings and goings.* **b.** Demise;

death. **2.** The condition underfoot as it affects one's headway in walking or riding. **3.** *Informal.* Progress or existence considered with regard to the conditions to be coped with. **4.** The activity of attending something. Used in combination: *partygoing.*
∼*adj.* **1.** Working; running: *in going order.* **2.** In full operation; flourishing: *a going concern.* **3.** Current; prevailing: *The going rates are low.* **4.** Available; to be found. Used after the noun: *the best products going.*

go·ing-o·ver (gō′ĭng-ō′vər) *n., pl.* **goings-over.** *Informal.* **1.** An examination; an inspection. **2.** A severe beating; a thrashing. **3.** A severe reprimand; scolding or rebuke.

go·ings-on (gō′ĭngz-ŏn′, -ôn′) *pl.n. Informal.* Events or behavior, especially when regarded as improper or mysterious.

goi·ter, goi·tre (goi′tər) *n. Pathology.* A chronic, noncancerous enlargement of the thyroid gland, visible as a swelling at the front of the neck, that may be due to underactivity or overactivity of the gland and may be associated with iodine deficiency. Also called "struma." See **exophthalmic goiter.** [French *goitre,* from Provençal *goitron,* from Vulgar Latin *gutturōnem* (unattested), from Latin *guttur*†, throat.] —**goi·trous** (goi′trəs) *adj.*

Go·lan Heights (gō′lən, -län′). Range of hills to the east of the Jordan River, disputed between Syria and Israel. Marking Syria's southern border after World War II, it was used from 1948 as a base from which to shell Israeli settlements. The heights were stormed by Israel during the last hours of the 1967 Middle East War and were subsequently colonized by Jewish settlers. They remain of vital strategic importance, and their administration is a key issue in Middle East peace negotiations.

Gol·con·da (gŏl-kŏn′də) *n.* A source of great riches, especially a mine. [After *Golconda,* India, city near Hyderabad, formerly noted for its diamonds.]

gold (gōld) *n.* **1.** *Symbol* **Au** A soft, yellow, corrosion-resistant element, the most malleable and ductile metal, occurring in veins and alluvial deposits and recovered by mining or by panning or sluicing. It is a good thermal and electrical conductor, is generally alloyed to increase its strength, and is used as an international monetary standard, in jewelry, for decoration, in dentistry, and as a plated coating on a wide variety of electrical and mechanical components. Atomic number 79, atomic weight 196.967, melting point 1,063.0°C, boiling point 2,966.0°C, specific gravity 19.32, valences 1, 3. **2. a.** Coins made of gold. **b.** A gold standard. **3.** Money; riches. **4.** A light olive-brown to dark yellow, or moderate, strong, to vivid yellow. **5.** Something regarded as having great value or goodness: *a heart of gold.* **6.** A gold medal.
∼*adj.* **1.** Of, pertaining to, or containing gold. **2.** Of the color of gold. **3.** Redeemable or secured by gold: *a gold bond.* [Middle English *gold,* Old English *gold.*]

Gold·bach's conjecture (gōld′bäkʜs′) *n. Mathematics.* The hypothesis that every even number greater than two is the sum of two prime numbers. It is generally thought to be true but so far is unproved. [After C. *Goldbach* (1690–1764), German mathematician.]

gold basis *n.* A gold standard as a basis for determining prices.

gold·beat·er's skin (gōld′bē′tərz) *n.* Treated animal membrane used to separate sheets of gold being hammered into gold leaf.

gold·beat·ing (gōld′bē′tĭng) *n.* The act, art, or process of beating sheets of gold into gold leaf. —**gold·beat·er** *n.*

Gold·berg (gōld′bərg), **Reuben Lucius,** known as "Rube" (1883–1970). U.S. cartoonist. He delighted his readers with several syndicated cartoon series and is perhaps best remembered for his drawings of zany and incredibly complex inventions that performed simple tasks. In 1948 he won a Pulitzer Prize for his political cartoons.

gold brick, gold·brick (gōld′brĭk′) *n.* **1.** A bar of gilded cheap metal that appears to be genuine gold. **2.** A fraudulent and worthless substitute. **3.** *Slang.* A person, especially a soldier, who avoids assigned duties or work; shirker.
∼*intr.v.* **-bricked, -bricking, -bricks.** *Slang.* To be a shirker.

gold bug *n.* A North American beetle, *Metriona bicolor,* with a metallic luster.

gold certificate *n.* A monetary note formerly issued to the public by the U.S. Treasury and redeemable in gold but now issued to Federal Reserve Banks to certify conformity with their legal reserve requirements.

Gold Coast. The name of Ghana before the country's independence (1957). The term was first applied by European traders to its coastline on the Gulf of Guinea, where gold was brought for sale from the forests inland.

gold·crest (gōld′krĕst) *n.* A small Eurasian songbird, *Regulus regulus,* with yellow-green plumage and an orange or yellow crest.

gold digger *n. Informal.* A person, especially a woman, who seeks gifts and expensive pleasures from others.

gold dust *n.* Gold in powder form, such as that found in placer mining.

gold·en (gōl′dən) *adj.* **1.** Of, pertaining to, made of, or containing gold: *a golden ring.* **2. a.** Having the color of gold or a yellow color suggestive of gold: *golden hair.* **b.** Suggestive of gold, as in richness or splendor: *a golden voice.* **3.** Of the greatest value or importance; precious. **4.** Marked by peace, prosperity, and often creativeness: *a golden year.* **5.** Very favorable or advantageous; excellent: *a golden opportunity.* **6.** Having a promising future; seemingly assured of success. **7.** Of, pertaining to, being, or marking a 50th anniversary. —**gold·en·ly** *adv.* —**gold·en·ness** *n.*

golden age *n.* **1.** *Greek & Roman Mythology.* The first age of the world, an untroubled and prosperous era during which humankind lived in ideal happiness. **2.** A period when a nation or some wide field of endeavor reaches its height. Compare **iron age, silver age.**

golden ager *n.* An elderly person, especially one of retirement age.

golden Al·ex·an·ders (ăl′ĭg-zăn′dərz) *n. Used with a singular or plural verb.* A plant, *Zizia aurea,* of eastern North America, having clusters of small yellow flowers.

golden anniversary *n.* A 50th anniversary, symbolized by gold.

golden aster *n.* Any of various North American plants of the genus *Chrysopsis,* having yellow, rayed flowers.

golden bantam *n.* A variety of corn having large, bright-yellow kernels on a relatively small ear.

golden calf *n.* **1.** A golden image of a sacrificial calf fashioned by Aaron and worshiped by the Israelites. Exodus 32. **2.** Wealth as an object of worship; mammon.

golden chain *n.* A shrub, the **laburnum** *(see).*

golden club *n.* An aquatic plant, *Orontium aquaticum,* of the eastern United States, having small golden-yellow flowers covering a clublike spadix.

Golden Delicious *n.* A variety of eating apple having greenish-yellow skin and sweet flesh.

golden eagle *n.* An eagle, *Aquila chrysaetos,* of mountainous areas of the Northern Hemisphere, having dark plumage with yellowish feathers on the head and neck.

gol·den·eye (gōl′dən-ī′) *n.* Either of two ducks, *Bucephala clangula* or *B. islandica,* of northern regions, having a short black bill, a rounded head, yellow eyes, and black and white plumage. [From their golden-yellow eyes.]

Golden Fleece *n. Greek Mythology.* The magic fleece of the winged ram, stolen by Jason and the Argonauts.

Golden Gate Bridge. Suspension bridge near San Francisco, California. It crosses the strait that links San Francisco Bay with the Pacific Ocean. The bridge was completed in 1937, and its central span of 1,280 meters (4,200 feet) was then the longest in the world.

golden glow *n.* A tall plant, *Rudbeckia laciniata hortensis,* cultivated for its yellow, many-rayed, double flowers.

Golden Horde *n.* The Mongol army that swept over eastern Europe in the 13th century and established a suzerain in Russia. [Translation of Tatar *altūn ordū,* from the color of the tent of their commander, Batu Khan.]

Golden Horn. *Turkish* **Ha·liç** (hä-lēch′). Inlet of the Bosporus in northwestern Turkey. It has served as the harbor for Istanbul since ancient times.

golden mean *n.* **1.** The course between extremes; moderation. **2.** The golden section.

golden oldie *n.* A recording, motion picture, or other form of entertainment that was very popular in the past.

golden pheasant *n.* A pheasant, *Chrysolophus pictus,* of China and Tibet, having a long tail and brilliantly colored plumage.

golden retriever *n.* A dog of a breed of retriever having a dense, wavy, cream or yellow coat.

gold·en·rod (gōl′dən-rŏd′) *n.* Any of various plants of the chiefly North American genus *Solidago,* having clusters of small yellow flowers that bloom in late summer or autumn.

golden rule *n.* **1.** The maxim or teaching that one should behave toward others as one would have others behave toward oneself. Matthew 7:12. **2.** Any basic important principle.

golden samphire *n.* A plant, the **samphire** *(see).*

gold·en·seal (gōl′dən-sēl′) *n.* A woodland plant, *Hydrastis canadensis,* of eastern North America, having small greenish-white flowers and a yellow root formerly used medicinally.

golden section *n.* A ratio between the two dimensions of a plane figure or the two divisions of a line such that the smaller is to the larger as the larger is to the sum of the two, roughly a ratio of three to five. The proportion, which is used in the fine arts, is considered particularly aesthetically pleasing. Also called "golden mean."

golden wattle *n.* Any of several yellow-flowered Australian trees or shrubs of the genus *Acacia*; especially, *A. pycnantha.*

gold-ex·change standard (gōld′ĭks-chānj′) *n.* A monetary system in which a country maintains its currency at par with the currency of another country on the gold standard.

gold-filled (gōld′fĭld′) *adj.* Made of a hard base metal with an outer layer of gold.

gold·finch (gōld′fĭnch′) *n.* **1.** A small Old World bird, *Carduelis carduelis,* having brownish plumage with red, yellow, and black markings. **2.** Any of several small New World birds of the genus *Spinus;* especially, *S. tristis,* of which the male has yellow and black plumage.

gold·fish (gōld′fĭsh′) *n., pl.* **-fishes** or collectively **goldfish. 1.** A freshwater fish, *Carassius auratus,* native to eastern Asia, characteristically having brassy or reddish coloring, and bred in many ornamental forms as an aquarium fish. **2.** Any of various similar aquarium fishes, especially the golden **orfe** *(see).*

goldfish bowl *n.* **1.** A **fish bowl** *(see).* **2.** A place or condition of exposure to public view.

gold foil *n.* Gold rolled or beaten into thin sheets thicker than gold leaf.

gold·i·locks (gōl′dē-lŏks′) *n.* **1.** A European plant, *Linosyrus vulgaris,* having narrow leaves and clusters of small yellow flowers. **2.** A Eurasian woodland plant, *Ranunculus auricomus,* similar and related to the buttercup. [Obsolete *goldy,* golden, from GOLD + LOCK(S).]

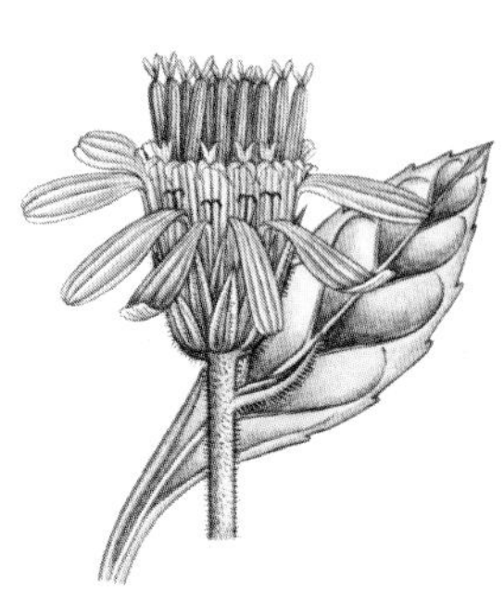

goldenrod *There are about 100 species of this herb, most of which are native to North America. The European goldenrod,* Solidago virgaurea *(above), was imported into Britain in Tudor times and used as a salve for wounds.*

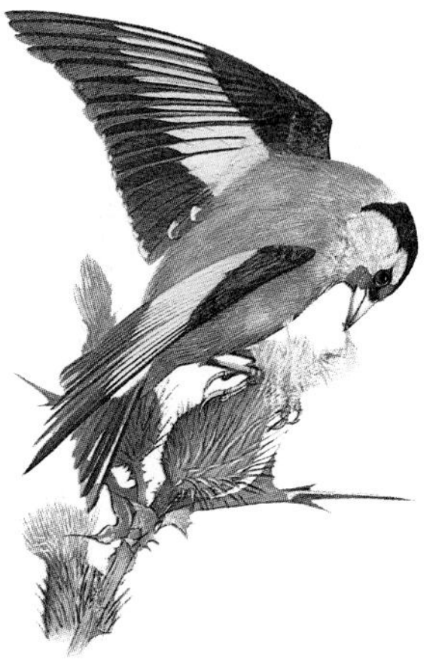

goldfinch *Among the smallest of finches,* Carduelis carduelis *(above), measures about 12 centimeters (4¾ inches) from head to tail. It feeds mainly on thistle seeds that it plucks with its pointed beak.*

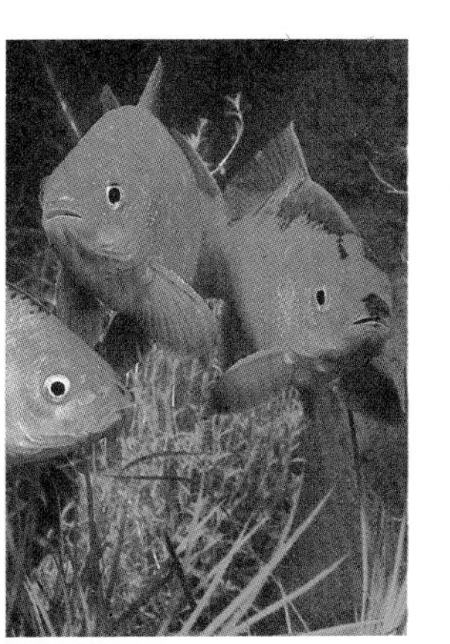

goldfish *The domesticated goldfish popular in aquariums and garden ponds was originally bred in China. Goldfish are descended from a grayish-yellow species of carp found in Europe and Asia.*

Gold·ing (gōl'dĭng), **William Gerald** (1911–). British novelist. He established his reputation with *Lord of the Flies* (1954). Later novels include *Pincher Martin* (1956), *Free Fall* (1959), and *The Scorpion God* (1971). He was awarded the Nobel Prize for literature (1983).

gold leaf *n.* Gold beaten into extremely thin sheets, used for gilding.

Gold·man (gōld'mən), **Emma** (1869–1940). U.S. anarchist agitator, born in Russia. In 1916 she was imprisoned for advocating birth control, in 1917 for opposing military conscription. In 1919 she was deported to Russia. She went to Spain during the Civil War and died in Canada in 1940. Her writings include *Anarchism and Other Essays* (1911) and *My Disillusionment in Russia* (1923).

gold medal *n.* A medal made of gold, or something looking like gold, awarded as a prize for coming in first in a race, competition, or the like. Compare **bronze medal, silver medal.**

gold mine *n.* **1.** A mine yielding gold ore. **2.** *Informal.* **a.** A source of great wealth or profit. **b.** An abundant source of something that is wanted: *a gold mine of information.*

gold-of-pleas·ure (gōld'əv-plĕzh'ər) *n.* A plant, *Camelina sativa,* native to Europe and Asia, having small yellow flowers and seeds rich in oil.

Gol·do·ni (gōl-dō'nē), **Carlo** (1707–93). Italian comic playwright. He wrote over 250 plays, 150 of which are comedies, including *The Mistress of the Inn* (1753), *The Fan* (1764), and *The Accomplished Maid* (1756). He lived in Paris after 1762 and died there a pauper.

gold plate *n.* **1.** Vessels, dishes, and utensils made of gold. **2.** A covering of gold, usually produced by electroplating.

gold-plate (gōld'plāt') *tr.v.* **-plated, -plating, -plates.** To cover with gold plate, usually by electroplating.

gold point *n.* **1.** The point in foreign-exchange rates at which it is no more expensive to import or export gold bullion in settling international accounts than to buy or sell bills of exchange. Also called "specie point." **2.** *Physics.* The melting point of gold, used as a fixed point for temperature scales.

gold reserve *n.* The reserve of gold bullion held by a government or central bank to redeem its notes.

gold rush *n.* A rush of migrants to an area where gold has been discovered, such as that to California in 1849.

Gold·schmidt process (gōld'shmĭt') *n.* A process for extracting metals by reducing the oxide with aluminum. [After Hans *Goldschmidt* (1861–1923), German chemist.]

gold·smith (gōld'smĭth') *n.* **1.** An artisan who fashions objects in gold. **2.** A tradesman who deals in gold articles.

Gold·smith (gōld'smĭth'), **Oliver** (*c.* 1728–74). Irish writer. He settled in London in 1756 and published his first work, *Enquiry into the Present State of Polite Learning in Europe* (1759). The publication of the satirical essays *The Citizen of the World* (1762) established him as a man of letters. His most famous works are his novel *The Vicar of Wakefield* (1766), the pastoral poem *The Deserted Village* (1770), and the dramatic comedy *She Stoops to Conquer* (1773).

goldsmith beetle *n.* Either of two scarabaeid beetles, *Cotalpa lanigera* or *Cetonia aurata,* having metallic greenish-yellow coloring.

gold standard *n.* A monetary standard under which the basic unit of currency is equal in value to and exchangeable in principle for a given amount of gold.

gold·stone (gōld'stōn') *n.* An **aventurine** *(see)* with gold-colored inclusions.

gold·thread (gōld'thrĕd') *n.* A low-growing woodland plant, *Coptis trifolia,* having white flowers and slender yellow roots.

Gold·wyn (gōld'wĭn), **Samuel,** born Samuel Goldfish (1882–1974). Polish-born U.S. film producer. In 1916 he established his own Goldwyn Pictures Corporation and then merged with Louis B. Mayer in 1924 to become Metro-Goldwyn-Mayer. Goldwyn produced a number of major films, including *Guys and Dolls* (1955) and *Porgy and Bess* (1959). He won an Academy Award for *The Best Years of Our Lives* (1946).

go·lem (gō'lĕm, -ləm) *n.* *Jewish Folklore.* An artificially created human being endowed with life by supernatural means.

golf (gôlf, gŏlf, gŏf, gôf) *n.* A game played on a large outdoor obstacle course having a series of usually 9 or 18 holes spaced far apart, the object being to propel a small ball by the use of a club into each hole with as few strokes as possible.

~*intr.v.* **golfed, golfing, golfs.** To play golf. [Middle English *golf†* (Scottish dialect).] —**golf·er** *n.*

golf ball *n.* **1.** A small, hard, dimpled ball used in golf. **2.** *Informal.* A revolving metal sphere on which the type is carried in many electric typewriters. **3.** A typewriter equipped with such a sphere.

golf club *n.* **1.** Any of a set of clubs having a slender shaft and a head of wood or iron, used in golf. **2. a.** An organization of golfers usually having its own golf course and premises. **b.** Such premises.

golf course *n.* A large tract of land laid out for golf. Also called "golf links."

Gol·gi (gōl'jē), **Camillo** (1844–1926). Italian physician. He established the existence of a complex of vesicles present in cells, now known as the Golgi apparatus. For his work on the structure of the nervous system he was awarded, with Santiago Ramón y Cajal (1852–1934), the Nobel Prize for physiology and medicine (1906).

Golgi apparatus *n.* A stack of membranous vesicles present in living cells and believed to function in the formation of secretions within the cell. Also called "Golgi body," "Golgi complex." [After Camillo GOLGI.]

gol·go·tha (gōl'gə-thə) *n.* **1.** A place of burial. **2.** A place or occasion of suffering or agony. [After GOLGOTHA.]

Gol·go·tha (gōl'gə-thə). The hill of Calvary where Jesus was crucified. [Late Latin, from Greek, from Aramaic *gulgŭltha,* skull (from the shape of the hill).]

gol·iard (gōl'yərd) *n.* Any of a class of wandering students in medieval Europe, who are supposed to have led a life of conviviality and debauchery and to have composed ribald and satirical Latin songs. [Middle English *goliard,* from Old French, glutton, trickster, from *gole,* throat, from Latin *gula,* gullet.] —**gol·iar·dic** (gōl-yär'dĭk) *adj.*

Go·li·ath (gə-lī'əth). The giant Philistine warrior who was slain by David with a stone and sling. I Samuel 17:4–51.

goliath beetle *n.* Any of several very large, herbivorous, scarabaeid beetles; especially, the African species *Goliathus giganteus,* which can reach a length of 20 centimeters (8 inches).

goliath frog *n.* The largest known frog, *Rana goliath,* which occurs in Africa and can reach a length of 35 centimeters (14 inches).

gol·li·wog, gol·li·wogg (gōl'ē-wŏg') *n.* A male doll with a black face and longish hair standing out from its head, usually made from soft material. [Originally the name of a doll designed by Florence Upton (died 1922) for a series of children's books by Bertha Upton (died 1912); possibly after POLLIWOG.]

golly *interj.* *Informal.* Used to express mild surprise or wonder. [Euphemism for GOD.]

GOM, G.O.M. Grand Old Man.

gombo. Variant of **gumbo.**

gom·broon (gŏm-brōon') *n.* A kind of Persian pottery. [After *Gombroon,* town in Iran.]

Gó·mez (gō'mĕz), **Juan Vicente** (*c.* 1857–1935). Venezuelan soldier and politician; president (1908–35). Once a cattle herdsman and almost illiterate, he gathered a guerrilla force around him that helped win the presidency for Cipriano Castro (*c.* 1858–1924). Castro made him vice president in 1899, but Gómez deposed him in 1908. He ruled by severe methods and established a police state. He also established the foundations of Venezuela's modern industrial economy.

Go·mor·rah (gə-môr'ə, -mŏr'ə). A city of ancient Palestine near Sodom.

Gom·pers (gŏm'pərz), **Samuel** (1850–1924). English-born U.S. labor leader who took part in the founding of the Federation of Organized Trades and Labor Unions (1881). When it was reorganized as the American Federation of Labor (1886), Gompers became its first president, an office he held until his death.

gom·pho·sis (gŏm-fō'sĭs) *n.* *Anatomy.* An immovable articulation consisting of a peg and rigid socket, such as a tooth and its bony socket. [New Latin, from Greek *gomphōsis,* from *gomphoun,* to fasten with bolts, from *gomphos,* bolt.]

Go·muł·ka (gō-mōol'kə, -mŭl'kə), **Władysław** (1905–82). Polish Communist leader. An active trade unionist, he was secretary of the Polish Workers' Central Committee (1943–49) and played a leading part in the resistance movement against the Germans. From 1945 to 1949 he was deputy premier of Poland but was purged for alleged "bourgeois nationalism" and sympathy with Tito. He was imprisoned without trial (1951–54) but readmitted to the party in 1956 and elected first secretary. He removed Stalinists from key positions, reduced the secret police terror, ended compulsory collectivization, and reached a compromise with the Church. In 1970 he resigned as first secretary in the wake of food riots.

go·mu·ti (gə-mōo'tē) *n.* **1.** A palm tree, *Arenga pinnata,* of southeast Asia, the sap of which yields sugar. **2.** The leaf fibers of this palm, used to make cord, rope, and the like. [Malay *gĕmuti.*]

–gon *suffix.* Indicates a figure having a specified number of sides and angles; for example, *nonagon.* [Greek *-gōnon,* from *-gonos,* -angled, from *gōnia,* angle.]

go·nad (gō'năd', gŏn'ăd') *n.* An organ in animals that produces gametes; especially, a testis or ovary. [New Latin, from Greek *gonos,* offspring, procreation, genitals.] —**go·nad·al, go·nad·ic** *adj.*

gon·a·do·trop·ic (gŏn'ə-dō-trŏp'ĭk, -trō'pĭk) *adj.* Also **gon·a·do·troph·ic** (-trŏf'ĭk, -trō'fĭk). Acting on or stimulating the gonads, as does a hormone.

gon·a·do·tro·pin (gŏn'ə-dō-trō'pĭn, -trŏp'ĭn) *n.* Also **gon·a·do·tro·phin** (-trō'fĭn). Any of several hormones that are secreted by the pituitary gland and stimulate activity of the ovaries and testes, as for example the **follicle-stimulating hormone** *(see).* Also called "gonadotropic hormone."

Gon·cha·rov (gŏn'chə-rôf'), **Ivan Alexandrovich** (1812–91). Russian novelist, famous for one novel, *Oblomov* (1858), a masterpiece of comedy.

Gon·court (gôN-kōor'), **Edmond Louis Antoine de** (1822–96) and his brother **Jules Alfred Huot de** (1830–70). French writers and literary critics. They are best known for their journal, published in nine volumes (1887–96). Edmond's will provided for the foundation of the Goncourt Academy, which annually awards the Goncourt Prize for literature.

Gond (gŏnd) *n.* A member of a people of Dravidian stock of central India.

Gon·dar (gŏn'dər). Town in northwest Ethiopia. It was a capital of Ethiopia, flourishing from *c.* 1630 to *c.*1860.

Gon·di (gŏn'dē) *n.* The Dravidian language of the Gonds.

gon·do·la (gŏnd'l-ə, gŏn-dō'lə) *n.* **1.** A narrow, lightweight barge having ends that curve up into a point and often a small cabin in the middle, propelled with a single oar from the stern, used on the canals of Venice. **2.** Any of various containers or vehicles suspended from a framework or larger vehicle, as: **a.** A cabin or basket suspended from a balloon or airship. **b.** A car or seat suspended

gondola *These long single-oared boats are the traditional form of transportation on the canals of Venice.*

from cables, as on a ski lift. **c.** A movable platform or container suspended from a building and used by builders and other workmen to gain access to outside walls and windows. **3.** An open, shallow freight car. Also called "gondola car." **4.** A flat-bottomed river boat. [Italian (Venetian dialect), *gondola*†, roll, rock.]

gon·do·lier (gŏnd'l-îr') *n.* The boatman of a gondola.

Gond·wa·na (gŏnd-wä'nə). Region of north-central India noted for its rock system and fossil flora. [Sanskrit *gondavana*, "Gond forest" : *gonda*, fleshy navel, name applied to the GOND + *vana*, forest.]

Gond·wa·na·land (gŏnd-wä'nə-lănd') *n.* A hypothetical southern portion of the earth's original land mass, Pangaea. Africa, South America, India, Arabia, Australia, Madagascar, New Guinea, the Malay Peninsula, Indonesia, and Antarctica are thought to have begun drifting apart, out of Gondwanaland, some 200 million years ago. See also **Laurasia.**

gone (gôn, gŏn). Past participle of **go.**
~*adj.* **1.** Past; bygone. **2.** Advanced beyond hope or recall. **3.** Dying or dead. **4.** Ruined; lost. **5.** *Informal.* **a.** Carried away; absorbed. **b.** Exhilarated; excited. **6.** Used up; exhausted. **7.** *Informal.* At a specified stage of a pregnancy: *four months gone.* —**gone on.** *Slang.* Infatuated with: *gone on the girl.*

gon·er (gôn'ər, gŏn'-) *n. Slang.* One who is ruined or doomed. [From GONE.]

gon·fa·lon (gŏn'fə-lən) *n.* A banner suspended from a crosspiece, especially as a standard in an ecclesiastical procession or as the ensign of a medieval Italian republic. [Italian *gonfalone*, standard, from Germanic.]

gon·fa·lon·ier (gŏn'fə-lə-nîr') *n.* **1.** The bearer of a gonfalon. **2.** The chief magistrate in any of several medieval Italian republics.

gong (gông, gŏng) *n.* **1. a.** A hanging rimmed metal disk that produces a loud, sonorous tone when struck with a padded mallet. **b.** See **tam-tam. 2.** A usually saucer-shaped bell that is struck with a mechanically operated hammer. **3.** *British Slang.* A medal. [Malay *gōng* (imitative).]

Gon·gor·ism (gŏng'gə-rĭz'əm) *n.* A florid, cluttered literary style. [Popularized by Luis de *Góngora y Argote* (1561-1627), Spanish poet.] —**Gon·go·ris·tic** (gŏng'gə-rĭs'tĭk) *adj.*

go·ni·a·tite (gō'nē-ə-tīt') *n.* Any of various extinct cephalopod mollusks of the genus *Goniatites*, the fossil remains of which are common constituents of Devonian and Carboniferous rocks. [Greek *gōnia*, angle (referring to the angular sutures in some species).]

go·nid·i·um (gō-nĭd'ē-əm) *n., pl.* **-ia** (-ē-ə). **1.** An asexually produced reproductive cell that separates from the parent body, as in certain colonial algae. **2.** An algal cell in the thallus of a lichen, so called because they were once thought to be the reproductive cells of the lichen. [New Latin : GON(O)- + Greek *-idion*, diminutive suffix.]

gonif. Variant of **ganef.**

go·ni·om·e·ter (gō'nē-ŏm'ə-tər) *n.* **1.** An optical instrument for measuring crystal angles. **2.** A radio receiver and directional antenna used as a system to determine the angular direction of incoming radio signals. [Greek *gōnia*, angle + -METER.] —**go·ni·o·met·ric** (gō'nē-ō-mĕt'rĭk), **go·ni·o·met·ri·cal** *adj.*

go·ni·om·e·try (gō'nē-ŏm'ə-trē) *n.* The science of measuring angles. [Greek *gōnia*, angle + -METRY.]

go·ni·on (gō'nē-ŏn') *n.* The point of the angle on either side of the lower jaw. [New Latin, from Greek *gōnia*, angle.]

go·ni·o·punc·ture (gō'nē-ō-pŭngk'chər) *n.* An operation for glaucoma in which fluid is drained from the eye by inserting a small knife through the cornea.

–gonium *suffix.* Indicates a reproductive cell or seed; for example, **oogonium.** [New Latin *gonium*, seed, cell, from Greek *gonos*, seed, procreation.]

gono-, gon- *prefix.* Indicates sexual, reproductive, or procreative; for example, **gonococcus, gonidium.** [New Latin *gono-*, from Greek, from *gonos*, seed, procreation.]

gon·o·coc·cus (gŏn'ə-kŏk'əs) *n., pl.* **-cocci** (-kŏk'sī). The bacterium, *Neisseria gonorrhoeae*, that causes gonorrhea. [New Latin : GONO- + -COCCUS.]

gon·o·cyte (gŏn'ə-sīt') *n.* **1.** An embryonic cell that develops into an ovum or a spermatozoon. **2.** An oocyte or spermatocyte. [GONO- + -CYTE.]

go-no-go (gō-nō'gō) *adj.* Of, pertaining to, or requiring the outcome of a parameter in order to stop or continue a course of action: *a go-no-go space launch.*

gon·o·phore (gŏn'ə-fôr', -fōr') *n.* A structure bearing or consisting of a reproductive organ or part, such as a reproductive cell or bud in a hydroid colony. [GONO- + -PHORE.] —**gon·o·phor·ic** (gŏn'ə-fôr'ĭk, -fōr'ĭk), **go·noph·o·rous** (gə-nŏf'ər-əs) *adj.*

gon·o·pore (gŏn'ə-pôr', -pōr') *n.* A reproductive aperture or pore, as in insects.

gon·or·rhe·a (gŏn'ə-rē'ə) *n.* An infectious disease of the genitourinary tract, rectum, and cervix, caused by the gonococcus, transmitted chiefly by sexual intercourse, and characterized by acute purulent urethritis with dysuria. [Late Latin *gonorrhoea*, from Greek *gonorrhoia* : GONO- + -RRHEA.] —**gon·or·rhe·al, gon·or·rhe·ic** *adj.*

–gony *suffix.* Indicates the production of; for example, **sporogony.** [Latin *-gonia*, from Greek, from *-goneia*, generation, from *gonos*, offspring, seed.]

Gon·za·ga (gən-zä'gə, -zăg'ə). Illustrious Italian princely house, whose members ruled Mantua from the 14th to the 18th century. The name comes from the village of Gonzaga, near Mantua, which Francesco Gonzaga (1466-1519) made into a center of learning and the arts.

Gon·za·les (gən-zä'ləs), **Richard Alonzo,** known as "Pancho" (1928-). U.S. tennis player. He won the U.S. lawn and clay-court championships for two years in succession (1948-49) before turning professional. He was the world professional champion every year but one between 1954 and 1961.

goo (gōō) *n. Informal.* **1.** A sticky moist substance. **2.** Sentimental drivel. [Perhaps short for BURGOO.] —**goo·ey** *adj.* —**goo·i·ly** *adv.*

goo·ber (gōō'bər) *n. Regional.* A **peanut** (see). Also called "goober pea." [Angolese *nguba.*]

good (gōōd) *adj.* **better, best. 1. a.** Having positive or desirable qualities; not bad or poor. **b.** Virtuous; morally admirable; upright. **2. a.** Serving the end desired; suitable; serviceable: *a good outdoor paint.* **b.** Worthy of proper treatment; not to be spoiled or wasted: *don't ruin good work.* **3. a.** Not spoiled or ruined; able to be used: *The milk is still good.* **b.** In excellent condition; whole; sound: *a good tooth.* **c.** Handsome or fine in appearance: *a good figure.* **4.** Superior to the average: *a good student.* **5. a.** Of high quality: *good books.* **b.** Discriminating: *good taste.* **c.** Well-tested or trustworthy: *a good brand of tuna.* **6.** Suitable for special or formal occasions: *his good clothes.* **7. a.** Beneficial; salutary: *a good night's rest.* **b.** Undisturbed or comfortable: *The patient had a good night.* **8.** Competent; skilled: *a good machinist; good at math.* **9.** Complete; thorough: *a good workout.* **10. a.** Safe; sure: *a good investment.* **b.** Valid or sound: *a good reason.* **c.** Genuine; real: *a good check.* **d.** Applicable; relevant: *his claim to the money was good.* **11. a.** Ample; substantial; considerable: *a good income.* **b.** Bountiful: *a good table.* **12.** Full: *a good mile from here.* **13. a.** Pleasant; enjoyable: *having a good time at the party.* **b.** Propitious; favorable: *good weather; a good omen.* **14. a.** Benevolent; cheerful; kind: *a good soul.* **b.** Loyal; staunch: *a good Socialist.* **15. a.** Well-behaved; obedient: *a good child.* **b.** Socially correct; proper: *good manners.* **c.** Kindly; well-disposed: *She's good to her husband.* **16.** Fertile: *good land.* **17.** Well-established; well-bred; of a high class: *a good family.* **18.** Physically pleasurable or materially enjoyable: *the good things in life.* **19.** Large; substantial: *a good distance away.* **20.** Used to introduce meeting and leave-taking formulas: *good morning; good evening; good night.* —**as good as.** Practically; virtually; nearly: *as good as new.* —**good and.** *Informal.* Very; entirely: *good and tired.* —**good for. 1.** Able to serve or continue performing for a specified period of time: *good for another year.* **2.** Able to be counted upon for producing something specified: *good for a laugh.* **3.** Worth in exchange: *a ticket good for two trips.* —**make good. 1.** To fulfill a promise, commitment, or the like; make valid. **2.** To compensate for or replace. **3.** To prove; verify. **4.** *Informal.* To succeed; do well.
~*n.* **1. a.** That which is good. **b.** The good, valuable, or useful part or aspect: *get the good out of something.* **c.** Benefit; real advantage: *Some good may yet come of it.* **2.** Welfare; benefit; well-being: *for the common good.* **3.** Goodness; virtue; merit: *There is much good in him.* —**come to no good.** To come to a bad end; prove worthless. —**for good.** For all time to come; permanently; forever: *She came home to stay for good.* —**no good.** *Informal.* **1.** Worthless. **2.** Futile; useless: *It's no good trying to coax him.* —**to the good. 1.** To one's benefit; for the best. **2.** In an advantageous financial position.
~*adv. Nonstandard.* Well. [Middle English *god, gode*, Old English *gōd.*]

> *Usage:* There is a clear distinction between the use of *good* and *well* following verbs. *Good* is an adjective that qualifies the subject of a linking verb, such as *be, feel, seem, smell, taste: It feels good; that tastes good. Well* is an adverb that qualifies the verb directly: *He dances well. He acts really well.* It is nonstandard to say or write *He dances good* or *He acts real good.*

good book *n.* Often **Good Book.** The Bible. Often preceded by *the.*

goodby, good-bye (gōōd'bī') *interj.* Used to express farewell on parting.
~*n., pl.* **good-bys, good-byes. 1.** An expression of farewell. **2.** An act of leave-taking: *lingering over their good-bys.* [Contraction of *God be with you.*]

good faith *n.* Integrity; sincerity of intent: *a promise made in good faith.*

good fellow *n.* A genial, companionable person.

good-fel·low·ship (gōōd'fĕl'ō-shĭp') *n.* Pleasant sociability; comradeship.

good-for-noth·ing (gōōd'fər-nŭth'ĭng) *n.* A person of little worth or usefulness.
~*adj.* Having little worth; useless.

Good Friday *n.* The Friday before Easter, observed by Christians in commemoration of the Crucifixion of Jesus.

good-heart·ed (gōōd'här'tĭd) *adj.* Kind and generous. —**good-heart·ed·ly** *adv.* —**good-heart·ed·ness** *n.*

Good Hope, Cape of. A promontory on the southwestern coast of Cape Province, in southern South Africa near Cape Town. It was circumnavigated by Bartolomeu Diaz (1488) and by Vasco da Gama (1497).

good-hu·mored (gōōd'hyōō'mərd) *adj.* Cheerful; amiable. —**good-hu·mored·ly** *adv.* —**good-hu·mored·ness** *n.*

goodie. Variant of **goody** (treat).

good·ish (gōōd'ĭsh) *adj.* **1.** Somewhat good. **2.** Somewhat large or big; goodly.

good-look·er (gōōd'lōōk'ər) *n. Informal.* A good-looking person, especially a woman.

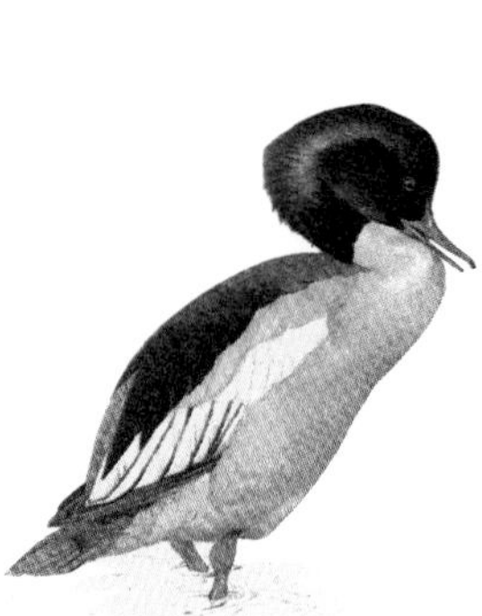

goosander *Mergus* merganser, *the goosander, is one of the few ducks that nest in tree holes. Common in the cooler regions of the Northern Hemisphere, it feeds largely on fish. It is an efficient swimmer, capable of staying underwater for more than a minute at a time.*

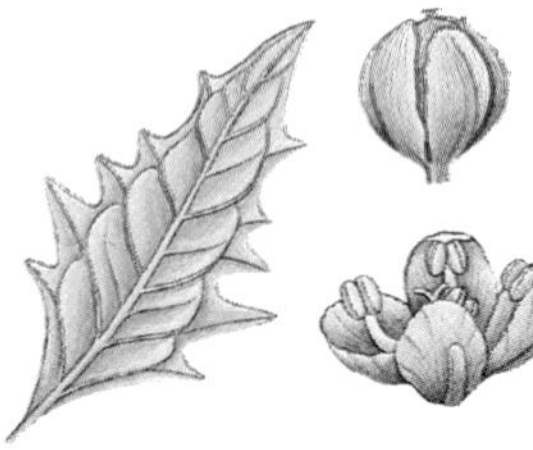

goosefoot *A plant that thrives in the nitrogen-rich soil near ponds and sewage farms. Its toothed leaf looks like a goose's foot. The red goosefoot,* Chenopodium rubrum, *is shown here.*

PRONUNCIATION KEY

ă, pat; ā, pay; âr, care;
ä, father, are; b, **bib**;
ch, **church**; d, **deed**; ĕ, pet;
ē, be; f, **fife**; g, **gag**; h, **hat**;
hw, **which**; ĭ, pit; ī, pie;
îr, **pier**; j, **judge**; k, **kick**;
l, **lid**, needle; m, **mum**;
n, no, sudden; ng, **thing**;
ŏ, pot; ō, toe; ô, **paw**, **for**;
oi, noise; ou, **out**; o͝o, **book**;
o͞o, **boot**; p, **pop**; r, **roar**;
s, sauce; sh, **ship**, **dish**;
t, tight; th, **thin**, **path**;
th, **this**, bathe; ŭ, cut; ûr, **fur**;
v, valve; w, **with**; y, **yes**;
z, zebra, **size**; zh, **vision**;
ə, about, item, edible,
gallop, circus, peaceful

IN FOREIGN WORDS:

à, *Fr.* **ami**; œ, *Fr.* **feu**, *Ger.* **schön**; ü, *Fr.* **tu**, *Ger.* **über**;
KH, *Ger.* **ich**, *Scot.* **loch**;
N, *Fr.* **bon**; y', *Fr.* **Compiègne**

STRESS MARKS:

Primary stress: ′
in·cite′ (ĭn-sīt′)
Secondary stress: ′
in′sight′ (ĭn′sīt′)

good-look·ing (go͝od′lo͝ok′ĭng) *adj.* Of a pleasing appearance; attractive; handsome.

good looks *pl.n.* Attractive appearance; handsomeness.

good·ly (go͝od′lē) *adj.* **-lier, -liest. 1.** Fairly large; considerable: *a goodly sum.* **2.** Of pleasing appearance; comely. **—good·li·ness** *n.*

good·man (go͝od′mən) *n., pl.* **-men** (-mĭn). *Archaic.* **1. a.** The male head of a household; the master. **b.** A husband. **2.** A courteous title of or form of address for a man not of gentle birth.

Good·man (go͝od′mən), **Benny,** originally Benjamin David Goodman (1909–86). U.S. clarinetist, known as the "King of Swing." In New York in 1935 he formed the Benny Goodman trio with Gene Krupa and Teddy Wilson; a year later Lionel Hampton made it a quartet. For at least 30 years Goodman maintained his reputation as one of the finest jazz musicians in the world.

good nature *n.* Cheerful, obliging disposition.

good-na·tured (go͝od′nā′chərd) *adj.* Having an easy-going, cheerful disposition. **—good-na·tured·ly** *adv.* **—good-na·tured·ness** *n.*

good·ness (go͝od′nĭs) *n.* **1.** The state or quality of being good; excellence; merit; worth. **2.** Virtuousness; moral rectitude. **3.** Kindness; benevolence; generosity. **4.** The good part of something; essence; strength.
~*interj.* Used as a euphemism for "god," often in phrases such as *Thank goodness* or *My goodness,* to express relief, surprise, or the like.

good offices *pl.n.* Favorable intervention, usually unobtrusive, on a person's behalf.

goods (go͝odz) *pl.n. Abbr.* **gds. 1.** Merchandise; wares. **2.** Portable personal property. **3.** *Chiefly British.* Merchandise to be transported; freight. Also used adjectivally: *a goods train.* **4.** *Economics.* Physical commodities, usually movable, and only consumed some time after production. Compare **services. 5.** *Used with a singular or plural verb.* Fabric; material. **—deliver the goods.** *Informal.* To produce what is expected; carry out a promise. **—get** (or **have**) **the goods on.** *Slang.* To obtain or have incriminating information or material against. **—the goods.** *Slang.* The real or genuine thing. [Plural of GOOD.]

Good Samaritan *n.* **1.** In a New Testament parable, the only passer-by to aid a man who had been beaten and robbed. Luke 10:30–37. **2.** A compassionate person who unselfishly helps another or others.

goods and chattels *pl.n.* Personal belongings.

Good Shepherd *n.* A name for Jesus. John 10:11–12.

good-sized (go͝od′sīzd′) *adj.* Of a fairly large size.

good-tem·pered (go͝od′tĕm′pərd) *adj.* Having an even or mild temper; not easily irritated. **—good-tem·pered·ly** *adv.* **—good-tem·pered·ness** *n.*

good turn *n.* An act or gesture that helps another person; a favor.

good·wife (go͝od′wīf′) *n., pl.* **-wives** (-wīvz′). *Archaic.* **1.** The female head of a household; the mistress. **2.** A courteous title of or form of address for a woman not of gentle birth.

good·will, good will (go͝od′wĭl′) *n.* **1.** Friendly or neighborly feeling; benevolence. Also used adjectivally: *a goodwill visit.* **2.** Cheerful acquiescence or willingness. **3.** *Accounting.* The good relationship of a business enterprise with its customers, regarded and assessed as an intangible asset.

Good·win Sands (go͝od′wĭn). Group of sandbanks in the Strait of Dover, lying *c.* 10 kilometers (6 miles) off the southeast coast of England. Shifting and partially exposed at low tide, they are extremely dangerous to shipping.

good·y[1], good·ie (go͝od′ē) *n., pl.* **-ies.** *Informal.* **1.** *Usually* **goodies.** Something attractive, interesting, or delectable; especially, something sweet to eat. **2.** A goody-goody. **3.** The virtuous character, as in a movie or play. Compare **baddy.**
~*adj. Informal.* Goody-goody.
~*interj.* Used to express childish delight.

goody[2] *n., pl.* **-ies.** *Archaic.* A polite title of or form of address for a married woman of humble rank. Often used with a surname. [Short for GOODWIFE.]

Good·year (go͝od′yîr′), **Charles** (1800–60). U.S. inventor. After experimenting for 10 years to find a method of raising the melting point of rubber, he accidentally came upon vulcanization when rubber mixed with sulfur dropped on a hot stove. The method was patented in 1844, but after failing to establish companies in Britain and France, Goodyear was imprisoned in Paris for debt in 1855 and died a pauper.

good·y-good·y (go͝od′ē-go͝od′ē) *adj.* Affectedly sweet or good; cloyingly sanctimonious.
~*n., pl.* **goody-goodies.** One who is affectedly good or virtuous.

goo·ey (go͞o′ē) *adj.* **-ier, -iest.** *Informal.* Thick and sticky. [From GOO.]

goof (go͞of) *n. Slang.* **1.** An incompetent, foolish, or stupid person. **2.** A careless mistake; slip.
~*v.* **goofed, goofing, goofs.** *Slang.* —*intr.* **1.** To make a silly mistake; blunder. **2.** To have aimless fun; fool about. Used with *about, around,* or *off.* —*tr.* **1.** To spoil; bungle. Often used with *up.* **2.** To give drugs to (a horse, for example); dope. **3.** To take or swallow (drugs). [Variant of dialect *goff,* from Old French *goffe,* awkward, from Medieval Latin *gufus*†, coarse.]

goof·ball (go͞of′bôl′) *n. Slang.* **1.** A barbiturate sleeping pill. **2.** An eccentric or deranged person.

goof-off (go͞of′ôf′, -ŏf′) *n.* One who shirks work or responsibility.

goof·y (go͞o′fē) *adj.* **-ier, -iest.** *Informal.* Silly; awkward; ridiculous: *a goofy hat.* **—goof·i·ly** *adv.* **—goof·i·ness** *n.*

goo·gol (go͞o′gŏl′) *n.* The number 10 raised to the power 100 (10^{100}); the number 1 followed by 100 zeros. [Coined by Edward *Kasner* (1878–1955), U.S. mathematician.]

goo·gol·plex (go͞o′gŏl-plĕks′) *n.* The number 10 raised to the power of one googol; the number 1 followed by 10^{100} zeros. [*googol* + du*plex.*]

gook (go͝ok, go͞ok) *n. Slang.* A dirty, sludgy, or slimy substance. [Possible alteration of GOO.]

Goo·la·gong Caw·ley (go͞o′lə-gông kô′lē), **Evonne** (1951–). Australian tennis player. She won the Wimbledon ladies' singles championship twice (1971 and 1980) and the doubles championship in 1974. Her record also includes three Australian singles championships (1974, 1975, and 1976).

goon (go͞on) *n.* **1.** *Slang.* A stupid or oafish person. **2.** *Informal.* A thug hired to commit acts of intimidation or violence. [From dialectal *gooney, gony*†, fool; popularized by the comic-strip character Alice the *Goon,* created by E.C. *Segar* (1894–1938).]

goo·ney bird (go͞o′nē) *n.* An albatross; especially, *Diomedea nigripes,* common on islands of the Pacific. [From dialectal *gooney,* fool. See **goon.**]

goop (go͞op) *n. Slang.* An ill-mannered person. [Coined by Gelett *Burgess* (1866–1951), U.S. humorist.]

goos·an·der (go͞os-ăn′dər) *n.* A duck, *Mergus merganser,* the male of which has a dark head and white body. [Probably GOOS(E) + Old Norse *önd* (stem *andar-*), duck.]

goose[1] (go͞os) *n., pl.* **geese** (gēs) or **gooses** (for sense 5). **1.** Any of various wild or domesticated water birds of the family Anatidae, and especially of the genera *Anser* and *Branta,* characteristically having a shorter neck than that of a swan and a shorter, more pointed bill than that of a duck. **2.** The female of such a bird, as distinguished from a gander. **3.** The flesh of such a bird, used as food. **4.** *Informal.* A silly person; simpleton. **5.** A tailor's pressing iron with a long curved handle. **—cook someone's goose.** *Informal.* To ruin someone's chances. [Goose, geese; Middle English *goos, gees,* Old English *gōs, gēs.*]

goose[2] *tr.v.* **goosed, goosing, gooses.** *Slang.* To jab (someone) between the buttocks with an upward thrust.
~*n., pl.* **gooses.** *Slang.* A jab between the buttocks. [Perhaps after GOOSE (bird), from the supposed resemblance of an upturned thumb to an outstretched goose's neck.]

goose barnacle *n.* Any of various barnacles of the genus *Lepas,* which are attached by a stalk to wood and other surfaces and have flattened shells. [So named from the belief that geese were born from barnacles.]

goose·ber·ry (go͞os′bĕr′ē, -bə-rē, go͞oz′-) *n., pl.* **-ries. 1.** A spiny shrub, *Ribes uva-crispa* (or *R. grossularia*), native to Eurasia, having lobed leaves, greenish flowers, and edible greenish or reddish berries. **2.** The fruit of this plant. **3.** Any of several plants bearing fruit similar to the gooseberry, such as the **Cape gooseberry** *(see).* [Perhaps GOOSE + BERRY.]

goose egg *n. Slang.* Zero, especially when written as a numeral to indicate that no points have been scored.

goose·fish (go͞os′fĭsh′) *n., pl.* **-fishes** or collectively **goosefish.** Any of several anglerfishes of the genus *Lophius,* such as *L. Americanus,* of Northern American Atlantic waters. Also called "monkfish."

goose flesh *n.* Momentary roughness of skin caused by erection of the papillae in response to cold or fear. Also called "goose bumps," "goose pimples."

goose·foot (go͞os′fo͝ot′) *n., pl.* **-foots.** Any of various usually weedy plants of the genus *Chenopodium,* having small greenish flowers. [From the shape of its leaves.]

goose grass *n.* A plant, **cleavers** *(see).*

goose·herd (go͞os′hûrd′) *n.* One who tends a flock of geese.

goose·neck (go͞os′nĕk′) *n.* **1.** A slender, curved object or part, such as the flexible shaft of a type of desk lamp. **2.** *Nautical.* A metal fitting joining a boom to a mast. **—goose·necked** *adj.*

goose step *n.* A military parade step performed by swinging each leg alternately sharply from the hips and keeping the knees locked.

goose-step (go͞os′stĕp′) *intr.v.* **-stepped, -stepping, -steps.** To execute or march in a goose step.

goos·y, goos·ey (go͞o′sē) *adj.* **-ier, -iest. 1.** Pertaining to or resembling a goose. **2.** *Informal.* Foolish; scatterbrained. **3.** *Informal.* Causing or affected with goose flesh.

G.O.P. Grand Old Party.

go·pher (gō′fər) *n.* **1.** Any of various short-tailed, burrowing mammals of the family Geomyidae, of North America, having fur-lined external cheek pouches. Also called "pocket gopher." **2.** A **ground squirrel** *(see),* especially one of the genus *Citellus.* **3.** Any of several burrowing tortoises of the genus *Gopherus;* especially, *G. polyphemus,* of the southeastern United States. In this sense, also called "gopher tortoise." [Shortening of earlier *magopher*†.]

gopher ball *n. Baseball.* A pitched ball that is hit for a home run.

gopher snake *n.* A **bull snake** *(see).*

go·pher·wood (gō′fər-wo͝od′) *n.* Also **gopher wood** (for sense 1). **1.** An unidentified wood, probably a kind of cypress, used in the construction of Noah's ark. Genesis 6:14. **2.** A tree, the **yellowwood** *(see).* [Hebrew *gōpher.*]

go·ral (gôr′əl, gōr′-) *n.* Either of two goat antelopes, *Naemorhedus goral* or *N. cranbrooki,* of mountainous regions of eastern Asia, having short, ridged, backward-curving horns in both sexes. [Hindi *gūral, goral,* perhaps from Sanskrit *gaura,* gaur.]

Gor·ba·chev (gôr′bə-chôf′), **Mikhail Sergeevich** (1931–). Soviet politician and leader. The success of his pioneering agrarian reforms earned him a place on the Central Committee in 1978 as secretary for agriculture. In 1980 he was elected to the Politburo, where be became a protégé of Yuri Andropov and an energetic advocate of economic and administrative reform. On the death of Konstantin Chernenko in 1985, he was elected General Secretary of the Communist Party.

gor·cock (gôr′kŏk′) *n.* The male of the red grouse. [From *gor-*† + COCK.]

Gor·di·an knot (gôr′dē-ən) *n.* **1.** An intricate knot tied by King Gordius of Phrygia and cut by Alexander the Great with his sword after hearing an oracle promise that whoever could undo it would be the next ruler of Asia. **2.** An exceedingly complicated problem or deadlock. **—cut the Gordian knot.** To solve a problem by resorting to prompt and bold measures.

Gor·di·mer (gôr′də-mər), **Nadine** (1923–). South African novelist and short-story writer, noted for her sensitive portrayals of interracial relationships. Among her best-known works are *The Soft Voice of the Serpent* (1953), *A Guest of Honor* (1970), and *July's People* (1981).

Gor·don (gôr′dn), **Charles George** (1833–85). British soldier who took part in the British capture of Peking (Beijing) in 1860. His later command of the Chinese army raised to put down the Taiping rebellion earned him the nickname of "Chinese Gordon." As governor general of Sudan, he died fighting the Mahdi when his garrison at Khartoum was overrun before a relief force could reach him.

Gordon setter *n.* A hunting dog of a breed originating in Scotland, having a silky black-and-tan coat. [After Alexander Gordon, the 4th Duke of *Gordon* (1743–1827).]

gore[1] (gôr) *tr.v.* **gored, goring, gores.** To pierce or stab with a horn or tusk. [Middle English *gōren,* to pierce, from *gore,* spear, Old English *gār.*]

gore[2] *n.* **1.** A triangular or tapering piece of cloth used as a part of a garment, such as a skirt, or in an umbrella or sail. **2.** A small triangular piece of land.
∼*tr.v.* **gored, goring, gores. 1.** To make or provide with a gore or gores. **2.** To cut into a gore. [Middle English *gore,* Old English *gāra,* triangular piece of land; akin to Old English *gār,* spear (from the triangular shape of the spearhead).]

gore[3] *n.* **1.** Blood, especially coagulated blood from a wound. **2.** *Informal.* Violence or killing, as in movie scenes. [Middle English *gore,* Old English *gor*†, dung, dirt.]

Go·ren (gôr′ən), **Charles Henry** (1901–). U.S. contract bridge authority. A lawyer and avid bridge player, he developed a revolutionary point-count system and soon abandoned his law practice to devote his time completely to bridge. His writings on the subject include *Contract Bridge Complete* (1951) and numerous newspaper columns.

gorge (gôrj) *n.* **1.** A deep, narrow passage with precipitous rocky sides, enclosed between mountains, usually a river valley or former river valley. **2.** A narrow entrance or passageway from the rear into the bastion or other outwork of a fortification. **3. a.** The contents of a stomach. **b.** *Archaic.* The throat; gullet. **4.** An instance of gluttonous eating; a gorging. **5.** A mass obstructing a narrow passage: *The shipping lane was blocked by an ice gorge.* **—make one's gorge rise.** To make one feel strong revulsion or violent anger.
∼*v.* **gorged, gorging, gorges.** —*tr.* **1.** To stuff; satiate; glut. Usually used reflexively. **2.** To devour greedily. —*intr.* To eat gluttonously. **—**See Synonyms at **satiate.** [Middle English, throat, from Old French, from Vulgar Latin *gurga* (unattested), variant of Latin *gurges,* whirlpool, throat.] **—gorg·er** *n.*

gor·geous (gôr′jəs) *adj.* **1.** Dazzlingly brilliant; resplendent; magnificent. **2.** Strikingly beautiful or attractive. **3.** *Informal.* Wonderful; delightful. [Middle English *gorgeouse,* showy, splendid, from Old French *gorgias*†, stylish, fine, elegant.] **—gor·geous·ly** *adv.* **—gor·geous·ness** *n.*

gor·ger·in (gôr′jər-ən) *n. Architecture.* The necking of a column. [French, from *gorge,* throat, GORGE.]

gor·get (gôr′jĭt) *n.* **1.** A piece of armor protecting the throat. **2.** An ornamental collar. **3.** The scarflike part of a wimple covering the neck and shoulders. **4.** A band or patch of distinctive color on the throat of an animal, especially a bird. **5.** A surgical instrument used to remove stones from the bladder. [Middle English, from Old French, diminutive of *gorge,* throat, GORGE.]

Gor·gon (gôr′gən) *n.* **1.** *Greek Mythology.* Any of the three sisters Stheno, Euryale, and the mortal Medusa who had terrifying teeth and claws, snakes for hair, and eyes which, if looked into, turned the beholder into stone. **2. gorgon.** A repulsively ugly or terrifying woman. [Middle English, from Latin *Gorgō* (stem *Gorgōn-*), from Greek, from *gorgos*†, terrible.] **—Gor·go·ni·an** *adj.*

gor·go·nei·on (gôr′gə-nē′ən) *n., pl.* **-neia** (-nē′ə). A representation of a Gorgon's head, especially one of Medusa. [Greek, from the neuter of *gorgoneios,* of a Gorgon, from *Gorgō,* GORGON.]

gor·go·ni·an (gôr-gō′nē-ən) *n.* Any of various corals of the order Gorgonacea, having a flexible, often branching skeleton of horny material.
∼*adj.* Of or belonging to the Gorgonacea. [Latin *Gorgonia,* coral, from *Gorgō,* GORGON.]

gor·gon·ize (gôr′gə-nīz′) *tr.v.* **-ized, -izing, -izes.** To have a paralyzing effect upon; petrify, as with fear. [From GORGON.]

Gor·gon·zo·la (gôr′gən-zō′lə) *n.* A pungent, blue-veined, cream-colored Italian cheese made of pressed cow's milk. [First made at *Gorgonzola,* village near Milan, Italy.]

go·ril·la (gə-rĭl′ə) *n.* **1.** A large anthropoid ape, *Gorilla gorilla,* of forests of equatorial Africa, having a stocky body and coarse, dark hair. **2.** A brutish or thuglike man. [New Latin (adopted 1847), from Greek *Gorillai*†, name of African tribe of hairy men.]

Gö·ring, Hermann. See **Goering.**

Gor·ky or **Gor·ki** (gôr′kē). Formerly **Nizh·ny Nov·go·rod** (nĭzh′nē nôv′gə-rŏd′). The second-largest city in the R.S.F.S.R., at the confluence of the Volga and Oka rivers in the central U.S.S.R. Under the czarist regime it was the site of historic trade fairs that continued until 1917. Maxim Gorky was born here, and the city was renamed in his honor in 1932.

Gorky or **Gorki, Maxim,** originally Alexey Maximovich Pyeshkov (1868–1936). Self-educated Russian writer, often considered the father of Soviet literature. His works include the play *The Lower Depths* (1902) and the novel *Mother* (1907).

gormand. Variant of **gourmand.**

gor·mand·ize (gôr′mən-dīz′) *v.* **-ized, -izing, -izes.** —*intr.* To eat gluttonously; gorge. —*tr.* To devour (food) gluttonously; gorge. ∼*n. Rare.* Variant of **gourmandise.** [From GOURMANDISE (obsolete sense "gluttony").] **—gor·mand·iz·er** *n.*

gorm·less (gôrm′ləs) *adj. British Informal.* Stupid; unable to deal with practical problems; blundering. [Variant of earlier *gaumless,* from dialect *gaum,* understanding, from Old English *gom, gome,* from Old Norse *gaumr,* heed.]

gorp (gôrp) *n.* A mixture of high-energy foods, such as dried fruit, nuts, and seeds, eaten as a snack. [Perhaps from slang *gorp,* to eat greedily.]

gorse (gôrs) *n.* Any of several spiny, thickset shrubs of the genus *Ulex;* especially, *U. europaeus,* native to Europe, having fragrant yellow flowers. Also called "furze," "whin." [Middle English *gorst, gors,* Old English *gorst, gors.*]

go·ry (gôr′ē, gōr′ē) *adj.* **-rier, -riest. 1.** Covered or stained with gore; bloody; bloodstained. **2.** Characterized by a great effusion of blood: *a gory battle.* **3.** Full of or characterized by bloodshed, slaughter, or acts of violence: *a gory narrative.* **—gor·i·ly** *adv.* **—gor·i·ness** *n.*

gosh (gŏsh) *interj. Informal.* Used to express mild surprise or delight. [Euphemistic variant of GOD.]

gos·hawk (gŏs′hôk′) *n.* **1.** A large hawk, *Accipiter gentilis,* having broad, rounded wings and gray or brownish plumage. **2.** Any of several similar or related hawks. [Middle English *goshawke,* Old English *gōshafoc* : *gōs,* GOOSE + *hafoc,* HAWK.]

Go·shen (gō′shən). Region of ancient Egypt on the eastern delta of the Nile, inhabited by the Israelites from the time of Joseph until the Exodus. Genesis 45:10.

gos·ling (gŏz′lĭng) *n.* **1.** A young goose. **2.** An inexperienced young person. [Middle English, earlier *gesling,* from Old Norse *gæslingr.* See **goose, -ling.**]

gos·pel (gŏs′pəl) *n.* **1.** *Sometimes* **Gospel.** The teachings of Jesus and the Apostles. **2. a. Gospel.** Any of the first four books of the New Testament describing the life, death, and resurrection of Jesus. **b.** A similar narrative. **3.** *Often* **Gospel.** A reading from any of these books included as part of a religious service. **4.** A teaching or doctrine of a religious teacher. **5.** A principle that is strongly advocated: *the gospel of hard work.* **6.** The infallibly accurate account of matters; the last word; *Don't take Freud as gospel.* Also used adjectivally: *the gospel truth.* **7.** Religious music of a style originated among blacks in the southern United States, characterized by evangelical lyrics and fervent singing, and much influenced by jazz. Also used adjectivally: *a gospel song.* [Middle English *gospel,* Old English *godspell,* "good news" (translation of Late Latin *evangelium,* EVANGEL) : *gōd,* GOOD + *spel,* news.]

gos·pel·er, gos·pel·ler (gŏs′pə-lər) *n.* **1.** One who teaches or professes faith in a gospel. **2.** A person who reads or sings the Gospel as part of a church service. [Middle English *gospeller,* Old English *godspellere,* from *godspellian,* to teach the gospel, from *godspell,* GOSPEL.]

gospel side, Gospel Side *n.* The left side of an altar or chancel. [So called from the practice in some churches of reading the Gospel and Epistle from different sides.]

gos·po·din (gŏs′pə-dēn′) *n., pl.* **-da** (-dä′). A courteous form of address used in the U.S.S.R. by Russians for non-Russians. [Russian, "master," "lord."]

gos·port (gŏs′pôrt′, -pōrt′) *n.* A flexible speaking tube used for communication between individual compartments or cockpits of an airplane. [After *Gosport,* England.]

gos·sa·mer (gŏs′ə-mər) *n.* **1.** A fine film of cobwebs often seen floating in the air or caught on bushes or grass. **2.** A soft, sheer, gauzy fabric. **3.** Anything delicate, light, or insubstantial.
∼*adj.* Also **gos·sa·mer·y** (-mə-rē). Light, thin, and delicate. [Middle English *gossomer, gosesomer* : perhaps *goos, gos,* GOOSE + *somer,* SUMMER (that is, early November (St. Martin's summer), when geese are eaten and gossamer is most in evidence).]

gos·san (gŏs′ən) *n. Geology.* An outcrop of quartz and iron oxides, often marking a sulfide ore. [Cornish *gossen,* from *gōs,* blood, from Old Cornish *guit* (referring to its russet color).]

Gosse (gŏs), **Sir Edmund William** (1849–1928). British critic and writer. He wrote essays and criticism and was chiefly responsible for introducing modern Scandinavian literature, especially that of Ibsen, to English readers. He is best known for his autobiographical work, *Father and Son,* published anonymously (1907).

gos·sip (gŏs′əp) *n.* **1. a.** Trifling, often groundless rumor, usually of a personal, sensational, or intimate nature. **b.** A friendly conversation on unimportant matters; chat. **c.** News of no great impor-

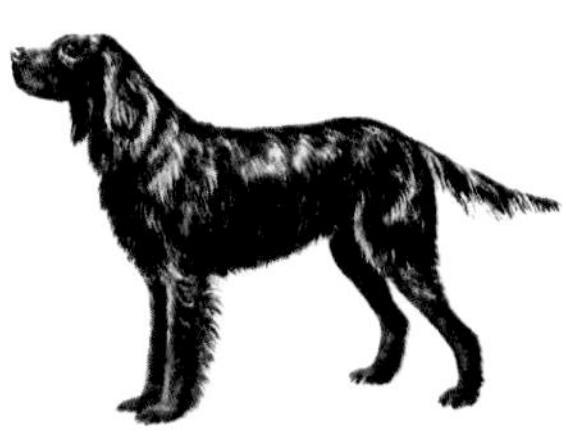

Gordon setter *This Scottish retriever was originally bred as a gun dog to collect game.*

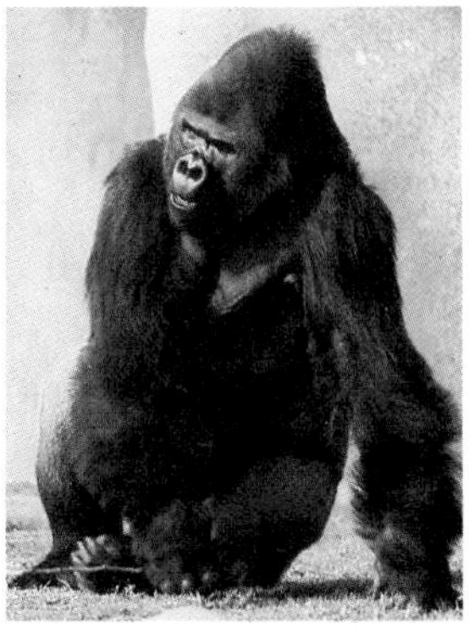

gorilla *Largely ground-dwelling, this African ape—which reaches 1.7 meters (5 feet 8 inches) in height—is, despite its fearsome appearance, a peaceful vegetarian.*

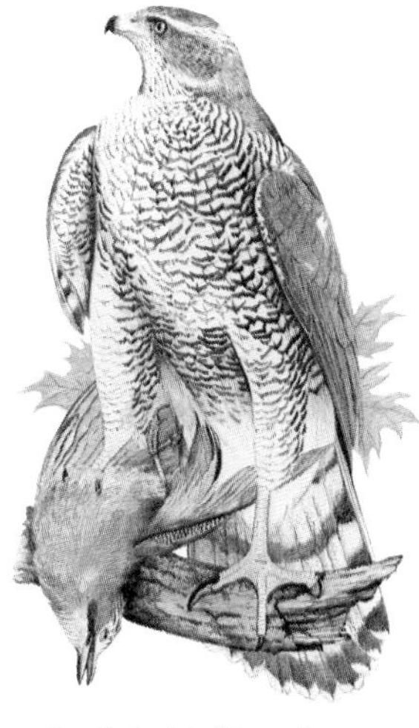

goshawk *An inhabitant of woodlands, the goshawk has short rounded wings and a long tail, enabling it to twist and turn at speed among trees to catch its prey. Because of its efficiency in catching large animals such as game birds and hares, it is often trained for falconry.*

PINNACLES OF CREATIVITY

Gothic architecture and carving marked a high point of European art

The term Gothic, now applied to four centuries of medieval European art, was originally coined during the Renaissance. The style reflected the intense religious formalism of the Middle Ages and was an attempt to express spiritual and mystical values while maintaining vitality and lightness.

The Gothic style was expressed predominantly architecturally, in cathedrals. Characteristic traits include stone tracery and ribs on walls and ceilings that serve to accentuate soaring pillars and high, pointed arches. The use of flying buttresses, which took from the walls and pillars much of the weight of the roof, enabled architects to lighten wall structure and incorporate huge stained-glass windows. The effect is of lightweight masonry shot through with light and color. Exteriors often had twin towers on the façade, lavishly decorated entrances, and rows of pinnacled flying buttresses.

The Gothic style made its appearance with the building of the abbey of Saint-Denis (1140–44), now a northern suburb of Paris, and reached a high point in Chartres Cathedral at the beginning of the 13th century. The style spread to Germany where Cologne Cathedral is a classic of Gothic style. In Britain an early example is Canterbury Cathedral, where, after a fire, the choir was rebuilt (1174–85) in a style inspired by the French Gothic cathedrals. English Gothic differed from the continental style in aiming for length rather than height. Because of this the building methods were different. French-style flying buttresses were not used. Later Gothic styles in Britain are termed Decorated (13th and 14th centuries) and Perpendicular (late 14th to 16th centuries). A unique feature of English Gothic architecture is fan vaulting. It was first used in the 14th century at Gloucester Cathedral.

The Gothic style also involved the development of sculpture. During the building of the abbey, Saint-Denis was a European center for metalworkers and stone sculptors, and their styles and techniques became international. Their hallmark was startling realism: portraits are lifelike, form is hinted at with exquisitely rendered draperies, and foliage is accurately recorded.

Stained glass and tapestry were also important art forms, as was painting, mainly in illuminated manuscripts, panels, and Italian frescoes. Gothic art culminated in the 1399 altarpiece by Melchior Broederlam at Dijon Cathedral and the manuscript prayer book, the *Très Riches Heures,* illuminated for the Duc de Berry in about 1411–16 by the Limbourg brothers. By then the Renaissance had begun in Italy.

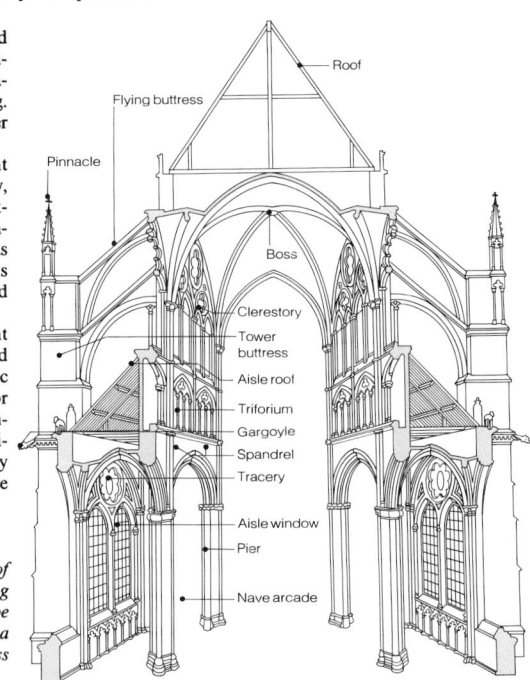

BUILT TO AMAZE *The Gothic cathedral was a web of stonework. Flying buttresses outside the building strengthened the structure, allowing the walls to be pierced by many windows and to soar past triforia and clerestories to high, pointed arches and cross vaulting delicately outlined by ribbed masonry.*

LIGHT AND SHADE *The high, vaulted nave of Amiens Cathedral, begun in 1220, shows a typical Gothic forest of pillars and interplay of light and shade.*

NOVEL REALISM *A 12th-century illumination for the Bible of Bury St. Edmunds shows Moses, Aaron, and the Numbering of the People with a novel realism.*

STONE MASTERPIECES *The faces and drapery in the 13th-century carved stone figures on Chartres Cathedral are masterpieces of Gothic sculpture.*

tance, as in a letter or article, written in a light style. **2.** A person who habitually talks about other people and their private affairs, especially in a disparaging way. **3.** *Archaic.* A close woman friend or companion. **4.** *Archaic.* A godparent.
~*intr.v.* **gossiped, -siping, -sips.** To engage in or spread gossip. —See Synonyms at **speak.** [Middle English *godsib,* godparent, godchild, close friend, Old English *godsibb* : *god,* GOD + *sibb,* kinsman.] —**gos·sip·er** *n.* —**gos·sip·y** *adj.*

gossip column *n.* A newspaper column that gives news of the private lives of famous people.

gos·sip·mong·er (gŏs′ĭp-mŭng′gər, -mŏng′gər) *n.* A person who spreads gossip.

gos·soon (gŏ-sōon′) *n. Irish.* A boy; especially, a servant boy. [French *garçon,* GARÇON.]

got. Past tense and past participle of **get.**

Gö·te·borg (yœ′tə-bôr′yə). Also **Goth·en·burg** (gŏth′ən-bûrg′, gŏt′n-). Chief port and second-largest city in Sweden, at the mouth of the Göta River on the southwest coast of the country and connected to Stockholm by the Göta Canal. The city has major oil refineries.

Goth (gŏth) *n.* **1.** A member of the Germanic people that originally occupied a region between the Baltic and the Black Sea, and that invaded the Roman Empire in the early centuries of the Christian era. See **Ostrogoth, Visigoth. 2.** An uncivilized or barbaric person. [Middle English *Gothes,* Goths, from Late Latin *Gothī* (singular *Gothus*), from Gothic *Gutans*† (unattested), tribal name.]
Goth. Gothic.
Goth·a (gō'tä). Town in southwest East Germany. It was once the residence of the dukes of Saxe-Coburg-Gotha. The *Almanach de Gotha,* published here (1761-1944), was an annual record of Europe's royal and aristocratic houses.
Goth·am¹ (gŏth'əm). Village of southern Nottinghamshire in England whose early inhabitants, the Wise Men of Gotham, are reputed by legend to have feigned stupidity in order to discourage King John from establishing a residence here.
Gotham². New York City. Used as a nickname. —**Goth·am·ite** *n.*
Gothenburg. See **Göteborg.**
Goth·ic (gŏth'ĭk) *adj. Abbr.* **Goth. 1. a.** Of or pertaining to the Goths or their language. **b.** Germanic; Teutonic. **2.** Of or pertaining to the Middle Ages; medieval. **3. a.** Of, pertaining to, or designating an architectural style prevalent in western Europe from the 12th to the 16th century, and characterized by pointed arches, rib vaulting, and flying buttresses. **b.** Of or pertaining to painting, sculpture, or other art forms prevalent in northern Europe from the 12th to the 16th century. **c.** Of or relating to an architectural style derived from medieval Gothic. **4.** *Sometimes* **gothic.** Of, pertaining to, or reminiscent of a literary style of fiction prevalent in the late 18th and early 19th centuries that emphasized the grotesque, mysterious, and desolate: *a Gothic novel.* **5.** *Sometimes* **gothic.** Barbarous; uncivilized; primitive; crude.
—*n. Abbr.* **Goth. 1.** The extinct East Germanic language of the Goths. **2.** Gothic art or architecture. **3.** *Often* **gothic.** *Printing.* **a.** A typeface, **black letter** *(see).* **b.** A typeface, **sans serif** *(see).* —**Goth·i·cal·ly** *adv.*
Gothic arch *n. Architecture.* A pointed arch, especially one with a jointed apex.
Goth·i·cism (gŏth'ĭ-sĭz'əm) *n.* **1.** Use of, imitation of, or an instance of Gothic style, as in architecture, art, or literature. **2.** A barbarous or crude manner or style.
Goth·i·cize (gŏth'ĭ-sīz') *tr.v.* **-cized, -cizing, -cizes.** To make Gothic.
Got·land or **Goth·land** or **Gott·land** (gŏt'lənd). The largest Swedish island, in the Baltic Sea to the east of the mainland. By tradition it is the original homeland of the Goths.
GO TO *n. Computer Science.* An instruction in programming language for the computer to leave the current sequence of instructions for another sequence at another point in the program.
got·ten. Past participle of **get.**
Göt·ter·däm·mer·ung (gərt'ər-dĕm'ə-rŭng') *n.* **1.** *Germanic Mythology.* The process of destruction of the ancient gods by the forces of evil. Also called "Twilight of the Gods." **2.** Any failure or slow destruction of some heroic person, magnificent enterprise, or the like.
Göt·ting·en (gœt'ĭng-ən). City in Lower Saxony in eastern West Germany, on the Leine Canal. It is famous for its university (founded 1734) and its influential Society of Sciences.
gouache (gwŏsh, gōō-äsh') *n.* **1.** A method of painting using opaque water colors mixed with a preparation of gum. **2.** An opaque water pigment prepared in such a way. **3.** A painting executed with such pigments. [French, from Italian *guazzo,* "puddle," from Latin *aquātiō,* watering, from *aquārī,* to bring water to, from *aqua,* water.]
Gou·da¹ (gou'də, gōō'-). Town in the South Holland province of the Netherlands, at the confluence of the Gouwe and Ijssel rivers. It has the largest market square in Holland.
Gouda² *n.* A mild, close-textured, pale yellow cheese made from whole or partially skimmed milk and often covered with a protective coating of wax. [Originally made in GOUDA.]
gouge (gouj) *n.* **1. a.** A chisel with a rounded, troughlike blade. **b.** A surgical instrument resembling this, used to cut and remove bone. **2.** A scooping or digging action, as with a gouge. **3.** A groove, hole, or indentation scooped with or as if with a gouge. **4.** *Informal.* **a.** An act of extortion or swindling. **b.** A large amount of money extorted. **5.** *Geology.* A deposit of clay, rock particles, or the like, in a fault or vein.
—*tr.v.* **gouged, gouging, gouges. 1.** To cut or scoop out with or as if with a gouge: *gouge a pattern in the sand.* **2.** To force out: *gouged out his eyes.* **3.** *Informal.* **a.** To extort from. **b.** To swindle. [Middle English *gouge,* from Old French, from Late Latin *gubia,* perhaps from Celtic, akin to Old Irish *gulban*†.] —**goug·er** *n.*
gou·lash (gōō'läsh, -lăsh) *n.* A stew of beef, lamb, or veal and vegetables, highly seasoned with paprika. Also called "Hungarian goulash." [Hungarian *gulyás (hus),* "herdsman('s meat)," from *gulya,* herd.]
Goul·burn (gōl'bərn). City in New South Wales in southeast Australia. Founded in 1833, it has two cathedrals and is a marketing center that serves a prosperous agricultural region.
Gould (gōōld), **Glenn** (1932-82). Canadian pianist. He first played with the Toronto Symphony Orchestra when he was 14 and was acclaimed for his performances of Bach, Beethoven, and Brahms.
goun·dou (gōōn'dōō') *n. Medicine.* A condition occurring in the tropics as a complication of yaws, in which bony swellings occur on either side of the nose. [From a West African name.]

Gou·nod (gōō-nō'), **Charles François** (1818-93). French composer. He wrote symphonies, oratorios, and songs but is mainly remembered for the operas *Faust* (1859) and *Romeo and Juliet* (1867) and for his church music.
gou·ra·mi (gōō-rä'mē, gōōr'ə-mē) *n., pl.* **-mis** or collectively **gourami.** Any of various freshwater fishes of the family Anabantidae, of southeastern Asia, many species of which are brightly colored and popular in home aquariums. *Osphronemus goramy* has been widely introduced and bred as a food fish. [Malay *gurāmi.*]
gourd (gôrd, gōrd, gōōrd) *n.* **1.** Any of several vines of the family Cucurbitaceae, such as the **bottle gourd** *(see),* related to the pumpkin, squash, and cucumber, and bearing fruits with a hard rind. **2.** The fruit of such a vine, such as a calabash, often of irregular and unusual shape. **3.** The dried and hollowed-out shell of one of these fruits, used as a drinking vessel or utensil. **4.** A small gourd-shaped bottle. [Middle English *gourde,* from Old French, from Latin *cucurbita,* probably of Mediterranean origin.]
gourde (gōōrd) *n. Abbr.* **g., G., gde. 1.** The basic monetary unit of Haiti, equal to 100 centimes. See feature at **currency. 2.** A coin worth one gourde. [French, feminine of *gourd,* heavy, from Latin *gurdus*†, heavy, dull, stupid.]
gour·mand, gor·mand (gōōr'mənd; *French* gōōr-mäN') *n.* A person who delights in eating well and heartily. [Middle English *gourmaunt,* glutton, from Old French *gourmand, gourmant*†.]
gour·mand·ise (gōōr'mən-dēz') *n.* Also *rare* **gor·mand·ize** (gôr'-). A taste and relish for good food. [Middle English, from Old French *gourmandise,* from GOURMAND.]
gour·met (gōōr-mā'; *French* gōōr-mĕ') *n.* A connoisseur of fine food and drink. Also used adjectively: *gourmet foods.* [French (influenced in sense by *gourmand*), from Old French *gromet, gourmet*†, wine-taster.]
gout (gout) *n.* **1.** *Pathology.* A disturbance of uric-acid metabolism, occurring predominantly in males, in which deposits of urates accumulate in the joints, especially those of the big toe, and cause arthritic attacks that may become chronic and produce deformity. **2.** A large blob or clot: *"and makes it bleed great gouts of blood"* (Oscar Wilde). [Middle English *goute,* from Old French, "drop" (from the belief that gout was caused by a flowing down of morbid humors), from Latin *gutta*†, drop.]
gout·weed (gout'wēd') *n.* A plant, **ground elder** *(see).*
gout·y (gou'tē) *adj.* **-ier, -iest. 1.** Of, relating to, or resembling gout. **2.** Suffering from or showing the effects of gout. —**gout·i·ly** *adv.* —**gout·i·ness** *n.*
gov. **1.** government. **2.** governor.
Gov. Governor.
gov·ern (gŭv'ərn) *v.* **-erned, -erning, -erns.** —*tr.* **1.** To control the actions or behavior of; guide; direct. **2.** To make and administer public policy for (a political unit); exercise sovereign authority in. **3.** To control the speed or magnitude of; regulate: *a valve governing fuel intake.* **4.** To keep under control; restrain. **5.** To decide; determine: *Chance usually governs the outcome of the game.* **6.** *Grammar.* **a.** To require (a noun or verb) to be in a particular case or mood. **b.** To require the use of (a specified case or mood). —*intr.* **1.** To exercise political authority. **2.** To have or exercise a predominating influence. [Middle English *governen,* from Old French *governer,* from Latin *gubernāre,* to direct, steer, from Greek *kubernan*†.] —**gov·ern·a·ble** *adj.*
gov·ern·ance (gŭv'ər-nəns) *n.* **1.** The act, process, or power of governing; government; authority. **2.** The system of government. **3.** The state of being governed.
gov·ern·ess (gŭv'ər-nĭs) *n.* **1.** A woman employed to educate and train the children of a private household. **2.** *Rare.* A woman who governs.
governing body *n.* A group of people responsible for the administration of a school, college, or similar institution.
gov·ern·ment (gŭv'ərn-mənt) *n. Abbr.* **gov., govt. 1.** The act or process of governing; especially, the administration of public policy in a political unit; political jurisdiction. **2.** The office, function, or authority of one who governs or a governing body. **3.** A system or policy by which a political unit is governed. **4.** Political science. **5.** A governing body or organization. **6.** An area within a single rule; a political unit. **7.** Influence; regulation; determination. **8.** *Grammar.* The affecting of a word's case or mood by another word. —**gov·ern·ment·al** *adj.* —**gov·ern·men·tal·ly** *adv.*
Government Issue *n. Abbr.* **GI, G.I.** Anything issued by the government or a government agency, such as U.S. Army equipment. —**government issue** *adj.*
gov·er·nor (gŭv'ər-nər, gŭv'nər) *n. Abbr.* **gov., Gov. 1.** A person who governs, especially: **a.** An official appointed to govern a colony or territory. **b.** The chief executive of a state in the United States. **2.** The manager or administrative head of an organization, business, or institution. **3.** A military commandant. **4.** *British Informal.* **a.** Used as a form of address, equivalent to *sir,* to a stranger, respected acquaintance, employer, or superior. **b.** One's father. **5.** *Machinery.* A feedback device on a machine or engine used to provide automatic control, as of speed, pressure, or temperature. [Middle English *governour,* from Old French *governeor,* from Latin *gubernātor,* from *gubernāre,* GOVERN.]
governor general *n., pl.* **governors general.** Also *Chiefly British* **gov·er·nor-gen·er·al** (gŭv'ər-nər-jĕn'ər-əl, -jĕn'rəl) *pl.* **governors-general** or **governor-generals.** *Abbr.* **Gov. Gen. 1.** *Often* **Governor General.** The highest-ranking representative of the Crown in some Commonwealth countries or formerly in a British

gourd *Gourds are fruit that are related to cucumbers and pumpkins. The dried shells of some species are used as containers for liquids. These are ornamental varieties.*

colony. **2.** A governor who has other, subordinate governors under his jurisdiction. **—gov·er·nor·gen·er·al·ship** *n.*

gov·er·nor·ship (gŭv′ər-nər-shĭp′) *n.* The office, term, or jurisdiction of a governor.

Gov. Gen. governor general.

govt. government.

gow·an (gou′ən) *n. Scottish.* A yellow or white wildflower, especially the daisy. [Dialect *gollan,* from Middle English, probably from Scandinavian; akin to Old Norse *gullinn,* golden.]

gowk (gôk) *n. British Regional.* A stupid person; fool. [Middle English *gowke,* from Old Norse *gaukr,* a cuckoo, from Germanic *gaukaz* (imitative).]

gown (goun) *n.* **1.** Any of various long, loose, flowing garments, such as a dressing gown or surgeon's protective coat. **2.** A long, usually formal, woman's dress. **3.** A distinctive outer robe worn on ceremonial occasions, as by scholars or clergymen. **4.** The academic community of a university town, as distinguished from the townspeople: *town and gown.* Compare **town.**
 ~*tr.v.* **gowned, gowning, gowns.** To dress in or invest with a gown. [Middle English *goune,* from Old French, from Late Latin *gunnā,* robe, fur.]

gowns·man (gounz′mən) *n., pl.* **-men** (-mĭn). One who wears a distinctive gown as a mark of profession or office.

Gow·on (gou′ən), **Yakubu** (1934–). Nigerian army officer and politician. Trained at the Sandhurst Military Academy in England, he took a commission in the Nigerian army (1954), becoming battalion commander (1966). After two coups (1966) he was appointed army commander in chief and head of the new military government. He led the federal forces in their successful war against the secessionist Biafran government (1967–70). He was deposed (1975).

Goy·a y Lu·ci·en·tes (goi′ə ē loō-sē-en′tēs), **Francisco José de** (1746–1828). Spanish painter and etcher. His best portraits, including *The Duchess of Alba,* were done mostly in the 1790's, his so-called "silver period." The war against France inspired some of his most powerful work, including 65 etchings, *The Disasters of the War* (1810–14).

G.P. **1.** general practitioner. **2.** Grand Prix.

G-par·i·ty (jē′păr′ə-tē) *n. Physics.* A quantum property of elementary particles that have zero strangeness and baryon number, conserved in strong interactions.

g.p.m. gallons per minute.

GPO **1.** general post office. **2.** Government Printing Office.

g.p.s. gallons per second.

GPU, G.P.U. Government Political Administration (Russian *Gosudarstvennoye Politicheskoye Upravlenie*): a former administrative branch of the Soviet government functioning as a policing and security organization in succession to the **Cheka** *(see)* and corresponding in broad outline to the later **KGB** *(see).*

gr. **1.** grade. **2.** gram. **3.** gross. **4.** group.

Gr. Greece; Greek.

Graaf·i·an follicle (grä′fē-ən) *n. Anatomy.* Any of the follicles in the mammalian ovary, containing a maturing ovum. [After Regnier de *Graaf* (1641–73), Dutch anatomist.]

grab¹ (grăb) *v.* **grabbed, grabbing, grabs.** —*tr.* **1.** To take or grasp suddenly; snatch; seize. **2.** To capture or restrain; arrest. **3.** To obtain or appropriate unscrupulously or forcibly. **4.** To consume hurriedly: *He grabbed a bite to eat.* **5.** *Slang.* To make an impression on; affect, especially in a positive or favorable way. —*intr.* To make a snatch: *He grabbed for the gun.*
 ~*n.* **1.** The act of grabbing; a sudden snatch. **2.** Anything grabbed. **3.** A mechanical device for gripping, for example, the jaws of an earth-moving machine. **—up for grabs.** *Informal.* Available for anyone to take. [Middle Dutch and Middle Low German *grabben.*] **—grab·ber** *n.*

grab² *n.* An Oriental coastal vessel with two or three masts. [Arabic *ghurāb,* raven, swift galley.]

grab bag *n.* **1.** A container filled with articles, such as party gifts, to be drawn at random. **2.** Any miscellaneous collection of often valuable items.

grab·ble (grăb′əl) *intr.v.* **-bled, -bling, -bles.** **1.** To feel around with the hands; grope. **2.** To sprawl on the ground on all fours. [Dutch *grabbelen,* frequentative of Middle Dutch *grabben,* GRAB (to seize).]

grab·by (grăb′ē) *adj.* **-bier, -biest.** Inclined to grab; greedy. **—grab·bi·ness** *n.*

gra·ben (grä′bən) *n.* A usually elongated depression of the earth's crust between two parallel faults. [German *Graben,* trench, from Old High German *grabo,* from *graban,* to dig.]

grab rope *n.* A rope for steadying oneself, as on a gangplank or an open deck.

Grac·chus (grăk′əs), **Tiberius Sempronius** (*c.* 163–133 B.C.) and **Caius Sempronius** (*c.* 153–121 B.C.), known as "the Gracchi." Roman statesmen. Tiberius was elected tribune of the people in 133. He passed a law to redistribute land but was killed in the same year during a riot. In 123 Caius was elected tribune, and when he proposed granting Roman citizenship to Latins, he too was killed in riots.

grace (grās) *n.* **1.** Seemingly effortless beauty or charm of movement, form, or proportion. **2.** A characteristic, quality, or accomplishment pleasing for its charm or refinement: *social graces.* **3.** Skill at avoiding the inept or clumsy course; a sense of fitness or propriety. **4. a.** A disposition to be generous or helpful; goodwill. **b.** Mercy; clemency. **5. a.** A favor rendered by one who need not do so. **b.** Kindly feeling; indulgence. **6.** Temporary immunity from penalties, granted after a deadline has been passed: *a period of grace before a new law is enforced.* **7.** *Theology.* **a.** Divine love and protection bestowed freely upon mankind. **b.** The state of being protected or sanctified by the favor of God. **c.** An excellence or power granted by God; an unmerited gift from God. **8.** A short prayer of blessing or thanksgiving said before or after a meal. **9.** *Usually* **Grace.** A title of or form of address for a duke, duchess, or archbishop. Used with *His, Her,* or *Your.* **10.** *Music.* A musical embellishment, such as an appoggiatura. **—fall from grace.** To lose the esteem in which one was formerly held, usually as a result of some misconduct. **—in someone's good** (or **bad**) **graces.** In (or out of) favor with; well (or unfavorably) regarded by. **—with (a) good** (or **bad**) **grace.** In a willing (or grudging) manner.
 ~*tr.v.* **graced, gracing, graces.** **1.** To honor or favor. **2.** To give beauty, elegance, or charm to. **3.** *Music.* To embellish with grace notes. [Middle English, from Old French, from Latin *grātia,* pleasure, favor, thanks, from *grātus,* favorable, pleasing.]

Grace, Princess. See Grace **Kelly.**

grace cup *n.* **1.** A cup used at the end of a meal, usually after grace, for the final toast. **2.** The final toast.

grace·ful (grās′fəl) *adj.* Showing grace of movement, style, form, or proportion. **—grace·ful·ly** *adv.* **—grace·ful·ness** *n.*
 Usage: *Graceful* and *gracious* are occasionally confused. *Graceful* refers to movement, style, or form: *a graceful pose/gesture.* *Gracious* refers to a state of mind, or the behavior characteristic of a state of mind, in which kindness, compassion, or warm courtesy feature.

grace·less (grās′lĭs) *adj.* **1.** Lacking grace; clumsy. **2.** Having no sense of propriety or decency. **—grace·less·ly** *adv.* **—grace·less·ness** *n.*

grace note *n. Music.* **1.** A musical note without melodic, harmonic, or time value, especially an appoggiatura, added as an embellishment. **2.** Any decorative flourish.

Grac·es (grā′sĭz) *pl.n. Greek Mythology.* Three sister goddesses, Aglaia, Euphrosyne, and Thalia, who dispense charm and beauty. Also called the "Three Graces."

grac·ile (grăs′il) *adj.* **1.** Gracefully slender. **2.** *Rare.* Graceful. [Latin *gracilis†,* slim, slender.] **—gra·cil·i·ty** (grə-sĭl′ə-tē) *n.*

gra·ci·o·so (grä′shē-ō′sō; *Spanish* grä-thyō′sō) *n., pl.* **-sos.** **1.** A clown or buffoon in Spanish comedies. **2.** *Obsolete.* A court favorite. [Spanish, "amusing (person)," clown, from Latin *grātiōsus,* GRACIOUS.]

gra·cious (grā′shəs) *adj.* **1.** Characterized by kindness and warm courtesy. **2.** Merciful; compassionate. **3.** Condescendingly courteous; indulgent. **4.** Leisurely; elegant: *a gracious dinner.* **5.** *Obsolete.* Fortunate; prosperous. —See Usage note at **graceful.**
 ~*interj.* Used to express surprise or wonder. [Middle English, from Old French, from Latin *grātiōsus,* favorable, pleasing, from Latin *grātia,* GRACE.] **—gra·cious·ly** *adv.* **—gra·cious·ness** *n.*

grack·le (grăk′əl) *n.* **1.** Any of several New World blackbirds of the family Icteridae, and especially of the genera *Quiscalus* or *Cassidix,* having iridescent blackish plumage. Also called "crow blackbird." **2.** Any of several Asian mynas of the genus *Gracula,* such as the Indian grackle, *G. religiosa.* [New Latin *Gracula,* from Latin *grāculus,* jackdaw.]

grad (grăd) *n. Informal.* A graduate of a school or college.

grad. **1.** grade. **2.** gradient. **3.** graduate; graduated.

grad·a·ble (grăd′ə-bəl) *adj.* **1.** Capable of or subject to being graded. **2.** *Linguistics.* Of, pertaining to, or designating a word such as *hot, warm,* or *cold,* which implicitly refers to a scale or standard and can be modified by *very* or *much,* for example, to indicate degree or extent.

gra·date (grā′dāt′) *v.* **-dated, -dating, -dates.** —*intr.* To pass imperceptibly from one degree, shade, or tone to another. —*tr.* **1.** To cause to pass imperceptibly from one degree, shade, or tone to another. **2.** To arrange according to or in grades. [Back-formation from GRADATION.]

gra·da·tion (grā-dā′shən) *n.* **1.** A series of gradual, successive stages; a systematic progression. **2.** Any of the degrees or stages in such a progression. **3.** Advancement by successive stages, tones, or shades, as from one color to another. **4.** The act of gradating or arranging in grades. **5.** *Geology.* The process of leveling land by filling in or wearing away existing features. **6.** *Linguistics.* An **ablaut** *(see).* [Latin *gradātiō* (stem *gradātiōn-*), from *gradus,* step, GRADE.] **—gra·da·tion·al** *adj.* **—gra·da·tion·al·ly** *adv.*

grade (grād) *n. Abbr.* **gr., grad.** **1.** A stage or degree in a process. **2.** A position in a scale of size or quality, as of eggs or meat. **3.** A group of persons or things all falling within the same limits; a class. **4.** A mark indicating a student's level of accomplishment. **5.** A class at an elementary school, or the pupils in it. **6.** A military, naval, or civil-service rank. **7.** A domestic animal produced by crossbreeding one of purebred stock with one of ordinary stock. **8.** A gradient (slope or degree of slope). **9.** *Abbr.* **grad.** A unit of angle equal to one hundredth of a right angle. It is indicated by a superscript g: $1^g = 0.9°$. **—at grade.** **1.** On the same level. **2.** At the same degree of inclination. **—make the grade.** *Informal.* **1.** To succeed; reach a goal. **2.** To meet a standard.
 ~*v.* **graded, grading, grades.** —*tr.* **1.** To arrange in steps or degrees; rank; sort. **2.** To arrange in a series or according to a scale. **3. a.** To determine the quality of (academic work, for example); evaluate. **b.** To give a grade to (a student, for example). **4.** To level or smooth to a desired or horizontal gradient. **5.** To gradate. **6.** To improve the quality of (livestock) by crossbreeding with purebred

stock. Often used with *up*. **7.** To effect a gradual change of shading in (colors or a colored area). *—intr.* To change or progress gradually. [French, from Latin *gradus*, step.]

–grade *suffix.* Indicates progression or movement; for example, **plantigrade, retrograde.** [French, from Latin *-gradus*, stepping, going, from *gradī*, to step, go.]

grade crossing *n.* An intersection of roads, railroad tracks, or a road and a railroad track at the same level. Also *British* "level crossing."

grade point or **grade index** *n.* A point assigned to a course credit, as in a university, that corresponds to the letter grade made in a course.

grade point average or **grade point index** *n.* The average grade earned, as by a student, figured by dividing the grade points earned by the number of credits attempted.

grad·er (grā′dər) *n.* **1.** One that grades. **2.** A machine that smooths a surface to the desired gradient and flatness, especially in road building. **3.** A student in a grade school: *a third grader.*

grade school *n.* An **elementary school** (see).

gra·di·ent (grā′dē-ənt) *n. Abbr.* **grad. 1.** An ascending or descending part of a road, railway, or the like; an incline. **2.** The degree of slope measured by the vertical change in height per horizontal distance traveled. **3.** *Physics.* The maximum rate at which a variable physical quantity changes in value per unit change in position. **4.** *Mathematics.* **a.** The slope of the tangent to a curve at a given point. **b.** A vector having coordinate components that are the partial derivatives of a function with respect to its variables. The gradient of a function f is written grad f. or ∇f. *—adj.* Of a consistent slope. [Perhaps from GRADE.]

gra·din (grā′dĭn; *French* grȧ-dăN′) *n.* Also **gra·dine** (grə-dēn′). **1.** Any of a series of steps or tiered seats, as in an amphitheater. **2.** A shelf next to an altar, for holding candles or ornaments. [French, from Italian *gradino*, diminutive of *grado*, step, GRADE.]

grad·u·al (grăj′ōō-əl) *adj.* **1.** Occurring in small stages or degrees or by even, continuous change. **2.** Moderate and regular: *a gradual slope.* *—n. Roman Catholic Church.* **1.** A book containing liturgical antiphons. **2.** An antiphon sung between the Epistle and the Gospel of the Tridentine Mass. [Middle English, from Medieval Latin *graduālis*, step by step, from Latin *gradus*, step, GRADE.] **—grad·u·al·ly** *adv.* **—grad·u·al·ness** *n.*

grad·u·al·ism (grăj′ōō-ə-lĭz′əm) *n.* The belief in or policy of advancing toward a goal, especially a political goal, by gradual, often slow stages. **—grad·u·al·ist** *n.* **—grad·u·al·is·tic** *adj.*

grad·u·and (grăj′ə-wănd′) *n. Chiefly British.* A student who is on the point of receiving a degree. [Medieval Latin *graduandus*, gerundive of *graduāre*, to GRADUATE.]

grad·u·ate (grăj′ōō-āt′) *v.* **-ated, -ating, -ates.** *Abbr.* **grad.** *—intr.* **1.** To be granted an academic degree or diploma. **2.** To change gradually, or by degrees. **3.** To progress to something more advanced: *From being stage manager, she graduated to directing.* *—tr.* **1.** To arrange or divide into categories, steps, or grades. **2.** To divide into marked intervals, especially for use in measurement. **3.** To grant a diploma or degree to. *—See Usage note below.* *—n.* (grăj′ōō-ĭt). *Abbr.* **grad.** **1.** One who has received an academic degree. **2.** A graduated container, such as a beaker or flask. *—adj.* (grăj′ōō-ĭt). **1.** Possessing an academic degree or diploma. **2.** Of, pertaining to, or designating studies beyond a bachelor's degree: *graduate courses.* [Middle English *graduaten*, from Medieval Latin *graduāre*, from Latin *gradus*, degree, step, GRADE.] **—grad·u·a·tor** *n.*

Usage: A strict traditionalist would insist that *she was graduated from college* is the only correct usage. But the usage *she graduated from college* is by now entirely acceptable, and the variant without a preposition, as in *she graduated college,* is rapidly gaining ground.

graduate school *n.* A school that offers studies beyond the bachelor's degree.

graduate student *n.* A student at a graduate school, especially one matriculated in a specific department and studying for a specific degree.

grad·u·a·tion (grăj′ōō-ā′shən) *n.* **1.** The conferring or receipt of an academic degree or diploma marking completion of studies. **2.** A ceremony at which degrees or diplomas are conferred. **3. a.** A division or interval on a graduated scale. **b.** A mark indicating the boundary of such an interval. **4.** An arrangement in or division into stages, intervals, or degrees.

grad·us (grā′dəs) *n., pl.* **-duses. 1.** A dictionary of prosody used as an aid in writing Latin or Greek poetry. **2.** A manual for developing a student's ability, especially a book of musical exercises. [Short for *Gradus ad Parnassum,* "step to Parnassus," dictionary of prosody formerly used in English public schools, from Latin *gradus*, step, GRADE.]

Grae·ae, Grai·ae (grē′ē′) *pl.n. Greek Mythology.* Three female deities personifying old age, who, with only one eye and one tooth among them, guarded their sisters, the Gorgons.

Graecism. Variant of **Grecism.**

Graecize. Variant of **Grecize.**

Graeco-. Variant of **Greco-.**

Graeco-Roman. Variant of **Greco-Roman.**

Graf (gräf) *n., pl.* **Grafen** (gräf′ən) A count. Used as a title of German, Austrian, or Swedish nobility corresponding to the English earl. [German, from Old High German *grāvo*.]

graf·fi·to (grə-fē′tō) *n., pl.* **-ti** (-tē). **1.** *Archaeology.* A crude drawing or inscription scratched on stone, plaster, or some other hard surface. **2.** *Usually* **graffiti.** Any scrawling written or drawn so as to be seen by the public, as on a wall or lavatory door, and often obscene or humorous. [Italian, diminutive of *graffio*, a scratching, from *graffiare*, to scratch, perhaps from *grafio*, a pencil, stylus, from Latin *graphium*, from Greek *graphion*, from *graphein*, to write.]

graft¹ (grăft, gräft) *tr.v.* **grafted, grafting, grafts. 1.** In horticulture: **a.** To unite (a shoot or bud) with a growing plant by insertion or placing in close contact. **b.** To join (a plant or plants) by such union. **2.** *Medicine.* To transplant or implant (tissue, for example) into a bodily part to replace a damaged part or compensate for a defect. **3.** To attach or incorporate, especially in an artificial way. *—n.* **1.** In horticulture: **a.** A detached shoot or bud united or to be united with a growing plant. **b.** The union or point of union of a detached shoot or bud with a growing plant by insertion or attachment. **c.** A plant produced by such union. **2.** *Medicine.* **a.** Material, especially tissue or an organ, surgically attached to or inserted into a bodily part to replace a damaged part or compensate for a defect. **b.** The procedure of transplanting such material. **c.** The configuration or condition resulting from such a procedure. **3.** Any act or product of attaching or incorporating. [Middle English *grafte, graff*, from Old French *grafe, grefe*, pencil, shoot for grafting (from its pencillike shape), from Latin *graphium*. See **graffito**.] **—graft·er** *n.*

graft² *n.* **1.** The unscrupulous use of one's position to derive profit or advantages; extortion. **2.** Money or an advantage gained or yielded under such circumstances. *—v.* **grafted, grafting, grafts.** *—tr.* To gain by graft. *—intr.* To practice graft. [Perhaps extended use of GRAFT (insertion, hence "additional activity").] **—graft·er** *n.*

graft·age (grăf′tĭj, gräf′-) *n.* The process and principles of making a horticultural graft.

graft copolymer *n. Chemistry.* A copolymer that has main chains of one type of monomer with side chains of the other monomer.

graft hybrid *n.* A plant produced by grafting in which the tissue of the scion mingles with that of the stock. It is a type of **chimera** *(see).*

gra·ham (grā′əm) *adj.* Made from or consisting of whole-wheat flour. [After Sylvester *Graham* (1794–1851), U.S. vegetarian who urged dietary reform.]

Gra·ham (grā′əm), **Martha** (c. 1894–). U.S. ballet dancer, teacher, and choreographer. She made her debut as a dancer in 1920 in Los Angeles and in 1930 founded the Dance Repertory Theatre in New York. Her full-length works include *Appalachian Spring* (1944) and *Clytemnestra* (1958).

Graham, Thomas (1805–69). British chemist. His investigation of gases and liquids led to the formulation of Graham's law. His work on colloids and crystalloids led to his discovery of dialysis.

Graham, William Franklin, known as "Billy" (1918–). U.S. evangelist. Ordained a minister in the Southern Baptist Church in 1939, he conducted his first intensive evangelical campaign in Los Angeles. Since then his evangelical tours have taken him throughout the world.

graham cracker *n.* A slightly sweet, usually rectangular cracker, made of whole-wheat flour.

Gra·hame (grā′əm), **Kenneth** (1859–1932). English writer. He wrote two volumes of autobiography, *The Golden Age* (1895) and *Dream Days* (1898) but is best known for his children's book *The Wind in the Willows* (1908).

Gra·ham Land (grā′əm). A part of the Antarctic Peninsula in Antarctica, bordering the Weddell Sea. Consisting chiefly of icebound rock, it was formerly a dependency of the Falkland Islands and now forms part of the British Antarctic Territory.

Graham's law *n. Physics.* The principle that the rates of diffusion of gases are inversely proportional to the square roots of their densities. Also called "Graham's law of diffusion." [Formulated by Thomas GRAHAM.]

Gra·hams·town (grā′əmz-toun′). Town and naval base in Cape Province in southern South Africa. Founded in 1820, it has two cathedrals and is the site of Rhodes University (established 1904).

Graiae. Variant of **Graeae.**

grail (grāl) *n. Often* **Grail. 1.** The cup or chalice in medieval legend used by Christ at the Last Supper and subsequently the object of many chivalrous quests. Also called "Holy Grail." **2.** The object of a prolonged endeavor. [Middle English *graal*, from Old French, from Medieval Latin *gradālis†*, dish.]

grain (grān) *n.* **1.** A small, hard seed or fruit, especially that produced by a cereal grass such as wheat, barley, rice, or oats. **2.** The seeds of such plants collectively, especially after having been harvested. **3.** Cereal grasses collectively: *a field of grain.* **4.** A relatively small discrete particle or crystalline mass: *a grain of sand.* **5.** *Aerospace.* A mass of solid propellant formed from a number of smaller pieces. **6.** The very smallest amount; a tiny quantity: *a grain of truth.* **7. a.** A unit of weight, one seven-thousandth of a pound in the avoirdupois, Troy, and apothecaries' systems. It is equal to 0.0648 gram. **b.** A metric unit of weight equal to 50 milligrams. It is used in weighing certain precious stones. In this sense, also called "metric grain." **8. a.** The arrangement, direction, or pattern of the fibrous tissue in wood. **b.** The arrangement, direction, or pattern of muscle fibers or meat. **9. a.** The outer side of a hide or piece of leather from which the hair or fur is removed. **b.** The pattern or markings on this side of leather. **10.** The pattern or markings on the skin. **11.** The pattern produced, as in stone, by the arrangement of particulate constituents. **12.** The relative size of the particles composing a substance or pattern: *a coarse grain.* **13.** Any painted, stamped, or printed design that imitates the pattern found in wood, leather, or stone. **14.** The direction or texture of fibers in a woven fabric. **15.** *Chemistry.* **a.** A state of fine crystallization. **b.** A small crystalline region in a polycrystalline solid. **16.** Temperament; nature; character. **17.** Any of the particles in a photographic emulsion that determine by their size the degree of the image's resolution. **18.** *Archaic.* Color; tint; hue. **19. a.** Cochineal or kermes. **b.** Red dye made from cochineal or kermes. **c.** Any fast dye. Not in current technical usage. —**against the grain.** In contradiction to one's natural disposition or character.

~*v.* **grained, graining, grains.** —*tr.* **1.** To form or cause to form into grains; granulate; crystallize. **2.** To paint, stamp, or print with a design imitating the grain of wood, leather, or stone. **3.** To give a granular or rough texture to. **4.** To remove the hair or fur from (hides) in preparation for tanning. —*intr.* To form into or become grains. [Middle English, from Old French, from Latin *grānum,* seed.] —**grain·er** *n.*

grain alcohol *n.* Alcohol *(see).*

grain elevator *n.* **1.** A building equipped with mechanical lifting devices, used for storing grain. **2.** The machine used for lifting grain, typically having an endless belt carrying a number of scoops.

grain·ing (grā′ĭng) *n.* **1.** The pattern of the grain in wood or leather. **2.** The application of an artificial grain or design to a surface, by painting, stamping, or printing. **3.** A fabric or surface patterned in this way. **4.** An artificially produced grainlike pattern.

grains (grānz) *n.* *Usually used with a singular verb.* An iron harpoon with two or more barbed prongs used for spearing fish. [Middle English *grein,* fork, from Old Norse *grein†,* branch, twig.]

grains of paradise *pl.n.* **1.** The pungent, aromatic seeds of either of two tropical African plants, *Aframomum melegueta* or *A. granum-paradisi,* used medicinally. **2.** The seeds of **cardamom** *(see).*

grain·y (grā′nē) *adj.* **-ier, -iest. 1.** Made of, full of, or resembling grain; granular. **2.** Resembling the grain of wood. **3.** In photography, speckled or poor in definition, as a result of large grains in the emulsion. Said of a photograph or photographic image.

gram¹, gramme (grăm) *n. Abbr.* **g, gm., gr.** A metric unit of mass and weight, equal to one thousandth (10^{-3}) of a kilogram (0.002205 pound). [French *gramme,* from Late Latin *gramma,* a small unit, from Greek, small weight, letter of the alphabet.]

gram² *n.* **1.** Any of several plants, such as a bean, *Phaseolus mungo,* or the chickpea, bearing seeds widely used as food in tropical Asia. **2.** The seeds of such a plant. [Portuguese *grão,* from Latin *grānum,* seed, GRAIN.]

–gram¹ *suffix.* Indicates something written or drawn; for example, **diagram, telegram.** [Latin *-gramma,* something written, from Greek, *-gramma, -grammos,* respectively from *gramma,* letter and *grammē,* line.]

–gram² *suffix.* Indicates a gram, as used in the metric system; for example, **kilogram.** [From GRAM (unit).]

gram. grammar; grammatical.

gra·ma (grä′mə) *n.* Any of various grasses of the genus *Bouteloua,* of western North America and South America, forming dense tufts or mats, and often used as pasturage. Also called "grama grass." [Spanish *grama,* from Latin *grāmina,* plural of *grāmen,* grass.]

gram·a·rye (grăm′ə-rē) *n. Archaic.* Occult learning; magic; necromancy. [Middle English *gramarie,* from Old French *gramaire,* GRAMMAR.]

gram-at·om (grăm′ăt′əm) *n.* The mass in grams of an element numerically equal to the atomic weight.

gram calorie *n.* A calorie *(see).*

gra·mer·cy (grə-mûr′sē, grăm′ər-sē) *interj. Archaic.* Used to express surprise or gratitude. [Middle English *gramercye, grand mercy,* great thanks, from Old French *grand merci : grand,* GRAND + *merci,* thanks, MERCY.]

gram flour *n.* Flour made from gram seeds.

gram·i·cid·in (grăm′ə-sīd′n) *n.* An antibiotic produced by a bacterium, *Bacillus brevis,* and used against most Gram-positive pathogenic bacteria. [GRAM-(POSITIVE) + -CID(E) + -IN.]

gram·i·ne·ous (grə-mĭn′ē-əs) *adj.* **1.** Of, pertaining to, or characteristic of grasses. **2.** Of or belonging to the family Gramineae, which includes the grasses. [Latin *grāmineus,* grassy, from *grāmen* (stem *grāmin-*), grass.]

gram·i·niv·or·ous (grăm′ə-nĭv′ər-əs) *adj.* Feeding on grasses, grain, or seeds. [Latin *grāmen* (stem *grāmin-*), grass + -VOROUS.]

gram·mar (grăm′ər) *n. Abbr.* **gram. 1.** The study of language as a systematically composed body of words that exhibit discernible regularity of structure (morphology), and their arrangement into sentences (syntax), sometimes including such aspects of language as the pronunciation of words (phonology), the meanings of words (semantics), and the history of words (etymology). **2. a.** The phenomena with which this study deals, as exhibited by a specific language at a specific time. **b.** The system of rules implicit in a language, viewed as a mechanism for generating all sentences possible in that language. **c.** A systematic description or listing of such rules. **3. a.** A normative or prescriptive system of rules setting forth the current standard of usage for teaching or reference purposes. **b.** A book containing such rules: *old-fashioned school grammars.* **4.** Writing or speech judged with regard to the rules or practice of grammar, especially syntax: *bad grammar.* **5. a.** The basic principles of any area of knowledge: *the grammar of music.* **b.** A book dealing with such principles. [Middle English, from Norman

French *gramere,* from Old French *gramaire,* from Latin *grammatica,* from Greek *grammatikē (tekhnē),* "(art) of the letters," from *grammatikos,* pertaining to letters, from *gramma,* letter.]

gram·mar·i·an (grə-mâr′ē-ən) *n.* A specialist in grammar.

grammar school *n.* **1.** An **elementary school** *(see).* **2.** *British.* A secondary preparatory school. **3.** A school stressing the study of classical languages.

gram·mat·i·cal (grə-măt′ĭ-kəl) *adj. Abbr.* **gram. 1.** Of or relating to grammar. **2.** Conforming to the rules of grammar. [Late Latin *grammaticālis,* from Latin *grammaticus,* from Greek *grammatikos,* pertaining to letters. See **grammar.**] —**gram·mat·i·cal·i·ty** (grə-măt′ĭ-kăl′ĭ-tē) *n.* —**gram·mat·i·cal·ly** *adv.*

grammatical gender *n.* The gender assigned to a word in the grammar of a language, as distinct from natural gender or sex. Compare **common gender, natural gender.**

gram·ma·tol·o·gy (grăm′ə-tŏl′ə-jē) *n.* The study and science of systems of graphic script. [French *grammatologie :* Greek *gramma* (stem *grammat-*), written character + -LOGY.] —**gram·ma·to·log·ic** (grăm′ə-tə-lŏj′ĭk), **gram·ma·to·log·i·cal** *adj.* —**gram·ma·tol·o·gist** *n.*

gramme. Variant of **gram** (metric unit).

gram-mo·lec·u·lar weight (grăm′mə-lĕk′yə-lər) *n. Chemistry.* A **mole** *(see).* Also called "gram molecule."

Gram-neg·a·tive (grăm′nĕg′ə-tĭv) *adj. Sometimes* **gram-negative.** Of, pertaining to, or designating a microorganism that does not retain the purple dye used in Gram's method.

gram·o·phone (grăm′ə-fōn′) *n.* A record player; phonograph. [Originally a trademark from earlier *graphophone,* inversion of PHONOGRAPH.]

Gram·pi·an Region (grăm′pē-ən). Since 1975 an administrative region of Scotland, bordering the North Sea in the northeast of the country. It incorporates the former counties of Aberdeen, Banff, Kincardine, and Moray. The southwest of the region is mountainous, lying in the Grampians. The terrain descends to arable lowlands in the northeast. Aberdeen is the administrative center.

Gram·pi·ans¹ (grăm′pē-ənz). Also **Grampian Mountains.** Mountain range extending across central Scotland, bounded to the north by the Great Glen and to the south by the central Lowlands. Its highest peak is Ben Nevis (1,344 meters; 4,406 feet), the highest mountain in Britain, and it also includes the peaks of the Cairngorms.

Grampians². A small range of mountains in Victoria state, southeast Australia. It forms the southwesterly extremity of the Great Dividing Range, its highest peak being Mt. William (1,166 meters; 3,827 feet).

Gram-pos·i·tive (grăm′pŏz′ə-tĭv) *adj. Often* **gram-positive.** Of, pertaining to, or designating a microorganism that retains the purple dye used in Gram's method.

gram·pus (grăm′pəs) *n.* **1.** A marine mammal, *Grampus griseus,* related to and resembling the dolphins but lacking a beaklike snout. **2.** Any of several similar cetaceans, such as the **killer whale** *(see).* **3.** *Informal.* A person who is short-winded and breathes heavily. [Middle English *graspeis,* from Old French *graspois, craspois,* from Medieval Latin *craspiscis : cras,* fat, from Latin *crassus* (see **crass**) + *piscis,* fish.]

Gram's method (grămz) *n.* A differential staining technique using the retention or lack of retention of a purple dye to classify bacteria. [After Hans Christian Joachim *Gram* (1855–1938), Danish physician.]

gran (grăn) *n. Informal.* A grandmother.

Gra·na·da (grə-nä′də). A historic city in southern Spain, the capital of Granada province. It has many fine examples of Moorish architecture, including the Alhambra. The city was the capital of the Muslim state of Granada, which, under the Nasrid dynasty (1238–1492), was the last Moorish stronghold in Spain.

gran·a·dil·la (grăn′ə-dĭl′ə) *n.* **1.** Any of various tropical American passionflowers; especially, *Passiflora quadrangularis,* bearing edible fruit. **2.** The egg-shaped, fleshy fruit of such a plant. In this sense, also called "passion fruit." [Spanish, diminutive of *granada,* pomegranate, from Vulgar Latin *grānāta* (unattested), from Latin *grānātum,* seedy, from *grānum,* GRAIN.]

Gra·na·dos (grə-nä′dōs), Enrique (1867–1916). Spanish composer whose most important compositions were for the piano. Among them was the set called *Goyescas* (1912–14), inspired by paintings of Goya.

gran·a·ry (grăn′ə-rē, grā′nə-) *n., pl.* **-ries. 1.** A building for storing threshed grain. **2.** A region yielding a copious quantity of grain. [Latin *grānārium : grānum,* GRAIN + -ARY.]

granary meal *n.* A mixture of malted wheat and rye, and sometimes wholemeal kernels, used in making *granary bread.* Also called "granary flour."

gran cas·sa (grän′käs′ə) *n., pl.* **gran casse** (käs′ē). *Music.* A bass drum. [Italian, "great drum."]

grand (grănd) *adj.* **grander, grandest. 1.** Large and impressive in size, scope, or extent. **2. a.** Magnificent; splendid. **b.** *Chiefly British Regional.* Wonderful; outstanding; very good. **3.** Rich and sumptuous: *grand furnishings.* **4.** Having higher rank than others of the same specified category: *grand duke.* **5.** The most important; principal; main: *grand ballroom.* **6.** Illustrious; outstanding: *a grand assemblage.* **7. a.** Pretentious. **b.** Calculated to impress: *a grand manner.* **8.** Dignified and admirable: *a grand old man.* **9.** Stately; regal. **10.** Lofty; noble: *a grand purpose.* **11.** *Music.* **a.** Written for a large ensemble. **b.** Complete in form; containing all the movements. **12.** Inclusive; complete: *grand total.*

~*n.* **1.** A **grand piano** *(see).* **2.** *Abbr.* **G** *Slang.* A thousand dollars.

[French, from Old French, from Latin *grandis†*, grand, full-grown.]
—**grand·ly** *adv.* —**grand·ness** *n.*

  Synonyms: *august, grandiose, imposing, magnificent, majestic, stately.*

grand– *prefix.* Indicates a family relationship or relative one generation removed from the relative specified; for example, **grandson**. [French, rendering Latin *magnus* in kinship terms of ascent (for example, *amita magna, grand-tante*), later extended in English to terms of descent as well (for example, *grandson*, but French *petit-fils*).]

gran·dam (grăn'dăm', -dəm) *n.* Also **gran·dame** (-dām', -dəm). 1. A grandmother. 2. An old woman. [Middle English *graundam*, from Norman French *graund dame*. See **grand, dame**.]

grand-aunt (grănd'ănt', -änt') *n.* A **great-aunt** *(see)*.

Grand Banks. A submerged plateau, rising from the continental shelf, off southeastern Newfoundland, Canada. It is *c.* 480 kilometers (300 miles) long and 640 kilometers (400 miles) wide.

Grand Canal. 1. Canal in China, longest in the world, extending *c.* 1,610 kilometers (1,000 miles) from Beijing to Hangzhou. It was begun in the 6th century B.C., and construction continued for 2,000 years. 2. The principal canal of Venice, Italy, a waterway in the shape of an *S* that passes through the heart of the city.

Grand Canyon. A vast ravine of the Colorado River in northwestern Arizona. The river's course has cut a canyon 451 kilometers (280 miles) long, exposing multicolored tiers of rock that have been spectacularly eroded by the weather. The canyon is at some points over 1.6 kilometers (1 mile) deep. The Grand Canyon, set aside by the U.S. government in 1908 as a national monument, was expanded in 1919 and designated **Grand Canyon National Park** (272,798 hectares; 673,575 acres). The park contains the most spectacular part of the canyon. **Grand Canyon National Monument** (80,303 hectares; 198,280 acres) is a primitive area adjoining the park on the west.

grand·child (grănd'chīld') *n., pl.* **-children** (-chĭl'drən). A child of a son or daughter.

Grand Cou·lee Dam (kōō'lē). A major dam on the Columbia River, in north-central Washington State. The reservoir has a capacity of 11,600 million cubic meters (15,080 million cubic yards) and is used for irrigation, hydroelectricity, and flood control.

grand·dad (grăn'dăd') *n. Informal.* A grandfather.

grand·dad·dy (grăn'dăd'ē) *n., pl.* **-dies.** *Informal.* 1. A grandfather. 2. An originator or pre-eminent figure: *the granddaddy of them all.*

grand·daugh·ter (grăn'dô'tər) *n.* The daughter of a son or daughter.

grand duchess *n. Abbr.* **G.D.** 1. The wife or widow of a grand duke. 2. A woman who is sovereign of a grand duchy. 3. The daughter of a czar or of one of his male descendants.

grand duchy *n. Abbr.* **G.D.** A territory ruled by a grand duke or a grand duchess.

grand duke *n. Abbr.* **G.D.** 1. A nobleman who is below a king in rank and is sovereign of a grand duchy. 2. A son or grandson of a czar.

grande dame (grän'däm', gränd-däm') *n., pl.* **grandes dames** *(pronounced as singular). French.* A woman revered as an authority or leading figure in her group or profession.

gran·dee (grăn-dē') *n.* 1. A nobleman of the highest rank in Spain or Portugal. 2. A person of eminence or high rank. [Spanish and Portuguese *grande*, "great (one)," from Latin *grandis*, GRAND.]

gran·deur (grăn'jər, -jōōr) *n.* 1. Greatness; splendor: *"The world is charged with the grandeur of God"* (Gerard Manley Hopkins). 2. Personal dignity or proud bearing, often of an unwarranted, self-important kind. [Middle English, from Old French, from *grand*, GRAND.]

grand·fa·ther (grănd'fä'thər) *n.* 1. The father of a mother or father. 2. A forefather; ancestor.

grandfather clause *n.* A clause in the constitutions of several Southern states prior to 1915, exempting from poll taxes and property and literacy requirements lineal descendants of persons who were registered voters before 1867.

grandfather clock *n.* A pendulum clock enclosed in a tall, narrow cabinet. Also called "longcase clock."

grand·fa·ther·ly (grănd'fä'thər-lē) *adj.* 1. Characteristic of or befitting a grandfather. 2. Having the qualities of a grandfather; kindly; indulgent; benevolent.

Grand Gui·gnol (grän'gēn-yōl') *n.* 1. A short, horrifying stage play. 2. A style typical of or resembling such a play in being sensational, violent, or macabre, often in a deliberately stylized way. [After *Le Grand Guignol*, a theater in Montmartre, Paris, that specialized in such plays.] —**Grand-Gui·gnol** *adj.*

gran·dil·o·quence (grăn-dĭl'ə-kwəns) *n.* Pompous or bombastic speech or expression. [Latin *grandiloquus*, speaking loftily : *grandis*, GRAND + *loquī*, to speak.] —**gran·dil·o·quent** *adj.* —**gran·dil·o·quent·ly** *adv.*

gran·di·ose (grăn'dē-ōs', grăn'dē-ōs') *adj.* 1. Characterized by greatness of scope or intent; grand. 2. Characterized by feigned or affected grandeur; pompous. —See Synonyms at **grand**. [French, from Italian *grandioso*, from *grande*, great, grand, from Latin *grandis*, GRAND.] —**gran·di·ose·ly** *adv.* —**gran·di·os·i·ty** (grăn'dē-ŏs'ə-tē), **gran·di·ose·ness** *n.*

gran·di·o·so (grăn'dē-ō'sō) *adv. Music.* In a grand and noble style. Used as a direction. [Italian, GRANDIOSE.] —**gran·di·o·so** *adj.*

grand jury *n. Law.* A jury of 12 to 23 persons convened in private session to evaluate accusations against persons charged with crime and to determine whether the evidence warrants bringing an indictment. Compare **petit jury.**

Grand Lama *n.* Either of two senior lamas, the **Dalai Lama** or the **Panchen Lama** *(both of which see)*.

grand larceny *n.* The theft of property of a value exceeding the amount constituting **petit larceny** *(see)*.

grand·ma (grănd'mä', grăn'mä', grăm'mä', grăm'ə) *n.* Also **grand·ma·ma** (grănd'mə-mä', -mä'mə). *Informal.* A grandmother.

grand mal (grăn mäl') *n.* A form of epilepsy characterized by severe seizures involving spasms and loss of consciousness. Compare **petit mal.** [French, "great illness" : GRAND + *mal*, illness, from Old French, bad, ill, from Latin *malus*.]

Grandma Moses. See Anna Mary Robertson **Moses.**

grand master *n.* 1. In chess, an **International Grand Master** *(see)*. 2. *Often* **Grand Master.** A title of or form of address for the head of any of various private and usually secret organizations, such as the Freemasons or Templars.

grand·moth·er (grănd'mŭth-ər) *n.* 1. The mother of a father or mother. 2. A female ancestor.

grand·moth·er·ly (grănd'mŭth'ər-lē) *adj.* 1. Characteristic of or befitting a grandmother. 2. Having the qualities of a grandmother; solicitous; indulgent.

grand·neph·ew (grănd'nĕf'yōō, -nĕv'yōō, grăn'-) *n.* A **great-nephew** *(see)*.

grand·niece (grănd'nēs, grăn'-) *n.* A **great-niece** *(see)*.

Grand Old Man *n. Abbr.* **G.O.M.** A man revered as a figure of long-standing eminence in his field.

Grand Old Party *n. Abbr.* **G.O.P.** The Republican Party.

grand opera *n.* A serious or melodramatic drama having the entire text set to music.

grand·pa (grănd'pä', grăm'pä', grăm'pə) *n.* Also **grand·pa·pa** (grănd'pə-pä', -pä'pə). *Informal.* A grandfather.

grand·par·ent (grănd'pâr'ənt, grăn'-) *n.* A parent of a mother or father; a grandmother or grandfather.

grand piano *n.* A piano having the strings strung in a horizontal harp-shaped frame supported usually on three legs and ranging in size from the baby grand to the concert grand. Compare **upright piano.**

Grand Prix (grän prē', grän prē') *n., pl.* **Grands Prix** or **Grand Prixes** (prēz', prē') *Abbr.* **G.P.** 1. Any of a series of international competitive races for sports cars of specific engine size over an exacting course, and counting toward the award of the driver's world championship each year. 2. Any of various other major races, as in cycling or horseracing, held annually. [French, big prize.]

Grand Rap·ids (răp'ĭdz). A city of southwest-central Michigan, on the Grand River. Founded in 1826, it developed as a lumber center and became famous for the manufacture of high-quality furniture, still a major industry.

grand sherif *n.* See **sherif** (sense 2).

grand siè·cle (grän sē-ěk'lə) *n. French.* The 17th century in France with reference to the arts, especially the classical period during the reign of Louis XIV. [Literally, "great age."]

grand·sire (grănd'sīr', -sər) *n. Archaic.* 1. A grandfather. 2. A male ancestor; forefather. 3. An old man.

grand slam *n.* 1. In bridge and other card games, the winning of all the tricks during the play of one hand. 2. In various sports, especially tennis and golf, the winning of all major events in a particular series or season. 3. *Baseball.* A home run hit when three runners are on base.

grand·son (grănd'sŭn', grăn'-) *n.* The son of a son or daughter.

grand·stand (grănd'stănd', grăn'-) *n.* 1. A roofed stand for spectators at a sports ground or race course, usually offering the best view and having the most expensive seats. 2. The spectators seated in such a stand.
~*intr.v.* **-standed, -standing, -stands.** To perform ostentatiously so as to impress an audience. —**grand·stand·er** *n.*

grandstand play *n.* A sports play or other action performed ostentatiously to impress onlookers.

grandstand view *n.* An unobstructed view.

Grand Te·ton National Park (tē'tŏn', tēt'n). Park, *c.* 125,800 hectares (310,440 acres), in northwestern Wyoming. It encompasses the most scenic portion of the snow-covered Teton Range, including its highest elevation, Grand Teton (*c.* 5,000 meters; 13,770 feet). The park has lakes, several glaciers, and a great variety of wildlife.

grand tour *n.* 1. Formerly, an extended tour of continental Europe considered as a part of the education of young men of the English upper class. 2. *Informal.* A comprehensive tour or inspection.

grand-un·cle (grănd'ŭng'kəl) *n.* A **great-uncle** *(see)*.

grange (grānj) *n.* 1. **Grange. a.** The Patrons of Husbandry, an association of farmers founded in the United States in 1867. **b.** One of its branch lodges. 2. *British.* A farm; especially, the residence and attached farm buildings of the farmer. 3. A feudal farm building used for storing grain paid as tithes. 4. *Archaic.* A granary. [Middle English, from Old French, from Medieval Latin *grānica*, from Latin *grānum*, GRAIN.]

grang·er (grān'jər) *n.* A member of a grange.

grang·er·ize (grān'jə-rīz') *tr.v.* **-ized, -izing, -izes.** 1. To illustrate (a book) with drawings, prints, or engravings taken from other books. 2. To mutilate (a book) by clipping out its illustrative material for such use. [After J. Granger (1723–1776), English biographer who published (1769) his *Biographical History of England* with blank pages where the reader could insert such illustrations.] —**grang·er·ism, grang·er·i·za·tion** *n.* —**grang·er·iz·er** *n.*

Grand Canyon *The great gorge of the Colorado River, in Arizona, has been formed by the river cutting its way down through the rock as the land around it rose.*

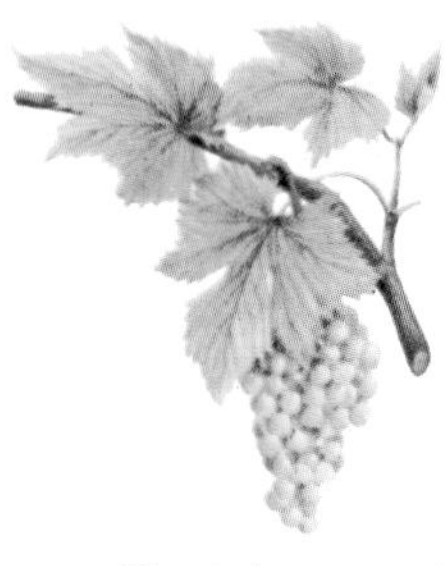

grape *Vines today are associated with warm and sunny climates, but in the Middle Ages, grapes were grown outdoors as far north as Yorkshire, England; and exploring Vikings found them on the North American coast somewhere between New England and Nova Scotia.*

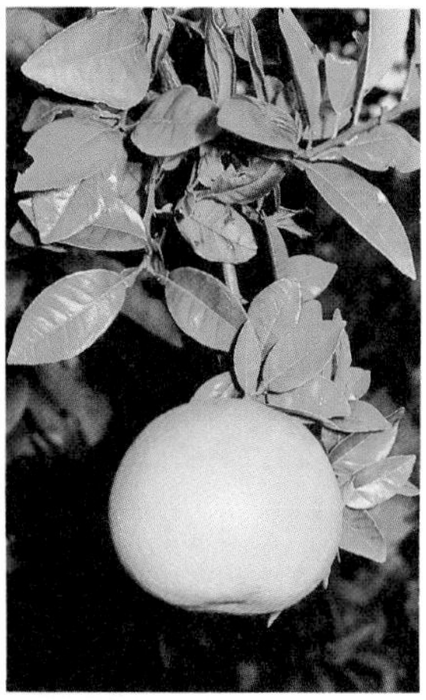

grapefruit *A segmented fruit originally from the Caribbean. As a source of vitamin C it is surpassed only by the orange and lemon.*

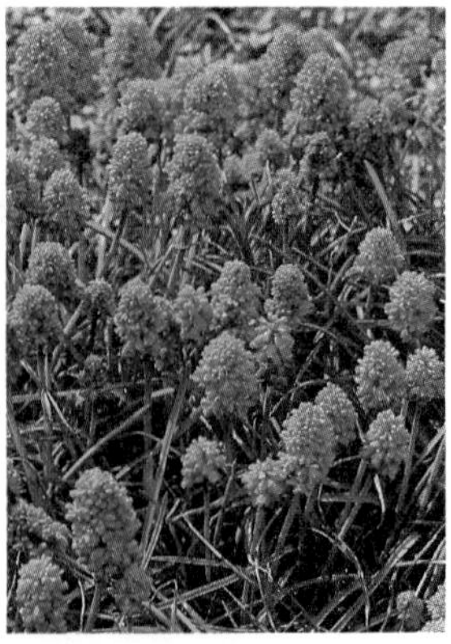

grape hyacinth *A small spring-blooming plant of the lily family.*

grani– *prefix.* Indicates grain; for example, **granivorous, graniform.** [Latin *grāni-,* from *grānum,* GRAIN.]

gra·nif·er·ous (grə-nĭf′ər-əs) *adj.* Bearing grain. [Latin *grānifer* : GRANI- + -FER.]

gran·i·form (grăn′ə-fôrm′) *adj.* Resembling a grain in form. [GRANI- + -FORM.]

gra·ni·ta (grə-nē′tə) *n.* A coarse-textured water ice. [Italian, "grained (ice)."]

gran·ite (grăn′ĭt) *n.* **1.** A common, coarse-grained, hard, and igneous rock consisting chiefly of quartz, orthoclase or microcline, and often mica, used in monuments and for building. **2.** Unyielding endurance; steadfastness; firmness. [Italian *granito,* "grained," from the past participle of *granire,* to impart a grained surface to, from *grano,* grain, from Latin *grānum,* GRAIN.] **—gra·nit·ic** (grə-nĭt′ĭk), **gran·it·oid** *adj.*

granite paper *n.* A paper containing a low proportion of colored mottling fibers.

gran·ite·ware (grăn′ĭt-wâr′) *n.* **1.** Enameled iron utensils. **2.** Earthenware with a speckled glaze resembling granite.

gra·niv·o·rous (grə-nĭv′ər-əs) *adj.* Feeding on grain and seeds. [GRANI- + -VOROUS.] **—gran·i·vore** (grăn′ə-vôr′, -vōr′) *n.*

gran·ny, gran·nie (grăn′ē) *n., pl.* **-nies. 1.** *Informal.* A grandmother. **2.** An old woman. **3.** A fussy or finicky person. **4.** *Southern U.S.* A midwife. [From obsolete *grannam,* variant of GRANDAM.]

granny glasses *pl.n.* A pair of small, round glasses with gold or steel rims.

granny knot *n.* Also **granny's knot.** A knot like a reef knot but with the second tie crossed incorrectly so that it readily comes undone. [Originally a sailor's disparaging term for such a knot.]

Granny Smith *n.* A variety of apple with a green skin and hard, crisp flesh, eaten cooked or raw.

grano– *prefix.* Indicates: **1.** Of or like granite; for example, **granolith. 2.** Granular; for example, **granophyre.** [German, from *Granit,* granite, from Italian *granito,* GRANITE.]

gran·o·di·o·rite (grăn′ō-dī′ə-rīt′) *n.* A coarse-grained acid igneous rock, intermediate between granite and diorite. It contains almost twice as much plagioclase as orthoclase.

gra·no·la (grə-nō′lə) *n.* Rolled oats mixed with various ingredients, such as dried fruit, brown sugar, and nuts, eaten especially as a breakfast cereal. [Originally a trademark.]

gran·o·lith (grăn′ə-lĭth′) *n.* A paving stone of crushed granite and cement. [GRANO- + -LITH.] **—gran·o·lith·ic** *adj.*

gran·o·phyre (grăn′ə-fīr′) *n.* A grained granite porphyry having a groundmass with irregular intergrowths of quartz and feldspar. [German *Granophyr* : GRANO- + *Porphyr,* porphyry, from Medieval Latin *porphyrium,* PORPHYRY.] **—gran·o·phyr·ic** (grăn′ə-fīr′ĭk) *adj.*

Gran Pa·ra·di·so (grän′ pär′ə-dē′zō). The highest mountain entirely within Italy, in the Alps near Aosta. It rises to 4,061 meters (13, 323 feet).

Gran Qui·vi·ra National Monument (grăn′ kĭ-vîr′ə). Area of 180 hectares (451 acres) in central New Mexico, including ruins of a Spanish mission and Indian pueblos.

grant (grănt, gränt) *tr.v.* **granted, granting, grants. 1.** To allow to have; consent to the fulfillment of: *grant a wish.* **2.** To permit or accord, as a favor or privilege: *grant a kiss.* **3. a.** To bestow; confer: *grant aid.* **b.** To transfer (property) by a deed; convey. **4.** To concede; acknowledge. **—take for granted. 1.** To consider as true or proven. **2.** To accept as being likely or probable; anticipate correctly. **3.** To accept the benefit of without due acknowledgment. ~*n.* **1.** The act of granting. **2.** Something granted. **3.** *Law.* A transfer of property by deed. **4.** One of several tracts of land in New Hampshire, Maine, and Vermont originally granted to an individual or group. —See Synonyms at **bonus.** [Middle English *graunten,* from Old French *gr(e)anter, creanter,* to insure, guarantee, from Vulgar Latin *crēdentāre* (unattested), from Latin *crēdēns* (stem *crēdent-*), present participle of *crēdere,* to believe, trust.] **—grant·a·ble** *adj.* **—grant·er** *n.*

Grant (grănt), **Cary,** stage name of Archibald Leach (1904–). U.S. film actor, born in England. In 1933 he played his first important role opposite Mae West in *She Done Him Wrong* and remained in films until 1969. His most famous films include *The Philadelphia Story* (1940), *Arsenic and Old Lace* (1944), *To Catch A Thief* (1955), and *North by Northwest* (1959).

Grant, Ulysses Simpson, originally Hiram Ulysses Grant (1822–85). 18th U.S. president and military commander. With the Illinois Volunteers he captured Fort Henry and Fort Donelson (1862), the first major Unionist victories in the Civil War, and after the victorious Vicksburg campaign (1862–63) he was made commander in chief of the Union army. He won the 1868 presidential election as the Republican candidate and was re-elected in 1872.

grant·ee (grăn-tē′, grän-) *n. Law.* One to whom a grant is made.

grant-in-aid (grănt′ĭn-ād′) *n., pl.* **grants-in-aid.** A grant made by a government or private organization to a lower level of government or local authority for the funding of public works, educational programs, or the like.

grant of probate *n. Law.* Authority given by a court to an executor to deal with the estate of a deceased person as provided for by the will.

gran·tor (grăn′tər, grăn′-) *n. Law.* One who makes a grant.

grants·man·ship (grănts′mən-shĭp′) *n.* The art of obtaining grants-in-aid. [GRANT + (GAME)SMANSHIP.]

gran·u·lar (grăn′yə-lər) *adj.* **1.** Composed of or appearing to be composed of granules or grains. **2.** Grainy. **—gran·u·lar·i·ty** *n.* **—gran·u·lar·ly** *adv.*

gran·u·late (grăn′yə-lāt′) *v.* **-lated, -lating, -lates.** —*tr.* **1.** To form into grains or granules. **2.** To make rough and grainy. —*intr.* **1.** To become granular or grainy. **2.** *Physiology.* To undergo granulation. **—gran·u·la·tive** *adj.* **—gran·u·la·tor, gran·u·lat·er** *n.*

gran·u·la·tion (grăn′yə-lā′shən) *n.* **1. a.** The act or process of granulating. **b.** The condition or appearance of being granulated. **2.** *Physiology.* **a.** The formation of small, fleshy, beadlike protuberances on the surface of a wound while healing. **b.** Any of these protuberances. Also called "granulation tissue."

gran·ule (grăn′yo͞ol) *n.* **1.** A small grain or pellet; a particle. **2.** *Astronomy.* Any of the smallest transient, brilliant markings visible in the photosphere of the sun. [Late Latin *grānulum,* diminutive of *grānum,* GRAIN.]

gran·u·lite (grăn′yə-līt′) *n.* A granular metamorphic rock often banded in appearance and composed chiefly of feldspar, quartz, and garnet. [GRANUL(E) + -ITE.] **—gran·u·lit·ic** (grăn′yə-lĭt′ĭk) *adj.*

gran·u·lo·cyte (grăn′yə-lō-sīt′) *n.* Any of a group of white blood cells having granules in their cytoplasm. [From GRANULE + -CYTE.] **—gran·u·lo·cyt·ic** (grăn′yə-lō-sĭt′ĭk) *adj.*

gran·u·lo·ma (grăn′yə-lō′mə) *n., pl.* **-mas** or **-mata** (-mə-tə). A mass of inflamed granulation tissue, usually associated with ulcerated infections. [New Latin : GRANUL(E) + -OMA.] **—gran·u·lom·a·tous** (grăn′yə-lŏm′ə-təs) *adj.*

gran·u·lose (grăn′yə-lōs′) *adj.* Having a surface covered with granules. [GRANUL(E) + -OSE.]

Gran·ville-Bark·er (grăn′vĭl′bär′kər), **Harley** (1877–1946). British actor, producer, dramatist, and critic. He was co-manager of the Royal Court Theatre (1904–07) and producer of a famous series of Shakespeare productions at the Savoy Theatre (1912–14). He is best remembered today for his drama criticism, especially the *Prefaces to Shakespeare* in six volumes (1927–47).

grape (grāp) *n.* **1.** Any of numerous woody vines of the genus *Vitis;* especially, *V. vinifera,* bearing clusters of edible fruit, and widely cultivated in many subspecies and varieties. Also called "grapevine." **2.** The fleshy, smooth-skinned, purple, red, or green fruit of such a vine, eaten raw or dried, and widely used in winemaking. **3.** Grapeshot. **—the grape.** Wine. [Middle English, from Old French, bunch of grapes, hook, from Germanic.] **—grap·ey, grap·y** *adj.*

grape fern *n.* Any of various ferns of the genus *Botrychium,* having a fertile frond bearing small, grapelike clusters of spore cases. One species, *B. lunaria,* is also called "moonwort."

grape·fruit (grāp′fro͞ot′) *n.* **1.** An evergreen tropical or semitropical tree, *Citrus paradisi,* cultivated for its edible fruit. **2.** The large, round fruit of this tree, having a yellow rind, or occasionally a pink and yellow rind, with a juicy, somewhat acid pulp. Also called "pomelo." [So called because the fruit grows in clusters.]

grape hyacinth *n.* Any of various plants of the genus *Muscari,* native to Eurasia, having narrow leaves and dense, spike-shaped clusters of rounded, usually blue flowers.

grape ivy *n.* An evergreen climbing shrub, *Rhoicissus rhomboidea,* native to Africa but widely grown as a house plant for its ornamental foliage.

grap·er·y (grā′pə-rē) *n., pl.* **-ies.** A building or plantation where grapes are grown.

grapes *n. Used with a singular verb.* An abnormal growth resembling a bunch of grapes on the pastern or fetlock of a horse.

grape·shot (grāp′shŏt′) *n.* A cluster of small iron balls formerly used as a cannon charge. [From its resemblance to a cluster of grapes.]

grape·stone (grāp′stōn′) *n.* A seed of a grape.

grape sugar *n.* **Dextrose** *(see).*

grape·vine (grāp′vīn′) *n.* **1.** A vine on which grapes grow. **2.** An informal, often secret means of transmitting information, gossip, or rumor from person to person: *heard it on the grapevine.* **3.** An information source.

graph (grăf, gräf) *n.* **1.** A drawing that expresses a relationship, often functional, between two sets of numbers as a set of points having coordinates that are plotted from a pair of axes and are determined by the relationship between the two sets. **2.** Any pictorial device, such as a pie chart or bar graph, used to display numerical relationships. Also called "chart." **3.** A representation of a quantity, as of a complex number, by a geometric object such as a point in a plane. **4.** A visual representation, such as a letter, of a phoneme or other speech unit.
~*tr.v.* **graphed, graphing, graphs. 1.** To represent by a graph. **2.** To plot (a function) on a graph. [Short for *graphic formula;* sense 4, from Greek *graphē,* writing.]

–graph *suffix.* Indicates: **1.** An apparatus that writes or records; for example, **telegraph, seismograph. 2.** Something drawn or written; for example, **lithograph, monograph.** [French *-graphe,* from Latin *-graphum,* from Greek *-graphon,* neuter of *-graphos,* written, from *graphein,* to write.]

graph·eme (grăf′ēm′) *n.* **1.** A letter of an alphabet. **2.** The sum of letters and letter combinations that represent a single phoneme. [Greek *graphēma,* letter, from *graphein,* to write.] **—gra·phe·mic** *adj.* **—gra·phe·mi·cal·ly** *adv.*

–grapher *suffix.* Indicates: **1.** A person who writes about or is skilled in a specified subject; for example, **geographer. 2.** One who employs a specified means to write, draw, or record; for example,

stenographer. [Late Latin *-graphus,* from Greek *-graphos,* from *graphein,* to write.]

graph·ic (grăf′ĭk) *adj.* Also **graph·i·cal** (-ĭ-kəl). **1.** Of or pertaining to written or pictorial representation. **2.** Of, pertaining to, or represented by or as if by a graph. **3.** Described in vivid detail; clearly outlined or set forth: *a graphic account.* **4.** Of or pertaining to the graphic arts. **5.** Of or pertaining to graphics. **6.** *Geology.* Having crystals resembling printed characters.
—*n* **1.** A graphic device, such as a picture or map, used for illustration. **2.** *Computer Science.* A graphic display generated by a computer or imaging device. [Latin *graphicus,* from Greek *graphikos,* from *graphē,* a writing, from *graphein,* to write.] —**graph·i·cal·ly** *adv.* —**graph·ic·ness** *n.*

graphic arts *pl.n.* **1.** The fine or applied visual arts that involve the application of lines and strokes to a two-dimensional surface. **2.** The reproductions made from blocks, plates, or type, such as engravings, etchings, woodcuts, and lithographs.

graph·ics (grăf′ĭks) *n. Used with a singular or plural verb.* **1.** The making of drawings in accordance with the rules of mathematics, as in engineering or architecture. **2.** Calculations, as of structural stress, from such drawings. **3.** The artwork accompanying written matter. **4.** *Computer Science.* The processing and displaying of data in pictorial form.

graph·ite (grăf′īt′) *n.* The soft, steel-gray to black, hexagonally crystallized allotrope of carbon, used in lead pencils, lubricants, paints and coatings, bricks, electrodes, crucibles, and rocket nozzles. Also called "black lead." [German *Graphit* : Greek *graphein,* to write + -ITE.] —**gra·phit·ic** (gră-fĭt′ĭk) *adj.*

graph·i·tize (grăf′ə-tīz′) *tr.v.* **-tized, -tizing, -tizes. 1.** To convert into graphite by a heating process. **2.** To coat or impregnate with graphite. —**graph·i·ti·za·tion** *n.*

graph·ol·o·gy (gră-fŏl′ə-jē) *n.* **1.** The study of handwriting, especially when employed as a means of analyzing the character of the writer. **2.** The study of writing systems. [Greek *graphē,* a writing (see **graphic**) + -LOGY.] —**graph·o·log·i·cal** (grăf′ə-lŏj′ĭ-kəl) *adj.* —**graph·ol·o·gist** *n.*

graph paper *n.* Paper ruled into small squares of equal size for use in drawing charts, graphs, or diagrams.

-graphy *suffix.* Indicates: **1.** A specified process or method of writing, recording, or describing; for example, **cacography, photography. 2.** A descriptive science of a specified subject or field; for example, **oceanography.** [Latin *-graphia,* from Greek, from *graphein,* to write.]

grap·nel (grăp′nəl) *n.* **1.** An iron shaft with claws at one end for grasping and holding; especially, one for drawing and holding an enemy ship alongside. Also called "grappling," "grappling-hook," "grappling iron." **2.** A small anchor with three or more flukes. [Middle English *grapenel,* from Norman French *grapenel* (unattested), diminutive of Old French *grapon,* anchor, hook, from Germanic.]

grap·pa (grä′pə; *Italian* gräp′pä) *n.* An Italian brandy distilled from the residue of pressed grapes. [Italian, "grape stalk," from Germanic.]

grap·ple (grăp′əl) *n.* **1.** Any instrument, such as a grapnel, used for grasping and holding. **2.** The act of grappling. **3. a.** A contest in which the participants attempt to clutch or grip each other. **b.** A grasp or grip in such a contest.
—*v.* **grappled, -pling, -ples.** —*tr.* **1.** To seize and hold with a grapnel. **2.** To seize firmly with the hands. —*intr.* **1.** To hold on to something with or as if with a grapnel. **2.** To attempt to resolve or overcome: *grapple with a problem; grapple with one's conscience.* [Middle English *grapel,* from Old French *grapil,* from Old Provençal, diminutive of *grapa,* hook, from Germanic.] —**grap·pler** *n.*

grap·to·lite (grăp′tə-līt′) *n.* Any of numerous extinct colonial marine animals chiefly of the orders Dendroidea and Graptoloidea, of the late Cambrian to Carboniferous periods. [Greek *graptos,* written, painted, from *graphein,* to write (see **graphic**) + -LITE (so called from the fossilized impressions resembling markings on slate).]

Gras·mere (grăs′mûr, gräs′-). A village in Cumbria in northwestern England, near Lake Grasmere. Set in the heart of the Lake District, it is famous for the beauty of its surroundings. Wordsworth lived there at Dove Cottage, which now houses a Wordsworth museum.

grasp (grăsp, gräsp) *v.* **grasped, grasping, grasps.** —*tr.* **1.** To take hold of or seize firmly with or as if with the hand. **2.** To hold firmly with or as if with the hand; clutch; clasp. **3.** To take in mentally; comprehend: *"It is this distinction between freedom and license that many parents cannot grasp"* (A.S. Neill). —See Synonyms at **apprehend.** —*intr.* **1.** To make a motion of seizing, snatching, or clutching. **2.** To show eager and prompt willingness or acceptance. Used with *at.*
—*n.* **1.** The act of grasping. **2.** A firm hold or grip. **3.** The ability or power to seize or attain; reach: *The directorship was within his grasp.* **4.** Understanding; comprehension: *an intuitive grasp of the problem.* [Middle English *graspen,* Old English *grapsan* (unattested), from Germanic.] —**grasp·er** *n.*

grasp·ing (grăs′pĭng, gräs′-) *adj.* Eager for gain; greedy; avaricious. —**grasp·ing·ly** *adv.* —**grasp·ing·ness** *n.*

grass (grăs, gräs) *n.* **1. a.** Any of numerous plants of the family Gramineae, characteristically having narrow leaves, hollow, jointed stems, and spikes or clusters of membranous flowers borne in smaller spikelets. **b.** Such plants collectively. **2.** Any of various plants, such as knotgrass, having slender leaves like those of the true grasses. **3.** An expanse of ground, such as a meadow or lawn, covered with grass or similar plants. **4.** Grazing land; pasture. **5.** *Slang.* Marijuana. **6.** A condition or place of retirement: *put a horse out to grass.* **7.** *Electronics.* The small variations in amplitude of an oscilloscope display due to electrical noise.
—*v.* **grassed, grassing, grasses.** —*tr.* **1.** To cover with grass; grow grass on. **2.** To feed (livestock) with grass. —*intr.* **1.** To become covered with grass. **2.** To graze. [Middle English *gras,* Old English *græs,* from Germanic.]

Grass (gräs), **Günter** (1927–). German poet, playwright, and novelist. Most of his novels are directly concerned with the social and political life of Germany. His two early novels, *The Tin Drum* (1959) and *Dog Years* (1963), are the most widely known.

grass cloth *n.* A material woven from rough natural plant fibers such as hemp or ramie.

grass court *n.* A tennis court with a cut grass surface.

grass-cut·ter (grăs′kŭt′ər, gräs′-) *n.* A West African water rat, *Thryonomis swinderianus,* with stiff, short fur.

Grasse (gräs). A town in the Alpes-Maritimes department of southern France, north of Cannes. Surrounded by extensive fields of flowers, it is famous for the manufacture of essences for perfume.

grass·finch (grăs′fĭnch′, gräs′-) *n.* Any of various Australian weaver finches of the genus *Poephila* and related genera, some species of which are kept as cage birds for their colorful plumage.

grass green *n.* A moderate yellow-green to strong or dark yellowish-green. —**grass-green** *adj.*

grass hockey *n. Canadian.* Field hockey as opposed to ice hockey.

grass·hop·per (grăs′hŏp′ər, gräs′-) *n.* **1.** Any of numerous insects of the families Locustidae (or Acrididae) (*short-horned grasshoppers*) and Tettigoniidae (*long-horned grasshoppers*), often destructive to plants and characteristically having long hind legs adapted for jumping. **2.** A cocktail consisting of crème de menthe, crème de cacao, and cream.

grass·land (grăs′lănd′, gräs′-) *n.* An area, such as a prairie or meadow, of grass or grasslike vegetation.

Gras·so (grăs′ō, grä′sō), **Ella Tambussi** (1919–81). U.S. public official. After serving as a state legislator (1952–59), Connecticut secretary of state (1959–70), and U.S. congresswoman (1970–75), she became the first American woman elected governor in her own right, filling that position from 1975 to 1980.

grass-of-Par·nas·sus (grăs′əv-pär-năs′əs, gräs′-) *n.* Any of various plants of the genus *Parnassia;* especially, *P. palustris,* having stalked basal leaves and a stem bearing a single white or yellowish flower.

grass parakeet *n.* Any of various small Australian parrots typically having a long tail and green plumage.

grass pink *n.* An orchid, *Calopogon pulchellus,* of marshy areas of eastern North America, having a single narrow leaf and a cluster of pinkish flowers.

grass·roots (grăs′ro͞ots′, -ro͝ots′, gräs′-) *pl.n.* **1.** People considered from a political viewpoint as constituting the basic voting population. **2.** The foundation or source of something; basis; origin.
—*adj.* **1.** Originating in or emerging from the people who make up the mass of an electorate: *a grassroots candidate; a grassroots policy.* **2.** Fundamental; basic.

grass-ski·ing (grăs′skē′ĭng, gräs′-) *n.* The sport of skiing down grassy slopes on specially adapted skis.

grass skirt *n.* A skirt made from lengths of flax or other grasses strung from a waistband and worn especially by the Polynesians.

grass snake *n.* Any of several greenish, nonvenomous snakes; especially, *Natrix natrix,* of Europe, or *Opheodrys vernalis,* of eastern North America.

grass tree *n.* Any of several woody-stemmed Australian plants of the genus *Xanthorrhoea,* having stiff, grasslike leaves and a spike of small white flowers. They yield a gum used in making varnishes.

grass widow *n.* **1.** A woman whose husband is habitually or temporarily absent. **2.** A woman who is divorced or separated from her husband. **3.** A woman who has had an illegitimate child. [Earliest sense, "unwed mother," probably with an allusion to a bed of straw or grass as a symbol of illicit sexual conduct.]

grass wren *n.* Any of various small Australian songbirds of the genus *Amytormis,* typically having a brown body and tail and a whitish breast.

grass·y (grăs′ē, gräs′ē) *adj.* **-ier, -iest. 1.** Covered with grass. **2.** Resembling or suggestive of grass, as in color or odor.

grate[1] (grāt) *v.* **grated, grating, grates.** —*tr.* **1.** To reduce to fragments, shreds, or powder by rubbing against an abrasive surface: *grate cabbage.* **2.** To cause to make a harsh grinding or rasping sound through friction. **3.** *Archaic.* To rub or wear away. —*intr.* **1.** To make a harsh rasping sound by or as if by scraping or grinding. **2.** To cause irritation or annoyance. Sometimes used with *on*: *grate on one's nerves.*
—*n.* A harsh, rasping sound made by scraping or rubbing: *the grate of a key in a lock.* [Middle English *graten,* from Old French *grater,* to scrape, from Germanic.] —**grat·ing·ly** *adv.*

grate[2] *n.* **1.** A framework of parallel or latticed bars used to hold the fuel in a stove, furnace, or fireplace. **2.** A similar framework used to block an opening; a grille; a grating. **3.** A fireplace. **4.** A perforated iron plate or screen for sieving and grading crushed ore.
—*tr.v.* **grated, grating, grates.** To equip with a grate. [Middle English, from Old French, grille, from Vulgar Latin *grata* (unattested), variant of Latin *crātis,* wickerwork, hurdle.]

grate·ful (grāt′fəl) *adj.* **1.** Appreciative of benefits received; thankful. **2.** Expressing gratitude. **3.** Affording pleasure or comfort; wel-

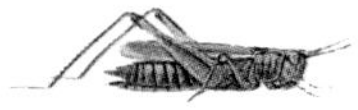

grasshopper *Around the world there are hundreds of species of grasshopper—a group that includes crickets and locusts. Most feed on plants and have long hind legs adapted for jumping. They are difficult to see in the grass where they live, but they can often be heard, since each species has a characteristic song, produced by rubbing the wings or legs together. The song is used by males to attract females and, less frequently, by females to attract males. The species shown here is* Omacestus viridulus.

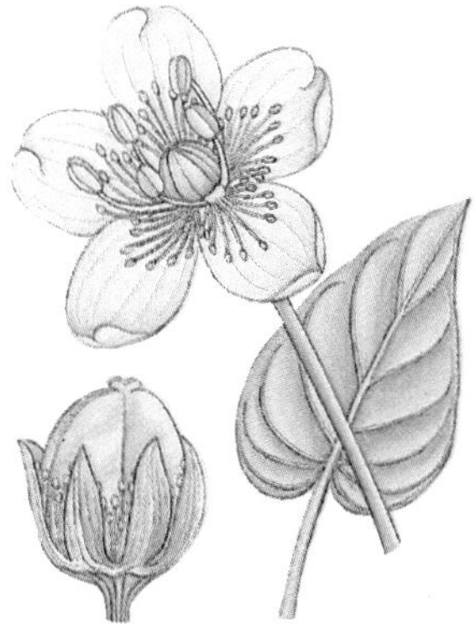

grass-of-Parnassus *This Northern Hemisphere wildflower is neither a grass nor grasslike; it is a marsh plant that takes its name from Mount Parnassus in Greece, the legendary home of the Muses. The species shown here is* Parnassia palustris.

PRONUNCIATION KEY

ă, pat; ā, pay; âr, care;
ä, father, are; b, bib;
ch, church; d, deed; ĕ, pet;
ē, be; f, fife; g, gag; h, hat;
hw, which; ĭ, pit; ī, pie;
îr, pier; j, judge; k, kick;
l, lid, needle; m, mum;
n, no, sudden; ng, thing;
ŏ, pot; ō, toe; ô, paw, for;
oi, noise; ou, out; o͝o, book;
o͞o, boot; p, pop; r, roar;
s, sauce; sh, ship, dish;
t, tight; th, thin, path;
th, this, bathe; ŭ, cut; ûr, fur;
v, valve; w, with; y, yes;
z, zebra, size; zh, vision;
ə, about, item, edible,
gallop, circus, peaceful

IN FOREIGN WORDS:

à, *Fr.* ami; œ, *Fr.* feu, *Ger.* schön; ü, *Fr.* tu, *Ger.* über; KH, *Ger.* ich, *Scot.* loch; N, *Fr.* bon; y′, *Fr.* Compiègne

STRESS MARKS:

Primary stress: ′
in·cite′ (ĭn-sīt′)
Secondary stress: ′
in′sight′ (ĭn′sīt′)

come: *"he left his home to enjoy the grateful air"* (Ronald Firbank). [From obsolete *grate*, agreeable, thankful, from Latin *grātus*, pleasing, favorable.] —**grate·ful·ly** *adv.* —**grate·ful·ness** *n.*

grat·er (grā′tər) *n.* **1.** One that grates. **2.** An implement with rough or sharp-edged slits and perforations on which to shred or grate foods.

grat·i·cule (grăt′ĭ-kyōōl′) *n.* **1.** A grid of meridians and parallels derived from a particular projection, used in drawing a map. **2.** *Optics.* A grid or pattern used to establish scale or position, placed in the eyepiece of an optical instrument. Also called "reticle," "reticule." [French, from Latin *crāticula*, gridiron, diminutive of *crātis*, wickerwork, hurdle.]

grat·i·fi·ca·tion (grăt′ə-fĭ-kā′shən) *n.* **1.** The act of gratifying. **2.** The condition of being gratified; satisfaction; pleasure. **3.** An instance or cause of gratification. **4.** *Archaic.* A reward; gratuity; bonus.

grat·i·fy (grăt′ə-fī′) *tr.v.* **-fied, -fying, -fies. 1.** To please or satisfy: *His achievement gratified his father.* **2.** To indulge; give in to (a desire, for example). **3.** *Archaic.* To requite; reward. [Middle English *gratifien*, to favor, from Old French, from Latin *grātificārī*, to reward, do favor to, from *grātus*, favorable, pleasurable.] —**grat·i·fi·er** *n.*

grat·i·fy·ing (grăt′ə-fī′ĭng) *adj.* Causing pleasure and satisfaction, as to the self-esteem: *a most gratifying sense of accomplishment.* —**grat·i·fy·ing·ly** *adv.*

gra·tin (grät′n, grăt′n; *French* grà-tăN′) *n.* A rich baked crust on dishes that have been topped with grated cheese or buttered crumbs. [French, from Old French, from *grater*, to GRATE (scrape).]

grat·ing[1] (grā′tĭng) *n.* **1.** A grille or network of bars set in a window or door or used as a partition; lattice; grate. **2.** *Physics.* **Diffraction grating** *(see).*

grat·ing[2] *adj.* **1.** Rasping or scraping in sound. **2.** Nerve-racking; irritating. —**grat·ing·ly** *adv.*

gra·tis (grăt′ĭs, grā′tĭs) *adv.* Freely; for nothing; without charge. ~*adj.* Free; gratuitous. [Middle English, from Latin *grātīs*, reduced form of *grātiīs*, without reward, as a favor, from *grātia*, favor, from *grātus*, favorable.]

grat·i·tude (grăt′ə-tōōd′, -tyōōd′) *n.* An appreciative awareness and thankfulness, as for kindness shown or a gift received. [Middle English, from Old French, from Medieval Latin *grātitūdō*, from *grātus*, favorable.]

gra·tu·i·tous (grə-tōō′ə-təs, -tyōō′-) *adj.* **1.** *Law.* Given or granted without return or recompense. **2.** Given or received without cost or obligation; free; gratis. **3.** Unnecessary or unwarranted; unjustified: *gratuitous criticism.* [Latin *grātuītus*, given as a favor, from *grātus*, favorable, pleasing.] —**gra·tu·i·tous·ly** *adv.* —**gra·tu·i·tous·ness** *n.*

gra·tu·i·ty (grə-tōō′ə-tē, -tyōō′-) *n., pl.* **-ties.** A material favor or gift, usually in the form of money, given in return for service; a tip. —See Synonyms at **bonus.** [Old French *gratuite*, from Medieval Latin *grātuitās* (stem *grātuitāt-*), present, gift, from Latin *grātuītus*, given free, GRATUITOUS.]

grat·u·lant (grăch′ōō-lənt) *adj. Archaic.* Congratulatory.

grat·u·late (grăch′ōō-lāt′) *tr.v.* **-lated, -lating, -lates.** *Archaic.* **1.** To greet with pleasure; welcome. **2.** To congratulate. [Latin *grātulārī*, to greet, salute, from *grātus*, pleasing, GRATEFUL.] —**grat·u·la·tion** *n.* —**grat·u·la·to·ry** (grăch′ōō-lə-tôr′ē, -tōr′ē) *adj.*

Gratz. See **Graz.**

grau·pel (grou′pəl) *n.* Precipitation consisting of pellets of snow. Also called "snow pellets," "soft hail." [German *Graupel*, diminutive of *Graupe*, hulled grain, groats, probably from Serbo-Croatian *krupa*.]

grav (grăv) *n.* A unit of acceleration equal to the acceleration of free fall or 9.807 meters per second per second. [Shortened from *gravity*.]

gra·va·men (grə-vā′mən) *n., pl.* **-vamina** (-văm′ə-nə). **1.** *Law.* **a.** The part of a charge or accusation that weighs most substantially against the accused. **b.** The essential part of a complaint. **2.** A grievance. [Late Latin *gravamen*, grievance, from Latin *grāvāre*, to weigh down, burden, from *gravis*, heavy, GRAVE.]

grave[1] (grāv) *n.* **1. a.** A hole dug in the ground to receive a corpse. **b.** A tombstone, mound, or other marker indicating such a burial place. **2.** Any place of burial or final laying to rest: *The sea was his grave.* **3.** The sign or marker of a burial place. **4.** *Poetic.* Death or extinction. —**dig one's own grave.** To be the cause of one's own failure or downfall. —**turn in one's grave.** To feel shock or disapproval at some modern event or action that runs counter to one's beliefs or ideas. Used of a dead person. [Middle English *grave*, Old English *græf*, from Germanic.]

grave[2] *adj.* **graver, gravest. 1.** Extremely serious; important; weighty: *a grave decision in a time of crisis.* **2.** Fraught with danger; critical: *in grave difficulties.* **3.** Grievous; dire: *a grave sin.* **4.** Dignified in conduct; sedate: *a grave procession.* **5.** Somber or worried: *a grave expression.* **6.** (*also* grăv). *Linguistics.* **a.** Written with or modified by the mark (`), as the *è* in *Sèvres.* **b.** Articulated toward the back of the oral cavity. —See Synonyms at **serious.** ~*n.* (*also* grăv). A grave accent (`), as one indicating a pronounced *e* for the sake of meter in the usually nonsyllabic ending *-ed* in English poetry. [Old French, from Latin *gravis*, heavy, weighty.] —**grave·ly** *adv.* —**grave·ness** *n.*

grave[3] *tr.v.* **graved, graven** (grā′vən), **graving, graves. 1.** To stamp or impress deeply; fix (words or ideas, for example) permanently. **2.** *Archaic.* To sculpt or carve; engrave: *"I wish I could grave my*

sonnets on an ivory tablet" (Oscar Wilde). [Grave, graven; Middle English *graven*, *graven*, Old English *grafan* (dig, engrave), *grafen*, from Germanic; akin to GRAVE (place of burial).]

grave[4] *tr.v.* **graved, graving, graves.** To clean (the bottom of a wooden ship) by removing barnacles and other accretions, and coating with pitch. [Middle English *graven*, probably from Old French *greve*, *grave*, sand, GRAVEL.]

gra·ve[5] (grä′vā) *adv. Music.* Slowly and solemnly. Used as a direction. [Italian, from Latin *gravis*, heavy, weighty, GRAVE.] —**gra·ve** *adj.*

grave·clothes (grāv′klōz′, -klōthz′) *pl.n.* The clothes or shroud in which a body is interred.

grave·dig·ger (grāv′dĭg′ər) *n.* A person whose occupation is digging graves.

grav·el (grăv′əl) *n.* **1.** Any unconsolidated mixture of rock fragments or pebbles. **2.** *Pathology.* Sandlike granular material occurring in the kidneys or bladder. ~*tr.v.* **graveled** or **-velled, -veling** or **-velling, -vels. 1.** To apply a surface of gravel to: *gravel a drive.* **2.** *Rare.* To confuse; perplex: *His inconsistencies gravel the reader.* **3.** *Informal.* To irritate. [Middle English, from Old French *gravele*, *gravelle*, diminutive of *grave*, *greve*, gravel, sand, pebbly shore, from Celtic.]

grav·el-blind (grăv′əl-blīnd′) *adj. Literary.* Having minimal vision; purblind. [GRAVEL + BLIND (by analogy with SANDBLIND).]

grav·el·ly (grăv′ə-lē) *adj.* **1.** Of, full of, or covered with gravel. **2.** Having a harsh rasping sound: *a gravelly voice.*

graven image *n.* An idol or fetish carved in wood or stone.

grav·er (grā′vər) *n.* **1.** A person who carves or engraves; a stone-carver. **2.** An engraver's cutting tool; a burin.

grave robber *n.* A person who plunders valuables from tombs or graves or who steals corpses, as for illicit dissection.

Graves (grāvz; *French* gräv) *n.* A dry, usually white wine produced near Bordeaux, in southwestern France. [After *Graves*, district in southwestern France.]

Graves (grāvz), **Robert Ranke** (1895–1985). British poet, novelist, and critic. As a war poet, he published *Over the Brazier* (1916) and *Fairies and Fusiliers* (1917) while serving in World War I. His novels include *I, Claudius* (1934) and a semiautobiographical work on the postwar generation, *Goodbye to All That* (1929). His major work of criticism was *The White Goddess* (1948).

Graves' disease (grāvz) *n. Pathology.* **Exophthalmic goiter** *(see).* [After Robert James *Graves* (1796–1853), Irish physician.]

grave·stone (grāv′stōn′) *n.* A stone placed over a grave as a marker; a tombstone.

grave·yard (grāv′yärd′) *n.* **1.** An area set aside as a burial ground, especially a small area around a church. **2.** An event or circumstance leading to the final ruin or failure of someone or something: *the graveyard of all our hopes.* **3.** A place for storing discarded or worn-out things, especially old automobiles.

graveyard shift *n.* **1.** A work shift that runs during the early morning hours, as from midnight to 8:00 A.M. **2.** The workers on an early-morning shift.

grav·id (grăv′ĭd) *adj.* **1.** Pregnant. **2.** Full of ripe eggs or distended by such fullness: *a fish gravid with roe.* [Latin *gravidus*, pregnant, from *gravis*, heavy.] —**gra·vid·i·ty** (grə-vĭd′ə-tē), **grav·id·ness** *n.* —**grav·id·ly** *adv.*

gra·vim·e·ter (grə-vĭm′ə-tər) *n.* **1.** Any instrument used to determine specific gravity. **2.** Any instrument used to measure the earth's gravitational field at a given point on its surface. [French *gravimètre* : Latin *gravis*, heavy, GRAVE + -METER.]

grav·i·met·ric (grăv′ə-mĕt′rĭk) *adj.* Also **grav·i·met·ric·al** (-rĭ-kəl). Of or pertaining to measurement by weight: *gravimetric analysis.* Compare **volumetric.** [Latin *gravis*, heavy, GRAVE + METRIC.] —**grav·i·met·ri·cal·ly** *adv.* —**gra·vim·e·try** (grə-vĭm′ə-trē) *n.*

graving dock *n.* A dry dock in which ships are repaired and their bottoms are graved.

grav·i·tate (grăv′ə-tāt′) *intr.v.* **-tated, -tating, -tates. 1.** To move in response to the force of gravity. **2.** To move downward. **3.** To be attracted by or as if by an irresistible force: *"My excuse must be that all Celts gravitate towards each other"* (Oscar Wilde). [New Latin *gravitare*, from *gravitās*, GRAVITY.] —**grav·i·tat·er** *n.*

grav·i·ta·tion (grăv′ə-tā′shən) *n.* **1.** *Physics.* **a.** The natural phenomenon of attraction between massive bodies. **b.** The action or process of moving under the influence of this attraction. **c.** The degree of such attraction. **2.** Any movement toward a source of attraction or place of settlement: *the gravitation of the middle classes to the suburbs.* —**grav·i·ta·tion·al, grav·i·ta·tive** (grăv′ə-tā′tĭv) *adj.* —**grav·i·ta·tion·al·ly** *adv.*

gravitational constant *n. Symbol* **G** The universal constant used in Newton's law of gravitation. It is equal to Fd^2/m_1m_2 where F is the gravitational force between two masses, m_1 and m_2, separated by a distance of d. It has the value 6.670×10^{-11} N m² kg⁻².

gravitational field *n.* The region of space in which one massive body exerts a force of attraction on another massive body. The force is inversely proportional to the square of the distance between the bodies and directly proportional to the product of their masses.

gravitational interaction *n.* The interaction that occurs between bodies as a result of their mass. It is the weakest of all forms of interaction. Compare **strong interaction, weak interaction, electromagnetic interaction.**

gravitational mass *n.* The mass of a body as determined by its response to a gravitational field, especially to the force of gravity. Compare **inertial mass.**

gravitational red shift *n.* See **red shift** (sense 2).
grav·i·ton (grăv′ə-tŏn′) *n.* A particle postulated to be the quantum of gravitational interaction, and presumed to have zero electric charge, zero rest mass, and spin 2. [GRAVIT(ATION) + -ON.]
grav·i·ty (grăv′ə-tē) *n.* **1.** *Physics.* **a.** The force of gravitation, being, for any two sufficiently massive bodies, directly proportional to the product of their masses and inversely proportional to the square of the distance between them; especially, the attractive gravitational force exerted by a celestial body, such as the earth on bodies on or near its surface. **b.** Loosely, gravitation. **c.** *Rare.* Weight. **2.** Grave nature or seriousness: *the gravity of their problem.* **3.** Solemnity or dignity of manner: *"With stern and austere gravity he persevered in his task"* (Sir Walter Scott). [Old French *gravite,* from Latin *gravitās* (stem *gravitāt-*), from *gravis,* heavy, serious, GRAVE.]
gravity cell *n.* An electrolytic cell with the electrodes in two different electrolytes, which are separated into two vertical layers as a result of differences in their relative densities.
gravity feed *n.* **1.** A method of supplying a fuel, lubricant, or other liquid to an engine, boiler, or plant, that relies on gravity rather than a pump. **2.** A system for providing a continuous supply of a powder or granular solid by allowing it to trickle from the base of a container, as, for example, the system used to supply fuel to a boiler.
gra·vure (grə-vyŏŏr′) *n.* **1.** A method of printing with etched plates or cylinders; intaglio printing. **2.** A tonal reproduction process using photomechanically prepared plates or cylinders to reproduce photographs on newsprint; photogravure. **3.** A plate or reproduction produced by gravure or used in the process. [French, from *graver,* to engrave, dig into, from Old French, from Frankish *graban* (unattested).]
gra·vy (grā′vē) *n., pl.* **-vies. 1. a.** The juices that drip from cooking meat. **b.** A sauce made by thickening and seasoning these juices. **2.** *Slang.* Money or profit easily or unexpectedly gained; especially, money in excess of that required for necessities. [Middle English *gravey,* perhaps a misreading of Old French *grané,* "(dish) seasoned with grains (of spice)," from *grain,* spice, GRAIN.]
gravy boat *n.* An elongated vessel with a lip, used for serving gravy.
gravy train *n. Slang.* An occupation or job that requires little effort while yielding considerable profit.
gray[1], **grey** (grā) *adj.* **1.** Of or pertaining to an achromatic color of any lightness between the extremes of black and white. **2. a.** Dull or dark, as from lack of light: *a gray, rainy day.* **b.** Lacking in cheer; gloomy. **3. a.** Having gray hair; hoary. **b.** Old, venerable, or ancient. **4.** Intermediate in character or position, especially in the area of morality or propriety.
∼*n.* **1.** An achromatic color of any lightness between the extremes of black and white. **2.** An object or animal of the color gray. **3.** *Sometimes* **Gray. a.** A member of the Confederate Army in the Civil War. **b.** The Confederate Army itself. Compare **blue.**
gray[2] *n. Abbr.* **Gy.** The SI unit of absorbed dose of ionizing radiation equal to the energy in joules absorbed by one kilogram of irradiated material. [After L.H. *Gray* (died 1965), British radiobiologist.]
Gray (grā), **Thomas** (1716–71). English poet. He was educated at Cambridge, where he spent most of his life as a scholar and professor of history and modern languages. His most famous poem, *Elegy Written in a Country Churchyard* (1751), won him the offer of the poet laureateship in 1757, which he declined.
gray·beard (grā′bîrd′) *n.* An old man.
gray eminence *n.* An **eminence grise** *(see).*
Gray Friar *n.* A **Franciscan** *(see).*
gray hen. Variant of **greyhen.**
gray·ish (grā′ĭsh) *adj.* Having a perceptible quality of grayness.
gray·lag goose (grā′lăg′) *n.* A gray goose, *Anser anser,* of marshy areas of the Old World. [Possibly GRAY + dialectal *lag,* last.]
gray·ling (grā′lĭng) *n., pl.* **-lings** or collectively **grayling. 1.** Any of several freshwater food fishes of the genus *Thymallus,* of the Northern Hemisphere, having a small mouth and a large dorsal fin. **2.** Any of several grayish or brownish butterflies of the family Satyridae, especially the European species *Eumenis semele.*
gray matter *n.* **1.** The brownish-gray nerve tissue of the brain and spinal cord, composed of nerve cells and fibers and some supportive tissue. **2.** *Informal.* Brains; intellect.
gray mullet *n.* A fish, the **mullet** *(see).*
Gray's Inn (grāz) *n.* One of the four legal societies forming the **Inns of Court** *(see)* in England.
gray squirrel *n.* A common squirrel, *Sciurus carolinensis,* of eastern North America, having gray or blackish fur and a very bushy tail.
gray·wacke (grā′wăk′, -wăk′ə) *n.* Any of various shale-containing dark-gray sandstones. [Partial translation of German *grauwacke* : *grau,* gray + *Wacke,* boulder.]
gray whale *n.* A whalebone whale, *Eschrichtius glaucus,* of Pacific waters, having grayish coloring with white blotches.
gray wolf *n.* The **timber wolf** *(see).*
Graz (gräts). Formerly **Gratz.** The second-largest city in Austria, on the Mur River in the southeast of the country. It is the capital of Styria province.
graze[1] *v.* **grazed, grazing, grazes.** —*intr.* **1.** To feed on growing grasses and herbage. **2.** To pasture livestock. —*tr.* **1.** To put (livestock) out to feed. **2.** To tend (feeding livestock) in a pasture. **3.** To feed on (pasture). [Middle English *grasen,* to feed on grass, Old English *grasian,* from *græs,* GRASS.] —**graz·er** *n.*
graze[2] *v.* **grazed, grazing, grazes.** —*tr.* **1.** To touch lightly in passing; skim; brush. **2.** To scrape or scratch slightly; abrade. —*intr.* To scrape or touch something lightly in passing.
∼*n.* **1.** A brushing or scraping along a surface. **2.** A scratch or abrasion resulting from such contact. [Perhaps from GRAZE (remove grass close to the ground).]
gra·zier (grā′zhər) *n.* A person who grazes and fattens cattle.
graz·ing (grā′zĭng) *n.* Land used for feeding; pasturage.
gra·zio·so (grä-tsyō′sō) *adv. Music.* Gracefully; smoothly. Used as a direction. [Italian, from Latin *grātiōsus,* GRACIOUS.] —**gra·zio·so** *adj.*
grease (grēs) *n.* **1.** Animal fat when melted or soft. **2.** Any thick oil or viscous lubricant. **3. a.** The oily substance present in raw wool; suint. **b.** Raw wool that has not been cleansed of this. In this sense, also called "grease wool," "wool in the grease."
∼*tr.v.* (grēs, grēz) **greased, greasing, greases. 1.** To coat, smear, lubricate, or soil with grease. **2.** To smear (a muffin tin, frying pan, or the like) with cooking fat. —**grease someone's palm.** *Slang.* To bribe. [Middle English *grese,* from Old French *graisse,* from Vulgar Latin *crassia* (unattested), from Latin *crassus,* fat.]
grease monkey *n. Informal.* A mechanic.
grease paint *n.* Theatrical make-up. Also called "paint."
grease·wood (grēs′wŏŏd′) *n.* **1.** A spiny shrub, *Sarcobatus vermiculatus,* of western North America, the oil from which has been used as fuel. **2.** Any of various similar or related plants, such as the **creosote bush** *(see).*
greas·y (grē′sē, -zē) *adj.* **-ier, -iest. 1.** Coated or soiled with grease. **2.** Containing grease, especially too much grease. **3.** Suggestive of or resembling something greased; slick; unctuous: *a greasy character.* —**greas·i·ly** *adv.* —**greas·i·ness** *n.*
greasy spoon *n. Informal.* A small, usually unsanitary restaurant that sells cheap food.
great (grāt) *adj.* **greater, greatest.** *Abbr.* **gt. 1.** Extremely large; bulky; big. **2.** Larger than others of the same kind: *the great auk.* **3.** Large in quantity or number: *A great throng awaited him.* **4.** Of considerable duration; extensive in time or distance. **5.** Extreme in magnitude, degree, or extent: *a great mistake.* **6.** Significant; important; meaningful: *A great work of art.* **7.** Chief or principal: *the great house on the estate.* **8.** Superior in quality or character; noble; excellent. **9.** Powerful; influential: *"Seek to be good, but aim not to be great"* (George Lyttelton). **10.** Eminent; distinguished: *a great leader.* **11.** Grand; aristocratic. **12.** *Archaic.* Pregnant. Used with *with*: *great with child.* **13.** *Informal.* Enthusiastic: *a great boxing fan.* **14.** *Informal.* Skillful: *She is great at algebra.* **15.** *Informal.* First-rate; very good: *a great book.* **16.** Used as an intensive, especially in exclamations: *great balls of fire!* **17.** *Archaic.* Capital; upper-case. Said of letters: *a great A.* **18.** Designating a family relationship or relative one generation removed from the relative specified. Used in combination: *a great-grandfather.*
∼*n.* **greats.** Outstanding individuals: *Many of the sport's greats were there.*
∼*adv. Informal.* Very well. [Middle English *grete,* Old English *great,* thick, coarse, from Germanic.] —**great·ness** *n.*
great ape *n.* Any large anthropoid ape, such as a gorilla or orangutan.
Great Ar·te·sian Basin (är-tē′zhən). Largest artesian area in the world. It lies in eastern Australia, between the Great Dividing Range and the Western Plateau and stretches northward to the Gulf of Carpentaria. The basin covers *c.* 1,750,000 square kilometers (676,250 square miles). It derives its water from the Eastern Highlands.
great auk *n.* A large, flightless sea bird, *Pinguinus impennis,* formerly common on northern Atlantic coasts but extinct since the middle of the 19th century.
great-aunt (grāt′ănt′, -änt′) *n.* A sister of one's grandparent. Also called "grand-aunt."
Great Au·stra·lian Bight (ô-strāl′yən bīt). A broad bay in the coast of southern Australia. It extends from West Cape in Western Australia to South West Cape in Tasmania.
Great Bar·ri·er Reef (băr′ē-ər). Largest coral reef in the world, in the Coral Sea off the coast of northeastern Australia. It extends from Torres Strait along the coast of Queensland almost to southern New Guinea, a distance of *c.* 2,012 kilometers (1,250 miles). Its banks of vividly colored corals teem with exotic fish and crustaceans, and there are coral islets overgrown with mangroves, palms, and flowering plants.
Great Basin. Region of the western United States, between the Wasatch Mts. and the Sierra Nevada. Covering an area of *c.* 518,000 square kilometers (200,000 square miles), it consists of steep-sided block mountains with broad plains between. Though not entirely arid, it includes Death Valley and the Mojave and Great Salt Lake deserts.
Great Bear *n. Astronomy.* A constellation, **Ursa Major** *(see).*
Great Bear Lake. Lake in north-central Mackenzie district in Northwest Territories, Canada. It is 31,800 square kilometers (12,275 square miles) in area, the largest lake in Canada.
Great Brit·ain (brĭt′n). *Abbr.* **G.B.** The largest island in Europe, in the northwest of the continent and separated from the mainland by the English Channel. The name has been used since 1707 to denote the political union of England, Scotland, and Wales. Great Britain includes the Isle of Man and Channel Islands, as well as the province of Northern Ireland. It is often loosely referred to as "Britain." See also **United Kingdom.**
great circle *n.* A circle that is the intersection of the surface of a

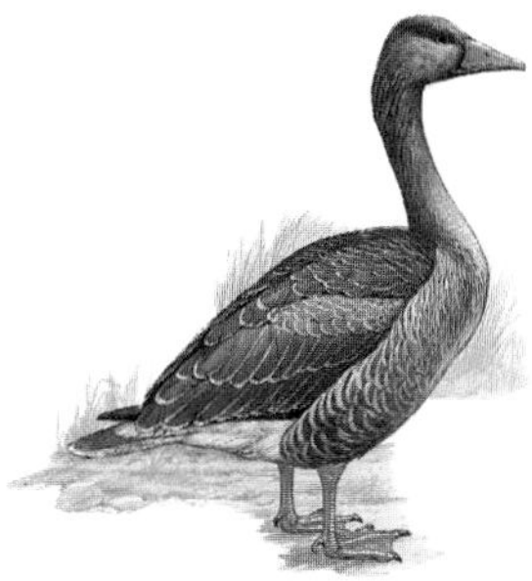

graylag goose *This European ancestor of the farmyard goose may have got its name from the fact that it lagged behind when other birds migrated. Graylags mate for life and repeat their courtship ritual whenever they meet after being separated for any length of time.*

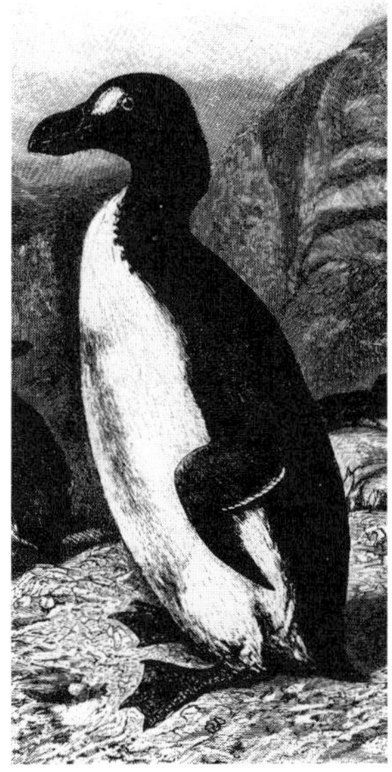

great auk *Ungainly and defenseless on land, the great auk was a fast, strong swimmer and lived on the fish that is caught around the shores of the North Atlantic. It was about 75 centimeters (2½ feet) tall, black and white like a penguin, and had very small wings that were useless for flying. It was hunted to extinction in the 19th century.*

sphere with a plane passing through the center of the sphere. Compare **small circle.**

great·coat (grāt′kōt′) n. A heavy overcoat.

Great Dane n. A very large and powerful dog of a breed developed in Germany, having a smooth, short coat and a narrow head.

Great Divide n. 1. See **Continental Divide** (sense 2). 2. The **Great Dividing Range.**

Great Dividing Range. Also **Great Divide.** Belt of highlands and plateaus in eastern Australia, extending roughly parallel to the coast, from the base of Cape York Peninsula to the Grampians. Acting as the watershed of the eastern seaboard, it is only partially mountainous but includes the Australian Alps, which rise to 2,228 meters (7,310 feet) at Mt. Kosciusko.

great·en (grāt′n) v. **-ened, -ening, -ens.** Archaic. —tr. To make great or greater; enlarge. —intr. To become great or greater.

Great·er, great·er (grā′tər) adj. Designating a city and its immediate suburbs: *Greater Los Angeles.*

Greater An·til·les (ăn-tĭl′ēz). Northern part of the chain of islands that separates the Caribbean Sea from the main body of the Atlantic Ocean. It includes Cuba, Jamaica, Hispaniola (Haiti and the Dominican Republic), and Puerto Rico, the four largest islands in the West Indies. See also **Lesser Antilles.** See map at **Latin America.**

greater doxology n. The **Gloria in excelsis Deo** (see).

Greater Man·ches·ter (măn′chĕs-tər, -chĭs-tər). Since 1974, a metropolitan county in northwestern England. It includes the cities of Manchester and Salford and the surrounding towns of Wigan, Bolton, Bury, Rochdale, Oldham, Ashton-Under-Lyne, and Stockport.

great·est (grāt′əst). Superlative of **great.**
~n. Informal. A wonderful or admirable person or thing. Preceded by *the: When I was a child I thought this book was just the greatest.*

Great Falls. City of north-central Montana, at the confluence of the Missouri and Sun rivers and near the falls that give the city its name. The city as oil and copper refineries and flour mills. It is often called "Electric City" because of the hydroelectric power plants in the vicinity.

Great Glen. Valley in northwest Scotland. It stretches for c. 97 kilometers (60 miles) from the Moray Firth to Loch Linnhe. The valley was formed by a fault in the earth's crust, and the glacial lakes that developed along the fault line, including Loch Ness, have a depth hundreds of feet below sea level.

great-grand·child (grāt′grănd′chīld′) n., pl. **-children** (-chīl′drən). Any of the children of a grandchild.

great-grand·daugh·ter (grāt′grăn′dô′tər, -grănd′dô′tər) n. Any daughter of a grandchild.

great-grand·fa·ther (grāt′grănd′fä′thər) n. The father of any grandparent.

great-grand·moth·er (grāt′grănd′mŭth′ər) n. The mother of any grandparent.

great-grand·par·ent (grāt′grănd′pâr′ənt) n. Either of the parents of any grandparent.

Great Dane *Bred originally for boar hunting in Germany about 400 years ago, this large dog is now bred as a domestic pet and for showing. A full-grown Great Dane may stand 75 centimeters (30 inches) tall at the shoulder and weigh 54 kilograms (120 pounds).*

great-grand·son (grāt′grănd′sŭn′) n. Any of the sons of a grandchild.

Great Grimsby. See **Grimsby.**

great gross n. Abbr. **g.gr.** A dozen gross.

great-heart·ed (grāt′här′tĭd) adj. 1. Noble or courageous in spirit; stouthearted. 2. Great in generosity; unselfish; magnanimous. —**great·heart·ed·ly** adv. —**great·heart·ed·ness** n.

great horned owl n. A large North American owl, *Bubo virginianus,* having brownish plumage and prominent ear tufts.

Great Lake. The largest natural freshwater lake in Australia, lying in the central uplands of Tasmania. It has a surface area of 142 square kilometers (54 square miles) but an average depth of only 13 meters (43 feet). It is used as a hydroelectric reservoir.

Great Lakes. Five freshwater lakes in central North America, forming part of the boundary between Canada and the United States. From east to west they are Lake Ontario, Lake Erie, Lake Huron, Lake Michigan, and Lake Superior, and together they form the world's largest area of fresh water. Only Lake Michigan is wholly in the United States. They were formed at the end of the last Ice Age, when their glacier-carved basins filled with water. The largest of the lakes, and the largest freshwater lake in the world, is Lake Superior; the smallest is Lake Erie, which is also the only one of the five whose depth does not extend below sea level.

great·ly (grāt′lē) adv. 1. In a style or manner befitting greatness; nobly. 2. To a great degree; very much; exceedingly.

great-neph·ew (grāt′nĕf′yōō, -nĕv′yōō) n. A son of a nephew or niece. Also called "grand-nephew."

great-niece (grāt′nēs′) n. A daughter of a nephew or niece. Also called "grand-niece."

great organ n. The principal manual, together with its pipes, of an organ that has more than one manual.

Great Ouse (ōōz). River in southern England, sometimes referred to simply as the Ouse. It rises in Northamptonshire and flows northeast for c. 250 kilometers (155 miles) until it empties into The Wash near King's Lynn, Norfolk.

Great Plains. Vast area of grassland in North America, stretching from the Mackenzie River delta in the north to southern Texas. The plains slope generally eastward from the foot of the Rocky Mts. to c. 100° W, where they merge with the wetter prairies. Most of the area is given over to ranches for cattle or sheep. Wheat is grown in the east where there is sufficient water, but soil erosion can be a problem, as in the Dust Bowl, created in the 1930's. The Great Plains have vast mineral resources, including oil, gas, coal, and gold.

Great Power n. A nation that has great military strength and economic influence; a superpower.

great primer n. Printing. Formerly, a size of type, 18-point.

Great Rebellion n. The **English Civil War** (see). Preceded by *the.*

Great Red Spot n. Astronomy. A feature of Jupiter, the **Red Spot** (see).

Great Rift Valley (rĭft). An extended geologic fault system, stretching for c. 6,400 kilometers (4,000 miles) from northern Syria, through the trough of the Red Sea and south as far as central Mozambique. For much of its length its traces have been lost by erosion, but in some parts, most spectacularly in southern Kenya, its cliffs rise thousands of feet. In Africa the valley has a western and eastern branch, with lakes and volcanoes.

Great Russian n. 1. A member of the main ethnic group of Russian-speaking people, inhabiting the central and northeastern U.S.S.R. 2. The language of these people that is the official Russian language.
~adj. Of or pertaining to this people or their language.

Great Salt Lake. A shallow saltwater lake in northeastern Utah. It is the largest saltwater lake in North America, with a surface area of c. 2,600 square kilometers (1,000 square miles). Its size and depth vary from year to year according to climatic conditions, but its average depth is c. 4 meters (13 feet).

Great Salt Lake Desert. A flat, arid region of northwestern Utah, southwest of Great Salt Lake. It is c. 177 kilometers (110 miles) long, barren of vegetation, and virtually uninhabitable.

Great Sand Dunes National Monument. Area in southern Colorado set aside to preserve large, high sand dunes in the Sangre de Christo Mts.

Great Sanhedrin n. The **Sanhedrin** (see).

Great Schism n. The division in the Roman Catholic Church from 1378 to 1417, when rival popes ruled at Rome and Avignon.

great seal n. Often **Great Seal.** The principal seal of a government, sovereign, or state, used to stamp very important official documents.

Great Slave Lake. Canada's second-largest lake, in southern Mackenzie district, Northwest Territories. It is the deepest lake in North America, reaching a depth of 615 meters (2,015 feet).

Great Smoky Mountains. Also **Great Smokies.** Part of the Appalachians on the North Carolina-Tennessee border, named for the smokelike haze that envelops them. They include many streams and waterfalls, hiking trails, luxuriant vegetation, and numerous recreation areas.

Great Spirit n. The principal deity in the religion of many North American Indian tribes.

Great St. Bernard Pass. See **St. Bernard Pass.**

Great Trek n. In South Africa, the migration, from the mid-1830's to the mid-1840's, of Boer farmers northward away from the Cape in order to find lands free from British rule. Preceded by *the.*

GREECE

(Map of Greece showing: BULGARIA, YUGOSLAVIA, MACEDONIA, Sérrai, Xánthi, Kaválla, Kastoria, Salonica (Thessaloniki), Thásos, Samothrace (Samothráki), TURKEY, ALBANIA, Smólikas 2637m, 2917m Mt Olympus (Ólimbos), Mt Athos 2033m, Lemnos (Límnos), 40°N, Corfu, Meteora, Lárisa, THESSALY, GREECE, Ioánnina, Northern Sporades, Lesbos (Lésvos), TURKEY, Levkás, Thermopylae, AEGEAN SEA, Agrínion, Delphi, Aliviérion, Euboea (Évvoia), Chios (Khíos), Kefallinia, Patras (Pátrai), Rhamnous, Marathon, 38°N, Corinth (Kórinthos), Asprópirgos, ATHENS (ATHÍNAI), Piraeus, Sounion, Ándros, Sámos, Olympia, Tiryns, Mycenae, Aegina (Aíyina), Tínos, Zákinthos, Loukás, Nauplia (Návplion), Delos (Dhílos), IONIAN SEA, Peloponnese (Pelopónnisos), Mistras, Sparta (Spárti), MIRTOAN SEA, Náxos, Cyclades, Cos (Kós), Sporades, Milos, Rhodes (Ródhos), 36°N, Cerigo (Kíthira), Santorini (Thíra), Dodecanese, Kárpathos, SEA OF CRETE, Kms 0 50 100 150, Miles 0 50 100, Canea, CRETE (KRÍTI), Iráklion, Knossos, Malia, Hagia Triada, Phaestos, MEDITERRANEAN SEA)

great-un·cle (grāt′ŭng′kəl) *n.* The uncle of one's father or mother. Also called "grand-uncle."

Great Vic·to·ri·a Desert (vĭk-tôr′ē-ə). Region, *c.* 725 kilometers (450 miles) wide, in southeastern Western Australia and western South Australia. It is bordered on the north by Gibson Desert and on the south by Nullarbor Plain.

Great Wall of Chi·na (chī′nə). A fortification, consisting of walls, watchtowers, and guard stations, extending 2,400 kilometers (1,500 miles) in a winding course across northern China from Gansu province to Hebei province. For most of its length it runs along the southern border of the Mongolian plain. It was built originally to keep out nomadic invaders from the north, and the first continuous wall was built in the 3rd century B.C. Most of the present wall was built during the Ming dynasty (1368–1644). The average height of the wall is 7.5 meters (25 feet) and the average thickness at the base is *c.* 7 meters (23 feet), although at most points it tapers to *c.* 3.5 meters (11 feet) at the top.

Great War *n.* **World War I** *(see).* Preceded by *the.*

great white shark *n.* A **white shark** *(see).*

Great Yar·mouth (yär′məth). Port and tourist resort in Norfolk, England. Built on a spit at the mouth of the Yare River, its fine harbor is one of the world's largest herring ports.

great year *n.* A period of 25,800 years that is one complete cycle of the equinoxes.

greave (grēv) *n.* Leg armor worn below the knee. [Middle English, from Old French *grevet*, shin.]

greaves (grēvz) *pl.n.* The unmelted residue left after animal fat or tallow has been rendered. [Low German *greven.*]

grebe (grēb) *n.* Any of various diving birds of the family Podicipedidae, that have lobed, fleshy membranes along each toe and a pointed bill. [French *grèbet*.]

Gre·cian (grē′shən) *adj.* **1.** Conforming to the styles and tastes of classical Greece. Said especially of architecture. **2.** Greek.
~*n.* A native of Greece. [Latin *Graecia,* Greece, from *Graecus,* GREEK.]

Grecian bend *n.* A posture in which the upper torso is thrust forward and the pelvis and buttocks backward, assumed by women of fashion in the late 19th century and often emphasized by wearing a bustle.

Grecian nose *n.* A long, straight nose extending in an unbroken line from the forehead.

Gre·cism, Grae·cism (grē′sĭz′əm) *n.* **1.** The style or spirit of Greek culture, art, or thought. **2.** Anything done in imitation of such style or spirit. **3.** An idiom of the Greek language.

Gre·cize, Grae·cize (grē′sīz′) *v.* **-cized, -cizing, -cizes.** —*tr.* To provide with or convert into a Greek form or style; Hellenize. —*intr.* To follow or adopt Greek culture, art, or thought. [French *gréciser,* from Latin *Graecizāre,* from Greek *Graekizein,* to speak Greek, from *Graikos,* GREEK.]

Greco, El. See **El Greco.**

Greco–, Graeco– *prefix.* Indicates Greek; for example, **Greco-Roman.** [From Latin *Graecus.*]

Gre·co-Ro·man, Grae·co-Ro·man (grē′kō-rō′mən, grĕk′ō-) *adj.* Of, relating to, or pertaining to both Greece and Rome: *Greco-Roman mythology.* [GRECO- + ROMAN.]

gree¹ (grē) *n. Scottish.* **1.** Superiority or victory. **2.** The prize or reward for victory. [Middle English, rank, from Old French *gre,* from Latin *gradus,* GRADE.]

gree² *intr.v.* **greed, greeing, grees.** *Northern British.* To be in harmony or agreement. [Aphetic variant of AGREE.]

gree³ *n. Obsolete.* Good will; favor. [Middle English, from Old French *gre,* from Late Latin *grātum,* from Latin *grātus,* pleasing, thankful.]

Greece (grēs). *Ancient Greek* **Hel·las** (hĕl′əs) *Modern Greek* **El·las** (ĕ-läs′). *Abbr.* **Gr.** Republic at the southern tip of the Balkan Peninsula. It comprises an indented, mountainous mainland whose ranges continue in numerous islands that make up a fifth of the country. Cereals, olives, and vines are the chief crops, and large numbers of sheep and goats are kept. Greece relies mainly on imported fuels, but oil has been discovered beneath the Aegean Sea. Tourism is a major industry, and the country has large merchant and fishing fleets. The Minoan civilization, Europe's first, flourished in Crete (*c.* 3000–1400 B.C.). Trade (*c.* 1100 B.C.) brought prosperity and heralded the Classical Age. Intercity strife allowed Philip II of Macedon to conquer most of Greece (338 B.C.), and his son Alexander (356–323 B.C.) ruled both Macedon and Greece and built a short-lived empire that was to spread Greek culture from Macedon and Egypt to India. The Romans conquered Greece (168–146 B.C.), and it was later part of the Byzantine Empire. It was conquered by the Ottoman Turks in the 15th century, but finally gained independence (1832) and a king (1833) after the Greek War of Independence. The army usurped power and deposed the king (1967) but was removed in 1974. Greece became a republic in 1975. The country became a full member of the European Economic Community (1981). It is also a strategic member of NATO but has strained relations with fellow member Turkey over its claims in the Aegean and Cyprus. Area, 131,944 square kilometers (50,944 square miles). Population, 9,600,000. Capital, Athens.

greed (grēd) *n.* A rapacious desire for more than one needs or deserves, as of food, wealth, or power; avarice. [Back-formation from GREEDY.]

greed·y (grē′dē) *adj.* **-ier, -iest. 1.** Excessively eager to acquire or possess something, especially in quantity; covetous; avaricious. **2.** Wanting to eat or drink more than one can reasonably consume; gluttonous; voracious. [Middle English *gredy,* Old English *grǣdig,* from Germanic *grǣdhuz* (unattested), hunger.] —**greed·i·ly** *adv.* —**greed·i·ness** *n.*

greegree. Variant of **grigri.**

Greek (grēk) *n.* **1.** *Abbr.* **Gk., Gr.** The language of the Hellenes, constituting the Hellenic group of Indo-European, chronologically divided into **Proto-Greek, Ancient Greek** with the **Koine, Late Greek, Medieval Greek,** and **Modern Greek** *(all of which see).* ***Note:*** Most frequently *Greek* is used to mean *Ancient Greek* or *Classical Greek,* as in the etymologies of this dictionary. **2.** *Abbr.* **Gk., Gr.** A native or inhabitant of Greece, or a descendant of such a person. **3.** *Informal.* Something unintelligible. Used chiefly in the phrase *It's Greek to me.* **4.** A member of the Greek Orthodox Church.
~*adj.* **1.** *Abbr.* **Gk., Gr.** Of, pertaining to, or designating Greece, the Hellenes, their language, or their culture. **2.** Of, pertaining to, or designating the Greek Orthodox Church. [Middle English *Grek,* Old English *Grēcas, Crēcas* (plural), from Germanic *Krēkaz* (unattested), from Latin *Graecus* (singular), from Greek *Graikos, Graikoi,* the name of a prehistoric tribe of Epirus, probably from Illyria.]

Greek Catholic *n.* **1.** A member of the Eastern Orthodox Church. **2.** A member of a Uniat Church.

Greek Church *n.* **1.** See **Eastern Church** (sense 1). **2.** The **Eastern Orthodox Church** *(see).* **3.** The **Greek Orthodox Church** *(see).*

Greek cross *n.* A cross formed by two bars of equal length crossing at the middle at right angles to each other.

Greek fire *n.* An incendiary chemical substance used in ancient and medieval times to set fire to enemy ships; specifically, the substance used by the Byzantine Greeks in the seventh century.

Greek god *n.* A handsome man, especially one whose looks seem to approach the Greek ideal of male beauty.

Greek Orthodox Church *n.* The established self-governing church of Greece, a part of the Eastern Orthodox Church, with its own chief bishop but recognizing the Patriarch of Constantinople as head. Also called "Greek Church."

Gree·ley (grē′lē), **Horace** (1811–72). U.S. journalist and politician. He founded and edited the *New Yorker* (1834–41), the *Log Cabin* (1840), and the *New York Tribune* (1841–72), a daily paper of high quality, through which he expressed his antislavery and moralistic views. In 1872 he unsuccessfully ran for president.

green (grēn) *n.* **1.** Any of a group of colors that may vary in lightness and saturation, whose hue is that of the emerald, or somewhat less yellow than that of growing grass; the hue of that portion of the spectrum lying between yellow and blue; one of the additive or light primaries; one of the psychological primary hues, evoked in the normal observer by radiant energy having a wavelength of approximately 530 nanometers. See **primary color. 2. a.** Something green in color. **b.** Green clothing. **3. greens.** Leafy plants or plant parts eaten as vegetables or in salads. **4. a.** A grassy area or lawn; especially, one used for a specified purpose: *a putting green; a bowling green.* **b.** A grass-covered area in the middle of a village. **5.** A green traffic light that signals that drivers may proceed.
~*adj.* **1.** Of the color green. **2.** Covered with green vegetation or foliage. **3.** Made with green or leafy vegetables: *a green salad.* **4.** Mild or temperate in climate. **5.** Fresh; youthful; vigorous. **6.** Not mature or ripe; young: *green bananas.* **7.** Pale and sickly in appearance; wan. **8.** Not yet fully processed, as: **a.** Not aged: *green wood.* **b.** Not cured or tanned: *green pelts.* **9.** Designating one of three quark colors, the others being red and blue. **10.** Lacking training, conditioning, or experience. **11.** Easily duped or deceived; gullible. **12.** *Informal.* Envious; jealous.
~*v.* **greened, greening, greens.** —*tr.* To make green. —*intr.* To become green. [Middle English *grene,* Old English *grēne,* from Germanic.] —**green·ish** *adj.* —**green·ly** *adv.* —**green·ness** *n.* —**green·y** *adj.*

green algae *pl.n.* Algae of the division Chlorophyta, which includes spirogyra, sea lettuce, and others having pronounced green coloring due to predominance of the pigment chlorophyll.

Green·a·way (grēn′ə-wā′), **Kate,** original name Catherine (1846–1901). English water colorist and illustrator. She excelled as an illustrator of her own children's books, such as *Under the Window* (1879), *A Day in a Child's Life* (1881), and *Kate Greenaway's Birthday Album* (1885).

green·back (grēn′băk′) *n. Informal.* **1.** A legal-tender note of U.S. currency. **2.** A dollar bill.

Greenback Party *n.* A former U.S. political party, organized in 1874, that advocated the use of inconvertible paper money.

green ban *n. Australian.* A refusal by a trade union to do work that may harm the environment.

green bean *n.* The **string bean** *(see).*

green belt *n.* An area of parks, farmland, or uncultivated land surrounding a town or city.

Green Beret *n.* A member of the U.S. Army Special Forces. [From the green beret that is part of the uniform.]

green·bot·tle (grēn′bŏt′l) *n.* A common insect, *Lucilia caesar,* related to the blowflies, that has a green metallic coloring and lays its eggs in decaying flesh.

green·bri·er (grēn′brī′ər) *n.* A plant, the **catbrier** *(see).*

green card *n.* **1.** A U.S. permit for aliens allowing unconditional residence and employment. **2.** An international insurance document for motorists.

green corn *n.* Young, tender ears of sweet corn.

green currency *n.* Formerly, any artificial currency unit, such as

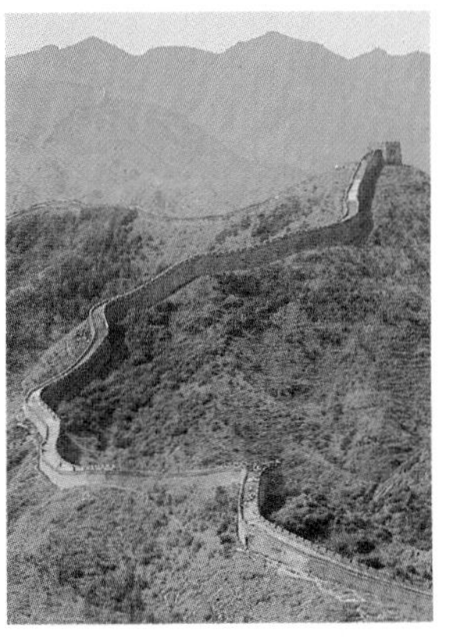

Great Wall of China *The Chinese emperor, Shih Huang Ti (259–210 B.C.), joined together several defensive wall sections to create the enormous barrier known as the Great Wall of China. This section of the present-day wall is near the Chinese capital, Beijing.*

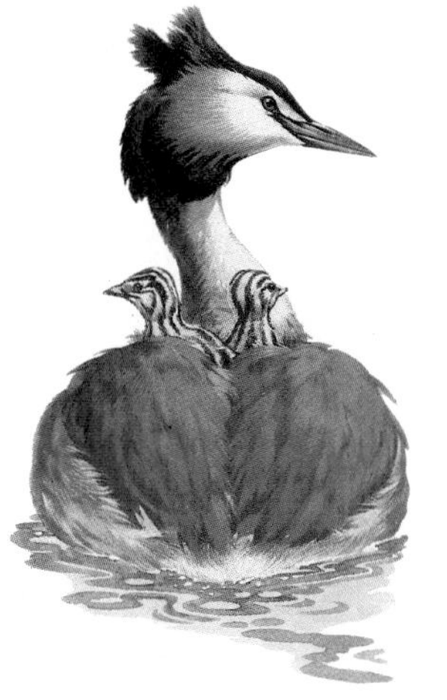

grebe *Species of grebe are found in all the world's continents except Antarctica. Most build floating nests of weeds, anchored to reeds in freshwater lakes and slow-flowing rivers, and young chicks are often carried on the parents' backs. This is the great crested grebe,* Podiceps cristatus.

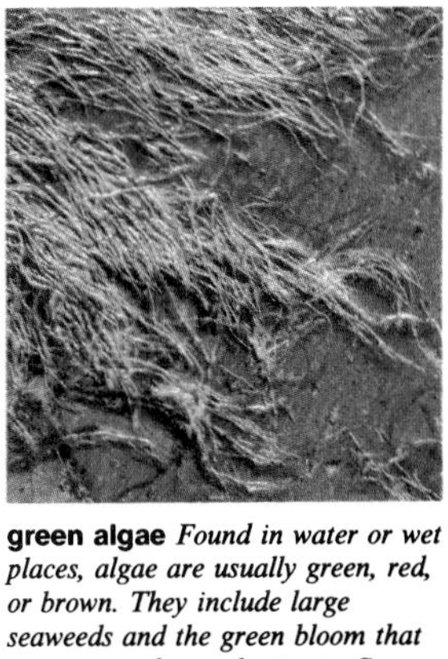

green algae *Found in water or wet places, algae are usually green, red, or brown. They include large seaweeds and the green bloom that appears on damp plant pots. Some species combine with fungi to form lichens.*

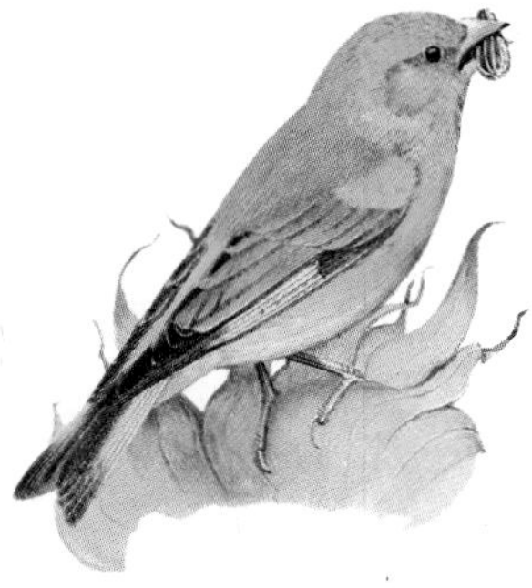

greenfinch *A farmland and garden bird of Europe and western Asia. It feeds on seeds that it cracks open with its short, stout beak.*

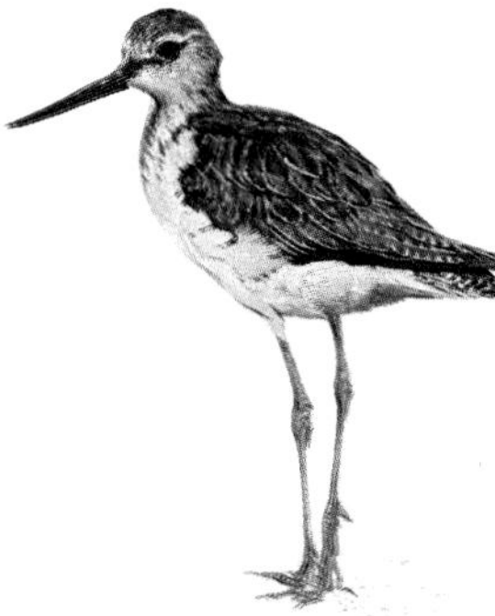

greenshank *The breeding grounds of the greenshank are found all through northern Europe and Asia. In winter the birds fly south to the Mediterranean and Africa. Greenshanks wade in fairly deep water, feeding on insects and small fish.*

PRONUNCIATION KEY

ă, pat; ā, pay; âr, care;
ä, father, are; b, bib;
ch, church; d, deed; ĕ, pet;
ē, be; f, fife; g, gag; h, hat;
hw, which; ĭ, pit; ī, pie;
îr, pier; j, judge; k, kick;
l, lid, needle; m, mum;
n, no, sudden; ng, thing;
ŏ, pot; ō, toe; ô, paw, for;
oi, noise; ou, out; o͝o, book;
o͞o, boot; p, pop; r, roar;
s, sauce; sh, ship, dish;
t, tight; th, thin, path;
th, this, bathe; ŭ, cut; ûr, fur;
v, valve; w, with; y, yes;
z, zebra, size; zh, vision;
ə, about, item, edible, gallop, circus, peaceful

IN FOREIGN WORDS:

à, *Fr.* ami; œ, *Fr.* feu, *Ger.* schön; ü, *Fr.* tu, *Ger.* über; KH, *Ger.* ich, *Scot.* loch; N, *Fr.* bon; y', *Fr.* Compiègne

STRESS MARKS:

Primary stress: ′
in·cite′ (ĭn-sīt′)
Secondary stress: ′
in′sight′ (ĭn′sīt′)

the green pound, used for agricultural transactions within the European Economic Community in order to protect Community prices from the currency fluctuations of the member nations. See **ECU.**

green dragon *n.* A plant, *Arisaema dracontium,* of eastern North America, having minute flowers at the base of a long stalk projecting from a narrow green bract. Also called "dragonroot."

Greene (grēn), **(Henry) Grahame** (1904–). British novelist and playwright. He writes both serious and light novels, the former marked by questions of morality and redemption (Greene is a convert to Roman Catholicism). Among his major works are *Brighton Rock* (1938) and *The End of the Affair* (1951). Other novels display Greene's interest in political and social troubles; for example, *The Quiet American* (1955) and *The Human Factor* (1978). He has also written short stories, plays, and film scripts such as *The Third Man* (1949).

green·er·y (grē′nə-rē) *n., pl.* **-ies. 1. a.** Green foliage; verdure. **b.** Such foliage used for decoration. **2.** A place where plants are grown.

green-eyed (grēn′īd′) *adj.* **1.** Having green eyes. **2.** Jealous.

green·finch (grēn′fĭnch′) *n.* A Eurasian bird, *Carduelis chloris* (or *Chloris chloris*), having green and yellow plumage.

green fingers *pl.n. Chiefly British Informal.* A **green thumb** *(see).*

green·fly (grēn′flī′) *n., pl.* **-flies** or collectively **greenfly.** A green aphid commonly occurring as a parasite on cultivated plants.

green·gage (grēn′gāj′) *n.* **1.** A variety of plum, *Prunus domestica italica,* whose fruit has yellowish-green skin and sweet flesh. **2.** The fruit of this tree. [GREEN + *gage,* after Sir William *Gage* (1777–1864), English botanist, who introduced it into England from France.]

green gland *n.* Either of a pair of excretory organs in certain crustaceans that discharges waste matter through an opening at the base of the antennae.

green·gro·cer (grēn′grō′sər) *n. Chiefly British.* A retailer of fresh fruit and vegetables. **—green·gro·cer·y** *n.*

green·head (grēn′hĕd′) *n.* **1.** A male mallard duck. **2.** Any of various green-headed Australian ants of the genus *Chalcopnera,* having a powerful sting.

green·heart (grēn′härt′) *n.* **1.** A tropical American tree, *Ocotea rodioei* (or *Nectandra rodioei*), having dark, greenish, durable wood. **2.** Any of various similar or related trees. **3.** The wood of such a tree.

green·horn (grēn′hôrn′) *n. Informal.* **1.** An inexperienced or immature person. **2.** A newcomer, especially to a country, who is unfamiliar with local ways. **3.** A gullible person. [Originally, a young animal with immature horns.]

green·house (grēn′hous′) *n.* **1.** A usually glass-enclosed structure used for cultivating plants that require controlled temperature and humidity. **2.** *Informal.* A part of an aircraft covered with a clear plastic bubble or shell.

greenhouse effect *n.* **1.** A heating effect that occurs in greenhouses as a result of solar radiation passing through the glass and heating the contents, which emit infrared radiation that cannot escape through the glass. **2.** The analogous effect that results from the absorption of solar radiation by the earth, its conversion and reemission in the infrared, the absorption of the infrared radiation by atmospheric ozone, water vapor, and carbon dioxide, and the consequent gradual rise in the temperature of the atmosphere.

green·ing (grē′nĭng) *n.* An apple of any of several varieties having green-skinned fruit, used chiefly in cooking.

green·keep·er (grēn′kē′pər) *n.* A person who looks after the greens of golf courses.

Green·land (grēn′lənd, -lănd′). *Danish* **Grøn·land** (grœn′län′). Island belonging to Denmark, lying mostly within the Arctic Circle. It is the largest island in the world. Most of the island is permanently ice-covered and uninhabited. The bulk of the population, which is of mixed Eskimo and European descent, is concentrated on the west coast. Fishing and fish processing are the principal industries and there is some mining. Greenland was discovered by Eric the Red in *c.* 960, but modern settlement of the island dates from the early 18th century, when it came under Danish control. It became an integral part of Denmark (1953), but gained internal home rule in 1979. It has great strategic importance, and there are U.S. air bases on it. Area, 2,175,000 square kilometers (840,000 square miles). Capital, Nuuk (formerly Godthåb). See map at **Arctic Ocean. —Green·land·er** *n.*

Greenland Sea. Arm of the Arctic Ocean, lying off the northeast coast of Greenland. It is the principal outlet of the Arctic Ocean into the Atlantic. Drifting ice floes make the northern part of the sea virtually unnavigable.

Greenland spar *n.* A mineral, **cryolite** *(see).*

Greenland whale *n.* An arctic whale, *Balaena mysticetus,* having a black body with a pale throat.

green leek *n.* Any of various green or mostly green Australian parrots.

green·let (grēn′lĭt) *n.* Any of various greenish birds of the genus *Hylophilus,* of Central and South America, related to the vireos.

green light *n.* **1.** The green-colored traffic light, meaning "go." **2.** Permission to proceed with a project or course of action.

green·ling (grēn′lĭng) *n.* Any of various food fishes of the family Hexagrammidae, of the northern Pacific.

green manure *n.* A growing crop, such as a clover or grass, that is plowed into soil to improve fertility.

green monkey *n.* Any of several African monkeys of the genus *Cercopithecus;* especially, *C. aethiops sabaeus,* having yellowish-gray fur with a greenish tinge.

green monkey disease *n.* **Marburg disease** *(see).*

Green Mountains. Range of the Appalachian Mts. extending 402 kilometers (250 miles) from southern Quebec through Vermont to western Massachusetts. Mt. Mansfield in Vermont is the highest peak (1,340 meters; 4,393 feet). It is one of the oldest ranges in North America.

Green·ock (grē′nək, grĭn′ək, grĕn′-). Burgh in Strathclyde Region in western Scotland, on the Firth of Clyde. It is a port, and shipping and shipbuilding are the chief industries.

green·ock·ite (grĕn′ə-kīt′) *n.* A yellow to brown or red mineral, essentially cadmium sulfide (CdS), used as a cadmium ore. [After Charles Cathcart, Lord *Greenock* (died 1859), British soldier.]

green onion *n.* See **scallion** (sense 1).

green pepper *n.* The unripened green fruit of various pepper plants, especially the sweet pepper, eaten raw or cooked.

green plover *n.* A bird, the **lapwing** *(see).*

green pound *n.* See **green currency.**

green revolution *n.* The increased agricultural production in developing countries resulting from the introduction of new high-yielding crop varieties and modern farming techniques.

green·room (grēn′ro͞om′, -ro͝om′) *n.* A waiting room in a theater, concert hall, television studio, or the like for the use of performers when off-stage. [From its being typically painted green.]

green·sand (grēn′sănd′) *n.* A sand or sediment given a dark greenish color by grains of glauconite.

green·shank (grēn′shăngk′) *n.* An Old World wading bird, *Tringa nebularia,* having greenish legs and a long bill.

green·sick·ness (grēn′sĭk′nĭs) *n. Pathology.* See **chlorosis** (sense 2). **—green·sick** *adj.*

green snake *n.* Any of several nonvenomous North American snakes of the genus *Opheodrys,* having a slender yellow-green body.

green soap *n.* A translucent, yellowish-green, soft or liquid soap made chiefly from vegetable oils, potassium hydroxide, oleic acid, glycerine, and purified water, used medicinally as a stimulant in chronic skin disorders. Also called "soft soap."

green·stick fracture (grēn′stĭk′) *n.* A fracture in a long bone of a child or young animal in which the bone is bent and splintered but not completely broken.

green·stone (grēn′stōn′) *n.* **1.** Any of various altered basic igneous rocks colored green by chlorite, hornblende, or epidote. **2.** The most common variety of jade, found in New Zealand and used for making tikis, ornaments, tools, or the like.

green·stuff (grēn′stŭf′) *n.* Green vegetables.

green·sward (grēn′swôrd′) *n. Poetic.* Turf on which the grass is green.

green tea *n.* Tea made from leaves that are not fermented before being dried. Compare **black tea.**

green thumb *n.* The ability to grow plants successfully. Also *chiefly British* "green fingers."

green turtle *n.* A large marine turtle, *Chelonia mydas,* having greenish flesh prized as food, used especially in turtle soup.

green vitriol *n.* A chemical compound, **ferrous sulfate** *(see).*

green·weed (grēn′wēd′) *n.* See **dyer's greenweed.**

Green·wich (grĭn′ĭj, grĕn′-). An ancient village, now a borough of Greater London in England. It is the site of the original Royal Observatory, designed by Sir Christopher Wren, through which passes the prime meridian, or longitude 0°. The Royal Naval College and the National Maritime Museum are also in the borough.

Greenwich mean time *n. Abbr.* **GMT, G.m.t.** Mean solar time for the meridian at Greenwich, England, used as a basis for calculating time throughout most of the world. Also called "Greenwich time," "universal time."

Greenwich meridian *n.* The **prime meridian** *(see)* that passes through Greenwich in England.

Greenwich Village. Village dating from colonial times, now a residential quarter of Lower Manhattan in New York City. Since the early 20th century it has been famous as an artists' quarter. It is also renowned for its cafés, restaurants, and nightclubs.

green·wood (grēn′wo͝od′) *n. Literary.* A wood or forest when the foliage is green.

greet[1] (grēt) *tr.v.* **greeted, greeting, greets. 1.** To address in a friendly and respectful way. **2.** To receive or welcome in a friendly manner. **3.** To receive with a specified reaction: *greet a joke with laughter.* **4.** To present itself to; be perceived by: *A din greeted our ears.* [Middle English *greten,* Old English *grētan,* from Germanic.] **—greet·er** *n.*

greet[2] *intr.v.* **greeted, greeting, greets.** *Archaic & Scottish.* To cry; weep.

greet·ing (grē′tĭng) *n.* **1.** An act or instance of greeting a person. **2.** *Usually* **greetings.** A gesture or word of welcome or salutation: *season's greetings.*

greg·a·rine (grĕg′ə-rīn′, -rĭn) *n.* Any of various sporozoan protozoans of the order Gregarinida, that are parasitic within invertebrates such as arthropods and annelids.
~adj. Of or belonging to the Gregarinida. [New Latin *Gregarina* (genus name), from Latin *gregārius,* GREGARIOUS.]

gre·gar·i·ous (grĭ-gâr′ē-əs) *adj.* **1.** Tending to move in or form a group with others of the same kind, in a herd, pack, or flock. **2.** Seeking and enjoying the company of others of one's kind; sociable. **3.** *Botany.* Growing in groups that are close together but not densely clustered or matted. [Latin *gregārius,* belonging to a flock, from *grex* (stem *greg-*), herd, flock.] —**gre·gar·i·ous·ly** *adv.* —**gre·gar·i·ous·ness** *n.*

grège, greige (grāzh) *n.* Light grayish-brown.

Gre·go·ri·an (grĭ-gôr'ē-ən, grĭ-gōr'-) *adj.* Pertaining to, associated with, or introduced by Pope Gregory I or Pope Gregory XIII.

Gregorian calendar *n.* The calendar now in use, introduced in 1582 by Pope Gregory XIII (1502–85), as a corrected form of the earlier **Julian calendar** *(see).* The Gregorian calendar stipulates that each ordinary year consists of 365 days and each leap year, or year whose number is divisible by four, of 366 days except for centenary years whose numbers are not divisible by 400.

Gregorian chant *n.* The monodic liturgical plainsong of the Roman Catholic Church, systematized during the papacy of Gregory I. Also called "plainsong."

Greg·o·ry I (grĕg'ə-rē), **Saint,** known as "the Great" (c. 540–604). Roman Doctor of the Church. As Pope Gregory I (590–604), he did much to increase papal authority and to establish the temporal independence of the papacy. He sent St. Augustine on a missionary expedition to Britain in 596.

grei·sen (grī'zən) *n.* A granitic rock composed chiefly of quartz and mica. [German *Greisen, Greissen,* from *greissen†,* to split.]

gre·mi·al (grē'mē-əl) *n.* In the Roman Catholic church, a silk cloth formerly placed on the lap of a bishop during Mass. [Medieval Latin *gremiāle,* from Latin *gremium,* lap.]

grem·lin (grĕm'lən) *n.* **1.** An imaginary gnomelike creature to whom mechanical problems in military aircraft were frequently attributed during World War II. **2.** Any source of trouble or mischief. [20th century : origin obscure, but influenced by GOBLIN.]

Gre·na·da (grə-nā'də). Independent island republic within the Commonwealth, in the southeastern Caribbean Sea. It was a British colony until 1974. It consists of the volcanic island of Grenada, the southernmost of the Windward Islands, and the smaller islands of the southern Grenadines. The economy is almost entirely agricultural. Area, 344 square kilometers (133 square miles). Population, 110,000. Capital, St. George's.

gre·nade (grə-nād') *n.* **1.** A missile containing priming and bursting charges, designed to be thrown by hand or fired from a launcher-equipped rifle. **2.** A glass container filled with a volatile chemical or a liquid that is dispersed when the glass is thrown and smashed. [French, from Old French *pome grenate,* POMEGRANATE (from its shape).]

gren·a·dier (grĕn'ə-dîr') *n.* **1. a.** A member of the British Grenadier Guards, the first regiment of the royal household infantry. **b.** Formerly, a soldier who threw grenades. **2.** Any of various deep-sea fishes of the family Macrouridae, having a long tapering tail and lacking a tail fin. In this sense, also called "rat-tail." **3.** Any of several African weaverbirds of the genus *Estrilda,* having a brightly colored plumage and bill. [French, "grenade thrower," from *grenade,* GRENADE.]

gren·a·dine¹ (grĕn'ə-dēn', grĕn'ə-dēn') *n.* A thin, openwork fabric of silk, wool, cotton, or synthetic material. [French *grenadine,* perhaps from *Granada,* in Spain.]

grenadine² *n.* A thick, sweet syrup made from pomegranates or red currants and used as flavoring, especially in mixed drinks. [French, from Old French *pome grenate,* POMEGRANATE.]

Gren·a·dines (grĕn'ə-dēnz', grĕn'ə-dēnz'). Group of some 600 small islands and islets in the Windward Islands, which lie between the Caribbean Sea and the main body of the Atlantic Ocean. The southern Grenadines, including Carriacou, the largest island, are part of Grenada, while the northern islands are part of St. Vincent and the Grenadines.

Gre·no·ble (grə-nō'bəl). City lying in the foothills of the Alps, on the Isère River, in southeastern France. It is the capital of Isère department and a marketing and industrial center. Grenoble is the principal hydroelectric center of France and an important center for nuclear research.

Gresh·am (grĕsh'əm), **Sir Thomas** (c. 1519–79). English banker, merchant, and financier. He made a fortune as a banker and was one of the founders of the Royal Exchange (completed in 1570).

Gresh·am's law (grĕsh'əmz) *n. Economics.* The theory that if two kinds of money in circulation have the same denominational value but different intrinsic values, the money with higher intrinsic value (called *good*) will be hoarded and eventually driven out of circulation by the money with lesser intrinsic value (called *bad*). [After Sir Thomas GRESHAM.]

gres·so·ri·al (grĕ-sôr'ē-əl, grĕ-sōr'-) *adj. Zoology.* Adapted for walking or having legs adapted for walking. Said of the ostrich and other flightless birds. [New Latin *gressōrius,* from *gressor,* one that walks, from Latin *gradī* (past participle *gressus*), to step, go.]

Gret·na Green (grĕt'nə grēn). Village in Dumfries and Galloway in Scotland, c. 2 kilometers (1.25 miles) from the English border. It was famous as a place where eloping lovers were married without residential qualifications or the consent of parents (1754–1856). After 1856 one of the parties had to have resided in Scotland for at least 21 days before the marriage. The services were usually performed by the local blacksmith, until such marriages were made illegal in 1940.

grew. Past tense of **grow.**

grey. Variant of **gray.**

Grey (grā), **Charles, 2nd Earl** (1764–1845). British politician. He became the acknowledged leader of the Whigs on the death of Charles James Fox in 1806. In 1830 he became prime minister and presided over the passing of the Great Reform Act (1832) and the

abolition of slavery throughout the British Empire (1833).

Grey, Lady Jane (1537–54). Queen of England for nine days. She was the great-granddaughter of Henry VII. On Edward VI's death (July 10, 1553) she was proclaimed queen, but the country rallied to Mary Tudor (Mary I), and after nine days Lady Jane was imprisoned. She was subsequently beheaded.

Grey, Zane (1872–1939). U.S. author. He wrote more than 60 books, which sold millions of copies during his lifetime. Most of his books were Westerns, such as *Riders of the Purple Sage* (1912), filled with self-reliant, righteous heroes, naive heroines, and ruthless villains. Many motion pictures were made from his books.

grey·hen (grā'hĕn') *n.* The female of the **black grouse** *(see).*

grey·hound (grā'hound') *n.* A large, slender dog of an ancient breed, having a smooth coat, a narrow head, and long legs, and capable of running swiftly. [Middle English *grehound,* Old English *grīghund : grīeg* (unattested), bitch + *hund,* dog, HOUND.]

grey·lag (grā'lăg') *n.* The **graylag goose** *(see).*

Grey of Fal·lo·don (făl'ə-dən), **Edward Grey, 1st Viscount** (1862–1933). British politician. As foreign secretary (1905–16), he was directly responsible for the Anglo-Russian entente (1907) and the secret Treaty of London (1915) that brought Italy into World War I.

grib·ble (grĭb'əl) *n.* Any of several small, wood-boring marine crustaceans of the genus *Limnoria;* especially, *L. lignorum,* which often damages underwater wooden structures. [Perhaps a diminutive of GRUB.]

grid (grĭd) *n.* **1.** A framework of parallel or crisscrossed bars; gridiron. **2.** A pattern of horizontal and vertical lines forming squares of uniform size on a map, chart, aerial photograph, or the like, used as a reference for locating points. **3.** *Electricity.* **a.** An interconnected system of electric cables and power stations that distributes electricity over a large area. **b.** A corrugated or perforated conducting plate in a storage battery. **c.** A network or coil of fine wires located between the anode and the cathode of a vacuum tube. **4.** A football field. [Short for GRIDIRON.]

grid bias *n.* The fixed voltage applied between the cathode and the grid of a vacuum tube.

grid·dle (grĭd'l) *n.* A thick, flat iron pan or other flat metal surface used for cooking by dry heat.
~*tr.v.* **griddled, -dling, -dles.** To cook on a griddle. [Middle English *gredil,* from Old French, from Vulgar Latin *crāticulum* (unattested), small grid, from Latin *crāticula,* diminutive of *crātis,* wickerwork.]

grid·dle·cake (grĭd'l-kāk') *n.* A pancake *(see).*

grid·i·ron (grĭd'ī'ərn) *n.* **1.** A flat framework of parallel metal bars used for grilling meat or fish. **2.** Any framework or network suggestive of a gridiron. **3.** A football field. **4.** A metal structure high above the stage of a theater, from which ropes or cables are strung to scenery and lights. [Middle English *gredire,* variant (influenced by *iren,* IRON) of *gredile, gredil,* GRIDDLE.]

grid·lock (grĭd'lŏk') *n.* A traffic jam in which no traffic can move in any direction because the vehicles have formed into intersecting crisscrossed lines. —**grid·locked** *adj.*

grief (grēf) *n.* **1.** Intense mental anguish; deep remorse, acute sorrow, or the like. **2.** A source of deep remorse or acute sorrow. —See Synonyms at **regret.** —**come to grief.** To meet with disaster; fail. [Middle English *gref,* from Old French *grief, gref,* from *grever,* GRIEVE.]

Grieg (grēg), **Edvard Hagerup** (1843–1907). Norwegian composer. He was inspired by Norwegian folk music, and many of its idioms occur in his music. His most famous works are the incidental music for *Peer Gynt* (1875) and a piano concerto (1868).

griev·ance (grē'vəns) *n.* **1. a.** An actual or supposed circumstance regarded as just cause for complaint or protest. **b.** A complaint or protestation based on such a circumstance. **2.** Indignation or resentment stemming from a feeling of having been wronged. —See Synonyms at **injustice.** [Middle English *grievaunce,* from Old French *grevance,* from *grever,* GRIEVE.]

grieve (grēv) *v.* **grieved, grieving, grieves.** —*tr.* **1.** To cause to be sorrowful or anguished; distress. **2.** *Archaic.* To hurt or harm. —*intr.* To be sorrowful; lament; mourn. [Middle English *greven,* from Old French *grever,* from Latin *gravāre,* to oppress, weigh upon, from *gravis,* heavy, weighty.] —**griev·ing·ly** *adv.*

griev·ous (grē'vəs) *adj.* **1. a.** Causing grief, pain, or anguish. **b.** Expressing grief; mourning. **2.** Serious or dire; grave. —**griev·ous·ly** *adv.* —**griev·ous·ness** *n.*

grievous bodily harm *n. Abbr.* **G.B.H.** In criminal law, serious physical harm inflicted by one person on another.

grif·fin, grif·fon, gry·phon (grĭf'ən) *n. Greek Mythology.* A fabulous beast with the head and wings of an eagle and the body of a lion. [Middle English *griffon,* from Old French *grifoun,* from Late Latin *grȳphus,* from Latin, from Greek *grups.*]

Grif·fith (grĭf'ĭth), **Arthur** (1872–1922). Irish nationalist leader. In 1905 he founded the Sinn Fein movement for Irish independence, and in 1918 he was elected to the British Parliament. With the other Sinn Fein members, he withdrew and established the Irish Dáil. He headed the Irish group that negotiated the 1921 treaty establishing the Irish Free State.

Griffith, D(avid) W(ark) (1875–1948). U.S. film director and producer. His revolutionary film *The Birth of a Nation* (1915) used the innovative techniques for which he is famous: the fade-in and fade-out, close-ups, moving-camera shots, flashbacks, and montage effects.

gridiron *A metal frame placed over a fire's glowing embers for cooking.*

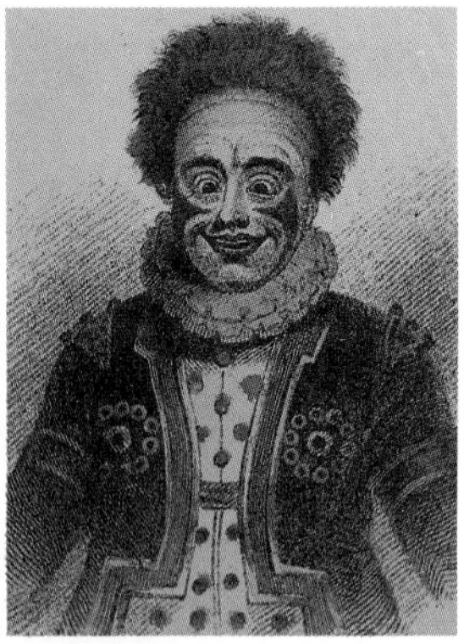

Grimaldi, Joseph *A portrait of Joseph Grimaldi (1779–1837), who was the first modern clown. He was the son of a Genoese harlequin who played in Italian commedia dell'arte.*

PRONUNCIATION KEY

ă, pat; **ā**, pay; **âr**, care; **ä**, father, are; **b**, bib; **ch**, church; **d**, deed; **ĕ**, pet; **ē**, be; **f**, fife; **g**, gag; **h**, hat; **hw**, which; **ĭ**, pit; **ī**, pie; **îr**, pier; **j**, judge; **k**, kick; **l**, lid, needle; **m**, mum; **n**, no, sudden; **ng**, thing; **ŏ**, pot; **ō**, toe; **ô**, paw, for; **oi**, noise; **ou**, out; **o͝o**, book; **o͞o**, boot; **p**, pop; **r**, roar; **s**, sauce; **sh**, ship, dish; **t**, tight; **th**, thin, path; ***th***, this, bathe; **ŭ**, cut; **ûr**, fur; **v**, valve; **w**, with; **y**, yes; **z**, zebra, size; **zh**, vision; **ə**, about, item, edible, gallop, circus, peaceful

IN FOREIGN WORDS:

à, *Fr.* ami; **œ**, *Fr.* feu, *Ger.* schön; **ü**, *Fr.* tu, *Ger.* über; **KH**, *Ger.* ich, *Scot.* loch; **N**, *Fr.* bon; **y'**, *Fr.* Compiègne

STRESS MARKS:

Primary stress: ′ **in·cite′** (ĭn-sīt′)
Secondary stress: ′ **in′sight′** (ĭn′sīt′)

grif·fon (grĭf′ən) *n.* **1.** Any of several breeds of dog having a wiry coat; especially, a small dog of a breed originating in Belgium, having a short, bearded muzzle. **2.** Any of several Old World vultures of the genus *Gyps,* especially *G. fulvus,* having black wings and a grayish body. **3.** Variant of **griffin.** [From *griffon,* variant of GRIFFIN.]

grift (grĭft) *n. Slang.* **1.** Money made dishonestly, as by a swindle. **2.** A swindle or confidence game.
~*intr.v.* **grifted, grifting, grifts.** *Slang.* To practice swindling or cheating. [Variant of GRAFT (money).] **—grift·er** *n.*

grig (grĭg) *n. Regional.* **1.** A grasshopper or cricket. **2.** A small eel. **3.** A lively merry person. [Middle English (originally "dwarf") : origin obscure.]

Gri·gnard reagent (grē-nyär′) *n. Chemistry.* Any of a group of reagents with the general formula RMgX, where R is an organic group and X is a halogen atom. They are used in the synthesis of organic compounds. [After Victor *Grignard* (1871–1935), French chemist.]

gri·gri, gree·gree, gris-gris (grē′grē) *n.* An African charm, fetish, or amulet. [17th century : of African origin.]

grill (grĭl) *v.* **grilled, grilling, grills.** *—tr.* **1.** To toast or fry on a gridiron or broil under a grill. **2.** To torture as if by subjecting to great heat. **3.** *Informal.* To question relentlessly; cross-examine. **4.** To mark or emboss with a gridiron. *—intr.* To undergo broiling.
~*n.* **1.** A part of a cooker that gives out intense downward heat, under which food may be cooked; a gridiron. **2.** Food cooked by grilling or broiling. **3.** A grillroom. **4.** Variant of **grille.** [French *griller,* from *gril, grille,* a grating, gridiron, from Old French *grille, grail,* from Vulgar Latin *grāticula* (unattested), variant of Latin *crāticula.* See **griddle.**]

gril·lage (grĭl′ĭj) *n.* A network or frame of crossed timbers serving as a foundation, usually on treacherous soil. [French, from *grille,* grating, GRILL.]

grille, grill (grĭl) *n.* **1.** A metal grating used as a screen, divider, barrier, or decorative element, as: **a.** In a window or gateway for observing callers. **b.** In a convent or prison for separating visitors. **c.** On a motor vehicle to protect the radiator. **2.** A square opening at the back of the hazard side of a tennis court. [French, grating, GRILL.]

grilled (grĭld) *adj.* **1.** Broiled under a grill. **2.** Having a grille.

Grill·par·zer (grĭl′pär′tsər), **Franz** (1791–1872). Austrian author. Often condemned by censors and rejected by the public, he wrote several tragic poems and plays, including *The Ancestress* (1817) and *The Waves of Sea and Love* (1831). Although unheralded at first, his plays were later considered among Austria's greatest dramas.

grill·room (grĭl′ro͞om′, -ro͝om′) *n.* A restaurant or room in a restaurant where grilled foods are served. Also called "grill."

grilse (grĭls) *n., pl.* **grilse.** A young salmon on its first return from the sea to fresh or brackish waters. [Middle English *grilles,* variant of *girsil,* perhaps from Old French *grisel,* gray. See **grizzle.**]

grim (grĭm) *adj.* **grimmer, grimmest. 1.** Unrelenting; rigid; stern. **2.** Uninviting or unnerving in aspect. **3. a.** Ghastly; sinister. **b.** Savagely ironic: *a grim jest.* **4.** *Archaic.* Ferocious; savage. **5.** *Informal.* Unpleasant; repellent: *a grim prospect.* **—**See Synonyms at **ghastly.** [Middle English *grim,* Old English *grim,* fierce, severe, from Germanic.] **—grim·ly** *adv.* **—grim·ness** *n.*

grim·ace (grĭm′ĭs, grĭ-mās′) *n.* A sharp contortion of the face expressive of pain, contempt, or disgust.
~*intr.v.* **grimaced, -macing, -maces.** To contort the facial features. [French *grimace,* earlier *grimache,* from Spanish *grimazo,* caricature, from *grima,* fright, from Germanic; akin to GRIM.]

Gri·mal·di (grĭ-mäl′dē), **Joseph** (1779–1837). English clown, one of the most famous clowns in history.

gri·mal·kin (grĭ-măl′kən, grĭ-môl′-) *n.* **1.** A cat; especially, an old female cat. **2.** A shrewish old woman. [Variant of *graymalkin* : GRAY + dialectal *malkin,* lewd woman, hussy, Middle English *Malkyn,* diminutive of *Mald,* pet form for *Matilda.*]

grime (grīm) *n.* Black dirt or soot; especially, such dirt clinging to or ingrained in a surface.
~*tr.v.* **grimed, griming, grimes.** To cover with dirt; begrime. [Middle English *grim(e),* from Middle Dutch *grīme.*]

Grimm (grĭm), **Jakob** (1785–1863) and his brother **Wilhelm** (1786–1859). German writers and philologists. They are famous for their collections of fairy tales (1812–14).

Grimm's Law *n. Phonetics.* A formula describing the regular changes undergone by Indo-European stop consonants represented in Germanic. It states that Indo-European *p, t,* and *k* become Germanic *f, th,* and *h;* Indo-European *b, d,* and *g* become Germanic *p, t,* and *k;* and Indo-European *bh, dh,* and *gh* become Germanic *b, d,* and *g.* [After Jakob GRIMM.]

grim reaper *n.* Death, viewed as an untimely destroyer of life, and based on the notion of Father Time wielding his scythe.

Grims·by (grĭmz′bē). Official name **Great Grims·by.** A town in the nonmetropolitan county of Humberside, at the mouth of the Humber River, in east-central England. It is one of the largest fishing ports in the world and supports a major frozen-food industry.

grim·y (grī′mē) *adj.* **-ier, -iest.** Covered or ingrained with grime. **—**See Synonyms at **dirty.** **—grim·i·ly** *adv.* **—grim·i·ness** *n.*

grin (grĭn) *v.* **grinned, grinning, grins.** *—intr.* To draw back the lips and bare the teeth, especially in a wide smile. *—tr.* To express with a grin. **—grin and bear it.** To put up with stoically; accept one's lot.
~*n.* **1.** The act of grinning. **2.** The expression on the face produced by grinning. [Middle English *grinnen,* Old English *grennian,* to grimace (in pleasure or displeasure); akin to *grānian,* to GROAN.] **—grin·ner** *n.* **—grin·ning·ly** *adv.*

grind (grīnd) *v.* **ground** (ground), **grinding, grinds.** *—tr.* **1. a.** To crush, pulverize, or powder with friction, especially by rubbing between two hard surfaces: *grind wheat into flour.* **b.** To shape, sharpen, or refine with friction: *grind a lens.* **2.** To rub (two surfaces) together; gnash: *grind the teeth.* **3.** To bear down on harshly; oppress. Often used with *down.* **4. a.** To operate by turning a crank: *grind an organ.* **b.** To produce (a tune, for example) by turning a crank. Used with *out.* **5.** To produce mechanically or without inspiration. Used with *out*: *publishers grinding out the same old stuff year after year.* **6.** To instill or teach by persistent repetition. Used with *into*: *grind the truth into their heads.* *—intr.* **1.** To perform the operation of grinding something. **2.** To be ground. **3.** To move with noisy friction; grate. **4.** *Informal.* To devote oneself to study or work. **5.** *Slang.* To rotate the pelvis in the manner of a striptease artist. Used chiefly in the phrase *bump and grind.*
~*n.* **1.** The act of grinding. **2.** A crunching or grinding noise. **3.** A specific grade or degree of pulverization, as of coffee beans: *coarse grind.* **4.** *Informal.* **a.** A laborious task, routine, or study: *tired of the daily grind of work and commuting.* **b.** One who works or studies excessively. [Grind, ground, ground; Middle English *grinden, grond, ygrounden;* Old English *grindan†, grond* (plural *grundon*), *gegrunden.*] **—grind·ing·ly** *adv.*

grin·de·li·a (grĭn-dē′lē-ə) *n.* **1.** Any plant of the genus *Grindelia,* having yellow, asterlike flowers, sometimes cultivated for ornament. **2.** The dried plants of certain species of grindelia, used medicinally in tonics, for example. [New Latin, after D.H. *Grindel* (1777–1836), Russian botanist.]

grind·er (grīn′dər) *n.* **1.** One that grinds; especially, a person who sharpens cutting edges. **2.** A grinding machine: *a coffee grinder*; *a meat grinder.* **3. a.** A molar. **b. grinders.** *Informal.* The teeth. **4.** See **hero** (sense 5).

grind·ing wheel (grīn′dĭng) *n.* An abrasive wheel usually consisting of a composite of hard particles, such as emery, bonded by a resin and used for grinding and sharpening tools.

grind·stone (grīnd′stōn′) *n.* **1.** A stone disk turned on an axle for grinding, polishing, or sharpening tools. **2.** A millstone. **—keep** (or **have**) **one's nose to the grindstone.** To work diligently and continuously.

grin·go (grĭng′gō) *n., pl.* **-gos.** In Latin America, a foreigner, especially an American or Englishman. Used contemptuously. [Spanish *gringo†,* unknown tongue, gibberish.]

grip[1] (grĭp) *n.* **1.** A tight hold; a firm grasp. **2.** The pressure or strength of such a grasp. **3. a.** A manner of grasping and holding something, such as a racket or golf club. **b.** A part for holding or grasping. **4.** A handshake. **5.** Mastery; command; understanding: *he has a good grip on French grammar.* **6.** A spasm or seizure, as of pain. **7. a.** A mechanical device that grasps and holds. **b.** A part designed to be grasped and held; handle. **8.** A small suitcase or valise. **9. a.** A stagehand who helps in shifting scenery. **b.** A member of a film production crew who adjusts sets and props and sometimes assists the cameraman. **10.** The degree of hold a tire has on the road. **—come to grips. 1.** To fight in hand-to-hand combat. **2.** To deal actively and conclusively, as with a problem. **—get a grip on oneself.** To be mentally in control of oneself. **—lose one's grip.** *Informal.* To lose control or mastery, especially of oneself.
~*v.* **gripped, gripping, grips.** *—tr.* **1.** To secure and maintain a tight hold on; seize firmly. **2.** To take hold of the mind or emotions of: *The audience was gripped by suspense.* *—intr.* To hold securely. [Middle English *grip,* partly Old English *gripa,* grasp, and partly Old English *gripa,* handful.]

grip[2]. Variant of **grippe.**

gripe (grīp) *v.* **griped, griping, gripes.** *—tr.* **1.** To cause sharp pain in the bowels of. **2.** *Archaic.* To grasp; seize. **3.** *Archaic.* To oppress or afflict. *—intr.* **1.** To have sharp pains in the bowels. **2.** *Informal.* To complain naggingly or petulantly; grumble. **3.** *Nautical.* To tend to turn into the wind. Used of a boat.
~*n.* **1. gripes.** Sharp, repeated pains in the bowels. **2.** *Informal.* A complaint. **3.** *Rare.* A grip; grasp. **4. gripes.** Ropes used to tie up a boat. **5.** *Archaic.* A handle. [Middle English *gripen,* Old English *grīpan,* from Germanic.] **—grip·er** *n.* **—grip·ing·ly** *adv.*

grippe, grip (grĭp) *n. Pathology.* **Influenza** *(see).* [French, from *gripper,* to seize, from Old French, from Frankish *grīpan* (unattested).]

grip·ping (grĭp′ĭng) *adj.* Holding one's undivided attention; riveting. **—grip·ping·ly** *adv.*

grip·sack (grĭp′săk′) *n.* A small suitcase.

Gris (grēs), **Juan,** born José Victoriano Gonzáles (1887–1927). Spanish cubist painter. He settled in Paris in 1906 and contributed especially to the development of synthetic cubism.

gri·saille (grĭ-zāl′; *French* grē-zä′y′) *n.* **1.** A style of monochromatic painting in shades of gray. **2.** A painting or design in this style. [French, from *gris,* gray, from Old French, from Frankish *gris* (unattested).]

gris·e·o·ful·vin (grĭz′ē-ō-fo͝ol′vən) *n.* An antibiotic used to treat ringworm and other fungal infections of the hair, skin, and nails. [New Latin, from *Penicillium griseofulvum dierckx,* fungus from which it was isolated : Medieval Latin *griseus,* gray + Latin *fulvus,* (reddish) yellow.]

gris·e·ous (grĭs′ē-əs, grĭz′-) *adj.* Mottled or grizzled with gray. [Medieval Latin *griseus,* from Germanic.]

gri·sette (grĭ-zĕt′) *n.* A French working girl, such as a shop assis-

tant, for example. [French, an inexpensive gray fabric for dresses, a woman wearing such a dress, from *gris,* gray. See **grisaille.**]

gris-gris. Variant of **grigri.**

gris·ly (grĭz′lē) *adj.* **-lier, -liest.** Horrifying; repugnant; gruesome. —See Synonyms at **ghastly.** [Middle English *grisly,* Old English *grislīc.*]

gri·son (grī′sən, grĭz′ən) *n.* Either of two carnivorous mammals, *Grison vittatus* or *G. cuja,* of Central and South America, having grizzled fur, a slender body, and short legs. [French, from Old French, gray animal, from *gris,* gray. See **grisaille.**]

gris·sin·i (grĭ-sē′nē) *pl.n.* Singular **grissine.** *Italian.* Long, slender, crisp sticks of bread.

grist (grĭst) *n.* **1.** Grain or a quantity of grain for grinding. **2.** Ground grain. —**grist for** (or **to**) **one's mill.** Something that can be used or turned to one's advantage. [Middle English *grist,* Old English *grīst.*]

gris·tle (grĭs′əl) *n.* Cartilage *(see),* especially when present in meat. [Middle English *gristil,* Old English *gristle,* from Germanic *gristil-* (unattested).]

gris·tly (grĭs′lē) *adj.* **-tlier, -tliest. 1.** Composed of or containing gristle. **2.** Resembling gristle. —**gris·tli·ness** *n.*

grist·mill (grĭst′mĭl′) *n.* A mill for grinding grain.

grit (grĭt) *n.* **1.** Minute rough granules, as of sand or stone. **2.** The texture or structure of stone to be used in grinding. **3.** A coarse hard sandstone, used for making grindstones and millstones. Also called "gritstone." **4.** *Informal.* Indomitable spirit; pluck. —*v.* **gritted, gritting, grits.** —*tr.* **1.** To clamp (the teeth) together, especially through anger or frustration. **2.** To cover or treat with grit. —*intr.* To make a grinding noise. [Middle English *grete,* Old English *grēot,* from Germanic.]

grith (grĭth) *n.* **1.** Protection or sanctuary provided by Old English law in certain circumstances, as when in a church or traveling on the king's highway. **2.** *Archaic.* Mercy or protection given in battle. [Middle English *grith,* Old English *grith,* from Old Norse *gridh†.*]

grits (grĭts) *pl.n.* **1.** Coarsely ground grain, especially oats or corn. **2.** Hominy grits *(see).* [Middle English *gryt,* bran, Old English *grytt,* from Germanic.]

grit·ty (grĭt′ē) *adj.* **-tier, -tiest. 1.** Containing or resembling grit. **2.** Showing resolution and fortitude; plucky. —See Synonyms at **brave.** —**grit·ti·ness** *n.*

Gri·vas (grē′väs′), **Georgios** (1898-1974). Cypriot soldier and politician, one of the principal advocates of Enosis (Cypriot union with Greece). He formed a guerrilla army, EOKA (National Organization for the Cyprus Struggle), to fight against British rule. He opposed the 1959 agreements that gave Cyprus independence and after 1964, as commander of the Cypriot National Guard, led the Greek Cypriots in the fighting against the Turkish Cypriots.

griv·et (grĭv′ĭt) *n.* A long-tailed African monkey, *Cercopithecus aethiops,* having a greenish-gray coat and tufts of white hair on the face. [French *grivet†.*]

griz·zle[1] (grĭz′əl) *v.* **-zled, -zling, -zles.** —*tr.* To make gray. —*intr.* To become gray. —*n.* **1.** The color gray. **2.** *Archaic.* Gray hair. **3. a.** The color of a roan animal. **b.** A roan animal. [Middle English *grisel,* gray, from Old French, diminutive of *gris,* gray, from Frankish *grīs* (unattested).]

griz·zle[2] *intr.v.* **-zled, -zling, -zles.** *Chiefly British.* **1.** To whimper; whine. **2.** To complain; grumble. [18th century (originally, to grin) : perhaps an ironic allusion to *patient Grizel* (Griselda), character in tales who exemplified the patient and uncomplaining wife.] —**griz·zler** *n.*

griz·zled (grĭz′əld) *adj.* **1.** Streaked with or partly gray. **2.** Having gray or graying hair.

griz·zly (grĭz′lē) *adj.* **-zlier, -zliest.** Grizzled. —*n., pl.* **grizzlies.** A grizzly bear.

grizzly bear *n.* The grayish form of the brown bear, *Ursus arctos,* of northwestern North America, sometimes considered a separate species, *U. horribilis.* Also called "grizzly."

gro. gross.

groan (grōn) *v.* **groaned, groaning, groans.** —*intr.* **1.** To voice a deep, wordless, prolonged sound expressive of pain, grief, annoyance, or disapproval. **2.** To produce a similar sound expressive of stress or strain: *The house groaned in the wind.* **3.** *Informal.* To complain or grumble, especially continually. **4.** To suffer oppression. —*tr.* To utter or convey with groaning. —*n.* The sound made in groaning; a moan. [Middle English *gronen,* Old English *grānian,* akin to *grennian,* to GRIN.] —**groan·er** *n.* —**groan·ing·ly** *adv.*

groat (grōt) *n.* A British silver fourpence piece used from the 14th to the 17th century. [Middle English *grote,* from Middle Dutch *groot,* "great" (referring to the thickness of the coin).]

groats (grōts) *pl.n.* **1.** Hulled, usually crushed grain, especially oats. **2.** Ground oat kernels boiled to a paste in water and used as food. [Middle English *grotes,* Old English *grotan.*]

gro·cer (grō′sər) *n.* A shopkeeper who sells foodstuffs and sundry household supplies. [Middle English, from Old French *grossier,* wholesale dealer, from Medieval Latin *grossārius,* from Latin *grossus,* thick, GROSS.]

gro·cer·y (grō′sə-rē) *n., pl.* **-ies. 1.** A store selling foodstuffs and household supplies. **2.** The occupation of a grocer. **3. groceries.** Goods sold by a grocer.

grog (grŏg) *n.* Alcoholic drinks; especially, rum diluted with water. [After Admiral Edward Vernon (1684-1757), nicknamed Old *Grog*

because of his habit of wearing a GROGRAM coat. He ordered that diluted rather than neat rum be served to his sailors.]

grog·gy (grŏg′ē) *adj.* **-gier, -giest.** Unsteady and dazed, as from sleep or drugs. [From GROG.] —**grog·gi·ly** *adv.* —**grog·gi·ness** *n.*

grog·ram (grŏg′rəm) *n.* **1.** A coarse, often stiffened fabric of silk, mohair, or wool, or a blend of these. **2.** A garment of this fabric. [Alteration of GROSGRAIN.]

groin (groin) *n.* **1.** *Anatomy.* The crease at the junction of the thighs with the trunk, together with the adjacent region. **b.** The external genital organs. **2.** *Architecture.* The curved edge at the junction of two intersecting vaults. **3.** A low wall built out into the sea to prevent erosion of the shore. —*tr.v.* **groined, groining, groins.** To provide or build with groins. [Earlier *gryne,* Middle English *grynde,* perhaps from Old English *grynde,* abyss, depression, from Germanic *grundja-* (unattested), from Common Germanic *grunduz* (unattested), GROUND.]

grom·met (grŏm′ĭt) *n.* **1. a.** A reinforced eyelet in cloth, leather, or the like, through which a fastener may be passed. **b.** A rubber or plastic ring set in a hole through metal, especially in the chassis of an electronic device, through which wires can be passed without chafing. **2.** *Nautical.* A rope or metal ring used for securing the edge of a sail. Also called "grummet." [Obsolete French *grom-(m)ette, gourmette,* bridle ring, from Old French *gourmel,* perhaps from Frankish *worm* (unattested), worm.]

grom·well (grŏm′wəl) *n.* **1.** Any of several plants of the genus *Lithospermum,* such as *L. officinale,* having small yellow or white flowers. **2.** Any of several similar or related plants. [Middle English *gromil,* from Old French, perhaps from Vulgar Latin *gruīnum milium* (unattested), "crane's millet" : Latin *gruīnus,* of a crane, from *grūs,* crane + *milium,* MILLET.]

Gro·my·ko (grə-mē′kō), **Andrey Andreyevich** (1909-). Soviet statesman. After joining the Communist Party in 1931, he was appointed ambassador to the United States (1943) and ambassador to the United Nations (1946-48). He served as a foreign minister from 1957 until his appointment as Soviet premier in 1983.

Gro·ning·en (grō′nĭng-ən). A province in the northeastern Netherlands. It is largely an agricultural region, but it acquired new industrial importance when vast reserves of natural gas were discovered in 1961. The provincial capital is the city of Groningen.

Grønland. See **Greenland.**

groom (grōōm, grŏŏm) *n.* **1.** A man or boy employed to take care of horses. **2.** A bridegroom. **3.** Any of several officers in an English royal household. **4.** *Archaic.* **a.** A man. **b.** A manservant. —*tr.v.* **groomed, grooming, grooms. 1.** To make (clothes, hair, or the like) neat and clean. **2.** To clean and brush (an animal). **3.** To train, as for a specified position: *groom a candidate for Congress.* [As "bridegroom," shortening of BRIDEGROOM; as "man," "servant," Middle English *grom†.*]

grooms·man (grōōmz′mən, grŏŏmz′-) *n., pl.* **-men** (-mĭn). The best man or an usher at a wedding.

groove (grōōv) *n.* **1.** A long, narrow furrow or channel, such as the spiral cut in a phonograph record. **2. a.** A situation or activity to which one is especially well suited; niche. **b.** A settled, humdrum routine; rut. **3.** *Slang.* Something that is very pleasing or satisfying. —*v.* **grooved, grooving, grooves.** —*intr. Slang.* **1.** To relax or let oneself move freely to the rhythm or beat of music, especially jazz. **2.** To settle easily or harmoniously into a situation, relationship, or the like. —*tr.* To cut a groove in. [Middle English *grofe,* from Middle Dutch *groeve,* ditch, from Germanic; akin to GRAVE.]

groov·er (grōō′vər) *n. Slang.* A person who grooves or is groovy.

groov·y (grōō′vē) *adj.* **-ier, -iest.** *Slang.* Pleasing; deeply satisfying. [From slang expression *in the groove,* playing (jazz) fluently, hence exciting, satisfying.]

grope (grōp) *v.* **groped, groping, gropes.** —*intr.* **1.** To reach about uncertainly; feel one's way. **2.** To search blindly or uncertainly: *rope for an answer.* —*tr.* **1.** To make (one's way) by groping. **2.** *Informal.* To touch or fondle sexually, usually in a clumsy manner. —*n.* The act or an instance of groping. [Middle English *gropen,* Old English *grāpian,* from Germanic.] —**grop·er** *n.* —**grop·ing·ly** *adv.*

Gro·pi·us (grō′pē-əs), **Walter** (1883-1969). German architect, founder of the Bauhaus school of architecture and one of the leading figures in the modern movement. He fled from Nazi Germany in 1934 and became professor of architecture at Harvard in 1938.

gros·beak (grōs′bēk′) *n.* Any of various finches of the genera *Hesperiphona, Pinicola,* and related genera, of Europe and America, having a thick, rounded bill. [Partial translation of French *grosbec* : Old French *gros,* thick, GROSS + *bec,* beak.]

gro·schen (grō′shən) *n., pl.* **groschen.** A coin equal to 1/100 of the schilling of Austria. See feature at **currency.** [German *Groschen,* from Middle High German *gros(se), grosche,* from Czech *grosh,* from Medieval Latin *(denārius) grossus,* "thick (penny)," from Latin *grossus,* thick, GROSS.]

gros·grain (grō′grān′) *n.* **1.** A heavy silk or rayon fabric with narrow ribs. **2.** A ribbon made of this. [French *gros grain,* "coarse grain" : Old French *gros,* thick, GROSS + GRAIN.]

gros point (grō) *n.* **1.** A large needlepoint stitch covering two vertical and two horizontal threads used, for example, in upholstery. **2.** Work done in this stitch. Compare **petit point.** [French, "large point."]

gross (grōs) *adj.* **grosser, grossest. 1. a.** Exclusive of deductions; total; entire. Compare **net. b.** Unmitigated in any way; utter.

grizzly bear *This variety of brown bear lives in western North America. Like other brown bears it has poor vision, but its sense of smell is acute.*

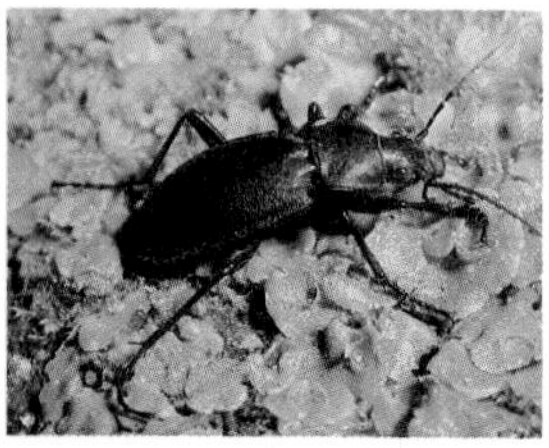

ground beetle *There are about 25,000 species of these fierce and worldwide predators. All hunt insects, including other beetles. Even the larvae are carnivorous, snapping up prey with clawlike jaws. The violet ground beetle, shown here, is so called because of the violet sheen on its wing cases.*

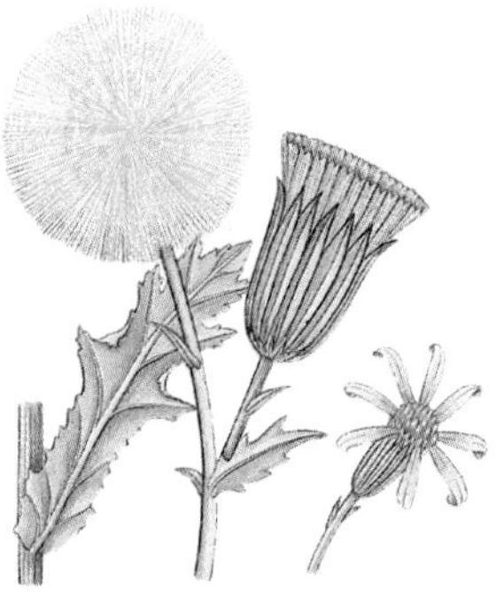

groundsel *In Anglo-Saxon times, this common weed was used in poultices—and its name comes from the Old English term* gundæswelgæ, *meaning "pus absorber." Groundsel seeds, carried on fine hairs, are spread by the wind.*

PRONUNCIATION KEY

ă, pat; ā, pay; âr, care; ä, father, are; b, bib; ch, church; d, deed; ĕ, pet; ē, be; f, fife; g, gag; h, hat; hw, which; ĭ, pit; ī, pie; îr, pier; j, judge; k, kick; l, lid, needle; m, mum; n, no, sudden; ng, thing; ŏ, pot; ō, toe; ô, paw, for; oi, noise; ou, out; o͝o, book; o͞o, boot; p, pop; r, roar; s, sauce; sh, ship, dish; t, tight; th, thin, path; *th*, this, bathe; ŭ, cut; ûr, fur; v, valve; w, with; y, yes; z, zebra, size; zh, vision; ə, about, item, edible, gallop, circus, peaceful

IN FOREIGN WORDS:

à, *Fr.* ami; œ, *Fr.* feu, *Ger.* schön; ü, *Fr.* tu, *Ger.* über; KH, *Ger.* ich, *Scot.* loch; N, *Fr.* bon; y', *Fr.* Compiègne

STRESS MARKS:

Primary stress: ′ **in·cite′** (ĭn-sīt′)
Secondary stress: ′ **in′sight′** (ĭn′sīt′)

2. Glaringly obvious; flagrant: *gross injustice.* **3. a.** Coarse; vulgar; obscene. **b.** Lacking sensitivity or discernment; unrefined. **c.** *Informal.* Offensive; distasteful. **4. a.** Overweight or corpulent, especially disgustingly so. **b.** Dense; profuse. **c.** Impenetrable; thick. Said especially of vegetation. **5.** *Pathology.* Visible to the naked eye: *a gross lesion.* —See Synonyms at **coarse, flagrant.**
∼*n., pl.* **grosses** (for sense 1) or **gross** (for sense 2). **1.** The entire body or amount; total. **2.** *Abbr.* **gr., gro. a.** Twelve dozen, used as a unit of measurement. **b.** A group of 144 or 12 dozen items. **—in the gross. 1.** Taken as a whole; in bulk. **2.** Wholesale.
∼*tr.v.* **grossed, grossing, grosses.** To earn as a total income or profit before deductions. **—gross out.** *Slang.* To fill with disgust. **—gross up.** To increase a net amount to its gross value before deductions. [Middle English, from Old French *gros,* thick, large, from Latin *grossus.*] **—gross·ly** *adv.* **—gross·ness** *n.*

gross domestic product *n. Abbr.* **GDP** The total market value of the goods and services produced within a country during a given period, excluding income derived from investments abroad.

gross national product *n Abbr.* **GNP** The total market value of all the goods and services produced by a nation during a given period, including income derived from investments abroad. Compare **national income.**

gros·su·lar·ite (grŏs′yə-lə-rīt′) *n.* A light-green, pink, gray, or brown garnet with composition $Ca_3Al_2(SiO_4)_3$, found alone or as a constituent part of the common garnet. [German *Grossularit,* "gooseberry stone" (from the color of certain kinds of garnet), from New Latin *Grossularia,* former genus of gooseberry, from Old French *groiselle, grosele,* gooseberry, from Middle Dutch *croesel,* "curly berry" (from its beard), diminutive of *kroes,* curled.]

grosz (grôsh) *n., pl.* **groszy** (grô′shē). A coin equal to 1/100 of the zloty of Poland. See feature at **currency.** [Polish, from Czech *grosh.* See **groschen.**]

Grosz (grōs), **George** (1893–1959). German painter, illustrator, and caricaturist. A leading member of the Berlin Dada movement, his reputation rests on the biting wit of his antibourgeois and antimilitarist drawings of the 1920's, executed with grotesque distortions. He became a U.S. citizen (1938).

grot (grŏt) *n. Poetic.* A grotto.

gro·tesque (grō-tĕsk′) *adj.* **1.** Characterized by ludicrous or incongruous distortion. **2.** Extravagant; outlandish; bizarre. **3.** Of or designating the grotesque in art or a work executed in this style. —See Synonyms at **fantastic.**
∼*n.* **1.** Anything thought to resemble the grotesque style in art. **2. a.** An artistic and decorative style developed in 16th-century Italy, characterized by incongruous combinations of monstrous human, animal, or natural forms. **b.** A work of art executed in this style. **3.** *Printing.* The family of 19th-century sans serif typefaces. [Earlier *crotescque,* from Old French *crotesque, grotesque,* from Old Italian *(pittura) grottesca,* "grottolike (painting)," from *grottesco,* of a grotto, from *grotta,* GROTTO.] **—gro·tesque·ly** *adv.* **—gro·tesque·ness** *n.*

gro·tes·que·rie, gro·tes·que·ry (grō-tĕs′kə-rē) *n., pl.* **-ries. 1.** The state of being grotesque; grotesqueness. **2.** Something grotesque.

Gro·ti·us (grō′shē-əs), **Hugo,** originally Huig de Groot (1583–1645). Dutch lawyer and writer. He wrote on politics, theology, and law. His *Of the Law of War and Peace* (1625) is generally considered to be the first comprehensive treatise on international law.

grot·to (grŏt′ō) *n., pl.* **-toes** or **-tos. 1.** A small cave or cavern. **2.** An artificial structure or excavation, as in a garden, resembling a cave or cavern. [Italian *grotta, grotto,* from Old Italian *grotta,* from Vulgar Latin *grupta* (unattested), variant of Latin *crypta,* vault, CRYPT.]

grot·ty (grŏt′ē) *adj.* **-tier, -tiest.** *Chiefly British Informal.* Unpleasant, grubby, or squalid. [From GROTESQUE.]

grouch (grouch) *intr.v.* **grouched, grouching, grouches.** To grumble or sulk.
∼*n.* **1.** A grumbling or sulky mood. **2.** A complaint; grudge. **3.** A habitually complaining or irritable person. [Middle English *grutchen,* to GRUDGE.]

grouch·y (grou′chē) *adj.* **-ier, -iest.** Inclined to grumbling and complaining; ill-humored; peevish; grumpy. **—grouch·i·ly** *adv.* **—grouch·i·ness** *n.*

ground[1] (ground) *n.* **1. a.** The solid surface of the earth. **b.** The floor of a body of water, especially the sea. **2. a.** Soil; earth: *level the ground for a lawn.* **b.** Land or earth having a specified characteristic: *high ground.* **3.** *Sometimes* **grounds.** An area of land designated for a specified purpose: *burial grounds.* **4. grounds.** The land surrounding or forming part of a house or other building: *The embassy has beautiful grounds.* **5.** *Often* **grounds.** The foundation for an argument, belief, or action; basis; premise. **6.** *Usually* **grounds.** The underlying condition prompting some action; cause; reason. Used with *for*: *grounds for suspicion.* **7.** An area of reference; a subject. **8. a.** A surrounding area; a background. **b.** The undecorated part of something. **9.** The preparatory coat of paint on which a picture is to be painted. **10. grounds.** The sediment at the bottom of a liquid, especially coffee. **11.** *Music.* A ground bass. **12.** *Electricity.* **a.** The position or portion of an electric current that is at zero potential with respect to the earth. **b.** A conducting connection to such a position or to the earth. **c.** A large conducting body, such as the earth, used as a return for electric currents and as an arbitrary zero of potential. **13.** Headway, progress, or advantage, as in a competition. —See Synonyms at **base. —cover ground. 1.** To travel a considerable distance. **2. a.** To make headway; accomplish a great deal. **b.** To deal with a subject fully. **—down to the ground.** *Chiefly British Informal.* Completely, absolutely: *His holiday plans suit me down to the ground.* **—from the ground up.** Leaving out nothing; completely; thoroughly. **—gain ground. 1.** To make progress. **2.** To gain favor or popularity. **—get off the ground. 1.** To get properly under way; have a successful beginning. Used of a project, idea, or the like. **2.** To cause to get off the ground. **—give ground.** To yield an advantage; give way. **—hold** (or **stand**) **one's ground.** To maintain one's position; not yield or retreat. **—on home ground.** In a familiar area or on a familiar subject. **—run into the ground. 1.** To work or push until exhausted. **2.** To overdo to the point of being tedious.
∼*adj.* **1.** Of, on, or near the ground. **2.** Living or used in or on the ground.
∼*v.* **grounded, grounding, grounds.** —*tr.* **1.** To place or set on the ground. **2.** To provide a basis for (an argument, theory, or the like); substantiate; justify. **3.** To supply with basic and essential information; instruct in fundamentals; school. **4.** To prevent (an aircraft or pilot) from flying. **5.** *Electricity.* To connect (an electric circuit) to a ground. **6.** *Nautical.* To run (a vessel) aground. **7.** To cover (a canvas or other surface) with a preparatory coat of paint. —*intr.* **1.** To hit or reach the ground. **2.** *Nautical.* To run aground. [Middle English *ground,* Old English *grund,* from Common Germanic *grunduz* (unattested).]

ground[2]**.** Past tense and past participle of **grind.**

ground ball *n. Baseball.* A batted ball that rolls or bounces along the ground. Also called "grounder."

ground bass *n.* A short musical bass passage or motif that is continually repeated under the changing harmonies and melodies of the upper range. Also called "basso ostinato," "ground."

ground beetle *n.* **1.** Any of numerous chiefly black or brown beetles of the family Carabidae, that often crawl under stones, logs, or debris. **2.** Any of various other beetles that live near the ground, such as any member of the family Tenebrionidae.

ground cherry *n.* Any of various chiefly New World plants of the genus *Physalis,* having round, fleshy fruit enclosed in a papery, bladderlike husk.

ground cover *n.* Low-growing plants that form a dense, extensive growth and tend to prevent soil erosion and discourage weeds.

ground crew *n.* A team of mechanics and technicians who maintain and service aircraft on the ground.

ground-ef·fect machine (ground′ĭ-fĕkt′) *n.* A vehicle designed for traveling over land or water by means of an air cushion.

ground elder *n.* A perennial herbaceous Eurasian plant, *Aegopodium podagraria,* widespread as a weed and on waste ground, having clusters of small white flowers and leaves composed of three leaflets. Also called "bishop's weed," "goutweed," "herb Gerard."

ground·er (ground′ər) *n. Baseball.* A ground ball.

ground floor *n.* The floor of a building at or nearly at ground level. **—get in on the ground floor.** To work with a project or business from its inception.

ground glass *n.* Glass that has been subjected to grinding or etching to diffuse light.

ground hemlock *n.* A low-growing yew, *Taxus canadensis,* of northeastern North America.

ground hog *n.* A rodent, the **woodchuck** *(see).*

Ground Hog Day *n.* February 2, traditionally the point that indicates an early or late spring. [From the legend that the ground hog emerges from hibernation on this day and returns to its burrow if it sees its shadow, presaging prolonged winter weather.]

ground·ing (ground′ĭng) *n.* A thorough knowledge of or training in the rudiments of a subject: *has a good grounding in math.*

ground ivy *n.* A creeping or trailing aromatic plant, *Glechoma hederacea,* native to Eurasia, having rounded, scalloped leaves and small purplish flowers. Also called "gill-over-the-ground."

ground·less (ground′lĭs) *adj.* Having no grounds or reasons; unjustified; unsubstantiated: *groundless optimism.* **—ground·less·ly** *adv.* **—ground·less·ness** *n.*

ground·ling (ground′lĭng) *n.* **1. a.** A plant or animal living on or close to the ground. **b.** A fish that lives at the bottom of the water. **2.** A person with uncultivated tastes. **3.** A spectator in the cheapest part of an Elizabethan theater.

ground loop *n.* A sharp, uncontrollable turn of an aircraft while taxiing, landing, or taking off.

ground·mass (ground′măs′) *n.* The fine-grained crystalline base of porphyritic rock, in which phenocrysts are embedded.

ground·nut (ground′nŭt′) *n.* **1.** A climbing vine, *Apios tuberosa,* of eastern North America, having compound leaves, clusters of fragrant brownish flowers, and small, edible tubers. **2.** Any of several other plants having underground tubers or nutlike parts. **3.** The tuber or nutlike part of such a plant. **4.** *Chiefly British.* The **peanut** *(see).*

ground pine *n.* **1.** A low-growing plant, *Ajuga chamaepitys,* native to the Old World, having narrow leaves, yellow flowers, and a resinous odor. **2.** A North American **club moss** *(see);* especially, *Lycopodium obscurum* or any similar species.

ground pink *n.* A plant, the **moss pink** *(see).*

ground plan *n.* **1.** A plan of a floor of a building as if seen from overhead. **2.** A preliminary or basic plan.

ground plum *n.* **1.** A plant, *Astragalus crassicarpus,* of the central and western United States, having purple or white flowers and green, plumlike, edible fruit. **2.** The fruit of this plant.

ground·print (ground′prĭnt′) *n.* In telecommunications, a **footprint** *(see).*

ground rent *n. Chiefly British.* **1.** Rent reserved on land by a lessor, usually for a stipulated lengthy term, to be used chiefly for building. **2.** Rent paid by the lessee of a flat to the freeholder, over a specified period of time.
ground rule *n.* Any basic rule of procedure modified or amended to fit a particular situation or event.
ground·sel[1] (ground′səl) *n.* Any of various plants of the genus *Senecio,* especially the Eurasian species *S. vulgaris,* having rayed, usually yellow flowers. [Middle English *groundeswele,* Old English *grundeswylige,* variant (influenced by *grund,* GROUND) of *gundæswelgæ,* "pus-absorber" (from its use to reduce abscesses) : *gund,* pus + *swelgan,* to swallow.]
groundsel[2]**.** Variant of **groundsill.**
groundsel tree *n.* A shrub, *Baccharis halimifoliar,* of coastal areas of the eastern United States, having white, plumelike fruiting clusters.
ground sheet *n.* **1.** A waterproof cover used to protect an area of ground, such as a football field. **2.** A waterproof sheet placed in a tent or under camp bedding as a protection against damp.
ground·sill (ground′sĭl′) *n.* Also **ground·sel** (ground′səl). The horizontal timber nearest the ground in the frame of a building. Also called "ground plate."
ground·speed, ground speed (ground′spēd′) *n. Aeronautics.* The speed of an airborne aircraft calculated in terms of the ground distance traversed in a given period of time. Compare **air speed.**
ground squirrel *n.* Any of various squirrellike rodents of the genus *Citellus* (or *Spermophilus*) and related genera, which live in underground burrows. Also called "gopher."
ground state *n. Physics.* The stationary state of least energy in a physical system.
ground stroke *n.* In tennis, a stroke played to a ball that has bounced.
ground substance *n. Anatomy.* The matrix of connective tissue, containing various cells and fibers.
ground swell *n.* **1.** An undulation of the ocean with deep rolling waves, often caused by a distant storm or earthquake. **2.** A sudden gathering of force, as of public opinion.
ground tissues *pl.n. Botany.* Plant tissues, such as pith and cortex, that are not specialized for a particular function.
ground water, ground·wa·ter (ground′wô′tər, -wŏt′ər) *n.* **1.** Any water beneath the earth's surface. **2.** A region of subsurface water beneath the water table, including underground streams. It forms the saturation zone in which all pore spaces are filled with water.
ground wave *n.* A radio wave that travels along the earth's surface. Compare **sky wave.**
ground·work (ground′wûrk′) *n.* A foundation or basis; preliminary work.
ground zero *n.* The point on the surface of the earth immediately below a nuclear explosion. Also called "hypocenter."
group (gro͞op) *n. Abbr.* **gr. 1.** An assemblage of persons or objects considered together: *a group of dinner guests; a group of Chinese porcelains.* **2.** Two or more figures that make up a unit or a design, as in sculpture or painting. **3.** A number of individuals or things considered together because of certain similarities. **4.** *Linguistics.* A subdivision of a linguistic family, less inclusive than a branch. **5.** A unit of two or more squadrons in an air force, smaller than a wing. **6.** Any class or collection of related objects or entities, as: **a.** Two or more atoms behaving or regarded as behaving as a single chemical unit. **b.** A vertical column in the periodic table of elements. Compare **period. c.** A geological stratigraphic unit, especially a unit consisting of two or more formations. **7.** *Mathematics.* A set together with a binary operation under which the set is closed and associative, and for which the set contains an identity element and an inverse for every element in the set. **8.** A small number of players, usually including a singer or singers, that perform popular or modern music.
~v. **grouped, grouping, groups.** *—tr.* To place or arrange in a group or groups. *—intr.* To form or be part of a group. [French *groupe,* from Italian *gruppo,* "knot," from Germanic.]
Usage: *Group,* as a collective noun, can be construed as singular or plural in determining the number of the verb it governs. A singular verb occurs when the persons or things in question are considered as one or as acting as one, or when they are related by membership in a class or category. A plural verb is possible when group refers to persons thought of as acting individually. The grammatical number of related pronouns and pronominal adjectives in turn agrees with that of the verb: *The group* (of persons) *is determined to retain its identity despite the merger. The group* (of persons) *were divided in their sympathies. This group* (of plants) *shows variation in coloring.*
group captain *n.* A commissioned officer in the Royal and Australian Air Forces, ranking between an air commodore and a wing commander, equivalent in rank to a colonel in the army and a captain in the navy.
group·er (gro͞o′pər) *n., pl.* **groupers** or collectively **grouper.** Any of various often large food and game fishes of the genera *Epinephelus, Mycteroperca,* and related genera, of warm seas. [Portuguese *garupa,* probably from a native South American name.]
group·ie (gro͞o′pē) *n. Informal.* **1.** A fan, usually female, of a rock or pop group who follows the group around on tours, usually in the hope of having personal contact with them. **2.** A sycophant or hanger-on.
group·ing (gro͞o′pĭng) *n.* **1.** The act or process of arranging in groups. **2.** A collection of objects arranged in a group.
group insurance *n.* Insurance covering members of a group under a single contract or under individual contracts, usually at reduced cost.
group·oid (gro͞o′poid′) *n. Algebra.* A nonempty set *G* together with a binary operation that associates with every pair of elements *x, y* in *G* a third element *z* in *G* denoted by *xy* or *x·y.*
group practice *n.* A medical or dental practice run by a group of associated physicians or dentists who share premises, secretarial help, and other resources.
group theory *n.* The branch of mathematics concerned with the properties of groups.
group therapy *n.* Psychotherapy involving more than one patient at a time, in which the changing interaction among the patients is part of the therapeutic process. Also called "group psychotherapy."
group·think (gro͞op′thĭngk′) *n.* **1.** Decision- and policy-making by a group, as a board of directors or a research team. **2.** The practice of conforming to group values or ethical standards.
grouse[1] (grous) *n., pl.* **grouse.** Any of various game birds of the family Tetraonidae, chiefly of the Northern Hemisphere, having mottled brown or grayish plumage. See **black grouse, red grouse.** [16th century : earlier *grewes,* perhaps plural of *grue* (unattested), perhaps from medieval Latin *grūtat.*]
grouse[2] *intr.v.* **groused, grousing, grouses.** *Informal.* To complain; carp; grumble.
~n. A complaint; grievance. [19th century : origin obscure.] **—grous·er** *n.*
grout (grout) *n.* **1. a.** A thin mortar used to fill cracks and crevices between masonry and around tiles. **b.** A finishing plaster. **2.** *Usually* **grouts.** *Chiefly British.* Sediment; lees. **3. a. grouts.** Groats. **b.** Wholemeal porridge.
~tr.v. **grouted, grouting, grouts.** To fill or finish with grout. Often used with *in: grout in tiles.* [Middle English *grout,* Old English *grūt,* akin to GRITS, GROATS.] **—grout·er** *n.*
grove (grōv) *n.* A small wood or group of trees lacking dense undergrowth. [Middle English *grove,* Old English *grāf*†.]
Grove (grōv), **Sir George** (1820–1900). British civil engineer and musicologist. His *Dictionary of Music and Musicians,* now a standard work, first appeared in four volumes between 1879 and 1889.
grov·el (grŭv′əl, grŏv′-) *intr.v.* **-eled, -eling, -els.** Also *chiefly British* **-elled, -elling. 1.** To humble oneself in a servile or demeaning manner; cringe. **2.** To lie or crawl in a prostrate position, often as a token of subservience or humility. **3.** To give oneself over to base pleasures. [Back-formation from obsolete *groveling,* prone, Middle English *gruflinge,* in prostrate position, from phrase *on grufe,* on the face, from Old Norse *ā grūfu* : *ā,* on + *grūfa*†, proneness.] **—grov·el·er** *n.* **—grov·el·ing·ly** *adv.*
grow (grō) *v.* **grew** (gro͞o), **grown** (grōn), **growing, grows.** *—intr.* **1. a.** To increase naturally in size or length, often in a specified direction. **b.** To increase in size by the addition of material through assimilation or accretion. **2. a.** To expand; gain: *The business grew under new management.* **b.** To increase in amount or degree: *membership is growing.* **c.** To become extended or intensified: *Her anxiety grew.* **3.** To develop and reach maturity. **4.** To be capable of growth; thrive; flourish: *plants that will grow in deep shade.* **5.** To become in a specified position in relation to something else or to each other, by or as if by the process of growth: *the edges of the wound grew together; we've grown apart recently.* **6.** To follow as a result of; originate. Usually used with *out: Their love grew out of friendship.* **7.** To develop by a gradual process or by degrees; become: *grow angry; grow cold; grow rich.* **8.** To come into existence; spring up: *Hostility grew between the two groups. —tr.* **1.** To cause to grow; cultivate: *grow tulips.* **2.** To let grow: *grow a beard.* **3.** To develop; put forth: *The plant has not grown any leaves yet.* **—**See Synonyms at **increase. —grow on** (or **upon**). To become more pleasurable, acceptable, or essential to: *a style that grows on one.* **—grow out of.** To outgrow. **—grow over.** To cover with growth: *a path grown over with moss.* **—grow up. 1.** To reach maturity; become an adult. **2.** To come into being; develop. [Grow, grew, grown; Middle English *growen, grewe, growen,* Old English *grōwan, grēow, grōwen,* from Germanic.] **—grow·er** *n.*
grow·ing (grō′ĭng) *adj.* **1.** Increasing in number or degree: *a growing desire to confess.* **2.** Of or associated with growth: *during the growing season.* **—grow·ing·ly** *adv.*
growing pains *pl.n.* **1.** Pains in the limbs and joints of children, often mistakenly attributed to rapid growth. **2.** Problems arising in the initial stages of an enterprise.
growing season *n.* The period of the year during which temperatures are high enough for the growth of a particular crop, usually regarded as the period between the last severe frost of spring and the first in the following autumn.
growl (groul) *v.* **growled, growling, growls.** *—intr.* **1.** To utter a growl. **2.** To speak in an angry or surly manner. *—tr.* To utter with a growl: *growl orders.*
~n. **1.** The low, guttural, menacing sound made by a dog or other animal, usually in anger. **2.** A sound suggestive of this. **3.** A gruff, surly utterance. [Perhaps imitative.]
growl·er (grou′lər) *n.* **1.** One that growls. **2.** A small iceberg or area of floe ice, large enough to be a danger to ships. **3.** *Electricity.* An electromagnetic device with two poles, used for magnetizing, demagnetizing, and finding short-circuited coils.
grown (grōn). Past participle of **grow.**
~adj. **1.** Having attained full growth; mature; adult. **2.** Produced

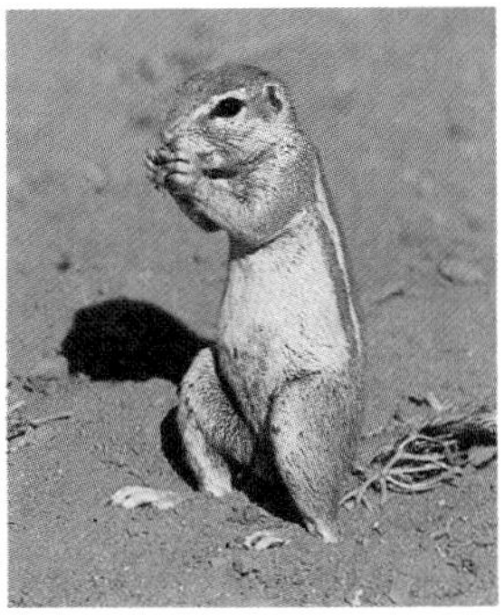

ground squirrel *Relatives of the tree-climbing squirrels, ground squirrels live in burrows in Eurasia, North America, and Africa. Those that store their food in cheek pouches are known as chipmunks in North America.*

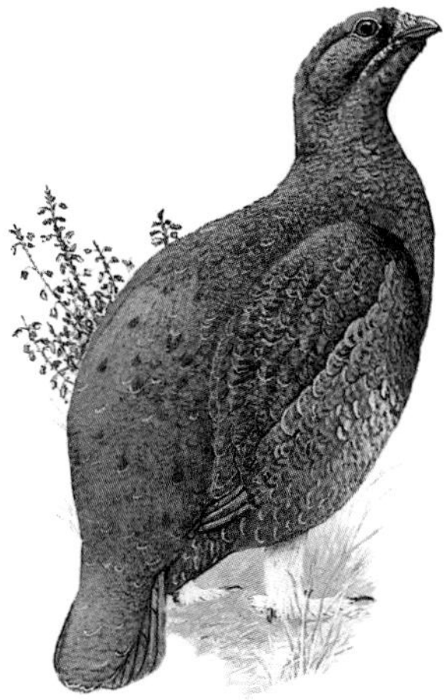

grouse *The red grouse, shown here, is the bird hunted on British moors during the grouse-shooting season. It is related to the willow grouse of Europe, Asia, and North America.*

or cultivated in a specified way or place. Used in combination: *home-grown vegetables.*

grown-up (grōn'ŭp') *adj.* **1.** Characteristic of or suitable for an adult. **2.** Being mature, fully-developed, or older than one's years in outlook, attitudes, or appearance. —*n.* An adult.

growth (grōth) *n.* **1. a.** The process of growing. **b.** A stage in the process of growing; size. **c.** Full development; maturity. **2.** Development from a lower or simpler to a higher or more complex form; evolution. **3.** An increase, as in size, number, value, or strength; extension or expansion: *population growth.* **4.** Something that grows or has grown: *a new growth of grass.* **5.** Broadly, an abnormal tissue formation, such as a tumor. **6.** The result of growth; production; cultivation.

growth company *n.* A company whose rate of growth significantly exceeds that of the average in its field or the overall rate of economic growth.

growth fund *n.* A mutual fund whose goal is capital appreciation.

growth hormone *n.* A hormone, secreted by the pituitary gland, that stimulates tissue growth, especially of the bones. Also called "somatotrophin." Compare **growth substance.**

growth ring *n.* An annual ring *(see).*

growth stock *n. Economics.* Shares that tend to increase in capital value rather than providing a high-interest income.

growth substance *n.* A substance produced by a plant that, in very small quantities, controls growth and development; a plant hormone. Also called "phytohormone." Compare **growth hormone.**

groyne. Variant of **groin** (sense 3).

grub (grŭb) *v.* **grubbed, grubbing, grubs.** —*tr.* **1.** To clear of roots and stumps by digging. **2.** To dig up by the roots. Often used with *up* or *out.* —*intr.* **1.** To dig in the earth; dig underground. **2. a.** To search laboriously; rummage. **b.** To toil arduously; drudge: *grub for a living.* —*n.* **1.** The thick, wormlike larva of certain beetles and other insects. **2.** *Informal.* Food. **3.** A dirty or unkempt person. **4.** A drudge. [Middle English *grubben,* Old English *grybban* (unattested).]

grub·ber (grŭb'ər) *n.* **1.** A person who grubs: *"The archaeologist is the last grubber among things mortal"* (Loren Eiseley). **2.** A grub hoe.

grub·by (grŭb'ē) *adj.* **-bier, -biest. 1.** Dirty; unkempt. **2.** Infested with grubs. **3.** Contemptible; beggarly. —**grub·bi·ly** *adv.* —**grub·bi·ness** *n.*

grub hoe *n.* A heavy hoe for grubbing up roots. Also called "grubbing hoe," "grubber."

grub screw *n.* A small headless screw used to secure a collar or other similar part to a shaft.

grub·stake (grŭb'stāk') *n.* Supplies or funds advanced to a mining prospector or a person starting a business, in return for a promised share of the profits. Also informally called "stake." —*tr.v.* **grubstaked, -staking, -stakes.** To supply with a grubstake. [GRUB (food) + STAKE (bet).] —**grub·stak·er** *n.*

Grub Street (grŭb) *n.* The world of impoverished writers and literary hacks. [From *Grub Street,* London, now Milton Street, formerly inhabited by such writers.]

grub·street (grŭb'strēt') *adj.* Turned out by hacks; poor; inferior: *a shelf of grubstreet novels.*

grudge (grŭj) *tr.v.* **grudged, grudging, grudges. 1.** To be reluctant to allow or grant. **2.** To show or feel reluctance about: *"His nature grudged thinking, for it crippled his speed in action"* (T.E. Lawrence). —*n.* **1.** A deep-seated feeling of resentment or rancor provoked by some incident or situation. **2.** The grounds for such a feeling. [Middle English *gruggen,* variant of *grutchen,* from Old French *grouchier†,* to murmur.] —**grudg·er** *n.*

grudg·ing (grŭj'ĭng) *adj.* Not offered willingly or spontaneously: *grudging praise.* —**grudg·ing·ly** *adv.*

gru·el (grōō'əl) *n.* **1.** A thin, watery porridge. **2.** *Chiefly British.* Severe punishment. [Middle English *gruel,* from Old French *gruel,* diminutive of *gru,* groats, oatmeal, from Frankish *grūt* (unattested).]

gru·el·ing, gru·el·ling (grōō'ə-lĭng) *adj.* Demanding and exhausting. —*n.* A grueling experience, especially punishment.

grue·some (grōō'səm) *adj.* Causing horror and repugnance; frightful and shocking: *the gruesome sight of the dismembered corpse.* —See Synonyms at **ghastly.** [From obsolete Scottish *grue,* to shiver, from Scandinavian.] —**grue·some·ly** *adv.* —**grue·some·ness** *n.*

gruff (grŭf) *adj.* **gruffer, gruffest.** Rough and stern in manner, voice, or appearance; harsh. [Dutch *grof,* from Middle Dutch, from Germanic.] —**gruff·ly** *adv.* —**gruff·ness** *n.*
    Synonyms: *bluff, blunt, brusque, crusty, curt.*

grum (grŭm) *adj.* **grummer, grummest.** Morose; sullen; glum. [Perhaps blend of GRIM and GLUM.]

grum·ble (grŭm'bəl) *v.* **-bled, -bling, -bles.** —*intr.* **1.** To mumble in discontent: *Bosses will always find something to grumble about.* **2.** To rumble or growl. —*tr.* To express in a grumbling, discontented manner. —*n.* **1. a.** A grumbling utterance. **b.** Grounds for grumbling. **2.** A rumble. [Frequentative of Middle English *grummen,* to grumble, perhaps from Middle Dutch *grommen.*] —**grum·bler** *n.* —**grum·bling·ly** *adv.* —**grum·bly** *adj.*

grum·met (grŭm'ĭt) *n. Nautical.* A grommet *(see).*

gru·mous (grōō'məs) *adj.* Also **gru·mose** (-mōs'). *Botany.* Formed

of or consisting of granular tissue, as certain roots are. [Latin *grūmus†,* little heap of earth.]

grump (grŭmp) *n. Informal.* **1. grumps.** A fit of ill temper. **2.** A surly, complaining person. [Imitative.]

grump·y (grŭm'pē) *adj.* **-ier, -iest.** Fretful and peevish; irritable; bad-tempered. [From dialectal *grump,* ill-tempered (imitative).] —**grump·i·ly** *adv.* —**grump·i·ness** *n.*

Grund·y·ism (grŭn'dē-ĭz'əm) *n.* Narrow-minded criticism of the morals of others. [After Mrs. *Grundy,* character in *Speed the Plough* (1798), a play by Thomas Morton (c. 1764–1838).]

Grü·ne·wald (grōō'nə-wōld', -vält'), **Matthias,** born Mathis Gothart Neithart (c.1475–1528). One of the great early German masters of northern European painting. He painted chiefly religious subjects, especially the Crucifixion of Christ.

grun·gy (grŭn'jē) *adj.* **-gier, -giest.** *Slang.* Being in a dirty, rundown, or inferior condition: *grungy old jeans.* [Origin unknown.]

grun·ion (grŭn'yən) *n.* A small fish, *Leuresthes tenuis,* of coastal waters of California and Mexico, that spawns along beaches during high spring tides. [Perhaps from Spanish *gruñón,* grumbler, from *gruñir,* to grumble, grunt, from Latin *grunnīre.*]

grunt (grŭnt) *v.* **grunted, grunting, grunts.** —*intr.* **1.** To utter a grunt. **2.** To make a deep, guttural sound. —*tr.* To utter or express (a reaction, for example) with a grunt: *he grunted approval.* —*n.* **1.** The deep, guttural sound characteristic of a pig. **2.** Any of various chiefly tropical marine fishes of the genus *Haemulon* and related genera, that produce grunting sounds. Also called "grunter." **3.** *Slang.* One who performs routine or mundane tasks. [Middle English *grunten,* Old English *grunnettan,* probably frequentative of *grunnian.*] —**grunt·ing·ly** *adv.*

grunt·er (grŭn'tər) *n.* **1.** One that grunts. **2.** *Informal.* A pig. **3.** A fish, the grunt.

grun·tled (grŭn'tld) *adj.* Extremely pleased; in a good mood. [Back-formation from DISGRUNTLED.]

Grus (grŭs) *n.* A constellation in the Southern Hemisphere near Indus and Phoenix. [New Latin, from Latin *grūs,* crane.]

Gru·yère (grōō-yâr', grē-; *French* grü-yâr') *n.* A pale yellow, firm-textured cheese with holes, made from whole milk. [Originally made in *Gruyère,* a district in Switzerland.]

Gruzinskaya S.S.R. See **Georgian S.S.R.**

gr. wt. gross weight.

gryphon. Variant of **griffin.**

grys·bok (grīs'bŏk') *n.* Either of two small African antelopes, *Raphicerus melanotis* or *R. sharpei,* having small, straight horns. [Afrikaans, "gray buck."]

GS, G.S. general staff.

G-string (jē'strĭng') *n.* **1.** A narrow strip of cloth passing between the legs and supported by a waistband, worn especially by striptease dancers. **2.** A string tuned to G on a musical instrument.

G-suit (jē'sōōt') *n.* A flight garment designed to counteract the effects of high acceleration by exerting pressure on parts of the body below the chest. Also called "anti-G suit." Compare **pressure suit.** [G, short for GRAVITY.]

gt. 1. gilt. **2.** great. **3.** *Medicine.* gutta.

gtd. guaranteed.

GTS gas turbine ship.

gua·ca·mo·le (gwä'kə-mō'lē) *n.* **1.** Any of a variety of Mexican or South American salads featuring avocado. **2.** A dip or spread of mashed avocado, tomato pulp, mayonnaise, and seasoning. [Mexican Spanish, from Nahuatl *ahuacamolli,* "avocado sauce" : *ahuacatl,* AVOCADO + *molli,* sauce.]

gua·cha·ro (gwä'chä-rō') *n., pl.* **-ros.** The oilbird *(see).* [American Spanish *guácharo,* from *guacho,* orphan, little bird, from Quechua *wáhcha,* diminutive of *wah,* strange.]

gua·co (gwä'kō) *n., pl.* **-cos.** Any of several tropical American plants used as an antidote against snakebites; especially, *Mikania guaco* or *Aristolochia serpentina.* [American Spanish, from a native word in South America.]

Gua·da·la·ja·ra (gwä'də-lə-här'ə). City and capital of Jalisco state, southwestern Mexico. It is the commercial center of a mining, industrial, and agricultural region. Situated at a height of more than 1,525 meters (5,000 feet) and surrounded by mountains, the city has a mild, dry climate and is a popular health resort.

Gua·dal·ca·nal (gwŏd'l-kə-năl'). Largest island in the Solomon Islands in the southwest Pacific Ocean. Its origin is volcanic; its dominant peak, Mt. Popomanasiu, which rises to a height of 2,331 meters (7,647 feet), is surrounded by jungle. Most of the population works on coastal coconut plantations. See map at **Pacific Ocean.**

Gua·de·loupe (gwä'də-lōōp'). An overseas department of France, one of the Leeward Islands in the Caribbean. It consists of two large islands, Basse Terre and Grande Terre, and several smaller islands. The capital is Basse-Terre. It was a French colony until 1946, when it was granted department status. See map at **Latin America.**

guai·a·col (gwī'ə-kôl', -kōl') *n.* A yellowish, oily, aromatic liquid, $C_7H_8O_2$, used chiefly as an expectorant and a local anesthetic. [GUAIAC(UM) + -OL.]

guai·a·cum (gwī'ə-kəm) *n.* **1.** A tree of the genus *Guaiacum;* especially, the **lignum vitae** *(see).* **2.** The wood of such a tree. **3.** A greenish-brown resin obtained from the lignum vitae, and used medicinally and in varnishes. [New Latin, from Spanish *guayacan,* from Taino.]

Guam (gwŏm). Unincorporated territory of the United States, the largest and most southerly of the Marianas Islands, in the North

Pacific Ocean. It has a mountainous interior and is fringed by coral reefs. Since 1954 it has been the site of the Pacific headquarters of the U.S. Strategic Air Command. Capital, Agana. See map at **Pacific Ocean.**

guan (gwän) *n.* Any of several birds of the genus *Penelope* and related genera, of the jungles of tropical America, related to and resembling the curassows. [American Spanish, from a native name in South America.]

gua·na·co (gwə-nä′kō) *n., pl.* **-cos.** A brownish South American mammal, *Lama guanicoe,* related to and resembling the domesticated llama. [Spanish, from Quechua *huanaco.*]

gua·nase (gwä′nāz′) *n.* An enzyme in the liver and spleen that catalyzes the removal of an amino group from guanine, which is thereby converted to xanthine. [GUAN(INE) + -ASE.]

guan·eth·i·dine (gwä-nĕth′ĭ-dēn′) *n.* A drug administered in the form of pills to reduce high blood pressure. [Blend of GUANIDINE + ETHYL.]

Guang·dong, Kuang-tung, or **Kwang-tung** (gwäng′dŏng′). Province of southeast China. It is hilly, and has more than 700 offshore islands. The province is a major producer of sugar cane, rice, silk, hemp, tea, tobacco, tropical and subtropical fruits, forest products, fish, and salt. It has reserves of tungsten, iron, uranium, and oil. Most of the people are Cantonese, and some 50 percent of overseas Chinese originated in the province, part of China since c. 200 B.C. Guangzhou (Canton) is the capital.

Guang·zhou, Kuang-chou, or **Kwang-chow** (gwäng′jō′). Also **Can·ton** (kăn-tŏn′). Port in southern China and the capital of Guangdong province. Situated on the Zhujiang (Pearl River) delta, it is the commercial and industrial center of southern China. The Portuguese, in the 16th century, and the British, in the 17th century, regularly used the port. The Opium War between Britain and China resulted in Guangzhou's becoming one of the first treaty ports (1842).

gua·ni·dine (gwä′nĭ-dēn′) *n.* A strong crystalline base, CH_5N_3, found in plant and animal tissues and used for organic syntheses. [GUAN(INE) + -ID(E) + -INE.]

gua·nine (gwä′nēn′) *n.* A purine, $C_5H_5N_5O$, that is a constituent of the nucleic acids DNA and RNA. [From GUANO, in which it is found.]

gua·no (gwä′nō) *n.* **1.** A substance composed chiefly of the dung of sea birds or bats, accumulated along certain coastal areas or in caves, and used as fertilizer. **2.** A similar artificially produced substance. [Spanish, from Quechua *huanu,* dung.]

gua·no·sine (gwä′nə-sēn′) *n.* A nucleoside consisting of guanine and the sugar ribose. [Blend of GUANINE + RIBOSE.]

Guan·tá·na·mo Bay (gwän-tä′nə-mō′). An inlet of the Caribbean on the southeastern coast of Cuba. U.S. Navy troops landed here (June 1898) in the Spanish-American War. In 1903 the United States leased a naval station on the bay.

guar (gwär) *n.* A legume, *Cyamopsis tetragonoloba,* adapted to semiarid regions and grown for its seeds and as forage. [Hindi *guār.*]

guar. guaranteed.

gua·ra·ni (gwär′ə-nē′) *n., pl.* **-nis** or **guarani. 1.** The basic monetary unit of Paraguay, equal to 100 céntimos. See feature at **currency. 2.** A note worth one guarani. [Spanish *guaraní,* GUARANI.]

Gua·ra·ni (gwär′ə-nē′) *n., pl.* **-nis** or collectively **Guarani. 1.** A member of a Tupi-Guaranian group of South American Indians of Paraguay, Bolivia, and southern Brazil. **2.** The Tupian language spoken by these peoples. [Spanish *guaraní,* a native tribal name.]

guar·an·tee (găr′ən-tē′) *n.* **1.** *Law.* **a.** A contract whereby a person undertakes to answer for the debt, default, or miscarriage of another. **b.** *Rare.* A person making or receiving such an undertaking. **2.** A formal undertaking whereby something is ensured; specifically, an undertaking by a manufacturer or vendor that his goods or services meet a certain standard. **3.** Something given or held as security. **4.** That which secures or ensures something: *Their name is a guarantee of quality.*
~*tr.v.* **guaranteed, -teeing, -tees. 1.** To assume responsibility for the debt, default, or miscarriage of; vouch for. **2.** To assume responsibility for the quality or execution of. **3.** To undertake to accomplish or secure: *He guaranteed to free the captives.* **4.** To ensure (a desired outcome, for example). **5.** To furnish security for. **6.** To express or declare with conviction. [Earlier *garante,* perhaps from Spanish, warrant. See **guaranty.**]

guar·an·tor (găr′ən-tər, -tôr′) *n.* **1.** A person who makes or gives a guarantee. **2.** A person who makes or gives a guaranty.

guar·an·ty (găr′ən-tē) *n., pl.* **-ties. 1.** An agreement by which one person assumes the responsibility of assuring payment or fulfillment of another's debts or obligations. **2.** That which guarantees something: *His record is a guaranty of his honesty.* **3.** Anything held or provided as security for the execution, completion, or existence of something. **4.** The provision of such security. **5.** A guarantor.
~*tr.v.* **guarantied, -tying, -ties.** To guarantee. [Old French *garantie,* from *garant,* warrant, from Frankish *wārjan* (unattested), to vouch for the truth of.]

guard (gärd) *v.* **guarded, guarding, guards.** —*tr.* **1.** To protect from harm; watch over; defend. **2. a.** To watch over to prevent escape or violence. **b.** To watch over to prevent mistakes, indiscretions, or the like: *guard one's words.* **3.** To keep watch at (a door or gate, for example) to supervise entries and exits. **4.** To supply with proper controls and checks; safeguard. **5.** To furnish (a device or object) with a protective piece. **6.** *Archaic.* To escort. —*intr.* To

take precautions; secure. Used with *against: guard against infection.*
—See Synonyms at **defend.**
~*n.* **1.** One that guards, keeps watch over, or protects. **2.** An individual or a group that stands watch or acts as a sentinel. **3.** One who supervises prisoners. **4.** A body of persons who form an escort or perform drill exhibitions on ceremonial occasions: *an honor guard.* **5. Guard.** *British.* A member of any of various regiments whose official duties include the ceremonial protection of the sovereign. **6.** *British.* A railway employee in charge of a train. **7.** *Football.* One of the two players on either side of the center. **8.** *Basketball.* A team member who plays the backcourt. **9.** A defensive position or stance in certain sports such as boxing or fencing. **10.** The act, condition, or duty of guarding: *"Have you had quiet guard?"* (Shakespeare). **11.** Something that gives protection; a safeguard: *a guard against tooth decay.* **12.** Any device or apparatus that prevents injury, damage, or loss. **13.** An attachment or covering put on a machine to protect the operator. **14.** A chain or band used to help safeguard a thing, such as a watch or bracelet, from loss. **15.** A guard ring. **16.** The portion of the hilt of a sword or of the handle of a knife or fork that protects the hand. **17.** The metal apparatus that encircles and guards the trigger of a firearm.
—**mount guard.** To go on duty. Said of a sentinel. —**off one's guard.** Unprepared; not alert. —**on one's guard.** Alert and watchful; cautious. —**stand guard. 1.** To act as a sentinel. **2.** To keep watch over someone or something.
~*adj.* Of, relating to, or acting as a guard: *guard duty.* [As verb, Middle English *garden,* from Old French *garder, guarder,* from Germanic. As noun, Middle English, from Old French *garde,* from *garder,* to guard.] —**guard·a·ble** *adj.* —**guard·er** *n.*

guar·dant, gar·dant (gär′dənt) *adj. Heraldry.* Designating an animal shown with its face turned toward the viewer. [Old French *gardant,* present participle of *garder,* to GUARD.]

guard cell *n. Botany.* Either of the paired epidermal cells that control the opening and closing of a stoma in plant tissue.

guard·ed (gär′dĭd) *adj.* Cautious; restrained; prudent: *guarded behavior.* —**guard·ed·ly** *adv.* —**guard·ed·ness** *n.*

guard hair *n.* Any of the coarse hairs that form a layer covering the underfur of certain mammals.

guard·house (gärd′hous′) *n.* **1.** A building that accommodates a military guard. **2.** A building used as a prison for military personnel guilty of minor offenses.

guard·i·an (gär′dē-ən) *n.* **1.** One who guards, protects, or defends. **2.** *Law.* A person who is legally responsible for the care and management of the person or property of one who is considered by law to be incompetent to manage his own affairs, such as a child during its minority. **3.** A superior in a Franciscan convent. [Middle English from Norman French, variant of Old French *gardien,* from *garder,* to GUARD.] —**guard·i·an·ship** *n.*

guardian angel *n. Roman Catholic Church.* An angel appointed to watch over a person.

guard·rail (gärd′rāl′) *n.* **1.** A protective rail, as on a staircase or next to a highway. **2.** An inner rail placed along the main rail of a railroad track at curves and crossings to prevent a train from jumping the tracks.

guard ring *n.* **1.** A ring used to prevent a more valuable ring from sliding off the finger. Also called "guard." **2.** An electrode in a computer or electron lens that counteracts distortion of the electric field at the edges of other electrodes.

guard·room (gärd′rōōm′, -rŏŏm′) *n.* **1.** A room used by guards on duty. **2.** A room in which prisoners are confined.

guards·man (gärdz′mən) *n., pl.* **-men** (-mĭn). **1.** One who acts as a guard. **2.** A member of the U.S. National Guard. **3.** *British.* A soldier in a regiment of household guards.

Guar·ne·ri (gwär-nâr′ē). Also **Guar·nie·ri** (-nyâr′ē). Italian family of violinmakers, whose workshops were in Cremona. The first member of the family to make violins was **Andrea** (c. 1626-98). The craft was carried on by each generation down to **Giuseppe** (c. 1687-1744), who is considered second only to the Stradivari family for the quality of his instruments.

Guar·ne·ri·us (gwär-nâr′ē-əs, -nîr′ē-əs) *n.* Any of the violins of superlative tone made by members of the Guarneri family in the 17th and 18th centuries.

Gua·te·ma·la (gwä′tə-mä′lə). Independent republic of Central America. It was the home of the Mayan civilization for 1,000 years before the Spanish conquest of 1524. It declared its independence from Spain in 1821. The country is chiefly agricultural, and coffee, cotton, beef, timber, and chicle are the chief exports. Nickel and petroleum are mined. An earthquake in 1976 killed more than 24,000 people. Area, 108,889 square kilometers (42,042 square miles). Population, 7,300,000. Capital, Guatemala City. See map at **Central American States.** —**Gua·te·ma·lan** *adj. & n.*

Guatemala City. Capital city of Guatemala, in a broad fertile plain in the southwestern part of the country. It is the largest city in Central America. It was founded in 1776 to replace Antigua as the capital, because its site was believed to be free of the danger of an earthquake. In 1917, however, an earthquake destroyed the city and it had to be rebuilt.

gua·va (gwä′və) *n.* **1.** Any of various tropical American and Asian shrubs and trees of the genus *Psidium;* especially, *P. guajava,* having white flowers and edible fruit. **2.** The pear-shaped fruit of this tree, having a yellow rind and pink flesh, and eaten fresh or preserved. [Spanish *guava, guayaba,* of South American Indian origin.]

Guayana. See **Guiana.**

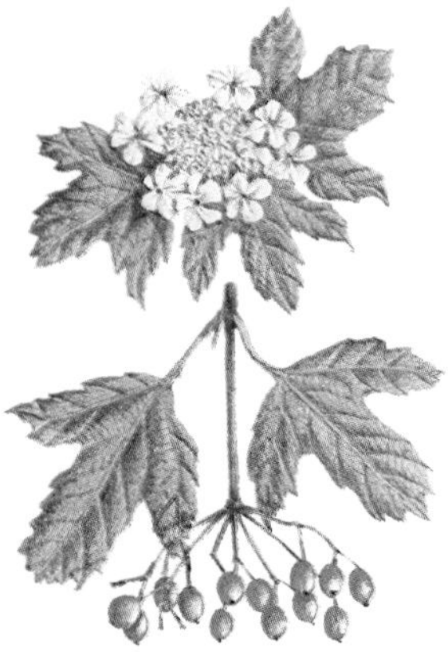

guelder rose *A shrub that is found both in the wild and in gardens. Its clusters of white flowers appear in June.*

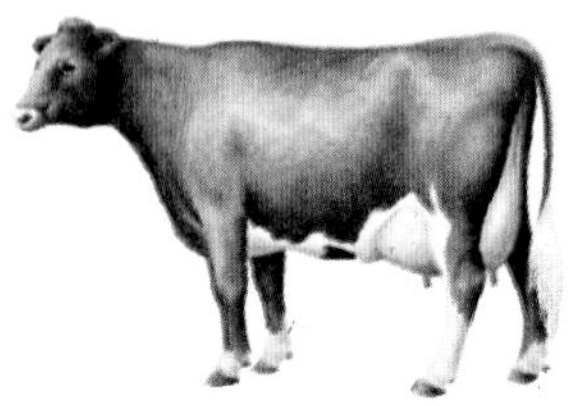

Guernsey *This breed of dairy cattle originated on the island of Guernsey in the English Channel and is the only breed permitted there. Guernsey cows produce very rich, yellowish milk.*

PRONUNCIATION KEY

ă, pat; ā, pay; âr, care;
ä, father, are; b, bib;
ch, church; d, deed; ĕ, pet;
ē, be; f, fife; g, gag; h, hat;
hw, which; ĭ, pit; ī, pie;
îr, pier; j, judge; k, kick;
l, lid, needle; m, mum;
n, no, sudden; ng, thing;
ŏ, pot; ō, toe; ô, paw, for;
oi, noise; ou, out; o͝o, book;
o͞o, boot; p, pop; r, roar;
s, sauce; sh, ship, dish;
t, tight; th, thin, path;
th, this, bathe; ŭ, cut; ûr, fur;
v, valve; w, with; y, yes;
z, zebra, size; zh, vision;
ə, about, item, edible, gallop, circus, peaceful

IN FOREIGN WORDS:

à, *Fr.* ami; œ, *Fr.* feu, *Ger.* schön; ü, *Fr.* tu, *Ger.* über; KH, *Ger.* ich, *Scot.* loch; N, *Fr.* bon; y', *Fr.* Compiègne

STRESS MARKS:

Primary stress: ′
in·cite′ (ĭn-sīt′)
Secondary stress: ′
in′sight′ (ĭn′sīt′)

Gua·ya·quil (gwī′ə-kēl′). City and chief port of Ecuador and capital of Guayas province. Its industries include tanning, sugar refining, and iron founding.

gua·yu·le (gwī-o͞o′lē) *n.* A woody plant or shrub, *Parthenium argentatum*, of the southwestern United States and Mexico, having sap sometimes used as a source of rubber. [American Spanish, from Nahuatl *cuauhuli* : *cuahuitl*, tree + *uli*, gum.]

gu·ber·nac·u·lum (go͞o′bər-năk′yo͞o-ləm) *n., pl.* **-la** (-lə). *Anatomy.* Either of two ligaments in the fetus that are attached to the gonads. In males they guide the testes into the scrotum. [New Latin, from Latin, rudder : *gubernāre*, to steer + *-culum*, diminutive suffix.]

gu·ber·na·to·ri·al (go͞o′bər-nə-tôr′ē-əl, -tōr′-, gyo͞o′-) *adj.* Of or relating to a governor. [Late Latin *gubernātorius*, from Latin *gubernātor*, GOVERNOR.]

gu·ber·ni·ya (go͞o-bĕr′nē-ə) *n.* **1.** An administrative subdivision of a soviet in the U.S.S.R. **2.** An administrative division equivalent to a province in Russia prior to 1917. [Russian, province, perhaps from Polish *gubernja*, from Latin *gubernāre*, GOVERN.]

guck (gŭk, go͝ok) *n. Slang.* A messy substance, such as sludge. [Perhaps GOO + MUCK.]

gudg·eon[1] (gŭj′ən) *n.* **1.** A small Eurasian freshwater fish, *Gobio gobio*, related to the carp and used as food and bait. **2.** Any of various similar fishes. **3.** An enticement; a bait. **4.** *Slang.* Someone who is easily duped; a gullible person.

~*tr.v.* **gudgeoned, -eoning, -eons.** *Slang.* To dupe; cheat. [Middle English *gojoun*, from Old French *goujon*, from Latin *gōbiō*, *gōbius*, GOBY.]

gudgeon[2] *n.* **1.** A metal pivot or journal at the end of a shaft or axle, around which a wheel or other device turns. **2.** The part of a hinge into which the pin fits. **3.** *Nautical.* The socket for the pintle of a rudder. **4.** A metal pin that joins two pieces of stone. [Middle English *gudyon*, from Old French *goujon*, diminutive of *gouge*, GOUGE (chisel).]

gudgeon pin *n.* See **wrist pin** (sense 2).

Gud·run (go͝od′ro͞on′). Also **Guth·run** (go͝o*th*′-), **Kud·run** (ko͝od′-). The daughter of the king of the Nibelungs and wife of Sigurd in the *Volsunga Saga.*

guel·der rose (gĕl′dər) *n.* A shrub, *Viburnum opulus*, native to Eurasia, having clusters of white flowers and small red fruit. [Originally grown in *Gelderland* (or *Guelderland*), a province of the east-central Netherlands.]

Guelph, Guelf (gwĕlf) *n.* A member of a strong faction in medieval Italy that supported the power of the pope and the city-states in a struggle against the German emperors and the Ghibellines. **—Guelph·ic** *adj.* **—Guelph·ism** *n.*

Guenevere. Variant of **Guinevere.**

gue·non (gə-nōn′; *French* gə-nôN′) *n.* Any of various African monkeys of the genus *Cercopithecus*, having long hind legs and a long tail. [French *guenon*†.]

guer·don (gûrd′n) *n. Poetic.* A reward; recompense.

~*tr.v.* **guerdoned, -doning, -dons.** *Poetic.* To reward. [Middle English, from Old French, from Medieval Latin *widerdōnum*, alteration (influenced by Latin *dōnum*, gift) of Old High German *widarlōn* : *widar*, again + *lōn*, reward, payment.]

Gue·ric·ke (gā′rĭ-kə), **Otto von** (1602–86). German physicist. His fame rests on his experiments in pneumatics, especially the invention of an air pump (*c.* 1650). He also invented a primitive machine to generate electricity.

Guer·ni·ca (gwâr′nĭ-kə). Historic town in the Basque region of northern Spain, in the province of Vizcaya. The severe air bombing of the town by German aircraft supporting the Nationalists in April 1937 provoked Picasso to paint the famous work *Guernica.*

guern·sey (gûrn′zē) *n., pl.* **-seys.** **1.** A knitted woolen sweater with a distinctive ribbed pattern across the shoulder, originally worn by seamen. **2.** *Australian.* A football jersey. [First worn by seamen on the island of GUERNSEY.]

Guern·sey[1] (gûrn′zē). An island and bailiwick in the English Channel. Guernsey Island itself is the second largest of the Channel Islands. The bailiwick includes all the Channel Islands except the largest, Jersey. The capital is St. Peter Port. Market gardening, dairy farming, and tourism are the chief industries.

Guernsey[2] *n., pl.* **-seys.** Any of a breed of brown and white dairy cattle originally developed on the Isle of Guernsey.

guer·ril·la, gue·ril·la (gə-rĭl′ə) *n.* A member of an irregular military unit, usually associated with a revolutionary movement, that seeks to overthrow a government or an occupying enemy by means of sudden acts of harassment.

~*adj.* Of or relating to guerrillas or their methods of fighting: *guerrilla warfare.* [Spanish *guerrilla*, diminutive of *guerra*, war, from Germanic.]

guess (gĕs) *v.* **guessed, guessing, guesses.** —*tr.* **1. a.** To predict (a result or event) with incomplete information. **b.** To assume, presume, or assert (a fact) without sufficient information. **2.** To estimate correctly on the basis of incomplete information. **3.** To suppose; judge. —*intr.* **1.** To make a conjecture. Often used with *at*: *We could only guess at his motives.* **2.** To make a correct guess. **3.** To suppose. —See Synonyms at **conjecture.**

~*n.* **1.** An act or instance of guessing. **2.** A conjecture arrived at by guessing. [Middle English *gessen*, perhaps from Scandinavian; akin to Old Swedish and Danish *gisse*.] **—guess·er** *n.*

guess·ti·mate, gues·ti·mate (gĕs′tə-mĭt) *n.* An estimate based more on intuition than on strict calculation. [GUESS + ESTIMATE.] **—guess·ti·mate** (gĕs′tə-māt′) *v.*

guess·work (gĕs′wûrk′) *n.* **1.** The process of making guesses. **2.** An estimate or judgment made by this process.

guest (gĕst) *n.* **1.** One who receives hospitality at the home or table of another. **2.** One to whom some entertainment or service is offered. **3.** A visitor, such as a foreign dignitary, to whom the hospitality of an institution, municipality, or government has been extended. **4.** The patron of a restaurant, hotel, boarding house, or the like. **5.** A contestant, performer, speaker, or other person appearing in a concert, television program, or the like. **6.** *Zoology.* A commensal organism; especially, an insect that lives in the nest or burrow of another species.

~*adj.* Of, for, or being a guest: *a guest conductor; a guest room.*

~*v.* **guested, guesting, guests.** —*tr.* To entertain as one's guest. —*intr.* To appear as a guest, especially on a television show. [Middle English *gest*, from Old Norse *gestr*.]

guest rope *n. Nautical.* **1.** An extra line used with the towline to steady a ship being towed. **2.** A rope dropped over the side of a ship for steadying or securing a smaller boat coming alongside. Also called "guess rope."

Gue·va·ra (gə-vär′ə), **Ernesto,** known as "Che" (1928–67). Latin-American revolutionary leader, born in Argentina. When Castro took power in Cuba (1959), Guevara was appointed president of the national bank, and was then minister of industry (1961–65). He later assisted revolutionary movements in other countries, but was captured by the Bolivian army and executed (1967). He wrote several books, among them a manual for revolutionaries, *Guerrilla Warfare* (1961).

guff (gŭf) *n. Slang.* Foolish talk; nonsense. [Originally, "puff," imitative.]

guf·faw (gə-fô′) *n.* A hearty or coarse burst of laughter.

~*intr.v.* **guffawed, -fawing, -faws.** To laugh explosively. [Imitative.]

Gug·gen·heim (go͝og′ən-hīm′). Family of U.S. industrialists and philanthropists. **Solomon** (1861–1949) established (1937) the foundation that built the Guggenheim Museum of Modern Art in New York in 1959.

Gui·a·na or **Gua·ya·na** (gē-ăn′ə, -ä′nə). Region on the north coast of South America, bounded by the Orinoco, Amazon, and Negro rivers. It consists of eastern Venezuela, Guyana, Surinam, French Guiana, and northern Brazil.

guid·ance (gīd′ns) *n.* **1.** An act or instance of guiding. **2.** Counseling, as on vocational, educational, or marital problems. **3.** Any of various processes or techniques by which missiles carrying sensing or information-processing equipment are guided in flight.

guide (gīd) *n. Abbr.* **g.** **1.** One who shows the way by leading, directing, or advising, usually by reason of greater experience with the course to be pursued. **2.** A person employed to guide a tour, group, or the like. **3. a.** Any sign or mark that serves to direct. **b.** An example, model, or criterion of accuracy to be followed. **4. a.** A guidebook. **b.** A book or manual that serves to instruct or to direct one's thinking. **5.** Any device, such as a ruler, line, ring, tab, or bar, that acts as an indicator or that regulates the motion of one's hand, a tool, or a machine part. **6. a.** A soldier stationed at the right or left of a column to control the alignment of the marchers, show the direction, or mark the point of pivot. **b.** A ship or vehicle on which other members of a convoy may align themselves.

~*v.* **guided, guiding, guides.** —*tr.* **1.** To show the way to; lead; direct. **2.** To direct the course of; steer: *guide a ship through a channel.* **3.** To manage the affairs of; govern. **4. a.** To influence the conduct or opinions of. **b.** To be a criterion for or motive of (an action, for example). —*intr.* To serve as a guide. [Middle English *g(u)ide*, from Old French, from Frankish *wītan*.] **—guid·a·ble** *adj.* **—guid·er** *n.*

guide·book (gīd′bo͝ok′) *n.* A handbook of information for travelers, tourists, students, or the like.

guided missile *n.* A missile capable of being guided while it is in flight. Compare **ballistic missile.**

guide dog *n.* A dog that has been specially trained to guide a blind person.

guide·line (gīd′līn′) *n.* **1.** *Printing.* A mark used to orient lettering, a drawing, or the like. **2.** *Usually* **guidelines.** A statement of policy or principles by a person or group having authority over an activity. **3.** Something serving as an example or source of instruction.

guide·post (gīd′pōst′) *n.* A post with a sign giving directions placed at an intersection or fork in a road; signpost.

guide rope *n.* **1.** A rope fastened to another rope that is lifting a load, to guide the rope and steady the load. **2.** A rope used to steady or moor an airship or balloon.

guide·word (gīd′wûrd′) *n.* A word or term that appears at the top of the page of a reference book, such as a dictionary, to indicate the first or last entry on the page.

gui·don (gī′dŏn′, gīd′n) *n. Military.* **1.** A small flag or pennant, often with a forked end, carried as a standard by a regiment or other military unit. **2.** The soldier bearing this standard. [French, from Italian *guidone*, from *guida*, GUIDE.]

guild, gild (gĭld) *n.* **1.** An association or corporation of persons of the same trade, pursuits, or interests formed for their mutual aid and protection, the maintenance of standards, or the furtherance of some purpose; especially, in medieval times, a society of merchants or artisans. **2.** *Ecology.* A group of plants having a characteristic mode of existence that involves some dependence upon other plant life, such as the lianas and epiphytes. [Middle English *gilde*, from Old Norse *gildi*, payment, fraternity, contribution.]

guil·der, gil·der (gĭl′dər) *n. Abbr.* **gld. 1.** The basic monetary unit of the Netherlands, Surinam, and the Netherlands Antilles, equal to 100 cents. See feature at **currency. 2.** A coin worth one guilder. Also called "gulden," "florin." [Middle English, alteration of Dutch *gulden,* GULDEN.]

guild·hall (gĭld′hôl′) *n.* **1.** The meeting hall of a guild or corporation, especially in medieval times. **2. a.** A town hall. **b. Guildhall.** The meeting hall of the Corporation of the City of London.

guilds·man (gĭldz′mən) *n., pl.* **-men** (-mĭn). A member of a guild.

guild socialism *n.* A type of socialism formerly advocated in England in which industry would be owned by the state but managed by a council of workers.

guilds·wom·an (gĭldz′wo͝om′ən) *n., pl.* **-women** (-wĭm′ĭn). A woman member of a guild.

guile (gīl) *n.* **1.** Cunning; craftiness. **2.** *Obsolete.* A trick; ruse. —See Synonyms at **artifice.**

∼*tr.v.* **guiled, guiling, guiles.** *Archaic.* To beguile; deceive. [Middle English *gile,* from Old French *guile,* from Germanic; akin to Old English *wigle,* divination, sorcery.]

guile·ful (gīl′fəl) *adj.* Full of guile; artfully deceitful; crafty. **—guile·ful·ly** *adv.* **—guile·ful·ness** *n.*

guile·less (gīl′lĭs) *adj.* Free of guile; simple; artless. —See Synonyms at **naive. —guile·less·ly** *adv.* **—guile·less·ness** *n.*

Guil·laume (gē-yōm′), **Charles Edouard** (1861–1938). Swiss physicist. For his discovery of the steel-nickel alloy called Invar he was awarded the Nobel Prize for physics (1920).

guil·le·mot (gĭl′ə-mŏt′) *n.* Any of several small sea birds of the genera *Uria* and *Cepphus,* of northern regions, having dark plumage with white markings. [French, diminutive of *Guillaume,* William.]

guil·loche (gĭ-lŏsh′, gē-yŏsh′) *n. Architecture.* An ornamental border formed of two or more bands interlaced in such a way as to repeat a design. [French *guillochis,* from *guillocher,* to decorate with guilloche, perhaps from Italian *ghiocciare,* dialectal variant of *gocciare,* to drip, trickle, from *goccia,* drop, from Latin *gutta.* See **gout.**]

guil·lo·tine (gĭl′ə-tēn′, gē′ə-) *n.* **1. a.** A machine with a heavy blade that falls freely between upright guides to behead a condemned prisoner. **b.** Any of various other machines used for execution by beheading. **c.** Execution by such a machine. Preceded by *the.* **2.** Any of various more or less similar cutting instruments, such as a surgical device used to remove tonsils. **3.** A device consisting of a long blade that is brought down onto a sheet of paper, metal, or the like to cut or trim it. **4.** *British.* A method of cutting off debate on a bill in Parliament by fixing beforehand a time for voting on successive stages. Compare **kangaroo closure.**

∼*tr.v.* **guillotined, -tining, -tines. 1.** To behead with a guillotine. **2.** To cut or trim with a guillotine. [After Joseph Ignace *Guillotin* (1738–1814), French doctor who proposed its use.] **—guil·lo·tin·er** *n.*

guilt (gĭlt) *n.* **1.** The fact of being responsible for an offense or wrongdoing. **2.** *Law.* Culpability for a crime or breach of regulations that carries a legal punishment or penalty. **3. a.** Remorseful awareness of having done something wrong. **b.** Feelings of remorse arising from a sense of inadequacy or imagined wrongdoing. **4.** *Rare.* Guilty behavior. [Middle English *gult, gilt,* Old English *gylt*†.]

guilt complex *n. Psychology.* An obsession with the idea of being to blame for something.

guilt·less (gĭlt′lĭs) *adj.* **1.** Free from guilt; blameless; innocent. **2.** Without knowledge or experience of something. **—guilt·less·ly** *adv.* **—guilt·less·ness** *n.*

guilt·y (gĭl′tē) *adj.* **-ier, -iest. 1.** Responsible for or chargeable with some reprehensible act. Often used with *of*: *guilty of cheating.* **2.** *Law.* Having committed a crime or a breach of regulations or having been adjudged to have done so: *plead guilty.* **3.** At fault; culpable: *the guilty party.* **4.** Suffering from or showing a sense of guilt: *a guilty conscience.* **—guilt·i·ly** *adv.* **—guilt·i·ness** *n.*

guimpe (gĭmp, gămp) *n.* **1.** A short-sleeved blouse worn under a jumper. **2.** A yoke insert for a low-necked dress. **3.** A starched cloth covering the neck and shoulders as part of a nun's habit. **4.** A trimming, **gimp** *(see).*

Guin. Guinea.

guin·ea (gĭn′ē) *n. Abbr.* **G., g. 1.** A former British gold coin worth one pound and one shilling. **2.** The sum of one pound and one shilling. [Originally made of gold from the *Guinea* coast of Africa.]

Guin·ea (gĭn′ē). *Abbr.* **Guin.** Formerly **French Guinea.** Independent republic on the west coast of Africa. The interior consists chiefly of highlands, although in the northeast the land descends to the Niger plains. The bulk of the labor force is employed in agriculture, but the major exports are bauxite and alumina. Guinea was a French colony from 1891 until 1958, when it gained its independence. Area, 245,856 square kilometers (94,925 square miles). Population, 5,150,000. Capital, Conakry. See map at **West African States.**

Guinea, Gulf of. Broad bay of the Atlantic Ocean formed by the large bend of the coast of west-central Africa. It extends, roughly, from the west coast of Ivory Coast to the Gabon estuary and includes the bights of Benin and Biafra.

Guin·ea-Bis·sau (gĭn′ē-bĭ-sou′). Formerly **Por·tu·guese Guinea** (pôr′chə-gēz′). Independent republic on the west coast of Africa. Except for the highlands on the border with Guinea, the land is low-lying. The chief exports are peanuts and peanut products, palm products, and copra. The country was a Portuguese colony from 1879 until 1974, when it gained its independence under the African Party for the Independence of Guinea and Cape Verde. There are plans to unite the two countries. Area, 36,125 square kilometers (13,948 square miles). Population, 780,000. Capital, Bissau. See map at **West African States.**

Guinea corn *n.* **Durra** *(see).*

guinea fowl *n.* Any of several pheasantlike birds of the family Numididae, native to Africa; especially, a widely domesticated species, *Numida meleagris,* having blackish plumage marked with many small white spots. Also called "guinea hen." [From the *Guinea* coast of Africa.]

guinea hen *n.* **1.** A female guinea fowl. **2.** The guinea fowl.

Guinea pepper *n.* **1.** A variety of the plant, *Capsicum frutescens,* from which cayenne pepper is made. **2.** The spicy fruit of an African tree, *Xylopia aethiopica,* which is made into a condiment.

guinea pig *n.* **1.** A domesticated rodent descended from the Brazilian or Peruvian cavy, *Cavia procellus,* having variously colored hair and no visible tail, and widely kept as pets and as experimental animals. **2.** Any person who is used as a subject for experimentation. [Probably from a confusion of GUIANA with the *Guinea* coast of Africa.]

guinea worm *n.* A long, threadlike nematode worm, *Dracunculus medinensis,* of tropical Asia and Africa, that is a subcutaneous parasite of man and other animals, causing ulcers on the arms, legs, and feet. [Probably from the *Guinea* coast of Africa.]

Guin·e·vere (gwĭn′ə-vîr′). Also **Guen·e·vere** (gwĕn′-). In Arthurian legend, the wife of King Arthur and the mistress of Lancelot. [Welsh *Gwenhwyvar,* perhaps "white phantom" : *gwyn,* white + *-hwyvar*†, phantom.]

Guin·ness (gĭn′ĭs), **Sir Alec** (1914–). English actor. He has played memorable roles in such films as *Kind Hearts and Coronets* (1949) in which he played eight parts, *The Lavender Hill Mob* (1951), *The Horse's Mouth* (1958), and *Lawrence of Arabia* (1962).

gui·pure (gĭ-pyo͝or′; *French* gē-pür′) *n.* **1.** A kind of coarse, large-patterned lace without a supporting net mesh. **2.** A trimming, **gimp** *(see).* [French, from Old French, from *guiper,* to cover with silk, wool, or the like, from Frankish *wīpan.*]

gui·ro (gwîr′ō) *n.* A percussion instrument consisting of a dried gourd with parallel grooves cut across it. It produces a rattling sound when a stick is drawn across it. [Spanish, gourd.]

guise (gīz) *n.* **1.** Outward appearance; aspect. **2.** False appearance; pretense. **3.** Mode of dress; garb: *in the guise of a beggar.* **4.** *Obsolete.* Custom; habit.

∼*v.* **guised, guising, guises.** —*tr. Archaic.* To costume. —*intr. Chiefly Scottish.* To go in disguise; masquerade. [Middle English, fashion, manner, from Old French, from Germanic.]

Guise (gēz). A powerful French ducal line of the 16th and 17th centuries.

guis·er (gī′zər) *n. Chiefly Scottish.* One who goes from door to door wearing mask and fancy dress at Halloween, performing for money, sweets, or the like. [From dialectal *guise,* to masquerade, from GUISE (noun).]

gui·tar (gĭ-tär′) *n.* A musical instrument similar to the lute, having a large flat-backed sound box generally in the shape of a violin, a long fretted neck, and usually six strings, played by strumming or plucking. [French *guitare,* from Old French, from Spanish *guitarra,* from Arabic *qītār,* from Greek *kithara,* lyre.] **—gui·tar·ist** *n.*

gui·tar·fish (gĭ-tär′fĭsh′) *n., pl.* **-fishes** or collectively **guitarfish.** Any of several bottom-dwelling marine fishes of the family Rhinobatidae having a guitar-shaped body.

Gui·try (gē-trē′), **Sacha** (1885–1957). French playwright, actor, and film director. The best known of the films he directed are *The Story of a Cheat* (1935) and *Pearls of the Crown* (1937).

Gu·ja·rat (go͞oj′ə-rät′). State in western India, lying on the Arabian Sea and including almost all of the Kathiawar peninsula. It was created in 1960 from the Gujarati-speaking parts of the former state of Bombay. The capital is Ahmadabad. Gujarat is the center of India's cotton-textile industry.

Gu·ja·ra·ti (go͞oj′ə-rä′tē) *n., pl.* **Gujarati. 1.** The Indic language spoken in Gujarat. **2.** A native or inhabitant of Gujarat or speaker of Gujarati.

gul (go͞ol) *n.* A motif in oriental carpets, typically a stylized compact device that is repeated at regular intervals in the central field. [Persian *gul*†, rose, flower.]

gu·lag (go͞o′läg′) *n. Often* **Gulag.** A forced labor camp or prison, used especially for political prisoners. [Russian *G*lavnoye *U*pravleniye Trudovykh *Lag*erei, Main Administration for Corrective Labor Camps.]

gu·lar (go͞o′lər, gyo͞o′-) *adj.* Of, pertaining to, or located on the throat. [Latin *gula,* throat.]

gulch (gŭlch) *n.* A small ravine, especially one cut by a torrent. [Origin obscure.]

gul·den (go͞ol′dən) *n., pl.* **guldens** or **gulden.** A monetary unit, the **guilder** *(see).* [Dutch *gulden (florijn),* golden (florin), from Middle Dutch.]

gules (gyo͞olz) *n. Heraldry.* The color red, indicated on a blazon by engraved vertical lines.

∼*adj. Heraldry.* Red. Usually used after the noun: *a lion gules.* [Middle English *goules,* from Old French *go(u)les,* red, red fur neckpiece, from the plural of *gole,* throat, from Latin *gula,* throat.]

gulf (gŭlf) *n.* **1.** *Abbr.* **G.** A large area of a sea or ocean partially enclosed by land; especially, a long landlocked portion of sea opening through a strait. **2.** A deep, wide chasm; abyss. **3.** A separating

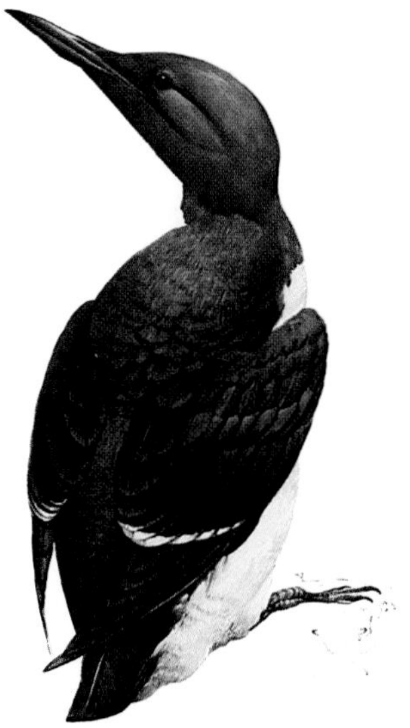

guillemot Uria aalge, *the guillemot, spends most of each year at sea, coming ashore in February to breed on cliff ledges. The birds, which breed on coasts across much of the Northern Hemisphere, do not build nests. Instead, the pear-shaped eggs are laid on bare rock.*

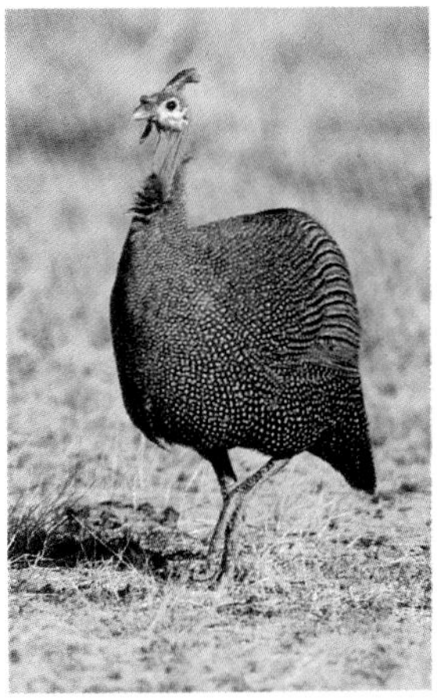

guinea fowl *Relatives of the domestic chicken, guinea fowls are native to Africa. This crowned guinea fowl—one of eight species of the bird—is in Etosha National Park in Namibia.*

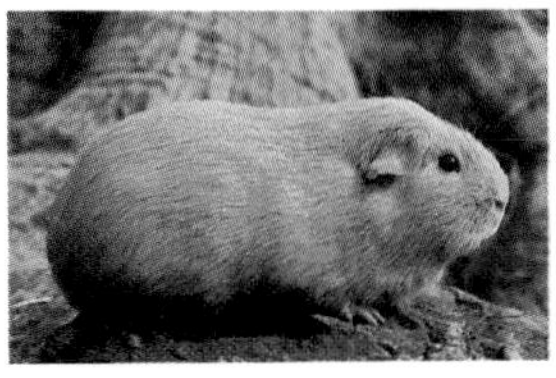

guinea pig *A tailless rodent introduced to Europe from Peru by the Spaniards soon after the discovery of America.*

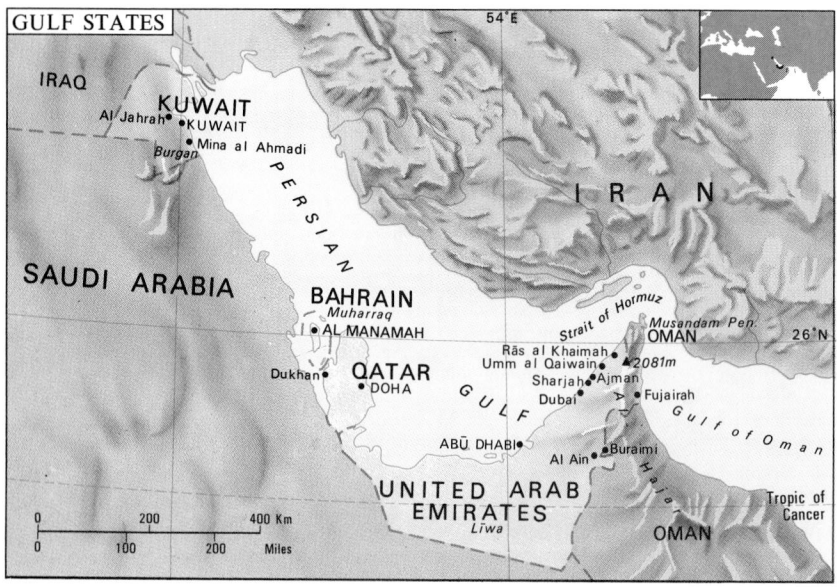

GULF STATES

Eurypharynx and *Saccopharynx,* which live on the sea bottom and can swallow prey much larger than themselves.

gum¹ (gŭm) *n.* **1. a.** Any of various viscous substances that are exuded by certain plants and trees and that dry into water-soluble, noncrystalline, brittle solids. **b.** Loosely, a similar plant exudate, such as a resin. **2.** Any of various adhesives made from such exudates or from some other sticky substance. **3. a.** Any of various trees, such as one of the genera *Eucalyptus, Liquidambar,* or *Nyssa,* that are a source of gum. Also called "gum tree." **b.** The wood of such a tree. Also called "gumwood." **4.** Chewing gum. ~*v.* **gummed, gumming, gums.** —*tr.* To cover, smear, seal, fill, or fix in place with gum. —*intr.* **1.** To exude or form gum. **2.** To become sticky or clogged with gum or a similar substance. —**gum up. 1.** To become clogged, as with gum. **2.** *Slang.* To ruin; bungle; spoil: *gum up the works.* [Middle English *gumme, gomme,* from Old French *gomme,* from Vulgar Latin *gumma* (unattested), from Latin *gummi, cummi,* from Greek *kommi,* from Egyptian *kemai.*]

gum² *n.* The firm connective tissue that is covered by mucous membrane and that envelops the bones of the jaw containing the tooth sockets and surrounds the bases of the teeth. Also called "gingiva." [Middle English *gome,* Old English *gōma,* palate, jaw.]

gum ac·croi·des (ə-kroi′dēz) *n.* A gum resin, **acaroid resin** *(see).* [New Latin *accroides,* from ACAROID.]

gum ammoniac *n.* A gum resin, **ammoniac** *(see).*

gum arabic *n.* A gum exuded by various African trees of the genus *Acacia,* especially *A. senegal,* and used in the preparation of pills and emulsions, the manufacture of mucilage and sweets, and in general as a thickener and colloidal stabilizer. Also called "acacia."

gum benzoin *n.* A gum resin, **benzoin** *(see).*

gum·bo, gom·bo (gŭm′bō) *n., pl.* **-bos. 1. a.** The mucilaginous pods of okra. **b. Okra** *(see).* **2.** A soup or stew thickened with okra and eaten especially in Africa, the Caribbean, and the southern United States. **3.** A fine silty soil, common in the southern and western United States, that forms an unusually sticky mud when wet. **4.** *Often* **Gumbo.** A patois spoken by some Blacks and Creoles in Louisiana and the French West Indies. [Louisiana French *gombo,* from Bantu.]

gum·boil (gŭm′boil′) *n.* A small boil or abscess on the gum, usually opening from the root of a tooth.

gum·bo-lim·bo (gŭm′bō-lĭm′bō) *n., pl.* **-bos.** An aromatic tree, *Bursera simaruba,* of Florida and the West Indies, having compound leaves and small white flowers. [Possibly GUMBO + *-limbo,* bird-lime (from its resin), from Bantu.]

gum·boot (gŭm′bōot′) *n.* A **Wellington boot** *(see).*

gum·drop (gŭm′drŏp′) *n.* A small candy made of flavored gum arabic or gelatin and coated with coarse granulated sugar.

gum·ma (gŭm′ə) *n., pl.* **-mas** or **gummata** (gŭm′ə-tə). A small, rubbery tumor formed in an advanced stage of syphilis. [New Latin, from Latin *gummi,* GUM.] —**gum·ma·tous** *adj.*

gum·mite (gŭm′īt′) *n.* A yellow to orange amorphous mineral consisting of hydrated uranium oxides. [German *Gummi,* GUM (referring to the gummy appearance of some types) + -ITE.]

gum·mo·sis (gŭ-mō′sĭs) *n.* The pathological formation of patches of gum on certain plants, such as sugar cane and certain fruit trees, resulting from attack by insects, microorganisms, or adverse weather conditions. [New Latin : Latin *gummi,* GUM + -OSIS.]

gum·mous (gŭm′əs) *adj.* Also **gum·mose** (-ōs′). **1.** Gumlike or composed of gum. **2.** Gummy.

gum·my (gŭm′ē) *adj.* **-mier, -miest. 1.** Consisting of or containing gum. **2.** Suffused with or yielding gum. **3.** Sticky; viscid. **4.** Coated with gum or something gumlike.

gum plant *n.* Any of several North American plants of the genus *Grindelia,* especially *G. squarosa,* having sticky leaves and bracts and yellow, rayed flowers.

gump·tion (gŭmp′shən) *n. Informal.* **1.** Basic common sense; practicality. **2.** Enterprise or initiative, especially when requiring courage or nerve. [18th century (Scottish) : origin obscure.]

gum resin *n.* A mixture of gum and resin that exudes from some trees and other plants.

gum·shoe (gŭm′shōo′) *n.* **1.** A rubber shoe or overshoe. **2.** A sneaker. **3.** *Slang.* A detective. ~*intr.v.* **gumshoed, -shoeing, -shoes.** *Slang.* To investigate stealthily; pry.

gum tree *n.* A tree, the **gum** *(see).*

gum·wood (gŭm′wŏod′) *n.* The wood of a gum tree. See **gum.**

gun (gŭn) *n.* **1.** A weapon consisting essentially of a metal tube from which a projectile is fired at high velocity. **2.** A cannon, as distinguished from a small firearm. **3.** A portable firearm. **4.** A device that shoots a projectile. **5.** A discharge of a gun as a signal or salute. **6.** One who carries or uses a gun, such as a member of a shooting party. **7.** A device that projects something under pressure or at great speed: *a grease gun; an electron gun.* —**go great guns.** *Informal.* To proceed with vigor or success. —**jump the gun. 1.** To begin a race before the starting signal. **2.** *Informal.* To act before the appropriate moment. —**stick to one's guns.** To hold fast to an opinion or appointed course of action. ~*v.* **gunned, gunning, guns.** —*tr.* **1.** To fire upon; shoot. Often used with *down.* **2.** *Informal.* To open the throttle of so as to accelerate: *gun an engine.* —*intr.* To hunt or shoot with a gun. —**gun for. 1.** To seek to catch, overcome, or destroy. **2.** To go after in earnest; set out to obtain: *gun for the best deal available.* [Middle English *gunne, gonne,* probably from *Gunna* (unattested), pet form of feminine name *Gunhild* (sometimes applied to a war engine),

---

distance or wide gap caused especially by a lack of understanding or communication. **4.** A whirlpool; eddy. ~*tr.v.* **gulfed, gulfing, gulfs.** To swallow; engulf. [Middle English *golf, goulf,* from Old French *golfe,* from Old Italian *golfo,* from Vulgar Latin *colp(h)us* (unattested), from Greek *kolpos, kolphos,* bosom, fold, bay.]

Gulf, the. See **Persian Gulf.**

Gulf States¹. The small, oil-rich Arab states on the Persian Gulf: Bahrain, Kuwait, Qatar, and the United Arab Emirates.

Gulf States². The five southern U.S. states that have coastlines on the Gulf of Mexico: Florida, Alabama, Mississippi, Louisiana, and Texas.

Gulf Stream *n.* A warm ocean current of the North Atlantic, issuing from the Gulf of Mexico and flowing east through the Straits of Florida, northeast along the southeastern coast of the United States, then east to merge with the North Atlantic Current.

gulf·weed (gŭlf′wēd′) *n.* Any of several brownish seaweeds of the genus *Sargassum,* especially *S. natans,* of tropical Atlantic waters, having rounded air bladders and often forming dense, floating masses. Also called "sargasso." [After the Gulf of Mexico, where it is found.]

gull¹ (gŭl) *n.* Any of various chiefly coastal aquatic birds of the subfamily Larinae, having long wings, webbed feet, and usually gray and white plumage. [Middle English *gull,* probably from Welsh *gwylan,* from Celtic *voilenno-* (unattested).]

gull² *n.* A gullible person; dupe; simpleton. ~*tr.v.* **gulled, gulling, gulls.** To deceive; cheat; dupe. [Probably from dialectal *gull,* unfledged bird, Middle English *golle, gulle,* probably from *gul,* yellow, pale, from Old Norse *gulr.*]

Gul·lah (gŭl′ə) *n.* **1.** Any of a group of Blacks inhabiting the Sea Islands and coastal area of South Carolina, Georgia, and northern Florida. **2.** The creolized English spoken by these people.

gul·let (gŭl′ĭt) *n.* **1.** *Anatomy.* The esophagus. **2.** The throat. **3.** A gully or ravine, especially one that serves as a water channel. **4.** A cut in the earth preliminary to mining or excavating. [Middle English *golet,* from Old French *goulet,* diminutive of *gole, goule,* throat, from Latin *gula.*]

gul·li·ble (gŭl′ə-bəl) *adj.* Able to be taken in; easily deceived or duped; credulous. [From GULL (dupe).] —**gul·li·bil·i·ty** *n.* —**gul·li·bly** *adv.*

Gull·strand (gŭl′strănd′), **Allvar** (1862–1930). Swedish ophthalmologist. For his experiments on the refraction of light in the eye he was awarded the Nobel Prize in 1911.

gul·ly¹ (gŭl′ē) *n., pl.* **-lies. 1.** A deep ditch or channel cut in the earth by running water, usually after a downpour. **2.** A gutter or channel. ~*tr.v.* **gullied, -lying, -lies.** To make a gully in. [Alteration of GULLET.]

gully² *n., pl.* **-lies.** *Chiefly Scottish.* A large knife. [Short for *gully knife : gully,* probably alteration of GULLET + KNIFE.]

gu·los·i·ty (gōo-lŏs′ə-tē, gyōo-) *n. Literary.* Gluttony. [Late Latin *gulōsitās* (stem *gulōsitāt-*), from Latin *gulōsus,* greedy, from *gula,* gullet.]

gulp (gŭlp) *v.* **gulped, gulping, gulps.** —*tr.* **1.** To swallow greedily or rapidly in large amounts. Usually used with *down: gulp down coffee.* **2.** To stifle by or as if by swallowing. —*intr.* **1.** To choke or gasp; swallow air, as in nervousness. **2.** To swallow food or drink in gulps. **3.** To make a noise in the throat when swallowing. ~*n.* **1.** The act of gulping. **2.** A large mouthful. **3.** A convulsive attempt to swallow; a catching of air in the throat. [Middle English *gulpen,* from Middle Dutch *gulpen* (imitative).] —**gulp·er** *n.* —**gulp·ing·ly** *adv.*

gulp·er eel (gŭl′pər) *n.* Any of various eellike fishes of the genera

from Old Norse *Gunnhildr* : *gunnr*, battle + *hildr*, war.]

gun·boat (gŭn′bōt′) *n.* A small armed vessel.

gunboat diplomacy *n.* Diplomacy that makes use of the threat of military intervention in order to achieve its purpose.

gun carriage *n.* A frame or structure upon which a gun is mounted for firing or maneuvering.

gun·cot·ton (gŭn′kŏt′n) *n.* An explosive, **nitrocellulose** *(see).*

gun dog *n.* A dog trained or bred to assist hunters, as in flushing or retrieving game.

gun·fight (gŭn′fīt′) *n.* Also **gun·fight·ing** (-ĭng). A duel or battle with firearms. —**gun·fight·er** *n.*

gun·fire (gŭn′fīr′) *n.* The firing of guns.

gun·flint (gŭn′flĭnt′) *n.* The piece of flint used to strike the igniting spark in a flintlock.

gung ho (gŭng′ hō′) *adj. Slang.* **1.** Unswervingly dedicated and loyal. **2.** Foolishly enthusiastic. [Pidgin English : probably Mandarin Chinese *gōng*, work + *hé*, together.]

gunk (gŭngk) *n. Informal.* A filthy, slimy, or greasy substance. [Originally a trade name for a degreasing compound, later extended to apply to any viscous substance.]

gun·lock (gŭn′lŏk′) *n.* A device for igniting the charge of a firearm.

gun·man (gŭn′mən) *n., pl.* **-men** (-mĭn). **1.** One armed with a gun. **2.** A desperado; an outlaw. **3.** A professional killer.

gun·met·al (gŭn′mĕt′l) *n.* **1.** An alloy of copper with ten percent tin and sometimes a few percent of zinc. **2.** Metal used for guns. **3.** Dark gray. —**gun·met·al** *adj.*

gun moll *n. Slang.* A girlfriend or woman accomplice of a gangster.

Gunn (gŭn), **Thomson William** (1929-). British poet. His work, which includes *My Sad Captains* (1961) and *Jack Straw's Castle* (1976), is marked by strictness of form, powerful imagery, and philosophical themes. He now lives chiefly in the United States.

Gun·nar (gōōn′är′). *Norse Mythology.* The husband of Brynhild, the brother-in-law of Sigurd, and the brother of Gudrun.

Gunn effect (gŭn) *n. Electronics.* The production of high-speed current fluctuations when voltage in excess of a critical level is applied to a semiconductor device, resulting in microwave generation. [After J.B. Gunn (b. 1928).]

gun·nel¹ (gŭn′əl) *n.* Any of various long, eellike fishes of the family Pholidae, of northern seas. [17th century : origin obscure.]

gunnel². Variant of **gunwale.**

gun·ner (gŭn′ər) *n.* **1.** A serviceman, especially a member of an aircraft crew, who aims or fires a gun. **2.** One who hunts with a gun. **3.** *British.* An artillery soldier, especially a private. **4.** A warrant officer in the navy having charge of ordnance.

gun·ner·y (gŭn′ə-rē) *n.* **1.** The art and science of constructing and operating guns. **2.** The use of guns.

gun·ny (gŭn′ē) *n.* **1.** A coarse fabric made of jute or hemp. **2.** Burlap. [Hindi *gōnī*, from Sanskrit *goṇī*, sack.]

gunny sack *n.* A sack made of burlap or gunny.

gun·point (gŭn′point′) *n.* The shooting end of a gun. —**at gunpoint.** Under the threat of being shot at.

gun·pow·der (gŭn′pou′dər) *n.* Any of various explosive powders used in blasting and to propel projectiles from guns; especially, a black explosive mixture of potassium nitrate, charcoal, and sulfur.

Gunpowder Plot *n.* A plot organized by Guy Fawkes to blow up Parliament and kill James I on November 5, 1605, in protest against the increasing repression of Roman Catholics in England. See **Guy Fawkes Day.**

gunpowder tea *n.* A type of green tea the leaves of which are rolled into pellets.

gun·room (gŭn′rōōm′, -rōōm′) *n.* The quarters of midshipmen and junior officers on a British warship.

gun·run·ner (gŭn′rŭn′ər) *n.* One that smuggles firearms and ammunition. —**gun·run·ning** *n. & adj.*

gun·ship (gŭn′shĭp′) *n.* An armed helicopter or other aircraft used to support troops and cover transport helicopters.

gun·shot (gŭn′shŏt′) *n.* **1.** Shot fired from a gun. **2.** A shooting of a gun. **3.** The range of a gun: *within gunshot.*

gun-shy (gŭn′shī′) *adj.* Afraid of gunfire. Said especially of gun dogs.

gun·sling·er (gŭn′slĭng′ər) *n. Slang.* A gunman. —**gun·sling·ing** *n. & adj.*

gun·smith (gŭn′smĭth′) *n.* One who makes or repairs firearms.

gun·stock (gŭn′stŏk′) *n.* See **stock** (sense 14.a).

Gun·ter's chain (gŭn′tərz) *n.* See **chain** (sense 9b). [After Edmund *Gunter* (1581-1626), English mathematician.]

Gun·ther (gŭn′tər). In the *Nibelungenlied,* a king of Burgundy whose wife Brunhild is won for him by Siegfried, who in return receives Kriemhild, Gunther's sister, as his wife. Identified with Gunnar.

gun·wale, gun·nel (gŭn′əl) *n.* The upper edge of a ship's side. [Middle English *gonnewale* : GUN + WALE (so called because it served formerly as a prop for the ship's guns).]

Guo·yü, Kuo·yü (kwô′yōō′) *n.* **Mandarin Chinese** *(see).* [Mandarin Chinese *guóyǔ yǔ* : *guó,* nation, national + *yǔ,* language.]

gup·py (gŭp′ē) *n., pl.* **-pies.** A small, brightly colored freshwater fish, *Poecilia reticulata* (or *Lebistes reticulatus*), of northern South America and adjacent islands of the West Indies, that is popular in home aquariums. [After R.J.L. *Guppy,* 19th-century clergyman of Trinidad who supplied the British Museum with the first specimen.]

Gur (gōōr) *n.* A group of languages of the Niger-Congo family spoken chiefly in Ghana and Upper Volta.

gur·gi·ta·tion (gûr′jə-tā′shən) *n.* A whirling motion, as of water;

ebullition. [Late Latin *gurgitāre,* to engulf, from Latin *gurges* (stem *gurgit-*), whirlpool, gulf.]

gur·gle (gûr′gəl) *v.* **-gled, -gling, -gles.** —*intr.* **1.** To flow in a broken, uneven current making intermittent low sounds. **2.** To make such sounds: *the baby gurgled with pleasure.* —*tr.* To express or pronounce with a gurgling sound. ~*n.* The act or sound of gurgling. [Probably from Medieval Latin *gurgulāre,* from Latin *gurguliō,* gullet.] —**gur·gling·ly** *adv.*

Gur·kha (gōōr′kə) *n., pl.* **-khas** or collectively **Gurkha. 1.** A member of a Rajput ethnic group that was driven out of India by the Muslims and is now predominant in Nepal. **2.** A soldier from Nepal serving in the British or Indian armies.

gur·nard (gûr′nərd) *n., pl.* **gurnards** or collectively **gurnard.** Also **gur·net** (gûr′nĭt). Any of various marine fishes of the family Triglidae, and especially of the Old World genus *Trigla,* having large, fingerlike, pectoral fins and a large, armored head. Compare **flying gurnard.** [Middle English, from Old French *gornart,* from Latin *grundīre, grunnīre,* to grunt (because it grunts when caught).]

gur·ney (gûr′nē) *n., pl.* **-neys.** A cot or stretcher on wheels. [Probably from the name *Gurney.*]

gur·ry (gûr′ē) *n.* Fish offal. [Origin unknown.]

gu·ru (gōōr′ōō, gōō-rōō′) *n. Often* **Guru.** A spiritual teacher or leader, as in the Hindu or Sikh religions. [Hindi *gurū,* "the venerable one," from Sanskrit *guruh,* heavy, venerable.]

gush (gŭsh) *v.* **gushed, gushing, gushes.** —*intr.* **1.** To flow forth suddenly and violently. **2.** To issue or emanate abundantly. **3.** To make an excessively demonstrative or affected display of sentiment or enthusiasm. —*tr.* To emit abundantly. ~*n.* **1.** A sudden, violent, or copious outflow: *a gush of tears.* **2.** An excessive, usually insincere, display of emotion. [Middle English *guschen, gosshen,* perhaps from Scandinavian, akin to Icelandic *gusa.*]

gush·er (gŭsh′ər) *n.* **1.** One that gushes. **2.** A gas or oil well with an abundant natural flow.

gush·y (gŭsh′ē) *adj.* **-ier, -iest.** Characterized by excessive, affected displays of sentiment or emotion.

gus·set (gŭs′ĭt) *n.* **1.** A triangular insert, as in a garment, for strengthening or enlarging. **2.** A triangular metal bracket used to strengthen a joist. [Middle English, from Old French *gousset,* armpit, piece of armor under the armpit, diminutive of *gousset†,* pod, shell.] —**gus·set·ed** *adj.*

gus·sy (gŭs′ē) *tr.v.* **-sied, -sying, -sies.** *Slang.* To dress smartly. Used with *up: all gussied up in her Sunday best.* [Origin obscure.]

gust¹ (gŭst) *n.* **1.** A violent, abrupt rush of wind, smoke, or the like. **2.** An abrupt outburst of emotion, as of rage. —See Synonyms at **wind.** [Old Norse *gustr.*]

gust² *n.* **1.** *Archaic.* Relish; gusto. **2.** *Obsolete.* Personal taste or inclination; liking. [Middle English *guste,* taste, from Latin *gustus.*]

gus·ta·tion (gŭs-tā′shən) *n.* The act or faculty of tasting; taste. [Latin *gustātiō* (stem *gustātiōn-*), from *gustāre,* to taste, from *gustus,* taste.]

gus·ta·to·ry (gŭs′tə-tôr′ē, -tōr′ē) *adj.* Also **gus·ta·tive** (-tĭv). Of or pertaining to the sense of taste.

Gus·ta·vus II (gŭs-tā′vəs), known as "Gustavus Adolphus" (1594-1632). King of Sweden (1611-32). As a general he fought successfully against Denmark, Russia, and Poland. He was drawn into the Thirty Years' War by his desire to assure Swedish control of the Baltic. He met his death at the Battle of Lützen (1632).

gus·to (gŭs′tō) *n.* **1.** Vigorous enjoyment; relish; zest. **2.** *Archaic.* Artistic style of execution. [Italian, from Latin *gustus,* taste.]

gus·ty (gŭs′tē) *adj.* **-tier, -tiest. 1.** Blowing in or characterized by gusts. **2.** Marked by sudden outbursts: *a gusty temperament.* —**gus·ti·ly** *adv.* —**gus·ti·ness** *n.*

gut (gŭt) *n.* **1.** The alimentary canal or a portion thereof; especially, the intestine or stomach. **2. guts.** The bowels; entrails; viscera. **3. guts.** The essential contents or part of something: *the guts of an old television set.* **4.** The intestines of some animals prepared as strings for musical instruments or as surgical sutures; catgut. **5. guts.** *Informal.* Courage; nerve. **6.** A narrow passage or channel. **7.** Fibrous material taken from the silk gland of a silkworm before it spins a cocoon, used for fishing tackle. —**hate someone's guts.** *Informal.* To detest or feel very hostile toward someone. ~*tr.v.* **gutted, gutting, guts. 1.** To remove the intestines or entrails of. **2.** To destroy the interior of: *fire gutted the house.* **3.** To extract the essential parts of (a book, article, or the like). ~*adj. Slang.* Arousing or aroused by basic emotions; visceral; instinctive: *a gut response.* [Middle English *gut,* Old English *guttas* (plural).]

gut·buck·et (gŭt′bŭk′ət) *n.* **1.** An early style of jazz, with a strong beat. Also called "barrelhouse." **2.** A homemade instrument, resembling a double bass, on which this music was originally played.

Gu·ten·berg (gōōt′n-bûrg′), **Johann** (*c.* 1397-1468). German printer. He was the first European to print with movable type set in molds. His Mazarin Bible of *c.* 1455 is believed to be the first book printed with movable type.

Guth·rie test (gŭth′rē) *n.* A blood test to determine the presence of the metabolic disease phenylketonuria in young children. [After Samuel *Guthrie* (1782-1848), U.S. chemist.]

Guthrun. Variant of **Gudrun.**

gut·less (gŭt′lĭs) *adj. Informal.* **1.** Lacking courage or drive. **2.** Insubstantial; weak. —**gut·less·ness** *n.*

guts·y (gŭt′sē) *adj.* **-ier, -iest.** *Informal.* **1.** Full of courage; daring;

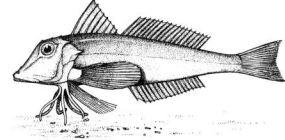

gurnard *A widely distributed inshore coastal fish. The gurnard uses its fingerlike pectoral rays to probe the seabed for the fish, small crabs, shrimp, and other shellfish on which it feeds.*

plucky. **2.** Earthy and uninhibited; raunchy: *a gutsy singing voice.* —**guts·i·ness** *n.*

gut·ta (gŭt′ə) *n., pl.* **guttae** (gŭt′ē′) **1.** *Architecture.* One of a group of small, droplike ornaments on a Doric entablature. **2.** *Abbr.* **gt.** *Medicine.* A drop. [Latin, drop.]

gut·ta-per·cha (gŭt′ə-pûr′chə) *n.* **1.** Any of several tropical trees of the genera *Palaquium* and *Payena,* having sap in the form of milky latex. **2.** A rubbery substance derived from the latex of these trees, used as electrical insulation and for waterproofing. [Malay *gĕtah percha* : *gĕtah,* sap + *percha,* strip of cloth.]

gut·tate (gŭt′āt′) *adj.* Also **gut·tat·ed** (-ā′tĭd) **1.** In the form of drops or having drops. **2.** *Biology.* Spotted as if by drops. [Latin *guttatus,* from *gutta,* drop.]

gut·ta·tion (gə-tā′shən) *n.* Loss of water from the surface of a plant in the form of liquid drops rather than vapor. [Latin *gutta,* drop.]

gut·ter (gŭt′ər) *n.* **1.** A channel for draining off water at the edge of a street or road. **2.** A pipe or trough for draining off water, fitted to the edge of a roof. **3.** A furrow or groove formed by running water. **4.** The trough on either side of a bowling alley. **5. a.** The space left for perforation, between stamps on a sheet. **b.** *Printing.* The white space between the facing pages of a book. **6.** An environment of poverty, vulgarity, or criminal activities; a slum.
~*v.* **guttered, -tering, -ters.** —*tr.* To form gutters or furrows in. —*intr.* **1.** To flow in channels or rivulets. **2.** To melt away through the channel formed by a burning wick. Said of candles. **3.** To burn with a low flame; flicker. [Middle English *guter, goter,* sewer, trough, drain, from Norman French *gotere,* from Vulgar Latin *guttāria* (unattested), from Latin *gutta,* drop.]

gut·ter·ing (gŭt′ər-ĭng) *n.* The drainpipes, gutters, and the like, fitted to the outside of a building to drain off rainwater.

gutter press *n.* The section of the popular press that seeks to reveal facts about people's personal lives in a sordid way.

gut·ter·snipe (gŭt′ər-snīp′) *n.* A street urchin.

gut·tur·al (gŭt′ər-əl) *adj.* **1.** Of or pertaining to the throat. **2.** Produced in the throat. **3.** *Phonetics.* Produced in or near the throat; velar or uvular. Not in technical usage.
~*n.* A guttural sound, such as a **velar** *(see).* [Old French, from Latin *guttur,* throat.] —**gut·tur·al·ism, gut·tur·al·i·ty, gut·tur·al·ness** *n.* —**gut·tur·al·ly** *adv.*

gut·tur·al·ize (gŭt′ər-ə-līz′) *tr.v.* **-ized, -izing, -izes.** *Phonetics.* To make guttural; velarize. —**gut·tur·al·i·za·tion** *n.*

guy¹ (gī) *n.* A rope, cord, or cable used for steadying, guiding, or holding something.
~*tr.v.* **guyed, guying, guys.** To fasten, guide, or hold with a guy. [Probably from Low German, akin to Dutch *gei,* brail.]

guy² (gī) *n.* **1.** *Informal.* A man; fellow. **2.** *British.* One who is odd or grotesque in appearance or dress. **3.** *Chiefly British.* An effigy of Guy Fawkes burned on Guy Fawkes Day. [After Guy FAWKES.]
~*tr.v.* **guyed, guying, guys.** To make fun of; mock.

Guy·an·a (gī-ăn′ə). Formerly **Brit·ish Gui·an·a** (brĭt′ĭsh gē-ăn′ə, -ä′nə). Independent republic within the Commonwealth, lying in northeastern South America. It was a British colony from 1814 until 1966, when it gained its independence. It became a republic in 1970. Bauxite has now overtaken sugar as its major export. Rice, gold, and diamonds are also exported. Some 51 percent of the population are of Asian origin (descendants of indentured laborers), and 33 percent are descendants of African slaves. Area, 214,969 square kilometers (83,000 square miles). Population, 800,000. Capital, Georgetown.

Guy Fawkes Day (gī′ fôks′) *n.* November 5, celebrated in England in commemoration of the **Gunpowder Plot** *(see).*

guy·ot (gē′ō′) *n.* A flat-topped submarine mountain. [After Arnold *Guyot* (1807–84), Swiss geographer and geologist.]

GUYANA

guz·zle (gŭz′əl) *v.* **-zled, -zling, -zles.** —*tr.* To eat or drink greedily or inordinately. —*intr.* To drink, especially alcoholic beverages, greedily or habitually. [Perhaps from Old French *gosiller,* vomit, from *gosier†,* throat.] —**guz·zler** *n.*

Gwent (gwĕnt). From 1974 a county of southeast Wales. It comprises the county of Monmouth excluding the Rhymney Valley, plus Brynmawr, formerly part of Brecknockshire. West Gwent with its chief towns (Newport, Pontypool, Ebbw Vale, and Cwmbran) is part of the South Wales industrial region. The east is fertile country crossed by the Usk and Wye rivers. The administrative center is Cwmbran.

Gwyn or **Gwynne** (gwĭn), **Eleanor,** known as "Nell" (1650–87). English actress, the mistress of Charles II. She bore Charles two sons, of whom the elder was made Duke of St. Albans.

Gwyn·edd (gwĭn′ĕth). From 1974 a county of northwest Wales. Created by the merger of the counties of Anglesey, Caernarvon, Merioneth, and that part of the Conwy Valley then in Denbighshire. Most of the land is within the Snowdonia National Park, and tourism is a major industry. The chief towns are the resorts of Llandudno, Bangor, and Conwy. The administrative center is Caenarvon.

gwyn·i·ad (gwĭn′ē-ăd) *n.* A freshwater fish, *Coregonus pennantii,* found in Lake Bala, Wales. It is a variety of whitefish. [Welsh, from *gwyn,* white.]

gybe. Variant of **jibe** (to swing).

gym (jĭm) *n.* **1.** A gymnasium. **2.** Gymnastics. **3.** A frame supporting structures used in outdoor play.

gym·kha·na (jĭm-kä′nə) *n.* **1.** An event at which various competitions are held to test the speed and skill of horses or ponies and their riders. **2.** An athletic competition or display. **3.** The place where such an event or competition is held. [Blend of GYM(NASIUM) + Hindi *(gend)-khānā,* "(ball) house," racket court, from *khāna,* house, from Persian *khāna†.*]

gym·na·si·um (jĭm-nā′zē-əm) *n., pl.* **-ums** or **-sia** (-zē-ə). **1.** A room or building equipped with ropes, mats, bars, and the like for gymnastics and sports. **2.** (gĭm-nä′zē-ŏŏm′). An academic high school in various central European countries, especially Germany. [Latin, *gymnasium,* school, from Greek *gumnasion,* from *gumnazein,* "to train naked," from *gymnastics,* from *gumnos,* naked.]

gym·nast (jĭm′năst′) *n.* One skilled in gymnastic exercises. [Greek *gumnastēs,* from *gumnazein,* to practice gymnastics. See **gymnasium.**]

gym·nas·tic (jĭm-năs′tĭk) *adj.* Of, pertaining to, or involving gymnastics. —**gym·nas·ti·cal·ly** *adv.*

gym·nas·tics (jĭm-năs′tĭks) *n.* **1.** *Used with a singular verb.* The practice of performing exercises that increase strength, suppleness, or agility, especially those performed with special apparatus in a gymnasium. **2.** *Used with a plural verb.* **a.** The exercises performed. **b.** Complex intellectual or artistic exercises: *mental gymnastics.*

gymno– *prefix.* Indicates bare or naked; for example, **gymnosperm.** [Greek *gumnos,* naked.]

gym·nos·o·phist (jĭm-nŏs′ə-fĭst′) *n.* Any of an ancient sect of Hindu ascetics who went naked or nearly naked. [French *gymnosophiste,* from Latin *gymnosophistae* (plural) from Greek *gumnosophistai* : *gumnos,* naked + *sophistēs,* SOPHIST.]

gym·no·sperm (jĭm′nə-spûrm′) *n.* Any plant of the class Gymnospermae, which includes the coniferous trees and other plants having seeds not enclosed within an ovary. [New Latin *Gymnospermae* : Greek *gumnos,* naked + -SPERM.] —**gym·no·sperm·ous** *adj.*

gym·nure (jĭm′noŏr′) *n.* An insectivorous mammal of the family Erinaceidae, of southeast Asia. Also called "hairy hedgehog." [New Latin *gymnura* : GYMNO- + -URA (tail).]

gy·nae·ce·um (jĭn′ə-sē′əm, gī′nə-) *n., pl.* **-cea** (-sē′ə). Also **gy·nae·ci·um** *pl.* **-cia** (-sē′ə). **1.** The women's quarters in an ancient Greek or Roman household. **2.** Variant of **gynoecium.** [Latin, from Greek *gunaikeion,* from *gunaikeios,* of women, from *gunē* (stem *gunaik-*), woman.]

gy·nan·dro·morph (jī-năn′drə-môrf′, gī-) *n.* An individual having male and female characteristics; especially, an insect with such characteristics resulting from an abnormality in the sex chromosomes. [GYNO- + ANDRO- + -MORPH.] —**gy·nan·dro·morph·ic, gy·nan·dro·morph·ous** *adj.* —**gy·nan·dro·morph·ism, gy·nan·dro·mor·phy** *n.*

gy·nan·drous (jī-năn′drəs, gī-) *n. Botany.* Having the stamens and pistil united to form a column. Said of such flowers as the orchid. [Greek *gunandros,* of doubtful sex : *gunē,* woman + *anēr* (stem *andr-*), man.]

gyn·ar·chy (jĭn′är′kē, jī′när′-, gī′-) *n., pl.* **-chies.** Gynecocracy. [GYNO- + -ARCHY.] —**gy·nar·chic** *adj.*

–gyne *suffix.* Indicates female reproductive organ: *trichogyne.*

gyneco–, gynec– or **gynaeco–, gynaec–** *prefix.* Indicates woman or women; for example, **gynecology.** [Greek, from *gunē* (stem *gunaik-*), woman.]

gy·ne·coc·ra·cy (jĭn′ĭ-kŏk′rə-sē, gī′nĭ-) *n., pl.* **-cies.** Government by women. [GYNECO + -CRACY.]

gynecol. gynecological; gynecology.

gy·ne·col·o·gy (gī′nĭ-kŏl′ə-jē, jī′-, jĭn′ə-) *n. Abbr.* **gyn., gynecol.** The medical study of disease in women, especially those diseases affecting the female reproductive organs and adjacent organs, such as the urinary tract. [GYNECO- + -LOGY.] —**gy·ne·co·log·i·cal** (gī′nĭ-kə-lŏj′ĭ-kəl), **gy·ne·co·log·ic** *adj.* —**gy·ne·col·o·gist** *n.*

gy·ne·co·mas·ti·a (gī′nĭ-kō-măs′tē-ə, jī-′, jĭn′ə-) *n.* Abnormal enlargement of the breasts in a man, due to hormone imbalance or hormone therapy. [New Latin : GYNECO- + Greek *mastis*, breast.]

gyn·e·cop·a·thy (jĭn´ĭ-kŏp´ə-thē, gī´nĭ-) *n. Pathology.* Any of various diseases peculiar to women.

gyn·i·at·rics (jĭn´ē-ăt´rĭks, gī´nē-) *n. Used with singular verb.* The treatment of diseases peculiar to women.

gyno–, gyn– *prefix.* Indicates: **1.** Woman or female; for example, **gynarchy, gynandromorph. 2.** Female reproductive organ; for example, **gynophore.** [Greek *guno-*, from *gunē*, woman.]

gy·noc·ra·cy (gī-nŏk´rə-sē) *n., pl.* **-cies.** Gynecocracy.

gy·no·di·oe·cious (gī´nō-dī-ē´shəs, jī´nō-) *adj. Botany.* Designating a species of plant in which female and hermaphrodite flowers are borne on separate plants. [GYNO- + DIOECIOUS.]

gy·noe·ci·um, gy·nae·ce·um (jī-nē´sē-əm, jī-) *n., pl.* **-cia** (-sē-ə). *Botany.* The female reproductive organs of a flower; the pistil or pistils collectively. [New Latin, alteration of GYNAECEUM.]

gy·no·mon·oe·cious (gī´nō-mŏn-ē´shəs, jī´nō-) *adj. Botany.* Designating a species of plant on which female and hermaphrodite flowers are borne on the same plant. [GYNO- + MONOECIOUS.]

gy·no·phore (jĭn´ə-fôr´, -fōr´, gī´nə-) *n. Botany.* A stalk in some plants that bears the pistil. [GYNO- + -PHORE.] **—gy·no·phor·ic** (jĭn´ə-fôr´ĭk, -fōr´-, jī´nə-, gī´-) *adj.*

–gynous *suffix.* Indicates: **1.** Women or females; for example, **monogynous. 2.** Female organs such as pistils; for example, **perigynous.** [New Latin *-gynus*, having pistils, from Greek *-gunos*, having a wife or wives, from *gunē*, woman.]

–gyny *suffix.* Indicates: **1.** The condition of having a specified number or kind of women or females; for example, **monogyny. 2.** The condition of having female organs or pistils; for example, **epigyny.** [Greek *gunē*, woman.]

gyp[1], gip (jĭp) *tr.v.* **gypped** or **gipped, gypping** or **gipping, gyps** or **gips.** *Informal.* To swindle, cheat, or defraud.
~*n.* **1.** The act or an instance of cheating; swindle. **2.** One who cheats; swindler. [Perhaps from GYP (servant).] **—gyp·per** *n.*

gyp[2] *n. British.* A servant who cleans students' rooms, especially at Cambridge University. [Perhaps from obsolete *gippo*, kitchen servant, short tunic, from obsolete French *jupeau*; akin to French *jupe*, skirt.]

gyp joint *n. Slang.* An establishment that makes a practice of overcharging or defrauding its clientele.

gyp·soph·i·la (jĭp-sŏf´ə-lə) *n.* Any of various plants of the genus *Gypsophila*, having small white or pink flowers, and including the baby's-breath. [New Latin *Gypsophila* : GYPSUM + -PHILA.]

gyp·sum (jĭp´səm) *n.* A white mineral, $CaSO_4 \cdot 2H_2O$, used in the manufacture of cements and plasters, especially plaster of Paris, and also in some fertilizers. [Latin, from Greek *gupsos*, from Semitic; akin to Hebrew *gephes*, plaster.] **—gyp·se·ous** (jĭp´sē-əs), **gyp·sif·er·ous** (jĭp-sĭf´ər-əs) *adj.*

Gyp·sy, Gip·sy (jĭp´sē) *n., pl.* **-sies. 1.** *Sometimes* **gypsy.** One of a nomadic Caucasoid people originally migrating from the border region between Iran and India to Europe in the 14th or 15th century and now living principally in Europe and the United States. **2.** The Indic language spoken by this people; Romany. **3.** *Often* **gypsy.** One that resembles a Gypsy in appearance or behavior, especially in having a wandering or carefree lifestyle.
~*adj. Often* **gypsy.** Of, pertaining to, or resembling Gypsies. [Shortening of EGYPTIAN, because they were believed to have come from Egypt.]

gypsy moth *n.* A moth, *Porthetria dispar*, native to the Old World, having hairy caterpillars that feed on foliage and are very destructive to trees.

gyp·sy·wort (jĭp´sē-wûrt´, -wôrt´) *n.* A Eurasian plant, *Lycopus eura-*

paeus, with hairy stems and leaves and white two-lipped flowers marked with purple dots.

gy·ral (jī´rəl) *adj.* **1.** Moving in a circular or spiral path; gyratory. **2.** Pertaining to a gyrus. **—gy·ral·ly** *adv.*

gy·rate (jī´rāt´) *v.* **-rated, -rating, -rates.** —*intr.* **1.** To revolve on or around a center or axis. **2.** To circle or spiral. —*tr.* To move in circles around a center: *gyrate your hips in time with the beat.* —See Synonyms at **turn.**
~*adj. Biology.* In rings; coiled. [Latin *gȳrāre*, from *gȳrus*, circle, from Greek *guros*, GYRE.] **—gy·ra·tion** *n.* **—gy·ra·tor** *n.* **—gy·ra·tor·y** (jī´rə-tôr´ē, -tōr´ē) *adj.*

gyre (jīr) *n.* **1.** The circular flow of water that occurs in each of the great ocean basins of the world, produced by the combined effects of prevailing winds and the earth's rotation. **2.** *Chiefly Poetic.* **a.** A ring or circle; vortex; spiral. **b.** A circular or spiral motion.
~*intr.v.* **gyred, gyring, gyres.** *Chiefly Poetic.* To gyrate. [Latin *gyrus*, from Greek *guros*, circle.]

gyr·fal·con, ger·fal·con (jûr´făl´kən, -fôl´kən, -fô´kən) *n.* A large falcon, *Falco rusticolus*, of northern regions, having various color phases ranging from black to white. [Middle English *gerfaucoun*, from Old French *gerfaucon*, from Old Norse *geirfalki*.]

gy·ro (jī´rō) *n., pl.* **-ros.** A gyroscope.

gyro– *prefix.* Indicates: **1.** Gyrating; for example, **gyroplane. 2.** Spiral; for example, **gyroscope. 3.** Gyroscope; for example, **gyrocompass.** [Latin, from Greek *guro-*, from *guros*, circle.]

gy·ro·com·pass (jī´rō-kŭm´pəs, -kŏm´pəs) *n.* A nonmagnetic navigational device in which the interaction of a gyroscope's angular momentum with the force produced by the earth's rotation is used to maintain a north-south orientation of the gyroscopic spin axis, thereby providing a stable directional reference.

gy·ro·mag·net·ic (jī´rō-măg-nĕt´ĭk) *adj.* Of, pertaining to, or resulting from the magnetic properties of a spinning, electrically charged particle.

gyromagnetic ratio *n.* The ratio of the magnetic moment to the intrinsic angular momentum of a spinning particle.

gyro pilot *n.* An automatic pilot incorporating a gyroscope to maintain a preset course and altitude.

gy·ro·plane (jī´rə-plān´) *n.* An aircraft such as a helicopter or autogyro with wings that rotate about a vertical axis.

gy·ro·scope (jī´rə-skōp´) *n.* **1.** A device consisting essentially of a spinning mass, typically a disk or wheel, the spin axis of which turns between two low-friction supports and maintains its angular orientation with respect to inertial coordinates when not subjected to external torques. **2.** Broadly, any spinning mass. Also called "gyro." [French : GYRO- + -SCOPE.] **—gy·ro·scop·ic** (jī´rə-skŏp´ĭk) *adj.* **—gy·ro·scop·i·cal·ly** *adv.*

gy·ro·sta·bi·liz·er (jī´rō-stā´bə-lī´zər) *n.* A device having a heavy gyroscope whose axis spins in a vertical plane to reduce the side-to-side rolling of a ship or aircraft.

gy·ro·stat (jī´rə-stăt´) *n.* A gyrostabilizer.

gy·ro·stat·ic (jī´rō-stăt´ĭk) *adj.* Of, pertaining to, or designating a gyroscope or gyrostatics. [GYRO- + -STAT + -IC.] **—gy·ro·stat·i·cal·ly** *adv.*

gy·ro·stat·ics (jī´rō-stăt´ĭks) *n. Used with a singular verb.* The study of rotating bodies.

gy·rus (jī´rəs) *n., pl.* **gyri** (jī´rī´). Any of the prominent, rounded, elevated convolutions on the surfaces of the cerebral hemispheres. [New Latin, from Latin, circle, GYRE.]

gyve (jīv) *n. Archaic.* A shackle or fetter, especially for the leg.
~*tr.v.* **gyved, gyving, gyves.** To shackle or fetter. [Middle English *gyve†*.]

gyroscope *A spinning flywheel that will hold itself in a stable plane regardless of how its frame is moved.*

H

hackle *The young bantam rooster raises its hackles—the long, narrow feathers on its neck—as part of its aggressive display, designed to make the bird appear larger than it really is. Dogs have hackles as well—special erectile hairs on the backs of their necks—that rise involuntarily if the animals are angry or frightened.*

Hackney *An English show horse, once used as a carriage horse and valued for its high-stepping trot. Developed in the 18th century, it was crossed with the Welsh pony to make a Hackney pony.*

haddock *A codlike fish found in the North Atlantic. It lives close to the sea bottom, feeding on mollusks and small fish.*

h, H (āch) *n., pl.* **h's** or **H's.** **1.** The eighth letter of the modern English alphabet. See feature at **alphabet. 2.** Any of the speech sounds represented by this letter. **3.** The eighth in a series. **4.** Something shaped like the letter H.

h, H, h., H. *Note:* As an abbreviation or symbol, *h* may be a small or a capital letter, with or without a period. Established forms or those generally preferred precede the definition. When no form is given, all four forms are in general use in that sense. **1.** H *Physics.* Hamiltonian. **2.** h., H. harbor. **3.** h., H. hard; hardness. **4.** h hecto-. **5.** h., H. height. **6.** H henry. **7.** h., H. high (gear). **8.** h, h. hit. **9.** h., H. *Music.* horn. **10.** h hour. **11.** h. hundred. **12.** h., H. husband. **13.** H The symbol for the element hydrogen. **14.** h The symbol for Planck's constant.

H *adj.* Designating a pencil or pencil lead that is hard. A number sometimes precedes *H* to indicate the degree of hardness, the hardest pencil being 6H. See **B, HB.**
~*n.* An H pencil.

ha, hah (hä) *interj.* Used to express surprise, wonder, triumph, puzzlement, or pique. [Middle English.]

ha hectare.

Haa·kon VII (hô′kən, -kōn′) (1872–1957). King of Norway (1905–57).

haar (här) *n. British Regional.* A cold fog or mist off the east coast of England or Scotland. [Probably from Old Norse *hárr,* HOAR.]

Haar·lem (här′ləm). City in the western Netherlands, the capital of North Holland province, on the Spaarne River near the North Sea. It was a major center of the golden age of Dutch painting in the 16th and 17th centuries. It is now famous for the culture and export of flowers and bulbs, especially tulips.

Hab. Habakkuk (Old Testament).

Ha·bak·kuk¹ (hə-băk′ək, hăb′ə-kŭk). Hebrew prophet of the late 7th century B.C.

Habakkuk² *n. Abbr.* **Hab.** A book of prophecies by Habakkuk in the Old Testament.

Habana. See Havana.

ha·ba·ne·ra (hä′bə-nâr′ə, ä′bə-) *n.* **1.** A slow Cuban dance. **2.** The music for this dance, in duple time, with a repetitive rhythmic pattern of a dotted eighth and sixteenth note pair followed by a pair of eighth notes. [Spanish *(danza) habanera,* "Havanan (dance)," from feminine of *habanero,* HABANERO.]

Ha·ba·ne·ro (hä′bə-nâr′ō, ä′bə-) *n., pl.* **-ros.** A native or inhabitant of Havana. [Spanish, from *La Habana,* HAVANA.]

hab. corp. habeas corpus.

hab·da·lah (hăv′dä-lä′) *n. Often* **Habdalah.** A Jewish religious ceremony observed at or marking the end of a Sabbath or holy day. [Hebrew *habdālāh,* separation.]

ha·be·as cor·pus (hä′bē-əs kôr′pəs) *n. Abbr.* **hab. corp.** *Law.* **1.** Any of a variety of writs that may be issued to bring a party before a court or judge, having as its function the release of a party from unlawful restraint. **2.** The right to demand such a writ. [Latin, "you shall have the body."]

hab·er·dash·er (hăb′ər-dăsh′ər) *n.* **1.** A dealer in men's furnishings such as shirts, hats, and socks. **2.** *British.* A dealer in sewing accessories and dressmaking materials. [Middle English *haberdassher,* probably from Norman French *haberdasser, hapertasser* (both unattested), from *hapertas†,* perhaps the name of a kind of cloth.]

hab·er·dash·er·y (hăb′ər-dăsh′ə-rē) *n., pl.* **-ies. 1.** The goods sold by a haberdasher. **2.** A shop or department selling these goods.

hab·er·geon (hăb′ər-jən) *n. Also* **hau·ber·geon** (hô′bər-jən). **1.** A short, sleeveless coat of mail. **2.** A hauberk. [Middle English, from Old French *haubergeon,* from *hauberc,* HAUBERK.]

Ha·ber process (hä′bər) *n.* An industrial process, first developed in 1908, for producing ammonia from hydrogen and atmospheric nitrogen by reacting the two gases together at a temperature of about 5000°C and a pressure of 20-50 megapascals. In the later **Haber-Bosch process** a method of making the hydrogen from water gas and steam was added. [After Fritz *Haber* (1868–1934), German chemist.]

hab·ile (hăb′ĭl) *adj. Rare.* Adroit; deft. [French, from Old French,

from Latin *habilis,* able, easily handled, from *habēre,* to hold, have.]

ha·bil·i·ment (hə-bĭl′ə-mənt) *n.* **1.** *Often* **habiliments. a.** The dress or garb associated with an office or occasion: *"shrouded from head to foot in the habiliments of the grave"* (Edgar Allan Poe). **b.** Clothes. **2.** *Rare.* Outfit; attire. [Middle English, from Old French *(h)abillement,* from *habiller,* to make fit, fit out, from HABILE.]

ha·bil·i·tate (hə-bĭl′ə-tāt′) *v.* **-tated, -tating, -tates.** —*tr.* **1.** To supply with the means; especially, to back (a mining operation) with working capital. **2.** *Rare.* To clothe. —*intr.* To qualify oneself for an office, especially as a teacher in a German university. [Late Latin *habilitāre* (past participle *habilitātus*), to qualify, from Latin *habilitās,* ability, from HABILE.] —**ha·bil·i·ta·tion** *n.*

hab·it (hăb′ĭt) *n.* **1. a.** A constant, often unconscious inclination to act in a particular way, acquired through frequent repetition over a long period. **b.** An established trend of the mind or character. **c.** *Psychology.* An automatic or mechanical reaction to a particular situation, acquired through frequently encountering it. **2.** *Often* **habits.** Customary manner or practice: *a man of ascetic habits.* **3.** An addiction, especially to a hard drug. **4.** *Rare.* Physical constitution. **5.** Characteristic appearance, form, or manner of growth, especially of a plant or crystal. Also called "habitus." **6. a.** A distinctive dress or costume, especially of a religious order. **b.** A riding habit.
~*tr.v.* **habited, -iting, -its. 1.** To clothe; dress. **2.** *Archaic.* To habituate. **3.** *Archaic.* To inhabit. [Middle English *(h)abit,* from Old French, from Latin *habitus,* from the past participle of *habēre,* to hold, have.]

> *Synonyms: custom, fashion, practice, usage, use.*

hab·it·a·ble (hăb′ə-tə-bəl) *adj.* Suitable to live in; inhabitable. [Middle English *abitable,* from Old French *(h)abitable,* from Latin *habitābilis,* from *habitāre,* to inhabit, reside, to have frequently, from *habēre* (past participle *habitus*), to have, hold.] —**hab·it·a·bil·i·ty, hab·it·a·ble·ness** *n.* —**hab·it·a·bly** *adv.*

hab·i·tant (hăb′ə-tənt; ä′bē-tän′ *for sense 2*) *n. Also* **ha·bi·tan** (ä′bē-tän′) (for sense 2). **1.** An inhabitant. **2.** An inhabitant of French descent in Canada or Louisiana belonging to the small farmer class. [Old French, from the present participle of *habiter,* to inhabit, from Latin *habitāre.* See **habitable.**]

hab·i·tat (hăb′ə-tăt′) *n.* **1.** The area or type of environment in which an organism or biological population normally lives or occurs. **2.** The place where a person or thing is most likely to be found. [Latin, "it dwells" (the first word in Latin descriptions of plant and animal species in old natural histories), third person singular present indicative of *habitāre,* to inhabit. See **habitable.**]

hab·i·ta·tion (hăb′ə-tā′shən) *n.* **1.** The act of inhabiting. **2.** The state of being inhabited. **3. a.** A natural environment or locality. **b.** A place of abode. [Middle English *habitacioun,* from Old French *habitation,* from Latin *habitātiō* (stem *habitātiōn-*), from *habitātus,* past participle of *habitāre,* to inhabit. See **habitable.**]

hab·it·ed (hăb′ə-tĭd) *adj.* **1. a.** Dressed. **b.** Attired in a habit. **2.** *Archaic.* Inhabited.

hab·it-form·ing (hăb′ĭt-fôr′mĭng) *adj.* **1.** Leading to psychological or physiological addiction: *a habit-forming drug.* **2.** Tending to become habitual.

ha·bit·u·al (hə-bĭch′ōō-əl) *adj.* **1. a.** Of the nature of a habit; done constantly or repeatedly. **b.** Being so by force of habit: *a habitual smoker.* **2.** Customary; constant; inveterate: *habitual rudeness.* **3.** Established by long use; usual. —See Synonyms at **usual.** —**ha·bit·u·al·ly** *adv.* —**ha·bit·u·al·ness** *n.*

ha·bit·u·ate (hə-bĭch′ōō-āt′) *tr.v.* **-ated, -ating, -ates. 1.** To accustom by frequent repetition or prolonged exposure. Often used reflexively. **2.** To cause to become psychologically dependent on a drug. [Late Latin *habituāre,* from Latin *habitus,* HABIT.] —**ha·bit·u·a·tion** *n.*

hab·i·tude (hăb′ə-tōōd′, -tyōōd′) *n.* A customary manner or way of behaving; a habit. [Middle English *(h)abitude,* from Old French *habitude,* from Latin *habitūdō,* condition, habit, from *habitus,* HABIT.]

ha·bit·u·é (hə-bĭch′ōō-ā′, hə-bĭch′ōō-ā′) *n.* A frequent visitor of a particular place, especially a place of entertainment. [French, from the past participle of *habituer*, to frequent, from Late Latin *habitu- āre*, to HABITUATE.]

hab·i·tus (hăb′ə-təs) *n., pl.* **habitus.** 1. Physical and constitutional characteristics, especially as related to susceptibility to a disease. 2. The habit of a plant or animal. See **habit** (sense 5). [New Latin, from Latin, appearance, HABIT.]

Habsburg. See **Hapsburg.**

ha·bu (hä′bōō) *n.* A large, venomous Japanese snake, *Trimeresurus flavoviridis*, found in the Ryukyu Islands. [Japanese.]

ha·ček (hä′chĕk′) *n.* A diacritical mark (ˇ) that resembles an in- verted circumflex and is used over certain letters, as č, to indicate quality of pronunciation. [Czech, *háček*.]

ha·chure (hă-shoor′, hăsh′oor′) *n.* Any of the short lines used to shade or to indicate slopes on relief maps and also to show their degree and direction. ~*tr.v.* (hă-shoor′) **hachured, -churing, -chures.** To make hachures on (a map). [French, from *hacher*, to engrave lines on, chop up. See **hash.**]

ha·ci·en·da (hä′sē-ĕn′də, ä′sē-) *n.* 1. In Spanish-speaking countries or areas influenced by Spain, a large estate; a plantation or large ranch. 2. The house of the owner of a hacienda; especially, in the southwestern United States, a low, sprawling house with a project- ing roof and wide porches. [Spanish, domestic work, landed prop- erty, from Latin *facienda*, things to be done, neuter plural gerundive of *facere*, to do.]

hack¹ (hăk) *v.* **hacked, hacking, hacks.** —*tr.* 1. a. To cut (branches or undergrowth, for example) with irregular and heavy blows or in a random manner. b. To chip, notch, chop off, or chop up roughly with a pick, knife, ax, or other tool. c. To make by cutting or chopping in such a way: *hacked a hole in the wood.* 2. To break up (earth) into clods or ridges. 3. a. To kick the shin of (an opponent), especially in field sports. b. To strike the arm of (an opponent) in basketball. 4. To destroy the quality of (a story or article, for exam- ple) by excessive cutting or bad editing. 5. *Informal.* To deal with successfully; cope with: *She tried living on her own but simply couldn't hack it.* —*intr.* 1. To chop or chip away at something. 2. To cough in short, dry-throated spasms. ~*n.* 1. A rough irregular cut or notch made by hacking. 2. A tool, such as a hoe or mattock, used for chopping or breaking up some- thing. 3. a. A kick or chopping blow. b. A wound from this. 4. A rough, dry cough. [Middle English *hacken*, from Old English *hac- cian*, to cut to pieces, from Germanic, of imitative origin.] —**hack· er** *n.*

hack² *n.* 1. A horse used for riding or driving; a hackney. 2. A broken-down horse for hire; a jade. 3. *Chiefly British.* A leisurely ride in the country on horseback. 4. A political hireling. 5. A per- son who hires himself out to do mediocre or routine work, espe- cially writing or journalism. 6. A carriage or hackney for hire. 7. *Informal.* a. A taxicab. b. A taxicab driver. ~*v.* **hacked, hacking, hacks.** —*tr.* 1. To let (a horse) out for hire. 2. *Informal.* To write as a hack or in the manner of a hack. 3. To make banal or hackneyed with indiscriminate use. —*intr.* 1. *Infor- mal.* To work as a hack, especially as a taxicab driver or a writer. 2. *Chiefly British.* To ride on horseback in the country at a leisurely pace. ~*adj.* 1. Working as a literary or journalistic hack: *a hack writer.* 2. Produced by or characteristic of a hack; banal; routine; commer- cial. [Short for HACKNEY.]

hack³ *n.* 1. A drying frame or rack, as for cheese, fish, or bricks. 2. A row of unfired bricks laid out to dry. 3. A feeding rack, espe- cially for hawks. ~*tr.v.* **hacked, hacking, hacks.** 1. To set out on a rack to dry. 2. To keep (hawks) at partial liberty. [Variant, influenced by HECK (frame), of HATCH (door).]

hack·a·more (hăk′ə-môr′, -mōr′) *n.* A rope or rawhide halter with a wide band that can be lowered over a horse's eyes, used to break in horses. [Alteration (influenced by HACK) of Spanish *jaquima*, head- stall of a halter, from Old Spanish *xaquima*, from Arabic *shakīmah*, bit of a bridle, restraint.]

hack·ber·ry (hăk′bĕr′ē) *n., pl.* **-ries.** 1. Any of various North Ameri- can trees or shrubs of the genus *Celtis*, having inconspicuous flow- ers and berrylike, often edible fruit. 2. The fruit of a hackberry. 3. The soft, yellowish wood of a hackberry. Also called "sugar- berry." [Variant of earlier *hagberry* : *hag*-, from Scandinavian, akin to Old Norse *heggr*, hackberry + BERRY.]

hack·but (hăk′bŭt′) *n.* Also **hag·but** (hăg′-). An obsolete type of gun, a harquebus *(see).* [Old French *haguebute, hacquebute*, from Middle Dutch *hakebusse*, HARQUEBUS.] —**hack·but·eer** (hăk′bə- tîr′), **hack·but·ter** (hăk′bŭt′ər) *n.*

hack·er (hăk′ər) *n.* 1. One that hacks. 2. An amateur computer en- thusiast. 3. Such an enthusiast who gains unauthorized access to other people's computer programs. [From HACK (to work as a hack) + -ER.]

hack·ie (hăk′ē) *n. Slang.* A taxicab driver. [From HACK (taxicab).]

hack·ing (hăk′ĭng) *adj.* Designating a cough or laughter that is rough, dry, and usually spasmodic.

hacking jacket *n.* A riding jacket with slits at the sides or back.

hack·le¹ (hăk′əl) *n.* 1. Any of the long, slender, often glossy feathers on the neck of a bird, especially a male domestic fowl. 2. **hackles.** The erectile hairs at the back of the neck, especially of a dog or similar animal. 3. a. A tuft of cock feathers trimming an artificial

fishing fly. b. A **hackle fly** *(see).* 4. A steel comb used for combing flax. —**get one's hackles up.** To make or be angry or ready to fight. —**make the hackles rise.** 1. To put in a fighting mood. 2. To cause a dog to bristle belligerently. ~*tr.v.* **hackled, -ling, -les.** 1. To trim (a fly) with a hackle. 2. To comb (flax) with a hackle. [Middle English *hakell, hekele, hechele*, HATCHEL.]

hackle² *v.* **-led, -ling, -les.** *Rare.* —*tr.* To chop roughly; mangle by hacking. —*intr.* To hack. [Frequentative of HACK (to cut).]

hackle fly *n.* An artificial fishing fly trimmed with hackles and usually without wings. Also called "hackle."

hack·ly (hăk′lē) *adj.* Nicked or notched; jagged; rough. [From HACKLE (to hack).]

hack·man (hăk′mən) *n., pl.* **-men** (-mĭn). The driver of a hack or hired carriage.

hack·ma·tack (hăk′mə-tăk′) *n.* A tree, the **tamarack** *(see).* [From Algonquian, akin to Abnaki *akemantak*, snowshoe wood.]

hack·ney (hăk′nē) *n., pl.* **-neys.** 1. **Hackney.** A horse of a trotting breed developed in England, having a gait characterized by pro- nounced flexion of the knee. 2. A horse suited for routine riding or driving; a hack. 3. A coach or carriage for hire. ~*tr.v.* **hackneyed, -neying, -neys.** 1. To overuse and cause to be- come banal and trite; cheapen. 2. To hire out; let. ~*adj.* 1. Banal; trite: *a hackney phrase.* 2. Hired: *a hackney car- riage.* [Middle English *hakenei*, probably after *Hakenei*, HACKNEY, where such horses were raised.]

Hack·ney (hăk′nē). Borough in the northeast of Greater London, England.

hack·neyed (hăk′nēd) *adj.* Overused so as to become stale or mean- ingless; trite; banal. —See Synonyms at **trite.**

hack·saw (hăk′sô′) *n.* A saw consisting of a tough, fine-toothed blade stretched taut in a frame, used for cutting metal.

hack·work (hăk′wûrk′) *n.* Commissioned work, as writing, done usually by formula and in conformance with commercial standards.

had. Past tense and past participle of **have.**

ha·dal (hād′l) *adj.* Of or designating the deepest parts of the oceans, especially those parts below about 6,000 meters (36,100 feet). [HADES (the nether world) + -AL.]

had·dock (hăd′ək) *n., pl.* **-docks** or collectively **haddock.** A food fish, *Melanogrammus aeglefinus*, of northern Atlantic waters, re- lated to and resembling the cod. [Middle English *haddok*, from Norman French *hadoc*, variant of Old French *(h)adot*†.]

hade (hād) *n. Geology.* The angle of inclination from the vertical of a vein, fault, or lode. ~*intr.v.* **haded, hading, hades.** To incline from the vertical. Used of a vein, fault, or lode. [Origin unknown.]

Ha·des¹ (hā′dēz). *Greek Mythology.* The god of the netherworld and dispenser of earthly riches; a brother of Zeus and husband of Per- sephone; identified with the Roman god Pluto.

Hades² *n.* 1. *Greek Mythology.* The netherworld kingdom of Hades, the abode of the shades of the dead. 2. *Often* **hades.** Hell. [Greek *Haidēs*.] —**Ha·de·an** *adj.*

Ha·dith (hə-dēth′) *n., pl.* **Hadith** or **-diths.** The body of traditions arising from or relating to Muhammad. [Arabic, "tradition."]

hadj, haj, hajj (hăj) *n.* A pilgrimage to Mecca made during Rama- dan as an objective of the religious life of a Muslim. [Arabic *ḥajj*, pilgrimage.]

hadj·i, haj·i, haj·ji (hăj′ē) *n.* 1. a. A Muslim who has made a pil- grimage to Mecca. b. A title used before the name of a Muslim who has made this pilgrimage. 2. A Christian of the Near East or Orient who has visited the Holy Sepulcher in Jerusalem. [Arabic *ḥājjī*, from *ḥajj*, HADJ.]

had·n't (hăd′ənt). Contraction of **had not.**

Ha·dri·an (hā′drē-ən) (A.D. 76–138). Roman emperor (117–138). As emperor he initiated plans to end distinctions between Rome and the provinces. He visited Britain (122), where he ordered the build- ing of Hadrian's Wall.

Hadrian IV. See **Adrian IV.**

Hadrian's Wall. Roman wall built by the emperor Hadrian between *c.* 122 and 126, and extended by Severus a century later, to fortify the northern boundary of Roman Britain. It stretched for *c.* 120 kilometers (75 miles) from Wallsend on the Tyne River to Bowness at the head of Solway Firth. Fragments of the wall and several stone blockhouses, or mile stations, remain.

had·ron (hăd′rŏn′) *n. Physics.* An elementary particle that can take part in a strong interaction. The elementary nature of hadrons is controversial; they are believed to consist of arrangements of quarks. [Greek *hadros*, thick + -ON.] —**had·ron·ic** (hă-drŏn′ĭk) *adj.*

had·ro·saur (hăd′rə-sôr′) *n.* Any of various amphibious dinosaurs of the genus *Anatosaurus* and related genera, which had webbed feet and a ducklike bill. [Greek *hadros*, thick, heavy + -SAUR.]

hadst. *Archaic.* Second person singular past indicative of **have.** Used with *thou.*

hae (hā, hă) *tr.v.* **haed, haen** (hān, hăn), **haeing, haes.** *Scottish.* To have.

ha·e·re mai, ha·e·re·mai (hä′ā-rā′ mä′ē) *interj. Australian & New Zealand.* Used to express welcome or a greeting. [Maori, "come hither."]

Ha·erh·pin. See **Harbin.**

haet (hāt) *n. Scottish.* A minute amount; a whit; a jot. [Contraction of *hae it!* take it!]

ha·fiz (hä′fĭz) *n.* 1. A Muslim who has memorized the Koran. 2. A

Hadrian *The Roman emperor who directed the building of Hadrian's Wall in Britain and the Pantheon in Rome was also an accomplished poet and musician.*

Hadrian's Wall *Designed to defend Roman Britain against attack from the north, Hadrian's Wall was constructed by the Roman legionaries who were later to patrol it. The ruins now average 1.8 meters (6 feet) in height, but the wall was originally as much as 4.5 meters (15 feet) high.*

title of respect used with the name of a Muslim who has accomplished this memorization. [Persian, from Arabic *hāfiz,* guard, watch, one who knows the Koran by heart, from *hafiza,* to watch, protect, memorize.]

Ha·fiz, Ha·fez (hä-fĭz′, -fĕz′) (*fl.* 14th century). Persian lyric poet. Educated in the classic Islamic tradition, he served as court poet to several Persian leaders. His innovative style revived the traditional Persian themes of love and wine. *The Divan,* a collection of about 700 of his poems, was first published in English in 1891.

haf·ni·um (hăf′nē-əm) *n. Symbol* **Hf** A brilliant, silvery, metallic element separated from ores of zirconium and used in nuclear reactor control rods, as a getter for oxygen and nitrogen, and in the manufacture of tungsten filaments. Atomic number 72, atomic weight 178.49, melting point 2,150°C, boiling point 5,400°C, specific gravity 13.29, valence 4. [New Latin, from *Hafnia,* Latin name for Copenhagen, from Danish *(København).*]

haft (hăft, häft) *n.* A handle or hilt; especially, a handle of a bladed instrument, such as a sword, knife, or sickle.
~*tr.v.* **hafted, hafting, hafts.** To fit or equip with a hilt or handle; set into a handle. [Middle English *haft,* Old English *hæft.*]

Haftarah. Variant of **Haphtarah.**

hag¹ (hăg) *n.* **1.** An old woman who is repulsive in appearance or manner; a crone. **2.** A witch; a sorceress. **3.** *Obsolete.* A female demon. **4.** A hagfish (*see*). [Middle English *hagge,* probably short for Old English *hægtesse†,* witch.] —**hag·gish** *adj.* —**hag·gish·ly** *adv.* —**hag·gish·ness** *n.*

hag² *n. Scottish & British Regional.* **1.** A boggy area on a moor. **2.** A piece of firmer ground in boggy land. **3.** A place where peat has been dug from a bog. [Middle English *hag,* gap, chasm, probably from Old Norse *högg,* gap, cutting blow.]

Hag. Haggai (Old Testament).

Ha·gar (hā′gər). The concubine of Abraham, mother of his son Ishmael and handmaiden to his wife Sarah, who, through jealousy for her own son Isaac, turned Hagar and Ishmael out of Abraham's household. Genesis 16–19.

hagbut. Variant of **hackbut.**

Ha·gen (hä′gən). In the *Nibelungenlied,* the murderer of Siegfried.

Ha·gen (hä′gən), **Walter Charles** (1892–1969). U.S. golfer. He won the U.S. Open championship twice (1914 and 1919), the British Open four times from 1922 to 1929, and the U.S. Professional Golfers' Association championship five times from 1921 to 1927.

hag·fish (hăg′fĭsh′) *n., pl.* **-fishes** or collectively **hagfish.** Any of various primitive, eel-shaped marine fishes of the family Myxinidae, having a jawless sucking mouth with rasping teeth with which they bore into and feed on other fishes. Also called "hag." [HAG (witch) + FISH.]

Hag·ga·dah, Hag·ga·da (hə-gä′də, -gô′də) *n., pl.* **-doth** (-dōt′, -dōth′). **1.** Traditional Jewish literature; especially, the nonlegal part of the Talmud. Compare **Halakah. 2.** The book containing the story of the Exodus and the ritual of the Seder, read at the Passover Seder. [Hebrew *haggādāh,* narration, telling, from *hagged,* to narrate, tell, from the Semitic root *ngd,* to rise, become conspicuous.] —**hag·gad·ic, Hag·gad·ic** (hə-gäd′ĭk, -gä′dĭk, -gô′dĭk) *adj.*

hag·ga·dist (hə-gä′dĭst, -gô′dĭst) *n.* **1.** A haggadic writer. **2.** A student of haggadic literature. —**hag·ga·dis·tic** (hăg′ə-dĭs′tĭk) *adj.*

Hag·ga·i¹ (hăg′ē-ī′, hăg′ī′). A Hebrew prophet of the 6th century B.C.

Haggai² *n. Abbr.* **Hag.** A book of the Old Testament attributed to Haggai.

hag·gard (hăg′ərd) *adj.* **1. a.** Appearing worn and exhausted from or as if from suffering, anxiety, or deprivation; gaunt: *"he looked as haggard as an actor by daylight"* (Henry James). **b.** Wild and unruly; uncontrolled. **2.** Wild and intractable. Said of a hawk used in falconry.
~*n.* An adult hawk captured for training. [French *hagard,* untamed hawk, wild hawk, perhaps from Germanic.] —**hag·gard·ly** *adv.* —**hag·gard·ness** *n.*

Synonyms: *careworn, wasted, worn.*

Hag·gard (hăg′ərd), **Sir (Henry) Rider** (1856–1925). British novelist. He served as a government official in the Transvaal (1875–81). His novels include *King Solomon's Mines* (1885), *She* (1887), and *Allan Quatermain* (1887).

hag·gis (hăg′ĭs) *n., pl.* **-gises** or **haggis.** A Scottish dish consisting of a mixture of the minced heart, lungs, and liver of a sheep or calf mixed with suet, onions, oatmeal, and seasonings, and traditionally boiled in the stomach of the animal. [Middle English *hageset†.*]

hag·gle (hăg′əl) *v.* **-gled, -gling, -gles.** —*intr.* **1.** To bargain, as over the price of something; wrangle: *"he preferred to be overcharged than to haggle"* (Somerset Maugham). **2.** To argue in an attempt to come to terms. —*tr.* **1.** To cut in a crude, unskillful manner; hack; mangle. **2.** *Archaic.* To harass or worry by wrangling. —See Synonyms at **argue.**
~*n.* An instance of haggling. [Frequentative of dialectal *hag,* to cut, from Middle English *haggen,* from Old Norse *höggva.*] —**hag·gler** *n.*

hag·i·ar·chy (hăg′ē-är′kē, hā′jē-) *n., pl.* **-chies.** Also **hag·i·oc·ra·cy** (hăg′ē-ŏk′rə-sē, hā′jē-) *pl.* **-cies** (for sense 1). **1.** Government by holy men, such as clerics. **2.** A hierarchy of saints. [HAGI(O)- + -ARCHY.]

hagio-, hagi- *prefix.* Indicates: **1.** A saint or body of saints; for example, *hagiology, hagiarchy.* **2.** A sacred or holy place; for example, *hagioscope.* [Late Latin, from Greek, from *hagios,* holy.]

Hag·i·og·ra·pha (hăg′ē-ŏg′rə-fə, hā′jē-) *n. Used with a singular or plural verb.* The third of the three ancient Jewish divisions of the Old Testament, containing those books not in the Law (Torah) or the Prophets, and comprising usually the Psalms, Proverbs, Job, the Song of Solomon, Ruth, Lamentations, Ecclesiastes, Esther, Daniel, Ezra, Nehemiah, and Chronicles. Also called "Writings." [Late Latin, from Greek : *hagio-,* sacred + *-graphos,* written.]

hag·i·og·ra·phy (hăg′ē-ŏg′rə-fē, hā′jē-) *n., pl.* **-phies. 1.** Biography of saints. **2.** Any idealizing or worshipful biography. [HAGIO- + -GRAPHY.] —**hag·i·og·ra·pher** *n.* —**hag·i·o·graph·ic** (hăg′ē-ə-grăf′-ĭk, hā′jē-), **hag·i·o·graph·i·cal** *adj.*

hag·i·ol·a·try (hăg′ē-ŏl′ə-trē, hā′jē-) *n. Theology.* Worship of the saints in a manner appropriate only to God. [HAGIO- + -LATRY.] —**hag·i·ol·a·ter** *n.* —**hag·i·ol·a·trous** *adj.*

hag·i·ol·o·gy (hăg′ē-ŏl′ə-jē, hā′jē-) *n., pl.* **-gies. 1.** Literature dealing with the lives of saints. **2.** A history of sacred writings. **3.** An authoritative list of saints. [HAGIO- + -LOGY.] —**hag·i·o·log·ic** (hăg′-ē-ə-lŏj′ĭk, hā′jē-), **hag·i·o·log·i·cal** *adj.* —**hag·i·ol·o·gist** *n.*

hag·i·o·scope (hăg′ē-ə-skōp′, hā′jē-) *n.* A small opening provided in an interior wall of a church to enable those in the transept to have a view of the main altar. Also called "squint." [HAGIO- + -SCOPE.] —**hag·i·o·scop·ic** (hăg′ē-ə-skŏp′ĭk, hā′jē-) *adj.*

hag·rid·den (hăg′rĭd′n) *adj.* **1.** Harassed or pursued by or as if by a witch. **2.** Tormented or harassed, as by nightmares or unreasoning fears.

Hague, The (hāg). *Dutch* **'s Gra·ven·ha·ge** (sкнrä′vən-hä′кнə). City in the western Netherlands, the capital of South Holland province, lying on the North Sea. Most of the Netherlands government's administrative offices are located here, as are the national legislature, the supreme court, and foreign embassies. It is also the site of the International Court of Justice.

Hague Tribunal *n.* Officially, the Permanent Court of Arbitration. A tribunal established at The Hague in 1899 for the peaceful settlement of international disputes.

hah. Variant of **ha.**

ha-ha¹ (hä′hä′) *n.* A sound made in imitation of laughter.
~*interj.* Also **haw-haw** (hô′hô′). Used to express amusement or scorn. [Middle English *ha ha,* from Old English.]

ha-ha² (hä′hä′) *n.* Also **haw-haw** (hô′hô′). A moat, walled ditch, or hedge sunk in the ground to serve as a fence without impairing the view. Also called "sunk fence." [French, apparently expressing surprise at finding such an unexpected obstacle.]

Hahn (hän), **Otto** (1879–1968). German chemist and physicist who discovered the process of nuclear fission. In 1938 he found that uranium atoms could be split in two when bombarded with neutrons, releasing atomic energy. Hahn received the Nobel Prize for chemistry (1944).

Hah·ne·mann (hä′nə-mən, -män′), **(Christian Friedrich) Samuel** (1755–1843). German physician; founder of homeopathy. He postulated that a disease should be treated with minute doses of a drug that induces comparable symptoms in a healthy subject. His *Organon of the Rational Art of Healing* (1810) set forth his views.

Hai·da (hī′də) *n., pl.* **-das** or collectively **Haida. 1.** Any of the North American Indian peoples inhabiting the Queen Charlotte Islands, British Columbia, and Prince of Wales Island, Alaska. **2.** A member of these peoples. **3.** The language of these peoples, the sole survivor of the Haida family of languages. **4.** A language family of the Na-Dene phylum. —**Hai·dan** *adj.*

Hai·fa (hī′fə). The chief city of northern Israel, on the Mediterranean Sea at the foot of Mt. Carmel. The old city was destroyed by Saladin in 1191; the prosperity of the modern city dates from the early 19th century. It is an industrial center and one of Israel's chief ports.

Haig (hāg), **Douglas, 1st Earl** (1861–1928). British commander in chief on the Western Front (1915–18). He went to France as commander of the First Army Corps and then became commander in chief. He was responsible for the costly assault at the Somme (1916). In 1918 he directed the counterattack that broke the Hindenburg Line.

haik, haick (hīk, hāk) *n.* A large piece of cotton, silk, or wool cloth, draped over the head and about the body, worn as an outer garment by Arabs. [Arabic *hā′ik,* from *hāka,* to weave.]

hai·ku (hī′kōo) *n., pl.* **haiku.** A Japanese lyric poem of a fixed, 17-syllable form that often simply points to a thing or pairing of things in nature that has moved the poet. Also called "hokku." [Japanese : *hai,* amusement + *ku,* sentence, verse.]

hail¹ (hāl) *n.* **1. a.** Precipitation in the form of pellets of ice and hard snow. **b.** A hailstone. **c.** *Archaic.* A hailstorm. **2.** Something suggestive of a shower of hail, as in force and quantity: *a hail of criticism; a hail of bullets.*
~*v.* **hailed, hailing, hails.** —*intr.* **1.** To precipitate as hail: *It's hailing outside.* **2.** To fall like hail. —*tr.* To pour down or forth: *hail oaths at someone.* [Middle English *hail, hagel,* Old English *hagol, hagalian.*]

hail² *v.* **hailed, hailing, hails.** —*tr.* **1. a.** To salute or greet; welcome. **b.** To greet or acclaim enthusiastically. **2.** To call out to in order to catch the attention of: *hail a cab.* —*intr.* To signal or call to a passing ship in greeting or to identify oneself. —**hail from.** To come or originate from: *He hails from Bombay.*
~*n.* **1.** The act of hailing. **2.** A shout made to greet or catch the attention of someone. **3.** The range within which a hail will be heard: *within hail.*
~*interj.* Used to express a greeting or tribute. [Middle English *hailen, haeilen,* from *(wæs)haeil,* "(be) healthy," hail, from Old

Norse *heill*, HALE, whole, healthy.] —**hail·er** *n.*

Hai·le Se·las·sie I (hī′lē sə-läs′ē, -lä′sē), born Ras Tafari (or Taffari) Makonnen (1891–1975). Emperor of Ethiopia (1930–36, 1941–74). After resisting the Italian invasion of his country (1936), he fled to England, returning with the Allies in 1941. His autocratic leadership brought opposition, and he was deposed in a military coup of 1974. He is revered as "the Lion of Judah, the Elect of God," by the Rastafarian cult of West Indians.

hail-fel·low (hāl′fĕl′ō) *adj.* Also **hail-fel·low-well-met** (hāl′fĕl′ō-wĕl′-mĕt′). Heartily friendly and congenial. [From the archaic greetings *Hail, fellow!* and *Hail, fellow! well met!*]

Hail Mary *n.* The *Ave Maria* (see).

hail·stone (hāl′stōn′) *n.* A hard pellet of snow and ice.

hail·storm (hāl′stôrm′) *n.* A storm with hail.

Hai·nan (hī′nän′). An island off the southern China coast, belonging to China and administratively part of Guangdong province. After Taiwan, it is the largest island off the China coast. The largest city and chief port is Haikou. The island is rich in minerals and the site of valuable rubber plantations.

Hai·naut (ā-nō′). *Flemish* **He·ne·gou·wen** (hā′nə-gou′wən). Low-lying province of southern Belgium, bordering on France. The capital is Mons, and the population is predominantly French-speaking.

Hai·phong (hī′fŏng′, -fông′). City in northeastern Vietnam, on the delta of the Song Hong (Red River) *c.* 16 kilometers (10 miles) inland from the Gulf of Tonkin. One of Southeast Asia's leading ports, it was severely damaged by bombing during the Vietnam War.

hair (hâr) *n.* **1. a.** Any of the cylindrical, often pigmented filaments characteristically growing from the epidermis of a mammal. **b.** A growth of such filaments, such as that forming the coat of an animal or covering the scalp of a human being. **2.** Any similar filamentous projection or bristle, such as a seta of an arthropod or an epidermal process of a plant. **3.** Fabric made from the hair of certain animals: *a coat of camel's hair.* **4.** A minute distance or narrow margin: *win by a hair.* **5.** A precise or exact degree: *calibrated to a hair.* —**get in someone's hair.** To upset or annoy someone. —**let one's hair down.** To drop one's reserve or inhibitions. —**split hairs.** To make petty and fine distinctions. —**turn a hair.** To reveal discomfiture or distress. Used in negative constructions: *accepted the challenge without turning a hair.*
~*adj.* **1.** Made of or with hair. **2.** For the hair: *a hair dryer.* [Middle English *haire, hare*, Old English *hǣr*, from Germanic *hǣram* (unattested).] See feature, next page.

hair·ball (hâr′bôl′) *n.* A small mass of hair swallowed by an animal, often causing indigestion or convulsions.

hair·breadth (hâr′brĕdth′) *adj.* Extremely close: *a hairbreadth escape.*
~*n.* Variant of **hairsbreadth.**

hair·brush (hâr′brŭsh′) *n.* A brush for grooming the hair.

hair clip *n.* A hinged clip that snaps together, used to hold the hair in place.

hair·cloth (hâr′klôth′, -klŏth′) *n.* A wiry fabric having usually a cotton or linen warp with a horsehair filler, used for upholstering and for stiffening and interlining garments.

hair·cut (hâr′kŭt′) *n.* **1.** A cutting of the hair. **2.** The style in which hair is cut.

hair·do (hâr′dōō′) *n., pl.* **-dos. 1.** A cutting or arranging of the hair, especially a woman's hair. **2.** The style in which the hair is arranged; coiffure.

hair·dress·er (hâr′drĕs′ər) *n.* A person who cuts or arranges people's hair, especially women's hair. —**hair·dress·ing** *n.*

haired (hârd) *adj.* Having hair, especially of a specified kind. Used chiefly in combination: *short-haired.*

hair follicle *n.* A tubular infolding of the epidermis that contains the root of a hair.

hair grass *n.* Any of various grasses having long, narrow stems and leaves, such as the tufted hair grass, *Deschampsia cespitosa.*

hair·grip (hâr′grĭp′) *n. Chiefly British.* A **bobby pin** (see).

hair·less (hâr′lĭs) *adj.* Having little or no hair.

hair·line (hâr′lĭn′) *n.* **1.** The outline of the growth of hair on the head, especially across the front. **2.** A very slender line. **3.** *Printing.* **a.** A very fine line on a typeface. **b.** A style of type using such lines. **4. a.** A textile design having thin, threadlike stripes. **b.** A fabric, usually a worsted, with such stripes. —**hair·line** *adj.*

hair·net (hâr′nĕt′) *n.* A very fine net worn to hold the hair in place.

hair piece *n.* A covering or bunch of human or artificial hair used to cover baldness or give shape to a hairstyle.

hair·pin (hâr′pĭn′) *n.* A thin, cylindrical strip of metal bent in a long U shape, used by women to secure a hairdo or a headdress.
~*adj.* Doubled back in a deep U: *a hairpin bend in the road.*

hair-rais·er (hâr′rā′zər) *n.* Something that causes wild excitement, terror, or thrills: *The ride in that sports car was a real hair-raiser.*

hair-rais·ing (hâr′rā′zĭng) *adj.* Horrifying; terrifying.

hairs·breadth, hair's-breadth (hârz′brĕdth′) *n.* Also **hair·breadth** (hâr′brĕdth′). A small space or distance; a narrow margin: *win by a hairsbreadth.*

hair seal *n.* Any of various seals of the family Phocidae, having a stiff, hairlike coat in the adult and ears visible only as small indentations.

hair sheep *n.* Any sheep of a breed having hair rather than wool and yielding a fine-grained hide.

hair shirt *n.* A coarse haircloth garment worn next to the skin by religious ascetics to mortify the flesh.

hail

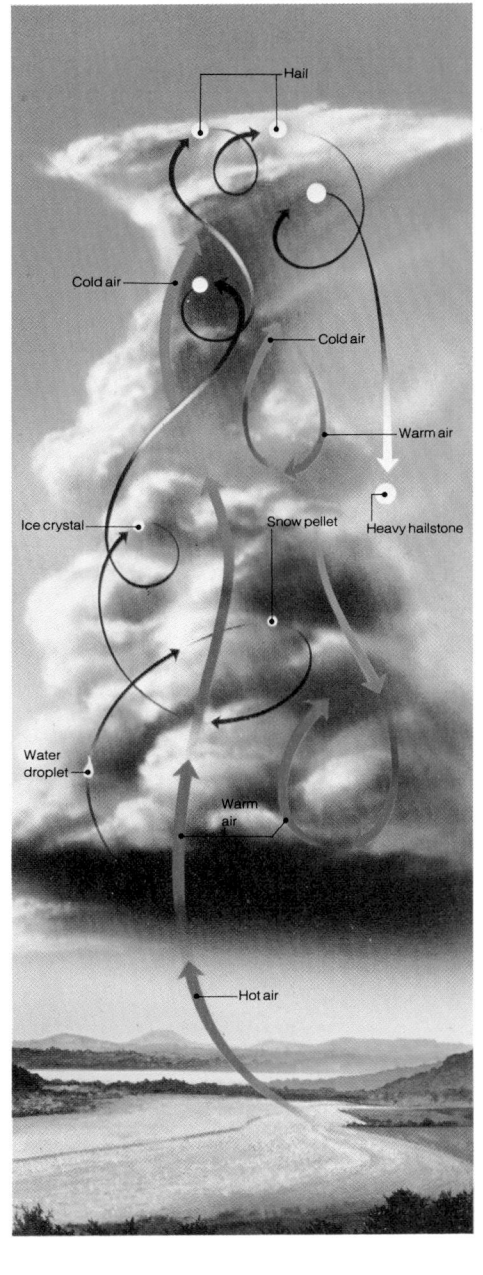

RAIN THAT FALLS AS ICE

How warm air builds bigger hailstones

In the topmost layer of a thundercloud—about 9 kilometers (6 miles) above the ground—the cold altitude means that the liquid cloud droplets turn to ice. But the warm, moist air at lower levels bubbles up in strong convection currents that keep the hailstones from falling until they are much larger and are heavier than air. In a turbulent cloud current small hailstones can be tossed up and down between the layers of moisture and ice many times, growing all the time. Very warm, moist air sets up a very strong updraft that helps to create the heaviest hailstones.

hairstreak *Hairstreak butterflies are so called because of the fine line across the undersides of their wings (upper illustration). This is the black hairstreak, which is widespread throughout the world.*

hair space *n. Printing.* The narrowest of the spaces used for separating words or letters.

hair·split·ting (hâr′splĭt′ĭng) *n.* The making of unreasonably fine distinctions; quibbling.
~*adj.* Concerned with subtle but petty distinctions. —**hair·split·ter** *n.*

hair·spring (hâr′sprĭng′) *n.* A fine coiled spring that regulates the movement of the balance wheel in a watch or clock.

hair·streak (hâr′strĕk′) *n.* Any of numerous butterflies of the sub-

hair

WHY HAIR TURNS WHITE

What hair is and how it gets its color

A hair is a structure of dead tissue growing from a follicle buried deep in the skin. Its hollow core is surrounded by a cortex strengthened by a sheath of keratin, a protein, and an outer cuticle of scales. The bulbous root is attached to the papillae, a layer of live cells supplied with blood vessels and nerves, from which the hair grows. Each hair follicle has oil glands and a muscle that, when it contracts, makes the hair stand on end. After growing 3 millimeters (.117 inch) a week for about three years, the hair falls out and is replaced.

Hair texture, abundance, rate of growth, and color are all hereditary. Melanin pigments in different forms and concentrations give human hair a range of colors varying from pale yellows through reds to blacks. Pigment is injected into the hair cortex from melanin cells in the papillae.

At a time preordained by genetic coding the papillae cease to inject melanin granules into the hair's cortex. Instead, there are minute air bubbles in the spaces between the transparent cells of the cortex. Light scattered by them makes the hair appear white.

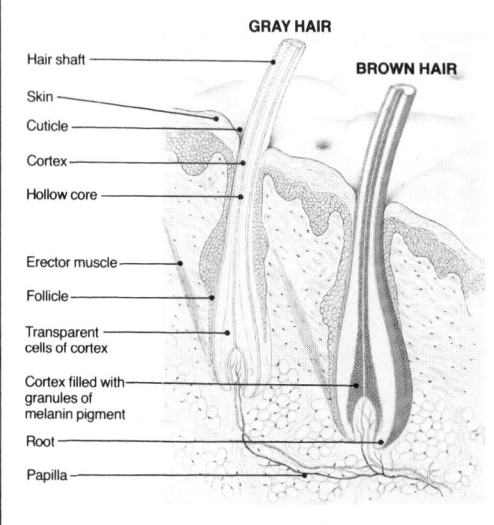

GRAY HAIR
BROWN HAIR

Hair shaft
Skin
Cuticle
Cortex
Hollow core
Erector muscle
Follicle
Transparent cells of cortex
Cortex filled with granules of melanin pigment
Root
Papilla

family Theclinae, having transverse streaks on the underwings and fine, hairlike projections on the hind wings.

hair stroke *n.* A very fine line in writing or printing, as a serif.

hair style *n.* The design or style in which hair is cut, set, or arranged. —**hair stylist** *n.*

hair transplant *n.* The grafting of strands of one's own hair onto a bald area of the scalp.

hair trigger *n.* A gun trigger adjusted to respond to a very slight pressure.

hair-trig·ger (hâr′trĭg′ər) *adj.* Responding to the slightest provocation: *a hair-trigger temper.*

hair·worm (hâr′wûrm′) *n.* **1.** Any of various slender, parasitic nematode worms of the genus *Trichostrongylus*, which infest the stomach and small intestine of cattle, sheep, and related animals. **2.** A **horsehair worm** (see).

hair·y (hâr′ē) *adj.* **-ier, -iest. 1.** Covered with hair or hairlike growths; hirsute: *a hairy arm.* **2.** Of or like hair: *a hairy coat.* **3.** *Slang.* Fraught with difficulties; hazardous: *a hairy escape.* —**hair·i·ness** *n.*

hairy frog *n.* A frog, *Astylosternus robustus,* of western Africa, the males of which grow hairlike filaments on the thighs during the breeding season.

hairy hedgehog *n.* A **gymnure** (see).

Hai·ti (hā′tē). Republic in the Caribbean, comprising the western third of the island of Hispaniola and the two small islands of Tortuga and Gonâve. A slave rebellion against French rule won the islanders their independence in 1804, and Haiti is thus the oldest independent black republic in the world. Political instability led to U.S. occupation (1915–34) and the repressive dictatorship (1957–71) of François Duvalier, "Papa Doc." His son, Jean Claude ("Baby Doc"), ruled from 1971 to 1986, when he fled the country after widespread civil unrest. Haiti is the poorest country in Latin America. Coffee is the mainstay of the economy, and bauxite and sugar are also exported. Area, 27,713 square kilometers (10,700 square miles). Population, 5,000,000. Capital, Port-au-Prince. See map at **Dominican Republic**.

Hai·tian (hā′shən, -tē-ən) *adj.* Of or pertaining to Haiti, its people, or its dialect.
~*n.* **1.** A native or inhabitant of Haiti. **2.** The French patois spoken by most Haitians. Also called "Haitian Creole."

haj, hajj. Variants of **hadj**.

haji, hajji. Variants of **hadji**.

ha·ka (hä′kä) *n. New Zealand.* A Maori war dance accompanied by chanting. [Maori.]

hake[1] (hāk) *n., pl.* **hakes** or collectively **hake. 1.** Any of various marine food fishes of the genus *Merluccius*, such as *M. merluccius*, related to and resembling the cod. **2.** Any of various other fishes, such as species of the American genus *Urophycis* or the Australian *Thyrsites atun.* [Middle English *hake*, perhaps from *hakefish*, from dialectal *hake*, Old Norse *haki*, hook (from the shape of its underjaw).]

hake[2] *n.* A wooden rack or frame for drying cheese, bricks, or fish. [Variant of HECK (frame).]

ha·ke·a (hä′kē-ə, hā′-) *n.* Any Australian tree of the genus *Hakea*, some species of which produce useful wood. [After C.L. von *Hake* (died 1818), German horticulturist.]

Ha·ken·kreuz (hä′kən-kroits′) *n.* The swastika used as a symbol of Nazi Germany or of anti-Semitism. [German, "hooked cross."]

ha·kim[1], **ha·keem** (hä′kēm′) *n.* A Muslim physician. [Arabic *ḥakīm*, wise, learned, philosopher, from *ḥakama*, to be wise, exercise authority.]

hakim[2] *n. pl.* **hakim** or **-kims.** A Muslim ruler, provincial governor, or judge. [Arabic *ḥākim*, governor, from *ḥakama*, to exercise authority.]

Hak·ka (häk′ə) *n., pl.* **-kas. 1.** A member of a Chinese people generally thought to have originated in central northern China, but now mostly scattered throughout southern China. **2.** A dialect of Chinese spoken by the Hakkas. [From dialectal pronunciation of Mandarin Chinese *kè jiā*, guest people, more recent migrants to a settled area.]

Hak·luyt (häk′lōōt′), **Richard** (c. 1552–1616). English geographer. He collected accounts of English voyages of exploration and published them in *Principal Navigations, Voyages, and Discoveries of the English Nation* (1589, 1598–1600).

Ha·la·fi·an (hə-lä′fē-ən) *adj.* Of, pertaining to, or designating a culture that flourished in parts of Syria and Iraq before 3500 B.C., characterized especially by its polychrome pottery. [After Tell *Halaf*, a site near the present village of Ras el 'Ain, in northeastern Syria near the Turkish border.]

Ha·la·kah, Hal·la·cha (hä′lä-ᴋʜä′, hä-lä′ᴋʜə) *n. Judaism.* The legal part of Talmudic literature, an interpretation of the laws of the Scriptures. Compare **Haggadah**. [Mishnaic Hebrew *halākhāh*, rule, tradition, from *hālakh*, to go.] —**Ha·lak·ic** (hə-läk′ĭk) *adj.*

ha·la·kist, ha·la·chist (hä′lə-kĭst, hə-lä′kĭst) *n.* Often **Halakist. 1.** A Hebrew judge or scholar who has written parts of the Halakah. **2.** A student or scholar of the Halakah.

ha·lal, hal·lal (hə-läl′) *tr.v.* **-lalled, -lalling, -lals** or **-lals.** To slaughter (animals) in the prescribed Muslim manner.
~*n.* Meat killed in this manner. Also used adjectively: *halal meat; a halal butcher.* [Arabic, "lawful."]

ha·la·la (hə-lä′lə) *n., pl.* **halala** or **-las.** A monetary unit of Saudi Arabia that is equal to 1/100 of the rial. See feature at **currency**. [Arabic.]

ha·la·tion (hā-lä′shən) *n.* **1.** A blurring or spreading of light around bright objects or areas on a photographic negative or print. **2.** A ring of light appearing around a bright object on a television screen. [HAL(O) + -ATION.]

halavah. Variant of **halvah**.

hal·berd (hăl′bərd) *n.* Also **hal·bert** (-bərt). A weapon of the 15th and 16th centuries having an axelike blade and a steel spike mounted on the end of a long shaft. [Middle English *halberd*, from Old French *hallebarde*, from Middle High German *helmbarde*, "handle axe" : *helm*, handle + *barte*, axe, hatchet, from Old High German *barta*.]

hal·ber·dier (hăl′bər-dîr′) *n.* A soldier, attendant, or guard armed with a halberd.

hal·cy·on (hăl′sē-ən) *n.* **1.** A fabled bird, identified with the kingfisher, that was supposed to have had the power to calm the wind and the waves during the winter solstice while it nested on the sea. **2.** *Poetic.* A kingfisher.
~*adj.* **1.** Calm and peaceful; tranquil. **2.** Prosperous; golden: *halcyon years.* [Middle English *alceon*, from Latin *(h)alcyon*, from Greek *(h)alkuōn*, a mythical bird, perhaps the kingfisher.]

halcyon days *pl.n.* **1.** Days of fine weather occurring near the winter solstice, especially the seven days before and the seven after, attributed by legend to the magical powers of the halcyon. **2.** A happy period of peace and tranquillity.

hale[1] (hāl) *adj.* **haler, halest.** Sound in health; not infirm; vigorous; robust. Used especially in the phrase *hale and hearty.* —See Synonyms at **healthy**. [Middle English *hal(e)*, Old English *hāl*, WHOLE.] —**hale·ness** *n.*

hale[2] *tr.v.* **haled, haling, hales. 1.** To compel to go; force: *hale a man into court.* **2.** *Archaic.* To pull, drag, draw, or hoist: *"The rope that haled the buckets from the well"* (Tennyson). [Middle English *halen*, from Old French *haler*, from Old Norse *hala*, from Middle Low German *halen*, to pull.]

Hale (hāl), **Edward Everett** (1822–1909). U.S. author and clergyman. A powerful preacher and prolific writer, he produced 150 literary works, many of which reflected his liberal Christian values.

Perhaps best known for his story "The Man Without a Country" (1863), he also served as the U.S. Senate chaplain from 1903 until his death.

Hale, Nathan (1755-76). U.S. soldier. A Connecticut schoolteacher turned Revolutionary War officer, he was captured by the British and sentenced to death for espionage. According to legend, his final words were "I only regret that I have but one life to lose for my country."

Haleb. See **Aleppo.**

ha·ler (hä′lər, -lĕr′) *n., pl.* **-lers** or **-leru** (-lə-rōō′). A monetary unit equal to ¹/₁₀₀ of the koruna of Czechoslovakia. See feature at **currency.** [Czech, from Middle High German *haller,* an early German silver coin, from *Hall,* town in Swabia where halers were once minted.]

half (hăf, häf) *n., pl.* **halves** (hăvz, hävz). **1. a.** Either of two equal parts that together constitute a whole. **b.** A part of something approximately equal to the remainder: *Half her life is spent dreaming.* **2.** *Informal.* A fifty-cent piece. **3.** *Sports.* **a.** Either of two playing periods into which a game is divided. **b.** The turn of one baseball team at bat. **4.** Either of two periods into which an event, such as a concert or play, may be divided. **5.** *Sports.* A halfback. **6.** *Golf.* A score equal to the opponent's score on a hole or a round. **7.** *Sports.* Either of the two sections of a playing field, considered as belonging to the team defending the goal in that section. **8.** Half an hour. Used in expressing time: *half past one.* **9.** *Chiefly British.* A school term; semester. **—and a half.** *Informal.* Of an exceptional kind: *a fight and a half.* **—by half.** By a considerable and often excessive amount. **—by halves. 1.** Partially; imperfectly. **2.** Reluctantly; unenthusiastically. **—go halves.** To share equally. **—in half.** Into halves.

~*adj.* **1.** Being a half, as in size, quantity, or the like: *a half smile.* **2.** Being approximately a half. **3.** Partial; incomplete. **4.** Having only one parent in common with another person.

~*adv.* **1.** To the extent of exactly or nearly 50 percent: *a half-empty tank.* **2.** Not completely or sufficiently; partly: *only half-prepared.* **3.** To some extent; somewhat: *I was half afraid she'd leave.* **4.** *Informal.* Tolerably; reasonably: *wanting a café with half-decent food.* **—not half. 1.** Not nearly: *not half as bad as I'd expected.* **2.** *British Informal.* Really. Used as an intensive: *He didn't half get angry.* [Middle English *half,* Old English *healf,* from Germanic.]

Usage: The phrases *a half, half of,* and *half a* are all correct, though they may differ slightly in meaning. For example, *a half day* is used when *day* has the special sense "a working day," and the phrase then means "four hours." *Half of a day* and *half a day* are not restricted in this way and can mean either four or twelve hours. When the accompanying word is a pronoun, however, the phrase with *of* must be used: *half of them.* The phrase *a half a,* though frequently heard, is held by some to be unacceptable.

half-a-crown. Variant of **half-crown.**

half-and-half (hăf′ənd-hăf′, häf′ənd-häf′) *adj.* Being half one thing and half another.

~*adv.* In equal portions.

~*n.* **1.** A mixture of two things in equal portions; especially, a mixture of equal parts of milk and cream. **2.** *British.* A blend of light ale and bitter.

half·back (hăf′băk′, häf′-) *n. Abbr.* **hb, hb. 1.** *Football.* One of the two players positioned near the flanks behind the line of scrimmage. **2.** One of several players in various sports stationed behind the forward line. **3.** The position played by a halfback.

half-baked (hăf′bākt′, häf′-) *adj.* **1.** Only partly baked; not cooked through. **2.** *Informal.* Not sufficiently thought out; ill-conceived; foolish: *a half-baked scheme.* **3.** *Informal.* Lacking good judgment or common sense: *a half-baked idiot.*

half-ball (hăf′bôl′, häf′-) *adj.* In billiards and snooker, designating a stroke aimed so as to make the cue ball hit the side of another ball.

half·beak (hăf′bēk′, häf′-) *n.* Any of various marine and freshwater fishes of the family Hemiramphidae, related to the flying fishes, and having the lower jaw extended beyond the upper jaw.

half binding *n.* A bookbinding in which the back and often the corners of the volume are bound in a material differing from the rest of the cover: *a half binding of leather.*

half blood, half-blood (hăf′blŭd′, häf′-) *n.* **1.** The relationship existing between persons having only one parent in common. **2.** A person existing in such a relationship. **3.** A half-breed. **4.** A half-blooded domestic animal.

half-blood·ed (hăf′blŭd′ĭd, häf′-) *adj.* **1.** Having only one parent in common. **2.** Having parents of different ethnic types. **3.** Having one parent of pedigreed stock and the other of unknown or mixed ancestry. Said of an animal.

half board *n.* A demi-pension *(see).*

half boot *n.* A low boot extending just above the ankle.

half-bound (hăf′bound′, häf′-) *adj.* Having a half binding. Said of a book.

half-bred (hăf′brĕd′, häf′-) *adj.* Having only one parent that is purebred; half-blooded.

half-breed (hăf′brēd′, häf′-) *n. Offensive Slang.* A person having parents of different ethnic types.

~*adj.* Half-blooded; hybrid.

half brother *n.* A brother related through one parent only.

half-butt (hăf′bŭt′, häf′-) *n.* In billiards and snooker, a cue that is shorter than a long butt though longer than an ordinary cue.

half-caste (hăf′kăst′, häf′käst′) *n.* A person of mixed racial descent;

especially, a Eurasian or a person of mixed white and black descent. **—half-caste** *adj.*

half cock *n.* The position of the hammer of a firearm when it is raised halfway and locked by a catch so that the trigger cannot be pulled. **—at half cock.** At a premature stage; before proper preparations are made.

half-cocked (hăf′kŏkt′, häf′-) *adj.* **1.** At the position of half cock. **2.** *Informal.* Inadequately prepared or conceived; not fully thought out.

~*adv. Informal.* Prematurely; hastily; carelessly: *fall halfcocked into an argument.*

half-crown (hăf′kroun′, häf′-) *n.* Also **half-a-crown** (hăf′ə-kroun′, hä′fə-). **1.** A British coin worth two shillings and sixpence, now no longer in circulation. **2.** The sum of two shillings and sixpence.

half-dead (hăf′dĕd′, häf′-) *adj. Chiefly British Informal.* Exhausted; very tired.

half dollar *n.* A U.S. or Canadian coin worth 50 cents.

half gainer *n.* A dive in which the diver springs from the board facing forward, rotates backward in the air in a half backward somersault, and enters the water headfirst, facing the board.

half-har·dy (hăf′här′dē, häf′-) *adj.* Designating a cultivated plant that can survive outside during winter except during a severe frost.

half-heart·ed (hăf′här′tĭd, häf′-) *adj.* Done with or possessing little interest or enthusiasm; uninspired: *a halfhearted attempt at painting.* **—half·heart·ed·ly** *adv.* **—half·heart·ed·ness** *n.*

half hitch *n.* A hitch made by looping a rope or strap around an object, and then back around itself, bringing the end of the rope through the loop.

half-hour (hăf′our′, häf′-) *n.* **1.** A period of 30 minutes. **2.** The point that marks 30 minutes after a given hour.

~*adj.* **1.** Lasting 30 minutes. **2.** Occurring on or indicating the half-hour: *a half-hour chime.* **—half-hour·ly** *adj. & adv.*

half hunter *n.* A pocket watch with a metal cover over all but the center part of the glass. Compare **hunter.**

half-in·te·gral (hăf′ĭn′tə-grəl, häf′-) *adj.* Having an integer as a numerator and 2 as a denominator. Said of a fraction.

half-jack (hăf′jăk′, häf′-) *n. South African Informal.* A flat half-bottle of alcohol.

half landing *n.* A landing that is halfway up a staircase.

half-length (hăf′lĕngkth′, -lĕngth′, häf′-) *n.* A portrait that shows only the upper half and hands of a person.

~*adj.* **1.** Of or denoting such a portrait. **2.** Of half the full length.

half-life (hăf′līf′, häf′-) *n., pl.* **-lives** (-līvz′). **1.** *Physics.* The time required for half the nuclei in a sample of a specific isotopic species to undergo **radioactive decay** *(see).* **2.** *Biology.* **a.** The time required by living tissue, an organ, or an organism to eliminate by biological processes half the quantity of a radioactive substance taken in. **b.** The time required for the radioactivity of material taken in by a living organism to be reduced to half its initial value by a combination of biological elimination processes and radioactive decay.

half-light (hăf′līt′, häf′-) *n.* The soft, subdued light found at dusk or dawn or in dimly lit interiors.

half-line (hăf′līn′, häf′-) *n.* A straight line extending in just one direction from a given point.

half-mast (hăf′măst′, häf′mäst′) *n.* The position about halfway up a mast or pole at which a flag is flown as a symbol of mourning for the dead or as a signal of distress.

~*tr.v.* **half-masted, -masting, -masts.** To place (a flag) at this position.

half measure *n.* An inadequate or halfhearted course of action.

half-moon (hăf′mōōn′, häf′-) *n.* **1.** The moon when only half its disk is illuminated. **2.** Something shaped like a half-moon, as the lunula of the fingernail.

~*adj.* (hăf′mōōn′, häf′-). Shaped like a half-moon: *half-moon spectacles.*

half nelson *n.* A wrestling hold in which one arm is passed under the opponent's arm from behind to the back of his neck. Compare **full nelson.**

half note *n. Music.* A note having one half of the value of a whole note. Also called "minim."

half-pen·ny (hā′pə-nē, hāp′nē) *n., pl.* **-nies** (for senses 1, 2); **half-pence** (hā′pəns) (for sense 3). Also **ha'pen·ny. 1.** A British coin worth half of a new penny. **2.** A British coin worth half an old penny, now no longer in circulation. **3.** The sum of half of a penny. **4.** A small or negligible amount.

half pint *n. Slang.* A small person or animal.

half-plate (hăf′plāt′, häf′-) *n.* A photographic plate measuring 6½ inches (16.5 centimeters) by 4¼ inches (10.8 centimeters).

half-price (hăf′prīs′, häf′-) *adv.* At a reduced price, usually half the full price. **—half-price** *adj.*

half relief *n.* **Mezzo-relievo** *(see).*

half sister *n.* A sister related through one parent only.

half-slip (hăf′slĭp′, häf′-) *n.* A woman's slip that extends from the waist to the hem of the outer garment.

half sole *n.* A shoe sole extending from the shank to the toe.

half-sole (hăf′sōl′, häf′-) *tr.v.* **-soled, -soling, -soles.** To fit or repair with a half sole.

half sovereign *n.* An obsolete British gold coin worth ten shillings.

half step *n.* **1.** *Music.* A **semitone** *(see).* **2.** A marching step of 15 inches at quick time and 18 at double time.

half tide *n.* **1.** The condition of the tide at a time halfway between high tide and low tide. **2.** The period during which this condition exists.

halo *A faint ring around the sun or moon, caused by refraction of light by particles in the upper atmosphere. Here the sun has been photographed on a hazy day.*

half-tim·bered (hăf′tĭm′bərd, häf′-) *adj.* Also **half-tim·ber** (-bər). *Architecture.* Having a wooden framework with plaster, brick, stone, or other masonry filling the spaces.

half-time (hăf′tīm′, häf′-) *n.* The interval between two halves in certain games. Also used adjectivally: *the half-time score.*

half title *n.* **1.** The title of a book printed at the top of the first page of the text or on a full page preceding the main title page. **2.** The title of a section of a book, consisting of only one line and printed on the leaf preceding the text of that section.

half tone *n. Music.* A **semitone** (see).

half-tone (hăf′tōn′, häf′-) *n.* **1.** *Art.* A tone or value halfway between a highlight and a dark shadow. **2.** *Photoengraving.* **a.** A picture in which the gradations of light are obtained by the relative darkness and density of tiny dots produced by photographing the subject through a fine screen. **b.** The technique or process that produces such pictures. **c.** The metal plate obtained by such a process. **d.** A picture made from such a plate.
~*adj.* Relating to, used in, or made by halftone.

half-track (hăf′trăk′, häf′-) *n.* A military motor vehicle, often lightly armored, with caterpillar treads in place of rear wheels. —**half-track, half-tracked** *adj.*

half-truth (hăf′trooth′, häf′-) *n.* A statement, especially one intended to deceive, that omits some of the facts necessary for a truthful description or account.

half volley *n.* **1.** A stroke, as in tennis, cricket, or similar games, in which the ball is hit immediately after it bounces off the ground. **2.** The position of the ball immediately after it bounces: *hit it on the half volley.*

half-way (hăf′wā′, häf′-) *adj.* **1.** Midway between two points or conditions; in the middle. **2.** Reaching or including only half of a portion; partial: *halfway measures.* —**half-way** *adv.*

halfway house *n.* **1.** An inn or other stopping place that marks the midpoint of a journey. **2.** A rehabilitation center where people who have left an institution, such as a mental hospital or prison, are helped to readjust to the outside world.

half-wit (hăf′wĭt′, häf′-) *n.* A stupid, foolish, or frivolous person; a simpleton. —**half-wit·ted** (hăf′wĭt′ĭd, häf′-) *adj.* —**half-wit·ted·ly** *adv.* —**half-wit·ted·ness** *n.*

hal·i·but (hăl′ə-bət, hŏl′-) *n., pl.* **-buts** or collectively **halibut.** Any of several large, edible flatfishes of the genus *Hippoglossus* and related genera, of northern Atlantic or Pacific waters. [Middle English *halybutte* : *hali, holi,* HOLY (it was eaten on holy days) + *butte,* flatfish, from Middle Dutch.]

Haliç. See **Golden Horn.**

Hal·i·car·nas·sus (hăl′ə-kär-năs′əs). Ancient Greek city of Caria, in southwestern Asia Minor. It was the site of the Mausoleum, a magnificent tomb constructed by the wife of Mausolus, the satrap of Caria (377-353 B.C.). The tomb was one of the Seven Wonders of the World.

Halicz. See **Galicia** (Central Europe).

hal·ide (hăl′īd′, -ĭd, hā′līd′, -lĭd) *n.* A binary chemical compound of a halogen with a more electropositive element or group. Also called "haloid." [HAL(O-) + -IDE.]

hal·i·dom (hăl′ə-dəm) *n. Obsolete.* **1.** Holiness; sanctity. **2.** A holy relic. **3.** A sanctuary. [Middle English *halidom,* Old English *hāligdōm* : *hālig,* HOLY + -DOM.]

Hal·i·fax[1] (hăl′ə-făks′). Town in the metropolitan county of West Yorkshire, in northern England. Since the Industrial Revolution it has been a center for the manufacture of carpets, textiles, and, more recently, machine tools.

Halifax[2]. Capital city of Nova Scotia, in eastern Canada. It is Canada's leading ice-free Atlantic port and the eastern terminus of the country's railroad network. It was founded in 1749 and named after George Montagu Dunk, 2nd Earl of Halifax (1716-71).

hal·ite (hăl′īt′, hā′līt′) *n.* **Rock salt** (see). [New Latin *halites* : HAL(O)- + -ITE.]

hal·i·to·sis (hăl′ə-tō′sĭs) *n.* Stale or foul-smelling breath. [New Latin : Latin *hālitus,* breath, from *hālāre†,* to breathe + -OSIS.]

hall (hôl) *n.* **1.** A large entrance hall or vestibule in a building; a lobby; a foyer **2.** A corridor or passageway leading from an entrance in a house, hotel, or other building. **3. a.** A building for public gatherings or entertainments, such as concerts, lectures, or plays. **b.** The large room in which such events are held. **4. a.** A large building belonging to a school used for assembly, entertainments, or the like. **b.** A large room in a college or university where meals are served and lectures or concerts occasionally held. **c.** *British.* A meal served in such a building. **d.** *British.* A sitting of such a meal: *second hall.* **5.** The main house on a landed estate; especially, the house of a nobleman. **6. a.** The house or castle of a medieval king, chieftain, or nobleman. **b.** The large principal room in such a house or castle, used for dining, entertaining, and sleeping. [Middle English *hal(le),* Old English *h(e)all.*]

hallah. Variant of **challah.**

hallal. Variant of **halal.**

Hall effect *n. Electronics.* An effect in which an electric potential difference is produced between two faces of a conductor carrying a current when a magnetic field is applied at right angles to the current. [After E.H. *Hall* (1855-1938), American physicist.]

Hal·lel (hä-lāl′, hä′lĕl′) *n. Judaism.* A chant of praise consisting of Psalms 113 to 118, used during Passover and on certain other Jewish holidays. [Hebrew *hallēl,* song of praise, praise, from *hallēl,* to praise.]

hal·le·lu·jah (hăl′ə-loo′yə) *interj.* Used, especially in religious contexts, to express praise or joy.
~*n.* **1.** The exclamation of "hallelujah." **2.** A musical composition expressing praise and based on the word "hallelujah." See **alleluia.** [Hebrew *hallelūyāh,* praise the Lord : *hallelū,* plural imperative of *hallēl,* to praise + *yāh,* short for YAHWEH.]

Hal·ley (hăl′ē), **Edmund** (1656-1742). British astronomer. He applied Newton's laws of motion to a particular comet of 1682, and in 1705 he correctly predicted its return in 1758.

Halley's comet *n.* A comet with a period of approximately 76 years, the first comet for which a return was successfully predicted. It appeared in 1910 and again in 1986. [After Edmund HALLEY.]

halliard. Variant of **halyard.**

hall·mark (hôl′märk′) *n.* **1.** A mark used in the United Kingdom to stamp gold, silver, or platinum articles that meet established standards of purity. Also called "platemark." **2.** Any mark indicating quality or excellence. **3.** Any conspicuous indication of the character or quality of something: *A sense of humor is the hallmark of humanity.*
~*tr.v.* **hallmarked, -marking, -marks.** To mark with a hallmark. [After Goldsmith's *Hall* in London, England, where gold and silver articles were appraised and stamped.]

hall of fame *n.* **1.** A room or building housing busts, plaques, or the like, honoring illustrious persons. **2.** A group of persons judged to be outstanding in a sport, profession, or other category.

hal·loo (hə-loo′) *interj.* Also **hal·loa** (hə-lo′). **1.** Used to gain someone's attention. **2.** Used to urge on hounds in a hunt.
~*n.* Also **halloa.** A shout or call of "halloo."
~*v.* **hallooed, -looing, -loos.** Also **hal·loa, -loaed, -loaing, -loas.** —*intr.* To shout "halloo"; call out. —*tr.* **1.** To urge on or pursue by calling "halloo" or shouting. **2.** To call out to. **3.** To utter with a loud shout. [Perhaps variant of earlier *hallow,* to shout so as to incite hounds, from Middle English *halowen,* from Old French *halloer* (imitative).]

hal·low (hăl′ō) *tr.v.* **-lowed, -lowing, -lows.** **1.** To make or set apart as holy; sanctify; consecrate. **2.** To honor as being holy; revere; adore. [Middle English *halowen,* Old English *hālgian,* from Germanic *hailag-* (unattested), HOLY.]

hal·lowed (hăl′ōd) *adj.* **1.** Made or set apart as being holy; sanctified; consecrated. **2.** Highly venerated; unassailable; sacrosanct.

Hal·low·een, Hal·low·e'en (hăl′ō-ēn′) *n.* The eve of All Saints' Day, falling on October 31 and celebrated by children who go in costume from door to door begging treats or playing pranks. [Short for *All Hallows Even.*]

Hal·low·mas, Hal·low·mass (hăl′ō-məs, -măs′) *n. Archaic.* The feast of All Saints' Day or Allhallowmas on November 1. [Short for ALLHALLOWMAS.]

hall porter *n. Chiefly British.* A porter in the lobby of a hotel or office building who looks after keys, takes messages, arranges porters to carry luggage, and the like.

Hall process *n.* The electrolytic reduction process by which aluminum is recovered from aluminum oxide. [After Charles Martin *Hall* (1863-1914), American chemist, who invented it.]

Hall·statt (hôl′stät′, häl′shtät′) *adj.* Of, designating, or pertaining to a dominant late Bronze Age and early Iron Age culture of central and western Europe, probably chiefly Celtic, that flourished from the 9th century B.C. to the 4th century B.C. [After *Hallstatt,* Austria, site of remains typical of the culture.]

hal·lu·ci·nate (hə-loo′sə-nāt′) *v.* **-nated, -nating, -nates.** —*intr.* To undergo hallucination. —*tr.* *Rare.* To cause to have hallucinations. [Latin *hallūcinārī, alūcinārī,* to wander in mind, from Greek *aluein,* to wander, be distraught.]

hal·lu·ci·na·tion (hə-loo′sə-nā′shən) *n.* **1.** False perception with a characteristically compelling sense of the reality of something not really present, as occurring in some psychological and neurological disorders and under the influence of certain drugs. **2.** The hallucinatory material so perceived. **3.** Any false or mistaken idea; a delusion.

hal·lu·ci·na·to·ry (hə-loo′sə-nə-tôr′ē, -tōr′ē) *adj.* **1.** Characterizing or characterized by hallucination. **2.** Inducing hallucination.

hal·lu·cin·o·gen (hə-loo′sə-nə-jən) *n.* A drug, such as mescaline or LSD, that induces hallucination. [HALLUCIN(ATION) + -GEN.] —**hal·lu·cin·o·gen·ic** (hə-loo′sə-nə-jĕn′ĭk) *adj.*

hal·lu·ci·no·sis (hə-loo′sə-nō′sĭs) *n.* Any abnormal condition or mental state characterized by hallucination. [New Latin : HALLUCIN(ATION) + -OSIS.]

hal·lux (hăl′əks) *n., pl.* **halluces** (hăl′yə-sēz′, hăl′ə-). **1.** The inner or first digit on the hind foot of a mammal; in man, the big toe. **2.** The homologous digit of a bird, reptile, or amphibian. In birds it is often directed backward. [New Latin, from Latin *hallux, (h)allus†,* big toe.]

hall·way (hôl′wā′) *n.* **1.** A corridor, passageway, or hall in a house or building. **2.** An entrance hall; a foyer; a vestibule.

halm. Variant of **haulm.**

ha·lo (hā′lō) *n., pl.* **-los** or **-loes. 1.** A luminous ring or disk of light surrounding the heads or bodies of sacred figures, as of saints in religious paintings; a nimbus. **2.** The aura of majesty or glory surrounding a person, thing, or event regarded with reverence, awe, or a similar sentiment. **3.** *Meteorology.* A circular band of light, sometimes colored, around the sun or moon, caused by the refraction and reflection of light by ice particles or water drops suspended in the intervening atmosphere. **4.** *Pathology.* Any of the colored rings seen around a light source by people with glaucoma or cataract

~*v.* **haloed, -loing, -los** or **-loes.** —*tr.* To adorn or invest with a halo. —*intr.* To form a halo. [Medieval Latin *halō,* from Latin *halōs,* from Greek *halōs†,* threshing floor, halo, disk of the sun or moon.]

halo–, hal– *prefix.* Indicates salt or the sea; for example, **halophyte, halite.** [French, from Greek, from *hals,* salt, sea.]

hal·o·bi·ont (hăl′ō-bī′ŏnt′) *n.* An organism that lives or grows in a saline environment. [HALO- + BIONT.]

hal·o·gen (hăl′ə-jən) *n.* Any of a group of five chemically related nonmetallic elements that includes fluorine, chlorine, bromine, iodine, and astatine. [Swedish : HALO- + -GEN.] **—ha·log·e·nous** (hə-lŏj′ə-nəs) *adj.*

hal·o·gen·ate (hăl′ə-jə-nāt′) *tr.v.* **-ated, -ating, -ates.** To treat or cause to combine with a halogen. **—hal·o·gen·a·tion** *n.*

hal·oid (hăl′oid′) *adj.* Derived from or resembling a halogen.
~*n.* A **halide** *(see).* [HAL(O)- + -OID.]

hal·o·per·i·dol (hăl′ō-pĕr′ə-dôl′, -dōl′) *n.* A tranquilizer used in the treatment of psychiatric disorders, including schizophrenia. [HALO- + (PI)PERID(INE) + -OL.]

hal·o·phil·ic (hăl′ə-fĭl′ĭk) *adj.* Designating organisms, especially bacteria, that grow best in a salty environment. [HALO- + -PHILIC.] **—hal·o·phile** (hăl′ə-fīl′) *n.*

hal·o·phyte (hăl′ə-fīt′) *n.* A plant that grows in saline soil, such as that of a salt marsh. [HALO- + -PHYTE.] **—hal·o·phyt·ic** (hăl′ə-fĭt′ĭk) *adj.*

hal·o·thane (hăl′ə-thān′) *n.* A general anesthetic administered by inhalation for inducing and maintaining anesthesia during surgery. [HALO- + (E)THANE.]

Hals (häls), **Frans** (*c.* 1580–1666). Dutch painter, noted for fine portraits, including *The Laughing Cavalier* (1624).

Hal·sey (hôl′zē, -sē), **William Frederick** (1882–1959). U.S. naval officer. During World War II he led American naval forces to several pivotal victories in the Pacific, including the battles of Guadalcanal (1942–43) and Leyte Gulf (1944). On September 2, 1945, the Japanese formally surrendered aboard the *Missouri,* his flagship.

halt[1] (hôlt) *n.* **1.** A suspension or cessation of movement or progress, particularly of marching; a stop or pause. **2.** *British.* A stopping place, without station facilities, used by trains on minor routes. **—call a halt to.** To put a stop to; end.
~*v.* **halted, halting, halts.** —*tr.* To cause to stop; arrest. —*intr.* To stop; pause.
~*interj.* Used as a command to stop, especially to marching troops. [German *Halt,* from Middle High German *halt,* from the imperative of *halten,* to stop, hold, from Old High German *haltan.*]

halt[2] *intr.v.* **halted, halting, halts. 1.** To be defective or to proceed poorly, as in the development of an argument in logic or in the rhythmical structure of a verse. **2.** To proceed or act with uncertainty or indecision; waver. **3.** *Archaic.* To limp or hobble, as a cripple.
~*n. Archaic.* The act of limping; lameness.
~*adj. Archaic.* Having a limp; lame; crippled. [Middle English *halten,* to be lame, Old English *healtian,* from Germanic.]

hal·ter[1] (hôl′tər) *n.* **1.** A device made of rope or leather straps that fits around the head or neck of an animal, particularly a horse or cow, and can be used to lead or secure it. **2.** A rope with a noose used for execution by hanging. **3.** Death or execution by hanging. **4.** A bodice for women that ties behind the neck and across the back, leaving the arms, shoulders, and back bare. Also used adjectivally or in combination: *a halter-necked dress.* **5.** Variant of **haltere.**
~*tr.v.* **haltered, -tering, -ters. 1.** To put a halter on; tie up with a halter. **2.** To put to death by hanging. [Middle English *halter,* Old English *hælftre.*]

hal·ter[2] (hôl′tər, hăl′-) *n., pl.* **halteres** (hôl-tîr′ēz, hăl-). Also **hal·tere** (-tîr′). Either of the small, clublike balancing organs that are the rudimentary hind wings of dipterous insects such as flies or mosquitoes. Also called "balancer." [New Latin, from Latin *haltēr,* leaden weights used in leaping exercises, from Greek, from *hallesthai,* to jump.]

halt·ing (hôl′tĭng) *adj.* **1.** Limping; lame. **2.** Imperfect; defective: *a halting argument.* **3.** Hesitant or wavering: *a halting voice; a halting translation.* **4.** Uneven; jerky: *halting rhythm.* **—halt·ing·ly** *adv.*

hal·vah, hal·va (häl-vä′, häl′vä) *n.* Also **ha·la·vah** (hä′lə-vä′). A confection of Turkish origin consisting of crushed sesame seeds and honey. [Yiddish *halva,* from Turkish *helva,* from Arabic *ḥalwā.*]

halve (hăv, häv) *tr.v.* **halved, halving, halves. 1.** To separate or divide into two equal portions or parts. **2.** To lessen or reduce by half; remove half of. **3.** *Informal.* To share equally; divide up. **4.** *Carpentry.* To join (two pieces of wood) by cutting off half of each at the joint so they will fit together smoothly. **5.** *Golf.* To play (a game or hole) using the same number of strokes as one's opponent. —*intr.* To divide into or form two equal parts.
~*n. Carpentry.* A joint made by halving. [Middle English *halven, halfen,* from *half,* HALF.]

halves. Plural of **half.**

hal·yard, hal·liard (hăl′yərd) *n.* A rope used to raise or lower a sail, flag, or yard. [Variant (influenced by YARD) of Middle English *halier,* from *halen,* to pull, HALE.]

ham (hăm) *n.* **1.** The thigh of the hind leg of certain animals, especially a hog. **2.** The meat of this part of a hog, often preserved by smoking or drying. **3.** The back of the knee. **4.** The back of the thigh. **5. hams.** The buttocks. **6.** *Slang.* **a.** An actor who overacts or a performer who exaggerates dramatic gestures, comic effects, or the like. Sometimes used adjectivally: *a ham actress.* **b.** Any person who, liking attention or acclaim, makes himself ridiculous or obnoxious. **7.** *Informal.* A licensed amateur radio operator.
~*v.* **hammed, hamming, hams.** —*intr.* To overact. —*tr.* To exaggerate or overdo (a role, line, or the like). Often used with *up.* [Middle English *ham(me),* Old English *ham(m).*]

Ham (hăm). The second of the three sons of Noah, considered in some traditions the ancestor of the Egyptians. Genesis 5:32.

ham·a·dry·ad (hăm′ə-drī′əd) *n., pl.* **-ads** or **-ades** (-ə-dēz′). **1.** *Greek & Roman Mythology.* A wood nymph living only as long as the tree of which she is the spirit and in which she lives. **2.** A snake, the **king cobra** *(see).* [Latin *Hamādryas* (stem *Hamādryad-*), from Greek *Hamadruas,* "one together with a tree" : *hama,* together with + *druas,* dryad, from *drus,* tree.]

ha·ma·dry·as (hăm′ə-drī′əs) *n.* A baboon, *Comopithecus* (or *Papio*) *hamadryas,* of northern Africa and Arabia, the adult male of which has a heavy mane. [New Latin, from Latin, HAMADRYAD.]

ha·mal, ham·mal (hə-mäl′, -môl′) *n.* A porter or bearer in certain Muslim countries. [Arabic *ḥammāl,* porter, from *ḥamala,* to carry.]

Ha·man (hā′mən). A chief minister of the Persian king Ahasuerus, who was hanged from his own gallows when his plot against the Jews was revealed by Esther. Esther 8:7.

ha·mate (hā′māt′) *adj.* Hooked at the tip. [Latin *hāmātus,* from *hāmus†,* hook.]

hamate bone *n.* A small hook-shaped bone in the wrist. Also called "unciform bone."

ham·ba (hăm′bə, hŭm′-) *interj. South African Slang.* Used as an expletive to scare or chase away a person or animal. Often considered offensive. [Nguni, imperative of *ukuhamba,* to go.]

Ham·ble·to·ni·an (hăm′bəl-tō′nē-ən) *n.* One of a strain of American trotting horses. [Named after the stallion *Hambletonian* (1849–76), from which the strain descended.]

Ham·burg (hâm′bûrg′, hăm′bo͝org′). City in northern West Germany, capital of and coextensive with the state of Hamburg. Situated on the Elbe River near its mouth on the North Sea, it is the chief port in West Germany.

ham·burg·er (hăm′bûr′gər) *n.* **1. a.** A patty of chopped beef, cooked by frying or broiling. **b.** A sandwich consisting of a hamburger patty in a roll or bun. **2.** Chopped meat, especially beef. [Short for *Hamburger steak,* after HAMBURG.]

hame (hām) *n.* Either of the two curved wooden or metal pieces of a harness that fit around the neck of a draft animal and to which the traces are attached. [Middle English, probably from Middle Dutch.]

Hame·lin (hăm′lən, -ə-lən). *German* **Ha·meln** (hä′məln). Town in Lower Saxony, West Germany, on the Weser River. It is the site of the legendary tale of the Pied Piper of Hamelin.

ham-fist·ed (hăm′fĭs′tĭd) *adj.* Ham-handed.

ham-hand·ed (hăm′hăn′dĭd) *adj. Informal.* **1.** Clumsy; maladroit. **2.** Having very large hands.

Ha·mil·car Bar·ca (hə-mĭl′kär′ bär′kə, hăm′əl-) (*c.* 270–228 B.C.). Carthaginian general and father of Hannibal. He led the Carthaginian forces during the final six years of the First Punic War (264–241). After signing a treaty with the Romans, he returned to Carthage and quelled a rebellion among his mercenary troops.

Ham·il·ton[1] (hăm′əl-tən). A burgh in Strathclyde Region, south-central Scotland, at the confluence of the Avon and Clyde rivers. It was near Hamilton that Rudolf Hess landed on his supposed peace mission flight from Germany in May 1941.

Hamilton[2]. Industrial city in Ontario, Canada, at the western end of Lake Ontario. It was originally settled by United Empire Loyalists in 1778 and has grown into one of Canada's largest cities and the country's leading producer of steel and iron.

Hamilton[3]. Capital of Bermuda, founded in 1790. Lying on Bermuda Island, it is a free port and tourist center.

Hamilton, Alexander (1755–1804). U.S. statesman. As the first secretary of the treasury (1789–95) he established the national bank and public credit system. He was mortally wounded in a duel with Aaron Burr.

Hamilton, Lady Emma, born Emma Lyon (*c.* 1761–1815). Mistress of Horatio Nelson. The daughter of a Cheshire blacksmith, she became the mistress of Charles Greville (1749–1809) and later married his uncle Sir William Hamilton (1730–1803), the British envoy to Naples. She met Nelson in 1793 and bore him a daughter in 1801. After her husband's death she lived with Nelson.

Ham·il·to·ni·an (hăm′əl-tō′nē-ən) *n. Symbol* **H 1.** *Physics.* A mathematical function that can be used systematically and with great generality to generate the equations of motion of a dynamic system, equal for many such systems to the sum of the kinetic and potential energies of the system expressed in terms of the system's coordinates and momenta treated as independent variables. **2.** A mathematical operator that generates such a function. [After William Rowan *Hamilton* (1805–65), Irish mathematician who formulated it.] **—Ham·il·to·ni·an** *adj.*

Ham·ite (hăm′īt′) *n.* **1.** One said to be descended from Ham. **2.** A member of a group of related peoples inhabiting northern and northeastern Africa, including the Berbers and the descendants of the ancient Egyptians.

Ha·mit·ic (hă-mĭt′ĭk) *adj.* Of or relating to Ham, the Hamites, or the language of the Hamites.
~*n.* A group of North African languages related to Semitic, including the Berber dialects, ancient Egyptian and its descendant, Coptic, and the Cushitic dialects spoken in Ethiopia.

Ham·i·to-Se·mit·ic (hăm′ə-tō-sə-mĭt′ĭk) *n.* A family of languages,

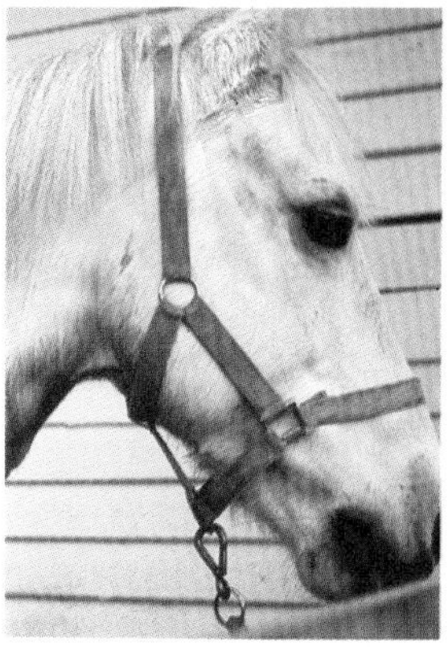

halter *An arrangement of leather straps for leading or restraining a horse or a pack animal.*

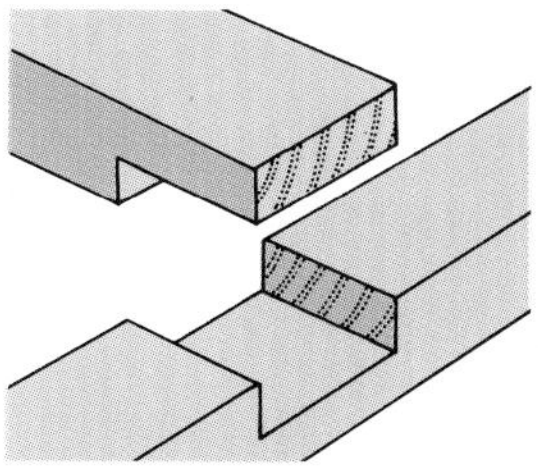

halve *A carpentry joint in which two pieces of wood—each chiseled out to half its thickness—are fitted together to form a union of the same thickness as the original pieces.*

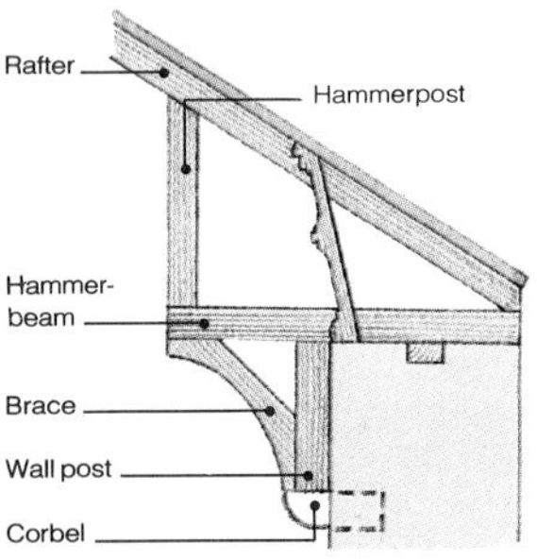

hammerbeam roof *The hammerbeam roof, using braced struts projecting from the walls to support the rafters, was common in England in the 15th century.*

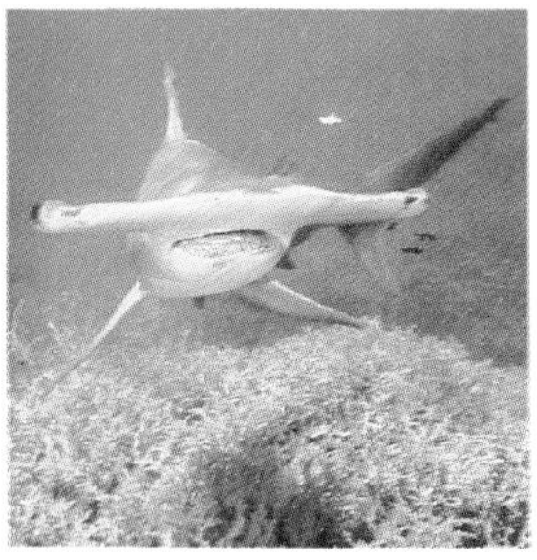

hammerhead *The broad head that gives this shark its name carries its eyes and nostrils. The shape of the head is believed to give it better vision and a directional sense of smell. There are nine species found all over the world, and all are considered dangerous.*

Afro-Asiatic *(see).* [HAMIT(IC) + SEMITIC.] **—Ham·i·to-Se·mit·ic** *adj.*

ham·let (hăm′lĭt) *n.* A small village. [Middle English, from Old French *hamelet,* diminutive of *hamel,* diminutive of *ham,* from Germanic.]

Ham·let (hăm′lĭt) *n.* An indecisive person. [After *Hamlet,* prince of Denmark, hero of Shakespeare's tragedy (1604).]

hammal. Variant of **hamal.**

Ham·mar·skjöld (hăm′ər-shōld′, -sho͝old′), **Dag Hjalmar Agne Carl** (1905–61). Swedish secretary-general of the United Nations (1953–61). During the Congo crisis he was killed in a plane crash over Zambia. He was posthumously awarded the Nobel Peace Prize in 1961.

ham·mer (hăm′ər) *n.* **1.** A hand tool used to exert an impulsive force by striking; especially, such a tool consisting of a handle with a perpendicularly attached head of a relatively heavy, rigid material, such as iron or hard rubber, used to drive nails or shape construction materials. **2.** Any tool or device of analogous function or action, as: **a.** The part of a gunlock that hits the primer or firing pin or explodes the percussion cap causing the gun to go off. **b.** One of the padded wooden pieces of a piano that strike the strings. **c.** Any part of an apparatus that strikes a gong or bell, as in a clock. **d.** A power tool that delivers blows with a weight. **3.** *Anatomy.* A bone, the **malleus** *(see).* **4.** *Sports.* A metal ball weighing 16 pounds and having a long wire or wooden handle by which it is thrown in track and field competition. **5.** A small mallet used by auctioneers. **—go (or come) under the hammer.** To be put up for auction. **—hammer and tongs.** With tremendous energy or effort; vigorously.

~*v.* **hammered, -mering, -mers.** *—tr.* **1. a.** To hit once or repeatedly with or as if with a hammer; strike; pound. **b.** To drive by hammering. **2.** To beat into a shape or flatten with a hammer. Often used with *out*: *He hammered the metal flat. The mechanic hammered out the dents.* **3.** To put together, fasten, or seal, particularly with nails, by hammering. **4.** To defeat (an opponent or enemy). **5.** To cause (ideas or information) to be absorbed by constant repetition: *She hammered the highway code into her pupils.* **6.** To subject to harsh criticism or relentless questioning. **7.** *British.* On the stock exchange, to declare (a broker) defaulted. *—intr.* **1.** To deal repeated blows with or as if with a hammer; pound; pummel: *branches hammering at the windows.* **2.** To beat in the manner of a hammer: *His pulse hammered.* **3.** To subject to repeated questioning or testing. Used with *away*: *hammered away at the examination candidates.* **4.** *Informal.* To work diligently; keep at something continuously. Often used with *away: He hammered away at his homework.* **—hammer out. 1.** To make by hammering. **2.** To settle or arrive at (a policy or agreement, for example) by vigorous discussion. [Middle English *hamer,* Old English *hamor.*] **—ham·mer·er** *n.*

hammer and sickle *n. Used with a singular verb.* **1.** An emblem of the Communist movement, consisting of a crossed hammer and sickle signifying the alliance of workers and peasants. **2.** *Informal.* Communism.

ham·mer·beam (hăm′ər-bēm′) *n.* A bracket projecting horizontally from the top of a wall and bearing the weight of the roof through the vertical hammerpost.

hammerbeam roof *n.* A roof whose weight is supported through a system of hammerbeams and hammerposts.

hammer drill *n.* A pneumatically operated drill for boring holes in stone in which the drilling bit is given a reciprocating motion.

ham·mered (hăm′ərd) *adj.* Created, shaped, or worked with or as if with a metalworker's hammer and often having indentations on the surface: *hammered gold.*

Ham·mer·fest (hä′mər-fĕst′). A town in northern Norway, on Kvaløy Island. Although it is the most northerly town in Europe, its harbor is ice-free the year round.

ham·mer·head (hăm′ər-hĕd′) *n.* **1.** The head of a hammer. **2.** Any of several large, predatory sharks of the genus *Sphyrna,* having the sides of the head elongated into large, fleshy extensions with the eyes at the ends. **3.** A wading bird, *Scopus umbretta,* of Africa and southwestern Asia, having brown plumage, a large, bladelike bill, and a long, backward-pointing crest. Also called "hammerkop." **4.** An African fruit bat, *Hypsignathus monstrosus,* with a hammer-shaped nose. **—ham·mer·head·ed** *adj.*

hammer lock *n.* A wrestling hold in which the opponent's arm is pulled behind his back and twisted upward.

ham·mer·post (hăm′ər-pōst′) *n.* A vertical post between a purlin and a hammerbeam.

ham·mer·smith (hăm′ər-smĭth′) *n.* One who works metals by hand with a hammer.

Ham·mer·stein (hăm′ər-stīn′), **Oscar II** (1895–1960). U.S. songwriter who collaborated with Richard Rodgers on a series of musicals. Their successes include *Oklahoma!* (1943), *South Pacific* (1949), *The King and I* (1951), and *The Sound of Music* (1959).

ham·mer·toe (hăm′ər-tō′) *n. Pathology.* A toe, usually the second, that is permanently bent downward.

Ham·mett (hăm′ĭt), **Dashiell** (1894–1961). U.S. author. He drew on his years at the Pinkerton detective agency in his highly acclaimed detective stories and novels, including *The Maltese Falcon* (1930). He later wrote several movies and also a radio serial about the tough, witty, and urbane Nick Charles, the hero of *The Thin Man* (1934).

ham·mock¹ (hăm′ək) *n.* A length of canvas, netting, or the like, hung between two supports, used for relaxation and formerly as a bed for sailors. [Spanish *hamaca,* from Taino.]

hammock². Variant of **hummock** (sense 2).

Ham·mu·ra·bi (hăm′ə-rä′bē) (died 1750 B.C.). King of Babylon (1792–1750 B.C.). He made Babylon the chief Mesopotamian kingdom and collated the laws of his people and of the Sumerians.

ham·my (hăm′ē) *adj.* **-mier, -miest. 1.** *Informal.* Characterized by exaggerated acting. **2.** Tasting or smelling of ham.

ham·per¹ (hăm′pər) *tr.v.* **-pered, -pering, -pers.** To prevent the free movement, action, or progress of; impede. **—See Synonyms at hinder.**

~*n. Nautical.* Necessary but encumbering equipment on a ship. [Middle English *hamperen*†.]

hamper² *n.* **1.** A large basket, typically of wickerwork, that usually has a cover. **2.** Such a basket or any other container packed with food and drink: *a Christmas hamper.* [Middle English *hampere,* variant of HANAPER.]

Hamp·shire (hămp′shîr′, -shər). Also **Hants** (hănts). County on the southern coast of England. It is crossed by chalk downs and is noted for sheep and dairy farming. Winchester, the ancient capital of Wessex, is the county town.

Hamp·stead (hămp′stĕd′, -stĭd). Residential district of northern London, noted for its heathland and intellectual community.

Hamp·ton (hămp′tən), **Lionel** (1913–). U.S. jazz musician. He was the first to popularize the vibraphone as a virtuoso solo instrument. He formed his own orchestra in 1940.

Hampton Roads. A channel of southeastern Virginia, connecting the James and Elizabeth rivers with Chesapeake Bay. One of the finest natural harbors in the world, it has been a major port since colonial times. It was the site of the Civil War battle (March 1862) between the ironclad ships *Monitor* and *Merrimack.*

ham·shack·le (hăm′shăk′əl) *tr.v.* **-led, -ling, -les. 1.** To hobble (an animal) by tying a rope or strap between one of the legs and the head. **2.** To hold back; hinder. [Perhaps from HAMPER (verb) + SHACKLE.]

ham·ster (hăm′stər) *n.* Any of several Eurasian rodents of the family Cricetidae; especially, *Mesocricetus auratus,* the golden hamster, having large cheek pouches and a short tail, popular as a pet and used in laboratory research. [German *Hamster,* from Old High German *hamustro,* from Slavic; akin to Old Slavic *chomĕstorŭ*†.]

ham·string (hăm′strĭng′) *n.* **1.** Either of two tendons at the rear hollow of the human knee. **2.** The large sinew in the back of the hock of a quadruped, such as a horse.

~*tr.v.* **hamstrung** (-strŭng′), **-stringing, -strings. 1.** To cut the hamstring of (an animal or person) and thereby cripple. **2.** To destroy or hinder the efficiency of (somebody or something); frustrate. [HAM (thigh) + STRING.]

Ham·sun (häm′sən), **Knut,** pen name of Knut Pedersen (1859–1952). Norwegian novelist. He wrote of individuals facing struggles of existence in works including *Hunger* (1890) and *The Growth of the Soil* (1917). In 1920 he won the Nobel Prize for literature.

ham·u·lus (hăm′yə-ləs) *n., pl.* **-li** (-lī′). A small hooklike projection or process, as at the end of a bone. [New Latin, from Latin *hāmulus,* little hook, diminutive of *hāmus*†, hook.]

ham·za, ham·zah (hăm′zə) *n.* A sign in Arabic orthography used to represent the sound of a glottal stop, transliterated in English as an apostrophe. [Arabic *hamza,* compression (of the windpipe), from *hamaza,* to press on, spur, goad.]

Han¹ (hän). A Chinese dynasty (206 B.C.–A.D. 220) noted for the unification and expansion of the national territory and for the promotion of literature and the arts.

Han² *n.* The Chinese as distinguished from other ethnic groups in China, such as the Manchus and the Mongols. **—Han** *adj.*

han·a·per (hăn′ə-pər) *n.* A wicker container or hamper used for storing documents. [Middle English *hanaper,* from Old French *hanapier,* case for holding goblets, from *hanap,* goblet, akin to Old English *hnæpp,* bowl, from Germanic *hnap* (unattested).]

hance (hăns) *n.* **1.** *Architecture.* **a.** The half arch that joins a lintel to a jamb. **b.** A **haunch** *(see).* **2.** *Nautical.* A curved rise or contour on a ship, as of the bulwarks. [Obsolete *ha(u)nce,* lintel, from *ha(u)nce,* to raise, from Middle English *hauncen,* probably short for *enhauncen,* to ENHANCE.]

Han·cock (hăn′kŏk′), **John** (1737–93). U.S. merchant, politician, and Revolutionary leader. A wealthy Bostonian, he protested against British rule, served in the Continental Congress (1775–80), and as its president was the first signer of the Declaration of Independence. He later served nine terms as governor of Massachusetts (1780–93).

hand (hănd) *n. Abbr.* **hd. 1.** The terminal part of the human arm below the wrist, consisting of the palm, four fingers, and an opposable thumb, used for grasping and holding. **2.** A homologous or similar part in other animals. **3.** A unit of length equal to four inches (10.16 centimeters), used especially to specify the height of a horse. **4.** Something suggesting the shape or function of the human hand. **5. a.** Any of the rotating pointers on the face of a mechanical clock. **b.** A pointer on any of various similar instruments, as a gauge or meter; a needle. **6.** A printer's mark, **index** *(see).* **7.** Lateral direction indicated according to the way in which one is facing: *at my right hand.* **8.** A style or individual sample of writing; handwriting; penmanship. **9.** A round of applause to signify approval; clapping. **10.** An act of physical assistance; help: *Give me a hand with these trunks.* **11.** *Card Games.* **a.** The cards held by a given player at any time: *a winning hand.* **b.** The number of cards dealt

each player; a deal. **c.** A player or participant: *a fourth hand for bridge.* **d.** A portion or section of a game during which all the cards dealt out are played: *a hand of poker.* **12.** A person who performs manual labor: *a factory hand.* **13.** A person who is part of a group or crew. **14.** Any participant in an activity. **15.** A person regarded in terms of a specialized skill or trait: *an old hand at drawing.* **16.** A source of information considered in terms of its immediacy or degree of reliability: *at first hand.* **17. a.** *Usually* **hands.** Possession, ownership, or keeping: *The books should be in her hands by noon.* **b.** *Often* **hands.** Power; jurisdiction; care: *out of my hands.* **c.** Doing or involvement; participation: *The hand of the Russians is evident here.* **d.** An influence or effect; a share: *I detect the professor's hand in your decision.* **18.** Permission or a promise, especially: **a.** A pledge to marry. **b.** A business agreement sealed by a clasp or handshake; one's word: *You have my hand on that.* **19.** Capacity for doing something that requires skill: *try one's hand at painting.* **20.** A manner or way of performing something; an emphasis; an approach: *a light hand with make-up.* **21.** The lower part of a pork shoulder. **22.** A large bunch of bananas. **—at hand. 1.** Close by; near; easily accessible. **2.** Near in time; imminent. **—at the hand (or hands) of.** Through the agency of. **—by hand. 1.** Using the hands as opposed to mechanical means: *sorted by hand.* **2.** Individually delivered, rather than handled by the Post Office. **—by one's own hand.** By one's own act or agency: *die by one's own hand.* **—change hands.** To pass into different ownership. **—come to hand.** To be or become available. **—eat out of someone's hand.** To accept someone's views, wishes, or orders meekly and without protest. **—force someone's hand.** To force someone to act prematurely or against his own wishes. **—from hand to hand.** From one person successively to another person. **—from hand to mouth. 1.** In dire poverty. **2.** On an unplanned, day-to-day basis. **—hand and foot. 1.** So as to prevent movement or escape: *tied up hand and foot.* **2.** With slavish devotion: *He waited on his master hand and foot.* **—hand in glove.** In close association or collusion. **—hand in hand. 1.** Holding each other's hand. **2.** In cooperation; jointly. **—hand over fist.** At a tremendous rate: *making money hand over fist.* **—hands down.** With no trouble; easily. **—hands off.** Do not touch. Keep away. **—have one's hands full.** To be unable to take on more duties or responsibilities because one is fully occupied. **—hold (or stay) one's hand.** To restrain oneself from proceeding with a planned punishment or action. **—in hand. 1.** Under control. **2.** Presently accessible. **3.** In preparation or being processed. **—keep one's hand in.** To practice or keep in practice. **—lay hands on.** To bless, ordain, or consecrate by touching. **—on hand.** Available. **—on (or upon) one's hands.** In one's possession, often as an imposed responsibility or burden. **—on the one hand.** As one point of view or side of an issue; in one respect. **—on the other hand.** As another or opposite point of view; from another standpoint. **—out of hand. 1.** Out of control. **2.** Abruptly and without proper consideration. **—play into the hands of.** To act or behave so as to give an advantage to (an opponent). **—show one's hand.** To reveal something previously hidden, such as one's motives or intentions. **—take in hand. 1.** To put under control or care. **2.** To deal with; treat. **—throw up one's hands.** To give up in despair; concede. **—to hand. 1.** Nearby. **2.** In one's possession. **—turn (or put) one's hand to.** To take up as an activity; work at. **—wash one's hands of.** To relinquish involvement in or responsibility for. **—with a heavy hand. 1.** In a clumsy or awkward manner. **2.** With great severity or emphasis. **—with a high hand.** In a presumptuous or cavalier fashion; overbearingly.
~adj. **1.** Of or pertaining to the hand. **2.** Made to be transported by hand: *hand luggage.* **3.** Performed or operated by hand; manual. **4.** Created by hand.
~tr.v. **handed, handing, hands. 1.** To give or pass with or as if with the hands; present: *Hand me your keys.* **2.** To aid, direct, or conduct with the hands: *The usher handed the patron to her seat.* **3.** *Nautical.* To roll up and secure (a sail); furl. **—hand down. 1.** To bequeath as an inheritance to or as if to one's heirs. **2.** To release or pronounce a court decision or verdict. **—hand in.** To turn in; submit: *hand in one's work.* **—hand it to.** *Informal.* To give credit to. **—hand on. 1.** To give to a successor. **2.** To pass on (a tradition, heirloom, or the like). **—hand over. 1.** To release into the possession of another; relinquish. **2.** To transfer one's responsibility, task, or the like to another. [Middle English *hand,* Old English *hand, hond,* from Germanic *handuz* (unattested).]

Hand (hănd), **(Billings) Learned** (1872–1961). U.S. jurist. As a district judge (1909–24) and federal judge (1924–51) he earned the respect of his peers, rendering decisions in nearly all fields of law. Although he was never a Supreme Court justice, his influence was such that he was sometimes called the tenth man of the high court.

hand·bag (hănd′băg′) *n.* **1.** A bag, usually a woman's, for carrying articles such as money, keys, and personal items; pocketbook; purse. **2.** A piece of small hand luggage.

hand·ball (hănd′bôl′) *n.* **1.** A game played by two or more players batting a ball against a wall with their hands, usually with a special glove. **2.** The small rubber ball used in this game.

hand·bar·row (hănd′băr′ō) *n.* A flat framework or litter having carrying poles at each end.

hand·bell (hănd′bĕl′) *n.* A bell to be rung by hand, especially one of a set tuned in a scale.

hand·bill (hănd′bĭl′) *n.* A printed sheet or pamphlet distributed by hand; a leaflet; a notice or advertisement.

hand·book (hănd′bo͝ok′) *n. Abbr.* **hdbk.** A manual or small reference book providing specific information or instruction about a subject, activity, place, or the like; a guide; a directory.

hand·brake (hănd′brāk′) *n.* **1.** A brake on a vehicle that is operated by a hand lever. **2.** The hand lever that operates such a brake.

hand·breadth (hănd′brĕdth′) *n.* Also **hand's-breadth** (hăndz′-), **hand's breadth.** A linear measurement approximating the width of the palm of the hand, from 2½ to 4 inches, or 6.25 to 10 centimeters.

hand·cart (hănd′kärt′) *n.* A small, usually two-wheeled cart pulled or pushed by hand.

hand·clap (hănd′klăp′) *n.* A beating together of the palms of one's hands, usually repeatedly, used to indicate applause, attract attention, or provide a rhythmic accompaniment to music.

hand·clasp (hănd′klăsp′, -kläsp′) *n.* An act of clasping the hand of another person, especially to show warmth or friendship.

hand·craft (hănd′krăft′, -kräft′) *n.* Variant of **handicraft.**
~tr.v. **handcrafted, -crafting, -crafts.** To make by hand.

hand·cuff (hănd′kŭf′) *n.* *Usually* **handcuffs.** A restraining device consisting of a pair of strong, connected hoops that can be tightened and locked about the wrists and used on one or both arms of a person in custody; a manacle. Also informally "cuff."
~tr.v. **handcuffed, -cuffing, -cuffs.** To restrain with handcuffs.

hand·ed (hăn′dĭd) *adj.* **1.** Having a hand or hands. **2.** Having a specified number or kind of hands, or a specified preference as regards a hand or hands. Used in combination: *one-handed; left-handed.* **3.** Involving a specified number of people. Used in combination: *a four-handed card game.*

hand·ed·ness (hăn′dĭd-nĭs) *n. Chemistry.* **Chirality** *(see).*

Han·del (hănd′l), **George Frederick** (1685–1759). German-born composer (naturalized British subject, 1726). Handel wrote many Italianate operas, including *Rinaldo* (1711). With *Saul* (1738) he moved from opera to Biblical oratorio, a medium he brought to perfection in *Messiah* (1742). Other works include the orchestral *Water Music* (1717). **—Han·del·i·an** (hăn-dē′lē-ən, -dēl′yən, -dĕl′ē-ən) *adj.*

hand·fast (hănd′făst′, -fäst′) *n. Archaic.* **1.** A secure grasp or grip. **2.** A handclasp used to signify a pledge, as a contract or a marriage.
~tr.v. **handfasted, -fasting, -fasts.** *Archaic.* **1.** To grip securely with the hand. **2.** To betroth or marry by joining the hands.

hand·feed (hănd′fēd′) *tr.v.* **-fed** (-fĕd′), **-feeding, -feeds. 1.** To feed (a person or animal) by hand. **2.** To feed (an animal) with regulated amounts of food at scheduled times.

hand·ful (hănd′fo͝ol′) *n., pl.* **-fuls. 1.** The quantity or number that can be held in the hand. **2.** A small but undefined quantity or number: *a handful of requests.* **3.** *Informal.* A person or thing too difficult to control or handle easily.

hand glass *n.* **1.** A small magnifying glass held in the hand. **2.** A mirror with a handle. **3.** A time glass used in timing the running out of a line used with a nautical log.

hand grenade *n.* A small grenade to be thrown by hand.

hand·grip (hănd′grĭp′) *n.* **1.** A grip by the hand or hands. **2.** Something suited to or facilitating a grip by the hand, as a handle or indentation. **3. handgrips.** Hand-to-hand fighting. **4.** A traveling bag; a holdall. In this sense, also called "grip."

hand·gun (hănd′gŭn′) *n.* A firearm that can be used with one hand; a pistol.

hand·held (hănd′hĕld′) *adj.* Designating a film camera that is carried rather than mounted.

hand·hold (hănd′hōld′) *n.* **1.** A grip by the hand or hands. **2.** Something that one can hold by the hand or hands for support, such as a branch or indentation on a rock surface.

hand·i·cap (hăn′dē-kăp′) *n.* **1.** A race or contest in which advantages or compensations are given to different contestants, according to their varied abilities or experience, to equalize the chances of winning. **2.** Such an advantage or penalty; especially, a handicap assigned to a golfer showing the number of strokes by which he is expected to exceed par for a given course. **3. a.** A deficiency, especially an anatomical, physiological, or mental deficiency, that prevents or restricts normal achievement. **b.** Any disadvantage, hindrance, or disability: *I find not being able to drive a handicap.*
~tr.v. **handicapped, -capping, -caps. 1.** To assign a handicap or handicaps to (a contestant). **2.** To put at a disadvantage; impede. [From the phrase *hand i' cap* ("hand in cap"), originally a lottery game in which players held forfeits in a cap.]

hand·i·cap·per (hăn′dē-kăp′ər) *n.* **1.** One who assigns handicaps. **2.** One who predicts the winners in a horse race, especially one who publishes such predictions as a guide for bettors.

hand·i·craft (hăn′dē-krăft′, -kräft′) *n.* Also **hand·craft** (hănd′krăft′, -kräft′). **1.** Skill and facility with the hands; workmanship. **2.** A particular trade or craft requiring skilled use of the hands, such as basketry. **3.** The work produced by such a trade or craft. [Middle English *handie-craft,* variant of *handcraft* : HAND + CRAFT.]

hand·i·crafts·man (hăn′dē-krăfts′mən, -kräfts′mən) *n., pl.* **-men** (-mĭn). A person skilled in handicraft; a craftsman.

hand·i·ly (hăn′dĭ-lē) *adv.* **1.** In a handy or easy manner; dexterously. **2.** Conveniently.

hand·i·ness (hăn′dē-nĭs) *n.* **1.** The quality of being handy; facility; expertise. **2.** The quality of being easy to use or readily accessible; convenience.

hand·i·work (hăn′dē-wûrk′) *n.* **1.** Work performed by hand or the objects produced by hand. **2.** That which is accomplished by a single person's efforts. **3.** The results of a person's actions. [Middle

PRONUNCIATION KEY
ă, pat; ā, pay; âr, care;
ä, father, are; b, bib;
ch, church; d, deed; ĕ, pet;
ē, be; f, fife; g, gag; h, hat;
hw, which; ĭ, pit; ī, pie;
îr, pier; j, judge; k, kick;
l, lid, needle; m, mum;
n, no, sudden; ng, thing;
ŏ, pot; ō, toe; ô, paw, for;
oi, noise; ou, out; o͝o, book;
o͞o, boot; p, pop; r, roar;
s, sauce; sh, ship, dish;
t, tight; th, thin, path;
th, this, bathe; ŭ, cut; ûr, fur;
v, valve; w, with; y, yes;
z, zebra, size; zh, vision;
ə, about, item, edible,
gallop, circus, peaceful

IN FOREIGN WORDS:
à, *Fr.* ami; œ, *Fr.* feu, *Ger.* schön; ü, *Fr.* tu, *Ger.* über; KH, *Ger.* ich, *Scot.* loch; N, *Fr.* bon; y′, *Fr.* Compiègne

STRESS MARKS:
Primary stress: ′
in·cite′ (ĭn-sīt′)
Secondary stress: ′
in′sight′ (ĭn′sīt′)

English *handiwork*, Old English *handgeweorc* : HAND + *geweorc*, work : *ge-*, collective prefix + *weorc*, WORK.]

hand·ker·chief (hăng'kər-chĭf) *n.* **1.** A small square of cotton, linen, or silk carried by a person for use in wiping the nose, mouth, or the like. **2.** A slightly larger piece of cloth worn as a decorative article; a kerchief; a scarf. [HAND + KERCHIEF.]

hand-knit (hănd'nĭt') *adj.* Also **hand-knit·ted** (-nĭt'ĭd). Knit by hand.
~*tr.v.* **hand-knitted, -knitting, -knits.** To knit by hand.

han·dle (hănd'l) *v.* **-dled, -dling, -dles.** —*tr.* **1.** To touch, lift, or turn with the hands. **2.** To operate with the hands; manipulate. **3.** To specialize in or have responsibility for; take charge of: *My colleague handles financial matters.* **4.** To deal with; process: *handle an application.* **5.** To manage, administer to, or represent: *handle a boxer.* **6.** To behave or act toward; treat. **7.** To confront or cope with, especially: **a.** To control or command: *handle a crowd.* **b.** To discuss or approach: *handle a problem.* —*intr.* To respond or react to control or manipulation; function under operation: *This bicycle handles well at high speed.*
~*n.* **1.** A part by means of which something such as a tool, object, or door is held or manipulated with the hand. **2.** An opportunity that may serve as an advantage for someone; a means; an opening. **3.** *Slang.* A person's name or title. —**fly off the handle.** *Informal.* To fly into a rage; become very angry suddenly. [Old English *handle* (noun), *handlian* (verb), from HAND.]
Usage: *handle, manipulate, wield, ply.* These verbs mean to use, operate, or manage things or, less often, persons. *Handle* can refer to management or control of tools, implements, persons, or nonphysical things such as problems and situations. In every case, unless it is qualified by an adverb, the term suggests competence in gaining an end or objective. *Manipulate* connotes skillful or artful management of physical things such as tools or instruments or of persons or personal affairs, in which case it often implies use of improper influence or fraud in gaining an end. *Wield* implies that one has full command of what is used, principally tools and implements, weapons, means of expression such as the pen, or intangibles such as authority and influence. The term likewise suggests that the means are used effectively. *Ply* refers principally to use of tools and to the regular and diligent pursuit of a given trade.

han·dle·bar (hănd'l-bär') *n.* *Usually* **handlebars.** A curved metal steering bar, as on a bicycle.

handlebar mustache *n.* A thick mustache that curls upward at the side of the lips.

han·dler (hănd'lər) *n.* **1.** One that handles. **2. a.** A person who trains or exhibits an animal, such as a dog. **b.** A person who acts as the trainer or second of a boxer.

han·dling (hănd'lĭng) *n.* **1.** A touching, feeling, or manipulating with the hands. **2.** The way in which a matter, especially a delicate one, is taken care of or treated; management. **3.** The way in which a subject is approached or discussed. **4.** The process of packing and distributing merchandise. **5.** *Law.* The act of receiving or selling stolen property.

hand·made (hănd'mād') *adj.* Made or prepared by hand rather than by machine.

hand·maid (hănd'mād') *n.* A female servant or attendant; a personal maid.

hand·maid·en (hănd'mād'n) *n.* **1.** A handmaid. **2.** That which serves or assists a higher cause: *Language is the handmaiden of thought.*

hand-me-down (hănd'mē-doun') *adj.* **1.** Handed down to one person after being used and discarded by another; secondhand. **2.** Of inferior quality; shabby.
~*n.* Something passed on from one person to another; especially, an item of clothing.

hand-off (hănd'ôf', -ŏf') *n.* A football play in which one player hands the ball to another.

hand organ *n.* A barrel organ operated by turning a crank.

hand out *tr.v.* To distribute (food, samples, or leaflets, for example); disseminate; proffer.

hand·out (hănd'out') *n.* **1.** Food, clothing, or money donated to a beggar or destitute person. **2.** A folder or leaflet distributed, especially as an accompaniment to a talk or lecture. **3.** A prepared news or publicity release.

hand-pick (hănd'pĭk') *tr.v.* **-picked, -picking, -picks. 1.** To gather or pick by hand. **2.** To select carefully, especially for a particular task or purpose.

hand·rail (hănd'rāl') *n.* A rail, as along a staircase, to be grasped with the hand for support.

hand·saw (hănd'sô') *n.* A saw that can be used with one hand.

hand's-breadth, hand's breadth. Variants of handbreadth.

hand·sel, han·sel (hăn'səl) *n. Chiefly British.* A gift to express good wishes at the beginning of a new year or enterprise.
~*tr.v.* **handseled** or **handselled, -seling** or **-selling, -sels.** *Chiefly British.* **1.** To give a handsel to. **2.** To inaugurate or initiate. [Middle English *hanselle*, Old English *handselen*, a giving into someone's hands, from Old Norse *handsal*, a giving of the hand : HAND + *sal*, a giving, payment.]

hand·set (hănd'sĕt') *n.* A portable telephone transmitter and receiver module.

hand·shake (hănd'shāk') *n.* **1.** The grasping of hands by two people as a gesture of greeting, leave-taking, congratulation, agreement, or the like. **2.** *Computer Science.* A dialogue between parts of a com-

puter system in which information is exchanged regarding the transmission and reception of data.

hands-off (hăndz'ôf', -ŏf') *adj.* Designating, pertaining to, or characterized by a policy of nonintervention.

hand·some (hăn'səm) *adj.* **1.** Having an attractive, pleasing, and dignified appearance: *a handsome man.* **2.** Impressively well made: *a handsome building.* **3. a.** Generous or liberal: *a handsome offer.* **b.** Considerable; plentiful: *a handsome reward.* **4.** Gracious; magnanimous: *a handsome gesture.* **5.** Marked by or requiring great skill or accomplishment: *a handsome piece of work.* —See Synonyms at **beautiful.** [Middle English *handsom,* easy to handle, handy : HAND + -SOME.] —**hand·some·ly** *adv.* —**hand·some·ness** *n.*

hands-on (hăndz'ŏn') *adj.* Of, pertaining to, or providing direct experience, especially of the manual operation of a computer system.

hand·spike (hănd'spīk') *n.* A heavy bar used as a lever.

hand·spring (hănd'sprĭng') *n.* A gymnastic feat in which the body is flipped completely forward or backward from an upright position, landing first on the hands, then on the feet.

hand·stand (hănd'stănd') *n.* The act of balancing on the hands with one's feet in the air.

hand-to-hand (hănd'tə-hănd') *adj.* At close quarters. —**hand-to-hand** *adv.*

hand-to-mouth (hănd'tə-mouth') *adj.* Characterized by constant financial difficulties. —**hand-to-mouth** *adv.*

hand-wash (hănd'wŏsh', -wôsh') *tr.v.* **-washed, -washing, -washes.** To wash (clothing or fabrics) by hand rather than in a machine.

hand·work (hănd'wûrk') *n.* Work done by hand rather than machine.

hand·writ·ing (hănd'rī'tĭng) *n.* **1.** Writing done with the hand rather than typed or printed. **2.** The writing characteristic of a particular person.

hand·writ·ten (hănd'rĭt'n) *adj.* Written by hand: *a handwritten invitation.*

hand·y (hăn'dē) *adj.* **-ier, -iest. 1.** Manually adroit. **2.** Readily accessible. **3.** Conveniently situated. **4.** Easy to use or handle. **5.** Supplying a need; useful: *The extra cash will be handy.* —See Synonyms at **dexterous.** [From HAND.]

Han·dy (hăn'dē), **William Christopher,** known as "W.C. Handy" (1873–1958). U.S. jazz composer and publisher. He wrote *St. Louis Blues* (1914).

hand·y·man (hăn'dē-măn') *n., pl.* **-men** (-mĕn'). **1.** A do-it-yourself enthusiast. **2.** One who does odd jobs or various small tasks; especially, one employed to do them.

hang (hăng) *v.* **hung** (hŭng) *or* **hanged** (for transitive sense 3 and intransitive sense 2), **hanging, hangs.** —*tr.* **1.** To fasten from above with no support from below; suspend. **2.** To suspend or fasten so as to allow free movement at or about the point of suspension: *hang a door.* **3.** To execute by suspending by the neck. **4.** To fix or attach at an appropriate angle: *hang a scythe to its handle.* **5.** To alter the hem of (a garment) so as to fall evenly at an appropriate height. **6.** To furnish, decorate, or appoint by suspending objects around or about: *hang a room with tapestries.* **7.** To hold or incline downward; let droop: *hang one's head in sorrow.* **8.** To attach to a wall: *hang wallpaper.* **9.** To deadlock (a jury) by failing to render a unanimous verdict. **10.** To leave (venison or other game) exposed to the air for some time to improve its flavor. **11. a.** To exhibit (pictures, as paintings) in an art gallery or museum. **b.** To exhibit the work of (a painter) in an art gallery or museum. **12.** *Baseball.* To throw (a pitch) so that it fails to break. —*intr.* **1.** To be attached from above with no support from below. **2.** To suffer death by hanging. **3. a.** To remain suspended or poised over a place or object; hover. **b.** To be suspended from a pivot and able to move freely. **4.** To attach oneself as an impediment or dependent; cling. Usually used with *on.* **5.** To incline downward; droop. **6.** To depend: *Everything hangs on your decision.* **7.** To pay strict or devoted attention: *hang on every word.* **8.** To remain unresolved or uncertain: *hang in the balance.* **9.** To fit or drape from the body in loose lines: *Her dress hangs awkwardly.* **10.** To be imminent; loom: *the threat hanging over us.* **11.** To be burdensome: *Time hung heavily on her hands.* —**hang around** (or **about**). *Informal.* **1.** To spend time in idleness; loiter. **2.** To remain; wait. —**hang back. 1.** To lag. **2.** To be averse; hold back. —**hang fire. 1.** To be slow in firing, as a gun. **2.** To delay. —**hang in.** *Informal.* To persevere. —**hang loose.** *Slang.* To remain calm; relax. —**hang on. 1.** To continue persistently or resolutely; persevere. **2.** To wait a while; be patient. **3.** To keep a telephone connection open; hold the line. —**hang one on. 1.** To strike (a person). **2.** *Slang.* To become drunk. —**hang together. 1.** To stand united; stick together. **2.** To constitute a coherent totality. —**hang tough.** *Informal.* To remain firmly resolved.
~*n.* **1.** The way in which something hangs. **2.** A downward inclination or slope. —**get the hang of.** *Informal.* **1.** To come to understand a process, argument, or the like. **2.** To develop the correct technique for doing something. —**not give** (or **care**) **a hang.** To be totally unconcerned or indifferent. [Hang, hung, hung; partly Middle English *hon, hong, hongen,* Old English *hōn* (transitive verb), to hang, suspend, *heng, hangen;* partly Middle English *hangen, hong, hanged,* Old English *hangian* (transitive and intransitive verb), to hang, be hung, suspend, *hangode, hanged;* partly Middle English *hingen,* from Old Norse *hanga* (transitive verb), to cause to hang.]
Usage: The usual past tense and past participle form of this

verb is *hung,* but in the context of capital punishment the form *hanged* is preferred: *The prisoner was hanged at six o'clock.* The use of *hung* in such a context would generally be considered nonstandard.

han·gar (hăng'ər) *n.* A large structure for housing, constructing, or maintaining aircraft. [French, from Old French, probably from Medieval Latin *angarium*†, shed for shoeing horses.]

hang·bird (hăng'bûrd') *n.* A bird, such as an oriole, that builds a hanging nest. Also called "hangnest."

Hangchow, Hang-chou. See **Hangzhou.**

hang·dog (hăng'dôg', -dŏg') *adj.* **1.** Shamefaced or guilty. **2.** Downcast; intimidated. —*n.* A sneaky or shamefaced person. [Originally, despicable person who was fit only to hang a dog.]

hang·er (hăng'ər) *n.* **1.** One that hangs. **2.** A contrivance to which something hangs or by which something is hung. **3.** A device around which a garment is draped for hanging from a hook or rod. **4.** A loop or strap by which something is hung. **5.** A bracket on a motor vehicle's spring shackle designed to hold it to the chassis. **6.** A decorative strip of cloth hung on a garment or wall.

hang·er-on (hăng'ər-ŏn', -ôn') *n., pl.* **hangers-on** (hăng'ərz-). A person who attaches himself to another, as from hope of gain.

hang-glide (hăng'glīd') *intr.v.* **-glided, -gliding, -glides.** To fly by means of a hang glider. —**hang-glid·ing** *n.*

hang glider *n.* **1.** A device resembling a kite from which a harnessed rider hangs while gliding from a height. **2.** The pilot of such a device.

hang·ing (hăng'ĭng) *n.* **1.** An act of killing by putting a noose around the victim's neck and allowing him to drop. **2.** A drapery hung over a wall or window. —*adj.* **1.** Situated on a sharp declivity. **2.** Projecting downward; overhanging. **3.** Suited for holding something that hangs. **4. a.** Susceptible to or meriting death by hanging: *a hanging crime.* **b.** Disposed to inflict the sentence of death by hanging: *a hanging judge.*

hanging indention *n.* The indention of every line in a paragraph except the first.

hanging valley *n.* A tributary valley that joins a main valley where the latter has been deepened, usually by glacial erosion. There is usually a steep fall from the floor of the tributary valley to that of the main valley.

hanging wall *n.* The wall of rock on the upper side of an inclined fault plane or mineral vein. Compare **footwall.**

hang·man (hăng'mən) *n., pl.* **-men** (-mĭn). One employed to execute condemned prisoners by hanging.

hang·nail (hăng'nāl') *n.* A small piece of dead skin at the side or the base of a fingernail that is partly detached from the rest of the skin. [By folk etymology from AGNAIL.]

hang out *intr.v.* **1.** To project downward. **2.** *Informal.* To reside or spend time. —*tr.v.* **1.** To spread out (washing, for example) to dry. **2.** To suspend for public display: *hang out a sign.* —**let it all hang out.** *Slang.* To be entirely uninhibited.

hang·out (hăng'out') *n. Informal.* A frequently visited place.

hang·o·ver (hăng'ō'vər) *n.* **1.** Unpleasant physical effects following the heavy consumption of alcohol; especially, a severe headache. **2.** A vestige; a holdover: *hangovers from prewar legislation.*

hang up *tr.v.* **1.** To replace (a telephone receiver) on its cradle. **2.** To retard, impede, or interrupt: *hang up a project.* **3.** To halt the movement or action of. **4.** *Informal.* To be a source of anxiety or preoccupation for: *Don't let it hang you up.* See **hung up.** —*intr.v.* **1.** To end a telephone conversation by replacing the receiver. **2.** To become halted or snagged. —**be hung up on.** *Informal.* To be obsessed or fixated by.

hang-up, hang·up (hăng'ŭp') *n. Informal.* **1. a.** A source of irritation or inhibition. **b.** An inhibition or fixation. **2.** An obstacle; an inconvenience.

Hang·zhou (häng'jō'). Formerly **Hang-chow, Hang-chou** (hăng'chou', häng'jō'). City in eastern China, the capital of Zhejiang province, at the head of Hangzhou Bay, an inlet of the East China Sea. Before being destroyed by Taiping rebels in 1861, it was renowned for its architecture. It is now a modern industrial city, important for its silk manufacture.

hank (hăngk) *n.* **1.** A coil or loop. **2.** *Nautical.* A ring on a stay attached to the head of a jib or staysail. **3.** A looped bundle, as of yarn. **4.** A length of yarn (768 meters; 840 yards) or fabric (512 meters; 560 yards). [Middle English, from Scandinavian; akin to Old Norse *hönk*†, hank, skein.]

han·ker (hăng'kər) *intr.v.* **-kered, -kering, -kers.** To have a longing; crave. Often followed by *after* or *for.* —See Synonyms at **yearn.** [Akin to dialectal *hank,* probably from Dutch (dialectal) *hankeren.*] —**han·ker·er** *n.*

han·ky, han·kie (hăng'kē) *n., pl.* **hankies.** *Informal.* A handkerchief (sense 1).

han·ky-pan·ky (hăng'kē-păng'kē) *n. Informal.* **1.** Devious or mischievous activity. **2.** Foolish talk or action. [Fanciful coinage, influenced by HOCUS-POCUS.]

Han·ni·bal (hăn'ə-bəl) (247–183 B.C.). Carthaginian soldier and statesman, the son of Hamilcar Barca. Hannibal crossed the Alps in 218 with about 35,000 men and 37 elephants and routed Roman armies at Trasimene and Cannae. He lacked the resources to attack Rome itself and was recalled to Africa in 203 to defend Carthage against an invasion by Scipio Africanus. Hannibal was defeated at Zama (202).

Han·no (hăn'ō), known as "the Great" (*fl.* 3rd century B.C.). Cartha-

ginian political leader. During the Second Punic War (218–201), he was opposed to Hamilcar Barca's and Hannibal's policy of foreign conquest. He eroded Hannibal's homeland support and after Hannibal's defeat negotiated a peace treaty with the Romans.

Han·no·ver (hä-nō'vər). *English* **Han·o·ver** (hăn'ō'vər). Capital city of Lower Saxony in northern West Germany, on the Leine River. It is an industrial and commercial center and the site of an important annual industrial fair.

Ha·noi (hä-noi', hă-). Capital of Vietnam, on the right bank of the Song Hong (Red River), in northern Vietnam. It is the country's major industrial city.

Han·o·ver (hăn'ō'vər). **1.** The family name of an electoral house of Germany (1692–1815). **2.** The family name of the royal family of Britain and Ireland (1714–1901).

Han·o·ve·ri·an (hăn'ō-vîr'ē-ən) *adj.* Of or pertaining to the city of Hannover or the electoral house or royal family of Hanover. —*n.* A heavy, strong horse of a breed developed by crossing German horses with Thoroughbreds.

Han·sard (hăn'sərd) *n. British & Canadian.* **1.** The official verbatim report of the proceedings and debates of Parliament. **2.** A similar report of the proceedings of various other legislative bodies. [After its first printer, Luke *Hansard* (1752–1828).]

hanse (hăns) *n.* **1. a.** A medieval merchant guild or trade association. **b.** The entrance fee to such a guild. **2. Hanse.** A town belonging to the Hanseatic League. Also called "Hanse town." **3. Hanse.** *Rare.* The Hanseatic League. [Middle English *hans,* from Old French *hanse,* from Middle Low German *hanse,* from Old High German *hansa,* troop, company, from Germanic *khansō* (unattested).] —**han·se·at·ic** (hăn'sē-ăt'ĭk) *adj.*

Han·se·at·ic League (hăn'sē-ăt'ĭk). A protective and commercial association of free towns in northern Germany and neighboring areas, formally organized in 1358 and dissolved in the 17th century.

hansel. Variant of **handsel.**

Han·sen's disease (hăn'sənz) *n.* **Leprosy** (*see*). [After G.H.A. *Hansen* (1841–1912), Norwegian physician who discovered the bacillus that causes leprosy.]

han·som (hăn'səm) *n.* A two-wheeled covered carriage with the driver's seat above and behind. Also called "hansom cab." [After Joseph A. *Hansom* (1803–82), English architect who designed it.]

Hants. See **Hampshire.**

Hanukah, Hanukkah. Variants of **Chanukah.**

han·u·man (hŭn'ə-măn', hä'nə-) *n., pl.* **-mans.** A monkey, *Presbytis entellus,* of southern Asia, having bristly hairs on the crown and the sides of the face. [Hindi, from Sanskrit *hanumant,* "having jaws," from *hanu,* jaw.]

hao. Variant of **chao.** [Vietnamese.]

hap (hăp) *n. Archaic.* **1.** Fortune; chance. **2.** A happening; an occurrence. —*intr.v.* **happed, happing, haps.** *Archaic.* To happen. [Middle English, from Old Norse *happ,* good luck, chance.]

ha·pax le·go·me·non (hā'păks' lə-gŏm'ə-nŏn') *n., pl.* **hapax legomena** (-ə-nə). A word or form that occurs only once in the recorded corpus of a given language. Often shortened to "hapax." [Greek, "a thing said only once."]

ha'penny. Variant of **halfpenny.**

hap·haz·ard (hăp-hăz'ərd) *adj.* **1.** Dependent upon or characterized by mere chance. **2.** Slipshod; untidy. —See Synonyms at **chance.** —*n.* Mere chance; fortuity. —*adv.* Casually; by chance. [HAP + HAZARD.] —**hap·haz·ard·ly** *adv.* —**hap·haz·ard·ness** *n.*

Haph·ta·rah, Haf·ta·rah (häf'tə-rä', häf-tôr'ə) *n., pl.* **-taroth** (-tə-rōt', -rōs', -tôr'ōt', -ōs'). *Judaism.* A reading selected from the Prophets, read in the synagogue service on the Sabbath. [Mishnaic Hebrew *haphṭārāh,* "conclusion," from *haphṭēr,* to conclude, discard, dismiss, from Hebrew *pāṭar,* separated, discharged.]

hap·less (hăp'lĭs) *adj.* Luckless; unfortunate.

haplite. Variant of **aplite.**

hap·log·ra·phy (hăp-lŏg'rə-fē) *n.* The shortening of the spelling of a word by the omission of a letter or syllable that should be repeated, as the spelling *deteriate* for *deteriorate.* [Greek *haplos,* single, simple (see **haploid**) + -GRAPHY.]

hap·loid (hăp'loid') *adj. Genetics.* Having the number of chromosomes present in the normal germ cell equal to half the number in the normal somatic cell. Compare **diploid.** —*n.* A haploid individual or cell. [Greek *haploeidēs,* single : *haplo(u)s,* single, simple : *ha-,* one + *-plo(u)s,* -fold + -OID.]

hap·loi·dy (hăp'loi'dē) *n. Genetics.* The state or condition of being haploid.

hap·lol·o·gy (hăp-lŏl'ə-jē) *n.* The shortening of a word by the omission of a sound or syllable in its pronunciation. [Greek *haplos,* single, simple (see **haploid**) + -LOGY.]

hap·lont (hăp'lŏnt') *n. Biology.* A haploid organism representing the vegetative phase of the life cycle of certain algae in which only the zygote is diploid. [HAPL(OID) + -ONT.]

hap·lo·sis (hăp-lō'sĭs) *n. Genetics.* Reduction of the diploid number of chromosomes by one half to the haploid number by meiosis. [New Latin : Greek *haplos,* single, simple (see **haploid**) + -OSIS.]

hap·ly (hăp'lē) *adv. Archaic.* **1.** By chance or accident. **2.** Perhaps.

ha'porth (hā'pərth) *n. British Informal.* A creature. Used in phrases like *you daft ha'porth.* [From *halfpennyworth.*]

hap·pen (hăp'ən) *intr.v.* **-pened, -pening, -pens.** **1.** To come to pass; come into being; take place. **2.** To befall or affect one. Used with *to: What happened to you?* **3. a.** To be the case by chance: *It*

hang glider *The hang glider was originally called a Rogallo wing, after its designer, who worked for the National Aeronautics and Space Administration (NASA). The pilot controls the glider with his own weight, moving himself against the fixed trapeze he holds to make the wing dive, climb, or turn.*

happens that I used to live out there. **b.** To chance: *She happened to be in.* **4.** To come upon someone or something by chance. Used with *on* or *upon.* **—happen by.** To appear by chance; turn up. [Middle English *happenen,* from HAP.]

Synonyms: *befall, betide, chance, occur, supervene.*

hap·pen·ing (hăp′ə-nĭng) *n.* **1.** An event. **2.** An improvised spectacle or performance. —See Synonyms at **occurrence.**

hap·pen·stance (hăp′ən-stăns′) *n.* Also **hap·pen·chance** (-chăns′, -chäns′). A chance circumstance. [HAPPEN + (CIRCUM)STANCE.]

hap·py (hăp′ē) *adj.* **-pier, -piest. 1.** Characterized by good luck; fortunate. **2. a.** Having, taking, or demonstrating pleasure or satisfaction; glad. **b.** Giving or causing pleasure or satisfaction: *a happy day.* **3.** Well-adapted; appropriate; felicitous: *a happy turn of phrase.* **4. a.** Characterized by a spontaneous or obsessive inclination to use something. Used in combination: *trigger-happy.* **b.** Enthusiastic about or involved with to a disproportionate degree. Used in combination: *money-happy.* —See Synonyms at **fit, glad.** [Middle English, from HAP.] **—hap·pi·ly** *adv.* **—hap·pi·ness** *n.*

hap·py-go-luck·y (hăp′ē-gō-lŭk′ē) *adj.* Taking things easily; trusting to luck; carefree.

happy hour *n.* A period of time, usually in the early evening, when drinks are served at reduced prices in bars or hotels.

happy hunting ground *n.* **1.** *Sometimes* **happy hunting grounds.** In North American Indian mythology, heaven or paradise. **2.** *Informal.* Any place or situation offering a plentiful supply of a particularly sought-after item or commodity: *Junk shops are a happy hunting ground for collectors of antiques.*

Haps·burg or **Habs·burg** (hăps′bûrg′, häps′bo͝org′). The dominant royal house in Europe from the late Middle Ages until the 20th century. The family name came from the castle of Hapsburg, built (1028) on the Aar River, Switzerland, by Werner I, bishop of Strasbourg. The Hapsburgs reached the height of their power in the 16th century under Charles V when Spain, with her European and American territories, was added to the family's possessions, creating a vast and unwieldy domain. Charles abdicated in 1558, dividing his empire between the two Hapsburg lines of Spain and Austria. The Spanish branch ceased to rule after 1700. In the 19th century the Napoleonic wars and Prussian and Italian nationalism weakened the Hapsburgs' grip on central Europe. The Hapsburg-ruled Austro-Hungarian Empire finally disintegrated after World War I.

hap·ten (hăp′tĕn′) *n.* Also **hap·tene** (-tēn′). *Biology.* An antigen that is incomplete and cannot by itself cause antibody formation but can neutralize specific antibodies when combined with one of the body's proteins. [German *Hapten* : Greek *haptein,* to fasten + -ENE.]

hap·ter·on (hăp′tə-rŏn′) *n., pl.* **-tera** (-tər-ə). The tissue in certain algae, especially the large seaweeds, that serves to attach the plant to a substrate. [From Greek *haptein,* to fasten.]

hap·tic (hăp′tĭk) *adj.* Of or pertaining to the sense of touch. [Greek *haptikos,* able to touch, from *haptein,* to touch, fasten.]

hap·to·nas·ty (hăp′tə-năs′tē) *n.* Movement of a plant part in response to touch, seen particularly in the leaves of insectivorous plants. [Greek *haptein,* to touch + -NASTY.]

hap·tot·ro·pism (hăp-tŏt′rə-pĭz′əm) *n. Biology.* **Thigmotropism** *(see).* [Greek *haptein,* to touch + TROPISM.]

ha·ra-ki·ri (hăr′ə-kîr′ē) *n.* Ritual suicide by disembowelment as formerly practiced by the Japanese upper classes when disgraced or under sentence of death, and still occasionally practiced today. Also called "seppuku." [Japanese.]

ha·rangue (hə-răng′) *n.* **1.** A long, pompous speech, especially one delivered before a gathering. **2.** A speech characterized by strong feeling or vehement expression; a tirade.

~v. **harangued, -ranguing, -rangued.** *—tr.* To deliver a harangue to. *—intr.* To deliver a harangue. [Middle English *arang,* from Old French *arenge, harangue,* from Medieval Latin *harenga,* perhaps from Germanic.] **—ha·rangu·er** *n.*

Ha·rap·pa (hə-răp′ə). Archaeological site of the Indus Valley civilization (*c.* 2500–1500 B.C.) in the Punjab, Pakistan. It has the remains of a well-laid-out city.

Ha·ra·re (hə-rä′rā). Formerly **Salis·bur·y** (sôlz′bĕr′ē, -brē). Capital and largest city of Zimbabwe, situated on the Mashonaland plateau in the northeast of the country. Founded in 1890, it has two cathedrals and a university (1970). Harare is an important tobacco-marketing center, and its manufactured products include processed food and tobacco, textiles and clothing, steel, chemicals, and furniture.

har·ass (hăr′əs, hə-răs′) *tr.v.* **-assed, -assing, -asses. 1.** To disturb or irritate persistently. **2.** To wear out; exhaust. **3.** To enervate (an enemy) by repeated attacks or raids. [French *harasser,* from Old French *harer,* to set a dog on, from *hare,* cry used to set a dog on, perhaps from Old High German *harên,* to call.] **—har·ass·er** *n.* **—har·ass·ment** *n.*

Synonyms: *badger, bait, hound, pester, plague, torment.*

Har·bin (här′bĭn). Also **Ha-erh-pin** (hä′ĕr′bĭn′). *Russian* **Khar·bin** (här-bĭn′, kär-). Capital of Heilongjiang province, northeastern China. Situated on the Songhua Jiang (Sungari River), it grew with the granting of a trade concession to Russia (1896). An important port and railroad junction, it is part of the Manchurian industrial region.

har·bin·ger (här′bĭn-jər) *n.* One that signals an approach; a forerunner: *"in a few minutes would appear the train's harbinger . . . a puff of white smoke"* (Vladimir Nabokov).

~tr.v. **harbingered, -gering, -gers.** To signal the approach of; presage. [Middle English *harbergere,* from Norman French and Old French, from *herbergier,* to provide lodging for, from *herberge,* lodging, from Old Saxon *heriberga,* lodging : *heri,* army + *berg-* (unattested), to protect.]

har·bor (här′bər) *n.* Also *chiefly British* **har·bour.** *Abbr.* **h., H. 1.** A sheltered part of a body of water deep enough to provide anchorage for ships; a port. **2.** Any protected place; a shelter; a refuge.

~v. **harbored, -boring, -bors.** Also *chiefly British* **har·bour, -boured, -bouring, -bours.** *—tr.* **1.** To give shelter to; protect; keep. **2.** To entertain or nourish (a thought or feeling). *—intr.* To shelter in or as if in a harbor. [Middle English *herberge, herber,* late Old English *herebeorg.* See **harbinger.**] **—har·bor·er** *n.*

har·bor·age (här′bər-ĭj) *n.* **1.** Shelter and anchorage for ships. **2.** Shelter; refuge. **3.** A place of shelter.

har·bor·mas·ter (här′bər-măs′tər, -mä′stər) *n.* An officer who oversees and enforces the regulations of a harbor.

harbor seal *n.* A hair seal, *Phoca vitulina,* of coastal waters of the Northern Hemisphere, having a spotted coat.

hard (härd) *adj.* **harder, hardest.** *Abbr.* **h., H. 1.** Resistant to pressure; not readily penetrated; firm; rigid. **2.** Physically toughened; rugged: *hard feet.* **3.** Strong-minded; not influenced by emotional considerations. **4.** Rigorous; stringent; demanding. **5.** Mentally and emotionally toughened; unfeeling. **6.** Characterized by an unwillingness to compromise or negotiate. **7.** Intense; forceful. **8.** Keen; penetrating. **9.** Assiduous; diligent; energetic: *a hard worker.* **10.** Difficult to accomplish, finish, or continue; strenuous; arduous. **11.** Difficult to understand, express, or convey; abstruse. **12.** Difficult to endure. **13.** Cruel; oppressive; unjust. **14.** Bitter; rancorous; harsh: *hard feelings.* **15.** Unpleasant because too bright, loud, or harsh: *a hard voice.* **16.** Uncompromisingly adhering to the principles of a specified political alignment: *on the hard left of the party.* **17.** Metallic, as opposed to paper. Said of money: *hard money.* **18. a.** Backed by bullion and having a stable exchange rate. Said of a currency. **b.** Being legal tender: *hard cash.* **19.** Demonstrably true: *hard facts.* **20.** Durable: *hard merchandise.* **21.** Consisting of rigid boards, usually covered with cloth, leather, or the like. Said of the binding of a book. **22.** Having a high alcoholic content; intoxicating. **23.** Containing dissolved substances, as salts, that interfere with the lathering action of soap. Said of water. **24.** *Phonetics.* **a.** Pronounced as a stop, as the *c* in *cake* and the *g* in *log.* **b.** Voiceless. Said of consonants. **c.** Not palatalized. Said of consonants in Slavic languages. **25.** *Physics.* Of relatively high energy; penetrating: *hard x-rays.* **26.** High in gluten content: *hard wheat.* **27.** Physically addictive: *hard drugs.* **—be hard on. 1.** To be unpleasant and difficult for. **2.** To deal with severely; be harsh with. **—hard up.** *Informal.* In need; poor.

~adv. **1.** Energetically; vigorously: *drink hard.* **2.** Intently; earnestly; persistently: *think hard.* **3.** With intensity or force. **4.** With difficulty; strenuously: *a fight hard won.* **5.** Close; near. Used with *by* or *upon.* **6.** Reluctantly: *die hard.* **7.** Toward or into a solid condition: *The cement will set hard within a day.* **8. a.** As much as possible: *Turn hard right.* **b.** *Nautical.* Completely; fully: *hard alee.* **—be hard put.** To have a good deal of difficulty in doing. **—go hard with.** To cause pain or distress to; gall: *This news will go hard with him.* **—hard at it.** Working busily. **—hard put.** Only just able: *She is hard put to make ends meet.*

~n. **1.** *British Slang.* Hard labor. **2.** *British.* A firm beach or foreshore. [Middle English *hard,* Old English *hard, heard.*]

Synonyms: *arduous, difficult, intricate, troublesome.*

hard-and-fast (härd′ən-făst′, -fäst′) *adj.* Rigidly applied; inflexible; allowing of no exceptions: *a hard-and-fast rule.*

hard·back (härd′băk′) *adj.* Having a binding or cover of rigid boards, usually covered with cloth, leather, or the like. Said of books. Also "hardbound," "hardcover."

~n. A hardback book.

hard·bake (härd′bāk′) *n. British.* Almond toffee.

hard·ball (härd′bôl′) *n.* **1.** Baseball. **2.** *Informal.* The use of any means, however ruthless, to attain an objective.

hard-bit·ten (härd′bĭt′n) *adj.* Toughened by experience; unsentimental.

hard·board (härd′bôrd′, -bōrd′) *n.* Thin wooden board manufactured from compressed wood pulp and sawdust.

hard-boiled (härd′boild′) *adj.* **1.** Cooked by boiling to a solid consistency. Said of an egg. **2.** *Informal.* **a.** Callous; unfeeling. **b.** Having no illusions; unromantic; cynical.

hard case *n.* **1.** A tough, unsentimental person. **2.** *British Informal.* A person who is persistently insolent or difficult to control.

hard cheese *n. British Informal.* Bad luck. Used interjectionally to express sympathy, sometimes ironically, at another's misfortune.

hard cider *n.* Fermented cider. Compare **sweet cider.**

hard coal *n.* **Anthracite** *(see).*

hard copy *n.* Material, as a computer printout, that may be read by the human eye, as distinguished from electronically stored data.

hard core *n.* **1.** The durable and resistant central part of a given entity; especially, the most intractable or die-hard nucleus of a group or organization: *the hard core of the secession movement.* **2.** A material used in constructing foundations for buildings, roads, and the like, consisting of broken bricks, stones, and other hard debris. **3.** *Informal.* Hard-core pornography.

hard-core, hard·core (härd′kôr′, -kōr′) *adj.* **1.** Stubbornly resistant or inveterate: *the hard-core criminal element.* **2.** Held to constitute an intractable social problem: *hard-core poverty.* **3.** Sexually very explicit and often dealing with sexual practices regarded as deviant: *hard-core pornography.*

hard court *n.* A tennis court with a hard surface, such as asphalt or concrete, rather than grass.

hard·cov·er (härd′kŭv′ər) *n. & adj.* **Hardback** (see).

Har·de·ca·nute (här′də-kə-nōōt′, -nyōōt′) (*c.* 1019–42). King of England (1040–42) and of Denmark (1035–42); the legitimate son of King Canute. His English throne was seized by Canute's illegitimate son, Harold I Harefoot. In 1040 Hardecanute claimed his throne after the usurper died.

hard·edge (härd′ĕj′) *n.* A style of abstract painting characterized by the sharp delineation of brightly colored geometric forms. —**hard·edge** *adj.*

hard·en (härd′n) *v.* **-ened, -ening, -ens.** —*tr.* **1.** To make firm or firmer; make solid or hard. **2.** To toughen mentally or physically; make rugged; inure. **3.** To make unfeeling or emotionally barren. **4.** To strengthen: *It hardened their opposition to the plan.* —*intr.* **1.** To become hard or hardened; set; fix; firm; freeze. **2.** *Economics.* **a.** To rise. Used of prices. **b.** To become stable. **3.** To become inured: *"But poor boys either harden early or are destroyed"* (T.H. White). —**harden off. 1.** To make (a cultivated plant) able to withstand outdoor conditions by gradually increasing exposure to a cold atmosphere. **2.** To become accustomed to outdoor conditions in this way. Used of plants. [Middle English, from HARD.]

hard·en·er (härd′n-ər) *n.* **1.** One that hardens. **2.** A substance added to varnish or paint to give a harder surface or finish. **3.** A substance added to certain glues to cause or hasten setting.

hard·en·ing (härd′n-ĭng) *n.* **1.** The act or process of becoming hard or harder. **2.** Something that hardens, such as a substance added to iron to yield steel.

hardening of the arteries *n.* **Arteriosclerosis** (see).

hard-fea·tured (härd′fē′chərd) *adj.* Having sharp or harsh features. Also *archaic* "hard-favored."

hard-fist·ed (härd′fĭs′tĭd) *adj.* Tightfisted; stingy; niggardly. —**hard-fist·ed·ness** *n.*

hard·hack (härd′hăk′) *n.* A woody plant, *Spiraea tomentosa,* of eastern North America, having leaves with rusty down on the undersides and spirelike clusters of small, rose-pink flowers. Also called "steeplebush." [HARD + HACK (cut).]

hard-hand·ed (härd′hăn′dĭd) *adj.* **1.** Having hands calloused or hardened by work. **2.** Heavy-handed; oppressive; tyrannical. —**hard-hand·ed·ness** *n.*

hard hat *n.* **1.** A lightweight protective helmet, usually of metal or reinforced plastic, worn by construction workers. **2.** *Informal.* A construction worker. **3.** *Informal.* A person with conservative or reactionary views; an ultraconservative. **4.** *Slang.* An extremely patriotic person.

hard-hat (härd′hăt′) *adj.* **1.** Designating an area on a building site where hard hats must be worn. **2.** Characterized by conservative or reactionary views. **3.** *Slang.* Extremely conservative.

hard·head (härd′hĕd′) *n., pl.* **-heads** or collectively **hardhead** (for sense 3). **1.** A shrewd and tough person. **2.** A stubborn, unmovable person. **3.** Any of several fishes having a bony head, especially a common croaker, *Micropogon undulatus,* of Atlantic waters.

hard·head·ed (härd′hĕd′ĭd) *adj.* **1.** Realistic; concerned with practical matters. **2.** Stubborn; willful. —**hard·head·ed·ly** *adv.* —**hard·head·ed·ness** *n.*

hard·heads (härd′hĕdz′) *n.* Used with a singular verb. A European plant, *Centaurea nigra,* with reddish-purple, thistlelike flowers.

hard·heart·ed (härd′här′tĭd) *adj.* Lacking in feeling, compassion, or sympathy; cold; pitiless. —**hard·heart·ed·ly** *adv.* —**hard·heart·ed·ness** *n.*

hard-hit (härd′hĭt′) *adj.* Badly or adversely affected.

hard-hit·ting (härd′hĭt′ĭng) *adj.* Effective; forceful.

har·di·hood (här′dē-hŏŏd′) *n.* **1.** Boldness and daring; audacity. **2.** Self-assured impudence or insolence.

Har·ding (här′dĭng), **Warren Gamaliel** (1865–1923). 29th U.S. president. An Ohio newspaperman turned politician, he moved from state politics to the U.S. Senate in 1914. Elected president in 1920, he made several misguided appointments that led to a corrupt administration. He died in San Francisco while on a national tour.

hard labor *n.* Compulsory physical labor imposed on convicted criminals.

hard landing *n.* The landing by impact of a spacecraft lacking devices such as retrorockets to slow it down.

hard line *n.* A firm, uncompromising policy, position, or stance.

hard-line (härd′līn′) *adj.* Characterized by a firm, uncompromising position or stance: *a hard-line foreign policy.* —**hard-lin·er** *n.*

hard·ly (härd′lē) *adv.* **1.** Barely; scarcely; just. **2.** To an almost negligible degree; almost not: *He could hardly make himself heard.* **3.** Probably not or almost surely not. **4.** Not in the prevailing circumstances: *I could hardly refuse.* **5.** Harshly. **6.** With difficulty. [Middle English *hardli,* boldly, hardily, Old English *h(e)ardlice* : HARD + -LY.]

Usage: **Hardly** has the force of a negative; therefore it is not used with another negative in standard English: *I could hardly see. I had hardly left.* Constructions such as *I couldn't hardly see* or *without hardly seeing* are often heard in colloquial speech but are not acceptable in formal speech or writing. Following clauses are introduced by *when* or *before: He had hardly left when/before the fire broke out.* The use of *than* or *until* in such constructions is not acceptable in standard English.

hard maple *n.* A tree, the **sugar maple** (see).

hard-mouthed (härd′mouth′, -mouthd′) *adj.* **1.** Not easily controlled by the bit. Said of a horse. **2.** Obstinate.

hard·ness (härd′nĭs) *n. Abbr.* **h., H. 1.** The quality or condition of being hard. **2.** The relative resistance of a mineral to scratching, as measured by the **Mohs scale** (see). **3.** The relative resistance of a metal to denting, scratching, or bending.

hard news *n.* News, as in a newspaper or television report, that deals with formal or serious topics and events.

hard-nosed (härd′nōzd′) *adj. Informal.* Hard-headed; tough-minded; practical: *a hard-nosed politician.*

hard of hearing *adj.* Deaf or slightly deaf.

hard pad *n.* A form of distemper in dogs.

hard palate *n.* The relatively hard, bony front part of the **palate** (see).

hard·pan (härd′păn′) *n.* **1.** A layer of hard subsoil or clay. **2.** Hard, unbroken ground. See **caliche. 3.** A foundation; bedrock.

hard-pressed (härd′prĕst′) *adj.* **1.** Closely pursued. **2.** Constantly troubled by harassment, economic difficulties, or the like. **3.** Barely able: *We'd be hard-pressed to find the time.*

hard rock *n.* A style of rock music characterized by an insistent beat and high volume.

hard rubber *n.* A relatively inelastic rubber made by vulcanization with 30 to 50 percent sulfur and usually some lime or magnesia as a filler.

hards (härdz) *n.* Used with a singular verb. The coarse refuse of flax or similar fiber. [Middle English *herdes, hurdes,* Old English *heordan* (plural).]

hard sauce *n.* A creamy sauce of butter and sugar with rum, brandy, or vanilla flavoring, served chilled with puddings, gingerbread, or fruitcakes.

hard-scrab·ble (härd′skrăb′əl) *adj.* Earning a bare subsistence, as on the land: *the sharecropper's hardscrabble life.*
~*n.* Barren or marginal farmland.

hard sell *n. Informal.* Aggressive, high-pressure selling or promotion. Compare **soft sell.**

hard-shell (härd′shĕl′) *adj.* Also **hard-shelled** (-shĕld′). **1.** Having a thick, heavy, or hardened shell. **2.** Unyieldingly orthodox; uncompromising; confirmed.
~*n.* A hard-shell clam or crab.

hard-shell clam *n.* The **quahog** (see).

hard-shell crab *n.* A marine crab with a fully hardened shell; especially, the edible species, *Cancer pagurus,* in this stage.

hard·ship (härd′shĭp′) *n.* **1.** Suffering or difficulty; adversity. **2.** A source or cause of privation or difficulty.

hard shoulder *n. British.* A reinforced or concreted strip at the side of a roadway on which vehicles may drive and stop only in emergencies.

hard-spun (härd′spŭn′) *adj.* Twisted tightly in spinning, often to the point of curling and looping. Said of yarn.

hard·stand (härd′stănd′) *n.* A hard-surfaced area, usually adjacent to an airstrip, for parking aircraft or ground vehicles.

hard·tack (härd′tăk′) *n.* A hard biscuit or bread made only with flour and water and formerly eaten by sailors. Also called "pilot bread," "sea biscuit," "sea bread," "ship's biscuit." [HARD + TACK (food).]

hard·top (härd′tŏp′) *n.* A car, often designed to resemble a convertible, having a fixed or detachable hard roof. —**hard·top** *adj.*

hard·ware (härd′wâr′) *n.* **1.** Metal goods and utensils such as locks, tools, and cutlery. **2. a.** A computer and the associated physical equipment directly involved in the performance of communications or data-processing functions. Compare **software, firmware. b.** Broadly, machines and other physical equipment directly involved in performing an industrial, technological, or military function. **3.** *Informal.* Heavy military weapons and equipment. **4.** *Informal.* Firearms; weapons.

hard water *n.* Water containing dissolved salts of calcium and magnesium; especially, water containing more than 85.5 parts per million of calcium carbonate. Compare **soft water.**

hard-wired (härd′wīrd′) *adj. Computer Science.* Designating or employing permanently wired circuits or components that are capable of logical decisions: *a hard-wired terminal.*

hard·wood (härd′wŏŏd′) *n.* **1.** The wood of a broad-leaved flowering tree as distinguished from that of a conifer. **2.** A broad-leaved flowering tree. Compare **softwood.**

har·dy[1] (här′dē) *adj.* **-dier, -diest. 1.** Robust; rugged; strong: *"a rude and hardy race, that lived mostly out of doors"* (Henry Thoreau). **2.** Courageous; intrepid; stouthearted. **3.** Brazenly daring; audacious; hotheaded. **4.** Capable of surviving unfavorable conditions such as cold weather or lack of moisture. Said chiefly of cultivated plants. —See Synonyms at **healthy.** [Middle English *hardy, hardi,* from Old French *hardi,* from the past participle of *hardir,* to become bold, make hard, from Germanic.] —**har·di·ly** *adv.* —**har·di·ness** *n.*

hardy[2] *n., pl.* **-dies.** A square-shanked chisel that fits into a square hole in an anvil. [Probably from HARD.]

Hardy, Oliver. See **Laurel and Hardy.**

Har·dy (här′dē), **Thomas** (1840–1928). British novelist and poet. A builder's son, he started his career as an architect and published his first short story in 1865. His Wessex novels, set in the southwest of England, include *Far from the Madding Crowd* (1874), *The Mayor of Casterbridge* (1886), *Tess of the d'Urbervilles* (1891), and *Jude the Obscure* (1896).

hardy hole *n.* The square hole in an anvil for inserting a hardy.

hardheads *Named for its knobby flower heads, this plant was formerly used by herbalists as an astringent. Its genus name,* Centaurea, *comes from the belief that Chiron, a centaur in Greek mythology, used the plant to heal wounds. Pictured above is* Centaurea nigra, *or black knapweed.*

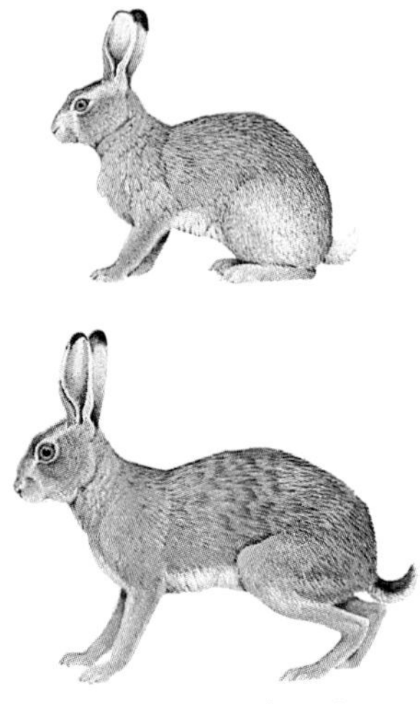

hare *The mad hares of March are male hares that stand on their hind legs and box each other to impress females during the mating season. The hare,* Lepus timidus *(above), is found in parts of northern Europe, Asia, and North America. The larger brown hare,* Lepus capensis *(bottom), is common in many parts of Africa and Asia.*

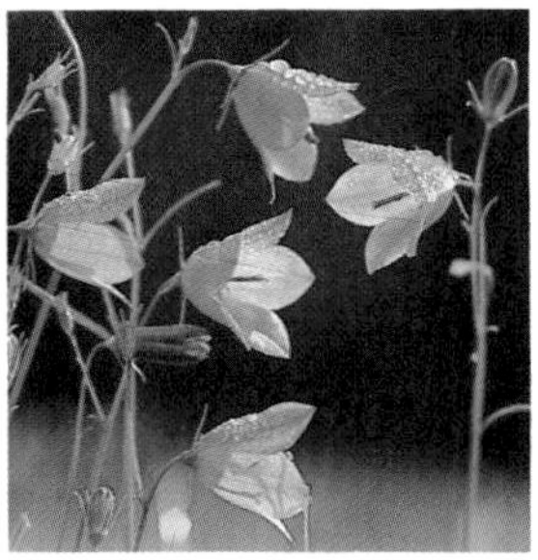

harebell *A member of the Campanulaceae family of bluebells and bellflowers, the harebell grows in dry, grassy places.*

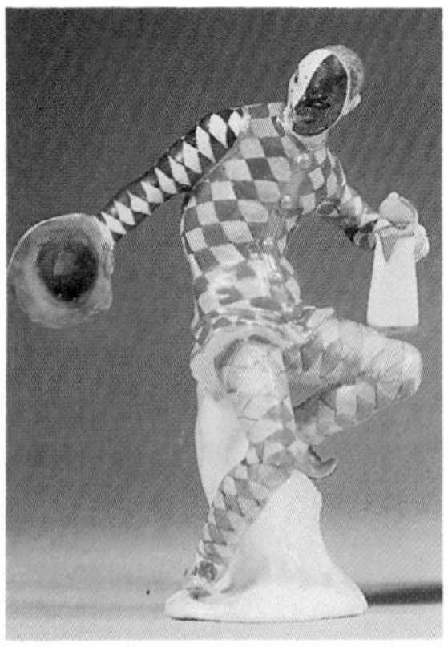

harlequin *A Meissen ceramic from about 1738. Harlequin began as a clownish peasant servant in the early Italian commedia dell'arte and survives in English pantomime today. He is amorous, yet faithful; he is clever, but credulous, because he is without guile. He gets out of trouble by means of his wit and his feline physical grace.*

hare (hâr) *n.* Any of various mammals of the family Leporidae, and especially of the genus *Lepus,* related to and resembling the rabbits but having longer ears, large hind feet, and long legs adapted for jumping. **—start** (or **raise**) **a hare.** *British.* To raise a matter for discussion.
~intr.v. **hared, haring, hares.** To run quickly: *He hared down the corridor.* [Middle English *hare,* Old English *hara,* from Germanic.]

hare and hounds *n.* A game in which one group of players leaves a trail of paper scraps for a pursuing group to follow.

hare•bell (hâr′bĕl′) *n.* A plant, *Campanula rotundifolia,* having slender stems and leaves and bell-shaped blue flowers. Also called "bluebell." [Middle English : HARE (perhaps because it grows in places frequented by hares) + BELL.]

hare•brained (hâr′brānd′) *adj.* Foolish; ill-considered: *harebrained schemes.*

Ha•re Krish•na (hä′rē krĭsh′nə, hăr′ē) *n.* A member of the International Society for Krishna Consciousness, a sect practicing a form of Hinduism dedicated to Krishna. [Hindi *hare,* invocation of God + *Krishna,* Krishna.]

hare•lip (hâr′lĭp′) *n.* A congenital fissure or pair of fissures in the upper lip, often associated with a cleft palate. **—hare•lipped** *adj.*

har•em (hâr′əm, hăr′-) *n.* **1.** A house or a section of a house reserved for women members of a Muslim household. **2.** The women occupying a harem; the wives, concubines, female relatives, and servants of a Muslim household. **3.** The wives and concubines collectively of a Muslim man, especially a wealthy one. **4.** A number of female animals, such as seals, that are the mates of a single male. [Arabic *ḥarīm,* sacred, forbidden place, from *ḥarama,* he prohibited.]

hare's-foot (hârz′fo͝ot′) *n.* A Eurasian plant, *Trifolium arvense,* having white or pink downy cloverlike flowers. Also called "hare's-foot clover."

Har•greaves (här′grēvz′), **James** (died 1778). British inventor of the spinning jenny (*c.* 1764). A weaver in Blackburn, Lancashire, Hargreaves developed his device to allow one operator to spin several threads at once.

har•i•cot (hăr′ĭ-kō′) *n.* **1.** The edible pod or seed of any of several beans, especially the string bean. **2.** A highly seasoned mutton or lamb stew with vegetables. [French, perhaps from Aztec *ayacotl* or Nahuatl *ayecotli.*]

har•i•jan (hăr′ə-jän′) *n.* A Hindu of the lowest caste; an **untouchable** *(see).* [Sanskrit, one devoted to Vishnu : *Hari,* Vishnu + *jana,* person. The use of the term in its present sense was introduced by Mahatma Gandhi.]

Ha•ri Rud (hä′rē ro͞od′). River, *c.* 1,125 kilometers (700 miles) long, rising in central Afghanistan and flowing west and then north into the steppes south of the Kara Kum desert in the Turkmen S.S.R. Its lower course forms part of the Afghanistan–U.S.S.R. border.

hark (härk) *v.* **harked, harking, harks.** *—intr.* To listen attentively; hearken. Often used with *to.* *—tr. Archaic.* To listen to; hear. **—hark back. 1.** To recall or return to an earlier time or point, as in a narrative or in reminiscing: *always harking back to his childhood.* **2.** To originate in or survive from: *This custom harks back to the Middle Ages.* [Middle English *herk(i)en,* Old English *heorcian* (unattested).]

harken. Variant of **hearken.**

harl[1] (härl) *n.* Filaments or fibers, as of hemp or flax. [Middle English *herle,* fiber, perhaps from Middle Low German *herle, harle*†.]

harl[2] *tr.v.* **harled, harling, harls.** *Scottish.* To roughcast. [Middle English, of obscure origin.]

Har•lem (här′ləm). A residential and business district of New York City, in Upper Manhattan. Though economically depressed, it is an important social and cultural center for black Americans.

har•le•quin (här′lə-kwən, -kən) *n.* **1. Harlequin.** A conventional buffoon of the commedia dell'arte, traditionally presented in a mask and parti-colored tights. **2.** A clown; a buffoon. **3.** A small duck, *Histrionicus histrionicus,* having a short bill and distinctive patterned plumage. In this sense, also called "harlequin duck."
~adj. Having a pattern of brightly colored diamond shapes like the costume of Harlequin. [Variant (influenced by obsolete French *harlequin*) of earlier *Harlicken, Harlaken,* from Old French *Herlequin, Hellequin,* leader of a troop of demon horsemen riding at night, probably from Old English *Herla cyning,* King *Herla,* a mythical figure who has been identified with Woden.]

har•le•quin•ade (här′lə-kwə-nād′) *n.* **1.** A comedy or pantomime in which Harlequin is the main attraction. **2.** A succession of farcical clownings; buffoonery.

harlequin bug *n.* A flat-bodied, brightly colored insect, *Murgantia histrionica,* that has a fetid odor, and is destructive to cabbage and other plants. Also called "calicoback," "fire bug."

Har•ley Street (här′lē). The London street in or around which many medical specialists have their private offices.

har•lot (här′lət) *n.* A promiscuous woman, especially a prostitute. [Middle English *harlot, herlot,* vagabond, itinerant jester, male servant, prostitute, from Old French *(h)arlot, herlot*†, young fellow, vagabond.] **—har•lot•ry** *n.*

Har•low (här′lō), **Jean,** stage name of Harlean Carpentier (1911–37). U.S. film actress. She won stardom with *Hell's Angels* (1930), in which she appeared as a wise-cracking sex symbol. Her other films include *Platinum Blonde* (1931) and *Bombshell* (1933).

harm (härm) *n.* **1.** Injury or damage, whether physical, psychological, or moral. **2.** Wrong; evil. **—in harm's way.** In danger; in a risky position. **—out of harm's reach** (or **way**). Out of danger; in a safe place.
~tr.v. **harmed, harming, harms.** To damage; injure; impair. —See Synonyms at **injure.** [Middle English *harm,* Old English *hearm,* from Germanic.]

har•mat•tan (här′mə-tăn′, här-măt′n) *n.* A dry, dusty wind that blows from the Sahara across western Africa. In the humid lands along the Gulf of Guinea its dryness is refreshing. Also called "the Doctor." [Twi *haramata,* probably from Arabic *ḥarām,* a forbidden or accursed thing, from the stem of *ḥarama,* to forbid, akin to *ḥaruma,* to be forbidden. See **harem.**]

harm•ful (härm′fəl) *adj.* Causing or capable of causing harm; damaging; injurious. **—harm•ful•ly** *adv.* **—harm•ful•ness** *n.*

harm•less (härm′lĭs) *adj.* **1.** Not harmful; not capable of harming. **2.** Inoffensive. **—harm•less•ly** *adv.* **—harm•less•ness** *n.*

har•mon•ic (här-mŏn′ĭk) *adj.* **1. a.** Of or pertaining to musical harmony as distinguished from melody or rhythm. **b.** Of or pertaining to harmonics. **2.** Characterized by harmony; concordant. **3. a.** *Mathematics.* Designating a function or series that can be expressed in terms of sines or cosines. **b.** Designating a function that appears in a harmonic series.
~n. **1.** *Acoustics.* A tone in the harmonic series of overtones produced by a fundamental tone. Also called "overtone," "partial," "partial tone." **2.** A tone produced on a stringed instrument by lightly touching an open or stopped vibrating string at a given fraction of its length so that both segments vibrate. **3.** *Physics.* A wave whose frequency is a whole-number multiple of that of another. [Latin *harmonicus,* from Greek *harmonikos,* from *harmonia,* HARMONY.] **—har•mon•i•cal•ly** *adv.*

har•mon•i•ca (här-mŏn′ĭ-kə) *n.* **1.** A small, rectangular musical instrument consisting of a row of free reeds set back in air holes, played by exhaling or inhaling. Also called "mouth organ." **2.** A **glass harmonica** *(see).* **3.** A musical instrument consisting of tuned strips of metal or glass fixed to a frame and struck with a hammer. [Variant (influenced by HARMONIC) of earlier *armonica,* from Italian, from *armonico,* harmonious, from Latin *harmonicus,* HARMONIC.]

harmonic analysis *n.* The representation of mathematical functions by means of linear operations, such as summation or integration, on characteristic sets of functions; especially, such representation by Fourier series.

harmonic mean *n.* The reciprocal of the arithmetic mean of the reciprocals of a given set of numbers.

harmonic minor scale *n. Music.* A minor scale with the seventh tone raised so that it lies only a semitone below the tonic. Compare **melodic minor scale.**

harmonic motion *n. Physics.* A form of periodic motion in which the displacement is symmetrical about a central point. See **simple harmonic motion.**

harmonic progression *n.* A sequence of quantities the reciprocals of which form an arithmetic progression; for example, 1, $1/3$, $1/5$, $1/7$, ...

har•mon•ics (här-mŏn′ĭks) *n. Used with a singular verb.* The theory or study of the physical properties and characteristics of musical sound.

harmonic series *n.* **1.** *Mathematics.* A series whose terms are in harmonic progression; for example, $1 + 1/3 + 1/5 + 1/7 + \dots$ **2.** *Acoustics.* A series of tones consisting of a fundamental tone and the overtones produced by it, whose frequencies are consecutive integral multiples of the frequency of the fundamental.

har•mo•ni•ous (här-mō′nē-əs) *adj.* **1.** Exhibiting accord in feeling or action; sympathetic: *a harmonious relationship.* **2.** Having component elements pleasingly or appropriately combined: *a harmonious structure.* **3.** Characterized by harmony of sound; melodious. **—har•mo•ni•ous•ly** *adv.* **—har•mo•ni•ous•ness** *n.*

har•mo•nist (här′mə-nĭst) *n.* **1.** A scholar who collates and seeks to harmonize the discrepancies in parallel passages of text, especially of the Gospels. **2. a.** One skilled in musical harmony. **b.** A composer or performer of music: *"The Ocean is a mighty harmonist"* (William Wordsworth). **3.** One of a school of ancient Greek musical theorists whose principles were based on the subjective effects of notes rather than on the mathematical relations between them. **4.** One who brings into consonance or accord; a harmonizer.

har•mo•nis•tic (här′mə-nĭs′tĭk) *adj.* **1.** Of or relating to harmony. **2.** Of or relating to the harmonizing of parallel passages of text. **—har•mo•nis•ti•cal•ly** *adv.*

har•mo•ni•um (här-mō′nē-əm) *n.* An organlike keyboard instrument that produces notes with free metal reeds vibrated by air forced from a bellows. [French, from *harmonie,* harmony, from Old French *armonie,* HARMONY.]

har•mo•nize (här′mə-nīz′) *v.* **-nized, -nizing, -nizes.** *—tr.* **1.** To bring into agreement or harmony; make harmonious. **2.** To provide harmony for (a melody). *—intr.* **1.** To be in agreement; be harmonious. **2.** To sing or play in harmony. —See Synonyms at **agree.** **—har•mo•niz•er** *n.*

har•mo•ny (här′mə-nē) *n., pl.* **-nies. 1.** Agreement in feeling, approach, action, disposition, or the like; sympathy; accord. **2.** The pleasing interaction or appropriate combination of the elements in a whole. **3.** *Music.* **a.** The study of the structure, progression, and relation of chords. **b.** The simultaneous combination of tones in a chord. **c.** A chord or chords added when writing or playing a melody to provide musical emphasis, background, or substance. **d.** The structure of a musical work or passage as considered from the point of view of its chordal characteristics and relationships. **4.** A combination of musical sounds considered to be pleasing; euphony. **5.** A collation of parallel passages from a text, especially the Gospels, with a commentary demonstrating their consonance and explaining their discrepancies. —See Synonyms at **proportion.** [Middle English *armonie,* from Old French *(h)armonie,* from Latin *harmonia,* from Greek, agreement, harmony, means of joining, from *harmos,* joint.]

har·ness (härʹnĭs) *n.* **1.** The equipment, consisting of straps and sometimes buckles, used by a draft animal to pull a vehicle or implement. **2.** Anything resembling a harness, such as the arrangement of straps used to hold a parachute to the body. **3.** A device that raises and lowers the warp threads on a loom. **4.** *Archaic.* Armor for a man or a horse. —**in harness.** On duty; at work. ~*tr.v.* **harnessed, -nessing, -nesses. 1. a.** To put a harness on (a draft animal). **b.** To attach (a draft animal) to a vehicle or implement by means of a harness. **2.** To bring under control and direct the force of: *If he can harness his energy, he will accomplish a great deal.* **3.** *Archaic.* To fit with armor; arm or equip for battle. [Middle English *harness, harnais,* baggage, equipment, trappings of a horse, from Old French *harneis,* military equipment, from Old Norse *hernest* (unattested), provisions for an army : *herr,* army + *nest,* provisions.] —**har·ness·er** *n.*

harnessed antelope *n.* Any of several African antelopes with markings resembling harness straps, such as the **bushbuck** *(see).*
harness hitch *n.* A type of knot forming a fixed loop in a rope.
harness race *n.* A horse race between pacers or trotters harnessed to sulkies.

Har·old I Hare·foot (härʹəld; hârʹfŏŏt′) (died 1040). Danish king of England (1037–40). He was the illegitimate son of King Canute and became king while Hardecanute, Canute's legitimate son, was preoccupied in Denmark. He died as Hardecanute was preparing to invade England and claim his throne.

Harold II (*c.* 1022–66). King of England (1066), the last of the Anglo-Saxon monarchs. He was the son of Godwin, Earl of Essex, and brother-in-law of Edward the Confessor. Shipwrecked in France (*c.* 1064), he was forced by the Normans to swear to support William of Normandy (William the Conqueror) in any claim on the English Crown. When Edward died in 1066, Harold succeeded him. He defeated the forces of his brother Tostig and Harold III Hardraade at Stamford Bridge, Yorkshire. He then rode south to meet William's Norman invasion and died at the Battle of Hastings (1066).

Harold III Hard·raa·de or **Haard·raa·de** (hôrʹrôʹdə) (1015–66). King of Norway (1046–66). In 1066 Hardraade invaded England, supporting Tostig against Harold II, and was killed at the Battle of Stamford Bridge.

harp (härp) *n.* **1.** A musical instrument consisting of an upright open triangular frame with 46 strings of graded lengths that are played by plucking with the fingers. **2.** Something similar to a harp in shape or sound. ~*v.* **harped, harping, harps.** —*intr.* To play a harp. —*tr. Archaic.* To give expression to; utter; refer to. —**harp on** (or **upon**). To talk or write about to an excessive and tedious degree; dwell upon. [Middle English *harp(e),* from Old English *hearpe,* from Germanic *harpōn-* (unattested).] —**harp·er** *n.*

Har·pers Ferry (härʹpərz). A town in eastern West Virginia, at the confluence of the Shenandoah and Potomac rivers. John Brown seized the U.S. arsenal here on October 16, 1859. The town is now a tourist center, with a national historic park and the John Brown Museum.

har·pins (härʹpĭnz′) *pl.n.* Also **har·pings** (-pĭngz). **1.** *Nautical.* The wooden supports of a ship under construction. **2.** The timbers used for strengthening the bow of a ship. [Perhaps from HARP.]

harp·ist (härʹpĭst) *n.* A person who plays the harp.

har·poon (här-pŏŏnʹ) *n.* A spearlike implement having a barbed head and attached rope that is hurled by hand or shot from a gun in hunting whales and large fish. ~*tr.v.* **harpooned, -pooning, -poons.** To strike, kill, or capture with or as if with a harpoon. [French *harpon,* from *harpe,* clamp, dog's claw, from Latin *harpē, harpa,* sickle, from Greek *harpē.*] —**har·poon·er, har·poon·eer** (härʹpŏŏ-nîrʹ) *n.*

harpoon gun *n.* A small cannonlike apparatus used to fire harpoons.

harp seal *n.* An earless seal, *Pagophilus groenlandicus,* found in the North Atlantic and Arctic oceans. [From the harp-shaped marking on its back.]

harp·si·chord (härpʹsĭ-kôrd′, -kôrd′) *n.* A keyboard instrument whose strings are plucked with quill or leather plectrums rather than being struck by hammers. [Obsolete French *harpechorde,* from Italian *arpicordo* : *arpi,* harp, from Late Latin *harpa,* from Germanic *harpōn-* (unattested), HARP + *corda,* string, from Latin *chorda,* from Greek *khordē.*] —**harp·si·chord·ist** *n.*

har·py (härʹpē) *n., pl.* **-pies. 1.** A predatory person. **2.** A shrewish woman. [From HARPY.]

Harpy *n., pl.* **-pies.** *Greek Mythology.* Any of several loathsome, voracious monsters having a woman's head and trunk and a bird's tail, wings, and talons. [French *harpie,* from Latin *harpȳia,* from Greek *harpuiai†,* "snatchers."]

harpy eagle *n.* A large eagle of South and Central America, *Harpia harpyja,* with an erectile head crest and mottled gray plumage. [From HARPY.]

har·que·bus (härʹkə-bəs, -kwə-bəs) *n.* Also **ar·que·bus** (ärʹ-). A heavy, portable matchlock gun invented during the 15th century.

Also called "hackbut." [Old French *(h)arquebuse,* from Middle Dutch *hakebusse* : *hake,* hook + *busse,* gun, from Late Latin *buxis,* BOX.]

har·ri·dan (härʹə-dən) *n.* A malicious, scolding woman. [Possibly from French *haridelle†,* gaunt woman.]

har·ri·er¹ (härʹē-ər) *n.* **1.** One that harries. **2.** Any of various slender, narrow-winged hawks of the genus *Circus,* such as *C. pygargus,* Montagu's harrier, that prey on small animals.

harrier² *n.* **1.** A small hound of a breed originally used in hunting hares. **2.** A cross-country runner. [From HARE.]

Har·ri·man (härʹə-mən), **(William) Averell** (1891–1986). U.S. diplomat. He was the son of a rail magnate and became ambassador to the Soviet Union (1943–46) and secretary of commerce (1946–48). He failed in 1956 to win the Democratic presidential nomination. He was governor of New York (1955–59).

Harris. See **Lewis with Harris.**

Har·ris (härʹĭs), **Joel Chandler** (1848–1908). U.S. author and journalist. While working for various Southern newspapers he developed a transcription of black plantation speech that he incorporated into *Uncle Remus: His Songs and His Sayings* (1880) and its many sequels.

Har·ris·burg (härʹĭs-bûrg′, hârʹ-). Capital of Pennsylvania, in the southeastern part of the state, on the Susquehanna River. It is an important railway junction and industrial center.

Har·ri·son (härʹĭ-sən), **Benjamin** (1833–1901). 23rd U.S. President (1889–93). A local politician and Civil War officer, he served in the U.S. Senate (1881–88) and then defeated the incumbent, Grover Cleveland, for the presidency. The Sherman Antitrust Act, the Sherman Silver Purchase Act, and the McKinley Tariff Act (all 1890) were important domestic developments during his administration.

Harrison, George (1943–). British pop musician, formerly lead guitarist with the Beatles. His best-known compositions include *Here Comes the Sun* and *My Sweet Lord.*

Harrison, Rex (1908–). English actor. A stage and motion-picture performer, he is perhaps best remembered for his portrayal of Professor Henry Higgins in the Broadway musical and film versions of *My Fair Lady,* for which he was awarded a Tony (1956) and an Academy Award (1964).

Harrison, William Henry (1773–1841). Ninth U.S. president (1841). After winning military fame in the Battle of Tippecanoe (1811) and the War of 1812, he served as a U.S. congressman (1816–18) and senator (1819–28) before unsuccessfully running for president in 1836. Four years later he was elected president and during his inaugural address caught a cold, which proved to be fatal thirty days later.

Harris tweed *n.* A trademark for a rough tweed fabric. [After *Harris* in the Outer Hebrides, where it is woven.]

Har·ro·gate (härʹō-gĭt, -gāt′). A residential town in North Yorkshire, England. It has been a spa since 1596 and is a popular vacation resort and retirement area.

har·row¹ (härʹō) *n.* A farm instrument consisting of a heavy frame with teeth or upright disks, used to break up and level plowed ground. ~*tr.v.* **harrowed, -rowing, -rows. 1.** To break up and level (soil or land) with a harrow. **2.** To inflict great distress or torment on the mind of; torment. [Middle English, from Old Norse *herfi.*]

harrow² *tr.v.* **-rowed, -rowing, -rows.** *Archaic.* To plunder or harry. [Middle English *harwen,* variant of *harien,* to HARRY.]

Har·row (härʹō). A residential borough of northwest Greater London. It is noted for one of England's most famous public schools, founded in 1571, whose former pupils include Byron, Lord Palmerston, and Sir Winston Churchill.

har·row·ing (härʹō-ĭng) *adj.* Extremely distressing.

har·rumph (hə-rŭmfʹ) *interj.* Used to express skepticism, disapproval, or discontent. ~*v.* **-rumphed, -rumphing, -rumphs.** —*intr.* To express skepticism, disapproval, or discontent by uttering "harrumph." —*tr.* To give vent to or express (skepticism or disapproval, for example) by uttering "harrumph." [Imitative.]

har·ry (härʹē) *tr.v.* **-ried, -rying, -ries. 1.** To raid, as in a war; sack; pillage. **2.** To disturb or annoy by constant attacks; harass. [Middle English *harien, herien,* from Old English *hergian,* from Germanic.]

harsh (härsh) *adj.* **harsher, harshest. 1.** Producing an unpleasant sensory response, as: **a.** Coarse in texture; rough: *harsh wool.* **b.** Disagreeable to the ear; grating: *a harsh voice.* **c.** Having a bitter or astringent taste: *cheap, harsh rum.* **d.** Visually jarring: *harsh colors.* **2.** Extremely severe or exacting; stern. —See Synonyms at **burdensome.** [Middle Low German *harsch,* "hairy," rough. See **hair, -ish.**] —**harsh·ly** *adv.* —**harsh·ness** *n.*

harsh·en (härʹshən) *v.* **-ened, -ening, -ens.** —*tr.* To make harsh. —*intr.* To become harsh.

harslet. Variant of **haslet.**

hart (härt) *n., pl.* **harts** or collectively **hart.** A male deer; especially, a male red deer over five years old. [Middle English *hert,* Old English *heor(o)t,* from Germanic.]

Hart (härt), **Lorenz Milton** (1895–1943). U.S. lyricist. He began collaborating with Richard Rodgers in 1919, and together they produced such memorable hits as "Manhattan," "Blue Moon," and "The Lady is a Tramp" and popular musicals that included *A Connecticut Yankee* (1927), *The Boys from Syracuse* (1938), and *Pal Joey* (1940).

Hart, Moss (1904–61). U.S. dramatist and librettist. He wrote Broadway hit comedies with George S. Kaufman, including *Once in*

harpy eagle *The harpy eagle of South and Central America eats monkeys, sloths, and peccaries (wild pigs).*

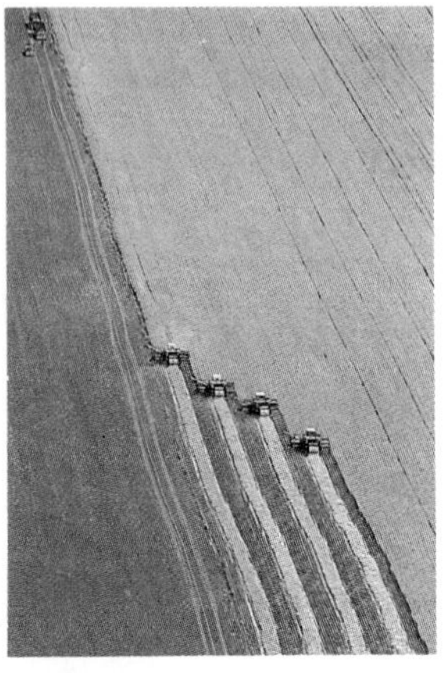

harvester *Modern harvesters on the vast wheat fields of the Middle West. The first horse-powered reaping machine was invented in 1826 by Patrick Bell, a Scottish clergyman.*

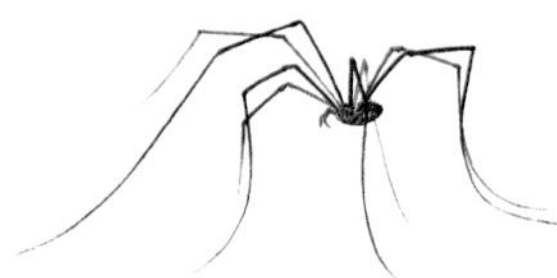

harvestman *The harvestman—a kind of spider—is commonly found in damp, shady woods of the Northern Hemisphere. It is also called daddy longlegs.*

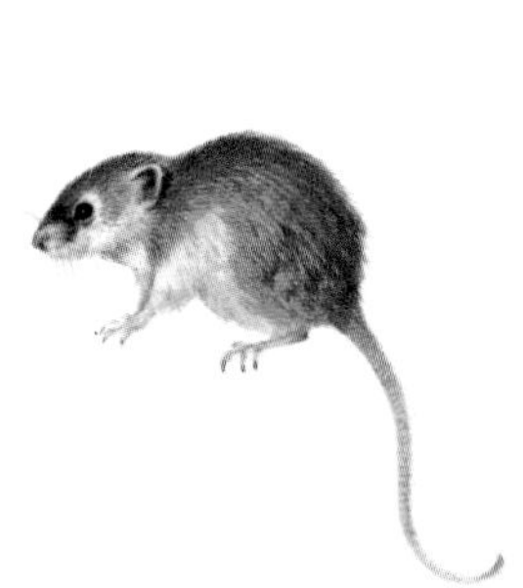

harvest mouse Micromys minutus, *the harvest mouse, makes its home in fields and hedgerows, climbing through and up tall grasses with the aid of its tail, which it uses as a fifth limb. As its scientific name suggests, it is one of the world's tiniest mammals. Fully grown, it is only about 60 millimeters (2$\frac{1}{2}$ inches) long and weighs a mere 5 grams ($\frac{1}{5}$ of an ounce).*

a Lifetime (1930) and *The Man Who Came to Dinner* (1939).

har·tal (här-täl′) *n.* A halting of work and business in India, usually as a political protest; a strike or boycott. [Hindi *hartāl,* from *hattāl,* "locking of shops" : *hāt,* shop, from Sanskrit *hatta,* shop, perhaps from *hatika,* gold, from *hari,* yellow + *tālā,* lock, bolt, from Sanskrit *tālā, tādā,* latch, probably from Dravidian.]

Harte (härt), **(Francis) Bret(t)** (1836–1902). U.S. author. As editor of *Overland Monthly* (1868–71) he contributed many tales about Californian mining towns. *The Luck of Roaring Camp and Other Sketches* (1870) is his best-known collection.

har·te·beest (här′tə-bēst′, härt′bēst′) *n., pl.* **-beests** or collectively **hartebeest.** Also **hart·beest** (härt′-). Either of two African antelopes, *Alcelaphus bucelaphus* or *A. lichtensteini,* having a brownish coat and ridged, outward-curving horns. [Obsolete Afrikaans, from Dutch *hartebeest, hertebeest : hert,* HART + *beest,* BEAST.]

Hart·ford (härt′fərd). Capital of Connecticut, in the central part of the state, on the Connecticut River. Traditionally a center for commerce and finance, it is of international importance in the field of insurance.

Hart·le·pool (härt′lē-po͞ol′, här′təl-). An industrial and fishing port in northeastern England. Situated on the Tees estuary, it is the main port of the Durham coal fields; its industries include shipbuilding, heavy engineering, clothing, and tourism.

Hart·nell (härt′nəl), **Sir Norman** (1901–79). British fashion designer. He designed utility wear during World War II and later became official dressmaker to Queen Elizabeth II. He was knighted in 1977.

har·tree (här′trē′) *n.* A unit of energy used in atomic physics equal to the ratio of the square of the charge on an electron (atomic unit of charge) to the radius of the first Bohr orbit of an atom (atomic unit of length). It has the value 4.850 × 10^{-18} joule. [After Douglas Rayner *Hartree* (1897–1958), British mathematician and physicist.]

harts·horn (härts′hôrn′) *n. Archaic.* **Sal volatile** *(see).* [Old English *heortes horn,* hart's horn.]

hart's-tongue (härts′tŭng′) *n.* An evergreen fern, *Phyllitis scolopendrium,* having narrow, undivided fronds. [So called from the shape of its fronds.]

har·um-scar·um (hâr′əm-skâr′əm) *adj.* Lacking a sense of responsibility; rash; reckless.
∼*adv.* With abandon; recklessly.
∼*n. Informal.* **1.** One who acts recklessly. **2.** Reckless behavior. [Perhaps from HARE + SCARE.]

Ha·run al-Ra·shid (hä-ro͞on′ äl′rä-shēd′) (A.D. *c.* 766–809). The fifth caliph of Baghdad (786–809) of the Abbassid dynasty. He figures in many tales of the *Arabian Nights* and symbolizes the golden age of Islamic rulers.

ha·rus·pex (hə-rŭs′pĕks′, hăr′ə-spĕks′) *n., pl.* **haruspices** (hə-rŭs′pə-sēz′). Also **a·rus·pex** (ə-rŭs′pĕks′). A priest in ancient Rome who practiced divination by the inspection of the entrails of animals. [Latin.]

Har·vard classification (här′vərd) *n.* A method of classifying stars that originally used the letters *A* to *P* to indicate the strength of the hydrogen absorption lines in their spectra but was later modified so that most stars could be classified, according to decreasing surface temperature, into seven groups known by the letters *O, B, A, F, G, K, M.* [After Harvard University, where it was developed.]

har·vest (här′vĭst) *n.* **1.** The act or process of gathering a crop, especially a grain crop. **2.** The crop thus gathered. **3.** The amount or measure of such a crop. **4.** The time or season of such gathering. **5.** The result or consequence of any action.
∼*v.* **harvested, -vesting, -vests.** —*tr.* **1.** To gather (a crop). **2.** To gather a crop from (a field or orchard, for example). **3.** To store; lay up. **4.** To receive (the benefits or consequences of an action). —*intr.* To gather a crop.
∼*adj.* Of or relating to a harvest: *a harvest supper.* [Middle English *hervest,* autumn, Old English *hærfest,* from Germanic.]

harvest bug *n.* The **chigger** *(see).*

har·vest·er (här′vĭ-stər) *n.* **1.** A person who harvests. **2.** A machine that harvests, especially a combine harvester.

harvest festival *n.* A service of thanksgiving on the completion of the harvest, held in a church or other building decorated with flowers, fruit, and vegetables.

harvest fly *n.* Any of several cicadas of the genus *Tibicen* that produce a shrill sound heard late in summer.

harvest home *n.* **1.** The completion of a harvest. **2. a.** The time of completing a harvest. **b.** A festival held at this time, especially a harvest supper. **c.** A song sung at this time.

har·vest·man (här′vĭst-mən) *n., pl.* **-men** (-mĭn). **1.** One who harvests. **2.** An arachnid, the **daddy longlegs** *(see).*

harvest mite *n.* An insect, the **chigger** *(see).*

harvest moon *n.* The full moon that occurs nearest to the autumnal equinox.

harvest mouse *n.* A very small Eurasian mouse, *Micromys minutus,* with reddish-brown fur and a prehensile tail, found in cornfields and hedgerows.

Har·vey (här′vē), **William** (1578–1657). English physician and anatomist who discovered the circulation of the blood. He became physician to James I and Charles I. His treatise *On the Motion of the Heart and the Blood* (1628) accurately described the circulation through the heart, lungs, arteries, and veins.

Har·well (här′wĕl′, -wəl). A village in Oxfordshire, England. An atomic research station was established here in 1947.

Har·wich (hăr′ĭj, -ĭch). A port in Essex, eastern England. Situated on the Stour estuary, it is an important passenger and commercial sea link with Denmark and the Netherlands.

Harz Mountains (härts). A mountain range in Central Europe. Extending from the Weser River in West Germany to the Elbe River in East Germany, it is the northernmost range of the European mountain system. Its forested slopes and mineral springs attract tourists.

has (hăz). Third person singular present indicative of **have.**

has-been (hăz′bĭn′) *n. Informal.* One that is no longer famous, popular, successful, or useful.

Has·dru·bal (hăz′dro͞o′bəl, hăz-dro͞o′-) (died 207 B.C.). Carthaginian general. Son of Hamilcar Barca and brother of Hannibal, he attempted to establish military dominance on the Iberian Peninsula during the Second Punic War. After a series of battles he retreated from present-day Spain and was ultimately defeated by Roman forces in 207 B.C.

Ha·šek (hä′shĕk′), **Jaroslav** (1883–1923). Czech novelist. He is best remembered for the novel *The Good Soldier Schweik* (1920–23).

hash[1] (hăsh) *n.* **1.** A dish of chopped or diced meat, especially meat that has been previously cooked, with potatoes and sometimes vegetables, usually browned and often baked. **2.** A jumble, hodgepodge, or mess. **3.** A reworking or restatement of material already familiar. **—make a hash of.** To make a mess of; botch. **—settle someone's hash.** *Informal.* To silence or subdue.
∼*tr.v.* **hashed, hashing, hashes. 1.** To chop into pieces; mince. **2.** *Informal.* To make a mess of; mangle. **3.** *Informal.* To discuss carefully; review. Often used with *over*: *hash over future plans.* [French *hachis,* from *hacher,* to chop up, from Old French *hachier,* from *hache,* ax, HATCHET.]

hash[2] *n. Slang.* **Hashish** *(see).*

hash house *n. Slang.* A cheap restaurant.

Hash·i·mo·to's disease (hăsh′ə-mō′tōz) *n.* An autoimmune disease resulting in chronic inflammation of the thyroid gland, with partial or total suppression of thyroid-hormone secretion. [After Hakaru *Hashimoto* (1881–1934), Japanese surgeon.]

hash·ish, hash·eesh (hăsh′ēsh′, -ĭsh) *n.* A purified resin prepared from the dried flowers of the hemp plant, smoked or chewed as a narcotic and hallucinogen. Also *slang* "hash." [Arabic *hashīsh,* hemp, dried grass.]

hash mark *n. Slang.* A service stripe on the sleeve of an enlisted person's uniform.

Hasidim. Variant of **Chassidim.**

has·let (hăs′lĭt, hăz′-) *n.* Also **hars·let** (här′slĭt). The heart, liver, and other edible viscera of an animal, especially hog viscera. [Middle English *hastelet, hastlet,* from Old French *hastelet,* diminutive of *haste,* spit, roast meat, perhaps from Latin *hasta,* spear.]

has·n't (hăz′ənt). Contraction of *has not.*

hasp (hăsp, häsp) *n.* A metal fastener having a hinged, slotted part that fits over a staple and may be secured by a pin, bolt, or padlock.
∼*tr.v.* **hasped, hasping, hasps.** To fasten or lock with a hasp. [Middle English *hasp,* Old English *hæsp(e), hæpse,* fastening, hinge, from Germanic *hasp-* (unattested).]

Has·sam (hăs′əm), **(Frederick) Childe** (1859–1935). U.S. painter. The leading American impressionist of his day, he used brilliant colors and bold brushwork to depict city street scenes and natural landscapes, including *Rainy Day in Boston* (1885) and *Allies Day, Fifth Avenue* (1917).

Has·san II (hä-săn′, hä-sän′) (1929–). King of Morocco (1961–). He succeeded his father, Muhammad V (reigned 1957–61).

Hassidim. Variant of **Chassidim.**

has·sle (hăs′əl) *n. Informal.* **1.** An argument or fight. **2.** Trouble; bother.
∼*v.* **hassled, -sling, -sles.** *Informal.* —*intr.* To argue or fight. —*tr.* To bother or harass: *street gangs hassling passers-by.* [Perhaps a blend of HAGGLE + TUSSLE.]

has·sock (hăs′ək) *n.* **1.** A thick cushion used as a footstool or for kneeling upon. **2.** A dense clump of grass; a tussock. [Middle English *hassok,* Old English *hassuc*†, clump of matted vegetation.]

hast (hăst). *Archaic.* Second person singular present indicative of **have.** Used with *thou.*

has·tate (hăs′tāt′) *adj.* Shaped like the head of an arrow or spear: *a hastate leaf.* [New Latin *hastatus,* from Latin *hasta,* spear.]

haste (hāst) *n.* **1.** Swiftness; rapidity. **2.** Eagerness or necessity to move swiftly; urgency. **3.** Careless or headlong hurrying; precipitateness. **—make haste.** To move or act swiftly; hurry.
∼*v.* **hasted, hasting, hastes.** —*intr.* To hasten. —*tr.* To cause to hurry; hasten. [Middle English, from Old French, from West Germanic *haisti-* (unattested), violence.]

has·ten (hā′sən) *v.* **-tened, -tening, -tens.** —*intr.* **1.** To move or act swiftly. **2.** To be eager or anxious. Used with an infinitive: *I hasten to point out that I was not actually present.* —*tr.* **1.** To cause to hurry; urge on. **2.** To bring about more quickly; accelerate: *events that hastened the downfall of the government.* —See Synonyms at **speed.**

Has·tings (hā′stĭngz). A coastal town in East Sussex, England. It was the most important of the Cinque Ports, with a long history of commercial and naval importance. Today it is a popular resort and residential town. William the Conqueror's victory at the Battle of Hastings (1066), fought nearby, ended Saxon rule in England and installed a Norman-French dynasty.

Hastings, Warren (1732–1818). The first governor-general of India (1774–85). He carried out land and legal reforms, facing the hostility of Sir Philip Francis (1740–1818), who tried to have him impeached for corruption. At the end of a long trial (1788–95) the House of Lords found Hastings not guilty.

hast·y (hā′stē) *adj.* **-ier, -iest.** **1.** Characterized by speed; swift; rapid. **2.** Done, made, or acting too quickly to be accurate or wise; rash: *Don't make a hasty decision.* **3.** Easily angered; irritable. —See Synonyms at **fast** and Usage note at **impetuous.** —**hast·i·ly** *adv.* —**hast·i·ness** *n.*

hasty pudding *n.* **1.** Cornmeal mush served with maple syrup, brown sugar, or other sweetening. **2.** *British.* A sweetened milk pudding made with flour, semolina, or tapioca.

hat (hăt) *n.* **1.** A covering for the head; especially, one having a shaped crown and brim. **2. a.** A hat of distinctive color and shape worn as a symbol of office. **b.** A role or office symbolized by or as if by the wearing of such a hat: *wore different hats as executive and homemaker.* —**at the drop of a hat.** At the slightest pretext or provocation. —**hat in hand.** In a servile or apologetic way. —**my hat!** Used to express surprise, disbelief, or rejection, as of a claim or report. —**pass the hat.** To take up a monetary collection. —**take one's hat off to.** To respect, admire, or congratulate. —**talk through one's hat. 1.** To talk nonsense. **2.** To bluff. —**throw** (or **toss**) **one's hat into the ring.** To enter a political race as a candidate for office. —**under one's hat.** Confidential; secret.
~*tr.v.* **hatted, hatting, hats.** To supply or cover with a hat. [Middle English *hat,* Old English *hæt(t),* from Germanic.]

hat·band (hăt′bănd′) *n.* A band of ribbon or cloth around the crown of a hat just above the brim.

hat·box (hăt′bŏks′) *n.* An often round box or case for a hat.

hatch¹ (hăch) *n.* **1. a.** An opening, as in the deck of a ship, in the floor or roof of a building, or in an airplane. **b.** The cover for such an opening. **c.** A hatchway. **d.** A ship's compartment. **2. a.** A Dutch door. **b.** The lower half of a Dutch door. **3.** A floodgate. —**down the hatch.** *Slang.* Down the throat; drink up. Used as a toast. —**under hatches.** *Chiefly British.* **1.** Below decks. **2.** Concealed. **3.** *Slang.* Dead. [Middle English *hacche, hecche,* Old English *hæc(c),* hatch, from Germanic *khak-* (unattested).]

hatch² *v.* **hatched, hatching, hatches.** —*intr.* **1.** To emerge from or break out of an egg. **2.** To crack open and release a young animal. Used of an egg. —*tr.* **1.** To produce (young) from an egg. **2.** To cause (an egg or eggs) to produce young. **3.** To originate or formulate; especially, to devise (a plot, for example) in secret.
~*n.* **1.** The act or an instance of hatching. **2.** The young hatched at one time; a brood. [Middle English *hacchen,* Old English *hæccan* (unattested).] —**hatch·er** *n.*

hatch³ *tr.v.* **hatched, hatching, hatches.** To shade by drawing or etching fine parallel or crossed lines on.
~*n.* Such a line. [Middle English *hachen,* from Old French *hach(i)er,* from *hache,* ax. See **hatchet.**]

hatch·back (hăch′băk′) *n.* **1.** An automobile with a sloping rear consisting of a door that opens upward. **2.** A door of this kind.

hatch·el (hăch′əl) *n.* A comb for separating flax fibers.
~*tr.v.* **hatcheled, -eling, -els.** Also *chiefly British* **-elled, -elling.** To separate (flax fibers) with a hatchel. [Middle English *hechele,* flax-comb. See **heckle.**]

hatch·er·y (hăch′ə-rē) *n., pl.* **-ies.** A place where eggs, especially those of fish or domestic fowl, are hatched.

hatch·et (hăch′ĭt) *n.* **1.** A small, short-handled ax for use in one hand. **2.** A tomahawk. —**bury the hatchet.** To stop fighting; make peace. —**dig up the hatchet.** To resume hostilities. [Middle English *hachet, hatchet,* small ax, from Old French *hachette,* diminutive of *hache,* ax, from Germanic.]

hatchet face *n.* A long, gaunt face with sharp features. —**hatch·et-faced** (hăch′ĭt-fāst′) *adj.*

hatchet job *n. Slang.* A malicious verbal attack, either spoken or written, intended to destroy the reputation of another.

hatchet man *n. Slang.* **1.** Someone who carries out unpleasant duties on behalf of another. **2.** A hired assassin. **3.** A harsh or malicious critic.

hatch·ing (hăch′ĭng) *n.* **1.** The fine lines used in graphic arts to show shading. **2.** The process of decorating with such lines.

hatch·ling (hăch′lĭng) *n.* A newly hatched bird, reptile, amphibian, or fish.

hatch·ment (hăch′mənt) *n. Heraldry.* A panel, usually diamond-shaped, bearing the coat of arms of a dead person. Also called "achievement." [Earlier *(h)achement, achiment,* perhaps short for ACHIEVEMENT.]

hatch·way (hăch′wā′) *n.* **1.** An opening, as in the deck of a ship, leading to a hold, compartment, or cellar. **2.** A ladder or stairway within a hatchway.

hate (hāt) *v.* **hated, hating, hates.** —*tr.* **1.** To feel hatred toward; loathe; detest. **2.** To find deeply distasteful or disagreeable; dislike: *hated having to borrow money.* —*intr.* To feel hatred.
~*n.* **1.** Strong dislike; animosity; hatred. **2.** An object of detestation or hatred: *a pet hate.* [Middle English, Old English *hatian,* (verb), from Germanic.] —**hate·a·ble, hat·a·ble** *adj.* —**hat·er** *n.*

hate·ful (hāt′fəl) *adj.* **1.** Inspiring hatred; detestable; despicable. **2.** Feeling or expressing hatred; malevolent. —**hate·ful·ly** *adv.* —**hate·ful·ness** *n.*
Synonyms: *abhorrent, detestable, obnoxious, odious, offensive, repellent.*

hath (hăth). *Archaic.* Third person singular present indicative of **have.**

Hath·a·way (hăth′ə-wā′), **Anne** (*c.* 1556–1623). Wife of William Shakespeare. She was born at Shottery, England, near Stratford, and married Shakespeare in 1582. She bore him three children: a daughter, Susanna, and the twins Hamnet and Judith. The farmhouse where she lived is preserved as a museum.

ha·tha yoga (hăth′ə, hŭt′ə) *n.* **1. Yoga** *(see).* **2.** A form of yoga concentrating on breathing exercises. [Sanskrit : *hatha,* force + YOGA.]

Hath·or (hăth′ôr′). The ancient Egyptian goddess of love, creation, happiness, and beauty, represented as having a cow's horns or head. [Greek *Hathōr,* from Egyptian *ḥt-ḥr.*]

Ha·thor·ic (hə-thôr′ĭk, -thŏr′ĭk) *adj.* **1.** Of or pertaining to the goddess Hathor. **2.** *Architecture.* Designating a column with a head of Hathor as its capital.

hat·pin (hăt′pĭn′) *n.* A long thick pin, usually with a decorative head, for securing a woman's hat to her hair.

ha·tred (hā′trĭd) *n.* Violent dislike or animosity; abhorrence. [Middle English *hatred, hatereden* : *hate, hete,* hate, Old English *hete* + *-reden,* Old English *rǣden,* condition.]

Hat·shep·sut (hăt-shĕp′so͞ot′). Also **Hat·shep·set** (-sĕt′). Queen of Egypt, reigned 1503–1482 B.C. On the death of her husband, King Thutmose II (*c.* 1512), she became regent for his son Thutmose III. In 1503 B.C. she bestowed the title pharaoh on herself and followed all the pharaonic customs, including the wearing of a false beard.

hat·ter (hăt′ər) *n.* One whose occupation is the manufacture, selling, or repair of hats. —**mad as a hatter.** Completely insane. [Idiom, referring to the symptoms, resembling insanity, caused by mercury poisoning, formerly a common disease of hatters, who used the metal in making hats.]

Hat·ter·as, Cape (hăt′ər-əs). Promontory on Hatteras Island, a low, sandy barrier bar in eastern North Carolina between the Atlantic Ocean and Pamlico Sound. Frequent storms drive ships landward, and the area around the cape is known as the Graveyard of the Atlantic.

hat trick *n.* **1.** The taking of three wickets in cricket by a bowler in three consecutive balls. **2.** Three consecutive wins, hits, or goals made by one player in one game, as in ice hockey. **3.** Any set of three victories or other notable achievements, especially when consecutive, in any field of endeavor. [The feat was once rewarded by the gift of a hat.]

haubergeon. Variant of **habergeon.**

hau·berk (hô′bûrk) *n.* A long tunic made of chain mail. [Middle English *hauberk,* from Old French *hauberc,* from Frankish *halsberg* (unattested), "neck protector": *hals,* neck + *berg-* (unattested), to protect.]

haugh (hôKH, hôf) *n. Scottish.* A low-lying meadow that is part of a river valley. [Middle English (Scottish) *holch, hawch,* Old English *healh,* corner of land.]

haugh·ty (hô′tē) *adj.* **-tier, -tiest.** Proud and vain to the point of arrogance; scornful and self-satisfied. —See Synonyms at **proud.** [From archaic *haught,* haughty, Middle English *haute,* from Old French *haut,* from Latin *altus,* high.] —**haugh·ti·ly** *adv.* —**haugh·ti·ness** *n.*

haul (hôl) *v.* **hauled, hauling, hauls.** —*tr.* **1.** To pull or drag forcibly; tug. **2.** To transport, as with a truck or wagon; cart. **3.** To change the course of (a ship); especially, to sail (a ship) closer into the wind. Often used with *up.* **4.** To bring before a court or other authority, especially for a reprimand. Often used with *up*: *hauled up before the directors.* —*intr.* **1.** To pull; tug. **2.** To provide transport for heavy goods; cart. **3. a.** To change compass bearing in a clockwise direction. Used of the wind. **b.** To blow from a direction nearer the bow of a ship. Used of the wind. Compare **veer. 4. a.** To sail, as on a certain course. **b.** To change the course of a ship. —**haul off. 1.** To steer a ship away from an object. **2.** To pull the arm back in order to deliver a blow.
~*n.* **1.** The act of pulling or dragging. **2.** The act of transporting or carting. **3.** The distance covered or time taken in traveling or transporting or in achieving something involving sustained effort: *the long haul to the South Pole.* **4.** Something that is pulled or transported; a load. **5.** Everything collected or acquired by a single effort; a take: *a haul of fish.* [Middle English *halen,* to pull, draw, from Old French *haler,* from Germanic.]

haul·age (hô′lĭj) *n.* **1.** The act, process, or business of hauling. **2.** The force required to haul something. **3.** The charge made for hauling something.

haul·er (hô′lər) *n.* Also *chiefly British* **haul·i·er** (hô′lē-ər). **1.** One that hauls. **2.** A company dealing in the transportation of goods by road.

haulm, halm (hôm) *n. Chiefly British.* **1.** The stems or stalks of peas, beans, potatoes, or grasses, used as litter for animals or for thatching. **2.** A single stalk of this kind. [Middle English *halm,* Old English *h(e)alm,* straw, stem.]

haulyard. Variant of **halyard.**

haunch (hônch, hŏnch) *n.* **1.** The hip, buttock, and upper thigh in humans and animals. **2.** The loin and leg of an animal, especially as used for food: *a haunch of venison.* **3.** *Architecture.* Either of the sides of an arch curving down from the apex to an impost. In this sense, also called "hance." —**sit on one's haunches.** To crouch down with the knees bent and the buttocks resting on the heels. [Middle English *ha(u)nche,* from Old French *hanche,* from Medieval Latin *hancha,* from Germanic *hanka* (unattested).]

haunt (hônt, hŏnt) *v.* **haunted, haunting, haunts.** —*tr.* **1.** To visit or appear to in the form of a ghost or other supernatural being. **2.** To visit often; frequent. **3.** To be frequently in the company of. **4.** To recur to continually; obsess: *The riddle continued to haunt her.* **5.** To linger or remain in; pervade. —*intr.* To recur or visit often; espe-

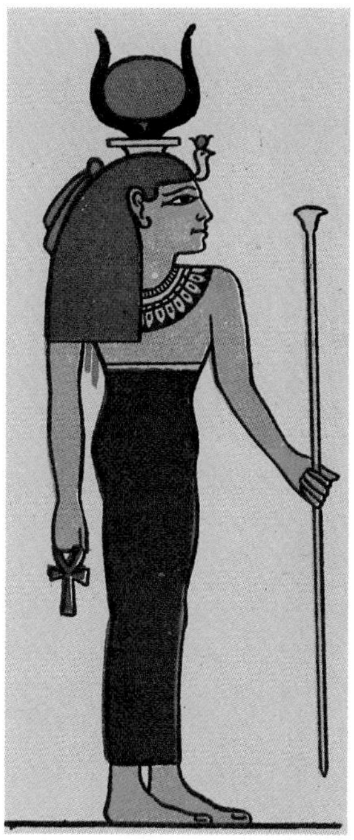

Hathor *At different times in ancient Egypt, Hathor was the wife of Horus and a goddess of love, associated with the sun god Ra and called the Lady of the West, or Underworld.*

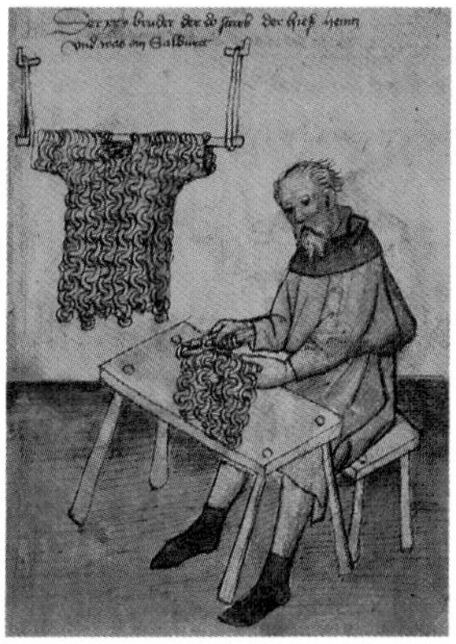

hauberk *An armorer making one of these chain mail tunics. Hauberks, which were worn by knights during the Hundred Years War (1338–1453) between England and France, were replaced by plate armor.*

cially, to appear habitually as a ghost or other supernatural being. ~*n.* (*also* hănt *for sense 2*). **1. a.** A place much frequented. **b.** A place where animals usually gather to feed. **2.** *Regional.* A ghost or other supernatural being. [Middle English *haunten,* from Old French *hanter,* from Germanic.]

haunt·ed (hôn′tĭd, hŏn′-) *adj.* **1.** Supposedly frequented by ghosts or other spectral beings: *a haunted house.* **2.** Obsessed by a constantly recurring memory or thought.

haunt·ing (hôn′tĭng, hŏn′-) *adj.* Continually recurring to the mind, especially in a poignant way; unforgettable. **—haunt·ing·ly** *adv.*

Haupt·mann (houpt′män′), **Gerhart Johann Robert** (1862–1946). German author. A prolific poet, playwright, and novelist, he wrote in several literary styles, although he was primarily known as a naturalist. His many works include *The Weavers* (1892), *Before Dawn* (1889), *Till Eulenspiegel* (1928), and *Atridentetralogie* (1941). In 1912 he was awarded a Nobel Prize for literature.

Hau·sa (hou′sə, -zə) *n., pl.* **Hausa. 1.** A member of a Negroid people of Niger and northern Nigeria. **2.** The language of this people, used widely as a trade language in Africa. **—Hau·sa** *adj.*

haus·frau (hous′frou′) *n.* A housewife, especially one who is houseproud. [German *Hausfrau.*]

Hauss·mann (hous′mən, ōs-män′), **Georges Eugène, Baron** (1809–91). French politician and town planner. He was responsible for rebuilding Paris during the time of Napoleon III.

haus·tel·lum (hô-stĕl′əm) *n., pl.* **haustella** (hô-stĕl′ə). The distal portion of the proboscis adapted as a sucking organ, seen in many insects, such as the bluebottle. [New Latin, from Latin *haustus,* past participle of *haurīre,* to draw, draw up.] **—haus·tel·late** (hô-stĕl′ĭt, hô′stə-lāt′) *adj.*

haus·to·ri·um (hô-stôr′ē-əm, -stōr′ē-əm) *n., pl.* **haustoria** (hô-stôr′ē-ə, -stōr′ē-ə). *Botany.* A specialized organ by which parasitic plants such as fungi obtain food from a host plant. [New Latin, from Latin *haustus,* past participle of *haurīre,* to draw, draw up.]

haut·boy (hō′boi′, ō′boi′) *n., pl.* **-boys.** Also **haut·bois** *pl.* **hautbois.** An oboe. [French *hautbois,* "high wood" (from its pitch) : *haut,* high, from Latin *altus* + *bois,* wood, from Germanic.]

haute cou·ture (ōt′ ko͞o-to͝or′) *n.* **1.** Exclusive fashions for women; high fashion. **2. a.** Leading clothes designers and dressmakers collectively. **b.** The clothes designed and made by these people. [French, "high sewing."]

haute cui·sine (ōt′ kwĭ-zēn′) *n.* Elaborate or skillful cooking; especially, that in the French tradition. [French, "high cooking."]

haute é·cole (ōt′ ā-kôl′) *n.* The art, techniques, or practice of expert horsemanship. [French, "high school."]

hau·teur (hō-tûr′) *n.* Haughtiness in bearing and attitude; arrogance. [French, from *haut,* high, pious, from Old French, from Latin *altus.*]

haut monde (ō mōɴd′, ō mŏnd′) *n.* Fashionable society. [French, "high world."]

Ha·van·a (hə-văn′ə). *Spanish* **La Ha·ba·na** (lä′ ä-vä′nä). Capital city of Cuba. Situated on the northwest coast, it has an excellent natural harbor and is one of the largest cities in the West Indies. It was founded in 1519 by the Spanish and has been prominent since 1552, when it became the country's capital. Since the revolution (1959) it has been extensively modernized, and an oil refinery has been built on the outskirts. The chief exports include tobacco (especially Havana cigars), sugar, rum, and clothing.

Havana cigar *n.* Any of several high-quality cigars made in Cuba, especially in Havana.

have (hăv) *v.* **had** (hăd) or *archaic* **hadst** (hădst), **having, has** (hăz). Present tense first person **have;** second person **have** or *archaic* **hast** (for singular); third person singular **has** or *archaic* **hath**; third person plural **have.** Used as an auxiliary verb before a past participle to form the present, past, and future perfect tenses, indicating completed or virtually completed action: *We had left before dawn. They have done it. I shall have finished by then.* —*tr.* **1. a.** To be in possession of as one's property; own: *have a big house.* **b.** To possess as a physical attribute: *have red hair.* **2. a.** To be related to: *have three aunts.* **b.** To be in a particular specified or implied relationship to: *has friends in high places; has a staff of 25.* **3.** To be in a position to make use of or enjoy: *have time to play.* **4.** To hold in one's mind; entertain: *have doubts.* **5.** To hold by law or entitlement. **6.** To bribe or buy off. **7.** To engage the attention of; captivate. **8.** To win a victory or advantage over: *He has you on that point.* **9.** *Informal.* To cheat, deceive, or trick. Often used in the passive: *I've been had.* **10.** To keep or put in a specified place, position, or condition: *have the carpet in the hall; had them eating out of his hand.* **11.** To accept or take: *I'll have the gray jacket.* **12.** To partake of; consume, as by eating or drinking. **13.** To obtain or receive. **14.** To be made of, consist of, or contain. **15.** To feel as an emotion: *has great love for her parents.* **16.** To exercise or bring into play. Used with *on*: *have mercy on me.* **17.** To allow; permit. Usually used in the negative: *I will not have the children out after dark.* **18. a.** To cause or arrange for (something to be done): *have the car fixed.* **b.** To order, invite, or compel: *have him go home; want to have you over for a drink.* **19.** To perform (an action) or take part in (an activity): *have a look at this; have the next dance.* **20.** To engage in. **21.** To carry out or stage: *have a party.* **22.** To be the subject of: *have a large funeral.* **23. a.** To experience; undergo. **b.** To enjoy: *have a good summer.* **24.** To suffer from (a disease or physical disability, for example): *She has multiple sclerosis.* **25.** To give birth to; bear: *She's going to have twins.* **26.** To be compelled: *have to go now.* **27.** To be scheduled for: *have an appointment at noon.* **28.** To be able to use; be in command of or competent in: *have the necessary technique; has no Latin.* **29.** To come to know; be informed about: *have it on good authority.* **30.** To receive as a guest: *She has her mother-in-law for a week.* **—had better** (or **best**). Ought to: *You had better go now.* **—had just as well.** Might as well. **—have at.** To attack. **—have done with.** To be through with; finish. **—have had it.** *Informal.* **1.** To have done everything that is possible or that will be permitted. **2.** To have endured all that one can. **3.** To be in a state beyond remedy, repair, or salvage. **—have it. 1.** To imply or state: *Talk has it they're getting a divorce.* **2.** To find or stumble on the answer or solution. **—have it in for.** To wish to harm, especially because of a grudge. **—have it out.** To settle decisively, especially by a full discussion or by a fight. **—have on. 1.** To be wearing. **2.** *Informal.* To be scheduled for or committed to. **—have someone on.** To deceive in a teasing, lighthearted way. **—have something coming.** *Informal.* To deserve whatever one receives: *He had that rebuke coming.* **—have something on someone.** To have well-supported suspicions or incriminating evidence regarding someone. **—let someone have it.** *Informal.* To attack (someone). **—not have any.** *Informal.* **1.** To refuse to tolerate. **2.** To refuse to become interested or involved. —See Usage note at **get.**

~*n.* A person or class enjoying material comforts as opposed to those who are poor: *The haves and the have-nots often have different political philosophies.* [Have, had, had, has; Middle English *haven* or *habben, hadde, had, has,* Old English *habban, hæfde, (ge)hæfd, hæbbe,* from Germanic *habhēn* (attested).]

have·lock (hăv′lŏk′, -lək) *n.* A cloth covering for a cap, having a flap to protect the back of the neck. [After Sir Henry *Havelock* (died 1857), British general in India.]

ha·ven (hā′vən) *n.* **1.** A harbor or anchorage; a port. **2.** A place of refuge; a sanctuary. —See Synonyms at **shelter.**

~*tr.v.* **havened, -vening, -vens.** *Rare.* To put into a haven. [Middle English, Old English *hæfen,* from Old Norse *höfn.*]

have-not (hăv′nŏt′) *n.* A person or class enjoying few or no material comforts. Used chiefly in the plural.

have·n't (hăv′ənt). Contraction of *have not.*

ha·ver (hā′vər) *intr.v.* **-vered, -vering, -vers. 1.** *British.* To dither; vacillate. **2.** *British Regional & Scottish.* To indulge in idle chatter; babble.

~*n.* *British Regional & Scottish.* Foolish or inconsequential talk; chitchat or nonsense. [18th century : origin obscure.]

hav·er·sack (hăv′ər-săk′) *n.* A canvas bag with straps worn over a shoulder or on the back to carry supplies on a hike or march. [French *havresac,* from German *Habersack,* originally bag for oats : *Haber,* oats + *Sack,* SACK.]

Ha·ver·sian canal (hə-vûr′zhən) *n.* *Anatomy.* Any of the fine interconnecting channels that carry the blood and nerve supply in bones. [After Clopton *Havers* (died 1702), English anatomist who discovered the channels.]

hav·er·sine (hăv′ər-sīn′) *n.* *Mathematics.* Half the value of a versed sine. [Blend of *half* + *versed* + *sine.*]

hav·il·dar (hăv′əl-där′) *n.* A noncommissioned officer in the Indian army corresponding to a sergeant. [Hindi, from Persian *hawāldār,* one having charge.]

hav·oc (hăv′ək) *n.* **1.** Destruction, as caused by a natural calamity or war; devastation. **2.** Confusion; disorder; muddle. **—cry havoc. 1.** *Archaic.* To signal an army to begin pillaging or collecting spoils. **2.** To sound an alarm. **—play havoc with.** To destroy, ruin, or make a mess of.

~*v.* **havocked, -ocking, -ocs.** *Poetic.* —*tr.* To destroy; devastate. —*intr.* To cause havoc. [Middle English *havok,* from Norman French, variant of Old French *havot*†, plunder, cry used to begin plunder.]

haw[1] (hô) *n.* A vocalized pause in speech.

~*intr.v.* **hawed, hawing, haws.** To pause in speaking. Used in the phrase *hem and haw.* See **hem** (short cough). [Imitative.]

haw[2] *n.* **1.** The fruit of a hawthorn. **2.** A hawthorn or similar tree or shrub. [Middle English *haw(e),* Old English *haga,* hawthorn, hedge, from Germanic.]

haw[3] *n.* The nictitating membrane, especially of a domesticated animal. [16th century : origin obscure.]

haw[4] *interj.* Used to command an animal to turn left. Compare **gee.**

~*intr.v.* **hawed, hawing, haws.** To turn to the left. [Origin unknown.]

Ha·wai·i (hə-wä′ē, -wä′yə, -wī′ə). Formerly **Sand·wich Islands** (sănd′wĭch, săn′-). A group of islands in the North Pacific; in 1959 it became the 50th state of the Union. Hawaii comprises more than 20 volcanic islands, including Maui, Kauai, Oahu (on which Honolulu, the state capital, is situated), and Hawaii, the principal and southernmost island of the group. Its economy depends on sugarcane and pineapple cultivation and on tourism. Since Capt. James Cook's discovery of the islands (1778), the population and culture have become a mix of European, Oriental, and Polynesian.

Ha·wai·ian (hə-wä′yən) *n.* **1.** A native or resident of Hawaii. **2.** The Polynesian language spoken by the inhabitants of Hawaii. **—Ha·wai·ian** *adj.*

Hawaiian guitar *n.* An electric guitar consisting of a long sounding board and six to eight steel strings that are plucked while being pressed with a steel bar.

haw·finch (hô′fĭnch′) *n.* A Eurasian bird, *Coccothraustes cocco-*

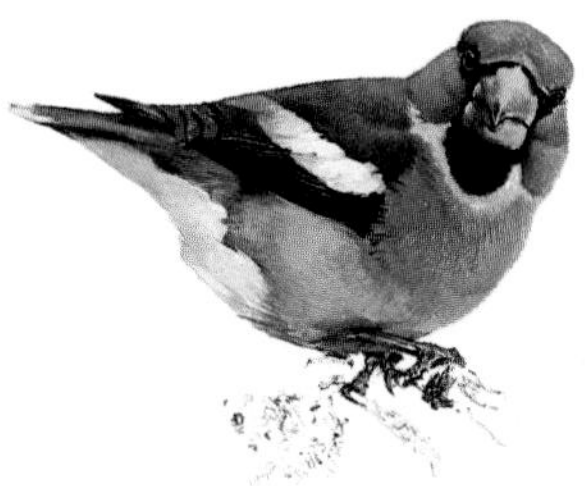

hawfinch *The thick beak of the hawfinch is operated by powerful muscles that enable it to crack open and eat large seeds and the hard stones of tree fruit such as cherries, sloes, and damsons. The birds, which also feed on holly berries and haws, are found in temperate latitudes across Europe and Asia.*

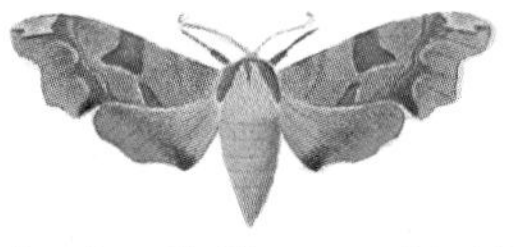

hawk moth *These powerful night fliers—some can fly at more than 50 kilometers (30 miles) per hour —get their name from the ability of some species to hover like a hawk while they suck nectar from flowers. The moths' wingspans range from 50 to 112 millimeters (2–4½ inches). This is the lime hawk moth, native to Britain, which feeds on the leaves of lime trees and elms.*

PRONUNCIATION KEY

ă, pat; ā, pay; âr, care;
ä, father, are; b, bib;
ch, church; d, deed; ĕ, pet;
ē, be; f, fife; g, gag; h, hat;
hw, which; ĭ, pit; ī, pie;
îr, pier; j, judge; k, kick;
l, lid, needle; m, mum;
n, no, sudden; ng, thing;
ŏ, pot; ō, toe; ô, paw, for;
oi, noise; ou, out; o͝o, book;
o͞o, boot; p, pop; r, roar;
s, sauce; sh, ship, dish;
t, tight; th, thin, path;
th, this, bathe; ŭ, cut; ûr, fur;
v, valve; w, with; y, yes;
z, zebra, size; zh, vision;
ə, about, item, edible, gallop, circus, peaceful

IN FOREIGN WORDS:

à, *Fr.* ami; œ, *Fr.* feu, *Ger.* schön; ü, *Fr.* tu, *Ger.* über;
KH, *Ger.* ich, *Scot.* loch;
ɴ, *Fr.* bon; y′, *Fr.* Compiègne

STRESS MARKS:

Primary stress: ′
in·cite′ (ĭn-sīt′)
Secondary stress: ′
in′sight′ (ĭn′sīt′)

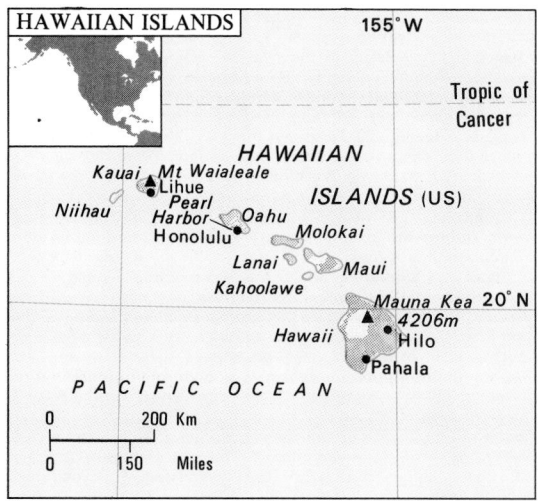

HAWAIIAN ISLANDS   155°W

thraustes, having a thick bill, brown, white, and black plumage, and a short tail. [HAW (fruit) + FINCH.]

haw-haw¹. Variant of **ha-ha** (laughter).

haw-haw². Variant of **ha-ha** (a ditch).

Haw-Haw, Lord. See William **Joyce.**

hawk¹ (hôk) *n.* **1.** Any of various birds of prey of the order Falconiformes, and especially of the genera *Accipiter* and *Buteo,* characteristically having a short, hooked bill and strong claws adapted for seizing. **2.** Any of various similar birds. **3.** A grasping, rapacious, or ruthless person who preys on others; a shark. **4. a.** One who favors an aggressive foreign policy. **b.** Broadly, one who takes a vigorous, uncompromising line on any matter of policy: *The hawks in the cabinet voted for further cuts in the education budget.* In this sense, compare **dove.**
~*v.* **hawked, hawking, hawks.** —*intr.* **1.** To hunt with trained hawks. **2.** To swoop and strike in the manner of a hawk. —*tr.* To hunt on the wing. Used of a bird. [Middle English *hauk,* Old English *h(e)afoc,* from Germanic.] —**hawk·er** *n.* —**hawk·ish** *adj.* —**hawk·ish·ly** *adv.* —**hawk·ish·ness** *n.*

hawk² *v.* **hawked, hawking, hawks.** —*intr.* To peddle; especially, to peddle wares by crying them in the streets. —*tr.* **1.** To carry (goods) about in the streets and offer them for sale by calling out; peddle. **2.** To spread (gossip, one's opinions, and the like). [Backformation from HAWKER.]

hawk³ *v.* **hawked, hawking, hawks.** —*intr.* To clear or attempt to clear the throat by coughing up phlegm. —*tr.* To clear the throat by coughing up (phlegm).
~*n.* An audible effort to clear the throat by expelling phlegm. [Imitative.]

hawk⁴ *n.* A small board with a handle on the underside, used to hold mortar or plaster. [17th century : origin obscure.]

hawk·er (hô′kər) *n.* A peddler, typically one who solicits business by calling at private houses. [Probably from Low German *höker,* from Middle Low German *höker,* from *höken,* to peddle, bend.]

hawk-eyed (hôk′īd′) *adj.* Having very sharp eyesight.

Haw·kins, Haw·kyns (hô′kĭnz), **Sir John** (1532–95). English naval administrator and officer. One of the most important seamen of his time, he directed the rebuilding of the royal fleet, which resulted in faster, better-armed ships that rebuffed the Spanish Armada (1588) and helped establish England as a major naval power.

hawk moth *n.* Any of various moths of the family Sphingidae, having a large body and long, narrow forewings and characteristically feeding while in flight on nectar from flowers. Also called "hummingbird moth," "sphinx moth."

Hawks (hôks), **Howard** (1896–1977). U.S. film director. His films include the thrillers *Scarface* (1932) and *The Big Sleep* (1946), the western *Red River* (1948), war films such as *The Dawn Patrol* (1930), and comedies, including *Bringing Up Baby* (1938).

hawk's-beard (hôks′bîrd′) *n.* Any of various plants of the genus *Crepis,* resembling the dandelion. [After its large bristly pappus.]

hawks·bill (hôks′bĭl′) *n.* A tropical sea turtle, *Eretmochelys imbricata,* valued as a source of tortoiseshell.

hawk·weed (hôk′wēd′) *n.* Any of various plants of the genus *Hieracium,* having yellow or orange dandelionlike flowers.

Ha·worth (hou′ərth). Village in West Yorkshire, England. It was here that the Brontë sisters lived and wrote; some of their novels, including *Wuthering Heights,* are set in the surrounding countryside. The parsonage that was their home has been preserved as a museum.

hawse (hôz) *n. Nautical.* **1.** The part of a ship where the hawseholes are located. **2.** A hawsehole or hawsepipe. **3.** The space between the bows of an anchored ship and her anchors. **4.** The arrangement of a ship's anchor cables when both starboard and port anchors are secured. [Middle English *halse,* probably from Old Norse *hals,* neck, ship's bow.]

hawse-hole (hôz′hōl′) *n. Nautical.* An opening in the bow of a ship through which a cable or hawser is passed.

hawse-pipe (hôz′pīp′) *n. Nautical.* A metal pipe running through a hawsehole through which a cable or hawser is passed.

haw-ser (hô′zər) *n. Nautical.* A cable or rope used in mooring or towing a ship. [Middle English *hauceour, hawser,* from Norman French *hauceour,* from Old French *haucier,* to lift, hoist, from Vulgar Latin *altiāre* (unattested), from Latin *altus,* high.]

haw-thorn (hô′thôrn′) *n.* Any of various thorny trees or shrubs of the genus *Crataegus,* especially *C. monogyna,* having white or pinkish flowers and reddish fruit. Also called "haw," "may," "may tree," "mayflower." [Middle English *haw(e)thorn,* Old English *hagathorn : haga,* HAW (fruit) + THORN.]

Haw-thorne (hô′thôrn′), **Nathaniel** (1804–64). U.S. novelist and short-story writer. He was born at Salem in Massachusetts and won fame with the novels *The Scarlet Letter* (1850) and *The House of the Seven Gables* (1851).

hay (hā) *n.* **1.** Grass or other plants such as clover or alfalfa, cut and dried for fodder. **2.** *Slang.* A trifling amount of money. Used only in negative phrases, especially in *that ain't hay.* —**hit the hay.** *Slang.* To go to bed. —**make hay while the sun shines.** To take full advantage of an opportunity.
~*v.* **hayed, haying, hays.** —*intr.* To convert grass into hay. —*tr.* **1.** To make (grass) into hay. **2.** To feed with hay. **3.** To put (land) under hay. [Middle English *hei, hay,* Old English *hīeg,* from Germanic.]

hay-box (hā′bŏks′) *n. Chiefly British.* A box filled with hay in which heated food can be left to continue cooking by retained heat.

hay-cock (hā′kŏk′) *n. Chiefly British.* A conical mound of hay in a field.

Hay·dn (hīd′n), **Franz Joseph** (1732–1809). Austrian composer. He wrote 104 symphonies and 84 string quartets, as well as operas and concertos. Among his works are the oratorios *The Creation* (1798) and *The Seasons* (1801). Mozart and Beethoven studied with him.

Hayes (hāz), **Helen** (1900–). U.S. actress. She has displayed her versatility and durability as an actress in a 50-year career encompassing stage, film, radio, and television performances, including her acclaimed portrayal of Queen Victoria in *Victoria Regina* (1933–34) and Oscar-winning performances in *The Sin of Madelon Claudet* (1935) and *Airport* (1970).

Hayes, Rutherford Birchard (1822–93). 19th U.S. president (1877–81). Winning the controversial election of 1876 by one electoral vote, he pacified the South by removing federal troops (1877), vetoed a bill restricting Chinese immigration (1879), and stemmed Congress's attempts to usurp presidential power.

hay fever *n.* An allergic condition of the upper respiratory tract and the eyes, characterized by a running nose, watering eyes, and sneezing due to histamine release caused by an abnormal sensitivity to certain airborne particles, notably pollen and dust.

hay-fork (hā′fôrk′) *n.* **1.** A long-handled pronged tool for moving hay; a pitchfork. **2.** A machine-operated fork for moving hay.

hay-loft (hā′lôft′, -lŏft′) *n.* A loft for storing hay.

hay-mak-er (hā′mā′kər) *n.* **1.** One who makes grass into hay. **2.** A machine that makes hay; especially, one that processes it so that it dries evenly and quickly. **3.** *Slang.* A powerful blow with the fist.

hay-mow (hā′mou′) *n.* **1.** A hayloft or haystack. **2.** The hay stored in a hayloft or haystack.

hay-rack (hā′răk′) *n.* **1.** A rack from which livestock eat hay. **2. a.** A rack fitted to a wagon for carrying hay. **b.** A wagon so fitted.

hay-rick (hā′rĭk′) *n.* A haystack.

hay-seed (hā′sēd′) *n.* **1.** Grass seed shaken out of hay. **2.** Pieces of chaff or straw that fall from hay. **3.** *Slang.* A country bumpkin.

hay-stack (hā′stăk′) *n.* A large stack of hay, usually built up into a cuboid shape with a ridged top.

hay-ward (hā′wôrd′) *n.* An officer formerly charged with the repair of fences and enclosures, and especially with the retention of cattle on the town common. [Middle English *hayward, heiward :* obsolete *heie,* hedge, fence, Old English *hege* + WARD.]

hay-wire (hā′wīr′) *n.* Wire used in baling hay.
~*adj. Informal.* **1.** Put together in a makeshift way. **2.** Not functioning properly; broken or in a state of disorder. **3.** Mentally confused or erratic; crazy. —**go haywire. 1.** To function improperly or fall into disorder. **2.** To break down mentally and act erratically. [Baling wire is often used for makeshift repair jobs.]

haz-ard (hăz′ərd) *n.* **1. a.** A source of potential loss or danger; a peril; a risk: *an occupational hazard.* **b.** Vulnerability to loss or danger: *at hazard.* **2.** A chance or accident. **3.** *Obsolete.* A gamble; a stake. **4.** A dice game resembling craps. **5.** Any of the openings in a court-tennis court through which the ball may be hit for points. **6.** A bunker or other obstacle on a golf course. —See Synonyms at **danger.**
~*tr.v.* **hazarded, -arding, -ards. 1.** To imperil; jeopardize. **2.** To run the risk of; expose oneself to. **3.** To venture (something); dare: *hazard a guess.* [Middle English *hasard, hazard,* from Old French *hasard,* from Spanish *azar,* throw of the dice, accident, from Arabic *al-zahr,* luck, chance.]

haz-ard-ous (hăz′ər-dəs) *adj.* **1.** Marked by danger; perilous. **2.** Depending on chance; risky.

hazard warning signal *n.* The simultaneous flashing of all the directional indicators on a motor vehicle, used as a warning to other road users when the vehicle has broken down or is otherwise obstructing traffic.

haze¹ (hāz) *n.* **1. a.** Atmospheric moisture, dust, smoke, and vapor suspended to form a partially opaque condition. **b.** *Meteorology.* The atmospheric condition so formed when visibility is less than

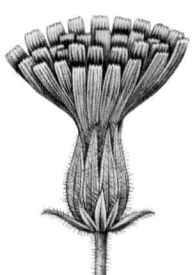

hawk's-beard *A European wildflower that is often confused with the dandelion because their blooms are so similar. Unlike the dandelion, the hawk's-beard holds its flowers on branching stems.*

hawksbill *Of about 230 species of turtle and tortoise, the hawksbill turtle is one of five marine varieties. These turtles rarely leave the water except to lay eggs in the sand on tropical beaches. The hatched young must find their own way to the water.*

hawkweed *A wildflower that grows in limestone cliffs and rocks, the hawkweed can produce ripe seed without fertilization. This leads to many mutations, making it difficult to identify different types.*

hawthorn *Hawthorns, or may trees, are widely used in Europe to form prickly, livestockproof hedges. The trees bear fleshy berries, or haws.*

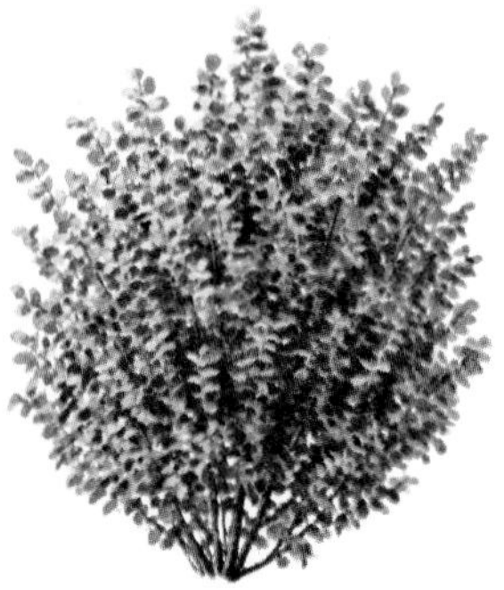

hazel *Mature hazels have been grown for centuries for their edible nuts. Young branches are also harvested because their straightness and flexibility make them ideal for fences and stakes.*

PRONUNCIATION KEY

ă, pat; ā, pay; âr, care;
ä, father, are; b, **bib**;
ch, **church**; d, **deed**; ĕ, pet;
ē, be; f, **fife**; g, **gag**; h, **hat**;
hw, **which**; ĭ, pit; ī, pie;
îr, pier; j, **judge**; k, **kick**;
l, lid, needle; m, **mum**;
n, no, sudden; ng, thing;
ŏ, pot; ō, **toe**; ô, **paw**, **for**;
oi, noise; ou, **out**; o͝o, **book**;
o͞o, boot; p, **pop**; r, roar;
s, sauce; sh, **ship**, **dish**;
t, tight; th, **thin**, **path**;
th, **this**, **bathe**; ŭ, **cut**; ûr, **fur**;
v, valve; w, **with**; y, **yes**;
z, zebra, size; zh, vision;
ə, about, item, edible, gallop, circus, peaceful

IN FOREIGN WORDS:

à, *Fr.* ami; œ, *Fr.* **feu**, *Ger.* **schön**; ü, *Fr.* **tu**, *Ger.* **über**;
KH, *Ger.* **ich**, *Scot.* loch;
N, *Fr.* bon; y', *Fr.* **Compiègne**

STRESS MARKS:

Primary stress: ′
in·cite′ (ĭn-sīt′)
Secondary stress: ′
in′sight′ (ĭn′sīt′)

1.24 miles (2 kilometers) but not less than 0.62 miles (1 kilometer). **c.** Indistinct visibility caused by rising heat: *a heat haze.* **2.** A vague or confused state of mind.
∼v. **hazed, hazing, hazes.** *—intr.* To become misty or hazy; blur. *—tr.* To make hazy. [Back-formation from HAZY.]

haze² *tr.v.* **hazed, hazing, hazes. 1.** *Nautical.* To persecute or punish with meaningless, difficult, or humiliating tasks. **2.** To initiate, as into a college fraternity, by exacting humiliating performances from or playing rough practical jokes upon. **3.** *Regional.* To drive (cattle or horses) with saddle horses. [Perhaps akin to Old French *haser*†, to insult, harass.] **—haz·er** *n.*

ha·zel (hā′zəl) *n.* **1.** Any of various shrubs or small trees of the genus *Corylus;* especially, *C. avellana,* of Europe, or *C. americana,* of North America, bearing edible nuts enclosed in a leafy husk. **2.** The nut of such a tree or shrub; a hazelnut. **3.** Light to strong brown or yellowish brown. [Middle English *hasel,* Old English *hæsel,* from Germanic.] **—ha·zel** *adj.*

hazel hen *n.* A Eurasian grouse, *Tetrastes bonasia,* having brownish-red plumage with gray and white markings. Also called "hazel grouse."

ha·zel·nut (hā′zəl-nŭt′) *n.* The edible nut of a hazel, having a smooth, hard brown shell. Also called "cob," "cobnut," "filbert."

Haz·litt (hăz′lĭt), **William** (1778–1830). British essayist and critic. He was a friend of Coleridge and Wordsworth. His works include *Characters of Shakespeare* (1817) and *The Spirit of the Age* (1825).

haz·y (hā′zē) *adj.* **-ier, -iest. 1.** Marked by the presence of haze; misty. **2.** Not clearly defined; vague; confused. [17th century (nautical) : origin obscure.] **—haz·i·ly** *adv.* **—haz·i·ness** *n.*

hazzan. Variant of **chazan.**

hb, hb. halfback.

Hb hemoglobin.

HB (āch′bē′) *adj.* Designating a pencil or pencil lead that is medium hard.
∼n. An HB pencil. [Abbreviation for *hard black.*]

H-beam (āch′bēm′) *n.* A steel joist or girder with an H-shaped cross section. Also called "H-girder."

H-bomb (āch′bŏm′) *n.* A **hydrogen bomb** *(see).*

H.C. 1. Holy Communion. **2.** House of Commons.

hd. 1. hand. **2.** head.

hdbk. handbook.

hdqrs. headquarters.

he¹ (hē) *pron.* The third person singular pronoun in the nominative case, masculine gender. **1.** Used to represent the male person, animal, or other being last mentioned or implied. **2.** Used to represent any person whose sex is not specified: *Everyone knows he is mortal.* —See Usage note at **me.**
∼n. A male animal or person: *Is the cat a he?* Often used in combination: *a he-cat.* [Middle English *he,* Old English *hĕ.*]

he² (hā) *n.* The fifth letter of the Hebrew alphabet. See feature at **alphabet.** [Hebrew *hē,* possibly "lattice window."]

he³ (hē) *interj.* Also **he-he** (hē′hē′). Used to express amusement or derision.

he⁴ (hē) *n.* A children's game, **tag** *(see).* [From HE (pronoun).]

He The symbol for the element helium.

HE, H.E. 1. high explosive. **2.** *Ecclesiastical.* His Eminence. **3.** His (or Her) Excellency.

head (hĕd) *n., pl.* **heads** or **head** (for sense 7b). *Abbr.* **hd. 1. a.** The upper or anterior vertebrate extremity, containing the brain and the eyes, ears, nose, mouth, and jaws. **b.** The analogous part of an invertebrate. **2.** The seat of the faculty of reason; intelligence, intellect, or mind. **3. a.** A mental facility or aptitude: *a head for mathematics.* **b.** A natural ability to deal with a specified thing or situation without losing one's self-control: *no head for drink; a good head for heights.* **4. a.** Poise; wits; composure: *Keep your head in a crisis.* **b.** Freedom to move or act without restraint. **5.** A portrait or representation of a head. **6.** Life: *a crime that cost him his head.* **7. a.** An individual considered as a unit: *a head count; The cost is $25 per head.* **b.** A single animal within a herd: *20 head of cattle.* **8.** The hair on the human head. **9. a.** One who occupies the foremost position; a leader, chief, or director: *the head of a big engineering company.* **b.** A headmaster or headmistress. **c.** The foremost or leading position: *at the head of the parade.* **10. a.** The difference in depth of a liquid at two given points. **b.** The measure of pressure at the lower point expressed in terms of this difference. **c.** Pressure, as of a liquid or vapor: *a head of steam.* **11.** The foam on an effervescent liquid. **12.** The breaking point or tip of a suppurating abscess, boil, or pimple. **13.** A turning point; a crisis: *bring matters to a head.* **14.** A projection, weight, or fixture at one end of an elongated object: *the head of a pin.* **15.** The operating part of a tool, machine, or other device, as: **a.** The working end of a hammer or ax. **b.** The operative part of a tape recorder or other device for recording and detecting stored information on magnetic tape or disks. **c.** The explosive part of a bomb, missile, or the like; a warhead. **16.** A rounded, compact mass of leaves, buds, or flowers, as of cabbage, lettuce, or cauliflower. **17.** *Botany.* A dense, compact cluster of flowers, as of composite plants or clover. **18.** The end of an object whose two ends are interchangeable, such as a drum. **19.** *Nautical.* **a.** The forepart of a vessel. **b.** The latrine of a vessel. **c.** The top part or upper edge of a sail. **20.** The source of a stream; a headwater. **21.** The upper end or extremity of something, as: **a.** The top of a staircase. **b.** The top of a page. **c.** The end of a bed where one's head lies. **d.** The end associated with a real or figurative head: *sitting at the head of the table.* **e.** The upper, landward end of a bay or lake. **22.** A high promontory, cape, or cliff rising above a body of water. **23.** A passage or gallery in a mine. **24.** *Astronomy.* The coma and nucleus of a comet. **25.** *Grammar.* The word in a construction that determines the syntactic character of the construction; for example, in the phrase *a lazy young boy, boy* is the head that determines that the whole structure functions as a noun. **26.** A **cylinder head** *(see).* **27. a.** A headline or heading. **b.** A distinct topic or category. **28.** Headway; progress. **29.** The head used as a rough unit of measure: *taller by a head; lost by a head.* **30.** *Informal.* A headache. **31.** *Slang.* A habitual user of drugs such as marijuana and LSD. **—bite someone's head off.** *Informal.* To speak angrily to someone. **—down by the head.** *Nautical.* With the bow lying lower in the water than the stern. **—go to one's head. 1.** To make lightheaded or drunk. **2.** To increase the pride or conceit of. **—head and shoulders above.** Far superior to. **—head or tail.** Something clear or unmistakable: *I couldn't make head or tail of the lecture.* **—in one's head.** In one's mind; internally: *did the sum in her head.* **—keep one's head above water.** To keep out of trouble, such as debt or poverty. **—off one's head.** Crazy; insane. **—off the top of one's head.** Impromptu; without careful consideration. **—on (or upon) one's head.** Within one's own responsibility, or at one's own risk: *"My deeds upon my head!"* (Shakespeare). **—one's head off.** *Informal.* Immoderately; inordinately; to extreme: *He snored his head off.* **—out of one's head. 1.** Delirious. **2.** Crazy. **3.** High on drugs or alcohol. **—over one's head. 1.** Beyond one's ability to understand or deal with: *a subject that is over his head.* **2.** To one higher in command: *go over the sergeant's head.* **3.** Notwithstanding the claims of others: *promoted over the heads of several senior managers.* **—put (or lay) heads together.** To combine forces or abilities. **—take it into one's head.** To make a sudden decision to do something, especially something unusual or irrational. **—turn someone's head. 1.** To infatuate someone, especially if the passion inspired is groundless or rash. **2.** To make someone conceited.
∼adj. **1.** Foremost in rank or importance: *the head librarian.* **2.** Placed at the top or front: *the head name on the list.* **3.** Coming from ahead or from the front: *head winds.*
∼v. **headed, heading, heads.** *—tr.* **1.** To be director or chief of; command: *head the committee.* **2.** To assume or be placed in the first or foremost position of: *head the line of march.* **3.** To aim or direct: *head the horse for home.* **4.** To remove the top of (a plant or tree). Often used with *down.* **5.** *Soccer.* To drive (the ball) by hitting it with the head. **6.** To place a head or heading on: *headed each column with a number.* **—head off. 1.** To block the progress of and force to change direction; intercept. **2.** To forestall or deflect (criticism, for example). *—intr.* **1.** To proceed or set out in a specified direction: *head for town.* **2.** To proceed toward or be destined for a specified, often undesirable condition: *headed for bankruptcy.* **3.** To form a head, as lettuce or cabbage. **4.** To originate; rise. Used of a stream or river. [Middle English *heved, he(f)d,* Old English *hēafod,* from Germanic.]

Head (hĕd), **Edith** (1898–1981). U.S. costume designer. Her first solo credit for designing motion-picture costumes was for *She Done Him Wrong* (1933). During her years as head designer for Paramount and Universal studios, she received 34 Academy Award nominations and won a record 8 Oscars for such movies as *All About Eve* (1950), *Sabrina* (1954), and *The Sting* (1973).

head·ache (hĕd′āk′) *n.* **1.** A pain in the head caused by mental or emotional stress, fatigue, or illness. **2.** *Informal.* Someone or something that annoys or bothers. **—head·ach·y** *adj.*

head·band (hĕd′bănd′) *n.* **1.** A band worn around the head. **2.** A cloth band attached to the top of the spine of a book.

head-bang (hĕd′băng′) *intr.v.* **-banged, -banging, -bangs.** To shake the head in a wild, frenzied manner while dancing to heavy-metal music. **—head-bang·ing** *n. & adj.*

head·board (hĕd′bôrd′, -bōrd′) *n.* A board, panel, or the like that forms the head, as of a bed.

head·case (hĕd′kās′) *n. British Slang.* A very stupid person; a dolt.

head·cheese (hĕd′chēz′) *n.* **1.** A jellied loaf or sausage containing chopped and boiled parts of the feet, head, and sometimes the tongue and heart of an animal, usually a hog. **2.** *Chiefly British.* **Brawn** *(see).*

head cold *n.* **Coryza** *(see).*

head·dress (hĕd′drĕs′) *n.* Anything worn on the head, as a covering or ornament.

head·ed (hĕd′ĭd) *adj.* **1.** Growing or grown into a head. **2.** Having a head or heads of the specified type or number. Used in combination: *three-headed.* **3.** Having a mental make-up of the specified type. Used in combination: *level-headed.*

head·er (hĕd′ər) *n.* **1.** One that fits a head on an object. **2.** One that removes a head from an object; especially, a machine that reaps the heads of grain and passes them into a wagon or receptacle. **3.** A pipe that serves as a central connection for two or more smaller pipes. **4.** A wooden beam in a floor or roof placed between two long beams and supporting the ends of one or more tailpieces. **5.** A brick laid across rather than parallel with a wall. Compare **stretcher. 6.** *Informal.* A headlong dive or fall. **7.** A raised tank or hopper that maintains a constant pressure or supply to some system, especially the small tank supplying water to a central-heating system. In this sense, also called "header tank."

head·fast (hĕd′făst′, -fäst′) *n.* A mooring rope or chain that secures the bow of a ship to the wharf.

head·first (hĕd′fûrst′) *adv.* Also **head·fore·most** (hĕd′fôr′mōst′, -məst, hĕd′fōr′-). **1.** With the head leading; headlong: *go headfirst down the stairs.* **2.** Impetuously; brashly. **—head·first** *adj.*

head gate *n.* A control gate upstream of a lock or canal.

head·gear (hĕd′gîr′) *n.* **1.** A covering, such as a hat or helmet, for the head. **2.** The part of a harness that fits about a horse's head. **3.** The rigging for hauling or lifting located at the head of a mine shaft. **4.** *Nautical.* The rigging on the forward sails.

head·hunt·ing (hĕd′hŭn′tĭng) *n.* **1.** The taking of human heads as trophies, practiced for religious purposes in some primitive societies. **2.** *Slang.* The attempt to recruit personnel, especially executive personnel. **3.** *Slang.* The process of eliminating or neutralizing political rivals. —**head·hunt·er** *n.*

head·ing (hĕd′ĭng) *n.* **1. a.** A word or words at the head of a chapter, paragraph, letter, or the like. **b.** A division or category. **2.** *Navigation.* The course or direction of movement of a ship or aircraft. **3.** *Mining.* **a.** A gallery or drift. **b.** The end of a gallery or drift.

head·lamp (hĕd′lămp′) *n.* A headlight.

head·land (hĕd′lənd, -lănd′) *n.* **1.** A point of land, usually high and with a sheer drop, extending out into a body of water; a promontory. **2.** The unplowed land at the end of a plowed furrow.

head·less (hĕd′lĭs) *adj.* **1. a.** Formed without a head. **b.** Decapitated. **2.** Without a leader or director. **3.** Witless; foolish.

head·light (hĕd′līt′) *n.* A powerful lamp, usually one of a pair, mounted on the front of a vehicle.

head·line (hĕd′līn) *n.* **1.** The title or caption of a newspaper article, set in large type, the size denoting the importance of the article. **2.** A line at the head of a page giving the title, author, page number, or the like. **3. headlines.** A brief résumé of the main items of interest at the beginning or end of a radio or television news bulletin. ~*tr.v.* **headlined, -lining, -lines.** **1.** To supply (an article or page) with a headline. **2.** To serve as the headliner of: *He headlines the bill.*

head·lin·er (hĕd′lī′nər) *n.* A performer who receives prominent billing; a star.

head·lock (hĕd′lŏk′) *n.* A wrestling hold in which the head of one wrestler is locked under the arm of the other.

head·long (hĕd′lông′, -lŏng′) *adv.* **1.** With the head leading; headfirst. **2.** Impetuously; rashly. **3.** At breakneck speed or with uncontrolled force. ~*adj.* **1.** Headfirst; done with the head leading: *a headlong fall.* **2.** Impetuous; rash. **3.** Uncontrollably forceful or fast. **4.** *Archaic.* Steep; sheer. —See Usage note at **impetuous.** [Middle English *hedlong,* variant of *hedling : hed,* HEAD + -LING.]

head·man (hĕd′măn′, -mən) *n., pl.* **-men** (-mĕn′, -mĭn). A chief or leader of a tribe or village.

head·mas·ter, head master (hĕd′măs′tər, -mä′stər) *n. Abbr.* **H.M.** A male school principal.

head·mis·tress, head mistress (hĕd′mĭs′trĭs) *n.* A female school principal.

head money *n.* **1.** A reward paid for the capture and delivery of a fugitive; a bounty. **2.** A poll tax.

head·most (hĕd′mōst′, -məst) *adj.* Leading; foremost. Said especially of a ship.

head note *n.* A note at the beginning of a page or document; especially, one prefixed to a report of a legal case that summarizes its contents.

head of state *n.* One, typically a monarch or president, who acts as the formal and ceremonial head of a nation as opposed to the head of the government. The head of state may either be a figurehead or have executive power, depending on the state's constitution.

head of the river *n. British.* **1.** Any of various rowing regattas; especially, one at which bumping races are held. **2.** The boat or crew holding the leading position in such a regatta.

head·on (hĕd′ŏn′, -ôn′) *adj.* **1.** Facing forward; frontal. **2.** With the front end exposed and receiving the impact: *a head-on collision.* **3.** Direct and uncompromising. —**head·on** *adv.*

head over heels *adv.* **1.** Rolling, as in a somersault. **2.** To the point of abandon; hopelessly: *head over heels in love.*

head·phone (hĕd′fōn′) *n.* A receiver, as for a telephone, radio, or record player, held to the ears by a band that fits over the head.

head·piece (hĕd′pēs′) *n.* **1.** A helmet, hat, or other headgear. **2.** A set of headphones; a headset. **3.** *Printing.* An ornamental design at the top of a page. **4.** *Archaic.* The head as the seat of intellect.

head·quar·ter (hĕd′kwôr′tər) *v.* **-tered, -tering, -ters.** *Informal.* —*intr.* To establish headquarters. —*tr.* To provide with headquarters. [Back-formation from HEADQUARTERS.]

> *Usage:* The verb *headquarter* is used informally in both transitive and intransitive senses: *The European correspondent will headquarter in Paris. The magazine has headquartered him in a building that houses many foreign journalists.* Neither of these examples is considered acceptable in formal writing.

head·quar·ters (hĕd′kwôr′tərz) *pl.n. Abbr.* **hdqrs., h.q., HQ, H.Q.** Sometimes used with a singular verb. **1.** The offices of a commander, as of a military unit, from which official orders are issued. **2.** Any center of operations: *Father makes the study his headquarters.*

> *Usage:* The noun *headquarters* is used with either a singular or plural verb. The plural is more common: *The headquarters are in New York.* But the singular is sometimes preferred when reference is to authority rather than to physical location: *Battalion headquarters has approved the retreat.*

head·race (hĕd′rās′) *n.* A watercourse that feeds water into a mill, water wheel, or turbine. Compare **tailrace.**

head·rest (hĕd′rĕst′) *n.* A support for the head, as at the back of a chair or car seat.

head·room (hĕd′rōōm′, -rŏŏm′) *n.* The vertical space in a room or

under a bridge, doorway, or the like; clearance.

heads (hĕdz) *n. Used with a singular verb.* The obverse side of a coin, often carrying a representation of a head. Compare **tails.**

head·sail (hĕd′səl, -sāl′) *n.* A sail, such as a jib, set forward of a foremast.

head·scarf (hĕd′skärf′) *n.* A scarf worn over the head, usually folded in a triangle and tied under the chin.

head sea *n.* Waves running directly against the course of a ship.

head·set (hĕd′sĕt′) *n.* A pair of headphones.

head·ship (hĕd′shĭp′) *n.* **1.** The position or office of the head or leader; primacy; command. **2.** *British.* The position of a headmaster or headmistress.

head shrinker *n.* **1.** *Slang.* A psychiatrist. **2.** A head-hunter who shrinks the heads of his victims.

heads·man (hĕdz′mən) *n., pl.* **-men** (-mĭn). Formerly, a public executioner who beheaded condemned prisoners.

head·spring (hĕd′sprĭng′) *n.* A fountainhead; a source.

head·stall (hĕd′stôl′) *n.* The section of a bridle that fits over the horse's head.

head·stand (hĕd′stănd′) *n.* An act of balancing on the head, usually supported by the hands, with one's feet in the air.

head start *n.* A start before other contestants in a race, or any comparable advantage.

head·stock (hĕd′stŏk′) *n.* A nonmoving part of a machine or powered tool that supports a revolving part, such as the spindle of a lathe.

head·stone (hĕd′stōn′) *n.* **1.** A memorial stone set at the head of a grave. **2.** *Architecture.* A keystone (see).

head·strong (hĕd′strông′, -strŏng′) *adj.* **1.** Inclined to insist on having one's own way; willful; obstinate. **2.** Resulting from willfulness or obstinacy. —See Synonyms at **obstinate, unruly.**

head·wait·er (hĕd′wā′tər) *n.* A waiter in charge of the other waiters in a restaurant, who often seats guests and generally serves as host. Also called "maître d'hôtel."

head·wa·ter (hĕd′wô′tər, -wŏt′ər) *n. Often* **headwaters.** The water from which a river rises; source.

head·way (hĕd′wā′) *n.* **1.** Forward movement or rate of forward movement, especially of a ship. **2.** Progress; advance. **3.** *Architecture.* Headroom; clearance. **4.** The distance in time or space between two vehicles traveling the same route.

head wind *n.* A wind blowing directly against the course of an aircraft or ship. Compare **tail wind.**

head·word (hĕd′wûrd′) *n.* A word placed at the beginning of a paragraph or forming a heading; especially, a word entered and defined in a dictionary or encyclopedia.

head·work (hĕd′wûrk′) *n.* Mental activity or work.

head·y (hĕd′ē) *adj.* **-ier, -iest. 1.** Tending to upset the balance of the senses or mental faculties; intoxicating. **2.** Exciting; exhilarating. **3.** Headstrong; obstinate. —**head·i·ly** *adv.* —**head·i·ness** *n.*

heal (hēl) *v.* **healed, healing, heals.** —*tr.* **1.** To restore to health; cure. **2.** To set right; repair: *healed the rift between us.* **3.** To rid of sin, anxiety, or the like; restore. —*intr.* **1.** To become whole and sound; return to health. **2.** To repair by natural processes, as by forming scar tissue. Used of cuts, wounds, and burns. [Middle English *helen,* Old English *hǣlen;* akin to WHOLE.] —**heal·a·ble** *adj.*

heal-all (hēl′ôl′) *n.* A plant, the self-heal (see).

heal·er (hē′lər) *n.* **1.** One that heals; especially, a physician. **2.** A person who aims to cure by spiritual, magical, or other nonmedical means.

health (hĕlth) *n.* **1.** The state of an organism with respect to functioning, disease, and abnormality at any given time. **2.** The state of an organism functioning normally without disease or abnormality. **3.** Broadly, any state of optimal functioning, well-being, or progress. **4.** A wish for someone's good health, expressed as a toast. [Middle English *helthe,* Old English *hǣlth.* See **whole, -th.**]

health farm *n.* A residential center where people go to improve their health and fitness by following diets, taking exercise, undergoing massage, and the like. Also called "health spa."

health food *n.* Food considered to be highly beneficial to the health; especially, food that has been organically grown and has not been overrefined or processed.

health·ful (hĕlth′fəl) *adj.* **1.** Conducive to good health; salutary. **2.** *Rare.* Healthy. —**health·ful·ly** *adv.* —**health·ful·ness** *n.*

health physics *n. Used with a singular verb.* The branch of medical physics concerned with protection from radiation.

health visitor *n. Chiefly British.* A nurse who visits old and sick people and those with young children in their homes.

health·y (hĕl′thē) *adj.* **-ier, -iest. 1.** Possessing good health. **2.** Conducive to good health; healthful: *healthy air.* **3.** Indicative of a rational or constructive frame of mind; sound: *a healthy attitude.* **4.** Indicative of or being in a sound and prosperous condition: *The firm's overseas operations are particularly healthy.* **5.** Sizable; considerable: *a healthy portion.* —**health·i·ly** *adv.* —**health·i·ness** *n.*

> *Synonyms:* hale, hardy, robust, sound, vigorous, well, well-preserved, wholesome.

Hea·ney (hē′nē), **Seamus Justin** (1939-). Irish poet born in Ulster. His poetry is typified by dense, earthy imagery and, increasingly, has shown a concern for the political crisis in Ulster. His books include *North* (1975) and *Field Work* (1979).

heap (hēp) *n.* **1.** A group of things haphazardly gathered or in disorder; a pile. **2.** *Often* **heaps.** *Informal.* A great deal; a lot. **3.** *Slang.* An old or run-down car; a jalopy. ~*tr.v.* **heaped, heaping, heaps. 1.** To put or throw in a heap; pile

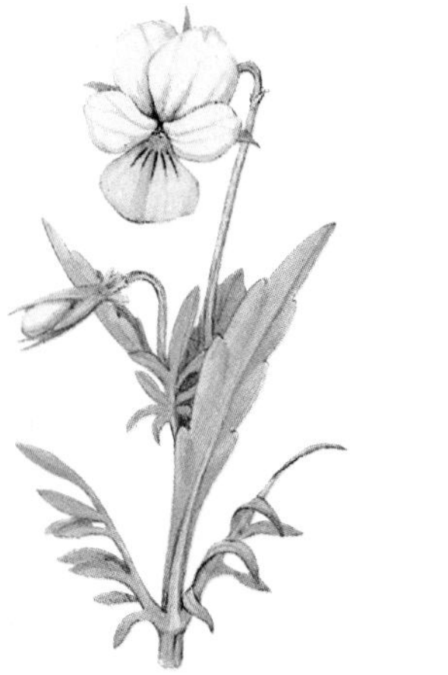

heartsease *In Shakespeare's play,* A Midsummer Night's Dream, *the fairy queen Titania falls in love with Bottom, the weaver, after the juice of heartsease is sprinkled onto her eyes. In North America this flower is more commonly known as Johnny-jump-up, or wild pansy.*

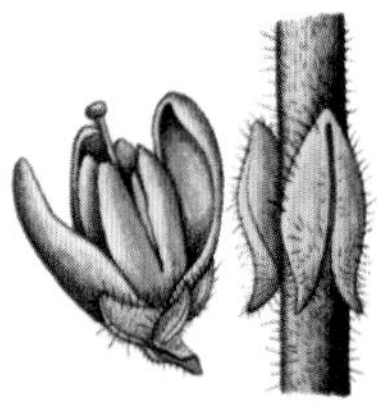

heather *Of the several species of heather, the true heather, or ling, is the most common. It grows on open moors and its young shoots are the main food of red grouse.*

PRONUNCIATION KEY

ă, pat; ā, pay; âr, care;
ä, father, are; b, bib;
ch, church; d, deed; ĕ, pet;
ē, be; f, fife; g, gag; h, hat;
hw, which; ĭ, pit; ī, pie;
îr, pier; j, judge; k, kick;
l, lid, needle; m, mum;
n, no, sudden; ng, thing;
ŏ, pot; ō, toe; ô, paw, for;
oi, noise; ou, out; o͝o, book;
o͞o, boot; p, pop; r, roar;
s, sauce; sh, ship, dish;
t, tight; th, thin, path;
th, this, bathe; ŭ, cut; ûr, fur;
v, valve; w, with; y, yes;
z, zebra, size; zh, vision;
ə, about, item, edible,
gallop, circus, peaceful

IN FOREIGN WORDS:

à, *Fr.* ami; œ, *Fr.* feu, *Ger.* schön; ü, *Fr.* tu, *Ger.* über; KH, *Ger.* ich, *Scot.* loch; N, *Fr.* bon; y', *Fr.* Compiègne

STRESS MARKS:

Primary stress: ′
in·cite′ (ĭn-sīt′)
Secondary stress: ′
in′sight′ (ĭn′sīt′)

up. **2.** To fill to overflowing: *heap a plate with vegetables; a heaping tablespoonful.* **3.** To bestow (praise, for example) in abundance; lavish. [Middle English *heap, hep(e),* Old English *hēap,* from Germanic.]

hear (hîr) *v.* **heard** (hûrd), **hearing, hears.** —*tr.* **1.** To perceive (sound) by the ear: *heard the siren of the fire engine.* **2.** To listen to attentively: *Hear me out.* **3.** To learn by the speech of others; be told: *I hear that you're sick.* **4.** To listen to in an official, professional, or formal capacity: *hear someone's confession; The fourth witness was heard in the afternoon.* **5.** To listen to with favor; give consideration to: *Lord, hear my plea.* **6.** To be present at and listen to: *heard an interesting lecture.* —*intr.* **1.** To be capable of perceiving sound: *The profoundly deaf cannot hear at all.* **2.** To receive a communication: *heard from them last week.* **3.** To be informed; learn: *I heard about your accident. I've never heard of him.* **—hear hear!** Used to express agreement with a speaker. **—not hear of.** To forbid mention or consideration of: *I won't hear of your going!* [Middle English *heren,* Old English *hīeran,* from Germanic.] **—hear·er** *n.*

hear·ing (hîr′ĭng) *n.* **1.** The sense by which sound is perceived; the capacity to hear. **2.** The range of audibility; earshot. **3.** An opportunity to be heard. **4.** *Law.* An opportunity for a person to put forward arguments or evidence to a judge or tribunal concerning a matter under investigation; especially, a preliminary examination, a trial, or an appeal.

hearing aid *n.* A small electronic apparatus that amplifies sound and is worn in or behind the ear to compensate for poor hearing. Also *British* "deaf-aid."

heark·en, hark·en (här′kən) *v.* **-ened, -ening, -ens.** —*intr.* To listen attentively; give heed. —*tr. Archaic.* To listen to; hear. [Middle English *herk(n)en,* Old English *he(o)rcnian,* from *he(o)rcian,* to HARK.]

hear·say (hîr′sā′) *n.* **1.** Information heard from another. **2.** *Law.* Evidence based on the reports of others rather than on a witness' own knowledge, and therefore generally not admissible as testimony. In this sense, also called "hearsay evidence."

hearse (hûrs) *n.* **1.** A vehicle for conveying a coffin. **2.** *Archaic.* A framelike structure over a coffin or tomb on which to hang epitaphs. [Middle English *herse,* harrow-shaped triangular frame for holding candles placed over a bier, from Old French, from Latin *hirpex* (stem *hirpic-*), harrow, rake, probably from Oscan (Samnite) *hirpus,* wolf (alluding to its teeth).]

Hearst (hûrst), **William Randolph** (1863–1951). U.S. newspaper and magazine publisher. Beginning with the San Francisco *Examiner* in 1887, he built the world's largest publishing empire, including 28 major newspapers, and pioneered popular journalism. Throughout his life he displayed a passion for collecting, buying everything from Egyptian mummies and Etruscan tombs to paintings, armor, entire rooms, and even a Spanish monastery. San Simeon, his "ranch" in western California, is now a popular tourist attraction.

heart (härt) *n.* **1. a.** *Anatomy.* The hollow, muscular organ in vertebrates that pumps blood through the circulatory system. It is divided vertically into two halves, each having an upper atrium and a lower ventricle. **b.** A similarly functioning structure in invertebrates. **2.** The approximate location of this organ in or on the body; the breast; the bosom. **3. a.** The heart thought of as the vital center of one's being, emotions, and sensibilities; the seat or repository of emotions: *decided with his heart rather than his head.* **b.** The heart thought of as the repository of one's deepest and sincerest feelings and beliefs: *an appeal from the heart; a subject near to his heart.* **4. a.** Character, disposition, or emotional constitution: *a man after my own heart.* **b.** One's prevailing mood or inclination: *a heavy heart; a change of heart. My heart wasn't in it.* **c.** Capacity for sympathy or generosity; compassion: *He has no heart.* **d.** Love; affection: *The child won her heart.* **5. a.** Courage; resolution; determination: *Don't lose heart.* **b.** The firmness of will or lack of feeling required for an unpleasant task or responsibility: *didn't have the heart to tell him.* **6.** A person esteemed as lovable, loyal, or courageous: *a dear heart.* **7. a.** The central or innermost part: *the heart of the financial district.* **b.** The compact central part of a cabbage, artichoke, or the like. **c.** The essential feature; the most vital part: *get to the heart of the problem.* **8.** *Chiefly British.* The condition of land with respect to fertility. Used chiefly in the phrase *in good heart.* **9.** A conventionalized two-lobed representation of the heart, usually colored red or pink. **10. a.** The red, heart-shaped symbol appearing on one of the four suits of playing cards. **b.** A card bearing this symbol. **c. hearts.** *Used with a singular or plural verb.* The suit of cards identified by this symbol. **11. hearts.** *Used with a singular verb.* A card game in which the objective is either to avoid hearts when taking tricks or to take all the hearts. **—at heart.** Essentially; fundamentally. **—break someone's heart.** To cause someone disappointment, sorrow, or grief. **—by heart.** By memory or rote. **—eat one's heart out. 1.** To undergo bitter, hopeless anguish or longing. **2.** To be consumed with envy. **—have one's heart in one's mouth.** To be anxious or apprehensive to an extreme. **—have one's heart in the right place. 1.** To mean well; have good intentions. **2.** To be an admirable and worthy person. **—in one's heart of hearts.** In one's truest feelings. **—take to heart.** To take seriously and be affected or troubled by. **—to one's heart's content.** To one's entire satisfaction, without limitation. **—wear one's heart on one's sleeve.** To show one's feelings clearly by one's behavior. [From Iago's comment "But I will wear my heart upon my sleeve / For daws to peck at . . ." in Shakespeare's *Othello* (1604), Act I, scene 1.] **—with all one's heart. 1.** With great willingness or pleasure. **2.** With the deepest feeling or devotion. ~*v.* **hearted, hearting, hearts.** —*tr. Archaic.* To encourage; hearten. —*intr.* To form a heart. Used of a cabbage, lettuce, or similar vegetable. [Middle English *he(o)rt, hart,* Old English *heorte.*]

heart·ache (härt′āk′) *n.* Emotional anguish; deep sorrow. —See Synonyms at **regret.**

heart attack *n.* **1.** An acute medical condition marked by a sudden severe pain in the chest, and sometimes also the arms and throat, resulting from abnormal functioning of the heart; especially, **coronary thrombosis** *(see).* See **myocardial infarction. 2.** An instance or episode of such a condition.

heart·beat (härt′bēt′) *n.* A single complete pulsation of the heart.

heart block *n.* Reduction or complete lack of coordination in the beating of the atria and ventricles of the heart.

heart·break (härt′brāk′) *n.* Intense sorrow or grief; crushing disappointment.

heart·break·ing (härt′brā′kĭng) *adj.* Causing heartbreak; acutely saddening or pitiful. **—heart·break·ing·ly** *adv.*

heart·bro·ken (härt′brō′kən) *adj.* Suffering from crushing grief or despair; having a broken heart. **—heart·bro·ken·ly** *adv.* **—heart·bro·ken·ness** *n.*

heart·burn (härt′bûrn′) *n.* A burning sensation in the stomach and esophagus, often accompanied by the eructation of small quantities of a highly acid fluid, caused by the regurgitation of stomach fluids; pyrosis. Also called "cardialgia."

heart disease *n.* Any organic or functional abnormality of the heart.

heart·ed (här′tĭd) *adj.* Having or showing a specified kind of disposition or emotional make-up. Used in combination: *heavy-hearted; false-hearted.*

heart·en (härt′n) *tr.v.* **-ened, -ening, -ens.** To give strength or hope to; encourage; cheer. **—heart·en·ing·ly** *adv.*

heart failure *n.* The partial mechanical failure of the heart as a pump, resulting in congestion of the lungs and liver, shortness and wheezing of breath, and edema in the legs.

heart·felt (härt′fĕlt′) *adj.* Deeply or sincerely felt; earnest. —See Synonyms at **sincere.**

hearth (härth) *n.* **1.** The floor of a fireplace, usually extending into a room and paved with brick, flagstone, or the like. **2.** The hearth thought of as the center of family life; the fireside; the home. **3.** *Metallurgy.* **a.** The lowest part of a blast furnace or cupola, from which the molten metal flows. **b.** The bottom of a reverberatory furnace where ore is exposed to the flame. **4.** The fireplace or brazier used by a blacksmith. [Middle English *herth,* Old English *heorth,* from Germanic.]

hearth·rug (härth′rŭg′) *n.* A rug laid on the floor in front of a fireplace.

hearth·stone (härth′stōn′) *n.* **1.** Stone used in the construction of a hearth. **2.** The fireside; home. **3.** A soft stone or powder used for scouring and whitening a hearth, steps, or the like.

heart·i·ly (härt′l-ē) *adv.* **1.** In a hearty manner; with warmth, enthusiasm, or good appetite. **2.** Thoroughly; completely: *heartily sick of all the complaining.*

heart·land (härt′lănd′) *n.* A central region; especially, one considered to be strategically, economically, or politically vital.

heart·less (härt′lĭs) *adj.* **1.** Without compassion; pitiless; cruel. **2.** *Archaic.* Without enthusiasm; spiritless. **—heart·less·ly** *adv.* **—heart·less·ness** *n.*

heart-lung machine (härt′lŭng′) *n.* A machine used during heart surgery that bypasses the heart and lungs and circulates oxygenated blood through the body.

heart murmur *n.* A sound, audible through a stethoscope placed over the heart, produced by turbulent blood flow and typically indicating some structural abnormality. Also called "bruit," "murmur."

heart-rend·ing (härt′rĕn′dĭng) *adj.* Causing anguish or deep sympathy; acutely moving.

heart-search·ing (härt′sûr′chĭng) *n.* An examination of one's innermost feelings.

hearts·ease, heart's-ease (härts′ēz′) *n.* **1.** Peace of mind. **2.** A plant, *Viola tricolor,* native to Eurasia, having small, spurred violet, yellow, or violet and yellow flowers. Also called "Johnny-jump-up," "love-in-idleness," "wild pansy." [Middle English *herts ease* : *herts,* genitive of *hert,* HEART + EASE.]

heart·sick (härt′sĭk′) *adj.* Sick at heart; profoundly disappointed; despondent. **—heart·sick·ness** *n.*

heart·some (härt′səm) *adj. British Regional.* **1.** Giving heart or spirit; encouraging. **2.** Cheerful; blithe.

heart·start·er (härt′stär′tər) *n. Australian Slang.* The first drink of the day, especially the first alcoholic drink.

heart·strick·en (härt′strĭk′ən) *adj.* Also **heart-struck** (-strŭk′). Overwhelmed with grief, dismay, or remorse.

heart·strings (härt′strĭngz′) *pl.n.* **1.** The deepest feelings or affections. Often used facetiously: *a performance geared to tug at the heartstrings.* **2.** In notions of anatomy held before the 17th century, sinews and tendons bracing and sustaining the heart.

heart·throb (härt′thrŏb′) *n.* **1.** A beat of the heart. **2.** An object of infatuation; an idol or sweetheart.

heart-to-heart (härt′tə-härt′) *adj.* Personal and candid; frank. ~*n.* A frank and intimate conversation.

heart-warm·ing (härt′wôr′mĭng) *adj.* **1.** Gratifying; encouraging. **2.** Moving.

heart·wood (härt′wŏŏd′) *n.* The older, inactive central wood of a tree or woody plant, usually darker and harder than the sapwood. Also called "duramen."

heart·worm (härt′wûrm′) *n.* A nematode worm, *Dirofilaria immitis,* parasitic in the heart and bloodstream of dogs and other mammals.

heart·y (här′tē) *adj.* **-ier, -iest. 1.** Expressed with warmth of feeling; exuberant and unrestrained: *a hearty welcome.* **2.** Complete or thorough; unequivocal: *hearty support.* **3. a.** Enjoying or requiring much food: *a hearty appetite.* **b.** Providing abundant nourishment; substantial: *a hearty bowl of soup.* —*n., pl.* **hearties.** A good fellow; a comrade; especially, a sailor.

heat (hēt) *n.* **1.** A form of energy associated with the motion of atoms or molecules. It is energy transferred as a result of a temperature difference, and is transmitted through solid and fluid media by conduction, through fluid media by convection, and through empty space by radiation. **2.** The perceptible, sensible, or measurable effect of such energy so transmitted; especially, a physiological sensation of being hot. **3.** An intense or pathological manifestation of such a perception or sensation; excessive warmth. **4.** The condition of being warm or hot. **5.** A hot season; hot weather. **6. a.** Intensity, as of color, appearance, emotion, or effect. **b.** The point or moment of greatest intensity: *in the heat of the argument.* **7.** A period or condition of sexual excitement in female mammals, **estrus** *(see).* **8. a.** A single course in a race or competition made up of several. **b.** A preliminary race or contest to determine finalists. **9.** *Slang.* **a.** Entanglement with or pursuit by the police. **b.** The police. **10.** *Informal.* Pressure or stress: *have to work harder when the heat is on.* **11.** *Slang.* Adverse reaction or comments: *took a lot of heat for his mistake.* —*v.* **heated, heating, heats.** —*tr.* **1.** To make warm or hot. **2.** To excite the feelings of; inflame. —*intr.* **1.** To become warm or hot. **2.** To become excited emotionally or intellectually. [Middle English *he(e)te,* Old English *hǣtu,* from Germanic.]

heat barrier *n.* **Thermal barrier** *(see).*

heat capacity *n.* The amount of heat required to raise the temperature of a body by one degree, either at constant pressure or at constant volume and without inducing chemical changes or change of phase. See **specific heat capacity.**

heat content *n.* A thermodynamic function, **enthalpy** *(see).*

heat death *n.* A state of maximum entropy in a closed system; especially, the hypothetical fate of the universe when it degenerates into a state in which no energy is available to do work.

heat·ed (hē′tĭd) *adj.* Marked by anger and emotion; impassioned: *a heated exchange.* —**heat·ed·ly** *adv.*

heat engine *n.* *Physics.* A device for obtaining mechanical work from heat, as by the expansion of a gas.

heat·er (hē′tər) *n.* **1.** An apparatus that heats or provides heat. **2.** Someone who heats something or tends a heating apparatus. **3.** *Electronics.* An electrically heated filament that indirectly heats the cathode in a valve. **4.** *Slang.* A pistol.

heat exchanger *n.* A device used to transfer heat from a fluid flowing on one side of a barrier to a fluid or fluids flowing on the other.

heat exhaustion *n.* A reaction to excessive heat, marked by prostration, weakness, and collapse resulting from dehydration. Also called "heat prostration." Compare **heat stroke.**

heath (hēth) *n.* **1.** Any of various usually low-growing shrubs of the genus *Erica* and related genera, native to the Old World, having small, evergreen leaves and small, urn-shaped pink or purplish flowers. Many species are also called "heather." **2.** An extensive tract of open, uncultivated land on sandy soil, covered with shrubby plants, especially heaths; a moor. **3.** Any of various butterflies of the genus *Coenonympha* in the family Satyridae. [Middle English *he(e)th, heath,* Old English *hǣth,* from Germanic.]

Heath (hēth), **Edward Richard George** (1916–). British politician. As leader of the Conservative Party he was prime minister from 1970 to 1974, when he lost support after calling for a mandate on his tough policy against unions. His administration was marked by Britain's entry into the Common Market (January 1973).

hea·then (hē′thən) *n., pl.* **heathens** or collectively **heathen. 1.** One who does not acknowledge the God of Judaism, Christianity, or Islam; especially, one who adheres to the polytheistic or animistic beliefs of a primitive people. **2.** One who is regarded as irreligious, uncivilized, or unenlightened. [Middle English *hethen,* Old English *hǣthen,* from Germanic, heath-dwelling, savage, from *haith-* (untested), HEATH.] —**hea·then** *adj.* —**hea·then·dom** (hē′thən-dəm), **hea·then·ism, hea·then·ry** *n.*

hea·then·ish (hē′thə-nĭsh) *adj.* **1.** Of or pertaining to heathens. **2.** Uncouth or barbarous in the manner ascribed to heathens. —**hea·then·ish·ly** *adv.* —**hea·then·ish·ness** *n.*

heath·er (hĕth′ər) *n.* **1.** A low-growing shrub, *Calluna vulgaris,* native to Eurasia, growing in dense masses and having small evergreen leaves and clusters of small, urn-shaped pinkish-purple flowers. Also called "ling." **2.** Any of several similar, related plants of the genus *Erica* or other genera; heath. **3.** Grayish purple to purplish red. [Middle English (Scottish) *hadder, hathir†,* assimilated to *he(e)th, heath,* HEATH.] —**heath·er** *adj.*

heath·er·y (hĕth′ə-rē) *adj.* **1.** Of or like heather. **2.** Covered with heather: *heathery hills.*

heath hen *n.* A form of the prairie chicken, *Tympanuchus cupido,* that became extinct in eastern North America during the first part of the 20th century.

Heath Rob·in·son (rŏb′ĭn-sən) *adj. British.* Ludicrously ingenious

---

heart

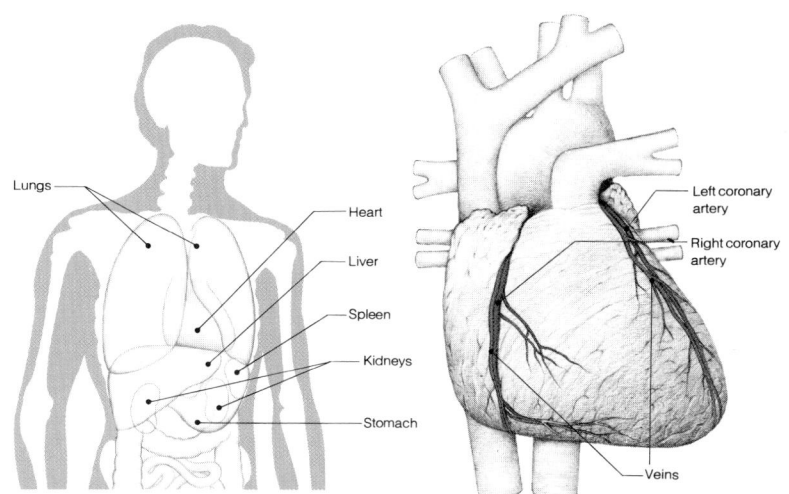

THE BODY'S STRONGEST MUSCLE
How the four-chambered heart pumps blood to every cell in the human body

Although it is only the size of a man's fist, the heart is the strongest of all the muscles. As it pumps blood around the body, it works twice as hard as the leg muscles of a sprinter or the arm muscles of a heavyweight boxing champion. It pumps through 4.5 liters (8 pints) of blood a minute and can increase the amount by at least five times during exertion. The heart consists of two pumps lying side by side. Each has an upper chamber, or atrium, and a lower chamber, or ventricle. The halves are separated by a wall of muscle called the septum.

THE HEART'S ROLE *The heart has to work nonstop to provide the body with a continuous supply of blood. The right side receives "used" blood from the veins and pumps it to the lungs to be oxygenated; oxygen-rich blood is then returned to the left side, which pumps it through the arteries.*

BLOOD SUPPLY *The heart needs its own supply of blood to keep it beating. Oxygen-rich blood is pumped to the chambers of the heart through the coronary arteries; once it has been used, the blood is returned to the right side of the heart through a network of veins.*

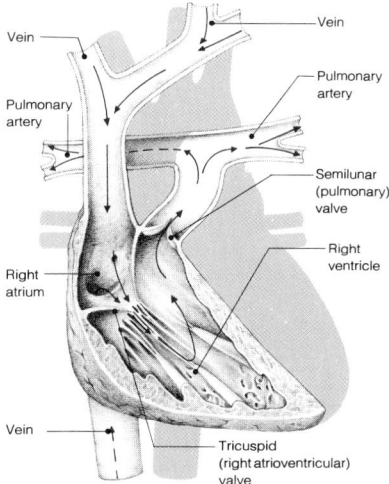

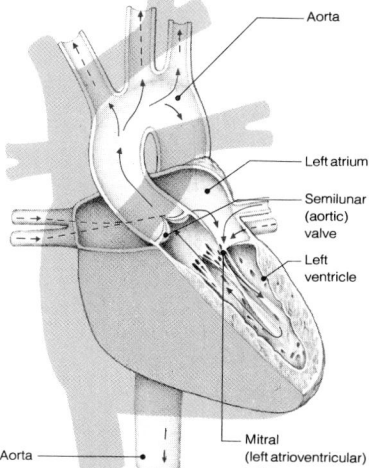

INCOMING BLOOD *Deoxygenated blood flows from the veins into the atrium on the right side of the heart. It then flows through the one-way tricuspid valve into the lower chamber, or ventricle. Contraction of the muscle surrounding the ventricle pumps the blood through the semilunar valve and along the pulmonary arteries to the lungs, where it receives oxygen.*

OUTGOING BLOOD *Oxygenated blood flows from the lungs into the left atrium before passing through the mitral valve into the ventricle below. Muscle surrounding the ventricle contracts and pumps the blood through the semilunar valve into the aorta. It is then circulated through the body's arteries and ultimately returned as deoxygenated blood to the right side of the heart.*

---

and complicated in design and construction. Said of a mechanical contrivance. [After Edward *Heath Robinson* (1872–1944), English cartoonist and book illustrator noted for his drawings of complicated contrivances.]

Heath·row (hēth′rō′). Site of London Airport. The principal air terminal of the United Kingdom, it is situated 24 kilometers (15 miles) west of central London.

heat lightning *n.* Intermittent flashes of light across the horizon on a hot summer evening, unaccompanied by thunder and thought to

FINAL DESTINATIONS FOR THE ELECT AND THE DAMNED

How different religions envisage life after death

Christian notions of heaven and hell grew out of the ancient Hebrew faith of Judaism. In Old Testament times, the Jews thought of heaven as the home of Yahweh, the God of Israel; only highly virtuous individuals, such as the prophet Elijah, were taken there. The rest of mankind, good and evil, slept in a gloomy underworld known as Sheol, where there was neither pleasure nor pain. Later Sheol—which resembled the classical Greek underworld of Hades—became in Jewish belief a place of rigorous punishment. Similarly, the Gehenna of the New Testament was a place for the wicked, while heaven became the destination of the righteous as well as the home of God.

The medieval church devised a fiery and detailed catalogue of torments for the damned, and some of these beliefs are still accepted by many Christians. Heaven, on the other hand, has usually been described only in vague terms as the place where believers are reunited for eternity with God. Most modern theologians prefer to speak of both heaven and hell as states or conditions of the soul, rather than places in any literal sense.

Other faiths have had more precise visions of paradise. For the Vikings of Scandinavia, for instance, heaven was Valhalla, the hall of the slain. Dead warriors, who were brought to Valhalla by the Valkyries, spent the day fighting. But their wounds were always healed in time for an evening of feasting with the god Odin. For devout Muslims, the Koran—the Islamic "Bible"—promises endless pleasure in heaven: shady gardens, cool fountains, beautiful women, and the wine that believers are forbidden on earth. Early Hindus also thought of paradise as earthly pleasures on an eternal scale; Vedic texts describe a realm of light with "music, sexual fulfillment, no pain and no care." Modern Hindus also believe in paradise, but it is reached only by the saintly and only after innumerable reincarnations.

Some faiths believe in multiple heavens. The largest branch of Buddhism, known as Mahayana Buddhism, teaches that there is a graded series of heavens. Buddhism also teaches, however, that man's ultimate goal is not paradise at all, but deliverance from the pain of life—the state of total blessedness called Nirvana, meaning extinction or, literally, "blowing out."

EASTERN TORMENT *The king of the underworld oversees the fate of sinners in a Japanese Buddhist view of hell. Beside him, a sinner sits in the scales of judgment; below, a liar has his tongue torn out.*

HEAVEN ON HIGH *Angels surround a dove symbolizing the Holy Spirit in an 18th-century painting on the ceiling of a German church.*

be cloud reflections of distant lightning. Also called "summer lightning."

heat of fusion *n.* The quantity of heat required to melt a given mass of a solid at a given temperature. See **latent heat.**

heat of vaporization *n.* The amount of heat required to convert a given mass of liquid into vapor at a given temperature. See **latent heat.**

heat pipe *n.* A device for conducting heat, consisting of a metal tube closed at both ends and containing volatile liquid at low pressure. Heat is carried down the tube by vaporized molecules of liquid and returns by capillary action through a wire-mesh coating inside the tube.

heat prostration *n.* Heat exhaustion *(see).*

heat pump *n.* An engine that transfers heat from a relatively low-temperature reservoir to one at a higher temperature, used for domestic heating.

heat rash *n.* Pathology. **Miliaria** *(see).*

heat-seal (hēt'sēl') *tr.v.* **-sealed, -sealing, -seals.** To seal by heating: *heat-sealed blood vessels.*

heat-seek·ing (hēt'sē'kĭng) *adj.* Designating or pertaining to missiles that home on a target by sensing the radiant heat emitted. —**heat-seek·er** *n.*

heat shield *n.* A barrier that prevents the heating of a space by absorbing, reflecting, or dissipating external heat; especially, a protective structure on a spacecraft or missile that dissipates heat on atmospheric re-entry by melting and vaporizing. Also called "ablator."

heat sink *n.* **1.** An environment having a much greater heat capacity and at a lower temperature than an object with which it is in thermal contact. **2.** Any device by means of which heat is absorbed or stored in or removed from a thermal system.

heat stroke *n.* A severe illness caused by exposure to excessively high temperatures and characterized by severe headache, high fever with a dry, hot skin, and, in serious cases, collapse and coma. Also called "sunstroke." Compare **heat exhaustion.**

heat-treat (hēt'trēt') *tr.v.* **-treated, -treating, -treats.** To subject (a material, especially a metal or alloy) to controlled changes of temperature in order to modify its properties.

heat wave *n.* A spell of unusually hot weather.

heave (hēv) *v.* **heaved** or *chiefly nautical* **hove** (hōv), **heaving, heaves.** —*tr.* **1.** To raise or lift with strenuous effort; hoist. **2. a.** To throw (a heavy object, for example) with great effort; hurl. **b.** To throw. **3.** To breathe or emit painfully or unhappily: *heaved a sigh.* **4.** Nautical. **a.** To raise (an anchor or net, for example). **b.** To pull on or haul (a rope or cable, for example). **5.** Geology. To cause (rock strata) to move in a horizontal direction. —*intr.* **1.** To rise up or swell, especially from turbulence; bulge; billow. **2.** Informal. To vomit or try to vomit. **3.** Nautical. **a.** To come to be in a specified position. Used of ships: *hove alongside; hove into view.* **b.** To pull on or haul a rope, cable, or the like: *heave around on the anchor.* **c.** To push or pull on a capstan bar or the like. —See Synonyms at **lift, throw.** —**heave to.** Nautical. **1.** To come to a stop. **2.** To bring (a ship) to a stop.
~*n.* **1.** The act or strain of heaving. **2.** Geology. The horizontal movement of rock strata displaced by a fault. **3.** Informal. A throw, especially one made with considerable effort. **4.** Dismissal; the heave ho. Preceded by *the.* [Heave, hove, hove; Middle English *hebben* or *heven, hove, hove,* Old English *hebban, hōf, hafen,* from Germanic.]

heave ho *interj.* Nautical. Used as a command to give a hard push or pull together.
~*n.* Also **heave-ho** (hēv'hō'). Slang. Dismissal, especially from a job. Preceded by *the.* [Originally used for heaving up an anchor.]

heav·en (hĕv'ən) *n.* **1.** Often **heavens.** The sky or universe as seen from the earth; the firmament. **2.** Often **Heaven. a.** In the Christian tradition, the abode of God, the angels, and the souls of those who are granted salvation. **b.** In a number of other religions and mythologies, a place of bliss where the souls of the blessed go after death. **3. a. Heaven.** Divine Providence: *May Heaven help you.* **b.** Often **heavens.** A euphemism for God, used in exclamations: *Good heavens!* **4. heavens.** The celestial powers; the gods: *The heavens favored the young ruler.* **5. a.** Supreme happiness; a state of bliss. **b.** A thing or place that is wonderful or enchantingly perfect; a sheer delight: *The lake was heaven.* —**move heaven and earth.** To do everything possible to bring something about. [Middle English *heven, hefen,* Old English *heofon, hefen.*]

heav·en·ly (hĕv'ən-lē) *adj.* **1.** Sublime; enchanting; lovely. **2.** Of or having to do with Heaven or the heavens; celestial. —**heav·en·li·ness** *n.*

heav·en-sent (hĕv'ən-sĕnt') *adj.* Occurring at an opportune time; providential.

heav·en·ward (hĕv'ən-wərd) *adv.* Also **heav·en·wards** (-wərdz). Toward heaven. —**heav·en·ward** *adj.*

heav·er (hē'vər) *n.* **1.** One that lifts or heaves. **2.** Nautical. A short bar used as a lever for twisting rope.

heaves (hēvz) *pl.n. Used with a singular or plural verb.* **1.** A pulmonary disease of horses, characterized by coughing and other serious respiratory irregularities. Also called "broken wind." **2.** Slang. A seizure of vomiting. Usually preceding by *the.*

heav·i·er-than-air (hĕv'ē-ər-thən-âr') *adj.* **1.** Denser than air. Said of a gas. **2.** Obtaining lift from aerodynamic forces rather than buoyancy. Said of an aircraft.

heav·i·ly (hĕv'ə-lē) *adv.* **1.** In a heavy manner. **2.** Very slowly and

with difficulty; laboriously: *walked heavily.* **3.** Greatly or severely: *heavily in debt.*

heav·i·ness (hĕv'ē-nĭs) *n.* The state or quality of being heavy.

Heav·i·side layer (hĕv'ē-sīd') *n.* A layer of the earth's atmosphere, the **E layer** *(see).* [After Oliver *Heaviside* (1850–1925), English physicist.]

heav·y (hĕv'ē) *adj.* **-ier, -iest. 1.** Having relatively great weight: *a heavy load.* **2.** Having relatively high density: *a heavy metal.* **3. a.** Of greater than average amount, volume, output, or the like; substantial: *heavy rainfall; a heavy turnout; heavy losses.* **b.** Of greater than average intensity, violence, or extent: *heavy fighting; heavy seas.* **4.** Dense or thick: *heavy fog.* **5. a.** Indulging to a great or habitual degree; chronic: *a heavy drinker.* **b.** Involved or participating on a large scale; prodigious: *a heavy investor.* **c.** Requiring or consuming relatively large quantities: *The car is heavy on oil.* **6. a.** Of great import or seriousness; grave: *heavy matters of state.* **b.** Ponderous; requiring effort to assimilate: *The report makes heavy reading.* **c.** Sad or painful: *heavy news.* **7. a.** Laborious; arduous: *a heavy day at work.* **b.** Burdensome; oppressive: *heavy taxes.* **8. a.** Copious: *a heavy breakfast.* **b.** Not easily or quickly digested: *an unusually heavy fruitcake.* **9.** Marked by a lack of fineness or gracefulness; coarse; inelegant: *heavy features; a heavy style of architecture.* **10.** Overcast: *heavy skies.* **11.** Dull and deep, suggesting great weight. Said of a sound: *fell with a heavy thump.* **12. a.** Clayey and tending to retain water. Said of soil. **b.** Spongy and tending to retard progress. Said of the going on a racecourse. **13.** Weighed with concern or sadness; despondent: *a heavy heart.* **14.** Lumbering; clumsy. **15.** Strong and pervasive; pungent: *a heavy odor.* **16. a.** Weighed down, as from being full; laden: *trees heavy with plums.* **b.** Showing weariness; listless: *heavy eyes.* **17.** Involving the large-scale extraction of raw materials or the manufacture of large commodities such as aircraft, motor vehicles, or armaments: *heavy industry.* **18.** Archaic. Gravid; in an advanced state of pregnancy. **19.** Theater. **a.** Of or pertaining to a serious or tragic dramatic role. **b.** Of or pertaining to the role of a villain. **20.** Physics. **a.** Designating an isotope with a mass greater than that of others found in the same element. **b.** Designating an atomic particle having a mass between that of pi mesons and protons. **21.** Bearing heavy arms or armor: *heavy cavalry.* **22.** Slang. **a.** Unpleasant or threatening: *a heavy scene.* **b.** Too intimate or demanding: *Don't get heavy with me.*
~*adv.* Heavily. —**hang heavy.** To pass slowly or tediously: *Time hung heavy on his hands.*
~*n., pl.* **heavies. 1.** A villain in a story or play. **2.** Informal. A ruffian; a tough: *a gang of heavies.* **3.** Informal. An important or influential person; a heavyweight. **4. a.** A serious or tragic role in a play. **b.** An actor playing such a role. **5.** Scottish. Heavy bitter beer. [Middle English *hevi,* Old English *hefig,* from Germanic.]
Synonyms: *cumbersome, hefty, massive, ponderous, unwieldy, weighty.*

heav·y-dut·y (hĕv'ē-dōō'tē, -dyōō'tē) *adj.* Made to withstand hard use or wear.

heav·y-foot·ed (hĕv'ē-fŏŏt'ĭd) *adj.* Having a heavy, lumbering gait. —**heav·y-foot·ed·ness** *n.*

heav·y-hand·ed (hĕv'ē-hăn'dĭd) *adj.* **1.** Clumsy. **2.** Tactless. **3.** Oppressive. —**heav·y-hand·ed·ly** *adv.* —**heav·y-hand·ed·ness** *n.*

heav·y-heart·ed (hĕv'ē-här'tĭd) *adj.* Melancholy; sad; depressed. —**heav·y-heart·ed·ly** *adv.* —**heav·y-heart·ed·ness** *n.*

heavy hydrogen *n.* An isotope of hydrogen with mass number greater than 1; especially, **deuterium** *(see).*

heav·y-lad·en (hĕv'ē-lād'n) *adj.* **1.** Laden with a heavy load. **2.** Burdened with cares; troubled.

heavy metal *n.* A style of rock music characterized by a heavy bass beat and the use of powerful amplification. —**heav·y-met·al** (hĕv'ē-mĕt'l) *adj.*

heav·y-set (hĕv'ē-sĕt') *adj.* Having a heavy, compact build.

heavy spar *n.* A mineral, **barite** *(see).*

heavy water *n.* Any of several isotopic varieties of water, especially **deuterium oxide** *(see),* consisting chiefly or exclusively of molecules containing hydrogen with mass number greater than 1 and used as a moderator in certain nuclear reactors.

heav·y·weight (hĕv'ē-wāt') *n.* **1.** One of above average weight. **2.** One that competes in the heaviest class; specifically, a boxer weighing more than 175 pounds (81 kilograms). **3.** Informal. A person of great importance or influence.

Heb. 1. Hebrew. **2.** Hebrews (New Testament).

heb·do·mad (hĕb'də-măd') *n.* **1.** A group of seven. **2.** A period of seven days; a week. [Latin *hebdomas* (stem *hebdomad-*), the number seven, seven days, from Greek, from *hepta,* seven.]

heb·dom·a·dal (hĕb-dŏm'ə-dəl) *adj.* Weekly. —**heb·dom·a·dal·ly** *adv.*

he·be (hē'bē) *n.* Any plant of the genus *Hebe,* which contains small evergreen shrubs with spikes of variously colored flowers, widely grown as garden ornamentals. Also called "shrubby veronica." [New Latin, after HEBE.]

He·be (hē'bē). Greek Mythology. The goddess of youth and spring, the cupbearer of Zeus. [Greek *Hēbē,* personification of *hēbē,* youth, youthful vigor.]

He·bei (hŭ'bā'). Also **Ho·pei, Ho·peh** (hō'bā'). Province of northeastern China, the oldest continuously civilized area in the world. Tianjin (Tientsin) is the capital.

he·be·phre·ni·a (hē'bə-frē'nə-ə, -frĕn'ə-ə) *n.* A schizophrenia, typically starting at puberty, characterized by foolish mannerisms, apa-

hebe *These evergreen shrubs, once known as veronicas, are popular garden plants in coastal regions because of their ability to withstand salt-laden winds. The species shown here is Hebe gauntleptii.*

hedgehog *When frightened, the hedgehog rolls up into a spiky ball. It feeds mostly on insects, worms, and occasionally snakes.*

hedge sparrow *Properly called the dunnock, this songbird is not related to the sparrow and can be distinguished from it by its insect-eater's bill, which is thin and pointed, whereas the seed-eating sparrow's bill is short and blunt.*

thy, delusions, hallucinations, senseless laughter, and regressive behavior. [Greek *hēbē,* youth + -PHRENIA.] **—he•be•phren•ic** (hē′bə-frĕn′ĭk, -frē′nĭk) *adj.*

heb•e•tate (hĕb′ə-tāt′) *tr.v.* **-tated, -tating, -tates.** To make blunt or dull. [Latin *hebetāre,* from *hebes*† (stem *hebet-*), blunt, dull.] **—heb•e•ta•tion** *n.* **—heb•e•ta•tive** *adj.*

heb•e•tude (hĕb′ə-to͞od′, -tyo͞od′) *n.* Dullness of mind; mental lethargy. [Late Latin *hebetūdo* : Latin *hebes* (stem *hebet-*), blunt, dull + -TUDE.] **—heb•e•tu•di•nous** (hĕb′ə-to͞od′n-əs, -tyo͞od′n-əs) *adj.*

Hebr. Hebrew.

He•bra•ic (hĭ-brā′ĭk) *adj.* Also **He•bra•i•cal** (-ĭ-kəl). Of, pertaining to, or characteristic of the Hebrews or their language or culture. [Middle English *Ebrayke,* from Late Latin *Hebraicus,* from Greek *Hebraikos,* from *Hebraios,* HEBREW.] **—He•bra•i•cal•ly** *adv.*

He•bra•ism (hē′brā-ĭz′əm, hē′brə-) *n.* **1.** A manner or custom characteristic of the Hebrews; especially, a Hebrew expression or idiom. **2.** The culture, spirit, or character of the Hebrew people. [From HEBRAIC.]

He•bra•ist (hē′brā′ĭst) *n.* A scholar of Hebrew. **—He•bra•is•tic** (hē′brā-ĭs′tĭk), **He•bra•is•ti•cal** *adj.* **—He•bra•is•ti•cal•ly** *adv.*

He•bra•ize (hē′brā-īz′) *v.* **-ized, -izing, -izes.** *—tr.* To make Hebraic in form or idiom. *—intr.* To use or adopt Hebraisms.

He•brew (hē′bro͞o) *n. Abbr.* **Heb., Hebr. 1.** A member of the Semitic people claiming descent from Abraham, Isaac, and Jacob; an Israelite; a Jew. **2. a.** The Semitic language of the ancient Hebrews, used in most of the Old Testament. **b.** Any of various later forms of this language, especially the form now spoken by the people of Israel.
~adj. Of or having to do with the Hebrews. [Middle English *Ebreu, Hebrewe,* from Old French *Ebreu,* from Latin *Hebraeus,* Hebraic, from Greek *Hebraios,* from Aramaic *'ibhray, 'ebhray,* from Hebrew *'ibhrī,* "he who came from across (the river)," from *'ēbher,* region across, from *ābhar,* to pass across or over.]

Hebrew calendar *n.* The **Jewish calendar** *(see).*

He•brews (hē′bro͞oz) *n. Abbr.* **Heb.** *Used with a singular verb.* A book of the New Testament; the Epistle to the Hebrews.

Hebrew Scriptures *pl.n.* The Pentateuch, the Prophets, and the Hagiographa, forming the covenant between God and the Jewish people that is the foundation and Bible of Judaism while constituting for Christians the **Old Testament** *(see).*

Heb•ri•des (hĕb′rə-dēz′). Also **Western Isles.** An archipelago of about 500 islands off the western coast of Scotland. It is divided into the Outer Hebrides, including Lewis, Harris, and the Uists; and the Inner Hebrides, including Skye, Mull, and Islay. **—Heb•ri•de•an** (hĕb′rə-dē′ən) *n. & adj.*

He•bron (hē′brən). *Arabic* **Al Kha•lil** (äl′ KHä-lēl′). Town on the Israeli-occupied West Bank of Jordan. It is one of the oldest inhabited cities in the world and is the traditional site of the tomb of Abraham.

Hec•a•te, Hek•a•te (hĕk′ə-tē). *Greek Mythology.* An ancient fertility goddess who later became identified with Persephone as queen of Hades and protectress of witches.

hec•a•tomb (hĕk′ə-tōm′, -to͞om′) *n.* **1.** In ancient Greece, a large-scale public offering to the gods, originally of 100 oxen. **2.** Any large-scale sacrifice. [Latin *hecatombē,* from Greek *hekatombē* : *hekaton,* hundred + *-bē,* from *bous,* ox.]

heck¹ (hĕk) *n.* Used as an intensive, as a euphemism for **hell** (sense 8): *ran like heck.*
~interj. Used as a euphemism for **hell.**

heck² *n. British Regional.* A frame or grating that obstructs the passage of fish in a river. [Middle English (northern dialect), variant of HATCH.]

heck•el•phone (hĕk′əl-fōn′) *n. Music.* A woodwind instrument of the oboe family having a pitch between that of the English horn and the bassoon. [German *Heckelphon,* after Wilhelm *Heckel* (1856–1909), German instrument maker.]

heck•le (hĕk′əl) *v.* **-led, -ling, -les.** *—tr.* **1.** To harass (a speaker or performer) persistently, as with questions, gibes, or objections; badger publicly. **2.** To comb (flax or hemp) with a hatchel. *—intr.* To engage in heckling a speaker or interrupting a public meeting. [Middle English *hekelen,* to comb flax, from *hekell, hechele,* flax-comb, hatchel, Old English *hæcel* (unattested).] **—heck•ler** *n.*

hec•tare (hĕk′târ′) *n. Abbr.* **ha** A metric unit of area equal to 100 ares or 2.471 acres. [French : HECT(O)- + ARE.]

hec•tic (hĕk′tĭk) *adj.* **1.** Characterized by feverish activity, confusion, or haste. See Usage note below. **2.** Of, relating to, or designating an undulating fever, as in diseases such as tuberculosis or septicemia. **3.** Consumptive; feverish. **4.** Flushed.
~n. **1.** A hectic fever. **2.** A person suffering from a hectic fever. [Middle English *etik,* from Old French *etique,* from Late Latin *hecticus,* from Greek *hektikos,* formed by habit, consumptive, hectic, from *hexis,* condition, habit, from *ekhein,* to have, hold, be in a certain condition.]

Usage: *Hectic* is well established in its general sense related to feverish activity, confusion, or haste. In earlier usage, that sense was sometimes deprecated as a loose extension of the term's meaning in medicine.

hecto–, hect– *prefix. Symbol* **h** Indicates 100; for example, **hectocotylus, hectare.** [French, from Greek *hekaton,* hundred.]

hec•to•cot•y•lus (hĕk′tō-kŏt′l-əs) *n., pl.* **-li** (-lī′). A modified arm of the male of certain cephalopods, such as the octopus, containing sperm and functioning as a reproductive organ. Also called "hectocotylus arm." [New Latin *Hectocotylus,* name given by G.L. Cuvier to the detached arm, which he thought was a parasitic worm : HECTO- + Greek *kotulē,* cup, hollow object (see **cotyledon**).]

hec•to•gram, hec•to•gramme (hĕk′tə-grăm′) *n. Abbr.* **hg** A metric unit of mass equal to 100 grams or 3.527 avoirdupois ounces. [French *hectogramme* : HECTO- + GRAM.]

hec•to•graph (hĕk′tə-grăf′, -gräf′) *n.* A machine using a glycerin-coated layer of gelatin to make copies of typed or written material. Also called "copygraph."
~tr.v. **hectographed, -graphing, -graphs.** To copy by means of a hectograph. [German *Hektograph* : HECTO- + -GRAPH.] **—hec•to•graph•ic** (hĕk′tə-grăf′ĭk) *adj.* **—hec•to•graph•i•cal•ly** *adv.*

hec•to•li•ter, hec•to•li•tre (hĕk′tə-lē′tər) *n. Abbr.* **hl 1.** A unit of capacity or volume, used in liquid measure, equal to 100 liters or 105.7 liquid quarts. **2.** A metric measure of capacity or volume, used in dry measure, equal to 100 liters or 90.8 dry quarts.

hec•to•me•ter, hec•to•me•tre (hĕk′tə-mē′tər) *n. Abbr.* **hm** A metric unit of length equal to 100 meters (about 328 feet).

hec•tor (hĕk′tər) *v.* **-tored, -toring, -tors.** *—tr.* To intimidate in a blustering way. *—intr.* To behave like a bully; swagger.
~n. A bully. [After HECTOR.]

Hec•tor (hĕk′tər). *Greek Legend.* A Trojan prince who led the forces of Troy in the Trojan War and was killed by Achilles. [Greek *Hektōr.*]

Hec•u•ba (hĕk′yo͞o-bə). *Greek Legend.* The wife of Priam and mother of Hector, Paris, and Cassandra.

he'd (hēd). **1.** Contraction of *he had.* **2.** Contraction of *he would.*

hed•dle (hĕd′l) *n.* One of a set of parallel cords or wires in a loom used to separate and guide the warp threads and make a path for the shuttle. [Probably altered from Middle English *helde,* heddle, Old English *hefeld,* from Germanic *hafjan* (unattested), to raise.]

hedge (hĕj) *n.* **1.** A row of closely planted shrubs or low-growing trees forming a fence or boundary. **2. a.** A line of objects or people forming a barrier. **b.** A means of protection or defense, especially against financial loss.
~v. **hedged, hedging, hedges.** *—tr.* **1.** To enclose or bound with or as if with a hedge or hedges. **2.** To restrict; hem in; confine. Often used with *in* or *about.* **3.** To counterbalance (a bet, for example) with other transactions so as to limit the risk of loss. *—intr.* **1.** To plant or cultivate a hedge or hedges. **2.** To take compensatory measures against possible loss. **3.** To avoid committing oneself, as by making cautious or ambiguous statements. [Middle English *hegge,* Old English *hegg, hecg* (unattested), from Germanic.] **—hedg•er** *n.* **—hedg•y** *adj.*

hedge garlic *n.* A plant, the **garlic mustard** *(see).*

hedge•hog (hĕj′hôg′, -hŏg′) *n.* **1.** Any of several small Old World mammals of the family Erinaceidae, and especially of the genus *Erinaceus,* having the back covered with dense, erectile spines and characteristically rolling into a ball for protection. **2.** Any of several similar spiny animals, as a porcupine. **3.** The spiny, burlike fruit of any of several plants. **4.** *Military.* An emplacement bristling with fortifications. [From Middle English *hedge hogge.*]

hedge•hop (hĕj′hŏp′) *intr.v.* **-hopped, -hopping, -hops.** To fly an aircraft close to the ground, rising above objects as they appear, as for spraying crops. **—hedge•hop•per** *n.*

hedge hyssop *n.* Any of various plants of the genus *Gratiola,* growing in damp places and having small yellow or whitish flowers.

hedge•row (hĕj′rō′) *n.* A row of bushes, shrubs, or trees forming a hedge.

hedge sparrow *n.* A European bird, *Prunella modularis,* of the family Prunellidae, having brownish plumage streaked with black. Also called "dunnock."

he•don•ic (hĭ-dŏn′ĭk) *adj.* **1.** Of, pertaining to, or marked by pleasure. **2.** Of or pertaining to hedonism or hedonics. [Greek *hēdonikos,* from *hēdonē,* pleasure.] **—he•don•i•cal•ly** *adv.*

he•don•ics (hĭ-dŏn′ĭks) *n. Used with a singular verb.* **1.** *Psychology.* The study of pleasant and unpleasant sensations. **2.** *Philosophy.* A branch of ethics that deals with the relation of pleasure to duty.

he•don•ism (hēd′n-ĭz′əm) *n.* **1.** Pursuit of or devotion to pleasure, especially the pleasures of the senses. **2.** The ethical doctrine that only that which is pleasant is intrinsically good. **3.** *Psychology.* The doctrine that behavior is motivated by the desire for pleasure and the avoidance of pain. [Greek *hēdonē,* pleasure (see **hedonic**) + -ISM.] **—he•don•ist** *n.* **—he•don•is•tic** (hēd′n-ĭs′tĭk) *adj.* **—he•don•is•ti•cal•ly** *adv.*

-hedral *suffix.* Indicates surfaces or faces of a given number; for example, **dihedral, polyhedral.** [From -HEDRON.]

-hedron *suffix.* Indicates a geometric figure having a given number of faces or surfaces; for example, **pentahedron, polyhedron.** [Greek *-edron,* from *hedra,* base, seat.]

hee•bie-jee•bies (hē′bē-jē′bēz) *pl.n. Slang.* A feeling of uneasiness or nervousness; the jitters. [Coined by Billy DeBeck (1890–1942), U.S. cartoonist, in his comic strip *Barney Google.*]

heed (hēd) *v.* **heeded, heeding, heeds.** *—tr.* To pay attention to; listen to and consider. *—intr.* To pay attention.
~n. Close attention or consideration. [Middle English *heden,* Old English *hēdan,* from Germanic.]

heed•ful (hēd′fəl) *adj.* Paying close attention; taking heed; mindful. **—heed•ful•ly** *adv.* **—heed•ful•ness** *n.*

heed•less (hēd′lĭs) *adj.* Paying little or no attention; not taking heed; unmindful. —See Synonyms at **careless, forgetful.** —See Usage note at **impetuous. —heed•less•ly** *adv.* **—heed•less•ness** *n.*

hee•haw (hē′hô′) *n.* **1.** The braying sound made by a donkey. **2.** A noisy laugh; a guffaw.

~*intr.v.* **heehawed, -hawing, -haws. 1.** To bray. **2.** To laugh noisily; guffaw. [Imitative.]

heel¹ (hēl) *n.* **1.** The rounded posterior portion of the human foot under and behind the ankle. **2.** A corresponding part in other vertebrates. **3.** That part of footwear, such as a sock, shoe, or stocking, that covers the heel. **4.** The built-up portion of a shoe or boot, supporting the heel. **5.** Either of the crusty ends of a loaf of bread. **6.** Something resembling the heel in position or shape; a lower, rearward surface, such as: **a.** The cushion of muscle on the palm of the hand below the thumb. **b.** The head of a golf club where it joins the shaft. **c.** The handle end of a violin bow. **d.** The lower end of a mast. **e.** The aft end of a ship's keel. **7.** *Horticulture.* The basal end of a cutting, tuber, or other plant part used in propagation. **8.** *Slang.* A callous or dishonorable man; a cad. **—cool one's heels.** To be kept waiting for a long time, especially out of deliberate rudeness. **—dig one's heels in.** To refuse to compromise or change one's position. **—down at the heels. 1.** Having one's shoe heels worn down. **2.** Shabby; run-down. **—lay by the heels.** To put in fetters or shackles; imprison or confine: "*If the king blames me for 't, I'll lay ye all/By the heels*" (Shakespeare). **—on** (or **upon**) **the heels of. 1.** Directly behind. **2.** Immediately following. **—show a clean pair of heels.** To run away. **—take to one's heels.** To flee; run away. **—to heel. 1.** Close behind; at one's heel. **2.** Under control; disciplined: *brought the rebellious prisoners to heel.* **—under the heel of.** Dominated or subjugated by.

~*interj.* Used when ordering a dog to keep close to the heel.

~*v.* **heeled, heeling, heels.** —*tr.* **1.** To furnish with a heel. **b.** To repair or replace the heels of (a shoe, for example). **2.** To follow upon the heels of; follow closely behind. **3. a.** In Rugby football, to kick (the ball) backward using the heel. **b.** In golf, to strike (the ball) with the heel of the club. —*intr.* **1.** To follow at one's heels: *taught the dog to heel.* **2.** To perform a dance step or movement with the heels. [Middle English *heel, he(e)le,* Old English *hēla,* from Germanic.] **—heel·less** *adj.*

heel² *v.* **heeled, heeling, heels.** —*intr.* To tip to one side; tilt; list. Used especially of ships. —*tr.* To cause (a ship) to list.

~*n.* A tilting or inclining to one side; a cant; a list. [Probably from obsolete *heeld,* to incline, Middle English *he(e)lden,* Old English *hieldan,* from Germanic.]

heel-and-toe (hēl'ən-tō') *adj.* Characterized by a stride in which the heel of one foot touches ground before the toe of the other foot is lifted, as in walking races.

~*intr.v.* **heel-and-toed, -toeing, -toes.** To operate the brake and accelerator of a car with the heel and toes of the same foot.

heel ball *n.* A colored wax used to stain and polish the edges of the soles and heels of shoes or to take brass rubbings.

heel bar *n. Chiefly British.* A small shop or a counter in a large shop where shoes are repaired while the customer waits.

heel bone *n.* The **calcaneus** (*see*).

heeled (hēld) *adj.* **1.** Having or fitted with heels. **2.** *Slang.* Provided with money. Used in combination: *well-heeled.*

heel·er (hē'lər) *n.* **1.** One who heels shoes. **2.** *Informal.* A **ward heeler** (*see*).

heel·post (hēl'pōst') *n.* The post to which a door or gate is hinged.

heel·tap (hēl'tăp') *n.* **1.** A layer of material added to the heel of a shoe; a lift. **2.** A small amount of alcoholic drink remaining in a container or drinking vessel.

heft (hĕft) *n.* Weight; heaviness; bulk.

~*tr.v.* **hefted, hefting, hefts. 1.** To determine or estimate the weight of by lifting. **2.** To hoist up; heave. [From HEAVE (by analogy with such pairs as *cleave, cleft.*)]

heft·y (hĕf'tē) *adj.* **-ier, -iest. 1.** Weighty; heavy. **2.** Large and powerful; bulky; muscular. **3.** Large in amount: *a hefty fine.* **—See** Synonyms at **heavy. —heft·i·ness** *n.*

He·gel (hā'gəl), **Georg Wilhelm Friedrich** (1770–1831). German philosopher. His main works, including *Encyclopedia of the Philosophical Sciences* (1817) and the *Philosophy of Right* (1821), proposed that truth is reached by a continuing dialectic: an initial *thesis,* when found unsatisfactory, generates an *antithesis;* these interact to form a *synthesis,* which may itself constitute a new thesis. Marx and Engels adapted the theory.

He·ge·li·an·ism (hā-gā'lē-ə-nĭz'əm) *n.* The monist, idealist philosophy of Hegel and his followers; especially, Hegel's doctrine of the "phenomenology of the mind," whereby all that exists must be mental, and therefore thought is reality; history, and especially the history of thought, represents the search for truth through **dialectic** (*see*). **—He·ge·li·an** *adj. & n.*

he·gem·o·ny (hĭ-jĕm'ə-nē, hĕj'ə-mō'nē) *n., pl.* **-nies.** Predominance; especially, the predominant influence of one state over others. [Greek *hēgemonia,* authority, rule, from *hēgemōn,* leader, from *hēgeisthai,* to lead.] **—heg·e·mon·ic** (hĕj'ə-mŏn'ĭk) *adj.*

He·gi·ra, He·ji·ra (hĭ-jī'rə, hĕj'ər-ə) *n.* **1.** The flight of Muhammad from Mecca to Medina in A.D. 622. **2.** The Muslim era, which is reckoned from this date. **3. hegira.** Any flight, as from danger. [Arabic *(al)hijrah,* emigration, flight, departure, from *hajara,* to leave, depart.]

he·gu·men (hĭ-gyoō'mən) *n.* Also **he·gu·me·nos** (-mə-nŏs') *n.* The head of a religious community in the Greek Orthodox Church. [Late Latin *hēgūmenus,* from Late Greek *hēgoumenos,* from Greek, leader, from *hēgeisthai,* to lead.]

heh (hā, hĕ) *interj.* **1.** Used to express surprise or inquiry, or to attract attention. **2.** Used to express malicious glee.

Hei·deg·ger (hī'dĕg'ər, -dĭ-gər), **Martin** (1889–1976). German phi-

losopher. His discussions on the "sense of being," which is the subject of *Being and Time* (1927), influenced Sartre and other existentialists.

Hei·del·berg (hīd'l-bûrg'). A city in West Germany, on the Neckar River, in the state of Baden-Württemberg. It was once the capital of the Palatinate. It has a spectacular ruined castle dating from the 13th century, and its university (1386) is the oldest in Germany.

Heidelberg man *n.* An extinct early member of the human species, suggested as being intermediate between *Homo erectus* and Neanderthal man, known primarily from a fossil jawbone found near Heidelberg, West Germany, in 1907.

heif·er (hĕf'ər) *n.* A young cow, especially one that has not yet given birth to a calf. [Middle English *heyfre, hayfre,* Old English *hēahfore†,* young ox.]

Hei·fetz (hī'fĭts), **Jascha** (1901–). U.S. violinist; born in Russia. Introduced to the violin at the age of three, he was considered the greatest living violinist just ten years later. After his American debut (1917) he moved to the United States and became a citizen (1925). He performed around the world, and recordings of his masterful technique and interpretation abound.

heigh (hā, hī) *interj. Archaic.* Used to express encouragement or to call attention.

heigh-ho (hī'hō', hā'-) *interj.* Used to express fatigue, melancholy, mild surprise, or disappointment.

height (hīt) *n.* Also *archaic* **heighth,** *obsolete* **highth** (hīth, hītth). *Abbr.* **h., H., hgt., ht 1. a.** The distance from the base to the top of something. **b.** The elevation of something above a given level; altitude. **2.** The condition or attribute of being sufficiently or relatively high or tall. **3.** The highest or uppermost point; the summit; the apex. **4. a.** The highest or most advanced stage or degree: *the height of stupidity; at the height of his fame.* **b.** The point of highest intensity; the climax: *the height of a storm.* **5.** *Often* **heights.** An eminence or area of high ground: *the Golan Heights.* **6.** *Obsolete.* High rank, estate, or degree. **7. a.** *Archaic.* Loftiness of mind. **b.** *Obsolete.* Arrogance; hauteur. [Middle English *he(i)ghth,* Old English *hēhthu, hīehthu.* See **high, -th.**]

height·en (hīt'n) *v.* **-ened, -ening, -ens.** —*tr.* **1.** To increase the quantity or degree of; intensify. **2.** To make high or higher; raise. —*intr.* **1.** To rise in degree or quantity; intensify. **2.** To become high or higher. **—height·en·er** *n.*

height-to-pa·per (hīt'tə-pā'pər) *n. Printing.* The height of type from foot to face, standardized at 0.9186 inch or 2.296 centimeters.

heil (hīl) *interj.* Hail! Used as a greeting, especially in the Nazi greeting *Heil Hitler!* [German.]

Hei·long·ji·ang (hā'lōong'jē-äng'). Northernmost province of China, formerly the northern part of Manchuria. Agriculture and forestry have been expanded since 1949, and its industries include oil refining, coal mining, and manufacturing. Its capital is Harbin.

Heilong Jiang. See **Amur.**

Hei·ne (hī'nə), **Heinrich** (1797–1856). German romantic poet. Heine lived after 1831 in Paris, where he supported a revolutionary literary movement known as Young Germany. He published several volumes of lyric poems, including *The Book of Songs* (1827).

hei·nous (hā'nəs) *adj.* Grossly wicked or reprehensible; abominable; odious; vile. [Middle English *heynous,* hateful, from Old French *haineus,* from *haïne,* hate, from *haïr,* to hate, from Frankish *hatjan* (unattested).] **—hei·nous·ly** *adv.* **—hei·nous·ness** *n.*

heir (âr) *n.* **1.** *Law.* A person who inherits or is entitled by law or by the terms of a will to inherit the estate of another. **2.** A person who succeeds or is in line to succeed to a hereditary rank, title, or office. **3.** One who is entitled or regarded as entitled to receive a heritage, as of ideas, from a predecessor; a successor. [Middle English *(h)eir, (h)air,* from Old French *(h)eir,* from Latin *hērēs.*] **—heir·dom** *n.* **—heir·ship** *n.*

heir apparent *n., pl.* **heirs apparent.** *Law.* An heir whose right to inheritance is indefeasible by law provided he survives his ancestor.

heir·ess (âr'ĭs) *n.* A female heir, especially one who inherits or is due to inherit great wealth.

heir·loom (âr'loōm') *n.* **1.** A valued possession passed down in a family through succeeding generations. **2.** *Law.* An article of personal property included in an inherited estate. [Middle English *heir lome* : HEIR + *lome,* utensil, tool, LOOM.]

heir presumptive *n., pl.* **heirs presumptive.** *Law.* An heir whose claim can be defeated by the birth of a closer relative before the death of the ancestor.

Hei·sen·berg (hī'zən-bûrg'), **Werner Karl** (1901–76). German physicist, one of the founders of quantum theory. For his **uncertainty principle** (*see*), which had a profound effect on physics, he was awarded the Nobel Prize in 1932.

Heisenberg uncertainty principle *n. Physics.* The **uncertainty principle** (*see*).

heist (hīst) *tr.v.* **heisted, heisting, heists.** *Slang.* To rob; steal. ~*n. Slang.* A robbery; a burglary. [Alteration of HOIST.]

hei·ti·ki (hā'tē'kē) *n. New Zealand.* A neck ornament of greenstone worn by Maoris. [Maori : *hei,* to hang + TIKI, amulet.]

Hejira. Variant of **Hegira.**

Hekate. Variant of **Hecate.**

Hel (hĕl). *Norse Mythology.* **1.** The daughter of Loki and the goddess of death. **2.** The underworld for the dead not killed in battle. [Old Norse *Hel.*]

He·La cell (hē'lä) *n.* Any of the cells of the first continuously cultured human carcinoma strain that are often used in the study of

helicopter *The rotor acts as a helicopter's wings as well as its propeller. The pilot controls the degree of lift by altering the angle of the blades to the air.*

hellebore *This highly poisonous evergreen, which flowers worldwide in woods in spring, is a relative of the popular garden Christmas rose.*

cellular processes. [After *Henrietta Lacks,* who donated such cells in 1951.]

held. Past tense and past participle of **hold** (to have in one's grasp).

hel·den·te·nor, Hel·den·te·nor (hĕl′dən-tə-nôr′, -nōr′) *n.* A singer with a powerful tenor voice suitable for heroic operatic parts. Also called "heroic tenor." [German : *Held,* hero, + *Tenor,* tenor.]

Hel·en (hĕl′ən). *Greek Legend.* The daughter of Zeus and Leda and wife of Menelaus. Her abduction by Paris led to the Trojan War.

Hel·e·na (hĕl′ə-nə). Capital of Montana, in the west-central part of the state. The city was founded after the discovery of gold (1864) at Last Chance Gulch. Today it is the commercial and shipping center of a mining and ranching area.

Helgoland. See **Heligoland.**

he·li·a·cal (hĭ-lī′ə-kəl) *adj.* Of or pertaining to the sun; especially, rising and setting with the sun. [From Late Latin *hēliacus,* from Greek *hēliakos,* from *hēlios,* the sun.]

he·li·an·thus (hē′lē-ăn′thəs) *n., pl.* **-thuses.** Any of various plants of the genus *Helianthus,* such as the sunflower and the Jerusalem artichoke, having large, yellow, daisylike flowers. [New Latin, from Greek *hēlios,* the sun + *anthos,* flower.]

hel·i·cal (hĕl′ĭ-kəl) *adj.* Of, pertaining to, or shaped like a helix. [Greek *helix* (stem *helik-*), HELIX.] **—hel·i·cal·ly** *adv.*

helical gear *n.* A gear in which the teeth are set in a helix around the axis.

he·li·ces. Alternate plural of **helix.**

hel·i·chrys·um (hĕl′ĭ-krĭs′əm) *n.* A plant of the genus *Helichrysum,* whose papery, daisylike flowers retain their form and color on drying. [New Latin, from Greek *helikhrusos* : *heli-,* spiral, HELIX + *khrusos,* gold.]

he·lic·i·ty (hē-lĭs′ə-tē, hĕ-) *n. Physics.* The component of the spin of a particle along its direction of motion. [Greek *helix* (stem *helik-*), HELIX + -ITY.]

hel·i·coid (hĕl′ĭ-koid′) *adj.* Arranged in or having the approximate shape of a flattened spiral.
~*n. Geometry.* A surface generated by a plane curve or a twisted curve that is rotated about a linear axis and at the same time is translated in the direction of the axis so that the two rates have a constant ratio. [Greek *helikoeidēs* : HELIX + -OID (shaped).]

hel·i·con (hĕl′ĭ-kŏn′, -kən) *n.* A large spiral brass tuba that fits around the player's shoulder. [After *Helicon,* a mountain in Boeotia sacred to the Muses.]

hel·i·cop·ter (hĕl′ĭ-kŏp′tər) *n.* An aircraft that derives its lift from blades that rotate about an approximately vertical central axis. [French *hélicoptère,* "spiral wing" : Greek *helix* (stem *helik-*), HELIX + -PTER.]

Hel·i·go·land (hĕl′ĭ-gō-lănd′). *German* **Hel·go·land** (hĕl′gō-lănd′, -länt′). A small island, belonging to West Germany, in the North Sea off the mouth of the Elbe River.

helio– *prefix.* Indicates the sun or of or by the sun; for example, **heliograph, heliotrope.** [Greek *hēlios,* the sun.]

he·li·o·cen·tric (hē′lē-ō-sĕn′trĭk) *adj.* **1.** Referred or relative to the sun. **2.** Having the sun as a center: *a heliocentric model of the universe.* **—he·li·o·cen·tric·i·ty** (hē′lē-ō-sĕn-trĭs′ə-tē) *n.*

heliocentric parallax *n. Astronomy.* **Annual parallax** *(see).*

He·li·o·gab·a·lus (hē′lē-ə-găb′ə-ləs, hē′lē-ō-), also **El·a·gab·a·lus** (ĕl′ə-găb′ə-ləs) (A.D. 204–22). Roman emperor (218–22). A priest of the pagan god Baal, he became emperor after the murder of his cousin Caracalla (217). His scandalous eccentricities and excesses and imposition of his religious beliefs caused unrest in Rome and led to a mutiny in which he was killed.

he·li·o·gram (hē′lē-ə-grăm′) *n.* A message sent by heliograph. [HELIO- + -GRAM.]

he·li·o·graph (hē′lē-ə-grăf′, -gräf′) *n.* **1.** An apparatus formerly used to photograph the sun. **2.** A signaling apparatus that reflects sunlight with a movable mirror to flash coded messages.
~*tr.v.* **heliographed, -graphing, -graphs.** To transmit (messages) by heliograph. [HELIO- + -GRAPH.] **—he·li·og·ra·pher** (hē′lē-ŏg′rə-fər) *n.* **—he·li·o·graph·ic** (hē′lē-ə-grăf′ĭk) *adj.* **—he·li·og·ra·phy** (hē′lē-ŏg′rə-fē) *n.*

he·li·o·gra·vure (hē′lē-ō-grə-vyo͝or′) *n.* **Photogravure** *(see).*

he·li·o·lith·ic (hē′lē-ə-lĭth′ĭk) *adj.* Of or designating a civilization characterized by sun worship and the erection of megaliths. [HELIO- + -LITHIC.]

he·li·om·e·ter (hē′lē-ŏm′ə-tər) *n.* A telescope equipped to measure small angular distances between celestial bodies. [French *héliomètre* : HELIO- + -METER.] **—he·li·o·met·ric** (hē′lē-ə-mĕt′rĭk), **he·li·o·met·ri·cal** *adj.* **—he·li·om·e·try** *n.*

He·li·os (hē′lē-ŏs′). *Greek Mythology.* The sun god, son of Hyperion, depicted as driving his four-horse chariot across the sky from east to west daily. [Greek *Hēlios,* from *hēlios,* the sun.]

he·li·o·stat (hē′lē-ə-stăt′) *n.* An instrument in which a mirror is automatically moved so that it reflects sunlight in a constant direction. [New Latin *heliostata* : HELIO- + -STAT.]

he·li·o·tax·is (hē′lē-ə-tăk′sĭs) *n. Biology.* The movement of an organism in response to the light of the sun. [New Latin : HELIO- + -TAXIS.] **—he·li·o·tac·tic** (hē′lē-ə-tăk′tĭk) *adj.*

he·li·o·ther·a·py (hē′lē-ə-thĕr′ə-pē) *n.* Medical therapy involving exposure to sunlight.

he·li·o·trope (hē′lē-ə-trōp′, hēl′yə-trōp′) *n.* **1.** Any of several plants of the genus *Heliotropium*; especially, *H. arborescens,* native to South America, having small, fragrant, purplish flowers. **2.** The **garden heliotrope** *(see).* **3.** Any of various plants that turn toward the sun. **4. Bloodstone** *(see).* **5.** Moderate, light, or brilliant violet to moderate or deep reddish purple. [New Latin *Heliotropium,* from Latin *hēliotropium,* from Greek *hēliotropion,* sundial, bloodstone, heliotrope : HELIO- + *tropos,* a turning (see **trope**).] **—he·li·o·trope** *adj.*

he·li·o·tro·pin (hē′lē-ə-trō′pĭn, -ŏt′rə-pĭn) *n. Chemistry.* **Piperonal** *(see).* [New Latin *Heliotropium,* HELIOTROPE + -IN.]

he·li·ot·ro·pism (hē′lē-ŏt′rə-pĭz′əm) *n. Biology.* Growth of a plant part toward or away from the light of the sun. [HELIO- + -TROPISM.] **—he·li·o·trop·ic** (hē′lē-ə-trŏp′ĭk) *adj.* **—he·li·o·trop·i·cal·ly** *adv.*

he·li·o·type (hē′lē-ə-tīp′) *n. Printing.* **1.** A photomechanically produced plate for pictures or type made by exposing a gelatin film under a negative, hardening it with chrome alum, and printing directly from it. **2.** The process of producing such a plate. **—he·li·o·type** *v.* **—he·li·o·typ·ic** (hē′lē-ə-tĭp′ĭk) *adj.*

he·li·o·zo·an (hē′lē-ə-zō′ən) *n.* Any of various aquatic protozoans of the order Heliozoa, having numerous stiff, radiating pseudopodia. [New Latin *Heliozoa* : HELIO- + -ZOAN.] **—he·li·o·zo·an** *adj.*

hel·i·port (hĕl′ə-pôrt′, -pōrt′) *n.* An airport for helicopters. [HELI(COPTER) + -PORT.]

he·li·um (hē′lē-əm) *n. Symbol* **He** A colorless, odorless, tasteless, inert gaseous element. It is used to inflate and so provide lift for balloons, as an inert component of various artificial atmospheres, in gaseous laser media, and as a superfluid in the form of helium II for extensive cryogenic research. Atomic number 2, atomic weight 4.0026, boiling point −268.6°C, liquid density at boiling point 7.62 pounds per cubic foot. [New Latin, from Greek *hēlios,* the sun (the element was first discovered in an examination of the solar spectrum).]

helium I *n. Symbol* **He I** Liquid helium existing as a normal fluid between the superfluid transition point of approximately 2.178° K at 1 atmosphere pressure and its boiling point of 4.2° K.

helium II *n. Symbol* **He II** Liquid helium existing as a superfluid below the transition point of approximately 2.178° K at 1 atmosphere and having extremely low viscosity and extremely high thermal conductivity.

he·lix (hē′lĭks) *n., pl.* **-lixes** or **helices** (hĕl′ə-sēz′, hē′lə-). **1.** A three-dimensional curve that lies on a cylinder or cone and cuts the elements at a constant angle. **2.** Any spiral form or structure. **3.** *Anatomy.* The folded rim of skin and cartilage around the outer ear. **4.** *Architecture.* A volute on a Corinthian or Ionic capital. **5.** Any terrestrial mollusk of the genus *Helix,* such as the garden snail, *H. aspersa.* [Latin, from Greek, spiral, spiral object.]

hell (hĕl) *n.* **1.** *Sometimes* **Hell.** The abode of the dead; the underworld where departed souls were believed to dwell; specifically, Sheol in the Hebrew Scriptures and Hades in the Greco-Roman tradition. **2.** *Sometimes* **Hell.** In the Christian tradition, the abode of condemned souls and devils; the place or state of eternal torture and punishment for the wicked after death, presided over by Satan and conventionally depicted as a place of everlasting fire. **3.** The infernal powers of evil and darkness. **4. a.** A place or state of great wickedness, torment, misery, or destruction. **b.** Torment; anguish. **c.** A cause or source of great misery or agony. **5. Hell.** *Christian Science.* Mortal belief; sin or error. **6.** *Archaic.* A gambling house. **7. a.** A tailor's receptacle for discarded material. **b.** A hellbox. **8. a.** A severe punishment or reprimand: *The boss gave me hell.* **b.** Turmoil; havoc; pandemonium: *All hell was let loose.* **9.** Used to express annoyance or surprise or as an intensive: *a hell of a good book. It hurts like hell.* **—for the hell of it.** Purely for the sake of amusement. **—hell and (**or **or) high water.** *Informal.* The ultimate ordeal, suffering, or deprivation: *I followed her through hell and high water. We're staying, come hell or high water.* **—hell to pay.** *Informal.* Bad trouble to be faced: *If we're caught doing this, there'll be hell to pay.* **—like hell.** *Informal.* Most assuredly not; never. Used for emphasis, especially in rejecting a possibility. **—raise (**or **kick up) hell.** *Slang.* To make a great fuss. **—the hell in.** *South African.* Extremely angry; furious. **—what the hell.** *Informal.* Used to express indifference or resignation.
~*intr.v.* **helled, helling, hells.** *Informal.* To behave riotously; carouse: *out all night helling around.*
~*interj. Slang.* Used to express acute anger, disgust, or impatience. [Middle English *hel(l),* Old English *hel(l),* from Germanic.]

he'll (hēl). **1.** Contraction of *he will.* **2.** Contraction of *he shall.*

Hel·lad·ic (hĕ-lăd′ĭk) *adj.* Of or pertaining to the Bronze Age culture on the mainland of Greece prior to 1100 B.C. [Latin *Helladicus,* from Greek *Helladikos,* from *Hellas* (stem *Hellad-*), HELLAS.]

Hel·las (hĕl′əs). The Greek name for Greece. [Greek, from *Hellēn*†, eponymous ancestor of the Greeks.]

hell·bend·er (hĕl′bĕn′dər) *n.* A large aquatic salamander, *Cryptobranchus alleganiensis,* of eastern and central North America.

hell-bent (hĕl′bĕnt′) *adj.* Impetuously or recklessly bent on doing, reaching, or achieving something. Used with *on* or *for.*

hell·box (hĕl′bŏks′) *n.* A printer's receptacle for broken or discarded type. Also called "hell."

hell·cat (hĕl′kăt′) *n.* **1.** A furious and evil woman; a witch. **2.** A fiendish person.

Hel·le (hĕl′ē). *Greek Mythology.* The daughter of a Greek king who, while fleeing with her brother from their stepmother, drowned in the Hellespont, thereafter named for her.

hel·le·bore (hĕl′ə-bôr′, -bōr′) *n.* **1.** Any of various plants of the genus *Helleborus,* native to Eurasia, most species of which are poisonous. See **Christmas rose. 2.** Any of various plants of the genus *Veratrum*; especially, *V. viride,* of North America, having large

PRONUNCIATION KEY

ă, pat; ā, pay; âr, care;
ä, father, are; b, bib;
ch, church; d, deed; ĕ, pet;
ē, be; f, fife; g, gag; h, hat;
hw, which; ĭ, pit; ī, pie;
îr, pier; j, judge; k, kick;
l, lid, needle; m, mum;
n, no, sudden; ng, thing;
ŏ, pot; ō, toe; ô, paw, for;
oi, noise; ou, out; o͝o, book;
o͞o, boot; p, pop; r, roar;
s, sauce; sh, ship, dish;
t, tight; th, thin, path;
th, this, bathe; ŭ, cut; ûr, fur;
v, valve; w, with; y, yes;
z, zebra, size; zh, vision;
ə, about, item, edible, gallop, circus, peaceful

IN FOREIGN WORDS:

à, *Fr.* ami; œ, *Fr.* feu, *Ger.* schön; ü, *Fr.* tu, *Ger.* über; KH, *Ger.* ich, *Scot.* loch; N, *Fr.* bon; y′, *Fr.* Compiègne

STRESS MARKS:

Primary stress: ′
in·cite′ (ĭn-sīt′)
Secondary stress: ′
in′sight′ (ĭn′sīt′)

leaves and greenish flowers and yielding a toxic alkaloid used medicinally. In this sense, also called "false hellebore," "Indian poke." [Middle English *ellebre,* from Old French, from Latin *elleborus,* from Greek *(h)elleboros,* perhaps "eaten by fawns" : *(h)ellos,* fawn + *-boros,* eaten, from *bibrōskein,* to eat, devour.]

hel·le·bor·in (hĕl′ə-bôr′ĭn, -bŏr′ĭn) *n.* A poisonous compound, $C_{28}H_{36}O_6$, extracted from a species of hellebore, *Helleborus viridis.* [HELLEBOR(E) + -IN.]

Hel·lene (hĕl′ēn) *n.* A Greek. [Greek *Hellēn.* See Hellas.]

Hel·len·ic (hĕ-lĕn′ĭk) *adj.* Of or relating to the ancient Greeks or their language; Greek. —*n.* The branch of the Indo-European language family that consists solely of Greek.

Hel·le·nism (hĕl′ə-nĭz′əm) *n.* **1.** An idiom, custom, or the like peculiar to the Greeks. **2.** The civilization and culture of ancient Greece. **3.** Admiration for or adoption of Greek ideas, style, or culture.

Hel·le·nist (hĕl′ə-nĭst) *n.* **1.** One in classical times who adopted the Greek language and culture, particularly a Jew of the Diaspora. **2.** A devotee or student of Greek civilization, language, or literature.

Hel·le·nis·tic (hĕl′ə-nĭs′tĭk) *adj.* **1.** Of or relating to Greek civilization, art, and culture from the death of Alexander the Great in 323 B.C. to the accession of Augustus (27 B.C.). **2.** Relating to the Hellenists.

Hel·le·nize (hĕl′ə-nīz′) *v.* **-nized, -nizing, -nizes.** —*intr.* To adopt Greek ways and speech; become Greek. —*tr.* To make Greek in character or culture. —**Hel·le·ni·za·tion** *n.* —**Hel·le·niz·er** *n.*

hel·ler¹ (hĕl′ər) *n., pl.* **heller.** One of several coins of small denomination formerly used in Austria and Hungary. [German *Heller,* from Middle High German *heller, haller,* HALER.]

hell·er² (hĕl′ər) *n. Regional.* A person who behaves recklessly or wildly. [From HELL.]

Hellespont. See Dardanelles.

hell·fire (hĕl′fīr′) *n.* The fires, torment, or punishment of hell. —*adj.* Preaching or zealously believing in the torments of hell: *an old-fashioned hellfire preacher.*

hell·fired (hĕl′fīrd′) *adj. Regional & Informal.* Extremely; very.

hell-for-leath·er (hĕl′fər-lĕth′ər) *adv. Informal.* At breakneck speed.

hell·gram·mite (hĕl′grə-mīt′) *n.* The large, brownish aquatic larva of the dobson fly, often used as fishing bait. Sometimes called "dobson." [Origin unknown.]

hell·hole (hĕl′hōl′) *n.* A hellish place, especially one of extreme wretchedness, squalor, or lewdness.

hell·hound (hĕl′hound′) *n.* **1.** A hound of hell; especially, Cerberus, watchdog of Hades. **2.** A devilish person; a fiend.

hel·lion (hĕl′yən) *n. Informal.* A mischievous, unrestrainable person, especially a young person or child. [Probably altered by assimilation to HELL from dialectal *hallion*†, scurvy person.]

hell·ish (hĕl′ĭsh) *adj.* **1.** Of, relating to, or worthy of hell; devilish. **2.** *Informal.* Awful; unpleasant; terrible: *hellish weather.* —**hell·ish·ly** *adv.* —**hell·ish·ness** *n.*

Hell·man (hĕl′mən), **Lillian** (1905-84). U.S. playwright. Her first play, *The Children's Hour* (1934), treated the then taboo subject of lesbianism. She also wrote *The Little Foxes* (1939) and *Watch on the Rhine* (1941). The first volume of her autobiography, *An Unfinished Woman,* won the National Book Award (1969).

hel·lo (hĕ-lō′, hə-) *interj.* Also **hul·lo** (hə-). **1.** Used to greet another, to answer the telephone, or to attract attention. **2.** Used to express surprise. —*n., pl.* **helloes.** Also **hullo.** A calling or greeting of "hello." —*v.* **helloed, -loing, -loes.** Also **hullo.** —*tr.* To say or call "hello" to. —*intr.* To call "hello." [Variant of earlier *hallo, hollo, holla,* stop!, from French *holà,* "ho there!"]

Hell's Angel *n.* One who belongs to a motorcycle gang of a type that originated in the United States, whose members wear denim, black leather, and various items of antisocial ornamentation and regalia, and are generally believed to behave in a violent and lawless manner.

Hell's Canyon. Greatest of the Snake River's many gorges, on the Idaho-Oregon border. It extends for *c.* 200 kilometers (125 miles) and reaches a maximum depth of *c.* 2,410 meters (7,900 feet).

helm¹ (hĕlm) *n.* **1.** *Nautical.* The tiller or wheel or the whole steering gear of a ship. **2.** A position of leadership or control: *at the helm.* —**ease the helm.** *Nautical.* To bring the helm somewhat toward midships in order to reduce strain on the rudder. —*tr.v.* **helmed, helming, helms.** To be at the helm of; steer; guide. [Middle English *helme,* Old English *helma.*]

helm² *n. Archaic.* A helmet. —*tr.v.* **helmed, helming, helms.** *Archaic.* To cover or furnish with a helmet. [Middle English *helm(e), healm,* Old English *helm.*]

hel·met (hĕl′mĭt) *n.* **1.** A piece of ancient, medieval, or modern armor, usually of metal, designed to protect the head. **2. a.** A head covering of hard material, such as leather, metal, or plastic, worn by policemen, firemen, cyclists, and others to protect the head. **b.** The headgear with a glass mask worn by deep-sea divers. **c.** A pith helmet; a topi. **d.** Any hat or headgear resembling a helmet, such as a balaclava. **3.** *Botany.* The hood-shaped sepal or corolla of some flowers. [Middle English, from Old French, diminutive of *helme, heaume,* helmet, from Frankish *helm* (unattested).] —**hel·met·ed** *adj.*

Helm·holtz (hĕlm′hōlts′), **Hermann Ludwig Ferdinand von** (1821-94). German physicist and physiologist. He formulated the mathematical law of the conservation of energy in 1847.

Helmholtz coils *pl.n. Physics.* Two identical flat coils carrying the same electric current in the same direction, mounted parallel at a distance apart equal to their radii. The arrangement produces a uniform magnetic field between the coils of known field strength. [Invented by H.L.F. von HELMHOLTZ.]

Helmholtz function *n. Symbol* **A** A measure of the thermodynamic free energy of a system, equal to the internal energy minus the product of thermodynamic temperature and entropy. Also called "Helmholtz free energy." [Devised by H.L.F. von HELMHOLTZ.]

hel·minth (hĕl′mĭnth′) *n.* A worm; especially, a parasitic intestinal nematode fluke, or tapeworm. [Greek *helmi(n)s* (stem *helminth-*), parasitic worm.]

hel·min·thi·a·sis (hĕl′mĭn-thī′ə-sĭs) *n.* A disease resulting from infestation with parasitic worms. [New Latin : HELMINTH + -IASIS.]

hel·min·thic (hĕl-mĭn′thĭk) *adj.* **1.** Of or pertaining to worms, especially parasitic intestinal worms. **2.** Tending to expel worms; anthelmintic. —*n.* A vermifuge or anthelmintic.

hel·min·thol·o·gy (hĕl′mĭn-thŏl′ə-jē) *n.* The scientific study of worms, especially parasitic worms. [HELMINTH + -LOGY.] —**hel·min·thol·o·gist** *n.*

helms·man (hĕlmz′mən) *n., pl.* **-men** (-mĭn). One who steers a ship.

Hé·lo·ïse (ĕl′ō-ēz′, ā′lō-ēz′) (*c.* 1098-1164). A young Frenchwoman who fell in love with her tutor, Peter Abelard. After she bore his child and secretly married him, her incensed family arranged to have him attacked and castrated. Their marriage ended; she became a nun, and he became a monk. Their story is a classic love tragedy.

hel·o·phyte (hĕl′ə-fīt′) *n.* A marsh plant. [Greek *helos,* marsh + -PHYTE.]

hel·ot (hĕl′ət, hē′lət) *n.* **1.** Helot. One of a class of serfs in ancient Sparta, neither a slave nor a free citizen. **2.** A serf; a bondsman. [Latin *Hēlōtes,* serfs, helots, from Greek *Heilōtes,* plural of *Heilōs*†.]

hel·ot·ism (hĕl′ə-tĭz′əm, hē′lə-) *n.* **1.** A system under which a particular section of the community, such as a religious or racial minority, is permanently oppressed and degraded. **2.** *Zoology.* Dulosis (see).

hel·ot·ry (hĕl′ə-trē, hē′lə-) *n.* **1.** The condition of serfdom. **2.** Helots as a class.

help (hĕlp) *v.* **helped** or *archaic* **holp** (hōlp), **helped** or *archaic* **holpen** (hōl′pən), **helping, helps.** —*tr.* **1. a.** To do something or provide something that will be of use to (someone) in achieving a purpose; give assistance to; aid: *I helped her to find the book.* **b.** To give assistance so as to enable (someone) to carry out an action more easily. Used elliptically with a preposition or an adverb: *He helped her into her coat. Help me down—I'm stuck.* **2.** To further the advancement or promote the interests of: *The party's disunity will only help its enemies.* **3.** To give relief to (one in difficulty or distress); succor. **4.** To alleviate or cure. **5.** To improve; benefit. **6.** To prevent, change, or rectify. Used with *can* or *cannot: I cannot help her laziness.* **7.** To refrain from; avoid. Used with *can* or *cannot: He cannot help laughing.* **8.** To serve in a shop or at table. —*intr.* To be of use or service; give assistance; aid. —See Synonyms at **improve.** —**cannot help but.** To be compelled to; be unable to avoid or resist: *He cannot help but do what they ask.* —**help oneself to.** To take (something) without asking permission. —**help out.** To help with a problem or difficulty. —**so help me God.** Used as an oath in solemn affirmation of what one has declared. —*n.* **1.** The act of helping; aid; assistance. **2.** Someone or something that helps: *You've been a great help.* **3.** Relief; remedy. **4.** Succor. **5. a.** A person employed to assist; especially, a farm worker or a domestic servant. **b.** Such employees collectively. **6.** *Rare.* A helping. —*interj.* Used to express an urgent need for assistance. [Middle English *helpen,* Old English *helpan,* from Germanic.] —**help·er** *n.*
Synonyms: *aid, assist, succor.*

help·ful (hĕlp′fəl) *adj.* Providing help; useful; beneficial. —**help·ful·ly** *adv.* —**help·ful·ness** *n.*

help·ing (hĕl′pĭng) *n.* A portion of food for one person.

helping hand *n.* Assistance; aid.

help·less (hĕlp′lĭs) *adj.* **1.** Unable to manage by oneself; defenseless; dependent. **2.** Lacking power or strength; impotent; ineffectual. **3.** Incapable of being remedied; hopeless: *a helpless situation.* **4.** Incapable of being controlled; involuntary: *helpless laughter.* —**help·less·ly** *adv.* —**help·less·ness** *n.*

help·mate (hĕlp′māt′) *n.* A helper or helpful companion, especially a spouse. [HELP + MATE (influenced by HELPMEET).]

help·meet (hĕlp′mēt′) *n.* A helpmate. [From *I will make an help meet for him* (Genesis 2:18, 20), "I will make a help suitable for him" : HELP + MEET (suitable).]

Hel·sin·ki (hĕl′sĭng′kē, hĕl-sĭng′-). *Swedish* **Hel·sing·fors** (hĕl′sĭng-fôrs′). Capital of Finland. Built on a promontory and several islands in the Gulf of Finland, it has two harbors, kept open by icebreakers during winter months. Its industries include paper, textiles, and shipbuilding.

hel·ter-skel·ter (hĕl′tər-skĕl′tər) *adv.* **1.** In disorderly haste; pell-mell. **2.** In confusion; haphazardly. —*adj.* **1.** Characterized by disorderly haste. **2.** Haphazard. —*n.* Chaos; confusion. [16th century : perhaps based on Middle English *skelte,* to hasten.]

helve (hĕlv) *n.* A handle of a tool, such as an ax, chisel, or hammer. [Middle English *helve, hilf,* Old English *hielf(e).*]

Helvetia. See Switzerland.

Hel·ve·tian (hĕl-vē′shən) *adj.* **1.** Of or relating to the Helvetii.

helmet *A Greek bronze helmet from Olympia, now in the British Museum, London. It dates from about 460 B.C.*

2. Swiss. [Latin *Helvētius,* of the HELVETII.] —**Hel·ve·tian** *n.*
Hel·vet·ic (hĕl-vĕt′ĭk) *adj.* Helvetian; Swiss.
~*n.* A Swiss Protestant; a Zwinglian.
Hel·ve·ti·i (hĕl-vē′shē-ī′) *pl.n.* A Celtic people inhabiting Switzerland during the time of Julius Caesar. [Latin.]
hem[1] (hĕm) *n.* **1.** An edge or border of a piece of cloth; especially, a finished edge for a garment, curtain, or the like, made by folding the selvage or raw edge under and stitching it down. **2.** The level of a hem; a hemline.
~*tr.v.* **hemmed, hemming, hems. 1.** To fold back and stitch down the edge of. **2.** To encircle and confine; enclose or restrict. Used with *in, about,* or *around*: *hemmed in by mountains.* [Middle English *hem(m),* Old English *hem(m).*] —**hem·mer** *n.*
hem[2]. A short cough or clearing of the throat made to gain attention, warn, fill a pause in speech, hide embarrassment, or the like. Often used as an interjection.
~*intr.v.* **hemmed, hemming, hems. 1.** To utter this sound. **2.** To hesitate in speaking. —**hem and haw.** To be hesitant and indecisive; equivocate. [Imitative.]
hem-[1], **hema-**. Variant of **hemo-**.
hem-[2]. Variant of **hemi-**.
he·ma·cy·tom·e·ter (hē′mə-sī-tŏm′ə-tər, hĕm′ə-) *n.* An instrument for estimating the number of blood cells in a measured volume of blood. [HEMA- + CYTO- + -METER.]
he·mag·glu·tin·ate (hē′mə-glōōt′n-āt′, hĕm′ə-) *tr.v.* **-ated, -ating, -ates.** To cause agglutination of (red blood cells). —**he·mag·glu·ti·na·tion** *n.*
he·mag·glu·ti·nin (hē′mə-glōōt′n-ĭn, hĕm′ə-) *n.* An antibody that causes agglutination of red blood cells containing or coated with the corresponding antigen. [HEM(O)- + AGGLUTININ.]
he·ma·gogue, he·ma·gog (hē′mə-gŏg′, -gōg′, hĕm′ə-) *n.* A drug or other agent that promotes the flow of blood, as in menstruation. [HEM(O)- + -AGOG(UE).]
he·mal (hē′məl) *adj.* **1.** Of or pertaining to the blood or blood vessels. **2.** Relating to or designating the side of the body that contains the heart. [HEM(O)- + -AL.]
he-man (hē′măn′) *n., pl.* **-men** (-mĕn′). *Informal.* A strong, muscular, virile man.
he·man·gi·o·ma (hĭ-măn′jē-ō′mə) *n., pl.* **-mas** or **-mata** (-mə-tə). A nonmalignant tumor of blood vessels, often seen on the skin as a type of birthmark. [HEM(O)- + ANGIOMA.]
hemat-. Variant of **hemato-**.
he·ma·te·in (hē′mə-tē′ĭn, hĕm′ə-, hē′mə-tēn′, hĕm′ə-) *n.* A dark-purple crystalline compound, $C_{16}H_{12}O_6$, used as an indicator and as a biological stain. [HEMAT(O)- + *-ein,* variant of -IN.]
he·ma·tem·e·sis (hē′mə-tĕm′ə-sĭs, hĕm′ə-) *n.* The vomiting of blood, often due to a bleeding gastric or duodenal ulcer. [HEMAT(O)- + Greek *emesis,* vomiting.]
he·mat·ic (hĭ-măt′ĭk) *adj.* Of, pertaining to, resembling, containing, or acting on blood.
~*n.* A remedy for anemia and other blood diseases. [Greek *haimatikos,* from *haima†* (stem *haimat-*), blood.]
he·ma·tin (hē′mə-tĭn, hĕm′ə-) *n.* A blue to blackish-brown powder, $C_{34}H_{32}N_4O_4FeOH$, that is the hydroxide of heme, containing ferric iron. [HEMAT(O)- + -IN.]
he·ma·tin·ic (hē′mə-tĭn′ĭk, hĕm′ə-) *adj.* Acting to increase the amount of hemoglobin in the blood.
~*n.* A hematinic drug used to treat iron-deficiency anemia. [HEMATIN + -IC.]
hem·a·tite (hĕm′ə-tīt′, hē′mə-) *n.* A blackish-red to brick-red mineral, essentially Fe_2O_3, the chief ore of iron. Also called "iron glance." [Latin *haematitēs,* from Greek *(lithos) haimatitēs,* "bloodlike (stone)," red iron ore, from *haima†* (stem *haimat-*), blood.]
hemato-, hemat- *prefix.* Indicates blood; for example, **hematology, hematin, hematic.** [Greek *haimato-,* from *haima†* (stem *haimat-*), blood.]
hem·a·to·blast (hĕm′ə-tō-blăst′, -blăst′, -hē′mə-, hĭ-măt′ə-) *n.* **1.** A platelet of the blood. **2.** An immature blood cell. [HEMATO- + -BLAST.] —**hem·a·to·blas·tic** (hĕm′ə-tə-blăs′tĭk, hē′mə, hĭ-măt′ə-) *adj.*
hem·a·to·cele (hĕm′ə-tō-sēl′, hē′mə-, hĭ-măt′ə-) *n.* A hemorrhage contained within a membranous cavity, especially in the testicle. [HEMATO- + -CELE.]
hem·a·to·crit (hĕm′ə-tō-krĭt′, hē′mə-, hĭ-măt′ə-) *n.* **1.** A centrifuge used to separate the cellular and other particulate matter of blood from the plasma. **2.** Packed cell volume *(see).* [HEMATO- + Greek *kritēs,* judge, from *krinein,* to decide, judge.]
hem·a·to·gen·e·sis (hĕm′ə-tō-jĕn′ə-sĭs, hē′mə, hĭ-măt′ə-) *n.* Hematopoiesis. [HEMATO- + -GENESIS.] —**hem·a·to·gen·ic** (hĕm′ə-tō-jĕn′ĭk, hē′mə, hĭ-măt′ə-) *adj.* —**hem·a·to·ge·net·ic** (hĕm′ə-tō-jə-nĕt′ĭk, hē′mə, hĭ-măt′ə-) *adj.*
he·ma·tog·e·nous (hē′mə-tŏj′ə-nəs, hĕm′ə-) *adj.* **1.** Producing blood. **2.** Originating or carried in the blood. [HEMATO- + -GENOUS.]
he·ma·toid (hē′mə-toid′, hĕm′ə-) *adj.* **1.** Bloody. **2.** Like blood. [Greek *haimatoeides* : HEMAT(O)- + -OID.]
he·ma·tol·o·gy (hē′mə-tŏl′ə-jē, hĕm′ə-) *n.* The science encompassing the generation, anatomy, physiology, pathology, and therapeutics of blood. [HEMATO- + -LOGY.] —**he·ma·to·log·i·cal** (hē′mə-tə-lŏj′ĭ-kəl, hĕm′ə-) *adj.* —**he·ma·to·log·i·cal·ly** *adv.* —**he·ma·tol·o·gist** (hē′mə-tŏl′ə-jĭst, hĕm′ə-) *n.*
he·ma·tol·y·sis (hē′mə-tŏl′ə-sĭs, hĕm′ə-) *n.* Biology. Hemolysis *(see).* [HEMATO- + -LYSIS.]

he·ma·to·ma (hē′mə-tō′mə, hĕm′ə-) *n., pl.* **-mas** or **-mata** (-mə-tə). *Pathology.* A localized swelling filled with blood. [HEMAT(O)- + -OMA.]
hem·a·to·poi·e·sis (hĕm′ə-tō-poi-ē′sĭs, hē′mə, hĭ-măt′ə-) *n.* The formation of blood in the body. Also called "hematogenesis," "hemopoiesis." [HEMATO- + -POIESIS.] —**hem·a·to·poi·et·ic** (hĕm′ə-tō-poi-ĕt′ĭk, hē′mə, hĭ-măt′ə-) *adj.*
he·ma·to·sis (hē′mə-tō′sĭs, hĕm′ə-) *n.* Oxygenation of venous blood in the lungs. [HEMAT(O)- + -OSIS.]
hem·a·tox·y·lin (hĕm′ə-tŏk′sə-lĭn, hē′mə-) *n.* A yellow or red crystalline compound, $C_{16}H_{14}O_6 \cdot 3H_2O$, the coloring principle of logwood, used in dyes, inks, and stains. [New Latin *Haematoxyl(on)* (plant genus) : *haemato-,* variant of HEMATO- + XYL(O)- + -IN.]
hem·a·to·zo·on (hĕm′ə-tō-zō′ŏn′, hē′mə-, hĭ-măt′ə-) *n., pl.* **-zoa** (-zō′ə). A parasitic protozoan or similar organism that lives in the blood. [HEMATO- + -ZOON.] —**hem·a·to·zo·ic** *adj.*
hem·a·tu·ri·a (hĕm′ə-tŏŏr′ē-ə, -tyŏŏr′ē-ə, hē′mə-) *n.* A condition in which blood or red blood cells are present in the urine. [HEMAT(O)- + -URIA.] —**hem·a·tu·ric** *adj.*
heme (hēm) *n.* The nonprotein, ferrous-iron-containing component of hemoglobin, having composition $C_{34}H_{32}FeN_4O_4$. [From HEMATIN.]
he·mel·y·tron (hē-mĕl′ə-trŏn′) *n., pl.* **-tra** (-trə). Also **hem·i·el·y·tron** (hĕm′ē-ĕl′ə-trŏn′). An insect forewing that is thickened at the base and membranous at the apex, characteristic of the true bugs. [HEM(I)- + ELYTRON.]
hem·er·a·lo·pi·a (hĕm′ər-ə-lō′pē-ə) *n.* A visual defect manifested as the inability to see as clearly in bright light as in dim light. Also called "day blindness." Compare **nyctalopia.** [New Latin, from Greek *hēmeralōps,* "day blind" : *hēmera,* day + *alaos†,* blind + -OPIA.]
hem·er·o·cal·lis (hĕm′ə-rō-kăl′ĭs) *n.* The day lily *(see).* [New Latin, from Latin, from Greek *hēmerokalles,* name of a kind of lily : *hēmera,* day + *kallos,* beauty.]
hemi-, hem- *prefix.* Indicates half; for example, **hemichordate, hemelytron.** Compare **demi-, semi-.** [Latin *hēmi-,* from Greek.]
–hemia. Variant of **-emia.**
hem·i·al·gi·a (hĕm′ē-ăl′jē-ə) *n.* Pain affecting one half of the body. [New Latin : HEMI- + -ALGIA.]
he·mic (hē′mĭk, hĕm′ĭk) *adj.* Of blood. [HEM(O) + -IC.]
hem·i·cel·lu·lose (hĕm′ĭ-sĕl′yə-lōs′, -lōz′) *n.* Any of several polysaccharides that are more complex than a sugar and less complex than cellulose, derived from plants and produced commercially from various seeds and other plant tissues.
hem·i·chor·date (hĕm′ĭ-kôr′dāt′) *n.* Any of various wormlike marine animals of the phylum or subphylum Hemichordata, having a primitive notochord and gill slits.
~*adj.* Of or belonging to the Hemichordata. [New Latin *Hemichordata* : HEMI- + CHORDATE.]
hem·i·cy·cle (hĕm′ĭ-sī′kəl) *n.* A semicircular structure or arrangement. [French *hémicycle,* from Latin *hēmicyclium,* from Greek *hēmikuklion* : HEMI- + *kuklos,* circle, CYCLE.]
hem·i·dem·i·sem·i·qua·ver (hĕm′ē-dĕm′ē-sĕm′ē-kwā′vər) *n. Chiefly British. Music.* A sixty-fourth note *(see).* [HEMI- + DEMISEMIQUAVER.]
hem·i·he·dral (hĕm′ĭ-hē′drəl) *adj.* Exhibiting only half the faces required for complete symmetry. Said of a crystal. [HEMI- + -HEDR(ON) + -AL.]
hem·i·hy·drate (hĕm′ĭ-hī′drāt′) *n.* A hydrate in which the molecular ratio of water molecules to anhydrous compound is 1:2. [HEMI- + HYDRATE.] —**hem·i·hy·drat·ed** *adj.*
hem·i·mor·phic (hĕm′ĭ-môr′fĭk) *adj.* Asymmetric at the axial ends. Said of a crystal. [HEMI- + -MORPHIC.]
hem·i·mor·phite (hĕm′ĭ-môr′fīt′) *n.* A mineral, **smithsonite.** [HEMIMORPH(IC) + -ITE.]
he·min (hē′mĭn) *n.* A brown or blue crystalline compound, $C_{34}H_{32}N_4O_4FeCl$, that is the chloride of heme and is used in identifying blood stains. [HEM(O)- + -IN.]
Hem·ing·way (hĕm′ĭng-wā′), **Ernest Miller** (1899-1961). U.S. novelist. He served in World War I with the Red Cross, then was a newspaper reporter in Toronto before settling in Paris with a group of expatriate U.S. writers, including Ezra Pound and Gertrude Stein. The novel *The Torrents of Spring* (1926) first revealed his clipped style. His major works are *The Sun Also Rises* (1926), *A Farewell to Arms* (1929), *For Whom the Bell Tolls* (1940), and *The Old Man and the Sea* (1952). He was awarded the Nobel Prize for literature in 1954.
hem·i·par·a·site (hĕm′ĭ-păr′ə-sīt′) *n.* **1.** An organism, such as mistletoe, that obtains some food from its host but also photosynthesizes. Also called "semiparasite." **2.** An organism that can live both parasitically and independently; a facultative parasite.
hem·i·ple·gi·a (hĕm′ĭ-plē′jē-ə) *n.* Paralysis of one side of the body only. Compare **paraplegia, quadriplegia.** [New Latin, from Middle Greek *hēmiplēgia* : HEMI- + -PLEGIA.] —**hem·i·ple·gic** *adj. & n.*
he·mip·ter·an (hĭ-mĭp′tər-ən) *n.* Also **he·mip·ter·on** (-tə-rŏn′). A hemipterous insect.
~*adj.* Of or belonging to the Hemiptera; hemipterous. [New Latin *Hemiptera* : HEMI- + -PTER.]
he·mip·ter·ous (hĭ-mĭp′tər-əs) *adj.* Of or belonging to the Hemiptera, a large group of insects characterized by piercing or sucking mouth parts in the form of a beak or rostrum. The group includes the **heteropterous** and **homopterous** bugs *(both of which see).*
hem·i·sphere (hĕm′ĭ-sfîr′) *n.* **1. a.** A half of a sphere bounded by a

great circle. **b.** A half of a symmetric, approximately spherical object as divided by a plane of symmetry: *cerebral hemisphere.* **2.** Either half of the celestial sphere as divided by the ecliptic, the celestial equator, or the horizon. **3.** Either the northern or southern half of the earth as divided by the equator or the eastern or western half as divided by a meridian. [Middle English *(h)emisper(i)e,* from Latin *hēmisphaerium,* from Greek *hēmisphairion* : HEMI- + *sphairion,* diminutive of *sphaira,* SPHERE.] **—hem·i·spher·ic** (hĕm′ə-sfîr′ĭk, -sfĕr′ĭk), **hem·i·spher·i·cal** *adj.* **—hem·i·spher·i·cal·ly** *adv.*

hem·i·stich (hĕm′ĭ-stĭk′) *n. Prosody.* **1.** Half a line of verse, especially when separated rhythmically from the rest of the line by a caesura. **2.** An incomplete or imperfect line of verse. [Latin *hēmistichium,* from Greek *hēmistikhion* : HEMI- + *stikhos,* line.]

hem·i·ter·pene (hĕm′ĭ-tûr′pēn′) *n.* Any of a group of hydrocarbons that have the formula C_5H_8. See **terpene.**

hem·line (hĕm′līn′) *n.* The height or level of the hem of a skirt, dress, or coat.

hem·lock (hĕm′lŏk′) *n.* **1. a.** A type of spruce tree of the genus *Tsuga,* native to North America, having small cones and short, flat needles. **b.** The wood of such a tree. **2. a.** Any of several poisonous plants of the genera *Conium* and *Cicuta,* such as the **poison hemlock** and **water hemlock** *(both of which see).* **b.** The poisonous alkaloid **coniine** *(see),* derived from the poison hemlock. [Old English *hymlic(e)*†.]

hemo–, hem–, hema– *prefix.* Indicates blood; for example, **hemocyte, hemin, hemacytometer.** [From Greek *haima*†, blood.]

he·mo·chro·ma·to·sis (hē′mə-krō′mə-tō′sĭs, hĕm′ə-) *n.* A hereditary disease in which excessive amounts of iron are absorbed by and stored in the body. Symptoms include diabetes, a bronze pigmentation of the skin, and severe damage to the liver and pancreas. Also called "bronze diabetes." [HEMO- + CHROMAT(O)- + -OSIS.]

he·mo·coel (hē′mə-sēl′, hĕm′ə-) *n.* The body cavity of arthropods and mollusks, consisting of a blood-filled expanded portion of the circulatory system. [HEMO- + Greek *koilos,* hollow.]

he·mo·cy·a·nin (hē′mə-sī′ə-nĭn, hĕm′ə-) *n.* A bluish, oxygen-bearing, copper-containing substance similar to hemoglobin, present in the blood of certain insects, crustaceans, and other invertebrates. [HEMO- + -CYAN(O) + -IN.]

he·mo·cyte (hē′mə-sīt′, hĕm′ə-) *n.* A cell in the blood. [HEMO- + -CYTE.]

he·mo·di·al·y·sis (hē′mō-dī-ăl′ə-sĭs, hĕm′ō-) *n.* A technique for removing waste products in the circulating blood of patients with kidney failure using the principle of **dialysis** *(see).* Blood is passed through a dialyzer (kidney machine) and the waste products filter through a semipermeable membrane.

he·mo·dy·nam·ics (hē′mō-dī-năm′ĭks, hĕm′ō-) *n.* The study of the circulation of the blood.

he·mo·flag·el·late (hē′mə-flăj′ə-lāt′, -lĭt, -flə-jĕl′ĭt, hĕm′ə-) *n.* A flagellate protozoan, as a trypanosome, that is parasitic in the blood.

he·mo·glo·bin (hē′mə-glō′bĭn, hĕm′ə-) *n. Abbr.* **Hb** The oxygen-bearing, iron-containing conjugated protein in vertebrate red blood cells, consisting of about 6 percent heme and 94 percent globin, and having as a typical formula $(C_{738}H_{1166}FeN_{203}O_{208}S_2)_4$. [Shortening of earlier *hematoglobulin* : HEMATIN + GLOBULIN.]

he·mo·glo·bi·nu·ri·a (hē′mə-glō′bə-no͝or′ē-ə, -nyo͝or′ē-ə, hĕm′ə-) *n.* The presence of hemoglobin in the urine. **—he·mo·glo·bi·nu·ric** *adj.*

he·mo·leu·ko·cyte (hē′mə-lo͞o′kə-sīt′, hĕm′ə-) *n.* A **leukocyte** *(see).*

he·mo·ly·sin (hē′mə-lī′sĭn, hĕm′ə-, hĭ-mŏl′ə-sĭn) *n.* An agent or substance, such as an antibody or bacterial toxin, that initiates destruction of red blood cells, thereby liberating hemoglobin. [HEMO- + LYSIN.]

he·mol·y·sis (hĭ-mŏl′ə-sĭs) *n.* The destruction of red blood cells, either in the body or in a blood sample. Also called "hematolysis." [HEM(O)- + -LYSIS.] **—he·mo·lyt·ic** (hē′mə-lĭt′ĭk) *adj.*

hemolytic disease of the newborn *n.* A condition in newborn babies resulting from destruction of the red blood cells of the fetus by antibodies from the mother's blood. It usually occurs because of incompatibility of maternal and fetal blood groups.

he·mo·phil·i·a (hē′mə-fĭl′ē-ə, hĕm′ə-) *n.* A hereditary blood coagulation disorder, principally affecting males but transmitted by females, characterized by excessive, sometimes spontaneous bleeding. [HEMO- + -PHILIA.]

he·mo·phil·i·ac (hē′mə-fĭl′ē-ăk′, hĕm′ə-) *n.* A person who suffers from hemophilia. Also called "bleeder."

he·mo·phil·ic (hē′mə-fĭl′ĭk, hĕm′ə-) *adj.* **1.** Pertaining to hemophilia. **2.** Growing well in blood, or in a culture containing blood, as do certain bacteria.

he·mo·pho·bi·a (hē′mə-fō′bē-ə, hĕm′ə-) *n.* A morbid fear of blood. [HEMO- + -PHOBIA.] **—he·mo·pho·bic** *adj.*

he·mo·poi·e·sis (hē′mə-poi-ē′sĭs, hĕm′ə-) *n. Physiology.* **Hematopoiesis** *(see).* [HEMO- + -POIESIS.]

he·mo·pro·tein (hē′mə-prō′tēn′) *n.* Any protein containing heme, such as hemoglobin, myoglobin, and cytochrome.

he·mop·ty·sis (hĭ-mŏp′tə-sĭs) *n.* The spitting up of blood from the lungs or bronchial tubes. [HEMO- + Greek *ptusis,* a spitting, from *ptuein,* to spit.]

hem·or·rhage (hĕm′ər-ĭj) *n.* Bleeding; especially, copious discharge of blood from the blood vessels.
~*intr.v.* **hemorrhaged, -rhaging, -rhages.** To bleed copiously in or as if in a hemorrhage. [Earlier *hemorrhagy,* from Old French *hemorragie,* from Latin *haemorrhagia,* from Greek *haimorrhagia* : HEMO- + -RRHAGIA.] **—hem·or·rhag·ic** (hĕm′ə-răj′ĭk) *adj.*

hem·or·rhoid (hĕm′ə-roid′) *n.* **1.** An itching or painful mass of dilated veins in swollen anal tissue. **2. hemorrhoids.** The pathological condition in which such swollen masses occur. In this sense, also called "piles." [Middle English *emeroudis,* from Old French *emeroyde,* from Latin *haemorrhoida,* from Greek *(phlebes) haimorrhoides,* bleeding (veins), from *haimorrhoos,* flowing with blood : HEMO- + *-rrhoos,* from *rhein,* to flow.]

hem·or·rhoid·al (hĕm′ə-roid′l) *adj.* **1.** Of or pertaining to hemorrhoids. **2.** *Anatomy.* Supplying the region of the rectum and anus. Said of certain arteries.

hem·or·rhoid·ec·to·my (hĕm′ə-roi-dĕk′tə-mē) *n., pl.* **-mies.** The removal of hemorrhoids by surgery.

he·mo·sid·er·in (hē′mō-sĭd′ər-ĭn) *n.* An iron-containing protein serving to store iron in the body. Excessive amounts are formed in certain disorders, such as hemochromatosis. [HEMO- + Greek *sideros,* iron + -IN.]

he·mo·sta·sis (hē′mə-stā′sĭs, hĕm′ə-) *n.* Also **he·mo·sta·sia** (-zhə, -zhē-ə, -zē-ə). The stopping of the flow or circulation of blood. [HEMO- + STASIS.]

he·mo·stat (hē′mə-stăt′) *n.* **1.** Any agent, such as a chemical, that stops bleeding. **2.** A clamplike instrument used in surgery to reduce or prevent bleeding. [HEMO- + -STAT.]

he·mo·stat·ic (hē′mə-stăt′ĭk) *adj.* Acting to stop the flow of blood or profuse bleeding.
~*n.* A hemostatic agent. [Late Greek *haimostatikos* : HEMO- + -STATIC.]

hemp (hĕmp) *n.* **1.** A tall plant, *Cannabis sativa,* native to Asia, having small greenish flowers and stems that yield a coarse fiber used in cordage. Also called "cannabis," "Indian hemp," "marijuana." **2.** The fiber of this plant. **3.** Any of various narcotic drugs, such as hashish, derived from this plant. **4. a.** Any of various similar or related plants, especially one yielding a fiber similar to that of *Cannabis sativa.* **b.** The fiber of such a plant. [Middle English *hemp(e),* Old English *hænep, henep,* from Germanic *hanipiz* (unattested); akin to Greek *kannabis.*]

hemp agrimony *n.* A Eurasian plant, *Eupatorium cannabinum,* having clusters of small reddish-purple flowers.

hemp agrimony *This tall riverside plant was used in medieval times as a purgative and a cure for jaundice.*

hemp·en (hĕm′pən) *adj.* Made of or resembling hemp.

hemp nettle *n.* Any of various Eurasian plants of the genus *Galeopsis;* especially, *G. tetrahit,* having white or reddish flowers.

hem·stitch (hĕm′stĭch′) *n.* **1.** A decorative stitch usually bordering a hem, as on a handkerchief, made by drawing out several parallel threads and catching together the cross threads in uniform groups, thus creating an open design. **2.** Needlework using this stitch. **—hem·stitch** *v.* **—hem·stitch·er** *n.*

hen (hĕn) *n.* **1.** A female bird; especially, the adult female of the domestic fowl. **2.** The female of certain aquatic animals, such as an octopus or a lobster. [Middle English *hen,* Old English *hen(n).*]

He·nan (hŭ′nän′). Also **Ho·nan, Ho-nan** (hō′-). Province of northeastern and central China. Traversed by the Huang He (Yellow River) and Huai He, which irrigate its densely populated and fertile central plain, it produces cereals and anthracite. The capital, Zhengzhou (Chengchow), is in the northwest of the province.

hen-and-chick·ens (hĕn′ən-chĭk′ənz) *n., pl.* **hens-and-chickens** (hĕnz′-). Any of several plants having many runners or offshoots; especially, the **houseleek** *(see).*

hen·bane (hĕn′bān′) *n.* A poisonous plant, *Hyoscyamus niger,* native to the Mediterranean region, having an unpleasant odor, clammy leaves, and funnel-shaped greenish-yellow flowers, and yielding a juice used medicinally. [Middle English, from HEN (fowl) + BANE (alluding to its poison).]

henbane *The yellow and purple summer flowers of this European wildflower have a nasty smell. The plant is very poisonous, but its seeds are used to make hyoscine, a drug used in the treatment of insomnia, rheumatism, and seasickness.*

hen·bit (hĕn′bĭt′) *n.* A plant, *Lamium amplexicaule,* native to Europe, having toothed leaves and small purplish-pink flowers. Also called "henbit dead nettle." [HEN + BIT (morsel).]

hence (hĕns) *adv.* **1. a.** For this reason; as a result; therefore: *handmade and hence expensive.* **b.** From this source: *She grew up in the Sudan, hence her interest in Nubian art.* **2. a.** From this time; from now: *A year hence he will have forgotten.* **b.** *Rare.* Henceforth: *Hence I'll trust no one.* **3. a.** Forth from this place; away from here. Usually used with an imperative: *Get thee hence!* **b.** Distant from here: *an inn two miles hence.* **c.** From this life: *depart hence.* **—from hence.** *Archaic.* From this place.
~*interj. Archaic.* Go; get out: "*Hence, loathed Melancholy*" (Milton). **—hence with!** Away with! [Middle English *hennes,* extended form of *henne,* hence, Old English *heonane,* from here, away.]

hence·forth (hĕns′fôrth′) *adv.* Also **hence·for·ward** (hĕns-fôr′wərd). From this time forth; from now on.

hench·man (hĕnch′mən) *n., pl.* **-men** (-mĭn). **1. a.** A loyal and trusted follower or subordinate. **b.** A person who supports a political figure chiefly out of self-interest. **2.** A member of a criminal gang. **3.** *Obsolete.* A page of honor to a prince or other person of high rank. [Middle English *hengestman, henx(st)man,* probably groom, squire : *hengest,* horse, stallion, from Old English, from Germanic *hangista-* (unattested) + MAN.]

hen·coop (hĕn′ko͞op′) *n.* A coop or cage for poultry.

hendeca– *prefix.* Indicates eleven; for example, **hendecahedron.** [Greek *hendeka,* eleven : *hen,* neuter of *heis,* one + *deka,* ten.]

hen·dec·a·gon (hĕn-dĕk′ə-gŏn′) *n.* A polygon with 11 sides. [HENDECA- + -GON.] **—hen·de·cag·o·nal** (hĕn′dĭ-kăg′ə-nəl) *adj.*

hen·dec·a·he·dron (hĕn-dĕk′ə-hē′drən) *n., pl.* **-drons** or **-dra** (-drə). A polyhedron with 11 plane surfaces. [HENDECA- + -HEDRON.] **—hen·dec·a·he·dral** *adj.*

hen·dec·a·syl·lab·ic (hĕn-dĕk′ə-sĭ-lăb′ĭk) *adj.* Containing eleven syllables.
~*n.* Also **hen·dec·a·syl·la·ble** (hĕn-dĕk′ə-sĭl′ə-bəl). A line of verse containing eleven syllables. [Latin *hendecasyllabus,* a hendecasyllable : Greek *hendeka,* eleven : *hen,* neuter of *heis,* one + *deka,* ten + *sullabē,* SYLLABLE.]

Hen·der·son (hĕn′dər-sən), **Arthur** (1863–1935). British Labour politician. He was an ironworker and trade union leader and was first elected to parliament in 1903. From 1932 until his death he was president of the World Disarmament Conference. He was awarded the Nobel Peace Prize in 1934.

hen·di·a·dys (hĕn-dī′ə-dĭs) *n.* A figure of speech in which two distinct words connected by a conjunction are used to express a single complex notion that would normally be expressed by an adjective and a noun; for example, in *He struck with steel and sword,* the phrase *steel and sword* is a hendiadys, used instead of *a steel sword.* [Medieval Latin, from Greek *hen dia duoin,* one by means of two : *hen,* neuter of *heis,* one + *dia,* through (see **dia-**) + *duoin,* genitive of *duō,* two.]

Hen·drix (hĕn′drĭks), **Jimi,** born James Marshall Hendrix (1942–70). U.S. rock musician. His innovative style of electric guitar playing changed the course of rock music. With his first major group, the Jimi Hendrix Experience, he recorded hits such as *Purple Haze* and *Foxy Lady,* which were his own compositions.

Henegouwen. See Hainaut.

hen·e·quen, hen·e·quin, hen·i·quen (hĕn′ə-kwən) *n.* **1.** A tropical American plant, *Agave fourcroydes,* having large, thick leaves that yield a coarse reddish fiber used in making rope and twine. **2.** The fiber obtained from this plant. [Spanish *henequén, jeniquén,* perhaps from Taino.]

henge (hĕnj) *n.* A structure of ritual significance belonging to the Neolithic or Bronze Age, circular in form and sometimes having stone or wooden posts. [Back-formation from STONEHENGE.]

Hen·gist (hĕn′gĭst) (died *c.* 488). Germanic chieftain. With his brother **Hor·sa** (hôr′sə), he led (A.D. 449) the Jutes who invaded southern Britain. They landed in the Isle of Thant, but were defeated at Aylesford, where Horsa was slain (*c.* 455). Hengist then conquered Kent, where he ruled from *c.* 455 to *c.* 488.

hen harrier *n.* The **marsh hawk** *(see).*

hen·house (hĕn′hous′) *n.* A chicken coop.

Hen·ie (hĕn′ē), **Sonja** (1913–69). Norwegian ice-skater. She was largely responsible for making ice-skating a popular, competitive sport. She was Norwegian champion at age 10, won Olympic gold medals in 1928, 1932, and 1936, and won 10 consecutive world championships between 1927 and 1936. In 1936 she settled in the United States, where she starred in ice shows and films.

Hen·ley (hĕn′lē), **William Ernest** (1849–1903). English editor and author. The editor of the *Scots Observer* (from 1889) and its successor, the *National Observer,* he published the early works of many aspiring English writers, including George Bernard Shaw, Thomas Hardy, and Rudyard Kipling.

Hen·ley-on-Thames (hĕn′lē-ŏn-tĕmz′). Town in Oxfordshire, in south-central England, on the Thames River. It is best known for its annual royal regatta, first held in 1839.

hen·na (hĕn′ə) *n.* **1.** A tree or shrub, *Lawsonia inermis,* of Asia and northern Africa, having fragrant white or reddish flowers. **2.** A reddish powder obtained from the leaves of this plant, used as a hair coloring and for dyeing leather. **3.** Moderate or strong reddish brown to strong brown.
~*tr.v.* **hennaed, -naing, -nas.** To dye (hair, for example) with henna. [Arabic *ḥinnā′.*] —**hen·na** *adj.*

henna wax *n.* A wax preparation derived from the henna plant and used as a noncolorant hair conditioner.

hen·ner·y (hĕn′ə-rē) *n., pl.* **-ies. 1.** A poultry farm. **2.** A coop or cage for poultry.

hen·o·the·ism (hĕn′ə-thē-ĭz′əm) *n.* Belief in one god, such as a special clan or tribal god, without denying the existence of others. Compare **monotheism.** [German *Henotheismus* : Greek *heno-,* from *hen,* neuter of *heis,* one + THEISM.] —**hen·o·the·ist** *n.* —**hen·o·the·is·tic** (hĕn′ə-thē-ĭs′tĭk) *adj.*

hen party *n. Informal.* A party or outing exclusively for women. Compare **stag party.**

hen·peck (hĕn′pĕk′) *tr.v.* **-pecked, -pecking, -pecks.** *Informal.* To dominate or harass (one's husband) with persistent nagging. [Back-formation from *henpecked,* alluding to a hen that attacks and dominates a rooster.]

Hen·ri (hĕn′rē), **Robert** (1865–1929). U.S. painter. After studying in Paris, he joined with a group of young painters, dubbed the Eight—or the Ashcan School by their detractors—who decried the artificiality and sentiment of traditional schools of art. Henri was also a well-known teacher, whose students included Edward Hopper.

Hen·ri·et·ta Ma·ri·a (hĕn′rē-ĕt′ə mə-rē′ə) (1609–69). Queen consort of Charles I of England, the daughter of Henry IV of France. She married Charles in 1625 and by remaining a Roman Catholic increased Charles's unpopularity with the Puritans.

hen·ry (hĕn′rē) *n., pl.* **-ries** or **-rys.** *Abbr.* **H** The unit of inductance in which an induced electromotive force of one volt is produced when the current is varied at the rate of one ampere per second. [After Joseph HENRY.]

Hen·ry I (hĕn′rē), also known as "Henry Beauclerc" (1068–1135). King of England (1100–35). He was the youngest son of William the Conqueror and succeeded his brother, William II.

Henry II¹ (1133–89). King of England (1154–89), son of Queen Ma-

tilda, and founder (through his father, Geoffrey, Count of Anjou) of the Angevin, or Plantagenet, royal line. Henry appointed Thomas Becket archbishop of Canterbury in 1162 but quarreled with him over the issue of the Crown's authority over the Church. This led to the murder of Becket in 1170.

Henry II² (1519–59). King of France (1547–59), the son of Francis I. He regained Calais from the English in 1558.

Henry III (1207–72). King of England (1216–72). He succeeded his father, King John. His reign was troubled by baronial opposition led by Simon de Montfort, whose representative parliament, called in 1265, is regarded as the first full English parliament.

Henry IV¹, also known as "Henry Bolingbroke" (1367–1413). King of England (1399–1413), eldest son of John of Gaunt and grandson of Edward III. He was banished from England by Richard II in 1398. The following year John of Gaunt died, and Richard confiscated his estates, to which Henry was heir. Henry returned, raised a military force, and compelled Richard to abdicate. Parliament confirmed his claim, and the Lancastrian dynasty was founded.

Henry IV², also known as "Henry of Navarre" (1553–1610). King of France (1589–1610), the son of Antoine de Bourbon and founder of the Bourbon royal line. He rid France of Spanish influence by his successful war against Spain (1595–98) and gave political rights to French Protestants in the Edict of Nantes (1598).

Henry V (1387–1422). King of England (1413–22), son of Henry IV. In the first years of his reign he suppressed the Lollards, executing their leader, Sir John Oldcastle, in 1417. He also reopened the Hundred Years' War, defeating the French at Agincourt (1415). By 1419 all of Normandy was once again in English hands.

Henry VI (1421–71). King of England (1422–61, 1470–71), only son of Henry V. He succeeded to the throne as a baby and for most of his reign exercised little control over the royal administration. The Yorkist victory at Northampton in 1460 left Henry a prisoner of his enemies. The following year Edward IV was proclaimed king. Henry, rescued from captivity, regained the throne in 1470. He was recaptured at the Battle of Barnet and murdered in the Tower of London in 1471.

Henry VII, also known as "Henry Tudor" (1457–1509). King of England (1485–1509), son of Edmund Tudor and founder of the Tudor line. He was head of the house of Lancaster after the death of Henry VI in 1471 and led the opposition to Richard III. In 1485 he defeated Richard at Bosworth Field and was acclaimed king. He married Elizabeth, daughter of Edward IV, and united the houses of York and Lancaster.

Henry VIII (1491–1547). King of England (1509–47), second son and successor of Henry VII. He married the first of his six wives, Catherine of Aragon, shortly after his accession in 1509. Her failure to deliver a male heir led to the divorce that compelled Henry to break with Rome by the Act of Supremacy in 1536. That same year he began the dissolution of the monasteries.

Henry, Joseph (1797–1878). U.S. physicist. He was the first director of the Smithsonian Institution, founded in 1846. He invented the electromagnetic telegraph and, independently of Michael Faraday, discovered electromagnetic induction, the principle on which the transformer and the dynamo are based.

Henry, O. See William Sydney **Porter.**

Henry, Patrick (1739–99). U.S. Revolutionary leader and orator. A member of the House of Burgesses (1765) and the Continental Congress (1774–76), he spurred the creation of the Virginia militia with the words "Give me liberty, or give me death" (1775). He also served as governor of Virginia and in the state legislature (1776–90).

Henry's law *n. Chemistry.* The principle that at equilibrium the amount of gas dissolved in a liquid is proportional to the gas pressure. [After William *Henry* (1774–1836), English chemist.]

Henry the Navigator (1394–1460). Prince of Portugal. In 1416 he established a headquarters for overseas exploration that laid the foundations of Portugal's overseas empire.

hep·a·rin (hĕp′ər-ĭn) *n.* A complex organic acid found especially in lung and liver tissue and having the ability in certain circumstances to prevent the clotting of blood. [New Latin *hepar,* liver, from Late Latin *hēpar,* from Greek + -IN.]

he·pat·ic (hĭ-păt′ĭk) *adj.* **1.** Of, pertaining to, or resembling the liver. **2.** Liver-colored. **3.** Of or belonging to the Hepaticae, a class of mosslike plants including the liverworts.
~*n.* **1.** A drug used to treat liver diseases. **2.** A plant of the class Hepaticae, a **liverwort** *(see).* [Middle English *epatik,* from Latin *hēpaticus,* of liver, from Greek *hēpatikos,* from *hēpar* (stem *hēpat-*), liver.]

he·pat·i·ca (hĭ-păt′ĭ-kə) *n.* Any of several woodland plants of the genus *Hepatica;* especially, *H. americana,* of eastern North America, having three-lobed leaves and white or lavender flowers. [New Latin *Hepatica,* from Medieval Latin *hēpatica,* liverwort, from Latin, feminine of *hēpaticus,* HEPATIC.]

hep·a·ti·tis (hĕp′ə-tī′tĭs) *n.* Inflammation of the liver due to infection or toxins, characterized by fever, weakness, and jaundice. [New Latin : Greek *hēpar* (stem *hēpat-*), liver + -ITIS.]

Hep·burn (hĕp′bûrn′, -bərn), **Katharine** (1909–). U.S. actress. She made her stage debut in 1928 and became a popular Hollywood film star. She has won an Oscar as best actress four times, for *Morning Glory* (1933), *Guess Who's Coming to Dinner* (1967), *The Lion in Winter* (1968), and *On Golden Pond* (1981).

hep·cat (hĕp′kăt′) *n. Slang.* A performer or devotee of swing and jazz during the 1940's.

He·phaes·tus (hĭ-fĕs′təs). *Greek Mythology.* The lame god of fire

henge *These prehistoric circles of free-standing stones or wooden uprights are thought to have been ceremonial centers in ancient Britain and France. The best-known example is Stonehenge, on Britain's Salisbury Plain. This one, dating from about 1800 B.C., is at Avebury in Wiltshire, England.*

HOW KNIGHTS WERE IDENTIFIED IN THE MIDDLE AGES

The symbol of gentility that grew from a simple means of identification

The use of pictures and emblems on shields, flags, and coats of arms was introduced into England from western Europe during the 12th century. But the exact date and place of origin of the heraldic system in western Europe is not known.

The earliest use was on the battlefield and in tournaments, or mock battles, as a means of identification for otherwise unrecognizable armor-clad knights. Bold symbols depicting a knight's name were embroidered on his surcoat, the garment worn over his armor, which became known as the coat of arms. Since few people could read or write at that time, this means of identification spread to the seals that were used to authenticate official documents. Heralds, the messengers of royal and noble households, whose duty it was to identify the knights, became interested in the colorful means of identification, and heraldry as it is known today began. Heraldic systems are similar throughout Europe, and a system akin to heraldry can be found in Japan.

In 1484 Richard III of England granted the heralds a charter incorporating them as a body within the Royal Household, now known as the College of Arms, or Heralds' College. The Kings of Arms (the senior heralds) grant arms on behalf of the Crown, and they also draw up the regulations regarding arms. Blazon, the language of heraldry, was invented by the early heralds and is still used to describe all coats of arms.

Originally arms were granted only to knights and nobles and were regarded as an honor. But during the 15th century the rich and powerful middle class that emerged from the crumbling feudal system were granted arms in recognition of their new "gentle" status, and since then a coat of arms has been regarded as the insignia of gentility. Arms are still granted to those who satisfy the Earl Marshal that they are eligible. Honorary arms can be granted to American citizens of English or British descent in the male line. Corporate bodies such as companies, banks, and local government authorities are also granted arms. The Kings of Arms' jurisdiction extends throughout the British Commonwealth.

HOW A COAT OF ARMS EVOLVES

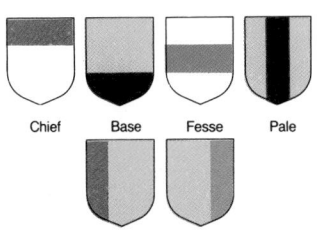

Chief | Base | Fesse | Pale

Dexter | Sinister

POSITIONS *In heraldic language, each area of the shield has its own name. The top is called the chief, the bottom is the base, the horizontal center is the fesse, the vertical center is the pale, the right side from the bearer's view is the dexter, and the left side is the sinister.*

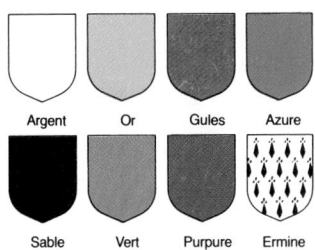

Argent | Or | Gules | Azure

Sable | Vert | Purpure | Ermine

TINCTURES *The colors, metals, and furs are called tinctures. The metals are argent (silver) and or (gold). Colors are gules (red), azure (blue), sable (black), vert (green), and purpure (purple). The furs are ermine and vair (squirrel).*

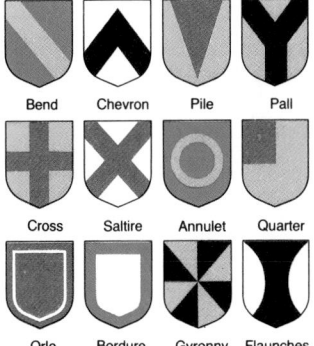

Bend | Chevron | Pile | Pall

Cross | Saltire | Annulet | Quarter

Orle | Bordure | Gyronny | Flaunches

FIRST GENERATION *A family's coat of arms can begin very simply, often with only one charge (the device on a shield) such as a chevron, cross, animal, or bird. The prominent geometric charges are called the ordinaries, and the less prominent geometric charges are called the subordi-*

naries. *If an ordinary is repeated on a shield, it must be a smaller form and is called a diminutive. Other charges are classified by the figures they depict, such as beasts, birds, or fish.*

Lion rampant | Lion passant reguardant | Leopard passant guardant | Boar passant

Talbot sejant | Stag's head cabossed | Unicorn statant | Eagle displayed

BEASTS AND BIRDS *In early heraldry few beasts were used other than the rampant or passant lion. Today various beasts and birds are used, and a variety of positions have been contrived for them.*

Bowes | Shakespeare | Cockburn | Trumpington

CANTING ARMS *Sometimes a family chooses a charge that is a pun on its surname. The Bowes Lyons, for instance, are represented by bows and lions, the Trumpingtons by trumpets. These are known as canting, or punning, arms.*

Per fesse | Per bend | Per bend sinister | Per pale

Per saltire | Per chevron | Barry | Quarterly

Paly | Barry nebuly | Bendy | Chevronny

PARTITION LINES *Some coats bear no charges and consist of a field divided by partition lines only. These lines run in the direction of almost any ordinary, which will often carry the word* per *before it.*

Label Eldest son | Crescent Second son | Mullet Third son | Martlet Fourth son

Annulet Fifth son | Fleur-de-lis Sixth son | Rose Seventh son | Cross moline Eighth son

INHERITING ARMS *Family arms are hereditary and pass from father to son. No two people can bear the same coat of arms, so the arms of sons must be differenced according to regulations laid down by the Kings of Arms. The eldest son has a label, the second a crescent, the third a mullet, the fourth a martlet, the fifth an annulet, and so on. The label is removed when the father dies and the eldest son inherits the coat. The differencing marks of younger sons are not removed. A younger son's eldest son differences the coat with a label until he inherits.*

Four quarterings | Six quarterings | Eight quarterings

QUARTERING *A shield is quartered, that is, divided into four, six, eight, or more portions, to accommodate coats of arms in-* herited from an heiress. *The quarterings read from dexter chief (top left when looking at the shield). The first quarter is the family coat, the next is the first acquired coat, the third quarter is the second acquired coat, and so on. If there is a blank at the end of the shield, then the family coat is repeated.*

THE ARMS OF A WOMAN

Lozenge | Impaling | Escutcheon of pretense

Daughters bear the same arms as their fathers, undifferenced, on a diamond-shaped figure known as a lozenge. But as a woman may not have a helmet, she cannot exhibit a crest. If a man has no sons, his daughters are his heraldic heiresses and may transmit their arms as a quartering to their descendants.

When a heraldic heiress marries, she places her arms on a small shield, known as an escutcheon of pretense, in the middle of her husband's shield. When a daughter who is not an heiress marries, she places her arms beside her husband's on a shield. This is known as impaling. If a woman is widowed, she bears her marital arms on a lozenge.

AN ACHIEVEMENT OF ARMS

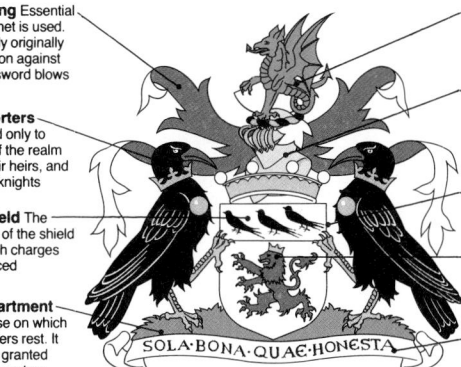

Mantling Essential if a helmet is used. Probably originally protection against sun or sword blows

Supporters Granted only to peers of the realm and their heirs, and certain knights

The Field The surface of the shield on which charges are placed

Compartment The base on which supporters rest. It may be granted with supporters

Crest A hereditary device fixed to the top of the helm, or helmet

Helmet A means of displaying the crest. Shape and position vary with rank

Shield The principal vehicle for displaying arms

Charge Any figure or emblem used in the shield or crest

Motto A guiding principle for those who bear the arms

SOLA·BONA·QUAE·HONESTA

Strictly, a coat of arms refers only to the shield and the devices (known as charges) borne on it, but in common usage the expression is used to refer to an achievement of arms, which is a representation of all the armorial devices to which the bearer is entitled.

herbs

PLANTS THAT CAN FLAVOR FOOD AND IMPROVE HEALTH
Nature's supply of seasonings and remedies

There are more than 50 herbs that are commonly used by cooks to add a special flavor to their dishes, and a well-stocked herb garden is indispensable to the master chef. Herbs are aromatic plants that can add flavor to bland food or disguise an unpleasant tang.

The use of herbs as medicine has an ancient history and is still common throughout the world—even in countries with sophisticated medical services. It is freely admitted that some herbs are medically useful; digitalis, for example, is obtained from foxgloves and

used in treating heart disease. Indeed many modern drugs are derived from herbs, and the value of herbalism is seldom dismissed outright; but there is not sufficient laboratory-tested proof of its claims for it to be accepted as a science.

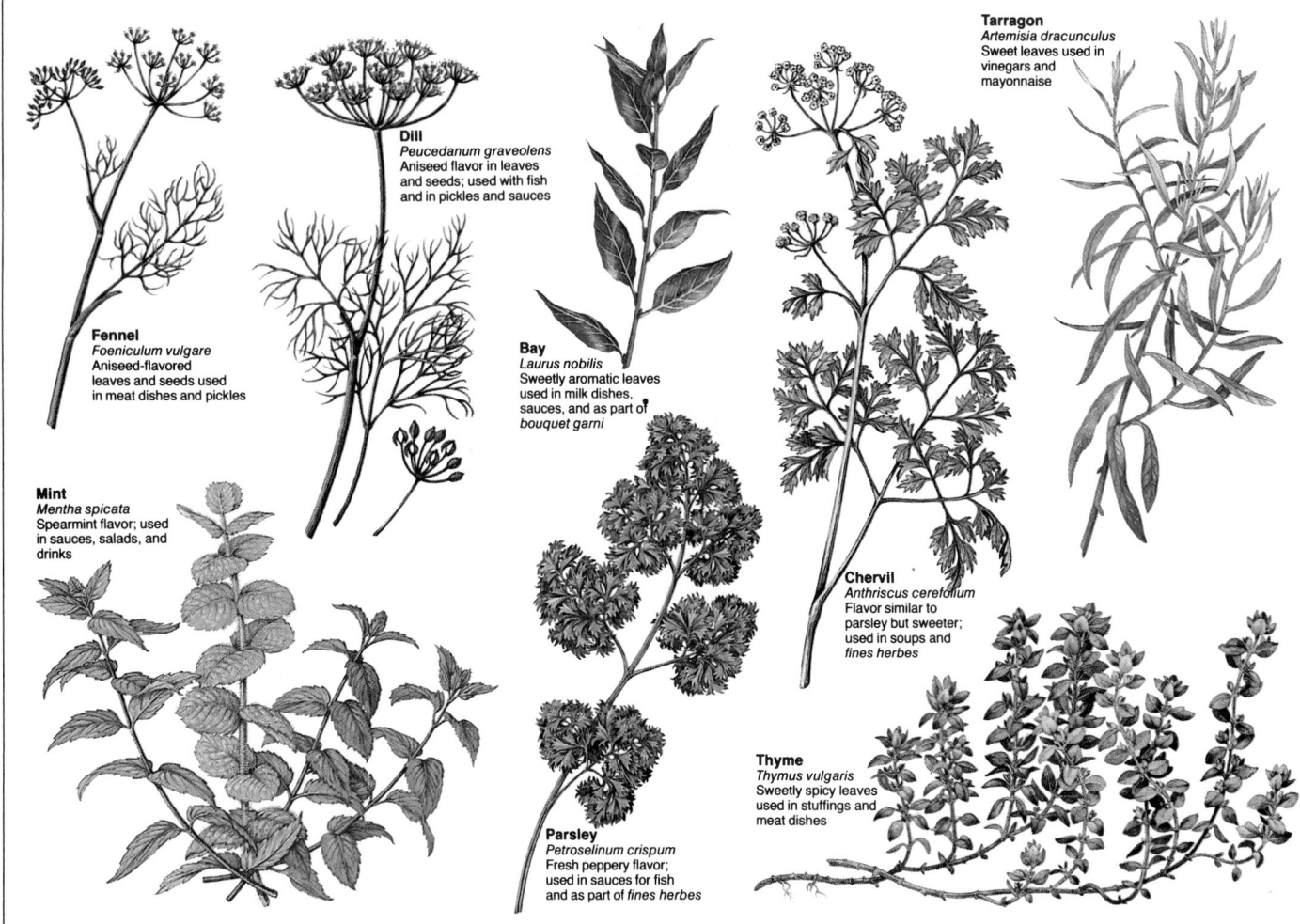

Tarragon
Artemisia dracunculus
Sweet leaves used in vinegars and mayonnaise

Dill
Peucedanum graveolens
Aniseed flavor in leaves and seeds; used with fish and in pickles and sauces

Fennel
Foeniculum vulgare
Aniseed-flavored leaves and seeds used in meat dishes and pickles

Bay
Laurus nobilis
Sweetly aromatic leaves used in milk dishes, sauces, and as part of *bouquet garni*

Mint
Mentha spicata
Spearmint flavor; used in sauces, salads, and drinks

Chervil
Anthriscus cerefolium
Flavor similar to parsley but sweeter; used in soups and *fines herbes*

Thyme
Thymus vulgaris
Sweetly spicy leaves used in stuffings and meat dishes

Parsley
Petroselinum crispum
Fresh peppery flavor; used in sauces for fish and as part of *fines herbes*

and metalworking; identified with the Roman god Vulcan.

Hep·ple·white (hĕp′əl-hwīt′) *adj.* Designating an English style of furniture of the late 18th century, noted for its light, graceful lines, its use of concave curves, and the shield or heart backs of its chairs. [After George HEPPLEWHITE.]

Hepplewhite, George (died 1786). English cabinetmaker. His elegant style, now much admired, was unfashionable in his day. His reputation rests on the designs in his *Cabinet-Maker and Upholsterer's Guide* (published in 1788).

hepta–, hept– *prefix.* Indicates seven; for example, **heptahedron, heptane.** [Greek *hepta,* seven.]

hep·tad (hĕp′tăd′) *n.* A group or series of seven. [Greek *heptas* (stem *heptad-*), the number seven, period of seven years, from *hepta,* seven.]

hep·ta·dec·a·no·ic acid (hĕp′tə-dĕk′ə-nō′ĭk) *n.* An organic acid, **margaric acid** *(see).*

hep·ta·gon (hĕp′tə-gŏn′) *n.* A polygon with seven sides and seven angles. [Greek *heptagonos,* having seven angles : HEPTA- + -GON.]

hep·tag·o·nal (hĕp·tăg′ə-nəl) *adj.* 1. Having seven sides and seven angles. 2. Of, pertaining to, or formed in heptagons. —**hep·tag·o·nal·ly** *adv.*

hep·ta·he·dral (hĕp′tə-hē′drəl) *adj.* 1. Having seven plane surfaces. 2. Of, pertaining to, or formed in heptahedrons. —**hep·ta·he·dral·ly** *adv.*

hep·ta·he·dron (hĕp′tə-hē′drən) *n.,* *pl.* **-drons** or **-dra** (-drə). A polyhedron with seven plane surfaces. [HEPTA- + -HEDRON.]

hep·ta·hy·drate (hĕp′tə-hī′drāt′) *n. Chemistry.* A hydrate in which the ratio of water molecules to anhydrous compound is 7:1.

hep·tam·er·ous (hĕp-tăm′ər-əs) *adj.* Having seven parts or arranged in groups of seven. Said especially of plant parts. [HEPTA- + -MEROUS.]

hep·tam·e·ter (hĕp-tăm′ə-tər) *n.* 1. A metrical unit consisting of seven feet. 2. A line of verse written in such meter. [HEPTA- + -METER.]

hep·tane (hĕp′tān′) *n.* A volatile, colorless, highly flammable liquid hydrocarbon, $CH_3(CH_2)_5CH_3$, obtained in the fractional distillation of petroleum, and used as a standard in determining octane ratings, as an anesthetic, and as a solvent. [HEPT(A)- (from the number of carbon atoms it possesses) + -ANE.]

hep·tan·gu·lar (hĕp-tăng′gyə-lər) *adj.* Having seven angles.

hep·tar·chy (hĕp′tär′kē) *n., pl.* **-chies. 1. a.** Government by seven persons. **b.** A state so governed. **2.** A state divided into seven units, each with its own ruler. **3.** *Often* **Heptarchy. a.** The informal confederation of the Anglo-Saxon kingdoms from the 5th to the 9th century, consisting of Kent, Sussex, Wessex, Essex, Northumbria, East Anglia, and Mercia. **b.** The historical period covering the existence of this confederation. [HEPT(A)- + -ARCHY.]

hep·ta·stich (hĕp′tə-stĭk′) *n.* A poem, stanza, or strophe consisting of seven lines. [HEPTA- + Greek *stikhos,* line of verse.]

Hep·ta·teuch (hĕp′tə-tōōk′, -tyōōk′) *n.* The first seven books of the Old Testament. [Greek *heptateukhos (biblos),* "(book) in seven volumes" : HEPTA- + *teukhos,* tool, case holding writing material, volume.]

hep·ta·va·lent (hĕp′tə-vā′lənt) *adj. Chemistry.* Having a valence of 7; septivalent.

hep·tode (hĕp′tōd′) *n.* A type of thermionic valve with seven electrodes: an anode, a cathode, and five grids. [HEPTA- + -ODE.]

Hep·worth (hĕp′wûrth′, -wərth), **Dame Barbara** (1903-75). English

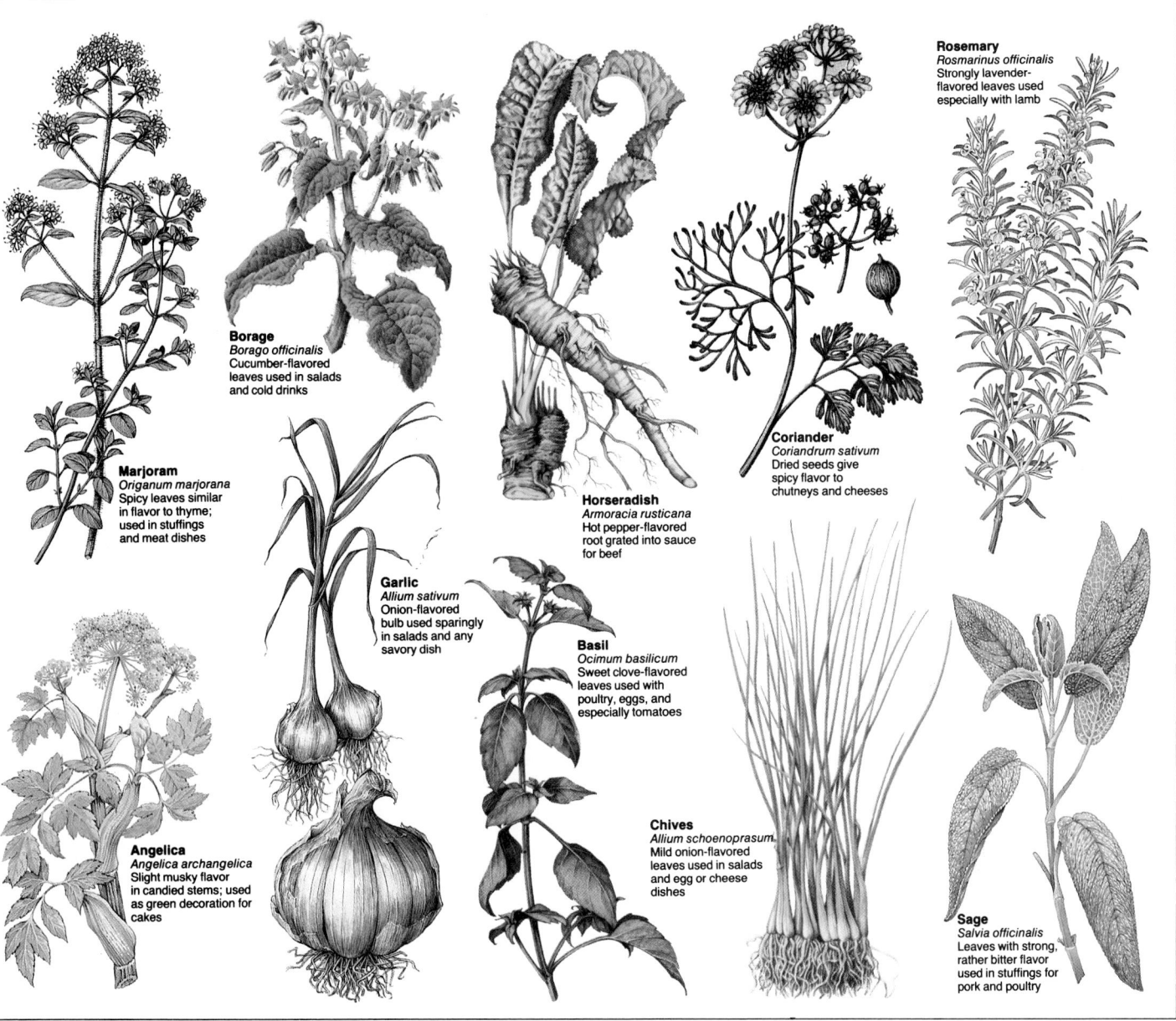

Marjoram
Origanum marjorana
Spicy leaves similar
in flavor to thyme;
used in stuffings
and meat dishes

Borage
Borago officinalis
Cucumber-flavored
leaves used in salads
and cold drinks

Horseradish
Armoracia rusticana
Hot pepper-flavored
root grated into sauce
for beef

Coriander
Coriandrum sativum
Dried seeds give
spicy flavor to
chutneys and cheeses

Rosemary
Rosmarinus officinalis
Strongly lavender-
flavored leaves used
especially with lamb

Garlic
Allium sativum
Onion-flavored
bulb used sparingly
in salads and any
savory dish

Basil
Ocimum basilicum
Sweet clove-flavored
leaves used with
poultry, eggs, and
especially tomatoes

Angelica
Angelica archangelica
Slight musky flavor
in candied stems; used
as green decoration for
cakes

Chives
Allium schoenoprasum
Mild onion-flavored
leaves used in salads
and egg or cheese
dishes

Sage
Salvia officinalis
Leaves with strong,
rather bitter flavor
used in stuffings for
pork and poultry

sculptor. Her works, like those of Henry Moore, explore the relationship between space and large rounded forms. She was made a dame in 1965.

her (hûr; *unstressed* hər, ər) *pron.* The objective case of the third person pronoun *she.* It is used: **1.** As the direct object of a verb: *They assisted her.* **2.** As the indirect object of a verb: *They offered her a lift.* **3.** As the object of a preposition: *This letter is addressed to her.* **4.** After *than* or *as* in comparisons in which the first term is in the objective case: *The judges praised him more than her.* **5.** *Informal.* In place of the reflexive pronoun *herself* as the indirect object of a verb: *She went to buy her a car.* **6.** In a certain informal style to refer to things not usually personified: *The engine's all right, so start her up.* **7.** In various elliptical, absolute, or interjectional phrases in which it is neither subject nor object: *Her and her fancy airs!*
~The possessive form of the pronoun *she.* Used attributively to indicate possession, agency, or reception of an action by the feminine person or entity spoken of: *her purse; pursuing her tasks; suffered her first rebuff.* —See Usage note at **me.** [Middle English *hire, her(e),* Old English *hire.*]

her. heraldry.

He·ra (hîr'ə). Also **He·re** (hîr'ē). *Greek Mythology.* The sister and consort of Zeus; identified with the Roman goddess Juno.

Heracles, Herakles. Variants of **Hercules.**

Her·a·cli·tus (hĕr'ə-klī'təs) (6th–5th century B.C.). Greek philosopher. He argued that strife and change are natural conditions of the universe. One of the most famous of his aphorisms is "All things are flowing."

Heraklion. See **Iráklion.**

her·ald (hĕr'əld) *n.* **1.** A person who proclaims important news; a messenger; an envoy. **2.** A person or thing that announces or gives indication of something to come; a harbinger; a precursor. **3.** *British.* An official responsible for regulating all matters and settling all questions relating to heraldry; an officer of arms. **4. a.** An official formerly charged with making royal proclamations and with bearing messages of state between sovereigns. **b.** An official who formerly made proclamations and conveyed challenges at a tournament.
~*tr.v.* **heralded, -alding, -alds. 1.** To proclaim; announce: "*the cocks that herald dawn all night*" (Malcolm Lowry). **2.** To usher in; inaugurate. [Middle English *herau(l)d,* from Old French *herau(l)t,* from Germanic.]

he·ral·dic (hə-răl'dĭk) *adj.* Of or pertaining to heralds or heraldry. —**he·ral·di·cal·ly** *adv.*

heraldic achievement *n. Heraldry.* A coat of arms, or representation of a coat of arms, complete with crest, motto, and supporters.

her·ald·ist (hĕr'əl-dĭst) *n.* One who practices or studies heraldry.

her·ald·ry (hĕr'əl-drē) *n., pl.* **-ries. 1.** *Abbr.* **her. a.** The profession of devising, granting, and blazoning arms, of tracing pedigrees, and of ruling on questions of precedence, as exercised by an officer of arms. **b.** A branch of knowledge dealing with the history and description in proper terms of armorial bearings and their accessories; armory. **2.** Armorial ensigns or similar insignia. **3.** Pomp and ceremony, especially as attended with armorial trappings; pageantry: *the heraldry of a royal progress.* See feature, page 785.

Heralds' College *n.* The **College of Arms** *(see).*

herb (ûrb, hûrb) *n.* **1.** An angiosperm plant that has a fleshy stem as distinguished from the woody tissue of shrubs and trees and that generally dies back at the end of each growing season; a herbaceous

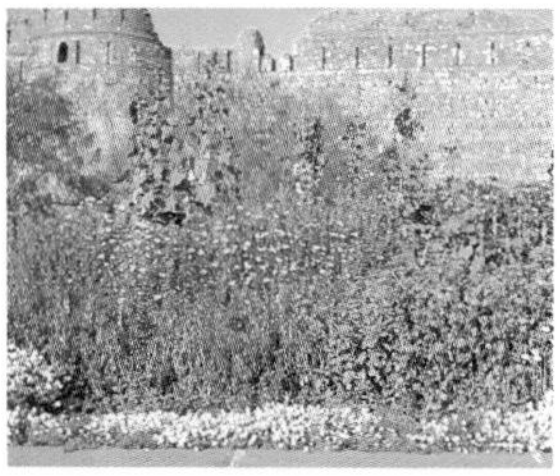

herbaceous border *A herbaceous border at Delhi Zoo in India. The English landscape gardener Gertrude Jekyll (1843–1932) was the great modern exponent of herbaceous gardens, in which perennial plants are arranged with taller species at the back, while colors and shapes are arranged to give changing patterns to the garden through the seasons.*

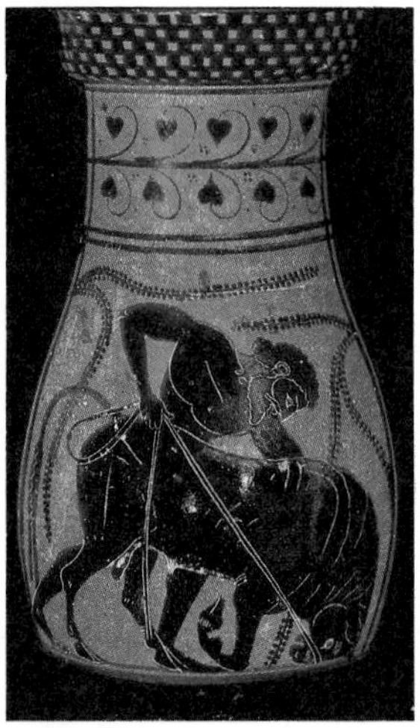

Hercules *One of the legendary 12 labors of Hercules, or Herakles, was capturing the mad bull of Crete. The episode is recalled on this Greek vase of about 500* B.C.

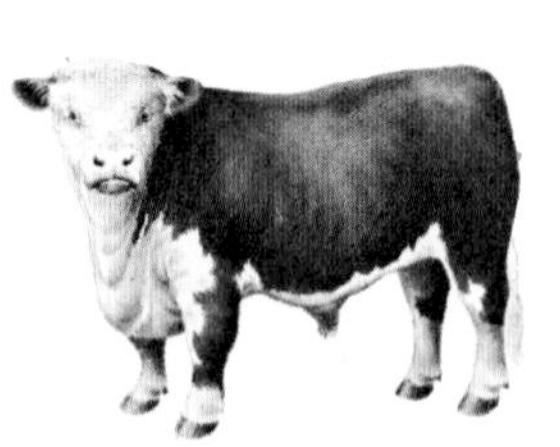

Hereford *Purebred Hereford cattle are always red and white. Cattle of other colors with white faces are crossbreeds. Herefords were originally developed in the Welsh border counties, including the former county of Herefordshire, but are now reared all over the world for beef.*

plant. **2.** Any of various often aromatic plants used especially in medicine or as seasoning. —See Note at **plant.** [Middle English *(h)erbe,* from Old French, from Latin *herba*†.]

her·ba·ceous (hûr-bā′shəs, ûr-) *adj.* **1.** Of, pertaining to, or characteristic of an herb as distinguished from a woody plant. **2.** Green and leaflike in appearance or texture. [Latin *herbāceus* : *herba,* HERB + -ACEOUS.]

herbaceous border *n.* A flower bed that contains herbaceous perennial plants rather than annuals or woody plants.

herb·age (ûr′bĭj, hûr′-) *n.* **1.** Herbaceous plant growth, especially grass or similar vegetation used for pasturage. **2.** The fleshy, often edible parts of plants. [Middle English *(h)erbage,* from Old French, from *(h)erbe,* HERB.]

herb·al (hûr′bəl, ûr′-) *adj.* Of, relating to, or containing herbs.
~*n.* A book about plants, especially those that are useful to man.

herb·al·ist (hûr′bə-lĭst, ûr′-) *n.* One who grows, collects, sells, or specializes in the use of herbs, especially medicinal herbs.

her·bar·i·um (hûr-bâr′ē-əm, ûr-) *n., pl.* **-iums** or **-ia** (-ē-ə). **1.** A collection of dried plants mounted and labeled for use in scientific study. **2.** A place or institution where such a collection is kept. [Late Latin *herbārium,* from Latin *herba,* HERB.]

herb bennet *n.* A hairy Eurasian plant, *Geum urbanum,* having small yellow flowers and an astringent root formerly used medicinally. Also called "bennet." [Middle English *herb beneit,* from Old French *herbe beneite* (or *benoite*), from Medieval Latin *herba benedicta,* "blessed herb" (from its medicinal properties) : Latin *herba,* HERB + *benedicta,* feminine past participle of *benedīcere,* to bless (see **benediction**).]

Her·bert (hûr′bərt), **George** (1593–1633). English poet, one of the metaphysical poets. None of his poems was published in his lifetime. They were collected in *The Temple* (1633).

herb Ge·rard (jə-rärd′) *n., pl.* **herbs Gerard.** A plant, **ground elder** *(see).* [After St. *Gerard,* whose name was invoked by those suffering from gout, for which the plant was formerly prescribed.]

her·bi·cide (hûr′bĭ-sīd′, ûr′-) *n.* A substance used to destroy plants, especially weeds. [HERB + -CIDE.] —**her·bi·cid·al** (hûr′bĭ-sīd′l, ûr′-) *adj.*

her·bi·vore (hûr′bə-vôr′, -vōr′, ûr′-) *n.* A herbivorous animal. [New Latin *Herbivora* (former designation of herbivores), from the neuter plural of *herbivorus,* HERBIVOROUS.]

her·biv·o·rous (hûr-bĭv′ər-əs, ûr-) *adj.* Feeding on plants; plant-eating. [New Latin *herbivorus* : HERB + -VOROUS.]

Herblock. See Herbert **Block.**

herb-of-grace (ûrb′əv-grās′, hûrb′-) *n., pl.* **herbs-of-grace.** *Archaic.* A plant, **rue** *(see).* [Probably from the association of rue (the plant) with rue (repentance).]

herb Paris *n., pl.* **herbs Paris.** A European plant, *Paris quadrifolia,* having a whorl of four leaves and a solitary yellow or greenish flower. [Probably Medieval Latin *herba paris,* "herb of a pair" (perhaps a reference to the two pairs of leaves on the whorl), assimilated to *Paris* : Latin *herba,* HERB + *paris,* genitive of *par,* equal.]

herb Robert *n., pl.* **herbs Robert.** A low-growing plant, *Geranium robertianum,* having divided leaves and small reddish-purple flowers. [Middle English *herbe Robert,* from Medieval Latin *herba Robertī,* "herb of Robert," variously supposed to be named after *Robert,* Duke of Normandy, Saint *Robert* (died 1067), French churchman, or Saint *Rupert,* 7th-century Bavarian ecclesiastic.]

Hercegovina. See **Bosnia and Hercegovina.**

Her·cu·la·ne·um (hûr′kyə-lā′nē-əm). Ancient town of southern Italy. Situated 8 kilometers (5 miles) southeast of Naples, on the slopes of Vesuvius, it was completely buried in the volcano's eruption (A.D. 79) and remained undiscovered until 1709.

her·cu·le·an (hûr′kyə-lē′ən, hər-kyo͞o′lē-ən) *adj.* **1.** Tremendously difficult or demanding: *a herculean task.* **2.** *Often* **Herculean.** Resembling Hercules in size, power, or courage: *Herculean strength.* **3. Herculean.** Of or relating to Hercules.

Her·cu·les[1] (hûr′kyə-lēz′). Also **Her·a·cles, Her·a·kles** (hĕr′ə-klēz′). *Greek & Roman Mythology.* The son of Zeus and Alcmene, a hero of extraordinary strength who won immortality by performing the 12 labors demanded by Hera.

Hercules[2] *n.* **1.** *Sometimes* **hercules.** A man of enormous strength. **2.** *Astronomy.* A constellation in the Northern Hemisphere near Lyra and Corona Borealis that contains the star Ras Algethi and the globular cluster M13. [After HERCULES.]

Her·cu·les′-club (hûr′kyə-lēz-klŭb′) *n.* A tree or shrub, *Aralia spinosa,* of the southeastern United States, having prickly compound leaves and large clusters of small white flowers. Also called "devil's walking stick."

Her·cyn·i·an (hûr-sĭn′ē-ən) *adj. Geology.* Designating or belonging to a phase in the late Paleozoic era (Carboniferous and Permian periods) characterized by mountain building. Also called "Variscan," "Armorican."

herd (hûrd) *n.* **1. a.** A group of cattle or other domestic animals of a single kind kept together. **b.** A number of wild animals of one species that remain together as a group: *a herd of elephants.* **2.** A number of people grouped together by some common factor: *a herd of stranded passengers.* **3.** *Archaic.* One who tends a herd; a herdsman. Now used chiefly in combination: *a goatherd.* —**the herd.** The multitude of common people regarded as undistinguished and easily led or influenced.
~*v.* **herded, herding, herds.** —*intr.* **1.** To congregate in a herd or group. **2.** To keep company; associate. —*tr.* **1. a.** To gather, tend, or drive (animals) in a herd. **b.** To gather or drive (people) as if in a herd. **2.** To place in a group. [Middle English *herd(e),* Old English *heord.*] —**herd·er** *n.*

her·dic (hûr′dĭk) *n.* A small horse-drawn cab having two wheels, side seats, and an entrance at the back. [After Peter *Herdic* (1824–1888), American carriage maker.]

herd instinct *n.* An instinct that impels people to come together in groups and to conform to the prevailing modes of thought and behavior of such groups.

herds·man (hûrdz′mən) *n., pl.* **-men** (-mĭn). A person who owns, breeds, or tends livestock.

here (hîr) *adv.* **1.** At or in this place: *Stop here.* **2.** At this time; now: *Let's adjourn the meeting here and resume after lunch.* **3.** At or on this point, detail, or item: *There is great disagreement here.* **4.** In the present life or condition. **5.** To this place; hither: *Come here.* **6.** Used for emphasis after an imperative: *Look here! Now you see here.* —**here and there.** In various places. —**neither here nor there.** Of no relevance or significance.
~*adj.* **1.** Existing in this place. Used for emphasis after a noun modified by a demonstrative pronoun: *Look at this word here. I'll have this one here.* **2.** *Nonstandard.* Used for emphasis between a demonstrative pronoun and a noun: *this here word.*
~*n.* This place: *He lives a mile from here. I left it near here.*
~*interj.* Used as a response to a roll call, as a command to an animal, as a way of calling attention, or as a rebuke or admonishment. —**here's to.** Used to propose a toast to a specified person or thing. [Middle English *her(e),* Old English *hēr.*]

Here. Variant of **Hera.**

here·a·bout (hîr′ə-bout′) *adv.* Also **here·a·bouts** (-ə-bouts′). In this general vicinity; around here.

here·af·ter (hîr-ăf′tər, -äf′tər) *adv.* **1.** Immediately following this in time, order, or place; after this. **2.** In a world to come; in the afterlife: *win salvation hereafter.*
~*n.* **1.** The future. **2.** The world to come; life after death: *belief in a hereafter.*

here·at (hîr-ăt′) *adv.* Because of this; at this.

here·by (hîr-bī′) *adv.* By virtue of this act, decree, bulletin, or document; by this means.

he·re·des. Plural of **heres.**

he·red·i·ta·ble (hə-rĕd′ə-tə-bəl) *adj.* Heritable.

her·e·dit·a·ment (hĕr′ə-dĭt′ə-mənt) *n. Law.* Any kind of property that can be inherited. [Medieval Latin *hērēditāmentum,* from Late Latin *hērēditāre,* to inherit, from Latin *hērēs* (stem *hērēd-*), heir.]

he·red·i·tar·i·an·ism (hə-rĕd′ə-târ′ē-ə-nĭz′əm) *n. Psychology.* The doctrine or school that regards heredity as the major factor in determining intelligence and behavior. Compare **environmentalism.** —**he·red·i·tar·i·an** *n. & adj.*

he·red·i·tar·y (hə-rĕd′ə-tĕr′ē) *adj.* **1.** *Law.* **a.** Descending from an ancestor to a legal heir; passing down by inheritance. **b.** Having title or possession through inheritance. **2.** Genetically transmitted or transmissible. **3. a.** Appearing in or characteristic of successive generations. **b.** Derived from or fostered by one's ancestors: *a hereditary prejudice.* **4.** Ancestral; traditional: *their hereditary home.* **5.** Of or pertaining to heredity or inheritance. —See Synonyms at **innate.** [Latin *hērēditārius,* from *hērēditās,* HEREDITY.] —**he·red·i·tar·i·ly** (hə-rĕd′ə-târ′ə-lē) *adv.* —**he·red·i·tar·i·ness** *n.*

he·red·i·tist (hə-rĕd′ə-tĭst) *n.* One who supports the theory that heredity rather than environment determines behavior.

he·red·i·ty (hə-rĕd′ə-tē) *n., pl.* **-ties.** **1.** The genetic transmission of characteristics from parents to offspring. **2.** The totality of characteristics and associated potentialities so transmitted to an individual organism. In this sense, compare **environment.** [Old French *heredite,* from Latin *hērēditās* (stem *hērēditāt-*), inheritance, from *hērēs* (stem *hērēd-*), heir.]

Her·e·ford (hĕr′ə-fərd, hûr′fərd) *n.* Any of a breed of beef cattle developed in Herefordshire, England, having a reddish coat with white markings.

Hereford and Worces·ter (wo͝os′tər). A county in west-central England, bordering Wales. It is traversed by the Wye, Avon, and Severn rivers, with the Malvern Hills in the center, and is mainly agricultural. The city of Worcester serves as the county town.

Her·e·ford·shire (hĕr′ə-fərd-shîr′, -shər). A former county of west-central England, now incorporated into Hereford and Worcester.

here·in (hîr-ĭn′) *adv.* In or into this; especially, in this book, document, or the like.

here·in·af·ter (hîr′ĭn-ăf′tər, -äf′tər) *adv.* In a following part of this document, statement, or book; after this.

here·in·be·fore (hîr′ĭn-bĭ-fôr′, -fōr′) *adv.* In a preceding part of this document, statement, or book; before this.

here·in·to (hîr-ĭn′to͞o) *adv.* Into this matter, circumstance, situation, or place; into this.

here·of (hîr-ŭv′, -ŏv′) *adv.* Pertaining to or concerning this.

here·on (hîr-ŏn′, -ôn′) *adv.* Hereupon.

He·re·ro (hə-râr′ō, hĕr′ə-rō′) *n., pl.* **Hereros** or collectively **Herero.** **1.** A member of a Negroid people living mainly in central Namibia. **2.** The Bantu language of this people.

he·res (hā′rās′) *n., pl.* **heredes** (hā-rā′dās′). *Law.* An heir. [Latin *hērēs.*]

here's (hîrz). Contraction of *here is.*

he·re·si·arch (hə-rē′zē-ärk′, hĕr′ə-sē-) *n.* The founder or chief proponent of a heresy or heretical movement. [Late Latin *haeresiarcha,* from Late Greek *hairesiarkhēs* : Greek *hairesis,* sect (see **heresy**) + -ARCH.]

her·e·sy (hĕr′ə-sē) *n., pl.* **-sies.** **1. a.** A belief or doctrine at variance with the orthodox doctrine of a religious system; especially, a belief or doctrine involving dissension from or denial of Christian dogma by a professed believer: *the Pelagian heresy.* **b.** Adherence to such dissenting belief or doctrine. **2. a.** A controversial or unorthodox opinion or doctrine in politics, philosophy, science, or other fields. **b.** Adherence to such unorthodox opinion. [Middle English *(h)eresie,* from Old French, from Late Latin *haeresis,* from Late Greek *hairesis,* from Greek, "a taking," school of thought, faction, from *hairein†,* to take, grasp, choose.]

her·e·tic (hĕr′ə-tĭk) *n.* A person who holds controversial or unorthodox opinions in any area; especially, one who publicly dissents from the officially accepted dogma of a religion. [Middle English *(h)eretik,* from Old French *(h)eretique,* from Late Latin *haereticus,* from Greek *hairetikos,* able to choose, factious, from *hairetos,* from *hairein,* to take, choose. See **heresy.**] **—he·ret·i·cal** (hə-rĕt′ĭ-kəl) *adj.* **—he·ret·i·cal·ly** *adv.*

here·to (hîr-tōo′) *adv.* To this place, document, matter, or proposition; to this: *Attached hereto is my voucher.*

here·to·fore (hîr′tə-fôr′, -fōr′) *adv.* Up to the present time; before this: *The discovery disproved all that we had heretofore believed.* [Middle English : HERE + *tofore, toforn,* before, Old English *tōforan* : TO + *foran,* before, from *fore,* FORE (in front).]

here·un·der (hîr-ŭn′dər) *adv.* **1.** In a following part of this document, statement, or book; after this. **2.** By the authority or under the powers of this decree, document, or the like.

here·un·to (hîr-ŭn′tōo) *adv.* Hereto.

here·up·on (hûr′ə-pŏn′, -pôn′) *adv.* Following instantly upon this; immediately after this; at this.

Her·e·ward the Wake (hĕr′ə-wərd thə wāk′) (*fl.* 1070). Anglo-Saxon folk hero. He led an English uprising against William the Conqueror in 1070, establishing himself and his followers on the Isle of Ely. William took control of the island in 1071, but Hereward escaped and is believed to have been pardoned later by William.

here·with (hîr-wĭth′, -wĭth′) *adv.* **1.** Along with this. **2.** By this means; hereby.

her·i·ot (hĕr′ē-ət) *n. Feudal law.* A death duty and later a tax on the expiry or abandoning of a holding paid by a tenant to his lord. It consisted commonly of the tenant's best beast and later of a money payment. [Middle English *heriet, heriot,* Old English *heregeatwe,* military equipment, "army-trappings" : *here,* army + *geatwa,* equipment, trappings.]

her·i·ta·ble (hĕr′ə-tə-bəl) *adj.* **1.** Capable of being inherited; passing by inheritance. **2.** Transmitted from one generation to another; hereditary. **3.** Capable of inheriting or of taking by inheritance. [Middle English *heretable,* from Old French *heritable,* from *heriter,* to inherit. See **heritage.**]

her·i·tage (hĕr′ə-tĭj) *n.* **1.** Property that is or can be inherited; an inheritance. **2.** Something other than property passed down from preceding generations; a legacy; a tradition. **3.** A condition or lot accruing to one through the circumstances of one's birth; a birthright: *a heritage of affluence and position.* [Middle English *(h)eritage,* from Old French, from *heriter,* to inherit, from Late Latin *hērēditāre,* from Latin *hērēs* (stem *hērēd-*), heir.]

her·i·tor (hĕr′ə-tər) *n.* An inheritor. [Middle English *heriter,* from Norman French, variant of Old French *heritier,* from Latin *hērēditārius,* HEREDITARY.]

her·i·tress (hĕr′ə-trĭs) *n.* Also **her·i·trix** (-trĭks). A female inheritor.

herl (hûrl) *n.* **1.** The barb of a feather used in trimming an artificial fly for angling. **2.** A fishing fly made with this. [Middle English *herle,* probably from Middle Low German *herle, harle†.*]

her·ma (hûr′mə) *n., pl.* **-mae** (-mē′, -mī′). Also **herm** (hûrm). In ancient Greece, a statue consisting of the head of the god Hermes mounted on a square stone post. [Latin, from Greek *hermēs,* from *Hermēs,* HERMES.]

her·maph·ro·dite (hər-măf′rə-dīt′) *n.* **1.** One having the sex organs and many of the secondary sex characteristics of both male and female. **2.** *Biology.* An organism, such as an earthworm, or a structure, such as a monoclinous flower, having both male and female reproductive organs. **3.** Anything consisting of a combination of diverse or contradictory elements. [Middle English *hermofrodite,* from Latin *hermaphrodītus,* from Greek *hermaphroditos,* after *Hermaphroditos,* Hermaphroditus, son of Hermes and Aphrodite who became united in one body with the nymph Salmacis.] **—her·maph·ro·dit·ic** (hər-măf′rə-dĭt′ĭk) *adj.* **—her·maph·ro·dit·i·cal·ly** *adv.*

hermaphrodite brig *n.* A two-masted vessel having a square-rigged foremast and a schooner-rigged mainmast. [It combines the characteristics of a brig and a schooner.]

hermaphrodite rig *n.* A jackass rig (*see*).

her·maph·ro·dit·ism (hər-măf′rə-dī′tĭz′əm) *n.* Also **her·maph·ro·dism** (-rə-dĭz′əm). The condition of being a hermaphrodite.

her·me·neu·tics (hûr′mə-nōo′tĭks, -nyōo′tĭks) *n. Used with a singular verb.* The science and methodology of interpretation, especially of Scriptural text. Compare **exegetics.** [New Latin *hermeneutica,* from Greek *hermēneutikē (tekhnē),* (art) of interpretation, from the feminine of *hermēneutikos,* interpreter, from *hermēneuein,* to interpret, from *hermēneus†,* interpreter.] **—her·me·neu·tic, her·me·neu·ti·cal** *adj.* **—her·me·neu·ti·cal·ly** *adv.*

Her·mes (hûr′mēz′). *Greek Mythology.* The god of commerce, invention, cunning, and theft, who also served as messenger and herald for the other gods, as the patron of travelers and rogues, and as the conductor of the dead to Hades; identified with the Roman god Mercury.

---

heredity

CHEMICAL CHAINS THAT GOVERN HEREDITY

Mingling characteristics down through the generations

Every living thing that results from sexual reproduction resembles its parents to some extent but is never an exact replica of either of them. A kitten looks like a cat and a nestling is recognizable as a bird because of genetic information contained in their chromosomes.

Chromosomes are microscopic structures in living cells. Each chromosome contains two chains of DNA (deoxyribonucleic acid) twisted around each other in a shape known as a "double helix." The varying chemical patterns along these chains are called genes, and it is through them that characteristics are passed on from one generation to another.

Chromosomes always occur in pairs (46 pairs in humans), but since one chromosome is inherited from the male parent and one from the female, the two members of a pair do not necessarily carry the same forms of genes. When preparing to produce a new generation, the chromosomes in the reproductive cells untwist and separate, only one from each pair going into each egg or sperm. So each new organism inherits an equal number of chromosomes from each parent, and they join to provide the full complement of new pairs.

If identical genes for one characteristic are inherited from each parent, then the offspring will have that characteristic. If the genes are not identical, the characteristic will be a blend of each or a "recessive" gene will give way to a "dominant" one. If one human parent's chromosome carries a gene for blue eyes and the other contributes a chromosome with the gene for brown eyes, the child will have brown eyes because brown is dominant. The recessive characteristic is suppressed but not lost, for it may reappear in subsequent generations. For example, a blue-eyed child may be born to two brown-eyed parents, each of whom has contributed a recessive gene for blue eyes.

Genes also "mutate" or alter—as a result of either external factors or internal chemical changes. Mutation is thought to be part of the mechanism of evolution by which species change and develop over thousands of years during which each generation may alter only slightly from its predecessor.

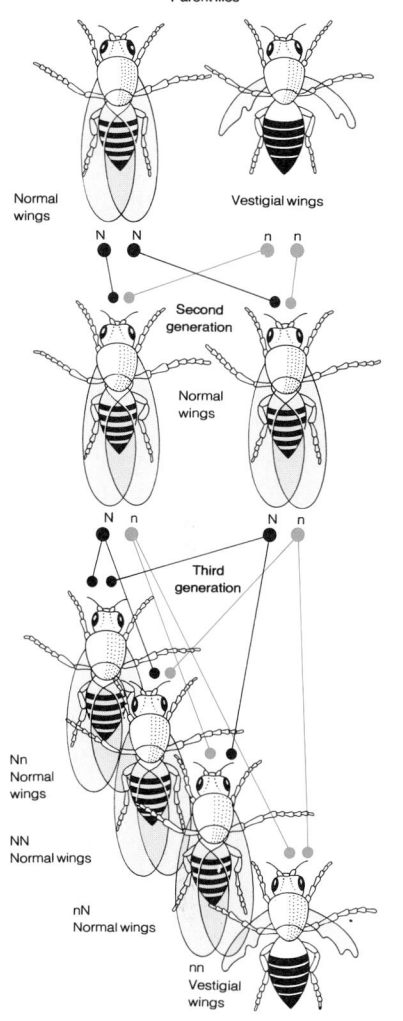

Parent flies

Normal wings

Vestigial wings

Second generation

Normal wings

Third generation

Nn Normal wings

NN Normal wings

nN Normal wings

nn Vestigial wings

POSSIBLE COMBINATIONS OF GENES *A dominant gene causes fruit flies to inherit normal wings, but a recessive gene giving vestigial wings may be inher-* *ited. Recessive genes from two flies with normal wings sometimes combine and produce offspring with vestigial wings.*

Hermes Tris·me·gis·tus (trĭs′mə-jĭs′təs). The Greek name for the Egyptian god Thoth, the supposed author of works on alchemy, astrology, and magic. [Latin, from Greek *Hermēs trismegistos,* "Hermes the thrice greatest."]

her·met·ic (hər-mĕt′ĭk) *adj.* Also **her·met·i·cal** (-ĭ-kəl). **1. a.** Completely sealed; especially, sealed against the escape or entry of air. **b.** Impervious to outside interference or influence; insulated; cloistered: *retreated to the hermetic confines of his room.* **2.** Hermetic. Of or relating to Hermes Trismegistus or to the works ascribed to him. **3.** Of or pertaining to the occult sciences, especially alchemy; magical; recondite. [New Latin *hermeticus,* from Latin *Hermes* (stem *Hermet-) Trismegistus,* HERMES TRISMEGISTUS. He is said to have invented a magic seal to make vessels airtight.] **—her·met·i·cal·ly** *adv.*

her·mit (hûr′mĭt) *n.* A person who has withdrawn from society and lives a solitary existence, especially for religious reasons; a recluse. [Middle English *(h)ermite,* from Old French, from Late Latin *erēmīta,* from Greek *erēmītēs,* "(one) of the desert," from *erēmia,* desert, solitude, from *erēmos,* deserted, solitary.] **—her·mit·ic** (hər-mĭt′ĭk), **her·mit·i·cal** (hər-mĭt′ĭ-kəl) *adj.* **—her·mit·i·cal·ly** *adv.*

her·mit·age (hûr′mə-tĭj) *n.* **1.** The habitation of a hermit or group of hermits. **2.** A place where one can live in seclusion; a retreat; a hideaway.

hermit crab *n.* Any of various crustaceans of the section Anomura within the order Decapoda, having a soft, unarmored abdomen, and occupying and carrying about the empty shell of a snail or other univalve mollusk.

hermit thrush *n.* A North American bird, *Hylocichla guttata,* having

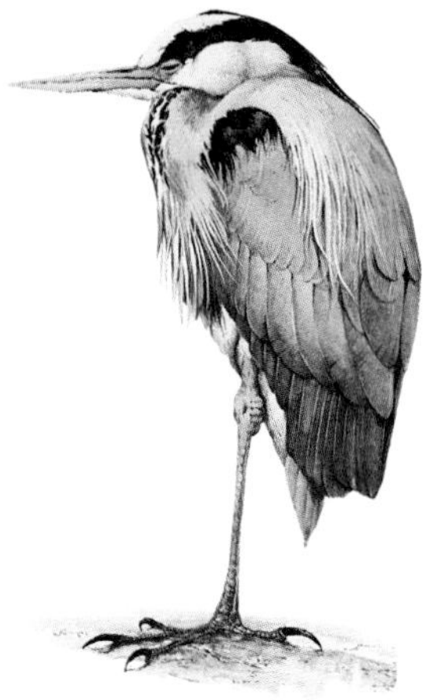

heron *These wading birds are native to Europe, Asia, and parts of Africa. They feed largely on fish, frogs, and rodents, waiting hunched on one leg for prey, then wading forward and stabbing downward with their long bills. This is* Ardea cinerea, *a species that is found in much of Europe, Asia, and the United States.*

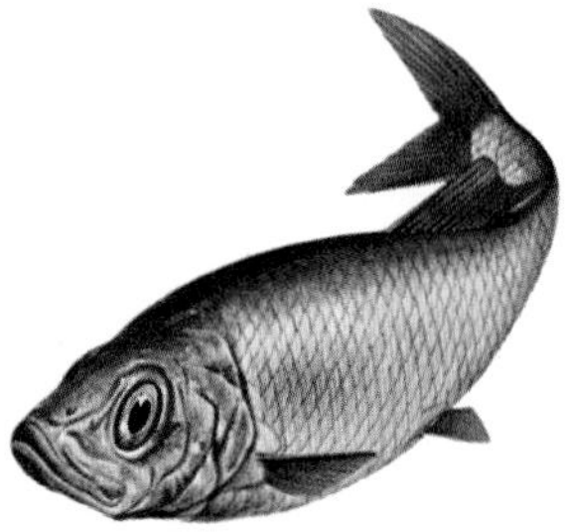

herring *The prime catch for fishing fleets in the Atlantic and Pacific oceans, herring live in large shoals that may contain up to 150 million fish. Overfishing has depleted stocks of herring in some areas.*

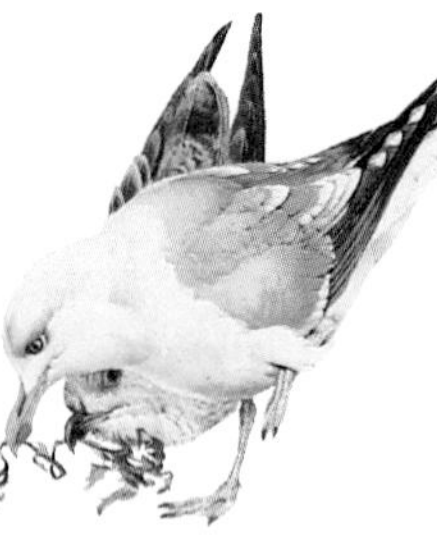

herring gull *This gull is found on coasts and inland waters in northern Europe and North America. It scavenges for food on garbage heaps and around fishing ports and harbors; it will also occasionally catch crabs and other shellfish, cracking them open by dropping them from the air.*

brownish plumage, a spotted breast, and a distinctive, melodious song.

hern (hûrn) *n. Archaic & Regional.* A heron. [Variant of HERON.]

her•ni•a (hûr′nē-ə) *n., pl.* **-as** or **-niae** (-nē-ē′). The protrusion of an organ, organic part, or any bodily structure through the wall that normally contains it. Hernia usually requires surgical treatment. Also called "rupture." [Middle English *hernia, hirnia,* from Latin *hernia.*] **—her•ni•al** *adj.*

her•ni•ate (hûr′nē-āt′) *intr.v.* **-ated, -ating, -ates.** To protrude through an abnormal bodily opening. [HERNI(A) + -ATE.] **—her•ni•a•tion** *n.*

he•ro (hîr′ō) *n., pl.* **-roes. 1.** In mythology and legend, a man, often born of one mortal and one divine parent, who is endowed with great courage and strength, celebrated for his bold exploits, and favored by the gods. **2.** Any man noted for feats of courage or nobility of purpose; especially, one who has risked or sacrificed his life: *heroes of forgotten wars.* **3.** A person who is greatly admired because of his special achievements or contributions in some event, field, or period: *The schoolboys discussed their football heroes.* **4.** The principal male character in a novel, poem, play, or the like. **5.** A very large sandwich made with a small loaf of crusty bread split lengthwise, containing lettuce, condiments, and a variety of meats and cheeses. In this sense, also called "grinder," "hero sandwich," "hoagie," "sub," "submarine." [Back-formation from Middle English *heroes* (plural), from Latin *hērōs* (plural *hērōēs*), a hero, from Greek *hērōs* (plural *hērōes*).]

Hero. *Greek Mythology.* A priestess of Aphrodite loved by Leander, who nightly swam the Hellespont to visit her; upon finding him drowned, Hero drowned herself.

Her•od (hĕr′əd), known as "Herod the Great" (*c.* 73–4 B.C.). King of Judea (37–4), son of Antipater II. He was named king of Judea by the Roman senate. He is said by St. Matthew to have ordered the killing of all children under the age of two in Bethlehem in order to destroy the infant Jesus.

Herod An•ti•pas (ăn′tĭ-păs′, -pəs) (died *c.* A.D. 40). Tetrarch of Galilee (4 B.C.–A.D. 39). Herod's marriage to his niece Herodias brought the disapproval of John the Baptist. The aggrieved Herodias persuaded her daughter, Salome, to ask for the Baptist's head as payment for dancing at Antipas' birthday celebration. Antipas complied, and the Baptist was executed.

He•rod•o•tus (hĭ-rŏd′ə-təs) (*c.* 484–425 B.C.). Greek historian, commonly known as the Father of History. His writing, chiefly concerning the Persian Wars, is the earliest known attempt at secular narrative history.

he•ro•ic (hĭ-rō′ĭk) *adj.* Also **he•ro•i•cal** (-ĭ-kəl). **1.** Of, relating to, or resembling the heroes of legend, especially of Greek and Roman legend. **2.** Having or displaying the qualities of a hero; courageous; noble: *heroic deeds.* **3.** Bold and daring, especially in the face of insurmountable odds; gallant: *a heroic attempt to halt the enemy's advance.* **4. a.** Impressive in size or scope; grand; grandiose: *a heroic undertaking.* **b.** *Fine arts.* Of a size somewhat larger than life: *heroic sculpture.* **5.** High-flown; ostentatious: *heroic language.* **6.** Of, pertaining to, or resembling heroic verse.
~*n.* **1.** A heroic verse or poem. **2. heroics.** Melodramatic behavior or language. **—he•ro•i•cal•ly** *adv.* **—he•ro•i•cal•ness** *n.*

heroic age *n.* The period in a nation's history, especially that of ancient Greece and Rome, when its legendary heroes are supposed to have lived.

heroic couplet *n.* A verse unit consisting of two rhymed lines in iambic pentameter.

heroic play *n.* A type of Restoration tragedy written in rhymed couplets and generally characterized by extravagant declamatory rhetoric.

heroic stanza *n.* An iambic pentameter quatrain rhymed *abab.* Also called "heroic quatrain."

heroic tenor *n.* A **Heldentenor** *(see).*

heroic verse *n.* Any of several verse forms suitable for and traditionally used in epic and dramatic poetry; especially, the dactylic hexameter in Greek and Latin and the iambic pentameter in English. Also called "heroic meter."

her•o•in (hĕr′ō-ĭn) *n.* A white, odorless, bitter crystalline compound, $C_{17}H_{17}NO(C_2H_3O_2)_2$, that is derived from morphine and is a highly addictive narcotic. Also called "diacetylmorphine." [From a trademark.]

her•o•ine (hĕr′ō-ĭn) *n.* **1.** A woman having or regarded as having heroic characteristics. **2.** The principal female character in a novel, poem, play, or the like. [Latin *hērōīna,* from Greek *hērōinē,* feminine of *hērōs,* HERO.]

her•o•ism (hĕr′ō-ĭz′əm) *n.* **1.** The condition or quality of being a hero. **2.** Heroic characteristics or conduct; courage; gallantry. —See Synonyms at **courage.**

he•ron (hĕr′ən) *n.* Any of various wading birds of the family Ardeidae, having a long neck, long legs, a long, pointed bill, and usually white or gray plumage. [Middle English *he(i)roun, hern(e),* from Old French *hairon,* from Frankish *haigro* (unattested).]

her•on•ry (hĕr′ən-rē) *n., pl.* **-ries. 1.** A place where herons nest and breed. **2.** A colony of herons or their nests.

hero worship *n.* **1.** Profound or excessive admiration for popular heroes or for other persons revered as ideals. **2.** Worship of the heroes of one's culture. **— he•ro-wor•ship** (hîr′ō-wûr′shĭp) *v.* **—he•ro-wor•ship•er** *n.*

herp. herpetology.

her•pes (hûr′pēz′) *n.* Any of several viral diseases causing eruptions of the skin or mucous membrane; especially, herpes simplex or herpes zoster. [Latin *herpēs,* from Greek, shingles, "a creeping," from *herpein,* to creep.] **—her•pet•ic** (hûr-pĕt′ĭk) *adj.*

herpes sim•plex (sĭm′plĕks′) *n.* A viral infection causing inflammation at junctions of the skin and mucous membrane, especially on the face. Also called "cold sore." See **genital herpes.** [New Latin, "simple herpes."]

her•pes•vi•rus (hûr′pēz-vī′rəs) *n.* Any of various DNA-containing animal viruses that produce herpes.

herpes zos•ter (zŏs′tər, zō′stər) *n.* A viral infection, **shingles** *(see).* [New Latin, "girdle herpes."]

herpetol. herpetology.

her•pe•tol•o•gist (hûr′pə-tŏl′ə-jĭst) *n.* A zoologist specializing in the study of reptiles and amphibians.

her•pe•tol•o•gy (hûr′pə-tŏl′ə-jē) *n. Abbr.* **herp., herpetol.** The scientific study of reptiles and amphibians as a branch of zoology. [Greek *herpeton,* "creeping thing," reptile, from *herpetos,* creeping, from *herpein,* to creep + -LOGY.] **—her•pe•to•log•ic** (hûr′pə-tə-lŏj′ĭk), **her•pe•to•log•i•cal** *adj.* **—her•pe•to•log•i•cal•ly** *adv.*

Herr (hĕr) *n., pl.* **Herren** (hĕr′ən). *Abbr.* **Hr.** A title of courtesy prefixed to the name or professional title of a German man, equivalent to the English *Mister.* [German, "Lord."]

Her•ren•volk (hĕr′ən-fōk′, -fôlk′) *n.* The **master race** *(see).* [German, "master race."]

Her•rick (hĕr′ĭk), **Robert** (1591–1674). English poet. Most of his work appeared in the collection *Hesperides* (1648).

her•ring (hĕr′ĭng) *n., pl.* **-rings** or collectively **herring.** Any of various fishes of the family Clupeidae; especially, a commercially important food fish, *Clupea harengus,* of Atlantic and Pacific waters. [Middle English *hering, heirreng,* Old English *hæring,* from West Germanic *hēringaz* (unattested).]

her•ring•bone (hĕr′ĭng-bōn′) *n.* **1.** A pattern consisting of rows of short, slanted parallel lines, with the direction of the slant alternating row by row, used in masonry, parquetry, and weaving. Also used adjectivally: *a herringbone brick pathway.* **2.** A twilled fabric woven in this pattern. Also used adjectivally: *a herringbone suit.* **3.** An embroidery stitch of one row of slanted parallel lines crossing another slanted in the opposite direction, so that each line is crossed symmetrically at top and bottom only. **4.** *Skiing.* A method of climbing a slope with the skis pointed outward.
~*v.* **herringboned, -boning, -bones.** —*tr.* To arrange in or decorate with a herringbone pattern. —*intr.* **1.** To produce this pattern. **2.** *Skiing.* To ascend a slope using the herringbone method. [From its resemblance to the skeletal structure of a herring.]

herringbone gear *n. Engineering.* A type of gearwheel in which two sets of teeth are cut on the rim, one set being at an angle to the other so that the teeth are V-shaped.

herring gull *n.* A common, widely distributed gull, *Larus argentatus,* having gray and white plumage with black wing tips. [From its habit of preying on herrings.]

hers (hûrz). Possessive pronoun, absolute form of *her.* **1.** Belonging to her; her own. Used predicatively: *The red boots are hers.* **2.** The one or ones belonging to her. Used substantively: *If you can't find your hat, take hers.* **—of hers.** Belonging or pertaining to her: *a friend of hers.* [Middle English *hirs, hires,* a double possessive from *hire,* HER.]

Her•schel (hûr′shəl), **Sir John Frederick William** (1792–1871). English mathematician and astronomer, son of Sir William. He extended his father's catalogue of double stars and nebulae.

Herschel, Sir William, born Friedrich Wilhelm Herschel (1738–1822). English astronomer, born in Germany. He settled in England in 1757, working as a music teacher and studying the sky in his spare time. In 1781 he discovered Uranus and was appointed astronomer to King George III. He also catalogued more than 800 double stars and some 2,500 nebulae.

her•self (hûr-sĕlf′) *pron.* A specialized form of the third person singular feminine pronoun. It is used: **1.** As a reflexive pronoun, forming the direct or indirect object of a verb or the object of a preposition: *hurt herself; gives herself the benefit of the doubt; talks to herself.* **2.** For emphasis after *she*: *She herself wasn't certain.* **3.** As an emphasizing substitute: *Herself in debt, she couldn't help us. It was addressed to her brother and herself.* **4.** As an indication of her real, normal, or healthy condition or identity: *She hasn't been herself lately.* **5.** *Chiefly Irish & Scottish.* An important or prominent woman, such as the mistress of a household. Sometimes used humorously.

Her•sey (hûr′sē), **John Richard** (1914–). U.S. author, born in China of missionary parents. He was a war correspondent during World War II, and his best-known works, such as *Hiroshima* (1946) and *A Bell for Adano* (Pulitzer Prize winner in 1945), reflect his feelings about man's inhumanity to man during that war.

Her•shey (hûr′shē), **Milton Snavely** (1857–1945). U.S. industrialist and philanthropist. In 1903 he acquired a site of 480 hectares (1,200 acres) near Lancaster, Pennsylvania, and formed his chocolate company. Later, as his personal fortune and the town of Hershey grew, he founded a home and school for orphan boys. The town is still populated mainly by the company's employees and is a popular tourist attraction.

Herst•mon•ceux, Hurst•mon•ceux (hûrst′mən-sōō′). Village in East Sussex, southeastern England. Its heavily restored castle (1440), one of the finest medieval brick buildings, has housed the Royal Observatory since its transfer from Greenwich in 1950.

Hert•ford•shire (här′fərd-shîr′, -shər, härt′-). Also **Herts** (härts, hûrts). County of southeastern England. Mainly low-lying but rising to the Chiltern Hills in the northwest, it is largely agricultural. Hertford is its county town.

hertz (hûrts) n., pl. **hertz.** Symbol **Hz** A unit of frequency equal to one cycle per second. [After Heinrich HERTZ.]

Hertz (hĕrtz), **Gustav** (1887–1975). German physicist. In 1925 he was awarded the Nobel Prize in physics for his work on the impact of electrons on atoms.

Hertz, Heinrich Rudolf (1857–94). German physicist. He succeeded in producing the first radio waves artificially.

Hertz·i·an wave (hûrt′sē-ən, hĕrt′-) n. A radio wave (see). [After Heinrich HERTZ.]

Hert·zog (hûrt′sōg′, -sôg′, hĕrt′-), **James Barry Munnik** (1866–1942). South African general in the Boer War. In 1924 he became South Africa's first National Party prime minister in an election pact with the Labour Party. He steered South Africa to greater independence from Britain until 1939.

Hertz·sprung-Rus·sell diagram (hĕrts′sprŭng-rŭs′əl) n. A graph of the logarithms of the luminosities of stars plotted against the logarithms of their surface temperatures. Points on the diagram fall into groups corresponding to different types of star. Also called "Russell diagram." See **main sequence.** [Developed by Ejnar *Hertzsprung* (1873–1967), Danish astronomer, and Henry N. *Russell* (1877–1957), American astronomer.]

Her·zl (hĕrt′səl), **Theodor** (1860–1904). Hungarian-born founder of the Zionist movement. He reported the Dreyfus affair in Paris for a Vienna newspaper and decided that Jewish assimilation in European society was impossible. In 1896 he advocated the establishment of a Jewish national state in his pamphlet *Der Judenstaat.* In 1897 he founded the Zionist World Congress and was its president until his death.

he's (hēz). **1.** Contraction of *he is.* **2.** Contraction of *he has.*

Hesh·van, Hesh·wan (ᴋʜĕsh′vən, hĕsh′-) n. The second month of the Hebrew calendar. Also called "Marcheshvan." See feature at **calendar.** [Hebrew *ḥeshwān,* short for *marḥeshwān.*]

He·si·od (hē′sē-əd, hĕs′ē-) (fl. c. 8th century B.C.). Greek poet. He wrote a long didactic poem on agriculture, *Works and Days,* and may have written the *Theogony,* a genealogy of the gods, and *The Shield of Heracles.*

hes·i·tan·cy (hĕz′ə-tən-sē) n., pl. **-cies. 1.** The state or quality of being hesitant; indecision. **2.** An instance of hesitating.

hes·i·tant (hĕz′ə-tənt) adj. Inclined or tending to hesitate; irresolute. **—hes·i·tant·ly** adv.

hes·i·tate (hĕz′ə-tāt′) intr.v. **-tated, -tating, -tates. 1. a.** To be slow to act or decide; hold back in uncertainty; waver. **b.** To be reluctant, especially out of propriety, scruples, or concern for others; have qualms; demur: *"Do you think she will hesitate to sacrifice you?"* (G.B. Shaw). **2.** To pause briefly in or as if in uncertainty: *hesitate on the way upstairs.* **3.** To speak haltingly; falter. [Latin *haesitāre,* to stick fast, be undecided, hesitate, frequentative of *haerēre* (past participle *haesum*), to hold or hang fast, stick.] **—hes·i·tat·er** n. **—hes·i·tat·ing·ly** adv.

> *Synonyms: falter, vacillate, waver.*

hes·i·ta·tion (hĕz′ə-tā′shən) n. **1.** The act or an instance of hesitating. **2.** A pause or faltering in speech. **—hes·i·ta·tive** adj. **—hes·i·ta·tive·ly** adv.

Hes·pe·ri·a (hĕ-spîr′ē-ə). Poetic. The Western Land. A name applied by the Greeks to Italy and by the Romans to Spain or regions beyond. [Latin, from Greek, from *hesperos, hesperios,* of evening, western, from *hesperos,* evening.]

Hes·pe·ri·an (hĕ-spîr′ē-ən) adj. Poetic. **1.** Of or pertaining to Hesperia or the west. **2.** Of or pertaining to the Hesperides.

Hes·per·i·des (hĕ-spĕr′ə-dēz′) pl.n. Greek Mythology. **1.** Three sisters who together with a dragon watched over the garden of the golden apples in the Islands of the Blest. **2.** Used with a singular verb. The garden of the golden apples. **3.** The Islands of the Blest, situated at the western end of the earth. [Latin *Hesperidēs,* from Greek *Hesperides,* plural of *Hesperis,* "western," daughter of the west, from *hesperos, hesperios,* of evening, western. See **Hesperia.**] **—Hes·per·id·i·an, Hes·per·id·e·an** (hĕs′pə-rĭd′ē-ən) adj.

hes·per·i·din (hĕ-spĕr′ə-dĭn) n. A white or colorless crystalline compound, $C_{28}H_{34}O_{15}$, occurring in citrus fruits, as oranges. [HESPERID(IUM) + -IN.]

hes·per·id·i·um (hĕs′pə-rĭd′ē-əm) n., pl. **-ia** (-ē-ə). Botany. A form of berry having a thickened, leathery rind and juicy pulp divided into segments, such as an orange, lemon, or other citrus fruit. [New Latin, after the golden apples in the garden of HESPERIDES.]

Hes·per·us (hĕs′pər-əs) n. **1.** The planet Venus in its appearance as the evening star. **2.** Any of various other stars or planets prominently visible in the early evening. [Latin, from Greek *hesperos,* western.]

Hess (hĕs), **Dame Myra** (1890–1965). British pianist. During World War II she organized daily lunchtime concerts at the National Gallery, London. She was made a dame in 1941.

Hess, Rudolf (1894–). German politician, born in Egypt. He joined Hitler in 1920 and took part in the Munich putsch, for which he was jailed. When Hitler became chancellor in 1933, he named Hess as his deputy führer. In 1939 Hess was named second in succession after Goering to the Nazi leadership. Hess flew to Scotland in May 1941, apparently in a bid to start peace talks with the British government. At the Nuremberg trials of 1946 he was sentenced to life imprisonment in Spandau Prison, Berlin, for war crimes.

Hess, Victor Franz (1883–1964). U.S. physicist, born in Austria.

He discovered cosmic rays, and shared the Nobel Prize for physics with Carl D. Anderson in 1936.

Hess, Walter Rudolf (1881–1973). Swiss physiologist. He shared the Nobel Prize in physiology and medicine with Moniz Antonio Egas (1874–1955) in 1949 for work on the separate control over body organs by different areas of the brain.

Hesse (hĕs). German **Hes·sen** (hĕs′ən). A state of West Germany. In the west-central part of the country, it consists mainly of forested uplands; there is some cattle raising, and potatoes, beets, and wheat are grown. The capital is Wiesbaden.

Hes·se (hĕs′ə), **Hermann** (1877–1962). German novelist and poet. He was a pacifist and, in 1914, moved to Switzerland, becoming a Swiss citizen in 1923. His novels, which explore psychological alienation, include *Steppenwolf* (1927) and *The Glass Bead Game* (1943). He was awarded the Nobel Prize for literature in 1946.

Hes·sian (hĕsh′ən) n. **1.** A native or inhabitant of Hesse. **2. a.** A Hessian mercenary in the British army in the Revolutionary War. **b.** Any mercenary. **3.** hessian. A coarse fabric; burlap. ~adj. Of or relating to Hesse or its people.

Hessian boot n. A high, tasseled man's boot introduced into England from Hesse in the early 19th century.

Hessian fly n. A small fly, *Mayetiola destructor,* having larvae that infest and destroy wheat and other grain plants. [Supposed to have been introduced to America by Hessian troops during the Revolutionary War.]

hes·site (hĕs′īt′) n. A black or gray mineral form of silver telluride, Ag_2Te. [German *Hessit,* after Henry *Hess,* 19th-century Swiss chemist.]

hessonite. Variant of **essonite.**

Hes·ti·a (hĕs′tē-ə). Greek Mythology. The goddess of the hearth, daughter of Cronus and Rhea; identified with the Roman goddess Vesta.

he·tae·ra (hĭ-tîr′ə) n., pl. **-ras** or **-taerae** (-tîr′ē′). Also **he·tai·ra** (-tîr′ə) pl. **-ras** or **-tairai** (-tîr′ī′). A courtesan or concubine; especially, in ancient Greece, one of a special class of cultivated female companions. [Greek *hetaira,* feminine of *hetairos,* companion.]

he·tae·rism (hĭ-tîr′ĭz′əm) n. Also **he·tai·rism** (-tîr′ĭz′əm). **1.** Concubinage. **2.** Anthropology. The practice of communal marriage supposed to have been characteristic of primitive societies. **—he·tae·rist** n.

hetero-, heter– prefix. Indicates other, another, or different; for example, **heterogamy, heterosexual.** [Greek *heteros,* other.]

het·er·o·cer·cal (hĕt′ə-rō-sûr′kəl) adj. Zoology. Pertaining to, designating, or characterized by a tail fin having two unequal lobes, with the vertebral column extending into the upper, usually larger lobe, as in sharks. Compare **homocercal.** [HETERO- + Greek *kerkos,* tail.]

het·er·o·chro·mat·ic (hĕt′ə-rō-krō-măt′ĭk) adj. **1.** Of or pertaining to different colors; varicolored. **2.** Consisting of different wavelengths or frequencies. **3.** Of or pertaining to heterochromatin. **—het·er·o·chro·ma·tism** (hĕt′ə-rō-krō′mə-tĭz′əm) n.

het·er·o·chro·ma·tin (hĕt′ə-rō-krō′mə-tĭn) n. Genetics. Chromosomal material exhibiting maximal staining in the nuclear meiotic interphase and lacking specific genetic activity. Compare **euchromatin.**

het·er·o·chro·mo·some (hĕt′ə-rō-krō′mə-sōm′) n. Genetics. **1.** An atypical chromosome, such as a sex chromosome. **2.** A chromosome composed primarily of heterochromatin.

het·er·o·clite (hĕt′ər-ə-klīt′) n. **1.** A word formed or inflected in an unusual way. **2.** Anything or anyone that departs from the normal or usual. [Late Latin, from Greek *heteroklitos,* irregularly inflected : HETERO- + Greek *klitos,* from *klinein,* to bend, inflect.] **—het·er·o·clite, het·er·o·clit·ic** (hĕt′ər-ə-klĭt′ĭk) adj.

het·er·o·cy·clic (hĕt′ə-rō-sī′klĭk, -sĭk′lĭk) adj. Chemistry. Of, pertaining to, or designating a chemical compound having a ring of atoms in its molecules that contains at least one atom of an element other than carbon. Compare **homocyclic.** ~n. Chemistry. A heterocyclic compound.

het·er·o·dac·tyl (hĕt′ə-rō-dăk′təl) adj. Designating a bird's foot on which the first and second toes point backward and the third and fourth forward. ~n. A bird having heterodactyl feet.

het·er·o·dont (hĕt′ər-ə-dŏnt′) adj. Having teeth of various different kinds. Said of most mammals. [HETERO(-) + -ODONT.]

het·er·o·dox (hĕt′ər-ə-dŏks′) adj. **1.** Not in agreement with accepted beliefs; especially, departing from an established religious doctrine or dogma. Compare **orthodox. 2.** Holding unorthodox opinions. [Late Latin *heterodoxus,* from Greek *heterodoxos,* differing in opinion : HETERO- + *doxa,* opinion, notion, from *dokein,* to expect, think.]

het·er·o·dox·y (hĕt′ər-ə-dŏk′sē) n., pl. **-ies. 1.** The condition or quality of being heterodox. **2.** A heterodox opinion or doctrine.

het·er·o·dyne (hĕt′ər-ə-dīn′) adj. Having alternating currents of two different frequencies that are combined to generate a current that has sum and difference frequencies, either of which may be used in radio or television receivers by proper tuning or filtering. ~tr.v. **heterodyned, -dyning, -dynes.** To combine (a radio-frequency wave) with a locally generated wave of different frequency in order to produce a new frequency equal to the sum or difference of the two. [HETERO- + DYNE.]

het·er·oe·cious (hĕt′ə-rē′shəs) adj. Spending alternate stages of a life cycle on different, unrelated hosts. Said of parasites such as rusts and tapeworms. [HETERO- + Greek *oikia*, house.] —**het·er·oe·cism** (hĕt′ə-rē′sĭz′əm) *n.*

het·er·o·gam·ete (hĕt′ə-rō-găm′ēt′, -gə-mēt′) *n.* Either of two conjugating gametes, such as the small, motile male spermatozoon and the larger, nonmotile female ovum, that differ in size, form, or behavior.

het·er·o·ga·met·ic (hĕt′ə-rō-gə-mĕt′ĭk) *adj.* Having a dissimilar pair of sex chromosomes, as in human males, or one unpaired sex chromosome, as in some male insects. Compare **homogametic.**

het·er·og·a·mous (hĕt′ə-rŏg′ə-məs) *adj.* **1.** *Biology.* Characterized by the fusion of unlike gametes in the reproductive process. **2.** *Botany.* Bearing flowers of different kinds, especially both male and female flowers, on one plant. [HETERO- + -GAMOUS.]

het·er·og·a·my (hĕt′ə-rŏg′ə-mē) *n.* **1.** Alternation of generations, one sexual, the other parthenogenetic, as in some aphids. **2.** A state in which uniting gametes are dissimilar in structure and size as well as in function. [HETERO- + -GAMY.] —**het·er·o·gam·ic** (hĕt′ə-rō-găm′ĭk) *adj.*

het·er·o·ge·ne·i·ty (hĕt′ə-rō-jə-nē′ə-tē) *n.* The quality or state of being heterogeneous; nonuniformity; dissimilarity.

het·er·o·ge·ne·ous (hĕt′ər-ə-jē′nē-əs, -jēn′yəs) *adj.* Also **het·er·o·ge·nous** (hĕt′ə-rōj′ə-nəs). **1.** Consisting of or involving parts that are unlike or without interrelation; having dissimilar constituents or elements; not homogeneous: *a heterogeneous collection of people.* **2.** Completely different; incongruous. **3.** *Physics & Chemistry.* Of, involving, or designating a system of two or more different phases: *a heterogeneous mixture; heterogeneous catalysis.* Compare **homogeneous.** —See Synonyms at **miscellaneous.** [Medieval Latin *heterogeneus,* from Greek *heterogenēs* : HETERO- + *genos,* kind.] —**het·er·o·ge·ne·ous·ly** *adv.* —**het·er·o·ge·ne·ous·ness** *n.*

het·er·o·gen·e·sis (hĕt′ə-rō-jĕn′ə-sĭs) *n.* Alternation of generations (see). —**het·er·o·ge·net·ic** (hĕt′ə-rō-jə-nĕt′ĭk) *adj.*

het·er·og·e·nous¹ (hĕt′ə-rōj′ə-nəs) *adj.* Also **het·er·o·gen·ic** (hĕt′ə-rō-jĕn′ĭk). Originating outside the body. [HETERO- + -GENOUS.] —**het·er·og·e·ny** *n.*

heterogenous². Variant of **heterogeneous.**

het·er·og·o·nous (hĕt′ə-rŏg′ə-nəs) *adj.* **1.** *Biology.* Characterized by the alternation of sexual and asexual generations. **2.** *Botany.* Designating plants in which the flowers differ from each other in the lengths of the stamens and styles. [HETERO- + -GON(Y) + -OUS.] —**het·er·og·o·ny** *n.*

het·er·o·graft (hĕt′ə-rō-grăft′, -gräft′) *n.* A type of tissue graft in which the donor and recipient are of different species. Also called "xenograft."

het·er·og·ra·phy (hĕt′ə-rŏg′rə-fē) *n., pl.* **-phies. 1.** Spelling that is inconsistent in respect of single sounds, as the spelling of modern English is; for example, the *-uf* sound is rendered very differently in the words *cuff* and *tough.* **2.** Spelling that departs from conventional usage. [HETERO- + -GRAPHY.]

het·er·og·y·nous (hĕt′ə-rōj′ə-nəs) *adj. Zoology.* Having two types of female, one able to reproduce sexually, the other infertile, as in ants. [HETERO- + -GYNOUS.]

het·er·o·junc·tion (hĕt′ə-rō-jŭngk′shən) *n. Electronics.* A junction between two semiconductors with different types of conductivity.

het·er·o·kar·y·on (hĕt′ə-rō-kăr′ē-ŏn′) *n.* A cell containing two or more nuclei of different types, or an organism made up of such cells. —**het·er·o·kar·y·ot·ic** (hĕt′ə-rō-kăr′ē-ŏt′ĭk) *adj.*

het·er·o·kar·y·o·sis (hĕt′ə-rō-kăr′ē-ō′sĭs) *n. Biology.* The presence of more than one type of nucleus in a single cell, as occurs in certain fungi. [HETERO- + KARY(O)- + -OSIS (condition).]

het·er·o·lec·i·thal (hĕt′ə-rō-lĕs′ə-thəl) *adj.* Having nonhomogeneous distribution of yolk in an ovum. Said of birds' eggs. Compare **isolecithal.** [HETERO- + Greek *lekithos,* yolk (see **lecithin**) + -AL.]

het·er·ol·o·gous (hĕt′ə-rŏl′ə-gəs) *adj.* **1.** Derived from a different species: *a heterologous graft.* **2.** Of or pertaining to cytological or histological elements not normally occurring in a designated part of the body. [HETERO- + -LOG(Y) + -OUS.]

het·er·ol·o·gy (hĕt′ə-rŏl′ə-jē) *n.* Lack of correspondence between bodily parts, as in structure, arrangement, or development, arising from differences in origin. [HETERO- + -LOGY.]

het·er·ol·y·sis (hĕt′ə-rŏl′ə-sĭs) *n., pl.* **-ses** (-sēz′). **1.** *Biology.* Dissolution of cells or protein components in one species by lytic agents of another. Compare **autolysis. 2.** *Chemistry.* A reaction in which the breaking of a chemical bond leads to the formation of a pair of ions with opposite charges. Also called "heterolytic fission." Compare **homolysis.** [New Latin : HETERO- + -LYSIS.] —**het·er·o·lyt·ic** (hĕt′ə-rō-lĭt′ĭk) *adj.*

het·er·om·er·ous (hĕt′ə-rŏm′ər-əs) *adj. Biology.* Having unequal or differing parts within the same structure or similar structures. [HETERO- + -MEROUS.]

het·er·o·mor·phic (hĕt′ə-rō-môr′fĭk) *adj.* Also **het·er·o·mor·phous** (-môr′fəs). **1.** Having a different shape, size, or function from the normal; atypical. **2.** Designating homologous chromosome pairs in which one differs from the other in size or shape. **3.** *Biology.* Having differing forms, as in different stages of an insect's life cycle. In this sense, compare **polymorphic.** [HETERO- + -MORPHIC.] —**het·er·o·mor·phism** *n.*

het·er·on·o·mous (hĕt′ə-rŏn′ə-məs) *adj.* **1.** Subject to external or foreign laws or domination; not autonomous. **2.** Differing in development or manner of specialization, as the dissimilar segments of certain arthropods. [HETERO- + Greek *nomos,* law + -OUS.] —**het·er·on·o·mous·ly** *adv.*

het·er·o·nym (hĕt′ə-rə-nĭm′) *n.* One of two or more words that have identical spelling but different meanings and pronunciations, as *row* (a line) and *row* (a fight). [Back-formation from HETERONYMOUS.]

het·er·on·y·mous (hĕt′ə-rŏn′ə-məs) *adj.* **1.** Of or pertaining to a heteronym. **2.** Designating names or terms that are different but have correspondence or interrelationship, as *master* and *mistress.* [Late Greek *heterōnumos* : HETERO- + Greek *onoma,* name.]

Het·er·o·ou·si·an (hĕt′ə-rō-ōō′sē-ən, -ou′sē-ən) *n.* Also **Het·er·ou·si·an** (hĕt′ə-rōō′sē-ən, -rou′sē-ən). A Christian holding that the substance and nature of God the Father and God the Son are different; an Arian. Compare **Homoiousian, Homoousian.**
~*adj.* Designating or pertaining to the Heteroousians or their beliefs. [Late Greek *hetero(o)usios,* of different substance : HETERO- + Greek *ousia,* substance, essence, from *ōn* (stem *ous-*), present participle of *einai,* to be.]

het·er·oph·o·ny (hĕt′ə-rŏf′ə-nē) *n. Music.* The simultaneous playing or singing of a single melody by two or more different instruments or singers. [HETERO- + -PHONY.]

het·er·o·pho·ri·a (hĕt′ər-ə-fôr′ē-ə, -fōr′ē-ə) *n.* A tendency to squint. [HETERO- + *-phoria,* tendency, act of bearing, from Greek *pherein,* to carry, bear.]

het·er·o·phyl·lous (hĕt′ə-rō-fĭl′əs) *adj. Botany.* Having unlike leaves on one plant. [HETERO- + -PHYLLOUS.] —**het·er·o·phyl·ly** (hĕt′ə-rō-fĭl′ē) *n.*

het·er·o·phyte (hĕt′ər-ə-fīt′) *n.* A plant, such as a parasite, that can obtain its nourishment from living or dead organic sources. [HETERO- + -PHYTE.]

het·er·o·plas·ty (hĕt′ər-ə-plăs′tē) *n., pl.* **-ties.** The surgical grafting of tissue obtained from another person or from a lower animal. [HETERO- + -PLASTY.]

het·er·op·ter·ous (hĕt′ə-rŏp′tər-əs) *adj.* Of or belonging to the insect order Heteroptera, which includes the true bugs, characterized by forewings and hind wings that differ from one another. [New Latin *Heteroptera* : HETERO- + -PTEROUS.]

het·er·o·sce·das·tic (hĕt′ə-rō-sĭ-dăs′tĭk) *adj. Statistics.* Pertaining to or designating variables for which all possible values do not have constant variance. [HETERO- + *scedastic,* from Greek *skedasis,* dispersion, scattering.]

het·er·o·sex·u·al (hĕt′ə-rō-sĕk′shōō-əl) *adj.* **1.** Characterized by attraction to the opposite sex. **2.** Of or pertaining to different sexes or to sexual relations between persons of the opposite sex.
~*n.* A heterosexual person. —**het·er·o·sex·u·al·i·ty** (hĕt′ə-rō-sĕk′shōō-ăl′ə-tē) *n.* —**het·er·o·sex·u·al·ly** *adv.*

het·er·o·sis (hĕt′ə-rō′sĭs) *n. Biology.* Increased vigor or other superior qualities arising from the crossbreeding of genetically different plants or animals. Also called "hybrid vigor." [New Latin, from Greek *heter(oi)ōsis,* alteration, transformation, from *heteroioun,* to alter, from *heteroios,* different in kind, from *heteros,* one of two, the other.]

het·er·os·po·rous (hĕt′ə-rŏs′pər-əs, -ər-ə-spôr′əs, -spōr′əs) *adj. Botany.* Producing microspores and megaspores. Said of seed plants and some ferns. [HETERO- + -SPOROUS.] —**het·er·os·po·ry** *n.*

het·er·o·tax·is (hĕt′ə-rō-tăk′sĭs) *n.* Also **het·er·o·tax·y** (hĕt′ər-ə-tăk′sē), **het·er·o·tax·i·a** (-tăk′sē-ə). Abnormal structural arrangement, as of organs of the body. [HETERO- + -TAXIS.] —**het·er·o·tac·tic** (hĕt′ə-rō-tăk′tĭk), **het·er·o·tac·tous** (hĕt′ə-rō-tăk′təs) *adj.*

het·er·o·thal·lic (hĕt′ə-rō-thăl′ĭk) *adj. Botany.* Producing male gametangia in one structure or plant and female gametangia in a different structure or plant, as in some algae and fungi. [HETERO- + Greek *thallos,* young shoot, THALLUS.] —**het·er·o·thal·lism** *n.*

het·er·o·to·pi·a (hĕt′ə-rō-tō′pē-ə) *n.* Also **het·er·ot·o·py** (-ə-rŏt′ə-pē). *Pathology.* Displacement of an organ or other part of the body from its normal position. —**het·er·o·top′ic** (hĕt′ə-rō-tŏp′ĭk) *adj.*

het·er·o·troph·ic (hĕt′ər-ə-trŏf′ĭk, -trō′fĭk) *adj.* Obtaining nourishment from organic substances, as do all animals and some plants. Compare **autotrophic.** [HETERO- + -TROPHIC.] —**het·er·o·troph·i·cal·ly** *adv.* —**het·er·o·troph·ism, het·er·ot·ro·phy** (hĕt′ə-rŏt′rə-fē) *n.*

het·er·o·typ·ic (hĕt′ə-rō-tĭp′ĭk) *adj.* **1.** *Biology.* Relating to or designating the first reduction division of meiosis. **2.** Of a different type or form. Compare **homeotypic.** [HETERO- + TYPIC(AL).]

het·er·o·zy·go·sis (hĕt′ə-rō-zī-gō′sĭs) *n.* **1.** Derivation from or union between genetically different gametes. **2.** The condition of being a heterozygote.

het·er·o·zy·gote (hĕt′ə-rō-zī′gōt′) *n.* An organism that has inherited different alleles for one or more genes; a hybrid. —**het·er·o·zy·gous** *adj.*

heth (KHāt, KHäth, KHĕt, KHĕth) *n.* The eighth letter of the Hebrew alphabet. See feature at **alphabet.** [Hebrew *hēth.*]

het·man (hĕt′mən) *n., pl.* **-mans.** A Cossack military leader. [Polish, probably from German *Hauptmann,* captain.]

het up (hĕt) *adj. Informal.* Angry or flustered; worked up. [Dialectal *het,* past participle of HEAT.]

heu·land·ite (hyōō′lən-dīt′) *n.* A white, red, or yellow zeolite mineral with composition $(Ca,Na,K)_6Al_{10}(Al,Si)Si_{29}O_{80}·25H_2O$. [After Henry Heuland, 19th-century English mineral collector.]

heu·ris·tic (hyōō-rĭs′tĭk) *adj.* **1.** Assisting the process of learning or discovery; guiding or furthering investigation: *I propose this theory purely as a heuristic device.* **2.** Designating an educational method in which the student is allowed or encouraged to learn independently through his own investigation. **3.** *Mathematics.* Designating a method of problem solving that relies on inductive reasoning from past experience in the absence of a relevant algorithm.
~*n.* A heuristic method or process. [From Greek *heuriskein,* to discover, find.] —**heu·ris·ti·cal·ly** *adv.*

heu·ris·tics (hyōō-rĭs'tĭks) *n. Used with a singular verb.* The science or study of heuristic methods and practices.

Heus·ler alloy (hoiz'lər, hyōōs'-) *n.* Any of a class of alloys of manganese, aluminum, zinc, and copper that are ferromagnetic even though their components are not. [After Conrad *Heusler,* 19th-century German chemist and mining engineer.]

He·ve·sy (hĕv'ə-shē), **Georg von** (1885–1966). Hungarian physicist and chemist. He used isotopes as tracers to investigate chemical processes and discovered the element hafnium. He was awarded the Nobel Prize for chemistry in 1943.

hew (hyōō) *v.* **hewed, hewn** (hyōōn) or **hewed, hewing, hews.** —*tr.* **1. a.** To make or shape with an ax, knife, or other cutting tool. Often used with *out: hew out a small canoe.* **b.** To form (a fissure, channel, or the like) by natural means, as by the action of lightning or dripping water. **2.** To cut down with an ax; fell. Used with *away, down, from,* or *off: hew down an oak.* **3.** To strike or cut; cleave; chop: *hewed in pieces.* —*intr.* **1.** To cut by repeated blows of an ax, sword, or the like. **2.** To adhere or conform: *hew to the line.* [Hew, hewn; Middle English *hewen, hewen,* Old English *hēawan, hēawen,* from Germanic.] —**hew·er** *n.*

hex (hĕks) *n.* **1.** An evil spell; a curse. **2.** A person or thing that exercises an evil or dominating influence. **3.** A witch. ~*tr.v.* **hexed, hexing, hexes.** **1.** To work evil on; bewitch. **2.** To wish or bring bad luck to, especially through superstitious means. [Pennsylvania Dutch, from German *Hexe,* witch, from Middle High German *hecse, häxe,* probably from Old High German *hagazussa, hagzissa.*]

hex. hexagon; hexagonal.

hexa-, hex- *prefix.* Indicates six; for example, **hexagram, hexane.** [Greek, from *hex,* six.]

hex·a·canth (hĕk'sə-kănth') *n. Zoology.* An **oncosphere** *(see).* [HEXA + Greek *akantha,* thorn, spine.]

hex·a·chlo·ro·eth·ane (hĕk'sə-klôr'ō-ĕth'ān', -klôr'ō-ĕth'ān') *n.* Also **hex·a·chlor·eth·ane** (-klôr-ĕth'ān', -klôr-ĕth'ān'). A colorless crystalline compound, Cl₃CCCl₃, that is used as a camphor substitute and in pyrotechnics, explosives, and veterinary medicine.

hex·a·chlo·ro·phene (hĕk'sə-klôr'ə-fēn', -klôr'ə-fēn') *n.* A white powder, (C₆HCl₃OH)₂CH₂, formerly used as a bactericidal agent in soaps, cosmetics, and skin medications.

hex·a·chord (hĕk'sə-kôrd') *n.* In medieval music, any of three diatonic sequences of six tones, the central interval being a semitone, and the others whole tones. [HEXA- + -CHORD.]

hex·ad (hĕk'săd') *n. H.G.* A group or series of six. [Late Latin *hexas* (stem *hexad-*), the number six, from Greek, from *hex,* six.] —**hex·ad·ic** (hĕk-săd'ĭk) *adj.*

hex·a·dec·a·nol (hĕk'sə-dĕk'ə-nôl', -nōl', -nŏl') *n.* **Cetyl alcohol** *(see).*

hex·a·dec·i·mal (hĕk'sə-dĕs'ə-məl) *adj.* Designating or pertaining to a number system with base 16, used in computer programming to represent groups of 4 bits. —*n.* **1.** A hexadecimal number. **2.** A hexadecimal notation.

hex·a·gon (hĕk'sə-gŏn') *n. Abbr.* **hex.** A polygon having six sides and six angles. [Late Latin *hexagōnum,* from Greek *hexagōnon,* from *hexagōnos,* six-angled : HEXA- + -GON.]

hex·ag·o·nal (hĕk-săg'ə-nəl) *adj. Abbr.* **hex.** **1.** Having six sides and six angles. **2.** Of, pertaining to, or formed in hexagons. **3.** *Chemistry & Geology.* Having three equal axes intersecting at 60° in one plane and one axis of variable length that is at right angles to the others. Said of crystals or crystal structures. —**hex·ag·o·nal·ly** *adv.*

hex·a·gram (hĕk'sə-grăm') *n.* **1.** A six-pointed star consisting of a regular hexagon with each of the sides extended to form equilateral triangles. **2.** A figure of six lines or sides. [HEXA- + -GRAM.]

hex·a·he·dral (hĕk'sə-hē'drəl) *adj.* **1.** Having six plane surfaces. **2.** Of, pertaining to, or formed in hexahedrons. [HEXAHEDR(ON) + -AL.] —**hex·a·he·dral·ly** *adv.*

hex·a·he·dron (hĕk'sə-hē'drən) *n., pl.* **-drons** or **-dra** (-drə). A polyhedron with six plane surfaces. [Greek *hexaedron,* from *hexaedros,* six-sided : HEXA- + -HEDRON.]

hex·a·hy·drate (hĕk'sə-hī'drāt') *n. Chemistry.* A crystalline substance that has six molecules of water of crystallization per molecule of the compound.

hex·am·er·ous (hĕk-săm'ər-əs) *adj.* **1.** Having six similar parts or divisions. **2.** *Botany.* Having flower parts, such as petals, sepals, and stamens, in sets of six. Also written *6-merous.* [HEXA- + -MEROUS.] —**hex·am·er·ism** *n.*

hex·am·e·ter (hĕk-săm'ə-tər) *n.* A line of verse consisting of six metrical feet. [Latin, from Greek *hexametron,* from *hexametros,* having six metrical feet : HEXA- + -METER.] —**hex·a·met·ric** (hĕk'sə-mĕt'rĭk), **hex·a·met·ri·cal** *adj.*

hex·a·mine (hĕk'sə-mēn') *n.* A colorless crystalline compound, C₆H₁₂N₇, used in solution as an antiseptic, especially for infections of the urinary tract. Also called "hexamethylenetetramine," "methenamine." [HEXA- + AMINE.]

hex·ane (hĕk'sān') *n.* **1.** A colorless, flammable liquid, CH₃(CH₂)₄CH₃, derived from the fractional distillation of petroleum and used as a solvent and as the working fluid in low-temperature thermometers. **2.** Any of a group of isomeric alkane hydrocarbons with the formula C₆H₁₄. [HEX(A)- + -ANE.]

hex·an·gu·lar (hĕk-săng'gyə-lər) *adj.* Having six angles.

hex·a·pla (hĕk'sə-plə) *n.* An edition of the Old Testament, compiled by Origen, having six versions of the text in separate columns. [Greek, neuter plural of *hexaplous,* sixfold : HEXA- + *plous,* -fold.]

hex·a·pod (hĕk'sə-pŏd') *n.* Any member of the class Insecta (or Hexapoda); an insect. ~*adj.* Also **hex·ap·o·dous** (hĕk-săp'ə-dəs). **1.** Of or belonging to the Hexapoda. **2.** Having six legs or feet. [New Latin *Hexapoda* : HEXA- + -POD.]

hex·ap·o·dy (hĕk-săp'ə-dē) *n.* A line of verse consisting of six metrical feet. [HEXA + *-pody,* from Greek *-podia,* condition of having a certain number of feet, from *pous* (stem *pod-*), foot.]

hex·a·stich (hĕk'sə-stĭk') *n.* A poem, stanza, or strophe consisting of six lines. [HEXA- + Greek *stikhos,* line of verse.]

Hex·a·teuch (hĕk'sə-tōōk', -tyōōk') *n.* The first six books of the Old Testament. [HEXA- + Greek *teukhos,* tool, case holding writing material, roll of papyrus, volume.]

hex·a·va·lent (hĕk'sə-vā'lənt) *adj. Chemistry.* Having a valence of 6; sexivalent.

hex·o·san (hĕk'sə-săn') *n.* Any of several polysaccharides that form a hexose on hydrolysis. [HEXOS(E) + -AN.]

hex·ose (hĕk'sōs') *n.* Any of various simple sugars, such as glucose, that have six carbon atoms per molecule. [HEX(A)- + -OSE.]

hex·yl (hĕk'səl) *n.* The hydrocarbon radical C₆H₁₃, having a valence of 1, especially the radical derived from normal hexane, CH₃(CH₂)₅. [HEX(A)- + -YL.]

hex·yl·re·sor·ci·nol (hĕk'səl-rə-zôr'sə-nôl', -nōl') *n.* A yellowish-white crystalline phenol, C₁₂H₁₈O₂, used as an antiseptic and anthelmintic.

hey (hā) *interj.* **1.** Used to express surprise, appreciation, wonder, or the like: *Hey, that's nice!* **2.** Used to attract attention: *Hey, you!* [Middle English *hei, hay.*]

hey·day (hā'dā') *n.* The period of greatest popularity, success, fashion, power, or the like; the prime. [Earlier *heyda,* probably an extension of HEY; akin to Low German *heida,* hurrah!]

Hey·er·dahl (hā'ər-däl', hī'-), **Thor** (1914–). Norwegian anthropologist and explorer. He led the Kon Tiki expedition on a raft across the Pacific Ocean from Peru to the Tuamotu Islands in 1947 to demonstrate that Polynesians might be of South American origin. In 1970 he crossed the Atlantic Ocean from Morocco to Barbados in a papyrus boat to show that the ancient Egyptians may have sailed to America.

hf high frequency.

Hf The symbol for the element hafnium.

hg hectogram.

Hg The symbol for the element mercury. [Latin *hydrargyrum.*]

HG, H.G. High German.

H-gird·er (āch'gûr'dər) *n.* An H-beam *(see).*

hgt. height.

H.H. **1.** His (or Her) Highness. **2.** His Holiness.

H-hour (āch'our') *n. Military.* Zero hour *(see).* [H, abbreviation for HOUR.]

hi (hī) *interj.* **1.** *Informal.* Used as a greeting. **2.** Used to attract attention. [Middle English *hy,* parallel form to HEY.]

HI Hawaii (used with a Zip Code).

hi·a·tus (hī-ā'təs) *n., pl.* **hiatuses** or **hiatus.** **1.** A gap or missing section; a lacuna. **2.** Any loss or interruption in time or continuity; a break. **3.** *Phonetics.* The immediate sequence of two vowel sounds each of which constitutes or belongs to a separate syllable. **4.** *Anatomy.* A separation, aperture, or fissure. [Latin *hiātus,* a gaping, gap, from the past participle of *hiāre,* to gape.]

hiatus hernia *n.* A hernia in which part of the stomach protrudes through the esophageal opening (hiatus) of the diaphragm.

Hi·a·wath·a (hī'ə-wŏth'ə, -wô'thə) (*fl.* 1570). An Onondagan chief who is credited with the organization of the Iroquois Confederacy. His name was also given to the hero of Longfellow's poem *The Song of Hiawatha* (1855).

hi·ba·chi (hī-bä'chē) *n., pl.* **-chis.** A portable charcoal-burning brazier with a grill, often used for cooking at table. [Japanese : *hi,* fire + *bachi,* bowl.]

hi·ber·nac·u·lum (hī'bər-năk'yə-ləm) *n., pl.* **-la** (-lə). Also **hi·ber·na·cle** (hī'bər-năk'əl). **1.** *Biology.* A case, covering, or structure in which an organism remains dormant for the winter. **2.** The shelter of a hibernating animal. [Latin *hibernāculum,* winter residence, from *hibernus,* winter.]

hi·ber·nal (hī-bûr'nəl) *adj.* Occurring in or pertaining to winter. [Latin *hibernālis,* from *hibernus,* winter.]

hi·ber·nate (hī'bər-nāt') *intr.v.* **-nated, -nating, -nates.** **1.** *Zoology.* To pass the winter in a dormant or torpid state. **2.** To be in an inactive or dormant state or period. [Latin *hibernāre,* to winter, from *hibernus,* winter.] —**hi·ber·na·tor** *n.*

hi·ber·na·tion (hī'bər-nā'shən) *n.* **1.** The action of hibernating. **2.** The state of torpidity or inactivity in which some organisms pass the winter. Compare **estivation.** **3.** Any state or period of inactivity likened to that of a wintering animal: "*Stirring suddenly from long hibernation I knew myself once more a poet*" (Robert Graves).

Hi·ber·ni·a (hī-bûr'nē-ə). *Poetic.* Ireland. [Latin, variant (influenced by *hībernus,* winter) of *I(u)verna, Juberna,* from Greek *Iernē.*] —**Hi·ber·ni·an** *adj.*

Hi·ber·ni·cism (hī-bûr'nə-sĭz'əm) *n.* Also **Hi·ber·ni·an·ism** (-nē-ə-nĭz'əm). An Irish idiom, trait, or custom.

hi·bis·cus (hī-bĭs'kəs) *n.* Any of various chiefly tropical plants, shrubs, or trees of the genus *Hibiscus,* having large, showy, variously colored flowers, several species of which are cultivated for ornament. [New Latin *Hibiscus,* from Latin, from Greek *hibiskos†,* marshmallow.]

hic (hĭk) *n.* The sound of a hiccup.

hibiscus *The hibiscus, the national flower of Hawaii, is a genus of about 300 species of flowers, shrubs, and trees. This is* Hibiscus syriacus, *a shrub that flowers in late summer.*

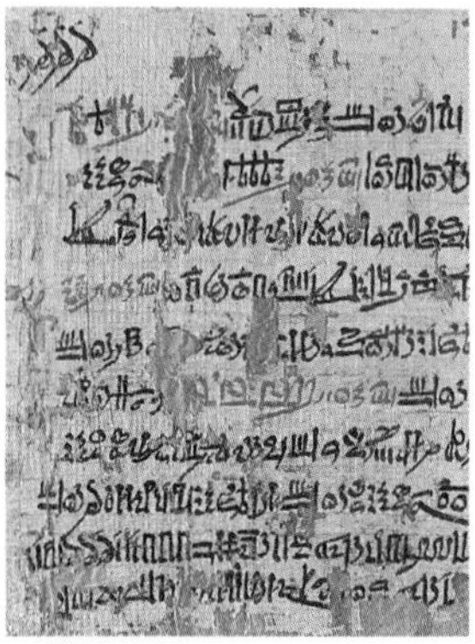

hieratic *Hieratic script used in a calendar dating from 1230 B.C. The Egyptian papyrus shows the days of the year as lucky (in black) or unlucky (in red).*

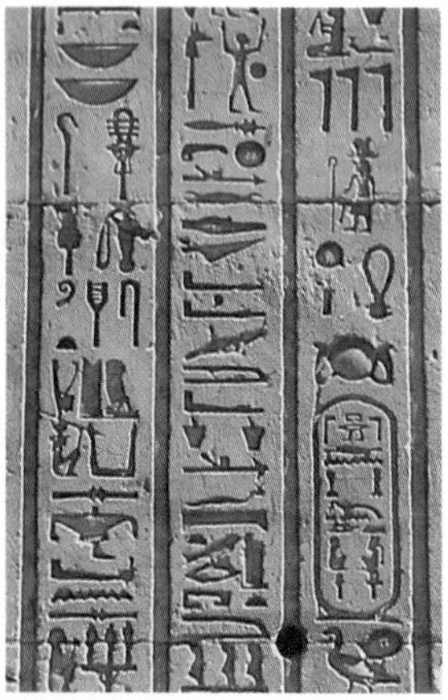

hieroglyphic *Pictographic Egyptian writing from a temple of Horus built between the third and first centuries B.C. at Edfu.*

PRONUNCIATION KEY

ă, pat; ā, pay; âr, **care**; ä, father, **are**; b, **bib**; ch, **church**; d, **deed**; ĕ, pet; ē, be; f, **fife**; g, **gag**; h, **hat**; hw, **which**; ĭ, pit; ī, pie; îr, **pier**; j, **judge**; k, **kick**; l, lid, needle; m, **mum**; n, no, sudden; ng, thing; ŏ, pot; ō, toe; ô, **paw**, for; oi, noise; ou, **out**; o͝o, **book**; o͞o, boot; p, **pop**; r, roar; s, sauce; sh, **ship**, **dish**; t, tight; th, **thin**, **path**; *th*, **this**, bathe; ŭ, cut; ûr, **fur**; v, valve; w, with; y, yes; z, zebra, size; zh, vision; ə, about, item, edible, gallop, circus, peaceful

IN FOREIGN WORDS:

à, *Fr.* ami; œ, *Fr.* **feu**, *Ger.* schön; ü, *Fr.* **tu**, *Ger.* **über**; KH, *Ger.* **ich**, *Scot.* **loch**; N, *Fr.* bon; y', *Fr.* Compiègne

STRESS MARKS:

Primary stress: ′
in·cite′ (ĭn-sīt′)
Secondary stress: ′
in′sight′ (ĭn′sīt′)

hic·cup, hic·cough (hĭk′əp) *n.* **1.** A spasm of the diaphragm resulting in a sudden, abortive inhalation that is stopped by a spasmodic closure of the glottis. In technical usage, also called "singultus." **2. hiccups.** An attack of hiccups. **3.** *Informal.* A slight difficulty or delay.
~v. **hiccupped, -cupping, -cups.** Also **hic·cough, -coughed, -coughing, -coughs.** *—intr.* **1.** To make a sound resembling that of a hiccup. **2.** To have an attack of hiccups. *—tr.* To say or express while hiccupping. [Earlier *hicket, hickop* (imitative).]

hic ja·cet (hĭk jā′sĭt, hēk yä′kĭt) *Abbr.* **H.J.** Here lies. Used in epitaphs on gravestones. [Latin.]

hick (hĭk) *n. Informal.* A gullible, provincial person; a yokel; a bumpkin.
~adj. Informal. Backward or unsophisticated: *a hick town.* [From *Hick,* an obsolete nickname for *Richard.*]

hick·ey (hĭk′ē) *n., pl.* **-eys.** *Informal.* **1.** Any device or contrivance; a gadget. **2.** A pimple, scar, or other mark on the skin. [20th century : origin obscure.]

Hick·ok (hĭk′ŏk′), **James Butler,** known as "Wild Bill Hickok" (1837–76). U.S. marshal and gunfighter.

hick·o·ry (hĭk′ə-rē) *n., pl.* **-ries. 1.** Any of several chiefly North American deciduous trees of the genus *Carya,* having hard, smooth nuts with an edible kernel. **2.** The hard, tough, heavy wood of any of these trees. **3.** The nut of any of these trees. **4.** A walking stick or switch made from hickory wood. [Shortening of earlier *pohickery,* from Virginian native name *pawcohiccora,* food prepared from crushed hickory nuts.]

Hicks (hĭks), **Edward** (1780–1849). U.S. primitive painter. A member of the Society of Friends, he became a noted back-country preacher, supporting himself by his paintings. His best-known work is *The Peaceable Kingdom,* of which nearly 100 versions exist.

hid. Past tense and alternate past participle of **hide** (to put out of sight).

hi·dal·go (hĭ-dăl′gō) *n., pl.* **-gos.** A member of the minor nobility in Spain. [Spanish, from Old Spanish *hijo dalgo,* "son of something (that is to say, property)" : *hijo,* son + *de,* of + *algo,* something.]

hid·den (hĭd′n). Past participle of **hide** (to put out of sight).
~adj. Not immediately apparent; having its true nature disguised: *hidden unemployment.*

hid·den·ite (hĭd′n-īt′) *n.* A transparent emerald-green variety of spodumene, used as a gemstone. [After William E. *Hidden* (1853–1918), American mineralogist.]

hide[1] (hīd) *v.* **hid** (hĭd), **hidden** (hĭd′n) or **hid, hiding, hides.** *—tr.* **1.** To put or keep out of sight; secrete. **2.** To prevent the disclosure or recognition of; conceal. **3.** To cut off or obstruct from sight; cover up. **4.** To avert (one's gaze) in shame or grief. *—intr.* **1.** To keep oneself out of sight. **2.** To seek refuge.
~n. British. A hunting **blind** *(see).* [Hide, hid, hidden or hid; Middle English *hiden, hid, hidden* (formed by analogy with RIDE, RIDDEN) or *hidd,* Old English *hȳdan, hȳdde, hīdd.*] **—hid·er** *n.*
Synonyms: *bury, cache, cloak, conceal, screen, secrete.*

hide[2] *n.* **1.** The skin of an animal; especially, the comparatively thick, tough skin or pelt of a large animal. **2.** *Informal.* The human skin.
~tr.v. **hided, hiding, hides.** *Informal.* To beat severely; flog. [Middle English *hyde, hide,* Old English *hȳd.*]

hide[3] *n.* An old English measure of land, usually the amount held to be adequate for one free family and its dependents, and varying from 60 to 120 acres. [Middle English *hide, hyde,* Old English *hīgid, hīd.*]

hide-and-seek (hīd′n-sēk′) *n.* Also **hide-and-go-seek** (-gō-sēk′). **1.** A children's game in which one player tries to find and catch others who are hiding. **2.** Any game or action involving evasion. **—hide-and-seek** *adj.*

hide·a·way (hīd′ə-wā′) *n.* **1.** A place of concealment; a hide-out. **2.** A secluded or isolated place.

hide·bound (hīd′bound′) *adj.* **1.** Having abnormally dry, stiff skin that adheres closely to the underlying flesh. Said of undernourished domestic animals such as cattle. **2.** Having the bark so contracted and unyielding as to hinder growth. Said of trees. **3.** Unduly adhering to the rules or to one's own opinions or prejudices; narrow-minded and inflexible.

hid·e·ous (hĭd′ē-əs) *adj.* **1.** Physically repulsive; revolting; ugly. **2.** Horrifying; appalling; terrifying. **3.** Repugnant to the moral sense; despicable; odious. [Middle English, from Norman French *hidous,* from Old French *hidous, hideus,* from *hi(s)de,* fear, horror, perhaps from Latin *hispidus,* rough, shaggy.] **—hid·e·ous·ly** *adv.* **—hid·e·ous·ness** *n.*

hide-out (hīd′out′) *n.* A place of shelter or concealment, especially for a person on the run.

hid·ey-hole, hid·y-hole (hī′dē-hōl′) *n.* A hiding place; hideaway.

hid·ing[1] (hī′dĭng) *n.* A state or place of concealment: *stayed in hiding until the coast was clear.*

hiding[2] *n. Informal.* **1.** A spanking or beating. **2.** A crushing defeat.

hi·dro·sis (hĭ-drō′sĭs) *n.* Perspiration, especially in excessive or abnormal amounts. [New Latin, from Greek *hidrōsis,* sweating, from *hidrōs,* sweat.]

hi·drot·ic (hĭ-drŏt′ĭk) *n.* Any drug or other agent that promotes sweating.
~adj. **1.** Stimulating sweating. **2.** Pertaining to sweating.

hie (hī) *intr.v.* **hied, hieing** or **hying, hies.** To go quickly; hasten; hurry. [Middle English *hien, hyghen,* Old English *hīgian,* to strive, exert oneself, hurry.]

hi·e·mal (hī′ə-məl) *adj.* Occurring in or pertaining to winter; hibernal. [Latin *hiemālis,* from *hiems,* winter.]

hi·er·arch (hī′ə-rärk′, hī′rärk′) *n.* **1.** One who occupies a position of authority in an ecclesiastical hierarchy. **2.** One who occupies a high position in a hierarchy. [Old French *hierarche,* from Medieval Latin *hierarcha,* from Greek *hierarkhēs,* president of sacred rites, high priest : HIER(O)- + -ARCH.]

hi·er·ar·chism (hī′ə-rär′kĭz′əm, hī′rär′-) *n.* Hierarchical practice or principles. **—hi·er·ar·chist** *n.*

hi·er·ar·chy (hī′ə-rär′kē, hī′rär′-) *n., pl.* **-chies. 1. a.** A body of persons organized or classified according to rank, capacity, or authority. **b.** A body of entities arranged in a graded series. **2.** Hierocracy. **3.** The body of clergy in a country or area, especially the bishops. [Middle English *ierarchie,* from Old French, from Medieval Latin *(h)ierarchia,* rule of a priest, from Greek *hierarkhia,* from *hierarkhēs,* HIERARCH.] **—hi·er·ar·chi·cal** (hī′ə-rär′kĭ-kəl, hī-rär′-), **hi·er·ar·chic** (-kĭk) *adj.* **—hi·er·ar·chi·cal·ly** *adv.*

hi·er·at·ic (hī′ə-răt′ĭk, hī-răt′-) *adj.* Also **hi·er·at·i·cal** (-ĭ-kəl) (for sense 1). **1.** Of or associated with sacred persons or offices; sacerdotal: *a hieratic gesture.* **2.** Designating or pertaining to a simplified cursive style of Egyptian hieroglyphics that was developed and chiefly used by the priestly class. Compare **demotic. 3.** Designating or pertaining to various styles of art that follow rules or conventions established by religious tradition, especially in ancient Egypt.
~n. **hieratic.** The hieratic script of ancient Egypt. [Latin *hierāticus,* from Greek *hieratikos,* from *hieratos* (unattested), from *hierasthai,* to be a priest, from *hiereus,* priest, from *hieros,* sacred, supernatural.] **—hi·er·at·i·cal·ly** *adv.*

hiero–, hier– *prefix.* Indicates sacred or holy; for example, **hierocracy, hierogram.** [Greek, from *hieros,* holy, sacred.]

hi·er·oc·ra·cy (hī′ə-rŏk′rə-sē, hī-rŏk′-) *n., pl.* **-cies.** Government by the clergy; ecclesiastical rule: *"Vermont will emerge next, because least . . . under the yoke of hierocracy"* (Thomas Jefferson). [HIERO- + -CRACY.] **—hi·er·o·crat·ic** (hī′ər-ə-krăt′ĭk, hī′rə-), **hi·er·o·crat·i·cal** (-ĭ-kəl) *adj.*

hi·er·o·dule (hī′ər-ə-do͞ol′, -dyo͞ol′, hī′rə-) *n.* A temple slave in the service of a particular deity. Used especially with reference to the ritual prostitution at the temple of Aphrodite in Corinth. [Late Latin *hierodūlus,* from Greek *hierodoulos* : HIERO- + *doulos*†, slave.] **—hi·er·o·du·lic** (hī′ər-ə-do͞o′lĭk, -dyo͞o′lĭk, hī′rə-) *adj.*

hi·er·o·glyph·ic (hī′ər-ə-glĭf′ĭk, hī′rə-) *adj.* Also **hi·er·o·glyph·i·cal** (-ĭ-kəl). **1.** Written in or pertaining to a system of writing used in ancient Egypt, in which figures or objects are used to represent words or sounds. **2.** Containing or inscribed with hieroglyphic pictures or symbols. **3.** Hard to read or decipher; illegible.
~n. **hieroglyphic.** Also **hi·er·o·glyph** (hī′ər-ə-glĭf′, hī′rə-). **1.** A picture or symbol used in hieroglyphic writing. **2. hieroglyphics.** Hieroglyphic writing. **3.** A picture or symbol with a hidden meaning; an emblem. **4. hieroglyphics.** Illegible or undecipherable writing. [Old French *hieroglyphique,* from Late Latin *hieroglyphicus,* from Greek *hierogluphikos,* written in hieroglyphics : HIERO- + *gluphē,* carving, engraving, from *gluphein,* to carve.] **—hi·er·o·glyph·i·cal·ly** *adv.* **—hi·er·o·glyph·ist** *n.*

hi·er·o·gram (hī′ər-ə-grăm′, hī′rə-) *n.* A sacred symbol. [HIERO- + -GRAM.]

hi·er·ol·o·gy (hī′ə-rŏl′ə-jē, hī-rŏl′-) *n., pl.* **-gies.** The sacred literature of a given people. [HIERO- + -LOGY.]

hi·er·o·phant (hī′ər-ə-fănt′, hī′rə-, hī-ĕr′ə-) *n.* **1.** In ancient Greece, an expounder of sacred mysteries, especially of the Eleusinian mysteries. **2.** An interpreter of esoteric or arcane knowledge: *"What did even the hierophants of science know of . . . evil?"* (Malcolm Lowry). [Late Latin *hierophanta, hierophantēs,* from Greek *hierophantēs,* interpreter of sacred mysteries : HIERO- + *phainein,* to reveal, show.] **—hi·er·o·phan·tic** (hī′ər-ə-făn′tĭk, hī′rə-) *adj.*

hifalutin. Variant of **highfalutin.**

hi-fi (hī′fī′) *n.* **1. High fidelity** *(see).* **2.** An electronic system or equipment for reproducing high-fidelity sound from radio, records, or magnetic tape. [*High fi*delity.] **—hi-fi** *adj.*

hig·gle (hĭg′əl) *intr.v.* **-gled, -gling, -gles.** To haggle; bargain. [Variant of HAGGLE.]

hig·gle·dy-pig·gle·dy (hĭg′əl-dē-pĭg′əl-dē) *adv.* In utter disorder or confusion.
~n., pl. **-dies.** A jumble; a muddle.
~adj. Topsy-turvy; jumbled. [Rhyming and jingling formation probably based on PIG (presumably from the manner in which pigs huddle together).]

high (hī) *adj.* **higher, highest. 1. a.** Extending, projecting, or placed far upward; tall; elevated. **b.** Extending farther upward than is usual: *a high forehead.* **2. a.** Having a specified elevation: *ten feet high.* **b.** Being at a specified level: *waist-high.* **3.** Being at or near its peak or culmination: *high noon.* **4.** Beginning to decompose, as meat; excessively gamy. **5.** Far removed in time; remote: *high antiquity.* **6.** Designating a sound produced by a relatively great frequency of vibrations: *a high note.* **7.** Situated far from the equator: *a high latitude.* **8.** Of great moment or importance, as: **a.** Preeminent in rank or standing: *the high priest; the high command.* **b.** Serious; weighty; grave: *high treason.* **9.** Lofty or exalted in quality, character, or style: *high moral standards; high culture.* **10. a.** Of relatively great quantity, magnitude, value, or degree: *a high temperature; high wage demands; a high vitamin content.* **b.** Of great force or violence: *high winds.* **11.** Luxurious: *high living.* **12.** Showing pride, arrogance, or disdain. **13.** Characterized by a state of excitement or euphoria; elated: *high spirits.* **14.** *Informal.* Intoxi-

cated by or as if by alcohol or a narcotic. **15.** At an advanced stage of development or complexity: *high finance.* **16. a.** Favorable: *a high opinion.* **b.** Well-regarded: *high standing.* **17.** *Phonetics.* Pronounced with part of the tongue close to the palate: *a high vowel.* **18.** *Usually* **High.** Of or pertaining to the High Church. **19.** Of, pertaining to, or being the gear in an automotive vehicle that produces the maximum speed.
~*adv.* **1.** At or to a high level: *rise very high.* **2.** In a high manner: *riding high; sing high; priced high.* **3.** *Nautical.* With full sails, sailing close to the wind.
~*n.* **1. a.** A high place, region, or level. **b.** A highest point: *The stock market reached a new high.* **2.** *Abbr.* **h., H.** The transmission gear of an automotive vehicle producing maximum speed. **3.** A center of high atmospheric pressure; anticyclone. **4.** *Informal.* Intoxication or euphoria induced by or as if by a stimulant or a narcotic. —**on high. 1.** At a high level or position. **2.** In heaven. [Middle English *hei, high,* Old English *hēah,* from Germanic.]
Synonyms: *elevated, lofty, tall, towering.*
high altar *n.* The principal altar in a church.
high and dry *adv.* **1.** In a helpless or destitute state. **2.** Out of water. Said of ships.
high and low *adv.* Here and there; everywhere: *searched high and low.*
high and mighty *adj.* Arrogant; domineering; disdainful.
high-ball (hī′bôl′) *n.* **1.** An iced drink consisting of alcoholic liquor and water, soda water, or the like, served in a tall glass. **2.** A railroad signal indicating full speed ahead.
~*intr.v.* **highballed, -balling, -balls.** To move ahead at full speed.
high-bind-er (hī′bīn′dər) *n.* **1.** A member of a former Chinese-American secret society of paid assassins and blackmailers. **2.** A gangster. **3.** A corrupt politician. [From the *High-binders,* a New York City gang (*c.* 1806).]
high blood pressure *n.* Hypertension.
high-born (hī′bôrn′) *adj.* Of noble birth.
high-boy (hī′boi′) *n.* A tall chest of drawers divided into two sections and supported on four legs. Compare **tallboy.**
high-brow (hī′brou′) *n.* *Informal.* One who has or affects superior learning or culture. Compare **middlebrow, lowbrow.** [Referring to a lofty forehead as a conventional sign of intellectual superiority.] —**high-brow, high-browed** *adj.*
high-bush cranberry (hī′boŏsh′) *n.* A North American shrub, *Viburnum trilobum,* having broad clusters of white flowers and scarlet fruit. Also called "cranberry bush."
high-chair (hī′châr′) *n.* A baby's feeding chair, usually with a detachable tray and mounted on tall legs.
High Church *n.* The branch of the Anglican Church that stresses the value of an episcopal hierarchy and sacramental ritual. Compare **Anglo-Catholic, Broad Church, Low Church.** —**High-Church** (hī′chûrch′) *adj.* —**High-Church-man** *n.*
high-class (hī′klăs′, -kläs′) *adj.* First-class; first-rate.
high-col-ored (hī′kŭl′ərd) *adj.* Extremely pink; florid. Said of the complexion.
high comedy *n.* Comedy marked by sophisticated characterizations and clever dialogue.
high court *n.* **Supreme Court** (see).
high day *n.* A holy day; a feast day.
high-def-i-ni-tion (hī′dĕf′ə-nĭsh′ən) *adj.* Designating a televized image with a high degree of clarity.
high-en-er-gy (hī′ĕn′ər-jē) *adj.* **1.** Of or relating to elementary particles with energies exceeding hundreds of thousands of electron volts. **2.** Yielding a large amount of energy upon undergoing chemical reaction. **3.** Vigorous; dynamic.
higher algebra *n.* The algebra of sets, groups, propositions, vectors, matrices, tensors, or the like, as opposed to the simple algebra of numbers.
higher criticism *n.* Critical study of Biblical texts with regard to such matters as their authorship, composition, editing, and compilation. Compare **lower criticism.**
higher education *n.* Education that takes place after attendance at secondary school, as at a college or university.
higher learning *n.* Education or scholastic attainment at the college or university level.
higher mathematics *n.* Mathematics involving advanced abstract ideas, including such topics as number theory, non-Euclidean geometry, topology, and analysis, as distinguished from simple arithmetic, algebra, geometry, and trigonometry.
high-er-up (hī′ər-ŭp′) *n.* *Informal.* One who has a higher rank, position, or status.
high explosive *n.* *Abbr.* **HE** A powerful, fast-acting explosive.
high-fa-lu-tin, hi-fa-lu-tin (hī′fə-loōt′n) *adj.* Also **high-fa-lu-ting** (-loōt′n, -loō′tĭng). *Informal.* Pompous or pretentious, especially in the use of language. [HIGH + *falutin,* perhaps variant of *fluting,* present participle of FLUTE.]
high fashion *n.* **Haute couture** (see).
high fidelity *n.* The electronic reproduction of sound, especially sound from broadcast, recorded, or taped sources, with minimal distortion. Also called "hi-fi." —**high-fi-del-i-ty** (hī′fĭ-dĕl′ə-tē, hī′fī-) *adj.*
high finance *n.* Complex financial dealings involving large sums of money.
high five *n.* A friendly or congratulatory slap with the open palm and the arm raised exchanged by two people.
high-fli-er, high-fly-er (hī′flī′ər) *n.* **1.** One that flies high. **2. a.** A

person of great ambition. **b.** A person expected by his superiors to go far. **3.** A very successful person, especially one who has a high status for his age.
high-flown (hī′flōn′) *adj.* **1.** Lofty; exalted. **2.** Pretentious.
high-fly-ing (hī′flī′ĭng) *adj.* **1.** Rising to a great height. **2.** Lofty in form or ambitions.
high frequency *n.* *Abbr.* **hf** A **radio frequency** (see) in the range between 3 and 30 megahertz.
High-gate (hī′gət, -gāt′). A residential district of northern London. In its cemetery are the graves of several famous people, including Karl Marx and George Eliot.
high gear *n.* **1.** See **high** (sense 2). **2.** A state of maximum activity, energy, or force.
High German *n.* **1.** *Abbr.* **HG, H.G.** The German language as spoken and written in southern Germany. See **Low German, Old High German, Middle High German. 2.** Any of various German dialects. [Translation of German *Hochdeutsch.*]
high-grade (hī′grād′) *adj.* Of superior quality.
high-hand-ed (hī′hăn′dĭd) *adj.* Arrogant or arbitrary in manner. —**high-hand-ed-ly** *adv.* —**high-hand-ed-ness** *n.*
high-hat (hī′hăt′) *n.* *Slang.* A snobbish or patronizing person. ~*tr.v.* (hī′hăt′) **high-hatted, -hatting, -hats.** *Slang.* To be condescending or supercilious toward. —**high-hat** *adj.*
High Holiday *n.* **1.** Rosh Hashanah. **2.** Yom Kippur.
highjack. Variant of **hijack.**
high jinks *pl.n.* Mischievous merriment; lively sport.
high jump *n.* **1.** An athletic event in which individual athletes compete to jump highest over an adjustable horizontal bar. **2.** Any of the jumps performed in such a competition.
high-keyed (hī′kēd′) *adj.* **1.** Excitable; nervous; high-strung. **2.** Bright in color; intense. **3.** Having a high pitch; shrill.
high-land (hī′lənd) *n.* **1.** Elevated land. **2. highlands.** A mountainous or hilly region or part of a country.
~*adj.* **1.** Of, relating to, or characteristic of such a region. **2. Highland.** Of or relating to the Highlands.
Highland cattle *n.* *Used with a plural verb.* A breed of long-horned cattle having shaggy, usually reddish-brown hair.
high-land-er (hī′lən-dər) *n.* **1.** One who lives in a highland area. **2. Highlander.** An inhabitant of the Highlands.
Highland fling *n.* An energetic reel or folk dance of the Highlands.
Highland pony *n.* A pony of a breed originating in the Scottish Highlands.
Highland Region. An administrative region of northern Scotland, formed from the former counties of Caithness, Sutherland, Ross and Cromarty, Inverness, Nairn, and parts of Argyll. Its administrative center is Inverness.
Highlands, the. That part of Scotland lying north of a line drawn from Dumbarton in the west northeastward to Stonehaven.
high-lev-el (hī′lĕv′əl) *adj.* **1.** Occurring, carried out, or situated at a high level. **2.** Being at a high level of importance: *a high-level official.*
high-level language *n.* *Computer Science.* A programming language that uses words and common mathematical symbols. Compare **low-level language.**
high life *n.* Also **high-life** (hī′līf′) (for sense 2). **1.** A fashionable or luxurious style of living. **2.** A style of West African music combining traditional African and American jazz elements. —**high-life** *adj.*
high-light (hī′līt′) *n.* **1.** In painting or photography, a brilliantly lighted area of the subject appearing as a luminous spot. **2.** An outstanding event or detail. **3.** *Usually* **highlights.** A bleached or light dyed streak in the hair.
~*tr.v.* **highlighted, -lighting, -lights. 1.** To give prominence to; focus attention upon. **2.** To add highlights to, as in painting. **3.** To dye or bleach (the hair) to produce highlights. **4.** To be the highlight of.
high-light-er (hī′lī′tər) *n.* **1.** A cosmetic in powder or cream form used to create highlights on the face. **2.** A felt-tipped pen with fluorescent ink used to pick out a word or passage in a text.
high-ly (hī′lē) *adv.* **1. a.** Extremely; very. Used as an intensive: *highly indignant.* **b.** To a greater than average degree: *highly paid.* **2.** Approvingly; favorably: *I think highly of his results.*
High Mass *n.* *Roman Catholic Church.* A sung Mass celebrated by a priest or prelate, sometimes assisted by a deacon and a subdeacon, and with full ceremonial.
high-mind-ed (hī′mīn′dĭd) *adj.* **1.** Characterized by morally lofty ideals or conduct; principled. **2.** *Archaic.* Disdainfully proud; arrogant; haughty. —**high-mind-ed-ly** *adv.* —**high-mind-ed-ness** *n.*
high muckamuck *n.* *Slang.* A **muckamuck** (see).
high-ness (hī′nĭs) *n.* **1.** The quality of being high, especially: **a.** Tallness; height. **b.** Greatness, as of degree or amount. **2.** A title of honor or form of address for any of various members of a royal family. Used with *His, Her, Your,* or *Their:* *Their Highnesses the Prince and Princess.*
high noon *n.* **1.** Exactly noon. **2.** The highest or most advanced stage or period: *was at the high noon of her creativity.*
high-oc-tane (hī′ŏk′tān′) *adj.* Having a high octane number.
high-pass filter (hī′păs′, -päs′) *n.* *Electronics.* A circuit that allows transmission of signals with frequencies above a given value, rejecting frequencies below this value.
high-pitched (hī′pĭcht′) *adj.* **1. a.** Having a high pitch to the ear. **b.** Tuned to a high pitch. **2.** Lofty; exalted, as a sermon might be. **3.** Steeply sloped, as a roof might be.
high place *n.* **1.** In early Semitic religions, a place of worship on top

Highland cattle *A hardy, shaggy-haired breed from the rugged uplands of Scotland. Highlands produce good beef even on poor pasture.*

Highland pony *A muscular breed of horse once widely used as a pack animal in the Scottish Highlands.*

high relief *A centaur battles with a human rival in a detail from a Greek frieze sculpted in this deeply cut style.*

hilt *The hilt, or handle, of an 11th-century Viking sword.*

of a hill. **2. high places.** Positions of power or influence, especially in public office: *corruption in high places.*

high point *n.* The single event or moment in a period of time, project, or the like, that stands out as particularly rewarding or revealing: *The high point of the concert was the oboe concerto.*

high-pow·ered (hī′pou′ərd) *adj.* **1.** Dynamic and highly motivated: *a high-powered salesman.* **2.** Intellectually demanding or impressive: *a high-powered seminar.* **3.** Capable of very great magnification. Said of optical instruments: *a high-powered telescope.*

high-pres·sure (hī′prĕsh′ər) *adj.* **1.** Of or pertaining to pressures higher than normal; especially, much higher than atmospheric pressure. **2.** Involving great psychological stress or great dedication of energy: *a high-pressure job.* **3.** *Informal.* Using aggressive and persistent persuasion in selling.
~*tr.v.* **high-pressured, -suring, -sures.** *Informal.* To convince or influence by using high-pressure methods of persuasion.

high priest *n.* **1.** *Judaism.* The senior priest serving in the temple, who alone could enter the holy of holies. **2.** Any of various other senior priests in various religions or sects. **3.** The unofficial leader or most influential figure of a fashion, theory, or movement: *the high priest of monetarism.*

high priestess *n.* A woman who functions or is regarded as a high priest.

high profile *n. Informal.* A conspicuous, well-publicized presence or stance. Compare **low profile.**

high relief *n.* A sculptural relief in which the modeled forms project from the background by at least half their depth. Also called "alto-relievo." [Translation of French *haut-relief.*]

high-rise (hī′rīz′) *adj.* Designating or being a building with many stories equipped with elevators. Compare **low-rise.**
~*n.* A high-rise building.

high·road (hī′rōd′) *n.* **1.** *Chiefly British.* A main road; a highway. **2.** A simple, direct, or sure path: *the highroad to happiness.*

high school *n.* **1.** A secondary school that includes grades 9 or 10 through 12. **2.** A secondary school that includes junior and senior high school, consisting of grades 7 through 12.

high seas *pl.n.* The open waters of an ocean or sea beyond the limits of national territorial jurisdiction.

high season *n.* Any of the periods during a year when attendance or demand is particularly high, as at a vacation resort.

high sign *n. Informal.* A gesture or other discreet signal given especially as a secret warning.

high·sound·ing (hī′soun′dĭng) *adj.* Impressive or pompous.

high-speed (hī′spēd′) *adj.* **1.** Moving, operating, or used at a high speed. **2.** Of, pertaining to, or designating photographic film that requires only a short exposure.

high-speed steel *n.* A type of steel that remains hard when hot, used for cutting tools for lathes, milling machines, and the like.

high-spir·it·ed (hī′spîr′ə-tĭd) *adj.* **1.** Having a proud or unbroken spirit; brave. **2.** Vivacious. —**high-spir·it·ed·ly** *adv.* —**high-spir·it·ed·ness** *n.*

high spot *n.* The best or most memorable part of a particular period of time: *Dinner was the high spot of the day.*

high-street (hī′strēt′) *adj. Chiefly British.* Of, pertaining to, or designating shops or other commercial enterprises of a kind typically found on a principal street: *a high-street grocer.*

high-strung (hī′strŭng′) *adj.* Constantly nervous and tense; easily excited or upset.

hight (hīt) *adj. Archaic.* Named; called. [Middle English *highten, hihten,* from *hehte, hight,* past tense of *hoten,* to call, be called, Old English *hātan* (past tense *heht*).]

high table *n. British.* The dining table, sometimes on a raised platform, in the dining hall of an institution, such as a university, at which senior members and their guests take their meals.

high-tail (hī′tāl′) *intr.v.* **-tailed, -tailing, -tails.** *Slang.* To move or depart in a great hurry; especially, to escape. —**hightail it.** To rush; hurry. [A reference to some animals who when startled raise their tails and flee.]

high tea *n. Chiefly British.* A substantial meal that typically includes tea, a hot course, and bread and butter, served in the late afternoon or early evening.

high tech (tĕk) *n.* **1.** A modern style of furnishings, fittings, and design in which industrial materials such as metal piping are used. **2.** High technology. —**high-tech** (hī′tĕk′) *adj.*

high technology *n.* Technology involving highly advanced or specialized systems or devices.

high-ten·sion (hī′tĕn′shən) *adj. Abbr.* **H.T.** Having or carrying a high voltage: *high-tension wires.*

high-test (hī′tĕst′) *adj.* **1.** Meeting the most exacting requirements. **2.** Of or pertaining to highly volatile, high-octane fuel.

high tide *n.* **1.** The tide at its full, when the water reaches its highest level. **2.** The time at which this occurs. **3.** A point of culmination; an acme.

high time *n.* **1.** A time almost too late; about time; fully time. **2.** *Informal.* A good time.

high-toned (hī′tōnd′) *adj.* **1.** Intellectually superior: *a high-toned lecture.* **2.** Socially superior: *a high-toned finishing school.* **3.** *Informal.* Having pretensions to elegance or slickness.

high treason *n.* Treason against one's state or sovereign.

highty-tighty. Variant of **hoity-toity.**

high-up (hī′ŭp′) *adj. Informal.* Of high position or status.
~*n. Informal.* A person who has a high rank or position.

High-veld (hī′vĕlt′, -fĕlt′). In South Africa, the savanna of the Afri-

can plateau above 1,500 meters (about 5,000 feet).

high water *n. Abbr.* **H.W., h.w.** **1.** High tide. **2.** The state of a body of water that has reached its highest level.

high-wa·ter mark (hī′wô′tər, -wŏt′ər) *n.* **1. a.** A mark indicating the highest level reached by a body of water. **b.** This level itself. **2.** The highest point of achievement; an apex.

high·way (hī′wā′) *n.* A main public road, especially one connecting towns and cities.

high·way·man (hī′wā′mən) *n., pl.* **-men** (-mĭn). A robber who holds up travelers on a highway.

H.I.H. His (or Her) Imperial Highness.

hi·jack, high·jack (hī′jăk′) *tr.v.* **-jacked, -jacking, -jacks.** **1.** To rob (a vehicle, such as a train or armored truck) by stopping it in transit. **2.** To steal (goods) from a vehicle by stopping it in transit. **3.** To seize or commandeer (a moving vehicle, such as an aircraft, ship, or car) by force or with threats of force, especially in an attempt to enforce political or other demands. **4.** To steal from (a person). **5.** To take control of using coercive or underhand methods: *The meeting was hijacked by a well-organized group of militants.*
~*n.* An act or instance of hijacking. [20th century : origin obscure.] —**hi·jack·er** *n.*

hike (hīk) *v.* **hiked, hiking, hikes.** —*intr.* **1. a.** To go on an extended walk, particularly for pleasure. **b.** To go on an extended march, especially over rough terrain; tramp. **2.** To go up, as prices. Often used with *up: The cost of living has hiked up again.* **3.** To be raised or hitched. Usually used with *up: Her coat has hiked up at the back.* —*tr.* **1.** To increase or raise in amount. Usually used with *up.* **2.** To pull, move, or raise with a sudden motion; hitch. Usually used with *up: He hiked up his pants.*
~*n.* **1.** A walk or march. **2.** A rise, as in prices. [19th century (dialect) : origin obscure.] —**hik·er** *n.*

hi·la. Plural of **hilum.**

hi·lar·i·ous (hĭ-lâr′ē-əs, hī-) *adj.* Boisterously funny, gay, or merry: *a hilarious joke.* [From Latin *hilarus, hilaris.* See **hilarity.**] —**hi·lar·i·ous·ly** *adv.* —**hi·lar·i·ous·ness** *n.*

hi·lar·i·ty (hĭ-lăr′ə-tē, hī-) *n.* Boisterous merriment. —See Synonyms at **mirth.** [Old French *hilarite,* from Latin *hilaritās,* from *hilaris, hilarus,* cheerful, from Greek *hilaros.*]

Hil·bert (hĭl′bərt), **David** (1862–1943). German mathematician. His work on integral equations laid the foundations of 20th-century functional analysis.

hill (hĭl) *n.* **1.** A well-defined, naturally elevated area of land smaller than a mountain. **2. hills. a.** A range or group of such elevations. **b.** *Informal.* Any remote rural area located in such elevated areas. **3.** A heap, pile, or mound, such as that formed by a living organism. Often used in combination: *anthill.* **4.** An incline, especially in a road; a slope. —**over the hill.** *Informal.* No longer young; past one's prime.
~*tr.v.* **hilled, hilling, hills.** **1.** To form into a hill, pile, or heap. **2.** To cover (a plant or plants) with a mound of soil. [Middle English *hill,* Old English *hyll.*] —**hill·er** *n.* —**hill·y** *adj.*

Hill (hĭl), **Archibald Vivian** (1886–1977). British physiologist and biochemist. He investigated heat production in muscles and nerves. In 1922 he shared the Nobel Prize in physiology and medicine with Otto Meyerhof.

Hil·la·ry (hĭl′ə-rē), **Sir Edmund Percival** (1919–). New Zealand mountaineer. Hillary and Tenzing Norgay became the first men to reach the summit of Mt. Everest in 1953.

hill·bil·ly (hĭl′bĭl′ē) *n., pl.* **-lies.** *Informal.* A person from the backwoods or a remote mountainous area.
~*adj.* Of or characteristic of the culture of such an area: *hillbilly music.* [HILL + *Billy,* a nickname for *William.*]

hill-fort (hĭl′fôrt′, -fōrt′) *n. Archaeology.* A fortified hilltop, showing traces of ramparts, ditches, and the like.

Hil·liard (hĭl′yərd), **Nicholas** (1537–1619). English miniature painter. He was appointed goldsmith, carver, and limner to Queen Elizabeth I.

hill myna *n.* A black songbird, *Gracula religiosa,* of India and the East Indies, that is kept as a cage bird for its ability to mimic human speech.

hill·ock (hĭl′ək) *n.* A small hill. [Middle English : HILL + -OCK.] —**hill·ock·y** *adj.*

hill·side (hĭl′sīd′) *n.* The side or slope of a hill.

hill station *n.* In India and various other Asian countries, a resort or settlement at a high altitude, frequented during the summer months because of its relatively cool climate.

hill·top (hĭl′tŏp′) *n.* The crest or top of a hill.

hilt (hĭlt) *n.* The handle of a weapon or tool, especially of a sword or dagger. —**to the hilt.** Completely.
~*tr.v.* **hilted, hilting, hilts.** To provide with a hilt. [Middle English *hilt,* Old English *hilt,* from Germanic *hilt-* (unattested).]

Hil·ton (hĭl′tən), **James** (1900–54). British novelist. He is best known for his books *Lost Horizon* (1933), set in the Tibetan lamasery of Shangri-La, and *Goodbye Mr. Chips* (1934), about an aging schoolmaster. Both were made into successful films.

hi·lum (hī′ləm) *n., pl.* **-la** (-lə). **1.** *Botany.* **a.** The scarlike mark on a seed, such as a bean, formed at the point where it was joined to the stalk connecting it to the placenta. **b.** The nucleus of a starch grain. **2.** *Anatomy.* Variant of **hilus.** [New Latin, from Latin *hīlum*†, trifle.]

hi·lus (hī′ləs) *n., pl.* **-li** (-lī′). Also **hi·lum** (hī′ləm), *pl.* **-la** (-lə). *Anatomy.* An indentation on the surface of an organ marking the point of entrance or exit of a blood vessel, nerve, or the like. [New Latin, from Latin, "a trifle."]

him (hĭm) *pron.* The objective case of the third person pronoun *he.* It is used: **1.** As the direct object of a verb: *They assisted him.* **2.** As the indirect object of a verb: *They offered him a lift.* **3.** As the object of a preposition: *This letter is addressed to him.* **4.** After *than* or *as* in comparisons in which the first term is in the objective case: *The judges praised her more than him.* **5.** *Informal.* In place of the reflexive pronoun *himself* as the indirect object of a verb: *He went to buy him a car.* **6.** In various elliptical, absolute, or interjectional phrases in which it is neither subject nor object: *Him and his sweet talk!* —See Usage note at **me.** [Middle English *him,* Old English *him.*]

H.I.M. His (or Her) Imperial Majesty.

Him·a·la·yas (hĭm'ə-lā'əz, hĭ-mäl'yəz). Also **Him·a·la·ya Mountains** (hĭm'ə-lā'ə, hĭ-mäl'yə). A mountain system of central Asia. The largest and highest chain in the world, it extends 2,415 kilometers (1,500 miles) across the northern Indian subcontinent from the Karakorum Range to the north-south section of the Brahmaputra River. Forming the southern edge of the central Asian plateau, it consists of a number of parallel ridges and is the source of the Indus, Ganges, and Brahmaputra river systems. Mt. Everest (8,848 meters; 29,028 feet), its highest peak, is the world's highest mountain. **—Him·a·la·yan** *adj.*

hi·mat·i·on (hĭ-măt'ē-ŏn') *n., pl.* **-ia** (-ē-ə). A long loose outer garment worn by men and women in ancient Greece. [Greek, diminutive of *hima* (stem *himat-*), garment, from *hennunai,* to clothe.]

Himm·ler (hĭm'lər), **Heinrich** (1900–45). German Nazi leader. In 1929 he was given command of the SS, the party's elite corps and Hitler's bodyguard. In 1936 he became head of the Third Reich's police forces and of the secret police, the Gestapo. He was also the commandant of the concentration and extermination camps. He was captured by British troops in May, 1945, and committed suicide by taking poison.

him·self (hĭm-sĕlf') *pron.* A specialized form of the third person singular masculine pronoun. It is used: **1.** As a reflexive pronoun, forming the direct or indirect object of a verb or the object of a preposition: *hurt himself; gives himself time; talks to himself.* **2.** For emphasis after *he*: *He himself wasn't certain.* **3.** As an emphasizing substitute: *In debt himself, he cannot help you. It was addressed to Kate and himself.* **4.** As an indication of his real, normal, or healthy condition or identity: *He hasn't been himself lately.* **5.** *Chiefly Irish & Scottish.* An important or prominent man, such as the head of a household. Sometimes used humorously. [Middle English *himself,* Old English *him selfum* : HIM + *selfum,* dative of *self,* SELF.]

Him·yar·ite (hĭm'yə-rīt') *n.* Also **Him·yar·it·ic** (hĭm'yə-rĭ-tĭk) (for sense 2). **1.** A member of an ancient people of southwestern Arabia. **2.** The Semitic language, closely related to Ethiopian, spoken by the ancient Himyarites.
~adj. Of, relating to, or characteristic of the Himyarites, their language, or their culture. [After *Himyar,* legendary ancient king in Yemen.] **—Him·yar·it·ic** *adj.*

Hi·na·ya·na (hē'nə-yä'nə) *n.* A branch of Buddhism, **Theravada** *(see).* Compare **Mahayana.** [Sanskrit *hīnayāna,* "lesser vehicle."] **—Hi·na·ya·nist** *n.* **—Hi·na·ya·nis·tic** (hē'nə-yə-nĭs'tĭk) *adj.*

Usage: Adherents of this school of Buddhism prefer the term *Theravada,* the term *Hinayana* having originally been a disparaging term coined by Mahayana Buddhists.

hind[1] (hīnd) *adj.* Also **hind·er** (hīn'dər). Located at or forming the back or rear; posterior: *hind legs.* [Middle English *hint,* perhaps from Old English *hinder,* behind, or *hindan,* from behind.]

hind[2] *n.* **1.** A female red deer. **2.** Any of several fishes of the genus *Epinephelus,* of Atlantic waters, related to and resembling the groupers. [Middle English *hinde,* Old English *hind.*]

hind[3] *n.* **1.** *Archaic British.* A peasant or farm laborer. **2.** *Archaic.* A rustic or country bumpkin. [Middle English, from Old English *hīwan.*]

hind·brain (hīnd'brān') *n.* The **rhombencephalon** *(see).*

Hin·de·mith (hĭn'də-mĭth, -mĭt), **Paul** (1895–1963). German violist and composer. He composed chamber music, instrumental works, and operas.

Hin·den·burg (hĭn'dən-bûrg'), **Paul Ludwig Hans Anton von** (1847–1934). German field marshal and politician, president of the Weimar Republic (1925–34). He appointed Hitler chancellor in January, 1933.

hin·der[1] (hĭn'dər) *v.* **-dered, -dering, -ders.** *—tr.* **1.** To hold back; be in the way of; hamper; delay. **2.** To obstruct or delay the progress of; prevent; stop. *—intr.* To be an obstacle or encumbrance. [Middle English *hindren,* Old English *hindrian,* from Germanic.] **—hin·der·er** *n.*

Synonyms: *balk, bar, block, dam, encumber, hamper, impede, obstruct, retard.*

hinder[2]. Variant of **hind** (rear).

hind·gut (hīnd'gŭt') *n.* **1.** The posterior portion of the colon in vertebrates. **2.** The posterior portion of the alimentary canal in arthropods. Compare **foregut.**

Hin·di (hĭn'dē) *n.* **1.** A group of vernacular Indic dialects spoken in northern India. **2.** A literary language based upon these dialects, now an official language and usually written in the Devanagari alphabet. **3.** A member of a cultural group of northern India speaking a Hindi dialect. [Hindi *Hindī,* from *Hind,* India, from Persian, from Old Persian *Hindu,* the river Indus. See **India.**] **—Hin·di** *adj.*

hind·most (hīnd'mōst') *adj.* Also **hind·er·most** (hīn'dər-). Farthest to the rear; most remote; last.

Hindostan. See **Hindustan.**

hind·quar·ter (hīnd'kwôr'tər) *n.* **1.** The posterior portion of a side of beef, lamb, or the like, including a hind leg and one or two ribs. **2.** *Usually* **hindquarters.** The posterior part of a quadruped, adjacent to the hind legs; the rump.

hin·drance (hĭn'drəns) *n.* **1.** The act of hindering. **2.** One that hinders; an impediment; an obstruction. —See Synonyms at **obstacle.** [Middle English *hind(e)raunce,* from *hindren,* to HINDER.]

hind·sight (hīnd'sīt') *n.* **1.** Perception or understanding of events after they have occurred. **2.** The rear sight of a firearm.

Hin·du (hĭn'dōō) *n.* Also *archaic* **Hin·doo. 1.** A believer in Hinduism. **2.** A native of India, especially northern India.
~adj. Also *archaic* **Hin·doo.** Of or pertaining to the Hindus or Hinduism. [Urdu, from Persian *Hindū,* from *Hind,* India. See **Hindi.**]

Hindu calendar *n.* The lunisolar calendar of the Hindus. The solar year is divided into 12 months in accordance with the successive entrances of the sun into the signs of the zodiac, the months varying in length from 29 to 32 days.

Hin·du·ism (hĭn'dōō-ĭz'əm) *n.* Also *archaic* **Hin·doo·ism.** A diverse body of religion, philosophy, and cultural practices native to and predominant in India, characterized broadly by beliefs in reincarnation and a supreme being of many forms and natures, by the view that opposing theories are aspects of one eternal truth, by a system of **caste** *(see),* and by the view that killing animals is wrong. See feature, next page.

Hindu Kush (kōōsh). Mountain range principally in northeastern Afghanistan. A western extension of the Himalayas, it extends 800 kilometers (500 miles) southwest from the Pamirs in the U.S.S.R. to include the Koh i Baba range in Afghanistan. The highest peak is Tirich Mir (7,692 meters; 25,236 feet) in Chitral, Pakistan.

Hin·du·stan (hĭn'dōō-stăn', -stän'). Also **Hin·do·stan** (-dō-). **1.** A historical region roughly occupying the part of the Indian subcontinent that lies to the north of the Deccan Plateau, characterized by the prevalence of Indic languages. **2.** The Indian subcontinent.

Hin·du·sta·ni (hĭn'dōō-stä'nē, -stăn'ē) *n.* **1.** A subdivision of the Indic branch of languages, including Urdu, Hindi, and other languages of northern India. **2.** A native of Hindustan.
~adj. Of or pertaining to Hindustani or Hindustan.

Hines (hīnz), **Earl Kenneth,** known as "Fatha" (1905–83). U.S. jazz musician. A leading jazz pianist for more than 50 years, he first gained national recognition through his recordings with Louis Armstrong in the 1920's. He organized and led several bands during the 1940's and continued to play until a week before his death.

hinge (hĭnj) *n.* **1.** A jointed or flexible device permitting turning or pivoting of a part, such as a door, lid, or flap, on a stationary frame. **2.** A structure or part similar to a hinge, especially: **a.** An anatomical joint between bones, such as the elbow. **b.** A joint that enables the valves of a bivalve mollusk to open and close. **3.** A small folded paper rectangle gummed on one side, used to fasten stamps, photographs, or the like in an album. **4.** A point, quality, or circumstance upon which subsequent situations or events depend.
~v. **hinged, hinging, hinges.** *—tr.* To attach by or equip with a hinge or hinges. *—intr.* **1.** To turn or hang, as on a hinge. **2.** To depend; be contingent. Usually used with *on* or *upon.* [Middle English *he(e)ng.*]

hin·ny[1] (hĭn'ē) *n., pl.* **-nies.** The hybrid offspring of a male horse and a female ass. Compare **mule.** [Latin *hinnus,* variant (influenced by *hinnīre,* to HINNY) of Greek *innos, ginnos*†.]

hinny[2] *intr.v.* **-nied, -nying, -nies.** *Rare.* To whinny; neigh. [Earlier *henny,* from Old French *hennir,* from Latin *hinnīre* (imitative).]

hint (hĭnt) *n.* **1.** A subtle suggestion or slight indication; an intimation. **2.** A statement or gesture conveying veiled information; a clue. **3.** A piece of useful advice, as on how to proceed with a task. **4.** A barely perceptible amount: *gin with a hint of vermouth.* **5.** *Obsolete.* An occasion; opportunity.
~v. **hinted, hinting, hints.** *—tr.* To make known by a hint; intimate. *—intr.* To give a hint or hints. Often used with *at*: *He hinted at the true purpose of his visit.* —See Synonyms at **suggest.** [Perhaps from obsolete *hent,* to grasp, seize, from Old English *hentan,* from Germanic.] **—hint·er** *n.*

hin·ter·land (hĭn'tər-lănd') *n.* **1.** The land lying inland from a coast. **2.** A region served by a port city and its facilities. **3.** A region remote from urban areas; back country. **4.** Any region, period, or situation that is remote or undefined. [German : *hinter,* behind, from Old High German *hintar* + *Land,* land.]

hip[1] (hĭp) *n.* **1.** The laterally projecting prominence of the pelvis or pelvic region from the waist to the thigh. **2.** The corresponding posterior part in quadrupeds. **3.** The hip joint. **4.** *Architecture.* The external angle formed by the meeting of two adjacent sloping sides of a roof. **—shoot from the hip.** *Slang.* To act or react impulsively and without proper thought. [Middle English *hip, hupe,* Old English *hype,* from Germanic.]

hip[2] *adj.* **hipper, hippest.** *Slang.* **1.** Aware of or in accordance with fashionable tastes and attitudes. **2.** Cognizant; aware. Used with *to*: *hip to the plan.* [Origin unknown.] **—hip·ness** *n.*

hip[3] *n.* The fleshy, berrylike fruit of a rose, consisting of an enlarged receptacle containing several small, hairy achenes. Also called "rosehip." [Middle English *hepe, hipe,* Old English *heope.*]

hip[4] *interj.* Used as a cheer or a signal for a cheer: *Hip, hip, hurrah!* [19th century : origin obscure.]

hip bath *n.* A **sitz bath** *(see).*

hip·bone (hĭp'bōn') *n.* The **innominate bone** *(see).*

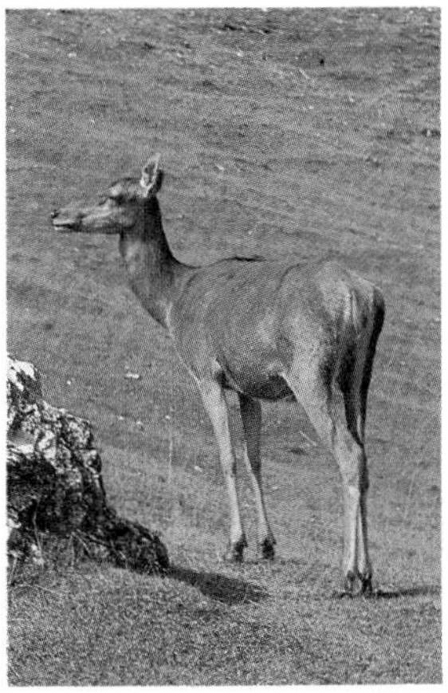

hind *An adult female red deer. This hind is a European red deer,* Cervus elaphus.

Hinduism

THE OLDEST FAITH ON EARTH

About 400 million people follow a religion that has no founder and no set creed

Alone among major world religions, Hinduism, the faith commanding the loyalty of 85 percent of India, has no one founder and no one authoritative scripture such as the Christian Bible or the Muslim Koran.

Instead, Hindu beliefs grew out of the fusion of two cultures when the Aryan people of central Asia settled in northern India in about 2000 B.C. among the original inhabitants of the subcontinent. The oldest surviving Hindu texts, the *Vedas*—which are largely a collection of Aryan hymns—date from about 1500 B.C., centuries before the rise of the other great world religions. Added later were scriptures such as the 4th-century B.C. epic poem the *Mahabharata* and the hundred-odd treatises on philosophic and mystical questions, such as the nature of reality and consciousness, known as the *Upanishads,* which were written after about 800 B.C.

At the heart of all these texts is the concept of reincarnation, the philosophical basis both for the Hindu emphasis on nonviolence and for the caste system that still pervades modern Indian society.

According to this concept, the souls of all living creatures are reborn in new bodies after death. Those who act virtuously in life are reborn in higher social castes; those whose actions (or karma) are evil return as lower-caste humans or even as animals. Release from this endless cycle of death and rebirth is possible only through arduous spiritual discipline. One such discipline—which is recommended in the *Bhagavad-gita* ("Song of the Lord"), contained in the epic *Mahabharata*—is the technique of physical control and meditation known as yoga (or union).

Hinduism's emphasis on respect for all life springs directly from this belief that every creature contains an immortal soul that is working out its own sacred destiny. It is for this reason that Hindus revere cows, for example, that many are vegetarian, and that Mahatma Gandhi's policy of nonviolent resistance to British rule in the 1930's and 1940's had such a powerful appeal. The Hindu sect of Jainism takes nonviolence still further; a Jain monk sweeps his path as he walks, so as not to harm even an insect.

The same belief in reincarnation also helps to explain the tenacious hold of the caste system, despite the banning by law of discrimination against the largest and lowest caste, the harijans, or untouchables. For the doctrine leads Hindus to believe that people are born into the caste they deserve as a result of their behavior in past lives.

Hinduism's 400 million adherents worship a total of more than 30 million gods and goddesses. But most of the great Hindu temples are now devoted to one of only two: the god of creation and destruction, Shiva; and a kindly god, Vishnu, who is believed to help men in times of special need.

BRAHMA *Once the supreme god in Hindu belief, Brahma has been replaced as a focus of worship since the 7th century A.D. by Shiva and Vishnu.*

SHIVA *An 11th-century bronze shows Shiva dancing in a ring of flames. The ring symbolizes the eternal cycle of creation, destruction, and rebirth.*

TEMPLE TO THE GODS *Every Hindu home has a shrine devoted to the family's favorite god, but major religious ceremonies usually take place in one of the temples. Many ceremonies attract thousands of pilgrims. Most Hindu temples have several covered shrines linked by open courtyards and decorated with elaborate and often painted carvings in wood, plaster, and stone. The enormous temple at Khajuraho (above), about 500 kilometers (300 miles) south of the Indian capital of New Delhi, has the tiered domes typical of Hindu architecture. It also contains a huge number of stone fertility sculptures of gods and humans making love.*

VISHNU *Like other Hindu gods, Vishnu has numerous incarnations, or avatars. In this 1870 print, Vishnu, who also appears as Rama and Krishna, is reclining on a serpent that represents eternity.*

hip-flask (hĭp′flăsk′, -fläsk′) *n.* A flask, usually containing liquor, designed to fit into a hip pocket.

hip girdle *n.* The **pelvic girdle** *(see).*

hip joint *n.* The ball-and-socket joint between the innominate bone of the pelvis and the femur.

hip-parch (hĭp′ärk′) *n.* An ancient Greek cavalry commander. [Greek *hipparkhos,* "horse leader" : *hippos,* horse + -ARCH.]

Hip-par-chus (hĭ-pär′kəs) (*fl.* 2nd century B.C.). Greek astronomer, the first of whom there is any record. Ptolemy constructed his geocentric view of the universe from observations made by Hipparchus, chiefly on Rhodes. His chart of the skies, in which 850 stars are placed, is the first known in history.

hip-pe-as-trum (hĭp′ē-ăs′trəm) *n.* Any plant of the South American genus *Hippeastrum,* some species of which are cultivated for their large, red, funnel-shaped flowers. [New Latin, from Greek *hippeus,* horseman (referring to the appearance of the leaves, which seem to ride one another) + *astron,* star (referring to shape of the flower).]

hipped¹ (hĭpt) *adj.* **1.** Having hips of a specified kind. Used in combination: *swivel-hipped; broad-hipped.* **2.** Having the hip dislocated. **3.** *Architecture.* Having a hip or hips. Said of a roof.

hipped² *adj.* Also **hip-pish** (hĭp′ĭsh). Melancholy; depressed. [Shortened variant of HYPOCHONDRIAC.]

hipped[3] *adj. Informal.* Obsessively absorbed. Used with *on*: *hipped on meditation.* [From HIP (aware).]

hip·pie, hip·py (hĭp′ē) *n., pl.* **-pies. 1.** A member of a loosely knit nonconformist movement of the 1960's and 1970's generally characterized by emphasis on nonviolence and universal love and a general rejection of the mores of conventional society, especially regarding dress, personal appearance, and living habits. **2.** Loosely, any young person who is exaggeratedly casual in dress, appearance, and behavior. [From HIP (aware).] **—hip·pie, hip·py** *adj.*

hip·po (hĭp′ō) *n., pl.* **-pos.** *Informal.* A hippopotamus.

hip·po·cam·pus (hĭp′ə-kăm′pəs) *n., pl.* **-pi** (-pī′, -pē′). **1.** *Anatomy.* Either of two ridges along each lateral ventricle of the brain that form part of the limbic system. **2.** *Greek & Roman Mythology.* A sea horse having the forelegs of a horse and the tail of a fish or dolphin. [Late Latin, from Greek *hippokampos* : *hippos,* horse + *kampos*†, sea monster.]

hip·po·cras (hĭp′ə-krăs′) *n.* A cordial made from wine and flavored with spices that was formerly used as a medicine. [Middle English *ypocras,* from Old French, from Medieval Latin *(vinum) Hippocraticum,* (wine) of Hippocrates (it was strained through a filter called Hippocrates' bag).]

Hip·poc·ra·tes (hĭ-pŏk′rə-tēz′) (*c.* 460–*c.* 370 B.C.). Greek physician, called the Father of Medicine. He played an important part in laying the foundations of scientific medicine and separating it from philosophical speculation and superstition. The Hippocratic oath, although it represented his ethical position, cannot be confidently attributed directly to him.

Hip·po·crat·ic oath (hĭp′ə-krăt′ĭk) *n.* An oath of ethical professional behavior taken by newly qualified doctors, attributed to Hippocrates.

Hip·po·crene (hĭp′ə-krēn′, hĭp′ə-krē′nē). *Greek Mythology.* A fountain on Mount Helicon, Greece, held sacred to the Muses and regarded as a source of poetic inspiration. [Latin *Hippocrēnē,* from Greek *Hippokrēnē* : *hippos,* horse (supposedly created by a stroke of Pegasus' hoof) + *krēnē*†, fountain.]

hip·po·drome (hĭp′ə-drōm′) *n.* **1.** An open-air stadium with an oval course for horse and chariot races in ancient Greece and Rome. **2.** An arena for horse and circus shows or similar entertainments. [Old French, from Latin *hippodromus,* from Greek *hippodromos* : *hippos,* horse + -DROME.]

hip·po·griff, hip·po·gryph (hĭp′ə-grĭf′) *n.* A mythological monster having the wings, claws, and head of a griffin and the body and hindquarters of a horse. [French *hippogriffe,* from Italian *ippogrifo* : *ippo-,* horse, from Latin *hippos,* from Greek + *grifo,* griffin, from Late Latin *grȳphus,* GRIFFIN.]

Hip·pol·y·ta (hĭ-pŏl′ə-tə). *Greek Mythology.* A queen of the Amazons, variously said to have been killed by Hercules in completion of one of his 12 labors or to have been conquered by him and given in marriage to Theseus of Athens.

Hip·pol·y·tus (hĭ-pŏl′ə-təs). *Greek Mythology.* A son of Theseus who spurned the advances of his stepmother, Phaedra, and was killed by Poseidon.

hip·po·pot·a·mus (hĭp′ə-pŏt′ə-məs) *n., pl.* **-muses** or **-mi** (-mī′). **1.** A large, chiefly aquatic African mammal, *Hippopotamus amphibius,* having dark, thick, almost hairless skin, short legs, and a broad, wide-mouthed muzzle. Also called "river horse." **2.** A similar but smaller animal, *Choeropsis liberiensis.* [Latin, from Late Greek *hippopotamos,* from Greek *hippos ho potamios,* "horse of the river" : *hippos,* horse + *potamos,* river.]

hip·py[1] (hĭp′ē) *adj.* **-pier, -piest.** Having broad or prominent hips. **—hip·pi·ness** *n.*

hippy[2]. Variant of **hippie.**

hip roof *n.* A roof having sloping edges and sides.

hip·ster[1] (hĭp′stər) *n. Slang.* One who is in touch with contemporary ideas and fashions, especially when unconventional. [HIP + -STER.]

hipster[2] *adj. Chiefly British.* Worn so as to hang from the hips and not the waist. Said especially of skirts, trousers, or slacks.

hip·sters (hĭp′stərz) *pl.n. Chiefly British.* Trousers or briefs whose waistline rests at hip level.

hi·ra·ga·na (hîr′ə-gä′nə) *n.* One of two sets of Japanese syllabaries of the kana system, having a cursive form. Also called "kana." See **katakana.** [Japanese, "flat kana."]

hir·cine (hûr′sīn′, -sĭn) *adj.* Of or characteristic of a goat, especially in having a strong odor or being lustful. [Latin *hircīnus,* from *hircus*†, he-goat.]

hire (hīr) *tr.v.* **hired, hiring, hires. 1.** To engage the services of (a person) for a fee; to employ. **2.** To arrange to use (a car, for example) on a temporary basis and for a fee; rent. **3.** To grant the services or allow the use of for remuneration; rent out. Often used with *out*: *I hire out my cottage for the summer. He hired himself out as a laborer.*

~n. **1.** Payment for services or the use of something. **2.** The act of hiring. **3.** The condition or fact of being hired. **—for hire.** Available for use or services in exchange for payment. [Middle English *hiren,* Old English *hȳr(i)an,* from Germanic (Low German area) *khūrjan* (unattested), from *khūrjō* (unattested), payment.] **—hir·a·ble, hire·a·ble** *adj.* **—hir·er** *n.*

hire·ling (hīr′lĭng) *n.* One who offers his services solely for payment; especially, a person willing to perform odious or offensive tasks for a fee; a mercenary.

hire-pur·chase (hīr′pûr′chĭs) *n. Abbr.* **H.P.** *British.* The **installment plan** *(see).*

Hi·ro·hi·to (hîr′ō-hē′tō) (1901–). Emperor of Japan (1926–). He has little political power, but in 1945 he influenced the Japanese government to accept unconditional surrender. In 1946 he renounced his divine status.

Hi·ro·shi·ge (hîr′ō-shē′gä′), **Ando** (1797–1858). Japanese artist. A master of color wood-block printing, he captured the serenity of the Japanese landscape with his idealistic, superbly composed works, including *Fifty-three Stages on the Tokaido* (1832).

Hi·ro·shi·ma (hîr′ə-shē′mə, hĭ-rō′shĭ-). A city in southern Japan, on the coast of Honshu. On August 6, 1945, it was almost entirely destroyed by an atomic bomb, the first city to become such a target. It has since been rebuilt as an industrial center and seaport, manufacturing textiles, rubber goods, and machinery.

hir·sute (hûr′so͞ot′, hîr′-, hər-so͞ot′) *adj.* **1.** Covered or coated with hair; hairy. **2.** Of, pertaining to, or consisting of hair. **3.** *Botany.* Covered with long, soft hairs: *hirsute stems.* [Latin *hirsūtus.*] **—hir·sute·ness** *n.*

hir·u·din (hîr-o͞od′n, hîr′ə-dən, -yə-dən) *n.* A substance extracted from the salivary glands of leeches and used as an anticoagulant. [Latin *hirudo, hirudin-,* a leech.]

hi·run·dine (hĭ-rŭn′dĭn, -dīn′) *adj.* Of, pertaining to, or characteristic of a swallow or the swallow family, Hirundinidae. [Latin *hirundo*†, a swallow + -INE.]

his (hĭz). The possessive form of the pronoun *he.* Used to indicate possession, agency, or reception of an action by the masculine being or person spoken of or an unspecified person considered to be male: **1.** Used attributively: *his wallet; pursuing his tasks; suffered his first rebuff. Each child should be accompanied by his mother.* **2.** Used absolutely: **a.** As a predicate adjective: *The black boots are his.* **b.** As a substantive: *If you can't find your hat, take his.* **—of his.** Belonging or pertaining to him: *a friend of his.* [Middle English *his,* Old English *his.*]

His·pan·ic (hĭ-spăn′ĭk) *adj.* **1.** Of, pertaining to, or characteristic of the language, people, and culture of Spain or Spain and Portugal. **2.** Of or pertaining to Latin America.

~n. A Latin American, especially one who has emigrated to the United States. [Latin *Hispānicus,* from *Hispānia,* SPAIN.]

his·pan·i·cist (hĭ-spăn′ə-sĭst) *n.* A student of or specialist in the language, culture, or literature of Spain.

his·pan·i·cize (hĭ-spăn′ə-sīz′) *tr.v.* **-cized, -cizing, -cizes.** To give a Spanish character to.

His·pan·io·la (hĭs′pən-yō′lə). Second-largest island of the West Indies. Lying between Cuba and Puerto Rico, it is divided into French-speaking Haiti to the west and the Spanish-speaking Dominican Republic to the east.

Hispano- *prefix.* Indicates: **1.** Spanish; for example, **Hispano-Arabian. 2.** Latin-American; for example, **Hispano-American.** [From Latin *Hispānus,* Spanish.]

his·pid (hĭs′pĭd) *adj.* Covered with stiff or rough hairs; bristly: *hispid stems.* [Latin *hispidus.*]

hiss (hĭs) *n.* **1.** A sharp, sibilant sound similar to a sustained *s,* such as that produced by breathing out through closed teeth or by gas escaping through a small gap. **2.** An expression of disapproval, contempt, or dissatisfaction conveyed by a hiss. **3.** Continuous unwanted noise, as from a loudspeaker.

~v. **hissed, hissing, hisses.** *—intr.* To make a hiss, especially as an expression of disapproval. *—tr.* **1.** To utter (words or sounds) with a hissing sound. **2.** To express disapproval, derision, or hatred for by hissing. [Middle English *hissen* (imitative).] **—hiss·er** *n.*

Hiss (hĭs), **Alger** (1904–). U.S. public official. Charged with espionage at the height of the Communist scare, he was convicted of perjury (1950) and served a four-year jail sentence while maintaining his innocence. His conviction remains a point of emotional debate and controversy.

hist (hĭst) *interj.* Used to attract attention, enjoin silence, or the like.

hist. 1. histology. **2.** historian; historical; history.

his·tam·i·nase (hĭ-stăm′ə-nās′, -naz′, hĭs′tə-mə-) *n.* An enzyme that occurs in the digestive system and is responsible for the inactivation of histamine. [HISTAMIN(E) + -ASE.]

his·ta·mine (hĭs′tə-mēn′, -mĭn) *n.* A white crystalline compound, $C_5H_9N_3$, found in plant and animal tissue, formed from histidine by the action of putrefactive bacteria. It stimulates gastric secretion, contracts smooth muscle, and is released during allergic reactions. [HIST(O)- + -AMINE.] **—his·ta·min·ic** (hĭs′tə-mĭn′ĭk) *adj.*

his·ti·dine (hĭs′tə-dēn′, -dĭn) *n.* A colorless crystalline amino acid, $C_6H_9N_3O_2$, used as a feed additive and dietary supplement. [HIST(O)- + -ID(E) + -INE.]

his·ti·o·cyte (hĭs′tē-ə-sīt′) *n.* A **macrophage** *(see)* found in connective tissue. [Greek *histion,* diminutive of *histos,* web + -CYTE.]

histo-, hist- *prefix.* Indicates bodily tissue; for example, **histamine, histolysis.** [Greek *histos,* web, beam, mast.]

his·to·chem·is·try (hĭs′tō-kĕm′ĭ-strē) *n.* The chemistry of cells and tissues. **—his·to·chem·i·cal** *adj.*

his·to·com·pat·i·bil·i·ty (hĭs′tō-kəm-păt′ə-bĭl′ə-tē) *n.* Compatibility between the various components of tissues, especially components of cell membranes, required for survival of tissue or organ transplants.

his·to·gen (hĭs′tə-jən′) *n.* Any of the parts of a plant that give rise to the epidermis, cortex, and vascular tissue. [HISTO- + -GEN.]

his·to·gen·e·sis (hĭs′tō-jĕn′ə-sĭs) *n.* The formation and development of bodily tissues. [New Latin : HISTO- + -GENESIS.] **—his·to·ge·net·ic** (hĭs′tō-jə-nĕt′ĭk), **his·to·gen·ic** (-jĕn′ĭk) *adj.* **—his·to·ge·net·i·cal·ly, his·to·gen·i·cal·ly** *adv.*

his·to·gram (hĭs′tə-grăm′) *n. Statistics.* A graphic representation of

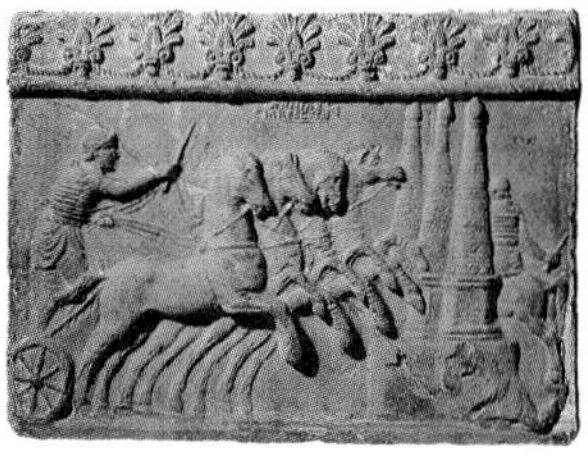

hippodrome *A chariot race taking place in a hippodrome. The Roman relief is probably first century* A.D.

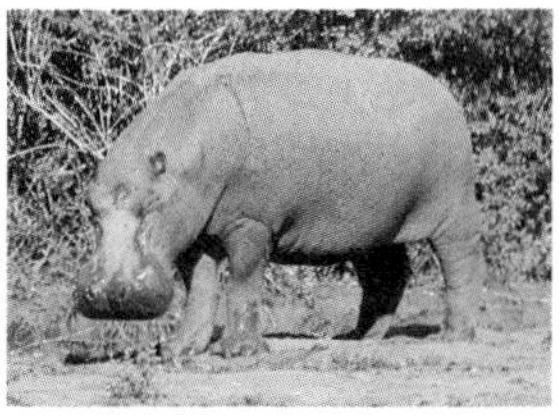

hippopotamus *Despite its massive weight—more than three tons—and short legs, a hippo can run faster than a man. Its favorite habitat, however, is water, where it lies partly submerged with only its eyes, ears, and nostrils projecting above the surface.*

PRONUNCIATION KEY

ă, pat; ā, pay; âr, care;
ä, father, are; b, bib;
ch, church; d, deed; ĕ, pet;
ē, be; f, fife; g, gag; h, hat;
hw, which; ĭ, pit; ī, pie;
îr, pier; j, judge; k, kick;
l, lid, needle; m, mum;
n, no, sudden; ng, thing;
ŏ, pot; ō, toe; ô, paw, for;
oi, noise; ou, out; o͝o, book;
o͞o, boot; p, pop; r, roar;
s, sauce; sh, ship, dish;
t, tight; th, thin, path;
th, this, bathe; ŭ, cut; ûr, fur;
v, valve; w, with; y, yes;
z, zebra, size; zh, vision;
ə, about, item, edible,
gallop, circus, peaceful

IN FOREIGN WORDS:

à, *Fr.* ami; œ, *Fr.* feu, *Ger.* schön; ü, *Fr.* tu, *Ger.* über; KH, *Ger.* ich, *Scot.* loch; N, *Fr.* bon; y′, *Fr.* Compiègne

STRESS MARKS:

Primary stress: ′
in·cite′ (ĭn-sīt′)
Secondary stress: ′
in′sight′ (ĭn′sīt′)

a frequency distribution in which the widths of contiguous vertical bars are proportional to the class widths of the variable and the heights of the bars are proportional to the class frequencies. [Greek *histos*, beam, mast + -GRAM.]

his·toid (hĭs'toid') *adj.* **1.** Resembling normal tissue. Said of some tumors. **2.** Consisting of one particular kind of tissue. [HISTO(O)- + -OID.]

his·tol·o·gy (hĭ-stŏl'ə-jē) *n. Abbr.* **hist. 1.** The anatomical study of the microscopic structure of animal and plant tissues. **2.** The microscopic structure of tissue. [French *histologie* : HISTO- + -LOGY.] **—his·to·log·i·cal** (hĭs'tə-lŏj'ĭ-kəl) *adj.* **—his·to·log·i·cal·ly** *adv.* **—his·tol·o·gist** *n.*

his·tol·y·sis (hĭ-stŏl'ə-sĭs) *n.* The breakdown and disintegration of organic tissue. [New Latin : HISTO- + -LYSIS.] **—his·to·lyt·ic** (hĭs'tə-lĭt'ĭk) *adj.* **—his·to·lyt·i·cal·ly** *adv.*

his·tone (hĭs'tōn') *n.* Any of several simple, water-soluble proteins, found especially in cell nuclei associated with nucleic acids, that can release on hydrolysis a high proportion of basic amino acids. [HIST(O)- + -ONE.]

his·to·pa·thol·o·gy (hĭs'tō-pə-thŏl'ə-jē) *n.* The histology of diseased tissue. **—his·to·path·o·log·i·cal** (hĭs'tō-păth'ə-lŏj'ĭ-kəl) *adj.*

his·to·phys·i·ol·o·gy (hĭs'tō-fĭz'ē-ŏl'ə-jē) *n.* The physiology of the microscopic functioning of bodily tissues. **—his·to·phys·i·o·log·i·cal** (hĭs'tō-fĭz'ē-ə-lŏj'ĭ-kəl) *adj.*

his·to·plas·mo·sis (hĭs'tō-plăz-mō'sĭs) *n.* A disease affecting the lungs that is caused by inhalation of spores of the fungus *Histoplasma capsulatum.*

his·to·ri·an (hĭ-stôr'ē-ən, hĭ-stōr'-) *n. Abbr.* **hist.** A writer or student of history; especially, one who is an authority on history.

his·to·ri·at·ed (hĭ-stôr'ē-ā'tĭd, hĭ-stōr'-) *adj.* Decorated with artistic designs: *a historiated initial.* [Medieval Latin *historiāre* (past participle *historiātus*), to tell a story in pictures, from *historia,* HISTORY.]

his·tor·ic (hĭ-stôr'ĭk, hĭ-stŏr'-) *adj.* **1. a.** Having importance in or influence on history; renowned. **b.** Likely to become important in history; having considerable contemporary significance: *a historic meeting.* **2. a.** Historical. **b.** Associated with events in history: *historic cities.* **3.** Of or designating tenses of verbs, especially in Latin or Greek, that refer to past time.

Usage: *Historic* and *historical* are differentiated in usage, although their senses overlap. *Historic* refers to what is important in history: *the historic first voyage to outer space.* It is also used of what is famous or interesting because of its association with persons or events in history: *a historic house. Historical* refers to whatever existed in the past, whether regarded as important or not: *a historical character.* Events are *historical* if they happened, *historic* only if they are regarded as important. *Historical* refers also to anything concerned with history or the study of the past: *a historical novel; historical discoveries.* The differentiation between the words is not complete. They are often used interchangeably: *historic times* or *historical times.*

his·tor·i·cal (hĭ-stôr'ĭ-kəl, hĭ-stŏr'-) *adj. Abbr.* **hist. 1.** Of, relating to, or of the nature of history as opposed to fiction or legend. **2. a.** Based on or concerned with events in history: *a historical novel.* **b.** Caused by events in history. **3.** Having considerable importance or influence in history; historic. **4.** *Linguistics.* **Diachronic** *(see).* —See Usage note at **historic. —his·tor·i·cal·ly** *adv.* **—his·tor·i·cal·ness** *n.*

historical geology *n.* The geologic study of the earth and its atmosphere from the time of its formation to the present day.

historical linguistics *pl.n.* The study of language development, especially that of a single variety, with emphasis on chronological change. Compare **comparative linguistics.**

historical materialism *n.* The Marxist theory, part of **dialectical materialism** *(see),* that states that society arises fundamentally from an economic base, and that it is characterized by a conflict of classes that will eventually result in a classless society.

historical method *n.* A method of analysis or exposition whereby a subject is considered in its origin and subsequent historical development.

historical present *n.* The present tense used as a literary device in the narration of events set in the past.

historical school *n.* A school of theorists, as in law or economics, stressing the influence of historical conditions.

his·tor·i·cism (hĭ-stôr'ə-sĭz'əm, hĭ-stŏr'-) *n.* **1.** The belief that inevitable processes are at work in history. **2.** The relativistic theory that all social and cultural phenomena are historically determined and that particular past events, cultures, or the like should be judged only in relation to other periods of history rather than in relation to one's own values. **3.** Veneration of the past or of tradition. **—his·tor·i·cist** *adj. & n.*

his·to·ric·i·ty (hĭs'tə-rĭs'ə-tē) *n.* Historical authenticity.

his·to·ri·og·ra·pher (hĭ-stôr'ē-ŏg'rə-fər, hĭ-stōr'-) *n.* **1.** One trained in or practicing historiography. **2.** A historian; especially, one officially appointed by a group or public institution.

his·to·ri·og·ra·phy (hĭ-stôr'ē-ŏg'rə-fē, hĭ-stōr'-) *n.* **1.** The principles or methodology of historical study. **2.** The writing of history. **3.** Historical literature. [Old French *historiographie,* from Greek *historiographia* : HISTORY + -GRAPHY.]

his·to·ry (hĭs'tə-rē) *n., pl.* **-ries. 1.** *Abbr.* **hist.** The branch of knowledge that records and analyzes past events. Sometimes used adjectivally: *a history book.* **2.** A chronological record of events, as of the life or development of a people, country, or institution. **3.** *Abbr.* **hist.** A narrative of events; a story; a chronicle. **4.** The events forming the subject matter of history. **5.** An interesting past: *a house with a history.* **6.** That which is not of current concern: *My youth is now history.* **7.** A drama based on historical events. **8. a.** A study or record of what has happened to a person or thing, especially from a particular point of view: *a patient's medical history.* **b.** A past or record marked by a particular characteristic: *has a history of violence.* **—make history.** To be of historic importance, especially by being the first of one's kind. [Latin *historia,* from Greek, inquiry, observation, from *histōr,* learned man.]

his·tri·on·ic (hĭs'trē-ŏn'ĭk) *adj.* Also **his·tri·on·i·cal** (-ĭ-kəl). **1.** Overemotional or dramatic; theatrical; affected. **2.** Of or pertaining to actors or acting. [Late Latin *histriōnicus,* theatrical, from *histriō*†, actor.] **—his·tri·on·i·cal·ly** *adv.*

his·tri·on·ics (hĭs'trē-ŏn'ĭks) *n.* **1.** *Used with a singular verb.* Theatrical arts. **2.** *Used with a plural verb.* Exaggerated emotional behavior calculated for effect.

hit (hĭt) *v.* **hit, hitting, hits.** *—tr.* **1.** To come in contact with forcefully; strike. **2.** To cause to make sudden and forceful contact; knock; bump: *hit her hand against the wall.* **3.** To deal a blow to. **4.** To strike with a missile: *He fired and hit the target.* **5.** To reach and affect adversely: *hit hard by the recession.* **6.** To come upon; arrive at; reach: *hit an all-time low.* **7.** To accord with; appeal to; suit: *The idea hit his fancy.* **8.** To propel with a blow. **9. a.** To make (a shot or stroke) when striking a ball in a game: *hit a volley.* **b.** *Baseball.* To succeed in getting (a base hit): *hit a triple.* **10.** *Informal.* To set out on or toward: *hit the road.* **11.** *Informal.* To resort to excessively: *hit the bottle.* **12.** *Informal.* To request or obtain money from: *The vagrant hit me for a dime. —intr.* **1. a.** To strike or deal a blow. Often used with *out.* **b.** *Informal.* To criticize or condemn. Used with *at* or *out at.* **2.** To come in contact; bump. **3.** To achieve or find something desired or sought, often by chance. Used with *on* or *upon.* **—hit it off.** *Informal.* To get along well together. **—hit the hay** (or **sack**). *Slang.* To go to bed. **—hit the nail on the head.** To be absolutely right. **—hit the roof** (or **ceiling**). To express anger, especially vehemently. **—hit the spot.** To give total satisfaction, as food or drink.

~n. **1.** A collision or impact. **2.** A successfully executed shot, blow, thrust, or throw. **3.** A show, song, performer, or the like that has popular success. Also used adjectivally: *a hit musical.* **4.** A bit of luck. **5.** An apt or effective jest, remark, or witticism. **6.** *Abbr.* **h, h.** *Baseball.* A base hit. **7.** *Slang.* **a.** A killing by a hit man. **b.** The target of such a killing. **8.** *Slang.* A dose of a narcotic drug. [Hit (infinitive, past tense, and past participle); Middle English *hitten, hitte, hit,* from Old Norse *hitta*†, to hit.] **—hit·ter** *n.*

hit-and-run (hĭt'n-rŭn') *adj.* **1.** Designating or involving the driver of a motor vehicle who after striking a pedestrian or another vehicle fails to stop. **2.** *Baseball.* Of or designating a play in which a man on base runs on the pitch and the batter attempts to hit the ball.

hitch (hĭch) *v.* **hitched, hitching, hitches.** *—tr.* **1.** To fasten or catch temporarily with a loop, hook, or noose; tie. **2.** To connect or attach, as to a vehicle. Often used with *up.* **3.** To move with jerks: *hitched his chair closer.* **4.** To raise by pulling or jerking. Often used with *up: hitch up one's trousers.* **5.** *Informal.* To obtain (a lift) by hitchhiking. **6.** *Slang.* To unite in marriage. Used chiefly in the phrase *get hitched. —intr.* **1.** To become entangled, snarled, or fastened. **2.** *Informal.* To hitchhike. **3.** To move haltingly, as with a limp. **4.** *Slang.* To become united in marriage.

~n. **1.** Any of various knots used for attaching a rope to a fixed object, such as a **harness hitch** or **half hitch** *(both of which see).* **2.** A short jerking motion; a tug. **3.** A hobble or limp. **4.** An impediment or delay: *a hitch in our plans for the party.* **5.** *Informal.* A lift obtained by hitchhiking. **6.** A term of service, especially of military service. [Middle English *hytchen*†.]

Hitch·cock (hĭch'kŏk'), **Alfred Joseph** (1899–1980). U.S. film director, born in London. He became a master of suspense. His first important film was *The 39 Steps* (1935). Other successes include *The Lady Vanishes* (1938), *Psycho* (1960), and *Family Plot* (1976).

hitch·hike (hĭch'hīk') *v.* **-hiked, -hiking, -hikes.** *—intr.* To travel by soliciting free lifts along a road. *—tr.* To solicit or get (a free lift) along a road. **—hitch·hik·er** *n.*

hitching post *n.* A post for temporarily tying up a horse or other animal.

hith·er (hĭth'ər) *adv.* To or toward this place: *Come hither.*

~adj. Located toward this side; nearer. [Middle English *hither,* Old English *hider.*]

hither and thither *adv.* Toward one place and then another as if in a state of turmoil; in all directions. Also "hither and yon."

hith·er·to (hĭth'ər-to͞o') *adv.* **1.** Until this time; up to now. **2.** *Archaic.* To this place; thus far.

hith·er·ward (hĭth'ər-wərd) *adv.* Also **hith·er·wards** (-wərdz). Hither.

Hit·ler (hĭt'lər), **Adolf** (1889–1945). Austrian-born founder of the German Nazi Party and chancellor of the Third Reich (1933–45). Hitler served in the German army in World War I. He joined the German Workers' Party and by 1921 had gained the leadership of it, renaming it the National Socialist German Workers' Party. Hitler was arrested after the "beer hall putsch" in Munich in 1923 and spent some months in prison, where he wrote the major part of *Mein Kampf.* By 1930 he had built the Nazi Party into the second-largest party in Germany. He lost the 1932 presidential election to Hindenburg, but a few months later the Nazis won most seats at a general election, and in January 1933 Hitler was appointed chancellor, bringing every German institution under the totalitarian con-

PRONUNCIATION KEY

ă, pat; ā, pay; âr, care;
ä, father, are; b, bib;
ch, church; d, deed; ĕ, pet;
ē, be; f, fife; g, gag; h, hat;
hw, which; ĭ, pit; ī, pie;
îr, pier; j, judge; k, kick;
l, lid, needle; m, mum;
n, no, sudden; ng, thing;
ŏ, pot; ō, toe; ô, paw, for;
oi, noise; ou, out; o͝o, book;
o͞o, boot; p, pop; r, roar;
s, sauce; sh, ship, dish;
t, tight; th, thin, path;
th, this, bathe; ŭ, cut; ûr, fur;
v, valve; w, with; y, yes;
z, zebra, size; zh, vision;
ə, about, item, edible,
gallop, circus, peaceful

IN FOREIGN WORDS:

à, *Fr.* ami; œ, *Fr.* feu, *Ger.* schön; ü, *Fr.* tu, *Ger.* über; KH, *Ger.* ich, *Scot.* loch; N, *Fr.* bon; y', *Fr.* Compiègne

STRESS MARKS:

Primary stress: '
in·cite' (ĭn-sīt')
Secondary stress: '
in'sight' (ĭn'sīt')

trol of the Nazi Party. In September 1939 Hitler's troops invaded Poland, causing the outbreak of World War II. By the spring of 1945 Germany faced defeat. On April 29 Hitler married his mistress, Eva Braun, and the next day they committed suicide.

hit list *n. Slang.* **1.** A list of potential murder victims as drawn up by a crime syndicate. **2.** A list of people or organizations against which some punitive action is to be taken. **3.** A list of projects, enterprises, or the like, from which support is to be withdrawn.

hit man *n. Slang.* One employed to commit murder; a hired assassin.

hit parade *n.* A list of the best-selling recorded songs over a given period.

hit-or-miss (hǐt′ər-mǐs′) *adj.* Random; haphazard; only occasionally effective.

Hit·tite (hǐt′īt′) *n.* **1.** A member of an ancient people living in Asia Minor and northern Syria about 2000–1200 B.C. **2.** An extinct Indo-European language spoken by these people. [Hebrew *Ḥittī,* from Hittite *Ḥatti.*] —**Hit·tite** *adj.*

hive (hīv) *n.* **1.** A natural or artificial structure for housing bees, especially honeybees. **2.** A colony of bees living in a hive. **3.** A place swarming with active people.
~*v.* **hived, hiving, hives.** —*tr.* **1.** To collect (bees) into a hive. **2.** To store (honey) in a hive. **3.** To store up; accumulate. Used with *up* or *away.* —*intr.* **1.** To enter a hive. **2.** To live together in close association. —**hive off. 1.** To leave in a large group, like bees forming a new hive. **2.** To assign or transfer (work or responsibilities, for example) elsewhere. **3.** *Chiefly British.* To dispose of (part of a nationalized company, for example) on the open market. [Middle English *hive,* Old English *hȳf.*]

hives (hīvz) *pl.n. Pathology.* Urticaria *(see).* [Origin unknown.]

H.J. hic jacet.

hl hectoliter.

H.L. House of Lords.

hm hectometer.

H.M. 1. headmaster. **2.** headmistress. **3.** His (or Her) Majesty.

H.M.S. 1. His (or Her) Majesty's Service. **2.** Her (or His) Majesty's Ship.

ho (hō) *interj.* Used to express surprise or joy, to attract attention to something sighted, or to urge onward: *Land ho! Westward ho!* [Middle English, partly from Old Norse *hō!* and partly from Old French *ho!,* halt!]

Ho The symbol for the element holmium.

HO, H.O. 1. Head Office. **2.** *British.* Home Office.

ho. house.

hoactzin. Variant of **hoatzin.**

hoa·gie (hō′gē) *n.* See **hero** (sense 5).

hoar (hôr, hōr) *adj.* Hoary.
~*n.* **1.** Hoariness. **2.** Hoarfrost. [Middle English *ho(o)r,* Old English *hār.*]

hoard (hôrd, hōrd) *n.* **1.** A hidden or stored fund or supply guarded for future use. **2.** A cache, as of ancient coins or jewels; a treasure. **3.** An accumulated store, as of facts or ideas.
~*v.* **hoarded, hoarding, hoards.** —*intr.* **1.** To gather or accumulate a hoard. **2.** To buy an unnecessarily large stock of, as of groceries, as a precaution against shortages. —*tr.* **1.** To accumulate or gather by saving or hiding. **2.** To keep an unnecessarily large stock of (goods) as a precaution against shortages. [Middle English *hord,* Old English *hord.*]

hoard·er (hôr′dər, hōr′-) *n.* One that hoards; especially, a person who never throws anything away.

hoard·ing (hôr′dĭng, hōr′-) *n. British.* **1.** A temporary wooden fence around a building or structure under construction or repair. **2.** A **billboard** *(see).* [Earlier *hoard,* a fence, from earlier *hourd,* from Norman French *hurdis,* from Old French *hourd,* scaffold, from Germanic.]

hoar·frost (hôr′frôst′, -frŏst′, hōr′-) *n.* Frozen dew that forms a white coating on a surface. Also called "hoar," "white frost."

hoarhound. Variant of **horehound.**

hoarse (hôrs, hōrs) *adj.* **hoarser, hoarsest. 1.** Low and grating in sound; husky; croaking. **2.** Having a husky, grating voice, often as a result of shouting or illness. [Middle English *hors,* from Old Norse *hārs* (unattested), variant of *hās,* from Germanic *hai(r)sa-* (unattested).] —**hoarse·ly** *adv.* —**hoarse·ness** *n.*

hoars·en (hôr′sən, hōr′-) *v.* **-ened, -ening, -ens.** —*tr.* To cause to be hoarse. —*intr.* To become hoarse.

hoar·y (hôr′ē, hōr′ē) *adj.* **-ier, -iest. 1.** Gray or white with or as if with age. **2.** Covered with grayish hair or down: *hoary leaves.* **3.** Very old; ancient. —**hoar·i·ness** *n.*

hoary cress *n.* A white-flowered perennial plant, *Cardaria* (or *Lepidium) draba,* native to the Mediterranean but widespread as a weed.

ho·at·zin (hō-ät′sĭn, wät-sēn′) *n.* Also **ho·act·zin** (hō-äkt′sĭn, wäkt′-sēn′). A brownish, crested bird, *Opisthocomus hoazin,* of tropical South America, having claws on the wings in the young. [American Spanish, from Nahuatl *uatzin,* pheasant.]

hoax (hōks) *n.* An act intended to deceive or trick, either as a practical joke or as a serious fraud.
~*tr.v.* **hoaxed, hoaxing, hoaxes.** To deceive or trick with a hoax. [Perhaps shortened variant of HOCUS.] —**hoax·er** *n.*

hob¹ (hŏb) *n.* **1.** A shelf or projection at the back or side of the inside of a fireplace, for holding things to be kept warm. **2.** A rotating tool used for cutting machine parts, such as gear teeth. [16th century : perhaps a variant of HUB (in the sense projection, lump).]

hob² *n.* A hobgoblin, sprite, or elf. —**play** (or **raise) hob.** To make mischief or trouble. Often used with *with.* [Middle English *hob,* from *Hobbe,* a nickname for *Robert* or *Robin.*]

Ho·ba meteorite (hō′bə) *n.* The world's largest meteorite (weighing 66 tons) discovered in 1920 near Grootfontein, Namibia. [From *Hoba West* farm, site of discovery.]

Ho·ban (hō′bən), **James** (*c.* 1762–1831). U.S. architect, born in Ireland. In 1792 he won a competition for the design of "the President's House" (today the White House), which he built from 1792 to 1799 and rebuilt after it was burned by the British in 1814. He was also one of the supervising architects for the U.S. Capitol.

Ho·bart (hō′bärt′). Capital and chief seaport of Tasmania, Australia. Built on a bight approximately 19 kilometers (12 miles) from the sea, it has an excellent natural harbor. Included among its exports are agricultural produce, timber, and wool. Its principal industries are zinc refining, flour milling, and chemicals.

Hobbes (hŏbz), **Thomas** (1588–1679). English political philosopher. He wrote *Leviathan* (1651), outlining his philosophy that individuals are essentially selfish.

Hobb·ism (hŏb′ĭz′əm) *n.* A theory promulgated by Thomas Hobbes, advocating powerful, especially monarchical government as the only means of adequately controlling the problems created by competing individual needs and interests.

hob·bit (hŏb′ĭt) *n.* Any of a race of fictional creatures, half the size of human beings. [After the characters in J.R.R. Tolkien's *The Hobbit* (1937) and *The Lord of the Rings* (1954–55).]

hob·ble (hŏb′əl) *v.* **-bled, -bling, -bles.** Also **hop·ple** (hŏp′əl), **-pled, -pling, -ples.** —*intr.* **1.** To walk or move awkwardly or with difficulty; limp. **2.** To proceed haltingly or unsteadily. —*tr.* **1.** To put a hobble on (an animal or its legs). **2.** To cause to limp. **3.** To hamper the action or progress of; restrain; impede.
~*n.* Also **hop·ple. 1.** An awkward, clumsy, or irregular walk or gait. **2.** A device, such as a rope or strap, used to tie the legs of an animal together in order to restrict its movement. **3.** *Archaic.* An unfortunate or awkward situation. [Middle English *hoblen,* of Low German origin, akin to Middle Dutch *hobbelen†,* to roll.]

hob·ble·bush (hŏb′əl-bŏosh′) *n.* A shrub, *Viburnum alnifolium,* of northeastern North America, having flat clusters of white flowers with the marginal flowers larger than the others. [From HOBBLE, because of the hindrance caused by its drooping branches.]

hob·ble·de·hoy (hŏb′əl-dē-hoi′) *n., pl.* **-hoys.** A gawky adolescent boy or girl. [16th century : origin obscure.]

hobble skirt *n.* A type of long skirt, popular between 1910 and 1914, that was so narrow below the knees that it restricted normal stride.

hob·by¹ (hŏb′ē) *n., pl.* **-bies. 1.** An occupation, activity, or interest, such as stamp collecting or gardening, engaged in primarily for pleasure; a pastime. **2.** *Regional.* A little horse; a nag. **3.** A hobbyhorse. **4.** An early kind of velocipede without pedals. [Middle English *hoby,* a hobbyhorse, something one pursues, perhaps from *Hobbin,* nickname for *Robin.*] —**hob·by·ist** *n.*

hobby² *n., pl.* **-bies.** Any of several small falcons of the genus *Falco;* especially, an Old World species, *F. subbuteo,* formerly used for hawking. [Middle English *hoby,* from Old French *hobé, hobet,* diminutive of *hobe†,* a small bird of prey.]

hob·by·horse (hŏb′ē-hôrs′) *n.* **1.** A child's toy consisting of a long stick with an imitation horse's head on one end. **2.** A rocking horse. **3. a.** A figure of a horse worn around the waist of a mummer or other performer pretending to ride a horse. **b.** A person wearing such a costume. **4.** An early form of bicycle; velocipede. **5.** A pet topic or idea about which one constantly talks; a subject that obsesses one.

hob·gob·lin (hŏb′gŏb′lĭn) *n.* **1.** A goblin variously represented as being mischievous or as ugly and evil. **2.** A bugbear. [HOB (elf) + GOBLIN.]

hob·nail (hŏb′nāl′) *n.* A short nail with a thick head used to protect the soles of shoes or boots. [HOB (projection, archaic sense peg) + NAIL.]

hob·nob (hŏb′nŏb′) *intr.v.* **-nobbed, -nobbing, -nobs.** To associate familiarly; socialize. Used with *with: He hobnobs with the rich.* [Originally *hob or nob,* (drink) to one another, from earlier *hab or nab,* hit or miss : perhaps Middle English *habbe,* present subjunctive of *habben,* to HAVE + *nabbe,* from *ne habble,* not to have.]

ho·bo (hō′bō) *n., pl.* **-boes** or **-bos. 1.** A tramp; a vagrant. **2.** A migratory, usually unskilled worker.
~*intr.v.* **hoboed, hoboing, -boes.** To live or wander about like a hobo. [19th century : origin obscure.] —**ho·bo·ism** *n.*

Hob·son-Job·son (hŏb′sən-jŏb′sən) *n.* The phonetic alteration of a word from another language into the sounds of an existing word in the language, as *compound,* "buildings enclosed by a barrier," from Malay *kampong.* [Anglo-Indian coinage, itself a Hobson-Jobson alteration (influenced by *Hobson* and *Jobson,* English surnames) of Arabic *yā Ḥasan, yā Ḥusayn!* O Hasan, O Husain! (ritual cry of mourning for Hasan and Husain, Muhammad's grandsons who were killed in battle).]

Hob·son's choice (hŏb′sənz) *n.* The option of accepting that which is offered or nothing; a choice with no real alternative. [After Thomas *Hobson* (died 1631), Cambridge, England, liveryman who required his customers to choose the next available horse.]

Ho Chi Minh (hō′ chē′ mĭn′), born Nguyen That Tanh (1890–1969). Founder and first president of North Vietnam (1954–69). After studying in Moscow, he founded the Indochinese Communist Party (1930) and returned to Vietnam to establish the Vietminh as a force

hobby *This member of the falcon family—which is found in Europe, Asia, and tropical Africa—is a spectacular flier. Capable of gliding upside-down and of looping the loop, it is fast enough to catch a dragonfly, a bat, or a swift in midair, and it will sometimes pluck and eat its kill on the wing.*

struggling for independence against French rule. In 1945, after Japan's surrender in World War II, he and his followers seized Hanoi, declaring independence. Forced to withdraw (1946), he led a jungle war that culminated in victory at Dien Bien Phu (1954). The Geneva Agreement that year established the new state of North Vietnam. Ho Chi Minh supported Vietcong guerrillas in the south, but died before the reunification of Vietnam.

Ho Chi Minh City. Formerly (until 1975) **Sai·gon** (sī-gŏn′). A port in southern Vietnam. On the Saigon River near the Mekong delta, it was successively the capital of Cochin China, French Indochina, and South Vietnam. The presence of U.S. forces during the Vietnamese War (1961-75) caused much social decay, exacerbated by their withdrawal and the republic's subsequent defeat.

hock¹ (hŏk) n. **1.** The tarsal joint of the hind leg of a horse or similar animal, corresponding to the human ankle. Also called "hough." **2.** A similar joint in the leg of a domestic fowl. —tr.v. **hocked, hocking, hocks.** To disable by cutting the tendons of the hock; hamstring. [Middle English *hoch,* Old English *hōh,* heel.]

hock² n. *Chiefly British.* **1.** Any of several white wines from the Rhine valley. **2.** Any of various white wines similar to German hock. [Short for obsolete *hockamore,* from German *Hochheimer (Wein),* wine of *Hochheim,* West Germany.]

hock³ tr.v. **hocked, hocking, hocks.** *Informal.* To pawn. —n. *Informal.* The state of being pawned. **—in hock.** *Informal.* In debt. [From Dutch *hok†,* prison.]

hock·ey (hŏk′ē) n. **1.** A game played on a field in which two opposing teams of 11 players, using curved sticks, try to drive a ball into the opponents' goal. Also called "field hockey." **2.** Ice hockey *(see).* [16th century : origin obscure.]

hockey stick n. A stick with one curved end, used in hockey.

Hock·ney (hŏk′nē), **David** (1937-). British artist. He developed a distinct style of fine figure drawing and also produced stage designs.

hock·shop (hŏk′shŏp′) n. *Informal.* A pawnshop.

ho·cus (hō′kəs) tr.v. **-cused** or **-cussed, -cusing** or **-cussing, -cuses** or **-cusses.** **1.** To fool or deceive; hoax; cheat. **2.** To stupefy, as with a drug. **3.** To adulterate (food or drink) with a drug. [Short for HOCUS-POCUS.]

ho·cus-po·cus (hō′kəs-pō′kəs) n. **1.** Nonsense words or phrases used as a formula by conjurers. **2.** A trick performed by a magician or juggler; sleight of hand. **3.** Any deception or chicanery. **4.** Any words or jargon used to mystify. —v. **hocus-pocused** or **-cussed, -cusing** or **-cussing, -cuses** or **-cusses.** —tr. To deceive; fool; cheat. —intr. To be deceptive. [17th century : mock Latin.]

hod (hŏd) n. **1.** An open container carried on a pole over the shoulder for transporting loads. **2.** A coal scuttle. [Perhaps variant of earlier dialectal *hot,* from Old French *hotte,* from Germanic.]

hodge-podge (hŏj′pŏj′) n. A mixture of dissimilar ingredients; jumble. [Middle English *hochepot,* from Old French. See **hotchpot.**]

Hodg·kin (hŏj′kĭn), **Thomas** (1798-1866). British doctor. In 1832 he identified the disease of lymphatic tissues since called Hodgkin's disease.

Hodgkin's disease n. A usually chronic, progressive, malignant disease marked by enlargement of the lymph nodes, spleen, and often of the liver and kidneys and occurring approximately twice as often in adult males as females. [After Thomas HODGKIN.]

hod·o·scope (hŏd′ə-skōp′) n. *Physics.* Any of various devices for indicating the paths of high-energy particles, used especially for investigating cosmic rays. [From Greek *hodos,* path, way + -SCOPE.]

hoe (hō) n. **1.** A tool with a flat blade attached at an angle to a long handle, used for weeding and breaking up the soil. **2.** A farming tool with a blade set at right angles to a short handle, used with a hacking action for digging. —v. **hoed, hoeing, hoes.** —tr. To weed, cultivate, or dig up with a hoe. —intr. To work with a hoe. [Middle English *howe,* from Old French *houe,* from Frankish *hauwa* (unattested).] **—ho·er** n.

hoe-cake (hō′kāk′) n. A thin cake made of cornmeal. [It was sometimes baked on the blade of a hoe.]

hoe-down (hō′doun′) n. **1.** A boisterous dance; especially, a square dance. **2.** The music for a hoe-down. **3.** A party at which hoe-downs are danced. [HOE + DOWN.]

Hoek Van Holland. See Hook of Holland.

Hof·fa (hŏf′ə), **James Riddle,** called "Jimmy" (1913-75?). U.S. labor leader. An aggressive labor organizer, he became president of the teamsters (1957) and threatened to organize all transportation workers into one union. He was convicted of misdealings (1964) and after several appeals was jailed (1967-71). In 1975 he was abducted from a Detroit restaurant and presumably was murdered.

Hoff·man (hŏf′mən, hŏf′-), **Dustin** (1937-). U.S. film actor, star of *The Graduate* (1967), *Midnight Cowboy* (1969), and *Straw Dogs* (1971). His performance in *Kramer vs. Kramer* (1979) won him an Academy Award.

Hof·manns·thal (hŏf′mənz-täl′, hôf′-), **Hugo von** (1874-1929). Austrian author. A poet, essayist, and dramatist, he established his reputation with lyric poems and equally beautiful plays, including *Yesterday* (1891) and *Death and the Fool* (1893).

hog (hŏg, hôg) n. Also **hogg** (for sense 4). **1.** A domesticated pig; especially, a castrated male pig weighing over 120 pounds. **2.** Any of various other mammals of the family Suidae, such as the boar or the wart hog. **3.** A self-indulgent, gluttonous, or vulgar person. **4.** *British.* A young sheep before its first shearing. **—go hog wild.** To react in an excited, immoderate, or irrational manner. —v. **hogged, hogging, hogs.** —tr. **1.** To keep or take more than one's share of. **2.** To cause (the back) to arch. **3.** To cut off (a horse's mane). —intr. To arch upward in the middle. Used of a ship's keel. [Middle English *hogge,* Old English *hogg,* from Celtic.]

ho·gan (hō′gän′, -gən) n. An earth-covered Navaho dwelling. [Navajo *hogan.*]

Ho·gan (hō′gən), **William Benjamin,** known as "Ben" (1912-). U.S. golfer. He won the U.S. Open championship in 1948, 1950, 1951, and 1953, the P.G.A. championship in 1948, and the British Open in 1953.

Ho·garth (hō′gärth′), **William** (1697-1764). British painter and engraver. In 1729 he started on *A Harlot's Progress,* a series of allegorical paintings. Other series included *A Rake's Progress* (1733) and *Marriage-à-la-Mode* (1745). His satirical paintings attacked the contradiction of luxury and squalor in society.

hog-back (hŏg′băk′, hôg′-) n. Also **hog's back.** A sharp ridge with steeply sloping sides, produced by the erosion of the broken edges of highly tilted strata.

hog cholera n. A highly infectious, often fatal viral disease of swine that is characterized by fever, diarrhea, and exhaustion. Also called "swine fever."

hog·fish (hŏg′fĭsh′, hôg′-) n., pl. **-fishes** or collectively **hogfish. 1.** A colorful fish, *Lachnolaimus maximus,* of warm Atlantic waters, having a long snout in the adult male. **2.** Any of several similar or related fishes, such as the **pigfish** *(see).*

Hogg (hŏg, hôg), **James** (1770-1835). Scottish poet. Originally a shepherd, he was discovered by Sir Walter Scott. His verse included *The Queen's Wake* (1813), and his prose *The Confessions of a Justified Sinner* (1824).

hog·gish (hŏg′ĭsh, hôg′ĭsh) adj. **1.** Coarsely self-indulgent or gluttonous. **2.** Filthy. **—hog·gish·ly** adv. **—hog·gish·ness** n.

Hog·ma·nay (hŏg′mə-nā′) n. *Chiefly Scottish.* New Year's Eve. [17th century (Scottish) : perhaps from Norman French *Hoguinané,* Old French *aguillanneuf†.*]

hog·nose snake (hŏg′nōz′, hôg′-) n. Also **hog·nosed snake** (-nōzd′). Any of several thick-bodied, nonvenomous North American snakes of the genus *Heterodon,* having an upturned snout.

hogs·head (hôgz′hĕd′, hŏgz′-) n. Abbr. **hhd 1.** Any of various units of volume or capacity ranging from 62.5 to 140 gallons; especially,

---

Hockney

AN ARTIST OF TODAY

Reflections and water fascinate a modern painter

David Hockney was born in England in 1937. As an art student he soon decided that abstract art was not the style for him, and has developed into a representational artist, working usually in flat, acrylic paint and in strong, light color. He has also executed series of etchings and has designed sets for the British Glyndebourne festival production of Stravinsky's opera *The Rake's Progress* and for New York City's Metropolitan Opera.

Hockney paints portraits, often double ones with each sitter apparently living in a world of his own. Subjects that particularly attract him are the movement of light and reflecting surfaces such as glass, tiles, and above all water.

A BIGGER SPLASH *This work, produced in California in 1967 using pale acrylic paints, shows the glittering leap of water thrown up by a diver's plunge into the pool. Water—in pools, showers, and sprinklers—is frequently a subject of Hockney's.*

a unit of capacity used in liquid measure in the United States, equal to 63 gallons (approximately 239 liters). **2.** A large barrel or cask with the capacity to hold a hogshead. [Middle English, "hog's head" (the reason for the name is obscure).]

hog-tie, hog·tie (hôg′tī′, hŏg′-) *tr.v.* **-tied, -tying** or **-tieing, -ties. 1.** To tie together the legs of. **2.** To impede or disrupt in movement or action.

hog·wash (hôg′wôsh′, hŏg′wŏsh′) *n.* **1.** Worthless, false, or ridiculous speech or writing. **2.** Garbage fed to hog; swill.

hog·weed (hôg′wēd′, hŏg′-) *n.* Any of various coarse, weedy plants.

Ho·hen·stau·fen (hō′ən-shtou′fən). Family of German rulers of the Holy Roman Empire (1138–1208, 1212–54), stemming from **Frederick** (died 1105) and his two sons, **Frederick II** (died 1147) and **Conrad** (1093–1152), who later became the German king and Holy Roman emperor (1138) and ruled until his death.

Ho·hen·zol·lern (hō′ən-zŏl′ərn, -tsô′lərn). A German royal family. It supplied the electors of Brandenburg from 1415, later extending control to Prussia (1618). Under Frederick I (reigned 1701–13) the Hohenzollerns' possessions were unified as the kingdom of Prussia. From 1871 to 1918 Hohenzollern monarchs ruled the German empire.

ho hum *interj.* Used to express a feeling of weariness, boredom, or dissatisfaction.

hoick (hoik) *tr.v.* **hoicked, hoicking, hoicks.** *Chiefly British.* To lift or bring up with a jerk. [Perhaps a variant of HIKE.]

hoi pol·loi (hoi′ pə-loi′) *n. Used with a plural verb.* The common people viewed from a position of social, economic, or intellectual advantage or privilege; the masses. Preceded by *the.* [Greek *hoi polloi,* the many, the masses : *hoi,* plural of *ho,* the + *polloi,* plural of *polus,* many.]

hoist (hoist) *tr.v.* **hoisted, hoisting, hoists.** To raise or haul up, particularly with the help of a mechanical apparatus. —See Synonyms at **lift.**

~*n.* **1.** An apparatus for lifting heavy or cumbersome objects. **2.** An act of hoisting. **3.** *Nautical.* **a.** The height or vertical dimension of a flag or of any square sail other than a course. **b.** A group of flags raised together as a signal. **c.** The inner edge of a flag, nearest to the pole. [Variant of dialectal *hoise,* from earlier *heise;* akin to Dutch *hijsen,* Low German *hissen*†.] **—hoist·er** *n.*

hoi·ty-toi·ty (hoi′tē-toi′tē) *adj.* Also **high·ty-tigh·ty** (hī′tē-tī′tē). **1. a.** Haughtily petulant. **b.** Pretentiously snobbish. **2.** Lightheaded; flighty.

~*n., pl.* **hoity-toities.** Also **high·ty-tigh·ty,** *pl.* **-ties 1.** Pretentious snobbery. **2.** Giddy behavior; flightiness. [Reduplication of *hoity,* from dialectal *hoit*†, to romp.]

hoke (hōk) *tr.v.* **hoked, hoking, hokes.** *Slang.* To give an artificial, false, or misleading quality to. [From HOKUM.]

hok·ey (hō′kē) *adj.* **-ier, -iest.** *Slang.* **1.** Corny; trite. **2.** Artificial; phony. **—hok·i·ly** *adv.* **—hok·i·ness** *n.*

ho·key-po·key (hō′kē-pō′kē) *n.* **1.** Hocus-pocus; chicanery. **2.** Inferior or cheap ice cream formerly sold by street venders.

Ho·kin·son (hō′kĭn-sən), **Helen Elna** (1893–1949). U.S. cartoonist. In more than 1,700 cartoons, she depicted middle-aged, usually nonplused women in stereotypical settings, such as garden-club meetings and choir practice. Published primarily in the *New Yorker,* her works were popular even among those she lampooned.

Hok·kai·do (hō-kī′dō). Northernmost of the four major islands that constitute Japan. It is the second largest of the islands, but the least populated. It was called Yezo until the Meiji restoration of 1868, when it was given its present name, which means "land of the northern sea." The interior of the island is largely mountainous and heavily forested and is rich in coal and iron. The northern part of the island is virtually uninhabited; the major cities, Sapporo, Hakodate, and Otaru, are all on the island's southwestern peninsula.

Hok·kien (hŏk-yĕn′) *n.* A dialect of Chinese spoken in Fujian province and also widely spoken in Taiwan and by people of Chinese origin in Southeast Asia.

hok·ku (hô′ko͞o) *n.* A Japanese poem, a **haiku** *(see).*

ho·kum (hō′kəm) *n.* **1.** Nonsense; bunk. **2.** Sentimental or clichéd material used in a play or movie as a means of obtaining a predictable audience response. [20th century : origin obscure.]

Ho·ku·sai (hō′ko͞o-sī′, hō′ko͞o-sī′) (1760–1849). Japanese artist. A master printmaker with unmatched technique, he captured both the serenity and the power of nature in his landscapes and historical scenes, such as *Thirty-six Views of Mt. Fuji* (1826–33).

hol–. Variant of **holo-.**

Hol·arc·tic (hō-lärk′tĭk, -lär′tĭk, hŏ-) *adj.* Of or designating the zoogeographic region that includes the northern areas of the earth and is divided into Nearctic and Palearctic regions. [HOL(O)- + ARCTIC.]

Hol·bein (hōl′bīn′), **Hans,** known as "Holbein the Younger" (*c.* 1497–1543). German painter. The son and pupil of **Hans Holbein the Elder** (*c.* 1465–1524), he worked in Basel and visited England in 1526. From *c.* 1536 he was court painter to Henry VIII. Holbein is noted for his portraits.

hold¹ (hōld) *v.* **held** (hĕld), **held** or *archaic* **holden** (hōl′dən), **holding, holds.** *—tr.* **1.** To have and keep, as in the hands, arms, or teeth; grasp; clasp. **2.** To support; keep up; bear: *This nail is too small to hold that mirror.* **3. a.** To maintain in a certain position or relationship; keep: *held his assailant at arm's length.* **b.** To maintain (oneself) in a specified posture or condition: *hold oneself erect.* **c.** To maintain in a steady or unchanged state: *hold prices down.* **4. a.** To contain; be filled by: *The jar holds one pint.* **b.** To accommodate; seat: *The church holds 500.* **5.** To keep or have (property, assets, or the like) in one's possession; own. **6. a.** To have or maintain for use; wield: *hold an advantage.* **b.** To have gained: *hold a certificate.* **7.** To maintain control over; restrain: *The dam held the flood waters. Hold your tongue!* **8. a.** To retain the attention or interest of: *She held the audience with her eyes.* **b.** To retain (a person's attention). **9. a.** To defend from attack; preserve: *hold the fort.* **b.** To keep despite a challenge: *held her seat at the last election.* **10. a.** To keep under restraint or in confinement: *held in custody.* **b.** To detain or delay: *Try to hold him until the police arrive.* **c.** To prevent from making further gains: *held to a draw.* **11.** To have the position of; occupy: *He holds the office of commander.* **12.** *Law.* **a.** To be the legal possessor of. **b.** To make (a person) fulfill the terms of a contract. Used with *to.* **c.** To adjudge or decree. **13.** To cause to fulfill an agreement or promise; bind: *They held him to his word.* **14. a.** To keep in one's mind or heart; harbor: *hold a grudge.* **b.** To regard in a specified manner: *hold her in contempt.* **15. a.** To have as an opinion or belief: *hold extreme views.* **b.** To assert; affirm: *hold that his hypotheses are incorrect.* **16.** To cause to take place; put on: *The race was held last month. Let's hold a party.* **17.** To assemble; convene: *held a meeting of the board.* **18.** To set aside; not sell or allocate: *The shop is holding the shoes until tomorrow.* **19.** To consume (alcohol) without noticeable effects: *He can't hold his liquor.* **20.** *Music.* To sustain (a note). **21.** *Computer Science.* To keep (data) on a storage device although it has been copied onto another location or another storage device. **22.** To keep (a telephone line) open. *—intr.* **1.** To maintain a grasp, clutch, or grip. **2. a.** To maintain a desired or accustomed position or condition: *Hold still!* **b.** To last; remain unchanged: *This weather won't hold.* **3.** To adhere closely; keep: *They held to a southwesterly course.* **4.** To stand up under stress, pressure, or opposition; last: *The platform will never hold under your weight.* **5.** To be valid, applicable, or true: *His theory still holds. The rule holds for all of us.* **6.** To wait while on the telephone; not hang up. —See Synonyms at **contain.** **—hold down. 1.** To keep in check; restrain; suppress. **2.** To work at and keep (a job). **—hold forth.** To talk at length; lecture. **—hold in.** To keep back, check, or suppress (an impulse or emotion, for example). **—hold it. 1.** To stop or wait. Usually used in the imperative. **2.** To maintain a position or pose; freeze. Used in the imperative. **—hold off. 1.** To prevent from reaching; keep at some distance: *hold off the enemy.* **2.** To defer or delay doing something; put off: *hold off buying a car until the spring.* **—hold on. 1.** To maintain one's grip; cling. **2.** To keep at; continue. **3.** To stop or wait for someone or something. **—hold one's own. 1.** To maintain one's ground or position; not falter. **2.** To prove oneself adequate or competent; be good enough. **—hold out. 1.** To present; offer. **2.** To last; stand up; endure. **3.** To refuse to surrender or give up; continue resisting. **—hold out for.** To insist upon or wait for, accepting no compromises. **—hold out on.** *Informal.* To refuse to give or divulge something expected or deserved. **—hold to.** To keep true or steadfast to; remain loyal or faithful to. **—hold together. 1.** To remain or cause to remain coherent or in one piece. **2.** To wear well or last a long time: *The old bike has held together well.* **—hold water.** To stand up under examination; be believable, valid, or tenable. **—hold with. 1.** To agree with. **2.** To be on the side of; support. **3.** To approve of; subscribe to.

~*n.* **1.** The act or a means of grasping; a grip; a clasp. **2.** A means of obtaining, retaining, or controlling something. **3.** Something held onto, as for support. **4.** A device that grips something so as to keep it in place. **5.** A strong psychological influence or power: *He seems to have a hold over her.* **6.** A means of influencing the behavior of a person, as through knowing discreditable information: *Finding the letter give him a hold on me.* **7.** A prison cell. **8.** *Archaic.* A fortified place; a stronghold. **9.** *Music.* **a.** The sustaining of a note longer than its indicated time value. **b.** The symbol designating this pause; a fermata. **10.** A temporary halt or pause: *There was a hold in the countdown.* **11.** A manner of gripping an opponent in wrestling: *a neck hold.* **—get hold of. 1.** To obtain. **2.** To establish contact with. **—no holds barred.** Without any restrictions; all methods allowed, regardless of fairness. [Hold, held, held, holden; Middle English *holden, heold, haldan, holden,* Old English *healdan, hēold, healden.*]

hold² *n.* **1.** *Nautical.* The interior of a ship below decks where cargo is stored. **2.** The place in an aircraft where the cargo is put. [Variant (influenced by HOLD) of Middle English *hole,* HOLE.]

hold·all (hōld′ôl′) *n.* A case or bag for carrying miscellaneous items, as when traveling.

hold back *tr.v.* **1.** To curb; restrain. **2.** To save for future use; keep apart or aside; retain. *—intr.v.* To refrain.

hold·back (hōld′băk′) *n.* A strap or iron placed between the shaft and the harness on a drawn wagon, allowing the horse to stop or back up.

hold·en. *Archaic.* Past participle of **hold** (to grasp).

hold·er (hōl′dər) *n.* **1.** A person who holds, possesses, or occupies something. Often used in combination: *a landholder; a shareholder.* **2.** A device for holding something. **3.** *Law.* One who legally possesses and is entitled to the payment of a check, bill, or promissory note.

hold·fast (hōld′făst′, -fäst′) *n.* **1.** Any of various devices used to fasten something securely. **2.** *Biology.* An organ or structure of attachment; especially, the **hapteron** *(see)* of certain seaweeds.

hold·ing (hōl′dĭng) *n.* **1.** Land rented or leased from another. **2.** *Of-*

PRONUNCIATION KEY

ă, pat; ā, pay; âr, care;
ä, father, are; b, bib;
ch, church; d, deed; ĕ, pet;
ē, be; f, fife; g, gag; h, hat;
hw, which; ĭ, pit; ī, pie;
îr, pier; j, judge; k, kick;
l, lid, needle; m, mum;
n, no, sudden; ng, thing;
ŏ, pot; ō, toe; ô, paw, for;
oi, noise; ou, out; o͝o, book;
o͞o, boot; p, pop; r, roar;
s, sauce; sh, ship, dish;
t, tight; th, thin, path;
th, this, bathe; ŭ, cut; ûr, fur;
v, valve; w, with; y, yes;
z, zebra, size; zh, vision;
ə, about, item, edible,
gallop, circus, peaceful

IN FOREIGN WORDS:

à, *Fr.* ami; œ, *Fr.* feu, *Ger.* schön; ü, *Fr.* tu, *Ger.* über; KH, *Ger.* ich, *Scot.* loch; N, *Fr.* bon; y′, *Fr.* Compiègne

STRESS MARKS:

Primary stress: ′
in·cite′ (ĭn-sīt′)
Secondary stress: ′
in′sight′ (ĭn′sīt′)

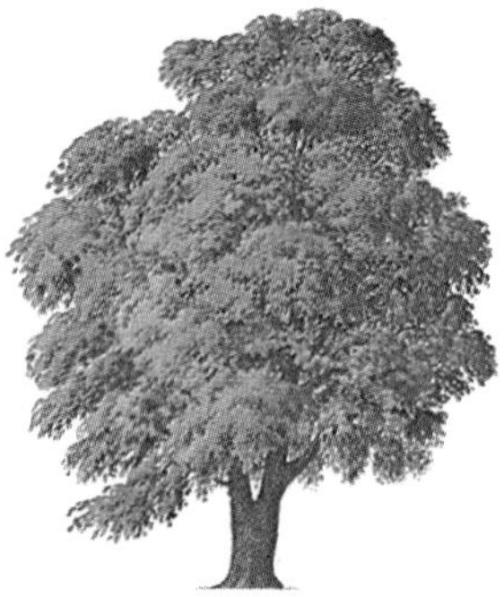

holm oak *Oaks are among the largest and most long-lived trees of European woodlands. The giant Major Oak in England's Sherwood Forest—said to have been used as a meeting place by the legendary outlaw Robin Hood—is 1,000 years old and still growing. Common oaks are deciduous, but the holm oak,* Quercus ilex *(above), is an evergreen.*

ten **holdings.** Legally possessed property, such as land, capital, or stocks.

holding company *n.* A company having partial or complete control of other companies.

holding operation *n.* A procedure intended only to keep a situation under control and prevent any deterioration.

holding pattern *n.* **1.** A fixed, usually circular pattern flown by an airplane awaiting clearance to land at an airport. **2.** A condition of waiting or delay.

hold over *tr.v.* **1.** To delay taking action or making a decision on. **2.** To postpone. **3.** To continue longer than expected: *hold over a movie for another week.* **4.** To use as a threat or for blackmail: *You can't hold my past over me like that.*

hold·o·ver (hōld'ō'vər) *n.* Someone or something that is held over, as an elected official kept in office after his term is over or an entertainer or entertainment continued beyond the original period of engagement.

hold up *tr.v.* **1.** To present; show: *Her work was held up as an example to all.* **2.** To hinder or interrupt; delay. **3.** To rob. *—intr.v.* To last; stand up; endure.

hold·up (hōld'up') *n.* **1.** A suspension of activity; a delay; an interruption. **2.** A robbery; especially, an armed robbery.

hole (hōl) *n.* **1.** A cavity in a solid. **2.** An opening or perforation through something; a gap; an aperture: *a hole in the clouds.* **3. a.** A deep place in water. **b.** A small, deep pond. **c.** A small bay; a cove. **4.** An animal's hollowed-out habitation, such as a burrow: *a rabbit hole.* **5.** *Informal.* An ugly, squalid, or depressing place or dwelling. **6.** A deep or isolated place of confinement; a dungeon. **7.** A fault or flaw; an error: *picked holes in the prosecution's argument.* **8.** *Informal.* A bad situation from which it seems difficult to extract oneself; a predicament. **9.** *Golf.* **a.** The small pit lined with a cup into which the ball must be hit. **b.** One of the 9 or 18 divisions of a golf course, from tee to cup. **10.** *Electronics.* A vacant electron energy state that is manifested as a charge defect in a crystalline solid, the defect behaving as a positive charge carrier with charge magnitude equal to that of the electron. **—hole in one.** *Golf.* The driving of the ball from the tee into the hole in only one stroke. **—in the hole.** *Informal.* In debt. **—make a hole in.** To use up a substantial amount of: *The trip made a big hole in my bank balance.*
~v. **holed, holing, holes.** *—tr.* **1.** To put a hole or holes in; puncture; perforate. **2.** To put, propel, or drive into a hole. *—intr.* To make a hole or holes. **—hole out.** *Golf.* To hit one's ball into the hole. **—hole up.** **1.** To hibernate in or as if in a hole. **2.** To shut oneself up, especially in cramped quarters: *They were all holed up in that tiny shack.* [Middle English *hol(e),* hole, ship's hold, Old English *hol,* hollow place.] **—hole·y** *adj.*
***Synonyms:** cavity, excavation, hollow, pit, pocket.*

hole-and-cor·ner (hōl'ən-kôr'nər) *adj. Informal.* Underhand; furtive: *hole-and-corner whispering.*

hole in the heart *n.* A congenital defect in which there is an opening between the right and left sides of the heart so that a proportion of the blood is not pumped to the lungs.

hole-in-the-wall (hōl'ĭn-*thə*-wôl') *n., pl.* **holes-in-the-wall.** A small, squalid, or out-of-the-way place. **—hole-in-the-wall** *adj.*

-holic, -aholic, -oholic *suffix.* Indicates addiction to or compulsive need or desire for; for example, **workaholic.** [Back-formation from *alcoholic.*]

hol·i·day (hŏl'ə-dā') *n.* **1.** A day on which custom or the law dictates a halting of general business activity to commemorate or celebrate a particular event. **2.** A religious feast day; a holy day. **3.** A day free from work that one may spend at leisure; a day off. **4.** *Often* **holidays.** *Chiefly British.* A period of time during which one is free from work, studies, or one's usual activities; vacation. **5.** A period of time spent away from home for recreation, as in a resort.
~adj. Of, suitable for, or characteristic of a holiday: *a holiday mood.*
~intr.v. **holidayed, -daying, -days.** *Chiefly British.* To take a holiday: *holidaying in the Bahamas.* [Middle English *holiday,* Old English *hāligdæg* : *hālig,* HOLY + *dæg,* DAY.]

Hol·i·day (hŏl'ə-dā'), **Billie,** original name Eleanora, known as "Lady Day" (1915–59). U.S. singer. With no formal music training, she blended her great natural ability and her experience of economic and social hardship into a sincere, individual, and moving jazz and blues singing career. Her autobiography, *Lady Sings the Blues* (1956), was also a successful motion picture (1972).

hol·i·day·mak·er (hŏl'ə-dā'mā'kər) *n. Chiefly British.* A person who is or is about to be on holiday; vacationer.

ho·li·er-than-thou (hō'lē-ər-*thən-thou'*) *adj.* Showing an attitude of superior virtue; self-righteously pious.

ho·li·ness (hō'lē-nĭs) *n.* **1.** The state or quality of being holy; sanctity. **2. Holiness.** A title or form of address for various high ecclesiastical dignitaries, especially the pope. Preceded by *His* or *Your.*

Hol·ins·hed (hŏl'ĭnz-hĕd', -ĭn-shĕd'), **Raphael** (died *c.* 1580). Also **Hol·lings·head** (-ĭngz-hĕd'). English chronicler. His *Chronicles* (1578), a history of England, Scotland and Ireland, form a valuable source of historical information, which was extensively used by Shakespeare and other Elizabethan dramatists.

ho·lism (hō'lĭz'əm) *n.* The theory that reality is made up of organic or unified wholes that are greater than the simple sum of their parts. [HOL(O)- + -ISM.] **—ho·list** *n.*

ho·lis·tic (hō-lĭs'tĭk) *adj.* **1.** Of or pertaining to holism. **2. a.** Emphasizing the importance of the whole and the interdependence of its parts. **b.** Concerned with entire systems rather than subdivisions or specialties: *holistic medicine; holistic ecology.* **—ho·lis·ti·cal·ly** *adv.*

hol·land (hŏl'ənd) *n.* A sturdy linen fabric used especially for upholstery. [After HOLLAND, where it was made.]

Holland. See **Netherlands.**

hol·lan·daise sauce (hŏl'ən-dāz', hŏl'ən-dāz') *n.* A creamy sauce of butter, egg yolks, and lemon or vinegar, served especially with fish or vegetables. [Translation of French *sauce Hollandaise,* Dutch sauce, from *Hollandaise,* feminine of *Hollandais,* Dutch, from *Hollande,* HOLLAND.]

Hol·land·er (hŏl'ən-dər) *n.* A native or inhabitant of the Netherlands; Dutchman.

Hol·lands (hŏl'əndz) *n.* A type of gin made in the Netherlands. Also called "Holland gin." [Dutch *Hollandsch,* from *hollandsch genever,* Dutch gin.]

hol·ler (hol'ər) *v.* **-lered, -lering, -lers.** *—intr.* **1.** To yell or shout; cry out; call. **2.** *Informal.* To complain loudly. *—tr.* To yell or shout (an utterance).
~n. A yell or shout; a loud call. [Originally a dialectal variant of HOLLO.]

Hol·ler·ith (hŏl'ə-rĭth') *n.* A code used for recording alphanumeric information on punch cards. Also called "Hollerith code." [After Herman *Hollerith* (1860–1929), U.S. inventor.]

Hollingshead, Raphael. See **Holinshead.**

hol·lo, hol·loa (hŏ-lō', hə-lō') *interj.* Used as a shout to catch a person's attention.
~n., pl. **hollos.** Also **hol·loa,** *pl.* **holloas.** A cry for attention.
~intr.v. **holloed, -loing, -los.** Also **hol·loa, -loaed, -loaing, -loas.** To shout; call out. [French *holà,* "ho there!"]

hol·low (hŏl'ō) *adj.* **-lower, -lowest.** **1.** Having a cavity, gap, or space within: *a hollow wall.* **2.** Being indented or concave; having depths or inclines: *hollow land.* **3.** Deeply recessed; sunken; fallen: *hollow cheeks.* **4.** Without substance or character; empty; superficial: *a hollow person.* **5.** Not genuine or real; specious: *hollow victories.* **6.** Having a reverberating sound; echoing: *hollow footsteps.* **7.** Cynical; false: *hollow laughter.* **8.** Hungry or unsatisfied.
~n. **1.** A cavity, gap, or space within something: *the hollow behind a wall.* **2.** An indented or concave surface or area; a shallow pocket: *the hollow of one's hand.* **3.** A valley or depression. —See Synonyms at **hole.**
~adv. Outright; thoroughly: *I was beaten hollow at chess.*
~v. **hollowed, -lowing, -lows.** *—tr.* **1.** To make hollow. Used with *out*: *hollow out a pumpkin.* **2.** To scoop or form by making hollow. Used with *out*: *hollow out a nest in the sand.* *—intr.* To become hollow. [Middle English *hol(e)we,* from *holh,* hole, Old English *holh,* hole, hollow place.] **—hol·low·ly** *adv.* **—hol·low·ness** *n.*

hol·low·ware (hŏl'ō-wâr') *n.* Serving pieces, especially of silver, such as bowls, jugs, and the like. Compare **flatware.**

hol·ly (hŏl'ē) *n., pl.* **-lies.** **1. a.** Any of numerous trees or shrubs of the genus *Ilex,* such as *I. opaca,* of eastern North America, or *I. aquifolium,* of Eurasia, often having bright-red berries and glossy, evergreen leaves with spiny margins. **b.** Branches or leaves of holly, traditionally used for Christmas decoration. **2.** Any of various similar or related plants. [Middle English *holi(n),* Old English *holen,* probably of Germanic origin.]

hol·ly·hock (hŏl'ē-hŏk') *n.* A tall plant, *Althaea rosea,* native to China and widely cultivated for its showy spikes of large, variously colored flowers. [Middle English *holihoc* : *holi,* HOLY + *hoc,* a mallow, Old English *hoc*†.]

Hol·ly·wood[1] (hŏl'ē-wŏŏd'). District of the city of Los Angeles, California. It has been the center of the U.S. film industry since before World War I. The Hollywood Bowl, a vast outdoor theater, is located in the foothills of the Santa Monica Mts.

Hollywood[2] *n.* The U.S. motion-picture industry or the somewhat meretriciously glamorous atmosphere often attributed to it.

Hollywood bed *n.* A mattress on a box spring supported by a metal frame or attached low legs.

holm (hōm, hōlm) *n. British.* **1.** An island in a river. **2.** Low land near a stream. [Middle English *holm,* from Old Norse *holmr,* islet, meadow.]

Holmes (hōmz, hōlmz), **Oliver Wendell** (1809–94). U.S. author. A professor of anatomy and physiology at Harvard (1847–82), he wrote humorous conversational pieces, including *The Autocrat of the Breakfast Table* (1858).

Holmes, Oliver Wendell, Jr. (1841–1935). U.S. jurist; Supreme Court justice (1902–32). One of the most influential justices in Supreme Court history, he combined his legal scholarship, philosophical mind, and fine literary style to form and express opinions that have shaped and changed the American concept of law.

hol·mic (hŏl'mĭk) *adj.* Pertaining to or containing holmium.

hol·mi·um (hŏl'mē-əm) *n. Symbol* **Ho** A relatively soft, malleable, stable rare-earth element occurring in gadolinite, monazite, and other rare-earth minerals. Atomic number 67, atomic weight 164.930, melting point 1,461°C, boiling point 2,600°C, specific gravity 8.803, valence 3. [From New Latin *Holmia,* Latinized form of Stockholm, Sweden.]

holm oak (hōm, hōlm) *n.* A tree, *Quercus ilex,* native to the Mediterranean region, having prickly evergreen leaves. Also called "holly oak," "ilex." [Middle English, variant of *holin,* HOLLY.]

holo-, hol- *prefix.* Indicates whole, entire, or entirely; for example, **holoblastic, Holarctic.** [Greek *holos,* whole, entire.]

hol·o·blas·tic (hŏl'ō-blăs'tĭk, hō'lō-) *adj.* Exhibiting or denoting cleavage in which the entire egg separates into individual blastomeres. Compare **meroblastic.** [HOLO- + -BLAST + -IC.]

hol·o·caust (hŏl′ə-kôst′, hō′lə-) *n.* **1.** Great or total destruction by fire; a conflagration. **2. a.** Any widespread, horrific destruction of human life. **b.** *Often* **Holocaust.** The mass killings of Jews by the Nazi regime during World War II. **3.** A sacrificial offering that is consumed entirely by flames; a burnt offering. —See Synonyms at **disaster.** [Middle English, from Old French *holocauste,* from Latin *holocaustum,* from Greek *holokauston,* from *holokaustos,* burnt whole : *holo-,* whole + *kaustos,* variant of *kautos,* burnt, from *kaein,* to burn.] —**hol·o·caus·tal** (hŏl′ə-kô′stəl, hō′lə-), **hol·o·caus·tic** (hŏl′ə-kô′stĭk, hō′lə-) *adj.*

Hol·o·cene (hŏl′ə-sēn′, hō′lə-) *adj. Geology.* Of, belonging to, or designating the geologic time or the rock system of the more recent of the two epochs of the Quaternary period, extending from the end of the Pleistocene to the present.
~*n. Geology.* The Holocene epoch or system of deposits. Preceded by *the.* Also called "Recent." [HOLO- + -CENE.]

hol·o·crine (hŏl′ə-krĭn, -krēn′, -krīn′, hō′lə-) *adj.* Pertaining to or designating a gland whose secretion is formed by the degeneration of the gland's cells, as sebaceous glands. Compare **merocrine.** [HOLO- + Greek *krinein,* to separate, divide.]

hol·o·en·zyme (hŏl′ō-ĕn′zīm′, hō′lō-) *n.* An enzyme in its active form, consisting of an apoenzyme and a coenzyme.

hol·o·gram (hŏl′ə-grăm′, hō′lə-) *n.* **1.** The pattern produced on a photosensitive medium that has been exposed by holography and then photographically developed. **2.** The photosensitive medium so exposed and so developed. Also called "holograph." [HOLO- + -GRAM.]

hol·o·graph (hŏl′ə-grăf′, -gräf′, hō′lə-) *n.* **1.** A document written wholly in the handwriting of the person whose signature it bears. **2.** A hologram.
~*tr.v.* **holographed, -graphing, -graphs. 1.** To produce an image of (a physical object) by holography. **2.** To form a hologram of (a physical object). [Late Latin *holographus,* entirely written by the signer, from Greek *holographos,* written in full : *holo-,* whole + -GRAPH.] —**hol·o·graph·ic** (hŏl′ə-grăf′ĭk, hō′lə-), **hol·o·graph·i·cal** (-ĭ-kəl) *adj.* —**hol·o·graph·i·cal·ly** *adv.*

ho·log·ra·phy (hō-lŏg′rə-fē, hə-) *n.* The technique of producing a three-dimensional image of an object by recording the wave pattern of light reflected from the object, especially by using lasers to record on a photographic plate the diffraction pattern from which a three-dimensional image can be projected. [HOLO- + -GRAPHY.] See feature, next page.

hol·o·he·dral (hŏl′ō-hē′drəl, hō′lō-) *adj.* Having as many planes as required for complete symmetry in a given crystal system. [HOLO- + -HEDRAL.]

hol·o·me·tab·o·lism (hŏl′ō-mə-tăb′ə-lĭz′əm, hō′lō-) *n.* Complete metamorphosis of a developing insect. —**hol·o·me·tab·o·lous** *adj.*

hol·o·phras·tic (hŏl′ə-frăs′tĭk, hō′lə-) *adj. Linguistics.* Expressing a set of ideas by means of a single word. [HOLO- + Greek *phrastikos,* indicative, expressive, from *phrazein,* to show.]

hol·o·phytic (hŏl′ō-fĭt′ĭk, hō′lō-) *adj.* Designating organisms, such as green plants, that manufacture their food by photosynthesis; autotrophic. [HOLO- + -PHYTIC.]

hol·o·plank·ton (hŏl′ō-plăngk′tən, hō′lō-) *n.* Microorganisms that are constituents of plankton for all stages of their life cycle.

hol·o·thu·ri·an (hŏl′ō-thŏŏr′ē-ən, hō′lō-) *n.* Any of various echinoderms of the class Holothuroidea, which includes the sea cucumbers. [New Latin *Holothuria* (genus), from Latin *holothūria,* water polyp, from Greek *holothourion*.] —**hol·o·thu·ri·an** *adj.*

hol·o·type (hŏl′ə-tīp′, hō′lə-) *n.* The single specimen used as the basis of the original published description of a taxonomic species. Also called "type specimen." [HOLO- + TYPE.] —**hol·o·typ·ic** (hŏl′ə-tĭp′ĭk, hō′lə-) *adj.*

hol·o·zo·ic (hŏl′ō-zō′ĭk, hō′lō-) *adj.* Obtaining nourishment by the ingestion of organic material, as do animals. [HOLO- + -ZOIC.]

holp. *Archaic.* Past tense of **help.**

hol·pen. *Archaic.* Past participle of **help.**

Holst (hōlst, hŏlst), **Gustav Theodore** (1874-1934). British composer, of part-Swedish descent. His best-known work is the orchestral suite *The Planets* (1914-16).

Hol·stein (hōl′stīn) *n.* Any of a breed of large black and white dairy cattle originally developed in Friesland. Also called "Friesian," "Holstein-Friesian." [After *Holstein,* West Germany.]

hol·ster (hōl′stər) *n.* **1.** A leather case shaped to hold a pistol and usually designed to be attached to a belt. **2.** A belt with loops or slots for carrying equipment such as small tools. [Dutch.] —**hol·stered** *adj.*

holt (hōlt) *n. Archaic.* **1.** A wood or grove; a copse. Often used in place names. **2.** A wooded hill. [Middle English *holt,* wood, Old English *holt*.]

ho·lus-bo·lus (hō′ləs-bō′ləs) *adv. Informal.* All together; all at once. [Perhaps based on *whole* and *bolus*.]

ho·ly (hō′lē) *adj.* **-lier, -liest. 1.** Belonging to, associated with, or consecrated to God or a divine power; sacred. **2.** Worthy of worship or high esteem; revered: *a holy book.* **3. a.** Living according to a religious or spiritual system; devout. **b.** Having great spiritual insight or wisdom; godly: *a holy man.* **c.** Morally blameless; saintly. **4.** Intended or set apart for a religious purpose: *a holy hour.* **5.** Solemnly undertaken; sacrosanct: *a holy pledge.* **6. a.** Formally associated with or pertaining to an established or organized religion. **b.** Religious in theme, depiction, or subject: *holy paintings.* **7.** Used as an intensive, especially in exclamations: *holy mackerel!* [Middle English *holy, holi, hali,* Old English *hālig,* from Germanic; akin to WHOLE.] —**ho·li·ly** *adv.* —**ho·li·ness** *n.*

Holy Alliance *n.* An agreement that was made by Russia, Prussia, and Austria in 1815 to govern by Christian principles.

Holy Ark *n.* The cabinet in a synagogue in which the scrolls of the Torah are kept.

Holy Bible *n.* The Bible.

Holy City *n.* **1.** Any city that is held to be sacred by a particular religion, as Jerusalem by the religions of Judaism, Christianity, and Islam. **2.** Heaven. Preceded by *the.*

Holy Communion *n. Abbr.* **H.C.** The Eucharist *(see).*

holy day *n.* A day set aside for a religious observance.

holy day of obligation *n. Roman Catholic Church.* A day other than a Sunday on which believers are required to attend Mass, as Christmas Day.

Holy Family *n.* The child Jesus together with Mary and Joseph. Preceded by *the.*

Holy Father *n.* One of the titles of the pope.

Holy Ghost *n.* The third person of the Christian Trinity. Also called "Holy Spirit."

Holy Grail *n.* The **Grail** *(see).*

Holy Innocents' Day *n.* December 28, a day commemorating the massacre of male infants by Herod after the birth of Jesus.

Holy Island. Also **Lin·dis·farne** (lĭn′dĭs-färn′). Island off the coast of Northumberland, in northeastern England. At low tide it is connected to the mainland. Celtic Christianity found its first home in England at the church and monastery built here by St. Aidan in 635. The Lindisfarne Gospels, also known as the Book of Durham, is an illuminated manuscript made on the island in the 7th century.

Holy Joe *n. Slang.* **1.** A pious or self-righteous person. **2.** A clergyman, especially a chaplain.

Holy Land. See Palestine.

Holy Office *n.* Official name, Congregation of the Holy Office. A congregation of the Roman Catholic Church that deals with such matters as the protection of the faith and morals.

holy of holies *n.* **1.** The innermost shrine of a Jewish tabernacle and temple. **2.** A place held to be especially sacrosanct. Also called "sanctum sanctorum."

holy orders *pl.n. Ecclesiastical.* **1.** *Used with a singular verb.* The sacrament or rite of ordination; the ceremony of admission into the priesthood or ministry. **2.** *Used with a plural verb.* The rank of an ordained Christian minister; clerical status. **3.** *Used with a plural verb.* Any of the grades of the ordained ministry of the Christian church, especially the priesthood and the diaconate. Also called "major orders." Compare **minor orders.**

holy place *n.* **1.** The outer chamber of the sanctuary in a Jewish temple. **2.** A place to which a pilgrimage is made.

Holy Roman Empire. *Abbr.* **H.R.E.** The loosely federated political entity of European Christendom, from the coronation of Otto I as Holy Roman emperor by the pope in 962 to the dissolution of the empire by Napoleon in 1806. The last emperor was Francis II (reigned 1792-1806). The term "Holy Roman Empire" did not come into use until several centuries after Otto's accession. From the outset the rule of the emperor was bedeviled by rivalry between the papal and the secular authority and after the 13th century by the rising ambitions of the nascent nation-states of Europe. After the election of Rudolf of Hapsburg as emperor in 1273, the imperial crown remained in Hapsburg hands, and the empire came to be little more than the Hapsburg domains, chiefly Austria and Spain.

holy rood *n.* **1.** A cross or crucifix; especially, one placed over a rood screen. **2. Holy Rood.** The cross upon which Jesus was crucified.

Holy Saturday *n.* The Saturday before Easter Sunday.

Holy Scripture *n.* The Old and New Testaments of the Bible. Also called "Holy Writ," "Scripture," "Scriptures."

Holy See *n. Roman Catholic Church.* **1.** The office or jurisdiction of the pope. **2.** The administrative officials of the Vatican.

Holy Sepulcher *n.* The tomb outside Jerusalem thought to be that of Jesus and regarded as a Christian shrine.

Holy Spirit *n.* The **Holy Ghost** *(see).*

ho·ly·stone (hō′lē-stōn′) *n.* A piece of soft sandstone used for scouring the wooden decks of a ship.
~*tr.v.* **holystoned, -stoning, -stones.** To scrub or scour with a holystone. [From its being used while kneeling.]

Holy Synod *n.* The administrative or governing body of any of the Eastern Orthodox churches.

Holy Thursday *n.* **1.** *Roman Catholic Church.* **Maundy Thursday** *(see).* **2.** *Anglican Church.* Ascension Day. See **ascension.**

holy water *n.* Water blessed by a priest and used in various ceremonies.

Holy Week *n.* The week before Easter Sunday.

Holy Writ *n.* Holy Scripture.

hom·age (hŏm′ĭj, ŏm′-) *n.* **1.** Ceremonial acknowledgment under feudal law by a vassal or tenant of allegiance to his lord. **2.** Honor or respect publicly expressed to a person or idea: *pay homage to our forefathers with this hymn.* —See Synonyms at **honor.** [Middle English, acknowledgment of a man's allegiance, from Old French, from Medieval Latin *homināticum,* from Latin *homō* (stem *homin-*), man.]

hom·bre (ŏm′brä′, -brē) *n. Slang.* A man; a fellow. [Spanish, from Latin *homō*.]

hom·burg (hŏm′bûrg′) *n.* A man's felt hat having a soft, dented crown and a shallow, slightly rolled brim. [First manufactured in *Homburg,* town near Wiesbaden, West Germany.]

Holstein *All over the world Holstein are used as dairy cattle. A Holstein cow may produce as much as 9,100 liters (2,000 gallons) of milk a year.*

THREE DIMENSIONS RECORDED IN TWO BY FILM AND LASERS

A technique whose full uses are still to be explored

Holography is a process that uses film and laser light to record and project three-dimensional images.

A holographic image can be produced only by laser light, which is one color and coherent—that is, all its waves are in phase. Holography was originally conceived in 1948 but did not become practicable until the invention of the laser in 1960. The first hologram was produced in the United States in 1963.

Two laser beams are used. One is bounced off an object, reflecting the shadings that give an impression of depth. The other is a reference beam. The two meet at the film, unfocused, where they interact to produce a complex pattern that holds all the information necessary to recreate the original image. This is done by reversing the process and bathing the film in laser light. The result is a pale, single-color but three-dimen-

sional image that changes as the observer moves. By using up to three lasers and plates, up to three colors can be produced.

Holography is used in scientific research and will find further uses, but its main impact on the public so far has been at exhibitions, where it is used to demonstrate how light can create images that appear to have the depth of real objects.

PRODUCING A HOLOGRAM

1. A continuous-wave gas laser directs a narrow beam of coherent light—pure light of a single wavelength—at a beam splitter

2. The beam splitter divides the beam at right angles into an object beam and a reference beam

3. Object beam

4. A mirror redirects the object beam toward the object

5. A concave lens expands the object beam passing through it

6. The object is bathed in light from the object beam and reflects light waves in all directions. The intensity of the waves varies with the shape and the surface character of the object

7. Some of the light waves travel toward the photographic plate

8. Reference beam

9. A mirror redirects the reference beam toward the photographic plate

10. A concave lens expands the reference beam passing through it

11. The converging reference beam light waves and the light waves reflected by the object overlap to set up interference (the two sets of light waves reinforce each other when the crests of the waves coincide and cancel each other out when the crests coincide with troughs)

12. The glass photographic plate with emulsion on one side records the interference as information on the depth and dimensions of the object. The object must be kept absolutely motionless while the plate is being exposed: otherwise the information provided by the interference will be obliterated

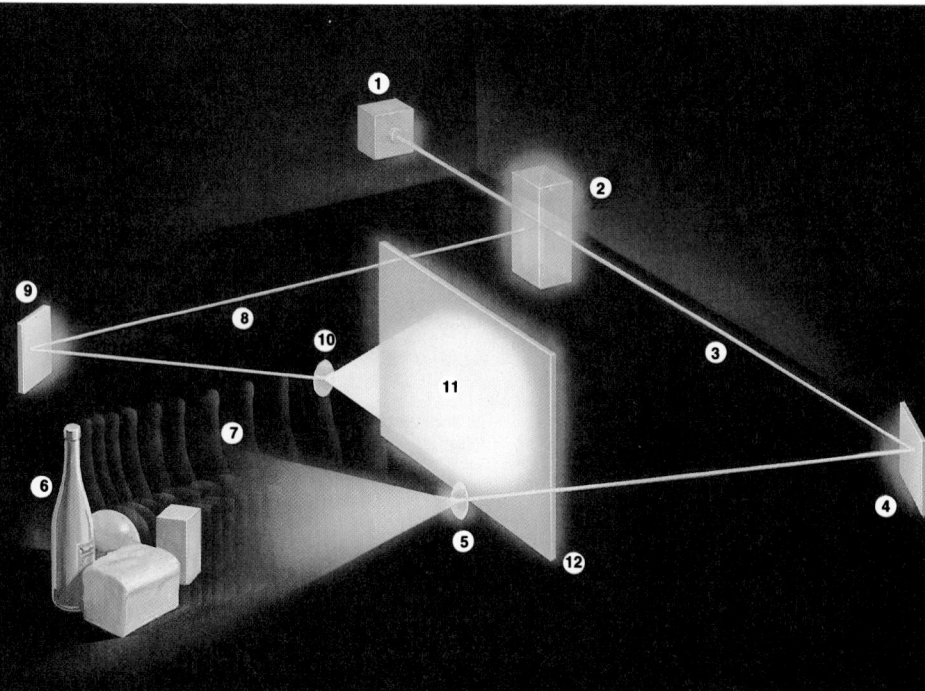

VIEWING THE IMAGE

1. After exposure, the photographic plate shows information on the recorded object as a hologram—a pattern of light and dark areas. The usual exposure time varies between one second and one minute, depending on laser power, emulsion sensitivity, and the amount of light reflected by the object

2. A source of coherent light is needed to reconstruct the hologram into an image of the object that is visible to the observer. A laser beam is directed through the plate at the same angle at which the reference beam struck it during exposure

3. A lens expands the reconstruction beam to flood the plate with light

4. An observer looking through the plate sees a three-dimensional image of the object behind it. So long as the light sources used in recording the object and in reconstructing the image are identical the image appears the same size, and at the same position and distance as the object recorded. As the observer moves from left to right around the image, its aspect alters just as that of the object would have altered

5. The three-dimensional image created by the reconstruction beam

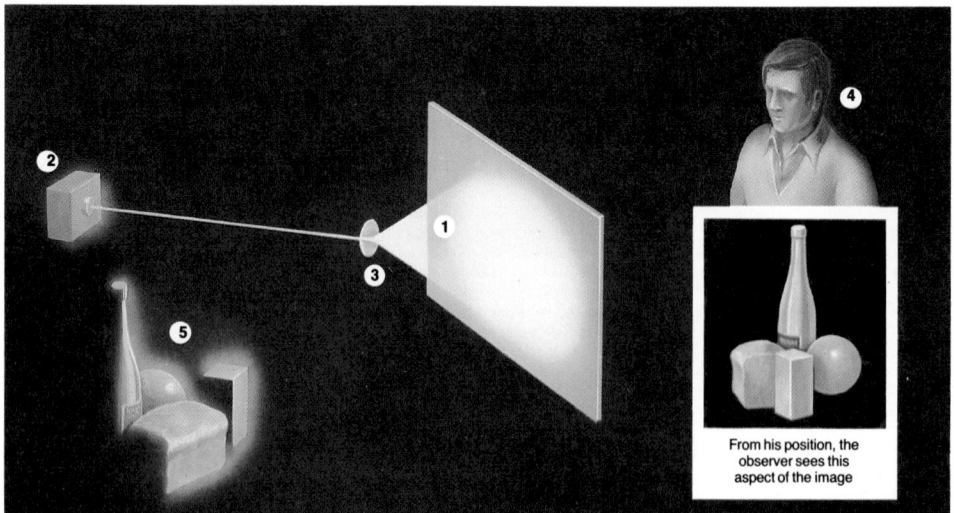

From his position, the observer sees this aspect of the image

home (hōm) *n.* **1.** A place where one lives; a residence; a habitation. **2.** The physical structure or the portion of it within which one lives, as a house or apartment. **3.** One's immediate family and its place of residence, considered as an environment to which one belongs: *house and home; didn't leave home till he was 21.* **4.** An environment or haven of shelter, happiness, or love. **5.** A place or condition valued as a refuge or place of origin. **6.** The place where one was born or spent one's early childhood, as a town, state, or country. **7.** The native habitat of a plant, animal, or the like. **8.** The place where something is discovered, founded, developed, or promoted; the source: *Boston, home of baked beans and cod.* **9.** A place where a group, such as a company or a sports team, is based or established. **10.** A goal or place of safety toward which players of a game, such as baseball, backgammon, or tag, progress. **11.** An institution providing temporary or permanent residential care, as for old people or those convalescing from illness: *a nursing home.* **—at home. 1.** In one's own house, environment, or city; not away or absent. **2.** Available to receive visitors: *a family that is home on*

Thursdays. **3.** At ease; relaxed and comfortable, as if in one's own home: *a speaker who seemed completely at home on the lecture platform.* **4.** Having or feeling an easy competence and familiarity: *at home in French.* —**close to home.** So as to affect an individual or group personally: *The prime minister's speech about war economies hit close to home.*

~*adj.* **1.** Of or pertaining to a home, especially to one's household or house: *home furnishings; home cooking.* **2.** Of or pertaining to one's country, place of birth, or nation; domestic. **3.** Of or pertaining to a base of operations or headquarters: *the home office of a worldwide company.* **4.** Going straight to the point; reaching the mark directly and accurately: *a home thrust.* **5.** Taking place or based at one's own headquarters: *a home game; the home team.*

~*adv.* **1.** At, to, or toward the direction of home: *finished work and headed home.* **2.** To the point at which something is directed; on target: *The arrow struck home.* **3. a.** To the furthest possible point or extent. **b.** To the center or heart of something; deeply: *The criticism struck home.* **4.** *Nautical.* Toward a vessel. —**bring home to.** To make clear to; cause to be understood by: *cannot seem to bring it home to him how important this is.* —**come home to.** To be brought home; become clear: *The real truth finally came home to him.* —**home free.** Free of tension or stress, especially after a difficult effort: *Once we get this heavy work done, we're home free.*

~*v.* **homed, homing, homes.** —*intr.* **1.** To go or return home, especially from a distance. Used especially of birds such as pigeons. **2.** To be guided to a target automatically, as by inertial guidance or heat sensing. —*tr.* To guide (a missile or aircraft) to a target automatically. —**home in.** To move, lead, or aim toward a goal. Used with *on: home straight in on the correct answer.* [Middle English *hom(e),* Old English *hām,* from Germanic.]

home base *n.* **1.** A base of operations; headquarters. **2.** An objective toward which players of a game progress; home. **3.** *Baseball.* The **plate** *(see).*

home·bod·y (hōm'bŏd'ē) *n., pl.* **-ies.** One who likes to stay or work at home; a domestic person.

home·bred (hōm'brĕd') *adj.* **1.** Produced, bred, or reared at home; domestic; indigenous. **2.** Not cultivated or sophisticated.

home·brew (hōm'brōō') *n.* An alcoholic beverage, especially beer, that is made at home. —**home-brewed** *adj.*

home·com·ing (hōm'kŭm'ĭng) *n.* **1.** A return to one's home or to a place where one formerly lived, worked, or studied. **2.** An annual event for visiting alumni at colleges and universities.

Home Counties. The counties of England nearest to London. Formerly the term covered Kent, Surrey, Middlesex, and Essex, but is now often used to include Buckinghamshire, Berkshire, Hertfordshire, and Sussex.

home economics *pl.n.* *Used with a singular verb.* The science or study of home management, including household budgets, purchase of food and clothing, child care, cooking, nutrition, and the like.

home front *n.* The civilian population of a country at war.

home-grown (hōm'grōn') *adj.* **1.** Grown or produced at home, as in one's own garden, district, or country. Said especially of fruit and vegetables. **2.** Produced or originating in one's home area: *our homegrown national hero.*

home guard *n.* **1.** A volunteer force formed to defend a homeland while the regular army is fighting elsewhere; especially, the force organized to defend Great Britain in the event of a German invasion in World War II. **2.** A member of such a force.

home·land (hōm'lănd') *n.* **1.** The land of one's allegiance; one's native land. **2.** The place of origin of a people. **3.** Any of the ten regions designated by the government of South Africa for the black population, in accordance with the policy of apartheid. Four of the homelands have already been granted self-governing status, namely, Transkei (1976), Bophuthatswana (1977), Venda (1979), and Ciskei (1980), but they have not been internationally recognized as independent states. The other homelands are Gazankulu, KaNgwane, KwaNdebele, Kwazulu, Lebowa, and Qwaqwa. In this sense, also called "Bantustan."

home·less (hōm'lĭs) *adj.* Having no home. —**home·less·ness** *n.*

home·ly (hōm'lē) *adj.* **-lier, -liest. 1.** Of a nature associated with or suited to the home; domestic; familiar: *a homely relaxed atmosphere.* **2.** Of a simple or unpretentious nature; uncomplicated or unsophisticated; plain: *"There is a sort of homely truth and naturalness in some books"* (Thoreau). **3.** Not attractive or good-looking; plain. Said of a person. —**home·li·ness** *n.*

home·made (hōm'mād') *adj.* **1.** Made or prepared in the home or on the premises; not bought: *homemade pie; a homemade dress.* **2.** Made or assembled by oneself. **3.** Crudely or simply made: *a homemade bomb.*

home·mak·er (hōm'mā'kər) *n.* A person who manages a household or who creates a homey environment.

homeo-, homoio- *prefix.* Indicates like or similar; for example, *homeostasis, homoiotherm.* [Latin *homoeo-,* from Greek *homoio-,* from *homoios,* similar, from *homos,* same.]

Home Office *n.* A department of the British government that deals with domestic affairs, especially law and order and immigration.

Home of the Hir·sel (hyōōm; hûr'səl), **Alec Douglas-Home, Baron,** born Alexander Frederick Douglas-Home (1903-). British prime minister (1963-64). He became a Conservative M.P. in 1931. In 1951 he succeeded his father as 14th Earl of Home and subsequently became foreign secretary (1960-63). In 1963 he succeeded Harold Macmillan as prime minister, renouncing his peerage to enter the Commons. He resigned the leadership of the Conservative

Party in 1965 and again became foreign secretary (1970-74).

ho·me·o·mor·phism (hō'mē-ō-môr'fĭz'əm, hŏm'ē-) *n.* **1.** *Chemistry.* A close similarity in the crystal forms of unlike chemical compounds. **2.** *Mathematics.* A one-to-one correspondence between the points of two geometric figures that is continuous in both directions. [Greek *homoiomorph(os),* of similar form : HOMEO- + -MORPH(OUS) + -ISM.] —**ho·me·o·mor·phous, ho·me·o·mor·phic** *adj.*

ho·me·op·a·thy (hō'mē-ŏp'ə-thē, hŏm'ē-) *n.* A system of medical treatment based on the use of minute quantities of remedies that in large doses produce effects similar to those of the disease being treated. Compare **allopathy.** [German *Homöopathie* : HOMEO- + -PATHY.] —**ho·me·o·path** (hō'mē-ə-păth', -păth', hŏm'ē-) *n.* —**ho·me·o·path·ic** (hō'mē-ə-păth'ĭk, hŏm'ē-) *adj.* —**ho·me·o·path·i·cal·ly** *adv.*

ho·me·o·sta·sis (hō'mē-ō-stā'sĭs, hŏm'ē-) *n.* A state of physiological equilibrium produced by a balance of functions and of chemical composition within an organism. [New Latin : HOMEO- + -STASIS.] —**ho·me·o·stat·ic** (hō'mē-ō-stăt'ĭk, hŏm'ē-) *adj.*

homeotherm. Variant of **homoiotherm.**

ho·me·o·typ·ic (hō'mē-ō-tĭp'ĭk, hŏm'ē-) *adj.* Relating to or designating the second nuclear division of **meiosis** *(see).* Compare **heterotypic.** [HOMEO- + TYPIC(AL).]

home plate *n.* In baseball, the **plate** *(see).*

hom·er¹ (hō'mər) *n.* **1.** A homing pigeon. **2.** *Baseball. Informal.* A home run. [From HOME.]

ho·mer² (hō'mər) *n.* An ancient Hebrew measure of capacity containing 10 ephahs (about 10 or 11 bushels) in dry measure or 10 baths (about 100 gallons) in liquid measure. [Hebrew *ḥomer.*]

Ho·mer (hō'mər) (8th century B.C.). Greek poet, supposed author of the epics *The Iliad* and *The Odyssey.* Both poems clearly derive from an orally transmitted tradition, describing the events of the Trojan War (c. 1200) and its aftermath. The epics mix fact with fantasy and embody the myths of ancient Greece.

Homer, Winslow (1836-1910). U.S. painter. Originally a magazine illustrator, he first painted rural life and Civil War battle scenes. During a trip to England (1881-82) he became fascinated with the sea, which he depicted in a series of realistic paintings such as *Eight Bells* (1886).

Ho·mer·ic (hō-mĕr'ĭk) *adj.* **1.** Of, pertaining to, or characteristic of the poet Homer, his works, or the legends and age of which he wrote. **2.** Heroic in proportion, degree, or character: *Homeric laughter.* —**Ho·mer·i·cal·ly** *adv.*

home rule *n.* *Abbr.* **H.R. 1.** The principle or practice of self-government in domestic matters in a dependent country or province. **2. Home Rule.** The movement in Ireland from 1870 until the 1920's to obtain self-government, the goal of the Irish Nationalists.

home run *n.* *Abbr.* **h.r.** *Baseball.* A hit that allows the batter to make a complete circuit of the bases and score a run.

home screen *n.* Television.

home·sick (hōm'sĭk') *adj.* Depressed by separation from one's family and home; longing for home. —**home·sick·ness** *n.*

home·spun (hōm'spŭn') *adj.* **1.** Spun or woven in the home. **2. a.** Made of a homespun fabric. **b.** Homemade. **3.** Simple and homely in character; unpretentious.

~*n.* **1.** A plain coarse woolen cloth made of homespun yarn. **2.** A similar sturdy fabric made on a power loom.

home·stead (hōm'stĕd') *n.* **1.** A house, especially a farmhouse, with adjoining buildings and land. **2.** *Law.* Property designated by a householder as his home and protected by law from forced sale to meet debts. **3.** Land claimed by a settler or a squatter, especially under the Homestead Act. **4.** The place where one's home is. **5.** *Australian & New Zealand.* The house of the owner or manager of a sheep or cattle station.

~*v.* **homesteaded, -steading, -steads.** —*intr.* To settle and farm land, especially under the Homestead Act. —*tr.* To claim and settle (land) as a homestead. —**home·stead·er** *n.*

Homestead Act *n.* An act passed by the U.S. Congress in 1862, promising ownership of a 160-acre tract of public land to a head of a family after he had cleared and improved the land and lived on it for five years.

Homestead National Monument. An area, 66 hectares (163 acres), in southeastern Nebraska, the site of the first farm claimed under the Homestead Act.

home·stretch (hōm'strĕch') *n.* **1.** The part of a racetrack from the last turn to the finish line. Also *British* "home straight." **2.** The final stages of an undertaking or journey.

home truth *n.* A fact about a person that is true but unpleasant. [From the adverbial sense of HOME, a truth that strikes home.]

home·ward (hōm'wərd) *adv.* Also **home·wards** (-wərdz). Toward home.

~*adj.* Directed toward home.

home·work (hōm'wûrk') *n.* **1.** Schoolwork that is to be done outside school hours, especially at home. **2.** Any preparatory work.

home·y, hom·y (hō'mē) *adj.* **homier, homiest.** *Informal.* Having a pleasant, homelike quality; cozy. —**hom·ey·ness** *n.*

hom·i·cid·al (hŏm'ĭ-sīd'l, hō'mə-) *adj.* **1.** Of or pertaining to homicide. **2.** Likely to commit homicide. —**hom·i·cid·al·ly** *adv.*

hom·i·cide (hŏm'ə-sīd', hō'mə-) *n.* **1.** The killing of one person by another. Compare **murder. 2.** A person who kills another person. [Middle English, from Old French, from Latin *homicīda,* killer, and *homicīdium,* killing : *homō,* man + *-cīda, -cīdium,* -CIDE (killer and killing).]

hom·i·let·ic (hŏm'ə-lĕt'ĭk) *adj.* Also **hom·i·let·i·cal** (-ĭ-kəl). **1.** Pertaining to or of the nature of a homily. **2.** Pertaining to homiletics. —**hom·i·let·i·cal·ly** *adv.*

hom·i·let·ics (hŏm′ə-lĕt′ĭks) *n. Used with a singular verb.* The art of preaching or writing sermons as a subject of theological study. [Greek *homilētikē*, art of conversing, from *homilētikos*, social, affable, from *homilētos*, conversation, from *homilein*, to consort with, from *homilos*, crowd. See **homily.**]

hom·i·ly (hŏm′ə-lē) *n., pl.* **-lies. 1.** A sermon, especially one intended to edify in a practical way rather than to expound religious doctrine. **2.** A tedious moralizing lecture or admonition. [Learned respelling of Middle English *omelie*, from Old French, from Late Latin *homīlia*, from Greek *homilia*, discourse, intercourse, association, from *homilos*, crowd : *homou*, together + *ilē†*, crowd.] —**hom·i·list** (hŏm′ə-lĭst) *n.*

hom·ing (hō′mĭng) *adj.* **1.** Of or pertaining to the ability, as of certain birds and fishes, to return home, especially from a great distance: *the homing instinct.* **2.** Assisting in guiding a missile or aircraft toward a target: *a homing guidance system.*

homing missile *n.* A missile that steers itself toward a target by means of an internal mechanism, such as a device that senses the target's heat radiation.

homing pigeon *n.* A domestic pigeon, such as one used for racing or for carrying messages, trained to return to its home roost. Also called "homer."

hom·i·nid (hŏm′ə-nĭd) *n.* Any primate of the family Hominidae, of which the human race, *Homo sapiens,* is the only extant species. ~*adj.* Of the Hominidae. [New Latin *Hominidae* : *Homo* (stem *homin-*), HOMO + -ID.]

hom·i·ni·za·tion (hŏm′ə-nə-zā′shən) *n.* The evolutionary development in human beings and their forebears of characteristics regarded as distinguishing humans from animals. [Latin *homō* (stem *homin-*), man + -IZ(E) + -ATION.]

hom·i·noid (hŏm′ə-noid′) *adj.* **1.** Of or belonging to the superfamily Hominoidea, which includes the apes and the human species. **2.** Resembling a human being; manlike. [New Latin *Hominoidea* : *Homo* (stem *homin-*), HOMO + -oidea, -OID.] —**hom·i·noid** *n.*

hom·i·ny (hŏm′ə-nē) *n.* Hulled and dried kernels of corn, prepared as food by boiling. [Perhaps of Algonquian origin.]

hominy grits *pl.n.* Hominy ground into a coarse white meal. Also called "grits."

ho·mo (hō′mō) *n.* Any member of the genus *Homo,* which includes one extant species, human beings. [New Latin *Homo,* from Latin *homō,* man.]

homo-, hom- *prefix.* Indicates same or like; for example, **homogamous, homodont.** [Latin, from Greek, from *homos,* same.]

Usage: Words beginning with the prefix *homo-* are often construed by folk etymology as being derived from Latin *homo,* meaning "man." For example, *homocentric* may be felt to be synonymous with *anthropocentric.* This is an error. There is no connection between Greek *homos,* "same," and Latin *homo,* "man." If analogous words were to be formed on Latin *homo,* the form would either be *homi-,* as in *homicide,* or *homini-,* as in *hominid.*

ho·mo·cen·tric (hō′mō-sĕn′trĭk, hŏm′ō-) *adj.* Having the same center. [New Latin *homocentricus,* from Greek *homokentros* : *homo-,* same + *kentron,* CENTER.]

ho·mo·cer·cal (hō′mō-sûr′kəl, hŏm′ō-) *adj.* Pertaining to, designating, or characterized by a tail fin having two symmetrical lobes extending from the end of the vertebral column, as in most bony fishes. Compare **heterocercal.** [HOMO- + -*cercal,* from Greek *kerkos,* tail.]

ho·mo·chro·mat·ic (hō′mō-krō-măt′ĭk, hŏm′ō-) *adj.* Of or characterized by one color; monochromatic. —**ho·mo·chro·ma·tism** (hō′mō-krō′mə-tĭz′əm) *n.*

ho·mo·cy·clic (hō′mō-sī′klĭk, -sĭk′lĭk) *adj. Chemistry.* Of, pertaining to, or designating a chemical compound having rings in its molecules formed of only one type of atom. Compare **heterocyclic.** ~*n.* A homocyclic compound.

ho·mo·dont (hō′mə-dŏnt′, hŏm′ə-) *adj.* Having teeth that are all of the same kind. Said of most vertebrates except mammals. [HOM(O)- + -ODONT]

ho·mo·e·rot·i·cism (hō′mō-ĭ-rŏt′ĭ-sĭz′əm) *n.* Also **ho·mo·er·o·tism** (-ĕr′ə-tĭz′əm). Sexual attraction for one's own sex; homosexuality. —**ho·mo·e·rot·ic** *adj.*

ho·mo·ga·met·ic (hō′mō-gə-mĕt′ĭk) *adj.* Having a similar pair of sex chromosomes, as in human females. Compare **heterogametic.**

ho·mog·a·mous (hō-mŏg′ə-məs) *adj. Botany.* **1.** Having flowers that are sexually alike in the same plant or inflorescence. **2.** Having stamens and pistils that mature simultaneously. [HOMO- + -GAMOUS.] —**ho·mog·a·my** (hō-mŏg′ə-mē) *n.*

ho·mo·ge·ne·i·ty (hō′mō-jə-nē′ə-tē, hŏm′ō-) *n.* The state or quality of being homogeneous.

ho·mo·ge·ne·ous (hō′mə-jē′nē-əs, -jēn′yəs, hŏm′ə-) *adj.* **1.** Like in nature or kind; similar; congruous. **2.** Uniform in structure or composition throughout. **3.** *Mathematics.* Consisting of terms of the same degree or elements of the same dimension. **4.** *Chemistry.* Having or involving only one phase. [Medieval Latin *homogeneus,* from Greek *homogenēs* : *homo-,* same + *-genēs,* born (see **-gen**) + -OUS.] —**ho·mo·ge·ne·ous·ly** *adv.* —**ho·mo·ge·ne·ous·ness** *n.*

ho·mog·e·nize (hə-mŏj′ə-nīz′, hō-) *tr.v.* **-nized, -nizing, -nizes. 1.** To make homogeneous. **2. a.** To reduce to particles and disperse throughout a fluid. **b.** To make uniform in consistency; especially, to render (milk) uniform in consistency by emulsifying the fat content. —**ho·mog·e·ni·za·tion** *n.* —**ho·mog·e·niz·er** *n.*

ho·mog·e·nous (hō-mŏj′ə-nəs, hə-) *adj.* **1.** *Biology.* Of or exhibiting homogeny. **2.** Homogeneous. [Medieval Latin *homogen(e)us,* HOMOGENEOUS.]

ho·mog·e·ny (hō-mŏj′ə-nē, hə-) *n. Biology.* Correspondence between organs or parts of different species, possibly of dissimilar function, due to common descent; homology. [Greek *homogeneia,* from *homogenēs,* HOMOGENEOUS.]

ho·mog·o·nous (hō-mŏg′ə-nəs, hə-) *adj.* Designating plants in which the stamens and styles are of the same length in all the flowers. [HOMO- + -GON(Y) + -OUS.] —**ho·mog·o·ny** *n.*

hom·o·graft (hŏm′ə-grăft′, -gräft′, hō′mə-) *n.* A graft of tissue obtained from a member of the same species as the individual receiving it.

hom·o·graph (hŏm′ə-grăf′, -gräf′, hō′mə-) *n.* A word that is spelled in the same way as another word but differs in meaning and origin and may differ in pronunciation. [HOMO- + -GRAPH.] —**hom·o·graph·ic** (hŏm′ə-grăf′ĭk, hō′mə-) *adj.*

homoio-. Variant of **homeo-.**

ho·moi·o·therm (hō-moi′ə-thûrm′) *n.* Also **ho·me·o·therm** (hō-mē′ə-thûrm′). A homoiothermic organism, such as a bird or mammal. [HOMOIO- + -THERM.]

ho·moi·o·ther·mic (hō-moi′ə-thûr′mĭk) *adj.* Also **ho·moi·o·ther·mal** (-məl), **ho·me·o·ther·mic** (hō-mē′ə-thûr′mĭk). Maintaining a relatively constant and warm body temperature that is independent of environmental temperature; warm-blooded. Compare **poikilothermic.**

Ho·moi·ou·si·an (hō′moi-ōō′sē-ən, -ou′sē-ən) *n.* In the 4th century, a Christian holding a modified version of the Arian view, to the effect that God the Father and Jesus the Son were of similar but not of the same substance. Compare **Heteroousian, Homoousian.** [Greek *homoiousios,* of similar substance : HOMOIO- + *ousia,* substance, from *ōn* (stem *ous-*), present participle of *einai,* to be.]

ho·mol·o·gate (hō-mŏl′ə-gāt′, hə-) *tr.v.* **-gated, -gating, -gates.** *Chiefly Scottish Law.* To ratify, assent to, or approve (a contract, deed, or the like). [Medieval Latin *homologāre,* from Greek *homologein,* to concur, agree, from *homologos,* HOMOLOGOUS.]

ho·mo·log·i·cal (hō′mə-lŏj′ĭ-kəl, hŏm′ə-) *adj.* Also **ho·mo·log·ic** (hō′mə-lŏj′ĭk). Homologous. —**ho·mo·log·i·cal·ly** *adv.*

ho·mol·o·gize (hō-mŏl′ə-jīz′, hə-) *tr.v.* **-gized, -gizing, -gizes. 1.** To make homologous. **2.** To show to be homologous. —**ho·mol·o·giz·er** *n.*

ho·mol·o·gous (hō-mŏl′ə-gəs, hə-) *adj.* **1.** Corresponding or similar in position, value, structure, or function. **2.** *Biology.* Corresponding in structure and evolutionary origin, as the flippers of a seal and the arms of a human being. Compare **analogous. 3.** *Genetics.* Designating two chromosomes that are similar in appearance, have the same linear sequence of genes, and pair during meiosis. One is derived from the male gamete and the other from the female gamete. **4.** *Chemistry.* Belonging to or being a series of organic compounds each successive member of which differs from the preceding member by a constant increment, especially by an added CH_2 group. **5.** *Mathematics.* Having the same effect or role in different functions or figures. [Greek *homologos,* agreeing : HOMO- + *logos,* word, proportion, from *legein,* to speak.]

hom·o·lo·graph·ic (hŏm′ə-lō-grăf′ĭk) *adj.* Maintaining the ratio of parts. [Irregularly from Greek *homalos,* even, level + GRAPHIC.]

homolographic projection *n.* An **equal-area projection** (see).

hom·o·logue, hom·o·log (hŏm′ə-lôg′, -lŏg′, hō′mə-) *n.* Something homologous; a homologous organ or part.

ho·mol·o·gy (hō-mŏl′ə-jē, hə-) *n., pl.* **-gies. 1.** The quality or condition of being homologous. **2.** A homologous relationship or correspondence. **3.** *Mathematics.* A topological classification of configurations into distinct types that imposes an algebraic structure or hierarchy on families of geometric figures. [Greek *homologia,* agreement, from *homologos,* HOMOLOGOUS.]

ho·mol·o·sine projection (hō-mŏl′ə-sīn′) *n.* An equal-area map projection in which the sinusoidal projection is used for latitudes between 40°N and 40°S and the Mollweide projection is used for higher latitudes. It is interrupted over ocean areas so that the continents appear with minimal distortion. [Irregularly from Greek *homalos,* even, flat + -INE.]

ho·mol·y·sis (hō-mŏl′ə-sĭs, hə-) *n. Chemistry.* A chemical reaction in which a bond breaks to give two electrically neutral free radicals. Also called "homolytic fission." Compare **heterolysis.** [HOMO- + -LYSIS.] —**ho·mo·lyt·ic** (hō′mə-lĭt′ĭk, hŏm′ə-) *adj.*

ho·mo·mor·phism (hō′mō-môr′fĭz′əm, hŏm′ō-) *n.* Similarity of external form, appearance, or size. [HOMO- + MORPH(O)- + -ISM.] —**ho·mo·mor·phic, ho·mo·mor·phous** *adj.*

hom·o·nym (hŏm′ə-nĭm′, hō′mə-) *n.* **1.** One of two or more words that have the same sound and often the same spelling but differ in meaning. Compare **homophone. 2. a.** A word that is used to designate several different things. **b.** A namesake. **3.** *Biology.* One of two or more identical but conflicting taxonomic designations independently proposed for members of different categories. [Latin *homōnymum,* from Greek *homōnumon,* from *homōnumos,* HOMONYMOUS.] —**hom·o·nym·ic** (hŏm′ə-nĭm′ĭk, hō′mə-) *adj.*

ho·mon·y·mous (hō-mŏn′ə-məs, hə-) *adj.* **1.** Having the same name. **2.** Of the nature of a homonym; homonymic. [Latin *homōnymus,* from Greek *homōnumos* : HOMO- + *onuma,* name.] —**ho·mon·y·mous·ly** *adv.*

ho·mon·y·my (hō-mŏn′ə-mē, hə-) *n.* The quality or condition of being homonymous.

Ho·mo·ou·si·an (hō′mō-ōō′sē-ən, -ou′sē-ən, hŏm′ō-) *n.* Also **Ho-**

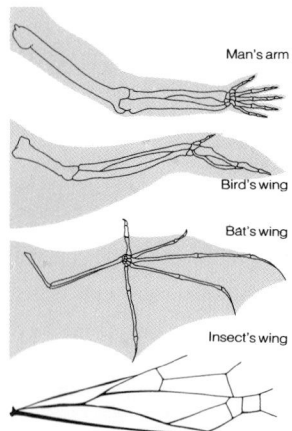

homologous *The human arm is homologous with bird and bat wings because, although it serves a different function, its structure and evolutionary history are similar. Bird, bat, and insect wings are analogous because they serve the same function—flight. The insect wing, however, has a different structure from that of the bird and bat and so is not homologous with them.*

Man's arm

Bird's wing

Bat's wing

Insect's wing

mou·si·an (hō-mo͞o′sē-ən, hō-mou′-). A Christian supporting the Council of Nicaea's Trinitarian definition of Jesus the Son of God as consubstantial with God the Father. Compare **Heteroousian, Homoiousian.** [Late Latin *homousiānus,* from *homousius,* consubstantial, from Greek *homoousios,* of identical substance : HOMO- + *ousia,* being (see **Homoiousian**).]

ho·mo·phile (hō′mə-fīl′) *adj.* **1.** Homosexual. **2.** Actively concerned with the rights and welfare of homosexuals. **—ho·mo·phile** *n.*

ho·mo·pho·bi·a (hō′mə-fō′bē-ə) *n.* Fear of homosexuals or of homosexuality. **—ho·mo·pho·bic** *adj.*

hom·o·phone (hŏm′ə-fōn′, hō′mə-) *n.* **1.** A word having the same sound as another word but differing from it in spelling, origin, and meaning; for example, English *sum* and *some* are homophones. Compare **homonym. 2.** A symbol, such as a letter or a group of letters, that represents the same sound as another; for example, English *kn* and *n* are homophones. [HOMO- + -PHONE.]

hom·o·phon·ic (hŏm′ə-fŏn′ĭk, hō′mə-) *adj.* Also **ho·moph·o·nous** (hō-mŏf′ə-nəs, hə-). **1.** Having the same sound. **2.** *Music.* Having or characterized by parts that move in unison to a single melodic line. [Greek *homophōnos,* having the same sound : HOMO- + *phōnē,* sound (see **-phone**).]

ho·moph·o·ny (hō-mŏf′ə-nē, hə-) *n.* **1.** The quality or condition of being homophonic. **2.** Homophonic music. Compare **polyphony, monophony.**

ho·mo·phy·ly (hō′mə-fī′lē, hŏm′ə-, hō-mŏf′ə-lē) *n.* Resemblance arising from common ancestry. [HOMO- + Greek *phulē,* tribe, PHYLE.] **—ho·mo·phyl·ic** (hō′mə-fĭl′ĭk, hŏm′ə-) *adj.*

ho·mo·plas·tic (hō′mə-plăs′tĭk, hŏm′ə-) *adj.* **1.** *Biology.* Of, pertaining to, or exhibiting superficial structural similarity arising from **convergence** *(see).* **2.** Of, pertaining to, or derived from a different individual of the same species: *a homoplastic graft.* [HOMO- + -PLASTIC.] **—ho·mo·plas·ti·cal·ly** *adv.*

ho·mo·pla·sy (hō′mə-plā′sē, -plăs′ē, hŏm′ə-) *n. Biology.* Superficial structural similarity arising from convergence or parallel evolution.

ho·mo·po·lar (hō′mə-pō′lər, hŏm′ə-) *adj. Chemistry.* Not ionic or polar; having uniform charge distribution. Said of covalent bonds.

ho·mop·ter·ous (hō-mŏp′tər-əs, hə-) *adj.* Also **ho·mop·ter·an** (-ən). Of or belonging to the order Homoptera, which includes insects such as the cicadas, aphids, and scale insects. [New Latin *Homoptera* : HOMO- + -PTEROUS.]

hom·or·gan·ic (hŏm′ôr-găn′ĭk, hō′môr-) *adj. Phonetics.* Designating two or more speech sounds, such as the alveolar consonants *t, d,* and *n,* formed in the same area or with the same organs of articulation. [HOM(O)- + ORGANIC.]

Ho·mo sa·pi·ens (hō′mō sā′pē-ənz, -ĕnz′) *n.* **1.** The taxonomic designation for modern human beings, the only extant species of the genus *Homo.* **2.** The human being as a thinking creature as distinguished from other organisms. [New Latin : HOMO + Latin *sapiēns,* SAPIENT.]

ho·mo·sce·das·tic (hō′mō-sĭ-dăs′tĭk, hŏm′ō-) *adj. Statistics.* Of or being variables for which all possible values have constant variance. [HOMO- + *scedastic,* from Greek *skedasis,* dispersion, scattering.] **—ho·mo·sce·das·tic·i·ty** (hō′mō-sĭ-dă-stĭs′ĭ-tē, hŏm′ō-) *n.*

ho·mo·sex·u·al (hō′mō-sĕk′sho͞o-əl, hō′mə-, hŏm′ə-) *adj.* **1.** Characterized by attraction to the same sex. **2.** Of or pertaining to sexual relations between persons of the same sex.
∼n. A homosexual person. **—ho·mo·sex·u·al·i·ty** (hō′mō-sĕk′sho͞o-ăl′ĭ-tē, hŏm′ō-) *n.*

ho·mos·po·rous (hō-mŏs′pər-əs, hō′mə-spôr′əs, -spōr′əs, hŏm′ə-) *adj. Botany.* Producing spores of one kind only. Said of certain ferns. [HOMO- + -SPOROUS.] **—ho·mos·po·ry** *n.*

ho·mo·tax·is (hō′mō-tăk′sĭs, hŏm′ō-) *n.* Similarity of arrangement and fossils in noncontemporaneous or widely separated geologic deposits. [New Latin : HOMO- + -TAXIS.] **—ho·mo·tax·ic** (hō′mō-tăk′sĭk, hŏm′ō-), **ho·mo·tax·i·al** (-tăk′sē-əl) *adj.*

ho·mo·thal·lic (hō′mō-thăl′ĭk, hŏm′ō-) *adj. Botany.* Having male and female reproductive structures in the same thallus, as in some fungi and algae. **—ho·mo·thal·lism** *n.*

ho·mo·zy·go·sis (hō′mō-zī-gō′sĭs, hŏm′ō-) *n.* The union of genetically identical gametes, resulting in the formation of a homozygote. **—ho·mo·zy·got·ic** (hō′mō-zī-gŏt′ĭk, hŏm′ō-) *adj.*

ho·mo·zy·gote (hō′mō-zī′gōt′, hŏm′ō-) *n.* An organism derived from the union of genetically identical gametes and having identical alleles for one or more genes. **—ho·mo·zy·gous** (hō′mō-zī′gəs, hō′mə-, hŏm′ō-, hŏm′ə-) *adj.*

ho·mun·cu·lus (hō-mŭng′kyə-ləs) *n., pl.* **-li** (-lī′). **1.** A diminutive man; a manikin. **2.** A fully formed individual believed by adherents of the early biological theory of preformation to be present in a sperm cell. [Latin, diminutive of *homō,* man.]

homy. Variant of **homey.**

hon. honorary.

Hon. 1. honorary. **2.** Honorable (title).

Honan, Ho-nan. See **Henan** (province), **Luoyang** (city).

hon·cho (hŏn′chō) *n., pl.* **-chos.** *Slang.* One who is in charge; leader or boss. [Japanese, squad leader: *han,* squad + *chō,* chief.]

Hondo. See **Honshu.**

Hon·du·ras (hŏn-do͝or′əs, -dyo͝or′əs). Republic of Central America, on the Gulf of Honduras, an inlet of the Caribbean. It gained its independence from Spain in 1821. The economy is predominantly agricultural, and the main exports are bananas, coffee, timber, and silver. Area, 112,088 square kilometers (43,266 square miles). Population, 3,700,000. Capital, Tegucigalpa. See map at **Central American States. —Hon·du·ran** *adj. & n.*

hone[1] (hōn) *n.* **1.** A fine-grained whetstone for giving a keen edge to razors and tools. **2.** A tool with a rotating abrasive tip for enlarging holes to precise dimensions.
∼tr.v. **honed, honing, hones.** To sharpen on or as if on a hone; give an edge to. [Middle English *hone,* Old English *hān,* stone, from Germanic.]

hone[2] *intr.v.* **honed, honing, hones.** *Informal.* **1.** To whine or moan. **2.** To hanker; yearn. Often used with *for* or *after.* [Old French *hoigner,* from *hon,* cry of discontent.]

Hon·eg·ger (ŏn′ə-gər, hŏn′-, ô′nĕ-gĕr′), **Arthur** (1892–1955). Swiss composer, born in France. A prolific proponent of the modern movement in French music, he brought his bold harmonic style to chamber, orchestral, and operatic music. Among his many works are *Pastorale d'été* (1921), *Pacific 231* (1924), and *Judith* (1926).

hon·est (ŏn′ĭst) *adj.* **1.** Not given to lying, cheating, stealing, or taking unfair advantage; truthful; trustworthy. **2. a.** Not characterized by deception or fraud; genuine. **b.** Not calculated or constructed to defraud: *honest dice.* **3.** Equitable; fair: *honest wages for an honest day's work.* **4. a.** Having or manifesting integrity and truth; not false: *honest reporting.* **b.** Sincere; candid; frank: *Give me your honest opinion.* **5. a.** Of guileless or ingenuous appearance; open: *"Flushed with purple grace/He shows his honest face."* (John Dryden). **b.** Unfeigned; undisguised: *honest pleasure.* **6. a.** Of good repute; respectable; decent. **b.** Unpretentious; unaffected: *honest country folk.* **7.** *Archaic.* Free from moral stain; virtuous; chaste. Usually said of a woman. [Middle English, from Old French *honeste,* from Latin *honestus,* honorable, from *honōs,* HONOR.]

honest broker *n.* A neutral mediator.

hon·est·ly (ŏn′ĭst-lē) *adv.* **1.** In an honest manner. **2.** Really; truly. Used as an intensifier: *I honestly don't know.*

hon·es·ty (ŏn′ĭ-stē) *n.* **1.** The quality or condition of being honest; integrity; trustworthiness. **2.** Truthfulness; sincerity: *in all honesty.* **3.** *Archaic.* Chastity. **4.** A plant, *Lunaria annua,* native to Eurasia, cultivated for its fragrant purplish flowers and round, flat, papery silver-white seed pods. In this sense, also called "satinpod."
Synonyms: *honor, integrity, probity, veracity.*

hone·wort (hōn′wûrt′, -wôrt′) *n.* **1.** A European plant, *Trinia glauca,* having clusters of small whitish flowers. **2.** Any of several similar and related plants. [*Hone-*† (meaning unknown) + WORT.]

hon·ey (hŭn′ē) *n., pl.* **-eys. 1.** A sweet yellowish or brownish viscid fluid produced by various bees from the nectar of flowers and used as food. **2.** A similar substance made by certain other insects. **3.** A sweet substance, such as the nectar of flowers. **4.** Sweetness. **5.** *Informal.* Sweet one; dear. Used as a term of endearment. **6.** *Informal.* A remarkably fine example: *a honey of a dress.*
∼tr.v. **honeyed** or **honied, -eying, -eys.** To sweeten with or as if with honey. [Middle English *hony,* Old English *hunig,* from Germanic.]

honey agaric *n.* The **honey mushroom** *(see).*

honey ant *n.* Any of various ants, such as one of the genus *Myrmecocystus,* that collect and store honeydew in the distensible abdomens of specialized workers.

honey badger *n.* A carnivorous mammal, *Mellivora capensis,* of Africa and Asia, having short legs and a thick coat. It feeds on honey and small animals. Also called "ratel."

honey bear *n.* A mammal, the **kinkajou** *(see).*

hon·ey·bee (hŭn′ē-bē′) *n.* Any of several social bees of the genus *Apis* that produce honey; especially, *A. mellifera,* widely domesticated as a source of honey and beeswax.

honey buzzard *n.* A European bird of prey, *Pernis apivorus,* having brown plumage with white streaks on the underparts. It feeds mainly on wasps and bee larvae.

hon·ey·comb (hŭn′ē-kōm′) *n.* **1.** A structure of hexagonal, thin-walled cells constructed from beeswax by honeybees to hold honey and eggs. **2.** Something suggesting this in structure or pattern.
∼tr.v. **honeycombed, -combing, -combs. 1.** To fill with cavities like a honeycomb: *castle walls honeycombed with little windows.* **2.** To penetrate thoroughly so as to weaken or undermine: *His story was honeycombed with lies.* **3.** To form in or cover with a honeycomb pattern.

hon·ey·creep·er (hŭn′ē-krē′pər) *n.* **1.** Any of various small, often brightly colored tropical American birds of the subfamily Dacninae, having a curved bill adapted for sucking nectar from flowers. **2.** Any of several similar birds of the family Drepanididae, of Hawaii.

hon·ey·dew (hŭn′ē-do͞o′, -dyo͞o′) *n.* **1.** A sweet, sticky substance excreted by various insects, especially aphids, on the leaves of plants. **2.** A similar sweet exudate on the leaves of plants. **3.** A honeydew melon.

honeydew melon *n.* A melon, a variety of *Cucumis melo,* having a smooth, yellow rind and greenish-white flesh.

hon·ey·eat·er (hŭn′ē-ē′tər) *n.* Any of various birds of the family Meliphagidae, of Australia and adjacent regions, having a curved bill and a long tongue adapted for sucking nectar from flowers.

hon·eyed, hon·ied (hŭn′ēd) *adj.* **1.** Containing, full of, or sweetened with honey. **2.** Ingratiating; sugary: *honeyed words.* **3.** Sweet; dulcet: *a honeyed voice.*

honey guide *n.* Any of various tropical Old World birds of the family Indicatoridae, some species of which lead animals or people to the nests of wild honeybees, where they eat the wax that remains after the honey has been removed.

honey locust *n.* **1.** A thorny tree, *Gleditsia triacanthos,* of eastern

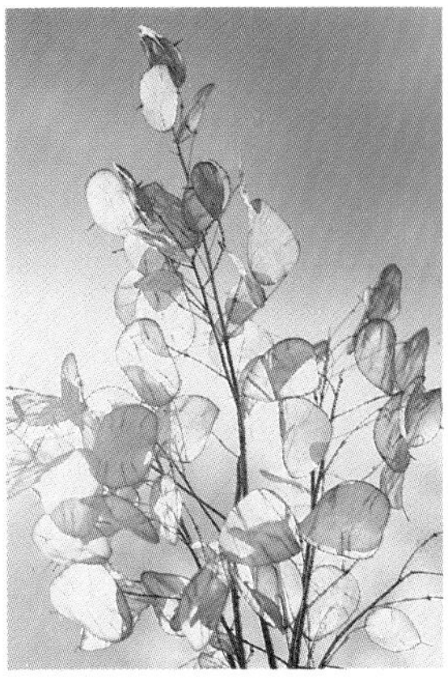
honesty Lunaria annua *has small fragrant purple flowers but is most prized for its silver, disklike seedpods (above), which are used in dried flower arrangements.*

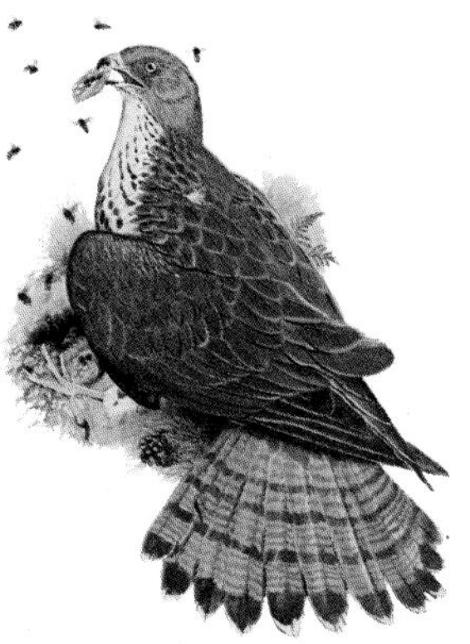
honey buzzard *Wasps and wild bees and their honey are the main diet of this bird of prey, though it also eats small frogs and lizards. Densely packed feathers on its head protect it from stings. Its breeding grounds are in Africa, Europe, and Asia.*

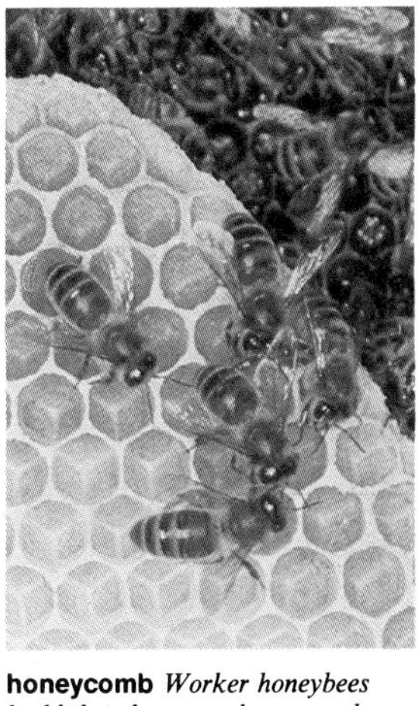
honeycomb *Worker honeybees build their hexagonal-patterned combs from beeswax secreted by their own bodies. The combs are used as nurseries for bee larvae and to store honey.*

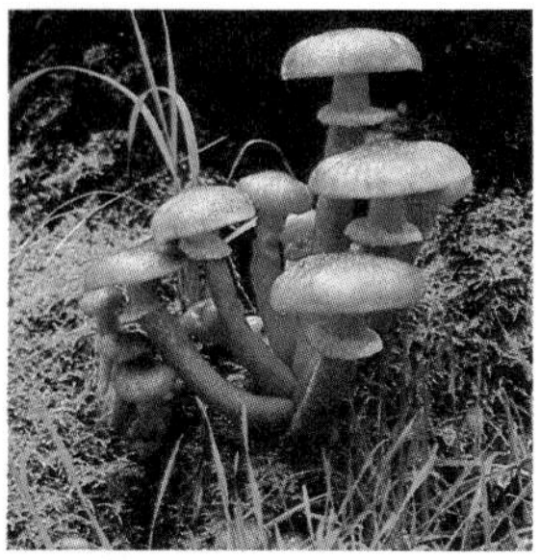

honey mushroom *Wood infected with this destructive fungus glows eerily in the dark. But its golden yellow mushrooms are safe to eat.*

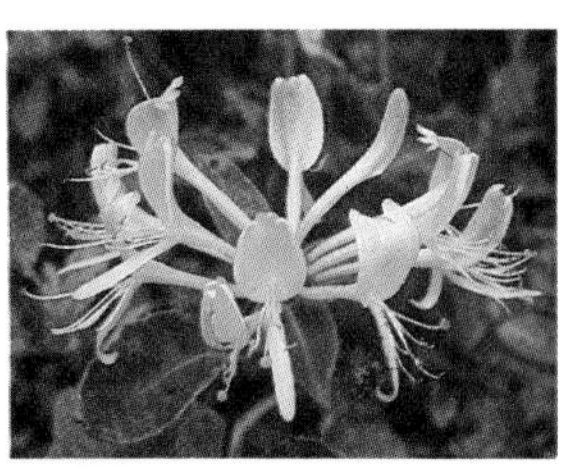

honeysuckle *A graceful and woody climber that is a popular and fragrant garden shrub. This species is* Lonicera periclymenum.

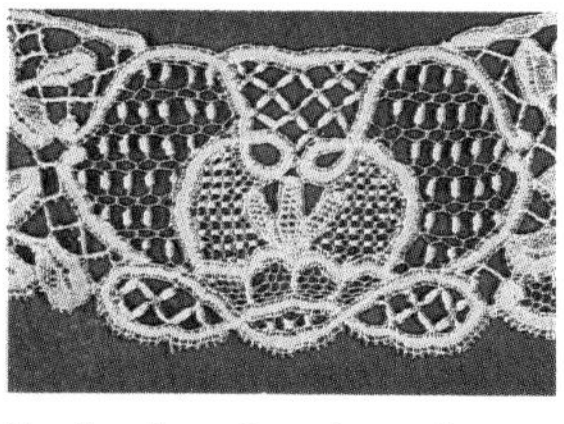

Honiton lace *One of several distinctive English styles of handmade lace. Honiton lace was employed to make the christening robe currently used by the British royal family; it was originally commissioned for one of Queen Victoria's children.*

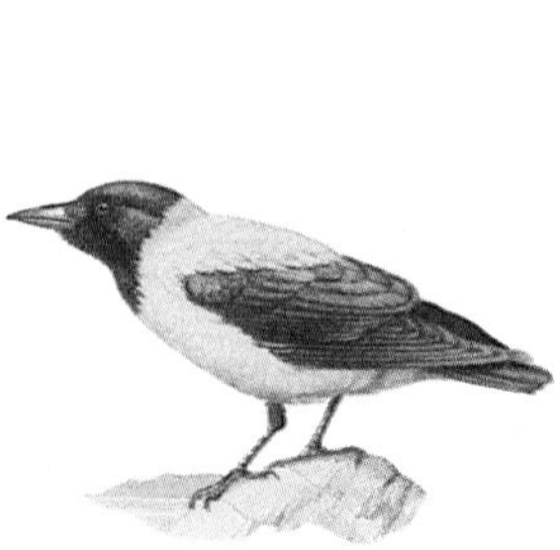

hooded crow *Like its close relative the carrion crow, with which it interbreeds, the hooded crow feeds on the flesh of dead animals. It has replaced the carrion crow in northern and eastern Europe and western Asia.*

North America, bearing long pods containing a sweet pulp. **2.** A similar tree, the **mesquite** *(see).*

hon·ey·moon (hŭn′ē-mo͞on′) *n.* **1.** A holiday taken by a newly married couple. Also used adjectivally: *the honeymoon suite.* **2.** A usually short-lived period of harmony and cooperation at the beginning of any joint undertaking or working relationship: *After a brief honeymoon, relations between the new governor and the state legislature quickly deteriorated.*
∼*intr.v.* **honeymooned, -mooning, -moons.** To spend a honeymoon. [HONEY + MOON (month), the first month of marriage being thought of as the sweetest.] **—hon·ey·moon·er** *n.*

honey mouse *n.* A small Australian marsupial, *Tarsipes spenserae,* having a long snout and tongue and prehensile tail. It climbs shrubs to feed on nectar. Also called "honey phalanger," "honeysucker."

honey mushroom *n.* A honey-colored mushroom, *Armillaria mellea,* that grows on tree stumps and is a serious pest of trees. Also called "honey agaric," "bootlace fungus."

hon·ey·suck·er (hŭn′ē-sŭk′ər) *n.* Any of various animals that feed on nectar, especially the honeyeater or the honey mouse.

hon·ey·suck·le (hŭn′ē-sŭk′əl) *n.* **1.** Any of various shrubs or vines of the genus *Lonicera,* having tubular, often very fragrant yellowish, white, or pink flowers. **2.** Any of various similar or related plants, such as any of certain Australian trees or shrubs of the genus *Banksia,* having dense spikes of flowers. **3.** A New Zealand tree, the **rewarewa** *(see).* [Middle English *honysoukel,* variant of *honysouke,* Old English *hunigsūce* : *hunig,* HONEY + *sūcan,* to SUCK.]

hong (hông, hŏng) *n.* A warehouse, factory, or foreign trading house in China. [Cantonese *hong,* corresponding to Mandarin Chinese *hang²,* profession, business establishment.]

Hong Kong (hŏng′ kŏng′, hông′ kông′). British crown colony in southern China, consisting of Hong Kong Island at the mouth of the Zhujiang (Pearl River) and about 230 islets in the South China Sea, Jiulong (Kowloon Peninsula), and the New Territories on the Chinese mainland. The island was ceded to Great Britain in the Treaty of Nanking (1842); part of Jiulong was acquired (1860); and the New Territories were leased to Great Britain for 99 years in 1898. Hong Kong is a free port and a major commercial, banking, and manufacturing center. Area, 1,045 square kilometers (403 square miles). Capital, Victoria (also called Hong Kong). See map at **China.**

honied. Variant of **honeyed.**

ho·ni soit qui mal y pense (ô′nē swä′ kē mäl′ ē päɴs′). Shamed be he who thinks evil of it. Used as the motto of the Order of the Garter. [French.]

Hon·i·ton lace (hŏn′ĭ-tən, hŭn′-) *n.* A type of bobbin lace consisting of floral sprigs sewn on net or joined by other lace. [After *Honiton,* Devonshire, England, where it was originally made.]

honk (hôngk, hŏngk) *n.* **1.** The raucous, resonant sound characteristically uttered by a wild goose. **2.** A similar sound, such as that made by an automobile horn.
∼*v.* **honked, honking, honks.** —*intr.* To emit a honk. —*tr.* To cause (a horn) to produce a honk. [Imitative.] **—honk·er** *n.*

hon·ky-tonk (hông′kē-tôngk′, hŏng′kē-tŏngk′) *n. Slang.* A cheap, noisy saloon or dance hall.
∼*adj.* Designating a type of ragtime usually played on a tinny old piano. [20th century : origin obscure.]

Hon·o·lu·lu (hŏn′ə-lo͞o′lo͞o). Capital of the state of Hawaii, on the island of Oahu. It is a crossroads of transport across the Pacific Ocean, as well as the economic center and leading port of Hawaii.

hon·or (ŏn′ər) *n.* Also *chiefly British* **hon·our. 1.** Esteem; respect; reverence: *the honor shown to him.* **2. a.** Reputation; good name. **b.** Credit: *It was to his honor that he refused the payment.* **3. a.** Glory; fame; distinction. **b.** A mark, token, or gesture of respect or distinction: *It is an honor to be seated next to the host.* **c.** A decoration or title conferred in recognition of distinguished conduct or achievement. **4.** Nobility of mind; probity; personal integrity. **5.** High rank; exalted position. **6.** One that imparts distinction by association: *He is an honor to our city.* **7.** Great privilege: *I have the honor to present the governor.* **8. Honor.** A title of respect used to or of mayors and judges. Preceded by *Your, His,* or *Her.* **9. a.** A code of principally male dignity, integrity, and pride maintained in some societies, as it was in feudal Europe, by force of arms. **b.** A woman's chastity or her reputation for chastity. **10. honors. a.** Special recognition for unusual academic achievement: *graduate with honors.* **b.** A course of study that is of a higher standard or more specialized or advanced than that taken by most students. Also used adjectivally: *an honors degree.* **11.** In golf, the right of teeing off first. **12. honors.** In card games, the four or five highest cards in the trump suit or in all suits. —See Synonyms at **honesty.** **—do the honors. 1.** To perform the social courtesies required of a host or hostess. **2.** To perform a particular social act such as filling glasses or carving a roast. **—(in) honor bound.** Constrained or obliged by one's moral or social standards. **—in honor of. 1.** As a sign of respect for. **2.** As a celebration of. **—on** (or **upon**) **one's honor.** With one's good name as a pledge.
∼*tr.v.* **honored, -oring, -ors.** Also *chiefly British* **hon·our, -oured, -ouring, -ours. 1. a.** To esteem; hold in respect. **b.** To show respect for. **2.** To confer distinction upon: *The ambassador honored us with her presence.* **3.** To accept or pay (a credit card or check, for example) as valid. **4.** To abide by (an agreement) or fulfill (an obligation): *Both parties claim to have honored their side of the bargain.* [Middle English *hono(u)r,* from Old French *honour,* from Latin *honour, honōs*† (stem *honōr-*).] **—hon·or·er** *n.*

Synonyms: *deference, homage, reverence, veneration.*

hon·or·a·ble (ŏn′ər-ə-bəl) *adj.* Also *chiefly British* **hon·our·a·ble. 1.** Deserving or winning honor and respect; creditable: *an honorable deed.* **2.** Bestowing honor; bringing distinction or recognition: *honorable service.* **3.** Possessing and characterized by honor: *"for Brutus is an honourable man"* (Shakespeare). **4.** Consistent with honor or good name: *the only honorable course.* **5. Honorable.** *Abbr.* **Hon. a.** Used with *the* as a title of respect for certain high officials. **b.** *British.* Used with *the* as a courtesy title for the children of barons and viscounts and the younger sons of earls. **c.** *British.* Used in the House of Commons as a title of respect when speaking of another member. **—hon·or·a·ble·ness** *n.* **—hon·or·a·bly** *adv.*

honorable discharge *n.* A discharge from the armed forces with a clean record.

honorable mention *n.* A written or spoken mention, as in a list, of one who has performed well in a competition but has not been awarded a prize.

hon·o·rar·i·um (ŏn′ə-râr′ē-əm) *n., pl.* **-ums** or **-ia** (-ē-ə). A voluntary fee paid to a person for professional services for which fees are not legally or traditionally required. [Latin, neuter of *honorārius,* HONORARY.]

hon·or·ar·y (ŏn′ə-rĕr′ē) *adj. Abbr.* **hon., Hon. 1.** Held, given, or conferred as a mark of honor without the usual prerequisites or privileges: *an honorary degree.* **2. a.** Holding an office or title given as an honor, without payment: *the honorary secretary of the association.* **b.** Voluntary; unpaid. **3.** Relying upon honor; not legally enforceable. Said of a duty or obligation.

hon·or·ee (ŏn′ə-rē′) *n.* One who receives an honor.

hon·o·rif·ic (ŏn′ə-rĭf′ĭk) *adj.* Conferring or showing respect or honor.
∼*n.* A title, phrase, or grammatical form conveying respect, used especially when addressing a social superior. [Latin *honorificus.* See **honor, -fic.**] **—hon·o·rif·i·cal·ly** *adv.*

ho·no·ris cau·sa (ō-nôr′ĭs kou′zə) *adv.* Conferred as a mark of honor. Said of an honorary degree. [Latin.]

honors list *n. British.* A list of persons on whom an honor, such as a peerage, is to be conferred.

honors of war *pl.n.* Certain courtesies granted a surrendering foe, such as the privilege of marching out bearing arms and colors.

honour. *Chiefly British.* Variant of **honor.**

honourable. *Chiefly British.* Variant of **honorable.**

Hon·shu (hŏn′sho͞o). Also **Hon·do** (hŏn′dō). The largest and economically most important of the four main islands that constitute Japan. It is predominantly mountainous and is the site of Japan's highest peak, Fujiyama (3,776 meters; 12,388 feet). Most of Japan's tea and silk comes from Honshu, and the island is also the industrial heartland of the country, with the Tokyo-Yokohama and Osaka-Kobe urban agglomerations.

hooch (ho͞och) *n. Slang.* Alcoholic liquor, especially when inferior or illicit. [Short for Alaskan *Hoochinoo,* a tribe that made a kind of distilled liquor.]

hood¹ (ho͝od) *n.* **1.** A loose covering for the head and neck, either attached to a cloak or jacket or separate. **2.** A draping of cloth hung from the shoulders of an academic gown that indicates the wearer's degree. **3.** A sack used to cover a falcon's head to keep it quiet. **4.** Something resembling a hood in shape or function, as: **a.** A metal cover or cowl for a hearth or stove. **b.** The hinged metal lid over an automobile engine. Also *British* "bonnet." **c.** A folding waterproof top for a carriage or baby carriage. **d.** An expanded part, crest, or marking on or near the head of an animal.
∼*tr.v.* **hooded, hooding, hoods.** To supply or cover with a hood. [Middle English *ho(o)d,* Old English *hōd,* from Germanic.]

hood² *n. Slang.* **1.** A hoodlum; a thug. **2.** A tough-looking youth. [Short for HOODLUM.]

-hood *suffix.* Indicates: **1.** The state, condition, or quality of being; for example, **manhood. 2.** All the members of a grouping of a specified nature; for example, **neighborhood.** [Middle English *-hod(e),* Old English *-hād,* originally an independent noun (condition, quality), from Germanic.]

Hood, Mount (ho͝od). A peak, 3,427 meters (11,235 feet) high, in the Cascade Range in northern Oregon. A symmetrical extinct volcano with glaciers and forested lower slopes, it is a popular mountain-climbing and skiing area.

Hood, Thomas (1799–1845). British poet. He is best known for his comic and topical verse, including *The Dream of Eugene Aram* (1831). *The Song of the Shirt* (1843) exposed the miseries of industrial work.

hood·ed (ho͝od′ĭd) *adj.* **1.** Covered with or having a hood. **2.** Shaped like a hood, cowl, or similar covering. **3.** *Zoology.* Having a crest, coloration, or skin formation suggesting a hood.

hooded crow *n.* A variety of the carrion crow that has a gray back and underparts and a black head, wings, and tail.

hooded seal *n.* A seal, *Cystophora cristata,* of northern seas, having a grayish, spotted coat and an inflatable hoodlike or bladderlike pouch in the region of the nose. Also called "bladdernose."

hood·lum (ho͝od′ləm, ho͞od′ləm) *n.* **1.** A gangster; a thug. **2.** A tough, destructive youth. [19th century : origin obscure.]

hood mold *n. Architecture.* A **dripstone** *(see).*

hoo·doo (ho͞o′do͞o) *n., pl.* **-doos. 1.** Voodoo. **2. a.** Bad luck. **b.** One that brings bad luck.
∼*tr.v.* **hoodooed, -dooing, -doos.** To bring bad luck to. [Perhaps variant of VOODOO.] **—hoo·doo·ism** *n.*

hood·wink (ho͝od′wĭngk′) *tr.v.* **-winked, -winking, -winks. 1.** To deceive; trick; take in. **2.** *Archaic.* To blindfold. **3.** *Obsolete.* To conceal. —See Synonyms at **deceive.** [HOOD + WINK.]

hoo·ey (ho͞o'ē) *n. Slang.* Nonsense.
~*interj. Slang.* Used as an exclamation of impatience or disbelief. [20th century : origin obscure.]

hoof (ho͝of, ho͞of) *n., pl.* **hoofs** or **hooves** (ho͞ovz, ho͝ovz). **1.** The horny sheath covering the toes or lower part of the foot of a mammal of the orders Perissodactyla and Artiodactyla, such as a horse, ox, or deer. **2.** The foot of such an animal, especially a horse. **3.** *Slang.* The human foot. —**on the hoof.** Alive; not yet slaughtered. Said especially of cattle.
~*v.* **hoofed, hoofing, hoofs.** —*tr.* To trample or kick with the hoofs. —*intr. Slang.* **1.** To dance. **2.** To go on foot; walk. Often used with *it*: *Let's hoof it instead of taking the bus.* [Middle English *hoof,* Old English *hōf,* from Germanic.]

hoof-and-mouth disease (ho͝of'ən-mouth', ho͞of'-) *n.* **Foot-and-mouth disease** *(see).*

hoof·bound (ho͝of'bound', ho͞of'-) *adj.* Afflicted with drying and contraction of the hoof, resulting in lameness. Said of a horse.

hoofed (ho͝oft, ho͞oft) *adj.* Having hoofs; ungulate.

hoof·er (ho͝of'ər, ho͞o'fər) *n. Slang.* A professional dancer; especially, a tap dancer.

Hoogh·ly or **Hug·li** (ho͞og'lē). River of northeastern India. It is the most westerly arm of the Ganges delta. Leaving the mainstream near the Bangladesh border, it flows 233 kilometers (145 miles) south to the Bay of Bengal. Constantly dredged to prevent silting, the Hooghly connects Calcutta to the sea.

hoo-ha (ho͞o'hä') *n. Informal.* A noisy fuss or uproar, especially one about nothing of importance; a hullabaloo. [Imitative.]

hook (ho͝ok) *n.* **1.** A curved or sharply bent device, usually of metal, used to catch, drag, suspend, or fasten something. **2.** A fishhook. **3.** A means of catching or ensnaring; a trap. **4.** Anything shaped like a hook, as: **a.** A curved or barbed plant or animal part. **b.** A short angled or curved line on a letter. **c.** The lip of a breaking wave. **d.** A sickle. **5. a.** A sharp bend or curve, as in a river. **b.** A spit of land with a sharply curved end. **6.** *Baseball.* A curve ball. **7.** *Boxing.* A short, swinging blow delivered with a crooked arm. **8.** *Golf.* A stroke that sends the ball to the left of a right-handed player or to the right of a left-handed player. **9.** *Basketball.* A hook shot. **10.** *Nautical.* An anchor. **11.** The part of a telephone on which the receiver sits or from which it is hung. —**by hook or (by) crook.** By whatever means possible, fair or unfair. —**get the hook.** *Slang.* To be dismissed or thrown out. —**hook, line, and sinker.** *Slang.* Without reservation; entirely; completely. —**off the hook.** *Slang.* Freed, as from blame, responsibility, or a vexatious obligation. —**on one's own hook.** *Informal.* By one's own efforts; on one's own account.
~*v.* **hooked, hooking, hooks.** —*tr.* **1. a.** To get hold of or catch with or as if with a hook. **b.** *Informal.* To snare. **c.** *Slang.* To steal; snatch. **d.** *Informal.* To please and make a fan of. **e.** *Slang.* To cause to become addicted. **2.** To fasten or hold up with or as if with a hook. Often used with *up.* **3.** To pierce or gore with the horns. Used especially of a bull. **4.** *Baseball.* To pitch (a ball) with a curve. **5.** *Boxing.* To hit with a hook. **6.** *Golf.* To drive (a ball) with a hook. **7.** To make (a rug, for example) by looping yarn through canvas with a type of crochet hook. —*intr.* **1.** To bend like a hook. **2.** To be fastened by means of a hook or a hook and eye. Used with *on, up,* and other adverbs. —**hook it.** *Slang.* To make a getaway; escape. [Middle English *ho(o)k,* Old English *hōc.*]

hook·ah (ho͝ok'ə) *n.* An Eastern smoking pipe designed with a long tube passing through an urn of water that cools the smoke as it is drawn through. Also called "narghile," "hubble-bubble," "water pipe." [Urdu, from Arabic *ḥuqqah,* small box, casket.]

hook and eye *n.* A clothes fastener consisting of a small blunt metal hook with a corresponding loop.

hook-and-lad·der truck (ho͝ok'ən-lăd'ər) *n.* A fire engine equipped with extension ladders and hooked poles.

Hooke (ho͝ok), **Robert** (1635–1703). English physicist, mathematician, and inventor. He was curator of experiments to the Royal Society (1662–1703) and defined Hooke's law. He invented the wheel barometer, improved astronomical instruments, and formulated the theory of planetary movement.

hooked (ho͝okt) *adj.* **1.** Bent or angled like a hook. **2.** Having a hook or hooks. **3.** Made by hooking yarn. **4.** *Slang.* **a.** Addicted to a narcotic. **b.** Liking something with an intensity that suggests addiction. Often used with *on*: *He was hooked on the place and went back every year.* —**hook·ed·ness** (ho͝ok'ĭd-nĭs) *n.*

hook·er[1] (ho͝ok'ər) *n.* **1.** A single-masted fishing smack used off southwestern England and Ireland. **2.** An old worn-out or clumsy ship, especially one that uses hooks and lines rather than nets. [Dutch *hoeker,* from *hoek,* hook, fishhook (as in *hoekboot,* hookboat), from Middle Dutch *hoec.*]

hooker[2] *n.* **1.** One that hooks. **2.** *Slang.* A prostitute.

Hook·er (ho͝ok'ər), **Sir Joseph Dalton** (1817–1911). British botanist. He wrote *Genera Plantarum* (1862–83), a global study of the distribution of plants.

Hooker, Richard (*c.* 1554–1600). English churchman and theologian. His great work, *Laws of Ecclesiastical Polity* (1594), helped formulate the tone and direction of Anglican theology.

Hooke's law *n.* The principle that the stress applied to a solid body produces a strain proportional to it provided that the elastic limit is not reached. [After Robert HOOKE.]

hook·nose (ho͝ok'nōz') *n.* An aquiline nose. —**hook·nosed** *adj.*

Hook of Hol·land (ho͝ok; hŏl'ənd). *Dutch* **Hoek van Hol·land** (ho͞ok' vän hôl'änt). Outer port of Rotterdam, in the Netherlands, on the North Sea. It is on Hook of Holland Cape and is connected by canal to Rotterdam.

hook shot *n.* A basketball shot made by arcing the far hand upward while standing or moving sideways to the basket.

hook up *tr.v.* **1.** To assemble or wire (a mechanism). **2.** To connect or link (a mechanism) to another mechanism or a source of power. Often used with *to*: *hooked up to the big central computer.* **3.** To fasten together with a hook or hooks. —*intr.v. Informal.* **1.** To form a tie or connection. Often used with *with.* **2.** To marry. Often used with *with.*

hook·up (ho͝ok'ŭp') *n.* **1.** A system of electric circuits and electrically powered equipment designed to operate together, as the linking of television or radio stations so that they can broadcast a special program together. **2.** A configuration of mechanical parts or devices acting as an integrated unit. **3.** A plan or schematic drawing of such a system. **4.** *Informal.* A connection, often between unlikely associates or factors.

hook·worm (ho͝ok'wûrm') *n.* Any of numerous small, parasitic nematode worms of the family Ancylostomatidae, having hooked mouth parts with which they fasten themselves to the intestinal walls of various hosts, including man, causing the disease ancylostomiasis.

hookworm disease *n.* **Ancylostomiasis** *(see).*

hook·y, hook·ey (ho͝ok'ē) *n. Informal.* Absence without leave; truancy. Used in the phrase *play hooky.* [Origin unknown.]

hoo·li·gan (ho͞o'lĭ-gən) *n. Informal.* A young ruffian; a thug. [19th century : perhaps variant of the Irish surname *Houlihan.*] —**hoo·li·gan·ism** *n.*

hoop (ho͞op, ho͝op) *n.* **1.** A circular band of metal or wood put around a cask or barrel to bind the staves together. **2.** Something resembling a hoop, as: **a.** A large wooden, plastic, or metal ring used as a toy or for circus animals to jump through. **b.** One of the lightweight circular supports for a hoop skirt. **c.** One of a pair of circular wooden or metal frames used to hold material taut for embroidery or similar needlework. **3.** A croquet wicket. **4.** In basketball and other games, the metal ring to which a net is attached to form the basket. —**go** (or **be put**) **through the hoop.** To undergo or be forced to undergo an ordeal or test.
~*tr.v.* **hooped, hooping, hoops.** To hold together or support with or as if with a hoop or hoops. [Middle English *hoop,* Old English *hōp,* from Germanic *hōpaz* (unattested).]

hoop·la (ho͞op'lä', ho͝op'-) *n.* **1.** A game in which small rings are thrown in an attempt to encircle an object and so win it. **2.** *Slang.* Boisterous, jovial commotion or excitement. **3.** *Slang.* Talk or publicity intended to mislead or confuse; ballyhoo. [French *houp-là*†.]

hoo·poe (ho͞o'po͞o, -pō) *n.* An Old World bird, *Upupa epops,* having distinctively patterned pinkish-brown plumage, a fanlike crest, and a slender, downward-curving bill. [Variant of obsolete *hoop,* from Old French *huppe,* from Latin *upupa* (imitative).]

hoop-pet·ti·coat narcissus (ho͞op'pĕt'ĭ-kōt', ho͝op'-) *n.* The **petticoat narcissus** *(see).*

hoop pine *n.* An Australian tree, *Araucaria cunninghamii,* having rough bark with hooplike cracks around its trunk and branches.

hoop skirt *n.* A long full skirt belled out with a series of connected hoops.

hoop snake *n.* Any of several American snakes, such as the mud snake, *Farancia abacura,* that supposedly grasp the tail in the mouth and move with a rolling, hooplike motion.

hooray. Variant of **hurrah.**

hoose·gow (ho͞os'gou') *n. Slang.* A jail. [Spanish *juzgado,* courtroom, from the past participle of *juzgar,* to judge, from Latin *jūdicāre,* to JUDGE.]

Hoo·sier (ho͞o'zhər) *n.* A nickname for a native or resident of Indiana. [Origin unknown.]

hoot[1] (ho͞ot) *v.* **hooted, hooting, hoots.** —*intr.* **1.** To utter the characteristic cry of an owl. **2.** To make a loud derisive or contemptuous cry; jeer. **3.** To sound an automobile horn. —*tr.* **1.** To shout down or drive off with jeering cries. Used especially with *down* or *off*: *hoot a speaker off a platform.* **2.** To express or convey by hooting: *hoot one's disgust.* **3.** To cause (an automobile horn) to sound.
~*n.* **1. a.** The characteristic cry of an owl. **b.** A sound suggesting an owl's cry; especially, the sound of an automobile horn. **2.** An inarticulate cry of contempt or derision. **3.** The least amount; a jot. Used chiefly in the phrase *not give a hoot.* **4.** *British Slang.* A very amusing person or thing. [Middle English *h(o)uten* (imitative).]

hoot[2] (ho͞ot, o͞ot) *interj.* Also **hoots** (ho͞ots, o͞ots). *Chiefly Scottish.* Used to express objection or annoyance. [Origin unknown.]

hoot·en·an·ny (ho͞ot'n-ăn'ē) *n., pl.* **-nies. 1.** A gathering of folk singers, typically with participation by the audience. **2.** *Informal.* An unidentified or unidentifiable gadget. [Origin unknown.]

hoot·er (ho͞o'tər) *n. Chiefly British.* **1.** The horn of an automobile or a device that makes a similar noise. **2.** *Slang.* The nose.

hoot owl *n.* Any of various owls having a hooting cry. Compare **screech owl.**

Hoo·ver (ho͞o'vər), **Herbert Clark** (1874–1964). 31st president of the United States (1929–33). He was orphaned at the age of 10 but became a millionaire through mining. After the Wall Street crash Hoover was unwilling to finance employment through federal intervention and lost the presidency to Franklin D. Roosevelt in 1932.

Hoover, J(ohn) Edgar (1895–1972). U.S. lawyer and director of the FBI (1924–72). He led the fight against gangsterism during the

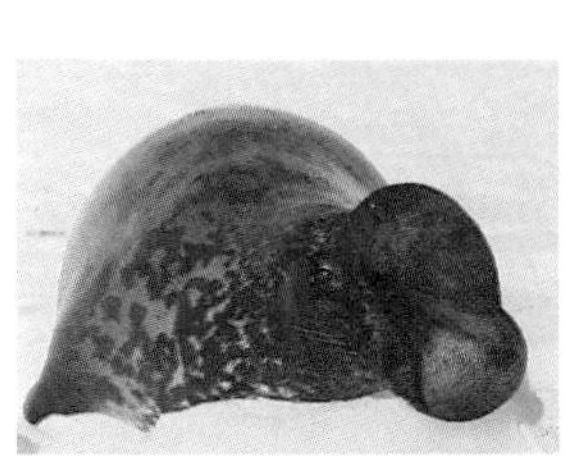

hooded seal *The male hooded seal can inflate its nose into a huge bladder (above), and is sometimes called the bladdernose. The bladder is inflated to impress rivals and cows during the mating season. Hooded seals live on arctic ice floes and grow to 3.5 meters (12 feet) long.*

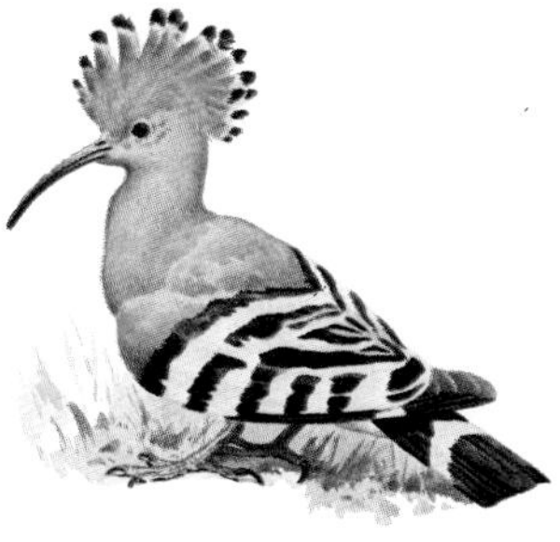

hoopoe *Widely distributed in Europe, Africa, and Asia, the hoopoe is an insect eater, related to the kingfisher.*

PRONUNCIATION KEY

ă, pat; ā, pay; âr, care;
ä, father, are; b, bib;
ch, church; d, deed; ĕ, pet;
ē, be; f, fife; g, gag; h, hat;
hw, which; ĭ, pit; ī, pie;
îr, pier; j, judge; k, kick;
l, lid, needle; m, mum;
n, no, sudden; ng, thing;
ŏ, pot; ō, toe; ô, paw, for;
oi, noise; ou, out; o͝o, book;
o͞o, boot; p, pop; r, roar;
s, sauce; sh, ship, dish;
t, tight; th, thin, path;
th, this, bathe; ŭ, cut; ûr, fur;
v, valve; w, with; y, yes;
z, zebra, size; zh, vision;
ə, about, item, edible, gallop, circus, peaceful

IN FOREIGN WORDS:

à, *Fr.* ami; œ, *Fr.* feu, *Ger.* schön; ü, *Fr.* tu, *Ger.* über; KH, *Ger.* ich, *Scot.* loch; N, *Fr.* bon; y', *Fr.* Compiègne

STRESS MARKS:

Primary stress: ′
in·cite′ (ĭn-sīt′)
Secondary stress: ′
in′sight′ (ĭn′sīt′)

Prohibition era (1919–33). In his later years Hoover was criticized for obsessive anticommunism.

Hoover Dam. Formerly **Boul·der Dam** (bōl'dər). Dam on the Colorado River between Nevada and Arizona. Built (1931–36) for hydroelectric power, flood control, and irrigation, it is 221 meters (726 feet) high and forms Lake Mead, 640 square kilometers (247 square miles), one of the world's largest reservoirs.

Hoo·ver·ville (hōō'vər-vĭl') *n.* A group of crudely built dwellings erected usually on the edge of a town to house the dispossessed and destitute during the depression of the 1930's. [(Herbert) HOOVER + -*ville*, from their prevalence during his administration.]

hooves. Alternate plural of **hoof.**

hop¹ (hŏp) *v.* **hopped, hopping, hops.** —*intr.* **1.** To move with light bounding skips or leaps: *The rabbit hopped across the field.* **2.** To jump on one foot. **3.** *Informal.* To move quickly, as: **a.** To board, get in, or mount something: *hopped on his bicycle and rode off.* **b.** To alight from, get out of, or dismount from something: *hopped out of bed and began to make breakfast.* **4.** To make a quick trip, especially by air: *hopped over to Europe on business.* **5.** *Informal.* To leave. **6.** To bounce after hitting, striking, or colliding with something: *The coin I dropped hopped around on the floor.* —*tr.* **1.** To skip or jump over: *hop the fence.* **2.** *Informal.* To jump aboard (a vehicle); get on: *hopped the train to town.* —*n.* **1.** A light springy jump or leap, especially on one foot. **2.** *Informal.* A dance; ball. **3.** A short distance. **4.** A short trip, especially by air. **5.** A ride; lift. **6.** A bounce taken by a batted baseball. —**on the hop.** *British Informal.* **1.** Very busy; active. **2.** Unprepared; without any warning: *caught on the hop by the unexpected snowfall.* [Middle English *hoppen*, Old English *hoppian*.]

hop² *n.* **1.** Any of several twining vines of the genus *Humulus;* especially, *H. lupulus,* having lobed leaves and green, conelike female flowers. **2. hops.** The dried, ripe female flowers of this plant, containing a bitter, aromatic oil and used as flavoring in brewing beer. **3. hops.** *Australian & New Zealand Slang.* Beer. —*v.* **hopped, hopping, hops.** —*tr.* To flavor with hops. —*intr.* To gather hops. —**hop up.** *Slang.* **1.** To increase the power or energy of. **2.** To stimulate with or as if with a narcotic. [Middle English *hoppe,* from Middle Dutch.]

hop·cal·ite (hŏp'kə-līt') *n.* A granular mixture of the oxides of copper, cobalt, manganese, and silver, used in gas masks to convert carbon monoxide to carbon dioxide. [*(Johns) Hop(kins University + University of) Cal(ifornia)* + -ITE.]

hop clover *n.* A clover, *Trifolium agrarium,* or one of a similar closely related species, native to Eurasia, having small yellow flower heads that resemble hops when withered.

hope (hōp) *v.* **hoped, hoping, hopes.** —*intr.* To entertain a wish for something with some expectation of its fulfillment: *hoping for a favorable reply.* —*tr.* **1.** To wish for with some confidence of fulfillment: *We hope to get there by Friday, but it depends on the weather.* **2.** To expect with confidence; trust: *I hope that this apology will satisfy your client.* —See Synonyms at **expect.** —**hope against hope.** To persist in hoping for something against the odds. —*n.* **1.** A wish or desire supported by some confidence of its fulfillment. **2.** A ground for expectation, optimism, or trust. **3.** That which is desired or anticipated. **4.** That in which one places one's confidence; one on whom hopes are centered: *She was our main hope for a gold medal at the games.* [Middle English *hopen,* Old English *hopian,* akin to Old Frisian *hopia*†.]

Hope (hōp), **Anthony,** pen name of Sir Anthony Hope Hawkins (1863–1933). British novelist. The most successful of his adventure stories was *The Prisoner of Zenda* (1894). He was knighted in 1918.

Hope, Bob, born Leslie Townes Hope (1903–). U.S. comedian, born in Britain. He costarred with Bing Crosby in the popular Road films, beginning with the *Road to Singapore* (1940).

hope chest *n.* A chest used by a young woman for the gradual collection of fine linens, silver, and other small household items in anticipation of marriage. Also *British* "bottom drawer."

hope·ful (hōp'fəl) *adj.* **1.** Having or manifesting hope. **2.** Inspiring hope; promising. —*n.* A person who aspires to success or who shows promise of succeeding. —**hope·ful·ness** *n.*

hope·ful·ly (hōp'fə-lē) *adv.* **1.** With hope; in a hopeful manner. **2.** It is to be hoped; let us hope: *Hopefully, nuclear weapons will never be used in war again.*

> **Usage:** The use of *hopefully* to mean "it is to be hoped," as in *Hopefully, we'll get there before dark,* is grammatically justified by analogy to the similar uses of *happily* and *mercifully.* However, this usage is by now such a bugbear to traditionalists that it is best avoided on grounds of civility, if not logic.

Hopeh, Ho·pei. See Hebei.

hope·less (hōp'lĭs) *adj.* **1.** Having no hope; despairing. **2.** Offering no hope; bleak. **3.** Incurable: *a hopeless case of cancer.* **4.** Insoluble; impossible: *a hopeless problem.* **5.** *Informal.* Totally lacking in competence or effectiveness: *As a comedian, he's hopeless.* —**hope·less·ly** *adv.* —**hope·less·ness** *n.*

hop garden *n.* A field in which hops are cultivated. Also called "hop yard."

hop·head (hŏp'hĕd') *n. Slang.* **1.** A drug addict. **2.** *Australian & New Zealand.* An alcoholic. [From obsolete slang *hop,* opium, probably from HOP (plant).]

hop hornbeam *n.* Any of several trees of the genus *Ostrya;* especially, *O. virginiana,* of eastern North America, having fruit resembling hops. Also called "ironwood."

hop *Since medieval times, when French monks perfected the technique, hops have been used to clarify, preserve, and flavor beer. Their young shoots taste like asparagus when cooked.*

horn *A forerunner of the modern French horn, known as a "natural" horn. With this type of brass horn, changes in key are achieved by inserting extra lengths of tubing— crooks—into the center of the hoop. The development in the early 19th century of valves that automatically alter the length of tubing gave the horn a much wider range.*

Ho·pi (hō'pē) *n., pl.* **Hopi** or **-pis.** **1.** A member of a Uto-Aztecan-speaking North American Indian tribe now inhabiting a reservation in northeastern Arizona. **2.** The language of this tribe. [Hopi *hópi,* peaceful.]

Hop·kins (hŏp'kĭnz), **Sir Frederick Gowland** (1861–1947). English biochemist. He is noted for his pioneer work on vitamins. He shared (1929) the Nobel Prize for medicine with Christiaan Eijkman.

Hopkins, Gerard Manley (1844–89). British poet. He converted to Roman Catholicism (1866) and became a Jesuit priest. None of his poems were published during his lifetime, but a posthumous collection (1918) influenced the interwar poets. Among his works are "The Windhover" and the long poem "The Wreck of the Deutschland."

Hopkins, Johns (1795–1873). U.S. financier and philanthropist. He amassed a fortune in banking and the railroad business. Aware of Baltimore's lack of emergency medical facilities and of his own lack of education, he gave $7 million for the founding of a free hospital and Johns Hopkins University.

Hopkins, Mark (1802–87). U.S. educator. Renowned as a teacher and administrator, he was president of Williams College in Williamstown, Massachusetts, from 1836 to 1872 and professor of intellectual and moral philosophy from 1872 until his death.

hop·lite (hŏp'līt') *n.* A heavily armed foot soldier of ancient Greece. [French, from Greek *hoplitēs,* from *hoplon*†, weapon.] —**hop·lit·ic** (hŏp-lĭt'ĭk) *adj.*

hop·per (hŏp'ər) *n.* **1.** One that hops; especially, a hopping insect. **2. a.** A large funnel into which materials, such as grain or fuel, are stored in readiness for dispensation and use. **b.** A freight car that is designed to discharge its load through the floor or by means of a hinged door. **c.** A barge that transports mud, silt, or the like away from a dredging operation and discharges it. **d.** A device for holding a stack of punched cards and feeding them into a computer. **3.** A receptacle in a legislature in which proposed bills are dropped.

Hop·per (hŏp'ər), **Edward** (1882–1967). U.S. painter. Sometimes called the painter of loneliness, he created calm, realistic depictions of stark city settings and lonesome roadside scenes. *Nighthawks* (1942), a haunting view of a late-night diner, is among his most famous works.

Hopper, Hedda (1890–1966). U.S. actress and columnist. After appearing on stage and in films, she began broadcasting (1936) and writing (1938) about the latest gossip from Hollywood. Known for her glittering array of exotic hats, she also carried on a celebrated feud with Louella Parsons for many years.

hop·ping (hŏp'ĭng) *adv.* Very; extremely. Used in the phrase *hopping mad.*

hopple. Variant of **hobble.**

hop·sack (hŏp'săk') *n.* Also **hop·sack·ing** (hŏp'săk'ĭng). **1.** A loosely woven, coarse fabric of cotton or wool used in clothing. **2.** A coarse fabric of hemp, jute, or the like used to make sacks. [Used by hop growers for bags.]

hop·scotch (hŏp'skŏch') *n.* A children's game in which players toss an object into succeeding sections of a figure such as a series of squares on the ground, then hop through the figure and back on one foot as they retrieve the object. [HOP + SCOTCH (line).]

hop, step, and jump *n.* An athletic event, the **triple jump** (*see*).

hop trefoil *n.* A Eurasian clover plant, *Trifolium campestre,* having yellow flower heads that when withered resemble the female flowers of the hop.

ho·ra, ho·rah (hôr'ə, hōr'ə) *n.* **1.** A traditional round dance of Romania and Israel. **2.** The music to which this dance is performed. [Modern Hebrew *hôrāh,* from Romanian *horā,* from Turkish *hora.*]

Hor·ace (hôr'ĭs, hŏr'-), born Quintus Horatius Flaccus (65–8 B.C.). Roman poet. His *Odes* and *Satires* express a humane philosophy.

ho·ra·ry (hôr'ə-rē, hōr'-) *adj.* **1.** Of an hour or the hours. **2.** Occurring once an hour. [Medieval Latin *hōrārius,* from Latin *hōra,* HOUR.]

Ho·ra·tian (hə-rā'shən) *adj.* Of, relating to, or characteristic of the poet Horace, marked in formal rigor, succinctness, or elegance.

Horatian ode *n.* An ode in which a fixed strophic pattern is followed. [After HORACE.]

horde (hôrd, hōrd) *n.* **1.** A throng or swarm, as of people, animals, or insects. **2.** A nomadic Mongol tribe. **3.** Any nomadic group. —*intr.v.* **horded, hording, hords.** To form or live in a horde. [Old French, from German *Horde,* from Polish *horda,* from Turkish *ordū,* camp. See also **Urdu.**]

Ho·reb (hôr'ĕb', hōr'-). A mountain generally identified in the Old Testament with Mt. Sinai.

hore·hound, hoar·hound (hôr'hound', hōr'-) *n.* **1.** An aromatic plant, *Marrubium vulgare,* native to Eurasia, having leaves covered with soft whitish hairs and yielding a bitter extract used as flavoring and as a cough remedy. Also called "white horehound." **2.** Any of several similar or related plants, such as the **black horehound** (*see*). [Middle English *horhoune,* Old English *hārhūne* : *hār,* HOAR + *hūne*†, horehound.]

ho·ri·zon (hə-rī'zən) *n.* **1.** The apparent intersection of the earth and sky as seen by an observer. Also called "apparent horizon," "visible horizon." **2.** *Astronomy.* **a.** The circular intersection of a plane tangent to the earth at the observer's station with the celestial sphere. Also called "sensible horizon." **b.** The intersection with the celestial sphere of a plane through the center of the earth and perpendicular to the line connecting the zenith and the nadir. Also called "rational horizon." **c.** The great circle of the celestial sphere at the intersection of the sensible and rational horizons at infinity, its plane passing through the center of the earth. Also called "celestial horizon." **3.** *Often* **horizons.** The range or limits of knowledge, experience, observation, or interest: *broaden one's horizons.* **4.** *Geology.* **a.** A specific position in a stratigraphic column, as the location of one or more fossils, that serves to identify the stratum with a particular period. **b.** A specific layer of soil in a cross section of land. **—on the horizon.** Emerging as a possibility; becoming apparent. [Middle English *orizon(te),* from Old French, from Late Latin *horīzōn,* from Greek *horizōn,* from the present participle of *horizein,* to divide, separate, from *horos*†, boundary, limit.]

hor·i·zon·tal (hôr'ə-zŏnt'l, hŏr'-) *adj.* **1.** Of, relating to, or near the horizon. **2.** Parallel to or in the plane of the horizon; level. Compare **vertical. 3.** Of, pertaining to, or involving those at the same rank, stage, or level in a hierarchy: *a horizontal study of sixth-graders throughout the country; horizontal job mobility.* Compare **vertical. 4.** Flat.
~*n.* Anything, such as a line, plane, or object, that is horizontal or assumed to be parallel with the horizon. [From Late Latin *horīzōn* (stem *horīzont-*), HORIZON.] **—hor·i·zon·tal·ly** *adv.*

hor·mone (hôr'mōn') *n.* **1.** A substance formed in an endocrine gland and conveyed by the bloodstream to a specific organ or tissue, whose function it modifies by means of its chemical activity. **2.** A compound produced by a plant that affects growth; a growth substance. **3.** Any of various synthetic compounds having effects similar to either of these substances. [Greek *hormōn,* from the present participle of *horman,* to urge on, from *hormē*†, impulse, onrush.] **—hor·mo·nal** (hôr-mō'nəl), **hor·mon·ic** (hôr-mŏn'ĭk) *adj.*

Hor·muz (hôr'mŭz', hôr-mo͞oz'). Also **Or·muz** (ôr'mŭz', ôr-mo͞oz'). An island, 44 square kilometers (17 square miles) in area, off the southern coast of Iran in the Strait of Hormuz, a strait linking the Persian Gulf with the Gulf of Oman.

horn (hôrn) *n.* **1.** Any of the hard, usually permanent structures projecting from the head of certain mammals, such as cattle, sheep, goats, or antelopes, consisting of a bony core covered with a sheath of keratinous material. **2.** A similar hard protuberance, such as an antler or a projection on the head of a giraffe or rhinoceros. **3.** A projecting structure or growth suggestive of a horn, such as the eyestalk of a snail. **4. a.** The hard, smooth, keratinous material forming the outer covering of the horns of cattle or related animals. **b.** A substance resembling this. **5.** A container made from a horn: *a powder horn.* **6.** *Archaic.* A symbol or source of strength. **7.** *Archaic.* A symbol of the cuckold. **8.** Anything resembling a horn in appearance, especially: **a.** A cornucopia. **b.** Either of the ends of a crescent moon. **c.** The point of an anvil. **d.** The pommel of a saddle. **e.** An ear trumpet. **f.** A device for projecting sound waves, as in a loudspeaker. **g.** A hollow, metallic, electromagnetic transmission antenna with a characteristically rectangular cross section. Also called "horn antenna." **9.** *Abbr.* **h., H.** *Music.* **a.** A wind instrument made of an animal horn. **b.** A wind instrument made of brass. **c.** A French horn. **d.** *Informal.* A wind instrument, especially the saxophone or trumpet. **10.** A signaling device, usually electrical, that produces a sound similar to that of a sounded animal horn: *a car horn.* **11.** *Aviation.* A short lever projecting from a control surface on an aircraft, to which is attached the cable, line, or rod by which the surface is operated. **12.** *Slang.* A telephone. **—blow** (or **toot**) **one's own horn.** To brag or boast about oneself. **—lock horns.** To become embroiled, as in argument or debate. **—on the horns of a dilemma.** Forced to choose between equally undesirable alternatives. **—pull** (or **draw**) **in one's horns. 1.** To restrain oneself; draw back. **2.** To take back a previous statement; recant. **3.** To economize.
~*tr.v.* **horned, horning, horns. 1.** To gore or wound with a horn. **2.** *Archaic.* To cuckold. **—horn in.** *Slang.* To join without being invited; intrude. [Middle English *horn,* Old English *horn,* from Germanic.] **—horn** *adj.* **—horn·less** *adj.* **—horn·like** *adj.*

Horn, Cape (hôrn). Most southerly point of South America, at Horn Island, Chile. It is also known as the Horn and is notorious for storms and heavy seas.

horn·beam (hôrn'bēm') *n.* **1.** Any of various trees of the genus *Carpinus*; especially, the Eurasian species, *C. betulus,* having smooth, grayish bark and hard, whitish wood. **2.** The wood of such a tree. Also called "ironwood." [From its tough, close-grained wood.]

horn·bill (hôrn'bĭl') *n.* Any of various tropical Old World birds of the family Bucerotidae, having a very large bill, often surmounted by an enlarged protuberance at the base.

horn·blende (hôrn'blĕnd') *n.* A common, greenish-black to black amphibole mineral, essentially calcium magnesium iron sodium aluminum aluminosilicate, found in igneous and metamorphic rocks. [German *Hornblende* : HORN + BLENDE.]

horn·book (hôrn'bo͝ok') *n.* **1.** A primer used formerly in teaching children to read, consisting of a single page protected by a transparent sheet of horn. **2.** A text that instructs in the basic skills or rudiments of a subject.

Horne (hôrn), **Lena** (1917–). U.S. singer. Noted for her versatile voice and classic beauty, she made her debut as a 16-year-old chorus dancer in Harlem and has since delighted audiences in nightclubs, Broadway musicals, motion pictures, and television productions.

Horne, Marilyn (1934–). U.S. operatic soprano. Renowned for her rich, wide-ranging voice, she became a principal performer at the Metropolitan Opera in New York City after her debut there as Adalgisa in *Norma* (1970).

horned (hôrnd) *adj.* **1.** Having a horn or horns. **2.** Having hornlike projections such as ear tufts: *a horned bird.*

horned owl *n.* Any of various owls of the genus *Bubo* that have prominent ear tufts.

horned poppy *n.* Any of various Eurasian poppies of the genera *Glaucium* and *Roemeria,* having variously colored flowers and long, curved seed capsules.

horned toad *n.* Any of several lizards of the genus *Phrynosoma,* of western North America and Central America, having hornlike projections on the head, a flattened, spiny body, and a short tail. Also called "horned lizard."

horned viper *n.* **1.** A venomous African snake, *Cerastes cornutus,* having a hornlike projection above each eye. Also called "sand viper." **2.** Any of various similar snakes of the genera *Cerastes* and *Pseudocerastes.*

hor·net (hôr'nĭt) *n.* Any of various large stinging wasps, especially *Vespa crabro,* characteristically building a large papery nest. [Middle English *hernet,* Old English *hyrnet.*]

hornet's nest *n.* A vehement or antagonistic response: *a provocative speech that stirred up a hornet's nest.*

horn·fels (hôrn'fĕlz') *n.* A hard, compact, metamorphic rock formed by the action of heat on clay rocks. Also called "hornstone." [German, "horn rock."]

hor·ni·to (hôr-nē'tō) *n., pl.* **-tos.** A low mound of volcanic origin, sometimes emitting smoke or vapor. [Spanish, diminutive of *horno,* oven, from Latin *furnus.*]

horn-mad (hôrn'măd') *adj.* Extremely angry; furious; enraged. [Originally "enraged enough to horn or gore someone."]

horn of plenty *n.* A **cornucopia** *(see).*

horn·pipe (hôrn'pīp') *n.* **1.** A musical instrument with a single reed, finger holes, and a bell and mouthpiece made of horn. **2.** A spirited British folk dance originally accompanied by a hornpipe. **3.** The music for such a dance.

horn-rimmed (hôrn'rĭmd') *adj.* Having rims or frames made of horn, tortoiseshell, or a material such as hard plastic made to resemble these. Said of eyeglasses.

horn silver *n.* A mineral, **cerargyrite** *(see).*

horn·swog·gle (hôrn'swŏg'əl) *tr.v.* **-gled, -gling, -gles.** *Regional Slang.* To deceive; bamboozle. [19th century : origin obscure.]

horn·tail (hôrn'tāl') *n.* Any of various sawflies of the family Siricidae, the female of which has a long, stout ovipositor with which it inserts its eggs into the wood of trees.

horn·wort (hôrn'wûrt', -wôrt') *n.* **1.** Any of several aquatic plants of the genus *Ceratophyllum,* forming submerged branching masses in quiet water. **2.** Any of various plants of the genus *Anthoceros.*

horn·y (hôr'nē) *adj.* **-ier, -iest. 1.** Having horns or similar projections. **2.** Made of horn. **3.** Resembling horn in hardness. **4.** *Slang.* Sexually aroused; in a state of sexual excitement. **—horn·i·ness** *n.*

hor·o·loge (hôr'ə-lōj', hŏr'-) *n.* A timepiece. [Middle English *horologe, orloge,* from Old French *orloge,* from Latin *hōrologium,* from Greek *hōrologion,* from *hōrologos,* "hour-teller" : *hōra,* HOUR + *legein,* to speak.]

Hor·o·lo·gi·um (hôr'ə-lō'jē-əm, hŏr'-) *n.* A constellation in the Southern Hemisphere near Hydrus, Eridanus, and Reticulum. [Latin *hōrologium,* HOROLOGE.]

ho·rol·o·gy (hô-rŏl'ə-jē, hō-) *n.* **1.** The science of measuring time. **2.** The art of making clocks and watches. [Middle English *horologie,* from Latin *hōrologium,* HOROLOGE.] **—ho·rol·o·gist** (hô-rŏl'ə-jĭst), **ho·rol·o·ger** (hô-rŏl'ə-jər) *n.* **—hor·o·log·ic** (hôr'ə-lŏj'ĭk, hŏr'-), **hor·o·log·i·cal** *adj.*

hor·o·scope (hôr'ə-skōp', hŏr'-) *n. Astrology.* **1.** The configuration of the planets and stars at a given moment, such as the moment of a person's birth. **2.** A diagram of the signs of the zodiac based on such a configuration. **3.** A forecast of a person's future based on such a diagram. [Old French, from Latin *hōroscopus,* from Greek *hōroskopos,* astrologer : *hōra,* HOUR + *skopos,* observer.]

ho·ros·co·py (hô-rŏs'kə-pē, hō-) *n., pl.* **-pies.** The casting and reading of horoscopes.

Hor·o·witz (hôr'ə-wĭts', hŏr'-), **Vladimir** (1904–). U.S. pianist, of Russian birth. He settled in the United States in 1940. Horowitz is famed as a brilliant technician and as a leading exponent of romantic pianism.

hor·ren·dous (hô-rĕn'dəs, hō-) *adj.* **1.** Hideous; horrifying; dreadful. **2.** *Informal.* Disagreeable; unpleasant. [Latin *horrendus,* from the gerundive of *horrēre,* to tremble.] **—hor·ren·dous·ly** *adv.*

hor·rent (hôr'ənt, hŏr'-) *adj. Archaic.* **1.** Bristling. **2.** Terrified; shuddering. [Latin *horrēns* (stem *horrent-*), present participle of *horrēre,* to tremble.]

hor·ri·ble (hôr'ə-bəl, hŏr'-) *adj.* **1.** Causing horror; dreadful: *"War is beyond all words horrible"* (Winston Churchill). **2.** Unpleasant; disagreeable; offensive. [Middle English, from Old French, from Latin *horrībilis,* from *horrēre,* to tremble.] **—hor·ri·ble·ness** *n.* **—hor·ri·bly** *adv.*

hor·rid (hôr'ĭd, hŏr'-) *adj.* **1.** Unpleasant; disagreeable. **2.** Unkind; nasty: *What a horrid thing to say!* **3.** Causing horror. **4.** *Archaic.* Bristling; rough: *"horrid with fern and intricate with thorn"* (John Dryden). [Latin *horridus,* from *horrēre,* to tremble.] **—hor·rid·ly** *adv.* **—hor·rid·ness** *n.*

hor·rif·ic (hô-rĭf'ĭk, hō-) *adj.* **1.** Causing horror; terrifying. **2.** *Informal.* Disagreeable. [Old French *horrifique,* from Latin *horrificus* : *horrēre,* to tremble + *-ficus,* -FIC.] **—hor·rif·i·cal·ly** *adv.*

hor·ri·fy (hôr'ə-fī', hŏr'-) *tr.v.* **-fied, -fying, -fies. 1.** To fill with horror; terrify. **2.** To cause unpleasant surprise to; shock. [Latin *horri-*

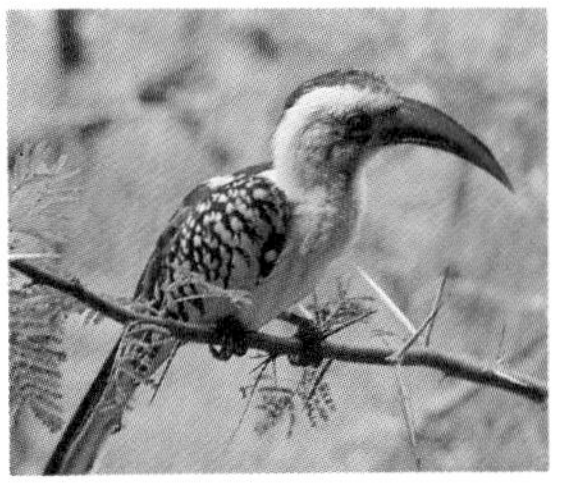

hornbill *Hornbills live in Africa and southern Asia. Unlike most birds they have long eyelashes. The huge beak is used to pick the fruit from trees.*

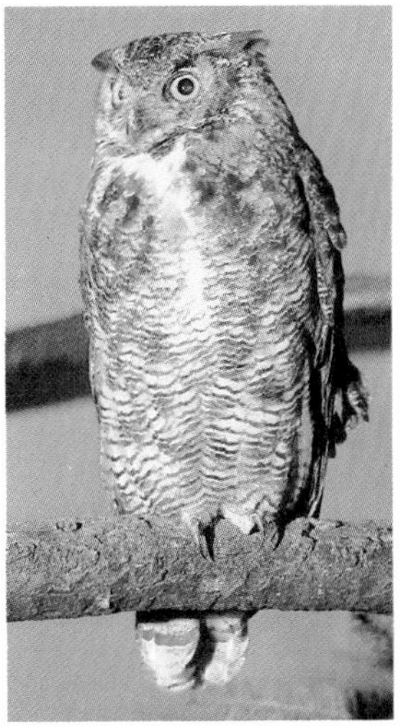

horned owl *The great horned owl,* Bubo virginianus, *can grow to nearly 60 centimeters (2 feet) tall and takes prey as large as rabbits and porcupines. It is widespread throughout North and South America.*

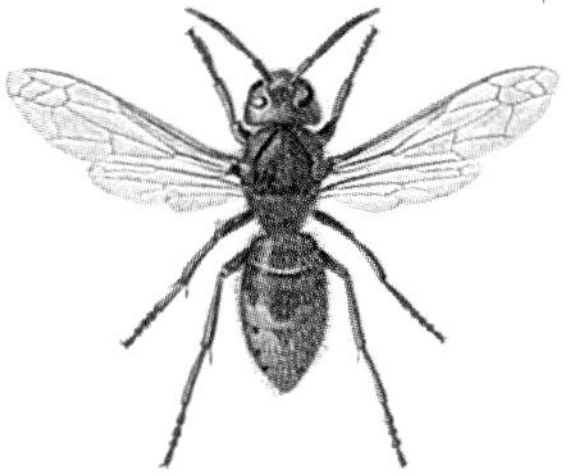

hornet Vespa crabro, *the giant hornet, can be more than 25 millimeters (1 inch) long, and even the smallest workers are larger than the queens of most other wasp species. Like common wasps, hornets live in colonies, often in hollow trees. Only the females have stings, but, despite a reputation for aggressiveness, hornets are relatively docile and rarely sting humans but the sting is a painful one.*

horse-brass *Ornaments have been used on animals since ancient times. Horse-brasses are probably of British origin, and their original purpose was to ward off evil spirits. Hundreds of different designs have been recorded.*

horsefly *Female horseflies live by sucking the blood of animals—mostly horses and cattle—though they will bite humans as well. The bite can be painful, but it is not normally dangerous. Male horseflies are harmless, feeding on flower nectar. Horsefly larvae live mostly in damp soil and feed on other small animals, commonly earthworms.*

horseradish *The horseradish originally came from central and western Asia but is now naturalized in the United States as well. Horseradish sauce is made from its grated root.*

---

horse

THE ANIMAL THAT WAS MAN'S MAIN POWER SOURCE
Horses bred for work, war, and sport

During most of civilized history man has used the horse as the source of greatest physical and military power and as the motive force in the most rapid means of transport. The horse was probably first domesticated during the Bronze Age by nomadic herdsmen of central Asia. Many breeds have been developed for different purposes. The breeds fall into three main types, according to their use: draft breeds, descended from the medieval warhorses and including the English Shire and the French Percheron; harness breeds such as the Hanoverian and the Hackney; and saddle breeds such as the Lipizzaner and the Thoroughbred.

The largest of all horse breeds is the·English Shire, which stands about 18 hands high. A hand is equivalent to 100 millimeters (4 inches) and a horse's height is measured to the top of the shoulder. The tiny Shetland pony is never more than 10½ hands high, but it is used as both draft and saddle horse. The Thoroughbred was descended from the ancient Arabian horse; it was bred for racing and stud. The Hanoverian was crossbred with the English Thoroughbred for George I (1714–27) and, like the hardy French and Belgian Ardennes and the East Prussian Trakehner (the pride of German horse breeding), was once a cavalry horse. All three are now bred mainly for sport.

Other flourishing breeds are the Friesian, which is indigenous to the Netherlands, one of Europe's oldest breeds, and a popular circus horse; the Austrian Lipizzaner, which excels in dressage at the Spanish Riding School in Vienna; and the Australian Waler, like the American Bronco, an excellent bucking horse. The Orlov, which was bred for trotting in pre-Revolutionary Russia, has declined because the studs were destroyed during the Revolution.

Trakehner 16 hands

Lipizzaner 16 hands

Friesian 13 hands

Waler Height variable

Thoroughbred 14½ –17 hands

Orlov 17 hands

Shetland 10½ hands

Percheron 16 hands

Shire 18 hands

Hanoverian 16 hands

Ardennes 15 hands

---

ficāre, from *horrificus,* HORRIFIC.] **—hor·ri·fi·ca·tion** (hôr′ə-fĭ-kā′shən) *n.*

hor·rip·i·la·tion (hô-rĭp′ə-lā′shən, hŏ-) *n.* The bristling of the body hair, as from fear or cold; goose flesh. [Late Latin *horripilātiō,* from Latin *horripilātus,* past participle of *horripilāre,* to bristle with hairs : *horrēre,* to bristle + *pilus,* hair.]

hor·ror (hôr′ər, hŏr′-) *n.* **1.** An intense and painful feeling of repugnance and fear; terror. **2.** Intense dislike; abhorrence; loathing: *has a horror of snakes.* **3. a.** The quality of causing horror. **b.** One that excites horror; a horrifying person or thing: *the horrors of war.* **4.** An unpleasant person, especially a child: *a little horror.* **5.** *Informal.* Something unpleasant, ugly, or disagreeable: *That hat is a real horror.* **6.** *Obsolete.* A bristling or shuddering condition.

~*adj.* Calculated to terrify the reader, listener, or watcher: *a horror story.* [Middle English *(h)orrour,* from Old French, from Latin *horror,* from *horrēre,* to tremble, bristle, be in horror.]

hor·rors (hôr′ərz, hŏr′-) *pl.n. Informal.* Intense nervous depression or anxiety: *had a bad case of the horrors.*

~*interj.* Used to express dismay, often humorously.

hor·ror-strick·en (hôr′ər-strĭk′ən, hŏr′-) *adj.* Also **hor·ror-struck** (-strŭk′). Horrified; filled with sudden fear or repugnance.

Horsa. See **Hengist.**

hors de com·bat (ôr′ də kôɴ-bä′) *adj.* Out of action; injured or disabled. [French.] **—hors de com·bat** *adv.*

hors d'oeuvre (ôr dûrv′; *French* ôr dœ′vrə) *n., pl.* **hors d'oeuvres** (ôr dûrvz′) or **hors d'oeuvre.** **1.** An appetizer served with drinks or before a meal. **2.** Any of various small dishes, such as spiced meat or specially garnished vegetables, served as a first course. [French, outside of the ordinary meal, side dish, "outside of work" : *hors,* outside, from Latin *forīs* + *de,* of + *oeuvre,* work, from Latin *opera,* from *opus* (stem *oper-*), work, OPUS.]

horse (hôrs) *n., pl.* **horses** or **horse.** **1. a.** A large, hoofed mammal, *Equus caballus,* having a short-haired coat, a long mane, and a long tail and domesticated since ancient times for riding and to pull vehicles or carry loads. **b.** An adult male of this species. **2.** A horse over a certain size, usually over 14½ hands high, as opposed to a pony. **3.** Any of various other equine mammals, such as the wild Asian species, **Przewalski's horse** *(see),* or certain extinct forms

related ancestrally to the modern horse. **4.** Mounted soldiers; cavalry: *a squadron of horse.* **5.** A supportive frame or device, such as a clothes horse or sawhorse. **6.** A gymnastic device having four legs and a padded body used for vaulting and other exercises. **7.** *Slang.* Heroin. **8. horses.** *Informal.* Horse racing or horse races. Preceded by *the*: *lost a fortune on the horses.* **9.** *Often* **horses.** Horsepower. **10.** *Geology.* **a.** A block of rock interrupting a vein and containing no minerals. **b.** A large block of displaced rock that is caught along a fault. **—a horse of another** (or **a different**) **color.** Another matter entirely; something else. **—be** (or **get**) **on one's high horse.** To be or become disdainful, superior, or conceited. **—flog** (or **beat**) **a dead horse. 1.** To continue to pursue an enterprise that has no hope of success. **2.** To dwell tiresomely on a subject that is no longer of interest. **—hold one's horses.** To check or rein one's eagerness; restrain oneself. **—the horse's mouth.** A source of information regarded as original or unimpeachable: *It's not just a rumor—I got the story straight from the horse's mouth.*
~*v.* **horsed, horsing, horses.** *—tr.* To provide with or place upon a horse. *—intr.* **1.** To mount or ride upon a horse. **2.** *Informal.* To indulge in horseplay. Usually used with *around* or *about.*
~*adj.* **1.** Of or pertaining to a horse. **2.** Mounted on a horse or horses. **3.** Drawn or operated by a horse or horses. [Middle English *hors,* Old English *hors,* from Germanic *hors-* (unattested).]

horse·back (hôrs′băk′) *n.* The back of a horse: *rode on horseback.* Also used adjectivally: *horseback riding.*
~*adv.* On horseback: *riding horseback.*

horse bean *n.* The **broad bean** *(see).*

horse·box (hôrs′bŏks′) *n.* A large van, or a trailer that can be pulled by a motor vehicle, used for transporting horses.

horse-brass, horse brass (hôrs′brăs′, -bräs′) *n.* A flat ornament made of brass and originally worn on a horse's harness to frighten away evil spirits.

horse·car (hôrs′kär′) *n.* **1.** A streetcar drawn by horses. **2.** A car for transporting horses.

horse chestnut *n.* **1.** Any of several trees of the genus *Aesculus*; especially, *A. hippocastanum,* native to Eurasia, having palmate leaves, erect clusters of pink or white flowers tinged with red, and brown, shiny nuts enclosed in a spiny bur. **2.** The nut of such a tree. In this sense, also called "conker." [Formerly used in treating ailments of horses.]

horse·flesh (hôrs′flĕsh′) *n.* **1.** Horses collectively; especially, racehorses considered in terms of their racing potential. **2.** The flesh of a horse; especially, edible horse meat.

horse·fly (hôrs′flī′) *n., pl.* **-flies.** Any of numerous large flies of the family Tabanidae, the females of which suck the blood of various mammals, including man, inflicting painful bites.

horse gentian *n.* Any of various plants of the genus *Triosteum,* having small purplish-brown flowers and leathery orange-yellow fruit. Also called "feverwort."

Horse Guards *pl.n.* **1.** A cavalry brigade of the household troops of the British royal family. **2.** The headquarters of the Horse Guards, in Whitehall, London.

horse·hair (hôrs′hâr′) *n.* **1.** The hair of a horse, especially from the mane or tail. **2.** Cloth made of horsehair, used chiefly in upholstery.
~*adj.* **1.** Made of horsehair. **2.** Covered or stuffed with horsehair.

horsehair worm *n.* Any of various slender aquatic worms of the phylum Nematomorpha, the larvae of which are parasitic within insects. Also called "hairworm." [These hairlike worms were once thought to have formed from horsehairs that dropped into drinking troughs.]

horse·hide (hôrs′hīd′) *n.* **1. a.** The hide of a horse. **b.** Leather made from this hide. **2.** *Informal.* A baseball.

horse latitudes *pl.n.* Either of two belts of latitudes located mostly over the oceans at about 30° to 35° north and south, having high barometric pressure, calms, light changeable winds, and fine weather. [18th century : perhaps alluding to the old nautical practice of throwing horses overboard to lighten becalmed ships.]

horse·laugh (hôrs′lăf′, -läf′) *n.* A loud, coarse, often mocking laugh; a guffaw.

horse·leech (hôrs′lēch′) *n.* Any of several large leeches of the genus *Haemopis.*

horse·less carriage (hôrs′lĭs) *n.* An automobile.

horse mackerel *n.* **1.** Any of several large, mackerellike marine fishes of the genus *Trachurus*; especially, *T. trachurus.* Also called "scad." **2.** Any of several tunas or related fishes.

horse·man (hôrs′mən) *n., pl.* **-men** (-mĭn). **1.** A man who rides a horse. **2.** One skilled at horsemanship.

horse·man·ship (hôrs′mən-shĭp′) *n.* The art and skill of riding a horse; equitation.

horse marine *n.* **1. a.** A marine assigned to the cavalry. **b.** A cavalryman assigned to a ship. **2.** One who is out of his element; a misfit.

horse·mint (hôrs′mĭnt′) *n.* Any of several coarse, aromatic plants such as *Mentha longifolia,* a European species of mint.

horse mushroom *n.* A large, edible mushroom, *Agaricus arvensis,* having a white cap with a grayish undersurface.

horse opera *n.* A film or other theatrical work about the American West; a Western.

horse·play (hôrs′plā′) *n.* Rowdy, rough play.

horse·pow·er (hôrs′pou′ər) *n. Abbr.* **hp 1.** A unit of power in the U.S. Customary System equal to 745.7 watts or 550 foot-pounds per second. **2.** The power exerted by a horse in pulling.

horse·pow·er-hour (hôrs′pou′ər-our′) *n.* A unit of work or energy equal to the work done by working at 1 horsepower for 1 hour, which is equivalent to 2.686 × 10^6 joules.

horse·rad·ish (hôrs′răd′ĭsh) *n.* **1.** A coarse plant, *Armoracia rusticana* (or *A. lapathifolia*), native to Eurasia, having a thick, whitish, pungent root. **2.** The grated root of this plant, often combined with vinegar or other ingredients and used as a condiment.

horse sense *n. Informal.* Common sense.

horse·shoe (hôrs′sho͞o′, hôrsh′-) *n.* **1.** A narrow U-shaped iron plate fitted and nailed to a horse's hoof. **2.** Something having a similar shape. Also used adjectivally: *a horseshoe magnet.* **3. horseshoes.** *Used with a singular verb.* A game in which players try to toss horseshoes so that they encircle a stake.
~*tr.v.* **horseshoed, -shoeing, -shoes.** To shoe (a horse).

horseshoe bat *n.* Any of various Old World insectivorous bats of the genus *Rhinolophus* and related genera, having a fleshy, horseshoe-shaped outgrowth around the nostrils that is used in echolocation.

horseshoe crab *n.* Any of various marine arthropods of the class Merostomata; especially, *Limulus polyphemus* (or *Xiphosura polyphemus*), of eastern North America, having a large, rounded body and a stiff, pointed tail. Also called "king crab."

horse·tail (hôrs′tāl′) *n.* Any of various nonflowering pteridophytic plants of the genus *Equisetum,* having a jointed, hollow stem and narrow, sometimes much reduced leaves.

horse-trad·ing (hôrs′trā′dĭng) *n.* Negotiation characterized by shrewd and vigorous bargaining.

horse·weed (hôrs′wēd′) *n.* A weedy North American plant of the fleabane family, *Erigeron canadensis,* having narrow leaves and numerous small white or greenish flowers.

horse·whip (hôrs′hwĭp′) *n.* A whip used to control a horse.
~*tr.v.* **horsewhipped, -whipping, -whips.** To beat with or as if with a horsewhip.

horse·wom·an (hôrs′wo͝om′ən) *n., pl.* **-women** (-wĭm′ĭn). **1.** A woman who rides a horse. **2.** A woman skilled at horsemanship.

horst (hôrst) *n.* A massive block of the earth's crust that lies between two parallel faults and is higher than the surrounding land. [German *Horst,* heap.]

hors·y, hors·ey (hôr′sē) *adj.* **-ier, -iest. 1. a.** Of, pertaining to, or characteristic of a horse. **b.** Suggestive of a horse in appearance. **2.** Devoted to horses and horsemanship: *the horsy set.*

hort. horticultural; horticulture.

hor·ta·tive (hôr′tə-tĭv) *adj.* Giving exhortation; urging strongly. [Late Latin *hortātīvus,* from Latin *hortātus,* past participle of *hortārī,* to exhort.] **—hor·ta·tive·ly** *adv.*

hor·ta·to·ry (hôr′tə-tôr′ē, -tōr′ē) *adj.* Hortative; urging strongly. [Late Latin *hortātōrius,* from *hortātus.* See **hortative.**]

hor·ti·cul·ture (hôr′tə-kŭl′chər) *n. Abbr.* **hort. 1.** The science or art of cultivating plants, especially those for ornamental use, or fruit and vegetables for food. **2.** The cultivation of a garden. [Latin *hortus,* garden + (AGRI)CULTURE.] **—hor·ti·cul·tur·al** (hôr′tə-kŭl′chər-əl) *adj.* **—hor·ti·cul·tur·al·ly** *adv.* **—hor·ti·cul·tur·ist** (hôr′tə-kŭl′chər-ĭst) *n.*

hor·tus sic·cus (hôr′təs sĭk′əs) *n.* A collection of dried plants; a herbarium. [Latin, "dry garden."]

Ho·rus (hôr′əs, hōr′-). The ancient Egyptian god of the sun and the sky, represented as having the head of a hawk.

Hos. Hosea (Old Testament).

ho·san·na (hō-zan′ə) *interj.* Used to express praise or adoration to God or the Messiah.
~*n.* **1.** A cry of "hosanna." **2.** A shout of fervent and worshipful praise. [Middle English, from Late Latin *(h)ōsanna,* from Greek, from Hebrew *hosha'nā,* "save us!"]

hose (hōz) *n., pl.* **hose** or *archaic* **hosen** (hō′zən) (for senses 1, 2); **hoses** (for sense 3). **1.** Stockings, socks, or pantyhose. **2. a.** A man's garment that covers the legs and hips and fastens to a doublet by points. **b.** Short full breeches reaching to the knees. **3.** A flexible tube for conveying fluids under pressure.
~*tr.v.* **hosed, hosing, hoses.** To water, drench, or wash with a hose. Often used with *down.* [Middle English *hose,* a stocking, Old English *hosa,* leg covering.]

Ho·se·a[1] (hō-zē′ə, -zā′ə). Hebrew Minor Prophet of the 8th century B.C.

Hosea[2] *n. Abbr.* **Hos.** A prophetic book of the Old Testament, attributed to Hosea.

ho·sier (hō′zhər) *n.* A maker of or dealer in hose and knitted underclothing. [Middle English *hosyer,* from *hose,* HOSE.]

ho·sier·y (hō′zhə-rē) *n.* **1. a.** Stockings and socks; hose. **b.** *British.* Stockings, socks, pantyhose, and underclothing. **2.** The business of a hosier.

hosp. hospital.

hos·pice (hŏs′pĭs) *n.* **1.** A shelter or lodging for travelers, children, or the destitute, often maintained by a monastic order. **2.** An institution that specializes in the care of the terminally ill. [French, from Old French, from Latin *hospitium,* hospitality, from *hospes* (stem *hospit-*), HOST (receiver of guests).]

hos·pi·ta·ble (hŏs′pə-tə-bəl, hŏ-spĭt′ə-bəl) *adj.* **1. a.** Welcoming guests with warmth and generosity. **b.** Well disposed toward strangers. **2.** Having an open and generous mind; receptive. **3.** Promoting well-being; agreeable: *a hospitable climate.* [New Latin *hospitabilis,* from Latin *hospitārī,* to be hospitable to, from *hospes* (stem *hospit-*), HOST (receiver of guests).] **—hos·pi·ta·bly** *adv.*

hos·pi·tal (hŏs′pə-təl, -pĭt′l) *n. Abbr.* **hosp. 1.** An institution providing medical or surgical care and treatment for people who are ill or

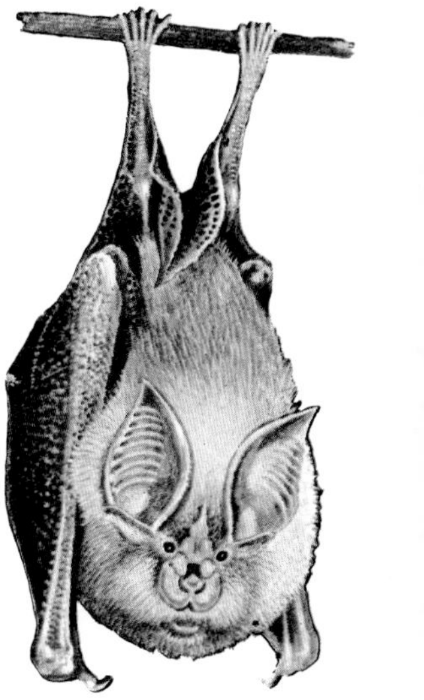

horseshoe bat *The horseshoe bat gets its name from the crescent-shaped flesh around its nose. The bat navigates in the dark by listening to the echoes of the high-pitched squeaks it emits through this fleshy area.*

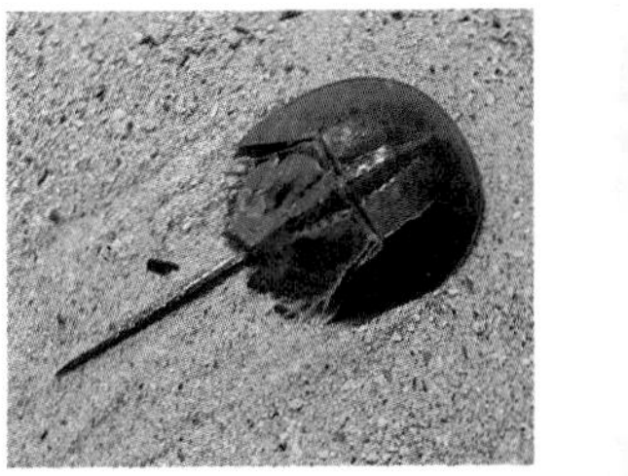

horseshoe crab *Fossil remains show that the horseshoe crab (also known as the king crab) has survived virtually unchanged for about 200 million years.*

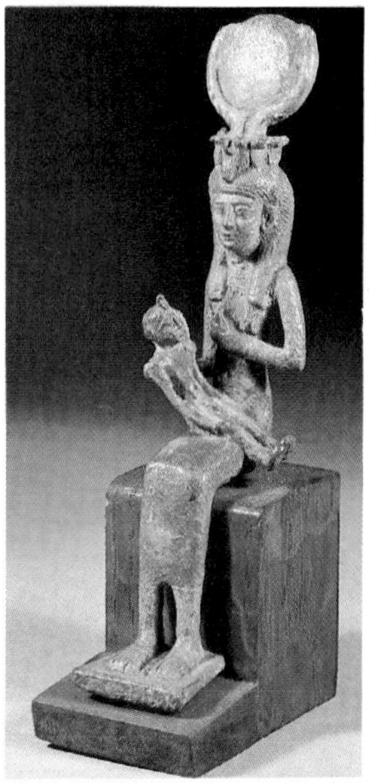

Horus *An Egyptian statue of Isis suckling Horus, the god of the sky whose eyes were the sun and the moon. In Egyptian mythology, Horus became ruler of a united Egypt and the pharaohs thought of themselves as his earthly representatives, using his name as the first of their titles.*

injured, obstetric treatment for pregnant women, psychiatric treatment for the mentally ill, and the like. See **day hospital, general hospital. 2.** *Archaic.* **a.** A hospice for travelers or pilgrims. **b.** A home, often charitable, for old people, the infirm, or foundlings. **3.** A repair shop for specified items: *a doll hospital.* [Middle English, hospice, from Old French, from Medieval Latin *hospitāle*, from Latin *hospitālis*, of a guest, from *hospes* (stem *hospit-*), HOST.]

hospital corner *n.* A method of folding sheets and blankets securely under the mattress at each corner of the foot of a bed, commonly used in making up beds in hospitals.

Hos·pi·tal·er, Hos·pi·tal·ler (hŏs′pə-tə-lər) *n.* **1.** A member of a military religious order founded among European crusaders in 11th-century Palestine. **2.** A member of any of several religious orders dedicated to the care of hospital patients. [Middle English *Hospitalier,* from Old French, from Medieval Latin *hospitāle,* hospice. See **hospital.**]

hos·pi·tal·i·ty (hŏs′pə-tăl′ə-tē) *n., pl.* **-ties. 1.** The act of being hospitable or a tendency toward being hospitable; welcoming and generous behavior toward guests or strangers. **2.** An instance of this. [Middle English *hospitalite,* from Old French, from Latin *hospitālitās* (stem *hospitālitāt-*), from *hospitālis,* of a guest. See **hospital.**]

hos·pi·tal·i·za·tion (hŏs′pə-tə-lĭ-zā′shən) *n.* **1. a.** The act of hospitalizing. **b.** The condition of being hospitalized. **2.** The length of time spent by a patient in a hospital. **3.** A form of insurance that partially or completely covers a patient's hospital expenses.

hos·pi·tal·ize (hŏs′pə-tə-līz′) *tr.v.* **-ized, -izing, -izes.** To put (a patient) into a hospital.

host¹ (hōst) *n.* **1.** One who receives or entertains guests in a social or business capacity. **2.** *Biology.* **a.** An organism that harbors and provides nourishment for a parasite. **b.** Any organism that supports another organism, as a commensal, or that supports part of another organism, as a tissue graft. **3.** The master of ceremonies of a radio or television program. **4.** A place or institution providing the venue for an organized event: *The city has been designated as host for the next Olympic Games.*
~*tr.v.* **hosted, hosting, hosts.** To serve as host for (a party or a television program, for example). [Middle English *(h)oste,* from Old French *host,* guest, from Latin *hospes* (stem *hospit-*), guest, host, stranger.]

host² *n.* **1.** A great number: *"a host of golden daffodils"* (William Wordsworth). **2.** An army. —See Synonyms at **multitude.** [Middle English, from Old French, from Medieval Latin *hostis,* army, from Latin, stranger, enemy.]

host³ *n. Often* **Host.** *Ecclesiastical.* The consecrated bread or wafer of the Eucharist. [Middle English *oste,* from Old French *oiste,* from Latin *hostia†,* sacrifice, victim.]

hos·ta (hŏ′stə) *n. Botany.* The **plantain lily** (see). [New Latin, genus name, after Nicolaus T. *Host* (d. 1834), Austrian botanist.]

hos·tage (hŏs′tĭj) *n.* **1.** A person taken, often by force, and held as security for the fulfillment of certain terms. **2.** Anything held as security. —**a hostage to fortune.** Something one has acquired and may lose. [Middle English *(h)ostage,* from Old French, either from *oste, hoste,* guest, HOST, or from Vulgar Latin *obsidāticum* (unattested), from Late Latin *obsidātus,* hostage (sense 2), from Latin *obses* (stem *obsid-*), a hostage : *ob-,* in the way of, in front of + *sedēre,* to sit.]

hos·tel (hŏs′təl) *n.* **1. a.** Any of various types of supervised, inexpensive lodging houses or residences for groups of people such as students, the homeless, or young travelers. **b.** A **youth hostel** (see). **2.** *Archaic.* An inn. [Middle English *(h)ostel,* from Old French, from Medieval Latin *hospitāle,* hospice. See **hospital.**]

hos·tel·er (hŏs′tə-lər) *n.* **1.** A traveler who stays at youth hostels. **2.** *Archaic.* An innkeeper.

hos·tel·ry (hŏs′təl-rē) *n., pl.* **-ries.** An inn.

host·ess (hō′stĭs) *n.* **1.** A woman who acts as a host. **2.** A woman whose occupation is greeting and assisting patrons, as in a restaurant or on an airplane.

hos·tile (hŏs′təl, -tīl′) *adj.* **1.** Of or pertaining to an enemy. **2.** Feeling or showing enmity or hatred; antagonistic. **3.** Inhospitable; unwelcoming: *a hostile environment.* [Old French, from Latin *hostīlis,* from *hostis,* HOST (enemy).] —**hos·tile·ly** *adv.*

hos·til·i·ty (hŏ-stĭl′ə-tē) *n., pl.* **-ties. 1.** The state of being hostile; antagonism; enmity. **2. a.** A hostile act or incident. **b. hostilities.** Overt warfare. —See Synonyms at **enmity.**

hostler. Variant of **ostler.**

hot (hŏt) *adj.* **hotter, hottest. 1. a.** Possessing great heat. **b.** Yielding much heat. **c.** Being at a high temperature. **2.** Warmer than is normal or desirable: *a hot forehead.* **3. a.** Causing a burning sensation because highly spiced: *a hot curry.* **b.** Heated and not having cooled down: *a hot drink.* **4. a.** Charged or energized with electricity: *a hot wire.* **b.** Radioactive, especially to a dangerous degree. **5.** Explosive; fiery: *a hot dispute; a hot temper.* **6.** Eager; excited; ardent: *in hot pursuit.* **7.** *Slang.* **a.** Recently stolen: *hot goods.* **b.** Wanted for criminal activity. **8.** Close to success or achievement: *hot on the trail.* **9.** *Informal.* Highly sensitive; dangerously controversial: *The issue proved too hot for the government to handle.* **10.** *Informal.* **a.** New; fresh: *hot off the press.* **b.** Currently popular: *one of the hottest young talents around.* **c.** Confidently expected to win: *the hot favorite.* **11.** *Slang.* Good or impressive. Usually used in the negative: *not so hot.* **12.** *Slang.* **a.** Performing with special skill or success. **b.** Lucky. **13.** *Slang.* Producing exciting emotional and physical reactions by means of strong rhythms and inspired improvisation. Said of jazz. **14.** Strong; striking; bright. Said of a

color. **15.** *Metallurgy.* At a temperature sufficiently high for metal to become soft enough to work or cast. Said of a process or a metal. —**hot under the collar.** *Informal.* Angry. —**in hot water.** *Informal.* In trouble. —**make it hot for.** *Informal.* To make things uncomfortable or dangerous for. [Middle English *hot,* Old English *hāt,* from Germanic.]

hot air *n. Informal.* Empty talk; boastful nonsense.

hot-air balloon (hŏt′âr′) *n.* A balloon consisting of a large fabric or plastic bag containing air, which is heated by a naked flame, and a passenger-carrying basket or gondola.

hot·bed (hŏt′bĕd′) *n.* **1.** A glass-covered bed of soil heated with fermenting manure or by electricity, used for the germination of seeds or for protecting tender plants. **2.** An environment conducive to rapid, excessively vigorous growth, especially of something bad: *a hotbed of intrigue.*

hot-blood·ed (hŏt′blŭd′ĭd) *adj.* **1.** Easily excited or angered. **2.** Passionate. **3.** Rash or reckless. —**hot-blood·ed·ness** *n.*

hot·box (hŏt′bŏks′) *n.* An overheated axle or journal box, as in a railway car, caused by excessive friction.

hot cake *n.* A pancake. —**go** (or **sell**) **like hot cakes.** To be in great demand.

hotch (hŏch) *v.* **hotched, hotching, hotches.** *Scottish.* —*tr.* To shake; jog. —*intr.* To fidget. [Perhaps from Old French *hocher, hochier,* perhaps from Frankish *hottisōn†* (unattested).]

hotch·pot (hŏch′pŏt′) *n. Law.* The gathering together of properties to secure an equal division of the total for distribution, as among the heirs of an intestate parent. [Middle English *hochepot,* from Old French : *hocher, hochier,* HOTCH + *pot,* pot, from (unattested) Vulgar Latin *pottus.*]

hotch·potch (hŏch′pŏch′) *n.* **1.** A hodgepodge. **2.** A stew made from many different ingredients. **3.** *Law.* A hotchpot. [Variant of HOTCHPOT.]

hot cross bun *n.* A sweet bun often made with raisins and marked on top with a cross of frosting traditionally eaten during Lent.

hot dipping *n.* The process of dipping metal objects in a second molten metal to give them a thin protective or decorative coating.

hot dog *n.* A frankfurter, typically served hot in a long, soft roll. ~*interj. Informal.* Used to express satisfaction or enthusiasm. [Perhaps from its fancied resemblance to a dachshund.]

hot-dog (hŏt′dôg′, -dŏg′) *intr.v.* **-dogged, -dogging, -dogs.** *Slang.* To do stunts or acrobatic feats, especially while skiing or surfing. —**hot-dog·ger** *n.*

ho·tel (hō-tĕl′) *n.* An establishment that provides accommodation and usually meals and other services for the public. [French *hôtel,* from Old French *hostel,* HOSTEL.]

ho·tel·ier (hō-tĕl′yər, ōt′l-yā′) *n.* A person who owns or manages a hotel or hotels. [French *hôtelier,* from Old French *hostelier,* innkeeper : *(h)ostel,* HOSTEL + *-ier,* -ER.]

hot flash *n.* A transient vasomotor symptom of the menopause, resulting from hormone imbalance, that involves dilation of the skin capillaries and the sensation of heat over all or part of the body. Also called "hot flush."

hot·foot (hŏt′fŏŏt′) *intr.v.* **-footed, -footing, -foots.** To go in haste. Used with *it.*
~*adv.* In haste.
~*n., pl.* **hotfoots.** A prank in which a match is stealthily inserted into the side of someone's shoe and lit. [Middle English (adverb), "with eager feet."]

hot·head (hŏt′hĕd′) *n.* One who is hotheaded.

hot·head·ed (hŏt′hĕd′ĭd) *adj.* **1.** Having a fiery temper. **2.** Impetuous; rash. —**hot·head·ed·ly** *adv.* —**hot·head·ed·ness** *n.*

hot·house (hŏt′hous′) *n., pl.* **-houses** (-hou′zĭz). A heated greenhouse or conservatory for plants requiring an even, relatively warm temperature.
~*adj.* **1.** Grown in a hothouse. **2.** Like or characteristic of a plant grown in a hothouse; delicate; sensitive.

hot line *n.* **1.** A direct communications link, as a telephone line, especially one between heads of government for use in time of crisis, as to prevent an accidental outbreak of war. **2.** A telephone facility that enables callers to talk confidentially to sympathetic listeners about personal problems.

hot·ly (hŏt′lē) *adv.* In an angry or fiery way; passionately: *answered hotly that he was innocent.*

hot-met·al printing (hŏt′mĕt′l) *n.* A method of printing using type cast from molten metal.

hot money *n.* Capital transferred from place to place at frequent intervals in order to achieve the maximum possible return.

hot pepper *n.* **1.** The pungent fruit of any of several varieties of *Capsicum frutescens.* **2.** A condiment made from such fruit.

hot plate *n.* **1.** An electrically heated plate for cooking or warming food. **2.** A table-top cooking device having one or two burners.

hot·pot (hŏt′pŏt′) *n. Chiefly British.* A stew of meat, especially lamb, with layers of potatoes, usually baked in a tight-lidded pot.

hot potato *n. Informal.* A highly controversial or sensitive issue: *The question of police accountability has become a political hot potato.*

hot-press (hŏt′prĕs′) *tr.v.* **-pressed, -pressing, -presses.** To subject (paper or cloth) to heat and pressure in order to extract oil.
~*n.* A machine for hot-pressing.

hot property *n. Informal.* A person or thing regarded as having great promise or potential.

hot rod, hot-rod (hŏt′rŏd′) *n. Slang.* A car rebuilt or remodeled for increased speed and acceleration. —**hot rodder** *n.*

hot seat *n. Slang.* **1.** A difficult or exposed position. **2.** The electric chair.

hot·shot (hŏt′shŏt′) *n. Slang.* An ostentatiously skillful person.

hot spot *n.* **1.** An area of high temperature in an engine or machine, either one that results from a malfunction or one that is used to vaporize fuel. **2.** A place full of danger, violence, or unrest. **3.** An area on the surface of the earth, away from a tectonic plate margin, that has a higher than average heat flow and that often gives rise to a volcano. **4.** An exciting, lively place, such as a nightclub.

hot spring *n.* A natural spring continuously discharging water that is above body temperature, or over 98°F (37°C).

Hot Springs. A city of west-central Arkansas, nearly coextensive with **Hot Springs National Park.** The city produces metal and electrical products and lumber. The springs were long used by Indians for medicinal purposes and were visited by Hernando de Soto in 1541. More than a million gallons of water a day, with an average temperature of 62°C (143°F), flow from 47 springs. The national park was established in 1921.

Hotspur. See **Percy, Sir Henry.**

Hot·ten·tot (hŏt′n-tŏt′) *n., pl.* **-tots** or collectively **Hottentot. 1.** A southern African people, held to be related to the Bantu and Bushmen. **2.** The language of this people. [Afrikaans.]

hot toddy *n.* A beverage, a **toddy** *(see).*

hot tub *n.* A very large, usually wooden tub in which a group of bathers can soak in hot water.

hot-wa·ter bottle (hŏt′wô′tər, -wŏt′ər) *n.* A container, usually made of rubber, designed to be filled with hot water and used to warm a part of the body or a bed.

hot-water crust *n.* A type of pie pastry made from flour, melted fat, and water.

Hou·dan (ho͞o′dăn′) *n.* A domesticated fowl having black and white plumage and a V-shaped comb. [French, developed in *Houdan,* a village near Paris, France.]

Hou·di·ni (ho͞o-dē′nē), **Harry,** born Ehrich Weiss (1874–1926). U.S. magician and showman. He was adept at escaping from chains, handcuffs, straitjackets, and padlocked containers.

Hou·don (ho͞o′dŏn′), **Jean Antoine** (1741–1828). French sculptor. He is especially noted for his statues of Washington and Voltaire and for his many portrait busts, including ones of Jefferson, Franklin, John Paul Jones, Rousseau, and Lafayette.

hough (hŏKH) *n. British.* **1.** A **hock** *(see).* **2.** A joint of meat, such as beef, from the hock or the part of the leg above it.
~*tr.v.* **houghed, houghing, houghs.** *British.* To hock or hamstring. [Middle English, from Old English *hōh,* heel, attested in *hōhsinu,* "hock-shin," hamstring.]

hound¹ (hound) *n.* **1.** A dog of any of various breeds used for hunting, characteristically having drooping ears, a short coat, and a deep, resonant voice. Also used in combination: *bloodhound; foxhound.* **2.** Any dog. **3.** A runner who pursues in the game of hare and hounds. **4.** A contemptible person; a scoundrel. **5.** One who eagerly pursues something: *a news hound.* **—follow the** (or **ride to**) **hounds.** To take part in a fox hunt.
~*tr.v.* **hounded, hounding, hounds. 1.** To pursue or harass relentlessly and tenaciously: *hounded by the press.* **2.** To incite to give chase; urge on. —See Synonyms at **harass.** [Middle English *h(o)und,* Old English *hund,* from Germanic.]

hound² *n.* **1.** Either of two projections at the side of a masthead that supports the trestletrees of large vessels or the rigging of smaller ones. **2.** Either of a pair of horizontal braces for reinforcing the running gear of a horse-drawn vehicle. [Middle English *hune, hownde,* probably from Old Norse *hūnn,* knob, knob at the top of a masthead.]

hound shark *n.* Any of various harmless edible sharks of the genus *Mustelus,* having flat teeth and well-developed spiracles. Also called "smooth hound," "soft-mouthed shark."

hound's-tongue (houndz′tŭng′) *n.* Any of several plants of the genus *Cynoglossum;* especially, *C. officinale,* native to Eurasia, having hairy leaves, small reddish-purple flowers, and prickly, clinging fruit. Also called "dog's tongue." [From the shape of its leaves.]

hound's-tooth check (houndz′to͞oth′) *n.* A patterned textile design consisting of small, broken checks. Also called "dog's-tooth check," "dogtooth check."

hour (our) *n. Abbr.* **h, hr 1.** The 24th part of a day. **2. a.** One of the points on a timepiece marking off 12 or 24 successive intervals of 60 minutes, from midnight to noon and noon to midnight, or from midnight to midnight. **b.** The time of day indicated by a 12-hour clock. **c. hours.** The time of day determined on a 24-hour basis: *1700 hours.* **3. a.** A customary time allotted for something: *dinner hour.* **b. hours.** A period in which a particular or specified activity takes place or is allowed to take place: *banking hours; drinking after hours.* **4. a.** The work that can be accomplished in an hour. **b.** The distance that can be traveled in an hour. **5. hours. a.** A time for daily liturgical devotion, as the canonical hours. **b.** The prayers recited during the canonical hours. **6. a.** A time of significance: *His hour had come.* **b.** The present time. Preceded by *the: the hero of the hour.* **7.** A time that is an exact number of hours, as one o'clock or six o'clock. Preceded by *the: I'll leave on the hour. The clock struck the hour.* **8. hours.** Times of rising and going to bed, working, and the like: *keeps late hours; works long hours.* **9.** An angle of 15° (a 24th part of the celestial equator), used as a measure of right ascension. **—till** (or **until**) **all hours.** Until very late at night. [Middle English *hour, (o)ure,* from Old French *(h)ore,* from Latin *hōra,* from Greek, time, season.]

hour angle *n.* The angle measured westward along the celestial equator from the celestial meridian of the observer to the hour circle passing through a celestial body.

hour circle *n.* A great circle passing through the poles of the celestial sphere and intersecting the celestial equator at right angles.

hour·glass (our′glăs′, -gläs′) *n.* An instrument for measuring time consisting of two glass chambers with a narrow connecting channel, and containing sand or mercury requiring an exact period of time, usually one hour, to trickle from one chamber to the other.
~*adj.* Shaped like an hourglass; narrow-waisted.

hour hand *n.* The indicator on a timepiece that shows the hour.

hou·ri (ho͝or′ē, ho͞or′ē) *n., pl.* **-ris. 1.** A voluptuous woman. **2.** One of the beautiful virgins of the Koranic paradise. [French, from Persian *ḥūrī,* from Arabic *ḥūr,* plural of *ḥaura‘,* gazellelike (dark-eyed).]

hour·ly (our′lē) *adj.* **1. a.** Occurring every hour. **b.** Frequent; continual. **2.** By the hour as a unit: *hourly pay.* **—hour·ly** *adv.*

Hou·sa·ton·ic (ho͞o′sə-tŏn′ĭk). River rising in the Berkshires in western Massachusetts and flowing *c.* 210 kilometers (130 miles) generally south through western Connecticut to Long Island Sound.

house (hous) *n., pl.* **houses** (hou′zĭz). *Abbr.* **ho. 1. a.** A structure serving as a dwelling for one or several families. **b.** A place of abode; a residence. **c.** Something that serves as an abode. **2.** A building used for shelter or storage. Often used in combination: *a warehouse; a henhouse.* **3.** A building having a particular function or providing a particular service to the public. Often used in combination: *a schoolhouse; a coffee-house.* **4.** A dwelling for a religious community. **5.** A household. **6.** *Often* **House.** A family line, including ancestors and descendants; especially, a royal or noble family: *the House of Orange.* **7.** A commercial firm: *a banking house.* Also used adjectivally: *house style; a house magazine.* **8.** A residential building for pupils at a boarding school. **9. a.** A place of entertainment, such as a theater. **b.** An audience at a theater. **10. a.** A hotel, restaurant, tavern, or club: *the specialty of the house.* Also used adjectivally: *the house wine.* **b.** *Slang.* A brothel. **11. a.** A legislative or deliberative assembly. **b.** The hall where such an assembly meets. **c.** A quorum of such an assembly. **12.** The people attending and voting in a formal debate: *spoke for the motion that this house would restore capital punishment.* **13.** *Astrology.* **a.** One of the 12 parts into which the heavens are divided. **b.** The sign of the zodiac indicating the seat or station of a planet in the heavens. Also called "mansion." **—bring the house down.** To cause wild and general applause; be an enormous popular success. **—keep house.** To look after a house and the people in it. **—like a house on fire. 1.** With great speed and effectiveness. **2.** Very well; superbly. **—on the house.** At the expense of the management or manager; free. **—put** (or **set**) **one's house in order.** To arrange one's affairs in an orderly manner.
~*v.* (houz) **housed, housing, houses.** —*tr.* **1.** To provide with a house or houses; furnish living quarters for: *The cottage housed ten boys.* **2.** To shelter, keep or store in or as if in a house. **3.** To contain; harbor. **4.** To fit into a socket or mortise. **5.** *Nautical.* To secure or stow safely. —*intr.* To lodge; dwell. [Middle English *h(o)us, house,* Old English *hūs,* from Germanic *hūsam* (unattested).]

house arrest *n.* Confinement to one's home enforced by administrative or judicial order.

house·boat (hous′bōt′) *n.* A barge or boat equipped for use as a home.

house·bound (hous′bound′) *n.* Unable to leave one's house, especially because of illness.

house·boy (hous′boi′) *n.* A male servant in a house.

house·break·ing (hous′brā′kĭng) *n.* The act of unlawfully breaking into another's house for the purpose of committing a felony. **—house·break·er** *n.*

house·bro·ken (hous′brō′kən) *adj.* **1.** Trained in habits of excretion appropriate for a house pet. **2.** Trained to be docile; compliant.

house·carl (hous′kärl′) *n.* A member of the bodyguard or household troops of a Danish or early English king or noble. [Old English *hūscarl,* from Old Norse *hūskarl* : *hūs,* house + *karl,* man.]

house·coat (hous′kōt′) *n.* A woman's garment resembling a dressing gown, used for informal wear at home.

house·craft (hous′krăft′, -kräft′) *n. Chiefly British.* Skill in the running of a household; household management.

house-dust mite (hous′dŭst′) *n.* A mite, *Dermatophagoides farinae,* that lives on shed scales of human skin and is common in the dust of mattresses and pillows. It can induce asthma or inflammation of the nasal mucous membranes in people who are allergic to it.

house·fa·ther (hous′fä′*th*ər) *n.* A male houseparent.

house finch *n.* A small finch, *Carpodacus mexicanus,* of western North America and Mexico, having a red head, throat, and breast. It is closely related to the **purple fich** *(see)* and often nests near dwellings.

house·fly (hous′flī′) *n., pl.* **-flies.** A common, widely distributed fly, *Musca domestica,* that frequents human dwellings and is a transmitter of a wide variety of diseases.

house·hold (hous′hōld′) *n.* A domestic establishment including the members of a family and others living under the same roof.
~*adj.* **1.** Of or pertaining to a household; domestic. **2.** Well-known; familiar: *has become a household name since his record-breaking run.* [Middle English HOUSE + *hold,* possession, property (from the verb).]

house·hold·er (hous′hōl′dər) *n.* One who owns or rents and occupies a house or apartment.

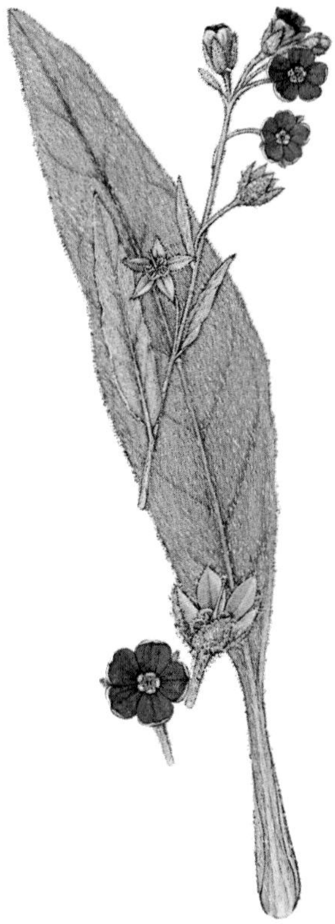

hound's-tongue *The shape and texture of the leaves of* Cynoglossum officinale *gave rise to its common English name. But the distinctive, unpleasant smell of the plant was also said to "tie the tongues of hounds"—that is, to keep them from barking. The juice of the leaves, boiled in hog lard, was once used to treat baldness.*

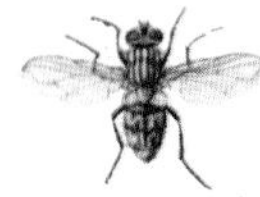

housefly *One of the most common insects in the home. Tiny suckers on the housefly's feet enable it to walk upside-down on ceilings.*

house martin *Originally house martins built their dome-shaped mud nests under overhanging cliffs or in caves, but they have adapted to the presence of man and now commonly nest under the eaves of houses—hence their name. They feed largely on flies and small beetles, catching them on the wing.*

e 3 in.
lus

house mouse Mus musculus, *the house mouse, is a rodent that has adapted to living in close company with man all over the world. It makes its nest in a wall near food stores and can produce as many as ten litters a year with up to seven young in each.*

house sparrow *Originally the house sparrow,* Passer domesticus, *was native only to Asia. But it spread westward into Europe, probably in the wake of Stone Age farmers, and now thrives near human settlements all over Europe and in much of North Africa. It has also been introduced into North America. The birds feed on seeds, insects, and—in built-up areas—on bread and scraps put out by humans.*

---

hovercraft

THE SHIP THAT FLIES
How a Hovercraft skims over land and sea

Hovercraft is a trademark and the popular description for an air-cushion vehicle—an amphibious craft that skims over land or sea on a bed of air created by a fan. Air is driven downward, beneath the vehicle, and is enclosed in a skirt, a rubberized fabric curtain that hangs down all around the base of the craft. The air lifts it to hover just above the surface of land or water. The craft can then be moved forward, backward, or sideways without encountering the drag that impedes a partly submerged ship.

The Hovercraft is thus swifter and more adaptable, useful for ferry work on short sea trips and ideal for work on difficult surfaces, such as swamps and ice-bound waters.

Air-cushion vehicles were pioneered in 1959 by the British Hovercraft Corporation and are now made all over the world. The technique has been applied to lawn mowers, and even to medical treatment—a severely burned patient is supported in a hover bed, which creates a cushion of sterile air under the body.

AT SEA *The most common use for the Hovercraft has been for short-distance ferry services. It is faster than conventional sea ferries and is quicker to load.*

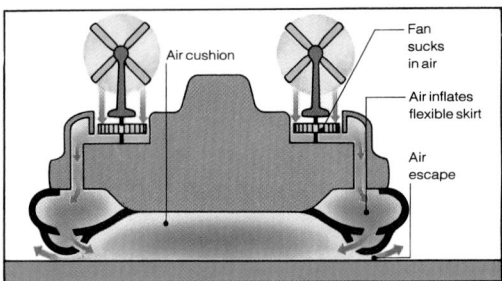

HOW IT WORKS *Powerful fans push air into the flexible skirt that surrounds the base of the craft, creating a cushion of air. This supports the craft over land or sea.*

Labels: Fan sucks in air; Air cushion; Air inflates flexible skirt; Air escape

---

household troops *pl.n.* The regiments of cavalry and infantry that escort and guard a sovereign and royal family.

house·hus·band (hous′hŭz′bənd) *n.* A man who stays at home and looks after the house and often the children while his wife earns the family income.

house·keep·er (hous′kē′pər) *n.* One who has charge of domestic tasks in a household.

house·keep·ing (hous′kē′pĭng) *n.* **1.** The management of a house and its occupants. **2.** Routine tasks that must be done to maintain an operation or system.

hou·sel (hou′zəl) *n. Archaic.* The Eucharist.
~*tr.v.* **houseled, -seling, -sels.** *Archaic.* To administer the Eucharist to. [Middle English *housel,* Old English *hūsl.*]

house·leek (hous′lēk′) *n.* Any of various plants of the genus *Sempervivum,* native to the Old World; especially, *S. tectorum,* having a basal rosette of fleshy leaves and a branching cluster of pinkish or purplish flowers. Also called "hen-and-chickens," "old-man-and-woman."

house·lights (hous′līts′) *pl.n.* The lights that illuminate the audience section of a concert hall, theater, or auditorium.

house·line (hous′lĭn′) *n. Nautical.* A small line formed of three strands, used for seizing. [From its use in housing larger ropes.]

house·maid (hous′mād′) *n.* A woman employed to do housework.

housemaid's knee *n.* A chronic, inflammatory swelling of the bursa of the knee anterior to the kneecap, caused by prolonged kneeling on hard floors.

house martin *n.* A Eurasian bird, *Delichon urbica,* having blue-black plumage with white markings and a forked tail.

house·mas·ter (hous′măs′tər, -mä′stər) *n.* A male teacher in charge of a residence hall at a boys' school.

house·mis·tress (hous′mĭs′trĭs) *n.* A female teacher in charge of a residence hall at a girls' school.

house·moth·er (hous′mŭ*th*′ər) *n.* A female houseparent.

house mouse *n.* Any of various Old World mice of the genus *Mus,* especially *M. musculus,* that have grayish fur and are widely distributed household pests.

house name *n.* An assumed name used by a journalist, as when writing several different articles in the same newspaper.

House of Burgesses *n.* The lower house of the legislature of colonial Virginia.

House of Commons *n. Abbr.* **H.C. 1. a.** The lower house of Parliament in the United Kingdom, having the main legislative powers and an elected membership. **b.** The members of the House of Commons collectively. In both senses, also called "Commons." **2.** The lower house of the Canadian parliament.

house of correction *n.* An institution housing persons convicted of minor criminal offenses.

house of God *n.* A church or chapel.

house of ill repute *n.* A brothel. Used euphemistically. Also called "house of ill fame."

House of Lords *n. Abbr.* **H.L. 1.** The upper house of Parliament in the United Kingdom, a nonelective chamber made up of members of the nobility and high-ranking clergy. **2.** The members of the House of Lords collectively. Also called "Lords."

House of Representatives *n. Abbr.* **H.R. 1.** The lower house of the U.S. Congress and of most state legislatures. **2.** In Australia,

the lower house of Parliament. **3.** In New Zealand, the legislative assembly.

house·par·ent (hous′pâr′ənt) *n.* A person in charge of a group of children living in a residential institution, especially a school.

house party *n.* **1.** A party at which guests stay overnight or for several days in a private home or other residence. **2.** The guests at a house party.

house physician *n.* **1.** A resident physician in a hospital. **2.** A physician employed by a hotel or other establishment.

house·plant (hous′plănt′, -plänt′) *n.* A plant that is grown indoors for ornament.

house·proud (hous′proud′) *adj.* Extremely fastidious about the cleaning, tidiness, and general appearance of a house.

house·rais·ing (hous′rā′zing) *n.* The construction of a house or its framework by a group of neighbors.

house·room (hous′rōōm′, -rŏŏm′) *n.* Room for lodging or storage in a house.

house·sit (hous′sĭt′) *intr.v.* **-sat** (-săt′), **-sitting, -sits.** To act as a house sitter.

house sitter *n.* A person who lives in and takes care of a house while the regular occupant is away.

house snake *n.* The **milk snake** *(see).*

Houses of Parliament *pl.n.* **1.** The British House of Commons and House of Lords collectively. **2.** The building where they meet.

house sparrow *n.* A small bird, *Passer domesticus,* native to the Old World but widely naturalized elsewhere, having brown and gray plumage, and a black throat in the male.

house·top (hous′tŏp′) *n.* The roof of a house. **—shout** (or **proclaim) from the housetops.** To make known publicly.

house·train (hous′trān′) *tr.v.* **-trained, -training, -trains.** To teach (a pet) to excrete outside the house or in a particular place.

house·warm·ing (hous′wôr′mĭng) *n.* A party to celebrate the occupancy of a new home. Also called "housewarming party."

house·wife (hous′wīf′ *for sense 1;* hŭz′ĭf *for sense 2) n., pl.* **-wives** (-wīvz′) (for sense 1); **housewifs** (hŭz′ĭfs) or **housewives** (hŭz′ĭvz) (for sense 2). **1.** A married woman who supervises the affairs of a household, especially one who has no outside employment. **2.** *Chiefly British.* A pocket container for sewing equipment.

house·wife·ly (hous′wīf′lē) *adj.* Of, pertaining to, or characteristic of a housewife; domestic. **—house·wife·li·ness** *n.*

house·wif·er·y (hous′wī′fə-rē, -wīf′rē) *n.* The function or duties of a housewife; housekeeping.

house·work (hous′wûrk′) *n.* The tasks performed in housekeeping, as cleaning or cooking.

hous·ing¹ (hou′zĭng) *n.* **1.** Buildings or other shelters in which people live, considered collectively. **2.** The provision of houses or dwellings. Also used adjectively: *housing policy.* **3. a.** Something that covers, protects, or guards. **b.** A frame, bracket, or box for holding or protecting a mechanical part: *a wheel housing.* **c.** An enclosing frame in which a shaft revolves. **4.** A hole, groove, or slot in a piece of wood for the insertion of another piece. **5.** A niche for a statue. **6.** The part of a mast that is below deck or of a bowsprit that is inside the hull.

housing² *n.* **1.** An ornamental or protective covering for a saddle. **2.** *Usually* **housings.** Trappings. [Middle English, from *house,* covering, from Old French *houce,* from Medieval Latin *hultia,* from Germanic.]

housing development *n.* A group of similarly designed houses or apartment buildings, usually under a single management.

housing project *n.* A publicly funded and administered housing development, usually for low-income families.

Hous·man (hous'mən), **A(lfred) E(dward)** (1859-1936). British poet. He was professor of Latin at Cambridge University, and published two volumes of poetry, *A Shropshire Lad* (1896) and *Last Poems* (1922), and an essay, *The Name and Nature of Poetry* (1933).

Hous·ton (hyōō'stən). A city in southeastern Texas, a deep-water port on the Houston Ship Canal. It is one of the world's leading oil centers and the third-busiest port in the United States. It is also an important center for space research.

Houston, Samuel (1793-1863). U.S. general and politician. Leaving an established political career in Tennessee, he became involved in the Texan struggle for independence from Mexico. He defeated Gen. Santa Anna (1836) and became president of the Republic of Texas (1836-38; 1841-44). When Texas was admitted to the Union, he served as U.S. senator (1845-59) and as governor (1859-61).

hout·ing (hou'tĭng) *n.* A European food fish, *Coregonus oxyrhynchus,* a species of whitefish that lives in the sea but spawns in rivers and lakes. [Dutch, from Middle Dutch *houtic†.*]

hove. *Chiefly Nautical.* Past tense and past participle of **heave.**

hov·el (hŭv'əl, hŏv'-) *n.* **1.** A small, miserable dwelling. **2.** An open, low shed. **3.** A cone-shaped building housing a kiln. [Middle English *hovel†.*]

hov·er (hŭv'ər, hŏv'ər) *intr.v.* **-ered, -ering, -ers. 1.** To fly, soar, or float, remaining roughly in one place, as if suspended: *gulls hovering over the waves.* **2.** To remain or linger in close proximity; move back and forth in or near a place. **3.** To be in a state of uncertainty; waver; vacillate: *hover between skepticism and belief.* —*n.* **1.** The condition of hovering. **2.** An act or instance of hovering. [Middle English *hoveren,* frequentative of *hoven†,* to hover, linger.] —**hov·er·er** *n.* —**hov·er·ing·ly** *adv.*

Hov·er·craft (hŭv'ər-krăft', -kräft', hŏv'-) *n.* A trademark for a vehicle capable of low-level flight over land or water on a cushion of air formed by the action of downward-directed fans. Also called "air-cushion vehicle."

hover fly *n.* Any fly of the family Syrphidae, having a hovering flight and typically having markings that mimic wasps or bees.

hov·er·port (hŭv'ər-pôrt', -pōrt', hŏv'-) *n.* A port for Hovercraft.

how¹ (hou) *adv.* **1.** In what manner or way: *He showed us how to work the machine. How did he react?* **2.** By what means; with what cause or explanation: *I don't know how you can afford it. How is it possible?* **3.** In what state or condition: *How do I look in this jacket?* **4.** To what extent, amount, or degree: *How do you like that? How much did it cost?* **5.** With what meaning: *How should I interpret this?* **6.** In what state of health or general well-being: *How are you? How is your mother?* **7.** Of what kind or quality: *How was the party?* **8.** By what name: *How is he called?* **9.** Used as an intensive: *How we laughed!* —**and how!** *Informal.* Very much so. —**how about?** What is your feeling or thought regarding? —**how come?** Why is it that? —**how is that?** or **how's that?** What? Usually used in requesting that something said be repeated: *How is that again?* —**how so?** Why is it so? —*conj.* **1.** Of the manner or style in which: *Be careful how you address the ambassador.* **2.** The fact that: *Remember how we used to go out drinking every night?* **3.** However; in whatever way: *As long as it gets done you can do it how you like.* —*n.* A manner or method of doing or performing: *learn the how of a procedure.* [Middle English *hou, how,* Old English *hū,* from Germanic.]

how² *interj.* Used to express greeting in presumed imitation of North American Indian speech. [From Sioux; akin to Dakota *háo* and Omaha *hau.*]

How·ard (hou'ərd), **Catherine** (c. 1520-42). English Catholic noblewoman who became the fifth wife of Henry VIII (1540). Her love affairs brought charges of treason from the Protestant faction at court, and she was executed.

Howard, Leslie, born Leslie Stainer (1893-1943). British stage and screen actor. He played the lead in the film *The Scarlet Pimpernel* (1934) and Ashley Wilkes in *Gone with the Wind* (1939).

Howard, Trevor Wallace (1916-). British actor. He made his screen debut in 1944. He starred in *Brief Encounter* (1946) and played Captain Bligh in *Mutiny on the Bounty* (1962).

how·be·it (hou-bē'ĭt) *adv. Archaic.* Be that as it may; nevertheless. —*conj. Obsolete.* Although.

how·dah (hou'də) *n.* A seat, usually fitted with a canopy and railing, placed on the back of an elephant or camel. [Urdu, from Persian *haudah,* from Arabic *haudaj,* litter.]

how do you do *interj.* Used in greeting a person formally, especially when being introduced for the first time.

how-do-you-do (hou'də-yə-dōō') *n.* Also **how-d'ye-do** (houd'-yə-dōō', hou'dē-). *Informal.* A difficult or embarrassing predicament. Usually used with *pretty, fine,* or *nice.*

how·dy (hou'dē) *interj. Regional.* Used to express greeting. [Short for *how do you do.*]

Howe (hou), **Elias** (1819-67). U.S. inventor. As an apprentice watchmaker he began to work at devising a sewing machine; he exhibited his first machine in 1845 and patented another in 1846. Over the next few years he brought several suits for infringement of patent, including a successful one against Isaac M. Singer.

Howe, Julia Ward (1819-1910). U.S. author, feminist, and philanthropist. Active in the woman suffrage movement, she was also concerned with peace. Her essay "Appeal to Womanhood Throughout the World" called for an international meeting of women to discuss peace. She is the author of "Battle Hymn of the Republic."

how-e'er (hou-âr'). *Poetic.* Contraction of *however.*

How·ells (hou'əlz), **William Dean** (1837-1920). U.S. author and editor. Editor (1866-71) and editor in chief (1871-81) of the *Atlantic Monthly,* he displayed his broad-minded yet discerning taste for literature by encouraging writers ranging from Mark Twain to Henry James. He also wrote many novels, such as *The Rise of Silas Lapham* (1885), poems, and books of travel, literary criticism, and memoirs.

how·ev·er (hou-ĕv'ər) *adv.* **1. a.** By contrast; on the other hand: *The first part was easy; the second stage, however, was considerably harder.* **b.** Nevertheless; in spite of that: *The tickets are expensive; however, I still think we should go.* **2.** By whatever manner or means: *However you come, come early.* **3.** To whatever degree or extent: *"I never am bored, however familiar the scene"* (Theodore Roethke). **4.** *Informal.* How. Used to add emphasis or show surprise: *However did he manage it?* —*conj.* **1.** In whatever way: *Dress however you like.* **2.** *Archaic.* Although; notwithstanding that. —See Usage note at **but.**

howf, howff (houf, hōf) *n. Scottish.* A popular meeting place, such as a tavern. [16th century : origin obscure.]

how·it·zer (hou'ĭt-sər) *n.* A cannon with a barrel longer than a mortar that delivers shells with medium velocities, either by a low or, more usually, by a high trajectory against targets that cannot be reached by flat trajectories. [Dutch *houwitser,* from German *Haubitze,* earlier *haufenitz,* from Czech *houfnice,* catapult.]

howl (houl) *v.* **howled, howling, howls.** —*intr.* **1.** To utter or emit a long, mournful, plaintive sound characteristic of wolves or dogs. **2.** To cry or wail loudly and uncontrollably, as in pain, sorrow, or anger. **3.** *Slang.* To laugh heartily. **4.** *Slang.* To go on a spree. —*tr.* To express or utter with a howl or howls. —**howl down.** To drown the sound of or silence (a speaker) by loud derisive calls and howls. —*n.* **1.** The sound of one that howls. **2.** A high-pitched whine produced in a sound system by electronic feedback. **3.** *Slang.* Something uproariously funny or absurd. [Middle English *houlen, howlen,* perhaps from Middle Dutch *hūlen.*]

howl·er (hou'lər) *n.* **1.** One that howls. **2.** Any of several monkeys of the genus *Alouatta,* of tropical America, having a long, prehensile tail and a loud, howling call. Also called "howler monkey." **3.** A device that produces a loud warning noise in an incorrectly replaced telephone receiver. **4.** *Slang.* An amusing, ridiculous, or stupid blunder.

how·let (hou'lĭt) *n. Archaic.* An owl or owlet. [Middle English *howlat,* diminutive of *(h)owle,* OWL.]

howl·ing (hou'lĭng) *adj. Informal.* Very great; tremendous: *The play is a howling success.*

how·so·ev·er (hou'sō-ĕv'ər) *adv.* **1.** To whatever degree or extent. **2.** By whatever means.

Hox·ha (hŏ'jə), **Enver** (1908-85). Albanian politician, the dominant figure in Albanian politics after independence (1946). He led his country's resistance forces in World War II and became prime minister (1946-54), then first secretary of the newly named (communist) Party of Labor.

hoy¹ (hoi) *n., pl.* **hoys. 1.** A small sloop-rigged coasting ship formerly used for transporting passengers or as a tender to a larger vessel. **2.** A heavy barge used for cargo. [Middle English, from Middle Dutch *hoei, hoede†.*]

hoy² *interj.* Used to attract attention or to drive or direct animals. [Middle English (expressive).]

hoy·a (hoi'ə) *n.* Any plant of the genus *Hoya;* especially, the **waxplant** *(see).* [After Thomas *Hoy,* 19th-century English gardener.]

hoy·den (hoid'n) *n.* A high-spirited, often impudent girl or woman. —*adj.* High-spirited; boisterous. [Originally, a rude youth, probably from Middle Dutch *heiden,* "heathen."]

Hoyle (hoil), **Edmond** (1672-1769). British author of the *Short Treatise on the Game of Whist* (1742), which defined the rules of the game and remained the standard authority until 1864. The expression "according to Hoyle" is used to mean "according to the rules."

Hoyle, Sir Fred (1915-). British astronomer. In 1948 he helped formulate the steady-state theory, which holds that the universe is expanding while the density of matter remains constant.

hp horsepower.

H.P. 1. hire purchase. **2.** Houses of Parliament.

HQ, h.q., H.Q. headquarters.

hr hour.

Hr. Herr.

h.r. home run.

H.R. 1. home rule. **2.** House of Representatives.

H.R.E. Holy Roman Emperor; Holy Roman Empire.

H.R.H. His (or Her) Royal Highness.

hrs hours.

Hrvatska. See **Croatia.**

H.S.H. His (or Her) Serene Highness.

Hsiamen. See **Xiamen.**

Hsi-an. See **Xi'an.**

Hsiang Chiang. See **Xiang Jiang.**

Hsi Chiang. See **Xi Jiang.**

Hsinking. See **Changchun.**

H.S.M. His (or Her) Serene Majesty.

ht height.

H.T. high tension.

hover fly *A harmless relative of the bluebottle that is commonly mistaken for a wasp or bee. The fly's maggotlike larvae feed on the sap-sucking garden pests called aphids.*

howdah *An 18th-century Mogul manuscript from India shows an English dignitary being carried in one of these seats.*

Hts. heights (in place names).

Hua Guo-feng or **Hua Kuo-feng** (hwä′ gwō′fŭng′) (1921–). Chinese prime minister (1976–80). In 1976 he succeeded Zhou En-lai as prime minister and Mao as chairman of the Communist Party. With Deng Xiao-ping, he initiated a program of modernization, increasing contacts with the West. He resigned in 1980.

Huang He, Hwang Ho (hwäng′ hē′). Also **Yellow River.** Major river of northern China, some 4,670 kilometers (2,900 miles) long. Its lower valley, a vast fertile alluvial plain, was the cradle of Chinese civilization. Since the Communists came to power (1949), the river has been much regulated, and the devastating floods that gave it the name China's Sorrow rarely occur.

hua·ra·che (wə-rä′chē, -chä, hə-) *n.* A flat-heeled sandal with an upper of woven leather strips. [Mexican Spanish *guarache, huarache†.*]

hub (hŭb) *n.* **1.** The center portion of a wheel, fan, or propeller. **2.** A center of activity or interest; a focal point. [16th century : probably a variant of HOB (lump, projection).]

Hub·ble (hŭb′əl), **Edwin Powell** (1889–1953). U.S. astronomer. In 1929, he published his discovery that the velocities of nebulae increased with distance. The Hubble constant is named after him.

hub·ble-bub·ble (hŭb′əl-bŭb′əl) *n.* **1.** A water pipe, the **hookah** (*see*). **2. a.** A bubbling sound. **b.** A confused sound, as of people talking; a hum. [Reduplication of BUBBLE.]

Hubble's constant *n.* The ratio of the velocity at which a distant galaxy is receding from the earth to its distance from the earth, approximately equal to about 50 to 100 kilometers per second per million parsecs. [After E.P. HUBBLE.]

hub·bub (hŭb′ŭb′) *n.* **1.** A confused babble of loud sounds and voices; a din; an uproar. **2.** Confusion; upheaval; tumult. —See Synonyms at **noise.** [Irish *hooboobbes,* akin to Old Irish *abú,* a war cry, from Old Irish *buide,* "victory," from Celtic *bod-io-†* (untested).]

hub·by (hŭb′ē) *n., pl.* **-bies.** *Informal.* A husband.

hub·cap (hŭb′kăp′) *n.* A round metal covering clamped over the hub of the wheel of a motor vehicle.

Hu·bei, Hu·peh, Hu·pei (hōō′bä′). Province in east-central China, consisting chiefly of an alluvial plain drained by the Chiang Jiang (Yangtze) and Han Shui. The capital is Wuhan.

hu·bris (hyōō′brĭs) *n.* Also **hy·bris** (hī′-). **1.** Overbearing pride or presumption; arrogance. **2.** In Greek tragedy, overbearing pride and insolence toward the gods, leading to personal downfall and ruin. [Greek *hubris,* insolence.] —**hu·bris·tic** (hyōō-brĭs′tĭk) *adj.*

huck (hŭk) *n.* Huckaback.

huck·a·back (hŭk′ə-băk′) *n.* A coarse absorbent cotton or linen fabric used especially for toweling. Also called "huck." [17th century : origin obscure.]

huck·le (hŭk′əl) *n.* The hip or haunch. [Diminutive of earlier *huck,* hip, haunch, from Middle English *huck-, huke-,* perhaps from Germanic; akin to Middle Low German *hūken,* to sit bent.]

huck·le·ber·ry (hŭk′əl-bĕr′ē) *n., pl.* **-ries. 1.** Any of various American shrubs of the genus *Gaylussacia,* related to the blueberries and bearing edible fruit. **2.** The glossy, blackish, many-seeded berry of such a bush. **3.** Any of various similar or related shrubs, such as the blueberry or whortleberry. [Probably variant of dialectal *hurtleberry,* WHORTLEBERRY.]

huck·ster (hŭk′stər) *n.* **1.** A person who sells wares in the street; a peddler; a hawker. **2.** A promoter of commercial products whose techniques are dubious or aggressive. **3.** *Slang.* A writer of advertising copy, as for television.
~*v.* **huckstered, -stering, -sters.** —*tr.* **1.** To sell; peddle. **2.** To haggle or bargain over. —*intr.* To haggle. [Middle English *huccstere,* perhaps from Middle Dutch *hokester.* See **hawker, -ster.**] —**huck·ster·ism** *n.*

Hud·ders·field (hŭd′ərz-fēld′). Industrial town in West Yorkshire, north-central England. It is the chief woolen textile manufacturing center of the region.

hud·dle (hŭd′əl) *n.* **1.** A densely packed group or crowd, as of people or animals. **2.** A confused array; a jumble. **3.** A brief gathering of a football team's players behind the line of scrimmage to prepare for the next play. **4.** *Informal.* A small private conference or meeting.
~*v.* **huddled, -dling, -dles.** —*intr.* **1.** To crowd together, as from cold or fear; nestle; snuggle. **2.** To draw oneself together; curl or hunch up; crouch. Often used with *up.* **3.** To gather in a football huddle. **4.** *Informal.* To gather in order to confer secretly; meet privately. —*tr.* **1.** To crowd together. **2.** To draw (oneself) together; hunch; crouch. Often used with *up.* **3.** *Chiefly British.* To bring or throw together hastily or carelessly. [16th century : perhaps from Low German; akin to HIDE (to conceal).]

Hu·di·bras·tic (hyōō′də-brăs′tĭk) *adj.* In the mock-heroic style of Samuel Butler's satire *Hudibras* (1663–78). [From *Hudibras,* by analogy with such words as *bombastic.*]

Hud·son (hŭd′sən), **Henry** (died 1611). English navigator. In 1609 he tried to find a northwest passage and discovered the river that bears his name. While he was returning from a second attempt in which he discovered Hudson Bay (1610–11), his crew mutinied. Hudson and his son were cast adrift in a boat and never seen again.

Hudson, Rock (1925–85). U.S. actor. A ruggedly handsome and popular leading man, he starred in many movies of the 1950's, including *The Magnificent Obsession* (1954) and *Pillow Talk* (1959). At the age of 60 he died of AIDS, heightening public awareness of that devastating disease.

Hudson Bay. Large inland sea in north-central Canada, connected to the Atlantic Ocean by the Hudson Strait. It covers an area of *c.* 1,230,000 square kilometers (475,000 square miles).

Hudson River. River in New York State, rising in the Adirondack Mts. and flowing south for *c.* 510 kilometers (315 miles) to Upper New York Bay at New York City.

Hudson's Bay Company *n.* A British company chartered in 1670 to participate in fur trading with the North American Indians in competition with the French in Canada.

Hudson seal *n.* Muskrat fur that is dyed, plucked, and sheared in imitation of sealskin. [After HUDSON BAY.]

hue (hyōō) *n.* **1.** The dimension of color that is referred to a scale of perceptions ranging from red to yellow, green, and blue, and circularly back to red. **2.** A particular gradation of color; a tint; a shade. **3.** Color: *all the hues of the rainbow.* **4.** Character; aspect: *the somber hue of a man of the cloth.* [Middle English *hewe,* complexion, appearance, Old English *hēo, hīw,* appearance, form, color, beauty.]

hue and cry *n.* **1.** Formerly: **a.** The pursuit of a criminal announced by loud shouts to alert others then legally obliged to aid in the chase. **b.** The loud shout used to arouse the pursuers. **2.** A public clamor, as of protest or demand; an outcry: *a big hue and cry over the latest spending cuts.* [Middle English *hew, heu,* from Old French *heu, hu,* an outcry, from *huer,* to cry out, shout (imitative).]

Hu·é (hyōō-ā′). Also **Hue** (hwä, wä). City in central Vietnam, on the Hué River. It is one of the most ancient towns of Vietnam, dating from the 3rd century B.C., and is a former capital of Annam. It was the seat of the Nguyen dynasty from the early 19th century but lost its historic status as the capital in 1887, when Saigon became the capital of Indochina.

hued (hyōōd) *adj.* Having a given hue, aspect, or character. Used in combination: *rosy-hued dawn.*

huff (hŭf) *n.* **1.** A fit of anger or annoyance; pique: *He stormed off in a huff.* **2.** In checkers, the removal of an opponent's checker from the board for failure to make a possible capture.
~*v.* **huffed, huffing, huffs.** —*intr.* **1.** To puff; blow. **2.** To speak or act with noisy, empty threats; bluster. Now used chiefly in the phrase *huff and puff.* **3.** To act or react indignantly; take offense. —*tr.* **1.** To puff or blow up; inflate. **2.** *Archaic.* To treat with insolence; bully; tease. **3.** To put in a huff; anger; annoy. **4.** In checkers, to make a huff. [Imitative of the sound of puffing.]

huff·ish (hŭf′ĭsh) *adj.* **1.** Peevish; sulky; in a huff. **2.** Arrogant; insolent. —**huff·ish·ly** *adv.* —**huff·ish·ness** *n.*

huff·y (hŭf′ē) *adj.* **-ier, -iest. 1.** Easily offended; sensitive; touchy. **2.** Irritated or annoyed; indignant. **3.** Arrogant; disdainful; haughty. —**huff·i·ly** *adv.* —**huff·i·ness** *n.*

hug (hŭg) *v.* **hugged, hugging, hugs.** —*tr.* **1.** To clasp or hold closely, especially in one's arms; embrace or enfold, as in affection. **2.** To ascribe steadfastly to (a belief or opinion, for example); cherish. **3.** To keep, remain, or be situated close to: *The old footpath winds inland, hugging the foot of the hill.* **4.** To be very pleased with (oneself); congratulate (oneself). —*intr.* To embrace or be in physical contact; cling together closely; snuggle.
~*n.* **1.** An affectionate, close embrace. **2.** A crushing embrace. [Scandinavian, akin to Old Norse *hugga,* to comfort, console, from Germanic *hugjan* (unattested).] —**hug·ga·ble** *adj.* —**hug·ger** *n.*

huge (hyōōj) *adj.* **huger, hugest.** Of exceedingly great size, extent, degree, or quantity; tremendous. —See Synonyms at **enormous.** [Middle English *huge, hoge,* shortened from Old French *ahuge, ahoge†.*] —**huge·ly** *adv.* —**huge·ness** *n.*

huge·ous (hyōō′jəs) *adj. Informal.* Huge. Used chiefly for humorous effect. —**huge·ous·ly** *adv.* —**huge·ous·ness** *n.*

hug·ger-mug·ger, hug·ger-mug·ger (hŭg′ər-mŭg′ər) *n.* **1.** Disorder; confusion; muddle. **2.** Concealment; secrecy.
~*adj.* **1.** Disordered; jumbled: *"worry out her financial problems in her own hugger-mugger way"* (Samuel Butler). **2.** Secret; surreptitious; clandestine: *hugger-mugger political deals.*
~*v.* **hugger-muggered, -gering, -gers.** —*tr.* To keep concealed or secret. —*intr.* To act in a surreptitious manner. [16th century : also *hucker mucker* and earlier *hoder moder,* all perhaps akin to Middle English *hoder,* huddle, and *mokere,* to hide.] —**hug·ger-mug·ger** *adv.*

Hughes (hyōōz), **Charles Evans** (1862–1948). U.S. jurist and statesman. He was appointed to the U.S. Supreme Court (1910), but resigned to make an unsuccessful bid for the presidency (1916). He served as secretary of state (1920–25) and in 1930 was appointed chief justice of the Supreme Court. Hughes was instrumental in defeating Franklin D. Roosevelt's "court-packing" plan (1937).

Hughes, Howard Robard (1905–76). U.S. film producer, aviator, and multimillionaire magnate. Among his films was *Hell's Angels* (1930). He founded the Hughes Aircraft Corporation, broke the airplane speed record (1935), and flew around the world in record time (1938). From 1950 he lived as a recluse.

Hughes, (James Mercer) Langston (1902–67). U.S. author. His first poem, "The Negro Speaks of Rivers," was published in 1921. After several years of drifting, he published collections of his poems, including *The Weary Blues* (1926) and *Shakespeare in Harlem* (1942). He also wrote dramas, biographies, and a series of newspaper columns.

Hughes, Richard Arthur Warren (1900–76). British novelist. His books include *A High Wind in Jamaica* (1929) and *In Hazard* (1938).

Hughes, Thomas (1822–96). British lawyer and author. His *Tom Brown's School Days* (1857) describes public-school life at Rugby under its famous headmaster Dr. Thomas Arnold.

Hugli. See **Hooghly.**

hug-me-tight (hŭg′mē-tīt′) *n.* A woman's close-fitting, usually knitted jacket, with or without sleeves.

Hu·go (hyo͞o′gō, ü-gō′), **Victor Marie** (1802–85). French poet, novelist, and dramatist. Shortly after Napoleon III seized power (1852), he went into exile in the Channel Islands, returning to France in 1870. His novels include *The Hunchback of Notre Dame* (1831), *Les Misérables* (1862), and *Toilers of the Sea* (1866).

Hu·gue·not (hyo͞o′gə-nŏt′, -nō′) *n.* A French Protestant of the 16th and 17th centuries. [French *huguenot,* assimilation (to *Hugues,* burgomaster of Geneva) of earlier (Genevan) French *eyguenot,* referring to those who opposed annexation by the Duke of Savoy, from Swiss German *Eidgenosse(n),* confederate(s), from Middle High German *eitgenōz* : *eit,* oath, from Old High German *eid* + *genōz,* companion, from Old High German *ginōz.*] **—Hu·gue·not, Hu·gue·not·ic** (hyo͞o′gə-nŏt′ĭk) *adj.* **—Hu·gue·not·ism** *n.*

huh (hŭ, hə) *interj.* Used to express surprise, interrogation, contempt, or indifference.

hu·ia (ho͞o′yə) *n.* An extinct New Zealand songbird, *Heteralocha acutirostris,* that had a beak that was strong and straight in the male and slender and curved in the female. [Maori.]

hu·la (ho͞o′lə) *n.* Also **hu·la-hu·la** (ho͞o′lə-ho͞o′lə). **1.** A Polynesian ethnic dance performed by men or women alone or together and characterized by undulating movements of the hips, arms, and hands, pantomiming a story. **2.** The music for this dance, composed typically of rhythmic drumbeats and chants. [Hawaiian.]

hula hoop *n.* A large, light hoop, often made of plastic, that is whirled around the body by the movement of the hips.

hulk (hŭlk) *n.* **1.** A heavy, unwieldy ship. **2. a.** The hull of an old, unseaworthy, or wrecked ship. **b.** An old or unseaworthy ship used as a prison or warehouse. **3. a.** A clumsy, awkward, or overweight person. **b.** A clumsy or bulky object.
∼*intr.v.* **hulked, hulking, hulks. 1.** To loom or rise in a towering or impressive fashion: *The big truck hulked out of the fog in front of our car.* **2.** *British Regional.* To move about in a lazy or clumsy manner. [Middle English *hulke,* Old English *hulc,* ship, from Medieval Latin *hulcus,* from Greek *holkas,* "ship that is towed," merchant vessel, from *helkein,* to pull, tow.]

hulk·ing (hŭl′kĭng) *adj.* Also **hulk·y** (hŭl′kē). Unwieldy, clumsy, or bulky; massive: *a hulking lumberjack.*

hull (hŭl) *n.* **1. a.** The enlarged calyx of a strawberry or similar fruit, usually green and easily detached. **b.** The dry outer covering of a fruit, seed, or nut; husk. **2.** *Nautical.* The main body of a ship, exclusive of masts, sails, yards, and rigging. **3.** The main body or frame of any of various other large vehicles, such as a tank, an airship, or a flying boat. **4.** The outer casing of a rocket, guided missile, or spaceship.
∼*tr.v.* **hulled, hulling, hulls. 1.** To remove the hull or hulls of (fruit or seeds). **2.** To pierce or break through the hull of (a ship, tank, or the like). [Middle English *hull, hole,* husk, from Old English *hulu;* akin to *helan,* to cover.]

Hull (hŭl). Also **King·ston up·on Hull** (kĭng′stən ə-pŏn hŭl′). City in Humberside, northeastern England, on the northern shore of the Humber estuary on the Hull River. It is one of Britain's largest ports and its busiest deep-sea fishing port.

hul·la·ba·loo, hul·la·bal·loo (hŭl′ə-bə-lo͞o′) *n., pl.* **-loos.** A great confused noise or din; an uproar. —See Synonyms at **noise.** [Earlier *hollo-ballo,* akin to the interjection HALLOO.]

hull down *adj.* **1.** So far away that the hull is below the horizon. Said of a ship. **2.** Concealed apart from the turret. Said of a tank.

hullo. Variant of **hello.**

hum[1] (hŭm) *v.* **hummed, humming, hums.** —*intr.* **1.** To utter a continuous low droning sound like that of the speech sound (m) when prolonged. **2. a.** To emit the continuous droning sound of an insect on the wing, or a similar sound. **b.** To move with such a sound. **3. a.** To give out a low, continuous drone blended of many sounds: *The avenue hummed with traffic.* **b.** To be full of activity. **4.** To produce a tune without opening the lips or forming words. —*tr.* To sing (a tune) without opening the lips or forming words.
∼*n.* **1.** A noise or tune produced by humming. **2.** A low-frequency continuous noise produced by an amplifier, usually as result of interference from the main frequency.
∼*interj.* (hŭm, hm) **1.** Uttered as a pause in speech or to indicate thought. **2.** Used to express surprise or displeasure. [Middle English *hummen* (imitative).] **—hum·mer** *n.*

hum[2] *tr.v.* **hummed, humming, hums.** *Australian.* To borrow; cadge. [Shortened from HUMBUG, to trick, deceive.]

hu·man (hyo͞o′mən) *adj.* **1.** Of, relating to, or characteristic of man or mankind: *the course of human events.* **2.** Having or manifesting the form, nature, or qualities characteristic of human beings, especially: **a.** Showing qualities characteristic of people as distinguished from machines, such as sympathy or fallibility: *human kindness. His mistake was only human.* **b.** Pertaining to or being a human being as distinguished from a lower animal; reasoning; moral. **c.** Pertaining to or being a human being as distinguished from a divine entity or infinite intelligence; mortal; earthly. **3.** Made up of people: *They formed a human bridge across the river.*
∼*n.* A human being; a person. [Middle English *humain(e), humayn(e),* from Old French *humain* (feminine *humaine*), from Latin *hūmānus,* akin to *homo* (stem *homin-*), man.] **—hu·man·ness** *n.*

Usage: *Human* (noun) is acceptable on all levels and in contexts not limited to the scientific or technical: *air not fit for humans to breathe.* In somewhat earlier usage, *human being* was often recommended as the better choice on a formal level, though *human* has a long history as a noun.

human being *n.* A member of the genus *Homo,* and especially of the species *Homo sapiens;* a person. —See Usage note at **human.**

hu·mane (hyo͞o-mān′) *adj.* **1.** Characterized by qualities of kindness, mercy, or compassion: *a humane judge.* **2.** Tending to evoke or promote these qualities; refining; civilizing: *a humane education.* **3.** Painless. Said especially of an agent or instrument for killing animals: *a humane drug.* [Middle English *humaine,* HUMAN.] **—hu·mane·ly** *adv.* **—hu·mane·ness** *n.*

human ecology *n.* See **ecology** (sense 2).

human engineering *n.* **1.** The industrial management of labor. **2.** The technology of efficient use of machines by human beings.

human interest *n.* The often sentimental preoccupation with the affairs or feelings of individuals, as in popular journalism. Also used adjectivally: *a human-interest story.*

hu·man·ism (hyo͞o′mə-nĭz′əm) *n.* **1.** Concern with the interests and needs of human beings. **2.** A philosophy or attitude that addresses itself exclusively to human as opposed to divine or supernatural concerns, often coupled with the belief that man is capable of reaching self-fulfillment without divine aid. **3.** The study of the humanities; cultured learning. **4. Humanism.** A cultural and intellectual movement of a secular character that occurred during the Renaissance following the rediscovery of the literature, art, and civilization of ancient Greece and Rome.

hu·man·ist (hyo͞o′mə-nĭst) *n.* **1.** A follower of the philosophy of humanism. **2.** One who is concerned with the study and welfare of human beings. **3.** One who studies the humanities; especially, a student of classical learning. **4. Humanist.** A student of the Renaissance or follower of Humanism.
∼*adj.* Also **hu·man·is·tic** (hyo͞o′mə-nĭs′tĭk). Of or relating to humanism or the humanities. **—hu·man·is·ti·cal·ly** *adv.*

hu·man·i·tar·i·an (hyo͞o-măn′ə-târ′ē-ən) *adj.* **1.** Concerned with the well-being of mankind and the alleviation of human suffering. **2.** Of or relating to humanitarianism.
∼*n.* One devoted to the promotion of human welfare and the advancement of social reforms; a philanthropist.

hu·man·i·tar·i·an·ism (hyo͞o-măn′ə-târ′ē-ə-nĭz′əm) *n.* **1.** The ideas, principles, or methods of humanitarians; philanthropy. **2.** *Ethics.* The belief that man's sole moral obligation is to work for the improved welfare of humanity. **3.** *Theology.* The belief or doctrine that Jesus was only human and not divine.

hu·man·i·ty (hyo͞o-măn′ə-tē) *n., pl.* **-ties. 1.** Human beings collectively; the human race; mankind. **2.** The condition, quality, or fact of being human; human nature; humanness. **3.** The quality of being humane; benevolence; kindness; mercy. **4.** A humane attribute or action. **5. humanities. a.** The study of the classical languages and literature of ancient Greece and Rome. **b.** Those branches of knowledge concerned with human beings and culture, as philosophy, literature, and the fine arts, as distinguished from the sciences. [Middle English *humanite,* from Old French, from Latin *hūmānitās* (stem *hūmānitāt-*), from *hūmānus,* HUMAN.]

hu·man·ize (hyo͞o′mə-nīz′) *v.* **-ized, -izing, -izes.** —*tr.* **1.** To make human; cause to have human characteristics or attributes. **2.** To make humane; imbue with human sympathy; civilize. —*intr.* **1.** To become human. **2.** To become humane. **—hu·man·i·za·tion** (hyo͞o′mə-nə-zā′shən) *n.* **—hu·man·iz·er** *n.*

hu·man·kind (hyo͞o′mən-kīnd′) *n.* The human race; mankind.

hu·man·ly (hyo͞o′mən-lē) *adv.* **1.** In a human way. **2.** By human means, capabilities, or powers. **3.** According to human experience or knowledge.

hu·man·oid (hyo͞o′mə-noid′) *adj.* Having human characteristics; especially, resembling a human being in appearance.
∼*n.* **1.** A humanoid being. **2.** A fictional synthetic man, an **android** *(see).*

Hum·ber (hŭm′bər). A river in Humberside, northeastern England, consisting of the estuary of the Trent and Ouse rivers and extending from their confluence for *c.* 60 kilometers (40 miles) to the North Sea. The fishing ports of Hull and Grimsby are on its northern and southern shores respectively.

Hum·ber·side (hŭm′bər-sīd′). From 1974 a nonmetropolitan county in northeastern England.

hum·ble (hŭm′bəl) *adj.* **-bler, -blest. 1.** Having or showing feelings of humility rather than of pride; aware of one's shortcomings; modest; meek. **2.** Showing deferential respect. **3. a.** Lacking high social status. **b.** Lowly; unpretentious: *a humble cottage.*
∼*tr.v.* **humbled, -bling, -bles. 1.** To curtail or destroy the pride of; humiliate. **2.** To give a lower condition or station to; abase. —See Synonyms at **degrade.** [Middle English *(h)umble,* from Old French *(h)umble,* from Latin *humilis,* low, lowly, base, from *humus,* ground, soil.] **—hum·ble·ness** *n.* **—hum·bler** *n.* **—hum·bly** *adv.*

Synonyms: *meek, modest, reserved, retiring.*

hum·ble·bee (hŭm′bəl-bē′) *n.* A bumblebee *(see).* [Middle English *humbylbee,* perhaps from Middle Low German *hummelbē* : *hummel,* bumblebee + *bē,* bee.]

humble pie *n.* Formerly, a pie made from the edible organs of a deer. **—eat humble pie.** To apologize for or admit one's faults abjectly in humiliating circumstances. [*Humble,* from earlier *humbles,* unexplained variant of *umbles;* see **numbles.** Phrase (influenced by HUMBLE, to humiliate) originally referred to eating the offal or least desirable part of a deer.]

Hum·boldt (hŭm′bōlt′). A river rising in northeastern Nevada and

hull *The green detachable part of soft fruit such as strawberries is thought to get its name because the leaves originally form a protective outer skin —like a ship's hull— around the flower buds that produce the fruit.*

flowing *c.* 485 kilometers (300 miles) west and southwest to the Humboldt Sink in western Nevada. Its length varies with the seasons.

Humboldt, (Friedrich Wilhelm Karl Heinrich) Alexander von (1769–1859). German explorer and geographer. He originated the study of the environment, ecology. His major work, *Kosmos,* is a physical description of the universe and a history of science (1845–62). The Humboldt Current (now called the Peru Current), off Peru's Pacific coast, was named after him.

Humboldt, (Karl) Wilhelm von (1767–1835). German statesman and philologist. He explored the relationship between language and culture.

Humboldt Bay. Sheltered inlet of the Pacific Ocean, *c.* 23 kilometers (14 miles) long and from 1.6 to 8 kilometers (1 to 5 miles wide), in northwestern California.

Humboldt Current. See **Peru Current.**

hum·bug (hŭm′bŭg′) *n.* **1.** Something intended to deceive; a hoax; a fraud. **2.** One who tries to trick or deceive others; an impostor; a charlatan. **3. a.** Nonsense; rubbish. **b.** Pretense or hypocrisy. **4.** *British.* A usually peppermint-flavored candy.
~*v.* **humbugged, -bugging, -bugs.** —*tr.* To deceive; trick; cheat. —*intr.* To practice trickery. [18th century : origin obscure.] —**hum·bug·ger** *n.* —**hum·bug·ger·y** (hŭm′bŭg′ə-rē) *n.*

hum·ding·er (hŭm′dĭng′ər) *n. Slang.* Someone or something extraordinary or superior; a marvel. [20th century : origin obscure.]

hum·drum (hŭm′drŭm′) *adj.* Without change, variety, or excitement; monotonous; ordinary. —See Synonyms at **boring.**
~*n.* Something or someone dull or unexciting. [Originally also *humtrum,* probably reduplication of HUM.]

Hume (hyōōm), **David** (1711–76). Scottish philosopher and historian. He argued that the perceptions of the mind were essentially impressions from sensations, emotions, and ideas.

hu·mec·tant (hyōō-mĕk′tənt) *n.* A substance that promotes retention of moisture.
~*adj.* Promoting moisture retention. [Latin *hūmectāns* (stem *hūmectant-*), present participle of *(h)ūmectāre,* to moisten, from *(h)ūmectus,* moist, from *(h)ūmēre,* to be moist.]

hu·mer·al (hyōō′mər-əl) *adj.* **1.** Pertaining to or located in the region of the humerus or the shoulder. **2.** Pertaining to or designating a body part analogous to the humerus. —**hu·mer·al** *n.*

humeral veil *n. Roman Catholic Church.* A shawllike vestment worn over the shoulders by a priest when carrying the Blessed Sacrament at benediction or in procession.

hu·mer·us (hyōō′mər-əs) *n., pl.* **-meri** (-mə-rī′). **1.** The long bone of the upper part of the arm, extending from the shoulder to the elbow. **2.** The corresponding bone in vertebrate animals. [New Latin, from Latin *umerus, humerus,* upper arm, shoulder.]

hu·mic (hyōō′mĭk) *adj.* Of, pertaining to, or derived from humus.

hu·mid (hyōō′mĭd) *adj.* Containing or marked by a high amount of moisture; oppressively damp: *humid weather.* —See Synonyms at **wet.** [Old French *humide,* from Latin *(h)ūmidus,* from *(h)ūmēre,* to be moist.] —**hu·mid·ly** *adv.*

hu·mid·i·fi·er (hyōō-mĭd′ə-fī′ər) *n.* An apparatus for increasing the humidity in a room, greenhouse, or other enclosed area.

hu·mid·i·fy (hyōō-mĭd′ə-fī′) *tr.v.* **-fied, -fying, -fies.** To make more humid; especially, to increase the amount of water vapor in (the air). —**hu·mid·i·fi·ca·tion** (hyōō-mĭd′ə-fĭ-kā′shən) *n.*

hu·mid·i·stat (hyōō-mĭd′ĭ-stăt′) *n.* An instrument designed to indicate or control the relative humidity of the air. Also called "hygrostat." [HUMIDI(TY) + -STAT.]

hu·mid·i·ty (hyōō-mĭd′ə-tē) *n.* **1.** Dampness, especially of the air. **2.** A measure of the amount of water vapor in the air. See **absolute humidity, relative humidity.** [Middle English *humidite,* from Old French, from Latin *hūmiditās* (stem *humiditāt-*), from *hūmidus,* HUMID.]

hu·mi·dor (hyōō′mə-dôr′) *n.* A case for the storage of cigars and other tobacco products, containing a device for keeping the humidity level constant. [From HUMID.]

hu·mil·i·ate (hyōō-mĭl′ē-āt′) *tr.v.* **-ated, -ating, -ates.** To lower the pride, dignity, or status of; humble or disgrace; degrade. —See Synonyms at **degrade.** [Late Latin *humiliāre,* from *humilis,* HUMBLE.] —**hu·mil·i·a·to·ry** (hyōō-mĭl′ē-ə-tôr′ē, -tōr′ē) *adj.*

hu·mil·i·a·tion (hyōō-mĭl′ē-ā′shən) *n.* **1.** The act of humiliating; degradation. **2.** The condition of being humiliated; disgrace; shame. **3.** A condition or circumstance that humiliates: *The child's unusual name was a humiliation to her at school.*

hu·mil·i·ty (hyōō-mĭl′ə-tē) *n.* The quality or condition of being humble; lack of pride; modesty. [Middle English *humilite,* from Old French *humilite,* from Latin *humilitās* (stem *humilitāt-*), from *humilis,* HUMBLE.]

hum·ming·bird (hŭm′ĭng-bûrd′) *n.* Any of numerous chiefly tropical New World birds of the family Trochilidae, usually very small and having a long, slender bill, wings capable of beating very rapidly, and often brilliantly colored plumage. [From the humming sound produced by the rapidly vibrating wings.]

hummingbird moth *n.* A moth, the **hawk moth** *(see),* that resembles a hummingbird.

hum·mock (hŭm′ək) *n.* Also **ham·mock** (hăm′ək) (for sense 2). **1.** A low mound or ridge of earth; a knoll. **2.** In the southern United States, a tract of forested land elevated above the level of an adjacent marsh. **3.** A ridge or hill of ice in an ice field. [16th century : origin obscure.] —**hum·mock·y** *adj.*

hum·mus, hum·mous (hŭm′əs) *n.* A puree of chickpeas and oil,

often flavored with garlic, sesame seed, and lemon, eaten as a sandwich spread or dip. [Arabic *ḥummuṣ,* chickpea.]

hu·mon·gous (hyōō-mŏng′gəs, -mŭng′gəs) *adj. Slang.* Extremely large; enormous. [Perhaps a blend of HUGE and MONSTROUS.]

hu·mor (hyōō′mər) *n.* Also *British* **hu·mour.** **1.** The quality of being laughable or comical; funniness: *He saw the humor of the situation.* **2.** Something designed to induce laughter or amusement: *a story full of humor.* **3.** The ability to perceive, enjoy, or express what is comical or funny: *a sense of humor.* **4.** In medieval physiology, any of the four fluids of the body, blood, phlegm, choler (or yellow bile), and black bile, the dominance of which was thought to determine a person's character and general health. Accordingly, one's disposition might be **sanguine, phlegmatic, choleric,** or **melancholy** *(all of which see).* **5.** A state of mind; a mood: *in a bad humor.* **6.** Disposition; character; temperament: *a girl of a most sullen humor.* **7. a.** A sudden, unanticipated whim. **b.** Capricious or peculiar behavior or action. **8.** *Physiology.* Any of various body fluids; especially, the **aqueous humor** or **vitreous humor** *(both of which see).* —See Synonyms at **mood, wit.** —**out of humor.** In a bad mood; irritable. ~*tr.v.* **humored, -moring, -mors.** Also *British* **hu·mour, -mouring, -mours.** **1.** To comply with the whims or wishes of (another); go along with; indulge. **2.** To adapt or accommodate oneself to. [Middle English *(h)umour,* fluid from an animal or plant, one of the four body fluids believed to affect mental disposition, from Norman French, from Latin *hūmor,* liquid, fluid.]

hu·mor·al (hyōō′mər-əl) *adj.* Pertaining to or arising from any of the bodily humors.

hu·mor·esque (hyōō′mə-rĕsk′) *n.* A whimsical or playful musical composition. [German *Humoreske,* from *Humor,* humor, from English HUMOR.]

hu·mor·ist (hyōō′mər-ĭst) *n.* **1.** A person with a sharp sense of humor. **2.** A performer or writer of comedy.

hu·mor·less (hyōō′mər-lĭs) *adj.* **1.** Devoid of a sense of humor. **2.** Said or done without humor: "*She winked at me but it was humorless; a wink of warning*" (Truman Capote). —**hu·mor·less·ly** *adv.* —**hu·mor·less·ness** *n.*

hu·mor·ous (hyōō′mər-əs) *adj.* **1.** Appealing to the sense of humor; funny; laughable; comical: *a humorous sight.* **2.** Characterized by or expressing humor; comic; witty; droll: *a humorous speaker.* **3.** *Archaic.* Capricious. **4.** *Obsolete.* Damp; moist. —**hu·mor·ous·ly** *adv.* —**hu·mor·ous·ness** *n.*

hump (hŭmp) *n.* **1.** A rounded mass or protuberance, such as the fleshy structure on the back of a camel or over the shoulders of some cattle. **2.** A deformity of the back, due in human beings to an abnormal curvature of the spine. **3.** A low mound of earth; a hummock. **4.** *British Slang.* A feeling of depression or extreme annoyance. Often preceded by *the.* —**over the hump.** Past the worst or most difficult part of something.
~*v.* **humped, humping, humps.** —*tr.* **1.** To make into a hump; arch; round. **2.** *Chiefly British Informal.* To carry (something large or heavy). **3.** *Slang* To exert (oneself) strenuously. —*intr.* **1.** To bend or arch so as to become a hump. **2.** *Slang.* To exert oneself. [Shortened from earlier *humpback(ed),* possibly a blend of earlier *crumpbacked* and HUNCHBACK(ED).]

hump·back (hŭmp′băk′) *n.* **1.** A person afflicted with an abnormally curved or humped back; a hunchback. **2.** An abnormally curved or humped back. **3.** A pathological condition, **kyphosis** *(see).* **4.** A whalebone whale, *Megaptera novaeangliae,* having a rounded back and long, knobby flippers. **5.** A salmon, *Oncorhynchus gorbuscha,* of the Pacific Ocean, the male of which has a humped back and hooked jaws. —**hump·backed** *adj.*

humpback bridge *n.* Also **humpbacked bridge.** A narrow bridge forming part of a road, having a steep incline and decline.

humped (hŭmpt) *adj.* Having a hump: *humped cattle.*

Hum·per·dinck (hōōmp′pər-dĭnk′, hŭm′-), **Engelbert** (1854–1921). German composer. He wrote the fairy-tale opera *Hänsel und Gretel* (1893).

humph (hŭmf) *interj.* Used to express doubt, displeasure, or contempt.

Hum·phrey (hŭm′frē), **Hubert Horatio** (1911–78). U.S. Democratic politician. He was vice president (1965–69) under Lyndon Johnson.

hummingbird *A blue-throated hummingbird,* Lampornis clemenciae—*a native of the Americas—hovers while it extracts nectar from a flower. Its wings, frozen here by high-speed photography, flap up to 200 times a second while it hovers, causing the humming sound for which the birds are named.*

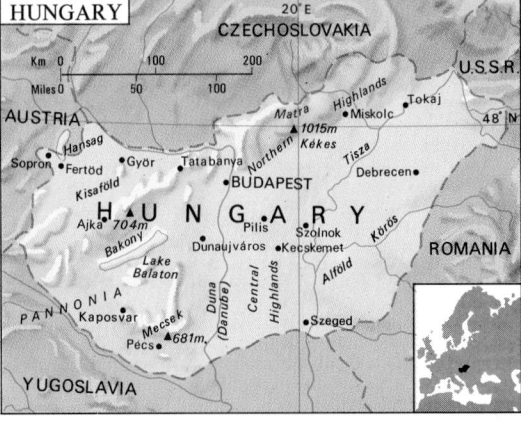

He was defeated for the presidency in 1968 by Richard Nixon and failed to win the Democratic nomination in 1972.

hump·ty (hŭmp'tē) *n. British.* A small, low, padded seat. [From *humpty* (adjective), hunchbacked; perhaps influenced by HUMPTY DUMPTY.]

Hump·ty Dump·ty (hŭmp'te dŭmp'tē) *n.* **1.** An egg-shaped character in a nursery rhyme who fell off a wall and broke into pieces. **2.** *Usually* **humpty dumpty.** *Informal.* A short, fat person.

hump·y (hŭm'pē) *adj.* **-ier, -iest. 1.** Covered with or containing humps. **2.** Resembling a hump.

hu·mus (hyōō'məs) *n.* A brown or black organic substance consisting of decayed vegetable and animal matter that provides nutrients for plants and increases the ability of soil to retain water. [Latin *humus,* earth, ground, soil.]

Hun (hŭn) *n.* **1.** Any of a fierce barbaric race of Asiatic nomads who invaded Europe in the late 4th century A.D. and, led by Attila, overran large parts of it in the mid-5th century. **2.** Often **hun.** A savage, uncivilized, or destructive person. [Old English *Hūne* and *Hūnas* (both plural), from Late Latin *Hūnī,* from Turki *Hun-yü.*]

Hun. Hungarian; Hungary.

Hu·nan, Hu-nan (hōō'nän'). Province in south-central China. Rich in mineral resources and forests, the province is especially famous for its cedar. Its capital is Changsha.

hunch (hŭnch) *n.* **1.** An intuitive feeling or guess about something; a premonition. **2.** A hump. **3.** A lump or chunk.

~v. **hunched, hunching, hunches.** *—tr.* To bend, arch, or draw up into a hump: *hunched his shoulders against the wind.* *—intr.* To draw oneself up closely into a crouched or cramped posture: *The scared child hunched in a corner.* [Origin unknown.]

hunch·back (hŭnch'băk') *n.* A person afflicted with an abnormally curved or hunched back. See **humpback.** **—hunch·backed** *adj.*

hun·dred (hŭn'drĭd) *n., pl.* **hundred** or **-dreds** (for senses 2, 4, and 5). *Abbr.* **h. 1. a.** The cardinal number that is ten more than ninety. **b.** A symbol representing this, such as 100 or C. **2.** A currency note worth 100 dollars: *I paid with a hundred and a ten.* **3.** The number in the third position left of the decimal point in an Arabic numeral. **4. a.** An unspecified large number: *I've been there hundreds of times.* **b.** The numbers between 100 and 999: *The dress was valued in the hundreds.* **5. hundreds.** A specified era of a hundred years: *the nineteen hundreds.* **6.** A former administrative division of some English and American counties. [Middle English *hundred,* Old English *hundred, hund,* from Germanic.] **—hun·dred** *adj. & pron.* **—hun·dred·fold** (hŭn'drĭd-fōld') *adj. & adv.*

hun·dredth (hŭn'drĭdth) *n.* **1.** The ordinal number 100 in a series. Also written 100th. **2.** One of 100 equal parts. **—hun·dredth** *adj. & adv.*

hun·dred·weight (hŭn'drĭd-wāt') *n., pl.* **hundredweight** or **-weights.** *Abbr.* **cwt. 1.** A unit of weight in the U.S. Customary System equal to 100 pounds. Also called "short hundredweight." **2.** A unit of weight in the British Imperial System equal to 112 pounds. Also called "long hundredweight."

Hundred Years' War *n.* A series of wars between England and France that lasted from 1337 until 1453.

hung (hŭng). Past tense and past participle of **hang.**

~adj. **1.** With no party having a working majority. Said of a legislative assembly: *a hung Congress.* **2.** So divided in opinion as to be unable to reach a verdict: *a hung jury.* —See Usage note at **hang.**

Hung. Hungarian; Hungary.

Hun·gar·i·an (hŭng-gâr'ē-ən) *adj. Abbr.* **Hun., Hung.** Of or relating to Hungary or its people, language, or culture.

~n. Abbr. **Hun., Hung. 1.** A citizen or native of Hungary. **2.** The Finno-Ugric language spoken in Hungary; Magyar.

Hungarian goulash *n.* **Goulash** *(see).*

Hungarian puli *n.* A dog, the **puli** *(see).*

Hun·ga·ry (hŭng'gə-rē). *Abbr.* **Hun., Hung.** *Hungarian* **Ma·gyar·or·szág** (mô'dyôr-ôr'säg'). Republic of central Europe. The country consists for the most part of plains, broken by the Danube and Tisza rivers. Hungary was part of the dual kingdom of Austria-Hungary from 1867 until 1918, when a Hungarian republic was proclaimed. The Communist Party seized power, and a new constitution, on the Soviet model, was established (1949). A counterrevolutionary uprising in Budapest (1956) was put down by Soviet troops. Area, 93,030 square kilometers (35,910 square miles). Population, 10,700,000. Capital, Budapest.

hun·ger (hŭng'gər) *n.* **1. a.** The weakness, debilitation, or pain caused by a prolonged lack of food; starvation. **b.** Mild discomfort or an uneasy sensation caused by a lack of food. **c.** A strong desire for food. **2.** A strong desire or craving for anything: *a hunger for affection.*

~v. **hungered, -gering, -gers.** *—intr.* **1.** To have a need or desire for food. **2.** To have a strong desire or craving for anything. Used with *after* or *for*: *In exile, he hungered for his native land.*

~tr. **1.** To cause to experience hunger; make hungry: *The thought of food hungered him even more.* **2.** To bring or reduce to the specified state because of hunger: *hungered the terrorists into submission.* —See Synonyms at **yearn.** [Middle English *hunger,* Old English *hungor, hungur,* from Germanic.]

hunger march *n.* A march or demonstration by the unemployed and poor to protest their condition. **—hunger marcher** *n.*

hunger strike *n.* A refusal to eat or a voluntary fast undertaken as a method of protest. **—hunger striker** *n.*

hung over *adj.* Suffering from a hangover.

hun·gry (hŭng'grē) *adj.* **-grier, -griest. 1.** Experiencing weakness, pain, or other discomfort from lack of food. **2.** Desiring or craving food. **3. a.** Strong desiring or craving anything: *hungry for recognition.* **b.** Using or requiring large quantities of something: *a fuel-hungry heating system.* **4.** Characterized by or expressing hunger, greed, or craving: *a hungry look.* **5.** Lacking richness or fertility: *hungry soil.* [Middle English *hungri,* Old English *hungri(g),* from *hungor,* HUNGER.] **—hun·gri·ly** *adv.* **—hun·gri·ness** *n.*

hung up *adj. Informal.* **1.** Delayed: *got hung up in rush-hour traffic.* **2.** Emotionally or psychologically disturbed or upset. **3.** Overinterested in or concerned with a subject: *hung up on punctuality.*

hunk (hŭngk) *n.* **1.** *Informal.* A large piece; a chunk: *a hunk of fresh bread.* **2.** *Slang.* A sexually appealing man, especially one with a powerful physique. [Probably akin to West Flemish *hunke*†, hunk of food.] **—hunk·y** *adj.*

hun·ker (hŭng'kər) *intr.v.* **-kered, -kering, -kers.** To squat close to the ground with the body leaning forward, the weight resting on the calves.

~n. **hunkers.** *Regional.* The haunches. [Scottish, from *hunker,* to squat, perhaps from Scandinavian; akin to Old Norse *hokra,* to crouch.]

hunks (hŭngks) *n., pl.* **hunks. 1.** An irritable or disagreeable old person. **2.** A stingy, covetous man; a miser. [17th century : origin obscure.]

hun·ky-do·ry (hŭng'kē-dôr'ē, -dōr'ē) *adj. Slang.* Perfectly all right; quite satisfactory; fine. [19th century : origin obscure.]

Hun·nish (hŭn'ĭsh) *adj.* **1.** Of or pertaining to the Huns or their language. **2.** *Sometimes* **hunnish.** Barbarous.

~n. The language of the Huns, variously classified as Turkic or Mongolian. **—Hun·nish·ness** *n.*

hunt (hŭnt) *v.* **hunted, hunting, hunts.** *—tr.* **1. a.** To pursue (game or other wild animals) for food or sport. See **hunting. b.** To seek out; track; search for. **c.** To search for (something deliberately hidden), as in a children's game: *hunt the thimble; hunt the slipper.* **2.** To search through (an area), as for game or prey. **3.** To make use of (hounds or horses, for example) in hunting. **4.** To drive out forcibly; chase away, especially by harassing. **5.** To harass persistently; persecute. *—intr.* **1.** To pursue game or other wild animals in order to capture or kill them. **2.** To conduct a diligent search; seek. Often used with *for.* **3.** *Aerospace.* **a.** To yaw back and forth about a flight path, as if seeking a new direction or another angle of attack. Used of aircraft, rockets, and space vehicles. **b.** To rotate up and down or back and forth without being deflected by the pilot. Used of a control surface or a rocket motor in gimbals. **4. a.** To oscillate about a selected value or setting. Used of a control system, electric motor, engine, carburetor, or the like. **b.** To swing back and forth or to oscillate. Used of an indicator on a display or measuring instrument. **—hunt down** (or **out**). To search for and locate. **—hunt up. 1.** To search for; seek. **2.** To hunt down.

~n. **1.** The act or sport of hunting game; the chase. **2. a.** A hunting expedition or outing. **b.** Those taking part in a hunt with horses and hounds. **3.** A diligent search or pursuit. [Middle English *hunten,* Old English *huntian,* from Germanic *huntjan* (unattested), akin to *hanthatjan* (unattested), to HENT.]

Hunt (hŭnt), **(James Henry) Leigh** (1784–1859). British radical essayist and journalist. He edited *The Examiner* from 1808 and was jailed (1813–15) for a libel on the Prince Regent.

Hunt, Richard Morris (1827–95). U.S. architect. A prolific architect, he oversaw the addition to the Louvre in Paris and designed many important works, such as the addition to the U.S. Capitol, the base of the Statue of Liberty, numerous academic buildings, and many mansions, including The Breakers in Newport, Rhode Island.

Hunt, (William) Holman (1827–1910). British artist who with Rossetti and Millais formed the Pre-Raphaelite Brotherhood. His works include *The Light of the World* (1854), *The Scapegoat* (1856), and *The Miracle of the Sacred Fire* (1898).

Hunt, William Morris (1824–79). U.S. painter. While studying in Europe he became influenced by and interested in contemporary French paintings, particularly the works of Millet. Through his Boston and Newport art schools and his own work he brought French painting to the attention of American artists and collectors.

hunt·er (hŭn'tər) *n.* **1.** One that hunts; especially, a person who hunts game for food or sport, or who captures wild animals. **2.** A horse bred or trained for use in hunting, typically a fast, strong jumper. **3.** A dog bred or trained for use in hunting. **4.** A person who searches for or seeks something. Usually used in combination: *a house hunter.* **5.** A watch with a hinged metal covering or case protecting the face and its glass covering. Compare **half hunter.**

hunt·er-gath·er·er (hŭn'tər-găth'ər-ər) *n.* A member of a group of primitive people, such as the Bushmen of the Kalahari, whose subsistence is based on hunting and collecting fruit and other plant foods.

hunt·er-kill·er (hŭn'tər-kĭl'ər) *adj.* Designating any of a class of submarines designed to locate, chase, and destroy enemy submarines.

hunter's moon *n.* The full moon following the harvest moon.

hunt·ing (hŭn'tĭng) *n.* **1.** The sport or activity of pursuing wild animals, especially: **a.** The sport of hunting wild animals, game birds, and the like with guns. **b.** *British.* The hunting of foxes or other vermin using packs of hounds but not guns. **2.** The act of conducting a serious search for something. Often used in combination: *job hunting; house hunting.*

~adj. Pertaining to or used in the sport of hunting: *a hunting horn.*

hunter *A horse bred for stamina and closely related to the Arab thoroughbreds of the racing world. Hunters are the traditional mounts for fox hunters.*

hurricane

RAGING SPIRALS OF WIND AND RAIN THAT TAKE THEIR POWER FROM HEAT AND MOISTURE

Hurricanes are born over the tropical seas near the equator

Hurricanes—or tropical cyclones or typhoons as they are also known—are powered by heat and moisture. They form near the equator over seas with a surface temperature of at least 27°C (81°F), a condition that occurs during the late summer "hurricane season." A rising column of warm, moist air forms a spiral system of clouds and strong winds. Technically, a hurricane exists when these winds reach a speed exceeding 32.7 meters a second (about 73 miles an hour).

Hurricanes drift slowly westward at about 16 kph (10 mph) with the trade winds and also veer away from the equator. When they leave the tropics or strike land, they dissipate, cut off from the warm seas that are the source of their energy. They are carefully monitored by weather satellites.

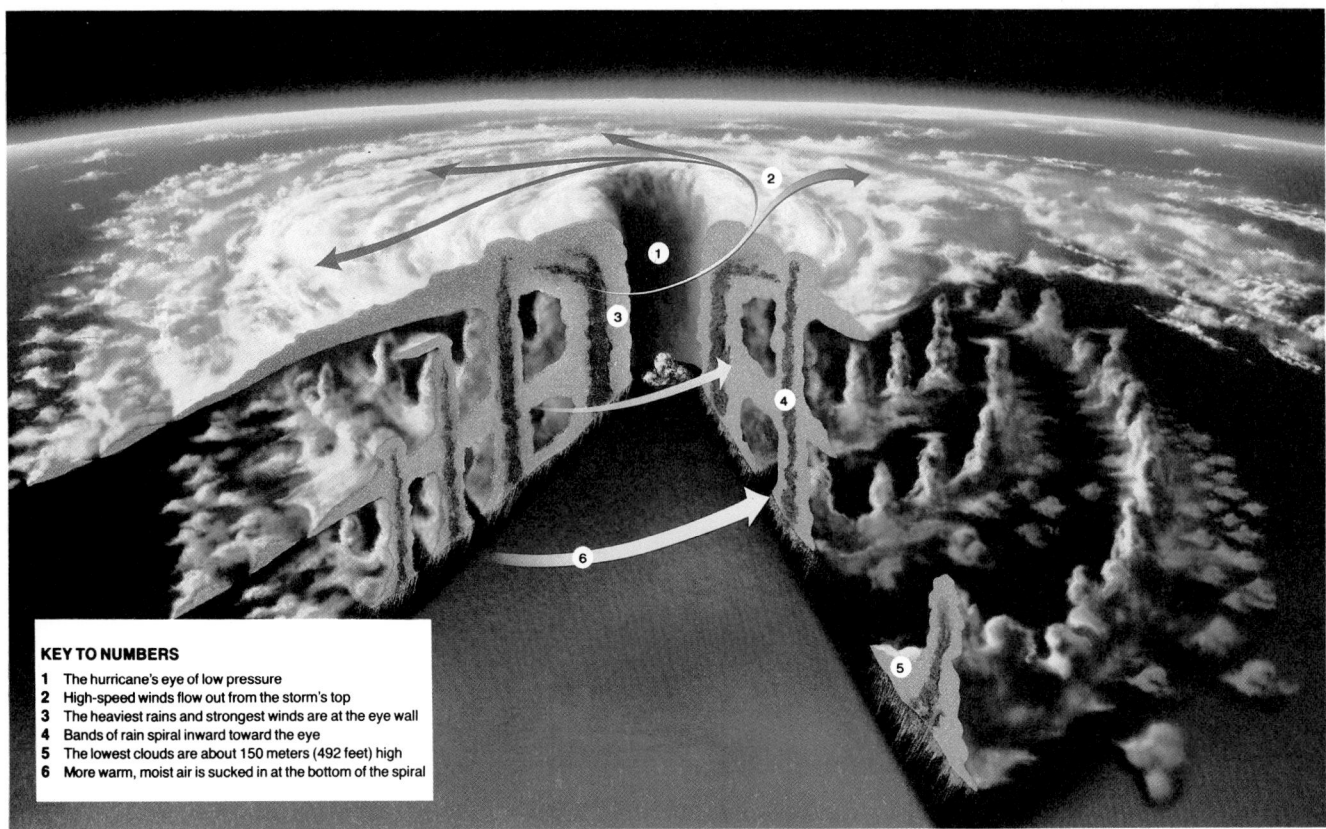

KEY TO NUMBERS
1. The hurricane's eye of low pressure
2. High-speed winds flow out from the storm's top
3. The heaviest rains and strongest winds are at the eye wall
4. Bands of rain spiral inward toward the eye
5. The lowest clouds are about 150 meters (492 feet) high
6. More warm, moist air is sucked in at the bottom of the spiral

SPIRAL OF WIND AND CLOUD *A hurricane builds up when warm, moist air begins to rise, forming cumulus clouds and allowing the prevailing trade winds to sweep in below. The system creates a spiral, twisting clockwise in the* *Northern Hemisphere and counterclockwise in the Southern. As the air rises, it cools and forms rain. The spiral forms an enormous catherine wheel up to 960 kilometers (600 miles) across, with winds increasing to about* *320 kph (200 mph) toward the center, or eye, which is a calm area of low pressure about 32 kilometers (20 miles) across. Many hurricanes contain as much energy as 400 twenty-megaton bombs.*

Hun·ting·don and Pe·ter·bor·ough (hŭn′tĭng-dən; pē′tər-bûr′ō, -bər-ə). Former county in east-central England, created in 1965 by the merger of the counties of Huntingdonshire and the Soke of Peterborough. In 1974 it was absorbed by the nonmetropolitan county of Cambridgeshire.

hunting ground *n.* **1.** The location of a hunt. **2.** An area regarded as a potential source of a sought-after object or objective.

hunting leopard *n.* The **cheetah** *(see).*

hunting lodge *n.* A small house or lodge occupied by hunters.

hunting spider *n.* The **wolf spider** *(see).*

hunt·ress (hŭn′trĭs) *n.* **1.** A woman or female that hunts. **2.** *Rare.* A mare used for hunting.

hunts·man (hŭnts′mən) *n., pl.* **-men** (-mĭn). **1.** A person who hunts; a hunter. **2.** One who manages a pack of foxhounds or other hunting dogs and handles them when they are out hunting.

Hu·on pine (hyōō′ŏn′) *n.* A coniferous tree, *Dacrydium franklinii,* of Southeast Asia, Australia, and Chile, having scalelike leaves and berrylike fruits. [After the *Huon* River, southern Tasmania.]

Hupeh, Hupei. See **Hubei.**

hur·dies (hûr′dēz′) *pl.n. Scottish.* The buttocks or haunches. [Origin unknown.]

hur·dle (hûrd′l) *n.* **1.** A light, portable barrier, usually consisting of two uprights between which a horizontal bar can be hung at varying heights and which must be jumped by competitors in certain races. **2. hurdles.** A race for horses or human runners in which a series of such hurdles are used. **3.** Any obstacle or problem that must be overcome. **4.** *Chiefly British.* A portable section of fencing made of intertwined branches or wattle and used chiefly for fencing in sheep. **5.** *British.* A frame or sledge formerly used to carry condemned traitors to their executions.
~*v.* **hurdled, -dling, -dles.** —*tr.* **1.** To jump over (a barrier) in or as if in a race. **2.** To enclose with hurdles. **3.** To overcome or successfully deal with (an obstacle or problem). —*intr.* To jump over barriers in or as if in a race. [Middle English *hurdel, hirdle,* Old English *hyrdel,* from Germanic.] —**hur·dler** *n.*

hur·dy-gur·dy (hûr′dē-gûr′dē) *n., pl.* **-dies. 1.** A medieval instrument shaped like a lute, played by street musicians with a crank that causes a resin-covered wheel to scrape across the strings. **2.** Any musical instrument played by turning a crank, such as a barrel organ. [Probably imitative.]

hurl (hûrl) *v.* **hurled, hurling, hurls.** —*tr.* **1.** To throw with great force; fling; pitch. **2.** To move or impel vigorously; thrust. **3.** To exclaim vehemently; shout out: *hurl abuse.* —*intr.* **1.** To play the game of hurling. **2.** To move with great speed, force, or violence; hurtle. —See Synonyms at **throw.**
~*n.* A forceful pitch or throw. [Middle English *h(o)urlen*†, to be driven with great force, throw, rush on.] —**hurl·er** *n.*

hurl·ey (hûr′lē) *n., pl.* **-ies. 1.** The stick used in the game of hurling. **2.** The game of hurling. [From HURL.]

hurl·ing (hûr′lĭng) *n.* A fast Irish game resembling lacrosse and hockey, played between teams of 15 with broad-bladed netless sticks and a hard ball. [From HURL.]

hurl·y-bur·ly (hûr′lē-bûr′lē) *n., pl.* **-lies.** Turbulence; commotion; disorder.
~*adj.* Full of noise or commotion. [Earlier *hurling and burling,* reduplication of *hurling,* tumult, from Middle English, gerund of HURL.]

Hu·ron (hyōōr′ən, -ŏn′) *n., pl.* **-rons** or collectively **Huron. 1.** A member of a confederation of four tribes of Iroquoian-speaking North American Indians formerly inhabiting the region east of Lake Huron and the St. Lawrence Valley. **2.** The Iroquoian language spoken among these tribes. [French, "one who has disheveled hair," boor, from *hure*, disheveled head, from Old French *hure*†.] —**Hu·ron** *adj.*

Huron, Lake. One of the five Great Lakes, on the border between the United States and Canada. It is the second largest of the group of lakes. It forms part of the Great Lakes-St. Lawrence seaway system and is navigated by ocean-going vessels.

hur·rah (hoō-rä′, -rô′) *interj.* Also **hoo·ray, hur·ray** (-rā′). Used as an exclamation of pleasure, approval, elation, or victory. —*n.* A shout of "hurrah." —*v.* **hurrahed, -rahing, -rahs.** Also **hoo·ray, hur·ray.** —*tr.* To applaud, cheer, or approve by shouting "hurrah." —*intr.* To shout "hurrah." [Alteration of HUZZA.]

hur·ri·cane (hûr′ə-kān′) *n.* **1. a.** A violent tropical cyclone originating in the Gulf of Mexico or Caribbean Sea, traveling north, northwest, or northeast from its point of origin, and usually involving heavy rains and thunder. **b.** A similar cyclone off the north of Australia. **2.** Wind exceeding 74 miles per hour, force 12 on the Beaufort scale. —See Synonyms at **wind.** [Earlier *furacano, haurachana*, from Spanish *huracan* and Portuguese *furacão*, both from Carib *huracan, furacan*.]

hurricane deck *n.* The upper deck on a ship such as a passenger steamer.

hurricane lamp *n.* A lamp consisting of a candle or electric bulb covered by a glass chimney.

hur·ried (hûr′ēd) *adj.* **1.** Obliged to move or act rapidly; rushed. **2.** Done in great haste: *a hurried tour.* —**hur·ried·ly** *adv.* —**hur·ried·ness** *n.*

hur·ry (hûr′ē) *v.* **-ried, -rying, -ries.** —*intr.* To move or act with haste. Often used with *up.* —*tr.* **1.** To cause to move or act rapidly or more rapidly; hasten: *hurry the children.* **2.** To cause to move or act too quickly; rush: *hurried them into marriage.* **3.** To hasten to completion; expedite: *This should hurry things along.* —See Synonyms at **speed.** —*n., pl.* **hurries. 1.** The act of hurrying; hastened progress. **2. a.** The need or wish to hurry: *There's no hurry.* **b.** A condition of urgency or eagerness: *Are you in a great hurry to leave?* [Perhaps from Middle English *horien.*]

Hurstmonceaux. See **Herstmonceaux.**

Hur·ston (hûr′stən), **Zora Neale** (*c.* 1901-60). U.S. author. In her several books and novels, including *Jonah's Gourd Vine* (1934) and *Seraph on the Suwanee* (1948), she wrote about black life with an originality and freshness that earned her critical acclaim. Her knowledge of anthropology added to the richness of her work.

hurt (hûrt) *v.* **hurt, hurting, hurts.** —*tr.* **1. a.** To cause physical damage or pain to; injure; wound. **b.** To produce a feeling of pain in (a person or living creature): *The tight collar hurt his neck.* **2.** To cause to suffer mental or emotional anguish; distress or offend. **3.** To harm; be prejudicial to; impair: *hurt his chances.* —*intr.* **1. a.** To have a feeling of pain or discomfort: *His leg hurts.* **b.** To produce a feeling of pain: *That collar hurts.* **2.** To cause distress, hardship, or damage: *The tax bill hurts.* —See Synonyms at **injure.** —*n.* **1.** Something that hurts; a pain, injury, or wound. **2.** Mental suffering; anguish. **3.** A wrong; damage; harm. [Middle English *hurten, hirten*, to strike, harm, from Old French *hurter*, from Gallo-Roman *hūrtare†* (unattested).]

hurt·er (hûr′tər) *n.* **1.** One that hurts. **2.** A concrete, stone, or iron block or post placed at the corner of a building to protect it from damage by passing traffic. [Middle English, shoulder of an axle against which the wheel hub strikes, from Old French *hurtoir*, from *herter*, to strike, knock against, HURT.]

hurt·ful (hûrt′fəl) *adj.* Causing hurt or injury; painful; damaging. —**hurt·ful·ly** *adv.* —**hurt·ful·ness** *n.*

hur·tle (hûrt′l) *v.* **-tled, -tling, -tles.** —*intr.* **1.** To move with or as if with great speed and often with a rushing or crashing noise: *The river hurtles over the waterfall.* **2.** To collide violently; crash. —*tr.* To throw or send forcibly or violently; hurl. [Middle English *hurtlen*, to dash one thing against another, collide, frequentative of *hurten*, to strike, HURT.]

Hus, Jan. See **John Huss.**

hus·band (hŭz′bənd) *n.* **1.** *Abbr.* **h., H.** A man joined to a woman in marriage; a woman's spouse. **2.** *Archaic.* A manager or steward. **3.** A prudent and thrifty manager, as of money: *He proved a careless husband of his resources.* —*tr.v.* **husbanded, -banding, -bands. 1.** To spend or use economically; budget; conserve: *husband one's energy.* **2.** *Archaic.* **a.** To marry. **b.** *Archaic.* To find a husband for. **3.** *Archaic.* To till (land). [Middle English *housbonde, hus(e)bonde*, husband, husbandman, Old English *hūsbonda*, master of a household, husband, from Old Norse *hūsbōndi* : *hūs*, house, from Germanic *hūsam* (unattested), HOUSE + *bōndi*, earlier *bōandi, būandi*, present participle of *bōa, būa*, to dwell.]

hus·band·man (hŭz′bənd-mən) *n., pl.* **-men** (-mĭn). One whose occupation is husbandry; a farmer. [Middle English *housbondeman : housbonde*, husbandman, HUSBAND + MAN.]

hus·band·ry (hŭz′bən-drē) *n.* **1. a.** The cultivation of plants or the raising of livestock; farming; agriculture. **b.** The application of scientific principles to a branch of farming, especially animal breeding: *animal husbandry.* **2.** The careful management of resources; conservation. [Middle English *housbondrie : housbonde*, husbandman, HUSBAND + -(E)RY.]

hush (hŭsh) *v.* **hushed, hushing, hushes.** —*tr.* **1.** To cause to be silent; to quiet. **2.** To quell or still; calm; soothe. **3.** To prevent from becoming publicly known; suppress; conceal: *tried to hush up the scandal.* —*intr.* To be or become silent or still. —*n.* A silence; stillness; quiet. —*interj.* Used to demand quiet or to calm a child. [Back-formation from earlier *husht* (interjection), from Middle English *huissht.*]

hush·a·by (hŭsh′ə-bī′) *interj.* Used to soothe a child or lull him to sleep. [HUSH + -*by* (as in *good-by*).]

hush-hush (hŭsh′hŭsh′) *adj. Informal.* Secret; confidential.

hush money *n. Informal.* A bribe or payment made to keep something secret.

husk (hŭsk) *n.* **1.** The membranous or green outer envelope of many fruits and seeds. **2.** The shell or outer covering of anything, especially when worthless. —*tr.v.* **husked, husking, husks.** To remove the husk or husks from. [Middle English *husk(e)*, probably from Middle Dutch *hūskijn*, diminutive of *hūs*, house, from Germanic *hūsam* (unattested), HOUSE.] —**husk·er** *n.*

husk·y¹ (hŭs′kē) *adj.* **-ier, -iest. 1.** Having a hoarse, often breathy quality, either naturally or from overuse or emotion: *"I listen to her voice which is dark, heavy, husky"* (Anaïs Nin). **2.** Like a husk. **3.** Full of husks. **4.** *Informal.* Rugged, strong, and burly. —*n., pl.* **huskies.** A husky person. [From HUSK.] —**husk·i·ly** *adv.* —**husk·i·ness** *n.*

hus·ky² (hŭs′kē) *n., pl.* **-kies. 1.** *Sometimes* **Husky.** A dog of a breed developed in Siberia for pulling sleds, having a dense, variously colored coat, small erect ears, and a bushy tail curled over the back. Also called "Siberian husky." **2.** A dog of any of several similar breeds of Arctic origin. [Probably a shortened variant of ESKIMO.]

Huss (hŭs), **John** (*c.* 1369-1415). Also **Jan Hus** (hoōs). Czech religious reformer. Huss attacked the corruption of the clergy and was excommunicated in 1412, when he denounced the bulls of the antipope John XXII. In exile he wrote *De Ecclesia*, which accorded the state the right to supervise the church. His death by burning made him a national hero.

hus·sar (hoō-zär′, -sär′) *n.* **1.** A member of a light cavalry regiment having dress uniforms, typically with much frogging. **2.** A horseman of the Hungarian light cavalry that was organized during the 15th century. [Hungarian *huszár*, "freebooter," hussar, from Old Serbian *husar, gusar*, from Old Italian *corsaro*, CORSAIR.]

Hus·sein Ibn Ta·lal (hoō-sān′ ĭb′ən tə-läl′) (1935-). King of Jordan from 1953. He succeeded his father, King Talal. Hussein has used diplomacy and a fiercely loyal militia to retain his throne. He suffered military defeat by Israel in 1967 and has since quelled Arab guerrilla attacks.

Huss·ite (hŭs′īt′, hoōs′-) *n.* A follower of John Huss. —*adj.* Of or pertaining to John Huss or his religious theories. —**Huss·it·ism** (hŭs′īt′īz′əm, hoōs′-) *n.*

hus·sy (hŭz′ē, hŭs′ē) *n., pl.* **-sies. 1.** A saucy or flippant girl. **2.** A lewd or sexually promiscuous woman. [Alteration of HOUSEWIFE.]

hust·ings (hŭs′tĭngz) *pl.n. Sometimes used with a singular verb.* **1.** *British.* A court formerly held in London. **2.** *British.* A platform from which (prior to the Ballot Act of 1872) candidates for Parliament addressed the electors. **3. a.** Any place or platform where political speeches are made. **b.** Political campaigning, especially in connection with an election: *a veteran of the hustings.* [Middle English *husting*, an assembly, Old English *hūsting*, from Old Norse *husthing*, "house assembly" : *hūs*, house, from Germanic *hūsam* (unattested), HOUSE + *thing*, assembly.]

hus·tle (hŭs′əl) *v.* **-tled, -tling, -tles.** —*tr.* **1.** To jostle or shove roughly. **2.** To hurry hurriedly or urgently: *hustle the prisoner onto a plane.* **3.** To hurry along; cause or urge to proceed hurriedly: *hustled the board into a quick decision.* **4.** *Slang.* **a.** To sell or obtain in undignified or unethical ways: *He hustles a few dollars by peddling racetrack tips.* **b.** To gain by energetic effort. —*intr.* **1.** To jostle and push. **2.** *Informal.* To work busily and quickly. **3.** *Slang.* To use vigorous, aggressive, or questionable means in order to make money. **4.** *Slang.* To solicit customers for or as a prostitute. —*n.* **1.** The act or an instance of hustling. **2.** *Slang.* A job or business, especially one that is undignified or unethical. **3.** *Informal.* Hurried activity: *the hustle and bustle of city streets.* [Originally to shake back and forth, from Middle Dutch *husselen*, frequentative of *hutsen*, to shake, from (unattested) Germanic *khut-* (probably imitative).] —**hus·tler** *n.*

Hus·ton (hyoō′stən), **John** (1906-). U.S. film director. He started his film career as a scriptwriter (1938) but later made successful action films, including *The Maltese Falcon* (1941), *The African Queen* (1951), and *The Man Who Would Be King* (1975).

hut (hŭt) *n.* **1.** A makeshift or crudely constructed dwelling or shelter. **2.** *Military.* A temporary structure for sheltering troops. —*v.* **hutted, hutting, huts.** —*tr.* To shelter or store in a hut. —*intr.* To live or take shelter in a hut. [Old French *hutte*, from Middle High German *hütte* or Old High German *hutt(e)a*.]

hutch (hŭch) *n.* **1.** A box, pen, or coop, usually having a wire-mesh side, for small animals, especially rabbits. **2.** A cupboard with storage drawers. **3.** A small house or hut. [Middle English *huche*, chest, from Old French *huche, huge*, from Medieval Latin *hutica†*.]

Hutch·in·son (hŭch′ĭn-sən), **Anne** (1591-1643). U.S. colonist and religious leader, born in England. After settling in Boston (1635), she was ostracized and later excommunicated for her religious beliefs. She moved to present-day Rhode Island with her family (1638) and then to Pelham Bay, Long Island, where she was killed by Indians.

hut-cir·cle (hŭt′sûr′kəl) *n. Archaeology.* A ring or partial ring of stones or earth indicating the site of a simple prehistoric dwelling.

hut·ment (hŭt′mənt) *n.* An encampment of huts; especially, a military camp.

Hut·ter·ite (hŭt′ə-rīt′, hōō′tə-) *n.* A member of an **Anabaptist** *(see)* sect originating in Moravia and now living in parts of Canada and the United States. Hutterites are mainly farmers and hold property in common. [After J. *Hutter*, 16th-century Moravian Anabaptist.]

Hut·ton (hŭt′n), **James** (1726–97). Scottish geologist and farmer. His principle of uniformitarianism (1785), describing the igneous origins of rocks and minerals, forms the basis of modern geology.

Hux·ley (hŭk′slē), **Aldous (Leonard)** (1894–1963). British novelist and essayist. In *Brave New World* (1932) he painted a grim picture of a future utopia, a scientifically organized society in which conventional human suffering has been eliminated. His fascination with mysticism shows in *Eyeless in Gaza* (1936) and in *Time Must Have a Stop* (1944).

Huxley, Sir Julian Sorell (1887–1975). British biologist and brother of Aldous. He was professor of zoology at King's College, London (1925–27), secretary of the Zoological Society of London (1935–42), and the first director general of UNESCO (1946–48). Huxley advocated the application of scientific principles to moral, social, and political issues.

Huxley, Thomas Henry (1825–95). British biologist who championed Darwin's theory of evolution. He was the grandfather of Aldous and Julian Huxley. His works include *Zoological Evidences as to Man's Place in Nature* (1863) and *Science and Culture* (1881).

Huy·gens (hī′gənz), **Christian** (1629–95). Dutch mathematician, astronomer, and physicist. He invented the micrometer (1655), discovered Saturn's rings (1655), pioneered the use of the pendulum in clocks (1657), and formulated Huygens' principle.

Huygens' principle *n. Physics.* The principle that any point on a wave front may be regarded as the source of a secondary wave and that the position of the wave front at any time is determined by the envelope at that time of the secondary waves arising from a previous wave front. [After Christian **Huygens**.]

huz·za, huz·zah (hə-zä′) *n. Archaic.* A shout of encouragement or triumph; a cheer.

~*interj. Archaic.* Used to express joy, encouragement, appreciation, or the like.

~*v.* **huzzaed, huzzaing, huzzas.** *Archaic.* —*intr.* To shout "huzza"; cheer. —*tr.* To cheer or encourage with shouts of huzza. [16th century : perhaps of nautical origin.]

H.V. high voltage.

H.W., h.w. high water.

Hwang Ho. See Huang He.

hwyl (hōō′īl) *n. Welsh.* Passionate poetic fervor; emotional eloquence.

hy·a·cinth (hī′ə-sĭnth) *n.* **1.** Any of several bulbous plants of the genus *Hyacinthus,* native to the Mediterranean region, having narrow leaves and a terminal cluster of variously colored, usually very fragrant flowers; especially, the widely cultivated species *H. orientalis.* **2.** Any of several similar or related plants, such as the **grape hyacinth** *(see).* **3.** A plant, perhaps a lily, gladiolus, or iris, that according to Greek mythology sprang from the blood of the slain Hyacinthus. **4.** A deep purplish blue to vivid violet. **5.** A reddish or cinnamon-colored variety of transparent zircon, used as a gemstone. Also called "jacinth." **6.** A blue semiprecious stone, perhaps aquamarine, known in antiquity. [Latin *hyacinthus,* from Greek *huakinthos,* wild hyacinth (connected by folk etymology with **Hyacinthus**), of Mediterranean origin.] —**hy·a·cin·thine** (hī′ə-sĭn′thĭn, -thīn′) *adj.*

hyacinth bean *n.* A twining vine, *Dolichos lablab,* of the Old World tropics, having purple or white flowers and edible pods and seeds.

Hy·a·cin·thus (hī′ə-sĭn′thəs). *Greek Mythology.* A beautiful youth loved but accidentally killed by Apollo, from whose blood Apollo caused the hyacinth to grow.

Hy·a·des (hī′ə-dēz′) *pl.n.* **1.** *Greek Mythology.* The five daughters of Atlas and sisters of the Pleiades, placed by Zeus in the heavens. **2.** *Astronomy.* A cluster of five stars in the constellation Taurus, supposed by ancient astronomers to indicate rain when they rose with the sun. [Latin, from Greek *Huades.*]

hyaena. Variant of **hyena.**

hy·a·lin (hī′ə-lĭn) *n.* Also **hy·a·line** (hī′ə-lĭn, -līn′). **1.** *Physiology.* The uniform matrix of hyaline cartilage. **2.** *Pathology.* A transparent substance occurring in certain degenerative skin conditions. [Greek *hualos*†, glass + -IN.]

hy·a·line (hī′ə-lĭn, -līn′) *adj.* Resembling glass; glassy; translucent or transparent.

~*n.* **1.** Something having a glassy or transparent appearance, as a clear sky or a calm lake. **2.** A glassy or transparent appearance. **3.** Variant of **hyalin.** [Late Latin *hyalinus,* from Greek *hualinos,* of crystal or glass, from *hualos, huelos*†, crystalline stone, glass.]

hyaline cartilage *n.* A common type of cartilage that has a glassy, translucent appearance and a bluish color, that in the adult is composed of cells in a seemingly homogeneous, translucent matrix, as in joints, and that in the fetus forms most of the skeleton.

hyaline membrane disease *n.* **Respiratory distress syndrome** *(see).*

hy·a·lite (hī′ə-līt′) *n.* A clear, colorless opal. [German *Hyalit,* from Greek *hualos*†, glass, crystal.]

hyalo-, hyal– *prefix.* Indicates glass or glassy material; for example, **hyaloplasm.** [Greek *hualos,* glass.]

hy·a·loid (hī′ə-loid′) *adj.* Glassy or transparent in appearance; hyaline. [Greek *hualoeidēs : hualos,* glass (see **hyaline**) + -OID.]

hyaloid membrane *n.* The transparent membrane that separates the vitreous humor of the eye from the retina.

hy·a·lo·plasm (hī′ə-lō-plăz′əm) *n.* The clear, fluid portion of cytoplasm, as distinguished from included granular and netlike components. [German *Hyaloplasma* : Greek *hualos*†, crystal + PLASM.] —**hy·a·lo·plas·mic** (hī′ə-lō-plăz′mĭk) *adj.*

hy·al·ur·on·ic acid (hī′əl-yōō-rŏn′ĭk) *n.* A mucopolysaccharide that is present in connective tissue and in the synovial fluid around joints. [HYAL(O)- + Greek *ouron,* urine.]

hy·al·ur·on·i·dase (hī′əl-yōō-rŏn′ə-dās′, -dāz′) *n.* An enzyme that breaks down hyaluronic acid, thereby making the fluid in which it is found less viscous. [HYAL(O)- + Greek *ouron,* urine + -ID + -ASE.]

hy·brid (hī′brĭd) *n.* **Abbr. hyb. 1.** *Genetics.* The offspring of genetically dissimilar parents or stock; especially, the offspring produced by breeding plants or animals of different varieties, species, or races. **2.** Something of mixed origin or composition. **3.** A word whose elements are derived from different languages. [Latin *hybrida, hibrida*†, hybrid, mongrel.] —**hy·brid** *adj.* —**hy·brid·ism** *n.* —**hy·brid·i·ty** *n.*

hybrid circuit *n.* An integrated electronic circuit formed from a number of distinct integrated circuits interconnected on a substrate. Compare **monolithic circuit.**

hybrid computer *n.* A computer that combines elements of both a digital and an analog computer; especially, one in which an analog input is converted to digital form for fast processing.

hy·brid·ize (hī′brĭ-dīz′) *v.* **-ized, -izing, -izes.** —*tr.* To cause to produce hybrids; crossbreed. —*intr.* To produce hybrids. —**hy·brid·i·za·tion** (hī′brĭ-də-zā′shən) *n.* —**hy·brid·iz·er** *n.*

hybrid vigor *n.* **Heterosis** *(see).*

hybris. Variant of **hubris.**

hy·da·thode (hī′də-thōd′) *n.* A microscopic epidermal structure in many plants through which water is excreted in the form of liquid drops. [Greek *hudōr* (stem *hudat-*), water + *hodos,* way.]

hy·da·tid (hī′də-tĭd′) *n.* **1.** A cyst formed as a result of infestation by a tapeworm, *Echinococcus granulosus,* in a larval stage. Also called "hydatid cyst." **2.** The encysted larva of *E. granulosus.* [Greek *hudatis* (stem *hudatid-*), watery vesicle, hydatid, from *hudōr* (stem *hudat-*), water.] —**hy·da·tid** *adj.*

hydatid disease *n.* The disease caused by the presence of hydatids in the liver, lungs, or brain, characterized by malignant tumors or tissue damage. Also called "echinococcosis," "echinococciasis."

Hyde. See **Jekyll and Hyde.**

Hyde Park¹ (hīd). Ancient park in central London, England, occupying 146 hectares (360 acres). It became a royal deer park under Henry VIII. Charles I opened it to the public in 1635.

Hyde Park². A village in southeastern New York, on the Hudson River. Settled c. 1740, it is the site of the Roosevelt estate, where Franklin D. Roosevelt was born and is buried. The national historic site includes his house and the Roosevelt Library.

Hy·der·a·bad¹ (hī′dər-ə-băd′, -bäd′). Former state in south-central India, since 1956 partitioned among the states of Karnataka, Maharashtra, and Andhra Pradesh. It is an almost entirely agricultural region, lying within the Deccan plateau. The city of Hyderabad, formerly the capital of the state of the same name, is now the capital of Andhra Pradesh.

Hyderabad². City of the province of Sind, in southern Pakistan. It is a manufacturing center and the third-largest city in Pakistan.

hy·dra¹ (hī′drə) *n., pl.* **-dras** or **-drae** (-drē′). Any of various small, freshwater polyps of the genus *Hydra* and related genera, having a naked, cylindrical body and an oral opening surrounded by tentacles. [New Latin *Hydra,* **Hydra** (so called because polyps may reproduce themselves from parts cut off).]

hydra² *n.* A multifarious source of evil, trouble, or destruction that cannot be eradicated by a single attempt. [After **Hydra**.]

Hy·dra¹ (hī′drə). *Greek Mythology.* A many-headed monster that sprouted two heads for each one cut off but was finally slain by Hercules, who cauterized each neck after severing its head. [Middle English *Ydre,* from Old French, from Latin *Hydra,* from Greek *Hudra,* from *hudra,* water serpent.]

Hydra². A constellation in the equatorial region of the southern sky near Cancer, Libra, and Centaurus. Also called the "Snake." [After **Hydra**.]

hy·drac·id (hī-drăs′ĭd) *n.* An acid, such as hydrocyanic acid, that contains no oxygen. [HYDR(O)- + ACID.]

hy·dran·gea (hī-drān′jə, -drăn′jə) *n.* Any of various shrubs or trees of the genus *Hydrangea,* cultivated for their large, flat-topped or rounded clusters of white, pink, or blue flowers. [New Latin, "water vessel" (from the cuplike shape of the seed pod) : HYDR(O)- + Greek *angos,* vessel, pitcher (see **angiology**).]

hy·drant (hī′drənt) *n.* An outlet from a water main consisting of an upright pipe with one or more nozzles or spouts. Also called "fire hydrant," "fireplug." [HYDR(O)- + -ANT.]

hy·dranth (hī′drănth′) *n. Zoology.* A polyp in a hydroid colony that is specialized for feeding. [HYDR(O)- + Greek *anthos,* flower.]

hy·drar·gy·rism (hī-drär′jə-rĭz′əm) *n.* Also **hy·drar·gy·ri·a** (hī′-drär-jĭr′ē-ə). *Pathology.* **Mercurialism** *(see).* [From New Latin *hydrargyrum,* from Latin *hydrargyros,* from Greek *hudrarguros,* "silver water" : HYDR(O)- + *aguros,* silver.]

hy·dras·tine (hī-drăs′tēn′, -tĭn) *n.* A poisonous white alkaloid, $C_{21}H_{21}NO_6$, obtained from the root of the goldenseal, *Hydrastis canadensis,* and formerly used to treat uterine hemorrhage. [From **Hydrastis**.]

hy·dras·tis (hī-drăs′tĭs) *n.* Any plant of the genus *Hydrastis,* having ornamental foliage and fruits, including the **goldenseal** *(see)*. [New Latin *Hydrastis* (genus) : HYDR(O)- + *-astis*†.]

hy·drate (hī′drāt′) *n.* A compound containing water combined in a definite ratio, the water being retained or regarded as being retained in its molecular state. ~*v.* **hydrated, -drating, -drates.** —*tr.* To combine with water; especially, to cause to form a hydrate. —*intr.* To become a hydrate. [HYDR(O)- + -ATE.] —**hy·dra·tion** (hī-drā′shən) *n.* —**hy·dra·tor** *n.*

hy·drat·ed (hī′drā′tĭd) *adj.* Chemically combined with water; especially, existing in the form of a hydrate.

hy·drau·lic (hī-drô′lĭk) *adj.* **1.** Of, involving, moved by, or operated by a fluid, especially water, under pressure. **2.** Of or pertaining to hydraulics. [Latin *hydraulicus,* from Greek *hudraulis,* a water organ invented by Ctesibius in the 2nd century B.C. : HYDR(O)- + *aulos,* tube, pipe.] —**hy·drau·li·cal·ly** *adv.*

hydraulic brake *n.* A brake in which the braking force is transmitted to the braking surface by a compressed fluid.

hydraulic cement *n.* A cement capable of solidifying under water. See **Portland cement.**

hydraulic press *n.* A machine in which a large force is exerted on the larger of two pistons in a pair of hydraulically coupled cylinders by means of a relatively small force applied to the smaller piston.

hydraulic ram *n.* **1.** A water pump in which the downward flow of naturally running water is intermittently halted by a valve so that the flow is forced upward through an open pipe into a reservoir. **2.** The large output piston of a hydraulic press.

hy·drau·lics (hī-drô′lĭks) *n. Used with a singular verb.* The physical science and technology of the static and dynamic behavior of fluids. Also called "fluid mechanics."

hydraulic suspension *n.* A form of motor-vehicle suspension in which springs are replaced by hydraulic devices consisting of a piston moving in a cylinder filled with fluid. See **hydroelastic suspension.**

hy·dra·zine (hī′drə-zēn′, -zĭn) *n.* A colorless, fuming, corrosive hygroscopic liquid, H_2NNH_2, used in jet and rocket fuels. [HYDR(O)- + AZ(O)- + -INE.]

hy·dra·zo·ic acid (hī′drə-zō′ĭk) *n.* A colorless, highly explosive liquid, HN_3, that forms explosive salts, called azides, when combined with heavy metals. [HYDR(O)- + AZO- + -IC.]

hy·dric (hī′drĭk) *adj.* **1.** Of, containing, or pertaining to hydrogen. **2.** Pertaining to, characterized by, or requiring considerable moisture. [HYDR(O)- + -IC.]

hy·dride (hī′drīd′) *n.* A compound of hydrogen with another, more electropositive element or group. [HYDR(O)- + -IDE.]

hy·dri·od·ic acid (hī′drē-ŏd′ĭk) *n.* A clear, colorless or pale-yellow aqueous solution of hydrogen iodide, HI, that is a strong acid and reducing agent. [HYDR(O)- + IODIC ACID.]

hy·dro¹ (hī′drō) *n., pl.* **hydros.** *British.* A hotel or similar establishment, especially at a spa resort, providing hydropathic treatment.

hydro² *adj. Informal.* Hydroelectric.

hydro-, hydr– *prefix.* Indicates: **1.** Water; for example, **hydrous, hydroelectric. 2.** Liquid; for example, **hydrometallurgy, hydrostatic. 3.** Composed of or combined with hydrogen; for example, **hydrochloride, hydrosulfide. 4.** Hydroid; for example, **hydrozoan.** [Greek *hudōr,* water.]

hy·dro·bro·mic acid (hī′drə-brō′mĭk) *n.* A clear, colorless or faintly yellow, highly acidic and corrosive aqueous solution of hydrogen bromide, HBr, used in the manufacture of bromides.

hy·dro·car·bon (hī′drə-kär′bən) *n.* Any of numerous organic compounds, such as benzene and methane, that contain only carbon and hydrogen.

hy·dro·cele (hī′drə-sēl′) *n.* A pathological accumulation of serous fluid in a bodily cavity, especially in the testicles. [Latin *hydrocēlē,* from Greek *hudrokēlē* : HYDRO- + -CELE.]

hy·dro·cel·lu·lose (hī′drō-sĕl′yə-lōs′, -lōz′) *n.* A gelatinous form of hydrated cellulose made by treating cellulose with acid, alkali, or water and used in making rayon, mercerized cotton, and paper.

hy·dro·ceph·a·lus (hī′drō-sĕf′ə-ləs) *n.* Also **hy·dro·ceph·a·ly** (-lē). A usually congenital condition in which an abnormal accumulation of cerebrospinal fluid in the cerebral ventricles causes enlargement of the skull and compression of the brain. In nontechnical usage, also called "water on the brain." [Late Latin, from Greek *hudrokephalon* : HYDRO- + -CEPHALUS.] —**hy·dro·ce·phal·ic** (hī′drō-sə-fāl′ĭk), **hy·dro·ceph·a·loid** (hī′drō-sĕf′ə-loid′), **hy·dro·ceph·a·lous** (hī′drō-sĕf′ə-ləs) *adj.*

hy·dro·chlo·ric acid (hī′drə-klôr′ĭk, -klōr′ĭk) *n.* A clear, colorless, fuming, poisonous, highly acidic aqueous solution of hydrogen chloride, HCl, used in petroleum production, as a chemical intermediate, and in ore reduction, food processing, pickling, and metal cleaning. Formerly called "spirits of salt."

hy·dro·chlo·ride (hī′drə-klôr′īd′, -klōr′īd′) *n.* A compound resulting or regarded as resulting from the reaction of hydrochloric acid with an organic base.

hy·dro·cor·al (hī′drə-kôr′əl, -kŏr′əl) *n.* Any of various colonial marine hydrozoans of the order Hydrocorallinae, having a limestone skeleton and resembling the coral. See **millepore.**

hy·dro·cor·ti·sone (hī′drō-kôr′tə-sōn′, -zōn′) *n.* A bitter, crystalline hormone, $C_{21}H_{30}O_5$, derived from the adrenal cortex and having activity and medical uses similar to those of **cortisone** *(see).* Also called "cortisol."

hy·dro·cy·an·ic acid (hī′drə-sī-ăn′ĭk) *n.* A colorless, volatile, extremely toxic, flammable aqueous solution of hydrogen cyanide,

HCN, used in the manufacture of dyes, fumigants, and plastics. Also called "prussic acid," "hydrogen cyanide."

hy·dro·dy·nam·ic (hī′drō-dī-năm′ĭk) *adj.* **1.** Of or pertaining to hydrodynamics. **2.** Of, pertaining to, or operated by the force of liquid in motion. —**hy·dro·dy·nam·i·cal·ly** *adv.*

hy·dro·dy·nam·ics (hī′drō-dī-năm′ĭks) *n. Used with a singular verb.* The dynamics of fluids, especially incompressible fluids, in motion. Also called "hydromechanics."

hy·dro·e·lec·tric (hī′drō-ĭ-lĕk′trĭk) *adj.* **1.** Generating electricity by conversion of the energy of running water. **2.** Using or involving electricity so generated. —**hy·dro·e·lec·tric·i·ty** (hī′drō-ĭ-lĕk′trĭs′ə-tē) *n.*

hy·dro·flu·or·ic acid (hī′drō-flŏŏ-ôr′ĭk, -ôr′ĭk, -flŏŏr′ĭk) *n.* A colorless, fuming, corrosive, dangerously poisonous aqueous solution of hydrogen fluoride, HF, used to etch or polish glass, pickle certain metals, and clean masonry.

hy·dro·foil (hī′drə-foil′) *n.* **1.** Any of a set of blades attached to the hull of a boat and aligned in the water at a small angle to the horizontal so that when the boat is in motion the fluid striking each blade's underside creates a high-pressure region below the blade, low pressure above it, and a resultant lift that raises the craft out of the water for efficient high-speed operation. **2.** A boat equipped with hydrofoils. In this sense, also called "hydroplane."

hy·dro·gen (hī′drə-jən) *n. Symbol* **H** A colorless, highly flammable gaseous element, the lightest of all gases and the most abundant element in the universe, used in the production of synthetic ammonia and methanol, in petroleum refining, in hydrogenation of organic materials, as a reducing atmosphere, in oxyhydrogen torches, and in rocket fuels. Atomic number 1, atomic weight 1.00797, melting point −259.14°C, boiling point −252.5°C, density 0.08988 gram per liter, valence 1. [French *hydrogène,* "water generating" (it forms water when oxidized) : HYDRO- + -GEN.] —**hy·drog·e·nous** (hī-drŏj′ə-nəs) *adj.*

hy·drog·en·ase (hī-drŏj′ə-nās′, -nāz′) *n.* An enzyme that catalyzes reduction reactions by causing the addition of hydrogen to a compound.

hy·dro·gen·ate (hī′drə-jə-nāt′, hī-drŏj′ə-) *tr.v.* **-ated, -ating, -ates.** To combine with or subject to the action of hydrogen; especially, to combine (an unsaturated compound) with hydrogen. —**hy·dro·gen·a·tion** (hī′drə-jə-nā′shən, hī-drŏj′ə-) *n.* —**hy·dro·gen·a·tor** *n.*

hydrogen bomb *n.* An explosive weapon of enormous destructive power, derived from the fusion of nuclei of various hydrogen isotopes in the formation of helium nuclei. Also called "fusion bomb," "H-bomb," "thermonuclear bomb."

hydrogen bond *n.* An essentially ionic weak chemical bond between a strongly electronegative atom and a hydrogen atom already bonded to another strongly electronegative atom.

hydrogen bromide *n.* An irritating colorless gas, HBr, used in the manufacture of barbiturates and synthetic hormones.

hydrogen chloride *n.* A colorless, fuming, corrosive, suffocating gas, HCl, used in the manufacture of plastics.

hydrogen cyanide *n.* Hydrocyanic acid *(see).*

hydrogen fluoride *n.* A colorless, fuming, mobile, corrosive liquid, or a highly soluble corrosive gas, HF, used in the manufacture of hydrofluoric acid, as a reagent, catalyst, and fluorinating agent, and in the refining of uranium and the preparation of many fluorine compounds.

hydrogen iodide *n.* A corrosive, colorless, suffocating gas, HI, used to manufacture hydriodic acid.

hydrogen ion *n.* **1.** The positively charged ion of hydrogen, H^+, formed by removal of the electron from atomic hydrogen. **2.** An ionized hydrogen molecule, H^+_2.

hy·dro·gen·ize (hī′drə-jə-nīz′, hī-drŏj′ə-) *tr.v.* **-ized, -izing, -izes.** To hydrogenate. —**hy·dro·gen·i·za·tion** *n.*

hy·dro·gen·ol·y·sis (hī′drō-jə-nŏl′ĭ-sĭs) *n.* The breaking of a chemical bond in an organic molecule with the simultaneous addition of a hydrogen atom to each of the resulting molecular fragments. [HYDROGEN + -LYSIS.]

hydrogen peroxide *n.* A colorless, heavy, strongly oxidizing liquid, H_2O_2, an essentially unstable compound, capable of reacting explosively with combustibles, and used principally in aqueous solution as an antiseptic, bleaching agent, oxidizing agent, oxidizer in rocket fuels, and laboratory reagent.

hydrogen sulfide *n.* A colorless, flammable, poisonous compound, H_2S, having a characteristic rotten-egg odor and used as a precipitator, purifier, and reagent.

hy·dro·ge·o·lo·gy (hī′drō-jē-ŏl′ə-jē) *n.* The scientific study of waters below the earth's surface and the geologic aspects of the surface waters and their interaction with the solid surface of the earth.

hy·dro·graph (hī′drə-grăf′, -gräf′) *n.* A graph showing seasonal variations of level, flow, or velocity in a body of water. [HYDRO- + -GRAPH.]

hy·drog·ra·phy (hī-drŏg′rə-fē) *n., pl.* **-phies. 1.** The scientific study, description, and analysis of the physical conditions, boundaries, flow, and related characteristics of oceans, seas, and coastlines, and their winds. **2. a.** The mapping of such bodies of water. **b.** Maps or charts of such bodies of water. [Old French *hydrographie* : HYDRO- + -GRAPHY.] —**hy·drog·ra·pher** *n.* —**hy·dro·graph·ic** (hī′drə-grăf′ĭk) *adj.* —**hy·dro·graph·i·cal·ly** *adv.*

hy·droid (hī′droid′ *n.* **1.** Any of numerous characteristically colonial hydrozoan coelenterates of the order Hydroida, having a polyp rather than a medusoid form as the dominant stage of the life cycle. The order includes the hydra, one of the few solitary hydroids.

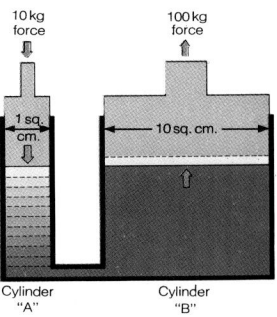

hydraulics *All hydraulic systems work on much the same principle as a lever. Moderate force exerted on a piston in a narrow liquid-filled cylinder (A) is transformed into much greater force on a broader piston in a connecting cylinder (B). If the second piston is ten times the area of the first, the force is multiplied tenfold but the second piston moves only one-tenth the distance.*

2. The asexual, hydralike polyp in the life cycle of any hydrozoan. ~*adj.* Of, pertaining to, or characteristic of a hydroid. [HYDR(A) (genus name) + -OID.]

hy·dro·ki·net·ic (hī′drō-kĭ-nĕt′ĭk, -kī-nĕt′ĭk) *adj.* **1.** Of or pertaining to hydrokinetics. **2.** Of or pertaining to the kinetic energy and motion of fluids.

hy·dro·ki·net·ics (hī′drō-kĭ-nĕt′ĭks, -kī-nĕt′ĭks) *n.* *Used with a singular verb.* The kinetics of fluids, especially incompressible fluids, in motion.

hy·dro·lase (hī′drə-lās′, -lāz′) *n.* Any of a group of enzymes that catalyze hydrolysis reactions by causing the addition or removal of a molecule of water. [HYDROL(YSIS) + -ASE.]

hydrologic cycle *n.* A water cycle (see).

hy·drol·o·gy (hī-drŏl′ə-jē) *n.* The scientific study of the properties, distribution, and effects of water and ice on the earth's land surface, in the soil and underlying rocks, and in the atmosphere. [New Latin *hydrologia* : HYDRO- + -LOGY.] —**hy·dro·log·ic** (hī′drə-lŏj′-ĭk), **hy·dro·log·i·cal** *adj.* —**hy·dro·log·i·cal·ly** *adv.* —**hy·drol·o·gist** (hī-drŏl′ə-jĭst) *n.*

hy·drol·y·sate (hī-drŏl′ə-sāt′, hī′drə-lī′sāt′) *n.* A product of hydrolysis. [HYDROLYS(IS) + -ATE.]

hy·drol·y·sis (hī-drŏl′ə-sĭs) *n.* Decomposition of a chemical compound by reaction with water, such as the dissociation of a dissolved salt or the catalytic conversion of glucose to starch. [HYDRO- + -LYSIS.] —**hy·dro·lyt·ic** (hī′drə-lĭt′ĭk) *adj.* —**hy·dro·lyt·i·cal·ly** *adv.*

hy·dro·lyte (hī′drə-līt′) *n.* A substance that is hydrolyzed. [HYDRO- + -LYTE.]

hy·dro·lyze (hī′drə-līz′) *v.* **-lyzed, -lyzing, -lyzes.** —*tr.* To subject to hydrolysis. —*intr.* To undergo hydrolysis. [From HYDROLYSIS.] —**hy·dro·lyz·a·ble** *adj.* —**hy·dro·ly·za·tion** (hī′drə-lī-zā′shən) *n.*

hy·dro·man·cy (hī′drə-măn′sē) *n.* Divination by means of signs appearing in water. [Middle English *ydromancy,* from Old French *hydromancie,* from Latin *hydromantīa,* from Greek *hydromanteia* (unattested) : HYDRO- + -MANCY.] —**hy·dro·man·cer** *n.* —**hy·dro·man·tic** (hī′drə-măn′tĭk) *adj.*

hy·dro·mag·net·ics (hī′drō-măg-nĕt′ĭks) *n.* *Used with a singular verb.* **Magnetohydrodynamics** (see).

hy·dro·me·chan·ics (hī′drō-mĭ-kăn′ĭks) *n.* *Used with a singular verb.* **Hydrodynamics** (see).

hy·dro·me·du·sa (hī′drō-mə-dōō′sə, -dyōō′sə) *n.,* *pl.* **-sas** or **-sae** (-sē′). A hydrozoan in its medusan stage. See **medusa.** —**hy·dro·me·du·san** *adj.*

hy·dro·mel (hī′drə-mĕl′) *n.* A liquid composed of honey and water that after fermentation is called mead. [Middle English *ydromel,* from Old French, from Late Latin *hydromel,* from Latin *hydromeli,* from Greek *hudromeli* : HYDRO- + *meli,* honey.]

hy·dro·met·al·lur·gy (hī′drō-mĕt′l-ûr′jē) *n.* The separation of metal from ores and ore concentrates by chemical reactions in aqueous solution, such as leaching, extraction, and precipitation. —**hy·dro·met·al·lur·gi·cal** (hī′drō-mĕt′l-ûr′jĭ-kəl) *adj.*

hy·dro·me·te·or (hī′drō-mē′tē-ər, -ôr′) *n.* A precipitation body, such as rain, snow, sleet, or hail, derived from the condensation of water in the atmosphere.

hy·dro·me·te·or·ol·o·gy (hī′drō-mē′tē-ə-rŏl′ə-jē) *n.* The meteorology of the occurrence, motion, and changes of atmospheric water.

hy·drom·e·ter (hī-drŏm′ə-tər) *n.* An instrument used to determine specific gravity; especially, a sealed, graduated tube, weighted at one end, that sinks in a fluid to a depth used as a measure of the fluid's specific gravity. —**hy·dro·met·ric** (hī′drə-mĕt′rĭk), **hy·dro·met·ri·cal** *adj.* —**hy·dro·met·ri·cal·ly** *adv.* —**hy·drom·e·try** (hī-drŏm′ə-trē) *n.*

hy·dro·ni·um (hī-drō′nē-əm) *n.* A hydrated hydrogen ion, H_3O^+. Also called "hydronium ion," "hydroxonium ion." [HYDR(O)- + (AMM)ONIUM.]

hy·drop·a·thy (hī-drŏp′ə-thē) *n.* The therapeutic use of water, both internally and externally. Also called "water cure." [HYDRO- + -PATHY.] —**hy·dro·path·ic** (hī′drə-păth′ĭk), **hy·dro·path·i·cal** *adj.* —**hy·dro·path·ist** (hī-drŏp′ə-thĭst), **hy·dro·path** (hī′drə-păth′) *n.*

hy·dro·per·i·car·di·um (hī′drō-pĕr′ĭ-kär′dē-əm) *n.* Excessive serous fluid within the pericardium.

hy·dro·phane (hī′drə-fān′) *n.* An opal that is almost opaque when dry, but transparent when wet. [HYDRO- + -PHANE.]

hy·dro·phil·ic (hī′drə-fĭl′ĭk) *adj.* Having an affinity for water; absorbing, tending to combine with, or capable of dissolving in or being wetted by water. [New Latin *hydrophilus,* HYDROPHILOUS.] —**hy·dro·phile** (hī′drə-fīl′) *n.*

hy·droph·i·lous (hī-drŏf′ə-ləs) *adj. Botany.* **1.** Growing or thriving in water; hydrophytic. **2.** Having water as a pollinating agent. [New Latin *hydrophilus* : HYDRO- + -PHILOUS.]

hy·droph·i·ly (hī-drŏf′ə-lē) *n. Botany.* Pollination by water. [HYDRO- + -PHILY.]

hy·dro·pho·bi·a (hī′drə-fō′bē-ə) *n.* **1.** Fear of water; especially, an abnormal aversion to drinking water. **2. Rabies** (see). [Late Latin, from Greek *hudrophobia* : HYDRO- + -PHOBIA.]

hy·dro·pho·bic (hī′drə-fō′bĭk, -fŏb′ĭk) *adj.* **1.** Antagonistic to, shedding, tending not to combine with, or incapable of dissolving in water. **2.** Of or exhibiting hydrophobia.

hy·dro·phone (hī′drə-fōn′) *n.* An electrical instrument for detecting or monitoring sound under water. [HYDRO- + -PHONE.]

hy·dro·phyte (hī′drə-fīt′) *n.* A plant that grows in an aquatic or very wet environment. Compare **mesophyte, xerophyte.** [HYDRO- + -PHYTE.] —**hy·dro·phyt·ic** (hī′drə-fĭt′ĭk) *adj.*

hydroplane *The hull of a high-performance boat is designed to provide lift so that at top speed the boat "planes" across the surface.*

hy·dro·plane (hī′drə-plān′) *n.* **1.** A seaplane. **2.** A motorboat designed so that the prow and much of the hull lift out of the water and skim the surface at high speeds. **3.** A hydrofoil (see). **4.** A horizontal rudder on a submarine.
~*intr.v.* **hydroplaned, -planing, -planes. 1.** To drive or ride in a hydroplane. **2. a.** To skim along on the surface of the water. **b.** To be or go out of control by skimming along the surface of a wet road. Used of an automobile.

hy·dro·pon·ics (hī′drə-pŏn′ĭks) *n.* *Used with a singular verb.* The cultivation of plants in gravel or other soilless substances through which water containing dissolved inorganic nutrients is pumped. Also called "aquiculture." [HYDRO- + (GEO)PONICS.] —**hy·dro·pon·ic** *adj.* —**hy·dro·pon·i·cal·ly** *adv.*

hy·dro·qui·none (hī′drō-kwĭ-nōn′, -kwĭn′ōn′) *n.* Also **hy·dro·quin·ol** (-kwĭn′ôl′, -ōl′). A white crystalline compound, $C_6H_4(OH)_2$, used as a photographic developer, antioxidant, stabilizer, and reagent.

hy·dro·scope (hī′drə-skōp′) *n.* An optical device used for viewing objects much below the surface of water. [HYDRO- + -SCOPE.] —**hy·dro·scop·ic** (hī′drə-skŏp′ĭk) *adj.*

hy·dro·ski (hī′drō-skē′) *n.* A form of hydrofoil on some seaplanes, used to provide extra lift to assist in taking off.

hy·dro·sol (hī′drə-sôl′, -sŏl′) *n.* A sol with water as the dispersing medium. [HYDRO- + SOL(UTION).] —**hy·dro·sol·ic** (hī′drə-sŏl′ĭk) *adj.*

hy·dro·sphere (hī′drə-sfîr′) *n.* The waters of the earth distinguished from the lithosphere and the atmosphere. —**hy·dro·spher·ic** (hī′drə-sfîr′ĭk, -sfĕr′ĭk) *adj.*

hy·dro·stat (hī′drə-stăt′, hī′drō-) *n.* A device that detects the presence or absence of water, used especially in steam boilers to prevent them from boiling dry. [HYDRO- + -STAT.]

hy·dro·stat·ic (hī′drə-stăt′ĭk) *adj.* Also **hy·dro·stat·i·cal** (-ĭ-kəl). Of or pertaining to hydrostatics. —**hy·dro·stat·i·cal·ly** *adv.*

hy·dro·stat·ics (hī′drə-stăt′ĭks) *n.* *Used with a singular verb.* The statics of fluids, especially incompressible fluids.

hy·dro·sul·fate (hī′drə-sŭl′fāt′) *n.* A salt formed by the union of sulfuric acid with an alkaloid or other organic base.

hy·dro·sul·fide (hī′drə-sŭl′fīd′) *n.* A chemical compound derived from hydrogen sulfide by replacement of one of the hydrogen atoms with a basic radical or base.

hy·dro·sul·fite (hī′drə-sŭl′fīt′) *n.* **1.** A salt of hyposulfurous acid. **2.** A bleaching agent, **sodium hydrosulfite** (see).

hy·dro·sul·fu·rous acid (hī′drō-sŭl-fyŏŏr′əs, -sŭl′fər-əs) *n.* **Hyposulfurous acid** (see).

hy·dro·tax·is (hī′drō-tăk′sĭs) *n. Biology.* Movement of an organism or cell in response to moisture. [New Latin : HYDRO- + -TAXIS.] —**hy·dro·tac·tic** (hī′drō-tăk′tĭk) *adj.*

hy·dro·ther·a·peu·tics (hī′drō-thĕr′ə-pyōō′tĭks) *n.* *Used with a singular verb.* Hydrotherapy. —**hy·dro·ther·a·peu·tic** *adj.*

hy·dro·ther·a·py (hī′drō-thĕr′ə-pē) *n.,* *pl.* **-pies.** The medical use of water in the treatment of certain diseases; especially, the exercising of diseased joints and muscles in remedial swimming pools. —**hy·dro·ther·a·pist** *n.*

hy·dro·ther·mal (hī′drō-thûr′məl) *adj.* **1.** Of or pertaining to hot water. **2.** *Geology.* **a.** Of or pertaining to hot magmatic emanations rich in water. **b.** Of or pertaining to the rocks, ore deposits, and springs produced by such emanations. —**hy·dro·ther·mal·ly** *adv.*

hy·dro·tho·rax (hī′drō-thôr′ăks′, -thōr′ăks′) *n.* The presence of serous fluid from the blood in one or both pleural cavities, often associated with cardiac failure.

hy·drot·ro·pism (hī-drŏt′rə-pĭz′əm) *n. Botany.* Growth of a plant part toward or away from water. [HYDRO- + -TROPISM.] —**hy·dro·trop·ic** (hī′drə-trŏp′ĭk) *adj.* —**hy·dro·trop·i·cal·ly** *adv.*

hy·drous (hī′drəs) *adj.* Containing water, especially that of crystallization or hydration. [HYDR(O)- + -OUS.]

hy·drox·ide (hī-drŏk′sīd′) *n.* A chemical compound containing the hydroxyl group. [HYDR(O)- + OXIDE.]

hydroxide ion *n.* The ion OH⁻, characteristic of basic hydroxides. Also called "hydroxyl ion."

hy·drox·o·ni·um ion (hī-drŏk-sō′nē-əm) *n.* **Hydronium** (see). [HYDROX(Y)- + -ONIUM (ION).]

hy·drox·y (hī-drŏk′sē) *adj.* Containing the hydroxyl group. Often used in combination: *hydroxyproline.* [From HYDROXYL.]

hy·drox·yl (hī-drŏk′sĭl) *n.* The univalent radical or group OH, characteristic of bases, certain acids, phenols, alcohols, carboxylic and sulfonic acids, and amphoteric compounds. [HYDR(O)- + OX(YGEN) + -YL.] —**hy·drox·yl·ic** (hī′drŏk-sĭl′ĭk) *adj.*

hy·drox·yl·a·mine (hī-drŏk′sə-lə-mēn′, hī′drŏk-sĭl′ə-mēn′) *n.* A colorless, crystalline compound, NH_2OH, explosive when heated above 130°C, that is used as a reducing agent and in organic synthesis.

hy·drox·y·pro·line (hī-drŏk′sĭ-prō′lēn′, -lĭn) *n.* An amino acid, $C_5H_9NO_3$, occurring in proteins, particularly collagen.

hy·drox·y·tryp·ta·mine (hī-drŏk′sĭ-trĭp′tə-mēn′, -mĭn) *n.* **Serotonin** (see).

hy·dro·zo·an (hī′drə-zō′ən) *n.* Any of numerous coelenterates of the class Hydrozoa, which includes the hydras, polyps, and Portuguese men-of-war. ~*adj.* Of, pertaining to, or belonging to the class Hydrozoa. [New Latin *Hydrozoa* : HYDRO- + -ZOAN.]

Hy·drus (hī′drəs) *n.* A southern constellation near Tucana and Mensa. [Latin, "water serpent," from Greek *hudros.*]

hy·e·na, hy·ae·na (hī-ē′nə) *n.* Any of several carnivorous mammals of the genera *Hyaena* or *Crocuta* of Africa and Asia, having powerful jaws and relatively short hind limbs. [Middle English *hyene*, from Latin *hyaena*, from Greek *huaina*, from *hus*, swine.]

hy·e·tal (hī′ə-təl) *adj.* Of or relating to rain or to rainy regions. [Greek *huetos*, rain, a heavy shower.]

hy·e·to·graph (hī′ə-tə-grăf′, -gräf′) *n.* **1.** A self-recording device for measuring rainfall. **2.** A rainfall chart. [Greek *huetos*, rain + -GRAPH.] **—hy·e·to·graph·ic** (hī′ə-tə-grăf′ĭk) *adj.* **—hy·e·tog·ra·phy** (hī′ə-tŏg′rə-fē) *n.*

Hy·gie·ia (hī-jē′ə). *Greek Mythology.* The goddess of health. [Greek *Hugieia*, from *hugiēs*, health, from *hugiēs*, healthy.]

hy·giene (hī′jēn′) *n.* **1.** The science of health and the prevention of disease. Also called "hygienics." **2.** Conditions and practices that serve to promote or preserve health. [French *hygiène*, earlier *hygiaine*, from New Latin *hygieina*, from Greek *hugieinē*, feminine of *hugieinos*, healthful, from *hugiēs*, healthy.]

hy·gi·en·ic (hī′jē-ĕn′ĭk, hī-jĕn′-) *adj.* **1.** Of or pertaining to hygiene. **2.** Sanitary. **3.** Tending to promote or preserve health. **—hy·gi·en·i·cal·ly** *adv.*

hy·gi·en·ics (hī′jē-ĕn′ĭks, hī-jĕn′-) *n. Used with a singular verb.* See **hygiene** (sense 1).

hy·gien·ist (hī-jē′nĭst, hī′jē′nĭst, hī-jĕn′ĭst) *n.* **1.** A specialist in hygiene. **2.** A **dental hygienist** (*see*).

hygro– *prefix.* Indicates wet, moist, or moisture; for example, **hygrograph.** [Greek *hugros*, wet, moist.]

hy·gro·graph (hī′grə-grăf′, -gräf′) *n.* An automatic hygrometer that records variations in atmospheric humidity. [HYGRO- + -GRAPH.]

hy·grom·e·ter (hī-grŏm′ə-tər) *n.* Any of several instruments that measure atmospheric humidity. [HYGRO- + -METER.] **—hy·gro·met·ric** (hī′grə-mĕt′rĭk) *adj.* **—hy·grom·e·try** (hī-grŏm′ə-trē) *n.*

hy·groph·i·lous (hī-grŏf′ə-ləs) *adj.* Growing in moist places. Said of certain plants. **—hy·gro·phile** (hī′grə-fīl′) *n.*

hy·gro·scope (hī′grə-skōp′) *n.* An instrument that measures changes in atmospheric moisture. [HYGRO- + -SCOPE.]

hy·gro·scop·ic (hī′grə-skŏp′ĭk) *adj.* Readily absorbing moisture, as from the atmosphere. [HYGROSCOP(E) + -IC.] **—hy·gro·scop·i·cal·ly** *adv.* **—hy·gro·sco·pic·i·ty** (hī′grə-skō-pĭs′ə-tē) *n.*

hy·gro·stat (hī′grə-stăt′) *n.* A **humidistat** (*see*). [HYGRO- + -STAT.]

hy·ing. Alternate present participle of **hie.**

hy·lic (hī′lĭk) *adj. Rare.* Of or pertaining to matter. [Late Latin *hylicus*, from Greek *hulikos*, from *hulē*, matter.]

hylo– *prefix.* Indicates matter; for example, **hylotheism.** [Greek *hulē*, matter, wood.]

hy·lo·mor·phism (hī′lə-môr′fĭz′əm) *n.* The philosophical doctrine that matter, as opposed to spirit, is the first cause of the universe. [HYLO- + -MORPHISM.]

hy·lo·the·ism (hī′lə-thē′ĭz′əm) *n.* The philosophical doctrine that matter and God are identical.

hy·lo·zo·ism (hī′lə-zō′ĭz′əm) *n.* The philosophical doctrine that life is a property or derivative of matter or that life and matter are inseparable. [Greek *hulē*, wood + ZO(O)- + -ISM.] **—hy·lo·zo·ic**, **hy·lo·zo·is·tic** (hī′lə-zō-ĭs′tĭk) *adj.* **—hy·lo·zo·ist** *n.*

hy·men (hī′mən) *n.* A membranous fold of tissue partly or completely blocking the external vaginal orifice. [Latin *hymēn*, from Greek *humēn*, membrane.] **—hy·men·al** *adj.*

Hy·men (hī′mən). *Greek Mythology.* The god of marriage. [Latin, from Greek *Humēn†.*]

hy·me·ne·al (hī′mə-nē′əl) *adj.* Of or pertaining to a wedding or marriage; nuptial.
~*n.* A wedding song or poem. [Latin *hymenaeus*, from Greek *humēnaios*, bridal song, wedding, from *Humēn*, HYMEN.]

hy·me·ni·um (hī-mē′nē-əm) *n., pl.* **-nia** (-nē-ə) *or* **-ums.** The spore-bearing layer of the fruiting body of certain fungi, containing basidia. [New Latin, from HYMEN.]

hy·me·nop·ter·an (hī′mə-nŏp′tər-ən) *n., pl.* **-tera** (-tər-ə) *or* **-terans.** Also **hy·me·nop·ter·on** (-tə-rŏn′) *pl.* **-tera** *or* **-terons.** Any insect of the order Hymenoptera, characteristically having two pairs of membranous wings and an ovipositor modified as a sting or drill, and including the bees, wasps, and ants.
~*adj.* Also **hy·me·nop·ter·ous** (-tər-əs). Of or belonging to the Hymenoptera. [New Latin *Hymenoptera*, from Greek *humenopteros*, "membrane-wing" : *humēn*, membrane, HYMEN + -PTEROUS.]

hymn (hĭm) *n.* **1.** A song of praise or thanksgiving to God. **2.** Any song of praise or joy; a paean.
~*v.* **hymned, hymning, hymns.** —*tr.* **1.** To praise, glorify, or worship in a hymn. **2.** To express in a hymn. —*intr.* To sing hymns. [Middle English *ymne, imne,* from Old French *ymne,* from Latin *hymnus,* from Greek *humnos†,* hymn, ode of praise of gods or heroes.]

hym·nal (hĭm′nəl) *n.* A book or collection of church hymns. Also called "hymnbook."
~*adj.* Of or pertaining to a hymn or hymns. [Middle English *hymnale,* from Medieval Latin *hymnāle,* from Latin *hymnus,* HYMN.]

hym·nist (hĭm′nĭst) *n.* Also **hym·no·dist** (hĭm′nə-dĭst) A composer of hymns.

hym·no·dy (hĭm′nə-dē) *n., pl.* **-dies.** **1.** The singing of hymns. **2.** The composing of hymns. **3.** The hymns of a particular period or church. [Medieval Latin *hymnōdia,* from Greek *humnōidia* : *humnos,* HYMN + *ōidē,* song.]

hym·nol·o·gy (hĭm-nŏl′ə-jē) *n.* **1.** The composition of hymns. **2.** The study of hymns. [Greek *humnologia,* "hymn-singing" : *humnōs,* HYMN + -LOGY.] **—hym·no·log·ic** (hĭm′nə-lŏj′ĭk), **hym·no·log·i·cal** *adj.* **—hym·nol·o·gist** (hĭm-nŏl′ə-jĭst) *n.*

hy·oid bone (hī′oid′) *n.* A U-shaped bone between the mandible and the larynx at the base of the tongue. Also called "hyoid." [French *hyoïde,* from New Latin *hyoides,* from Greek *huoeides,* "in the form of an upsilon" : *hu,* name of the letter upsilon + -OID.] **—hy·oid, hy·oid·e·an** (hī-oi′dē-ən) *adj.*

hy·o·man·dib·u·lar (hī′ō-măn-dĭb′yə-lər) *n.* A U-shaped bone in fishes that attaches the jaw to the skull. [*Hyo-,* from Greek *hu,* upsilon (referring to the shape of the bone) + MANDIBULAR.]

hy·o·scine (hī′ə-sēn′) *n.* A drug, **scopolamine** (*see*). [German *Hyoscin,* from New Latin *Hyoscyamus,* genus of henbane from which it is obtained, from Greek *huoskuamos* : *huos,* genitive of *hus,* pig + *kuamos†,* bean.]

hy·o·scy·a·mine (hī′ə-sī′ə-mēn′) *n.* A poisonous white crystalline alkaloid, $C_{17}H_{23}NO_3$, isomeric with atropine and used as an antispasmodic, analgesic, and sedative. [New Latin *Hyoscyamus.* See **hyoscine.**]

hyp. **1.** hypotenuse. **2.** hypothesis.

hyp–. Variant of **hypo-.**

hyp·a·bys·sal (hĭp′ə-bĭs′əl, hī′pə-) *adj.* Solidifying chiefly as a minor intrusion, especially as a dike or sill, before reaching the earth's surface. Said of rocks. [HYP(O)- + ABYSSAL.]

hy·pae·thral (hī-pē′thrəl) *adj.* Open to the sky; roofless: *an ancient hypaethral temple.* [Latin *hypaethrus,* from Greek *hupaithros* : *hupo-,* beneath + *aithēr,* sky.]

hypesthesia. Variant of **hypoesthesia.**

hy·pan·thi·um (hī-păn′thē-əm, hī-) *n., pl.* **-thia** (-thē-ə). The cup-shaped or flattened floral receptacle of various plants, having the gynoecium at the center and the other flower parts around the rim. [New Latin : HYP(O)- + ANTH(O)- + -IUM.] **—hy·pan·thi·al** *adj.*

hype¹ (hīp) *n. Slang.* **1.** Deception. **2.** Deceptively inflated advertising or promotion. **3.** A promotional gimmick or campaign.
~*tr.v.* **hyped, hyping, hypes.** *Slang.* To publicize, promote, or exploit by touting and often overrating: *hyping a new film.* [20th century (originally, to shortchange, swindle) : origin obscure.]

hype² *n. Slang.* **1.** A hypodermic injection, syringe, or needle. **2.** A drug addict.
~*tr.v.* **hyped, hyping, hypes.** *Slang.* To stimulate with or as if with an injection of a drug. Sometimes used with *up: The pep talk hyped up the team.* [Short for HYPODERMIC.]

hyper– *prefix.* Indicates: **1.** Over, above, or in great amount; for example, **hypersonic. 2.** In abnormal excess; for example, **hyperacid. 3.** To an excessive degree; for example, **hypercritical.** [Greek *huper,* over, above, beyond, exceeding.]

hy·per·a·cid·i·ty (hī′pər-ə-sĭd′ə-tē) *n.* Excessive acidity, especially of the gastric juices in the stomach. **—hy·per·ac·id** (hī′pər-ăs′ĭd) *adj.*

hy·per·ac·tive (hī′pər-ăk′tĭv) *adj.* Excessively or abnormally active.

hyperaemia Variant of **hyperemia.**

hyperaesthesia Variant of **hyperesthesia.**

hy·per·bar·ic (hī′pər-băr′ĭk) *adj.* Of, pertaining to, producing, operating at, or occurring at pressures higher than normal atmospheric pressure: *a hyperbaric chamber.* [HYPER- + BAR(O)- + -IC.]

hy·per·bo·la (hī-pûr′bə-lə) *n., pl.* **-las** *or* **-lae** (-lē). *Geometry.* A plane curve having two branches, formed by: **1.** A conic section intersecting both halves of a right circular cone. **2.** The locus of points related to two given points such that the difference in the distances of each point from the two given points is a constant. [New Latin, from Greek *huperbolē,* "a throwing beyond," excess (when a hyperbola is formed from a conic section, the angle made by the base of the cone and the intersecting plane is greater than the angle formed by a parabola), from *huperballein,* "to throw beyond," exceed : *huper-,* beyond + *ballein,* to throw.]

hy·per·bo·le (hī-pûr′bə-le) *n.* Exaggeration or extravagant statement used as a figure of speech, as *I could sleep for a year* or *This book weighs a ton.* [Earlier *yperbole,* from Latin *hyperbolē,* from Greek *huperbolē,* excess. See **hyperbola.**]

hy·per·bol·ic (hī′pər-bŏl′ĭk) *adj.* Also **hy·per·bol·i·cal** (-ĭ-kəl). **1.** Of, pertaining to, or employing hyperbole. **2.** *Mathematics.* **a.** Of, pertaining to, or having the form of a hyperbola. **b.** Based on or having a metric that is a hyperbola: *hyperbolic geometry.* **c.** Of or pertaining to a hyperbolic function: *hyperbolic cosine.* **—hy·per·bol·i·cal·ly** *adv.*

hyperbolic function *n. Mathematics.* Any of a set of six functions that are related, for a real variable *z*, to the hyperbola in a manner analogous to the relationship of the trigonometric functions to a circle, including: **1.** *Symbol* **sinh** The *hyperbolic sine,* defined by the equation $\sinh z = \frac{1}{2}(e^z - e^{-z})$. **2.** *Symbol* **cosh** The *hyperbolic cosine,* defined by the equation $\cosh z + \frac{1}{2}(e^z + e^{-z})$. **3.** *Symbol* **tanh** The *hyperbolic tangent,* defined by the equation $\tanh z + \sinh z/\cosh z$. **4.** *Symbol* **coth** The *hyperbolic cotangent,* defined by the equation $\coth z + \cosh z/\sinh z$. **5.** *Symbol* **sech** The *hyperbolic secant,* defined by the equation $\operatorname{sech} z = 1/\cosh z$. **6.** *Symbol* **cosech** *or* **csch** The *hyperbolic cosecant,* defined by the equation $\operatorname{cosech} z = 1/\sinh z$.

hyperbolic paraboloid *n.* See **paraboloid.**

hy·per·bo·lism (hī-pûr′bə-lĭz′əm) *n.* **1.** The use of hyperbole. **2.** A hyperbole.

hy·per·bo·lize (hī-pûr′bə-līz′) *v.* **-lized, -lizing, -lizes.** —*intr.* To use hyperbole; exaggerate. —*tr.* To express with hyperbole; exaggerate.

hy·per·bo·loid (hī-pûr′bə-loid′) *n. Geometry.* Either of two quadric surfaces having a finite center with certain plane sections that are hyperbolas and others that are ellipses or circles.

hy·per·bo·re·an (hī′pər-bôr′ē-ən, -bōr′ē-ən, -bə-rē′ən) *adj.* **1.** Of or pertaining to the far north; arctic. **2.** Very cold; frigid. [Latin *Hyperborei,* HYPERBOREAN.]

Hy·per·bo·re·an (hī′pər-bôr′ē-ən, -bōr′ē-ən, -bə-rē′ən) *n. Greek Mythology.* A member of a people known to the ancient Greeks from the earliest times, living in an unidentified country in the far north and renowned as pious and divinely favored adherents of the cult of Apollo. —*adj.* Of or pertaining to the Hyperboreans. [Latin *Hyperborei,* from Greek *Huperboreoi* (plural) : *huper-,* beyond, extreme + *boreios,* northern, from *Boreas,* "north wind," north.]

hy·per·cap·ni·a (hī′pər-kăp′nē-ə) *n.* The presence of an abnormally high carbon dioxide concentration in the blood. Also called "hypercarbia." [HYPER- + *-capnia,* from Greek *kapnos,* smoke.]

hy·per·cat·a·lex·is (hī′pər-kăt′l-ĕk′sĭs) *n.* The addition of one or more syllables in excess of the normal number in the last foot of a line of verse. [New Latin : HYPER- + *catalexis,* omission in the last foot of a line, from Greek *katalēxis,* from *katalēgein,* to leave off (see **catalectic**).] —**hy·per·cat·a·lec·tic** (hī′pər-kăt′l-ĕk′tĭk) *adj.*

hy·per·charge (hī′pər-chärj′) *n. Symbol* **Y** *Physics.* A quantum number numerically equal to twice the average electric charge of a particle multiplet or, equivalently, to the sum of the strangeness and the baryon number.

hy·per·cor·rec·tion (hī′pər-kə-rĕk′shən) *n.* Mispronunciation of words or use of incorrect grammatical constructions as a result of trying to avoid nonstandard speech forms. —**hy·per·cor·rect** (hī′pər-kə-rĕkt′) *adj.* —**hy·per·cor·rect·ly** *adv.*

hy·per·crit·i·cal (hī′pər-krĭt′ĭ-kəl) *adj.* Overcritical; especially, excessively critical about trivial matters. —**hy·per·crit·i·cal·ly** *adv.* —**hy·per·crit·i·cism** (hī′pər-krĭt′ə-sĭz′əm) *n.*

hy·per·du·li·a (hī′pər-dōō′lē-ə, -dyōō′lē-ə) *n.* In the Roman Catholic and Eastern Orthodox churches, the special reverence given to the Virgin Mary. Compare **dulia, latria.** [Medieval Latin : HYPER- + DULIA.] —**hy·per·du·lic** (hī′pər-dōō′lĭk, -dyōō′lĭk), **hy·per·du·li·cal** (-lĭ-kəl) *adj.*

hy·per·e·mi·a, hy·per·ae·mi·a (hī′pər-ē′mē-ə) *n.* The presence of an excessive amount of blood in the vessels supplying a particular organ of the body. [HYPER- + -EMIA.] —**hy·per·e·mic** (hī′pər-ē′mĭk) *adj.*

hy·per·es·the·sia, hy·per·aes·the·sia (hī′pər-ĕs-thē′zhə, -zhē-ə) *n. Pathology.* Abnormally high sensitivity, especially of the skin, to touch, heat, cold, or pain. [New Latin : HYPER- + ESTHESIA.] —**hy·per·es·thet·ic** (hī′pər-ĕs-thĕt′ĭk) *adj.*

hy·per·eu·tec·tic (hī′pər-yōō-tĕk′tĭk) *adj. Chemistry.* Having the minor component present in a larger amount than in the eutectic composition of the same components. Said of mixtures.

hy·per·ex·ten·sion (hī′pər-ĭk-stĕn′shən) *n.* Extension of a limb beyond normal limits, usually as part of an orthopedic exercise.

hy·per·fine structure (hī′pər-fīn′) *n. Abbr.* **hfs** *Physics.* The splitting of a spectral line into two or more components as a result of the spin or magnetic moment of the atomic nucleus.

hy·per·ga·my (hī-pûr′gə-mē) *n.* The practice or state of being married to a person of equal or superior rank, caste, or class. [HYPER- + -GAMY.] —**hy·per·ga·mous** *adj.*

hy·per·gly·ce·mi·a (hī′pər-glī-sē′mē-ə) *n.* The presence of an abnormally high concentration of glucose in the blood, as occurs in diabetes. —**hy·per·gly·ce·mic** (hī′pər-glī-sē′mĭk) *adj.*

hy·per·gol·ic (hī′pər-gŏl′ĭk) *adj.* Igniting spontaneously on contact with an oxidizer. Said of a rocket fuel. [German *Hypergol* : HYP(ER)- + Greek *ergon,* work + -OL(E) + -IC.]

hy·per·i·cum (hī-pĕr′ĭ-kəm) *n.* Any plant of the genus *Hypericum,* which includes **Saint John's wort** and **rose of Sharon** *(both of which see).* [New Latin *Hypericum* (genus), from Greek *hupereikon* : HYPER- + *ereikē,* heath.]

hy·per·in·su·lin·ism (hī′pər-ĭn′sə-lə-nĭz′əm) *n.* The presence of abnormally large quantities of insulin in the blood, resulting in hypoglycemia.

Hy·pe·ri·on[1] (hī-pîr′ē-ən). *Greek Mythology.* A Titan, the son of Gaea and Uranus and father of Helios, the sun god.

Hyperion[2]. One of the smallest satellites of the planet Saturn.

hy·per·ker·a·to·sis (hī′pər-kĕr′ə-tō′sĭs) *n.* Hypertrophy of the horny, outer layer of the skin. [New Latin : HYPER- + Greek *keras* (stem *kerat-*), horn + -OSIS.] —**hy·per·ker·a·tot·ic** (hī′pər-kĕr′ə-tŏt′ĭk) *adj.*

hy·per·ki·ne·sia (hī′pər-kĭ-nē′zhə, -zhē-ə) *n.* Also **hy·per·ki·ne·sis** (-nē′sĭs). Pathologically excessive restlessness, occurring particularly in children as a symptom of certain disorders. [New Latin : HYPER- + Greek *kinēsis,* movement, from *kinein,* to move.] —**hy·per·ki·net·ic** (hī′pər-kĭ-nĕt′ĭk) *adj.*

hy·per·mar·ket (hī′pər-mär′kĭt) *n. Chiefly British.* A very large self-service store, similar to a supermarket but usually selling a wider variety of goods. [From French *hypermarché.* See **hyper-, market.**]

hy·per·me·ter (hī-pûr′mə-tər) *n.* **1.** A verse or metric line having one or more syllables in excess of the normal number. **2.** An extra syllable. —**hy·per·met·ric** (hī′pər-mĕt′rĭk), **hy·per·met·ri·cal** *adj.*

hy·per·me·tro·pi·a (hī′pər-mə-trō′pē-ə) *n. Pathology.* Hyperopia *(see).* [New Latin, from Greek *hupermetros,* beyond measure, excessive : *huper-,* beyond, excessive + *metron,* measure + -OPIA.] —**hy·per·me·trop·ic** (hī′pər-mə-trŏp′ĭk), **hy·per·me·trop·i·cal** *adj.* —**hy·per·me·tro·py** (hī′pər-mĕt′rə-pē) *n.*

hy·perm·ne·sia (hī′pərm-nē′zhə, -zhē-ə) *n.* Unusually exact or vivid memory. [New Latin : HYPER- + (A)MNESIA.]

hy·per·mo·til·i·ty (hī′pər-mō-tĭl′ə-tē) *n.* Abnormally increased movement, especially of the stomach or intestines.

hy·per·ne·phro·ma (hī′pər-nĭ-frō′mə) *n., pl.* **-mas** or **-mata** (-mə-tə). A type of malignant tumor of the kidney.

hy·per·on (hī′pə-rŏn′) *n. Physics.* A subatomic particle with mass greater than the nucleon, decaying into a nucleon or another hyperon and lighter particles and having $2I + 1$ charge states, where I is the isospin of the particle multiplet. [HYPER- + -ON.]

hy·per·o·pi·a (hī′pə-rō′pē-ə) *n.* A pathological condition of the eye in which entering light rays are focused behind the retina because of a refractive error or because of flattening of the globe of the eye, so that vision is better for distant than for near objects. Also called "hypermetropia," "farsightedness," "long-sightedness." [New Latin : HYPER- + -OPIA.] —**hy·per·ope** (hī′pə-rōp′) *n.* —**hy·per·op·ic** (hī′pə-rŏp′ĭk) *adj.*

hy·per·os·to·sis (hī′pər-ŏ-stō′sĭs) *n.* Excessive or abnormal thickening or growth of bone tissue. [New Latin : HYPER- + OST(EO)- + -OSIS.] —**hy·per·os·tot·ic** (hī′pər-ŏ-stŏt′ĭk) *adj.*

hy·per·par·a·site (hī′pər-păr′ə-sīt′) *n.* An organism that is parasitic on or in another parasite. —**hy·per·par·a·sit·ic** (hī′pər-păr′ə-sĭt′ĭk) *adj.*

hy·per·par·a·thy·roid·ism (hī′pər-păr′ə-thī′roi-dĭz′əm) *n.* An abnormal increase in the activity of the parathyroid glands.

hy·per·phys·i·cal (hī′pər-fĭz′ĭ-kəl) *adj.* Beyond the physical or material; supernatural.

hy·per·pi·tu·i·ta·rism (hī′pər-pī-tōō′ə-tə-rĭz′əm, -tyōō′ə-tə-rĭz′əm) *n.* Pathologically excessive production of anterior pituitary hormone, especially growth hormones, resulting in acromegaly or gigantism. —**hy·per·pi·tu·i·tar·y** (hī′pər-pī-tōō′ə-tĕr′ē, -tyōō′ə-tĕr′ē) *adj.*

hy·per·plane (hī′pər-plān′) *n. Mathematics.* A plane, or an analogue of a plane, with more than three dimensions.

hy·per·pla·sia (hī′pər-plā′zhə, -zhē-ə) *n.* An abnormal increase in the number of cells in an organ or tissue with consequent enlargement of the affected part. [New Latin : HYPER- + -PLASIA.] —**hy·per·plas·tic** (hī′pər-plăs′tĭk) *adj.*

hy·per·ploid (hī′pər-ploid′) *adj. Genetics.* Having a chromosome number in excess of an exact multiple of the normal haploid number. [HYPER- + -PLOID.] —**hy·per·ploid·y** *n.*

hy·perp·ne·a (hī′pərp-nē′ə, hī′pər-) *n.* Abnormally deep and rapid breathing, as after exercise. [New Latin : HYPER- + Greek *pnoia,* breath, from *pnein,* to breathe.]

hy·per·py·rex·i·a (hī′pər-pī-rĕk′sē-ə) *n.* Abnormally high fever, with a body temperature of 106°F (41.1°C) or above; hyperthermia. —**hy·per·py·rex·i·al, hy·per·py·ret·ic** (hī′pər-pī-rĕt′ĭk) *adj.*

hy·per·sen·si·tive (hī′pər-sĕn′sə-tĭv) *adj.* **1.** Abnormally sensitive; especially, oversensitive. **2.** Liable to respond abnormally to the presence of an antigen or drug. —**hy·per·sen·si·tive·ness, hy·per·sen·si·tiv·i·ty** (hī′pər-sĕn′sə-tĭv′ə-tē) *n.*

hy·per·son·ic (hī′pər-sŏn′ĭk) *adj.* Of or pertaining to speed equal to or exceeding five times the speed of sound. —**hy·per·son·i·cal·ly** *adv.* —**hy·per·son·ics** *n.*

hy·per·space (hī′pər-spās′) *n. Mathematics.* Space with more than three dimensions; especially, a four-dimensional space.

hy·per·sthene (hī′pərs-thēn′) *n.* A green, brown, or black splintery, cleavable pyroxene mineral, essentially $(Fe,Mg)_2Si_2O_6$. [French *hypersthène* : HYPER- + Greek *sthenos,* strength.] —**hy·per·sthen·ic** (hī′pərs-thĕn′ĭk) *adj.*

hy·per·ten·sion (hī′pər-tĕn′shən) *n.* **1.** Abnormally high arterial blood pressure. **2.** *Informal.* A state of high emotional tension. —**hy·per·ten·sive** (hī′pər-tĕn′sĭv) *adj. & n.*

hy·per·ther·mi·a (hī′pər-thûr′mē-ə) *n.* Unusually high fever; hyperpyrexia. [New Latin : HYPER- + THERM(O)- + -IA.] —**hy·per·therm·al** (hī′pər-thûr′məl) *adj.*

hy·per·thy·roid·ism (hī′pər-thī′roi-dĭz′əm) *n.* Overactivity of the thyroid gland, resulting in excessive production of thyroid hormones. See **thyrotoxicosis.** —**hy·per·thy·roid** *adj. & n.*

hy·per·ton·ic (hī′pər-tŏn′ĭk) *adj.* **1.** *Pathology.* Having extreme muscular or arterial tension. **2.** *Chemistry.* Having the higher osmotic pressure of two solutions. —**hy·per·to·ni·a** (hī′pər-tō′nē-ə), **hy·per·to·nic·i·ty** (hī′pər-tō-nĭs′ə-tē) *n.*

hy·per·tro·phy (hī-pûr′trə-fē) *n.* Also **hy·per·tro·phi·a** (hī′pər-trō′fē-ə). *Pathology.* Abnormal enlargement of an organ or part as a result of the enlargement without increase in number of its constituent cells. —*v.* **hypertrophied, -phying, -phies.** —*tr.* To cause to grow abnormally large. —*intr.* To grow abnormally large. [HYPER- + -TROPHY.] —**hy·per·troph·ic** (hī′pər-trŏf′ĭk, -trō′fĭk) *adj.*

hy·per·ven·ti·la·tion (hī′pər-vĕnt′l-ā′shən) *n.* Abnormally fast or deep respiration in which excessive quantities of air are taken in, causing buzzing in the ears, tingling of extremities, and sometimes fainting. —**hy·per·ven·ti·late** (hī′pər-vĕnt′l-āt′) *v.*

hy·per·vi·ta·min·o·sis (hī′pər-vī′tə-mə-nō′sĭs) *n.* Any of various abnormal conditions resulting from excessive vitamin intake.

hy·pha (hī′fə) *n., pl.* **-phae** (-fē). Any of the threadlike filaments forming the mycelium of a fungus. [New Latin, from Greek *huphē,* web.] —**hy·phal** *adj.*

hy·phen (hī′fən) *n.* A punctuation mark (-) used to connect the parts of a compound word or name and used between syllables, especially of a word that is split over two consecutive lines. —*tr.v.* **hyphened, -phening, -phens.** To hyphenate. [Late Latin, from Late Greek *huphen,* a sign written below two consecutive letters to show that they belong to the same word, from Greek, in the same word : *hupo-,* under + *hen,* neuter of *heis,* one.]

hy·phen·ate (hī′fə-nāt′) *tr.v.* **-ated, -ating, -ates.** To divide or connect (syllables, words, names, or word elements) with a hyphen. —**hy·phen·a·tion** (hī′fə-nā′shən) *n.*

hy·phen·at·ed (hī′fə-nā′tĭd) *adj. Informal.* Of foreign birth or mixed national origin: *German-Americans and other hyphenated Americans.*

hy·phen·ize (hī′fə-nīz′) *tr.v.* **-ized, -izing, -izes.** To hyphenate. —**hy·phen·i·za·tion** (hī′fə-nə-zā′shən) *n.*

hyp·na·gog·ic, hyp·no·gog·ic (hĭp′nə-gŏj′ĭk, -gō′jĭk) *adj.* **1.** Inducing sleep. **2.** Of or pertaining to the state of drowsiness preceding sleep. [French *hypnagogique* : HYPN(O)- + Greek *agōgos,* leading, from *agein,* to lead.]

hypno–, hypn– *prefix.* Indicates: **1.** Sleep; for example, **hypnopompic. 2.** Hypnosis; for example, **hypnoanalysis, hypnotherapy.** [Greek *hupnos,* sleep.]

hyp·no·a·nal·y·sis (hĭp′nō-ə-năl′ə-sĭs) *n.* A psychoanalytic technique in which hypnosis is used to elicit unconscious material from a patient.

hyp·no·gen·e·sis (hĭp′nō-jĕn′ə-sĭs) *n.* The process of inducing or entering a hypnotic state or sleep. —**hyp·no·ge·net·ic** (hĭp′nō-jə-nĕt′ĭk) *adj.* —**hyp·no·ge·net·i·cal·ly** *adv.*

hyp·noid (hĭp′noid′) *adj.* Also **hyp·noid·al** (hĭp-noid′l). Of or resembling hypnosis or sleep. [HYPN(O)- + -OID.]

hyp·nol·o·gy (hĭp-nŏl′ə-jē) *n.* The scientific study of sleep. [HYPNO- + -LOGY.] —**hyp·no·log·ic** (hĭp′nə-lŏj′ĭk), **hyp·no·log·i·cal** *adj.* —**hyp·nol·o·gist** *n.*

hyp·no·pe·di·a (hĭp′nə-pē′dē-ə) *n.* A method of teaching in which information heard while the learner is asleep is supposed to be retained. [HYPNO- + Greek *paideia,* education, from *pais* (stem *paid-*), boy.] —**hyp·no·pe·dic** *adj.*

hyp·no·pho·bi·a (hĭp′nə-fō′bē-ə) *n.* Abnormal fear of sleep. [New Latin : HYPNO- + -PHOBIA.] —**hyp·no·pho·bic** *adj.*

hyp·no·pom·pic (hĭp′nə-pŏm′pĭk) *adj.* Of or pertaining to the partially conscious state preceding complete awakening. [HYPNO- + Greek *pompē,* a sending off, procession, POMP + -IC.]

Hyp·nos (hĭp′nŏs′). Also **Hyp·nus** (hĭp′nəs). *Greek Mythology.* The god of sleep. [Greek *Hupnos.*]

hyp·no·sis (hĭp-nō′sĭs) *n., pl.* **-ses** (-sēz′). **1.** An artificially induced sleeplike condition in which an individual is extremely responsive to suggestions made by the hypnotist. **2.** Hypnotism. **3.** Any sleeplike condition. [New Latin : Greek *hupnos,* sleep + -OSIS.]

hyp·no·ther·a·py (hĭp′nō-thĕr′ə-pē) *n.* Treatment for mental or physical illness based on or using hypnosis.

hyp·not·ic (hĭp-nŏt′ĭk) *adj.* **1. a.** Of, involving, or inducing hypnosis. **b.** Resembling hypnosis or inducing a state that resembles hypnosis; mesmerizing: *hypnotic music.* **c.** Of, pertaining to, or practicing hypnotism. **2.** Inducing sleep; soporific.
∼*n.* **1. a.** A person who is hypnotized. **b.** A person who can be hypnotized. **2. a.** An agent that causes sleep; a soporific. **b.** An agent used to produce a hypnotic state. [French *hypnotique,* from Late Latin *hypnōticus,* from Greek *hupnōtikos,* sleepy, from *hupnoun,* to put to sleep, from *hupnos,* sleep.] —**hyp·not·i·cal·ly** *adv.*

hyp·no·tism (hĭp′nə-tĭz′əm) *n.* **1.** The theory or practice of inducing hypnosis. **2.** An act of inducing hypnosis.

hyp·no·tist (hĭp′nə-tĭst) *n.* A person who induces hypnosis.

hyp·no·tize (hĭp′nə-tīz′) *tr.v.* **-tized, -tizing, -tizes. 1.** To put in a state of hypnosis. **2.** To fascinate; entrance. —**hyp·no·tiz·a·ble** *adj.* —**hyp·no·ti·za·tion** (hĭp′nə-tə-zā′shən) *n.* —**hyp·no·tiz·er** *n.*

hy·po[1] (hī′pō) *n.* In photography, **sodium thiosulfate** *(see).* [Short for HYPOSULFITE.]

hypo[2] *n., pl.* **-pos.** *Informal.* A hypodermic syringe or injection.

hypo–, hyp– *prefix.* Indicates: **1.** Below or beneath; for example, **hypodermic. 2.** At a lower point; for example, **hypogenous. 3.** Abnormally low; for example, **hypoglycemia. 4.** Deficient; for example, **hypoxia. 5.** Partial or incomplete; for example, **hypoesthesia. 6.** *Chemistry.* Designating an acid containing a low amount of oxygen; for example, **hypophosphorous acid.** [Greek *hupo-,* from *hupo,* under, from under, beneath.]

hy·po·a·cid·i·ty (hī′pō-ə-sĭd′ə-tē) *n.* **1.** *Chemistry.* Slight acidity. **2.** *Medicine.* Below normal acidity.

hy·po·bar·ic (hī′pə-băr′ĭk) *adj.* Below normal pressure. [HYPO- + BAR(O)- + -IC.] —**hy·po·bar·ism** *n.*

hy·po·blast (hī′pə-blăst′, -bläst′) *n. Embryology.* The **endoblast** *(see).* [HYPO- + -BLAST.] —**hy·po·blas·tic** (hī′pə-blăs′tĭk) *adj.*

hy·po·caust (hī′pə-kôst′, hĭp′ə-) *n.* In ancient Rome, a space under the floor where heat from a furnace was accumulated to heat a room or a bath. [Latin *hypocaustum,* from Greek *hupokauston,* from *hupokaiein,* to burn underneath : *hupo-,* under + *kaiein,* to burn.]

hy·po·cen·ter (hī′pō-sĕn′tər) *n.* **Ground zero** *(see).*

hy·po·chlo·rite (hī′pə-klôr′īt′, -klōr′īt′) *n.* A salt or ester of hypochlorous acid.

hy·po·chlo·rous acid (hī′pə-klôr′əs, -klōr′əs) A weak, unstable acid, HOCl, occurring only in solution and used as a bleach, oxidizer, deodorant, and disinfectant.

hy·po·chon·dri·a (hī′pə-kŏn′drē-ə) *n.* **1.** The persistent neurotic conviction that one is or is likely to become ill, sometimes involving experiences of real pain, when illness is neither actually present nor likely. Also called "hypochondriasis." **2.** Plural of **hypochondrium.** [Originally a region of the abdomen (formerly held to be the seat of melancholy), from Late Latin, from Greek *hupokhondria,* plural of *hupokhondrion,* belly, abdomen, from *hupokhondrios,* under the cartilage of the breastbone : *hupo-,* under + *khondros,* cartilage.]

hy·po·chon·dri·ac (hī′pə-kŏn′drē-ăk′) *n.* A person afflicted with hypochondria.
∼*adj.* **1.** Pertaining to or afflicted with hypochondria. **2.** *Anatomy.* Pertaining to or located in the hypochondrium. —**hy·po·chon·dri·a·cal** (hī′pə-kən-drī′ə-kəl) *adj.* —**hy·po·chon·dri·a·cal·ly** *adv.*

hy·po·chon·dri·um (hī′pə-kŏn′drē-əm) *n., pl.* **-dria** (-drē-ə). The upper lateral region of the abdomen, below the ribs. [New Latin, from Greek *hupokhondrion,* abdomen. See **hypochondria.**]

hy·poc·o·rism (hī-pŏk′ə-rĭz′əm, hī-, hī′pə-kôr′ĭz′əm, -kōr′ĭz′əm) *n.* **1.** A name of endearment or a pet name. **2.** The use of such names. **3.** A euphemism. [Late Latin *hypocorisma,* from Greek *hupokorisma,* from *hupokorizesthai,* to call by endearing names : *hupo-,* below, beneath + *korizesthai,* to caress, from *koros,* boy, and *korē,* girl.] —**hy·po·co·ris·tic** (hī′pə-kə-rĭs′tĭk), **hy·po·co·ris·ti·cal** *adj.* —**hy·po·co·ris·ti·cal·ly** *adv.*

hy·po·cot·yl (hī′pə-kŏt′l) *n. Botany.* The part of the axis of a plant embryo or seedling plant that is below the cotyledons. [HYPO- + COTYL(EDON).] —**hy·po·cot·yl·ous** (hī′pə-kŏt′l-əs) *adj.*

hy·poc·ri·sy (hĭ-pŏk′rə-sē) *n., pl.* **-sies. 1.** The feigning of beliefs, feelings, or virtues that one does not hold or possess; gross insincerity. **2.** An instance of such insincerity. [Middle English *ipocrisie, ypocrisy,* from Old French *ypocrisie,* from Late Latin *hypocrisis,* from Greek *hupokrisis,* playing of a part on the stage, from *hupokrinein,* to separate gradually, answer, answer one's fellow actor, play a part : *hupo-,* under + *krinein,* to separate.]

hyp·o·crite (hĭp′ə-krĭt′) *n.* A person given to hypocrisy. [Middle English *ipocrite, ypocrite,* from Old French *ypocrite,* from Late Latin *hypocrita,* from Greek *hupocritēs,* actor, hypocrite, from *hupokrinein,* to play a part. See **hypocrisy.**]

hyp·o·crit·i·cal (hĭp′ə-krĭt′ĭ-kəl) *adj.* **1.** Characterized by hypocrisy; pretended or feigned: *hypocritical praise for someone she really despises.* **2.** Being a hypocrite: *a hypocritical rogue.* —**hyp·o·crit·i·cal·ly** *adv.*

hy·po·cy·cloid (hī′pō-sī′kloid′) *n. Geometry.* The plane locus of a point fixed on a circle that rolls on the inside circumference of a fixed circle.

hy·po·der·mal (hī′pə-dûr′məl) *adj.* **1.** Of or pertaining to the hypodermis. **2.** Lying below the epidermis.

hy·po·der·mic (hī′pə-dûr′mĭk) *adj.* **1.** Of or pertaining to the layer just beneath the epidermis. **2.** Pertaining to the hypodermis. **3.** Injected beneath the skin.
∼*n.* **1.** A hypodermic needle or syringe. **2.** A hypodermic injection. [HYPO- + DERM(ATO)- + -IC.] —**hy·po·der·mi·cal·ly** *adv.*

hypodermic injection *n.* A subcutaneous, intramuscular, or intravenous injection by means of a hypodermic syringe and needle.

hypodermic needle *n.* **1.** A hollow needle used with a hypodermic syringe. **2.** A hypodermic syringe complete with needle.

hypodermic syringe *n.* A tubular, piston-operated syringe fitted with a hypodermic needle for hypodermic injections, withdrawing blood, and the like.

hy·po·der·mis (hī′pə-dûr′mĭs) *n.* Also **hy·po·derm** (hī′pə-dûrm′). **1.** *Zoology.* An epidermal layer of cells that secretes an overlying chitinous cuticle, as in arthropods. **2.** *Botany.* A layer of cells lying immediately below the epidermis in certain plants, usually serving to support or protect tissue beneath it. [New Latin : HYPO- + *dermis,* DERMA (skin).]

hy·po·es·the·sia (hī′pō-ĕs-thē′zhə, -zhē-ə) *n.* Also **hy·pes·the·sia** (hī′pĕs-thē′zhə, -zhē-ə). *Pathology.* Partial loss of sensation; diminished sensibility. [New Latin : HYPO- + (AN)ESTHESIA.]

hy·po·eu·tec·tic (hī′pō-yōō-tĕk′tĭk) *adj. Chemistry.* Having the minor component present in a smaller amount than in the eutectic composition of the same components. Said of mixtures, especially alloys.

hy·po·gas·tri·um (hī′pō-găs′trē-əm) *n., pl.* **-tria** (-trē-ə). The lowest of the three median regions of the abdomen. [New Latin, from Greek *hupogastrion* : HYPO- + GASTR(O)- + -IUM.] —**hy·po·gas·tric** *adj.*

hy·po·ge·al (hī′pə-jē′əl) *adj.* Also **hy·po·ge·an** (-ən), **hy·po·ge·ous** (-əs). **1.** Located under the earth's surface; underground. **2.** *Botany.* Designating germination in which the cotyledons remain below the surface of the ground. [Late Latin *hypogēus,* from Greek *hupogaios* : HYPO- + *gē, gaia,* earth.]

hyp·o·gene (hĭp′ə-jēn′) *adj.* Formed or situated below the earth's surface. Said of rocks. [HYPO- + (EPI)GENE.]

hy·pog·e·nous (hī-pŏj′ə-nəs) *adj. Botany.* Developing or growing on a lower surface, as fungi on leaves. [HYPO- + -GENOUS.]

hyp·o·ge·um (hĭp′ə-jē′əm, hī′pə-) *n., pl.* **-gea** (-jē′ə). **1.** A subterranean chamber of an ancient building. **2.** An ancient subterranean burial chamber, such as a catacomb. [Latin *hypogēum,* from Greek *hupogaion,* from *hupogaios,* HYPOGEAL.]

hy·po·glos·sal (hī′pə-glŏs′əl) *adj.* **1.** Located under the tongue. **2.** *Anatomy.* Of or pertaining to the hypoglossal nerve.
∼*n.* The hypoglossal nerve. [New Latin *hypoglossus,* hypoglossal nerve : HYPO- + Greek *glōssa,* tongue.]

hypoglossal nerve *n.* The twelfth cranial nerve, which supplies motor fibers to the muscles of the tongue.

hy·po·gly·ce·mi·a (hī′pō-glī-sē′mē-ə) *n.* An abnormally low level of sugar in the blood. —**hy·po·gly·ce·mic** *adj.*

hy·pog·y·nous (hī-pŏj′ə-nəs) *adj. Botany.* Having or characterizing floral parts or organs that are below and not in contact with the ovary. [HYPO- + -GYNOUS.] —**hy·pog·y·ny** *n.*

hy·poid gear (hī′poid′) *n.* A gear in which the shapes of the teeth are hypocycloids, used for applications in which a high surface load is desirable. [Shortened from HYPOCYCLOID.]

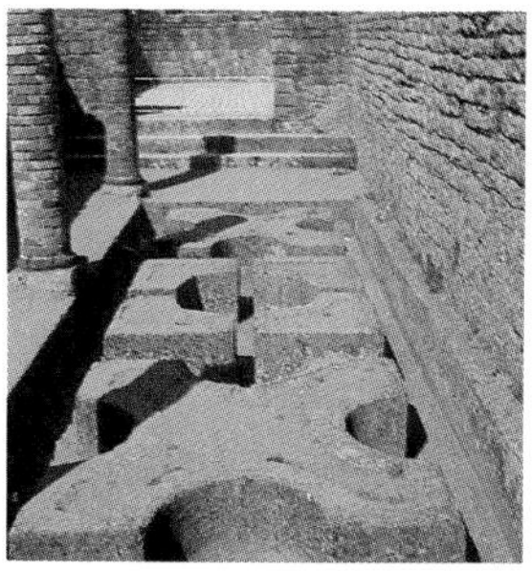

hypocaust *The underfloor heating system used by the Romans, in which a central furnace circulated warm air through concealed sunken channels. The channels shown here, exposed in the ruins of the Roman baths at Conimbriga (now Coimbra), Portugal, date from the second century A.D.*

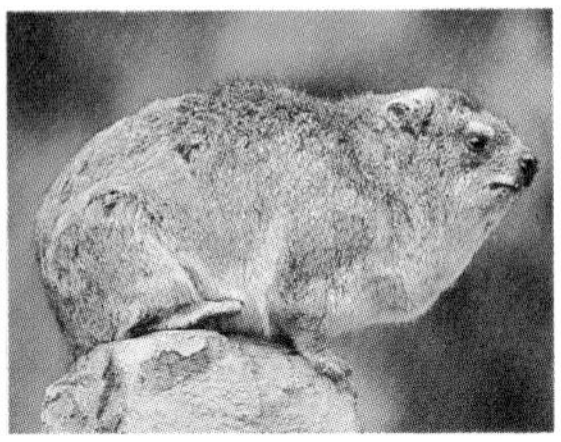

hyrax *Although hyraxes look like rodents, they have no close relatives. The nearest is thought to be the elephant. The animals, which grow to between 30 and 50 centimeters (12–20 inches) long, are native to Africa and southwestern Asia and have hooflike nails on most of their toes.*

PRONUNCIATION KEY

ă, pat; ā, pay; âr, care;
ä, father, are; b, bib;
ch, church; d, deed; ĕ, pet;
ē, be; f, fife; g, gag; h, hat;
hw, which; ĭ, pit; ī, pie;
îr, pier; j, judge; k, kick;
l, lid, needle; m, mum;
n, no, sudden; ng, thing;
ŏ, pot; ō, toe; ô, paw, for;
oi, noise; ou, out; o͝o, book;
o͞o, boot; p, pop; r, roar;
s, sauce; sh, ship, dish;
t, tight; th, thin, path;
th, this, bathe; ŭ, cut; ûr, fur;
v, valve; w, with; y, yes;
z, zebra, size; zh, vision;
ə, about, item, edible, gallop, circus, peaceful

IN FOREIGN WORDS:

à, *Fr.* ami; œ, *Fr.* feu, *Ger.* schön; ü, *Fr.* tu, *Ger.* über; KH, *Ger.* ich, *Scot.* loch; N, *Fr.* bon; y', *Fr.* Compiègne

STRESS MARKS:

Primary stress: ′
in·cite′ (ĭn-sīt′)
Secondary stress: ′
in′sight′ (ĭn′sīt′)

hy·po·lim·ni·on (hī′pō-lĭm′nē-ŏn′, -ən) *n., pl.* **-nia** (-nē-ə). The lower, colder layer of a lake or other body of water that is divided into two layers at different average temperatures. [HYPO- + Greek *limnion,* diminutive of *limnē,* lake.]

hy·po·ma·ni·a (hī′pə-mā′nē-ə, -mān′yə) *n.* A mild state of mania involving slightly abnormal elation and overactivity. —**hy·po·man·ic** (hī′pə-măn′ĭk, -mā′nĭk) *adj.*

hy·po·nas·ty (hī′pə-năs′tē) *n.* An upward bending of leaves or other plant parts, resulting from growth of the lower side. [German *Hyponastie* : HYPO- + -NASTY.] —**hy·po·nas·tic** (hī′pə-năs′tĭk) *adj.*

hy·po·ni·trite (hī′pə-nī′trīt′) *n.* A salt or ester of hyponitrous acid.

hy·po·ni·trous acid (hī′pə-nī′trəs) *n.* An unstable white crystalline acid, $H_2N_2O_2$.

hy·po·nym (hī′pə-nĭm′) *n.* A word that includes the meaning of another, more general word, such that the two can never be entirely interchangeable; for example, *cabbage* is a hyponym of *vegetable.* [HYP(O)- + -ONYM.] —**hy·pon·y·mous** (hī-pŏn′ə-məs) *adj.* —**hy·pon·y·my** (hī-pŏn′ə-mē) *n.*

hy·po·phos·phite (hī′pō-fŏs′fīt′) *n.* A salt of hypophosphorous acid.

hy·po·phos·pho·rous acid (hī′pō-fŏs′fər-əs, -fŏs-fôr′əs, -fōr′əs) *n.* A clear, colorless or slightly yellow oily liquid, H_3PO_2, used in the preparation of hypophosphites.

hy·poph·y·sis (hī-pŏf′ə-sĭs) *n., pl.* **-ses** (-sēz′). *Anatomy.* The **pituitary gland** *(see).* [New Latin, outgrowth, from Greek *hupophusis,* attachment underneath, growth, from *hupophuein,* to grow up under : *hupo-,* under + *phuein,* to bring forth, grow.] —**hy·po·phys·e·al** (hī′pə-fĭz′ē-əl, hī-pŏf′ə-sē′əl) *adj.*

hy·po·pi·tu·i·ta·rism (hī′pō-pĭ-to͞o′ə-tə-rĭz′əm, hī′pō-pĭ-tyo͞o′-) *n.* Deficient or diminished production of pituitary hormones. —**hy·po·pi·tu·i·tar·y** (hī′pō-pĭ-to͞o′ə-tĕr′ē, -tyo͞o′ə-tĕr′ē) *adj.*

hy·po·pla·sia (hī′pō-plā′zhə, -zhē-ə) *n. Pathology.* Incomplete or arrested development of an organ or part. [New Latin : HYPO- + -PLASIA.] —**hy·po·plas·tic** (hī′pō-plăs′tĭk) *adj.*

hy·po·ploid (hī′pō-ploid′) *adj. Genetics.* Having a chromosome number less by only a few chromosomes than a multiple of the normal haploid number. [HYPO- + -PLOID.] —**hy·po·ploid·y** *n.*

hy·po·pne·a (hī′pō-nē′ə) *n.* Abnormally slow and shallow breathing. [New Latin : HYPO- + Greek *pnoē,* breathing, from *pnein,* to breathe.]

hy·po·sen·si·tiv·i·ty (hī′pō-sĕn′sə-tĭv′ə-tē) *n.* Also **hy·po·sen·si·tive·ness** (-sĕn′sə-tĭv-nĭs). Less than normal sensitivity. —**hy·po·sen·si·tive** *adj.*

hy·po·sen·si·tize (hī′pō-sĕn′sə-tīz′) *tr.v.* **-tized, -tizing, -tizes.** To make less sensitive; desensitize. —**hy·po·sen·si·ti·za·tion** (hī′pō-sĕn′sə-tə-zā′shən) *n.*

hy·pos·ta·sis (hī-pŏs′tə-sĭs) *n., pl.* **-ses** (-sēz′). **1.** *Philosophy.* That which underlies something else; substance or essence as distinguished from attributes or qualities. **2.** *Theology.* **a.** Any of the persons of the Trinity as distinguished from the single nature of the godhead. **b.** The essential person of Christ in which his human and divine natures are united. **3.** *Medicine.* The accumulation of blood or fluid in a part of the body, such as the lungs, that is caused by poor circulation. **4.** *Genetics.* A condition in which the action of one gene conceals or suppresses the action of another gene that is not its allele. [Late Latin, substance, from Greek *hupostasis,* "a standing under," origin, substance, existence : *hupo-,* under + *stasis,* a standing.] —**hy·po·stat·ic** (hī′pə-stăt′ĭk), **hy·po·stat·i·cal** *adj.* —**hy·po·stat·i·cal·ly** *adv.*

hypostatic union *n. Theology.* The union of Christ's human and divine natures in one hypostasis or person. [Greek *hupostatikos,* of substance, from *hupostatos,* standing under, from *huphistasthai,* to stand under : *hupo-,* under + *histasthai,* middle voice of *histanai,* to cause to stand.]

hy·pos·ta·tize (hī-pŏs′tə-tīz′) *tr.v.* **-tized, -tizing, -tizes. 1.** To symbolize (a concept) in a concrete form. **2.** To ascribe material existence to. [Greek *hupostatos,* standing under. See **hypostatic union.**] —**hy·pos·ta·ti·za·tion** (hī-pŏs′tə-tə-zā′shən) *n.*

hy·po·sthe·ni·a (hī′pəs-thē′nē-ə) *n.* Abnormal lack of strength; extreme weakness. [New Latin : HYPO- + Greek *sthenos,* strength.] —**hy·po·sthen·ic** (hī′pəs-thĕn′ĭk) *adj.*

hyp·o·style (hĭp′ə-stīl′, hī′pə-) *n.* A building having a roof or ceiling supported by rows of columns, as in ancient Egyptian architecture. [Greek *hupostulos,* resting upon pillars set underneath : *hupo-,* under + *stulos,* pillar.] —**hyp·o·style** *adj.*

hy·po·sul·fite (hī′pō-sŭl′fīt′) *n.* **Sodium thiosulfate** *(see).*

hy·po·sul·fu·rous acid (hī′pō-sŭl-fyo͝or′əs, -sŭl′fər-əs) *n.* An unstable acid, $H_2S_2O_4$, known only in aqueous solution and used as a bleaching and reducing agent. Also called "hydrosulfurous acid."

hy·po·tax·is (hī′pə-tăk′sĭs) *n.* The subordination of one clause to another by means of a connective, as in *I shall despair if you don't come.* Compare **parataxis.** [Greek *hupotaxis,* subjection, submission, from *hupotassein,* to arrange under : *hupo-,* under + *tattein,* to arrange.] —**hy·po·tac·tic** (hī′pə-tăk′tĭk) *adj.*

hy·po·tension (hī′pō-tĕn′shən) *n.* Abnormally low arterial blood pressure. —**hy·po·ten·sive** (hī′pō-tĕn′sĭv) *adj.*

hy·pot·e·nuse (hī-pŏt′n-o͞os′, -yo͞os′) *n. Abbr.* **hyp** The side of a right triangle opposite the right angle. [Latin *hypotēnūsa,* from Greek *hupoteinousa,* line subtending the right angle, hypotenuse, from *hupoteinein,* to stretch under : *hupo-,* under + *teinein,* to stretch.]

hypoth. hypothesis.

hy·po·thal·a·mus (hī′pō-thăl′ə-məs) *n.* The part of the brain that lies below the thalamus and regulates bodily temperature, hunger, thirst, and other autonomic activities. —**hy·po·tha·lam·ic** (hī′pō-thə-lăm′ĭk) *adj.*

hy·poth·ec (hī-pŏth′ĭk) *n.* In Roman and Scots law, a security granted a creditor on the property of a debtor without transfer of possession or title. [French *hypothèque,* from Late Latin *hypothēca,* pledge, mortgage, from Greek *hupothēkē,* from *hupotithenai,* "to place under," put down as a deposit : *hupo-,* under + *tithenai,* to place.] —**hy·poth·e·car·y** (hī-pŏth′ĭ-kĕr′ē) *adj.*

hy·poth·e·cate (hī-pŏth′ĭ-kāt′) *tr.v.* **-cated, -cating, -cates.** *Law.* To pledge (property) as security to a creditor without transfer of title or possession; mortgage. [Medieval Latin *hypothēcāre,* from Late Latin *hypothēca,* HYPOTHEC.] —**hy·poth·e·ca·tion** (hī-pŏth′ĭ-kā′shən) *n.* —**hy·poth·e·ca·tor** *n.*

hy·po·ther·mal (hī′pō-thûr′məl) *adj.* **1.** *Geology.* Of, pertaining to, or designating high-temperature deposits derived from magmatic emanations forced under pressure into pre-existing rock openings. **2.** Of, pertaining to, or characterized by hypothermia.

hy·po·ther·mi·a (hī′pō-thûr′mē-ə) *n.* **1.** Abnormally low body temperature caused by exposure to cold. **2.** The deliberate lowering of body temperature to reduce metabolic rate during surgery. [HYPO- + Greek *thermē,* heat + -IA.]

hy·poth·e·sis (hī-pŏth′ə-sĭs) *n., pl.* **-ses** (-sēz′). *Abbr.* **hyp., hypoth. 1.** An assertion subject to verification or proof, as: **a.** A proposition stated as a basis for argument or reasoning. **b.** A premise from which a conclusion is drawn. **c.** A conjecture that accounts, within a theory or set of coherent beliefs, for a set of facts and that can be used as a basis for further investigation. **2.** An assumption used as the basis for action. [Late Latin, from Greek *hupothesis,* proposal, suggestion, supposition, from *hupotithenai,* "to place under," propose, suppose : *hupo-,* under + *tithenai,* to place.]

hy·poth·e·size (hī-pŏth′ə-sīz′) *v.* **-sized, -sizing, -sizes.** —*tr.* To assert as a hypothesis. —*intr.* To form a hypothesis or hypotheses.

hy·po·thet·i·cal (hī′pə-thĕt′ĭ-kəl) *adj.* Also **hy·po·thet·ic** (-thĕt′ĭk). **1.** Of or based on a hypothesis. **2. a.** Suppositional; conjectural; uncertain. **b.** Conditional; contingent. **3.** Existing as an idea or possibility but not actual: *That's only a hypothetical case.* [Late Latin *hypotheticus,* from Greek *hupothetikos,* from *hupothesis,* HYPOTHESIS.] —**hy·po·thet·i·cal·ly** *adv.*

hypothetical imperative *n.* In the philosophy of Immanuel Kant, a principle of conduct arising from expediency or necessity rather than from moral law. Compare **categorical imperative.**

hy·po·thy·roid (hī′pō-thī′roid′) *adj.* Affected by or manifesting hypothyroidism.
∼*n.* A person affected by hypothyroidism.

hy·po·thy·roid·ism (hī′pō-thī′roi-dĭz′əm) *n.* Also **hy·po·thy·roid·e·a** (hī′pō-thī-roi′dē-ə). **1.** Insufficient production of thyroid hormones. **2.** A pathological condition resulting from severe thyroid insufficiency; especially, **myxedema** or **cretinism** *(both of which see).* [HYPO- + THYROID + -ISM.]

hy·po·ton·ic (hī′pō-tŏn′ĭk) *adj.* **1.** *Pathology.* Having less than normal muscular or arterial tone or tension. **2.** *Chemistry.* Having the lower osmotic pressure of two fluids. —**hy·po·to·nic·i·ty** (hī′pō-tə-nĭs′ə-tē) *n.*

hy·po·tro·choid (hī′pə-trō′koid′) *n. Geometry.* The locus of a point anywhere on the radius, or radius extended, of a circle that rolls inside a fixed circle. A hypotrochoid for which the moving point is on the circumference of the rolling circle is a hypocycloid.

hy·po·xan·thine (hī′pō-zăn′thēn′, -thĭn) *n.* A white powder, $C_5H_4N_4O$, that is an intermediate in the metabolism of purines.

hy·pox·i·a (hī-pŏk′sē-ə) *n.* Deficiency in the amount of oxygen reaching bodily tissues. [New Latin : HYP(O)- + OX(Y)- + -IA.] —**hy·pox·ic** *adj.*

hypso– *prefix.* Indicates height; for example, **hypsometry.** [Greek *hupsos,* height, summit.]

hyp·sog·ra·phy (hĭp-sŏg′rə-fē) *n.* **1.** The scientific study of the earth's topologic configuration above sea level, especially the measurement and mapping of land elevations. **2.** A representation or description of such features, as on a map or in an atlas. **3.** Hypsometry. [HYPSO- + -GRAPHY.] —**hyp·so·graph·ic** (hĭp′sə-grăf′ĭk), **hyp·so·graph·i·cal** *adj.*

hyp·som·e·ter (hĭp-sŏm′ə-tər) *n.* An instrument that estimates land elevations in mountainous regions from the boiling points of liquids. [HYPSO- + -METER.]

hyp·som·e·try (hĭp-sŏm′ə-trē) *n.* The measurement of elevation relative to sea level. [HYPSO- + -METRY.] —**hyp·so·met·ric** (hĭp′sə-mĕt′rĭk), **hyp·so·met·ri·cal** *adj.* —**hyp·so·met·ri·cal·ly** *adv.* —**hyp·som·e·trist** (hĭp-sŏm′ə-trĭst) *n.*

hy·rax (hī′răks′) *n., pl.* **-raxes** or **-races** (-rə-sēz′). Any of several herbivorous mammals of the family Procaviidae of Africa and adjacent Asia, resembling the rodents but more closely related to the hoofed mammals. Also called "dassie" and, especially in the Old Testament, "cony." [New Latin, from Greek *hurax*†, shrew mouse.]

hy·son (hī′sən) *n.* A type of Chinese green tea, the leaves of which are twisted or curled. [Cantonese *hei chon,* corresponding to Mandarin Chinese *xī chūn,* "bright spring," after the name of a famous tea grower, *Li Xi-chun.*]

hys·sop (hĭs′əp) *n.* **1.** A woody plant, *Hyssopus officinalis,* native to Asia, having spikes of small blue flowers and aromatic leaves used in perfumery and as a condiment. **2.** Any of several similar or related plants. **3.** An unidentified plant mentioned in the Bible as the source of twigs used for sprinkling in certain Hebraic purificatory rites. Exodus 12:22. [Middle English *ysop,* from Old English *hysope* and Old French *ysope*, both from Latin *hyssōpus*, from Greek *hussō-pos*, from Semitic, akin to Hebrew *'ezōbh*.]

hys·ter·ec·to·mize (hĭs′tə-rĕk′tə-mīz′) *tr.v.* **-mized, -mizing, -mizes.** To perform a hysterectomy on.

hys·ter·ec·to·my (hĭs′tə-rĕk′tə-mē) *n., pl.* **-mies.** The removal of either the whole of the uterus or the body of the uterus but not the cervix. [HYSTER(O)- + -ECTOMY.]

hys·ter·e·sis (hĭs′tə-rē′sĭs) *n., pl.* **-ses** (-sēz′). *Physics.* The failure of a property that has been changed by an external agent to return to its original value when the cause of the change is removed. See **magnetic hysteresis.** [New Latin, from Greek *husterēsis*, a shortcoming, from *husterein*, to be behind, come later, from *husteros*, later, behind.] **—hys·ter·et·ic** (hĭs′tə-rĕt′ĭk) *adj.*

hysteresis loop *n. Physics.* A closed curve obtained by plotting a graph of the magnetic induction of a ferromagnetic substance (as ordinate) against the external magnetic field. The shape of the curve is characteristic of the magnetic properties of the material and shows the ease with which it is magnetized and the ability to retain magnetization.

hys·ter·i·a (hĭ-stĕr′ē-ə, -stîr′ē-ə) *n.* **1.** A neurosis characterized by susceptibility to suggestion, emotional instability, amnesia, and other mental aberrations. **2.** Excessive or uncontrollable fear or other strong emotion. [New Latin, from Latin *hystericus*, HYSTERIC.]

hys·ter·ic (hĭ-stĕr′ĭk) *n.* A person suffering from hysteria. ~*adj.* Hysterical. [Latin *hystericus*, from Greek *husterikos*, suffering in the womb (hysteria was once thought to be caused by uterine disturbances), from *hustera*, womb.]

hys·ter·i·cal (hĭ-stĕr′ĭ-kəl) *adj.* **1.** Of, characterized by, or arising from hysteria: *hysterical paralysis.* **2.** Having or prone to having hysterics. **3.** *Informal.* Extremely funny. **—hys·ter·i·cal·ly** *adv.*

hys·ter·ics (hĭ-stĕr′ĭks) *n. Usually used with a singular verb.* **1.** An attack of hysteria. **2.** *Informal.* **a.** A fit of uncontrollable laughing. **b.** A fit of wild anger: *He'll have hysterics if he finds out.*

hystero–, hyster– *prefix.* Indicates: **1.** Womb or uterus; for example, **hysterectomy. 2.** Hysteria; for example, **hysterogenic.** [Greek *hustera*, womb.]

hys·ter·o·gen·ic (hĭs′tə-rō-jĕn′ĭk) *adj.* Causing hysteria. [HYSTERO- + -GENIC.]

hys·ter·oid (hĭs′tə-roid′) *adj.* Also **hys·ter·oid·al** (hĭs′tə-roid′l). Resembling hysteria. [HYSTER(O)- + -OID.]

hys·ter·on prot·er·on (hĭs′tə-rŏn′ prŏt′ə-rŏn′) *n.* **1.** A figure of speech in which the natural or rational order of its terms is reversed, as *bred and born* instead of *born and bred.* **2.** *Logic.* The fallacy of assuming as a premise a proposition following something yet to be proved. [Late Latin, from Greek *husteron proteron,* "latter first" : *husteron,* neuter of *husteros,* latter + *proteron,* neuter of *proteros,* first, former.]

hys·ter·ot·o·my (hĭs′tə-rŏt′ə-mē) *n., pl.* **-mies.** Surgical incision into the uterus. [New Latin *hysterotomia* : HYSTERO- + -TOMY.]

hys·tric·o·morph (hĭ-strĭk′ə-môrf′) *n.* Any rodent belonging to the suborder *Hystricomorpha,* which includes the porcupines, chinchillas, guinea pigs, and agoutis. [Greek *hustrix* (stem *hustrik-*), porcupine + -MORPH.] **—hys·tric·o·morph, hys·tric·o·morph·ic** (hĭ-strĭk′ə-môr′fĭk) *adj.*

Hz hertz (unit of frequency).

I

ibex *These wild goats live in the mountains of Europe, Asia, and North Africa. The one shown here is a male European ibex.*

i, **I** (ī) *n., pl.* **i's** or **I's. 1.** The ninth letter of the modern English alphabet. See feature at **alphabet. 2.** Any of the speech sounds represented by this letter. **3.** Something shaped like an I. **4.** The ninth in a series. **—dot one's i's and cross one's t's.** To pay rigorous attention to detail; be exhaustively comprehensive.

i, I, i., I. *Note:* As an abbreviation or symbol, *i* may be a small or a capital letter, with or without a period. Established forms or those generally preferred precede the definition. When no form is given, all four forms are in general use in that sense. **1. i, I** *Electricity.* current. **2. i** *Mathematics.* imaginary unit; the square root of −1. **3. i.** incisor. **4. I.** independence; independent. **5. I.** institute. **6. i.** interest. **7. I.** international. **8. i.** intransitive. **9. I** The symbol for the element iodine. **10. i., I.** island; isle. **11. I** isospin. **12. i, I** The Roman numeral for one.

I (ī) *pron.* The first person singular pronoun in the nominative case. **1.** Used to represent the speaker or writer. **2.** Sometimes used in a conditional construction depending on the elliptically understood clause *if I were you,* to express advice or indirect injunction: *I wouldn't go out without a coat today.* **—See Usage note at me.**
~*n., pl.* **I's.** The self; the ego. [Middle English *i, ich,* Old English *ic,* from Germanic *eka* (unattested).]

i–¹. Variant of **y–.**

i–². Variant of **in–** (not).

–i *suffix.* Indicates a specified region, national origin, or people; for example, **Kashmiri, Pakistani, Tandoori.** [Adjective suffix in Semitic and Indo-Iranian languages.]

–i– *infix.* Used to connect the elements of a compound word, especially when they are of Latin origin; for example, **patrilineal, homicide.** [From or by analogy with French *-i-,* from Latin.]

IA Iowa (used with a Zip Code).

i.a. in absentia.

–ia¹ *suffix.* Indicates: **1.** Diseases and disorders; for example, **alexia, diphtheria. 2.** Plants or genera of plants; for example, **poinsettia, begonia. 3.** Zoological classes; for example, **Amphibia. 4.** Areas and countries; for example, **Manchuria.** [New Latin, from Latin and Greek, suffix of feminine abstract nouns.]

–ia² *suffix.* Indicates collective nouns; for example, **trivia, genitalia.** [New Latin, from Latin, neuter plural of *-ius,* and from Greek, neuter plural of *-ios.*]

I·a·coc·ca (ī′ə-kō′kə), **Lido Anthony,** known as "Lee" (1924–). U.S. business executive. He has served as president of the Ford Motor Company (1970–78) and as president and later chairman of the Chrysler Corporation (from 1978). As chairman of the Statue of Liberty-Ellis Island Foundation he organized the campaign to restore and refurbish the statue for its centennial in 1986.

IAEA International Atomic Energy Agency.

–ial *suffix.* Indicates of, pertaining to, or characterized by; for example, **managerial, residential.** [Middle English, from Old French *-ial, -iel,* from Latin *-iālis : -i-,* stem + *-ālis,* -AL.]

i·amb (ī′ămb′) *n.* **1.** A metrical foot consisting of a short syllable followed by a long (in quantitative verse), or an unstressed syllable followed by a stressed (in accentual verse). Also called "iambic," "iambus." There are four iambs in the following line: "*I-am′bics march′ from short′ to long′*" (Coleridge). **2.** A line of verse consisting of such feet. Compare **trochee.** [French *iambe,* from Latin *iambus,* IAMBUS.]

i·am·bic (ī-ăm′bĭk) *adj.* **1.** Consisting of iambs or characterized by their predominance: *iambic pentameter.* **2.** Employing this rhythm: *the iambic poets of antiquity.*
~*n.* **1.** An iamb. **2.** *Usually* **iambics.** A verse, stanza, or poem written in iambs. [Latin *iambicus,* from Greek *iambikos,* from *iambos,* IAMBUS.]

i·am·bus (ī-ăm′bəs) *n., pl.* **-buses** or **-bi** (-bī′). An iamb. [Latin, from Greek *iambos†.*]

–ian¹ *suffix.* Indicates: **1.** Of or belonging to; for example, **Bostonian. 2.** Characteristic of or resembling; for example, **Johnsonian.** [Old French *-ien,* from Latin *-iānus : -i-,* stem + *-ānus,* -AN.]

–ian² *suffix.* Indicates: **1.** Admirer or follower of; for example, **Chaucerian. 2.** One skilled in or a specialist, for example, **pediatri-**cian, logistician. **3.** One belonging to a certain period of time or place; for example, **Edwardian.** [From –IAN.]

–iana. Variant of **-ana** (a collection).

IAS *Aeronautics.* indicated air speed.

–iasis *suffix.* Indicates a pathological condition; for example, **teniasis.** [New Latin, from Greek, suffix of action.]

I.A.T.A., IATA International Air Transport Association.

i·at·ric (ī-ăt′rĭk) *adj.* Also **i·at·ri·cal** (-rĭ-kəl). *Rare.* Pertaining to medicine or physicians; medical. [Greek *iatrikos,* from *iatros,* physician, healer, from *iasthai†,* to heal, cure.]

–iatric *suffix.* Indicates a specified kind of patient or medical treatment; for example, **geriatric.** [From IATRIC.]

–iatrics *suffix.* Indicates medical treatment; for example, **pediatrics.** [From IATRIC.]

i·at·ro·gen·ic (ī-ăt′rə-jĕn′ĭk) *adj.* Induced in a patient by a doctor's actions or treatment: *an iatrogenic disease.* [Greek *iatros,* physician (see **iatric**) + -GENIC.]

–iatry *suffix.* Indicates medical treatment; for example, **psychiatry.** [French *-iatrie,* from New Latin *-iatria,* from Greek *iatreia,* the art of healing, from *iatros,* physician. See **iatric.**]

ib. ibidem.

I.B.A. Independent Broadcasting Authority (in Britain).

I·ba·dan (ē-bä′dän). A city in southwestern Nigeria, *c.* 130 kilometers (80 miles) north of Lagos. It is the second-largest city in the country and one of the oldest settlements in Africa.

Ib·ár·ru·ri Gó·mez (ĭ-bär′ōōr-ē gō′mĕz), **Dolores** (1895–). Spanish Communist leader. Her oratory in the Spanish Civil War won her the nickname of La Pasionaria ("the passionflower"). She sought refuge in the U.S.S.R. (1939), but returned to Spain in 1977.

I-beam (ī′bēm′) *n.* A steel beam or girder with a cross section formed like the capital letter I.

I·be·ri·a (ī-bîr′ē-ə). **1.** The ancient name for the region roughly corresponding to the eastern part of modern Georgian S.S.R. **2.** An ancient name for the Iberian Peninsula.

I·be·ri·an (ī-bîr′ē-ən) *adj.* **1. a.** Of or pertaining to the ancient ethnological group or groups that inhabited the Iberian Peninsula. **b.** Of or pertaining to the language or culture of these groups. **2. a.** Of or pertaining to the Iberian Peninsula. **b.** Broadly, Spanish, or Spanish and Portuguese. **3.** Of or pertaining to ancient Iberia in the Caucasus, to its inhabitants, their language, or their culture.
~*n.* **1. a.** A member of the ancient Caucasoid people that inhabited the Iberian Peninsula. **b.** The language of this people. **2.** An inhabitant of the Iberian Peninsula. **3.** An inhabitant of ancient Iberia in the Caucasus.

Iberian Peninsula. Land mass of extreme southwestern Europe, comprising Spain and Portugal, separated from the rest of Europe by the Pyrenees and from Africa by the Strait of Gibraltar.

Ibero– *prefix.* Indicates the Iberian Peninsula or Iberian; for example, *Ibero-Celtic.*

I·ber·ville (ē-bĕr-vēl′), **Pierre Le Moyne, Sieur d'** (1661–1706). French explorer and naval officer; born in Canada. After several years of defending interests in the Hudson Bay region, he explored the Mississippi delta and founded the first permanent settlement in the Louisiana Territory (1699).

i·bex (ī′bĕks′) *n., pl.* **ibexes, ibices** (ī′bĭ-sēz′), or collectively **ibex.** Any of several wild goats of the genus *Capra,* of mountainous regions of the Old World; especially, having long, ridged, backward-curving horns. Also called "steinbok." [Latin, perhaps of Alpine origin.]

I·bib·i·o (ĭ-bĭb′ē-ō) *n., pl.* **-os** or collectively **Ibibio. 1.** A member of a people of southeastern Nigeria. **2.** The Niger-Congo language of this people. **—I·bib·i·o** *adj.*

ibid. ibidem.

i·bi·dem (ĭb′ə-dĕm′, ĭ-bī′dəm) *adv. Abbr.* **ib., ibid.** *Latin.* In the same place. Used in footnotes and bibliographies to refer to the book, chapter, article, or page cited just before.

–ibility. Variant of **–ability.**

i·bis (ī′bĭs) *n., pl.* **ibises** or collectively **ibis.** Any of various long-billed, mainly tropical, wading birds of the family Threskiornithidae, such as the sacred ibis, *Threskiornis aethiopica.* See **wood ibis.** [Latin *ībis,* from Greek *ibis,* from Egyptian *hīb.*]

I·bi·za or **I·vi·za** (ē-vē′zə). The third largest of the Balearic Islands, in the Mediterranean Sea, and the one nearest the east coast of Spain. Ibiza is also the name of the largest town. The island is a popular tourist resort.

-ible. Variant of **-able.**

ibn-Ga·bi·rol (ĭb′ən-gə-bîr′əl), **Solomon ben Yehuda,** also known as "Avicebrón" (*c.* 1021–58). Jewish philosopher and poet. He was a leading contributor to the growth of Jewish culture in Moorish Spain; his Neo-Platonist philosophy, particularly in *Fons Vitae,* had great influence on Jews and Christians.

ibn-Rushd. See **Averroës.**

ibn Saud (soud) (*c.* 1880–1953). Founder and first king of modern Saudi Arabia, which he ruled from 1932 until his death. His long struggle to gain control of central Arabia began in 1902. It continued against the Turks, with British support during World War I, and against rival Arab factions in the 1920's. The discovery of oil in 1936, which later brought great wealth, occurred in his reign.

ibn-Sina. See **Avicenna.**

I·bo (ē′bō) *n., pl.* **Ibos** or collectively **Ibo. 1.** A member of a Negroid people of Nigeria. **2.** The Kwa language spoken by this people.

Ib·sen (ĭb′sən), **Henrik** (1828–1906). Norwegian dramatist and poet, whose plays created a major scandal in his lifetime because of their realism but are now acclaimed as classics. His chief works include *A Doll's House* (1879), *Ghosts* (1881), and *An Enemy of the People* (1882). Other major plays are *Hedda Gabler* (1890) and *The Master Builder* (1892).

-ic, -ical *suffix.* Indicates: **1.** Of, pertaining to, or characteristic of; for example, **seismic, Gaelic, geological, metrical. 2.** *Chemistry.* Having or taking a valence higher than in corresponding *-ous* compounds; for example, **ferric.** Compare **-ous. —**See Usage note at **classic.** [Middle English *-ic, -ik,* from Latin *-icus.*]

IC integrated circuit.

ICA 1. Institute of Contemporary Arts. **2.** International Cooperation Administration.

ICAO International Civil Aviation Organization.

Ic·a·rus¹ (ĭk′ər-əs). *Greek Mythology.* The son of Daedalus, who, in escaping from Crete on artificial wings made for him by his father, flew so close to the sun that the wax with which his wings were fastened melted, so that he fell into the Aegean Sea and drowned.

Icarus² *n. Astronomy.* A small asteroid, the one that passes closest to the sun. [After ICARUS.]

ICBM intercontinental ballistic missile.

ice (īs) *n.* **1.** Water frozen solid. **2.** A surface, layer, or mass of frozen water. **3. a.** Pieces of ice, as those put in a drink, for example, to chill it. **b.** Anything resembling frozen water, such as **dry ice** *(see).* **4.** A dessert consisting of sweetened and flavored crushed ice. **5.** *Slang.* Diamonds. **6. a.** The skating surface in an ice rink. **b.** The playing field in ice hockey. **7.** *Astronomy.* A mixture of solid water, carbon dioxide, other gases, and dust, forming the nucleus of a comet. **—break the ice.** To dispel the initial mood of reserve or formality of a social situation. **—cut no ice.** *Informal.* To have no influence or effect; make no impression. **—on ice. 1.** In a refrigerator or freezer. **2.** *Informal.* **a.** In reserve or readiness. **b.** Put aside; shelved; postponed. **c.** Held incommunicado. **d.** Certain to be won. Said of games. **—on thin ice.** In a risky situation; on uncertain ground.

~*v.* **iced, icing, ices.** *—tr.* **1.** To coat with ice. **2.** To cause to become ice; freeze. **3. a.** To chill by setting in or as if in ice. **b.** To put ice in (a drink, for example). **4.** To cover or decorate (a cake) with icing. *—intr.* To turn into, or become coated with, ice; freeze. Often used with *over* or *up.* [Middle English *is,* Old English *īs,* from Germanic.]

I.C.E. Institute of Civil Engineers.

Ice. Iceland; Icelandic.

ice age *n.* **1.** A **glacial period** *(see).* **2. Ice Age.** The Pleistocene or glacial epoch.

ice ax *n.* An ax used by mountaineers for cutting steps in ice.

ice bag *n.* A small waterproof bag used as an **ice pack** *(see).*

ice barrier *n.* A section of the ice sheet covering Antarctica that extends beyond the coastline. Also called "barrier."

ice·berg (īs′bûrg′) *n.* **1.** A massive floating body of ice broken away from a glacier or ice sheet. Also called "berg." **2.** *Slang.* One who appears to be cold or aloof. [Probably partial translation of Danish and Norwegian *isberg* : *is,* ice + *berg,* mountain.]

iceberg lettuce *n.* A type of lettuce characterized by its light green coloring, crisp leaves, and compact head.

ice·blink (īs′blĭngk′) *n.* A yellowish glare in the sky over an ice field. Also called "blink."

ice-blue (īs′blo͞o′) *n.* A pale greenish blue. **—ice-blue** *adj.*

ice·boat (īs′bōt′) *n.* **1.** A boatlike vehicle set on runners that sails on ice. **2.** An icebreaker.

ice·bound (īs′bound′) *adj.* **1.** Locked in by ice: *an icebound ship.* **2.** Jammed or covered over by ice: *an icebound harbor.*

ice·box (īs′bŏks′) *n.* **1.** An insulated chest or box in which ice is put to cool and preserve food. **2.** A refrigerator.

ice·break·er (īs′brā′kər) *n.* **1.** A sturdy ship built for breaking a passage through icebound waters. Also called "iceboat." **2.** A protective pier or dock apron used as a buffer against floating ice.

ice bucket *n.* **1.** A small insulated bucket with a lid, containing ice for adding to drinks. **2.** A somewhat larger bucket of this sort, used without a lid to cool bottles placed inside it.

ice cap *n.* An extensive perennial cover of ice and snow, smaller than an ice sheet.

ice-cold (īs′kōld′) *adj.* Very cold; freezing cold.

ice cream *n.* **1.** A smooth, sweet, cold food prepared from a frozen mixture of milk products and sometimes egg yolks and flavored in a variety of ways. **2.** Such a food, but with animal fat or seaweed products used as substitutes for milk products.

ice-cream cone (īs′krēm′) *n.* **1.** A conical wafer used to hold a scoop of ice cream. **2.** This wafer with the ice cream in it.

ice-cream soda *n.* A refreshment consisting of ice cream scoops in a mixture of soda water and flavoring syrup.

iced (īst) *adj.* **1.** Covered over with ice. **2.** Chilled with ice. **3.** Decorated or coated with icing.

ice·fall (īs′fôl′) *n.* **1.** A broken, tumbled mass of ice where a glacier becomes steeper. **2.** An avalanche of ice.

ice field *n.* **1.** A large, level expanse of floating ice. **2.** A large expanse of ice on land.

ice floe *n.* A flat expanse of floating ice, smaller than an ice field.

ice foot *n.* A belt or ledge of ice that forms along the shoreline in Arctic regions.

ice hockey *n.* A game played on ice in which two opposing teams of skaters, using curved sticks, try to drive a flat disk, or puck, into the opponents' goal. Also called "hockey."

ice·house (īs′hous′) *n.* A building, often underground, formerly used for storing ice and preserving it by natural means.

Icel. Iceland; Icelandic.

Ice·land (īs′lənd). *Abbr.* **Ice., Icel.** An island republic in the North Atlantic Ocean, just south of the Arctic Circle. Much of the island is of volcanic origin and there are *c.* 200 volcanoes, several of which are still active, as well as a number of geysers and lakes of boiling mud. Less than 2 percent of the land is cultivated, and the economy is heavily dependent on the cod-fishing industry. Area, 102,819 square kilometers (39,698 square miles). Population, 230,000. Capital, Reykjavík. See map at **Western Europe.**

Ice·land·er (īs′lən-dər) *n.* A native of Iceland.

Ice·land·ic (īs-lăn′dĭk) *adj. Abbr.* **Ice., Icel.** Of or pertaining to Iceland, its inhabitants, their language, or their culture.

~*n.* The North Germanic language spoken in Iceland, specifically: **1.** This language as spoken since the 16th century. **2. Old Icelandic** *(see).*

Iceland moss *n.* A brittle, grayish-brown, edible lichen, *Cetraria islandica,* of Arctic regions and northern Europe.

Iceland poppy *n.* **1.** An Arctic poppy, *Papaver nudicaule,* widely cultivated for its white or yellow flowers. **2.** Any of several similar Arctic poppies.

Iceland spar *n.* A doubly refracting, transparent, crystalline form of calcite used in experiments on optical polarization.

ice machine *n.* A machine that freezes water into ice cubes.

ice milk *n.* A smooth, sweet, cold food prepared from a frozen mixture of milk products, usually containing less than half the butterfat of ice cream.

ice needle *n.* Any of the thin ice crystals that float high in the atmosphere in certain conditions of clear, cold weather.

ice-out (īs′out′) *n.* The thawing of ice on a body of water.

ice pack *n.* **1.** A bag or folded cloth filled with crushed ice and applied to sore or swollen parts of the body. Also called "pack." **2.** A container filled with a liquid of high thermal capacity that can be frozen, used to keep food or other materials cool.

ice pick *n.* A pointed awl for chipping or breaking ice.

ice plant *n.* A plant, *Mesembryanthemum* (or *Cryophytum*) *crystallinum,* native to southern Africa, having fleshy leaves and stems covered with glistening encrustations, and white or pink flowers.

ice point *n.* The temperature at which pure water and ice are in equilibrium in a mixture at one atmosphere of pressure; the melting point of ice, or freezing point of water, under normal atmospheric pressure. Compare **steam point.**

ice rink *n.* **1.** A building housing a level ice surface for skating. **2.** The ice surface itself. Also called "skating rink."

ice-scour·ing (īs′skour′ĭng) *n. Geology.* The erosion of rock by glacial ice. **—ice-scoured** *adj.*

ice sheet *n.* A vast, continuous expanse of land ice, such as that covering the Antarctic continent. See **glacier.**

ice shelf *n.* A thick, floating ice sheet attached to a coastline.

ice show *n.* An entertainment, such as a variety show, performed by skaters on ice.

ice skate *n.* **1.** A metal runner or blade that is fitted to the sole of a shoe for skating on ice. **2.** A shoe or light boot with such a runner permanently fixed to it.

ice-skate (īs′skāt′) *intr.v.* **-skated, -skating, -skates.** To skate on ice. **—ice-skat·er** *n.*

ice storm *n.* A storm in which rain or snow freezes on contact.

ice wall *n.* A cliff of ice forming the seaward margin of an ice sheet.

ice water *n.* **1. a.** Very cold drinking water. **b.** Such water containing ice. **2.** Melted ice.

ICFTU International Confederation of Free Trade Unions.

ich (ĭk) *n.* A contagious disease of tropical aquarium fishes, caused by a protozoan, *Ichthyophthirius multifiliis,* and characterized by small white pustules on the body. [Short for New Latin *Ichthyophthirius,* genus name : ICHTHYO- + Greek *phtheir,* louse.]

I ching (ē′ chĭng′) *n.* A classical book of ancient China whose philosophy seeks to explain nature and human nature in terms of changing balances. As a form of fortune-telling, the book is used to explain each of 64 hexagrams, one of which is chosen at random by

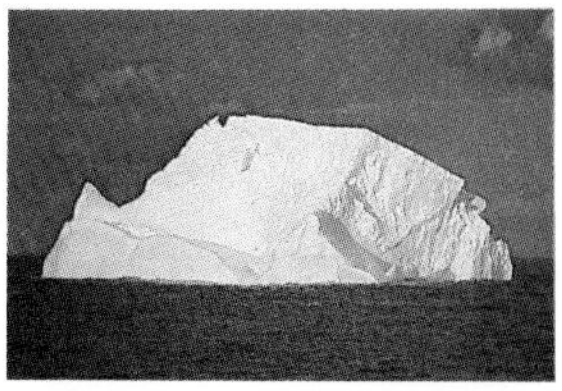

iceberg *Water is less dense at its freezing point than just above it. As a result, an iceberg floats. However, only about a quarter of a berg is visible; the rest is below the sea's surface.*

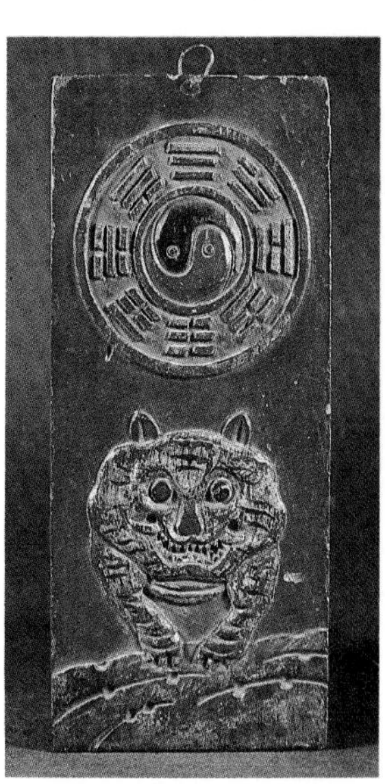

I Ching *This lacquered board, bearing symbols from the* I Ching, *or "Book of Changes," was meant to be hung in a doorway to keep out devils. The central circle encloses the fishlike symbols for yin and yang, the feminine and masculine forces that shape the universe in Chinese thought. Around them are the eight trigrams, or divinatory categories, used in the* I Ching. *Each trigram is made up of three solid (masculine) or broken (feminine) bars, representing all the possible combinations of the two forces.*

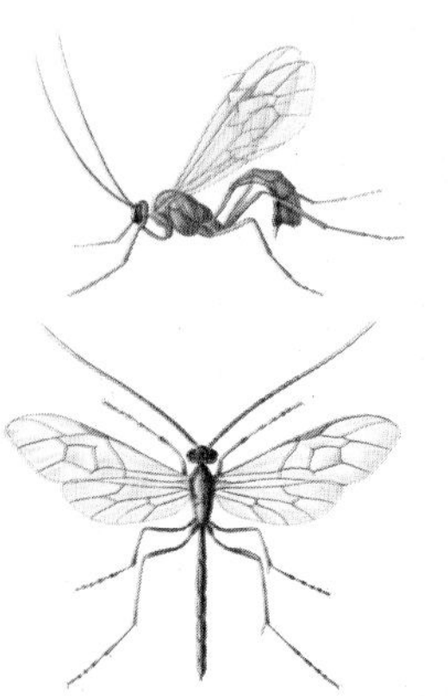

ichneumon fly *Worldwide, there are about 40,000 species of this parasitic insect. The fly (seen here from above and from the side) injects its eggs into the larvae, or caterpillars, of other insects—often butterflies and moths. When the eggs hatch, the ichneumon larvae feed on the caterpillar's body from the inside, eventually killing it.*

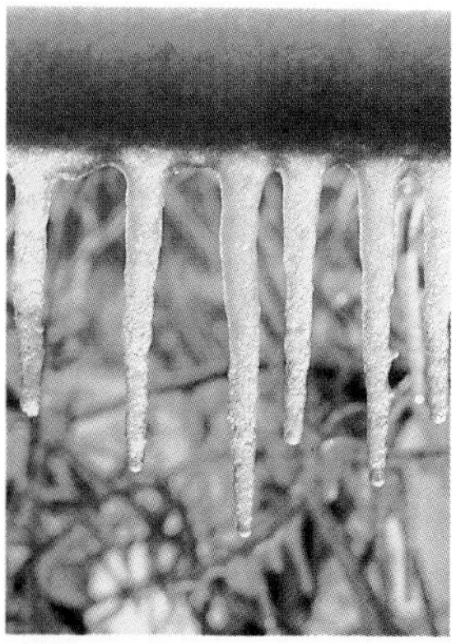

icicle *These long spikes of ice are formed by dripping water.*

the person consulting it. [Chinese, "book of changes."]

ich·neu·mon (ĭk-no͞o′mən, -nyo͞o′mən) *n.* A mongoose of the genus *Herpestes*; especially, *H. ichneumon,* of Africa. [Latin, from Greek *ikhneumōn,* "tracker," a weasel that hunts out crocodile eggs, from *ikhneuein,* to track, from *ikhnos*†, track.]

ichneumon fly *n.* Any of various wasplike insects of the family Ichneumonidae, having larvae that are parasitic on the larvae of other insects. Also called "ichneumon wasp."

ich·nite (ĭk′nīt′) *n.* A fossilized footprint. Also called "ichnolite." [Greek *ikhnos,* footstep, track (see **ichneumon**) + -ITE.]

ich·nog·ra·phy (ĭk-nŏg′rə-fē) *n., pl.* **-phies.** **1.** The art or process of drawing up ground plans. **2.** A ground plan of a building. [French *ichnographie,* from Latin, from Greek *ikhnographia* : *ikhnos,* track + *-graphia,* -GRAPHY.]

i·chor (ī′kôr′, ī′kər) *n.* **1.** *Greek Mythology.* The rarefied fluid said to run in the veins of the gods. **2.** A fluid likened to blood. **3.** *Pathology.* A watery, acrid discharge from a wound or ulcer. [Greek *ikhōr*†.] **—i·chor·ous** (ī′kər-əs) *adj.*

ich·thy·ic (ĭk′thē-ĭk) *adj.* Of, pertaining to, or characteristic of fishes. [Greek *ikhthus,* fish. See **ichthyo-**.]

ichthyo-, ichthy- *prefix.* Indicates fish; for example, **ichthyology, ichthyornis.** [Latin, from Greek *ikhthuo-,* from *ikhthus,* fish.]

ich·thy·o·fau·na (ĭk′thē-ə-fô′nə) *n.* The fish of a particular region.

ich·thy·oid (ĭk′thē-oid′) *adj.* Also **ich·thy·oid·al** (ĭk′thē-oid′l). Characteristic of or resembling a fish.

~*n.* A fish or fishlike vertebrate. [Greek *ikhthuoeidēs* : ICHTHY(O)- + -OID.]

ich·thy·ol·o·gy (ĭk′thē-ŏl′ə-jē) *n. Abbr.* **ichthyol., ichth.** A branch of zoology specializing in the study of fishes. [ICHTHYO- + -LOGY.] **—ich·thy·o·log·ic** (ĭk′thē-ə-lŏj′ĭk), **ich·thy·o·log·i·cal** *adj.* **—ich·thy·ol·o·gist** *n.*

ich·thy·oph·a·gous (ĭk′thē-ŏf′ə-gəs) *adj.* Feeding on fish; fish-eating. [Greek *ikhthuophagos* : ICHTHYO- + -PHAGOUS.] **—ich·thy·oph·a·gy** (ĭk′thē-ŏf′ə-jē) *n.*

ich·thy·or·nis (ĭk′thē-ôr′nĭs) *n.* Any of various extinct, fish-eating birds of the genus *Ichthyornis,* that existed during the Cretaceous period. [New Latin "fish bird" : ICHTHY(O)- + Greek *ornis,* bird.]

ich·thy·o·saur (ĭk′thē-ə-sôr′) *n.* Also **ich·thy·o·saur·us** (ĭk′thē-ə-sôr′əs) *pl.* **-sauri** (-sôr′ī′), **-sauruses.** Any of various extinct fishlike marine reptiles of the order Ichthyosauria, of the Triassic to the Cretaceous periods. [New Latin *Ichthyosaurus* : ICHTHYO- + -SAUR.]

ich·thy·o·sis (ĭk′thē-ō′sĭs) *n.* A congenital skin disease, characterized by dry, thickened, scaly skin. Also called "xeroderma." [New Latin : ICHTHY(O)- + -OSIS.]

–ician *suffix.* Indicates a person who practices or is a specialist in a specified field; for example, **beautician, phonetician.**

i·ci·cle (ī′sĭ-kəl) *n.* A tapering spike of ice formed by the freezing of dripping or falling water. [Middle English *isikel* : *is,* ICE + *ikel,* icicle, Old English *gicel.*]

i·ci·ly (ī′sĭ-lē) *adv.* In an icy or chilling manner.

i·ci·ness (ī′sē-nĭs) *n.* The condition or quality of being icy.

ic·ing (ī′sĭng) *n.* **1.** A covering for cakes, cookies, and other baked goods, made from sugar, butter, water, and egg whites or milk, and often flavored and cooked. **2.** The formation of ice; especially, the formation of ice from moisture in the atmosphere, as on an aircraft or ship. **3.** The act of intentionally shooting the puck far out of defensive territory in ice hockey.

ick·y (ĭk′ē) *adj. Slang.* **1.** Sticky; cloying. **2.** Sentimental; mawkish. **3.** Nasty; unpleasant. [20th century : origin obscure.]

ICJ International Court of Justice.

Ick·nield Way (ĭk′nēld′). Prehistoric road in England. It ran southwest from the Wash, along the line of the Chiltern Hills and the Berkshire Downs, to Salisbury Plain.

i·con, i·kon (ī′kŏn′) *n.* Also **ei·kon** (for sense 2). **1.** An image; a representation. **2.** A representation or picture of a sacred Christian personage, itself regarded as sacred, especially in the tradition of the Eastern Churches. **3.** An important and enduring symbol. [Latin *īcōn,* from Greek *eikōn,* likeness, image.]

i·con·ic (ī-kŏn′ĭk) *adj.* **1.** Pertaining to or having the character of an icon. **2.** Having a conventional style. Said of certain memorial statues and busts, such as the ancient statues of victorious athletes.

Iconium. See **Konya.**

icono– or **icon–** *prefix.* Indicates likeness, image; for example, **iconolatry.** [Greek *eikono-,* from *eikōn,* image, ICON.]

i·con·o·clasm (ī-kŏn′ə-klăz′əm) *n.* The action or doctrine of an iconoclast.

i·con·o·clast (ī-kŏn′ə-klăst′) *n.* **1.** A destroyer of sacred images, specifically: **a.** Any of the opponents of the use and veneration of icons in the Eastern Churches during the 8th and 9th centuries A.D. **b.** A Protestant in the 16th and 17th centuries who opposed the veneration of sacred images and traditions. **2.** One who attacks and seeks to overthrow traditional or popular ideas or institutions. [Medieval Latin *īconoclāstēs,* from Medieval Greek *eikonoklastēs,* "image breaker" : ICONO- + -CLAST.] **—i·con·o·clas·tic** (ī-kŏn′ə-klăs′tĭk) *adj.* **—i·con·o·clas·ti·cal·ly** *adv.*

i·co·nog·ra·phy (ī′kə-nŏg′rə-fē) *n., pl.* **-phies.** **1. a.** Pictorial illustration of a given subject. **b.** The collected representations illustrating a subject. **2. a.** A given set of symbolic forms bearing the meaning of a stylized work of art. **b.** The conventions defining these symbolic forms and governing their interrelationship. [Greek *eikonographia,* description, sketch, "drawing of images" : ICONO- + -GRAPHY.] **—i·con·o·graph·ic** (ī-kŏn′ə-grăf′ĭk), **i·con·o·graph·i·cal** *adj.*

i·co·nol·a·try (ī′kə-nŏl′ə-trē) *n.* The worship of images or icons. [ICONO- + -LATRY.] **—i·co·nol·a·ter** *n.*

i·co·nol·o·gy (ī′kə-nŏl′ə-jē) *n., pl.* **-gies.** **1.** The branch of art history dealing with the description, analysis, and interpretation of icons or iconic representations. **2.** Symbolic representation. [French *iconologie* : ICONO- + -LOGY.] **—i·con·o·log·i·cal** (ī-kŏn′ə-lŏj′ĭ-kəl) *adj.* **—i·co·nol·o·gist** *n.*

i·con·o·scope (ī-kŏn′ə-skōp′) *n.* A television-camera tube equipped for rapid scanning of an information-storing, photoactive mosaic by a beam of electrons. [Originally a trademark : ICONO- + -SCOPE.]

i·co·nos·ta·sis (ī′kə-nŏs′tə-sĭs) *n., pl.* **-ses** (-sēz′). The screen dividing the sanctuary from the main body of an Eastern Church. [Late Greek *eikonostasion,* shrine, "place where images stand" : ICONO- + Greek *stasis,* a standing.]

i·co·sa·he·dron (ī-kō′sə-hē′drən) *n., pl.* **-dra** (-drə) or **-drons.** A polyhedron having 20 faces. A regular icosahedron has faces that are equilateral triangles. [Greek *eikosaedron* : *eikosi,* twenty.] **—i·co·sa·he·dral** *adj.*

–ics *suffix.* Indicates: **1.** *Used with a singular verb.* The science or art of; for example, **graphics, poetics.** **2.** *Used with a plural verb.* The act, practices, or activities of; for example, **acrobatics, athletics.** **3.** *Used with a plural verb.* Characteristic properties or operations of; for example, **mechanics, dynamics.** [From -IC, originally used to render the Greek plural noun ending *-ika,* as in *mathēmatika,* MATHEMATICS.]

ICSH interstitial-cell stimulating hormone.

ic·ter·ic (ĭk-tĕr′ĭk) *adj.* **1.** Pertaining to or having jaundice. **2.** Used to treat jaundice.

~*n.* A remedy for jaundice.

ic·ter·us (ĭk′tər-əs) *n. Pathology.* **Jaundice** *(see).* [New Latin, from Greek *ikteros*†, jaundice.]

ic·tus (ĭk′təs) *n., pl.* **-tuses** or **ictus.** **1.** A metrical or rhythmical stress in verse. **2.** *Pathology.* A sudden attack; a fit; a stroke. [Latin, blow, stroke, from the past participle of *īcere*†, to strike.]

ICU intensive care unit.

i·cy (ī′sē) *adj.* **icier, iciest.** **1.** Containing or covered with ice; frozen; slippery: *an icy road.* **2.** Resembling ice; cold or slippery. **3.** Bitterly cold; freezing. **4.** Chilling in manner; frigid: *an icy smile.*

id (ĭd) *n. Psychoanalysis.* That division of the psyche associated with instinctive impulses and demands for immediate satisfaction of primitive needs. See **ego, superego.** [New Latin (translation of German *es,* it), from Latin, it, neuter of *is,* he.]

ID Idaho (used with a Zip Code).

Id. Idaho.

I'd (īd). **1.** Contraction of *I had.* **2.** Contraction of *I would.* **3.** Contraction of *I should.*

–id *suffix.* Indicates: **1.** *Zoology.* A member of a family; for example, **hominid.** **2.** *Chemistry.* Variant of **-ide.** [Partly from New Latin -IDAE and partly from French *-ide,* from Latin *-is* (stem *-id-*), feminine patronymic suffix.]

id. idem.

i.d. inside diameter.

I.D. **1.** identification. **2.** intelligence department.

IDA International Development Association.

I·da, Mount (ī′də). Mountain in central Crete associated with the worship of Zeus. It rises to 2,456 meters (8,058 feet) and is the highest mountain on the island.

–idae *suffix.* Indicates taxonomic names of families in zoology; for example, **Hominidae.** [New Latin. See **-id.**]

I·da·ho (ī′də-hō′). State in the northwestern United States, one of the group of Rocky Mt. states. The capital and largest city is Boise. It is noted for its unspoilt natural beauty, two-fifths of the state being covered by natural forest. Hell's Canyon, also known as "Grand Canyon of the Snake," is at one point 2,401 meters (7,900 feet) below the mountain peaks and is the deepest gorge in North America. The economy is largely agricultural, beef and dairy farming being the most important activities. **—I·da·ho·an** *adj. & n.*

ID card (ī′dē′) *n.* A card that gives identifying information, such as name, age, and organizational membership, about a person, who then carries the card and uses it to establish his or her identity. Also called "identity card."

–ide, –id *suffix.* Used to form the names of chemical compounds, especially salts derived from acids that contain no oxygen; for example, **chloride.** [German *-id,* from French *-ide* (first used in *oxide,* OXIDE), from *acide,* ACID.]

i·de·a (ī-dē′ə) *n.* **1.** That which comes into existence in the mind as a product of mental activity, such as thought or knowledge; a thought; a conception: *many good ideas.* **2.** An opinion, conviction, or principle produced after thought or observation: *Upon what do you base your political ideas?* **3.** A plan, scheme, or method. **4.** The gist or significance of a specific action or situation. **5.** A notion; a fancy. **6.** *Obsolete.* A mental image of something remembered. **7.** *Music.* A theme or motif. **8.** *Philosophy.* **a.** In the philosophy of Plato, an archetype of which a corresponding being in phenomenal reality is an imperfect replica. **b.** In the philosophy of Kant, a concept of reason that is transcendent but nonempirical. **c.** In the philosophy of Hegel, absolute truth, the complete and ultimate product of reason. [Latin, from Greek, form, model, class, notion.]

Synonyms: *concept, conception, notion, thought.*

i·de·al (ī-dē′əl, ī-dēl′) *n.* **1.** A conception of something in its absolute perfection. **2.** One regarded as a standard or model of perfection.

3. An ultimate object of endeavor; a goal. **4.** A worthy principle or aim. **5.** That which exists only in the mind.
~adj. **1.** Conforming to an ultimate form of perfection or excellence. **2.** Considered the best of its kind. **3.** Completely or highly satisfactory. **4.** Existing only in the mind; visionary; imaginary. **5.** Of, pertaining to, or consisting of ideas or mental images. **6.** *Philosophy.* **a.** Existing as an archetype or pattern, especially as a Platonic idea. **b.** Of or pertaining to idealism. [French *idéal,* from Late Latin *ideālis,* from Latin *idea,* model, IDEA.]
Synonyms: *archetype, exemplar, model, standard.*

ideal gas *n. Physics.* A hypothetical gas that obeys the gas laws. In kinetic theory, a model of such a gas is a large number of particles of negligible size, moving randomly and making elastic collisions with the walls of the container.

ideal gas law *n. Physics.* **Gas equation** *(see).*

i·de·al·ism (ī-dē'ə-lĭz'əm) *n.* **1.** The envisaging of things in an ideal form. **2.** Pursuit of one's ideals. **3.** An idealizing treatment of a subject in literature or art. **4.** The theory that the object of external perception, in itself or as perceived, consists of ideas. In this sense, compare **materialism, realism.**

i·de·al·ist (ī-dē'ə-lĭst) *n.* **1.** One whose conduct is influenced by idealism. **2.** One who is unrealistic and impractical; a visionary. **3.** An artist or writer whose work is imbued with idealism. **4.** An adherent of any system of philosophical idealism.

i·de·al·is·tic (ī-dē'ə-lĭs'tĭk) *adj.* Pertaining to or having the nature of an idealist or idealism. **—i·de·al·is·ti·cal·ly** *adv.*

i·de·al·i·ty (ī'dē-ăl'ə-tē) *n., pl.* **-ties. 1.** The state or quality of being ideal. **2.** Existence in idea only.

i·de·al·ize (ī-dē'ə-līz') *v.* **-ized, -izing, -izes.** *—tr.* **1. a.** To regard as ideal. **b.** To treat (a person or thing) as if ideal. **2.** To depict or imagine as ideal. *—intr.* **1.** To render something as an ideal. **2.** To conceive an ideal or ideals. **—i·de·al·i·za·tion** (ī-dē'ə-lə-zā'shən) *n.* **—i·de·al·iz·er** *n.*

i·de·al·ly (ī-dē'ə-lē) *adv.* **1.** In conformity with an ideal; perfectly. **2.** In ideal conditions; theoretically.

i·de·ate (ī-dē'āt') *v.* **-ated, -ating, -ates.** *—tr.* To form an idea of; imagine; conceive. *—intr.* To conceive mental images; think. [IDEA.] **—i·de·a·tion** (ī'dē-ā'shən) *n.* **—i·de·a·tion·al** *adj.*

i·dée fixe (ē-dā fēks') *n., pl.* **idées fixes** *(pronounced as singular).* A fixed idea; an obsession.

i·dée re·çue (ē-dā rə-sü') *n., pl.* **idées reçues** *(pronounced as singular).* A received idea; an opinion that is held out of respect for convention rather than from conviction. [French.]

i·dem (ī'dĕm'). *Abbr.* **id.** The same. Used to indicate a reference previously mentioned. [Latin *īdem* (masculine), *idem* (neuter), the same, from *id,* it, neuter of *is,* he.]

i·dem·po·tent (ī'dĕm-pō'tənt, ī-dĕm'pə-tənt) *adj. Mathematics.* Unchanged by multiplication by itself. Said of matrices, functions, operators, and the like. [Latin *idem,* same + POTENT.]

i·den·tic note (ī-dĕn'tĭk) *n.* A diplomatic communication with wording that has been agreed upon by two or more governments, copies of which are dispatched simultaneously on behalf of these governments. [Medieval Latin *identicus,* IDENTICAL.]

i·den·ti·cal (ī-dĕn'tĭ-kəl) *adj.* **1.** Being the same. **2.** Being exactly alike or equal. —See Synonyms at **same.** [Medieval Latin *identicus,* from Late Latin *identitās,* IDENTITY.] **—i·den·ti·cal·ly** *adv.* **—i·den·ti·cal·ness** *n.*
Usage: Standard English recommends that the preposition following *identical* should be *with (That picture is identical with the one in my office),* but *to* is becoming increasingly common.

identical twin *n.* Either of a pair of twins of the same sex developed from a single fertilized ovum that split in half. Identical twins have identical genetic constitutions and show pronounced mutual resemblance. Also called "monozygotic twin."

i·den·ti·fi·ca·tion (ī-dĕn'tə-fĭ-kā'shən) *n.* **1.** The act of identifying. **2.** The state of being identified. **3.** *Abbr.* **I.D.** Proof of one's identity, such as a document, for example. **4.** *Psychology.* **a.** An individual's recognition of a personal or group identity. **b.** The transferal of response to an object considered identical to another. **5.** The recognition of oneself in another character, such as one in fiction or public life, with consequently strong sympathy for the character and concern for his or her fate.

identification card *n.* An **ID card** *(see).*

i·den·ti·fy (ī-dĕn'tə-fī') *v.* **-fied, -fying, -fies.** *—tr.* **1. a.** To establish the identity of. **b.** To ascertain the origin, nature, or definitive characteristics of: *His accent was difficult to identify.* **c.** To determine and select: *identify the best method.* **2.** To determine the taxonomic classification of. **3.** To consider as identical; equate. **4.** To associate with. **5.** *Psychology.* To associate or affiliate (oneself) closely with a person or group. **6.** To imagine (oneself) as another person, such as a literary character or a prominent figure. *—intr.* To establish an identification with another or others: *The reader often identifies with the hero of a novel.* [Medieval Latin *identificāre* : Late Latin *identitās,* IDENTI(TY) + -FY.] **—i·den·ti·fi·a·ble** (ī-dĕn'tə-fī'ə-bəl) *adj.* **—i·den·ti·fi·er** *n.*
Usage: When used in the sense of "to see oneself as similar or identical to," the verb *identify* may be used with or without the reflexive pronoun, as in *I identified myself with the hero* or *I identified with the hero.* Used technically, in the field of psychology, *identify* expresses close association with a person or group and lacks the reflexive pronoun, as in *He identifies with his father.*

i·den·ti·ty (ī-dĕn'tə-tē) *n., pl.* **-ties. 1.** The collective aspect of the set of characteristics by which a thing is definitively recognizable or known. **2.** The set of behavioral or personal characteristics by which an individual is recognizable as a member of a group. **3.** The name or nature of a person or thing: *reveal one's identity.* **4.** The quality or condition of being exactly the same as something else. **5.** The quality or condition of being or remaining the same. **6.** The personality of an individual regarded as a persisting entity. **7.** *Mathematics.* **a.** An equality satisfied by all values of the variables for which the expressions involved in the equality are defined. **b.** A member of a set that combines with other members and leaves them unchanged for a particular operation; for example, the integer 1 is the identity for real numbers under multiplication. Also called "identity element." [Late Latin *identitās,* from Latin *idem,* the same, IDEM.]

identity card *n.* An **ID card** *(see).*

identity crisis *n. Psychology.* A period of disorientation and anxiety resulting from difficulties experienced in resolving personal conflicts, adjusting to social demands and pressures, or the like.

identity matrix *n.* A square matrix with numeral 1's along the diagonal from upper left to lower right and 0's in all other positions.

identity sign *n.* A mathematical symbol ($\equiv$), used to denote identity rather than equality.

ideo– *prefix.* Indicates idea; for example, **ideogram.** [French *idéo-,* from Greek *idea,* form, notion.]

id·e·o·gram (ĭd'ē-ə-grăm', ī'dē-) *n.* Also **id·e·o·graph** (-grăf', -gräf'). **1.** A character or symbol representing an idea or thing without indicating pronunciation, as the characters in Chinese. **2.** A graphic symbol; for example, &, %, @. [IDEO- + -GRAM.]

id·e·og·ra·phy (ĭd'ē-ŏg'rə-fē, ī'dē-) *n.* **1.** The representation of ideas by graphic symbols. **2.** The use of ideograms to express ideas. [IDEO- + -GRAPHY.] **—id·e·o·graph·ic** (ĭd'ē-ə-grăf'ĭk) *adj.*

i·de·o·log·i·cal (ī'dē-ə-lŏj'ĭ-kəl, ĭd'ē-) *adj.* **1.** Of or relating to ideology. **2.** Of or concerned with ideas. **—i·de·o·log·i·cal·ly** *adv.*

i·de·ol·o·gist (ī'dē-ŏl'ə-jĭst, ĭd'ē-) *n.* **1.** An advocate or adherent of a given ideology. **2.** A student of ideologies. **3.** *Archaic.* A visionary; a theorist.

i·de·o·logue (ī'dē-ə-lŏg', ĭd'ē-) *n.* An advocate of a given ideology, especially one of its official exponents. [French *idéologue,* back-formation from *idéologie,* IDEOLOGY.]

i·de·ol·o·gy (ī'dē-ŏl'ə-jē, ĭd'ē-) *n., pl.* **-gies. 1.** The body of ideas reflecting the needs and aspirations of an individual, group, or culture. **2.** A set of doctrines or beliefs that form the basis of a political, economic, or other system. [French *idéologie* : IDEO- + -LOGY.]

i·de·o·mo·tor (ī'dē-ə-mō'tər, ĭd'ē-) *adj.* Of or being a motor response to an ideational rather than a sensory stimulus.

ides (īdz) *n. Used with a singular or plural verb.* In the ancient Roman calendar, the 15th day of March, May, July, or October or the 13th day of the other months. [Middle English *idus, ides,* from Old French *ides,* from Latin *īdūs*†.]

id est (ĭd ĕst'). *Abbr.* **i.e.** *Latin.* That is.

idio– *prefix.* Indicates individuality, peculiarity, isolation, or distinctness; for example, **idiolect.** [Greek, from *idios*†, personal, peculiar, separate.]

id·i·o·blast (ĭd'ē-ō-blăst') *n.* A specialized plant cell that differs from the cells around it. [IDIO- + -BLAST.] **—id·i·o·blast·ic** (ĭd'-ē-ō-blăs'tĭk) *adj.*

id·i·o·cy (ĭd'ē-ə-sē) *n., pl.* **-cies. 1.** A condition of subnormal intellectual development or ability, characterized by an intelligence quotient in the range 20–50. No longer in technical usage. Compare **imbecility. 2.** Extreme folly or stupidity. **3.** A foolish or stupid utterance or deed.

id·i·o·gram (ĭd'ē-ə-grăm') *n.* A **karyotype** *(see).* [IDIO- + -GRAM.]

id·i·o·lect (ĭd'ē-ə-lĕkt') *n.* The speech of an individual, considered as a linguistic pattern unique among speakers of his language or dialect. [IDIO- + (DIA)LECT.] **—id·i·o·lect·al** (ĭd'ē-ə-lĕk'təl), **id·i·o·lect·ic** (id'ē-ə-lĕk'tĭk) *adj.*

id·i·om (ĭd'ē-əm) *n.* **1.** An expression or phrase that has a meaning of its own that is not apparent from the meanings of its individual words; for example, *to make friends,* meaning "to become acquainted," and *to do away with,* meaning "to dispose of," are English idioms. **2.** The specific grammatical, syntactical, and structural character of a given language. **3.** A regional speech or dialect. **4.** A specialized vocabulary used by a particular group of people; jargon: *legal idiom.* **5.** A style of artistic expression characteristic of a given individual, school, period, or medium. [Old French *idiome,* from Late Latin *idiōma,* from Greek, peculiarity, idiom, from *idiousthai,* to make one's own, from *idios*†, own, personal.]

id·i·o·mat·ic (ĭd'ē-ə-măt'ĭk) *adj.* **1.** Peculiar to or characteristic of a given language. **2.** Resembling or having the nature of an idiom. **3.** Using many idioms; fluent and natural: *spoke idiomatic French.* **—id·i·o·mat·i·cal·ly** *adv.*

id·i·o·mor·phic (ĭd'ē-ə-môr'fĭk) *adj.* Occurring as crystals. Said of minerals. [Greek *idiomorphos,* having one's own form : IDIO- + -MORPHOUS.] **—id·i·o·mor·phic·al·ly** *adv.* **—id·i·o·mor·phism** *n.*

id·i·op·a·thy (ĭd'ē-ŏp'ə-thē) *n. Medicine.* A disease of unknown origin or cause. [Greek *idiopathia,* disease having its own origin : IDIO- + -PATHY.] **—id·i·o·path·ic** (ĭd'ē-ō-păth'ĭk) *adj.*

id·i·o·plasm (ĭd'ē-ō-plăz'əm) *n.* A hypothetical structural unit of germ plasm. **—id·i·o·plas·mic, id·i·o·plas·mat·ic** (ĭd'ē-ō-plăz-măt'-ĭk) *adj.*

id·i·o·syn·cra·sy (ĭd'ē-ō-sĭng'krə-sē) *n., pl.* **-sies. 1.** A structural or behavioral characteristic peculiar to an individual or group. **2.** A physiological or temperamental peculiarity. **3.** Unusual hypersensitivity to a drug or food. —See Synonyms at **eccentricity.** [Greek

PRONUNCIATION KEY

ă, pat; ā, pay; âr, care; ä, father, are; b, bib; ch, church; d, deed; ĕ, pet; ē, be; f, fife; g, gag; h, hat; hw, which; ĭ, pit; ī, pie; îr, pier; j, judge; k, kick; l, lid, needle; m, mum; n, no, sudden; ng, thing; ŏ, pot; ō, toe; ô, paw, for; oi, noise; ou, out; o͝o, book; o͞o, boot; p, pop; r, roar; s, sauce; sh, ship, dish; t, tight; th, thin, path; *th,* this, bathe; ŭ, cut; ûr, fur; v, valve; w, with; y, yes; z, zebra, size; zh, vision; ə, about, item, edible, gallop, circus, peaceful

IN FOREIGN WORDS:

à, *Fr.* ami; œ, *Fr.* feu, *Ger.* schön; ü, *Fr.* tu, *Ger.* über; KH, *Ger.* ich, *Scot.* loch; N, *Fr.* bon; y', *Fr.* Compiègne

STRESS MARKS:

Primary stress: '
in·cite' (ĭn-sīt')
Secondary stress: '
in'sight' (ĭn'sīt')

idiosunkrasia : IDIO- + *sunkrasis*, a mingling, mixture, temperament : *syn*-, together + *krasis*, mixture, CRASIS.] —**id·i·o·syn·crat·ic** (ĭd'ē-ō-sĭn-krăt'ĭk) *adj.* —**id·i·o·syn·crat·i·cal·ly** *adv.*

id·i·ot (ĭd'ē-ət) *n.* **1.** A mentally deficient person, having an intelligence quotient in the 20 to 50 range, and classified as severely subnormal. No longer in technical usage. **2.** A very stupid person. [Middle English, from Old French *idiote*, from Latin *idiōta*, ignorant person, from Greek *idiōtēs*, private person, plebeian, layman, ignorant person, from *idios†*, peculiar, private.]

id·i·ot·ic (ĭd'ē-ŏt'ĭk) *adj.* Very stupid. —**id·i·ot·i·cal·ly** *adv.*

idiot light *n.* A light on the instrument panel of an automobile that gives forewarning, as of an overheated engine.

-idium *suffix.* Indicates a small structure or form; for example, **nephridium.** [New Latin, from Greek *-idion.*]

i·dle (ĭd'l) *adj.* **idler, idlest. 1.** Not employed; inactive: *Cancellation of the meeting left her idle.* **2.** Avoiding employment; lazy; shiftless. **3.** Not in operation or working order: *idle machinery.* **4.** Empty; pointless: *idle talk.* **5.** Unfounded; baseless: *idle rumors.* —See Synonyms at **inactive.**
~*v.* **idled, idling, idles.** —*intr.* **1.** To pass time without working or in avoiding work. **2.** To move lazily and without purpose. **3.** To run at a slow speed or out of gear. Used of a motor or a machine. —*tr.* **1.** To pass (time) without working or in avoiding work; waste. Often used with *away*: *idle the afternoon away.* **2.** To cause to be unemployed or inactive. **3.** To cause (a motor or machine) to idle. [Middle English *idel*, idle, void, empty, Old English *īdel*, from West Germanic *īdal* (unattested).] —**i·dle·ness** *n.* —**i·dly** *adv.*

idle character *n.* An alphanumeric or digital character that is transmitted over a communications line but does not appear in the output of the receiving terminal.

idle pulley *n.* A pulley on a shaft that rests on or presses against a drive belt to guide it or take up slack. Also called "idler," "idler pulley," "idle wheel."

i·dler (ĭd'lər) *n.* **1.** One that idles. **2.** An idle wheel or idle pulley. **3.** A sailor exempt from night watch.

idle wheel *n.* **1.** A gear, wheel, or roller interposed between two similar parts to convey motion from one to the other without change in speed or direction of motion. Also called "idler." **2.** An idle pulley.

I·do (ī'dō) *n.* An artificial language based on Esperanto. [Esperanto, offspring, from Greek *-id*, "daughter of."]

id·o·crase (ĭd'ō-krās', ī'dō-) *n.* A green, brown, yellow, or blue mineral, essentially $Ca_{10}Al_4(Mg,Fe)_2(Si_2O_4)_2(SiO_4)_5(OH)_4$. Also called "vesuvianite." [French : Greek *eidos*, form, shape + *krasis*, mixture.]

i·dol (ī'dl) *n.* **1. a.** An image used as an object of worship. **b.** A false god. **2.** One that is the object of deep love or devotion. **3.** *Archaic.* Something visible but without substance. [Middle English *idol, idel*, from Old French *idole, idele*, from Late Latin *īdōlum*, from Greek *eidōlon*, image, form, apparition, from *eidos*, form.]

i·dol·a·ter (ī-dŏl'ə-tər) *n.* **1.** One who worships idols. **2.** One who blindly admires or adores another. [Middle English *idolatrer*, from Old French *idolatre*, from Late Latin *īdōlolatrēs*, from Greek *eidōlolatreia* : *eidōlon*, IDOL + *-latrēs*, worshiper.]

i·dol·a·trize (ī-dŏl'ə-trīz') *tr.v.* **-trized, -trizing, -trizes.** To make an idol of. —See Synonyms at **revere.**

i·dol·a·trous (ī-dŏl'ə-trəs) *adj.* **1.** Given to idolatry. **2.** Constituting idolatry. —**i·dol·a·trous·ly** *adv.* —**i·dol·a·trous·ness** *n.*

i·dol·a·try (ī-dŏl'ə-trē) *n., pl.* **-tries. 1.** The worship of idols. **2.** Blind admiration of or devotion to something or someone. [Middle English, from Old French, from Medieval Latin *īdōlatrīa*, from Greek *eidōlolatreia* : *eidōlon*, IDOL + *-latreia*, -LATRY.]

i·dol·ize (ī'dl-īz') *tr.v.* **-ized, -izing, -izes. 1.** To regard with blind admiration or devotion. **2.** To worship as an idol. —See Synonyms at **revere.** —**i·dol·i·za·tion** (ī'dl-ə-zā'shən) *n.* —**i·dol·iz·er** *n.*

i·do·lum (ī-dō'ləm) *n., pl.* **-la** (-lə). **1.** An image in the mind. **2.** A fallacy. [Latin, IDOL.]

Idun. Variant of **Ithunn.**

i·dyll, i·dyl (ī'dl) *n.* **1.** A short poem describing a picturesque episode or scene of rustic life. **2.** A scene or event of rural simplicity. **3.** A delightful and simple episode in life or literature. **4.** A piece of calm pastoral music. [Latin *īdyllium*, from Greek *eidullion*, diminutive of *eidos*, form, picture.]

i·dyl·lic (ī-dĭl'ĭk) *adj.* **1.** Of, pertaining to, or having the nature of an idyll. **2.** Having a natural charm and picturesqueness. —**i·dyl·li·cal·ly** *adv.*

i·dyl·list (ī'dl-ĭst) *n.* A writer of idylls.

-ie. Variant of **-y.**

i.e. id est.
Usage: The abbreviations *i.e.* and *e.g.* are not interchangeable, though they are sometimes confused. The distinction can easily be made by reference to their meanings: *i.e.* stands for the Latin *id est*, meaning "that is"; *e.g.* stands for the Latin *exempli gratia*, meaning "for example." Thus, *i.e.* always gives a fuller explanation of what precedes it: *the manager, i.e. the man in charge,* whereas *e.g.* introduces an example, or set of examples: *the people in charge, e.g. supervisors, stewards.* It is unacceptable to use such expressions as: *schoolchildren, i.e. five-year-olds and six-year-olds,* when what follows the abbreviation is an example rather than an explanation.

if (ĭf) *conj.* **1.** Used to introduce a conditional clause, meaning: **a.** In the event that: *If I were to go, I would be late.* **b.** Granting that: *Even if that's true, what should we do?* **c.** On condition that: *She will sing only if she is paid.* **d.** Whenever: *I always go if she asks me.*

e. Although: *They are gifted, if inexperienced.* **2.** Used to introduce an indirect question, meaning whether: *Ask if he will come.* **3.** Used to introduce an exclamatory clause, indicating: **a.** A wish: *If she had only come earlier!* **b.** Surprise, anger, or a similar emotion: *If she ever does that again!* —**if not. 1.** Though perhaps not: *certainly comfortable, if not rich.* **2.** And possibly even: *a millionaire, if not a billionaire.*
~*n.* A possibility, condition, or stipulation. [Middle English *(y)if*, Old English *gif*.]
Usage: Both *if* and *whether* may be used to introduce an indirect question, but *whether* is slightly more formal. It is also more likely whenever more than one condition is being expressed and linked by *or*: *He asked whether John would arrive on time or whether he would be late.* Sometimes it is necessary to use *whether* in order to avoid ambiguity: *Tell me if you want an answer,* for example, could mean either "Tell me whether you want an answer," or "If you expect an answer, there is something you should tell me."

IF, i.f. intermediate frequency.

IFC International Finance Corporation.

I·fe (ē'fā). City in southwestern Nigeria, a leading center for the marketing and exporting of cocoa. It is believed to be the oldest settlement of the Yoruba tribe, dating from *c.* 1300. Terra-cotta and bronze sculptures made there in that period are considered some of the finest treasures of West African art.

if·fy (ĭf'ē) *adj. Informal.* Doubtful; uncertain. [From IF.] —**if·fi·ly** *adv.* —**if·fi·ness** *n.*

I formation *n. Football.* An alignment of the offensive team in which all the backs line up in single file behind the center.

IG, I.G. inspector general.

I-gird·er (ī'gûr'dər) *n.* A girder with an I-shaped cross section.

ig·loo (ĭg'lōō) *n., pl.* **-loos.** An Eskimo house, traditionally dome-shaped and built of blocks of ice or hard snow. [Eskimo *iglu, igdlu,* house.]

ign. ignition.

Ig·na·ti·us Loy·o·la (ĭg-nā'shəs loi-ō'lə), **Saint** (1491-1556). Spanish soldier and priest who founded the Society of Jesus (the Jesuits) in 1534.

ig·ne·ous (ĭg'nē-əs) *adj.* **1.** Of, pertaining to, or characteristic of fire. **2.** *Geology.* **a.** Formed by solidification from a molten or partially molten state. Said of rocks. **b.** Of or pertaining to rock so formed; pyrogenic. [Latin *igneus*, from *ignis*, fire.]

ig·nis fat·u·us (ĭg'nĭs făch'ōō-əs) *n., pl.* **ignes fatui** (ĭg'nēz' făch'ōō-ī'). **1.** A phosphorescent light that hovers or flits over swampy ground at night, caused by spontaneous combustion of methane and other gases emitted by rotting organic matter. Also called "friar's lantern," "will-o'-the-wisp." **2.** Something that misleads or deludes; a deception. [Medieval Latin, "foolish fire."]

ig·nite (ĭg-nīt') *v.* **-nited, -niting, -nites.** —*tr.* **1. a.** To cause to burn. **b.** To set fire to. **2.** To arouse or kindle. —*intr.* To begin to burn; catch fire. [Latin *ignīre*, to set on fire, from *ignis*, fire.] —**ig·nit·a·ble, ig·nit·i·ble** *adj.* —**ig·nit·er, ig·ni·tor** *n.*

ig·ni·tion (ĭg-nĭsh'ən) *n.* **1.** The act of igniting or the point at which this occurs. **2.** *Abbr.* **ign. a.** An electrical system, typically powered by a battery or magneto, that provides the spark to ignite the fuel mixture in an internal-combustion engine. **b.** A switch or other device that activates this system.

ignition point *n.* The minimum temperature at which a substance will continue to burn without additional external heat.

ig·ni·tron (ĭg-nī'trŏn', ĭg'nə-) *n.* A single-anode, mercury-vapor rectifier in which current passes as an arc between the anode and a mercury-pool cathode, used in power rectification. [Latin *ignis*, fire + -TRON.]

ig·no·ble (ĭg-nō'bəl) *adj.* **1.** Not having an honorable character or purpose; contemptible. **2.** Not of the nobility; common. —See Synonyms at **mean** (base). [Latin *ignōbilis* : *in*-, not + *nōbilis*, NOBLE.] —**ig·no·bil·i·ty** (ĭg'nō-bĭl'ə-tē), **ig·no·ble·ness** *n.* —**ig·no·bly** *adv.*

ig·no·min·i·ous (ĭg'nō-mĭn'ē-əs) *adj.* **1.** Characterized by shame or disgrace. **2.** Deserving disgrace or shame; despicable. **3.** Degrading; debasing. —**ig·no·min·i·ous·ly** *adv.* —**ig·no·min·i·ous·ness** *n.*

ig·no·min·y (ĭg'nə-mĭn'ē, -mə-nē) *n., pl.* **-ies. 1.** Dishonor; infamy. **2.** That which causes dishonor; a disgraceful act or disgraceful conduct. —See Synonyms at **disgrace.** [Latin *ignōminia* : *in*-, not + *nōmen* (stem *nōmin*-), name, reputation.]

ig·no·ra·mus (ĭg'nə-rā'məs) *n., pl.* **-muses.** An ignorant person. [New Latin, from Latin, "we do not know," from *īgnōrāre*, to be ignorant, IGNORE.]

ig·no·rance (ĭg'nər-əns) *n.* The condition of being ignorant; lack of knowledge.

ig·no·rant (ĭg'nər-ənt) *adj.* **1.** Without education or knowledge. **2.** Exhibiting lack of education or knowledge. **3.** Unaware or uninformed: *ignorant of what had happened.* **4.** *Nonstandard.* Ill-mannered. [Middle English *ignoraunt*, from Old French *ignorant*, from Latin *īgnōrāns* (stem *īgnōrant*-), present participle of *īgnōrāre*, to be ignorant, IGNORE.] —**ig·no·rant·ly** *adv.*
Synonyms: uneducated, unlearned, unlettered, untaught, untutored.

ig·no·ra·ti·o e·len·chi (ĭg'nə-rā'shē-ō ĭ-leng'kī) *n. Latin.* The procedure of disproving an extraneous proposition rather than one actually advanced. ["Ignoring of proof," translation of Greek *elenkhou agnoia*.]

ig·nore (ĭg-nôr′) *tr.v.* **-nored, -noring, -nores.** To refuse to pay attention to; disregard. —See Synonyms at **refuse.** [French *ignorer,* from Latin *ĭgnōrāre,* not to know, disregard.] —**ig·nor·a·ble** *adj.* —**ig·nor·er** *n.*

ig·no·tum per ig·no·ti·us (ĭg-nō′təm pər ĭg-nō′tē-əs) *n. Latin.* An explanation that is more confusing than that which it purports to explain. ["The unknown by means of the more unknown."]

I·go·rot (ĭg′ə-rŏt′, ē′gə-) *n., pl.* **-rots** or collectively **Igorot.** Also **I·gor·ro·te** (ē′gôr-rō′tā). **1.** A member of any of several related peoples of mountainous northern Luzon in the Philippines. **2.** The Malayo-Polynesian language of these people.

I·gua·çu Falls (ē′gwä-sōō′). Falls in the Iguaçu River, on the Argentina-Brazil border near the Paraguay line. There are two main sections composed of hundreds of waterfalls, the highest of which is 64 meters (210 feet).

i·gua·na (ĭ-gwä′nə) *n.* Any of various large tropical American lizards of the family Iguanidae, often having spiny projections along the back. [Spanish, from Arawak *iwana.*]

i·guan·o·don (ĭ-gwä′nə-dŏn′) *n.* Any of various large dinosaurs of the genus *Iguanodontidae,* of the Jurassic and Cretaceous periods. [New Latin *Iguanodon* : IGUAN(A) + -ODON.]

IGY International Geophysical Year.

ih·ram (ē-räm′) *n.* **1.** The sacred dress of Muslim pilgrims, consisting of two lengths of white cotton. **2.** The sacred state in which the pilgrim exists while wearing this dress. [Arabic *ihrām,* "prohibition," from *harama,* he prohibited. See **harem.**]

IHS A graphic symbol for Jesus. [From ΙΗΣΟΤΣ or IHSOUS, Jesus (in Greek capitals).]

Ijs·sel or **IJs·sel** or **Ys·sel** (ī′səl). River, *c.* 116 kilometers (72 miles) long, of the Netherlands, flowing from the Lower Rhine River northward to the Ijsselmeer.

Ijs·sel·meer or **IJs·sel·meer** or **Ys·sel·meer** (ī′səl-mâr′). Lake of the northwestern Netherlands. It was formed in 1932 from the Zuider Zee by the Wieringen-Friesland Barrage. A program of land reclamation has reduced its area by two thirds, increasing the land area of the Netherlands by *c.* 6 percent.

i·ke·ba·na (ē′kä-bä′nä, ĭk′ə-bä′nə) *n.* The Japanese art of formal flower arrangement with special regard to balance, harmony, and form. [Japanese, "living flowers."]

Ikhnaton. See **Akhenaton.**

ikon. Variant of **icon.**

ilang-ilang. Variant of **ylang-ylang.**

IL Illinois (used with a Zip Code).

ILA International Longshoremen's Association.

-ile *suffix.* Indicates relationship with, similarity to, or capability of; for example, **prehensile, virile.** [Middle English, from Old French, from Latin *-ilis.*]

il·e·ac (ĭl′ē-ăk′) *adj.* **1.** Of or pertaining to ileus. **2.** Of or pertaining to the ileum; ileal.

Île-de-France (ēl-də-fräNs′). A region and former province in north-central France, occupying the Paris basin in the Seine lowland, with Paris as its center.

Île du Diable. See **Devil's Island.**

il·e·i·tis (ĭl′ē-ī′tĭs) *n.* Inflammation of the ileum. [New Latin : IL-E(UM) + -ITIS.]

il·e·os·to·my (ĭl′ē-ŏs′tə-mē) *n., pl.* **-mies.** The surgical formation of an artificial opening through the abdominal wall into the ileum so that the intestinal contents can be discharged without passing through the colon. [ILEO- + -STOMY.]

il·e·um (ĭl′ē-əm) *n., pl.* **-ea** (-ē-ə). The lower portion of the small intestine, extending from the jejunum to the cecum. [New Latin, from Latin *īlium, īleum†,* groin, flank.] —**il·e·al** *adj.*

il·e·us (ĭl′ē-əs) *n.* Intestinal obstruction due to loss of peristalsis or to mechanical obstruction, causing colic, vomiting, and toxemia. [Latin *īleus,* from Greek *(e)ileos,* "a twisting," from *eilein, illein,* to roll, wind.]

i·lex (ī′lĕks′) *n.* **1.** Any of various trees or shrubs of the genus *Ilex;* a holly. **2.** The **holm oak** (see). [Latin *īlex,* holm oak, of Mediterranean origin.]

I.L.G.W.U. International Ladies' Garment Workers' Union.

Il·i·ad (ĭl′ē-əd) *n.* A Greek epic poem attributed to Homer, recounting the siege of Troy.

il·i·um (ĭl′ē-əm) *n., pl.* **-ia** (-ē-ə). The uppermost and widest of three bones constituting one of the lateral halves of the pelvis. [New Latin, from Latin *īlium, īleum†,* groin, flank.] —**il·i·ac** (ĭl′ē-ăk′) *adj.*

ilk[1] (ĭlk) *n.* **1.** Type or kind: *people of that ilk.* Sometimes used humorously. **2.** *Scottish.* Used following a name in the phrase *of that ilk* to indicate that the one named resides on an estate bearing the same name: *Duncan of that ilk.* —See Synonyms at **type.** [Middle English *ilke, ilk,* Old English *ilca,* same.]

ilk[2]. Variant of **ilka.**

il·ka (ĭl′kə) *adj.* Also **ilk** (ĭlk). *Scottish.* Each; every. [Middle English *ilka(n),* each one : *ilk, ech,* EACH + *a,* A.]

ill (ĭl) *adj.* **worse, worst. 1.** Not healthy; sick. **2.** Not normal; unsound: *ill health.* **3.** Resulting in suffering; distressing. **4.** Characterized by animosity or an unpleasant disposition: *ill humor.* **5.** Boding evil; unpropitious. **6.** Disreputable; wicked: *a house of ill repute.* **7.** *Archaic & Regional.* Difficult; hard: *He's ill to please.* —See Synonyms at **sick.**
~adv. **worse, worst. 1.** In an ill manner; badly. **2.** Scarcely or with difficulty. *Note:* The adverb *ill* combines with many adjectives, usually derived from the participles of verbs, to form attributive modifiers before nouns: *an ill-regulated life; an ill-deserving man.* In such

use, the elements are joined with a hyphen. However, when *ill* modifies an adjective coming after the noun or pronoun, the two words are written separately: *His life was ill regulated. The man is ill deserving.*
~n. **1.** Evil; wrongdoing. **2.** Disaster or harm. **3.** A physical or moral trouble. [Middle English *ill(e),* from Old Norse *illr†,* bad.]

I'll (ĭl). **1.** Contraction of *I will.* **2.** Contraction of *I shall.*

ill. illustrated; illustration; illustrator.

Ill. Illinois (state).

ill-ad·vised (ĭl′əd-vīzd′) *adj.* Unwise; foolish. —**ill-ad·vis·ed·ly** (ĭl′-əd-vī′zĭd-lē) *adv.*

ill-as·sort·ed (ĭl′ə-sôr′tĭd) *adj.* Poorly matched: *They are an ill-assorted couple.*

ill-at-ease (ĭl′ət-ēz′) *adj.* Nervous; uncomfortable.

il·la·tion (ĭ-lā′shən) *n.* **1.** The act of inferring or drawing conclusions. **2.** A conclusion drawn; a deduction. [Late Latin *illātiō* (stem *illātiōn-*) from Latin, "a carrying in," deduction, from *illātus* (past participle of *inferre,* to bring in) : *in-,* in + *-lātus,* "carried."]

il·la·tive (ĭl′ə-tĭv, ĭ-lā′-) *adj. Grammar.* **1.** Expressing or preceding an inference: *"Therefore" is an illative word.* **2.** Designating a case in Finnish and Hungarian that expresses movement or direction toward. —**il·la·tive** *n.*

ill-be·haved (ĭl′bĭ-hāvd′) *adj.* Ill-mannered.

ill-be·ing (ĭl′bē′ĭng) *n.* A condition of being lacking in prosperity, happiness, or health.

ill-bod·ing (ĭl′bō′dĭng) *adj.* Portending evil; inauspicious.

ill-bred (ĭl′brĕd′) *adj.* **1.** Badly brought up; ill-mannered; impolite. **2.** Not thoroughbred.

ill-con·sid·ered (ĭl′kən-sĭd′ərd) *adj.* Unwise; foolish.

ill-de·fined (ĭl′dĭ-fīnd′) *adj.* Not defined clearly.

ill-dis·posed (ĭl′dĭs-pōzd′) *adj.* **1.** Having an unfriendly or hostile attitude. **2.** Unwilling.

il·le·gal (ĭ-lē′gəl) *adj.* **1.** Prohibited by law. **2.** Prohibited by official rules. —**il·le·gal·ly** *adv.*

il·le·gal·i·ty (ĭl′ē-găl′ə-tē) *n., pl.* **-ties. 1.** The state or quality of being illegal. **2.** An illegal act.

il·le·ga·lize (ĭ-lē′gə-līz′) *tr.v.* **-ized, -izing, -izes.** To make illegal. —**il·le·gal·i·za·tion** (ĭ-lē′gə-lə-zā′shən) *n.*

il·leg·i·ble (ĭ-lĕj′ə-bəl) *adj.* Not legible or decipherable. —**il·leg·i·bil·i·ty** (ĭ-lĕj′ə-bĭl′ə-tē), **il·leg·i·ble·ness** *n.* —**il·leg·i·bly** *adv.*

il·le·git·i·ma·cy (ĭl′ĭ-jĭt′ə-mə-sē) *n.* **1.** The condition or quality of being illegitimate. **2.** Bastardy.

il·le·git·i·mate (ĭl′ĭ-jĭt′ə-mĭt) *adj.* **1.** Against the law; illegal. **2.** Born to unmarried parents. **3.** Improper; unfair. **4.** Incorrectly deduced. —**il·le·git·i·mate·ly** *adv.*

ill-fat·ed (ĭl′fā′tĭd) *adj.* **1.** Destined for misfortune; doomed. **2.** Marked by or causing misfortune; unlucky.

ill-fa·vored (ĭl′fā′vərd) *adj.* **1.** Having an ugly or unattractive face. **2.** Objectionable; offensive. —**ill-fa·vored·ly** *adv.* —**ill-fa·vored·ness** *n.*

ill feeling *n.* Feelings of animosity or rancor.

ill-found·ed (ĭl′foun′dĭd) *adj.* Having no factual basis.

ill-got·ten (ĭl′gŏt′n) *adj.* Obtained in an evil manner or by dishonest means. Used chiefly in the phrase *ill-gotten gains.*

ill humor *n.* An irritable state of mind; surliness.

ill-hu·mored (ĭl′hyōō′mərd) *adj.* Irritable and surly. —**ill-hu·mored·ly** *adv.* —**ill-hu·mored·ness** *n.*

ill-judged (ĭl′jŭjd′) *adj.* Unwise; foolish.

il·lib·er·al (ĭ-lĭb′ər-əl) *adj.* **1.** Narrow-minded; bigoted. **2.** Ungenerous, mean, or stingy. **3.** *Archaic.* **a.** Lacking liberal culture. **b.** Ill-bred; ungentlemanly; vulgar. [Latin *illīberālis : in-,* not + *līberālis,* LIBERAL.] —**il·lib·er·al·i·ty** (ĭ-lĭb′ə-răl′ə-tē), **il·lib·er·al·ness** *n.* —**il·lib·er·al·ly** *adv.*

il·lic·it (ĭ-lĭs′ĭt) *adj.* Not sanctioned by custom or law; illegal; unlawful. —See Usage note at **elicit.** [Latin *illicitus,* not allowed : *in-,* not + *licitus,* LICIT.] —**il·lic·it·ly** *adv.* —**il·lic·it·ness** *n.*

il·lim·it·a·ble (ĭ-lĭm′ĭ-tə-bəl) *adj.* Incapable of being limited or circumscribed; limitless. —See Synonyms at **infinite.** —**il·lim·it·a·bil·i·ty** (ĭ-lĭm′ĭ-tə-bĭl′ə-tē), **il·lim·it·a·ble·ness** *n.* —**il·lim·it·a·bly** *adv.*

Il·li·noi·an (ĭl′ə-noi′ən) *adj.* Of or pertaining to the third glacial stage in North America. [After the state of *Illinois.*]

Il·li·nois[1] (ĭl′ə-noi′, -noiz′) *Abbr.* **Ill.** State in the north-central United States. The capital is Springfield; the largest city is Chicago. Its fertile prairies make it a leading agricultural state. It also has rich mineral reserves and is a leading producer of coal and fluorspar. —**Il·li·nois·an** (ĭl′ə-noi′ən) *n. & adj.*

Illinois[2]. River, 439 kilometers (273 miles) long, formed by the confluence of the Des Plaines and Kankakee rivers in northeastern Illinois and flowing southwest to the Mississippi. It is an important commercial waterway.

Illinois[3] *n., pl.* **Illinois. 1.** A member of a confederacy of Algonquian-speaking Indian peoples that inhabited Illinois and parts of Iowa, Wisconsin, and Missouri. **2.** The Algonquian language of the Illinois and Miami peoples.

il·liq·uid (ĭ-lĭk′wĭd) *adj.* **1.** Incapable of being readily converted into cash: *illiquid assets.* **2.** Lacking in cash or liquid assets: *not bankrupt but just illiquid.* [IN-, not + LIQUID.] —**il·li·quid·i·ty** (ĭl′ĭ-kwĭd′-ə-tē) *n.*

il·lit·er·ate (ĭ-lĭt′ər-ĭt) *adj.* **1.** Unable to read or write. **2. a.** Marked by inferiority to an expected standard of familiarity with language and literature. **b.** Violating prescribed standards of speech or writing. **3.** Ignorant of the fundamentals of a specified art or branch of knowledge: *musically illiterate.*

iguana *The iguanas are one of the biggest families of lizards, with some 700 species. They occur mainly in tropical America and many, like this common iguana, live in trees.*

~*n.* One who is illiterate. [Latin *illiterātus* : *in-*, not + *literātus*, LITERATE.] —**il·lit·er·a·cy** (ĭ-lĭt'ər-ə-sē) *n.* —**il·lit·er·ate·ly** *adv.* —**il·lit·er·ate·ness** *n.*

ill-man·nered (ĭl'măn'ərd) *adj.* Lacking or indicating a lack of good manners; impolite; rude. —**ill-man·nered·ly** *adv.*

ill nature *n.* A disagreeable, irritable, or malevolent disposition.

ill-na·tured (ĭl'nā'chərd) *adj.* Disagreeable; surly. —**ill-na·tured·ly** *adv.* —**ill-na·tured·ness** *n.*

ill·ness (ĭl'nĭs) *n.* **1. a.** Sickness of body or mind. **b.** A sickness; a disease. **2.** *Obsolete.* Evil; wickedness.

il·log·ic (ĭ-lŏj'ĭk) *n.* The lack of logic.

il·log·i·cal (ĭ-lŏj'ĭ-kəl) *adj.* **1.** Contradicting or disregarding the principles of logic. **2.** Without logic; senseless. —**il·log·i·cal·i·ty** (ĭ-lŏj'ĭ-kăl'ə-tē), **il·log·i·cal·ness** *n.* —**il·log·i·cal·ly** *adv.*

ill-o·mened (ĭl'ō'mənd) *adj.* Marked by bad omens.

ill-sort·ed (ĭl'sôr'tĭd) *adj.* Badly matched; ill-assorted.

ill-starred (ĭl'stärd) *adj.* Ill-fated; unlucky.

ill-tem·pered (ĭl'tĕm'pərd) *adj.* **1.** Having a bad temper; irritable. **2.** *Archaic.* Out of sorts; unwell. —**ill-tem·pered·ly** *adv.*

ill-timed (ĭl'tīmd') *adj.* Done or occurring at an inappropriate time; untimely.

ill-treat (ĭl'trēt') *tr.v.* **-treated, -treating, -treats.** To maltreat. —See Synonyms at **abuse.** —**ill-treat·ment** *n.*

il·lude (ĭ-lōōd') *tr.v.* **-luded, -luding, -ludes.** To deceive; trick. [Latin *illūdere,* to trick, sport with, from *lūdus,* game.]

il·lume (ĭ-lōōm') *tr.v.* **-lumed, -luming, -lumes.** *Poetic.* To illuminate. [Shortened from ILLUMINE.]

il·lu·min·ance (ĭ-lōō'mə-nəns) *n. Physics.* See **illumination** (sense 8).

il·lu·mi·nant (ĭ-lōō'mə-nənt) *n.* Something that gives off or provides light.

il·lu·mi·nate (ĭ-lōō'mə-nāt') *v.* **-nated, -nating, -nates.** —*tr.* **1.** To provide with light; turn or focus light upon. **2.** To decorate or hang with lights. **3.** To make understandable; clarify. **4.** To enable to understand; enlighten. **5.** *Literary.* To endow with fame or splendor; celebrate. **6.** To adorn (a text, page, or initial letter) with ornamental designs, miniatures, or lettering in brilliant colors or precious metals. —*intr.* To become lighted; glow.

~*n.* (ĭ-lōō'mə-nĭt). One who has or professes to have an unusual degree of enlightenment. [Latin *illūmināre* : *in-,* in + *lūmināre,* to light up, from *lūmen,* light.]

il·lu·mi·na·ti (ĭ-lōō'mə-nä'tē) *pl.n.* **1.** Persons claiming to be unusually enlightened with regard to some subject. **2. Illuminati. a.** The members of a secret society of freethinkers and republicans that flourished in Germany during the late 18th century. Also called "Illuminaten." **b.** Persons regarded as atheists, libertines, or radical republicans during the 18th century (such as the French Encyclopedists, the Freemasons, or the freethinkers). **3. Illuminati.** The members of a heretical sect of 16th-century Spain, who claimed special religious enlightenment. [Latin *illūmināti,* "enlightened ones," plural of *illūminātus,* past participle of *illūmināre,* ILLUMINATE.]

il·lu·mi·na·tion (ĭ-lōō'mə-nā'shən) *n.* **1.** The act of illuminating. **2.** The state of being illuminated. **3.** A light source. **4.** *Often* **illuminations.** Lights used as decoration. **5.** Spiritual or intellectual enlightenment. **6.** Clarification; elucidation. **7. a.** The art or act of decorating a text, page, or initial letter with ornamental designs, miniatures, or lettering. **b.** An example of this art. **8.** *Physics.* The luminous flux per unit area at any point on a surface exposed to incident light.

il·lu·mi·na·tive (ĭ-lōō'mə-nā'tĭv) *adj.* Causing or able to cause illumination.

il·lu·mi·na·tor (ĭ-lōō'mə-nā'tər) *n.* **1.** One that illuminates. **2.** A device for producing, concentrating, or reflecting light. **3.** A person who illuminates manuscripts, texts, or the like.

il·lu·mine (ĭ-lōō'mĭn) *v.* **-mined, -mining, -mines.** —*tr.* To illuminate; give light to. —*intr.* To be or become illuminated. [Middle English *illuminen,* from Latin *illūmināre,* to ILLUMINATE.] —**il·lu·mi·na·ble** *adj.*

il·lu·mi·nism (ĭ-lōō'mə-nĭz'əm) *n.* **1.** Belief in or proclamation of a special personal enlightenment. **2. Illuminism.** The ideas and principles of various groups of illuminati. [ILLUMIN(ATI) + -ISM.] —**il·lu·mi·nist** *n.*

illus. illustrated; illustration; illustrator.

ill-use (ĭl'yōōz') *tr.v.* **-used, -using, -uses.** To maltreat.

~*n.* (ĭl'yōōs'). Also **ill-us·age** (ĭl'yōō'sĭj). Bad or unjust treatment.

il·lu·sion (ĭ-lōō'zhən) *n.* **1. a.** An erroneous perception of reality. **b.** An erroneous concept, belief, or ideal. **c.** Loosely, a delusion. **2.** The condition of being deceived by erroneous perceptions or beliefs. **3.** Something that causes an erroneous belief or perception. **4.** *Art.* Illusionism. **5.** A fine transparent silk or tulle, used for dresses or trimmings. **6.** A conjuring trick. —See Usage note at **delusion.** [Middle English *illusioun,* from Old French *illusion,* from Late Latin *illūsiō* (stem *illūsiōn-*), from Latin, a mocking, jeering, from *illūdere* (past participle *illūsus*), to mock, jeer at : *in-,* against + *lūdere,* to play, from *lūdus,* game.] —**il·lu·sion·al, il·lu·sion·ar·y** (ĭ-lōō'zhə-něr'ē) *adj.*

il·lu·sion·ism (ĭ-lōō'zhə-nĭz'əm) *n.* **1.** The doctrine that the material world is an immaterial product of the senses. **2.** The use of illusionary techniques and devices in art or decoration. —**il·lu·sion·is·tic** (ĭ-lōō'zhə-nĭs'tĭk) *adj.*

il·lu·sion·ist (ĭ-lōō'zhə-nĭst) *n.* **1.** An adherent of the doctrine of illusionism. **2.** A conjuror or ventriloquist. **3.** An artist whose work is marked by illusionism.

il·lu·sive (ĭ-lōō'sĭv) *adj.* Of, pertaining to, or of the nature of an illusion; lacking reality; illusory. [From ILLUSION.] —**il·lu·sive·ly** *adv.* —**il·lu·sive·ness** *n.*

il·lu·so·ry (ĭ-lōō'sə-rē, -zə-rē) *adj.* Tending to deceive; of the nature of an illusion; illusive.

il·lus·trate (ĭl'ə-strāt', ĭ-lŭs'trāt') *v.* **-trated, -trating, -trates.** —*tr.* **1. a.** To clarify by use of examples, comparisons, or the like. **b.** To clarify by serving as an example, comparison, or the like. **2.** To provide (a publication) with explanatory or decorative pictures, photographs, diagrams, or the like. **3.** *Obsolete.* To illuminate. —*intr.* To present a clarification, example, or explanation. [Latin *illūstrāre* : *in-,* in + *lūstrāre,* to make bright, enlighten.] —**il·lus·tra·tor** *n.*

il·lus·tra·tion (ĭl'ə-strā'shən) *n. Abbr.* **ill., illuṣ. 1. a.** The action of clarifying or explaining. **b.** The state of being clarified or explained. **2.** Material used to clarify or explain. **3. a.** A picture, photograph, or diagram used to clarify or to decorate a text. **b.** Such visual matter collectively: *a book lacking illustration.* **4.** *Obsolete.* Illumination. —See Synonyms at **example.**

il·lus·tra·tive (ĭ-lŭs'trə-tĭv, ĭl'ə-strā'tĭv) *adj.* Acting as an illustration. —**il·lus·tra·tive·ly** *adv.*

il·lus·tri·ous (ĭ-lŭs'trē-əs) *adj.* Renowned; famous; celebrated. [Latin *illūstris,* shining, clear, probably back-formation from *illūstrāre,* ILLUSTRATE.] —**il·lus·tri·ous·ly** *adv.* —**il·lus·tri·ous·ness** *n.*

il·lu·vi·a·tion (ĭ-lōō'vē-ā'shən) *n.* The deposition in an underlying soil layer of colloids, soluble salts, and mineral particles leached out of an overlying soil layer. [IN- (in) + (AL)LUVI(UM) + -ATION.] —**il·lu·vi·al** (ĭ-lōō'vē-əl) *adj.*

ill will *n.* Unfriendly feeling; hostility; enmity.

il·ly (ĭl'lē) *adv. Rare.* Badly; ill.

Il·lyr·i·a (ĭ-lîr'ē-ə). *Latin* **Il·lyr·i·cum** (-ĭ-kəm). Ancient region of the Balkan Peninsula, of vague extent. The name is most commonly used for the region extending from the Adriatic coast of northern Albania to the Dinaric Alps.

Il·lyr·i·an (ĭ-lîr'ē-ən) *n.* **1.** A member of a people inhabiting Illyria. **2.** The Indo-European language of the Illyrians.

~*adj.* Of, pertaining to, or characteristic of the Illyrians or their language.

il·men·ite (ĭl'mə-nīt') *n.* A lustrous black-to-brownish titanium ore, essentially a mixed ferrous and titanium oxide, $FeO·TiO_2$. [German *Ilmenit*; first found in *Ilmen,* range in the Ural Mountains.]

ILO International Labor Organization.

I·lo·ca·no (ē'lō-kä'nō) *n., pl.* **-nos** or collectively **Ilocano.** Also **I·lo·ka·no.** **1.** A member of a people inhabiting northwestern Luzon in the Philippines. **2.** The Austronesian language of these people.

~*adj.* Of, pertaining to, or characteristic of the Ilocano or their language. [Spanish, from *iloko,* native name in the Philippines.]

I.L.P. Independent Labour Party (in Great Britain).

ILS *Aeronautics.* instrument landing system.

im-. Variant of **in-.**

I.M. 1. intramuscular. **2.** International Master (in chess).

I'm (īm). Contraction of *I am.*

im·age (ĭm'ĭj) *n.* **1.** A reproduction of the appearance of someone or something; especially, a sculptured likeness. **2.** A duplicate, counterpart, or other representative reproduction of an object, such as: **a.** An optical reproduction formed by a lens or mirror. **b.** A photographic reproduction, either visible or undeveloped (*latent image*). **c.** A reproduction of a picture on a television screen. **3.** One that closely resembles another; a double: *He is the image of his uncle.* **4. a.** The opinion or concept of someone or something that is held by the public. **b.** The character projected by someone or something to the public, especially by the mass media. **5.** A personification of something specified: *He is the image of health.* **6.** A mental picture of something not real or present. **7. a.** A comparison or metaphor: *Plato's image of the cave.* **b.** A figure, usually recurrent, in art or literature that has a symbolic value: *the image of the Fool in Shakespeare.* **8.** *Mathematics.* The function of a specific variable or the value of the function for a specific value of the variable. **9.** *Obsolete.* An apparition. **10.** *Computer Science.* An exact duplication of data in a file onto another medium.

~*tr.v.* **imaged, -aging, -ages. 1.** To make or produce a likeness of; copy or portray. **2.** To mirror or reflect. **3.** To symbolize or typify. **4.** To picture mentally; imagine or recall. **5.** To describe, especially so as to call up a mental picture. [Middle English, from Old French, from Latin *imāgō*; akin to *imitārī,* IMITATE.]

image converter *n.* A device for converting invisible electromagnetic radiation, such as infrared or ultraviolet radiation, into a visible optical image. Also called "image tube."

image intensifier *n.* A device for increasing the intensity of a faint optical image, generally using photoemission of electrons from a cathode and acceleration of these electrons onto a screen.

im·age-ma·ker (ĭm'ĭj-mā'kər) *n. Informal.* One who employs skillful publicity and advertising to create a favorable public image of a person or organization. —**im·age-ma·king** *n.*

image orthicon *n.* An orthicon (see).

im·age·ry (ĭm'ĭj-rē) *n., pl.* **-ries. 1.** The production of mental pictures or images. **2. a.** The employment of comparisons or vivid descriptions in writing or speaking to produce mental images. **b.** Any metaphorical representation, as in literature or art. **3. a.** Representative images, particularly statues or icons. **b.** The art of making such images. [Middle English *imagerie,* from Old French, from *image,* IMAGE.]

im·ag·i·na·ble (ĭ-măj'ə-nə-bəl) *adj.* Capable of being conceived of by the imagination: *chose the worst time imaginable for a vacation.* **—im•ag•i•na•bly** *adv.*

im•ag•i•nal (ĭ-măʹgə-nəl, ĭ-mäʹ-) *adj.* Of or relating to an imago. [New Latin *imago* (stem *imagin-*), IMAGO.]

im•ag•i•nar•y (ĭ-măjʹə-nĕrʹē) *adj.* **1.** Having existence only in the imagination; unreal. **2.** *Mathematics.* **a.** Of, pertaining to, or being the coefficient of the imaginary unit in a complex number. **b.** Of, pertaining to, involving, or being an imaginary number. **c.** Involving only a complex number of which the real part is zero. ~*n., pl.* **imaginaries.** *Mathematics.* An imaginary number. **—im•ag•i•nar•i•ly** *adv.* **—im•ag•i•nar•i•ness** *n.*

imaginary number *n.* A **complex number** *(see)* in which the real part is zero and the coefficient of the imaginary unit is not zero. Also called "imaginary."

imaginary unit *n.* *Symbol* **i** The square root of -1.

im•ag•i•na•tion (ĭ-măjʹə-nāʹshən) *n.* **1. a.** The formation of a mental image or concept of that which is not real or present. **b.** A mental image or idea. **2.** The ability or tendency to form such mental images or concepts. **3. a.** The mental faculty permitting visionary and creative thought. **b.** Visionary and creative thought. **4.** *Archaic.* **a.** An unrealistic idea or notion; a fancy. **b.** A plan or scheme. **—im•ag•i•na•tion•al** *adj.*

im•ag•i•na•tive (ĭ-măjʹə-nə-tĭv, -nāʹtĭv) *adj.* **1.** Having a strong imagination, especially a creative imagination. **2.** Tending to indulge in the fanciful or in make-believe. **3.** Created by, indicative of, or characterized by imagination or creativity. **—im•ag•i•na•tive•ly** *adv.* **—im•ag•i•na•tive•ness** *n.*

im•ag•ine (ĭ-măjʹən) *v.* **-ined, -ining, -ines.** *—tr.* **1.** To form a mental picture or image of; create in the mind. **2.** To suppose; conjecture. **3.** To believe (something that has no basis in reality): *imagines himself to be an artist.* *—intr.* **1.** To employ the imagination. **2.** To make a guess; conjecture. [Middle English *imaginen,* from Old French *imaginer,* from Latin *imāginārī,* to picture to oneself, from *imāgō,* IMAGE.] **—im•ag•in•er** *n.*

im•a•gism (ĭmʹə-jĭzʹəm) *n.* A literary movement among British and U.S. poets, launched about 1912, to promote free verse and precise imagery. **—im•a•gist** *n.* **—im•a•gis•tic** (ĭmʹə-jĭsʹtĭk) *adj.*

i•ma•go (ĭ-māʹgō) *n., pl.* **-goes** or **imagines** (ĭ-măjʹə-nēzʹ). **1.** An insect in its sexually mature adult stage after metamorphosis. **2.** *Psychoanalysis.* An often idealized image of a person, usually a parent, formed in childhood and persisting into adulthood. [New Latin, from Latin *imāgō,* IMAGE.]

i•mam (ĭ-mämʹ) *n.* Also **i•maum** (ĭ-mämʹ, ĭ-mômʹ). **1.** A prayer leader of Islam. **2.** A Muslim scholar; especially, an authority on Islamic law. **3. Imam. a.** A title accorded to Muhammad and his four immediate successors. **b.** Any of the leaders regarded by the Shiites as successors of Muhammad. **c.** Any of various religious and temporal leaders claiming descent from Muhammad. [Arabic *imām,* leader, from *amma,* he led.]

i•mam•ate (ĭ-mäʹmātʹ) *n.* **1.** The office of an imam. **2.** A country governed by an imam.

i•ma•ret (ĭ-mäʹrĕt) *n.* An inn or hostel for pilgrims in Turkey. [Turkish, from Arabic *imārah,* hospice, "cultivated land," from *amara,* he built.]

im•bal•ance (ĭm-bălʹəns) *n.* A lack of balance or proportion.

im•be•cile (ĭmʹbə-sĭl, -səl) *n.* **1.** A feeble-minded person. **2.** A dolt. **3.** A person affected by imbecility. No longer in technical usage. ~*adj.* Also **im•be•cil•ic** (ĭmʹbə-sĭlʹĭk). **1.** Deficient in mental ability. **2.** Stupid. [Old French *imbecille,* from Latin *imbēcillus,* "without support," feeble : *in-,* not + *bacillum,* diminutive of *baculum,* staff, rod.] **—im•be•cile•ly** *adv.*

im•be•cil•i•ty (ĭmʹbə-sĭlʹə-tē) *n.* A condition of moderate to severe subnormal intellectual development, characterized by an intelligence quotient in the upper range of idiocy. No longer in technical usage. Compare **idiocy.**

imbed. Variant of **embed.**

im•bibe (ĭm-bībʹ) *v.* **-bibed, -bibing, -bibes.** *—tr.* **1.** To drink (especially alcoholic drink). **2.** To absorb or take in as if by drinking: *"the whole body . . . imbibes delight through every pore"* (Thoreau). **3.** To receive and absorb into the mind. **4.** *Obsolete.* To permeate; saturate. *—intr.* To drink. [Middle English *enbiben,* to absorb, from Old French *embiber,* from Latin *imbibere,* to drink in : *in-,* in + *bibere,* to drink.] **—im•bib•er** *n.*

im•bi•bi•tion (ĭmʹbĭ-bĭshʹən) *n.* **1.** *Chemistry.* The absorption or adsorption of a liquid by a solid or a gel. **2.** In photography, the absorption of a dye by gelatin. **3.** *Rare.* The act of imbibing. [IMBIBE + -TION.]

im•bri•cate (ĭmʹbrĭ-kātʹ, -kĭt) *adj.* **1.** Having the edges overlapping in a regular pattern, as tiles on a roof, the scales of a fish, or bracts or sepals of a plant. **2.** Covered or ornamented with a pattern or design of overlapping parts or edges. ~*v.* (ĭmʹbrĭ-kātʹ) **imbricated, -cating, -cates.** *—tr.* To overlap in a regular pattern. *—intr.* To be arranged with regular overlapping edges. [Latin *imbricātus,* past participle of *imbricāre,* to cover with roof tiles, from *imbrex* (stem *imbric-*), roof tile, from *imber* (stem *imbr-*), rain.]

im•bri•ca•tion (ĭmʹbrĭ-kāʹshən) *n.* **1.** A regular overlapping of edges. **2.** A pattern or design having such overlapping.

im•bro•gli•o (ĭm-brōlʹyō) *n., pl.* **-glios. 1.** A confused or difficult situation; a predicament; an entanglement. **2.** *Rare.* A confused heap; a tangle. [Italian *imbroglio* : probably *in-,* in + *broglio,* grove, bush, from Old French *breuil,* from Late Latin *brogilus,* from Gaulish *brogilos* (unattested), from *brogos, broga*†, field.]

im•brue (ĭm-bro͞oʹ) *tr.v.* **-brued, -bruing, -brues.** Also **em•brue** (ĕm-). *Rare.* **1.** To stain or dye. Used of blood. **2.** To soak or saturate. [Middle English *enbrewen, enbrowen,* from Old French *embruer, embrouer,* to soak : *en-,* in + *breu,* broth, from Germanic.]

im•brute (ĭm-bro͞otʹ) *v.* **-bruted, -bruting, -brutes.** *Rare.* *—tr.* To cause to become brutal. *—intr.* To become brutal.

im•bue (ĭm-byo͞oʹ) *tr.v.* **-bued, -buing, -bues. 1.** To inspire, permeate, or pervade. **2.** To make thoroughly wet; saturate, as with stain or dye. [Latin *imbuere,* to moisten, stain.]

IMF, I.M.F. International Monetary Fund.

Im•ho•tep (ĭm-hōʹtĕp) (*fl. c.* 2650 B.C.). Egyptian architect, astrologer, physician, and chief minister to Pharoah Djoser (*c.* 2686–2613 B.C.). He is thought to have designed the first pyramid at Saqqara.

im•id•az•ole (ĭmʹĭd-ăzʹōl, -ə-zōlʹ) *n.* Any of a group of heterocyclic nitrogen compounds, especially the white crystalline base, $C_3H_4N_2$; 1,3-diazole. Also called "glyoxaline." [IMID(E) + AZOLE.]

im•ide (ĭmʹĭdʹ, -ĭd) *n.* A compound derived from ammonia containing the divalent group —CO•NH•CO— combined with two other radicals. [Alteration of AMIDE.]

im•ine (ĭ-mēnʹ, ĭmʹĭn) *n.* A compound derived from ammonia containing the divalent NH group combined with alkyl or other radicals. [Alteration of AMINE.]

im•i•no acid (ĭ-mēʹnō) *n.* An organic compound, such as proline or hydroxyproline, similar to an amino acid and also a constituent of proteins, but containing an imino group (-NH) rather than an amino group (C-NH_2).

i•mip•ra•mine (ĭ-mĭpʹrə-mēnʹ, ĭmʹə-präʹmēn) *n.* A water-soluble compound, $C_{19}H_{24}N_2$, used medically as an antidepressant. [IM(IDE) + PR(OPYL) + AMINE.]

im•i•tate (ĭmʹə-tātʹ) *tr.v.* **-tated, -tating, -tates. 1.** To model oneself on the behavior or actions of. **2. a.** To copy the appearance, mannerisms, or speech of; mimic. **b.** To copy the literary, artistic, or musical style of. **3.** To copy; reproduce. **4.** To resemble. [Latin *imitārī*† (past participle *imitātus*).] **—im•i•ta•tor** *n.*

Synonyms: *ape, copy, mimic, parody, simulate.*

im•i•ta•tion (ĭmʹə-tāʹshən) *n.* **1.** An act of imitating. **2.** Something derived or copied from an original. **3.** *Music.* The repetition of a phrase or sequence often with variations in key, rhythm, and voice. **—im•i•ta•tion•al** *adj.*

im•i•ta•tive (ĭmʹə-tāʹtĭv) *adj.* **1.** Of or involving imitation. **2.** Not original; derivative; copied. **3.** Tending to imitate. **4.** Onomatopoeic. **—im•i•ta•tive•ly** *adv.* **—im•i•ta•tive•ness** *n.*

im•mac•u•la•cy (ĭ-măkʹyə-lə-sē) *n.* The quality or condition of being immaculate; immaculateness.

im•mac•u•late (ĭ-măkʹyə-lĭt) *adj.* **1.** Free from stain or blemish; spotless; pure. **2.** Free from fault or error. **3.** Impeccably clean. **4.** Having no markings or spots. Said of plants and animals. [Middle English *immaculat,* from Latin *immaculātus* : *in-,* not + *maculātus,* past participle of *maculāre,* to stain, blemish, from *macula,* spot.] **—im•mac•u•late•ly** *adv.* **—im•mac•u•late•ness** *n.*

Immaculate Conception *n.* **1.** The Roman Catholic doctrine that the Virgin Mary was conceived in her mother's womb free from all stain of original sin. Compare **virgin birth. 2.** The day, December 8, on which this is celebrated.

im•ma•nent (ĭmʹə-nənt) *adj.* **1.** Existing or remaining within; inherent. **2.** Restricted entirely to the mind; subjective. Compare **transeunt. 3.** Present throughout the universe. Said of God. Compare **transcendent.** [Late Latin *immanēns* (stem *immanent-*), present participle of *immanēre,* to remain in : Latin *in-,* in + *manēre,* to remain.] **—im•ma•nence** *n.* **—im•ma•nent•ly** *adv.*

im•ma•nent•ism (ĭmʹə-nən-tĭzʹəm) *n.* Any of various religious theories postulating that a deity or abstract spirit is immanent in the world.

Im•man•u•el, Em•man•u•el (ĭ-mănʹyo͞o-əl) *n.* **1.** The child whose birth was prophesied by Isaiah, as a sign that Judah would not be destroyed. Isaiah 7:14. **2.** A name applied to Jesus. Matthew 1:23. [Hebrew, "God with us."]

im•ma•te•ri•al (ĭmʹə-tîrʹē-əl) *adj.* **1.** Having no material body or form. **2.** Of no importance or relevance; inconsequential. **—im•ma•te•ri•al•ly** *adv.* **—im•ma•te•ri•al•ness** *n.*

im•ma•te•ri•al•ism (ĭmʹə-tîrʹē-ə-lĭzʹəm) *n.* A metaphysical doctrine asserting that things only have an existence through perception by the mind. **—im•ma•te•ri•al•ist** *n.*

im•ma•te•ri•al•i•ty (ĭmʹə-tîrʹē-ălʹə-tē) *n., pl.* **-ties. 1.** The state or quality of being immaterial. **2.** Something immaterial.

im•ma•te•ri•al•ize (ĭmʹə-tîr-ē-ə-līzʹ) *tr.v.* **-ized, -izing, -izes.** To render immaterial.

im•ma•ture (ĭmʹə-tyo͝orʹ, -to͝orʹ, -cho͝orʹ) *adj.* **1.** Not fully grown or developed. **2.** Behaving with less than normal maturity. **3.** Not having a chance to achieve a mature state due to constant erosion. Said of soils. **4.** *Informal.* Childish; silly. [Latin *immātūrus* : *in-,* not + *mātūrus,* MATURE.] **—im•ma•ture•ly** *adv.* **—im•ma•tur•i•ty** (ĭmʹə-tyo͝orʹə-tē), **im•ma•ture•ness** *n.*

im•meas•ur•a•ble (ĭ-mĕzhʹər-ə-bəl) *adj.* **1.** Incapable of being measured. **2.** Vast; limitless. **—im•meas•ur•a•bil•i•ty** (ĭ-mĕzhʹər-ə-bĭlʹə-tē), **im•meas•ur•a•ble•ness** *n.* **—im•meas•ur•a•bly** *adv.*

im•me•di•a•cy (ĭ-mēʹdē-ə-sē) *n., pl.* **-cies. 1.** The condition or quality of being immediate; directness. **2.** Something immediate. **3.** Immediate or direct perception; intuitiveness. **4.** *Philosophy.* Direct consciousness as opposed to that involving an intermediary such as memory.

im•me•di•ate (ĭ-mēʹdē-ĭt) *adj.* **1.** Acting or occurring without mediation or interposition; direct: *immediate consequence.* **2.** Directly ap-

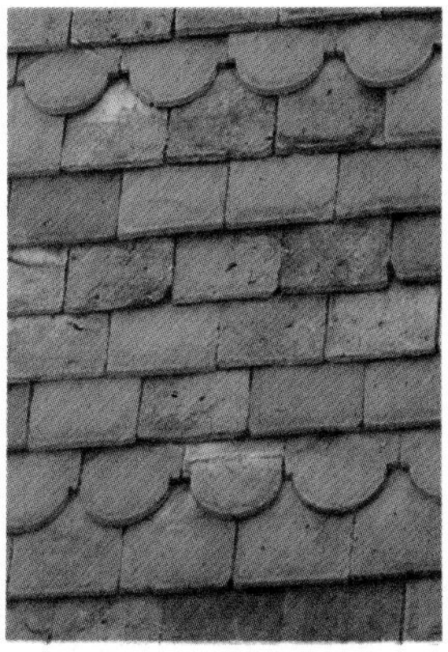

imbricate *An imbricated, or overlapping, clay tile wall in Sussex, England.*

prehended or perceived; intuitive: *immediate awareness.* **3.** Next in line or relation: *the immediate successor.* **4.** Occurring without delay: *an immediate response.* **5.** Of or near the present time: *the immediate future.* **6.** Close at hand; near: *the immediate vicinity.* **7.** Of direct concern or importance. [Late Latin *immediātus* : Latin *in-,* not + *mediātus,* past participle of *mediāre,* to be in the middle, MEDIATE.] —**im·me·di·ate·ness** *n.*

immediate constituent *n. Linguistics. Abbr.* **I.C.** Any of the main grammatical divisions into which a word, phrase, or sentence can be most immediately divided; for example, the immediate constituents of *the watch has stopped* are *the watch* and *has stopped.*

im·me·di·ate·ly (ĭ-mē′dē-ĭt-lē) *adv.* **1.** Without intermediary; directly. **2.** Without delay. **3.** Nearby.
~*conj.* As soon as; directly.
> *Usage:* immediately, instantly, forthwith, directly, promptly, presently. *These adverbs mean with little or no delay. They are arranged in approximate order of intensity.* Immediately *and* instantly *imply no delay whatever, as between request and response.* Forthwith, directly, *and* promptly *all stress readiness of response but with a brief interval prior to fulfillment of the action involved.* Presently *has the mere force of soon.*

im·med·i·ca·ble (ĭ-mĕd′ĭ-kə-bəl) *adj.* Incurable.

Im·mel·mann turn (ĭm′əl-mən, -män′) *n.* A maneuver in which an airplane first completes half a loop then half a roll in order to gain altitude and change direction in flight simultaneously. [After Max *Immelmann* (1890–1916), German pilot.]

im·me·mo·ri·al (ĭm′ə-môr′ē-əl, -mōr′ē-əl) *adj.* Reaching beyond the limits of memory, tradition, or recorded history. Used chiefly in the phrase *from time immemorial.* [Medieval Latin *immemoriālis* : Latin *in-,* not + *memoriālis,* memorial, from *memoria,* MEMORY.] —**im·me·mo·ri·al·ly** *adv.*

im·mense (ĭ-mĕns′) *adj.* **1.** Extremely large; huge. **2.** Boundless. **3.** *Informal.* Very great: *immense pleasure.* —See Synonyms at **enormous.** [Old French, from Latin *immēnsus,* immeasurable : *in-,* not + *mēnsus,* past participle of *mētīrī,* to measure.] —**im·mense·ly** *adv.* —**im·mense·ness** *n.*

im·men·si·ty (ĭ-mĕn′sə-tē) *n., pl.* **-ties. 1.** The quality or state of being immense. **2.** Something immense. **3.** *Informal.* A very large amount.

im·men·sur·a·ble (ĭ-mĕn′shər-ə-bəl) *adj. Rare.* Immeasurable.

im·merge (ĭ-mûrj′) *v.* **-merged, -merging, -merges.** *Archaic.* —*tr.* To immerse. —*intr.* To submerge or disappear in or as if in a liquid. [Latin *immergere,* IMMERSE.] —**im·mer·gence** *n.*

im·merse (ĭ-mûrs′) *tr.v.* **-mersed, -mersing, -merses. 1.** To cover completely in a liquid; submerge. Used with *in.* **2.** To baptize by submerging in water. **3.** To involve profoundly; absorb. Used with *in: a scholar immersed in the past.* [Latin *immergere* (past participle *immersus*), to dip in : *in-,* in + *mergere,* to dip.]

im·mer·sion (ĭ-mûr′zhən, -shən) *n.* **1.** An act of immersing. **2.** The condition of being immersed. **3.** Baptism performed by totally submerging a person in water. **4.** Absorption: *her total immersion in politics.* **5.** *Astronomy.* The obscuring of a celestial body by another or by the shadow of another, as in an eclipse or occultation. Also called "ingress."

immesh. Variant of **enmesh.**

im·me·thod·i·cal (ĭm′ə-thŏd′ĭ-kəl) *adj.* Not methodical. —**im·me·thod·i·cal·ly** *adv.*

im·mi·grant (ĭm′ĭ-grənt) *n.* **1.** One who enters a country to settle permanently. Compare **emigrant. 2.** An organism living or growing in a place to which it has recently migrated. —**im·mi·grant** *adj.*

im·mi·grate (ĭm′ĭ-grāt′) *v.* **-grated, -grating, -grates.** —*intr.* To enter and settle in a country or region of which one is not a native. —*tr.* To bring in or introduce as immigrants. —See Usage note at **migrate.** [Latin *immigrāre,* to remove into, go in : *in-,* in + *migrāre,* to remove, MIGRATE.]

im·mi·gra·tion (ĭm′ĭ-grā′shən) *n.* **1.** The act, process, or an instance of immigrating. **2. a.** The area in a port or airport where passengers arriving from abroad have their passports and visas checked. **b.** The government officials in charge of this process.

im·mi·nence (ĭm′ə-nəns) *n.* Also **im·mi·nen·cy** (-nən-sē) *pl.* **-cies. 1.** The quality or condition of being imminent. **2.** Something imminent.

im·mi·nent (ĭm′ə-nənt) *adj.* **1.** About to occur; impending. **2.** *Archaic.* Jutting out; overhanging. —See Usage note at **eminent.** [Latin *imminēns* (stem *imminent-*), present participle of *imminēre,* to project over or toward, threaten : *in-,* toward + *-minēre,* to project.] —**im·mi·nent·ly** *adv.*

im·min·gle (ĭ-mĭng′gəl) *v.* **-gled, -gling, -gles.** *Archaic.* —*intr.* To intermingle; blend. —*tr.* To blend.

im·mis·ci·ble (ĭ-mĭs′ə-bəl) *adj.* Incapable of mixing or blending. Said of two or more liquids. —**im·mis·ci·bil·i·ty** (ĭ-mĭs′ə-bĭl′ə-tē) *n.* —**im·mis·ci·bly** *adv.*

im·mit·i·ga·ble (ĭ-mĭt′ĭ-gə-bəl) *adj. Rare.* Incapable of being mitigated. —**im·mit·i·ga·bly** *adv.*

im·mit·tance (ĭ-mĭt′əns) *n.* Electrical impedance or admittance. [IM(PEDANCE) + (AD)MITTANCE.]

im·mix (ĭ-mĭks′) *tr.v.* **-mixed, -mixing, -mixes.** *Rare.* To commingle; blend. [Back-formation from Middle English *immixte,* mixed in, from Latin *immixtus,* past participle of *immiscēre,* to mix in : *in-,* in + *miscēre,* to mix.] —**im·mix·ture** (ĭ-mĭks′chər) *n.*

im·mo·bile (ĭ-mō′bəl, -bēl′) *adj.* **1. a.** Unable to move. **b.** Incapable of being moved. **2.** Not moving; motionless. **3.** Not fluid; viscous. Said of liquids. [Middle English *inmobile,* from Latin *immōbilis* :

in-, not + *mōbilis,* MOBILE.] —**im·mo·bil·i·ty** (ĭm′ō-bĭl′ə-tē) *n.*

im·mo·bil·ism (ĭ-mō′bə-lĭz′əm) *n.* A highly reactionary political stance. —**im·mo·bil·ist** *n. & adj.*

im·mo·bi·lize (ĭ-mō′bə-līz′) *tr.v.* **-lized, -lizing, -lizes. 1.** To render immobile. **2.** To impede movement or use of: *immobilize troops.* **3.** *Medicine.* To fix (a broken limb, for example) so that no movement is possible. **4. a.** *Finance.* To withdraw (specie) from circulation and reserve as security for other money. **b.** To convert (floating capital) into fixed capital. —**im·mo·bi·li·za·tion** (ĭ-mō′bə-lə-zā′shən) *n.* —**im·mo·bi·liz·er** *n.*

im·mod·er·ate (ĭ-mŏd′ər-ĭt) *adj.* Not moderate; extreme. —See Synonyms at **excessive.** [Middle English *immoderat,* from Latin *immoderātus* : *in-,* not + *moderātus,* MODERATE.] —**im·mod·er·ate·ly** *adv.* —**im·mod·er·ate·ness, im·mod·er·a·tion** (ĭ-mŏd′ə-rā′shən) *n.*

im·mod·est (ĭ-mŏd′ĭst) *adj.* **1.** Lacking modesty. **2. a.** Contrary to conventional standards of sexual propriety. **b.** Morally offensive. **3.** Arrogant. [Latin *immodestus* : *in-,* not + *modestus,* MODEST.] —**im·mod·est·ly** *adv.* —**im·mod·es·ty** *n.*

im·mo·late (ĭm′ə-lāt′) *tr.v.* **-lated, -lating, -lates. 1.** To kill as a sacrifice. **2.** To destroy or renounce for the sake of something else. [Latin *immolāre,* to sacrifice, originally "to sprinkle with sacrificial meal" : *in-,* on + *mola,* meal.] —**im·mo·la·tion** (ĭm′ə-lā′shən) *n.* —**im·mo·la·tor** *n.*

im·mor·al (ĭ-môr′əl, ĭ-mŏr′-) *adj.* **1.** Contrary to established morality, especially in sexual matters. **2.** Morally dissolute. **3.** Unethical or unfair. **4.** Tending to corrupt. —**im·mor·al·ly** *adv.*

im·mor·al·ist (ĭ-môr′ə-lĭst, -mŏr′-) *n.* One who advocates immorality.

im·mo·ral·i·ty (ĭm′ô-răl′ə-tē, ĭm′ə-) *n., pl.* **-ties. 1.** The quality or condition of being immoral. **2.** An immoral act. **3.** Immoral behavior; especially, sexual promiscuity.

im·mor·tal (ĭ-môr′tl) *adj.* **1.** Not subject to death. **2.** Having eternal fame; imperishable. **3.** Of or pertaining to immortality.
~*n.* **1.** One not subject to death. **2.** One whose fame is enduring. **3.** *Often* **Immortals.** The gods of ancient Greece and Rome. **4. Immortal.** A member of the French Academy. [Middle English, from Latin *immortālis* : *in-,* not + *mortālis,* MORTAL.] —**im·mor·tal·ly** *adv.*

im·mor·tal·i·ty (ĭm′ôr-tăl′ə-tē) *n.* **1.** The quality or condition of being immortal. **2.** Endless life. **3.** Enduring fame.

im·mor·tal·ize (ĭ-môrt′l-īz′) *tr.v.* **-ized, -izing, -izes. 1.** To make immortal. **2.** To give permanent fame to.

im·mor·telle (ĭm′ôr-tĕl′) *n.* Any plant with flowers that retain their color when dried. [French, from the feminine of *immortel,* from Latin *immortālis,* IMMORTAL.]

im·mo·tile (ĭ-mōt′l) *adj.* Not motile. Said of living organisms. —**im·mo·til·i·ty** (ĭm′ō-tĭl′ə-tē) *n.*

im·mov·a·ble, im·move·a·ble (ĭ-mōō′və-bəl) *adj.* **1. a.** Incapable of being moved. **b.** Incapable of movement. **2.** Not capable of alteration. **3.** Unyielding in principle, purpose, or adherence; steadfast. **4.** Showing no sign of emotional stress; unimpressionable. **5.** *Law.* Not liable to be physically removed: *immovable property.* **6.** Occurring on the same date each year. Said of feast days and holidays.
~*n.* **1.** One that is incapable of movement. **2.** Usually **immovables.** Immovable property, such as real estate. Compare **movable.** —**im·mov·a·ble·ness, im·mov·a·bil·i·ty** (ĭ-mōō′və-bĭl′ə-tē) *n.* —**im·mov·a·bly** *adv.*

im·mune (ĭ-myōōn′) *adj.* **1.** *Biology.* **a.** Having immunity to infection. **b.** Relating to or conferring immunity. **2.** Exempt, as from an obligation or a duty. **b.** Not affected or responsive: *immune to tears.* **3.** Protected from danger. [Latin *immūnis.*] —**im·mune** *n.*
> *Usage:* In the senses of "exempt" and "protected from," *immune* is followed by *from* (*immune from tax, immune from commercial pressures*). In the senses of "resistant to a disease" and "not affected by or responsive to," *immune* is followed by *to* (*immune to diphtheria, immune to their entreaties*).

im·mu·ni·ty (ĭ-myōō′nə-tē) *n., pl.* **-ties. 1.** The quality or condition of being immune. **2.** An inherited, acquired, or induced resistance to a specific pathogen, especially by the production of antibodies or by inoculation.

im·mu·nize (ĭm′yə-nīz′) *tr.v.* **-nized, -nizing, -nizes.** To render immune. —**im·mu·ni·za·tion** (ĭm′yə-nə-zā′shən) *n.*
> *Usage: Immunize* is followed by *against* (*to immunize someone against a particular disease*).

immuno- *prefix.* Indicates immune response or immunity; for example, *immunogenetics, immunogenic.* [From IMMUNE.]

im·mu·no·as·say (ĭm′yə-nō-ăs′ā, ĭm-yōō′-) *n.* A method of identifying substances, particularly proteins, by studying the antibodies they induce when injected into an animal.

im·mu·no·chem·is·try (ĭm′yə-nō-kĕm′ĭ-strē) *n.* The chemistry of immunological phenomena, as of antigen stimulation of tissue or of antigen-antibody reactions.

im·mu·no·e·lec·tro·pho·re·sis (ĭm′yə-nō-ĭ-lĕk′trə-fə-rē′sĭs, ĭm-yōō′-) *n.* The separation of antigens by electrophoresis with identification through specific immunological reactions.

im·mu·no·ge·net·ics (ĭm′yə-nō-jə-nĕt′ĭks) *n. Used with a singular verb.* The study of the interrelation between immunity to disease and genetic make-up.

im·mu·no·gen·ic (ĭm′yə-nō-jĕn′ĭk) *adj.* Producing immunity.

im·mu·no·glob·u·lin (ĭm′yə-nō-glŏb′yə-lĭn) *n.* Any one of a group of structurally similar proteins that show antibody activity.

im·mu·nol·o·gy (ĭm′yə-nŏl′ə-jē) *n.* The study of immunity to disease. [IMMUNO- + -LOGY.] —**im·mu·no·log·ic** (ĭm′yə-nə-lŏj′ĭk), **im-**

mu·no·log·i·cal *adj.* **—im·mu·no·log·i·cal·ly** *adv.*

im·mu·no·sup·pres·sive (ĭm′yə-nō-sə-prĕs′ĭv) *adj.* Tending to suppress a natural immune response of an organism to an antigen. ∼*n.* An immunosuppressive drug.

im·mu·no·ther·a·py (ĭm′yə-nō-thĕr′ə-pē, ĭm-yo͞o′-) *n.* **1.** The treatment of disease by use of antigenic preparations. **2.** The treatment of disease or infection by immunosuppressive techniques. **—im·mu·no·ther·a·pist** *n.*

im·mure (ĭ-myo͝or′) *tr.v.* **-mured, -muring, -mures. 1.** To confine within walls; imprison. **2.** To build into a wall; entomb in a wall. **3.** To shut (oneself) away in seclusion. [Medieval Latin *immūrāre* : Latin *in-*, in + *mūrus*, wall.] **—im·mure·ment** *n.*

im·mu·ta·ble (ĭ-myo͞o′tə-bəl) *adj.* Not mutable; not susceptible to change; ageless. [Middle English, from Latin *immūtābilis* : *in-*, not + *mūtābilis*, MUTABLE.] **—im·mu·ta·bil·i·ty** (ĭ-myoo′tə-bĭl′ə-tē), **im·mu·ta·ble·ness** *n.* **—im·mu·ta·bly** *adv.*

imp (ĭmp) *n.* **1.** A mischievous child. **2.** A mischievous elf. **3.** A small or young demon. **4.** *Archaic.* A descendant.
∼*tr.v.* **imped, imping, imps. 1.** To graft (new feathers) onto the wing of a falcon to repair damage or to increase flying capacity. **2.** *Archaic.* To furnish with wings. [Middle English *impe*, scion, offspring, child, Old English *impa*, young shoot, sapling, from *impian*, to graft on, from Common Romance *impotare* (unattested), from Medieval Latin *impotus*, graft, from Greek *emphutos*, implanted, from *emphuein*, to implant : *en-*, in + *phuein*, plant.]

imp. 1. imperative. **2.** imperfect. **3.** imperial. **4.** import; imported; importer. **5.** important. **6.** imprimatur.

Imp. 1. imperator. **2.** imperatrix.

im·pact (ĭm′păkt′) *n.* **1.** The striking of one body against another; a collision. **2.** The effect of one thing upon another. **3.** The influence or force of a person, thing, or idea.
∼*tr.v.* (ĭm-păkt′) **impacted, -pacting, -pacts.** To pack firmly together. [Latin *impactus*, past participle of *impingere*, to dash or strike against, IMPINGE.] **—im·pac·tion** (ĭm-păk′shən) *n.*

im·pact·ed (ĭm-păk′tĭd) *adj.* **1.** Wedged together at the broken ends. Said of a fractured bone. **2. a.** Placed in the alveolus in a manner prohibiting eruption into a normal position. Said of a tooth. **b.** Driven upward into the alveolar process or surrounding tissue. Said of a tooth.

im·pair (ĭm-pâr′) *tr.v.* **-paired, -pairing, -pairs.** To make worse by lessening strength, value, quantity, or quality; damage: *The accident impaired her voice. The storm impaired communications.* —See Synonyms at **injure.** [Middle English *empairen*, from Old French *empeirer*, from Vulgar Latin *impējōrāre* (unattested), to make worse : *in-* (intensive) + Late Latin *pējōrāre*, to make or become worse, from Latin *pējor*, worse.] **—im·pair·ment** *n.*

im·pa·la (ĭm-pä′lə) *n.* An African antelope, *Aepyceros melampus*, having a reddish coat, and ridged, curved horns in the male. [Zulu.]

im·pale, em·pale (ĭm-pāl′) *tr.v.* **-paled, -paling, -pales. 1. a.** To pierce with a sharp stake or point. **b.** To torture or kill by impaling. **2.** To render helpless as if by impaling. **3.** *Heraldry.* To display (arms) on either side of a vertical line on a shield. [Medieval Latin *impālāre* : Latin *in-*, in + *pālus*, stake, pole.] **—im·pale·ment** *n.* **—im·pal·er** *n.*

im·pal·pa·ble (ĭm-păl′pə-bəl) *adj.* **1. a.** Not perceptible to the touch; intangible. **b.** So fine that individual grains cannot be felt. Said of powder. **2.** Not easily perceived or grasped by the mind. **—im·pal·pa·bil·i·ty** (ĭm-păl′pə-bĭl′ə-tē) *n.* **—im·pal·pa·bly** *adv.*

im·pan·el (ĭm-păn′əl) *tr.v.* **-eled, -eling, -els** or *chiefly British* **-elled, -elling.** Also **em·pan·el** (ĕm-). To enroll (a jury) upon a panel or list. **—im·pan·el·ment** *n.*

im·par·i·syl·la·bic (ĭm-păr′ə-sĭ-lăb′ĭk) *adj.* Not having the same number of syllables in all its forms. Said of nouns or verbs in inflected languages.

im·par·i·ty (ĭm-păr′ə-tē) *n., pl.* **-ties.** Inequality; disparity; dissimilarity. [Late Latin *imparitās* (stem *imparitāt-*), from Latin *impār*, not equal : *in-*, not + *pār*, equal.]

im·park (ĭm-pärk′) *tr.v.* **-parked, -parking, -parks. 1.** To confine (deer, for example) in a park. **2.** To enclose (land) for a park. **—im·par·ka·tion** (ĭm-pär-kā′shən) *n.*

im·part (ĭm-pärt′) *tr.v.* **-parted, -parting, -parts. 1.** To grant a share of; bestow. **2.** To make known; disclose. —See Synonyms at **reveal.** [Latin *impartīre*, to cause to share in, share with : *in-*, in + *partīre*, to share, divide, from *pars* (stem *part-*), part, share.] **—im·part·a·ble** *adj.* **—im·part·er** *n.* **—im·part·ment** *n.*

im·par·tial (ĭm-pär′shəl) *adj.* Not partial; unprejudiced; fair. —See Synonyms at **fair. —im·par·ti·al·i·ty** (ĭm-pär′shē-ăl′ə-tē), **im·par·tial·ness** *n.* **—im·par·tial·ly** *adv.*

im·part·i·ble (ĭm-pär′tə-bəl) *adj. Law.* Not partible; indivisible. Said of land. [Late Latin *impartibilis* : Latin *in-*, not + *partībilis*, PARTIBLE.] **—im·part·i·bil·i·ty** (ĭm-pär′tə-bĭl′ə-tē) *n.* **—im·part·i·bly** *adv.*

im·pass·a·ble (ĭm-păs′ə-bəl) *adj.* Unable to be traversed. **—im·pass·a·bil·i·ty** (ĭm-păs′ə-bĭl′ə-tē), **im·pass·a·ble·ness** *n.* **—im·pass·a·bly** *adv.*

im·passe (ĭm′păs′) *n.* **1.** A situation where no further progress can be made; a deadlock. **2.** A road or passage having no exit; a dead end; a cul-de-sac. [French : Old French *in-*, not, in- + *passer*, to PASS.]

im·pas·si·ble (ĭm-păs′ə-bəl) *adj.* **1. a.** Not subject to suffering or pain. **b.** Incapable of being injured: *"The Godhead is impassible."* (Aldous Huxley). **2.** Impassive. [Middle English, from Old French, from Late Latin *impassibilis* : *in-*, not + *passibilis*, PASSIBLE.] **—im·pas·si·bil·i·ty** (ĭm-păs′ə-bĭl′ə-tē), **im·pas·si·ble·ness** *n.* **—im·pas·si·bly** *adv.*

im·pas·sion (ĭm-păsh′ən) *tr.v.* **-sioned, -sioning, -sions.** To arouse the passions of. [Italian *impassionare* : *in-*, in, from Latin + *passione*, passion, from Late Latin *passiō*, PASSION.]

im·pas·sioned (ĭm-păsh′ənd) *adj.* Filled with passion; ardent.

im·pas·sive (ĭm-păs′ĭv) *adj.* **1.** Devoid of or not subject to emotion; apathetic. **2.** Revealing no emotion; expressionless. **3.** Incapable of physical sensation. [IN- (not) + Latin *passīvus*, capable of feeling, PASSIVE.] **—im·pas·sive·ly** *adv.* **—im·pas·sive·ness, im·pas·siv·i·ty** (ĭm′pə-sĭv′ə-tē) *n.*

im·paste (ĭm-pāst′) *tr.v.* **-pasted, -pasting, -pastes. 1.** To make into a paste. **2.** To apply pigment thickly to. [Italian *impastare* : *in-*, in, + *pasta*, PASTE.]

im·pas·to (ĭm-păs′tō, -päs′tō) *n.* **1.** The application of thick layers of pigment. **2.** The layers of pigment thus applied. [Italian, from *impastare*, IMPASTE.]

im·pa·tience (ĭm-pā′shəns) *n.* **1.** The inability to wait patiently. **2.** The inability to endure irritation. **3.** Restive eagerness, desire, or anticipation. [Middle English *impacience*, from Old French *impatience*, from Latin *impatientia*, from *impatiēns* (stem *impatient-*), not patient : *in-*, not + *patiēns*, PATIENT.]

im·pa·ti·ens (ĭm-pā′shəns, -shənz, -shē-ənz) *n.* Any plant of the genus *Impatiens*, which includes the jewelweed. [New Latin *Impatiens*, from Latin *impatiēns*, IMPATIENT (so called because the ripe pods burst open when touched).]

im·pa·tient (ĭm-pā′shənt) *adj.* **1.** Lacking patience, as in enduring delay or imperfection. **2.** Restively eager. **—im·pa·tient·ly** *adv.*

im·peach (ĭm-pēch′) *tr.v.* **-peached, -peaching, -peaches. 1. a.** To accuse of a crime, especially a crime against the state such as treason. **b.** To charge with improper conduct in office before a proper tribunal: *President Andrew Johnson was impeached in the House, but acquitted by the Senate.* **2.** To challenge or discredit; attack. [Middle English *empeachen*, to impede, accuse, from Old French *empe(s)cher*, impede, from Late Latin *impedicāre*, to entangle, put in fetters : Latin *in-*, in + *pedica*, fetter.] **—im·peach·a·ble** *adj.* **—im·peach·er** *n.* **—im·peach·ment** *n.*

im·pearl (ĭm-pûrl′) *tr.v.* **-pearled, -pearling, -pearls.** *Archaic.* **1.** To form into pearls. **2.** To adorn with or as if with pearls.

im·pec·ca·ble (ĭm-pĕk′ə-bəl) *adj.* **1.** Without flaw; faultless. **2.** Not to be doubted: *impeccable sources.* **3.** *Rare.* Not capable of sin. [Latin *impeccābilis*, not liable to sin : *in-*, not + *peccāre*, to sin.] **—im·pec·ca·bil·i·ty** (ĭm-pĕk′ə-bĭl′ə-tē) *n.* **—im·pec·ca·bly** *adv.*

im·pe·cu·ni·ous (ĭm′pĭ-kyo͞o′nē-əs) *adj.* Lacking money; penniless. [IN- (not) + obsolete *pecunious*, rich, Middle English *pecunyous*, from Latin *pecūniōsus*, from *pecūnia*, money.] **—im·pe·cu·ni·ous·ly** *adv.* **—im·pe·cu·ni·ous·ness, im·pe·cu·ni·os·i·ty** (ĭm′pĭ-kyo͞o′nē-ŏs′ə-tē) *n.*

im·pe·dance (ĭm-pē′dəns) *n.* **1.** *Symbol* **Z** A measure of the total opposition to current flow in an alternating-current circuit, equal to the ratio of the rms electromotive force in the circuit to the rms current produced by it, and usually represented in complex notation as $Z = R + iX$, where R is the ohmic resistance and X is the reactance. **2.** An analogous measure of resistance to an alternating effect, such as the resistance to vibration of the medium in sound transmission *(acoustic impedance)* or to vibration by an applied force *(mechanical impedance).* [From IMPEDE.]

impedance matching *n.* The use of electric circuits, transmission lines, and other devices to make the impedance of a load equal to the internal impedance of the source of power, thereby making possible the most efficient transfer of power.

im·pede (ĭm-pēd′) *tr.v.* **-peded, -peding, -pedes.** To obstruct the way of; hinder the progress of; block. —See Synonyms at **hinder.** [Latin *impedīre*, to entangle, fetter.] **—im·ped·er** *n.*

im·ped·i·ment (ĭm-pĕd′ə-mənt) *n.* **1.** A hindrance; an obstruction. **2.** Something that impedes, as: **a.** An organic defect, especially one preventing clear articulation: *a speech impediment.* **b.** *Law.* Something that obstructs the making of a legal contract. —See Synonyms at **obstacle.** [Latin *impedīmentum*, from *impedīre*, IMPEDE.] **—im·ped·i·men·tal** (ĭm-pĕd′ə-mĕnt′l), **im·ped·i·men·tar·y** (ĭm-pĕd′ə-mĕn′tə-rē) *adj.*

im·ped·i·men·ta (ĭm-pĕd′ə-mĕn′tə) *pl.n.* Objects, such as provisions, baggage, or military equipment, that impede or encumber. [Latin *impedīmenta*, plural of *impedīmentum*, IMPEDIMENT.]

im·pel (ĭm-pĕl′) *tr.v.* **-pelled, -pelling, -pels. 1.** To urge to action, as through moral pressure or necessity; compel; constrain. **2.** To drive forward; propel. [Latin *impellere*, to drive on or against : *in-*, against + *pellere*, to drive.]

im·pel·lent (ĭm-pĕl′ənt) *adj.* Impelling.
∼*n.* One that impels.

im·pel·ler (ĭm-pĕl′ər) *n.* **1.** One that impels. **2.** *Mechanics.* **a.** A rotating device used to force a gas in a given direction under pressure. **b.** A rotor or rotor blade in such a device.

im·pend (ĭm-pĕnd′) *intr.v.* **-pended, -pending, -pends. 1.** To hang or hover menacingly. **2.** To be about to take place. **3.** *Archaic.* To overhang. [Latin *impendēre* : *in-*, against + *pendēre*, to hang.]

im·pen·dent (ĭm-pĕn′dənt) *adj. Rare.* Impending.

im·pend·ing (ĭm-pĕn′dĭng) *adj.* Due to happen soon; imminent.

im·pen·e·tra·ble (ĭm-pĕn′ə-trə-bəl) *adj.* **1.** Not capable of being penetrated or entered. **2.** Incomprehensible; inscrutable; unfathomable. **3.** Impervious to argument or sentiment. **4.** *Physics.* Incapable of occupying space already occupied by matter. Said of bodies or particles. [Middle English *impenetrabel*, from Old French

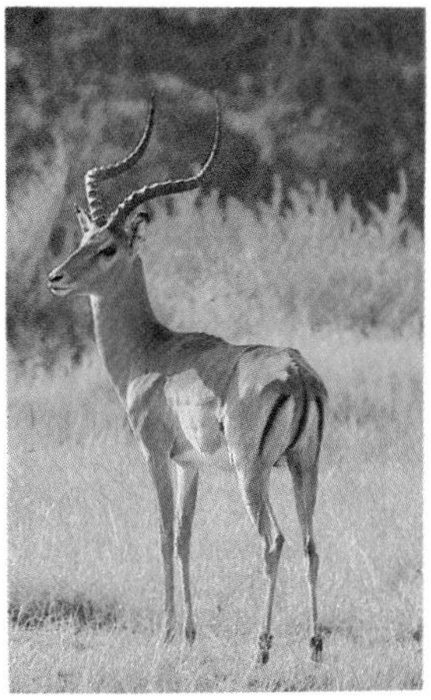

impala *When alarmed, the impala takes flight in bounding leaps up to 9 meters (30 feet) long and 3 meters (10 feet) high. Impalas live in large herds in East Africa. Only the males possess horns.*

PRONUNCIATION KEY

ă, pat; ā, pay; âr, care; ä, father, are; b, bib; ch, church; d, deed; ĕ, pet; ē, be; f, fife; g, gag; h, hat; hw, which; ĭ, pit; ī, pie; îr, pier; j, judge; k, kick; l, lid, needle; m, mum; n, no, sudden; ng, thing; ŏ, pot; ō, toe; ô, paw, for; oi, noise; ou, out; o͝o, book; o͞o, boot; p, pop; r, roar; s, sauce; sh, ship, dish; t, tight; th, thin, path; *th*, this, bathe; ŭ, cut; ûr, fur; v, valve; w, with; y, yes; z, zebra, size; zh, vision; ə, about, item, edible, gallop, circus, peaceful

IN FOREIGN WORDS:

à, *Fr.* ami; œ, *Fr.* feu, *Ger.* schön; ü, *Fr.* tu, *Ger.* über; KH, *Ger.* ich, *Scot.* loch; N, *Fr.* bon; y′, *Fr.* Compiègne

STRESS MARKS:

Primary stress: ′ **in·cite′** (ĭn-sīt′)
Secondary stress: ′ **in′sight′** (ĭn′sīt′)

impenetrable, from Latin *impenetrābilis* : *in-,* not + *penetrābilis,* PENETRABLE.] —**im·pen·e·tra·bil·i·ty** (ĭm-pĕn'ə-trə-bĭl'ə-te), **im·pen·e·tra·ble·ness** *n.* —**im·pen·e·tra·bly** *adv.*

im·pen·i·tent (ĭm-pĕn'ə-tənt) *adj.* **1.** Not penitent; unrepentant. **2.** Hardened; resolute. [Late Latin *impaenitēns* (stem *impaenitent-*) : Latin *in-,* not + *paenitēns,* PENITENT.] —**im·pen·i·tence** *n.* —**im·pen·i·tent** *n.* —**im·pen·i·tent·ly** *adv.*

imper. imperative.

im·per·a·tive (ĭm-pĕr'ə-tĭv) *adj. Abbr.* **imp., imper.** **1.** Expressing a command or plea; peremptory. **2.** Assuming the power or authority to command or control. **3.** *Grammar.* Of or designating the mood that expresses a command or request. **4.** Extremely important; essential. **5.** Obligatory; mandatory. —See Synonyms at **urgent.** —*n. Abbr.* **imp., imper.** **1.** *Grammar.* **a.** The imperative mood. **b.** A verb form of the imperative mood. **2. a.** A command; an order. **b.** Something that is important or essential. **c.** An obligation. [Late Latin *imperātīvus,* from Latin *imperāre,* "to prepare against (an occasion)," hence to command : *in-,* against + *parāre,* to prepare.] —**im·per·a·tive·ly** *adv.* —**im·per·a·tive·ness** *n.*

im·pe·ra·tor (ĭm'pĕ-rä'tôr, -tōr', -rä'tər) *n.* **1.** A title given to a victorious commander in ancient Rome. **2.** *Abbr.* **Imp.** An emperor, especially of the Roman Empire. [Latin *imperātor,* EMPEROR.]

im·pe·ra·trix (ĭm'pĕ-rä'trĭks', -rä'trĭks') *n. Abbr.* **Imp.** An empress. [Latin.]

im·per·cep·ti·ble (ĭm'pər-sĕp'tə-bəl) *adj.* **1.** Not perceptible. **2.** Barely perceptible; slight or subtle. —**im·per·cep·ti·bil·i·ty** (ĭm'pər-sĕp'tə-bĭl'ə-tē), **im·per·cep·ti·ble·ness** *n.* —**im·per·cep·ti·bly** *adv.*

im·per·cep·tive (ĭm'pər-sĕp'tĭv) *adj.* Not perceptive; lacking perception. —**im·per·cep·tiv·i·ty** (ĭm'pər-sĕp-tĭv'ə-tē), **im·per·cep·tive·ness** *n.*

im·per·cip·i·ent (ĭm'pər-sĭp'ē-ənt) *adj.* Imperceptive. —**im·per·cip·i·ence** *n.*

im·per·fect (ĭm-pûr'fĭkt) *adj. Abbr.* **imp., imperf.** **1. a.** Not perfect; having some flaw or defect. **b.** Incomplete. **2.** Of or designating the tense of a verb that shows, usually in the past, an action or condition as incomplete, continuous, or coincident with another action. **3.** *Botany.* **a.** Having either stamens or a pistil only: *imperfect flowers.* **b.** Designating fungi in which the sexual reproductive stage has not been discovered or has been lost during evolution. **4.** *Law.* Not legally enforceable because of a technical defect. **5.** *Music.* **a.** Designating a cadence ending on the dominant rather than the direct chord of the tonic. **b.** Of or designating intervals other than the fourth, fifth, and octave. —*n. Abbr.* **imp., imperf.** **1.** The imperfect tense. **2.** A verb in this tense. [Middle English *imperfit,* from Old French *imparfait,* from Latin *imperfectus* : *in-,* not + *perfectus,* PERFECT.] —**im·per·fect·ly** *adv.* —**im·per·fect·ness** *n.*

imperfect competition *n.* Monopolistic competition *(see).*

im·per·fec·tion (ĭm'pər-fĕk'shən) *n.* **1.** The quality or condition of being imperfect. **2.** Something imperfect; a defect; a flaw. —See Synonyms at **blemish.**

im·per·fec·tive (ĭm'pər-fĕk'tĭv) *adj. Grammar.* Of or designating a verb in the imperfective aspect. —*n. Grammar.* **1.** The imperfective aspect. **2.** A verb in the imperfective aspect.

imperfective aspect *n.* An aspect of verbs that expresses action without regard to its beginning or completion. Compare **perfective aspect.** See **aspect.**

im·per·fo·rate (ĭm-pûr'fər-ĭt) *adj.* **1.** Not perforated. **2.** Not perforated into detachable rows. Said of stamps and sheets of stamps. **3.** *Anatomy.* Lacking a normal opening. Said of a bodily part. —*n.* An imperforate stamp.

im·pe·ri·al[1] (ĭm-pîr'ē-əl) *adj. Abbr.* **imp.** **1. a.** Of or pertaining to an empire or a sovereign, especially an emperor or empress. **b.** Of or pertaining to the British Empire. **2.** Designating a nation or government having sovereign rights over colonies or dependencies. **3. a.** *Obsolete.* Having supreme authority; sovereign. **b.** Regal; majestic. **4.** Outstanding in size or quality. **5.** Of or pertaining to the British Imperial system of weights and measures. —*n.* **1. Imperial.** A supporter or a soldier of the Holy Roman Empire. **2.** An emperor or empress. **3.** A dome with a pointed top. **4.** Something outstanding in size or quality. **5. a.** A size of paper, usually 23 by 33 inches. **b.** A size of book; especially, *imperial octavo* (7½ by 11 inches) or *imperial quarto* (11 by 15 inches). **6.** Formerly, a Russian gold coin. [Middle English *emperial, imperial,* from Old French, from Late Latin *imperiālis,* from Latin *imperium,* command, EMPIRE.] —**im·pe·ri·al·ly** *adv.*

imperial[2] *n.* A pointed beard grown from the lower lip and chin. [French *impériale,* IMPERIAL (after Napoleon III, who wore one).]

im·pe·ri·al·ism (ĭm-pîr'ē-ə-lĭz'əm) *n.* **1.** The policy of extending a nation's authority by territorial acquisition or by the establishment of economic and political hegemony over other nations. **2.** The system, policies, or practices of an imperial government. **3.** The imposing of its will on others by a country or powerful organization, as in social, cultural, or other matters. Used derogatorily. —**im·pe·ri·al·ist** *n. & adj.* —**im·pe·ri·al·is·tic** (ĭm-pîr'ē-ə-lĭs'tĭk) *adj.* —**im·pe·ri·al·is·ti·cal·ly** *adv.*

Imperial jade *n.* A light-green jade derived from gem-quality jadeite.

imperial moth *n.* A large New World moth, *Eacles imperialis,* having yellow wings with purplish or brownish markings.

Imperial system *n.* The system of weights and measures used in Great Britain and various other countries, using units of weights such as the ounce, pound, and stone; units of length such as the inch, foot, yard, and mile; and units of volume such as the pint, quart, and gallon.

Imperial Valley. Fertile region in southeastern California, extending southward into northwestern Mexico. It has a long growing season (more than 300 days), can support two crops a year with irrigation, and is an important source of winter fruits and vegetables and cotton, grains, and dairy products.

im·per·il (ĭm-pĕr'əl) *tr.v.* **-iled, -iling, ils** or *chiefly British* **-illed, -illing.** To put in peril; endanger. —**im·per·il·ment** *n.*

im·pe·ri·ous (ĭm-pîr'ē-əs) *adj.* **1.** Domineering; overbearing. **2.** *Obsolete.* Regal; imperial. **3.** *Rare.* Urgent; pressing. —See Synonyms at **dictatorial.** [Latin *imperiōsus,* from *imperium,* IMPERIUM.] —**im·pe·ri·ous·ly** *adv.* —**im·pe·ri·ous·ness** *n.*

im·per·ish·a·ble (ĭm-pĕr'ĭ-shə-bəl) *adj.* Not perishable. —**im·per·ish·a·bil·i·ty** (ĭm-pĕr'ĭ-shə-bĭl'ə-tē), **im·per·ish·a·ble·ness** *n.* —**im·per·ish·a·bly** *adv.*

im·pe·ri·um (ĭm-pîr'ē-əm) *n., pl.* **-ria** (-ē-ə). **1.** Absolute rule; supreme power. **2.** A sphere of power or dominion; an empire. [Latin, EMPIRE.]

im·per·ma·nent (ĭm-pûr'mə-nənt) *adj.* Not permanent; not lasting or durable. —**im·per·ma·nence, im·per·ma·nen·cy** *n.*

im·per·me·a·ble (ĭm-pûr'mē-ə-bəl) *adj.* **1.** Not permeable. **2.** *Physics.* Not allowing the passage of fluids. **3.** *Geology.* Not allowing water or other fluid to pass through it easily. Said of rock. [Late Latin *impermeābilis* : *in-,* not + *permeābilis,* PERMEABLE.] —**im·per·me·a·ble·ness** *n.* —**im·per·me·a·bly** *adv.*

im·per·mis·si·ble (ĭm'pər-mĭs'ə-bəl) *adj.* Not permissible. —**im·per·mis·si·bil·i·ty** (ĭm'pər-mĭs'ə-bĭl'ə-tē) *n.* —**im·per·mis·si·bly** *adv.*

im·per·script·i·ble (ĭm'pər-skrĭp'tə-bəl) *adj.* Not supported by written authority; unrecorded.

im·per·son·al (ĭm-pûr'sə-nəl) *adj.* **1.** *Grammar.* **a.** Pertaining to or designating a verb or construction that expresses the action of an unspecified agent and is used in the third person singular without a separate subject (as *methinks*) or a purely nominal subject (as *snowed* in *it snowed*). **b.** Indefinite. Said of pronouns. **2.** Not personal; not related or connected to a person or persons: *impersonal possessions.* **3.** Exhibiting little or no individuality or personality. **4.** Lacking sympathy or human warmth. —**im·per·son·al·i·ty** (ĭm-pûr'sə-năl'ə-tē) *n.* —**im·per·son·al·ly** *adv.*

im·per·son·al·ize (ĭm-pûr'sə-nə-līz') *tr.v.* **-ized, -izing, -izes.** To make impersonal.

im·per·son·ate (ĭm-pûr'sə-nāt') *tr.v.* **-ated, -ating, -ates.** **1.** To act the character or part of, especially in order to entertain. **2.** To assume the identity of for unlawful purposes. **3.** *Archaic.* To embody; personify. [IN- (in) + PERSON + -ATE.] —**im·per·son·ate** (ĭm-pûr'sə-nĭt) *adj.* —**im·per·son·a·tion** (ĭm-pûr'sə-nā'shən) *n.* —**im·per·son·a·tor** *n.*

im·per·ti·nence (ĭm-pûrt'n-əns) *n.* Also **im·per·ti·nen·cy** (-ən-sē) *pl.* **-cies.** **1.** The quality of being impertinent; insolence. **2.** Irrelevance. **3.** An impertinent act, person, or statement.

im·per·ti·nent (ĭm-pûrt'n-ənt) *adj.* **1.** Impudent; presumptuous; rude. **2.** Not pertinent; irrelevant. [Middle English, irrelevant, from Old French, from Late Latin *impertinēns* (stem *impertinent-*) : Latin *in-,* not + *pertinēns,* PERTINENT.] —**im·per·ti·nent·ly** *adv.*

im·per·turb·a·ble (ĭm'pər-tûr'bə-bəl) *adj.* Not capable of being perturbed; calm. —See Synonyms at **cool.** —**im·per·turb·a·bil·i·ty** (ĭm'pər-tûr'bə-bĭl'ə-tē), **im·per·turb·a·ble·ness** *n.* —**im·per·turb·a·bly** *adv.*

im·per·vi·ous (ĭm-pûr'vē-əs) *adj.* **1.** Incapable of being penetrated, as by water or light. **2.** Not affected; unable to be influenced: *impervious to her charm.* [Latin *impervius* : *in-,* not + *pervius,* PERVIOUS.] —**im·per·vi·ous·ly** *adv.* —**im·per·vi·ous·ness** *n.*

im·pe·ti·go (ĭm'pə-tī'gō, -tē'gō) *n.* A contagious skin disease characterized by pustules that burst and form characteristic thick yellow crusts. [Latin *impetīgō,* "an attack," from *impetere,* to assail, attack. See **impetus.**]

im·pe·trate (ĭm'pə-trāt') *tr.v.* **-trated, -trating, -trates.** *Theology.* **1.** To obtain by entreaty or petition. **2.** To beseech. [Latin *impetrāre,* to accomplish : *in-* (intensive) + *patrāre,* to father, achieve, accomplish, from *pater,* father.] —**im·pe·tra·tion** (ĭm'pə-trā'shən) *n.* —**im·pe·tra·tor** *n.*

im·pet·u·ous (ĭm-pĕch'ōō-əs) *adj.* **1.** Characterized or prompted by sudden energy, emotion, or the like; impulsive; brash. **2.** Having great impetus; rushing with violence: *impetuous, heaving waves.* [Middle English, from Old French *impetueux,* from Latin *impetuōsus,* from *impetus,* IMPETUS.] —**im·pet·u·os·i·ty** (ĭm-pĕch'ōō-ŏs'ə-tē), **im·pet·u·ous·ness** *n.* —**im·pet·u·ous·ly** *adv.*

Usage: **impetuous, heedless, hasty, headlong, sudden.** These adjectives describe persons and their actions and decisions when marked by abruptness or lack of deliberation. *Impetuous* suggests impulsiveness, impatience, or lack of thoughtfulness. *Heedless* implies carelessness or lack of a sense of responsibility or proper regard for the consequences of action. *Hasty* and *headlong* both stress hurried action, and the latter especially implies recklessness. *Sudden* is applied to action or to personal attributes, such as moods, that make themselves apparent abruptly or unexpectedly.

im·pe·tus (ĭm'pə-təs) *n., pl.* **-tuses.** **1. a.** An impelling force; an impulse. **b.** Something that incites; a stimulus. **2.** Loosely, the force associated with a moving body. [Latin, attack, from *impetere,* to assail, attack : *in-,* against + *petere,* to go toward, seek, attack.]

im·pi·e·ty (ĭm-pī′ə-tē) n., pl. **-ties.** **1.** The quality or state of being impious. **2.** An impious act. **3.** Undutifulness.

im·pinge (ĭm-pĭnj′) intr.v. **-pinged, -pinging, -pinges.** **1.** To encroach; trespass. Used with on or upon. **2.** To collide; strike; dash. Used with on, upon, or against. [Latin impingere, to push against : in-, against + pangere, to fasten, drive in.] **—im·pinge·ment** n. **—im·ping·er** n.

impingement attack n. Metallurgy. Erosion of a metal surface that is in contact with a turbulent fluid containing small gas bubbles or solid particles.

im·pi·ous (ĭm′pē-əs, ĭm-pī′-) adj. **1.** Not pious; lacking reverence; profane. **2.** Lacking due respect. [Latin impius : in-, not + pius, PIOUS.] **—im·pi·ous·ly** adv. **—im·pi·ous·ness** n.

imp·ish (ĭm′pĭsh) adj. Of or like an imp; mischievous. —See Synonyms at **playful.** **—imp·ish·ly** adv. **—imp·ish·ness** n.

im·pla·ca·ble (ĭm-plăk′ə-bəl, ĭm-plā′kə-) adj. **1.** Not placable; incapable of appeasement; inexorable. **2.** Unalterable; inflexible. [Latin implācābilis : in-, not + plācābilis, PLACABLE.] **—im·pla·ca·bil·i·ty** (ĭm-plăk′ə-bĭl′ə-tē), **im·pla·ca·ble·ness** n. **—im·pla·ca·bly** adv.

im·plant (ĭm-plănt′, -plänt′) tr.v. **-planted, -planting, -plants.** **1.** To entrench or set in firmly, as in the ground; infix. **2.** To establish decisively, as in the mind or consciousness; instill; ingrain. **3.** Medicine. To insert or embed surgically, as in grafting. ~n. (ĭm′plănt′, -plänt′) Something implanted; especially, an implanted drug, device, or piece of tissue.

im·plan·ta·tion (ĭm′plăn-tā′shən) n. **1.** An act or instance of implanting. **2.** The condition of being implanted. **3.** An implanted object. **4.** The attachment and embedding of the fertilized ovum in the uterine wall.

im·plau·si·ble (ĭm-plô′zə-bəl) adj. Not plausible. **—im·plau·si·bil·i·ty** (ĭm-plô′zə-bĭl′ə-tē), **im·plau·si·ble·ness** n. **—im·plau·si·bly** adv.

im·plead (ĭm-plēd′) tr.v. **-pleaded, -pleading, -pleads.** To sue or prosecute in a court of law. [Middle English impleden, from Old French empleid(i)er : en- (intensive) + pleid(i)er, PLEAD.]

im·ple·ment (ĭm′plə-mənt) n. **1.** A tool, utensil, or instrument. **2.** An article used to outfit or equip. **3.** A means employed to achieve a given end; an agent. **4.** In Scottish law, performance of a contract or an obligation. —See Synonyms at **tool.** ~tr.v. (ĭm′plə-mĕnt′) **implemented, -menting, -ments.** **1.** To put into practical effect; carry out: implement the new procedures. **2.** To supply with implements. [Middle English, from Late Latin implēmentum, a filling up, supplement, from Latin implēre, to fill up, fulfill : in- (intensive) + plēre, to fill.] **—im·ple·men·ta·tion** (ĭm′plə-mĕn-tā′shən) n.

im·pli·cate (ĭm′plĭ-kāt′) tr.v. **-cated, -cating, -cates.** **1.** To involve intimately or incriminatingly. **2.** Archaic. To entangle; entwine. [Latin implicāre : in-, in + plicāre, to fold.]

im·pli·ca·tion (ĭm′plĭ-kā′shən) n. **1.** The act of implicating or the condition of being implicated. **2.** The act of implying or the condition of being implied. **3.** That which is implied, especially: **a.** An indirect suggestion. **b.** An inference.

im·pli·ca·tive (ĭm′plĭ-kā′tĭv) adj. Also **im·pli·ca·to·ry** (ĭm′plĭ-kə-tôr′ē, -tōr′ē) **1.** Having a tendency to implicate. **2.** Of or pertaining to implication. **—im·pli·ca·tive·ly** adv.

im·plic·it (ĭm-plĭs′ĭt) adj. **1.** Implied or understood although not directly expressed: His anger was implicit. **2.** Inherent or contained in the nature of something although not directly expressed. Used with in: Suspicion is implicit in such a tone of voice. **3.** Having no doubts or reservations; unquestioning: Her trust in him was implicit. **4.** Mathematics. Pertaining to or designating a function of two or more variables of the form f (x, y) = 0. For example, in 2xy + 1 = 0, x is an implicit function of y. [Latin implicitus, earlier implicātus, involved, entangled, from the past participle of implicāre, to involve, IMPLICATE.] **—im·plic·it·ly** adv. **—im·plic·it·ness** n.

im·plied (ĭm-plīd′) adj. Suggested, involved, or understood although not clearly or openly expressed.

im·plode (ĭm-plōd′) v. **-ploded, -ploding, -plodes.** —intr. To undergo implosion. —tr. **1.** To cause implosion in. **2.** Phonetics. To pronounce by implosion. [IN- (in) + (EX)PLODE.]

im·plore (ĭm-plôr′, -plōr′) v. **-plored, -ploring, -plores.** —tr. **1.** To appeal to in supplication; entreat; beseech: I implore you to have mercy on the defendant. **2.** To plead or beg for urgently: I implore your mercy. —intr. To make an earnest appeal. —See Synonyms at **beg.** [Latin implōrāre, to invoke with tears : in-, in + plōrāre, to weep, bewail, lament (perhaps imitative).] **—im·plo·ra·tion** (ĭm′plô-rā′shən) n. **—im·plor·er** n. **—im·plor·ing·ly** adv.

im·plo·sion (ĭm-plō′zhən) n. **1.** A more or less violent collapse inward, as of a highly evacuated glass vessel. **2.** Phonetics. The stopping of the breath while breathing in to form a stop consonant. Compare plosion. [IN- + (EX)PLOSION.]

im·plo·sive (ĭm-plō′sĭv) adj. Phonetics. Pronounced by implosion. ~n. Phonetics. A consonant pronounced by implosion.

im·ply (ĭm-plī′) tr.v. **-plied, -plying, -plies.** **1.** To say or express indirectly; suggest: Her use of "we" implied that she was speaking for others. **2.** To involve or suggest by logical necessity; entail: His aims imply a good deal of energy. —See Synonyms at **suggest.** [Middle English implien, emplien, from Old French emplier, from Latin implicāre, infold, involve, IMPLICATE.]
Usage: It is a common mistake to confuse imply (to state or express something indirectly) with infer (to deduce, or draw a conclusion from what is stated). The speaker or writer implies: Your report implies that the mechanism was faulty. The listener or reader

infers: I infer from your report that the mechanism was faulty.

im·pol·i·cy (ĭm-pŏl′ə-sē) n., pl. **-cies.** **1.** The state of or an instance of being impolitic. **2.** A bad policy.

im·po·lite (ĭm′pə-līt′) adj. Not polite; discourteous; rude. [Latin impolītus, unpolished : in-, not + polītus, polished, POLITE.] **—im·po·lite·ly** adv. **—im·po·lite·ness** n.

im·pol·i·tic (ĭm-pŏl′ə-tĭk) adj. Not wise or expedient; not politic. **—im·pol·i·tic·ly** adv. **—im·pol·i·tic·ness** n.

im·pon·der·a·ble (ĭm-pŏn′dər-ə-bəl) adj. Incapable of being weighed, measured, or evaluated with precision. ~n. Something that is imponderable; an indeterminable factor: Public support is a great imponderable. **—im·pon·der·a·ble·ness** n. **—im·pon·der·a·bly** adv.

im·po·nent (ĭm-pō′nənt) n. One who imposes a duty. [From IMPOSE, by analogy with opponent.] **—im·po·nent** adj.

im·port (ĭm-pôrt′, -pōrt′, ĭm′pôrt′, -pōrt′) v. **-ported, -porting, -ports.** —tr. **1.** To bring or carry in from an outside source; especially, to bring in (goods) from a foreign country for trade or sale. Compare export. **2.** To mean; signify. **3.** To imply. **4.** Archaic. To have importance for. —intr. To be significant. —See Synonyms at **mean** (convey sense). ~n. (ĭm′pôrt′, -pōrt′). **1.** Abbr. **imp.** Something imported. **2. a.** The business of importing. **b.** Importation. **3.** Meaning; signification. **4.** Importance; significance. —See Synonyms at **importance, meaning.** [Middle English importen, from Latin importāre, to carry in : in-, in + portāre, to carry.] **—im·port·a·bil·i·ty** (ĭm-pôrt′ə-bĭl′ə-tē) n. **—im·port·a·ble** adj. **—im·port·er** n.

im·por·tance (ĭm-pôr′təns) n. **1.** The condition or quality of being important; significance; consequence. **2.** Personal status; standing. **3.** Obsolete. An important matter.
Synonyms: consequence, import, moment, significance, weight.

im·por·tant (ĭm-pôr′tənt) adj. Abbr. **imp.** **1.** Having a great effect or being of great concern; significant: an important decision to many people. **2.** Holding or considered as holding a high position in people's estimation. **3.** Self-important. [Old French, from Old Italian importante, from Medieval Latin importāns (stem important-), present participle of importāre, to mean, be significant, from Latin, to carry in, IMPORT.] **—im·por·tant·ly** adv.
Usage: The following sentence may be written with the adjective important: The truth is evident; more important, it will prevail. It may also be written with an adverb: The truth is evident; more importantly, it will prevail. Most grammarians prescribe the adjective form, in which important stands for "what is important," but the use of importantly is now very common.

im·por·ta·tion (ĭm′pôr-tā′shən, ĭm′pōr-) n. **1.** The act, occupation, or business of importing. **2.** Something imported; an import.

im·por·tu·nate (ĭm-pôr′chŏŏ-nĭt) adj. **1.** Stubbornly or unreasonably persistent in request or demand. **2.** Urgent; pressing. **—im·por·tu·nate·ly** adv. **—im·por·tu·nate·ness** n.

im·por·tune (ĭm′pôr-tōōn′, -tyŏŏn′, ĭm-pôr′chən) tr.v. **-tuned, -tuning, -tunes.** **1.** To beset with repeated and insistent requests. **2.** To solicit, especially for immoral purposes. **3.** Obsolete. To ask for insistently and repeatedly. **4.** Obsolete. To annoy; vex. —See Synonyms at **beg.** ~adj. Importunate. [Medieval Latin importūnārī, to be troublesome, from Latin importūnus, "without a port," difficult of access, unfit, unsuitable : in-, not + portus, port, harbor.] **—im·por·tune·ly** adv. **—im·por·tun·er** n.

im·por·tu·ni·ty (ĭm′pôr-tōō′nə-tē, -tyōō′nə-tē) n., pl. **-ties.** **1. a.** The act of importuning. **b.** The state or quality of being importunate. **2.** importunities. Insistent demands or requests.

im·pose (ĭm-pōz′) v. **-posed, -posing, -poses.** —tr. **1.** To establish or apply as compulsory; levy: The amount of duties imposed now constitutes a protective tariff. **2.** To lay (something burdensome) upon another or others: impose extra duties. **3.** To obtrude or force (oneself, for example) upon another or others. **4.** Printing. To arrange (type or plates) in the correct order and lock them into a chase. **5.** To pass off (something) on others: He imposed a fraud on his company. **6.** To lay (hands) on the head of a person receiving certain sacraments. Used of a bishop or priest. —intr. **1.** To take unfair advantage of something or someone. Used with on or upon: imposed on his host by staying late. **2.** To make an impression, often fraudulently. Used with on or upon. [Old French imposer, from Latin impōnere (past participle impositus), to put on : in-, on + pōnere, to put, place.] **—im·pos·er** n.

im·pos·ing (ĭm-pō′zĭng) adj. Impressive, as in size or appearance. —See Synonyms at **grand.**

imposing stone n. Printing. A stone or metal slab on which material to be printed is arranged. Also called "imposing table."

im·po·si·tion (ĭm′pə-zĭsh′ən) n. **1.** The act of imposing. **2.** Something imposed, as a tax, undue burden, or fraud. **3.** A burdensome or unfair demand, as upon someone's time. **4.** Printing. The arrangement of printed matter to form a sequence of pages.

im·pos·si·bil·i·ty (ĭm-pŏs′ə-bĭl′ə-tē) n., pl. **-ties.** **1.** The condition or quality of being impossible. **2.** Something impossible.

im·pos·si·ble (ĭm-pŏs′ə-bəl) adj. **1.** Not capable of existing or happening. **2.** Having little likelihood of happening or being accomplished. **3.** Untrue or ridiculously exaggerated: an impossible claim. **5.** Not capable of being dealt with or tolerated: an impossible request; an impossible child. [Middle English, from Old French, from Latin impossibilis : in-, not + possibilis, POSSIBLE.] **—im·pos·si·bly** adv.

im·post¹ (ĭm′pōst′) n. **1.** Something imposed or levied, as a tax or duty. **2.** The weight a horse must carry in a handicap race. [Old French, from Medieval Latin *impositum,* from Latin *impositus,* past participle of *impōnere,* IMPOSE.]

impost[2] *n. Architecture.* The uppermost part of a column or pillar supporting an arch, usually projecting from a wall like a bracket. [French *imposte,* from Italian *imposta,* from Latin, feminine past participle of *impōnere,* IMPOSE.]

im·pos·tor (ĭm-pŏs′tər) *n.* A person who deceives, especially by assuming a false identity. [Old French *imposteur,* from Late Latin *impos(i)tor,* from Latin *impōnere* (past participle *impositus*), IMPOSE.]

im·pos·ture (ĭm-pŏs′chər) *n.* Deception or fraud; especially, assumption of a false identity. [Late Latin *impostura,* from Latin *impos(i)tus,* past participle of *impōnere,* IMPOSE.]

im·po·tent (ĭm′pə-tənt) *adj.* **1.** Lacking physical strength or vigor; weak. **2.** Powerless; ineffectual. **3.** Incapable of sexual intercourse. Said of males. Compare **frigid**. **4.** *Obsolete.* Lacking self-restraint. —See Synonyms at **sterile**. [Middle English, from Old French, from Latin *impotēns* : *in-,* not + *potēns,* POTENT.] **—im·po·tence, im·po·ten·cy** *n.* **—im·po·tent·ly** *adv.*

im·pound (ĭm-pound′) *tr.v.* **-pounded, -pounding, -pounds. 1.** To confine in or as if in a pound. **2.** To seize and retain, especially in legal custody. **3.** To accumulate (water) in a reservoir. **—im·pound·age, im·pound·ment** *n.* **—im·pound·er** *n.*

im·pov·er·ish (ĭm-pŏv′ər-ĭsh) *tr.v.* **-ished, -ishing, -ishes. 1.** To diminish or exhaust the wealth of; reduce to poverty. **2.** To deprive of natural richness or strength. —See Usage note at **deplete**. [Middle English *enpoverisen,* from Old French *empovrir* (present stem *empovriss-*), to make poor : *en-* (causative) + *povre,* POOR.] **—im·pov·er·ish·ment** *n.*

im·prac·ti·ca·ble (ĭm-prăk′tĭ-kə-bəl) *adj.* **1.** Not capable of being done or carried out. **2.** Unfit for use or passage, as a road may be. **3.** *Archaic.* Unmanageable; intractable. —See Usage note at **impractical**. **—im·prac·ti·ca·bil·i·ty** (ĭm-prăk′tĭ-kə-bĭl′ə-tē), **im·prac·ti·ca·ble·ness** *n.* **—im·prac·ti·ca·bly** *adv.*

im·prac·ti·cal (ĭm-prăk′tĭ-kəl) *adj.* **1.** Unwise to implement or maintain in practice. **2.** Incapable of dealing efficiently with practical matters, especially financial or mechanical matters. **3.** Not in accord with experience or common sense. Impracticable. **—im·prac·ti·cal·i·ty** (ĭm-prăk′tĭ-kăl′ə-tē), **im·prac·ti·cal·ness** *n.*

Usage: There is a certain overlap of usage between *impracticable* and *impractical,* but generally the senses are distinct. *Impracticable* applies to something that is not capable of being carried out or put into practice. *Impractical* refers to that which is not sensible or prudent. A plan may be *impractical* if it involves undue cost or effort and still not be *impracticable.* The distinction between these words is subtle, and *impractical* is often used where *impracticable* would be more precise.

im·pre·cate (ĭm′prə-kāt′) *tr.v.* **-cated, -cating, -cates.** To invoke evil or a curse upon. [Latin *imprecārī* : *in-,* on + *precārī,* to pray, entreat.] **—im·pre·ca·tor** *n.* **—im·pre·ca·to·ry** (ĭm′prə-kə-tôr′ē, -tōr′ē) *adj.*

im·pre·ca·tion (ĭm′prə-kā′shən) *n.* **1.** The act of imprecating. **2.** A curse.

im·pre·cise (ĭm′prĭ-sīs′) *adj.* Not precise; inexact. **—im·pre·cise·ly** *adv.* **—im·pre·ci·sion** (ĭm′prĭ-sĭzh′ən) *n.*

im·preg·na·ble[1] (ĭm-prĕg′nə-bəl) *adj.* **1.** Able to resist capture or entry by force: *an impregnable castle.* **2.** Unable to be shaken, refuted, or criticized: *impregnable convictions.* [Middle English *imprenable,* from Old French : *in-,* not + *prenable,* PREGNABLE.]

impregnable[2] *adj.* Able to be impregnated. [From IMPREGNATE.]

im·preg·nate (ĭm-prĕg′nāt′) *tr.v.* **-nated, -nating, -nates. 1.** To make pregnant; inseminate. **2.** To fertilize (an ovum, for example). **3.** To fill throughout or saturate. **4.** To permeate or imbue.
~*adj.* Impregnated; made pregnant. [Late Latin *impregnāre* : Latin *in-,* in + *praegnās,* PREGNANT.] **—im·preg·na·tion** *n.* **—im·preg·na·tor** *n.*

im·pre·sa (ĭm-prā′zə) *n.* Also **im·prese** (ĭm-prēz′). An emblem or device with a motto. [French *impresse,* from Italian *impresa,* undertaking, emblem. See **impresario**.]

im·pre·sa·ri·o (ĭm′prə-sär′ē-ō′, -sâr′ē-ō′) *n., pl.* **-sarios** or **-sari** (-sär′ē). **1.** One who sponsors or produces entertainments, especially theatrical and musical ones. **2.** A manager; producer. [Italian, undertaker, manager, from *impresa,* undertaking, chivalric deed, emblem, from the feminine of *impreso,* past participle of *imprendere,* to undertake, from Vulgar Latin *imprendere* (unattested). See **emprise**.]

im·pre·scrip·ti·ble (ĭm′prĭ-skrĭp′tə-bəl) *adj. Law.* Immune from prescription; inalienable. **—im·pre·scrip·ti·bly** *adv.*

im·press[1] (ĭm-prĕs′) *tr.v.* **-pressed, -pressing, -presses. 1.** To produce or apply with pressure. **2.** To mark or stamp with or as if with pressure. **3.** To produce a vivid perception or image of. **4.** To affect or influence deeply or forcibly. **5.** To emphasize; stress. **6.** To transmit a force or motion to. —See Synonyms at **affect**.
~*n.* (ĭm′prĕs′). **1.** The act of impressing. **2.** A mark or pattern produced by impressing. **3.** A stamp or seal meant to be impressed. **4.** A characteristic quality. [Middle English *impressen,* from Latin *imprimere* (past participle *impressus*) : *in-,* in + *premere,* to press.]

im·press[2] *tr.v.* **-pressed, -pressing, -presses. 1.** Formerly, to compel (a person) to serve in a military force. **2.** To confiscate (property).
~*n.* Impressment. [IN- (intensive) + PRESS (to force into service).]

im·press·i·ble (ĭm-prĕs′ə-bəl) *adj.* Susceptible to being impressed. **—im·press·i·bly** *adv.*

im·pres·sion (ĭm-prĕsh′ən) *n.* **1.** The act or process of impressing. **2.** The effect, mark, or imprint made on a surface by pressure. **3. a.** An effect, image, or feeling retained as a consequence of experience. **b.** An effect produced by an event or action. **4.** A vague notion, remembrance, or belief. **5.** An imitation or mimicking of another person or thing, especially when done by a professional entertainer. **6.** *Printing.* **a.** All the copies of a publication printed at one time from the same set of type. **b.** A single copy of this printing. **c.** A print taken from an engraving or from type. **7.** In dentistry, an imprint of the teeth and surrounding tissue in material such as wax or plaster, used as a mold in making dentures or inlays. —See Synonyms at **opinion**.

im·pres·sion·a·ble (ĭm-prĕsh′ən-ə-bəl) *adj.* Readily influenced; suggestible. **—im·pres·sion·a·bil·i·ty, im·pres·sion·a·ble·ness** *n.*

Im·pres·sion·ism (ĭm-prĕsh′ə-nĭz′əm) *n. Sometimes* **impressionism. 1.** A theory or style of painting originating and developed in France during the 1870's, characterized chiefly by concentration on the general impression produced by a scene or object and by the use of unmixed primary colors and small strokes to simulate actual reflected light. **2.** A literary style characterized generally by the use of details and mental associations to evoke subjective and sensory impressions rather than the re-creation of objective reality. **3.** A musical style of the late 19th and early 20th centuries, using unusual harmonies to evoke suggestions of mood, place, and natural phenomena. **—Im·pres·sion·ist** *n.* & *adj.*

im·pres·sion·ist·ic (ĭm-prĕsh′ə-nĭs′tĭk) *adj.* **1.** Of or pertaining to impressionism. **2.** Of or pertaining to a subjective, sketchy approach or attitude: *an impressionistic survey of recent history.*

im·pres·sive (ĭm-prĕs′ĭv) *adj.* Making a strong, favorable impression; awesome or stirring. **—im·pres·sive·ly** *adv.* **—im·pres·sive·ness** *n.*

im·press·ment (ĭm-prĕs′mənt) *n.* The act or policy of impressing men or property for public service or use: *army ranks swelled by impressment.*

im·pres·sure (ĭm-prĕsh′ər) *n. Archaic.* An impression.

im·prest (ĭm-prĕst′) *n.* An advance or loan of government or public funds toward the performance of some service for the government. [Probably from Italian *imprestare,* to make a loan to : *in-,* toward, from Latin + *prestare,* to lend, from Latin *praestāre,* to pay, give, from *praestō,* at hand (see **presto**).]

im·pri·ma·tur (ĭm′prə-mā′tər, -mä′tər) *n.* **1.** *Abbr.* **imp.** Official approval or license to print or publish, especially under conditions of censorship. **2.** Broadly, any official sanction. [Latin, let it be printed, from Latin *imprimere,* to print, IMPRESS.]

im·pri·mis (ĭm-prī′mĭs) *adv. Archaic.* In the first place. [Middle English, from Latin *in prīmīs,* among the first (things) : *in,* in + *prīmīs,* ablative plural of *prīmus,* first.]

im·print (ĭm-prĭnt′) *v.* **-printed, -printing, -prints.** —*tr.* **1.** To produce or impress (a mark or pattern) on a surface. **2.** To stamp or produce a mark on. **3.** To establish firmly or impress, as on the mind or memory. **4.** To subject (a young animal) to imprinting. —*intr.* To become imprinted. Used of young animals.
~*n.* (ĭm′prĭnt′). **1.** A mark or pattern produced by imprinting. **2.** A distinguishing manifestation: *the imprint of defeat.* **3. a.** The publisher's name, often with the date, address, and edition of a publication, printed at the bottom of a title page. **b.** The printer's name, usually placed on the copyright page. [Middle English *imprenten,* from Old French *empreinter,* from *empreinte,* impression, from *empreindre,* to print, from Latin *imprimere,* to IMPRESS.]

im·print·ing (ĭm′prĭnt′ĭng) *n.* A learning process occurring early in the life of certain animals, whereby the young recognize and associate with members of their own species or with a surrogate parent.

im·pris·on (ĭm-prĭz′ən) *tr.v.* To put in or as if in prison. [Middle English *inprisonen, emprisonen,* from Old French *emprisoner* : *en-* (causative) + *prison,* PRISON.] **—im·pris·on·ment** *n.*

im·prob·a·bil·i·ty (ĭm-prŏb′ə-bĭl′ə-tē) *n., pl.* **-ties. 1.** The condition of being improbable. **2.** Something improbable.

im·prob·a·ble (ĭm-prŏb′ə-bəl) *adj.* Not probable; doubtful or unlikely. [Latin *improbābilis* : *in-,* not + *probābilis,* PROBABLE.] **—im·prob·a·ble·ness** *n.* **—im·prob·a·bly** *adv.*

im·pro·bi·ty (ĭm-prō′bə-tē) *n.* Lack of probity; dishonesty. [Latin *improbitās,* from *improbus,* dishonest : *in-,* not + *probus,* honest, good.]

im·promp·tu (ĭm-prŏmp′to͞o, -tyo͞o) *adj.* Not rehearsed; improvised. —See Synonyms at **extemporaneous**.
~*adv.* In the manner of improvisation; spontaneously.
~*n.* Something made or done impromptu; specifically, a musical composition that is improvisatory in style. [French, from Latin *in promptū,* at hand : *in,* in + *promptū,* ablative of *promptus,* ready, PROMPT.]

im·prop·er (ĭm-prŏp′ər) *adj.* **1.** Not suited to the circumstances or intention. **2.** Not in keeping with propriety; indecorous: *improper conduct.* **3.** Not consistent with fact or rule; incorrect: *improper reasoning.* **4.** Irregular or abnormal. [Old French *impropre,* from Latin *improprius* : *in-,* not + *proprius,* one's own, PROPER.] **—im·prop·er·ly** *adv.* **—im·prop·er·ness** *n.*

Usage: *improper, unbecoming, unseemly, indelicate, indecent, indecorous.* These adjectives mean in violation of accepted standards of what is right or proper. *Improper* can apply to any act or statement contrary to such standards, but often refers to unethical conduct, violation of etiquette, or morally offensive behavior. *Unbecoming* suggests what is beneath the standard implied by one's character or position. What is *unseemly* or *indelicate* violates good

PRONUNCIATION KEY

ă, pat; ā, pay; âr, care;
ä, father, are; b, bib;
ch, church; d, deed; ĕ, pet;
ē, be; f, fife; g, gag; h, hat;
hw, which; ĭ, pit; ī, pie;
îr, pier; j, judge; k, kick;
l, lid, needle; m, mum;
n, no, sudden; ng, thing;
ŏ, pot; ō, toe; ô, paw, for;
oi, noise; ou, out; o͝o, book;
o͞o, boot; p, pop; r, roar;
s, sauce; sh, ship, dish;
t, tight; th, thin, path;
th, this, bathe; ŭ, cut; ûr, fur;
v, valve; w, with; y, yes;
z, zebra, size; zh, vision;
ə, about, item, edible, gallop, circus, peaceful

IN FOREIGN WORDS:

à, *Fr.* ami; œ, *Fr.* feu, *Ger.* schön; ü, *Fr.* tu, *Ger.* über; KH, *Ger.* ich, *Scot.* loch; N, *Fr.* bon; y′, *Fr.* Compiègne

STRESS MARKS:

Primary stress: ′
in·cite′ (ĭn-sīt′)
Secondary stress: ′
in′sight′ (ĭn′sīt′)

Impressionism

THE IMPRESSIONISTS' QUEST TO CAPTURE THE FLEETING MOMENT
The style that opened the way for 20th-century art

Impressionism, the most revolutionary art movement of the second half of the 19th century, flouted the conventions of academic painting in a way that at first baffled but finally delighted the art-loving public. Inspired by Edouard Manet, the Impressionists were mainly Frenchmen, with a core consisting of Claude Monet, Auguste Renoir, Edgar Degas, Camille Pissarro, and the Englishman Alfred Sisley. They worked largely outdoors in order to avoid the contrived effects of studio work. The Impressionists developed a technique of applying dabs of color to build up an impression of what the eye sees, rather than trying to fill in every detail precisely. The "inner eye" of the painter became more important than making political or social statements. The Impressionists would represent a particular color by applying dabs of several pure colors to the canvas, allowing the eye of the beholder standing at a distance to blend them together. Compared to the work of traditional artists, the Impressionists' paintings seemed sketchlike and perhaps careless. Their aim was to capture the fleeting image and to recreate light, atmosphere, and movement in all their natural brilliance.

The group dissolved after 1886, but their influence lived on, revolutionizing European painting and preparing the way for the diverse styles of the 20th century.

IMPRESSION: SUNRISE *This painting by Claude Monet, exhibited at the Impressionists' first group show in Paris in 1874, was to give the group their name . . . and to add a word to the vocabulary of art. The name was first used mockingly by the French critic Louis Leroy.*

THE RED ROOFS *The colors seem to vibrate on the canvas in Camille Pissarro's painting, of which a part is shown above. His aim was not to define precisely but to use swift brushstrokes to give an instant impression.*

LE MOULIN DE LA GALETTE *The Moulin was a popular Montmartre entertainment spot for young Parisians and their girls. Auguste Renoir immortalized the gaiety and bustle of a Sunday afternoon dance there in the 1870's. His use of dappled light is typical of Impressionism.*

---

taste; *indelicate* suggests immodesty, coarseness, or tactlessness. *Indecent* refers to what is offensive or harmful morally. *Indecorous* implies violation of the manners of polite society.

improper fraction *n.* A fraction that is greater than or equal to one, such as $9/5$, $217/4$, $12/12$. Compare **proper fraction.**

improper integral *n.* An integral having at least one nonfinite limit or having an integrand that becomes infinite between the limits of integration.

im·pro·pri·ate (ĭm-prō′prē-āt′) *tr.v.* **-ated, -ating, -ates.** To transfer (church property, tithes, or the like) into lay hands. [Medieval Latin *impropriāre,* from *proprius,* own.] **—im·pro·pri·a·tion** *n.* **—im·pro·pri·a·tor** *n.*

im·pro·pri·e·ty (ĭm′prə-prī′ə-tē) *n., pl.* **-ties. 1.** The quality or condition of being improper. **2.** An improper act. **3.** An improper or unacceptable usage in speech or writing.

im·prove (ĭm-prōōv′) *v.* **-proved, -proving, -proves.** —*tr.* **1.** To ad-

vance to a better state or quality; make better. **2.** To increase the productivity or value of (property or land, for example). —*intr.* **1.** To become or get better. **2.** To make beneficial additions or changes: *improve on the translation.* [Earlier *improwe,* from Norman French *emprouer,* to turn to profit : Old French *en-* (causative) + *prou,* profit, from Late Latin *prōde,* advantageous (see **proud**).] **—im·prov·a·bil·i·ty** *n.* **—im·prov·a·ble** *adj.* **—im·prov·er** *n.*

Synonyms: ameliorate, better, enhance, help.

im·prove·ment (ĭm-prōōv′mənt) *n.* **1.** The act of improving. **2.** The state of being improved. **3. a.** A change or addition that improves. **b.** A person or thing that incurs a change for the better.

Usage: Improvement may be followed by *in* or *on,* depending on the context. To say that there is an *improvement in* something is simply to say that "something has improved." *Improvement on* is used only in the context of comparison: *That is a great improvement on yesterday's performance.*

im·prov·i·dent (ĭm-prŏv′ə-dənt) *adj.* **1.** Not providing for the future; thriftless. **2.** Rash; incautious. **—im·prov·i·dence** *n.* **—im·prov·i·dent·ly** *adv.*

im·pro·vi·sa·tion (ĭm-prŏv′ə-zā′shən, ĭm′prə-və-) *n.* **1.** The act of improvising. **2.** Something improvised, especially a dramatic skit. **—im·pro·vi·sa·tion·al** *adj.*

im·prov·i·sa·tor (ĭm-prŏv′ə-zā′tər) *n.* One who improvises; especially, one who improvises music or verse, for example. **—im·pro·vi·sa·to·ri·al** (ĭm-prŏv′ə-zə-tôr′ē-əl, -tōr′ē-əl) *adj.* **—im·pro·vi·sa·to·ry** (ĭm′prə-vī′zə-tôr′ē, -tōr′ē) *adj.*

im·pro·vise (ĭm′prə-vīz′) *v.* **-vised, -vising, -vises.** *—tr.* **1.** To invent, compose, or recite without preparation. **2.** To make or provide from available materials. *—intr.* To invent, compose, recite, or execute something spontaneously or without preparation. [French *improviser,* from Italian *improvvisare,* from *improvviso,* unforeseen, impromptu, from Latin *imprōvīsus,* : *in-,* not + *prōvīsus,* past participle of *prōvīdere,* to foresee, PROVIDE.] **—im·pro·vis·er** *n.*

im·pro·vised (ĭm′prə-vīzd′) *adj.* **1.** Invented, composed, or recited spontaneously or without preparation. **2.** Made with whatever was available at the time. —See Synonyms at **extemporaneous.**

im·pru·dence (ĭm-pro͞od′ns) *n.* **1.** The quality or condition of being imprudent. **2.** An imprudent act.

im·pru·dent (ĭm-pro͞od′dənt) *adj.* Not prudent; unwise or injudicious; rash. [Middle English, from Latin *imprūdēns* : *in-,* not + *prūdēns,* PRUDENT.] **—im·pru·dent·ly** *adv.*

im·pu·dent (ĭm′pyə-dənt) *adj.* **1.** Impertinent; rude; disrespectful. **2.** *Obsolete.* Immodest. —See Synonyms at **shameless.** [Middle English, from Latin *impudēns* : *in-,* not + *pudēns* (stem *pudent-*), present participle of *pudēre,* to be ashamed.] **—im·pu·dence, im·pu·den·cy** *n.* **—im·pu·dent·ly** *adv.*

im·pu·dic·i·ty (ĭm′pyo͞o-dĭs′ə-tē) *n. Archaic.* Immodesty; shamelessness. [Old French *impudicite,* from Latin *impudicus,* immodest : *in-,* not + *pudicus,* modest, from *pudēre,* to be ashamed.]

im·pugn (ĭm-pyo͞on′) *tr.v.* **-pugned, -pugning, -pugns.** To oppose or attack as false; criticize; challenge. [Middle English *impugnen,* from Old French *impugner,* from Latin *impugnāre,* to fight against : *in-,* against + *pugnāre,* to fight.] **—im·pugn·a·ble** *adj.* **—im·pugn·er** *n.* **—im·pugn·ment** *n.*

im·pu·is·sance (ĭm-pyo͞o′ə-səns, ĭm-pwĭs′əns) *n.* Lack of power or effectiveness; weakness; impotence. **—im·pu·is·sant** *adj.*

im·pulse (ĭm′pŭls′) *n.* **1.** An impelling force or the motion it produces; a thrust; a push; momentum; impetus. **2.** A sudden inclination or urge; a desire; whim: *an impulse to speak up.* **3.** A motivating propensity; a drive; an instinct. **4.** *Physics.* The product of the average value of a force and the time during which it acts, equal in general to the change in momentum produced by the force in this time interval. **5.** *Physiology.* A **nerve impulse** *(see).* [Latin *impulsus,* from the past participle of *impellere,* IMPEL.]

impulse buying *n.* The purchasing of goods as a result of a sudden urge rather than deliberate planning.

impulse turbine *n.* A type of turbine that is driven by jets of fluid directed onto the blades, used especially in the generation of hydroelectricity.

im·pul·sion (ĭm-pŭl′shən) *n.* **1.** The act of impelling or the condition of being impelled. **2.** An impelling force; a thrust. **3.** Motion produced by an impelling force. **4.** An urging; compulsion.

im·pul·sive (ĭm-pŭl′sĭv) *adj.* **1.** Inclined to act on impulse rather than thought. **2.** Produced as a result of impulse; precipitate; uncalculated: *an impulsive act.* **3.** Having force or power to impel or incite; forceful. **4.** *Physics.* Acting within brief time intervals. Said especially of a force. —See Synonyms at **spontaneous.** **—im·pul·sive·ly** *adv.* **—im·pul·sive·ness** *n.*

im·pu·ni·ty (ĭm-pyo͞o′nə-tē) *n., pl.* **-ties.** **1.** Exemption from punishment or penalty. **2.** Immunity or preservation from recrimination, retribution, regret, or the like. [Latin *impūnitās* (stem *impūnitāt-*), from *impūnis,* not punished : *in-,* not + *poena,* penalty, pain, from Greek *poina, poinē,* expiation, punishment.]

im·pure (ĭm-pyo͝or′) *adj.* **1.** Not pure or clean; contaminated. **2.** Not purified by religious rite; defiled. **3.** Immoral or obscene; unchaste. **4.** Mixed with another substance; alloyed; adulterated. **5.** Being a composite of more than one color, or mixed with black or white. Said of color. **6.** Deriving from more than one source, style, or convention; bastardized. Said of the arts. **7.** Containing improper usages or foreign elements. Said of language. **—im·pure·ly** *adv.* **—im·pure·ness** *n.*

im·pu·ri·ty (ĭm-pyo͝or′ə-tē) *n., pl.* **-ties.** **1.** The quality or condition of being impure: *moral impurity.* **2. a.** Something that is impure. **b.** Something that renders something else impure; a contaminant. **3.** *Electronics.* An element added in small controlled amounts to a pure crystal of another element in order to produce or modify semiconductor properties.

im·put·a·ble (ĭm-pyo͞o′tə-bəl) *adj.* Capable of being ascribed or imputed; attributable. **—im·put·a·bil·i·ty** *n.* **—im·put·a·bly** *adv.*

im·pu·ta·tion (ĭm′pyo͞o-tā′shən) *n.* **1.** The act of imputing. **2.** Something imputed or ascribed.

im·pu·ta·tive (ĭm-pyo͞o′tə-tĭv) *adj.* Characterized by or arising from imputation. **—im·pu·ta·tive·ly** *adv.*

im·pute (ĭm-pyo͞ot′) *tr.v.* **-puted, -puting, -putes.** **1.** To ascribe (a crime or fault) to another. **2.** To attribute to a cause or source. **3.** *Theology.* To attribute (wickedness or merit) to a person. —See Synonyms at **attribute.** [Middle English *inputen,* from Old French *imputer,* from Latin *imputāre,* to bring into the reckoning : *in-,* in, into, + *putāre,* to reckon, compute, consider.]

in (ĭn) *prep.* **1. a.** Within the confines of; inside: *in the safe.* **b.** Within the area covered by: *playing in the mud; We live in Spain.* **c.** *Informal.* Into: *came in my office.* **2.** On or affecting some part of: *He was hit in the head.* **3. a.** As a part, aspect, or property of: *a delay in delivery.* **b.** Within the scope or context of: *in the story; in physics.* **c.** Included as part of: *in the first batch.* **d.** Resulting from the operations of: *in her imagination.* **4. a.** During the course of or before the expiration of: *ready in a few minutes.* **b.** At the time of: *in winter.* **5. a.** At the position of: *put in command.* **b.** Closely associated with, especially in a professional way or as an occupation: *in banking.* **6.** After the pattern or form of: *going around in circles.* **7.** To or at the condition or situation of; into: *in trouble.* **8.** As an expression of; out of; by way of: *said in anger; in answer to the question.* **9. a.** During or as part of the act or process of: *in hot pursuit.* **b.** While affected by: *in his delirium.* **10.** With the attribute of: *in silence.* **11. a.** By means of: *paid in cash.* **b.** Made with or through the medium of; using: *a text written in French.* **12.** Within the category or class of: *the latest thing in fashion.* **13.** With reference to; as regards: *in my opinion; equal in speed.* **14.** Wearing: *in pajamas.* **15.** Used to indicate ratio, rate, or number: *a one in five chance; killed in their hundreds.* **—in all.** Taking the whole sum into account: *ten dollars in all.* **—in on.** Involved or associated with: *in on the latest project.* **—in that.** Inasmuch as; since.
~adv. **1.** To or toward the inside or a center; inward: *He stepped in; the group closed in.* **2.** Toward a particular or appropriate destination or location: *sailed in; news is coming in.* **3.** Into a given place or position: *Let her in.* **4. a.** Present or as being present: *tell me when he's going to be in; count me in.* **b.** Indoors: *time to go in.* **5.** Into a given activity together: *joined in and sang.* **6.** Inward: *caved in.* **7.** So as to blend with or be part of something: *mix in.* **8.** So as to achieve a state of popularity or power: *skirts are coming back in; the Democrats got in.* **—all in.** *Informal.* Very tired; exhausted. **—in for.** About to experience something, usually something unpleasant: *He's in for a shock.* **—in with.** On familiar or friendly terms with: *get in with the boss.*
~adj. **1.** Fashionable; popular; prestigious: *the in place to go.* **2.** Exclusive or private; appealing to a clique: *a member of the in crowd; telling in jokes.* **3.** Having power; incumbent: *the in party.*
~n. **1.** *Often* **ins.** Those in power or having the advantage. **2.** *Informal.* A means of access or favor. **—ins and outs.** **1.** The twists and turns, as of a road. **2.** The intricacies of an activity, situation, or process. [Middle English *in,* Old English *in, inn.*]

In The symbol for the element indium.

IN Indiana (used with a Zip Code).

in–[1] *prefix.* Also **i-** (before *g*), **il-** (before *l*), **im-** (before *b, m, p*), **ir-** (before *r*). Indicates not, lacking, or without; for example, **inaction.** —See Usage notes at **non–, un–.** [Middle English, from Old French, from Latin.]

in–[2] *prefix.* Also **il-** (before *l*), **im-** (before *b, m, p*), **ir-** (before *r*). Indicates: **1.** In, into, within, or inward; for example, **incretion, intubation.** **2.** Intensive action; for example, **impress, implant, inosculate.** **3.** Causative function (with basic meaning "to cause to become," "to put in"); for example, **integrate, impound, imperil.** Compare **en-**[1]. [Middle English, from Old French, from Latin, from *in,* in, within. In borrowed Latin compounds, *in-* indicates (in addition to the above senses): 1. On, upon, as in **inunction.** 2. Toward, to, as in **irradiate, imminent.** 3. Against, as in **impugn, infest.**]

in–[3] *comb. form.* Indicates found or taking place within a specified context: for example, **in-flight, in-service.**

-in[1] *suffix.* Also **-ein** (for sense 1). Indicates: **1.** A neutral chemical compound, such as glyceride or protein, as distinguished from an alkaloid or basic substance; for example, **globulin, phthalein.** **2.** Enzyme; for example, **pancreatin.** **3.** Names of drugs and other pharmaceutical products; for example, **penicillin, aspirin.** **4.** Certain other individual chemical compounds; for example, **glycerin.** [French *-ine,* from Latin *-īna,* feminine of *-īnus,* belonging to. See **-ine.**]

-in[2] *comb. form.* Indicates organized participatory activity: **phone-in; love-in.**

in. inch or inches.

-ina *suffix.* Indicates feminine names or titles: for example, **Georgina, czarina.**

in·a·bil·i·ty (ĭn′ə-bĭl′ə-tē) *n.* Lack of ability or means.

in ab·sen·ti·a (ĭn ăb-sĕn′shē-ə, -shə) *adv.* In absence; while or although not present: *The prisoner was sentenced in absentia by the judge.*

in·ac·ces·si·ble (ĭn′ăk-sĕs′ə-bəl) *adj.* **1.** Not accessible; difficult to approach or reach. **2.** Difficult to obtain. **—in·ac·ces·si·bil·i·ty** *n.* **—in·ac·ces·si·bly** *adv.*

in·ac·cu·ra·cy (ĭn-ăk′yər-ə-sē) *n., pl.* **-cies.** **1.** The quality or condition of being inaccurate. **2.** An error or mistake.

in·ac·cu·rate (ĭn-ăk′yər-ĭt) *adj.* **1.** Not accurate. **2.** Mistaken or incorrect. **—in·ac·cu·rate·ly** *adv.* **—in·ac·cu·rate·ness** *n.*

in·ac·tion (ĭn-ăk′shən) *n.* Lack or absence of action or activity.

in·ac·ti·vate (ĭn-ăk′tə-vāt′) *tr.v.* **-vated, -vating, -vates.** To render inactive. **—in·ac·ti·va·tion** *n.*

in·ac·tive (ĭn-ăk′tĭv) *adj.* **1.** Not active or not tending to be active. **2. a.** Not functioning; being out of use. **b.** Retired from or not engaged in military duty or service. **3. a.** *Chemistry.* Not readily participating in chemical reactions. **b.** *Biology.* Having no significant effect on or interaction with living organisms. **c.** *Medicine.* Quiescent. Said especially of a disease. **d.** *Physics.* Displaying little

PRONUNCIATION KEY

ă, pat; ā, pay; âr, care;
ä, father, are; b, bib;
ch, church; d, deed; ĕ, pet;
ē, be; f, fife; g, gag; h, hat;
hw, which; ĭ, pit; ī, pie;
îr, pier; j, judge; k, kick;
l, lid, needle; m, mum;
n, no, sudden; ng, thing;
ŏ, pot; ō, toe; ô, paw, for;
oi, noise; ou, out; o͝o, book;
o͞o, boot; p, pop; r, roar;
s, sauce; sh, ship, dish;
t, tight; th, thin, path;
th, this, bathe; ŭ, cut; ûr, fur;
v, valve; w, with; y, yes;
z, zebra, size; zh, vision;
ə, about, item, edible,
gallop, circus, peaceful

IN FOREIGN WORDS:

à, *Fr.* ami; œ, *Fr.* feu, *Ger.* schön; ü, *Fr.* tu, *Ger.* über; KH, *Ger.* ich, *Scot.* loch; N, *Fr.* bon; y′, *Fr.* Compiègne

STRESS MARKS:

Primary stress: ′
in·cite′ (ĭn-sīt′)
Secondary stress: ′
in′sight′ (ĭn′sīt′)

or no radioactivity. **—in·ac·tive·ly** adv. **—in·ac·tive·ness, in·ac·tiv·i·ty** n.

Synonyms: *dormant, idle, inert, passive, supine, torpid.*

in·ad·e·qua·cy (ĭn-ăd′ĭ-kwə-sē) n., pl. **-cies.** **1.** The quality or condition of being inadequate. **2.** A failing or lack; defect.

in·ad·e·quate (ĭn-ăd′ĭ-kwĭt) adj. **1.** Not adequate; insufficient. **2.** Not able; incapable. **3.** Socially awkward or ill-at-ease; gauche. **—in·ad·e·quate·ly** adv.

in·ad·mis·si·ble (ĭn′əd-mĭs′ə-bəl) adj. Not admissible or allowed: *inadmissible evidence.* **—in·ad·mis·si·bil·i·ty** n. **—in·ad·mis·si·bly** adv.

in·ad·ver·tence (ĭn′əd-vûr′təns) n. Also **in·ad·ver·ten·cy** (-tən-sē) pl. **-cies.** **1.** The quality of being inadvertent. **2.** An instance of being inadvertent; a mistake; oversight. [Medieval Latin *inadvertentia* : Latin *in-,* not + *advertēns,* present participle of *advertēre,* to ADVERT.]

in·ad·ver·tent (ĭn′əd-vûr′tənt) adj. **1.** Not duly attentive; negligent. **2.** Accidental; unintentional. [Back-formation from INADVERTENCE.] **—in·ad·ver·tent·ly** adv.

in·ad·vis·a·ble (ĭn′əd-vī′zə-bəl) adj. Unwise; not recommended. **—in·ad·vis·a·bil·i·ty** n.

-inae suffix. Indicates the names of zoological subfamilies.

in ae·ter·num (ĭn ē-tûr′nəm) adv. *Latin.* Forever; to eternity.

in·al·ien·a·ble (ĭn-āl′yə-nə-bəl) adj. Not to be removed or transferred to another; not alienable: *inalienable rights.* **—in·al·ien·a·bil·i·ty** n. **—in·al·ien·a·bly** adv.

in·al·ter·a·ble (ĭn-ôl′tər-ə-bəl) adj. Not alterable; unchangeable. **—in·al·ter·a·bil·i·ty** n. **—in·al·ter·a·bly** adv.

in·am·o·ra·ta (ĭn-ăm′ə-rä′tə, ĭn′ăm-) n., pl. **-tas.** A woman with whom one is in love. [Italian, from feminine of *inamorato,* past participle of *inam(m)orare,* to inspire love in, enamor : *in-,* in, into + *amore,* love, from Latin *amor,* love, from *amāre,* to love.]

in·am·o·ra·to (ĭn-ăm′ə-rä′tō, ĭn′ăm-) n., pl. **-tos.** A man with whom one is in love. [Italian, from the past participle of *inam(m)orare,* enamor. See **inamorata.**]

in·and·in (ĭn′ən-ĭn′) adv. Repeatedly within the same or closely related stocks: *to breed pigs in-and-in.* **—in·and·in** adj.

in·and·out (ĭn′ənd-out′) adj. Involving the purchase and sale of a single security within a short period of time.

in·ane (ĭn-ān′) adj. Lacking intelligence, sense, or substance; empty; silly: *an inane comment.* **—See Synonyms at foolish.**
~ n. Rare. Something that is empty; specifically, the empty void of infinite space. [Latin *inānis†,* empty, vain.] **—in·ane·ly** adv.

in·an·i·mate (ĭn-ăn′ə-mĭt) adj. **1.** Not animate; not having the qualities associated with active, living organisms. **2.** Not exhibiting life; appearing lifeless or dead. **3.** Not animated or energetic; listless; spiritless. **—See Usage note at dead. —in·an·i·mate·ly** adv. **—in·an·i·mate·ness** n. **—in·an·i·ma·tion** n.

in·a·ni·tion (ĭn′ə-nĭsh′ən) n. **1.** Exhaustion, as from lack of nourishment. **2.** The condition or quality of being spiritually or mentally empty. [Middle English, from Late Latin *inānītiō* (stem *inānītiōn-*), from *inānīre,* to make empty, from *inānis,* empty, INANE.]

in·an·i·ty (ĭn-ăn′ə-tē) n., pl. **-ties.** **1.** The condition or quality of being inane. **2.** An inane or absurd act or remark.

in·ap·peas·a·ble (ĭn′ə-pē′zə-bəl) adj. Incapable of being appeased.

in·ap·pel·la·ble (ĭn′ə-pĕl′ə-bəl) adj. *Law.* Incapable of being appealed against: *an inappellable decision.* [Obsolete French *inappelable,* from *appeler,* to APPEAL.]

in·ap·pe·tence (ĭn-ăp′ə-təns) n. Also **in·ap·pe·ten·cy** (-tən-sē). Lack of appetite or desire. **—in·ap·pe·tent** adj.

in·ap·pli·ca·ble (ĭn-ăp′lĭ-kə-bəl) adj. Not applicable. **—in·ap·pli·ca·bil·i·ty** n. **—in·ap·pli·ca·bly** adv.

in·ap·po·site (ĭn-ăp′ə-zĭt) adj. Not pertinent; unsuitable. **—in·ap·po·site·ly** adv. **—in·ap·po·site·ness** n.

in·ap·pre·ci·a·ble (ĭn′ə-prē′shə-ə-bəl) adj. Not appreciable; insignificant; negligible. **—in·ap·pre·ci·a·bly** adv.

in·ap·pre·ci·a·tive (ĭn′ə-prē′shə-tĭv, -shē-ā′tĭv) adj. Feeling or showing no appreciation; unappreciative. **—in·ap·pre·ci·a·tive·ly** adv. **—in·ap·pre·ci·a·tive·ness** n.

in·ap·proach·a·ble (ĭn′ə-prō′chə-bəl) adj. Not approachable; inaccessible. **—in·ap·proach·a·bil·i·ty** n. **—in·ap·proach·a·bly** adv.

in·ap·pro·pri·ate (ĭn′ə-prō′prē-ĭt) adj. Not appropriate; unsuitable. **—in·ap·pro·pri·ate·ly** adv. **—in·ap·pro·pri·ate·ness** n.

in·apt (ĭn-ăpt′) adj. **1.** Not appropriate; unsuitable. **2.** Unskillful; inept.

Usage: *Inapt* and *inept* are frequently interchangeable, but there is a tendency in modern English to differentiate their contexts of use. *Inept* generally applies to clumsiness of language or behavior: *an inept remark, inept handling of the situation. Inapt* tends to be used more with abstract ideas and has the sense of something inappropriate: *an inapt comparison* would be one which did not make its intended point. *Unapt* is also used in this way.

in·ap·ti·tude (ĭn-ăp′tə-tŏŏd′, -tyŏŏd′) n. **1.** Inappropriateness. **2.** Lack of skill; ineptitude.

in·arch (ĭn-ärch′) tr.v. **-arched, -arching, -arches.** To graft by joining independently growing scions that have not been removed from the parent stock. [IN + ARCH.]

in·arm (ĭn-ärm′) tr.v. **-armed, -arming, -arms.** *Rare.* To embrace.

in·ar·tic·u·late (ĭn′är-tĭk′yə-lĭt) adj. **1.** Uttered without the use of normal words or syllables; incomprehensible. **2. a.** Unable to speak; speechless. **b.** Unable to speak with clarity or eloquence. **3.** Unable to be expressed in words: *inarticulate sorrow.* **4.** *Biology.*

Not having joints or segments. **—in·ar·tic·u·late·ly** adv. **—in·ar·tic·u·la·cy, in·ar·tic·u·late·ness** n.

in·ar·tis·tic (ĭn′är-tĭs′tĭk) adj. **1.** Not conforming to the principles or criteria of art. **2.** Not artistic; not appreciating or possessing skill in art. **—in·ar·tis·ti·cal·ly** adv.

in·as·much as (ĭn′əz-mŭch′) conj. **1.** Because of the fact that; since. **2.** To the extent that; insofar as. **—See Usage note at insofar.**

in·at·ten·tion (ĭn′ə-tĕn′shən) n. Lack of attention, notice, or regard; heedlessness; neglect.

in·at·ten·tive (ĭn′ə-tĕn′tĭv) adj. Showing a lack of attention; negligent. **—in·at·ten·tive·ly** adv. **—in·at·ten·tive·ness** n.

in·au·di·ble (ĭn-ô′də-bəl) adj. Incapable of being heard; not audible. **—in·au·di·bil·i·ty** n. **—in·au·di·bly** adv.

in·au·gu·ral (ĭn-ô′gyər-əl) adj. Of, pertaining to, or characteristic of an inauguration.
~ n. A speech or address made at an inauguration.

in·au·gu·rate (ĭn-ô′gyə-rāt′) tr.v. **-rated, -rating, -rates.** **1.** To admit (a president, prime minister, or the like) into office by a formal ceremony. **2.** To begin or start officially. **3.** To open or begin use of formally with a ceremony; dedicate. **—See Synonyms at begin.** [Latin *inaugurāre,* to take omens from the flight of birds, to consecrate, install : *in,* in + *augurāre,* to augur, from *augur,* soothsayer.] **—in·au·gu·ra·tor** n.

in·au·gu·ra·tion (ĭn-ô′gyə-rā′shən) n. **1.** A formal beginning or introduction. **2.** Formal introduction to an office or position of power.

Inauguration Day n. The day, January 20, on which the newly elected president of the United States is installed in office.

in·aus·pi·cious (ĭn′ô-spĭsh′əs) adj. Not auspicious; ill-omened. **—in·aus·pi·cious·ly** adv. **—in·aus·pi·cious·ness** n.

in between prep. Between two things, limits, or the like. **—in between** adv.

in·be·tween (ĭn′bĭ-twēn′) adj. Intermediate.
~ n. An intermediate or intermediary: *conservatives, radicals, and in-betweens.*

in·board (ĭn′bôrd′, -bōrd′) adj. **1.** *Nautical.* Within the hull or toward the center of a ship: *an inboard engine.* **2.** *Aeronautics.* Designating either of the two engines that are closest to the fuselage in an aircraft with four or more wing-mounted engines. **3.** Toward the center of a machine.
~ n. A motor attached to the inside of the hull of a boat. Compare **outboard motor.** [IN + BOARD.] **—in·board** adv.

in·born (ĭn′bôrn′) adj. **1.** Possessed by an organism at birth. **2.** Inherited or hereditary. **—See Synonyms at innate.**

in·bound (ĭn′bound′) adj. Homeward bound or incoming.

in·bounds (ĭn′boundz′) adj. *Basketball.* Of or pertaining to a means of putting the ball in play by having one player standing out of bounds pass it to another player on the court.

in·breathe (ĭn′brēth′) tr.v. **-breathed, -breathing, -breathes.** **1.** To breathe in; inhale. **2.** *Rare.* To inspire.

in·bred (ĭn′brĕd′) adj. **1.** Produced by inbreeding. **2.** Innate; deep-seated. **—See Synonyms at innate.**

in·breed (ĭn′brēd′) tr.v. **-bred** (-brĕd′), **-breeding, -breeds.** **1.** To produce by the continued breeding of closely related individuals. **2.** To breed or develop within; engender. **—in·breed·ing** adj. & n.

inc. **1.** income. **2.** incorporated. **3.** increase. **4.** including. **5.** inclusive.

Inc. incorporated.

In·ca (ĭng′kə) n., pl. **-cas** or collectively **Inca.** **1.** A member of the group of Quechuan Indian peoples who ruled Peru before the Spanish conquest. **2.** A king or other member of the royal family of this group of peoples. [Spanish, from Quechua *inka,* king, prince.] See feature, next page.

in·cal·cu·la·ble (ĭn-kăl′kyə-lə-bəl) adj. **1.** Not calculable; indeterminate. **2.** Incapable of being foreseen; unpredictable; uncertain: *the incalculable consequences of her actions.* **—in·cal·cu·la·bil·i·ty, in·cal·cu·la·ble·ness** n. **—in·cal·cu·la·bly** adv.

in·ca·les·cent (ĭn′kə-lĕs′ənt) adj. *Chemistry.* Growing warm; increasing in temperature. [Latin *incalescēns* (stem *incalescent-*), present participle of *incalescere* : IN- + *calescere,* grow warm, from *calēre,* be warm.] **—in·ca·les·cence** n.

in camera (ĭn kăm′ər-ə) adv. **1.** In secret, private, or closed session. **2.** *Law.* In private with a judge rather than in open court; in the chambers of a judge. [Latin, "in the chamber."]

in·can·desce (ĭn′kən-dĕs′) v. **-desced, -descing, -desces.** *—intr.* To become incandescent. *—tr.* To cause to become incandescent. [Latin *incandēscere,* to become white with heat, glow : *in-* (intensive) + *candēscere,* to become white, glow, from *candēre,* to be white, shine.]

in·can·des·cence (ĭn′kən-dĕs′əns) n. **1.** The emission of visible light by a hot object. **2.** The light emitted by an incandescent object. **3.** A high degree of emotion, intensity, brilliance, or the like: *his rhetoric reached incandescence.* **—See Synonyms at blaze.**

in·can·des·cent (ĭn′kən-dĕs′ənt) adj. **1.** Emitting a visible white glow as a result of being heated. **2.** Very intense, brilliant, or bright: *incandescent eyes; incandescent anger.* **—See Synonyms at bright. —in·can·des·cent·ly** adv.

incandescent lamp n. An electric lamp in which a filament is heated to incandescence by an electric current.

in·can·ta·tion (ĭn′kăn-tā′shən) n. **1. a.** Ritual recitation or chanting of charms or spells to produce a magical effect. **b.** The casting of these spells. **2.** The formulaic words, phrases, or sounds used in this manner. [Middle English *incantacioun,* from Old French *incanta-*

Inca

EMPIRE PERCHED ON THE SPINE OF THE ANDES
State ownership and benefits 500 years ago

Most of the world's major empires have been based in valleys and lowlands, where broad rivers ease trade and communications. Uniquely, the Incas created an empire in the heights, an empire that stretched along the Andean spine of South America for nearly 5,000 kilometers (3,125 miles), from present-day Ecuador southward to Chile and Argentina.

The name Inca, which now refers to a whole culture, was originally the title given to its chief by a small tribe that settled near Cuzco in Peru in about A.D. 1000.

In about 1438, a military and administrative genius called Pachacuti became Inca. In little more than 50 years, he and his son Topa forged the mountain tribes into a tightly organized society whose ruler was worshiped as the earthly representative of the sun god Viracocha.

The Incas made no use of the wheel for transport and they had no writing. But relay runners carrying messages in the form of knotted cords could reach anywhere in the empire within a week. Everything was owned by the state apart from a few personal possessions, and the peasants were drafted in their thousands to terrace the steep hillsides and to work on roads, irrigation schemes, and temples. In return, the state provided them with food when they grew old or were sick.

But the huge empire, of perhaps 16 million people, did not last. It fell to the Spanish in 1530 after the conquistador Francisco Pizarro, at the head of a mere 180 men, kidnapped and killed the Inca Atahualpa.

HIGH CITADEL *Machu Picchu, set on high cliffs in the Andes near Cuzco, was one of the few Inca cities never found by the Spanish. Abandoned by the Incas in the 16th century, its granite temples and terraced fields were rediscovered by U.S. explorer Hiram Bingham in July 1911.*

tion, from Late Latin *incantātiō* (stem *incantātiōn-*), enchantment, spell, from Latin *incantāre,* ENCHANT.] —**in·can·ta·tion·al** *adj.*

in·can·ta·to·ry (ĭn-kăn'tə-tôr'ē, -tōr'ē) *adj.* **1.** Of or pertaining to incantation. **2.** Of or producing a monotonously regular sound: *incantatory verse.*

in·ca·pa·ble (ĭn-kā'pə-bəl) *adj.* **1.** Not capable; lacking the requisite ability or power. **2.** Not admitting of or susceptible to: *incapable of improvement.* **3.** *Law.* Lacking legal qualifications or requirements; ineligible: *incapable of holding office.* —**in·ca·pa·bil·i·ty, in·ca·pa·ble·ness** *n.* —**in·ca·pa·bly** *adv.*

in·ca·pac·i·tate (ĭn'kə-păs'ə-tāt') *tr.v.* **-tated, -tating, -tates. 1.** To deprive of strength or ability. **2.** To make legally ineligible; disqualify. —**in·ca·pac·i·tant** *n.* —**in·ca·pac·i·ta·tion** *n.*

in·ca·pac·i·ty (ĭn'kə-păs'ə-tē) *n., pl.* **-ties. 1.** Lack of strength or ability; disability; helplessness. **2.** *Law.* That which renders legally ineligible; a disqualification.

incapsulate. Variant of **encapsulate.**

in·car·cer·ate (ĭn-kär'sə-rāt') *tr.v.* **-ated, -ating, -ates. 1.** To put in jail. **2.** To shut in; confine. [Latin *incarcerāre* : *in-,* in + *carcer,* prison, enclosed place.] —**in·car·cer·a·tion** *n.* —**in·car·cer·a·tor** *n.*

in·car·na·dine (ĭn-kär'nə-dīn', -dĕn', -dĭn) *adj.* **1.** Flesh-colored. **2.** Blood-red.
~*n.* A color resembling flesh or blood.
~*tr.v.* **incarnadined, -dining, -dines.** To make the color of blood or flesh. [Old French *incarnadin,* from Old Italian *incarnadino, incarnatino,* from *incarnato,* flesh-colored, from Late Latin *incarnāre,* IN-CARNATE.]

in·car·nate (ĭn-kär'nĭt) *adj.* **1. a.** Invested with bodily nature and form: *a god incarnate.* **b.** Embodied or personified: *wisdom incarnate.* **2.** Incarnadine.
~*tr.v.* (ĭn-kär'nāt') **incarnated, -nating, -nates. 1.** To give bodily, especially human, form to. **2.** To embody or personify. **3.** To actu-

alize; realize. [Late Latin *incarnāre,* to make flesh : Latin *in-* (causative) + *carō* (stem *carn-*), flesh.]

in·car·na·tion (ĭn'kär-nā'shən) *n.* **1.** A manifestation or the act of making a divinity, spirit, or the like manifest in bodily form. **2. Incarnation.** *Theology.* The embodiment of God in the human form of Jesus. **3.** Any bodily manifestation of a supernatural being. **4.** One held to personify a given abstract quality or idea.

incase. Variant of **encase.**

in·cau·tious (ĭn-kô'shəs) *adj.* Not cautious; rash. —**in·cau·tious·ly** *adv.* —**in·cau·tious·ness** *n.*

in·cen·di·ar·y (ĭn-sĕn'dē-ĕr'ē) *adj.* **1. a.** Causing or capable of causing fire. **b.** Producing intense fire. Said of a military weapon. **c.** Of or involving arson. **2.** Tending to inflame or produce anger or violence; inflammatory.
~*n., pl.* **incendiaries. 1.** One who sets fire to property; an arsonist. **2.** One who stirs up violent feelings or quarrels. **3.** An incendiary bomb. [Latin *incendiārius,* from *incendium,* burning, fire, from *incendere,* to set on fire.] —**in·cen·di·a·rism** *n.*

incendiary bomb *n.* A bomb used to start a fire. Also called "fire bomb," "incendiary."

in·cense[1] (ĭn-sĕns') *tr.v.* **-censed, -censing, -censes.** To cause to be angry or indignant; outrage. [Middle English *encensen,* from Old French *incenser,* from Latin *incendere* (past participle *incensus*), to set on fire, enrage.] —**in·cense·ment** *n.*

in·cense[2] (ĭn'sĕns') *n.* **1.** An aromatic substance, as a gum or wood, that burns with a pleasant odor. **2.** The smoke or odor produced by the burning of such a substance. **3.** Broadly, any pleasant smell. **4.** Adulation; praise; admiration.
~*tr.v.* **incensed, -censing, -censes. 1.** To perfume with incense. **2.** To burn incense in front of, especially as a ritual act. [Middle English *insens, encens,* from Old French *encens,* from Late Latin *incensum,* neuter past participle of Latin *incendere,* to set on fire.]

in·cen·tive (ĭn-sĕn'tĭv) *n.* Something inciting to action or effort, such as the fear of punishment or the expectation of reward.
~*adj.* Inciting; motivating. [Middle English, from Latin *incentīvum,* from the neuter of *incentīvus,* that sets the tune, inciting, from *incinere* (past participle *incentus*), to sing, sound : *in-* (intensive) + *canere,* to sing.]

in·cept (ĭn-sĕpt') *tr.v.* **-cepted, -cepting, -cepts. 1.** *Biology.* To take in (food); ingest. **2.** Formerly, to take the degree of master or doctor at a university. [Latin *inceptus,* begun, attempted, past participle of *incipere,* to begin : IN- + *capere,* to take.]

in·cep·tion (ĭn-sĕp'shən) *n.* The beginning of something. —See Synonyms at **origin.** [Latin *inceptiō* (stem *inceptiōn-*), from *incipere,* to take in hand, begin : *in-,* in + *capere,* to take.]

in·cep·tive (ĭn-sĕp'tĭv) *adj.* **1.** Incipient; beginning. **2.** *Grammar.* Expressing an action, state, or occurrence in its initial phase. Used of certain verbs, for example, *start* or *wake.*
~*n.* An inceptive verb.

in·cer·ti·tude (ĭn-sûr'tə-tōōd', -tyōōd') *n.* **1.** Uncertainty; doubt. **2.** Insecurity or instability. [Old French, from Late Latin *incertitūdō* : *in-,* not + *certitūdō,* CERTITUDE.]

in·ces·sant (ĭn-sĕs'ənt) *adj.* Continuing without respite or interruption; unceasing. —See Synonyms at **continual.** [Late Latin *incessāns* : *in-,* not + *cessāns* (stem *cessant-*), present participle of *cessāre,* CEASE.] —**in·cess·an·cy, in·cess·ant·ness** *n.* —**in·ces·sant·ly** *adv.*

in·cest (ĭn'sĕst') *n.* **1.** Sexual union between persons who are so closely related that their marriage is illegal or contrary to custom. **2.** The crime committed by such closely related persons who marry, cohabit, or copulate illegally. [Middle English, from Latin *incestus,* "unchaste," "impure" : *in-,* not + *castus,* CHASTE.]

in·ces·tu·ous (ĭn-sĕs'chōō-əs) *adj.* **1.** Of or involving incest. **2.** Having committed incest. **3.** Resulting from incest. **4.** Excessively introspective or mutually involved: *an incestuous group of friends.* —**in·ces·tu·ous·ly** *adv.* —**in·ces·tu·ous·ness** *n.*

inch[1] (ĭnch) *n. Abbr.* **in. 1.** A unit of length in the U.S. Customary and British Imperial systems, equal to $1/12$ of a foot or 25.4 millimeters. **2.** A unit of pressure equal to the pressure required to balance a column of mercury one inch high in a barometer. **3.** A depth of water or snow that would cover a surface with a layer one inch deep: *two inches of rain.* **4.** A very small amount or distance: *wouldn't budge an inch.* —**by inches.** Gradually; by small degrees. —**every inch.** In every respect: *every inch a gentleman.* —**inch by inch.** Very gradually. —**within an inch of.** Almost to the point of. —**within an inch of one's life. 1.** Close to death. **2.** Thoroughly; soundly: *beat him within an inch of his life.*
~*v.* **inched, inching, inches.** —*intr.* To move slowly or by small degrees. —*tr.* To cause to move in such a manner. [Middle English *inch(e),* Old English *ince, ynce,* from Latin *unica,* twelfth part, inch, ounce, from *ūnus,* one.]

inch[2] *n. Scottish.* A small island, especially one near the seacoast. Used in place names. [Middle English *inch, ynche,* from Scottish Gaelic *innis,* akin to Old Irish *inist.*]

inch·meal (ĭnch'mēl') *adv.* Gradually; little by little. [*inch* + *piecemeal.*]

in·cho·ate (ĭn-kō'ĭt) *adj.* **1.** In an initial or early stage; just beginning; incipient. **2.** Immature; imperfect. [Latin *inchoātus,* past participle of *inchoāre, incohāre,* to begin, originally "to harness" : *in-,* in + *cohum,* strap fastening the plough beam to the yoke.] —**in·cho·ate·ly** *adv.*

in·cho·a·tion (ĭn'kō-ā'shən) *n.* A beginning; start; origin.

in·cho·a·tive (ĭn-kō′ə-tĭv) *adj. Grammar.* Inceptive. Used of certain verbs. —**in·cho·a·tive** *n.*
In·chon (ĭn′chŏn′). City of northwestern South Korea, on the Yellow Sea. It has an ice-free harbor, and its fishing is an important industry. During the Korean War U.S. troops landed at Inchon (1950) to launch the UN drive northward.
inch·worm (ĭnch′wûrm′) *n.* A **measuring worm** *(see).*
in·ci·dence (ĭn′sə-dəns) *n.* **1.** An act, instance, or manner of occurring or affecting; an occurrence. **2.** The extent or frequency of the occurrence of something. **3.** *Physics.* The arrival of incident radiation or of an incident projectile at a surface.
in·ci·dent (ĭn′sə-dənt) *n.* **1.** A definite, distinct occurrence; an event. **2.** An event that is subordinate to another. **3.** Something contingent upon or related to something else. **4. a.** A relatively minor occurrence or event that precipitates a public crisis. **b.** An event involving violence or hostilities. —See Synonyms at **occurrence.**
—adj. **1.** Tending to arise or occur as a minor concomitant. Used with *to*: *"There is a professional melancholy . . . incident to the occupation of a tailor"* (Charles Lamb). **2.** Related to or dependent on another thing. **3.** *Law.* Contingent upon or related to something else. **4.** *Physics.* Falling upon; striking. [Middle English, from Old French, from Latin *incidēns* (stem *incident-*), present participle of *incidere,* to fall upon, happen to : *in-,* on + *cadere,* to fall.]
in·ci·den·tal (ĭn′sə-dĕnt′l) *adj.* **1.** Occurring as a fortuitous or minor concomitant: *incidental expenses.* **2.** Attending or related. Often used with *to*: *action incidental to the main plot.* **3.** Following upon incidentally. Often used with *upon.*
—n. Usually **incidentals.** A minor concomitant circumstance, event, expense, or the like.
in·ci·den·tal·ly (ĭn-sə-dĕnt′l-ē) *adv.* **1.** Casually; by chance. **2.** Parenthetically; by the way.
incidental music *n.* Music that accompanies the action of a play, film, or the like.
in·cin·er·ate (ĭn-sĭn′ə-rāt′) *v.* **-ated, -ating, -ates.** *—tr.* To consume by burning to ashes. *—intr.* To burn or burn up. [Medieval Latin *incinerāre* : Latin *in-,* in, into + *cinis* (stem *ciner-*), ashes.] —**in·cin·er·a·tion** *n.*
in·cin·er·a·tor (ĭn-sĭn′ə-rā′tər) *n.* One that incinerates; especially, a furnace or other apparatus for burning waste.
in·cip·i·ent (ĭn-sĭp′ē-ənt) *adj.* In an initial or early stage; just beginning to exist or appear. [Latin *incipiēns* (stem *incipient-*), beginning, present participle of *incipere,* to take in hand, begin : *in-,* in + *capere,* to take.] —**in·cip·i·en·cy, in·cip·i·ence** *n.* —**in·cip·i·ent·ly** *adv.*
in·ci·pit (ĭn′sĭ-pĭt) *n.* A beginning; specifically, an introductory word of a medieval manuscript.
in·cise (ĭn-sīz′) *tr.v.* **-cised, -cising, -cises. 1.** To cut into or mark with a sharp instrument. **2.** To cut (designs or writing, for example) into a surface; engrave; carve. [Old French *inciser,* from Latin *incīdere* (past participle *incīsus*) : *in-,* into, in + *caedere,* to cut.]
in·cised (ĭn-sīzd′) *adj.* **1.** Cut into; engraved; carved. **2.** Made with or as if with a sharp instrument. **3.** Deeply notched.
in·ci·sion (ĭn-sĭzh′ən) *n.* **1.** The act of incising. **2.** A surgical cut into soft tissue. **3.** A notch, as in the edge of a leaf. **4.** Incisiveness.
in·ci·sive (ĭn-sī′sĭv) *adj.* **1.** Cutting; penetrating. **2.** Trenchant; marked by directness, clarity, and decisiveness: *incisive comments.* [Medieval Latin *incīsīvus,* from Latin *incisus,* past participle of *incīdere,* INCISE.] —**in·ci·sive·ly** *adv.* —**in·ci·sive·ness** *n.*
Synonyms: *biting, crisp, cutting, mordant, trenchant.*
in·ci·sor (ĭn-sī′zər) *n.* A tooth adapted for cutting, located at the front of the mouth. In man there are four incisors in each jaw.
in·cite (ĭn-sīt′) *tr.v.* **-cited, -citing, -cites.** To provoke to action, stir up, or urge on. —See Synonyms at **provoke.** [Old French *inciter,* from Latin *incitāre,* to urge, set in violent motion : *in-* (intensive) + *citāre,* frequentative of *ciēre, cīre,* to set in violent motion, rouse, provoke.] —**in·ci·ta·tion** (ĭn′sī-tā′shən) *n.* —**in·cite·ment** *n.* —**in·cit·er** *n.*
in·ci·vil·i·ty (ĭn′sĭ-vĭl′ĭ-tē) *n., pl.* **-ties. 1.** Coarse or ill-mannered behavior; rudeness. **2.** An act of incivility.
incl. including; inclusive.
in·clem·ent (ĭn-klĕm′ənt) *adj.* **1.** Wild; stormy. Said of weather. **2.** *Rare.* Severe or unmerciful. [Latin *inclēmēns* : *in-,* not + *clēmēns,* CLEMENT.] —**in·clem·en·cy** *n.* —**in·clem·ent·ly** *adv.*
in·clin·a·ble (ĭn-klī′nə-bəl) *adj.* **1.** Disposed; inclined. Often used with *to.* **2.** Favorably disposed; amenable. Often used with *to.*
in·cli·na·tion (ĭn′klə-nā′shən) *n.* **1.** An attitude or disposition toward something. **2.** A trend or general tendency toward a particular aspect, condition, or character: *an inclination to be serious.* **3.** Something for which one has a preference or leaning: *an inclination to garden.* **4.** The act of inclining. **5.** The state of being inclined. **6.** A deviation from a definite direction, especially from a horizontal or vertical. **7.** The degree of deviation from a horizontal or vertical. **8.** *Mathematics.* The angle between a line on a graph and the positive limb of the *x*-axis. **9.** *Astronomy.* The angle between the plane of a planet's orbit and that of the ecliptic. **10. Magnetic dip** *(see).* —See Synonyms at **tendency.**
in·cline (ĭn-klīn′) *v.* **-clined, -clining, -clines.** *—intr.* **1.** To deviate from a horizontal or vertical; lean; slant; slope. **2.** To have or express a mental tendency; be disposed: *inclines to an opposite view.* **3.** To tend toward a particular state or condition. **4.** To lower or bend the head or body, as in a nod or bow. *—tr.* **1.** To cause to lean, slant, or slope; place at an inclination. **2.** To influence (someone or something) to have a certain preference, leaning, or disposition; dispose. **3.** To bend or lower in a nod or bow.
—n. (ĭn′klīn′). An inclined surface; a slope or gradient. [Middle English *inclinen, enclinen,* from Old French *encliner,* from Latin *inclīnāre* : *in-,* toward + *-clīnāre,* to bend, lean.] —**in·clin·er** *n.*
in·clined (ĭn-klīnd′) *adj.* **1.** Having a preference or tendency; disposed. Often used with *to.* **2.** Sloping, slanting, or leaning.
inclined plane *n.* **1.** A plane surface inclined to the horizontal. **2.** A simple machine, such as an inclined track or plank, allowing a load to be raised or lowered by rolling or sliding.
in·cli·nom·e·ter (ĭn′klə-nŏm′ə-tər) *n.* **1.** An instrument used to determine **magnetic dip** *(see);* a dip circle. **2.** An instrument for showing the inclination of an aircraft or ship relative to the horizontal. Also called "dip needle." **3.** *Machinery.* A **clinometer** *(see).*
inclose. *Rare.* Variant of **enclose.**
in·clude (ĭn-klo͞od′) *tr.v.* **-cluded, -cluding, -cludes. 1.** To have as a part or member; be made up of, at least in part; contain. **2.** To contain as a minor or secondary element. **3.** To cause to be a part of something; consider with or put into a group, class, or total. [Middle English *includen,* from Latin *inclūdere,* to shut in : *in-,* in + *claudere,* to close.] —**in·clud·a·ble, in·clud·i·ble** *adj.*
Synonyms: *comprehend, comprise, embrace, involve.*
in·clud·ed (ĭn-klo͞o′dĭd) *adj.* **1.** *Botany.* Not protruding beyond a surrounding part. Said of stamens that do not project from a corolla. **2.** *Geometry.* Formed by and between two intersecting straight lines: *an included angle.*
in·clu·sion (ĭn-klo͞o′zhən) *n.* **1.** The act of including or the state of being included. **2.** Something included. **3.** *Mineralogy.* Any solid, liquid, or gaseous foreign body enclosed in a mineral or rock. **4.** *Biology.* Any nonliving mass in cytoplasm. **5.** *Mathematics.* A relationship between two sets valid only when the members of one set are all members of the other. [Latin *inclūsiō* (stem *inclūsiōn-*), from *inclūdere* (past participle *inclūsus*), to INCLUDE.]
inclusion body *n.* Any of various abnormal structures in a cell nucleus or cytoplasm having characteristic staining properties and associated especially with the presence of viruses.
in·clu·sive (ĭn-klo͞o′sĭv) *adj. Abbr.* **incl. 1.** Taking everything into account; including everything; comprehensive. **2.** Including the specified extremes or limits as well as the area between them. Often used after the noun: *23–84 inclusive.* **3.** *Logic.* Designating a disjunction that needs only one of its elements to be true for it to be valid. [Medieval Latin *inclūsīvus,* from Latin *inclūdere* (past participial stem *inclūs-*), to INCLUDE.] —**in·clu·sive·ly** *adv.* —**in·clu·sive·ness** *n.*
inclusive of *prep.* Taking into consideration or account; including: *the whole family, inclusive of the grandparents.*
in·co·er·ci·ble (ĭn′kō-ûr′sə-bəl) *adj.* Not subject to coercion.
incog. incognito.
in·cog·i·tant (ĭn-cŏj′ə-tənt) *adj. Rare.* Thoughtless; unthinking; inconsiderate. [Latin *incōgitāns* : *in-,* not + *cōgitāns* (stem *cōgitant-*), present participle of *cōgitāre,* to think about, COGITATE.]
in·cog·ni·ta (ĭn-kŏg′nə-tə, ĭn′kŏg-nē′tə) *adv.* With one's identity disguised or concealed. Used of a woman.
—n. A woman who is incognito. —**in·cog·ni·ta** *adj.*
in·cog·ni·to (ĭn-kŏg′nə-tō, ĭn′kŏg-nē′tō) *adv.* With one's identity disguised or concealed: *travel incognito.*
—n. Abbr. **incog. 1.** One who is incognito. **2.** The anonymity or disguised appearance assumed by one who is incognito. [Italian, from Latin *incognitus,* unknown : *in-,* not + *cognitus,* past participle of *cognōscere,* to know (see **cognition**).] —**in·cog·ni·to** *adj.*
in·cog·ni·zant (ĭn-kŏg′nə-zənt) *adj.* Lacking knowledge or awareness of something; unaware. —**in·cog·ni·zance** *n.*
in·co·her·ent (ĭn′kō-hîr′ənt) *adj.* **1.** Not coherent; disordered; unconnected; inharmonious. **2.** Characterized by an inability to think or express thoughts in a clear or orderly manner: *incoherent with grief.* —**in·co·her·ence, in·co·her·en·cy** *n.* —**in·co·her·ent·ly** *adv.* —**in·co·her·ent·ness** *n.*
in·com·bus·ti·ble (ĭn′kəm-bŭs′tə-bəl) *adj.* Incapable of burning.
—n. An incombustible object or material. [Middle English, from Medieval Latin *incombustibilis* : Latin *in-,* not + *combūrere* (past participle *combustus*), to burn up (see **combust**).] —**in·com·bus·ti·bil·i·ty** (ĭn′kəm-bŭs′tə-bĭl′ə-tē) *n.* —**in·com·bus·ti·bly** *adv.*
in·come (ĭn′kŭm′) *n. Abbr.* **inc. 1.** The amount of money or its equivalent received during a period of time, such as a year, in exchange for labor or services, from the sale of goods or property, or as profit from financial investments. **2.** *Archaic.* An influx. [Middle English, a coming in, entry : IN + *comen,* COME.]
income group *n.* A section of a population having roughly the same income.
in·com·er (ĭn′kŭm′ər) *n.* One that comes in; especially, a person who is not considered to be integrated with his new environment.
income tax *n.* A graduated tax levied on annual income.
in·com·ing (ĭn′kŭm′ĭng) *adj.* **1. a.** Coming in; entering or arriving: *incoming telephone calls.* **b.** Coming in as profits. **2.** About to come in; next in succession: *the incoming president.*
—n. **1.** The act of coming in; an entrance; an arrival. **2.** *Usually* **incomings.** Income; revenue.
in·com·men·su·ra·ble (ĭn′kə-mĕn′shər-ə-bəl, -sər-ə-bəl) *adj.* **1.** Having no common quality upon which to make a comparison; incapable of being measured or judged comparatively; incommensurate. **2.** *Mathematics.* **a.** Having no common measure; not having the same units. **b.** Not having a common factor other than one.
—n. Something that is incommensurable. —**in·com·men·su·ra·bil·i·ty** *n.* —**in·com·men·su·ra·bly** *adv.*

PRONUNCIATION KEY

ă, pat; ā, pay; âr, care;
ä, father, are; b, bib;
ch, church; d, deed; ĕ, pet;
ē, be; f, fife; g, gag; h, hat;
hw, which; ĭ, pit; ī, pie;
îr, pier; j, judge; k, kick;
l, lid, needle; m, mum;
n, no, sudden; ng, thing;
ŏ, pot; ō, toe; ô, paw, for;
oi, noise; ou, out; o͝o, book;
o͞o, boot; p, pop; r, roar;
s, sauce; sh, ship, dish;
t, tight; th, thin, path;
th, this, bathe; ŭ, cut; ûr, fur;
v, valve; w, with; y, yes;
z, zebra, size; zh, vision;
ə, about, item, edible,
gallop, circus, peaceful

IN FOREIGN WORDS:

à, *Fr.* ami; œ, *Fr.* feu, *Ger.* schön; ü, *Fr.* tu, *Ger.* über; KH, *Ger.* ich, *Scot.* loch; N, *Fr.* bon; y′, *Fr.* Compiègne

STRESS MARKS:

Primary stress: ′
in·cite′ (ĭn-sīt′)
Secondary stress: ′
in′sight′ (ĭn′sīt′)

in·com·men·su·rate (ĭn′kə-mĕn′shər-ĭt, -sər-ĭt) adj. **1. a.** Not commensurate; unequal; disproportionate: *a reward incommensurate with his efforts*. **b.** Inadequate. **2.** Incommensurable. —**in·com·men·su·rate·ly** adv. —**in·com·men·su·rate·ness** n.

in·com·mode (ĭn′kə-mōd′) tr.v. **-moded, -moding, -modes.** To cause to be inconvenienced; disturb. [French *incommoder,* from Old French, from Latin *incommodāre,* from *incommodus,* inconvenient : *in-,* not + *commodus,* convenient.]

in·com·mo·di·ous (ĭn′kə-mō′dē-əs) adj. Inconvenient or uncomfortable, as by affording insufficient room. —**in·com·mo·di·ous·ly** adv. —**in·com·mo·di·ous·ness** n.

in·com·mod·i·ty (ĭn′kə-mŏd′ə-tē) n., pl. **-ties.** Rare. **1.** Inconvenience; discomfort. **2.** Something that is inconvenient.

in·com·mu·ni·ca·ble (ĭn′kə-myōō′nĭ-kə-bəl) adj. **1.** Not communicable; that cannot be told or shared. **2.** Rare. Incommunicative. —**in·com·mu·ni·ca·bil·i·ty** n. —**in·com·mu·ni·ca·bly** adv.

in·com·mu·ni·ca·do (ĭn′kə-myōō′nĭ-kä′dō) adj. Without the means or right of communicating with others, as one held in solitary confinement. [Spanish, past participle of *incomunicar,* to deny communication : *in-,* not, from Latin + *comunicar,* to communicate, from Latin *commūnicāre,* COMMUNICATE.] —**in·com·mu·ni·ca·do** adv.

in·com·mu·ni·ca·tive (ĭn′kə-myōō′nĭ-kā′tĭv, -kə-tĭv) adj. Not communicative; reticent. —**in·com·mu·ni·ca·tive·ly** adv. —**in·com·mu·ni·ca·tive·ness** n.

in·com·mut·a·ble (ĭn′kə-myōō′tə-bəl) adj. **1.** Incapable of being exchanged. **2.** Not changeable; unalterable. —**in·com·mut·a·bil·i·ty,** **in·com·mut·a·ble·ness** n. —**in·com·mut·a·bly** adv.

in·com·pa·ra·ble (ĭn-kŏm′pər-ə-bəl) adj. **1.** Incapable of being compared; incommensurable. **2.** Above all comparisons; unsurpassed; matchless. —**in·com·pa·ra·bil·i·ty,** **in·com·pa·ra·ble·ness** n. —**in·com·pa·ra·bly** adv.

in·com·pat·i·bil·i·ty (ĭn′kəm-păt′ə-bĭl′ə-tē) n., pl. **-ties. 1.** The state or quality of being incompatible; lack of harmony or consistency; disagreement; incongruity. **2. incompatibilities.** Mutually exclusive or antagonistic qualities or things.

in·com·pat·i·ble (ĭn′kəm-păt′ə-bəl) adj. **1.** Not compatible, as in being: **a.** Unable to live or work together. **b.** Not consistent with something else. **2.** Incapable of being held simultaneously by one person, as offices, ranks, or the like. **3.** Logic. Incapable of being simultaneously true; mutually exclusive. **4.** Medicine. **a.** Designating blood transfusions or tissue grafts that evoke adverse reactions in the recipient due to antibody formation. **b.** Designating drugs that in combination do not produce their desired therapeutic effects. **5.** Botany. **a.** Not capable of self-fertilization. **b.** Not capable of forming a viable graft union. —See Synonyms at **inconsistent.** ~n. Usually **incompatibles.** An incompatible element, person, object, or the like. [Medieval Latin *incompatibilis* : *in-,* not + *compatibilis,* COMPATIBLE.] —**in·com·pat·i·ble·ness** n. —**in·com·pat·i·bly** adv.

in·com·pe·tent (ĭn-kŏm′pə-tənt) adj. **1.** Not competent; not able or not in a position to act. **2.** Lacking competence; clumsy or very inefficient. **3.** Law. Not qualified to act in law. ~n. An incompetent person. —**in·com·pe·tence, in·com·pe·ten·cy** n. —**in·com·pe·tent·ly** adv.

in·com·plete (ĭn′kəm-plēt′) adj. **1.** Not complete. **2.** Not fully formed. **3.** Football. Not caught or not caught in bounds. Used of a forward pass. —**in·com·plete·ly** adv. —**in·com·plete·ness, in·com·ple·tion** n.

in·com·pli·ant (ĭn′kəm-plī′ənt) adj. Not compliant; unyielding. —**in·com·pli·ance, in·com·pli·an·cy** n. —**in·com·pli·ant·ly** adv.

in·com·pre·hen·si·ble (ĭn′kəm-prĭ-hĕn′sə-bəl, ĭn-kŏm′-) adj. **1.** Incapable of being understood or comprehended, as: **a.** Unintelligible. **b.** Unknowable; unfathomable. **2.** Archaic. Without limits; boundless. —**in·com·pre·hen·si·bil·i·ty, in·com·pre·hen·si·ble·ness** n. —**in·com·pre·hen·si·bly** adv.

in·com·pre·hen·sion (ĭn′kŏm-prĭ-hĕn′shən, ĭn-kŏm′-) n. Lack of comprehension or understanding.

in·com·pre·hen·sive (ĭn′kŏm-prĭ-hĕn′sĭv, ĭn-kŏm′-) adj. Not apprehensive or all-inclusive; limited in range or scope. —**in·com·pre·hen·sive·ly** adv. —**in·com·pre·hen·sive·ness** n.

in·com·press·i·ble (ĭn′kəm-prĕs′ə-bəl) adj. Incapable of being compressed. —**in·com·press·i·bil·i·ty** n.

in·com·put·a·ble (ĭn′kəm-pyōō′tə-bəl) adj. Incapable of being computed or calculated. —**in·com·put·a·bil·i·ty** n.

in·con·ceiv·a·ble (ĭn′kən-sē′və-bəl) adj. Incapable of being conceived or thought of; unbelievable. —**in·con·ceiv·a·bil·i·ty, in·con·ceiv·a·ble·ness** n. —**in·con·ceiv·a·bly** adv.

in·con·cin·ni·ty (ĭn′kən-sĭn′ĭ-tē) n. Lack of congruity or harmony; unsuitability. [Latin *inconcinnitas,* awkwardness, from *inconcinnus,* awkward : *in-,* not + *concinnus,* skillfully put together.]

in·con·clu·sive (ĭn′kən-klōō′sĭv) adj. Not conclusive; not allowing a proper conclusion to be drawn. —**in·con·clu·sive·ly** adv. —**in·con·clu·sive·ness** n.

in·con·den·sa·ble, in·con·den·si·ble (ĭn′kən-dĕn′sə-bəl) adj. Incapable of being condensed; especially, that cannot be reduced to a solid or liquid. —**in·con·den·sa·bil·i·ty** (ĭn′kən-dĕn′sə-bĭl′ə-tē) n.

in·con·dite (ĭn-kŏn′dīt, -dīt′) adj. Rare. Badly constructed; crude. Said of literary or artistic compositions. [Latin *inconditus* : *in-,* not + *conditus,* past participle of *condere,* to put together.] —**in·con·dite·ly** adv.

in·con·form·i·ty (ĭn′kən-fôr′mə-tē) n. Resistance to or lack of conformity; nonconformity.

in·con·gru·ent (ĭn-kŏng′grōō-ənt) adj. **1.** Not congruent. **2.** Incongruous. —**in·con·gru·ence** n. —**in·con·gru·ent·ly** adv.

in·con·gru·i·ty (ĭn′kŏng-grōō-ĭ-tē, ĭn′kən-) n., pl. **-ties. 1.** The state or quality of being incongruous. **2.** That which is incongruous.

in·con·gru·ous (ĭn-kŏng′grōō-əs) adj. **1.** Inharmonious or incompatible with the surroundings; incongruent: *a plan incongruous with good sense.* **2.** Made up of disparate, inconsistent, or discordant parts or qualities. **3.** Not consistent with what is correct, appropriate, or logical; out-of-place: *an incongruous remark.* —See Synonyms at **inconsistent.** [Latin *incongruus* : *in-,* not + *congruus,* CONGRUOUS.] —**in·con·gru·ous·ly** adv. —**in·con·gru·ous·ness** n.

in·con·nec·tor (ĭn′kə-nĕk′tər) n. A flow-chart symbol that indicates continuation of a broken line of flow.

in·con·sec·u·tive (ĭn′kən-sĕk′yōō-tĭv, -sĕk′yə-) adj. Not consecutive; not in a logical sequence.

in·con·se·quent (ĭn-kŏn′sə-kwənt) adj. **1.** Not obtained as a result. **2.** Not derived from the premises or obtained by logic or reason; irrelevant. **3.** Proceeding without logical sequence; haphazard. **4.** Out of character with the nature or style of something. **5.** Unimportant; insignificant. [Late Latin *inconsequēns* : Latin *in-,* not + *consequēns,* CONSEQUENT.] —**in·con·se·quence** n. —**in·con·se·quent·ly** adv.

in·con·se·quen·tial (ĭn-kŏn′sə-kwĕn′shəl) adj. **1.** Without consequence; lacking importance; petty. **2.** Inconsequent. **3.** Designating the behavior of a person who disregards the consequences of his or her behavior. —**in·con·se·quen·ti·al·i·ty** (ĭn-kŏn′sə-kwĕn′shē-ăl′ə-tē), **in·con·se·quen·tial·ness** n. —**in·con·se·quen·tial·ly** adv.

in·con·sid·er·a·ble (ĭn′kən-sĭd′ər-ə-bəl) adj. Too small or unimportant to merit attention or consideration; trivial. —**in·con·sid·er·a·ble·ness** n. —**in·con·sid·er·a·bly** adv.

in·con·sid·er·ate (ĭn′kən-sĭd′ər-ĭt) adj. Not considerate; thoughtless of others. [Latin *inconsiderātus* : *in-,* not + *consīderātus,* CONSIDERATE.] —**in·con·sid·er·ate·ly** adv. —**in·con·sid·er·ate·ness, in·con·sid·er·a·tion** n.

in·con·sis·ten·cy (ĭn′kən-sĭs′tən-sē) n., pl. **-cies.** Also **in·con·sis·tence** (-təns) (for sense 1). **1.** The state or quality of being inconsistent; lack of consistency or uniformity; incongruity. **2.** Something that is inconsistent.

in·con·sis·tent (ĭn′kən-sĭs′tənt) adj. **1.** Not consistent, especially: **a.** Erratic. **b.** Incongruous. **c.** Contradictory. **d.** Illogical. **2.** Mathematics. Designating two or more equations that do not have one set of values of the variable in common. —**in·con·sis·tent·ly** adv.

  Synonyms: discordant, incompatible, incongruous.

in·con·sol·a·ble (ĭn′kən-sō′lə-bəl) adj. Incapable of being consoled or solaced; deeply despondent. —**in·con·sol·a·bil·i·ty** (ĭn′kən-sō′lə-bĭl′ə-tē), **in·con·sol·a·ble·ness** n. —**in·con·sol·a·bly** adv.

in·con·so·nant (ĭn-kŏn′sə-nənt) adj. Lacking harmony, agreement, or compatibility; discordant. —**in·con·so·nance** n. —**in·con·so·nant·ly** adv.

in·con·spic·u·ous (ĭn′kən-spĭk′yōō-əs) adj. Not readily noticeable. —**in·con·spic·u·ous·ly** adv. —**in·con·spic·u·ous·ness** n.

in·con·stan·cy (ĭn-kŏn′stən-sē) n., pl. **-cies. 1.** Fickleness; faithlessness. **2.** Unreliability; instability. **3.** An act or instance of being inconstant.

in·con·stant (ĭn-kŏn′stənt) adj. **1.** Not constant. **2.** Fickle. —See Synonyms at **faithless.** —**in·con·stant·ly** adv.

in·con·sum·a·ble (ĭn′kən-sōō′mə-bəl) adj. **1.** Incapable of being consumed. **2.** Satisfying an economic requirement without being consumed, as currency. —**in·con·sum·a·bly** adv.

in·con·test·a·ble (ĭn′kən-tĕs′tə-bəl) adj. Incapable of being contested; unquestionable. —**in·con·test·a·bil·i·ty** (ĭn′kən-tĕs′tə-bĭl′ə-tē), **in·con·test·a·ble·ness** n. —**in·con·test·a·bly** adv.

in·con·ti·nent (ĭn-kŏn′tə-nənt) adj. **1.** Not continent; unrestrained; uncontrolled. Often said of sexual behavior. **2.** Incapable of holding back, containing, or retaining. Usually used with *of: incontinent of anger.* **3.** Incapable of controlling the passage of urine or feces. [Middle English, from Old French, from Latin *incontinēns,* unrestrained : *in-,* not + *continēns,* restrained, CONTINENT.] —**in·con·ti·nence** n.

in·con·ti·nent·ly (ĭn-kŏn′tə-nənt-lē) adv. **1.** In an incontinent manner. **2.** Archaic. Immediately; straightaway.

in·con·trol·la·ble (ĭn′kən-trō′lə-bəl) adj. Rare. Not controllable; difficult to restrain.

in·con·tro·vert·i·ble (ĭn′kŏn-trə-vûr′tə-bəl) adj. Not able to be contradicted; indisputable; unquestionable. —**in·con·tro·vert·i·bil·i·ty** (ĭn-kŏn′trə-vûr′tə-bĭl′ə-tē), **in·con·tro·vert·i·ble·ness** n. —**in·con·tro·vert·i·bly** adv.

in·con·ven·i·ence (ĭn′kən-vēn′yəns) n. **1.** The state or quality of being inconvenient; lack of ease or comfort; trouble; difficulty. **2.** Something that causes difficulty, trouble, or discomfort; an inconvenient thing or situation. ~tr.v. **inconvenienced, -iencing, -iences.** To cause inconvenience to; trouble; bother.

in·con·ven·i·ent (ĭn′kən-vēn′yənt) adj. Not convenient, especially: **1.** Not accessible or handy. **2.** Difficult, awkward, or troublesome. [Middle English, from Old French, from Latin *inconveniēns* : *in-,* not + *conveniēns,* CONVENIENT.] —**in·con·ven·i·ent·ly** adv.

in·con·vert·i·ble (ĭn′kən-vûr′tə-bəl) adj. Incapable of being converted, changed, or exchanged; especially, designating currency not redeemable for another currency or for gold or silver. —**in·con·vert·i·bil·i·ty, in·con·vert·i·ble·ness** n. —**in·con·vert·i·bly** adv.

in·con·vin·ci·ble (ĭn′kən-vĭn′sə-bəl) adj. Incapable of being convinced.

in·co·or·di·nate (ĭn′kō-ôrd′n-ĭt, -āt′) *adj.* **1.** Not of the same order. **2.** Uncoordinated. —**in·co·or·di·nate·ly** *adv.*

in·co·or·di·na·tion (ĭn′kō-ôrd′n-ā′shən) *n.* **1.** Lack of coordination. **2.** The inability to exercise normal voluntary control of relatively complex muscular movement.

in·cor·po·rate¹ (ĭn-kôr′pə-rāt′) *v.* **-rated, -rating, -rates.** —*tr.* **1.** To unite with or blend indistinguishably into something already in existence. **2.** To cause to merge or combine together into a united whole. **3.** To admit as a member to a corporation or similar organization. **4.** To cause to form into a legal corporation. **5.** *Rare.* To give substance or material form to; embody; substantiate. —*intr.* **1.** To become united or combined into an organized body. **2.** To form a legal corporation.
~*adj.* (ĭn-kôr′pər-ĭt). **1.** Combined into one united body; merged. **2.** Formed into a legal corporation. [Middle English *incorporaten,* from Late Latin *incorporāre,* to form into a body : Latin *in-* (intensive) + *corporāre,* to form into a body (see **corporate**).] —**in·cor·po·ra·tion** *n.* —**in·cor·po·ra·tive** *adj.* —**in·cor·po·ra·tor** *n.*

in·cor·po·rate² (ĭn-kôr′pər-ĭt) *adj. Rare.* Incorporeal. [Late Latin *incorporātus,* not in the body, spiritual : Latin *in-,* not + *corporātus,* embodied, CORPORATE.]

in·cor·po·rat·ed (ĭn-kôr′pə-rā′tĭd) *adj.* **1.** United into one body; combined. **2.** *Abbr.* **Inc., inc.** Organized and maintained as a legal business corporation.

in·cor·po·ra·ting (ĭn-kôr′pə-rā′tĭng) *adj. Linguistics.* Polysynthetic.

in·cor·po·re·al (ĭn′kôr-pôr′ē-əl, -pōr′ē-əl) *adj.* **1.** Lacking material form or substance. **2.** Spiritual. **3.** *Law.* Lacking material substance but existing in the eyes of the law; intangible, such as a right or patent might be. [Latin *incorporeus* : *in-,* not + *corporeus,* CORPOREAL.] —**in·cor·po·re·al·ly** *adv.*

in·cor·po·re·i·ty (ĭn-kôr′pə-rē′ə-tē) *n.* Immateriality. [Latin *incorporeus,* INCORPOREAL.]

in·cor·rect (ĭn′kə-rĕkt′) *adj.* Not correct, especially: **1.** Erroneous. **2.** Improper; inappropriate. —**in·cor·rect·ly** *adv.* —**in·cor·rect·ness** *n.*

in·cor·ri·gi·ble (ĭn-kôr′ə-jə-bəl, ĭn-kŏr′-) *adj.* **1.** Incapable of being corrected or reformed: *an incorrigible liar.* **2.** Firmly rooted; impossible to eliminate; ineradicable: *incorrigible innocence.*
~*n.* A person or animal that will not be tamed or corrected. [Middle English, from Late Latin *incorrigibilis* : Latin *in-,* not + *corrigere,* to CORRECT.] —**in·cor·ri·gi·bil·i·ty, in·cor·ri·gi·ble·ness** *n.* —**in·cor·ri·gi·bly** *adv.*

in·cor·rupt (ĭn′kə-rŭpt′) *adj. Rare.* **1.** Not corrupt or immoral. **2.** Not decayed; unspoiled. **3.** Free from error or deterioration. Said of a text or manuscript. [Middle English, from Latin *incorruptus* : *in-,* not + *corruptus,* CORRUPT.] —**in·cor·rupt·ly** *adv.* —**in·cor·rupt·ness** *n.*

in·cor·rupt·i·ble (ĭn′kə-rŭp′tə-bəl) *adj.* **1.** Incapable of being morally corrupted, as by bribery; honest. **2.** Not subject to decay or decomposition. —**in·cor·rupt·i·bil·i·ty** *n.* —**in·cor·rupt·i·bly** *adv.*

in·cras·sate (ĭn-krăs′ĭt, -āt′) *adj.* Also **in·cras·sat·ed** (-ā′tĭd). *Biology.* Thickened; enlarged. Said especially of cell walls. [Late Latin *incrassāre* (past participle *incrassātus*), become thick, from *crassus,* thick.]

in·crease (ĭn-krēs′) *v.* **-creased, -creasing, -creases.** —*intr.* **1.** To become greater or larger. **2.** To multiply; reproduce. **3.** *Literary.* To advance, as in power or attainment; thrive; prosper. —*tr.* To make greater or larger.
~*n.* (ĭn′krēs′) *Abbr.* **inc., incr. 1.** The act of increasing; enlargement; multiplication. **2.** The amount of such increase; an increment: *a tax increase of ten percent.* **3.** *Archaic.* Crops and other produce. —**on the increase.** Increasing. [Middle English *encresen,* from Old French *encreistre* (present stem *encreiss-*), from Latin *incrēscere,* to grow in or on : *in-,* in + *crēscere,* to grow.] —**in·creas·a·ble** *adj.* —**in·creas·er** *n.* —**in·creas·ing·ly** *adv.*
Synonyms: *augment, enlarge, expand, extend, grow, magnify.*

in·cre·ate (ĭn′krē-āt′, ĭn-krē′ĭt) *adj. Archaic.* Existing without having been created. Said especially of divine beings. —**in·cre·ate·ly** *adv.*

in·cred·i·bil·i·ty (ĭn-krĕd′ə-bĭl′ə-tē) *n., pl.* **-ties. 1.** The condition or quality of being incredible. **2.** Something incredible.

in·cred·i·ble (ĭn-krĕd′ə-bəl) *adj.* **1.** Too implausible to be believed; unbelievable. **2.** Hard to believe; astonishing. **3.** *Informal.* Marvelous; wonderful. [Middle English, from Latin *incrēdibilis* : *in-,* not + *crēdibilis,* CREDIBLE.] —**in·cred·i·ble·ness** *n.* —**in·cred·i·bly** *adv.*
Usage: *Incredible* and *incredulous* are sometimes confused, but there is a clear distinction between them. *Incredible* means simply "unbelievable"; *incredulous* means "disbelieving" or "skeptical." A story may be *incredible*; the skeptical person to whom it is told is *incredulous.*

in·cre·du·li·ty (ĭn′krə-do͞o′lə-tē, -dyo͞o′lə-tē) *n.* Also **in·cred·u·lous·ness** (ĭn-krĕj′ə-ləs-nĭs). Disbelief.

in·cred·u·lous (ĭn-krĕj′ə-ləs) *adj.* **1.** Disbelieving; skeptical. **2.** Expressing disbelief: *an incredulous stare.* —See Usage note at **incredible.** [Latin *incrēdulus* : *in-,* not + *crēdulus,* CREDULOUS.] —**in·cred·u·lous·ly** *adv.*

in·cre·ment (ĭn′krə-mənt) *n.* **1.** An increase in number, size, or extent; growth; enlargement. **2.** Something added or gained; especially, an increase in salary awarded to an employee according to his progress, along a salary scale. **3.** A small increase in quantity. **4.** *Mathematics.* A small positive or negative change in a variable.
~*tr.v.* (-mĕnt′) **incremented, -menting, -ments.** To add a small amount to, often at regular intervals. [Middle English, from Latin *incrēmentum,* from *incrēscere,* to INCREASE.] —**in·cre·men·tal** *adj.* —**in·cre·men·tal·ly** *adv.*

in·cre·men·tal·ism (ĭn′krə-mĕn′tl-ĭz′əm) *n.* Social or political gradualism. —**in·cre·men·tal·ist** *n.*

incremental plotter *n.* A device for plotting graphs from the output of a computer.

in·cres·cent (ĭn-krĕs′ənt) *adj.* Waxing. Said of the moon. Compare **decrescent.** [Latin *incrēscēns,* present participle of *incrēscere,* to INCREASE.]

in·cre·tion (ĭn-krē′shən) *n.* **1.** Secretion directly into the bloodstream, characteristic of endocrine glands. **2.** The product of such secretion; a hormone. [IN- (in) + (SE)CRETION.]

in·crim·i·nate (ĭn-krĭm′ə-nāt′) *tr.v.* **-nated, -nating, -nates. 1.** To charge with or involve in a crime or other wrongful act. **2.** To indicate the guilt of. [Late Latin *incrīmināre* : Latin *in-,* in + *crīmen* (stem *crīmin-*), CRIME.] —**in·crim·i·na·tion** *n.* —**in·crim·i·na·to·ry** (ĭn-krĭm′ə-nə-tôr′ē, -tōr′ē) *adj.*

in·cross (ĭn′krôs′, -krŏs′) *n.* An organism produced as a result of continuous inbreeding.
~*v.* **incrossed, -crossing, -crosses.** —*tr.* To produce by continuous inbreeding. —*intr.* To produce an incross.

incrust. Variant of **encrust.**

in·crus·ta·tion (ĭn′krŭs-tā′shən) *n.* **1.** An encrusting; a hard coating; especially, a deposit of a fine material. **2.** A facing of marble or mosaic on a building. **3.** A scab or other concretion on a surface. [French or from Late Latin *incrustātiō,* from Latin *incrustāre,* to ENCRUST.]

in·cu·bate (ĭn′kyə-bāt, ĭng′-) *v.* **-bated, -bating, -bates.** —*tr.* **1.** To warm (eggs), as by bodily heat, so as to promote embryonic development and the hatching of young; brood. **2.** To maintain (a bacterial culture or an embryo, for example) at optimum environmental conditions for development, especially in an incubator. **3.** To cause to develop; foment. —*intr.* **1.** To brood eggs. **2.** To develop in favorable conditions. Used of eggs, embryos, bacteria, and the like. **3.** To undergo incubation. [Latin *incubāre,* to hatch, lie down upon : *in-,* on + *cubāre,* to lie down.] —**in·cu·ba·tive** *adj.*

in·cu·ba·tion (ĭn′kyə-bā′shən, ĭng′-) *n.* **1.** The act of incubating or the state of being incubated. **2.** *Medicine.* **a.** The development of an infection from the time an organism is first exposed to it up to the time of the first appearance of signs or symptoms. **b.** The time between exposure to an infection and the first appearance of signs or symptoms. In this sense, also called "incubation period." —**in·cu·ba·tion·al** *adj.*

in·cu·ba·tor (ĭn′kyə-bā′tər, ĭng′-) *n.* One that incubates, especially: **1.** A cabinet in which a uniform temperature can be maintained, used in growing bacterial cultures or hatching eggs. **2.** An apparatus for maintaining an infant, especially a premature infant, in an environment of controlled temperature, humidity, and oxygen.

in·cu·bus (ĭn′kyə-bəs, ĭng′-) *n., pl.* **-buses** or **-bi** (-bī′). **1.** An evil spirit believed to descend upon and have sexual intercourse with sleeping women. Compare **succubus. 2.** A nightmare. **3.** Something oppressively or nightmarishly burdensome. [Middle English, from Late Latin, from Latin *incubāre,* to lie down upon, INCUBATE.]

in·cu·des. Plural of **incus.**

in·cul·cate (ĭn-kŭl′kāt′) *tr.v.* **-cated, -cating, -cates.** To teach or impress by forceful urging or frequent repetition; instill: *inculcate a code of ethics.* [Latin *inculcāre,* to trample in, impress upon : *in-,* in + *calcāre,* to trample, from *calx* (stem *calc-*), heel.] —**in·cul·ca·tion** *n.* —**in·cul·ca·tor** *n.*

in·cul·pa·ble (ĭn-kŭl′pə-bəl) *adj.* Not culpable; free from guilt; blameless.

in·cul·pate (ĭn-kŭl′pāt′) *tr.v.* **-pated, -pating, -pates.** To incriminate; cause blame to be attached to. [Late Latin *inculpāre* : *in-,* on + *culpāre,* to blame, from Latin *culpa,* fault, CULPA.] —**in·cul·pa·tion** *n.* —**in·cul·pa·to·ry** (ĭn-kŭl′pə-tôr′ē, -tōr′ē) *adj.*

in·cult (ĭn-kŭlt′) *adj. Archaic.* **1.** Not cultured; uncultivated. **2.** Not tilled or cultivated. [Latin *incultus,* uncultivated : *in-,* not + *cultus,* past participle of *colere,* to till.]

in·cum·ben·cy (ĭn-kŭm′bən-sē) *n., pl.* **-cies. 1.** The condition or quality of being incumbent. **2.** Something that is incumbent. **3.** The holding and administering of an office or ecclesiastical benefice. **4.** The term of such a benefice or office.

in·cum·bent (ĭn-kŭm′bənt) *adj.* **1.** Lying, leaning, or resting upon something else. **2.** Imposed as an obligation or duty; required; obligatory. **3.** Holding a specific office or ecclesiastical benefice.
~*n.* A person who holds an office or ecclesiastical benefice. [Middle English, from Latin *incumbēns* (stem *incumbent-*), present participle of *incumbere,* to lean upon : *in-,* on + *cumbere,* to lean, recline.] —**in·cum·bent·ly** *adv.*

in·cu·nab·u·lum (ĭn′kyo͞o-năb′yə-ləm) *n., pl.* **-la** (-lə). **1.** A book printed from movable type before 1501. Also called "incunable." **2.** An artifact of an early period. **3. incunabula.** The earliest stages in the development of something. [Latin *incūnābula* (plural), swaddling clothes, cradle, infancy : *in-,* in + *cūnābula,* infancy, origin, cradle, from *cūnae,* cradle.] —**in·cu·nab·u·lar** *adj.*

in·cur (ĭn-kûr′) *tr.v.* **-curred, -curring, -curs. 1.** To meet with; run into. **2.** To become liable or subject to as a result of one's own actions; bring upon oneself. [Latin *incurrere,* to run into, come upon : *in-,* in + *currere,* to run.]

in·cur·a·ble (ĭn-kyo͝or′ə-bəl) *adj.* **1.** Not curable. Said of a disease. **2.** Broadly, not susceptible to modification.
~*n.* A person suffering from an incurable disease. —**in·cur·a·bil·i·ty, in·cur·a·ble·ness** *n.* —**in·cur·a·bly** *adv.*

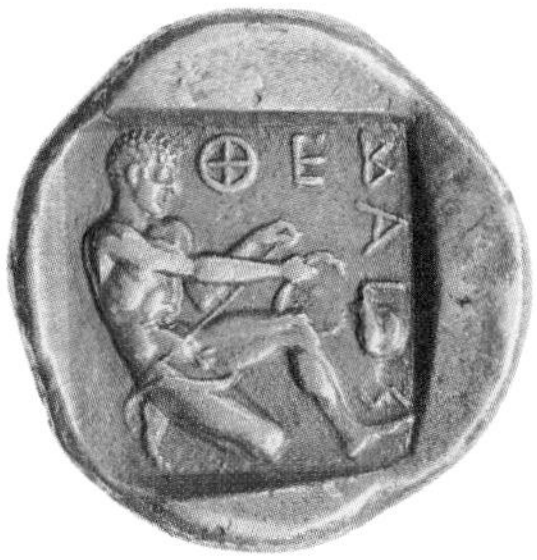

incuse *The most common example of this patterned impression is a coin. This one is from Thebes in Greece and dates from the fifth century* B.C. *The outline of the stamping tool can be seen.*

PRONUNCIATION KEY

ă, pat; ā, pay; âr, care;
ä, father, are; b, bib;
ch, church; d, deed; ĕ, pet;
ē, be; f, fife; g, gag; h, hat;
hw, which; ĭ, pit; ī, pie;
îr, pier; j, judge; k, kick;
l, lid, needle; m, mum;
n, no, sudden; ng, thing;
ŏ, pot; ō, toe; ô, paw, for;
oi, noise; ou, out; o͝o, book;
o͞o, boot; p, pop; r, roar;
s, sauce; sh, ship, dish;
t, tight; th, thin, path;
th, this, bathe; ŭ, cut; ûr, fur;
v, valve; w, with; y, yes;
z, zebra, size; zh, vision;
ə, about, item, edible,
gallop, circus, peaceful

IN FOREIGN WORDS:

à, *Fr.* ami; œ, *Fr.* feu, *Ger.* schön; ü, *Fr.* tu, *Ger.* über; KH, *Ger.* ich, *Scot.* loch; N, *Fr.* bon; y', *Fr.* Compiègne

STRESS MARKS:

Primary stress: ʹ
in·citeʹ (ĭn-sītʹ)
Secondary stress: ʹ
inʹsightʹ (ĭnʹsītʹ)

in·cu·ri·ous (ĭn-kyo͝orʹē-əs) *adj.* **1.** Not curious; uninterested. **2.** Not arousing interest; lacking novelty. **3.** Heedless; negligent. —See Synonyms at **indifferent.** [Latin *incūriōsus,* indifferent : *in-,* not + *cūriōsus,* CURIOUS.] **—in·cu·ri·os·i·ty** (ĭn-kyo͝orʹē-ŏsʹĭ-tē), **in·cu·ri·ous·ness** *n.* **—in·cu·ri·ous·ly** *adv.*

in·cur·rent (ĭn-kûrʹənt) *adj.* Affording passage to an inflowing current. Said of anatomical ducts and vessels. [Latin *incurrēns* (stem *incurrent-*), present participle of *incurrere,* to run into, INCUR.]

in·cur·sion (ĭn-kûrʹzhən, -shən) *n.* **1.** A sudden attack on or invasion of hostile territory; a raid. **2.** An entering into. [Middle English, from Old French, from Latin *incursiō* (stem *incursiōn-*), from *incurrere* (past participle *incursus*), to run into, attack, INCUR.]

in·cur·vate (ĭn-kûrʹvātʹ) *tr.v.* **-vated, -vating, -vates.** To bend (something) into an inward curve.
∼*adj.* (ĭn-kûrʹvātʹ, -vĭt). Curved, especially inward. [Latin *incurvāre* (past participle *incurvātus*) : *in-,* in + *curvāre,* to bend, from *curvus,* CURVE.] **—in·cur·va·tion** *n.* **—in·cur·va·ture** (ĭn-kûrʹvə-cho͝orʹ) *n.*

in·curve (ĭn-kûrvʹ) *v.* **-curved, -curving, -curves.** —*intr.* To bend into an inward curve. —*tr.* To incurvate.
∼*n.* (ĭnʹkûrvʹ). An inward curve. [Latin *incurvāre,* INCURVATE.]

in·cus (ĭngʹkəs) *n., pl.* **incudes** (ĭng-kyo͞oʹdēz). An anvil-shaped bone in the mammalian middle ear. Also called "anvil." Compare **malleus, stapes.** [Latin *incūs,* anvil, from *incūdere* (past participle *incūsus*), to forge with a hammer : *in-,* in + *cūdere,* to strike, stamp.]

in·cuse (ĭn-kyo͞ozʹ, -kyo͞osʹ) *adj.* Hammered, stamped, or pressed in. Said of a design or feature of a design on a coin.
∼*n.* A design impressed in such a manner.
∼*tr.v.* **incused, -cusing, -cuses. 1.** To impress (a design) on a coin. **2.** To impress (a coin) with a design. [Latin *incūsus,* past participle of *incūdere,* to beat or stamp in. See **incus.**]

Ind (ĭnd) *n.* **1.** *Archaic.* India. **2.** *Obsolete.* The Indies.

ind. 1. independence; independent. **2.** index. **3.** indicative. **4.** indigo. **5.** indirect. **6.** industrial; industry.

Ind. 1. Independent. **2.** India. **3.** Indian. **4.** Indiana. **5.** Indies.

in·da·ba (ĭn-däʹbə) *n.* **1.** A conference or meeting of indigenous tribes in southern Africa to discuss a serious issue. **2.** *South African Informal.* **a.** A discussion. **b.** A personal concern. [Zulu, "business, affair."]

in·da·mine (ĭnʹdə-mēnʹ, -mĭn) *n.* Any of a group of organic bases that form unstable bluish or greenish salts used as dyes, especially the base, $NH_2C_6H_4N:C_6H_4:NH$, used to produce the dye safranine. Also called "phenylene blue." [*ind*(igo) + *amine.*]

in·debt·ed (ĭn-dĕtʹĭd) *adj.* **1.** Owing gratitude or recognition for something: *indebted to her for her help.* **2.** Owing money. [Middle English *endetted,* from Old French *endette,* from the past participle of *endetter,* to involve in debt, oblige : *en-,* in + *dette,* DEBT.]

in·debt·ed·ness (ĭn-dĕtʹĭd-nĭs) *n.* **1.** The state of being indebted. **2.** That which is owed to another.

in·de·cen·cy (ĭn-dēʹsən-sē) *n., pl.* **-cies. 1.** The state or quality of being indecent. **2.** Something that is indecent.

in·de·cent (ĭn-dēʹsənt) *adj.* **1.** Offensive to good taste; unseemly. **2.** Offensive to public moral values; immodest. —See Synonyms at **improper. —in·de·cent·ly** *adv.*

indecent assault *n.* The act or offense of making a sexual attack other than rape on a person who has not consented.

indecent exposure *n.* The act or offense of indecently exposing one's body, especially the genitals, to public view.

in·de·ci·pher·a·ble (ĭnʹdĭ-sīʹfər-ə-bəl) *adj.* Incapable of being deciphered, especially by being illegible. **—in·de·ci·pher·a·bil·i·ty, in·de·ci·pher·a·ble·ness** *n.*

in·de·ci·sion (ĭnʹdĭ-sĭzhʹən) *n.* Irresolution; indecisiveness.

in·de·ci·sive (ĭnʹdĭ-sīʹsĭv) *adj.* **1.** Not decisive; inconclusive. **2.** Prone to or characterized by indecision; vacillating; hesitant. **3.** Not clearly defined; indefinite. **—in·de·ci·sive·ly** *adv.* **—in·de·ci·sive·ness** *n.*

in·de·clin·a·ble (ĭnʹdĭ-klīʹnə-bəl) *adj.* Having no set of grammatical inflections; not declinable.

in·de·com·pos·a·ble (ĭnʹdē-kəm-pōʹzə-bəl) *adj.* Not capable of being split into component parts.

in·dec·o·rous (ĭn-dĕkʹər-əs) *adj.* Lacking propriety or good taste; unseemly. —See Usage note at **improper. —in·dec·o·rous·ly** *adv.* **—in·dec·o·rous·ness** *n.*

in·de·cor·um (ĭnʹdĭ-kôrʹəm, -kōrʹəm) *n.* **1.** Lack of decorum; lack of propriety or good taste. **2.** An instance of indecorous behavior.

in·deed (ĭn-dēdʹ) *adv.* **1.** Without a doubt; certainly; truly. **2.** In fact; in reality. **3.** Admittedly; unquestionably. **4.** What is more.
∼*interj.* Used to express surprise, skepticism, or irony. [Middle English *in dede,* in reality : *in,* IN + *dede,* DEED.]

indef. indefinite.

in·de·fat·i·ga·ble (ĭnʹdĭ-fătʹə-gə-bəl) *adj.* **1.** Untiring; tireless. **2.** Unremitting. [Latin *indēfatīgābilis* : *in-,* not + *dēfatīgāre,* to tire out : *dē-* (intensive) + *fatīgāre,* to FATIGUE.] **—in·de·fat·i·ga·bil·i·ty, in·de·fat·i·ga·ble·ness** *n.* **—in·de·fat·i·ga·bly** *adv.*

in·de·fea·si·ble (ĭnʹdĭ-fēʹzə-bəl) *adj.* Not capable of being annulled or made void. **—in·de·fea·si·bil·i·ty** *n.* **—in·de·fea·si·bly** *adv.*

in·de·fec·ti·ble (ĭnʹdĭ-fĕkʹtə-bəl) *adj.* **1.** Having the ability to resist defect or failure; permanent; lasting. **2.** Without flaw or defect; perfect. **—in·de·fec·ti·bil·i·ty** *n.* **—in·de·fec·ti·bly** *adv.*

in·de·fen·si·ble (ĭnʹdĭ-fĕnʹsə-bəl) *adj.* Not capable of being defended, especially: **1.** Inexcusable. **2.** Invalid; untenable. **3.** Vulnerable to attack. **—in·de·fen·si·bil·i·ty, in·de·fen·si·ble·ness** *n.* **—in·de·fen·si·bly** *adv.*

in·de·fin·a·ble (ĭnʹdĭ-fīʹnə-bəl) *adj.* Not capable of being defined, described, or analyzed.
∼*n.* A word, concept, or quality that cannot be defined. **—in·de·fin·a·ble·ness** *n.* **—in·de·fin·a·bly** *adv.*

in·def·i·nite (ĭn-dĕfʹə-nĭt) *adj. Abbr.* **indef. 1.** Not definite, especially: **a.** Unclear; vague. **b.** Lacking precise limits. **c.** Uncertain; undecided. **2.** *Grammar.* Not specifying whether an action is complete or continuous. Said of verb tenses. **3.** *Botany.* Indeterminate. [Latin *indēfīnītus* : *in-,* not + *dēfīnītus,* DEFINITE.] **—in·def·i·nite·ly** *adv.* **—in·def·i·nite·ness** *n.*

indefinite article *n. Grammar.* An article, as English *a* or *an,* that does not fix or immediately fix the identity of the noun modified. Compare **definite article.**

indefinite integral *n. Mathematics.* The set of all functions of which a given function is the derivative, usually represented by $\int f(x)dx + C$, where $\int f(x)dx$ is any member of the set and C is an arbitrary constant. Compare **definite integral.**

indefinite pronoun *n. Grammar.* A pronoun, for example *any* or *some,* that does not specify the identity of its object.

in·de·his·cent (ĭnʹdĭ-hĭsʹənt) *adj.* Not splitting open at maturity: *indehiscent fruit.* Compare **dehiscent. —in·de·his·cence** *n.*

in·del·i·ble (ĭn-dĕlʹə-bəl) *adj.* **1.** Incapable of being removed, erased, or washed away. **2.** Making a mark not easily erased or washed away: *an indelible laundry pencil.* **3.** Permanent; enduring: *indelible memories.* [Latin *indēlēbilis* : *in-,* not + *dēlēbilis,* that can be obliterated, from *dēlēre,* to obliterate, DELETE.] **—in·del·i·bil·i·ty, in·del·i·ble·ness** *n.* **—in·del·i·bly** *adv.*

in·del·i·ca·cy (ĭn-dĕlʹĭ-kə-sē) *n., pl.* **-cies. 1.** The quality or condition of being indelicate. **2.** An instance of indelicate speech or behavior; a crudity.

in·del·i·cate (ĭn-dĕlʹĭ-kĭt) *adj.* **1. a.** Offensive to propriety. **b.** Coarse; tasteless. **2.** Tactless. —See Usage note at **improper. —in·del·i·cate·ly** *adv.* **—in·del·i·cate·ness** *n.*

in·dem·ni·fi·ca·tion (ĭn-dĕmʹnə-fĭ-kāʹshən) *n.* **1.** The act of indemnifying or the condition of being indemnified. **2.** Something that indemnifies, such as a sum paid in compensation.

in·dem·ni·fy (ĭn-dĕmʹnə-fīʹ) *tr.v.* **-fied, -fying, -fies. 1.** To protect against possible damage, legal suit, or bodily injury; insure. **2.** To compensate for incurred damage or hurt. [Latin *indemnis,* uninjured (see **indemnity**) + -FY.] **—in·dem·ni·fi·er** *n.*

in·dem·ni·ty (ĭn-dĕmʹnə-tē) *n., pl.* **-ties. 1.** Insurance or other security against possible damage, loss, or hurt. **2.** A legal exemption from prosecution or liability for damages resulting from one's actions. **3.** Compensation for damage, loss, or hurt incurred; indemnification. —See Synonyms at **reparation.** [Middle English *indempnyte,* from Old French *indemnite,* from Late Latin *indemnitās* (stem *indemnitāt-*), from Latin *indemnis,* unhurt, uninjured : *in-,* not + *damnum,* hurt, harm.]

in·de·mon·stra·ble (ĭnʹdĭ-mŏnʹstrə-bəl) *adj.* Incapable of being proved or demonstrated. Said especially of axiomatic truths. **—in·de·mon·stra·bil·i·ty** *n.* **—in·de·mon·stra·bly** *adv.*

in·dene (ĭnʹdēnʹ) *n.* A colorless organic liquid, C_9H_8, obtained from coal tar and used in preparing synthetic resins.

in·dent[1] (ĭn-dĕntʹ) *v.* **-dented, -denting, -dents.** —*tr.* **1.** To cut or tear (a document with two or more copies) along an irregular line so that the parts can later be matched for establishing authenticity. **2.** To draw up (a deed or other document) in duplicate or triplicate. **3. a.** To notch or serrate the edge of; make jagged. **b.** To form indentations in: *a deeply indented coastline.* **4. a.** To make notches, grooves, or holes in (wood, for example) for the purpose of mortising. **b.** To fit or join together by or as if by mortising. **5.** To set in from the margin (the first line of a paragraph, for example). **6.** *Chiefly British.* To order (goods) by an indent. **7.** To bind (an apprentice) by indenture. —*intr.* **1.** To form an indentation. **2.** *Chiefly British.* To draw up or order an indent for something.
∼*n.* (ĭn-dĕntʹ, ĭnʹdĕntʹ). **1.** An indenture. **2.** *Chiefly British.* An official requisition or purchase order for goods. **3.** An indention. [Middle English *indenten, endenten,* to make a toothlike incision into, from Old French *endenter* : *en-,* in + *dent,* tooth, from Latin *dēns* (stem *dent-*).] **—in·dent·er, in·den·tor** *n.*

in·dent[2] *tr.v.* **-dented, -denting, -dents. 1.** To push in or press down upon so as to form a dent or impression. **2.** To make a dent in.
∼*n.* (ĭn-dĕntʹ, ĭnʹdĕntʹ). An indentation.

in·den·ta·tion (ĭnʹdĕn-tāʹshən) *n.* **1.** The act of indenting or the condition of being indented. **2. a.** A notch or jagged cut in an edge. **b.** A series of notches or jagged cuts. **3.** A deep recess in a border, coastline, or other boundary. **4.** *Printing.* An indention.

in·den·tion (ĭn-dĕnʹshən) *n.* **1.** *Printing.* The blank space between a margin and the beginning of an indented line. **2.** Indentation. **3.** *Archaic.* A dint or dent.

in·den·ture (ĭn-dĕnʹchər) *n.* **1.** *Law.* A deed or contract executed between two or more parties. **2.** *Usually* **indentures.** A contract binding one party into the service of another for a stipulated term. **3.** *Archaic.* A document having indented edges. **4.** An official or authenticated inventory, list, or voucher. **5.** *Archaic.* Indentation.
∼*tr.v.* **indentured, -turing, -tures. 1.** To bind by indenture. **2.** *Archaic.* To form an indentation in. [Middle English *indenture, endenture,* from Old French *endenture,* from *endenter,* INDENT.]

in·de·pend·ence (ĭnʹdĭ-pĕnʹdəns) *n. Abbr.* **ind. 1.** The state or quality of being independent. **2.** The point in time at which a state attains national independence: *has made great strides since independence.* **3.** *Archaic.* Sufficient income for self-support; a sufficiency.

In·de·pend·ence (ĭn′dĭ-pĕn′dəns). City in western Missouri, a suburb of Kansas City. In the mid-19th century it was the departure point for expeditions along the Santa Fe, Oregon, and California trails.

Independence Day *n.* **1.** In the United States, a public holiday (July 4) celebrating the anniversary of the adoption of the Declaration of Independence in 1776. **2.** A similar holiday in other countries, celebrating the attainment of national independence.

in·de·pend·en·cy (ĭn′dĭ-pĕn′dən-sē) *n., pl.* **-cies.** **1.** Independence. **2.** An independent territory or state. **3. Independency.** The Independent movement in England; Congregationalism.

in·de·pend·ent (ĭn′dĭ-pĕn′dənt) *adj. Abbr.* **ind. 1.** Politically autonomous; self-governing. **2. a.** Free from the influence, guidance, or control of another or others. **b.** Self-reliant; not seeking or relying on help or guidance from others. **3.** Not contingent upon another person or thing. **4.** Affiliated with or loyal to no one political party or organization: *the independent vote.* **5.** Not dependent on or affiliated with a larger or controlling group, system, or the like; separate: *an independent brewery.* **6.** Financially self-sufficient; self-supporting. **7.** Not having to work for a living; wealthy in one's own right. **8.** Providing a sufficient income upon which to live: *independent means.* **9.** *Mathematics.* **a.** Not dependent on other variables: *independent variable.* **b.** Of or pertaining to a system of equations, no one of which is necessarily satisfied by a set of values of the independent variables that satisfy all the others. **c.** Of, pertaining to, or designating an outcome of a trial of a chance experiment the probability of which does not depend on the outcome of any other trial of the chance experiment. ~*n. Abbr.* **ind.** One that is independent; especially, a voter or politician who does not pledge allegiance to any one political party. —**in·de·pend·ent·ly** *adv.*

In·de·pend·ent (ĭn′dĭ-pĕn′dənt) *n.* **1.** A member of a movement in England in the 17th century advocating the political and religious independence of individual congregations. **2.** *British.* A Congregationalist. —**In·de·pend·ent** *adj.*

independent clause *n.* A main clause *(see).*

independent school *n.* A school which is not maintained or controlled by central government or a local authority, and which usually charges fees.

in-depth (ĭn′dĕpth′) *adj.* Detailed; thorough: *an in-depth study.*

in·de·scrib·a·ble (ĭn′dĭ-skrīb′ə-bəl) *adj.* **1.** Incapable of description; undefinable. **2.** Beyond description. —**in·de·scrib·a·bil·i·ty, in·de·scrib·a·ble·ness** *n.* —**in·de·scrib·a·bly** *adv.*

in·de·struc·ti·ble (ĭn′dĭ-strŭk′tə-bəl) *adj.* Not capable of being destroyed. —**in·de·struc·ti·bil·i·ty, in·de·struc·ti·ble·ness** *n.* —**in·de·struc·ti·bly** *adv.*

in·de·ter·mi·na·ble (ĭn′dĭ-tûr′mə-nə-bəl) *adj.* **1.** Not capable of being fixed or measured; not ascertainable. **2.** Incapable of being finally settled or decided. —**in·de·ter·mi·na·bly** *adv.*

in·de·ter·mi·na·cy (ĭn′dĭ-tûr′mə-nə-sē) *n.* The state or quality of being indeterminate. [From INDETERMINATE.]

in·de·ter·mi·nate (ĭn′dĭ-tûr′mə-nĭt) *adj.* **1. a.** Not precisely or quantitatively determined. **b.** Incapable of being so determined. **c.** Lacking clarity or precision. **d.** Not capable of clear interpretation; inconclusive; ambiguous. **e.** Not known in advance. **2.** *Botany.* **a.** Not terminating in a flower and continuing to grow at the apex: *an indeterminate inflorescence.* **b.** Not fixed in number, being too numerous to count: *indeterminate stamens.* **3.** *Mathematics.* **a.** Designating an equation containing more than one variable that has an unlimited number of solutions. **b.** Having no numerical meaning: $0 \div 0$ is indeterminate. **c.** Designating a structure or framework consisting of forces that cannot be analyzed into a set of vectors. **4.** *Physics.* Designating an effect that appears to have no cause or does not obey a causal law. [Middle English *indeterminat,* from Late Latin *indēterminātus* : Latin *in-,* not + *dēterminātus,* DETERMINATE.] —**in·de·ter·mi·nate·ly** *adv.* —**in·de·ter·mi·nate·ness, in·de·ter·mi·na·tion** *n.*

indeterminate sentence *n.* A sentence whose length is determined by the prisoner's conduct while in prison.

indeterminate vowel *n. Phonetics.* See **schwa** (sense 1).

in·de·ter·min·ism (ĭn′dĭ-tûr′mə-nĭz′əm) *n.* The philosophical doctrine that human actions are not necessarily predetermined by physiological and psychological factors. —**in·de·ter·min·ist** *n. & adj.* —**in·de·ter·min·is·tic** *adj.*

in·dex (ĭn′dĕks′) *n., pl.* **-dexes** or **indices** (-də-sēz′) (for senses 5 and 6). **1.** Anything that serves to guide, point out, or otherwise facilitate reference, as: **a.** *Abbr.* **ind.** An alphabetized listing of names, places, and subjects included in a printed work that gives for each item the page on which it may be found. **b.** A series of notches cut into the edge of a book for easy access to chapters or other divisions; a thumb index. **c.** Any table, file, or catalogue which enables a reference to be located. **2.** Anything that reveals or indicates; a sign; token: *"Her face . . . was a fair index to her disposition"* (Samuel Butler). **3.** A character (☞) used in printing to call attention to a particular· paragraph or section. Also called "fist," "hand." **4.** Something that serves as an indicator or pointer, as in a scientific instrument. **5.** *Mathematics.* **a.** A number or symbol, often written as a subscript or superscript to a mathematical expression, that indicates an operation to be performed on, an ordering relation involving, or a use of the associated expression. **b.** A number indicating a specific property of a particular material: *refractive index.* **6.** A formula indicating the current level of something, such as prices, by reference to a standard, usually taken to be 100: *cost-of-living index.* **7.** An index finger. ~*tr.v.* **indexed, -dexing, -dexes. 1.** To compile an index for. **2.** To enter (an item) in an index. **3.** To indicate or signal. **4.** To make index-linked. [Latin *index* (plural *indicēs),* forefinger, indicator.]

in·dex·a·tion (ĭn′dĕk-sā′shən) *n.* **1.** An act of indexing. **2.** The act of relating salaries, pensions, and the like to the cost-of-living index. Also called "index-linking."

index finger *n.* The finger next to the thumb; the forefinger.

In·dex Li·bro·rum Pro·hib·i·to·rum (ĭn′dĕks′ lĭ-brôr′əm prō-hĭb′ə-tôr′əm, lĭ-brōr′əm prō-hĭb′ə-tōr′əm) *n.* A list formerly published by Church authority for Roman Catholics, restricting or forbidding the reading of certain books. Also shortened to "Index." [New Latin, "index of prohibited books."]

in·dex-linked (ĭn′dĕks′lĭngkt′) *adj.* Directly related to the cost-of-living index. Said of salaries, pensions, and the like. —**in·dex-link·ing** *n.*

index number *n.* A number indicating change in magnitude, as of price, wage, employment, or production shifts, relative to the magnitude at some given point usually taken as 100.

index of refraction *n.* **Refractive index** *(see).*

In·di·a (ĭn′dē-ə). *Abbr.* **Ind.** Independent republic of southern Asia. Much of India came under British domination in the mid-18th century. Its government, initially in the hands of the East India Company, was transferred to the Crown (1858) following the Indian Mutiny (1857–58). India became independent in 1947, when the country was partitioned and the Muslim areas of the east and northwest were made into the new nation of Pakistan. India has three main natural divisions: the triangular Deccan plateau of the south, the northern plains, and the Himalayas. The whole peninsula south of the Himalayas is often referred to as the "Indian subcontinent." The northern plains, which are crossed by the Indus, Ganges, and Brahmaputra rivers, form the world's largest alluvial lowland and the most densely populated part of the country. India's population is exceeded only by that of China. Although 40 percent of the national income is derived from agriculture, especially rice and wheat, India is also rich in mineral reserves. Its iron ore is the basis of rapidly expanding steel, machinery, and transport equipment industries. India is one of the leading producers of mica, coal, manganese, and aluminum, but still relies on imported oil. Area, 3,288,000 square kilometers (1,269,496 square miles). Population, 713,800,-000. Capital, Delhi (also New Delhi). See map, next page.

India ink *n.* **1.** A black pigment made from lampblack mixed with a binding agent and molded into cakes or sticks. **2.** A liquid ink made from this. [Formerly thought to be a product of India.]

In·di·a·man (ĭn′dē-ə-mən) *n., pl.* **-men** (-mĭn). A large merchant ship formerly used on trade routes to India.

In·di·an (ĭn′dē-ən) *n. Abbr.* **Ind. 1.** A native or inhabitant of India or of the East Indies. **2.** A member of any of the aboriginal peoples of North America, South America, or the West Indies. **3.** Loosely, any of the languages spoken by the American Indians. ~*adj.* **1.** Of or pertaining to India or the East Indies, their culture, their languages, or their people. **2.** Of or pertaining to the aboriginal people of North America, South America, or the West Indies.

In·di·an·a (ĭn′dē-ăn′ə). *Abbr.* **Ind.** State in the north-central United States. The capital and largest city is Indianapolis. Arable farming and cattle raising remain important, but Indiana is now a major manufacturing state and producer of petroleum. —**In·di·an·i·an** *n. & adj.*

Indiana Dunes National Lakeshore. A conservation and recreation area occupying 3,488 hectares (8,720 acres) in northwestern Indiana along the southern shore of Lake Michigan.

Indian agent *n.* An official representing the United States government in dealings with American Indians, especially on reservations.

Indian almond *n.* A tree, *Terminalia catappa,* of tropical Asia, having fruit with edible seeds. Also called "myrobalan."

In·di·an·ap·o·lis (ĭn′dē-ə-năp′ə-lĭs). Largest city and capital of the state of Indiana, on the White River in the middle of the state. In the center of a rich agricultural region, it is a major grain and livestock market and food-processing center.

Indian bean *n.* A tree, the **catalpa** *(see).*

Indian club *n.* A bottle-shaped wooden club used in juggling or other gymnastic exercises.

Indian corn *n.* See **corn.**

Indian file *n.* **Single file** *(see).*

Indian giver *n. Informal.* One who gives something as a gift to another and then takes or demands it back.

Indian hemp *n.* **1.** A plant, **hemp** *(see).* **2.** A North American plant, *Apocynum cannabinum,* whose stem fibers were formerly used by Indians for making matting and ropes.

Indian licorice *n.* The **rosary pea** *(see).*

Indian millet *n.* **Durra** *(see).*

Indian mulberry *n.* A small tree, *Morinda citrifolia,* of Indonesia and Australia from which red and yellow dyes are obtained.

Indian Mutiny. A revolt by native Indian troops in 1857–58 leading to the end of the rule of the East India Company and the subsequent administration of India by the British Crown.

Indian National Congress *n.* One of the main political parties in India, founded in 1885, which has frequently been the governing party since India's independence.

Indian Ocean. World's third-largest ocean, occupying an area of *c.* 73,427,000 square kilometers (28,350,000 square miles) and having a width of *c.* 6,400 kilometers (4,000 miles) at the equator. It ex-

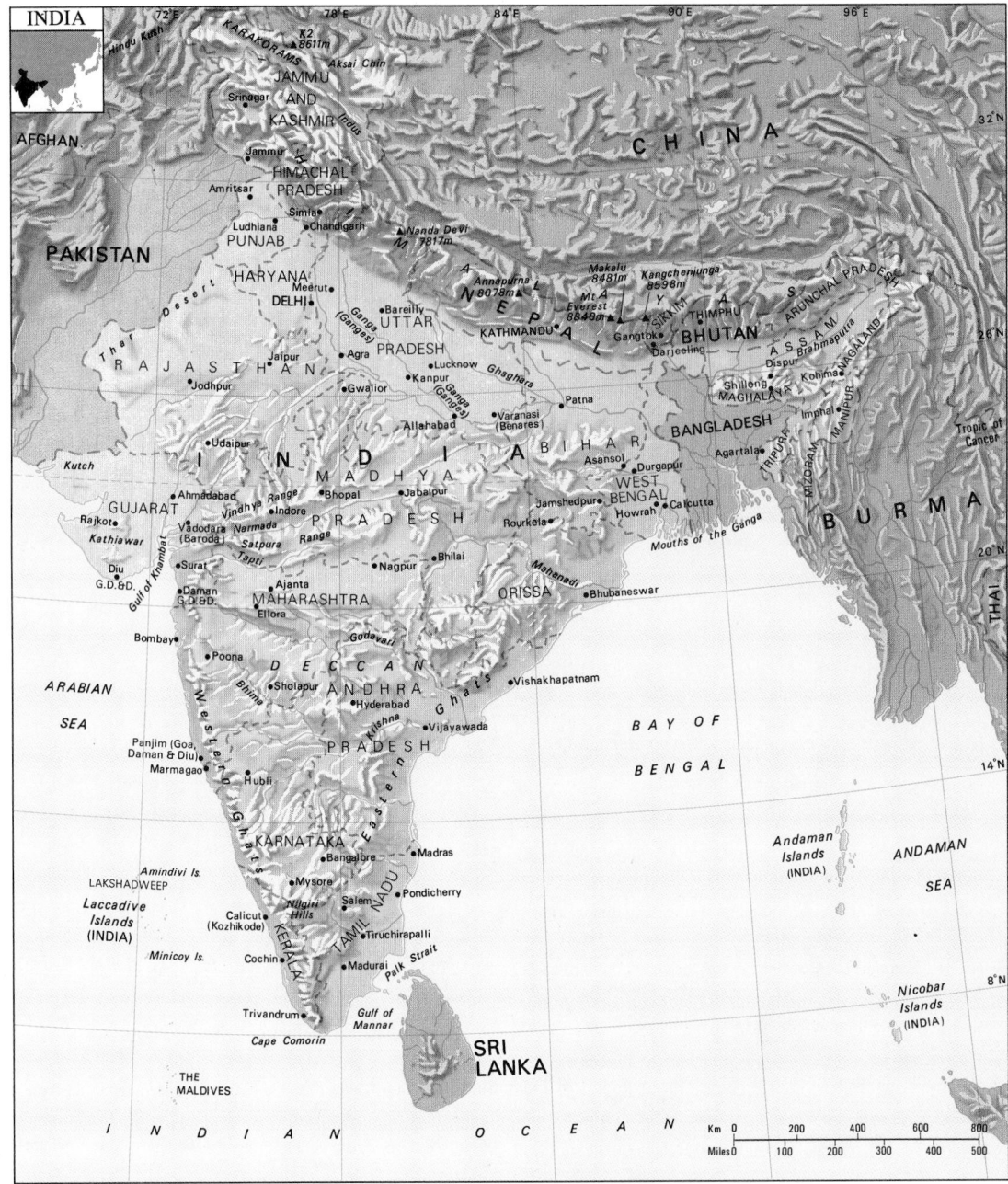

tends from southern Asia to the Antarctic and from east Africa to southeastern Australia. It is divided into eastern and western halves by the Mid-Oceanic Ridge, a few peaks of which emerge as islands. The average depth of the ocean is *c.* 3,400 meters (11,000 feet).

Indian paintbrush *n.* Any of various plants of the genus *Castilleja,* having spikes of flowers surrounded by showy, brightly colored bracts. Also called "painted cup."

Indian pipe *n.* A waxy white or sometimes pinkish saprophytic woodland plant, *Monotropa uniflora,* having scalelike leaves and a solitary, nodding flower.

Indian poke *n.* A species of **hellebore** (see).

Indian pudding *n.* A pudding made of cornmeal and milk and sweetened with molasses.

Indian red *n.* An iron oxide used as a paint and cosmetic pigment.

Indian rope trick *n.* The feat of climbing an unsupported rope, which some Indians are supposed to be able to perform.

Indian summer *n.* **1.** A period of mild weather occurring in late autumn or early winter. **2.** A pleasant, tranquil, or flourishing period occurring during the end of a condition or period, such as the late stage of one's life.

Indian Territory. An area occupying part of the modern state of Oklahoma. It was set aside in 1834 by the government as a homeland for five Indian tribes expelled from the east. After 1889 the land was forcibly repurchased and the surviving Indians placed on reservations.

Indian tobacco *n.* A poisonous North American plant, *Lobelia inflata,* having light-blue flowers and rounded seed pods.

Indian turnip *n.* **1.** A plant, the **jack-in-the-pulpit. 2.** The acrid tuber of this plant.

Indian wrestling *n.* A contest of strength between two people who clasp each other's hand with the elbow resting on a table, the winner being the one who forces his opponent's hand down to the table.

India paper *n.* **1.** A thin, uncoated, delicate paper made of vegetable fiber, used especially for taking impressions of engravings. **2. Bible paper** (see).

India rubber *n.* See **rubber** (sense 1). —**In·di·a·rub·ber** *adj.*

In·dic (ĭn′dĭk) *adj.* **1.** Of, pertaining to, or constituting the Indic languages. **2.** Of or pertaining to India, its people, or their culture. ~*n.* A branch of the Indo-European languages that comprises Sanskrit and its modern descendants (including Hindi and Urdu), and Pali, Prakrit, and Dard.

in·di·can (ĭn′dĭ-kăn′) *n.* **1.** A compound, $C_8H_6NOSO_2OH$, excreted, usually in the form of its potassium salt, in the urine. **2.** A glycoside, $C_{14}H_{17}NO_6$, occurring in the indigo plant. [Latin *indicum,* IN-DIGO + -AN.]

in·di·cant (ĭn′dĭ-kənt) *n.* Something that serves to indicate. [Latin *indicāns* (stem *indicant-*), present participle of *indicāre,* to INDICATE.]

in·di·cate (ĭn′dĭ-kāt′) *tr.v.* **-cated, -cating, -cates. 1. a.** To demonstrate or point out with precision: *indicate a route.* **b.** To state or exhibit in complete detail. **c.** To show a reading of. Used of instruments. **2.** To serve as a sign, symptom, or token of; signify. **3.** To suggest or demonstrate the necessity, expedience, or advisability of:

The symptoms indicate immediate surgery. **4.** To state, disclose, or express briefly. [Latin *indicāre*, to show, from *index*, forefinger, indicator, INDEX.] —**in·di·ca·to·ry** (ĭn-dĭk′ə-tôr′ē, -tōr′ē) *adj.*

in·di·ca·tion (ĭn′dĭ-kā′shən) *n.* **1.** The action of indicating. **2. a.** Something that indicates; a sign, token, or symptom. **b.** Something indicated as necessary or expedient. **3.** The reading shown on a measuring instrument. —See Synonyms at **sign.**

in·dic·a·tive (ĭn-dĭk′ə-tĭv) *adj.* **1.** Serving to point out or indicate: *indicative of their cynical attitude.* **2.** *Abbr.* **ind.** *Grammar.* Pertaining to or designating a verb mood used to indicate that the denoted act or condition is an objective fact. Compare **subjunctive.** ~*n. Abbr.* **ind.** *Grammar.* **1.** The indicative mood. **2.** A verb in this mood. —**in·dic·a·tive·ly** *adv.*

in·di·ca·tor (ĭn′dĭ-kā′tər) *n.* **1. a.** A device that indicates, such as a pointer or index. **b.** A circumstance or characteristic that serves to indicate: *all the usual indicators of a weak economy.* **2.** Any of various meters, gauges, or other instruments that are used to monitor the operation or condition of an engine, furnace, electrical network, reservoir, or other physical system. **3.** The needle, dial, or other registering device on such an instrument. **4.** An indicator board. **5.** An accurate measuring instrument used to measure small linear distances or to check that a component has the correct dimensions. Also called "dial gauge." **6.** A plant species that requires special conditions of soil, temperature, and the like, and therefore indicates these conditions in places where it grows. Also called "indicator species." **7.** *Chemistry.* Any of various substances, such as litmus or phenolphthalein, that indicate the presence, absence, or concentration of a substance, or the degree of reaction between two or more substances, by means of a characteristic change, especially in color.

indicator board *n.* A board displaying information; especially, one in a railroad station or airport showing departure and arrival times. Also called "indicator."

indicator diagram *n.* A graph or oscilloscope record showing the variation of pressure and volume within the combustion chamber of an internal-combustion engine or steam engine.

in·di·ces. Alternate plural of **index.**

in·di·ci·a (ĭn-dĭsh′ē-ə, -dĭsh′ə) *pl.n.* **1.** Identifying marks or indications; signs. **2.** Markings on bulk mailings used as a substitute for stamps or cancellations. [Latin, plural of *indicium*, sign, from *indicāre*, to INDICATE.]

in·dict (ĭn-dīt′) *tr.v.* **-dicted, -dicting, -dicts.** To accuse formally of a crime or other offense; charge. [Alteration (influenced by obsolete *indict*, to proclaim) of Middle English *enditen*, to accuse, from Anglo-French *enditer*, to dictate, INDITE.] —**in·dict·ee** (ĭn′dī-tē′) *n.* —**in·dict·er, in·dic·tor** *n.*

in·dict·a·ble (ĭn-dīt′ə-bəl) *adj. Law.* **1.** Liable to be indicted. **2.** Rendering a person liable to indictment. Said of a crime.

in·dic·tion (ĭn-dĭk′shən) *n.* **1.** A 15-year cycle used as a chronological unit for tax purposes in ancient Rome and incorporated in some medieval systems. **2.** *Archaic.* A proclamation. [Middle English *indiccioun*, from Late Latin *indictiō* (stem *indictiōn-*), "proclamation" (of Diocletian, fixing a 15-year assessment of property tax), from *indīcere*, to proclaim, INDITE.]

in·dict·ment (ĭn-dīt′mənt) *n.* **1.** The act of indicting or the state of being indicted. **2.** *Law.* A written statement charging a party with the commission of a crime.

Indies. See **East Indies, West Indies.**

in·dif·fer·ence (ĭn-dĭf′ər-əns) *n.* **1.** Lack of interest or concern. **2.** The quality of being indifferent.

in·dif·fer·ent (ĭn-dĭf′ər-ənt) *adj.* **1.** Having no particular interest or concern; apathetic. **2.** Unaffected; insensible: *indifferent to their pleas.* **3.** Showing no partiality, bias, or marked preference. **4.** Not mattering one way or the other; of no great importance; insignificant. **5.** Of average quality, extent, or degree. **6.** Being neither good nor bad; mediocre. **7.** Not active or involved; neutral. **8.** *Biology.* **a.** Undifferentiated, as cells or tissue. **b.** Occurring in two or more ecological communities. Said of a species. —See Synonyms at **average.** [Middle English, from Old French, from Latin *indifferēns* : *in-*, not + *differēns*, DIFFERENT.] —**in·dif·fer·ent·ly** *adv.*

Synonyms: *apathetic, detached, incurious, unconcerned.*

Usage: The usual preposition following this word is *to* (*He was indifferent to her advances*) but *as to* is sometimes used, especially in the context of abstract ideas (*He was indifferent as to the consequences of his action*), and *about* is often heard in less formal usage (*I'm indifferent about money*).

in·dif·fer·ent·ism (ĭn-dĭf′ər-ən-tĭz′əm) *n.* The belief that religions are all of like validity. —**in·dif·fer·ent·ist** *n.*

in·di·gen (ĭn′də-jən, -jěn′) *n.* Also **in·di·gene** (-jēn′). One that is native or indigenous to an area. [Latin *indigena*, native.]

in·di·gence (ĭn′də-jəns) *n.* Want or neediness.

in·dig·e·nous (ĭn-dĭj′ə-nəs) *adj.* **1.** Occurring or living naturally in an area; not introduced; native. **2.** Intrinsic; innate. [From Latin *indigena*, native.] —**in·dig·e·nous·ly** *adv.* —**in·dig·e·nous·ness** *n.*

in·di·gent (ĭn′də-jənt) *adj.* **1.** Lacking the means of subsistence; impoverished; needy. **2.** *Archaic.* Lacking or deficient in something specified. Usually used with *of.* ~*n.* A destitute or needy person. [Middle English, from Old French, from Latin *indigēns* (stem *indigent-*), present participle of *indigēre*, to lack : *indi-*, strengthened form of *in-*, in + *egēre*, to lack, want.] —**in·di·gent·ly** *adv.*

in·di·gest·ed (ĭn′dī-jěs′tĭd, ĭn′dī-) *adj.* **1.** Not carefully thought over or considered. **2.** Shapeless or chaotic.

in·di·gest·i·ble (ĭn′dī-jěs′tə-bəl, ĭn′dī-) *adj.* **1.** Difficult or impossible

INDIAN OCEAN

to digest. **2.** Difficult for the mind to assimilate, especially because of poor expression or presentation. —**in·di·gest·i·bil·i·ty** *n.* —**in·di·gest·i·bly** *adv.*

in·di·ges·tion (ĭn′dī-jěs′chən, ĭn′dī-) *n.* **1.** The inability to digest food. **2.** Discomfort or illness resulting from this; dyspepsia.

in·dign (ĭn-dīn′) *adj. Obsolete.* **1.** Unworthy. **2.** Shameful; disgraceful. [Middle English *indigne*, from Old French, from Latin *indignus* : *in-*, not + *dignus*, worthy.]

in·dig·nant (ĭn-dĭg′nənt) *adj.* Characterized by or filled with indignation; outraged. [Latin *indignāns* (stem *indignant-*), present participle of *indignārī*, to regard as unworthy, from *indignus*, unworthy, INDIGN.] —**in·dig·nant·ly** *adv.*

in·dig·na·tion (ĭn′dĭg-nā′shən) *n.* Anger aroused by something unjust, mean, or unworthy. —See Synonyms at **anger.** [Middle English *indignacioun*, from Latin *indignātiō* (stem *indignātiōn-*), from *indignārī*, to regard as unworthy. See **indignant.**]

in·dig·ni·ty (ĭn-dĭg′nə-tē) *n., pl.* **-ties. 1. a.** Humiliating, degrading, or abusive treatment of an individual. **b.** An offense to dignity; an affront. **2.** *Obsolete.* The want of dignity or honor. [Latin *indignitās* (stem *indignitāt-*), from *indignus*, unworthy, INDIGN.]

in·di·go (ĭn′dĭ-gō′) *n., pl.* **-gos** or **-goes. 1.** Any of various plants of the genus *Indigofera*, some of which yield a blue dyestuff. **2.** Any of several similar or related plants. **3.** A blue dye obtained from indigo or other plants or produced synthetically. **4.** *Abbr.* **ind.** Dark blue to grayish purplish blue. [Earlier *indico*, from Spanish, from Latin *indicum*, from Greek *indikon (pharmakon)*, "Indian (dye)," from *Indikos*, Indian, from *India*, INDIA.] —**in·di·go** *adj.*

indigo bunting *n.* A small bird, *Passerina cyanea*, of North and Central America, the male of which has deep-blue plumage.

indigo snake *n.* A nonvenomous bluish-black snake, *Drymarchon corais*, of the southern United States and northern Mexico.

in·di·go·tin (ĭn-dĭg′ə-tĭn, ĭn′dĭ-gō′-) *n.* A dark blue, crystalline compound, $C_{16}H_{10}N_2O_2$, the principal coloring matter of indigo. [INDIGO + -IN.]

in·di·rect (ĭn′-dĭ-rěkt′, -dī-rěkt′) *adj. Abbr.* **ind. 1. a.** Not taking a direct course; roundabout. **b.** Not proceeding or operating directly: *an indirect connection.* **2.** Not descending in a straight line of succession. Said of an inheritance or title. **3. a.** Not straight to the point; circumlocutory. **b.** Evasive; devious. **4.** Not directly planned for; secondary: *indirect benefits.* **5.** Pertaining to or characteristic of indirect speech; oblique. —**in·di·rect·ly** *adv.* —**in·di·rect·ness** *n.*

indirect discourse or **speech** *n.* A construction giving an account of a previous statement without quoting it verbatim, introduced by a verb such as *say* or *tell,* sometimes followed by *that,* and having appropriate changes in person and tense; for example, *She said that he had left.* Also called "indirect speech," "reported speech." Compare **direct speech.**

in·di·rec·tion (ĭn′dĭ-rĕk′shən, ĭn′dī-) *n.* **1.** The quality or state of being indirect. **2.** Lack of direction; aimlessness. **3.** Lack of straight-forwardness; deviousness.

indirect lighting *n.* Illumination by reflected or diffused light.

indirect object *n.* A grammatical object indirectly affected by the action of a verb; for example, *me* in *Sing me a song* and *the rabbit* in *He feeds the rabbit lettuce.* Compare **direct object.**

indirect passive *n.* A passive construction in which the subject corresponds to the indirect or prepositional object in an active construction; for example, *they* in the sentence *They were given the papers.*

indirect tax *n.* A tax levied on goods or services rather than individuals and collected through the vendor. Compare **direct tax.**

in·dis·cern·i·ble (ĭn′dĭ-sûr′nə-bəl) *adj.* **1.** Not able to be discerned or perceived. **2.** Barely discernible or perceptible. —**in·dis·cern·i·bly** *adv.*

in·dis·ci·pline (ĭn-dĭs′ə-plĭn′) *n.* Lack of discipline; unruly behavior.

in·dis·creet (ĭn′dĭs-krēt′) *adj.* **1.** Lacking discretion; injudicious. **2.** Too frank; inclined to reveal more than is wise. —**in·dis·creet·ly** *adv.* —**in·dis·creet·ness** *n.*

in·dis·crete (ĭn′dĭs-krēt′) *adj.* Not divided or divisible into separate parts; unified.

in·dis·cre·tion (ĭn′dĭs-krĕsh′ən) *n.* **1.** Lack of discretion. **2.** An indiscreet act or remark.

in·dis·crim·i·nate (ĭn′dĭs-krĭm′ə-nĭt) *adj.* **1.** Wanting in discrimination or discernment: *indiscriminate admiration of power.* **2.** Random; haphazard. **3.** Confused; motley. **4.** Not restricted or restrained; promiscuous. —**in·dis·crim·i·nate·ly** *adv.* —**in·dis·crim·i·nate·ness** *n.*

in·dis·crim·i·na·tion (ĭn′dĭs-krĭm′ə-nā′shən) *n.* The condition or quality of being indiscriminate. —**in·dis·crim·i·na·tive** *adj.*

in·dis·pen·sa·ble (ĭn′dĭs-pĕn′sə-bəl) *adj.* **1.** Incapable of being dispensed with; essential; required. **2.** Incapable of being set aside or escaped; inevitable. —See Synonyms at **necessary.**
~*n.* An indispensable person or thing. —**in·dis·pen·sa·bil·i·ty,** **in·dis·pen·sa·ble·ness** *n.* —**in·dis·pen·sa·bly** *adv.*

in·dis·pose (ĭn′dĭs-pōz′) *tr.v.* **-posed, -posing, -poses. 1.** To make averse; disincline. **2.** To render unfit; disqualify. **3.** To cause to be or feel ill; sicken.

in·dis·posed (ĭn′dĭs-pōzd′) *adj.* **1.** Mildly ill. **2.** Disinclined; unwilling. —See Synonyms at **sick.**

in·dis·po·si·tion (ĭn′dĭs-pə-zĭsh′ən) *n.* **1.** Disinclination; unwillingness. **2.** A minor ailment.

in·dis·put·a·ble (ĭn′dĭs-pyōō′tə-bəl) *adj.* Beyond doubt; undeniable. —**in·dis·put·a·ble·ness** *n.* —**in·dis·put·a·bly** *adv.*

in·dis·sol·u·ble (ĭn′dĭ-sŏl′yə-bəl) *adj.* **1.** Impossible to break or undo; binding: *an indissoluble contract.* **2.** Incapable of being dissolved, disintegrated, or decomposed. —**in·dis·sol·u·bil·i·ty,** **in·dis·sol·u·ble·ness** *n.* —**in·dis·sol·u·bly** *adv.*

in·dis·tinct (ĭn′dĭs-tĭngkt′) *adj.* **1.** Not clearly delineated; blurred. **2.** Faint; dim. **3.** Difficult to understand or make out: *indistinct speech.* —**in·dis·tinct·ly** *adv.* —**in·dis·tinct·ness** *n.*

in·dis·tinc·tive (ĭn′dĭs-tĭngk′tĭv) *adj.* Lacking distinctive qualities; not distinctive. —**in·dis·tinc·tive·ly** *adv.* —**in·dis·tinc·tive·ness** *n.*

in·dis·tin·guish·a·ble (ĭn′dĭs-tĭng′gwĭ-shə-bəl) *adj.* Not distinguishable, especially: **1.** Difficult or impossible to perceive or make out. **2.** So similar as to be incapable of being distinguished from another

or each other. —**in·dis·tin·guish·a·bil·i·ty,** **in·dis·tin·guish·a·ble·ness** *n.* —**in·dis·tin·guish·a·bly** *adv.*

in·dite (ĭn-dīt′) *tr.v.* **-dited, -diting, -dites. 1.** To write; compose. **2.** To set down in writing. **3.** *Obsolete.* To dictate. [Middle English *enditen,* to compose, write down, from Norman French *enditer,* from Vulgar Latin *indictāre* (unattested), frequentative of Latin *indīcere* (past participle *indictus*), to proclaim : *in-,* toward + *dīcere,* to pronounce.] —**in·dite·ment** *n.* —**in·dit·er** *n.*

in·di·um (ĭn′dē-əm) *n. Symbol* **In** A soft, malleable, silvery-white metallic element found primarily in ores of zinc and tin, used as a plating over silver in making mirrors, in plating aircraft bearings, and in compounds for transistors. Atomic number 49, atomic weight 114.82, melting point 156.61°C, boiling point 2,000°C, specific gravity 7.31, valencies 1, 2, 3. [New Latin, from Latin *indicum,* INDIGO (from the indigo-blue color of its spectrum).]

in·di·ver·ti·ble (ĭn′dĭ-vûr′tə-bəl, -dī-) *adj.* Incapable of being diverted or turned aside. —**in·di·ver·ti·bly** *adv.*

in·di·vid·u·al (ĭn′də-vĭj′ōō-əl) *adj.* **1. a.** Of or pertaining to a single human being. **b.** By or for one person: *an individual portion.* **2.** Existing as a distinct entity; single; separate. **3.** Distinguished by particular characteristics; peculiar to one person; distinctive. **4.** *Obsolete.* Indivisible; inseparable. —See Synonyms at **characteristic, single.**
~*n.* **1. a.** A single human being considered separately from his group or from society. **b.** A single organism as distinguished from a group or colony. **2.** An independent, strong-willed person. **3.** A person. [Middle English *indyvyduall,* separate, indivisible, from Medieval Latin *indīviduālis,* from Latin *indīviduus,* indivisible : *in-,* not + *dīviduus,* divisible, from *dīvidere,* to DIVIDE.] —**in·di·vid·u·al·ly** *adv.*

Usage: Individual (noun) in the sense of "a person" is fittingly used when a single human being is distinguished from a group or mass by contrast or by stress on a special quality: *the individual's right to dissent from a majority view; an individual to the core.* Careful writers and stylists avoid the use of the term *individual* as a substitute for *person: Two individuals were arrested for the crime.*

in·di·vid·u·al·ism (ĭn′dĭ-vĭj′ōō-ə-lĭz′əm) *n.* **1.** Individuality. **2.** The assertion of one's uniqueness; egoism. **3.** An individual peculiarity or foible. **4.** *Economics.* **a.** The theory that a citizen should have freedom in his economic pursuits and should succeed by his own initiative. **b.** The practice of this: *rugged individualism.* **5.** The doctrine that the interests of the individual should take precedence over the interests of the state or social group. **6.** *Philosophy.* The doctrine that reality is composed of individual entities.

in·di·vid·u·al·ist (ĭn′dĭ-vĭj′ōō-ə-lĭst) *n.* **1.** One who asserts his individuality by his independence of thought and action. **2.** One who advocates individualism. —**in·di·vid·u·al·ist, in·di·vid·u·al·is·tic** *adj.* —**in·di·vid·u·al·is·ti·cal·ly** *adv.*

in·di·vid·u·al·i·ty (ĭn′dĭ-vĭj′ōō-ăl′ə-tē) *n., pl.* **-ties. 1.** The quality of being individual; distinctness. **2.** The aggregate of distinguishing attributes of a person or thing. **3.** A single, distinct entity. **4.** *Archaic.* Indivisibility.

in·di·vid·u·al·ize (ĭn′dĭ-vĭj′ōō-ə-līz′) *tr.v.* **-ized, -izing, -izes. 1.** To give individuality to. **2.** To consider individually; specify; particularize. **3.** To modify to suit a particular individual. —**in·di·vid·u·al·i·za·tion** *n.*

in·di·vid·u·ate (ĭn′də-vĭj′ōō-āt′) *tr.v.* **-ated, -ating, -ates. 1.** To individualize. **2.** To form into a separate and distinct entity.

in·di·vid·u·a·tion (ĭn′də-vĭj′ōō-ā′shən) *n.* **1.** The act or process of individuating; specifically, the process by which social individuals become differentiated one from the other. **2.** The condition of being individuated; individuality.

in·di·vis·i·ble (ĭn′də-vĭz′ə-bəl) *adj.* **1.** Incapable of being divided. **2.** *Mathematics.* Incapable of being divided exactly. —**in·di·vis·i·bil·**

INDONESIA

i·ty, in·di·vis·i·ble·ness *n.* —in·di·vis·i·bly *adv.*

Indo– *prefix.* Indicates India or East Indian; for example, **Indochina.**

In·do-Ar·y·an (ĭn′dō-âr′ē-ən) *adj.* **1.** Belonging to or characteristic of any of the Indo-European-speaking peoples of the Indian subcontinent. **2.** Indo-Iranian.
~*n.* **1.** Any of the Indo-Aryan peoples. **2.** An Indo-Iranian.

In·do·chi·na (ĭn′dō-chī′nə). Region of Southeast Asia. It includes Burma, Thailand, Laos, Kampuchea, Vietnam, and the Malay Peninsula. See **French Indochina.** —**In·do·chi·nese** *n. & adj.*

in·doc·ile (ĭn-dŏs′əl) *adj.* Difficult to control or instruct; not docile. —**in·do·cil·i·ty** *n.*

in·doc·tri·nate (ĭn-dŏk′trə-nāt′) *tr.v.* **-nated, -nating, -nates. 1.** To instruct in a body of doctrine. **2.** To teach to accept a system of thought uncritically. —**in·doc·tri·na·tion** *n.*

In·do-Eu·ro·pe·an (ĭn′dō-yŏŏr′ə-pē′ən) *adj.* **1.** Belonging to or constituting a family of languages that includes the Germanic, Celtic, Italic, Baltic, Slavic, Greek, Armenian, Hittite, Tocharian, Iranian, and Indic groups. **2.** Belonging to or constituting Proto-Indo-European. **3.** Of, pertaining to, or characteristic of cultural traits appearing to be common to or widely distributed among peoples who speak Indo-European languages, and presumed to be inherited from the original speakers of Proto-Indo-European.
~*n.* **1.** The Indo-European family of languages. **2. Proto-Indo-European** *(see).* **3.** A member of any of the peoples who speak Indo-European languages. **4.** A member of the presumed prehistoric people who spoke Proto-Indo-European. [Named after the geographical extremities of the distribution of the languages : INDO– + EUROPEAN.]

In·do-Eu·ro·pe·an·ist (ĭn′dō-yŏŏr′ə-pē′ə-nĭst) *n.* A historical linguist specializing in the study of Indo-European.

In·do-Ger·man·ic (ĭn′dō-jər-măn′ĭk) *adj.* Indo-European.
~*n.* Indo-European. [Translation of German *indogermanisch.*]

In·do-Hit·tite (ĭn′dō-hĭt′īt′) *n.* Indo-European together with Hittite. Used by those who do not consider Hittite to be itself within the Indo-European family proper.

In·do-I·ra·ni·an (ĭn′dō-ĭ-rā′nē-ən, -ī-rä′nē-ən) *adj.* Belonging to or constituting the branch of Indo-European made up of the Indic and the Iranian language groups.
~*n.* The Indo-Iranian branch of Indo-European.

in·dole, in·dol (ĭn′dōl′) *n.* A white crystalline compound, C_8H_7N, obtained from coal tar and used in perfumery, medicine, and as a flavoring. [IND(IGO) + -OLE.] —**in·dol·ic** *adj.*

in·dole·a·ce·tic acid (ĭn′dōl-ə-sē′tĭk). **IAA.** An organic compound, $C_{10}H_9NO_2$, which is the most common of the group of substances that regulate plant growth (auxins).

in·dole·a·ce·to·ni·trile (ĭn′dōl-ə-sē′tō-nī′trĭl) *n.* Abbr. **IAN.** A common auxin, $C_{10}H_8N_2$.

in·dole·am·ine (ĭn′dō-lăm′ēn, ĭn′dō-lə-mēn′) *n.* Any of various derivatives of indole containing an amine group.

in·do·lent (ĭn′də-lənt) *adj.* **1.** Averse to work or activity; habitually lazy. **2.** *Pathology.* **a.** Causing little or no pain: *an indolent tumor.* **b.** Slow to heal; persistent: *an indolent ulcer.* [Late Latin *indolēns,* painless : Latin *in-,* not + *dolēns* (stem *dolent-*), present participle of *dolēre,* to give pain, feel pain.] —**in·do·lence** *n.*

In·dol·o·gy (ĭn-dŏl′ə-jē) *n.* The study of Indian history, languages, and culture. [INDO– + -LOGY.] —**In·dol·o·gist** *n.*

in·do·meth·a·cin (ĭn′dō-mĕth′ə-sĭn) *n.* A drug, $C_{19}H_{16}ClNO_4$, that relieves pain and inflammation and is used particularly in the treatment of rheumatoid arthritis. [INDO(LE) + METH- + AC(ETIC ACID) + -IN.]

in·dom·i·ta·ble (ĭn-dŏm′ə-tə-bəl) *adj.* Incapable of being overcome, subdued, or vanquished; unconquerable. [Late Latin *indomitābilis,* untamable : Latin *in-,* not + *domitāre,* frequentative of *domāre* (past participle *domitus*), to tame.] —**in·dom·i·ta·bly** *adv.*

In·do·ne·si·a (ĭn′də-nē′zhə, -shə). Formerly **Dutch East Indies** (dŭch ēst ĭn′dēz). Republic in southeastern Asia, the fifth-largest nation in the world and the world's largest Muslim nation. It consists of more than 13,000 islands lying between the Indian and Pacific oceans. Despite fertile land, prolific sea fisheries, and abundant minerals, Indonesia is still one of the world's poorest countries because of lack of development. The chief agricultural product is rice, and cash crops include tea, rubber, copra, coffee, and sugar. Indonesia also exports petroleum, petroleum products, and tin. It gained its independence from the Netherlands in 1949 under Ahmed Sukarno. He was removed by a bloody military coup (1965), and since then Gen. Suharto has reversed his Communist policies. Area, 1,904,345 square kilometers (735,077 square miles). Population, 147,400,000. Capital, Jakarta, on the island of Java.

In·do·ne·si·an (ĭn′də-nē′zhən, -shən) *n.* **1.** A native or inhabitant of Indonesia. **2.** A member of a hypothetical non-Malay race of Indonesia, Malaysia, and the Philippines, having both Mongoloid and Polynesian characteristics. **3.** The official language of Indonesia, **Bahasa Indonesia** *(see).*
~*adj.* Of or pertaining to Indonesia, its people, or their language.

Indonesian Borneo. See **Kalimantan.**

in·door (ĭn′dôr′, -dōr′) *adj.* **1.** Of, pertaining to, or situated in the interior of a house or other building: *an indoor pool.* **2.** Carried on or used indoors: *indoor games.* [Short for earlier *within-door* : WITHIN + DOOR.]

in·doors (ĭn-dôrz′, -dōrz′) *adv.* In or into a house or other building. [Short for earlier *withindoors* : WITHIN + DOORS.]

in·do·phe·nol (ĭn′dō-fē′nôl) *n.* A green or blue organic dye, OH $C_6H_4NC_6H_4O$, or its derivatives.

indorse. Variant of **endorse.**

In·dra (ĭn′drə). *Hinduism.* A principal Vedic deity associated with rain and thunder. [Sanskrit *Indraḥ†.*]

in·draft (ĭn′drăft′, -dräft) *n.* **1.** A pulling or drawing inward. **2.** An inward flow or current: *an indraft of cold air.*

in·drawn (ĭn′drôn′) *adj.* **1.** Drawn in. **2.** Introspective; aloof.

in·dri (ĭn′drē) *n., pl.* **-dris.** A large lemur, *Indri indri,* of Madagascar, having silky fur and a short tail. [Malagasy *indry!* look! (mistakenly assumed to be the animal's name).]

in·du·bi·ta·ble (ĭn-dyōō′bə-tə-bəl, ĭn-dyōō′-) *adj.* Too obvious to be doubted; unquestionable. —**in·du·bi·ta·bil·i·ty** *n.* —**in·du·bi·ta·bly** *adv.*

in·duce (ĭn-dōōs′, -dyōōs′) *tr.v.* **-duced, -ducing, -duces. 1.** To lead or move by influence or persuasion; prevail upon: *finally induced him to give up smoking.* **2.** To stimulate the occurrence of; especially, to hasten (childbirth) artificially, as by the use of drugs. **3.** To infer by inductive reasoning. **4.** *Physics.* To produce (an electric current or magnetic effect) by induction. —See Synonyms at **persuade.** [Middle English *inducen,* from Latin *indūcere* : *in-,* in + *dūcere,* to lead.] —**in·duc·er** *n.* —**in·duc·i·ble** *adj.*

in·duce·ment (ĭn-dōōs′mənt, ĭn-dyōōs′-) *n.* **1.** The act or process of inducing: *the inducement of sleep.* **2.** That which induces; an incentive; a motive. **3.** An introductory or background statement explaining the main allegations in a legal proceeding.

in·duct (ĭn-dŭkt′) *tr.v.* **-ducted, -ducting, -ducts. 1. a.** To place ceremoniously or formally in an office or benefice; install. **b.** To introduce, as to facts or knowledge; initiate. **c.** To admit to military service. **2.** *Physics.* To induce. [Middle English *inducten,* from Medieval Latin *indūcere* (past participle *inductus*), from Latin, to lead in, INDUCE.]

in·duc·tance (ĭn-dŭk′təns) *n.* **1.** The property of an electric circuit that enables an electromagnetic force to be generated as a result of a change of current in the same circuit *(self-inductance)* or in a nearby circuit with which it is magnetically linked *(mutual inductance).* **2.** A measure of this property in henries. **3.** A circuit element that introduces this property.

in·duc·tile (ĭn-dŭk′təl) *adj.* Unyielding; not pliant or ductile.

in·duc·tion (ĭn-dŭk′shən) *n.* **1.** The act of inducting or of being inducted. **2.** *Electricity.* **a.** The generation of electromotive force in a closed circuit by a varying magnetic flux through the circuit. **b.** The charging of an isolated conducting object by momentarily earthing it while a charged body is nearby. **3. a.** *Logic.* A principle of reasoning to a conclusion about all the members of a class from examination of only a few members of the class; broadly, reasoning from the particular to the general. Compare **deduction.** **b.** A conclusion reached by this method. **4.** *Mathematics.* A deductive method of proof in which verification of a proposition consists of proving the first case and the case immediately following an arbitrary case for which the proposition is assumed to be correct. **5.** The act of inducing. **6.** *Archaic.* A preface or preamble.

induction coil *n.* A transformer, often used in the ignition systems of gasoline engines, in which an interrupted, low-voltage direct current in the primary is converted into an intermittent, high-voltage current in the secondary.

induction hardening *n.* A method of hardening the surface of a metal component by inducing eddy currents in it to heat it rapidly, then rapidly cooling it.

induction heating *n.* A method of heating a conducting material by inducing electric currents within it as a result of applying an alternating magnetic field to it.

induction motor *n.* A brushless electric motor in which an alternating current fed to the stator induces a current in the windings of the rotor. Rotation occurs as a result of the interaction of the magnetic field of the stator with that of the rotor.

in·duc·tive (ĭn-dŭk′tĭv) *adj.* **1.** Of or utilizing induction: *inductive method.* **2.** *Electricity.* Of or arising from inductance: *inductive reactance.* **3.** Causing or influencing; inducing. —**in·duc·tive·ly** *adv.* —**in·duc·tive·ness** *n.*

inductive statistics *n.* The branch of statistics involving generalizations, predictions, estimations, and decisions from data initially presented.

in·duc·tor (ĭn-dŭk′tər) *n.* **1.** A person who inducts, as into office. **2.** *Electricity.* Symbol **L** A device that functions by or introduces inductance into a circuit.

indue. Variant of **endue.**

in·dulge (ĭn-dŭlj′) *v.* **-dulged, -dulging, -dulges. —tr. 1.** To yield to the desires and whims of (oneself or another), especially to an excessive degree; humor; pamper. **2.** To gratify or yield to: *indulge a craving for chocolate.* **3.** To grant an ecclesiastical indulgence or dispensation to. —*intr.* **1.** To allow oneself some special pleasure; indulge oneself. Used with *in: indulge in an afternoon nap.* **2.** *Informal.* To consume an excessive amount of alcohol. —See Synonyms at **pamper.** [Latin *indulgēre†,* to be forbearing, grant a favor.] —**in·dulg·er** *n.*

in·dul·gence (ĭn-dŭl′jəns) *n.* **1.** The act of indulging or the fact of being indulgent; tolerance, forbearance, or absence of restraint. **2. a.** The act of indulging in something. **b.** Something indulged in: *Sports cars are an expensive indulgence.* **3. a.** Something granted as a favor or privilege. **b.** Permission to extend the time of payment or performance, as in business. **4.** *Roman Catholic Church.* The remission of temporal punishment due for a sin after the guilt has been

Indus Valley

INDIA'S FIRST GREAT CIVILIZATION

Wealth from farming and foreign trade 4,000 years ago

As long ago as 2400 B.C. a wealthy city-based civilization flourished in the valley of the River Indus, in present-day Pakistan. At its peak it covered an area greater than that of ancient Egypt, had its own writing system, and traded with regions 2,560 kilometers (1,600 miles) away—for example, southern Mesopotamia. Its greatest centers were the capitals of Harappa and Mohenjo-Daro, excavated in the 1920's by the British archaeologist Sir John Marshall.

Its economy was based on agriculture— wheat, barley, rice, and cotton. Terra-cotta pots and models have survived, many bearing inscriptions; but the writing system has not yet been deciphered. About 1750 B.C. the cities were abandoned—possibly because the Indus River burst its banks and brought a flood; possibly because the region was under attack by light-skinned nomads from the northwest, the Aryans, whom many claim invaded India from 2000–1000 B.C. The conquered people became known as Dasyu ("dark-skinned"), and this distinction in color may have been the origin of India's caste system.

PRIESTLY RULER *One of the finds uncovered at Mohenjo-Daro in the 1920's was a soapstone bust (right) of one of the city's priest-kings.*

MOHENJO-DARO *In the foreground of the ruins stands a building that was once a granary. The city was built to a plan, with blocks of buildings laid out in a grid pattern and every house connected to main drainage.*

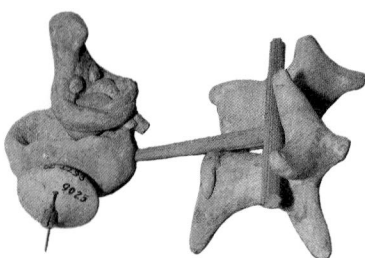

TOY FROM THE PAST *Indus Valley potters made terra-cotta models of everyday objects. This tiny bullock cart was probably used as a child's toy. Similar carts are still used in the area today.*

SACRED BULL *This soapstone seal from the Indus Valley civilization is thought to have had some religious significance. The writing on the seal has not yet been deciphered.*

forgiven. **5.** A royal dispensation during the reigns of Charles II and James II of England granting special religious freedom to the Nonconformists and the Roman Catholics. ~*tr.v.* **indulgenced, -gencing, -gences.** *Roman Catholic Church.* To grant an indulgence to.

in·dul·gent (ĭn-dŭl'jənt) *adj.* Showing, characterized by, or given to indulgence; lenient: *an indulgent employer.* —See Synonyms at **thoughtful.** —**in·dul·gent·ly** *adv.*

in·du·line (ĭn'də-lēn') *n.* Also **in·du·lin** (-lĭn). Any of a group of blue or black synthetic azine dyestuffs used for coloring varnishes and dyeing wool.

in·dult (ĭn-dŭlt') *n.* A temporary exemption from the common law of the Roman Catholic Church granted by the pope. [Middle English, from Medieval Latin *indultum,* from Latin *indultus,* past participle of *indulgēre†,* INDULGE.]

in·du·pli·cate (ĭn-dōō'plĭ-kĭt, ĭn-dyōō'-) *adj. Botany.* Having the edges folded or turned inward but not overlapping. Said of the parts of a bud. [IN- (in, inward) + Latin *duplicātus,* doubled up, DUPLICATE.]

in·du·rate (ĭn'dōō-rāt', ĭn'dyōō-) *v.* **-rated, -rating, -rates.** —*tr.* **1.** To make hard; harden. **2.** To make callous. —*intr.* **1.** To harden. **2.** To become obdurate. ~*adj.* (ĭn'dōō-rĭt, ĭn'dyōō-). Hardened; obstinate; unfeeling. [Latin *indūrāre,* to harden : *in-* (intensive) + *dūrāre,* to harden, from *dūrus,* hard.] —**in·du·ra·tion** *n.* —**in·du·ra·tive** *adj.*

In·dus¹ (ĭn'dəs). Chief river of Pakistan, rising near Mt. Kailas. in Tibet and flowing to the Arabian Sea southeast of Karachi. It is *c.* 3,060 kilometers (1,900 miles) long. The Indus Valley is the most populous part of Pakistan. Its alluvial plains were the site of the early Indus Valley civilization that flourished from *c.* 2500 B.C. to *c.* 1500 B.C.

Indus² *n.* A constellation in the Southern Hemisphere near Tucana and Pavo.

in·du·si·um (ĭn-dōō'zē-əm, -zhē-əm, ĭn-dyōō'-) *n., pl.* **-sia** (-zē-ə, -zhē-ə). An enclosing membrane, such as that covering and protecting the sorus of a fern. [Latin, tunic, from Greek *endusis,* from *enduein,* to sink or slip into, put on : *en-,* in + *duein,* to sink.]

in·dus·tri·al (ĭn-dŭs'trē-əl) *adj. Abbr.* **ind. 1.** Of, pertaining to, or derived from industry: *an industrial exhibition.* **2.** Having highly developed industries: *an industrial nation.* **3.** Employed, required, or used in industry: *industrial diamonds.* **4.** Involving or concerning workers in industry: *industrial relations.* ~*n.* **industrials.** Shares in industrial companies. —**in·dus·tri·al·ly** *adv.*

industrial action *n. Chiefly British.* Any action, such as striking or boycotting, taken by workers to protest against working conditions, managerial policy, or the like.

industrial archaeology *n.* The study of machines, methods, and sites characteristic of the early history of the Industrial Revolution.

industrial arts *pl.n. Used with a singular verb.* A subject of study in schools aimed at developing the manual and technical skills required to work with tools and machinery.

industrial design *n.* The study or practice of designing manufacturable products.

industrial disease *n.* An occupational disease characteristic of workers in a particular industry, for example **asbestosis** *(see).*

in·dus·tri·al·ism (ĭn-dŭs'trē-ə-lĭz'əm) *n.* An economic system in which industries are dominant.

in·dus·tri·al·ist (ĭn-dŭs'trē-ə-lĭst) *n.* A person, such as the owner, the managing director, or a large shareholder of an industrial enterprise, who has a substantial interest in the running and profits of that enterprise.

in·dus·tri·al·ize (ĭn-dŭs'trē-ə-līz') *v.* **-ized, -izing, -izes.** —*tr.* **1.** To develop industry in, especially on an extensive scale. **2.** To organize as an industry. —*intr.* To become industrial. —**in·dus·tri·al·i·za·tion** *n.*

industrial melanism *n.* **Melanism** *(see).*

industrial park *n.* An area usually located on the outskirts of a city and zoned for a group of industries and businesses.

industrial psychology *n.* Psychology applied to such problems of industry as personnel selection, training, and efficiency. —**industrial psychologist** *n.*

industrial relations *n.* **1.** *Used with a plural verb.* The relations that exist between the management and workers in an enterprise. **2.** *Used with a singular verb.* The art or study of managing these relations, especially from the point of view of improving them.

industrial revolution *n.* **1.** Social and economic changes brought about when extensive mechanization of production systems results in a shift from home manufacturing to large-scale factory production. **2. Industrial Revolution.** A period of such change beginning in the middle of the 18th century in England. Preceded by *the.*

industrial union *n.* A union to which all the workers of a particular industry can belong regardless of their trade. Compare **craft union.**

in·dus·tri·ous (ĭn-dŭs'trē-əs) *adj.* **1.** Diligently active; assiduous in work or study. **2.** *Obsolete.* Skillful; clever. —See Usage note at **busy.** [Latin *industriōsus,* from *industria,* skill, INDUSTRY.] —**in·dus·tri·ous·ly** *adv.* —**in·dus·tri·ous·ness** *n.*

in·dus·try (ĭn'də-strē) *n., pl.* **-tries.** *Abbr.* **ind. 1.** The commercial production and sale of goods, including the extraction and processing of raw materials and construction. **2.** A particular branch of manufacture and trade: *the textile industry.* **3. a.** Industrial management as distinguished from the work force. **b.** Manufacturing enterprises as distinguished from agriculture. **4.** Diligence; assiduity.

5. Study or interest in a specifed subject, cause, or the like, especially when considered exploitative. —See Usage note at **business**. [Middle English *industrie*, skill, diligence, from Old French, from Latin *industria*.]

in·dwell (ĭn-dwĕl′) *v.* **-dwelt** (-dwĕlt′), **-dwelling, -dwells.** —*intr.* **1.** To abide as a divine inner spirit, force, or principle. Usually used with *in.* **2.** To exist within permanently. Used with *in.* —*tr.* To abide within as a divine spirit, force, or principle. —**in·dwell·er** *n.*

-ine[1] *suffix.* Indicates of, pertaining to, or belonging to; for example, **Ursuline, elephantine.** [Middle English *-ine, -in,* from Old French *-in,* from Latin *-īnus, -inus,* from Greek *-inos.*]

-ine[2] *suffix. Chemistry.* **1.** Indicates a halogen element; for example, **chlorine, astatine. 2.** Indicates any of various nitrogen-containing compounds, such as: **a.** An amine; for example, **cadaverine. b.** An amino acid; for example, **glycine. c.** An alkaloid; for example, **strychnine. d.** An azine; for example, **induline. 3.** Variant of **-in** (sense 1). [Middle English *-ine,* -INE (pertaining to).]

-ine[3] *suffix.* Indicates of or resembling; for example, **opaline.** [Middle English *-ine,* -INE (pertaining to).]

in·e·bri·ant (ĭn-ē′brē-ənt) *adj.* Intoxicating. —*n.* An intoxicant.

in·e·bri·ate (ĭn-ē′brē-āt′) *tr.v.* **-ated, -ating, -ates. 1.** To make drunk; intoxicate. **2.** To exhilarate or stupefy with or as if with alcohol. —*adj.* (ĭn-ē′brē-ĭt). Intoxicated. —*n.* (ĭn-ē′brē-ĭt). An intoxicated person; especially, a drunkard. [Latin *inēbriāre* : *in-* (intensive) + *ēbriāre* (past participle *ēbriātus*), to intoxicate, from *ēbrius.*] —**in·e·bri·a·tion** *n.*

in·e·bri·at·ed (ĭn-ē′brē-ā′tĭd) *adj.* Exhilarated or confused by or as if by alcohol; intoxicated; drunk.

in·e·bri·e·ty (ĭn′ĭ-brī′ə-tē) *n.* Drunkenness; intoxication.

in·ed·i·ble (ĭn-ĕd′ə-bəl) *adj.* Not suitable for consumption; not edible. —**in·ed·i·bil·i·ty** *n.*

in·ed·it·ed (ĭn-ĕd′ĭ-tĭd) *adj.* **1.** Not edited. **2.** Not published.

in·ed·u·ca·ble (ĭn-ĕj′ə-kə-bəl) *adj.* Not able to be educated; unable to learn.

in·ef·fa·ble (ĭn-ĕf′ə-bəl) *adj.* **1.** Beyond expression; indescribable or unspeakable: *ineffable delight.* **2.** Not to be uttered; taboo: *the ineffable name of the Deity.* [Middle English, from Old French, from Latin *ineffābilis* : *in-,* not + *effābilis,* EFFABLE.] —**in·ef·fa·bil·i·ty, in·ef·fa·ble·ness** *n.* —**in·ef·fa·bly** *adv.*

in·ef·face·a·ble (ĭn′ĭ-fā′sə-bəl) *adj.* Not effaceable; indelible. —**in·ef·face·a·bil·i·ty** *n.* —**in·ef·face·a·bly** *adv.*

in·ef·fec·tive (ĭn′ĭ-fĕk′tĭv) *adj.* **1.** Not effective; having no effect. **2.** Incompetent; not performing to the required standard. —**in·ef·fec·tive·ly** *adv.* —**in·ef·fec·tive·ness** *n.*

in·ef·fec·tu·al (ĭn′ĭ-fĕk′chōō-əl) *adj.* **1.** Not effectual; inadequate. **2.** Powerless; lacking in force or competence: *an ineffectual king.* —**in·ef·fec·tu·al·i·ty, in·ef·fec·tu·al·ness** *n.* —**in·ef·fec·tu·al·ly** *adv.*

in·ef·fi·ca·cious (ĭn′ĕf-ĭ-kā′shəs) *adj.* Not producing a desired effect or result. —**in·ef·fi·ca·cious·ly** *adv.* —**in·ef·fi·ca·cious·ness** *n.*

in·ef·fi·ca·cy (ĭn-ĕf′ĭ-kə-sē) *n.* The state or quality of being inefficacious.

in·ef·fi·cient (ĭn′ĭ-fĭsh′ənt) *adj.* **1.** Wanting in ability; incompetent. **2.** Wasteful of time, energy, or materials. **3.** Not producing the intended result. —**in·ef·fi·cien·cy** *n.* —**in·ef·fi·cient·ly** *adv.*

in·e·las·tic (ĭn′ĭ-lăs′tĭk) *adj.* Not elastic; unyielding; unadaptable. —See Synonyms at **stiff.** —**in·e·las·tic·i·ty** (ĭn′ĭ-lă-stĭs′ə-tē) *n.*

in·el·e·gant (ĭn-ĕl′ə-gənt) *adj.* **1.** Lacking elegance or polish. **2.** Coarse; vulgar. [Old French, from Latin *inēlegāns* : *in-,* not + *ēlegāns,* ELEGANT.] —**in·el·e·gance** *n.* —**in·el·e·gant·ly** *adv.*

in·el·i·gi·ble (ĭn-ĕl′ə-jə-bəl) *adj.* **1.** Not qualified; not fulfilling the necessary conditions: *ineligible to enter the competition.* **2.** Not worthy of being chosen. —*n.* A person who is not eligible. —**in·el·i·gi·bil·i·ty** *n.* —**in·el·i·gi·bly** *adv.*

in·el·o·quent (ĭn-ĕl′ə-kwənt) *adj.* Not eloquent; not fluent or vivid in expression. —**in·el·o·quence** *n.* —**in·el·o·quent·ly** *adv.*

in·e·luc·ta·ble (ĭn′ĭ-lŭk′tə-bəl) *adj.* Not to be avoided or overcome; inevitable. [Latin *inēluctābilis* : *in-,* not + *ēluctārī,* to struggle out : *ex-,* out + *luctārī,* to struggle.] —**in·e·luc·ta·bil·i·ty** *n.* —**in·e·luc·ta·bly** *adv.*

in·ept (ĭn-ĕpt′) *adj.* **1.** Not apt or fitting; unsuitable; inappropriate: *an inept comparison.* —See Usage note at **inapt. 2.** Not sensible; foolish: *an inept remark.* **3.** Awkward; clumsy; incompetent. —See Synonyms at **awkward.** [Latin *ineptus* : *in-,* not + *aptus,* APT.] —**in·ept·ly** *adv.* —**in·ept·ness** *n.*

in·ep·ti·tude (ĭn-ĕp′tə-tōōd′, -tyōōd′) *n.* **1.** The quality of being inept. **2.** An inept act or remark.

in·e·qua·ble (ĭn-ĕk′wə-bəl) *adj.* Not uniform; unevenly distributed.

in·e·qual·i·ty (ĭn′ĭ-kwŏl′ə-tē) *n., pl.* **-ties. 1.** The condition of being unequal. **2.** Lack of equality, as of opportunity, distribution of wealth, or the like. **3.** Unevenness; lack of smoothness or regularity. **4.** Variability; changeability. **5.** An instance of being unequal. **6.** *Mathematics.* An algebraic statement that a quantity is greater than another quantity or that it is less than another quantity.

in·eq·ui·ta·ble (ĭn-ĕk′wə-tə-bəl) *adj.* Not equitable; unfair; unjust. —**in·eq·ui·ta·ble·ness** *n.* —**in·eq·ui·ta·bly** *adv.*

in·eq·ui·ty (ĭn-ĕk′wə-tē) *n., pl.* **-ties. 1.** Lack of equity; injustice; unfairness. **2.** An instance of injustice or unfairness.

in·e·rad·i·ca·ble (ĭn′ĭ-răd′ĭ-kə-bəl) *adj.* That cannot be uprooted, eradicated, or erased. —**in·e·rad·i·ca·ble·ness** *n.* —**in·e·rad·i·ca·bly** *adv.*

Industrial Revolution

TRANSFORMATION OF THE WORLD ECONOMY
The causes and effects of change

The complex of changes in British economic, social, and political life, which are collectively called the Industrial Revolution, had their roots in the development of overseas trade, in the founding of financial institutions, and in the formation of traditions of religious and intellectual freedom. The impetus to the transition from an agricultural to an industry-based economy came, however, from the unprecedented rise in world population that began in the 18th century. It created a reserve of labor and a steady expansion of demand for manufactured goods. A healthy foreign trade caused an increase in national wealth: more people were in paid employment and had money to save. Consequently, financial institutions accumulated funds to invest in new industries hungry for capital to manufacture industrial and consumer goods incorporating scientific or technical innovations. Textile machinery such as Crompton's "mule" (1779), which mechanized spinning, concentrated industry in factories, staffed with cheap labor often working in squalid, dangerous conditions. Whole cities of slums grew around them.

The Industrial Revolution spread from Britain to Europe and America during the 19th century, and to Asia, Australia, and Africa during the 20th. The distressing effects of social dislocation were gradually mitigated by social legislation, the development of social institutions, trade unions, and the welfare state, and an overall increase in wealth.

COALBROOKDALE *In 1703 a Shropshire ironmaster, Abraham Darby, first smelted pig iron with coke instead of costly charcoal at the Coalbrookdale ironworks (above). Iron and steel became cheaper, inventions such as the steam engine were mass-produced, and thus industrial output increased vastly.*

NIGERIA *In parts of Asia, South America, and Africa, industrialization is just beginning. Oil discoveries in Nigeria (left) are increasing national wealth.*

in·er·ra·ble (ĭn-ĕr′ə-bəl, -ûr′ə-bəl) *adj.* Inerrant. —**in·er·ra·bil·i·ty, in·er·ra·ble·ness** *n.* —**in·er·ra·bly** *adv.*

in·er·rant (ĭn-ĕr′ənt, ĭn-ûr′-) *adj.* Making no errors; unerring. —**in·er·ran·cy** *n.*

in·ert (ĭn-ûrt′) *adj.* **1.** Inherently unable to move or act. **2.** Resisting motion or action; sluggish. **3.** *Chemistry.* **a.** Exhibiting no chemical activity; totally unreactive. **b.** Exhibiting chemical activity under special or extreme conditions only. —See Synonyms at **inactive.** [Latin *iners* (stem *inert-*), inactive, unskilled : *in-,* not + *ars,* skill, ART.] —**in·ert·ly** *adv.* —**in·ert·ness** *n.*

inert gas *n.* Any of the elements helium, neon, argon, krypton, xenon, and radon that were formerly thought to be completely inert but which are now known to form some compounds. Also called "noble gas," "rare gas."

in·er·tia (ĭn-ûr′shə) *n.* **1.** *Physics.* **a.** The tendency of a body to resist acceleration. **b.** The tendency of a body at rest to remain at rest or of a body in motion to stay in motion in a straight line unless disturbed by an external force. **2.** Resistance or disinclination to motion, action, or change. **3.** *Medicine.* Reduction or absence of activity in certain smooth muscles: *uterine inertia.* [New Latin, from Latin, lack of skill, idleness, from *iners,* INERT.]

in·er·tial (ĭn-ûr′shəl) *adj.* **1.** Of or pertaining to inertia. **2.** Arising from or depending upon the effects of inertia. **3.** Referred to an inertial frame of reference.

inertial frame *n.* Any frame of reference relative to which the Newtonian law of motion, that a mass *m* subjected to a force *F* moves in accordance with the equation $F = ma$, where *a* is the acceleration, is valid. Also called "inertial system," "Newtonian frame."

inertial guidance *n.* Guidance of a missile in which data from a gyroscope and an accelerometer are used by a computer to maintain a predetermined course.

inertial mass *n.* The mass of a body as determined by its momentum. Compare **gravitational mass**.

inertial platform *n.* The devices used in inertial guidance and their mounting platform.

in·er·tia-reel seat belt (ĭn-ûr′shə-rēl′) *n.* A type of seat belt used in cars, in which the belt is only restrained from unwinding from a metal drum when the car is decelerating. The occupant of the seat therefore has freedom of movement except during a collision or very sharp braking.

inertia selling *n. British.* The illegal sending of unrequested goods to people in the hope that they will not be returned and payment can be demanded.

inertia welding *n.* The welding together of two metal parts caused by the heat of friction when a spinning part is pressed against a stationary part.

in·es·cap·a·ble (ĭn′ə-skā′pə-bəl) *adj.* That cannot be escaped; unavoidable; inevitable. —**in·es·cap·a·bil·i·ty** *n.* —**in·es·cap·a·bly** *adv.*

in·es·cutch·eon (ĭn′ə-skŭch′ən) *n. Heraldry.* A small escutcheon placed at the center of a larger escutcheon.

in es·se (ĭn ĕs′ē) *adj. Latin.* In actual existence. Compare **in posse**.

in·es·sen·tial (ĭn′ə-sĕn′shəl) *adj.* **1.** Not essential; unnecessary. **2.** Without essence.
~*n.* Something inessential. —**in·es·sen·ti·al·i·ty** (ĭn′ə-sĕn′shē-ăl′ə-tē) *n.*

in·es·ti·ma·ble (ĭn-ĕs′tə-mə-bəl) *adj.* **1.** Incapable of being estimated or computed; indeterminable: *inestimable damage.* **2.** Of incalculable value. —**in·es·ti·ma·bly** *adv.*

in·ev·i·ta·ble (ĭn-ĕv′ĭ-tə-bəl) *adj.* **1.** Incapable of being avoided or evaded. **2.** That cannot be prevented; certain to take place. **3.** Invariably appearing or occurring; predictable: *made the inevitable jokes about the bridegroom.*
~*n.* Something that is inevitable. Preceded by *the.* —**in·ev·i·ta·bil·i·ty, in·ev·i·ta·ble·ness** *n.* —**in·ev·i·ta·bly** *adv.*

in·ex·act (ĭn′ĭg-zăkt′) *adj.* Not exact; not quite accurate or precise. —**in·ex·act·ly** *adv.* —**in·ex·act·ness** *n.*

in·ex·act·i·tude (ĭn′ĭg-zăk′tə-tōōd′, -tyōōd′) *n.* Lack of exactness.

in·ex·cus·a·ble (ĭn′ĭk-skyōō′zə-bəl) *adj.* Not excusable; unpardonable. —**in·ex·cus·a·bil·i·ty, in·ex·cus·a·ble·ness** *n.* —**in·ex·cus·a·bly** *adv.*

in·ex·haust·i·ble (ĭn′ĭg-zô′stə-bəl) *adj.* **1.** Incapable of being exhausted or used up. **2.** Unfailing; tireless; indefatigable. —**in·ex·haust·i·bil·i·ty, in·ex·haust·i·ble·ness** *n.* —**in·ex·haust·i·bly** *adv.*

in·ex·is·tent (ĭn′ĭg-zĭs′tənt) *adj.* Not existent; nonexistent. —**in·ex·ist·ence, in·ex·ist·en·cy** *n.*

in·ex·o·ra·ble (ĭn-ĕk′sər-ə-bəl) *adj.* **1.** Not capable of being persuaded by entreaty; unyielding: *"and more inexorable far/Than empty tigers or the roaring sea"* (Shakespeare). **2.** Relentless; unremitting. [Latin *inexōrābilis : in-,* not + *exōrābilis,* from *exōrāre,* to move by entreaty, from *ex-,* completely + *ōrāre,* to plead.] —**in·ex·ora·bil·i·ty, in·ex·o·ra·ble·ness** *n.* —**in·ex·o·ra·bly** *adv.*

in·ex·pe·di·ent (ĭn′ĭk-spē′dē-ənt) *adj.* Not expedient; inadvisable. —**in·ex·pe·di·ence, in·ex·pe·di·en·cy** *n.* —**in·ex·pe·di·ent·ly** *adv.*

in·ex·pen·sive (ĭn′ĭk-spĕn′sĭv) *adj.* Not expensive; fairly cheap. —**in·ex·pen·sive·ly** *adv.* —**in·ex·pen·sive·ness** *n.*

in·ex·pe·ri·ence (ĭn′ĭk-spîr′ē-əns) *n.* Lack of experience.

in·ex·pe·ri·enced (ĭn′ĭk-spîr′ē-ənst) *adj.* Lacking experience and the knowledge gained from experience.

in·ex·pert (ĭn-ĕk′spûrt′) *adj.* Not expert; not skillful or adept. —**in·ex·pert·ly** *adv.* —**in·ex·pert·ness** *n.*

in·ex·pi·a·ble (ĭn-ĕk′spē-ə-bəl) *adj.* **1.** Not capable of being expiated or atoned for: *inexpiable crimes.* **2.** *Archaic.* Implacable; unrelenting. —**in·ex·pi·a·ble·ness** *n.* —**in·ex·pi·a·bly** *adv.*

in·ex·pli·ca·ble (ĭn-ĕk′splĭ-kə-bəl, ĭn′ĭk-splĭk′ə-bəl) *adj.* Not explicable; not capable of being explained or accounted for. —**in·ex·pli·ca·bil·i·ty, in·ex·pli·ca·ble·ness** *n.* —**in·ex·pli·ca·bly** *adv.*

in·ex·plic·it (ĭn′ĭk-splĭs′ĭt) *adj.* Not explicit; indefinite; vague.

in·ex·press·i·ble (ĭn′ĭk-sprĕs′ə-bəl) *adj.* Not capable of being expressed; indescribable: *inexpressible joy.* —**in·ex·press·i·bil·i·ty, in·ex·press·i·ble·ness** *n.* —**in·ex·press·i·bly** *adv.*

in·ex·pres·sive (ĭn′ĭk-sprĕs′ĭv) *adj.* **1.** Expressing little or nothing. **2.** *Archaic.* Inexpressible. —**in·ex·pres·sive·ly** *adv.* —**in·ex·pres·sive·ness** *n.*

in·ex·pug·na·ble (ĭn′ĭk-spŭg′nə-bəl, -spyōō′nə-) *adj.* Not expugnable; impregnable. —**in·ex·pug·na·bly** *adv.*

in·ex·pung·i·ble (ĭn′ĭk-spŭn′jə-bəl) *adj.* Incapable of being expunged or obliterated.

in·ex·ten·si·ble (ĭn′ĭk-stĕn′sə-bəl) *adj.* Not extensible; unable to be extended.

in ex·ten·so (ĭn ek-stĕn′sō, ĭk-) *adv. Latin.* At full length; in full: *His article was published in extenso.*

in·ex·tin·guish·a·ble (ĭn′ĭk-stĭng′gwĭ-shə-bəl) *adj.* Not capable of

being extinguished or quenched. —**in·ex·tin·guish·a·ble·ness** *n.* —**in·ex·tin·guish·a·bly** *adv.*

in·ex·tir·pa·ble (ĭn′ĭk-stûr′pə-bəl) *adj.* Incapable of being eradicated or destroyed.

in ex·tre·mis (ĭn ek-strē′mĭs, ĭk-) *adv.* **1.** At the point of death. **2.** In grave difficulties. [Latin, "in the last (straits)."]

in·ex·tri·ca·ble (ĭn-ĕk′strĭ-kə-bəl) *adj.* **1. a.** Incapable of being disentangled or untied. **b.** Too intricate or complicated to solve. **2. a.** Firmly resisting one's attempts at escape or resolution: *an inextricable quandary.* **b.** Incapable of being freed: *The screws were rusted in and quite inextricable.* —**in·ex·tri·ca·bil·i·ty, in·ex·tri·ca·ble·ness** *n.* —**in·ex·tri·ca·bly** *adv.*

inf. 1. infantry. **2.** inferior. **3.** infinitive. **4.** influence. **5.** information.

Inf. infantry.

in·fal·li·bil·ism (ĭn-făl′ə-bə-lĭz′əm) *n. Roman Catholic Church.* The principle of the pope's infallibility. —**in·fal·li·bil·ist** *n.*

in·fal·li·ble (ĭn-făl′ə-bəl) *adj.* **1.** Incapable of erring; entirely dependable: *an infallible source of information.* **2.** Incapable of failing; certain: *an infallible antidote.* **3.** Incapable of error in expounding doctrine on faith or morals. Said especially of the pope speaking ex cathedra. [French, from Medieval Latin *infallibilis : in-,* not + *fallibilis,* FALLIBLE.] —**in·fal·li·bil·i·ty, in·fal·li·ble·ness** *n.* —**in·fal·li·bly** *adv.*

in·fa·mous (ĭn′fə-məs) *adj.* **1.** Having an exceedingly bad reputation; notorious. **2.** Causing or deserving infamy; loathsome; grossly shocking: *an infamous deed.* **3.** *Law.* **a.** Formerly, deprived of all or some civil rights as a result of being convicted of certain serious crimes. **b.** Designating a crime, such as treason or perjury, that entailed this deprivation. —See Synonyms at **mean** (base). [Middle English, from Medieval Latin *infamōsus,* from Latin *infāmis : in-,* not + *fāma,* FAME.] —**in·fa·mous·ly** *adv.* —**in·fa·mous·ness** *n.*

in·fa·my (ĭn′fə-mē) *n., pl.* **-mies. 1.** Evil fame or reputation. **2.** The condition of being infamous. **3.** An infamous act. —See Synonyms at **disgrace**. [Middle English *infamye,* from Old French *infamie, infame,* from Latin *infāmia,* from *infāmis,* INFAMOUS.]

in·fan·cy (ĭn′fən-sē) *n., pl.* **-cies. 1.** The state or period of being an infant. **2.** The earliest years or stage of something: *television in its infancy.* **3.** *Law.* The state or period of being a minor.

in·fant (ĭn′fənt) *n.* **1.** A child in the earliest period of its life; a baby. **2.** *Law.* One under the legal age of majority; a minor.
~*adj.* **1.** Of or being in infancy. **2.** Intended for infants or very young children. **3.** Young and growing: *an infant enterprise.* [Middle English *enfaunt,* from Old French *enfant,* from Latin *infāns,* "(one) unable to speak" : *in-,* not + *fāns* (stem *fant-*), present participle of *fārī,* to speak.]

in·fan·ta (ĭn-făn′tə) *n.* **1.** A daughter of a Spanish or Portuguese king. **2.** The wife of an infante. [Spanish, feminine of *infante,* INFANTE.]

in·fan·te (ĭn-făn′tā) *n.* Any son of a Spanish or Portuguese king other than the heir to the throne. [Spanish and Portuguese, "infant," from Latin *infāns,* INFANT.]

in·fan·ti·cide (ĭn-făn′tĭ-sīd′) *n.* **1. a.** The killing of an infant. **b.** *Law.* The killing by its mother of a child under one year old. **2.** A person who kills an infant. **3.** The practice of killing infants. [Late Latin *infanticidium* (killing) and *infanticida* (killer) : Latin *infāns,* INFANT + *-cidium, -cida,* -CIDE.] —**in·fan·ti·cid·al** *adj.*

in·fan·tile (ĭn′fən-tīl′, -tĭl) *adj.* **1.** Of or pertaining to infants or infancy. **2.** Lacking maturity, sophistication, or reasonableness. **3.** *Pathology.* Designating diseases occurring in adults that are recognizable in childhood: *infantile paralysis.* [French, from *infantilis,* from *infāns,* INFANT.]

infantile autism *n. Psychology.* See **autism** (sense 2).

infantile paralysis *n. Pathology.* **Poliomyelitis** (see).

in·fan·til·ism (ĭn′fən-tə-lĭz′əm) *n.* **1.** A state of arrested development in an adult, characterized by a retention of infantile mentality accompanied by stunted growth and sexual immaturity. **2.** Childish behavior or speech.

in·fan·til·ize (ĭn-făn′tə-līz′) *tr.v.* **-ized, -izing, -izes.** To treat (a person, especially an adolescent) as if still at an early stage of development.

infant mortality rate *n.* The number of deaths of infants aged under one year for every 1000 live births, occurring in any one year.

in·fan·try (ĭn′fən-trē) *n., pl.* **-tries.** *Abbr.* **Inf., inf.** The branch of an army made up of units trained to fight on foot. [French *infanterie,* from Italian *infanteria,* from *infante,* youth, foot soldier, from Latin *infāns,* INFANT.]

in·fan·try·man (ĭn′fən-trē-mən) *n., pl.* **-men** (-mĭn). A soldier serving in the infantry.

infant school *n. British.* A school for children aged between approximately five and seven years. Compare **junior school**.

in·farct (ĭn-färkt′, ĭn′färkt′) *n.* Also **in·farc·tion** (ĭn-färk′shən). A dead area of tissue resulting from failure of local blood supply. [New Latin *infarctus,* from Latin *infarctus, infartus,* past participle of *infarcīre,* to stuff in, cram : *in-,* in + *farcīre,* to stuff.] —**in·farct·ed** *adj.*

in·farc·tion (ĭn-färk′shən) *n.* **1.** Death of an organ or part of an organ that occurs when its blood supply is obstructed by a blood clot or embolus. **2.** An infarct.

in·fat·u·ate (ĭn-făch′ōō-āt′) *tr.v.* **-ated, -ating, -ates. 1.** To cause to behave foolishly. **2.** To inspire with powerful but foolish and unreasoning passion or attraction.

~*adj.* (ĭn-făch′o͞o-ĭt, -āt′). *Archaic.* Infatuated. [Latin *infatuāre* : *in-* (causative) + *fatuus,* FATUOUS.]

in·fat·u·at·ed (ĭn-făch′o͞o-ā′tĭd) *n.* Possessed by a powerful, unreasoning, often short-lived, passion or attraction. —**in·fat·u·at·ed·ly** *adv.*

in·fat·u·a·tion (ĭn-făch′o͞o-ā′shən) *n.* **1.** The state or an instance of being infatuated. **2.** An object of extravagant, short-lived passion. —See Synonyms at **love.**

in·fau·na (ĭn′fô-nə) *n., pl.* **-nas** or **-nae** (-nē). The mass of aquatic animals that live just beneath the bed of a sea, lake, or river. [Danish *ifauna* : IN- + FAUNA.]

in·fea·si·ble (ĭn-fē′zə-bəl) *adj.* Not feasible; impracticable.

in·fect (ĭn-fĕkt′) *tr.v.* **-fected, -fecting, -fects. 1.** To contaminate with pathogenic microorganisms. **2.** To communicate a disease to (another person). **3.** To invade and produce infection in. **4.** To corrupt; contaminate. **5.** To affect as if by contagion. [Middle English *infecten,* from Latin *inficere* (past participle *infectus*), to work in, dye, taint : *in-,* in + *facere,* to do.]

in·fec·tion (ĭn-fĕk′shən) *n.* **1.** Invasion of the body by pathogenic microorganisms. **2.** An instance of such invasion. **3.** The pathological state resulting from such invasion, characterized by inflammation and tissue damage due to the action of toxins produced by the microorganisms. **4.** An agent or contaminated substance responsible for such invasion. **5.** An infectious disease. **6. a.** Moral contamination or corruption, as by the communication of harmful influences. **b.** The communication or spreading from one to another of ideas, emotions, or the like, as if by contagion.

in·fec·tious (ĭn-fĕk′shəs) *adj.* **1.** Capable of causing infection. **2.** Capable of being transmitted by infection without actual contact; communicable. Said of a disease. Compare **contagious. 3.** Caused by a microorganism. Said of a disease. **4.** Tending to spread or affect others easily: *an infectious chuckle.* —**in·fec·tious·ly** *adv.* —**in·fec·tious·ness** *n.*

infectious enterohepatitis *n.* In veterinary medicine, **blackhead.**

infectious hepatitis *n.* See **hepatitis.**

infectious mononucleosis *n.* An acute, contagious, febrile disease, **mononucleosis** *(see).* Also called "glandular fever."

in·fec·tive (ĭn-fĕk′tĭv) *adj.* Capable of producing infection; infectious. —**in·fec·tive·ness, in·fec·tiv·i·ty** *n.*

in·fe·lic·i·tous (ĭn′fə-lĭs′ə-təs) *adj.* **1.** Not happy; unfortunate; sad. **2.** Inappropriate; inapt, as in style or manner of expression. —**in·fe·lic·i·tous·ly** *adv.*

in·fe·lic·i·ty (ĭn′fə-lĭs′ə-tē) *n., pl.* **-ties. 1.** The quality or condition of being infelicitous. **2.** Something inappropriate or inapt. [Middle English *infelicite,* from Latin *infēlīcitās,* from *infēlix,* unhappy : *in-,* not + *fēlix,* happy.]

in·fer (ĭn-fûr′) *v.* **-ferred, -ferring, -fers.** —*tr.* **1.** To conclude from evidence; deduce. **2.** To have as a necessary or logical consequence. —See Usage note at **imply.** —*intr.* To draw inferences. —See Synonyms at **conjecture.** [Old French *inferer,* from Latin *inferre,* to bring in, introduce, deduce : *in-,* in- + *ferre,* to bear.] —**in·fer·a·ble** *adj.* —**in·fer·a·bly** *adv.*

in·fer·ence (ĭn′fər-əns) *n.* **1.** The act or process of inferring. **2.** Something inferred; a conclusion based on a premise. **3.** *Logic.* A process of reasoning consisting of forming conclusions from premises.

in·fer·en·tial (ĭn′fə-rĕn′shəl) *adj.* Derived or capable of being derived from inference. —**in·fer·en·tial·ly** *adv.*

in·fe·ri·or (ĭn-fîr′ē-ər) *adj. Abbr.* **inf. 1. a.** Low or lower in quality, status, or estimation. **b.** Mediocre; second-rate. **2.** Low or lower in order, degree, or rank. **3.** Situated under or beneath. **4.** *Botany.* Located below the perianth and other floral parts. Said of an ovary. **5.** *Printing.* Set below the normal line. Said of type. **6.** *Astronomy.* **a.** Orbiting between the sun and the earth: *an inferior planet.* **b.** Lying below the horizon.

~*n.* **1.** A person of lesser rank or status than another. **2.** *Printing.* An inferior character. [Middle English, from Latin *īnferior,* comparative of *īnferus,* low.] —**in·fe·ri·or·i·ty** (ĭn′fîr-ē-ôr′ə-tē, -ŏr′ə-tē) *n.*

inferior court *n.* A court of law of lower rank than another, usually with a limited jurisdiction, the decisions of which are subject to appeal to a superior court.

inferiority complex *n.* A neurotic condition resulting from a persistent, unrealistic sense of inadequacy, characterized by withdrawal or by compensatory and often aggressive attempts to attract attention.

in·fer·nal (ĭn-fûr′nəl) *adj.* **1.** Of or pertaining to the world of the dead in classical mythology. **2.** Of, pertaining to, or characteristic of hell or those in it. **3.** Abominable; damnable: *Stop that infernal racket!* [Middle English, from Old French, from Late Latin *īnfernālis,* from *īnfernus,* hell, from Latin, lower.] —**in·fer·nal·ly** *adv.*

infernal machine *n. Archaic.* An explosive device maliciously designed to harm or destroy.

in·fer·no (ĭn-fûr′nō) *n., pl.* **-nos. 1.** *Often* **Inferno.** Hell. **2.** Any place or situation likened to hell; especially, a conflagration. [Italian, hell, from Late Latin *īnfernus.* See **infernal.**]

in·fer·tile (ĭn-fûrt′l) *adj.* **1.** Not fertile; unproductive; barren. **2.** Incapable of producing offspring. —See Synonyms at **sterile.** —**in·fer·til·i·ty** (ĭn′fər-tĭl′ə-tē) *n.*

in·fest (ĭn-fĕst′) *tr.v.* **-fested, -festing, -fests. 1.** To inhabit or overrun in large numbers so as to be harmful or unpleasant. **2.** To invade and live on or within a living organism. Said of animal parasites, such as ticks and tapeworms. [Middle English *infesten,* to attack, molest, trouble, from Old French *infester,* from Latin *infestāre,* from *infestus,* hostile.] —**in·fes·ta·tion** *n.*

in·feu·da·tion (ĭn′fyo͞o-dā′shən) *n.* In feudal society: **1.** The process of granting legal possession of an estate. **2.** The deed used for this.

in·fib·u·late (ĭn-fĭb′yə-lāt′, -yo͞o-lāt′) *tr.v.* **-lated, -lating, -lates.** To enclose or fasten (especially, the female genitals) with a clasp or stitches to prevent sexual intercourse. [Latin *infībulāre* : IN- + *fībula,* clasp.] —**in·fib·u·la·tion** *n.*

in·fi·del (ĭn′fə-dəl, -dĕl′) *n.* **1.** One who has no religious beliefs. **2.** One who is an unbeliever with respect to a particular religion, especially Christianity or Islam. [Middle English *infydel,* from Old French *infidel,* from Latin *infidēlis,* unfaithful : *in-,* not + *fidēs,* faith.] —**in·fi·del** *adj.*

in·fi·del·i·ty (ĭn′fə-dĕl′ə-tē) *n., pl.* **-ties. 1.** Lack of fidelity or loyalty. **2.** Unfaithfulness to a sexual partner, especially a spouse. **3.** An act of disloyalty or sexual unfaithfulness. **4.** Lack of religious faith, especially in Christianity or Islam.

in·field (ĭn′fēld′) *n.* **1.** A field located near a farmhouse. **2.** *Baseball.* **a.** The area of the field enclosed by the foul lines and the arc of the outfield grass just beyond the bases. **b.** The defensive positions of first base, second base, third base, and shortstop. Compare **outfield. 3.** The area inside a racetrack or running track.

in·field·er (ĭn′fēl′dər) *n. Baseball.* A player who plays in the infield.

in·fight·ing (ĭn′fī′tĭng) *n.* **1.** Rivalry or competition, often bitter, between members of the same group or organization: *political infighting.* **2.** In boxing, hitting at close range, especially in order to tire out one's opponent. —**in·fight·er** *n.*

in·fil·trate (ĭn-fĭl′trāt′, ĭn′fĭl-) *v.* **-trated, -trating, -trates.** —*tr.* **1.** To pass (a liquid or gas) into something through its interstices. **2.** To permeate with a liquid or gas passed through interstices. **3.** To send (troops, for example) surreptitiously into enemy-held territory. **4.** To gain entry or cause to gain entry to (an organization or political party, for example) surreptitiously, and with subversive intent. —*intr.* To gain entrance gradually or surreptitiously.

~*n.* Any substance that accumulates gradually in bodily tissues.

in·fil·tra·tion (ĭn′fĭl-trā′shən) *n.* **1.** The act or process of infiltrating. **2.** The state of being infiltrated. **3.** Something that infiltrates. —**in·fil·tra·tive** (ĭn-fĭl′trə-tĭv) *adj.* —**in·fil·tra·tor** *n.*

infin. infinitive.

in·fi·nite (ĭn′fə-nĭt) *adj.* **1.** Having no boundaries or limits. **2.** Immeasurably or uncountably large. **3.** *Mathematics.* **a.** Existing beyond or being greater than any arbitrarily large value. **b.** Unlimited in spatial extent. **c.** Of or designating a set capable of being put into one-to-one correspondence with a proper subset of itself. **4.** Continuing endlessly in time, space, extent, or magnitude. **5.** All-encompassing; total: *God's infinite love.*

~*n.* Something infinite; infinity. Preceded by *the.* —**the Infinite (Being).** God. [Middle English *infinit,* from Old French, from Latin *infīnītus* : *in-,* not + *fīnītus,* FINITE.] —**in·fi·nite·ly** *adv.* —**in·fi·nite·ness** *n.*

Synonyms: *boundless, countless, eternal, illimitable, innumerable, limitless, measureless, numberless.*

in·fin·i·tes·i·mal (ĭn′fə-nə-tĕs′ə-məl) *adj.* **1.** Immeasurably or incalculably minute. **2.** Loosely, very small; minute. **3.** *Mathematics.* Capable of having values arbitrarily close to zero. —See Synonyms at **small.**

~*n.* **1.** An infinitesimal amount or quantity. **2.** *Mathematics.* A function having values arbitrarily close to zero. [New Latin *infinitesimus* : Latin *infīnītus,* INFINITE + *-esimus,* ordinal suffix.] —**in·fin·i·tes·i·mal·ly** *adv.*

infinitesimal calculus *n.* Differential and integral calculus.

in·fin·i·tive (ĭn-fĭn′ə-tĭv) *n. Abbr.* **inf., infin.** *Grammar.* **1.** A verb form that is not inflected to indicate person, number, or tense. **2.** Such a verb form used in English: **a.** To serve as a substantive while retaining some verbal aspects, such as modification by adverbs and connection with an object, preceded by *to;* for example, *To go willingly is to show strength.* **b.** To form verb phrases, preceded by *to;* for example, *He wished to go.* In this usage, the *to* may be dropped with certain verbs; for example, *He may go.*

~*adj.* Of, pertaining to, or using the infinitive. [Late Latin *infīnītīvus,* "unlimited" (because it has no definite numbers or persons), from Latin *infīnītus,* INFINITE.] —**in·fin·i·ti·val** (ĭn′fə-nə-tī′vəl)

in·fin·i·tude (ĭn-fĭn′ə-to͞od′, -tyo͞od′) *n.* **1.** The state or quality of being infinite. **2.** An infinite quantity, number, or extent.

in·fin·i·ty (ĭn-fĭn′ə-tē) *n., pl.* **-ties. 1.** The quality or condition of being infinite. **2.** Unbounded space, time, or quantity. **3.** An indefinitely large number or amount. **4.** *Mathematics.* The limit that a function f is said to approach at $x = a$ when for x close to a, $f(x)$ is larger than any preassigned number. **5.** A point that is sufficiently far away from a lens or mirror for it to be assumed that light emitted by it will fall in parallel rays on the lens or mirror.

in·firm (ĭn-fûrm′) *adj.* **1.** Weak in body, especially from old age; feeble. **2.** Lacking moral firmness; irresolute. —See Synonyms at **weak.** [Middle English *infirme,* from Latin *infirmus* : *in-,* not + *firmus,* FIRM.] —**in·firm·ly** *adv.* —**in·firm·ness** *n.*

in·fir·ma·ry (ĭn-fûr′mə-rē) *n., pl.* **-ries.** A place for the care of the sick or injured; especially, a hospital or dispensary. [Medieval Latin *infirmāria,* from Latin *infirmus,* INFIRM.]

in·fir·mi·ty (ĭn-fûr′mə-tē) *n., pl.* **-ties. 1.** A disability, especially one caused by an illness or old age. **2.** Bodily weakness; frailty. **3.** Moral weakness.

in·fix (ĭn-fĭks′) *tr.v.* **-fixed, -fixing, -fixes. 1.** To fix into another.

PRONUNCIATION KEY

ă, pat; ā, pay; âr, care;
ä, father, are; b, bib;
ch, church; d, deed; ĕ, pet;
ē, be; f, fife; g, gag; h, hat;
hw, which; ĭ, pit; ī, pie;
îr, pier; j, judge; k, kick;
l, lid, needle; m, mum;
n, no, sudden; ng, thing;
ŏ, pot; ō, toe; ô, paw, for;
oi, noise; ou, out; o͝o, book;
o͞o, boot; p, pop; r, roar;
s, sauce; sh, ship, dish;
t, tight; th, thin, path;
th, this, bathe; ŭ, cut; ûr, fur;
v, valve; w, with; y, yes;
z, zebra, size; zh, vision;
ə, about, item, edible,
gallop, circus, peaceful

IN FOREIGN WORDS:

à, *Fr.* ami; œ, *Fr.* feu, *Ger.* schön; ü, *Fr.* tu, *Ger.* über;
KH, *Ger.* ich, *Scot.* loch;
N, *Fr.* bon; y′, *Fr.* Compiègne

STRESS MARKS:

Primary stress: ′
in·cite′ (ĭn-sīt′)
Secondary stress: ′
in′sight′ (ĭn′sīt′)

2. To fix in the mind; inculcate; instill. **3.** *Grammar.* To insert (a morphological element) as an infix.
~*n.* (ĭn′fĭks′). *Grammar.* **1.** An inflectional or derivational element inserted into the body of a word; for example, an infix *-n-* is added to the Old Latin verb root *frag-,* "break," to form the imperfective *frang-,* "is breaking." **2.** An intermediate letter or sound, in English usually a vowel, that connects the elements of a compound word; for example, the *-o-* in *meritocracy* is an infix. [Latin *infigere* (past participle *infixus*) : *in-,* in + *fīgere,* to FIX.]

infl. influence; influenced.

in fla·gran·te de·lic·to (ĭn flə-grän′tē də-lĭk′tō) *adv. Law.* In the actual act of committing an offense; red-handed. [Latin, with the crime still blazing.]

in·flame (ĭn-flām′) *v.* **-flamed, -flaming, -flames.** —*tr.* **1.** To set on fire; kindle. **2. a.** To arouse or excite into a state of strong emotion or passion. **b.** To arouse (strong emotion or passion) in. **3.** To intensify intolerably: *"inflamed to madness an already savage nature"* (Robert Graves). **4.** To produce inflammation in. —*intr.* **1.** To catch fire. **2.** To become excited or aroused. **3.** To be affected by inflammation. [Middle English *inflamen,* from Old French *enflammer,* from Latin *inflammāre* : *in-* (intensive) + *flammāre,* to set on fire, from *flamma,* FLAME.]

in·flam·ma·ble (ĭn-flăm′ə-bəl) *adj.* **1.** Tending to ignite easily and burn rapidly; flammable. **2.** Quickly or easily aroused to strong emotion; passionate. —See Usage note at **flammable.**
~*n.* Something flammable. [French, from Medieval Latin *inflammābilis,* from Latin *inflammāre,* to INFLAME.] **—in·flam·ma·bil·i·ty, in·flam·ma·ble·ness** *n.* **—in·flam·ma·bly** *adv.*

in·flam·ma·tion (ĭn′flə-mā′shən) *n.* **1.** The act of inflaming or the state of being inflamed. **2.** Localized heat, redness, swelling, and pain as a result of irritation, injury, or infection.

in·flam·ma·to·ry (ĭn-flăm′ə-tôr′ē, -tōr′ē) *adj.* **1.** Arousing strong emotion, especially anger or aggression. **2.** Characterized or caused by inflammation.

in·fla·ta·ble (ĭn-flā′tə-bəl) *adj.* Having to be inflated for use: *an inflatable rubber raft.*
~*n.* Any object that can be inflated; especially, a large inflatable object made of sturdy material and used for children to play on.

in·flate (ĭn-flāt′) *v.* **-flated, -flating, -flates.** —*tr.* **1.** To fill and swell with a gas. **2.** To cause to increase unduly: *Success inflated his ego.* **3.** *Economics.* To raise or expand abnormally, as prices, wages, or circulating currency. —*intr.* To become inflated. [Latin *inflāre,* to blow into : *in-,* in + *flāre,* to blow.] **—in·flat·er, in·fla·tor** *n.*

in·flat·ed (ĭn-flā′tĭd) *adj.* **1.** Distended or expanded by or as if by gas or air. **2.** Unduly increased or puffed up: *inflated ideas.* **3.** Increased or raised to abnormal economic levels: *inflated wages.* **4.** Resulting from inflation. **5.** *Botany.* Hollow and enlarged: *an inflated calyx.* **—in·flat·ed·ness** *n.*

in·fla·tion (ĭn-flā′shən) *n.* **1.** The act of inflating or the state of being inflated. **2.** *Economics.* A continuing increase in available currency and credit beyond the proportion of available goods, or an increase in the costs of production, resulting in a sharp and continuing rise in price levels and a fall in the purchasing power of money. Compare **deflation.** See **cost-push, demand-pull.**

in·fla·tion·ar·y (ĭn-flā′shə-nĕr′ē) *adj. Economics.* Pertaining to or tending to cause inflation.

inflationary spiral *n. Economics.* Continually increasing inflation attributed to the mutually reinforcing effects of rising costs, wages, or the like interacting with rising prices.

in·fla·tion·ist (ĭn-flā′shə-nĭst) *n.* One who advocates inflation by increasing the supply of available currency and credit. **—in·fla·tion·ism** *n.*

in·fla·tion-proof (ĭn-flā′shən-pro͞of′) *adj.* Increasing in value at the same rate as inflation: *an inflation-proof investment.*
~*tr.v.* **inflation-proofed, -proofing, -proofs.** To make the value of (pensions, wages, or the like) rise at the same rate as inflation.

in·flect (ĭn-flĕkt′) *v.* **-flected, -flecting, -flects.** —*tr.* **1.** To turn from a course or alignment; bend. **2.** To alter (the voice) in tone or pitch; modulate. **3.** *Grammar.* To alter (a word) as by conjugating or declining. —*intr. Grammar.* To be modified by inflection. [Middle English *inflecten,* from Latin *inflectere,* to bend, warp, change : *in-* (intensive) + *flectere,* to bend.] **—in·flec·tive** *adj.* **—in·flec·tor** *n.*

in·flec·tion (ĭn-flĕk′shən) *n.* Also *chiefly British* **in·flex·ion.** **1.** The act of inflecting or a state of being inflected. **2.** An alteration in pitch or tone of the voice. **3.** *Grammar.* **a.** An alteration of the form of a word, usually by means of affixes, to indicate different grammatical and syntactical relations, such as the declension of nouns, adjectives, and pronouns or the conjugation of verbs. **b.** An element added to a word to denote a grammatical function, such as the *s* in *apples* indicating the plural form or the *'s* in *girl's* indicating the possessive case. **c.** An inflected form of a word. **4.** *Mathematics.* A change in direction of a geometric curve, occurring at a point (the *point of inflection*) at which the curvature of the curve changes sign. **—in·flec·tion·al** *adj.* **—in·flec·tion·al·ly** *adv.*

in·flexed (ĭn-flĕkst′) *adj.* Bent or curved inward or downward, as petals or sepals. [Latin *inflexus,* past participle of *inflectere,* to bend, INFLECT.]

in·flex·i·ble (ĭn-flĕk′sə-bəl) *adj.* **1.** Not flexible; stiff; rigid. **2.** Incapable of being changed; unalterable: *inflexible rules.* **3.** Rigidly adhering to a purpose or stance; unyielding. —See Synonyms at **stiff.** **—in·flex·i·bil·i·ty, in·flex·i·ble·ness** *n.* **—in·flex·i·bly** *adv.*
Synonyms: *adamant, inexorable, obdurate, unyielding.*

in·flict (ĭn-flĭkt′) *tr.v.* **-flicted, -flicting, -flicts.** **1.** To deal or give (a blow, wound, or the like). Used with *on* or *upon.* **2.** To impose (someone or something considered unpleasant): *"malignant Nature, who reserves the right to inflict upon her children the most terrifying jests"* (Thornton Wilder). [Latin *inflīgere* (past participle *inflictus*) : *in-,* on + *flīgere,* to strike.] **—in·flict·er, in·flic·tor** *n.* **—in·flic·tive** *adj.*

in·flic·tion (ĭn-flĭk′shən) *n.* **1.** The act or process of inflicting. **2.** Something inflicted, such as blows or punishment.

in-flight (ĭn′flīt′) *adj.* **1.** Carried out or made while in flight: *in-flight refueling.* **2.** Provided for use or enjoyment while in flight: *in-flight entertainment.*

in·flo·res·cence (ĭn′flə-rĕs′əns) *n.* **1.** *Botany.* **a.** A characteristic arrangement of flowers on a single main stalk. **b.** The part of a plant consisting of the flower-bearing stalk. **2.** A flowering. [New Latin *inflorescentia,* from Late Latin *inflōrēscere,* to begin to flower : Latin *in-* (intensive) + *flōrēscere,* to begin to flower (see **florescence**).]

in·flow (ĭn′flō′) *n.* **1.** The act or process of flowing in or into. **2.** Something that flows in; an influx.

in·flu·ence (ĭn′flo͞o-əns) *n. Abbr.* **inf., infl.** **1.** A power indirectly or intangibly affecting a person or a course of events. **2.** Power to sway or affect, based on prestige, wealth, ability, character, or position. **3.** A person or thing exercising such power. **4.** An effect or change produced by such power. **5.** *Astrology.* **a.** An occult ethereal fluid believed to flow from the stars to affect the fate of humankind. **b.** The occult power emanating from the stars. **—under the influence.** *Informal.* Intoxicated, especially with alcohol.
~*tr.v.* **influenced, -encing, -ences.** **1.** To have power over; affect. **2.** To cause a change in the nature or development of; have a modifying effect upon. —See Synonyms at **affect.** [Middle English, from Old French, from Medieval Latin *influentia,* "a flowing in," from Latin *influēns* (stem *influent-*), present participle of *influere,* to flow in : *in-,* in + *fluere,* to flow.] **—in·flu·enc·er** *n.*

in·flu·ent (ĭn′flo͞o-ənt) *adj.* Flowing in.
~*n.* Something that flows in; especially, a tributary. [Middle English, from Latin *influēns,* flowing in. See **influence.**]

in·flu·en·tial (ĭn′flo͞o-ĕn′shəl) *adj.* Having or exercising influence. **—in·flu·en·tial·ly** *adv.*

in·flu·en·za (ĭn′flo͞o-ĕn′zə) *n.* An acute infectious viral disease characterized by inflammation of the respiratory tract, fever, muscular pain, and irritation in the intestinal tract. Also called "flu," "grippe." [Italian, influence, hence "intangible visitation," epidemic (specifically the European epidemic of influenza of 1743), from Medieval Latin *influentia,* INFLUENCE.]

in·flux (ĭn′flŭks′) *n.* **1.** A flowing in of substance. **2.** A sudden invasion or arrival of many people or things: *an influx of visitors.* **3.** The mouth of a river or stream. [Late Latin *influxus,* from Latin, past participle of *influere,* to flow in. See **influence.**]

influx control *n.* In South Africa, the legal control exercised on the movement by black people into urban areas.

in·fo (ĭn′fō′) *n. Informal.* Information.

in·fold (ĭn-fōld′) *tr.v.* **-folded, -folding, -folds.** **1.** To fold inward. **2.** Variant of **enfold.** **—in·fold·er** *n.* **—in·fold·ment** *n.*

in·form (ĭn-fôrm′) *v.* **-formed, -forming, -forms.** —*tr.* **1. a.** To impart information to. **b.** To acquaint (oneself) with knowledge of a subject. **2.** To give form or character to; be the formative principle of. **3.** To animate or inspire with a particular quality or character; imbue. **4.** *Archaic.* To form or shape (the mind or character) by teaching or training. —*intr.* To disclose or provide information, usually of an incriminating nature. Used with *on* or *against.* [Middle English *enfourmen,* from Old French *enfourmer,* from Latin *informāre,* to give form to, form an idea of : *in-* (intensive) + *formāre,* to form, from *forma,* FORM.]

in·for·mal (ĭn-fôr′məl) *adj.* **1.** Not performed or made according to prescribed regulations or forms; unofficial; irregular: *an informal truce.* **2.** Completed or performed without ceremony or formality: *an informal gathering.* **3.** Of, for, or pertaining to ordinary everyday use; casual; relaxed: *informal clothes.* **4.** Belonging to the usage of spoken or written language as used in face-to-face communication by familiar equals and considered inappropriate in certain cultural contexts, as in the standard written prose of ceremonial and official communications. **—in·for·mal·ly** *adv.*

in·for·mal·i·ty (ĭn′fôr-măl′ə-tē) *n., pl.* **-ties.** **1.** The state or quality of being informal. **2.** An informal act.

in·form·ant (ĭn-fôr′mənt) *n.* **1.** One who discloses information; an informer. **2.** A person who gives information about a subject of study; especially, a speaker of a particular language or dialect used as a source of linguistic evidence in research.

in·for·mat·ics (ĭn′fər-măt′ĭks) *n. Used with a singular verb.* Information science.

in·for·ma·tion (ĭn′fər-mā′shən) *n. Abbr.* **inf.** **1.** The act of informing or the condition of being informed; communication of knowledge. **2.** Knowledge derived from study, experience, or instruction. **3.** Knowledge of a specific event or situation; news; word. **4.** A service or agency supplying facts or news. **5.** *Law.* A formal accusation of a crime made by a public officer rather than by indictment by a grand jury. **6.** A nonaccidental signal used as an input to a computer or communications system. —See Synonyms at **knowledge.** **—in·for·ma·tion·al** *adj.*

information retrieval *n.* The branch of computer science concerned with the classification, storage, and retrieval of information by computers and associated electronic devices.

information science *n.* The science concerned with gathering, classifying, storing, retrieving, manipulating, and evaluating informa-

PRONUNCIATION KEY

ă, pat; ā, pay; âr, care;
ä, father, are; b, bib;
ch, church; d, deed; ĕ, pet;
ē, be; f, fife; g, gag; h, hat;
hw, which; ĭ, pit; ī, pie;
îr, pier; j, judge; k, kick;
l, lid, needle; m, mum;
n, no, sudden; ng, thing;
ŏ, pot; ō, toe; ô, paw, for;
oi, noise; ou, out; o͝o, book;
o͞o, boot; p, pop; r, roar;
s, sauce; sh, ship, dish;
t, tight; th, thin, path;
th, this, bathe; ŭ, cut; ûr, fur;
v, valve; w, with; y, yes;
z, zebra, size; zh, vision;
ə, about, item, edible,
gallop, circus, peaceful

IN FOREIGN WORDS:

à, *Fr.* ami; œ, *Fr.* feu, *Ger.* schön; ü, *Fr.* tu, *Ger.* über;
KH, *Ger.* ich, *Scot.* loch;
N, *Fr.* bon; y′, *Fr.* Compiègne

STRESS MARKS:

Primary stress: ′
in·cite′ (ĭn-sīt′)
Secondary stress: ′
in′sight′ (ĭn′sīt′)

tion, especially by means of computers. Also called "informatics."
information technology *n.* The technology used in information science.
information theory *n.* The theory of the probability of transmission of messages with a given degree of accuracy when the items of information constituting the messages are subject, with certain probabilities, to transmission failure, distortion, and accidental additions.
in·form·a·tive (ĭn-fôr′mə-tĭv) *adj.* Also **in·form·a·to·ry** (-tôr′ē, -tōr′ē). Providing or disclosing information; instructive.
in·formed (ĭn-fôrmd′) *adj.* **1.** Knowledgeable; educated. **2.** Reflecting or resulting from thorough knowledge of a subject: *an informed opinion.*
in·form·er (ĭn-fôr′mər) *n.* **1.** One who informs against others, often for payment. **2.** An informant.
in·fra (ĭn′frə) *adv. Latin.* Below; specifically, in a subsequent part of the text. Compare **supra.**
infra– *prefix.* Indicates: **1.** Below, beneath, inferior to; for example, **infrared, infrasonic. 2.** After, later; for example, **infralapsarianism.** [Latin *infrā,* below, beneath.]
in·fract (ĭn-frăkt′) *tr.v.* **-fracted, -fracting, -fracts.** To break (a rule, law, or agreement); infringe; violate. [Latin *infringere* (past participle *infractus*), to destroy, INFRINGE.] **—in·frac·tor** *n.*
in·frac·tion (ĭn-frăk′shən) *n.* The act or an instance of breaching or violating; infringement; violation. —See Synonyms at **breach.**
in·fra dig (ĭn′frə dĭg′) *adj. Informal.* Beneath one's dignity. [Latin *infrā dignitātem.*]
in·fra·lap·sar·i·an·ism (ĭn′frə-lăp-sâr′ē-ə-nĭz′əm) *n.* The chiefly Calvinist predestinarian doctrine that it was only after the Fall that God elected some from the fallen to be saved by a redeemer. Also called "sublapsarianism." [From INFRA- + Latin *lapsus,* to fall, LAPSE.] **—in·fra·lap·sar·i·an** *n. & adj.*
in·fran·gi·ble (ĭn-frăn′jə-bəl) *adj.* **1.** Unbreakable. **2.** Inviolable. [Old French, from Late Latin *infrangibilis* : Latin *in-,* not + *frangere,* to break.] **—in·fran·gi·bil·i·ty** *n.* **—in·fran·gi·bly** *adv.*
in·fra·or·bit·al (ĭn′frə-ôr′bĭ-təl) *adj. Anatomy.* Located or occurring beneath the orbit.
in·fra·red (ĭn′frə-rĕd′) *adj.* **1.** Of, pertaining to, or designating electromagnetic radiation having wavelengths greater than those of visible light and shorter than those of microwaves; radiation with wavelengths between 0.8 micrometer and 1 millimeter. **2.** Generating, using, or sensitive to such radiation. **—in·fra·red** *n.*
in·fra·son·ic (ĭn′frə-sŏn′ĭk) *adj.* Generating or using waves or vibrations with frequencies below that of audible sound.
in·fra·sound (ĭn′frə-sound′) *n.* A wave phenomenon having the general characteristics of sound waves except that its frequency range is below that of sound.
in·fra·struc·ture (ĭn′frə-strŭk′chər) *n.* **1.** An underlying base or supporting structure. **2.** The basic facilities, equipment, services, and installations needed for the growth and functioning of a country, community, operation, or organization.
in·fre·quent (ĭn-frē′kwənt) *adj.* **1.** Not frequent; rare. **2.** Not steady; irregular; occasional: *an infrequent guest.* **—in·fre·quence, in·fre·quen·cy** *n.* **—in·fre·quent·ly** *adv.*
in·fringe (ĭn-frĭnj′) *v.* **-fringed, -fringing, -fringes.** —*tr.* To break or ignore the terms or obligations of (an oath, agreement, law, or the like); disregard; violate. —*intr.* To go beyond the limits of something; trespass; encroach. Used with *on* or *upon.* [Latin *infringere* : *in-* (intensive) + *frangere,* to break.] **—in·fring·er** *n.*
in·fringe·ment (ĭn-frĭnj′mənt) *n.* **1.** A violation, as of a law, regulation, or agreement; a breach. **2.** An encroachment, as of a right or privilege. —See Synonyms at **breach.**
in·fun·dib·u·li·form (ĭn′fən-dĭb′yə-lə-fôrm′) *adj. Botany.* Funnel-shaped.
in·fun·dib·u·lum (ĭn′fən-dĭb′yə-ləm) *n., pl.* **-la** (-lə). Any of various funnel-shaped bodily passages or parts; especially, the conical stalk connecting the pituitary gland to the hypothalamus at the base of the brain. [Latin, funnel, from *infundere,* to pour in, INFUSE.] **—in·fun·dib·u·lar, in·fun·dib·u·late** *adj.*
in·fu·ri·ate (ĭn-fyoor′ē-āt′) *tr.v.* **-ated, -ating, -ates. 1.** To make furious; enrage. **2.** To annoy or irritate intensely: *an infuriating delay.* ~*adj.* (ĭn-fyoor′ē-ĭt). *Archaic.* Furious. [Medieval Latin *infuriāre,* to enrage : Latin *in-* (intensive) + *furiāre,* to enrage, from *furia,* FURY.] **—in·fu·ri·at·ing·ly** *adv.*
in·fuse (ĭn-fyooz′) *v.* **-fused, -fusing, -fuses.** —*tr.* **1.** To put in or introduce into by or as if by pouring. Used with *into.* **2.** To pervade or imbue, as with a quality or emotion. Used with *with.* **3.** To instill or inculcate (a quality). Used with *into.* **4.** To steep or soak without boiling, in order to extract soluble elements or active principles. —*intr.* To undergo infusion. [Middle English *infusen,* from Old French *infuser,* from Latin *infundere* (past participle *infūsus*), to pour in : *in-,* in + *fundere,* to pour.] **—in·fus·er** *n.*
in·fus·i·ble¹ (ĭn-fyoo′zə-bəl) *adj.* Incapable of being fused or melted; resistant to heat. **—in·fus·i·bil·i·ty, in·fus·i·ble·ness** *n.*
infusible² *adj.* Capable of being infused. **—in·fus·i·bil·i·ty, in·fus·i·ble·ness** *n.*
in·fu·sion (ĭn-fyoo′zhən) *n.* **1.** The act or process of infusing. **2.** A liquid product obtained by infusing. **3.** An admixture. **4.** The introduction of a solution into a vein by slow injection.
in·fu·sion·ism (ĭn-fyoo′zhə-nĭz′əm) *n. Theology.* The Christian doctrine that a pre-existing soul of divine origin is infused into the body at conception or birth. Compare **creationism. —in·fu·sion·ist** *n. & adj.*

in·fu·so·ri·al (ĭn′fyoo-sôr′ē-əl, -sōr′ē-əl) *adj.* **1.** Of or pertaining to infusorians. **2.** Containing or consisting of infusorians.
in·fu·so·ri·an (ĭn′fyoo-sôr′ē-ən, -sōr′ē-ən) *n.* Any of numerous microscopic organisms, especially of the phylum Protozoa or the order Rotifera, occurring in stagnant water or in infusions containing organic material. No longer in technical usage. [New Latin *Infusoria,* "found in infusions."] **—in·fu·so·ri·an** *adj.*
–ing¹ *suffix.* Indicates: **1.** The present participle of verbs; for example, **going, seeing, hoping. 2.** Participial adjectives; for example, **striking, gripping. 3.** Adjectives resembling participial adjectives but not derived from verbs; for example, **swashbuckling. 4.** Adjectives used adverbially as intensives, in the sense "to the point of"; for example, **dripping** wet. [Middle English *-inge, -ing,* variants of *-end, -ind,* Old English *-ende,* related to Latin *-āns,* -ANT.]
–ing² *suffix.* Indicates: **1.** The act, process, or art of performing a specified action; for example, **dancing, thinking. 2.** The thing or substance used in performing such an action; for example, **coating, wadding. 3.** Something that is to undergo such an action; for example, **washing, mending. 4.** The result of such an action; for example, **peeling, opening, drawing. 5.** Something that belongs to, is connected with, used in making, or has the character of; for example, **lagging, boarding. 6.** An action upon or involving; for example, **sounding, berrying.** [Middle English *-ing,* Old English *-ung, -ing.*]
–ing³ *suffix.* Indicates the possession of a certain quality or nature; for example, **sweeting, wilding.** [Middle English *-ing,* Old English *-ing, -ung,* of, belonging to, descended from.]
in·gath·er (ĭn-găth′ər) *tr.v.* **-ered, -ering, -ers. 1.** To reap or gather in (especially, a harvest). **2.** To collect, gather together, or gather back (dispersed people or objects). Used especially in the phrase *the ingathering of the exiles,* with reference to the founding of the state of Israel. **—in·gath·er·er** *n.*
Inge (ĭnj), **William** (1913-73). U.S. playwright. He wrote several popular and critically acclaimed dramas about the hopes and fears of small-town Midwesterners. Among his most successful works were *The Dark at the Top of the Stairs* (1957) and his Pulitzer Prize winner, *Picnic* (1953).
Inge (ĭng), **William Ralph** (1860-1954). English religious leader. His brilliant but pessimistic sermons and articles won him the nickname "the Gloomy Dean."
in·gem·i·nate (ĭn-jĕm′ĭ-nāt′) *tr.v.* **-nated, -nating, -nates.** To urge or reiterate constantly.
Ing·en·housz (ĭng′ən-hous), **Jan** (1730-99). Dutch scientist who discovered the principle of photosynthesis (1779). He demonstrated that plants absorb carbon dioxide in daylight and release oxygen at night.
in·gen·i·ous (ĭn-jēn′yəs) *adj.* **1.** Having or arising from an inventive or cunning mind; characterized by ingenuity; clever: *an ingenious idea; an ingenious gadget.* **2.** *Obsolete.* Having genius; brilliant. —See Synonyms at **clever.** [French *ingénieux,* from Latin *ingeniōsus,* from *ingenium,* inborn talent, skill.] **—in·gen·i·ous·ly** *adv.* **—in·gen·i·ous·ness** *n.*

Usage: Ingenious and *ingenuous* are often confused in everyday use because of the similarity of their spelling. *Ingenious* means "clever," "original" (*an ingenious plot; an ingenious solution to a problem*); *ingenuous* means "innocent," "naive" (*an ingenuous manner; his behavior was ingenuous*). The noun *ingenuity* has come to mean "ingeniousness" and not, as might have been expected, "ingenuousness."

in·gé·nue (ăn′zhə-noo′, -nyoo′; *French* ăN-zhā-nü′) *n.* **1.** An artless, innocent girl or young woman. **2.** An actress playing an ingénue. [French, feminine of *ingénu,* guileless, artless, from Latin *ingenuus,* INGENUOUS.]
in·ge·nu·i·ty (ĭn′jə-noo′ə-tē, -nyoo′ə-tē) *n., pl.* **-ties. 1.** Inventive skill or imagination; cleverness. **2.** The state of being ingeniously contrived. **3.** *Usually* **ingenuities.** An ingenious or imaginative device: *"sophistication in the ingenuities of language"* (T.S. Eliot). **4.** *Archaic.* Ingenuousness. [Latin *ingenuitās,* frankness, innocence (but influenced in meaning by INGENIOUS), from *ingenuus,* INGENUOUS.]
in·gen·u·ous (ĭn-jĕn′yoo-əs) *adj.* **1.** Without sophistication or worldliness; artless; innocent. **2.** Open or honest; frank; candid. —See Synonyms at **frank, naive.** —See Usage note at **ingenious.** [Latin *ingenuus,* native, free-born, noble, honest, frank.] **—in·gen·u·ous·ly** *adv.* **—in·gen·u·ous·ness** *n.*
In·ger·soll (ĭng′gər-sôl′, -sōl′, -səl), **Robert Green** (1833-99). U.S. politician and lecturer. A Civil War officer and later attorney general of Illinois (1867-69), he is primarily known as a lecturer and adamant proponent of scientific and humanistic rationalism, a view based on the theories of Charles Darwin.
in·gest (ĭn-jĕst′) *tr.v.* **-gested, -gesting, -gests. 1.** To take (food, for example) in by or as if by swallowing. **2.** To take in (air). Used of a jet engine. [Latin *ingerere* (past participle *ingestus*), to carry in : *in-,* in + *gerere,* to bear, carry.] **—in·ges·tion** *n.* **—in·ges·tive** *adj.*
in·ges·ta (ĭn-jĕs′tə) *pl.n.* Ingested matter, especially food. [New Latin, from Latin, neuter plural of *ingestus,* past participle of *ingerere,* to INGEST.]
in·gle (ĭng′gəl) *n.* **1.** A fire upon a hearth. **2.** A fireplace.
in·gle·nook (ĭng′gəl-nook′) *n.* A space by or beside a large fireplace, often with seats inside it facing each other. [*Ingle,* Scottish, probably from Scots Gaelic *aingeal,* fire + NOOK.]
in·glo·ri·ous (ĭn-glôr′ē-əs, ĭn-glōr′-) *adj.* **1.** Ignominious; dishonorable. **2.** Obscure; unknown. [Latin *inglōrius* : *in-,* not + *glōria,* GLORY.] **—in·glo·ri·ous·ly** *adv.* **—in·glo·ri·ous·ness** *n.*

ingot *A 24-karat gold ingot weighing 1 kilogram (2.2 pounds). It was made in Chiasso, Switzerland.*

PRONUNCIATION KEY

ă, pat; ā, pay; âr, care; ä, father, are; b, bib; ch, church; d, deed; ĕ, pet; ē, be; f, fife; g, gag; h, hat; hw, which; ĭ, pit; ī, pie; îr, pier; j, judge; k, kick; l, lid, needle; m, mum; n, no, sudden; ng, thing; ŏ, pot; ō, toe; ô, paw, for; oi, noise; ou, out; o͝o, book; o͞o, boot; p, pop; r, roar; s, sauce; sh, ship, dish; t, tight; th, thin, path; *th*, this, bathe; ŭ, cut; ûr, fur; v, valve; w, with; y, yes; z, zebra, size; zh, vision; ə, about, item, edible, gallop, circus, peaceful

IN FOREIGN WORDS:

à, *Fr.* ami; œ, *Fr.* feu, *Ger.* schön; ü, *Fr.* tu, *Ger.* über; KH, *Ger.* ich, *Scot.* loch; N, *Fr.* bon; y', *Fr.* Compiègne

STRESS MARKS:

Primary stress: ′
in·cite′ (ĭn-sīt′)
Secondary stress: ′
in′sight′ (ĭn′sīt′)

in·go·ing (ĭn′gō′ĭng) *adj.* Entering; coming in.
in·got (ĭng′gət) *n.* **1.** A mass of metal shaped for convenient storage or transportation. **2.** A casting mold for metal. [Middle English *ingot,* mass of metal, "something poured into (the mold)" : *in,* IN + Old English *goten,* past participle of *geotan,* to pour.]
ingot iron *n.* A form of low-carbon steel containing small quantities of other elements.
ingraft. Variant of **engraft.**
in·grain, en·grain (ĭn-grān′) *tr.v.* **-grained, -graining, -grains. 1.** To impress indelibly on the mind or nature; fix; infuse. Used with *in, into,* and *on.* **2.** *Archaic.* To cause (a dye or stain) to sink indelibly into the fiber of something.
~*adj.* (ĭn′grān′) **1.** Deeply rooted; instilled. **2.** Dyed in the yarn before weaving or knitting. **3.** Made of fiber or yarn dyed before weaving. Said especially of rugs.
~*n.* **1.** Yarn or fiber dyed before manufacture. **2.** Any article made of ingrained yarns, such as a carpet. [IN- (in) + GRAIN (dye).]
in·grained (ĭn-grānd′) *adj.* **1.** Deeply infused; imbued; deep-seated: *ingrained faults.* **2.** Deeply worked into the grain, pores, or the like: *ingrained mud.* **3.** Complete; utter: *an ingrained cad.*
in·grate (ĭn′grāt′) *n.* An ungrateful person.
~*adj. Archaic.* Ungrateful. [Middle English *ingrat,* from Latin *ingrātus,* ungrateful : *in-,* not + *grātus,* pleasing, thankful.]
in·gra·ti·ate (ĭn-grā′shē-āt′) *tr.v.* **-ated, -ating, -ates.** To bring (oneself) deliberately into the good graces or favor of another. [IN- (in) + Latin *grātia,* GRACE.] **—in·gra·ti·at·ing·ly** *adv.* **—in·gra·ti·a·tion** *n.* **—in·gra·ti·a·to·ry** (ĭn-grā′shē-ə-tôr′ē, -tōr′ē) *adj.*
in·grat·i·tude (ĭn-grăt′ə-to͞od′, -tyo͞od′) *n.* Lack of gratitude; ungratefulness. [Middle English, from Old French, from Medieval Latin *ingrātitūdō* : *in-,* not + *grātitūdō,* GRATITUDE.]
in·gra·ves·cent (ĭn′grə-vĕs′ənt) *adj.* Gradually increasing in severity. Said of a disease. [Latin *ingravescēns* (stem *ingravescent-*), present participle of *ingravescere,* to become heavier, from *gravis,* heavy, GRAVE.] **—in·gra·ves·cence** *n.*
in·gre·di·ent (ĭn-grē′dē-ənt) *n.* **1.** Something added or required to form a mixture or compound: *ingredients for onion soup.* **2.** A component or constituent: *Hard work is an ingredient of success.* [Middle English, "something that enters into a mixture," from Latin *ingrediēns* (stem *ingredient-*), present participle of *ingredī,* to enter into. See **ingress.**]
In·gres (ăN′grə), **Jean Auguste Dominique** (1780–1867). French artist, who led the French classical school of painting after the death of Jacques Louis David. He is noted for his superb draftsmanship and his historical paintings, drawings, and mythological works.
in·gress (ĭn′grĕs′) *n.* Also **in·gres·sion** (ĭn-grĕsh′ən) (for sense 1). **1.** A going in or entering. **2.** The right or permission to enter. **3.** A means or place of entering. **4.** *Astronomy.* **Immersion** *(see).* [Middle English *ingresse,* from Latin *ingressus,* from the past participle of *ingredī,* to enter into : *in-,* in, into + *gradī,* to step.]
in·gres·sive (ĭn-grĕs′ĭv) *adj.* **1.** Of or pertaining to entering. **2.** Of or designating a speech sound pronounced with an inhalation of breath.
~*n.* An ingressive speech sound. **—in·gres·sive·ness** *n.*
in-group (ĭn′gro͞op′) *n.* A group united by common beliefs, attitudes, and interests, characteristically excluding outsiders.
in·grow·ing (ĭn-grō′ĭng) *adj.* Growing inward; especially, designating a toenail that grows into the surrounding flesh.
in·grown (ĭn′grōn′) *adj.* **1.** Grown abnormally into the flesh: *an ingrown toenail.* **2.** Grown within; innate: *an ingrown habit.*
in·growth (ĭn′grōth′) *n.* **1.** The act of growing inward. **2.** Something that grows inward or within.
in·gui·nal (ĭng′gwə-nəl) *adj.* Of, pertaining to, or located in the groin. [Latin *inguinālis,* from *inguen* (stem *inguin-*), groin.]
ingulf. Variant of **engulf.**
in·gur·gi·tate (ĭn-gûr′jə-tāt′) *tr.v.* **-tated, -tating, -tates.** To swallow greedily or in excessive amounts; gorge. [Latin *ingurgitāre* : *in-,* in + *gurges* (stem *gurgit-*), whirlpool, abyss.] **—in·gur·gi·ta·tion** *n.*
INH isoniazid.
in·hab·it (ĭn-hăb′ĭt) *v.* **-ited, -iting, -its.** —*tr.* To live or reside in. —*intr. Archaic.* To dwell. [Middle English *enhabiten,* from Old French *enhabiter,* from Latin *inhabitāre* : *in-,* in + *habitāre,* to dwell, frequentative of *habēre* (past participle *habitus*), to have, possess.] **—in·hab·it·a·bil·i·ty** *n.* **—in·hab·it·a·ble** *adj.* **—in·hab·i·ta·tion** *n.* **—in·hab·it·er** *n.*
in·hab·i·tan·cy (ĭn-hăb′ə-tən-sē) *n., pl.* **-cies.** Occupancy.
in·hab·i·tant (ĭn-hăb′ə-tənt) *n.* A person or animal that inhabits a place; a permanent resident.
in·hab·it·ed (ĭn-hăb′ə-tĭd) *adj.* Having inhabitants; populated.
in·ha·lant (ĭn-hā′lənt) *adj.* Used in or for inhaling.
~*n.* Something that is inhaled, such as a medicine.
in·ha·la·tion (ĭn′hə-lā′shən) *n.* **1.** The act or an instance of inhaling. **2.** A medicinal preparation that is inhaled.
in·ha·la·tor (ĭn′hə-lā′tər) *n.* A device that produces a vapor to ease breathing or to medicate the respiratory system. Also called "inhaler."
in·hale (ĭn-hāl′) *v.* **-haled, -haling, -hales.** —*tr.* To draw in by breathing. —*intr.* **1.** To breathe in. **2.** To draw cigarette smoke into the lungs. [Latin *inhālāre* : *in-,* in + *hālāre,* to breathe (see **halitosis**).]
in·hal·er (ĭn-hā′lər) *n.* **1.** One that inhales. **2.** An inhalator. **3.** A respirator.
in·har·mon·ic (ĭn′här-mŏn′ĭk) *adj.* Not harmonic; discordant.
in·har·mo·ni·ous (ĭn′här-mō′nē-əs) *adj.* **1.** Not in harmony; discordant. Said of sounds. **2.** Not in accord or agreement. **—in·har·mo·ni·ous·ly** *adv.* **—in·har·mo·ni·ous·ness** *n.*
in·haul (ĭn-hôl′) *n.* Also **in·haul·er** (ĭn-hô′lər). *Nautical.* A rope used to draw in a ship's sail.
in·here (ĭn-hîr′) *intr.v.* **-hered, -hering, -heres.** To be inherent or innate. Used with *in.* [Latin *inhaerēre* : *in-,* in + *haerēre,* to stick, remain fixed.] **—in·her·ence** (ĭn-hîr′əns, -hĕr′əns), **in·her·en·cy** *n.*
in·her·ent (ĭn-hîr′ənt, -hĕr′ənt) *adj.* Existing as an essential or characteristic constituent or attribute; intrinsic. [Latin *inhaerēns* (stem *inhaerent-*), present participle of *inhaerēre,* INHERE.] **—in·her·ent·ly** *adv.*
in·her·it (ĭn-hĕr′ĭt) *v.* **-ited, -iting, -its.** —*tr.* **1.** To receive (property, a title, or the like) from a parent, ancestor, or another person by legal succession or will. **2.** To receive or take over from a predecessor. **3.** *Biology.* To receive (a character or characteristic) genetically from a parent or ancestor. **4.** To come into possession of; possess. —*intr.* To succeed as an heir; take possession of an inheritance. [Middle English *enheriten,* from Old French *enheriter,* from Late Latin *inhērēditāre* : *in-* (intensive) + *hērēditāre,* to inherit, from *hērēs* (stem *hērēd-*), heir.] **—in·her·i·tor** *n.* **—in·her·i·trix** (ĭn-hĕr′ĭ-trĭks) *n.*
in·her·it·a·ble (ĭn-hĕr′ə-tə-bəl) *adj.* **1.** Capable of being inherited. **2.** Capable of inheriting; having the right to inherit. **3.** *Law.* Capable of being transferred by a will from one generation to a later generation. **—in·her·it·a·bil·i·ty** *n.* **—in·her·i·ta·bly** *adv.*
in·her·i·tance (ĭn-hĕr′ə-təns) *n.* **1.** The act or right of inheriting. **2.** That which is inherited or to be inherited; legacy; bequest. **3.** Anything regarded as a heritage: *the cultural inheritance of Rome.* **4.** *Biology.* **a.** The process of genetic transmission of characters or characteristics. **b.** The configuration of characters or characteristics so inherited.
inheritance tax *n.* A tax on inherited property.
in·hib·it (ĭn-hĭb′ĭt) *tr.v.* **-ited, -iting, -its. 1.** To restrain or hold back (an impulse, natural reaction, or the like). **2.** To prohibit or forbid, especially in ecclesiastical law. **3.** *Psychology.* To cause inhibition in. **4.** To act as an inhibitor. —See Synonyms at **restrain.** [Middle English *inhibiten,* from Latin *inhibēre* (past participle *inhibitus*), to restrain, hold in : *in-,* in + *habēre,* to have, hold.] **—in·hib·it·a·ble** *adj.* **—in·hib·it·ed** *adj.* **—in·hib·i·tive, in·hib·i·to·ry** (ĭn-hĭb′ĭ-tôr′ē, -tōr′ē) *adj.*
in·hi·bi·tion (ĭn′hĭ-bĭsh′ən, ĭn′ĭ-) *n.* **1.** The act of inhibiting or the state of being inhibited. **2. a.** *Psychology.* Restraint of an instinctive impulse or the condition inducing such restraint. **b.** Any emotion, idea, habit, or the like, which holds back one's impulses or desires. **3.** The prevention or reduction of the functioning of an organ or part by affecting its nerve supply.
in·hib·i·tor, in·hib·it·er (ĭn-hĭb′ə-tər) *n.* One that inhibits, as: **1.** A substance used to retard or halt a chemical reaction, such as rusting; anticatalyst. **2.** An inert substance added to another substance to inhibit some reaction. **3.** An impurity in a solid that inhibits luminescence. **4.** A substance, such as a drug, that prevents or reduces a physiological action.
in·ho·mo·ge·ne·ous (ĭn-hŏm′ə-jĕn′ē-əs, -hōm-ə-) *adj.* Not homogeneous; lacking in uniformity: *an inhomogeneous magnetic field.* **—in·ho·mo·gen·e·i·ty** (ĭn-hŏm′ə-jə-nē′ə-tē, -nā′ə-) *n.*
in·hos·pi·ta·ble (ĭn-hŏs′pĭ-tə-bəl, ĭn′hŏ-spĭt′ə-bəl) *adj.* **1.** Displaying no hospitality; unfriendly. **2.** Not affording shelter or sustenance; barren. **—in·hos·pi·ta·ble·ness** *n.* **—in·hos·pi·ta·bly** *adv.* **—in·hos·pi·tal·i·ty** (ĭn-hŏs′pĭ-tăl′ə-tē) *n.*
in-house (ĭn′hous′) *adj.* Working, originating, or produced within an organization or group: *an in-house editor, not a freelance.* **—in-house** *adv.*
in·hu·man (ĭn-hyo͞o′mən) *adj.* **1.** Not possessing desirable human qualities; lacking kindness or pity; barbarous; brutal. **2.** Not of ordinary human form or type. —See Synonyms at **cruel.** [Latin *inhūmānus* : *in-,* not + *hūmānus,* HUMAN.] **—in·hu·man·ly** *adv.* **—in·hu·man·ness** *n.*
in·hu·mane (ĭn′hyo͞o-mān′) *adj.* Not humane; lacking in pity or compassion. **—in·hu·mane·ly** *adv.*
in·hu·man·i·ty (ĭn′hyo͞o-măn′ə-tē) *n., pl.* **-ties. 1.** Lack of pity or compassion. **2.** An inhumane or cruel act.
in·hume (ĭn-hyo͞om′) *tr.v.* **-humed, -huming, -humes.** To place in a grave; bury; inter. [Latin *inhumāre* : *in-,* in + *humus,* earth, ground.] **—in·hu·ma·tion** *n.* **—in·hum·er** *n.*
in·im·i·cal (ĭn-ĭm′ĭ-kəl) *adj.* **1.** Not conducive; harmful; adverse: *habits inimical to good health.* **2.** Unfriendly; hostile; antagonistic: *"a voice apparently cold and inimical"* (Arnold Bennett). [Late Latin *inimīcālis,* from Latin *inimīcus,* enemy : *in-,* not + *amīcus,* friend.]
in·im·i·ta·ble (ĭn-ĭm′ĭ-tə-bəl) *adj.* Defying imitation; matchless; unique. **—in·im·i·ta·bil·i·ty** *n.* **—in·im·i·ta·bly** *adv.*
in·i·on (ĭn′ē-ən) *n.* The projecting point of the occipital bone at the base of the skull, used as a measuring point in craniometry. [Greek, back of the head.]
in·iq·ui·tous (ĭ-nĭk′wə-təs) *adj.* **1.** Of the nature of iniquity; wicked; sinful. **2.** *Informal.* Disgraceful; scandalous: *an iniquitous waste of money.* **—in·iq·ui·tous·ly** *adv.* **—in·iq·ui·tous·ness** *n.*
in·iq·ui·ty (ĭ-nĭk′wə-tē) *n., pl.* **-ties. 1.** Moral turpitude or sin; wickedness: *"the human mind, since the Fall, was nothing but a sink of iniquity"* (Henry Fielding). **2.** A grossly immoral act; a sin. [Middle English *iniquite,* from Old French, from Latin *iniquitās* (stem *iniquitāt-*), from *inīquus,* unjust : *in-,* not + *aequus,* just, EQUAL.]
init. initial.

in·i·tial (ĭ-nĭsh′əl) *adj. Abbr.* **init. 1.** Occurring or existing at the beginning or outset; first. **2.** Occurring first in a word, syllable, or the like.
~*n. Abbr.* **init. 1. a.** The first letter of a person's name, used as a shortened signature or for identification. **b. initials.** The first letters of each part of a person's full name, used as a shortened signature or for identification. **2.** The first letter of a word. **3.** A large, often highly decorated letter set at the beginning of a chapter, verse, paragraph, or the like.
~*tr.v.* **initialed, -tialing, -tials.** Also *chiefly British* **-tailled, -tialling.** To mark or sign with one's own initial or initials, especially in order to indicate approval or authorization. [Latin *initiālis,* from *initium,* beginning.] **—in·i·tial·ly** *adv.*

i·ni·tial·ism (ĭ-nĭsh′ə-lĭz′əm) *n.* An abbreviation of a phrase consisting of the initial letter of each word in the phrase; distinguishable from an acronym in that it is not pronounced as a single word; for example **C.I.A., B.B.C.**

in·i·tial·ize (ĭ-nĭsh′ə-līz′) *tr.v.* **-ized, -izing, -izes.** *Computer Science.* To set to a starting position or value. **—in·i·tial·i·za·tion** *n.* **—in·i·tial·iz·er** *n.*

in·i·ti·ate (ĭ-nĭsh′ē-āt′) *tr.v.* **-ated, -ating, -ates. 1.** To begin or originate. **2.** To introduce (a person) to a new field, interest, skill, or the like. **3.** To admit into membership, as with ceremonies or ritual. —See Synonyms at **begin.**
~*adj.* (ĭ-nĭsh′ē-ĭt). Initiated.
~*n.* (ĭ-nĭsh′ē-ĭt). **1.** One who has been initiated. **2.** A novice; beginner. [Latin *initiāre,* from *initium,* beginning. See **initial.**] **—in·i·ti·a·tor** *n.*

in·i·ti·a·tion (ĭ-nĭsh′ē-ā′shən) *n.* **1.** The act of initiating or the fact of being initiated. **2.** A ceremony, ritual, test, or period of instruction by which a new member is admitted to an organization, office, or status or to knowledge.

in·i·ti·a·tive (ĭ-nĭsh′ē-ə-tĭv, -ē′ā-tĭv, -nĭsh′ə-tĭv) *n.* **1. a.** The ability or instinct to initiate and follow through a plan or task; enterprise and determination. **b.** The right or power to initiate: *has the initiative.* **2.** The first step or action; the opening move: *take the initiative; new peace initiatives.* **3. a.** The power or right to introduce a new legislative measure. **b.** The right and procedure by which citizens can propose a law by petition and ensure its submission to the electorate, as in many U.S. states and in Switzerland. **—on one's own initiative.** Without instruction or coercion; unprompted.
~*adj.* **1.** Of, pertaining to, or requiring initiative: *an initiative test.* **2.** Used to initiate; initiatory. **—in·i·ti·a·tive·ly** *adv.*

in·i·ti·a·to·ry (ĭ-nĭsh′ē-ə-tôr′ē, -tōr′ē) *adj.* **1.** Introductory; initial. **2.** Used to initiate; initiative.

inj. injection.

in·ject (ĭn-jĕkt′) *tr.v.* **-jected, -jecting, -jects. 1.** To force or drive (a fluid) into something. **2.** *Medicine.* **a.** To introduce (a fluid) into the skin, subcutaneous tissue, muscle, blood vessels, or a bodily cavity by means of a syringe. **b.** To introduce a fluid into (a part of the body) in this way. **3.** To introduce (a new element) into consideration: *inject a note of humor into the negotiations.* **4.** To place (a satellite, rocket, or the like) in an orbit, trajectory, or stream. [Latin *inicere, injicere* (past participle *injectus*), to throw or put in : *in-,* in + *jacere,* to throw.]

in·ject·a·ble (ĭn-jĕk′tə-bəl) *adj.* Able to be injected. Said of a drug.
~*n.* A drug or medicine that can be injected directly into the bloodstream.

in·jec·tion (ĭn-jĕk′shən) *n. Abbr.* **inj. 1.** The act or an instance of injecting. **2.** A fluid that is injected. **3.** Broadly, anything injected.

injection molding *n.* **1.** A process for making molded articles by forcing a liquid under pressure into a mold. **2.** An article made by such a process.

in·jec·tor (ĭn-jĕk′tər) *n.* **1.** A device used to force water into a steam boiler. **2.** A device for spraying atomized fuel into the combustion chamber of an internal-combustion engine.

in·ju·di·cious (ĭn′jo͞o-dĭsh′əs) *adj.* Lacking judgment or discretion. **—in·ju·di·cious·ly** *adv.* **—in·ju·di·cious·ness** *n.*

In·jun (ĭn′jən) *n. Informal & Regional.* A North American Indian. [Facetious respelling of INDIAN.]

in·junc·tion (ĭn-jŭngk′shən) *n.* **1.** The act of enjoining. **2.** That which is enjoined; a command, directive, or order. **3.** *Law.* A court order enjoining or prohibiting a party from a specific course of action. [Late Latin *injunctiō,* from Latin *injungere* (past participle *injunctus*), to enjoin : *in-,* in + *jungere,* to join.] **—in·junc·tive** *adj.*

in·jure (ĭn′jər) *tr.v.* **-jured, -juring, -jures. 1.** To cause harm or damage to; hurt. **2.** To commit an injustice or offense against; wrong. [Back-formation from INJURY.] **—in·jur·er** *n.*
Synonyms: *damage, harm, hurt, impair, mar, wound.*

in·ju·ri·ous (ĭn-jo͝or′ē-əs) *adj.* **1.** Harmful or damaging. **2.** Slanderous; libelous. **—in·ju·ri·ous·ly** *adv.* **—in·ju·ri·ous·ness** *n.*

in·ju·ry (ĭn′jə-rē) *n., pl.* **-ries. 1.** Damage of or to a person, property, reputation, or thing. **2.** A specific damage or wound: *a leg injury.* **3.** Injustice. **4.** *Law.* Any wrong or damage done to persons, property, reputation, or rights that gives grounds for legal action. —See Synonyms at **injustice.** [Middle English *injurie,* from Norman French, from Latin *injūria,* injustice, wrong, from *injūrius,* unjust, wrongful : *in-,* not + *jūs* (stem *jūr-*), right, law.]

in·jus·tice (ĭn-jŭs′tĭs) *n.* **1.** The fact, practice, or quality of being unjust; lack of justice. **2.** An unjust act; a wrong. [Middle English, from Old French, from Latin *injūstitia,* from *injūstus,* unjust : *in-,* not + *jūstus,* JUST.]
Synonyms: *grievance, injury, wrong.*

ink (ĭngk) *n.* **1.** A pigmented liquid or paste used especially for writing or printing. **2.** A dark liquid secreted by cuttlefish and other cephalopods for protective concealment.
~*tr.v.* **inked, inking, inks.** To mark or stain with ink. **—ink in.** To retrace the pencil lines of (a drawing) in ink. **—ink up.** To put ink onto (a printing machine) to prepare for printing. [Middle English *enke,* from Old French *enke, enque,* from Late Latin *encaustum,* from Greek *enkauston,* purple ink, from *enkaiein,* to paint in encaustic.] **—ink·er** *n.*

In·ka·tha (ĭn-kä′tə) *n.* A Zulu national liberation movement founded in 1928 whose aim is a single multiracial South Africa.

ink·ber·ry (ĭngk′bĕr′ē) *n., pl.* **-ries. 1.** A shrub, *Ilex glabra,* of eastern North America, having black, berrylike fruit. **2. Pokeweed** *(see).* **3.** The fruit of either of these plants.

ink·blot (ĭngk′blŏt′) *n.* **1.** A blotted pattern of spilled ink. **2.** Such a pattern used in the Rorschach test.

ink·horn (ĭngk′hôrn′) *n.* A small container made of horn or similar material, formerly used to hold writing ink.
~*adj.* Pedantic; recondite: *an inkhorn term.*

ink·ling (ĭngk′lĭng) *n.* **1.** A hint or intimation. **2.** A vague idea or notion. [Middle English *inklet,* to mutter.]

ink pad *n.* An ink-soaked cushion used to ink a rubber stamp. Also called "pad."

ink sac *n.* A gland near the anus in an octopus or other cephalopod mollusk that secretes ink.

ink·stand (ĭngk′stănd′) *n.* **1.** A tray or rack for bottles of ink, pens, and other writing implements. **2.** An inkwell.

ink·well (ĭngk′wĕl′) *n.* A small ink reservoir into which a pen is dipped for filling.

ink·y (ĭng′kē) *adj.* **-ier, -iest. 1.** Of or containing ink. **2.** Dark or murky. **3.** Stained or smeared with ink. **—ink·i·ness** *n.*

inky cap *n.* Any of various mushrooms of the genus *Coprinus,* having gills that dissolve into a dark liquid on maturing.

inky cap *A group of mostly edible fungi that grow in open woodlands from spring until autumn and are easily identifiable by their dark caps. This is the shaggy inky cap,* Coprinus comatus, *which is edible and particularly tasty when young.*

inlace. Variant of **enlace.**

in·laid (ĭn′lād′, ĭn-lād′) *adj.* **1.** Set into a surface in a decorative pattern. **2.** Decorated with a pattern set into a surface.

in·land (ĭn′lənd) *adj.* **1.** Of, pertaining to, or located in the interior part of a land mass. **2.** Operating or applying within the borders of a country, region, or state; domestic: *inland trade.*
~*adv.* In, toward, or into the interior of a land mass.
~*n.* (-lănd′, -lənd). The interior of a country, region, or state.

inland drainage *n.* **Internal drainage** *(see).*

Inland Empire. An agricultural region of the northwestern United States between the Cascade Range and the Rocky Mts., comprising portions of eastern Washington, northeastern Oregon, northern Idaho, and western Montana.

in·land·er (ĭn′lən-dər, -lăn′-) *n.* A person who lives in or near the center of a land mass, especially in a large continent such as Australia.

Inland Passage. See **Inside Passage.**

inland sea *n.* An isolated, landlocked expanse of water, with no outlet to the world's main seas.

Inland Sea. An arm of the Pacific Ocean, enclosed by the Japanese islands of Honshu, Shikoku, and Kyushu, except for a narrow channel connecting it to the Sea of Japan. Within it are *c.* 950 small islands, about two-thirds of which form the Inland Sea National Park.

in-law (ĭn′lô′) *n.* Any relative by marriage. [From -IN-LAW.]

-in-law *comb. form.* Indicates relation through marriage; for example, **sister-in-law.**

in·lay (ĭn-lā′, ĭn′lā′) *tr.v.* **-laid, -laying, -lays. 1.** To set (pieces of wood, ivory, or the like) into a surface, usually at the same level, to form a design. **2.** To decorate (a surface) with wood, ivory, or the like.
~*n.* (ĭn′lā′). **1.** An article, material, or substance that has been inlaid. **2.** A design, pattern, or decoration made by inlaying. **3.** *Dentistry.* A solid filling of gold, porcelain, or the like, fitted to a cavity in a tooth and cemented in place. **4.** A piece of tissue, such as bone, surgically inserted into an organ or part to repair a defect. **—in·lay·er** *n.*

in·let (ĭn′lĕt′, -lĭt) *n.* **1.** A relatively narrow channel or pocket of water. **2.** A stream or bay leading inland, as from the ocean; an estuary. **3.** A narrow passage of water between two islands. **4.** An entry or drainage passage, as to a culvert. **5.** Something that is inserted, let in, or inlaid. **6.** A way or means of entering; especially, a valve or part through which a fluid enters a machine, engine, or the like. Also used adjectivally: *inlet manifold; inlet valve.*
~*tr.v.* **inletted, -letting, -lets.** To insert; let in.

in·li·er (ĭn′lī′ər) *n.* An older rock formation completely surrounded by newer strata.

in loc. cit. Variant of **loc. cit.**

in lo·co pa·ren·tis (ĭn lō′kō pə-rĕn′tĭs) *adv. Latin.* In the position or place of a parent.

in·ly (ĭn′lē) *adv. Poetic.* Inwardly.

in·ly·ing (ĭn′lī′ĭng) *adj.* Positioned within or inside.

in·mate (ĭn′māt′) *n.* **1.** A resident in a building or dwelling. **2.** A person confined to an institution such as a prison or mental hospital. [Perhaps INN (influenced by IN) + MATE.]

in me·di·as res (ĭn mā′dē-äs′ rās′; ĭn mē′dē-əs rēz′) *adv. Latin.* Into the middle of things. Used chiefly of the classical literary or dramatic device whereby an author starts a narrative by plunging the audience into the middle of an objective sequence of events. [Taken from the passage *"in medias res . . . auditorem rapit,"* "(the poet) plunges his hearer . . . into the middle of things" (Horace, *Ars Poetica*).]

in me·mo·ri·am (ĭn mə-môr′ē-əm, mə-môr′-) *prep. Latin. Abbr.* **in mem.** In memory of; as a memorial to. Used in epitaphs.

inmesh. Variant of **enmesh.**

in·mi·grant (ĭn′mĭ′grənt) *n.* A person who moves to another area within the same country.

in·mi·gra·tion (ĭn′mĭ-grā′shən) *n.* The movement of people to another area within the same country.

in·most (ĭn′mōst′) *adj.* Innermost.

inn (ĭn) *n.* **1.** A public lodging house serving food and drink to travelers; hotel. **2.** A tavern or restaurant. **3.** *British.* Formerly, a hall of residence for students. [Middle English *inn*, Old English *inn*.]

in·nards (ĭn′ərdz) *pl.n. Informal.* **1.** Internal bodily organs; viscera. **2.** Broadly, any inner parts, as of machinery. [Variant of INWARDS.]

in·nate (ĭ-nāt′, ĭn′āt′) *adj.* **1.** Possessed at birth; inborn. **2.** Possessed as an essential characteristic; inherent. **3.** Of or produced by thought as distinguished from experience: *innate ideas.* [Middle English *innat*, from Latin *innātus*, past participle of *innāscī*, to be born in : *in-*, in + *nāscī*, to be born.] —**in·nate·ly** *adv.* —**in·nate·ness** *n.*

Synonyms: congenital, hereditary, inborn, inbred

in·ner (ĭn′ər) *adj.* **1.** Located further inside: *an inner room.* **2. a.** Occurring within. **b.** Closer to the center; more secret or exclusive: *inner circles of government.* **3.** Less apparent; underlying: *the inner meaning of a poem.* **4.** Pertaining to the soul or mind: *an inner struggle.* **5.** *Chemistry.* Designating a cyclic compound formed by the reaction of one functional group in a molecule with another in the same molecule. [Middle English *inner*, Old English *innera, innra.*]

inner city *n.* The older, central part of a city, especially when characterized by crowded, run-down, low-income districts. —**in·ner·cit·y** *adj.*

in·ner-di·rect·ed (ĭn′ər-dĭ-rĕk′tĭd, -dī-) *adj.* Guided by personal principles rather than those shared by society at large: *an inner-directed personality.* Compare **other-directed.** —**in·ner-di·rec·tion** *n.*

inner ear *n.* The **internal ear** (*see*).

Inner Hebrides. See **Hebrides.**

inner man *n.* The mind, soul, or spirit.

Inner Mon·go·li·an Autonomous Region (mŏng-gō′lē-ən) Autonomous region in northeast China. Since the coming of Communist rule in China in 1949 it has had limited powers of self-government within the Chinese state. Most of the Mongols in China live here, although they form less than 10 percent of the region's population. It comprises largely steppelands and arid near-desert; stock-raising is the chief economic activity. Its capital is Hohhot (Huhehot).

in·ner·most (ĭn′ər-mōst′) *adj.* **1.** Situated or occurring farthest within. **2.** Most intimate: *innermost feelings.*

inner planet *n.* Any of the planets Mercury, Venus, Earth, or Mars, with orbits inside the asteroid belt. Compare **outer planet.**

inner product *n. Mathematics.* **Scalar product** (*see*).

inner space *n.* **1.** Space at or near the earth's surface, especially space beneath the sea. **2.** The subconscious or spiritual part of the self.

Inner Temple *n.* In England, one of the four legal societies forming the **Inns of Court** (*see*).

inner tube *n.* The inflatable rubber tube that fits inside the outer casing of a pneumatic tire.

in·ner·vate (ĭ-nûr′vāt′, ĭn′ər-) *tr.v.* **-vated, -vating, -vates.** **1.** To supply (a bodily part) with nerves. **2.** To stimulate (a nerve or bodily part). [IN- + NERV(E) + -ATE.] —**in·ner·va·tion** *n.*

in·nerve (ĭ-nûrv′) *tr.v.* **-nerved, -nerving, -nerves.** To give nervous energy to; stimulate.

In·ness (ĭn′ĭs), **George** (1825–94). U.S. landscape painter. He began his career as a romantic artist in the manner of the Hudson River School, but later developed a personal style that subordinated details of form and local color to a freer, more intimate atmospheric effect. His best-known work is *Peace and Plenty.*

in·ning (ĭn′ĭng) *n.* **1.** In baseball, one of nine divisions or periods of a regulation game, in which each team has a turn at bat as limited by three outs. **2.** *Archaic.* **a.** The reclamation of flooded or marshy land. **b.** *Often* **innings.** Land that has been reclaimed. [From IN.]

in·nings (ĭn′ĭngz) *n., pl.* **innings. 1.** The period or division of a game of cricket during which one team bats. **2.** The play or the number of runs of a batsman during his turn at batting: *He had a magnificent innings.* **3.** Any period of opportunity and action: *She will get her innings soon.* [From *in* (verb), to go in.]

inn·keep·er (ĭn′kē′pər) *n.* One who owns or manages an inn.

in·no·cence (ĭn′ə-səns) *n.* **1.** The state, quality, or virtue of being innocent. **2.** A plant, **bluets** (*see*).

in·no·cent (ĭn′ə-sənt) *adj.* **1.** Uncorrupted by evil, malice, or wrongdoing; sinless; untainted; pure: *as innocent of evil as a babe.* **2. a.** Not guilty of a specific crime; legally blameless: *found innocent on all charges.* **b.** Not responsible for or guilty of something wrong or unethical: *innocent of negligence.* **3.** Not dangerous or harmful; not serious: *an innocent prank.* **4.** Not experienced or worldly; credulous; naive: *innocent tourists.* **5.** Not exposed to or familiar with something; devoid. Used with *of: innocent of learning.* **6.** Betraying or suggesting no deception or guile; simple; artless: *an innocent smile.* —See Synonyms at **naive.**

~*n.* **1.** A person who is free of evil or sin; one who is pure or

uncorrupted. **2.** A simple, guileless, inexperienced, or unsophisticated person; one who is vulnerable or credulous: *an innocent abroad.* **3.** A very young child. [Middle English, from Old French, from Latin *innocēns* : *in-*, not + *nocēns* (stem *nocent-*), present participle of *nocēre*, to harm, hurt.] —**in·no·cent·ly** *adv.*

Innocent III, Pope, born Lotario di Segni (*c.* 1161–1216). He became pope in 1198. Innocent III raised the papacy to new heights of power through his intervention in European politics. He also organized the Fourth Crusade and the suppression of the Albigenses. His acceptance of St. Dominic and St. Francis of Assisi sanctioned the works of these itinerant preachers.

in·noc·u·ous (ĭ-nŏk′yōō-əs) *adj.* **1.** Having no adverse effect; harmless: *an innocuous snakebite.* **2.** Inoffensive; unobjectionable: *an innocuous speech.* [Latin *innocuus* : *in-*, not + *nocuus*, harmful, from *nocēre*, to harm.] —**in·noc·u·ous·ly** *adv.* —**in·noc·u·ous·ness** *n.*

in·nom·i·nate (ĭ-nŏm′ə-nĭt) *adj.* **1.** Having no specific name. **2.** Anonymous. [Late Latin *innōminātus* : Latin *in-*, not + *nōminātus*, past participle of *nōmināre*, to name, NOMINATE.]

innominate artery *n.* A short artery that arises from the aortic arch and divides in the neck to form the right common carotid and right subcarian arteries.

innominate bone *n. Anatomy.* A large flat bone forming the lateral half of the pelvis, consisting of the fused ilium, ischium, and pubis. Also called "hip bone."

innominate vein *n.* Either of a pair of veins in the neck formed by the union of the internal jugular and subclavian veins. The innominate veins join to form the superior vena cava.

in·no·vate (ĭn′ə-vāt′) *v.* **-vated, -vating, -vates.** —*tr.* To begin or introduce (something new). —*intr.* To begin or introduce something new; be inventive. [Latin *innovāre*, to renew : *in-* (intensive) + *novāre*, to make new, renew, from *novus*, new.] —**in·no·va·tive** *adj.* —**in·no·va·to·ry** *adj.* —**in·no·va·tor** *n.*

in·no·va·tion (ĭn′ə-vā′shən) *n.* **1.** The act of innovating. **2.** That which is newly introduced; a change. —**in·no·va·tion·al** *adj.*

Inns·bruck (ĭnz′brook′). City in western Austria, the capital of Tirol province. It is a popular summer and winter resort and was the site of the 1964 and 1976 Winter Olympics.

Inns of Court *pl.n.* **1.** The four legal societies in England founded at the beginning of the 14th century, consisting of Gray's Inn, Lincoln's Inn, the Inner Temple, and the Middle Temple, which have the exclusive right to grant law students admission to the bar as lawyers. **2.** The buildings housing these societies.

in·nu·en·do (ĭn′yōō-ĕn′dō) *n., pl.* **-does. 1.** An indirect, oblique, or subtle implication, often derogatory in nature. **2.** *Law.* **a.** An interpretation, as in a libel suit, of allegedly libelous or slanderous material. **b.** Any explanation of a word or charge. [Latin *innuendō*, by hinting, from *innuendum*, gerund of *innuere*, to nod to, signal to : *in*, toward + *-nuere*, to nod.]

Innuit. Variant of **Inuit.**

in·nu·mer·a·ble (ĭ-nōō′mər-ə-bəl, ĭ-nyōō′-) *adj.* Also **in·nu·mer·ous** (-mər-əs). Too many to be counted or numbered. —See Synonyms at **infinite.** —**in·nu·mer·a·bil·i·ty, in·nu·mer·a·ble·ness** *n.* —**in·nu·mer·a·bly** *adv.*

in·nu·tri·tion (ĭn′nōō-trĭsh′ən, ĭn′nyōō-, ĭn′yōō-) *n.* Lack of nutrition; poor nourishment. —**in·nu·tri·tious** *adj.*

in·ob·serv·ance (ĭn′əb-zûr′vəns) *n.* **1.** Lack of heed or attention; disregard. **2.** Nonobservance, as of a law or custom. —**in·ob·serv·ant** *adj.*

in·oc·u·la·ble (ĭn-ŏk′yə-lə-bəl) *adj.* **1.** Transmissible by inoculation. **2.** Susceptible to a disease transmitted by inoculation. [From INOCULATE.] —**in·oc·u·la·bil·i·ty** *n.*

in·oc·u·late (ĭ-nŏk′yə-lāt′) *tr.v.* **-lated, -lating, -lates. 1.** To introduce the virus of a disease or other antigenic material into the body of (a person or animal) in order to immunize, cure, or experiment: *inoculated against polio.* **2.** To communicate a disease to by transferring its virus or other causative agent. **3.** To implant (microorganisms or infectious material) into a medium suitable for their growth. **4.** To introduce nitrogen-fixing bacteria or mycorrhizal fungi into (the soil) to enhance plant growth. **5.** To influence (someone) with ideas, opinions, or the like. [Middle English, from Latin *inoculāre*, to engraft : *in-*, in + *oculus*, eye, bud.] —**in·oc·u·la·tive** *adj.* —**in·oc·u·la·tor** *n.*

in·oc·u·la·tion (ĭ-nŏk′yə-lā′shən) *n.* **1.** The act, process, or an instance of inoculating. **2.** Inoculum.

in·oc·u·lum (ĭ-nŏk′yə-ləm) *n.* **1.** The material used in an inoculation. Also called "inoculant," "inoculation." **2.** Fungal spores, bacteria, or other pathogens that initiate an outbreak of plant disease.

in·o·dor·ous (ĭn-ō′də-rəs) *adj.* Having no odor.

in·of·fen·sive (ĭn′ə-fĕn′sĭv) *adj.* Giving no offense; harmless; unobjectionable. —**in·of·fen·sive·ly** *adv.* —**in·of·fen·sive·ness** *n.*

in·of·fi·cious (ĭn′ə-fĭsh′əs) *adj. Law.* Contrary to natural affection or moral duty. Said of a will in which the testator unreasonably disinherits the rightful heirs. [Latin *inofficiōsus* : *in-*, not + *officiōsus*, dutiful, OFFICIOUS.] —**in·of·fi·cious·ly** *adv.*

in·op·er·a·ble (ĭn-ŏp′ər-ə-bəl) *adj.* **1.** Not operable. **2.** Not susceptible to surgery. Said especially of malignant tumors. —**in·op·er·a·bly** *adv.*

in·op·er·a·tive (ĭn-ŏp′ər-ə-tĭv) *adj.* Not working or functioning; not taking effect: *inoperative measures.*

in·op·por·tune (ĭn-ŏp′ər-tōōn′, -tyōōn′) *adj.* Not opportune; ill-timed; inappropriate. —**in·op·por·tune·ly** *adv.* —**in·op·por·tune·ness** *n.*

in·or·di·nate (ĭn-ôrd′n-ĭt) *adj.* **1.** Exceeding reasonable limits; immoderate; unrestrained: *inordinate desires.* **2.** Not regulated; disorderly. —See Synonyms at **excessive.** [Middle English *inordinat,* from Latin *inordinātus* : *in-,* not + *ōrdinātus,* past participle of *ōrdināre,* to set in order, from *ōrdō* (stem *ōrdin-*), order.] **—in·or·di·na·cy, in·or·di·nate·ness** *n.* **—in·or·di·nate·ly** *adv.*

in·or·gan·ic (ĭn′ôr-găn′ĭk) *adj. Abbr.* **inorg. 1. a.** Involving neither organic life nor the products of organic life. **b.** Not composed of organic matter; especially, mineral. **2.** Of or pertaining to the chemistry of noncarbon compounds not usually classified as **organic** *(see).* **3.** Not arising in normal growth; artificial. **4.** Lacking system or structure. **—in·or·gan·i·cal·ly** *adv.*

inorganic chemistry *n.* The branch of chemistry that deals with the formation, structure, and properties of compounds of elements other than carbon, usually considered to include some simple carbon compounds such as carbon dioxide and carbonate salts. Compare **organic chemistry.**

in·os·cu·late (ĭn-ŏs′kyə-lāt′) *v.* **-lated, -lating, -lates.** —*tr.* **1.** To unite (blood vessels, nerve fibers, or ducts) by small openings. **2.** To make continuous; blend (as fibers, for example). —*intr.* **1.** To open into one another. **2.** To unite so as to be continuous; blend. **3.** To communicate by means of small channels or openings. Used of blood vessels, nerve fibers, and the like. [IN- + Latin *ōsculāre,* to provide with an opening, from *ōsculum,* little mouth, opening, diminutive of *ōs,* mouth.] **—in·os·cu·la·tion** *n.*

in·o·si·tol (ĭn-ō′sə-tōl′, -tôl′, -tŏl′) *n.* One of nine isomeric alcohols, $C_6H_6(OH)_6$; especially, one found in plant and animal tissue and classified as a member of the vitamin B complex. [Greek *īs* (genitive *īnos*), tendon, sinew, muscle + -IT(E) + -OL.]

in·o·trop·ic (ē′nə-trō′pĭk, -trŏp′ĭk, ī′nə-) *adj.* Affecting the contraction of muscles, especially heart muscle: *Digitalis is an inotropic drug.* [Greek *īs* (stem *īn-*), tendon + -TROPIC.]

in·pa·tient (ĭn′pā′shənt) *n.* A patient living or staying in a hospital. Compare **outpatient.**

in per·so·nam (ĭn pər-sō′nəm) *adv. Law.* Against a person. Said of a proceeding. Compare **in rem.** [Latin.] **—in per·so·nam** *adj.*

in pet·to (ēn pĕt′tō) *adv.* Secretly; privately. Said of appointments of cardinals by the pope undisclosed in consistory. [Italian, "in the breast."] **—in pet·to** *adj.*

in-phase (ĭn′fāz′) *adj. Physics.* Designating or pertaining to two or more waves, alternating signals, or other periodically varying quantities for which the maximum (and minimum) values of each quantity occur at the same time.

in pos·se (ĭn pŏs′ē) *adj. Latin.* Possible but not actual; potential. Compare **in esse.** [Literally, in possibility.]

in pro·pri·a per·so·na (ĭn prō′prē-ə pûr-sō′nə) *adv. Latin.* In one's own person; in one's self.

in·put (ĭn′po͝ot′) *n.* **1.** Anything put into a system or expended in its operation to achieve a result or output, especially: **a.** Energy, work, or power used to drive a machine. **b.** Current, electromotive force, or power supplied to an electric circuit, network, or device. **c.** Information put into a communications system for transmission or into a data-processing system for processing. **d.** The entirety of basic resources, including materials, equipment, and funds, required to complete a project. **2.** A position, terminal, or station at which any such input enters a system. **3.** Contribution to or participation in a common effort: *a discussion with input from all members of the group.* **4.** Information in general.
∼*tr.v.* **input** or **inputted, -putting, -puts.** To insert (data) into a data-processing system.

in·put-out·put (ĭn′po͝ot-out′po͝ot′) *adj.* **1.** Designating the equipment forming part of a computer system that controls the passage of information into or out of the system. **2.** Concerned with or pertaining to the passage of information into or out of a computer. **2.** Designating an analysis of the input into a system in relation to output, especially in terms of economics.

in·quest (ĭn′kwĕst′) *n.* **1.** A judicial inquiry concerning some matter, usually before a jury; especially, an investigation into the cause of someone's death held before a jury and a coroner. **2.** A jury making such an inquiry. **3.** An investigation. [Middle English *enquest,* from Old French *enqueste,* from Vulgar Latin *inquesta* (unattested), from the feminine past participle of *inquaerere* (unattested), to INQUIRE.]

in·qui·e·tude (ĭn-kwī′ə-to͞od′, -tyo͞od′) *n.* **1.** Restlessness. **2.** Uneasiness; disquietude. [Middle English, from Late Latin *inquiētūdō,* from Latin *inquiētus,* restless : *in-,* not + *quiētus,* QUIET.]

in·qui·line (ĭn′kwə-līn′, -lĭn) *n.* An animal that characteristically lives commensally in the burrow or dwelling place of an animal of another kind. [Latin *inquilīnus,* tenant, dweller.] **—in·qui·line** *adj.* **—in·qui·lin·ism** (ĭn′kwə-lə-nĭz′əm), **in·qui·lin·i·ty** (ĭn′kwə-lĭn′ə-tē) *n.* **—in·qui·lin·ous** (ĭn′kwə-lī′nəs) *adj.*

in·quire (ĭn-kwīr′) *v.* **-quired, -quiring, -quires.** Also **en·quire** (ĕn-). —*intr.* **1. a.** To put a question. **b.** To request information. Used with *about* or *after; inquire after another's health.* **2.** To make an inquiry; look into; investigate. Used with *into.* —*tr.* **1.** To ask about. **2.** To ask: *"I am free to inquire what a work of art means to me"* (Bernard Berenson). —See Synonyms at **ask.** [Middle English *enquiren, enqueren,* from Old French *enquerrer,* from Vulgar Latin *inquaerere* (unattested), variant of Latin *inquīrere* : *in-* (intensive) + *quaerere,* to seek, ask.] **—in·quir·er** *n.* **—in·quir·ing·ly** *adv.*

in·quir·y (ĭn-kwīr′ē, ĭn′kwə-rē) *n., pl.* **-ies.** Also **en·quir·y** (ĕn-, ĕn′-). **1.** The act of inquiring. **2.** A question; query. **3.** A close examination of some matter in a quest for information or truth.

in·qui·si·tion (ĭn′kwə-zĭsh′ən) *n.* **1.** The act of inquiring into a matter; investigation. **2. a.** A judicial inquiry. **b.** The verdict of a judicial inquiry. **3. Inquisition.** A former tribunal in the Roman Catholic Church directed at the suppression and punishment of heresy. See **Spanish Inquisition. 4.** Any inquisitorial investigation or scrutiny. [Middle English *inquisicioun,* from Old French *inquisition,* from Latin *inquīsītiō* (stem *inquīsītiōn-*), from *inquīrere* (past participle *inquīsītus*), to INQUIRE.] **—in·qui·si·tion·al** *adj.*

in·quis·i·tive (ĭn-kwĭz′ə-tĭv) *adj.* **1.** Unduly curious and inquiring; prying. **2.** Eager to learn. —See Usage note at **curious. —in·quis·i·tive·ly** *adv.* **—in·quis·i·tive·ness** *n.*

in·quis·i·tor (ĭn-kwĭz′ə-tər) *n.* **1.** One who enquires; a questioner. **2.** One who investigates officially. **3. Inquisitor.** A member of the Inquisition.

in·quis·i·to·ri·al (ĭn-kwĭz′ə-tôr′ē-əl, -tōr′ē-əl) *adj.* **1.** Pertaining to, resembling, or having the function of an inquisitor. **2.** *Law.* Designating a form of criminal procedure, often conducted in secrecy, in which one party acts as both prosecutor and judge. Compare **accusatorial. 3.** Involving or imposing browbeating interrogation. **—in·quis·i·to·ri·al·ly** *adv.*

in re (ĭn rē′) *prep. Law.* In the matter or case of; with regard to. [Latin.]

in rem (ĭn rĕm′) *adv. Law.* Against a thing, as a property, status, or right. Compare **in personam.** [Latin.] **—in rem** *adj.*

I.N.R.I. Jesus of Nazareth, King of the Jews. Used as an inscription on a crucifix. [Latin *Iesus Nazarenus Rex Iudaeorum.*]

in·road (ĭn′rōd′) *n.* **1.** A hostile invasion; raid; incursion. **2.** *Often* **inroads.** An encroachment; an intrusion: *Her work made inroads on her free time.* [IN + ROAD (obsolete sense "raid").]

in·rush (ĭn′rŭsh′) *n.* A sudden rushing in; an irruption; influx.

ins. 1. inspector. **2.** insulated; insulation. **3.** insurance.

in·sal·i·vate (ĭn-săl′ə-vāt′) *tr.v.* **-vated, -vating, -vates.** To mix (food) with saliva in chewing. **—in·sal·i·va·tion** *n.*

in·sa·lu·bri·ous (ĭn′sə-lo͞o′brē-əs) *adj.* Not salubrious; unhealthy: *an insalubrious climate.* **—in·sa·lu·bri·ty** *n.*

in·sane (ĭn-sān′) *adj.* **1.** Of, exhibiting, or suffering from insanity. **2.** Characteristic of, used by, or for the insane. **3.** Very foolish; rash; wild. [Latin *insānus* : *in-,* not + *sānus,* SANE.] **—in·sane·ly** *adv.* **—in·sane·ness** *n.*

in·san·i·tar·y (ĭn-săn′ə-tĕr′ē) *adj.* Not sanitary; unhealthy: *insanitary conditions.*

in·san·i·ty (ĭn-săn′ə-tē) *n., pl.* **-ties. 1.** Persistent mental disorder or derangement. **2.** Unsoundness of mind sufficient to exempt a person from legal responsibility for his actions. **3. a.** Extreme foolishness; total folly. **b.** Something foolish.
Synonyms: *dementia, lunacy, madness, mania.*

in·sa·tia·ble (ĭn-sā′shə-bəl, -shē-ə-bəl) *adj.* Incapable of being satiated or satisfied: *an insatiable lust for power.* [Middle English *insaciable,* from Old French, from Latin *insatiābilis* : *in-,* not + *satiāre,* to SATIATE.] **—in·sa·tia·bil·i·ty, in·sa·tia·ble·ness** *n.* **—in·sa·tia·bly** *adv.*

in·sa·ti·ate (ĭn-sā′shē-ĭt) *adj.* Not satisfied; never satisfied; insatiable. **—in·sa·ti·ate·ly** *adv.* **—in·sa·ti·ate·ness** *n.*

in·scribe (ĭn-skrīb′) *tr.v.* **-scribed, -scribing, -scribes. 1.** To write, print, carve, or engrave (words or letters) on or in a paper, stone, wood, or other surface. **2.** To mark or engrave (a surface) with words or letters. **3.** To enter (a name) on a list or in a register. **4.** To write an inscription, such as a message or autograph, on (a book or photograph, for example) as an informal dedication to another. **5.** *Geometry.* To enclose (a polygon or polyhedron) within a closed configuration of lines, curves, or surfaces so that every vertex of the enclosed figure is incident on the enclosing configuration. **6.** *British.* To issue (loan stocks) in the form of shares whose holders' names are registered: *inscribed securities.* [Latin *inscrībere* : *in-,* in + *scrībere,* to write.] **—in·scrib·a·ble** *adj.* **—in·scrib·er** *n.*

in·scrip·tion (ĭn-skrĭp′shən) *n.* **1.** The act or an instance of inscribing. **2.** That which is inscribed, such as the wording on a coin or monument, or a dedication of a book or work of art. [Middle English *inscripcioun,* from Latin *inscriptiō* (stem *inscriptiōn-*), a writing in or upon, from *inscrībere* (past participle *inscriptus*), to INSCRIBE.] **—in·scrip·tion·al, in·scrip·tive** *adj.* **—in·scrip·tive·ly** *adv.*

in·scru·ta·ble (ĭn-skro͞o′tə-bəl) *adj.* Not able to be fathomed or understood; impenetrable; enigmatic: *an inscrutable look.* **—in·scru·ta·bil·i·ty, in·scru·ta·ble·ness** *n.* **—in·scru·ta·bly** *adv.*

in·sect (ĭn′sĕkt′) *n.* **1.** Any of numerous usually small invertebrate animals of the class Insecta (or Hexapoda), having an adult stage characterized by three pairs of legs, a segmented body with three major divisions, and usually two pairs of wings. **2.** Loosely, any of various similar invertebrate animals such as the spider, centipede, or tick. **3.** One who is small or contemptible. [Latin *insectum (animale),* "segmented (animal)" (translation of Greek *entomon;* see **entomo-**), from *insectus,* past participle of *insecāre,* to cut into : *in-,* in + *secāre,* to cut.] See feature, next page.

in·sec·tar·i·um (ĭn′sĕk-târ′ē-əm) *n., pl.* **-ums** or **-ia** (-ē-ə). Also **in·sec·tar·y** (ĭn′sĕk-tĕr′ē) *pl.* **-ies.** A place in which living insects are kept or bred.

in·sec·ti·cide (ĭn-sĕk′tə-sīd′) *n.* A substance used to kill insects. **—in·sec·ti·ci·dal** (ĭn-sĕk′tə-sīd′l) *adj.*

in·sec·ti·vore (ĭn-sĕk′tə-vôr′, -vōr′) *n.* **1.** Any of various mammals of the order Insectivora, characteristically feeding on insects, and including the shrews, moles, and hedgehogs. **2.** An organism that feeds on insects. [New Latin *Insectivora* (order) : Latin *insectum,* INSECT + *-vorus,* -VOROUS.]

in·sec·tiv·o·rous (ĭn′sĕk-tĭv′ər-əs) *adj.* **1.** Feeding on insects.

insect

CREATURES WHOSE NUMBERS DOMINATE THE EARTH
The common features of a million diverse species

More than three-quarters of the known living species of animal are insects. Nearly a million species have so far been named throughout the world, and there may be millions more species still to be discovered, chiefly in the tropics. The name insect means "segmented." An insect's body is made up of three parts: the head, the thorax, which is composed of 3 segments, and the abdomen, which has 11 segments. On the thorax are wings and three pairs of legs.

Apart from these common features, insects are a widely varied class. They range in size from the microscopic feather-winged beetles to the Goliath beetle of West Africa, which is nearly 150 millimeters (6 inches) long. Most species are less than 6 millimeters (¼ inch) long.

Their methods of reproduction are sexual but very diverse. Their lifespan varies from as little as two hours for an adult mayfly to more than 15 years for a queen ant. Among the most familiar insects are beetles, butterflies, moths, ants, bees, wasps, grasshoppers, and flies.

Most insects use their six legs for crawling, but some use the first pair of legs to grab their prey. Some aquatic insects have legs modified for swimming, for example the flattened "oars" of water boatmen. The speed at which insect species use their wings varies widely. The gently fluttering butterfly beats its wings only ten times a second, but the mosquito's wingbeats are so rapid—about 300 a second—that they cause a high-pitched hum.

AN INSECT'S SUIT OF ARMOR

The insect's body is made up of sections covered by a hard outer skeleton, like a suit of armor. The eye is made up of thousands of lenses each of which picks up part of a scene to register on the insect's brain as an image made up of dots.

HOW AN INSECT SEES

One eye unit

Lens concentrates light on retinal rod

Screen of pigment isolates each unit from its neighbors

Lens

Retina

Retinal rod creates image

Nerve fiber takes image to brain

Mosaic of thousands of eye units

THE LIFE CYCLE OF A FLY

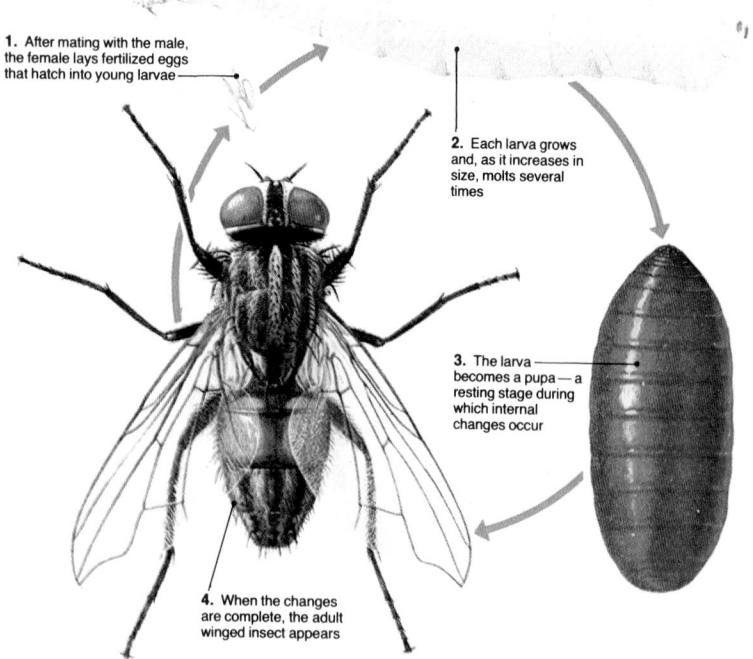

1. After mating with the male, the female lays fertilized eggs that hatch into young larvae

2. Each larva grows and, as it increases in size, molts several times

3. The larva becomes a pupa—a resting stage during which internal changes occur

4. When the changes are complete, the adult winged insect appears

A fly exists in four stages: egg, larva, pupa, and adult insect. Because its skin does not stretch, a growing larva sheds its skin several times; it emerges each time larger and with a new skin.

2. *Botany.* Capable of trapping and absorbing insects, as the pitcher plant or Venus's flytrap. [INSECT + -VOROUS.]

insectivorous bat *n.* Any of various bats of the suborder Microchiroptera, characteristically having large ears and feeding on insects.

in·se·cure (ĭn′sĭ-kyŏŏr′) *adj.* **1.** Not secure or safe; inadequately guarded or protected. **2.** Not firm or firmly fixed; unstable; shaky.

3. Apprehensive or lacking self-confidence: *felt insecure in company.* —**in·se·cure·ly** *adv.* —**in·se·cu·ri·ty, in·se·cure·ness** *n.*

in·sel·berg (ĭn′zəl-bûrg′) *n.* A domed hill or hard rock rising steeply from the surrounding region. [German : *Insel*, island + *Berg*, mountain.]

in·sem·i·nate (ĭn-sĕm′ə-nāt′) *tr.v.* **-nated, -nating, -nates.** **1.** To sow seed in. **2.** To introduce semen into the uterus of. **3.** To introduce (ideas) into the mind of another. [Latin *insēminīre : in-,* in + *sēminīre,* to plant, from *sēmen* (stem *sēmin-*), seed, SEMEN.] —**in·sem·i·na·tion** *n.* —**in·sem·i·na·tor** *n.*

in·sen·sate (ĭn-sĕn′sāt′, -sĭt) *adj.* **1. a.** Lacking sensation; inanimate. **b.** Unconscious. **2.** Lacking sensibility; inhuman; unfeeling. **3.** Lacking sense; foolish. —**in·sen·sate·ly** *adv.*

in·sen·si·ble (ĭn-sĕn′sə-bəl) *adj.* **1.** Deprived of the power of feeling; unconscious. **2.** Imperceptible; inappreciable: *an insensible change.* **3. a.** Insusceptible; unaffected: *insensible to the cold.* **b.** Unaware; unmindful: *I am not insensible of your concern.* **c.** Not emotionally affected; unfeeling; indifferent: *insensible to their cries of pain.* **4.** *Archaic.* Lacking intelligence; irrational. —**in·sen·si·bil·i·ty** *n.* —**in·sen·si·bly** *adv.*

in·sen·si·tive (ĭn-sĕn′sə-tĭv) *adj.* **1.** Lacking sensation; not physically sensitive. **2.** Lacking sensitivity; unfeeling, unresponsive, or tactless. —**in·sen·si·tiv·i·ty, in·sen·si·tive·ness** *n.* —**in·sen·si·tive·ly** *adv.*

in·sen·ti·ent (ĭn-sĕn′shənt) *adj.* Without sensation or consciousness; inanimate. —**in·sen·ti·ence** *n.*

in·sep·a·ra·ble (ĭn-sĕp′ər-ə-bəl) *adj.* **1.** Incapable of being separated. **2.** Always together; intimate. —**in·sep·a·ra·bil·i·ty, in·sep·a·ra·ble·ness** *n.* —**in·sep·a·ra·bly** *adv.*

in·sert (ĭn-sûrt′) *tr.v.* **-serted, -serting, -serts.** **1.** To put or set into, between, or among another or other things. **2.** To introduce into the body or text of something; interpolate.
~*n.* (ĭn′sûrt). Something inserted; especially, printed material, such as a map or advertising feature, inserted in a book or magazine. [Latin *inserere* (past participle *insertus) : in-,* in + *serere,* to sow, plant.] —**in·sert·er** *n.*

in·sert·ed (ĭn-sûr′tĭd) *adj.* **1.** Joined to another part, as stamens to a corolla. **2.** *Anatomy.* Attached to the bone or other part that it moves. Said of a muscle.

in·ser·tion (ĭn-sûr′shən) *n.* **1.** The act of inserting. **2.** Something inserted, such as an advertisement in a newspaper. **3.** *Anatomy.* A point or mode of attachment of a muscle to a bone. **4.** A strip of lace, embroidery, or other trimming to be inserted in a garment, tablecloth, or the like. **5.** *Botany.* The point at which one part is attached to another. —**in·ser·tion·al** *adj.*

in·ser·vice (ĭn′sûr′vĭs) *adj.* Occurring while one is employed or in the context of one's work: *in-service training.*

in·ses·so·ri·al (ĭn′sə-sôr′ē-əl, -sōr′ē-əl) *adj. Rare.* Perching or adapted for perching: *insessorial claws.* [Late Latin *insessor,* "one that perches," from Latin *insidēre* (past participle *insessus*), to sit upon : *in-,* on + *sedēre,* to sit.]

in·set (ĭn-sĕt′) *tr.v.* **-set, -setting, -sets.** To insert; set in.
~*n.* (ĭn′sĕt). **1.** Something set in, as: **a.** A small map or illustration set within a larger one. **b.** A leaf or group of pages inserted in a publication. **c.** A piece of material set into a dress as trimming. **2.** An inflow, as of water.

in·shore (ĭn′shôr′, -shōr′) *adj.* **1.** Situated or taking place close to the shore. **2.** Coming toward the shore. —**in·shore** *adv.*

inshrine. Variant of **enshrine.**

in·side (ĭn-sīd′, ĭn′sīd′) *n.* **1.** The inner or interior part. **2.** An inner side or surface. **3.** The middle part; the part away from the edge: *the inside of the path.* **4. insides.** *Informal.* **a.** The inner organs; the entrails. **b.** The inner parts or workings. **5.** A position affording access to exclusive or confidential information. —**inside out. 1.** With the inner surface turned out; reversed. **2.** Completely; thoroughly: *knows her subject inside out.* —**on the inside.** In a position of confidence or influence.
~*adj.* **1.** Situated within; interior. **2.** For the interior. **3.** Involving or coming from those having access to exclusive knowledge: *inside information.* **4.** *Baseball.* Passing too near the body of the batter. Said of a pitch.
~*adv.* (ĭn-sīd′). **1.** Into or in the interior; within. **2.** *British Slang.* In or into prison. **3.** In one's inner feelings or nature: *made me feel good inside.*
~*prep.* (ĭn-sīd′). **1. a.** Within: *inside an hour.* **b.** Less than: *His running time is well inside the record.* **2.** Into: *to go inside the house.* —**inside of.** Within the boundaries or limits of.

inside job *n.* A crime committed by, or with the complicity of, someone who works or lives where the crime is committed.

Inside Passage. Also **In·land Passage** (ĭn′land). Natural, protected waterway, *c.* 1,530 kilometers (950 miles) long, off the coast of British Columbia and southeast Alaska. Its scenic wonders include snow-capped mountains, waterfalls, glaciers, and narrow channels.

in·sid·er (ĭn-sī′dər) *n.* **1.** An accepted member of a clique. **2.** One who has access to exclusive or confidential information.

inside track *n.* **1.** In a curved race track, the path next to the inner rail. **2.** An advantageous position in a competition.

in·sid·i·ous (ĭn-sĭd′ē-əs) *adj.* **1.** Working or spreading harmfully in a subtle or stealthy manner: *insidious disease.* **2.** Intended or seeking to entrap with guile: *insidious argument.* **3.** Wily; treacherous. [Latin *insidiōsus,* "lying in wait for," from *insidiae,* ambush, from *insidēre,* to sit in or on, lie in wait for. See **insessorial.**] **—in·sid·i·ous·ly** *adv.* **—in·sid·i·ous·ness** *n.*

in·sight (ĭn′sīt′) *n.* **1.** The capacity to discern the true nature of a situation; penetration. **2.** An elucidating glimpse. **3.** *Psychology.* **a.** In behavioral studies, the sudden perception by an animal of a solution to a problem or difficulty. **b.** In psychoanalysis, a patient's perception of his own mental condition.

in·sight·ful (ĭn′sīt′fəl, ĭn-sīt′-) *adj.* Showing or having insight; perceptive. **—in·sight·ful·ly** *adv.*

in·sig·ni·a (ĭn-sĭg′nē-ə) *n., pl.* **insignia** or **-as.** Also **in·sig·ne** (-nē). **1.** A badge of office, rank, membership, or nationality; an emblem. **2.** A distinguishing sign: *the insignia of success.* [Latin, plural of *insigne,* sign, mark, from *insignis,* distinguished, marked : *in-,* in + *signum,* SIGN.]

Usage: This word is now generally used as a singular, with plural forms being either *insignia* or *insignias.* The original singular, *insigne,* is rare and is restricted to technical contexts.

in·sig·nif·i·cant (ĭn′sĭg-nĭf′ĭ-kənt) *adj.* **1. a.** Trivial; unimportant. **b.** Lacking significant features or character. **c.** Contemptible. **2.** Small; trifling. **—in·sig·nif·i·cance, in·sig·nif·i·can·cy** *n.* **—in·sig·nif·i·cant·ly** *adv.*

in·sin·cere (ĭn′sĭn-sîr′) *adj.* Not sincere; hypocritical. **—in·sin·cere·ly** *adv.* **—in·sin·cer·i·ty** (ĭn′sĭn-sĕr′ə-tē) *n.*

in·sin·u·ate (ĭn-sĭn′yo͞o-āt′) *v.* **-ated, -ating, -ates.** *—tr.* **1.** To introduce gradually, subtly, artfully, or insidiously. **2.** To convey or imply with oblique hints and allusions; hint covertly: *insinuated that I wasn't telling the truth.* *—intr.* To make insinuations. —See Synonyms at **suggest.** [Latin *insinuāre,* to wind one's way into : *in-,* in + *sinuāre,* to curve, from *sinus,* curve, SINUS.] **—in·sin·u·a·tive** *adj.* **—in·sin·u·a·tor** *n.*

in·sin·u·at·ing (ĭn-sĭn′yo͞o-ā′tĭng) *adj.* **1.** Provoking gradual doubt or suspicion; suggestive: *insinuating remarks.* **2.** Ingratiating: *a silky insinuating voice.* **—in·sin·u·at·ing·ly** *adv.*

in·sin·u·a·tion (ĭn-sĭn′yo͞o-ā′shən) *n.* **1.** The act or practice of insinuating. **2.** An artfully indirect suggestion.

in·sip·id (ĭn-sĭp′ĭd) *adj.* **1.** Lacking flavor or zest; unpalatable: *insipid food.* **2.** Lacking excitement or the ability to excite; spiritless; dull; unstimulating: *an insipid character.* [Late Latin *insipidus* : Latin *in-,* not + *sapidus,* SAPID.] **—in·si·pid·i·ty** (ĭn′sĭ-pĭd′ə-tē), **in·sip·id·ness** *n.* **—in·sip·id·ly** *adv.*

in·sist (ĭn-sĭst′) *v.* **-sisted, -sisting, -sists.** *—intr.* To emphasize or keep resolutely to an assertion, demand, or course of action. Usually used with *on* or *upon*: *insisted on her rights*; *insisted on paying the bill.* *—tr.* To assert or demand positively and persistently: *He insisted that he was right.* [Latin *insistere,* to stand on, persist : *in-,* on + *sistere,* to cause to stand, stand firm.] **—in·sis·tence, in·sis·ten·cy** *n.*

in·sis·tent (ĭn-sĭs′tənt) *adj.* **1.** Persistent; pertinacious. **2.** Demanding notice: *insistent hunger.* **—in·sis·tent·ly** *adv.*

in si·tu (ĭn sī′to͞o, sĭt′o͞o) *adv. Latin.* In (its original) place.

insnare. Variant of **ensnare.**

in·so·bri·e·ty (ĭn′sə-brī′ə-tē) *n.* Lack of sobriety; intemperance.

in·so·far (ĭn′sō-fär′) *adv.* To such an extent.

Usage: The writing of this form as a single word, followed by *as,* is now widespread, though it is still criticized by traditionalist writers on usage, who recommend separate words: *in so far as.*

insofar as *conj.* To the extent that.

in·so·late (ĭn′sō-lāt′) *tr.v.* **-lated, -lating, -lates.** To expose to sunlight, as for bleaching. [Latin *insōlāre* : *in-,* in + *sōl,* sun.]

in·so·la·tion (ĭn′sō-lā′shən) *n.* **1.** Exposure to sunlight, as for therapeutic purposes. **2. Sunstroke** *(see).* **3. a.** The solar radiation falling on the earth or another planet. **b.** The rate of delivery of such radiation per unit surface area.

in·sole (ĭn′sōl′) *n.* **1.** The inner sole of a shoe or boot. **2.** An extra strip of material put inside a shoe for comfort or protection.

in·so·lence (ĭn′sə-ləns) *n.* **1.** The quality of being insolent. **2.** An instance of insolent behavior.

in·so·lent (ĭn′sə-lənt) *adj.* **1.** Presumptuous and insulting in manner or speech; arrogant. **2.** Audaciously impudent; impertinent. [Middle English, from Latin *insolēns,* perhaps originally "unusual," "quaint" : *in-,* not + *solēns* (stem *solent-*), present participle of *solēre,* to use (see **obsolete**).] **—in·so·lent·ly** *adv.*

in·sol·u·ble (ĭn-sŏl′yə-bəl) *adj.* **1. a.** Incapable of being dissolved in water. **b.** Incapable of being dissolved in the specified solvent. **2.** Not able to be solved or explained. [Middle English *insolible,* from Latin *insolūbilis* : *in-,* not + *solvere,* to SOLVE.] **—in·sol·u·bil·i·ty, in·sol·u·ble·ness** *n.* **—in·sol·u·bly** *adv.*

in·solv·a·ble (ĭn-sŏl′və-bəl) *adj.* Incapable of being solved. **—in·solv·a·bil·i·ty** *n.* **—in·solv·a·bly** *adv.*

in·sol·vent (ĭn-sŏl′vənt) *adj.* **1.** Unable to meet debts or discharge liabilities; bankrupt. **2.** Pertaining to bankruptcy or bankrupt persons.

∼n. One who is insolvent. **—in·sol·ven·cy** *n.*

in·som·ni·a (ĭn-sŏm′nē-ə) *n.* Chronic inability to sleep. [Latin, from *insomnis,* sleepless : *in-,* not + *somnus,* sleep.] **—in·som·ni·ous** *adj.*

in·som·ni·ac (ĭn-sŏm′nē-ăk′) *n.* A person suffering from insomnia.

∼adj. Causing or exhibiting insomnia.

in·so·much as (ĭn′sō-mŭch′ăz′) *conj.* **1.** To such extent or degree. **2.** Since; inasmuch. [Middle English *in so muche,* translation of Old French *en tant (que).*]

in·sou·ci·ance (ĭn-so͞o′sē-əns) *n.* Lack of concern; lighthearted indifference.

in·sou·ci·ant (ĭn-so͞o′sē-ənt) *adj.* Blithely indifferent; carefree. [French : *in-,* not + *souciant,* present participle of *soucier,* to trouble, upset (reflexively, "to care"), from Latin *sollicitāre,* to agitate, vex (see **solicit**).] **—in·sou·ci·ant·ly** *adv.*

insoul. Variant of **ensoul.**

insp. inspector.

in·span (ĭn-spăn′, ĭn′spăn′) *v.* **-spanned, -spanning, -spans.** *Chiefly South African.* *—tr.* **1.** To harness (a draft animal) as to a wagon. **2.** To prepare (a wagon, for example) for a journey. *—intr.* **1.** To inspan a draft animal. **2.** To prepare for a journey, as by making a wagon ready. [Afrikaans, from Middle Dutch *inspannen,* from *spannen,* to yoke.]

in·spect (ĭn-spĕkt′) *tr.v.* **-spected, -specting, -spects.** **1.** To examine carefully and critically, especially for flaws. **2.** To review or examine officially: *inspecting the troops.* [Latin *inspectāre,* frequentative of *inspicere* (past participle *inspectus*), to look into : *in-,* in + *specere,* to look.] **—in·spect·ive** *adj.*

in·spec·tion (ĭn-spĕk′shən) *n.* **1.** The act of inspecting. **2.** An examination, scrutiny, or review, especially one of a formal or official character: *an inspection of the troops.* **—in·spec·tion·al** *adj.*

in·spec·tor (ĭn-spĕk′tər) *n. Abbr.* **ins., insp.** **1.** One who inspects; especially, an official whose job it is to examine and supervise the running of a particular operation, institution, or organization, and to ensure that the appropriate rules and standards are maintained. **2.** A police officer of the rank next below superintendent and above sergeant. **—in·spec·to·ral, in·spec·to·ri·al** (ĭn′spĕk-tôr′ē-əl, -tōr′ē-əl) *adj.* **—in·spec·tor·ship** *n.*

in·spec·tor·ate (ĭn-spĕk′tər-ĭt) *n.* **1.** The office or duties of an inspector. **2.** A staff of inspectors. **3.** An inspector's district.

inspector general *n., pl.* **inspectors general.** **1.** A person in charge of a staff of inspectors or a system of inspection. **2.** An officer having investigative powers in the armed forces.

insphere. Variant of **ensphere.**

in·spi·ra·tion (ĭn′spə-rā′shən) *n.* **1.** Stimulation of the mental or emotional faculties to a high level of feeling, animation, or creative activity. **2.** The condition of being so stimulated. **3.** Someone or something perceived as the source of such stimulation: *His example was an inspiration to us all.* **4.** Something that is inspired, such as an idea or action. **5.** *Theology.* Divine guidance or influence exerted directly upon the mind and soul of humankind. **6.** The act of breathing in; inhalation.

in·spi·ra·tion·al (ĭn′spə-rā′shən-əl) *adj.* **1.** Of or pertaining to inspiration. **2.** Providing or intended to convey inspiration. **3.** Resulting from inspiration. **—in·spi·ra·tion·al·ly** *adv.*

in·spi·ra·tor (ĭn′spə-rā′tər) *n.* **1.** An inhaler. **2.** A respirator.

in·spir·a·to·ry (ĭn-spīr′ə-tôr′ē, -tōr′ē) *adj.* Pertaining to or used for the drawing in of air.

in·spire (ĭn-spīr′) *v.* **-spired, -spiring, -spires.** *—tr.* **1.** To animate the mind or emotions of; serve as a source of inspiration to: *inspired by his rousing speech.* **2.** To stimulate or impel to a particular feeling or action: *inspired her to be brave.* **3. a.** To elicit; bring forth: *a woman capable of inspiring love.* **b.** To suggest or bring about; serve as a source of inspiration for: *a whole poem inspired by that fleeting smile.* **4. a.** To affect, guide, or arouse by divine influence. **b.** To communicate by divine influence: *oratory inspired by God.* **5.** To inhale (air). **6.** *Archaic.* **a.** To breathe upon. **b.** To breathe life into. *—intr.* **1.** To rouse latent energies, ideals, or reverence. **2.** To inhale. [Middle English *inspiren,* from Old French *inspirer,* from Latin *inspīrāre,* to breathe into : *in-,* into + *spīrāre,* to breathe.] **—in·spir·er** *n.* **—in·spir·ing·ly** *adv.*

in·spired (ĭn-spīrd′) *adj.* Resulting from or as if from inspiration: *an inspired guess; an inspired performance.*

in·spir·it (ĭn-spĭr′ĭt) *tr.v.* **-ited, -iting, -its.** To instill courage or life into; animate; enliven.

in·spis·sate (ĭn-spĭs′āt′, ĭn′spĭ-sāt′) *v.* **-sated, -sating, -sates.** *—tr.* To cause to thicken, as by boiling or evaporation; condense. *—intr.* To thicken. [Late Latin *inspissāre* : Latin *in-* (intensive) + *spissāre,* to thicken, from *spissus*†, thick.] **—in·spis·sa·tion** *n.* **—in·spis·sa·tor** (ĭn-spĭs′ā′tər) *n.*

inst. **1.** instance. **2.** instant. **3.** institute; institution. **4.** instrument.

Inst. institute; institution.

in·sta·bil·i·ty (ĭn′stə-bĭl′ə-tē) *n., pl.* **-ties.** Lack of stability, firmness, or steadiness: *emotional instability.*

in·stall, in·stal (ĭn-stôl′) *tr.v.* **-stalled, -stalling, -stalls** or **-stals.** **1.** To set (a machine, for example) in position and connect or adjust for use. **2.** To put in an office, rank, or position, especially with ceremonies. **3.** To settle in the place or condition specified; establish. Often used reflexively: *He installed himself by the window.* [Old French *installer,* from Medieval Latin *installāre* : *in-* (causative) + *stallum,* place, stall.] **—in·stall·er** *n.*

in·stal·la·tion (ĭn′stə-lā′shən) *n.* **1.** The act of installing or the state of being installed. **2.** A system of machinery or other apparatus set up for use. **3.** A military base or camp.

in·stall·ment[1], **in·stal·ment** (ĭn-stôl′mənt) *n.* **1.** One of several successive payments in settlement of a debt. **2.** A portion of anything issued at intervals. **3.** A chapter, episode, or part of a work presented serially. [Variant of earlier *estallment,* from Norman French *estalement,* from *estaler,* to fix (as payments), from *estal,* place, fixed position, from Old High German *stal,* place, stall.]

installment[2], **instalment** *n.* The act of installing (sense 2) or state of being installed.

installment plan *n.* A credit system by which payment for merchandise is made in installments over a fixed period of time.

in·stance (ĭn′stəns) *n. Abbr.* **inst.** **1.** A case or example. **2.** A legal

PRONUNCIATION KEY

ă, pat; ā, pay; âr, care; ä, father, are; b, bib; ch, church; d, deed; ĕ, pet; ē, be; f, fife; g, gag; h, hat; hw, which; ĭ, pit; ī, pie; îr, pier; j, judge; k, kick; l, lid, needle; m, mum; n, no, sudden; ng, thing; ŏ, pot; ō, toe; ô, paw, for; oi, noise; ou, out; o͝o, book; o͞o, boot; p, pop; r, roar; s, sauce; sh, ship, dish; t, tight; th, thin, path; *th,* this, bathe; ŭ, cut; ûr, fur; v, valve; w, with; y, yes; z, zebra, size; zh, vision; ə, about, item, edible, gallop, circus, peaceful

IN FOREIGN WORDS:

à, *Fr.* ami; œ, *Fr.* feu, *Ger.* schön; ü, *Fr.* tu, *Ger.* über; KH, *Ger.* ich, *Scot.* loch; N, *Fr.* bon; y′, *Fr.* Compiègne

STRESS MARKS:

Primary stress: ′ in·cite′ (ĭn-sīt′)
Secondary stress: ′ in′sight′ (ĭn′sīt′)

proceeding or process; a suit: *a court of first instance.* **3.** A specified step in a procedure or list of considerations: *Apply in the first instance to the personnel manager.* **4. a.** Prompting; request: *He called at the instance of his wife.* **b.** *Archaic.* Urgent solicitation. —See Synonyms at **example.** —**for instance.** For example.
~*tr.v.* **instanced, -stancing, -stances.** **1.** To offer as an example; cite. **2.** To demonstrate or show by being an example of; exemplify. [Middle English *instaunce,* from Old French *instance,* from Latin *instantia,* presence, perseverance, urgency, from *instāns,* INSTANT.]
in·stan·cy (ĭn′stən-sē) *n.* **1.** Urgency. **2.** *Rare.* Immediateness.
in·stant (ĭn′stənt) *n. Abbr.* **inst.** **1.** A very brief time; a moment: *He arrived in an instant.* **2.** A particular point in time: *the instant she arrives.* —See Synonyms at **moment.**
~*adj. Abbr.* **inst.** **1.** Immediate: *instant attention.* **2.** Imperative; urgent: *an instant need.* **3.** Of the current month: *my letter of the fifth instant.* Compare **proximo, ultimo.** **4.** Prepared or devised so as to be made usable or accessible rapidly and with minimal effort: *instant soup; instant history.*
~*adv. Poetic.* Instantly. [Middle English, urgent, immediate, from Old French, from Latin *instāns* (stem *instant-*), present participle of *instāre,* to stand upon, be present, persist : *in-,* upon + *stāre,* to stand.]
in·stan·ta·ne·ous (ĭn′stən-tā′nē-əs) *adj.* **1.** Occurring or completed without perceptible delay. **2.** Occurring or applying at a specific instance of time. Said of changing physical quantities that are considered at a given instance: *instantaneous pressure.* [Medieval Latin *instantāneus,* from Latin *instāns,* urgent. INSTANT.] —**in·stan·ta·ne·ous·ly** *adv.* —**in·stan·ta·ne·ous·ness** *n.*
in·stan·ter (ĭn-stăn′tər) *adv.* Instantly. [Medieval Latin, from Latin, urgently, from *instāns,* urgent, INSTANT.]
in·stant·ly (ĭn′stənt-lē) *adv.* **1.** At once. **2.** *Archaic.* Urgently. —See Synonyms at **immediately.**
~*conj.* As soon as: *tell me instantly she comes.*
instant replay *n.* A recording of an event, such as a sports play, on videotape for playback, especially in slow motion, as soon as the event is completed. Also *British* "action replay."
in·star (ĭn′stär) *n.* **1.** An insect or other arthropod between molts, as during metamorphosis. **2.** This stage of development. [New Latin, from Latin *instar*†, form, likeness (referring to the successive forms of the arthropod after each molt, as *first instar, second instar,* and so on).]
in·state (ĭn-stāt′) *tr.v.* **-stated, -stating, -states.** To put in office; install. [IN- (causative) + STATE (rank).] —**in·state·ment** *n.*
in sta·tu quo (ĭn stā′cho͞o kwō′; stă′-, stăch′o͞o-) *adv. Latin.* In the same state or condition as before.
in·stau·ra·tion (ĭn′stô-rā′shən) *n. Archaic.* **1.** Renovation; restoration. **2.** Institution; establishment. [Latin *instaurātiō* (stem *instaurātiōn-*), from *instaurāre,* to restore.] —**in·stau·ra·tor** *n.*
in·stead (ĭn-stĕd′) *adv.* In the place of that previously mentioned or implied; as an alternative or substitute: *Planning to drive, he walked instead.* —**instead of.** In lieu of; rather than: *"Instead of eating monkeys/They are eating Christians"* (T.S. Eliot). [Middle English *in sted (of)* : IN + STEAD.]
in·step (ĭn′stĕp′) *n.* **1.** The arched, middle section of the human foot. **2.** The part of a shoe, stocking, or the like, covering the instep. [Probably IN + STEP.]
in·sti·gate (ĭn′stĭ-gāt′) *tr.v.* **-gated, -gating, -gates.** **1.** To urge on; goad; incite, especially to wrongdoing. **2.** To foment; stir up. [Latin *instīgāre* : *in-* (intensive) + *stīgāre,* to spur on.] —**in·sti·ga·tion** *n.* —**in·sti·ga·tive** *adj.* —**in·sti·ga·tor** *n.*
in·still (ĭn-stĭl′) *tr.v.* **-stilled, -stilling, -stills.** Also *chiefly British* **in·stil, -stilled, -stilling, -stils.** **1.** To introduce or impart by gradual, persistent efforts; implant. **2.** To pour in drop by drop. [Latin *instillāre,* to drip in : *in-,* in + *stillāre,* to drip, from *stilla*†, drop.] —**in·stil·la·tion** (ĭn′stə-lā′shən) *n.* —**in·still·er** *n.* —**in·still·ment, in·stil·ment** *n.*
in·stinct (ĭn′stĭngkt′) *n.* **1. a.** The innate aspect of behavior that is unlearned, complex, and normally adaptive. **b.** A powerful intuition or impulse. **2.** An innate aptitude: *an instinct for picking a winner.*
~*adj.* (ĭn-stĭngkt′). *Archaic.* Imbued or charged with something, such as energy. [Middle English, from Latin *instinctus,* instigation, from the past participle of *instinguere,* to instigate, urge on : *in-,* on + *stinguere,* to prick, incite.] —**in·stinc·tu·al** *adj.*
in·stinc·tive (ĭn-stĭngk′tĭv) *adj.* **1.** Of or pertaining to instinct. **2.** Arising from instinct. —See Synonyms at **spontaneous.** —**in·stinc·tive·ly** *adv.*
in·sti·tute (ĭn′stə-to͞ot′, -tyo͞ot′) *tr.v.* **-tuted, -tuting, -tutes.** **1. a.** To establish, organize, and set in operation. **b.** To initiate; begin. **2.** To establish or invest in a position; especially, to install (a clergyman) in a position of spiritual authority.
~*n.* **1.** Something instituted, especially: **a.** An authoritative rule or precedent. **b. institutes.** A digest of the principles or rudiments of some subject, especially law. **2.** *Abbr.* **inst., Inst.** **a.** An organization or association set up to promote some cause. **b.** An educational institution. **c.** The building or buildings of such an organization or institution. **3.** A short, intensive workshop or seminar on one specific subject. [Middle English *instituten,* from Latin *instituere,* to establish, ordain : *in-,* in + *statuere,* to set up, from *stāre* (past participle *status*), to stand.] —**in·sti·tu·tor** *n.*
in·sti·tu·tion (ĭn′stə-to͞o′shən, -tyo͞o′shən) *n. Abbr.* **inst., Inst.** **1.** The act of instituting. **2. a.** A relationship or behavioral pattern of importance in the life of a community or society: *the institution of marriage.* **b.** *Informal.* An ever-present feature; a fixture: *His corny jokes were a family institution.* **3.** An organization or establishment set up to perform a specific charitable, religious, educational, or other public service. **4.** The building or buildings housing such an organization. **5.** A place of confinement, such as a mental hospital.
in·sti·tu·tion·al (ĭn′stə-to͞o′shə-nəl, -tyo͞o′shə-nəl) *adj.* **1.** Of or pertaining to institutions. **2.** Organized through institutions or as an institution: *institutional religion.* **3.** Characteristic or suggestive of an institution, especially in being uniform, dull, or unimaginative: *institutional furniture.* **4.** Of or pertaining to the principles or institutes of a subject such as law. —**in·sti·tu·tion·al·ly** *adv.*
in·sti·tu·tion·al·ism (ĭn′stə-to͞o′shə-nə-lĭz′əm, ĭn′stə-tyo͞o′-) *n.* **1.** Belief in established forms, such as those of a religion, sometimes to the virtual exclusion of other considerations. **2.** The provision of institutional care or maintenance for those in need. —**in·sti·tu·tion·al·ist** *n. & adj.*
in·sti·tu·tion·al·ize (ĭn′stə-to͞o′shə-nə-līz′, ĭn′stə-tyo͞o′-) *tr.v.* **-ized, -izing, izes.** **1.** To make into an institution; give legal or institutional status to. **2.** To confine (a person) in an institution. **3.** To expose to the harmful effects of long-term confinement in an institution, producing apathy, dependence, and boredom. —**in·sti·tu·tion·al·i·za·tion** *n.*
instr. **1.** instruction; instructor. **2.** instrument; instrumental.
in·stroke (ĭn′strōk′) *n.* An inward stroke, especially a piston stroke moving away from the crankshaft.
in·struct (ĭn-strŭkt′) *v.* **-structed, -structing, -structs.** —*tr.* **1.** To furnish with knowledge; teach; educate. **2.** To provide with authoritative directions; give orders to. **3.** *Law.* To provide (a jury) with a full elucidation of the points of law in a particular case. —*intr.* To serve as an instructor. —See Synonyms at **command, teach.** [Middle English *instructen,* from Latin *instruere* (past participle *instructus*), to build, prepare, instruct : *in-,* in + *struere,* to build.]
in·struc·tion (ĭn-strŭk′shən) *n. Abbr.* **instr.** **1.** The act, practice, or profession of instructing; education. **2. a.** Imparted knowledge. **b.** An imparted or acquired item of knowledge; a lesson. **3. instructions.** Directions; orders. **4.** *Computer Science.* A part of a program that causes the computer to perform a specific operation. —**in·struc·tion·al** *adj.*
in·struc·tive (ĭn-strŭk′tĭv) *adj.* Conveying knowledge or information. —**in·struc·tive·ly** *adv.* —**in·struc·tive·ness** *n.*
in·struc·tor (ĭn-strŭk′tər) *n. Abbr.* **instr.** **1.** One who instructs; a teacher. **2. a.** An academic rank below that of assistant professor. **b.** One who holds such a rank. —**in·struc·tor·ship** *n.*
in·stru·ment (ĭn′strə-mənt) *n. Abbr.* **inst., instr.** **1.** A means by which something is done; agency. **2.** One used to accomplish some purpose. **3.** A mechanical implement; tool. **4.** A device for recording or measuring; especially, such a device functioning as part of a control system, as in an aircraft, for example. **5.** A device for producing or playing music: *a stringed instrument.* **6.** A legal document. —See Synonyms at **tool.**
~*tr.v.* **instrumented, -menting, -ments.** **1.** To provide or equip with instruments. **2.** To arrange (music) for instruments. [Middle English, from Latin *instrūmentum,* implement, equipment, tool, from *instruere,* to prepare, equip, INSTRUCT.]
in·stru·men·tal (ĭn′strə-mĕnt′l) *adj.* **1.** Serving as a means or instrument; contributing decisively to some outcome. **2.** Of, pertaining to, or accomplished with an instrument or tool. **3.** Performed on or written for a musical instrument or instruments rather than the voice. **4.** *Grammar.* Of or designating a case in Russian, Sanskrit, and certain other inflected languages, used typically to express means, agency, or accompaniment.
~*n.* **1.** The instrumental case. **2.** A form or construction in this case. —**in·stru·men·tal·ly** *adv.*
in·stru·men·tal·ism (ĭn′strə-mĕnt′l-ĭz′əm) *n.* A pragmatic theory that ideas are instruments that function as guides of action, their validity being measured by the success of the action.
in·stru·men·tal·ist (ĭn′strə-mĕnt′l-ĭst) *n.* **1.** One who plays a musical instrument. **2.** A student or advocate of instrumentalism.
in·stru·men·tal·i·ty (ĭn′strə-mĕn-tăl′ə-tē) *n., pl.* **-ties.** **1.** The quality or circumstance of being instrumental. **2.** Agency; means.
in·stru·men·ta·tion (ĭn′strə-mĕn-tā′shən) *n.* **1. a.** The application or use of instruments in the performance of some work. **b.** Instruments collectively. **2.** The study and practice of arranging music for instruments. **3.** The study, development, and manufacture of instruments, as for scientific use. **4.** Instrumentality.
instrument flying *n.* The flying of an aircraft using only the recording instruments and radio instructions from the ground, without visual observation.
instrument panel *n.* A mounted array of instruments used to monitor performance. Also called "instrument board."
in·sub·or·di·nate (ĭn′sə-bôrd′n-ĭt) *adj.* Not submissive to authority; rebellious.
~*n.* An insubordinate person. —**in·sub·or·di·nate·ly** *adv.* —**in·sub·or·di·na·tion** *n.*
Usage: *insubordinate, rebellious, mutinous, factious, seditious.* These adjectives are applied to persons or their actions and mean in opposition to, and usually in defiance of, established authority. *Insubordinate* implies failure to recognize or accept the authority of a superior. *Rebellious* implies open defiance of authority to which one is subject. *Mutinous,* a still stronger term, pertains to uprising against lawful authority, especially that of a naval or military command. *Factious* describes what promotes divisiveness, dissension, or

disunity within a group or organization. *Seditious* applies principally to the stirring up of resistance against a government.

in·sub·stan·tial (ĭn′səb-stăn′shəl) *adj.* **1.** Lacking substance; imaginary. **2.** Not firm; unsubstantial. **—in·sub·stan·ti·al·i·ty** (ĭn′səb-stăn′shē-ăl′ə-tē) *n.*

in·suf·fer·a·ble (ĭn-sŭf′ər-ə-bəl) *adj.* Not endurable; intolerable. **—in·suf·fer·a·ble·ness** *n.* **—in·suf·fer·a·bly** *adv.*

in·suf·fi·cien·cy (ĭn′sə-fĭsh′ən-sē) *n., pl.* **-cies. 1.** The quality or state of being insufficient. **2.** A lack or deficiency, as of some requisite thing or quality. **3.** *Medicine.* Inability of an organ to function properly.

in·suf·fi·cient (ĭn′sə-fĭsh′ənt) *adj.* Not sufficient; inadequate: *insufficient evidence.* **—in·suf·fi·cient·ly** *adv.*

in·suf·flate (ĭn-sŭf′lāt′, ĭn′sə-flāt′) *tr.v.* **-flated, -flating, -flates. 1.** To blow or breathe into or upon. **2.** To treat medically by blowing a powder, gas, or vapor into a bodily cavity. [Late Latin *insufflāre* : Latin *in-,* into + *sufflāre,* to blow.] **—in·suf·fla·tor** *n.*

in·suf·fla·tion (ĭn′sə-flā′shən) *n.* **1.** The act or an instance of insufflating. **2.** *Ecclesiastical.* A ritual breathing upon a person or thing as a symbol of the influence of the Holy Spirit.

in·su·lar (ĭn′sə-lər, ĭns′yə-) *adj.* **1.** Of, pertaining to, or constituting an island. **2.** Characteristic or suggestive of the isolated life of an island, especially: **a.** Circumscribed and detached in outlook and experience. **b.** Narrow; prejudiced. **3.** *Anatomy.* Designating isolated tissue or an island of tissue. [Late Latin *īnsulāris,* from Latin *īnsula,* island, ISLE.] **—in·su·lar·ism, in·su·lar·i·ty** (ĭn′sə-lăr′ə-tē, ĭns′yə-) *n.* **—in·su·lar·ly** *adv.*

in·su·late (ĭn′sə-lāt′, ĭns′yə-) *tr.v.* **-lated, -lating, -lates. 1. a.** To detach; isolate. **b.** To shield (a person), as from unpleasant realities. **2.** To prevent the passage of heat, electricity, or sound into or out of (a body or region), especially by interposition of an appropriate material. [Originally "to convert into an island," from Latin *īnsula,* island, ISLE.]

in·su·la·tion (ĭn′sə-lā′shən, ĭns′yə-) *n.* **1.** The act of insulating or state of being insulated. **2.** Material used in insulating.

in·su·la·tor (ĭn′sə-lā′tər, ĭns′yə-) *n.* **1.** A material that insulates; especially, a substance that is a poor conductor of heat, electricity, or sound. **2.** A device that insulates.

in·su·lin (ĭn′sə-lən, ĭns′yə-) *n.* **1.** A polypeptide hormone secreted by the islands of Langerhans in the pancreas and functioning to regulate carbohydrate metabolism by controlling blood glucose levels. **2.** A preparation derived from the pancreas of the pig or the ox for use in the medical treatment of diabetes. [Latin *īnsula,* island.]

insulin shock *n.* **1.** Acute hypoglycemia that typically results from an overdose of insulin given to a diabetic and may lead to coma. Also called "insulin reaction." **2.** Such a condition formerly induced artificially for therapeutic purposes in schizophrenics.

in·sult (ĭn-sŭlt′) *v.* **-sulted, -sulting, -sults.** —*tr.* **1. a.** To speak to or treat in a callous or contemptuous way. **b.** To reveal a disdainful estimate of: *The paper's political analysis insults its readers' intelligence.* **2.** *Archaic.* To make an attack upon; assault. —*intr. Obsolete.* To behave arrogantly. —See Synonyms at **offend.**
—*n.* (ĭn′sŭlt). **1.** An offensive action or remark; an affront. **2.** A slur; an aspersion: *Your refusal to confide is an insult to my discretion.* **3.** *Medicine.* An injury, irritation, or trauma. [French *insulter,* to triumph over, behave arrogantly, from Latin *insultāre,* to leap on, jump over : *in-,* on, upon + *saltāre,* frequentative of *salīre,* to jump.]

in·su·per·a·ble (ĭn-sōō′pər-ə-bəl) *adj.* Incapable of being overcome; insurmountable: *an insuperable barrier.* **—in·su·per·a·bil·i·ty, in·su·per·a·ble·ness** *n.* **—in·su·per·a·bly** *adv.*

in·sup·port·a·ble (ĭn′sə-pôr′tə-bəl, -pōr′tə-bəl) *adj.* **1.** Unbearable; intolerable. **2.** Lacking grounds or defense; unjustifiable: *an insupportable claim.* **—in·sup·port·a·ble·ness** *n.* **—in·sup·port·a·bly** *adv.*

in·sup·press·i·ble (ĭn′sə-prĕs′ə-bəl) *adj.* That cannot be suppressed; irrepressible.

in·sur·ance (ĭn-shŏŏr′əns) *n. Abbr.* **ins. 1. a.** The act, business, or process of insuring persons or property. **b.** The state of being insured. **2.** A contract binding a company to indemnify an insured party against stipulated loss, damage, or injury in return for premiums paid. Also called "insurance policy." **3.** The sum for which such a contract insures something. **4.** The periodical premium paid for this indemnification. **5.** A protective measure or device: *took an umbrella as an insurance against rain.*

in·sur·ant (ĭn-shŏŏr′ənt) *n.* One who is insured.

in·sure (ĭn-shŏŏr′) *v.* **-sured, -suring, -sures.** —*tr.* **1.** To cover with insurance: *Am I insured if I drive your car?* **2.** To make sure or certain; ensure. **3.** To make safe or secure. Used with *from* or *against*: *Nowadays a degree doesn't insure you against unemployment.* —*intr.* To buy or sell insurance. —See Usage note at **assure.** [Middle English *insuren, ensuren,* to guarantee, from Norman French *enseurer,* perhaps variant of Old French *ass(e)urer,* to ASSURE.] **—in·sur·a·bil·i·ty** *n.* **—in·sur·a·ble** *adj.*

in·sured (ĭn-shŏŏrd′) *n., pl.* **insured.** One covered by insurance.

in·sur·er (ĭn-shŏŏr′ər) *n.* One who insures; an underwriter.

in·sur·gence (ĭn-sûr′jəns) *n.* **1.** Uprising. **2.** An act of revolt.

in·sur·gen·cy (ĭn-sûr′jən-sē) *n.* **1.** The quality or state of being insurgent. **2.** Insurgence.

in·sur·gent (ĭn-sûr′jənt) *adj.* Rising in revolt against civil authority or a government in power.
—*n.* **1.** One who revolts against authority. **2.** A member of a political party who rebels against its leadership. [Latin *insurgēns* (stem *insurgent-*), present participle of *insurgere,* to rise up : *in-* (intensive) + *surgere,* to rise, SURGE.]

in·sur·mount·a·ble (ĭn′sər-moun′tə-bəl) *adj.* Incapable of being surmounted; insuperable: *struggling against insurmountable difficulties.* **—in·sur·mount·a·bly** *adv.*

in·sur·rec·tion (ĭn′sə-rĕk′shən) *n.* An act or instance of open revolt against civil authority or a constituted government. —See Synonyms at **rebellion.** [Middle English *insurrecioun,* from Old French *insurrection,* from Latin *insurrectiō* (stem *insurrectiōn-*), from *insurgere* (past participle *insurrectus*), to rise up. See **insurgent.**] **—in·sur·rec·tion·al** *adj.* **—in·sur·rec·tion·ar·y** *adj. & n.* **—in·sur·rec·tion·ist** *n.*

in·sus·cep·ti·ble (ĭn′sə-sĕp′tə-bəl) *adj.* Not susceptible; unaffected.

int. 1. interest. **2.** interior. **3.** internal. **4.** international. **5.** interval.

in·tact (ĭn-tăkt′) *adj.* **1.** Not impaired in any way. **2.** Having all parts; whole. [Middle English *intacte,* untouched, from Latin *intactus* : *in-,* not + *tactus,* past participle of *tangere,* to touch.] **—in·tact·ness** *n.*

in·ta·glio (ĭn-tăl′yō; *Italian* ĭn-tä′lyō) *n., pl.* **-glios** or **-tagli** (-tăl′yē; *Italian* -tä′lyē). **1. a.** A figure or design incised into the surface of hard metal or stone. **b.** The art or process of making intaglios. **2.** Something, such as a gemstone, carved in intaglio. Compare **cameo. 3.** Printing done with a plate bearing an image in intaglio. **4.** A die incised to produce a design in relief. [Italian, from *intagliare,* to engrave : *in-,* in + *tagliare,* to cut, from (unattested) Vulgar Latin *tālliāre* (see **tailor**).] **—in·ta·glia·ted** *adj.*

in·take (ĭn′tāk′) *n.* **1.** An opening by which a fluid is admitted into a container or conduit. **2.** An airway into a mine. **3. a.** The act of taking in. **b.** A person, thing, or quantity that is taken in or received: *an intake of energy; a fresh intake of members.*

in·tan·gi·ble (ĭn-tăn′jə-bəl) *adj.* **1.** Incapable of being perceived by touch; impalpable. **2.** Imprecisely defined or identified; elusive: *intangible ideas.* **—in·tan·gi·bil·i·ty, in·tan·gi·ble·ness** *n.* **—in·tan·gi·ble** *n.* **—in·tan·gi·bly** *adv.*

in·tar·si·a (ĭn-tär′sē-ə) *n.* **1.** A mosaic worked in wood. **2.** The art or process of making such mosaics. **3. a.** A knitting technique by which large patches of different color are juxtaposed in stocking stitch to form an asymmetrical design, keeping several yarns on the needle at once and joining them by overlapping behind the work. **b.** Work produced or decorated by this method. [Perhaps IN(LAY) + *tarsia,* an inlaid mosaic, from Arabic *tarṣī.*]

in·te·ger (ĭn′tə-jər) *n.* **1.** Any member of the set of positive whole numbers (1, 2, 3, . . .), negative whole numbers (−1, −2, −3, . . .), and zero (0). **2.** Any intact unit or entity. [Latin, whole, complete, perfect, virtuous.]

in·te·gra·ble (ĭn′tə-grə-bəl) *adj. Mathematics.* Capable of being integrated. Said of a function.

in·te·gral (ĭn′tə-grəl) *adj.* **1. a.** Essential for completion; necessary to the whole. **b.** Forming a constituent or intrinsic part; not separate: *a house with an integral garage.* **2.** Whole; entire; intact. **3.** *Mathematics.* **a.** Expressed or expressible as or in terms of integers. **b.** Expressed as or involving integrals.
—*n.* **1.** A complete unit; a whole. **2.** *Mathematics.* The limit of a sum of terms as the number of terms tends to infinity and the terms tend to zero. There are two types: the **definite integral** and the **indefinite integral** *(both of which see).* [Middle English, from Late Latin *integrālis,* making up a whole, from Latin *integer,* whole.] **—in·te·gral·i·ty** *n.* **—in·te·gral·ly** *adv.*

integral calculus *n.* The mathematical study of integration, the properties of integrals, and their applications.

integral domain *n. Mathematics.* A commutative ring with unity having no proper divisors of zero, that is, having no nonzero elements *a, b* such that $a \cdot b = 0$, where 0 is the additive identity.

in·te·grand (ĭn′tə-grănd′) *n.* A mathematical function or equation to be integrated. [Latin *integrandus,* from *integrāre,* to INTEGRATE.]

in·te·grant (ĭn′tə-grənt) *adj.* Integral; constituent. [Latin *integrāns* (stem *integrant-*), present participle of *integrāre,* to INTEGRATE.]

in·te·grate (ĭn′tə-grāt′) *v.* **-grated, -grating, -grates.** —*tr.* **1.** To make into a whole by bringing all parts together; unify. **2.** To unite with or incorporate into a larger body or unit; especially, to cause (members of an ethnically or culturally distinct group) to be assimilated into a society. **3.** To desegregate. **4.** *Mathematics.* To calculate the integral of (a function). **5.** To bring about the harmonious integration of (personality traits): *an integrated personality.* —*intr.* To become integrated or undergo integration. [Latin *integrāre,* to make complete, from *integer,* whole.] **—in·te·gra·tive** *adj.*

in·te·grat·ed circuit (ĭn′tə-grā′tĭd) *n. Abbr.* **IC.** An electronic circuit made of a number of components connected in a single small package, either by fixing small separate components on a ceramic wafer or by building them into the surface of a silicon chip.

in·te·gra·tion (ĭn′tə-grā′shən) *n.* **1. a.** An act or the process of integrating. **b.** The state of becoming integrated. **c.** Desegregation. **2.** The organization of the psychological or social traits and tendencies of a personality into a harmonious whole. **3.** *Physiology.* The processing of information received by the nervous system in such a way that a flexible and coordinated response is made.

in·te·gra·tor (ĭn′tə-grā′tər) *n.* **1.** One that integrates. **2.** An instrument for mechanically calculating definite integrals.

in·teg·ri·ty (ĭn-tĕg′rə-tē) *n.* **1.** Strict adherence to a code of moral values, artistic principles, or other standards; complete sincerity or honesty. **2.** The state of being unimpaired; soundness. **3.** Completeness; unity. —See Synonyms at **honesty.** [Middle English *integrite,* from Old French, from Latin *integritās* (stem *integritāt-*), completeness, purity, from *integer,* whole. See **integer.**]

in·teg·u·ment (ĭn-tĕg′yōō-mənt) *n.* An outer covering or coat, such

intarsia *An ambitious type of inlay work developed in 15th-century Italy. A veneer is inlaid with pieces of different colors to make a pattern or elaborate picture. This example is from a cloister ceiling in the monastery of San Juan de los Reyes in Toledo, Spain.*

PRONUNCIATION KEY

ă, pat; ā, pay; âr, care;
ä, father, are; b, bib;
ch, church; d, deed; ĕ, pet;
ē, be; f, fife; g, gag; h, hat;
hw, which; ĭ, pit; ī, pie;
îr, pier; j, judge; k, kick;
l, lid, needle; m, mum;
n, no, sudden; ng, thing;
ŏ, pot; ō, toe; ô, paw, for;
oi, noise; ou, out; ŏŏ, book;
ōō, boot; p, pop; r, roar;
s, sauce; sh, ship, dish;
t, tight; th, thin, path;
th, this, bathe; ŭ, cut; ûr, fur;
v, valve; w, with; y, yes;
z, zebra, size; zh, vision;
ə, about, item, edible, gallop, circus, peaceful

IN FOREIGN WORDS:

à, *Fr.* ami; œ, *Fr.* feu, *Ger.* schön; ü, *Fr.* tu, *Ger.* über; KH, *Ger.* ich, *Scot.* loch; N, *Fr.* bon; y′, *Fr.* Compiègne

STRESS MARKS:

Primary stress: ′
in·cite′ (ĭn-sīt′)
Secondary stress: ′
in′sight′ (ĭn′sīt′)

as the skin of an animal, the coat of a seed, or the membrane enclosing an organ. [Latin *integumentum,* from *integere,* to cover : *in-,* on + *tegere,* to cover.] **—in·teg·u·ment·al, in·teg·u·men·ta·ry** *adj.*

in·tel·lect (ĭn'tə-lĕkt') *n.* **1. a.** The ability to learn and reason as distinguished from the ability to feel or will; the capacity for knowledge and understanding. **b.** The ability to think abstractly or profoundly. **2. a.** A person of great intellectual ability. **b.** The intellectual members of a group. —See Synonyms at **mind.** [Middle English, from Old French, from Latin *intellectus,* perception, comprehension, from the past participle of *intellegere,* to perceive, choose between. See **intelligent.**]

in·tel·lec·tion (ĭn'tə-lĕk'shən) *n.* **1.** The act or process of exercising the intellect; mental activity. **2.** A thought or idea. [Middle English *intelleccioun,* understanding, from Latin *intellectiō* (stem *intellectiōn-*), from *intellectus,* INTELLECT.]

in·tel·lec·tive (ĭn'tə-lĕk'tĭv) *adj.* Of, pertaining to, or generated by the intellect. **—in·tel·lec·tive·ly** *adv.*

in·tel·lec·tu·al (ĭn'tə-lĕk'cho͞o-əl) *adj.* **1. a.** Of or pertaining to the intellect. **b.** Rational rather than emotional: *an intellectual debate.* **2.** Appealing to or requiring the exercise of the intellect. **3. a.** Having superior intelligence. **b.** Involved in activity requiring the use of the intellect. **c.** Given to or marked by the creative use of the intellect, as expressed in abstract thought, study, and developed artistic and literary tastes. —See Synonyms at **intelligent.**

~n. **1.** An intellectual person. **2.** One belonging to an intellectual group or class, and involved in mental rather than manual labor. **—in·tel·lec·tu·al·i·ty** *n.* **—in·tel·lec·tu·al·ly** *adv.*

in·tel·lec·tu·al·ism (ĭn'tə-lĕk'cho͞o-ə-lĭz'əm) *n.* **1.** Devotion to the exercise or development of the intellect, especially to the extent of disregarding emotional or spiritual factors. **2.** The doctrine that knowledge is the product of pure reason; rationalism. **—in·tel·lec·tu·al·ist** *n.* **—in·tel·lec·tu·al·is·tic** *adj.*

in·tel·lec·tu·al·ize (ĭn'tə-lĕk'cho͞o-ə-līz') *tr.v.* **-ized, -izing, -izes. 1.** To make rational. **2.** To treat in an intellectual way, especially at the expense of an emotional response or interpretation. **—in·tel·lec·tu·al·i·za·tion** *n.*

in·tel·li·gence (ĭn-tĕl'ə-jəns) *n.* **1. a.** The capacity to acquire and apply knowledge. **b.** The faculty of thought and reason. **c.** Superior powers of mind. **2. a.** *Often* **Intelligence.** An intelligent being, especially one that is incorporeal, such as an angel. **b. Intelligence.** *Christian Science.* "The primal and eternal quality of . . . God" (Mary Baker Eddy). **3.** Received information; news. **4. a.** Secret information, especially about an enemy. **b.** The work of gathering such information. **c.** An agency, staff, or office employed in such work. —See Synonyms at **mind.**

intelligence quotient *n. Abbr.* **IQ, I.Q.** An index of an individual's tested mental ability as compared to the rest of the population, usually arrived at by dividing an individual's mental age by his chronological age and multiplying by 100.

in·tel·li·genc·er (ĭn-tĕl'ə-jən-sər) *n. Archaic.* **1.** One who conveys news; an informant. **2.** A secret agent, informer, or spy.

intelligence test *n.* A standardized test used to establish an intelligence level rating by measuring an individual's ability to form concepts, solve problems, and perform other intellectual operations.

in·tel·li·gent (ĭn-tĕl'ə-jənt) *adj.* **1.** Having intelligence. **2.** Having a high degree of intelligence; mentally acute. **3.** Showing intelligence; perceptive and sound. **4.** Guided or motivated by the intellect; rational. **5.** Designating or pertaining to a computer terminal that can be used or programmed to perform logical operations as well as the input and output of data. [Latin *intelligēns* (stem *intelligent-*), present participle of *intellegere, intelligere,* to perceive, choose between : *inter-,* between + *legere,* to gather, choose.] **—in·tel·li·gen·tial** (ĭn-tĕl'ə-jĕn'shəl) *adj.* **—in·tel·li·gent·ly** *adv.*

Synonyms: *bright, brilliant, clever, intellectual, knowing, quick-witted, smart.*

in·tel·li·gent·si·a (ĭn-tĕl'ə-jĕnt'sē-ə, -gĕnt'sē-ə) *n. Used with a singular or plural verb.* The class within a society consisting of those who are cultured, well-educated, or intellectual. [Russian *intelligyentsia,* from Polish *inteligiencja,* from Latin *intelligentia,* intelligence, from *intelligēns,* INTELLIGENT.]

in·tel·li·gi·ble (ĭn-tĕl'ə-jə-bəl) *adj.* **1.** Comprehensible. **2.** Capable of being apprehended by the intellect alone. [Middle English, from Latin *intelligibilis,* from *intelligere,* to perceive. See **intelligent.**] **—in·tel·li·gi·bil·i·ty** *n.* **—in·tel·li·gi·bly** *adv.*

In·tel·sat (ĭn'tĕl-săt') *n. I*nternational *Tel*ecommunications *Sat*ellite Consortium: an international organization formed in 1964, whose member countries cooperate in establishing and promoting nonmilitary satellite communications.

in·tem·per·ance (ĭn-tĕm'pər-əns) *n.* Lack of temperance or restraint, as in the indulgence of an appetite or passion.

in·tem·per·ate (ĭn-tĕm'pər-ĭt) *adj.* Not temperate or moderate; excessive. **—in·tem·per·ate·ly** *adv.* **—in·tem·per·ate·ness** *n.*

in·tend (ĭn-tĕnd') *tr.v.* **-tended, -tending, -tends. 1.** To have in mind; plan: *She intended to leave.* **2.** To design for a specific purpose or destine for a particular use. **3.** To signify; mean. [Middle English *entenden,* from Old French *entendre,* from Latin *intendere,* to stretch toward, direct one's mind to : *in,* toward + *tendere,* to stretch, tend.]

in·ten·dance (ĭn-tĕn'dəns) *n.* **1.** The function of an intendant; management; superintendence. **2.** An intendancy.

in·ten·dan·cy (ĭn-tĕn'dən-sē) *n., pl.* **-cies. 1.** The position or function of an intendant. **2.** Intendants collectively. **3.** The district supervised by an intendant in Latin America.

in·ten·dant (ĭn-tĕn'dənt) *n.* **1.** Formerly, a provincial or colonial administrative official of France, Spain, or Portugal. **2.** A district administrator in some countries of Latin America. **3.** *Archaic.* A manager or superintendent. [French, from Old French, "director," administrator, from Latin *intendēns* (stem *intendent-*), present participle of *intendere,* to direct one's mind to, INTEND.]

in·tend·ed (ĭn-tĕn'dĭd) *adj.* **1.** Planned; intentional. **2.** Prospective; future.

~n. Informal. A person's prospective husband or wife.

in·tend·ment (ĭn-tĕnd'mənt) *n.* The true meaning or intention of something as fixed by law.

in·ten·er·ate (ĭn-tĕn'ə-rāt') *tr.v.* **-ated, -ating, -ates.** To make tender; soften. [IN- (causative) + Latin *tener,* TENDER + -ATE.] **—in·ten·er·a·tion** *n.*

in·tense (ĭn-tĕns') *adj.* **1.** Of great intensity; extreme in degree, concentration, or extent. **2.** Involving or showing strain: *made an intense effort to finish on time.* **3. a.** Deeply felt; profound. **b.** Tending to feel deeply: *an intense writer.* [Middle English, from Old French, from Latin *intensus,* stretched tight, from the past participle of *intendere,* to stretch toward, INTEND.] **—in·tense·ly** *adv.* **—in·tense·ness** *n.*

in·ten·si·fi·er (ĭn-tĕn'sə-fī'ər) *n.* **1.** One that intensifies. **2.** An intensive. **3.** *Photography.* A substance added to an emulsion to increase its sensitivity.

in·ten·si·fy (ĭn-tĕn'sə-fī') *v.* **-fied, -fying, -fies.** *—tr.* **1.** To make intense or more intense. **2.** To increase the contrast of (a photographic image). *—intr.* To become intense or more intense. [INTENSE + -FY.] **—in·ten·si·fi·ca·tion** *n.*

in·ten·sion (ĭn-tĕn'shən) *n.* **1.** *Logic.* The sum of the properties or attributes connoted by a term. Compare **extension. 2.** Intensity. [Latin *intensiō* (stem *intensiōn-*), from *intensus,* INTENSE.]

in·ten·si·ty (ĭn-tĕn'sə-tē) *n., pl.* **-ties. 1.** Exceptionally great concentration, power, or force. **2.** *Physics.* **a.** The measure of effectiveness of a force field given by the force per unit test element. **b.** The energy transferred by a wave per unit time across a unit area perpendicular to the direction of propagation.

in·ten·sive (ĭn-tĕn'sĭv) *adj.* **1.** Of, pertaining to, or characterized by intensity. **2.** Pertaining to or being a linguistic intensive. **3.** Concentrated and exhaustive: *intensive study.* **4.** Designating or pertaining to a method of land cultivation calling for large-scale employment of capital and labor and designed to increase productivity. **5.** *Physics.* Having the same value for any subdivision of a thermodynamic system. Said of pressure, for example. **6.** Having a greater than average requirement of the specified resource. Used in combination: *labor-intensive; an energy-intensive system.*

~n. A linguistic element that intensifies the effect of a word or phrase but has itself little or no semantic content; for example, in the sentence *She is terribly pretty, terribly* is an intensive.

intensive care *n.* Continuous and carefully monitored medical treatment given to patients who are seriously ill, especially in a specialized section (*intensive-care unit*) of a hospital.

in·tent (ĭn-tĕnt') *n.* **1.** That which is intended; aim; purpose. **2.** The state of mind prevailing at the time of an action: *acted with malicious intent.* **3.** Meaning; purport. —See Synonyms at **intention. —to all intents and purposes.** Practically; virtually.

~adj. **1.** Firmly fixed; concentrated. **2.** Having the attention applied; engrossed. **3.** Having the mind fastened upon some purpose. [Middle English *entent,* from Old French, from Latin *intentus,* a stretching out, from the alternate past participle of *intendere,* to stretch toward, INTEND.] **—in·tent·ly** *adv.* **—in·tent·ness** *n.*

in·ten·tion (ĭn-tĕn'shən) *n.* **1.** A plan of action; a design. **2. a.** An aim that guides action; object. **b. intentions.** Purpose in regard to marriage: *honorable intentions.* **3.** *Logic.* **a.** A concept derived from an object of thought. **b.** The general connotation or concept of something. **4.** *Medicine.* The course or manner of healing of a surgical wound. **5.** *Archaic.* Import; meaning. **6.** *Archaic.* Intentness. [Middle English *entencioun,* from Old French *entention,* from Latin *intentiō* (stem *intentiōn-*), "a stretching out," from *intendere,* to stretch toward, INTEND.]

Synonyms: *aim, end, goal, intent, object, objective, purpose.*

in·ten·tion·al (ĭn-tĕn'shə-nəl) *adj.* **1.** Done deliberately; intended: *an intentional slight.* **2.** Having to do with logical intention or connotation. —See Synonyms at **voluntary. —in·ten·tion·al·i·ty** (ĭn-tĕn'shə-năl'ə-tē) *n.* **—in·ten·tion·al·ly** *adv.*

in·ter (ĭn-tûr') *tr.v.* **-terred, -terring, -ters.** To place (a dead body) in a grave; bury. [Middle English *enteren,* from Old French *enterrer,* from Vulgar Latin *interrāre* (unattested) : Latin *in,* in + *terra,* earth, ground.]

inter– *prefix.* Indicates: **1.** Between or among; for example, **intercollegiate, international. 2.** Mutually or together; for example, **interact, intermingle. *Note:*** Many compounds other than those entered here may be formed with *inter-.* In forming compounds, *inter-* is normally joined with the following element without space or hyphen: *intercontinental.* However, if the second element begins with a capital letter, it is separated with a hyphen: *inter-American.* In Latin phrases used in English, the Latin preposition remains a separate word: *inter alia.* [Middle English *inter-, entre-,* from Old French, from Latin *inter-,* from *inter,* between, among. In borrowed Latin compounds, *inter-* indicates: 1. Between, among, as in **interregnum.** 2. Mutually, each other, as in **intersect.** 3. At intervals, as in **intermit.** 4. Preventively, destructively, as in **internecine.**]

inter. intermediate.
in·ter·act (ĭn′tər-ăkt′) *intr.v.* **-acted, -acting, -acts.** To act on each other.
in·ter·ac·tion (ĭn′tər-ăk′shən) *n.* **1.** The action, state, or result of interacting. **2.** *Physics.* Any of four fundamental ways in which elementary particles and bodies can influence each other, characterized by the strength and range of such interaction and classified as strong, weak, electromagnetic, and gravitational.
in·ter·ac·tive (ĭn′tər-ăk′tĭv) *adj.* **1.** Acting on each other. **2.** *Computer Science.* Designating or pertaining to a system in which information and instructions can be continuously transferred between computer and operator.
in·ter a·li·a (ĭn′tər ā′lē-ə) *adv. Latin.* Among other things.
in·ter a·li·os (ĭn′tər ā′lē-ōs′) *adv. Latin.* Among other persons.
in·ter·a·tom·ic (ĭn′tər-ə-tŏm′ĭk) *adj.* Occurring or operating between atoms.
in·ter·brain (ĭn′tər-brān′) *n.* A part of the brain, the **diencephalon** *(see).*
in·ter·breed (ĭn′tər-brēd′) *v.* **-bred** (-brĕd), **-breeding, -breeds.** —*intr.* **1.** To breed with another kind or species; crossbreed; hybridize. **2.** To breed within a narrow range or with closely related types or individuals; inbreed. —*tr.* To cause to interbreed.
in·ter·ca·lar·y (ĭn-tûr′kə-lĕr′ē) *adj.* **1.** Added to the calendar to make the calendar year correspond to the solar year. Said of a day or a month. **2.** Having such a day or month added. Said of a year. **3.** Interpolated; constituting an insertion. **4.** Designating nonlocalized plant growth occurring in regions other than the apical meristems, as at internodes and leaf bases. [Latin *intercalārius,* from *intercalāre,* to INTERCALATE.]
in·ter·ca·late (ĭn-tûr′kə-lāt′) *tr.v.* **-lated, -lating, -lates.** **1.** To add (a day or month) to a calendar. **2.** To insert, interpose, or interpolate. [Latin *intercalāre,* to proclaim the insertion of a day : *inter-,* among, between + *calāre,* to call.] **—in·ter·ca·la·tion** *n.* **—in·ter·ca·la·tive** *adj.*
in·ter·cede (ĭn′tər-sēd′) *intr.v.* **-ceded, -ceding, -cedes.** **1.** To plead on another's behalf: *interceded with the father for the child.* **2.** To act as mediator in a dispute. [Latin *intercēdere,* to come between : *inter-,* between + *cēdere,* to go.] **—in·ter·ced·er** *n.*
in·ter·cel·lu·lar (ĭn′tər-sĕl′yə-lər) *adj. Biology.* Among or between cells.
in·ter·cept (ĭn′tər-sĕpt′) *tr.v.* **-cepted, -cepting, -cepts.** **1. a.** To stop, deflect, or interrupt the progress or intended course of: *intercepted a message; intercepted her at the airport.* **b.** In ball games such as football, hockey or the like, to cut off, or take possession of (a ball) by anticipating an opponent's pass. **2.** *Archaic.* **a.** To cut off from access or communication. **b.** To prevent. **3.** *Mathematics.* To cut off or bound a part of (a line, plane, surface, or solid).
—*n.* (ĭn′tər-sĕpt′). *Mathematics.* **1.** A point of interception. **2.** A line segment formed by an intercept; for example, the distance from the origin of coordinates along a coordinate axis to the point at which a line, curve, or surface intersects the axis. [Latin *intercipere* (past participle *interceptus*), to intercept, seize in transit : *inter,* preventively + *capere,* to take, seize.] **—in·ter·cep·tion** *n.* **—in·ter·cep·tive** *adj.*
in·ter·cep·tor, in·ter·cep·ter (ĭn′tər-sĕp′tər) *n.* One that intercepts; especially, a fast-climbing, highly maneuverable fighter plane designed to intercept enemy aircraft.
in·ter·ces·sion (ĭn′tər-sĕsh′ən) *n.* **1.** Entreaty in favor of another; especially, a prayer or petition to God on behalf of another. **2.** Mediation in a dispute. [Old French, from Latin *intercessiō* (stem *intercessiōn-*), from *intercēdere* (past participle *intercessus*), INTERCEDE.] **—in·ter·ces·sion·al** *adj.* **—in·ter·ces·sor** *n.* **—in·ter·ces·so·ry** *adj.*
in·ter·change (ĭn′tər-chānj′) *v.* **-changed, -changing, -changes.** —*tr.* **1.** To switch each of (two things) into the place of the other. **2.** To give and receive mutually; exchange. **3.** To cause to succeed each other; alternate: *interchanging wit with wisdom in the course of conversation.* —*intr.* **1.** To change places with each other. **2.** To succeed each other; alternate.
—*n.* (ĭn′tər-chānj′). **1.** The act or process or an instance of interchanging, especially: **a.** A switch of places. **b.** An exchange. **2.** Alternation. **3.** A highway intersection designed to permit traffic to move freely from one road to another. [Middle English *entrechaungen,* from Old French *entrechangier* : INTER- + *changier,* to CHANGE.] **—in·ter·chang·er** *n.*
in·ter·change·a·ble (ĭn′tər-chān′jə-bəl) *adj.* Capable of being interchanged; admitting transposition. **—in·ter·change·a·bil·i·ty, in·ter·change·a·ble·ness** *n.* **—in·ter·change·a·bly** *adv.*
in·ter·col·le·giate (ĭn′tər-kə-lē′jĭt, -jē-ĭt) *adj.* Involving or representing two or more colleges.
in·ter·co·lum·ni·a·tion (ĭn′tər-kə-lŭm′nē-ā′shən) *n. Architecture.* **1.** The open spaces between the columns in a colonnade. **2.** The system whereby they are spaced.
in·ter·com (ĭn′tər-kŏm′) *n. Informal.* An internal communication system, as between two rooms. [Short for INTERCOMMUNICATION.]
in·ter·com·mu·ni·cate (ĭn′tər-kə-myōō′nə-kāt′) *intr.v.* **-cated, -cating, -cates.** **1.** To communicate with each other. **2.** To be connected or adjoined, as rooms. **—in·ter·com·mu·ni·ca·tion** *n.* **—in·ter·com·mu·ni·ca·tive** *adj.*
in·ter·com·mun·ion (ĭn′tər-kə-myōōn′yən) *n.* The practice by members of different Christian denominations of receiving communion at each other's eucharistic services or at a common service.
in·ter·con·nect (ĭn′tər-kə-nĕkt′) *v.* **-nected, -necting, -nects.** —*intr.* To be connected one to the other. —*tr.* To connect (one thing with another). **—in·ter·con·nec·tion** *n.*
in·ter·con·ti·nen·tal (ĭn′tər-kŏn′tə-nĕnt′l) *adj.* **1.** Extending from one continent to another: *intercontinental flight.* **2.** Carried on between continents: *intercontinental warfare.* **3.** Capable of flight from one continent to another: *intercontinental ballistic missile.*
in·ter·cos·tal (ĭn′tər-kŏst′l) *adj.* Located or occurring between the ribs. [New Latin *intercostalis* : Latin *inter-,* between + *costa,* rib.]
in·ter·course (ĭn′tər-kôrs′, -kōrs′) *n.* **1.** Interchange between persons or groups; communication. **2. Sexual intercourse** *(see).* [Middle English *intercurse,* from Old French *entrecours,* from Latin *intercursus,* past participle of *intercurrere,* to run between : *inter-,* between + *currere,* to run.]
in·ter·crop (ĭn′tər-krŏp′) *v.* **-cropped, -cropping, -crops.** —*intr.* To grow a secondary crop between the rows of a principal crop. —*tr.* To plant such a crop between (another crop).
—*n.* (ĭn′tər-krŏp′). A secondary crop grown between the rows of a principal crop.
in·ter·cross (ĭn′tər-krŏs′) *n.* A **crossbreed** *(see).* **—in·ter·cross** *v.*
in·ter·cur·rent (ĭn′tər-kûr′ənt) *adj.* **1.** Occurring as an interruption in a process. **2.** *Pathology.* Occurring during the course of an existing disease. [Latin *intercurrēns* (stem *intercurrent-*), present participle of *intercurrere,* to run between. See **intercourse.**]
in·ter·cut (ĭn′tər-kŭt′) *tr.v.* **-cut, -cutting, -cuts.** To insert (a scene or camera shot) into a film sequence, so as to achieve dramatic contrast or to make it appear that two or more actions are taking place simultaneously.
in·ter·de·nom·i·na·tion·al (ĭn′tər-də-nŏm′ə-nā′shən-əl) *adj.* Of or involving different religious denominations.
in·ter·den·tal (ĭn′tər-dĕnt′l) *adj.* **1.** Located between the teeth. **2.** *Phonetics.* Pronounced with the tip of the tongue protruding between the teeth, as (th) in *that* or (th) in *thumb.*
—*n. Phonetics.* A consonant pronounced in this manner.
in·ter·de·pen·dent (ĭn′tər-də-pĕn′dənt) *adj.* Dependent on each other. **—in·ter·de·pen·dence** *n.* **—in·ter·de·pen·dent·ly** *adv.*
in·ter·dict (ĭn′tər-dĭkt′) *tr.v.* **-dicted, -dicting, -dicts.** **1.** To prohibit or place under an ecclesiastical or legal sanction. **2.** To cut or destroy (an enemy line of communication) by firepower so as to halt an enemy's advance.
—*n.* (ĭn′tər-dĭkt′). **1.** An authoritative prohibition or legal injunction. **2.** A Roman Catholic ecclesiastical censure whereby an offending person or district is excluded from participation in most sacraments and from Christian burial. [Learned respelling of Middle English *entrediten,* to announce ecclesiastical censure, from Old French *entredire* (past participle *entredit*), from Latin *interdīcere,* to forbid : *inter-,* preventively + *dīcere,* to say.] **—in·ter·dic·tion** *n.* **—in·ter·dic·tive, in·ter·dic·to·ry** *adj.* **—in·ter·dic·tive·ly** *adv.* **—in·ter·dic·tor** *n.*
in·ter·dis·ci·pli·nar·y (ĭn′tər-dĭs′ĭ-plĭ-nĕr′ē) *adj.* Concerned with two or more academic disciplines usually considered distinct: *an interdisciplinary degree.*
in·ter·est (ĭn′trĭst, -tər-ĭst) *n.* **1. a.** A feeling of curiosity, fascination, or absorption. **b.** The cause of any such feeling. **c.** The quality or aspect of something that enables it to cause any such feeling. **2.** *Often* **interests.** Advantage; self-interest. **3. a.** A right, claim, or legal share in something. **b.** *Usually* **interests.** Something in which such a right, claim, or share is held. **4. a.** Involvement with or participation in something. **b.** A leisure activity or pursuit: *What are your interests?* **5. a.** *Abbr.* **i., int.** A charge for a financial loan, usually a percentage of the amount loaned. **b.** An excess or bonus beyond what is expected or due: *She returned his ardor with interest.* **6.** *Usually* **interests.** A group of persons sharing an interest in an enterprise, industry, or segment of society. **—in the interest** (or **interests**) **of.** For the sake of; on behalf of.
—*tr.v.* **interested, -esting, -ests.** **1.** To arouse the curiosity or hold the attention of. **2.** To cause to become involved or concerned. **3.** *Archaic.* To concern or affect. [Middle English, variant (influenced by Old French *interest,* damage) of *interesse,* concern, share, from Norman French, substantive use of Latin *interesse,* "to be in between," to matter, be of concern : *inter-,* between + *esse,* to be.]
in·ter·est·ed (ĭn′trĭ-stĭd, -tər-ĭ-stĭd, -tə-rĕs′tĭd) *adj.* **1.** Having or showing curiosity, fascination, or concern. **2.** Possessing a right, claim, or share; personally concerned: *the interested parties.* **3.** Influenced by considerations of personal gain; self-seeking. **—in·ter·est·ed·ly** *adv.* **—in·ter·est·ed·ness** *n.*
in·ter·est·ing (ĭn′trĭ-stĭng, -tər-ĭ-stĭng, -tə-rĕs′tĭng) *adj.* Arousing or holding attention; absorbing. **—in·ter·est·ing·ly** *adv.*
in·ter·face (ĭn′tər-fās′) *n.* **1.** A surface forming a common boundary between adjacent bodies, liquids, or regions. **2.** A link between two circuits or parts, especially in a computer. **3.** The meeting point or boundary at which two theories, systems, groups of people or the like meet and affect each other.
—*v.* **interfaced, -facing, faces.** —*tr.* To connect (material) with or through an interface. —*intr.* To become interfaced. **—in·ter·fa·cial** (ĭn′tər-fā′shəl) *adj.*
in·ter·fac·ing (ĭn′tər-fās′ĭng) *n.* A strip of firm fabric sewn between the layers of a garment to thicken or stiffen it.
in·ter·fas·cic·u·lar (ĭn′tər-fə-sĭk′yə-lər) *adj. Botany.* Occurring between fascicles: *interfascicular cambium.*
in·ter·fere (ĭn′tər-fîr′) *intr.v.* **-fered, -fering, -feres.** **1.** To be a hindrance or obstacle. Often used with *with.* **2.** To intervene or intrude in the affairs of others; meddle. **3.** In various sports, to impede an opponent contrary to the rules of the game. **4.** To strike one hoof

PRONUNCIATION KEY
ă, pat; ā, pay; âr, care;
ä, father, are; b, bib;
ch, church; d, deed; ĕ, pet;
ē, be; f, fife; g, gag; h, hat;
hw, which; ĭ, pit; ī, pie;
îr, pier; j, judge; k, kick;
l, lid, needle; m, mum;
n, no, sudden; ng, thing;
ŏ, pot; ō, toe; ô, paw, for;
oi, noise; ou, out; ŏŏ, book;
ōō, boot; p, pop; r, roar;
s, sauce; sh, ship, dish;
t, tight; th, thin, path;
th, this, bathe; ŭ, cut; ûr, fur;
v, valve; w, with; y, yes;
z, zebra, size; zh, vision;
ə, about, item, edible,
gallop, circus, peaceful

IN FOREIGN WORDS:
à, *Fr.* ami; œ, *Fr.* feu, *Ger.* schön; ü, *Fr.* tu, *Ger.* über;
KH, *Ger.* ich, *Scot.* loch;
N, *Fr.* bon; y′, *Fr.* Compiègne

STRESS MARKS:
Primary stress: ′
in·cite′ (ĭn-sīt′)
Secondary stress: ′
in′sight′ (ĭn′sīt′)

against the opposite hoof or leg while moving. Used of a horse. **5.** *Physics.* To produce interference with another wave. **6.** *Electronics.* To inhibit or prevent clear reception of broadcast signals. [Old French *(s')entreferir,* to strike each other : INTER- + *ferir,* to strike, from Latin *ferīre.*] **—in·ter·fer·er** *n.* **—in·ter·fer·ing·ly** *adv.*

Synonyms: *meddle, tamper, tinker.*

in·ter·fer·ence (ĭn′tər-fîr′əns) *n.* **1. a.** The act, process, or an instance of interfering. **b.** Something that interferes. **2. a.** *Football.* The blocking of defensive tacklers to protect the ball carrier. **b.** *Sports.* The illegal obstruction or hindrance of the ball or of an opposing player. **3.** *Physics.* The phenomenon of two or more waves of the same frequency combining to form a wave in which the disturbance at any point is the algebraic or vector sum of the disturbances due to the interfering waves at that point. **4.** *Electronics.* **a.** The inhibition or prevention of clear reception of broadcast signals. **b.** The distorted portion of a received signal. **—in·ter·fer·en·tial** (ĭn′tər-fə-rĕn′shəl) *adj.*

in·ter·fe·rom·e·ter (ĭn′tər-fə-rŏm′ə-tər) *n.* **1.** Any of several optical, acoustic, or radio-frequency instruments that use interference phenomena between a reference wave and an experimental wave, or between two parts of an experimental wave, to determine wavelengths, wave velocities, distances, and directions. **2.** A type of radio telescope in which the received waves are collected by two separate antennae, connected so as to combine the signals. See **aperture synthesis.** [INTERFER(E) + -METER.]

in·ter·fer·on (ĭn′tər-fîr′ŏn) *n.* A protein produced in response to, and acting to prevent replication of, an infectious viral form within a cell. [INTERFER(E) + -ON.]

in·ter·fer·tile (ĭn′tər-fûrt′l) *adj.* Able to interbreed.

in·ter·fluve (ĭn′tər-flo͞ov′) *n.* The region of higher land between two rivers that are in the same drainage system. [INTER- + Latin *fluvius,* river. See **fluvial.**] **—in·ter·flu·vi·al** *adj.*

in·ter·fuse (ĭn′tər-fyo͞oz′) *v.* **-fused, -fusing, -fuses.** *—tr.* **1.** To fuse or blend. **2.** To spread throughout; diffuse. *—intr.* **1.** To become fused or blended. **2.** To become diffused.

in·ter·ga·lac·tic (ĭn′tər-gə-lăk′tĭk) *adj.* Between galaxies.

in·ter·gla·ci·al (ĭn′tər-glā′shəl) *n.* A comparatively short period of warmth during an overall period of glaciation. **—in·ter·gla·ci·al** *adj.*

in·ter·grade (ĭn′tər-grād′) *intr.v.* **-graded, -grading, -grades.** To merge or grow into each other in a series of stages, forms, or types, Used especially of biological species.

∼n. (ĭn′tər-grād′). A transitional step, grade, or form. **—in·ter·gra·da·tion** *n.* **—in·ter·gra·di·ent** (ĭn′tər-grā′dē-ənt) *adj.*

in·ter·im (ĭn′tər-ĭm) *n.* An interval of time between one event, process, or period and another.

∼adj. Belonging to, made, or taking place during an interim; temporary, provisional, or partial: *interim measures; an interim payment.* [Latin, in the meantime, from *inter,* among, at intervals.]

in·te·ri·or (ĭn-tîr′ē-ər) *adj. Abbr.* **int. 1.** Of, pertaining to, or located on the inside; inner. **2.** Of or pertaining to one's mental or spiritual being. **3.** Situated away from a coast or border; inland.

∼n. Abbr. **int. 1.** The internal portion or area of something, especially of a building; the inside. **2.** One's mental or spiritual being. **3. a.** A representation of the inside of a building or room, as in a painting. **b.** A film scene that is shot indoors. **4.** The inland part of a given political or geographical entity. **5. Interior.** The internal or domestic affairs of a country. [Latin, comparative of *inter,* in, within.] **—in·te·ri·or·i·ty** (ĭn-tîr′ē-ôr′ə-tē, -ŏr′ə-tē) *n.* **—in·te·ri·or·ly** *adv.*

interior angle *n.* **1.** Any of four angles formed between two straight lines cut by a transversal. **2.** The angle formed inside a polygon by two adjacent sides.

interior decorator *n.* One who plans and executes the layout and decoration of an architectural interior. Also called "interior designer." **—interior decoration** *n.*

interior monologue *n.* In literature, the direct representation of a character's thoughts and feelings, as opposed to a narrative description of them.

interj. interjection.

in·ter·ject (ĭn′tər-jĕkt′) *tr.v.* **-jected, -jecting, -jects.** To interpose parenthetically or by way of an interruption. [Latin *interjicere* (past participle *interjectus*), to throw between : *inter-,* between + *jacere,* to throw.] **—in·ter·jec·tor** *n.* **—in·ter·jec·to·ry** *adj.*

in·ter·jec·tion (ĭn′tər-jĕk′shən) *n.* **1.** An exclamation; an ejaculation. **2.** *Abbr.* **interj. a.** A part of speech consisting of an exclamatory word capable of standing alone; for example, *oh!* or *ahem!* **b.** A word, phrase, or other sound used exclamatorily and capable of standing alone; for example, *Heavens!* or *Shut up!* **—in·ter·jec·tion·al** *adj.* **—in·ter·jec·tion·al·ly** *adv.*

in·ter·lace (ĭn′tər-lās′) *v.* **-laced, -lacing, -laces.** *—tr.* **1.** To connect together by or as if by weaving; interweave. **2.** To intersperse. **3.** *Electronics.* To scan (a television picture, for example) in two stages, each composed of alternate lines. *—intr.* To intertwine. Used with *with.* **—in·ter·lace·ment** *n.*

In·ter·la·ken (ĭn′tər-lä′kən). Town in Switzerland on the Aar River, between Thun and Brienz lakes. It is the tourist center of the Bernese Alps.

in·ter·lam·i·nate (ĭn′tər-lăm′ə-nāt′) *tr.v.* **-nated, -nating, -nates. 1.** To insert (a layer) between other layers. **2.** To arrange in alternating layers. **—in·ter·lam·i·nar** *adj.* **—in·ter·lam·i·na·tion** *n.*

in·ter·lard (ĭn′tər-lärd′) *tr.v.* **-larded, -larding, -lards. 1.** To modify or diversify by interspersing with something different or foreign. **2.** To be interspersed through; occur in repeatedly. [Old French *entrelarder,* to alternate layers of fat and lean : INTER- + *larder,* to insert fat, cover with lard, from LARD.]

in·ter·leaf (ĭn′tər-lēf′) *n., pl.* **-leaves** (-lēvz′). A blank leaf inserted between the regular pages of a book.

in·ter·leave (ĭn′tər-lēv′) *tr.v.* **-leaved, -leaving, -leaves. 1.** To provide (a book) with an interleaf or interleaves. **2.** To insert (an interleaf) into a book. **3.** To arrange in alternating layers.

in·ter·line¹ (ĭn′tər-līn′) *tr.v.* **-lined, -lining, -lines. 1.** To insert (writing) between printed or written lines. **2.** To insert words between the lines of (a text). **—in·ter·lin·e·a·tion** (ĭn′tər-lĭn′ē-ā′shən) *n.*

interline² *tr.v.* **-lined, -lining, -lines.** To fit with an interlining.

in·ter·lin·e·ar (ĭn′tər-lĭn′ē-ər) *adj.* **1.** Inserted between the lines of a text. **2.** Written or printed with different languages or versions in alternating lines.

In·ter·lin·gua (ĭn′tər-lĭng′gwə) *n.* An artificially devised international language comprising elements of both English and the Romance languages. [Italian : INTER- + *lingua,* language.]

in·ter·lin·ing (ĭn′tər-lī′nĭng) *n.* An extra lining between the outer fabric and the ordinary lining of a garment.

in·ter·lock (ĭn′tər-lŏk′) *v.* **-locked, -locking, -locks.** *—tr.* **1.** To unite firmly or join closely, as by hooking or dovetailing. **2.** To arrange or connect (separate parts of a system) so that they cannot be operated independently. **3.** *Computer Science.* To prevent initiation of new operations until current operations are completed. *—intr.* To engage or be joined firmly.

∼n. (ĭn′tər-lŏk′). **1.** A mechanism that ensures that a particular activity cannot take place until a prescribed sequence of operations has been carried out. **2.** A fabric knitted with interlocking stitches.

in·ter·lo·cu·tion (ĭn′tər-lō-kyo͞o′shən) *n.* Conversation. [Latin *interlocūtiō* (stem *interlocūtiōn-*) from *interloquī* (past participle *interlocūtus*), to speak between : *inter-,* between + *loquī,* to speak.]

in·ter·loc·u·tor (ĭn′tər-lŏk′yə-tər) *n.* **1.** Someone who takes part in a conversation. **2.** A partner in such a dialogue. **3.** The performer in a minstrel show who is placed midway between the end men and engages in banter with them.

in·ter·loc·u·to·ry (ĭn′tər-lŏk′yə-tôr′ē, -tōr′ē) *adj.* **1.** Made during the course of a suit, divorce trial, or the like: *an interlocutory decree.* **2.** Interspersed, as into a text or talk. **3.** Of, pertaining to, or resembling a conversation.

in·ter·lope (ĭn′tər-lōp′) *intr.v.* **-loped, -loping, -lopes. 1.** To violate the legally established trading rights of others. **2.** To interfere in the affairs of others; intrude. —See Synonyms at **intrude.** [Back-formation from *interloper* : INTER- + Dutch *loper,* running, from Middle Dutch, from *loopen,* to run.] **—in·ter·lo·per** *n.*

in·ter·lude (ĭn′tər-lo͞od′) *n.* **1.** An intervening episode, feature, or period of time. **2. a.** A short farcical entertainment performed between the acts of a medieval mystery or morality play. **b.** A 16th-century genre of comedy derived from this. **c.** An entertainment between the acts of a play. **3.** A short musical piece inserted between the parts of a longer composition. [Middle English *enterlude,* from Medieval Latin *interlūdium,* performance between acts : Latin *inter-,* between + *lūdus,* play.]

in·ter·lun·a·tion (ĭn′tər-lo͞o-nā′shən) *n.* The period during which the moon is invisible, occurring between the old and new moon. **—in·ter·lu·nar** (ĭn′tər-lo͞o′nər) *adj.*

in·ter·mar·ry (ĭn′tər-măr′ē) *intr.v.* **-ried, -rying, -ries. 1.** To marry a member of another group. **2.** To be bound together by the marriages of members. **3.** To marry within one's own family, tribe, or clan. **—in·ter·mar·riage** *n.*

in·ter·me·di·a·cy (ĭn′tər-mē′dē-ə-sē) *n.* **1.** The state of being intermediate. **2.** The act of intermediating.

in·ter·me·di·ar·y (ĭn′tər-mē′dē-ĕr′ē) *n., pl.* **-ies. 1.** One who acts as a mediator. **2.** One that acts as an agent between persons or things; a means. **3.** An intermediate state or stage.

∼adj. **1.** Acting as a mediator. **2.** In between; intermediate.

in·ter·me·di·ate (ĭn′tər-mē′dē-ĭt) *adj. Abbr.* **inter. 1.** Lying or occurring at a point, degree, or level between two extremes; in between; in the middle. **2.** *Geology.* Designating a class of igneous rocks containing less than ten percent free quartz, some feldspar, and about 52 to 66 percent silica.

∼n. Abbr. **inter. 1.** One that is intermediate. **2.** An intermediary. **3.** *Chemistry.* A substance formed as a necessary stage in the change from reactants to products during a chemical reaction.

∼intr.v. (ĭn′tər-mē′dē-āt′) **intermediated, -ating, -ates.** To act as an intermediary; mediate. [Medieval Latin *intermediātus,* from Latin *intermedius* : *inter-,* between + *medius,* middle.] **—in·ter·me·di·ate·ly** *adv.* **—in·ter·me·di·ate·ness** *n.* **—in·ter·me·di·a·tion** *n.* **—in·ter·me·di·a·tor** *n.*

in·ter·ment (ĭn-tûr′mənt) *n.* The act or ritual of interring.

in·ter·mez·zo (ĭn′tər-mĕt′sō, -mĕd′zō) *n., pl.* **-zos** or **-zi** (-sē, -zē). **1.** A brief musical, theatrical, or dance performance during an interval; an entr'acte. **2. a.** A short movement separating the major sections of a symphonic work. **b.** An independent instrumental composition having the character of such a movement. [Italian, from Latin *intermedius,* INTERMEDIATE.]

in·ter·mi·na·ble (ĭn-tûr′mə-nə-bəl) *adj.* Tiresomely protracted; endless. —See Synonyms at **continual.** **—in·ter·mi·na·bly** *adv.*

in·ter·min·gle (ĭn′tər-mĭng′gəl) *v.* **-gled, -gling, -gles.** *—tr.* To mix or mingle. *—intr.* To mix or mingle with one another.

in·ter·mis·sion (ĭn′tər-mĭsh′ən) *n.* **1. a.** The act of intermitting. **b.** The state of being intermitted. **2.** A respite; a temporary cessation. **3.** The period between the separate acts or parts of a play,

PRONUNCIATION KEY

ă, pat; ā, pay; âr, care;
ä, father, are; b, bib;
ch, church; d, deed; ĕ, pet;
ē, be; f, fife; g, gag; h, hat;
hw, which; ĭ, pit; ī, pie;
îr, pier; j, judge; k, kick;
l, lid, needle; m, mum;
n, no, sudden; ng, thing;
ŏ, pot; ō, toe; ô, paw, for;
oi, noise; ou, out; o͝o, book;
o͞o, boot; p, pop; r, roar;
s, sauce; sh, ship, dish;
t, tight; th, thin, path;
th, this, bathe; ŭ, cut; ûr, fur;
v, valve; w, with; y, yes;
z, zebra, size; zh, vision;
ə, about, item, edible,
gallop, circus, peaceful

IN FOREIGN WORDS:

à, *Fr.* ami; œ, *Fr.* feu, *Ger.* schön; ü, *Fr.* tu, *Ger.* über; KH, *Ger.* ich, *Scot.* loch; N, *Fr.* bon; y′, *Fr.* Compiègne

STRESS MARKS:

Primary stress: ′
in·cite′ (ĭn-sīt′)
Secondary stress: ′
in′sight′ (ĭn′sīt′)

internal-combustion engine

THE ENGINE THAT PUT THE WORLD ON WHEELS
Rotary motion from a series of explosions

Every invention changes the world to some extent, but none has done so more than the internal-combustion engine. Gasoline-driven and diesel-powered automobiles, airplanes, modern tractors, submarines, tanks, and many other forms of transport were all made possible by it. Gas turbines and jet engines also operate by internal combustion.

Its name comes from the fact that fuel is burned inside the engine, rather than in a separate chamber—as in a steam engine, for example. The idea of burning an explosive mixture of gases to drive a piston to and fro was first put into practice in 1856 by two Italians, Eugenio Barsanti and Felice Matteucci, using a mixture of coal gas and air. Since then the idea has been steadily refined. In 1876 the German manufacturer Nikolaus August Otto built the first successful engine based on the four-stroke cycle (see below). Otto's engine was gas-fueled. It was the Ger-

man engineer Gottlieb Daimler who in 1883 made an engine that could run on gasoline. It was more powerful and, being portable, made the automobile feasible. In the diesel engine, developed in Germany in 1892 by Rudolf Diesel, the fuel-air mixture is not detonated by a spark from a spark plug but ignites because of the heat produced by compression.

All conventional engines face the problem that the reciprocating (up and down) movement of the piston has to be converted into rotary movement of a shaft to make it turn wheels or a propeller. This problem is solved by using connecting rods to link pistons and shaft. The connecting rods pump up and down like the legs of a cyclist. Several pistons operate in turn; this produces continuous rotation of the shaft, which in turn makes each piston perform its cycle of strokes before the next spark from the plug.

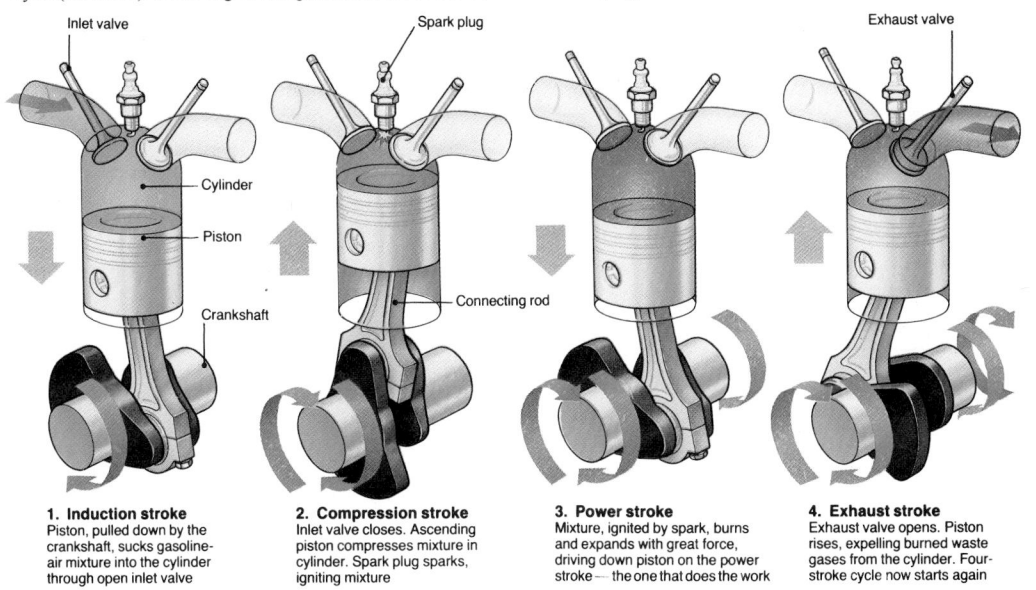

1. Induction stroke
Piston, pulled down by the crankshaft, sucks gasoline-air mixture into the cylinder through open inlet valve

2. Compression stroke
Inlet valve closes. Ascending piston compresses mixture in cylinder. Spark plug sparks, igniting mixture

3. Power stroke
Mixture, ignited by spark, burns and expands with great force, driving down piston on the power stroke — the one that does the work

4. Exhaust stroke
Exhaust valve opens. Piston rises, expelling burned waste gases from the cylinder. Four-stroke cycle now starts again

---

film, or other entertainment. [Latin *intermissiō* (stem *intermissiōn-*), from *intermittere*, to INTERMIT.]

in·ter·mit (ĭn′tər-mĭt′) v. **-mitted, -mitting, -mits.** —*intr.* To cease activity temporarily or repeatedly. —*tr.* To suspend (activity) temporarily or repeatedly; interrupt. [Latin *intermittere*, to interrupt at intervals : *inter-*, at intervals + *mittere*, to send, let go.] —**in·ter·mit·tence** *n.*

in·ter·mit·tent (ĭn′tər-mĭt′ənt) *adj.* Stopping and starting at intervals. —See Synonyms at **periodic.** —**in·ter·mit·tent·ly** *adv.*

intermittent current *n.* A periodically interrupted unidirectional electric current.

intermittent fever *n.* A fever, such as malaria, in which periods of improvement alternate with periods of deterioration.

in·ter·mix (ĭn′tər-mĭks′) v. **-mixed, -mixing, -mixes.** —*tr.* To mix together. —*intr.* To be or become mixed together. [Back-formation from earlier *intermixt*, from Latin *intermixtus*, past participle of *intermiscēre*, to mix together : *inter-*, mutually + *miscēre*, to mix.]

in·ter·mix·ture (ĭn′tər-mĭks′chər) *n.* **1.** The process of intermixing or the state of being intermixed. **2.** Something composed of various ingredients; a mixture. **3.** Something added to a mixture; an admixture.

in·ter·mo·lec·u·lar (ĭn′tər-mə-lĕk′yə-lər) *adj.* Occurring or operating between molecules.

in·tern, in·terne (ĭn′tûrn′) *n.* An advanced student or recent graduate undergoing supervised practical training, especially medical training in a hospital. ~*v.* **interned, -terning, -terns.** —*intr.* (ĭn′tûrn′). To train or serve as an intern. —*tr.* (ĭn-tûrn′). To detain or confine, especially in wartime. [French *interner*, to confine, from *interne*, inmate, resident assistant physician, from Old French, from Latin *internus*, INTERNAL.] —**in·tern·ship** *n.*

in·ter·nal (ĭn-tûr′nəl) *adj.* **1.** Of, relating to, or located within the limits or surface of something; inner; interior. **2.** Emanating from, belonging to, or dependent on the nature of something; intrinsic; inherent: *the internal contradictions of his theory.* **3.** Located, acting, or effective within the body. **4.** Pertaining to mental or spiritual life, as opposed to material things; subjective. **5.** Of or relating to

the domestic affairs of a country. **6.** Of or involving those who belong to a group or organization, as opposed to those outside it: *the party's internal squabbles; an internal appointment.* **7. a.** Designating an examination set and marked by the teaching institution itself, rather than by a public examinations board. **b.** Designating an examiner from one's own educational institution, as opposed to one brought in from outside. **8.** Designating a medical examination of the vagina or uterus. ~*n. Informal.* An internal medical examination. [New Latin *internalis*, from Latin *internus*, from *inter*, in, within.] —**in·ter·nal·i·ty** *n.* —**in·ter·nal·ly** *adv.*

in·ter·nal-com·bus·tion engine (ĭn-tûr′nəl-kəm-bŭs′chən) *n.* An engine, such as a piston engine or a gas turbine, in which fuel is burned within the engine proper rather than in an external furnace as in a steam engine.

internal drainage *n.* A system of drainage with no outlet to the sea. Also called "inland drainage."

internal ear *n.* The portion of the ear that includes the semicircular canals, the vestibule, and the cochlea. Also called "inner ear," "labyrinth."

internal energy *n. Symbol* **U** A thermodynamic property of a system equal to the total kinetic and potential energies of all the molecules present. It is the quantity that changes when the system alters or suffers external work without energy transfer from or to its surroundings.

in·ter·nal·ize (ĭn-tûr′nə-līz′) *tr.v.* **-ized, -izing, -izes.** **1.** To take (external conditions, values, or the like) into one's consciousness as part of one's own thinking; assimilate. **2.** To keep within oneself; repress: *internalize feelings of aggression.* —**in·ter·nal·i·za·tion** *n.*

internal medicine *n.* The medical study and treatment of nonsurgical constitutional diseases in adults.

Internal Revenue Service *n. Abbr.* **I.R.S.** The U.S. government department responsible for the collection of federal taxes.

internal rhyme *n.* Rhyme within a single line of verse, or between lines of verse, in which at least one of the rhyming syllables is not at the end of a line.

internal secretion *n. Physiology.* A secretion of an endocrine gland discharged directly into the blood.

in·ter·na·tion·al (ĭn′tər-năsh′ən-əl) *adj. Abbr.* **int., intl., internat.**
1. Of, pertaining to, or involving two or more nations or nationalities: *an international incident.* **2.** Ordered, demanded, or controlled by a group of nations: *an international commission.* **3.** Equally accessible to all nations: *international waters.*
~*n. Sports.* **1.** A contest or match between representative teams of two or more nations. **2.** A member of any such team. —**in·ter·na·tion·al·ly** *adv.*

in·ter·na·tion·al (ĭn′tər-năsh′ən-əl) *n.* **1.** Any of several socialist organizations of international scope formed during the late 19th and early 20th centuries; especially: **a.** The *First International* (International Workingmen's Association), organized (1864) by Marx and Engels to associate the trade unions of all nations. **b.** The *Second International* (Socialist International), an association formed (1889) to promote the unity of socialist parties in various countries. **c.** The *Third International* (Communist International), organized (1919) by the Bolsheviks to coordinate the activities of communist movements throughout the world. In this sense, also called "Comintern." **d.** The *Fourth International* formed (1937) by followers of Trotsky in opposition to Stalin and the Third International. **2.** The Internationale.

International Bank for Reconstruction and Development *n.* The official name for the **World Bank** *(see).*

international candle *n. Physics.* See **candle** (sense 3a).

International Court of Justice *n. Abbr.* **ICJ** The main judicial body of the United Nations, founded in 1945 and based in The Hague. Also called "World Court."

International Criminal Police Organization *n.* See **Interpol.**

International Date Line *n.* The date line *(see).*

In·ter·na·tio·nale (ĭn′tər-năsh′ən-əl; *French* ăn-tĕr-nä-syô-näl′) *n.* A revolutionary song adopted at different times by various syndicalist and Communist movements as an international socialist anthem. Preceded by *the.* [French, "the International."]

International Grand Master *n.* In chess, a player of the highest ranking, as certified by the World Chess Federation (F.I.D.E.). Also called "grand master."

in·ter·na·tion·al·ism (ĭn′tər-năsh′ən-ə-lĭz′əm) *n.* **1.** The state or quality of being international in character, principles, concern, or attitude. **2.** The policy or principle of cooperation among nations, especially in politics and economics. —**in·ter·na·tion·al·ist** *n.*

in·ter·na·tion·al·ize (ĭn′tər-năsh′ə-nə-līz′) *tr.v.* **-ized, -izing, -izes.** **1.** To make international. **2.** To put under international control. —**in·ter·na·tion·al·i·za·tion** *n.*

International Labor Organization *n. Abbr.* **ILO** A specialized agency of the United Nations originally established in 1919 to standardize and improve international labor conditions.

international law *n.* A set of rules generally regarded and accepted as binding in relations between states and nations. Also called "law of nations."

International Master *n.* In chess, a player of the highest ranking but one, as certified by the World Chess Federation (F.I.D.E.). Also called "master."

International Monetary Fund *n. Abbr.* **IMF** An international financial organization set up (1945) by the United Nations to regulate the exchange values of currencies, and thereby promote international trade. Loans are made to member nations in difficulties with their balance of payments, often with strict conditions attached.

International Phonetic Alphabet *n. Abbr.* **IPA, I.P.A.** A phonetic alphabet sponsored by the International Phonetic Association to provide a uniform, universally comprehensible system of letters and symbols for writing the speech sounds of all languages.

international pitch *n. Music.* **Concert pitch** *(see).*

International Practical Temperature Scale *n. Abbr.* **IPTS** A temperature scale based on 11 fixed points with agreed methods of determining temperatures between these points. It ranges from 13.81 K (triple point of hydrogen) to 1337.58 K (melting point of gold).

international time zone. See **time zone.**

interne. Variant of **intern.**

in·ter·ne·cine (ĭn′tər-nēs′ēn′, -ən, -nē′sīn′) *adj.* **1.** Mutually destructive; ruinous or fatal to both sides. **2.** Characterized by bloodshed or carnage. **3.** Carried on within a nation or organization: *internecine struggles.* [Latin *internecīnus,* from *interneciō,* massacre, from *internecāre,* to slaughter, massacre : *inter* (intensive) + *necāre,* to kill.]

in·tern·ee (ĭn′tûr-nē′) *n.* One who is interned, especially during a war.

in·ter·neu·ron (ĭn′tər-nŏŏr′ŏn′, -nyŏŏr′-) *n. Physiology.* A neuron that acts as a link between motor neurons and sensory neurons in a reflex arc. —**in·ter·neu·ro·nal** (-nŏŏr′ə-nəl, -nyŏŏr′-, -nŏŏ-rō′-, -nyŏŏ-) *adj.*

in·ter·nist (ĭn-tûr′nĭst) *n.* A doctor who specializes in internal medicine. [INTERN(AL MEDICINE) + -IST.]

in·tern·ment (ĭn-tûrn′mənt) *n.* The act of interning or the state of being interned.

in·ter·node (ĭn′tər-nōd′) *n.* A section or part between two nodes, as of a nerve or stem. —**in·ter·no·dal** (ĭn′tər-nōd′l) *adj.*

in·ter·nun·ci·o (ĭn′tər-nŭn′shē-ō′, -sē-ō′) *n., pl.* **-os.** A Vatican diplomatic envoy or representative ranking just beneath a nuncio. [Italian *internunzio,* from Latin *internuntius,* go-between : *inter-,* between + *nūntius,* messenger, NUNCIO.] —**in·ter·nun·cial** *adj.*

in·ter·o·cep·tor (ĭn′tə-rō-sĕp′tər) *n. Physiology.* A specialized sensory nerve receptor responding to stimuli originating in internal

organs. [From INTER(IOR) + (RE)CEPTOR.] —**in·ter·o·cep·tive** *adj.*

in·ter·of·fice (ĭn′tər-ô′fĭs, -ŏf′ĭs) *adj.* Taking place between offices, especially of an organization: *an interoffice memo.*

in·ter·par·ti·cle (ĭn′tər-pär′tĭ-kəl) *adj.* Occurring or existing between particles.

in·ter·pel·late (ĭn′tər-pĕl′āt′, ĭn-tûr′pə-lāt′) *tr.v.* **-lated, -lating, -lates.** In some legislative bodies, to question formally about government policy or action. [Latin *interpellāre,* to interrupt by speaking.] —**in·ter·pel·lant** *n. & adj.* —**in·ter·pel·la·tion** *n.* —**in·ter·pel·la·tor** *n.*

in·ter·pen·e·trate (ĭn′tər-pĕn′ə-trāt′) *v.* **-trated, -trating, -trates.** —*tr.* **1.** To penetrate thoroughly; permeate. **2.** To penetrate (each other). —*intr.* To penetrate mutually. —**in·ter·pen·e·tra·tion** *n.* —**in·ter·pen·e·tra·tive** *adj.*

in·ter·per·son·al (ĭn′tər-pûr′sə-nəl) *adj.* Occurring between or involving two or more people: *interpersonal relations.*

in·ter·phase (ĭn′tər-fāz′) *n. Biology.* A period or stage between two successive mitotic divisions of a cell nucleus.

in·ter·plan·e·tar·y (ĭn′tər-plăn′ə-tĕr′ē) *adj.* Between planets.

in·ter·play (ĭn′tər-plā′) *n.* Reciprocal action and reaction; interaction.
~*intr.v.* **interplayed, -playing, -plays.** To act or react on each other; interact.

in·ter·plead (ĭn′tər-plēd′) *intr.v.* **-pleaded, -pleading, -pleads.** *Law.* To go to court together in order to settle a point in which a third party is involved. [Norman French *entrepleder* : INTER- + *pleder,* to plead, from Old French *plaidier, pleidier,* to PLEAD.]

in·ter·plead·er (ĭn′tər-plē′dər) *n. Law.* **1.** A legal procedure to determine which of two persons bringing the same suit against a third person is the rightful claimant. **2.** One who interpleads.

In·ter·pol (ĭn′tər-pōl′) *n.* An international police organization comprising the police forces of over 100 countries and concentrating on international crimes. The General Secretariat is in Paris. Also officially called "International Criminal Police Organization."

in·ter·po·late (ĭn-tûr′pə-lāt′) *v.* **-lated, -lating, -lates.** —*tr.* **1.** To insert or introduce between other things or parts; interpose; interject. **2.** To insert (additional or false material) in a text. **3.** To change or falsify (a text) by introducing new or false material. **4.** *Mathematics.* To determine a value of (a function) between known values by a procedure different from that specified by the function itself. —*intr.* To make insertions, additions, or interjections. [Latin *interpolāre* : *inter-,* between + *polīre,* to adorn, furbish, POLISH.] —**in·ter·po·la·tion** *n.* —**in·ter·po·la·tive** *adj.* —**in·ter·po·la·tor** *n.*

in·ter·pose (ĭn′tər-pōz′) *v.* **-posed, -posing, -poses.** —*tr.* **1.** To place in an intervening position; insert or introduce between parts. **2.** To introduce or interject (a remark, question, or digression) during a conversation or speech. **3.** To exert (influence or authority) in order to interfere, obstruct, or intervene: *interpose one's veto.* —*intr.* **1.** To come between; intervene. **2.** To introduce a remark, question, or argument; interrupt. [Old French *interposer,* from Latin *interpōnere* (past participle *interpositus*), to place between : *inter-,* between + *pōnere,* to put, place.] —**in·ter·pos·er** *n.* —**in·ter·po·si·tion** (ĭn′tər-pə-zĭsh′ən) *n.*

in·ter·pret (ĭn-tûr′prĭt) *v.* **-preted, -preting, -prets.** —*tr.* **1.** To clarify the meaning of; elucidate. **2.** To explain or perceive the significance of; construe: *interpreted his grunt as a refusal.* **3.** To represent the meaning or character of (a piece of music or a dramatic role, for example). **4.** To translate. —*intr.* **1.** To offer an explanation. **2.** To act as an interpreter. —See Synonyms at **explain.** [Middle English *interpreten,* from Old French *interpreter,* from Latin *interpretārī,* from *interpres,* interpreter, negotiator.] —**in·ter·pret·a·bil·i·ty, in·ter·pret·a·ble·ness** *n.* —**in·ter·pret·a·ble** *adj.*

in·ter·pre·ta·tion (ĭn-tûr′prə-tā′shən) *n.* **1.** The act or process of interpreting; elucidation. **2.** The result of interpreting; an explanation or inference. **3.** A concept of a work of art as expressed by the character and style of its representation or performance. —**in·ter·pre·ta·tion·al** *adj.*

in·ter·pre·ta·tive (ĭn-tûr′prə-tā′tĭv) *adj.* Also **in·ter·pre·tive** (-prə-tĭv). Expository; explanatory. —**in·ter·pre·ta·tive·ly** *adv.*

in·ter·pret·er (ĭn-tûr′prə-tər) *n.* **1.** One who translates orally the words of parties communicating with each other in different languages. **2.** One who makes and expounds an interpretation: *medieval interpreters of Aristotle.* **3.** *Computer Science.* A program or circuit for changing from the language in which instructions are written into machine code for use by the computers.

in·ter·ra·cial (ĭn′tər-rā′shəl) *adj.* Involving or existing between members of different racial groups: *interracial tension.*

in·ter·reg·num (ĭn′tər-rĕg′nəm) *n., pl.* **-nums** or **-na** (-nə). **1.** The interval of time between the end of a sovereign's reign and the accession of a successor. **2.** A period of temporary suspension of the usual functions of government or control. **3.** Any gap in continuity. [Latin *interrēgnum* : *inter-,* between + *rēgnum,* REIGN.] —**in·ter·reg·nal** *adj.*

in·ter·re·late (ĭn′tər-rĭ-lāt′) *v.* **-lated, -lating, -lates.** —*tr.* To place in mutual relationship. —*intr.* To come into mutual relationship. —**in·ter·re·la·tion** *n.* —**in·ter·re·la·tion·ship** *n.*

in·ter·rex (ĭn′tər-rĕks′) *n., pl.* **interreges** (ĭn′tər-rē′jēz′). One who holds supreme state power during an interregnum. [Latin *interrex* : *inter-,* between + *rēx,* king.]

interrog. interrogative.

in·ter·ro·gate (ĭn-tĕr′ə-gāt′) *tr.v.* **-gated, -gating, -gates.** **1.** To question closely and formally; especially, to subject to prolonged and systematic questioning, sometimes with the use of threats or force. **2.** To obtain specific information from (a computer or data store) by program. —See Synonyms at **ask.** [Latin *interrogāre,* to consult, question : *inter-,* between + *rogāre,* to ask.] —**in·ter·ro·gat·ing·ly** *adv.* —**in·ter·ro·ga·tion** *n.* —**in·ter·ro·ga·tion·al** *adj.* —**in·ter·ro·ga·tor** *n.*

interrogation point *n.* A question mark (sense 1) *(see).* Also called "interrogation mark."

in·ter·rog·a·tive (ĭn′tə-rŏg′ə-tĭv) *adj.* Abbr. **interrog. 1.** Having the form or character of a question; asking or serving to ask a question: *an interrogative raising of the eyebrows.* **2.** Designating a word or form used in asking a question: *an interrogative pronoun.* Compare **demonstrative, relative.**
~*n.* **1.** A word or form used in asking a question. **2.** An interrogative sentence or expression. **3.** A question mark. —**in·ter·rog·a·tive·ly** *adv.*

in·ter·rog·a·to·ry (ĭn′tə-rŏg′ə-tôr′ē, -tōr′ē) *adj.* Interrogative.
~*n., pl.* **-ries.** *Usually* **interrogatories.** *Law.* A formal statement of questions that one party to a civil action may require the rival party to answer under oath. —**in·ter·rog·a·tor·i·ly** *adv.*

in·ter·rupt (ĭn′tə-rŭpt′) *v.* **-rupted, -rupting, -rupts.** —*tr.* **1. a.** To break the continuity or uniformity of. **b.** To be in the way of; obstruct (a view, for example). **2.** To hinder or stop the action or discourse of (someone) by breaking in. —*intr.* To break in upon an action or discourse. —See Synonyms at **intrude.**
~*n.* *Computer Science.* A signal or code for temporarily interrupting the processing of one computer program in order to process a different program. [Middle English *interrupten,* from Latin *interrumpere* (past participle *interruptus*), to break in : *inter,* between + *rumpere,* to break.] —**in·ter·rup·tion** *n.* —**in·ter·rup·tive** *adj.*

in·ter·rupt·ed (ĭn′tə-rŭp′tĭd) *adj.* **1.** Broken in continuity; discontinuous. **2.** *Botany.* Having an uneven arrangement, as of leaflets along a stem. —**in·ter·rup·ted·ly** *adv.*

in·ter·rupt·er, in·ter·rup·tor (ĭn′tə-rŭp′tər) *n.* **1.** One that interrupts. **2.** A device for periodically and automatically opening or closing an electric circuit.

in·ter se (ĭn′tər sē′, sā′) *adv.* *Latin.* Between or among themselves.

in·ter·sect (ĭn′tər-sĕkt′) *v.* **-sected, -secting, -sects.** —*tr.* To divide or penetrate (a line or space, for example) by cutting across or through. —*intr.* **1.** To cut across or overlap each other. **2.** To form an intersection. [Latin *intersecāre* (past participle *intersectus*) : *inter-,* mutually + *secāre,* to cut.]

in·ter·sec·tion (ĭn′tər-sĕk′shən) *n.* **1. a.** The act or process of intersecting. **b.** A place where things intersect; especially, a place where two or more roads cross. **2.** *Mathematics.* **a.** The point or locus of points common to two or more geometric figures. **b.** A set every member of which is an element of each of two or more given sets.

in·ter·sex (ĭn′tər-sĕks′) *n.* An intersexual individual.

in·ter·sex·u·al (ĭn′tər-sĕk′shōō-əl) *adj.* **1.** Existing or occurring between the sexes. **2.** Having sexual characteristics intermediate between those of a typical male and a typical female. —**in·ter·sex·u·al·i·ty** *n.* —**in·ter·sex·u·al·ly** *adv.*

in·ter·space (ĭn′tər-spās′) *tr.v.* **-spaced, -spacing, -spaces.** To make or occupy a space between.
~*n.* (ĭn′tər-spās′). A space between two things; an interval. —**in·ter·spa·tial** (ĭn′tər-spā′shəl) *adj.*

in·ter·sperse (ĭn′tər-spûrs′) *tr.v.* **-spersed, -spersing, -sperses. 1.** To scatter or distribute among other things at irregular intervals. **2.** To supply or diversify with things distributed at irregular intervals. [Latin *interspergere* (past participle *interspersus*), to scatter among : *inter-,* among + *spargere,* to scatter.] —**in·ter·spers·ed·ly** (ĭn′tər-spûr′sĭd-lē) *adv.* —**in·ter·sper·sion** (ĭn′tər-spûr′zhən, -shən) *n.*

in·ter·state (ĭn′tər-stāt′) *adj.* Involving, existing between, or connecting two or more states.
~*n.* A major road running between two states.

in·ter·stel·lar (ĭn′tər-stĕl′ər) *adj.* Between the stars.

in·ter·stice (ĭn-tûr′stĭs) *n., pl.* **-stices** (-stī-sēz′, -sĭz). A narrow or small space between things or parts; hole; crevice. [French, from Late Latin *interstitium,* from Latin *intersistere* (past participle *interstitus*), to stand in the middle of : *inter-,* in the middle of, between + *sistere,* to stand.]

in·ter·sti·tial (ĭn′tər-stĭsh′əl) *adj.* **1.** Of or occurring in interstices. **2.** Affecting or based on interstices.
~*n.* **1.** Any of various cells occurring in the spaces between tissues or organs, especially those interspersed between the seminiferous tubules of the testis. **2.** An atom or ion in a crystal, in a position between two normal lattice positions. —**in·ter·sti·tial·ly** *adv.*

in·ter·sti·tial-cell stimulating hormone (ĭn′tər-stĭsh′əl-sĕl′) *n.* Abbr. **ICSH** A luteinizing hormone *(see).*

interstitial compound *n.* *Chemistry.* A solid compound in which atoms of a nonmetal such as carbon or boron occupy interstitial positions in a metal lattice.

in·ter·strat·i·fy (ĭn′tər-străt′ə-fī′) *tr.v.* **-fied, -fying, -fies.** To alternate or vary with other strata. Used in the passive. —**in·ter·strat·i·fi·ca·tion** *n.*

in·ter·tex·ture (ĭn′tər-tĕks′chər) *n.* **1.** The act of interweaving or the state of being interwoven. **2.** Something interwoven.

in·ter·tid·al (ĭn′tər-tīd′l) *adj.* Of, pertaining to, or designating the region between the extremes of high and low tide.

in·ter·tri·bal (ĭn′tər-trī′bəl) *adj.* Existing or carried on between tribes.

in·ter·tri·go (ĭn′tər-trī′gō) *n.* Inflammation of two moist skin surfaces that are in contact and between which there is friction, as may occur on the inside of the thighs.

in·ter·trop·i·cal (ĭn′tər-trŏp′ĭ-kəl) *adj.* *Geography.* **1.** Between or within the tropics. **2.** Of or pertaining to the tropics.

in·ter·twine (ĭn′tər-twīn′) *v.* **-twined, -twining, -twines.** —*tr.* To twist or braid together. —*intr.* To interweave with one another; become entwined. —**in·ter·twine·ment** *n.*

in·ter·ur·ban (ĭn′tər-ûr′bən) *adj.* Pertaining to or connecting urban areas: *an interurban bus.*

in·ter·val (ĭn′tər-vəl) *n.* Abbr. **int. 1.** A space between two objects, points, or units. **2.** The temporal duration between two instants, events, or states. **3.** *Mathematics.* **a.** A set consisting of all the numbers between a pair of given numbers, either including the end points *(closed interval)* or excluding the end points *(open interval).* **b.** A line segment representing such a set. **c.** A set of numbers greater than or less than a given number and including or excluding the given number. **4.** *Chiefly British.* A short pause between the acts of a play, parts of a concert, and the like; an intermission. **5.** *Music.* The difference in pitch between two notes on a given scale. —**at intervals. 1.** Intermittently; now and then. **2.** Separated by spaces. [Middle English *intervalle,* from Latin *intervallum,* space between ramparts : *inter-,* between + *vallum,* rampart.]

in·ter·vene (ĭn′tər-vēn′) *intr.v.* **-vened, -vening, -venes. 1.** To enter, appear, or have an effect as an extraneous element: *At this point fate intervened.* **2.** To come, appear, or lie between two things. **3.** To occur or come between two periods or points of time. **4.** To come in or between so as to mediate, prevent, or otherwise affect an outcome. Often used with *between* or *in.* **5.** To interfere, usually through force or threat of force, in the affairs of another nation. **6.** *Law.* To enter into a suit as a third party for the protection of an alleged interest. [Latin *inter-,* between + *venīre,* to come.] —**in·ter·ven·er** *n.* —**in·ter·ven·shon** *n.*

in·ter·ven·tion·ism (ĭn′tər-vĕn′shə-nĭz′əm) *n.* **1.** The policy of intervening in the affairs of another sovereign state. **2.** Government action designed to control or influence domestic economic activity, as through nationalization of industries. —**in·ter·ven·tion·ist** *adj. & n.*

in·ter·ver·te·bral disk (ĭn′tər-vûr′tə-brəl, -vûr′tē′-) *n.* *Anatomy.* Any of the flexible plates of fibrocartilage connecting adjacent vertebrae in the spinal column.

in·ter·view (ĭn′tər-vyōō′) *n.* **1. a.** A face-to-face meeting. **b.** Such a meeting arranged for a particular purpose, especially the assessment of a candidate for a job or award. **2. a.** A conversation between a reporter and a person from whom he seeks facts or statements. **b.** An account or reproduction of such a conversation.
~*v.* **interviewed, -viewing, -views.** —*tr.* To have an interview with. —*intr.* To undergo an interview: *Some people don't interview well.* [Earlier *entervewe,* from Old French *entrevue,* from *entrevu,* past participle of *(s')entrevoir,* to see each other : *entre-,* INTER- + *voir,* to see, from Latin *vidēre.*] —**in·ter·view·ee** *n.* —**in·ter·view·er** *n.*

in·ter·vo·cal·ic (ĭn′tər-vō-kăl′ĭk) *adj.* *Phonetics.* Immediately followed and immediately preceded by a vowel.

in·ter·volve (ĭn′tər-vŏlv′) *tr.v.* **-volved, -volving, -volves.** To wind or coil together.

in·ter·weave (ĭn′tər-wēv′) *tr.v.* **-wove** (-wōv′) or *rare* **-weaved, -woven** (-wō′vən) or *rare* **-wove, -weaving, -weaves. 1.** To weave together. **2.** To intermix.

in·tes·tate (ĭn-tĕs′tāt′, -tĭt) *adj.* **1.** Having made no legal will: *died intestate.* **2.** Not disposed of by a legal will. Said of property.
~*n.* One who dies without a legal will. [Middle English, from Latin *intestātus* : *in-,* not + *testātus,* TESTATE.] —**in·tes·ta·cy** (ĭn-tĕs′tə-sē) *n.*

intestinal flora *n.* All the harmless and beneficial bacteria that live in the intestinal tract.

intestinal fortitude *n.* Courage; endurance.

in·tes·tine¹ (ĭn-tĕs′tən) *n.* The portion of the **alimentary canal** *(see)* extending from the stomach to the anus. See **small intestine, large intestine.** [Latin *intestīnum,* from *intestīnus,* internal, from *intus,* within.] —**in·tes·ti·nal** *adj.* —**in·tes·ti·nal·ly** *adv.*

intestine² *adj.* Involving or restricted to the people of a country; internal; internecine: *intestine conflicts.*

in·ti·ma (ĭn′tə-mə) *n., pl.* **-mae** (-mē′) or **-mas.** *Anatomy.* The innermost layer of an organ or part, especially the wall of a lymphatic vessel, artery, or vein. [New Latin, from Latin, feminine of *intimus,* innermost.]

in·ti·ma·cy (ĭn′tə-mə-sē) *n., pl.* **-cies. 1.** The condition of being intimate. **2.** An instance of being intimate. **3.** *Sometimes* **intimacies.** Sexual intercourse. Used formally or euphemistically. [From INTIMATE.]

in·ti·mate¹ (ĭn′tə-mĭt) *adj.* **1.** Marked by close acquaintance, association, or familiarity: *an intimate friend.* **2. a.** Pertaining to or indicative of one's deepest nature. **b.** Very personal; private; secret. **3.** Essential; innermost. **4.** Characterized by informality and privacy: *an intimate nightclub.* **5.** Involved in a sexual relationship. —See Synonyms at **familiar.**
~*n.* A close friend or confidant. [Late Latin *intimātus,* past participle of *intimāre,* to put in, announce, INTIMATE (to hint).] —**in·ti·mate·ly** *adv.* —**in·ti·mate·ness** *n.*

in·ti·mate² (ĭn′tə-māt′) *tr.v.* **-mated, -mating, -mates. 1.** To communicate with a hint or other indirect sign; imply subtly. **2.** To announce; proclaim. —See Synonyms at **suggest.** [Late Latin *intimāre,* to make known or announce (one's inmost thoughts), from Latin *intimus,* inmost, deepest.] —**in·ti·ma·ter** *n.* —**in·ti·ma·tion** *n.*

in·tim·i·date (ĭn-tĭm′ə-dāt′) *tr.v.* **-dated, -dating, -dates. 1.** To make timid; frighten. **2.** To discourage, silence, or inhibit by or as if by threats. —See Synonyms at **threaten.** [Medieval Latin *intimidāre* : Latin *in-* (causative) + *timidus,* TIMID.] —**in·tim·i·da·tion** *n.* —**in·tim·i·da·tor** *n.* —**in·tim·i·da·to·ry** (ĭn-tĭm'ə-də-tôr'ē, -tōr'ē) *adj.*

in·tinc·tion (ĭn-tĭngk'shən) *n. Ecclesiastical.* The administration of the Eucharist by dipping the host into the wine before offering it to the communicant. [Late Latin *intinctiō* (stem *intinctiōn-*), from Latin *intingere* (past participle *intinctus*), to dip in : *in-,* in + *tingere,* to moisten, dye.]

in·tine (ĭn'tēn') *n.* The inner layer of the cell wall surrounding a grain of pollen. Also called "endosporium." [Latin *inti(mus),* innermost + -INE.]

in·tit·ule (ĭn-tĭt'yōōl) *tr.v.* **-uled, -uling, -ules.** *British.* To give a title to (an Act of Parliament). [Old French *intituler,* from Late Latin *intitulāre* : Latin *in-,* in + *titulus,* TITLE.]

intl. international.

in·to (ĭn'tōō) *prep.* **1.** To the inside or middle part of; to a point within. **2.** To the action or occupation of: *go into banking.* **3.** To the condition, state, or form of: *break into pieces; get into debt.* **4.** So as to be in or within: *enter into an agreement.* **5.** To a time or place in the course of: *well into the week.* **6.** Against: *ram into a tree.* **7.** Toward; in the direction of: *look into the distance.* **8.** As a divisor of: *Two into eight is four.* **9.** *Informal.* Interested in or involved with: *They are into vegetarianism.* [Middle English *into,* Old English *intō* : IN + TO.]

in·tol·er·a·ble (ĭn-tŏl'ər-ə-bəl) *adj.* **1.** Insupportable; unbearable. **2.** *Informal.* Extremely annoying; maddening. —**in·tol·er·a·bil·i·ty, in·tol·er·a·ble·ness** *n.* —**in·tol·er·a·bly** *adv.*

in·tol·er·ance (ĭn-tŏl'ər-əns) *n.* **1.** The quality or condition of being intolerant. **2.** Inability to withstand or consume: *an intolerance to certain drugs.*

in·tol·er·ant (ĭn-tŏl'ər-ənt) *adj.* **1.** Not tolerant of different characteristics or habits in others; bigoted. **2.** Irritable; short-tempered. **3.** Unable or indisposed to endure. —**in·tol·er·ant·ly** *adv.*

in·to·nate (ĭn'tō-nāt') *tr.v.* **-nated, -nating, -nates. 1.** To intone. **2.** To utter with a particular intonation.

in·to·na·tion (ĭn'tō-nā'shən) *n.* **1. a.** The act of intoning or chanting. **b.** An intoned utterance. **2.** A manner of producing musical notes, especially with regard to accuracy of pitch. **3. a.** The use of pitch as an element of meaning in language: *a questioning intonation.* **b.** A characteristic pattern of rising and falling pitch in speaking: *a lilting intonation in his voice.* **4.** *Music.* The opening phrase of a plainsong composition, sung as a solo part.

in·tone (ĭn-tōn') *v.* **-toned, -toning, -tones.** *—tr.* **1.** To recite in a singing voice. **2.** To utter in a monotone. *—intr.* **1.** To speak with a given intonation. **2.** To sing a plainsong intonation. [Middle English *entonen,* from Old French *entoner,* from Medieval Latin *intonāre,* to utter in a musical tone : Latin *in-,* in + *tonus,* TONE.] —**in·ton·er** *n.*

in to·to (ĭn tō'tō) *adv. Latin.* Totally; altogether.

in·tox·i·cant (ĭn-tŏk'sĭ-kənt) *n.* An agent that intoxicates; especially, an alcoholic drink. —**in·tox·i·cant** *adj.*

in·tox·i·cate (ĭn-tŏk'sĭ-kāt') *tr.v.* **-cated, -cating, -cates. 1.** To induce, especially by the effect of ingested alcohol, any of a series of progressively deteriorating states ranging from exhilaration to stupefaction; make drunk. **2.** To stimulate or excite: *"a man whom life intoxicates, who has no need of wine"* (Anaïs Nin). **3.** To poison. [Medieval Latin *intoxicāre,* to put poison in, poison : Latin *in-,* in + *toxicum,* poison.] —**in·tox·i·ca·tion** *n.* —**in·tox·i·ca·tive** *adj.* —**in·tox·i·ca·tor** *n.*

intr. intransitive.

intra– *prefix.* Indicates in, within, or inside of; for example, **intracranial, intramuscular.** *Note:* Many compounds other than those entered here may be formed with *intra-.* In forming compounds, *intra-* is normally joined with the following element without space or hyphen: *intraorbital.* However, if the second element begins with a capital letter or with the letter *a,* it is separated with a hyphen: *intra-European, intra-atomic.* [Late Latin, from Latin *intrā,* within.]

in·tra·a·tom·ic (ĭn'trə-ə-tŏm'ĭk) *adj.* Within an atom.

in·tra·car·di·ac (ĭn'trə-kär'dē-ăk') *adj.* Within the heart.

in·tra·car·ti·lag·i·nous (ĭn'trə-kär'tə-lăj'ə-nəs) *adj.* Within cartilage.

in·tra·cel·lu·lar (ĭn'trə-sĕl'yə-lər) *adj.* Occurring or situated within a cell or cells.

In·tra·coast·al Waterway (ĭn'trə-kō'stəl). A shipping passage, 3,950 kilometers (2,455 miles) long, partly manmade, partly artificial, between the U.S. Atlantic coast from Trenton, New Jersey, to Key West, Florida, and along the Gulf of Mexico to Brownsville, Texas, on the Rio Grande. The waterway, used by pleasure and commercial craft, was authorized by Congress in 1919.

in·tra·cra·ni·al (ĭn'trə-krā'nē-əl) *adj.* Within the skull.

in·trac·ta·ble (ĭn-trăk'tə-bəl) *adj.* **1.** Difficult to manage or govern; stubborn. **2.** Difficult to mold or manipulate. **3.** Difficult to deal with or solve. **4.** Difficult to alleviate, remedy, or cure. —See Synonyms at **unruly.** —**in·trac·ta·bil·i·ty, in·trac·ta·ble·ness** *n.* —**in·trac·ta·bly** *adv.*

in·tra·cu·ta·ne·ous (ĭn'trə-kyōō-tā'nē-əs) *adj.* Within the skin: *an intracutaneous injection.*

in·tra·der·mal (ĭn'trə-dûr'məl) *adj.* Within the skin; intracutaneous.

in·tra·dos (ĭn-trā'dŏs', -dŏs') *n., pl.* **intrados** (-dōz', -dōz') or **-doses.** *Architecture.* The inner curve of an arch. [French, "inside back" : INTRA- + *dos,* back, from Old French, from Latin *dorsum.*]

in·tra·ga·lac·tic (ĭn'trə-gə-lăk'tĭk) *adj.* Occurring or situated within one galaxy.

in·tra·mo·lec·u·lar (ĭn'trə-mə-lĕk'yə-lər) *adj.* Within a molecule.

in·tra·mu·ral (ĭn'trə-myōōr'əl) *adj.* **1.** Existing or carried on within the bounds of an institution, especially a university. **2.** *Anatomy.* Within the wall of a cavity or organ. —**in·tra·mu·ral·ly** *adv.*

in·tra·mus·cu·lar (ĭn'trə-mŭs'kyə-lər) *adj.* Within muscle.

in·tran·si·gent (ĭn-trăn'sə-jənt) *adj.* Refusing to moderate a position; uncompromising. [French *intransigeant,* from Spanish *los intransigentes,* "the uncompromising" (name of a party of extreme republicans) : *in-,* not, from Latin + *transigente,* present participle of *transigir,* to compromise, from Latin *trānsigere,* to drive through, come to an understanding : *trāns-,* through + *agere,* to drive.] —**in·tran·si·gence, in·tran·si·gen·cy** *n.* —**in·tran·si·gent** *n.* —**in·tran·si·gent·ly** *adv.*

in·tran·si·tive (ĭn-trăn'sə-tĭv) *adj. Abbr.* **intr., i. 1.** *Grammar.* Designating a verb or verb construction that does not require a direct object to complete its meaning; for example; the verb *triumph* is always intransitive, and the verb *win* is sometimes intransitive. **2.** *Logic.* Designating or characterizing a relationship such that if A and B have the relationship, and B and C have the relationship then it is not true that A and C have the relationship; for example, if A is the uncle of B, and B is the uncle of C, it is not true to say that A is the uncle of C, and therefore "is the uncle of" is an intransitive relationship. Compare **transitive.** *~n.* An intransitive verb. [Late Latin *intransitīvus* : *in-,* not + *transitīvus,* TRANSITIVE.] —**in·tran·si·tive·ly** *adv.* —**in·tran·si·tive·ness** *n.*

in·tra·nu·cle·ar (ĭn'trə-nōō'klē-ər, -nyōō'klē-ər) *adj.* Within a nucleus.

in·tra·psy·chic (ĭn'trə-sī'kĭk) *adj.* Existing or taking place within the psyche: *intrapsychic conflict.* —**in·tra·psy·chi·cal·ly** *adv.*

in·tra·spe·cif·ic (ĭn'trə-spə-sĭf'ĭk) *adj.* Occurring within a species: *intraspecific selection.*

in·tra·state (ĭn'trə-stāt') *adj.* Within the boundaries of a state.

in·tra·tel·lu·ric (ĭn'trə-tə-lōōr'ĭk) *n. Geology.* Formed or found below the earth's surface. Said of rocks.

in·tra·u·ter·ine (ĭn'trə-yōō'tər-ĭn, -tə-rīn') *adj.* Within the uterus.

intrauterine device *n. Abbr.* **IUD, I.U.D.** A piece of metal or plastic, often in the shape of a loop, ring, or spiral, inserted into the uterus as a contraceptive.

in·tra·va·sa·tion (ĭn-trăv'ə-sā'shən) *n.* The entry of foreign matter into a blood vessel. [INTRA- + VAS + -ATION.]

in·tra·vas·cu·lar (ĭn'trə-văs'kyə-lər) *adj.* Within the blood vessels or lymphatics.

in·tra·ve·na·tion (ĭn'trə-vē-nā'shən) *n.* The entry of foreign matter into a vein.

in·tra·ve·nous (ĭn'trə-vē'nəs) *adj. Abbr.* **IV** Within or into a vein or veins. *~n., pl.* **intravenouses.** An intravenous injection, drip, or transfusion. —**in·tra·ve·nous·ly** *adv.*

in-tray (ĭn'trā') *n.* A tray, usually on an office desk, for incoming mail, documents needing attention, and the like.

intreat. Variant of **entreat.**

intrench. Variant of **entrench.**

intrenchment. Variant of **entrenchment.**

in·trep·id (ĭn-trĕp'ĭd) *adj.* Resolutely courageous; fearless; bold. —See Synonyms at **brave.** [French, *intrépide,* from Latin *intrepidus* : *in-,* not + *trepidus,* agitated, alarmed.] —**in·tre·pid·i·ty** (ĭn'-trə-pĭd'ə-tē) *n.* —**in·trep·id·ly** *adv.*

in·tri·ca·cy (ĭn'trĭ-kə-sē) *n., pl.* **-cies. 1.** The condition or quality of being intricate. **2.** Something intricate.

in·tri·cate (ĭn'trĭ-kĭt) *adj.* **1.** Having many elements in a complex arrangement; convoluted. **2.** Soluble or comprehensible only with painstaking effort; complicated. —See Synonyms at **complex, hard.** [Middle English, from Latin *intrīcātus,* past participle of *intrīcāre,* to entangle : *in-,* in + *trīcae,* trifles, troubles, perplexities.] —**in·tri·cate·ly** *adv.* —**in·tri·cate·ness** *n.*

in·tri·gant, in·tri·guant (ĭn'trē-gänt', ăn-trē-gäN') *n.* One who intrigues; a plotter. [French, "intriguing," from Italian *intrigante,* present participle of *intrigare,* to INTRIGUE.]

in·trigue (ĭn'trēg', ĭn-trēg') *n.* **1.** A covert maneuver to achieve an unavowed purpose; a secret or underhand scheme. **2.** The use of or involvement in such schemes. **3.** A clandestine love affair. **4. a.** The quality of exciting interest or curiosity; allurement. **b.** Mystery; suspense. —See Synonyms at **conspiracy.** *~v.* (ĭn-trēg') **intrigued, -triguing, -trigues.** *—intr.* To engage in covert schemes; plot. *—tr.* **1.** To insinuate (one's way, for example) by scheming. **2.** To arouse the interest or curiosity of. [French, from Italian *intrigo,* from *intrigare,* to perplex, from Latin *intrīcāre,* to entangle. See **intricate.**] —**in·tri·guer** *n.* —**in·trigu·ing·ly** *adv.*

in·trin·sic (ĭn-trĭn'sĭk) *adj.* Also *archaic* **in·trin·si·cal** (-sĭ-kəl). **1.** Belonging to the essential nature of a thing; inherent: *"the exploitive and oppressive relationships intrinsic to capitalism"* (E.P. Thompson). **2.** *Anatomy.* Situated within or belonging solely to a body part, as certain nerves and muscles are. [Old French *intrinseque,* inner, from Late Latin *intrinsecus,* inward, from Latin, inwardly, on the inside : *intrim* (unattested), inward, from *intrā,* within + *secus,* alongside.] —**in·trin·si·cal·ly** *adv.*

intrinsic factor *n. Biochemistry.* A protein secreted in the stomach that is essential for the absorption of vitamin B_{12}.

intrinsic semiconductor *n.* A semiconductor that has no dopant added, having equal numbers of current-carrying holes and electrons.

in·tro (ĭn'trō') *n. Informal.* An introduction.

intro– *prefix.* Indicates: **1.** In or into; for example, **introjection.**

2. Inward; for example, **introvert.** [Latin, from *intrō,* to the inside, inwardly.]

intro., introd. introduction; introductory.

in·tro·duce (ĭn′trə-do͞os′, -dyo͞os′) *tr.v.* **-duced, -ducing, -duces.** **1.** To identify and present; especially: **a.** To present to an audience. **b.** To make (a stranger) known to another person. Often used with *to.* **c.** To make (strangers) acquainted. **2.** To present and recommend (a plan, for example) for consideration. **3.** To bring into currency, use, or practice; institute. **4.** To bring in and establish: *introduce exotic birds.* **5.** To insert or inject. **6.** To make (a person) acquainted with something new: *introduced them to sailing.* **7.** To preface; open. [Latin *intrōdūcere,* to lead in : *intrō-,* in + *dūcere,* to lead.] **—in·tro·duc·er** *n.* **—in·tro·duc·i·ble** *adj.*

in·tro·duc·tion (ĭn′trə-dŭk′shən) *n. Abbr.* **intro., introd. 1.** An act of introducing. **2.** The state of being introduced. **3.** A means of presenting one person to another, such as a personal presentation or formal letter. **4.** Something recently introduced; an innovation. **5.** Anything spoken, written, or otherwise presented in introducing, especially: **a.** A preface, as in a book. **b.** A short preliminary movement in a musical work. **6.** A basic instructive text or course of study. [Middle English *introduccion,* from Old French *introduction,* from Latin *intrōductiō* (stem *intrōductiōn-*), from *intrōdūcere,* to INTRODUCE.]

in·tro·duc·to·ry (ĭn′trə-dŭk′tə-rē) *adj.* Also **in·tro·duc·tive** (-tĭv). *Abbr.* **intro., introd.** Serving to introduce. **—in·tro·duc·to·ri·ly** *adv.*

in·tro·gres·sion (ĭn′trə-grĕsh′ən) *n. Genetics.* The introduction of genetic material to one gene pool from another by hybridization. Also called "introgressive hybridization." [INTRO- + *-gression* (as in *digression*).]

in·tro·it, In·tro·it (ĭn-trō′ĭt) *n. Ecclesiastical.* **1.** A hymn or psalm sung at the opening of a service, especially in the Anglican Church. **2.** *Roman Catholic Church.* The beginning of the proper of the Mass, usually consisting of a psalm verse, antiphon, and the Gloria Patri followed by the repeated verse. [Middle English, "entrance," beginning, from Old French *introït,* from Latin *introitus,* from the past participle of *introīre,* to go in, enter : *intrō-,* into + *īre,* to go.]

in·tro·jec·tion (ĭn′trə-jĕk′shən) *n.* **1.** The unconscious incorporation into one's personality of the characteristics of another person or of an inanimate object. **2.** The incorporation or adoption of any attitude or belief. [INTRO- + (PRO)JECTION.] **—in·tro·ject** *v.*

in·tro·mis·sion (ĭn′trə-mĭsh′ən) *n.* **1.** Introduction; admission. **2.** *Biology.* The introduction of one organ or part into another, such as the penis into the vagina. [Medieval Latin *intrōmissiō* (stem *intrōmissiōn-*), from Latin *intrōmittere,* to INTROMIT.] **—in·tro·mis·sive** *adj.*

in·tro·mit (ĭn′trə-mĭt′) *tr.v.* **-mitted, -mitting, -mits.** To cause or permit to enter; introduce or admit. [Middle English *intromitten,* from Latin *intrōmittere,* to send or put in, introduce : *intrō-,* in + *mittere,* to send.] **—in·tro·mit·tent** *adj.* **—in·tro·mit·ter** *n.*

in·trorse (ĭn-trôrs′) *adj. Botany.* Facing inward; turned toward the axis. Said especially of anthers that shed their pollen toward the flower. [Latin *introrsus,* contracted from *intrōversus,* turned inward : *intrō-,* inward + *versus,* past participle of *vertere,* to turn.]

in·tro·spect (ĭn′trə-spĕkt′) *intr.v.* **-spected, -specting, -spects.** To turn one's thoughts inward; examine one's own feelings. [Latin *intrōspicere* (past participle *intrōspectus*), to look into : *intrō-,* into + *specere,* to look.]

in·tro·spec·tion (ĭn′trə-spĕk′shən) *n.* Contemplation of one's own thoughts and sensations; self-examination.

in·tro·spec·tive (ĭn′trə-spĕk′tĭv) *adj.* **1.** Of, pertaining, or given to introspection. **2.** Given to private thought; contemplative. **—in·tro·spec·tive·ly** *adv.* **—in·tro·spec·tive·ness** *n.*

in·tro·ver·sion (ĭn′trə-vûr′zhən, -shən) *n.* **1. a.** The directing of one's thoughts and interests inward, especially to an excessive degree, accompanied by absence of interest in or aptitude for dealing with the external world and other people. **b.** A disposition toward introversion. Compare **extroversion. 2.** *Medicine.* The turning inward of a hollow organ. **—in·tro·ver·sive** *adj.*

in·tro·vert (ĭn′trə-vûrt′) *v.* **-verted, -verting, -verts.** *—tr.* **1.** To turn or direct inward. **2.** To concentrate (one's thoughts or feelings) inward upon themselves. **3.** To turn (a tubular organ or part) inward upon itself. *—intr.* To exhibit introversion.
~n. (ĭn′trə-vûrt′). **1.** A person whose manner and behavior are characterized by introversion. Compare **extrovert. 2.** An anatomical structure, such as the intestine, that is turned inward upon itself.
~adj. Characterized by introversion; introverted. [New Latin *introvertere* : INTRO- + Latin *vertere,* to turn.]

in·trude (ĭn-tro͞od′) *v.* **-truded, -truding, -trudes.** *—tr.* **1.** To interpose (oneself or something) without invitation or permission, or quite inappropriately. **2.** *Geology.* To force (molten rock) into existing rocks. *—intr.* To come in rudely or inappropriately; enter as an improper or unwanted element: *intruding on a private conversation.* [Latin *intrūdere,* to thrust in : *in-,* in + *trūdere,* to thrust.] **—in·trud·er** *n.*

Synonyms: *interlope, interrupt, obtrude.*

in·tru·sion (ĭn-tro͞o′zhən) *n.* **1.** The act or an instance of intruding, or the state of being intruded upon. **2.** An inappropriate or unwelcome addition: *"The fields were a timid intrusion on a landscape hardly marked by man"* (Doris Lessing). **3.** *Law.* Illegal entry upon or appropriation of the property of another. **4.** *Geology.* **a.** The forcing of molten rock into existing rocks. **b.** The intrusive mass so produced.

in·tru·sive (ĭn-tro͞o′sĭv) *adj.* **1.** Intruding or tending to intrude. **2.** *Geology.* Designating igneous rock forced into existing rocks while in molten state; irruptive. **3.** *Linguistics.* Constituting an **epenthesis** *(see).* —See Usage note at **curious. —in·tru·sive·ly** *adv.* **—in·tru·sive·ness** *n.*

intrust. Variant of **entrust.**

in·tu·bate (ĭn′to͞o-bāt′, -tyo͞o-bāt′) *tr.v.* **-bated, -bating, -bates.** *Medicine.* To insert a tube into (an organ or passage); cannulate. **—in·tu·ba·tion** *n.*

in·tu·it (ĭn-to͞o′ĭt, -tyo͞o′ĭt) *v.* **-ited, -iting, -its.** *—tr.* To know or sense by intuition. *—intr.* To acquire knowledge by intuition. [Back-formation from INTUITION.]

in·tu·i·tion (ĭn′to͞o-ĭsh′ən, ĭn′tyo͞o-) *n.* **1. a.** The act or faculty of knowing without the use of rational processes; immediate cognition. **b.** Knowledge so gained; a perceptive insight. **2.** A capacity for guessing accurately; sharp insight. **3.** A sense of something not evident or deducible; impression; notion. —See Synonyms at **reason.** [Middle English *intuycion,* contemplation, from Old French *intuition,* from Late Latin, view, contemplation, from Latin *intuērī,* to look at or toward, contemplate : *in-,* on, toward + *tuērī,* to look at, watch.]

in·tu·i·tion·al (ĭn′to͞o-ĭsh′ən-əl, ĭn′tyo͞o-) *adj.* Of, pertaining to, or based on intuition. **—in·tu·i·tion·al·ly** *adv.*

in·tu·i·tion·al·ism (ĭn′to͞o-ĭsh′ən-ə-lĭz′əm, ĭn′tyo͞o-) *n. Philosophy.* Intuitionism. **—in·tu·i·tion·al·ist** *n.*

in·tu·i·tion·ism (ĭn′to͞o-ĭsh′ən-ĭz′əm, ĭn′tyo͞o-) *n.* **1.** The theory that basic truths are known by intuition rather than reason. **2.** The theory that objects of perception are known to be real by intuition. **3.** *Philosophy.* The theory that ethical principles are known to be valid and universal through intuition. **4.** The theory that mathematical statements are true or false only if they can be proved to be so. **—in·tu·i·tion·ist** *n. & adj.*

in·tu·i·tive (ĭn-to͞o′ə-tĭv, ĭn-tyo͞o′-) *adj.* **1.** Of, pertaining to, or arising from intuition; intuitional. **2.** Known or perceived through intuition. **3.** Possessing or demonstrating intuition. **—in·tu·i·tive·ly** *adv.* **—in·tu·i·tive·ness** *n.*

in·tu·i·tiv·ism (ĭn-to͞o′ə-tĭ-vĭz′əm, ĭn-tyo͞o′-) *n. Philosophy.* The theory of intuitionism in ethics. **—in·tu·i·tiv·ist** *n.*

in·tu·mesce (ĭn′to͞o-mĕs′, ĭn′tyo͞o-) *intr.v.* **-mesced, -mescing, -mesces.** To swell or expand; enlarge. [Latin *intumēscere,* to swell up : *in-* (intensive) + *tumēscere,* to begin to swell, from *tūmere,* to swell.]

in·tu·mes·cence (ĭn′to͞o-mĕs′əns, ĭn′tyo͞o-) *n.* **1.** The process or condition of swelling. **2.** A swollen organ or part. **—in·tu·mes·cent** *adj.*

in·turn (ĭn′tûrn′) *n.* A curving inward. **—in·turned** *adj.*

in·tus·sus·cept (ĭn′təs-sə-sĕpt′) *tr.v.* **-cepted, -cepting, -cepts.** *Pathology.* To fold or turn inward; invaginate. [Probably back-formation from INTUSSUSCEPTION.] **—in·tus·sus·cep·tive** *adj.*

in·tus·sus·cep·tion (ĭn′təs-sə-sĕp′shən) *n.* **1.** *Pathology.* Invagination; especially, an infolding of one part of the intestine into another. **2.** *Botany.* The deposition of molecules into a cell wall, thereby increasing the surface area. [New Latin *intussusceptio* : Latin *intus,* within + *susceptiō* (stem *susceptiōn-*), taking up, from *suscipere,* to take up : *sub-,* up from under + *capere,* to take, seize.]

intwine. Variant of **entwine.**

intwist. Variant of **entwist.**

In·u·it, In·nu·it (ĭn′yə-wət) *n., pl.* **-its** or collectively **Inuit, Innuit. 1.** An Eskimo of North America and Greenland as distinguished from one of Asia and the Aleutian Islands. **2.** The language of these Eskimos.

in·u·lin (ĭn′yə-lĭn) *n.* A fructose polysaccharide, $(C_6H_{10}O_5)_3$ or $(C_6H_{10}O_5)_4$, stored as a food reserve in the roots of many plants.

in·unc·tion (ĭn-ŭngk′shən) *n.* The process of applying and rubbing in an ointment. [Middle English, from Latin *inunctiō* (stem *inunctiōn-*), from *inunguere,* to smear oil on, anoint : *in-,* on + *unguere,* to smear, anoint.]

in·un·date (ĭn′ŭn-dāt′) *tr.v.* **-dated, -dating, -dates. 1.** To cover with water, especially flood water; overflow. **2.** To overwhelm as if with a flood; swamp: *inundated with requests.* [Latin *inundāre,* "to flow in" : *in-,* in + *undāre,* to flow, from *unda,* wave.] **—in·un·da·tion** *n.* **—in·un·da·tor** *n.* **—in·un·da·to·ry** (ĭn-ŭn′də-tôr′ē, -tōr′ē) *adj.*

in·ure, en·ure (ĭn-yo͝or′) *v.* **-ured, -uring, -ures.** *—tr.* To make used to something unpleasant by prolonged subjection. Usually used in the passive, and with *to*: *He became inured to the flies and mosquitoes.* *—intr.* To come into operation; take effect, especially in law. [Middle English *enewren* : *en-* (causative) + *ure,* use, custom, from Old French *uevre, euvre,* custom, work, from Latin *opera,* work.] **—in·ure·ment** *n.*

in·urn (ĭn-ûrn′) *tr.v.* **-urned, -urning, -urns.** *Archaic.* **1.** To put or seal (ashes of the dead, for example) in an urn. **2.** To bury or entomb.

in u·ter·o (ĭn yo͞o′tə-rō) *adj. Latin.* In the womb. **—in u·ter·o** *adv.*

in·u·tile (ĭn-yo͞ot′l, -tīl) *adj.* Useless. [Middle English, from Old French, from Latin *inūtilis* : *in-,* not + *ūtilis,* useful, from *ūtī*†, to use.] **—in·u·tile·ly** *adv.* **—in·u·til·i·ty** (ĭn′yo͞o-tĭl′ə-tē) *n.*

inv. 1. invented; invention; inventor. **2.** invoice.

in va·cu·o (ĭn văk′yo͞o-ō′) *adj. Latin.* **1.** In a vacuum. **2.** In isolation; considered without reference to related evidence. **—in va·cu·o** *adv.*

in·vade (ĭn-vād′) *v.* **-vaded, -vading, -vades.** *—tr.* **1.** To enter (a territory, for example) by force in order to conquer or overrun. **2.** To encroach or intrude upon; violate: *to invade someone's privacy.*

intrusion *Bands of a pale volcanic rock known as lamprophyre divide darker areas of slate near the northern coast of Cornwall, England. The markings were created when molten lamprophyre welled up from the earth's interior through cracks in the slate, then cooled and hardened, filling the cracks. Rocks that are forced into layers of other rocks in this way are said to be intrusive.*

PRONUNCIATION KEY

ă, pat; ā, pay; âr, care;
ä, father, are; b, **bib;**
ch, **church;** d, **deed;** ĕ, pet;
ē, be; f, **fife;** g, **gag;** h, **hat;**
hw, **which;** ĭ, pit; ī, pie;
îr, pier; j, **judge;** k, **kick;**
l, lid, needle; m, **mum;**
n, no, sudden; ng, **thing;**
ŏ, pot; ō, toe; ô, **paw, for;**
oi, noise; ou, **out;** o͝o, **book;**
o͞o, boot; p, **pop;** r, **roar;**
s, sauce; sh, **ship, dish;**
t, **tight;** th, **thin, path;**
th, **this, bathe;** ŭ, **cut;** ûr, **fur;**
v, valve; w, **with;** y, **yes;**
z, zebra, **size;** zh, vision;
ə, about, item, edible,
gallop, circus, peaceful

IN FOREIGN WORDS:

à, *Fr.* ami; œ, *Fr.* **feu,** *Ger.* schön; ü, *Fr.* **tu,** *Ger.* **über;**
KH, *Ger.* **ich,** *Scot.* **loch;**
N, *Fr.* bon; y′, *Fr.* **Compiègne**

STRESS MARKS:

Primary stress: ′
in·cite′ (ĭn-sīt′)
Secondary stress: ′
in′sight′ (ĭn′sīt′)

3. To overrun or infest: *The kitchen was invaded by ants.* **4.** To enter and spread harm through: *Infection has invaded the membranes.* —*intr.* To make an invasion. [Middle English *invaden,* from Latin *invādere,* "to go in" : *in-,* in + *vādere,* to go.] —**in·vad·er** *n.*

in·vag·i·nate (ĭn-văj′ə-nāt′) *v.* **-nated, -nating, -nates.** —*tr.* **1.** To enclose in or as in a sheath. **2.** To turn within; introvert. —*intr.* To become enclosed or turned within itself. [Medieval Latin *invāgīnāre* : Latin *in-,* in + *vāgīna,* sheath.] —**in·vag·i·na·ble** *adj.*

in·vag·i·na·tion (ĭn-văj′ə-nā′shən) *n.* **1.** The act or process of invaginating or the condition of being invaginated. **2.** Something invaginated, as an organ or part. **3.** The infolding of an outer layer of cells to form a cavity, especially as in the embryonic development of the gastrula from the blastula.

in·va·lid[1] (ĭn′və-lĭd) *n.* A chronically ill or disabled person.
~*adj.* **1.** Disabled by illness or injury; sickly or infirm. **2.** Of, pertaining to, or for invalids.
~*v.* **invalided, -liding, -lids.** —*tr.* **1.** To make an invalid of; disable physically. **2.** *Chiefly British.* To release or exempt from duty because of ill health. —*intr.* To become invalided. [Latin *invalidus,* not strong, ineffective : *in-,* not + *validus,* strong, VALID.]

in·val·id[2] (ĭn-văl′ĭd) *adj.* **1.** Null; legally ineffective. **2.** Falsely based or reasoned; unjustified: *an invalid conclusion.* [Latin *invalidus,* ineffective, INVALID (infirm).] —**in·val·id·ly** *adv.*

in·val·i·date (ĭn-văl′ə-dāt′) *tr.v.* **-dated, -dating, -dates. 1.** To make legally ineffective or void. **2.** To undermine or destroy the force or effectiveness of (an argument, for example). —See Synonyms at **nullify.** —**in·val·i·da·tion** *n.* —**in·val·i·da·tor** *n.*

in·va·lid·ism (ĭn′və-lĭd-ĭz′əm) *n.* The condition of being chronically ill or disabled.

in·val·i·di·ty[1] (ĭn′və-lĭd′ə-tē) *n.* The condition or quality of being void or unjustifiable; lack of validity.

invalidity[2] *n.* The condition of being ill or disabled, usually for a long period of time. Also used adjectivally: *invalidity benefit.*

in·val·u·a·ble (ĭn-văl′yo͞o-bəl) *adj.* **1.** Of inestimable use or help; indispensable; much appreciated: *an invaluable service.* **2.** Having extremely high value; priceless: *invaluable paintings.* —See Synonyms at **costly.** —**in·val·u·a·bly** *adv.*

In·var (ĭn-vär′) *n.* A trademark for an iron alloy containing 36 percent nickel, with an extremely low coefficient of expansion, and used chiefly in measuring rods and tapes, pendulums, balance wheels, tuning forks, and in temperature-regulating devices.

in·var·i·a·ble (ĭn-vâr′ē-ə-bəl) *adj.* Not changing or subject to change; constant.
~*n.* Something that does not change; especially, a mathematical expression or a physical quantity. —**in·var·i·a·bil·i·ty, in·var·i·a·ble·ness** *n.* —**in·var·i·a·bly** *adv.*

in·var·i·ant (ĭn-vâr′ē-ənt) *adj.* **1.** Not varying; constant. **2.** Unaffected by a given mathematical operation, such as a transformation of coordinates.
~*n.* An invariant quantity, function, configuration, or system. —**in·var·i·ance** *n.*

in·va·sion (ĭn-vā′zhən) *n.* **1.** The act or an instance of invading; especially, entrance by force. **2.** The onset of something injurious or harmful, as of a disease. **3.** Any intrusion or encroachment. [Middle English *invasioune,* from Old French *invasion,* from Late Latin *invāsiō* (stem *invāsiōn-*), from Latin *invādere,* to INVADE.]

in·va·sive (ĭn-vā′sĭv) *adj.* **1.** Tending to spread; especially, tending to invade healthy tissue. **2.** *Archaic.* Of, relating to, or given to armed aggression.

in·vec·tive (ĭn-vĕk′tĭv) *n.* Vehement accusation or abuse; denunciation; vituperation. [Middle English *invectiff,* abusive, vituperative, from Old French *invectif,* from Late Latin *invectīva (ōrātiō),* "abusive (speech)," from Latin *invehere,* to attack, INVEIGH.] —**in·vec·tive** *adj.* —**in·vec·tive·ly** *adv.* —**in·vec·tive·ness** *n.*

in·veigh (ĭn-vā′) *intr.v.* **-veighed, -veighing, -veighs.** To give vent to angry censure; protest vehemently; rail. Used with *against.* [Latin *invehī,* passive infinitive of *invehere,* to carry in, sail into, assail, attack : *in-,* in + *vehere,* to carry.] —**in·veigh·er** *n.*

in·vei·gle (ĭn-vē′gəl, ĭn-vā′-) *tr.v.* **-gled, -gling, -gles. 1.** To lead astray or win over by deceitful flattery or persuasion: *She inveigled me into joining her plot.* **2.** To obtain by cajolery. —See Synonyms at **lure.** [Earlier *invegle,* from Norman French *envegler,* alteration of Old French *aveugler,* to blind, from *aveugle,* blind, from Medieval Latin *ab oculīs,* without eyes : Latin *ab,* out of + *oculus,* eye.] —**in·vei·gle·ment** *n.* —**in·vei·gler** *n.*

in·vent (ĭn-vĕnt′) *tr.v.* **-vented, -venting, -vents. 1.** To conceive of or devise (something entirely new); produce (an invention). **2.** To fabricate; make up. [Middle English *inventen,* to come upon, find, from Latin *invenīre* (past participle *inventus*) : *in-,* on + *venīre,* to come.] —**in·vent·i·ble** *adj.*

in·ven·tion (ĭn-vĕn′shən) *n. Abbr.* **inv. 1.** The act or process of inventing. **2.** A new device or process developed from study and experimentation. **3.** A mental fabrication; a falsehood or fictitious story. **4.** Skill in inventing; inventiveness. **5.** A short musical piece developing a single theme contrapuntally. **6.** *Archaic.* A discovery; a finding. —**in·ven·tion·al** *adj.*

in·ven·tive (ĭn-vĕn′tĭv) *adj.* **1.** Of or characterized by invention or imagination: *an inventive spy-story.* **2.** Adept or skillful at inventing; creative; ingenious. —**in·ven·tive·ly** *adv.* —**in·ven·tive·ness** *n.*

in·ven·tor (ĭn-vĕn′tər) *n.* Also **in·vent·er.** *Abbr.* **inv.** One who conceives or devises a previously unknown device, method, or process.

in·ven·to·ry (ĭn′vən-tôr′ē, -tōr′ē) *n., pl.* **-ries. 1.** A detailed list of things, such as articles or goods in one's possession. **2.** The process of making such a list. **3.** The items so listed. **4.** The total quantity of goods and materials held by an organization or company. **5.** Broadly, an evaluation or survey.
~*tr.v.* **inventoried, -rying, -ries. 1.** To make an inventory of. **2.** To include in an inventory. [Medieval Latin *inventōrium,* list, altered from Late Latin *inventārium,* "a finding out," "enumeration," from Latin *invenīre,* to come upon, find, INVENT.] —**in·ven·to·ri·al** *adj.* —**in·ven·to·ri·al·ly** *adv.*

in·ve·rac·i·ty (ĭn′və-răs′ə-tē) *n., pl.* **-ties. 1.** Lack of veracity; untruthfulness. **2.** An untruth; a falsehood.

In·ver·car·gill (ĭn′vər-kär′gĭl). A city in New Zealand on the southeast coast of South Island. It is the center of a dairy and agricultural district and has food-processing industries.

In·ver·ness[1] (ĭn′vər-nĕs′). Royal burgh in northeast Scotland. The administrative center of the Highland Region, it supports distilling, tweed-manufacturing, sawmilling, tourism, and some coal shipping from its port at the head of the Moray Firth.

Inverness[2]. Formerly the largest county in Scotland. It lay between the western Cairngorms and the Outer Hebrides, and was absorbed into the Highland Region in 1975.

Inverness[3] *n. Often* **inverness. 1.** A loose overcoat with a detachable cape. **2.** The cape of such a coat. Also called "Inverness cape." [First popularized in INVERNESS.]

in·verse (ĭn-vûrs′, ĭn′vûrs′) *n.* **1.** That which is opposite, as in sequence or character; the reverse. **2.** *Mathematics.* An element in a set that yields the identity element of the set when combined with another element in a binary operation; especially: **a.** The reciprocal of a designated quantity. **b.** The negative of a designated quantity.
~*adj.* **1.** Reversed in order, nature, or effect. **2.** Turned upside down; inverted. **3.** *Mathematics.* Pertaining to an inverse. Said of relationships, proportions, or functions. [Latin *inversus,* past participle of *invertere,* to INVERT.] —**in·verse·ly** *adv.*

in·ver·sion (ĭn-vûr′zhən, -shən) *n.* **1.** The act of inverting or the state of being inverted. **2.** An interchange of position, especially of adjacent objects in a sequence. **3.** A change in normal word order, such as the placing of a verb before its subject. **4.** *Music.* **a.** A rearrangement of notes in which upper and lower voices are transposed, as in counterpoint, or in which each interval in a single melody is applied in the opposite direction. **b.** An interval, chord, or melody resulting from such rearrangement. **5.** Homosexuality. **6.** *Medicine.* The turning inward or inside out of an organ or part. **7.** *Genetics.* A type of chromosome mutation in which a chromosome segment is inserted in reverse order. **8.** *Chemistry.* Conversion from the dextrorotatory to the levorotatory or from the levorotatory to the dextrorotatory form. **9.** *Meteorology.* A state in which the air temperature increases with increasing altitude, holding surface air down. [Latin *inversiō* (stem *inversiōn-*), from *invertere,* to INVERT.] —**in·ver·sive** *adj.*

in·vert (ĭn-vûrt′) *v.* **-verted, -verting, -verts.** —*tr.* **1.** To turn inside out or upside down. **2.** To reverse the position, order, or condition of. **3.** To subject to inversion. —*intr.* To be subjected to inversion.
~*n.* (ĭn′vûrt′) **1.** Something inverted. **2.** A homosexual. [Latin *invertere,* to turn inside out or upside down : *in-,* in, inward + *vertere,* to turn.] —**in·vert·i·ble** *adj.*

in·ver·tase (ĭn′vûr-tās′) *n.* A plant and animal enzyme that catalyzes the conversion of sucrose to glucose and fructose. Also called "sucrase," "saccharase."

in·ver·te·brate (ĭn-vûr′tə-brĭt, -brāt′) *adj.* **1.** Having no backbone or spinal column; not vertebrate. **2.** Lacking strength of character; spineless.
~*n.* An invertebrate animal. [New Latin *Invertebrata,* neuter plural of *invertebratus,* having no backbone : IN- (no) + VERTEBRATE.]

in·vert·ed comma (ĭn-vûr′tĭd) *n. Chiefly British.* A **quotation mark** *(see).*

inverted mordent *n. Music.* A **pralltriller** *(see).*

inverted snobbery *n.* **1.** The conscious affirmation of values, tastes, or habits characteristic of one's lower-class background, or the affectation of values, tastes, or habits supposedly characteristic of a class lower than one's own. **2.** A sense of social exclusiveness resulting from such an image of oneself.

in·vert·er (ĭn-vûr′tər) *n.* **1.** One that inverts. **2.** *Electronics.* A device used to convert direct current into alternating current. **3.** *Computer Science.* A logic component, a **NOT gate** *(see).*

invert sugar *n.* A hygroscopic mixture of equal parts of glucose and fructose resulting from the hydrolysis of sucrose and used chiefly in brewing and in medicine. [Commercially produced by inversion of sucrose.]

in·vest (ĭn-vĕst′) *v.* **-vested, -vesting, -vests.** —*tr.* **1.** To commit (money or capital) in order to gain profit or interest, as by purchasing property or shares. **2.** To spend or utilize (time, money, or effort) for future advantage or benefit. Often used with *in.* **3.** To endow with rank, authority, or power. **4.** To inaugurate with ceremony; install in office. **5.** To provide with some enveloping or pervasive quality. **6.** *Rare.* To clothe; adorn. **7.** To cover completely; envelop; shroud. **8.** *Military. Rare.* To surround with hostile troops or ships; besiege. —*intr.* **1.** To invest money; make an investment. Often used with *in.* **2.** *Informal.* To buy. Used with *in.* [Old French *investir,* from Medieval Latin *investīre,* from Latin, to clothe in, surround : *in-,* in + *vestīre,* to clothe, from *vestis,* clothes.] —**in·ves·tor** *n.*

in·ves·ti·gate (ĭn-vĕs′tĭ-gāt′) *v.* **-gated, -gating, -gates.** —*tr.* To observe or inquire into in detail; examine systematically. —*intr.* To make an investigation. [Latin *investīgāre,* to trace out, search into :

PRONUNCIATION KEY

ă, pat; ā, pay; âr, care;
ä, father, are; b, bib;
ch, church; d, deed; ĕ, pet;
ē, be; f, fife; g, gag; h, hat;
hw, which; ĭ, pit; ī, pie;
îr, pier; j, judge; k, kick;
l, lid, needle; m, mum;
n, no, sudden; ng, thing;
ŏ, pot; ō, toe; ô, paw, for;
oi, noise; ou, out; o͝o, book;
o͞o, boot; p, pop; r, roar;
s, sauce; sh, ship, dish;
t, tight; th, thin, path;
th, this, bathe; ŭ, cut; ûr, fur;
v, valve; w, with; y, yes;
z, zebra, size; zh, vision;
ə, about, item, edible,
gallop, circus, peaceful

IN FOREIGN WORDS:

à, *Fr.* ami; œ, *Fr.* feu, *Ger.* schön; ü, *Fr.* tu, *Ger.* über;
KH, *Ger.* ich, *Scot.* loch;
N, *Fr.* bon; y′, *Fr.* Compiègne

STRESS MARKS:

Primary stress: ′
in·cite′ (ĭn-sīt′)
Secondary stress: ′
in′sight′ (ĭn′sīt′)

in-, in + *vestīgāre*, to trace, track, from *vestīgium*, trace, footprint, VESTIGE.] —**in·ves·ti·ga·ble**, **in·ves·ti·ga·tive**, **in·ves·ti·ga·to·ry** (ĭn-věs′tĭ-gə-tôr′ē, -tōr′ē) *adj.* —**in·ves·ti·ga·tor** *n.*

in·ves·ti·ga·tion (ĭn-věs′tĭ-gā′shən) *n.* The act, process, or an instance of investigating; an inquiry.

investigative journalism *n.* The gathering of news, especially news of crime, corruption, official mismanagement, or controversial plans, by means of investigation. —**investigative journalist** *n.*

in·ves·ti·tive (ĭn-věs′tə-tĭv) *adj.* Of or pertaining to investiture.

in·ves·ti·ture (ĭn-věs′tə-chŏor′) *n.* 1. The act or formal ceremony of conferring upon a person the authority and symbols of a high office. 2. *Chiefly British.* An act or formal ceremony of conferring honors or awards, especially one performed by a sovereign. 3. *Archaic.* A thing that covers or adorns, as a garment. [Middle English, from Medieval Latin *investītūra*, from *investīre*, INVEST.]

in·vest·ment (ĭn-věst′mənt) *n.* 1. The act of investing or the state of being invested. 2. An amount invested. 3. Property or another possession acquired or invested in for future income or benefit. 4. Investiture. 5. *Archaic.* A garment; vestment. 6. An outer covering or layer. 7. *Rare.* A siege.

investment trust *n.* Also **investment company.** *Finance.* A company that invests its capital, acquired by the issue of shares, solely in other companies.

in·vet·er·ate (ĭn-vět′ər-ĭt) *adj.* 1. Firmly established by long standing; deep-rooted. 2. Persisting in an ingrained habit; habitual: *an inveterate liar.* [Latin *inveterātus*, past participle of *inveterāre*, to render old : *in-* (causative) + *vetus* (stem *veter-*), old.] —**in·vet·er·a·cy** (ĭn-vět′ər-ə-sē), **in·vet·er·ate·ness** *n.* —**in·vet·er·ate·ly** *adv.*

in·vi·a·ble (ĭn-vī′ə-bəl) *adj.* Nonviable; especially, biologically incapable of growth or reproduction: *an inviable seed.*

in·vid·i·ous (ĭn-vĭd′ē-əs) *adj.* 1. Tending to rouse ill will or animosity; offensive: *an invidious clause in the contract.* 2. Containing or implying a slight; unfairly discriminatory. [Latin *invidiōsus*, envious, hostile, from *invidia*, ENVY.] —**in·vid·i·ous·ly** *adv.* —**in·vid·i·ous·ness** *n.*

in·vig·or·ate (ĭn-vĭg′ə-rāt′) *tr.v.* **-at·ed, -at·ing, -ates.** To impart vigor, strength, or vitality to: *"A few whiffs of the raw, strong scent of phlox invigorated her"* (D.H. Lawrence). [IN- (causative) + VIGOR + -ATE.] —**in·vig·or·at·ing·ly**, **in·vig·or·a·tive·ly** *adv.* —**in·vig·or·a·tion** *n.* —**in·vig·or·a·tive** *adj.* —**in·vig·or·a·tor** *n.*

in·vin·ci·ble (ĭn-vĭn′sə-bəl) *adj.* 1. Unconquerable; unbeatable. 2. Incapable of being surmounted; insuperable. [Middle English, from Latin *invincibilis* : *in-*, not + *vincibilis*, VINCIBLE.] —**in·vin·ci·bil·i·ty**, **in·vin·ci·ble·ness** *n.* —**in·vin·ci·bly** *adv.*

in vi·no ve·ri·tas (ĭn vē′nō věr′ĭ-täs′). *Latin.* When drunk, one speaks the truth. [Latin, "in wine (there is) truth."]

in·vi·o·la·ble (ĭn-vī′ə-lə-bəl) *adj.* 1. Safe from or secured against violation or profanation; kept sacred. 2. Impregnable to assault, trespass, or disturbance. —**in·vi·o·la·bil·i·ty**, **in·vi·o·la·ble·ness** *n.* —**in·vi·o·la·bly** *adv.*

in·vi·o·late (ĭn-vī′ə-lĭt) *adj.* Not violated; intact: *an inviolate shrine.* [Middle English *inviolat*, from Latin *inviolātus* : *in-*, not + *violātus*, past participle of *violāre*, VIOLATE.] —**in·vi·o·la·cy** (ĭn-vī′ə-lə-sē), **in·vi·o·late·ness** *n.* —**in·vi·o·late·ly** *adv.*

in·vis·cid (ĭn-vĭs′ĭd) *adj.* 1. Having no viscosity. 2. Of or pertaining to an inviscid fluid.

in·vis·i·ble (ĭn-vĭz′ə-bəl) *adj.* 1. Incapable of being seen; not visible. 2. Not accessible to view; hidden. 3. a. Not easily noticed or detected; inconspicuous. b. Hidden from public view. 4. *Economics.* a. Not published in financial statements: *an invisible asset.* b. Designating items of international trade consisting of services rather than goods: *invisible exports.* ~*n.* 1. One that is invisible. 2. **invisibles.** *Economics.* Imports and exports of services such as tourism, banking, or insurance, as opposed to goods. —**in·vis·i·bil·i·ty**, **in·vis·i·ble·ness** *n.* —**in·vis·i·bly** *adv.*

invisible ink *n.* Ink that is colorless and invisible until treated by a chemical, heat, or special light. Also called "sympathetic ink."

in·vi·ta·tion (ĭn′vĭ-tā′shən) *n.* 1. The act of inviting. 2. A spoken or written request for one's presence or participation. 3. An allurement, enticement, or attraction.

in·vi·ta·tion·al (ĭn′vĭ-tā′shən-əl) *adj.* Restricted to invited participants: *an invitational golf tournament.*

in·vi·ta·to·ry (ĭn-vī′tə-tôr′ē, -tōr′ē) *n., pl.* **-ries.** A psalm or other piece sung as an invitation to prayer in church services. [Middle English *invytatory*, from Medieval Latin *invītātōrium*, from the neuter of Late Latin *invītātōrius*, inviting, antiphonal, from Latin *invītāre*, INVITE.]

in·vite (ĭn-vīt′) *v.* **-vit·ed, -vit·ing, -vites.** —*tr.* 1. To request the presence or participation of. 2. To request politely or formally. 3. To tend to bring on; provoke. 4. To lure; entice; tempt. —*intr.* To give an invitation. ~*n.* (ĭn′vīt′). *Informal.* An invitation. [Old French *inviter*, from Latin *invītāre*†.]

in·vit·ing (ĭn-vī′tĭng) *adj.* Attractive; tempting: *an inviting dessert.* —**in·vit·ing·ly** *adv.* —**in·vit·ing·ness** *n.*

in vi·tro (ĭn vē′trō) *adj.* Designating biological processes made to occur in an artificial environment outside the living organism: *in vitro fertilization.* [New Latin, "in glass."] —**in vi·tro** *adv.*

in vi·vo (ĭn vē′vō) *adj.* Designating biological processes or experiments conducted or occurring within the living organism. [New Latin, "in a living body."] —**in vi·vo** *adv.*

in·vo·cate (ĭn′və-kāt′) *tr.v.* **-cat·ed, -cat·ing, -cates.** *Archaic.* To in-

voke. [Latin *invocāre*, INVOKE.] —**in·voc·a·tive** (ĭn-vŏk′ə-tĭv) *adj.* —**in·vo·ca·tor** *n.*

in·vo·ca·tion (ĭn′və-kā′shən) *n.* 1. The act of invoking; especially, an appeal to a higher power for assistance. 2. A prayer or other formula used in invoking, as at the opening of a religious service. 3. a. A conjuring or calling up of a spirit by incantation. b. The incantation used in conjuring. [Middle English, from Old French, from Latin *invocātiō* (stem *invocātiōn-*), from *invocāre*, INVOKE.] —**in·vo·ca·tion·al** *adj.*

in·voc·a·to·ry (ĭn-vŏk′ə-tôr′ē, -tōr′ē) *adj.* Of, pertaining to, or having the nature of an invocation.

in·voice (ĭn′vois′) *n. Abbr.* **inv.** A detailed list of goods supplied or sent or services rendered, with an account of all costs; a bill. ~*tr.v.* **invoiced, -voic·ing, -voices.** 1. To list on an invoice. 2. To present an invoice to. [Originally *invoyes*, plural of *invoy*, invoice, from Old French *envoy*, a sending, shipment of goods. See **envoi.**]

in·voke (ĭn-vōk′) *tr.v.* **-voked, -vok·ing, -vokes.** 1. To call upon (a higher power) for assistance. 2. To appeal to; petition. 3. To call for (help, for example) earnestly; solicit. 4. To summon (a spirit, for example) with incantations; conjure up. 5. To cite in support or justification of one's cause. [Old French *invoquer*, from Latin *invocāre*, "to call upon" : *in-*, in, on + *vocāre*, to call.] —**in·vo·ca·ble** *adj.* —**in·vok·er** *n.*

in·vo·lu·cel (ĭn-vŏl′yŏo-sĕl′) *n. Botany.* A secondary involucre, as at the base of an umbellule in a compound umbel. [New Latin *involucellum*, diminutive of *involucrum*, INVOLUCRE.]

in·vo·lu·crate (ĭn′və-lōo′krĭt, -krāt′) *adj. Botany.* Having an involucre.

in·vo·lu·cre (ĭn′və-lōo′kər) *n.* Also **in·vo·lu·crum** (-lōo′krəm) *pl.* **-cra** (-krə). *Botany.* A whorl or series of leaflike scales or bracts beneath or around a flower or flower cluster. [New Latin *involucrum*, from Latin, wrapper, case, envelope, from *involvere*, to enwrap, INVOLVE.] —**in·vo·lu·cral** *adj.*

in·vo·lu·crum (ĭn′və-lōo′krəm) *n., pl.* **-cra** (-krə). 1. An enveloping sheath or envelope. 2. *Botany.* Variant of **involucre.** [New Latin, INVOLUCRE.]

in·vol·un·tar·y (ĭn-vŏl′ən-tĕr′ē) *adj.* 1. Not desired; enforced: *involuntary exile.* 2. Performed without conscious willing; unintentional. 3. *Physiology.* Not subject to conscious control: *an involuntary muscle.* —See Synonyms at **spontaneous.** —**in·vol·un·tar·i·ly** *adv.* —**in·vol·un·tar·i·ness** *n.*

in·vo·lute (ĭn′və-lōot′) *adj.* Also **in·vo·lut·ed** (-lōo′tĭd). 1. Intricate; complex. 2. *Botany.* Having the margins rolled inward. 3. Having whorls that obscure the axis or other volutions, as the shell of a cowry. ~*n. Mathematics.* The locus of a fixed point on a tangent line as it rolls but does not slide around a fixed curve. ~*intr.v.* (ĭn′və-lōot′) **involuted, -lut·ing, -lutes.** To become involute. [Latin *involutus*, past participle of *involvere*, to enwrap, INVOLVE.]

in·vo·lu·tion (ĭn′və-lōo′shən) *n.* 1. The act of involving or the state of being involved. 2. Anything that is internally complex or involved. 3. *Grammar.* A complicated construction. 4. *Mathematics.* The multiplying of a quantity by itself a specified number of times; raising to a power. In this sense, compare **evolution.** 5. *Physiology.* The shrinking of an organ, as of the womb after childbirth, or as a result of old age. [Latin *involūtiō* (stem *involūtiōn-*), from *involvere*, INVOLVE.]

in·volve (ĭn-vŏlv′) *tr.v.* **-volved, -volv·ing, -volves.** 1. To contain or include as a part. 2. To have as a necessary feature or consequence; imply. 3. To draw in as an associate or participant; embroil; implicate. 4. To occupy or engross completely; absorb. 5. To make complex or intricate; complicate. 6. *Poetic.* To wrap; envelop: *a castle involved in mist.* 7. *Archaic.* To wind or coil about. 8. *Mathematics.* To raise (a number) to a specified degree. Not in technical usage. —See Synonyms at **include.** [Middle English *involven*, from Latin *involvere*, to enwrap, "roll in" : *in-*, in + *volvere*, to roll, turn.] —**in·volve·ment** *n.* —**in·volv·er** *n.*

in·volved (ĭn-vŏlvd′) *adj.* 1. Complicated; intricate. 2. Involute; twisted. 3. Confused; tangled. 4. Associated; implicated; concerned. Used with *in: involved in a conspiracy.* 5. Having a romantic or sexual relationship. Used with *with.* —See Synonyms at **complex.**

in·vul·ner·a·ble (ĭn-vŭl′nər-ə-bəl) *adj.* 1. Immune to attack; impregnable: *an invulnerable position.* 2. Incapable of being damaged, injured, or wounded. [Latin *invulnerābilis* : *in-*, not + *vulnerāre*, to wound (see **vulnerable**).] —**in·vul·ner·a·bil·i·ty**, **in·vul·ner·a·ble·ness** *n.* —**in·vul·ner·a·bly** *adv.*

in·ward (ĭn′wərd) *adj.* 1. Located inside; inner. 2. Directed or moving toward the interior. 3. Existing in thought or mind. 4. Intimate; familiar. Used with *with.* ~*adv.* Also **in·wards** (-wərdz). 1. Toward the inside or center. 2. Toward the mind or the self: *thoughts turned inward.* ~*n.* 1. An inner or central part. 2. An inner essence or spirit. 3. **inwards.** Entrails; innards. [Middle English *inward*, Old English *inweard.*]

in·ward·ly (ĭn′wərd-lē) *adv.* 1. On or in the inside; within. 2. Within one's own mind or thoughts: *inwardly alarmed.* 3. Privately; to oneself: *inwardly laughing.* 4. *Archaic.* Intimately; closely.

in·ward·ness (ĭn′wərd-nĭs) *n.* 1. Intimacy; familiarity. 2. a. Self-preoccupation; introspection. b. Concern with the spiritual aspect of life. 3. Essential or fundamental nature. 4. Internal quality or essence.

in·weave (ĭn-wēv′) *tr.v.* **-wove** (-wōv′) or **-weaved, -woven** (-wō′vən) or rare **-wove, -weaving, -weaves.** To weave into a fabric or design.

in·wrought (ĭn-rôt′) *adj.* **1.** Worked or woven in, as thread might be. **2.** Having a pattern worked or woven in, as a fabric might.

in·ya·la (ĭn-yä′lə) *n.* An antelope, the **nyala** (*see*).

I·o¹ (ī′ō). *Greek Mythology.* A maiden who was loved by Zeus and transformed by him or by Hera into a heifer.

Io² *n.* The innermost of Jupiter's four large satellites, and the second nearest to the surface of the planet.

IOC International Olympic Committee.

i·o·date (ī′ə-dāt′) *tr.v.* **-dated, -dating, -dates.** To iodize. —*n.* A salt of iodic acid. [IOD(O)- + -ATE.]

i·od·ic acid (ī-ŏd′ĭk) *n.* A colorless or white crystalline powder, HIO₃, used as an antiseptic and deodorant. [French *iodique,* from *iode,* IODINE.]

i·o·dide (ī′ə-dīd′) *n.* A binary compound of iodine with a more electropositive atom or group. [IOD(O)- + -IDE.]

i·o·dine (ī′ə-dīn′, -dĭn, -dēn′) *n. Symbol* **I 1.** A lustrous, grayish-black, corrosive, poisonous halogen element having radioactive isotopes, especially I-131, used as tracers and in thyroid disease diagnosis and therapy. Its compounds are used as germicides, antiseptics, and dyes. Atomic number 53, atomic weight 126.9044, melting point 113.5°C, boiling point 184.35°C, specific gravity (solid, 20°C) 4.93, valences 1, 3, 5, 7. **2.** A **tincture** (*see*) of iodine and sodium iodide, NaI, or potassium iodide, KI, used as an antiseptic for wounds. [French *iode,* from Greek *iōdēs, ioeidēs,* violet-colored : *ion,* violet, of Mediterranean origin + -INE.]

i·o·dism (ī′ə-dĭz′əm) *n.* Poisoning by iodine or iodine compounds. [IOD(O)- + -ISM.]

i·o·dize (ī′ə-dīz′) *tr.v.* **-dized, -dizing, -dizes.** To treat or combine with iodine or an iodide. [IOD(O)- + -IZE.]

iodo-, iod– *prefix.* Indicates iodine; for example, **iodoform, iodide.** [French *iode,* IODINE.]

i·o·do·form (ī-ō′də-fôrm′, ī-ŏd′ə-) *n.* A yellowish iodine compound, CHI₃, used as an antiseptic. [IODO- + FORM(YL).]

i·o·dom·e·try (ī′ə-dŏm′ə-trē) *n. Chemistry.* A form of volumetric analysis for the estimation of the strength of iodine solutions by titration against sodium thiosulfate, using starch as an indicator. [IODO- + -METRY.] —**i·o·do·me·tric** (ī′ə-dō-mĕt′rĭk) *adj.*

i·o·do·phor (ī-ō′də-fôr′) *n.* A substance consisting of iodine and a solubilizing agent that releases free iodine when in solution. [IODO- + -PHOR(E).]

i·o·dop·sin (ī′ə-dŏp′sĭn) *n.* A light-sensitive pigment in retinal cones of the eye.

i·o·lite (ī′ə-līt′) *n.* A blue silicate mineral, Al₃(Mg,Fe)₂AlSi₅O₁₈, occurring chiefly in metamorphic rocks. Also called "cordierite."

i·o moth (ī′ō) *n.* A large yellowish moth, *Automeris io,* of North America, having prominent eyelike spots on the hind wings. [After *Io,* who was tormented by gadflies sent by Hera as a punishment.]

i·on (ī′ən, ī′ŏn′) *n.* An atom, group of atoms, or molecule that has acquired a net electric charge by gaining electrons in or losing electrons from an initially electrically neutral configuration. [Greek *ion,* "going particle" (referring to the passage of ions to either of the electrodes in electrolysis), neuter present participle of *ienai,* to go.]

–ion *suffix.* Indicates: **1.** An act or process or the outcome of an act or process; for example, **indention. 2.** A state of being; for example, **cohesion.** [Middle English *-io(u)n,* from Old French *-ion,* from Latin *-iō* (stem *-iōn-*).]

I·o·na (ī-ō′nə). Small island of the Inner Hebrides. Of religious importance since St. Columba founded a monastery there (563), it is also the burial place of many of the monarchs of Scotland, Ireland, Norway, and Denmark. It is rich in Celtic remains.

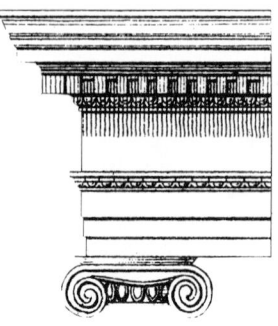

Ionic order *The scroll, or volute, of Ionic capitals has its source in natural spiral forms such as the Egyptian lotus, the nautilus shell, and rams' horns.*

ion engine *n.* A rocket engine that develops thrust by expelling ions rather than gaseous combustion products. Also called "ion rocket." See **ionic propulsion.**

Io·nes·co (yə-nĕs′kō, ē′ə-), **Eugene** (1912–). Romanian-born French playwright, whose play, *The Bald Soprano* (1956), marked a new era in the Theater of the Absurd. He continued to stress his rejection of realism in plays such as *Rhinoceros* (1960) and *Exit the King* (1963).

ion exchange *n.* A reversible chemical reaction between a solid and a solution by means of which ions may be interchanged, used in water softening and separation of radioactive isotopes.

I·o·ni·a (ī-ō′nē-ə). A region on the western coast of Asia Minor. An ancient Greek settlement, it was probably colonized (*c.* 1100 B.C.) by refugees from Achaea. The Ionians became the cultural leaders of the Greek world between the 8th and 6th centuries B.C. Conquered by the Lydians (550 B.C.) and by the Persians (546 B.C.), they were eclipsed following their unsuccessful revolt (499–494 B.C.).

I·o·ni·an (ī-ō′nē-ən) *adj.* **1.** Of or pertaining to Ionia or the Ionians. **2.** *Music.* Of or designating an authentic mode represented by the scale of C on a keyboard instrument. —*n.* A member of a Hellenic people who settled in Attica and on the northern coast of the Peloponnese in about 1100 B.C. and founded colonies in Asia Minor.

Ionian Islands. Chain of Greek islands in the Ionian Sea. They extend from Corfu, off the west coast of Greece and Albania, southward to Zante (Zákinthos), off the southwest Greek coast, and include Paxoi, Levkás, Cephalonia (Kefallinía), and Ithaca, the legendary home of Odysseus.

Ionian Sea. Area of the central Mediterranean. Bounded by Sicily and southern Italy in the west, the Strait of Otranto in the north, and Greece in the east, it includes the Ionian Islands.

i·on·ic (ī-ŏn′ĭk) *adj.* Of, containing, or involving ions.

I·on·ic (ī-ŏn′ĭk) *adj.* **1.** Ionian. **2.** Pertaining to the Ionic order. **3.** In Greek verse: **a.** Designating a metrical foot consisting of two long syllables followed by two short ones, or two short syllables followed by two long ones. **b.** Designating a verse or meter having such feet. —*n.* **1.** The ancient Greek dialect of Ionia, belonging to Attic-Ionic, early developed as a medium for scientific and historical prose. **2.** In Greek verse, an Ionic foot, verse, or meter.

ionic bond *n.* A chemical bond characteristic of salts and formed by the complete transfer of one or more electrons from one kind of atom to another. Also called "electrovalent bond."

ionic crystal *n.* A crystal formed of an array of positive and negative ions held together by electrostatic forces.

Ionic order *n.* An order of classical Greek architecture characterized by fluted columns and two opposed volutes in the capital. Compare **Corinthian order, Doric order.**

ionic propulsion *n.* Propulsion by the reactive thrust of a high-speed beam of similarly charged ions ejected by an ion engine. Also called "ion propulsion."

ion implantation *n.* A technique for introducing controlled amounts of impurity into a material, usually into a semiconductor, by bombarding it with ions of the impurity.

i·on·i·za·tion (ī′ə-nə-zā′shən) *n.* **1.** The formation of one or more ions by the addition of electrons to or the removal of electrons from an electrically neutral atomic or molecular configuration, by heat, electrical discharge, radiation, or chemical reaction. **2.** The state or condition of being ionized.

ionization chamber *n.* A gas-filled enclosure fitted with electrodes between which electric current flows upon ionization of the gas by incident radiation, the electrodes being maintained at a potential difference just sufficient to collect ions thus produced without causing further ionization.

ionization potential *n.* The energy required to remove completely the weakest bound electron from its ground state in an atom or molecule so that the resulting ion is also in its ground state.

i·on·ize (ī′ə-nīz′) *v.* **-ized, -izing, -izes.** —*tr.* To convert totally or partially into ions. —*intr.* To become converted totally or partially into ions.

ionizing radiation *n.* Radiation capable of producing ionization, including energetic charged particles such as alpha and beta rays, and electromagnetic radiation such as x-rays, and neutrons.

i·o·none (ī′ə-nōn′) *n.* Either of two yellowish to colorless liquid isomers, C₁₃H₂₀O, having a strong odor of violets and used in perfumes. [Greek *ion,* violet (see **iodine**) + -ONE.]

i·on·o·sphere (ī-ŏn′ə-sfîr′) *n.* An electrically conducting set of layers of the earth's atmosphere, extending from altitudes of approximately 60 to 400 kilometers (35 to 250 miles) and more, caused by ionization of rarefied atmospheric gases by incident solar radiation; the D, E, and F layers. [ION + -SPHERE.]

i·on·o·spher·ic wave (ī-ŏn′ə-sfîr′ĭk) *n. Electronics.* A **sky wave** (*see*).

ion propulsion *n.* Ionic propulsion.

ion rocket *n.* **1.** A rocket using ionic propulsion. **2.** An **ion engine** (*see*).

ion trap *n.* A magnet mounted to the neck of a kinescope to prevent ions from striking the kinescope screen.

I.O.O.F. Independent Order of Oddfellows.

i·o·ta (ī-ō′tə) *n.* **1.** The ninth letter in the Greek alphabet, written I, ι. Transliterated in English as *I, i.* See feature at **alphabet. 2.** A very

---

IRAN AND IRAQ

Map labels: TURKEY · SYRIA · JORDAN · SAUDI ARABIA · NEUTRAL TERRITORY · IRAQ · IRAN · U. S. S. R. · AFGHANISTAN · PAK. · KUWAIT · BAHRAIN · QATAR · OMAN · CASPIAN SEA · Tabrīz · Lake Urmia · Rasht · Mashhad (Meshed) · Nineveh · Mosul · Sulaymānīyah · Arbil · Kirkūk · TEHRĀN · Mt. Damāvand 5601m. · Elburz Mts · 3600m · Qahremānshahr · Kermānshāh · Samarra · Bisitun · Qom · Dasht-e-Kavir · Hamadān · Arāk · BAGHDAD · Al Kūt · Esfahān (Isfahan) · Karbalā · Al Hillah · Babylon · 4548m · Ahvāz · Khorramshahr · (Khūninshahr) · Ur · Basra · Ābādān · Kermān · Dasht-e-Lut · Persepolis · Shīrāz · Bandar Abbās · Zagros Mountains · Makran · Syrian Desert · Mesopotamia · Euphrates · Karun · Shatt al Arab · Persian Gulf · Gulf of Oman · Tigris · Kurdistan · 50°E · 60°E · 40 N · 30°N · 0 400 800 Km · 0 200 400 Miles

small amount. Often used in the phrase *not one iota*. [Greek *iōta*, of Semitic origin; akin to Hebrew *yōdh*, YOD.]

i·o·ta·cism (ī-ō′tə-sĭz′əm) *n.* The conversion of other vowel sounds in Greek to the sound of iota. [Late Latin *iotacismus*, from Greek *iotakismos*, from *iōta*, IOTA.]

IOU (ī′ō-yōō′) *n., pl.* **IOU's, IOUs.** A promise to pay a debt. [Short for *I owe you.*]

–ious *suffix.* Indicates characterized by or full of; for example, **sagacious, edacious.** [Middle English, partly from Latin *-ius,* and partly from Old French *-ieus, -ieux,* from Latin *-iōsus : -i-,* stem + *-ōsus,* -OUS.]

I·o·wa¹ (ī′ə-wə). State in the north-central United States, between the Mississippi and Missouri rivers. It was part of the Louisiana Purchase. Almost 95 percent of its gently undulating land is given over to agriculture. The capital, Des Moines, is a meat-processing center. —**I·o·wan** *adj. & n.*

Iowa². River, 530 kilometers (329 miles) long, rising in the lakes of northern Iowa and flowing southeast to the Mississippi River.

Iowa³ *n., pl.* **-was** or collectively **Iowa. 1.** A member of a Siouan-speaking North American Indian people formerly inhabiting the region of Minnesota, Iowa, and Missouri. **2.** The Siouan language of this people. —**I·o·wa** *adj.*

IPA, I.P.A. 1. International Phonetic Alphabet. **2.** International Phonetic Association. **3.** isopropyl alcohol.

ip·e·cac (ĭp′ə-kăk′) *n.* Also **ip·e·cac·u·an·ha** (ĭp′ə-kăk′yōō-ăn′ə). **1.** A low-growing South American shrub, *Cephaelis ipecacuanha.* **2.** A medicinal extract from the dried roots of this shrub used as an expectorant and to induce vomiting. [Shortened from Portuguese *ipecacuanha,* from Tupi *ipekaaguéne.*]

Iph·i·ge·ni·a (ĭf′ə-jə-nī′ə, -nē′ə). *Greek Mythology.* The daughter of Clytemnestra and Agamemnon, offered as a sacrifice to Artemis to enable the Greek fleet to sail for Troy.

ip·o·moe·a (ĭp′ə-mē′ə) *n.* Any tropical or subtropical climbing plant of the genus *Ipomoea,* such as the sweet potato and morning glory, having trumpet-shaped flowers. [New Latin, from Greek *ips* (stem *ipo-*), worm + *homoios,* like.]

ip·pon (ĭp′pŏn′) *n.* In judo, a full scoring point, resulting directly in victory. [Japanese, "point."]

ip·se dix·it (ĭp′sē dĭk′sĭt) *n., pl.* **ipse dixits. 1.** An unsupported assertion, usually by a person of authority or standing. **2.** An arbitrary statement; dictum. [Latin, he himself said (it), translation of Doric Greek *autos epha,* expression used by the Pythagoreans of sayings of Pythagoras.]

ip·si·lat·er·al (ĭp′sə-lăt′ər-əl) *adj.* On or affecting the same side of the body. [Irregularly from Latin *ipse,* self + LATERAL.]

ip·sis·si·ma ver·ba (ĭp-sĭs′ə-mə vûr′bə) *pl.n.* The very words. [Latin.]

ip·so fac·to (ĭp′sō făk′tō) *adv.* By the fact itself; by that very fact: *An alien, ipso facto, has no right to a U.S. passport.* [Latin.]

ip·so ju·re (ĭp′sō jōōr′ē) *adv.* By the law itself. [Latin.]

Ips·wich (ĭp′swĭch′). Town and port in Suffolk, eastern England, at the head of the Orwell estuary. It is the administrative center for the county and supports engineering and chemical industries.

IPTS International Practical Temperature Scale.

IQ, I.Q. intelligence quotient.

Ir The symbol for the element iridium.

Ir. Irish.

ir-¹. Variant of **in-¹.**

ir-². Variant of **in-².**

IRA individual retirement account.

I.R.A., IRA *n.* Irish Republican Army: a secret Irish Nationalist organization formed to oppose the partition of Ireland, active in anti-British terrorist acts in the 1930's and 1940's, and again in the 1970's and 1980's. In 1969 it split into the **Official** and **Provisional** wings (*both of which see*). See **Sinn Fein.**

i·ra·de (ĭ-rä′dĕ) *n.* A decree by a Muslim ruler. [Turkish, from Arabic *'irāda,* will.]

I·rá·kli·on (ĭ-rä′klē-ôn′). Also **He·rak·li·on** (hĭ-răk′lē-ən). *Italian* **Can·di·a** (kăn′dē-ə). Port on the north coast of the island of Crete, Greece. It is the island's chief port and exports wine, olive oil, and fruit. It is noted for its Venetian fortifications, the relics of 15th- and 16th-century Venetian rule.

I·ran (ĭ-răn′, -rän′). Formerly **Per·sia** (pûr′zhə, -shə). Country of western Asia. Mountainous and sparsely populated, its geographical position has made it a crossroads for trade and culture and a target for conquest. Overrun by many, including Alexander the Great (*c.* 325 B.C.) and the Arabs (7th century A.D.), who introduced Islam, Persia was always able eventually to overthrow or absorb each occupation and re-establish its own power. By the late 18th century, however, it had declined into a buffer state between Russia, Turkey, and British India. In World War II the country (known since 1935 as Iran) was occupied jointly by Russia and Britain, who installed Muhammad Reza Pahlavi as shah (1941). Despite massive U.S. aid, the shah was overthrown (1979) by a revolution led by the Muslim fundamentalist leader, Ayatollah Khomeini. Ninety percent uncultivated, the country is economically dependent on its vast oil reserves, up to 10 percent of the world's total. Area, 1,648,000 square kilometers (636,290 square miles). Population, 37,500,000. Capital, Tehran.

I·ra·ni·an (ĭ-rā′nē-ən) *adj.* Of or pertaining to Iran, its inhabitants, or their language.

~*n.* **1.** A native or inhabitant of Iran. **2. a.** A group of languages including Persian, Kurdish, and Pashto, spoken principally in Iran,

Afghanistan, and west Pakistan, and forming a subbranch of the Indo-Iranian branch of the Indo-European language family. **b.** The modern Persian language as spoken in Iran; Farsi.

I·raq (ĭ-răk′, ē-räk′). Republic of western Asia. Its area includes the geographical location of ancient Mesopotamia, on the fertile plain between the Tigris and Euphrates rivers. Wrested from the Turkish empire and established as an independent kingdom (1921), it joined the Arab League (1945) and following the assassination of the king (1958) became a socialist republic. In 1980 it began an inconclusive war with Iran. Iraq's economy rests heavily on oil, which accounts for over 90 percent of its exports. Area, 434,924 square kilometers (167,924 square miles). Population 12,800,000. Capital, Baghdad. See map at **Iran.**

I·ra·qi (ē-rä′kē) *adj.* Of or pertaining to Iraq, its inhabitants, or their language.

~*n., pl.* **-qis** or collectively **Iraqi. 1.** A native or inhabitant of Iraq. **2.** The Arabic dialect spoken in Iraq.

i·ras·ci·ble (ĭ-răs′ə-bəl, ī-răs′-) *adj.* **1.** Prone to outbursts of temper; easily angered. **2.** Characterized by or resulting from anger. [Old French, from Late Latin *īrāscibilis,* from Latin *īrāscī,* to get angry, from *īra,* anger, IRE.] —**i·ras·ci·bil·i·ty, i·ras·ci·ble·ness** *n.* —**i·ras·ci·bly** *adv.*

i·rate (ī-rāt′, ī′rāt′) *adj.* **1.** Angry; enraged. **2.** Characterized or occasioned by anger: *an irate phone call.* [Latin *īrātus,* from *īra,* anger, IRE.] —**i·rate·ly** *adv.*

IRBM Intermediate Range Ballistic Missile.

ire (īr) *n.* Wrath; anger. —See Synonyms at **anger.** [Middle English, from Old French, from Latin *īra,* anger.]

ire·ful (īr′fəl) *adj.* Full of ire; angry; wrathful. —**ire·ful·ly** *adv.* —**ire·ful·ness** *n.*

Ire·land (īr′lənd). *Irish* **Ei·re** (âr′ə). Second largest of the British Isles. Its fertile central lowlands contain many peat bogs and are surrounded by several low mountain ranges, including the mountains of Mourne, Wicklow, Kerry, and Ox. Once occupied by a number of Celtic kingdoms, after the 12th century it fell increasingly under English domination. Following violence and unrest during and after World War I the predominantly Roman Catholic southern 26 counties became an autonomous state, the 6 northern counties remaining within the United Kingdom as the province of Northern Ireland.

Ireland, Republic of. Country of northwestern Europe. After much bitter fighting and civil unrest the Anglo-Irish Treaty (1921) paved the way for the 26 southern counties of Ireland to become the Irish Free State (1922). In 1937 a new constitution with full sovereignty was adopted by plebiscite, and the people called their country Eire.

It left the Commonwealth in 1949 and since then has been known officially as the Republic of Ireland. Mainly agricultural, its economy rests chiefly on beef and dairy cattle, sheep, pig, and poultry farming, two-thirds of the land being used for crop or pasture. Distilling, brewing, food processing, and electronics, chemicals, and textile manufacture are also important. The republic has been a member of the European Economic Community since 1973. Area, 70,283 square kilometers (27,136 square miles). Population, 3,500,000. Capital, Dublin.

I·re·ne (ī-rē′nē). *Greek Mythology.* The goddess of peace. [From Greek *eirēnē,* peace.]

i·ren·ic, ei·ren·ic (ī-rĕn′ĭk, ī-rē′nĭk) *adj.* Also **i·ren·i·cal, ei·ren·i·cal** (ī-rĕn′ĭk-əl, ī-rē′-). Promoting peace; conciliatory; pacific. [Greek *eirēnikos,* from *eirēnē†,* peace.] —**i·ren·i·cal·ly** *adv.*

irenicon. Variant of **eirenicon.**

i·ren·ics (ī-rĕn′ĭks, ī-rē′nĭks) *n. Used with a singular verb.* The branch of theology dealing with the promotion of peace and unity among Christian churches.

Ire·ton (īr′tən), **Henry** (1611–51). English Parliamentary general during the English Civil War (1642–51). Ireton married Cromwell's daughter and later helped bring Charles I to trial, being one of the signatories of his death warrant.

Irian Jaya. See **West Irian.**

ir·i·da·ceous (ĭr′ĭ-dā′shəs) *adj.* Of or pertaining to the iris family. [From New Latin *Iridacea,* iris family, from *Iris,* type genus, from Latin, iris.]

ir·i·dec·to·my (îr′ə-dĕk′tə-mē, ĭr′ə-) *n., pl.* **-mies.** The surgical removal of part of the iris of the eye. [Latin *īris* (stem *īrido-*), IRIS + -ECTOMY.]

ir·i·des·cent (îr′ə-dĕs′ənt) *adj.* Producing a display of lustrous, rainbowlike colors. [Latin *īris* (stem *īrid-*), rainbow, IRIS + -ESCENT.] —**ir·i·des·cence** *n.*

i·rid·ic (ī-rĭd′ĭk, ī-rĭd′-) *adj.* Pertaining to the iris of the eye.

i·rid·i·um (ī-rĭd′ē-əm, ī-rĭd′-) *n. Symbol* **Ir** A very hard and brittle, exceptionally corrosion-resistant, whitish-yellow metallic element occurring in platinum ores and used principally to harden platinum and in high-temperature materials, electrical contacts, and wear-resistant bearings. Atomic number 77, atomic weight 192.2, melting point 2,410°C, boiling point 4,527°C, specific gravity 22.42 (17°C), valences 3, 4. [New Latin, from Latin *īris* (stem *īrid-*), rainbow, IRIS (from the variety of colors it gives in solutions).]

ir·i·dos·mine (îr′ə-dŏz′mĭn, -dŏs′mĭn, ĭr′ə-) *n.* An alloy, **osmiridium** *(see).* [German *Iridosmin* : IRID(IUM) + OSM(IUM) + -INE.]

i·ris (ī′rĭs) *n., pl.* **irises** or **irides** (ī′rə-dēz′, îr′ə-). **1.** The pigmented, round, contractile membrane of the eye, situated between the cornea and lens, and perforated by the pupil. **2.** Any of numerous plants of the genus *Iris,* having sword-shaped leaves and variously colored flowers. **3.** *Rare.* A rainbow or rainbowlike display of colors. [Middle English *iris, yris,* rainbow, kind of prismatic crystal, from Latin *īris,* from Greek *iris,* rainbow, iris of the eye.]

I·ris (ī′rĭs). *Greek Mythology.* The goddess of the rainbow and messenger of the gods.

iris diaphragm *n.* A diaphragm that can be adjusted to vary the diameter of a central aperture, commonly used on cameras to regulate the amount of light admitted to a lens.

I·rish (ī′rĭsh) *adj. Abbr.* **Ir.** Of or pertaining to Ireland, its people, or their language.

—*n. Abbr.* **Ir. 1.** *Used with a plural verb.* **a.** The inhabitants of Ireland. **b.** People of immediate Irish descent. **2.** The Celtic language spoken in Ireland; Irish Gaelic. **3.** The English spoken in Ireland. **4.** *Informal.* Fieriness of temper or passion; high spirit. [Middle English *Irisc(h),* from Old English *Īras,* the Irish.]

Irish bull *n.* An apparently consistent but actually illogical or inconsistent statement.

Irish coffee *n.* A drink of sweetened hot coffee and Irish whiskey, topped with thick cream.

Irish elk *n.* A large extinct European deer of the genus *Megaloceros,* of the Pliocene and Pleistocene epochs, having palmate antlers.

Irish English *n.* English as spoken by the Irish.

Irish Gaelic *n.* The Goidelic language of Ireland, an official language of the Republic of Ireland. Also called "Erse," "Irish."

I·rish·ism (ī′rĭsh-ĭz′əm) *n.* An Irish idiom or custom.

I·rish·man (ī′rĭsh-mən) *n., pl.* **-men** (-mĭn). A man of Irish birth, citizenship, or descent.

Irish moss *n.* An edible North Atlantic seaweed, *Chondrus crispus,* that yields a mucilaginous substance used medicinally and in preparing jellies. Also called "carrageen."

Irish Republic. 1. The free state proclaimed by Irish rebels against British rule during the abortive Easter Rebellion in Dublin (1916). **2.** The Republic of Ireland. Used erroneously.

Irish Republican Army *n.* The **I.R.A.** *(see).*

Irish Sea. An arm of the Atlantic Ocean. It separates Britain from Ireland and is connected to the Atlantic by the North Channel in the north and by St. George's Channel in the south.

Irish setter *n.* A setter having a silky reddish-brown coat. Also called "red setter."

Irish stew *n.* A stew of meat and vegetables.

Irish terrier *n.* A terrier having a wiry brown coat.

Irish water spaniel *n.* A retriever having a dark curly coat and a characteristic topknot.

Irish whiskey *n.* A whiskey made in Ireland by the distillation of barley.

Irish wolfhound *n.* A large dog of an ancient breed, having a rough, shaggy coat.

I·rish·wom·an (ī′rĭsh-wŏŏm′ən) *n., pl.* **-women** (-wĭm′ĭn). A woman of Irish birth, citizenship, or descent.

i·ri·tis (ī-rī′tĭs) *n.* Inflammation of the iris of the eye. [New Latin : IR(IS) + -ITIS.]

irk (ûrk) *tr.v.* **irked, irking, irks.** To vex; weary; irritate. —See Synonyms at **annoy.** [Middle English *irken, yrken,* perhaps from Old Norse *yrkja,* to work.]

irk·some (ûrk′səm) *adj.* Causing annoyance or bother; wearisome; tedious: *irksome restrictions.* —See Synonyms at **boring.** —**irk·some·ly** *adv.* —**irk·some·ness** *n.*

IRO International Refugee Organization.

i·ro·ko (ī-rō′kō) *n.* **1.** A tropical tree, *Chlorophora excelsa.* **2.** The wood of this tree, often used as a substitute for teak. [Yoruba.]

i·ron (ī′ərn) *n.* **1.** *Symbol* **Fe** A silvery-white, lustrous, malleable, ductile, magnetic or magnetizable, metallic element occurring abundantly in combined forms, notably in hematite, limonite, magnetite, and taconite, and used alloyed in a wide range of important structural materials. Atomic number 26, atomic weight 55.847, melting point 1,535°C, boiling point 3,000°C, specific gravity 7.874 (20°C), valences 2, 3, 4, 6. **2.** Great hardness or strength; firmness: *a will of iron.* **3.** An implement made of iron alloy or similar metal; especially, a bar heated for use in branding, cauterizing, or soldering. **4.** Any of various golf clubs with a metal head, numbered from one or two to nine or ten according to the degree of slant of the face of the club. **5.** A metal appliance with a handle and a weighted flat bottom, used when heated to press wrinkles from fabric. **6.** *Informal.* A harpoon. **7. irons. a.** Fetters; shackles. **b.** Stirrups. **8.** Iron taken as a dietary supplement in the form of a tonic, pill, or other medication. —**have many irons in the fire.** To be engaged in many undertakings simultaneously. —**in irons. 1.** Fettered. **2.** *Nautical.* Lying head to the wind and unable to turn either way. —**pump iron.** *Informal.* In body building, to exercise with weights. —**strike while the iron is hot.** To seize an opportunity to act.

—*adj.* **1.** Made of or containing iron. **2.** Extremely hard and strong: *an iron fist.* **3.** Hardy; robust: *an iron constitution.* **4.** Inflexible; unyielding: *an iron will.* **5.** Base; degraded.

—*v.* **ironed, ironing, irons.** —*tr.* **1. a.** To press and smooth (clothing, for example) with a heated iron. **b.** To remove (creases) by pressing. Sometimes used with *out.* **2.** *Rare.* To put in irons; fetter. **3.** To fit or clad with iron. —*intr.* **1.** To iron clothes. **2.** To be capable of being ironed: *this fabric irons well.* —**iron out.** To settle through discussion or compromise; work out: *iron out our problems.* [Middle English *yren, yron, iren,* Old English *īren,* earlier *īsern, īsen.*]

iron age *n. Classical Mythology.* The last of the ages of the history of the world, a very degenerate age, and supposedly the one we are in now. Compare **golden age, silver age.**

Iron Age *n.* The generally prehistoric period succeeding the Bronze Age, characterized by the introduction and spread of iron tools and weapons, beginning in the Middle East around the 12th century B.C., and in Europe around the 8th century B.C.

i·ron·bark (ī′ərn-bärk′) *n.* Any of several Australian trees of the genus *Eucalyptus,* often having hard, rough bark.

iron blue *n.* Any of various light- and heat-resistant, semitransparent blue pigments of powerful tinctorial strength, used chiefly in permanent industrial finishes, printing inks, and artists' colors.

i·ron·bound (ī′ərn-bound′) *adj.* **1.** Bound with iron. **2.** Rigid and unyielding. **3.** Bound with rocks and cliffs, as a coast.

i·ron·clad (ī′ərn-klăd′) *adj.* **1.** Sheathed with iron plates for protection. **2.** Rigid: *an ironclad rule.* **3.** Fully protected from attack; unshakeable: *an ironclad argument.*

—*n.* A 19th-century warship having sides armored with metal plates.

Iron Cross *n.* A medal formerly awarded to German soldiers for the highest degree of bravery.

Iron Curtain *n.* A barrier that prevents free exchange or communication; specifically, the political and ideological barrier between the Soviet bloc and western Europe after World War II. [Popularized (1946) by Winston Churchill.]

iron glance *n.* A mineral, **hematite** *(see).*

iron gray *n.* A dark gray with a slightly greenish tinge.

iron hand *n.* Rigorous or despotic control: *ruling with an iron hand.* —**i·ron·hand·ed** (ī′ərn-hăn′dĭd) *adj.*

iron horse *n. Informal.* A railroad locomotive.

i·ron·ic (ī-rŏn′ĭk) *adj.* Also **i·ron·i·cal** (ī-rŏn′ĭ-kəl). **1.** Characterized by or constituting irony. **2.** Given to the use of irony. —See Usage note at **sarcastic.** —**i·ron·i·cal·ly** *adv.* —**i·ron·i·cal·ness** *n.*

i·ron·ing (ī′ər-nĭng) *n.* **1.** The pressing of clothes with a heated iron. **2.** The clothing to be pressed or that has been pressed.

ironing board *n.* A long narrow padded board on a collapsible support, used as a working surface for ironing.

i·ron·ist (ī′rə-nĭst) *n.* A notable user of irony, especially a writer. —**i·ron·ize** *v.*

iron lung *n.* An airtight tank in which the entire body except the head is enclosed and by means of which pressure is regularly increased and decreased to provide artificial respiration. Also called "respirator."

iron maiden *n.* A medieval torture device, consisting of a coffinlike case lined with iron spikes, in which the victim was enclosed.

i·ron·mas·ter (ī′ərn-măs′tər, -mäs′tər) *n. Chiefly British.* A manufacturer of iron.

i·ron·mon·ger (ī′ərn-mŭng′gər, -mŏng′gər) *n. Chiefly British.* A hardware merchant, selling metal tools and utensils.

i·ron·mon·ger·y (īʹərn-mŭngʹgə-rē, -mŏngʹgə-rē) *n., pl.* **-ies.** *Chiefly British.* **1.** Ironware. **2.** The shop or business of an ironmonger. **3.** *Slang.* Firearms.

iron oxide *n.* Any of various oxides of iron, such as ferrous oxide.

iron pyrites *n.* A mineral, **pyrite** *(see).*

iron rations *pl.n.* Emergency rations, especially those carried by a soldier.

i·ron·sides (īʹərn-sīdzʹ) *n., pl.* **ironsides. 1.** A person with great stamina or powers of endurance. **2.** An ironclad ship.

i·ron·smith (īʹərn-smĭthʹ) *n.* One who works in iron; a blacksmith.

i·ron·stone (īʹərn-stōnʹ) *n.* **1.** Any of several kinds of iron ore with admixtures of silica and clay. **2.** A hard white pottery.

i·ron·ware (īʹərn-wârʹ) *n.* Iron utensils and other products made of iron.

i·ron·weed (īʹərn-wēdʹ) *n.* Any plant of the genus *Vernonia,* having clusters of purplish flowers.

i·ron·wood (īʹərn-wŏŏdʹ) *n.* **1.** Any of various trees having very hard wood, such as the **hornbeam** and the **hop hornbeam** *(both of which see).* **2.** The wood of such a tree.

i·ron·work (īʹərn-wûrkʹ) *n.* **1.** Iron objects, such as gratings or gates, especially when made by hand. **2.** The craft or profession of making such objects.

i·ron·work·er (īʹərn-wûrʹkər) *n.* **1.** A person who makes ironwork. **2.** A person who works in an ironworks.

i·ron·works (īʹərn-wûrksʹ) *n., pl.* **ironworks.** *Usually used with a singular verb.* A building or establishment where iron is smelted or where heavy iron products are made.

i·ro·ny[1] (īʹrə-nē) *n., pl.* **-nies. 1.** The use of words to convey the opposite of their literal meaning. **2.** An expression or utterance marked by such a deliberate contrast between apparent and intended meaning. **3.** A literary style employing such contrasts for humorous or rhetorical effect. **4.** Incongruity between what might be expected and what actually occurs: *the irony of being run over by an ambulance.* **5.** An occurrence, result, or circumstance notable for such incongruity. **6. Dramatic irony** *(see).* **7. Socratic irony** *(see).* —See Synonyms at **wit.** [Latin *īrōnia,* from Greek *eirōneia,* dissembling, feigned ignorance, from *eirōn,* dissembler, "one who says less than he thinks," from *eirein,* to say.]

i·ron·y[2] (īʹər-nē) *adj.* Of, like, or containing iron.

Ir·o·quoi·an (îrʹə-kwoiʹən) *n.* **1.** A family of North American Indian languages spoken in Canada and the eastern United States by such peoples as the Iroquois, Cherokee, Conestoga, Erie, and Wyandot. **2.** A member of a people using a language of this family.
~*adj.* **1.** Of or designating this language family. **2.** Of or pertaining to the Iroquois or their culture.

Ir·o·quois (îrʹə-kwoiʹ, -kwoizʹ) *n., pl.* **Iroquois. 1.** A member of any of several Iroquoian-speaking North American Indian peoples formerly inhabiting New York State, and forming the confederacy known as the *Five Nations,* including the Cayuga, Mohawk, Oneida, Onondaga, and Seneca peoples. After 1722 the confederacy was joined by the Tuscaroras to form the *Six Nations.* **2.** Any of the languages spoken among these peoples. —**Ir·o·quois** *adj.*

ir·ra·di·ance (ĭ-rāʹdē-əns) *n. Symbol* **E** *Physics.* The radiant flux or radiation reaching a surface per unit area. Compare **radiance.**

ir·ra·di·ant (ĭ-rāʹdē-ənt) *adj.* Sending forth radiant light. [Latin *irradiāns* (stem *irradiant-*), present participle of *irradiāre,* IRRADIATE.]

ir·ra·di·ate (ĭ-rāʹdē-ātʹ) *v.* **-ated, -ating, -ates.** —*tr.* **1. a.** To expose to radiation. **b.** To treat with radiation. **2.** To emit in a manner analogous to the emission of light. **3.** To make intellectually interesting or spiritually radiant; clarify; illumine. —*intr. Archaic.* **1.** To send forth rays; radiate. **2.** To become radiant. [Latin *irradiāre,* to shine forth : *in-,* toward + *radiāre,* to shine, RADIATE.] —**ir·ra·di·a·tive** *adj.* —**ir·ra·di·a·tor** *n.*

ir·ra·di·a·tion (ĭ-rāʹdē-āʹshən) *n.* **1.** The act of irradiating or the condition of being irradiated. **2.** *Medicine.* Therapy or treatment by exposure to radiation.

ir·rad·i·ca·ble (ĭ-rădʹĭ-kə-bəl) *adj.* Incapable of being uprooted or destroyed. [Medieval Latin *irradicabilis* : Latin *in-,* not + Latin *radix,* root.] —**ir·rad·i·ca·bly** *adv.*

ir·ra·tion·al (ĭ-răshʹən-əl) *adj.* **1. a.** Not endowed with reason. **b.** Affected by loss of usual or normal mental clarity; incoherent, as, for example, from shock. **c.** Contrary to reason; illogical: *an irrational dislike.* **2.** In Greek and Latin verse: **a.** Designating a syllable whose length does not fit the metrical pattern. **b.** Designating a metrical foot containing such a syllable. **3.** *Mathematics.* Incapable of being expressed as an integer or a ratio or quotient of integers. —**ir·ra·tion·al·ly** *adv.* —**ir·ra·tion·al·ness** *n.*

ir·ra·tion·al·i·ty (ĭ-răshʹə-nălʹə-tē) *n., pl.* **-ties.** Also **ir·ra·tion·al·ism** (ĭ-răshʹən-ə-lĭzʹəm). **1.** The state or quality of being irrational. **2.** An irrational idea or action.

irrational number *n. Mathematics.* A member of the set of real numbers that is not a member of the set of rational numbers; a number that cannot be expressed as an integer or an exact ratio of two integers; for example, the number π (pi).

Ir·ra·wad·dy (îrʹə-wäʹdē). The chief river of Burma. Rising in the Patkai hills in the northeastern part of the country, it flows 2,010 kilometers (1,250 miles) south to the Bay of Bengal. Its delta, west of the Gulf of Martaban, is a major rice-growing area.

ir·re·claim·a·ble (îrʹĭ-klāʹmə-bəl) *adj.* Incapable of being reclaimed: *irreclaimable wasteland.* —**ir·re·claim·a·bil·i·ty, ir·re·claim·a·ble·ness** *n.* —**ir·re·claim·a·bly** *adv.*

ir·rec·on·cil·a·ble (ĭ-rĕkʹən-sīʹlə-bəl, ĭ-rĕkʹən-sīʹ-) *adj.* **1.** Not capable of being reconciled; implacably hostile. **2.** Incompatible; incongruous.
~*n.* **1.** A person who will not compromise or adjust. **2. irreconcilables.** Conflicting ideas or beliefs that cannot be brought into harmony. —**ir·rec·on·cil·a·bil·i·ty** *n.* —**ir·rec·on·cil·a·bly** *adv.*

ir·re·cov·er·a·ble (îrʹĭ-kŭvʹər-ə-bəl) *adj.* Incapable of being recovered; irreparable: *irrecoverable losses.* —**ir·re·cov·er·a·ble·ness** *n.* —**ir·re·cov·er·a·bly** *adv.*

ir·re·cu·sa·ble (îrʹĭ-kyōōʹzə-bəl) *adj.* Not subject to challenge or objection; unexceptionable; undeniable. [French *irrécusable,* from Late Latin *irrecūsābilis* : *in-,* not + *recūsābilis,* that should be rejected, from Latin *recūsāre,* to reject.] —**ir·re·cu·sa·bly** *adv.*

ir·re·deem·a·ble (îrʹĭ-dēʹmə-bəl) *adj.* **1.** Incapable of being bought back or paid off: *an irredeemable annuity.* **2.** Not convertible into coin: *irredeemable banknotes.* **3.** Incapable of being remedied. **4.** Incapable of being saved or reformed.
~*n.* A bond, annuity, or similar investment that cannot be redeemed before it matures. —**ir·re·deem·a·bil·i·ty** *n.* —**ir·re·deem·a·bly** *adv.*

ir·re·den·tist (îrʹĭ-dĕnʹtĭst) *n.* One who advocates the recovery of lands of which his nation has been deprived, or of territory culturally or historically related to his nation but now subject to a foreign government. [Italian *irredentista,* from *(Italia) irredenta,* "unredeemed (Italy)" (Italian-speaking areas subject to other countries), from *irredento,* not redeemed : *in-,* not, from Latin + *redento,* redeemed, from Latin *redemptus,* past participle of *redimere,* REDEEM.] —**ir·re·den·tism** *n.* —**ir·re·den·tist** *adj.*

ir·re·duc·i·ble (îrʹĭ-dōōʹsə-bəl, -dyōōʹsə-bəl) *adj.* **1.** Incapable of being reduced to a desired, simpler, or smaller form or amount. **2.** *Medicine.* Incapable of being replaced in a normal position. Said especially of a hernia. —**ir·re·duc·i·bil·i·ty, ir·re·duc·i·ble·ness** *n.* —**ir·re·duc·i·bly** *adv.*

ir·ref·ra·ga·ble (ĭ-rĕfʹrə-gə-bəl) *adj.* Incapable of being refuted or controverted; indisputable. [Late Latin *irrefrāgābilis* : Latin *in-,* not + *refrāgārī,* to oppose, akin to *frangere,* to break.] —**ir·ref·ra·ga·bil·i·ty** *n.* —**ir·ref·ra·ga·bly** *adv.*

ir·re·fran·gi·ble (îrʹĭ-frănʹjə-bəl) *adj.* **1.** Incapable of being violated or broken; indestructible. **2.** *Physics.* Incapable of being refracted. —**ir·re·fran·gi·bil·i·ty** *n.* —**ir·re·fran·gi·bly** *adv.*

ir·ref·u·ta·ble (ĭ-rĕfʹyə-tə-bəl, îrʹĭ-fyōōʹtə-bəl) *adj.* Incapable of being refuted or disproved; incontrovertible: *irrefutable arguments.* —**ir·ref·u·ta·bil·i·ty** *n.* —**ir·ref·u·ta·bly** *adv.*

irreg. irregular; irregularly.

ir·re·gard·less (îrʹĭ-gärdʹlĭs) *adv. Nonstandard.* Regardless.

ir·reg·u·lar (ĭ-rĕgʹyə-lər) *adj. Abbr.* **irreg. 1.** Not according to rule, accepted order, or general practice. **2.** Not conforming to legality, moral law, or social convention: *an irregular marriage.* **3.** Not straight, uniform, or symmetrical: *a path of irregular width; irregular facial features.* **4.** Of uneven rate, occurrence, or duration: *an irregular heartbeat; irregular attendance.* **5.** Deviating from type; asymmetrically arranged or atypical. **6.** *Botany.* Having differing floral parts, especially petals. **7.** Falling below the manufacturer's standard or usual specifications; flawed; imperfect. **8.** *Grammar.* Departing from the usual set of inflectional forms; for example, the verb *be* is an irregular verb. **9.** Not belonging to a permanent, organized military force: *irregular troops.*
~*n.* **1.** A person or thing that is irregular. **2.** A soldier, such as a guerrilla, who is not a member of a regular military force. —**ir·reg·u·lar·ly** *adv.*

ir·reg·u·lar·i·ty (ĭ-rĕgʹyə-lărʹə-tē) *n., pl.* **-ties. 1.** The quality or state of being irregular. **2.** That which is irregular. **3.** Constipation.

ir·rel·a·tive (ĭ-rĕlʹə-tĭv) *adj.* **1.** Having no correlative relationship; unconnected. **2.** Irrelevant. —**ir·rel·a·tive·ly** *adv.*

ir·rel·e·vance (ĭ-rĕlʹə-vəns) *n.* Also **ir·rel·e·van·cy** (-vən-sē) *pl.* **-cies. 1.** The quality or state of being irrelevant. **2.** That which is irrelevant.

ir·rel·e·vant (ĭ-rĕlʹə-vənt) *adj.* **1.** Having no applications or effects in a specified circumstance; unrelated to the subject under discussion or the matter to be dealt with. **2.** Lacking in contemporaneity; failing to deal with current concerns. —**ir·rel·e·vant·ly** *adv.*

ir·re·lig·ion (îrʹĭ-lĭjʹən) *n.* Hostility or indifference to religion.

ir·re·lig·ious (îrʹĭ-lĭjʹəs) *adj.* Indifferent or hostile to religion; ungodly. —**ir·re·lig·ious·ly** *adv.* —**ir·re·lig·ious·ness** *n.*

ir·rem·e·a·ble (ĭ-rĕmʹē-ə-bəl, ĭ-rēʹmē-) *adj. Archaic.* Affording no possibility of return. [Latin *irremeābilis* : *in-,* not + *remeāre,* to return : *re-,* back + *meāre,* to go.]

ir·re·me·di·a·ble (îrʹĭ-mēʹdē-ə-bəl) *adj.* Impossible to remedy, correct, or repair; incurable. —**ir·re·me·di·a·bly** *adv.*

ir·re·mis·si·ble (îrʹĭ-mĭsʹə-bəl) *adj.* **1.** Not remissible; unpardonable. **2.** In need of doing; unavoidable; obligatory. —**ir·re·mis·si·bil·i·ty** *n.* —**ir·re·mis·si·bly** *adv.*

ir·re·mov·a·ble (îrʹĭ-mōōʹvə-bəl) *adj.* **1.** Not physically removable. **2.** Not liable to removal from office. —**ir·re·mov·a·bil·i·ty** *n.* —**ir·re·mov·a·bly** *adv.*

ir·rep·a·ra·ble (ĭ-rĕpʹə-rə-bəl) *adj.* Incapable of being repaired, rectified, or amended; beyond repair: *irreparable harm.* —**ir·rep·a·ra·bil·i·ty, ir·rep·a·ra·ble·ness** *n.* —**ir·rep·a·ra·bly** *adv.*

ir·re·peal·a·ble (îrʹĭ-pēʹlə-bəl) *adj.* Not capable of being repealed.

ir·re·place·a·ble (îrʹĭ-plāʹsə-bəl) *adj.* Incapable of being replaced because so valuable.

ir·re·pres·si·ble (îrʹĭ-prĕsʹə-bəl) *adj.* Not capable of being repressed; impossible to control or restrain. —**ir·re·pres·si·bil·i·ty, ir·re·pres·si·ble·ness** *n.* —**ir·re·pres·si·bly** *adv.*

ironstone *A sedimentary rock rich in iron minerals. It is an important source of iron ore.*

ir·re·proach·a·ble (ĭr′ĭ-prō′chə-bəl) *adj.* Not meriting any reproach; beyond reproach; perfect. —**ir·re·proach·a·bil·i·ty, ir·re·proach·a·ble·ness** *n.* —**ir·re·proach·a·bly** *adv.*

ir·re·sis·ti·ble (ĭr′ĭ-zĭs′tə-bəl) *adj.* **1.** Impossible to resist. **2.** Having an overpowering appeal: *an irresistible urge to dance.* **3.** Very attractive; alluring: *an irrestible woman.* —**ir·re·sis·ti·bil·i·ty, ir·re·sis·ti·ble·ness** *n.* —**ir·re·sis·ti·bly** *adv.*

ir·res·o·lu·ble (ĭ-rĕz′əl-yə-bəl, ĭr′ĭ-zŏl′-) *adj.* Not capable of being solved.

ir·res·o·lute (ĭ-rĕz′ə-lōōt′) *adj.* **1.** Unresolved as to action or procedure. **2.** Lacking in resolution; vacillating; wavering; indecisive. —**ir·res·o·lute·ly** *adv.* —**ir·res·o·lute·ness, ir·res·o·lu·tion** *n.*

ir·re·solv·a·ble (ĭr′ĭ-zŏl′və-bəl) *adj.* **1.** Incapable of being solved or resolved. **2.** Not capable of being separated into component parts; irreducible.

ir·re·spec·tive (ĭr′ĭ-spĕk′tĭv) *adj. Archaic.* Characterized by disregard; heedless. —**irrespective of.** Regardless of; without consideration of.

~*adv. Informal.* Regardless; without considering: *We advised him against it but he carried on irrespective.* —**ir·re·spec·tive·ly** *adv.*

ir·re·spir·a·ble (ĭr′ĭ-spīr′ə-bəl, ĭ-rĕs′pər-) *adj.* Not fit for breathing; not respirable.

ir·re·spon·si·ble (ĭr′ĭ-spŏn′sə-bəl) *adj.* **1.** Not mentally or financially fit to assume responsibility. **2.** Showing no sense of responsibility or due care; reckless; untrustworthy. **3.** *Archaic.* Not liable to be called to account by a higher authority.

~*n.* An irresponsible person. —**ir·re·spon·si·bil·i·ty, ir·re·spon·si·ble·ness** *n.* —**ir·re·spon·si·bly** *adv.*

ir·re·spon·sive (ĭr′ĭ-spŏn′sĭv) *adj.* **1.** Not responsive, as to treatment or stimuli. **2.** Not responding or answering readily. —**ir·re·spon·sive·ly** *adv.* —**ir·re·spon·sive·ness** *n.*

ir·re·triev·a·ble (ĭr′ĭ-trē′və-bəl) *adj.* **1.** Not capable of being retrieved or recovered. **2.** Beyond help or repair. —**ir·re·triev·a·bil·i·ty, ir·re·triev·a·ble·ness** *n.* —**ir·re·triev·a·bly** *adv.*

ir·rev·er·ence (ĭ-rĕv′ər-əns) *n.* **1.** Absence of reverence or due respect. **2.** A disrespectful act or remark.

ir·rev·er·ent (ĭ-rĕv′ər-ənt) *adj.* **1.** Lacking in reverence; disrespectful: *an irreverent person.* **2.** Proceeding from irreverence: *an irreverent act.* —**ir·rev·er·ent·ly** *adv.*

ir·re·vers·i·ble (ĭr′ĭ-vûr′sə-bəl) *adj.* **1.** Incapable of being reversed. **2.** *Chemistry.* **a.** Designating or pertaining to a chemical reaction that takes place almost completely in one direction. **b.** Designating or pertaining to a change in which intermediate stages do not attain thermodynamic equilibrium. —**ir·re·vers·i·bil·i·ty, ir·re·vers·i·ble·ness** *n.* —**ir·re·vers·i·bly** *adv.*

ir·rev·o·ca·ble (ĭ-rĕv′ə-kə-bəl) *adj.* Incapable of being retracted or revoked; irreversible. —**ir·rev·o·ca·bil·i·ty, ir·rev·o·ca·ble·ness** *n.* —**ir·rev·o·ca·bly** *adv.*

ir·ri·ga·ble (ĭr′ĭ-gə-bəl) *adj.* Capable of irrigation; able to be irrigated.

ir·ri·gate (ĭr′ĭ-gāt′) *tr.v.* **-gated, -gating, -gates.** **1. a.** To supply (dry land) with water by means of ditches, pipes, or streams. **b.** To water or provide (land) with water. Used of a river, stream, or the like. **2.** To wash out (a cavity or wound) with water or a medicated fluid. **3.** To make fertile or vital by or as if by watering. [Latin *irrigāre,* to lead water to : *in-,* in + *rigāre,* to wet, water.] —**ir·ri·ga·tion** *n.* —**ir·ri·ga·tion·al** *adj.* —**ir·ri·ga·tor** *n.*

ir·ri·ta·bil·i·ty (ĭr′ə-tə-bĭl′ə-tē) *n.* **1.** The quality or state of being irritable; testiness; petulance. **2.** *Medicine.* Excessive sensitivity. **3.** *Biology.* The capacity to respond to stimuli.

ir·ri·ta·ble (ĭr′ə-tə-bəl) *adj.* **1.** Easily annoyed; ill-tempered. **2.** *Medicine.* Abnormally sensitive. **3.** *Biology.* Responsive to stimuli. [Latin *irritābilis,* from *irritāre,* IRRITATE.] —**ir·ri·ta·ble·ness** *n.* —**ir·ri·ta·bly** *adv.*

ir·ri·tant (ĭr′ə-tənt) *adj.* Causing physical or mental irritation.

~*n.* Something that causes irritation. [Latin *irritāns* (stem *irritant-*), present participle of *irritāre,* IRRITATE.]

ir·ri·tate (ĭr′ə-tāt′) *tr.v.* **-tated, -tating, -tates.** **1. a.** To annoy; vex. **b.** To provoke. **2.** To chafe or inflame. —See Synonyms at **annoy.** [Latin *irritāre†.*] —**ir·ri·tat·ing·ly** *adv.* —**ir·ri·ta·tive** (ĭr′ə-tā′tĭv) *adj.* —**ir·ri·ta·tor** *n.*

ir·ri·ta·tion (ĭr′ə-tā′shən) *n.* **1.** The act of irritating. **2.** A source of irritation. **3.** The condition of being irritated; vexation. **4.** *Medicine.* Incipient inflammation, soreness, roughness, or irritability of a bodily part.

ir·ro·ta·tion·al (ĭr′ō-tā′shən-əl) *adj.* Not rotating or involving rotation.

ir·rupt (ĭ-rŭpt′) *intr.v.* **-rupted, -rupting, -rupts.** **1.** To break or burst in; make an incursion or invasion. **2.** *Ecology.* To increase irregularly in number. Used of a human or animal population. [Latin *irrumpere* (past participle *irruptus*) : *in-,* in + *rumpere,* to break, burst.] —**ir·rup·tion** *n.*

ir·rup·tive (ĭ-rŭp′tĭv) *adj.* **1.** Irrupting or tending to irrupt. **2.** *Geology.* Intrusive. **3.** Characterized by irruption.

IRS Internal Revenue Service.

Ir·tysh (ĭr′tĭsh). River in western Siberia in the U.S.S.R. It rises in Xinjiang Uigur Zizhiqu in China and flows *c.* 4,260 kilometers (2,650 miles) to join the Ob River.

Ir·ving (ûr′vĭng), **Sir Henry,** born John Henry Brodribb (1838–1905). Great Shakespearean actor. His productions, particularly those at London's Lyceum Theatre, won him the first theatrical knighthood to be awarded to an Englishman (1895).

Irving, Washington (1783–1859). U.S. diplomat and writer. His

best-known work is *The Sketch Book* (1819–20), containing the classic stories "Rip Van Winkle" and "The Legend of Sleepy Hollow."

is (ĭz). The third person singular present indicative of the verb **be.**

is. island; isle.

Is. **1.** Isaiah (Old Testament). **2.** island; isle.

is-. Variant of iso-.

Isa. Isaiah (Old Testament).

I·saac (ī′zək). A Hebrew patriarch, the son of Abraham and Sarah and the father of Jacob and Esau. Genesis 21:1–4. [Late Latin *Isaacus,* from Greek *Isaak,* from Hebrew *Yiṣḥāq,* "he laughs."]

I·sa·bel·la I of Castile (ĭz′ə-bĕl′ə), also called "the Catholic" (1451–1504). Queen of Castile. Her marriage to Ferdinand of Aragon (1469) led to the eventual unification of Spain. She was the patron of Christopher Columbus.

i·sa·go·gic (ī′sə-gŏj′ĭk) *adj.* Pertaining to or designating studies, especially Bible studies, of an introductory kind. [Latin, from Greek *eisagōgikos,* introductory, from *eisagōgē,* introduction : *eis,* into + *agōgē,* leading, from *agein,* to lead.]

i·sa·gog·ics (ī′sə-gŏj′ĭks) *pl.n.* Introductory studies, especially of the Bible.

I·sa·iah¹ (ī-zā′ə, ī-zī′ə). Also in Douay Bible **I·sa·ias** (ī-zā′yəs, ī-zī′-əs). A Hebrew prophet of the 8th century B.C. [Hebrew *Yǝsha‘yāh(u),* "salvation of the Lord" : *yēsha‘, yǝshū‘āh,* salvation + *yāh(u),* the Lord.]

Isaiah² *n. Abbr.* **Is., Isa.** A book in the Old Testament attributed to Isaiah, though now considered to be the work of three writers.

i·sal·lo·bar (ī-săl′ə-bär′) *n. Meteorology.* A line on a weather map connecting places exhibiting equal changes in barometric pressure within a given period of time. [IS(O)- + ALLO- + Greek *baros,* weight.]

ISBN *n.* International Standard Book Number; a number assigned under an international system to each newly published book, to facilitate ordering and identification.

is·che·mi·a (ĭ-skē′mē-ə) *n. Pathology.* A local anemia caused by mechanical obstruction of the blood supply. [New Latin *ischaemia,* from Greek *iskhaimos,* stanching, stopping blood : *iskhein,* to keep back, hold, restrain + *haima,* blood.]

is·chi·um (ĭs′kē-əm) *n., pl.* **-chia** (-kē-ə). *Anatomy.* The lowest of three major bones composing each half of the pelvis. [Latin, hip joint, from Greek *iskhion†.*]

-ise. Variant of **-ize.**

is·en·trop·ic (ī′sĕn-trŏp′ĭk, -trō′pĭk) *adj.* Without change in entropy; at constant entropy. [IS(O)- + ENTROP(Y) + -IC.]

I·seult, Y·seult (ĭ-sōōlt′). Also **I·sol·de** (ĭ-sōl′də, ĭ-zōl′-). **1.** A legendary Irish princess who married Mark, the king of Cornwall, and had a doomed love for his nephew, Tristan. **2.** A legendary princess of Brittany, whom Tristan in some accounts married.

Is·fa·han (ĭs′fə-hän′, -hän′). Formerly **As·pa·da·na** (ăs′pə-dä′nə). City in central Iran and the capital of the Isfahan province. It is noted for its carpet manufacturing and metalwork. It was the capital of Persia under Shah Abbas the Great (*c.* A.D. 1600).

–ish *suffix.* Indicates: **1. a.** Having the nationality of; for example, **Swedish, Finnish.** **b.** Having the qualities or character of; for example, **childish, sheepish. c.** Tending to or preoccupied with; for example, **bookish, selfish. d.** Somewhere near or approximately. Used informally in naming hours or years: *She's fortyish.* **2.** Somewhat or rather; for example, **greenish.** [Middle English *-is(c)h,* Old English *-isc,* from Common Germanic *-iskaz* (unattested), corresponding to Greek *-iskos,* diminutive noun suffix.]

Ish·er·wood (ĭsh′ər-wōōd′), **Christopher** (1904–86). English novelist, best known for his portrayals of Berlin in the early 1930's in works such as *Mr. Norris Changes Trains* (1935) and *Goodbye to Berlin* (1939), on which the musical *Cabaret* is based.

Ish·ma·el¹ (ĭsh′mē-əl). The son of Abraham by Sarah's handmaid, Hagar. Genesis 16:1–16. [Late Latin *Ismaël,* from Hebrew *Yishmā‘ēl,* "God hears" : *yishmā,* he hears, from *shāma‘,* he heard + *'Ēl,* God.]

Ishmael² An outcast. [From ISHMAEL, referring to Abraham's expulsion of Ishmael and Hagar after the birth of Isaac (Genesis 21:14).]

Ish·ma·el·ite (ĭsh′mē-ə-līt′) *n.* **1.** A member of a group of desert-dwelling people believed by the ancient Hebrews to be descended from Ishmael. **2.** An outcast. —**Ish·ma·el·it·ism** *n.*

Ish·tar (ĭsh′tär′). *Assyrian & Babylonian Mythology.* The goddess of love, fertility, and war; identified with the Phoenician Astarte. [Akkadian *Ishtar,* akin to Hebrew *'Ashtōreth,* ASHTORETH.]

i·sin·glass (ī′zĭng-glăs′, -gläs′, ī′zən-) *n.* **1.** A transparent, almost pure gelatin prepared from the air bladder of certain fishes, such as the sturgeon. **2.** A mineral, **muscovite** *(see).* [Alteration (influenced by GLASS) of obsolete Dutch *huizenblas,* from Middle Dutch *huusblase* : *huus,* sturgeon, from Germanic *hūsōn-* (unattested) + *blase,* bladder.]

I·sis¹ (ī′sĭs). *Egyptian Mythology.* A goddess of fertility, and sister and wife of Osiris.

Isis². See **Oxford.**

isl. island; isle.

Is·lam (ĭs′ləm, ĭz′-, ĭs-läm′) *n.* **1.** A religion based upon the teachings of the prophet Muhammad, believing in one God (Allah) and in Paradise and Hell, and having a body of law set forth in the Koran and the Sunna; the Muslim religion. **2. a.** All those nations of the world, especially in Asia and Africa, whose populations are Muslim; the Muslim world. **b.** Islamic civilization. **3.** Muslims collectively. [Arabic *islām,* "submission (to God)," from *aslama,* he

A RELIGION BUILT ON THE DIRECT WORD OF ALLAH

Muhammad's followers observe five obligations

Islam is based on the teachings of the Koran (or Qur'an), claimed by believers to be the direct word of Allah, that is, God, and revealed to the prophet Muhammad in the 7th century A.D. It spread rapidly from Mecca in northwest Arabia across North Africa and the Middle East, and into Spain, part of Russia, and eventually India and Indonesia. Today its followers number about 600 million.

Standing in the tradition of both Christianity and Judaism, Islam promises that the faithful follower will go to Paradise and the nonbeliever to Hell. Allah is the creator of the universe and a loving but just god, and Abraham and Jesus are included in the Islamic prophets. Islam has five obligations, or pillars, that the faithful must observe—to believe in Allah and Muhammad, to pray five times daily while facing Mecca, to give money to charity, to fast between sunrise and sunset during the month of Ramadan, and to visit the holy shrine at Mecca at least once in a lifetime if circumstances permit.

The Koran also has a political message, as it details how men should live in a community and permits the waging of holy war (jihad) against nonbelievers. After the death of Muhammad, Islam split into two groups, the Sunni Muslims today numbering 536 million and the Shiite Muslims numbering 40 million.

THE KAABA SHRINE *In the Great Mosque in Mecca lies this cube-shaped building containing the Black Stone, most sacred of Islamic objects, said to have been given by Gabriel to Abraham.*

ISLAMIC ART *The Koran forbids the representation of Allah, the human form, and animals, so an abstract style developed. This tile mural is from the Jum'a Mosque, Isfahan.*

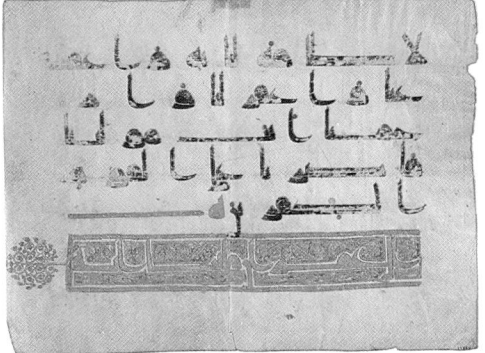

THE DIVINE WORD *After Muhammad's death, the revelations he received from God through the angel Gabriel were written down as the sacred text, the Koran. It is about as long as the New Testament in the Bible, with 114 chapters, called suras, which are placed in order according to length.*

The Koran is believed to be the direct word of God. The suras received while Muhammad was at Mecca concern spiritual truths, those he received later at Medina concern political and moral questions. The Koran teaches that there is only one God and that no intermediaries between God and man are necessary. For this reason no Islamic priesthood has developed. The text on the left is in Naskh script, the general text for Arabic manuscripts. The text above is written in Kufic.

surrendered, he resigned himself, from *salama,* he was safe.] —**Is·lam·ic** *adj.*

Is·la·ma·bad (ĭs-lä′mə-bäd′, ĭz-). A new city in north Pakistan, the national capital since 1967.

Is·lam·ism (ĭs′lə-mĭz′əm, ĭz′-) *n.* The religious faith, principles, or cause of Islam. —**Is·lam·ist** *n.*

Is·lam·ize (ĭs′lə-mīz′, ĭz′-) *tr.v.* **-ized, -izing, -izes. 1.** To convert to Islam. **2.** To impose the laws and practices of Islam on. —**Is·lam·i·za·tion** *n.*

is·land (ī′lənd) *n.* **1.** *Abbr.* **i., l., is., Is., isl.** A land mass, especially one smaller than a continent, entirely surrounded by water. **2.** Anything completely isolated or regarded as resembling such an isolated land mass. **3.** A traffic island *(see).* **4.** *Anatomy.* A tissue or cluster of cells separated from surrounding tissue by a groove or differing from surrounding tissue in structure.
~*tr.v.* **islanded, -landing, -lands. 1. a.** To make into or as if into an island; insulate. **b.** To place on an island. **2.** To dot or intersperse with or as if with islands. [Middle English *eland, ilond, ylond* (influenced by ISLE), Old English *ī(e)gland, īland.*]

is·land·er (ī′lən-dər) *n.* An inhabitant of an island.

is·land-hop·ping (ī′lənd-hŏp′ĭng) *n.* The making of short boat trips or short-haul flights to a number of islands in the same area.

islands of Lang·er·hans (läng′ər-häns′) *pl.n.* Also **islets of Lang·er·hans.** Irregular masses of small endocrine cells that lie in the interstitial tissue of the pancreas and secrete insulin and glucagon. [After Paul *Langerhans* (1847–88), German doctor.]

Islands of the Blest *pl.n. Greek Mythology.* See **Hesperides.**

Islas Baleares. See **Baleric Islands.**

Islas Malvinas. See **Falkland Islands.**

Is·lay (ī′lä). Island lying off the west coast of Scotland, the most southerly of the Inner Hebrides. Its comparative prosperity is due chiefly to an established whiskey-distilling industry.

isle (īl) *n. Abbr.* **i., l., is., Is., isl.** An island, especially a small one. Used poetically and in place names. [Middle English *i(s)le,* from Old French, from Latin *īnsula†.*]

is·let (ī′lĭt) *n.* A little island.

ism (ĭz′əm) *n. Informal.* A distinctive doctrine, system, or theory. [From -ISM.]

-ism *suffix.* Indicates: **1.** An action, practice, or process; for example, **terrorism, favoritism. 2.** A state or condition of being; for example, **pauperism, parallelism. 3.** A characteristic behavior or quality; for example, **heroism, individualism. 4.** A distinctive usage or feature, especially of language; for example, **malapropism, Latinism. 5.** A doctrine, theory, system, or principle; for example, **Platonism, expressionism, capitalism, pacifism.** [Middle English *-isme,* from Old French, from Latin *-ismus,* from Greek *-ismos,* suffix used to form nouns of action from verbs in *-izein,* -IZE.]

Is·ma·il·i, Is·ma·i·li (ĭs′mä-īl′ē) *n.* Also **Is·ma·il·i·an** (ĭs′mä-īl′ē-ən). A Muslim of a Shiite sect. [Arabic *Isma'īlīy,* after *Isma'īl* (died A.D. 760), son of the sixth Imam Jafar.]

is·n't (ĭz′ənt). Contraction of *is not.*

ISO International Standards Organization.

iso-, is- *prefix.* Indicates: **1.** Equal, identical, or similar; for example, **isallobar, isogon. 2.** *Chemistry.* Isomeric; for example, **isopropyl alcohol.** [Greek, from *isos†,* equal.]

i·so·ag·glu·ti·na·tion (ī′sō-ə-glōōt′n-ā′shən) *n.* The agglutination of red blood cells by the serum of another individual of the same species.

i·so·ag·glu·tin·in (ī′sō-ə-glōōt′n-ĭn) *n.* An isoantibody that causes agglutination of red blood cells.

i·so·ag·glu·tin·o·gen (ī′sō-ăg′lōō-tĭn′ə-jən) *n.* An isoantigen that on exposure to its isoantibody induces agglutination of the red blood cells to which it is attached. [ISOAGGLUTIN(IN) + -GEN.]

i·so·am·yl acetate (ī′sō-ăm′əl) *n.* A colorless compound, $(CH_3)_2CHCH_2CH_2OOCCH_3$, used as a solvent and a flavoring.

i·so·an·ti·bod·y (ī′sō-ăn′tē-bŏd′ē) *n., pl.* **-ies.** An antibody that occurs in only some individuals of a species and reacts specifically with the corresponding isoantigen from a different individual of the same species.

i·so·an·ti·gen (ī′sō-ăn′tī-jən, -jĕn′) *n.* An antigen that occurs in only some individuals of a species and never in those having cells that contain the corresponding isoantibody.

i·so·bar (ī′sə-bär′) *n.* **1.** A line on a map connecting points of equal atmospheric pressure. **2.** *Physics.* Any of two or more nuclides having the same mass number but different atomic numbers. [ISO- + Greek *baros,* weight.] —**i·so·bar·ic** *adj.*

i·so·bath (ī′sō-băth′, -bäth′) *n.* A line on a chart connecting points of equal water depth. [Greek *isobathēs,* of equal depth : ISO- + *bathēs,* depth.]

i·so·bu·tane (ī′sō-byōō′tān) *n.* An isomer of **butane** *(see).*

i·so·chor, i·so·chore (ī′sō-kôr′, -kōr′) *n.* A line on a graph showing how the temperature of fluid kept at constant volume varies with pressure. [ISO- + Greek *khōros,* space, place.]

i·so·chro·mat·ic (ī′sō-krō-măt′ĭk) *adj.* **1. a.** Having the same color. **b.** Of uniform color. **2.** *Photography.* Orthochromatic.

i·soch·ro·nal (ī-sŏk′rə-nəl) *adj.* Also **i·soch·ro·nous** (-nəs), **i·so·chron·ic** (ī′sō-krŏn′ĭk). **1.** Equal in duration. **2.** Characterized by or occurring at equal intervals of time. [Greek *isokhronos,* ISOCHRONOUS.] —**i·soch·ro·nal·ly** *adv.* —**i·soch·ro·nism** (ī-sŏk′rə-nĭz′əm) *n.*

i·soch·ro·nize (ī-sŏk′rə-nīz′) *tr.v.* **-nized, -nizing, -nizes.** To make isochronal.

i·soch·ro·ous (ī-sŏk′rō-əs) *adj.* Having the same color throughout. [ISO- + -CHROOUS.]

i·so·cli·nal (ī′sə-klī′nəl) *adj.* Also **i·so·clin·ic** (ī′sə-klĭn′ĭk). **1.** Having the same inclination or angle of dip. **2.** *Geology.* Designating folds having limbs parallel to each other.
~*n.* Also **i·so·clin·ic.** An isoclinal line.

i·so·cline (ī′sə-klīn′) *n.* An anticline or syncline with its limbs so tightly folded as to have the same dip. [ISO- + -CLINE.]

isoclinic line *n.* Also **isoclinal line.** A line on a map connecting points of equal magnetic dip.

i·soc·ra·cy (ī-sŏk′rə-sē) *n.* A form of government in which all have equal power. [ISO- + -CRACY.] —**i·so·crat·ic** (ī′sō-krăt′ĭk, ĭ′sə-) *adj.*

i·so·cy·an·ide (ī′sō-sī′ə-nīd′) *n. Chemistry.* **1.** An organic compound containing the group –NCO. Also called "carbylamine." **2.** A salt containing the ion NCO^-.

i·so·di·a·met·ric (ī′sō-dī′ə-mĕt′rĭk) *adj.* **1.** Having equal diameters. **2.** Designating a crystal that has three equal axes.

i·so·di·a·phere (ī′sō-dī′ə-fîr′) *n.* Any of two or more nuclides that have the same difference between their total number of constituent neutrons and constituent protons. [ISO- + -diaphere, from Greek *diapherein,* to differ, "carry across" : DIA- + *pherein,* to carry.]

i·so·di·mor·phism (ī′sō-dī-môr′fĭz-əm) *n.* Isomorphism between crystalline forms of two dimorphic substances.

i·so·dy·nam·ic (ī′sō-dī-nǎm′ĭk) *adj.* **1.** Having equal force or strength. **2.** Designating an imaginary line drawn on the earth's surface that connects points of equal horizontal magnetic intensity.

i·so·e·lec·tric (ī′sō-ĭ-lĕk′trĭk) *adj.* Having equal electric potential.

isoelectric point *n. Chemistry.* The pH value of a solution in which a given substance, especially an amino acid or protein, forms neutral zwitterions or neutral colloidal particles.

i·so·e·lec·tron·ic (ī′sō-ĭ-lĕk-trŏn′ĭk) *adj.* Having equal numbers of electrons or the same electronic configuration.

i·so·en·zyme (ī′sō-ĕn′zīm) *n.* Also **i·so·zyme** (ī′sō-zīm′). Any one of the variant forms of a given enzyme. Isoenzymes catalyze the same type of reaction but differ slightly in physical and immunological properties. —**i·so·en·zy·mic** *adj.*

i·so·gam·ete (ī′sō-găm′ēt′, -gə-mēt′) *n.* A gamete that is morphologically indistinguishable from one with which it unites. —**i·so·ga·met·ic** (ī′sō-gə-mĕt′ĭk) *adj.*

i·sog·a·my (ī-sŏg′ə-mē) *n.* Sexual union of isogametes, such as occurs in certain algae, fungi, and protozoans. [ISO- + -GAMY.] —**i·sog·a·mous** *adj.*

i·sog·e·nous (ī-sŏj′ə-nəs) *adj.* Also **i·so·ge·nic** (ī′sə-jĕn′ĭk) (for sense 2). *Biology.* **1.** Having a similar origin. Said, for example, of organs derived from the same embryonic tissue. **2.** Genetically identical. [ISO- + -GENOUS.] —**i·sog·e·ny** *n.*

i·so·ge·o·therm (ī′sō-jē′ō-thĕrm′) *n. Geology.* An imaginary line below the earth's surface connecting points of equal temperature. [ISO- + GEO- + Greek *thermē,* heat.]

i·so·gloss (ī′sə-glôs′, -glŏs′) *n.* A geographical boundary line delimiting the area in which a given linguistic feature occurs. [ISO- + Greek *glōssa,* language, tongue.] —**i·so·gloss·al** *adj.*

i·so·gon (ī′sə-gŏn′) *n.* An equiangular polygon. [ISO- + -GON.]

i·so·gon·ic (ī′sə-gŏn′ĭk) *adj.* Also **i·sog·o·nal** (ī-sŏg′ə-nəl). Having equal angles.
~*n.* Also **i·sog·o·nal.** An isogonic line.

isogonic line *n.* A line on a map connecting points of equal magnetic declination.

i·so·graft (ī′sō-grăft′) *n.* A tissue graft in which the donor and recipient are genetically identical, as, for example, by being identical twins. Also called "syngraft."

i·so·gram (ī′sə-grăm′) *n.* An isopleth *(see).*

i·so·hel (ī′sō-hĕl′) *n.* A line drawn on a map connecting points receiving equal sunlight. [ISO- + Greek *hēlios,* sun.]

i·so·he·mo·ly·sin (ī′sō-hē′mə-lī′sən, -hĕm′ə-, -hī-mŏl′ī-sĭn) *n.* Hemolysin obtained from the serum of an individual injected with red blood cells from another individual of the same species.

i·so·he·mol·y·sis (ī′sō-hə-mŏl′ī-sĭs) *n.* Hemolysis resulting from the action of isohemolysin.

i·so·hy·et (ī′sō-hī′ət) *n.* A line drawn on a map connecting points receiving equal rainfall. [ISO- + Greek *huetos,* rain.]

i·so·la·ble (ī′sə-lə-bəl, ĭs′ə-) *adj.* Capable of being isolated.

i·so·late (ī′sə-lāt′, ĭs′ə-) *tr.v.* **-lated, -lating, -lates. 1. a.** To separate from a group or whole and set apart. **b.** To identify; pick out. **2.** To place in quarantine. **3.** *Chemistry.* To obtain (a substance) in an uncombined form. **4.** To obtain (a species or strain of bacterium or fungus, especially a pathogen) in a pure form. **5.** To render free of external influence; insulate. [Back-formation from *isolated,* from French *isolé,* from Italian *isolato,* from Late Latin *īnsulātus,* converted into an island, from Latin *īnsula,* island.] —**i·so·la·tor** *n.*

i·so·lat·ed (ī′sə-lā′tĭd, ĭs′ə-) *adj.* **1.** Having undergone isolation. **2.** Infrequent; sporadic: *an isolated incident.* **3.** Lacking in or having failed to maintain human contact; psychologically cut off from others.

isolated point *n.* An acnode *(see).*

i·so·lat·ing (ī′sə-lā′tĭng, ĭs′ə-) *adj.* Pertaining to or designating languages that have no inflections but convey each unit of meaning through a separate word.

isolating mechanism *n. Biology.* Any factor that prevents the breeding of one population with another. Isolating mechanisms encourage the evolution of the separated populations into new varieties and species.

i·so·la·tion (ī′sə-lā′shən, ĭs′ə-) *n.* **1.** The act of isolating. **2.** The condition of being isolated, especially psychologically isolated from others. **3.** Separation or quarantine imposed on a person having or suspected of having a highly infectious or contagious disease. Also used adjectivally: *isolation ward; isolation hospital.* —**in isolation.** Considered apart from context, surrounding factors, relationships, or the like. —See Synonyms at **solitude.**

i·so·la·tion·ism (ī'sə-lā'shə-nĭz'əm, ĭs'ə-) *n.* A national policy of remaining aloof from political or economic relations with other countries. —**i·so·la·tion·ist** *n. & adj.*

Isolde. Variant of **Iseult.**

i·so·lec·i·thal (ī'sə-lĕs'ə-thəl) *adj. Biology.* Having the yolk evenly distributed throughout the egg. Said of the eggs of mammals and some other vertebrates. Compare **heterolecithal.**

i·so·leu·cine (ī'sə-lōō'sēn') *n.* An essential amino acid, $C_6H_{13}NO_2$, isomeric with leucine.

i·so·line (ī'sə-līn') *n.* An **isopleth** (*see*).

i·sol·o·gous (ī-sŏl'ə-gəs) *adj.* Designating two or more organic compounds that have a similar structure but contain some different atoms of the same valence. [ISO- + (HOMO)LOGOUS.]

i·so·mag·net·ic (ī'sō-măg-nĕt'ĭk) *adj.* 1. Designating or pertaining to points of equal magnetic induction. 2. Designating an imaginary line on the earth's surface connecting points of equal magnetic intensity.

i·so·mer (ī'sə-mər) *n.* 1. *Chemistry.* **a.** A compound having the same percentage composition and molecular weight as another compound but differing in chemical or physical properties. **b.** Such a compound so differing because of the manner of linkage of its constituent atoms. Also called "structural isomer." **c.** Such a compound so differing because of the manner of arrangement of its constituent atoms in space. Also called "stereoisomer." **d.** A stereoisomer manifesting one of two structures that rotate the plane of polarization of polarized light either to the left or to the right. Also called "optical isomer." **e.** A stereoisomer having no effect on polarized light but exhibiting isomerism because of a structural asymmetry about a double bond in the molecule. Also called "geometric isomer." 2. *Physics.* An atom whose nucleus can exist in any of several bound excited states for a measurable period of time. In this sense, also called "nuclear isomer." [Greek *isomerēs*, equally divided, equal : ISO- + *meros*, part.] —**i·so·mer·ic** *adj.*

i·som·er·ase (ī-sŏm'ə-rās') *n.* Any of a group of enzymes that catalyze the conversion of one isomer into another.

i·som·er·ism (ī-sŏm'ə-rĭz'əm) *n.* 1. The phenomenon of the existence of isomers. 2. The complex of chemical and physical phenomena characteristic of or attributable to isomers. 3. The state or condition of being an isomer.

i·som·er·ize (ī-sŏm'ə-rīz') *v.* **-ized, -izing, -izes.** —*tr.* To cause to change into an isomeric form. —*intr.* To become an isomeric form. —**i·som·er·i·za·tion** *n.*

i·som·er·ous (ī-sŏm'ər-əs) *adj.* 1. Having an equal number of parts or markings. 2. Having or designating floral whorls with equal numbers of parts. [ISO- + -MEROUS.]

i·so·met·ric (ī'sə-mĕt'rĭk) *adj.* Also **i·so·met·ri·cal** (-rĭ-kəl). 1. Of or exhibiting equality in dimensions or measurements. 2. *Crystallography.* Of or being a crystal system of three equal and mutually orthogonal axes. 3. *Physiology.* Of or involving muscular contraction occurring when the ends of the muscle are fixed in place so that increase in tension occurs without appreciable decrease in length. ~*n.* A line connecting isometric points. [Greek *isometros*, of equal measure : ISO- + *metron*, measure.]

i·so·met·rics (ī'sə-mĕt'rĭks) *n. Used with a singular verb.* Exercise involving isometric contraction, used to build up muscles and improve fitness. Also called "isometric exercise."

i·so·me·tro·pi·a (ī'sō-mə-trō'pē-ə) *n.* Equality of refraction in both eyes. [New Latin : Greek *isometros*, of equal measure, ISOMETRIC + -OPIA.]

i·som·e·try (ī-sŏm'ə-trē) *n.* Equality of measure. [ISO- + -METRY.]

i·so·morph (ī'sə-môrf') *n.* An object, organism, or group exhibiting isomorphism. [ISO- + -MORPH.]

i·so·mor·phism (ī'sə-môr'fĭz'əm) *n.* 1. *Biology.* Similarity in form, as in different kinds of organisms or cells. 2. *Mathematics.* A one-to-one correspondence between the elements of two sets such that the result of an operation on elements of one set corresponds to the result of the analogous operation on their images in the other set. 3. *Crystallography.* The existence or an instance of the existence of two or more different substances having closely similar crystalline structure, crystalline dimensions, and chemical composition. 4. Structural similarity due to resemblance of corresponding parts. —**i·so·mor·phic, i·so·mor·phous** *adj.*

i·so·oc·tane (ī'sō-ŏk'tān') *n.* A highly flammable liquid, $(CH_3)_3CCH_2CH(CH_3)_2$, used to determine the octane numbers of fuels.

i·so·ni·a·zid (ī'sə-nī'ə-zĭd) *n. Abbr.* **INH** A soluble, colorless, crystalline compound, $C_6H_7N_3O$, usually administered orally for the treatment of tuberculosis. [From *iso*nicotinic acid hydr*azide*.]

i·so·pi·es·tic (ī'sō-pī-ĕs'tĭk) *adj.* Marked by or indicating equal pressure; isobaric. ~*n.* An isobar. [ISO- + Greek *piestos*, capable of being compressed, from *piezein*, to press tight, compress.]

i·so·pleth (ī'sə-plĕth') *n.* A line on a map connecting places at which some geographical or meteorological feature is the same. Also called "isogram," "isoline." [Greek *isoplēthēs*, of equal number : ISO- + *plēthos*, great number.]

i·so·pod (ī'sə-pŏd') *n.* Any of numerous crustaceans of the order Isopoda, which includes the woodlice and gribbles. ~*adj.* Of or belonging to the Isopoda. [New Latin *Isopoda*, "those

having pairs of legs" : ISO- + *-poda*, plural of -POD.]

i·so·pren·a·line (ī'sə-prĕn'ə-lĭn) *n.* A drug that is used in the treatment of asthma and similar conditions to dilate the air passages.

i·so·prene (ī'sə-prēn') *n.* A colorless volatile liquid, $CH_2:CHC(CH_3):CH_2$, used chiefly to make synthetic rubber. [ISO- + PR(OPYL) + -ENE.]

i·so·pro·pyl alcohol (ī'sə-prō'pəl) *n.* A clear, colorless, mobile flammable liquid, $(CH_3)_2CHOH$, used in antifreeze compounds, lotions and cosmetics, and as a solvent for gums, shellac, and essential oils. [ISO- + PROPYL.]

i·sos·ce·les (ī-sŏs'ə-lēz') *adj. Geometry.* Having two equal sides: *isosceles triangle; isosceles trapezoid.* [Late Latin *isosceles,* from Greek *isoskelēs,* "having equal legs" : ISO- + *skelos,* leg.]

i·so·seis·mic (ī'sō-sīs'mĭk) *adj.* Also **i·so·seis·mal** (-məl). *Geology.* Of, pertaining to, or exhibiting equal seismic intensities.

i·sos·mot·ic (ī'sŏz-mŏt'ĭk, ī'sŏs-) *adj. Chemistry.* Of or exhibiting equal osmotic pressure; isotonic. [IS(O)- + OSMOTIC.]

i·so·spin (ī'sə-spĭn') *n. Symbol* **I** A quantum number that is related to the number of charge states of a subatomic particle by the equation $2I + 1 = M$, where M is the number of such states. Also called "isotopic spin." [Short for *isotopic spin.*]

i·sos·ta·sy (ī-sŏs'tə-sē) *n. Geology.* A theoretical state of equilibrium of the earth's crust in which the crust rests on a denser underlying medium and has equal pressure at all points. [ISO- + Greek *stasis,* a standing, standstill.]

i·so·ster·ic (ī'sō-stĕr'ĭk) *adj.* Designating two molecules, such as CO_2 and N_2O, that have the same number of atoms and the same configuration of valence electrons.

i·so·tac·tic (ī'sō-tăk'tĭk) *adj. Chemistry.* Designating a polymer in which the groups attached to the main chain are not arranged regularly, although the same irregularity is repeated along the chain. Compare **syndiotactic.** [ISO- + -TACTIC.]

i·so·therm (ī'sə-thûrm') *n.* 1. A line drawn on a weather map or chart linking all points of equal atmospheric temperature. 2. A line on a graph connecting points of equal temperature. [French *isotherme,* having the same temperature : ISO- + -THERM.]

i·so·ther·mal (ī'sə-thûr'məl) *adj.* 1. Of, pertaining to, or indicating equal temperatures. 2. Of or designating changes of pressure and volume at constant temperature. 3. Of or pertaining to an isotherm. ~*n.* An isotherm.

i·so·tone (ī'sə-tōn') *n.* One of two or more atoms, the nuclei of which have the same number of neutrons but different numbers of protons. [ISO- + Greek *tonos,* stretching, TONE.]

i·so·ton·ic (ī'sə-tŏn'ĭk) *adj.* 1. Of equal tension. Said of two or more muscles. 2. Isosmotic. 3. *Music.* Of equal tone; of equal intervals of the well-tempered scale. [ISO- + Greek *tonos,* tension, stretching, TONE.]

i·so·tope (ī'sə-tōp') *n.* Any of two or more atoms, the nuclei of which have the same number of protons but different numbers of neutrons. Compare **nuclide.** [ISO- + Greek *topos,* place, "position in the periodic table" (see **topic**).] —**i·so·top·ic** (ī'sə-tŏp'ĭk) *adj.* —**i·so·top·ic·al·ly** *adv.*

i·so·tron (ī'sə-trŏn') *n.* An instrument for separating small quantities of isotopes by ionizing them and applying an electric field to the ions. [ISO- + -TRON.]

i·so·trop·ic (ī'sə-trŏp'ĭk) *adj.* Also **i·so·tro·pous** (ī-sŏt'rə-pəs). 1. Identical in all directions; invariant with respect to direction. 2. *Biology.* Lacking predetermined axes. Said of certain ova. [ISO- + -TROPIC.] —**i·sot·ro·py** (ī-sŏt'rə-pē), **i·sot·ro·pism** (ī-sŏt'rə-pĭz'-əm) *n.*

isozyme. Variant of **isoenzyme.**

I-spy (ī'spī') *n.* A game in which one player secretly chooses an object in his field of vision and specifies its initial letter, leaving the other players to guess what it is.

Is·ra·el[1] (ĭz'rē-əl). *Abbr.* **Isr.** Republic of western Asia and the world's only state with Judaism as the official religion. The country was created as a United Nations mandate (1947) from the former British League of Nations mandate of Palestine as a homeland for Jews. It declared its independence in 1948. Largely regarded as invaders by the native Palestinians, many of whom now live as refugees in neighboring countries, the Iraelis have four times (1948, 1956, 1967, 1973) defeated surrounding Arab states. In 1982 the Israelis invaded southern Lebanon to secure their northern border against guerrillas of the Palestine Liberation Organization. Israel has few natural resources, but with U.S. aid large areas of desert have been reclaimed and an industrial economy built up. The chief exports are cut diamonds, textiles, fruit, and vegetables. Area, 20,770 square kilometers (8,017 square miles). Population, 3,900,-000. Capital, Jerusalem. See map, next page.

Israel[2] *n.* 1. The descendants of Jacob. 2. The whole Hebrew people, past, present, and future, regarded as the chosen people of Jehovah by virtue of the covenant of Jacob. 3. Any group considered or considering itself to be God's chosen people or the inheritors of God's covenant with Jacob, especially the Christian Church or any of various Christian sects. [Latin *Israēl,* from Greek, from Hebrew *Yisrā'ēl,* the name given to Jacob by the angel with whom he wrestled (Genesis 32:28), "he who struggles with God."]

Is·rae·li (ĭz-rā'lē) *adj.* Of or relating to the state of Israel or its people. ~*n., pl.* **Israeli** or **-lis.** A native or inhabitant of the state of Israel.

Is·ra·el·ite (ĭz'rē-ə-līt') *n.* 1. A Hebrew. 2. A member of any of various Christian groups regarded as heirs of the covenant of Jacob.

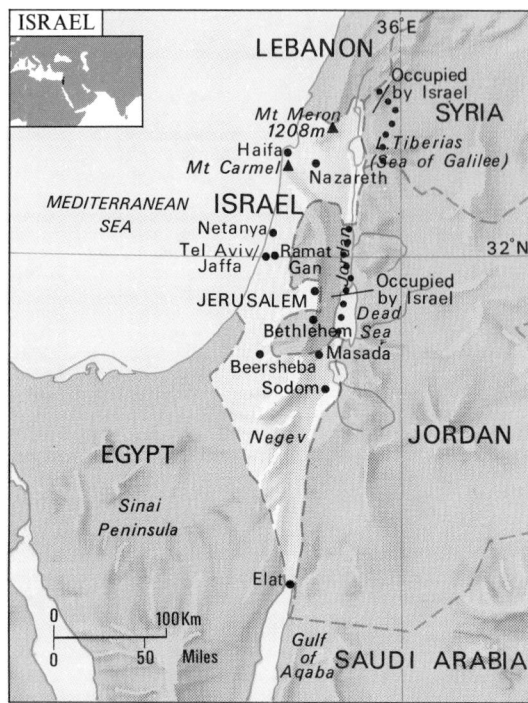

~adj. Also **Is·ra·el·it·ic** (ĭz'rē-əl-ĭt'ĭk). Of or relating to Israel or the Israelites.

Is·sa·char¹ (ĭs'ə-kär'). One of the patriarchs of Israel, son of Jacob and Leah. Genesis 30:18.

Issachar² n. The tribe descended from Issachar.

Is·sei (ēs'sā') n., pl. **-seis** or collectively **Issei**. A Japanese immigrant to the United States or Canada. [Japanese, first generation, from Chinese (Mandarin) *yi¹ shi⁴ : yi¹*, first + *shi⁴*, generation.]

is·su·a·ble (ĭsh'ōō-ə-bəl) adj. **1.** Capable of issuing or being issued. **2.** Capable of being established as an issue; open to debate or litigation. **3.** Authorized for issue.

is·su·ance (ĭsh'ōō-əns) n. An act of issuing; issue.

is·su·ant (ĭsh'ōō-ənt) adj. *Archaic & Heraldry.* Emerging; issuing or proceeding from.

is·sue (ĭsh'ōō) n. **1. a.** An act or instance of flowing, passing, or giving out. **b.** An act of circulating, distributing, or publishing by an office or official group: *government issue of new bonds.* **2.** Something produced, published, or offered, as: **a.** An item or set of items, such as stamps or coins, made available at one time by a government department or other organization. **b.** A new set of bonds, shares, or the like made available for purchase at the same time. **c.** All the copies of a periodical printed for publication at the same time. **d.** The contents of these copies: *in the June issue of Reader's Digest.* **3.** An allocation; that which is given out: *an issue of ammunition.* **4.** The result of an action or series of events. **5.** Something proceeding from a specified source: *suspicions that were the issue of a deranged mind.* **6. a.** A point of discussion, debate, or dispute. **b.** A matter of wide public concern. **c.** The essential point; crux: *the real issue.* **d.** A point of dispute in a legal action: *an issue of fact; an issue of law.* **e.** A culminating point leading to a decision; a result. Used chiefly in legal contexts: *bring a case to an issue.* **7.** A place of egress; an outlet: *a lake with no issue to the sea.* **8.** Children; offspring or descendants. Used chiefly in legal contexts. **9.** *Pathology.* **a.** A discharge, as of blood. **b.** A suppurating sore. **10.** *Archaic.* Termination; close. **—at issue. 1.** In question; in dispute. **2.** At variance; in disagreement. **—force the issue.** To make decisive action unavoidable. **—join issue.** To enter into controversy. **—take issue with.** To take an opposing point of view; disagree with.

~v. **issued, -suing, -sues. —intr. 1.** To go or come forth; emerge. **2.** To accrue as proceeds or profit: *Little money issued from the stocks.* **3.** To be circulated or published. **4.** To originate or be derived. Used with *from.* **5.** To terminate or result. Used with *in.* **—tr. 1.** To cause to flow out; emit. **2.** To circulate, allocate, or distribute, especially in an official capacity: *The school issued uniforms to the players.* **3.** To publish. **4.** To make public; announce: *issue a stern warning.* [Middle English, from Old French *(e)issue,* from Vulgar Latin *exūta* (unattested), "exit," altered from Latin *exita,* feminine of *exitus,* past participle of *exīre,* to go out : *ex-,* out + *īre,* to go.] **—is·su·er** n.

-ist suffix. Indicates: **1.** A person who does, makes, produces, operates, plays, or sells a specified thing; for example, **dramatist, lobbyist, motorist, organist, tobacconist. 2.** A person who is skilled, trained, or employed in a specified field; for example, **machinist, radiologist, industrialist. 3.** An adherent or proponent of a doctrine, system, or school of thought; for example, **anarchist, federalist, Platonist. 4.** A person characterized by a certain trait or predilection; for example, **romanticist, sadist. 5.** A person having a disparaging or hostile attitude toward a particular social group on the basis of a specified characteristic; for example, **sexist, ageist, racist.** [Middle English *-iste,* from Old French, from Latin *-ista, -istēs,* from Greek *-istēs,* agential suffix for verbs in *-izein,* -IZE.]

Is·tan·bul (ĭs'tän-bōōl', ĭs'tän-). Formerly (before 1930) **Con·stan·ti·no·ple** (kŏn'stăn-tə-nō'pəl). Largest city and chief port of Turkey. It is a major manufacturing, cultural, and tourist center, with many museums, including Hagia Sophia and the Seraglio (royal palace).

isth·mi·an (ĭs'mē-ən) adj. **1.** Of, pertaining to, or forming an isthmus. **2. Isthmian.** Of or pertaining to the Isthmus of Corinth, especially with regard to the biennial pan-Hellenic games held there in antiquity. **3. Isthmian.** Of or pertaining to the Isthmus of Panama.

isth·mus (ĭs'məs) n., pl. **-muses** or **-mi** (-mī'). **1.** A narrow strip of land connecting two larger masses of land. **2.** *Anatomy.* **a.** A narrow strip of tissue joining two larger organs or parts of an organ. **b.** A narrow passage connecting two larger cavities. [Latin, from Greek *isthmos†.*]

-istics suffix. Indicates study of a specified subject; for example, **statistics, cladistics.**

is·tle, ix·tle (ĭs'lē, ĭst'-) n. A plant, **pita** *(see).* [Mexican Spanish *ixtle,* from Nahuatl *ichtli.*]

Is·tri·a (ĭs'trē-ə). Peninsula of the northwest Yugoslavian coast. It separates the Gulf of Venice from the Bay of Kvarner in the Adriatic Sea.

it (ĭt) pron. The third person singular pronoun, neuter gender in the nominative or objective case. **1.** Used to represent the thing, non-human being, or person whose sex is unknown or disregarded, last mentioned or implied. **2.** Used without a previously understood antecedent or consequent as **a.** The formal subject of an impersonal verb: *It is raining.* **b.** The object, having little meaning, of various verbs: *Live it up.* **3.** Used to represent a word, phrase, or clause that follows: *It is he. It's certain that she'll win.* **4.** Used to represent a situation, topic for consideration, or any other item of discourse that the speaker assumes the hearer will comprehend without antecedent: *Always try to do it right the first time.* **5.** Used to represent all the experience that can be endured or desired: *He'd had it; he resigned.* **6.** Used to represent the crucial moment on which an outcome depends: *This is it! he thought, as the plane's engine sputtered.* **7.** Used to represent a human life: *The old man's eyes closed; it was all over.*

~n. **1.** The player who chases the others in a game of tag. **2.** *Informal.* An important person. Usually used derogatorily, especially in such phrases as *he thinks he's it.* **3.** *Informal.* **a.** Sexual intercourse. **b.** *Rare.* Sexual attractiveness. [Middle English *(h)it, (h)yt,* Old English *hit, hyt.*]

It. Italian; Italy.

i.t.a., I.T.A. n. *I*nitial *t*eaching *a*lphabet: a 44-letter phonetic alphabet used in teaching young children to read.

it·a·col·u·mite (ĭt'ə-kŏl'yə-mīt') n. A variety of sandstone that is slightly flexible when cut into thin slabs. Also called "flexible sandstone." [Found in *Itacolumi,* a mountain in Brazil.]

it·a·con·ic acid (ĭt'ə-kŏn'ĭk) n. A white crystalline substance, $CH_2:C(COOH)CH_2COOH$, obtained by the fermentation of carbohydrates and used in the manufacture of synthetic resins. [Anagram of *aconitic.*]

ital. italic.

Ital. Italian; Italy.

Italia. See **Italy.**

I·tal·ian (ĭ-tăl'yən) adj. Abbr. **It., Ital.** Pertaining to Italy, its people, their culture, or their language.

~n. Abbr. **It., Ital. 1.** A native or citizen of Italy, or a person of Italian descent. **2.** The Romance language of Italy and one of the three official languages of Switzerland. [Middle English, from Italian *Italiano,* from *Italia,* ITALY.]

I·tal·ian·ate (ĭ-tăl'yə-nāt', -nĭt) adj. Italian in character. [Italian *Italianato,* from *Italiano,* ITALIAN.]

Italian East Africa. Former Italian colony in East Africa. It comprised Italian Somaliland (now part of Somalia); Eritrea (another Italian colony, now part of Ethiopia); and Abyssinia (the rest of Ethiopia, conquered by the Italians in 1935-36). The territory was captured by Allied and Ethiopian forces in 1941 and broken up.

Italian greyhound n. A dog of a breed of small greyhound having a long, narrow skull, a deep, narrow chest, and sloping hindquarters.

Italian hand n. A forward-slanting script employed by 15th-century Italian calligraphers and used as a model for modern, especially English penmanship. Also called "Italian handwriting."

I·tal·ian·ism (ĭ-tăl'yə-nĭz'əm) n. **1.** An Italian custom, trait, or expression. **2.** A quality characteristic of Italy or its people.

I·tal·ian·ize (ĭ-tăl'yə-nīz') v. **-ized, -izing, -izes. —tr.** To give an Italian aspect to. **—intr.** To become Italian; adopt Italian speech, manners, or customs. **—I·tal·ian·i·za·tion** n.

Italian sandwich n. See **hero** (sense 5).

Italian Somaliland. See **Somalia.**

Italian sonnet n. A Petrarchan sonnet *(see).*

Italian vermouth n. A sweet, aromatic wine distilled and flavored with herbs.

i·tal·ic (ĭ-tăl'ĭk, ī-tăl'-) adj. Abbr. **ital. 1.** Of, pertaining to, or being a style of printing type patterned upon a Renaissance script with the letters slanting to the right, now chiefly used to set off a word or passage within a text printed in roman type, indicating that the word or passage is emphatic, in a foreign language, or has a structurally independent function within the main text: *This sentence is*

ITALY

printed in italic type. Compare **roman. 2.** Pertaining to or designating a modern style of handwriting similar to Italian hand.
~*n.* **1.** Italic handwriting. **2. a.** Often **italics.** Italic type or print. **b.** An italic character. [Introduced in the Aldine Virgil printed in Venice in 1501, which was dedicated to Italy.]
I·tal·ic (ĭ-tăl′ĭk) *adj.* **1.** Of or pertaining to ancient Italy or its peoples. **2.** Of or pertaining to a branch of Indo-European languages that includes the Latino-Faliscan and Osco-Umbrian groups.
~*n.* The Italic branch of the Indo-European family of languages. [Latin *Italicus,* from Greek *Italikos,* from *Italia,* Italy, from Latin.]
i·tal·i·cize (ĭ-tăl′ĭ-sīz′) *v.* **-cized, -cizing, -cizes.** —*tr.* **1.** To print in italic type. **2.** To underscore (written matter) with a single line to indicate italics. —*intr.* To print or put words in italics; use italics. —**i·tal·i·ci·za·tion** *n.*
It·a·ly (ĭt′ə-lē). *Abbr.* **It., Ital.** Italian **I·ta·li·a** (ē-tä′lyä). Republic of southern Europe. It includes Sardinia to the west. The mainland peninsula's spine is formed by the Appenines, the only lowlands of any size being the fertile Po River valley in the northeast. After the fall of the Western Roman Empire (A.D. 476), Italy was dominated by successive foreign powers until its unification (1870) under the Piedmontese royal family. A republic was declared (1946) following the country's defeat in World War II. Industries, especially textiles and motor vehicles, are concentrated in the north, with much of the south being economically depressed. Rich in cultural heritage and with many holiday resorts, much of the country is heavily depend-

ent on tourism. Italy is a founder member of the European Economic Community. Area, 301,225 square kilometers (116,303 square miles). Population, 57,100,000. Capital, Rome.
itch (ĭch) *n.* **1.** An irritating or tickling skin sensation, causing a desire to scratch. **2.** Any of various contagious skin diseases, such as scabies, marked by intense irritation, eruptions, and itching. **3.** A restless desire or craving: *an itch for foreign travel.*
~*v.* **itched, itching, itches.** —*intr.* **1.** To feel, have, or produce an itch. **2.** To have a persistent, restless craving. —*tr.* To cause to itch. [Middle English *(y)icchen,* Old English *giccan,* from Germanic *juk-* (unattested).] —**itch·i·ness** *n.* —**itch·y** *adj.*
–ite¹ *suffix.* Indicates: **1.** A person who is: **a.** A native or resident of a specified place; for example, *New Jerseyite.* **b.** A member of a tribe or family; for example, **Ammonite. c.** An adherent of a doctrine, idea, way of life, or the like; for example, **socialite. d.** A supporter of someone specified, or their views; for example, **Luddite. 2.** *Biology.* A part of an organ or body; for example, **somite. 3.** A fossil; for example, **trilobite. 4.** A mineral or rock; for example, **graphite. 5. a.** An explosive; for example, **gelignite. b.** A commercial product; for example, **Lucite.** [Middle English, from Old French, from Latin *-ita, -itēs,* from Greek *-itēs.*]
–ite² *suffix.* Indicates a salt or ester of an acid whose adjectival denomination ends in *-ous;* for example, **sulfite.** [French, arbitrarily altered from -ATE.]
i·tem (ī′təm) *n.* **1.** A single article listed on a bill or unit included in

ivory *An ivory saltcellar with two chambers, carved in West Africa in the 16th century by a Benin craftsman. It shows two Portuguese dignitaries with their attendants, surmounted by a ship.*

ivy *The ivy genus,* Hedera, *is a group of evergreen climbers that grow throughout the temperate zones of the Northern Hemisphere. Ivy was once believed to have magical powers, and its use as a Christmas decoration stems from the belief that it would ward off goblins.*

a collection, enumeration, or series and specified separately. **2.** A separate matter for consideration, such as a topic or proposal listed on an agenda. **3.** An entry in an account. **4. a.** A bit of information; detail. **b.** A short piece in a newspaper or magazine. **5.** A member of a set of minimal units: *a lexical item.*
~*tr.v.* **itemed, iteming, items.** *Archaic.* To itemize.
~*adv.* Also; likewise. Used to introduce each article in an enumeration or list. [Middle English, also, likewise, from Latin, from *ita,* so.]

i·tem·ize (ī′tə-mīz′) *tr.v.* **-ized, -izing, -izes.** To set down item by item; list. **—i·tem·i·za·tion** *n.* **—i·tem·iz·er** *n.*

it·er·ate (ĭt′ə-rāt′) *tr.v.* **-ated, -ating, -ates.** To say or perform again; repeat. [Latin *iterāre,* from *iterum,* again.] **—it·er·ant** *adj.* **—it·er·a·tion, it·er·ance** *n.*

it·er·a·tive (ĭt′ə-rā′tĭv, -ər-ə-tĭv) *adj.* **1.** Repetitious. **2.** *Grammar.* Frequentative.

Ith·a·ca (ĭth′ə-kə). *Greek* **I·thá·ki** (ē-thä′kē). An island of Greece, one of the Ionian Islands. It is mountainous and has little arable land.

I·thunn, I·thun (ē′*th*o͝on′). Also **I·dun** (-do͝on′). *Norse Mythology.* The wife of Bragi, goddess of youth and spring. [Old Norse *Idhunn,* probably from *idh,* again, anew.]

i·tin·er·an·cy (ī-tĭn′ər-ən-sē, ĭ-tĭn′-) *n.* Also **i·tin·er·a·cy** (-ər-ə-sē). A state or system of itinerating, especially in the role or office of public speaker, minister, or judge.

i·tin·er·ant (ī-tĭn′ər-ənt, ĭ-tĭn′-) *adj.* Traveling from place to place, especially to perform some duty or work: *an itinerant preacher.*
~*n.* One who so travels. [Late Latin *itinerāns* (stem *itinerant-*), present participle of *itinerārī,* ITINERATE.]

i·tin·er·ar·y (ī-tĭn′ə-rĕr′ē, ĭ-tĭn′-) *n., pl.* **-ies. 1.** A route or proposed route of a journey. **2.** An account or record of a journey. **3.** A travelers' guidebook.
~*adj.* **1.** Of or pertaining to a journey or to a route. **2.** Traveling from place to place; itinerant. [Middle English *itinerarie,* from Late Latin *itinerārium,* course of travel, from *itinerārius,* of traveling, from Latin *iter* (stem *itiner-*), journey.]

-itis *suffix.* Indicates inflammation of or inflammatory disease; for example, **laryngitis, bronchitis.** [New Latin, from Greek *-itis,* feminine of *-itēs,* -ITE (pertaining to, native).]

it'll (ĭt′l). **1.** Contraction of *it will.* **2.** Contraction of *it shall.*

ITO International Trade Organization.

-itol *suffix. Chemistry.* Indicates an alcohol containing more than one hydroxyl group; for example, **mannitol.** [-ITE + -OL.]

its (ĭts). The possessive form of the pronoun *it.* Used to indicate possession, agency, or reception of an action by the thing, nonhuman being, or person whose sex is not known or disregarded, spoken of: *its forepaw.* [Originally *it's* : IT + *-'s,* possessive ending.]

it's (ĭts). **1.** Contraction of *it is.* **2.** Contraction of *it has.*

it·self (ĭt-sĕlf′) *pron.* A specialized form of the third person singular neuter pronoun. It is used: **1.** As a reflexive pronoun, forming the direct or indirect object of a verb or the object of a preposition: *This record player turns itself off.* **2.** For emphasis, after a noun or *it*: *The trouble is in the machine itself.* **3.** As an emphasizing substitute: *Itself in difficulties, the bank could not help us.* **4.** As an indication of its real identity or normal, healthy condition: *The computer is acting itself again since the program was corrected.* **—in itself.** Considered in isolation: *in itself, quite a good idea.* [Middle English *itself,* Old English *hit self* : IT + SELF.]

it·sy-bit·sy (ĭt′sē-bĭt′sē) *adj.* Also **it·ty-bit·ty** (ĭt′ē-bĭt′ē). *Informal.* Very small; tiny. [Baby-talk reduplication of LITTLE (influenced by BIT).]

ITU International Telecommunication Union.

-ity *suffix.* Indicates a state or quality; for example, **authenticity, jollity.** [Middle English *-it(i)e,* from Old French *-ite,* from Latin *-itās* : thematic vowel *-i-* + *-tās* (stem *-tāt-*), -TY.]

IUD *n.* An **intrauterine device** *(see).*

-ium *suffix.* Indicates: **1.** *Chemistry.* **a.** A metallic chemical element; for example, **californium, unnilquadium. b.** A positive ion formed from a group or molecule; for example, **ammonium, hydroxonium. 2.** A biological or anatomical structure; for example, **pericardium.** [New Latin, from Latin, from Greek *-ion,* diminutive suffix.]

IV, i.v. intravenous; intravenously.

I·van III (ī′vən), born Ivan Vasilyevich, called "the Great" (1440–1505). Grand Prince of Muscovy (1462–1505), whose successful campaigns against the Tatars laid the foundations for eventual Russian unity. He also set up a strong central government.

Ivan IV, born Ivan Vasilyevich, called "the Terrible" (1530–84). First ruler of Russia to be proclaimed czar (1547). He greatly expanded the Russian state by war and conquest, but his later pathological fear of treachery led him to the violent suppression of suspected opposition.

I've (īv). Contraction of *I have.*

-ive *suffix.* Indicates having a tendency toward or inclination to perform some action; for example, **degenerative, disruptive.** [Middle English *-if, -ive,* from Old French *-if* (feminine *-ive*), from Latin *-īvus* (feminine *-īva,* neuter *-īvum*).]

Ives (īvz), **Charles Edward** (1874–1954). U.S. composer. Many of his works anticipated those of later 20th-century musicians in their abandonment of conventional tonality. His *Third Symphony* (1904–11) won the 1947 Pulitzer Prize.

Ives, James Merritt (1824–95). U.S. lithographer. Hired as a bookkeeper for Nathaniel Currier's lithography business (1852), he was recognized for his artistic talents, contributing many of his own drawings and directing the complicated printing process. He became a partner in the business (1857), creating the renowned American lithograph team of Currier & Ives.

IVF in vitro fertilization.

i·vied (ī′vēd) *adj.* Overgrown or covered with ivy.

Iviza. See **Ibiza.**

i·vo·ry (ī′və-rē, īv′rē) *n., pl.* **-ries. 1. a.** The hard, smooth, yellowish-white dentine forming the main part of the tusks of the elephant, and used as an ornamental material. **b.** A similar substance forming the tusks or teeth of certain other animals, such as the walrus. **2.** A tusk, especially an elephant's tusk. **3.** A substance, such as a plant product, resembling ivory. **4.** Pale or grayish yellow to yellowish white. **5.** *Often* **ivories.** An article made of ivory. **6.** *Usually* **ivories.** *Slang.* **a.** Piano keys. **b.** Dice. **c.** The teeth.
~*adj.* **1.** Made of or resembling ivory. **2.** Of the color ivory. [Middle English *ivor(ie), yvory,* from Old French *ivurie, ivoire,* from Vulgar Latin *eboreus* (unattested), from neuter of Latin *eboreus,* of ivory, from *ebur* (stem *ebor-*), ivory.]

i·vo·ry-bill (ī′və-rē-bĭl′, īv′rē-) *n.* The ivory-billed woodpecker.

i·vo·ry-billed woodpecker (ī′və-rē-bĭld′, īv′rē-) *n.* A large, probably extinct North American woodpecker, *Campephilus principalis,* having a white bill.

ivory black *n.* A black pigment prepared from charred ivory.

Ivory Coast. Republic in West Africa, on the Gulf of Guinea. Ceded to France (1842), it became an independent republic in 1960. It was once the center of the slave and ivory trade and is now Africa's largest exporter of timber and coffee. Area, 322,463 square kilometers (124,503 square miles). Population, 7,900,000. Capital, Abidjan. See map at **West African States.**

ivory gull *n.* An Arctic gull, *Pagophila eburnea.*

ivory nut *n.* The hard seed of the American ivory palm, *Phytelephas macrocarpa,* yielding an ivorylike substance.

ivory tower *n.* A place or attitude of retreat; especially, a preoccupation with lofty, remote, or intellectual considerations rather than with practical everyday life. [Translation of French *tour d'ivoire,* first used by C.A. Sainte-Beuve with reference to Alfred de Vigny, who was anxious to preserve the purity of his inspiration unmixed with practical matters.]

i·vy (ī′vē) *n., pl.* **ivies. 1.** Any of several woody, climbing or trailing plants of the genus *Hedera,* native to the Old World, especially *H. helix,* having lobed, evergreen leaves and berrylike black fruit. **2.** Any of various other climbing or creeping plants, such as ground ivy or poison ivy. [Middle English *ivi, ivye,* Old English *īfig,* from Germanic *ibahs* (unattested), obscurely related to Latin *ibex,* "climber," IBEX.]

Ivy League *n.* An association of eight traditional and prestigious universities in the northeastern United States, comprising Brown, Columbia, Cornell, Dartmouth, Harvard, Princeton, the University of Pennsylvania, and Yale.
~*adj.* Of or resembling the traditions of the Ivy League, especially in being conservative and restrained in style. [Referring to the ivy-covered university buildings.] **—Ivy Leaguer** *n.*

i·wis, y·wis (ĭ-wĭs′) *adv. Archaic.* Certainly; assuredly. [Middle English *iwis(se), gewis,* Old English *gewis,* certain.]

I·wo Ji·ma (ē′wō jē′mə). The largest of the Volcano Islands. Lying in the Pacific Ocean, 1,200 kilometers (750 miles) south of Tokyo, it has been part of Japan since 1887 and was the scene of fierce fighting during World War II.

IWW, I.W.W. Industrial Workers of the World.

Ix·i·on (ĭk-sī′ən). *Greek Mythology.* A Thessalian king whom Zeus punished for his temerity in seeking Hera's love by having him bound to a perpetually revolving wheel in Hades.

ix·o·di·a·sis (ĭk′sō-dī′ə-sĭs) *n.* Any disease caused by infestation with ticks. [New Latin, from Greek *ixōdēs,* resembling birdlime, sticking, from *ixos,* birdlime + -IASIS.]

ixtle. Variant of **istle.** See **pita.**

I·yar, Iy·yar (ē-yär′, ē′yär) *n.* The eighth month of the year on the Hebrew calendar. See feature at **calendar.** [Hebrew *iyyār.*]

iz·ar (ĭ-zär′) *n.* A long cotton outer garment, usually white, worn by women in many Muslim countries. [Arabic *'izār, 'izr,* veil, covering.]

-ization *suffix.* Indicates action, process, or result of doing or making; for example, *colonization.* [-IZ(E) + -ATION.]

-ize *suffix.* Indicates: **1. a.** To cause to be or to become; make into; for example, **dramatize. b.** To make conform with; make like for example, **Hellenize, Anglicize. c.** To treat or regard as; for example, **idolize. 2.** To cause to acquire a specified quality; for example, **legalize, modernize, sterilize. 3.** To become or become similar to; for example, **crystallize, oxidize, materialize. 4. a.** To subject to; for example, **jeopardize, anesthetize. b.** To affect with; for example, **magnetize, galvanize. 5.** To do or follow some practice; for example, **pasteurize, bowdlerize.** [Old French *-iser,* Latin *-izāre,* Greek *-izein.*]

Iz·mir (ĭz-mîr′). Formerly **Smyr·na** (smûr′nə). City and port in western Turkey. At the head of the Gulf of Izmir, an inlet of the Aegean Sea, it is the commercial center of the Levant, with strong Greek connections.

iz·zard (ĭz′ərd) *n. Archaic.* The letter *z.* [Earlier *ezed,* probably from Old French *et zède,* "and zed."]

J

j, J (jā) *n., pl.* **j's** or **J's.** **1.** The tenth letter of the modern English alphabet. See feature at **alphabet. 2.** Any of the speech sounds represented by this letter. **3.** Anything shaped like the letter J. **4.** The Roman numeral for 1, a substitute for i or I in the final position used especially in prescriptions. **5.** The tenth in a series.

j, J, j., J. *Note:* As an abbreviation or symbol, *j* may be a small or capital letter, with or without a period. Established forms or those generally preferred precede the definition. When no form is given, all four forms are in general use in that sense. **1.** J jack (playing card). **2.** J. Japan; Japanese. **3.** J current density. **4.** J joule. **5.** J. journal. **6.** J. judge; justice.

ja (yä) *interj. South African Informal.* Yes. [Afrikaans.]

J.A. judge advocate.

jaap (yäp) *n. South African.* Also **ja·pie** (yä'pē). A simple-minded, innocent person; a country bumpkin. [Afrikaans, from *Jaap,* pet form of *Jakob, Jacob.*]

jab (jăb) *v.* **jabbed, jabbing, jabs.** —*tr.* **1.** To poke abruptly, especially with something sharp. **2.** To stab or pierce. **3.** To thrust into or against something with a rough, abrupt movement. **4.** To punch with short blows. —*intr.* **1.** To make an abrupt jabbing motion. **2.** To deliver a quick punch.
~*n.* **1.** A quick stab or blow. **2.** *Boxing.* A short straight punch. [Variant of JOB.]

jab·ber (jăb'ər) *v.* **-bered, -bering, -bers.** —*intr.* To talk rapidly, unintelligibly, or idly. —*tr.* To utter rapidly or unintelligibly.
~*n.* Rapid or babbling talk. [Middle English *jaberen* (imitative).] —**jab·ber·er** *n.*

jab·ber·wock·y (jăb'ər-wŏk'ē) *n.* **1.** Nonsense verse. **2.** Unintelligible speech or writing; nonsense; gibberish. [Title of a poem in Lewis Carroll's *Through the Looking-Glass* (1871).]

jab·i·ru (jăb'ə-rōo') *n.* **1.** A large tropical American wading bird, *Jabiru mycteria,* having white plumage and a dark, naked head and neck. **2.** A similar Australian bird, *Xenorhyncus asiaticus.* Also called "black-necked stork." **3.** Any of various other similar birds, such as the **saddlebill** *(see).* [Portuguese *jabirú,* from Tupi-Guarani.]

jab·o·ran·di (jăb'ə-răn'dē) *n., pl.* **-dis. 1.** Either of two tropical American shrubs, *Pilocarpus jaborandi* or *P. microphyllus.* **2.** The dried leaves of these shrubs, which yield **pilocarpine** *(see).* [Portuguese, from Tupi-Guarani *jaburandi.*]

jab·ot (zhă-bō', jă-) *n.* A cascade of frills down the front of a shirt, blouse, or bodice. [French, from Auvergne or Limousin dialect, akin to Old French dialectal *gave,* throat, from a Romance root *gab-* (unattested), crop, gullet, perhaps from Gaulish.]

jac·a·mar (jăk'ə-mär') *n.* Any of various tropical American birds of the family Galbulidae, related to the woodpeckers. [French, from Tupi-Guarani *jacamaciri.*]

ja·ça·na (zhä'sə-nä') *n.* Any of several tropical marsh birds of the family Jacanidae, having long toes adapted for walking on floating vegetation. Also called "lily-trotter." [From Portuguese *jaçaná,* from Tupi-Guarani *jasaná.*]

jac·a·ran·da (jăk'ə-răn'də) *n.* **1.** Any of several trees of the genus *Jacaranda,* native to tropical America, having clusters of pale purple flowers. **2.** The wood of such a tree. **3.** Any similar wood, or the tree yielding it. [Portuguese *jacarandá,* from Tupi-Guarani.]

ja·cinth (jā'sĭnth, jăs'ĭnth) *n.* **1.** A reddish-orange variety of zircon, **hyacinth** *(see).* **2.** *Obsolete.* A hyacinth plant or flower. [Middle English *iacynth, iacin(c)t,* from Old French *iacinte* or Medieval Latin *jacintus,* from Latin *hyacinthus,* HYACINTH.]

jack (jăk) *n.* **1.** *Usually* **Jack.** A man; a fellow; a chap. Often used in direct address. **2. a.** *Archaic.* One who does odd jobs. **b.** One who works in the specified manual trade. Used in combination: *lumberjack; steeplejack.* **3.** A sailor; a tar. **4.** *Abbr.* **J** A playing card showing the figure of a young man or prince and ranking below a queen; a knave. **5. a.** Any of several devices or contrivances replacing human labor. Often used in combination: *bootjack.* **b.** A usually portable device for raising heavy objects, especially one for raising a motor vehicle when changing a tire, by means of force applied with a lever, screw, or hydraulic press. **c.** A wooden wedge for cleaving rock. **d.** A support or brace; especially, the iron crosstree on a topgallant masthead. **e.** A device that turns a spit for roasting meat. **6.** The male of certain animals, especially the ass. **7.** Any of several food and game fishes chiefly of the genus *Caranx,* of Atlantic and Pacific waters. **8.** A piece of wood holding the leather or quill pluck in a harpsichord or the hammer in other keyboard instruments, such as the piano. **9.** Any of the metal pieces used in the game of **jacks** *(see).* Also called "jackstone." **10.** A socket that accepts a plug at one end and attaches to an electric circuit at the other. **11.** A jacklight. **12.** A small flag flown at the bow of a ship, usually to indicate nationality. **13.** *Slang.* Money. —**every man jack.** Every single person of a group.
~*v.* **jacked, jacking, jacks.** —*tr.* To hunt or fish for with a jacklight. —*intr.* To jacklight. —**jack up. 1.** To raise with or as if with a jack. **2.** *Informal.* To increase (prices, for example). **3.** To bolster confidence in; support. **4.** *New Zealand.* To arrange; set up; put in order. **5.** *Australian.* To refuse to cooperate; resist or rebel.
~*adj. Australian Informal.* Tired or dissatisfied. Used with *of: jack of it all.* [Transferred use of the name *Jack,* familiar form of *John,* used to represent "any man."]

jack·al (jăk'əl, -ôl') *n.* **1.** Any of several doglike carnivorous mammals of the genus *Canis,* of Africa and Asia, that feed on carrion or prey on other animals. **2.** An accomplice or lackey characterized by the greed and baseness attributed to the jackal. [Turkish *chakāl,* from Persian *shagāl,* from Persian *shagāl,* *shaghāl*†.]

jack·a·napes (jăk'ə-nāps') *n.* **1.** A conceited, cheeky young man. **2.** A mischievous child. **3.** *Archaic.* A monkey or ape. [Earlier, "an ape," originally (c. 1450) *Jack Napes,* perhaps referring to the nickname of William de la Pole, 1st Duke of Suffolk, whose badge was a figure of a tame ape's ball and chain.]

jack·ass (jăk'ăs') *n.* **1.** A male ass or donkey. **2.** A foolish or stupid person; a blockhead. **3.** An Australian bird, the **kookaburra** *(see).* [JACK (male) + ASS.]

jackass penguin *n.* The northernmost of penguins, *Spheniscus demersus,* found especially on the islets off the west coast of Africa, so called because of its donkeylike braying.

jackass rig *n. Nautical.* Any nonstandard combination of square rig and fore-and-aft rig on a sailing ship having two or more masts. Also called "hermaphrodite rig."

jack·boot (jăk'bōot') *n.* **1.** A stout military boot extending to or above the knee. **2.** Oppressive, bullying behavior. Also used adjectivally: *jackboot tactics.*

jack·daw (jăk'dô') *n.* A Eurasian bird, *Corvus monedula,* related to and resembling the crow, having a black and gray plumage. Also called "daw."

jack·e·roo, jack·a·roo (jăk'ə-rōo') *n., pl.* **-roos.** *Australian Informal.* An apprentice hand on a sheep or cattle ranch.
~*intr.v.* **jackerooed, -rooing, -roos.** To work as a jackeroo. [Blend of JACK (man) and KANGAROO.]

jack·et (jăk'ĭt) *n.* **1.** A short coat, usually waist- or hip-length, worn by men or women. **2.** Any of various coverings worn on the upper part of the body. Used in combination: *a straitjacket.* **3.** The coat of certain animals. **4.** An outer covering or casing, especially: **a.** The skin of a baked potato. **b.** A **dust jacket** *(see).* **c.** Insulation covering a steam pipe, wire, boiler, or the like. **d.** A paper or thin cardboard envelope for a phonograph record.
~*tr.v.* **jacketed, -eting, -ets.** To supply or cover with a jacket. [Middle English *jaket,* from Old French *jacquet, jaquet,* diminutive of *jaque,* short jacket, perhaps from the name *Jacques.*]

Jack Frost *n.* Frost or cold weather personified.

jack·fruit (jăk'frōot') *n.* **1.** A tree, *Artocarpus heterophyllus,* of tropical Asia, bearing large, edible fruit. **2.** The fruit of this tree, resembling breadfruit. [Portuguese *jaca,* from Malayalam *chakka* + FRUIT.]

jack·ham·mer (jăk'hăm'ər) *n.* A hand-held pneumatic machine for drilling rock.

jack-in-the-box (jăk'ĭn-thə-bŏks') *n., pl.* **jack-in-the-boxes** or **jacks-in-the-box.** A toy consisting of a usually grotesque puppet that springs up out of a box when the lid is opened.

jackal *The common, or Indian, jackal (above) is one of several species of this doglike mammal found in the warmer parts of Asia and Africa. Jackals are mostly scavengers, feeding on the carcasses left by the larger carnivores such as lions, but also hunt in packs for birds and small animals.*

jack-in-the-box *A favorite toy of European children in the 19th century. The earliest versions, dating back to the 16th century, were modeled on Punch and Judy and known as "Punch boxes."*

jack-in-the-pul-pit (jăk'ĭn-*th*ə-pŏŏl'pĭt, -pŭl'pĭt) *n., pl.* **jack-in-the-pulpits** or **jacks-in-the-pulpit**. A plant, *Arisaema triphyllum*, of eastern North America, having a leaflike spathe enclosing a clublike spadix. Also called "Indian turnip."

Jack Ketch *n. Archaic British.* A hangman. [After John KETCH.]

jack-knife (jăk'nīf') *n., pl.* **-knives** (-nīvz) or **-knifes** (for senses 2,3). **1.** A large pocketknife. **2.** A dive executed by jumping headfirst and then bending the body at the waist and, with the legs straight, touching the feet with the hands before straightening out to enter the water, hands first. **3.** An uncontrollable maneuver of a tractor-trailer truck, in which the trailer swings round at an angle, usually of less than 90°, to the tractor or cab.
~*v.* **jackknifed, -knifing, -knifes.** —*tr.* To fold or double like a jackknife. —*intr.* **1.** To bend or fold up like a jackknife. **2.** To make a jackknife dive. **3.** To go out of control by performing a jackknife. Used of a vehicle. [Probably JACK + KNIFE.]

jack-light (jăk'līt') *n.* A light used as a lure in night hunting or fishing.
~*intr.v.* **jacklighted, -lighting, -lights.** To hunt or fish with a jacklight.

jack mackerel *n.* A food and game fish, *Trachurus symmetricus*, of Pacific coastal waters. Also called "saurel."

jack-of-all-trades (jăk'əv-ôl'trādz) *n., pl.* **jacks-of-all-trades.** A person who can do many different kinds of work.

jack-o'-lan-tern (jăk'ə-lăn'tərn) *n.* **1. a.** A lantern made from a hollowed pumpkin with a carved face. **b.** A commercial imitation of this. **2.** A phosphorescent light over marshy ground or a similar phenomenon; an **ignis fatuus** *(see)* or similar phenomenon.

jack-plane (jăk'plān') *n.* A bench plane for rough surfacing. [JACK + PLANE.]

jack plug *n.* A usually single-pronged electrical plug for use with a jack.

jack-pot (jăk'pŏt') *n.* **1. a.** The accumulated stakes in a kind of poker that requires one to hold a pair of jacks or better in order to open the betting. **b.** Any cumulative pool or kitty in various games and competitions. **2.** A top prize or reward. —**hit the jackpot.** *Informal.* To experience great success or sudden good fortune. [JACK (playing card) + POT.]

jack rabbit *n.* Any of several large long-eared, long-legged hares of the genus *Lepus*, of western North America. [JACK(ASS) (from its long ears) + RABBIT.]

Jack Russell terrier *n.* A dog of a breed developed from the fox terrier, having a smooth, white coat with black and tan markings, short legs, and a stocky body. Also called "Jack Russell." [After John *Russell* (1795-1883), English clergyman known as the "sporting parson."]

jacks (jăks) *n. Used with a singular verb.* A game played with a set of six-pointed metal pieces and a small ball, the object being to pick up the pieces in various combinations while bouncing and catching the ball. Also called "jackstones." [Shortened from *jackstones* : JACK (man) + STONE.]

jack-screw (jăk'skrōō') *n.* A jack for lifting, operated by a screw. Also called "jack."

jack-shaft (jăk'shăft', -shäft') *n.* An auxiliary or intermediate shaft that transmits motion from a motor to a machine.

jack-snipe (jăk'snīp') *n., pl.* **-snipes** or collectively **jacksnipe. 1.** A Eurasian wading bird, *Limnocryptes minima*, having brownish plumage and a long bill. **2.** Any of several similar birds. [JACK + SNIPE.]

Jack-son (jăk'sən). Capital of Mississippi since 1821, situated on the Pearl River. The city was the scene of bitter fighting during the Civil War and of civil rights agitation after World War II.

Jackson, Andrew (1767-1845). Seventh U.S. president. He became a national hero after his defense of New Orleans against the British in 1815 and was elected president in 1828 and 1832.

Jackson, Jesse Louis (1941-). U.S. civil rights leader and politician. A Baptist minister, he directed national antidiscrimination efforts (1966-77). In the 1980's he made controversial diplomatic missions as a private citizen, denounced U.S. ties with South Africa, and sought the 1984 Democratic presidential nomination.

Jackson, Thomas Jonathan (1824-63). U.S. Confederate general in the Civil War. He won his nickname—"Stonewall"—for his resistance to Union forces at Bull Run (1861). He was accidentally killed by his own troops at Chancellorsville (1863).

jack-stay (jăk'stā') *n.* **1.** A stay for racing or cruising vessels used to steady the mast against the strain of the gaff. **2.** A rope, rod, or batten along the upper side of a yard, gaff, or boom to which a sail is fastened. **3.** A rope or rod running vertically on the forward side of the mast on which the yard moves.

jack-stone (jăk'stōn') *n.* **1.** jackstones. *Used with a singular verb.* The game of **jacks** *(see).* **2.** See **jack** (sense 9).

jack-straw (jăk'strô') *n.* **1.** jackstraws. *Used with a singular verb.* A game played with a pile of straws or thin sticks, with the players attempting in turn to remove a single stick without disturbing the others. Also called "spilikins." **2.** One of the straws or sticks used in this game. [JACK + STRAW.]

Jack Tar, Jack tar *n.* A sailor. [*Jack* (name) + TAR.]

Jack the Ripper. An unknown murderer who killed and mutilated a number of prostitutes in the East End of London in 1888.

Ja-cob (jā'kəb). Hebrew patriarch; son of Isaac and grandson of Abraham; father of 12 sons, ancestors of the 12 tribes of Israel.

Jac-o-be-an (jăk'ə-bē'ən) *adj.* **1.** Of or pertaining to the reign of James I of England or his times. **2.** Pertaining to or designating an architectural style of 17th-century England, blending late Gothic and Palladian elements.
~*n.* Any prominent figure of this period. [New Latin *Jacobaeus*, from *Jacobus*, JAMES.]

Jac-o-be-than (jăk'ə-bē'thən) *adj.* Pertaining to, suggestive of, or designating a style, especially in architecture, characteristic of the reigns of Elizabeth I and James I. Often used humorously. [Blend of JACOBEAN + ELIZABETHAN, coined (1933) by Sir John Betjeman.]

Jac-o-bin (jăk'ə-bĭn) *n.* **1.** A member of the most radical republican group during the French Revolution, led by Robespierre, which overthrew the Girondins in 1793 and instituted the Reign of Terror. **2.** A leftist or extreme left-wing revolutionary. Often used derogatorily. **3.** A French Dominican friar. [French, from Late Latin *Jacōbus*, after the church of *Saint-Jacques*, Paris, near which the Jacobin friars built their first convent. The French political group was founded (1789) in this convent.] —**Jac-o-bin-ic, Jac-o-bin-i-cal** *adj.* —**Jac-o-bin-ism** *n.*

Jac-o-bin-ize (jăk'ə-bĭ-nīz') *tr.v.* **-ized, -izing, -izes.** To imbue with or convert to revolutionary ideas characteristic of the Jacobins.

Jac-o-bite (jăk'ə-bīt') *n.* A supporter of James II of England or of the Stuart pretenders after 1688. [From New Latin *Jacobus*, JAMES.] —**Jac-o-bit-i-cal** (jăk'ə-bĭt'ĭ-kəl) *adj.* —**Jac-o-bit-ism** *n.*

Jacobite Rebellion *n.* **1.** The failed Jacobite uprising (1715-16) led by the Earl of Mar in support of James Edward Stuart, the Old Pretender. Also called the "Fifteen." **2.** The later Jacobite uprising (1745-46) led by Charles Edward Stuart, the Young Pretender, in which all hopes of restoring the Stuarts to the throne were finally crushed. Also called the "Forty-Five."

Jac-ob-sen (yăk'əb-sən), **Arne** (1902-71). Danish designer. His severely functional style, such as his three-legged stacking stool, influenced much modern design. He summed up his work in the motto "economy plus function equals style."

Jacob's ladder *n.* **1.** *Nautical.* A rope or chain ladder with rigid rungs. **2.** A widely cultivated garden plant, *Polemonium caeruleum*, having blue flowers and numerous paired leaflets. [From the ladder seen by the patriarch JACOB in a dream. Genesis 28:12.]

ja-co-bus (jə-kō'bəs) *n., pl.* **-buses.** A gold coin issued during the reign of James I. [New Latin *Jacobus*, JAMES.]

jac-o-net (jăk'ə-nĕt') *n.* A light, cotton cloth with a soft finish used especially for bandages and poulticing. [Urdu *jagannāthī*, first made in *Jagannath* (now Puri), India.]

Jac-quard (jăk'ärd', jə-kärd') *adj.* Made on or pertaining to a Jacquard loom.
~*n.* A fabric with an intricately woven pattern made on a Jacquard loom. Also called "Jacquard weave." [After Joseph Marie JACQUARD.]

Jac-quard (zhä-kär'), **Joseph Marie** (1752-1834). French silk weaver. His invention of the Jacquard loom (c. 1801) made it possible to weave complex patterns automatically. The silk workers of his native Lyons smashed his machines, but by 1812 some 11,000 looms were in use and they were adopted worldwide.

Jacquard loom *n.* A loom fitted with perforated cards to facilitate the weaving of a figured fabric. [After Joseph Marie JACQUARD.]

Jac-que-rie (zhä-krē') *n.* **1.** The uprising of the French peasants against the nobility in 1358. **2.** *Often* **jacquerie.** A violent peasant revolt. [French, from Old French, from *jacques*, "peasant," from *Jacques*, James.]

jac-ta-tion (jăk-tā'shən) *n.* **1.** Bragging; boasting. **2.** *Pathology.* Jactitation. [Latin *jactātiō* (stem *jactātiōn*-), from *jactāre*, "to toss about," discuss, boast, frequentative of *jacere* (past participle *jactus*), to throw.]

jac-ti-ta-tion (jăk'tə-tā'shən) *n.* **1.** *Law.* A false boast or claim, especially of marriage, detrimental to the interests of another. **2.** *Pathology.* Extreme restlessness or tossing in bed, often associated with a high fever. In this sense, also called "jactation." [Medieval Latin *jactitātiō* (stem *jactitātiōn*-), a false assertion made to the injury of another, from *jactitāre*, frequentative of Latin *jactāre*, to boast, declare publicly. See **jactation**.]

Ja-cuz-zi (jə-kōō'zē, jä-) *n.* A trademark for a deep bath with a device that makes the water swirl around.

jade[1] (jād) *n.* **1.** Either of two distinct minerals, **nephrite** and **jadeite** *(both of which see)*, that are generally pale green or white and are used mainly as gemstones or in carved ornaments. **2.** A dull yellowish-green. [French *jade*, *ejade*, from Spanish *(piedra de) ijada*, "(stone of the) flank" (from the belief that it was a cure for renal colic), from Vulgar Latin *iliata* (unattested), flanks, from Latin *īlia*, plural of *īlium*, flank, ILEUM.] —**jade** *adj.*

jade[2] *n.* **1.** A broken-down or useless horse; a nag. **2.** A worthless or disreputable woman.
~*v.* **jaded, jading, jades.** —*tr.* To exhaust or wear out. —*intr.* To become weary or spiritless. [Middle English *jade†*, a broken-down horse.]

jad-ed (jā'dĭd) *adj.* **1.** Wearied; spiritless as through fatigue: "*My father's words had left me jaded and depressed*" (William Styron). **2.** Dulled by surfeit; sated: "*the sickeningly sweet life of the amoral, jaded, bored upper classes*" (John Simon). —See Synonyms at **tired.** [From JADE (verb).] —**jad-ed-ly** *adv.* —**jad-ed-ness** *n.*

jade-ite (jā'dīt') *n.* A rare, emerald to light-green, white, red-brown, yellow-brown, or violet jade, NaAlSi$_2$O$_6$, used as a gem and for ornamental carvings. Also called "jade." [French : JADE + -ITE.]

j'a-doube (zhä-dōōb') *interj. French.* Used in chess to express the

jack rabbit *The North American jack rabbit is, in fact, a hare. Its large ears perform two functions: they improve its ability to hear approaching predators, and they help it to lose excess body heat and so keep cool in the desert.*

intention not to move a piece that one is about to touch. [Literally "I adjust."]

jae·ger (yā′gər; *also* jä′gər *for sense 1*) *n.* **1.** Any of several sea birds of the genus *Stercorarius* that snatch food from other birds. See **skua. 2.** A huntsman or hunting attendant. [German *Jäger,* "hunter."]

Jaf·fa (jăf′ə). *Hebrew* **Ja·fo** (yä′fô). *Arabic* **Ya·fa** (yäf′ə). Ancient city of west-central Israel. Founded by the Phoenicians, it was taken by the Israelites in the 6th century B.C. The city fell to the Arabs (A.D. 636), to the Crusaders (1126 and 1191), and to the Ottoman Turks (16th century). It became part of Tel Aviv–Jaffa in 1950.

Jaffa orange *n.* A variety of orange having a large, thick-skinned fruit. Also called "jaffa." [After JAFFA, near which it was originally grown.]

jag¹ (jăg) *n.* **1.** A sharp projection; a barb. **2. a.** A hanging flap along the edge of a garment. **b.** A slash or slit in a garment exposing material of a different color.
—*tr.v.* **jagged, jagging, jags. 1.** To cut jags in; notch. **2.** To cut unevenly; make (an edge) ragged. **3.** *Scottish.* To prick; jab sharply. [Middle English *jagge*†.]

jag² *n.* **1.** *Slang.* **a.** A bout of drinking, drug taking, or the like. **b.** Any period of indulgence in an activity: *a crying jag.* **2.** *Regional.* A small load or portion. [16th century : origin obscure.]

jag·ad·gu·ru (jŭg′əd-gŏŏ-rŏŏ′, -gŏŏ′rŏŏ) *n.* A title for a revered Hindu guru. [Hindi, from Sanskrit *jagadguru,* "father of the world," title appled to Brahma, Vishnu, and Shiva : *jagat-,* world + GURU.]

Jagannath. Variant of **Juggernaut.**

jag·ged (jăg′ĭd) *adj.* **1.** Toothed or serrated; having jags. **2.** Roughly torn; having a ragged edge. —See Synonyms at **rough.** —**jag·ged·ly** *adv.* —**jag·ged·ness** *n.*

Jag·ger (jăg′ər), **Michael Philip,** known as "Mick" (1943–). English rock singer and songwriter, lead singer of the Rolling Stones. He has also appeared as a film actor.

jag·ger·y (jăg′ə-rē) *n.* Unrefined sugar made from palm sap. [From Indo-Portuguese *jagara,* from Kanarese *sharkare,* from Sanskrit *śarkarā*†, "gravel," sugar.]

jag·gy (jăg′ē) *adj.* **-gier, -giest.** Having jags; jagged.

jag·u·ar (jăg′wär′, -yŏŏ-är′) *n.* A large feline mammal, *Panthera onca,* of tropical America, having a tawny coat spotted with black rosettelike markings. [Spanish *jaguar, yaguar* and Portuguese *jaguar,* from Tupi-Guarani *jaguara, yaguara.*]

ja·gua·ron·di, ja·gua·run·di (jăg′wə-rŭn′dē, jä′gwə-) *n., pl.* **-dis.** A long-tailed grayish-brown wild cat, *Felis yagouaroundi,* of tropical America. [American Spanish and Portuguese, from Tupi-Guarani.]

Jah (jä) *n.* Yahweh; God. Used especially by Rastafarians. [Shortened from Hebrew, YAHWEH.]

Jahveh, Jahweh. Variants of **Yahweh.**

Jahvist, Jahwist. Variants of **Yahwist.**

jai a·lai (hī′ lī′, hī′ ə-lī′, hī′ ə-lī′) *n.* An extremely fast court game popular in Spain, Latin America, and the Philippines, in which players use a long hand-shaped basket strapped to the wrist to propel the ball against a wall. Also called "pelota."

jail (jāl) *n.* Also *chiefly British* **gaol.** A place for the confinement of persons in lawful detention; a prison.
—*tr.v.* **jailed, jailing, jails.** Also *chiefly British* **gaol.** To detain in custody; imprison. [*Jail* and *gaol,* respectively from Middle English *jaiole* and *gayole,* from Old French *jaiole* and Old Northern French *gaiole,* both from Vulgar Latin *gaviola* (unattested), variant of *caveola* (unattested), diminutive of Latin *cavea,* a hollow, den, coop.]

jail·bird (jāl′bûrd′) *n. Informal.* A prisoner or ex-convict; especially, one who has a long record of imprisonment.

jail·break (jāl′brāk′) *n.* An escape from prison. —**jail·break·er** *n.*

jail·er, jail·or (jā′lər) *n.* Also *chiefly British* **gaol·er.** A keeper of or guard in a jail.

jail fever *n.* A virulent type of typhus fever, formerly endemic in crowded and dirty prisons.

jail·house (jāl′hous′) *n.* A jail.

Jain (jīn) *n.* Also **Jai·na** (jī′nə). A believer in or follower of Jainism. [Hindi *jaina,* from Sanskrit *jainas,* from *jinas,* saint, "overcomer," from *jayati,* to conquer.] —**Jain, Jai·na** *adj.*

Jain·ism (jī′nĭz′əm) *n.* An ascetic religion of India, founded in the 6th century B.C. It teaches that the soul is immortal and will be reincarnated until it reaches perfection and is liberated. The deity of Jainism consists not of a single supreme being but of the collection of these perfect liberated souls.

Jai·pur (jī′pŏŏr′). The capital of Rajasthan state, northwestern India. Founded in 1728, it was the capital of the Rajput state of Jaipur and came under British protection in 1818.

Ja·kar·ta or **Dja·kar·ta** (jə-kär′tə). Formerly **Ba·ta·vi·a** (bə-tā′vē-ə). The capital of Indonesia, situated on the northwestern coast of Java. Founded by the Dutch (c. 1619), it became an important center of the Dutch East India Company. Renamed Jakarta on independence in 1949, the city has fine buildings, a Roman Catholic cathedral, and a university (founded 1950). Its port, Tandjung Priok, exports oil, rubber, timber, and tea.

jake (jāk) *adj. Slang.* Fine; suitable; all right: *That's jake with me.* [Origin unknown.]

jakes (jāks) *n. Used with a singular verb. Regional.* A privy. [Perhaps from the French name *Jacques.*]

Ja·kob·son (yä′kəb-sən, jä′-), **Roman** (1896–1982). U.S. linguist. He was a principal founder (1926) of the Prague School and a major influence on contemporary linguistics. His works include *Funda-*

mentals of Language (with Morris Halle, 1956).

jal·ap (jăl′əp) *n.* **1.** A Mexican plant, *Exogonium purga,* having a tuberous rootstock that is dried, powdered, and used medicinally as a cathartic. **2.** Any of several similar or related plants. **3.** The dried rootstock of such a plant. [French *jalap,* from Mexican Spanish *jalapa,* short for *(purga de) Jalapa,* "(purgative of) Jalapa," capital of Veracruz state, Mexico.]

ja·lop·y (jə-lŏp′ē) *n., pl.* **-ies.** *Informal.* An old, dilapidated car. [20th century : origin obscure.]

ja·lou·sie (jăl′ŏŏ-sē; *chiefly British* zhăl′ŏŏ-zē′) *n.* A blind or shutter having adjustable horizontal slats for regulating the passage of air and light. [French, "jealousy" (probably because one sees through it without being seen).]

jam¹ (jăm) *v.* **jammed, jamming, jams.** —*tr.* **1.** To drive or wedge forcibly; squeeze into a tight position. **2. a.** To force or push suddenly: *jam the lid down.* **b.** To apply (brakes) suddenly. Used with *on.* **3. a.** To cause to be stuck in a position so that movement or extrication is difficult or impossible: *Her skirt was jammed in the bicycle wheel.* **b.** To cause to lock in an unworkable position: *jam the typewriter keys.* **4.** To fill or pack to excess; cram: *He jammed the drawer with old socks.* **5.** To block, congest, or clog: *The drain was jammed by debris.* **6.** To crush or bruise between two bodies or surfaces: *jammed her finger in the door.* **7.** *Electronics.* To interfere with or prevent the clear reception of (broadcast signals) by electronic means. —*intr.* **1.** To become wedged; stick. **2.** To become inoperable because of jammed parts. **3.** To force into or through a limited space. **4.** To play in a jam session.
—*n.* **1.** The act of jamming or the condition of being jammed. **2.** A crush or congestion of people or things in a limited space: *a traffic jam.* **3.** A **jam session** *(see).* **4.** *Informal.* A predicament: *in a jam with the police.* [18th century : imitative.]

jam² *n.* **1.** A preserve made from whole fruit boiled to a pulp with sugar. **2.** *British.* Something that is pleasant or comes as a bonus: *always promised jam tomorrow.* [Probably from JAM (act of jamming).]

Jam. James (New Testament).

Ja·mai·ca (jə-mā′kə). An island in the Caribbean Sea. Its central uplands rise to 2,256 meters (7,402 feet) in the Blue Mts. to the east. The island was discovered by Columbus (1494), settled by the Spanish, but taken by the British in 1655. Jamaica became a major center of the slave trade with extensive sugar plantations. In 1962 the island became an independent Commonwealth state. In the election of 1980, with high unemployment and much street violence, the left-wing Michael Manley, in power since 1972, was replaced as prime minister by the pro-Western Edward Seaga, and much-needed foreign investment capital became available. The island once depended on exports of bananas, but bauxite is now by far the main export. Tourism and sugar are also important. Area, 10,991 square kilometers (4,243 square miles). Population, 2,200,-000. Capital, Kingston. —**Ja·mai·can** *n. & adj.*

jamb (jăm) *n.* A vertical post or piece forming the side of a door or window frame. [Middle English *jambe,* from Old French, "leg," from Late Latin *gamba,* hoof, from Greek *kampē,* joint.]

jam·ba·lay·a (jŭm′bə-lī′ə) *n.* A Creole dish consisting of rice with shrimp, chicken, turkey, or similar ingredients. [Louisiana French, from Provençal *jambalaia* (a stew of chicken and rice).]

jam·beau (jăm′bō) *n., pl.* **-beaux** (-bōz). A piece of armor for the leg below the knee. Also called "jambe." [Middle English, from Norman French *jambeau* (unattested), from Old French *jambe,* leg.]

jam·bo·ree (jăm′bə-rē′) *n.* **1.** A lively celebration. **2.** A large assembly, often international, especially of Scouts or Guides. [19th century : origin obscure.]

James¹ (jāmz). **1.** Also **Da·ko·ta** (də-kō′tə). River rising in central North Dakota and flowing 1,142 kilometers (710 miles) generally southeast to the Missouri River in southeastern South Dakota. **2.** River rising in western Virginia and flowing 547 kilometers (340 miles) generally east to Chesapeake Bay.

James² *n. Abbr.* **Jam., Jas.** The 20th book of the New Testament, attributed to St. James the Less.

James IV of Scotland (1473–1513). King of Scotland from 1488.

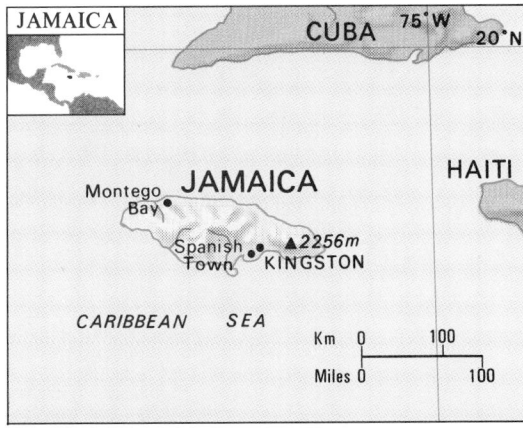

jaguar *The largest American cat, the jaguar is a predator like the tigers of Asia. It lives mostly in forests in South America and was revered as a god by pre-Columbian peoples from Mexico to Peru.*

He led Scotland to its greatest military defeat—at Flodden (1513) against the English, in which he died with many of his nobles.

James V of Scotland (1512–42). King of Scotland from 1513. He allied himself with the Church and people to curb the nobility, but in 1542 dissent between the king and his nobles allowed the English to overwhelm the Scottish army at Solway Moss.

James VI of Scotland and I of England (1566–1625). King of Scotland from 1567 and first Stuart king of England from 1603, when he succeeded the childless Elizabeth I. James believed in the divine right of kings and quarreled with Parliament, sowing the seeds of civil war.

James VII of Scotland and II of England (1633–1701). Last Stuart king to rule both countries (1685–88). His fervent Roman Catholicism almost denied him accession. A rebellion against him by the Duke of Monmouth (1685) was unsuccessful, but in 1688 seven leading political figures invited William of Orange to invade the country. James was deserted by his own troops and fled to France.

James, Henry (1843–1916). U.S. novelist and critic. He settled in England in 1876, and his early novels, *The American* (1877), *The Portrait of a Lady* (1881), and *The Bostonians* (1886), deal with the impact of European civilization on Americans. His other works include *The Turn of the Screw* (1898), *The Ambassadors* (1903), and *The Golden Bowl* (1904). **—James·i·an** *n. & adj.*

James, Jesse Woodson (1847–82). U.S. outlaw. He was a Confederate guerrilla during the Civil War. After the war he organized an armed band of brigands and spent the next 15 years robbing banks and trains in the West. James was murdered in St. Louis, Missouri, by Robert Ford, a member of his own gang.

James, Saint[1], called "the Less." Described by St. Paul (Galatians 1:19) as the brother of Jesus, he is considered to be the author of the Epistle of James and 1st bishop of Jerusalem.

James, Saint[2], called "the Greater." One of the Twelve Apostles; son of Zebedee and brother of John; traditionally supposed to have been martyred by Herod Agrippa (*c.* A.D. 44).

James, Saint[3]. One of the Twelve Apostles; often identified with St. James the Less.

James, William (1842–1910). U.S. psychologist and philosopher, brother of Henry James. He developed the theory of pragmatism and is noted for his pioneering study *The Varieties of Religious Experience* (1902).

Jame·son (jām′sən), **Sir Leander Starr** (1853–1917). South African politician. His disastrous raid into the Boer Transvaal Republic (1895) led to the fall of Cecil Rhodes. Jameson later became prime minister of Cape Colony (1904–08).

James·town (jāmz′toun). Ruined village on the James River in Virginia. It was the first permanent English settlement in the New World (founded 1607).

jam·mer (jăm′ər) *n.* A device for jamming broadcast signals.

Jam·mu and Kash·mir (jŭm′ōō; kăsh-mîr′; kăsh′mîr′) *n.* A state in northern India, in the Indian part of Kashmir. The Himalayan and Karakoram ranges lie in the north and east of the state. There are two capitals: Jammu (winter) and Srinagar (summer).

jam·my (jăm′ē) *adj.* **-mier, -miest.** **1.** Covered with jam. **2.** *British Informal.* **a.** Lucky. **b.** Easy or pleasant: *a jammy job.*

jam·packed (jăm′păkt′) *adj. Informal.* Full, crowded, or crammed: *an article jam-packed with new ideas.*

jam·pan (jăm′păn′) *n.* A type of sedan chair, used in parts of India, that is carried by four people. [Bengali *jhāmpān.*]

jam session *n.* An informal gathering at which musicians, especially jazz musicians, play improvised music together, usually for their own enjoyment.

Jam·shid, Jam·shyd (jăm-shēd′) *n. Persian Mythology.* A king who drank a cup of the elixir of life. He was punished for boasting that he was immortal by being made human, after which he became a great ruler for 700 years.

Jan. January.

Ja·ná·ček (yän′ə-chĕk), **Leoš** (1854–1928). Czech composer, influenced by folk music. His works include the operas *Jenůfa* (1904), *Kátya Kabanová* (1921), and the *Glagolitic Mass* (1926).

Ja·na·ta (jŭn′ə-tä′) *n.* A political coalition that held power in India between 1977 and 1979. [Hindi, "group of the people."]

jan·gle (jăng′gəl) *n.* A harsh, discordant, metallic sound.
~*v.* **jangled, -gling, -gles.** —*intr.* **1.** To make a jangle. **2.** *Archaic.* To wrangle; dispute. —*tr.* **1.** To cause (something metallic) to jangle: *jangled the bells.* **2.** To grate on or jar (the nerves). [Middle English *janglen,* from Old French *jangler,* probably from Germanic, akin to Middle Dutch *jangelen†.*] **—jan·gler** *n.*

jan·is·sar·y (jăn′ĭ-sĕr′ē) *n., pl.* **-ies.** Also **jan·i·zar·y** (-zĕr′ē). A soldier in an elite guard of Turkish troops organized in the 14th century and abolished in 1826. [French *janissaire,* from Turkish *yeniçeri : yeni,* new + *çeri,* militia.]

jan·i·tor (jăn′ə-tər) *n.* **1.** One who attends to the cleaning or maintenance of a building. **2.** *Archaic.* A doorman. [Latin *jānitor,* from *jānua,* door, from *jānus,* arched passage.] **—jan·i·to·ri·al** (jăn′ə-tôr′-ē-əl, -tōr′ē-əl) *adj.*

Jan·sen (jăn′sən, yän′-), **Cornelis Otto** (1585–1638). Dutch theologian. He founded a reform movement in the Roman Catholic Church known as Jansenism. In the *Augustinus* (1640) he argued against the concept of a state of grace. His movement was condemned as heretical by Pope Innocent X in 1653.

Jan·sen·ism (jăn′sə-nĭz′əm) *n.* The heretical theological principles of Cornelis Jansen, which emphasize predestination, deny free will,

Janus A Roman coin portraying the double-headed deity Janus, who was the god of doorways, gates, and arches.

and maintain that human nature is incapable of good. **—Jan·sen·ist** *n. & adj.* **—Jan·sen·is·tic** *adj.*

Jan·sky (jăn′skē), **Karl Guthe** (1905–50). U.S. engineer. He discovered in 1931 that the stars transmit radio waves, thereby laying the foundations of the science of radio astronomy.

Jan·u·ar·y (jăn′yōō-ĕr′ē) *n., pl.* **-ies.** *Abbr.* **Jan.** The first month of the year in the Gregorian calendar. January has 31 days. See feature at **calendar.** [Middle English *Januarie,* from Latin *Jānuārius (mensis),* "(month) of Janus," from JANUS.]

Ja·nus (jā′nəs). *Mythology.* An ancient Roman god of gates and doorways, depicted with two faces looking in opposite directions, whose festival month was January.

Ja·nus·faced (jā′nəs-fāst′) *adj.* Hypocritical; two-faced.

Jap. Japan; Japanese.

ja·pan (jə-păn′) *n.* **1.** A black enamel or lacquer of a type originating in the Orient, used to produce a durable glossy finish. **2.** Any object decorated and varnished in the Japanese manner.
~*adj.* Relating to or varnished with japan.
~*tr.v.* **japanned, -panning, -pans.** **1.** To enamel with japan. **2.** To coat with a glossy finish. [From JAPAN, from Malay *Japang,* from Chinese *Jih-pun : jih,* sun + *pun,* origin.]

Ja·pan (jə-păn′). *Japanese* **Nip·pon** (nĭp′pŏn′) or **Ni·hon** (nē-hōn′). *Abbr.* **J., Jap.** Nation consisting of several islands in the North Pacific Ocean lying off the mainland of east Asia. The four main islands, Honshu, Shikoku, Kyushu, and Hokkaido, are mountainous. The highest peak is Fujiyama (3,776 meters; 12,388 feet). Japan has been ruled from the 5th century A.D. by emperors of the Yamoto dynasty, though legends trace their origins back to the 7th century B.C. The native Shinto religion was challenged by Buddhism after the 6th century A.D. From the 12th to 19th centuries, real power lay in the hands of the shoguns, feudal warlords whose dominance ended with the accession of the emperor Meiji (Mutsuhito). During his reign (1868–1912), Japan opened its doors to Western trade and industrial technology. Victory in the Russo-Japanese war (1904–05) encouraged expansion into Asia, and Japan occupied Korea and parts of China during the first half of the 20th century. One of the Axis powers in World War II, Japan surrendered in 1945 after atomic bombs were dropped on Hiroshima and Nagasaki. In 1946 the emperor Hirohito renounced the imperial claim to divinity, remaining head of state in a constitutional monarchy. A highly industrialized country with few natural resources, Japan depends on imported oil, although nuclear power should soon provide a third of its energy. It is the world's leading fishing nation, and relies on imports of food, and exports, particularly of motor vehicles, electric and electronic products, ships, synthetic fibers, and steel. Area, 372,313 square kilometers (143,713 square miles). Population, 117,100,000. Capital, Tokyo.

Japan clover *n.* A leguminous plant, *Lespedeza striata,* native to Asia, cultivated as a forage plant and for soil improvement.

Japan Current. *Japanese* **Ku·ro·shi·o** (kōō′rō-shē′ō). A warm ocean

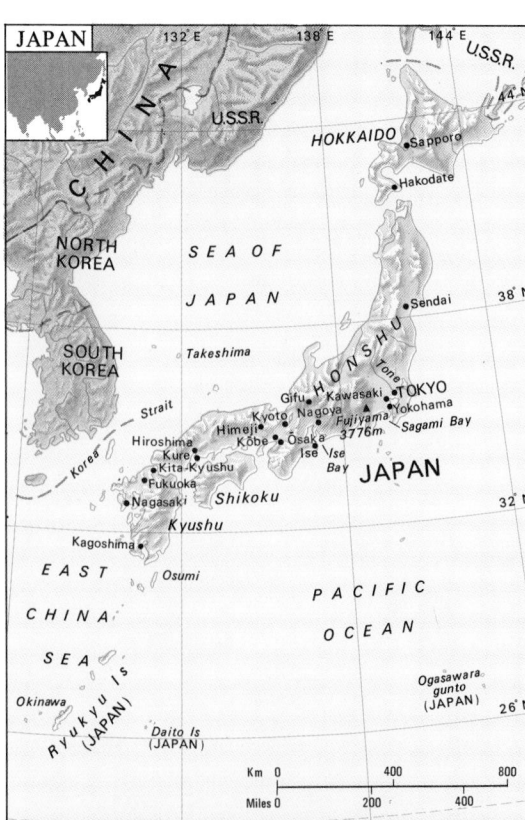

current flowing northeast from the Philippine Sea past southeastern Japan to the North Pacific.

Jap·a·nese (jăp′ə-nēz′, -nēs′) *adj. Abbr.* **J., Jap.** Of or pertaining to Japan, or to the people, language, or culture of Japan.
~*n., pl.* **Japanese. 1.** A native or inhabitant of Japan, or a descendant of one. **2.** *Abbr.* **J., Jap.** The language of Japan, having no proven affinities to any other language.

Japanese andromeda *n.* An ornamental shrub, *Pieris japonica,* native to Japan, having small, early-blooming white flowers.

Japanese beetle *n.* A metallic-green and brownish beetle, *Popillia japonica,* native to eastern Asia, the larvae and adults of which are serious plant pests in North America.

Japanese cedar *n.* A tree, the **cryptomeria** *(see),* or its wood.

Japanese iris *n.* A plant, *Iris kaempferi,* native to Asia, and cultivated in many varieties for its large, flat, showy flowers.

Japanese ivy *n.* **Boston ivy** *(see).*

Japanese lantern *n.* A paper lantern; a Chinese lantern.

Japanese leaf *n.* A plant, the **Chinese evergreen** *(see).*

Japanese maple *n.* A shrub or small tree, *Acer palmatum,* native to eastern Asia and widely cultivated for its decorative foliage.

Japanese quince *n.* See **japonica** (sense 1).

Japanese river fever *n. Pathology.* **Scrub typhus** *(see).*

Japanese spurge *n.* A plant, **pachysandra** *(see).*

Japan paper *n.* A strong fibrous paper made in Japan, and often used for printing etchings.

Japan Trench *n.* A depression in the floor of the North Pacific off northeastern Japan, extending from the Bonin to the Kurile islands and reaching depths of over 30,000 feet.

Japan wax *n.* A pale-yellow, solid wax obtained from the berries of certain plants of the genus *Rhus* and used in wax matches, soaps, food packaging, and as a substitute for beeswax.

jape (jāp) *v.* **japed, japing, japes.** *Archaic.* —*intr.* To joke or quip. —*tr.* To joke about; make sport of.
~*n.* A joke or quip. [Middle English *japen,* to trick, joke, from Old French *japper,* to yap (imitative).] —**jap·er** *n.* —**jap·er·y** *n.*

Ja·pheth (jā′fĭth). Also **Ja·phet** (-fĭt). The second son of Noah, in some traditions considered the ancestor of the Caucasian race. Genesis 5:32.

Ja·phet·ic (jə-fĕt′ĭk) *adj.* **1.** Of or pertaining to Japheth or his descendants. **2.** Designating a discredited linguistic grouping that attempted to associate Basque, Etruscan, and sometimes Sumerian and Elamite with the Indo-European languages.

japie. Variant of **jaap.**

ja·pon·i·ca (jə-pŏn′ĭ-kə) *n.* **1.** A shrub, *Chaenomeles speciosa,* native to Japan, that has quincelike fruit and is cultivated for its red flowers. Also called "flowering quince," "Japanese quince." **2.** A shrub, the **camellia** *(see).* [New Latin, "Japanese," from *Japonia,* JAPAN.]

Jaques-Dal·croze (zhäk′dăl-krōz′), **Emile** (1865–1950). Swiss composer. He developed eurhythmics, an expression of the rhythm of music through physical movement.

jar¹ (jär) *n.* **1.** A cylindrical glass or earthenware vessel with a wide mouth and usually without handles. **2.** The contents of such a vessel; a jarful. **3.** *British Informal.* A glass of beer. [French *jarre,* from Provençal *jarra,* from Arabic *jarrah,* large earthen vase.]

jar² (jär) *v.* **jarred, jarring, jars.** —*intr.* **1.** To make or utter a harsh, discordant sound. **2.** To have an unpleasant or disturbing effect; grate: *His voice jarred on her nerves.* **3.** To shake or shiver from impact. **4.** To clash or conflict. —*tr.* **1.** To cause to make a harsh, discordant sound. **2.** To bump or cause to move or shake from impact. **3.** To startle or unsettle; shock.
~*n.* **1.** A jolt; a shock. **2.** A harsh or grating sound. [16th century : probably imitative.]

jar·di·nière (järd′n-îr′; *French* zhär-dē-nyär′) *n.* **1.** A large, decorative stand or pot for plants. **2.** Diced, cooked vegetables served as a garnish with meat. [French, feminine of *jardinier,* gardener, from *jardin,* garden, from Old French from Vulgar Latin *gardīnus* (unattested), GARDEN.]

jar·ful (jär′fŏŏl) *n., pl.* **-fuls. 1.** The amount a jar will hold. **2.** The contents of a jar.

jar·gon¹ (jär′gən) *n.* **1.** The specialized or technical language of a trade, profession, class, or fellowship; cant: *"She could not follow the ugly academic jargon"* (Virginia Woolf). Compare **argot, slang. 2.** A hybrid language or dialect; pidgin. **3.** Nonsensical, incoherent, or meaningless utterance; gibberish: *"Wholly a blessed time: when jargon might abate, and . . . genuine speech begin"* (Thomas Carlyle).
~*intr.v.* **jargoned, -goning, -gons.** To speak in or use jargon. [Middle English *iargoun, gargoun,* meaningless chatter, from Old French *jargoun, gargon,* "twittering" (probably imitative).] —**jar·gon·ize** *v.* —**jar·gon·is·tic** *adj.*

jar·gon² (jär′gŏn′) *n.* Also **jar·goon** (-gŏŏn′). A smoky, yellow, or colorless variety of zircon. [French, ZIRCON.]

jarl (yärl) *n.* A chieftain or nobleman of the medieval Scandinavians. [Old Norse, from Common Germanic *erilaz* (unattested), EARL.]

Jarls·berg (yärlz′bûrg) *n.* A mild, pale-yellow Norwegian cheese. [After *Jarlesberg,* Norway, an estate west of Oslo.]

jar·o·site (jär′ə-sīt′) *n.* A yellow to brown mineral, KFe₃(SO₄)₂(OH)₆, occurring in masses or hexagonal crystals. [After *Barranco Jaroso,* Almeria, Spain, where it was first found.]

jar·rah (jär′ə) *n.* An Australian eucalyptus tree, *Eucalyptus marginata,* widely grown for its hard, red-brown timber. [From a native Australian language.]

Jar·row (jär′ō). An industrial town in Tyne and Wear, northeast

England, on the Tyne River. The early historian the Venerable Bede lived at Jarrow in a 7th-century monastery, whose ruins survive. In the 20th century Jarrow developed important shipyards and steelworks, whose collapse during the 1930's Depression led to 80 percent local unemployment. The Jarrow March (1936) of the unemployed to London is famous in trade union history.

Jar·ry (zhǎ-rē′), **Alfred** (1873–1907). French writer. His play *Ubu Roi* (1896), which made fun of the bourgeoisie, is regarded as perhaps the earliest example of the Theater of the Absurd.

Jas. James (New Testament).

jas·mine (jăz′mən) *n.* Also **jes·sa·mine** (jĕs′ə-mĭn). **1.** Any of several shrubs of the genus *Jasminum;* especially, *J. officinalis,* native to Asia, having fragrant white flowers used in making perfume. See **winter jasmine. 2.** Any of several other plants or shrubs having fragrant flowers, such as the frangipani *(red jasmine).* **3.** Light to brilliant yellow. [French *jasmin,* from Arabic *yās(a)mīn,* from Persian *yasmīn, yāsman*†.]

Ja·son (jā′sən). *Greek Mythology.* The leader of the Argonauts in quest of the Golden Fleece; husband of Medea.

jas·pé (jăs′pā) *adj.* Being randomly colored like jasper. [French.]

jas·per (jăs′pər) *n.* **1.** An opaque variety of quartz, reddish, brown, or yellow in color. **2.** Chalcedony, especially green chalcedony. [Middle English *jaspre,* from Old French *jasp(r)e,* from Latin *jaspis,* from Greek *iaspis,* from Semitic, akin to Assyrian *ashpū,* Aramaic *yashb,* and Hebrew *yashpāh.*]

Jasper National Park. Second-largest national park in Canada, established in 1907 in the Rocky Mountains of Alberta. It has glaciers, hot springs, and game preserves.

Jas·pers (yäs′pərs), **Karl Theodor** (1883–1969). German philosopher and psychologist, advocate of existentialism. His works include *Philosophie* (1932).

jasper ware *n.* A fine stoneware invented by Josiah Wedgwood, often colored by metallic oxides with raised designs in white.

Jat (jät, jŏt) *n.* A member of an Indo-Aryan people of the Punjab and Uttar Pradesh. [Hindi *jāṭ*†.]

ja·to (jā′tō) *n.* **1.** A takeoff aided by an auxiliary jet or rocket. **2.** An auxiliary unit providing thrust for such a takeoff. [From *JATO,* acronym for *jet-assisted takeoff.*]

jaun·dice (jôn′dĭs, jän′-) *n.* **1.** Yellowish discoloration of the skin and white of the eyes due to excess bile pigment in the blood. It is caused by any of several pathological conditions such as hepatitis, in which normal processing of bile is interrupted. Also called "icterus." **2.** A state of jealousy or bitterness. [Middle English *jaun-(d)is,* from Old French *jaunice,* from *jaune,* yellow, from Latin *galbinus,* greenish yellow, pale green, from *galbus*†.]

jaun·diced (jôn′dĭst, jän′-) *adj.* **1.** Affected with jaundice. **2.** Affected by envy, cynicism, prejudice, or hostility; embittered. **3.** Yellow or yellowish.

jaunt (jônt, jänt) *n.* A short trip or excursion, usually taken for pleasure; an outing.
~*intr.v.* **jaunted, jaunting, jaunts.** To make a short journey, especially for pleasure. [16th century : origin obscure.]

jaunting car *n.* A light, open cart with seats hung back to back over its two wheels, once commonly used in Ireland. Also called "jaunty car."

jaun·ty (jôn′tē, jän′-) *adj.* **-tier, -tiest. 1.** Having or expressing a buoyant or self-confident air; carefree. **2.** Crisp and dapper in appearance; smart. [Earlier *jentee, jantee,* elegant, "genteel," from French *gentil.*] —**jaun·ti·ly** *adv.* —**jaun·ti·ness** *n.*

Jau·rès (zhō-rĕs′), **Jean Léon** (1859–1914). French journalist and politician, leader of the French Socialist Party before World War I. In 1914 Jaurès argued for arbitration rather than armed conflict between the Triple Entente and the Triple Alliance. He was assassinated on July 31 by a fanatical nationalist.

Jav. Javanese.

ja·va (jăv′ə, jä′və) *n. Informal.* Brewed coffee. [From JAVA.]

Ja·va (jä′və, jăv′ə). The most populous island of Indonesia, situated between the Indian Ocean and the Java Sea. From the 1st century A.D. a distinctive Hindu-Javanese civilization flourished for 16 centuries. Java was later converted to Islam, and was colonized by the Dutch from the 17th century. The island became part of the Republic of Indonesia in 1950. It has well-irrigated soil producing rice, sugar, tea, and kapok. Java also has reserves of oil and is an important producer of textiles. The most industrialized of the Indonesian islands, Java includes the nation's three largest cities: Jakarta (the capital), Surabaya, and Bandung.

Java man *n.* A type of primitive man, **Pithecanthropus** *(see).*

Jav·a·nese (jăv′ə-nēz′, -nēs′) *adj. Abbr.* **Jav.** Of or pertaining to Java, or to the people, language, or culture of Java.
~*n., pl.* **Javanese.** *Abbr.* **Jav. 1.** A native or inhabitant of Java. **2.** The Indonesian language spoken in Java.

Java sparrow *n.* A small, grayish weaverbird, *Padda oryzivora,* native to tropical Asia and often kept as a cage bird.

jave·lin (jăv′lən, jăv′ə-) *n.* **1.** A light spear thrown with the hand and used as a weapon. **2.** A metal or metal-tipped spear, weighing 800 grams (1 pound 12 ounces) for men, 600 grams (1 pound 5 ounces) for women, used in contests of distance throwing. **3.** The athletic field event in which such a spear is thrown. [French *javeline,* from Old French, variant of *javelot,* from Celtic.]

Ja·velle water, Ja·vel water (zhə-vĕl′) *n.* An aqueous solution of potassium or sodium hypochlorite, used as a disinfectant and bleaching agent. [From *Javel,* former French town, now part of Paris.]

jay *The harsh cry of the common jay (above) can be heard throughout much of the Northern Hemisphere. Acorns are one of the jay's main foods—it buries them in the autumn, then digs them up to eat during the winter.*

jaw (jô) *n.* **1.** Either of two bony or cartilaginous structures in most vertebrates forming the framework of the mouth and holding the teeth. See **mandible, maxilla. 2. a.** The anatomical parts forming the wall of the mouth and serving to open and close it. **b.** The corresponding parts in insects and other invertebrate animals. **3. jaws.** A mechanical device resembling the jaws, such as the gripping parts of a vise or the hinged parts of a mechanical grab. **4. jaws.** The walls or narrow mouth of a pass, canyon, or cavern. **5. jaws.** A dangerous situation or confrontation: *the jaws of death.* **6.** *Informal.* **a.** Impudent argument or expression of opposition: *Don't give me any jaw.* **b.** Idle chatter. **c.** A moralizing lecture. —*intr.v.* **jawed, jawing, jaws.** *Informal.* To talk or chat, especially at tedious length. [Middle English *iawe, iowe,* from Old French *joe*†.]

ja·wan (jə-wän′) *n.* A soldier in the Indian Army, especially a private. [Urdu, "young man."]

jaw·bone (jô′bōn′) *n.* Any bone of the jaw; especially, the bone of the lower jaw. See **mandible.**

jaw·break·er (jô′brā′kər) *n.* **1.** *Slang.* A word that is difficult to pronounce. **2.** A kind of very hard candy.

jay (jā) *n.* **1.** Any of various often crested birds of the family Corvidae, usually having a loud, harsh call. The Eurasian jay, *Garrulus glandarius,* is brownish-pink with blue and white wings and a black and white crest. **2.** A noisy or talkative person; a chatterbox. **3.** *Slang.* A gullible or inexperienced person. [Middle English, from Old French, from Late Latin *gāius* and *gāia*†.]

Ja·ya Peak (jī′ə). Also **Mount Su·kar·no** (sŏŏ-kär′nō). Highest mountain in Indonesia (5,039 meters; 16,532 feet), situated in the Maoke range of West Irian.

jay·walk (jā′wôk′) *intr.v.* **-walked, -walking, -walks.** To cross a street illegally or recklessly. [From JAY (inexperienced person).] —**jay·walk·er** *n.*

jazz (jăz) *n.* **1.** A kind of native American music first played extemporaneously by black bands in Southern towns at the turn of the century. In most styles it has syncopated rhythms with solo and ensemble improvisations on basic tunes and chord patterns, and, in more recent styles, a highly sophisticated harmonic idiom. **2.** Big-band dance music, popular especially in the 1920's and 1930's. **3.** *Slang.* Animation; enthusiasm. **4.** *Slang.* Extreme exaggeration; nonsense: *all that jazz about his big deals.* —**and all that jazz.** *Slang.* And so on; and all that sort of thing. —*v.* **jazzed, jazzing, jazzes.** —*tr.* **1.** To play in a jazz style. **2.** *Slang.* To lie or exaggerate to. —*intr.* **1.** To play or dance to jazz. **2.** *Slang.* To lie or exaggerate. —**jazz up.** *Informal.* **1.** To play or arrange (music) in a more lively or improvised way, as by a jazz arrangement. **2.** To make more interesting; enliven. [20th century; origin obscure.] —**jazz·er** *n.*

jazz ballet *n.* **1.** A choreographed dance work performed to jazz music. **2.** This style of dancing.

jazz-rock (jăz′rŏk′) *n.* Music that blends jazz elements and the heavy repetitive rhythms of rock.

jazz·y (jăz′ē) *adj.* **-ier, -iest. 1.** Resembling jazz; rhythmical. **2.** *Slang.* Showy; vivid; flashy. —**jazz·i·ly** *adv.* —**jazz·i·ness** *n.*

J.C. 1. Jesus Christ. **2.** Julius Caesar.

J.C.D. 1. Doctor of Canon Law. [Latin *Juris Canonici Doctor*] **2.** Doctor of Civil Law. [Latin *Juris Civilis Doctor*]

J.C.S. Joint Chiefs of Staff.

jct. junction.

J.D. 1. Doctor of Laws. [Latin *Jurum Doctor*] **2.** juvenile delinquent.

jeal·ous (jĕl′əs) *adj.* **1.** Fearful or wary of being supplanted; apprehensive of loss of position or affection. **2.** Resentful or bitter in rivalry; envious. Often used with *of.* **3.** Possessively watchful; vigilant. **4.** Protective; solicitous. Used with *of* or *for: jealous for his daughter's welfare.* **5.** Concerning or arising from feelings of envy, apprehension, or bitterness: *jealous thoughts.* **6.** In religious contexts, intolerant of disloyalty or infidelity: *a jealous God.* [Middle English *gelus, ielus,* jealous, zealous for, from Old French *gelos, jelous,* from Medieval Latin *zēlōsus,* from Late Latin *zēlus,* from Greek *zēlos,* zeal.] —**jeal·ous·ly** *adv.* —**jeal·ous·ness** *n.*

jeal·ous·y (jĕl′ə-sē) *n., pl.* **-ies. 1.** A jealous attitude, especially toward a rival. **2.** Close watchfulness.

jean (jēn) *n.* **1.** A heavy, strong, twilled cotton, used in making trousers, uniforms, and work clothes. **2. jeans.** Trousers made of denim, jean, or some other hard-wearing fabric. In this sense, also called "blue jeans." [Earlier *iene fustian, geane fustian,* from Middle English *Jene, Gene,* Genoa, where it was first made.] —**jean** *adj.*

Jeanne d'Arc. See **Joan of Arc.**

Jeans (jēnz), **Sir James Hopwood** (1877–1946). British astronomer, physicist, and mathematician. He was noted for his work on the kinetic theory of gases and his investigations into the relationships between mathematical concepts and the natural world.

Jedda. See **Jiddah.**

Jeep (jēp) *n.* A trademark for a small, originally military motor vehicle with four-wheel drive, suitable for use on rough terrain. [Originally *G.P.*, "general purpose."]

jeer (jîr) *v.* **jeered, jeering, jeers.** —*intr.* To speak or shout derisively; mock. Often used with *at.* —*tr.* To deride; taunt. —*n.* Often **jeers.** A scoffing or taunting remark or shout. [Middle English *geere*†.] —**jeer·er** *n.* —**jeer·ing·ly** *adv.*

Jef·fers (jĕf′ərz), **(John) Robinson** (1887–1962). U.S. poet. Most of his narrative and lyric poems have a California setting, reflecting the many years he spent living on the coast near Carmel. Among his works are *Californians* (1916), *Tamar* (1924), *Cawdor* (1928), and *Solstice* (1935).

Jef·fer·son (jĕf′ər-sən), **Thomas** (1743–1826). Third president of the United States (1801–09). In 1776 Jefferson drafted the Declaration of Independence. As president, he acquired the Louisiana Purchase from France (1803). He was also a scholar, scientist, educator, lawyer, diplomat, political philosopher, and architect. Jefferson designed his own home, Monticello, and many buildings for the University of Virginia.

Jefferson City. Capital of Missouri. It is in the central part of the state on the south bank of the Missouri River. The city was a small river village when it was chosen as the capital in 1821; today the state government is the major employer.

jehad. Variant of **jihad.**

Jehan. See **Shah Jahan.**

Je·ho·vah (jī-hō′və). God, especially in Christian translations of the Old Testament. [From the Hebrew Tetragrammaton YHWH with the addition of the vowel points of ADONAI.]

Jehovah's Witnesses *n.* A religious sect founded in the United States during the late 19th century, the followers of which practice active evangelism, preach the imminent approach of the millennium, and are strongly opposed to war and to the authority of organized government in matters of conscience.

Je·ho·vist (jī-hō′vĭst) *n.* The author of portions of the Hexateuch, Yahwist (see).

je·june (jə-jōōn′) *adj.* **1.** Childish; immature; unsophisticated. **2.** Lacking in substance; insipid; dull: *"and there pour forth jejune words and useless empty phrases"* (Anthony Trollope). **3.** Not nourishing; insubstantial. [From Latin *jējūnus,* hungry, fasting.] —**je·june·ly** *adv.* —**je·june·ness** *n.*

je·ju·num (jə-jōō′nəm) *n., pl.* **-na** (-nə). The section of the small intestine between the duodenum and the ileum. [Medieval Latin *jējūnum (intestīnum),* "the fasting (intestine)," translation of Greek *nēstis,* the jejunum, from *nēstis,* fasting, so named because it was always found (in dissection) empty.] —**je·ju·nal** *adj.*

Je·kyll and Hyde (jĕk′əl, jē′kəl; hīd) *n. Informal.* A person who has two distinct alternating personalities. [After *The Strange Case of Dr. Jekyll and Mr. Hyde* (1886), novel by R.L. Stevenson.] —**Je·kyll-and-Hyde** *adj.*

jell (jĕl) *v.* **jelled, jelling, jells.** —*intr.* **1.** To become firm or gelatinous; congeal. **2.** *Informal.* To take shape or fall into place; become clear and definite; crystallize: *My ideas on the subject haven't jelled yet.* —*tr.* To cause to jell. [Back-formation from JELLY.]

jel·la·ba, jel·la·bah (jĕl′ə-bə) *n.* Also **djel·la·ba.** A long, loose garment with a hood worn by men, especially in North Africa. [Arabic.]

Jel·li·coe (jĕl′ĭ-kō), **John Rushworth Jellicoe, 1st Earl,** (1859–1935). British naval officer and governor of New Zealand

---

jellyfish

THE STINGING SEA CREATURE

The primitive jellyfish stuns its prey with poison

Jellyfish are found in all the oceans of the world, mostly near the coast. About 200 species have been identified. They range in diameter from 1.5 millimeters (¹/₁₆ inch) to 2 meters (6½ feet).

The creatures are not fish but primitive animals consisting of two bell-shaped layers of cells, separated by a thick layer of jelly. The jelly is made up almost entirely of water, and jellyfish soon dry out if they are stranded on beaches in the sun.

The bell-shaped body is fringed with stinging tentacles. When a jellyfish is touched by food or an enemy, cells in the tentacles shoot needlelike threads into the victim. Through these threads the jellyfish injects a poison that stings and stuns. Inside the fringe of tentacles there are usually four longer ones, which surround the mouth and convey food to it.

Jellyfish eggs are fertilized by sperm from smaller jellyfish drawn into the creature's mouth along with the food. The earliest development of the fertilized eggs takes place in pouches at the side of the mouth. Later, larvae are released from the pouches and settle on weeds or stones. They become polyps, from which small jellyfish bud off to grow into adults.

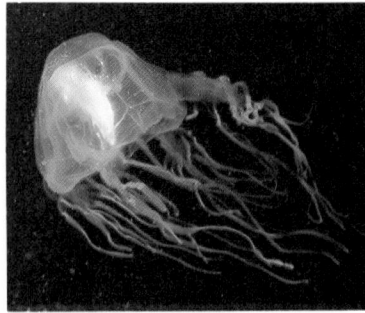

MOVEMENT *The sea wasp (Chironex fleckeri), a deadly jellyfish found off the coast of Queensland, Australia, moves itself along by contracting the two bell-shaped layers of cells.*

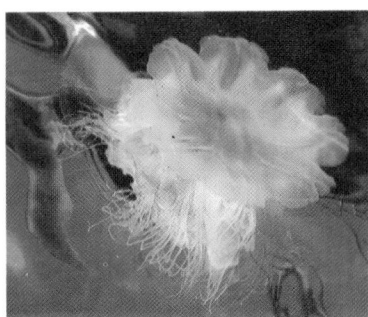

FEEDING *The tentacles of the lion's mane jellyfish (Cynea capillata) wait for food—plankton, fish, or shrimp. The fringe tentacles stun the prey and the central tentacles carry it to the mouth.*

(1920–24). He was commander in chief of the fleet that fought the Germans at Jutland (1916).

jel·lied (jĕl′ēd) *adj.* **1.** Chilled or otherwise congealed into jelly. **2.** Coated with jelly. **3.** Prepared or cooked within jelly.

jel·li·fy (jĕl′ə-fī′) *v.* **-fied, -fying, -fies.** —*intr.* To become jelly. —*tr.* To make into jelly. **—jel·li·fi·ca·tion** *n.*

jel·ly[1] (jĕl′ē) *n., pl.* **-lies. 1.** A soft, semisolid food substance with a resilient consistency, made by the setting of a liquid containing pectin or gelatin, or by the addition of gelatin or a similar substance to a liquid, especially: **a.** A fruit-flavored dessert set with gelatin. **b.** A preserve made from fruit juice and sugar set with pectin and used as a jam. **c.** A savory food such as aspic or calf's-foot jelly. **2.** Any substance with the consistency of jelly, such as a petroleum ointment. **3.** Anything similar or likened to jelly.
∼*v.* **jellied, -lying, -lies.** —*tr.* **1.** To make into or cause to become jelly. **2.** To set or prepare with jelly. —*intr.* To become jelly; set. [Middle English *geli, gely,* from Old French *gelee,* frost, jelly, from Vulgar Latin *gelāta* (unattested), from Latin, feminine past participle of *gelāre,* to freeze.]

jelly[2] *n. British Slang.* Gelignite.

jel·ly·bean (jĕl′ē-bēn′) *n.* A small bean-shaped candy with a hardened sugar coating over a chewy center.

jel·ly·fish (jĕl′ē-fĭsh′) *n., pl.* **-fishes** or collectively **jellyfish. 1.** Any of numerous usually free-swimming marine coelenterates of the class Scyphozoa, characteristically having a gelatinous, tentacled, often bell-shaped medusoid stage as the dominant or only phase of its life cycle. **2.** Any of various similar or related coelenterates or other organisms. **3.** *Informal.* A person who lacks force of character, resilience, or self-control.

jem·a·dar (jĕm′ə-där′) *n.* A native officer of the former British army in India with a rank corresponding to lieutenant. [Urdu *jama'dār* : Persian *jama'at,* body of men, from Arabic *jam',* collection + *dār,* holder, from Old Persian.]

jem·be (jĕm′bē) *n. East African.* A short-handled hoe with the blade set at right angles, used with a swinging, overarm motion to break up the soil. [Swahili.]

jemmy. *Chiefly British.* Variant of **jimmy.**

Je·na (yā′nə). An East German town situated on the Saale River. Fichte, Hegel, and others taught at its university (founded 1557–58). The town is also the headquarters of the Zeiss optical firm, founded in 1846. Napoleon defeated the Prussians at Jena (1806).

je ne sais quoi (zhə′nə-sā-kwä′, -sē-) *n. French.* An indefinable or unspecifiable distinctive quality. [Literally, "I don't know what."]

Jenghiz Khan. See **Genghis Khan.**

Jen·kins (jĕng′kĭnz, jĕn′-), **Roy Harris** (1920–). British politician. He was home secretary (1965), Chancellor of the Exchequer (1967–70), and president of the European Commission (1977–81). Jenkins was a founding member of the Social Democratic Party (launched 1981) and its first elected leader (1982–83).

Jen·ner (jĕn′ər), **Edward** (1749–1823). British physician and pioneer of vaccination. In 1796 he found that smallpox could be prevented by inoculation with the substance from cowpox lesions.

jen·net, gen·et (jĕn′ĭt) *n.* **1.** A small Spanish saddle horse. **2.** A female donkey or ass; a jenny. [Middle English *jennett, genett,* from Old French *genet,* from Spanish *jinete,* light horseman, from Arabic *Zenetī,* Berber tribe famed for horsemanship.]

jen·ny (jĕn′ē) *n., pl.* **-nies. 1.** A female donkey or ass. **2.** A female wren. **3.** A spinning jenny. **4.** A hand-operated machine for bending sheet metal at an angle. [From *Jenny,* pet form of *Jane.*]

je·on (jā′ôn′, jā-ôn′) *n., pl.* **jeon.** A monetary unit, the **jun** *(see).*

jeop·ard·ize (jĕp′ər-dīz′) *tr.v.* **-ized, -izing, -izes.** To expose to loss of or injury to; make vulnerable or precarious; imperil.

jeop·ard·y (jĕp′ər-dē) *n., pl.* **-ies. 1.** Danger or risk of loss or injury; peril; vulnerability. **2.** *Law.* The defendant's risk or danger of conviction when put on trial. —See Synonyms at **danger.** [Middle English *jeopartie,* even chance, from Old French *jeu parti,* "divided play, even chance" : *jeu,* game, from Latin *jocus,* jest, game + *parti,* past participle of *partir,* to divide, from Latin *partīre,* from *pars* (stem *part-*), PART.]

Jeph·thah (jĕf′thə, jĕp′-). A judge of Israel who sacrificed his daughter to fulfill a rash vow. Judges 11–12.

je·quir·i·ty bean (jĭ-kwĭr′ə-tē) *n.* The **rosary pea** *(see)* or any of its seeds. [From Tupi-Guarani *jekiritī.*]

Jer. Jeremiah (Old Testament).

jer·bo·a (jər-bō′ə) *n.* Any of various small, leaping rodents of the family Dipodidae, of desert regions of Asia and northern Africa, having long hind legs and a long, tufted tail. Also called "desert rat." [New Latin, from Medieval Latin *jerbōa,* from Arabic *yerbō', yarbu',* flesh of the loins (from the animal's highly developed thighs).]

jer·e·mi·ad (jĕr′ə-mī′əd) *n.* An elaborate and prolonged lamentation or a tale of woe. [French *jérémiade,* after *Jérémie,* JEREMIAH (the prophet who lamented the decline of morals).]

Jer·e·mi·ah[1] (jĕr′ə-mī′ə). Also in Douay Bible **Jer·e·mi·as** (-əs). A Major Prophet of the 7th and 6th centuries B.C. [Late Latin *Jeremias,* from Hebrew *Yirmayāh(ū),* "the Lord is exalted."]

Jeremiah[2] *n.* Also in Douay Bible **Jeremias.** *Abbr.* **Jer.** A book in the Old Testament containing the prophecies of Jeremiah.

Jeremiah[3] *n. Sometimes* **jeremiah.** A person given to bewailing the evils of the day or prophesying disasters to come. [After the Old Testament prophet.]

jer·e·pi·go (jĕr′ə-pē′gō) *n.* In South Africa, a sweet fortified red or white wine. [Portuguese *cheripiga.*]

Je·rez (de la Fron·te·ra) (hē-rāth′ dē lä frōn-tār′ä). A city in southwest Spain, situated on the Guadalete River in Andalusia. It is famous for the making of sherry, whose name derives from that of the city.

Jer·i·cho (jĕr′ĭ-kō′). Ancient city near the modern village of Al Ariha, just north of the Dead Sea, in the part of Jordan occupied by Israel in 1967. The earliest remains date back to before 7000 B.C. and probably represent the world's oldest known settlement. By the time the Israelites under Joshua captured Jericho (*c.* 1300 B.C.) it was a thriving Canaanite town. Herod the Great destroyed it (*c.* 30 B.C.) and later rebuilt it with a great fortress and palace in Hellenistic style.

jerk[1] (jûrk) *v.* **jerked, jerking, jerks.** —*tr.* **1.** To move (something) with a sharp, sudden, abrupt motion; give an abrupt thrust, push, pull, or twist to: *He jerked his head as a signal.* **2.** To throw or toss with a quick, abrupt motion. **3.** In weightlifting, to raise (the weight) from the height of the shoulder to above the head. **4.** To utter abruptly or sharply. Used with *out.* —*intr.* **1.** To move in sudden abrupt motions; jolt: *The train jerked ahead.* **2.** To make spasmodic motions: *His legs jerked from fatigue.*
∼*n.* **1.** A sudden, abrupt motion, such as a yank, tug, or twist. **2.** A jolting or lurching motion. **3.** *Physiology.* A sudden spasmodic, muscular movement, especially a reflex movement. **4. jerks.** Violent convulsive twitching and shaking, often resulting from excitement. **5. jerks.** *Informal.* **Chorea** *(see).* **6.** *Slang.* A stupid, objectionable, or fatuous person. [16th century : perhaps imitative.] **—jerk·er** *n.*

jerk[2] *tr.v.* **jerked, jerking, jerks.** To cut (meat) into long strips and dry in the sun or cure by exposing to smoke. [Back-formation from JERKY (cured meat).]

jer·kin (jûr′kən) *n.* **1.** A man's or woman's sleeveless and collarless jacket. **2.** A short, close-fitting coat or jacket, usually of leather, worn in former times. [16th century : origin obscure.]

jerk·y[1] (jûr′kē) *adj.* **-ier, -iest.** Characterized by jerks or jerking. **—jerk·i·ly** *adv.* **—jerk·i·ness** *n.*

jerky[2] *n.* Cured meat, **charqui** *(see).* [Earlier *jerkin beef,* from CHARQUI.]

jer·o·bo·am (jĕr′ə-bō′əm) *n.* An outsize wine bottle of varying capacity, usually holding about 4/5 of a gallon. [Humorously after *Jeroboam I,* king of northern Israel, who was a "mighty man of valor" (I Kings 11:28).]

Je·rome (jə-rōm′), **Saint,** born Sophronius Eusebius Hieronymus (*c.* 340–420). Dalmatian priest, scholar, and Doctor of the Church. His *Vulgate* was the first authentic Latin translation of the Bible from Hebrew.

Jer·ry (jĕr′ē) *n., pl.* **-ries.** *Chiefly British Slang.* A German; especially, a German soldier. [Alteration of GERMAN.]

jer·ry-build (jĕr′ē-bĭld′) *tr.v.* **-built** (-bĭlt′), **-building, -builds.** To build shoddily, flimsily, and cheaply. [19th century : origin obscure.] **—jer·ry-build·er** *n.*

jerry can *n.* A flat-sided can for storing or transporting liquids, used especially for motor fuels and having a capacity of between 20 and 23 liters (4.4 and 5 gallons). [*Jerry,* perhaps short for JEROBOAM.]

jer·sey (jûr′zē) *n., pl.* **-seys. 1.** A soft, plain-knitted fabric used for clothing. **2.** A knitted pullover shirt worn as a uniform in certain sports. **3.** A close-fitting knitted garment for the upper part of the body, usually made of wool. [Originally worn by the fishermen of JERSEY.]

Jer·sey[1] (jûr′zē). The largest of the Channel Islands, situated in the English Channel to the west of Normandy. The island was annexed by the Normans in A.D. 933, and French influence has persisted since autonomy was granted in 1204. Dairy goods, potatoes, and tomatoes are important products. The capital is St. Helier.

Jersey[2] *n.* Any of a breed of fawn-colored dairy cattle developed on the island of Jersey.

Jersey City. Coastal city in New Jersey, near the mouth of the Hudson River. It is connected to Manhattan by the Hudson River tunnels. Its industries include oil refining, chemicals, and paper.

Je·ru·sa·lem (jə-ro͞o′sə-ləm, -zə-ləm). *Arabic* **Al Quds** (äl ko͝ots). The capital of Israel, situated in the east of the country. Of immense historical and religious importance, it was the royal city of King David in the 10th century B.C. and was destroyed by Nebuchadnezzar in the 6th century. Subsequently rebuilt, it was occupied by Alexander the Great (332 B.C.). Jerusalem was taken by Pompey (65 B.C.), and Jesus Christ was crucified there under the Roman procurator Pontius Pilate. The city was in Islamic hands (7th–11th centuries A.D.) and made capital of a Crusader kingdom (1099) by Godfrey of Bouillon. Reconquered by Saladin (1187), Jerusalem remained in Islamic hands, apart from brief intervals (1229–39, 1243–44), until World War I. In 1917 the city was captured from the Turks by the British. In 1948 it was divided between Israel and Jordan. Israel occupied the Jordanian sector in the Six-Day War (1967), and its status remains disputed today. Jerusalem has innumerable mosques, churches, and synagogues, as well as holy places of great historical importance, such as the Western, or Wailing, Wall, sacred to the Jews as the major surviving part of the 2nd Hebrew Temple. The Mount of Olives and 4th-century Church of the Holy Sepulcher are among the many Christian sites, while the 7th-century Dome of the Rock is sacred to Islam.

Jerusalem artichoke *n.* **1.** A North American sunflower, *Helianthus tuberosus,* having yellow, rayed flowers and widely cultivated

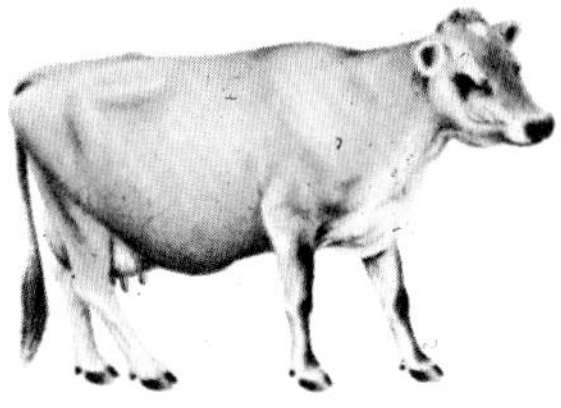

Jersey *These fine-boned dairy cattle originated on the British Channel Island of Jersey and are the only breed permitted there. They yield a rich milk high in butterfat, the oily substance from which butter is made.*

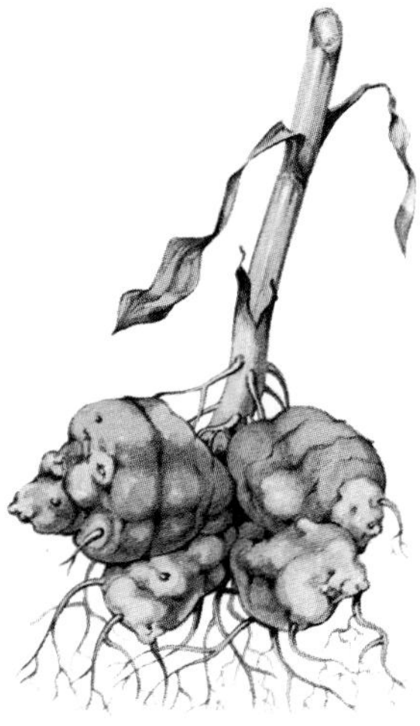

Jerusalem artichoke *The underground potatolike tubers of this plant, originally native to the United States, are eaten as a vegetable.*

PRONUNCIATION KEY

ă, pat; ā, pay; âr, care;
ä, father, are; b, bib;
ch, church; d, deed; ĕ, pet;
ē, be; f, fife; g, gag; h, hat;
hw, which; ĭ, pit; ī, pie;
îr, pier; j, judge; k, kick;
l, lid, needle; m, mum;
n, no, sudden; ng, thing;
ŏ, pot; ō, toe; ô, paw, for;
oi, noise; ou, out; o͝o, book;
o͞o, boot; p, pop; r, roar;
s, sauce; sh, ship, dish;
t, tight; th, thin, path;
th, this, bathe; ŭ, cut; ûr, fur;
v, valve; w, with; y, yes;
z, zebra, size; zh, vision;
ə, about, item, edible, gallop, circus, peaceful

IN FOREIGN WORDS:

à, *Fr.* ami; œ, *Fr.* feu, *Ger.* schön; ü, *Fr.* tu, *Ger.* über; KH, *Ger.* ich, *Scot.* loch; N, *Fr.* bon; y′, *Fr.* Compiègne

STRESS MARKS:

Primary stress: ′
in·cite′ (ĭn-sīt′)
Secondary stress: ′
in′sight′ (ĭn′sīt′)

for its edible tubers. **2.** The tuber of this plant, eaten as a vegetable. Also called "artichoke." [*Jerusalem*, alteration (by folk etymology) of Italian *girasole*, sunflower, GIRASOL.]

Jerusalem Bible *n.* A translation of the Bible into various modern European languages, initiated by the Biblical School of Jerusalem and used especially in the Roman Catholic Church.

Jerusalem cherry *n.* A small shrub, *Solanum pseudo-capsicum*, native to the Old World, bearing inedible reddish fruit and used as a house plant.

Jerusalem cross *n.* A cross with four arms, each terminating in a crossbar.

jess (jĕs) *n.* A short strap fastened around the leg of a hawk or other bird used in falconry, and to which a leash may be fastened. —*tr.v.* **jessed, jessing, jesses.** To put jesses on (a hawk). [Middle English *ges(se)*, from Old French *ges*, "a throwing," "something thrown around," from Vulgar Latin *jectus* (unattested), variant of Latin *jactus*, from *jacere*, to throw.]

jessamine. Variant of **jasmine.**

Jes·se (jĕs′ē). Father of King David. I Samuel 16.

Jesse tree *n.* A pictorial representation of the genealogy of Christ, proceeding from the stem of Jesse, found in church carvings and paintings, stained-glass windows, and manuscript illuminations.

POWER IN THE AIR FROM ESCAPING EXHAUST

The jet's transformation of the internal-combustion engine

The world's first jet aircraft was German—the Heinkel HE 178, test-flown in August 1939. It beat the jet plane of the English engineer Frank Whittle into the air by two years. But it is Whittle's design on which all postwar jet engines have been based. Whittle, who can therefore be regarded as the father of the jet airplane, took out his first jet engine patent in 1931 and by 1937 had built a prototype engine that was successfully tested.

The jet engine utilizes internal combustion, but in a new way. Air entering at the front has its pressure increased by about 20 times by a rotary compressor. Heated by the compression, the air passes into a combustion chamber, where it ignites injected fuel, usually kerosene. The resulting superheated gases expand rapidly and take the only way of escape open to them—through a constricting nozzle at the back. They

escape at a tremendous velocity, thrusting the aircraft forward with a force equal and opposite to the rearward thrust of the exhaust from the engine. As the gases rush toward the nozzle, they spin a turbine that drives the compressor.

World War II and the postwar boom in air travel brought great technological advances to the jet engine. The first flying prototypes developed a thrust of 450–900 kilograms (1,000–2,000 pounds). Today's turbofan bypass jets, used in jumbo jet aircraft, can deliver a thrust of 22,500 kilograms (50,000 pounds).

The jet engine has not only transformed air travel. It has also been used to power Hovercraft and ships. Most of the major car manufacturers have experimented with gas turbine (jet) engines, and since 1970 the Greyhound bus company has run over 2 million miles with experimental gas turbine buses.

TURBOFAN BYPASS JET

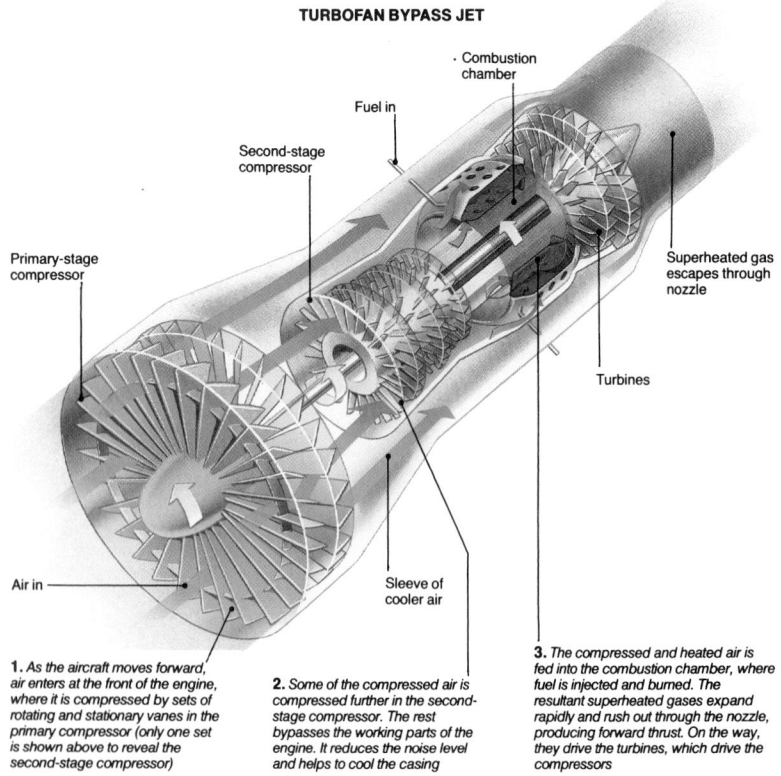

Combustion chamber

Fuel in

Second-stage compressor

Primary-stage compressor

Superheated gas escapes through nozzle

Turbines

Air in

Sleeve of cooler air

1. *As the aircraft moves forward, air enters at the front of the engine, where it is compressed by sets of rotating and stationary vanes in the primary compressor (only one set is shown above to reveal the second-stage compressor)*

2. *Some of the compressed air is compressed further in the second-stage compressor. The rest bypasses the working parts of the engine. It reduces the noise level and helps to cool the casing*

3. *The compressed and heated air is fed into the combustion chamber, where fuel is injected and burned. The resultant superheated gases expand rapidly and rush out through the nozzle, producing forward thrust. On the way, they drive the turbines, which drive the compressors*

[After JESSE, father of David and ancestor of Christ, whose birth, in Christian belief, is prophesied by Isaiah: "And there shall come forth a rod out of the stem of Jesse, and a branch shall grow out of his roots" (Isaiah 11:1).]

jest (jĕst) *n.* **1.** Something said or done to provoke amusement and laughter. **2.** A humorous or frivolous tone or mood: *spoken in jest.* **3.** A jeering remark; a taunt. **4.** An object of ridicule; a laughing stock. **5.** *Obsolete.* A notable exploit. —See Synonyms at **joke.** ~*v.* **jested, jesting, jests.** —*intr.* **1.** To act or speak playfully; make sport; joke. **2.** To make witty or amusing remarks. **3.** To utter scoffs or jeers; gibe. —*tr.* To make fun of; ridicule. [Middle English *geste*, deed, tale, from Old French *geste, jeste*, from Latin *gesta*, exploits, from *gerere*, to do.]

jest·er (jĕs′tər) *n.* One given to jesting; especially, a clown or buffoon employed by a king or nobleman at medieval courts.

Je·su (jē′zōō; *Latin* yā′sōō). *Poetic.* A form of the name *Jesus* used in addressing Him in hymns and prayers. [Late Latin.]

Jes·u·it (jĕzh′ōō-ĭt, jĕz′yōō-) *n.* **1.** A member of the Society of Jesus, a Roman Catholic order founded by St. Ignatius Loyola in 1534, active in missionary and other work. **2.** *Often* **jesuit.** One given to excessively subtle debating or legalistic arguments. Used derogatorily. [French *Jésuite*, from New Latin *Jesuita*, from JESUS.] —**Jes·u·it·i·cal** *adj.* —**Jes·u·it·i·cal·ly** *adv.*

Je·sus (jē′zəs), also called, in various contexts, "Jesus Christ," "Christ," "Christ Jesus," and "Jesus of Nazareth" (*c.* 4 B.C.–*c.* A.D. 29). Son of Mary; founder of Christianity; regarded by Christians as the son of God and the Messiah. ~*interj.* Also **Jesus Christ.** Used as an oath or to express outrage or surprise. [Late Latin *Jēsūs*, from Greek *Iēsous*, from Hebrew *yēshūa'*, from *Yəhōshūa'*, JOSHUA.]

Jesus freak *n.* A member of a movement among young Christians adapting traditional evangelicalism to a pop culture.

jet¹ (jĕt) *n.* **1.** A dense, black lignite that takes a high polish and is used for jewelry. **2.** A deep, dark black. [Middle English *ge(e)t, jeet*, from Norman French *geet*, Old French *jaiet*, from Latin *gagātēs*, from Greek *gagatēs*, "stone of *Gagai*" (town in Lycia).] —**jet** *adj.*

jet² *n.* **1.** A high-velocity fluid stream forced under pressure out of a small-diameter opening or nozzle. **2.** Something emitted in or as if in such a stream: *a jet of sparks.* **3.** An outlet, such as a spout or nozzle, for emitting such a stream. **4. a.** A jet-propelled vehicle; especially, a jet-propelled aircraft. **b.** A jet engine. ~*v.* **jetted, jetting, jets.** —*intr.* **1.** To spurt or squirt out in a jet or jets. **2.** To travel by jet aircraft. —*tr.* To propel outward or squirt, as under pressure. [Old French *jeter*, to spout forth, "to throw," from Vulgar Latin *jectāre* (unattested), from Latin *jactāre*, frequentative of Latin *jacere* (past participle *jactus*), to throw.]

jet black *n.* The color of jet; a deep dark black.

je·té (jə-tā′) *n.* A ballet step executed by springing from one leg to the other, with a backward kick of the first leg. [French, from past participle of *jeter*, to throw.]

jet engine *n.* **1.** Any engine that develops thrust by ejecting a jet, especially by ejecting a jet of gaseous combustion products. **2.** Such an engine, especially a gas turbine, equipped to consume atmospheric oxygen and used mainly to propel aircraft.

jet·foil (jĕt′foil′) *n.* A hydrofoil propelled by a jet engine.

jet lag *n.* The psychological dislocation and disruption of bodily rhythms caused by high-speed travel across several time zones by aircraft.

jet·lin·er (jĕt′lī′nər) *n.* A large passenger-carrying jet aircraft.

jet pipe *n.* A pipe or duct fitted to the rear end of a jet engine, through which the exhaust gases are discharged.

jet·port (jĕt′pôrt′, -pōrt′) *n.* An airport equipped for jet aircraft.

jet·pro·pelled (jĕt′prə-pĕld′) *adj.* Propelled or powered by one or more jet engines.

jet propulsion *n.* Propulsion derived from the high-velocity expulsion of fluid or gas in a jet; especially, propulsion by jet engines.

jet·sam (jĕt′səm) *n.* **1.** Cargo or equipment thrown overboard to lighten a ship in distress. **2.** Discarded cargo or equipment found washed ashore. Used in the phrase *flotsam and jetsam.* Compare **flotsam. 3.** Discarded odds and ends. [Earlier *jetson*, from JETTISON.]

jet set *n.* A social set made up of people who are rich, sophisticated, and who spend much of their time traveling from one place to another. —**jet-set·ter** *n.*

jet stream *n.* **1.** A high-altitude, narrow airstream in the troposphere, generally moving from a westerly direction. It may reach speeds of more than 400 kilometers, or 250 miles per hour. **2.** A high-speed stream of emitted fluid; a jet.

jet·ti·son (jĕt′ĭ-sən, -zən) *tr.v.* **-soned, -soning, -sons. 1.** To cast off or overboard. **2.** To discard or abandon (something unwanted or burdensome). ~*n.* **1.** The act of jettisoning. **2.** Jetsam. [From Middle English *jetteson*, a throwing overboard, from Norman French *getteson*, from Latin *jactātiō* (stem *jactātiōn*-), from *jactāre*, to throw. See **jet** (to propel).]

jet·ton (jĕt′ŏn) *n.* A stamped or engraved counter used especially as a chip in casinos. [French *jeton*, from *jeter*, to throw, add up (accounts).]

jet·ty¹ (jĕt′ē) *n., pl.* **-ties. 1.** A pier, groin, mole, or other structure projecting into a body of water to influence the current or tide or to protect a harbor or shoreline. **2.** A wharf. [Middle English *jette*, from Old French *jetee*, a jutting, projection, from the feminine past

participle of *jeter,* to throw, project. See **jet** (to propel).]
jetty² *adj.* Resembling jet, especially in color. —**jet·ti·ness** *n.*
jeu d'es·prit (zhœ dĕs-prē′) *n., pl.* **jeux d'esprit** (*pronounced as singular*). *French.* A display or stroke of wit, especially in literature.
jeu·nesse do·rée (zhœ-nĕs′ dô-rā′) *n. French. Used with a singular or plural verb.* Fashionable and wealthy young people. [Literally, "gilded youth."]
Jew (jōō) *n.* **1.** An adherent of Judaism in its religious or cultural aspects. **2.** A descendant of the Hebrew people. [Middle English *Giw, Ju,* from Old French *giu, juiu,* from Latin *Jūdaeus,* from Greek *Ioudaios,* from Aramaic *Yəhūdāy* and Hebrew *Yəhūdī,* after the tribe of *Yəhūdāh,* JUDAH.]
Jew-bait·ing (jōō′bā′tǐng) *n.* Systematic persecution of Jews. —**Jew-bait·ing** *adj.* —**Jew-bait·er** *n.*
jew·el (jōō′əl) *n.* **1.** A costly ornament of precious metal or gems used as an adornment. **2.** A precious stone; a gemstone. **3.** A small gem or gem substitute used as a bearing in a watch. **4.** A person or thing that is treasured or esteemed. **5.** A decorative glass boss in a stained glass window.
~*tr.v.* **jeweled, -eling, -els** or *chiefly British* **-elled, -elling. 1.** To adorn with jewels. **2.** To fit (a watch, for example) with jewels. [Middle English *iuel, gewel,* from Norman French *juel,* perhaps from *jeu,* game, jest, from Latin *jocus.*]
jew·el·fish (jōō′əl-fĭsh′) *n., pl.* **-fish** or **-fishes** or collectively **jewelfish.** A small, brilliantly colored freshwater cichlid fish, *Hemichromis bimaculatus,* of tropical Africa, popular in home aquariums.
jew·el·er (jōō′ə-lər) *n.* Also *chiefly British* **jew·el·ler. 1.** A person who makes, repairs, or deals in jewelry. **2.** A person who is skilled in the art of cutting, polishing, and setting gemstones.
jeweler's rouge *n.* Finely powdered ferric oxide, used as a metal polish.
jew·el·ry (jōō′əl-rē) *n.* Also *chiefly British* **jew·el·ler·y. 1.** Jewels collectively. **2.** Any objects, such as bracelets, rings, necklaces, or the like, worn or used for adornment.
jew·el·weed (jōō′əl-wēd′) *n.* Any of several plants of the genus *Impatiens,* having yellowish, spurred flowers and seed pods that burst open at a touch when ripe. Also called "touch-me-not."
Jew·ess (jōō′ĭs) *n.* A Jewish woman or girl. Sometimes considered offensive. —See Usage note at **-ess.**
jew·fish (jōō′fĭsh′) *n. pl.* **-fishes** or collectively **jewfish.** Any of several large, dark marine fishes of the family Serranidae, such as *Epinephelus itajara,* of tropical Atlantic waters, and the Australian **mulloway** *(see).*
Jew·ish (jōō′ĭsh) *adj.* Of, concerning, or characteristic of the Jews, their customs, or their religion.
~*n.* Yiddish. Not in technical usage. —**Jew·ish·ly** *adv.* —**Jew·ish·ness** *n.*
Jewish Autonomous Region. Also **Bi·ro·bi·dzhan** (bǐr′ō-bǐ-jän′, -jän′). An autonomous region of the Russian S.F.S.R., created in 1934 as a Siberian area of settlement for Soviet Jews. Its remoteness and severe climate discouraged colonization, and Jews remain in the minority.
Jewish calendar *n.* The lunisolar calendar used by the ancient Hebrews and for religious purposes today, calculating the date from the supposed year of creation, 3761 B.C. and based on a meteoric cycle of 19 years, with the 3rd, 6th, 8th, 11th, 14th, 17th, and 19th years of each cycle designated leap years. Also called "Hebrew calendar." See feature at **calendar.**
Jew·ry (jōō′rē) *n.* **1.** Jews collectively; the Jewish people. **2.** The district of a medieval city inhabited by Jews.
jew's-ear (jōōz′ĭr′) *n.* An edible fungus, *Auricularia auricula,* having a brown or flesh-colored saucer-shaped fruiting body and growing on wood.
jew's-harp, jews'-harp (jōōz′härp′) *n.* A small musical instrument with a lyre-shaped metal frame that is held between the teeth when played, and a projecting steel tongue that is plucked to produce a soft, twanging sound. [Earlier *jew's trump,* perhaps alteration (influenced by JEW) of Dutch *jeugdtromp,* children's trumpet.]
jez·e·bel (jĕz′ə-bĕl′, -bəl) *n. Sometimes* **Jezebel.** A shamelessly immoral or scheming woman. [After JEZEBEL.]
Jez·e·bel (jĕz′ə-bĕl′, -bəl). Also in Douay Bible **Jez·a·bel.** Phoenician princess of the 9th century B.C. who as Ahab's wife and queen of Israel encouraged idolatry and the killing of the prophets of Israel. I Kings 16:31, 18:3.
JHVH, JHWH. Variants of YHWH.
-ji *suffix. Indian.* Used with a person's name as a sign of respect; for example, *Gandhiji.* [Hindi.]
Jiang, Jie·shi (jyäng′ jā′shə), also **Chiang Kai-shek** (chăng′ kī-shĕk′) (1887-1975). Chinese general and statesman. He joined the army and was active in the 1911 revolution. In 1918 he joined the Guomindang (Nationalist People's Party), and became its leader after the death of Sun Zhongshan (Sun Yat-sen) in 1925. In 1926 he allied his forces with the Communists against the Chinese warlords, but a year later purged left-wingers from his own forces, and the alliance broke up (1928). Later he waged war on the Communists. After World War II civil war broke out again (1946-49), and when the Guomindang was defeated Jiang withdrew to Taiwan. He was president of Taiwan until his death.
Jiang Qing (jyäng′ chĭng′), also **Chiang Ch'ing** (chăng′ chĭng′) (1914–). Wife of Mao Ze-dong (Tse-tung). She was an actress before she married him in 1939. After his death (1976) she was arrested, expelled from the Chinese Communist Party, and given a suspended death sentence for plotting rebellion.

Jiang·su or **Chiang·su** or **Kiang·su** (jyäng′sōō′). Province of eastern China. It largely comprises the deltas of the Huang He and Chang Jiang, and is one of the country's smallest and most densely populated provinces. Nanjing is the capital.
Jiang·xi or **Chiang·hsi** or **Kiang·si** (jyäng′sē′). Province of central southern China. It is a major rice-growing area, with resources of coal, uranium, tin, and lead. The capital is Nanchang. The southern part of the province was held by Mao Ze-dong's Communists (1930-34) during the war against the Guomindang, and it was from here that the Long March was begun.
jiao (jou) *n., pl.* **jiao.** A monetary unit, the *fen (see).*
jib¹ (jĭb) *n.* **1.** A triangular sail stretching from the foretopmast head to the jib boom and in small craft to the bowsprit or the bow. **2. a.** The arm of a mechanical crane. **b.** The boom of a derrick. —**the cut of someone's jib.** *Informal.* Someone's appearance, style, or manner. [17th century : origin obscure.]
jib² *intr.v.* **jibbed, jibbing, jibs. 1.** To draw back, balk, or show reluctance. Often used with *at.* **2.** To stop short and turn restively from side to side; shy. Used of an animal.
~*n.* Also **jib·ber** (jĭb′ər). An animal that jibs. [19th century : origin obscure.]
jibbah. Variant of **jubbah.**
jib boom *n.* A spar forming a continuation of the bowsprit.
jibe¹ (jĭb) *v.* **jibed, jibing, jibes.** Also **gybe.** —*intr.* To shift a fore-and-aft sail from one side of a vessel to the other while sailing before the wind; to jib. —*tr.* To cause to jibe.
~*n.* The act of jibing. [From obsolete Dutch *gijben†.*]
jibe² *intr.v.* **jibed, jibing, jibes.** *Informal.* To be in accord; harmonize; agree. [19th century : origin obscure.]
jibe³. Variant of **gibe** (taunt).
Jibuti. See Djibouti.
Jid·dah (jĭd′ə). Also **Jed·da** (jĕd′ə) or **Jud·dah** (jŭd′ə). A Red Sea port in western Saudi Arabia. It serves Mecca, which lies about 74 kilometers (46 miles) inland.
jif·fy (jĭf′ē) *n., pl.* **-fies.** Also **jiff** (jĭf). *Informal.* A moment; no time at all: *I'll be there in a jiffy.* —See Synonyms at **moment.** [18th century : origin obscure.]
jig (jĭg) *n.* **1. a.** Any of various lively kicking or leaping dances, usually in 6/8 time. **b.** A piece of music for such a dance. Also called "gigue." **2.** A joke or trick. **3.** A fishing lure, usually made of metal and having one or more hooks, that darts or bobs about when pulled through the water. **4.** An apparatus for cleaning or separating ore by agitation in water. **5.** A device for guiding a tool or for holding machine work in place.
~*v.* **jigged, jigging, jigs.** —*intr.* **1.** To dance or play a jig. **2.** To move or bob up and down jerkily and rapidly. **3.** To operate a jig, as in fishing, machine work, or refining ore. —*tr.* **1.** To shake or jerk up and down or to and fro. **2.** To machine with the aid of a jig. **3.** To separate or clean (ore) by shaking a jig. [16th century : origin obscure.]
jig·ger¹ (jĭg′ər) *n.* **1.** A person who jigs or operates a jig. **2. a.** A small measure for alcoholic drinks, especially spirits. **b.** A small quantity of alcoholic drink. **3.** A short golf club with an iron head. **4.** In fishing, mining, or mechanics, a jig. **5.** Any device that operates with a jerking or jolting motion, such as a drill. **6.** *Nautical.* **a.** A light tackle. **b.** A small sail, set in the stern of a yawl, for example. **c.** A boat having such a sail. **d.** A jigger mast *(see).* **7.** *Informal.* Any trivial article or device whose name eludes one. **8.** A rest for a billiard cue.
jigger² *n.* **1.** A mite, the **chigger** *(see).* **2.** A flea, the **chigoe** *(see).*
jig·gered (jĭg′ərd) *adj. Slang.* **1.** Very surprised. Used as a mild oath: *I'll be jiggered.* **2.** Exhausted; tired out.
jigger mast *n. Nautical.* **1.** The short after mast from which the jigger sail is set on a ketch or yawl. Also called "mizzenmast." **2.** The fourth mast aft on a four-masted ship. Also called "jigger."
jig·ger·y-po·ker·y (jĭg′ə-rē-pō′kə-rē) *n.* Underhand scheming or behavior; trickery. [From Scottish dialect *joukery-pawkery,* based on dialect *jouk†,* to duck, dodge.]
jig·gle (jĭg′əl) *v.* **-gled, -gling, -gles.** —*intr.* To move or rock lightly up and down or to and fro in an unsteady, jerky manner. —*tr.* To cause to move in this manner.
~*n.* A jiggling motion. [Frequentative of JIG (verb).]
jig·saw (jĭg′sô′) *n.* **1.** A saw, often power-driven, with a narrow, vertical reciprocating blade, used to cut sharp curves. **2.** A jigsaw puzzle.
jigsaw puzzle *n.* A puzzle consisting of a picture pasted on cardboard or wood and cut into numerous interlocking pieces, the object being to reassemble the picture by fitting the pieces together. Also called "jigsaw," "picture puzzle."
ji·had, je·had (jĭ-häd′) *n.* **1.** A Muslim holy war against infidels. **2.** A crusade. [Arabic *jihād.*]
Ji·lin or **Ki·rin** (jē′lĭn). Province of northeast China. It lies on the fertile Manchurian Plain and is a major cereal producer. It also has extensive coal and iron deposits, the basis of a large industrial region centered on the cities of Changchun (the capital) and Jilin.
jil·la·roo (jĭl′ə-rōō) *n., pl.* **-roos.** *Australian Informal.* A female jackeroo. [Alteration of JACKEROO, with allusion to *Jack and Jill.*]
jilt (jĭlt) *tr.v.* **jilted, jilting, jilts.** To reject or cast aside (a lover), especially after an engagement.
~*n.* A woman who discards a lover. [17th century : origin obscure.]
jim-crow, Jim-Crow (jĭm′krō′) *adj. Slang.* **1.** Favoring or promoting the segregation of blacks: *jim-crow policies.* **2.** For blacks only:

jet *This hard black stone, which has been modeled into jewelry at least since Roman times, is a type of coal. These pieces were made in Britain during the Roman occupation.*

a jim-crow waiting room. Usually considered offensive in both senses. [From JIM CROW.]

Jim Crow *n. Slang.* **1. a.** The systematic practice of segregating and suppressing black people. **b.** A black person. Used derogatorily in both senses. **2.** A device for straightening iron bars or rails. [After *Jim Crow,* a character in an act by Thomas D. Rice (1808–60), U.S. entertainer who based it on an anonymous 19th-century song called "Jim Crow."] —**Jim-Crow·ism** *n.*

Ji·mé·nez (hē-mě′něs), **Juan Ramón** (1881–1958). Spanish poet. His best-known work is *Platero y Yo* (1917), relating his wanderings through Andalusia with his donkey. In 1956 he received the Nobel Prize for literature.

jim-jams (jĭm′jămz′) *pl.n. Slang.* **1.** A state of extreme nervousness; the jitters. **2.** Delirium tremens. [Whimsical reduplication.]

jim·my (jĭm′ē) *n., pl.* **-mies.** Also *chiefly British* **jem·my** (jěm′ē). A short crowbar with curved ends, especially when regarded as a burglar's tool. —*tr.v.* **jimmied, -mying, -mies.** Also *chiefly British* **jemmy.** To pry open with or as if with a jimmy. [From the pet name of *James.*]

Jimmy *n. Scottish Informal.* Used as a humorous form of address to a man whose name is not known by the speaker. [Pet form of *James,* considered as a very common Scottish name.]

jim·son·weed (jĭm′sən-wēd′) *n.* A coarse, poisonous plant, *Datura stramonium,* having large, trumpet-shaped white or purplish flowers and prickly fruit. Also called "stramonium," "thorn apple." [From archaic *Jamestown weed,* named for JAMESTOWN, Virginia.]

Ji·nan or **Chi·nan** or **Tsi·nan** (jē′nän′). Capital of Shandong province, northeast China, situated in the Huang He valley. A rail and marketing center of a rich farming area, its products include iron and steel, flour, textiles, chemicals, and agricultural machinery.

Jinghiz Khan. See **Genghis Khan.**

jin·gle (jĭng′gəl) *v.* **-gled, -gling, -gles.** —*intr.* **1.** To make a repeated tinkling or ringing metallic sound. **2.** To have the sound of a verse jingle. —*tr.* To cause to jingle. —*n.* **1. a.** The tinkling sound produced by light bits of metal striking together: *the jingle of sleigh bells.* **b.** Something resembling or suggesting this. **2.** A simple, repetitious, catchy rhyme or song, especially one used in an advertisement. [Middle English *ginglen* (probably imitative).]

jin·go (jĭng′gō) *n., pl.* **-goes.** One who vociferously supports his country, especially one who supports a belligerent foreign policy; an uncritical patriot; a chauvinist. Also used adjectivally: *jingo policies.* —**by jingo.** Used to express surprise or for emphasis. [From the refrain of a music-hall song sung in England by supporters of Benjamin Disraeli's policy against Russia in 1878: *"We don't want to fight, yet by Jingo! if we do,/ We've got the ships, we've got the men, and got the money too."* Originally used in conjuring, perhaps euphemistic for *by Jesus.*] —**jin·go·ish** *adj.* —**jin·go·ism** *n.* —**jin·go·ist** *n.* —**jin·go·is·tic** *adj.*

jink (jĭngk) *intr.v.* **jinked, jinking, jinks.** To make a quick evasive turn, especially when flying or playing Rugby football. —*n.* **1.** A sudden evasive turn. **2. jinks.** Boisterous play; frolic. Used chiefly in the phrase *high jinks.* [18th century (originally Scottish): perhaps imitative of quick movement.]

Jin·men or **Chin·men** (jĭn′měn′, chěn′mün′). Also **Que·moy** (kē-moi′). Island group, a possession of Taiwan, lying in the Taiwan Strait close to the mainland of China. It remained in Nationalist hands after 1949 and is still a military base. Its bombardment from the mainland (1949–58) served only to strengthen defense ties between Taiwan and the United States.

Jin·nah (jĭn′ə), **Mohammed Ali** (1876–1948). First governor-general of Pakistan. When India was about to achieve independence from Britain, Jinnah feared the Muslim minority would be kept from power by the Hindus, and he insisted on a Muslim homeland. Pakistan was established in 1947.

jin·ni, jin·ee (jĭn′ē, jĭ-nē′) *n., pl.* **jinn** (jĭn). Also **djin·ni, djin·ny,** *pl.* **djinn.** In Muslim legend, a spirit capable of assuming human or animal form and exercising supernatural influence over men. [Arabic *jinnīy.*]

jin·rick·sha (jĭn-rĭk′shô) *n.* Also **jin·rik·i·sha.** A rickshaw *(see).* [Japanese : *jin,* man + *riki,* power + *sha,* vehicle.]

jinx (jĭngks) *n. Informal.* Something or someone believed to bring bad luck or misfortune. —*tr.v.* **jinxed, jinxing, jinxes.** *Informal.* To bring bad luck to. [Perhaps from *Jynx,* genus name of the wryneck, from Greek *iunx,* wryneck (a bird used in magic), from *iuzein,* to call, cry.]

ji·pi·ja·pa (hē′pē-hä′pä) *n.* A palmlike plant, *Carludovica palmata,* of Central and South America, having long-stalked, fanlike leaves used to make Panama hats. [Spanish, after *Jipijapa,* Ecuador.]

jit·ney (jĭt′nē) *n., pl.* **-neys.** *Informal.* **1.** A small bus or automobile that transports passengers on a route for a small fare. **2.** *Archaic.* A nickel. [Origin unknown.]

jit·ter (jĭt′ər) *intr.v.* **-tered, -tering, -ters.** *Informal.* To be nervous or uneasy; fidget. [20th century : origin obscure.] —**jit·ter·y** *adj.*

jit·ter·bug (jĭt′ər-bŭg′) *n. Slang.* **1.** A fast dance performed to quick-tempo jazz or swing music and consisting of various two-step patterns embellished with twirls and throws, especially popular in the 1940's. **2.** A person who does such a dance. **3.** A highly nervous person. —*intr.v.* **jitterbugged, -bugging, -bugs.** To dance the jitterbug. [JITTER + BUG.]

jit·ters (jĭt′ərz) *pl.n. Informal.* A fit of nervousness; anxiety.

jiujitsu, jiujutsu. Variants of **jujitsu.**

Jiu·long or **Chiu-lung** (jyŏ′lŏng′). Also **Kow·loon** (kou′lōon′). A port and peninsula on mainland China, forming part of the British crown colony of Hong Kong. It was ceded to Britain in 1860.

jive (jīv) *n. Slang.* **1. a.** A style of lively, fast jazz music. **b.** A fast, jerky dance, similar in style to rock'n'roll, originally performed to jive music and later to rock'n'roll music. **2. a.** Glib or deceptive talk: *Don't give me that jive.* **b.** The jargon of jazz musicians and enthusiasts. [20th century : origin obscure.] —**jive** *v.*

j.n.d. *Psychology.* just noticeable difference.

jnr., Jnr. junior.

jnt. joint.

jo, joe (jō) *n., pl.* **joes.** *Scottish.* A sweetheart. [16th century : variant of JOY.]

Joan of Arc (jōn; ärk), **Saint** (1412–31). *French* **Jeanne d'Arc** (zhän därk′). French heroine, known as the Maid of Orléans. She led the French resistance that forced the English to raise the siege of Orléans (1429). The same year, aged 17, she led an army of 12,000 to Rheims and had the dauphin crowned Charles VII. She was captured and sold to the English (1430) by the Burgundians and tried for heresy and sorcery. Joan was burned at the stake in Rouen (1431). She was beatified (1909) and canonized (1920).

job¹ (jŏb) *n.* **1.** An action requiring some exertion; a task; an undertaking. **2.** An activity performed in exchange for payment; especially, one performed regularly as one's trade, occupation, or profession. **3. a.** A specific piece of work to be done for a set fee. **b.** The object to be worked on. **c.** Anything resulting from or produced by work. **4.** A position in which one is employed. **5. a.** An assigned or assumed duty or responsibility: *It was her job to get her younger brother ready for school.* **b.** Anything that must be done: *Stitching up her cuts was a very messy job.* **6.** *Informal.* A difficult or strenuous task: *We had a job getting the piano up the stairs.* **7.** *Informal.* A thing that is notable of its kind: *driving a nice little red job.* **8.** *Chiefly British Informal.* A state of affairs: *It's a good job you called the fire brigade.* **9.** *Informal.* A criminal act, especially a robbery: *pull a bank job.* **10.** Something done ostensibly in the public interest, but actually for private gain or advantage. —See Synonyms at **task.** —**just the job.** *Chiefly British.* Precisely what is or was required. —**lie down on the job.** *Informal.* To neglect the responsibilities of one's job. —**on the job.** *Informal.* **1.** Working at one's occupation or task; at work. **2.** Paying close attention to one's work or responsibilities. —*v.* **jobbed, jobbing, jobs.** —*intr.* **1.** To do odd jobs or piecework: *a jobbing builder.* **2.** To act as a middleman or jobber. **3.** To exploit a position of trust for private advantage. —*tr.* **1. a.** To purchase (merchandise) from manufacturers and sell it to retailers. **b.** *Chiefly British.* To buy and sell (stocks and shares) as a jobber. **2.** To arrange for (contracted work) to be done in portions by others; subcontract. **3.** To transact (official business) dishonestly for private profit. [Originally a piece of work, perhaps from obsolete *job†,* "piece."]

job² *v.* **jobbed, jobbing, jobs.** *Archaic.* —*tr.* To jab. —*intr.* To make a jab. —*n. Archaic.* A jab. [Middle English *jobben†.*]

Job¹ (jōb). In the Old Testament, an upright man whose faith in God survived the test of repeated calamities, and who is taken as a model of patient endurance: *the patience of Job.* [Hebrew *Iyyobh,* "hated, persecuted," from *ayabh,* to be hostile.]

Job² *n.* A book of the Old Testament, recounting the story of Job.

job·ber (jŏb′ər) *n.* **1.** One who buys merchandise from manufacturers and sells it to retailers. **2.** A person who does piecework or odd jobs. **3.** A public official who exploits his position for personal gain. **4.** *Chiefly British.* A middleman in the exchange of stocks and securities among brokers; a stockjobber.

job·ber·y (jŏb′ə-rē) *n.* Corruption among public officials. [From JOB (to seek graft).]

job·hold·er (jŏb′hōl′dər) *n.* One who has a regular job.

job-hop (jŏb′hŏp′) *intr.v.* **-hopped, -hopping, -hops.** To change jobs frequently. —**job-hop·per** *n.*

job·less (jŏb′lĭs) *adj.* Unemployed. —**job·less·ness** *n.*

job lot *n.* **1.** Miscellaneous goods sold in one lot. **2.** Any collection of unsorted and usually inferior items.

job reservation *n.* In South Africa, the practice of limiting various categories of employment to particular race groups, thereby effectively excluding blacks from many trades and professions.

Job's comforter *n.* One who discourages or saddens while seemingly offering sympathy or comfort. [From JOB, who was treated in such a way by his friends.]

job·shar·ing (jŏb′shâr′ĭng) *n.* A practice whereby the responsibility for a job is shared between two alternating part-time workers.

Job's-tears (jōbz′tîrz′) *n.* Used with a singular or plural verb. **1.** A grass, *Coix lacryma-jobi,* of tropical Asia, having edible seeds enclosed in beadlike modified leaves. **2.** The seeds of this plant. **3.** The beadlike, seed-containing structures of this plant, used for ornamentation.

Jo·cas·ta (jō-kăs′tə). *Greek Legend.* A Theban queen who unknowingly married her own son Oedipus.

jock¹ (jŏk) *n. Informal.* A jockey. [Short for JOCKEY.]

jock² *n.* **1.** A jockstrap *(see).* **2.** *Slang.* **a.** A male athlete, especially in college. **b.** A virile and promiscuous man; a playboy.

Jock (jŏk) *n. Scottish.* A Scotsman. Often used as a familiar, humorous, or derogatory form of address. [Scottish form of *Jack.*]

jock·ey (jŏk′ē) *n., pl.* **-eys.** A person who rides horses in races, especially as a profession.

~v. **jockeyed, -eying, -eys.** —*tr.* **1.** To ride (a horse) as jockey. **2.** To direct or maneuver by cleverness or skill. **3.** To trick; outwit. —*intr.* **1.** To ride a horse in a race. **2.** To maneuver for a certain position or advantage. **3.** To employ trickery; cheat; swindle. [Originally "lad," diminutive of Scottish *Jock,* JACK (a man).]

jock·strap, jock strap (jŏk′străp′) *n.* An elastic support for the male genitals, sometimes employing a rigid metallic cup, worn especially in athletic or other strenuous activity. Also called "athletic supporter," "jock." [Slang *jock,* "penis," earlier *jockum*† + STRAP.]

jo·cose (jō-kōs′) *adj.* **1.** Given to good-humored joking; merry. **2.** Characterized by joking; humorous. [Latin *jocōsus,* from *jocus,* jest, joke.] —**jo·cose·ly** *adv.* —**jo·cos·i·ty** (jō-kŏs′ə-tē) *n.*

joc·u·lar (jŏk′yə-lər) *adj.* **1.** Given to or characterized by joking. **2.** Meant in jest; facetious. —See Synonyms at **jolly.** [Latin *joculāris,* from *joculus,* diminutive of *jocus,* jest, joke.] —**joc·u·lar·i·ty** *n.* —**joc·u·lar·ly** *adv.*

joc·und (jŏk′ənd, jō′kənd) *adj.* Having a cheerful disposition or quality; merry. [Middle English, from Old French, from Late Latin *jōcundus,* from Latin *jūcundus,* agreeable, pleasant, from *juvāre,* to entertain, delight, AID.] —**joc·und·ly** *adv.* —**jo·cund·i·ty** *n.*

Jodh·pur (jŏd′pŏŏr′). A city in northwestern India, in Rajasthan state. Founded in 1459, it became the capital of a large princely state and now has a university (founded 1962).

jodh·pur boots (jŏd′pər) *pl.n.* Short ankle-high leather boots worn with jodhpurs for riding.

jodh·purs (jŏd′pərz) *pl.n.* Wide-hipped riding breeches of heavy cloth, fitting tightly at the knees and ankles. [From JODHPUR.]

Jo·do (jō′dō′) *n.* Pure Land Buddhism (see). [Japanese.]

Joe Blow *n. Informal.* The average man; the man in the street.

Jo·el[1] (jō′əl). A Hebrew Minor Prophet.

Joel[2] *n.* A book of the Old Testament containing Joel's prophecies of the judgment of Judah.

jo·ey (jō′ē) *n., pl.* **-eys. 1.** *Australian.* **a.** A young kangaroo or other young animal. **b.** A young child. **2.** *New Zealand.* An opossum. [Native Australian name.]

jog[1] (jŏg) *v.* **jogged, jogging, jogs.** —*tr.* **1.** To jar or move by shoving, bumping, or jerking. **2.** To give a slight push or shake to; nudge. **3.** To stimulate; stir (one's memory, for example). —*intr.* **1.** To ride at a steady, slow trot. **2.** To run at a moderate pace, especially for exercise. **3.** To proceed in a leisurely, monotonous, or uneventful way.
~*n.* **1.** A slight jolt or shake. **2.** A nudge. **3.** A slow, steady pace; a trot. [Middle English (probably imitative).] —**jog·ger** *n.*

jog[2] *n.* **1.** A protruding or receding part in a surface or line. **2.** An abrupt change in direction.
~*intr.v.* **jogged, jogging, jogs.** To turn sharply; veer. [Perhaps variant of JAG.]

jog·ging (jŏg′ĭng) *n.* Exercise that consists of running at a slow, regular pace or alternately running and walking.

jog·gle[1] (jŏg′əl) *v.* **-gled, -gling, -gles.** —*tr.* To shake or jar repeatedly. —*intr.* To move with a shaking or jolting motion.
~*n.* A shaking or jolting motion. [Frequentative of JOG.]

joggle[2] *n.* **1.** A joint between two pieces of building material formed by a notch and a fitted projection. **2.** The notch or the projecting piece used in such a joint.
~*tr.v.* **joggled, -gling, -gles.** To join or attach by means of a joggle. [From JOG (protruding part).]

Jog·ja·kar·ta (jŏg′yə-kär′tə). Also **Djok·ja·kar·ta** (jŏk′-). A city in Indonesia, situated in south-central Java. Palaces and temples have been located in the surrounding area since the 8th century B.C. and include the magnificent Buddhist monument of Borobudur. Founded in 1755, Jogjakarta was the capital of the Indonesian Republic (1946–49). It has a university (founded 1949) and markets tea, tobacco, and handicrafts.

jog trot *n.* **1.** A moderate, steady, jolting pace; a jog. **2.** A regular, humdrum way of living or of doing something.

Jo·han·nes·burg (jō-hăn′ĭs-bûrg′, yō-hä′nĭs-). The largest city in South Africa, situated in the Transvaal in the northeast of the country. It lies on the Witwatersrand and was founded in 1886 when gold was discovered. Now the center of the world's largest gold field, Johannesburg is at the heart of South Africa's most highly industrialized region.

Jo·han·nine (jō-hăn′īn, -ən) *adj.* Pertaining to or designating those parts of the New Testament attributed to St. John. [From Latin *johannīnus,* from *Johannes,* JOHN.]

john (jŏn) *n. Slang.* **1.** A toilet. **2.** A prostitute's customer. [From *John* (masculine name).]

John[1] (jŏn) *n.* **1.** A book of the New Testament, the fourth Gospel, attributed to St. John. **2.** Any of three New Testament Epistles attributed to St. John.

John[2], also known as "John Lackland" (c. 1167–1216). King of England from 1199. He was the youngest son of Henry II and intrigued against his father and then his brother, Richard I. Under him, the English lost most of their possessions in France. The barons rose against John and forced him to set his seal on the Magna Carta (1215), a cornerstone of English liberty.

John, Augustus Edwin (1878–1961). British painter. He often painted gypsies, as in *Encampment on Dartmoor* (1906). He painted portraits of his wife Dorelia, of George Bernard Shaw (1914), Thomas Hardy (1923), and Dylan Thomas (c. 1936). He was elected to the Royal Academy in 1928.

John, Saint, also known as "the Evangelist," "the Divine." One of the Twelve Apostles; reputed author of the 4th Gospel, three epistles, and the Book of Revelation.

John XXIII, Pope, born Angelo Giuseppe Roncalli (1881–1963). He became pope in 1958. He called a general council of the Church, the first for almost a century, and worked for world peace and Christian unity. See **Vatican Council.**

John Bar·ley·corn (bär′lē-kôrn′) *n.* A personification of malt liquor or of alcoholic beverages in general.

John Birch Society (bûrch) *n.* An ultraconservative anticommunist organization established in the United States by Robert H.W. Welch, Jr., in 1958. [Named after *John Birch* (died 1945), U.S. intelligence officer.]

John Bull *n.* **1.** A personification of England or the English. **2.** A typical Englishman. [After *The History of John Bull* (1712), a satire by John ARBUTHNOT.]

John Doe *n.* **1.** A name formerly used in U.S. legal proceedings to designate a fictitious or unidentified person. **2.** An average citizen; the man in the street. Also called "Richard Roe."

John Do·ry (dôr′ē, dōr′ē) *n.* Any fish of the family Zeidae; especially, *Zenopsis ocellata,* of the western Atlantic, or *Zeus faber,* of the eastern Atlantic and Mediterranean, having spiny fins and a laterally compressed body.

John Han·cock (hăn′kŏk) *n. Informal.* A person's signature. [After John HANCOCK, whose signature appears prominently on the Declaration of Independence.]

Johnny Appleseed. See John **Chapman.**

john·ny·cake (jŏn′ē-kāk′) *n.* **1.** Corncake (see). **2.** *Australian.* A thin cake made with wheat meal or flour, often cooked on the embers of a campfire.

John·ny-come-late·ly (jŏn′ē-kŭm-lāt′lē) *n., pl.* **-lies.** *Informal.* A newcomer or latecomer, especially a recent adherent to a cause or fashion.

John·ny-jump-up (jŏn′ē-jŭmp′ŭp′) *n.* A plant, the **heartsease** (see). [From its quick growth.]

John·ny-on-the-spot (jŏn′ē-ŏn-thə-spŏt′, -ôn′-) *n. Informal.* A person who is available and ready to act when necessary.

John·ny Reb (jŏn′ē rĕb′) *n. Informal.* A Confederate soldier during the Civil War.

John of Gaunt (1340–99). Duke of Lancaster, fourth son of Edward III. He effectively ruled England during his father's last years and in the first years of Richard II's reign.

John of the Cross, Saint, born Juan de Yepes y Álvarez (1542–91). Spanish monk, mystic, and poet. He tried to restore austerity to Carmelite life. Friction among the Carmelites led to his imprisonment (1577) and finally retreat to a life of solitude. He was canonized in 1726.

John o'Groats (jōn′ ə-grōts′). Location in the extreme northeast of Scotland, named after John de Groat, a Dutchman, who built an octagonal house there in the 16th century. The northern extremity of Britain is popularly marked by John o'Groats.

John Paul II, Pope, born Karol Wojtyla (1920–). The first Polish-born pope. He was archbishop of Kraków before his election in 1978 as the first non-Italian pope since the Dutch-born Adrian VI (reigned 1522–23).

Johns (jŏnz), **Jasper** (1930–). U.S. artist. He aims to remove the boundary between art and real life, and has made bronze casts of light bulbs, toothbrushes, and beer cans.

John·son (jŏn′sən), **Amy** (1903–41). Pioneer British aviator. She was the first woman to fly solo from London to Australia (1930). She drowned after bailing out into the Thames estuary while on war service.

Johnson, Andrew (1808–75). 17th U.S. president (1865–69). A Southerner who remained loyal to the Union during the Civil War, Johnson was elected vice president in 1864 and succeeded the assassinated Abraham Lincoln. He pursued a policy of conciliation toward the defeated Confederate states to the point of readmitting them to the Union without requiring political reforms or ensuring civil rights for freed slaves.

Johnson, Lyndon Baines (1908–73). 36th U.S. president. Johnson succeeded to the office after John F. Kennedy's assassination (1963). He launched a welfare program, termed the Great Society, and overwhelmingly won the presidential election in 1964. He faced increasing criticism over the mounting involvement in Vietnam and did not stand for re-election in 1968.

Johnson, Samuel, known as "Dr. Johnson" (1709–84). British writer and lexicographer. His works include *Dictionary of the English Language* (1755) and *Lives of the Poets* (1779–81).

John·so·ni·an (jŏn-sō′nē-ən) *adj.* Of, resembling, or relating to Samuel Johnson or his writings.
~*n.* An admirer or student of Samuel Johnson or his work.

Johnson grass *n.* A coarse grass, *Sorghum halepense,* native to the Mediterranean area, cultivated for forage but often a troublesome weed. [Developed by William *Johnson,* 19th-century U.S. agriculturalist.]

John the Baptist, Saint. Son of Elizabeth and Zacharias; cousin of Jesus, whom he baptized; executed by Herod Antipas.

Jo·hore or **Jo·hor** (jō-hôr′, -hōr′). A state in Malaysia, situated in the south of the Malay Peninsula. Its extensive forests produce rubber, copra, and palm oil, and there are important reserves of tin and bauxite. The capital, Johore Baharu, is connected to Singapore by a causeway.

joie de vi·vre (zhwä′ də vē′vrə) *n.* Hearty or carefree enjoyment of life. [French, "joy of living."]

join (join) *v.* **joined, joining, joins.** —*tr.* **1.** To put or bring together; unite or make continuous: *The children joined hands in a circle.* **2.** To put or bring into close association or relationship: *joined in marriage.* **3.** *Geometry.* To connect (points), as with a straight line. **4.** To form a junction with; combine with. **5.** To become a part or member of (a club, society, or the like). **6.** To take a place among, in, or with; enter into the company of: *I shall join you later.* **7.** *Informal.* To adjoin. —*intr.* **1.** To come or act together; form a connection, junction, or alliance. Often used with *with.* **2.** To become a member of a group. **3.** To take part; participate. Used with *in: He joined in the singing.* —**join up.** To enlist, especially in the armed forces.
~*n.* A joint; a junction. [Middle English *joinen,* from Old French *joindre* (stem *joign-*), from Latin *jungere.*]
   Synonyms: *associate, combine, connect, consolidate, link, relate, unite.*
   Usage: The use of *together* following this verb is often felt to be redundant: *He joined (together) the two wires.* The longer form does have a certain value in adding emphasis, however, and it is well established in a few fixed phrases, for example: *whom God hath joined together. . . .*

join•der (join'dər) *n.* **1.** The act of joining. **2.** *Law.* **a.** A joining of causes of action or defense in a suit. **b.** A joining of parties in a suit. **c.** The formal acceptance of an issue offered. [From French *joindre* (mistaken as a substantive), to JOIN.]
join•er (joi'nər) *n.* **1.** One that joins. **2.** *Chiefly British.* A person who makes furniture, house fittings, door frames, or the like. **3.** *Informal.* A person given to joining groups, organizations, or causes.
join•er•y (joi'lə-rē) *n. Chiefly British.* **1.** The skill or craft of a joiner. **2.** Work done by a joiner, such as the fittings in a house.
joint (joint) *n.* Abbr. **jnt. 1. a.** A point or position at which two or more things are joined. **b.** A configuration in or by which two or more things are joined. **2.** The manner of joining. **3. a.** *Anatomy.* A point of connection or articulation between two or more bones, consisting of cartilage and connective tissue. **b.** A similar connection between segments in the body or leg of an arthropod. **4.** *Botany.* A point on a stem from which a leaf or branch may grow; a node. **5.** *Geology.* A fracture or crack in a rock mass along which no movement has occurred. **6.** A large cut of meat, such as the shoulder or leg, used for roasting. **7.** *Slang.* A cheap or disreputable gathering place, such as a nightclub or bar. **8.** *Slang.* Any dwelling or public establishment. Often used humorously. **9.** *Slang.* A marijuana cigarette. —**out of joint. 1.** Dislocated, as a bone. **2.** Not harmonious; inconsistent. **3.** Out of order; unsatisfactory.
~*adj.* **1.** Shared by or common to two or more: *a joint belief. The divorced couple received joint custody of the children.* **2.** Sharing with another or others: *joint heirs.* **3.** Formed, created, involving, or characterized by cooperation or united action: *a joint effort.* **4.** Involving both houses of a legislature: *a joint session.* **5.** *Law.* Regarded as one legal body united in identity of interest, ownership, or liability.
~*tr.v.* **jointed, jointing, joints. 1.** To combine or attach at a joint or joints. **2.** To provide or construct with joints. **3.** To cut (meat) into joints. [Middle English, from Old French, from the past participle of *joindre,* to JOIN.] —**joint•ly** *adv.*
Joint Chiefs of Staff *pl.n.* The principal military advisory group to the President of the United States, that is composed of the chiefs of the Army, Navy, and Air Force, and the commandant of the Marine Corps.
joint•ed (join'tĭd) *adj.* **1.** Having a joint or joints. **2.** Having a specified type of joint. Often used in combination: *double-jointed.*
joint•er (join'tər) *n.* **1.** One that joints; especially, a machine or tool used in making joints. **2.** A sharp triangular device connected to the beam of a plow to bury trash.
joint resolution *n.* A resolution passed by both houses of a bicameral legislature and eligible to become a law if signed by the chief executive or passed over his veto. Compare **concurrent resolution.**
joint stock *n.* Stock or capital funds of a company held jointly or in common by the owners.
joint-stock company (joint'stŏk') *n.* A business with a separate legal identity whose capital is held in shares by joint owners, each of whom enjoys limited liability.
join•ture (join'chər) *n. Law.* An estate settled on a woman by her husband, by an arrangement that takes effect in the event of her widowhood.
~*tr.v.* **jointured, -turing, -tures.** *Law.* To arrange a jointure for. [Middle English, from Old French, from Latin *junctūra,* JUNCTURE.]
joist (joist) *n.* Any of the parallel horizontal beams set from wall to wall to support the boards of a floor or ceiling.
~*tr.v.* **joisted, joisting, joists.** To construct with joists. [Middle English *gyste, giste,* from Old French *giste,* beam supporting a bridge, from Latin *jacitum,* from the past participle of *jacēre,* to lie down.]
jo•jo•ba (hə-hō'bə) *n.* A flowering shrub, *Simmondsia californica,* of southwestern North America, whose seeds contain a high proportion of liquid wax used in lubrication, polishes, pharmaceuticals, and cosmetics.
joke (jōk) *n.* **1.** An amusing story, especially one with a punch line. **2.** An amusing or jesting remark; a witticism, quip, or pun. **3.** A mischievous trick; a prank. **4. a.** An amusing or ludicrous incident or situation. **b.** The amusing aspect of something: *couldn't see the joke.* **5.** Something not to be taken seriously; triviality: *His accident was no joke.* **6.** An object of amusement or derision; a laughingstock.
~*v.* **joked, joking, jokes.** —*intr.* **1.** To tell or play jokes; to jest. **2.** To speak in fun; be facetious. —*tr.* To make fun of; to tease. [Latin *jocus,* jest, joke.] —**jok•ing•ly** *adv.*
   Synonyms: *crack, gag, jest, quip, sally, wisecrack, witticism.*
jok•er (jō'kər) *n.* **1. a.** A person who tells or plays jokes; a clown; a prankster. **b.** An insolent person who seeks to make a show of cleverness. **2.** A playing card, usually printed with a picture of a jester, used in certain games as the highest ranking card or as a wild card. **3.** An unpredictable person or factor that may prove troublesome. Used chiefly in the phrase *joker in the pack.* **4.** *Slang.* A fellow; a man. **5.** A minor clause in a document, such as a legislative bill, that voids or changes its original purpose.
jo•lie laide (zhŏl'ē lĕd') *n., pl.* **jolies laides.** *French.* A woman or girl whose features are not conventionally pretty but are nonetheless attractive. [Literally, "pretty ugly."]
Jo•li•et or **Jol•li•et** (jō'lē-ĕt', jō'lē-ĕt'), **Louis** (1645-1700). French-Canadian explorer of America. Traveling with six companions in birchbark canoes, he explored the Mississippi from its confluence with the Wisconsin River to its juncture with the Arkansas River (1673).

---

joint

JOINTS: DESIGNED FOR DIFFERENT DEGREES OF MOVEMENT
Cartilage, ligament, and fluid to protect against wear and tear

Wherever two bones come into contact in the body there is a joint. It may be fixed, like the joints in the skull, but what most people think of as joints are movable, like the joints in the limbs.

The bone endings in joints are lined with elastic, pearly white tissue called cartilage, and between them is a smooth, thin layer of tissue called the synovial membrane. This produces a lubricant, synovial fluid, that acts like oil in a machine: the two bony surfaces never touch but are kept apart by a thin layer of fluid.

Tough, fibrous bands of tissue—ligaments—are attached to the bones on either side of a joint, giving stability and limiting the range of movement. The range of possible movement also depends on the design of the joint.

A hinged joint, as in the fingers, elbows, and knees, allows movement backward and forward and some degree of rotation. A pivot joint, as in the top of the neck, allows nodding and some rotary movement. A ball-and-socket joint, as in the shoulders, allows the maximum flexibility of movement. A sliding joint, as in the ankles and wrists, allows a range of movements similar to those of a ball-and-socket joint but more limited in flexibility.

HINGED JOINT

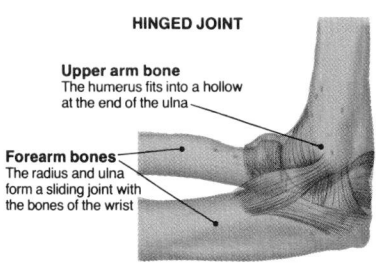

Upper arm bone
The humerus fits into a hollow at the end of the ulna

Forearm bones
The radius and ulna form a sliding joint with the bones of the wrist

In a hinged joint, the ends of the bones are connected across the joint by strong ligaments that allow bending in one plane only.

BALL-AND-SOCKET JOINT

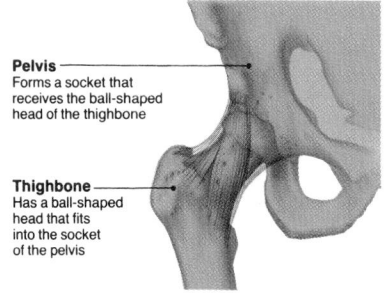

Pelvis
Forms a socket that receives the ball-shaped head of the thighbone

Thighbone
Has a ball-shaped head that fits into the socket of the pelvis

In a ball-and-socket joint, the rounded end of one bone fits into a hollow in the other, allowing swiveling movements in any plane.

SLIDING JOINT

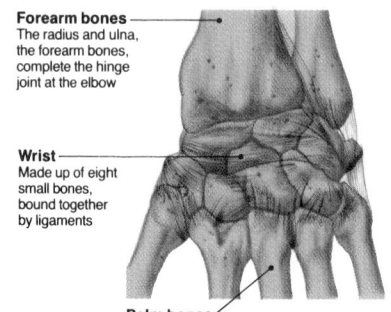

Forearm bones
The radius and ulna, the forearm bones, complete the hinge joint at the elbow

Wrist
Made up of eight small bones, bound together by ligaments

Palm bones
Have hinged and rotating joints where they meet the wristbones

Sliding joints have meeting surfaces that are almost flat, allowing the surfaces to slide over one another in a range of movements.

PIVOT JOINT

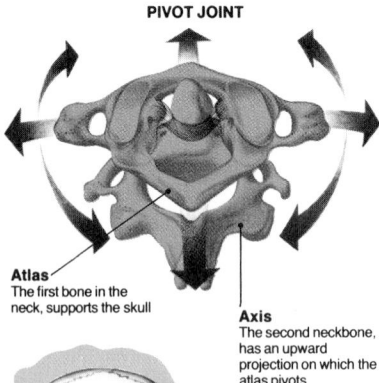

Atlas
The first bone in the neck, supports the skull

Axis
The second neckbone, has an upward projection on which the atlas pivots

Atlas

Axis

At the top of the neck, the atlas and the axis bones form between them a pivot joint, giving the head a range of movements based on the ability to nod back and forth and to rotate from side to side.

Jo·liot-Cu·rie (zhô-lyō′kü-rē′), **(Jean) Frédéric** (1900–58), born Jean Frédéric Joliot, and **Irène** (1897–56). French physicists. Irène Joliot-Curie was the daughter of Pierre and Marie Curie. She married Frédéric Joliot, her mother's assistant, who added Curie to his name. Together they discovered artificial radioactivity, for which they won the 1935 Nobel Prize for chemistry. Both died of cancer, after lifelong exposure to radioactivity.

jol·li·fi·ca·tion (jŏl′ə-fĭ-kā′shən) n. Festivity; revelry; merrymaking. [From JOLLY.]

jol·li·fy (jŏl′ə-fī′) v. **-fied, -fying, -fies.** —tr. To cause to become jolly; cheer up. —intr. To make merry; celebrate.

jol·li·ty (jŏl′ə-tē) n. Gaiety; merriment.

jol·ly (jŏl′ē) adj. **-lier, -liest. 1.** Full of merriment and good spirits; fun-loving; gay. **2.** Exhibiting or occasioning happiness or mirth; cheerful; festive. **3.** Greatly pleasing; enjoyable.
~adv. British Informal. Very; extremely: a jolly good cook.
~tr.v. **jollied, -lying, -lies. 1.** To keep amused or diverted for one's own purposes; humor. Often used with up or along. **2.** To poke fun at good-naturedly; tease. [Middle English jolif, joli, from Old French, gay, pleasant, probably from Old Norse jōl, name of the midwinter festival, yule, from Common Germanic jegol (unattested), YULE.] —**jol·li·ly** adv. —**jol·li·ness** n.
　　Synonyms: blithe, convivial, jocular, jovial, merry.

jol·ly-boat (jŏl′ē-bōt′) n. A small boat kept by the stern of a larger ship. [Probably an alteration of earlier jolywat†.]

Jolly Rog·er n. A black flag bearing the emblematic white skull and crossbones of a pirate ship.

Jol·son (jōl′sən), **Al,** born Asa Yoelson (1886–1950). U.S. singer, born in Russia. He imitated black singers. His hits include "My Mammy" and "Sonny Boy." He starred in *The Jazz Singer,* the first major film with synchronized sound (1927).

jolt (jōlt) v. **jolted, jolting, jolts.** —tr. **1.** To shake or cause to move with a sudden jerk or blow. **2.** To bump into; jostle. **3.** To put into a specified condition by or as if by a jolt: *He was jolted out of his reverie by a police siren.* —intr. To proceed in an irregular, bumpy, or jerky fashion.
~n. **1.** A sudden jarring or jerking, as from a blow. **2.** An abrupt or unexpected shock or reversal: *a jolt to his complacency.* [16th century : origin obscure.] —**jolt·er** n. —**jolt·i·ly** adv. —**jolt·y** adj.

Jomada. Variant of **Jumada.**

Jo·nah¹ (jō′nə). An Old Testament prophet who was thrown overboard during a storm at sea caused by his disobedience to God. He was swallowed by a great fish and disgorged unharmed three days later. [Hebrew *Yōnāh,* "the moaning one," dove, pigeon, akin to *ānāh,* "moan."]

Jonah² n. A book of the Old Testament containing the story of Jonah.

Jonah³ n. One thought to bring bad luck. [After JONAH.]

Jon·a·than¹ (jŏn′ə-thən). Eldest son of King Saul of Israel and friend of David. I Samuel 20.

Jonathan² n. A variety of red, late-ripening apple. [After *Jonathan* Hasbrouck (died 1846), U.S. jurist.]

Jonathan³ n. **Brother Jonathan** (see).

Jones (jōnz), **(Alfred) Ernest** (1879–1958). British psychoanalyst, a follower of Sigmund Freud. Jones was instrumental in developing the use of psychoanalysis in Britain and North America.

Jones, (Everett) LeRoi. See Imamu Amiri Baraka.

Jones, Inigo (1573–1652). English architect. Jones studied in Italy and brought the Palladian classical style to England. Among the buildings he designed are the Queen's House, Greenwich, and the Banqueting Hall, Whitehall, London. He also introduced the use of movable scenery and the proscenium arch into England.

Jones, John Luther, known as "Casey" (1864–1900). U.S. railroad engineer. He died at the throttle while trying to stop his train from crashing into the rear of another train. All the passengers aboard Jones's train were saved. A friend wrote the well-known ballad about his heroic death.

Jones, John Paul, born John Paul (1747–92). U.S. naval hero, born in Scotland. He settled in Virginia and on the outbreak of the American Revolution gained a commission from Congress. In command of a French force he raided the British coast in 1779, destroying two British warships. Jones later became an admiral in the Russian navy. He died in Paris.

Jones, Mary Harris, known as "Mother Jones" (1830–1930). U.S. labor leader. From 1871 until shortly before her death, she traveled around the country, appearing wherever workers were striking against unfair management. She was known for her fiery speeches.

Jones, Robert Tyre, known as "Bobby" (1902–71). U.S. golfer. He was the only golfer ever to win the "Grand Slam," the British and U.S. amateur and open golf championships in the same year (1930).

jong (yŏng) n. South African Informal. Used as a familiar term of address to a man, woman, or child. [From Cape Dutch *jonger,* boy.]

jon·gleur (jŏng′glər; French zhôn-glœr′) n. A wandering minstrel and storyteller in medieval England and France. [French, from Old French, variant of *jogleur,* JUGGLER.]

jon·quil (jŏng′kwĭl, jŏn′-) n. A widely cultivated plant, *Narcissus jonquilla,* having long, narrow leaves and short-tubed, fragrant yellow flowers. [New Latin *jonquilla,* from Spanish *junquillo,* diminutive of *junco,* rush, reed, from Latin *juncus†.*]

Jon·son (jŏn′sən), **Ben(jamin)** (1572–1637). English playwright and poet. His plays include *Volpone* (c. 1606), *The Alchemist* (1610), and *Bartholomew Fair* (1614).

jook. Variant of **juk.**

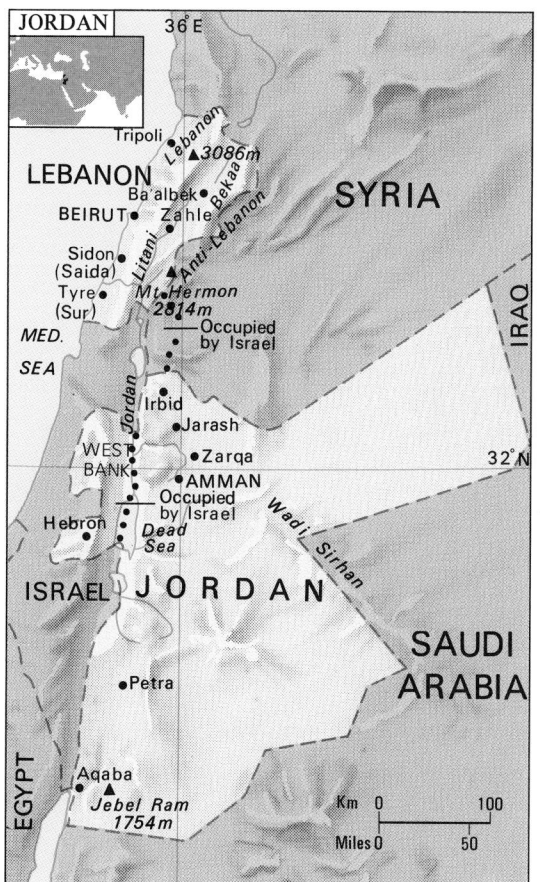

JORDAN 36 E
Tripoli
LEBANON ▲3086m SYRIA
Ba'albek Bekaa
BEIRUT• Zahle
Sidon (Saida)
Tyre (Sur) Mt. Hermon 2814m
MED. SEA ——Occupied by Israel
Irbid
Jarash
WEST BANK •Zarqa 32°N
•AMMAN
Occupied by Israel
Hebron Dead Sea
ISRAEL JORDAN
SAUDI ARABIA
•Petra
Wadi Sirhan
IRAQ
Litani Lebanon Anti-Lebanon
Jordan
EGYPT ‖ ●Aqaba
▲ Jebel Ram 1754m
Km 0 ———— 100
Miles 0 —— 50

Jop·lin (jŏp′lĭn), **Scott** (1868–1917). U.S. pianist and composer. He developed a style of ragtime blending European musical forms and southern black rhythms. His most famous work is "Maple Leaf Rag" (1899).

Jor·dan (jôrd′n). River flowing south from Syria and Lebanon, partially marking the border between Israel and Jordan and emptying into the Dead Sea. St. John the Baptist baptized his followers in the river, which is 320 kilometers (199 miles) long.

Jordan, Hash·e·mite Kingdom of (hăsh′ə-mīt′). Formerly **Trans·jor·dan** (trăns′jôrd′n, trănz′-). A largely desert Arab state in southwest Asia. Most of its fertile land lies in the Jordan River valley and West Bank (Jordanian territory west of the Jordan, occupied by Israel since the Six-Day War of 1967). However, with foreign aid, the cultivated area is expanding. Jordan, then part of the Nabataean empire, fell to the Romans (c. A.D. 110), and later to the Arabs, Crusaders, and Turks (1516). After the Arab Revolt against the Turks in World War I, Transjordan, a British mandate east of the Jordan, led by the Hashemite family, was established (1923). Its independence became effective in 1948. The same year, Transjordan occupied the West Bank, adopting its present name in 1949. Resident units of the Palestine Liberation Organization provoked a civil war in 1970–71. Jordan assisted Syria in the Yom Kippur War (1973) and supported Iraq against Iran in 1980. King Hussein, ruler since 1952, has been a mediating influence between the militant Arab states and the West. Jordan relies on exports of phosphates, vegetables, and fruit. Area, 97,740 square kilometers (37,738 square miles) including the West Bank. Population, 2,150,000. Capital, Amman. —**Jor·da·ni·an** (jôr-dā′nē-ən) n. & adj.

Jordan almond n. A large variety of almond from Málaga, Spain, used widely in confectionery. [By folk etymology from Middle English *jardin,* probably from Old French *jardin,* from Vulgar Latin *gardīnus* (unattested), GARDEN + ALMOND.]

jo·rum (jôr′əm) n. **1.** A large drinking bowl. **2.** The amount such a bowl contains. [Perhaps after *Joram* (II Samuel 8:10), who brought vessels of silver, gold, and brass to King David.]

jo·seph (jō′zəf) n. A long riding coat with a small cape, worn by women in the 18th century. [Probably after Joseph's (son of Jacob) "coat of many colors" (Genesis 37:3).]

Jo·seph¹ (jō′zəf). Son of Jacob and Rachel, sold into slavery in Egypt. Genesis 3; 37; 41; 45.

Joseph². Husband of Mary the mother of Jesus. Matthew 1:16.

Joseph, Chief (c. 1840–1904). Nez Percé leader. In 1877 he led his people on a retreat to Canada to avoid relocation by the U.S. government. Chief Joseph and some 750 Nez Percé were captured by U.S. troops about 30 miles south of the Canadian border.

Jo·seph (jō′zəf, zhō′zĕf′), **Père,** born François le Clerc du Tremblay (1577–1638). French Capuchin friar and diplomat. Known as

the *Eminence Grise* (Gray Eminence), he was a close friend and adviser of Cardinal Richelieu.
Jo·sé·phine (jō′zə-fēn′, zhō-zā-fēn′), born Marie Joséphine Rose Tascher de la Pagerie (1763–1814). Wife of Napoleon I, Empress of France (1804–09). Born in Martinique, she married Napoleon in 1796 after the execution of her first husband, Viscount Beauharnais. Her failure to bear a child led Napoleon to repudiate their marriage in 1809, although she continued to advise him.
Joseph of Ar·i·ma·the·a (âr′ə-mə-thē′ə, ăr′-). An Israelite who provided a tomb for Jesus; the subject of many legends.
Joseph's coat *n.* A tropical plant, *Amaranthus tricolor,* cultivated for its variously colored foliage.
Jo·seph·son (jō′zəf-sən, -zĭf-), **Brian David** (1940–). British physicist. He predicted theoretically the Josephson effect and Josephson junction. He shared the 1973 Nobel Prize for physics with Leo Esaki and Ivar Giaever for this work.

Joshua tree Yucca brevifolia *is the tallest and most treelike of the yuccas, growing to a height of about 10 meters (more than 30 feet). Yuccas are native to Mexico and the southern United States.*

Josephson effect *n. Physics.* Any of certain electrical phenomena observed at very low temperatures at a junction between two superconducting materials separated by a thin insulating layer. Under such conditions a direct current can flow with no applied voltage up to a critical value. A small direct voltage across the junction can cause an alternating current to flow. [Predicted theoretically by B.D. JOSEPHSON in 1962.]
Josephson junction *n. Physics.* A junction in which two superconductors at very low temperature are separated by a thin insulating layer such that Josephson effects can be observed. Josephson junctions are used in physics for accurate measurement of magnetic fields and definition of physical quantities and, in particular, for high-speed switches in advanced computers.
Josephson memory *n.* A computer memory consisting of a number of interconnected Josephson junctions, which are switched between conducting and superconducting states by variations in magnetic field.
Jo·se·phus (jō-sē′fəs), **Flavius** (A.D. 37–*c.* 100). Jewish general and historian. He was governor of Galilee and took part in the Jewish revolt against the Romans. His *History of the Jewish War* is the major source of information about the siege of Masada (72–73).
josh (jŏsh) *v.* **joshed, joshing, joshes.** *Informal.* —*tr.* To tease (someone) good-humoredly. —*intr.* To banter; joke.
∼*n.* A teasing or joking remark. [19th century : origin obscure.]
Josh. Joshua (Old Testament).
Josh·u·a[1] (jŏsh′o͞o-ə) Also in Douay Bible **Jos·u·e** (-yo͞o-ē). Successor of Moses in the Exodus.
Joshua[2] *n.* Also in Douay Bible **Josue.** *Abbr.* **Josh.** An Old Testament book with the narrative of Joshua.
Joshua tree *n.* A treelike plant, *Yucca brevifolia,* of the southwestern United States, having sword-shaped leaves and greenish-white flowers. [From the greatly extended branches, recalling the outstretched arm of the prophet Joshua as he pointed with his spear to the city of Ai. Joshua 8:18.]
Jo·si·ah (jō-sī′ə). Also in Douay Bible **Jo·si·as** (-əs). King of Judah (*c.* 638–*c.* 608 B.C.).
Jos·quin des Prés or **des Prez** (zhōs-kăɴ′ dā prā′) (*c.* 1450–1521). Flemish composer. His musical style bridged the early and later Renaissance periods. He helped to introduce the northern polyphonic manner to Italy.
joss (jŏs) *n.* An image of a Chinese god. [Pidgin English, from Portuguese *deos,* god, from Latin *deus.*]
joss house *n.* A Chinese temple or shrine.
joss stick *n.* A stick of fragrant tinder mixed with clay and burned as incense.
jos·tle (jŏs′əl) *v.* **-tled, -tling, -tles.** —*intr.* **1.** To come in contact or collide repeatedly, as in a crowd; knock or push together. **2.** To make one's way by pushing or elbowing. **3.** To vie for an advantage or favorable position. **4.** To be in close proximity. —*tr.* **1. a.** To force (one's way) by pushing, shoving, and elbowing. **b.** To push or shove roughly or unceremoniously. **2.** To come into close contact or collision with. **3.** To vie with for an advantage or favorable position. **4.** To be in close proximity with: *"books written in all languages by men and women of all tempers, races, and ages jostle each other on the shelf"* (Virginia Woolf).
∼*n.* A rough shove or push. [Earlier *justle,* from Middle English *justlen,* to come against in combat, frequentative of *justen,* from Old French *juster,* to JOUST.]
jot (jŏt) *n.* The smallest bit or particle; an iota.
∼*tr.v.* **jotted, jotting, jots.** To write down briefly and hastily: *jot down an address.* [Earlier *iote,* from Latin *iōta,* from Greek, IOTA.]
jot·ter (jŏt′ər) *n. British.* A small pad or notebook for notes or messages.
jot·ting (jŏt′ĭng) *n. British.* A brief note or memorandum.
Jo·tun·heim (yô′to͞on-hām′). Also **Jö·tunn·heim** (yœ′-), **Jo·tunn·heim·r** (-hā′mər). *Norse Mythology.* **Utgard** *(see).*
jou·al (zho͞o-äl′, zhwäl) *n. Canadian.* Uneducated, nonstandard, or dialectal Canadian French. [Respelling of French *cheval,* horse, as it would sound in nonstandard or dialectal Canadian French.]
Jou·bert (zho͞o′bâr′), **Petrus Jacobus,** known as "Piet" (1834–1900). Afrikaner statesman and commandant general of the Boer forces. Favoring political equality for British immigrants, he three times failed against Paul Kruger in bids for the presidency of the Transvaal (1883, 1893, 1898).
joule (jo͞ol) *n. Abbr.* **J** The International System unit of energy, equal to the work done when a current of 1 ampere is passed through a resistance of 1 ohm for 1 second. This is equivalent to the work done when the point of application of a force of 1 newton is displaced 1 meter in the direction of the force. [After James P. JOULE.]
Joule (jo͞ol), **James Prescott** (1818–89). British physicist who was the first to measure the mechanical equivalent of heat. A brewer by trade, he performed a number of experiments to prove that a given amount of electrical energy will always produce the same amount of heat. He provided Helmholtz with the evidence for the law of conservation of energy.
Joule's law *n.* **1.** The principle that the heat generated by an electric current passing through a wire is equal to the product of the potential difference between the ends of the wire, the current flowing through it, and the time for which it flows. **2.** The principle that the internal energy of a gas at a constant temperature is independent of the volume of the gas. This law applies only to ideal gases; in real gases the internal energy varies with volume as a result of intermolecular forces.
Joule-Thom·son effect (jo͞ol-tŏm′sən) *n.* The fall in temperature of a gas when it expands through a small hole, caused by work being done against the intermolecular forces within the gas. Also called "Joule-Kelvin effect."
jounce (jouns) *v.* **jounced, jouncing, jounces.** —*intr.* To move with bumps and jolts. —*tr.* To cause to jounce.
∼*n.* A rough, jolting bounce. [Middle English *jouncen*†.]
jour. **1.** journal; journalist. **2.** journeyman.
jour·nal (jûr′nəl) *n. Abbr.* **J., jour. 1.** A daily record of occurrences or transactions, especially: **a.** A personal record of experiences and reflections; a diary. **b.** An official record of daily proceedings, as of a legislative body. **c.** A ship's log. **2.** *Bookkeeping.* **a.** A daybook. **b.** A book of original entry in a double-entry system, listing all transactions and indicating the accounts to which they belong. **3. a.** A newspaper. **b.** A periodical presenting news or containing scholarly articles on a particular subject: *a medical journal.* **c.** Used as part of the title of certain newspapers or periodicals. **4.** The part of a shaft or axle supported by a bearing. [Middle English, from Old French *jurnal, jornal,* from *journal, jornel,* "daily," from Late Latin *diurnālis,* diurnal, from Latin *diurnus,* daily, from *diēs,* day.]
journal box *n.* A housing enclosing a journal and its bearings.
jour·nal·ese (jûr′nə-lēz′, -lēs′) *n.* The slick, superficial style of writing often held to be characteristic of newspapers and magazines. [JOURNAL + -ESE.]
jour·nal·ism (jûr′nə-lĭz′əm) *n.* **1. a.** The collecting, reporting, writing, photographing, editing, and publishing of news or articles for any of the media, especially for newspapers and magazines. **b.** The business or occupation of working in the news media. **2.** Material written for publication in a newspaper or magazine. **3.** A style of writing associated with newspapers and magazines, characterized by direct presentation of facts or occurrences with little attempt at analysis or interpretation. **4.** Newspapers and magazines collectively. **5.** An academic course in journalism. **6.** Written material of current interest or wide popular appeal.
jour·nal·ist (jûr′nə-lĭst) *n.* **1.** *Abbr.* **jour.** A person whose occupation is journalism. **2.** A person who keeps a journal.
jour·nal·is·tic (jûr′nə-lĭs′tĭk) *adj.* Pertaining to or characteristic of journalism or journalists. —**jour·nal·is·ti·cal·ly** *adv.*
jour·nal·ize (jûr′nə-līz′) *v.* **-ized, -izing, -izes.** —*tr.* To record in a journal. —*intr.* To keep a journal. —**jour·nal·iz·er** *n.*
jour·ney (jûr′nē) *n., pl.* **-neys. 1. a.** An act of traveling from one place to another; a trip. **b.** A long overland trip as distinguished from a voyage or a flight. **2. a.** The distance traveled on a journey. **b.** The time required for such a trip. **3.** A process of transition or progress: *our journey through life.*
∼*v.* **journeyed, -neying, -neys.** —*intr.* To travel; make a trip. —*tr.* To travel over or through. [Middle English *journey, jorne,* period of travel, a day's traveling, from Old French *jornee,* from Vulgar Latin *diurnāta* (unattested), from Latin *diurnum,* daily portion, neuter of *diurnus,* daily, from *diēs,* day.] —**jour·ney·er** *n.*
jour·ney·man (jûr′nē-mən) *n., pl.* **-men** (-mĭn). **1.** *Abbr.* **jour.** One who has fully served an apprenticeship in a trade or craft and is a qualified worker in another's employ. **2.** Any competent workman. [Middle English : JOURNEY (in the dialectal sense of "a day's work") + MAN.]
jour·ney·work (jûr′nē-wûrk′) *n.* **1.** The work of a journeyman. **2.** Menial or routine work.
joust (jŭst, joust, jo͞ost) *n.* Also **just** (jŭst). **1.** A combat with lances between two mounted knights or men-at-arms; a tilting match. **2.** *Usually* **jousts.** A series of these matches; a tournament. **3.** Any combat or exchange suggestive of a joust.
∼*intr.v.* **jousted, jousting, jousts.** Also **just.** To engage in such combat or exchange; tilt. [Middle English, from Old French *juste, jouste,* from *juster,* to join battle, joust, from Vulgar Latin *juxtāre* (unattested), to come together, from Latin *juxtā,* close together.]
Jove (jōv) *n.* **1.** The god **Jupiter** *(see).* **2.** *Poetic.* The planet Jupiter. —**by Jove.** A mild oath used to express surprise or to give emphasis. [Middle English, from Latin *Jov-,* stem of the oblique cases of Old Latin *Jovis.*]
jo·vi·al (jō′vē-əl) *adj.* Marked by hearty conviviality. —See Synonyms at **jolly.** [Originally "born under the influence of Jupiter" (the planet, regarded as the source of happiness), from French *jovial,* from Italian *gioviale,* from *Giove,* Jove, from Latin *Jov-.*] —**jo·vi·al·i·ty** *n.* —**jo·vi·al·ly** *adv.*
Jo·vi·an (jō′vē-ən) *adj.* **1.** Of, pertaining to, or resembling the god Jove. **2.** Of, relating to, or occurring on the planet Jupiter.

Jow·ett (jou′ĕt, -ĭt), **Benjamin** (1817–93). British classical scholar and master of Balliol College, Oxford (1870–93). His work *The Interpretation of Scripture* (1860) provoked charges of heresy from orthodox Anglicans. He also published classical translations, the most notable being of Plato's *Dialogues.*

jowl¹ (joul) *n.* **1.** The jaw, especially the lower jaw. **2.** The cheek. [Middle English *chawle, chauel,* Old English *ceafl.*]

jowl² *n.* **1.** The flesh under the lower jaw, especially when plump or flaccid. **2.** A similar fleshy part, such as a dewlap or a wattle. [Middle English *cholle,* probably Old English *ceole, ceolu,* throat.]

joy (joi) *n.* **1.** A condition or deep feeling of pleasure or delight; happiness; gladness. **2.** The expression or manifestation of such a feeling. **3.** A source or object of pleasure or satisfaction. —See Synonyms at **pleasure.**
∼*v.* **joyed, joying, joys.** —*intr.* To take pleasure; rejoice. —*tr. Archaic.* **1.** To fill with joy. **2.** To enjoy. [Middle English *joy(e),* from Old French *joie, joye,* from Vulgar Latin *gaudia* (unattested), from Latin, plural of *gaudium,* gladness, delight, from *gaudēre,* to rejoice.]

joy·ance (joi′əns) *n.* **1.** Enjoyment; delight. **2.** Merrymaking; festivity. [JOY + -ANCE.]

Joyce (jois), **James Augustine Aloysius** (1882–1941). Irish novelist, poet, and dramatist. He lived in Europe from 1904, publishing his first collection of stories, *Dubliners,* in 1914 and his first, largely autobiographical novel, *Portrait of the Artist as a Young Man,* in 1916. He is best known for *Ulysses* (1922), a novel that minutely describes the events of a single day in Dublin and is noted for its linguistic innovation. **—Joy·ce·an** (joi′sē-ən) *adj.*

Joyce, William, also known as "Lord Haw-Haw" (1906–46). Nazi propagandist, born in the United States of Irish parentage. During World War II he made propaganda broadcasts from Germany, delivered in the upper-class accent that earned him his nickname. He was tried in Britain and executed for treason after the war.

joy·ful (joi′fəl) *adj.* Feeling, causing, or expressing joy. —See Synonyms at **glad. —joy·ful·ly** *adv.* **—joy·ful·ness** *n.*

joy·less (joi′lĭs) *adj.* Destitute of joy; cheerless; dismal. **—joy·less·ly** *adv.* **—joy·less·ness** *n.*

joy·ous (joi′əs) *adj.* Feeling or causing joy; joyful. —See Synonyms at **glad. —joy·ous·ly** *adv.* **—joy·ous·ness** *n.*

joy ride *n.* **1.** A ride taken in a car, especially a stolen car, simply for fun and often for the thrills provided by reckless driving. **2.** A hazardous, reckless, and often costly venture. **—joy-ride** (joi′rīd′) *v.*

joy·stick (joi′stĭk′) *n. Informal.* **1.** The control stick of an aircraft. **2.** A manual control device linked to a computer, used especially in making moves in a video game.

J.P. justice of the peace.

J particle, j psi particle *n.* The **psi particle** *(see).*

jr., Jr. junior.

J.S.D. Doctor of Juristic Science. [Latin *Juris Scientiae Doctor*]

Juan Car·los (hwän kär′lōs, -lōs) (1938–). King of Spain (1975–). Acceding to the throne on the death of Franco, he helped restore parliamentary democracy. His declared opposition to an attempted military coup (February 1981) contributed to its failure.

Juan de Fu·ca Strait (hwän′də fyo͞o′kə, wän′). Inlet of the Pacific Ocean, *c.* 160 kilometers (100 miles) long, between northwestern Washington State and Vancouver Island, British Columbia.

ju·ba (jo͞o′bə) *n.* A group dance, probably of West African origin, characterized by complex rhythmic clapping and body movements and practiced on plantations in the southern United States during the 18th and 19th centuries. [Probably from Zulu.]

Ju·bal (jo͞o′bəl). A descendant of Cain and the reputed inventor of musical instruments. Genesis 4:21.

jub·bah (jo͝ob′ə) *n.* Also **jib·bah** (jĭb′ə). A long, loose, open, outer garment with sleeves, worn by Muslims and Parsees. [Arabic.]

ju·be (jo͞o′bē) *n.* A loft or rood screen and gallery that separate the choir from the nave in a church. [French *jubé,* from Medieval Latin, opening word of the prayer *Jube, Domine, benedicere,* bid, Lord, a blessing : perhaps applied to the structure because the prayer was recited there by the deacon.]

ju·bi·lant (jo͞o′bə-lənt) *adj.* Filled with or expressing great joy, especially through success or triumph. [Latin *jūbilāns* (stem *jūbilant-*), present participle of *jūbilāre,* to JUBILATE.] **—ju·bi·lance, ju·bi·lan·cy** *n.* **—ju·bi·lant·ly** *adv.*

ju·bi·late (jo͞o′bə-lāt′) *intr.v.* **-lated, -lating, -lates.** To rejoice; exult. [Latin *jūbilāre,* to raise a shout of joy.]

Ju·bi·la·te (jo͞o′bə-lä′tē, -lä′-) *n.* **1.** The 100th Psalm in the King James Bible, or the 99th in the Vulgate and the Douay Bible. **2.** A musical setting of the Jubilate. **3.** The third Sunday after Easter. **4.** A song or outburst of joy and triumph. [Latin *jūbilāte!,* rejoice! (the first word in the Jubilate), imperative of *jūbilāre,* to JUBILATE.]

ju·bi·la·tion (jo͞o′bə-lā′shən) *n.* **1.** The state of being jubilant; exultation. **2.** A celebration or other expression of joy.

ju·bi·lee (jo͞o′bə-lē′) *n.* **1. a.** A special anniversary; especially, a 25th, 50th, 60th, or 75th anniversary. **b.** The celebration of such an anniversary. **2.** A season or occasion of joyful celebration. **3.** Jubilation; rejoicing. **4.** In the Old Testament, a year of rest to be observed by the Israelites every 50th year, during which slaves were to be set free, alienated property restored to its former owners, and the land left untilled. Leviticus 25:8–17. **5.** *Roman Catholic Church.* A year during which plenary indulgence may be obtained by the performance of certain pious acts. It is usually granted at intervals of 25 years. [Middle English, from Old French *jubilé,* from Late Latin *jūbilaeus (annus),* "(year) of jubilee," alteration (influenced by Latin *jūbilāre,* to JUBILATE) of Late Greek *iōbēlaios,* from *iōbēlos,* jubilee, from Hebrew *yōbhēl,* "ram's horn" (used to proclaim the jubilee), originally, "leading animal," akin to *hōbhīl,* to lead, conduct.]

Jud. **1.** Judges (Old Testament). **2.** Judith (Apocrypha).

J.U.D. Doctor of Canon and Civil Law. [Latin *Juris Utriusque Doctor,* "Doctor of either law"]

Ju·dae·a or **Ju·de·a** (jo͞o-dē′ə). The southern part of ancient Palestine. The Kingdom of Judah, located here, lay south of Israel. Under David, the two kingdoms were united, the Judaean city of Jerusalem becoming his capital. Judah became independent in *c.* 922 B.C., later falling to the Assyrians, Babylonians, Greeks, and Persians. In A.D. 135 it was absorbed into the Roman province of Syria. **—Ju·dae·an, Ju·de·an** *n. & adj.*

Ju·dah¹ (jo͞o′də). Also in Douay Bible **Ju·da.** Son of Jacob and Leah; ancestor of one of the twelve tribes of Israel. [Hebrew *Yəhūdāh,* "praised."]

Judah² *n.* The tribe of Israel descended from Judah.

Judah³. An ancient kingdom in southern Palestine, occupied by the tribes of Judah and Benjamin and governed by the descendants of Solomon. I Kings 11:31, 12:17–21. See **Judaea.**

Ju·da·ic (jo͞o-dā′ĭk) *adj.* Also **Ju·da·i·cal** (-ĭ-kəl). Of or pertaining to Jews or Judaism. [Latin *Jūdaicus,* from Greek *Ioudaikos,* from *Ioudaios,* JEW.] **—Ju·da·i·cal·ly** *adv.*

Ju·da·i·ca (jo͞o-dā′ĭ-kə) *pl.n.* Books, documents, and artifacts representing the literature, history, and culture of the Jewish people. [Latin, "Jewish matters."]

Ju·da·ism (jo͞o′dē-ĭz′əm) *n.* **1.** The monotheistic religion of the Jewish people, tracing its origins to Abraham, having its spiritual and ethical principles embodied chiefly in the Old Testament and the Talmud. **2.** Conformity to the traditional ceremonies and rites of the Jewish religion. **3.** The cultural, spiritual, and social way of life of the Jewish people. **4.** The Jewish people. [Late Latin *Jūdaismus,* from Greek *Ioudaismos,* from *Ioudaios,* JEW.] **—Ju·da·ist** *n.* **—Ju·da·is·tic** *adj.* See feature, next page.

Ju·da·ize (jo͞o′dē-īz′) *v.* **-ized, -izing, -izes.** —*tr.* To bring into conformity with or convert to Judaism. —*intr.* To adopt Jewish customs and beliefs. **—Ju·da·i·za·tion** *n.* **—Ju·da·iz·er** *n.*

Ju·das¹ (jo͞o′dəs), called "Judas Iscariot." One of the Twelve Apostles, who betrayed Jesus for 30 pieces of silver. [Late Latin *Jūdas,* from Greek *Ioudas,* from Hebrew *Yəhūdāh,* JUDAH.]

Judas², known as "Saint Jude" to distinguish him from Judas Iscariot. One of the Twelve Apostles.

Judas³ *n.* **1.** One who betrays under the appearance of friendship. **2.** *Usually* **judas.** A one-way peephole in a door. [From JUDAS (Iscariot).]

Judas Maccabeus. See **Maccabeus.**

Judas tree *n.* Any of various trees of the genus *Cercis;* especially, the ornamental Eurasian species *C. siliquastrum,* having clusters of pinkish-red flowers that appear before the leaves. Also called "redbud." [From a belief that Judas Iscariot hanged himself on it.]

Juddah. See **Jiddah.**

jud·der (jŭd′ər) *intr.v.* **-dered, -dering, -ders.** *Chiefly British.* To shake, shudder, or vibrate violently.
∼*n. Chiefly British.* A juddering movement, especially in a mechanical system. [Probably from JAR + SHUDDER.]

Jude (jo͞od) *n.* The Epistle of Jude, a book of the New Testament often attributed to Saint Jude.

Judea. See **Judaea.**

Judeo-. *prefix.* Indicates Judaism; for example, *Judeo-Christian.* [From Latin *judaeus,* Jewish.]

Ju·de·o-Ger·man (jo͞o-dā′ō-jûr′mən) *n.* **Yiddish** *(see).*

Ju·de·o-Span·ish (jo͞o-dā′ō-spăn′ĭsh) *n.* **Ladino** *(see).*

Judg. Judges (Old Testament).

judge (jŭj) *v.* **judged, judging, judges.** —*tr.* **1. a.** To pass judgment upon in a court of law. **b.** To sit in judgment upon; try; hear. **2.** To determine authoritatively after deliberation, especially: **a.** To decide or settle (a controversy, for example). **b.** To appraise discriminatingly as an expert: *"You can always judge the quality of a cook or restaurant by roast chicken"* (Julia Child). **c.** To declare after deliberation: *They judged her a witch.* **d.** To choose the winners of (a competition). **3.** To form an appraisal or estimate of: *judge character; judge distances.* **4.** To criticize; censure. **5.** To consider, especially as a result of careful thought; conclude: *judged that the moment was right.* —*intr.* **1.** To act or decide as a judge; pass judgment. **2.** To form an opinion or estimation; make a critical determination or appraisal.
∼*n.* **1.** *Abbr.* **J.** A public official who hears and decides cases brought before a court of law for the purpose of administering justice; justice; magistrate. **2.** An appointed arbiter in a contest or competition. **3.** One who makes critical judgments: *He's a poor judge of character.* **4.** A leader of the Israelites during a period of about 400 years between the death of Joshua and the accession of Saul. [Middle English *jugen,* from Old French *jugier,* from Latin *jūdicāre,* from *jūdex* (stem *jūdic-*), judge.]
Synonyms: *arbiter, arbitrator, referee, umpire.*

judge advocate *n., pl.* **judge advocates.** *Abbr.* **J.A.** **1.** A commissioned officer in the U.S. Army assigned to the Judge Advocate General's Corps. **2.** A staff officer serving as legal adviser to a commander. **3.** An officer acting as prosecutor at a court-martial.

Judge Advocate General *n., pl.* **Judge Advocates General** or **Judge Advocate Generals.** A major general in the U.S. Army or Air Force who serves as senior legal officer.

Judg·es (jŭj′əz) *n. Used with a singular verb. Abbr.* **Jud., Judg.** A

Judas tree *Pink flowers appear on the Judas tree's bare branches in early spring. It is said to be blushing for Judas Iscariot who, according to some folk tradition, hanged himself from one of the trees, but its name may simply refer to the biblical province of Judah, now Judaea, where it grows wild.*

PRONUNCIATION KEY
ă, pat; ā, pay; âr, care;
ä, father, are; b, bib;
ch, church; d, deed; ĕ, pet;
ē, be; f, fife; g, gag; h, hat;
hw, which; ĭ, pit; ī, pie;
îr, pier; j, judge; k, kick;
l, lid, needle; m, mum;
n, no, sudden; ng, thing;
ŏ, pot; ō, toe; ô, paw, for;
oi, noise; ou, out; o͝o, book;
o͞o, boot; p, pop; r, roar;
s, sauce; sh, ship, dish;
t, tight; th, thin, path;
th, this, bathe; ŭ, cut; ûr, fur;
v, valve; w, with; y, yes;
z, zebra, size; zh, vision;
ə, about, item, edible, gallop, circus, peaceful

IN FOREIGN WORDS:
à, *Fr.* ami; œ, *Fr.* feu, *Ger.* schön; ü, *Fr.* tu, *Ger.* über; KH, *Ger.* ich, *Scot.* loch; N, *Fr.* bon; y′, *Fr.* Compiègne

STRESS MARKS:
Primary stress: ′
in·cite′ (ĭn-sīt′)
Secondary stress: ′
in′sight′ (ĭn′sīt′)

Judaism

THE ONE GOD OF ABRAHAM
Ancient faith that binds the Jewish people

Judaism is the world's oldest surviving monotheistic religion, and from it both Christianity and Islam have arisen.

Jewish history tells that 4,000 years ago God made a covenant with Abraham, the father of the Jewish nation. He promised the land of Canaan (later called Palestine) to the Jews if Abraham would spread to all mankind the lesson that there is one God. Famine drove the Jews from Canaan to Egypt, where they became slaves. Moses was called by God to lead them back to their promised land. When they reached Mount Sinai, God (Yahweh or Jehovah) appeared to Moses, renewed the covenant made with Abraham, and revealed to Moses the Law, which included the Ten Commandments. This is regarded as the foundation of Judaism.

More formal shape was given to the religion during the latter part of the 6th century B.C., when the Jews returned to Palestine from a period of exile in Babylon. The Law and other sacred writings were studied and interpreted by rabbis, or teachers, and a detailed social code grew up.

The principles of Judaism are contained in the Torah, or Law—incorporated in the Hebrew Bible, the Old Testament, as the first five books—and in the Talmud, the ancient commentary on the Law. One God is the creator of the universe who cares for and saves the world. Obedience to the sacred teachings will win redemption. Jews hope for God to send a messiah, an ideal ruler, who will bring all mankind under just and divine rule. Christians believe that Jesus was this messiah.

Even before the Christian era, most Jews lived outside Palestine. Of today's 13 million Jews, 6 million live in the United States, 3 million in Israel, and half a million in Britain.

FOUND IN A CATACOMB *Hebrew ritual objects are portrayed on the base of a 2nd-century* A.D. *gold goblet found in a Jewish catacomb in Rome. The original objects are thought to have come from the Jewish Temple in Jerusalem, when it was desecrated by Antiochus IV of Syria about 170* B.C.

THE SAVING OF THE JEWS *The story of Esther—who married Ahasuerus, a 6th century B.C. Persian king, and persuaded him to prevent a massacre of her fellow Jews—is told in this 18th-century illuminated scroll. The annual Feast of Lots, or Purim, is named after the lots drawn to choose the proposed day of slaughter. At Purim, Jews exchange gifts and make donations to the poor.*

TO THE PROMISED LAND *Throughout their bondage in Egypt the Jews never lost faith in God or in His Covenant made with Abraham that one day they would live in the Promised Land. This picture (left) in a 15th-century Jewish prayer book shows Moses leading his people across the Red Sea back to Palestine, their earlier home, that famine had forced them to leave.*

book of the Old Testament containing the history of the Israelites during the rule of the judges.

judge·ship (jŭj′shĭp) *n.* The office, duties, or jurisdiction of a judge.

judg·mat·ic (jŭj-măt′ĭk) *adj.* Also **judg·mat·i·cal** (-ĭ-kəl). *Informal.* Judicious. [From JUDGMENT.] —**judg·mat·i·cal·ly** *adv.*

judg·ment (jŭj′mənt) *n.* Also **judge·ment. 1. a.** The capacity to appraise, discriminate, and compare, and so arrive at a sound evaluation; discernment. **b.** The capacity to make reasonable decisions, especially in regard to the practical affairs of life; good sense; wisdom. **c.** The exercise of such a capacity. **2.** A formal decision, as of an arbiter in a contest. **3.** A discriminating appraisal; an authoritative opinion. **4.** Estimation: *make a judgment of the distance.* **5.** An assertion of something believed; idea; opinion: *It's my judgment that we ought to leave soon.* **6.** Criticism; censure. **7.** *Law.* **a.** A verdict by a court of law; a judicial decision. **b.** A court act creating or affirming an obligation, such as a debt. **c.** A writ in witness of such an act. —See Synonyms at **opinion, reason.** [Middle English *jugement,* from Old French, from *jugier,* to JUDGE.]

judg·ment·al (jŭj-měn′tl) *adj.* **1.** Of, pertaining to, or involving a judgment. **2.** Given to making judgments, especially moral judgments.

Judgment Day *n.* **1.** In Judaism, Christianity, and Islam, the day of God's final judgment upon mankind. **2.** Any day of reckoning or final judgment. Also called "Day of Judgment."

ju·di·ca·ble (jōō′dĭ-kə-bəl) *adj.* **1.** Capable of being judged. **2.** Liable to be judged. [Late Latin *jūdicābilis,* from Latin *jūdicāre,* to JUDGE.]

ju·di·ca·tive (jōō′dĭ-kā′tĭv, -kə-tĭv) *adj.* Having the capacity to judge; judicial. [Medieval Latin *jūdicātivus,* from Latin *jūdicāre,* to JUDGE.]

ju·di·ca·tor (jōō′dĭ-kā′tər) *n.* One who acts as judge. [Late Latin *jūdicātor,* from Latin *jūdicāre,* to JUDGE.]

ju·di·ca·to·ry (jōō′dĭ-kə-tôr′ē, -tōr′ē) *n., pl.* **-ries. 1.** A court of justice; a tribunal. **2.** A system of courts of law for the administration of justice; a judiciary.
—*adj.* Of or pertaining to the administration of justice. [Medieval Latin *jūdicātōrium,* from Latin *jūdicāre,* to JUDGE.]

ju·di·ca·ture (jōō′dĭ-kə-chōōr′) *n.* **1.** The administering of justice. **2.** The position, function, or authority of a judge. **3.** A court of law. **4.** A system of law courts and their judges. [Old French, from Medieval Latin *jūdicātūra,* from Latin *jūdicāre,* to JUDGE.]

ju·di·cial (jōō-dĭsh′əl) *adj.* **1.** Of, pertaining to, or proper to courts of law or to the administration of justice: *the judicial branch of the government.* Compare **executive, legislative. 2.** Decreed by or proceeding from a court of justice. **3.** Pertaining or appropriate to the office of a judge. **4.** Characterized by or expressing judgment. **5.** *Theology.* Proceeding from a divine judgment. [Middle English, from Old French, from Latin *jūdiciālis,* from *jūdicium,* judgment, from *jūdex* (stem *jūdic-*), JUDGE.] **—ju·di·cial·ly** *adv.*

judicial separation *n.* A court order recognizing that husband and wife are living apart and regulating their mutual rights and liabilities. Also called "legal separation."

ju·di·ci·ar·y (jo͞o-dĭsh′ē-ĕr′ē) *adj.* Of or pertaining to courts, judges, or judicial decisions.
~n., pl. **judiciaries. 1.** The judicial branch of government. Compare **executive, legislature. 2.** A system of courts of justice. **3.** Judges collectively. [Latin *jūdiciārius,* from *jūdicium,* judgment. See **judicial.**]

ju·di·cious (jo͞o-dĭsh′əs) *adj.* Having or exhibiting sound judgment. [Old French *judicieux,* from Latin *jūdicium.* See **judicial.**] **—ju·di·cious·ly** *adv.* **—ju·di·cious·ness** *n.*

Ju·dith¹ (jo͞o′dĭth). In the Apocrypha, a Jewish woman who rescued her people by slaying the Assyrian general Holofernes.

Judith² *n.* A book of the Apocrypha and the Douay Bible relating the story of Judith.

ju·do (jo͞o′dō) *n.* A modern form of jujitsu applying principles of balance and leverage, often played as a sport. [Japanese *jūdō* : *jū,* soft (see **jujitsu**) + *dō,* way.] **—ju·do·ist** *n.*

ju·do·gi (jo͞o-dō′gə) *n.* A white costume worn by judo players, consisting of loose trousers and a loose-sleeved jacket fastened by a belt. [Japanese.]

ju·do·ka (jo͞o′dō-kä) *n.* One who practices judo; judo player. [Japanese.]

Ju·dy (jo͞o′dē) *n., pl.* **-ies.** A character in a puppet show. See **Punch.**

jug (jŭg) *n.* **1.** A small pitcher. **2. a.** A vessel of earthenware, glass, or metal with a lip or spout, a handle, and sometimes a stopper or cap, made for holding and pouring liquids. **b.** The contents of a jug. **c.** The amount of liquid a jug will hold. **3.** *British Informal.* A glass for beer or some other alcoholic drink, especially one with a handle. **4.** *Slang.* Jail.
~tr.v. **jugged, jugging, jugs. 1.** To stew (a hare, for example) in an earthenware vessel. **2.** *Slang.* To put in jail. [From *Jug,* pet form of *Joan* or *Judith.*]

ju·ga. A plural of **jugum.**

ju·gal (jo͞o′gəl) *adj.* Of or pertaining to the zygomatic bone.
~n. The zygomatic bone. Also called "jugal bone."

ju·gate (jo͞o′gāt′) *adj.* Joined in or forming a pair or pairs. Said especially of compound leaves. [From New Latin *jugum,* yoke, from Latin.]

jug band *n.* A country-and-western musical group playing improvised instruments, such as empty jugs and washboards.

JUG·FET (jŭg′fĕt) *n. Electronics.* A type of field-effect transistor in which the gate is a p-n junction with the conducting channel. [*Ju*nction-*G*ate *F*ield-*E*ffect *T*ransistor.]

jug·ger·naut (jŭg′ər-nôt′) *n.* **1.** Anything that draws blind and destructive devotion, or to which people are ruthlessly sacrificed, such as a belief or institution. **2.** *British.* A very large, heavy motor vehicle, especially a long-distance truck. [From JUGGERNAUT.]

Jug·ger·naut (jŭg′ər-nôt′) *n.* **1.** *Hinduism.* Also **Jag·an·nath** (jŭg′ə-nät′, -nôt′). A title of the deity Vishnu. **2.** A huge car or wagon on which an idol of the god Vishnu is drawn in procession; specifically, such a vehicle used in an annual procession in Puri, in the Indian state of Orissa. [From Hindi *Jagannath,* from Sanskrit *Jagannātha* : *jagat-,* world + *nāthás,* lord.]

jug·gle (jŭg′əl) *v.* **-gled, -gling, -gles.** *—tr.* **1.** To keep (two or more balls, plates, or other objects) in the air at one time by alternately tossing and catching. **2.** To keep (more than one activity) in motion or progress at one time. **3.** To attempt to balance or otherwise cope with: *juggle a handbag and glass at a cocktail party.* **4.** To manipulate, especially in order to deceive: *juggle figures in a ledger.* *—intr.* **1.** To perform the tricks of a juggler. **2.** To use trickery to deceive.
~n. **1.** An act of juggling. **2.** A piece of trickery for some dishonest purpose. [Middle English *jogelen,* from Old French *jogler,* from Latin *joculārī,* to jest. See **juggler.**]

jug·gler (jŭg′lər) *n.* **1.** An entertainer who performs tricks of dexterity; especially, one who juggles balls or other objects. **2.** One who uses tricks, deception, or fraud. [Middle English *iugelere, iugelour,* jester, magician, from Old French *joglere, juglere,* from Latin *joculātor,* from *joculārī,* to jest, from *joculus,* diminutive of *jocus,* jest, joke.]

jug·gler·y (jŭg′lə-rē) *n., pl.* **-ies. 1.** The art or performance of a juggler. **2.** Trickery; deception.

Jugoslavia. See **Yugoslavia.**

jug·u·lar (jŭg′yə-lər) *adj.* **1.** Of, pertaining to, or located in the region of the neck or throat. **2.** Of, designating, or having pelvic fins in front of the pectoral fins.
~n. A jugular vein. [Late Latin *jugulāris,* from Latin *jugulum,* collarbone, diminutive of *jugum,* yoke.]

jugular vein *n.* Any of several veins in the neck. The *internal jugular* is a large paired vein conveying blood from the brain, face, and neck to the subclavian vein. The *external jugular* is a smaller paired vein taking blood from the face, scalp, and neck to the subclavian vein.

ju·gum (jo͞o′gəm) *n., pl.* **-ga** (-gə) or **-gums.** A paired or yokelike structure, such as a pair of opposite leaflets, a ridge or furrow connecting two parts of a bone, or a lobe joining the bases of the forewings and hind wings of certain insects. [New Latin, from Latin *jugum,* yoke.]

juice (jo͞os) *n.* **1. a.** Any fluid naturally contained in plant or animal tissue. **b.** Any bodily secretion. **c.** Any extracted fluid, especially that of a fruit. **2. a.** The essence or animating spirit of something. **b.** Vigorous life and vitality. **3.** *Slang.* **a.** Electric current. **b.** Fuel for an engine. **4.** *Slang.* Alcoholic drink. **—stew in one's own juice.** To suffer from problems of one's own making.
~tr.v. **juiced, juicing, juices. 1.** To extract the juice from. **2.** *Slang.* To make lively. Used with *up.* [Middle English *iuys, jus,* from Old French *jus,* from Latin *jūs,* broth, sauce, juice.]

juic·er (jo͞o′sər) *n.* A kitchen appliance for extracting juice from fruits and vegetables.

juic·y (jo͞o′sē) *adj.* **-ier, -iest. 1.** Full of juice; succulent. **2.** Richly interesting; suggestive; racy: *a juicy bit of gossip.* **—juic·i·ly** *adv.* **—juic·i·ness** *n.*

ju·jit·su (jo͞o-jĭt′so͞o) *n.* Also **ju·jut·su, jiu·jit·su, jiu·jut·su.** A Japanese art of self-defense or hand-to-hand combat based on maneuvers that seek to turn an opponent's weight and strength against himself. [Japanese *jūjitsu* : *jū,* soft, yielding, + *jitsu,* art.]

ju·ju (jo͞o′jo͞o′) *n.* **1.** An object used as a fetish, charm, or amulet in West Africa. **2.** The supernatural power ascribed to such an object. [Probably of West African origin.] **—ju·ju·ism** *n.*

ju·jube (jo͞o′jo͞ob′) *n.* **1. a.** Any of several spiny trees of the genus *Ziziphus;* especially, *Z. jujuba,* native to the Old World, having small yellowish flowers and dark red fruit. **b.** The fleshy, edible fruit of this tree. Also called "Chinese date." **2.** A fruit-flavored, usually chewy candy or lozenge. [Middle English *iuiube,* from Old French *jujube* or Medieval Latin *jujuba,* both from Latin *zizyphum,* from Greek *zizuphon*†.]

juk, jook (jo͝ok) *tr.v.* **juked** or **jooked, juking** or **jooking, jukes** or **jooks.** *West Indian Informal.* To prick; jab.
~n. West Indian Informal. A prick or jab. [West African, probably Fulani *jukka,* to spur, poke.]

juke box (jo͞ok) *n.* A coin-operated phonograph, typically encased in an illuminated and decorated cabinet and equipped with push buttons for the selection and playing of records. [From earlier *jukehouse,* a brothel, from Gullah, disorderly.]

Jul. July.

ju·lep (jo͞o′lĭp) *n.* **1.** A **mint julep** *(see).* **2.** A sweet syrupy drink, especially one to which medicine may be added. [Middle English *iulep,* from Old French *julep,* from Arabic *julāb,* from Persian *gulāb,* "rose water" : *gul,* rose + *āb,* water.]

Jul·ian (jo͞ol′yən), known as "Julian the Apostate," born Flavius Claudius Julianus (A.D. 331–363). Roman emperor (361–363). He was brought up as a Christian, but on succeeding to the throne he began to take measures to restore the official dominance of the old Roman religion. He died in battle.

Ju·li·an·a (jo͞o′lē-ăn′ə), born Juliana Louise Emma Maria Wilhelmina (1909–). Queen of the Netherlands (1948–80). She married Prince Bernard (1911–) in 1937 and came to the throne after the abdication of her mother, Wilhelmina. In 1980 Juliana abdicated in favor of her daughter Beatrix.

Julian calendar *n.* The calendar introduced by Julius Caesar in Rome in 46 B.C., that fixed the length of the year at 365 days, with an extra day every fourth, or leap, year. It was eventually replaced by the Gregorian calendar. See feature at **calendar.**

ju·li·enne (jo͞o′lē-ĕn′; *French* zhü-lyĕn′) *adj.* Cut into thin strips about the size of a matchstick: *julienne potatoes.*
~n. Consommé or broth garnished with strips of julienne vegetables. [From French *à la julienne,* probably from the given name *Julien* or *Jules.*]

Jul·ius II (jo͞ol′yəs), born Giuliano della Rovere (1443–1513). Pope (1503–13). A soldier and statesman more than a spiritual leader, he restored papal authority in central Italy through campaigns against Venice and formed the Holy League to expel the French from Italy. He ordered the reconstruction of St. Peter's in Rome and commissioned Michelangelo to decorate the Sistine Chapel and Raphael to decorate his papal apartments.

Julius Caesar. See **Caesar.**

Ju·ly (jo͞o-lī′, jo͞o-) *n., pl.* **-lys.** *Abbr.* **Jul.** The seventh month of the year according to the Gregorian calendar. July has 31 days. See feature at **calendar.** [Middle English *Julie,* from Norman French, from Latin *Jūlius (mēnsis),* (month of) Julius Caesar.]

Ju·ma (jo͞o′mä) *n.* The Islamic Sabbath, falling on Friday.

Ju·ma·da, Jo·ma·da (jo͞o-mä′dä) *n.* **1.** The fifth month of the year in the Muslim calendar, having 30 days. **2.** The sixth month of the year in the Muslim calendar, having 29 days. See feature at **calendar.** [Arabic *Jumādā.*]

jum·ble¹ (jŭm′bəl) *v.* **-bled, -bling, -bles.** *—intr.* To move, mix, or mingle in a confused, disordered manner. *—tr.* **1.** To stir or mix in a disordered mass. **2.** To muddle; confuse.
~n. **1.** A confused or disordered mass: *a jumble of disconnected ideas.* **2.** A disordered state; muddle. **3.** *Chiefly British.* Goods to be sold at a jumble sale. [16th century : perhaps imitative.]

jumble² *n.* A light, thin, crisp, biscuit, variously flavored with fruit or almonds and usually tightly rolled. [17th century (originally, a cake made in rings) : perhaps from earlier *gimmal,* variant of GIMBALS.]

jumble sale *n. Chiefly British.* A rummage sale.

jum·bo (jŭm′bō) *n., pl.* **-bos. 1.** An unusually large person, animal, or thing. **2.** *Informal.* A jumbo jet.

juggernaut *Modern British trailer trucks get their popular name from their resemblance to the huge wagon used to carry the statue of the Hindu god Jagannath in Indian festivals.*

Juggernaut *Devotees of the Hindu god Vishnu are said to have hurled themselves to death under the wheels of the huge wagon (above) used to carry the god's statue during processions. One of Vishnu's titles—Jagannath, or Juggernaut, meaning "Lord of the world"—has passed into English as the word for an overwhelming force that advances and crushes whatever is in its path.*

jumping jack *A wooden doll, suspended on twisted strings in a frame. The doll somersaults over the strings when the sides of the frame are moved apart. Toys based on the same principle have been popular for at least 200 years.*

junco *These finches are found in conifer forests throughout western North America. This is the Oregon junco.*

~*adj.* Larger than average: *a jumbo box of detergent.*
Jum·bo (jŭm′bō). A name for an elephant, as used by children and in folktales. [Probably from the second element of MUMBO JUMBO.]
jumbo jet *n.* A large jet airliner.
jum·buck (jŭm′bŭk′) *n. Australian Informal.* A sheep. [From a native Australian name.]
Jum·na (jŭm′nə). Also **Ya·mu·na** (yä′mə-nə). A river in northern India. It rises in the Himalayas of Uttar Pradesh and flows roughly south through Delhi to its confluence with the Ganges. The juncture of the two rivers is known as the Prayag, a place of pilgrimage in Hindu religion. The Jumna is 1,385 kilometers (860 miles) long.
jump (jŭmp) *v.* **jumped, jumping, jumps.** —*intr.* **1. a.** To spring off the ground or other base by a muscular effort of the legs and feet: *jumped three feet into the air.* **b.** To perform this movement repeatedly or rhythmically, as for exercise. **2. a.** To move or propel oneself, legs downward, down, off, out, or into something. **b.** To involve or commit oneself enthusiastically: *He jumped into the political fray.* **c.** To parachute from an aircraft. **3.** To spring or pounce with the intent to upbraid or censure. Used with *on* or *at*: *He jumped on me for saying such a thing.* **4.** To form judgments hastily or haphazardly. Used with *to*: *jump to conclusions.* **5.** To grab at eagerly; respond with alacrity. Used with *at*: *jump at the chance.* **6.** To start involuntarily: *You made me jump.* **7.** To rise suddenly and pronouncedly: *Prices jumped.* **8. a.** To skip over space or material, leaving a break in continuity. **b.** To be displaced vertically or laterally because of improper alignment: *The film jumped during projection.* **9.** *Computer Science.* To move from one set of instructions in a program to another farther ahead or behind rather than moving sequentially. **10.** *Checkers.* To move over an opponent's playing piece. **11.** *Bridge.* To make a jump bid. **12.** To be in agreement; coincide. **13.** *Slang.* To have a lively, pulsating quality: *a nightclub that jumps.* **14.** *Physics.* To change from one quantum state to another. —*tr.* **1.** To leap over or across: *jump a gate.* **2.** To leap aboard or jump on (a vehicle) illegally: *jump a train.* **3.** *Slang.* To spring upon in sudden attack: *The muggers jumped him.* **4.** To cause to leap: *jump a horse over a hurdle.* **5.** To cause to increase suddenly and markedly. **6.** To miss out; skip: *The typewriter jumped a space.* **7.** To drive through or move away from (traffic lights), before they change to green. **8.** *Bridge.* To raise (a partner's bid) by more than is necessary. **9.** *Checkers.* To take (an opponent's piece) by moving over it with one's own. **10.** To leave (a course or track) through mishap: *The train jumped the rails.* **11.** To leave or abandon without authorization: *jump ship; jump bail.* **—jump to it.** *Informal.* To set about a task promptly and eagerly. ~*n.* **1.** The act of jumping; leap. **2. a.** The space or distance covered by a leap: *a jump of seven feet.* **b.** A descent by parachute from an aircraft. **3.** A hurdle, fence, barrier, or span to be jumped. **4.** An athletic event featuring skill in jumping: *the high jump.* **5.** A sudden, pronounced rise, as in price or salary. **6.** A step or level: *a jump ahead of the others.* **7.** A major transition, as from one career to another. **8.** A short trip: *just a hop, skip, and a jump to the shore.* **9.** A break in continuity, as in a film. **10.** *Checkers.* A move made by jumping. **11. a.** An involuntary nervous movement, as when startled. **b. jumps.** *Informal.* The fidgets. **12.** *Physics.* A change between two quantum states. **13.** *West African.* A dance with live music. [16th century : probably imitative.]
jump bid *n. Bridge.* A bid at a higher level than that required to exceed the preceding bid.
jumped-up (jŭmpt′ŭp′) *adj. Informal.* Having risen from a humble to a significant position.
jump·er[1] (jŭm′pər) *n.* **1.** One that jumps. **2.** A type of coasting sled. **3.** *Electricity.* A short length of wire used temporarily to complete or by-pass a circuit. **4.** A bit or other boring device in a hammer drill.
jumper[2] *n.* **1.** A sleeveless dress worn over a blouse or sweater. **2.** *Chiefly British.* **a.** A jersey or sweater. **b.** Loosely, any knitted top. [Probably from British dialectal *jump, jup,* man's loose jacket, woman's underbodice, from French *juppe,* variant of *jupe,* skirt, from Arabic *jubbah,* JUBBAH.]
jumper cable *n.* A **booster cable** *(see).*
jumping bean *n.* A seed, as of certain Mexican shrubs or plants of the genera *Sebastiania* and *Sapium,* containing the larva of a moth, *Carpocapsa* (or *Enarmonia*) *saltitans,* the movements of which cause the seed to jerk or roll.
jumping jack *n.* A toy figure with jointed limbs that can be made to dance by pulling an attached string or frame.
jumping mouse *n.* Any of various small rodents of the family Zapodidae, having a long tail and long hind legs.
jump·ing-off place (jŭm′pĭng-ôf′, -ŏf′) *n.* **1.** A very remote place. **2.** A starting point for an enterprise. Also called "jumping-off point."
jump jet *n.* A fixed-wing jet aircraft in which the engine ducts can be rotated so that the aircraft can take off and land vertically.
jump lead *n. Chiefly British.* A **booster cable** *(see).*
jump-off (jŭmp′ôf′, -ŏf′) *n.* In show-jumping, a round that decides which of two or more horses previously tying for first place is the winner.
jump seat *n.* **1.** A portable or folding seat in an aircraft or in a car between the front and rear seats. **2.** A small rear seat in a sports car.
jump shot *n. Basketball.* A shot made by a player at the highest point of a jump.
jump-start (jŭmp′stärt′) *tr.v.* **-started, -starting, -starts. 1.** To start (a car engine) by pushing or rolling and suddenly releasing the clutch. **2.** To start (a car engine) using jump leads.
~*n.* The process of jump-starting.
jump suit *n.* **1.** A parachutist's uniform. **2.** Also **jump·suit** (jŭmp′sōōt′). A one-piece garment with legs, reaching from neck to ankles, and usually made of a close-fitting, stretch fabric.
jump-up (jŭmp′ŭp′) *n.* A West Indian festival dance.
jump·y (jŭm′pē) *adj.* **-ier, -iest. 1.** Characterized by fitful, jerky movements. **2.** Easily unsettled or alarmed; nervous or on edge, as with apprehension. **—jump·i·ness** *n.*
jun (jōōn) *n., pl.* **jun.** A coin equal to 1/100 of the won of North Korea. Also called "jeon." See feature at **currency.** [Korean.]
Jun. 1. June. **2.** Also **jun.** junior.
junc. junction.
jun·co (jŭng′kō) *n., pl.* **-cos.** Any of various North American finches of the genus *Junco,* having predominantly gray plumage. [Spanish, "rush," junco. See **jonquil.**]
junc·tion (jŭngk′shən) *n.* **1.** The act or process of joining or the condition of being joined. **2.** *Abbr.* **jct., junc.** The place where two things join or meet; specifically, the place where two roads or railway routes join or cross paths. **3.** A transition layer or boundary between two different materials or between physically different regions in a single material, especially: **a.** A connection between conductors or sections of a transmission line. **b.** The interface between a region of predominantly positive charge carriers and another of predominantly negative charge carriers in a semiconductor. **c.** A mechanical or alloyed contact between different metals or other materials, as in a thermocouple. [Latin *junctiō* (stem *junctiōn-*), from *junctus,* past participle of *jungere,* to join.] **—junc·tion·al** *adj.*
junction box *n.* An enclosed panel used to connect or branch electric circuits without making permanent splices.
junction transistor *n.* A common type of transistor in which contact is made between regions of different conductivity type.
junc·ture (jŭngk′chər) *n.* **1.** The act of joining, or the condition of being joined. **2.** The line or point where two things are joined; junction; joint; hinge. **3.** A point or interval in time; especially, a crisis or similar turning point. **4.** The transition or mode of transition from one sound to another in speech. [Middle English, from Latin *junctūra,* from *junctus,* past participle of *jungere,* to join.]
June (jōōn) *n. Abbr.* **Jun.** The sixth month of the year according to the Gregorian calendar. June has 30 days. See feature at **calendar.** [Middle English, from Old French *juin,* from Latin *Jūnius (mēnsis),* (month consecrated to) the goddess JUNO.]
Ju·neau (jōō′nō). The capital of Alaska, on the Gastineau Channel, in the southeastern Alaska Panhandle. The city developed as a boom town after gold was discovered nearby in 1880.
June beetle *n.* Any of various North American beetles of the subfamily Melolonthinae, having larvae that are often destructive to crops. Also called "June bug," "May beetle."
June·ber·ry (jōōn′bĕr′ē) *n., pl.* **-ries.** The **shadbush** *(see),* or its fruit.
Jung (yŏŏng), **Carl Gustav** (1875–1961). Swiss psychiatrist, a pioneer of psychoanalysis. He worked with Freud but developed his own approach to psychoanalysis, based in part on his study of schizophrenia. Jung coined the terms "introvert" and "extrovert" to define psychological types. His best-known work is *Psychology of the Unconscious* (1912). **—Jung·i·an** *n. & adj.*
Jung·frau (yŏŏng′frou′). One of the highest peaks (4,158 meters; 13,632 feet) in the Swiss Alps, situated in the Bernese Oberland overlooking Interlaken. Its summit was first scaled in 1811.
jun·gle (jŭng′gəl) *n.* **1.** Land densely overgrown with tropical vegetation and trees. **2.** Any dense thicket or growth. **3.** *Slang.* A hobo camp or place of rendezvous. **4.** A milieu characterized by intense, often ruthless competition. **5.** Any maze, entanglement, or confusion, especially one that is fruitless or leads nowhere. [Originally, "wasteland," from Hindi and Marathi *jaṅgal,* from Sanskrit *jāṅgala*†, "dry," desert.] **—jun·gly** *adj.*
jungle fever *n.* A pernicious malaria occurring in the East Indies.
jungle fowl *n.* Any of several birds of the genus *Gallus,* of southeastern Asia; especially, *G. gallus,* considered to be the ancestor of the common domestic fowl.
jungle gym *n.* A structure of poles and bars on which children can play. [Originally a trademark.]
jungle juice *n. Slang.* Alcoholic drink, especially when homemade.
jun·ior (jōōn′yər) *adj. Abbr.* **Jnr., jnr., Jr., jr., Jun., jun. 1.** Designed for or including youthful persons: *a junior tennis match; junior dress sizes.* **2.** Lower in rank or shorter in length of tenure: *the junior senator.* **3.** Younger. Used especially after a name to denote the younger of two persons who share the same name, such as a father and son: *William Jones, Jr.* **4.** Designating the third or penultimate year of a U.S. high school or college. **5.** *British.* Of or pertaining to school children between the ages of 7 and 11.
~*n.* **1.** A younger person or individual. **2.** A person lesser in rank or length of service; subordinate. **3.** An undergraduate in the third or penultimate year of a high school or college. **4.** *British.* A schoolchild between the ages of 7 and 11. [Latin *jūnior,* from preclassical *juvenior* (unattested), comparative of *juvenis,* young.]
junior college *n.* An educational institution offering a two-year course that is generally the equivalent of the first two years of a four-year undergraduate course.
junior high school *n.* A school intermediate between grammar school and high school, and generally including the seventh, eighth, and sometimes ninth grades. Also called "junior high."

junior lightweight *n.* A professional boxer who weighs between 126 and 130 pounds (57 and 59 kilograms).
junior middleweight *n.* A professional boxer who weighs between 147 and 154 pounds (66.5 and 70 kilograms).
junior school *n. British.* A school for children aged between 7 and 11. Compare **infant school.**
junior welterweight *n.* A professional boxer who weighs between 135 and 140 pounds (61 and 63.5 kilograms).
ju•ni•per (jo͞o′nə-pər) *n.* Any of various evergreen coniferous trees or shrubs of the genus *Juniperus* in the cypress family (Cupressaceae), having spine-tipped needles and aromatic, bluish-gray, berrylike cones. An oil from the berries of *J. communis* is used to flavor gin. [Middle English *junipere,* from Latin *jūniperus* †.]
junk¹ (jŭngk) *n.* **1.** Scrapped materials such as glass, rags, paper, or metals that can be converted into usable stock. **2.** *Informal.* **a.** Anything worn-out or fit to be discarded. **b.** Something of inferior quality; something cheap or shoddy. **c.** Anything meaningless, fatuous, or unbelievable; nonsense. **3.** *Slang.* A narcotic drug; especially, heroin. **4.** *Nautical.* **a.** Hard salt beef. **b.** Old cordage, reused for gaskets, oakum, and mats.
∼*tr.v.* **junked, junking, junks.** To throw away or discard as useless; scrap. [Originally (until the 20th century) a nautical term meaning old, worn-out pieces of rope or cable, from Middle English *jonke* †.]
junk² *n.* A flat-bottomed ship used in China and Southeast Asia with a high poop and battened sails. [Chiefly from Portuguese *junco* and Dutch *jonk,* from Malay *jong,* sea-going ship.]
Jun•ker (yo͝ong′kər) *n.* A member of the Prussian landed aristocracy, especially of its ultrareactionary section. [German, from Old High German *junchērro* : *jung,* young + *hērro,* comparative of *hēr,* worthy, exalted.] —**Jun•ker•dom** *n.*
jun•ket (jŭng′kĭt) *n.* **1.** A sweet food made from flavored milk set with rennet. **2.** A party, banquet, or outing. **3.** A trip or excursion, especially one taken by an official and underwritten with public funds.
∼*intr.v.* **junketed, -keting, -kets. 1.** To hold a party or banquet. **2.** To make an excursion using public funds. [Middle English *jonket,* a kind of egg custard served on rushes or made in a rush mat, from *junket,* rush basket, from Old Northern French *jonquette,* from *jonc,* rush, from Latin *juncus.* See **jonquil.**] —**jun•ket•er** *n.* —**jun•ket•ing** *n.*
junk food *n. Informal.* Food that has been processed so as to be easily prepared and that is often of low nutritional value.
junk•ie, junk•y (jŭng′kē) *n., pl.* **-ies.** *Slang.* A drug addict, especially one using heroin.
Ju•no (jo͞o′nō). *Roman Mythology.* The principal Roman goddess, wife and sister of Jupiter, patroness primarily of marriage and the well-being of women, identified with the Greek goddess Hera. [Latin *Jūno* †.]
Ju•no•esque (jo͞o′nō-ĕsk′) *adj.* Having the stately bearing and imposing beauty of the goddess Juno.
jun•ta (ho͝on′tə, ho͞on′-, jŭn′-) *n.* **1.** A group of military officers holding state power in a country after a coup d'état. **2.** A council or small legislative body in a government, especially in Central and South American countries. **3.** Variant of **junto.** [Spanish and Portuguese, from Vulgar Latin *juncta* (unattested), "joined," from Latin, feminine past participle of *jungere,* to join.]
jun•to (jŭn′tō) *n., pl.* **-tos.** Also **jun•ta.** A small, usually secret group or committee that gathers for some common interest or aim; cabal; clique; faction. [Variant of JUNTA.]
Ju•pi•ter¹ (jo͞o′pə-tər) *Roman Mythology.* The supreme god, patron of the Roman state, brother and husband of Juno, identified with the Greek god Zeus. Also called "Jove." [Middle English, from Latin *Jūpiter, Jūppiter,* Old Latin *Jovis Pater,* "Jove Father."]
Jupiter² *n. Astronomy.* The fifth planet from the sun, the largest and most massive in the solar system, having a diameter of approximately 142,000 kilometers (88,700 miles), a mass approximately 318 times that of earth, and a sidereal period of revolution about the sun of 11.86 years at a mean distance of 773 million kilometers (483 million miles). [After JUPITER.] See feature, next page.
ju•ra. Plural of **jus.**
Ju•ra Mountains (jo͝or′ə). A mountain range in eastern France and western Switzerland. It forms a natural boundary between the two countries. Crêt de la Neige (1,723 meters; 5,653 feet) is the highest point.
ju•ral (jo͝or′əl) *adj.* **1.** Of or pertaining to law. **2.** Of, pertaining to, or arising from rights and obligations. [From Latin *jūs* (stem *jūr-*), right, law.] —**ju•ral•ly** *adv.*
Ju•ras•sic (jo͞o-răs′ĭk) *adj. Geology.* Of, belonging to, or designating the time and deposits of the second period of the Mesozoic era, characterized by the existence of dinosaurs and primitive mammals and birds.
∼*n. Geology.* The Jurassic period. Preceded by *the.* [French *jurassique,* after the JURA MOUNTAINS.]
ju•rat (jo͝or′ăt′) *n.* A certification on an affidavit declaring when, where, and before whom it was sworn. [Latin *jūrātum (est),* "(it has been) sworn," from *jūrāre,* to swear. See **jury.**]
Jur. D. Doctor of Law. [Latin *Juris Doctor*]
ju•rid•i•cal (jo͞o-rĭd′ĭ-kəl) *adj.* Also **ju•rid•ic** (-ĭk). Of or pertaining to the law and its administration. [From Latin *jūridicus* : *jūs* (stem *jūr-*), law + *dīcere,* to say.] —**ju•rid•i•cal•ly** *adv.*
juridical days *pl.n.* The days on which courts are in session. Compare **dies non.**
ju•ris•con•sult (jo͝or′əs-kŏn′sŭlt′) *n.* A person learned in law; jurist. [Latin *jūrisconsultus* : *jūris,* genitive of *jūs,* law + *consultus,* past participle of *consulere,* to CONSULT.]
ju•ris•dic•tion (jo͝or-əs-dĭk′shən) *n.* **1.** The right and power to interpret and apply the law. **2.** Authority or control. **3.** The extent of authority or control. **4.** The territorial range of authority or control. [Middle English *jurisdiccioun,* from Old French *juridiction,* from Latin *jūrisdictiō* (stem *jūrisdictiōn-*) : *jūris,* genitive of *jūs,* law + *dictiō,* declaration (see **diction**).] —**ju•ris•dic•tion•al** *adj.* —**ju•ris•dic•tion•al•ly** *adv.*
ju•ris•pru•dence (jo͝or′əs-pro͞od′əns) *n.* **1.** The philosophy of law or the formal science of law. **2.** A division or department of law. **3.** A system or body of laws. [Originally "skill in law," from Late Latin *jūrisprūdentia* : *jūris,* genitive of *jūs,* law + *prūdentia,* foresight, knowledge, from *prūdēns,* knowing, PRUDENT.] —**ju•ris•pru•den•tial** *adj.* —**ju•ris•pru•den•tial•ly** *adv.*
ju•ris•pru•dent (jo͝or′əs-pro͞od′ənt) *n.* One who is versed in jurisprudence. —**ju•ris•pru•dent** *adj.*
ju•rist (jo͝or′əst) *n.* **1.** A person who is skilled in the law; especially, one who studies or writes about legal matters. **2. a.** A judge. **b.** A lawyer. [Old French, from Medieval Latin *jūrista,* from Latin *jūs* (stem *jūr-*), law.]
ju•ris•tic (jo͞o-rĭs′tĭk) *adj.* Also **ju•ris•ti•cal** (-tĭ-kəl). **1.** Of or pertaining to a jurist or to jurisprudence. **2.** Of or pertaining to law or legality. —**ju•ris•ti•cal•ly** *adv.*
ju•ror (jo͝or′ər, -ôr′) *n.* **1. a.** A person serving as a member of a body sworn to hear and deliver a verdict on a case. **b.** A person called or designated for jury duty. **2.** A person who serves on any body acting in a capacity analogous to that of a jury, as when judging the entries in a competition. [Middle English *juroure,* from Norman French *jurour,* from Latin *jūrātor,* "swearer," from *jūrātus,* past participle of *jūrāre,* to swear. See **jury.**]
ju•ry¹ (jo͝or′ē) *n., pl.* **-ries. 1.** A group of persons forming a body sworn to give a verdict on some matter; specifically, a body of persons summoned by law and sworn to hear and deliver a verdict upon a case presented in court. See **grand jury, petit jury. 2.** A group of persons forming a committee to judge, for example, a competition and award prizes. [Middle English *jurie,* from Norman French *juree,* from Old French *juree,* oath, inquest, from Latin *jūrāta,* "thing sworn," from the feminine past participle of *jūrāre,* to swear, from *jūs* (stem *jūr-*), law.]
jury² *adj. Nautical.* Intended or designed for emergency or temporary use; makeshift: *a jury rig.* [Perhaps ultimately from Old French *ajurie,* aid.]
jury box *n.* The enclosed area in a court where the jury sits.
ju•ry•man (jo͝or′ē-mən) *n., pl.* **-men** (-mĭn). A man serving on a jury; a male juror.
ju•ry-rigged (jo͝or′ē-rĭgd′) *adj. Nautical.* Rigged for emergency or temporary use.
ju•ry•wom•an (jo͝or′ē-wo͝om′ĭn) *n., pl.* **-women** (-wĭm′ĭn). A woman serving on a jury; a female juror.
jus (yo͞os) *n., pl.* **jura** (yo͞o′rə). *Latin.* **1.** Right; justice; law. **2.** A given right; a legal power.
jus gen•ti•um (gĕn′tē-əm) *n. Latin.* The law of nations; international law.
Jus•sieu (zhü-syœ′). A family of eminent French botanists. **Antoine de Jussieu** (1686–1758) was a director of the Jardin des Plantes in Paris, and his younger brother **Bernard de Jussieu** (*c.* 1699–1777) worked at the Jardins du Roi. **Joseph de Jussieu** (1704–79), the youngest of the brothers, lived for many years in South America and introduced the garden heliotrope into Europe. **Antoine Laurent de Jussieu** (1748–1836), their nephew, was professor of botany at the Paris Museum of Natural History, and his *Genera Plantarum* (1789) was a major work of plant classification that remains fundamental to modern botany.
jus•sive (jŭs′ĭv) *adj. Grammar.* Expressing or used to express a command.
∼*n. Grammar.* A word, mood, or construction used to express command. [From Latin *jussus,* past participle of *jubēre,* to command.]
just¹ (jŭst) *adj.* **1.** Honorable and fair in one's dealings and actions. **2.** Consistent with moral right; fair; equitable. **3.** Properly due or merited: *just deserts.* **4.** Legally valid or correct; lawful: *just title.* **5.** Suitable; fitting. **6.** Well-founded; justified; legitimate: *just resentment.* **7.** Exact; accurate: *a just measure.* **8.** Upright before God; righteous. —See Synonyms at **fair.**
∼*adv.* (jŭst; *unstressed* jəst, jĭst). **1.** Precisely; exactly: *That's just what I was going to say.* **2.** At the exact moment of: *Just as I was leaving, he turned up.* **3.** Only a moment ago: *He has just come.* **4.** By a narrow margin; barely: *You have just missed Tom.* **5.** But a little distance: *You'll find it just down the road.* **6.** Merely; only: *I just meant that I agree.* **7.** Conceivably; possibly: *There's just a chance she won't notice.* **8.** Simply; certainly. Used as an intensive: *It's just beautiful!* —**just about. 1.** On the point of: *I was just about to go.* **2.** Almost; very nearly: *I've just about had enough.* —**just now. 1.** At this very moment. **2.** Only a moment ago. —**just so. 1.** Carried out, arranged, or presented with due regard for neatness, accuracy, tidiness, or the like. **2.** Used to express agreement. [Middle English *just(e),* from Old French *juste,* from Latin *jūstus.*] —**just•ly** *adv.* —**just•ness** *n.*
just². Variant of **joust.**
Just (jŭst), **Ernest Everett** (1883–1941). U.S. embryologist. He researched the cellular processes of marine organisms and pioneered

juniper *The leaves and branches of this conifer were once burned with beech wood to preserve hams, and its berries are used in certain sauces and to flavor gin.*

junk *The traditional Chinese flat-bottomed boat has a large rudder that serves partly as a keel. The sails open and close like a fan.*

the study of the surface properties of cells. His major work is *Biology of the Cell Surface* (1939).

jus·tice (jŭs′tĭs) *n.* **1.** Moral rightness; equity. **2.** The quality of being just, fair, or in conformity with what is right or legal: *recognized the justice of our cause.* **3.** Good reason: *He's very angry, and with justice.* **4.** Fair handling; due reward or treatment. **5.** The administration and procedure of law. **6.** *Abbr.* **J.** A judge. **7.** A justice of the peace. —**bring to justice.** To effect the arrest and trial of (a lawbreaker). —**do justice to.** **1.** To approach with proper appreciation; enjoy fully. **2.** To show to full advantage: *The picture doesn't do justice to her eyes.* [Middle English, from Old French, from Latin *jūstitia,* from *jūstus,* JUST.] —**jus·tice·ship** *n.*

Justice, Department of. The legal department of the executive branch of the U.S. government, headed by the Attorney General and having as its jurisdiction the legal representation of the government, the enforcement of antitrust and civil-rights laws, and the supervision of immigration and naturalization.

justice of the peace *n. Abbr.* **J.P.** A magistrate of the lowest level of the state court system, having authority chiefly to act upon minor offenses, commit cases to a higher court for trial, perform marriages, and administer oaths.

jus·ti·ci·a·ble (jŭ-stĭsh′ə-bəl) *adj.* Appropriate for or subject to court trial; liable to be brought before a court of law. [French, from Old French, from *justicier,* to try, from *justice,* JUSTICE.]

jus·ti·ci·ar (jŭ-stĭsh′ē-ər) *n.* Also **jus·ti·ci·a·ry** (-ē-ĕr′ē). Formerly, an English legal officer who acted for the king in his absence.

jus·ti·ci·ar·y (jŭ-stĭsh′ē-ĕr′ē) *adj.* Pertaining to the administration of the law. ~*n., pl.* **justiciaries. 1.** One who administers the law. **2.** Variant of **justiciar.** [Medieval Latin *jūstitiārius,* from Latin *jūstitia,* JUSTICE.]

jus·ti·fi·a·ble (jŭs′tə-fī′ə-bəl) *adj.* Capable of being justified. —**jus·ti·fi·a·bil·i·ty, jus·ti·fi·a·ble·ness** *n.* —**jus·ti·fi·a·bly** *adv.*

jus·ti·fi·ca·tion (jŭs′tə-fĭ-kā′shən) *n.* **1.** The act of justifying. **2.** The condition or fact of being justified. **3.** A fact, circumstance, or evidence that justifies; a ground for defense.

jus·ti·fi·ca·tive (jŭ-stĭf′ĭ-kā-tĭv) *adj.* Also **jus·ti·fi·ca·to·ry** (-tôr′ē, -tōr′ē). Serving as justification.

jus·ti·fi·er (jŭs′tə-fī′ər) *n.* **1.** One that justifies. **2.** *Printing.* A space that varies as necessary to justify a line.

JUPITER: THE GIANT AMONG THE PLANETS

The "space fossil" inside a swirling shroud of multicolored gases

Jupiter is much the largest of the planets, with a diameter through its equator of 142,800 kilometers (88,700 miles). It is twice as massive as the other eight planets put together. Jupiter is regarded by astronomers as a kind of space fossil, for its enormous mass and powerful gravity have retained even the lightest of the gases from which all the planets were originally formed. Jupiter is thought to resemble Earth as it was before it solidified.

Because of its great distance from the sun—at 778,300,000 kilometers (483,600,000 miles) it is five times as far as Earth is from the sun—Jupiter takes 11.86 Earth-years to make an orbit and complete its year. But its rotation on its own axis is rapid, taking less than ten hours. The speed of rotation—44,800 kilometers (28,000 miles) an hour—has caused Jupiter to become flattened at the poles.

It is believed that Jupiter has a central rocky core surrounded by layers of liquid hydrogen, which are in turn overlaid by a deep, gaseous atmosphere. Only the multicolored cloud tops can be seen from Earth. These are bitterly cold, about –150°C (–238°F), but Jupiter is certainly hot at its core, perhaps as hot as 30,000°C (about 54,000°F). It emits more heat than it can receive from the sun—perhaps as a result of slow contraction under its own gravity. No manned craft can approach the planet because of the intense zones of radiation surrounding it.

The gaseous surface is streaked by dark belts and bright zones; the dark belts are regions of descending gas, the bright zones regions of ascending gas. The colors are vivid and there is one remarkable feature, the Great Red Spot, whose color may be due to the presence of phosphorus. Jupiter has a family of 16 satellites—four as large as planets.

Planet location guide

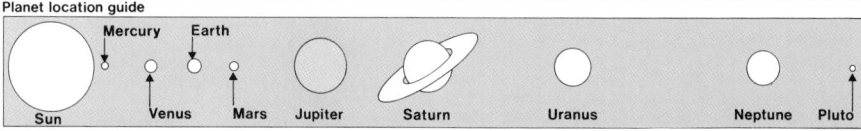

Sun   Mercury   Venus   Earth   Mars   Jupiter   Saturn   Uranus   Neptune   Pluto

THE MOONS OF JUPITER *This composite picture shows Jupiter (upper right) and its four largest satellites. Io (upper left) is red, slightly larger than Earth's moon, and has active volcanoes. Europa (center) is a little smaller than Io and has a smooth, icy crust. Ganymede (lower left), with a diameter of 5,000 kilometers (about 3,100 miles), is larger even than the planet Mercury, and Callisto (lower right) also is much larger than Earth's moon. Ganymede and Callisto are both icy and cratered. The satellites are shown in the correct relative positions.*

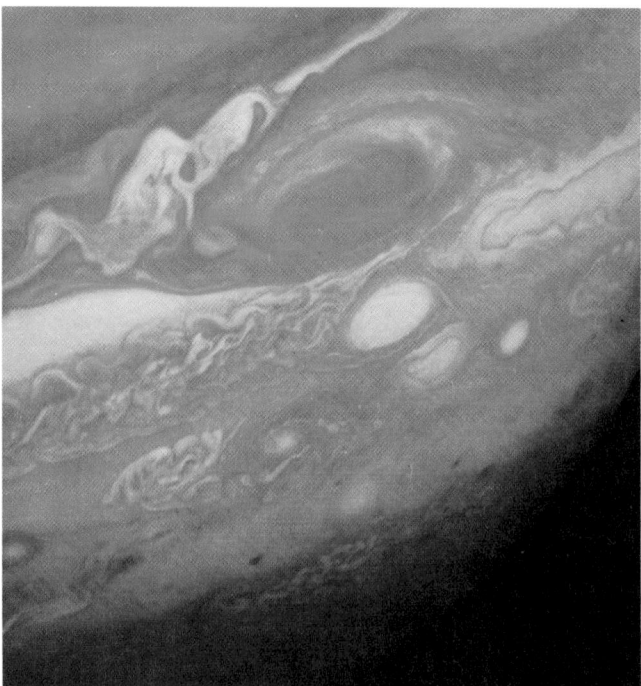

GREAT RED SPOT *This dramatic view of Jupiter's Great Red Spot was taken by a U.S. Voyager spacecraft in 1979 from a distance of 9.2 million kilometers (more than 5 million miles). The oval-shaped spot on the photograph seems to be a whirling storm of colored gas. It may be phosphorus that causes the spot's red color. The spot, which stands out among the vivid clouds of gas surrounding Jupiter, is enormous. It is 48,000 kilometers (about 30,000 miles) across at its greatest dimension—so large that Earth could fall into it without touching the sides.*

jus·ti·fy (jŭs′tə-fī′) v. **-fied, -fying, -fies.** —tr. **1.** To demonstrate or prove to be just, right, or valid. **2.** To show to be well-founded; warrant. **3.** To declare free of blame; absolve. **4.** *Theology.* To free (man) of the guilt and penalty attached to grievous sin. Said only of God. **5.** *Law.* **a.** To demonstrate good reason for (an action taken). **b.** To prove to be qualified to act as a bondsman. **6.** *Printing.* To adjust or space (a line of type) to the proper length. —intr. *Printing.* To be or become properly spaced and of the correct length. Said of a line of type. [Middle English *justifien,* originally, to judge, punish, from Old French *justifier,* from Late Latin *jūstificāre,* to do justice toward, to forgive, pardon : *jūstus,* JUST + *facere,* to do.]

Jus·tin·i·an I (jŭs-tĭn′ē-ən), known as "the Great" (A.D. 483-565). Byzantine emperor (527-65). He held the eastern frontier of his empire against the Persians and with the brilliant generalship of Belisarius reconquered former Roman territories in Africa, Italy, and Spain. A devout if autocratic Christian, he also achieved the temporary unity of the Eastern and Western churches and built the great cathedral of St. Sophia in Constantinople. As an administrator, he revised Roman law according to a system known as the Justinian Code.

Justinian Code n. The codification of Roman law made by order of Justinian I and published in A.D. 529.

jut (jŭt) intr.v. **jutted, jutting, juts.** To project, usually sharply, beyond the limits of the main body; protrude. Often used with *out:* "He had a sharp crooked nose jutting out of a lean dancer's face" (Graham Greene). ~n. Something that protrudes; projection. [Variant of JET (to project).] —**jut·ting·ly** adv.

jute (jōōt) n. **1.** Either of two Asian plants, *Corchorus capsularis* or *C. olitorius,* yielding a fiber used for sacking and cordage. **2.** The fiber obtained from such a plant. **3.** The coarse fabric made from the fiber of this plant. [Bengali *jhōṭo, jhuṭo,* from Sanskrit *jūṭa†,* twisted hair (of ascetics and Shiva).]

Jute (jōōt) n. A member of any of several Germanic tribes, some of whom invaded Britain and settled in Kent in the 5th century A.D. —**Jut·ish** adj.

Jut·land (jŭt′lənd). *Danish* **Jyl·land** (yül′län). A peninsula of northern Europe, almost entirely flat, situated between the North and Baltic seas. Mainland Denmark occupies the northern part, the southern region lying in West Germany. The Battle of Jutland (1916), fought in the North Sea off the Danish coast between the British and German fleets, was the largest naval engagement of World War I. Though the Germans inflicted the greater losses, they failed to break British control of the seas and afterward remained in the harbor until the end of the war.

juv. juvenile.

Ju·ve·nal (jōō′və-nəl), born Decimus Junius Juvenalis (c. A.D. 60-140). Roman satirical poet. He is remembered for his 16 *Satires* (probably written after A.D. 100), which denounce the extravagance, snobbery, and corruption of the privileged classes in Rome.

ju·ve·nes·cent (jōō′və-nĕs′ənt) adj. Becoming young or youthful. [JUVEN(AL) + -ESCENT.] —**ju·ve·nes·cence** n.

ju·ve·nile (jōō′və-nəl, -nīl′) adj. Abbr. **juv. 1.** Young; youthful. **2.** Not fully developed; not yet adult. Said of animals and plants or their parts. **3.** Characteristic of youth or children; immature: *juvenile behavior.* **4.** Intended for or appropriate to children or young persons: *juvenile fashions.* ~n. Abbr. **juv. 1. a.** A young person; child. **b.** A young animal that has not reached sexual maturity. **c.** A plant bearing the juvenile form of foliage. **2.** An actor who plays roles of children or young persons. **3.** A children's book. —See Synonyms at **young.** [Latin *juvenīlis,* from *juvenis,* young, a youth.] —**ju·ve·nile·ly** adv. —**ju·ve·nile·ness** n.

juvenile court n. A court dealing with children and young offenders.

juvenile delinquent n. Abbr. **J.D.** A child or adolescent who exhibits antisocial or criminal behavior. —**juvenile delinquency** n.

juvenile hormone n. An insect hormone that prevents metamorphosis into the adult form and maintains larval characteristics.

ju·ve·nil·i·a (jōō′və-nĭl′ē-ə) pl.n. Works, particularly written or artistic works, produced in childhood or youth. [Latin *juvenīlia,* neuter plural of *juvenīlis,* JUVENILE.]

ju·ve·nil·i·ty (jōō′və-nĭl′ə-tē) n., pl. **-ties. 1.** The quality or condition of being foolishly juvenile; immaturity. **2.** The quality or condition of being young or youthful. **3.** juvenilities. Juvenile or immature acts or characteristics. **4.** Young persons collectively.

ju·ve·noc·ra·cy (jōō′və-nŏk′rə-sē) n. Rule or influence by young people. [Latin *juvenis,* young person + -CRACY.]

jux·ta·pose (jŭk′stə-pōz′) tr.v. **-posed, -posing, -poses.** To place or situate side by side or close together, especially so as to produce or exhibit a contrasting effect. [French *juxtaposer,* probably from JUXTAPOSITION.]

jux·ta·po·si·tion (jŭk′stə-pə-zĭsh′ən) n. The act of juxtaposing or the state of being juxtaposed. [French : Latin *juxtā,* close together + POSITION.] —**jux·ta·po·si·tion·al** adj.

Jylland. See Jutland.

PRONUNCIATION KEY

ă, pat; ā, pay; âr, care; ä, father, are; b, bib; ch, church; d, deed; ĕ, pet; ē, be; f, fife; g, gag; h, hat; hw, which; ĭ, pit; ī, pie; îr, pier; j, judge; k, kick; l, lid, needle; m, mum; n, no, sudden; ng, thing; ŏ, pot; ō, toe; ô, paw, for; oi, noise; ou, out; ŏŏ, book; ōō, boot; p, pop; r, roar; s, sauce; sh, ship, dish; t, tight; th, thin, path; th, this, bathe; ŭ, cut; ûr, fur; v, valve; w, with; y, yes; z, zebra, size; zh, vision; ə, about, item, edible, gallop, circus, peaceful

IN FOREIGN WORDS:

à, *Fr.* ami; œ, *Fr.* feu, *Ger.* schön; ü, *Fr.* tu, *Ger.* über; KH, *Ger.* ich, *Scot.* loch; N, *Fr.* bon; y′, *Fr.* Compiègne

STRESS MARKS:

Primary stress: ′ in·cite′ (ĭn-sīt′) Secondary stress: ′ in′sight′ (ĭn′sīt′)

K

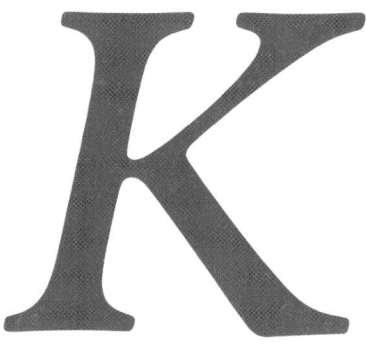

kabuki *Richly embroidered costumes are worn by the actors for historical scenes in Japanese kabuki plays. Plain costumes are worn for scenes from everyday life. The actors do not have masks as they do in No plays; instead they wear elaborate make-up.*

kale *Curled kale, shown here, is one of two types of this vegetable. The other is mossy kale. Both are related to the cabbage.*

k, K (kā) *n., pl.* **k's** or **K's. 1.** The 11th letter of the modern English alphabet. See feature at **alphabet. 2.** Any of the speech sounds represented by this letter. **3.** The 11th in a series; 10th when *J* is omitted. **4.** *Informal.* Thousand: *a job that pays $40k.* **5.** *Computer Science.* A unit of storage capacity equal to 1024 words, bytes, or bits.

k, K, k., K. *Note:* As an abbreviation or symbol, *k* may be a small or a capital letter, with or without a period. Established forms or those generally preferred precede the definition. When no form is given, all four forms are in general use in that sense. **1. K** kaon. **2. k** karat. **3. K a.** kelvin (temperature unit). **b.** Kelvin (temperature scale). **4. k** kilo-. **5. k., K.** king. **6. K** *Chess.* king. **7. K.** *Card Games.* king. **8. k., K.** knight. **9. K.** Köchel number. **10. k., K.** kopeck. **11. k., K.** koruna. **12. k., K.** krona. **13. k., K.** krone. **14. k** The symbol for the Boltzmann constant.

K The symbol for the element potassium. [New Latin *kalium.*]

K2. See **Godwin-Austen, Mount.**

ka (kä) *n.* A spirit believed by the ancient Egyptians to dwell in a man or statue. [Egyptian.]

Kaa·ba, Caa·ba (kä′bə) *n.* A Muslim shrine in Mecca that houses a sacred black stone said to have been given to Abraham by the archangel Gabriel and toward which followers of Muhammad face when praying. [Arabic *ka'bah,* "square building," from *ka'b, ka'ba,* cube.]

kab. Variant of **cab** (measure).

kabala, kabbala. Variants of **cabala.**

ka·bel·jou (kä′bəl-you′, käb′əl-) *n., pl.* **-jous** or collectively **kabeljou.** *South African.* An edible codlike fish, *Argyrosmus hololepidotus,* of the family Sciaenidae. [Afrikaans, from Dutch *kabeljauw,* from Germanic.]

ka·bob (kə-bŏb′) *n.* **Shish kebab** *(see).*

ka·bu·ki (kə-bōō′kē) *n.* A type of popular Japanese drama, evolved from the older No theater, in which elaborately costumed performers, usually male, enact both tragedies and comedies using stylized movements, dances, and songs. [Japanese, "art of singing and dancing" : *kabu,* singing and dancing + *ki,* art.]

Ka·bul (kä′bōol) *n.* Capital of Afghanistan. It commands the northeast trade route into Pakistan and has frequently been occupied by foreign invaders during its 3,000-year history, most recently by Soviet forces. From 1504 to 1526 it was the capital of the Mogul Empire. It became Afghanistan's capital in 1773.

Ka·byle (kə-bīl′) *n., pl.* **-byles** or collectively **Kabyle. 1.** A member of one of the Berber tribes inhabiting Tunisia or Algeria. **2.** The Hamitic Berber dialect spoken by these people.

ka·chi·na (kə-chē′nə) *n.* A doll that represents one of the rainbringing ancestral spirits of the Hopi. [Hopi *qacina,* supernatural.]

Ká·dár (kä′där), **János** (1912–). First secretary of the Hungarian Communist Party (1956–). He joined the invading Soviet forces during the 1956 revolution and was prime minister (1956–58, 1961–65).

Kaddafi, Muammar. See **Quaddafi.**

Kad·dish (kä′dĭsh) *n. Judaism.* A prayer in praise of God said in daily synagogue services and by mourners after the death of a close relative. [Aramaic *qaddīsh,* holy.]

kaf·fee·klatsch (kŏ′fē-kläch′, kä′fē-kläch′) *n.* A casual gathering for coffee and conversation. [German *Kaffee,* COFFEE + *Klatsch,* chat.]

kaf·fir, ka·fir (kăf′ər) *n.* A variety of sorghum, *Sorghum vulgare caffrorum,* of Africa, cultivated in dry regions for its grain and as fodder. Also called **"kaffircorn."** [From KAFFIR.]

Kaf·fir, Ka·fir (kăf′ər) *n., pl.* **-firs** or collectively **Kaffir, Kafir. 1. a.** A member of any of the Bantu-speaking tribes inhabiting South Africa. **b.** The language spoken by these people; Xhosa. **2.** A non-Muslim. Used derogatorily by Muslims. **3.** A black African, especially one living in southern Africa. Used derogatorily. **4.** Variant of **Kafir** (Iranian people). **5. Kaffirs.** On the London Stock Exchange, South African mining shares. [Arabic *kafir,* "infidel," present participle of *kafara,* to deny, be skeptical.]

kaf·fir·corn (kăf′ər-kôrn′) *n.* A variety of sorghum, **kaffir** *(see).*

kaffir lily *n.* A bulbous plant, *Schizostylis coccinea,* native to South

Africa, that is widely cultivated as a garden plant for its showy autumn-blooming pink or red flowers.

kaf·fi·yeh (kä-fē′ə, kä-) *n.* Also **kef·fi·yeh** (kĕ-). A headdress, usually worn by Arab men, consisting of a folded triangle of material held in place with a cord. [Arabic, perhaps from Late Latin *cofea,* COIF.]

Ka·fir (kăf′ər) *n., pl.* **-firs** or collectively **Kafir. 1.** A member of a people of ancient Iranian stock living in northeastern Afghanistan. **2.** Variant of **Kaffir.**

Kaf·i·ri (kăf′ə-rē) *n.* The Indic language of the Iranian Kafirs.

Kaf·ka (käf′kä), **Franz** (1883–1924). Czech novelist. He wrote enigmatic stories in which individuals were constantly threatened by a nightmarishly impersonal world. Most of his work, including *The Trial* (1925) and *The Castle* (1926), was published posthumously.

Kaf·ka·esque (käf′kə-ĕsk′, käf′-) *adj.* **1.** Of, pertaining to, or characteristic of Franz Kafka or of his writings. **2.** Characterized by surreal distortion and by the evocation of a sinister impersonal force controlling human affairs.

kaftan. Variant of **caftan.**

Ka·fu·e (kä-fōō′ā). River of central Zambia. It flows 960 kilometers (600 miles) from the Zaire border to join the Zambezi. The Kafue Dam provides two thirds of Zambia's hydroelectric power.

Ka·go·shi·ma (kä′gō-shē′mä). Port and naval base on Kagoshima Bay, southern Kyushu, Japan. The first European missionary to Japan, St. Francis Xavier, landed here in 1549.

kagoule. Variant of **cagoule.**

kaiak. Variant of **kayak.**

Kai·feng (kī′fŭng′). A city in northwestern Henan, China. It is a commercial, agricultural, and industrial center. The Huang He, just to the north, has frequently flooded the city. Founded in the 3rd century B.C., it was capital of the Song (Sung) dynasty (960–1127).

kail. Variant of **kale.**

Kai·las (kī-läs′). Peak and pilgrimage site in the Kailas Range of southwestern Tibet. It rises to *c.* 6,795 meters (22,280 feet).

kail·yard (kāl′yärd′) *n. Scottish.* A vegetable garden. [Scottish *kail,* kale + YARD.]

Kail·yard School (kāl′yärd′) *n.* A group of writers who make considerable use of Scots dialect in their works about Scottish life. [From KAILYARD.]

kain, kane, cain (kān) *n.* Tax or rent payments made in kind. [Middle English *cain,* from Scottish Gaelic *cáin,* rent, fine, probably from Late Latin *canōn,* tribute, decree, from Latin, rule, law, CANON.]

kai·nite (kī′nīt′, kā′-) *n.* A mineral, essentially $KCl \cdot MgSO_4 \cdot 3H_2O$, found in potash deposits and used mainly as fertilizer and as a source of potassium compounds. [German *Kainit* : Greek *kainos,* new, recently formed + -ITE.]

kai·ser, Kai·ser (kī′zər) *n.* Any of the emperors of the Holy Roman Empire (A.D. 800–1806), of Austria (1804–1918), or of Germany (1871–1918). [German *Kaiser,* from Old High German *Keisar,* from Latin *Caesar,* CAESAR.]

kai·ser·in, Kai·ser·in (kī′zər-ĭn) *n.* The wife of a kaiser; an empress. [German, feminine of *Kaiser,* KAISER.]

ka·ka (kä′kə) *n.* A brownish or greenish parrot, *Nestor meridionalis,* of New Zealand. [Maori, imitative of its cry.]

ka·ka·po (kä′kə-pō′) *n., pl.* **-pos.** A ground-dwelling owllike nocturnal parrot, *Strigops habroptilus,* of New Zealand, having greenish plumage. [Maori KAKA (parrot) + *po,* night.]

ka·ke·mo·no (kä′kə-mō′nō) *n., pl.* **-nos.** A Japanese scroll painting on silk or paper that is hung vertically. [Japanese, "hanging thing," scroll : *kake,* hanging + *mono,* thing.]

ka·la·a·zar (kä′lə-ə-zär′) *n.* A chronic, usually fatal disease that occurs in Asia, especially in India, is caused by a protozoan parasite, *Leishmania donovani,* and is characterized by irregular fever, enlargement of the spleen and liver, hemorrhages, and extreme emaciation. [Hindi *kālā-āzār* : *kālā,* black, from Sanskrit *kālaḥ,* blue-black, black, from Dravidian + *āzār,* disease, from Persian *āzār†.*]

Ka·la·ha·ri Desert (kä′lə-här′ē). Arid, sand-covered plateau between the Zambezi and Orange rivers in southern Africa. It occupies most of Botswana and parts of South Africa and Namibia and is inhabited by Bushmen and Hottentots.

Kal·a·ma·zoo (kăl′ə-mə-zōō′). A city of southwest Michigan, on the Kalamazoo River at its confluence with Portage Creek. It is an industrial and commercial center in a fertile farm area. The city has a large paper industry.

kal·an·cho·e (kăl′ən-kō′ē, kə-lăng′kō-ē) *n.* Any of various small tropical shrubs of the genus *Kalanchoe,* having clusters of variously colored, often red flowers on tall stems, that are cultivated as a house plant. [French, ultimately from Cantonese *goh leung choi* (Mandarin *gāo liáng cái*), tall cool plant.]

Ka·lash·ni·kov (kə-lăsh′nĭ-kôf′) *n.* A trademark for an automatic rifle, designed in the U.S.S.R., that is operated by gas, has a caliber of 7.62 millimeters, and has a high degree of accuracy over ranges of up to 300 meters. Also called "AK 47."

kale, kail (kāl) *n.* **1.** A variety of cabbage, *Brassica oleracea acephala,* eaten as a vegetable or used for livestock feed, having ruffled or crinkled leaves that do not form a tight head. Also called "borecole." **2.** *Scottish.* **a.** A cabbage. **b.** Broth containing cabbage. **3.** *Slang.* Money. [Middle English (northern dialect) *cal(e),* variant of COLE.]

ka·lei·do·scope (kə-lī′də-skōp′) *n.* **1.** A tube in which patterns of colors are optically produced and viewed for amusement; especially, one in which a pair of angled mirrors reflect light transmitted through loose bits of colored glass contained at one end, causing them to appear as symmetrical designs when viewed at the other. **2.** A constantly changing set of colors. **3.** A series of changing phases or events. [Greek *kalos,* beautiful + *eidos,* form + -SCOPE.] —**ka·lei·do·scop·ic** (kə-lī′də-skŏp′ĭk), **ka·lei·do·scop·i·cal** (-ĭ-kəl) *adj.* —**ka·lei·do·scop·i·cal·ly** *adv.*

kalends. Variant of **calends.**

ka·li (kā′lē, kăl′ē) *n.* A plant, the **saltwort** *(see).*

Ka·li (kä′lē). In Hindu mythology, Devi, considered as the goddess of death and destruction.

Kal·i·man·tan (kăl′ə-män′tän′, kä′lə-). Also **Indonesian Borneo.** The Indonesian section of the island of Borneo, occupying two thirds of the island. It is densely forested and produces timber.

Ka·lim·ba (kə-lĭm′bə) *n.* An African musical instrument in the shape of a wooden box set with metal bars that are plucked with the fingers. [Of African origin.]

Ka·li·nin (kə-lē′nĭn), **Mikhail Ivanovich** (1875–1946). President of the supreme council of the U.S.S.R. (1937–46). He was born a peasant, took part in the 1917 revolution, and joined the politburo in 1926. He was a founder of *Pravda* (1912).

Ka·li·nin·grad (kə-lē′nĭn-grăd′). Also (until 1946) **Kö·nigs·berg** (kā′nĭgz-bûrg′). A port in northwest U.S.S.R. It was founded (1255) by the Teutonic Knights and eventually became the capital of East Prussia.

Ka·li·yu·ga (kä′lə-yōō′gə) *n. Hindu Mythology.* The fourth and present age of the world, characterized by moral degeneration.

kal·li·din (kăl′ə-dĭn) *n.* A type of kinin *(see).*

kal·li·kre·in (kăl′ĭ-krē′ĭn, kə-lĭk′rē-ĭn) *n.* Any of several enzymes that act on globulins in the blood to synthesize the kinins bradykinin and kallidin.

kal·mi·a (kăl′mē-ə) *n.* An evergreen shrub of the genus *Kalmia,* which includes the **mountain laurel** *(see).*

Kal·muck (kăl′mŭk′, kăl-mŭk′) *n., pl.* **-mucks** or collectively **Kalmuck.** Also **Kal·muk** or **Kal·myk** (kăl′mĭk, kăl-mĭk′) **1.** A member of one of the Buddhist Mongol peoples originally inhabiting northwestern China and later migrating westward to the lower Volga. **2.** The Mongolian language spoken by the Kalmucks.

ka·long (kä′lông, -lŏng, kə-lông′, -lŏng′) *n.* An East Indian fruit bat, *Pteropus vampyrus,* having a wingspan of over 4 feet. [Javanese.]

kalpak. Variant of **calpac.**

kalsomine. Variant of **calcimine.**

Ka·ma (kä′mə). In Hindu mythology, the god of erotic love, son of Brahma and husband of Rati.

kam·a·cite (kăm′ə-sīt′) *n.* A nickel-iron alloy found in certain meteorites. [Obsolete German *Kamacit,* from Greek *kamax* (stem *kamak-*), shaft.]

ka·ma·la (kä′mə-lə, kăm′ə-, kŭm′ə-) *n.* **1.** An Asian tree, *Mallotus philippinensis,* that bears a hairy, capsular fruit. **2.** A powder obtained from the capsules of the kamala tree that is used as a dye and was formerly used to treat tapeworm and ringworm infestations. [Sanskrit *kamala,* probably from Dravidian, akin to Kanarese *kōmale.*]

Ka·ma·su·tra (kä′mə-sōō′trə) *n.* A treatise in Sanskrit (4th–7th century A.D.) setting forth rules for erotic love and marriage in accordance with Hindu law. [Sanskrit, "book on love" : *kāma,* love, desire + *sūtram,* manual.]

Kam·chat·ka Peninsula (kăm-chăt′kə). A peninsula of Far Eastern U.S.S.R., occupying 269,878 square kilometers (104,200 square miles) between the Sea of Okhotsk and the Bering Sea and Pacific Ocean.

kame (kām) *n.* A mound or long, low ridge of sand and gravel deposited during the melting of glacial ice. [Scottish, from Middle 255lish *camb,* northern variant of COMB.]

Ka·me·ha·me·ha I (kä-mā′hä-mä′hä), called "the Great" (1753?–1819). First king of the Sandwich (now Hawaiian) Islands. He first became king of Hawaii Island and then through conquest gained control of all the islands. Kamehameha founded a dynasty that lasted until 1872.

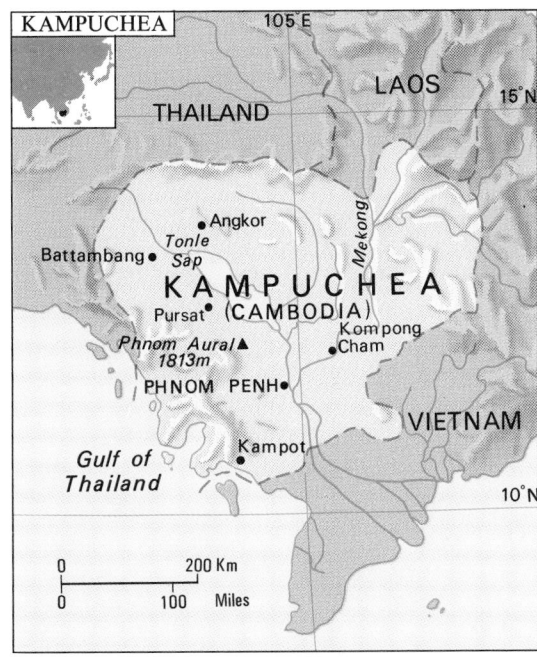

KAMPUCHEA

ka·mi (kä′mē) *n., pl.* **kami.** A divinity or god in the Shinto religion. [Japanese, "god."]

ka·mi·ka·ze (kä′mĭ-kä′zē) *n.* **1.** During World War II, a Japanese pilot trained to make a suicidal crash attack on a target such as a naval vessel. **2.** An airplane loaded with explosives to be piloted in a suicide attack. ~*adj.* **1.** Of, pertaining to, resembling, or being a kamikaze: *enemy pilots receiving kamikaze training.* **2.** *Informal.* Courting disaster; reckless or suicidal: *a kamikaze cab driver.* [Japanese, "divine wind" : *kami,* KAMI + *kaze,* wind.]

Kam·pa·la (käm-pä′lə). The capital of Uganda, on Lake Victoria. It was founded by the British near Mengo, the seat of the kabaka (king) of Buganda. It became the country's capital in 1962.

kam·pong (kăm′pông′, kăm′-) *n.* A compound or village in Malaysia. [Malay.]

Kam·pu·che·a (käm′pə-chē′ə). Formerly **Cam·bo·di·a** (kăm-bō′-dē-ə). Republic of Southeast Asia. Its fertile basin is drained by the Mekong River, and the Khmer Empire flourished here (500–1450). Cambodia became part of French Indochina in 1863 and was a battleground for foreign powers after French withdrawal (1953). From 1971–75 the country was known as the Khmer Republic. During the regime of Pol Pot, leader of the successful communist Khmer Rouge (1976–79), the country was known as Democratic Kampuchea, and some 3,000,000 people are estimated to have died of starvation or to have been killed. The Vietnamese occupied Kampuchea in 1978, and insurgency continued. Much of the country has been ruled by the pro-Vietnamese Heng Samrin since 1979. Warfare has severely disrupted Kampuchea's agriculture-based economy, and the country relies on imports of food and fuel, and foreign aid. Area, 181,035 square kilometers (69,880 square miles). Population, 5,200,000. Capital, Phnom Penh. —**Kam·pu·che·an** *n. & adj.*

kamsin. Variant of **khamsin.**

ka·na (kä′nə) *n.* Either of two Japanese syllabaries, **hiragana** or **katakana** *(both of which see).* Compare **kanji.** [Japanese, "pseudocharacters" (as distinguished from *kanji,* which are regarded as originally Chinese characters) : *ka,* false + *na,* name, character.]

Ka·na·ka (kə-nä′kə, -năk′ə) *n.* **1.** A native of the South Sea Islands. **2.** A native of Hawaii. [Hawaiian, "person."]

kan·a·my·cin (kăn′ə-mī′sĭn) *n.* An antibiotic, $C_{18}H_{36}O_{11}N_4$, obtained from the soil actinomycete bacterium *Streptomyces kanamyceticus* and used to treat a wide range of bacterial infections. [New Latin *Streptomycetes kanamyceticus* (specific epithet of the bacterium).]

Kanchenjunga. See **Kangchenjunga, Mount.**

Kan·da·har or **Qan·da·har** (kän′də-här′). A city in southern Afghanistan. It is the center of a fertile region and lies on the trade route between Pakistan and the U.S.S.R.

Kan·din·sky (kăn-dĭn′skē), **Wassily** (1866–1944). Russian abstract painter, who worked in Germany. He considered form and color capable of spiritual expression. Kandinsky was appointed professor of the Bauhaus School in Weimar (1922). He was a member of the *Blaue Reiter,* a group of German expressionist painters.

Kan·dy (kăn′dē). Formerly **Can·dy.** A city in the central tea-growing district of Sri Lanka. It was the seat of the Singhalese kings until the British occupation in 1815.

kane. Variant of **kain.**

Kanea. See **Canea.**

kangaroo *The red kangaroo (above) is the largest species of this group of Australian marsupials. It can travel at 50 kilometers (30 miles) per hour and jump 9 meters (30 feet) in a single bound.*

kapok *The traditional stuffing for toys, cushions, and life jackets is made from silky fibers that surround the seeds of the tropical silk-cotton tree,* Ceiba pentandra.

PRONUNCIATION KEY

ă, pat; ā, pay; âr, care;
ä, father, are; b, bib;
ch, church; d, deed; ĕ, pet;
ē, be; f, fife; g, gag; h, hat;
hw, which; ĭ, pit; ī, pie;
îr, pier; j, judge; k, kick;
l, lid, needle; m, mum;
n, no, sudden; ng, thing;
ŏ, pot; ō, toe; ô, paw, for;
oi, noise; ou, out; o͝o, book;
o͞o, boot; p, pop; r, roar;
s, sauce; sh, ship, dish;
t, tight; th, thin, path;
th, this, bathe; ŭ, cut; ûr, fur;
v, valve; w, with; y, yes;
z, zebra, size; zh, vision;
ə, about, item, edible, gallop, circus, peaceful

IN FOREIGN WORDS:

à, *Fr.* ami; œ, *Fr.* feu, *Ger.* schön; ü, *Fr.* tu, *Ger.* über; KH, *Ger.* ich, *Scot.* loch; N, *Fr.* bon; y', *Fr.* Compiègne

STRESS MARKS:

Primary stress: ′
in·cite′ (ĭn-sīt′)
Secondary stress: ′
in′sight′ (ĭn′sīt′)

kan·ga, khan·ga (kăng′gə, kăng′ə) *n.* A piece of brightly colored cloth worn as a garment by women in East Africa.

kan·ga·roo (kăng′gə-ro͞o′) *n., pl.* **-roos.** Any of various herbivorous marsupials of the family Macropodidae, of Australia and adjacent areas, characteristically having short forelimbs, large hind limbs adapted for leaping, and a long, tapered tail. [Probably from a native name in Queensland, Australia.]

kangaroo closure *n.* A form of closure in a parliamentary debate in which the speaker limits discussion to selected amendments. Compare **guillotine.**

kangaroo court *n.* **1.** A mock court set up in violation of established legal procedure. **2.** A court characterized by dishonesty or incompetence. [By allusion to its irregular procedures, suggesting the leaps of a kangaroo.]

kangaroo paw *n.* Any of various plants of the Australian genus *Anigozanthus,* having swordlike leaves and clusters of tubular flowers that when unopened resemble a kangaroo's paws.

kangaroo rat *n.* Any of various long-tailed rodents of the genera *Dipodomys* and *Microdipodops,* of arid areas of western North America, having long hind legs adapted for jumping.

kangaroo vine *n.* A climbing or trailing vine, *Cissus antarctica,* native to Australia and widely grown as a house plant for its glossy green foliage.

Kang·chen·jun·ga, Mount (kăng′chən-jŭng′gə). Also **Kan·chen·jun·ga** (kăn′-) or **Kin·chin·jun·ga** (kĭn′hĭn-). The world's third-highest peak (8,598 meters; 28,215 feet), on the India-Nepal border. It was first climbed in 1955.

kan·ji (kän′jē) *n., pl.* **kanji** or **-jis. 1.** A Japanese system of writing based upon borrowed or modified Chinese characters. **2.** A character used in the kanji system of writing. Compare **kana.** [Japanese, from Chinese (Mandarin) *hànzi* : *hàn,* Chinese (originally a dynastic name) + *zì,* word.]

Kan·na·da (kä′nə-də) *n.* A Dravidian language spoken chiefly in the state of Karnataka, in southern India. **—Kan·na·da** *adj.*

Ka·no (kä′nō). A city in northern Nigeria, capital of Kano state. It was once the terminus of a major Sahara caravan route and is still a trade center.

Kan·pur (kän′po͝or). *English* **Cawn·pore** (kôn′pôr). The largest city in Uttar Pradesh in northern India, on the Ganges River. It is a communications junction and manufacturing center. Its British garrison was massacred (1857) during the Indian Mutiny.

Kan·sas (kăn′zəs). *Abbr.* **Kans.** State of the central United States, in the Great Plains. Its main products are agricultural. It joined the Union in 1861 after a bloody fight between free staters and proslavery groups. Topeka is the capital.

Kansas City. Either of a pair of twin cities in the central United States. Kansas City, Kansas, is west of the Kansas River; the much larger Kansas City, Missouri, lies to its east.

Kansu. See **Gansu.**

Kant (kănt, känt), **Immanuel** (1724–1804). German idealist philosopher. In the *Critique of Pure Reason* (1781) Kant argued that reason was the means by which the phenomena of experience are translated into understanding. He put forward his system of ethics based on the categorical imperative in the *Critique of Practical Reason* (1788). **—Kant·i·an** *n. & adj.* **—Kant·i·an·ism** *n.*

kan·tar (kăn-tär′) *n.* Any of various units of weight used in some eastern Mediterranean countries. [Arabic *qinṭār,* ultimately from Latin *centēnārius,* of a hundred, from *centum,* hundred.]

kan·zu (kăn′zo͞o) *n.* A long, usually white garment worn by men in Africa. [Swahili.]

ka·o·lin (kā′ə-lĭn) *n.* A fine white to yellowish or grayish clay, mostly kaolinite, used as an adsorbent in medicine and in ceramics and refractories and as a filler or coating for paper and textiles. Also called "china clay," "porcelain clay," "terra alba." [French, from Mandarin Chinese *gaō lĭng,* name of a hill in Jiangxi Province where it was first obtained, "high mountain" : *gaō,* high + *lĭng,* mountain, peak.]

ka·o·lin·ite (kā′ə-lĭ-nīt′) *n.* A mineral, essentially $Al_2O_3 \cdot 2SiO_2 \cdot 2H_2O$, the principal constituent of kaolin.

ka·on (kā′ŏn′) *n. Symbol* **K** *Physics.* **1.** Either of two elementary particles in the meson family, a neutral particle, K zero, or a positively charged particle, K plus, having strangeness quantum number −1. **2.** Either of two corresponding antiparticles, K zero bar or K minus. [*ka,* the letter *k* + (MES)ON.]

ka·pell·meis·ter (kə-pĕl′mī′stər, kä-, kă-) *n., pl.* **kapellmeister.** Often **Kapellmeister.** The musical director of a choir or orchestra, especially at the court of an 18th-century German prince. [German, from *Kapelle,* choir + *Meister,* master.]

kaph, caph (käf, kôf) *n.* The 11th letter in the Hebrew alphabet. Transliterated in English as *K, k,* or *kh.* See feature at **alphabet.** [Hebrew *kāph,* "palm of the hand."]

ka·pok (kā′pŏk′) *n.* A silky fiber obtained from the fruit of the silk-cotton tree and used for insulation and as padding in pillows, mattresses, and life preservers. [Malay.]

kap·pa (kăp′ə) *n.* The tenth letter in the Greek alphabet, written Κ, κ. Transliterated in English as *K, k.* See feature at **alphabet.** [Greek, from Semitic, akin to Hebrew *kāph,* KAPH.]

ka·put (kə-po͝ot′, -po͞ot′, kä-) *adj. Informal.* **1.** Destroyed; wrecked. **2.** Not functioning; out of order. [German *kaputt,* from French *capot,* as in the expression *être capot,* to have lost all tricks at cards, "be hoodwinked," from *capot,* cloak with hood, from *cape,* CAPE (garment).]

kar·a·bi·ner (kăr′ə-bē′nər) *n.* An oblong steel ring that is snapped to the eye of a piton and through which a rope is run, used in mountaineering. [German *Karabiner(haken),* "carbine hook" (originally used to fasten carbines to a belt) : *Karabiner,* carbine, from French *carabine,* CARBINE + *Haken,* hook.]

Ka·ra·chi (kə-rä′chē). Largest city and chief port and naval base of Pakistan, on the Arabian Sea. It was the national capital from 1947 to 1959.

Ka·ra·jan (kär′ə-yän′), **Herbert von** (1908–). Austrian conductor. He founded the Salzburg Easter Festival in 1967.

Kar·a·kal·pak (kăr′ə-käl-päk′) *n.* **1.** A native or inhabitant of the Kara-Kalpak A.S.S.R. **2.** The language spoken by the Karakalpaks. **—Kar·a·kal·pak** *adj.*

Kar·a-Kal·pak Autonomous Soviet Socialist Republic (kăr′-ə-käl-päk′). Autonomous region in Central Asian U.S.S.R. It comprises parts of the Kyzul Kum desert and the Amu Darya delta on the Aral Sea. Many of the people are Karakalpak Muslims.

Kar·a·ko·ram Range (kăr′ə-kôr′əm). Range of mountains in central Asia, stretching through Jammu and Kashmir to Tibet. It includes Mt. Godwin-Austen, which at 8,611 meters (28,250 feet) is the world's second-highest mountain.

kar·a·kul, car·a·cul (kăr′ə-kəl) *n.* **1.** Any of a breed of sheep native to central Asia, having wool that is curled and glossy in the young and wiry and coarse in the adult. Also called "broadtail." **2.** Fur made from the pelt of a karakul lamb. Compare **broadtail, Persian lamb.** [Originally bred near *Kara Kul,* "black lake," lake in Tadzhik S.S.R.]

Ka·ra·man·lis (kär′ə-män-lēs′), **Constantine** (1907–). Greek prime minister (1955–63, 1974–80). In 1963 he resigned and went to Paris, returning after the fall of the Greek military government (1974). He was elected president in 1980.

Ka·ra Sea (kär′ə). Shallow section of the Arctic Ocean, off northwestern U.S.S.R. The ice-locked sea is an important fishing ground, but is navigable only during August and September.

kar·at, car·at (kăr′ət) *n. Abbr.* **kt.** A unit of measure for the fineness of gold, equal to 1/24 of the total amount of pure gold in an alloy. [Old French *carat,* unit of weight for precious stones, CARAT.]

ka·ra·te (kə-rä′tē) *n.* A Japanese art of self-defense in which sharp blows and kicks are struck at an opponent's body. [Japanese : *kara,* empty + *te,* hand.]

Ka·re·li·an (kə-rē′lē-ən, -rēl′yən) *n.* **1.** A native or inhabitant of the Karelian A.S.S.R. **2.** The Finnish dialect spoken by the Karelians. **—Ka·re·li·an** *adj.*

Karelian Autonomous Soviet Socialist Republic. Also **Ka·re·li·a** (kə-rē′lē-ə, -rēl′yə). Administrative region of northwest U.S.S.R.. It lies between the White Sea and Finland and is rich in timber and mineral deposits.

Karelian Isthmus. An isthmus in the U.S.S.R., between the Gulf of Finland and Lake Ladoga. From 1917 the greater part, the north, was Finnish, but this was ceded to the U.S.S.R. in 1944.

Ka·ren (kə-rĕn′) *n., pl.* **-rens** or collectively **Karen. 1.** A member of a Thai people living in south Burma. **2.** Any of the languages of this people.

Ka·ri·ba, Lake (kə-rē′bə). A reservoir on the Zambia-Zimbabwe border. It was formed on the Zambezi River after the building of the Kariba Dam (1955–59), which provides hydroelectricity for the Copper Belt in Zambia and also parts of Zimbabwe.

Kar·loff (kär′lôf′, -lŏf′), **Boris,** born William Pratt (1887–1969). British film actor. He played the monster in *Frankenstein* (1931) and starred in many horror films.

Kar·lo·vy Va·ry (kär′lō-vē vä′rē). *German* **Karls·bad** (kärlz′băd′). Famous spa in Bohemia in Czechoslovakia. Its hot medicinal springs were popular with European royalty and aristocrats before World War I.

Karls·ruh·e or **Carls·ruh·e** (kärlz′ro͞o′ə). Canal port and industrial city in West Germany and capital of the former state of Baden.

kar·ma (kär′mə, kûr′-) *n.* **1.** *Hinduism & Buddhism.* The sum of a person's actions during the successive phases of his existence, regarded as determining his destiny in future incarnations. **2.** Fate; destiny. [Sanskrit *karman* (nominative *karma*), act, deed, work, from *karoti,* he makes, he does.] **—kar·mic** (kär′mĭk, kûr′-) *adj.*

Kar·nak (kär′năk). Village in central Egypt on the Nile River. It is the site of ancient Thebes, with its Great Temple of Amen.

Kar·na·ta·ka (kär′nə-tä′kə). Formerly **My·sore** (mī-sôr′). State of India, on the Arabian Sea coast. It produces most of the world's sandalwood. Bangalore is the capital.

Kärn·ten (kĕrn′tən). *English* **Ca·rin·thi·a** (kə-rĭn′thē-ə). State of southern Austria. It produces cereals and livestock and has deposits of magnesite, iron ore, zinc, and lead. Klagenfurt is the capital.

ka·ross (kə-rŏs′) *n.* A simple cloak made from animal skins that is worn by southern African tribesmen. [Afrikaans *karos,* perhaps from Dutch *kuras,* from French *cuirasse,* CUIRASS.]

kar·ri (kăr′ē) *n.* **1.** A eucalyptus tree, *Eucalyptus diversicolor,* of western Australia. **2.** The hard red timber of the karri. [Native Australian name.]

kar·roo, ka·roo (kə-ro͞o′) *n.* Any arid plateau of southern Africa. [Afrikaans *karo,* of Hottentot origin.]

Kar·roo or **Ka·roo** (kə-ro͞o′). Plateau of southern South Africa. It is divided by the Groot-Swartberge Range into the lower, southern Little Karroo and the higher Great Karroo. It is a grazing and fruit-growing area.

Karroo System. Vast system of rocks found in Africa south of the equator. Dating from the Permo-Carboniferous to late Triassic periods, it comprises nonmarine sediments, with coal and oil deposits, and volcanic rocks. The system is noted for its reptilian fossils.

karst (kärst) *n.* A barren limestone or dolomitic region in which erosion has produced fissures, sinkholes, underground streams, and caverns. [German.]

karyo-, caryo- *prefix.* Indicates the nucleus of a living cell; for example, **karyogamy, karyotype.** [New Latin, from Greek *karuon,* kernel, nut.]

kar·y·og·a·my (kăr′ē-ŏg′ə-mē) *n.* The coming together and fusing of two gamete nuclei. [KARYO- + -GAMY.]

kar·y·o·ki·ne·sis (kăr′ē-ō-kə-nē′sĭs) *n.* A form of cell division, **mitosis** *(see).* —**kar·y·o·ki·net·ic** (kăr′ē-ō-kə-nĕt′ĭk) *adj.*

kar·y·o·lymph (kăr′ē-ə-lĭmf′) *n.* The clear homogeneous liquid portion of nuclear protoplasm.

kar·y·o·plasm (kăr′ē-ə-plăz′əm) *n.* Nuclear protoplasm, **nucleoplasm** *(see).* [KARYO- + -PLASM.] —**kar·y·o·plas·mic** (kăr′ē-ə-plăz′-mĭk) *adj.*

kar·y·o·some (kăr′ē-ə-sōm′) *n.* **1.** An aggregation of chromatin in a resting nucleus during mitosis. **2.** A cell nucleus. [KARYO- + -SOME (body).]

kar·y·o·type (kăr′ē-ə-tīp′) *n.* A photomicrograph of metaphase chromosomes of a given species in a standard array showing their number, size, and shape. Also called "idiogram." —**kar·y·o·typ·ic** (kăr′ē-ə-tĭp′ĭk), **kar·y·o·typ·ic·al** (-ĭ-kəl) *adj.*

Kasan. See **Kazan.**

Kasbah. Variant of **Casbah.**

ka·sha (kä′shə, kăsh′ə) *n.* A dish of eastern European origin consisting of buckwheat groats. [Russian *kasha,* from Old Slavonic *kāsyā* (unattested).]

Kash·mir or **Cash·mere** (kăsh′mîr, kăsh-mîr′). Former princely state on the northwestern border of India. A Hindu-led region with a largely Muslim population, it became a source of conflict between India and Pakistan after Indian independence (1947) and was partitioned in 1949, becoming Jammu and Kashmir, an Indian state, and Azad Kashmir under Pakistani control. Sporadic fighting continued until 1972.

Kashmir goat. Variant of **Cashmere goat.**

Kash·mir·i (kăsh-mîr′ē, kăzh-) *n., pl.* **-miris** or collectively **Kashmiri.** **1.** A native or inhabitant of Kashmir. **2.** An Indic language spoken in Jammu and Kashmir. —**Kash·mir·i** *adj.*

kash·ruth, kash·rut (kä-shrооth′, -shrооt′) *n.* **1.** The body of Jewish dietary laws. **2.** The state of being kosher. [Hebrew, "appropriateness."]

Kas·sel or **Cas·sel** (kä′səl). City in Hesse in eastern West Germany. The city was chartered in 1198.

kat, khat (kät) *n.* An evergreen shrub, *Catha edulis,* native to Africa and Arabia, whose leaves have narcotic properties and are chewed or used to make a tea. [Arabic *qāt.*]

kat·a·bat·ic wind (kăt′ə-băt′ĭk) *n.* A cold flow of air traveling downward. [Greek *katabatikos,* affording a means of descent, from *katabos,* descending, steep, from *katabainein,* to go down + *-ikos,* -IC.]

ka·ta·ka·na (kä′tə-kä′nə, kät′ə-kän′ə) *n.* A phonetic Japanese syllabary used for writing foreign words or documents, such as telegrams. Also called "kana." See **hiragana.** [Japanese : *kata,* one, one-sided + KANA.]

ka·thak (kə-täk′) *n.* A classical dance of northern India that uses complex rhythmic patterns and contains elements of mimed narrative. [Bengali, "storyteller," from Sanskrit *kathayati,* he tells.]

ka·tha·ka·li (kä′tə-kä′lē) *n.* A vigorous classical dance of Kerala in southern India that is performed by men wearing elaborate costumes and make-up and is based on episodes from Hindu literary texts. [Malayalam, drama : *katha,* story, from Sanskrit *kathā,* talk + *kali,* play.]

Ka·tha·rev·u·sa, Ka·tha·rev·ou·sa (kä′thə-rĕv′ə-sä′) *n.* The literary and official form of Modern Greek, showing many morphological and lexical features restored from Classical Greek. Compare **Dhimotiki.** [Modern Greek *kathareuousa,* from Greek, feminine present participle of *kathareuein,* to be pure, from *katharos,* pure.]

Kath·man·du or **Kat·man·du** (kăt′män-dоо′, kät′-). Capital of Nepal. It was founded in the 8th century on the Baghmati River and became the capital when taken by the Gurkhas in 1768.

Kat·mai National Monument (kăt′mī). A nearly inaccessible region, 1,130,815 hectares (2,792,137 acres), in southern Alaska. The area includes Mt. Katmai, an active volcano, the Valley of the Ten Thousand Smokes, glacier-covered peaks, and crater lakes.

Ka·to·wi·ce (kä′tō-vēt′sĕ). City in southern Poland, producing coal, and iron and steel. It was part of Germany until the partition of Silesia (1921).

Kat·te·gat or **Cat·te·gat** (kăt′ĭ-găt′). Strait between Sweden and Jutland, Denmark, connecting with the North Sea via the Skagerrak and with the Baltic Sea via the Øresund, Store Baelt, and Lille Baelt.

ka·ty·did (kā′tē-dĭd′) *n.* Any of various green, long-horned insects of the predominantly tropical family Tettigoniidae, related to the grasshoppers and the crickets, with specialized organs on the wings of the male that produce a distinctive shrill sound when rubbed together. [Imitative.]

Kauff·mann (kouf′män′), **(Maria Anna) Angelica** (1741-1807). Swiss painter. She worked chiefly in England, often contributing small works to rooms designed by the Adam brothers.

Kauf·man (kôf′mən), **George Simon** (1889-1961). U.S. playwright and director. Working alone or collaborating with writers like Marc Connolly (1890-1980), Edna Ferber, and Moss Hart, he wrote or directed such Broadway hits as *Dulcy* (1921), *Dinner at Eight*

(1932), and the Pulitzer Prize winner *Of Thee I Sing* (1931).

Ka·un·da (kä-оōn′də), **Kenneth David** (1924-). Zambian President (1964-). He led his country (formerly Northern Rhodesia) to full independence under the name of Zambia (1964). He has been influential in the Organization of African Unity.

kau·ri (kou′rē) *n.* **1. a.** Any of several coniferous trees of the genus *Agathis;* especially, *A. australis,* of New Zealand, having white, close-grained, durable wood. **b.** The wood of such a tree. In both senses, also called "kauri pine." **2.** A resin obtained from a kauri or from deposits of fossilized exudations of a kauri and used in varnishes and enamels. In this sense, also called "kauri gum," "kauri resin." [Maori *kauri.*]

ka·va (kä′və) *n.* **1.** A shrub, *Piper methysticum,* of tropical Pacific islands, the dried roots of which are used to make an intoxicating drink. **2.** The beverage made from kava. [Tongan *kava,* "bitter."]

Ka·wa·sa·ki (kä′wə-sä′kē). City in Japan, part of the Tokyo Bay industrial complex. Its industries include shipbuilding, engineering, and oil refining.

kay (kā) *n.* The letter *k.*

Kay (kā), **Sir.** *Arthurian Legend.* The rude, boastful foster brother and steward of King Arthur.

kay·ak, kai·ak (kī′ăk′) *n.* **1.** A watertight Eskimo canoe made of skins stretched over a light wooden frame and having a deck covering that closes around the waist of the paddler. Compare **umiak. 2.** A lightweight and highly maneuverable, usually canvas-covered canoe similar in construction to a kayak. [Eskimo *qajaq.*]

Kaye (kā), **Danny** (1913-). U.S. entertainer. After several years of entertaining in upstate New York resorts, he received parts in Broadway productions such as *Lady in the Dark* (1941). He also starred in several movies, including *The Secret Life of Walter Mitty* (1947) and *Hans Christian Andersen* (1952).

kay·o (kā-ō′, kā′ō) *n., pl.* **-os.** *Slang.* A knockout in boxing. ~*tr.v.* **kayoed, -oing, -os.** *Slang.* To knock out. [Pronunciation of K.O., abbreviation of *knock out.*]

Ka·zakh (kə-zăk′, -zäk′) *n., pl.* **-zakhs** or collectively **Kazakh.** Also **Ka·zak. 1.** A member of a Turkic people dwelling in the Kazakh S.S.R. and in northwestern China. **2.** The Turkic language of this people. —**Ka·zakh** *adj.*

Kazakh Soviet Socialist Republic. Also **Ka·zakh·stan** (kə-zăk′-stän′). Second-largest republic of the U.S.S.R. The world's first fast-breeder nuclear reactor was built here on the Mangyshlak Peninsula. Alma Ata is the capital.

Ka·zan or **Ka·san** (kə-zän′). City in European U.S.S.R., on the Volga River. It was capital of a Tatar khanate until captured by Russia in 1552. Tolstoy and Lenin studied at its university.

Ka·zan (kə-zăn′, -zän′), **Elia,** born Elia Kazanjoglous (1909-). U.S. stage and film director, born in Turkey of Greek parents. He directed Tennessee Williams's *A Streetcar Named Desire* (1947) and the films *On the Waterfront* (1954) and *East of Eden* (1955).

Ka·zan·tza·kis (kä′zənt-sä′kēs), **Nikos** (1885-1957). Greek writer. Among his novels are *Zorba the Greek* (1946) and *Christ Recrucified* (1954).

ka·zoo (kə-zоō′) *n., pl.* **-zoos.** A toy musical instrument with a membrane that produces a sound when a player hums or sings into the mouthpiece. [Probably imitative of its sound.]

kb kilobar.

KB *Chess.* king's bishop.

K.B. 1. King's Bench. **2.** Knight Bachelor.

K.B.E. Knight (Commander of the Order) of the British Empire.

KBP *Chess.* king's bishop's pawn.

kc kilocycle.

K.C. 1. King's Counsel. **2.** Knights of Columbus.

kcal kilocalorie.

kcs, kc/s kilocycles per second.

K.D., k.d. *Finance.* knocked down.

ke·a (kē′ə) *n.* A brownish-green parrot, *Nestor notabilis,* of mountainous areas of New Zealand, that normally eats insects but sometimes kills sheep by slashing them and eating their fat and flesh. [Maori, imitative of its cry.]

Kean (kēn), **Edmund** (c. 1787-1833). British actor. He was hailed as a great tragic actor for his roles as Shylock at the Drury Lane Theatre (1814), as Richard III, and as Iago.

Kea·ton (kē′tən), **Buster,** born Joseph Francis Keaton (1895-1966). U.S. film actor. His skill as a mime artist made him a great comedian of the silent screen. His films include *The Navigator* (1924).

Keats (kēts), **John** (1795-1821). English poet. His collection *Lamia and Other Poems* (1820) includes "The Eve of St. Agnes" and the famous odes "To a Nightingale," "To Autumn," "To Psyche," and "On a Grecian Urn." He died of tuberculosis at the age of 26. —**Keats·i·an** *adj. & n.*

ke·bab, ke·bob (kə-bŏb′) *n.* Shish kebab *(see).*

Ke·ble (kē′bəl), **John** (1792-1866). British clergyman. He delivered a sermon in Oxford (1833) defending Catholic principles in the Church of England, so initiating the Oxford Movement.

Kechua. Variant of **Quechua.**

keck (kĕk) *intr.v.* **kecked, kecking, kecks.** To make the sound of vomiting. [Imitative.]

ked (kĕd) *n.* Any of various wingless parasitic flies; especially, the sheep ked, *Melophagus ovinus,* and the deer ked, *Liptoptena cervi.* [16th century : origin obscure.]

kedge (kĕj) *n.* A light anchor used for warping a vessel. ~*v.* **kedged, kedging, kedges.** —*tr.* To move (a ship) by pulling on a rope attached to an anchor lowered some distance away.

katydid *The katydid,* Pterophylla camellifolia, *rubs its wings together to produce its high-pitched song. The sound, which is made only by males, is designed to attract females.*

kayak *Now much used in sport, the watertight Eskimo kayak was originally developed for hunting in very cold waters.*

—*intr.* To move by means of a kedge. Used of a ship. [From *kedge,* earlier *cadge,* to warp a ship, perhaps from Middle English *caggen*†, to tie, bind.]

kedg·er·ee (kĕj′ə-rē′, kĕj′ə-rē′) *n.* **1.** A dish of rice, lentils, onions, eggs, and spices served in India. **2.** A dish consisting of flaked fish, boiled rice, and eggs. [Hindi *khichṛī,* from Sanskrit *khiccā*†.]

keef. Variant of **kif.**

keek (kēk) *intr.v.* **keeked, keeking, keeks.** *Scottish.* To peek; peep. ~*n. Scottish.* A look, especially a quick one; peek. [Middle English *kike,* probably from Middle Dutch *kiken,* to peep.]

keel¹ (kēl) *n.* **1.** The main structural member of a ship, running lengthwise along the center line from bow to stern and forming the backbone of the vessel to which the frames are attached. **2.** A ship. **3.** A structure that resembles a ship's keel in function or shape, such as the member extending lengthwise at the bottom of an aircraft fuselage. **4.** *Biology.* A structure having a longitudinal ridge suggestive of a ship's keel, as: **a.** The anterior part of the breastbone of a flying bird. **b.** A pair of united petals in certain flowers, as those of the pea. **—on an even keel.** In an unimpaired or stable condition; steady.
~*v.* **keeled, keeling, keels.** —*tr.* To cause (a vessel) to capsize. —*intr.* **1.** To roll on her keel; capsize. Used of a ship. **2.** To collapse or fall in or as if in a faint: *He keeled over when he was told about the disaster.* [Middle English *ke(o)le,* from Old Norse *kjölr.*] **—keeled** *adj.*

keel² *n.* **1. a.** A barge, especially one for carrying coal on the Tyne in England. **b.** The amount carried by such a barge. **2.** A British unit of weight formerly used for coal and equal to 21.2 tons. [Middle English *kele,* from Middle Dutch *kiel,* ship.]

keel³ *tr.v.* **keeled, keeling, keels.** *Archaic & Regional.* To cool (a hot liquid, for example), especially by stirring in order to prevent boiling over. Used chiefly in the phrase *keel the pot.* [Middle English *kelen,* Old English *cēlan.*]

keel·boat (kēl′bōt′) *n.* A large, covered, flat-bottomed boat with a keel but without sails, used for river transport.

keel·haul (kēl′hôl′) *tr.v.* **-hauled, -hauling, -hauls.** **1.** To punish by dragging under the keel of a ship from one side to the other or from stem to stern. **2.** To castigate; scold severely. [Dutch *kielhalen* : Middle Dutch *kiel,* keel of a ship + *halen,* to pull, haul.]

Keeling Islands. See **Cocos Islands.**

keel·son (kĕl′sən, kēl′-) *n.* Also **kel·son** (kĕl′-). *Nautical.* A timber or girder placed parallel with and bolted to the keel of a ship for additional strength. [Probably from Low German *kielswīn* : Middle Low German *kiel,* keel of a ship + *swīn,* swine, "timber."]

keen¹ (kēn) *adj.* **keener, keenest.** **1.** Having a fine, sharp cutting edge or point: *a keen razor.* **2.** Intellectually acute; penetrating: *a keen mind.* **3.** Acutely sensitive: *a keen sense of hearing.* **4.** Vivid; intense: *"His entire body hungered for keen sensation, something exciting"* (Richard Wright). **5.** Bitter; piercing: *a keen wind.* **6.** Marked by sharp dispute: *a keen discussion.* **7. a.** Ardent; enthusiastic: *a keen chess player.* **b.** Eagerly desirous: *keen on going.* **8.** *Slang.* Splendid; fine: *We saw a keen movie.* —See Synonyms at **eager, sharp.** [Middle English *kene,* Old English *cēne,* wise, bold, powerful, from Common Germanic *kōnjaz* (unattested).] **—keen·ly** *adv.* **—keen·ness** *n.*

keen² *n.* A loud wailing lamentation for the dead.
~*intr.v.* **keened, keening, keens.** To wail or lament loudly, especially for the dead. [Irish Gaelic *caoine,* lamentation, from *caoinim,* I wail, from Old Irish *coīnim,* from Common Celtic *koinyo-* (unattested), to wail.]

keen·er (kē′nər) *n.* One who keens; especially, a professional mourner at an Irish funeral.

keep (kēp) *v.* **kept** (kĕpt), **keeping, keeps.** —*tr.* **1.** To retain possession of: *keep the change; kept his nerve.* **2.** To store; put customarily: *Where do you keep your saw?* **3.** To take in one's charge temporarily: *Keep this for me until I return.* **4. a.** To provide with the necessities of life; support: *"There's little to earn and many to keep"* (Charles Kingsley). **b.** To support (a mistress or lover) financially. Used chiefly in the past participle: *a kept woman.* **5. a.** To supply with room and board for a charge: *keep boarders.* **b.** To raise and feed: *keep chickens.* **6.** To have the resources to retain for pleasure or use: *"It is not too much for me now, in degree or cost, to keep a coach"* (Samuel Pepys). **7.** To have in ready supply: *I always keep plenty of flour and sugar on hand.* **8.** To be in charge of; manage or tend: *keeps a large garden.* **9. a.** To maintain by making regular entries in: *kept a diary.* **b.** To enter (data) in a book: *keep financial records.* **10.** To cause to continue in a specified state, condition, or course of action: *kept us all guessing; keep her away.* **11. a.** To preserve and protect; maintain: *kept up the house and grounds.* **b.** To withhold for the time being; reserve: *keep some for tomorrow.* **12.** To restrain from leaving; detain: *What kept you? The teacher kept us after school.* **13.** To cause to remain; confine: *keep in quarantine.* **14.** To prevent or deter: *used an insulated bucket to keep the ice cubes from melting.* **15. a.** To observe habitually: *keep late hours.* **b.** To observe in an appropriate or prescribed manner: *keep the Sabbath.* **16.** To adhere to; fulfill: *keep a schedule; keep one's word.* **17.** To refrain from divulging: *keep a secret; keep one's own counsel.* **18.** To associate with habitually: *She kept bad company.* —*intr.* **1.** To remain in a specified state, condition, or course of action; stay: *keep in line; keep quiet.* **2. a.** To persevere in; continue to do: *keep guessing; kept on talking.* **b.** To continue in a direction or course: *keep to the left.* **3.** To be with respect to health: *How are you keeping?* **4. a.** To remain fresh or unspoiled: *The dessert won't keep.* **b.** To continue being withheld: *I've got some interesting gossip, but it'll keep till tomorrow.* —See Synonyms at **observe.** **—keep at it.** To persevere in an action or work. **—keep back.** To refuse to tell or give; withhold. **—keep down.** **1.** To maintain control over: *tried to keep costs down.* **2.** To prevent from progressing, accomplishing, or succeeding. **—keep off.** To refrain from approaching; stay away from. **—keep one's distance.** To continue in an attitude of aloofness. **—keep one's eyes open** (or **peeled**). To be alert or watchful: *keep your eyes open for danger.* **—keep one's nose clean.** To stay out of trouble: *He could have been elected if he'd kept his nose clean.* **—keep pace.** To stay even: *tried to keep pace with inflation.* **—keep to oneself.** **1.** To shun the company of others. **2.** To refrain from sharing or divulging: *He's keeping the news to himself.* **—keep up.** **1.** To maintain in good condition. **2.** To persevere in; carry on: *keep up traditions; can't keep this up forever.* **3.** To continue at the same level or pace: *Don't walk so fast; I can't keep up.* **4.** To remain informed or in touch: *keep up with current research.* **5.** To cause to stay up late at night. **6.** To match one's competitors, colleagues, neighbors, or associates in success or lifestyle: *unsuccessfully tried to keep up with his partners.*
~*n.* **1.** Care; charge: *The child is in my keep for the day.* **2.** The means by which one is supported; the necessities of life: *earn one's keep.* **3.** The main tower or donjon of a medieval castle; stronghold. —See Synonyms at **livelihood.** **—for keeps.** **1.** For an indefinitely long period: *He gave it to me for keeps.* **2.** Seriously and permanently: *We're separating for keeps.* [Middle English *kepen,* Old English *cēpan*†, to seize, hold, guard.]
Synonyms: *maintain, reserve, retain, withhold.*

keep·er (kē′pər) *n.* **1.** One who keeps, especially: **a.** An attendant, guard, or warden, as in a museum or art gallery. **b.** One who has the charge or care of something, as animals in a zoo or circus. **2.** A device for keeping something in place. **3.** A small piece of iron placed across the poles of a permanent magnet when it is not in use in order to complete the magnetization.

keep·ing (kē′pĭng) *n.* **1.** Custody; care; guardianship. **2.** Harmony; conformity: *remarks out of keeping with the occasion.*

keep·net (kēp′nĕt′) *n.* A cylindrical net, open at one end and suspended in the water, into which anglers put fish to keep them alive.

keep·sake (kēp′sāk′) *n.* Something given or kept as a reminder of the giver; a memento.

kees·hond (kās′hŏnt′) *n., pl.* **-honden** (-hŏn′dən) or **-honds.** A dog of a small breed originating in the Netherlands, having a thick grayish-black coat. [Dutch : probably *Kees,* nickname for *Cornelis,* from Latin *Cornēlius*†, name of a Roman gens + *hond,* dog.]

Kee·wa·tin (kē-wāt′n). An administrative district, 590,934 square kilometers (228,160 square miles), in the Northwest Territories, Canada, north of Manitoba and including Hudson and James bays.

kef. Variant of **kif.**

Ke·fau·ver (kē′fô′vər), **(Carey) Estes** (1903–63). U.S. legislator. A Democratic congressman (1939–49) and senator (1949–63) from Tennessee, he gained wide recognition for his investigations into organized crime (1950–51), which were the first televised Senate hearings. He was nominated as Adlai Stevenson's running mate in 1956.

keffiyeh. Variant of **kaffiyeh.**

ke·fir (kĕ-fîr′) *n.* A creamy drink made of fermented cow's milk. [Russian, of Caucasian origin.]

Kef·la·vík (kĕp′lä-vēk′). A fishing port in southwest Iceland. Its international airport, built by the United States in World War II as Meeks Field, has also been a NATO base since 1951.

keg (kĕg) *n.* **1.** A small cask or barrel, usually with a capacity of five to ten gallons. **2.** An aluminum container for transporting and storing beer. [Earlier *cag,* Middle English *kag,* from Old Norse *kaggi*†.]

keg·ler (kĕg′lər) *n.* A person who bowls; bowler. [German *Kegler,* from *kegeln,* to bowl, from *Kegel,* bowling pin, from Old High German *kegil*†, stick, peg.]

keis·ter (kē′stər) *n. Slang.* The buttocks. [Origin unknown.]

ke·ku·lé formula (kā′kə-lā′) *n. Chemistry.* A structural formula for benzene in which the six carbon atoms are positioned at the corners of a regular hexagon and linked by alternate double and single bonds. [After KEKULÉ VON STRADONITZ.]

Ke·ku·lé von Stra·do·nitz (kā′ko͞o-lā′ fən shträ′dō-nĭts′), **(Friedrich) August** (1829–96). German chemist. He carried out important research concerning the structure and combining power of atoms and in 1865 formulated the structure of benzene.

Kel·ler (kĕl′ər), **Helen Adams** (1880–1968). U.S. writer and lecturer. She was deaf and blind from early childhood, but learned to read, write, and speak. She is noted for her work for the blind.

Kells (kĕlz). Market town in County Meath, Republic of Ireland. *The Book of the Kells,* an 8th-century illuminated Gospel, is said to have been written at a monastery founded here by St. Columba in the 6th century.

kel·ly green (kĕl′ē) *n.* A strong yellowish green. [From the Irish name *Kelly* (green being a color associated with Ireland).]

Kel·ly (kĕl′ē), **Grace Patricia** (1929–82). U.S. film actress. She starred in several films, including *High Noon* (1952), *To Catch a Thief* (1955), and *Country Girl* (1954), for which she won an Academy Award. In 1956 she gave up her career to marry Prince Rainier III of Monaco.

ke·loid, che·loid (kē′loid′) *n.* A mass of fibrous connective tissue, usually at the site of a scar. [French *kéloïde* : Greek *khēlē,* claw, CHELA + -OID.] **—ke·loid·al** (kē-loid′l) *adj.*

PRONUNCIATION KEY

ă, pat; ā, pay; âr, care;
ä, father, are; b, bib;
ch, church; d, deed; ĕ, pet;
ē, be; f, fife; g, gag; h, hat;
hw, which; ĭ, pit; ī, pie;
îr, pier; j, judge; k, kick;
l, lid, needle; m, mum;
n, no, sudden; ng, thing;
ŏ, pot; ō, toe; ô, paw, for;
oi, noise; ou, out; o͝o, book;
o͞o, boot; p, pop; r, roar;
s, sauce; sh, ship, dish;
t, tight; th, thin, path;
th, this, bathe; ŭ, cut; ûr, fur;
v, valve; w, with; y, yes;
z, zebra, size; zh, vision;
ə, about, item, edible, gallop, circus, peaceful

IN FOREIGN WORDS:

à, *Fr.* ami; œ, *Fr.* feu, *Ger.* schön; ü, *Fr.* tu, *Ger.* über; KH, *Ger.* ich, *Scot.* loch; N, *Fr.* bon; y′, *Fr.* Compiègne

STRESS MARKS:

Primary stress: ′
in·cite′ (ĭn-sīt′)
Secondary stress: ′
in′sight′ (ĭn′sīt′)

kelp (kĕlp) *n.* **1.** Any of various brown, often very large seaweeds of the order Laminariales. Also called "oarweed." **2.** The ash of kelp, used as a source of potash and iodine. Also called "varec." [Middle English *cúlpet*.]

kel·pie¹ (kĕl'pē) *n.* A water spirit in Scottish legend, usually having the shape of a horse and causing or rejoicing in drownings. [18th century : origin obscure.]

kelpie² *n.* A sheep dog of a breed that originated in Australia and was developed from the Scottish collie. Also called "barb." [From *Kelpie*, the name of an early specimen of the breed.]

kelson. Variant of **keelson.**

kelt (kĕlt) *n.* A salmon that is in an exhausted condition after spawning. [Middle English : origin obscure.]

Kelt. Variant of **Celt.**

Keltic. Variant of **Celtic.**

kel·vin (kĕl'vĭn) *n. Symbol* **K** The unit of thermodynamic temperature, equal to ¹/₂₇₃.₁₆ of the thermodynamic temperature of the triple point of water. [After Baron KELVIN.]

Kel·vin (kĕl'vĭn) *adj. Abbr.* **K** Of, pertaining to, or designating an **absolute scale** *(see)* of temperature whose zero point is approximately −273.15°C.

Kelvin, William Thomson, 1st Baron (1824–1907). British physicist and inventor. He established the Kelvin scale of temperature and supervised the laying of a cable across the Atlantic (1866). He also did important work in thermodynamics.

Kemal Atatürk. See **Atatürk.**

Kem·ble (kĕm'bəl). British theatrical family, founded by **Roger Kemble** (1722–1802). His sons, **John Philip Kemble** (1757–1823) and **Charles Kemble** (1775–1854), were both distinguished actors, and his eldest daughter was Sarah Siddons. **Frances Ann Kemble**, known as "Fanny" (1809–93), was the daughter of Charles Kemble.

kempt (kĕmpt) *adj.* Neat; tidy. [Probably back-formation from UN-KEMPT.]

ken (kĕn) *v.* **kenned** or **kent** (kĕnt), **kenning, kens.** —*tr.* **1.** *Chiefly Scottish.* To know (a person, fact, or thing). **2.** *Chiefly Scottish.* To recognize. **3.** *Archaic.* To descry; make out. —*intr. Chiefly Scottish.* To have an understanding of something.
~*n.* **1.** Range of knowledge or understanding: *beyond my ken.* **2.** Range of vision; view. [Middle English *kennen*, Old English *cennan*, to make known (probably influenced in sense by Old Norse cognate *kenna*, to know).]

Ken·dal green (kĕn'dəl) *n.* **1.** A coarse green woolen fabric similar to tweed. **2.** The color of this fabric. [Originally manufactured at *Kendal*, England.]

ken·do (kĕn'dō) *n.* A traditional Japanese martial art in which two contestants wearing protective armor fight with bamboo swords. [Japanese *kendō*, "the art of fencing," from Chinese *jiàn*, sword + *daò*, way.]

Kennedy, Cape. See **Canaveral, Cape.**

Ken·ne·dy (kĕn'ə-dē), **Edward Moore** (1932–). U.S. Democratic politician. He is the youngest of the Kennedy brothers and was elected to the Senate (1962). He campaigned unsuccessfully for the Democratic presidential nomination in 1980.

Kennedy, John Fitzgerald (1917–63). 35th president of the United States (1961–63), the youngest president ever to be elected and also the first Roman Catholic president. He studied at Harvard, where he wrote *Why England Slept*, a study of the English failure to judge adequately the Nazi threat, which became a best seller. After a distinguished war career in the navy he entered the House of Representatives (1947) and the Senate (1952). He executed (although he did not plan) the disastrous attempt by Cuban exiles to invade Cuba (1961), but caused Khrushchev to back down over his attempt to establish Soviet nuclear missiles there in 1962. A liberal in domestic policy, he established the Peace Corps, fought for slum clearance and cheap public housing, and raised the minimum wage. He agreed to a partial Test Ban Treaty with the U.S.S.R. (1963) and insisted on continued U.S. access to West Berlin. He was assassinated in Dallas, Texas on November 22, 1963.

Kennedy, Joseph Patrick (1888–1969). U.S. multimillionaire and father of the Kennedy brothers. He made a fortune from banking and the stock market and became U.S. ambassador to Britain (1937–40). He resigned because he opposed aid to the Allies.

Kennedy, Robert Francis (1925–68). U.S. Democratic politician. He was attorney general (1961) during the presidency of his brother John F. Kennedy. He was elected to the Senate (1964) and was campaigning for the Democratic nomination for the presidency when he was assassinated (June 1968).

ken·nel¹ (kĕn'əl) *n.* **1.** A shelter for a dog or cat. **2.** A pack of dogs, especially hounds. **3.** An establishment where dogs are bred, trained, or boarded. **4.** The lair of a wild animal, as a fox.
~*v.* **kenneled** or **-nelled, -neling** or **-nelling, -nels.** —*tr.* To keep or place in or as if in a kennel. —*intr.* To stay or take cover in or as if in a kennel. [Middle English *kenel*, from Old Northern French *kenil* (unattested), variant of Old French *chenil*, from Vulgar Latin *canile* (unattested), from Latin *canis*, dog.]

kennel² *n.* A gutter along a street. [Variant of *cannel*, Middle English *canel, canal*, CANAL.]

Ken·nel·ly (kĕn'ə-lē), **Arthur Edwin** (1861–1939). U.S. electrical engineer. At the same time as Oliver Heaviside, he correctly predicted the existence of an ionized layer in the upper atmosphere, the Kennelly-Heaviside layer.

Ken·nel·ly-Heav·i·side layer (kĕn'ə-lē-hĕv'ē-sīd') *n.* The **E** layer *(see)* of the ionosphere.

Ken·ne·saw Mountain National Battlefield Park (kĕn'ə-sô'). Park in northwestern Georgia, site of a Civil War battle during Gen. William T. Sherman's advance on Atlanta (1864).

ken·ning (kĕn'ĭng) *n.* A metaphorical, usually compound expression used especially in Old English and Old Norse poetry; for example, *storm of swords* is a kenning for *battle*. [Old Norse *kenning*, "naming," symbol, from *kenna*, to know, name (with a kenning).]

Ken·ny (kĕn'ē), **Elizabeth** (1886–1952). Australian pioneer of polio treatment. She applied hot towels to affected limbs instead of wrapping them in plaster casts, the traditional treatment.

ke·no (kē'nō) *n.* A game of chance that is similar to lotto but uses balls rather than counters. [Probably from French *quine*, set of five (winning numbers), back-formation from Old French *quines*, five each, from Latin *quīnī* (accusative *quīnas*).]

ke·no·sis (kə-nō'sĭs) *n. Theology.* Christ's relinquishment of the form of God in becoming man and suffering death. Philippians 2:5-8. [Late Greek *kenōsis*, from Greek, an emptying, from *kenoun*, to empty, from *kenos*, empty.] —**ke·not·ic** (kə-nŏt'ĭk) *adj.*

Ken·sing·ton and Chel·sea (kĕn'zĭng-tən; chĕl'sē). Since 1965 a royal borough of Greater London.

ken·speck·le (kĕn'spĕk'əl) *adj. Scottish.* Easily recognized; conspicuous. [From dialectal *kenspeck*, from Scandinavian; akin to Old Norse *kennispeki*, power of recognition. See **ken.**]

kent. Alternate past tense and past participle of **ken.**

Kent (kĕnt). A county of southeast England, called "the Garden of England" for its hop and fruit crops. The Saxon kingdom of Kent was the first to be converted to Christianity (597) by St. Augustine. The administrative center is Maidstone.

Kent, Rockwell (1882–1971). U.S. artist. A world traveler, he published several collections of his stark woodcuts and other works, including *Wilderness: A Journal of Quiet Adventure in Alaska* (1920), which established his reputation as an artist and writer. He also illustrated special editions of *Moby Dick* (1930) and other classics.

ken·te (kĕn'tē, -tā') *n.* **1.** A brightly colored cloth of Ghana, woven in strips. **2.** A large cloth made up of such strips, worn as dress in the style of a toga by Ghanaian men. [Probably from Akan.]

ken·ti·a palm (kĕn'tē-ə) *n.* A palm, *Howea belmoreana* (or *Kentia belmoreana*), often grown as a house plant. Also called "sentry palm."

Kent·ish (kĕn'tĭsh) *adj.* Of, relating to, or inhabiting Kent, England.
~*n.* The dialect originally spoken in Kent, England.

Kentish glory *n.* A large, handsome European moth, *Endromis versicolora.*

kent·ledge (kĕnt'lĭj) *n. Nautical.* Pig iron used as permanent ballast. [Old French *quintelage*, ballast, from *quintal*, hundredweight, from Medieval Latin *quintale*, from Arabic *qinṭār*, KANTAR.]

Ken·tuck·y (kən-tŭk'ē) *Abbr.* **Ky.** A state of central United States. Known as the "Bluegrass State" because of the rich pastures of bluegrass in its central area, it also has coal deposits, and heavy industry has been developed at Louisville. Frankfort is its capital.

Kentucky bluegrass *n.* See **bluegrass.**

Kentucky coffee tree *n.* A deciduous North American tree, *Gymnocladus dioica*, having flat, pulpy pods containing seeds formerly used as a coffee substitute. Also called "coffee tree."

Kentucky Derby *n.* An annual horse race for three-year-olds run since 1875 at Churchill Downs in Louisville, Kentucky.

Ken·ya (kĕn'yə). East African republic lying across the equator. The fertile southwest highlands are Africa's major source of coffee and tea, the country's main exports, along with pyrethrum and sisal. Tourism is a major industry. Kenya was proclaimed a British col-

Kerry *An Irish breed of dairy cow, moderate in size and milk yield but easy to raise. It is productive even on poor pasture.*

kestrel *Mice, rats, and voles form the main diet of this common bird of prey. Kestrels hunt by hovering high in the air while they watch for prey, then closing in and pouncing. They are found all over Europe, Africa, and Asia and have been known to make their nests even in the center of large cities.*

ony in 1920. The savage Mau Mau rebellion of the Kikuyu (1952–60) hastened independence (1963) under Jomo Kenyatta, and stability and prosperity ensued. However, the world recession of the 1970's and a disastrous drought in 1980 severely strained the economy. Area, 582,646 square kilometers (224,901 square miles). Population, 15,300,000. Capital, Nairobi. **—Ken·yan** *n. & adj.*

Kenya, Mount. Extinct volcano in Kenya. It is Africa's second-highest mountain (5,200 meters; 17,058 feet).

Ken·yat·ta (kĕn-yä′tə), **Jomo Kamau** (1894–1978). First president of independent Kenya (1964–78). In 1947 he became leader of the Kenya African Union. He was a suspected organizer of the Mau Mau rebellion (1952) and was imprisoned by the British (1952–61). Kenyatta negotiated independence and was elected prime minister.

Ke·ogh plan (kē′ō) *n.* A retirement plan for the self-employed. [After Eugene J. *Keogh* (born 1907).]

kep (kĕp) *tr.v.* **kepped, kepping, keps.** *British Regional.* To catch. [Variant of KEEP (in obsolete sense, to "seize, hold").]

ke·pi (kā′pē, kĕp′ē) *n., pl.* **-is.** A French military cap with a flat, circular top and a visor. [French *képi,* from Swiss German *käppi,* diminutive of German *Kappe,* cap.]

Kep·ler (kĕp′lər), **Johannes** (1571–1630). German astronomer, founder of modern astronomy. His three laws, based on the observations made by his teacher Tycho Brahe, made sense of the theory that the planets revolve around the sun.

Kep·ler's laws (kĕp′lərz) *pl.n.* Three laws describing planetary motion, published by Kepler between 1609 and 1619: the path of a planet is an ellipse with the sun at one focus; a line from the sun to a planet sweeps out equal areas in equal time periods; the square of the orbital period of a planet is proportional to the cube of its average distance from the sun.

kept. Past tense and past participle of **keep.**

Ker·a·la (kĕr′ə-lə). The most densely populated state in India. It lies in the southwest part of the country, between the Western Ghats and the coast. Though poor and undeveloped, Kerala has the highest literacy rate in India.

ker·a·tec·to·my (kĕr′ə-tĕk′tə-mē) *n., pl.* **-mies.** Surgical removal of all or part of the cornea.

ker·a·tin (kĕr′ə-tĭn) *n.* A tough, fibrous protein containing sulfur and forming the outer layer of epidermal structures such as hair, nails, horns, and hoofs. [Greek *keras* (stem *kerat-*), horn + -IN.] **—ke·rat·i·nous** (kə-răt′n-əs) *adj.*

ker·a·tin·ize (kĕr′ə-tĭ-nīz′) *v.* **-ized, -izing, -izes.** *—tr.* To form keratin in or on. *—intr.* To form a keratinous layer. **—ker·a·tin·i·za·tion** *n.*

ker·a·ti·tis (kĕr′ə-tī′tĭs) *n.* Inflammation of the cornea.

kerato–, kerat– *prefix. form.* Indicates: **1.** Horny tissue, especially of the skin; for example, **keratin. 2.** The cornea of the eye; for example, **keratitis.**

ker·a·to·sis (kĕr′ə-tō′sĭs) *n., pl.* **-ses** (-sēz′). A horny growth or condition of the skin, as a wart.

kerb. *British.* Variant of **curb.**

ker·chief (kûr′chĭf, -chēf′) *n.* **1.** A square scarf, often worn around the neck or as a head covering. **2.** A handkerchief. [Middle English *c(o)urchef, kercheffe,* from Old French *couvrechef, cuerchief,* "head covering" : *co(u)vrir,* to COVER + *ch(i)ef,* head, from Latin *caput.*]

Ke·ren·sky (kə-rĕn′skē), **Aleksandr Feodorovich** (1881–1970). Russian politician. He was head of government between the two Russian revolutions in 1917, but was expelled by the Bolsheviks because of his moderate policies. He lived in the United States from 1940 until his death.

kerf (kûrf) *n.* **1.** A groove or notch made by a saw, ax, or the like. **2.** The cut end of a tree that has been felled. [Middle English *kyrf, kerf,* Old English *cyrf,* act of cutting.]

ker·fuf·fle (kər-fŭf′əl) *n. Chiefly British Informal.* A fuss or commotion. [20th century : origin obscure.]

Kérkyra. See **Corfu.**

ker·ma (kûr′mə) *n. Physics.* The sum of all the initial kinetic energies of particles produced in a given sample by ionizing radiation divided by the mass of the sample. [*k*inetic *e*nergy *r*eleased in *ma*tter.]

ker·mes (kûr′mēz) *n.* **1.** A red dyestuff prepared from the dried bodies of female scale insects of the genus *Kermes,* especially the Eurasian species *K. ilices.* **2.** A small evergreen Eurasian oak, *Quercus coccifera,* on which kermes scale insects live. [French *kermès,* short form for *alkermès,* from Spanish *alkermez,* from Arabic *al-qirmiz,* "the kermes," from Sanskrit *kṛmi-ja-,* (red dye) produced by a worm : *kṛmi-,* worm + *ja-,* born, produced.]

ker·mis, ker·mess, kir·mess (kûr′mĭs) *n.* **1.** An outdoor fair in the Low Countries. **2.** A fund-raising fair or carnival. [Dutch *kermis(se),* from Middle Dutch *kercmisse* : *kerke, kerc,* church, from West Germanic *kirika* (unattested), from Late Greek *kurikon,* CHURCH + *misse,* Mass.]

kern¹, kerne (kûrn) *n.* **1.** A medieval Scottish or Irish foot soldier. **2.** A country bumpkin; yokel. [Middle English *kerne,* from Middle Irish *ceithern,* from Old Irish, band of foot soldiers, possibly from *cath,* battle, troop.]

kern² *n. Printing.* The portion of a character or typeface that projects beyond the body or shank.
~tr.v. **kerned, kerning, kerns.** *Printing.* To provide (a character or typeface) with a kern. [French *carne,* corner, salient angle, from Latin *cardō* (stem *cardin-*), hinge.]

kern³ *n. Engineering.* The middle part of a wall, column, or other supporting structure regarded as the part subject to compressive forces. [Perhaps from German *Kern,* nucleus.]

Kern (kûrn), **Jerome David** (1885–1945). U.S. songwriter. He wrote more than 50 stage and film musicals and more than a thousand songs. His most successful musical was *Showboat* (1927), and his songs include "Ol' Man River" and "Smoke Gets in Your Eyes."

ker·nel (kûr′nəl) *n.* **1.** A grain or seed, as of a cereal grass, enclosed in a hard husk. **2.** The inner, usually edible part of a nut or fruit stone. **3.** The most material and central part; essence or core: *"that hard kernel of gaiety that never breaks"* (Evelyn Waugh). [Middle English *kirnel, kernell,* Old English *cyrnel,* seed, kernel, diminutive of *corn,* corn, berry, seed.]

kernel sentence *n.* In generative grammar, any of a small number of basic and irreducible sentence types from which all other sentences may be formed or derived.

kern·ite (kûr′nīt′) *n.* A colorless to white crystalline mineral, $Na_2B_4O_7 \cdot 4H_2O$, that is a major source of boron. [Found in *Kern* County, California.]

ker·o·gen (kĕr′ə-jən) *n.* A bituminous material found in shale that produces hydrocarbons similar to petroleum when heated. Oil shale is rich in kerogen. [Greek *kēros,* wax + -GEN.]

ker·o·sene, ker·o·sine (kĕr′ə-sēn′, kĕr′ə-sēn′, kăr′ə-sēn′, kăr′ə-sēn′) *n.* A thin oil distilled from petroleum or shale oil and used as a fuel and alcohol denaturant. Also called "coal oil" and in British usage "paraffin." [Greek *kēros,* wax (see **ceruse**) + -ENE (from the use of paraffin in its distillation).]

Ke·rou·ac (kĕr′o͞o-ăk′), **Jack** (1922–69). U.S. writer and leading figure of the beat generation. His mainly autobiographical books include *On the Road* (1957), *Dharma Bums* (1958), and *Desolation Angels* (1965).

Kerr cell (kûr) *n.* A cell consisting of a transparent liquid to which a strong electric field can be applied to stop the passage of light through the cell. The device, which depends for its action on the electrical Kerr effect, is used for producing short pulses of light for laser experiments, high speed photography, and the like. [After John *Kerr* (1824–1907), British physicist.]

Kerr effect *n. Physics.* **1.** The production of double refraction in certain transparent solids or liquids by application of a strong electric field. **2.** The slight elliptical polarization of light that is reflected from the surface of strongly magnetized material. [After John *Kerr* (1824–1907), British physicist.]

Ker·ry¹ (kĕr′ē). A county on the southwest coast of the Republic of Ireland. Its mountains and lakes are a tourist attraction. Its county town is Tralee.

Kerry² *n., pl.* **-ries.** Any of a breed of small, black dairy cattle originally raised in the county of Kerry, Ireland.

Kerry blue terrier *n.* Any of a breed of terriers of Irish origin, having a dense, wavy bluish-gray coat.

Kerry Hill *n.* A large, broad-bodied sheep of a breed originally from the Kerry Hills of Wales.

ker·sey (kûr′zē) *n., pl.* **-seys. 1.** A woolen fabric, often ribbed, formerly used for hose and trousers. **2.** A twilled woolen fabric, sometimes with a cotton warp, used for coats. **3.** *Often* **kerseys.** A garment, as a coat, made of kersey. [Middle English, probably after *Kersey,* a village in Suffolk, England.]

ker·sey·mere (kûr′zē-mîr′) *n.* A type of fine woolen cloth with a twill weave. Also called "cassimere." [Altered from CASSIMERE (by association with KERSEY).]

ke·ryg·ma (kə-rĭg′mə) *n., pl.* **ke·ryg·ma·ta** (-mə-tə). *Theology.* The proclamation of religious truths, especially as taught in the Gospels. [Greek, proclamation, from *kērussein,* to proclaim.] **—ker·yg·mat·ic** (kĕr′ĭg-măt′ĭk) *adj.*

Ke·sey (kē′zē), **Ken Elton** (1935–). U.S. novelist. He wrote *One Flew Over the Cuckoo's Nest* (1962, filmed 1975), set in a mental ward, and *Sometimes A Great Notion* (1964, filmed 1971).

Kes·sel·ring (kĕs′əl-rĭng′), **Albert** (1887–1960). German military commander. In World War II he led blitzkrieg operations against Poland, France, the U.S.S.R., and Britain. He was convicted of war crimes and sentenced to death, but was reprieved and freed (1952).

kes·trel (kĕs′trəl) *n.* **1.** A small Old World falcon, *Falco tinnunculus,* with brown and gray plumage, that is noted for its habit of hovering while searching for prey. Also called "windhover" in British usage. **2.** Any of several Old World falcons. [Middle English *castrell,* alteration of Old French *cresserelle, crecelle,* "rattle," kestrel (from its cry), from Vulgar Latin *crepicella* (unattested), diminutive formation from Latin *crepitāre,* to rattle, creak, crackle, frequentative of *crepāre,* to crack.]

ketch (kĕch) *n.* A two-masted fore-and-aft-rigged sailing vessel with a mizzen or jigger mast situated aft of a taller mainmast but forward of the rudder. Compare **yawl.** [Earlier *catch,* Middle English *cache,* probably from *cachen, cacchen,* to hunt, CATCH.]

Ketch (kĕch), **John,** known as "Jack" (died 1686). English executioner, famous for his cruelty and incompetence. He bungled the execution of, among others, the Duke of Monmouth (1685). The name has passed into English folklore and is still given to the hangman in Punch and Judy puppet shows.

ketch·up (kĕch′əp, kăch′-) *n.* Also **catch·up** (kăch′əp, kĕch′-), **cat·sup** (kăt′səp, kăch′əp, kĕch′-) A condiment consisting of a thick, smooth, spicy sauce usually made from tomatoes. [Malay *kichap,* from Chinese (Amoy) *kôechiap* "brine of fish" : *kôe* (Mandarin *qui*), a kind of fish + *chiap* (Mandarin *zhī*), juice.]

ke·tene (kē′tēn′) *n.* A pungent, toxic, colorless gas, H_2CCO, used chiefly as an acetylation agent. [KET(O)- + -ENE.]

keto–, ket– *prefix. Chemistry.* Indicates a ketone or ketonic properties; for example, **ketosis.** [From KETONE.]

ke·to·e·nol tautomerism (kē′tō-ē′nôl′, -nōl′, -nŏl′) *n. Chemistry.* A type of tautomerism involving an equilibrium between the keto and enol forms of a molecule, occurring because of migration of a hydrogen atom.

ke·to form (kē′tō) *n. Chemistry.* A structural form of an organic compound in which its molecules contain a ketone group (CO) linked to an adjacent carbon atom.

ke·to·gen·e·sis (kē′tō-jĕn′ə-sĭs) *n.* The formation of ketone bodies, as in diabetes. —**ke·to·gen·ic** (kē′tō-jĕn′ĭk) *adj.*

ke·to·hex·ose (kē′tō-hĕk′sōs, -sōz′) *n.* A ketose sugar that has six carbon atoms in its molecules.

ke·tone (kē′tōn) *n.* Any of a class of organic compounds having a carbonyl group linked to a carbon atom of two hydrocarbon radicals and having the general formula $R_1(CO)R_2$, where R_1 may be the same as R_2. [German *Keton,* from *Aketon, Azeton,* ACETONE.] —**ke·ton·ic** (kē-tŏn′ĭk) *adj.*

ketone body *n.* Any of several substances, such as acetoacetic acid, increasing in the blood during starvation and in certain diabetic and other pathological conditions. Also called "acetone body."

ketone group *n. Chemistry.* A carbonyl group (CO) linked to two carbon atoms, as in a ketone.

ke·to·nu·ri·a (kē′tō-nōor′ē-ə, -nyŏor′ē-ə) *n.* The presence of ketone bodies in the urine.

ke·to·pen·tose (kē′tō-pĕn′tōs, -tōz′) *n.* A ketose sugar that has five carbon atoms in its molecules.

ke·tose (kē′tōs, -tōz′) *n.* Any of various carbohydrates containing a ketone group in each molecule. Compare **aldose.** [KET(O)- + -OSE.]

ke·to·sis (kē-tō′sĭs) *n.* A pathological accumulation of ketone bodies in the body. [New Latin : KET(O)- + -OSIS.] —**ke·tot·ic** (kē-tŏt′ĭk) *adj.*

ke·to·ste·roid (kē′tō-stîr′oid′, -stĕr′oid′) *n.* A steroid containing a steroid group.

ket·tle (kĕt′l) *n.* **1.** A metal pot, usually with a lid, for boiling or stewing. **2.** A teakettle. **3.** A kettledrum. **4.** A depression left in a mass of glacial drift, apparently formed by the melting of an isolated block of glacial ice. **5.** A pothole. **6.** Any of various large vessels used for industrial processes such as refining metals and distilling. —**kettle of fish. 1.** A troublesome, awkward, or embarrassing situation. **2.** A matter to be reckoned with: *Making money and keeping it are two quite different kettles of fish.* [Middle English *ketel,* from Old Norse *ketill,* from Common Germanic *katilaz* (unattested), from Latin *catillus,* small bowl or dish, from *catīnus†,* bowl, dish, pot.]

ket·tle·drum (kĕt′l-drŭm′) *n.* A large copper or brass hemispherical drum with a parchment head that can be tuned by adjusting the tension.

keV kiloelectron volt.

kev·el (kĕv′əl) *n.* A sturdy cleat or pin for securing the heavier cables of a ship. [Middle English *kevile,* peg, from Old North French *keville,* from Late Latin *clāvicula,* bolt, bar, from Latin, small key, from *clāvis,* key.]

Kew Gardens (kyōo). The Royal Botanic Gardens at Kew in the London borough of Richmond. Founded in 1759, they were presented to the nation in 1841.

key¹ (kē) *n., pl.* **keys. 1.** An implement designed to open a lock; especially, a usually metal notched and grooved implement that is inserted into and turned to open or close a lock. **2. a.** Something that is a means of access, control, or possession. **b.** An essential ingredient or element; requisite: *A good diet is the key to a long life.* **3. a.** A small instrument for winding a spring, as of a clock. **b.** A slotted metal strip used to open cans. **4. a.** An explanation of a set of symbols or abbreviations. **b.** A set of answers to a test or puzzle. **c.** A table, gloss, or cipher for decoding or interpreting. **d.** Something that serves to explain or interpret. **5.** A device, as a pin or wedge, inserted to lock together mechanical or structural parts. **6.** The keystone in the crown of an arch. **7. a.** A button or lever, as on a typewriter, that is pressed with the finger to operate a machine. **b.** A button or lever on a musical instrument, such as a clarinet or piano, that is pressed with the fingers to produce or modulate a sound. **8.** *Music.* **a.** A tonal system consisting of seven notes in fixed relationship to a tonic, having a characteristic key signature and being since the Renaissance the structural foundation of the bulk of Western music; tonality. **b.** The principal tonality of a musical work: *an étude in the key of E.* **9.** The pitch of a voice or other sound: *She spoke in a high key.* **10. a.** A characteristic tone or level of intensity, as of a speech, theatrical performance, or sales campaign. **b.** The general tone or intensity of color in a picture, as a painting. **11.** *Botany.* A **samara** (see). **12.** *Biology.* A list of taxonomic characters used on a presence or absence system to identify plants and animals. **13.** The roughness of a surface that provides a bond for the application of another finish, such as plaster. **14.** *Slang.* A kilogram of a drug, especially heroin or marijuana. —**in** (or **out of**) **key.** In tune or out of tune with other factors. ~*tr.v.* **keyed, keying, keys. 1.** To lock together with or as if with a key. **2.** To furnish (an arch) with a keystone. **3.** To supply with a key. **4.** To regulate the pitch of (a musical instrument). **b.** To bring into tune or harmony; coordinate: *The speech was keyed to the occasion.* **5.** To supply an explanatory key for. **6.** To roughen (a surface) so as to provide a bond for a subsequent finish. —**key up.** To raise in pitch or intensity; make tense, nervous, or excited.

~*adj.* Of crucial importance: *Mining is a key industry in many countries.* [Middle English *key(e), kay,* Old English *cǣg(e)†.*]

key² *n.* A low offshore island or reef, especially in the Gulf of Mexico. [Spanish *cayo,* CAY.]

Key (kē), **Francis Scott** (1799–1843). U.S. lawyer and poet. After witnessing the British attack on Baltimore on the night of September 13, 1814, and seeing the American flag still flying on the following morning, he wrote "Defense of Fort M'Henry," a patriotic poem soon after set to music and renamed "The Star-Spangled Banner." In 1931 Congress officially adopted the song as the national anthem.

key·board (kē′bôrd′, -bōrd′) *n.* A set of keys, as on a piano, an organ, or a typewriter. Also used adjectively: *keyboard instruments.* ~*tr.v.* **keyboarded, -boarding, -boards.** To set (copy) by means of a keyed typesetting machine. —**key·board·er** *n.* See feature, next page.

Keyes (kīz, kĕz), **Frances Parkinson** (1885–1970). U.S. author. Primarily remembered for her critically ill-received but highly popular novels, including *Dinner at Antoine's* (1948), that provided a glimpse into the lives of wealthy, urbane characters, she was also a magazine editor and wrote widely on religious subjects.

key fruit *n.* A **samara** (see). [From its shape.]

key·hole (kē′hōl′) *n.* The hole in a lock into which a key fits.

keyhole saw *n.* A narrow saw with a fine-toothed blade used for cutting small curves.

key money *n.* Payment made by a prospective tenant to a landlord to assure tenancy of an apartment or house.

Keynes (kānz), **John Maynard, 1st Baron** (1883–1946). Influential British economist who believed that high unemployment could be due to insufficient consumer spending rather than inflated wage levels and that government intervention was then necessary. At the Bretton Woods Agreement (1944) he was instrumental in establishing the International Monetary Fund and the International Bank for Reconstruction and Development.

Keynes·i·an (kān′zē-ən) *adj.* Of or pertaining to the economic theories or policies of John M. Keynes. ~*n.* A supporter of Keynes's economic theories or policies. —**Keynes·i·an·ism** *n.*

key·note (kē′nōt′) *n.* **1.** The tonic of a musical key. **2.** A prime or crucial element: *saw simplicity as the keynote of the plan.* **3.** An underlying or prevailing tone, spirit, or idea: *Pessimism was the keynote of the novel.* ~*tr.v.* **keynoted, -noting, -notes.** To give or set the keynote of.

keynote speech *n.* An opening address, as at a political convention, that outlines the issues to be considered.

key·punch (kē′pŭnch′) *n.* A keyboard machine that is used to punch holes in cards or tapes for data-processing systems. ~*tr.v.* **keypunched, -punching, -punches.** To punch holes in (cards or tape) with a keypunch. —**key·punch·er** *n.*

key signature *n.* The group of sharps or flats placed to the right of the clef on a musical staff to identify the key.

key·stone (kē′stōn′) *n.* **1.** *Architecture.* The central wedge-shaped stone of an arch that locks the others together. **2.** An essential part on which other parts depend.

key·stroke (kē′strōk′) *n.* A single depression of a key of a typewriter, typesetting machine, keypunch, or other keyboard device.

key·way (kē′wā′) *n., pl.* **-ways. 1.** A slot in a wheel hub or shaft for a key. **2.** The keyhole of a cylinder lock.

Key West (kē′ wĕst′). Seaport and resort at the western tip of the Florida Keys in the United States, a site of U.S. naval and air bases.

key word, key·word (kē′wûrd′) *n.* **1.** A word serving as a key to a cipher or code. **2.** A significant word or quality. **3.** A word used as an index to other words or information.

kg kilogram.

K.G. Knight of the (Order of the) Garter (in Britain).

KGB, K.G.B. (kā′jē′bē′) *n.* An intelligence agency of the Soviet Union. [Russian *Komityet Gosudarstvyennoi Byezopasnosti,* commission of state security.]

Kha·cha·tu·ri·an (kä′chä-tōor′ē-ən, kăch′ə-), **Aram Ilyich** (1903–78). Russian musician. He composed concertos for piano (1936) and violin (1940), three symphonies (1934, 1943, and 1947), and the ballets *Gayaneh* (1942) and *Spartacus* (1954).

Khadafy, Muammar. See Qaddafi.

kha·di (kä′dē) *n.* Also **khad·dar** (kä′dər). A plain, hand-woven cotton fabric of India. [Hindi.]

khak·i (kăk′ē, kä′kē) *n., pl.* **khakis. 1.** A color ranging from light olive brown to yellowish brown. **2.** A sturdy wool or cotton cloth of the color khaki. **3.** *Often* **khakis.** A military uniform of khaki cloth. [Urdu *khākī,* dusty, dust-colored, from *khāk,* dust, from Persian *khāk†.*] —**khak·i** *adj.*

Kha·lid (kä-lēd′, KHä-), **Ibn Abdul Aziz** (1913–82). Fourth king of Saudi Arabia. He succeeded after the assassination of his half-brother King Faisal (1975).

khalif. Variant of **caliph.**

Khalkidhiki. See Chalcidice.

Khalkis. See Chalcis.

kham·sin, kham·seen, kam·sin (kăm-sēn′) *n.* A generally southerly hot wind from the Sahara that blows across Egypt and the southeast Mediterranean from March to early May. [Arabic *(rīh al-)khamsīn,* (wind of the) 50 (days), from *khamsūn,* 50.]

khan¹ (kän, kăn) *n.* **1.** A ruler, an official, or an important person in India and some central Asian countries. **2.** Formerly, a title given to the rulers of Mongol, Tatar, or Turkish tribes who succeeded

THE KEYBOARD'S GROWTH FROM THE CLAVICHORD TO THE SYNTHESIZER

The device that allows a musician to play many notes at once

The piano is the best known and most popular of the keyboard instruments. When depressed, each key activates a light hammer that strikes a string, causing it to vibrate and produce the required note; the strings are of different lengths and sizes to give varied pitch. By using both hands on a keyboard, a musician can play up to ten notes at the same time.

With most keyboard instruments—from the 16th-century clavichord to the modern synthesizer—the keys are depressed with the fingers. But the organ (the largest and most complex of the group) also has a pedal keyboard that is depressed with the feet, so more than ten notes can be played at once.

Before the first piano was built in Italy at the beginning of the 18th century, the main keyboard instrument was the harpsichord. Its strings are mechanically plucked instead of struck, which means that the volume and tone cannot be varied by finger touch. Unlike the piano, it has no "loud" pedal for use in sustaining a note.

The United States has the largest keyboard instrument in the world—a 20th-century organ in Atlantic City, New Jersey. It has seven keyboards that control more than 33,000 pipes.

Clavichord
The strings of this soft-toned instrument are struck by metal tongues that stay in contact as long as the keys are depressed, so they can be used to create a vibrato

Harpsichord
A prominent solo and ensemble instrument from the 16th to the early 19th centuries, it is now used mainly for early music performances

Spinet
This wing-shaped instrument, similar to the harpsichord, has also been revived for early music

Electric Organ
Portable electric organs now rival pianos as family musical instruments. They have no pipes but create sounds by generating electronic signals

Piano Accordion
Metal reeds are vibrated by bellows pushed and pulled by the player. Note selection is by studs (left hand) and keys (right hand)

Upright Piano
The first successful instrument was made in London in 1811. Vertical rather than horizontal strings took less space, allowing small pianos to enter the home

Grand Piano
The strings are horizontal. The "loud" pedal (right foot) increases note duration; the "soft" pedal (left foot) lessens the volume either by bringing the hammers nearer to the string or by causing fewer strings to be struck for each note

Synthesizer
It can simulate all keyboard instrument sounds and a wide variety of other sounds, from rainfall to sirens

Genghis Khan, as well as to emperors of China. [Middle English *caan, c(h)an,* from Old French, from Medieval Latin *caanus,* from Turkish *khān,* contraction of *khāqān,* sovereign, ruler.]

khan² *n.* A caravanserai or inn in certain countries of Asia. [Middle English, from Arabic and Persian *khān,* inn.]

khan·ate (kä′nāt′, kăn′āt′) *n.* The realm or position of a khan.

khanga. Variant of **kanga.**

Khaniá. See **Canea.**

Kharbin. See **Harbin.**

kha·rif (kə-rēf′) *n.* A crop harvested at the end of autumn in India and neighboring countries. Compare **rabi.** [Urdu, from Arabic *kharafa,* to gather.]

Khar·kov (kär′kôf′, -kôv′). A city in western U.S.S.R., formerly capital of the Ukraine (1919–34).

Khar·toum (kär-tōōm′). *Arabic* **al-Kartum** or **Al Khartum.** Capital of Sudan. Founded as an army camp by Muhammad Ali (1821), it was destroyed by Mahdists in 1885, when Gen. Charles Gordon was killed defending it. Gen. H.H. Kitchener recaptured the city in 1898 and replanned it.

khat. Variant of **kat.**

Khayyám, Omar. See **Omar Khayyám.**

khe·dive (kə-dēv′) *n. Often* **Khedive.** A Turkish viceroy ruling Egypt between 1867 and 1914. [French *khédive,* from Turkish *hidiv,* from Persian *khidīw,* prince.]

khi. Variant of **chi.**

Khmer (kə-mâr′) *n., pl.* **Khmers** or collectively **Khmer. 1.** A member of a people of Kampuchea whose culture flourished during the Middle Ages. **2.** The Mon-Khmer language of this people.

Khmer Republic. See **Kampuchea.**

Khmer Rouge (rōōzh) *n.* A Communist movement in Kampuchea. Khmer Rouge guerrillas fought against the U.S.-backed government of General Lon Nol in the early 1970's. They eventually seized power in 1975 under the leadership of Pol Pot and remained in control until the end of 1978. See **Kampuchea.** [French, "red Khmer."]

Khoi·san (koi′sän′) *n.* A family of languages of southwestern Africa, including those of the Bushmen and Hottentots, that is characterized by clicks.

Kho·mei·ni (kō-mā′nē), **Ayatollah Ruholla** (c. 1902–). Iranian leader and head of the Shiite Muslims. He was arrested in 1964 and exiled for his opposition to Shah Reza Pahlavi. When the shah fled to Egypt (1979), Khomeini returned to Tehran (1979) amid wild celebrations. He established a new constitution giving himself supreme power.

Khor·ram·shahr (кнōōr′äm-shär′). Town in Khuzestan, western Iran. It is at the confluence of the Karun River and the Shatt al Arab and is a major port and oil-refining center.

khoum (kōōm, kŏŏm) *n.* A monetary unit equal to ⅕ of the ouguiya of Mauritania. See feature at **currency.** [Native word.]

Khrush·chev (krōōsh-chôf′, -chôv′), **Nikita Sergeyevich** (1894–1971). Soviet leader (1955–64). He was political head of the Ukraine (1938–49) under Stalin. He succeeded Georgi Malenkov as first secretary of the All Union Party (1953). He later denounced Stalin (1956). He was deposed (1964) after the Cuban missile crisis (1962) and the failure of economic reforms.

Khufu. See **Cheops.**

khur·ta, kur·ta (kŏŏr′tə) *n.* A long, loose-fitting, collarless shirt worn in India. [Hindi.]

khus·khus (kŭs′kəs, kōōs′kōōs′) *n.* **1.** An aromatic perennial Indian grass, *Vetiveria zizanioides* (or *Andropogon squarrosus*). **2.** The root of this plant, used to make fans, mats, and the like. [Hindi.]

Khu·ze·stan (kōō′zī-stän′). Province in southwest Iran. A fertile region producing dates, citrus fruits, melons, cotton, and rice, it is also rich in petroleum and has many refineries. More than half the population is Arab.

Khy·ber Pass (kī′bər). Main mountain pass between Afghanistan and Pakistan, frequently fought over. Its gorge runs 53 kilometers (33 miles) through the Safid Koh range and for 8 kilometers (5 miles) is no more than 180 meters (c. 600 feet) wide.

kHz kilohertz.

ki·ang (kē-äng′) *n.* A Tibetan variety of the wild ass, *Equus hemionus kiang.* [Tibetan *rkyan.*]

Kiangsi. See **Jiangxi.**

Kiangsu. See **Jiangsu.**

kib·ble¹ (kĭb′əl) *n.* An iron bucket used, as in wells or mines, for hoisting water, ore, or rubbish to the surface. [German *Kübel;* akin to Old English *cyfel,* from Medieval Latin *cupellus,* a measure for corn, diminutive of *cuppa,* CUP.]

kibble² *tr.v.* **-bled, -bling, -bles.** To crush or grind (grain, for example) coarsely. [18th century : origin obscure.]

kib·butz (kĭ-bōōts′, -bŏŏts′) *n., pl.* **kibbutzim** (kĭb′ŏŏt-sēm′, kĭb′ŏŏt-). A collective farm or settlement in modern Israel. [Hebrew *qibbūtz,* "gathering," from *qibbētz,* he gathered.]

kibe (kīb) *n.* An ulcerated chilblain, especially one on the heel. [Middle English *kybe,* perhaps from Welsh *cibi, cibwst*†.]

kib·itz·er (kĭb′ĭt-sər) *n. Informal.* **1.** An onlooker at a card game who gives unwanted advice to the players. **2.** A person who offers unwanted advice; a meddler. [Yiddish, from German *Kiebitz,* plover, busybody.] —**kib·itz** *v.*

kib·lah (kĭb′lə) *n.* **1.** The direction toward which Muslims face when they pray. **2.** A niche in the wall of a mosque indicating this direction. [Arabic *qiblah,* from *qābilah,* he lay opposite.]

ki·bosh (kī′bŏsh′, kī-bŏsh′) *n. Informal.* Something that checks or

stops: *put the kibosh on that reckless plan.* [Origin unknown.]

Kibris. See **Cyprus.**

kick (kĭk) *v.* **kicked, kicking, kicks.** —*intr.* **1.** To strike out with the foot or feet. **2.** To recoil, as a gun does when fired. **3.** *Informal.* To object vigorously; protest or rebel. **4. a.** To score or gain ground by kicking a ball. **b.** *Football.* To punt. —*tr.* **1.** To strike with the foot. **2.** To drive or move by striking with the foot. **3.** To spring back against suddenly, as a gun when fired. **4.** To score (a goal or point) by kicking a ball. **5.** *Slang.* To free oneself of (an addiction, as smoking). —**kick around.** *Informal.* **1.** To treat badly; abuse. **2.** To give consideration or thought to (an idea). **3.** To move from place to place. **4.** To lie neglected or unobserved: *There's a pen kicking around here somewhere.* —**kick in.** *Slang.* To contribute (one's share). —**kick out.** *Informal.* To throw out; dismiss. —**kick up. 1.** To cause to be propelled upward with force: *tires kicking up gravel.* **2.** To stir up (trouble): *kicking up a row.* **3.** To show signs of disorder: *His ulcer began to kick up.* —**kick up one's heels.** *Informal.* To cast off one's inhibitions and have a good time. —**kick upstairs.** To promote to a higher yet less desirable position. ~*n.* **1. a.** A vigorous thrust or blow with the foot. **b.** The thrusting motion of the legs in swimming. **2.** The jolting recoil of a gun. **3.** *Slang.* Power, force, or resilience: *still a lot of kick in that engine.* **4.** *Slang.* Stimulating or intoxicating impact: *quite a kick in that martini.* **5.** *Slang.* A feeling of excitement or pleasure: *got a kick out of the show.* **b. kicks.** Fun; thrills: *just for kicks.* **6.** *Slang.* A temporary, often obsessive interest or enthusiasm: *on a health-food kick.* **7.** *Slang.* Complaint; protest. **8. a.** An act or instance of kicking a ball. **b.** A kicked ball. **c.** The distance spanned by a kicked ball: *a 47-yard kick.* **9.** A sudden momentary increase in pressure that forces drilled mud back up the bore of an oil or gas well. [Middle English *kiken, kyken*†.]

kick back *intr.v.* **1.** To recoil unexpectedly and violently. **2.** *Slang.* To pay a kickback. **3.** To suffer a sudden momentary increase in pressure. Used of an oil or gas well.

kick·back (kĭk′băk′) *n.* **1.** A sharp response or reaction; a repercussion. **2.** *Slang.* A percentage payment to a person able to influence or control a source of income, as by confidential arrangement or coercion.

kick·er (kĭk′ər) *n.* **1.** A person, animal, or thing that kicks. **2.** *Informal.* A sudden, surprising turn of events; twist. **3.** A tricky or concealed condition; pitfall. **4.** A condition that imposes an automatic increase, as in a pension plan.

kick off *intr.v.* **1.** *Sports.* To begin or resume play with a kickoff. **2.** To start; begin. **3.** *Slang.* To die.

kick·off (kĭk′ôf′, -ŏf′) *n.* **1. a.** A place kick in football or soccer with which play is begun. **b.** The time at which a game is due to begin. **2.** A beginning.

kick pleat *n.* A short pleat at the hem of a skirt that enables the wearer to walk more easily.

kick·shaw (kĭk′shô′) *n.* **1.** A trinket or trifle; gewgaw. **2.** A fancy food; delicacy. [Earlier *kickshose, quelkchose,* from French *quelquechose,* something.]

kick sorter *n. Physics.* A device for sorting a train of pulses according to their height, used to investigate the pulses from a radiation counter to determine the energy spectrum of the incident radiation.

kick·stand (kĭk′stănd′) *n.* A swiveling metal bar on the base of a two-wheeled vehicle, as a motorcycle or bicycle, that keeps it upright when not in use.

kick-start (kĭk′stärt′) *tr.v.* **-started, -starting, -starts.** To start (an engine) by using a kick starter.

kick starter *n.* A device, as a pedal, for starting an engine, as of a motorcycle, that is activated by a downward push of the foot.

kick turn *n.* A stationary turn made in skiing by lifting one ski and positioning it in the intended direction and then lifting and positioning the other to be parallel with it.

kick·y (kĭk′ē) *adj.* **-ier, -iest.** *Slang.* Providing a kick by being unusual or unconventional. —**kick·i·ness** *n.*

kid (kĭd) *n.* **1. a.** A young goat. **b.** The young of a similar animal, such as an antelope. **2.** The flesh of a young goat. **3. a.** Leather made from the skin of a young goat. **b.** An article made of this leather. **4.** *Informal.* **a.** A child. **b.** A young person. ~*adj.* **1.** Made of kid. **2.** *Informal.* Younger: *my kid brother.* ~*v.* **kidded, kidding, kids.** —*tr. Informal.* **1.** To mock playfully; tease. **2.** To deceive in fun; fool. —*intr.* **1.** *Informal.* To engage in teasing or good-humored fooling. **2.** To bear young. Used of a goat or an antelope. [Middle English *kide, kyde,* from Old Norse *kidh,* young goat, from Germanic *kidhja-* (unattested).] —**kid·der** *n.*

Kidd (kĭd), **William,** known as "Captain Kidd" (1645–1701). Scottish pirate. He sailed in 1696 with a commission to defend ships of the East India Company. He was to be paid according to ships taken, so he turned pirate, attacking friendly ships. Kidd was brought from America to London, found guilty, and hanged.

Kid·der·min·ster (kĭd′ər-mĭn′stər) *n.* An ingrain carpet. [After Kidderminster, England, where it was originally made.]

Kid·dush (kĭd′əsh, kĭ-dōōsh′) *n. Judaism.* A traditional blessing and prayer recited over bread or a cup of wine on the eve of the Sabbath or a festival. [Hebrew *qiddūsh,* sanctification, from *qiddesh,* he sanctified.]

kid·dy, kid·die (kĭd′ē) *n., pl.* **-dies.** *Informal.* A small child.

kid glove *n.* A glove made of fine, soft leather, especially kidskin. —**handle with kid gloves.** To treat tactfully and cautiously.

kid·nap (kĭd′năp′) *tr.v.* **-napped** or **-naped, -napping** or **-naping, -naps.** To abduct and detain (a person or animal) unlawfully, often

kidney

KIDNEYS: THE BODY'S "FILTER PLANT"

A system of 2¹/₂ million microscopic filters that purify the blood

The kidneys are the body's purification unit—a filtering system that cleanses the bloodstream of waste products. Nearly 70 liters (15 gallons) of blood an hour flow through the kidneys. Reddish brown organs, each about the size of a fist, they contain between them some 2¹/₂ million microscopic filter loops called nephrons. Incoming blood from the renal artery passes through the nephrons and is returned to the bloodstream, with its cargo of cells, proteins, vitamins, and other essential substances. Molecules of dissolved waste matter, however, are too large to pass through the nephrons. Along with surplus water, they are collected in the form of urine and funneled to the bladder for later expulsion from the body.

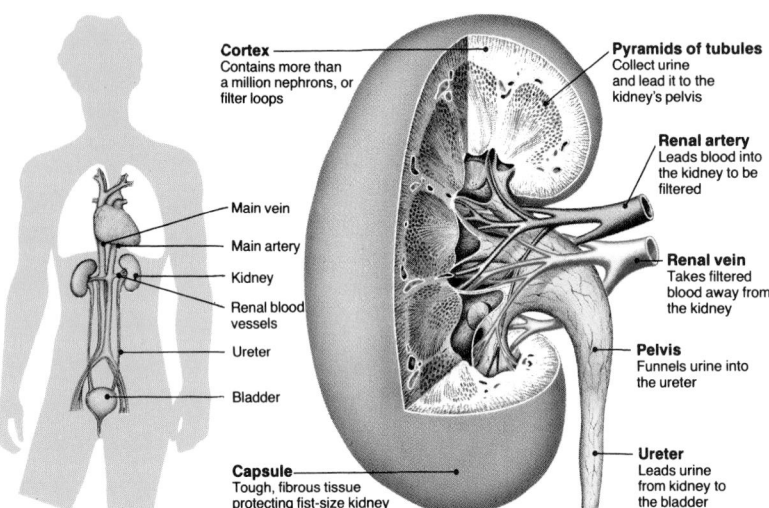

Cortex
Contains more than a million nephrons, or filter loops

Pyramids of tubules
Collect urine and lead it to the kidney's pelvis

Renal artery
Leads blood into the kidney to be filtered

Renal vein
Takes filtered blood away from the kidney

Pelvis
Funnels urine into the ureter

Ureter
Leads urine from kidney to the bladder

Main vein

Main artery

Kidney

Renal blood vessels

Ureter

Bladder

Capsule
Tough, fibrous tissue protecting fist-size kidney

CLEANSING THE BLOODSTREAM *The kidneys lie to the back of the abdomen. Blood enters them through the renal arteries and flows to the nephrons, or filter loops; each kidney contains about* 1¹/₄ *million nephrons. Filtered blood is returned to the circulation through the renal veins, and waste products, such as urea, are secreted as urine and channeled along the ureter to the bladder.*

Kilauea *The lava-spouting central crater of Kilauea is called Halemaumau, or "house of everlasting fire," and is said to be the home of Hawaii's fire goddess, Pele. Kilauea, whose name means "rising smoke cloud," is one of the world's largest active volcanoes.*

for ransom. [Back-formation from *kidnapper* : KID (child) + obsolete *napper*, thief, from *nap*, to seize, probably from Scandinavian; akin to Swedish *nappa†*, to snatch.] —**kid·nap·per, kid·nap·er** *n.*
kid·ney (kĭd′nē) *n., pl.* **-neys. 1.** *Anatomy.* Either of a pair of organs in the dorsal region of the vertebrate abdominal cavity, functioning to maintain proper water balance, regulate acid-base concentration, and excrete metabolic wastes as urine. **2.** The kidney of certain animals, eaten as food. **3.** An excretory organ of certain invertebrates. **4. a.** Disposition; temperament. **b.** Kind, sort, or class. [Middle English *kidenei, kydney* : possibly *kiden-* (an obscure element) + *ei*, egg, Old English *æg.*]
kidney bean *n.* **1.** A bean, *Phaseolus vulgaris,* cultivated in many forms for its edible seeds. **2.** The reddish seed of the kidney bean.
kidney machine *n.* An apparatus for filtering waste products and water from the blood of a patient whose kidneys have ceased to function. Also called "artificial kidney."
kidney stone *n. Pathology.* A renal **calculus** (see).
kidney vetch *n.* A plant, *Anthyllis vulneraria,* native to Europe, having grayish-green leaves and small yellow flowers. [Formerly used to treat kidney disorders.]
kid·skin (kĭd′skĭn′) *n.* Soft leather made from the skin of a young goat.
kid stuff *n. Informal.* **1.** Something very easy or uncomplicated. **2.** Something suitable only for children.
kief. Variant of **kif.**
Kiel (kēl). Capital of Schleswig-Holstein, West Germany. It is a Baltic seaport and was an important naval base (1871–1945).
kiel·ba·sa (kĕl-bä′sə, kĭl-, kēl-) *n.* A smoked Polish sausage. [Polish.]
Kiel Canal. Canal in West Germany. It runs 98 kilometers (61 miles) from Kiel to the Elbe estuary, connecting the Baltic with the North Sea.
kier (kîr) *n.* A vat for boiling, dyeing, or bleaching cloth or yarn. [Earlier *keare,* from Old Norse *ker,* tub, akin to Old High German *char,* Gothic *kas†,* vessel.]
Kier·ke·gaard (kîr′kə-gärd′), **Søren Aabye** (1813–55). Danish philosopher. He opposed Hegel's idea that truth was absolute and attacked the reliance on ritual and dogma in Christianity. His books include *Either-Or* (1843) and *Stages on Life's Way* (1845). —**Kier·ke·gaard·i·an** *adj. & n.*
kie·sel·guhr (kē′zəl-gŏor′) *n. Mineralogy.* **Diatomite** (see). [German : *Kiesel,* pebble + *Guhr,* earthy deposit from water.]
kie·ser·ite (kē′zə-rīt′) *n.* A whitish to yellowish hydrous magnesium

sulfate mineral, used as a source of Epsom salts. [German *Kieserit,* after Dietrich G. *Kieser* (died 1862), German physicist.]
Ki·ev (kē-ĕv′). City in the southwest U.S.S.R. At the confluence of the Dnieper, Pripet, and Dvina rivers, it is the capital of the Ukraine and the U.S.S.R.'s third-largest city. It is the traditional center of Russian Christianity.
kif, keef, kief (kĭf, kēf) *n.* Also **kef** (kĕf, kēf, kāf). **1.** Indian hemp or other related material prepared for smoking, especially in Maghreb. **2.** The odd euphoria often associated with its use. [Arabic *kayf,* euphoria, enjoyment.]
Kikládhes. See **Cyclades.**
Ki·ku·yu (kĭ-kōō′yōō) *n., pl.* **-yus** or collectively **Kikuyu. 1. a.** A member of a Bantu people of Kenya. **b.** The Bantu language of this people. **2. kikuyu.** A hardy grass, *Pennisetum clandestinum,* used for lawns and pasture in southern Africa and central America.
Ki·lau·e·a (kē′lou-ā′ə). Volcanic crater of Hawaii. On the southeast slopes of Mauna Loa, it is one of the largest craters in the world (*c.* 3 kilometers; 2 miles across) still volcanically active.
Kil·dare (kĭl-dâr′). County of the Republic of Ireland. The Bog of Allen lies in the north. Kildare, a market town, was founded by St. Bride in A.D. 490. Naas, in the northeast, is the county town.
kil·der·kin (kĭl′dər-kĭn) *n.* **1.** A cask. **2.** An English measure of capacity that is equal to approximately 68 liters, or 18 gallons. [Middle English *kilderkyn,* earlier *kyn(d)erkyn,* from Middle Dutch *kinderkin, kinnekijn,* diminutive of *kintal,* hundredweight, from Medieval Latin *quintāle,* from Arabic *qinṭār,* KANTAR.]
ki·lim (kē-lēm′) *n.* An oriental tapestry-woven rug or other textile piece. [Turkish, from Persian *kilīm†.*]
Kil·i·man·ja·ro (kĭl′ə-mən-jär′ō). Extinct volcano in northern Tanzania. It has two peaks, Mt. Kibo (5,895 meters; 19,340 feet), Africa's highest peak, and Mt. Mawenzi (5,354 meters; 17,564 feet). The surrounding plain is a wildlife preserve.
Kil·ken·ny¹ (kĭl-kĕn′ē). County of the Republic of Ireland. In the southeast of the country in the province of Leinster, it is ringed by hills and drains toward Waterford harbor in the southeast.
Kilkenny². County town of Kilkenny, it was once the capital of the ancient kingdom of Ossory and is one of Ireland's oldest settlements.
kill (kĭl) *v.* **killed, killing, kills.** —*tr.* **1. a.** To put to death; slay. **b.** To deprive of life: *Famine killed thousands.* **2.** To put an end to; extinguish. **3.** To destroy a vitally essential quality in: *Too much garlic killed the taste of the meat.* **4.** *Informal.* To pass (time) idly or unproductively. **5.** *Informal.* To consume entirely; finish off: *kill a bottle of whiskey.* **6.** *Informal.* To cause extreme pain or discomfort to: *My shoes are killing me.* **7.** *Informal.* To mark for deletion; rule out. **8.** *Informal.* To thwart passage of; veto: *kill a congressional bill.* **9.** *Informal.* To cause to stop; turn off: *killed the engine.* **10.** *Informal.* To exhaust by overexertion. **11.** *Informal.* To destroy the effect of (a color, for example) by contrast; neutralize. **12. a.** To hit (a ball) with great force. **b.** In a racket game, as tennis, to hit (a ball) with such force as to make a return impossible. —*intr.* **1.** To be fatal; cause death or extinction: *Excessive speed kills.* **2.** To commit murder. —**kill off.** To destroy in such large numbers as to render extinct.
~*n.* **1.** The act or moment of killing. **2.** An animal killed, especially in hunting. —**in at the kill.** Present at the moment of triumph. [Middle English *kullen, killen, kellen,* Old English *cyllan* (unattested).]
Kil·lar·ney (kĭ-lär′nē). Market town and tourist center in County Kerry, in the Republic of Ireland.
kill·deer (kĭl′dîr′) *n., pl.* **-deers** or collectively **killdeer.** A New World bird, *Charadrius vociferus,* of inland ponds, streams, and fields, having a distinctive cry. [Imitative of its cry.]
killed spirits *n.* A solution of zinc chloride that is used as a flux for soldering and is made by adding zinc to hydrochloric acid. [Referring to the action of zinc as killing or neutralizing hydrochloric acid.]
kill·er (kĭl′ər) *n.* **1.** One that kills; especially, a murderer. **2.** The killer whale.
killer whale *n.* A black and white predatory whale, *Orcinus orca,* of cold seas. Also called "grampus," "orc."
kil·lick (kĭl′ĭk) *n.* Also **kil·lock** (-ək). A small anchor, especially one made of a stone in a wooden frame. [Origin unknown.]
kil·li·fish (kĭl′ĭ-fĭsh′) *n., pl.* **-fishes** or collectively **killifish.** Any of numerous small fishes of the family Cyprinodontidae, chiefly of fresh and brackish waters of warm regions. [Origin unknown.]
kill·ing (kĭl′ĭng) *n.* **1.** A murder; homicide. **b.** A murder. **2.** An animal killed in hunting; quarry. **3.** *Informal.* A sudden large profit: *made a killing on the stock market.*
~*adj.* **1.** Designed or apt to kill; fatal. **2.** Exhausting: *a killing ordeal.* **3.** *Informal.* Hilarious. —**kill·ing·ly** *adv.*
kill·joy (kĭl′joi′) *n.* A person who spoils the enthusiasm or fun of others.
Kil·mer (kĭl′mər), **(Alfred) Joyce** (1886–1918). U.S. author. A respected journalist and lecturer, he published his first book of verse, *Summer of Love,* in 1911. His other books, including *Trees and Other Poems* (1914), were published before he volunteered to fight in World War I (1917). He was killed on a French battlefield.
kiln (kĭln, kĭl) *n.* Any of various types of ovens for hardening, burning, or drying substances such as grain, meal, or clay; especially, a brick-lined oven used to bake or fire ceramics.
~*tr.v.* **kilned, kilning, kilns.** To process in a kiln. [Middle English *kylne,* Old English *cyline, cylen,* from Latin *culīna,* kitchen, irregular

variant of *coquīna,* cookery, from *coquīnus,* of cooking, from *coquere,* to cook.]

Kil·ner jar (kĭl′nər) *n.* A trademark for a glass jar having a tightly fitting lid that is used in preserving and bottling.

ki·lo (kē′lō) *n., pl.* **-los.** **1.** A kilogram. **2.** A kilometer.

kilo– *prefix. Symbol* **k** Indicates 1,000 (10^3); for example, **kilowatt, kilocalorie.** [French, arbitrarily from Greek *khilioi,* thousand.]

kil·o·cal·o·rie (kĭl′ə-kăl′ə-rē) *n. Abbr.* **kcal** A kilogram calorie.

kil·o·cy·cle (kĭl′ə-sī′kəl) *n. Abbr.* **kc** **1.** A unit equal to 1,000 cycles. **2.** Loosely, 1,000 cycles per second.

kil·o·gram, kil·o·gramme (kĭl′ə-grăm′) *n. Abbr.* **kg** **1.** The fundamental unit of mass in the International System, equal to the mass of a prototype block of platinum–iridium kept at the International Bureau of Weights and Measures at Sèvres, France, that is equal to about 2.20462 pounds. **2.** A force equal to a kilogram weight, or the product of a kilogram mass with the acceleration of gravity.

kilogram calorie *n.* See **calorie** (sense 3).

kil·o·gram-me·ter (kĭl′ə-grăm-mē′tər) *n.* A meter-kilogram-second unit of work equal to the work performed by a one-kilogram force acting through a distance of one meter.

kil·o·hertz (kĭl′ə-hûrts′) *n. Abbr.* **kHz** One thousand hertz.

kil·o·me·ter (kĭl′ə-mē′tər, kĭ-lŏm′ə-tər) *n. Abbr.* **km** One thousand meters, approximately 0.62137 mile. **—kil·o·met·ric** (kĭl′ə-mĕt′rĭk) *adj.*

kil·o·ton (kĭl′ə-tŭn′) *n.* **1.** One thousand tons. **2.** An explosive force equivalent to that of 1,000 tons of TNT.

kil·o·volt (kĭl′ə-vōlt′) *n. Abbr.* **kV** One thousand volts.

kil·o·watt (kĭl′ə-wŏt′) *n. Abbr.* **kW** One thousand watts.

kil·o·watt-hour (kĭl′ə-wŏt′our′) *n. Abbr.* **kWh** A unit of electric power consumption indicating the total energy developed by a power of one kilowatt acting for one hour.

kilt (kĭlt) *n.* A knee-length skirt with deep pleats, usually of a tartan wool, worn especially as part of formal dress for men in the Scottish Highlands.
~tr.v. **kilted, kilting, kilts.** To tuck up around the body. [From the dialectal verb *kilt,* to fasten up, tuck up, Middle English (northern dialect) *kilten,* from Scandinavian, akin to Danish *kilte,* to tuck up, Old Norse *kjalta†,* shirt.] **—kilt·ed** *adj.*

kil·ter (kĭl′tər) *n.* Good condition or proper form: *The radio was out of kilter.* [17th century : origin obscure.]

Kim·ber·ley (kĭm′bər-lē). A city in central South Africa. In Cape Province, south of the Vaal River, it was founded (1871) as a diamond-mining camp and is still a major mining center.

kim·ber·lite (kĭm′bər-līt′) *n.* A type of rock that is found especially in South Africa and that often contains diamonds. [KIMBERLEY + -ITE¹.] **—kim·ber·lit·ic** (kĭm′bər-lĭt′ĭk) *adj.*

Kim Il Sung (kĭm′ ĭl′ sŭng′, so͝ong′), born Kim Song Ju (1912–). North Korean political and military leader. He led the Korean People's army against Japan (1932–45) and became leader of Soviet-dominated North Korea in 1945. He proclaimed the Democratic People's Republic of Korea in 1948 and remained its premier until 1972, when he became its president.

ki·mo·no (kə-mō′nə, -nō) *n., pl.* **-nos.** **1.** A long, loose, wide-sleeved Japanese robe, worn with a broad sash. **2.** A loose dressing gown that is similar to a kimono. [Japanese, "thing for wearing" : *ki,* to wear + *mono,* person, thing.]

kin (kĭn) *n.* One's relatives collectively; family; kindred; kinsfolk.
~adj. Related; akin. [Middle English *kin(n), kyn,* Old English *cyn(n).*]

-kin *suffix.* Indicates small or diminutive; for example, **lambkin.** [Middle English, from Middle Dutch *-kin, -kijn,* from West Germanic *-kin* (unattested).]

ki·na (kē′nə) *n., pl.* **kina** or **-nas.** The basic monetary unit of Papua New Guinea, equal to 100 toea. [Native name.]

ki·nase (kī′nās′, -nāz′) *n.* An enzyme or metal ion that activates the inactive precursor of another enzyme. [KIN(ETIC) + -ASE.]

Kin·car·dine (kĭn-kär′dən). Also **Kin·car·dine·shire** (-shîr, -shər). Former county of eastern Scotland, incorporated into Grampian Region (1975).

Kinchinjunga. See **Kangchenjunga, Mount.**

kind¹ (kīnd) *adj.* **kinder, kindest.** **1.** Of a friendly, generous, and hospitable nature; warmhearted and good. **2.** Showing sympathy, generosity, or thoughtfulness: *a kind act; his kind remarks about your work.* **3.** Humane; considerate: *kind to animals.* **4.** Forbearing; tolerant: *very kind about the broken window.* **5.** Generous; liberal: *Fate has been kind to her.* **6.** Not harmful; beneficial: *a soap kind to the skin.* [Middle English *kynde, kind,* Old English *gecynde,* natural, innate.]
Synonyms: *benevolent, benign, caring, compassionate, kindhearted, kindly.*

kind² *n.* **1.** A class or category of similar or related individuals: *the kind of people who are cheerful in the morning.* —See Usage note at **sort.** **2.** A specific type; variety: *What kind of dog is that?* **3.** A rough, often not very good approximation to the thing specified: *a kind of shelter; gave us soup of a kind.* —See Synonyms at **type.** **—all kinds of.** *Informal.* Plenty of; ample: *We have all kinds of time to finish the job.* **—in kind.** **1.** With produce or commodities rather than with money: *pay in kind.* **2.** In the same manner or with something equivalent; accordingly: *returned the slight in kind.* **—kind of.** *Informal.* Somewhat: *I'm kind of hungry.* [Middle English *kynd(e), kind(e),* Old English *cynd, gecynd(e),* birth, nature, race.]

kin·der·gar·ten (kĭn′dər-gärt′n) *n.* A program or class for four- to six-year-old children that serves as an introduction to school. [German *Kindergarten,* "children's garden."]

kind·heart·ed (kīnd′här′tĭd) *adj.* Having or proceeding from a kind heart; sympathetic, generous, and helpful. —See Synonyms at **kind.** **—kind·heart·ed·ly** *adv.* **—kind·heart·ed·ness** *n.*

kin·dle (kĭnd′l) *v.* **-dled, -dling, -dles.** *—tr.* **1.** To set fire to; cause to start burning; ignite. **2.** To cause to glow; light up: *The sunset kindled the skies.* **3. a.** To inflame; excite. **b.** To arouse; inspire: *"no spark had yet kindled in him an intellectual passion"* (George Eliot). *—intr.* **1.** To catch fire; burst into flame. **2.** To become bright; glow. **3.** To become inflamed; be aroused or stirred up. [Middle English *kind(e)len,* from Old Norse *kynda,* to kindle, catch fire (but influenced in form by Old Norse *kyndill,* torch), akin to Middle High German *künden†,* to set on fire.] **—kin·dler** *n.*

kind·less (kīnd′lĭs) *adj.* **1.** Heartless. **2.** *Obsolete.* Inhuman.

kind·li·ness (kīnd′lē-nĭs) *n.* **1.** The quality of being kindly. **2.** A kindly deed; a good turn; a kindness.

kin·dling (kĭnd′lĭng) *n.* Easily ignited material, such as dry sticks of wood, used to start a fire.

kind·ly (kīnd′lē) *adj.* **-lier, -liest.** **1.** Having a sympathetic, helpful, or benevolent nature; customarily showing kindness: *a kindly old soul.* **2.** Expressive of a sympathetic, helpful, or benevolent nature or impulse: *a kindly interest.* **3.** Agreeable; pleasant. **4.** *Archaic.* **a.** Lawful; legitimate. **b.** Native-born. **c.** Natural to its kind. —See Synonyms at **kind.**
~adv. **1.** Out of kindness: *He kindly overlooked their mistake.* **2.** In a kind manner; graciously; cordially: *She spoke kindly to him.* **3.** Pleasantly; agreeably: *The sun shone kindly.* **4.** As a matter of courtesy; please: *Would you kindly refrain from doing that?* **5.** *Obsolete.* In a way or course that is natural; fittingly. **—take kindly to.** **1.** To be receptive or favorably disposed to: *doesn't take kindly to people who criticize him.* **2.** To be naturally attracted or fitted to; thrive on.

kind·ness (kīnd′nĭs) *n.* **1.** The quality or state of being kind: *We relied upon their kindness.* **2.** An instance of kind behavior: *You did him a great kindness when you hired him.*

kin·dred (kĭn′drĭd) *n.* **1.** Connection by blood or marriage; kinship. **2. a.** A group of related persons, as a family, clan, or tribe. **b.** A person's relatives; kinfolk.
~adj. **1.** Of the same ancestry or family: *kindred clans.* **2.** Having a similar or related origin, nature, or character: *kindred emotions; a kindred spirit.* [Middle English *kin(d)red(e), kinraden* : KIN + *-rede,* from Old English *rǣden,* condition, rule, from *rǣdan,* to advise, rule, read.] **—kin·dred·ness** *n.*

kine. *Archaic.* Plural of **cow.**

kin·e·mat·ics (kĭn′ə-măt′ĭks) *n. Used with a singular verb. Physics.* A branch of mechanics concerned with the study of motion exclusive of the influences of mass and force. Compare **dynamics, statics.** [Greek *kinēma* (stem *kinēmat-*), motion, from *kinein,* to move.]

kin·e·mat·ic viscosity (kĭn′ə-măt′ĭk) *n. Symbol* ν *Physics.* The viscosity of a fluid divided by its density.

kin·e·scope (kĭn′ə-skōp′) *n.* **1.** A cathode-ray tube in a television receiver that translates received electrical signals into a visible picture on a luminescent screen. **2.** A film of a transmitted television program.
~tr.v. **kinescoped, -scoping, -scopes.** To make a kinescope of (a transmitted television program). [KINE(TIC) + -SCOPE.]

ki·ne·sics (kə-nē′sĭks, -zĭks, kī-) *n. Used with a singular verb.* The study of nonlinguistic bodily movements, as facial expressions and gestures, as a systematic mode of communication. [Greek *kinēsis,* motion + -ICS.] **—ki·ne·sic** (kə-nē′sĭk, -zĭk, kī-) *adj.*

ki·ne·si·ol·o·gy (kə-nē′sē-ŏl′ə-jē, kə-nē′zē-) *n.* The study of locomotion in relation to the structure and working of human muscles. [Greek *kinēsis,* movement + -LOGY.] **—ki·ne·si·ol·o·gist** *n.*

-kinesis *suffix.* Indicates: **1.** Division; for example, **cytokinesis.** **2.** Movement or motion; for example, **photokinesis.** [New Latin, from Greek *kinēsis,* movement, from *kinein,* to move.]

kin·es·the·sia (kĭn′ĭs-thē′zhə, kī′nĭs-) *n.* The sensation of bodily position, presence, or movement resulting chiefly from stimulation of sensory nerve endings in muscles, tendons, and joints. [New Latin, from Greek *kinein,* to move + AESTHESIA.] **—kin·es·the·tic** (kĭn′ĭs-thĕt′ĭk, kī′nĭs-) *adj.*

ki·net·ic (kĭ-nĕt′ĭk, kī-) *adj.* Of, relating to, or produced by motion. [Greek *kinētikos,* from *kinētos,* moving, from *kinein,* to move.] **—ki·net·i·cal·ly** *adv.*

kinetic art *n.* Art or art objects that move, have moving parts, or depend on a moving observer for their effect.

kinetic energy *n.* Energy associated with motion, equal for a body in pure translational motion at nonrelativistic speeds to half the product of its mass and the square of its speed. Compare **potential energy.**

ki·net·ics (kĭ-nĕt′ĭks, kī-) *n.* **1.** *Used with a singular verb. Physics.* The study of all aspects of motion, comprising both kinematics and dynamics. **2.** *Used with a singular verb. Physics.* The study of the relationship between motion and the forces affecting motion. **3.** *Used with a singular verb. Chemistry.* The study of the rates of chemical reactions. **4.** *Used with a plural verb. Physics.* The general motion of a particle or system. **5.** *Used with a plural verb. Chemistry.* The rate of a given chemical reaction, especially as affected by changes in temperature, concentration, or the like.

kinetic theory *n.* A theory of the behavior of matter, especially of pressure-volume-temperature relationships in gases, based in its simplest form on the identification of heat with the kinetic energy

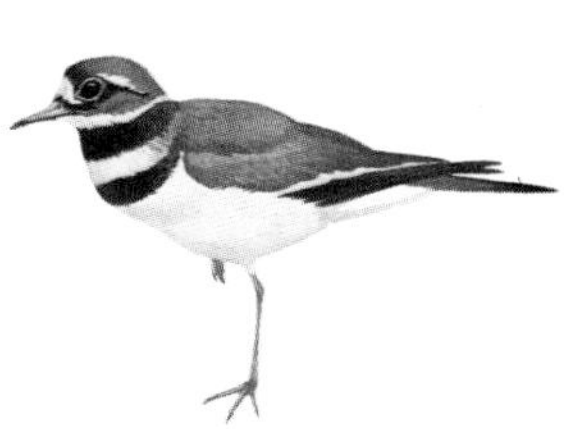

killdeer *This wader was named in imitation of its call. It is easily identified by its double breast markings. A relative of the sandpiper, the killdeer is a migratory bird of North America but is sometimes seen in Europe when high winds blow it off course.*

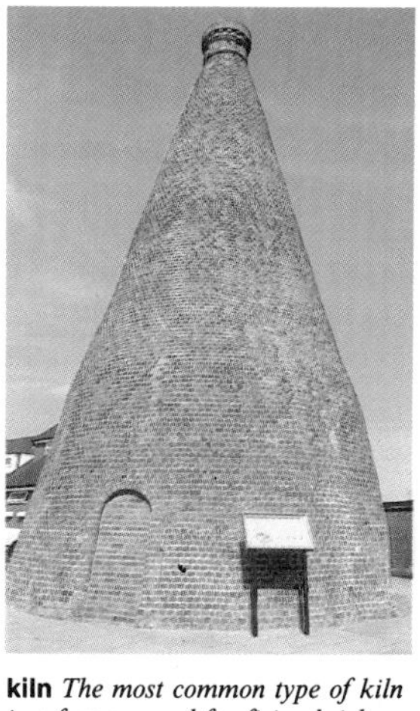

kiln *The most common type of kiln is a furnace used for firing bricks or pottery, in which the minimum working temperature is about 900° C (1650° F). The brick pottery kiln pictured is called a bottle kiln.*

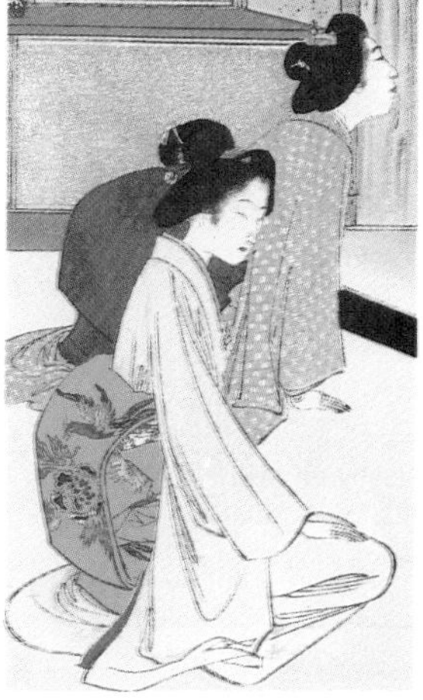

kimono *The kimono is derived from a loose robe worn by Japanese peasants in the 16th century. In the 17th century it became fashionable among wealthy townsfolk and merchants, who turned its simple shape into the backdrop for sumptuous decoration. It is fastened with a wide sash called an obi.*

of a substance's rapid, randomly moving molecules and on statistical analysis of this motion for large numbers of molecules.

ki·ne·tin (kī′nə-tĭn) *n.* An artificial cytokinin. [Greek *kinētos,* moving + -IN.]

kinfolk, kinfolks. Variants of **kinsfolk.**

king (kĭng) *n.* **1.** *Abbr.* **k., K.** A male monarch. **2.** One that is supreme or pre-eminent in a particular category, class, or sphere: *The lion is considered to be the king of the jungle.* **3. King.** God or Christ. **4.** *Abbr.* **K.** A playing card bearing a picture of a king. **5. a.** *Abbr.* **K** The principal chess piece, which can move one square in any direction and must be protected against checkmate. **b.** A piece in checkers that has reached the opponent's side of the board and been crowned and can then move both backward and forward. [Middle English *king,* Old English *cyning.*]

King (kĭng), **Billie Jean,** born Billie Jean Moffitt (1943–). U.S. tennis player. She has won 20 titles at Wimbledon (6 singles, 10 women's doubles, and 4 mixed doubles). She also won the U.S. Championship in 1967, 1971, 1972, and 1974.

King, Coretta Scott (1922–). U.S. civil-rights leader. Trained as a singer, she married Martin Luther King in 1953 and first became involved in the civil-rights movement in 1955. Since her husband's death (1968), she has continued to work for peace and for nonviolent social change.

King, Martin Luther, Jr. (1929–68). U.S. clergyman and civil-rights leader. He organized the Southern Christian Leadership Council to press for black rights (1957) and led a civil-rights march on Washington (1963). King was assassinated by James Earl Ray in Memphis, Tennessee. His books include *Why We Can't Wait* (1964) and *Where Do We Go From Here: Chaos or Community?* (1967). He was awarded the Nobel Peace Prize in 1964.

King, William Lyon Mackenzie (1874–1950). Liberal politician and Canada's longest-serving prime minister (1921–26, 1926–30, and 1935–48).

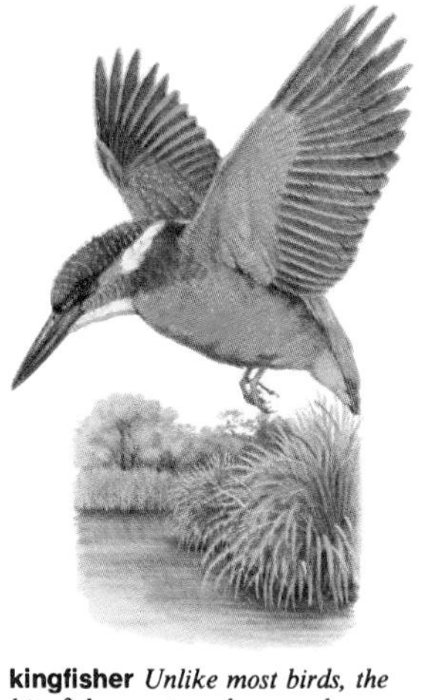

kingfisher *Unlike most birds, the kingfisher nests underground, tunneling out a riverbank burrow that can be up to 1 meter (3.28 feet) long. The birds feed mainly on fish, which they snatch from the water, carry to a perch, and kill by beating them against a branch. They then swallow the fish head first so that the scales and fins lie flat. Kingfishers —which are found in Europe, Asia, and Africa—are seldom preyed upon by other birds because their flesh is foul-tasting.*

king·bolt (kĭng′bōlt′) *n.* A vertical bolt used for such purposes as joining the body of a wagon to the front axle and usually serving as a pivot. Also called "kingpin."

King Charles spaniel *n.* A variety of toy spaniel having a curly black and tan coat and long ears. [After King CHARLES II of England.]

king cobra *n.* A large venomous snake, *Ophiophagus hannah,* of tropical Asia. Also called "hamadryad."

king crab *n.* **1.** A large crab, *Paralithodes camtschatica,* of coastal waters of Alaska, Japan, and Siberia, valued commercially for its edible flesh. **2.** A marine arthropod, the **horseshoe crab** *(see).*

king·craft (kĭng′krăft′, -kräft′) *n.* The art or method used by a king to rule; especially, the use of cunning in the exercise of royal power.

king·cup (kĭng′kŭp′) *n. Chiefly British.* Any of several plants having cup-shaped yellow flowers; especially, the **marsh marigold** *(see).*

king·dom (kĭng′dəm) *n.* **1.** A government, territory, state, or population that is nominally or actually ruled by a king or queen. **2. a.** The eternal spiritual sovereignty of God. **b.** The realm over which this sovereignty extends. **3.** An area, province, or realm in which one thing is dominant: *the kingdom of the imagination.* **4. a.** The broadest, most inclusive taxonomic category of organisms having certain basic characteristics: *the plant kingdom.* **b.** Any such large general category of natural forms: *the mineral kingdom.* [Middle English *kingdom,* Old English *cyningdōm* : KING + -DOM.]

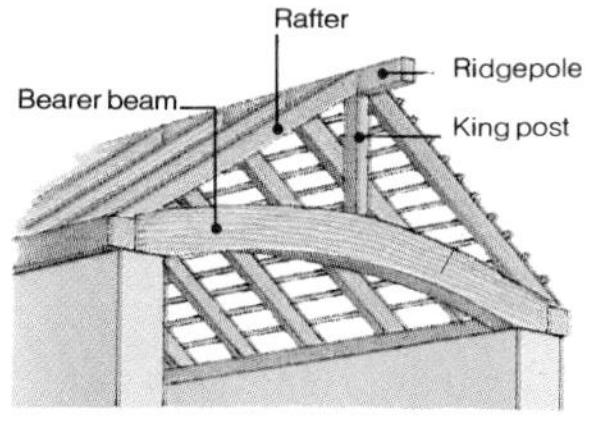

king post *The central roof beam rising from a horizontal beam to the ridge.*

kingdom come *n.* **1.** The next world: *a bomb that could blow us all to kingdom come.* **2.** The end of time; forever: *You can scream till kingdom come, but he won't take any notice.* [From the phrase *Thy kingdom come* in The Lord's Prayer.]

king·fish (kĭng′fĭsh′) *n., pl.* **-fishes** or collectively **kingfish. 1. a.** Any of several food and game fishes of the genus *Menticirrhus,* indigenous to warm Atlantic waters. **b.** Any of several similar or related fishes. **2.** *Informal.* A pre-eminent or powerful person, especially a prominent political leader.

king·fish·er (kĭng′fĭsh′ər) *n.* Any of various birds of the family Alcedinidae, characteristically having a crested head; especially, *Alcedo atthis,* which has blue-green and orange plumage. [Originally *king's fisher,* Middle English *kyngys fischare.*]

King James Bible *n.* An Anglican translation of the Bible from Hebrew and Greek into English published in 1611 under the auspices of James I. Also called "Authorized Version," "King James Version."

king·klip (kĭng′klĭp′) *n., pl.* **kingklip.** *Chiefly South African.* Either of two edible marine fishes of the Ophidiidae family, *Xiphiurus capensis* or *Hoplobrotula gnathopus.* [Afrikaans, from Dutch *koning,* KING + *klip,* stone.]

King Lear. See **Lear.**

king·let (kĭng′lĭt) *n.* **1.** Either of two small grayish North American birds, *Regulus satrapa* or *R. calendula,* with a yellowish or reddish patch on the crown of the head. **2.** A petty or insignificant king.

king·ly (kĭng′lē) *adj.* **-lier, -liest. 1.** Having the status or rank of king. **2.** Of or pertaining to a king; regal: *kingly power.* **3.** Like or suitable for a king; majestic.
~*adv.* As a king; royally. **—king·li·ness** *n.*

king mackerel *n.* A food and game fish, *Scomberomorus cavalla,* of warm Atlantic waters. Also called "cavalla," "cero."

king·mak·er (kĭng′mā′kər) *n.* **1.** One who has control over who is king. **2.** One with sufficient political power to influence the selection of a candidate for office.

king-of-arms (kĭng′əv-ärmz′) *n., pl.* **kings-of-arms.** The title of the highest-ranking heraldic officer in the United Kingdom.

king·pin (kĭng′pĭn′) *n.* **1.** In bowling, the foremost or central pin of the arrangement of pins to be knocked down. **2.** The most important or essential person or thing in an enterprise or system. **3. a.** A hardened steel pin in the steering system of a motor vehicle that does not have independent front suspension. **b.** A **kingbolt** *(see).*

king post, king·post (kĭng′pōst′) *n.* A supporting post extending vertically from a crossbeam to the apex of a triangular truss. Compare **queen post.**

king prawn *n.* Any of various large edible prawns of the genus *Enaeus.*

Kings (kĭngz) *n. Used with a singular verb.* **1.** Either of the two Old Testament books, I Kings or II Kings, that tell the history of the kings of Israel and Judah. **2.** Any of a group of four books, I, II, III, and IV Kings, in the Douay version of the Old Testament that correspond to I Samuel, II Samuel, I Kings, and II Kings in the King James Bible.

King's Bench *n.* A division of the British superior court system that hears criminal and civil cases. Used when the monarch is a male.

King's Counsel *n. Abbr.* **K.C.** A barrister appointed as counsel to the British crown. Used when the monarch is a male.

King's English *n.* Spoken or written English that is considered a standard of good usage.

King's evil, king's evil *n.* A disease, **scrofula** *(see).* [From the belief that scrofula could be healed by the king's touch.]

king·ship (kĭng′shĭp′) *n.* **1.** The position, power, province, or prerogative of a king. **2.** The period or tenure of a king; reign. **3.** A monarchy. **4.** The domain ruled by a king; kingdom. **5.** The style of a king; majesty.

king-size (kĭng′sīz′) *adj.* Also **king-sized** (-sīzd′). Larger or longer than a standard or usual size: *king-size cigarettes; a king-size bed.*

Kings·ley (kĭngz′lē), **Charles** (1819–75). English author. He was professor of modern history at Cambridge (1860–69) and chaplain to Queen Victoria (1873). Kingsley wrote the adventure novels *Westward Ho!* (1855) and *Hereward the Wake* (1865) and the children's book *Water Babies* (1863).

king snake *n.* Any of various nonvenomous New World snakes of the genus *Lampropeltis,* having yellow or reddish markings.

King·ston¹ (kĭngz′tən). The capital and chief port of Jamaica. Founded in 1693 following the destruction of Port Royal by earthquake, it became the capital in 1872.

Kingston². A city on Lake Ontario, Canada, connected to Ottawa by the Rideau Canal. It stands on the site of Fort Frontenac and was the capital of Canada from 1841 to 1844.

Kingston upon Hull. See **Hull.**

Kingston upon Thames (tĕmz). Royal borough in southwest Greater London. The Coronation Stone near the Guildhall is a relic of the days (901–78) when Saxon kings were crowned here.

king·wood (kĭng′wo͝od′) *n.* **1.** A South American tree, *Dalbergia cearensis,* having hard, fine-textured, purplish-brown wood used in cabinetmaking. **2.** The wood of this tree.

ki·nin (kī′nĭn) *n.* Any of a class of polypeptides found in the blood that act in the contraction of smooth muscle and the dilation of blood vessels. [Greek *kinein,* to move + -IN.]

kink (kĭngk) *n.* **1.** A tight curl or a sharp twist in a line or wirelike material that is typically caused by the tensing of a looped section. **2.** A painful muscle spasm, as in the neck or back; a crick. **3.** A quirk of personality. **4.** A clever or eccentric idea or notion. **5.** A slight difficulty or flaw, as in a plan or system. **6.** *Chiefly British.* A sexual peculiarity or deviation.
~*v.* **kinked, kinking, kinks.** —*tr.* To cause to have a kink or kinks. —*intr.* To form kinks. [Low German *kinke,* a twist in a rope, from Middle Low German *kinke*†.]

kink·a·jou (kĭng′kə-jo͞o′) *n.* An arboreal mammal, *Potos flavus,* of tropical America, having brownish fur and a long, prehensile tail. Also called "honey bear," "potto." [French *quincajou,* from Algonquian; akin to Ojibwa *quingwâage,* wolverine.]

kink·y (kĭng′kē) *adj.* **-ier, -iest. 1.** Tightly curled; frizzy: *kinky hair.* **2.** *Informal.* **a.** Marked by or making use of a perverted eroticism. **b.** Marked by sexual perversion. **—kink·i·ly** *adv.* **—kink·i·ness** *n.*

kin·ni·kin·nick, kin·ni·kin·nic (kĭn′ĭ-kĭ-nĭk′) *n.* **1.** A tobaccolike preparation made from the dried leaves or bark of various plants and used for smoking, especially by American Indians. **2.** A plant having leaves or bark used in such a preparation, as the **bearberry** *(see).* [Algonquian; akin to Natick *kinukkinuk,* mixture.]

ki·no (kē′nō) *n., pl.* **-nos.** A reddish resin obtained from several Old World tropical trees of the genera *Pterocarpus* and *Butea* and used to treat dysentery and diarrhea. [A West African word, akin to Mandingo *keno.*]

Kin·ross (kĭn-rôs′). Also **Kin·ross-shire** (-shîr, -shər). Former county of east-central Scotland. It is now part of Tayside Region.

kin selection *n.* The theory that natural selection in animal populations may operate through the mechanism of cooperation among a group of related individuals, which ensures that the average fitness for survival of the group is increased, although one member's individual fitness may be decreased through apparently altruistic behavior.

Kin·sey (kĭn′zē), **Alfred Charles** (1894–1956). U.S. zoologist. He worked at the Institute of Sex Research, Harvard, and published *Sexual Behavior in the Human Male* (1948) and *Sexual Behavior in the Human Female* (1953), pioneer studies of their kind.

kins·folk (kĭnz′fōk′) *pl.n.* Also *informal* **kin·folk** (kĭn′fōk′), **kin·folks** (-fōks′). Members of one's family; kindred.

Kin·sha·sa (kĭn-shä′sə). Formerly **Lé·o·pold·ville** (lē′ə-pōld′vĭl′, lā′-). Capital of Zaire. An ancient settlement on the Zaire River, it was founded by Henry M. Stanley (1881).

kin·ship (kĭn′shĭp′) n. **1.** The state of being related by blood. **2.** The state of being related in character, origin, or the like; similarity.

kins·man (kĭnz′mən) n., pl. **-men** (-mĭn). A male relative.

kins·wom·an (kĭnz′wŏŏm′ən) n., pl. **-women** (-wĭm′ĭn). A female relative.

ki·osk (kē′ŏsk′, kē-ŏsk′) n. **1.** A small, sometimes ornamental structure used as a newsstand or refreshment booth. **2.** Chiefly British. A booth for a public telephone; a telephone booth. **3.** An open gazebo or pavilion. **4.** A cylindrical structure on which advertisements are posted. [French kiosque, from Turkish köshk, pavilion, from Persian kūshk†, palace.]

kip¹ (kĭp) n., pl. **kip.** The basic monetary unit of Laos, equal to 100 at. See feature at **currency.** [Thai.]

kip² n. The untanned hide of a small or young animal, such as a calf. [Obsolete Dutch kip, bundle (of hides), from Middle Dutch; akin to Old Norse kippi†, bundle.]

kip³ n. British Slang. **1. a.** Sleep. **b.** A period of sleep. **2.** A place to sleep, such as a room or bed. **3.** A rooming house.
~intr.v. **kipped, kipping, kips.** British Slang. To sleep or prepare to sleep: Can we kip down here? [Danish kippet†, cheap inn.]

kip⁴ n. Engineering. A 1,000-pound unit of weight, used to express loads. [KI(LO)- + P(OUND).]

Kip·ling (kĭp′lĭng), **(Joseph) Rudyard** (1865–1936). Indian-born British poet and novelist. His first volume of poetry, Departmental Ditties (1886), was followed by Plain Tales from the Hills (1888). His later works include the two Jungle Books (1894–95), Kim (1901), and the Just So Stories (1902). He received the Nobel Prize for literature (1907).

kip·per (kĭp′ər) n. **1.** A male salmon or sea trout in the spawning season. **2.** A herring that has been split, salted, and smoked.
~tr.v. **kippered, -pering, -pers.** To cure (fish) by splitting, salting, and smoking. [Middle English kypre, Old English cypera, perhaps from coper, COPPER (from the color of the fish).]

Kipp's apparatus (kĭps) n. Chemistry. A laboratory apparatus for the controlled production of a gas by the action of a liquid on a solid, used especially to prepare hydrogen sulfide by the action of sulfuric acid on iron sulfide. [After P.J. Kipp (1808–64), Dutch chemist.]

kir (kĭr) n. A drink consisting of white wine flavored with cassis. [After Canon Kir, former mayor of Dijon, France, who is said to have invented the drink.]

Kir·giz, Kir·ghiz (kĭr-gēz′) n., pl. **-gizes, -ghizes** or collectively **Kirgiz, Kirghiz. 1.** A member of a Turkic people living principally in the Kirgiz S.S.R. of the Soviet Union. **2.** The Turkic language of this people.

Kirgiz or **Kirghiz Soviet Socialist Republic.** Republic of the U.S.S.R. Bounded on the southeast by China, it is almost entirely mountainous, with the Tian Shan on the Chinese border. It is rich in mineral deposits, especially coal, lead, mercury, antimony, and uranium, of which it is one of the U.S.S.R.'s major producers. The capital, Frunze, is on a Trans-Siberian Railway spur line.

Ki·ri·ba·ti (kĭr′ə-bä′tē). Formerly **Gil·bert Islands** (gĭl′bərt). Republic in the western Pacific. It includes the Phoenix Islands, the southern Line Islands, and Ocean Island (Banaba). Formerly part of the Gilbert and Ellice Islands Colony, Kiribati gained independence from the United Kingdom in 1979. The same year the phosphate deposits of Banaba became exhausted, and the country now depends on copra exports and British aid. Fishing and tourism are expanding. Area, 886 square kilometers (342 square miles). Population, 56,000. Capital, Betio (on Tarawa). See map at **Pacific Ocean.**

ki·ri·ga·mi (kĭr′ĭ-gä′mē) n. The Japanese art of making ornamental designs by cutting and folding paper. Compare **origami.** [Japanese : kiri, to cut + -gami, from kami, paper.]

Kirin. See **Jilin.**

kirk (kûrk) n. **1.** Chiefly Scottish. A church. **2. Kirk.** Chiefly British. The Presbyterian Church of Scotland. [Middle English kirk(e), from Old Norse kirkja, from Old English cir(i)ce, CHURCH.]

Kirk·cal·dy (kûr-kôl′dē). Royal burgh of east-central Scotland. In the former county of Fife, it is a port and coal-mining center on the Firth of Forth.

Kirk·cud·bright (kûr-kōō′brē). Former county of southwest Scotland, incorporated into Dumfries and Galloway Region (1975).

Kirk·wall (kûrk′wôl). Royal burgh of north Scotland. On Mainland (Pomona) Island in the Orkney Islands, it is the islands' largest town, chief port, and administrative center.

Kir·man (kər-män′, kîr′-) n. A Persian rug with an elaborate border pattern and muted colors. [After Kirman, province of Iran.]

kirmess. Variant of **kermis.**

kirsch (kîrsh) n. A colorless brandy made from the fermented juice of cherries. [German Kirsch(wasser), "cherry (water)," from Old High German kirsa, cherry, from Vulgar Latin cerasia (unattested).]

kir·tle (kûrt′l) n. **1.** A knee-length tunic or coat formerly worn by men. **2.** A woman's long dress or skirt. [Middle English kirtel, Old English cyrtel, from Germanic kurtilaz (unattested), "short coat," diminutive of kurt- (unattested), short, from Latin curtus, cut short.]

kish (kĭsh) n. Metallurgy. Graphite formed on the surface of molten iron when the iron contains large amounts of carbon. [Perhaps alteration of German Kies, gravel.]

Kish (kĭsh). A city of ancient Mesopotamia. Excavated in the

1920's, it revealed its pre-Sumerian origins when the earliest existing example of writing was discovered here—a precuneiform tablet dating from 3500 B.C.

kish·ke (kĭsh′kə) n. A food, **derma** (see). [Yiddish, probably from Russian kishka, gut.]

Kis·lev (kĭs′ləf) n. The third month of the Hebrew year. See feature at **calendar.** [Hebrew kislēw.]

kis·met (kĭz′mĕt′, -mĭt) n. Fate; fortune. [Turkish kismet, from Arabic qismah, lot, from qasama, he divided, he allotted.]

kiss (kĭs) v. **kissed, kissing, kisses.** —tr. **1.** To touch or caress with the lips as a sign of sexual passion, affection, greeting, or respect. **2.** To touch lightly; brush against: The mist kissed the flowers. **3.** To touch or hit against (another billiard ball) lightly. —intr. **1.** To touch or caress each other with the lips. **2.** To meet with a light, gentle touch. —**kiss good-by.** To be forced to undergo the loss of. —**kiss off.** Informal. To get rid of; dismiss.
~n. **1.** A caress or touch with the lips. **2.** A slight or gentle touch. **3.** A gentle impact between billiard balls. **4. a.** A small piece of candy, especially of chocolate. **b.** A baked confection made of meringue. [Middle English kissen, cussen, Old English cyssan.]

kiss-curl (kĭs′kûrl′) n. A small, almost circular curl of hair lying flat against the cheek, forehead, or nape of the neck.

kiss·er (kĭs′ər) n. **1.** A person who kisses. **2.** Slang. The mouth or face.

kissing bug n. An assassin bug, Melanolestes picipes, that inflicts a painful bite, often on the lips of a sleeping person.

kissing cousin n. A distant relative known well enough to be kissed when greeted.

kissing disease n. Informal. Mononucleosis.

Kis·sin·ger (kĭs′ĭn-jər), **Henry Alfred** (1923–). U.S. foreign policy adviser. He was born in Germany and fled the Nazis (1938) to live in the United States. Under presidents Richard Nixon and Gerald Ford he was executive secretary of the National Security Council (1969) and secretary of state (1973). He helped negotiate the Vietnam cease-fire (1973), for which he shared the Nobel Peace Prize (1973) with the North Vietnamese negotiator, Le Duc Tho.

kissing gate n. British. A gate that is partially enclosed in a U- or V-shaped structure on the side opposite the hinge so as to allow only one person to pass through at a time.

kiss of death n. Something that is ultimately ruinous, disastrous, or fatal: He offered to help, but assistance from an incompetent person would have been the kiss of death. [From the kiss of Judas that betrayed Jesus.]

kiss of life n. Mouth-to-mouth resuscitation.

kiss of peace n. A ceremonial gesture, as a kiss or a handshake, used as a sign of unity and brotherhood among those celebrating and attending the Eucharist.

kist¹ (kĭst) n. Chiefly Scottish & South African. A large, lidded chest. [Middle English, from Old Norse kista, CHEST.]

kist². Variant of **cist** (coffin).

kit¹ (kĭt) n. **1. a.** A set of instruments or equipment used for a specific job or purpose: a survival kit; a travel kit. **b.** A collection of clothing and other personal effects, as for travel or a sporting activity. **c.** A container, as a box, bag, or rucksack, for such a set or collection. **2.** A set of parts or materials to be assembled: a model airplane kit. **3.** A packaged set of related materials: a sales kit. **4.** British Regional. A wooden tub or barrel for holding water or foodstuffs. —**the (whole) kit and caboodle.** Informal. The entire collection or lot.
~tr.v. **kitted, kitting, kits.** Chiefly British. To equip; provide with a kit or outfit. Usually used with out or up. [Middle English kytt, kitt, wooden tub, from Middle Dutch kittet, jug, tankard.]

kit² n. A kitten or other young fur-bearing animal. [Short for KITTEN.]

kit³ n. New Zealand. A basket, especially one woven from flax. [Maori kete, bag.]

kit⁴ n. A small three-stringed violin. [Origin unknown.]

kit bag, kit·bag (kĭt′băg′) n. A traveling bag, such as a rucksack; especially, a long narrow canvas bag used by servicemen.

kitch·en (kĭch′ən) n. **1.** A room or area in which food is cooked or prepared. **2.** The facilities and equipment used in the preparation and serving of food. **3.** The staff that prepares, cooks, and serves food. [Middle English kichene, kuchene, Old English cycene, from West Germanic kocina (unattested), from Late Latin coquīna, from Latin, feminine of coquīnus, of cooking, from coquere, to cook.]

kitchen cabinet n. An unofficial but influential group of advisers to the head of a government.

Kitch·e·ner of Khar·toum and of Broome (kĭch′ə-nər; kär-tōōm′; brōōm), **Horatio Herbert, 1st Earl** (1850–1916). British soldier and statesman. As commander in chief of the Egyptian army, he won back the Sudan for Egypt at the Battle of Omdurman (1898). He brought the Boer War (1899–1902) to a conclusion. As secretary for war in World War I he recruited 3,000,000 volunteers for the armed forces. He was killed on board H.M.S. Hampshire when it was mined.

kitch·en·ette (kĭch′ə-nĕt′) n. A small kitchen.

kitchen garden n. A garden in which vegetables and fruits are grown for household consumption.

kitchen midden n. A refuse heap or mound of the Mesolithic or later prehistoric periods, containing numerous artifacts, shells, and often animal bones. [Midden, Middle English myddyng, from Scandinavian; akin to Danish mødding.]

kitchen police n. Abbr. **KP 1.** Enlisted military personnel assigned

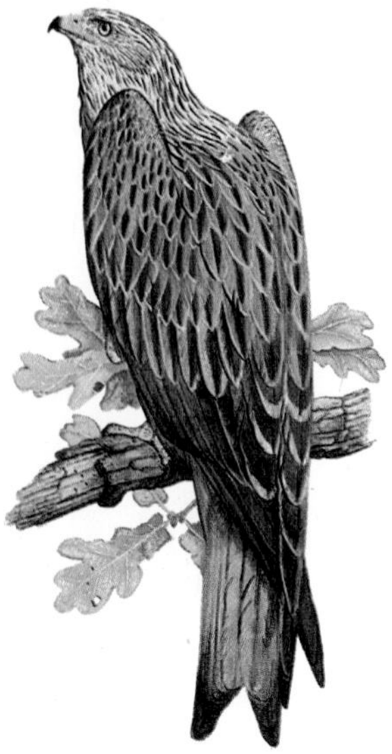

kite *The hovering, gliding flight of this hawk gave the name to the manmade kite. The red kite (above) used to scavenge the streets of Tudor London, but it has now vanished from cities and inhabits the woods and parklands of Europe and parts of the Middle East.*

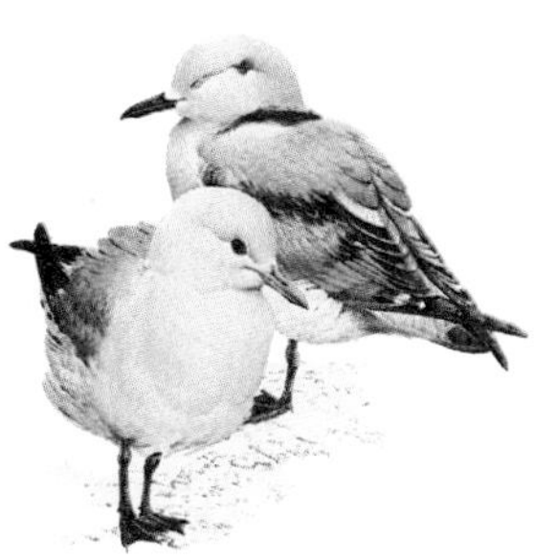

kittiwake *The kittiwake, which is a type of gull, spends most of its life at sea, following the movements of fish and ships, and rarely comes ashore except to breed. It lays its eggs in cup-shaped nests on cliff ledges around the northern coasts of Europe, Asia, and North America.*

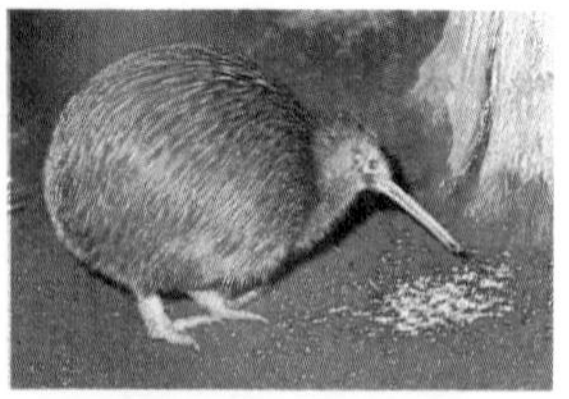

kiwi *The flightless national bird of New Zealand. The kiwi lays the largest egg in proportion to its size of any bird: the bird weighs little more than 3 kilograms (about 7 pounds), yet it produces an egg of about 500 grams (1 pound).*

to work in the kitchen. **2.** The work of the kitchen police.

kitch·en-sink (kĭch′ən-sĭngk′) *adj. Chiefly British.* Portraying working-class domestic life realistically and unromantically: *kitchen-sink drama.*

kitch·en·ware (kĭch′ən-wâr′) *n.* Utensils for use in the kitchen, such as pots and pans.

kite (kīt) *n.* **1.** A light framework covered with cloth, plastic, or paper that is designed to climb and hover in a steady breeze at the end of a long string. **2.** Any of the highest sails of a ship, used only in a light wind. **3.** Any of various predatory birds of the subfamilies Milvinae and Elaninae, having a long, often forked tail. **4.** A negotiable paper, as a check, that represents a fictitious financial transaction and is used temporarily to sustain credit or raise money. **5.** *Geometry.* A quadrilateral that has two pairs of equal adjacent sides. **—fly a kite.** To stop bothering or urging: *Finally I told him to go fly a kite.*
~*v.* **kited, kiting, kites.** —*intr.* **1.** To fly like a kite; soar or glide. **2.** To get money or credit with a kite. —*tr.* To use a kite to sustain credit or raise money. [Middle English *kyte, kete,* kite (bird), Old English *cȳta,* from Common Germanic *kūtja-* (unattested), probably imitative of its cry.]

kith and kin (kĭth′ ən kĭn′) *pl.n.* Friends and neighbors. [Middle English *kith, kyth,* Old English *cȳth(the), cȳththu,* "knowledge," "acquaintance," friend.]

Kíthira. See **Cythera.**

kitsch (kĭch) *n.* **1.** Vulgarity, sentimentality, and pretentious bad taste, especially in the arts, sometimes achieved deliberately for effect or fun. **2.** Examples or an example of kitsch. [German, from *kitschen*†, to put together (a work of art) sloppily.] **—kitsch, kitsch·y** *adj.*

kit·ten (kĭt′n) *n.* A young cat. **—have kittens.** *Informal.* To be very angry, nervous, or upset.
~*intr.v.* **kittened, -tening, -tens.** To bear kittens. [Middle English *kitoun,* from Old North French *caton* (unattested), diminutive of *cat,* cat, from Late Latin *cattus,* CAT.]

kit·ten·ish (kĭt′n-ĭsh) *adj.* Playful; coy. **—kit·ten·ish·ly** *adv.*

kit·ti·wake (kĭt′ē-wāk′) *n.* Either of two gulls, *Rissa tridactyla* or *R. brevirostris,* of northern regions. [Imitative of its cry.]

kit·tle (kĭt′l) *adj. Scottish.* Requiring careful handling; tricky; delicate. [Scottish *kittle,* to tickle, Middle English (Scottish) *kytyllen,* probably from Old Norse *kitla.*]

kit·ty¹ (kĭt′ē) *n., pl.* **-ties. 1.** In some card games, a sum of money contributed by each player at the start of a hand, all of which is won by the winner of that hand. **2.** A pool of money, especially one contributed to equally by a group of people and used to buy something that they all share. [Originally "small bowl," diminutive of KIT (tub).]

kitty² *n., pl.* **-ties.** *Informal.* A kitten or cat. [From *kit,* short for KITTEN.]

ki·va (kē′və) *n.* An underground or partly underground room in a Pueblo Indian village, used by the men especially for ceremonies or councils. [Hopi.]

Kivu, Lake (kē′vo͞o). Africa's highest lake. It lies at 1,459 meters (4,788 feet) on the Zaire-Rwanda border, in the western arm of the Great Rift Valley.

ki·wi (kē′wē) *n.* **1.** Any of several nocturnal flightless birds of the genus *Apteryx,* of New Zealand, having vestigial wings and a long, slender bill. **2. a.** A vine, *Actinidia chinensis,* native to Asia, bearing hairy, edible fruit. **b.** The fruit of this vine. In this sense, also called "Chinese gooseberry," "kiwi fruit." **3. Kiwi.** *Informal.* A New Zealander. [Maori.]

K.K.K. Ku Klux Klan.

Klai·pe·da (klī′pə-də). *German* **Me·mel** (mā′məl). Ice-free Baltic port and industrial city in Lithuanian S.S.R. A strategic fortress, it was held by the Prussians from 1635 until 1919. The city fell to the Russians in 1945.

Klam·ath (klăm′əth). River, *c.* 425 kilometers (265 miles) long, rising in the Klamath Mts. of southwestern Oregon and flowing across northwestern California to the Pacific Ocean. It is used for irrigation and is a source of hydroelectric power.

Klan (klăn) *n.* The **Ku Klux Klan** *(see).*

Klans·man (klănz′mən) *n., pl.* **-men** (-mĭn). A member of the Ku Klux Klan.

Klax·on (klăk′sən) *n.* A trademark for a loud horn formerly used on automobiles. [From Greek *klazein,* to roar.]

Klee (klā), **Paul** (1879–1940). Swiss painter. His works, mainly small abstracts, are reminiscent of doodles or children's art, as in *Twittering Machine, The Zoo,* and *Fish Magic.*

Kleen·ex (klē′nĕks′) *n.* A trademark for a soft cleansing tissue.

Klein bottle (klīn) *n.* A one-sided topologic surface having no inside or outside, formed by inserting the small open end of a tapered tube through the side of the tube and making it contiguous with the larger open end. Compare **Möbius strip.** [After Felix *Klein* (1849–1925), German mathematician.]

Kleist (klīst), **Heinrich von** (1777–1811). German dramatist. In his plays, including *The Broken Pitcher* (1808) and other works, he created characters torn between reason and emotion and between heroism and cowardice. Largely unrecognized in his lifetime, he is now ranked among Germany's most profound and influential dramatists.

Klem·pe·rer (klĕm′pər-ər), **Otto** (1885–1973). German conductor. He conducted several orchestras in Germany, but left in 1933 and went on to conduct many major orchestras all over the world.

klep·to·ma·ni·a (klĕp′tə-mā′nē-ə, -mān′yə) *n.* An obsessive impulse to steal, especially in the absence of economic necessity or personal desire. [New Latin : Greek *kleptein,* to steal + -MANIA.] **—klep·to·ma·ni·ac** (klĕp′tə-mā′nē-ăk′) *n.*

klieg light (klēg) *n.* A powerful carbon-arc lamp producing an intense light and used especially in making movies. [Invented by the brothers John H. *Kliegl* (1869–1959) and Anton T. *Kliegl* (1872–1927), lighting experts.]

Klimt (klĭmt), **Gustav** (1862–1918). Austrian art nouveau painter. He achieved fame as a portrait and landscape painter of great exotic and erotic sensibility. His mosaics and paintings are characterized by large predominant patterns of gold, as in *The Kiss.*

Kline (klīn), **Franz Joseph** (1919–62). U.S. painter. Establishing his particular brand of abstract expressionism after seeing his black-and-white sketches magnified by a projector, he used bold, controlled sweeps of black on a white field in most of his works. Late in his career he began using colors.

klip·spring·er (klĭp′sprĭng′ər) *n.* A small, hoofed African antelope, *Oreotragus oreotragus,* having large ears. [Afrikaans, "cliff springer" : Dutch *klip,* cliff, from Middle Dutch *klippe,* from Germanic *klibam* (unattested), CLIFF + *springer,* from *springen,* to leap, from Middle Dutch.]

Klon·dike (klŏn′dīk′). A region of the Yukon Territory, Canada. It was the scene of a famous gold rush (1897–98); the gold yield, however, has steadily declined since 1910. It takes its name from the Klondike River, a tributary of the Yukon.

kloof (klo͝of) *n.* In South Africa, a deep ravine. [Afrikaans, from Dutch, from Middle Dutch *clove,* cleft.]

klutz (klŭts) *n. Slang.* **1.** A clumsy or dull-witted person. **2.** A bungler. [German *Klotz,* clod, "block," from Middle High German *kloz,* block, lump.]

kly·stron (klī′strŏn′) *n.* An electron tube used to amplify or generate radio waves of microwave range frequencies by means of velocity modulation. [Greek *klustēr,* syringe, clyster pipe, from *kluzein,* to wash out + (ELECTR)ON.]

km kilometer.

K-mes·on (kā′mĕz′ŏn′, -mē′zŏn′, -mĕs′ŏn′, -mē′sŏn′) *n. Physics.* A type of meson, a **kaon** *(see).*

km/h kilometers per hour.

kn. *Nautical.* knot.

knack (năk) *n.* **1.** A clever, expedient way of doing something. **2.** A specific skill or talent for doing something, especially one difficult to explain or teach. [Middle English *knak(ke),* probably identified with *knak,* sharp blow, from Dutch and Low German *knak.*]

knack·er (năk′ər) *n. British.* **1.** A person who buys useless or worn-out horses and slaughters them to sell their hides or meat. **2.** A person who buys up discarded structures and dismantles them to sell the materials. **3.** *Slang.* A testicle.
~*tr.v.* **knackered, -ering, -ers.** *British Slang.* To wear out; exhaust. [Originally "harness maker," saddler, probably from Scandinavian, akin to Old Norse *hnakkur,* saddle.] **—knack·er·y** *n.*

knack·wurst, knock·wurst (nŏk′wûrst′, -wo͝orst′) *n.* A short, thick sausage resembling a frankfurter. [German *Knackwurst,* "sausage whose skin cracks open when bitten" : *knacken,* to crack, from Middle High German + *Wurst,* sausage, WURST.]

knap¹ (năp) *v.* **knapped, knapping, knaps.** —*tr.* **1.** *British Regional.* To strike sharply; rap. **2.** To break or chip (flints, for example) with a sharp blow. **3.** *British Regional.* To chatter about. —*intr. British Regional.* To deliver a sharp blow. [Middle English *knappen,* probably from Low German, akin to Middle Dutch *cnappen,* Low German *knappen.*]

knap² *n. Regional.* The crest of a hill; a summit. [Middle English *knap,* Old English *cnæpp.*]

knap·sack (năp′săk′) *n.* A case or bag, usually of canvas or leather, worn on the back to carry supplies and equipment, especially on a hike or march. [Low German *knappsack* : probably *knappen,* to snap, bite, eat + *sack,* bag, from Middle Low German, from Germanic, from Latin *saccus,* SACK (bag).]

knap·weed (năp′wēd′) *n.* Any of various plants of the genus *Centaurea,* having purplish, thistlelike flowers. [Middle English *knopwed* : KNOP (from the knobby head of its flower) + WEED.]

knar (när) *n.* A knot or protuberance on a tree or in wood. [Middle English *knarre,* probably from Scandinavian; akin to Norwegian *knart.*]

knave (nāv) *n.* **1.** An unprincipled, crafty man. **2.** In card games, the jack. [Middle English *knave,* Old English *cnafa,* boy, lad, from Common Germanic *knabōn-* (unattested).]

knav·er·y (nā′və-rē) *n., pl.* **-ies. 1.** Dishonest or crafty dealing. **2.** A piece of mischief or trickery.

knav·ish (nā′vĭsh) *adj.* Like or characteristic of a knave; dishonest and unprincipled. **—knav·ish·ly** *adv.* **—knav·ish·ness** *n.*

knawel (nôl) *n.* A low-growing, weedy plant, *Scleranthus annuus,* native to Eurasia, having narrow leaves and inconspicuous green flowers. [German *Knäuel,* knot, knob, ball of yarn, from Middle High German *kniuwel, kliuwel(in),* from Old High German *kliuwilin,* from *kliuwa,* ball.]

knead (nēd) *tr.v.* **kneaded, kneading, kneads. 1.** To mix and work (a substance) into a uniform mass; especially, to fold, press, and stretch (dough) with the hands. **2.** To make (bread or pottery, for example) by kneading. **3.** To squeeze, press, or roll with the hands, as in massaging. **4.** To blend together or manipulate as if by kneading. [Middle English *kneden,* Old English *cnedan.*] **—knead·er** *n.*

knee (nē) *n.* **1. a.** *Anatomy.* The joint of the human leg that is the

articulation for the tibia and fibula with the femur and is covered in front by the patella. **b.** The region of the leg around this joint, especially at the front. **c.** A corresponding joint of a leg of a vertebrate, as the forelimb of a hoofed animal. **2.** The part of a garment, as trousers or stockings, that covers the knee. **3.** Something resembling the knee in action, as a pivoted device, or in shape, as a bent pipe. **4.** A woody projection arising from the roots of some swamp-growing trees: *cypress knees.* **—to one's knees.** Into a state of submission or defeat.
~*tr.v.* **kneed, kneeing, knees.** To strike with the knee. [Middle English *kne(e), kn(e)ow,* Old English *cnēo.*]

knee breeches *pl.n.* Breeches extending to or just below the knee.

knee·cap (nē′kăp′) *n.* **1.** A bone, the **patella** *(see).* **2.** A kneepad.

knee-deep (nē′dēp′) *adj.* **1.** Reaching to the knees; knee-high. **2.** Submerged to the knees. **3.** Deeply occupied or engaged.

knee-high (nē′hī′) *adj.* As tall or high as the knee.
~*n.* (nē′hī′). A stocking that extends to just below the knee.

knee·hole (nē′hōl′) *n.* A space or opening for the knees, as under a desk or counter. Also used adjectivally: *a kneehole desk.*

knee jerk *n.* A sudden involuntary reflex kick forward produced by a smart tap to the tendon below the patella as the leg hangs relaxed at a right angle to the thigh.

knee-jerk (nē′jûrk′) *adj. Informal.* **1.** Automatic: *Unrest is often a knee-jerk reaction to authoritarianism.* **2.** Marked by or reacting with unthinking predictability: *knee-jerk pessimism.*

kneel (nēl) *intr.v.* **knelt** (nĕlt) or **kneeled, kneeling, kneels.** To fall or rest on bent knees. [Middle English *kne(w)len,* Old English *cnēowlian.* Knelt (past tense and past participle) is an analogous formation after FEEL, FELT.]

knee-length (nē′lĕngkth′, -lĕngth′) *adj.* Reaching the knee or just below the knee: *knee-length socks.*

kneel·er (nē′lər) *n.* **1.** One who kneels. **2.** Something, as a stool, cushion, or board, to kneel on.

knee·pad (nē′păd′) *n.* A protective covering for the knee. Also called "kneecap."

knell (nĕl) *v.* **knelled, knelling, knells.** —*intr.* **1.** To ring or sound, especially for a funeral; toll. Used of a bell. **2.** To produce a mournful or ominous sound. —*tr.* To signal, summon, or proclaim by tolling.
~*n.* **1.** The slow, solemn sounding of a bell, as at a funeral; a tolling. **2.** An omen or signal of disaster, failure, or extinction. [Middle English *knillen, knellen,* Old English *cnyllan.*]

Knel·ler (nĕl′ər), **Sir Godfrey** (1646–1723). British portrait painter, born in Germany. He moved to England in 1675 and soon acquired the patronage of the powerful Duke of Monmouth. Later patrons included Charles II, James II, William III, and Anne.

Knes·set (kə-nĕs′ĕt′) *n.* The Israeli parliament. [Hebrew (Mishnaic) *Kəneseth,* "assembly," from *kānas,* he gathered.]

knew. Past tense of **know.**

Knick·er·bock·er (nĭk′ər-bŏk′ər) *n.* **1.** A descendant of the Dutch settlers of New York. **2.** A New Yorker. **3. knickerbockers.** Full breeches gathered and banded just below the knee. Also called "knickers." [From Diedrich *Knickerbocker,* fictitious Dutch settler and pretended author of Washington Irving's *History of New York* (1809).]

knick·ers (nĭk′ərz) *pl.n.* **1.** Long bloomers formerly worn as underwear by women and girls. **2.** *British.* Underpants worn by women and girls. **3.** Knickerbockers.

knick-knack, nick-nack (nĭk′năk′) *n.* A small ornamental article; a trinket. [Reduplication of KNACK (device).]

knick·point (nĭk′point′) *n.* A place in the long or longitudinal profile of a river valley where the slope changes. [Partial translation of German *Knickpunkt.*]

knife (nīf) *n., pl.* **knives** (nīvz). **1.** A cutting instrument or weapon consisting of a sharp blade with a handle. **2.** A sharp cutting edge; blade. **—under the knife.** *Informal.* Undergoing surgery.
~*v.* **knifed, knifing, knifes.** —*tr.* **1.** To use a knife on, especially to cut, stab, or wound. **2.** *Informal.* To hurt, defeat, or betray by underhand means. —*intr.* To cut or slash a way through with or as if with a knife: *The lifeboat knifed through the surf.* [Middle English *knyf, knif,* Old English *cnīf.*]

knife-edge (nīf′ĕj′) *n.* **1.** The cutting edge of a blade. **2.** A sharp mountain ridge. **3.** A sharp, knifelike edge, such as a sharp pleat or fold. **4.** A wedge of metal used as a low-friction fulcrum for a balancing beam or lever. **5.** A position of extreme precariousness.

knife pleat *n.* One of a series of narrow, flat pleats all lying in one direction and often overlapping.

knife switch *n.* A type of electric switch in which flat, hinged metal blades are pushed between fixed contact clips.

knight (nīt) *n. Abbr.* **k., K., Knt, Kt** **1.** The holder of a nonhereditary rank conferred by a sovereign in recognition of personal merit or services rendered to the country and in Britain bearing the title *Sir* before the Christian name. **2.** A member of any of several orders or brotherhoods that call their members knights. **3.** A medieval tenant giving military service as a mounted man-at-arms to a feudal landholder. **4.** A medieval gentleman-soldier, usually of high birth, raised by a sovereign to privileged military status after training as a page and squire. **5. a.** A defender, champion, or zealous upholder of a cause or principle. **b.** The devoted champion of a lady. **6.** A chess piece usually having the shape of a horse's head that can be moved two squares horizontally and one vertically or two vertically and one horizontally.
~*tr.v.* **knighted, knighting, knights.** To give (a person) a knighthood; make a knight of. [Middle English *cniht, knyght,* Old English *cniht,* originally "boy," "lad," "servant," from West Germanic *knihtas* (unattested).]

knight bachelor *n., pl.* **knights bachelor.** One who holds a knighthood but does not belong to any special order, such as the Garter.

knight banneret *n.* A **banneret** *(see).*

knight errant *n., pl.* **knights errant.** **1.** A knight of medieval romance who wandered in search of adventure. **2.** One given to adventurous or quixotic conduct. **—knight-er·rant·ry** (nīt′ĕr′ən-trē) *n.*

knight·head (nīt′hĕd′) *n.* Either of two timbers rising from the keel of a sailing ship to support the inner end of the bowsprit. [They were sometimes adorned with a carved knight's head.]

knight·hood (nīt′ho͝od′) *n.* **1.** The rank or dignity of a knight. **2.** The behavior of or qualities befitting a knight; chivalry. **3.** Knights as a body or class.

knight·ly (nīt′lē) *adj.* Of, pertaining to, or befitting a knight. **—knight·li·ness** *n.*

knight marshal *n., pl.* **knights marshal.** A royal court official, a **marshal** *(see).*

Knight of Co·lum·bus (kə-lŭm′bəs) *n.* A member of a benevolent society of Roman Catholic men.

Knight of Pyth·i·as (pĭth′ē-əs) *n.* A member of a secret fraternal order founded for philanthropic purposes.

Knights of the Round Table *pl.n. Arthurian Legend.* The knights of the court of King Arthur.

Knight Templar *n., pl.* **Knights Templars.** *Abbr.* **K.T.** A member of an order of knights founded in 1119 to protect pilgrims in the Holy Land during the second Crusade and suppressed between 1311 and 1314. Also called "Templar."

knish (kə-nĭsh′) *n.* A piece of dough stuffed with potato, cheese, or meat and baked or fried. [Yiddish, from Russian, akin to Ukrainian *knyš,* Polish *knysz*†.]

knit (nĭt) *v.* **knit** or **knitted, knitting, knits.** —*tr.* **1. a.** To make (a fabric or garment) by intertwining yarn or thread in a series of connected loops either on a machine or by hand with knitting needles: *knit a pair of mittens.* **b.** To make (yarn or thread) into a fabric or garment by knitting. **2. a.** To join closely; unite securely: *a tightly knit community.* **b.** To cause to grow together securely: *wore a cast and kept my arm immobile to knit the broken bone.* **3.** To draw (the brows) together in wrinkles; furrow. —*intr.* **1. a.** To make a fabric or garment by intertwining yarn or thread in a series of connected loops. **b.** To make a plain stitch; knit using a plain stitch. **2.** To come or grow together securely. Used especially of fractured bones. **3.** To come together in wrinkles or furrows.
~*n.* **1.** A fabric or garment made by knitting. **2.** The method, style, or way in which a garment has been knitted: *a loose knit.* [Middle English *knitten,* Old English *cnyttan,* to tie in a knot.] **—knit·ter** *n.*

knit·ting (nĭt′ĭng) *n.* **1.** The process of producing something knitted. **2.** Knitted work.

knitting needle *n.* A long, thin, pointed rod used in knitting.

knit·wear (nĭt′wâr′) *n.* Knitted clothing, especially sweaters.

knives. Plural of **knife.**

knob (nŏb) *n.* **1. a.** A rounded protuberance on a surface or extremity. **b.** A rounded handle, as on a drawer or door. **c.** A rounded control switch or dial. **2.** *Chiefly British.* A small rounded piece, as of butter. **3.** A prominent rounded hill or mountain. [Middle English *knobbe,* from Middle Low German, tree knot, knob.] **—knobbed** *adj.* **—knob·by** *adj.*

knob·bly (nŏb′lē) *adj.* **-blier, -bliest.** Having or covered with small knoblike protrusions; knobby: *knobbly knees.*

knob·ker·rie (nŏb′kĕr′ē) *n.* A short club with one knobbed end, used as a weapon by South African tribesmen. [Afrikaans *knopkierie* : *knop,* knob, from Middle Dutch *cnoppe* + *kieri,* club, from Hottentot *kīrri,* a stick.]

knock (nŏk) *v.* **knocked, knocking, knocks.** —*tr.* **1.** To strike with a hard blow; hit. **2.** To affect in a specified way by or as if by knocking: *knocked him senseless; knocked the china to bits.* **3.** To cause to collide: *knocked my head against the shelf.* **4.** To produce by hitting or striking: *She knocked a hole in the wall.* **5.** To instill with or as if with blows: *Try to knock some sense into his head.* **6.** *Slang.* To criticize adversely; disparage. **7.** *British Slang.* To astonish. —*intr.* **1.** To strike a sharp, audible blow or series of blows, as at a door when requesting admittance; rap. **2.** To collide; bump. **3. a.** To make a pounding or clanking noise, as of a laboring or defective engine. **b.** To emit a characteristic metallic sound as a result of faulty combustion. Used of a gasoline engine. **—knock around** (or **about**). *Informal.* **1.** To be rough or brutal with; maltreat. **2.** To discuss or consider. **3.** To travel around, often aimlessly. **—knock cold.** To knock out. **—knock dead.** *Slang.* To affect strongly and usually positively: *a virtuoso performance that knocked the audience dead.* **—knock for a loop.** To surprise tremendously; astonish. **—knock off. 1.** *Informal.* **a.** To take a break or rest from; stop. **b.** To cease work. **2.** *Informal.* To make, accomplish, or consume hastily or easily. **3.** *Informal.* To eliminate; deduct: *The grocer knocked off a little from the bill.* **4.** *Slang.* To kill. **5.** *Slang.* To hold up or rob. **6.** *Informal.* To copy the design or production of. **—knock out of the box.** *Baseball.* To force the removal of (an opposing pitcher) by heavy hitting. **—knock together.** To make or assemble quickly or carelessly.
~*n.* **1.** An instance of knocking; a blow. **2.** The sound of a sharp tap on a hard surface; a rap. **3. a.** A pounding, clanking noise made by an engine, especially one in poor operating condition. **b.** A characteristic metallic sound emitted by an engine as a result of faulty

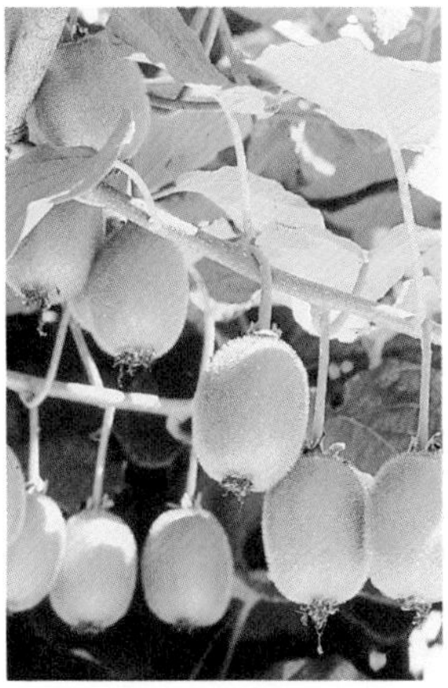

kiwi *The kiwi fruit, also called the Chinese gooseberry, is harvested from an Asian climbing bush,* Actinidia chinensis.

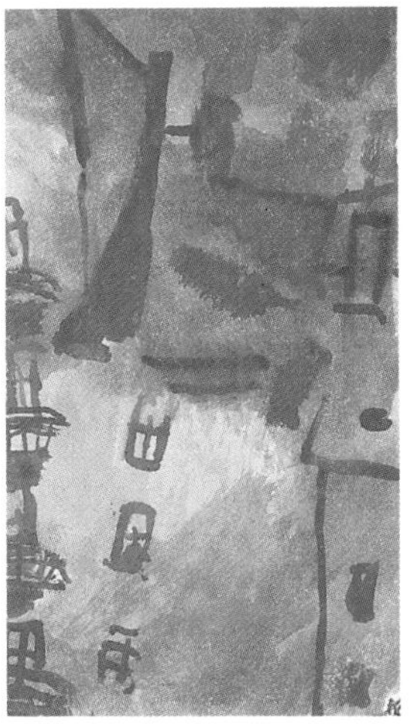

Klee painting Sun in the Courtyard. *Klee developed his own symbolic language for his childlike pictures, describing them as being like musical compositions that used colors in place of notes.*

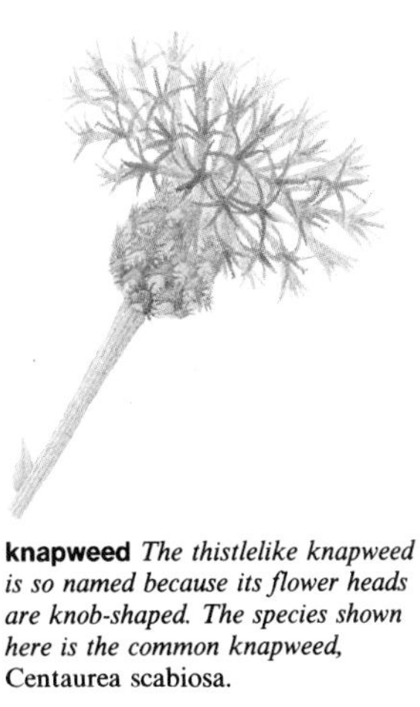

knapweed *The thistlelike knapweed is so named because its flower heads are knob-shaped. The species shown here is the common knapweed,* Centaurea scabiosa.

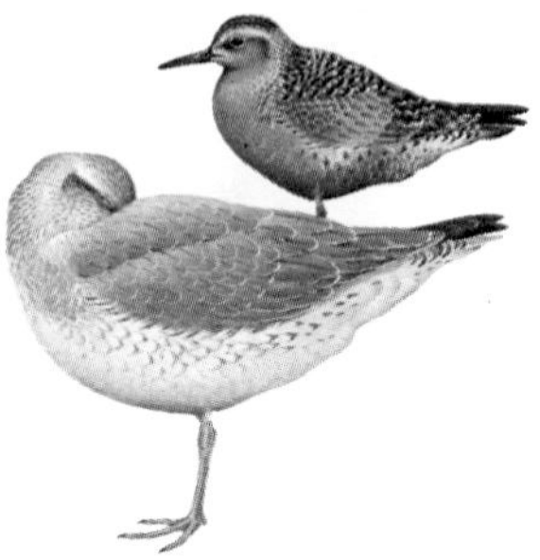

knot *A wader that breeds in the Arctic and winters along the shores of northern Europe. The adult birds have a brick-red plumage in summer and autumn, which changes to gray and white in winter.*

PRONUNCIATION KEY

ă, pat; ā, pay; âr, care; ä, father, are; b, bib; ch, church; d, deed; ĕ, pet; ē, be; f, fife; g, gag; h, hat; hw, which; ĭ, pit; ī, pie; îr, pier; j, judge; k, kick; l, lid, needle; m, mum; n, no, sudden; ng, thing; ŏ, pot; ō, toe; ô, paw, for; oi, noise; ou, out; o͝o, book; o͞o, boot; p, pop; r, roar; s, sauce; sh, ship, dish; t, tight; th, thin, path; *th*, this, bathe; ŭ, cut; ûr, fur; v, valve; w, with; y, yes; z, zebra, size; zh, vision; ə, about, item, edible, gallop, circus, peaceful

IN FOREIGN WORDS:

à, *Fr.* ami; œ, *Fr.* feu, *Ger.* schön; ü, *Fr.* tu, *Ger.* über; KH, *Ger.* ich, *Scot.* loch; N, *Fr.* bon; y', *Fr.* Compiègne

STRESS MARKS:

Primary stress: ′ in·cite′ (ĭn-sīt′)
Secondary stress: ′ in′sight′ (ĭn′sīt′)

combustion. **4.** *Slang.* A criticism or insult; a cutting remark. **5.** *Informal.* A misfortune, setback, or trouble: *has taken a few knocks over the years.* [Middle English *knokken,* Old English *cnocian.*]

knock·a·bout (nŏk′ə-bout′) *n.* A small sloop with a mainsail, a jib, and a keel but no bowsprit.
~*adj.* **1.** Rough; boisterous; rowdy. **2.** Appropriate for rough wear or use.

knock back *tr.v. Informal.* **1.** To drink (alcohol, for example) quickly or in large quantities. **2.** *British.* To cost; especially, to cost (a person) a large amount of money. **3.** *British.* To surprise and disconcert. **4.** *British.* To reject, refuse, or rebuff.

knock·back (nŏk′băk′) *n. British.* A rejection, refusal, or rebuff.

knock down *tr.v.* **1.** To disassemble into parts, as for storage or shipping. **2.** To declare as sold at an auction, as by striking a blow with a gavel. **3.** *Informal.* To reduce, as in price. **4.** *Slang.* To receive as wages; earn.

knock·down (nŏk′doun′) *adj.* **1.** Strong enough to knock down or overwhelm; powerful: *a knockdown blow.* **2.** Designed to be assembled and disassembled quickly and easily: *knockdown furniture.* **3.** *Informal.* Extremely low; cheap: *knockdown prices.*
~*n.* **1.** The act of knocking down; a toppling or overwhelming. **2.** An overwhelming blow or shock. **3.** Something designed to be assembled and disassembled quickly and easily. **4.** *Australian Informal.* An introduction to a person.

knock·down-drag·out (nŏk′doun-drăg′out′) *adj.* Marked by roughness, violence, and acrimony: *had a knockdown-dragout fight.*

knock·er (nŏk′ər) *n.* One that knocks, especially: **a.** An often decorative fixture used for knocking on a door. **b.** *Slang.* One who constantly criticizes. **—on the knocker.** **1.** *British Informal.* From door to door; especially, as a door-to-door salesman: *working on the knocker.* **2.** *Australian Informal.* Punctually; promptly.

knock·er-up (nŏk′ər-ŭp′) *n., pl.* **knockers-up.** *British.* **1.** One who goes from door to door, as a salesman or a political canvasser. **2.** Formerly, one whose job was to wake people up, as for work, by going from house to house knocking on windows.

knock·ing-shop (nŏk′ĭng-shŏp′) *n. British Slang.* A brothel.

knock-knee (nŏk′nē′) *n.* An abnormal condition in which one knee is turned toward the other or in which each is turned toward the other. **—knock-kneed** *adj.*

knock·off (nŏk′ôf′, -ŏf′) *n. Informal.* A usually less expensive copy, as of a dress.

knock out *tr.v.* **1.** To render unconscious. **2.** *Boxing.* To defeat (an opponent) by knocking him to the canvas for a count of ten. **3.** To bring to an end; eliminate: *City ordinances knocked out real-estate speculation.* **4.** *Informal.* To exert or exhaust (oneself or another) to the utmost. **5.** *Informal.* To delight or amaze: *We've been really knocked out by the book's success.* **6.** *Informal.* To render useless or inoperative: *The earthquake knocked out all electricity and telephone service.*

knock·out (nŏk′out′) *n.* **1. a.** The act of knocking out. **b.** The state of being knocked out. **c.** A blow that induces unconsciousness. **d.** The knocking out of an opponent. **2.** *Slang.* Something very impressive or attractive.
~*adj.* Effecting a knockout.

knockout drops *pl.n. Slang.* A solution, as of chloral hydrate, put into a drink to render the drinker unconscious.

knock up *intr.v.* To hit a ball in practice for a period before starting to play a game, as of tennis or squash. —*tr.v.* **1.** To make or assemble quickly or carelessly. **2.** *British Informal.* To exhaust; wear out. **3.** *British.* To wake up, as by knocking at a door. **4.** *Cricket.* To score (runs) quickly. **5.** *Slang.* To make pregnant.

knock-up (nŏk′ŭp′) *n.* A practice session or warm-up period before a game, as of tennis or squash, starts.

knockwurst. Variant of **knackwurst.**

knoll (nōl) *n.* A small rounded hill or mound; a hillock. [Middle English *knol(le),* Old English *cnoll.*]

knop (nŏp) *n.* A decorative knob or boss, as on the end of the handle of a spoon. [Middle English *knoppe,* probably from Middle Low German or Middle Dutch.]

Knos·sos or **Cnos·sos** (nŏs′əs). City of ancient Crete. Just south of modern Iráklion, it was occupied from *c.* 3000 B.C. and by the time of its destruction, probably by earthquake (*c.* 1400 B.C.), it was, as the center of Minoan culture, one of the leading cities of the ancient world. The legends of the Labyrinth, the Minotaur, and Atlantis probably originated here. It was excavated and extensively restored between 1899 and 1935.

knot[1] (nŏt) *n.* **1.** A more or less complex, compact intersection of interlaced material, as cord, ribbon, or rope. **2.** A fastening made by tying together lengths of material, as rope, in a prescribed way. **3.** A decorative bow of ribbon, fabric, or braid. **4.** A unifying tie or bond, especially a marriage bond. **5.** A tight cluster of persons or things. **6.** A difficulty; a problem. **7. a.** A hard place or node on a plant, especially on a tree, at a point from which a stem or branch grows. **b.** The circular, contrastingly dark-colored cross section of such a node as it appears cross-grained on a piece of cut lumber. **8.** A growth on or enlargement of a gland, muscle, or the like. **9.** *Nautical.* **a.** A division on a log line used to measure the speed of a ship. **b.** *Abbr.* **kn., kt.** A unit of speed of ships or aircraft, one nautical mile per hour, about 1.85 kilometers or 1.15 statute miles per hour. **c.** A distance of one nautical mile. **—tie (up) in knots.** To make (a person) very tense or confused. **—tie the knot.** *Slang.* **1.** To get married. **2.** To perform a marriage ceremony.
~*v.* **knotted, knotting, knots.** —*tr.* **1.** To tie in or fasten with a knot. **2.** To snarl or entangle. **3.** To cause to form knots. —*intr.* **1.** To become snarled or entangled. **2.** To form a knot. [Middle English *knot(te),* Old English *cnotta.*]
Usage: In nautical usage *knot* is a unit of speed, not of distance, and has a built-in meaning of "per hour." Therefore, a ship would strictly be said to travel at ten knots (not ten knots per hour).

knot[2] *n.* A shore bird, *Calidris canutus,* related to the sandpipers, having plumage that is grayish and mottled in winter and brick-red in summer and a short, black bill. [Middle English, origin obscure.]

knot garden *n.* A formal garden having the flower beds arranged in an intricate, usually geometric pattern.

knot·grass (nŏt′grăs′, -gräs′) *n.* **1.** A low-growing, weedy plant, *Polygonum aviculare,* having very small greenish flowers. Also called "allseed." **2.** Any of several similar plants.

knot·hole (nŏt′hōl′) *n.* A hole in a piece of timber where a knot has dropped out or been removed.

knot·ted (nŏt′ĭd) *adj.* **1.** Tied or fastened in or with a knot. **2.** Intricate; knotty. **3.** Characterized by or full of knots; gnarled: *a knotted branch.*

knot·ty (nŏt′ē) *adj.* **-tier, -tiest.** **1.** Tied or tangled in knots: *a knotty cord.* **2.** Covered with knots or knobs; gnarled: *knotty hands.* **3.** Difficult to understand or solve; intricate and puzzling: *a knotty problem.* —See Synonyms at **complex.** **—knot·ti·ness** *n.*

knot·weed (nŏt′wēd′) *n.* Any of several plants of the genus *Polygonum,* having jointed stems and inconspicuous flowers.

knout (nout) *n.* A leather scourge formerly used for flogging criminals, especially in Russia.
~*tr.v.* **knouted, knouting, knouts.** To flog with a knout. [French, from Russian *knut,* from Old Norse *knūtr,* knot.]

know (nō) *v.* **knew** (no͞o, nyo͞o), **known** (nōn), **knowing, knows.** —*tr.* **1.** To perceive directly with the senses or mind; apprehend with clarity or certainty: *didn't know the answer.* **2.** To be certain of; regard or accept as true beyond doubt: *I just know he's telling the truth.* **3.** To be capable of; have the skill to: *Do you know how to swim?* **4.** To have a thorough or practical understanding of, as through experience or study: *knows the rules of bridge.* **5. a.** To have personal experience of: *has never known real hunger.* **b.** To be subjected to or limited by: *grief that knows no bounds.* **6.** To recognize the character or quality of: *knew him for a liar.* **7.** To be able to distinguish; recognize: *Do you know him from his twin brother?* **8.** To be acquainted or familiar with: *We know them, but we wouldn't call them friends.* **9.** To see, hear, or experience: *I've never known her to lose her temper. He's known to have the habit of being late.* **10.** *Archaic.* To have sexual intercourse with: *"And Adam knew Eve his wife; and she conceived"* (Genesis 4:1). —*intr.* **1.** To possess knowledge, understanding, or information about something: *Mother knows best.* **2.** To be cognizant or aware: *We knew about what he had done.* **—in the know.** Possessing correct or exclusive information. [Know, knew, known; Middle English *knowen, knew, knowe(n),* Old English *(ge)cnāwan, (ge)cnēow, (ge)cnāwen.*] **—know·a·ble** *adj.* **—know·er** *n.*
Usage: In negative constructions, *know* may be followed by clauses introduced by *that, whether,* or *if,* but not by *as*: *I don't know that/whether/if* (not *as*) *he can come.*

know-all (nō′ôl′) *n. British Informal.* A know-it-all.

know-how (nō′hou′) *n. Informal.* The knowledge, skill, or ingenuity required to do something correctly.

know·ing (nō′ĭng) *adj.* **1.** Possessing knowledge, intelligence, or understanding. **2.** Suggestive of secret or private information: *a knowing glance.* **3.** Having or showing clever awareness and resourcefulness; shrewd. **4.** Planned; deliberate: *knowing complicity in the plot.* —See Synonyms at **intelligent.** **—know·ing·ly** *adv.* **—know·ing·ness** *n.*

know-it-all (nō′ĭt-ôl′) *n. Informal.* A person who believes himself to be exceptionally well-informed and displays his knowledge in an arrogant or outspoken fashion.

knowl·edge (nŏl′ĭj) *n.* **1.** The state or fact of knowing. **2.** Familiarity, awareness, or understanding gained through experience or study. **3.** That which is known, as: **a.** The sum or range of what has been perceived, discovered, or inferred. **b.** Specific information about something. **4.** Learning; erudition: *men of knowledge.* **5.** *Archaic.* Sexual intercourse; copulation. Now used only in the legal phrase *carnal knowledge.* **—to one's knowledge.** **1.** So far as one knows. **2.** Known to one as a certain fact. [Middle English *knowlege, know(e)lech,* from *cnawlechen, know(e)lechen,* to confess, recognize, Old English *cnāwlǣcan* (unattested), from *cnāwan,* to KNOW.]
Synonyms: *enlightenment, erudition, information, learning, lore, scholarship, wisdom.*

knowl·edge·a·ble (nŏl′ĭ-jə-bəl) *adj.* Possessing or showing knowledge or intelligence; sharp and well informed.

known (nōn). Past participle of **know.**
~*adj.* Proved or generally recognized: *a known crook; the only known case of recovery from the disease.*
~*n.* Something that is known: *proceed from the known to the unknown.*

know-noth·ing (nō′nŭth′ĭng) *n.* **1. Know-Nothing.** A member of a mid-19th-century American political movement that was antagonistic toward immigrants and Roman Catholics. **2.** An ignoramus. **3.** An agnostic. **4.** An anti-intellectual.

Knox (nŏks), **John** (*c.* 1505–72). Leader of the Scottish Reformation. He became chaplain to Edward VI (1551), but after the accession of the Roman Catholic Mary Tudor (1553) he fled to Geneva, where he was influenced by Calvin. After Mary's death (1558),

Knox returned to Scotland (1559), and by 1560 the Confession of Faith was drawn up and Protestantism became the established religion in Scotland, despite the subsequent efforts of Mary Queen of Scots.

Knox·ville (nŏks′vĭl′) Industrial port in eastern Tennessee. On the Tennessee River, it was settled in 1786 and was twice state capital (1796–1812, 1817–19). It is the seat of the Tennessee Valley Authority.

Knt knight.

knuck·le (nŭk′əl) *n.* **1.** *Anatomy.* **a.** A joint or region around a joint of a finger, especially one of the joints connecting the fingers to the hand. **b.** Any of the rounded protuberances formed by the bones in such a joint. **2.** A cut of meat centering on the carpal joint, as of a pig. **3.** The part of a hinge through which the pin passes. **4.** A joint between two members of a structure or mechanism in which the two components are at an angle to each other. **5. knuckles.** A weapon consisting of a metal strip or chain with holes or links into which the fingers fit. **—near** (or **close to**) **the knuckle.** Approaching what is conventionally regarded as indecent.
~*tr.v.* **knuckled, -ling, -les. 1.** To press, rub, or hit with the knuckles of the fist: *"They stared gaping, and knuckling their brows"* (Mary Renault). **2.** To shoot (a marble) with the thumb over the bent forefinger. **—knuckle down.** *Informal.* To apply oneself earnestly to a task: *knuckled down to work.* **—knuckle under.** To yield to pressure; give in. [Middle English *knokel,* from Middle Low German *knökel.*]

knuck·le·bone (nŭk′əl-bōn′) *n.* **1.** A knobbed bone, as of a knuckle or joint. **2. knucklebones.** *Used with a singular verb.* A game formerly played by tossing knucklebones.

knuck·le-dust·ers (nŭk′əl-dŭs′tərz) *pl.n. Slang.* A weapon consisting of a piece of metal that fits snugly over the knuckles; knuckles.

knuck·le·head (nŭk′əl-hĕd′) *n.* A fool or idiot.

knuckle joint *n.* A hinged, flexible joint formed by the juncture of two rods or projections, one inside the other and the two locked by a pin that functions as an axle.

knuckle sandwich *n. Slang.* A punch in the mouth.

knur, knurr (nûr) *n.* A bump or knot, as on a tree trunk. [Middle English *knorre,* swelling, from Germanic, akin to Middle Low German and Middle High German *knorre,* knot, knob.]

knurl (nûrl) *n.* **1.** A knob, knot, or similar protuberance. **2.** Any of a series of small ridges or beads along the edge of a metal object, as a thumbscrew, to aid in gripping. [Probably from KNUR (influenced by GNARL).] **—knurl·y** *adj.*

KO (kā′ō′) *tr.v.* **KO'd, KO'ing, KO's.** Also **K.O., k.o.** *Slang.* To knock out, as in boxing.
~*n.* (kā-ō′, kā′ō′) *pl.* **KO's.** *Slang.* In boxing, a **knockout** *(see).*

ko·a (kō′ə) *n.* **1.** A Hawaiian tree, *Acacia koa.* **2.** The hard, reddish wood of this tree, used especially for making furniture. [Hawaiian.]

ko·a·la (kō-ä′lə) *n.* An arboreal marsupial, *Phascolarctos cinereus,* of Australia, having grayish fur and feeding chiefly on the leaves and bark of eucalyptus trees. Also called "koala bear." [Earlier *koola,* from the native Australian name *kūlla.*]

ko·an (kō′än′) *n.* In Zen Buddhism, a problem or riddle that aims to break down logical reasoning. [Japanese.]

Ko·be (kō′bē). City in south Honshu in Japan. On Osaka Bay at the eastern end of the Inland Sea, it has major shipbuilding facilities and produces sugar, rubber, and ferrous metals.

København. See **Copenhagen.**

Ko·blenz or **Co·blenz** (kō′blĕnts). A city in West Germany, founded by the Romans (1st century A.D.) at the confluence of the Rhine and Moselle rivers. The center of the Moselle wine trade, it also produces pianos, furniture, clothing, and paper.

ko·bo (kō′bō) *n., pl.* **kobo.** A Nigerian coin equal to 1/100 of a naira. See feature at **currency.** [Alteration of English *copper* (penny).]

ko·bold (kō′bôld′) *n.* In German folklore: **1.** A mischievous household elf. **2.** A gnome that haunts underground places such as mines and caves. [German *Kobold,* from Middle High German *kobolt.*]

Koch (kōKH), **Robert** (1843–1910). German bacteriologist. He discovered the cholera bacillus and the bacterial origin of anthrax. He was awarded the Nobel Prize (1905) for his work on tuberculosis.

Köch·el number (kœ′KHəl) *n. Abbr.* **K.** A number that has been assigned to each of the compositions of Mozart. [After Ludwig *Köchel* (1800–77), Austrian musicologist who catalogued Mozart's compositions.]

Ko·dály (kō′dī′), **Zoltan** (1882–1967). Hungarian composer. His works include the opera *Háry János* (1926), *Te Deum* (1936), and *Missa Brevis* (1945).

Ko·di·ak (kō′dē-ăk′). An island in the Shelikof Strait off the southern coast of Alaska. It was settled by Russians (1784) as a whale- and seal-hunting center.

Kodiak bear *n.* A form of the brown bear, *Ursus arctos,* of islands and coastal areas of Alaska, sometimes considered a separate species. [After KODIAK island.]

ko·el (kō′əl) *n.* A cuckoo, *Eudynamys scolopacea,* found in India, southeast Asia, and Australia, that lays its eggs in the nests of crows. [Hindi, from Sanskrit *kokila.*]

Koest·ler (kĕst′lər, kĕs′-), **Arthur** (1905–83). Hungarian-born British author and journalist. Educated in Vienna, he became a communist, but his novel *Darkness at Noon* (1940) shows his disillusionment with communism as practiced in the U.S.S.R. While reporting the Spanish Civil War he narrowly escaped execution by Franco. In his later works, such as *The Sleepwalkers* (1959) and *The Ghost in the Machine* (1968), he explores various philosophical aspects of science and psychology.

kof·ta (kôf′tə, kŏf′-) *n.* A dish served in India in which the ingredients, usually chopped meat or vegetables together with spices, are formed into balls and served in a sauce. [Urdu.]

kohl (kōl) *n.* A preparation used chiefly in Muslim and Asian countries as a cosmetic around the eyes. [Arabic *kuḥl, koḥl,* powder of antimony. See also **alcohol.**]

Kohl (kōl), **Helmut** (1930–). West German politician. He became chancellor in 1982.

kohl·ra·bi (kōl-rä′bē, -răb′ē) *n., pl.* **-bies.** A plant, *Brassica caulorapa,* with a thickened stem that is eaten as a vegetable. Also called "turnip cabbage." [German *Kohlrabi* (influenced by *Kohl,* cabbage), from Italian *cavoli rape,* plural of *cavolo rapa* : *cavolo,* cole, cabbage, from Latin *caulis* + *rapa,* turnip, from Latin *rāpa, rāpum.*]

Koi·ne (koi-nā′, koi′nā′) *n.* **1.** A dialect of Greek that developed primarily from Attic and eventually replaced the local dialects, becoming the common language of the Hellenistic world from which the later stages of Greek are descended. **2. koine.** A language common to people speaking different languages; a lingua franca. [Greek *koinē (dialektos),* "common (language)," from *koinos,* common.]

Ko·kosch·ka (kə-kôsh′kə), **Oskar** (1886–1980). Austrian-born expressionist painter, skilled at portraits and landscapes. He left Nazi Germany and settled in England and later in Switzerland.

kok-sa·ghyz (kōk′sə-gēz′, -gĭz′, kŏk′-) *n.* A dandelion, *Taraxacum kok-saghyz,* of central Asia, having fleshy roots that yield a form of rubber. [Russian *kok-sagyz,* from Turkish *kok-sagiz* : *kok,* root + *sagiz,* rubber.]

kola. Variant of **cola** (nut-bearing tree).

kola nut. Variant of **cola nut.**

Kol·chak (kôl′chŏk′), **Alexandr Vasilyevich** (1874–1920). Russian admiral. He was commander of the Black Sea fleet during World War I, and after the 1917 October Revolution he led the White Russians against the Bolsheviks. He was recognized by the Allies as head of the provisional Russian government (1918–20), but was captured and shot by the Bolsheviks.

ko·lin·sky (kə-lĭn′skē) *n., pl.* **-skies. 1.** Any of several minks of northern Eurasia, especially *Mustela siberica.* **2.** The tawny fur of such an animal. [Russian *kolinskiĭ,* "(mink) of Kola," from *Kola,* district in northwestern U.S.S.R.]

kol·khoz, kol·koz (kŏl-kôz′) *n., pl.* **-khozes** or **-khozy** (-kô′zē). A Soviet collective farm. [Russian, contraction of *kollektivnoe khozyaistvo* : *kollektivnoe,* neuter of *kollektivny,* collective + *khozyaistvo,* household, farm.]

Kol·lon·tai (kŏ-lŏn-tī′), **Aleksandra Mikhailovna** (1872–1952). Russian revolutionary and author. Despite her privileged social position, she joined the Social-Democratic Worker's Party (1898) and after the October Revolution (1917) used her political influence to advocate social changes.

Koll·witz (kôl′vĭts′, kôl′wĭts′), **Käthe** or **Kaethe** (1867–1945). German artist. Profoundly affected by her contact with the poor, the death of her son in battle (1914), and the growing violence in the world, she used her sculptures and prints, including *The Living to the Dead* (1919), to eloquently denounce war and social injustice. During World War II, her grandson was killed in battle (1942) and her studio was bombed, destroying much of her work (1943).

Köln (kœln). *English* **Co·logne** (kə-lōn′). City and port on the west bank of the Rhine in North Rhine-Westphalia in West Germany. It is a major industrial city, producing iron and steel, machinery, chemicals, textiles, and eau de cologne.

Kol Ni·dre (kōl nĭd′rā, -rə, kôl) *n. Judaism.* The opening prayer recited on the eve of Yom Kippur, containing a declaration of the annulment of all personal vows of the preceding year. [Aramaic *kol nidhrē,* "all vows," from its opening words.]

Komenský, Jan. See John Amos **Comenius.**

Ko·mo·do dragon (kə-mō′dō) *n.* A large monitor lizard, *Varanus komodoensis,* of the Indonesian islands of Komodo and Flores. It is the largest living lizard, growing up to 10 feet (3 meters) long.

kom·so·mol (kŏm′sə-môl′, -mŏl′) *n.* In the Soviet Union, a communist youth organization. [Russian, acronym of *Kommunistichesky Soyuz Molodyozhi,* Communist Union of Youth.]

kon·fyt (kən-fīt′) *n. South African.* Crystallized or preserved fruit, often in syrup. [Afrikaans, from Dutch *konfijt,* preserves.]

Kong-fu-zi or **Kong-zi.** See **Confucius.**

Kon·go[1] (kŏng′gō). A powerful African state founded in the 14th century. It covered the area now occupied by Angola, Congo, and Zaire.

Kongo[2] *n., pl.* **Kongos** or collectively **Kongo. 1.** A member of a Bantu people of the region of the lower Congo River. **2.** The Bantu language of the Kongo.

kon·go·ni (kŏng-gō′nē) *n.* A large east African antelope, *Alcelaphus buselaphus,* that is a species of hartebeest. [Swahili.]

Königsberg. See **Kaliningrad.**

ko·ni·ol·o·gy (kō′nē-ŏl′ə-jē) *n.* The scientific study of atmospheric dust and its effects. [Greek *konia,* dust + -LOGY.]

Kon·ka·ni (kŏng′kə-nē, kông′-) *n.* An Indic language related to Marathi and spoken on the west coast of India south of Maharashtra and north of Kerala. [Marathi *koṅkaṇī,* from *Koṅkaṇ,* Konkan, region of western India.]

Kon·stanz (kôn′stänts). *English* **Con·stance** (kŏn′stəns). Port in Baden-Württemberg in West Germany, on Lake Constance. Its industries include chemicals, electrical equipment, textiles, and tourism.

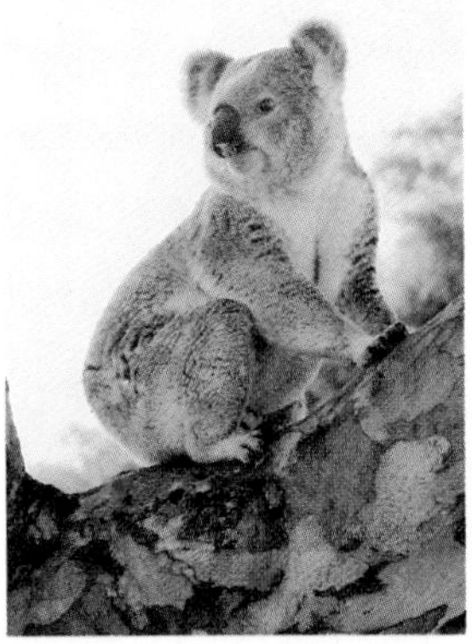

koala *These bearlike Australian marsupials feed almost exclusively on the leaves of eucalyptus trees. Their name comes from an aboriginal phrase meaning "no drink"—because the animals never take a drink, getting all the water they need from the juice of the leaves they eat.*

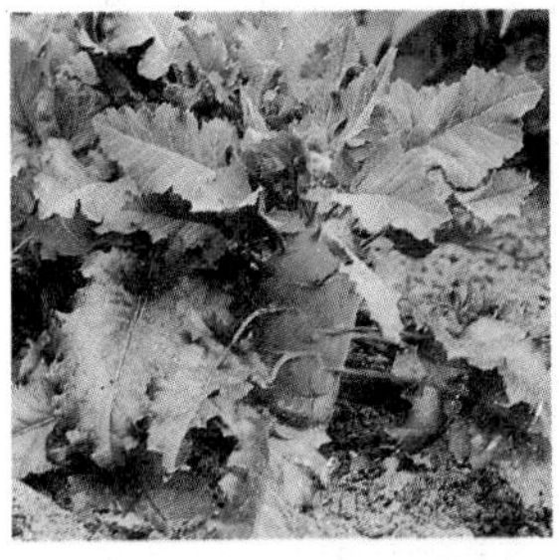

kohlrabi *This nutty-flavored vegetable is thought to have been brought to western Europe by the Crusaders. Both its turniplike stem and cabbagelike top are edible. Botanically, it is related to the cabbage, cauliflower, and Brussels sprout, though it resembles none of them.*

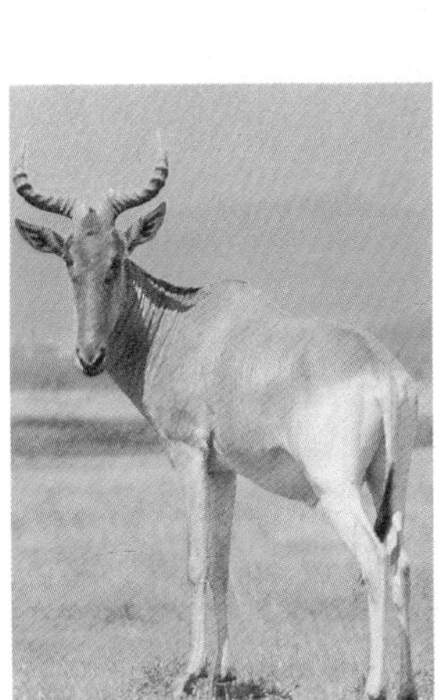

kongoni *The kongoni is one of about six species of hartebeest inhabiting the open plains of East Africa.*

Kon·ya (kôn-yä′). *Latin* **I·co·ni·um** (ī-kō′nē-əm). Capital of Konya province in central Turkey. It markets grains, sugar, flax, fruit, and livestock and produces carpets, silk goods, and cotton. In the 13th century the order of the dancing dervishes was founded in the city.

koodoo. Variant of **kudu.**

kook (kŏŏk) *n. Slang.* An amusingly eccentric or zany person. [Perhaps from CUCKOO.] —**kook·i·ness** *n.* —**kook·y** *adj.*

kook·a·bur·ra (kŏŏk′ə-bûr′ə) *n.* A large kingfisher, *Dacelo novaeguineae* (or *D. gigas*), of Australia and adjacent areas, having a call resembling raucous laughter. Also called "jackass," "laughing jackass." [Native Australian name.]

kop (kŏp) *n. South African.* An isolated hill or peak. [Afrikaans, "head, hill."]

ko·peck, co·peck, co·pek (kō′pĕk′) *n. Abbr.* **k., K.** A coin equal to ¹⁄₁₀₀ of the rouble of the U.S.S.R. See feature at **currency.** [Russian *kopyeika,* from *kopye,* lance (from the figure of the czar with a lance in his hand originally stamped on the coin), from *kopat',* to hack.]

Kopernik, Mikolaj. See Nicolaus **Copernicus.**

kop·pa (kŏp′ə) *n.* A letter occurring in certain early forms of the Greek alphabet, later mostly replaced by **kappa** (*see*). Transliterated in English as *q.* [Greek, from Semitic, akin to Hebrew *qōph,* КОРН.]

kop·pie, kop·je (kŏp′ē) *n. South African.* A small, isolated hill. [Afrikaans, diminutive of KOP.]

Ko·ran (kə-rän′, -răn′, kô-, kō-) *n.* The sacred text of Islam, believed to contain the revelations made by Allah to Muhammad. Also called "Alcoran." [Arabic *qur'ān,* reading, recitation, from *qara'a,* to read, recite.] —**Ko·ran·ic** (kə-răn′ĭk, kô-, kō-) *adj.*

Kor·da (kôr′də), **Sir Alexander** (1893–1956). Hungarian-born British film producer. His productions include *The Scarlet Pimpernel* and *The Third Man.*

kookaburra *This Australian bird is also known as the "laughing jackass." Its call starts as a low chuckle that rises sharply in volume and pitch. In a group, each bird begins its call a few notes behind its neighbor, so producing an uncanny effect of uncontrollable laughter.*

KOREA   126° E
USSR
Kaema
CHINA   NORTH KOREA
• Chongjin
▲ Pai - t'ou - shan 2744m
• Sinuiju
Hamhung •
Hungnam •
Korea PYONGYANG • Chungsan
Bay Kyomipo •
• Wonsan
SEA
OF
38° N
JAPAN
Kaesong •
SŎUL (SEOUL) •
Inchon •
Takeshima (JAP.)
YELLOW SEA
SOUTH KOREA
Taejon •
Taegu • • Kyongju
Kwangju • Masan • • Pusan
Mokpo •
JAPAN
Km 0   200
Miles 0   100
Cheju do (S. KOREA)

Ko·re·a (kə-rē′ə, kō′-). *Korean* **Cho·son** (chō′sŏn′). *Japanese* **Cho·sen** (chō′sĕn′). Peninsula in northeast Asia. Extending southward between the Yellow Sea and the Sea of Japan, it is mainly mountainous. Civilized from *c.* 1200 B.C., it was united under the kingdom of Silla (A.D. 668), and despite a Mongol invasion (13th century) it survived until a Japanese occupation (1910–45). Following World War II the Soviet- and U.S.-occupied zones became separate republics; the northern, Soviet-sponsored republic invaded the south (1950), which resisted with the aid of U.N. forces. The border was established by treaty (1953), dividing the peninsula into South Korea and North Korea.

Korea, North. Officially, Democratic People's Republic of Korea. Asian republic. Lying north of the 1953 cease-fire line, it has the bulk of the peninsula's mineral resources. With Soviet aid it has built up its industries and intensified the cultivation of its limited fertile land. Its chief exports are metals. Area, 120,538 square kilometers (46,528 square miles). Population, 17,900,000. Capital, Pyongyang.

Korea, South. Officially, Republic of Korea. Asian republic. It has few natural resources apart from coal, iron ore, and graphite. Though more than a third of the population is still engaged in

agriculture, the republic has developed its industries with U.S. aid, and its growth rates in the 1970's were among the world's highest. Area, 98,484 square kilometers (38,015 square miles). Population, 37,500,000. Capital, Seoul.

Ko·re·an (kə-rē′ən, kō-, kō̄-) *adj.* Of or pertaining to Korea, its inhabitants, or their language.
~*n.* **1.** A native or inhabitant of Korea. **2.** The language of Korea, unclassified linguistically but containing many words of Chinese origin.

Korean War *n.* A war (1950–53) between North Korea, helped by China, and South Korea, helped by U.N. forces consisting of mainly U.S. troops.

korf·ball (kôrf′bôl′, kôrf′-) *n.* A game of Dutch origin that resembles basketball and is played by teams of both sexes. [Dutch *korfbal,* basketball.]

Kórinthos. See **Corinth.**

Kort·rijk (kôrt′rīk). *French* **Cour·trai** (kŏŏr-trā′). City of West Flanders province in Belgium, on the Leie (Lys) River. It was a major center of the medieval cloth industry of Flanders.

ko·ru·na (kôr′ə-nä′, kôr′-) *n., pl.* **-ny** (-nē) or **-nas.** *Abbr.* **k., K. 1.** The basic monetary unit of Czechoslovakia, equal to 100 halers. See feature at **currency. 2.** A coin worth one koruna. [Czech, "crown," from Latin *corōna,* CROWN.]

Kos. See **Cos.**

Kos·ci·us·ko (kŏs′ē-ŭs′kō). Australia's highest mountain (2,228 meters; 7,310 feet). Part of the Snowy Mts. of southeast New South Wales, it is a winter sports center. It is named after the Polish patriot Thaddeus Kosciusko (1746–1817).

ko·sher (kō′shər) *adj.* **1.** Conforming to or prepared in accordance with Jewish dietary laws, as: **a.** Slaughtered or prepared for eating according to rabbinic law; ritually pure: *kosher meat.* **b.** Restricted to the use of such food: *They keep a kosher house.* **c.** Specializing in the preparation or sale of such food: *a kosher delicatessen.* Compare **tref. 2.** *Slang.* **a.** Proper; correct. **b.** Genuine; legitimate. —**keep kosher.** To obey the Jewish dietary laws.
~*n.* Food prepared and served in accordance with the Jewish dietary laws.
~*tr.v.* **koshered, -shering, -shers.** To make kosher. [Yiddish, from Hebrew *kāshēr,* proper.]

Kos·suth (kŏs′ōōth′), **Lajos** (1802–94). Hungarian revolutionary leader. He aimed for Hungarian independence from Austria, declaring the Hapsburg dynasty invalid. He was appointed provisional governor of the 1849 Hungarian Republic, but after Russian intervention, he fled to Turkey.

Ko·sy·gin (kə-sē′gĭn), **Alexei Nikolayevich** (1904–80). Soviet premier (1964–80). He was deputy chairman of the Council of Ministers (1940–53), but he lost his position after Stalin's death (1953). He became premier on the fall of Khrushchev.

ko·to (kō′tō) *n., pl.* **-tos.** A Japanese musical instrument that has 13 strings stretched over an oblong box. [Japanese.]

koumis, koumiss. Variants of **kumiss.**

Kous·se·vits·ky (kŏŏ′sə-vĭt′skē), **Sergei** (1874–1951). Russian-born U.S. conductor. He left Russia in 1920 and eventually settled in the United States. He set up the Koussevitsky Music Foundation (1942) to encourage new composers.

Ko·vacs (kō′văks′), **Ernie** (1919–62). U.S. comedian. A zany and popular performer, he brought his unique brand of comedy to a series of live television shows (1950–57), a format that favored his inventive visual gags. He also played a few dramatic roles and published a novel, *Zoomar* (1957).

ko·whai (kō′wī′) *n.* A New Zealand tree, *Sophora tetraptera,* with sweet-smelling golden flowers. [Maori.]

Kowloon. See **Jiulong.**

kow·tow (kou-tou′, kou′tou′) *n.* **1.** A Chinese salutation in which the forehead is touched to the ground as an expression of respect, worship, or submission. **2.** An obsequious act.
~*intr.v.* **kowtowed, -towing, -tows. 1.** To perform a kowtow. **2.** To show servile deference; fawn: *Even the conductor kowtowed to the board of directors.* [Mandarin Chinese *ké tóu* : *ké,* to knock, bump + *tóu,* head.]

Kozhikode. See **Calicut.**

KP 1. *Chess.* king's pawn. **2.** kitchen police.

Kr The symbol for the element krypton.

KR *Chess.* king's rook.

kr. 1. krona. **2.** krone.

kraal, craal (krôl, kräl) *n.* **1.** A village of rural black people in southern Africa, typically consisting of huts surrounded by a stockade. **2.** An enclosure for livestock in southern Africa.
~*tr.v.* **kraaled, kraaling, kraals.** To put or keep (livestock) in a kraal. [Afrikaans, "enclosure for cattle," from Portuguese *curral,* possibly of Hottentot origin. See also **corral.**]

Krafft-E·bing (kräft′ĕb′ĭng, kräft′-), **Baron Richard von** (1840–1902). German neurologist and psychiatrist. He studied paranoia, epilepsy, and sexual deviance. He is best known today for his work *Psychopathia Sexualis* (1886).

kraft (kräft, kräft) *n.* A tough wrapping paper made from sulfate wood pulp. [German *Kraft,* force, strength, from Old High German, from Germanic *kraftaz* (unattested). See also **craft.**]

krait (krīt) *n.* Any of several brightly colored venomous snakes of the genus *Bungarus,* of southeastern Asia. [Hindi *karait†.*]

Kra·ka·to·a (krăk′ə-tō′ə). Also **Kra·ka·tau** (-tou′). Small volcanic island, in the Strait of Sunda west of Java and east of Sumatra. It was blown apart (1883) by one of the largest volcanic eruptions ever recorded, causing a tsunami that killed more than 36,000 people.

kra·ken (krä′kən) *n.* A legendary sea monster said to dwell in Norwegian waters. [Dialectal Norwegian : *krake†*, kraken + *-n*, suffix used as the definite article.]

Kra·ców or **Cra·cow** (krä′kou′, kräk′ou′). City and river port in southern Poland, on the Vistula River. Founded in the 8th century, it was the national capital from 1305 to 1595 and remains an important cultural center. Its university (1364) is one of the oldest in Europe. Kraków produces metals, machinery, chemicals, clothing, and rolling stock.

Kra·mer (krä′mər), **Stanley E.** (1913–). U.S. filmmaker. He has produced and directed dramatic films that deal with emotionally charged social conflicts, such as racism, the threat of nuclear war, and religious prejudice. Among his important works are *The Defiant Ones* (1958), *On the Beach* (1959), and *Inherit the Wind* (1960).

kra·me·ri·a (krə-mîr′ē-ə) *n.* A dried root, the **rhatany** *(see)*. [New Latin (Linnaeus), after J.G.H. *Kramer*, 18th-century Austrian botanist.]

krans (kräns, kränz) *n. South African.* An overhanging, sheer wall of rock; a precipice. [Afrikaans.]

K ration *n.* A U.S. Army emergency field ration used in World War II and consisting of a single packaged meal.

kraton. Variant of **craton.**

kraut (krout) *n.* Sauerkraut.

Krebs (krĕbz), **Sir Hans Adolf** (1900–81). British biochemist, born in Germany. He discovered the Krebs cycle. He shared the Nobel Prize for medicine (1953) with Fritz Lipmann (1899–).

Krebs cycle (krĕbz) *n.* A series of enzymatic reactions that constitute the second stage of respiration in aerobic organisms, involving the breakdown of acetyl units, especially during respiration, to provide the main source of energy for cells in the form of ATP. Also called "citric acid cycle," "tricarboxylic acid cycle." [After Hans KREBS.]

Krem·lin (krĕm′lĭn) *n.* **1. a.** The citadel of an ancient Russian town or city. **b.** The citadel of Moscow, housing the offices of the Soviet government. **2.** The Soviet government. [French, from Russian *kreml'*, citadel, of Tatar origin.]

Krem·lin·ol·o·gy (krĕm′lə-nŏl′ə-jē) *n.* The study and analysis of the politics of the Soviet government. **—Krem·lin·ol·o·gist** *n.*

kreu·zer (kroit′sər) *n.* Any of several small coins of low value formerly used in Austria and Germany. [German *Kreuzer*, from Middle High German *kriuzer*, from *kriuze*, a cross (the coins were originally stamped with a cross), from Old High German *krūzi*, from Latin *crux*, CROSS.]

Kriem·hild (krēm′hĭld′, -hĭlt′). Also **Kriem·hil·de** (krēm-hĭl′də). In the Nibelungenlied, the wife of Siegfried and avenger of his murder.

krill (krĭl) *pl.n.* Small marine crustaceans of the order Euphausiacea, constituting the principal food of whalebone whales. [Norwegian *kril†*, young of fish.]

krim·mer (krĭm′ər) *n.* A gray, curly fur made from the pelts of lambs of the Crimean region. [German *Krimmer*, from *Krim*, the Crimean peninsula.]

Kri·o (krē′ō) *n., pl.* **-os. 1.** A creolized language based on English and spoken in Sierra Leone. **2.** A native speaker of Krio. [Alteration of CREOLE.]

kris, creese (krēs) *n.* A sword of Malayan origin having a wavy double-edged blade. [Malay *kěris.*]

Krish·na (krĭsh′nə). *Hinduism.* The eighth and principal avatar of the deity Vishnu, often depicted as a handsome young man playing a flute. [Hindi, "the black one," from Sanskrit *kṛṣṇáh*, black, dark blue, dark.] **—Krish·na·ism** *n.*

Kris·tian·sand (krĭs′chən-sănd′). Seaport of southern Norway. On the Skagerrak, it has shipbuilding, fishery, and timber industries.

Kríti. See **Crete.**

kro·na¹ (krō′nə) *n., pl.* **-nor** (-nôr′, -nər). *Abbr.* **k., K., kr. 1.** The basic monetary unit of Sweden, equal to 100 öre. See feature at **currency. 2.** A coin worth one krona. [Swedish, "crown," from Old Swedish *krūna, krōna*, from Latin *corōna*, wreath, CROWN.]

krona² *n., pl.* **-nur** (-nər). *Abbr.* **k., K., kr. 1.** The basic monetary unit of Iceland, equal to 100 aurar. See feature at **currency. 2.** A coin worth one króna. [Icelandic *króna*, from Old Norse *krūna*, crown, from Middle Low German *krōne*, from Latin *corōna*, CROWN.]

kro·ne (krō′nə) *n., pl.* **-ner** ((-nər).) *Abbr.* **k., K., kr. 1.** The basic monetary unit of Denmark and Norway, equal to 100 øre. See feature at **currency. 2.** A coin worth one krone. [Danish *krone* and Norwegian *krune*, "crown," from Old Norse *krūna*, from Latin *corōna*, CROWN.]

Kronos. Variant of **Cronos.**

Kron·shtadt (krŏn′shtät). *German* **Kron·stadt** (krŏn′stät′). Seaport and naval base of the U.S.S.R. on the island of Kotlin in the Gulf of Finland. Its importance declined in the 19th century after the construction of a deep-water canal to St. Petersburg.

Kro·pot·kin (krə-pŏt′kĭn), **Prince Pyotr Alexeyevich** (1842–1921). Russian anarchist revolutionary. He joined the anarchist movement in 1872 and was imprisoned in Russia (1874–76), but escaped. He settled in England in 1886.

KRP *Chess.* king's rook's pawn.

Kru (kroō) *n., pl.* **Krus** or collectively **Kru. 1.** A member of a Negro people living mainly on the coast of Liberia. **2.** The language of these people.

Kru·ger (kroō′gər), **(Stephanus Johannes) Paulus**, known as "Oom Paul" (1825–1904). Afrikaner leader of South Africa. His nationalist policies as president of the Transvaal Republic from 1883 led to the second Boer War (1899–1902). He fled the advancing British in 1900 and died in exile in Switzerland.

Kruger National Park. A wildlife preserve in northeast South Africa. Extending along the Mozambique border of the Transvaal, it occupies an area of 21,000 square kilometers (8,106 square miles). It originated as the Sabi Game Reserve, established by President Kruger in 1898 and opened to the public in 1928.

kru·ger·rand (kroō′gər-rănd′, -ränd′) *n.* A coin containing one troy ounce of pure gold, minted in South Africa but widely used by investors or speculators in gold. [Afrikaans, after S.J.P. KRUGER, whose portrait appears on the obverse + *rand*, rand.]

krummhorn. Variant of **crumhorn.**

Krung Thep (kroōng tĕp). *English* **Bang·kok** (băng′kŏk′). Capital and chief port of Thailand, on the Chao Phraya near the Gulf of Thailand. It is the country's main cultural, commercial, and industrial center and one of the leading cities of Southeast Asia, with an international jewelry market. Within the city are the royal palace and more than 400 Buddhist temples.

Kru·pa (kroō′pə), **Gene** (1909–73). U.S. musician. A renowned jazz drummer, he became famous with Benny Goodman's band (1935–38) for his virtuoso swing technique, flamboyant playing style, and flair for exciting solo work. He formed his own band in 1938 but continued to play with Goodman and others.

Krupp (krŭp). German family of arms manufacturers, whose factories in Essen were founded in the early 19th century and are still in production.

kryp·ton (krĭp′tŏn′) *n. Symbol* **Kr** A whitish, inert gaseous element used chiefly in gas-discharge lamps, fluorescent lamps, and electronic flash tubes. Atomic number 36, atomic weight 83.80, melting point -156.6°C, boiling point -152.30°C, density 3.73 kg per m³ (0°C). [New Latin, "hidden (element)," from Greek *krupton*, neuter of *kruptos*, hidden, from *kruptein*, to hide.]

KS Kansas (used with a Zip Code).

Ksha·tri·ya (kə-shăt′rē-ə, -chăt′rē-ə) *n.* **1.** A Hindu caste that includes the professional, governing, and military occupations. **2.** A member of the Kshatriya caste. See **caste.** [Sanskrit *kṣatriya*, "ruling, ruler," from *kṣatra*, rule, dominion, from *kṣayati*, he possesses, he rules.]

Kt knight.

kt. 1. karat. **2.** *Nautical.* knot.

K.T. Knight Templar.

Kua·la Lum·pur (kwä′lə loōm′poōr′). The capital of Malaysia, on the Kelang River. It is the commercial center of a tin-mining and rubber-growing area.

Kuang-chou. See **Guangzhou.**

Kuang-tung. See **Guangdong.**

Ku·blai Khan (koō′blī kän′) (1215–94). First Mongol emperor of China. He was a grandson of Gengis Khan and became khan in 1259. He founded the Yuan dynasty (1279) and made Buddhism the state religion. Marco Polo spent 17 years at Kublai Khan's court.

Ku·brick (koō′brĭk, kyoō′-), **Stanley** (1928–). U.S. film director. His films include *Lolita* (1962), *Dr. Strangelove* (1963), *2001: A Space Odyssey* (1969), *A Clockwork Orange* (1971), and *The Shining* (1980).

ku·chen (koō′kən, -кнən) *n.* A yeast-raised coffee cake originally from Germany that contains fruits and nuts and is usually sprinkled with sugar and spices. [German *Kuchen*, from Middle High German *kuoche*, cake, from Old High German *kuocho.*]

ku·dos (kyoō′dŏs′, -dŏs′, koō′-) *n., pl.* **kudos.** Acclaim or prestige as a result of achievement or position: *The prize gave him little material benefit but did bring kudos.* [Originally British university slang, from Greek *kudos*, glory, fame.]

Usage: Kudos is one of those words, like *congeries,* that look like plurals but are etymologically singular, and so it is correctly used with a singular verb: *Kudos is due her.*

ku·du, koo·doo (koō′doō) *n.* Either of two African antelopes, *Tragelaphus strepsiceros* or *T. imberbis*, having a brownish coat with narrow white vertical stripes and long, spirally curved horns in the male. [Afrikaans *koedoe*, from Xhosa *iqudu.*]

kud·zu (koōd′zoō) *n.* A vine, *Pueraria lobata*, native to Japan, that has compound leaves and clusters of reddish-purple flowers and is grown for fodder and forage. [Japanese *kuzu.*]

Ku·fic, Cu·fic (koō′fĭk, kyoō′-) *adj.* Designating or pertaining to an early form of the Arabic alphabet used for making fine copies of the Koran. [Arabic *Al Kufah*, town in south-central Iraq, where such copies of the Koran were made.] **—Ku·fic** *n.*

Ku Klux Klan (koō′ klŭks′ klän′, kyoō′-) *n. Abbr.* **K.K.K. 1.** A secret society organized in the South after the Civil War to reassert white supremacy by terroristic methods. **2.** A secret fraternal organization founded in Georgia in 1915 and dedicated to maintaining legal and de facto segregation of blacks. [Said to be Greek *kuklos*, circle, CYCLE + *klan*, from CLAN.] **—Ku Klux·er** (koō klŭk′sər, kyoō) *n.* **—Ku Klux·ism** *n.*

kuk·ri (koōk′rē) *n.* A large knife with a blade broadening to the point, used especially by the Gurkhas. [Hindi.]

ku·lak (koō-lăk′, -läk′, kyoō-, koō′läk′, -läk′, kyoō′-) *n.* **1.** In Czarist Russia and during the October Revolution, a rich peasant or village usurer notorious as an exploiter. **2.** One of a class of Russian peasants after the revolution who opposed the collectivization of farms and later had their property confiscated or were themselves liquidated. [Russian, "fist," "tight-fisted person," from Turkic, akin to Turkish *kol*, arm.]

Krishna *The eighth and most important incarnation (avatar) of Vishnu, one of the principal gods of Hinduism. Krishna is a slayer of demons, a flute player, and a lover. This illustration, showing the blue-skinned god with his favorite mistress, Radha, dates from 1647.*

kudu *One of the largest antelopes, the kudu stands 1.3 meters (4½ feet) tall at the shoulder. It lives mainly in the savannah of southern and eastern Africa in small herds.*

Külek Bŏgazi. See **Cilician Gates.**

Kul·tur (kŏŏl-tŏŏr′) n. Culture; especially, the authoritarian and chauvinistic aspects of German culture and civilization as idealized by the exponents of German imperialism during the period 1900–45. [German, from Latin *cultūra,* CULTURE.]

Kul·tur·kampf (kŏŏl-tŏŏr′kämpf′) n. **1.** The struggle (1872–87) between the Roman Catholic Church and the German government for control over civil marriage and school and church appointments. **2.** Any conflict between secular and religious authorities. [German, "culture struggle."]

Kum. See **Qom.**

Ku·mas·i (kŏŏ-mä′sē). Formerly **Coo·mas·sie.** The second-largest city of Ghana. Capital of the Ashanti region west of Lake Volta, it is the country's major center for cocoa production and an important transport junction. The Golden Stool, the historical symbol of the Ashanti nation, is kept here.

ku·miss, kou·mis, kou·miss (kŏŏ-mĭs′, kŏŏ′mĭs) n. The fermented milk of a mare or camel, drunk by certain peoples of western and central Asia. [Russian *kumys,* from Kazan Tatar *kumyz.*]

küm·mel (kĭm′əl, kü′məl) n. A colorless liqueur flavored with caraway seeds or cumin. [German *Kümmel,* "cumin seed," from Old High German *kumil, kumīn,* from Latin *cumīnum,* CUMIN.]

kum·quat, cum·quat (kŭm′kwŏt′) n. **1.** Any of several trees or shrubs of the genus *Fortunella,* native to China, having small, edible, orangelike fruit. **2.** The citrus fruit of the kumquat, with an acid pulp and a thin, edible rind often used in preserves. [Cantonese *kam kwat, gam gwat,* corresponding to Mandarin Chinese *jīn jú,* "golden orange."]

Kun (kŏŏn), **Béla** (1885–c. 1939). Hungarian Communist leader. He formed the Hungarian Communist Party and became president of a coalition (1919), promising his allies Soviet support for war against Romania, but no support came. Kun fled to Vienna and then to the U.S.S.R., where he was executed in one of Stalin's purges.

Kunene. See **Cunene.**

kung fu (kŭng fŏŏ′, kŏŏng) n. A martial art originating in China and resembling karate. [From Chinese *gōng fu,* skill.]

Kun·ming, K'un·ming (kŏŏn′mĭng′). Ancient walled city of southwest China. It is the capital of Yunnan province and the seat of Yunnan University.

kunz·ite (kŏŏnt′sīt′) n. A transparent lilac-colored variety of spodumene, used as a gemstone. [After George F. *Kunz* (1856–1932), gem expert.]

Kuo·yü, Guo·yü (gwô′yü′, kŏŏ′yŏŏ′) n. **Mandarin Chinese** (see). [Mandarin Chinese *gúoyŭ* : *gúo,* nation, national + *yŭh,* language.]

Kurd (kûrd, kŏŏrd) n. A member of a formerly nomadic Muslim people living chiefly in Kurdistan.

Kurd·ish (kûr′dĭsh, kŏŏr′-) adj. Of or pertaining to the Kurds, their culture, or their language.
~n. The northwestern Iranian language of the Kurds.

Kurd·i·stan (kûr′dĭ-stän′). Area of western Asia. Lying west and southwest of the Caspian Sea, it was split among southeast Turkey, north Syria, north Iraq, northwest Iran, and south U.S.S.R. with the dissolution of the Ottoman Empire (1918). Its inhabitants, the Kurds, have been fighting in all these countries for the establishment of an independent state.

Ku·ro·sa·wa (kŏŏr′ō-sä′wə), **Akira** (1910–). Japanese film director. His *Rashomon* won the 1951 Venice Film Festival Grand Prize and gave Japanese films international status. His work deals with traditional Japanese institutions, as in *The Seven Samurai* (1954) and *Kagemusha* (1980).

Kuroshio. See **Japan Current.**

kur·ra·jong (kûr′ə-jŏng′, -jông′) n. **1.** An Australian tree, *Brachychiton populneum,* having evergreen leaves and yellowish or reddish flowers. **2.** Any of several other Australian trees, such as the green kurrajong, *Hibiscus heterophyllus,* that have edible leaves and shoots. [Native Australian name.]

Kursk (kŏŏrsk). Industrial city in the U.S.S.R. In 1943 Soviet forces routed a German army here in the world's largest tank battle.

kurta. Variant of **khurta.**

kur·to·sis (kər-tō′sĭs) n. *Statistics.* A deviation from the normal distribution curve in which the curve remains symmetrical but is either too sharp at the peak values (*positive kurtosis*) or too flat at the peak values (*negative kurtosis*). [Greek *kurtōsis,* convexity, curvature, from *kurtos,* convex.]

ku·ru (kŏŏr′ōō) n. A fatal neurological disease caused by a virus, occurring in New Guinea and characterized by tremors affecting the whole body. [New Guinea native name.]

ku·rus (kə-rŏŏsh′) n., pl. **kurus.** A monetary unit, the Turkish piaster, equal to 1/100 of the lira (or pound) of Turkey. See feature at **currency.** [Turkish.]

Kush. See **Cush.**

Kushitic. Variant of **Cushitic.**

Ku·wait (kŏŏ-wāt′). Sheikhdom of western Asia. On the east coast of the Arabian Peninsula, it was settled in 1756 and was a British protectorate from 1899 to 1961. Oil was discovered in 1938 and Kuwait is now one of the world's major oil-producing countries, with oil accounting for 80 percent of its exports. Its per capita income is one of the highest in the world. Area, 17,818 square kilometers (6,878 square miles). Population, 1,400,000. Capital, Kuwait. See map at **Gulf States.** **—Ku·wai·ti** n. & adj.

Kuy·by·shev (kwē′bə-shĕf′, -shĕv′). Formerly (before 1935) **Sa·ma·**

ra (sə-mär′ə). Industrial city and river port on the Volga, in the U.S.S.R. It was the capital of the U.S.S.R. (1941–42) while Moscow was under German attack.

Kuz·bas (kŏŏz-bäs′). Also **Kuz·netsk Basin** (kŏŏz-nyĕtsk′). Major industrial area of the U.S.S.R., in western Siberia.

kV kilovolt.

kvass, kvas (kə-väs′) n. A fermented Russian beverage similar to beer, made from rye or barley. [Russian *kvas.*]

kvetch (kə-vĕch′) intr.v. **kvetched, kvetching, kvetches.** *Slang.* To complain or find fault in a persistent, querulous manner.
~n. *Slang.* A chronic and annoying complainer. [Yiddish, from German *quetschen,* to crush, squeeze, from Middle High German *quetzen.*]

kW kilowatt.

Kwa (kwä) n. A branch of the Niger-Congo language family that includes Ibo, Yoruba, and other languages of West Africa. **—Kwa** adj.

kwa·cha (kwä′chə) n. **1.** The basic monetary unit of Zambia, equal to 100 ngwee. **2.** The basic monetary unit of Malawi, equal to 100 tambala. See feature at **currency.** [Native word in Zambia.]

Kwangchow. See **Guangzhou.**

Kwangtung. See **Guangdong.**

kwan·za (kwän′zə) n., pl. **kwanza** or **-zas.** The basic monetary unit of Angola, equal to, 100 lweis. See feature at **currency.** [Swahili.]

kwa·shi·or·kor (kwä′shē-ôr′kôr′) n. Severe malnutrition caused by protein deficiency, occurring especially in African children, and characterized by anemia, edema, potbelly, depigmentation of the skin, and loss of hair or change in hair color. [Native word in Ghana.]

kWh kilowatt-hour.

KWIC (kwĭk) n. An index, usually generated by computer, in which key words are extracted together with the context in which the words appear. [*k*eyword *i*n *c*ontext.]

KY Kentucky (used with a Zip Code).

Ky. Kentucky.

ky·ack (kī′ăk′) n. A packsack that hangs on either side of a packsaddle. [Origin unknown.]

ky·a·nite (kī′ə-nīt′) n. Also **cy·a·nite** (sī′-). A bluish, greenish, or colorless mineral, essentially Al_2SiO_5, used as a refractory. [German *Zyanit* : *zyan(o)-,* CYANO- + -ITE.]

ky·a·nize (kī′ə-nīz′) tr.v. **-nized, -nizing, -nizes.** To treat (wood) with mercuric chloride in order to preserve it. **—ky·a·ni·za·tion** n.

kyat (chät) n. **1.** The basic monetary unit of Burma, equal to 100 pyas. See feature at **currency.** **2.** A coin worth one kyat. [Burmese.]

kyle (kīl) n. In Scotland, a narrow strait, as between two islands. [Gaelic *caol,* narrow.]

ky·lin (kē′lĭn) n. A mythical animal used as a decoration on Chinese and Japanese pottery. [Mandarin Chinese *qílín* : *qí,* male + *lín,* female.]

ky·lix (kī′lĭks, kĭl′ĭks) n., pl. **kylikes** (kī′lĭ-kēz′, kĭl′ĭ-). Also **cy·lix** (sī′-līks, sĭl′ĭks), pl. **cylices** (sī′lĭ-sēz′, sĭl′ĭ-). A shallow, typically tall-stemmed drinking cup with two handles, used in ancient Greece. [Greek *kulix,* cup.]

ky·loe (kī′lō) n. Any of a breed of long-horned, long-haired beef cattle from northwest Scotland. [19th century : origin obscure.]

ky·mo·graph (kī′mə-grăf′, -gräf′) n. An instrument for recording variations in pressure, especially in blood pressure. [*Kymo-,* variant of *cymo-,* from CYME + -GRAPH.]

Kymric. Variant of **Cymric.**

Kymry. Variant of **Cymry.**

Kyo·to (kē-ō′tō, kyō′-). City in south-central Honshu, Japan. On the Kamo River, it is the capital of Kyoto prefecture and was Japan's capital from A.D. 794 until 1868, though its importance declined after the eclipse of the emperors by the shoguns (1192). It is the center of Buddhism in Japan and has many historic buildings. Noted for craft industries, including brocades, porcelain, and lacquerware, it also manufactures chemicals, textiles, and machinery.

ky·pho·sco·li·o·sis (kī′fō-skō′lē-ō′sĭs) n. Abnormal curvature of the spine both forward and sideways. [New Latin, from *kypho-,* from *kyphosis* + *scoliosis.*]

ky·pho·sis (kī-fō′sĭs) n. Abnormal rearward curvature of the spine, caused by bone disease, bad posture, or congenital deformity. Also called "humpback," "hunchback." [Greek *kuphōsis,* from *kuphos,* bent, hunchbacked.] **—ky·phot·ic** (kī-fŏt′ĭk) adj.

Kypros. See **Cyprus.**

Kyr·i·e e·le·i·son (kîr′ē-ā′ ĭ-lā′ə-sŏn′, -sən) n. A liturgical prayer in some Christian churches beginning with or composed of the words "Lord, have mercy." [Late Latin, from Greek *Kurie eleēson,* "Lord, have mercy" : *Kurie,* vocative of *kurios,* lord, master, "powerful (one)," from *kuros,* power, supreme authority + *eleēson,* aorist imperative of *elein,* to show mercy, from *eleos,* pity, mercy (see **alms**.)]

Kyu·shu (kyōō′shōō). One of the four main islands of Japan. The most southerly, the third largest, and most densely populated of Japan's islands, it lies to the east of the Korea Strait and is joined to Honshu, across the Shimonoseki Strait, by a road and rail bridge. Much of the island is mountainous, forcing a concentration of agriculture around the Chikugo River in the northwest. Its industries have developed around important coal fields in the north.

Ky·zyl Kum (kə-zĭl′ kŏŏm′). Desert in the U.S.S.R., lying across the Kazakhstan-Uzbekistan border. It is the country's major atomic-testing ground.

l, L (ĕl) *n., pl.* **l's** or **L's. 1.** The 12th letter of the modern English alphabet. See feature at **alphabet. 2.** Any of the speech sounds represented by this letter. **3.** Anything shaped like the letter L. **4.** The Roman numeral for 50. **5.** The 12th in a series; 11th when *J* is omitted.

l, L, l., L. *Note:* As an abbreviation or symbol, *l* may be a small or a capital letter, with or without a period. Established forms or those generally preferred precede the definition. When no form is given, all four forms are in general use in that sense. **1. l., L.** lake. **2. L** lambert. **3. L** large. **4. L.** Latin. **5. l.** left. **6. l.** length. **7. L.** lodge (society). **8. L.** licentiate (in titles). **9. l., L.** line. **10. L.** Linnaean. **11. l.** lira. **12. l** liter. **13. L** *Electricity.* inductor. **14. L** *Physics.* latent heat.

l– *prefix. Chemistry.* Indicates a levorotatory compound. Usually written in italics: for example, "*l*-glucose." Compare **d–.**

L– *prefix. Chemistry.* Indicating an optically active compound with a molecular structure derived from or related to the structure of levorotatory glyceraldehyde: for example "L-alanine." Compare **D–.** An isomer designated L– may itself be levorotatory (*l*-) but is not necessarily so.

la¹ (lä) *n.* **1.** The syllable used to represent the sixth tone of the diatonic scale. **2.** The tone A.

la² *interj. Archaic.* Used to express emphasis or to indicate surprise. [Perhaps variant of LO.]

La¹ The symbol for the element lanthanum.

La² (lä) *n.* **1.** A respectful title prefixed to the surname of an eminent female artiste: *La Sutherland.* **2.** A title facetiously prefixed to the surname of a woman who is regarded as formidable, temperamental, or troublesome. [Feminine definite article of Romance languages.]

LA Louisiana (used with a Zip Code).

La. Louisiana.

L.A. 1. Legislative Assembly. **2.** Library Association. **3.** local agent. **4.** Los Angeles.

laa·ger, la·ger (lä′gər) *n. Chiefly South African.* **1.** A defensive encampment encircled by wagons or armored vehicles. **2.** A narrow and protective social or intellectual environment.
~v. laagered, -gering, -gers. —*tr.* To form into a laager. —*intr.* To camp in a laager. [Afrikaans *lager,* from Dutch *leger,* camp, LAIR.]

laager mentality *n.* An attitude or policy of isolationism and inflexible opposition to change, especially as thought by its opponents to characterize the ruling Afrikaners of South Africa.

lab (lăb) *n. Informal.* A **laboratory** (see).

lab. laboratory.

Lab. 1. Labor. **2.** Labrador.

lab·a·rum (lăb′ər-əm) *n., pl.* **-ara** (-ər-ə). **1.** The banner adopted by Constantine the Great after his conversion to Christianity, combining the Roman military standard and Christian symbols. **2.** Any banner, especially an ecclesiastical one. [Late Latin *labarum*†.]

lab·da·num (lăb′də-nəm) *n.* Also **lad·a·num** (lăd′n-əm). A resinous exudation of certain Old World plants of the genus *Cistus,* yielding a fragrant essential oil used in flavorings and perfumes. [Medieval Latin, from Latin *lādanum,* from Greek *ladanon, lēdanon,* from *lēdon,* shrub from which labdanum exudes, from Semitic.]

Labe. See **Elbe.**

la·bel (lā′bəl) *n.* **1.** Anything functioning as a means of identification; especially: **a.** A piece of paper, card, or the like attached to an article such as a parcel or suitcase to designate its origin, owner, and destination. **b.** A piece of paper or similar material attached to a container such as a bottle or packet, providing printed or written information about the contents. **2.** A term serving to describe or categorize; an epithet. **3.** The brand or trademark of a particular company, especially of a record company. **4.** A molding over a door or window; a dripstone. **5.** The heraldic device distinguishing an eldest son, consisting of a horizontal band across the upper part of the shield with a set of usually three downward projections. **6.** *Chemistry.* A radioactive element in a compound, used to trace the pathway of the compound through a system.
~tr.v. labeled or **labelled, -beling** or **-belling, -bels. 1.** To attach a label to. **2.** To describe, classify, or designate. **3.** To make an atom in (a molecule or compound) radioactive so that the pathway of the molecule or compound can be traced through a system. [Middle English, label, narrow strip, from Old French, ribbon, strip, from Germanic.] —**la·bel·er, la·bel·ler** *n.*

la·bel·lum (lə-bĕl′əm) *n., pl.* **-bella** (-bĕl′ə). **1.** The often enlarged lip of an orchid. **2.** The lobe at the top of a fly's proboscis. [New Latin, from Latin, "small lip," diminutive of *labrum,* lip.]

la·bi·al (lā′bē-əl) *adj.* **1.** Of or pertaining to the lips or labia. **2.** Resembling or serving as a lip. **3.** *Music.* Producing tones by the impact of a stream of air upon the edge of a lip, as in a flute or the flue pipes of an organ. **4.** *Phonetics.* Formed mainly by closing or partly closing the lips.
~n. A labial sound, such as (b), (m), (v), (w), or a rounded vowel. [Medieval Latin *labiālis,* from Latin *labium,* lip.] —**la·bi·al·ly** *adv.*

la·bi·al·ize (lā′bē-ə-līz′) *tr.v.* **-ized, -izing, -izes.** *Phonetics.* To round (a vowel); make labial. —**la·bi·al·ism, la·bi·al·i·za·tion** *n.*

la·bi·a ma·jo·ra (lā′bē-ə mə-jôr′ə, -jōr′ə) *pl.n.* Two rounded folds of tissue that form the external lateral boundaries of the vulva. [New Latin, "greater lips."]

labia mi·no·ra (lā′bē-ə mə-nôr′ə, -nōr′ə) *pl.n.* Two narrow folds of tissue enclosed within the cleft of the labia majora. Also called "nympha." [New Latin, "lesser lips."]

la·bi·ate (lā′bē-īt, -āt′) *adj.* **1.** Having lips or liplike parts. **2.** *Botany.* **a.** Having or designating flowers with the corolla divided into two liplike parts. **b.** Of or belonging to the family Labiatae, which includes the mints.
~n. A labiate plant. [New Latin *labiatus,* from Latin *labium,* lip.]

la·bile (lā′bīl, -bəl) *adj.* Constantly liable to undergo change or fluctuation; unstable. [Late Latin *lābilis,* from Latin *lābī,* to slide.] —**la·bil·i·ty** *n.*

labio– *prefix.* Indicates formed with the lips (and another organ); for example, **labiodental.** [Latin *labium,* lip.]

la·bi·o·den·tal (lā′bē-ō-dĕnt′l) *adj. Phonetics.* Articulated with the lip or lips and teeth.
~n. *Phonetics.* A labiodental sound, such as (f) or (v).

la·bi·o·na·sal (lā′bē-ō-nā′zəl) *adj. Phonetics.* Simultaneously labial and nasal.
~n. *Phonetics.* A labionasal sound.

la·bi·o·ve·lar (lā′bē-ō-vē′lər) *adj. Phonetics.* Simultaneously labial and velar.
~n. *Phonetics.* A labiovelar sound, such as (w).

la·bi·um (lā′bē-əm) *n., pl.* **-bia** (-bē-ə). **1.** *Anatomy.* Any of four folds of tissue of the female external genitalia. See **labia majora, labia minora. 2.** *Zoology.* A liplike structure, such as the appendage forming the lower lip in insects. **3.** *Botany.* Any of the liplike divisions of a labiate corolla. [New Latin, from Latin, lip.]

la·bor (lā′bər) *n.* Also *chiefly British* **la·bour. 1.** Physical or mental exertion of a practical nature, as distinguished from exertion for the sake of pleasure or recreation; work. **2.** A specific task, especially one requiring physical effort. **3.** The contribution made by workers to the production of goods and provision of services in a community; work done for wages as distinguished from work done for profit. **4.** The class of people who make such a contribution; workers collectively, as distinguished from management and employers. **5. Labor.** A political party claiming to represent the interests of this class, especially in Great Britain. **6. a.** The physical effort involved in giving birth; parturition. **b.** An instance or period of such effort: *a long labor; a difficult labor.* —See Synonyms at **work.**
~v. labored, -boring, -bors. —*intr.* **1.** To expend great physical or mental effort; work; toil. **2.** To strive painstakingly or strenuously for a particular end. **3. a.** To proceed slowly; plod. **b.** To pitch and roll. Used of a ship. **4.** To be hampered. Used with *under: laboring under a misconception.* **5.** To undergo the pains of childbirth. —*tr.* **1.** To deal with in exhaustive detail; treat laboriously: *labor a point.* **2.** To cultivate; till. [Middle English, from Old French, from Latin *labor.*]

lab·o·ra·to·ry (lăb′rə-tôr′ē, -tōr′ē; *British* lə-bŏr′ə-tə-rē) *n., pl.* **-ries.**

938

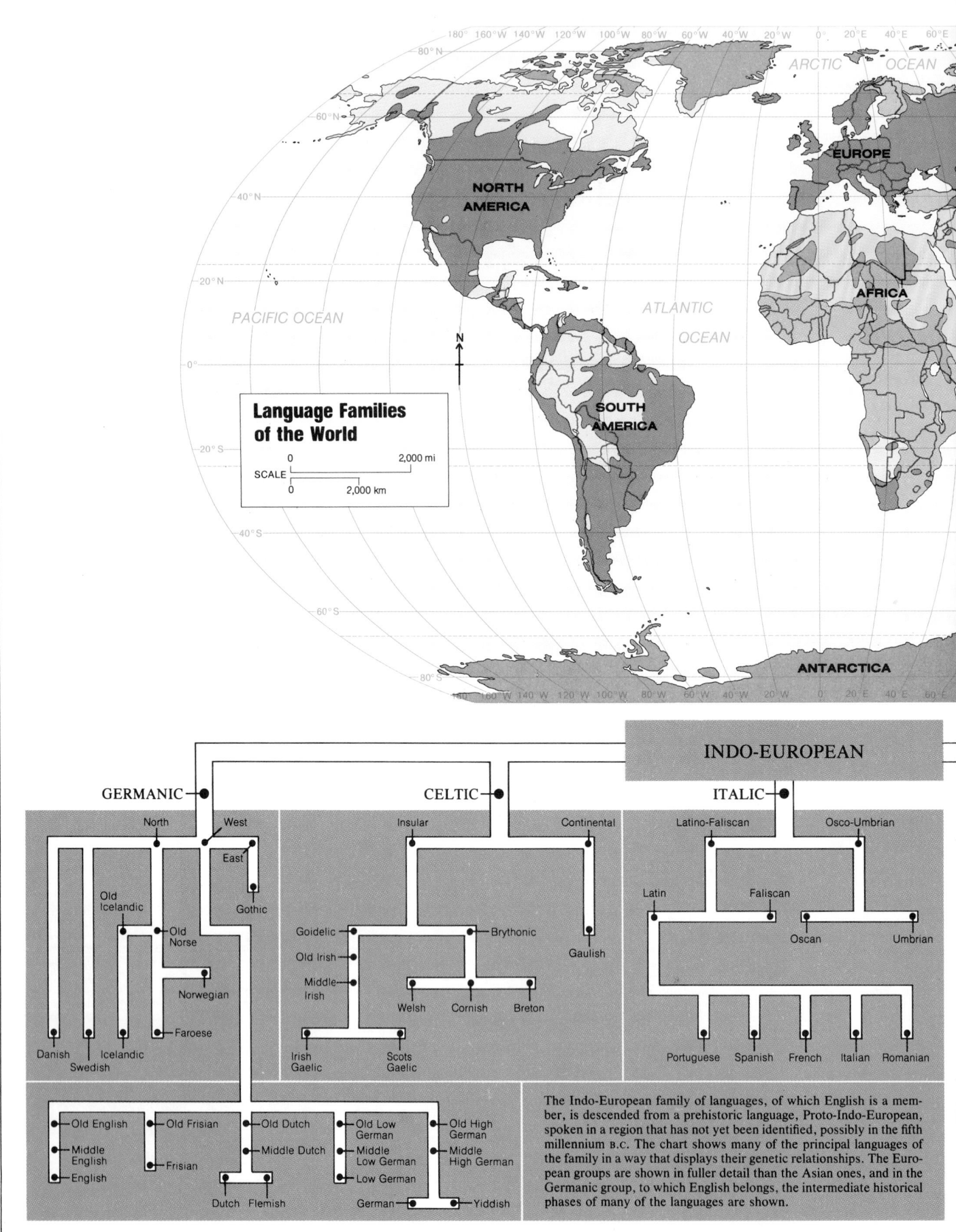

Language Families of the World

SCALE

0 — 2,000 mi
0 — 2,000 km

INDO-EUROPEAN

GERMANIC

North — West — East

Old Icelandic
Old Norse
Norwegian
Faroese
Danish — Swedish — Icelandic
Gothic

Old English — Old Frisian — Old Dutch — Old Low German — Old High German
Middle English — Frisian — Middle Dutch — Middle Low German — Middle High German
English — Low German
Dutch — Flemish — German — Yiddish

CELTIC

Insular — Continental

Goidelic — Brythonic
Old Irish
Middle Irish
Welsh — Cornish — Breton
Gaulish
Irish Gaelic — Scots Gaelic

ITALIC

Latino-Faliscan — Osco-Umbrian

Latin — Faliscan
Oscan — Umbrian
Portuguese — Spanish — French — Italian — Romanian

The Indo-European family of languages, of which English is a member, is descended from a prehistoric language, Proto-Indo-European, spoken in a region that has not yet been identified, possibly in the fifth millennium B.C. The chart shows many of the principal languages of the family in a way that displays their genetic relationships. The European groups are shown in fuller detail than the Asian ones, and in the Germanic group, to which English belongs, the intermediate historical phases of many of the languages are shown.

LANGUAGE FAMILIES OF THE WORLD

KEY

Indo-European: see chart below

Ural-Altaic: Finnish, Magyar, Turkish, Tungus, Manchu, Mongolian, the languages of the Samoyeds

Dravidian: Tamil, Telegu, Malayalam, Kannada

Sino-Tibetan: Chinese, Tibetan, Burmese

Mon-Khmer: Mon, Khmer, other languages of Southeast Asia

Japanese and Korean

Austronesian: Bahasa Indonesia, Javanese, Bahasa Malaysia, Tagalog, languages of Micronesia, Melanesia, Polynesia

Afro-Asiatic: a family of languages of southwestern Asia and northern Africa, including Hebrew and Arabic

Nilo-Saharan: a family of languages of northern and central Africa

Niger-Kordofanian: a family of languages of sub-Saharan Africa, including Swahili

All others

Uninhabited area

— International boundary

The map shows where the major language families of the world are found. Beside the family names in the key, some languages of each family are named or the area covered by the family is described. See also feature at **language.**

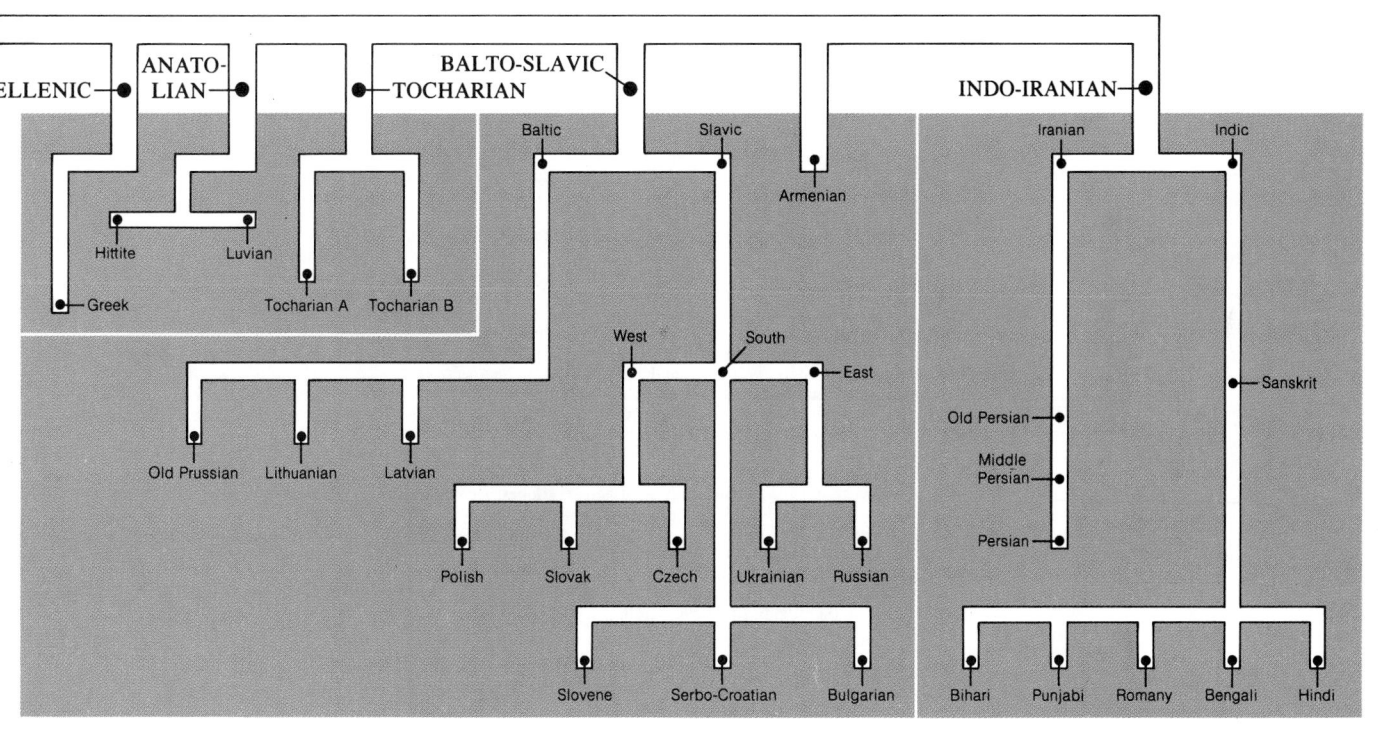

Labrador retriever *Fishermen introduced this North American breed into Europe in the early 19th century. Labradors, which usually have black- or fawn- colored fur, were once trained as retrievers and used to pick up shot game. Today they are often kept as pets or used as guide dogs for the blind.*

lace *Making lace by hand was an important European industry from the Renaissance to World War I. These examples of handmade English lace are from Devon—one of the few centers where the craft still survives despite competition from modern textile machinery.*

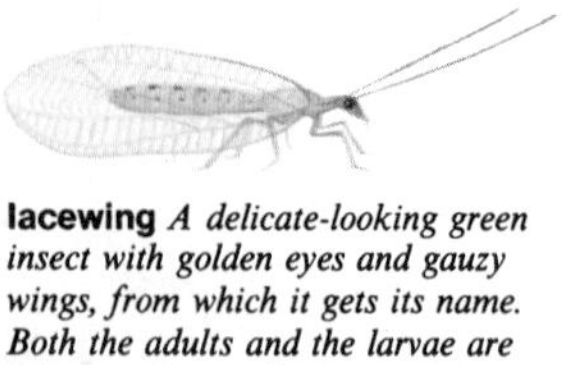

lacewing *A delicate-looking green insect with golden eyes and gauzy wings, from which it gets its name. Both the adults and the larvae are fierce predators, feeding mainly on aphids.*

Abbr. **lab. 1.** A room or building equipped for scientific experimentation, research, or testing. Also used adjectivally: *laboratory conditions; a laboratory assistant.* **2.** A place where drugs and chemicals are manufactured. **3.** Any place equipped for study, practice, or testing, such as a **language laboratory** *(see).* Also informally called "lab." [Medieval Latin *labōrātōrium,* workshop, from Latin *labōrātus,* past participle of *labōrāre,* to LABOR.]

labor camp *n.* **1.** A penal settlement where the prisoners undertake forced labor. **2.** A camp for migrant workers.

Labor Day *n.* The first Monday in September, a legal holiday observed in the United States and Canada in honor of the working class.

la·bored (lā′bərd) *adj.* **1.** Done or produced with labor or difficulty: *labored breathing.* **2.** Showing evidence of labor; lacking natural ease; overworked.

la·bor·er (lā′bər-ər) *n.* A person who performs physical work, especially of an unskilled nature.

la·bor-in·ten·sive (lā′bər-ĭn-tĕn′sĭv) *adj.* Requiring a high degree of human as opposed to mechanical work.

la·bo·ri·ous (lə-bôr′ē-əs, lə-bōr′-) *adj.* **1.** Requiring long, hard work. **2.** Hard-working; industrious. **3.** Not fluent or spontaneous; labored: *a laborious explanation.* [Middle English, from Old French *laborieus,* from Latin *labōriōsus,* from *labor,* LABOR.] **—la·bo·ri·ous·ly** *adv.* **—la·bo·ri·ous·ness** *n.*

la·bor·ite (lā′bə-rīt′) *n.* Also *chiefly British* **la·bour·ite. 1.** A member or supporter of a labor movement or union. **2. Laborite.** A member of a political party representing labor.

labor of love *n.* A task performed for the enjoyment it brings to oneself or another.

la·bor-sav·ing (lā′bər-sā′vĭng) *adj.* Designed to reduce or eliminate the labor required to carry out a task.

labor union *n.* An organization of wage earners formed for the purpose of serving their class interests with respect to wages and working conditions; a trade union.

labour. *Chiefly British.* Variant of **labor.**

Labour Party *n.* **1.** A British political party, formed in 1900 from the Independent Labour Party and various trade unions, cooperative societies, and other socialist bodies, and claiming to represent the interests of workers. **2.** Any of several similar parties in other countries, especially in the Commonwealth.

Lab·ra·dor[1] (lăb′rə-dôr′) *Abbr.* **Lab.** Peninsula of eastern Canada, divided between Quebec and Newfoundland provinces. A high plateau, with barren tundra in the north and coniferous forest in the south, it has large mineral, forest, and hydroelectric resources. **—Lab·ra·dor·i·an** *n. & adj.*

Labrador[2]**.** The mainland part of Newfoundland province, Canada.

Labrador Current. Also **Arctic Current.** A cold ocean current flowing southward from Baffin Bay along the coast of Labrador to unite with the Gulf Stream over the Grand Banks off southeastern Newfoundland.

lab·ra·dor·ite (lăb′rə-dôr′īt′, -dô-rīt′) *n.* A plagioclase feldspar, found in igneous rocks, and characterized by brilliant colors in some specimens. [After LABRADOR.]

Labrador retriever *n.* A dog of a breed originating in Newfoundland, having a short, dense, black or yellow-brown coat and a tapering tail.

la·bret (lā′brĕt) *n.* An ornament inserted in a perforation in the lip. [Latin *labrum,* lip + -ET.]

la·brum (lā′brəm) *n., pl.* **-bra** (-brə). A lip or liplike structure, such as the upper lip in insects. [New Latin, from Latin, lip.]

La Bru·yère (lä brōō-yâr′), **Jean de** (1645–96). French writer. His single work, *Caractères de Théophraste, Traduits du Grec, avec les Caractères et les Mœurs de ce Siècle* (1688–96), satirized society under Louis XIV.

la·bur·num (lə-bûr′nəm) *n.* Any of several poisonous trees or shrubs of the genus *Laburnum;* especially, *L. anagyroides,* cultivated for its drooping clusters of yellow flowers. Also called "golden chain." [Latin *laburnum,* perhaps from Etruscan.]

lab·y·rinth (lăb′ə-rĭnth′) *n.* **1. a.** An intricate structure of interconnecting passages; a maze **b. Labyrinth.** *Greek Mythology.* The maze in which the Minotaur was confined. **2.** Something highly intricate or tortuous in character, composition, or construction. **3.** *Anatomy.* **a.** A group of communicating anatomical cavities. **b.** The internal ear, comprising the semicircular canals, vestibule, and cochlea. **4.** *Electronics.* A loudspeaker housing containing a number of air chambers, used to reduce the production of standing waves and improve the quality of sound reproduction. [Learned respelling of Middle English *laborintus,* from Latin *labyrinthus,* from Greek *laburinthos,* probably akin to *labrus,* LABYRIS.]

labyrinth fish *n.* Any small freshwater fish of the family Anabantidae, of tropical Africa and Asia, having a lunglike breathing organ.

lab·y·rin·thi·an (lab′ə-rĭn′thē-ən) *adj.* Labyrinthine.

lab·y·rin·thine (lăb′ə-rĭn′thĭn, -thēn′) *adj.* **1.** Of, pertaining to, or constituting a labyrinth. **2.** Intricate; complicated.

lab·y·rinth·o·dont (lăb′ə-rĭn′thə-dŏnt′) *n.* Any primitive extinct amphibian of the subclass Labyrinthodontia, having hollow teeth convoluted in cross-section.
~*adj.* Of or pertaining to the Labyrinthodontia. [New Latin *Labyrinthodontia* : LABYRINTH + -ODONT.]

lab·y·ris (lăb′ə-rĭs) *n.* Also **lab·rys** (lăb′rĭs). **1.** In ancient Minoan civilization, a sacred double-headed ax. **2.** A similarly-shaped modern feminist symbol of strength, especially of lesbian solidarity. [Greek *labrus,* double-headed ax.]

lac[1] (lăk) *n.* A resinous secretion of the **lac insect** *(see),* used in making shellac. [Dutch *lak* or French *laque,* from Hindi *lākh,* from Prakrit *lakkha,* from Sanskrit *lākshā.*]

lac[2], **lakh** *n.* In India: **1.** The sum of 100,000: *12 lacs of rupees.* **2.** A very large number. [Hindi *lākh,* from Sanskrit *laksha.*]

La Camargue. See **Camargue, La.**

Laccadive, Minicoy, and Amindivi Islands. See **Lakshadweep.**

lac·co·lith (lăk′ə-lĭth′) *n.* A mushroom-shaped body of igneous rock intruded between layers of sedimentary rock. [Greek *lakkos,* cistern (referring to the shape) + -LITH.]

lace (lās) *n.* **1.** A delicate fabric woven of silk, cotton, nylon, or other thread in an open weblike pattern. **2.** A cord or ribbon threaded through eyelets or around hooks on two opposite edges, as of a shoe or garment, for drawing and tying them together. **3.** Gold or silver braid ornamenting an officer's uniform.
~*v.* **laced, lacing, laces.** *—tr.* **1.** To thread a cord through the eyelets or around the hooks of: *laced her shoes.* **2. a.** To draw together and tie the laces of. Used with *up.* **b.** To pinch in the waist of by tightening corset laces. **3.** To intertwine: *lace shoots of a plant through a trellis.* **4.** To apply lace to. **5.** To add spirits to (a drink). **6.** To streak with color. **7.** *Informal.* To give a beating to; thrash. *—intr.* To be fastened with a lace. **—lace into.** To attack; assail. [Middle English *lace, laas, las,* braid, cord, from Old French *laz, las,* from Vulgar Latin *lacium* (unattested), from Latin *laqueus,* noose, trap, probably related to *lacere,* to allure.] **—lac·er** *n.*

Lacedaemon. See **Laconia.**

lac·er·ate (lăs′ə-rāt′) *tr.v.* **-ated, -ating, -ates. 1.** To tear (especially flesh) roughly or jaggedly. **2.** To distress deeply.
~*adj.* Also **lac·er·at·ed** (-rā′tĭd). **1.** Torn; mangled. **2.** Deeply wounded; distressed. **3.** Having jagged, deeply cut edges: *lacerate leaves.* [Latin *lacerāre,* from *lacer,* torn, rent, mangled.] **—lac·er·a·tion** *n.* **—lac·er·a·tive** *adj.*

La·cer·ta (lə-sûr′tə) *n.* A constellation in the Northern Hemisphere near Cygnus and Andromeda. [New Latin, from Latin, LIZARD.]

la·cer·til·i·an (lăs′ər-tĭl′ē-ən) *adj. Rare.* Of, pertaining to, or characteristic of lizards and closely related reptiles. [From New Latin *Lacertilia,* a former suborder of lizardlike reptiles, from Latin *lacerta,* LIZARD.]

lace·wing (lās′wĭng′) *n.* Any of various greenish or brownish insects of the families Chrysopidae and Hemerobiidae, having four gauzy wings, threadlike antennae, and larvae that feed on insect pests such as aphids. [From the texture of the wings.]

lach·es (lăch′ĭz, lā′chĭz) *n., pl.* **laches.** *Law.* Culpable negligence; especially, delay in asserting a right or a claim. [Middle English *lachesse,* from Norman French, Old French, from *lasche,* lax, from Vulgar Latin *lascus* (unattested), from Latin *laxus,* LAX.]

Lach·e·sis (lăk′ə-sĭs) *Greek Mythology.* One of the three **Fates** *(see).* She determines the length of the thread of life. [Greek *Lakhesis,* "disposer of lots," from *lakhein,* aorist infinitive of *lankhanein*†, to obtain by lot.]

Lach·ry·ma Chris·ti (lăk′rə-mə krĭs′tē) *n.* A dryish white or occasionally red wine produced from grapes grown on the southern slopes of Vesuvius. [Latin, "tear of Christ."]

lach·ry·mal, lac·ri·mal (lăk′rə-məl) *adj.* **1.** Of or pertaining to tears. **2.** Of or pertaining to the lachrymal glands.
~*n.* **1.** A lachrymatory. **2. lachrymals.** The lachrymal glands. [Medieval Latin *lachrymālis, lacrimālis,* from Latin *lacrima, lacruma,* tear.]

lachrymal duct *n.* The short duct in the inner corner of the eyelid through which tears are drained into the nasal cavity. Also called "tear duct."

lachrymal gland *n.* A gland that lies beneath the upper eyelid in humans and many vertebrates and secretes tears.

lach·ry·ma·tor (lăk′rə-mā′tər) *n.* Any substance that induces an excessive flow of tears; especially, **tear gas** *(see).* [Latin *lacrima,* tear + -OR.]

lach·ry·ma·to·ry (lăk′rə-mə-tôr′ē, -tōr′ē) *n., pl.* **-ries.** Formerly, a vase or phial for holding the tears of mourners.
~*adj.* Of, pertaining to, or causing tears. [Medieval Latin *lachrymatōrium,* from Late Latin *lacrimatōrius,* of tears, from Latin *lacrimāre,* to cry, from *lacrima,* tear.]

lach·ry·mose (lăk′rə-mōs′) *adj.* **1.** Weeping or inclined to weep; tearful. **2.** Causing tears; sorrowful. **3.** Lugubrious; morose. [Latin *lacrimōsus,* from *lacrima,* tear.] **—lach·ry·mose·ly** *adv.*

lac·ing (lā′sĭng) *n.* **1.** *British.* A course of stone or brick built into a stone or rubble wall so as to bind the facing to the core. **2.** *Informal.* A thrashing.

la·cin·i·ate (lə-sĭn′ē-āt′) *adj.* Also **la·cin·i·a·ted** (-ā′tĭd). *Biology.* **1.** Fringed. **2.** Having edges cut into narrow, fringelike segments or lobes: *laciniate petals.* [Latin *lacinia,* fringe, tuft.] **—la·cin·i·a·tion** *n.*

lac insect *n.* Any of various insects of the subfamily Lacciferinae; especially, *Laccifer lacca,* of southern Asia, the female of which secretes the resinous substance lac.

lack (lăk) *n.* **1.** A deficiency or want: *a lack of money.* **2.** A need.
~*v.* **lacked, lacking, lacks.** *—tr.* To be entirely without or have too little of (a thing or quality). *—intr.* **1.** To be wanting or deficient. Used with *in* or *for.* **2.** *Archaic.* To be missing. [Middle English *lac, lacke,* perhaps from Middle Dutch, deficiency, fault.]

Usage: Intransitive *lack,* followed by *for,* has attracted criticism: *They lack for nothing; You will not be lacking for support.* In both examples, the transitive use of *lack* provides an alternative: *They lack nothing; You will not lack support.*

lack·a·dai·si·cal (lăk′ə-dā′zĭ-kəl) *adj.* Lacking spirit or enthusiasm; languid. [From earlier *lackadaisy,* extended form of LACKADAY.] —**lack·a·dai·si·cal·ly** *adv.* —**lack·a·dai·si·cal·ness** *n.*

lack·a·day (lăk′ə-dā′) *interj. Archaic.* Used to express regret or disapproval. [From the phrase *alack the day.*]

lack·ey (lăk′ē) *n., pl.* **-eys.** Also **lac·quey,** *pl.* **-queys. 1.** A liveried male servant; a footman. **2.** A servile follower; a toady.
~*tr.v.* **lackeyed, -eying, -eys.** Also **lac·quey, -queyed, -queying, -queys.** To attend as a lackey. [French *laquais,* from Old French, from Catalan *alacay,* akin to Spanish ALCALDE.]

lack·lus·ter (lăk′lŭs′tər) *adj.* Also *chiefly British* **lack·lus·tre.** Lacking luster, brightness, or vitality; dull.

La·clos (lä-klō′), **Pierre Choderlos de** (1741–1803). French writer and general. His novel, *Les Liaisons Dangereuses* (1782), is a study of moral and sexual corruption. He died fighting in Italy.

La·co·ni·a (lə-kō′nē-ə). Also **Lac·e·dae·mon** (lăs′ĭ-dē′mən). Ancient region of the southern Peloponnese, Greece. Sparta, its capital, dominated the area before the rise of the Achaean League in the 3rd century B.C. —**La·co·ni·an** *adj. & n.*

la·con·ic (lə-kŏn′ĭk) *adj.* Expressed in or using few words; terse; succinct. —See Synonyms at **concise.** [Latin *laconicus,* from Greek *Lakōnikos,* of or resembling the Laconians or Spartans (known for their brevity of speech: a famous anecdote concerns Philip of Macedon's warning, "If I enter Laconia, I shall raze Sparta to the ground," to which the Spartans returned the laconic message "If", from *Lakōn†,* native of Laconia, Spartan.] —**la·con·i·cal·ly** *adv.*

lac·o·nism (lăk′ə-nĭz′əm) *n.* Also **la·con·i·cism** (lə-kŏn′ĭ-sĭz′əm). **1.** Succinctness of expression. **2.** A laconic expression.

La Co·ru·ña (lä kō-rōō′nyə). City in northwestern Spain, capital of La Coruña province. It is an Atlantic port and a summer resort.

lac·quer (lăk′ər) *n.* **1.** Any of various clear or colored synthetic coatings, made by dissolving cellulose derivatives together with plasticizers and pigments in a mixture of volatile solvents, and used to give wood and metal surfaces a high gloss. **2.** Any glossy, often resinous material used as a surface coating, such as the exudation of the lacquer tree. **3.** A baked-on finish on the inside of food and drink cans.
~*tr.v.* **lacquered, -quering, -quers. 1.** To coat with lacquer. **2.** To give a sleek, glossy finish to. [Earlier *lacker,* from obsolete French *lacre,* sealing wax, variant of Portuguese *laca,* LAC (resin).] —**lac·quer·er** *n.*

lacquer tree *n.* A tree, *Rhus verniciflua,* of eastern Asia, having a toxic exudation from which a black lacquer is obtained. Also called "varnish tree."

lacrimal. Variant of **lachrymal.**

lac·ri·ma·tion (lăk′rə-mā′shən) *n.* The secretion of tears, especially in excess.

lacrimator. Variant of **lachrymator.**

la·crosse (lə-krôs′, -krŏs′) *n.* A team game of American Indian origin played with long-handled sticks fitted with nets for catching, carrying, and throwing the ball. [Canadian French, from French *(le jeu de) la crosse,* (the game of) the hooked stick, from Old French *crosse, croce,* staff, crosier, from Germanic.]

lac·tal·bu·min (lăk′tăl-byōō′mən) *n.* The albumin contained in milk. [LACT(O)- + ALBUMIN.]

lac·tam (lăk′tăm) *n.* Any of various amides containing the group -CONH-. [LACT(ONE) + AM(IDE).]

lac·ta·ry (lăk′tə-rē) *adj.* Of or pertaining to milk. [Latin *lactārius,* from *lac* (stem *lact-*), milk.]

lac·tase (lăk′tās′) *n.* An enzyme occurring in certain yeasts and in the intestinal juices of mammals that catalyzes the conversion of lactose into glucose and galactose. [LACT(O)- + -ASE.]

lac·tate (lăk′tāt′) *intr.v.* **-tated, -tating, -tates.** To secrete or produce milk.
~*n.* A salt or ester of lactic acid. [Latin *lactāre,* to suckle, from *lac* (stem *lact-*), milk.] —**lac·ta·tion** *n.*

lac·te·al (lăk′tē-əl) *adj.* **1.** Of, pertaining to, or like milk; milky. **2.** *Anatomy.* Of or pertaining to the lacteals.
~*n. Anatomy.* Any of numerous minute lymph-carrying vessels that convey chyle from the intestine to the thoracic duct. [Latin *lacteus,* of milk, from *lac* (stem *lact-*), milk.] —**lac·te·al·ly** *adv.*

lac·tes·cent (lăk-tĕs′ənt) *adj.* **1.** Becoming milky. **2.** Milky. **3.** *Biology.* Secreting or yielding a milky juice. Said of certain plants and insects. [Latin *lactescēns* (stem *lactescent-*), present participle of *lactescēre,* to become milky, from *lactēre,* to be milky, from *lac* (stem *lact-*), milk.] —**lac·tes·cence** *n.*

lac·tic (lăk′tĭk) *adj.* Pertaining to or derived from milk. [French *lactique,* from Latin *lac* (stem *lact-*), milk.]

lactic acid *n.* A hygroscopic syrupy liquid, $C_3H_6O_3$, present in sour milk, molasses, various fruits, and wines, and used in foods and beverages as an acidulant, flavoring, and preservative, and in adhesives, plasticizers, and pharmaceuticals.

lac·tif·er·ous (lăk-tĭf′ər-əs) *adj.* **1.** Producing, secreting, or conveying milk. **2.** *Botany.* Yielding latex or a similar milky juice; laticiferous. [Late Latin *lactifer* : LACT(O)- + -FEROUS.]

lac·ti·fuge (lăk′tə-fyōōj′) *n.* Any drug or other agent used to suppress the secretion of milk in mothers not breast-feeding their babies. [LACTI- + -FUGE.]

lacto-, lact- *prefix.* Indicates milk; for example, **lactoprotein.** [French, from Late Latin, from Latin *lac* (stem *lact-*), milk.]

lac·to·ba·cil·lus (lăk′tō-bə-sĭl′əs) *n., pl.* **-cilli** (-sĭl′ī′). Any of various bacilli of the genus *Lactobacillus* that ferment carbohydrates to produce lactic acid.

lac·to·fla·vin (lăk′tə-flā′vĭn, lăk′tə-flā′-) *n. Chemistry.* **Riboflavin** (see).

lac·to·gen·ic (lăk′tə-jĕn′ĭk) *adj.* Inducing lactation: *lactogenic hormone.* [LACTO- + -GENIC.]

lac·tone (lăk′tōn′) *n.* A cyclic ester of a hydroxyl acid, formed by removing the constituents of water from a molecule of the acid. [LACT(O)- + -ONE.] —**lac·ton·ic** *adj.*

lac·to·pro·tein (lăk′tō-prō′tēn′, -prō′tē-ən) *n.* Any protein normally present in milk.

lac·tose (lăk′tōs′) *n.* A white crystalline disaccharide, $C_{12}H_{22}O_{11}$, occurring in milk and used in pharmaceuticals, infant foods, bakery products, and confections. Also called "milk sugar," "sugar of milk." [French : LACT(O)- + -OSE.]

la·cu·na (lə-kyōō′nə) *n., pl.* **-nae** (-nē) or **-nas. 1.** An empty space or missing part, especially in an ancient manuscript; a gap. **2.** *Biology.* A cavity or depression. [Latin *lacūna,* pool. See **lagoon.**] —**la·cu·nal, la·cu·nar·y** *adj.*

la·cu·nar (lə-kyōō′nər) *n., pl.* **-nars** or **lacunaria** (lăk′yōō-nâr′ē-ə). *Architecture.* **1.** A ceiling or soffit decorated with a pattern of recessed panels. **2.** A panel in such a pattern.
~*adj. Biology.* Of, pertaining to, or containing lacunae. [Latin *lacūnar,* from *lacūna,* cavity, cleft, pool. See **lagoon.**]

la·cus·trine (lə-kŭs′trən) *adj.* **1.** Of or pertaining to a lake. **2.** Living or growing in or along the edges of lakes. [French *lacustre,* of a lake, from Latin *lacus,* LAKE (influenced in form by Latin *palūster,* marshy, from *palus,* swamp).]

lac·y (lā′sē) *adj.* **-ier, -iest.** Of, pertaining to, or resembling lace. —**lac·i·ness** *n.*

lad (lăd) *n.* **1.** A boy or young man. **2.** *Informal.* A man of any age. Used familiarly. **3.** *British.* A person of any age who looks after horses: *a stable lad.* [Middle English *ladde†.*]

ladanum. Variant of **labdanum.**

lad·der (lăd′ər) *n.* **1.** A device consisting of two long structural members crossed by parallel, equally spaced rungs, used for climbing up or down. **2.** A length of unraveled stitches, as in a stocking. Also called "run." **3. a.** A means of ascent and descent: *ascending the social ladder.* **b.** A series of ranked stages or levels: *high on the executive ladder.* **4.** *Sports.* A competition in a game, such as squash or tennis, in which each competitor tries to beat the competitor above him and so take his place. [Middle English *ladder,* Old English *hlǣd(d)er.*]

lad·der·back (lăd′ər-băk′) *n.* **1.** A chair back consisting of two upright posts connected by horizontal slats. **2.** A chair with this type of back. —**lad·der·back** *adj.*

lad·die (lăd′ē) *n.* A young lad.

lade (lād) *v.* **laded, laden** (lād′n) or **laded, lading, lades.** —*tr.* **1. a.** To load with or as if with cargo. **b.** To ship (cargo). **2.** To take up or remove water with a ladle or the like; bale. —*intr.* To take on cargo. [Lade (infinitive), laden (past participle); Middle English *laden, laden,* Old English *hladan, gehladen.*]

lad·en (lād′n) *adj.* **1.** Weighed down with a load; heavy. **2.** Oppressed; burdened: *laden with grief.* **3.** Saturated or suffused. Also used in combination: *a guilt-laden atmosphere.*

la·di·da (lä′dē-dä′) *adj. Informal.* Affectedly genteel; pretentious.
~*n. Informal.* A person showing such affectation. [Imitative of affected speech.]

ladies' man. Variant of **lady's man.**

la·dies'-tress·es, la·dy's-tress·es (lā′dēz-trĕs′ĭz) *n.* Used with a singular or plural verb. Any of various orchids of the genus *Spiranthes,* having a spike of small white flowers usually in a spiral.

La·din (lə-dēn′) *n.* **1.** The Rhaeto-Romanic dialect spoken in southeast Switzerland, contiguous parts of northern Italy, and the Tyrol. It is a distinct Romance language. **2.** An inhabitant of this region who speaks Ladin. [Italian *Ladino,* from Latin *Latīnus,* LATIN.]

lad·ing (lā′dĭng) *n.* **1.** An act of loading. **2.** Cargo; freight: *a bill of lading.*

La·di·no (lə-dē′nō) *n.* A Romance language, derived from Spanish with Hebrew elements and modifications, spoken by Sephardic Jews, especially in the Balkans. Also called "Judeo-Spanish." [Spanish, "Latin," from Latin *Latīnus,* LATIN.]

la·dle (lād′l) *n.* **1.** A long-handled spoon with a deep bowl for serving liquids. **2.** A large container used to transfer molten metals.
~*tr.v.* **ladled, -dling, -dles. 1.** To lift out or convey with a ladle. **2.** To distribute (money or food, for example) liberally. Used with *out.* [Middle English *ladel,* Old English *hlædel,* from *hladan,* to draw out, LADE.]

Lad·o·ga, Lake (lăd′ə-gə, lä′də-). Largest freshwater lake in Europe, in northwest U.S.S.R. It covers 18,130 square kilometers (7,000 square miles).

la·dy (lā′dē) *n., pl.* **-dies. 1. a.** A woman having the refined habits, gentle manners, and other characteristics typically associated with breeding, culture, and high station; the female equivalent of a gentleman. **b.** A well-behaved young girl: *She's a perfect little lady.* **2. a.** An adult female. Used as a polite term, especially in her presence: *Would you ask the lady to wait?* **b.** *Informal.* Madam. Used in direct address: *Can I help you, lady?* **3.** A woman considered especially from the point of view of some specified ability or quality: *She's a very dynamic lady.* **4. a.** A woman to whom a man is romantically attached; a ladylove. **b.** *Informal.* A wife or mistress. **5. Lady.** A term prefixed to the title of certain positions of office when such a position is held by a woman: *the Lady Mayor.* **6. Lady.** *British.* The general feminine title of nobility and of other rank, used in the following specific ways: **a.** For the wife or widow of a

lacquer *A lacquered tray from an 18th-century Chinese picnic set, now in the Victoria and Albert Museum, London.*

ladybug *There are more than 3,000 species of ladybug, and almost all are among the most beneficial insects, eating countless numbers of aphids, greenflies, and other pests. In California they are gathered by the thousands in their breeding grounds and sold to farmers who use them to clean their crops.*

lady's-slipper *This species of wildflower grows in many parts of the United States. It is the state flower of Minnesota.*

knight or baronet: *Lady Smith* (wife of Sir Harry Smith). **b.** Semiformally for a marchioness, countess, viscountess, or baroness: *Lady Salisbury* (the Marchioness of Salisbury). **c.** As the usual style for the wife or widow of a baron: *Lady Snow* (wife of Lord Snow); **d.** As a courtesy title for the daughter of a duke, marquis, or earl: *Lady Hester Stanhope* (daughter of Earl Stanhope); **e.** As a courtesy title for the wife or widow of a younger son of a duke or marquis: *Lady John Russell* (wife of Lord John Russell, third son of the Duke of Bedford). ***Note:*** In direct address, *my lady* and *your ladyship* are deferential substitutes for any of the above. With all except **a**, the formal usage (as in addressing a letter), is *The Lady Snow, The Lady Ruthven,* and the like. [Middle English *la(ve)di, lafdi,* Old English *hlǣfdige,* "kneader of bread," lady : *hlǣf,* LOAF + *dig-* (unattested), knead.]

la·dy·bug (lā'dē-bŭg') *n.* Any of numerous small beetles of the family Coccinellidae, often reddish with black spots. Also called "lady beetle," "ladybird." [After OUR LADY.]

Lady Chapel *n. Sometimes* **lady chapel.** A chapel in a church or cathedral dedicated to the Virgin Mary.

la·dy·fin·ger (lā'dē-fĭng'gər) *n.* Also **la·dys·fin·ger** (lā'dēz-). A small, oval sponge cake, suggestive of a finger.

lady in waiting *n., pl.* **ladies in waiting.** A lady of a court appointed to serve or attend a queen or princess. Also called "lady of the bedchamber."

la·dy-kill·er (lā'dē-kĭl'ər) *n. Slang.* A man reputed to be exceptionally successful and often ruthless with women.

la·dy·like (lā'dē-līk') *adj.* **1.** Characteristic of or befitting a lady; refined; well-bred. **2.** Unduly sensitive to matters of propriety or decorum. **3.** Effeminate. Said of a man.

la·dy·love (lā'dē-lŭv') *n.* A beloved woman; a sweetheart.

lady of the house *n.* The female head of a household.

la·dy·ship (lā'dē-shĭp') *n. Sometimes* **Ladyship.** Used in addressing or referring to a woman holding the title of Lady. Used with *Your* or *Her.* See Note at **lady.**

lady's man *n.* Also **ladies' man.** A man who enjoys and attracts the company of ladies.

lady's mantle *n.* Any of various plants of the genus *Alchemilla,* having clusters of small greenish flowers.

la·dy's-slip·per (lā'dēz-slĭp'ər) *n.* Any of various orchids of the genus *Cypripedium,* having variously colored flowers with an inflated, pouchlike lip.

la·dy's-smock (lā'dēz-smŏk') *n.* A plant, the **cuckooflower** *(see).*

lady's-tresses. Variant of **ladies'-tresses.**

Laën·nec (lā-nĕk'), **René Théophile Hyacinthe** (1781–1826). French physician who invented the stethoscope.

La·er·tes (lā-ûr'tēz). *Greek Mythology.* The father of Odysseus.

La·e·trile (lā'ə-trĭl) *n.* A trademark for a cyanide-containing compound extracted from the seeds of peaches and related plants and used experimentally in the treatment of cancer.

La·fa·yette (lä'fē-ĕt', lăf'ē-), **Marie Joseph Paul Yves Roch Gilbert du Motier, Marquis de** (1757–1834). French soldier and politician. He served on George Washington's staff in the American Revolution. In France he took part in the 1789 and 1830 revolutions. He designed the modern French flag.

La Fa·yette (lä fē-ĕt'), **Marie Madeleine Pioche de la Vergne, Comtesse de** (1634–93). French writer. Her novel *La Princesse de Clèves* (1678) examines the conflicts between passion and duty in marriage.

Laf·fite or **La·fitte** (lä-fēt'), **Jean** (*c.* 1780–1826). French pirate. After convincing the skeptical Americans of his allegiance during the War of 1812, he and his 1,000 men fought valiantly in the Battle of New Orleans (1815) in return for an official pardon for their crimes on the high seas. Laffite then returned to his buccaneering ways, plundering treasure ships along the Spanish Main.

La Fol·lette (lə fŏl'ət), **Robert Marion** (1885–1925). U.S. politician and reformer. A progressive Wisconsin lawyer, he served as congressman (1885–91), governor (1900–06), and U.S. senator (1906–25), introducing reform policies that became the goals of progressives nationwide. He ran unsuccessfully for president in 1924.

La·fon·taine (lə-fŏn-tān', -fôN-tĕn'), **Henri-Marie** (1854–1943). Belgian jurist and statesman. He was president of the International Peace Bureau (1907–43) and was awarded the Nobel Peace Prize in 1913.

La Fon·taine (lä fôN-tĕn'), **Jean de** (1621–95). French poet, who collected the fables of Aesop and others in his *Fables* (1668–94).

lag[1] (lăg) *v.* **lagged, lagging, lags.** *—intr.* **1.** To fail to keep up a pace; fall behind; straggle; loiter. Often used with *behind.* **2.** To proceed or develop slowly or abnormally slowly. **3.** To fail, weaken, or slacken gradually; flag. **4.** *Billiards.* To determine the order of play by successively hitting the cue ball against the end rail, the ball rebounding closest to the head rail indicating the player to shoot first. *—tr.* **1.** To fall or lag behind. **2.** To shoot, throw, or pitch (a marble or coin, for example) at a mark.
~*n.* **1.** One that lags. **2.** The act, process, or condition of lagging. **3.** A condition of slowness or retardation. **4.** An extent or duration of lagging; a time lag: *"he wondered darkly at how great a lag there was between his thinking and his actions"* (Thomas Wolfe). **5.** Any interval between events or phenomena. [Probably from *lag* (noun), last person; compare dialect *fog, seg, lag,* fanciful distortions of *first, second, last* in children's games.] **—lag·ger** *n.*

lag[2] *n.* Any covering for a cylindrical object, especially the insulating covering of a hot-water cylinder, steam pipes, or the like.
~*tr.v.* **lagged, lagging, lags.** To furnish or cover with lagging. [Perhaps from Scandinavian, akin to Swedish *lagg,* barrel stave.] **—lag·ger** *n.*

lag[3] *tr.v.* **lagged, lagging, lags.** *Slang.* **1.** To arrest. **2.** To send to prison.
~*n. Slang.* **1.** A convict. Used especially in the phrase *an old lag.* **2.** A term of imprisonment. [19th century : origin obscure.]

lag·an (lăg'ən) *n.* Also **li·gan** (lī'gən), **lag·end** (lăg'ənd). *Law.* Cargo or equipment thrown into the sea from a ship in distress, often attached to a float or buoy to enable it to be recovered. [Old French, perhaps from Old Norse *lögn* (stem *lagn-*), dragnet.]

Lag b'O·mer (läg' bō'mər) *n.* A Jewish holiday, originally an agricultural festival, celebrated on the 33rd day after the second day of Passover, on the 18th day of Iyar. [Hebrew, "33rd (day) of the Omer."]

la·ge·na (lə-jē'nə) *n.* The structure in the inner ear of fishes and amphibians that is homologous to the cochlea of higher vertebrates. [Latin, from Greek *lagēnos,* flask (referring to the shape).]

la·ger[1] (lä'gər) *n.* A light, usually effervescent beer of a type originally brewed in Germany, that contains a relatively small amount of hops. [Short for German *Lager(bier),* (beer) for storing, from *lager,* store, lair, from Old High German *legar,* lair.]

lager[2]**.** Variant of **laager.**

La·ger·löf (lä'gər-ləv), **Selma** (1858–1940). Swedish novelist. She wrote *Gösta Berlings Saga* (1891) and in 1909 became the first woman to win the Nobel Prize for literature.

lag·gard (lăg'ərd) *adj.* Lagging behind or tending to lag behind; dawdling; straggling. [LAG (fall behind) + -ARD.] **—lag·gard** *n.* **—lag·gard·ly** *adv.* **—lag·gard·ness** *n.*

lag·ging (lăg'ĭng) *n.* **1.** Insulation used to prevent heat diffusion from steam pipes, boilers, and the like. **2.** A wooden frame built to support the sides of an arch until the keystone is positioned. [From LAG (insulating covering).]

la·gniappe (lăn-yăp', lăn'yăp') *n.* **1.** A small gift presented to a customer with his purchase by a store owner. **2.** *Informal.* An extra or unexpected gift; a gratuity. [Louisiana French, from American Spanish *la ñapa* : *la,* the + *ñapa,* lagniappe, from Quechua *yápa,* addition.]

lag·o·morph (lăg'ə-môrf') *n.* Any of various gnawing mammals of the order Lagomorpha, which includes the rabbits and hares. [New Latin *Lagomorpha* : Greek *lagōs,* hare + -MORPH.] **—lag·o·mor·phic** *adj.*

la·goon (lə-gōōn') *n.* Also **la·gune, la·gu·na** (-gōō'nə). A body of salt water separated from the sea by sand or shingle bars or coral reefs. [French *lagune* and Italian or Spanish *laguna,* from Latin *lacūna,* pool, cavity, from *lacus,* LAKE.]

La·gos (lā'gŏs', -gəs). Capital and largest city of Nigeria, on the Gulf of Guinea. A new one is currently being developed at Abuja. Lagos consists of four islands and four mainland sections, joined to one another by bridges and causeways. It is Nigeria's chief port and industrial center.

lag screw *n.* A heavy screw having a square bolt head. [Originally used in securing barrel staves. See **lag** (insulate).]

Lag·ting, Lag·thing (läg'tĭng) *n.* The upper house in the Storthing, or parliament, of Norway. [Norwegian : *lag,* society, from Old Norse, due place (influenced in meaning by plural *lög,* law) + *ting,* parliament, from Old Norse *thing,* parliament, assembly.]

La Guar·di·a (lə gwär'dē-ə), **Fiorello Henry** (1882–1947). U.S. politician. He was a U.S. congressman (1917–21, 1923–33) and mayor of New York City (1934–45).

La·hore (lə-hôr', -hōr'). A city in east-central Pakistan, the capital of Punjab province and Pakistan's second-largest city. It is notable for its architecture.

Lahr (lär), **Bert** (1895–1967). U.S. entertainer. At the age of 15 he joined a vaudeville troupe, the start of a show-business career that encompassed Broadway productions, such as *Hold Everything* (1928), and many dramatic and motion-picture roles, including the much-loved Cowardly Lion in *The Wizard of Oz* (1939).

la·ic (lā'ĭk) *adj.* Also **la·i·cal** (-ĭ-kəl). Of or pertaining to the laity; secular.
~*n.* A layman. [Late Latin *lāicus,* LAY.] **—la·i·cal·ly** *adv.*

la·i·cize (lā'ĭ-sīz') *tr.v.* **-cized, -cizing, -cizes.** **1.** To free from ecclesiastical control; give over to laymen. **2.** To secularize. **—la·i·ci·za·tion** *n.*

laid. Past tense and past participle of **lay** (verb).

laid-back (lād'băk') *adj. Informal.* Relaxed; easy-going.

laid lines *pl.n.* The close thin lines detectable in laid paper, produced by the parallel wires of the mold.

laid paper *n.* **1.** A paper made on wire molds that give it a characteristic watermark of fine lines. Compare **wove paper. 2.** A machine-made paper imitating this.

lain. Past participle of **lie** (to recline).

Laing (lăng, lāng), **Ronald David** (1927–). British psychiatrist. His controversial theories about the nature of sanity are outlined in *The Politics of Experience* (1967). His other books include *The Divided Self* (1960) and a book of poetry, *Knots* (1970).

lair (lâr) *n.* **1.** The den or dwelling of a wild animal. **2.** *British.* An enclosure for cattle to stay in on their way to market. **3.** *Obsolete.* A resting place; a couch. **4.** *Informal.* A place of hiding or seclusion.
~*v.* **laired, lairing, lairs.** *—tr.* To put in a lair. *—intr.* To retreat to or lie in a lair. [Middle English *lair, leir,* Old English *leger.*]

laird (lârd) *n.* In Scotland, the owner of a landed estate. [Scottish, variant of LORD.]

lais·sez-al·ler, lais·ser-al·ler (lĕs'ā-ä-lā') *n.* An absence of constraint; uncontrolled freedom. [French, "let go."]

lais·sez-faire, lais·ser-faire (lĕs′ā-fâr′) *n.* **1.** The doctrine that government should not interfere with commerce. **2.** *Informal.* Noninterference in the affairs of others. [French, "allow (them) to do."] —**lais·sez-faire** *adj.* —**lais·sez-faire·ism** *n.*

lais·sez-pas·ser, lais·ser-pas·ser (lĕs′ā-pă-sā′) *n.* A pass; especially, a permit allowing one to enter a restricted area. [French, "allow (them) to pass."]

la·i·ty (lā′ə-tē) *n., pl.* **-ties. 1.** Laymen collectively, as distinguished from the clergy. **2.** All those persons outside a given profession, art, or other specialized field; nonprofessionals. [From LAY (non-clergy).]

La·ius (lā′əs). *Greek Mythology.* The king of Thebes who was killed by his own unwitting son, Oedipus.

lake¹ (lāk) *n. Abbr.* L., l. **1.** A large inland body of fresh or salt water. **2.** A scenic pond, as in a park. **3.** A large pool of any liquid. [Middle English *lac,* from Old French *lac,* from Latin *lacus,* basin for water.]

lake² *n.* A pigment consisting of organic coloring matter with an inorganic base or carrier. [Variant of LAC (resin).]

lake³ *tr.v.* **laked, laking, lakes.** To cause (blood) to become a homogeneous solution by releasing hemoglobin from erythrocytes, as by suspending the erythrocytes in water. [From LAKE (pigment).]

Lake District. Scenic district and tourist area of northwest England, lying between Morecambe Bay and the Solway Firth. It includes the Cumbrian Mts. and 15 lakes, among them Windermere, Ullswater, and Derwent Water. The Lake District National Park, covering *c.* 32,375 hectares (80,000 acres), was established in 1951.

lake dwelling *n.* A dwelling built on piles in a shallow lake, especially in prehistoric times. —**lake dweller** *n.*

lake herring *n.* **1.** A fish, the **powan** *(see).* **2.** A North American food fish, *Coregonus artedii* (or *Leucichthys artedii*), of the Great Lakes region, related to the whitefishes. See **cisco.**

Lake Plac·id (plăs′ĭd). Village in northeastern New York State. It is on Mirror Lake in the Adirondack Mts. and was the site of the Winter Olympic Games in 1932 and 1980.

Lake Poets *pl.n.* Coleridge, Wordsworth, and Southey, grouped as a school because they lived for a time in the Lake District.

lak·er (lā′kər) *n.* **1.** A lake fish, such as the lake trout. **2.** A ship used on lakes.

Lake Suc·cess (sək-sĕs′). A village in southeastern New York, on northwestern Long Island. It is a residential community and was the temporary home of the United Nations Security Council (1946–51).

lake trout *n.* A freshwater food fish, *Salvelinus namaycush,* of the Great Lakes. Also called "Mackinaw trout," "togue."

lakh. Variant of **lac** (sum of money).

Lak·shad·weep (lək-shäd′wēp). Formerly **Lac·ca·dive, Mi·ni·coy, and A·min·di·vi Islands** (lăk′ə-dīv′; mĭn′ĭ-koi′; ŭm′ən-dē′vē). Indian territory off the coast of Kerala, comprising 27 coral islands, 10 of which are inhabited. The total area is only 32 square kilometers (12 square miles). Administered as separate island groups by Britain (1877–1947), it became a single territory, the Laccadive, Minicoy, and Amindivi Islands, in 1956. The name was changed to Lakshadweep in 1973.

lak·y (lā′kē) *adj.* **-ier, -iest.** Of the color of lake or of blood.

-lalia *suffix.* Indicates a speech defect; for example, **echolalia.** [New Latin, from Greek *lalia,* from Greek *lalein,* to babble.]

La·lique (lə-lēk′), **René** (1860–1945). French jeweler and glassmaker, who applied art nouveau designs to crystalware.

Lal·lan (lăl′ən) *n.* Also **Lal·lans** (lăl′ənz). *Scottish.* **1.** The Lowlands of Scotland. **2.** The dialect of Scottish English spoken in the Lowlands. [Scottish, variant of LOWLANDS.] —**Lal·lan, Lal·lans** *adj.*

lal·la·tion (lă-lā′shən) *n.* The pronunciation of the sound (l) as (r). [Latin *lallāre,* to make lulling sounds.]

lam¹ (lăm) *v.* **lammed, lamming, lams.** *Slang.* —*tr.* To thrash; wallop. —*intr.* To strike. Used with *into* or *out.* [Of Scandinavian origin, akin to Old Norse *lemja,* to flog, make lame by beating.]

lam² (lăm) *intr.v.* **lammed, lamming, lams.** *Slang.* To escape, as from prison. —*n. Slang.* Flight. —**on the lam.** In flight, especially from the law. [Origin obscure.]

lam. laminated.

Lam. Lamentations (Old Testament).

la·ma (lä′mə) *n.* A Buddhist monk of Tibet or Mongolia. [Tibetan *bla-ma,* superior one.]

La·ma·ism (lä′mə-ĭz′əm) *n.* The religion of Tibet and Mongolia and neighboring areas, a form of Mahayana Buddhism with an admixture of animism, characterized by elaborate rituals. [From LAMA (priest).] —**La·ma·ist** *n. & adj.* —**La·ma·is·tic** *adj.*

La Man·cha (lə män′chə). Region and former province of central Spain. A bleak plateau noted for its windmills, it was the setting for Cervantes' novel, *Don Quixote de la Mancha.*

La Manche. See **English Channel.**

La·marck (lə-märk′), **Jean Baptiste Pierre Antoine de Monet, Chevalier de** (1744–1829). French naturalist. His idea of human evolution influenced Darwin's theory, but Lamarck also believed that acquired characteristics could be inherited, a belief since discredited.

La·marck·i·an (lə-mär′kē-ən) *adj.* Of or relating to Lamarck or Lamarckism. —*n.* A supporter of Lamarckism.

La·marck·ism (lə-mär′kĭz′əm) *n.* The theory that adaptive responses to environment cause structural changes capable of being inherited. Compare **Darwinism.** See **acquired characteristic.** [Developed by Chevalier de LAMARCK.]

La·mar·tine (lä-mär-tēn′), **Alphonse Marie Louis de** (1790–1869). French romantic poet who was briefly minister of foreign affairs in 1848.

la·ma·ser·y (lä′mə-sĕr′ē) *n., pl.* **-ies.** A Lamaist monastery.

La·maze (lə-mäz′) *adj.* Relating to or being a method of childbirth in which the mother is prepared physically and psychologically to give birth without the use of drugs. [After Fernand *Lamaze* (1890–1957).]

lamb (lăm) *n.* **1.** A young sheep, especially one not yet weaned. **2.** The flesh of a young sheep used as meat. **3.** Lambskin. **4. a.** A sweet, mild-mannered person; a dear. **b.** One who is easily cheated; a dupe. **5.** A member of a Christian flock. —**the Lamb.** Christ. Also called "Lamb of God." —*intr.v.* **lambed, lambing, lambs.** To give birth to a lamb. [Middle English, Old English, from Germanic *lambiz-* (unattested).]

Lamb (lăm), **Charles,** known as "Elia" (1775–1834). English essayist. He and his sister, **Mary Ann Lamb** (1764–1847), wrote *Tales from Shakespeare* (1807) for children.

lam·baste, lam·bast (lăm-bāst′) *tr.v.* **-basted, -basting, -bastes** or **-basts.** *Slang.* **1.** To give a thrashing to; whip; beat. **2.** To attack verbally; berate or criticize. [Perhaps LAM (beat) + BASTE (beat).]

lamb·da (lăm′də) *n.* The 11th letter in the Greek alphabet, written Λ, λ. Transliterated in English as *L, l.* See feature at **alphabet.** [Greek *lambda,* of Semitic origin, akin to Hebrew *lāmedh,* LAMED.]

lambda particle *n. Symbol* Λ *Physics.* An electrically neutral subatomic particle in the baryon family, having a mass 2,183 times that of the electron and a mean lifetime of approximately 2.5×10^{-10} second. [From LAMBDA.]

lambda point *n.* **1.** The temperature at which the transition from helium I to superfluid helium II occurs, approximately 2.19° K. **2.** The temperature of any phase transition in which the specific heat capacity regarded as a function of temperature has a logarithmic singularity.

lamb·doid (lăm′doid′) *adj.* Also **lamb·doi·dal** (lăm-doid′l). Designating the deeply serrated suture in the skull between the two parietal bones and the occipital bone. [French *lambdoïde,* from Greek *lambdoeidēs,* "lambda-shaped" : LAMBDA + -OID.]

lam·bent (lăm′bənt) *adj.* **1.** Flickering lightly and gently over a surface: *lambent flames.* **2.** Flitting over subjects with effortless brilliance: *a lambent wit.* **3.** Having a gentle glow; luminous. —See Synonyms at **bright.** [Latin *lambēns* (stem *lambent-*), present of *lambere,* to lick, tap.] —**lam·ben·cy** *n.* —**lam·bent·ly** *adv.*

lam·bert (lăm′bərt) *n. Symbol* L A unit of illumination equal to one lumen per square centimeter. [After J.H. *Lambert* (1728–77), German physicist.]

lamb·kin (lăm′kĭn) *n.* **1.** A small lamb. **2.** A small endearing child. [Middle English *lambkin* : LAMB + -KIN.]

lam·bre·quin (lăm′bər-kĭn, -brə-kĭn) *n.* **1. a.** A piece of material worn over a helmet in medieval times. **b.** A heraldic representation of this; **mantling** *(see).* **2.** A scalloped band of color ornamenting the top of a piece of porcelain. [French, from Dutch *lamperkin* (unattested), diminutive of *lamper,* veil, from Middle Dutch *lampert†.*]

lamb·skin (lăm′skĭn) *n.* **1.** The skin of a lamb, especially when dressed without removing the fleece, as for a garment. **2.** Leather made from the dressed hide of a lamb.

lamb's-let·tuce (lămz′lĕt′əs) *n.* A plant, **corn salad** *(see).*

lamb's-quar·ters, lamb's quarters (lămz′kwôr′tərz) *n.* Used with a singular or plural verb. A species of **pigweed** *(see).*

lamb's wool *n.* **1.** Wool shorn from a lamb. **2.** A fabric or yarn made from this wool.

lame¹ (lām) *adj.* **lamer, lamest. 1.** Disabled or crippled in one or more limbs, especially in a leg or foot so that walking is impaired. **2.** Weak and ineffectual; unsatisfactory: *a lame excuse.* —*tr.v.* **lamed, laming, lames. 1.** To cause to become lame. **2.** To make ineffective; disable. [Middle English *lame,* Old English *lama.*] —**lame·ly** *adv.* —**lame·ness** *n.*

lame² *n.* A thin metal plate such as an overlapping plate in medieval armor. [Old French, from Latin *lāmina,* thin plate.]

la·mé (lă-mā′) *n.* A fabric in which are woven metallic threads, often of gold or silver. [French, from adjective, "worked with silver and gold thread," from Old French *lame,* thin metal plate, LAME.]

la·med, la·medh (lä′mĕd′, -mĭd) *n.* The 12th letter in the Hebrew alphabet. See feature at **alphabet.** [Hebrew *lāmedh,* "ox goad" (from the shape of the letter).]

lame duck *n. Informal.* **1.** An official or body during the period between an election defeat and the inauguration of a successor. **2.** An ineffectual, helpless, or disabled person. **3.** A company that is chronically unable to achieve profitability. **4.** A speculator on a stock market who is unable to meet all his obligations.

la·mel·la (lə-mĕl′ə) *n., pl.* **-mellae** (-mĕl′ē) or **-las. 1.** A thin scale, plate, or layer; especially: **a.** Any of the gills of a mushroom. **b.** Any of the concentric layers of calcified material of which bone is formed. **c.** Any of the layers of membranes in a plant chloroplast. **2.** A thin layer of a fluid. **3.** A wooden, metal, or concrete member forming the frame of a vaulted roof. [New Latin, from Latin *lāmella,* diminutive of *lāmina,* thin plate.] —**la·mel·lar** *adj.* —**la·mel·lar·ly** *adv.*

la·mel·late (lăm′ə-lāt′, lə-mĕl′āt′) *adj.* Also **lam·el·la·ted** (lăm′ə-lā′-

lanceolate *A botanical term describing the narrow leaves of shrubs and trees that taper gently to a point like the head of a lance. These leaves are from a willow tree.*

PRONUNCIATION KEY

ă, pat; ā, pay; âr, care;
ä, father, are; b, bib;
ch, church; d, deed; ĕ, pet;
ē, be; f, fife; g, gag; h, hat;
hw, which; ĭ, pit; ī, pie;
îr, pier; j, judge; k, kick;
l, lid, needle; m, mum;
n, no, sudden; ng, thing;
ŏ, pot; ō, toe; ô, paw, for;
oi, noise; ou, out; o͝o, book;
o͞o, boot; p, pop; r, roar;
s, sauce; sh, ship, dish;
t, tight; th, thin, path;
th, this, bathe; ŭ, cut; ûr, fur;
v, valve; w, with; y, yes;
z, zebra, size; zh, vision;
ə, about, item, edible,
gallop, circus, peaceful

IN FOREIGN WORDS:

à, *Fr.* ami; œ, *Fr.* feu, *Ger.* schön; ü, *Fr.* tu, *Ger.* über; KH, *Ger.* ich, *Scot.* loch; N, *Fr.* bon; y', *Fr.* Compiègne

STRESS MARKS:

Primary stress: ′
in·cite′ (ĭn-sīt′)
Secondary stress: ′
in′sight′ (ĭn′sīt′)

tĭd). **1.** Having, composed of, or arranged in thin layers or lamellae. **2.** Resembling a lamella. **—lam·el·la·tion** *n.*

lamelli– *prefix.* Indicates a lamella or lamellae; for example, **lamellibranch.** [From LAMELLA.]

la·mel·li·branch (lə-mĕl′ə-brăngk′) *n.* Any of the mollusks of the class Pelecypoda (or Lamellibranchia), having a hinged bivalve shell and including the clams, mussels, and oysters.
~adj. Of or pertaining to lamellibranchs. [New Latin *Lamellibranchia,* "plate gilled" : LAMELLI- + BRANCHIA.]

la·mel·li·corn (lə-mĕl′ə-kôrn′) *n.* A beetle of the superfamily Lamellicornia (or Scarabaeoidea), which includes the scarabs and other beetles having antennae tipped with movable leaflike plates. [New Latin *Lamellicornia,* "plate horned" : LAMELLI- + Latin *cornū,* horn.] **—la·mel·li·corn** *adj.*

la·mel·li·form (lə-mĕl′ə-fôrm′) *adj.* Having the form of a thin plate or lamella. [LAMELLI- + -FORM.]

la·ment (lə-mĕnt′) *v.* **-mented, -menting, -ments.** *—tr.* **1.** To express grief for or about; mourn over: *lament a death.* **2.** To regret deeply; deplore. *—intr.* **1.** To grieve. **2.** To wail; complain.
~n. **1.** An expression of sorrow or grief; a lamentation. **2.** A song or poem expressing grief; an elegy; a dirge. [French *lamenter,* from Old French, from Latin *lāmentārī,* from *lāmentum,* expression of sorrow.] **—la·ment·er** *n.*

la·men·ta·ble (lə-mĕn′tə-bəl, lăm′ən-) *adj.* **1.** To be lamented; deplorable; highly regrettable. **2.** *Archaic.* Exhibiting sorrow or grief; mournful. —See Synonyms at **pathetic.** **—la·men·ta·bly** *adv.*

lam·en·ta·tion (lăm′ən-tā′shən) *n.* **1.** The act of lamenting. **2.** An instance of such expression of grief; a lament.

Lam·en·ta·tions (lăm′ən-tā′shənz) *n. Used with a singular verb. Abbr.* **Lam.** A book of the Old Testament, attributed to Jeremiah.

la·ment·ed (lə-mĕn′tĭd) *adj.* Mourned for. **—la·ment·ed·ly** *adv.*

la·mi·a (lā′mē-ə) *n., pl.* **-mias** or **-miae** (-ē′). **1.** *Greek Mythology.* A monster, represented as a serpent with the head and breasts of a woman, reputed to prey upon humans and suck their blood. **2.** A sorceress; a vampire. [Middle English, from Latin, from Greek.]

lam·i·na (lăm′ə-nə) *n., pl.* **-nae** (-nē′) or **-nas. 1.** A thin plate, sheet, or layer, as of bone or mineral. **2.** *Botany.* The expanded area, or blade, of a leaf or thallus. **3.** *Zoology.* A scalelike or platelike structure, such as any of the thin layers of sensitive tissue in the hoof of a horse. **4.** *Geology.* A narrow bed of rock. [New Latin, from Latin *lāmina,* thin plate.] **—lam·i·nar, lam·i·nal** *adj.*

lam·i·nar flow (lăm′ə-nər) *n.* Nonturbulent flow of a viscous fluid in layers near a boundary, as of lubricating oil in bearings. Compare **streamline flow, turbulent flow.**

lam·i·nar·i·a (lăm′ə-nâr′ē-ə, -nĕr′ē-ə) *n.* Any seaweed of the genus *Laminaria,* having large, brown, leathery fronds. See **kelp.** [New Latin, from Latin *lamina,* tissue, plate. See **lamina.**]

lam·i·nate (lăm′ə-nāt′) *v.* **-nated, -nating, -nates.** *—tr.* **1.** To beat or compress into a thin plate or sheet. **2.** To divide into thin layers. **3.** To make by uniting several layers. **4.** To cover with thin sheets. *—intr.* To split into thin layers or sheets.
~adj. (lăm′ə-nĭt, -nāt′). Also **lam·i·nose** (-nōs′), **lam·i·nous** (-nəs). Consisting of, arranged in, or covered with a lamina or laminae.
~n. A laminated product, such as plywood. [LAMIN(A) + -ATE.] **—lam·i·na·tor** *n.*

lam·i·nat·ed (lăm′ə-nā′tĭd) *adj.* **1.** Composed of layers bonded together. **2.** Arranged in laminae; laminate.

laminated glass *n.* See **safety glass.**

laminated iron *n.* Thin sheets of iron or a steel-silicon alloy shaped to form the core of a transformer to reduce the eddy current losses that occur with a solid iron core.

lam·i·na·tion (lăm′ə-nā′shən) *n.* **1.** The process or state of being laminated. **2.** Something laminated. **3.** A lamina.

lam·i·ni·tis (lăm′ə-nī′tĭs) *n.* Inflammation of the sensitive laminae in the hoof of a horse. Also called "founder." [New Latin : LAMIN(A) + -ITIS.]

Lam·mas (lăm′əs) *n.* **1.** *Roman Catholic Church.* A festival on August 1 commemorating St. Peter's deliverance from prison. **2.** A harvest festival formerly held in England on August 1 when bread baked from the season's first ripe grain was consecrated. In this sense, also called "Lammas Day." [Middle English *Lammasse,* Old English *hlāfmæsse* : *hlāf,* LOAF + *mæsse,* MASS.] **—Lam·mas·tide** *n.*

lam·mer·gei·er, lam·mer·gey·er (lăm′ər-gī′ər) *n.* A large predatory bird, *Gypaetus barbatus,* of mountainous regions of the Old World, having black bristles around the bill. Also called "bearded vulture" and sometimes "ossifrage." [German *Lämmergeier* : *Lämmer,* genitive plural of *Lamm,* lamb, from Old High German *lamb,* from Germanic *lambiz-* (unattested), LAMB + *Geier,* vulture, from Old High German *gīr.*]

lamp (lămp) *n.* **1. a.** Any of various devices that generate light, heat, or therapeutic radiation. **b.** A vessel containing oil, paraffin, or alcohol burned through a wick for illumination. **2.** *Poetic.* A star, planet, meteor, or other celestial body regarded as lighting the heavens. **3.** *Literary.* That which illumines the mind or the soul. [Middle English *lampe,* from Old French, from Latin *lampas,* from Greek, torch, from *lampein,* to shine.]

lamp·black (lămp′blăk′) *n.* A gray or black pigment made from the soot of incompletely burned carbonaceous materials, used as a pigment, and in matches, explosives, lubricants, and fertilizers. Also called "blacking."

Lam·pe·du·sa (lăm′pə-do͞o′zə), **Giuseppe Tomasi di** (1896–1957). Italian novelist. His best-known work, *The Leopard* (1958), published posthumously, deals with his own experience of the Sicilian aristocracy in decline at the beginning of the century.

lam·per eel (lăm′pər) *n.* The **lamprey** *(see).* [Variant of LAMPREY.]

lam·pern (lăm′pərn) *n.* A European lamprey, *Lampetra fluviatilis,* that migrates up rivers from the sea to spawn. [Middle English *laumprun,* from Old French, from *lampreie,* LAMPREY.]

lam·pi·on (lăm′pē-ən) *n.* An oil-burning lamp, often of colored glass, for outdoor use. [French, from Italian *lampione,* augmentative of *lampa,* lamp, from Old French *lampe,* LAMP.]

lamp·light (lămp′līt′) *n.* The light shed by a lamp.

lamp·light·er (lămp′lī′tər) *n.* **1.** Formerly, a person employed to light and extinguish street lamps. **2.** Something, such as a torch or taper, used to light lamps.

lam·poon (lăm-po͞on′) *n.* **1.** A bitingly satirical piece of writing that is strongly personal in its flavor and ridicule. **2.** A light, good-humored satire. —See Synonyms at **caricature.**
~tr.v. **lampooned, -pooning, -poons.** To assail in a satirical composition; write a lampoon concerning. [French, perhaps from *lampons,* let us drink (used as a refrain in 17th-century poetry), first person plural imperative of *lamper,* to gulp down, guzzle, from Germanic.] **—lam·poon·er, lam·poon·ist** *n.* **—lam·poon·er·y** *n.*

lamp·post (lămp′pōst′) *n.* A post supporting a street lamp.

lam·prey (lăm′prē) *n., pl.* **-preys.** Any of various primitive elongated freshwater or anadromous fishlike vertebrates of the family Petromyzontidae, characteristically having a jawless sucking mouth with a rasping tongue. Also called "lamper eel." [Middle English *lamprei,* from Old French *lampreie,* from Medieval Latin *lamprēda*†. See also **limpet.**]

lam·pro·phyre (lăm′prə-fīr′) *n.* Any of several intermediate igneous rocks comprising feldspar and ferromagnesian minerals that occur as dikes and minor intrusions. [Greek *lampros,* bright + *-phyre,* from PORPHYRY.]

lamp·shade (lămp′shād′) *n.* Any of various protective or ornamental coverings used for screening a light bulb.

lamp shell *n.* A marine invertebrate, a **brachiopod** *(see).* [From the shape of one of the valves in certain species.]

La·na·i (lä-nä′ē, lə-nī′). Island, 365 square kilometers (141 square miles) of central Hawaii, west of Maui. Pineapple growing is important to the island's economy.

Lan·ark (lăn′ərk). Town in south-central Scotland, on the Clyde River. At New Lanark, nearby, Robert Owen built a model industrial village for his mill hands in the early 19th century.

la·nate (lā′nāt′) *adj. Biology.* Covered with or consisting of woolly hairs. [Latin *lānātus,* from *lāna,* wool.]

Lancang Jiang. See **Mekong.**

Lan·ca·shire¹ (lăng′kə-shîr, -shər). Nonmetropolitan county in northwestern England. In the late 18th and early 19th centuries it was the greatest cotton-manufacturing region in the world. Preston is the administrative center, and Lancaster is the county town. Since 1974 the Liverpool and Manchester areas, Lancashire's old industrial heartland, have been formed into the metropolitan counties of Merseyside and Greater Manchester.

Lancashire² *n.* A white, crumbly, English cheese made from cow's milk. [Originally made in LANCASHIRE.]

Lan·cas·ter¹ (lăng′kə-stər). The family name of the English royal family (1399–1461).

Lancaster². County town of Lancashire, northwest England, on the Lune River. It stands on the site of a Roman military station.

Lan·cas·tri·an (lăng-kăs′trē-ən) *adj.* **1.** Of or pertaining to the English royal house of Lancaster. **2.** Of or pertaining to Lancashire or its inhabitants.
~n. **1.** A member of the Lancastrian faction in the Wars of the Roses (1455–85). **2.** An inhabitant of Lancashire.

lance (lăns, läns) *n.* **1.** A thrusting weapon with a long wooden shaft and a sharp metal head, used by horsemen. **2.** A similar implement for spearing fish or killing whales. **3.** A lancer. **4.** A lancet.
~tr.v. **lanced, lancing, lances. 1.** To pierce with a lance. **2.** *Archaic.* To fling; hurl. **3.** To make an incision in with a lancet; cut into: *lance a boil.* [Middle English *la(u)nce,* from Old French *lance,* from Latin *lancea*†.]

lance corporal *n. Abbr.* **L/Cpl. 1.** In the U.S. Marine Corps, an enlisted man ranking above a private first class and below a corporal. **2.** In the British Army, a noncommissioned officer of the lowest rank. [From obsolete *lancepesade,* from Old French *lancepessade,* from Old Italian *lancia spezzata,* old soldier, "broken lance" : *lancia,* LANCE + *spezzata,* feminine past participle of *spezzare,* to break in pieces.]

lance·let (lăns′lĭt, läns′-) *n.* Any of various small, flattened marine organisms of the genus *Amphioxus* and subphylum Cephalochordata, allied to the vertebrates but having a notochord rather than a true vertebral column. Also called "amphioxus."

Lan·ce·lot, Laun·ce·lot (lăn′sə-lət, -lŏt′, län′-). *Arthurian Legend.* A knight of the Round Table whose love affair with Queen Guinevere resulted in a war with King Arthur.

lan·ce·o·late (lăn′sē-ə-lāt′) *adj.* Narrow and tapering at each end: *lanceolate leaves.* [Late Latin *lanceolātus,* from Latin *lanceola,* diminutive of *lancea,* LANCE.]

lanc·er (lăn′sər, län′-) *n.* **1.** Formerly, a cavalryman armed with a lance. **2.** A soldier belonging to a regiment that was originally armed with lances. [French *lancier,* from Old French, from LANCE.]

lanc·ers (lăn′sərz, län′-) *n.* Also **lan·ciers** (lăn′sîrz, län′-). *Used with a singular verb.* **1.** A form of quadrille for 8 or 16 couples. **2.** The music for this dance.

lance sergeant *n.* In certain regiments of the British Army, a corporal.

lan·cet (lăn′sĭt, län′-) *n.* **1.** A surgical knife with a short, wide, pointed, double-edged blade. **2.** *Architecture.* **a.** A lancet arch. **b.** A lancet window. [Middle English *lancette,* from Old French, diminutive of *lance,* LANCE.]

lancet arch *n. Architecture.* An arch that is narrow and pointed like the head of a spear. Also called "lancet."

lancet fish *n.* Either of two large marine fishes, *Alepisaurus ferox,* of the Atlantic, or *A. richardsoni,* of the Pacific, having long, sharp teeth and a large dorsal fin.

lancet window *n. Architecture.* A tall narrow window set in a lancet arch. Also called "lancet."

lance·wood (lăns′wo͝od′, läns′-) *n.* **1.** Any of several tropical American trees, such as one of the genera *Calycophyllum* or *Mimusops,* having hard, durable, uniformly grained wood. **2.** The wood of such a tree.

lan·cin·at·ing (lăn′sə-nā′tĭng) *adj.* Acute; stabbing. Said of a pain.

land (lănd) *n.* **1.** The solid ground of the earth, especially as distinguished from the sea. **2. a.** The soil; the earth: *till the land.* **b.** Any tract of ground considered in terms of its potential or nature: *desert land; prime building land.* **c. lands.** *South African.* An area of land used for the cultivation of crops. **d.** The rural as opposed to the urban life: *back to the land.* **3. a.** A nation. **b.** A district or region inhabited by a particular people. **c. lands.** Territorial possessions. **d.** A sphere or domain: *no longer in the land of the living.* **4.** Public or private landed property; real estate. **5.** *Law.* Any tract of land that may be owned, together with everything growing or constructed upon it. **b.** A landed estate. **6. a.** Any of the raised strips in a field that is divided by furrows. **b.** The raised portion of a grooved surface. —**how the land lies.** The nature of the prevailing state of affairs.
~*v.* **landed, landing, lands.** —*tr.* **1. a.** To bring to and unload on land: *land cargo.* **b.** To set or bring down on land or other surface: *land an aircraft.* **2.** To cause to arrive; bring to a specified place or condition: *His dealings landed him in jail.* **3. a.** To catch and pull in (a fish). **b.** *Informal.* To win; secure: *land a big contract.* **4.** To deliver: *land a blow on the head.* —*intr.* **1. a.** To come to shore. **b.** To disembark. **2. a.** To descend toward and settle on the ground or other surface. **b.** To meet or come to rest on a surface in a specified way: *landed on her feet.* **3.** To reach a specified place or condition in the end; finish up: *We took the wrong bus and landed 12 blocks from home. You'll land in court if you carry on this way.* [Middle English, Old English.]

Land (lănd), **Edwin Herbert** (1909–). U.S. inventor. He developed a light-polarizing plastic film, and, naming the material Polaroid, incorporated it into lenses for cameras and sunglasses. He also conducted optic research for the military and invented the one-step photographic process (1948), making possible a line of instant cameras.

–land *suffix.* Indicates: **1.** A region of a specified quality or kind; for example, **grassland.** **2.** A realm of a specified nature; for example, **dreamland.**

lan·dau (lăn′dô′, -dou′) *n.* **1.** A four-wheeled closed carriage with passenger seats facing front and back and a roof made in two sections for lowering or detaching. **2.** An early type of car with a roof similar to this. [First manufactured in *Landau,* Bavaria.]

lan·dau·let, lan·dau·lette (lăn′dô-lĕt′) *n.* **1.** A small landau. **2.** An early type of car having a collapsible roof over the back seat and an open driver's seat.

land bank *n.* A bank that issues long-term loans on real estate in return for mortgages.

land breeze *n.* Wind blowing from the land toward the sea or a lake center in the early part of the day, most commonly in the tropics.

land bridge *n.* **1.** A tract of land once thought to have connected one continent to another, providing a passage for migrating animals and thereby influencing their distribution. **2.** A tract of land, such as the Panama isthmus, joining two continents.

land crab *n.* Any terrestrial crab of the tropical family Gecarinidae, having a large, square body.

land·ed (lăn′dĭd) *adj.* **1.** Owning land: *landed gentry.* **2.** Consisting of land or real estate: *a landed estate.*

land·fall (lănd′fôl′) *n.* **1.** The sighting or reaching of land on a voyage or flight. **2.** The land sighted or reached.

land·fill (lănd′fĭl′) *n.* **1.** A method of rehabilitating land in which garbage and trash are buried in low-lying ground to build it up. **2.** Land that has been rehabilitated by landfill.

land·form (lănd′fôrm′) *n.* Any physical feature of the earth's surface, such as a mountain or river valley.

land grant *n.* A government grant of public land for a railroad, highway, or state college.

land-grant (lănd′grănt′, -gränt′) *adj.* Being a state educational institution given land by the Federal government under provision of the Morrill Act of 1862 on the condition that it offer courses in agriculture and the mechanical arts.

land·grave (lănd′grāv′) *n.* **1.** In medieval Germany, a count having jurisdiction over a particular territory. **2.** The title of certain German princes. [German *Landgraf,* from Middle High German *lantgrāve* : *lant,* land, + *grāve,* count.]

land·gra·vi·ate (lănd-grā′vē-ĭt, -āt′) *n.* The office, jurisdiction, or territory of a landgrave.

land·gra·vine (lănd′grə-vēn′) *n.* **1.** The wife or widow of a land-

grave. **2.** A woman who is the ruler of a landgraviate. [German *Landgräfin,* from Middle High German *lantgrævinne,* from *lantgrāve,* LANDGRAVE.]

land·hold·er (lănd′hōl′dər) *n.* A person who owns or holds land. —**land·hold·ing** *n. & adj.*

land·ing (lăn′dĭng) *n. Abbr.* **ldg. 1. a.** The act or process of coming to land or rest, especially after a sea voyage or flight. **b.** A termination, especially of a sea voyage or flight. **2.** A site for landing. **3. a.** An intermediate platform on a flight of stairs. **b.** The area at the top or bottom of a staircase.

landing beam *n.* A radio beam transmitted from an airfield to enable incoming aircraft to make a landing using instruments only.

landing craft *n. Abbr.* **L.C.** A flat-bottomed naval craft specifically designed to convey troops and equipment from ship to shore.

landing field *n.* A tract of land providing a runway for aircraft.

landing gear *n.* The undercarriage of an aircraft, designed to support the weight of the craft and its load on the ground.

landing strip *n.* An aircraft runway without airport facilities.

land·la·dy (lănd′lā′dē) *n., pl.* **-dies. 1.** A woman who owns and rents or leases land, commercial property, or residential units. **2.** A woman who runs a boarding house or inn. **3.** *Chiefly British.* A woman who is a publican or the wife of a publican.

länd·ler (lĕnt′lər) *n.* **1.** An Austrian country dance for couples in triple time. **2.** The music for this dance. [German, from dialectal *Landl,* Upper Austria, where the dance originated.]

land·less (lănd′lĭs) *adj.* Owning or having no land.

land line *n.* **1.** A telephone or telegraph link consisting of a cable laid over land rather than under the sea. **2.** A radio link.

land·locked (lănd′lŏkt′) *adj.* **1.** Surrounded or nearly surrounded by land. **2.** Confined to inland waters, as certain salmon are.

land·lord (lănd′lôrd′) *n.* **1.** A person who owns and leases land or buildings. **2.** A man who runs a boarding house or inn. **3.** *Chiefly British.* A man who is a publican; a publican.

land·lord·ism (lănd′lôr-dĭz′əm) *n.* **1.** A system of land management in which ownership of land is vested in a private individual or group that leases it at a fixed rate to tenants. **2.** The advocacy of such a system.

land·lub·ber (lănd′lŭb′ər) *n.* A person with little or no experience of the sea or seamanship.

land·mark (lănd′märk′) *n.* **1.** A fixed marker, such as a concrete block, indicating a boundary line. **2.** A prominent and identifying natural or man-made feature of a landscape. **3.** An event marking an important stage of development or a turning point in history.

land·mass (lănd′măs′) *n.* Any large area of land, such as a continent.

land mine *n.* An explosive mine laid usually just below the surface of the ground.

land office *n.* A government office that handles and keeps records of any sale or transfer of public land.

land-of·fice business (lănd′ô′fĭs, -ŏf′ĭs) *n.* A thriving, extensive, or rapidly moving business.

land of milk and honey *n.* A region or country offering the promise of a high standard of living and material comforts. [Referring to the Promised Land and God's promise to Moses to lead the Israelites "unto a land flowing with milk and honey" (Exodus 3:8).]

Land of Nod *n. Informal.* Sleep. [Punning phrase from NOD (to fall asleep) and the biblical Land of Nod: "And Cain . . . dwelt in the land of Nod, on the East of Eden" (Genesis 4:16).]

Land of the Midnight Sun *n.* **1.** Land lying north of the Arctic Circle. It has at least one day in summer when the sun does not set. **2.** Any region or country whose borders lie within this area, especially Lapland.

Land of the Rising Sun *n.* Japan.

Lan·don (lăn′dən), **Alfred Mossman** (1887–). U.S. politician. A Kansas oilman and progressive Republican, he was elected governor (1932 and 1934) despite a nationwide sweep by the Democrats. Nominated to oppose Franklin D. Roosevelt in the 1936 presidential election, he was soundly defeated but was later appointed by Roosevelt to represent the United States at the Pan-American Conference of 1938.

Lan·dor (lăn′dôr′, -dər), **Walter Savage** (1775–1864). British writer. He is best known for his *Imaginary Conversations of Literary Men and Statesmen* (1824–29), written in Florence.

land·own·er (lănd′ō′nər) *n.* One who owns land. —**land·own·er·ship** *n.* —**land·own·ing** *n. & adj.*

land-poor (lănd′po͝or′) *adj.* Owning much unprofitable land but lacking the capital to improve or maintain it.

Land·race (lănd′rās′) *n.* A pig of a white, lop-eared breed, yielding good-quality bacon and pork. [Danish : *land,* LAND + *race,* breed, RACE.]

land·scape (lănd′skāp′) *n.* **1.** A wide view or vista of natural scenery: *a desert landscape.* **2.** A painting, photograph, or other pictorial representation depicting such scenery. **3.** The branch of art dealing with the representation of natural scenery. **4. a.** A locality as seen with regard to its natural and man-made features: *an industrial landscape.* **b.** The scenery or appearance, natural or as modified by man, characteristic of a particular locality: *the New England landscape.* **5.** An extensive mental view; a prospect; a vista: *whole landscapes of thought.*
~*v.* **landscaped, -scaping, -scapes.** —*tr.* To adorn or improve (grounds) by contouring the land and planting flowers, shrubs, or trees. —*intr.* To arrange grounds artistically as a profession. [Dutch *landschap,* from Middle Dutch *landschap, lantscap,* land-

Landrace *A northern European breed of pig reared for its bacon. It is widely used for crossing as well as pure breeding.*

scape, region : *land,* land + *-schap, -scap,* suffix indicating condition.]

landscape architecture *n.* The decorative and functional alteration, planning, and planting of a piece of land, especially with reference to the siting of buildings. **—landscape architect** *n.*

landscape gardening *n.* The planning and planting of gardens or grounds in order to obtain a picturesque or harmonious result. **—landscape gardener** *n.*

land·scap·ist (lănd′skă′pĭst) *n.* A painter of landscapes.

Land·seer (lănd′sîr′), **Sir Edwin Henry** (1802–73). British painter. His paintings, often depicting animals, were popular with both Queen Victoria and the public, combining sentimentality with photographic realism.

Land's End. Rugged, westernmost peninsula of Cornwall and of England. It is the furthest point on the mainland of Great Britain from John o' Groats, which is traditionally considered to be its northernmost point.

land·side (lănd′sīd′) *n.* The flat side of a plow opposite the furrow.

lands·knecht (länts′kə-nĕkt′) *n.* A European mercenary soldier in the 16th or 17th century; especially, a German foot soldier armed with a pike or lance. Also called "lansquenet." [German *Landsknecht* : *land* + *knecht,* soldier, KNIGHT.]

land·slide (lănd′slīd′) *n.* **1. a.** The dislodging and fall of a mass of earth or rock or both. **b.** The dislodged mass. Also *chiefly British* "landslip." **2. a.** An overwhelming majority of votes for a political party or candidate. **b.** An election that sweeps a party or person into office. **c.** Any great victory.

land·slip (lănd′slĭp′) *n. Chiefly British.* A landslide.

lands·man¹ (lăndz′mən) *n., pl.* **-men** (-mĭn). One who lives and works on land as distinguished from a seaman.

lands·man² (länts′mən) *n., pl.* **landsleit** (länts′līt′). A fellow Jew coming from one's own district or town in Eastern Europe. [Yiddish, compatriot, from Middle High German *lantsman* : Old High German *lant,* land + *man,* man.]

Land·stei·ner (lănd′stī′nər), **Karl** (1868–1943). Austrian physician. Noted for his discovery of blood groups (1900) and for devising the ABO classification that enabled blood transfusions to be made, he also discovered the Rh factor, and was the first to isolate the poliomyelitis virus. He was awarded the Nobel Prize in 1930.

Land·tag (länt′täk′) *n.* **1.** A legislative assembly of a West German state. **2.** In some German states in the 19th century, a diet or assembly. [German, "land-day."]

land·ward (lănd′wərd) *adv.* Also **land·wards** (-wərdz). Toward the land or the interior.

~*adj.* Being toward the land.

Land·wehr (länt′vâr′) *n.* In German-speaking countries, a trained military reserve. [German, "land defense."]

land yacht *n.* A wind-powered vehicle having wheels and sails and used on flat ground, such as beaches. **—land yachting** *n.*

lane (lān) *n.* **1. a.** A narrow way or passage between walls, hedges, or fences. **b.** A narrow road, as in the country. **2.** Any narrow passage, course, or track, such as: **a.** A prescribed course for ships or aircraft. **b.** Any of two or more strips delineated on a road or highway to accommodate a single line of traffic. **c.** Any of a set of parallel courses marking the bounds for contestants in a race, especially a swimming or running race. **d.** A bowling alley. [Middle English, Old English, akin to Old Frisian *lana,* Middle Dutch *lāne*†.]

lang (lăng) *adj. Scottish.* Long.

lang. language.

Lang (lăng), **Fritz** (1890–1976). German film director. After pioneering the German film industry with such films as *Metropolis* (1926) and *M* (1931), he moved to Hollywood, where he made many Westerns and thrillers, noted for their somberness of tone.

Lange (läng), **Dorothea** (1895–1965). U.S. photographer. In the 1930's she lived with migratory workers in the Dust Bowl of the Great Plains—particularly those of Oklahoma—and produced an eloquent photographic study of their lives. Her first exhibition, in 1934, established her reputation as a documentary photographer.

Langerhans, islets of *pl.n.* **Islets of Langerhans** *(see).*

Lang·land (lăng′lənd), **William** (c.1332–1400). English poet. Probably a minor cleric, he is credited with the authorship of *The Vision of William concerning Piers the Plowman* (earliest complete known edition, 1392), one of the greatest literary works of medieval England. Its religious allegory is combined with social comment on inequality and clerical abuse.

lang·lauf (läng′louf′) *n.* A cross-country ski run. [German *Langlauf,* "long race" : *lang,* long, from Old High German + *Lauf,* a running, from Old High German *hlouf,* a leap, from *hlouffan,* to leap.] **—lang·lauf** *v.* **—lang·lauf·er** *n.*

lang·ley (lăng′lē) *n.* A unit of illumination used to measure temperature, as of a star, equal to one gram calorie per square centimeter of irradiated surface. [After S.P. LANGLEY.]

Lang·ley (lăng′lē), **Samuel Pierpoint** (1834–1906). U.S. astronomer and aviation pioneer. Through his solar radiation research and his book *The New Astronomy* (1888), he helped advance and popularize astronomy. His unmanned, steam-powered aircrafts were the first successful heavier-than-air flying machines (1896). From 1887 to 1906 he directed the Smithsonian Institute.

Lan·go·bard (lăng′gō-bärd′) *n., pl.* **-bardi** (-bär′dē). A Lombard *(see).* **—Lan·go·bar·dic** *adj.*

lan·gouste (län-gōōst′) *n.* The **spiny lobster** *(see).* [French, from Old French, from Old Provençal *langosta,* from Vulgar Latin *la-*

custa (unattested), perhaps variant of Latin *lŏcusta,* lobster, LOCUST.]

lan·gous·tine (làn′gōōs-tēn′) *n.* A **Dublin Bay prawn** *(see).* [French, diminutive of LANGOUSTE.]

lan·grage (lăng′grĭj) *n.* Also **lan·grel** (-grəl), **lan·gridge** (-grĭj). A type of shot consisting of scrap iron loaded into a case, formerly used in naval warfare to damage sails and rigging.

lang·syne, lang syne (lăng-sīn′, -zīn′) *adv. Scottish.* Long ago.

~*n. Scottish.* Time long past; times past. [Middle English *lang sine* : *lang,* LONG + *sine,* contraction of *sithen,* SINCE.]

Lang·try (lăng′trē), **Lillie,** born Emilie Charlotte le Breton (1853–1929). British actress. Known as the "Jersey Lily," she was already a society figure before making her stage debut (1881). She was for a time the mistress of Edward, Prince of Wales.

lan·guage (lăng′gwĭj) *n. Abbr.* **lang. 1. a.** The aspect of human behavior that involves the use of vocal sounds in meaningful patterns and, when they exist, corresponding written symbols to form, express, and communicate thoughts and feelings. **b.** The faculty in human beings which enables them to communicate in this way. **2.** A pattern of such behavior, historically established among a social or cultural group, involving a grammar and vocabulary that offers substantial communication only among its users: *the English language.* **3.** Any method of communicating ideas, as by a system of signs, symbols, gestures, or the like: *the language of algebra; body language.* **4.** The transmission of meaning, feeling, or intent by significance of act or manner: *"There's language in her eye"* (Shakespeare). **5.** The special vocabulary and usages of a scientific, professional, or other group. **6.** A characteristic style of speech or writing: *Miltonic language.* **7. a.** Speech or writing which uses vulgar or abusive terms: *Watch your language!* **b.** A particular manner of utterance or choice of words: *gentle language.* **8.** The manner or means of communication between living creatures other than man: *the language of dolphins.* **9. a.** *Often* **languages.** A language, especially a foreign language, as a subject of study: *He did languages at the university.* **b.** Linguistics. **10.** *Law.* The wording of a document or statute as distinct from its spirit. **11.** A computer programming code enabling human language to be translated into a form intelligible to computers. **—speak the same language.** To have the same background, experience, or understanding as another person. [Middle English *langage,* from Old French, from Gallo-Roman *linguāticum* (unattested), from Latin *lingua,* tongue, language.]

language laboratory *n.* A room designed for learning foreign languages, using audiovisual equipment such as tape recorders and a monitoring device that enables the teacher to listen and speak to students individually or all together.

langue (läng) *n. Linguistics.* Language considered as an abstract pattern or system shared by a speech community, as opposed to **parole** *(see),* the actual instances of its use in speech or writing. Compare **competence.** [French (specialized sense introduced by Saussure), tongue, language.]

langue de chat (də shä′) *n.* A thin, flat, finger-shaped, sweet biscuit or piece of chocolate. [French, "cat's tongue."]

langue d'oc (dôk′) *n.* The Romance language spoken in and around Provence and the Roussillon surviving in Provençal and Occitan. [French, from Old French, "language of *oc.*" *Oc* is the word for "yes" in Provençal.]

Langue·doc (läng-dôk′). Wine-producing region of southern France, formerly a province, lying on the Mediterranean Sea to the west of the Rhône. Its largest city is Toulouse.

langue d'o·ïl (läng dô-ēl′) *n.* The Romance language of Gaul north of the Loire on which modern French is based. [French, "language of *oïl.*" *Oïl* is the word for "yes" in northern medieval French.]

lan·guet (lăng′gwĭt, lăng-gwĕt′) *n.* A tonguelike thing or part. [Middle English, from Old French *languette,* diminutive of *langue,* tongue, language, from Latin *lingua.*]

lan·guid (lăng′gwĭd) *adj.* **1.** Lacking energy or vitality; faint; weak. **2.** Showing little or no spirit or animation; listless. **3.** Slow of movement; sluggish. [Old French *languide,* from Latin *languidus,* from *languēre,* to LANGUISH.] **—lan·guid·ly** *adv.* **—lan·guid·ness** *n.*

lan·guish (lăng′gwĭsh) *intr.v.* **-guished, -guishing, -guishes. 1. a.** To become weak or feeble; sag with loss of strength or vigor; flag. **b.** To continue in a state of apathy, debility, or suffering; exist under miserable or disheartening conditions. **c.** To be left ignored or neglected. **2.** To fall off; fade. **3.** To become listless as with longing; pine. Often used with *for.* **4.** To affect a mawkish air of nostalgia, tenderness, or wistfulness. [Middle English *languishen,* from Old French *languir* (stem *languiss-*), from Vulgar Latin *languīre* (unattested), from Latin *languēre,* to be faint or weak.] **—languish·er** *n.* **—lan·guish·ment** *n.*

lan·guish·ing (lăng′gwĭ-shĭng) *adj.* **1.** Becoming weak; fading. **2.** Slow; lingering. **3.** Expressing languor; full of sentimentality. **—lan·guish·ing·ly** *adv.*

lan·guor (lăng′gər) *n.* **1.** Physical or mental lassitude; sluggishness. **2.** Oppressive quiet or stillness. **3.** An atmosphere or feeling of soft or wistful tenderness. **4.** *Archaic.* Debility; sickness. —See Synonyms at **lethargy.** [Middle English, from Old French, from Latin, from *languēre,* to LANGUISH.] **—lan·guor·ous** *adj.* **—lan·guor·ous·ly** *adv.* **—lan·guor·ous·ness** *n.*

lan·gur (lŭng-gōōr′) *n.* Any of various slender, long-tailed, leaf-eating Asian monkeys of the genus *Presbytis* and related genera. Also called "leaf monkey." [Hindi *langūr,* perhaps from Sanskrit *lāngūla*†, "tailed."]

laniard. Variant of **lanyard.**

language

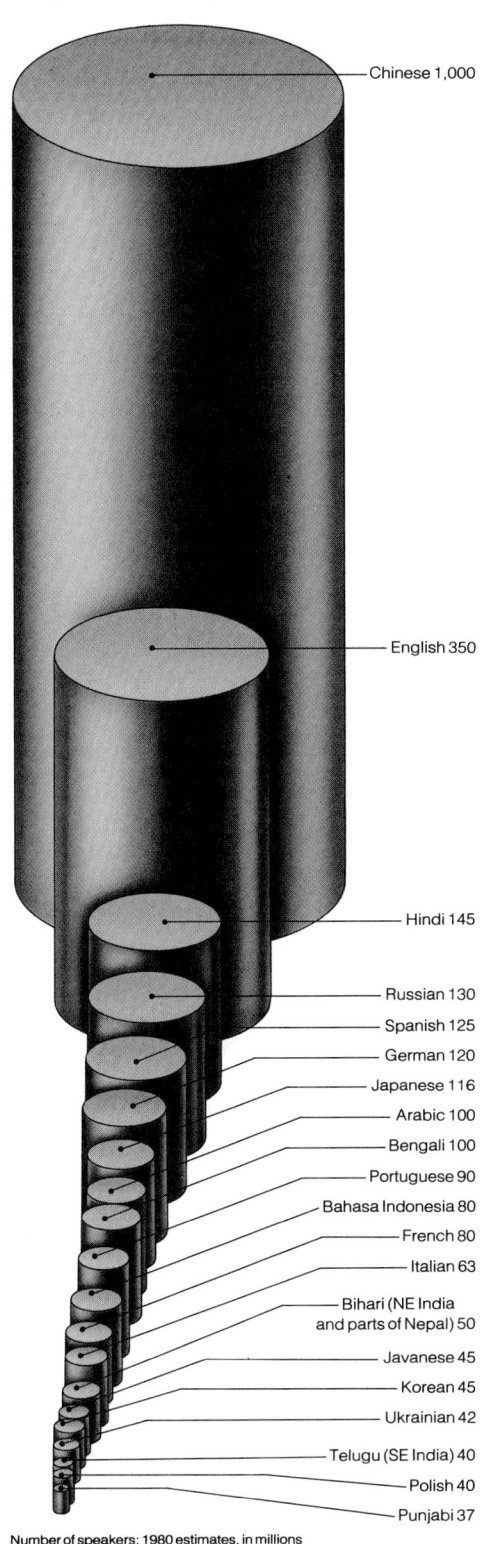

THE TONGUES OF MEN

The 20 most widely spoken languages in the world

Chinese is spoken by the largest number of people, but many dialects, such as Mandarin and Cantonese, are mutually unintelligible when spoken, and could almost be regarded as separate languages. On this basis, English is the most widely spoken language. Like Spanish and Portuguese, it has spread far beyond its land of origin.

Chinese 1,000

English 350

Hindi 145

Russian 130

Spanish 125

German 120

Japanese 116

Arabic 100

Bengali 100

Portuguese 90

Bahasa Indonesia 80

French 80

Italian 63

Bihari (NE India and parts of Nepal) 50

Javanese 45

Korean 45

Ukrainian 42

Telugu (SE India) 40

Polish 40

Punjabi 37

Number of speakers; 1980 estimates, in millions

---

la·ni·ar·y (lă′nē-ĕr′ē) *adj.* Adapted for tearing. Said of teeth, especially canines.
~*n., pl.* **laniaries.** A laniary tooth; a canine. [Latin *laniāre,* to tear.]

La·nier (lə-nîr′), **Sidney** (1842–81). U.S. author. Unable to support himself as a writer despite the publication of his novel *Tiger-Lilies* (1867), he studied law and joined his father's firm. Tuberculosis forced his retirement but provided him the time to write poetry, including "The Marshes of Glynn" (1878), and works of criticism.

la·nif·er·ous (lə-nĭf′ər-əs) *adj. Biology.* Having wool or woollike hair. [Latin *lānifer,* "wool-bearing" : *lāna,* wool + -FEROUS.]

lank (lăngk) *adj.* **1.** Long and lean; gaunt. **2.** Long, straight, and limp: *lank hair.* —See Usage note at **lean.** [Old English *hlanc,* loose, hollow, from Germanic.] —**lank·ly** *adv.* —**lank·ness** *n.*

lank·y (lăng′kē) *adj.* **-ier, -iest.** Tall, thin, and ungainly. —See Usage note at **lean.** —**lank·i·ly** *adv.* —**lank·i·ness** *n.*

lan·ner (lăn′ər) *n.* **1.** A falcon, *Falco biarmicus,* of Africa and the Mediterranean region. **2.** *Archaic.* The female of this species, used in falconry. [Middle English *laner,* from Old French *lanier (faucon),* cowardly (falcon), scornful application of *lanier,* weaver, from Latin *lānārius,* wool worker, from *lāna,* wool.]

lan·ner·et (lăn′ə-rĕt′) *n. Archaic.* A male lanner, smaller than the female, used in falconry. [Middle English *lanerette,* from Old French *laneret,* diminutive of *lanier,* LANNER.]

lan·o·lin, lan·o·line (lăn′ə-lən) *n.* A yellowish-white fatty substance obtained from wool and used in soaps, cosmetics, and ointments. Also called "wool fat." [German *Lanolin* : Latin *lāna,* wool + -OL (hydrocarbon) + -IN.]

la·nose (lā′nōs′) *adj.* Having woolly hair. [Latin *lānōsus,* from *lāna,* wool.] —**la·nos·i·ty** *n.*

Lan·sing (lăn′sĭng). Capital of Michigan, in the southern part of the state. The city grew after the arrival of the railroad (1870's) and the beginning of the automobile industry (1897). Automobiles and automobile parts are its major manufactures.

lans·que·net (lăns′kə-nĕt′) *n.* **1.** A card game involving betting. **2.** A landsknecht *(see).* [French.]

lan·ta·na (lăn-tā′nə) *n.* Any of various aromatic, chiefly tropical shrubs of the genus *Lantana,* having dense clusters of small, variously colored flowers. [New Latin *Lantana†.*]

lan·tern (lăn′tərn) *n.* Also *obsolete* **lant·horn** (lănt′hôrn′, lăn′tərn). **1.** A case that has transparent or translucent sides for holding and protecting a light, and is either fixed or portable. **2.** The room at the top of a lighthouse where the light is located. **3.** *Architecture.* A structure built on top of a roof with open or windowed walls to let in light and air. **4.** A slide projector. [Middle English *lanterne,* from Old French, from Latin *lanterna,* from Greek *lamptēr,* lantern, torch, from *lampein,* to shine.]

lantern fish *n.* Any of numerous small deep-sea fishes of the family Myctophidae, having phosphorescent light organs on the body.

lantern fly *n.* Any of various chiefly tropical insects of the subfamily Fulgorinae, having an enlarged, elongated head. [They were once erroneously thought to be luminous.]

lantern jaw *n.* **1.** A protruding, usually square-shaped, lower jaw. **2. lantern jaws.** Long thin jaws with sunken cheeks. —**lan·tern-jawed** *adj.*

lantern slide *n.* A photographic slide for projection, used in a magic lantern.

lantern wheel *n.* A small pinion consisting of circular disks connected by cylindrical bars that serve as teeth, used now chiefly in inexpensive clocks. Also called "lantern pinion."

lan·tha·nide (lăn′thə-nīd′) *n.* Also **lan·tha·non** (-nŏn′). A rare-earth element *(see).* [LANTHAN(UM) + -IDE.]

lanthanide series *n.* The set of chemically related elements with atomic numbers from 57 to 71; the rare-earth elements.

lan·tha·num (lăn′thə-nəm) *n. Symbol* **La** A soft, silvery-white, malleable, ductile, metallic, rare-earth element, obtained chiefly from monazite and bastnaesite, used in glass manufacture and with other rare earths in carbon lights for motion-picture and television studio lighting. Atomic number 57, atomic weight 138.91, melting point 920°C, boiling point 3,469°C, specific gravity 5.98 to 6.186, valence 3. [New Latin, from Greek *lanthanein,* to hide (from the finding of lanthanum concealed in cerium oxide).]

Lan-ts'ang Chiang. See **Mekong.**

la·nu·gi·nous (lə-nōō′jə-nəs, lə-nyōō′-) *adj.* Also **la·nu·gi·nose** (-nōs′). Covered with soft, short hair; downy. [Latin *lānūginōsus,* from *lānūgō,* down, LANUGO.] —**la·nu·gi·nous·ness** *n.*

la·nu·go (lə-nōō′gō, lə-nyōō′-) *n., pl.* **-gos.** Fine, soft hair, such as that covering a fetus. [Latin *lānūgō,* down, from *lāna,* wool.]

lan·yard, lan·iard (lăn′yərd) *n.* **1.** *Nautical.* A short rope or gasket for seizing a ladder, for example, or to secure rigging. **2.** A cord worn around the neck for carrying a knife, keys, or a whistle. **3.** A cord with a hook at one end used to fire a cannon. [Middle English *lanyer,* from Old French *laniere, lasniere,* from *lasne,* thong, strap : perhaps *laz,* LACE + *nasle,* string, from Germanic.]

Lao (lou) *n., pl.* **Lao** or collectively **Lao.** Also **La·o·tian** (lā-ō′shən, lou′shən). **1.** A member of a Buddhist people of Thai stock living in the area of the Mekong River in Laos and Thailand. **2.** The Thai language of this people, the official language of Laos.
~*adj.* Of the Lao or their language.

La·oc·o·on (lā-ŏk′ō-ŏn′). *Greek Mythology.* A Trojan priest of Apollo who was killed with his two sons by two sea serpents for having warned his people against the Trojan horse.

La·od·i·ce·a (lā-ŏd′ĭ-sē′ə). Name given to several cities built in Asia and Asia Minor by the Greek Seleucid dynasty in the 3rd century B.C. The chief one, Laodicea ad Lycum, near present-day Denizli in western Turkey, was a prosperous market town on the Roman trading route from the Orient and an early center of Christianity. —**La·od·i·ce·an** *n. & adj.*

La·od·i·ce·an (lā-ŏd'ə-sē'ən) *adj.* Indifferent or lukewarm, especially in religion. [After *Laodicea ad Lycum,* whose early church is reproved in Revelation 3:14–16 as being "lukewarm, and neither hot nor cold."] —**La·od·i·ce·an** *n.*

La·om·e·don (lā-ŏm'ə-dŏn'). *Greek Mythology.* The founder and king of Troy and father of Priam.

La·os (lä'ŏs, lous). Country in Southeast Asia. It is largely mountainous and forested, most of the population living in the Mekong River valley. Rice dominates the economy; teak and tin are exports. Laos was part of French Indochina, becoming fully independent in 1953. Pathet Lao Communists fought two civil wars (1953–54, 1960–73) and finally swept away the 600-year monarchy in 1975. The country aided the Vietnamese invasion of Kampuchea (1979), and by 1980 there was a massive Vietnamese presence in Laos, still racked by guerrilla activity. Area, 236,800 square kilometers (91,428 square miles). Population, 3,720,000. Capital, Vientiane (Viangchan). —**La·o·tian** (lā-ō'shən) *adj. & n.*

Lao-tse or **Lao Zi** (lou'dzŭ') (*c.* 6th century B.C.). Chinese philosopher. In legend he is a hermit from the Imperial Court who became deified as the founder of Taoism and author of Tao-te-Ching (Way of Life). [Chinese, "old master."]

lap¹ (lăp) *n.* **1.** The front region or area of a seated person extending from the lower trunk to the knees. **2. a.** The portion of a garment that covers this area. **b.** The front part of a skirt or dress used to hold or carry something. **c.** A hanging or flapping part of a garment. **3.** A hollow or depressed area, as in the land. **4.** A secure place or environment: *in the lap of luxury.* —**in someone's lap.** Under someone's responsibility. —**in the lap of the gods.** To be decided by fate or some impersonal power. [Middle English *lappe,* Old English *læppa,* flap of a garment, from Germanic.]

lap² *v.* **lapped, lapping, laps.** —*tr.* **1.** To fold, wrap, or wind over or around something: *lap pie crust over a filling.* **2.** To envelop in something; enwrap; swathe: *lapped in sables.* **3. a.** To place a thing) so as to overlap another. **b.** To lie partly over (something underneath); project onto or over the edge of. **4.** In cabinetmaking, to join as by scarfing. **5.** To get ahead of (an opponent) in a race by one or more complete circuits of the course. **6.** To polish until smooth, especially to hone (two mating parts against each other) with or without an abrasive. **7.** To convert (cotton or other fibers) into a sheet or layer. —*intr.* **1.** To fold or wind around something. **2.** To extend beyond an edge; overlap.
~*n.* **1.** A part that overlaps. **2. a.** One complete turn or circuit, especially of a racecourse or racetrack. **b.** A segment or stage of a race, journey, or comparable undertaking. **3.** A length, as of rope, required to encircle a drum or wheel, for example. **4.** A continuous band, layer, or sheet of cotton, flax, or other fibers ready for further processing. **5.** A wheel, disk, or slab of leather or metal, either stationary or rotating, for polishing stone, glass, or the like. [Middle English *lappen,* probably from *lappe,* LAP (as of a garment).]

lap³ *v.* **lapped, lapping, laps.** —*tr.* **1.** To take in (a liquid or food) with the tongue. Often used with *up.* Usually used of animals, especially dogs and cats. **2.** To wash against with a gentle intermittent slapping sound. Used of waves or a body of water. —*intr.* **1.** To drink by lifting a liquid with the tongue. **2.** To dash or slap softly

against a shore or other surface. —**lap up.** *Informal.* To receive eagerly and uncritically: *lap up praise.*
~*n.* **1.** The act or process of lapping. **2.** A watery food for animals. **3.** An amount ingested by a lap. **4.** The sound of lapping water. [Middle English *lappen,* Old English *lapian.*] —**lap·per** *n.*

lap·a·ro·scope (lăp'ə-rə-skōp') *n.* A surgical instrument that is inserted through the abdominal wall to inspect the abdominal organs. [Greek *lapara,* flank, from *laparos,* soft + -SCOPE.] —**lap·a·ros·co·py** (lăp'ə-rŏs'kə-pē) *n.*

lap·a·rot·o·my (lăp'ə-rŏt'ə-mē) *n., pl.* **-mies.** Surgical incision into the abdominal wall, either as a prelude to further surgery or to aid diagnosis. [Greek *lapara,* flank, from *laparos,* soft + -TOMY.]

La Paz (lə păz', päz'). Administrative capital of Bolivia, founded in 1548. Independence from Spain was declared here in 1809, and it became the capital in 1898. At 3,577 meters (11,735 feet) it is the world's highest capital.

lap·board (lăp'bôrd', -bōrd') *n.* A flat board to hold on the lap as a substitute for a table or desk.

lap dissolve *n.* A cinematic technique of overlapping a fade-out and a fade-in so that one scene dissolves into the next.

lap dog *n.* **1.** A small, easily held dog kept as a pet. **2.** *Informal.* A person prepared to do another's bidding out of uncritical love or admiration. Used derogatorily.

la·pel (lə-pĕl') *n.* Either of two parts of a garment, such as a jacket, that are an extension of the collar and fold back against the breast. [From LAP (flap of a garment).]

lap·ful (lăp'fŏŏl') *n.* As much as the lap can support or hold.

lap·i·dar·i·an (lăp'ə-dâr'ē-ən) *adj.* Cut in or inscribed on stone. [Latin *lapidārius,* of stone, from *lapis* (stem *lapid-*), stone, perhaps akin to Greek *lepas,* of Mediterranean origin.]

lap·i·dar·y (lăp'ə-dĕr'ē) *n., pl.* **-ies.** **1.** A person who works at cutting, polishing, or engraving gemstones. **2.** A dealer in precious or semiprecious stones.
~*adj.* **1.** Of or pertaining to precious stones or the art of working with them. **2.** Engraved in stone. **3.** Elegant and concise: *lapidary prose.* [Latin *lapidārius,* stoneworker, from *lapis* (stem *lapid-*), stone. See **lapidarian.**]

lap·i·date (lăp'ə-dāt') *tr.v.* **-dated, -dating, -dates.** To pelt with stones or stone to death. [Latin *lapidāre,* to stone, from *lapis* (stem *lapid-*), stone.] —**lap·i·da·tion** *n.*

la·pid·i·fy (lə-pĭd'ə-fī') *v.* **-fied, -fying, -fies.** —*tr.* To turn into stone. —*intr.* To become stone. [French *lapidifier,* from Medieval Latin *lapidificāre* : *lapis* (stem *lapid-*), stone + -*ficāre,* -FY.]

la·pil·lus (lə-pĭl'əs) *n., pl.* **-pilli** (-pĭl'ī'). *Usually* **lapilli.** A small solidified fragment of lava. [Latin *lapillus,* small stone, diminutive of *lapis,* stone. See **lapidarian.**]

lap·is laz·u·li (lăp'ĭs lăz'yŏŏ-lē) *n.* **1.** An opaque, azure-blue to deep-blue gemstone of lazurite. **2.** A mineral, **lazurite** (*see*). [Middle English, from Medieval Latin : Latin *lapis,* stone (see **lapidarian**) + Medieval Latin *lazuli,* genitive of *lazulum,* lapis lazuli, from Arabic *lāzaward,* from Persian *lāzhuward†.*]

Lap·ith (lăp'ĭth) *n., pl.* **-ithae** (-ə-thē') or **-iths.** *Greek Mythology.* One of a Thessalonian tribe who, at the disastrous wedding of the Lapith king, defeated the drunken centaurs.

lap joint *n.* A joint in which the ends or edges are overlapped and fastened together. —**lap-joint·ed** *adj.*

La·place (lə-pläs'), **Pierre Simon, Marquis de** (1749–1827). French mathematician and astronomer. His speculation, in *Mécanique Céleste* (1798–1825), that the solar system evolved from a rotating nebula is thought to be broadly correct.

Laplace operator *n. Mathematics.* Symbol ∇^2 The differential operator $\partial^2/\partial x^2 + \partial^2/\partial y^2 + \partial^2/\partial z^2$. Also called "Laplacian." [After P.S. de LAPLACE.]

Lap·land or **Lapp·land** (lăp'lănd') Vast region of northern Europe, largely within the Arctic Circle. It includes sections of Norway, Sweden, Finland, and the U.S.S.R. The region is rich in mineral and forest resources, aquatic and land fowl, fish, and reindeer. —**Lap·land·er, Lapp·land·er** *n.*

La Pla·ta (lä plä'tä). City in eastern Argentina, the capital of Buenos Aires province, 8 kilometers (5 miles) inland from Ensenada, its port on the Río de la Plata. It is Argentina's leading oil-refining center.

lap of honor *n.* A celebratory circuit made of a racetrack or other sports ground by the winner or winners of a sports event.

Lapp (lăp) *n.* Also **Lap·pish** (lăp'ĭsh) (for sense 2). **1.** A member of a people of nomadic tradition who inhabit Lapland. Also called "Laplander." **2.** The Finno-Ugric language of this people.
~*adj.* Of the Lapps or their language.

lap·pet (lăp'ĭt) *n.* **1.** A decorative flap, streamer, or loose fold on a garment or headdress. **2.** A flaplike structure, such as the wattle of a bird. [From LAP (fold or flap).]

Lappland. See **Lapland.**

lapse (lăps) *intr.v.* **lapsed, lapsing, lapses. 1. a.** To fall away by degrees; decline; vanish: *My enthusiasm soon lapsed.* **b.** To subside gradually; drift: *lapse into dreaminess.* **c.** To drop in standard or quality, usually temporarily. **d.** To cease practicing or adhering to a belief, custom, or the like: *a lapsed Catholic.* **2.** To elapse: *Years had lapsed since we last met.* **3. a.** *Law.* To pass to another through neglect or omission. Said of a right or privilege, a benefice, or an estate. **b.** To become void or ineffective.
~*n.* **1.** The act of lapsing; a gradual or imperceptible falling or sliding away. **2. a.** A minor slip or failure: *a lapse of the memory.* **b.** A fall from rectitude; moral error. **3.** A slipping into a lower

lapwing *Vanellus vanellus, the lapwing or peewit of Europe and Asia, nests on the ground and feeds mainly on insects in farmland, moors, and coastal marshes.*

larch *These deciduous conifers, originally mountain trees from central Europe, grow in mild lowland climates. Because they do not cast heavy shadows, they are often used to shelter hardwood saplings in planted forests. This is the European larch,* Larix decidua.

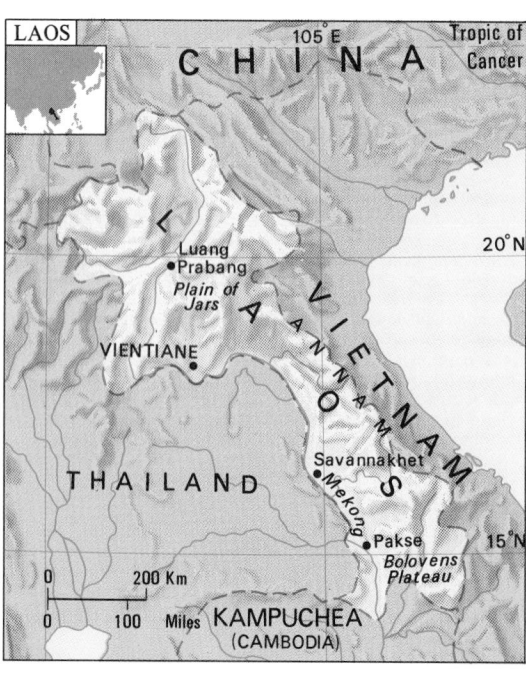

state or degree; a decline: *his lapse into premature senility.* **4. a.** The passage of time. **b.** An interval. **5.** *Law.* The termination of a right, interest, or privilege through disuse, a death, or other failure. **6.** An abandonment of a practice, especially of religious faith. **7.** A failure to renew membership of an organization. [Latin *lapsus,* error, a sliding, from *lābī* (past participle *lapsus*), to slide.] **—laps·er** *n.*

lapse rate *n.* The rate of change of a meteorological parameter with increasing height, such as the rate of change of atmospheric temperature for every 100 meters increase in altitude.

lap·strake (lăp′strāk′) *adj.* Also **lap·streak** (-strēk′). *Nautical.* Built with each strake overlapping the one below; clinker-built.
∼*n.* Also **lap·streak.** A clinker-built boat. [LAP (to overlap) + STRAKE.]

lap·sus (lăp′səs) *n., pl.* **-sus.** A lapse; a slip.

lapsus lin·guae (lĭng′gwī′) *n., pl.* **lapsus linguae.** A slip of the tongue; an inappropriate word or group of words uttered unintentionally. [Latin.]

La·pu·tan (lə-pyōō′tən) *adj.* Impractical and visionary; absurd. [After *Laputa,* a country in Swift's *Gulliver's Travels* (1726) devoted to absurdly visionary schemes.]

lap·wing (lăp′wĭng′) *n.* Any of several Eurasian birds of the genus *Vanellus,* related to the plovers; especially, *V. vanellus,* having a narrow crest. Also called "peewit," "pewit," "green plover." [Middle English *lapwinge,* variant (influenced by *winge,* wing, and *lappen,* to overlap) of *lappewinke,* Old English *hlēapewince* : *hlēapan,* to LEAP + *-wince* (unattested), WINK (referring to its way of flying).]

lar (lär) *n., pl.* **lares** (lâr′ēz) or **lars.** *Sometimes* **Lar.** A tutelary deity or spirit of an ancient Roman household. [Latin *Lār*†.]

Lar·a·mie (lăr′ə-mē), **Jacques** (died 1821). Fur trapper in Colorado and southeastern Wyoming, probably born in Canada. He is reputed to be the first to reach the upper course of the Laramie River. Though he figures importantly in legends of the West, little is known about him.

lar·board (lär′bərd) *n. Nautical.* The port side.
∼*adj. Nautical.* On the port side. [Middle English *lathebord, lad(d)borde,* probably "the loading side" (but influenced by STARBOARD) : *laden,* to load, LADE + *bord,* ship's side, BOARD.]

lar·ce·ny (lär′sə-nē) *n., pl.* **-nies.** *Law.* The felonious taking and removing of another's personal property with the intent of permanently depriving the owner. See **grand larceny, petit larceny.** [Middle English, from Old French *larcin,* from Latin *latrōcinium,* military service for pay, freebooting, from *latrō,* mercenary soldier, from Greek *latron,* pay.] **—lar·ce·nist, lar·ce·ner** *n.* **—lar·ce·nous** *adj.* **—lar·ce·nous·ly** *adv.*

larch (lärch) *n.* **1.** Any of several coniferous trees of the genus *Larix,* such as *L. decidua,* the European larch, having deciduous needles and heavy, durable wood. **2.** The wood of a larch. [German *Lärche,* from Middle High German *larche, lerche,* from Old High German *larihha* (unattested), from Latin *larix*† (stem *laric-*).]

lard (lärd) *n.* The white solid or semisolid rendered fat of a pig.
∼*tr.v.* **larded, larding, lards. 1.** To cover or coat with fat. **2.** To insert strips of bacon or the like in (lean meat or poultry) before cooking. **3.** To enrich (speech or writing) with witticisms, quotations, or similar additions. Often used derogatorily. [Middle English, from Old French, from Latin *lārdum, lāridum*†.] **—lard·y** *adj.*

lar·der (lär′dər) *n.* A small room, cupboard, or the like where meat and other foods are kept. [Middle English, from Old French *lardier,* from *lard,* LARD.]

larder beetle *n.* A small black beetle, *Dermestes lardarius,* found in houses, where it feeds on bacon and other fatty foods.

Lard·ner (lärd′nər), **Ringgold Wilmer,** known as "Ring" (1885–1933). U.S. journalist and author. A nationally syndicated sportswriter, he turned to fiction and wrote several humorous books, including *You Know Me, Al* (1916) and *Gullible's Travels* (1917). He also wrote for the theater, collaborating on *Elmer the Great* (1928) and *June Moon* (1929).

lar·don (lärd′n) *n.* Also **lar·doon** (lär-dōōn′). A strip of fat for larding meat. [French, from Old French, from *lard,* LARD.]

lares and penates *pl.n.* Esteemed household possessions. [From two kinds of Roman household gods. See **lar, penates.**]

large (lärj) *adj.* **larger, largest.** *Abbr.* **L, lg., lge. 1.** Of considerable size, extent, quantity, capacity, or amount; big; not small: *a large house.* **2.** Important; on a considerable scale: *a large steel producer.* **3. a.** Of wide scope or capacity: *a large mind.* **b.** Having breadth or sweep; comprehensive. **4. a.** Liberal; generous: *a large heart.* **b.** Prodigal. **5. a.** Pretentious; big. Said of speech or manners. **b.** *Rare.* Unrestrained; loose; gross. Said of speech or language. **6.** *Nautical.* Designating a favorable wind. **—at large. 1.** At liberty; free. **2.** At length; copiously: *He spoke at large on the housing problem.* **3.** As an entity or whole; in general. **—in the large.** On a broad scale. [Middle English, from Old French, from Latin *largus*†, generous, bountiful.] **—large·ness** *n.*

large calorie *n.* A unit of heat, a **calorie** *(see).*

large-heart·ed (lärj′här′tĭd) *adj.* Having a generous disposition; sympathetic. **—large-heart·ed·ness** *n.*

large intestine *n.* The portion of the intestine that extends from the ileum to the anus, forming an arch around the convolutions of the small intestine, and including the cecum, colon, and rectum.

large·ly (lärj′lē) *adv.* **1.** In a large manner; on a large scale. **2.** To a large extent; mainly.

large-mind·ed (lärj′mīn′dĭd) *adj.* Having a breadth of ideas; of liberal views; open-minded. **—large-mind·ed·ness** *n.*

large·mouth bass (lärj′mouth′) *n.* A North American freshwater food and game fish, *Micropterus salmoides.*

larg·er-than-life, larger than life (lärj′ər-*th*ən-līf′) *adj.* Seeming to belong to the world of fiction rather than to real life; possessing extraordinary qualities.

large-scale (lärj′skāl′) *adj.* **1.** Of large scope; extensive. **2.** Drawn or made large to show detail. Said of maps and models.

lar·gesse, lar·gess (lär-jĕs′, lär′jĭs, -jĕs′) *n.* **1. a.** Generosity, especially as displayed by an important person on a great occasion. **b.** The money, favors, or gifts bestowed. **2.** Generosity of attitude. [Middle English, from Old French, from *large,* generous, LARGE.]

lar·ghet·to (lär-gĕt′ō) *adv. Music.* Moderately slow in tempo. Used as a direction.
∼*n., pl.* **larghettos.** *Music.* A larghetto movement or passage.
∼*adj. Music.* Moderately slow. [Italian, diminutive of LARGO.]

larg·ish (lär′jĭsh) *adj.* Fairly large.

lar·go (lär′gō) *adv. Music.* In a slow, solemn manner. Used as a direction.
∼*adj. Music.* Slow and solemn.
∼*n., pl.* **largos.** *Music.* A largo movement or passage. [Italian, slow, "broad," from Latin *largus,* LARGE.]

lar·i·at (lăr′ē-ət) *n.* **1.** A long rope with a running noose for catching wild livestock; a lasso. **2.** A rope for picketing grazing horses or mules. [Spanish *la reata,* lasso, rope for tying mules : *la,* the + *reatar,* to tie again : *re-,* again, from Latin + *atar,* to tie, from Latin *aptāre,* to fit, from *aptus,* APT.]

Lá·ri·sa (lä′rē-sä). Also **La·ris·sa** (lə-rĭs′ə). Capital of ancient Thessaly in Greece. It now produces silk and tobacco.

lark[1] (lärk) *n.* **1.** Any of various chiefly Old World birds of the family Alaudidae, having a sustained, melodious song. See **skylark. 2.** Any of several similar birds, such as the meadowlark. [Middle English *larke,* Old English *lāwerce, lǣwerce,* from West Germanic *larw(a)rikōn* (unattested).]

lark[2] *n. Informal.* **1.** A carefree adventure. **2.** A harmless prank. **3.** An amusing situation or event: *What a lark!*
∼*intr.v.* **larked, larking, larks.** *Informal.* **1.** To play or have fun. Often used with *about* or *around.* **2.** To play tricks. [Probably variant of dialectal *lake,* to play, from Middle English *leiken,* from Old Norse *leika.*]

lark·spur (lärk′spûr′) *n.* Any of various plants of the genus *Delphinium,* having spurred, variously colored flowers.

lark·y (lär′kē) *adj.* **-ier, -iest. 1.** Ready for an adventure or harmless prank; carefree. **2.** Resulting from a lark.

Lar·mor precession (lär′môr, lăr′mər) *n.* The precession of the orbit of an electron in an atom subjected to a magnetic field. The frequency of the precession (the *Larmor frequency*) is $eH/4\pi mv$, where H is the field strength and $m,e,$ and v are the mass, charge, and velocity of the electron respectively. [After Sir Joseph *Larmor* (1857–1942), British physicist.]

La Roche·fou·cauld (lä rôsh-fōō-kō′), **François, Duc de** (1613–80). French moralist. He wrote *Maximes* (1664), a collection of cynical epigrams suggesting that people are ruled by self-interest.

La Ro·chelle (lä rô-shĕl′). City in western France, on the Bay of Biscay. It is the chief French Atlantic fishing port. During the 16th-century Wars of Religion it was the most important stronghold of the Protestant Huguenots.

La·rousse (lə-rōōs′), **Pierre** (1817–75). French lexicographer, who compiled the *Grand Dictionnaire Universel du XIXe Siècle* (1866–76). The company he founded still publishes reference books.

lar·ri·gan (lăr′ĭ-gən) *n. Sometimes* **Larrigan.** A moccasin with knee-high leggings made of oiled leather. [17th century : origin obscure.]

lar·rup (lăr′əp) *tr.v.* **-ruped, -ruping, -rups.** *Regional.* To beat; flog.
∼*n. Regional.* A blow. [19th century : origin obscure.]

Lars Por·se·na (lärz pôr′sĭ-nə) (*c.* 6th century B.C.). Etruscan king who, in Roman legend, attacked Rome after the proclamation of the Republic (509 B.C.) but failed to restore the Roman monarchy.

lar·um (lăr′əm) *n. Archaic.* An alarm. [Short for ALARUM.]

lar·va (lär′və) *n., pl.* **-vae** (-vē). **1.** The wingless, often wormlike form of a newly hatched insect before metamorphosis. **2.** The newly hatched stage of any of various animals that undergo metamorphosis, differing markedly in appearance from the adult. [Latin *lārva*†, disembodied spirit, mask.] **—lar·val** *adj.*

lar·vi·cide (lär′vĭ-sīd′) *n.* An insecticide designed to kill larval pests. [LARV(A) + -CIDE.] **—lar·vi·ci·dal** *adj.*

laryng-. Variant of **laryngo-.**

la·ryn·ge·al (lə-rĭn′jē-əl, -jəl, lăr′ən-jē′əl) *adj.* Also **la·ryn·gal** (lə-rĭng′gəl). **1.** Of, pertaining to, affecting, or near the larynx. **2.** *Phonetics.* Produced in or with the larynx; glottal.
∼*n.* **1.** A part of the larynx. **2.** *Phonetics.* A laryngeal sound. **3.** Any of a set of sounds reconstructed for Proto-Indo-European, of uncertain character (but originally thought to be laryngeal in nature), manifested in various environments, typically involving loss of the original sound in most languages of the family. [New Latin *laryngeus,* from *larynx* (stem *laryng-*), LARYNX.]

lar·yn·gec·to·my (lăr′ən-jĕk′tə-mē) *n., pl.* **-mies.** Surgical removal of part or all of the larynx, as for the treatment of laryngeal cancer. [LARYNG(O)- + -ECTOMY.]

la·ryn·ges. Alternate plural of **larynx.**

lar·yn·gi·tis (lăr′ən-jī′tĭs) *n.* Inflammation of the larynx, causing hoarseness and sometimes temporary loss of speech. [New Latin : LARYNG(O)- + -ITIS.] **—lar·yn·git·ic** (lăr′ən-jĭt′ĭk) *adj.*

laryngo-, laryng- *prefix.* Indicates the larynx or pertaining to the

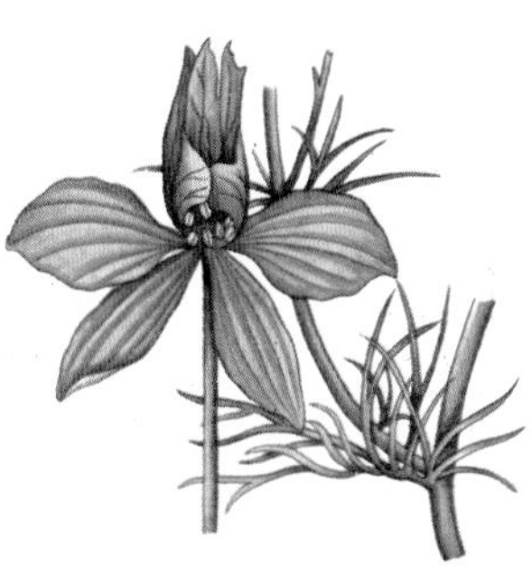

larkspur *The tall spikes of these originally Mediterranean flowers bear showers of blooms in shades of pink, white, or blue, yielding a blue dye from which blue ink was formerly made.*

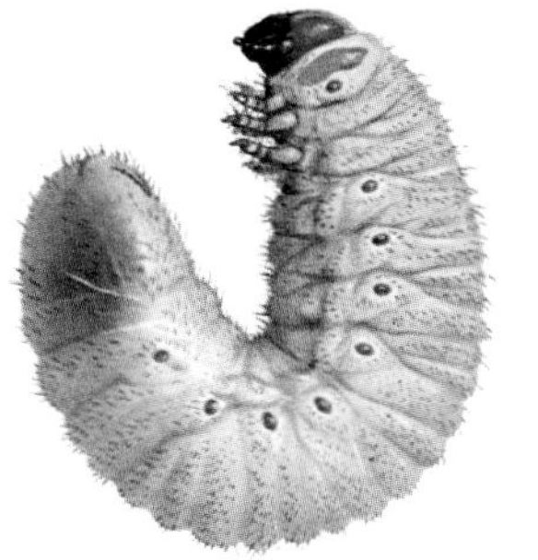

larva *The second stage in the four-stage life cycle of most advanced insects. The four stages are egg, larva, pupa, and adult. This is the larva of a dung beetle.*

PRONUNCIATION KEY

ă, pat; ā, pay; âr, care;
ä, father, are; b, bib;
ch, church; d, deed; ĕ, pet;
ē, be; f, fife; g, gag; h, hat;
hw, which; ĭ, pit; ī, pie;
îr, pier; j, judge; k, kick;
l, lid, needle; m, mum;
n, no, sudden; ng, thing;
ŏ, pot; ō, toe; ô, paw, for;
oi, noise; ou, out; ŏŏ, book;
ōō, boot; p, pop; r, roar;
s, sauce; sh, ship, dish;
t, tight; th, thin, path;
th, this, bathe; ŭ, cut; ûr, fur;
v, valve; w, with; y, yes;
z, zebra, size; zh, vision;
ə, about, item, edible, gallop, circus, peaceful

IN FOREIGN WORDS:

à, *Fr.* ami; œ, *Fr.* feu, *Ger.* schön; ü, *Fr.* tu, *Ger.* über; KH, *Ger.* ich, *Scot.* loch; N, *Fr.* bon; y′, *Fr.* Compiègne

STRESS MARKS:

Primary stress: ′
in·cite′ (ĭn-sīt′)
Secondary stress: ′
in′sight′ (ĭn′sīt′)

larynx; for example, **laryngoscope, laryngitis.** [New Latin, from Greek *larungo-*, from *larunx* (stem *larung-*), LARYNX.]

la·ryn·go·graph (lə-rĭng′gə-grăf′, -gräf′) *n.* An instrument used to observe the functioning of the vocal cords by means of electrodes placed on the surface of the neck. [LARYNGO- + -GRAPH.] —**la·ryn·go·graph·ic** *adj.* —**lar·yn·gog·ra·phy** (lăr′ĭng-gŏg′rə-fē) *n.*

lar·yn·gol·o·gy (lăr′ĭng-gŏl′ə-jē) *n.* The medical study or treatment of the larynx and its diseases. [LARYNGO- + -LOGY.] —**lar·yn·go·log·i·cal** (lăr′ĭng-gə-lŏj′ĭ-kəl) *adj.* —**lar·yn·gol·o·gist** *n.*

la·ryn·go·scope (lə-rĭng′gə-skōp′) *n.* A tubular instrument used to observe the interior of the larynx. [LARYNGO- + -SCOPE.] —**la·ryn·go·scop·ic, la·ryn·go·scop·i·cal** *adj.* —**la·ryn·go·scop·i·cal·ly** *adv.* —**lar·yn·gos·co·py** (lăr′ĭng-gŏs′kə-pē) *n.*

lar·yn·got·o·my (lăr′ĭng-gŏt′ə-mē) *n., pl.* -**mies.** Surgical incision into the larynx. [LARYNGO- + -TOMY.]

lar·ynx (lăr′ĭngks) *n., pl.* **la·ryn·ges** (lə-rĭn′jēz) or -**ynxes.** The upper part of the respiratory tract between the pharynx and the trachea, having cartilaginous walls and containing the vocal cords. [New Latin, from Greek *larunx†*.]

la·sa·gna, la·sa·gne (lə-zän′yə) *n.* **1.** Flat wide noodles. **2.** A dish made by baking such noodles in layers with minced meat, tomatoes, and cheese. [Italian, from Latin *lasanum*, cooking pot, originally "chamber pot," from Greek *lasanon†*.]

La Salle (lə săl′), **Robert Cavelier, Sieur de** (1643–87). French explorer. He led expeditions to North America and claimed Louisiana for France (1682). He was murdered by mutineers on his final expedition.

las·car (lăs′kər) *n.* A sailor from the East Indies. [Hindi *lashkarī*, soldier, from *lashkar*, army, from Persian, from Arabic *al-'askar*, the army.]

Las Ca·sas (läs kä′səs), **Bartolomé de** (1474–1566). Spanish planter in the West Indies, who joined the Dominican order and campaigned for the abolition of Indian slavery.

Las·caux (lă-skō′). Cave near Montignac in southwest France, lying above the Vézère valley in the Dordogne. Discovered in 1940, it is one of the most important sites of prehistoric cave art in Europe. The paintings, mostly of animals, are from the late Aurignacian period.

larynx

THE MEDIUM OF SPEECH

How sounds are formed in the larynx

The larynx is often known as the voice box because spoken sounds are formed there. As air is expelled from the lungs, it passes through the larynx, where it provides the energy for speech. If the vocal cords are tensed, the passage of air makes them vibrate and produce a buzzing, or voiced, sound that is then shaped into spoken words by the tongue, teeth, and lips. In adolescent boys, the larynx enlarges in response to the male sex hormone, and the treble voice of childhood "breaks," or deepens.

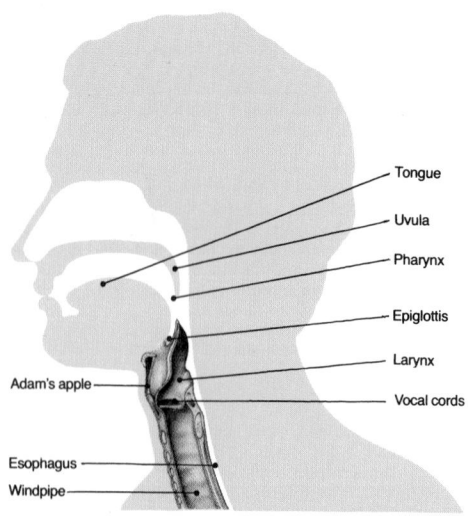

Tongue

Uvula

Pharynx

Epiglottis

Larynx

Adam's apple

Vocal cords

Esophagus

Windpipe

ANATOMY OF THE LARYNX *The larynx is a structure of cartilage, muscles, and ligaments in the windpipe. It sticks out slightly in the front of the neck to form the Adam's apple and contains the vocal cords. Muscles control the length and tension of the cords, which can be vibrated by air passing through them to make sounds. To ensure that foods and fluids pass down the esophagus rather than down the windpipe to the lungs, the epiglottis— a valvelike flap of cartilage behind the tongue—closes during the act of swallowing.*

las·civ·i·ous (lə-sĭv′ē-əs) *adj.* **1.** Of or characterized by lust; lewd; lecherous. **2.** Exciting sexual desires. [Late Latin *lascīviōsus*, from Latin *lascīvia*, licentiousness, wantonness, from *lascīvus*, wanton, lustful.] —**las·civ·i·ous·ly** *adv.* —**las·civ·i·ous·ness** *n.*

lase (lāz) *intr.v.* **lased, lasing, lases.** To function as a laser; emit coherent radiation by the action of a laser. [Back-formation from LASER.]

la·ser (lā′zər) *n.* **1.** Any of several devices that convert incident electromagnetic radiation of mixed frequencies to one or more discrete frequencies of highly amplified and coherent visible radiation. Also called "optical maser." **2.** Any such device, including the **maser** *(see),* the output of which is in an invisible region of the electromagnetic spectrum. [*L*ight *a*mplification by *s*timulated *e*mission of *r*adiation.]

lash¹ (lăsh) *n.* **1.** A stroke or blow with or as if with a whip, rope, or the like. **2.** The thin stinging part or parts of a whip; the thongs. **3.** A remark that insults, reprimands, or ridicules. **4.** A powerful or violent impact: *the lash of rain on the windows.* **5.** An eyelash.
~*v.* **lashed, lashing, lashes.** —*tr.* **1.** To strike with or as if with a whip. **2.** To strike against with force or violence: *waves lashing the sides of the ship.* **3.** To move or wave rapidly to and fro: *a lion lashing his tail.* **4.** To make a vehement verbal or written attack on. **5.** To incite or urge as with lashes. —*intr.* **1.** To move a limb, tail, or the like rapidly or suddenly. **2.** To make a sudden or violent attack. Used with *at* or *against.* —**lash out. 1.** To make a sudden or violent attack. **2.** To express vehement criticism. **3.** To kick out violently. Used of a horse. [Middle English *lashe†*.] —**lash·er** *n.*

lash² *tr.v.* **lashed, lashing, lashes.** To secure or bind, as with a rope, cord, or chain. [Middle English *lasshen*, from Old French *lac(h)ier*, from Latin *laqueāre*, to ensnare, from *laqueus*, snare.] —**lash·er** *n.*

lash·ing (lăsh′ĭng) *n.* **1.** Something used for securing or binding, such as a rope or cord. **2.** A beating or flogging.

lash·ings (lăsh′ĭngz) *pl.n. Chiefly British.* Lavish quantities. [From LASH (whip) in an obsolete sense "lavish."]

Las·ki (lăs′kē), **Harold Joseph** (1893–1950). British socialist and political theorist. He was a professor at the London School of Economics.

Las Pal·mas (läs päl′məs). Capital of Spain's Las Palmas province in the Canary Islands, on the Isla de Gran Canaria. It was founded in 1478 and named after the palm trees growing there. Las Palmas was an important station for Spanish trade ships on the African-South American route. Today it is a major tourist resort.

La Spe·zia (lä spä′tsyä). Seaport in northwest Italy, lying on the Gulf of La Spezia. It has been an important fortified town since the Middle Ages and is today the largest naval station and arsenal in Italy.

lass (lăs) *n.* **1.** A girl or young woman. **2.** A sweetheart. [Middle English *lasce, lasse†*.]

Lassa. See Lhasa.

Las·sa fever (lăs′ə, lä′sə) *n.* A severe viral disease of central West Africa, typically causing fever, headache, and muscular pain and often leading to death from heart or kidney failure.

las·si (lăs′ē, lŭs′ē) *n.* A sweet or salty cold drink, originating in India, made from yoghurt or buttermilk and spices. [Hindi.]

las·sie (lăs′ē) *n.* A lass. [Diminutive of LASS.]

las·si·tude (lăs′ə-tōōd′, -tyōōd′) *n.* A state of exhaustion or torpor. —See Synonyms at **lethargy.** [Latin *lassitūdō*, from *lassus*, tired, weary.]

las·so (lăs′ō) *n., pl.* -**sos** or -**soes.** A long rope or leather thong with a running noose at one end used especially to catch horses and cattle.
~*tr.v.* **lassoed, -soing, -sos** or -**soes.** To catch with or as if with a lasso; rope. [Spanish *lazo*, from Latin *laqueus*, snare.]

last¹ (lăst, läst). Alternate superlative of **late.**
~*adj.* **1.** Being or coming after all others: *last on the list.* **2.** Being the only remaining part of a collection or sequence: *my last stamp.* **3.** Most recent; latest: *last year.* **4.** Highest; greatest; utmost: *the last degree.* **5.** Most valid, authoritative, or conclusive: *The boss always has the last say.* **6.** Least appropriate; most unexpected: *the last man we suspected.* **7.** The lowest in rank, size, or importance: *the last prize.* **8.** Final or ultimate, as just before death: *famous last words.* —See Usage note at **first.** —**every last.** *Informal.* All; omitting none: *He took every last cigarette.* —**last but not least.** Important or significant although coming at the end.
~*adv.* **1.** After all others, as in chronology or sequence: *They left last.* **2.** Most recently: *last heard of in May.* Often used in combination: *the last-mentioned item.*
~*n.* **1.** One that is last: *the last of the Plantagenets.* **2.** The end: *He held out until the last.* **3.** The final mention or appearance of something: *I fear we haven't seen the last of her.* **4.** The person or thing most recently mentioned: *You need glue, string, and paper, the last being the most important.* **5.** The last instance or occasion of something: *This day will be your last.* —**at (long) last.** After a considerable length of time; finally. —**breathe one's last.** To die. [Middle English *last*, Old English *latost*, superlative of *laet, late*, LATE.]
　　Synonyms: eventual, final, terminal, ultimate.

last² *v.* **lasted, lasting, lasts.** —*intr.* **1.** To continue in existence; go on: *The war lasted for four years.* **2.** To remain in good condition; endure: *Clay lasts longer than paper.* **3.** To endure or get through: *His strength won't last.* **4.** To remain in adequate supply: *Will our water last?* —*tr.* **1.** To be adequate or sufficient for: *Five dollars will last me till tomorrow.* **2.** To endure throughout: *He didn't last the course.* **3.** To take or go on for (a specified time): *It lasts half an*

laser

THE ELEMENTAL POWER OF THE LASER

A beam of intensely pure light that can slice through metal or perform eye surgery

In the laser, man has at his service a device that unlocks an elemental power of nature—the power of light. The laser's beam of intensely pure light can cut through metal or pierce diamond, the hardest natural substance on earth.

The first laser—*Light Amplification by means of Stimulated Emission of Radiation*—was built by the American physicist T. H. Maiman in 1960. But the principles on which the laser depends had been established when the century was young, by physicists unraveling the secrets of the atom. In 1913 Niels Bohr, a Dane, pointed out that atoms exist only in certain states, each with its own energy level. If an atom

changes from a high-energy level to a low-energy level, it gives out surplus energy in the form of radiation. Some atoms give off this excess energy spontaneously. Others, as was observed in 1917 by the German-born physicist Albert Einstein, can be triggered into changing their energy state if they are bombarded with radiation from an outside source. This is known as the stimulated emission of radiation.

For the laser he built in 1960, Maiman used a rod of artificial ruby. Atoms in the rod were excited by high-intensity light from outside and were stimulated to give off pure red light in brief, penetrating pulses. The pulsed ruby laser is still the most powerful type of

laser, producing light with 10 million times the intensity of sunlight. It was followed by the gas laser, which is less powerful but emits a continuous beam of light, rather than very short pulses.

Laser light differs from ordinary light in several ways. Whereas ordinary white light is made up of light of different wavelengths (that is, colors), laser light is of a single wavelength. Instead of spreading out on all directions from its source like light from the sun or from an electric light bulb, pure laser light stays concentrated, with a beam that is almost perfectly parallel. It is this concentration of energy that makes the laser so powerful.

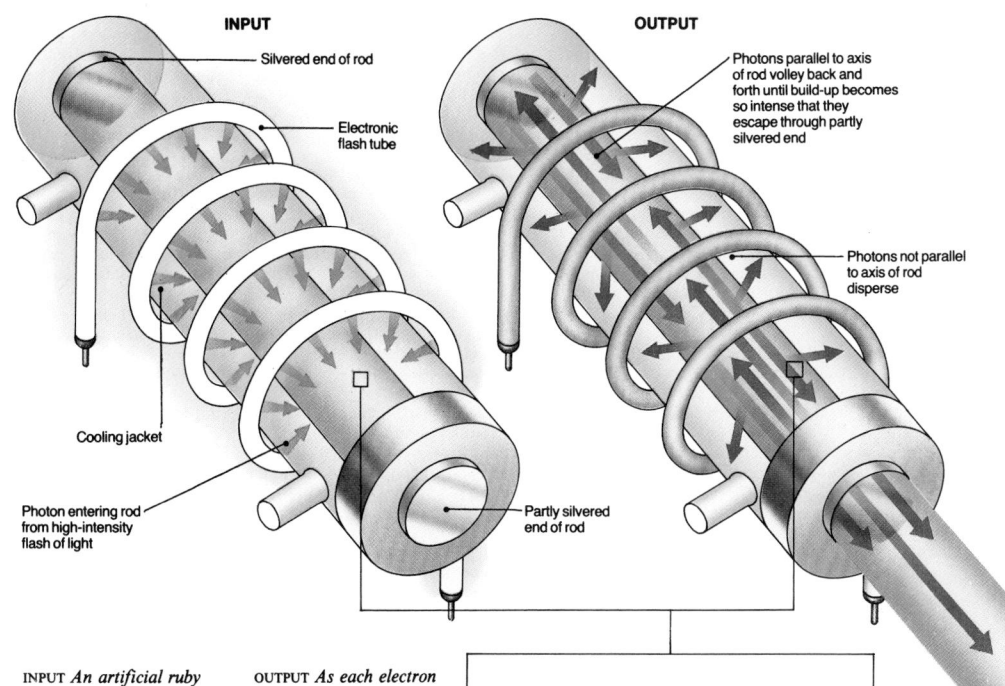

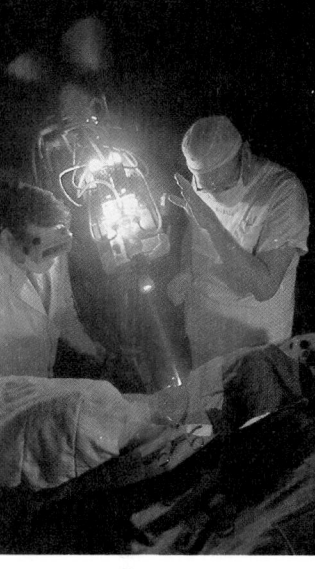

LASERS IN ACTION

Producing bursts of light energy that last for only a few millionths of a second, but are 10 million times more powerful than the light from the sun the ruby laser is used in eye surgery and also (above) in the treatment of skin cancer.

The accurately focused laser beam burns away cancerous cells, but without causing damage to surrounding tissue. Laser scalpels can make fine incisions and at the same time heat-seal the blood vessels to reduce bleeding.

In industry, lasers are used for cutting and welding and to guide tunnel-boring machinery on a perfectly straight line. In telecommunications, they are used in fiber optics; and they help to create three-dimensional photographs in holography. Sending out a laser pulse and measuring the time that elapses before its reflection returns, provides a very accurate way of measuring distances. The distance from earth to moon, for instance, can be calculated to the nearest meter.

INPUT *An artificial ruby rod, about 160 millimeters (6 inches) long and 12 millimeters (1/2 inch) across, is silvered at one end and partly silvered at the other. Encompassing the rod is a high-intensity electronic flash tube. When the tube flashes on, chromium atoms in the ruby become excited. This causes the outer electrons to jump from their ground state of energy to a high-energy level; they fall back, first to an intermediate state, then to the ground state from which they originally jumped.*

OUTPUT *As each electron falls back from an intermediate to a ground state, it emits a photon of light energy. Some photons collide with electrons still in the intermediate state. The electrons release photons that travel in exactly the same direction as the "striker" photon. Other electrons are struck and release more photons. A chain reaction develops. The silvered ends reflect back and forth those photons traveling parallel to the rod's axis until a hot red beam builds up and flashes out from the partly silvered end.*

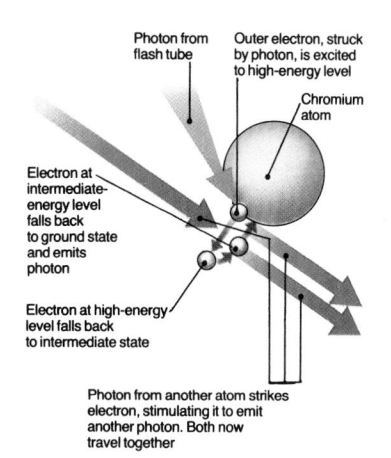

---

hour. [Middle English *lasten*, Old English *lǣstan*.] **—last·er** *n.*

last³ *n.* A block or form shaped like a human foot, used by shoemakers in making or repairing shoes.
~*tr.v.* **lasted, lasting, lasts.** To mold or shape on a last. **—stick to one's last.** To do the work to which one is accustomed. [Middle English *laste*, Old English *lǣste*, from *lāst*, sole, footprint.]

last⁴ *n.* Chiefly British. A unit of weight or volume varying for different commodities and in different districts, and approximating 80 bushels, 640 gallons, or 2 tons. [Middle English *last*, "load," "burden," Old English *hlæst*.]

last-ditch (lăst'dĭch') *adj.* Of or designating a final desperate effort:

a last-ditch attempt to save the company.

Las·tex (lăs'tĕks) *n.* A trademark for a yarn having a core of elastic rubber wound with rayon, nylon, silk, or cotton threads. [(E)LAS-(TIC) + TEX(TILE).]

last honors *pl.n.* Observances or signs of respect at a funeral. Also called "funeral honors."

last hurrah *n.* A last appearance or effort, especially at the end of a career.

last·ing¹ (lăs'tĭng, läs'-) *adj.* Continuing for a long time; durable. **—last·ing·ly** *adv.* **—last·ing·ness** *n.*

lasting² *n.* A durable twilled fabric.

lateen *In a lateen rig, the luff, or leading edge of the sail, is attached to a very long spar, not the mast. Lateen-rigged boats, like this one on the Nile, are still common in many parts of the world.*

Last Judgment *n.* According to the Bible, the final judgment by God of all mankind. Preceded by *the.*

last·ly (lăst′lē) *adv.* In the end; in conclusion; finally.

last minute *n.* The moment or time immediately before an event or deadline: *She always does everything at the last minute.* Also called "last moment." **—last-min·ute** (lăst′mĭn′ĭt) *adj.*

last name *n.* A surname.

last post *n. Sometimes* **Last Post.** *Military.* **1.** A bugle call blown as a signal for the hour for retiring to bed. **2.** A bugle call blown at funerals.

last resort *n.* A final measure or course of action open to one.

last straw *n.* An additional difficulty, irritation, or trouble that stretches one's tolerance or endurance beyond the limit. Preceded by *the.* [Based on the proverbial phrase, *It's the last straw that breaks the camel's back.*]

Last Supper *n.* Christ's supper with his disciples on the night before his Crucifixion, at which he instituted the Eucharist. Preceded by *the.* Also called the "Lord's Supper."

last thing *adv. Informal.* As the last or final action: *She'll do that last thing before she leaves.*

last word *n.* **1.** The final statement in a verbal argument. **2. a.** A conclusive or authoritative statement or treatment: *the last word in car safety.* **b.** The power or authority of ultimate decision. **3.** *Informal.* The newest in fashion; the latest thing. Preceded by *the.*

Las Ve·gas (läs vā′gəs). City in southern Nevada. Set in a remote ranching and mining region, it is the leading gambling city in the country and the site of many famous nightclubs.

lat. latitude.

Lat. Latin.

lat·a·ki·a (lăt′ə-kē′ə) *n.* A grade of Turkish tobacco. [After *Latakia,* Syrian port in a tobacco-growing region.]

latch (lăch) *n.* **1.** A fastening or lock, typically a bar that falls into a groove or cavity and is lifted by a lever. **2.** A small spring-lock for an outside door that can be opened from the outside by a key. *~v.* **latched, latching, latches.** *—tr.* To close or lock with a latch. *—intr.* To have a latch for closing or locking. **—latch on.** *Informal.* **1.** To attach oneself; cling. Used with *to.* **2.** To understand; perceive: *The fool still hasn't latched on.* Often used with *to.* **3.** To single out (an idea, for example). Used with *to: latched on to idealism as the key to his work.* [Middle English *lache,* from *lachen,* to latch, seize, Old English *læccan,* to grasp.]

latch·et (lăch′ĭt) *n. Archaic.* A thong used to fasten a shoe or sandal. [Middle English, from Old French *lachet, lacet,* shoestring, from *las,* noose, snare.]

latch·key (lăch′kē′) *n.* **1.** A key for opening a latch, especially one on an outside door or gate. **2.** A symbol of freedom from parental authority.

latchkey child *n.* A child who has a key to his home because both parents are out working when he returns from school.

latch·string (lăch′strĭng′) *n.* A cord attached to a latch and often passed through a hole in the door to allow lifting of the latch from the outside.

late (lāt) *adj.* **later** or *rare* **latter** (lăt′ər), **latest** or **last** (lăst, läst). **1.** Coming or occurring after the correct, usual, or expected time; delayed. **2. a.** Beginning at, occurring at, or lasting until a relatively advanced hour or time: *a late breakfast.* **b.** Occurring, being, or continuing towards the end: *the late 19th century.* **c.** Coming from near the end of a period or life: *a late Rembrandt.* **d.** At an advanced hour at night: *It was very late by then.* **3.** Taking longer than usual to reach a given stage: *a late developer.* **4.** Having recently begun or occurred; just previous to the present: *the latest developments.* **5.** Being the immediate past occupant of a position or place; former. **6.** Dead, especially recently deceased: *the late Mr. Foster.* —See Synonyms at **tardy.**
~adv. **later, latest. 1.** After the correct, usual, or expected time; tardily. **2. a.** At a relatively advanced time: *undertaken late in his life.* **b.** At an advanced hour of the night: *called very late.* **c.** Far into a period of time. **3.** In the recent past: *As late as last week, he was still alive.* **—of late.** In the near past; lately. [Middle English, Old English *læt.*] **—late·ness** *n.*

lat·ed (lā′tĭd) *adj. Poetic.* Belated. [From LATE.]

la·teen (lă-tēn′) *adj. Nautical.* **1.** Designating a triangular sail hung on a long yard attached to a short mast. **2.** Rigged with such a sail. *~n.* A lateen-rigged boat. [French *(voile) Latine,* "Latin (sail)" (from its use in the Mediterranean), from Old French, feminine of *Latin,* LATIN.]

Late Greek *n.* Greek during the early Byzantine Empire, from about the fourth to about the seventh century A.D.

Late Latin *n.* Latin from the third to the seventh century A.D.

late·ly (lāt′lē) *adv.* Not long ago; recently.

La Tène (lä tĕn′) *adj.* Pertaining to or designating an Iron Age European civilization dating from the fifth to the first century B.C. [After *La Tène,* on Lake Neuchâtel, Switzerland, where the remains were first discovered.]

la·tent (lā′tənt) *adj.* Present or potential, but not manifest: *latent talent.* [Latin *latēns* (stem *latent-*), present participle of *latēre,* to lie hidden, be concealed.] **—la·ten·cy** *n.* **—la·tent·ly** *adv.*

Synonyms: *dormant, potential, quiescent.*

latent heat *n. Symbol* **L** The quantity of heat absorbed or released by a substance undergoing a change of state, as by ice changing to water or water to steam.

latent image *n.* In photography, an invisible image produced in an emulsion after exposure but before development.

latent period *n.* **1.** The incubation period of an infectious disease. **2.** The interval between stimulus and response.

lat·er (lā′tər). Comparative of **late.**
~adj. Subsequent.

lat·er·al (lăt′ər-əl) *adj.* **1.** Of, pertaining to, or situated at or on the side or sides. **2.** *Phonetics.* Designating a sound produced by breath passing along one or both sides of the tongue.
~n. **1.** A lateral part, projection, passage, or appendage. **2.** *Phonetics.* A lateral sound, such as (l). [Latin *laterālis,* from *latus*† (stem *later-*), side.] **—lat·er·al·ly** *adv.*

lateral inversion *n.* Inversion between right and left, such as that which occurs in the formation of an image in a plane mirror.

lateral line *n.* A linear series of sensory pores and tubes for sensing sound and vibration, as along the side of a fish.

lateral pass *n. Football.* A pass thrown sideways, parallel to the line of scrimmage.

Lat·er·an (lăt′ər-ən) *n.* **1.** The church of Saint John Lateran, the cathedral church of the pope as bishop of Rome. **2.** The palace, now a museum, adjoining this church. Preceded by *the.* [Latin *Laterana,* district of ancient Rome, residence of the family Plautii *Laterani.*]

la·te·ra rec·ta. Plural of **latus rectum.**

lat·er·ite (lăt′ə-rīt′) *n.* A reddish-brown earthy substance, the residue produced by leaching of the soil in tropical regions, consisting of a preponderance of hydrated iron oxide with some hydrated aluminum oxide. Compare **bauxite.** [Latin *later*†, brick, tile + -ITE.]

lat·est (lā′tĭst). Alternate superlative of **late.**
~adj. Most recent, modern, or up-to-date.
~n. Informal. The most recent or up-to-date news, fashion, or the like. Preceded by *the.*

la·tex (lā′tĕks) *n., pl.* **latices** (lăt′ə-sēz′) or **-texes. 1.** The usually milky, viscous sap of certain trees and plants, such as the rubber tree, that coagulates on exposure to air. **2.** An emulsion of rubber or plastic globules in water, used in paints, adhesives, and other products. [New Latin, from Latin *latex,* fluid.] **—la·tex** *adj.*

latex paint *n.* A paint having a binder that is a latex. Also called "rubber-base paint."

lath (lăth, läth) *n., pl.* **laths** (lăthz, läthz, lăths, läths). **1.** A narrow, thin strip of wood or metal, used especially in making a supporting structure for plaster, shingles, slates, or tiles. **2.** Any other building material, such as a sheet of metal mesh, used for similar purposes. **3.** A slat. **4.** Lathing.
~tr.v. **lathed, lathing, laths.** To build, cover, or line with laths. [Middle English *lat, lathe,* Old English *lætt.*]

lathe (lāth) *n.* **1.** A machine on which a piece of wood or metal, for example, is spun on a horizontal axis and shaped by a fixed cutting or abrading tool. **2.** A potter's wheel.
~tr.v. **lathed, lathing, lathes.** To cut or shape on a lathe. [Perhaps Middle English *lath,* Old Danish *lad,* supporting stand, perhaps a special use of *lad,* pile, from Old Norse *hladh.*]

lath·er (lăth′ər) *n.* **1.** A light foam formed by soap or detergent agitated in water. **2.** Froth formed by profuse sweating, as on a horse. **—in a lather.** *Informal.* Highly excited or upset; agitated.
~v. **lathered, -ering, -ers.** *—tr.* **1.** To put lather on; coat with lather. **2.** *Informal.* To give a beating to; whip. *—intr.* **1.** To produce lather; foam. **2.** To become coated with lather. Used especially of horses. [Revival of Old English *lēathor,* washing soda.] **—lath·er·er** *n.* **—lath·er·y** *adj.*

lath·ing (lăth′ĭng, läth′-) *n.* **1.** The act or process of building with laths. **2.** A structure made of laths. Also called "lath."

lath·y (lăth′ē, läth′ē) *adj.* **-ier, -iest.** Tall and thin like a lath.

la·ti·ci·fer (lā-tĭs′ə-fər) *n.* A cell or vessel containing latex, found in such plants as rubber, poppy, and euphorbia. [New Latin, from *latex* (stem *latic-*) + -FER.]

lat·i·cif·er·ous (lăt′ə-sĭf′ər-əs) *adj.* Secreting or exuding latex. [New Latin *latex* (stem *latic-*), LATEX + -FEROUS.]

lat·i·fun·di·um (lăt′ə-fŭn′dē-əm) *n., pl.* **-dia** (-dē-ə). A landed estate, especially one in the ancient Roman world or in Latin America. [Latin *lātifundium* : *lātus,* broad + *fundus,* estate, bottom.]

Lat·in (lăt′n) *adj.* **1.** *Abbr.* **L., Lat.** Of or pertaining to Latium, its people, or its culture. **2.** Of or pertaining to ancient Rome, its people, or its culture. **3.** Of, pertaining to, or composed in the language of ancient Rome and Latium. **4.** Of or pertaining to those countries or peoples using Romance languages, especially the countries of Latin America. **5.** Of or pertaining to the Roman Catholic Church, as distinguished from the Eastern Orthodox Church.
~n. Abbr. **L., Lat. 1.** The ancient Italic dialect of Latium or the language into which it evolved, which through the political and cultural expansion of Rome became the dominant language of the Western Roman Empire, and survived into the Middle Ages as a language of learning and state documents, and until modern times as the official language of the Roman Catholic Church. See **Late Latin, Medieval Latin, New Latin, Old Latin, Vulgar Latin. 2.** A native or resident of ancient Latium. **3.** A member of a Latin people, especially of Latin America. **4.** A Roman Catholic.

Latin alphabet *n.* The **Roman alphabet** *(see).*

Latin America. A division of the Americas, consisting broadly of the countries of Central and South America (specifically those speaking Romance languages), together with Mexico. The region constitutes the fourth largest of the world's major divisions, with 14 percent of its land and 8 percent of its people. Latin America's backbone of young fold mountains, the Sierra Madre of Mexico and the Andes, is earthquake-prone and forms part of the Pacific's

LATIN AMERICA

UNITED STATES OF AMERICA

A T L A N T I C

O C E A N

Bermuda (UK)

30°N

Tropic of Cancer

GULF OF MEXICO

Sierra Madre Occidental

Gulf of California

Baja California

Rio Grande

Sierra Madre Oriental

C. San Lucas

MEXICO

Yucatán

Straits of Florida

BAHAMAS

CUBA

Greater Antilles

JAMAICA

Turks & Caicos Is (UK)

Hispaniola

HAITI

DOMINICAN REP.

Puerto Rico (US)

Virgin Is (US) (UK)

Anguilla (UK)

Montserrat (UK)

ANTIGUA

Guadeloupe (FR.)

DOMINICA

Martinique (FR.)

ST LUCIA

BARBADOS

ST VINCENT & THE GRENADINES

GRENADA

TRINIDAD & TOBAGO

Leeward Is

Lesser Antilles

St Kitts & Nevis

Windward Is

CARIBBEAN SEA

Curaçao (NETH.)

Citlaltepetl 5699m

Popocatepetl 5452m

Ixtacihuatl

Isthmus of Tehuantepec

BELIZE

GUATEMALA

HONDURAS

EL SALVADOR

NICARAGUA

L. Nicaragua

COSTA RICA

PANAMA

Canal Zone (US)

VENEZUELA

Llanos

Orinoco

Caroni

GUYANA

SURINAM

FRENCH GUIANA

Angel Fall

Guiana Highlands

Cuquenán Falls

Dam

COLOMBIA

ECUADOR

Galapagos Is (ECUADOR)

Cotopaxi 5896m

Negro

Putumayo

Amazon

Equator

Huascaran 6768m

Ucayali

Purus

Selvas

La Montaña

Madeira

Tapajos

Xingu

Tocantins

B R A Z I L

Mato Grosso

Brazilian

Serra Geral de Goias

S. Francisco

Highlands

Serra do Espinhaço

Ancohuma 7014m

Illimani 6402m

L. Titicaca

BOLIVIA

Altiplano

Mamore

Urubupungá Dam

Paraguay

Campos

PACIFIC

OCEAN

Easter I. (CHILE)

Llullaillaco 6723m

Atacama Desert

Gran Chaco

PARAGUAY

Tropic of Capricorn

Pissis 6858m

Ojos del Salado 7084m

Bonete 6872m

Salinas Grandes

Parana

Entre Rios

Serra do Mar

L. Patos

URUGUAY

30°S

Tupungato 6800m

Aconcagua 6960m

Juan Fernandez Is (CHILE)

A N D E S

A R G E N T I N A

Pampas

Plate

Colorado

Negro

Bio Bio

Patagonia

A T L A N T I C

O C E A N

S. Georgia (UK)

Falkland Is (UK)

Tierra del Fuego

Strait of Magellan

Cape Horn

Drake Passage

60°S

0   1000   2000 Km
0   500   1000   Miles

Equatorial scale

90°W   60°W

"Ring of Fire," with active volcanoes. To the east lie highland blocks, and vast lowlands drained by great rivers such as the Amazon and Paraná. The region has some of the driest places on earth—some 20 percent is thorn forest, savanna, steppe, or desert—but it also has more tropical rain forest than any other region. The forest covers 30 percent of the area and supplies more than 15 percent of the world's hardwoods. Less than 25 percent of Latin America is cultivated; 34 percent of its workers are in agriculture. It produces much of the world's coffee, sugar cane, and bananas and also beef and wool. The area has vast reserves of silver, copper, high-grade iron ore, bauxite, chrome, and nickel. It has little coal but considerable oil and gas, soon to supply most of the energy for its increasing industrialization, especially in Mexico and Brazil. The region's basic problems persist, however: a shortage of arable land, overpopulation and the drift of people to the cities, social disparities, and political instability.

Lat·in·ate (lăt′n-āt′) *adj.* Imitative of the style of Latin or using many Latinisms: *Latinate English prose.*

Latin Church *n.* The Roman Catholic Church.

Latin cross *n.* A cross with the lower limb longest.

Lat·in·ism (lăt′n-ĭz′əm) *n.* An idiom, structure, or word derived from or in imitation of Latin.

Lat·in·ist (lăt′n-ĭst) *n.* A Latin scholar.

La·tin·i·ty (lə-tĭn′ə-tē) *n.* **1.** The use of Latin. **2.** The manner in

lattice *A latticed window in the Tower of London.*

which Latin is used in speaking or writing; Latin style.

Lat·in·ize (lăt′n-īz′) *v.* **-ized, -iz·ing, -iz·es.** —*tr.* **1.** To translate into Latin. **2.** To transliterate into the characters of the Latin alphabet; Romanize. **3.** To cause to adopt or acquire Latin characteristics or customs. **4.** To cause to follow or resemble the Roman Catholic Church in dogma or practices. —*intr.* To use Latinisms. —**Lat·in·i·za·tion** *n.* —**Lat·in·i·zer** *n.*

Latin Quarter. A section of Paris on the left bank of the Seine, a center for university students for many centuries.

Latin square *n. Mathematics.* A set of *n* numbers or symbols arranged in a square array of *n* rows and *n* columns such that each number or symbol occurs only once in each row and column. Such squares are used for the statistical analysis of variability.

lat·ish (lă′tĭsh) *adj. Informal.* Fairly late. —**lat·ish** *adv.*

lat·i·tude (lăt′ə-tōōd′, -tyōōd′) *n. Abbr.* **l., L., lat. 1.** Extent; breadth; range. **2.** Freedom from normal restraints, limitations, or regulations. **3.** *Geography.* The angular distance north or south of the equator, measured in degrees along a meridian, as on a map, globe, or the celestial sphere. **4.** A region of the earth considered in relation to its distance from the equator: *temperate latitudes.* **5.** The range of values or conditions over which something operates or is effective; for example, the range of exposures over which a photographic film yields usable images. [Middle English, from Latin *lātitūdō,* from *lātus,* wide, broad.] —**lat·i·tu·din·al** *adj.*

lat·i·tu·di·nar·i·an (lăt′ə-tōōd′n-âr′ē-ən, -tyōōd′n-âr′ē-ən) *adj.* Favoring freedom of thought and behavior, especially in religion.

—*n.* A latitudinarian person. [Latin *lātitūdō* (stem lātitūdin-), LATI-TUDE + -ARIAN.] —**lat·i·tu·di·nar·i·an·ism** *n.*

La·ti·um (lā′shē-əm). **1.** An ancient country in west-central Italy. **2.** See **Lazio.**

La Tour (lə tōōr′), **Georges de** (1593–1652). French painter. He specialized in genre painting and religious subjects, and is famous for the dramatic lighting of his night scenes, as in *La Madeleine à la Veilleuse.*

la·tri·a (lə-trī′ə) *n.* In the Roman Catholic and Eastern Orthodox churches, the special reverence due to God alone. Compare **dulia, hyperdulia.** [Latin, from Greek *latreia,* worship.]

la·trine (lə-trēn′) *n.* A lavatory, as in a barracks or camp. [French, from Latin *latrīna,* contraction of *lavātrīna,* bath.]

La·trobe (lə-trōb′), **Benjamin Henry** (1764–1820). U.S. engineer and architect; born in England. Immigrating in 1796, he began a career that established architecture as a profession in America. Among his many achievements are the Baltimore Cathedral (1804–18) and the chambers of the U.S. Congress and Supreme Court.

-latry *suffix.* Indicates the worship of; for example, **idolatry.** [Greek *latreia,* service, worship.]

lat·ten (lăt′n) *n.* **1.** An alloy formerly made of or made to resemble brass, hammered thin, and used in the manufacture of church vessels. **2.** Any thin sheet of metal, especially of tin. [Middle English *laton,* from Old French *leiton, laton,* from Arabic *lāṭūn,* copper, from Turkish dialectal *altan,* gold.]

---

latitude and longitude

THE GRID LINES ON THE GLOBE
A method of locating precisely any place on earth

For purposes of navigation and geography, the earth's surface is divided into degrees, minutes, and seconds of latitude and longitude.

An imaginary line from the equator to the center of the earth and another from the North Pole (or from the South Pole) to the center of the earth would meet at an angle of 90°. This angle is divided into degrees, from 0° at the equator to 90°N at the North Pole (or 90°S at the South Pole). The same degree reading is given to every point on the globe's surface that is at the same angle to these imaginary lines. Each degree is subdivided into 60 minutes, and each minute into 60 seconds. A circle joining the points with the same degree reading forms a line parallel to the equator; it is called a parallel, or a line of latitude. Every place on that line has the same latitude.

A line of longitude joins places at which the sun is at its highest point in the sky at the same time. It is a noon, or midday, line, hence the term meridian, from the Latin *meridies,* "midday." Each meridian runs from Pole to Pole, and is half a Great Circle. In the same way that latitude is measured as angles north

and south of the equator (latitude 0°), longitude is measured as angles east and west of the Prime Meridian (longitude 0°), which passes through Greenwich, England. Longitude therefore represents difference in time on earth. Noon occurs an hour earlier for each 15° of longitude to the east of the Prime Meridian, and an hour later for each 15° to the west. Traveling eastward, an hour must be added to Greenwich time for each 15° of longitude to obtain local time. Traveling westward, an hour must be subtracted for each 15° of longitude. The 180° meridian is the International Date Line for most of its length. Travelers going eastward across this line set the calendar back a day; travelers going westward set it forward a day.

FIXING LATITUDE AND LONGITUDE *An imaginary line inclined at 15° above a line from the earth's center to the equator would meet the globe surface at what we call the latitude 15°N. Similarly, an imaginary line at a horizontal angle of 15° to a line between the earth's center and the Prime Meridian would meet the globe surface at what we call the longitude 15° (W or E).*

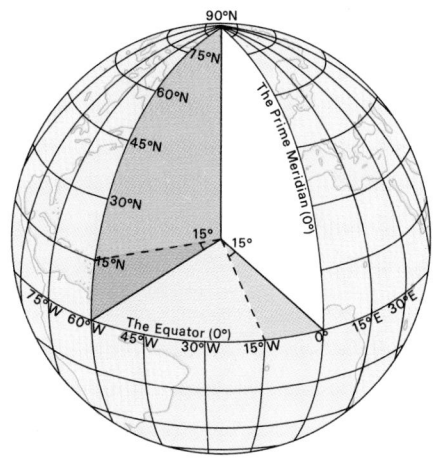

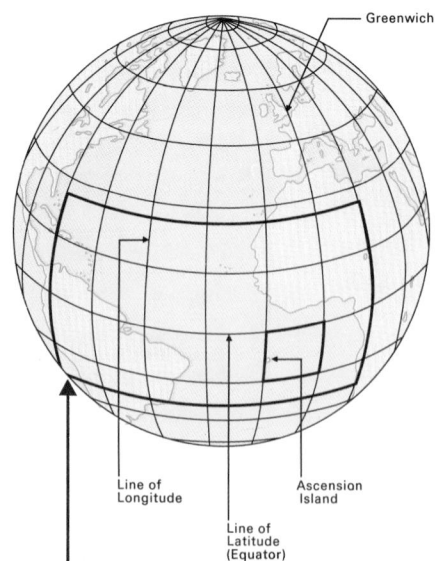

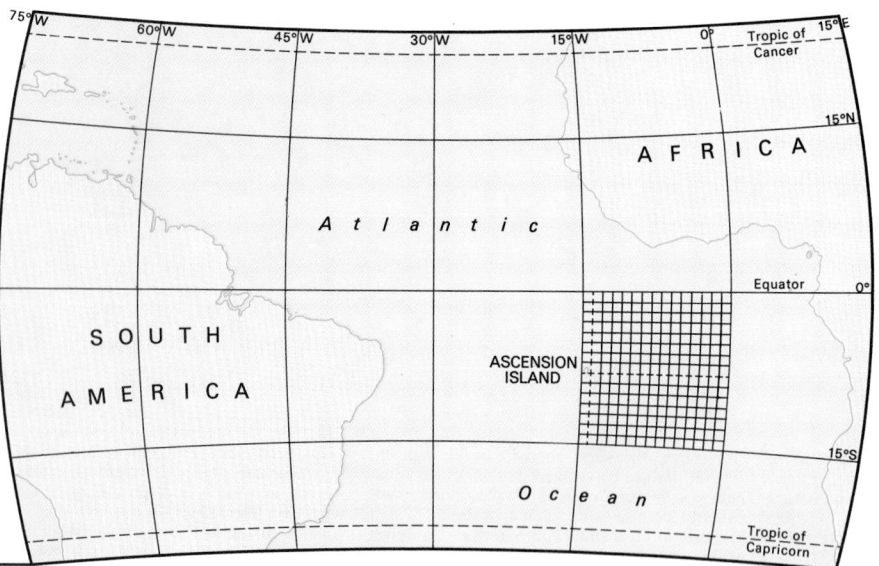

LOCATING ASCENSION ISLAND *The island is about 88 square kilometers (34 square miles) in area. It is located at 14°22′W and 7°57′S; that is, 14 degrees 22 minutes west of the Prime Meridian and 7 degrees 57 minutes south of the equator. A degree of longitude at* the equator is about 111 kilometers (69 miles); a degree of latitude anywhere is about 111 kilometers. By giving position not just in degrees but accurate to the minute and second, it is possible to locate precisely an airport on the island.

lat·ter (lăt′ər). *Rare.* Alternate comparative of **late.**
~*adj.* **1.** Designating the second of two persons or things mentioned. **2.** Further advanced in time or sequence; later. **3.** Closer to the end: *the latter part of the book.*
~*n.* The second of two persons or things mentioned. [Middle English, Old English *lætra,* comparative of *læt,* LATE.]
Usage: *Latter* is appropriate only in referring to the second of two previously mentioned entities: *We could travel by car or train—the latter would be quicker. Latter* is sometimes loosely used to refer to the last-mentioned item in a sequence of three or more (*We could travel by car, train or boat—the latter would be quicker*), but correct usage prefers an alternate form, such as *the last-named, the last of these,* or simply *the last.* Similarly, *latter* is not acceptable when only one item is referred to: *We could travel by car—the latter is very convenient.*
lat·ter-day (lăt′ər-dā′) *adj.* Belonging to present or recent time; modern.
Latter-day Saint *n.* A **Mormon** *(see).*
lat·ter·most (lăt′ər-mōst′) *adj.* Last.
lat·tice (lăt′ĭs) *n.* **1.** An open framework made of strips of metal, wood, or other material interwoven to form regular, patterned spaces. **2.** A screen, window, gate, or the like made of such a framework. **3.** Something, such as a heraldic bearing, that resembles such a framework. **4.** *Physics.* A regular, periodic configuration of points, particles, or objects throughout an area or space; especially, the arrangement of ions or molecules in a crystalline solid.
~*tr.v.* **latticed, -ticing, -tices.** To construct or furnish with a lattice or latticework. [Middle English *latis,* from Old French *lattis,* from *latte,* lath, from Germanic, akin to Old English *lætt,* LATH.]
lat·tice·work (lăt′ĭs-wûrk′) *n.* **1.** A lattice or something resembling a lattice; trelliswork. **2.** A structure made of lattices.
la·tus rec·tum (lăt′əs rĕk′təm, lā′təs) *n., pl.* **latera recta** (lăt′ər-ə rĕk′tə, lā′tər-ə). In geometry, a chord through the focus of a parabola, hyperbola, or ellipse parallel to a transverse axis. [New Latin, "straight side."]
Lat·vi·a (lăt′vē-ə). Constituent republic of the U.S.S.R., on the Baltic Sea. It consists largely of a fertile lowland, although there are numerous lakes and hills to the east. Latvia came under Russian control in the 18th century. From 1918 to 1940 it was an independent republic, but during World War II it was annexed by the U.S.S.R. Its capital is Riga.
Lat·vi·an (lăt′vē-ən) *adj.* Of or pertaining to Latvia, its people, or its language.
~*n.* **1.** A native or inhabitant of Latvia. **2.** The Baltic language of these people. In this sense, also called "Lettish."
lau·an (lo͞o′än′, lə-wän′) *n.* Timber obtained from any of various trees native to the Philippines, such as *Shorea,* having light yellow to brown, close-grained wood. [Tagalog *lawaan.*]
laud (lôd) *tr.v.* **lauded, lauding, lauds.** To give praise or express devotion to; glorify. —See Synonyms at **praise.**
~*n.* **1.** Praise; glorification. **2.** A hymn or song of praise. **3.** *Usually* **Lauds.** *Ecclesiastical.* **a.** An early-morning church service at which psalms of praise are sung. **b.** The service of prayers following the matins and constituting with them the first of the seven canonical hours. [Latin *laudāre,* to praise, from *laus* (stem *laud-*), praise.] **—laud·er** *n.*
Laud (lôd), **William** (1573–1645). Archbishop of Canterbury (1633–45). His attempts to introduce the Book of Common Prayer into Scotland led to the Bishops' Wars and his eventual imprisonment and execution by Parliament.
laud·a·ble (lô′də-bəl) *adj.* Deserving approbation; commendable; praiseworthy. **—laud·a·bil·i·ty, laud·a·ble·ness** *n.* **—laud·a·bly** *adv.*
lau·da·num (lôd′n-əm) *n.* A tincture of opium. [New Latin *laudanum* (coined by Paracelsus), possibly from Latin *lādanum, labdanum,* resin, LABDANUM.]
laud·a·tion (lô-dā′shən) *n.* The act of lauding; praise.
laud·a·tive (lô′də-tĭv) *adj.* Laudatory.
laud·a·to·ry (lô′də-tôr′ē, -tōr′ē) *adj.* Including, expressing, or bestowing praise; eulogistic. [Late Latin *laudātōrius,* from Latin *laudāre* (past participle *laudātus*), to praise, LAUD.]
Lau·der (lô′dər), **Sir Harry,** born Hugh MacLennan (1870–1950). Scottish music-hall star who created the comic figure of a wry but sentimental Highlander.
laugh (lăf, läf) *v.* **laughed, laughing, laughs.** —*intr.* **1.** To express emotion, typically mirth, by a series of inarticulate sounds, characteristically with the mouth open in a wide smile. **2.** To produce sounds or cries resembling laughter. **3.** To manifest or appear to manifest joy in any way. —*tr.* **1.** To drive, induce, or effect with or by laughter: *They laughed him off the stage.* **2.** To utter or express by or as if by laughing: *laughing their appreciation.* **—be laughing.** *Informal.* To be in a position of good fortune, satisfaction, or easy success. **—laugh at. 1.** To exhibit amusement at. **2.** To poke fun at; ridicule; deride. **3.** To refuse to consider seriously. **—laugh down.** To silence with laughter. **—laugh off** (or **away**). To dismiss lightly (especially, something unpleasant or painful), by or as if by laughing.
~*n.* **1.** A burst or sound of laughter. **2.** *Informal.* Something amusing, improbable, or ridiculous; a joke or absurdity: *That's a laugh.* **—have the last laugh.** To enjoy vindication. [Middle English *laughen,* Old English *hliehhan, hlæhhan.*] **—laugh·er** *n.* **—laugh·ing·ly** *adv.*
laugh·a·ble (lăf′ə-bəl, läf′-) *adj.* Causing or deserving laughter or derision. **—laugh·a·ble·ness** *n.* **—laugh·a·bly** *adv.*
laughing gas *n.* An anesthetic, **nitrous oxide** *(see).*
laughing hyena *n.* The **spotted hyena** *(see).*
laughing jackass *n.* A bird, the **kookaburra** *(see).*
laugh·ing·stock (lăf′ĭng-stŏk′, läf′-) *n.* An object of jokes or ridicule; a butt; a fool.
laugh·ter (lăf′tər, läf′-) *n.* **1.** The act of laughing. **2.** The sound produced by laughing. **3.** The experience or appearance of joy, merriment, amusement, or the like. **4.** *Archaic.* A cause or subject for laughter. [Middle English, Old English *hleahtor.*]
Laugh·ton (lôt′n), **Charles** (1899–1962). British actor. Among many starring Hollywood roles was his screen triumph as Captain Bligh in *Mutiny on the Bounty* (1935).
launce (lăns, läns, lôns) *n.* A fish, the **sand eel** *(see).* [Perhaps variant of LANCE.]
Launcelot. Variant of **Lancelot.**
launch[1] (lônch, länch) *v.* **launched, launching, launches.** —*tr.* **1.** To move or set in motion with force; propel: *launch a missile; launched a volley of snowballs.* **2.** To slide or lower (a boat) into the water, especially for the first time. **3.** To put into action; inaugurate; initiate. **4.** To set or start (a person or group) on a particular course of action. **5.** To engage (oneself) vigorously and enthusiastically in a new activity. **6.** To introduce (a new book, film, product, or the like) to the public through a publicity campaign. —*intr.* **1.** To begin a new project or venture; especially, to widen or extend one's current activities or enterprises. Usually used with *out: The company is launching out into plastics this year.* **2.** To make a rousing or enthusiastic beginning. Used with *into* or *forth into: The whole crowd launched into song.* **3.** To start talking or writing, especially eagerly and at length. Used with *on* or *forth* or *into: launched forth into a tirade.*
~*n.* An act of launching. Also used adjectivally: *a launch complex.* [Middle English *launchen,* to hurl, pierce, from Old North French *lancher,* variant of Old French *lancier,* from *lance,* LANCE.]
launch[2] *n.* **1.** A large ship's boat formerly sloop-rigged but now powered. **2.** Any large, open motorboat. [Portuguese *lancha,* from Malay, akin to Malay *lancharan,* boat.]
launch·er (lôn′chər, län′-) *n.* One that launches, such as: **1.** A device for firing grenades. **2.** A device for firing rockets.
launching pad *n.* Also **launch pad.** The base or platform from which a rocket or space vehicle is launched.
launch vehicle *n. Aerospace.* A **booster** *(see).*
laun·der (lôn′dər, län′-) *v.* **-dered, -dering, -ders.** —*tr.* **1.** To wash, or wash and iron (clothes, linen, or the like). **2.** To pass (money from a dubious source) through a bank or other intermediary, in order to obscure its origin. —*intr.* **1.** To withstand washing in a specified way: *This material launders well.* **2.** To wash, or wash and iron, clothes or linens.
~*n.* In mining, a wooden trough for water, used for washing ore. [From obsolete *launder,* launderer, from Middle English *launder,* variant of *lavender,* from Old French *lavandier,* from Vulgar Latin *lavandārius* (unattested), from Latin *lavanda,* things that need washing, from the gerundive of *lavāre,* to wash, LAVE.] **—laun·der·er** *n.*
laun·dress (lôn′drĭs, län′-) *n.* A woman who launders clothes, linen, or the like, as an occupation.
Laun·dro·mat (lôn′drə-măt′, län′-) *n.* A trademark for a commercial establishment equipped with washing machines and dryers, usually coin-operated and self-service.
laun·dry (lôn′drē, län′-) *n., pl.* **-dries. 1.** Soiled or laundered clothes and linens; washing. **2.** A place where laundering is done. [From obsolete *launder,* launderer. See **launder.**]
laun·dry·man (lôn′drē-mən) *n., pl.* **-men** (-mĭn). **1.** A man who makes collections and deliveries for a commercial laundry. **2.** A man who works in a laundry.
laun·dry·wom·an (lôn′drē-wo͝om′ən) *n., pl.* **-women** (-wĭm′ən). A woman who is a laundry worker.
Laur·as·i·a (lô-rā′shə, -zhə). Ancient supercontinent that formed the northern land mass of the world when the single continent of Pangaea split into two sections at the end of the Paleozoic era. It comprised North America, Greenland, Europe, and Asia (excluding the Indian subcontinent), and itself split during the Mesozoic era into North America and Eurasia.
lau·re·ate (lôr′ē-ĭt) *adj.* **1.** Worthy of laurels for one's achievements; pre-eminent. **2.** Crowned or decked with laurel as a mark of honor. **3.** Honored for achievement in a field. **4.** *Archaic.* Made of laurel sprigs, as a wreath or crown.
~*n.* **1.** A poet laureate. **2.** One honored with a crown of laurel. **3.** One who has received an honor or award: *a Nobel laureate.* [Latin *laureātus,* crowned with laurel, from *laurea,* laurel tree or crown, from *laureus,* of laurel, from *laurus,* LAUREL.] **—lau·re·ate·ship** *n.*
lau·rel (lôr′əl, lŏr′-) *n.* **1.** A shrub or tree, *Laurus nobilis,* native to the Mediterranean region, having aromatic evergreen leaves and small blackish berries. Also called "bay." **2.** Any of several similar or related shrubs or trees, such as **California laurel, cherry laurel, mountain laurel,** and **spurge laurel** *(all of which see).* **3.** *Usually* **laurels.** Leaves or twigs of a laurel, especially *L. nobilis,* formed into a wreath and conferred as a mark of honor in ancient times upon poets, heroes, and victors in athletic contests. **4. laurels.** Honor and glory won for achievement. **—look to one's laurels.** To protect one's position of eminence against rivals. **—rest on one's laurels.** To be content with past achievements and to cease striving.
~*tr.v.* **laureled** or **-relled, -reling** or **-relling, -rels.** To crown with laurel. [Middle English *lorel, laurer,* laurel tree, from Old French

launcher *A rocket being fired from a hand-held launcher. Since the bazooka of World War II was developed as an antitank weapon, light rocket launchers have been increasingly important in every modern army.*

laurel *A common garden shrub, it can stand shade and damp and even neglect and still produce its shiny black berries.*

PRONUNCIATION KEY

ă, pat; ā, pay; âr, care;
ä, father, are; b, bib;
ch, church; d, deed; ĕ, pet;
ē, be; f, fife; g, gag; h, hat;
hw, which; ĭ, pit; ī, pie;
îr, pier; j, judge; k, kick;
l, lid, needle; m, mum;
n, no, sudden; ng, thing;
ŏ, pot; ō, toe; ô, paw, for;
oi, noise; ou, out; o͝o, book;
o͞o, boot; p, pop; r, roar;
s, sauce; sh, ship, dish;
t, tight; th, thin, path;
th, this, bathe; ŭ, cut; ûr, fur;
v, valve; w, with; y, yes;
z, zebra, size; zh, vision;
ə, about, item, edible,
gallop, circus, peaceful

IN FOREIGN WORDS:

à, *Fr.* ami; œ, *Fr.* feu, *Ger.* schön; ü, *Fr.* tu, *Ger.* über; KH, *Ger.* ich, *Scot.* loch; N, *Fr.* bon; y′, *Fr.* Compiègne

STRESS MARKS:

Primary stress: ′
in·cite′ (ĭn-sīt′)
Secondary stress: ′
in′sight′ (ĭn′sīt′)

lavender *This fragrant shrub has been associated for centuries with traditional flower gardens.*

lorier, from *lor,* laurel, from Latin *laurus,* perhaps of Mediterranean origin.]

Lau·rel and Har·dy (lôr′əl, lŏr′-; här′dē). Film comedy team, the first great innovative comedians of talking films. **Stan Laurel,** born Arthur Stanley Jefferson (1890–1965), was British, **Oliver Hardy** (1892–1957), American. They made many short films between 1926 and 1945. *The Music Box* (1932) won an Academy Award.

Lau·ren·tian Mountains (lô-rĕn′shən). A low-lying range in southern Quebec, Canada, extending from the St. Lawrence River to Hudson Bay. Its highest point is Mt. Tremblant (961 meters; 3,150 feet). The region is a popular resort area.

lau·ric acid (lôr′ĭk, lŏr′-) *n.* A fatty acid, $C_{12}H_{24}O_2$, obtained chiefly from coconut oil, and used in making soaps, cosmetics, insecticides, and alkyd resins. Also called "dodecanoic acid." [Latin *laurus,* LAUREL (from its occurrence in some laurel).]

lau·rus·ti·nus (lôr′ə-stī′nəs) *n.* A Mediterranean shrub, *Viburnum tinus,* often grown for ornament, having glossy, dark green foliage and flattish clusters of small pink or white flowers. [New Latin : Latin *laurus,* laurel + *tinus,* name of a plant (probably laurustinus), probably from Germanic.]

lau·ryl alcohol (lôr′əl, lŏr′-) *n.* A white crystalline solid, $C_{12}H_{26}O$, used in the manufacture of detergents. [LAURIC ACID + -YL.]

Lau·sanne (lō-zăn′, -zän′). A city in western Switzerland, on Lake Geneva. It is the trading and marketing center of a fertile agricultural region and also a popular resort and conference center.

lav. lavatory.

la·va (lä′və, lăv′ə) *n.* **1.** Molten rock that issues from a volcano or a fissure in the earth's surface. **2.** The same rock when cooled and solidified. [Italian, lava stream from Vesuvius, stream caused by rain, from *lavare,* to wash, from Latin *lavāre,* to wash, LAVE.]

la·va·bo (lə-vā′bō, -vä′bō) *n., pl.* **-boes. 1.** *Often* **Lavabo. a.** In the Roman Catholic and Anglican churches, the ceremonial washing of the celebrant's hands after the offertory of the Mass. **b.** The psalm passage formerly recited at this point. **2.** The basin or small towel used in this ritual. **3.** A washbowl and water tank with a spout used for ablutions in medieval monasteries. [Latin *lavābo,* "I shall wash" (first word in Psalm 26:6), from *lavāre,* to wash, LAVE.]

lav·age (lăv′ĭj; *French* là-vàzh′) *n. Medicine.* A washing, especially of a hollow organ, such as the stomach or lower bowel, with repeated injections of water. [French, a washing, from Old French, from *laver,* to wash, from Latin *lavāre,* to wash, LAVE.]

La·val (lə-văl′), **Pierre** (1883–1945). French politician. He twice served as prime minister (1931–32, 1935–36). Following the surrender of France he became premier of the Vichy government (1942). He was executed for treason for collaborating with the Germans.

la·va-la·va (lä′və-lä′və) *n.* A rectangular strip of printed cotton cloth tied around the waist and worn as a skirt by Polynesians, especially Samoans. [Samoan.]

lav·a·liere (lăv′ə-lîr′) *n.* Also **la·val·lière** (là-và-lyâr′). A pendant worn on a chain around the neck. [French *lavallière,* after Louise de *La Vallière,* a mistress of Louis XIV.]

la·va·tion (lă-vā′shən, lā-) *n.* The process of washing; a cleansing. [Latin *lavātiō* (stem *lavātiōn-*), from *lavāre,* LAVE.]

lav·a·to·ry (lăv′ə-tôr′ē, -tōr′ē) *n., pl.* **-ries.** *Abbr.* **lav. 1.** A room equipped with washing and often toilet facilities. **2.** A basin or bowl, especially one permanently installed with running water, for washing. **3.** A toilet. **4.** *Ecclesiastical.* The ritual washing of the celebrant's hands; lavabo. [Middle English *lavatorie,* from Late Latin *lavātorium,* washing place, washing vessel, from Latin *lavāre,* to wash, LAVE.] **—la·va·to·ri·al** *adj.*

lave (lāv) *v.* **laved, laving, laves.** *—tr.* **1.** To wash; bathe. **2.** To lap or wash against: *The stream laved the rocks.* *—intr.* To bathe oneself: *"In her chaste current oft the Goddess laves"* (Pope). [Middle English *laven,* from Old French *laver,* from Latin *lavāre.*]

lav·en·der (lăv′ən-dər) *n.* **1.** Any of various aromatic Old World plants of the genus *Lavandula;* especially, *L. officinalis* (or *L. spica* or *L. vera*), having clusters of small purplish flowers and yielding an oil used in perfumery. **2.** The fragrant dried leaves, stems, and flowers of such a plant. **3.** Any of various similar or related plants, such as **sea lavender** and **spike lavender** *(both of which see).* **4.** Pale to light bluish purple, to very light or pale violet. [Middle English *lavendre,* from Norman French, from Medieval Latin *lavendula, livendula*†.] **—lav·en·der** *adj.*

la·ver[1] (lā′vər) *n.* **1.** A large basin used in ancient Judaism by the priest for ablutions before making a sacrificial offering. **2.** *Archaic.* A stone basin or trough used for washing. **3.** *Archaic.* The baptismal font or the water in it. [Middle English *laver, lavor,* from Old French *laveoir,* perhaps from Late Latin *lavātorium,* LAVATORY.]

la·ver[2] (lä′vər) *n.* Any of several edible seaweeds of the genus *Porphyra.* [New Latin, from Latin *laver*†.]

La·ver (lā′vər), **Rodney George,** known as "Rod" (1938–). Australian tennis player. He was Wimbledon champion in 1961, 1962, 1968, and 1969. He won the world's four major singles titles in 1962 as an amateur and in 1969 as a professional.

la·ver bread (lä′vər) *n.* The fronds of laver seaweed dipped in oatmeal, fried and eaten, especially in Wales.

La Vé·ren·drye (lä vā-räN-drē′), **Pierre Gaultier de Varennes, Sieur de** (1685–1749). French Canadian explorer. In search of a route to the Pacific, he and his sons established a chain of trading posts between present-day Rainy Lake, Ontario, and Winnipeg, Manitoba, that opened western Canada to further exploration and broke the economic stronghold of the British Hudson Bay Company.

lav·er·ock (lăv′ər-ək) *n. Scottish & Archaic.* A skylark. [Middle English *laverok,* Old English *lǣwerce,* LARK.]

lav·ish (lăv′ĭsh) *adj.* **1.** Extravagant; prodigal. **2.** Characterized by or produced with extravagance and profusion: *a lavish buffet.* **3.** Showing unrestrained generosity: *a lavish present.* —See Synonyms at **ornate.**

~tr.v. **lavished, -ishing, -ishes.** To give or pour forth unstintingly: *the loving care they lavished on the work.* [Middle English *lavas,* from noun, "an outpouring," profusion, from Old French *lavasse,* torrent of rain, from *laver,* to wash, LAVE.] **—lav·ish·er** *n.* **—lav·ish·ly** *adv.* **—lav·ish·ness** *n.*

La·voi·sier (lä-vwä-zyā′, lə-vwä′zē-ā′), **Antoine Laurent** (1743–94). French chemist and father of modern chemistry. He isolated the major constituents of air, disproved the phlogiston theory by explaining the role of oxygen in combustion, and organized the classification of compounds. He was guillotined during the French Revolution for having held various government posts.

law (lô) *n. Abbr.* **l., L. 1.** A rule established by authority, society, or custom. **2. a.** The body of rules governing the affairs of people within a community or among states; a legal system: *the law of nations.* **b.** The condition of social order or justice resulting from the existence of a legal system in a society. **c.** A declaration or position which is not to be questioned or disputed: *His word is law.* **3.** A set of rules or customs dealing with a specified area of a legal system: *the law of contracts; criminal law.* **4.** In Britain: **a.** The body of rules and principles originally followed by the common law courts, as opposed to those which were administered by the courts of equity. **b.** That part of the law which arises out of legislation; statute law as opposed to common law. **5. a.** The system of courts, judicial processes, and legal officers giving effect to the laws of a society: *resort to the law in defense of one's interests.* **b.** An impromptu system of justice, usually illegal, substituted for established juridical procedure: *gang law.* **6.** The science and study of law; jurisprudence. **7.** Knowledge of law: *His law is good.* **8.** The profession of a lawyer. **9. Law. a.** *Often* **Laws.** A code of behavior of divine origin: *Mosaic Law.* **b.** In the Old Testament, the Pentateuch and the precepts laid down in it. **10. a.** *Often* **laws.** Principles of conduct conceived to be of natural origin: *the laws of decency.* **b.** A way of life: *law of the jungle.* **11.** *Often* **laws.** A code of principles and regulations observed by a profession or association or by sportsmen: *the law of the turf.* **12. a.** *Often* **laws.** A formulation of the observed recurrence, order, relationship, or interaction of natural phenomena: *laws of motion.* **b.** A generalization based on the observation of repeated events: *Parkinson's law.* **13.** *Mathematics.* A general principle or rule that is obeyed in all cases to which it is applicable. **14.** *Often* **laws.** The rules of an art; principles or elements: *the laws of harmony; the laws of grammar.* **15.** *Slang.* The police or a policeman. Preceded by *the.* **—be a law unto oneself.** To disregard established laws and conventions; make one's own rules. **—go to law.** To take a complaint to court for settlement. **—lay down the law.** To speak in a firm, authoritarian way. **—take the law into one's own hands.** To redress a wrong or proceed by one's own methods rather than proper authority. [Middle English *law(e),* binding custom or practice, Old English *lagu,* code of rules.]

law-a·bid·ing (lô′ə-bī′dĭng) *adj.* Abiding by the law.

law and order *n. Used with a singular or plural verb.* **1.** A state of peace in a law-abiding society. **2.** The use or advocacy of stringent measures to reduce crime and eliminate violence in a society.

law·break·er (lô′brā′kər) *n.* A person who breaks the law. **—law·break·ing** *n. & adj.*

law·ful (lô′fəl) *adj.* **1.** Within the law; allowed by law: *lawful methods.* **2.** Established or recognized by the law; legally acknowledged: *the lawful heir.* **3.** Legally sanctioned; legitimate: *a lawful marriage.* **—law·ful·ly** *adv.* **—law·ful·ness** *n.*

law·giv·er (lô′gĭv′ər) *n.* **1.** One who gives a code of laws to a people. **2.** A lawmaker; a legislator. **—law·giv·ing** *n. & adj.*

law·less (lô′lĭs) *adj.* **1. a.** Unrestrained by law; disobedient: *a lawless person.* **b.** Unbridled: *lawless passion.* **2.** Heedless of or contrary to the law: *a lawless act.* **3.** Not governed by law: *the lawless border.* **—law·less·ly** *adv.* **—law·less·ness** *n.*

law·mak·er (lô′mā′kər) *n.* One who drafts or helps to enact laws; a legislator. **—law·mak·ing** *n. & adj.*

law·man (lô′măn′) *n., pl.* **-men** (-mĕn′). A law enforcement officer, such as a sheriff.

law merchant *n., pl.* **laws merchant.** The rules and regulations applied to trade and commerce, drawn from the customs of merchants in the past; commercial law.

lawn[1] (lôn) *n.* A usually closely mown plot or area planted with grass or similar plants. [Variant of obsolete *laund,* from Middle English *launde, lawnde,* from Old French *launde,* heath, from Germanic.] **—lawn·y** *adj.*

lawn[2] *n.* A very fine fabric of cotton or linen. [Middle English, probably from *Laon,* France, linen-manufacturing town.] **—lawn·y** *adj.*

lawn bowling *n.* A game played on a level lawn, or bowling green, by rolling a wooden ball as close as possible to a target ball, the jack. Also called "bowling."

lawn mower *n.* A machine with a revolving blade or blades for cutting grass.

lawn tennis *n.* **1.** Tennis played on a grass court. **2.** Tennis.

law of averages *n.* The assertion that what happens at one extreme will be counteracted by what happens at the other, thus maintaining an average.

law of large numbers *n. Mathematics.* **Bernoulli's law** *(see).*

Law of Moses *n.* **Mosaic Law** *(see).*

law of nations *n.* **International law** *(see).*

Law•rence (lôr′əns, lŏr′-), **David Herbert** (1885–1930). British novelist, short-story writer, essayist, and poet. Among his novels are *Sons and Lovers* (1913) and *Women in Love* (1920). The sex scenes in his work aroused controversy: publication of *Lady Chatterley's Lover* (1928) was not allowed in Britain until 1961.

Lawrence, Ernest Orlando (1901–58). U.S. physicist. He designed the cyclotron, a particle accelerator, and was awarded the Nobel Prize in physics (1939).

Lawrence, Gertrude (1898–1952). British actress. She formed a memorable partnership with her childhood friend Noël Coward, notably in his play *Private Lives* (1930). She later appeared in films such as *The King and I* (1951).

Lawrence, James (1781–1813). U.S. naval officer. After distinguished service in the Tripolitan War, he was promoted to captain in the War of 1812. During his reckless attack on the H.M.S. *Shannon,* which was blockading Boston Harbor, he lost his vessel and his life, but not before uttering his famous war cry, "Don't give up the ship!"

Lawrence, Thomas Edward, also known as "T.E. Lawrence," "T.E. Shaw," and Lawrence of Arabia (1888–1935). British soldier and writer. He was sent in 1916 to organize Arab insurgency in the Turkish empire and led a legendary guerrilla action. He wrote a philosophical record of the desert campaign, *The Seven Pillars of Wisdom* (1926). Lawrence was killed in a motorcycle accident.

law•ren•ci•um (lô-rĕn′sē-əm, lō-) *n. Symbol* **Lw** A synthetic transuranic element having a single isotope with mass number 257 and a half-life of 38 seconds. [After E. O. LAWRENCE.]

law stationer *n.* **1.** A person who sells stationery required by lawyers. **2.** *Chiefly British.* A person who engrosses legal documents.

law•suit (lô′so͞ot′) *n.* A case brought before a court, usually a civil case.

law term *n.* **1.** A word or expression used in legal contexts. **2.** A period of time appointed for the sitting of a law court.

law•yer (lô′yər) *n.* **1.** One whose profession is to give legal advice and assistance to clients and represent them in court. **2.** *British.* Loosely, a solicitor. **3.** A student or teacher of law. **4.** *Regional.* A freshwater fish, the **burbot** *(see).* [Middle English *lawyere,* from *lawe,* LAW.] **—law•yer•ly** *adj.*

Usage: *lawyer, attorney, counselor, counsel, solicitor, barrister, advocate.* These nouns denote members of the legal profession. *Lawyer* is the general and most comprehensive term for one authorized to manage the legal affairs of a client, give legal advice, and represent clients in court. *Attorney* is often used interchangeably with *lawyer* but in a narrower sense refers to a legal agent for a client in the transaction of business. In a still narrower sense, *attorney* denotes anyone legally appointed to transact another's business. *Counselor* and *counsel* are terms for persons who give legal advice and serve as trial lawyers; *counsel* is also applied to a team of lawyers employed in conducting a case. *Solicitor,* especially in Britain and some other Commonwealth countries, refers to a lawyer who gives legal advice, acts as a legal agent, represents clients in lower courts, and prepares cases for trial in higher courts. *Barrister,* in England and some other Commonwealth countries, refers to a lawyer who represents and argues cases for clients in higher courts. *Advocate* is largely restricted to military usage. In Scotland, France, and South Africa, it has the approximate sense of trial lawyer.

lax (lăks) *adj.* **1. a.** Showing little concern; remiss; negligent: *lax about paying bills.* **b.** Not strict; unenforced. **2.** Not taut, firm, or compact; slack. **3.** Loose and not easily retained or controlled. Said of bowel movements. **4.** *Phonetics.* Pronounced with the muscles of the tongue and jaw partially relaxed; wide. Said of certain vowel sounds, such as *e* in *let* or *i* in *hide.* Compare **tense.** —See Synonyms at **careless.** [Middle English, from Latin *laxus,* slack, loose.] **—lax•a•tion** *n.* **—lax•i•ty, lax•ness** *n.* **—lax•ly** *adv.*

lax•a•tive (lăk′sə-tĭv) *n. Medicine.* A drug that stimulates evacuation of the bowels. Also called "cathartic," "purgative."
~adj. **1.** Stimulating evacuation of the bowels. **2.** Unrestrained. [Middle English *laxatif,* from adjective, "producing looseness," from Old French, from Latin *laxātīvus,* from *laxāre,* to relax, from *laxus,* loose, LAX.]

Lax•ness (läks′nĕs′), **Halldór Kiljan** (1902–). Icelandic novelist, writing in the epic tradition of his country. He was awarded the Nobel Prize (1955).

lay[1] (lā) *v.* **laid** (lād), **laying, lays.** *—tr.* **1.** To cause to lie; put in a recumbent position: *lay a child in its crib.* **2.** To place or rest in a particular state or position: *lay the books on the table.* **3.** To put or set down, especially for a particular purpose or as a basis: *lay a trail; lay foundations.* **4.** To produce and deposit: *lay eggs.* **5. a.** To cause to settle or subside: *The fog laid the wind.* **b.** To scotch (a rumor, for example). **c.** To exorcise (a ghost). **6.** To put or apply: *lay an ear to the door.* **7.** To assign or attribute: *laid the blame on him.* **8.** To put in a setting; locate: *laid the story in Italy.* **9.** To bury; sink in the ground: *lay a cable.* **10.** To place in the proper position or spot: *lay a carpet; lay bricks.* **11. a.** To arrange in a required order for use; make ready: *lay a trap; lay a fire.* **b.** To arrange knives, forks, place mats, and the like on (a table). **12.** To devise; make: *lay plans.* **13.** To apply in a thick layer or coat: *lay paint on a canvas.* **14.** To place or give (importance): *lay stress on clarity.* **15.** To impose as a burden or punishment. Usually used with *upon*: *lay a penalty upon him.* **16.** To put forth for examination; present; submit. Often used with *before: lay a case before a committee.* **17.** To place (a bet); stake; wager: *lay ten dollars on a horse.* **18.** To bring or deliver forcefully: *laid a blow on his jaw.* **19.** *Archaic.* To take possession of; annex. **20.** *Military.* To aim (a gun or cannon). **21. a.** To place together (strands) to be twisted into rope. **b.** To make in this manner. Used with *up: lay up cable.* **22.** To inlay: *The floor was laid in semiprecious stones.* **23.** To bring (a ship) to a specified position: *lay the vessel alongside the dock.* **24.** In hunting, to put (hounds) on a scent. *—intr.* **1.** To produce and deposit eggs. **2. a.** *Nonstandard.* To lie; recline. **b.** *Nautical.* To lie in a specified position: *The ship laid aft.* **—lay about one.** To hit out in all directions; fight vigorously. **—lay aloft.** *Nautical.* To go up into the rigging of a ship. **—lay aside. 1.** To put off to one side; abandon: *lay aside all hope.* **2.** To put aside for the future; save. **3.** To disregard for the moment. **—lay away. 1.** To reserve for the future; save. **2.** To hold (merchandise) for future delivery. **—lay bare.** To expose to view; reveal. **—lay down. 1.** To store (wine or provisions), especially in a cellar. **2.** To place (a bet); wager. **3.** To relinquish or sacrifice (one's hopes or life, for example). **4.** To begin the construction of (a ship, railroad, or the like). **5.** To make or formulate (a rule, principle, or the like). **6.** To convert (land) into pasture: *lay down a field with grass.* **7.** To put down (a chart, diagram, or the like) on paper. **—lay down one's arms.** To surrender. **—lay down one's life.** To sacrifice one's life. **—lay down the law. 1.** To assert authoritatively what is to be done or observed. **2.** To scold vehemently. **—lay hold of.** To seize; grasp. **—lay in.** To obtain and store (provisions or supplies). **—lay into.** To attack, either physically or verbally. **—lay it on.** *Informal.* **1.** To be effusive with praise, flattery, excuses, or the like. **2.** To inflict blows on; strike. **—lay on. 1.** To provide (refreshments or entertainment, for example). **2.** To install the necessary pipes and fittings for supplying (gas, electricity, or water). **—lay oneself open.** To make oneself vulnerable; expose oneself, as to criticism, blame, or the like. **—lay open. 1.** To cut open. **2.** To expose; reveal. **—lay to. 1.** To apply oneself vigorously. **2.** *Nautical.* **a.** To bring (a sailing ship) to a stop in open water, steadying her with a jib or other small sail. **b.** To remain stationary, facing into the wind. **—lay to rest.** To bury. **—lay waste.** To ravage (land, for example).
~n. **1.** A share of the profits of a whaling or fishing expedition allotted in place of wages. **2. a.** The direction the strands of a rope or cable are twisted in: *a left lay.* **b.** The amount of such twist. **3.** The position, way, or direction in which something, such as land, lies. **4.** *Chiefly British Slang.* A line of activity, especially one of a questionable nature. **—in lay.** In a period of ovulation. Said of laying hens. **—lay of the land. 1.** The nature, surface, or form of an area of land. **2.** *Informal.* An arrangement. [Lay, laid, laid; Middle English *leggen, leide, leid,* Old English *lecgan, lēde, gelēd.*]

Usage: *Lay* (to put, place, or prepare) and *lie* (to recline or be situated) are frequently confused. *Lay* is a transitive verb and takes an object. *Lay* and its principal parts (*laid, laying*) are correctly used in the following examples: *He laid* (not *lay*) *the newspaper on the table. The table was laid for four. Lie* is an intransitive verb and does not take an object. *Lie* and its principal parts (*lay, lain, lying*) are correctly used in the following examples: *She often lies* (not *lays*) *down after lunch. When I lay* (not *laid*) *down I fell asleep. The rubbish had lain* (not *laid*) *there a week. I was lying* (not *laying*) *in bed when he called. The valley lies to the east.* There are a few exceptions to these rules. The idioms *lay low, lay for,* and the nautical use of *lay,* as in *lay at anchor,* though intransitive, are well established.

lay[2] *adj.* **1.** Pertaining to, coming from, or serving the laity; secular: *a lay preacher.* **2.** Nonprofessional; not formally qualified or trained. **3.** Of or typical of the average or common man: *a lay opinion.* [Middle English *laie,* from Old French *lai,* from Late Latin *lāicus,* from Greek *laikos,* from *laos*†, the people.]

lay[3] *n.* A ballad. [Middle English, from Old French *lai,* akin to Provençal *lais*†.]

lay[4]. Past tense of **lie** (recline).

lay•a•bout (lā′ə-bout′) *n. Chiefly British.* One who avoids work; a lazy person; an idler.

lay brother *n.* A man who has taken religious vows but who is not ordained and is usually employed in manual duties.

lay by *tr.v.* **1.** To keep on hand for future needs; save. **2.** To lay (a sailing vessel) to. *—intr.v.* To lay to. Used of a sailing vessel.

lay-by (lā′bī′) *n., pl.* **-bys. 1.** *Chiefly British.* **a.** An area beside a main road where vehicles can stop without obstructing other traffic. **b.** A similar area on a canal or beside a railroad for boats or railroad cars. **2.** *Australian & New Zealand.* A method of reserving an article in a shop by paying a deposit: *put a dress on lay-by.*

lay clerk *n. Chiefly British.* A lay male member of a cathedral or church choir.

lay day *n. Commerce.* A day in port allowed to the lessee of a ship without charge; a free day. [From LAY (verb).]

lay•er (lā′ər) *n.* **1. a.** A single thickness, coating, or stratum spread out or covering a surface. **b.** A superimposed level: *layers of meaning.* **2.** One that lays; specifically, a hen. **3.** *Horticulture.* A stem covered with soil for rooting while still part of a living plant.
~v. **layered, -ering, -ers.** *—tr.* **1.** To cut (hair) into layers. **2.** *Horticulture.* To propagate (a plant) by layering. *—intr.* **1.** To separate or split into layers. **2.** *Horticulture.* To take root as a result of layering. [Middle English *leyer,* from *leyen, leggen,* to LAY.]

layer cake *n.* A usually iced cake of two or more layers separated by a filling, such as jelly or cream.

lay•ered (lā′ərd) *adj.* **1.** Having or arranged in layers. **2.** Consisting

PRONUNCIATION KEY

ă, pat; ā, pay; âr, care;
ä, father, are; b, bib;
ch, church; d, deed; ĕ, pet;
ē, be; f, fife; g, gag; h, hat;
hw, which; ĭ, pit; ī, pie;
îr, pier; j, judge; k, kick;
l, lid, needle; m, mum;
n, no, sudden; ng, thing;
ŏ, pot; ō, toe; ô, paw, for;
oi, noise; ou, out; o͝o, book;
o͞o, boot; p, pop; r, roar;
s, sauce; sh, ship, dish;
t, tight; th, thin, path;
th, this, bathe; ŭ, cut; ûr, fur;
v, valve; w, with; y, yes;
z, zebra, size; zh, vision;
ə, about, item, edible,
gallop, circus, peaceful

IN FOREIGN WORDS:

à, *Fr.* ami; œ, *Fr.* feu, *Ger.* schön; ü, *Fr.* tu, *Ger.* über; KH, *Ger.* ich, *Scot.* loch; N, *Fr.* bon; y′, *Fr.* Compiègne

STRESS MARKS:

Primary stress: ′
in•cite′ (ĭn-sīt′)
Secondary stress: ′
in′sight′ (ĭn′sīt′)

of one garment or layer of fabric worn over another: *the layered look; a layered skirt.*

lay·er·ing (lā′ər-ĭng) *n.* Also **lay·er·age** (-ĭj). The process of rooting branches, twigs, or stems that are still attached to a parent plant, as by placing a specially treated part in moist soil.

lay·ette (lā-ĕt′) *n.* Clothing and other accessories for a newborn baby. [French, from Old French, diminutive of *laie*, box, from Middle Dutch *laeget.*]

lay figure *n.* **1.** A jointed model of the human body used by artists, especially to demonstrate the arrangement of drapery. Also called "mannequin." **2.** A subservient person.

lay·man (lā′mən) *n., pl.* **-men** (-mĭn). **1.** A member of a congregation as distinguished from the clergy. **2.** One who does not have special or advanced training or skill.

lay off *tr.v.* **1.** To suspend (workers) from employment, especially during a slack period. **2.** To mark off; chart the boundaries of. **3.** *Informal.* **a.** To desist from (an activity): *lay off shouting.* **b.** To leave (a person or thing) alone. —*intr.v. Informal.* To desist.

lay·off (lā′ôf′, -ŏf′) *n.* **1.** The suspension or dismissal of employees. **2.** The interval for which employment has been suspended.

lay out *tr.v.* **1.** To put or spread out in readiness, as for wear, packing, display, or inspection. **2. a.** To arrange according to plan: *laid out the grounds of the castle.* **b.** To set out (an argument, for example). **3.** *Informal.* To spend or invest (money), especially on a large scale. **4.** To clothe and prepare (a corpse) for burial. **5.** *Informal.* To knock down; especially, to knock unconscious. **6.** *Informal.* To put (oneself) to a lot of trouble.

lay·out (lā′out′) *n.* **1.** The laying out of something. **2.** The arrangement, plan, or structuring of something laid out; the overall picture or form: *the layout of a factory.* **3. a.** The arrangement and juxtaposition of printed matter, photographs, or the like, as for a newspaper or magazine page. **b.** A dummy, sketch, or paste-up for matter to be printed. **4.** A diagram showing how something, such as a machine, is constructed.

lay over *intr.v.* To stop at some place in the course of a journey because of scheduling requirements.

lay·o·ver (lā′ō′vər) *n.* A stop, usually of short duration, imposed by the scheduling of a carrier or carriers.

lay reader *n.* A layman in the Anglican or Roman Catholic church authorized by a bishop to preach and conduct certain services. Also called "reader."

lay·shaft *n.* A secondary shaft to which motion is transmitted from the main shaft in a gear box.

lay sister *n.* A woman who has taken religious vows but who is not ordained and is usually employed in manual labors.

lay up *tr.v.* **1.** To stock (supplies) for future needs. **2.** *Informal.* To confine as an invalid. **3.** To put (a ship) in dock, as for repairs.

lay·up (lā′ŭp′) *n. Basketball.* A usually one-handed, banked shot made close to the basket after driving in.

lay·wo·man (lā′wŏom′ən) *n., pl.* **-women** (wĭm′ən). A woman who is not a member of the clergy.

la·zar (lā′zər, lăz′ər) *n. Archaic.* A beggar afflicted with some loathsome disease, especially leprosy; a leper. [Middle English, from Medieval Latin *Lazarus*, LAZARUS.]

laz·a·ret·to (lăz′ə-rĕt′ō) *n., pl.* **-tos.** Also **laz·a·ret, laz·a·rette** (lăz′ə-rĕt′). **1.** Formerly, a hospital treating contagious diseases. Also called "lazar house," "pest house." **2.** A building or ship used as a quarantine station. **3.** A storage space between the decks of a ship. [Italian *lazaretto*, from *lazzaro*, leper, beggar, from Medieval Latin *Lazarus*, LAZARUS.]

Laz·a·rus (lăz′ər-əs). **1.** The brother of Mary and Martha whom Jesus raised from the dead. John 11:1-44. **2.** The diseased beggar in the parable of the rich man and the beggar. Luke 16:19-31.

Lazarus, Emma (1849-87). U.S. author and philanthropist. A poet, author, and translator, she is best remembered for her eloquent expression of the problems of immigrants and persecuted peoples. Her poem "The New Colossus" is inscribed on the base of the Statue of Liberty, which celebrated its centennial in 1986.

laze (lāz) *v.* **lazed, lazing, lazes.** —*intr.* To be lazy; loaf. —*tr.* To spend (time) in loafing. Often used with *away.*
~*n.* Time spent in idleness. [Back-formation from LAZY.]

la·zu·li (lăz′yŏo-lē) *n.* **Lapis lazuli** (see).

laz·u·lite (lăz′yŏo-līt′) *n.* A relatively rare, deep sky-blue or azure mineral, essentially (Mg,Fe)Al₂(PO₄)₂(OH)₂, in which iron usually replaces some of the magnesium. [Medieval Latin *lazulum*, LAPIS LAZULI + -ITE.]

laz·u·rite (lăz′yŏo-rīt′) *n.* A relatively rare, azure, violet-blue, or Prussian blue mineral, NA₄₅Al₃Si₃O₁₂S. Also called "lapis lazuli." [German *Lasurit*, from Medieval Latin *lazur*, from Arabic *lāzaward*, LAPIS LAZULI.]

la·zy (lā′zē) *adj.* **-zier, -ziest. 1.** Resistant to work or exertion; given to idleness; slothful. **2.** Slow-moving; sluggish: *a lazy river.* **3.** Conducive to languor or indolence: *a lazy day.* [Perhaps from Low German and akin to *lasich*, idle.] —**la·zi·ly** *adv.* —**la·zi·ness** *n.*

la·zy·bones (lā′zē-bōnz′) *n., pl.* **-bones.** *Informal.* A lazy person.

lazy eye *n.* Amblyopia.

lazy Su·san (sŏo′sən) *n.* A revolving tray for condiments or food.

lazy tongs *pl.n.* Tongs having a jointed extensible framework operated by scissorlike handles for grasping an object at a distance.

lb pound [Latin *libra.*]

l.b. *Cricket.* leg bye.

l.c. 1. letter of credit. **2.** in the place cited. [Latin *loco citato*] **3.** *Printing.* lower-case.

L.C. 1. landing craft. **2.** Library of Congress.

L/C letter of credit.

LCD (ĕl′sē′dē′) *n.* A **liquid crystal display** (see).

l.c.d., L.C.D. lowest common denominator.

l.c.m., L.C.M. lowest common multiple.

LCT. local civil time.

L/Cpl. lance-corporal.

ld. 1. *Printing.* lead. **2.** load.

Ld. 1. Limited. **2.** Lord (English title).

LD lethal dose. LD₅₀ is an index of toxicity indicating the amount of poison that causes the death of 50 percent of a batch of experimental organisms.

L-D converter (ĕl′dē′) *n. Metallurgy.* A converter for producing steel by blowing oxygen through a water-cooled pipe into molten pig iron, thus burning off some of the carbon. [From *Linz-Donawitz*, after two towns in Austria where the method was first used.]

L-do·pa (ĕl-dō′pə) *n.* An amino acid, $C_9H_{11}NO_4$, that occurs naturally in the body and is used to treat Parkinson's disease. Also called "levodopa." [From *L-dihydroxyphenylalanine.*]

lea¹ (lē, lā) *n.* Also **ley** (lā, lē). *Poetic.* **1.** Grassland; meadow. **2.** Land sown temporarily with grass. [Middle English *ley(e)*, Old English *lēah, lēa.*]

lea² (lē) *n.* A measure of yarn that is 300, 200, 120, or 80 yards (275, 183, 110, or 73 meters) depending on the type. [Middle English *lee*, perhaps from French *lier*, from Latin *ligāre*, to bind.]

lea. 1. league (unit of distance). **2.** leather.

leach (lēch) *v.* **leached, leaching, leaches.** —*tr.* **1.** To remove soluble constituents from (a substance) by the action of a percolating liquid. **2.** To remove (soluble constituents) from a substance in this way. —*intr.* **1.** To be dissolved and washed out by a percolating liquid. **2.** To lose or yield soluble matter to a percolating liquid. ~*n.* **1.** The process of leaching. **2.** A porous, perforated, or sievelike vessel that holds material to be leached. **3.** The substance through which a liquid is leached. **4.** The solution thus leached. [Variant of obsolete *letch*, to wet, probably ultimately from Old English *leccan*, to moisten.] —**leach·er** *n.*

leach·ing (lē′chĭng) *n. Geology.* Separation and removal of soluble components from soil by percolating water. Also called "chemical weathering."

Lea·cock (lē′kŏk′), **Stephen Butler** (1869-1944). British-born Canadian humorist. He was a professor of economics at McGill University, Montreal, while writing humorous essays and books.

lead¹ (lēd) *v.* **led** (lĕd), **leading, leads.** —*tr.* **1. a.** To show the way to by going in advance; conduct, escort, or direct. **b.** To show (the way) by going in advance or by setting an example. **2.** To guide physically, as by taking by the hand or by holding by a rope: *lead a horse.* **3.** To serve as a route for; conduct on a particular course: *The path led him to a cemetery.* **4. a.** To cause to follow some course of action or line of thought; induce: *led him to believe otherwise.* **b.** To influence the answer of a (witness) by phrasing a question in a certain way. **5. a.** To direct the performance or activities of: *lead a battalion.* **b.** To inspire the conduct of: *lead the nation.* **6.** To assume leadership in; steer; guide: *lead a discussion.* **7.** To be at the head of: *His name led the list.* **8.** To have an advance over: *led the field in aerodynamics.* **9.** To pursue; live: *leading a hectic life.* **10.** In card games, to begin a round of play by putting down (a card): *led an ace.* **11.** To aim in front of (a moving target). **12.** *Chiefly British.* To be the principal first violinist in (an orchestra). **13.** To guide (a partner) when dancing. **14.** To be the main channel for (water, electricity, or the like). —*intr.* **1.** To be first; be ahead: *leading by a length.* **2.** To go first as a guide. **3.** To act as commander, director, or conductor. **4.** To guide a partner in dance steps. **5.** To be guided: *The horse leads easily.* **6.** To afford a passage, course, or route: *a door leading into the kitchen.* **7.** To tend toward a certain goal or result. Used with *to: led to complications.* **8.** To make the initial play, as in a card game. **9.** *British.* To be the principal first violinist in an orchestra. **10.** *Boxing.* To deliver attacking punches with a specified fist: *leading with his left.* **11.** To begin a presentation in a given way: *led with the election news.* **12.** In dancing, to start off on a specified foot: *leading with your right foot.* **13.** *Music.* To have a lead in a piece of music. —**lead astray.** To lead into error or wrongdoing. —**lead on.** To draw along; lure; entice, especially by deception. —**lead up to. 1.** To result in by a series of steps. **2.** To proceed toward (one's true purpose or subject) with preliminary remarks.
~*n.* **1.** The first place; the foremost position. **2.** The margin by which one is ahead: *he was losing his lead.* **3. a.** A piece of information of possible use in a search: *several good leads for a job.* **b.** A clue; a hint. **4.** Command; leadership: *take the lead.* **5.** An example; a precedent. **6. a.** The principal role in a dramatic production. **b.** The person playing such a part. **7.** *Journalism.* **a.** The opening line or paragraph of a news story. **b.** A prominently displayed news story. **8.** In card games: **a.** The first play. **b.** The prerogative of making or turn to make the first play. **c.** The card played. **9.** In boxing: **a.** The arm with which a boxer usually leads. **b.** A punch using this arm. **10.** A leash, rope, or strap for leading an animal. **11.** *Nautical.* The direction in which a rope runs. **12.** *Mining.* A deposit of gold ore in an old riverbed. **b.** A lode. **13.** A wire or cable for making an electrical connection. **14.** The act of aiming ahead of and firing at a moving target. **15.** *Music.* A major part at the beginning of a piece of music for an instrument or voice. **16.** A stream or other channel leading up to a mill. [Middle English *leden*, Old English *lǣdan, lǣdde, lǣded.*]

lead[2] (lĕd) *n.* **1.** *Symbol* **Pb** A soft, malleable, ductile, bluish-white, dense metallic element, extracted chiefly from galena and used in containers and pipes for corrosives, in solder and type metal, bullets, radiation shielding, paints, and antiknock compounds. Atomic number 82, atomic weight 207.19, melting point 327.5°C, boiling point 1,744°C, specific gravity 11.35, valences 2, 4. **2.** A lump of lead suspended by a line, used to make soundings to determine the depth of water. **3. leads.** *British.* **a.** A flat or slightly pitched roof covered with sheets of lead. **b.** The sheets of lead used for such a roof. **4.** Bullets from or for firearms; shot. **5. leads.** Strips of lead used in fitting windows with small panes or stained glass pieces. **6.** *Printing. Abbr.* **ld.** A thin strip of type metal used to separate lines of type. **7. a.** Any of various, often graphitic, compositions used as the writing substance in pencils. **b.** A thin stick of such material.
~*adj.* Containing or made of lead.
~*v.* **leaded, leading, leads.** —*tr.* **1.** To cover, line, weight, fill, or treat with lead. **2.** *Printing.* To provide space between (lines of type) with leads. **3.** To secure (window glass) with leads. —*intr.* To become filled, covered, or clogged with lead. [Middle English *lead, lœd,* Old English *lēad,* from West Germanic *lauda* (unattested), akin to Gaelic *luaidh*†.]

lead acetate (lĕd) *n.* A poisonous white crystalline compound, $Pb(C_2H_3O_2)_2 \cdot 3H_2O$, used in dyes, waterproofing compounds, and varnishes. Also called "sugar of lead."

lead arsenate (lĕd) *n.* A poisonous white crystalline compound, $Pb_3(AsO_4)_2$, used in insecticides and herbicides.

lead carbonate (lĕd) *n.* A poisonous white amorphous powder, $PbCO_3$, used as a paint pigment.

lead chromate (lĕd) *n.* A poisonous yellow crystalline compound, $PbCrO_4$, used as a paint pigment.

lead·en (lĕd'n) *adj.* **1.** Made of or containing lead. **2.** Heavy and inert like lead. **3.** Dull and listless; sluggish. **4.** Burdened; weighted down; depressed: *a leaden heart.* **5.** Dull, dark gray: *a leaden sky.* **—lead·en·ly** *adv.* **—lead·en·ness** *n.*

lead·er (lē'dər) *n.* **1.** A person who leads others along a way; a guide. **2.** One in charge or in command of others. **3.** The head of a political party or organization. **4.** *British.* **Leader. a.** A member of the House of Commons who is responsible for organizing the program of parliamentary business. Also called "Leader of the House of Commons." **b.** A peer who has a similar function in the House of Lords. Also called "Leader of the House of Lords." In both senses, also called "Leader of the House." **5. a.** The principal performer in an orchestra, quartet, choir, or the like; especially, a principal first violinist who represents the orchestra to the conductor and often plays solos. **b.** The conductor of an orchestra, band, or choral group. **6.** The foremost horse, dog, or other animal in a harnessed team. **7.** *British.* The senior counsel, usually a King's Counsel, who conducts a case in court. **8.** *Chiefly British.* The main editorial article in a newspaper or periodical. Also called "leading article." **9. leaders.** *Printing.* Dots or dashes in a row leading the eye across a page, as in an index entry. **10.** A pipe for conveying rainwater from the roof to the ground. **11.** A short length of gut, wire, or the like by which the hook is attached to a fishing line. **12.** *Botany.* The growing apex or main shoot of a shrub or tree. **13.** A tab on the end of a film or tape, used to thread it.

lead·er·ship (lē'dər-shĭp') *n.* **1.** The position, office, or term of a leader. **2.** A group of leaders. **3.** The capacity to be a leader; ability to lead.

lead glance *n.* A mineral, **galena** *(see).*

lead glass *n.* **Flint glass** *(see).*

lead-in (lĕd'ĭn') *n.* **1.** An introduction, as to a subject or program. **2.** The part of an antenna or aerial that leads to an electronic transmitter or receiver.

lead·ing[1] (lē'dĭng) *adj.* **1.** Major; principal: *a leading factor.* **2.** At the head; in the lead; foremost: *the leading candidate.* **3.** Playing a lead or principal role in a theatrical production: *a leading lady.* **4.** Phrased to elicit a desired response: *a leading question.* —See Synonyms at **chief. —lead·ing·ly** *adv.*

lead·ing[2] (lĕd'ĭng) *n.* **1.** A border or rim of lead, as around a windowpane. **2.** *Printing.* The spacing between lines.

leading edge (lē'dĭng) *n.* **1.** The edge of a sail that faces the wind. **2.** The front edge of an aircraft propeller blade or wing.

leading light (lē'dĭng) *n. Informal.* A person of great importance or value, especially to a group or undertaking.

leading-rein *n.* A rope or rein attached to a horse's bridle or halter by which to lead it.

leading tone (lē'dĭng) *n. Music.* The seventh note, or degree, of a scale, a half tone below the tonic; a subtonic.

lead lights (lĕd) *pl.n.* Also **lead·ed lights** (lĕd'ĭd). Windows made up of small pieces of glass held together by lead strips.

lead line (lĕd) *n. Nautical.* A sounding line with a lump of lead on it used to determine the depth of water.

lead monoxide (lĕd) *n. Chemistry.* **Litharge** *(see).*

lead off (lĕd) *intr.v.* **1.** To make the initial play or move; start. **2.** *Baseball.* To be the first batter in an inning or a line-up.

lead-off (lĕd-ôf', -ŏf') *n.* **1.** An opening play or move; a start; a beginning. **2.** A person or thing that starts something.

lead pencil (lĕd) *n.* A pencil that contains a thin stick of graphite as its marking substance.

lead·plant (lĕd'plănt', -plänt') *n.* A shrub, *Amorpha canescens,* of central North America, having leaves covered with whitish hairs. [Once thought to indicate the presence of lead.]

lead poisoning (lĕd) *n.* Acute or chronic poisoning by lead or any of its salts, the acute form causing severe gastroenteritis, and the chronic form anemia, abdominal pain, constipation, partial paralysis, and convulsions. Also called "plumbism," "saturnism."

lead screw *n.* A threaded screw along the bed of a lathe, used to drive the tool carriage along at a controlled rate, as in cutting threads.

leads·man (lĕdz'mən) *n., pl.* **-men** (-mĭn). *Nautical.* The man who uses the lead line in taking soundings.

lead tetraethyl (lĕd) *n.* **Tetraethyl lead** *(see).*

lead-time (lēd'tim') *n.* The time needed or available between the decision to start a project and the completion of the work.

Lead·ville (lĕd'vĭl'). A town of central Colorado, in the Rocky Mts. at an altitude of *c.* 3,110 meters (10,200 feet). Gold was discovered nearby in 1860. The first vein was exhausted two years later, but silver was found in 1877.

leadwort Plumbago capensis, *one of twelve species in the leadwort genus.*

lead·wort (lĕd'wûrt', -wôrt') *n.* **1.** Any of various plants of the genera *Plumbago* or *Ceratostigma,* having clusters of variously colored flowers. **2.** Any of several similar plants. Also called "plumbago." [Some species were thought to cure lead poisoning.]

leaf (lēf) *n., pl.* **leaves** (lēvz). *Abbr.* **l., L. 1.** A usually green, flattened structure of vascular plants, characteristically consisting of a blade-like expansion attached to a stem, and functioning as a principal organ of photosynthesis and transpiration. **2.** A leaflike organ or structure. **3.** Leaves collectively; foliage. **4.** The leaves of a plant used or processed for a specific purpose: *tobacco leaf.* **5.** Any of the sheets of paper bound in a book, each side of which constitutes a page. **6.** Metal in the form of a very thin sheet: *gold leaf.* **7.** A hinged or removable section for a table top. **8.** A hinged or otherwise movable section of a folding door, shutter, or gate. **9.** Any of the metal strips forming a leaf spring. **—in leaf.** Having sprouted or produced leaves; green with foliage. **—turn over a new leaf.** To make a significant change in one's life by mending one's ways.
~*intr.v.* **leafed, leafing, leafs. 1.** To produce leaves; put forth foliage. **2.** To turn pages rapidly; glance: *leafed through the catalogue.* [Middle English *le(e)f,* Old English *lēaf.*] See feature, next page.

leaf·age (lē'fĭj) *n.* Leaves; foliage.

leaf beet *n.* A vegetable, **chard** *(see).*

leaf-cut·ter ant (lēf'kŭt'ər) *n.* Any of various ants of the genus *Atta,* native to South America, that cut away leaf pieces to use them as fertilizer for their fungus gardens.

leaf-cutter bee *n.* Any of various carpenter bees of the genus *Megachile* that use pieces of leaf to construct the walls of their egg cells. *M. centuncularis* is a pest of garden roses.

leaf fat *n.* A dense fat that collects around the kidneys of certain animals, notably pigs.

leaf·hop·per (lēf'hŏp'ər) *n.* Any of numerous insects of the family Cicadellidae, that suck juices from plants.

leaf insect *n.* Any of various chiefly Asiatic insects of the genus *Phyllium* and related genera, that resemble leaves.

leaf insect *Related to stick insects, leaf insects live in the forests of tropical Asia and New Guinea, camouflaged from predators by their resemblance to leaves. The insect's eggs are also protected by camouflage: they resemble plant seeds.*

leaf-lard *n.* High-grade lard made from the leaf fat of a pig.

leaf·less (lēf'lĭs) *adj.* Having or putting forth no leaves.

leaf·let (lēf'lĭt) *n.* **1.** Any of the segments of a compound leaf. **2.** A small leaf or leaflike part. **3.** A printed, usually folded sheet of paper for distribution, such as an advertising circular.
~*v.* **leafleted** or **leafletted, -leting** or **-letting, -lets.** —*intr.* To distribute leaflets. —*tr.* **1.** To distribute leaflets in (an area). **2.** To distribute leaflets to (people).

leaf miner *n.* Any of numerous small flies and moths that in the larval state dig into and feed on leaf tissue.

leaf mold *n.* Humus or compost consisting of decomposed leaves and other organic material.

leaf spot *n.* Any of various plant diseases resulting in well-defined darkened areas on the leaves.

leaf spring *n.* A composite spring, used especially in vehicle suspensions, consisting of several layers of flexible metallic strips joined to act as a single unit.

leaf·stalk (lēf'stôk') *n.* The stalk by which a leaf is attached to a stem; a petiole.

leaf·worm (lēf'wûrm') *n.* See **cotton leafworm.**

leaf·y (lē'fē) *adj.* **-ier, -iest. 1.** Having or covered with leaves. **2.** Consisting of leaves. **3.** Leaflike. **—leaf·i·ness** *n.*

league[1] (lēg) *n. Abbr.* **l., L. 1.** An association of states, organizations, or individuals formed to promote common interests; an alliance. **2.** An association of sports teams or clubs that play one another. **3.** *Informal.* A class of competition; a level: *out of his league.* **—in league.** Allied; in close cooperation.
~*v.* **leagued, leaguing, leagues.** —*intr.* To come together for a common purpose; unite. —*tr.* To bring together under a common agreement; join. [Middle English *ligg,* from Old French *ligue,* from Italian *liga, lega,* from *legare,* to bind, from Latin *ligāre.*]

league[2] *n. Abbr.* **lea. 1. a.** A unit of distance equal to three statute miles. **b.** Any of various other units of about the same length. **2.** A square league. [Middle English *leg(h)e,* from Late Latin *leuca, leuga,* perhaps from Gaulish.]

League of Nations. An international organization of nations established in 1920 to promote world peace and dissolved in 1946.

lea·guer[1] (lē'gər) *n. Archaic.* **1.** A siege; beleaguerment. **2.** A besieging army or its camp.
~*tr.v.* **leaguered, -guering, -guers.** To besiege; beleaguer. [Dutch *leger,* camp, siege, from Middle Dutch, camp, lair.]

leaguer[2] *n.* A person who belongs to a league.

leaf shape

DIFFERENT SHAPES BUT IDENTICAL FUNCTION

How leaves have adapted to their native habitats

Although leaves differ widely in appearance, the main function they perform is the same—to provide food for the plant. A leaf does this by photosynthesis, the process in which it uses light and its own green coloring, chlorophyll, to make food from the carbon dioxide and water the plant has absorbed.

The shape of its leaves is the result of a plant's evolution in its native habitat—its individual adaptation to carry out photosynthesis with maximum efficiency. A plant may have many small leaves or fewer large ones and they are arranged in a mosaic that secures the greatest possible exposure of leaf surface to light and air. Plants that grow in shade usually have a large leaf area

to obtain whatever light is available.

A leaf's second function is to control the plant's loss of water through stomata, or pores, on its underside. In many plants leaves alter their shape by curling at the edges when the weather is dry to reduce the exposed area of the underside and so cut down water loss. Some plants have made the alteration of shape permanent—heathers, thyme, coniferous trees, and other plants have adapted to the exposed conditions of their native habitats by evolving small, narrow leaves to reduce water loss. Succulent plants, such as houseleeks, have evolved thick leaves to store water, and cacti have reduced their leaves to stems.

SIMPLE LEAVES

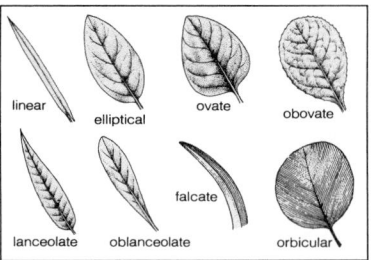

COMPOUND LEAVES

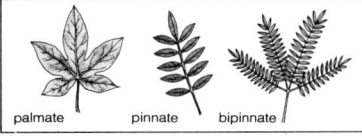

VENATION

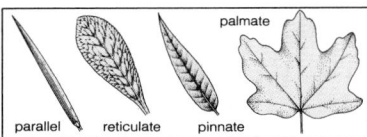

LEAF BASE

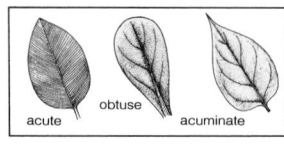

LEAF APEX

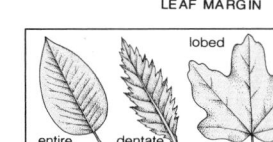

LEAF MARGIN

IDENTIFICATION *Leaves are either simple (with a single blade) or compound (with separate leaflets), but their actual shape, design of veins (venation), and position on the stem vary greatly. Terms devised by botanists describe these variations and help to identify the plant.*

Le·ah (lē′ə). The first wife of Jacob. Genesis 29:16–23. [Hebrew, "wild cow."]

Lea·hy (lā′hē), **William Daniel** (1875–1959). U.S. naval officer and diplomat. Serving from the Spanish-American War through World War II, he rose from the rank of ensign to admiral of the fleet, the second American to achieve that rank.

leak (lēk) *n.* **1.** An escape from normal or proper confinement; especially, an accidental escape from a container or conduit. **2.** Something escaping normal or proper confines, such as: **a.** A liquid or gas abnormally flowing out of a pipe or reservoir. **b.** An electric current diverted through faulty insulation. **c.** Light or other radiation passing through an accidental opening. **3.** A flaw, crack, hole, or passage through which an escape occurs. **4.** The path followed by the escaping material. **5. a.** A disclosure of confidential information, either intentional or deliberate. **b.** The information disclosed. **c.** The source of such information. **—spring a leak.** To contract or develop an opening or other flaw that allows the escape or entrance of a substance. ~*v.* **leaked, leaking, leaks.** —*intr.* **1.** To permit the escape or passage of something through a hole, crack, or similar opening. **2.** To escape or pass through such an opening. **3.** To become publicly known through a breach of secrecy. Often used with *out: The news leaked out.* —*tr.* **1.** To permit (a substance) to escape or pass through a hole, crack, or similar opening. **2.** To disclose (information) without authorization or official sanction. [Middle English *leke,* perhaps from Old Norse *leki.*]

leak·age (lē′kĭj) *n.* **1.** The process or an instance of leaking. **2.** That which escapes by leaking. **3.** An allowance made for loss of stock by leaking, as in commerce.

Lea·key (lē′kē), **Louis Seymour Bazett** (1903–72). British paleontologist. He influenced evolutionary theory with his account and

analysis of the discovery, by his wife, **Mary Leakey** (1913–), of the 1.75-million-year-old *Zinjanthropus* skull at Olduvai Gorge in Tanzania. Mary Leakey and his son **Richard Leakey** (1944–) have continued his research.

leak·y (lē′kē) *adj.* **-ier, -iest.** Having leaks or tending to leak.

lean¹ (lēn) *v.* **leaned** or **leant** (lĕnt), **leaning, leans.** —*intr.* **1.** To bend or slant away from the vertical. **2.** To incline the weight of the body so as to be supported: *leaning against the railing.* **3.** To rely for assistance or support: *Lean on me for help.* **4.** To have a tendency or preference. Used with *to* or *toward: She leans toward the group approach.* **5.** *Informal.* To exert pressure. Used with *on: Their boss is leaning on them.* —*tr.* **1.** To set or place so as to be resting or supported. **2.** To cause to incline: *Lean your head back.* **—lean over backward.** To put oneself to great inconvenience to achieve something. ~*n.* A tilt or inclination away from the vertical. [Middle English *lenen,* Old English *hleonian, hlinian.*]
Usage: Leaned is the usual past tense and participle form in American English, *leant* in British English; the former is more widespread in the English-speaking world, especially in written English. Many users of British English write *leaned,* but say (lĕnt).

lean² *adj.* **leaner, leanest. 1.** Not fleshy or fat; thin. **2.** Containing little or no fat. Said of meat. **3.** Not productive or abundant: *lean years.* **4. a.** Lacking mineral value: *lean ore.* **b.** Lacking a high proportion of combustible material; containing much air: *lean fuel.* ~*n.* Meat with little or no fat. [Middle English *lene,* Old English *hlæne,* from Germanic *hlainjaz* (unattested).] **—lean·ly** *adv.* **—lean·ness** *n.*
Usage: lean, spare, skinny, scrawny, lank, lanky, rawboned, gaunt. These adjectives describe persons who are thin of body. *Lean* and *spare* often suggest desirable absence of flesh in one who is athletic and vigorous; sometimes, however, they have no particular connotation. *Skinny* and *scrawny* imply unattractive thinness associated with underdevelopment or undernourishment. *Lank* describes one who is thin in proportion to height, and *lanky* one who is thin, tall, and loose-jointed. *Rawboned* suggests the lankiness or spareness of an outdoorsman. *Gaunt* implies thinness that gives undue prominence to the bones and may suggest illness or hardship.

Lean (lēn), **David** (1908–). British film director. His work includes *The Bridge on the River Kwai* (1957) and *Lawrence of Arabia* (1962), both of which won Academy Awards.

Le·an·der (lē-ăn′dər). *Greek Mythology.* Youth who loved Hero and drowned while swimming the Hellespont one night to be with her.

lean·ing (lē′nĭng) *n.* A tendency; a proclivity; an inclination.

leant. Alternate past tense and past participle of **lean** (verb). —See Usage note at **lean.**

lean-to (lēn′tōō′) *n., pl.* **-tos. 1.** A shed with a single-pitch roof attached to the side of a building. **2.** A shelter made from planks or branches raised in the front on poles.

leap (lēp) *v.* **leaped** or **leapt** (lĕpt, lēpt), **leaping, leaps.** —*intr.* **1.** To jump off the ground with a spring of the legs. **2.** To jump forward; vault; bound. **3.** To move quickly, abruptly, or impulsively: *leaps from one loyalty to another.* —*tr.* **1.** To jump over; hurdle: *leap the brook.* **2.** To cause to jump: *leap a horse.* ~*n.* **1.** The act of springing up or forward; a vault; a bound. **2.** The distance cleared in a forward spring. **3.** An abrupt or precipitous passage, shift, or transition. **4.** Something, such as a fence, that is or is to be leaped. **—a leap in the dark.** A course of action or a risk taken without knowing what the consequences will be. **—by leaps and bounds.** Very quickly and by large degrees. [Middle English *le(a)pen,* Old English *hlēapan.*] **—leap·er** *n.*
Usage: Leaped is the usual past tense and participle form in American English, *leapt* in British English; the former is more widespread in the English-speaking world, especially in written English. Many users of British English write *leaped,* but say (lĕpt).

leap·frog (lēp′frôg′, -frŏg′) *n.* A game in which one player kneels or bends over while the next in line jumps over him straddle-legged. ~*v.* **leapfrogged, -frogging, -frogs.** —*tr.* **1.** To jump over in or as if in leapfrog. **2.** *Military.* To advance (two military units) by engaging one with the enemy while moving the other to a forward position. —*intr.* To move forward or progress by or as if by alternating leaps.

leapt. Alternate past tense and past participle of **leap.** **—See Usage note at leap.**

leap year *n.* **1.** A year in the Gregorian calendar having 366 days, with the extra day, February 29, intercalated to compensate for the quarter-day difference between an ordinary year and the astronomical year. A year whose number is divisible by 4 is a leap year, except centennial numbers, which are leap years only when divisible by 400. See feature at **calendar. 2.** An intercalary year in any calendar.

Lear (lîr) *n.* A foolish, self-deceiving father, especially one whose behavior has tragic consequences. [After *King Lear,* hero of Shakespeare's tragedy (1605).]

Lear, Edward (1812–88). British artist and writer. He was a skilled painter of birds, but is famous for the whimsical humor of his limericks and such works as his first *Book of Nonsense* (1846).

learn (lûrn) *v.* **learned** or **learnt** (lûrnt), **learning, learns.** —*tr.* **1.** To gain knowledge, comprehension, or mastery of through experience or study. **2.** To fix in the mind or memory; memorize: *learned the poem by heart.* **3.** To acquire through experience: *learned humility in the hands of his captors.* **4.** To become informed of; find out. **5.** *Obsolete.* To give information of. **6.** *Nonstandard.* To teach. —*intr.* **1.** To gain knowledge, comprehension, or skill. **2.** To become informed. Used with *of* or *about.* [Middle English *lernen,* Old English *leornian.*] —**learn·er** *n.*

Usage: *Learned* is the usual past tense and participle form in American English, *learnt* in British English; the former is more widespread in the English-speaking world, especially in written English. *Learned* pronounced as one syllable (lûrnd) should not be confused with the adjective *learned* (as in *a learned historian),* which is pronounced as two syllables (lûr′nĭd). • *Learn* in the sense of "to teach, impart knowledge" has no status in standard English: *She taught (*not *learned) him English.*

learn·ed (lûr′nĭd) *adj.* **1.** Having or demonstrating profound knowledge or scholarship; erudite; scholarly. **2.** Scholarly or directed toward scholars: *a learned journal.*

learn·ing (lûr′nĭng) *n.* **1.** Instruction; education. **2.** Acquired wisdom, knowledge, or skill. **3.** *Psychology.* The process of development through experience that leads to relatively permanent changes in behavior. —See Synonyms at **knowledge.**

learning curve *n.* A graph representing progress in learning, usually showing a fairly steady increase, especially at the beginning, and then leveling off toward the end.

learning disability *n.* A condition held to be associated with neurological dysfunction that is characterized by inability to master a skill, as reading or numerical calculation.

learn·ing-dis·a·bled (lûr′nĭng-dĭs-ā′bəld) *adj.* Having a learning disability.

learnt. Alternate past tense and past participle of **learn.** —See Usage note at **learn.**

lease (lēs) *n.* **1. a.** A contract granting use or possession of property for a specified period in exchange for rent. **b.** The legal document granting such use or possession. **2.** The term or duration of use or possession granted by such a contract. **3.** Property used or possessed by contract in exchange for rent. —**a new lease on life.** Renewed strength, enthusiasm, or usefulness.

~tr.v. **leased, leasing, leases. 1.** To grant use or possession of by lease. **2.** To use or possess by lease. [Middle English *les,* from Anglo-French, from *lesser,* to lease, from Old French *laissier,* to let go, leave, from Latin *laxāre,* to let go, loosen, from *laxus,* LAX.] —**leas·a·ble** *adj.*

lease-back (lēs′băk′) *n.* The leasing of property by a new owner back to the previous owner: *sale and lease-back.*

lease·hold (lēs′hōld′) *n.* **1.** Use or possession by lease. **2.** Property held under a lease for a term of years. Compare **freehold.**

~adj. Designating property held under a lease for a term of years.

lease·hold·er (lēs′hōl′dər) *n.* A person who uses or possesses property through a lease.

leash (lēsh) *n.* **1.** A chain, rope, or strap attached to the collar or harness of an animal and used to hold it in check or lead it. **2.** A control or check kept on something, as if by a leash. **3.** In hunting, a group of three animals, such as hounds, foxes, or hares. —**straining at the leash.** Eager and impatient to start.

~tr.v. **leashed, leashing, leashes.** To restrain with or as if with a leash. [Middle English *lees, leshe,* from Old French *laisse,* from *laissier,* to loosen, let (a dog run slack). See **lease.**]

leash law *n.* An ordinance requiring that dogs be kept on a leash when not restricted to their owners' property.

leas·ing (lē′sĭng) *n. Archaic.* A lie, or the act of lying; falsehood. [Middle English *le(e)sing,* Old English *lēasung,* from *lēasian,* to lie, from *lēas,* untrue, false.]

least (lēst). Alternate superlative of **little.**

~adj. **1.** Lowest in importance or rank. **2.** Smallest in magnitude, amount, or degree. **3.** Slightest; remotest: *He hasn't the least notion.*

~adv. To or in the smallest degree or amount. —**at least. 1.** According to the lowest possible assessment; no less than. **2.** In any event; anyway: *You might at least answer.*

~n. The smallest or slightest degree, amount, or the like. —**at the (very) least.** At the lowest calculation; as a minimum. —**in the least.** At all: *I don't mind in the least.* [Middle English *leest, least,* Old English *lǣst,* from Germanic *loisiz* (unattested), little. See **less.**]

least common denominator *n. Mathematics.* The **lowest common denominator** *(see).*

least common multiple *n. Mathematics. Abbr.* **l.c.m.** The least quantity that is exactly divisible by each of two or more designated quantities; for example, 12 is the least common multiple of 2, 3, 4, and 6. Also called "lowest common multiple."

least flycatcher *n.* A small, grayish North American bird, *Empidonax minimus.*

least squares *n. Used with a singular verb.* A method of determining the line or curve that best fits an experimental set of data, using the criterion that the sums of the squares of deviations of experimental points from curve ordinates be a minimum.

least·wise (lēst′wīz′) *adv.* Also *regional* **least·ways** (-wāz′). *Informal.* Anyway; at least.

leat (lēt) *n. British.* An open ditch or trench that conducts water to a mill, mining works, or the like. [Old English *-gelǣt* (as in *wætergelǣt,* watercourse), from the root of LET.]

leath·er (lĕth′ər) *n. Abbr.* **lea. 1.** The dressed or tanned hide of an animal, usually with the hair removed. **2.** Any of various articles made of leather, such as a strap or boot. **3.** The flap of a dog's ear.

~adj. Of or made of leather.

~tr.v. **leathered, -ering, -ers. 1. a.** To cover with leather. **b.** To add leather parts to. **2.** *Informal.* To beat with or as if with a leather strap. [Middle English *lether, leder,* Old English *lether.*]

leath·er·back (lĕth′ər-băk′) *n.* A large, chiefly tropical marine turtle, *Dermochelys coriacea,* having a leathery, ridged carapace.

leath·er·ette (lĕth′ə-rĕt′) *n.* An imitation leather. [Originally a trademark.]

leath·er·head (lĕth′ər-hĕd′) *n.* The **friarbird** *(see).*

leath·er·jack·et (lĕth′ər-jăk′ĭt) *n.* A fish, *Oligoplites saurus,* of Atlantic and Pacific waters, having tough, leathery skin and venomous spines on the anal fin.

leath·ern (lĕth′ərn) *adj. Archaic.* **1.** Made of or covered with leather. **2.** Resembling leather.

leath·er·neck (lĕth′ər-nĕk′) *n. Slang.* A marine. [Referring to the U.S. marine uniform that formerly had a leather neckband.]

leath·er·wood (lĕth′ər-wo͝od′) *n.* **1.** A shrub, *Dirca palustris,* of eastern North America, having tough, pliable bark and small yellow flowers. **2.** A shrub, the **titi** *(see).*

leath·er·y (lĕth′ə-rē′) *adj.* Having the texture or appearance of leather; tough or weathered: *leathery hands.*

leave[1] (lēv) *v.* **left** (lĕft), **leaving, leaves.** *—tr.* **1.** To go out of or away from. **2.** To go without taking or removing. Often used with *behind: left his book behind on the train.* **3. a.** To cause to remain as a consequence or aftereffect: *left a trail of smoke.* **b.** To bring to a specified state or condition: *left her in a rage.* **4. a.** To forgo moving, changing, proceeding with, or interfering with; let remain: *Leave the dishes in the sink.* **b.** To allow (a person or thing) to do something without intervening: *left the house to burn down.* **c.** To postpone: *leave packing till the morning.* **5.** To have remaining alive after one's death: *He leaves a son.* **6.** To give as or as if as a bequest. **7.** To submit to another to be done, acted upon, or accomplished: *Leave the hard work for Jones to do.* **8.** To abandon; forsake: *She's leaving home.* **9.** To give (information) to be acted upon at a later stage: *I left my number with his wife.* **10.** To have as remainder: *6 from 12 leaves 6.* *—intr.* To depart; set out; go. —**leave alone.** To refrain from disturbing, upsetting, or dealing with. —**leave be.** To refrain from interfering with, changing, or disturbing. —**leave it at that.** To stop at the point indicated and do or say no more. —**leave much to be desired.** To fall far short of the appropriate standard or quality. —**leave off. 1.** To stop; cease. **2.** To stop doing or using: *leave off smoking.* —**leave out. 1.** To omit. **2.** To disregard or ignore, especially in social matters. [Leave, left, left; Middle English *leven, left, lefte,* Old English *lǣfan, lǣfde, lǣfed.*]

Usage: *Leave* and *let* are interchangeable only when they are followed by a noun or pronoun and *alone*: *Leave* (or *let*) *John alone.* The intended sense here is "refrain from disturbing or interfering," and both *leave alone* and *let alone* are capable of expressing it acceptably. Some writers and speakers use only *let alone* in such examples and restrict *leave alone* to the sense of "depart and leave one in solitude." However, in the following sentences, considered as examples in writing, *leave alone* is acceptable in the sense of "refrain from disturbing": *Leave him alone and he will produce. Left alone, he was quite productive. Leave* is not interchangeable with *let* in other senses of "allow" or "permit," as illustrated in the following examples. In all of them, only *let* is acceptable: *Let me be. Let him go. Let us not quarrel. Let it lie.*

leave[2] *n.* **1.** Permission: *With your leave, I must go.* **2.** Official permission, as for military personnel, to be absent from work or duty for a considerable length of time: *leave of absence.* **3.** The duration of absence granted by such permission. **4.** Formal or verbal farewell: *took leave of her with a heavy heart.* —**on leave.** Absent with official permission. [Middle English *leve,* Old English *lēaf.*]

leave[3] *intr.v.* **leaved, leaving, leaves.** To put forth foliage; leaf. [Middle English *leven,* from *le(e)f,* LEAF.]

leaved (lēvd) *adj.* **1.** Having or bearing a leaf or leaves. **2.** Having a specified number or kind of leaves. Usually used in combination: *three-leaved; wide-leaved.*

leav·en (lĕv′ən) *n.* **1. a.** A substance, such as yeast, added to batters and doughs to produce fermentation. **b.** A portion of fermented dough used to produce fermentation in a new batch of dough. **2.** Any element or influence that works to lighten or enliven the whole.

~tr.v. **leavened, -ening, -ens. 1.** To add yeast or some other fermenting agent to. **2.** To produce fermentation in. **3.** To pervade with a lightening or enlivening influence: *leavened with a gentle humor.* [Middle English *levain,* from Old French, probably from Latin *levāmen,* alleviation, hence (in Vulgar Latin) "that which raises," from *levāre,* to raise.]

Leav·en·worth (lĕv′ən-wûrth′). A city in northeastern Kansas, on the Missouri River. It has varied industries and is the commercial center of a farm and livestock area. Fort Leavenworth is nearby.

Leavenworth, Henry (1783–1834). U.S. soldier. After the War of 1812 he served almost continuously on the frontier, building Forts Snelling and Leavenworth and commanding the entire southwestern frontier after 1834. He died of bilious fever while attempting to negotiate peace between warring Indian tribes.

leaves. Plural of **leaf.**

leave-tak·ing (lēv′tā′kĭng) *n.* **1.** A departure or farewell. **2.** An act of saying farewell.

leav·ings (lē′vĭngz) *pl.n.* Scraps or remains; leftovers; residue. —See Usage note at **remainder.**

Leb·a·non (lĕb′ə-nən). Small country in the Middle East. It has few resources, but developed as a regional center of international finance, trade, and tourism. Unlike other Arab countries, it has a large Christian population. It also has many Palestinian refugees. Lebanon was created as a French League of Nations mandate in 1920 and proclaimed its independence in 1941. It played a minor

PRONUNCIATION KEY

ă, pat; ā, pay; âr, care; ä, father, are; b, bib; ch, church; d, deed; ĕ, pet; ē, be; f, fife; g, gag; h, hat; hw, which; ĭ, pit; ī, pie; îr, pier; j, judge; k, kick; l, lid, needle; m, mum; n, no, sudden; ng, thing; ŏ, pot; ō, toe; ô, paw, for; oi, noise; ou, out; o͝o, book; o͞o, boot; p, pop; r, roar; s, sauce; sh, ship, dish; t, tight; th, thin, path; *th,* this, bathe; ŭ, cut; ûr, fur; v, valve; w, with; y, yes; z, zebra, size; zh, vision; ə, about, item, edible, gallop, circus, peaceful

IN FOREIGN WORDS:

à, *Fr.* ami; œ, *Fr.* feu, *Ger.* schön; ü, *Fr.* tu, *Ger.* über; KH, *Ger.* ich, *Scot.* loch; N, *Fr.* bon; y′, *Fr.* Compiègne

STRESS MARKS:

Primary stress: ′ **in·cite′** (ĭn-sīt′)
Secondary stress: ′ **in′sight′** (ĭn′sīt′)

role in the 1948 and 1956 Arab-Israeli wars, but did not participate in those of 1967 and 1973. Civil war between rival groups occurred in 1958, 1969, 1973, 1975-76, when a Syrian peace-keeping force entered the country, and again in 1977. To counter PLO attacks on northern Israel, the Israelis occupied southern Lebanon in 1978, after which a U.N. peace-keeping force took over, and again in 1982, when more than 10,000 PLO guerrillas were evacuated, mainly from Beirut, under U.S., French, and Italian supervision. The country is still beset by civil and religious strife. Area, 10,400 square kilometers (4,014 square miles). Population, 3,200,000. Capital, Beirut. See map at **Jordan.** —**Leb·a·nese** *n. & adj.*

le·bens·raum (lā′bəns-roum′) *n.* **1.** Additional territory deemed, especially by the Nazis, to be necessary to a nation for its economic well-being. **2.** Broadly, any extra space needed to facilitate working or living. [German, "living space."]

Le Brun (lə brœn′), **Charles** (1619–90). Artist to Louis XIV. He decorated Versailles, directed the Gobelins works (1663), responsible for royal furnishings, and was a founder of the Académie de

France (1666), set up to enable French artists to study abroad.

Le Cap. See **Cap-Haïtien.**

Le Car·ré (lə kă-rā′), **John,** born David John Moore Cornwell (1931–). British writer of espionage novels. These include *The Spy Who Came in from the Cold* (1963), *Tinker, Tailor, Soldier, Spy* (1974), and *Smiley's People* (1980).

lech, letch (lĕch) *n. Informal.* **1.** A strong desire or craving, especially of a sexual nature. **2.** A lecherous act.
~*intr.v.* **leched** or **letched, leching** or **letching, leches** or **letches.** *Informal.* To behave in a lecherous manner. Often used with *after.* [Back-formation from LECHER.]

Le Cha·te·lier's principle (lə shä-tə-lyā′) *n. Chemistry.* The principle that if a chemical reaction is at equilibrium and the conditions (such as pressure, temperature, or concentration) are changed, then there will be a compensating change in the position of equilibrium tending to restore the original conditions. [After H.L. *Le Châtelier* (1850–1936), French chemist.]

lech·er (lĕch′ər) *n.* A man given to excessive sexual cravings or indulgence. [Middle English *lech(o)ur,* from Old French *lecheor, lecheur,* from *lechier,* to live in debauchery, lick, from Frankish *likkōn* (unattested).]

lech·er·ous (lĕch′ər-əs) *adj.* Given to, characterized by, or inciting lechery. —**lech·er·ous·ly** *adv.* —**lech·er·ous·ness** *n.*

lech·er·y (lĕch′ə-rē) *n.* **1.** Excessive indulgence in sexual activity. **2.** Prurience; lasciviousness.

lec·i·thin (lĕs′ə-thən) *n.* Any of a group of phosphatides found in all plant and animal tissues, produced commercially from egg yolks, soybeans, and corn, and used in the processing of foods, pharmaceuticals, cosmetics, paints and inks, and rubber and plastics. [Greek *lekithos†,* egg yolk + -IN.]

lec·i·thin·ase (lĕs′ə-thə-nās′, -nāz′) *n.* Any of several enzymes that break down lecithin.

Le Cor·bu·sier (lə kôr-bōō-zyā′), pseudonym of Charles-Edouard Jeanneret-Gris (1887–1965). Swiss-born French architect. His design and use of modular housing units has greatly influenced modern town planning.

lec·tern (lĕk′tərn) *n.* **1.** A reading desk with a slanted top holding the books from which Scriptural passages are read during a church service. **2.** Broadly, any stand that serves as a support for notes or books, especially those of a speaker. [Middle English *lectorn, lettron,* from Old French *lettrun,* from Medieval Latin *lectrīnum,* from *lectrum,* from Latin *lectus,* past participle of *legere,* to read.]

lec·tion (lĕk′shən) *n.* **1.** A variant reading or transcription of a text as given in a particular edition or copy. **2.** A reading from Scripture that forms a part of a church service. [Latin *lectiō* (stem *lectiōn-*), "a reading," from *legere,* to read. See **lection.**]

lec·tion·ar·y (lĕk′shə-nĕr′ē) *n., pl.* **-ies.** A book containing lessons or a list of lessons from Scripture to be read at services. [Late Latin *lectiōnārium,* from Latin *lectiō,* LECTION.]

lec·tor (lĕk′tər) *n.* **1. a.** A cleric of the second lowest of the four minor orders in the early Christian church and formerly in the Roman Catholic Church, having the office of reading the sacred books in church. **b.** In the Roman Catholic Church, an ordinand who has been admitted to one of the first stages of the priestly ministry. **2.** A person who reads aloud certain of the Scriptural passages used in a church service; a reader. **3.** A lecturer or reader in certain universities. [Late Latin, from Latin, "reader," from *legere,* to read. See **lecture.**] —**lec·tor·ship** *n.*

lec·ture (lĕk′chər) *n.* **1.** An exposition of a given subject delivered before an audience or class for the purpose of instruction; a discourse. **2.** A method of teaching by discourse, especially as opposed to teaching by conversation or seminar. **3.** A sober admonition or correction; a solemn scolding.
~*v.* **lectured, -turing, -tures.** —*intr.* To deliver a lecture. —*tr.* **1.** To give a lecture to (a class or audience). **2.** To scold soberly and at length. [Middle English, "a reading," from Old French, from Medieval Latin *lectūra,* from *lectus,* past participle of *legere,* to read.]

lec·tur·er (lĕk′chər-ər) *n.* **1.** A person who gives a lecture. **2. a.** A teacher in a college or university ranking below a reader or professor. **b.** The rank or position of such a teacher.

lec·ture·ship (lĕk′chər-shĭp′) *n.* **1.** The status or position of a lecturer. **2.** An endowment or foundation supporting a series or course of lectures.

led. Past tense and past participle of **lead.**

LED (ĕl′ē-dē′, lĕd) *n. Electronics.* A semiconductor device that emits light when a voltage is applied, used extensively in visual displays on calculators, digital measuring instruments, and the like. [*l*ight-*e*mitting *d*iode.]

Le·da (lē′də). *Greek Mythology.* A queen of Sparta and the mother, by Zeus in the form of a swan, of Helen and Pollux, and by her husband Tyndareus, of Castor and Clytemnestra.

Led·bet·ter (lĕd′bĕt′ər), **Huddie,** known as "Leadbelly" (1888–1949). U.S. musician. A talented, original singer and guitarist, he led a nomadic life until the 1930's, when he began to record much of his music, including "Good Night, Irene."

le·der·ho·sen (lā′dər-hō′zən) *pl.n.* Men's leather shorts worn as part of traditional Tyrolean or Bavarian costume. [German, "leather trousers."]

ledge (lĕj) *n.* **1.** A horizontal projection forming a narrow shelf on a wall. **2.** A cut or projection forming a shelf on a cliff or rock wall. **3.** A ridge or rock shelf under water. **4.** A level of rock bearing ore; a vein. [Middle English *legge,* a raised strip or bar, perhaps from

---

Le Corbusier

CONCRETE "MACHINES" FOR LIVING IN
Building high with 20th-century materials

Le Corbusier was the name adopted by Charles Edouard Jeanneret, born at La Chaux-de-Fonds, Switzerland, in 1887. He trained as a designer-engraver at the local art school and went on to become one of the most influential figures in 20th-century architecture.

The most powerful advocate of the modernist architectural school, he believed that in the machine age housing must be functional, or utilitarian. "A house is a machine for living in," he said. He produced undecorated buildings modeled on factory architecture, despite his professed fascination with the "ceaseless inexhaustible miracle of proportion."

Le Corbusier studied in Paris in 1908–9, with Auguste Perret, pioneer of building in reinforced concrete. There Le Corbusier learned the techniques of reinforced concrete that he was to employ so frequently. Throughout the 1920's and 1930's he worked with his cousin Pierre Jeanneret, designing such buildings as the five-story Swiss pavilion at the University of Paris, made of concrete and raised on stilts. His design for

the Ville Contemporaine, a town for three million people, was never built, but it inspired other architects with its pedestrian walkways, roof gardens, courtyards, elevated highways, and recreation areas. His pre-World War II work is self-contained and abstract, showing classical influence, but his later work shows more interest in the environment.

His Unité d'Habitation in Marseille (1946–52) is a 17-story residential block built on stilts and designed to blend with the mountain background. Other projects include the town of Chandigarh, Punjab, India, built to replace Lahore—lost through partition in 1947. Chandigarh is only a partial success because it is not sufficiently adapted to Indian customs.

Le Corbusier built to heights unknown in Europe for domestic architecture and was a powerful influence on the building of high-rise dwellings in postwar Europe. Although he was a pioneer in the use of modern materials, his buildings have been criticized, chiefly for the isolation they impose on their inhabitants.

A SACRED TASK *Le Corbusier's pilgrimage chapel at Ronchamp, Vosges, France, completed in 1952, is his most unconventional work. Its thick roof hangs over the white walls, producing remarkable acoustic effects. The towers act as funnels for light and the irregularly placed windows contain stained glass. A strip of stained glass also runs along the very top of the walls, causing lines of light to climb and descend the interior walls as the sun moves across the sky.*

leggen, to lay, Old English *lecgan.*] **—ledged, ledg·y** *adj.*

ledg·er (lĕj′ər) *n.* **1. a.** A book in which the monetary transactions of a business are recorded as debits and credits. **b.** A book to which the record of accounts is transferred as final entry from original listings. **2.** A slab of stone laid flat over a grave. **3.** A horizontal timber in scaffolding, attached to the uprights and supporting the putlogs. **4.** In fishing, ledger bait, ledger line, or ledger tackle. [Middle English *legger,* book fixed in one place, probably from Middle Dutch *legger, ligger,* respectively from *leggen,* to lay, and *liggen,* to lie.]

ledger bait *n.* Fishing bait that is designed to rest on the bottom.

ledger board *n.* The top railing of a fence or balustrade.

ledger line, leg·er line (lĕj′ər) *n.* **1.** *Music.* A short line placed above or below a staff to accommodate notes higher or lower than the staff's range. **2.** A fishing line used with ledger bait.

ledger tackle *n.* Fishing tackle used with ledger bait.

Le Duc Tho (lā′ dŭk′ tō′). (1911–). Vietnamese politician who negotiated the North Vietnamese–U.S. cease-fire (1973) with Henry Kissinger. Both were awarded the Nobel Peace Prize (1973), but Le Duc Tho refused it.

Led·yard (lĕd′yərd), **John** (1751–89). U.S. explorer. He sailed with Capt. Cook (1776) and later tried unsuccessfully to find financing for further expeditions to the northwestern coast of America. While attempting to walk across Siberia (1787), he was arrested by order of Empress Catherine. He died in Cairo on his way to explore the sources of the Niger River.

lee (lē) *n.* **1. a.** *Nautical.* The side or quarter away from the direction from which the wind blows; the side sheltered from the wind. **b.** Any place sheltered from the wind. **2.** Cover; shelter: *under the lee of a large tree.*
~adj. Located on or moving in the direction of the side toward which the wind blows: *the lee side of a ship.* Compare **weather.** [Middle English *le(e),* from Old English *hlēo,* covering, shelter.]

Lee (lē), **Ann,** known as "Mother Ann" (1736–84). English religious leader in America. She founded the American Shakers, a religious movement based on communal living, celibacy, frugality, and industry.

Lee, Charles (1731–82). U.S. Revolutionary general, born in England. A major general in the Continental Army, he disliked and disobeyed George Washington and his military record raised doubts about his allegiance.

Lee, Gypsy Rose (1914–70). U.S. entertainer and author. A renowned ecdysiast (a term coined specifically for her by H.L. Mencken), she also wrote best-selling mystery novels, such as *The G-String Murders* (1941).

Lee, Henry, known as "Light-Horse Harry" (1756–1818). U.S. Revolutionary statesman and commander. A brilliant cavalry officer, he later served in the Continental Congress (1785–88), as governor of Virginia (1792–95), and as U.S. congressman (1799–1801).

Lee, Richard Henry (1732–94). U.S. Revolutionary leader. A member of the Virginia House of Burgesses (1758–75), the Continental Congress (1774–79 and 1784–87), and the U.S. Senate (1789–92), he profoundly affected the founding and early development of the United States.

Lee, Robert Edward (1807–70). Commander of the Confederate armies in the Civil War. He led the troops who captured John Brown at Harpers Ferry in 1859. Loyalty to his native Virginia led him to resign from the Union Army in April 1861. As a Confederate general, he won victories at Bull Run (1862), Fredericksburg (1862), and Chancellorsville (1863). Lee was appointed Confederate commander in chief in February 1865, two months before surrendering to Gen. Ulysses S. Grant at Appomattox.

lee·board (lē′bôrd′, -bōrd′) *n.* Either of a pair of movable boards or plates attached to the sides of certain flat-bottomed sailing vessels that is lowered into the water on the lee side when the vessel is sailing to windward to prevent its drifting leeward.

leech¹ (lēch) *n.* **1.** Any of various chiefly aquatic bloodsucking or carnivorous annelid worms of the class Hirudinea, having suckers at each end of the body. One species, *Hirudo medicinalis,* was formerly used by physicians to bleed patients. **2.** One who preys on or clings to another; a parasite. **3.** *Archaic.* A physician.
~tr.v. **leeched, leeching, leeches.** *Medicine.* **1.** To bleed (someone) with leeches. **2.** To drain in a parasitic way: *leeched them penniless.* **3.** *Archaic.* To heal. [Middle English *leche,* from Old English *lǽce,* leech; akin to Middle Dutch *leke*† and *lǽce,* physician.]

leech² *n.* *Nautical.* **1.** Either vertical edge of a square sail. **2.** The after edge of a fore-and-aft sail. [Middle English *leche,* earlier *liche,* probably from Middle Low German *līk,* leech line.]

Leeds (lēdz). City in West Yorkshire, north England, on the Aire River. It is a center of the wool industry.

leek (lēk) *n.* **1.** A plant, *Allium porrum,* related to the onion and having a cylindrical bulb that is the base of the flat, overlapping leaves. **2.** The blanched leaves of this plant, used as food. **3.** Any of various similar wild plants of the genus *Allium.* [Middle English *le(e)k,* Old English *lēac.*]

leer (lîr) *intr.v.* **leered, leering, leers.** To look or glance slyly, lasciviously, or with hostile intent: *leered at her with a dirty grin.*
~n. A sly or lascivious look. [Probably from obsolete *leer,* cheek, Middle English *ler(e),* Old English *hlēor.*]

leer·y (lîr′ē) *adj.* **-ier, -iest.** *Informal.* Suspicious or distrustful; wary. [From LEER, sly look.]

lees (lēz) *pl.n.* The sediment or dregs of an alcoholic drink, such as wine. [Plural of obsolete *lee,* sediment, from Middle English *lie,* from Old French, from Medieval Latin *lia,* from Celtic.]

lee shore *n.* A shore toward which the wind is blowing and toward which a ship is likely to be driven.

leet (lēt) *n.* **1.** A former manorial court in England. Also called "court-leet." **2.** The jurisdiction of this court. [Middle English *lete,* from Norman French *lete* and Medieval Latin *leta*†.]

Leeu·wen·hoek (lā′wən-ho͝ok′), **Anton van** (1632–1723). Dutch naturalist. He was a pioneer in microscopy.

lee·ward (lē′wərd, lo͞o′ərd) *adj.* Located on or moving in the direction of the side toward which the wind is blowing.
~n. **1.** The lee direction. **2.** The lee side or quarter.
~adv. Toward the lee side. Compare **windward.**

Lee·ward Islands¹ (lē′wərd). Northern group of the Lesser Antilles in the West Indies, extending from Puerto Rico to the Windward Islands. The chief islands or groups are the Virgin Islands, Guadeloupe, Anguilla, Antigua, St. Kitts-Nevis, and Montserrat.

Leeward Islands². The western group of the Society Islands, part of French Polynesia.

lee·way (lē′wā′) *n.* **1.** The drift of a ship or aircraft to leeward of true course. **2.** A margin of freedom or variation, as of activity, time, or expenditure; latitude.

left¹ (lĕft) *adj.* **1. a.** Designating, belonging to, or located on the side of the body in which most of the heart is located and which has the hand that is weaker in most people: *left arm.* **b.** Designating or located on the corresponding side of anything that can be said to have a front: *the bird's left wing.* **c.** Designating or located on that side of anything which an observer facing it perceives to be on or toward his left side. **2.** *Often* **Left.** Of, belonging to, or toward the political or intellectual Left.
~n. **1. a.** The left side or direction: *My house is on the left.* **b.** That which is on or toward the left-hand side. **2.** A turn in the direction of the left hand or side: *took a left at the traffic lights.* **3.** *Often* **Left. a.** The individuals and groups pursuing generally egalitarian political goals by reformist or revolutionary means, as opposed to broadly conservative, established, or reactionary interests. **b.** A stance of favoring such goals, considered as part of a roughly measurable political continuum: *moving further to the Left.* **4.** In boxing, the left hand or a blow struck by the left hand.
~adv. On or toward the left side or direction. [Middle English *luft, lift, left,* Old English *left, lyft* (attested only in *lyftādl,* paralysis, "left-disease"), akin to Middle Dutch *luft, lucht*†, weak, useless.]

left². Past tense and past participle of **leave.**

Left Bank. A district in Paris on the left or southern bank of the Seine River, noted for its artistic and bohemian atmosphere.

left-hand (lĕft′hănd′) *adj.* **1.** Of, pertaining to, or located on the left. **2.** Moving or turning to the left: *a left-hand turn.* **3.** Intended for the left hand or a left-handed person.

left-hand·ed (lĕft′hăn′dĭd) *adj.* **1.** Having more power or skill in the left hand, or using the left hand more easily than the right: *a left-handed pitcher.* **2.** Executed with the left hand. **3.** Designed for wear on or use by the left hand. **4.** Awkward; clumsy; maladroit. **5.** Obliquely derisive; dubious; insincere: *a left-handed compliment.* **6.** Of, pertaining to, or born of a morganatic marriage. **7.** Turning or spiraling from right to left; counterclockwise.
~adv. With the left hand. **—left-hand·ed·ly** *adv.* **—left-hand·ed·ness** *n.*

left-hand·er (lĕft′hăn′dər) *n.* **1.** One who is left-handed or uses the left hand. **2.** A blow with the left hand.

left·ism (lĕf′tĭz′m) *n.* *Often* **Leftism.** The ideology of the political Left. **—left·ist** *n.* & *adj.*

left·o·ver (lĕft′ō′vər) *adj.* Of or designating something that has been left as an unused remnant or portion.

left·o·vers (lĕft′ō′vərz) *pl.n.* An unused portion or remnant of something, especially of food.

left wing *n.* **1.** The troops on the left-hand side of an army. **2.** In ball games such as soccer or hockey: **a.** An attacking player on the far left-hand side of a team. **b.** The position of such a player. **3.** *Often* **Left Wing.** The radical or leftist faction of a group or party. **—left-wing** *adj.* **—left-wing·er** *n.*

left·y (lĕf′tē) *n., pl.* **-ies.** *Informal.* **1.** A left-handed person. **2.** A person on the political Left.

leg (lĕg) *n.* **1.** A limb or appendage of an animal, used for locomotion or support. **2.** The lower or hind limb in man and primates. **3.** The edible back part of the hindquarter of an animal such as a chicken or sheep. **4.** Any supporting part resembling a leg in shape or function: *a table leg.* **5.** Either or any of the branches of a forked or jointed object, such as a pair of compasses. **6.** Any part of a garment, especially of a pair of trousers, that covers all or part of the leg. **7.** *Geometry.* Either side of a right-angled triangle that is not the hypotenuse. **8. a.** A stage of a journey, course, or race: *ran the first leg quickly.* **b.** A stage of a sporting contest that counts toward the final result: *won the first leg but lost the second.* **9.** *Nautical.* The distance traveled by a sailing vessel on a single tack. **10.** *Cricket.* The right side of the field when the batsman is right-handed, or vice versa. **—give a leg up.** To assist by boosting or providing support. **—not have a leg to stand on.** To have no justifiable or logical basis for a defense or proposition. **—on one's last legs.** On the verge of failure, exhaustion, collapse, or death. **—pull someone's leg.** *Informal.* To tease, make fun of, or fool someone. **—shake a leg.** *Slang.* To hasten; hurry. Often used in the imperative. **—stretch one's legs.** To stand or walk, especially after sitting for a long time.
~intr.v. **legged, legging, legs.** *Informal.* To walk or run, especially

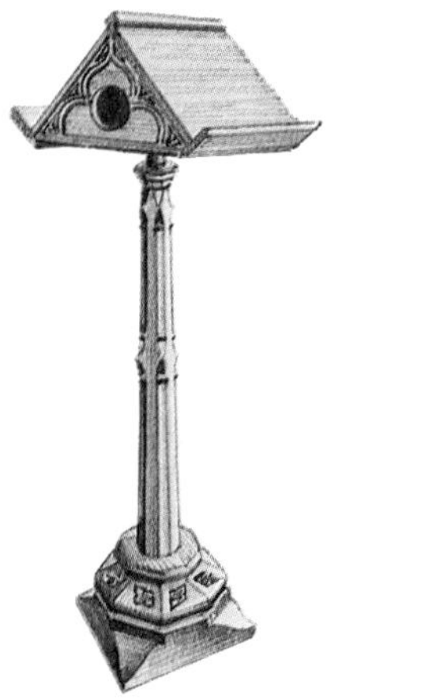

lectern *In medieval Christian churches, pairs of lecterns, or ambos, were often built into the sanctuary—one for the Epistle reading and another for the Gospel. Others, like this doublesided lectern dating from 1500 in Suffolk, England, were freestanding.*

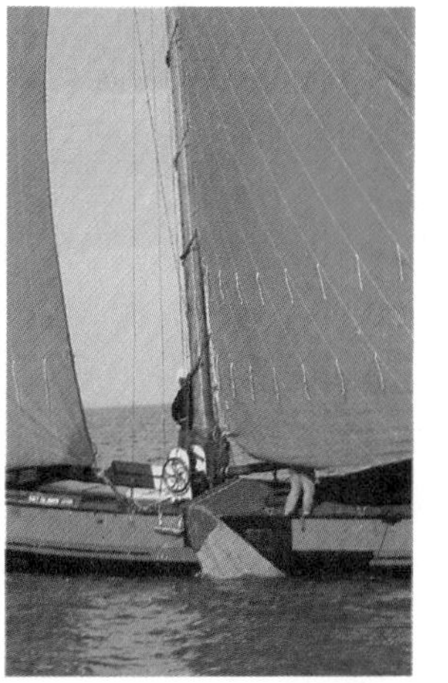

leeboard *On a flat-bottomed vessel the leeboard helps to compensate for the absence of a keel when sailing close to the wind.*

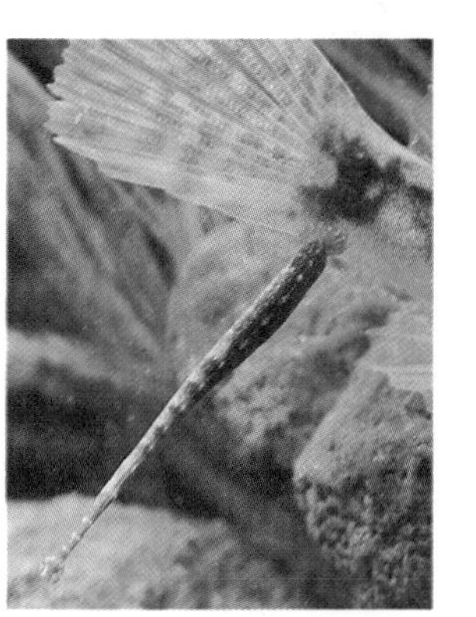

leech *These parasitic worms have suckers at one or both ends of their bodies by which they fasten onto other animals and feed on their blood. Here a leech has attached itself to the tail of a bullhead fish. Leeches were once widely used by doctors to draw off blood from human patients in the belief that this would speed the patients' recovery from a variety of illnesses.*

so as to escape. Usually used with *it*: *We legged it to the station.* [Middle English *leg, legge,* from Old Norse *leggr†.*]

leg. 1. legal. 2. legate. 3. *Music.* legato. 4. legislation; legislative; legislature.

leg·a·cy (lĕg′ə-sē) *n., pl.* **-cies.** 1. Money or property bequeathed to someone by will. 2. Something handed down from an ancestor or predecessor, or from the past: *a legacy of madness.* [Middle English *legacie,* from Old French, from Medieval Latin *lēgantia,* from Latin *lēgāre,* to depute, commission, bequeath.]

le·gal (lē′gəl) *adj. Abbr.* **leg.** 1. Of, pertaining to, or concerned with law: *legal papers.* 2. a. Authorized by or based on law: *a legal act.* b. Established by law; statutory. 3. In conformity with or permitted by law. 4. Recognized or enforced by law rather than by equity. 5. In terms of or created by the law: *a legal offense.* 6. Applicable to or characteristic of lawyers or their profession: *legal advice.* 7. *Theology.* a. Of or pertaining to Mosaic law. b. Of or pertaining to salvation through works rather than through faith. [Old French, from Latin *lēgālis,* from *lēx* (stem *lēg-*), law.] **—le·gal·ly** *adv.*

legal age *n.* The age of legal responsibility. See **age.**

legal cap *n.* A white writing paper, often ruled, measuring 8½ by 13 to 16 inches and generally used by lawyers.

le·gal·ese (lē′gə-lēz′, -lēs′) *n.* The specialized vocabulary of the legal profession.

legal holiday *n.* Any holiday authorized by law and characterized by limit or ban on work or official business.

le·gal·ism (lē′gə-lĭz′əm) *n.* 1. Strict, literal adherence to law. 2. *Theology.* Adherence to the doctrine of salvation by works rather than by faith. **—le·gal·ist** *n.* **—le·gal·is·tic** *adj.* **—le·gal·is·ti·cal·ly** *adv.*

le·gal·i·ty (lē-găl′ə-tē) *n., pl.* **-ties.** 1. The state or quality of being legal; lawfulness. 2. Adherence to or observance of the law. 3. A requirement of law: *Legalities prevented the merger.*

le·gal·ize (lē′gə-līz′) *tr.v.* **-ized, -izing, -izes.** To make legal or lawful. **—le·gal·i·za·tion** *n.*

legal memory *n. Law.* The period of time required for certain customs to attain legal significance.

legal pad *n.* A ruled pad of writing paper that measures 8½ by 14 inches.

legal reserve *n.* The sum of money that a bank or insurance company is required by law to set aside as security.

legal separation *n.* **Judicial separation** *(see).*

legal tender *n.* Currency that may legally be offered in payment of a debt and that a creditor must accept.

leg·ate (lĕg′ĭt) *n. Abbr.* **leg.** 1. An official emissary; especially, an official representative of the pope. 2. In Roman history: a. The deputy of a general. b. The deputy of a provincial governor. c. During the empire, a provincial governor. [Middle English, from Old French, from Latin *lēgātus,* from the past participle of *lēgāre,* to depute, commission, send on an embassy.] **—leg·ate·ship** *n.* **—leg·a·tine** *adj.*

leg·a·tee (lĕg′ə-tē′) *n.* The inheritor of a legacy.

le·ga·tion (lə-gā′shən) *n.* 1. The sending of a legate. 2. The mission on which a legate is sent. 3. a. A diplomatic mission in a foreign country, ranking below an embassy. b. The legate and staff of such a mission. 4. The position or office of a legate. 5. The premises occupied by a legation. [Middle English *legacioun,* from Old French *legation,* from Latin *lēgātiō* (stem *lēgātiōn-*), from *lēgātus,* LEGATE.]

le·ga·to (lə-gä′tō) *adv. Abbr.* **leg.** *Music.* In an even, smooth style. Used as a direction.
~n., pl. **legatos.** A smooth, even style, performance, or passage. [Italian, connected, continuous, bound, from *legare,* to bind, from Latin *ligāre.*] **—le·ga·to** *adj.*

leg·a·tor (lə-gā′tər, lĕg′ə-tôr′) *n.* A person who makes a will; a testator. [Latin *lēgātōr,* from *lēgāre,* to bequeath. See **legacy.**] **—leg·a·tor·i·al** *adj.*

leg bye *n. Abbr.* **l.b.** *Cricket.* A run scored when a bowled ball is deflected off the batsman's legs or any other part of his body except his hands.

leg·end (lĕj′ənd) *n.* 1. a. An unverified popular story handed down from earlier times. b. A story of the life of a saint. 2. A body or collection of such stories. 3. A romanticized or popularized myth of modern times. 4. A person who achieves legendary fame: *He was a legend in his own lifetime.* 5. An inscription or title on an object, such as a coat of arms or coin. 6. An explanatory caption accompanying a map, chart, or illustration. [Middle English *legende,* originally, story of a saint's life, from Old French, from Medieval Latin *legenda,* "things for reading," from Latin *legendus,* gerundive of *legere,* to collect, gather, read.]

leg·en·dar·y (lĕj′ən-dĕr′ē) *adj.* 1. Of, constituting, based on, or of the nature of a legend. 2. Famous or described in legend. 3. Celebrated or notorious to such an extent as to form the basis of a legend.

Lé·ger (lā-zhā′), **Fernand** (1881-1955). French painter. One of the early cubists, his obsession with machinery led to his being called "the primitive of the machine age."

leg·er·de·main (lĕj′ər-də-mān′) *n.* 1. **Sleight of hand** *(see).* 2. Any deception or trickery; hocus-pocus. [Middle English *legerdemayn,* from Old French *leger de main,* "light of hand" : *leger,* light, from Vulgar Latin *leviārius* (unattested), from Latin *levis* + *main,* hand, from Latin *manus.*]

leger line. Variant of **ledger line.**

le·ges. Plural of **lex.**

leg·ged (lĕg′ĭd, lĕgd) *adj.* 1. Having a leg or legs. 2. Having a specified number or kind of legs. Used in combination: *bowlegged; six-legged.*

leg·gings (lĕg′ĭngz) *pl.n.* Coverings for the legs, as of canvas or leather, usually extending from the knee to the foot.

leg·gy (lĕg′ē) *adj.* **-gier, -giest.** 1. Having disproportionately long legs: *a leggy colt.* 2. *Informal.* Having attractively long and slender legs. 3. Having long, spindly, often leafless stems.

leg·horn (lĕg′hôrn′, -ərn) *n.* 1. The dried and bleached straw of an Italian variety of wheat. 2. A plaited fabric made from this straw. 3. A hat made from this fabric. 4. *Often* **Leghorn.** A domestic fowl of a breed of Mediterranean origin, noted for prolific production of eggs. [After LEGHORN.]

Leghorn. See **Livorno.**

leg·i·ble (lĕj′ə-bəl) *adj.* Capable of being read or deciphered. [Middle English *legibille,* from Late Latin *legibilis,* from Latin *legere,* to read.] **—leg·i·bil·i·ty, leg·i·ble·ness** *n.* **—leg·i·bly** *adv.*

le·gion (lē′jən) *n.* 1. The major unit of the ancient Roman army consisting of 3,000 to 6,000 infantry troops and 100 to 200 cavalrymen. 2. *Sometimes* **legions.** Any large number; a multitude: *He surveyed the massed, singing legions.* 3. *Usually* **Legion.** Any of several honorary or military organizations: *the Foreign Legion; the British Legion.* See Synonyms at **multitude.**
~adj. Very numerous; abundant: *Examples are legion.* [Middle English *legioun,* from Old French *legion,* from Latin *legiō,* from *legere,* "to gather," levy troops.]

le·gion·ar·y (lē′jə-nĕr′ē) *adj.* Of, pertaining to, or constituting a legion.
~n., pl. **legionaries.** A soldier of a legion.

legionary ant *n.* An army ant *(see).*

le·gion·naire (lē′jə-nâr′) *n.* A member of a legion. [French *légionnaire,* from Old French *legion,* LEGION.]

Legionnaires' disease *n.* A serious, often fatal, bacterial infection of the lungs, characterized by fever, chest pain, dry cough, and breathlessness. [First identified when it struck members attending an American Legion convention in Philadelphia (1976).]

Legion of Honor *n.* A high French civilian and military decoration, instituted in 1802.

Legion of Merit *n.* A U.S. military decoration awarded for exceptionally meritorious conduct in the performance of outstanding services.

legis. legislation; legislative; legislature.

leg·is·late (lĕj′ĭs-lāt′) *v.* **-lated, -lating, -lates.** *—intr.* 1. To pass a law or laws. 2. *Informal.* To make provision by taking prior measures. Used with *for: You can't legislate for a rainy day.* *—tr.* To create or bring about by legislation; enact into law. [Back-formation from LEGISLATOR.]

leg·is·la·tion (lĕj′ĭs-lā′shən) *n. Abbr.* **leg., legis.** 1. The act or procedure of legislating; lawmaking. 2. A law or laws made by such a procedure.

leg·is·la·tive (lĕj′ĭs-lā′tĭv) *adj. Abbr.* **leg., legis.** 1. Of or pertaining to legislation. 2. Resulting from or decided by legislation. 3. Having the power to create laws; designed to legislate: *a legislative body.* 4. Of or pertaining to a legislature. Compare **executive, judicial.**
~n. The legislative body of a government. **—leg·is·la·tive·ly** *adv.*

legislative assembly *n. Sometimes* **Legislative Assembly.** 1. A bicameral legislature, as in some U.S. states. 2. A unicameral legislature, as in a Canadian province. 3. The lower house of a bicameral legislature, as in Australia.

legislative council *n. Sometimes* **Legislative Council.** 1. The upper house of a bicameral legislature, as in Australia. 2. A unicameral legislature, as in certain dependent states or territories.

leg·is·la·tor (lĕj′ĭs-lā′tər) *n.* 1. A person who creates or enacts laws. 2. A member of a legislative body. [Latin *lēgis lātor,* "proposer of law" : *lēgis,* genitive of *lēx,* law + *lātor,* bearer, proposer, from *lātus,* "carried," past participle of *ferre,* to bear, carry.] **—leg·is·la·to·ri·al** *adj.*

leg·is·la·ture (lĕj′ĭs-lā′chər) *n. Abbr.* **leg., legis.** An official body of persons having the responsibility and power to legislate for a political unit, such as a nation or state.

le·gist (lē′jĭst) *n.* A specialist in law. [Medieval Latin *lēgista,* from Latin *lēx,* law.]

le·git (lə-jĭt′) *n. Slang.* Legitimate drama; stage plays collectively as opposed to films and musicals.
~adj. Slang. Legitimate.

le·git·i·ma·cy (lə-jĭt′ə-mə-sē) *n.* The quality or fact of being legitimate.

le·git·i·mate (lə-jĭt′ə-mĭt) *adj.* 1. In compliance with the law; lawful. 2. In accordance with traditional or established patterns and standards. 3. Based on logical reasoning; reasonable: *a legitimate solution.* 4. Authentic; genuine. 5. Born in wedlock. 6. Of, pertaining to, or ruling by hereditary right. 7. Of, pertaining to, or designating stage plays as opposed to films, musicals, music-hall, and the like.
~tr.v. (lə-jĭt′ə-māt′) **legitimated, -mating, -mates.** 1. To justify as legitimate; authorize. 2. To make, establish, or declare legitimate. [Middle English, born in wedlock, from Medieval Latin *lēgitimātus,* past participle of *lēgitimāre,* to make lawful, from Latin *lēgitimus,* lawful, legal, from *lēx* (stem *lēg-*), law.] **—le·git·i·mate·ly** *adv.* **—le·git·i·ma·tion** *n.*

le·git·i·mist (lə-jĭt′ə-mĭst) *n.* A person who believes in or supports legitimate authority; especially, a supporter of rule by hereditary right. **—le·git·i·mism** *n.* **—le·git·i·mist, le·git·i·mis·tic** *adj.*

le·git·i·mize (lə-jĭt′ə-mīz′) *tr.v.* Also **le·git·i·ma·tize** (-mə-tīz′). To make or claim to be legitimate or acceptable.

leghorn *Leghorn chickens, which are descended from Mediterranean birds, were first bred in the United States in the mid-19th century. They are excellent egg layers, but are too light to make good table birds.*

leg·less (lĕg′lĭs′) *adj.* **1.** Without legs. **2.** *Slang.* So drunk as to be unable to walk.

leg·man (lĕg′măn) *n., pl.* **-men** (-mĕn). **1.** A news reporter who gathers news in person away from the office, interviewing people and visiting the scenes of incidents. **2.** A person employed to deliver messages, run errands, and perform other tasks requiring legwork.

Leg·o (lĕg′ō) *n.* A trademark for any of various construction sets consisting of small, plastic interlocking toy bricks.

leg-of-mut·ton (lĕg′ə-mŭt′n, lĕg′əv-) *adj.* Resembling a leg of mutton in shape; tapering sharply from one large end to a point or smaller end, as in a sleeve or sail.

leg·room (lĕg′ro͞om′, -ro͝om′) *n.* Space that enables one to stretch one's legs, as in a car or movie theater.

leg·ume (lĕg′yo͞om′, lə-gyo͞om′) *n.* **1.** A pod, such as that of a pea or bean, that splits into two halves with the seeds attached to the lower edge of one of the halves. **2.** Such a pod or seed, used as food. **3.** Any plant of the family Leguminosae, characteristically bearing such pods. [French *légume,* from Latin *legūmen*†, pulse, bean.]

le·gu·mi·nous (lə-gyo͞o′mə-nəs) *adj.* **1.** Of, belonging to, or characteristic of the family Leguminosae, which includes peas, beans, clover, alfalfa, and other plants. **2.** Resembling or of the nature of a legume. [New Latin *leguminosus,* from Latin *lugūmen,* bean, LEGUME.]

leg·work (lĕg′wûrk′) *n. Informal.* Work, such as collecting information, that involves walking or traveling about.

Le·hár (lā′här′), **Franz** (1870–1948). Hungarian composer of light operas. His first success was *Viennese Ladies* (1902). His most popular work remains *The Merry Widow* (1905).

Le Ha·vre (lə hä′vrə). Commercial port on the north coast of France, on the Seine estuary. One of France's leading ports, it handles much transatlantic trade and is the main port for transatlantic liners. The city is built around one of the largest central squares in Europe, the Place de l'Hôtel de Ville.

Leh·mann (lā′mən), **Lotte** (1888–1976). German soprano. She sang chiefly with the Vienna State Opera (1914–38), then settled in the United States, singing at the Metropolitan Opera, New York. She created the role of Ariadne in Richard Strauss's *Ariadne auf Naxos,* and Strauss wrote *Arabella* especially for her.

lehr (lîr) *n.* A long oven for annealing glass. [17th century : origin obscure.]

le·hu·a (lā-ho͞o′ə) *n.* A tree, *Metrosideros collina,* of Hawaii and other Pacific islands, having showy red flowers. [Hawaiian.]

lei[1] (lā, lā′ē) *n., pl.* **leis.** A garland of flowers. [Hawaiian.]

lei[2]. Plural of **leu.**

Leib·nitz or **Leib·niz** (līb′nĭts′), **Baron Gottfried Wilhelm von** (1646–1716). German philosopher and mathematician. He devised the infinitesimal calculus independently of Newton. His philosophy includes the theories that the universe is made of indivisible units called monads and—since God disposes these in the best possible combination—that we live in the best possible world. **—Leib·nizt·i·an, Leib·niz·i·an** *adj.*

Leices·ter[1] (lĕs′tər). City in central England, the county town of Leicestershire. It has been an industrial center, chiefly associated with hosiery and shoe manufacturing, since the 14th century.

Leicester[2] *n.* **1.** A sheep of a breed developed in Leicestershire, having long, fine wool. **2.** A hard, flaky, orange-colored cheese. In this sense, also called "red Leicester."

Leicester, Robert Dudley, 1st Earl of (*c.* 1532–88). English courtier and favorite of Elizabeth I. In 1553 he helped place his sister-in-law, Lady Jane Grey, on the throne. He was condemned to death, but pardoned. He was a confidant of Elizabeth, who shortly after her accession made him a privy councillor (1559) and later captain general of her armies (1587).

Leices·ter·shire (lĕs′tər-shîr′, -shər). Nonmetropolitan county in central England. Although Leicester and other towns in the western part of the county are industrial centers, Leicestershire remains primarily an agricultural county, the home of Stilton cheese.

Lei·den or **Ley·den** (līd′n). City in South Holland, Netherlands. The Leyden jar was invented at its famous university, founded (1575) by William of Orange.

Leigh (lē), **Vivien,** born Vivien Hartley (1913–67). English actress. She won an Academy Award as best actress for her roles in *Gone with the Wind* (1939) as Scarlett O'Hara and in *A Streetcar Named Desire* (1951) as Blanche Dubois. She was the second wife of Laurence Olivier.

Leins·dorf (līnz′dôrf′), **Erich** (1912–). U.S. conductor, born in Austria. He made his U.S. debut as an assistant conductor of the Metropolitan Opera (1938). He later conducted the Cleveland Symphony Orchestra, the New York City Opera Company, and the Boston Symphony Orchestra.

Lein·ster (lĕn′stər). Province in the east of the Republic of Ireland, consisting of the counties of Carlow, Dublin, Kildare, Kilkenny, Leix, Longford, Louth, Meath, Offaly, Westmeath, Wexford, and Wicklow. The major city is Dublin.

Leip·zig (līp′sĭg, -sĭk). City in south-central East Germany, one of the great historic industrial and cultural centers of Europe and now the second-largest city in East Germany. Originally a Slav settlement called Lipsk, it developed by the early Middle Ages into a major trading and commercial town, famous from the 15th to the mid-20th centuries for its book and music publishing. Its university was founded in 1409. At the Battle of Leipzig in 1813, the armies of Russia, Prussia, and Austria inflicted a decisive defeat on the army of Napoleon.

leish·man·i·a·sis (lēsh′mə-nī′ə-sĭs) *n.* **1.** Infection with flagellate protozoans of the genus *Leishmania.* **2.** A disease, such as kala-azar or various ulcerative skin diseases, caused by such infection. [New Latin, from *Leishmania,* genus of protozoans, identified by Sir William B. *Leishman* (1865–1926), British medical officer.]

leis·ter (lēs′tər) *n.* A three-pronged spear used for catching fish, such as salmon.
~*tr.v.* **leistered, -tering, -ters.** To spear (a fish) with a leister. [Old Norse *ljōstr,* from *ljōsta*†, to strike.]

lei·sure (lē′zhər, lĕzh′ər) *n.* Freedom from time-consuming duties, responsibilities, or activities. —See Synonyms at **rest.** **—at leisure. 1.** Having free time. **2.** Not employed, occupied, or engaged. **3.** Unhurried. **—at one's leisure.** When one has free time; at one's convenience.
~*adj.* **1.** Not spent in work or compulsory activity; free. **2.** Having much leisure; leisured. [Middle English *leisour, leiser,* freedom, opportunity, from Norman French *leisour,* variant of Old French *leisir,* to be permitted, from Latin *licēre*†, to be lawful, be permitted.]

lei·sured (lē′zhərd, lĕzh′ərd) *adj.* **1.** Having much leisure: *the leisured classes.* **2.** Unhurried; leisurely.

lei·sure·ly (lē′zhər-lē, lĕzh′ər-) *adj.* Without haste; unhurried: *a leisurely meal.*
~*adv.* In a steady, relaxed manner; slowly. **—lei·sure·li·ness** *n.*

leit·mo·tif, leit·mo·tiv (līt′mō-tēf′) *n.* **1.** *Music.* A thematic passage, as in Wagnerian opera, associated with a specific character, thing, or element. **2.** A dominant theme or recurring image or use of words, as in a novel. [German *Leitmotiv,* "leading motif."]

Lei·trim (lē′trĭm). County in the north of the Republic of Ireland, having a short border with Northern Ireland. The county town is Carrick on Shannon. The County is divided by Lough Allen into a lowland southern half and a mountainous northern half.

Leix (lēsh). County in the central part of the Republic of Ireland, occupying the valleys of the Upper Nore and Upper Barrow rivers. The county town is Port Laoise.

lek[1] (lĕk) *n.* **1.** The basic monetary unit of Albania, equal to 100 quintars. **2.** A coin worth one lek. See feature at **currency.** [Albanian.]

lek[2] *n.* An area used for courtship display and mock fighting by certain male birds, especially the black grouse. [Probably from Scandinavian; akin to Swedish *lek,* sport, play, Old Norse *leikr,* play; compare LAIK.]

lek·ker (lĕk′ər) *adj. South African Informal.* **1.** Very good-tasting; delicious. **2.** Very pleasing, attractive, or enjoyable. **3.** Slightly drunk; tipsy. [Afrikaans, from Dutch.]

Le·ly (lē′lē), **Sir Peter** (1618–80). Dutch painter. He worked in England from *c.* 1643 and in 1660 was appointed principal painter to Charles II, recording in portraits the Restoration court.

LEM (lĕm) *n. Aerospace.* A *l*unar *e*xcursion *m*odule.

lem·an (lĕm′ən, lē′mən) *n. Archaic.* **1.** A lover. **2.** A mistress. [Middle English *leofman, lemman* : *lef, leof,* dear, from Old English *lēof* + MAN.]

Léman, Lac. See **Geneva, Lake.**

Le Mans (lə mäN′). City in northwest France, capital of Sarthe department, on the Sarthe River. It was settled from pre-Roman times and was for a time the Merovingian capital. Its Romanesque cathedral is renowned for its flamboyant flying buttresses. Since 1906 Le Mans has been the site of an annual 24-hour motor race.

Lemberg. See **Lvov.**

lem·ma[1] (lĕm′ə) *n., pl.* **-mas** or **lemmata** (lĕm′ə-tə). **1.** *Logic.* A subsidiary proposition assumed to be valid and used to demonstrate a principal proposition. **2.** A theme, argument, or subject indicated in a title. **3.** A glossed word in a glossary or other listing. [Latin, from Greek *lēmma,* anything received, argument, proof, from *lambanein* (past perfect *eilēmmai*), to grasp, take.]

lemma[2] *n., pl.* **-mas** or **lemmata.** *Botany.* The outer, lower bract enclosing the flower in a grass spikelet. [Greek *lemma,* rind, husk, from *lepein,* to peel.]

lem·ma·tize (lĕm′ə-tīz′) *tr.v.* **-ized, -izing, -izes.** To arrange (words in a text) in such a way that all words which are inflected or variant forms of the same word are grouped together. [Latin *lemma* (stem *lemmat-*), proposition (see LEMMA) + -IZE.]

lem·ming (lĕm′ĭng) *n.* **1.** Any of various volelike rodents of the genus *Lemmus* and related genera, of northern regions, such as the European species *L. lemmus,* noted for its mass migrations as a result of periodic population increases. **2.** A person who willfully follows a disastrous course of action; a self-destructive person. [Norwegian *lemming, lemende,* akin to Swedish *lemmel*†.]

lem·nis·cate (lĕm-nĭs′kĭt) *n. Geometry.* **1.** A plane curve that is the locus of the foot of a perpendicular from the origin to a tangent moving on a rectangular hyperbola. The curve, which has two symmetrical lobes, has the equation $(x^2 + y^2) = a^2 (x^2 - y^2)$, where a is the greatest distance from the node to the curve. Also called "lemniscate of Bernoulli." **2.** A plane curve that is the locus of the vertex of a triangle with the side opposite the vertex of fixed length and the other two sides having a constant product (k) equal to one quarter of the square of the fixed side. Its equation is $[(x + a)^2 + y^2][(x - a)^2 + y^2] = k^4$, where a is one half of the length of the fixed side. Also called "lemniscate of Cassini." [Greek *lēmniskos,* fillet, ribbon.]

lem·nis·cus (lĕm-nĭs′kəs) *n., pl.* **-nisci** (-nĭs′ī′, -nĭs′kē). A bundle of sensory nerve fibers located in the brain. [New Latin, from Latin *lēmniscus,* ribbon, from Greek *lēmniskos*†.]

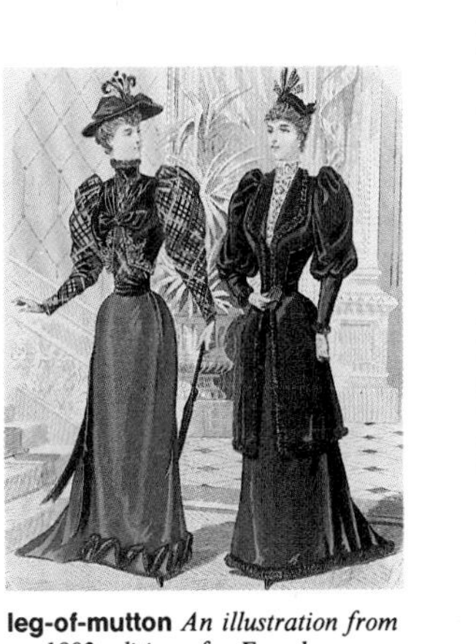

leg-of-mutton *An illustration from an 1892 edition of a French magazine called* Salon de la Mode, *showing leg-of-mutton sleeves on the dresses.*

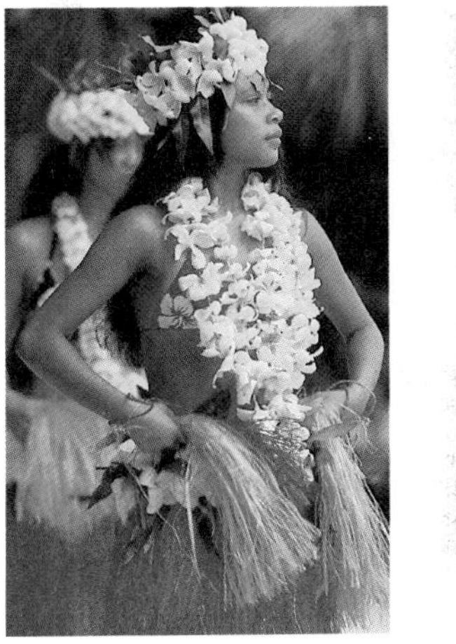

lei *Garlands of beads, shells, or flowers have been used by Hawaiians since ancient times as symbols of welcome and farewell.*

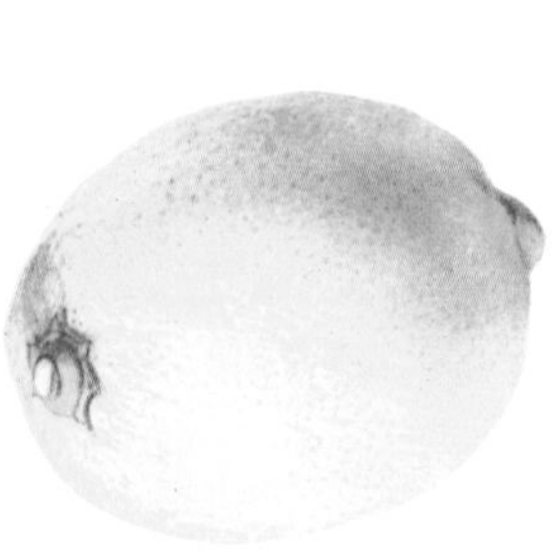

lemon *Citrus limon, the lemon tree, was introduced into Europe after it was discovered in Palestine by the Crusaders. The tree can grow up to 6 meters (20 feet) high.*

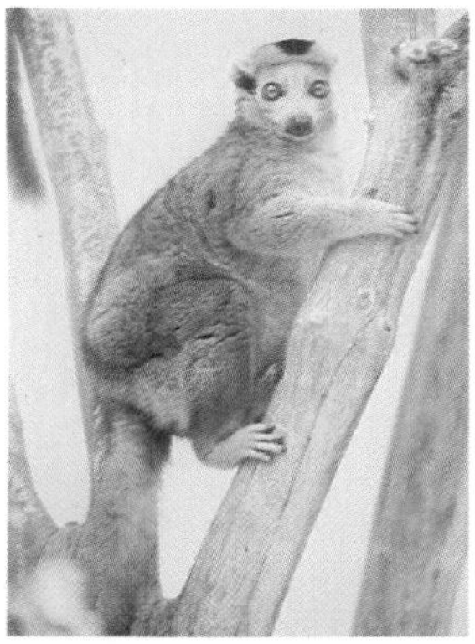

lemur *Found chiefly in Madagascar, the lemur is a primitive primate that lives mainly in trees and feeds on fruit, vegetation, and insects. It gets its name from the Latin word for ghosts*—lemures—*because of its pallid face.*

PRONUNCIATION KEY

ă, pat; ā, pay; âr, care;
ä, father, are; b, bib;
ch, church; d, deed; ĕ, pet;
ē, be; f, fife; g, gag; h, hat;
hw, which; ĭ, pit; ī, pie;
îr, pier; j, judge; k, kick;
l, lid, needle; m, mum;
n, no, sudden; ng, thing;
ŏ, pot; ō, toe; ô, paw, for;
oi, noise; ou, out; o͝o, book;
o͞o, boot; p, pop; r, roar;
s, sauce; sh, ship, dish;
t, tight; th, thin, path;
th, this, bathe; ŭ, cut; ûr, fur;
v, valve; w, with; y, yes;
z, zebra, size; zh, vision;
ə, about, item, edible, gallop, circus, peaceful

IN FOREIGN WORDS:

à, *Fr.* ami; œ, *Fr.* feu, *Ger.* schön; ü, *Fr.* tu, *Ger.* über; KH, *Ger.* ich, *Scot.* loch; N, *Fr.* bon; y', *Fr.* Compiègne

STRESS MARKS:

Primary stress: ′
in·cite′ (ĭn-sīt′)
Secondary stress: ′
in′sight′ (ĭn′sīt′)

lem·on (lĕm′ən) *n.* **1.** A spiny evergreen tree, *Citrus limon,* native to Asia, widely cultivated for its yellow, egg-shaped fruit. **2.** The fruit of this tree, having an aromatic rind and acid, juicy pulp. **3. Lemon yellow** *(see).* **4.** *Informal.* Something or someone that is or proves to be defective, inadequate, or unsuitable. [Middle English *lymon,* from Old French *limon,* from Arabic *laymūn,* variant of *līmūn,* from Persian *līmūn*†.] **—lem·on** *adj.*

lem·on·ade (lĕm′ə-nād′) *n.* A cold drink made of lemon juice or flavoring, water, and sugar. [French *limonade* : obsolete *limon,* LEMON + -ADE.]

lemon balm *n.* A plant, **balm** *(see).*

lemon curd *n.* A sweet, viscous, yellow spread used in tarts or on sandwiches, prepared from lemons, sugar, butter, and eggs. Also called "lemon cheese."

lemon drop *n.* A small, hard, lemon-flavored candy.

lemon geranium *n.* A widely cultivated plant, *Pelargonium limoneum* (or *P. mellisimum*), having lemon-scented leaves and small, pale purple flowers.

lem·on·grass (lĕm′ən-grăs′, -gräs′) *n.* Any of several tropical grasses of the genus *Cymbopogon;* especially, *C. citratus,* yielding an aromatic oil used in perfumery and as flavoring.

lemon sole *n.* An edible marine flatfish, *Microstomus kitt* (or *Limanda limanda*), having a variegated brown body. Also called "lemon dab." [French *limande,* from Old French, irregularly from *lime,* file, lemon sole (from its shape), from Latin *lima,* file.]

lemon verbena *n.* An aromatic plant, *Lippia citriodora,* native to South America, cultivated for its fragrant foliage and flowers.

lem·on·wood (lĕm′ən-wo͝od′) *n.* A tree, the **degame** *(see),* or its wood.

lem·on·y (lĕm′ə-nē) *adj.* Having the characteristic odor or flavor of lemons.

lemon yellow *n.* Brilliant, vivid yellow to greenish yellow. **—lem·on-yel·low** *adj.*

lem·pi·ra (lĕm-pîr′ə) *n.* **1.** The basic monetary unit of Honduras, equal to 100 centavos. **2.** A coin or note worth one lempira. See feature at **currency.** [After *Lempira,* indigenous Indian leader who resisted the Spanish.]

le·mur (lē′mər) *n.* Any of several arboreal primates chiefly of the family Lemuridae, of Madagascar and adjacent islands, having large eyes, soft fur, and a long tail. [New Latin, coined by Linnaeus after Latin *lemurēs,* LEMURES, from the ghostly appearance of its face and its nocturnal habits.]

lem·u·res (lĕm′yo͞o-rēz′) *pl.n.* In ancient Rome, the spirits of the dead considered as frightening specters. [Latin *lemurēs.*]

Le·na (lē′nə). Easternmost of the major rivers of Siberia, rising near Lake Baikal and flowing northeast for 4,300 kilometers (2,670 miles) into the Arctic Ocean. It broadens into a vast delta *c.* 400 kilometers (250 miles) wide.

Le Nain (lə năN′), **Antoine** (*c.* 1588–1648) and **Mathieu** (*c.* 1607–77). French painters. The brothers worked in Paris after *c.* 1630, painting mostly peasant scenes. They signed their paintings without initials, so it is difficult to separate their work.

Len·a·pe (lĕn′ə-pē) *n.* Also **Len·i-Len·a·pe** (lĕn′ē-), **Len·ni-Len·a·pe.** A tribe, the **Delaware** *(see).*

lend (lĕnd) *v.* **lent** (lĕnt), **lending, lends.** *—tr.* **1.** To give out or allow the use of (something) temporarily on the condition that it or its equivalent in kind will be returned. **2.** To provide (money) temporarily on the condition that the amount borrowed will be returned, often with an interest fee. **3.** To contribute or impart, especially a desirable attribute or quality; add: *She lent elegance to the proceedings.* **4.** To put at another's service or needs; give. **5.** To accommodate or offer (itself) to something; be suited to. Used reflexively: *This medium lends itself to many styles.* *—intr.* To make a loan or loans. —See Usage note at **loan.** [Middle English *len(d)en,* Old English *lǣnan,* to lend, give.] **—lend·er** *n.*

lending library *n.* A library from which books may be borrowed or rented for a fee. Also called "circulating library."

lend-lease (lĕnd′lēs′) *n.* The aid program during World War II through which the United States provided food, munitions, and other goods to strategic countries threatened by Germany and Italy.
~tr.v. **lend-leased, -leasing, -leases.** To provide (aid) to a country, as under the provisions of the Lend-Lease Act (1941).

le·nes. Plural of **lenis.**

L'En·fant (län-fäN′), **Pierre Charles** (1754–1825). U.S. architect; born in France. Chosen by George Washington to survey and plan Washington, D.C. (1791), he proposed radial boulevards and a system of parks that, because of their high cost and his impudence, were not completed at that time. In the 1890's his plan was reconsidered and recommended for the city's central region.

length (lĕngkth, lĕngth) *n. Abbr.* **l. 1.** The state, quality, or fact of being long. **2. a.** The measurement of the extent of something along its greatest dimension. **b.** The measurement of the extent of something from back to front as distinguished from its width or height. **3.** A piece of something, often of a standard size, normally measured along the greatest dimension: *a length of cloth.* **4.** A unit of measurement based on the approximate extent from front to back of an animal or vehicle in a race: *The boat won by two lengths.* **5.** The extent of a thing from start to finish as measured by space, pages, or words: *the length of a story.* **6.** The amount of time between particular moments; a duration; a period. **7.** The distance between particular points or locations: *the length of their journey.* **8.** The state or quality of extending greatly in time or space. **9.** *Phonetics.* **a.** The quantity or duration of a vowel. **b.** Loosely, the quality of a vowel. **10.** In verse, the quantity or duration of a syllable. **11.** *Cricket.* The distance in front of the batsman at which the ball strikes the pitch: *bowled a good length.* **12.** The longer side or dimension of a swimming pool, or the distance from end to end: *swam ten lengths.* **—at length. 1.** After some time; eventually. **2.** For a considerable time; fully. **—go to any** (or **great**) **length** (or **lengths**). To take great trouble. **—keep at arm's length.** To refuse to become closely associated with.
~adj. **1.** Extending up to or down to a specified part or point. Used in combination: *shoulder-length hair.* **2. a.** Having a specified length. Used in combination: *a full-length opera.* **b.** Being as long as something specified. Used in combination: *a book-length manuscript.* [Middle English *lengthe,* Old English *lengthu.*]

length·en (lĕngk′thən, lĕng′-) *v.* **-ened, -ening, -ens.** *—tr.* To make longer. *—intr.* To become longer. **—length·en·er** *n.*

length·wise (lĕngkth′wīz′, lĕngth′-) *adv.* Also **length·ways** (-wāz′). In or along the direction of a length: *He cut the cloth lengthwise.* **—length·wise** *adj.*

length·y (lĕngk′thē, lĕng′-) *adj.* **-ier, -iest.** Of considerable length, especially in time; drawn-out. **—length·i·ly** *adv.* **—length·i·ness** *n.*

le·ni·en·cy (lē′nē-ən-sē, lēn′yən-) *n., pl.* **-cies.** Also **le·ni·ence** (lē′nē-əns, lēn′yəns). **1.** The condition or quality of being lenient. **2.** A lenient action. —See Synonyms at **mercy.**

le·ni·ent (lē′nē-ənt, lēn′yənt) *adj.* **1.** Merciful, restrained, or forgiving; gentle or understanding. **2.** Not austere or strict; liberal; generous: *lenient rules.* **3.** *Archaic.* Soothing or relaxing. [Latin *lēniēns* (stem *lēnient-*), present participle of *lēnīre,* to soothe, make soft, from *lēnis,* soft.] **—le·ni·ent·ly** *adv.*

Le·nin (lĕn′ĭn, -ēn′), **Vladimir Ilich,** born Vladimir Ilich Ulyanov, also known as "Nikolai Lenin" (1870–1924). Russian revolutionary leader. He was exiled to Siberia for subversive activities in 1895. In 1900 he went abroad to study Marx's theories, returning briefly to Russia during the abortive 1905 revolution. Lenin was in Switzerland in 1917 when the revolution broke out in Russia, and the German government secretly helped him travel to Petrograd. On November 7 (October 25 by the Russian calendar) he led the Bolshevik overthrow of Kerensky's government and was head of the Soviet government until his death following a stroke.

Len·in·grad (lĕn′ĭn-grăd′). Formerly **St. Pe·ters·burg** (sānt pē′tərz-bûrg′), **Pet·ro·grad** (pĕt′rō-grăd′). City in the western U.S.S.R., on the banks and delta islands of the Neva River, at the head of the Gulf of Finland. It is the U.S.S.R.'s second-largest city and a leading seaport and commercial and industrial center. It was founded in 1703 by Peter the Great as St. Petersburg and was the capital of Russia from 1712 until 1918. From 1914 until 1924 it was called Petrograd. The city was laid out on classical lines by French and Italian architects: its central thoroughfare is the celebrated Nevsky Prospect. The city is also the site of the famous Hermitage Museum.

Len·in·ism (lĕn′ə-nĭz′əm) *n.* The theory and practice of proletarian revolution as developed by Lenin. See **Marxism-Leninism. —Len·in·ist** *n. & adj.*

Lenin Peak. Highest peak in the Trans-Alai Range of mountains, in southwest Asian U.S.S.R. It rises to 7,134 meters (23,405 feet) and is the third-highest mountain in the U.S.S.R.

le·nis (lē′nĭs, lā′-) *adj. Phonetics.* Articulated with little or no aspiration; weak; soft. The consonants *b* and *d* are lenis compared with *p* and *t.* Compare **fortis.**
~n., pl. **lenes** (lē′nēz, lā′-). *Phonetics.* A speech sound pronounced with little or no aspiration; a lenis consonant. [Latin *lēnis,* soft, mild, smooth.]

len·i·tive (lĕn′ə-tĭv) *adj.* Capable of easing pain or discomfort.
~n. A lenitive medicine. [Old French *lenitif,* from Medieval Latin *lēnītīvus,* from Latin *lēnīre,* to soothe, soften, from *lēnis,* soft.]

len·i·ty (lĕn′ə-tē) *n., pl.* **-ties. 1.** The state, condition, or quality of being lenient; leniency. **2.** A lenient action. [Latin *lēnitas* (stem *lēnitāt-*), gentleness, mildness, from *lēnis,* soft, mild.]

Len·non (lĕn′ən), **John** (1940–80). English pop musician, one of the Beatles. He and Paul McCartney wrote most of the group's songs during the 1960's. Lennon married the singer Yoko Ono in 1969. He was murdered in New York by Mark Chapman.

le·no (lē′nō) *n., pl.* **-nos. 1.** A weaving of a type in which the warp yarns are paired and twisted. **2.** A fabric having such a weave. [Probably from French *linon,* fine linen, from *lin,* flax, linen, from Latin *līnum.*]

lens (lĕnz) *n.* **1.** A carefully ground or molded piece of glass, plastic, or other transparent material, in which either or both opposite surfaces are curved such that light rays are refracted to converge or diverge and form an image. **2.** A combination of two or more such lenses, sometimes with other optical devices such as prisms, used to form an image for viewing or photographing. Also called "compound lens." **3.** Any device that causes radiation other than light to converge or diverge by an action analogous to that of an optical lens. **4.** A transparent, biconvex body of the eye between the iris and the vitreous humor, that focuses light rays entering through the pupil to form an image on the retina. In this sense, also called "crystalline lens." **5.** A combination of electrodes or magnets used to converge or diverge a beam of electrons or other charged particles. Also called "electron lens." [New Latin, from Latin *lēns,* LENTIL (from the resemblance of an optical lens to a lentil seed).]

lent. Past tense and past participle of **lend.**

Lent (lĕnt) *n.* The 40 weekdays before Easter (beginning on Ash Wednesday), observed as a season of penitence. [Middle English *lente, lenten,* originally "spring," Old English *lencten,* probably from

THE DEVICE THAT FOCUSES REFLECTED RAYS OF LIGHT

Manipulating the lens to capture sharper images

A lens has one or more curved surfaces that refract, or bend, light rays passing through it to form an image on a surface beyond the lens—the retina of the eye or a movie screen, for example. The distance from the lens to the focal plane is known as the focal length.

In cameras, telescopes, and similar devices, the lens is turned on a screw-thread mounting to adjust the focal length and so focus the images of objects at various distances. In a human eye, focal length is adjusted by muscles that alter the lens curvature.

Light rays of different colors are bent by different amounts as they pass through a curved surface; this causes a distortion of the image, known as "chromatic aberration." In cameras, sharper images are obtained by arranging two or more lenses so that the aberration of one cancels out the aberration of the other. Such an arrangement is collectively called an achromatic lens. A zoom lens may contain 20 separate lenses.

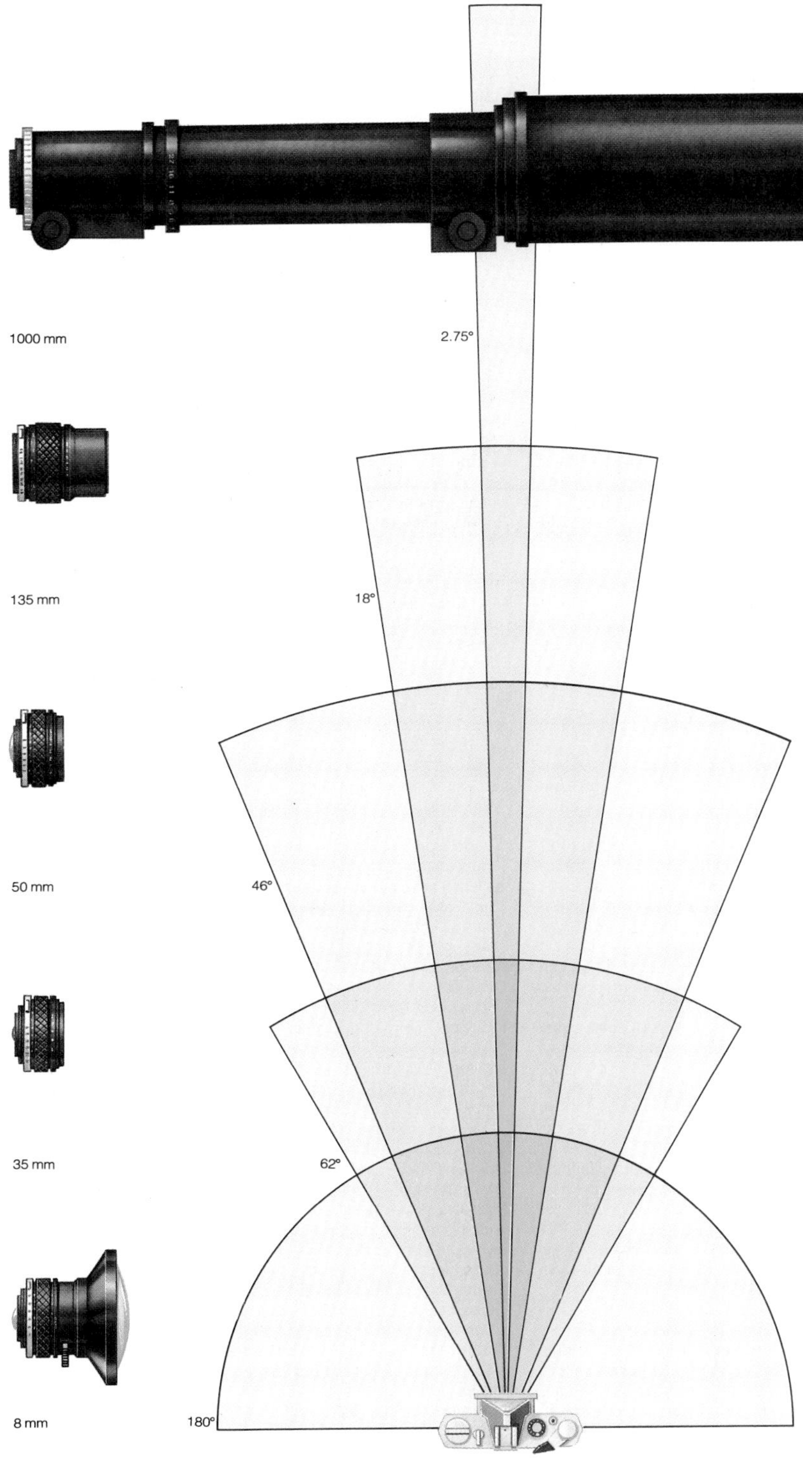

1000 mm

2.75°

135 mm

18°

50 mm

46°

35 mm

62°

8 mm

180°

THE EFFECT OF CHANGING THE LENS *The usual camera lens provides a 45° field of view, similar to what can be seen with one eye. Different sizes of lens can be fitted according to the size of the image being recorded and the focal length it requires. The field of view reduces as the focal length increases. The pictures on the right were taken from the same point, using a 35-millimeter camera fitted in turn with the five lenses shown above.*

Germanic *lang-* (unattested), LONG (referring to the lengthening days of spring).]

Lent·en (lĕn′tən) *adj.* **1.** Of or pertaining to Lent. **2.** Characteristic of or appropriate to Lent; meager; somber: *Lenten fare; a Lenten face.*

len·tic (lĕn′tĭk) *adj.* Of, pertaining to, or designating ecological communities living in still water. Compare **lotic**. [Latin *lentus,* slow, still.]

len·ti·cel (lĕn′tə-sĕl′) *n. Botany.* Any of the small pores on the surface of the stems of woody plants, allowing the passage of gases to and from the interior tissue. [New Latin *lenticella,* diminutive of Latin *lēns* (genitive *lentis*), LENTIL.] —**len·ti·cel·late** *adj.*

len·tic·u·lar (lĕn-tĭk′yə-lər) *adj.* **1. a.** Shaped like a biconvex lens. **b.** Shaped like a lentil seed. **2.** Of or pertaining to a lens, especially that of the eye. [Latin *lenticulāris,* like a lentil, from *lenticula,* LENTIL (compare **lens**).]

len·ti·go (lĕn-tī′gō) *n., pl.* **-tigines** (-tĭj′ə-nēz′). **1.** A freckle. **2.** A nevus. [Latin *lentīgo,* freckles, from *lēns,* LENTIL.] —**len·tig·i·nous** (lĕn-tĭj′ə-nəs), **len·tig·i·nose** (-nōs′) *adj.*

len·til (lĕn′təl) *n.* **1.** A leguminous plant, *Lens esculenta* (or *L. culinaris*), native to the Old World, having pods containing edible seeds. **2.** The round, brown or orange, flattened seed of this plant. [Middle English, from Old French *lentille,* from Vulgar Latin *lentīcula* (unattested), variant of Latin *lenticula,* diminutive of *lēns*†, lentil.]

len·tisk (lĕn′tĭsk) *n.* The **mastic tree** *(see).* [Middle English, from Latin *lentīscus*†.]

len·to (lĕn′tō) *adv. Music.* Slowly. Used as a direction.
~*adj. Music.* Slow.
~*n. Music.* A lento passage. [Italian, from Latin *lentus,* slow.]

len·toid (lĕn′toid′) *adj.* Lenticular.

Len·ya (lĕn′yə), **Lotte,** born Karoline Wilhemine Blamauer (1898–1981). Austrian singer and actress. In 1926 she married Kurt Weill, who composed *The Seven Deadly Sins* for her.

Lenz's law (lĕn′səs) *n. Physics.* The principle that if the magnetic flux linked with a circuit changes, the current induced in the circuit flows in such a way as to produce a field opposing the change. [After Heinrich Friedrich Emil *Lenz* (1804–65), German physicist.]

Le·o¹ (lē′ō) *n.* **1.** A constellation in the Northern Hemisphere near Cancer and Virgo, containing the bright star Regulus. **2. a.** The fifth sign of the **zodiac** *(see).* Also called the "Lion." **b.** One born under this sign. [New Latin, from Latin *leō,* LION.]

Leo² *n.* A name for a lion, as used by children and in folk tales. [Latin, "lion."]

Leo I, Saint, known as "Leo the Great" (c. 400–61). Italian pope (440–61). His negotiations with Attila in 452 and Gaiseric the Vandal in 455 saved Rome from Barbarian invasion. *The Leonian Sacramentary,* the oldest existing form of the Roman missal, is named after him.

Leo Minor *n.* A constellation in the Northern Hemisphere near Leo and Ursa Major.

Le·ón (lā-ōn′). Capital of León province in northwest Spain. It was the capital of the medieval kingdom of León and is today a major tourist center.

Le·o·nar·do da Vin·ci (lē′ə-när′dō də vĭn′chē), (1452–1519). Italian artistic and scientific genius of the Renaissance. He trained in Florence under Verrocchio and became engineer and adviser to Duke Ludovico Sforza in Milan, Cesare Borgia in Florence, and finally Francis I in Amboise in France. Few of his paintings survive, but among these are *The Virgin of the Rocks* (1485) and *Mona Lisa* (or *La Gioconda*) (1503).

Le·on·ca·val·lo (lā′ōn-kə-vä′lō), **Ruggiero** (1858–1919). Italian composer. He wrote several operas, including *I Pagliacci* (1892), in the style of Italian *verismo,* or realism.

le·one (lē-ōn′) *n.* **1.** The basic monetary unit of Sierra Leone, equal to 100 cents. **2.** A note worth one leone. See feature at **currency.** [From SIERRA LEONE.]

Le·o·nid (lē′ə-nĭd) *n., pl.* **-nids** or **Leonides** (lē-ōn′ĭ-dēz′). Any of the meteors constituting the shower that recurs annually in mid-November. [New Latin *Leōnidēs,* from Latin *Leō,* lion (the meteors seem to radiate from the constellation Leo).]

Le·on·i·das I (lē-ōn′ə-dəs) (died 480 B.C.). King of Sparta. He led a handful of Spartans and Thespians in the heroic defense of the pass at Thermopylae in 480 B.C. during the Persian Wars. He was killed in the battle.

le·o·nine (lē′ə-nīn′) *adj.* Of, pertaining to, or characteristic of a lion: *a leonine sigh.* [Middle English, from Old French *leonin(e),* from Latin *leonīnus,* from *leō* (stem *leōn-*), LION.]

Le·o·nine (lē′ə-nīn′) *adj.* Of or pertaining to any of the popes called Leo. [Latin *leonīnus,* of Leo.]

Leonine verse *n.* **1.** A Latin verse of a type written in the Middle Ages, usually consisting of alternating hexameters and pentameters, each line having internal rhyme. **2.** A similar verse in English poetry. [After *Leo* or *Leonius,* medieval poet who used this verse.]

leop·ard (lĕp′ərd) *n.* **1.** A large feline mammal, *Panthera pardus,* of Africa and Asia, having a tawny coat with dark rosettelike markings. There is also a black color variant. See **panther. 2.** Any of several similar felines, such as the cheetah or the snow leopard. **3.** The pelt or fur of a leopard. **4.** *Heraldry.* A lion in side view, having one forepaw raised and the head facing the observer. [Middle English *leopard, leupard,* from Old French, from Late Latin *leopardus,* from Late Greek *leopardos, leontopardos,* "lion pard" (it

leopard *A large cat found throughout Africa and most of Asia, the leopard hunts at night, feeding on monkeys, rodents, birds, and dogs. It is normally solitary and generally waits in a tree to ambush its prey.*

was thought to be a hybrid) : *leōn* (genitive *leontos*), LION + *pardos,* PARD.]

leop·ard·ess (lĕp′ər-dĭs) *n.* A female leopard.

Le·o·par·di (lā′ə-pär′dē), **Count Giacomo** (1798–1837). Italian poet. His *Canti* (1816–36) combine patriotic appeals against Austrian rule with lyrical nature poetry.

leopard lily *n.* A tall plant, *Lilium pardalinum,* of the western United States, having orange-red, dark-spotted flowers and long stamens.

leopard moth *n.* A moth, *Zeuzera pyrina,* having black-spotted white wings and larvae that damage trees by boring into the wood.

leop·ard's-bane (lĕp′ərdz-bān′) *n.* **1.** Any of several plants of the genus *Doronicum,* especially *D. plantagineum,* having rayed yellow flowers. **2.** Any of several similar or related plants.

Le·o·pold II (lē′ə-pōld′) King of the Belgians (1865–1909). In 1885 he was given personal rule of the Congo Free State, established in that year at an international congress at Berlin. He imposed slavery on the natives in rubber plantations and was forced by public opinion to hand over control to the Belgian government in 1908.

Léopoldville. See **Kinshasa.**

le·o·tard (lē′ə-tärd′) *n.* A skin-tight, one-piece garment that covers the torso, worn especially by dancers, gymnasts, or the like. [After Jules *Léotard,* 19th-century French acrobat who popularized it.]

Le·pan·to, Battle of (lĭ-păn′tō; *Italian* lē-pän′tō). A naval battle (1571) in a strait between the Gulf of Corinth (Lepanto) and the Ionian Sea, in which Ottoman sea power was temporarily destroyed by a Christian armada.

Lep·cha (lĕp′chə) *n., pl.* **-chas** or collectively **Lepcha. 1.** A member of a Mongoloid people living in Sikkim, India. **2.** The Tibeto-Burman language of this people.

lep·er (lĕp′ər) *n.* **1.** A person afflicted with leprosy. **2.** One who is spurned on moral or social grounds. [Middle English, from *leper,* leprosy, from Old French *lepre,* from Late Latin *lepra,* from Greek *lepra,* from *lepros,* scaly, from *lepos, lepis,* a scale.]

lepido-, lepid- *prefix.* Indicates a scale or flake; for example, **lepidopteran.** [Greek *lepis* (stem *lepid-*), scale.]

le·pid·o·lite (lĭ-pĭd′l-īt′) *n.* A lilac or pink to gray mica, $K_2Li_3Al_4Si_7O(OH,F)_3$, used as a lithium ore and in glass and ceramic production. [German *Lepidolith*: LEPIDO- + -LITH.]

lep·i·dop·ter·an (lĕp′ə-dŏp′tər-ən) *n., pl.* **-terans** or **-tera** (-tə-rə). Also **lep·i·dop·ter·on** (-tə-rŏn′, -tər-ən) *pl.* **-terons** or **-tera** (-tə-rə). A lepidopterous insect. [New Latin *Lepidoptera,* "scale-winged ones" : LEPIDO- + -PTER.] —**lep·i·dop·ter·an** *adj.*

lep·i·dop·ter·ist (lĕp′ə-dŏp′tər-ĭst) *n.* An entomologist specializing in the study of butterflies and moths.

lep·i·dop·ter·ous (lĕp′ə-dŏp′tər-əs) *adj.* Of or belonging to the order Lepidoptera, which includes insects such as the butterflies and moths, having four wings covered with small scales, and with caterpillars forming the larval stage.

lep·i·dote (lĕp′ə-dōt′) *adj.* Covered with small scales. [Greek *lepidōtos,* from *lepis,* scale.]

Le·pon·tine Alps (lə-pŏn′tən ălps). A section of the Alps in southern Switzerland and along the Swiss–Italian border. The highest peak is Monte Leone (3,563 meters; 11,683 feet).

lep·o·rine (lĕp′ə-rīn′, -ər-ən) *adj.* Of or characteristic of hares. [Latin *leporīnus,* from *lepus* (stem *lepor-*), hare.]

lep·re·chaun (lĕp′rə-kôn′, -kŏn′) *n.* In Irish folklore, any of a race of elves who are cobblers and have hidden treasure. [Earlier *lubrican,* from Irish *lupracán, leipracán,* from Middle Irish *luchrupán,* from Old Irish *luchorpán* : *lū,* small + *corp,* body, from Latin *corpus.*]

lep·ro·sar·i·um (lĕp′rə-sâr′ē-əm) *n., pl.* **-ums** or **-saria** (-ē-ə). A hospital for the treatment of lepers. [Medieval Latin, from Late Latin *leprōsus,* LEPROUS.]

lep·rose (lĕp′rōs′) *adj.* Scurfy or scaly; leprous. [Late Latin *leprōsus,* LEPROUS.]

lep·ro·sy (lĕp′rə-sē) *n.* A chronic, infectious, granulomatous disease occurring chiefly in tropical and subtropical regions, caused by a bacillus, *Mycobacterium leprae,* and ranging in severity from noncontagious and spontaneously remitting forms to contagious, malignant forms with progressive anesthesia, paralysis, ulceration, nutritive disturbances, gangrene, and mutilation. Also called "Hansen's disease." [From LEPROUS.] —**lep·rot·ic** *adj.*

lep·rous (lĕp′rəs) *adj.* **1.** Having leprosy. **2.** Of, pertaining to, or resembling leprosy. **3.** *Biology.* Having or consisting of loose, scurfy scales. [Middle English *lepro(u)s,* from Late Latin *leprōsus,* from *lepra,* leprosy. See **leper.**] —**lep·rous·ly** *adv.* —**lep·rous·ness** *n.*

-lepsy *suffix.* Indicates a fit or seizure; for example, **narcolepsy.** [Greek *-lēpsia,* from *lēpsis,* taking, seizure, from *lambanein* (future stem *lēps-*), to take, seize.]

lepto-, lept- *prefix.* Indicates slender, thin, fine; for example, **leptocephalus, lepton.** [Greek *leptos,* peeled, fine, small, thin, from *lepein,* to peel.]

lep·to·ceph·a·lus (lĕp′tə-sĕf′ə-ləs) *n., pl.* **-li** (-lī′). Any of the slender, transparent larvae of eels and certain other fishes. [New Latin, "slender-headed" : LEPTO- + -CEPHALOUS.]

lep·ton¹ (lĕp′tŏn′) *n., pl.* **-ta** (-tə). **1.** A monetary unit equal to 1/100 of the drachma of Greece. See feature at **currency. 2.** An ancient Greek coin. [Modern Greek, from Greek, small coin, from *leptos,* fine, small, from *lepein,* to peel.]

lepton² *n., pl.* **-tons.** Any of a family of elementary particles including the electron, the muon, the tau particle, and their associated neutrinos, all having spin equal to ½ and masses less than those of the mesons. [LEPT(O)- + -ON.]

lepton number *n. Symbol* **L** *Physics.* A quantum number equal to the number of leptons in an interaction minus the number of antileptons. Each type of lepton has its own quantum number that is separately conserved.

lep·to·some (lĕp′tə-sōm′) *n. Physiology.* A person with a slender, thin, or frail body. [German *Leptosom* : LEPTO- + -SOME (body).] —**lep·to·so·mat·ic** *adj.*

lep·to·spi·ro·sis (lĕp′tō-spī-rō′sĭs) *n.* An infectious disease caused by bacteria of the genus *Leptospira* that may be transmitted to humans by contact with rodents, dogs, and other mammals and is characterized by fever and either jaundice or meningitis. [New Latin *Leptospira* (LEPTO- + Greek *speira*, coil) + -OSIS.]

lep·to·spo·ran·gi·ate (lĕp′tō-spə-răn′jē-ĭt) *adj.* Of or pertaining to ferns in which the sporangium develops from a single cell. Compare **eusporangiate.**

lep·to·tene (lĕp′tə-tēn′) *n. Biology.* The first stage of prophase in mitosis and meiosis when the nuclear material becomes visible as slender single-stranded threads. [LEPTO- + -*tene,* from Greek *taina,* band, thread.]

Lep·us (lē′pəs) *n.* A constellation in the Southern Hemisphere near Orion and Columba. [New Latin, from Latin, hare.]

Lé·ri·da (lā′rī-də). Capital of Lérida province, Catalonia, northeast Spain. An ancient fortified city on the Segre River, it was taken by Julius Caesar (49 B.C.). The city commanded the approaches to Barcelona during the Spanish Civil War and fell to the Nationalists in 1938 after a nine-month battle.

Ler·mon·tov (lĕr′mən-tôf′, -tôv′), **Mikhail Yuryevich** (1814–41). Russian writer. He wrote the novel *A Hero of Our Time* (1840), and many poems. He was killed in a duel.

Ler·ner (lûr′nər), **Alan Jay** (1918–86). U.S. lyricist. He wrote musicals with the composer Frederick Loewe, including *Brigadoon* (1947) and *My Fair Lady* (1956).

Le·sage (lə-säzh′), **Alain René** (1668–1747). French writer. His novel *Gil Blas de Santillane* (1715–35) was one of the earliest examples of modern realistic fiction.

les·bi·an (lĕz′bē-ən) *n. Sometimes* **Lesbian.** A female homosexual. ~*adj. Sometimes* **Lesbian.** Of or pertaining to female homosexuals. [After LESBOS, alluding to the supposed homosexuality of Sappho who lived there.] —**les·bi·an·ism** *n.*

Les·bi·an (lĕz′bē-ən) *n.* **1.** A native or resident of Lesbos. **2.** The Ancient Greek dialect of Lesbos, belonging to Aeolic, used in the lyric poetry of Sappho. ~*adj.* **1.** Of or pertaining to Lesbos or its people. **2.** Of or pertain-

---

Leonardo da Vinci

THE MAN WHO WANTED TO KNOW EVERYTHING
How curiosity drove the artist who became the world's greatest designer

Leonardo da Vinci was one of the outstanding figures of the Renaissance—not only an artist of rare power but a pioneering scientist as well. His devouring curiosity drove him to explore fields as diverse as anatomy, botany, geology, meteorology, physics, mathematics, geometry, and music. His architectural drawings explored design problems in buildings, harbors, irrigation systems and canals, but no building by him survives. He foretold the future with sketches of submarines, diving suits, tanks, parachutes, flying machines, machine guns, and cluster bombs. All these ideas and observations were recorded in voluminous notebooks; 7,000 pages survive, many annotated by the left-handed designer in mirror writing. Born in Vinci, a village near Florence, in 1452, Leonardo was the illegitimate son of a lawyer and a peasant girl. He died in France in 1519.

TANK PROTOTYPE *Leonardo's hand-cranked tank was never made, but its design foreshadowed the first tanks that were built some 400 years later.*

MASTER DRAFTSMAN *Few of Leonardo's major artistic works have survived complete and undamaged. Some, like The Adoration of the Magi (begun in 1481), were never finished. Others, like The Last Supper (1497), a mural in a Milan monastery, have deteriorated because Leonardo used unorthodox techniques. This drawing—of the Virgin and Child with St. Anne and John the Baptist—is a rare exception.*

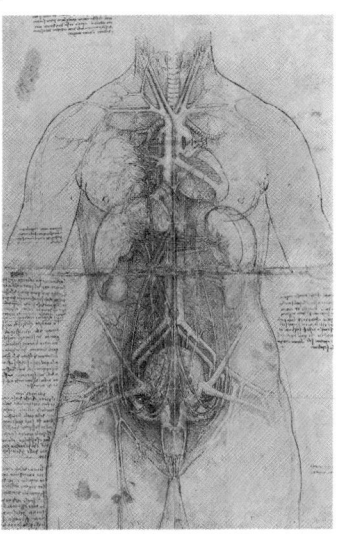

ANATOMY OF ART *To sketch the internal layout of the human body, Leonardo dissected more than 30 corpses. Detailed notes on his painstaking observations are jotted down in his characteristic right-to-left mirror writing.*

PRONUNCIATION KEY

ă, pat; ā, pay; âr, care;
ä, father, are; b, bib;
ch, church; d, deed; ĕ, pet;
ē, be; f, fife; g, gag; h, hat;
hw, which; ĭ, pit; ī, pie;
îr, pier; j, judge; k, kick;
l, lid, needle; m, mum;
n, no, sudden; ng, thing;
ŏ, pot; ō, toe; ô, paw, for;
oi, noise; ou, out; o͝o, book;
o͞o, boot; p, pop; r, roar;
s, sauce; sh, ship, dish;
t, tight; th, thin, path;
th, this, bathe; ŭ, cut; ûr, fur;
v, valve; w, with; y, yes;
z, zebra, size; zh, vision;
ə, about, item, edible,
gallop, circus, peaceful

IN FOREIGN WORDS:

à, *Fr.* ami; œ, *Fr.* feu, *Ger.*
schön; ü, *Fr.* tu, *Ger.* über;
KH, *Ger.* ich, *Scot.* loch;
N, *Fr.* bon; y′, *Fr.* Compiègne

STRESS MARKS:

Primary stress: ′
in·cite′ (ĭn-sīt′)
Secondary stress: ′
in′sight′ (ĭn′sīt′)

ing to the Ancient Greek dialect of Lesbos. **3.** Of, pertaining to, or characteristic of Sappho or her poetry.

Les•bos (lĕz′bəs, -bŏs). *Greek* **Lés•vos** (lāz′vôs). Mountainous Greek island off western Turkey, the home of Sappho and Aristotle.

lese majesty (lēz) *n.* Also *French* **lèse ma•jes•té** (lĕz mȧ-zhĕs-tā′). **1.** An offense or crime committed against the ruler or supreme power of a state; treason. **2.** The act or an instance of affronting another's dignity or overstepping authority. [Old French *lese-majeste,* from Latin *laesa mājestās,* "violated majesty" : *laesa,* past participle of *laedere,* to injure, damage, offend + MAJESTY.]

le•sion (lē′zhən) *n.* **1.** A wound or injury. **2.** A circumscribed pathological alteration of tissue or an organ. **3.** A point or patch of a skin disease. [Middle English *lesioun,* from Old French *lesion,* from Latin *laesiō* (stem *laesiōn-*), from *laedere*†, to injure, damage.]

Le•so•tho (lə-sō′tō). Formerly **Ba•su•to•land** (bə-so͞o′tō-lănd′). Independent Commonwealth country, surrounded by South Africa. It became a British protectorate in 1868 and an independent kingdom in 1966. It is mountainous but produces wheat and corn. Area, 30,355 square kilometers (11,720 square miles). Population, 1,400,000. Capital, Maseru. See map at **South Africa.**

les•pe•de•za (lĕs′pə-dē′zə) *n.* Any plant of the genus *Lespedeza,* which includes the bush clovers. [New Latin; named after Vincente Manuel de *Céspedes,* misspelled *Léspedes* (died 1785), Spanish governor of East Florida.]

less (lĕs). Alternate comparative of **little.**
~*adj.* **1.** Not as great in extent, quantity, magnitude, or degree: *takes less sugar; needs less attention.* **2.** Lower in importance, esteem, or rank: *No less a person than a marquis is considered.* **—no less. 1.** Used, sometimes ironically, as a comment on a preceding statement, when surprised or impressed: *She's going to Harvard, no less.* **2.** None other: *The surprise guest turned out to be no less than the President himself.* —See Usage note at **few.**
~*adv.* To a smaller extent, degree, or frequency.
~*n.* A smaller amount.
~*prep.* Minus; subtracting: *Five less one is four.* [Middle English *less(e),* Old English *lǣssa* (adjective) and *lǣs* (adverb and noun), from Germanic *loisiz* (unattested), little.]

-less *suffix.* Indicates: **1.** Lack of, free of, not having, or without; for example, **toothless, sleepless, blameless. 2.** Not acting or able to be acted upon in a specified way; for example, **tireless, ceaseless, countless.** [Middle English *-les(se),* Old English *-lēas,* from *lēas,* lacking, free from.]

les•see (lĕ-sē′) *n.* One holding a lease. [Middle English, from Norman French *lessee,* variant of Old French *lesse,* past participle of *lesser,* to LEASE.] **—les•see•ship** *n.*

less•en (lĕs′ən) *v.* **-ened, -ening, -ens.** —*tr.* **1.** To cause to decrease; make less. **2.** To make little of; minimize; belittle. —*intr.* To become less; decrease. —See Synonyms at **decrease.** [Middle English *lessenen,* from *lesse,* LESS.]

Les•seps (lĕs′əps), **Ferdinand Marie, Vicomte de** (1805–94). French engineer and diplomat. He planned and supervised construction of the Suez Canal, opened in 1869. His company began building the Panama Canal in 1881 but went bankrupt in 1888. The canal was completed by the U.S. government.

less•er (lĕs′ər) *adj.* Smaller or less in size, amount, value, or importance, especially in a comparison of two elements. [Middle English double comparative, from LESS.]

Lesser An•til•les (ăn-tĭl′ēz). A chain of islands in the West Indies, forming a barrier between the Atlantic Ocean and the Caribbean Sea. They are made up of the Leeward and Windward islands. See map at **Latin America.**

lesser brethren *pl.n.* Those members of a group regarded as less important than the other members.

lesser celandine *n.* A plant, *Ranunculus ficaria,* having heart-shaped leaves and yellow flowers. Also called "pilewort."

lesser doxology *n.* The **Gloria Patri** *(see).*

lesser panda *n.* See **panda.**

Les•sing (lĕs′ĭng), **Doris May** (1919–). English novelist, born in Iran. She published her first novel, *The Grass is Singing,* in 1950, and her works include the semiautobiographical *Children of Violence* (1952–69), a five-volume series.

Lessing, Gotthold Ephraim (1729–81). German dramatist and critic. He wrote the plays *Minna von Barnhelm* (1763) and *Nathan der Weise* (1779), which advocated tolerance.

les•son (lĕs′ən) *n.* **1.** Something to be learned. **2. a.** A period of instruction; a class: *a tennis lesson.* **b.** The material taught in one such period. **3. a.** An experience or observation that imparts beneficial new knowledge or wisdom. **b.** The knowledge or wisdom learned in such a manner. **4.** A reprimand or punishment. **5.** A reading from the Bible or other sacred writing as part of a religious service.
~*tr.v.* **lessoned, -soning, -sons.** *Rare.* **1.** To teach a lesson or lessons to; instruct. **2.** To reprimand or punish. [Middle English *lesso(u)n,* a reading, lesson, from Old French *lecon,* from Latin *lectiō,* LECTION.]

les•sor (lĕs′ôr′, lĕ-sôr′) *n.* One who lets property under a lease; a landlord. [Middle English *lessour,* from Norman French, from *lesser,* to LEASE.]

lest (lĕst) *conj.* **1.** So as to prevent the possibility that; for fear that: *Tiptoe lest the guard should hear you.* **2.** That. Used after phrases denoting fear, worry, or the like: *anxious lest he should become ill.* [Middle English *leste,* short for *les the,* whereby less, Old English *thȳ lǣs the,* from *lǣs,* LESS.]

Lésvos. See **Lesbos.**

let¹ (lĕt) *tr.v.* **let, letting, lets. 1.** Used as an auxiliary followed by an infinitive omitting *to:* **a.** To grant permission to; allow: *She let him continue.* **b.** To cause to. Used with *know* or *hear: He let me know the results.* **2.** Used as an auxiliary in the imperative: **a.** In order to convey a command, request, or proposal: *Let's finish the job!* **b.** In order to convey a warning or threat: *Just let her try!* **c.** In order to convey an assumption or hypothesis: *Let x equal y.* **d.** In order to convey acceptance of or resignation to the inevitable: *Let death come!* **3.** To permit to move or change in a specified manner: *let the dog through.* **4.** To rent or lease: *let a room to a bachelor.* **5.** To assign (a contract for work, for example): *let the construction job to a new firm.* **—let alone.** Not to speak of; much less: *Don't whisper, let alone speak.* **—let in.** To permit to enter. **—let in for.** To involve in: *let them in for a lot of trouble.* **—let in on. 1.** To take into one's confidence; inform: *Were they let in on the secret?* **2.** To allow to participate: *Let him in on the robbery.* **—let into. 1.** To permit to enter or be inserted into. **2.** To take into one's confidence; inform. **—let off. 1.** To emit or release: *let off steam.* **2.** To excuse or dismiss: *let the workmen off early.* **3.** To give little or no punishment to for an offense: *He was let off with a year on probation.* **4.** To detonate or fire: *let off a bomb.* **—let on. 1.** To allow it to be known: *Don't let on that you helped me.* **2.** To pretend. **—let out. 1.** To release from confinement. **2.** To give forth; emit: *The dog let out a yelp.* **3.** To make known (a secret, for example); reveal: *Who let that story out?* **4.** To increase the size of (a garment, for example). **5.** To rent or lease (buildings, land, or the like). [Middle English *leten,* Old English *lǣtan,* to leave behind, leave undone.]
Usage: In colloquial speech *let's* has come increasingly to be used as a mere indicator that a suggestion is being proffered, and its connection with the more formal *let us* has become correspondingly attenuated, so that one hears usages like *let's us go, don't let's get all excited,* and *let's get yourself ready for the doctor.* These usages are best avoided in formal writing. See also Usage note at **leave.**

let² *n.* **1.** An obstacle. Used chiefly in the phrase *without let or hindrance.* **2.** *Sports.* **a.** In certain games such as tennis or squash, a small irregularity in the play that causes the point to be replayed. **b.** A point replayed for this reason.
~*tr.v.* **letted** or **let, letting, lets.** *Archaic.* To obstruct or hinder. [Middle English *let(te),* a hindrance, from *letten,* to hinder, prevent, Old English *lettan.*]

-let *suffix.* Indicates: **1.** Diminutive size or minor status; for example, **booklet, starlet. 2.** An article worn on some part of the body; for example, **bracelet, anklet.** [Middle English *-lette,* from Old French *-elet* : noun ending *-el* + *-et(te),* -ETTE.]

letch. Variant of **lech.**

let down *tr.v.* **1.** To take down; lower: *let down the sails.* **2.** To fail to satisfy; disappoint: *The mayor let down the electorate.* **3.** To undo so as to add length: *let down a dress; let down her hair.*

let•down (lĕt′doun′) *n.* **1.** A slowing down, relaxing, or decrease, as of effort or energy. **2.** *Informal.* A disappointment. **3.** The descent made by an aircraft in order to land.

le•thal (lē′thəl) *adj.* **1.** Sufficient to cause or capable of causing death. **2.** Of, pertaining to, or causing death. —See Synonyms at **fatal.** [Latin *lethālis,* from *lēthum,* death, variant of *lētum.*] **—le•thal•i•ty** (lē-thăl′ĭ-tē) *n.* **—le•thal•ly** *adv.*

lethal dose *n.* See **LD.**

lethal gene *n.* A gene that, under certain conditions, brings about the death of the organism carrying it, usually when its effect is not masked by a normal dominant gene.

lethargic encephalitis *n. Pathology.* **Encephalitis lethargica** *(see).*

leth•ar•gy (lĕth′ər-jē) *n.* **1.** Sluggish indifference or slowness; a feeling of laziness or lack of arousal. **2.** A state of unconsciousness resembling deep sleep, from which an individual can be roused but into which he at once relapses. [Middle English *litargie, letargie,* from Old French *litargie,* from Latin *lēthargia,* drowsiness, from Greek, from *lēthargos,* forgetful, from *lēthē,* forgetfulness.] **—le•thar•gic** *adj.* **—le•thar•gi•cal•ly** *adv.*
Synonyms: *languor, lassitude, sluggishness, torpor.*

Le•the (lē′thē) *n. Greek Mythology.* **1.** The river of forgetfulness in Hades. **2.** Oblivion; loss of memory. [Greek *lēthē,* forgetfulness (later personified).] **—Le•the•an** *adj.*

Le•to (lē′tō′) *Greek Mythology.* A consort of Zeus and the mother of Apollo and Artemis.

let's (lĕts). Contraction of *let us.*

Lett (lĕt) *n.* A Latvian.

let•ter (lĕt′ər) *n.* **1.** A written symbol or character representing a speech sound; a component of an alphabet. **2.** A written or printed communication directed to an individual or organization. **3.** *Often* **letters.** A formal or legal document giving information or granting rights to its bearer or recipient. **4.** The literal meaning of something: *the letter of the law.* **5.** *Printing.* **a.** A piece of type that prints a single character. **b.** A specific style of type. **c.** The characters in one style of type. **6. letters.** Literary culture or learning; literature as a discipline or profession. Used with a singular verb. **7.** An emblem in the shape of the initial of a school awarded to athletes. **—to the letter.** Precisely as directed, as when following orders.
~*v.* **lettered, -tering, -ters.** —*tr.* **1.** To write letters on. **2.** To write in letters. —*intr.* To win an athletic letter. [Middle English *letter, lettre,* from Old French *lettre,* from Latin *littera,* letter (of the alphabet), letter, document (in plural only).] **—let•ter•er** *n.*

letter bomb *n.* An explosive device that is thin enough to fit into a

PRONUNCIATION KEY

ă, pat; ā, pay; âr, care;
ä, father, are; b, bib;
ch, church; d, deed; ĕ, pet;
ē, be; f, fife; g, gag; h, hat;
hw, which; ĭ, pit; ī, pie;
îr, pier; j, judge; k, kick;
l, lid, needle; m, mum;
n, no, sudden; ng, thing;
ŏ, pot; ō, toe; ô, paw, for;
oi, noise; ou, out; o͝o, book;
o͞o, boot; p, pop; r, roar;
s, sauce; sh, ship, dish;
t, tight; th, thin, path;
th, this, bathe; ŭ, cut; ûr, fur;
v, valve; w, with; y, yes;
z, zebra, size; zh, vision;
ə, about, item, edible,
gallop, circus, peaceful

IN FOREIGN WORDS:

à, *Fr.* ami; œ, *Fr.* feu, *Ger.* schön; ü, *Fr.* tu, *Ger.* über;
KH, *Ger.* ich, *Scot.* loch;
N, *Fr.* bon; y′, *Fr.* Compiègne

STRESS MARKS:

Primary stress: ′
in•cite′ (ĭn-sīt′)
Secondary stress: ′
in′sight′ (ĭn′sīt′)

large envelope and is designed to explode when the envelope is opened.

let·ter·box (lĕt′ər-bŏks′) *n.* **1.** A mailbox (see). **2.** A slot in a front door, usually covered with a flap, through which mail is delivered.

letter card *n.* A card, often with a printed stamp, that has gummed edges and can be folded and sent as a letter.

letter carrier *n.* A person who delivers the mail.

let·tered (lĕt′ərd) *adj.* **1. a.** Educated to read and write; literate. **b.** Erudite; learned. **2.** Of or pertaining to literacy or learning. **3.** Inscribed or marked with letters.

let·ter·head (lĕt′ər-hĕd′) *n.* **1.** The printed heading at the top of a sheet of writing paper, usually a person's address or the name and address of an organization. **2.** Paper with such a printed heading.

let·ter·ing (lĕt′ər-ĭng) *n.* **1.** The act, process, or art of forming or inscribing with letters. **2.** The letters themselves.

letter of advice *n.* A letter containing specific information about a commercial transaction, as from a consignor to a consignee.

letter of credit *n.* *Abbr.* **l.c., L/C** A letter issued by a bank authorizing the bearer or person named to draw a stated amount of money from it or its branches, or from associated banks or agencies.

let·ter-per·fect (lĕt′ər-pûr′fĭkt) *adj.* Correct in every detail; word-perfect.

let·ter·press (lĕt′ər-prĕs′) *n.* **1. a.** The process of printing from a raised inked surface. **b.** Anything printed in this fashion. **2.** The text itself as distinct from illustrations or other ornamentation.

let·ters (lĕt′ərz) *n.* *Used with a singular verb.* Literary culture or learning; literature as a discipline or profession: *a man of letters.*

letters of administration *pl.n.* A legal document entrusting an individual with the administration of a deceased person's estate.

letters of credence *pl.n.* Also **letter of credence.** An official document conveying the credentials of a diplomatic envoy to a foreign government. Also called "letters credential."

letters of marque *pl.n.* Also **letter of marque.** **1.** A document issued by a nation allowing a private citizen to seize citizens or goods of another nation. **2.** A document issued by a nation allowing a private citizen to equip a ship with arms in order to attack enemy ships. Also called "letters of marque and reprisal." [Middle English, from Old French *marque*, reprisal, from Old Provençal *marca*, from *marcar*, to seize as a pledge, from Germanic.]

letters patent *pl.n.* *Law.* A document issued by a government granting a patent to an inventor.

letters testamentary *pl.n.* *Law.* A document issued by a probate court or officer informing executors of a will of their appointment and authority.

Let·tish (lĕt′ĭsh) *adj.* Of or pertaining to the Latvians or their language.
   ~*n.* A language, Latvian (see).

let·tre de ca·chet (lĕt′rə də kă-shā′) *n.,* *pl.* **lettres de cachet** (*pronounced as singular*). Formerly, a document issued or sanctioned by the French sovereign, granting powers of arrest or banishment without trial. [French, "letter with a seal."]

let·tuce (lĕt′əs) *n.* **1.** Any of various plants of the genus *Lactuca;* especially, *L. sativa,* cultivated for its edible leaves. **2.** The leaves of *L. sativa,* eaten as salad. **3.** Any of various plants resembling lettuce, such as the sea lettuce. [Middle English *letus(e),* from Old French *laituës,* plural of *laituë,* from Latin *lactūca,* from *lac* (stem *lact-*), milk (from its milky juice).]

let up *intr.v.* **1.** To diminish; slacken; lessen. **2.** To stop.

let·up (lĕt′ŭp′) *n.* **1.** A slackening of pace, force, intensity, or effort; a slowdown. **2.** A temporary stop; a pause.

le·u (lĕ′o͞o) *n.,* *pl.* **lei** (lā′ī) **1.** The basic monetary unit of Romania, equal to 100 bani. **2.** A coin worth one leu. See feature at **currency.** [Romanian, "lion," from Latin *leō* (stem *leōn-*), LION.]

leu·cine (lo͞o′sēn′) *n.* An essential amino acid, $C_6H_{13}NO_2$, derived from the hydrolysis of protein by pancreatic enzymes. [LEUC(O)- + -INE.]

leu·cite (lo͞o′sīt′) *n.* A white or gray mineral, consisting essentially of $KAl(SiO_3)_2$. [German *Leucit* : LEUC(O)- + -ITE.]

leuco-. Variant of **leuko-.**

leu·co·plast (lo͞o′kə-plăst′) *n.* Also **leu·co·plas·tid** (lo͞o′kə-plăs′tĭd). A colorless plastid in the cytoplasm of plant cells, around which starch collects. [LEUCO- + PLAST(ID).]

leu·ke·mi·a (lo͞o-kē′mē-ə) *n.* Any of a group of usually fatal diseases of the reticuloendothelial system, involving uncontrolled proliferation of leukocytes, which suppress the production of normal blood cells. [New Latin : LEUK(O)- + -EMIA.]

leuko-, leuk-, leuco– *prefix.* Indicates: **1.** White or colorless; for example, leukoderma, leucoplast. **2.** Leukocyte; for example, leukopenia, leukemia. [New Latin, from Greek *leukos,* clear, white.]

leu·ko·cyte (lo͞o′kə-sīt′) *n.* Any of the white or colorless nucleated cells occurring in blood. Also called "hemoleukocyte," "white blood cell," "white cell," "white corpuscle." [LEUKO- + -CYTE.] —**leu·ko·cyt·ic** (lo͞o′kə-sĭt′ĭk) *adj.*

leu·ko·cy·to·sis (lo͞o′kō-sī-tō′sĭs) *n.,* *pl.* **-ses** (-sēz′). A large increase in the number of leukocytes in the blood, generally in response to infection. [New Latin : LEUKOCYT(E) + -OSIS.] —**leu·ko·cy·tot·ic** (lo͞o′kō-sī-tŏt′ĭk) *adj.*

leu·ko·der·ma (lo͞o′kō-dûr′mə) *n.* Partial or total lack of skin pigmentation. Also called "vitiligo." [New Latin : LEUKO- + -DERMA.] —**leu·ko·der·mal, leu·co·der·mic** *adj.*

leu·ko·ma (lo͞o-kō′mə) *n.* A dense, white opacity of the cornea of the eye. [New Latin, from Greek *leukōma* : LEUK(O)- + -OMA.]

leu·ko·pe·ni·a (lo͞o′kə-pē′nē-ə) *n.* An abnormally low number of

leukocytes in the blood. [New Latin : LEUKO- + -PENIA.]

leu·ko·poi·e·sis (lo͞o′kō-poi-ē′sĭs) *n.* The formation and development of leukocytes. Also called "leukocytopoiesis." [New Latin : LEUKO- + -POIESIS.] —**leu·ko·poi·et·ic** (lo͞o′kō-poi-ĕt′ĭk) *adj.*

leu·kor·rhe·a (lo͞o′kə-rē′ə) *n.* A whitish or yellowish vaginal discharge containing mucus, which in excessive amounts may indicate infection of the lower reproductive tract. [New Latin : LEUKO- + -RRHEA.]

lev (lĕf) *n.,* *pl.* **leva** (lĕv′ə). *Abbr.* **L. 1.** The basic monetary unit of Bulgaria, equal to 100 stotinki. **2.** A coin worth one lev. See feature at **currency.** [Bulgarian, "lion," from Old Bulgarian *livu,* probably from Old High German *lewo,* from Latin *leō,* LION.]

Lev. Leviticus (Old Testament).

Lev·al·loi·si·an (lĕv′ə-loi′zē-ən) *adj.* Of or pertaining to a western European stage in lower Paleolithic culture distinguished by the method of striking off flake tools from pieces of flint. [After *Levallois*-Perret, district near Paris.]

lev·al·lor·phan (lĕv′ə-lôr′făn′, -fən) *n.* A drug used to counteract the slowing in breathing caused by narcotic pain relievers without reducing their analgesic effects. [*Levorotatory* + *all*yl + m*orph*ine + *-an* (unsaturated carbon compound).]

le·vant[1] (lə-vănt′) *n.* A type of heavy, coarse-grained morocco leather often used in bookbinding. Also called "Levant morocco." [Originally imported from the LEVANT.]

levant[2] *intr.v.* **-vanted, -vanting, -vants.** To run away or abscond, usually leaving unpaid debts behind. [Perhaps from slang "run (or throw) a levant," perhaps from LEVANT, as in French *faire voile en Levant,* "sail to the Levant."]

Le·vant (lə-vănt′). The countries bordering on the eastern Mediterranean. [Middle English *levaunt,* "the Orient," from Old French *levant,* "rising" (said of the sun), present participle of *lever,* to rise, raise.]

le·vant·er (lə-văn′tər) *n.* **1.** One who levants; an absconder. **2.** A strong easterly wind in the extreme west Mediterranean area. In this sense, also called "levante." **3. Levanter.** A Levantine.

le·van·tine (lə-văn′tĭn, lĕv′ən-tēn′, -tĭn′) *n.* A strong, closely woven silk fabric. [Originally made in the LEVANT.]

Le·van·tine (lə-văn′tĭn, lĕv′ən-tēn′, -tĭn′) *adj.* Of or pertaining to the Levant.
   ~*n.* **1.** A native or resident of the Levant. **2.** A ship from the Levant.

le·va·tor (lə-vā′tər) *n.,* *pl.* **levatores** (lĕv′ə-tôr′ēz, -tōr′ēz) **1.** *Anatomy.* Any muscle that raises a part of the body. **2.** A surgical instrument for lifting the depressed part of a fractured skull. [New Latin, from Latin *levāre,* to raise.]

lev·ee[1] (lĕv′ē) *n.* **1.** A natural embankment built up by a river. **2.** An embankment raised to prevent a river from overflowing. **3.** A small ridge or raised area bordering an irrigated field. **4.** A landing place on a river; a pier. [French *levée,* from Old French *levee,* "raising," from the past participle of *lever,* to raise.]

lev·ee[2] (lĕv′ē, lə-vē′) *n.* **1.** A reception held by a monarch or other high-ranking person on rising from bed. **2.** A formal reception, as at a royal court. [French *levé,* variant of *lever,* rising, from *lever,* to rise.]

lev·el (lĕv′əl) *n.* **1. a.** Relative position or rank on a scale, as in a hierarchy, society, or other grouping. Also used in combination and adjectivally: *high-level talks between diplomats.* **b.** Loosely, any grade or step in a series or position on a range: *a deeper level of meaning; at the spiritual level.* **c.** A natural or proper position, place, or stage: *finally found her own level.* **2.** An amount, degree, standard, or value achieved: *a level of output; sound levels.* **3.** Position along a vertical axis; elevation; height: *the level of the windows.* **4. a.** A horizontal line or plane at right angles to the plumb or vertical. **b.** The position or height of such a line or plane: *eye level.* **5. a.** A flat, horizontal surface. **b.** A layer, as of land or rock. **6.** A tract of land of uniform elevation. **7. a.** An instrument for ascertaining whether a surface is horizontal, consisting essentially of an encased, liquid-filled tube containing an air bubble that moves to a center window when the instrument is set on a horizontal plane. Also called "spirit level." **b.** Such a device combined with a telescope, used in surveying. **c.** A computation of the difference in elevation between two points, using a spirit level. —**on a level with.** Equal to. —**on the level.** *Informal.* Without deception.
   ~*adj.* **1.** Having a flat, smooth surface. **2.** On a horizontal plane. **3.** Being at the same height as another; even. **4.** Poured or measured into a container so as to be even with its rim: *a level teaspoonful.* **5.** Being of the same degree or rank as another; equal. **6.** Without abrupt variations; uniform; consistent. —**one's level best.** The best one is capable of doing.
   ~*v.* **leveled** or **-levelled, -eling** or **-elling, -els.** —*tr.* **1.** To make horizontal, flat, or even. Often used with *off.* **2.** To tear down; raze. **3.** To knock down with or as if with a blow. **4.** To put (two persons or things) in the same rank, degree, or plane. **5.** To aim along a horizontal plane: *leveled a gun at my head.* **6.** To direct (a gaze or remark, for example) emphatically or forcefully toward someone. **7.** To measure the different elevations of (a tract of land) with a level. —*intr.* **1.** To render persons or things equal, as in rank, importance, or size. **2.** To achieve or come to a level. **3.** To aim a weapon horizontally. **4.** *Informal.* To be frank. Used with *with: Level with me on what happened.* —**level off** (or **out**). **1.** To move toward stability or consistency. **2.** To maneuver an aircraft into horizontal flight after gaining or losing altitude.
   ~*adv.* Along a flat or even line or plane. [Middle English *level,*

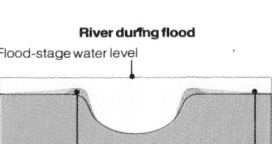

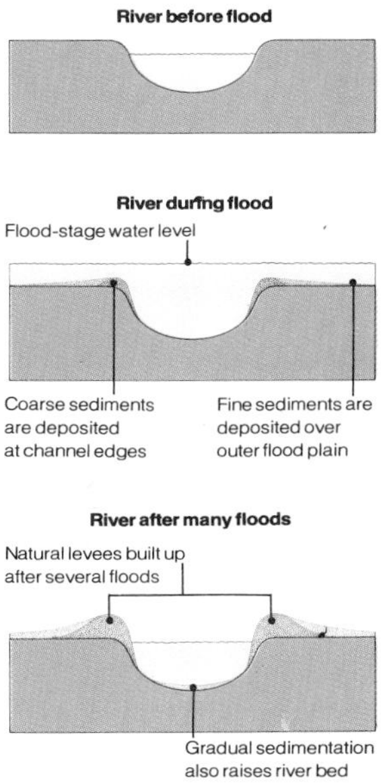

River before flood

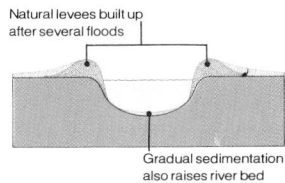

River during flood
Flood-stage water level

Coarse sediments are deposited at channel edges   Fine sediments are deposited over outer flood plain

River after many floods
Natural levees built up after several floods

Gradual sedimentation also raises river bed

levee *Rivers that flood regularly can create natural levees. Each time the river bursts its banks, fine sediment is spread over the flood plain, but coarse sediment builds up along the banks. In places, natural levees along the Mississippi have built up to a height of 12 meters (40 feet) above the river's lowest level.*

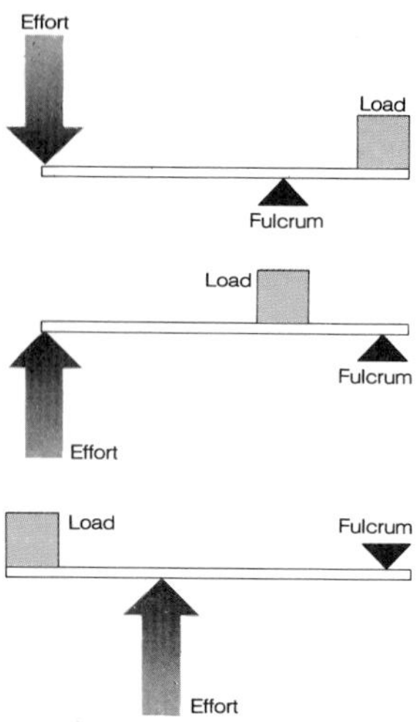

lever *There are three basic types of lever that differ according to the relative positions of the pivot (or fulcrum), the effort, and the load. In the first type (top), effort and load are on opposite sides of the fulcrum—as in a crowbar or seesaw. In the second (center), the load is between effort and fulcrum—as in a wheelbarrow. In the third (bottom), the effort is between load and fulcrum. The forearm is an example; the elbow joint is the fulcrum and the effort is exerted by the biceps muscle that pulls on the bones of the forearm to raise a load in the hand.*

livel, from Old French *livel,* from Vulgar Latin *libellum* (unattested), variant of Latin *lībella,* level, water level, plummet line, diminutive of *lībra,* "a pound," balance, level.] **—lev•el•ly** *adv.* **—lev•el•ness** *n.*
Synonyms: *even, flat, flush, plane, smooth.*

level crossing *n. British.* A **grade crossing** *(see).*

lev•el•er, lev•el•ler (lĕv′ə-lər) *n.* **1.** One that levels. **2.** One who advocates the abolition of social inequalities.

lev•el•head•ed (lĕv′əl-hĕd′ĭd) *adj.* Characteristically self-composed; sensible; calm. **—lev•el•head•ed•ly** *adv.* **—lev•el•head•ed•ness** *n.*

leveling rod *n.* A graduated pole or stick with a movable marker, used with a surveyor's level to measure differences in elevation. Also called "leveling pole," "leveling staff."

Lev•el•ler (lĕv′ə-lər) *n.* A member of an English radical political movement active in the 1640's that advocated universal male suffrage, parliamentary democracy, and religious tolerance.

level of significance *n.* The probability of a false rejection of the null hypothesis in a statistical test.

le•ver (lĕv′ər, lē′vər) *n.* **1.** A simple **machine** *(see)* consisting of a rigid body, typically a metal bar, pivoted on a fixed fulcrum. **2.** A projecting handle used to adjust or operate a mechanism. **3.** A means of advancement or accomplishment.
~v. **levered, -vering, -vers.** *—tr.* To move or lift with a lever. *—intr.* To use a lever. [Middle English *lever, levour,* from Old French *levier, leveor,* from *lever,* to raise, from Latin *levāre,* from *levis,* light.]

le•ver•age (lĕv′ər-ĭj, lē′vər-) *n.* **1.** The action of a lever. **2.** The mechanical advantage of a lever. **3.** Positional advantage; power to act effectively; influence.

lev•er•et (lĕv′ər-ĭt) *n.* A young hare, especially one less than a year old. [Middle English, from Norman French, diminutive of *levre,* variant of Old French *lievre,* hare, from Latin *lepus* (stem *lepor-*).]

Le•ver•rier (lə-vĕ-ryā′), **Urbain Jean Joseph** (1811–77). French astronomer. He discovered the planet Neptune in 1846, independently of its discovery by the English astronomer, J.C. Adams.

Lé•vesque (lə-vĕk′), **René** (1922–). Canadian politician. In 1967 he cofounded the Parti Québecois, a French-Canadian separatist party. He became premier of Quebec in 1976.

Le•vi[1] (lē′vī′). A son of Jacob and Leah. Genesis 29:34.

Levi[2] *n.* A tribe of Israel descended from Levi.

lev•i•a•ble (lĕv′ē-ə-bəl) *adj.* **1.** Liable to be levied, as a tax is. **2.** Liable to be taxed or to have a levy imposed, as imports might be.

le•vi•a•than (lə-vī′ə-thən) *n.* **1.** A monstrous sea creature mentioned in the Old Testament. Job 41:1. **2.** Any very large animal. **3.** Anything unusually large for its kind. [Middle English, from Late Latin, from Hebrew *libhyāthān.*]

lev•i•gate (lĕv′ĭ-gāt′) *tr.v.* **-gated, -gating, -gates. 1.** To make into a smooth, fine powder, as by grinding when moist. **2.** To suspend in a liquid. **3.** To make smooth; polish.
~adj. (lĕv′ĭ-gāt′, -gĭt) *Botany.* Smooth; glabrous. [Latin *lēvigāre* : *lēvis,* smooth + *agere,* to do, make.] **—lev•i•ga•tion** *n.*

lev•in (lĕv′ən) *n. Archaic.* Lightning. [Middle English *leven(e),* probably from Scandinavian; akin to Old Swedish *liughn(elder),* lightning (flash).]

lev•i•rate (lĕv′ə-rāt′, -ər-ĭt) *n.* The practice of marrying the widow of one's brother, as required by ancient Hebrew law. Compare **sororate.** [Latin *lēvir,* husband's brother.] **—lev•i•rat•ic, lev•i•rat•i•cal** *adj.*

Le•vis (lē′vīz′) *pl.n.* A trademark for snugly fitting trousers of heavy denim with rivets reinforcing points of strain.

Lé•vi-Strauss, Claude (lĕv′ē strous′) (1908–). French social anthropologist, born in Belgium. He is a leading exponent of the theory of structuralism and believes that there are similar underlying patterns of social life in all cultures, resulting from the unconscious structure of the human mind.

lev•i•tate (lĕv′ə-tāt′) *v.* **-tated, -tating, -tates.** *—intr.* To rise into the air and float, in apparent defiance of gravity. *—tr.* **1.** To cause to rise into the air and float. **2.** To support (a patient with severe burns) on an **air bed** *(see).* [From LEVITY.] **—lev•i•ta•tion** *n.* **—lev•i•ta•tor** *n.*

Le•vite (lē′vīt′) *n.* A member of the tribe of Levi, the men of which were assistants to the Temple priests.

Le•vit•i•cal (lə-vĭt′ĭ-kəl) *adj.* Also **Le•vit•ic** (-vĭt′ĭk). **1.** Of or pertaining to the Levites. **2.** Of or pertaining to Leviticus.

Le•vit•i•cus (lə-vĭt′ĭ-kəs) *n. Abbr.* **Lev.** The third book of the Old Testament, containing the Hebrew ceremonial laws.

lev•i•ty (lĕv′ə-tē) *n., pl.* **-ties. 1.** Lightness of speech or manner, especially when inappropriate; frivolity. **2.** Changeableness; inconstancy. **3.** *Archaic.* Lack of weight; lightness; buoyancy. [Latin *levitās* (stem *levitat-*), from *levis,* light.]

levo- *prefix.* Indicates: **1.** Toward the left-hand side; for example, **levorotatory. 2.** A levorotatory chemical compound; for example, **levulose.** [Latin *laevus,* left.]

le•vo•do•pa (lē′və-dō′pə) *n.* Also *rare* **lae•vo•do•pa. L-dopa** *(see).*

le•vo•ro•ta•tion (lē′vō-rō-tā′shən) *n.* A counterclockwise rotation; a rotation to the left, especially of the plane of polarized light.

le•vo•ro•ta•to•ry (lē′vō-rō′tə-tôr′ē, -tōr′ē) *adj.* Also **le•vo•ro•ta•ry** (-rō′tə-rē). **1.** In optics, turning or rotating the plane of polarization of light to the left or counterclockwise. **2.** *Chemistry.* Of or pertaining to a solution that rotates the plane of polarized light in this way. Compare **dextrorotatory.**

lev•u•lose (lĕv′yə-lōs′) *n.* A sugar, **fructose** *(see).* [LEVO- + -ULE + -OSE.]

lev•y (lĕv′ē) *v.* **-ied, -ying, -ies.** *—tr.* **1.** To impose or collect (a tax, for example). **2.** To conscript into military service. **3.** To declare, begin, or wage (a war). *—intr.* To confiscate property, especially in accordance with a legal judgment.
~n., pl. **levies. 1.** The act or process of levying. **2. a.** The money, property, or number of soldiers levied. **b.** *Usually* **levies.** The men or troops levied. [Middle English *leve(e), levie,* from Old French *levee,* a raising, from *lever,* to raise.] **—lev•i•er** *n.*

lewd (lōōd) *adj.* **lewder, lewdest. 1.** Licentious; lustful. **2.** Obscene; indecent. **3.** *Obsolete.* Wicked. [Middle English *lew(e)d,* originally, ignorant, vulgar, Old English *lǣwede†,* lay (nonclergy).] **—lewd•ly** *adv.* **—lewd•ness** *n.*

lew•is (lōō′ĭs) *n.* A dovetailed iron tenon made of several parts and designed to fit into a dovetail mortise in a large stone so that it can be lifted by a hoisting apparatus. Also called "lewisson."

Lew•is (lōō′ĭs), **Cecil Day** (1904–72). British poet and author. In *Revolution in Writing* (1935), he attempted to reconcile Marxism with the liberal artistic tradition. He also wrote detective stories under the pseudonym Nicholas Blake.

Lewis, Clive Staples (1898–1963). British author and critic. His works include the medieval study *The Allegory of Love* (1936) and the autobiographical *Surprised by Joy* (1954).

Lewis, John Llewellyn (1880–1969). U.S. labor leader. President of the United Mine Workers of America (1920–60), a founder of the Committee for Industrial Organization (1935), and president of the Congress of Industrial Organization (1936–40), he strove to unionize unorganized fields of labor and to increase the power of unions.

Lewis, Meriwether (1774–1809). U.S. explorer and soldier. With William Clark, he explored the American northwest in search of a land passage to the Pacific (1804–06). Their success strengthened the American claim to the Oregon region. After the expedition he served as governor of the Louisiana Territory (1806–09).

Lewis, (Harry) Sinclair (1855–1951). U.S. novelist. He satirized middle-class America in his 22 novels, including *Main Street* (1920), *Babbit* (1922), and *Elmer Gantry* (1927). In 1930 he became the first American to win a Nobel Prize for literature.

Lewis, (Percy) Wyndham (1884–1957). English painter and author, born in the United States. In 1914–15 he edited with Ezra Pound the organ of the vorticist movement, *Blast.* His writings include *The Apes of God* (1930) and *Self-Condemned* (1954).

Lewis acid *n. Chemistry.* A compound capable of accepting a pair of electrons from a donor to form a coordinate bond. See **acid.** [After Gilbert Newton *Lewis* (1875–1946), U.S. chemist.]

Lewis base *n. Chemistry.* A compound capable of donating a pair of electrons to an acceptor to form a coordinate bond. See **base.** [After G.N. *Lewis* (see **Lewis acid**).]

lew•is•ite (lōō′ĭ-sīt′) *n.* An oily, colorless to violet or brown liquid, $C_2H_2AsCl_3$, used to make a highly toxic military gas. [After Winford Lee *Lewis* (died 1943), American chemist.]

Lewis with Har•ris (hăr′ĭs). Largest and most northerly island in the Outer Hebrides off northwest Scotland, now part of Western Isles Region. Lewis is low-lying, Harris mountainous.

lex (lĕks) *n., pl.* **leges** (lē′jēz). A law or system of laws. [Latin *lēx.*]

lex. lexicon.

lex•eme (lĕk′sēm′) *n.* An abstract linguistic unit, posited as the smallest vocabulary unit in the semantic system of a language, consisting typically of: **1.** A word root abstracted from its inflections, such as *run-* in the group *runs, running, runner.* **2.** A set consisting of a word together with all its inflections and derivations. **3.** An idiomatic phrase that makes no sense when broken down into its components, such as *to kick the bucket* ("to die").

lex•i•cal (lĕk′sĭ-kəl) *adj.* **1.** Of or pertaining to the vocabulary, words, or morphemes of a language. **2.** Of, pertaining to, or appropriate to lexicography or a lexicon. [From LEXICON.]

lex•i•cog•ra•pher (lĕk′sĭ-kŏg′rə-fər) *n.* One who writes, compiles, or edits a dictionary.

lex•i•cog•ra•phy (lĕk′sĭ-kŏg′rə-fē) *n.* The writing or compilation of a dictionary or dictionaries. [LEXICO(N) + -GRAPHY.] **—lex•i•co•graph•ic** (lĕk′sĭ-kə-grăf′ĭk), **lex•i•co•graph•i•cal** *adj.* **—lex•i•co•graph•i•cal•ly** *adv.*

lex•i•col•o•gy (lĕk′sĭ-kŏl′ə-jē) *n.* The study of the lexical component of language. [LEXICO(N) + -LOGY.] **—lex•i•co•log•i•cal** (lĕk′-sĭ-kə-lŏj′ĭ-kəl) *adj.* **—lex•i•co•log•i•cal•ly** *adv.* **—lex•i•col•o•gist** *n.*

lex•i•con (lĕk′sĭ-kŏn′) *n. Abbr.* **lex. 1.** A dictionary, especially of an ancient language such as Latin or Hebrew. **2.** A vocabulary of terms used in or of a particular profession, subject, or style; a specialized list of terms: *the lexicon of the sports page.* **3.** *Linguistics.* The morphemes of a language. [New Latin, from Greek *lexikon (biblion),* (book) pertaining to words, from *lexis,* speech, word, phrase, from *legein,* to speak.]

lex•ig•ra•phy (lĕk-sĭg′rə-fē) *n.* A system of writing, such as that of Chinese, in which each word is represented by a single character or symbol. [Greek *lexis,* word (see **lexis**) + -GRAPHY.] **—lex•i•graph•ic** *adj.* **—lex•i•graph•i•cal•ly** *adv.*

Lex•ing•ton[1] (lĕk′sĭng-tən). A city of north-central Kentucky, in the Bluegrass Country. It is a railroad shipping point and market center for a farming, ranching, and horse-raising area.

Lexington[2]. Town in eastern Massachusetts, outside Boston. The first battle of the Revolution was fought here on April 19, 1775. There are a number of 17th-century buildings in the area.

lex•is (lĕk′sĭs) *n.* Vocabulary; the total set of words in a language. [Greek, word, from *legein,* to speak.]

ley. Variant of **lea** (meadow).

Leyden. See **Leiden.**

Ley·den jar (līd′n) *n.* An early form of capacitor, consisting of a glass jar lined inside and out with tinfoil and having a conducting rod connected to the inner foil lining and passing out of the jar through an insulated stopper. [After LEIDEN (Leyden), where it was invented (1745).]

ley farming (lē, lā) *n.* The rotation, or alternate growing, of crops and grass on arable land.

Ley·land cypress (lā′lənd) *n.* A fast-growing hybrid conifer tree, *Cupressocyparis leylandii.* [After C. J. *Leyland* (1849–1926), British botanist.]

ley lines *pl.n.* Straight lines linking hilltops, tumuli, church sites, and other traditional places of sanctity in the British Isles. They sometimes appear to correspond with prehistoric tracks. [From LEY, variant of LEA (grassland) : the lines are supposed to have demarcated ancient meadows.]

Ley·te (lā′tē, -tā). Island, one of the Visayans, in the east-central Philippines. In World War II the island was occupied by the Japanese (1942) and was later the site of the first U.S. landing (October 1944) in the campaign to recover the Philippines. In Leyte Gulf, an inlet of the Pacific between Leyte and the island of Smar, U.S. naval forces destroyed the Japanese fleet.

lf, l.f. **1.** *Printing.* lightface. **2.** low frequency.

LG, L.G. Low German.

lg., lge. large.

Lha·sa or **Las·sa** (lä′sə, läs′ə). Capital of Tibet Autonomous Region, southwest China. Formerly the center of Tibetan Buddhism, it had numerous monasteries, temples, and convents, many of which were closed or razed following the Tibetan revolt against the Chinese in 1959. Until 1904 Lhasa was closed to foreign visitors and known as the "Forbidden City."

Lhasa ap·so (äp′sō) *n.* A small dog of a Tibetan breed, having a long, straight coat. [LHASA + Tibetan *apso,* Lhasa apso.]

li (lē) *n., pl.* **li.** A traditional Chinese measure of distance, today standardized at 547 yards (500 meters). [Chinese *lĭ.*]

Li The symbol for the element lithium.

li·a·bil·i·ty (lī′ə-bĭl′ə-tē) *n., pl.* **-ties. 1.** Something for which one is liable; an obligation or debt. **2. liabilities.** The financial obligations entered in the balance sheet of a business enterprise. Compare **assets. 3.** A hindrance; a handicap. **4.** Likelihood.

li·a·ble (lī′ə-bəl) *adj.* **1.** Legally obliged; responsible. Used with *for: liable for military service.* **2.** Susceptible; subject. Used with *to: liable to fainting spells.* **3.** Likely; apt. Used with an infinitive: *You're liable to get hurt if you fall for her.* —See Synonyms at **responsible.** [Middle English, perhaps from Norman French *liable* (unattested), from Old French *lier,* to bind, from Latin *ligāre.*]

li·aise (lē-āz′) *intr.v.* **-aised, -aising, -aises.** To contact and communicate, often on a regular or official basis; effect a liaison. Often used with *with* or *between.* [Back-formation from LIAISON.]

li·ai·son (lē′ā-zŏn′, lē-ā′zŏn′, lē′ə-; *French* lyĕ-zôN′) *n., pl.* **-sons. 1.** An instance or means of communication between bodies, groups, or units. **2. a.** A close relationship. **b.** A sexual relationship. **3.** The pronunciation of the usually silent final consonant of a word when followed by a word beginning with a vowel. **4.** In cookery, a thickening agent, such as egg yolks or cream, for sauces, soups, or the like. [French *liaison,* "binding," from Old French, from *lier,* to bind.]

li·an·a (lē-ăn′ə, -ä′nə) *n.* Also **li·ane** (-än′). Any of various high-climbing, usually woody vines common in the tropics. [French *liane,* perhaps from Latin *ligāre,* to bind.]

li·ang (lē-äng′) *n., pl.* **liang** or **liangs.** A former Chinese unit of weight, equivalent to ¹⁄₁₆ of the catty, approximately 1¹⁄₃ ounces. [Mandarin Chinese *liang³.*]

Liao·ning (lyou′nǐng′). Province of northeastern China, on the Bo Hai. The province is rich in coal, iron ore, and other minerals and is highly industrialized. The major crop is soybeans. Its capital is Shenyang.

li·ar (lī′ər) *n.* One who tells lies.

li·as (lī′əs) *n.* **1.** A pale gray, clayey limestone, usually found with clays and shales, particularly in southwest England. Also used adjectively: *lias limestone.* **2. Lias.** The earliest series of rocks formed in the Jurassic period, consisting of beds of sandstone, clay, lias limestone, and shale, and often containing ammonite fossils. [Middle English, from Old French *liois,* a kind of limestone, probably from Germanic.] —**li·as, li·as·sic** *adj.*

lib (lĭb) *n. Informal.* Liberation. Often used as an abbreviation in titles such as *animal lib* or *women's lib.*

lib. 1. liberal. **2.** librarian; library.

Lib. Liberal.

li·ba·tion (lī-bā′shən) *n.* **1. a.** The pouring of a liquid offering as a religious ritual. **b.** The liquid poured. **2.** *Informal.* An intoxicating drink. [Middle English *libacioun,* from Latin *lībātiō* (stem *lībātiōn-*), from *lībāre,* to taste, pour out as an offering.]

lib·ber (lĭb′ər) *n. Informal.* A proponent of liberation: *a women's libber.* [From LIB.]

Lib·by (lĭb′ē), **Willard Frank** (1908–80). U.S. chemist. He developed the method of radiocarbon dating. Libby won the Albert Einstein Award (1959) and the Nobel Prize in chemistry (1960).

li·bec·ci·o (lē-běch′ē-ō′; *Italian* lē-bět′chō) *n.* A southwest wind in Italy. [Italian, from Latin *Libs,* the southwest wind, from Greek *Lips†* (stem *lib-*).]

li·bel (lī′bəl) *n. Law.* **a.** Any written, printed, or pictorial statement that damages a person by defaming his character or reputation. **b.** The act of presenting such a statement to the public.

Compare **slander. 2.** Any slighting statement. **3.** The written claims presented by a plaintiff to an ecclesiastical court. ~*tr.v.* **libeled** or **libelled, -beling** or **-belling, -bels. 1.** To make or publish a defamatory statement about. **2.** To speak slightingly of. **3.** To make a claim or bring an action against in an ecclesiastical court. —See Synonyms at **malign.** [Middle English, formal written claim of a plaintiff, from Old French *libel,* from Latin *libellus,* a little book, diminutive of *liber,* book.] —**li·bel·ist, li·bel·er** *n.*

li·bel·ant, li·bel·lant (lī′bə-lənt) *n.* The plaintiff in a case of ecclesiastical libel.

li·bel·ee, li·bel·lee (lī′bə-lē′) *n.* The defendant in a case of ecclesiastical or admiralty libel.

li·bel·ous, li·bel·lous (lī′bə-ləs) *adj.* Containing or constituting a libel; defamatory. —**li·bel·ous·ly** *adv.*

Lib·er·a·ce (lĭb′ə-rä′chē), **(Wladziu)** (1919–) U.S. pianist and entertainer. He has performed around the globe, captivating audiences with his virtuosity and amusing them with his flamboyant costumes and style.

lib·er·al (lĭb′ər-əl, lĭb′rəl) *adj. Abbr.* **lib. 1.** Having, expressing, or following social or political views or policies that favor nonrevolutionary progress and reform. **2. a.** Having, expressing, or following views or policies that favor the freedom of individuals to act or express themselves in a manner of their own choosing. **b.** Having, expressing, or following a belief in laissez-faire economic policies. **3. Liberal.** *Abbr.* **Lib.** Of, designating, or belonging to a Liberal political party. **4.** Of, pertaining to, or designating a wide cultural education, as opposed to a technical or specialized one. **5.** Tolerant of the ideas or behavior of others. **6. a.** Tending to give freely; generous: *a liberal benefactor.* **b.** Generously given; bountiful: *a liberal helping.* **7.** Not strict or literal: *a liberal translation.* ~*n.* **1.** A person with liberal ideas or opinions. **2. Liberal.** *Abbr.* **Lib.** A member of a Liberal political party. [Middle English, from Old French, from Latin *līberālis,* of freedom, from *līber,* free.] —**lib·er·al·ly** *adv.* —**lib·er·al·ness** *n.*

liberal arts *pl.n.* Academic disciplines, such as languages, history, philosophy, and pure science, that provide information of general cultural concern, as distinguished from narrow practical training.

lib·er·al·ism (lĭb′ər-ə-lĭz′əm, lĭb′rə-) *n.* Liberal views and policies, especially with regard to social or political questions.

lib·er·al·i·ty (lĭb′ə-răl′ə-tē) *n., pl.* **-ties. 1.** The quality or state of being liberal. **2.** A generous gift.

lib·er·al·ize (lĭb′ər-ə-līz′, lĭb′rə-) *v.* **-ized, -izing, -izes.** —*tr.* To make liberal or more liberal. —*intr.* To become liberal or more liberal. —**lib·er·al·i·za·tion** *n.*

Liberal Party *n.* A political party advocating liberalism; especially, a party formed in Great Britain in the 19th century.

liberal studies *n. Usually used with a singular verb.* An arts course consisting of literature, social studies, and the like, taken by students undergoing further education whose main courses are usually technical, professional, or scientific.

lib·er·ate (lĭb′ə-rāt′) *tr.v.* **-ated, -ating, -ates. 1.** To free, as from oppression, repression, bondage, or foreign control. **2.** *Chemistry.* To release from combination. Used especially of gases. **3.** *Slang.* To obtain by looting; steal. In this sense, used ironically. [Latin *līberāre,* from *līber,* free.] —**lib·er·a·tion** *n.* —**lib·er·a·tion·ist** *n.* —**lib·er·a·tor** *n.*

liberation theology *n.* A school of theology, especially prevalent in the Catholic Church in Latin America, seeing in the Gospel a call to liberate people from political and material oppression.

Li·be·ri·a (lī-bîr′ē-ə). Africa's oldest independent republic, founded as a home for freed U.S. slaves early in the 19th century. Most Liberians are subsistence farmers, although the country exports iron ore, rubber, rice, coffee, and sugar. Area, 111,369 square kilometers (43,000 square miles). Population, 1,900,000. Capital, Monrovia. See map at **West African States.** —**Li·be·ri·an** *n. & adj.*

lib·er·tar·i·an (lĭb′ər-târ′ē-ən) *n.* **1.** One who believes in freedom, especially individual freedom, of action and thought. **2.** One who believes in free will as opposed to determinism. [From LIBERTY.] —**lib·er·tar·i·an** *adj.* —**lib·er·tar·i·an·ism** *n.*

lib·er·tine (lĭb′ər-tēn′) *n.* **1.** One who acts without moral or sexual restraint; a dissolute person. **2.** One standing in defiance of established moral precepts. ~*adj.* Morally or sexually unrestrained. [Middle English *libertyn* (only in the sense "freed slave"), from Latin *lībertīnus,* from *lībertus,* set free, from *līber,* free.]

lib·er·tin·ism (lĭb′ər-tē-nĭz′əm) *n.* Also **lib·er·tin·age** (-tē′nĭj). **1.** Sexual promiscuity. **2.** *Rare.* Freedom of thought.

lib·er·ty (lĭb′ər-tē) *n., pl.* **-ties. 1. a.** The condition of being not subject to restriction or control. **b.** The right to act in a manner of one's own choosing. **2.** The state of not being in confinement or servitude. **3.** Permission or right to do a specific thing; a privilege. **4.** *Often* **liberties.** A social action regarded as more familiar than polite convention permits: *Is it a liberty to address you by your first name?* **b.** A statement, attitude, or action not warranted by conditions or actualities: *a historical novel that takes liberties with chronology.* **5.** Authorized leave from naval duty. —**at liberty. 1.** Not in confinement or under constraint; free. **2.** Not occupied or in use. [Middle English *liberte,* from Old French, from Latin *lībertās* (stem *lībertāt-*), from *līber,* free.]

liberty cap *n.* **1.** A brimless cap that fits snugly around the head and has a soft conical crown. Compare **Phrygian cap. 2.** A **magic mushroom** *(see).* [Adopted as a symbol of liberty during the

French Revolution. In ancient Rome such caps were presented to slaves when they were freed.]

liberty hall *n. Informal.* **1.** A place in which one can behave as one likes. **2.** A state of absolute freedom.

Liberty Island. Island, *c.* 4 hectares (10 acres), in Upper New York Bay, southwest of Manhattan. The Statue of Liberty was placed on the island in 1885–86, using the star-shaped Fort Wood (built in 1841 as a harbor defense) as a base. Formerly called Bedloe's Island, the island was renamed by Congress in 1956.

Liberty Ship *n.* A large American cargo ship of a type produced in large numbers during World War II.

li·bid·i·nous (li-bĭd′n-əs) *adj.* Characterized by or having lustful desires; licentious; lascivious. [Middle English *lybydynous,* from Latin *libīdinōsus,* from *libīdō,* desire, LIBIDO.]

li·bi·do (li-bē′dō, -bī′dō) *n., pl.* **-dos. 1.** The psychic and emotional energy associated with instinctual biological drives. **2. a.** Sexual desire. **b.** Manifestation of the sexual drive. [Latin *libīdō,* desire, lust.] **—li·bid·i·nal** (li-bĭd′n-əl) *adj.*

Li Bo. See **Li Po.**

li·bra (li′brə *for sense 1;* lē′brä *for sense 2*) *n., pl.* **-brae** (-brē′) (for sense 1) *or* **-bras** (-bräs) (for sense 2). **1.** A unit of weight in ancient Rome corresponding to a pound and equivalent to approximately 12 ounces. **2.** A former gold coin of Peru. [Latin *lībra,* "pound," balance.]

Li·bra (li′brə, lē′-) *n.* **1.** A constellation in the Southern Hemisphere near Scorpius and Virgo. **2. a.** The seventh sign of the **zodiac** (*see*). Also called the "Balance," the "Scales." **b.** One born under this sign. [New Latin, from Latin *lībra,* "pound," balance. See **libra.**] **—Li·bran** *n. & adj.*

li·brar·i·an (li-brâr′ē-ən) *n. Abbr.* **lib. 1.** A person in charge of a library. **2.** One trained or employed in library administration. **—li·brar·i·an·ship** *n.*

li·brar·y (li′brĕr′ē) *n., pl.* **-ies.** *Abbr.* **lib. 1.** A repository for literary and artistic materials, such as books, periodicals, newspapers, pamphlets, and prints, kept for reading or reference. **2.** A collection of such material, especially when systematically arranged for reference or borrowing. **3. a.** An institution or foundation maintaining such a collection. **b.** A room in a private home set aside to house such a collection. **4.** A series or set of books issued by a publisher. **5.** A collection of standard computer programs. [Middle English *librarie,* from Old French *librairie,* from Vulgar Latin *librāriā* (unattested), alteration of Latin *librāria (taberna),* book (shop), from *liber†,* book.]

library edition *n.* A special edition of a book, usually large, strongly bound, and of superior quality.

Library of Congress classification *n.* A system of classification of books and other publications using a notation of letters of the alphabet and numbers. Compare **Dewey decimal system.** [After the *Library of Congress,* the national library of the United States in Washington, D.C., founded in 1800.]

library science *n.* The principles, practice, or study of library administration and care.

library tape *n.* **1.** A magnetic tape stored separately from the computer from which it was generated. **2.** A magnetic tape containing a listing of library tapes.

li·brate (li′brāt′) *intr.v.* **-brated, -brating, -brates. 1.** To oscillate; undergo libration. **2.** To balance; hover. [Latin *librāre* (past participle *librātus*), from *libra,* balance.] **—li·bra·to·ry** (li′brə-tôr′ē, -tōr′ē) *adj.*

li·bra·tion (li-brā′shən) *n.* A real or apparent very slow oscillation of a satellite as viewed from its parent celestial body.

li·bret·tist (li-brĕt′ĭst) *n.* The author of a libretto.

li·bret·to (li-brĕt′ō) *n., pl.* **-tos** *or* **-bretti** (-brĕt′ē). The text of an opera or other dramatic musical work. [Italian, diminutive of *libro,* book, from Latin *liber* †.]

Li·bre·ville (lē′brə-vēl′). Capital and chief port of Gabon, lying on the Gabon River estuary. It was founded as a French trading post and renamed Libreville (1848) after freed slaves were settled here.

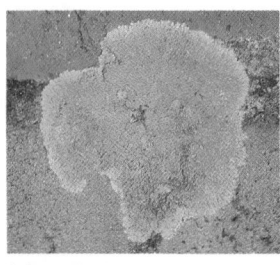

lichen *The lichens—symbiotic plants formed by a partnership between fungi and algae—can survive and flourish in almost any climate. Some thrive even under snow, providing an important food source for animals such as reindeer.*

Lib·y·a (lĭb′ē-ə). Republic in North Africa, the first independent state created by the United Nations (1951). Oil discoveries brought great prosperity in the 1970's, and the nationalized oil industry remains the basis of the economy. In 1969 King Idris I was deposed by Col. Muammar el-Qaddafi, and the country has since been run as an Islamic state. Area, 1,759,540 square kilometers (679,362 square miles). Population, 2,900,000. Capital, Tripoli.

Lib·y·an (lĭb′ē-ən) *adj.* Of or pertaining to Libya, its people, or their language.
~*n.* **1.** A native or resident of Libya. **2.** The extinct Hamitic language used in ancient Libya.

lice. Plural of **louse.**

li·cense (li′səns) *n.* Also *Chiefly British* **li·cence. 1.** Official or legal permission to do or own a specified thing. **2.** Proof of permission granted, usually in the form of a document, card, or plate: *a driver's license.* Compare **certificate. 3.** Deviation from normal rules, practices, or methods in order to achieve a certain end or effect: *artistic license.* **4.** An instance of such deviation. **5.** Freedom from strict rules, especially concerning behavior or speech. **6.** Excessive or undisciplined freedom constituting an abuse of a privilege. **7.** Lust; licentiousness.
~*tr.v.* **licensed, -censing, -censes. 1.** To give or yield permission to or for. **2.** To grant a license to or for; authorize. **3.** To obtain a license for: *Have you licensed the car yet?* [Middle English *licence,* from Old French *licence,* from Latin *licentia,* freedom, from *licēre,* to be lawful, be permitted. See **leisure.**] **—li·cens·a·ble** *adj.* **—li·cen·ser, li·cen·sor** *n.*

licensed practical nurse *n. Abbr.* **LPN, L.P.N.** A nurse who has completed a practical nursing program and who is licensed by a state to provide routine patient care under the direction of a registered nurse or a physician.

licensed premises *pl.n. British.* A place, such as a public house or hotel, licensed to sell alcohol to be consumed there. Compare **off-license.**

licensed vocational nurse *n. Abbr.* **LVN, L.V.N.** A licensed practical nurse who is permitted to practice in California or Texas.

li·cen·see (li′sən-sē′) *n.* One to whom a license is granted; especially, one licensed to sell beer and spirits.

li·cen·ti·ate (li-sĕn′shē-ĭt, -āt′) *n.* **1. a.** A person who is granted a license by an authorized body to practice a specific profession. **b.** A person licensed to preach, especially in the Presbyterian Church. **2.** *Abbr.* **L. a.** A degree from certain European universities ranking below that of a doctorate. **b.** One holding such a degree. [Medieval Latin *licentiātus,* from *licentiāre,* to allow, from Latin *licentia,* freedom, LICENSE.]

li·cen·tious (li-sĕn′shəs) *adj.* **1.** Lacking moral discipline or sexual restraint. **2.** Having no regard for accepted rules or standards. [Latin *licentiōsus,* from *licentia,* freedom, dissoluteness, LICENSE.] **—li·cen·tious·ly** *adv.* **—li·cen·tious·ness** *n.*

lichee. Variant of **litchi.**

li·chen (li′kən) *n.* **1.** Any of numerous plants consisting of a fungus, usually of the class Ascomycetes, in close combination with certain algae, characteristically forming a crustlike, scaly, or branching growth on rocks or tree trunks. **2.** *Pathology.* Any of various skin eruptions occurring typically in lichenlike patches.
~*tr.v.* **lichened, -chening, -chens.** To cover with lichen or lichens. [Latin *līchēn,* from Greek *leikhēn,* "licker," from *leikhein,* to lick.] **—li·chen·ose, li·chen·ous** *adj.*

li·chen·in (li′kə-nĭn) *n.* A white, starchlike, gelatinous compound, $C_6H_{10}O_5$, obtained from a lichen, Iceland moss. [LICHEN + -IN.]

li·chen·ol·o·gy (li′kə-nŏl′ə-jē) *n.* The botanical study of lichens. **—li·chen·ol·o·gist** *n.*

lich gate, lych gate (lĭch) *n.* A roofed gateway to a churchyard used originally to rest biers before burial. [Middle English *lycheyate* : *lich,* body, corpse, Old English *līc* + *gate, yate,* GATE.]

Lich·ten·stein (lĭk′tən-stīn′), **Roy** (1923–). U.S. painter and sculptor. He is a leading exponent of pop art.

lic·it (lĭs′ĭt) *adj.* Within the law; legal. [Middle English, from Latin *licitus,* from the past participle of *licēre,* to be permitted. See **leisure.**] **—lic·it·ly** *adv.* **—lic·it·ness** *n.*

lick (lĭk) *v.* **licked, licking, licks.** *—tr.* **1.** To pass the tongue over or along. **2.** To lap up. **3.** To move or flicker over like a tongue: *The waves licked the rocks lining the shore.* **4.** *Informal.* To thrash; whip. **5.** *Informal.* To get the better of; defeat. *—intr.* To pass over something with or as if with the tongue: *The flames licked at our feet.* **—lick into shape.** To bring into satisfactory condition or appearance. **—lick one's chops.** To anticipate delightedly. **—lick one's wounds.** To recuperate after a defeat.
~*n.* **1.** The act or process of licking. **2.** A small quantity; a bit: *a lick of paint.* **3.** A place frequented by animals that lick the exposed natural salt deposits. **4.** *Informal.* A blow. **5.** *Informal.* Speed; pace: *at a good lick.* **—lick and a promise.** A superficial effort made without care or enthusiasm. [Middle English *licken,* Old English *liccian.*] **—lick·er** *n.*

lick·er·ish, li·quor·ish (lĭk′ər-ĭsh) *adj. Archaic.* **1.** Lascivious; lecherous. **2.** Relishing pleasurable sensations. **3.** Greedy. **4.** Arousing hunger; appetizing. [Alteration of Middle English *lickerous,* from Norman French *likerous* (unattested), variant of Old French *lecheres,* from *lecheor,* LECHER.]

lick·e·ty-split (lĭk′ə-tē-splĭt′) *adv. Informal.* With great speed. [From LICK and SPLIT.]

lick·ing (lĭk′ĭng) *n. Informal.* **1.** A beating or spanking. **2.** A resounding defeat.

LIBYA

MALTA   20° E

TUNISIA   MEDITERRANEAN SEA

TRIPOLI
Al Azīzīyah   •Homs (Al Khums)
Jabal •Gharyan   •Misratah   Benghazi
Nafusah   Gulf of Sirte   Jabal al Akhdar

30° N

TRIPOLITANIA

CYRENAICA   EGYPT

ALGERIA   L I B Y A   LIBYAN DESERT

Sabhah

FEZZAN   S A H A R A

Al Kufrah

Tropic of Cancer

CHAD

NIGER   20° N
0   400   800 Km
0   200   400 Miles

lick·spit·tle (lĭk'spĭt'l) n. A fawning underling; a toady. —**lick·spit·tle** adj.

lic·o·rice (lĭk'ər-ĭs, -ĭsh) n. Also chiefly British **li·quo·rice**. 1. A plant, Glycyrrhiza glabra, of the Mediterranean region, having blue flowers and a sweet, distinctively flavored root. 2. The root of this plant, used as a flavoring in candy, drinks, tobacco, and medicines. 3. A candy made from or flavored with this root. 4. Any of various plants resembling or tasting like licorice, especially the wild licorice, Astragalus glycyphyllos. [Middle English licoris, licorice, from Norman French lycorys and Old French licoresse, licorece, from Late Latin liquirītia, alteration (influenced by Latin liquor, LIQUOR) of Greek glukurrhiza, "sweetroot" : glukus, sweet + rhiza, root.]

lic·tor (lĭk'tər) n. A Roman functionary who carried fasces in attendance on a magistrate. [Middle English littour, from Latin lictor.]

lid (lĭd) n. 1. A removable or sometimes hinged cover for any hollow receptacle. 2. An eyelid. 3. Biology. A flaplike covering, such as an operculum. 4. A curb or restraint: put the lid on crime. 5. Slang. A hat. —**flip one's lid**. Slang. To lose one's composure. [Middle English, Old English hlid, covering, gate, opening.] —**lid·ded** adj.

li·dar (lī'där) n. A type of radar using a directional laser or maser beam. [Light + radar.]

Li·di·ce (lĭd'ə-sē, -ät-sē'). Mining village west of Prague, Czechoslovakia, destroyed in 1942 by the German army in retaliation for the assassination of Nazi chief Reinhard Heydrich (1904–42). The men were killed and the women and children deported. After the war a new village was built, the old site maintained as a memorial.

lid·less (lĭd'lĭs) adj. 1. Having no lid. 2. Having no eyelids. Said of animals. 3. Archaic. Sleepless; watchful.

li·do (lē'dō) n., pl. **-dos**. 1. An open-air swimming pool for public use, often providing other recreational facilities. 2. A bathing beach. [Italian, beach of sand or silt separated from the mainland by a lagoon, such as the LIDO, from Latin litus, shore.]

Li·do (lē'dō). A long, narrow, sandy island in northeastern Italy, separating the Venetian lagoon from the Adriatic Sea. It is a fashionable beach resort.

li·do·caine (lī'də-kān') n. A local anesthetic administered by injection or direct application for dental and minor surgical operations. [From acetanilide + (CO)CAINE.]

lie¹ (lī) intr.v. **lay** (lā), **lain** (lān), **lying**, **lies**. 1. To be in or place oneself in a prostrate or recumbent position; rest; recline. Often used with down. 2. a. To be placed on or supported by a surface that is usually horizontal. b. To float at anchor. Used of a ship. 3. To be or remain in a specified condition: The conflict lies dormant. 4. To exist; be inherent: Her good nature lies within her. 5. To be located: The spring lies several miles beyond this village. 6. To be buried or entombed. 7. To extend: Our land lies between these trees and the river. 8. Archaic. To stay for a night or short while: The regiment is lying not far from here. 9. To remain on the ground. Used of game birds. 10. Law. To be admissible or maintainable. —See Usage note at lay. —**lie down**. To remain impassive in the face of provocation: She won't take those insults lying down. —**lie low**. To keep oneself or one's plans hidden. —**lie off**. Nautical. To anchor away from the shore or from another ship. —**lie over**. To remain and wait until a future time. —**lie to**. Nautical. To remain stationary while facing the wind. —**lie with**. 1. To be decided by, dependent upon, or up to: The choice lies with you. 2. Archaic. To have sexual intercourse with. ~n. 1. The manner or position in which something is situated. 2. A lair or hiding place of an animal. 3. Golf. The position of a ball that has come to a stop. [Lie, lay, lain; Middle English lien or lig(g)en, lay, lie(y)en, Old English licgan, læg, legen.]

lie² n. 1. A false statement or piece of information deliberately presented as being true; a falsehood. 2. Anything meant to deceive or give a wrong impression. —**give the lie to**. 1. To prove to be untrue; belie. 2. To accuse of lying; contradict. ~v. **lied**, **lying**, **lies**. —intr. 1. To present false information with the intention of deceiving. 2. To convey a false image or impression: Appearances often lie. —tr. To put in a specific condition through deceit: lied themselves into trouble. [Middle English ligen, lien, Old English lēogan.]

Lie (lē), **Trygve Halvdan** (1896–1968). Norwegian politician and first secretary-general of the United Nations (1946–53).

Lieb·frau·milch (lēp'frou-mĭlKH') n. German. A white wine from the Rhine region. [German : Liebfrau, the Virgin Mary (to whom the convent where the wine was first produced was dedicated) + Milch, milk.]

Lie·big (lē'bĭk), **Justus, Baron von** (1803–73). German chemist. He discovered chloral and later revealed the importance in plant growth of atmospheric nitrogen and carbon dioxide and of soil minerals.

Liebig condenser n. Chemistry. A simple laboratory condenser, usually of glass, having a straight central tube surrounded by a jacket through which cold water is passed. [After Justus von LIEBIG.]

Lieb·knecht (lēp'knĕkt'), **Karl** (1871–1919). German politician. Expelled from the Social Democratic Party in 1916, he engaged in illegal antiwar activity with Rosa Luxemburg in the Spartacusbund, which later became the German Communist Party. In 1919 he led an unsuccessful uprising and was murdered and arrested by army officers.

Liech·ten·stein (lĭkH'tən-shtīn'). Small, landlocked Alpine principality in central Europe. It has a currency and customs union with neighboring Switzerland, which looks after its defense and foreign affairs. Area, 157 square kilometers (61 square miles). Population, 25,000. Capital, Vaduz.

lied (lēd; German lēt) n., pl. **lieder** (lē'dər). A German song in the style of a ballad for solo voice and piano. [German Lied, song, from Old High German liod.]

Lie·der·kranz (lē'dər-kränts', -kränts') n. A trademark for a soft cheese resembling a mild Limburger. [German, "song collection."]

lie detector n. A polygraph (see) used to detect lying in a person undergoing interrogation.

lief (lēf) adv. Archaic. Readily; willingly: as lief go now as later. ~adj. Archaic. 1. Beloved; dear. 2. Ready or willing. [Middle English le(e)f, lif, from le(e)f, "beloved," Old English lēof.]

liege (lēj) n. 1. A lord or sovereign in feudal law. 2. A vassal or subject owing allegiance and services to a lord or sovereign under feudal law. ~adj. 1. Of, pertaining to, or designating the relationship between a vassal or subject and his lord. 2. Entitled to the loyalty and services of his vassals or subjects. Said of a feudal lord. 3. Bound to give such allegiance and services to a lord or monarch. Said of a feudal vassal or subject. 4. Loyal. [Middle English li(e)ge, lege, from Old French li(e)ge, from Medieval Latin lēticus, laeticus, from lētus, lītus, serf, from Germanic.]

Li·ège (lē-ĕzh'). Flemish **Luik** (loik). City on the Meuse River, Belgium. It is a center of the country's steel, engineering, and arms industries.

liege·man (lēj'mən) n., pl. **-men** (-mĭn). 1. A feudal vassal or subject. 2. A loyal supporter or follower.

lie in intr.v. Archaic. To be in confinement for childbirth.

lien (lēn, lē'ən) n. Law. The right to take and hold or sell the property of a debtor as security or payment for a debt. [Old French l(o)ien, bond, tie, from Latin ligāmen, from ligāre, to bind.]

li·e·nal (lī-ē'nəl) adj. Of or pertaining to the spleen. [Latin liēn, spleen.]

li·en·ter·y (lī'ən-tĕr'ē) n. Diarrhea in which the feces contain undigested food. [French, lientérie, from Greek leienteria : leios, smooth + entera, intestine.]

li·erne (lē-ûrn') n. Architecture. A reinforcing rib used in Gothic vaulting to connect the intersections and bosses of the primary ribs. [French, from Old French, from lier, to bind, from Latin ligāre.]

lieu (lōō) n. Place; stead. Used chiefly in the phrase in lieu of. [Middle English liue, from Old French lieu, from Latin locus, place, LOCUS.]

lieu·ten·ant (lōō-tĕn'ənt; British lĕf-tĕn'ənt) n. Abbr. **Lieut., Lt.** Military. 1. One of two ranks held by commissioned officers: a. A second lieutenant, the lowest-ranking commissioned officer. b. A first lieutenant, an officer ranking above a second lieutenant and below a captain. 2. U.S. Navy. One of two ranks held by commissioned officers: a. A lieutenant junior grade, ranking between a lieutenant senior grade and an ensign. b. A lieutenant senior grade, ranking between a lieutenant commander and a lieutenant junior grade. 3. British & Canadian Navy. A commissioned officer ranking between a lieutenant commander and a sublieutenant, equivalent in rank to a captain in the army. 4. One who is second in command to and sometimes acts in place of a superior; a deputy. [Originally, "officer who acts for a superior," from Middle English lieutenaunt, vice regent, from Old French lieutenant : lieu, LIEU + tenant, present participle of tenir, to hold; from Vulgar Latin tenīre (unattested), from Latin tenēre.] —**lieu·ten·an·cy** n.

lieutenant colonel n. Abbr. **Lt. Col.** Military. A commissioned officer ranking between a colonel and a major.

lieutenant commander n. Abbr. **Lt. Comdr.** A commissioned naval officer ranking between a commander and a lieutenant.

lieutenant general n. Abbr. **Lt. Gen.** A commissioned army officer ranking between a general and a major general.

lieutenant governor n. Abbr. **Lt. Gov.** 1. An elected state official ranking just below the governor. 2. The appointed head of government of a Canadian province.

Li·far (lē-fär', lē'fär), **Serge** (1905–). Russian dancer and choreographer. After moving to France to further his dance studies, he became premier danseur and ballet master of the Paris Opéra Ballet (1929), a position he used to advance his theories of choreography and to stage ballets such as Promethée (1929) and Phèdre (1950).

life (līf) n., pl. **lives** (līvz). 1. The property or quality manifested in functions such as metabolism, growth, response to stimulation, and reproduction, by which living organisms are distinguished from dead organisms or from inanimate matter. 2. The characteristic state or condition of a living organism. 3. Living organisms collectively: plant life. 4. A living being, especially a person, contrasted with one no longer alive: lives lost in battle. 5. The interval between the birth or inception of an organism and its death. 6. a. The remainder of one's life: paralyzed for life. Also used adjectively: a life sentence. b. Slang. A sentence of life imprisonment. 7. The period of one's life that has already passed: She has suffered from rheumatism all her life. 8. The interval or amount of time during which anything exists or functions: the operating life of a machine. 9. a. A spiritual state regarded as a transcending of death. b. Salvation. 10. An account of a person's life; a biography: lives of the saints. 11. a. Human activities, relationships, and interests collectively: everyday life. b. A career; prospects: made a new life for herself in Australia. c. A mode of activity or existence: country life. 12. A pleasant, easy, or luxurious manner of existence: That's the life. 13. An animating force; a source of vitality. 14. Animation, spirit,

Life Guards *One of the two mounted regiments in the Household Division —the section of the British Army that forms the monarch's personal bodyguard. The Life Guards are seen here parading near Buckingham Palace in London.*

or liveliness: *full of life.* **15.** Strength or freshness of flavor. **16.** In fine arts: **a.** A living person or model regarded as an artistic subject: *painted from life.* Also used adjectivally: *life drawing.* **b.** Actual environment or reality; nature. **17. Life.** *Christian Science.* God. **—as big** (or **large**) **as life. 1.** Life-size. **2.** *Informal.* Physically real; living; vital. **—bring to life. 1.** To cause to regain consciousness. **2.** To put spirit into; animate. **3.** To make lifelike. **—come to life. 1.** To regain consciousness. **2.** To become or seem to become animated; grow lively or lifelike. **—for dear life.** Desperately or urgently. **—for life. 1.** Until the end of one's life. **2.** So as to save one's life. **—for the life of one.** *Informal.* Though trying hard. Used with negative expressions: *For the life of me I couldn't remember her name.* **—not on your life.** *Informal.* Not for any reason; definitely not. **—take someone's life.** To kill. **—the good life.** An affluent, luxurious lifestyle. **—the life of Riley.** *Informal.* An easy or good lifestyle. **—the life of the party.** An animated or amusing person who is the center of attention at a social gathering. **—to save one's life.** No matter how hard one tries: *I can't dance to save my life.* **—to the life.** Exactly or closely resembling a model or original. **—true to life.** Not deviating from reality; faithfully representing real life. [Middle English *lif(e),* Old English *līf.*]

life belt *n.* A large ring of buoyant material designed to keep a person afloat.

life•blood (līf′blŭd′) *n.* **1.** Blood regarded as essential for life. **2.** The indispensable vital part of a thing.

life•boat (līf′bōt′) *n.* **1.** A boat carried on a ship to sustain persons abandoning the ship. **2.** A boat used for rescuing people at sea.

life buoy *n.* See **buoy** (sense 2).

life cycle *n.* **1.** The course of developmental changes through which an organism passes from its inception as a fertilized zygote to the mature state in which another zygote may be produced. **2.** A progression through a series of differing stages of development, as in insect metamorphosis.

life estate *n.* Property that a person can hold during his lifetime, but may not sell or bequeath to anyone else.

life expectancy *n.* The statistically determined number of years that an individual is expected to live.

life•guard (līf′gärd′) *n.* An expert swimmer trained and employed to safeguard swimmers or bathers. Also called "lifesaver."

Life Guards *pl.n.* A British regiment, formerly a cavalry corps and now armored in combat and forming part of the mounted section of the sovereign's personal bodyguard. **—Life Guardsman** *n.*

life history *n.* **1.** The history of changes undergone by an organism from inception or conception to death. **2.** The developmental history of an individual or group in society.

life instinct *n. Psychology.* An instinct that includes the impulses for self-preservation and reproduction.

life insurance *n.* Insurance that guarantees a specific sum of money to a beneficiary when the insured dies or to the insured if he lives beyond a certain age.

life interest *n.* Interest payable to a person during his lifetime, which lapses when he dies.

life jacket *n.* An inflatable sleeveless jacket designed to keep the wearer afloat in water.

life•less (līf′lĭs) *adj.* **1.** Having no life; inanimate. **2.** Having lost life; dead. **3.** Incapable of sustaining life; not inhabited by living beings. **4.** Lacking vitality or animation; dull; listless. —See Usage note at **dead. —life•less•ly** *adv.* **—life•less•ness** *n.*

life•like (līf′līk′) *adj.* **1.** Resembling a living thing. **2.** Accurately representing real life. **—life•like•ness** *n.*

life line *n.* **1.** An anchored line thrown as a support to someone falling or drowning. **2.** A line shot to a ship in distress either to connect it with the shore or for hauling aboard other lifesaving devices such as heavier lines or breeches buoys. **3.** A line used to raise and lower deep-sea divers. **4. a.** Any means or route by which necessary supplies are transported. **b.** Any person or thing that provides continuous or sustained support in times of difficulty or distress. **5.** A diagonal line crossing the palm of the hand and alleged to indicate the length and major events of one's life.

life•long (līf′lông′, -lŏng′) *adj.* Continuing for a lifetime.

life peer *n. British.* A peer whose title is bestowed for a lifetime only and lapses at death. **—life peerage** *n.*

life preserver *n.* **1.** A buoyant device, usually in the shape of a ring, belt, or jacket, designed to keep a person afloat in the water. **2.** *British.* A weapon, such as a club or bludgeon.

lif•er (lī′fər) *n. Slang.* A prisoner serving a life sentence.

life raft *n.* A raft usually made of wood or inflatable material and used in an emergency at sea.

life•sav•er (līf′sā′vər) *n.* **1.** One that saves a life. **2.** A **lifeguard** *(see).* **3.** One that provides help in a minor crisis or emergency. **4.** A life preserver shaped like a ring.

life•sav•ing, life-sav•ing (līf′sā′vĭng) *n.* A set of skills or techniques for rescuing and resuscitating the victims of accidents, especially victims of drowning.

∼*adj.* **1.** Of or pertaining to the techniques studied in lifesaving: *a lifesaving medal.* **2. a.** Saving life. **b.** Providing help in a minor crisis or emergency.

life science *n.* Any of the fields of science dealing with the structure and function of organisms, such as botany, zoology, biochemistry, genetics, or immunology. Compare **physical science.**

life-size (līf′sīz′) *adj.* Also **life-sized** (-sīzd′). Being of the same size as the person, animal, or thing represented.

life span *n.* The period of time during which an organism or machine remains alive or functional under normal conditions.

life•style, life-style (līf′stīl′) *n.* A way of life or style of living that reflects the attitudes and values of an individual or a culture.

life-sup•port system (līf′sə-pôrt′, -pōrt′) *n.* **1.** The equipment that provides a viable environment where this would not normally be possible, as in a spacecraft or below the sea. **2.** Hospital equipment that artificially sustains life.

life•time (līf′tīm′) *n.* **1.** The period of time during which an individual is alive. **2.** The interval or amount of time during which an object, property, process, or phenomenon exists or functions. **3.** *Physics.* The average time of existence of an unstable particle or nucleus. Also called "mean life."

∼*adj.* Continuing or lasting for such a period of time: *a lifetime guarantee.*

life•work (līf′wûrk′) *n.* Also **life's work.** The chief work or creation of one's lifetime.

lift (lĭft) *v.* **lifted, lifting, lifts.** *—tr.* **1.** To direct or carry from a lower to a higher position; raise; elevate: *lift the suitcase; lift one's eyes.* **2.** To pick up for the purpose of moving or removing: *lift the child from the playpen.* **3. a.** To take back or remove; revoke; rescind: *lift a ban.* **b.** To bring an end to (a blockade or siege) by removing forces. **c.** To cease (artillery fire) on an area. **4.** To raise in condition, rank, esteem, or value; exalt: *Her courage lifted her in their eyes.* **5.** To remove (plants) from the ground for transplanting. **6.** To project or sound in loud, clear tones: *lifted their voices in song.* **7.** *Informal.* To steal; pilfer. **8.** *Informal.* To plagiarize. **9.** To pay off or clear (a debt or mortgage, for example). **10.** To perform cosmetic surgery on (the face or breasts), especially to remove wrinkles or sag. **11.** *Golf.* **a.** To hit (the ball) very high into the air. **b.** To pick up (the ball) in the hand to put in a better position. **12.** To carry (a passenger or goods) in a vehicle. *—intr.* **1.** To rise; ascend. **2.** To disappear or disperse by or as if by rising: *The clouds had lifted.* **3.** To use force or energy in or as if in lifting something. **4.** To yield to upward force: *The window won't lift.* **5.** To stop temporarily.

∼*n.* **1.** The act or process of raising or rising to a higher position. **2.** Power or force available for raising: *the lift of a pump.* **3.** An amount or weight raised or capable of being raised at one time; a load. **4.** The extent or height to which something is raised; the amount of elevation. **5.** The distance or space through which something is raised. **6.** A rising of the level of the ground. **7.** A rising of spirits; a mood of exhilaration or happiness. **8.** A raised, high, or erect position: *the lift of her chin.* **9.** A machine or device designed to pick up, raise, or carry something. **10.** Any of the layers of leather, rubber, or other material making up the heel of a shoe. **11. a.** *Chiefly British.* See **elevator** (sense 1). **b.** An apparatus for transporting people up and down a mountain; a **chair lift** *(see).* **12.** A ride given in a vehicle to help someone reach a destination. **13.** Any kind of assistance or help. **14.** A set of pumps used in a mine. **15.** *Aeronautics.* **a.** The component of the total aerodynamic force acting on an airfoil, or on an entire aircraft or winged missile, perpendicular to the relative wind and normally exerted in an upward direction, opposing the pull of gravity. **b.** The upward force on a balloon, airship, or the like. [Middle English *liften,* from Old Norse *lypta.*] **—lift•er** *n.*

Synonyms: *boost, elevate, heave, hoist, raise.*

lifting body *n.* An aircraft or spacecraft that has no wings and gains lift by the action of aerodynamic forces on its body.

lift off *intr.v.* To commence flight. Used of a rocket or other craft.

lift•off (lĭft′ôf′, -ŏf′) *n.* **1.** The initial movement by which a rocket or other craft commences flight. **2.** The instant at which this occurs.

lift pump *n.* A simple pump for lifting a liquid to a higher level, typically having a piston with a valve in the base moving vertically in a cylinder.

lig•a•ment (lĭg′ə-mənt) *n.* **1.** *Anatomy.* A sheet or band of tough, fibrous tissue connecting two or more bones or cartilages, or supporting an organ, fascia, or muscle. **2.** Any unifying or connecting tie or bond. [Middle English, from Latin *ligāmentum,* bond, bandage, from *ligāre,* to bind.] **—lig•a•men•tal, lig•a•men•ta•ry, lig•a•men•tous** *adj.*

ligan. Variant of **lagan.**

lig•and (lĭg′ənd, lī′gənd-) *n. Chemistry.* An atom, ion, group, or molecule that is linked to a central atom in an inorganic coordination compound. [Latin *ligandum,* gerund of *ligāre,* to bind.]

li•gase (lī′gās′) *n.* An enzyme that catalyzes the linkage of molecules, using ATP as an energy source. [Latin *ligāre,* to bind + -ASE.]

li•gate (lī′gāt′) *tr.v.* **-gated, -gating, -gates.** To tie up, bind, or constrict with a ligature. [Latin *ligāre,* to bind.]

li•ga•tion (lī-gā′shən) *n.* **1.** The act of binding or applying a ligature. **2.** The state of being bound. **3.** Something that binds; a ligature.

lig•a•ture (lĭg′ə-cho͝or′) *n.* **1.** The act of tying together, binding, or constricting. **2.** A cord, wire, or bandage used for tying, binding, or constricting. **3.** Something that unites; a bond. **4.** In surgery, a thread, wire, cord, or the like, applied in a tight loop, as to close vessels, tie off ducts, or constrict a growth. **5.** A character or type combining two or more letters, such as *fi.* **6.** *Music.* **a.** A group of notes intended to be played or sung as one phrase. **b.** A curved line indicating such a phrase; a slur.

∼*tr.v.* **ligatured, -turing, -tures.** To ligate. [Middle English, from Latin *ligātūra,* from *ligāre,* to bind.]

li•ger (lī′gər) *n.* A hybrid produced by the mating of a female tiger and a male lion. [Blend of *li*on + *tiger.*]

PRONUNCIATION KEY

ă, pat; ā, pay; âr, care;
ä, father, are; b, bib;
ch, church; d, deed; ĕ, pet;
ē, be; f, fife; g, gag; h, hat;
hw, which; ĭ, pit; ī, pie;
îr, pier; j, judge; k, kick;
l, lid, needle; m, mum;
n, no, sudden; ng, thing;
ŏ, pot; ō, toe; ô, paw, for;
oi, noise; ou, out; o͝o, book;
o͞o, boot; p, pop; r, roar;
s, sauce; sh, ship, dish;
t, tight; th, thin, path;
th, this, bathe; ŭ, cut; ûr, fur;
v, valve; w, with; y, yes;
z, zebra, size; zh, vision;
ə, about, item, edible,
gallop, circus, peaceful

IN FOREIGN WORDS:

à, *Fr.* ami; œ, *Fr.* feu, *Ger.* schön; ü, *Fr.* tu, *Ger.* über; KH, *Ger.* ich, *Scot.* loch; N, *Fr.* bon; y′, *Fr.* Compiègne

STRESS MARKS:

Primary stress: ′
in·cite′ (ĭn-sīt′)
Secondary stress: ′
in′sight′ (ĭn′sīt′)

light¹

LIGHT: THE VISIBLE PART OF A VERY WIDE SPECTRUM

Light is a part of the same phenomenon as radio waves and x-rays

Light is that part of the electromagnetic spectrum to which the eye is sensitive. Electromagnetic energy travels in waves at about 300,000 kilometers (about 186,000 miles) per second in a vacuum, which is thought to be the ultimate speed limit in the universe. The spectrum extends from radio waves of very low frequency to gamma rays from radioactive substances, of very high frequency and dangerous to living things.

Within its narrow part of the spectrum, light varies in color—depending on the frequency, or wavelength, of its waves—from comparatively low-frequency red

through orange, yellow, green, and blue to high-frequency violet. Isaac Newton demonstrated in 1666 that white light can be separated into its different colors by passing it through a glass prism. This happens because each color (wavelength) is refracted at a different angle.

A rainbow is a spectrum of light produced by the natural prism of raindrops in the atmosphere. Color results from the absence or the absorption of other wavelengths. A red object appears red because other colors are absorbed and only red is reflected.

When a light source—for example, a distant galaxy—is receding at a very great speed, the light waves from it are effectively lengthened and appear redder than they should. This "red shift" indicates that the universe is still expanding.

Each chemical element has its own characteristic pattern of lines in the spectrum—a kind of identifying "fingerprint" of colors emitted or absorbed by its atoms. Because of this the composition of heavenly bodies can be discovered by analyzing the light that comes from them.

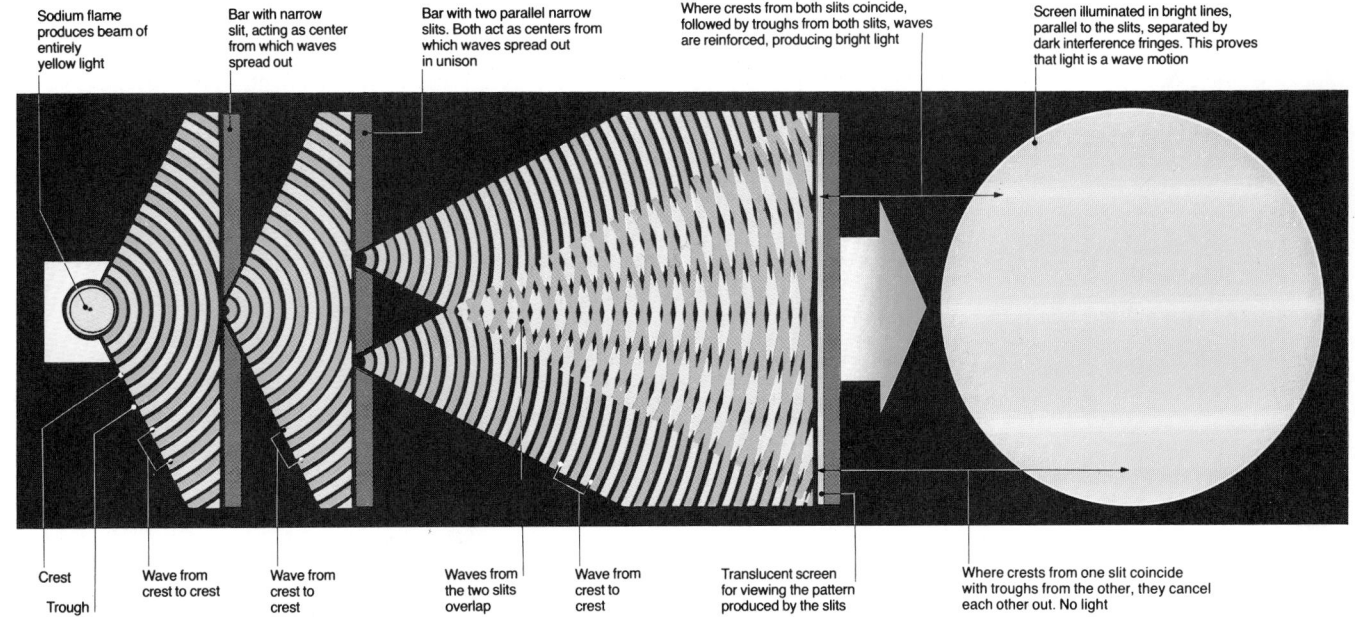

Sodium flame produces beam of entirely yellow light

Bar with narrow slit, acting as center from which waves spread out

Bar with two parallel narrow slits. Both act as centers from which waves spread out in unison

Where crests from both slits coincide, followed by troughs from both slits, waves are reinforced, producing bright light

Screen illuminated in bright lines, parallel to the slits, separated by dark interference fringes. This proves that light is a wave motion

Crest
Trough

Wave from crest to crest

Wave from crest to crest

Waves from the two slits overlap

Wave from crest to crest

Translucent screen for viewing the pattern produced by the slits

Where crests from one slit coincide with troughs from the other, they cancel each other out. No light

PROOF THAT LIGHT TRAVELS IN WAVES *Newton thought that light was a steady stream of particles; his contemporary Christiaan Huygens thought it had a wave motion. They were both right. Light consists of moving quanta* (packets) *of photons (particles of pure energy). And Thomas Young, an English physicist, proved in 1802 that it does have a wave motion. In his experiment* (above), *the parallel beams of light should have produced* *a brighter area where they overlapped if light were a steady stream. Instead, they produced bright bands separated by dark bands, the result of two sets of waves coinciding or canceling each other out.*

light¹ (līt) *n.* **1.** *Physics.* **a.** Electromagnetic radiation that has a wavelength in the range from about 3,900 to about 7,700 angstroms and that may be perceived by the normal, unaided human eye. **b.** Loosely, other electromagnetic radiation that is close to light in wavelength, but not visible: *ultraviolet light.* **2.** The sensation of the perception of such radiation; brightness. **3. a.** A source of illumination, such as the sun or an electric lamp. **b.** The illumination derived from such a source: *by the light of the moon.* **c.** The particular quality or amount of such illumination: *I moved the lamp to get better light.* **d.** The path by which light reaches a person: *You're standing in my light.* **4.** Daylight. **5.** Dawn; daybreak. **6. a.** Something that admits light, such as a window. **b.** *Often* **lights.** Daylight falling on a window. See **ancient lights. 7.** A means or agent, such as a match or cigarette lighter, for igniting something. **8. a.** Something that provides clarification or elucidation: *shed some light on the problem.* **b.** A state of understanding or awareness, especially as derived from a particular source: *saw the light; in the light of experience.* **9.** The state of being visible, publicly available, or generally known; public attention or awareness: *bring new facts to light.* **10.** A way of regarding something; an angle; an aspect: *saw the situation in a new light.* **11.** *Archaic & Poetic.* Eyesight. **12. lights.** One's individual opinions, choices, or life philosophy: *acted according to their own lights.* **13.** A person who inspires or is adored by another: *Her son is the light of her life.* **14.** A prominent or distinguished person, especially one serving as an example for others; a notable or luminary: *the brighter lights of Irish art.* **15.** An expression of the eyes, usually indicative of animation or liveliness. **16. a.** Spiritual illumination. **b. Light.** In Quaker doctrine, the guiding spirit or divine presence in each person. **17. a.** The representation of light in art. **b.** An area of pronounced illumination in a painting or photograph. **18. a.** A traffic light. **b.** A lighthouse beacon. —**in (the) light of.** In consideration of; in relation to. —**see the light (of day). 1.** To be born; come into existence. **2.** To become known to the public. **3.** To comprehend or perceive the meaning of something. —**shed** (or **throw**) **light on.** To provide information about; make more comprehensible.
~*v.* **lighted** or **lit** (līt), **lighting, lights.** —*tr.* **1.** To set on fire; ignite; kindle. **2.** To cause to give out light; make luminous. **3.** To provide, cover, or fill with light; illuminate. **4.** To guide or direct with or as if with lights. **5.** To enliven or animate: *a smile lighting her face.* —*intr.* To start to burn; be ignited or kindled: *Green wood will not light easily.* —See Usage note at **light². —light up. 1.** To become or cause to become light, radiant, or bright. **2.** To become or cause to become animated or cheerful. **3.** *Informal.* To start smoking a cigarette, cigar, or pipe.
~*adj.* **lighter, lightest.** *Abbr.* **lt. 1.** Having a greater rather than lesser degree of **lightness** (see). Said of a color. **2.** Characterized by or filled with light; radiant; bright. **3.** Pale, as if mixed with white; fair: *a light complexion.* [Middle English *liht, light,* Old English *lēoht, līht.*]

light² *adj.* **lighter, lightest. 1.** Of relatively low weight; not heavy. **2.** Of low weight in proportion to bulk; of relatively low density. **3.** Of less than the correct, standard, or lawful weight; underweight: *a light pound.* **4.** Exerting little pressure; having relatively little force or impact: *a light kick.* **5. a.** Having relatively little volume, quantity, or intensity: *a light rain; light traffic.* **b.** Moderate; abstemious: *a light eater; a light smoker.* **6. a.** Having little importance or value; insignificant: *light chatter.* **b.** Characterized by frivolity; silly; trivial. **7.** Intended as entertainment; not serious or profound: *a light comedy.* **8.** Free from worries or troubles; blithe. **9.** Having little moral discipline; wanton. **10.** Suffering from mild delirium or faintness; dizzy. **11.** Moving quickly and easily; graceful; nimble. **12. a.** Designed for ease and quickness of movement; having a slim structure and little weight: *light aircraft.* **b.** Designed to carry relatively small loads: *a light truck.* **13.** Concerned with the production of relatively small consumer goods: *light industry.* **14.** Performed or endured without significant difficulty or effort: *Many hands make light work.* **15.** Easily disturbed or awakened: *a light sleeper.* **16.** *Military.* Carrying little equipment or arms: *a light brigade.*

17. Characterized by lightness and elegance in design or construction; not ponderous or massive. **18.** Easily digested. **19.** Having a spongy or flaky texture; well-leavened: *light pastries.* **20.** Having a loose, porous consistency; not packed together or solid: *light earth.* **21.** Containing a relatively small amount of alcohol: *a light wine.* **22.** Faint; not bold. Said of type. **23.** In phonetics and prosody, designating a vowel or syllable pronounced with little or no stress. **24.** *Informal.* Lacking an adequate supply of something. Used with *on.* —**make light of.** To regard or treat as insignificant or petty. —*adv.* **1.** Lightly. **2.** Without additional weight or burdens; in an unencumbered manner: *traveling light.*

~*intr.v.* **lighted** or **lit** (lĭt), **lighting, lights. 1.** To get down, as from a mount or vehicle; dismount; alight. **2.** To descend to the ground after flight; perch; land. **3.** To come upon unexpectedly; strike suddenly, as a blow or stroke of luck may. Often used with *on* or *upon*: *Misfortune lighted upon her.* **4.** To come upon an object or idea by chance or accident. Used with *on* or *upon.* —**light into.** *Informal.* To attack verbally or physically; assail. —**light out.** *Informal.* To leave hastily; run off. [Middle English *liht, light,* Old English *lēoht, līht.*]

Usage: Generally, *lit* is the past tense and past participle of both **light¹** and **light².** *Lighted* is used only in a few special senses; for example, when **light¹** means "provide with light: *I was lighted along the corridor by candles.* When **light²** is used in the phrases *light on* or *light upon,* meaning "discover," *lighted* and *lit* are both possible: *We lighted* (or *lit*) *upon an old map.* In adjectival use, *lighted* is the usual form, although *lit* is sometimes found, especially if there is a preceding adverb: *a lighted cigarette,* but *a well-lit arcade.*

light adaptation *n.* The process in which the eye adapts to increased illumination. —**light·a·dapt·ed** *adj.*

light air *n.* A wind whose speed is 0.3 to 1.5 meters per second, force 1 on the Beaufort scale.

light breeze *n.* A wind whose speed is 1.6 to 3.3 meters per second, force 2 on the Beaufort scale.

light bulb *n.* An electric lamp in which a filament is heated to incandescence by an electric current.

light-emitting diode *n.* See **LED.**

light·en¹ (lĭt'n) *v.* **-ened, -ening, -ens.** —*tr.* **1. a.** To make light or lighter; illuminate; brighten. **b.** To make (a color) lighter. **2.** *Archaic.* To enlighten mentally or spiritually, as by imparting knowledge or wisdom to. —*intr.* **1.** To become light or lighter; brighten. **2.** To be luminous; glow; shine. **3.** To produce or give off flashes of lightning. —See Usage note at **lightning.**

lighten² *v.* **-ened, -ening, -ens.** —*tr.* **1.** To make less heavy, as by a reduction in weight or load. **2.** To lessen the oppressiveness, trouble, or severity of. **3.** To relieve of cares or worries; gladden. —*intr.* **1.** To become lighter. **2.** To become less oppressive, severe, or troublesome. **3.** To become cheerful. —See Synonyms at **relieve.**

light·er¹ (lī'tər) *n.* **1.** One that lights or ignites something. **2.** A mechanical device for lighting a cigarette, cigar, or pipe.

lighter² *n. Nautical.* A large barge used to transport goods over short distances or to deliver to or unload from a larger cargo ship unable to navigate in shallow water.

~*v.* **lightered, -ering, -ers.** —*tr.* To convey (cargo) in a lighter. —*intr.* To use a lighter to transport cargo. [Middle English, from Middle Dutch *lichter* (unattested), from *lichten,* to lighten, unload.]

light·er·age (lī'tər-ĭj) *n.* **1.** The transport of goods on a lighter. **2.** The fee charged for such service.

light·er-than-air (lī'tər-thən-âr') *adj.* Having a weight less than that of the air displaced. Said of certain aircraft.

light·face (līt'fās') *n. Printing. Abbr.* **lf** A typeface or font of characters having relatively thin, light lines. Compare **boldface.** —**light·face, light·faced** *adj.*

light-fin·gered (līt'fĭng'gərd) *adj.* **1.** Having quick and nimble fingers. **2.** Skilled at or given to petty thievery. —**light·fin·gered·ly** *adv.* —**light-fin·gered·ness** *n.*

light flyweight *n. Boxing & Wrestling.* A fighter weighing not more than 48 kilograms (106 pounds).

light-foot·ed (līt'fŏŏt'ĭd) *adj.* Also *poetic* **light-foot** (-fŏŏt'). Treading with light and nimble ease. —**light-foot·ed·ly** *adv.* —**light-foot·ed·ness** *n.*

light-head·ed (līt'hĕd'ĭd) *adj.* **1.** Delirious, giddy, or faint: *light-headed with wine.* **2.** Frivolous; silly. —**light-head·ed·ly** *adv.* —**light-head·ed·ness** *n.*

light-heart·ed (līt'här'tĭd) *adj.* **1.** Blithe; carefree; gay. **2.** Not serious: *a light-hearted look at the week's news.* —See Synonyms at **glad.** —**light-heart·ed·ly** *adv.* —**light-heart·ed·ness** *n.*

light heavyweight *n. Boxing & Wrestling.* A fighter weighing between 72.5 and 79.5 kilograms (160 and 175 pounds).

light·house (līt'hous') *n.* A tall structure topped by a powerful light used as a beacon or signal to aid marine navigation.

light·ing (lī'tĭng) *n.* **1.** The state of being lighted; illumination. **2. a.** The method or equipment used to provide artificial illumination. **b.** The illumination so provided.

lighting-up time (lī'tĭng-ŭp') *n. British.* The time by which vehicles must have their lights on along public highways.

light·ly (līt'lē) *adv.* **1.** With little weight or force; gently. **2.** To a slight extent or amount; sparingly; little: *use lightly.* **3.** With buoyancy or ease; quickly and gracefully. **4.** In a carefree manner; cheerfully; blithely: *take the bad news lightly.* **5.** Without enough care or serious consideration; thoughtlessly; indifferently. **6.** Depreciatingly; slightingly.

lighthouse *Beacons have been used at least since Roman times to warn shipping away from dangerous waters. This modern lighthouse marks the rocks below Beachy Head on England's Sussex coast.*

lightning

SHOWER POWER

How rain generates the awesome voltage of lightning

When drops of water falling through a thundercloud strike other drops, some of the energy in each is transformed into an electric charge. The charges are minute at first, but powerful updrafts in the cloud keep lifting the drops, so that they collide again and again. The charges build up, turning the cloud into a gigantic battery. Within about 15 minutes, the total charge becomes so great—many millions of volts—that it overcomes the insulating effect of the air.

The electricity is discharged as an enormous spark that grounds itself to the nearest spot on the ground. Lightning travels in a forked path, but sometimes it is seen as a sheet—which is a reflection of forked lightning occurring elsewhere. The spark heats the surrounding air to more than 16,000°C (about 28,800°F)—three times hotter than the sun's surface—causing it to expand explosively and generate the shock wave we hear as thunder.

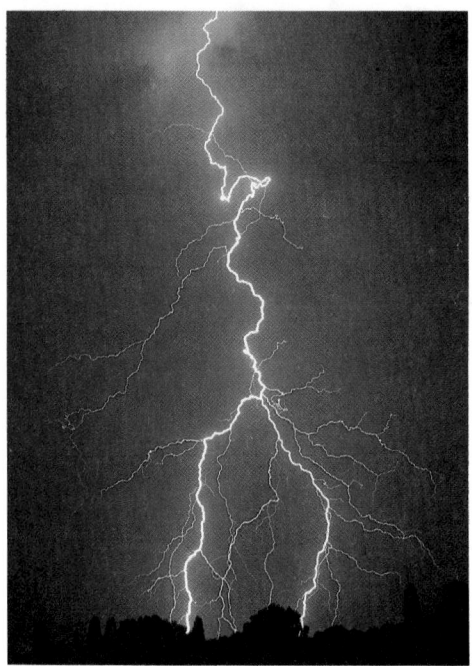

FORKED LIGHTNING *A bolt of lightning can arc across a gap of up to 8 kilometers (5 miles). The spark forks as it flashes through the sky, hunting for the easiest path to the earth. Then, once one or more of the branches makes contact, the bolt discharges itself and the side branches fade in midair.*

light meter *n. Photography.* An **exposure meter** *(see).*

light-mind·ed (līt'mīn'dĭd) *adj.* Frivolous, silly, or inane; giddy. —**light-mind·ed·ly** *adv.* —**light-mind·ed·ness** *n.*

light·ness¹ (līt'nĭs) *n.* **1.** The dimension of the color of an object by which the object appears to reflect or transmit more or less of the incident light, varying from black to white for surface colors, and from black to colorless for transparent volume colors. **2.** The relative paleness of an object or the brightness of a place.

lightness² *n.* **1.** The state or quality of having little weight or force. **2.** Ease or quickness of style or movement; agility; nimbleness. **3.** Freedom from worry or trouble; blitheness; gaiety. **4.** Lack of appropriate seriousness; levity.

light·ning (līt'nĭng) *n.* A large-scale natural electric discharge in the atmosphere in the form of a visible flash of light.

~*intr.v.* **lightninged** (-nĭngd), **-ninging, -nings.** To discharge a flash or flashes of lightning. Sometimes used impersonally.

~*adj.* Moving with extreme alacrity; very fast or sudden, like a flash of lightning. [Middle English *light(e)ning,* from *lightenen,* to illuminate, from **LIGHT** (illumination).]

Usage: Lightning and *lightening* are sometimes confused in spelling, on account of their similar pronunciations. *Lightning* is the noun (as in *thunder and lightning*); *lightening* is a participle form of the verbs *lighten¹* and *lighten².* Note that it is possible, though rare, to use *lighten¹* to refer to the process that produces lightning: *It was thundering and lightening by the time I returned.*

lightning arrester *n.* A protective device for electrical equipment that reduces excessive voltage resulting from lightning to a safe level by grounding the discharge.

lightning bug *n.* A firefly.

lightning rod *n.* A grounded metal rod placed high on a structure to prevent damage by conducting lightning to the ground.

light opera *n.* An **operetta** *(see).*

light pen *n. Computer Science.* A photoelectric device shaped like a pen, used to sense and amend data or lines on a visual-display unit.

light ratio *n. Astronomy.* The ratio of the brightness of a star to that of any other star one magnitude fainter, approximately 2.512.

lights (līts) *pl.n.* The lungs, especially of sheep, pigs, or bullocks, used chiefly as pet food. [Middle English *lihte,* from *liht,* LIGHT (not heavy).]

light•ship (līt′shĭp′) *n.* A ship with a powerful light or warning signals anchored in dangerous waters to alert other vessels.

light show *n.* A display of moving colored lights or slides projected onto a screen or wall, especially in a discotheque.

light•some[1] (līt′səm) *adj.* **1.** Providing light; illuminating; luminous. **2.** Covered with or full of light; bright. **—light•some•ly** *adv.* **—light•some•ness** *n.*

lightsome[2] *adj.* **1.** Light, nimble, or graceful in movement; buoyant. **2.** Carefree; blithe; cheerful. **3.** Frivolous; silly. **—light•some•ly** *adv.* **—light•some•ness** *n.*

lights out *n. Used with a singular verb.* The time when all lights must be extinguished for the night, as in a military camp, boarding school, or the like.

light-struck (līt′strŭk′) *adj.* Fogged by accidental exposure. Said of photosensitive materials.

light water *n.* Ordinary water as distinguished from heavy water.

light•weight (līt′wāt′) *n.* **1.** A person, animal, or thing that weighs relatively little. **2.** A person of little ability, intelligence, influence, or importance. **3.** *Boxing & Wrestling.* A fighter weighing between 57 and 61 kilograms (126 and 135 pounds).
~adj. Weighing relatively little; not heavy: *lightweight wool.*

light•wood (līt′wo͝od′) *n.* Dry, easily ignited, often resinous wood, as of a pine, used for kindling or fuel.

light-year, light year (līt′yîr′) *n.* The distance that light covers traveling in a vacuum for a period of one year, approximately 9.4607 × 10^{12} kilometers (5.878 × 10^{12} miles).

lign aloes (līn) *n.* Also **lign-al•oes** (lī-năl′ōz, lĭg-). *Archaic.* The wood of a tree, *Aquilaria agallocha,* mentioned in the Old Testament. Numbers 24:6. [Middle English *ligne aloes,* from Late Latin *lignum aloēs,* "wood of the aloe" : Latin *lignum,* wood + *aloēs,* genitive of *aloē,* ALOE.]

lig•ne•ous (lĭg′nē-əs) *adj.* Consisting of or having the texture or appearance of wood; woody. Said of a plant. [Latin *ligneus,* from *lignum,* wood.]

ligni–, ligno–, lign– *prefix.* Indicates wood; for example, **lignocellulose, lignin.** [Latin *lignum,* wood.]

lig•ni•fy (lĭg′nə-fī′) *v.* **-fied, -fying, -fies.** *—intr.* To form or turn into wood through the formation and deposit of lignin in cell walls. *—tr.* To make woody or woodlike by the deposit of lignin. [French *lignifier* : LIGNI- + -FY.] **—lig•ni•fi•ca•tion** *n.*

lig•nin (lĭg′nĭn) *n.* The chief noncarbohydrate constituent of wood, a polymer that functions as a natural binder and support for the cellulose fibers of woody plants. [LIGN(I)- + -IN.]

lig•nite (lĭg′nīt′) *n.* A low-grade, brownish-black coal. Also called "brown coal." [French : LIGN(I)- + -ITE.] **—lig•nit•ic** (lĭg-nĭt′ĭk) *adj.*

lig•no•cel•lu•lose (lĭg′nō-sĕl′yə-lōs′) *n.* Any combination of lignin and cellulose that strengthens plant cells.

lig•num vi•tae (lĭg′nəm vī′tē) *n., pl.* **lignum vitaes. 1.** Either of two tropical American trees, *Guaiacum officinale* or *G. sanctum,* having evergreen leaves and heavy, durable, resinous wood. **2.** The wood of either of these trees, used for machine bearings. **3.** Any of several similar or related trees. [New Latin, from Late Latin, "tree or wood of life" : *lignum,* wood + *vītae,* genitive of *vīta,* life.]

lig•ro•in (lĭg′rō-ən) *n.* A volatile, flammable fraction of petroleum boiling in the range 70–130°C and used chiefly as a solvent. Also called "benzine." [20th century : origin obscure.]

lig•u•la (lĭg′yə-lə) *n., pl.* **-lae** (-lē′) or **-las.** A strap-shaped structure, especially a mouthpart in certain insects. [New Latin, LIGULE.]

lig•u•late (lĭg′yə-lĭt, -lāt′) *adj.* **1.** Strap-shaped. **2.** Having a ligule or ligula. [New Latin *ligula,* LIGULE + -ATE.]

lig•ule (lĭg′yo͞ol) *n.* A straplike structure, such as a ray flower of a daisy or a sheathlike organ at the base of a grass leaf. [New Latin *ligula,* from Latin, tongue of a shoe, shoe-strap, variant of *lingula,* from *lingua,* tongue.]

lig•ure (lĭg′yo͝or′) *n.* A precious stone of ancient Israel. Exodus 28:19. [Middle English *lugre, ligurie,* from Late Latin *ligūrius,* from Greek *ligurion*†, a precious stone.]

Li•gu•ria (lĭ-gyo͝or′ē-ə). Region of northwest Italy, on the Ligurian Sea, a section of the Mediterranean between Liguria and Corsica. The port of Genoa is the capital. **—Li•gu•ri•an** *adj. & n.*

lik•a•ble, like•a•ble (lī′kə-bəl) *adj.* Pleasing; attractive. **—lik•a•bil•i•ty, lik•a•ble•ness** *n.*

like[1] (līk) *v.* **liked, liking, likes.** *—tr.* **1.** To find pleasant; enjoy. **2.** To feel an attraction, tenderness, or affection for; be fond of. **3.** To want, wish, or prefer. **4.** To feel toward or respond to; view; regard: *How do you like that!* **5.** *Obsolete.* To agree with; suit or please: *This likes me not.* *—intr.* To have an inclination or preference; desire; choose; wish: *If you like, we can go fishing.*
~n. **likes.** Preferences or predilections. Used in the phrase *likes and dislikes.* [Middle English *lik(i)en,* Old English *līcian,* to please, be sufficient.] **—lik•er** *n.*

Synonyms: *dote, enjoy, fancy, love, relish.*

Usage: *Like* is often followed by an infinitive form of the verb, which may be preceded by a noun or pronoun: *I would like you to travel by bus.* The insertion of *for* (*I would like for you to travel by bus*) is often heard in informal American English, and occasionally in some other English dialects, but it is not considered standard. The forms *would have/should have liked* are usually followed by a simple infinitive form (*They would have liked to go*), rather than by a perfect infinitive as in *They would have liked to have gone;* the double use of *have* is considered unnecessary.

like[2] *prep.* **1.** Possessing the characteristics of; resembling closely; similar to. **2. a.** In the same way as: *to live like pigs.* **b.** In the typical manner of: *It's not like you to take offense.* **3.** Desirous of; disposed to: *He felt like swimming.* **4.** As if the probability exists for; indicative of: *It looks like a bad season for the Yankees.* **5.** Such as; for example: *The better wines, like claret, cost more.*
~adj. **1.** Possessing the same or almost the same characteristics; similar: *on this and like occasions.* **2.** Having equivalent value or quality. Usually used in negative phrases: *There's nothing like an open fire.* **3.** Alike: *They are as like as two brothers.*
~adv. **1.** *Informal.* In the manner of being; as if: *He ran like crazy.* **2.** *Informal.* Probably; likely: *Like as not she'll change her mind.* **3.** *Nonstandard.* Used to provide emphasis or a pause: *Like let's get going.*
~n. **1.** Similar or related persons or things. Used with *the: He was subject to fevers, coughs, asthma, and the like.* **2.** *Often* **likes.** *Informal.* An equivalent or similar person or thing; an equal or match: *I've never seen the likes of this before.*
~conj. Nonstandard. **1.** In the same way that; as: *She talks just like you do.* **2.** As if: *He acts like he owns the place.* [Middle English *lic, lik,* Old English *līc* (unattested), short for *gelīc.*]

Usage: *Like* as a conjunction is not appropriate to formal usage, especially written usage, except in certain constructions noted below. On other levels it occurs frequently, especially in casual speech and in writing representing speech. In formal usage the conjunctive *like* is most acceptable when it introduces an elliptical clause in which a verb in not expressed: *He took to politics like a fish to water. The dress looked like new.* Both examples, which are generally acceptable on a formal level, employ such elliptical, or shortened, expressions following *like.* If they were recast to include full clauses containing verbs, *like* would preferably be replaced, in formal usage, by *as, as if,* or *as though*: *took to politics as a fish takes to water; dress looked as if it were new.* The examples that follow illustrate the difference. All employ *like* to introduce full clauses containing verbs; all are termed unacceptable by many users; and in every case a more desirable construction is indicated: *He manipulates an audience like* (preferably *as*) *a virtuoso commands a musical instrument. The engine responds now like* (preferably *as*) *good machinery should. It looks like* (preferably *as if*) *they will be finished earlier than usual. He had no authority, but he always acted like* (preferably *as if*) *he did.* The restriction on *like* as a conjunction does not affect its other uses. Fear of misusing *like* often causes writers to use *as* in its place in constructions where *like* is not only acceptable but clearly called for. It is always used acceptably when it functions prepositionally, followed by a noun or pronoun as object: *works like a charm; sings like an angel: looking for a girl like me* (not *I*); *spoke like one who had authority* (but not *like he had authority*). Used prepositionally, *like* indicates comparison; in modern usage *as,* in place of *like,* would imply the assumption of another role: *He behaved like* (not *as*) *a child. She treated him like* (not *as*) *a fool. John, like* (not *as*) *his grandfather earlier, chose to ignore politics.* See also Usage note at **as.**

like[3] *v.* Also **liked** (līkt). *Nonstandard.* To be just on the point of; be or come near to. Used as a verbal auxiliary: *I like to have killed him when he said that.*

-like *suffix.* Indicates: **1.** A resemblance or similarity to something specified; for example, **lifelike. 2.** A characteristic of or appropriateness to something specified; for example, **childlike, ladylike.** [From LIKE (preposition).]

like•li•hood (līk′lē-ho͝od′) *n.* The state of being likely; probability.

like•ly (līk′lē) *adj.* **-lier, -liest. 1.** Having, expressing, or exhibiting an inclination or probability; apt. Used with an infinitive: *They are likely to become angry with him.* **2.** That can with reasonable confidence be expected to occur; probable: *the likely outcome; More rain is likely.* **3.** Within the realm of credibility; seeming to be true; plausible: *a likely excuse.* **4.** Apparently appropriate or suitable for a purpose: *called all the likely shops.* **5.** Apparently capable of doing well or becoming successful; promising: *a likely lad.* **6.** Attractive; pleasant; enjoyable.
~adv. Probably. [Middle English *likely,* from Old Norse *līkligr,* from *līkr,* like.]

Usage: As an adverb, *likely* normally requires a qualifying word, such as *quite, very,* or *most*: *I will very likely arrive by six.* If you do not wish to use a qualifying word, it is preferable to use an alternative word, such as *probably.*

like-mind•ed (līk′mīn′dĭd) *adj.* Of the same turn of mind.

lik•en (lī′kən) *tr.v.* **-ened, -ening, -ens.** To see, mention, or show as being like or similar; compare. [Middle English *lik(n)en,* from *lik,* LIKE (adjective).]

like•ness (līk′nĭs) *n.* **1.** The state or quality of resembling or being like something. **2.** An imitative appearance; a semblance or guise.

PRONUNCIATION KEY

ă, pat; ā, pay; âr, care;
ä, father, are; b, bib;
ch, church; d, deed; ĕ, pet;
ē, be; f, fife; g, gag; h, hat;
hw, which; ĭ, pit; ī, pie;
îr, pier; j, judge; k, kick;
l, lid, needle; m, mum;
n, no, sudden; ng, thing;
ŏ, pot; ō, toe; ô, paw, for;
oi, noise; ou, out; o͝o, book;
o͞o, boot; p, pop; r, roar;
s, sauce; sh, ship, dish;
t, tight; th, thin, path;
th, this, bathe; ŭ, cut; ûr, fur;
v, valve; w, with; y, yes;
z, zebra, size; zh, vision;
ə, about, item, edible, gallop, circus, peaceful

IN FOREIGN WORDS:

à, *Fr.* ami; œ, *Fr.* feu, *Ger.* schön; ü, *Fr.* tu, *Ger.* über;
KH, *Ger.* ich, *Scot.* loch;
N, *Fr.* bon; y′, *Fr.* Compiègne

STRESS MARKS:

Primary stress: ′
in•cite′ (ĭn-sīt′)
Secondary stress: ′
in′sight′ (ĭn′sīt′)

lilac *There are 30 species of the lilac genus,* Syringa, *as well as many cultivated varieties. This is* Syringa vulgaris, *or common lilac, thought to come originally from the Romanian province of Transylvania.*

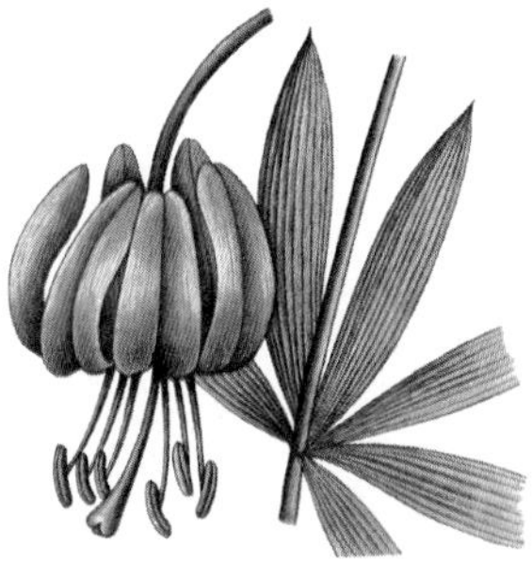

lily *This genus of 80 species and numerous garden hybrids is represented throughout the temperate zone of the Northern Hemisphere. The species shown here, with its large turbanlike flowers—*Lilium martagon, *or the Turk's-cap lily—is native to the mountains of central Europe and Russia.*

3. A pictorial, graphic, or sculptured representation of someone or something; an image.

Synonyms: *affinity, analogy, resemblance, similarity, similitude.*

like·wise (līk′wīz′) *adv.* **1.** In the same way; similarly. **2.** As well; also; too. —See Synonyms at **also.**

Usage: *Likewise* is considered to be an adverb (*She did likewise*) in standard English, and its occasional informal use as a conjunction attracts criticism: *Her speech, likewise her manner, upset me.*

lik·ing (lī′kĭng) *n.* **1.** The state or act of someone who likes. **2.** A feeling of attraction, tenderness, or love; fondness; affection. **3.** Preference; inclination; taste: *Was the meal to your liking?*

li·ku·ta (lē-ko͞o′tä) *n., pl.* **makuta** (mä-). A coin equal to 1/100 of the zaire of Zaire. See feature at **currency.** [Native word in Zaire.]

li·lac (lī′lək, -lŏk′, -lăk′) *n.* **1.** Any of various shrubs of the genus *Syringa;* especially, *S. vulgaris,* widely cultivated for its clusters of fragrant purplish or white flowers. **2.** Pale purple; mauve. [Obsolete French, from Spanish, from Arabic *līlak,* from Persian, variant of *nīlak,* from *nīl,* indigo, blue.] —**li·lac** *adj.*

li·lan·ge·ni (lĭ-läng′gĕ-nē) *n., pl.* **emalangeni** (ĕm′ə-). The standard monetary unit of Swaziland. See feature at **currency.** [Swazi : *li-,* singular prefix + *-langeni,* money.]

lil·i·a·ceous (lĭl′ē-ā′shəs) *adj.* Of, pertaining to, or belonging to the Liliaceae, a family of flowering plants including lilies, tulips, and onions. [Late Latin *līliāceus,* from *līlium,* lily.]

Li·li·en·thal (lē′lē-ən-täl′), **Otto** (1848–96). German aeronautical pioneer. His theoretical essays on aviation, monoplane and biplane glider designs, and more than 2,000 flights in his crafts greatly contributed to the quest for controlled powered flight. He was mortally wounded when a glider he was piloting crashed.

Lil·ith (lĭl′ĭth) *n.* **1.** In ancient Semitic legend, an evil female spirit or demon alleged to haunt lonely, deserted places and attack children. **2.** In Hebrew folklore, the first wife of Adam, believed to have been in existence before the creation of Eve. **3.** A witch in medieval legend. [Hebrew *līlīth.*]

Li·li·u·o·ka·la·ni (lē-lē′o͞o-ō-kä-lä′nē), born Lydia Kamekeha (1838–1917). Hawaiian queen (1891–93). Hawaii's last governing sovereign, she bitterly opposed annexation to the United States. Yielding to powerful local support for the move, she abdicated the throne to avoid possible bloodshed.

Lille (lēl). Capital of Nord department, northern France. It is a commercial, cultural, and manufacturing center, long known for its textile products.

Lil·lie (lĭl′ē), **Beatrice** (1898–). British actress and singer, born in Canada. She made her London stage debut in 1914 and her first film, *Exit Smiling,* in 1926.

Lil·li·pu·tian (lĭl′ə-pyo͞o′shən) *n.* **1.** A very small person or being. **2.** A person of little intelligence, worth, or significance.

~*adj.* **1.** Very small; diminutive. **2.** Trivial; petty. [After *Lilliput,* the land of tiny people, in Swift's *Gulliver's Travels* (1726).]

Li·long·we (lē-lông′wā′). Capital of Malawi, in the western highlands, in a fertile agricultural area.

lilt (lĭlt) *n.* **1.** A light, happy tune or song. **2.** A cheerful or lively manner of speaking marked by a pleasantly varied cadence. **3.** A light, springing manner of moving or walking.

~*v.* **lilted, lilting, lilts.** —*tr.* To say, sing, or play in a cheerful, rhythmic manner. —*intr.* To speak, sing, or play with liveliness or rhythm. [Middle English *lulten*†, to sound, sing.]

lil·y (lĭl′ē) *n., pl.* **-ies. 1.** Any of various plants of the genus *Lilium,* having showy, variously colored, often trumpet-shaped flowers. **2.** Any of various similar or related plants, such as the tiger lily or the water lily. **3.** The flower of such a plant. [Middle English *lilie,* Old English, from Latin *līlium,* akin to Greek *leirion,* probably of Mediterranean origin.]

lil·y-liv·ered (lĭl′ē-lĭv′ərd) *adj.* Cowardly; timid.

lily of the valley *n., pl.* **lilies of the valley.** A plant, *Convallaria majalis,* having a spike of fragrant, bell-shaped white flowers.

lily pad *n.* Any of the broad, floating leaves of a water lily.

lil·y-trot·ter (lĭl′ē-trŏt′ər) *n.* A bird, the **jaçana** *(see).*

lil·y-white (lĭl′ē-hwīt′, -wīt′) *adj.* **1.** White as a lily. **2.** Beyond reproach; blameless; pure.

lim. limit.

Li·ma (lē′mə). Capital of Peru, founded in 1535 by Francisco Pizarro. It is now an industrial center and the site of oil-refining and diversified manufacturing industries. Its port is Callao.

li·ma bean (lī′mə) *n.* **1.** Any of several varieties of a tropical American plant, *Phaseolus lunatus* (or *P. limensis*), having flat pods containing large, light-green, edible seeds. **2.** The seed of such a plant. See **butter bean.** [After LIMA.]

lim·a·cine (lĭm′ə-sēn′, lī′mə-) *adj.* Of, pertaining to, or resembling a slug. [New Latin *limacinus* : Latin *līmax* (stem *līmac-*), slug, snail, from *līmus,* slime + -INE.]

li·ma·çon (lĭm′ə-sŏn′; *French* lē-mə-sôN′) *n.* In geometry, a type of curve: the locus of a point on a straight line such that the point is always a fixed distance from the intersection of the line with a fixed circle as the line rotates about a point on the circle. [French, snail (named by Pascal with reference to the shape).]

limb[1] (lĭm) *n.* **1.** Any of the jointed appendages of a person or an animal, used for locomotion or grasping, such as an arm, leg, wing, or flipper. **2.** Any of the larger branches of a tree. **3.** Any extension or projecting part, as of a building or a mountain range. **4.** One that is considered to be an extension, member, or representative of a larger body, group, or the like. **5.** *Geology.* Either of the sides of a fold in rock strata, away from the central axis. **6.** *Informal.* An impish or naughty child. **—out on a limb.** *Informal.* In a difficult, awkward, or vulnerable position.

~*tr.v.* **limbed, limbing, limbs.** To dismember. [Middle English *lim, lymm,* Old English *lim;* akin to Old Norse *limr*†.] —**limb·less** *adj.*

limb[2] *n.* **1.** *Astronomy.* The circumferential edge of the apparent disk of a celestial body. **2.** The edge of a graduated arc or circle used in an instrument to measure angles. **3.** *Botany.* The expanded tip of a petal or the expanded upper part of a united corolla. [French *limbe,* from Latin *limbus*†, border, hem, seam.]

lim·bate (lĭm′bāt′) *adj. Botany.* Having an edge of a different color. [Late Latin *limbātus,* bordered, from *limbus*†, border.]

lim·ber[1] (lĭm′bər) *adj.* **1.** Bending or flexing readily; pliable. **2.** Capable of moving, bending, or contorting easily; agile; supple.

~*v.* **limbered, -bering, -bers.** —*tr.* To make limber. Often used with *up.* —*intr.* To make oneself limber. Used with *up*: *The football players limbered up before the game.* [16th century : perhaps from LIMBER (vehicle).] —**lim·ber·ly** *adv.* —**lim·ber·ness** *n.*

limber[2] *n.* A two-wheeled horse-drawn vehicle that carries ammunition and behind which a field gun may be towed.

~*v.* **limbered, -bering, -bers.** —*tr.* To fasten a limber to (a gun). Often used with *up.* —*intr.* To fasten a limber and a gun together. Often used with *up.* [Middle English *lymo(u)r,* shaft of a carriage, perhaps from Medieval Latin *limōnārius,* of a shaft, from *limō,* shaft, perhaps from Celtic.]

limber[3] *n. Nautical.* A channel on either side of the keelson into which water drains and can then be pumped away. [French *lumière,* hole, limber (literally, light).]

lim·bic system (lĭm′bĭk) *n.* The part of the brain governing basic activities, such as self-preservation, reproduction, and the expression of fear and rage. [French *limbique,* from *limbe,* LIMBUS.]

lim·bo[1] (lĭm′bō) *n., pl.* **-bos. 1.** *Often* **Limbo.** *Theology.* The abode of just souls kept from Heaven through circumstance, such as lack of baptism. **2.** A region or condition of oblivion or neglect. **3.** A state or place of confinement. **4.** An intermediate state, usually of an unpleasant or unsatisfactory nature. [Middle English, from Medieval Latin *in limbō,* "(region) on the border (of hell)" : *in,* on + *limbus*†, border.]

limbo[2] *n., pl.* **-bos.** A West Indian dance in which the performer has to pass under a low bar, bending his knees and leaning backward. [20th century : origin obscure.]

Lim·burg·er, Lim·bourg·er (lĭm′bûr′gər) *n.* A soft, often pungen, white cheese made with herbs, originally produced in Limburg province, Belgium.

lim·bus (lĭm′bəs) *n., pl.* **-bi** (-bī′). *Biology.* A distinctive border or edge. [Latin *limbus*†, border, hem, seam.]

lime[1] (līm) *n.* **1.** A spiny, evergreen tree, *Citrus aurantifolia,* native to Asia, having fragrant white flowers, and egg-shaped fruit with a green rind and acid juice used as flavoring. **2.** The fruit of this tree. [French, from Provençal *limo,* from Arabic *līmah.*]

lime[2] *n.* Any of several Old World linden trees of the genus *Tilia,* having sweet-scented flowers. [Variant of *line,* dialectal variant of obsolete *lind,* LINDEN.]

lime[3] *n.* **1. a. Calcium oxide** *(see).* **b. Calcium hydroxide** *(see).* **2.** A sticky substance smeared on twigs to catch birds; birdlime.

~*tr.v.* **limed, liming, limes. 1.** To treat with lime. **2.** To smear with birdlime. **3.** To catch or snare with or as with birdlime. [Middle English *lim,* Old English *līm.*]

lime·ade (līm-ād′) *n.* A sweetened beverage of lime juice and plain or carbonated water.

lime green *n.* A bright yellowish green. —**lime-green** *adj.*

lime·kiln (līm′kĭl′, -kĭln′) *n.* A furnace used to reduce naturally occurring forms of calcium carbonate to lime.

lime·light (līm′līt′) *n.* **1.** An early type of stage light in which lime was heated to incandescence producing brilliant illumination. **2.** The brilliant light so produced. Also called "calcium light." **3.** The state of being at the center of public attention. Used especially in the phrase *in the limelight.*

li·men (lī′mən) *n., pl.* **-mens** or **limina** (lĭm′ə-nə). The threshold of a physiological or psychological response. [Latin *līmen,* threshold, akin to *līmes,* boundary, LIMIT.] —**lim·i·nal** (lĭm′ə-nəl) *adj.*

lime pit *n.* A pit containing lime and water in which hides are soaked to remove the hair before they are tanned.

lim·er·ick (lĭm′ər-ĭk) *n.* A light humorous or nonsensical verse of five anapestic lines usually with the rhyme scheme *aabba.* [From the line "Will you come up to Limerick?" (the refrain of a convivial verse in a similar form).]

Lim·er·ick[1] (lĭm′ər-ĭk). County in Munster province, Republic of Ireland. Its fertile pastures support dairy and beef cattle.

Limerick[2]. Port on the Shannon River, the county town of County Limerick, Republic of Ireland. It was founded by the Vikings on an island on the river. It has long been noted for its lace.

li·mes (lī′mēz′) *n., pl.* **limites** (lĭm′ə-tēz′). A fortified boundary, as of the Roman Empire. [Latin *limes,* boundary, LIMIT.]

lime·stone (līm′stōn′) *n.* A sedimentary rock, chiefly $CaCO_3$. The chief mineral is calcite, but dolomite may also be present. It is used as building stone, and in the manufacture of lime, carbon dioxide, and cement.

lime-twig (līm′twĭg′) *n.* **1.** A twig covered with birdlime to catch birds. **2.** A snare.

lime·wa·ter (līm′wô′tər, -wŏt′ər) *n.* A clear, colorless, alkaline, aqueous solution of calcium hydroxide, used in calamine lotion and other skin preparations and as an antacid. It is used in a laboratory test for carbon dioxide, which causes it to go milky.

lim·ey (lĭ'mē) *n., pl.* **-eys.** *Slang.* **1.** A British person. **2.** A British sailor. [From earlier *lime-juicer,* American term for a British sailor or ship (the drinking of lime juice as an antiscorbutic was compulsory in the Royal Navy).] **—lim·ey** *adj.*

li·mic·o·line (lī-mĭk'ə-līn', -lĭn) *adj.* Of, pertaining to, or designating shore birds, such as sandpipers, of the suborder Charadrii. [New Latin *Limicolae* (former order name), "mud dwellers" : Latin *līmus,* slime, mud + *-colae,* from *-colus,* -COLOUS.]

lim·it (lĭm'ĭt) *n. Abbr.* **lim. 1.** The point, edge, or line beyond which something is no longer possible or allowable; the final or furthest confines or extent of something. **2.** *Usually* **limits.** The boundary surrounding a specific area; bounds: *within the city limits.* **3.** The maximum or minimum amount or number allowed: *an overdraft limit of $300; no minimum age limit.* **4.** *Informal.* Someone or something that goes beyond the limits of forbearance or acceptability. Preceded by *the.* **5.** *Archaic.* A region or section enclosed within or as if within boundaries. **6.** *Mathematics.* **a.** A number that is approached by a function as the variable approaches zero, infinity, or some other number. **b.** A value that a sequence or series approaches as the number of terms approaches infinity. **7.** Either of the two values between which a definite integral is defined. —See Synonyms at **boundary. —off limits.** Out of bounds.
~*tr.v.* **limited, -iting, -its. 1.** To confine or restrict within a limit or limits. **2.** To specify; fix definitely. [Middle English *limite,* from Latin *līmes*† (stem *līmit-*), border between fields, boundary.] **—lim·it·a·ble** *adj.* **—lim·i·ta·tive** *adj.* **—lim·it·er** *n.*
Synonyms: *bound, circumscribe, confine, restrict.*

lim·i·tar·y (lĭm'ə-tĕr'ē) *adj.* **1. a.** Of or pertaining to a limit or boundary. **b.** Limiting; restrictive. **2.** Limited.

lim·i·ta·tion (lĭm'ə-tā'shən) *n.* **1.** The act of limiting or the state of being limited. **2.** A restriction. **3.** A shortcoming. **4.** *Law.* A limited period during which, by statute, an action may be brought.

lim·it·ed (lĭm'ə-tĭd) *adj. Abbr.* **Ld., ltd., Ltd. 1. a.** Having a limit or limits. **b.** Confined or restricted. **2. a.** Not attaining the highest goals or achievement: *a limited success.* **b.** Having only moderate talent or range of ability: *a rather limited writer.* **3.** Having governmental or ruling powers restricted by enforceable limitations, as a constitution or legislative body might. **4.** Designating transport facilities, such as trains or buses, that make few stops and carry relatively few passengers. **—lim·i·ted·ly** *adv.* **—lim·i·ted·ness** *n.*

limited edition *n.* An edition, as of a book or print, limited to a stated number of copies.

limited liability company *n. British.* A public or private company in which the liability of a shareholder for the company's debts is limited to his actual investment, such that his other assets are not affected if the company fails.

lim·i·ter (lĭm'ə-tər) *n. Electronics.* A circuit that cuts off an alternating signal and restricts it to a predetermined maximum or minimum value. Also called "clipper."

li·mi·tes. Plural of **limes.**

lim·it·less (lĭm'ĭt-lĭs) *adj.* **1.** Having no limit or limits. **2.** Unconfined or unrestricted. —See Synonyms at **infinite.**

limit point *n. Mathematics.* A limit.

lim·i·trophe (lĭm'ə-trōf') *adj.* Near or on a frontier. Said of a country or region. [French, from Late Latin *limitrophus,* from Latin *līmes* (stem *limit-*), boundary + Greek *-trophos,* supporting, feeding (referring to frontier land devoted to supporting troops guarding the border).]

limn (lĭm) *tr.v.* **limned, limning, limns.** *Archaic.* **1.** To describe. **2.** To depict by painting or drawing. [Middle English *limnen,* to illuminate (manuscripts), shortened from *luminen,* from Old French *luminer,* from Latin *lūmināre,* from *lūmen,* light.] **—lim·ner** (lĭm'nər) *n.*

lim·net·ic (lĭm-nĕt'ĭk) *adj.* Of or occurring in the water of lakes or ponds to the level of light penetration. [Greek *limnē*†, pool, lake.]

lim·nol·o·gy (lĭm-nŏl'ə-jē) *n.* The scientific study of the life and phenomena of lakes, ponds, and streams. [Greek *limnē,* pool, lake + -LOGY.] **—lim·no·log·i·cal** *adj.* **—lim·no·log·i·cal·ly** *adv.* **—lim·nol·o·gist** *n.*

lim·o (lĭm'ō) *n., pl.* **-mos.** *Informal.* A limousine.

Li·moges[1] (lĭ-mōzh'). Capital of Haute-Vienne department, west-central France, on the Vienne River. It is famous for its ceramics.

Limoges[2] *n.* A variety of fine porcelain made at Limoges. Also called "Limoges ware."

lim·o·nene (lĭm'ə-nēn') *n.* A liquid, $C_{10}H_{16}$, with a characteristic lemonlike fragrance, used as a solvent, wetting agent, and dispersing agent, and in the manufacture of resins. [French *limon,* lime, from Old French, LEMON + -ENE.]

li·mo·nite (lī'mə-nīt') *n.* A widely occurring yellowish-brown to black natural iron oxide, essentially $FeO(OH) \cdot nH_2O$, used as an ore of iron. [German *Limonit,* "meadow ore," bog iron ore : Greek *leimōn*†, meadow + -ITE.] **—li·mo·nit·ic** (lī'mə-nĭt'ĭk) *adj.*

lim·ou·sine (lĭm'ə-zēn', lĭm'ə-zēn') *n.* **1.** Formerly, a large car with an enclosed passenger compartment and an open but roofed driver's seat. **2.** Any large and luxurious car. [Originally a cloak popular in *Limousin,* former province of France, which the projecting roof was thought to resemble.]

limp (lĭmp) *intr.v.* **limped, limping, limps. 1.** To walk lamely, especially with irregularity, when or as if one leg is weaker or shorter than the other. **2.** To move or proceed haltingly or unsteadily.
~*n.* An irregular, jerky, or awkward way of walking.
~*adj.* **limper, limpest. 1.** Lacking or having lost rigidity; flaccid; flabby. **2.** Lacking vitality, vigor, or strength of character; weak. **3.** Not stiffened; paperbacked. Said of a bookbinding. [Probably shortened from obsolete *limphalt,* lame, ultimately from Old English *lemphealt, læmpihalt.*] **—limp·ly** *adv.* **—limp·ness** *n.*

lim·pet (lĭm'pĭt) *n.* **1.** Any of numerous, generally marine gastropod mollusks, as of the families Acmaeidae and Patellidae, characteristically having a tent-shaped shell and adhering to rocks of tidal areas. **2.** One who clings persistently. **3.** A type of explosive designed to cling to the hull of a ship and detonate on contact or signal. [Middle English *lempet,* Old English *lempedu,* from Medieval Latin *lamprēda,* LAMPREY.]

lim·pid (lĭm'pĭd) *adj.* **1.** Characterized by transparent clearness; pellucid. **2.** Easily intelligible; clear. Said especially of literary style. **3.** Calm and untroubled; serene. [French *limpide,* from Latin *limpidus*†.] **—lim·pid·i·ty, lim·pid·ness** *n.* **—lim·pid·ly** *adv.*

limp·kin (lĭmp'kĭn) *n.* A brownish wading bird, *Aramus guarauna,* of warm, swampy regions of the New World, having a distinctive, wailing call. Also called "courlan." [LIMP (referring to its movements) + -KIN.]

Lim·po·po (lĭm-pō'pō). River in southern Africa. It flows 1,600 kilometers (1,000 miles) from a source near Pretoria, Transvaal, South Africa, to the Indian Ocean north of Maputo, Mozambique.

lim·u·lus (lĭm'yə-ləs) *n., pl.* **-li** (-lī'). A horseshoe crab; especially, *Limulus polyphemus.* [New Latin, from Latin, diminutive of *limus,* sidelong.]

lim·y (lī'mē) *adj.* **-ier, -iest.** Of, resembling, or containing lime.

lin. 1. lineal. **2.** linear.

lin·ac (lĭn'ăk') *n. Physics.* A **linear accelerator** *(see).* [From *lin*ear *ac*celerator.]

lin·age, line·age (lī'nĭj) *n.* **1.** The number of lines of printed or written material. **2.** Payment for written work according to the number of such lines.

lin·al·o·ol (lĭ-năl'ō-ôl', -ōl') *n.* Also **lin·al·ol** (lĭn'ə-lôl', -lōl'). A colorless, fragrant liquid, $C_{10}H_{18}O$, distilled from the oils of rosewood, bergamot, and other plants and trees, and used in perfume manufacture. [Earlier *linaloe,* fragrant wood of a Mexican tree, from Mexican Spanish *lináloe,* from Spanish, from Late Latin *lignum aloēs,* "wood of the aloe" : Latin *lignum,* wood + *aloē,* ALOE.]

linch·pin (lĭnch'pĭn') *n.* **1.** A locking pin inserted in the end of a shaft, as in an axle to prevent a wheel from slipping off. **2.** A central or cohesive element: *the linchpin of the family.* [Middle English *lynspin* : *lins,* linchpin, Old English *lynis,* akin to Old Saxon *lunisa*† + PIN.]

Lin·coln[1] (lĭng'kən). County town and market center of Lincolnshire, England, on the Witham River. It is a hub of rail and road transportation.

Lincoln[2]. The capital of Nebraska, in the southeastern part of the state. It is the railroad, trade, and industrial center for a large grain and livestock area.

Lincoln, Abraham (1809–65). 16th president of the United States (1861–65). From 1836 he practiced law in Illinois, until he became a Whig congressman (1847–49). Lincoln opposed slavery and in 1856 joined the new Republican Party, winning the 1860 presidential election. He vigorously led the North in the Civil War and in 1863 issued the Emancipation Proclamation, freeing the slaves in the areas still under Confederate control. He was re-elected president in 1864, and during its 1864–65 session Congress approved the 13th Amendment to the Constitution, abolishing slavery. Lincoln was assassinated in April 1865, only a few days after the war's end, at Ford's Theater in Washington, by John Wilkes Booth.

Lincoln, Mount. Peak, 4,357 meters (14,284 feet) high, in central Colorado, highest elevation of Park Range of the Rocky Mts.

Lincoln green *n.* **1.** A yellowish- or brownish-green color. **2.** Cloth of this color, which Robin Hood and his men are supposed to have worn. [After LINCOLN, England, where the cloth was originally made.] **—Lincoln-green** *adj.*

Lincoln Red *n.* Any of a breed of short-horned, red-coated beef cattle developed in eastern England.

Lin·coln·shire (lĭng'kən-shĭr', -shər). Largely flat county in eastern England, intersected by canals and dikes. Much of its fenland has been drained for agricultural use. Lincoln is its county town.

Lincoln's Inn *n.* One of the four **inns of Court** *(see).*

linc·tus (lĭngkt'təs) *n.* A liquid, syrupy medicine taken to relieve coughs. [Latin, from the past participle of *lingere,* to lick.]

Lind (lĭnd), **Jenny,** known as "the Swedish Nightingale" (1820–87). Swedish soprano. After 1852 she lived mainly in London.

lin·dane (lĭn'dān') *n.* A white poisonous powder used as a weed killer and insecticide. It is an isomer of hexachlorocyclohexane. [After T. van den *Linden,* 20th-century Dutch chemist.]

Lind·bergh (lĭnd'bûrg', lĭn'-), **Anne Spencer Morrow** (1906–). U.S. aviator and author. After marrying Charles Lindbergh (1929) she became an accomplished pilot in her own right. Among her successful books are *North to the Orient* (1935) and *The Flower and the Nettle* (1976).

Lindbergh, Charles Augustus, known as "Lucky Lindy" (1902–74). U.S. pilot. In May 1927 he made the first solo nonstop transatlantic flight, from New York to Paris.

lin·den (lĭn'dən) *n.* Any of various trees of the genus *Tilia,* having heart-shaped leaves and yellowish, often fragrant flowers, and often planted for shade. [Perhaps from Middle English *linden,* made of linden wood, Old English *linden,* from *linde,* the linden.]

Lindisfarne. See **Holy Island.**

Lind·say (lĭn'zē, lĭnd'-), **(Nicholas) Vachel** (1879–1931). U.S. poet. A peripatetic poet, he roamed the South and the Midwest, writing

linden *The common linden, or lime, tree grows to a height of over 30 meters (100 feet). Its fragrant yellow-white flowers bloom in late June and July.*

PRONUNCIATION KEY

ă, pat; ā, pay; âr, care;
ä, father, are; b, bib;
ch, church; d, deed; ĕ, pet;
ē, be; f, fife; g, gag; h, hat;
hw, which; ĭ, pit; ī, pie;
îr, pier; j, judge; k, kick;
l, lid, needle; m, mum;
n, no, sudden; ng, thing;
ŏ, pot; ō, toe; ô, paw, for;
oi, noise; ou, out; ŏŏ, book;
ōō, boot; p, pop; r, roar;
s, sauce; sh, ship, dish;
t, tight; th, thin, path;
th, this, bathe; ŭ, cut; ûr, fur;
v, valve; w, with; y, yes;
z, zebra, size; zh, vision;
ə, about, item, edible,
gallop, circus, peaceful

IN FOREIGN WORDS:

à, *Fr.* ami; œ, *Fr.* feu, *Ger.* schön; ü, *Fr.* tu, *Ger.* über; KH, *Ger.* ich, *Scot.* loch; N, *Fr.* bon; y', *Fr.* Compiègne

STRESS MARKS:

Primary stress: ʹ
in·cite' (ĭn-sīt')
Secondary stress: ʹ
in'sight' (ĭn'sīt')

and trading his poems for room and board. His original rhythmic style, typified in the collections *General William Booth Enters into Heaven* (1913) and *The Congo* (1914), earned him wide popularity.

line[1] (līn) *n. Abbr.* **l., L.** **1.** In geometry: **a.** The locus of a point having one degree of freedom; a curve. **b.** A set of points (x, y) that satisfy the linear equation $ax + by + c = 0$, where a and b are not both zero. **2.** A thin, continuous mark, such as that made by a pen, pencil, or brush applied to a surface. **3.** A similar mark cut or scratched into a surface. **4.** An indentation or crease in the skin, especially on the face or palm; a wrinkle. **5.** *Sports.* **a.** A mark on a playing court or field indicating a boundary of play. **b.** A mark or imaginary point at which a race starts or ends. **6.** A border or boundary: *the county line.* **7.** Any demarcation: *a picket line.* **8.** A contour or outline. **9.** In art: **a.** A mark used to define a shape or represent a contour. **b.** Any of the marks that make up the formal design of a picture. **10.** A cable, rope, string, cord, or wire, such as: **a.** One used on a ship. **b.** One used for catching fish. **c.** A clothes line. **d.** A string or cord used, as by builders or surveyors, for taking measurements, leveling, or straightening. **e.** A cable transmitting electric power of telecommunications signals: *telephone lines.* **11.** An open or functioning telephone connection. **12. a.** A system of public transport, as by ship, aircraft, or bus, usually over a definite route. **b.** A company owning or managing such a system. Sometimes used in combination: *an airline.* **13. a.** A railroad track. **b.** A particular section of a railroad network: *the Boston to New York line.* **14.** A course of progress or movement: *the line of flight.* **15. a.** A general method, manner, or course of procedure: *different lines of thought.* **b.** A manner or course of procedure determined by a specified factor: *development along Communist lines; a society divided along tribal lines.* **16.** An official or prescribed policy: *the party line.* **17.** A state of alignment, conformity, or agreement: *brought the front wheels into line; a wages agreement in line with recent settlements.* **18. a.** One's trade or occupation. **b.** The range of one's competence or preferred activity: *not really in my line.* **19.** Merchandise of a similar or related nature: *This store carries a line of small tools.* **20.** A group of persons or things arranged in a row or series, especially abreast. **21.** A series of persons, especially belonging to the same family, who succeed each other chronologically: *comes from a long line of bankers.* **22. a.** A row of words printed or written across a page or a column. **b.** A unit of verse made up of such a row, or formed of a certain number of metrical feet characteristic of the verse. **c. lines.** *British.* A usually specified number of lines of prose or verse to be written out by a pupil as a punishment. **23.** A brief letter; a note. **24.** *Often* **lines.** The dialogue of a play or other theatrical presentation: *learning his lines.* **25.** A calculated or glib way of speaking, usually to obtain some undeclared end. **26.** A hint or snippet of information: *tried to get a line on their secret plans.* **27.** A horizontal demarcation in bridge dividing categories of points scored: *Points above the line do not count toward game.* **28.** *Music.* Any of the five parallel marks composing a staff. **29.** *Military.* **a.** A formation in which elements, such as troops, tanks, or ships, are arranged abreast of each other. **b.** The battle area closest to the enemy. **c.** The troops in this area. **d.** A bulwark or trench. **e.** An extended system of such fortifications or defenses. **f. Line.** *British Army.* The regular numbered regiments, as distinguished from the Guards and auxiliary units. Preceded by *the.* **30.** The equator. Preceded by *the*: *crossed the line.* **31.** Any of the horizontal bands that make up a television picture. **32.** The course followed when hunting a fox. **33.** A unit of magnetic flux, one **maxwell** *(see).* **34.** The proportion of an insurance risk assumed by a particular underwriter or company. **—all along the line. 1.** In every place. **2.** At every stage or moment. **—draw the line (at).** To refuse to go as far as or beyond; consider as unacceptable. **—hold the line. 1.** To keep open a telephone connection. **2.** To maintain a firm position. **—in line for.** Likely or due to receive: *in line for promotion.* **—in the line of duty.** As a part of one's responsibilities in a given job. **—keep in line.** To keep in order; restrain. **—lay** (or **put**) **on the line.** *Informal.* **1.** To make payment. **2.** To jeopardize; put at risk: *put his reputation on the line.* **3.** To be candid or explicit: *He sure laid it on the line.* **—read between the lines.** To deduce the implicit rather than explicit meaning of a statement. **—shoot a line.** To try to deceive by lying or exaggerating. **—toe the line.** To obey the rules; conform.
~*v.* **lined, lining, lines.** —*tr.* **1.** To mark or incise with a line or lines. **2.** To represent or depict with a line or lines. **3.** To place in a series or row. Often used with *up.* **4.** To form a bordering line along: *Small stalls lined the alleys.* —*intr.* To form a line. Usually used with *up.* See **line up.** [Middle English *ligne, line,* cord, stroke, mark, line, partly from Old French *ligne,* from Vulgar Latin *linja* (unattested), from Latin *līnea,* thread, line, from *līnum,* flax, and partly from Old English *līne,* cord, rope, series, representing a Common Germanic borrowing of Latin *līnea.*]

line[2] *tr.v.* **lined, lining, lines. 1.** To sew or fit a covering to the inside surface of: *a coat lined with fur.* **2.** To cover the inner surface of: *Moisture lined the cave's walls.* **3.** To fill plentifully, as with money or food. [Middle English *linen,* from *line,* flax, Old English *līn,* from Germanic *līnam* (unattested), from Latin *līnum,* flax.]

lin·e·age[1] (lĭn′ē-ĭj) *n.* **1.** Direct descent from a particular ancestor; ancestry. **2.** Derivation. **3.** The descendants of a certain ancestor considered as the founder of the line. [Middle English *linage,* from Old French *li(g)nage,* from *ligne,* LINE.]

lineage[2]. Variant of **linage.**

lin·e·al (lĭn′ē-əl) *adj. Abbr.* **lin. 1.** Belonging to or being in the direct line of descent from an ancestor. Compare **collateral. 2.** Derived from or pertaining to a particular line of descent: *the lineal rights of royalty.* **3.** Linear. [Middle English, from Old French, from Late Latin *līneālis,* from Latin *līnea,* LINE.] **—lin·e·al·ly** *adv.*

lin·e·a·ment (lĭn′ē-ə-mənt) *n.* **1.** A distinctive shape, contour, or line, especially of the face. **2.** A definitive or characteristic mark or feature. [Middle English *liniament,* from Latin *līneāmentum,* from *līneāre,* to make straight, from *līnea,* LINE.]

lin·e·ar (lĭn′ē-ər) *adj. Abbr.* **lin. 1.** Of, pertaining to, or resembling a line or lines; straight. **2.** *Geometry.* **a.** In, of, describing, described by, or related to a straight line. **b.** Having only one dimension. **3.** *Art.* Characterized chiefly by forms and shapes that are precisely defined by line. Compare **painterly. 4.** Narrow and elongated: *a linear leaf.* **5.** Designating a form of script made up of lines rather than pictorial symbols. See **Linear A, Linear B.** [Latin *līneāris,* from *līnea,* LINE.] **—lin·e·ar·ly** *adv.*

Linear A *n.* A partly linear, partly pictographic script used in Crete from about 1900 to 1500 B.C.

linear accelerator *n.* An electron, proton, or heavy-ion **accelerator** *(see)* in which the paths of the particles accelerated are essentially straight lines rather than circles or spirals. Also called "linac."

linear algebra *n.* **1.** A branch of mathematics dealing with the theory of systems of linear equations, matrices, vector spaces, determinants, and linear transformations. **2.** A mathematical ring and vector space with scalars from an associated field, the multiplication of which is of the form $(aA)(bB) = (ab)(AB)$ where a and b are scalars and A and B are vectors.

Linear B *n.* A syllabic script, probably a modification of Linear A, used in Mycenaean Greek documents from the 14th to the 12th century B.C. and deciphered by Michael Ventris in 1952.

linear equation *n.* An algebraic equation, such as $x + y + 5 = 0$, in which the highest degree term in the variable or variables is of the first degree.

linear measure *n.* **1.** Measurement of length. **2.** A unit or system of units for measuring length. Also called "long measure."

linear momentum *n. Physics.* **Momentum** *(see).*

linear motor *n.* A type of electric motor in which the moving and stationary parts are linear and parallel so that a current causes motion along a line. Commonly, the moving part, which may be a vehicle, such as a locomotive, contains horizontal coils that induce a voltage in a long metal rail.

linear perspective *n.* See **perspective** (sense 1).

linear programming *n. Mathematics.* A technique using successive approximations to find the optimum value of a function that is subject to linear constraints, used extensively in planning industrial processes, economic models, and the like.

lin·e·a·tion (lĭn′ē-ā′shən) *n.* **1.** A marking or outlining with lines. **2.** An outline. **3.** An arrangement of lines.

line·back·er (līn′băk′ər) *n. Football.* Any of three defensive players forming a second line of defense usually just behind the ends and tackles. **—line·back·ing** *n.*

line breeding *n.* Selective inbreeding to perpetuate certain qualities or characteristics in a strain of stock.

line cut *n.* A letterpress printing plate made from a line drawing by a photoengraving process. Also called "line engraving."

line drawing *n.* A drawing made with lines only, especially one used as copy for a line engraving.

line drive *n. Baseball.* A batted ball hit sharply so that its path roughly describes a straight line. Also called "liner."

line engraving *n. Printing.* **1.** A metal plate, used in intaglio printing, on the surface of which design lines have been hand engraved. **2.** The process of making such an engraving. **3.** A print made from such an engraving. **4.** A line cut.

Line Islands (līn). Group of small islands in the central Pacific Ocean. Eight of them are part of Kiribati. The other three are uninhabited and are dependencies of the United States.

line·man (līn′mən) *n., pl.* **-men** (-mĭn). **1.** One who installs or repairs telephone, telegraph, or other electric power lines. **2.** One who inspects and repairs railroad tracks. **3.** *Football.* A player positioned on the forward line.

lin·en (lĭn′ən) *n.* **1.** Thread made from fibers of the flax plant. **2.** Cloth woven from this thread. **3.** Garments or other articles, such as sheets and tablecloths, made from this or similar cloth. ~*adj.* **1.** Made of flax or linen. **2.** Resembling linen. [Middle English, Old English *līnen, linnen,* "made of flax" (not used of linen cloth), from Germanic *līnin* (unattested), from *līnam* (unattested), flax, from Latin *līnum.*]

line of credit *n.* A **credit line** *(see).*

line of fire *n.* The flight path of a bullet or other missile discharged from a firearm.

line of force *n. Physics.* An imaginary line in a field of force, any tangent to which gives the direction of the field at the point of tangency.

line of scrimmage *n. Football.* See **scrimmage.**

line of sight *n.* An imaginary line from the eye to the object being looked at. Also called "line of vision."

lin·e·o·late (lĭn′ē-ə-lāt′) *adj. Biology.* Marked with fine lines. [New Latin *lineolatus,* from Latin *līneola,* diminutive of *līnea,* LINE.]

line printer *n.* A fast printer that prints characters a whole line at a time, used especially for printing the output from computers.

lin·er[1] (lī′nər) *n.* **1.** One that draws or makes a line or lines. **2.** A commercial ship or aircraft, especially one carrying passengers on a regular route. **3. Eyeliner** *(see).* **4.** *Baseball.* A **line drive** *(see).*

PRONUNCIATION KEY

ă, pat; ā, pay; âr, care;
ä, father, are; b, bib;
ch, church; d, deed; ĕ, pet;
ē, be; f, fife; g, gag; h, hat;
hw, which; ĭ, pit; ī, pie;
îr, pier; j, judge; k, kick;
l, lid, needle; m, mum;
n, no, sudden; ng, thing;
ŏ, pot; ō, toe; ô, paw, for;
oi, noise; ou, out; o͝o, book;
o͞o, boot; p, pop; r, roar;
s, sauce; sh, ship, dish;
t, tight; th, thin, path;
th, this, bathe; ŭ, cut; ûr, fur;
v, valve; w, with; y, yes;
z, zebra, size; zh, vision;
ə, about, item, edible,
gallop, circus, peaceful

IN FOREIGN WORDS:

à, *Fr.* ami; œ, *Fr.* feu, *Ger.* schön; ü, *Fr.* tu, *Ger.* über; KH, *Ger.* ich, *Scot.* loch; N, *Fr.* bon; y′, *Fr.* Compiègne

STRESS MARKS:

Primary stress: ′
in·cite′ (ĭn-sīt′)
Secondary stress: ′
in′sight′ (ĭn′sīt′)

liner² *n.* **1.** One who makes or puts in linings. **2.** Something used as a lining: *a wastebasket liner.*
lines·man (līnz′mən) *n., pl.* **-men** (-mĭn). *Sports.* An official assisting the referee or umpire, as in soccer or tennis, whose main duty is to indicate when the ball has gone out of play.
line spectrum *n.* A spectrum consisting of a set of discrete, fairly narrow lines.
line squall *n.* A band of extremely stormy weather with gusting winds, hail, and thunderstorms, associated with a cold front.
line storm *n.* A violent storm or series of storms of rain and wind popularly supposed to take place during the equinoxes.
line up *intr.v.* To form or take a place in a line. *—tr.v.* **1.** To put into line or into alignment. **2.** To assemble, organize, or prepare: *lined up a lot of evidence against him.*
line-up, line·up (līn′ŭp′) *n.* **1.** A line of persons formed for inspection or identification. **2.** A group or arrangement of people or things brought together for a particular purpose: *an interesting line-up of acts for the show; in the team's line-up for tonight's game.*
ling¹ (lĭng) *n., pl.* **lings** or collectively **ling.** Any of various marine food fishes related to or resembling the cod, such as *Molva molva,* of northwest European waters. [Middle English *leng(e),* probably of Low German origin; akin to Dutch *lenghe, linghe.*]
ling² *n.* A plant, **heather** *(see).* [Middle English *lyng,* from Old Norse.]
-ling¹ *suffix.* Indicates: **1.** The young of a specified animal; for example, **duckling, gosling. 2.** A smaller, lesser, or inferior version; for example, **princeling, underling. 3.** One produced by or under the care or control of; for example, **earthling, nursling, hireling.** Often used derogatorily. [Middle English, Old English, from Common Germanic *-linga-* (unattested) : noun ending *-ilaz* (unattested) + patronymic ending *-inga-.*]
-ling² *suffix.* Indicates: **1.** Direction or position; for example, **sideling, flatling. 2.** Condition; for example, **darkling.** [Middle English, from Old English, from West Germanic *-ling-, -lang-* (unattested).]
ling. linguistics.
lin·gam (lĭng′gəm) *n.* Also **lin·ga** (-gə). A stylized phallus worshiped as a symbol of the Hindu god Shiva. [Sanskrit *liṅgaṁ,* "distinctive mark," penis.]
ling·cod (lĭng′kŏd′) *n., pl.* **-cods** or collectively **lingcod.** A food fish, *Ophiodon elongatus,* of northern Pacific waters.
lin·ger (lĭng′gər) *v.* **-gered, -gering, -gers.** *—intr.* **1.** To delay departure; be slow and reluctant to leave; tarry. **2.** To hover between life and death for some time before dying. **3.** To remain, in dilute form; be slow in disappearing: *The smell of frying lingered on; The memory still lingers.* **4.** To delay; procrastinate. **5.** To proceed slowly; saunter. *—tr. Archaic.* To prolong; protract. Used with *on* or *out.* —See Synonyms at **stay.** [Middle English (northern dialect) *lengeren,* frequentative of *lengen,* to tarry, from Old Norse *lengja.*] **—lin·ger·er** *n.* **—lin·ger·ing·ly** *adv.*
lin·ge·rie (län′zhə-rā′, lăn′zhə-rē; *French* lăNzh-rē′) *n.* **1.** Women's underwear and night wear. **2.** *Archaic.* Linen articles, especially garments. [French, "linen garments," from *linge,* linen, from Latin *līneus,* made of linen, from *līnum,* flax.]
lin·go (lĭng′gō) *n., pl.* **-goes.** *Informal.* Language that is distinctive, unintelligible, or unfamiliar through being foreign or a jargon. [Portuguese *lingoa,* "tongue," language, from Latin *lingua.*]
lin·gua (lĭng′gwə) *n., pl.* **-guae** (-gwē′). A tongue or tonguelike organ. [Latin.]
lingua fran·ca (frăng′kə) *n., pl.* **linguae francae** (-kē) or **lingua francas. 1.** Any hybrid language used as a medium of communication between peoples of different languages. **2.** Any mutually intelligible medium of communication. **3. Lingua franca.** A mixture of Italian with French, Spanish, Arabic, Greek, and Turkish, formerly spoken in eastern Mediterranean ports. [Italian, "the Frankish tongue."]
lin·gual (lĭng′gwəl) *adj.* **1.** Of, pertaining to, or resembling the tongue or a tonguelike organ. **2.** *Phonetics.* Formed with the tongue in conjunction with other organs of speech. **3.** *Rare.* Linguistic. *~n. Phonetics.* A sound that is pronounced with the tongue in conjunction with other organs of speech, such as the sounds (t), (l), or (n). **—lin·gual·ly** *adv.*
lin·gui·form (lĭng′gwə-fôrm′) *adj.* Having the form of a tongue.
lin·gui·ni (lĭng-gwē′nē) *n.* **1.** *Used with a singular or plural verb.* Pasta in the form of long, thin, flat strands. **2.** A dish consisting of or containing such pasta. [Italian, plural of *linguino,* "small tongue," from *lingua,* tongue, from Latin.]
lin·guist (lĭng′gwĭst) *n.* **1.** A person who speaks several languages fluently. **2.** A student of a language or languages. **3.** A specialist in linguistics. **4.** *West African.* The spokesman of a chief, especially in Ghana. [Latin *lingua,* tongue, language.]
lin·guis·tic (lĭng-gwĭs′tĭk) *adj.* Of or pertaining to language or linguistics. **—lin·guis·ti·cal·ly** *adv.*
linguistic form *n.* Any meaningful unit of speech, such as an affix, word, phrase, or sentence. Also called "form."
lin·guis·tics (lĭng-gwĭs′tĭks) *n. Used with a singular verb. Abbr.* **ling.** The science of language; the study of the nature and structure of human speech.
lin·gu·late (lĭng′gyə-lāt′) *adj.* Tongue-shaped. [Latin *lingulātus,* from *lingula,* diminutive of *lingua,* tongue.]
lin·i·ment (lĭn′ə-mənt) *n.* A medicinal fluid applied to the skin by rubbing as an anodyne or to relieve stiffness. [Middle English *lynyment,* from Late Latin *linīmentum,* from Latin *linere,* to anoint.]
li·nin (lī′nən) *n.* The filamentous, achromatic material in the nucleus of a cell that interconnects the chromatin granules. [Latin *līnum,* flax + -IN.]
lin·ing (lī′nĭng) *n.* **1. a.** An interior covering or coating. **b.** Material that may be used for such covering or coating. **2.** The act or process of applying a lining to something.
link¹ (lĭngk) *n.* **1.** Any of the rings or loops forming a chain. **2.** Anything resembling a chain link in its physical arrangement or its connecting function, such as a cuff link or a loop in crochet. **3.** Anything that connects or provides a connection, such as: **a.** Something constituting a causal relation: *the link between stress and heart disease.* **b.** A system of transport or communications, as between two or more points: *a satellite link; the Boston to Washington shuttle link.* **c.** A single unit or element in such a system: *the islanders' only link with the outside world.* **d.** A passage, continuity, or progression, as in music, prose, or a broadcast. **4.** A unit of length used in surveying, equal to 0.01 chain or 20.1 centimeters (7.92 inches). **5.** A rod or lever transmitting motion in a machine. *~v.* **linked, linking, links.** *—tr.* **1.** To connect or couple with or as if with links. **2.** To intertwine: *link arms. —intr.* To become connected with or as with links. —See Synonyms at **join.** [Middle English, from Old Norse *hlenkr* (unattested), variant of *hlekkr,* link, ring.]
link² *n.* A torch formerly used at night for lighting one's way in the streets. [Perhaps from Medieval Latin *linchinus,* variant of *lichinus,* from Latin *lychnus,* from Greek *lukhnos,* lamp.]
link·age (lĭng′kĭj) *n.* **1.** The act or process of linking. **2.** The state or condition of being linked. **3.** A system of interconnected machine elements, such as rods, springs, and pivots, used to transmit power or motion. **4.** *Electricity.* A measure of the induced voltage in a circuit caused by a magnetic flux, and equal to the flux multiplied by the number of turns in the coil that surrounds it. **5.** *Genetics.* The occurrence of genes together on the same chromosome such that they are likely, in proportion to their proximity, to be inherited together rather than independently. **6.** In international relations, a bargaining tactic whereby apparently diverse issues are combined so that agreement on one is dependent on agreement on another or others.
link·boy (lĭngk′boi′) *n.* A boy hired to carry a torch to light persons along dark streets.
linked (lĭngkt) *adj.* **1.** Connected, especially by or as if by links. **2.** Intertwined: *linked arms.* **3.** *Genetics.* Exhibiting linkage.
linking verb *n.* A verb, such as *appear, be, feel, grow,* or *seem,* that connects a subject and a predicate adjective or predicate nominative; a copula.
link·man (lĭnk′mən) *n., pl.* **-men** (-mĭn). *British.* A person responsible for providing continuity between different items in a radio or television broadcast.
links (lĭngks) *pl.n.* **1.** A golf course. **2.** *Chiefly Scottish.* Relatively flat or undulating ground, sandy and turf-covered, along a seashore. [Middle English, from Old English *hlincas,* plural of *hlinc,* ridge.]
linn (lĭn) *n. Chiefly Scottish.* **1.** A waterfall. **2.** A steep ravine. [Scottish Gaelic *linne.*]
Lin·nae·us (lĭ-nē′əs, -nā′-), **Carolus,** also known as "Karl Linné" (after 1761 "von Linné") (1707–78). Swedish biologist. He created the system of classification of plants and animals used today. In his *Systema Naturae* (1735) and *Species Plantarum* (1753), animals and plants were described by genus and species. **—Lin·nae·an, Lin·ne·an** *adj.*
lin·net (lĭn′ĭt) *n.* **1.** A small Old World songbird, *Acanthis cannabina,* having brownish plumage. **2.** A similar bird, *Carpodacus mexicanus,* of western North America. [Old French dialectal *linette,* from *lin,* flax (the bird feeds on linseed), from Latin *līnum.*]

linnet *Though linseed is the linnet's favorite food, it feeds on other plants as well. But its numbers are declining as the increasing use of weedkillers depletes its food supply.*

li·no·cut (lī′nə-kŭt′) *n.* **1.** A print taken from a block of linoleum on which a design has been carved with a gouging tool. **2.** The technique of producing such prints.
lin·o·le·ic acid (lĭn′ə-lē′ĭk) *n.* A clear to straw-colored liquid, $C_{18}H_{32}O_2$, an important component of drying oils and an essential fatty acid in the human diet, being obtained from vegetable seed oils and some animal fats. [Greek *linon,* flax + OLEIC ACID (so called because found in linseed oil).]
lin·o·len·ic acid (lĭn′ə-lĕn′ĭk) *n.* A colorless liquid, $C_{18}H_{30}O_2$, an important component of natural drying oils and an essential fatty acid in the human diet, being obtained from vegetable oils. [Arbitrarily from LINOLEIC ACID.]
li·no·le·um (lĭ-nō′lē-əm) *n.* A durable, washable material made in sheets by pressing a mixture of heated linseed oil, rosin, powdered cork, and pigments onto a burlap or canvas backing, used chiefly as a floor covering. [Latin *līnum,* flax + *oleum,* OIL.]
Li·no·type (lī′nə-tīp′) *n.* A trademark for a machine that can set an entire line of type on a single metal slug and that is operated by a keyboard similar to that of a typewriter. **—Li·no·type** *v.* **—Li·no·typ·er, Li·no·typ·ist** *n.*
lin·sang (lĭn′săng′) *n.* Any of several Asian or African catlike carnivorous mammals of the genera *Poiana* and *Prionodon,* having a spotted coat and a long striped tail. [Malay.]
lin·seed (lĭn′sēd′) *n.* The seed of flax, especially when used as the source of linseed oil. [Middle English, Old English *līnsǣd* : Old English *līn,* flax, from Latin *līnum* + SEED.]
linseed oil *n.* A golden-yellow, amber, or brown oil that thickens and hardens on exposure to air, extracted from the seeds of flax, and used as a drying oil in paints and varnishes, and in linoleum, printing inks, and synthetic resins.
lin·sey-wool·sey (lĭn′zē-wo͝ol′zē) *n., pl.* **-seys.** A coarse fabric of

lintel *A massive lintel above the shoulder-high main entrance to the Church of the Nativity, Bethlehem.*

lion *Unlike most wild cats, which are solitary animals, the lion lives in groups, known as prides. It spends up to 20 hours a day asleep and may feed only once or twice a week. Once found all over Asia, Africa, and Europe, lions are now largely confined to eastern and southern Africa.*

PRONUNCIATION KEY

ă, pat; ā, pay; âr, care;
ä, father, are; b, bib;
ch, church; d, deed; ĕ, pet;
ē, be; f, fife; g, gag; h, hat;
hw, which; ĭ, pit; ī, pie;
îr, pier; j, judge; k, kick;
l, lid, needle; m, mum;
n, no, sudden; ng, thing;
ŏ, pot; ō, toe; ô, paw, for;
oi, noise; ou, out; o͝o, book;
o͞o, boot; p, pop; r, roar;
s, sauce; sh, ship, dish;
t, tight; th, thin, path;
th, this, bathe; ŭ, cut; ûr, fur;
v, valve; w, with; y, yes;
z, zebra, size; zh, vision;
ə, about, item, edible,
gallop, circus, peaceful

IN FOREIGN WORDS:

à, *Fr.* ami; œ, *Fr.* feu, *Ger.* schön; ü, *Fr.* tu, *Ger.* über; KH, *Ger.* ich, *Scot.* loch; N, *Fr.* bon; y', *Fr.* Compiègne

STRESS MARKS:

Primary stress: ′
in·cite′ (ĭn-sīt′)
Secondary stress: ′
in′sight′ (ĭn′sīt′)

cotton or linen woven with wool. [Middle English *lynsy-wolsye* : probably after *Lindsey,* village in Suffolk (where it was originally manufactured) + WOOL.]

lin·stock (lĭn′stŏk′) *n.* A long forked stick for holding a match, formerly used to fire cannon. [Dutch *lontstok* : *lont,* match, wick, akin to Middle Low German *lunte*† + *stok,* stick.]

lint (lĭnt) *n.* **1.** Downy material obtained by scraping linen cloth and used for dressing wounds. **2.** The mass of soft fibers surrounding the seeds of unginned cotton. **3.** Clinging bits of fiber and fluff; fuzz. [Middle English *lynet,* from Latin *linteum,* linen cloth, from *linteus,* made of linen, from *līnum,* flax.]

lin·tel (lĭnt′l) *n.* The horizontal beam that forms the upper member of a window or door frame and supports part of the structure above it. [Middle English, from Old French *lintel, lintier,* from Vulgar Latin *līmitāris* (unattested), alteration (influenced by Latin *līmes,* stem *līmit-,* boundary, LIMIT) of Latin *līmināris,* of a threshold, from *līmen,* threshold, LIMEN.]

lint·er (lĭn′tər) *n.* **1.** A machine that removes the short fibers that cling to cotton seeds after the first ginning. **2. linters.** The fibers thus removed.

lint·white (lĭnt′hwīt′, -wīt′) *n. Poetic.* A linnet. [Middle English *lynkwhyte,* Old English *līnetwige,* "linseed eater" : *līn,* flax + *-twige,* "plucker," "eater," from West Germanic *twig-* (unattested), to pluck.]

Linz (lĭnts). Capital of Upper Austria, on the Danube River. It is an iron and steel center and major port.

li·on (lī′ən) *n., pl.* **lions** or collectively (senses 1, 2) **lion. 1.** A large, carnivorous feline mammal, *Panthera leo,* of Africa and India, having a short tawny coat and a long, heavy mane around the neck and shoulders in the male. **2.** Any of several related animals considered to resemble a lion in some way. **3.** A person resembling a lion, as in bravery or ferocity. **4.** One whose eminence, as in arts and letters, has led to social prestige; a sought-after celebrity. **5.** A heraldic representation of a lion, the national emblem of Great Britain. **6. Lion.** *Astronomy.* The constellation and sign of the zodiac, **Leo** *(see).* Preceded by *the.* **—beard the lion in his den.** To face or defy the opposition in its own territory or home. **—twist the lion's tail.** To irritate or insult the nation or government of Great Britain. [Middle English *li(o)un, leoun,* from Norman French *liun* and Old French *lion,* both from Latin *leō* (stem *leōn-*), from Greek *leōn,* perhaps from Semitic.]

li·on·ess (lī′ə-nĭs) *n.* A female lion. [Middle English *leonesse,* from Old French *lionnesse,* from *lion,* LION.]

li·on-heart·ed (lī′ən-här′tĭd) *adj.* Extraordinarily courageous.

li·on·ize (lī′ə-nīz′) *tr.v.* **-ized, -izing, -izes.** To look upon or treat (a person) as a celebrity. **—li·on·i·za·tion** *n.* **—li·on·iz·er** *n.*

lion's share *n.* The largest or best part of a whole.

lip (lĭp) *n.* **1.** *Anatomy.* Either of two fleshy, muscular folds that together surround the opening of the mouth. **2.** Any structure or part that similarly encircles or bounds an orifice, as: **a.** *Anatomy.* A labium. **b.** The margin of flesh around a wound. **c.** Either of the margins of the aperture of a gastropod shell. **d.** The rim of a vessel, bell, crater, or the like. **3.** *Botany.* Any of the protruding divisions of an irregular corolla or calyx, either paired, as in the snapdragon, or single, as in an orchid. **4.** The tip of a pouring spout. **5.** *Slang.* Insolent talk. **6.** *Music.* The ability to shape the lips properly in playing a brass instrument; embouchure. **—bite one's lip. 1.** To hold back one's anger or other feeling. **2.** To show vexation. **—button one's lip.** *Slang.* To stop talking. **—smack one's lips.** To relish or gloat over something anticipated or remembered.
~*tr.v.* **lipped, lipping, lips. 1. a.** To touch the lips to. **b.** *Poetic.* To kiss. **2.** To utter; especially, to whisper or murmur. **3.** To lap. Used of water. **4.** To serve as a lip or rim to. **5.** *Golf.* To hit the ball so that it stops just at the edge of (the hole). [Middle English *lip(pe),* Old English *lippa.*]

Li·pa·ri Islands (lĭp′ə-rē). Formerly **Ae·o·li·an Islands** (ē-ō′lē-ən). Italian islands lying north of Sicily, in the Tyrrhenian Sea. They are volcanic and include Lipari, Vulcano, Stromboli, and Salina.

lip·ase (lĭp′ās′, lī′pās′) *n.* An enzyme that hydrolyzes fats to form glycerol and fatty acids. [LIP(O)- + -ASE.]

lip gloss *n.* A clear or colored cosmetic grease used to add shine to the lips.

lip·id (lĭp′ĭd, lī′pĭd) *n.* Also **lip·ide** (lĭp′īd′, lī′pīd′). Any of numerous fats and fatlike materials that are generally insoluble in water but soluble in common organic solvents, that are related to the fatty-acid esters, and that together with carbohydrates and proteins constitute the principal structural material of living cells. [French *lipide* : LIP(O)- + -ID.]

Lip·iz·za·ner, Lip·pi·zan·er (lĭp′ət-sän′ər) *n.* Any of a breed of nearly white horses, used by the Spanish Riding School in Vienna and trained in feats of dressage. [German, after *Lippiza,* Yugoslavia, where the breed was developed.]

Li Po (lē′pō′, lē′bō′) or **Li Bo** (lē′bō′) (1701–62). Chinese poet. One of China's greatest poets, he lived an episodic life, serving as court poet, wandering for long periods of time, and studying Taoism, all while writing the romantic and sometimes wine-inspired verses that earned him great repute.

lipo–, lip– *prefix.* Indicates fat or fatty; for example, **lipolysis, lipoma.** [New Latin, from Greek *lipos,* fat.]

li·po·gen·e·sis (lĭp′ə-jĕn′ə-sĭs) *n.* The synthesis of fatty acids in living cells. [LIPO- + -GENESIS.]

lip·oid (lĭp′oid′) *adj.* Also **lip·oi·dal** (lĭ-poid′l). Resembling fat; fatty. [LIP(O)- + -OID.] **—lip·oid** *n.*

li·pol·y·sis (lĭ-pŏl′ə-sĭs) *n.* The hydrolysis of fats or lipids. [LIPO- + -LYSIS.]

li·po·ma (lĭ-pō′mə) *n., pl.* **-mata** (-mə-tə) or **-mas.** A benign tumor of fatty cells. [LIP(O)- + -OMA.] **—li·pom·a·tous** (lĭ-pŏm′ə-təs) *adj.*

lip·o·pro·tein (lĭp′ō-prō′tēn′, -tē-ĭn) *n.* A conjugated protein consisting of a simple protein combined with a lipid group.

lip·o·some (lĭp′ə-sōm′) *n.* A small sac consisting of a synthetic membrane made of phospholipid, used to convey relatively toxic drugs to target organs or cancerous tumors. [LIPO- + -SOME.]

lip·o·trop·ic (lĭp′ō-trŏp′ĭk, -trō′pĭk, lī′pō-) *adj.* Preventing abnormal or excessive accumulation of fat in the liver. [LIPO- + -TROPIC.] **—li·pot·ro·pism, li·pot·ro·py** (lĭ-pŏt′rə-pē) *n.*

lipped (lĭpt) *adj.* **1.** Having a lip or lips. **2.** Having a specified number or kind of lips: *thin-lipped.*

Lip·pi (lĭp′ē), **Filippino** (*c.* 1457–1504). Florentine painter. He completed (*c.* 1480) Masaccio's frescoes in the Brancacci Chapel, Florence. He also painted the *Vision of St. Bernard* (*c.* 1486), and the *Madonna Enthroned.*

Lippi, Fra Filippo, also known as "Fra Lippo" (*c.* 1406–69). Florentine painter, father of Filippino. He left the Carmelite order to become a pupil of Masaccio. His paintings, such as the *Annunciation* (*c.* 1438) and the *Coronation of the Virgin* (*c.* 1441), display a bold three-dimensional style.

Lippizaner. Variant of **Lipizzaner.**

lip-read (lĭp′rēd′) *v.* **-read** (-rĕd′), **-reading, -reads.** *—tr.* To interpret (another's utterance) by lip reading. *—intr.* To use lip reading.

lip reading *n.* A technique used, especially by the deaf, to understand unheard speech by interpreting lip and facial movements. **—lip reader** *n.*

lip service *n.* Superficial respect or agreement.

lip·stick (lĭp′stĭk′) *n.* A stick of waxy or creamy lip coloring enclosed in a small cylindrical case.

lip-synch (lĭp′sĭngk′) *v.* **-synched, -synching, -synchs.** *—intr.* To move the lips in synchronization with recorded sound, as lyrics to a song. *—tr.* To move the lips in synchronization with: *lip-synched the song perfectly.* [LIP + SYNCH(RONIZE).]

Lip·tau·er (lĭp′tou′ər) *n.* **1.** A soft cheese originating in Hungary. **2. a.** A cheese spread made of Liptauer and paprika. **b.** An imitation spread made with cream cheese or cottage cheese. [German, after *Liptau* (Liptow), Hungary.]

liq. 1. liquid. **2.** liquor.

li·quate (lī′kwāt′) *tr.v.* **-quated, -quating, -quates.** To separate (the metals in an alloy) by melting some constituents while leaving others solid. [Latin *liquāre,* to melt, dissolve.] **—li·qua·tion** *n.*

liq·ue·fac·tion (lĭk′wə-făk′shən) *n.* **1.** The process of liquefying. **2.** The state of being liquefied.

liq·ue·fi·er (lĭk′wə-fī′ər) *n.* A device that liquefies; especially, an apparatus for liquefying gases.

liq·ue·fy, liq·ui·fy (lĭk′wə-fī′) *v.* **-fied, -fying, -fies.** *—tr.* To cause to become liquid, especially: **1.** To melt (a solid) by heating. **2.** To condense (a gas) by cooling. *—intr.* To become liquid. **—**See Synonyms at **melt.** [Old French *liquefier,* from Latin *liquefacere* : *liquēre,* to be liquid + *facere,* to make.] **—liq·ue·fa·cient** *n.*

li·ques·cent (lĭ-kwĕs′ənt) *adj.* Becoming or tending to become liquid; melting. [Latin *liquescēns* (stem *liquescent-*), present participle of *liquescere,* to become liquid, from *liquēre,* to be liquid.] **—li·ques·cence, li·ques·cen·cy** *n.*

li·queur (lĭ-kûr′, -kyo͝or′) *n.* **1.** A sweet syrupy alcoholic beverage, often with a brandy base, usually drunk in small quantities at the end of a meal. **2.** A mixture of sugar and wine used for inducing the second fermentation in the making of champagne. [French, from Old French *licour,* liquid, LIQUOR.]

liq·uid (lĭk′wĭd) *n. Abbr.* **liq. 1.** The state of matter in which a substance exhibits a characteristic readiness to flow, little or no tendency to disperse, and relatively high incompressibility. **2.** Matter or a specific body of matter in this state. **3.** *Phonetics.* A liquid consonant.
~*adj.* **1.** Of or being a liquid. **2.** Liquefied, especially: **a.** Melted by heating: *liquid wax.* **b.** Condensed by cooling: *liquid oxygen.* **3.** Clear; shining: *liquid eyes.* **4.** Flowing and clear; musical: *a liquid voice.* **5.** *Phonetics.* Designating a consonant, especially (l) or (r), that is produced without friction and can be prolonged like a vowel. **6.** Flowing gracefully in motion. **7.** Readily converted into cash: *liquid assets.* [Middle English *liquide* (adjective), from Old French, from Latin *liquidus,* from *liquēre,* to be liquid.] **—liq·uid·ly** *adv.*

liquid air *n.* Air in the liquid state, condensed from the gas by cooling and sometimes pressure, and used as a refrigerant.

liq·uid·am·bar (lĭk′wĭd-ăm′bər) *n.* A tree of the genus *Liquidambar,* such as the sweet gum. [New Latin *Liquidambar,* "liquid amber" (from its aromatic resin) : LIQUID + Medieval Latin *ambar,* ambergris, AMBER.]

liq·ui·date (lĭk′wə-dāt′) *v.* **-dated, -dating, -dates.** *—tr.* **1.** To pay off or settle (a debt, claim, or obligation). **2.** To wind up the affairs of (a business, a bankrupt estate, or the like) by determining the liabilities and applying the assets to their discharge. **3.** To convert (assets) into cash. **4.** To abolish. **5.** To dispose of; kill, especially by impersonal means: *The double agent was liquidated.* *—intr.* To go into liquidation. [Late Latin *liquidāre,* to make clear, melt, from Latin *liquidus,* LIQUID.] **—liq·ui·da·tion** *n.* **—liq·ui·dat·or** *n.*

liquid crystal *n.* Any of various liquids in which the atoms or molecules have partial order and are regularly arrayed in either one dimension or two dimensions, the order giving rise to optical properties, such as anisotropic scattering, associated with the crystals.

liquid crystal display *n.* A digital display, as in electronic calculators, containing liquid crystal between sheets of glass, becoming readable when a voltage is applied. Also called "LCD."

liquid glass *n.* **Sodium silicate** (*see*).

li·quid·i·ty (lĭ-kwĭd′ə-tē) *n., pl.* **-ties. 1.** The condition or quality of being liquid. **2.** The condition of having sufficient cash or liquid assets to pay debts or assume obligations.

liquidity preference *n. Economics.* A preference, influenced by factors such as income level and interest rates, for keeping one's assets in the form of money rather than investing them.

liq·uid·ize (lĭk′wə-dīz) *v.* **-ized, -izing, -izes.** —*tr.* To make liquid. —*intr.* To become liquid.

liquid measure *n.* **1.** A unit or system of units of liquid capacity. **2.** A measure for liquids.

liquid oxygen *n.* A pale blue liquid produced by distilling liquid air and used as a rocket fuel. Boiling point -182.9°C. Also called "lox."

liq·uor (lĭk′ər) *n. Abbr.* **liq. 1.** Alcoholic drink made by distillation or fermentation. **2.** A liquid substance, such as broth or juice, which has been used in cooking. **3.** *Pharmacy.* An aqueous solution of a nonvolatile substance. **4.** A solution, emulsion, or suspension for industrial use. **5.** Warm water used in brewing. ~*tr.v.* **liquored, -uoring, -uors. 1. a.** To treat (leather) with grease. **b.** To steep (malt, for example) in warm water. **2.** *Slang.* To cause to become drunk with alcoholic spirits. Used with *up.* [Middle English *lic(o)ur*, liquid, beverage, from Old French, from Latin *liquor*, from *liquēre*, to be liquid.]

liquorice. *Chiefly British.* Variant of **licorice.**

liquorish. Variant of **lickerish.**

li·ra (lîr′ə; *Italian* lē′rä) *n., pl.* **lire** (lîr′ā; *Italian* lē′rā) or **-ras.** *Abbr.* **l. 1.** The standard monetary unit of Italy, equal to 100 centesimi. **2.** The standard monetary unit of Turkey, equal to 100 kurus or piastres. **3.** A coin or note worth one lira. See feature at **currency.** [Italian, from Latin *lībra*, balance, measure.]

lir·i·o·den·dron (lîr′ē-ə-dĕn′drŏn) *n., pl.* **-drons** or **-dra.** Any of various trees of the genus *Liriodendron* in the family Magnoliaceae, especially the tulip tree, *L. tulipifera* of North America, or *L. chinense* from China. [New Latin, from Greek *leirion*, lily + *dendron*, tree.]

lir·i·pipe (lîr′ə-pīp′) *n.* A long scarf or cord attached to and hanging from a hood. [Medieval Latin *liripipium* †.]

Lis·bon (lĭz′bən). *Portuguese* **Lis·bo·a** (lēzh-vō′ə). Capital and chief port of Portugal, on the Tagus estuary. It exports wine, cork, and canned fish and produces textiles, chemicals, and paper. Voyages of discovery in the 15th and 16th centuries made it one of Europe's wealthiest cities. The city was rebuilt after an earthquake destroyed it in 1755.

li·sen·te (lē-sĕn′tä) *n., pl.* **lisente** (pronounced as singular). A monetary unit equal to 1/100 of the loti of Lesotho. See feature at **currency.** [Sotho, from English CENT.]

lisle (līl) *n.* **1.** A fine, smooth, tightly twisted cotton thread used especially for hosiery and underwear. Also called "lisle thread." **2.** Fabric knitted of lisle. [From *Lisle,* earlier form of LILLE, where it was originally made.]

lisp (lĭsp) *n.* **1.** A speech defect or mannerism characterized by the failure to produce normal sibilants, especially by the substitution of the sounds (th) and (*th*) for the sibilants (s) and (z). **2.** A sound suggestive of a lisp, such as the rustling of leaves. ~*v.* **lisped, lisping, lisps.** —*intr.* **1.** To speak with a lisp. **2.** To speak imperfectly, as a child does. —*tr.* To pronounce or express with a lisp. [Middle English *(w)lispen,* Old English *wlispian* (attested only in compound *awlispian*), from *wlisp,* a lisping, akin to Old High German *lisp* (imitative).] —**lisp·er** *n.*

lis pen·dens (lĭs′ pĕn′dĕnz′) *n., pl.* **lites pendentes** (lī′tēz′ pĕn-dĕn′tēz′). *Law.* A pending suit, usually concerning property, notice of which may be officially registered so that a prospective purchaser will know litigation is in progress. [Latin, "pending lawsuit."]

Lis·sa·jous figure (lē′sə-zhoō′) *n.* A type of curve: the locus of a point that moves with two simple harmonic motions in mutually perpendicular directions, the shape depending on the frequencies and relative phase of the motions. Lissajous figures can be formed from two electrical signals on an oscilloscope and used to measure frequency and phase. [After Jules *Lissajous* (1822–80), French physicist.]

lis·some, lis·som (lĭs′əm) *adj.* **1.** Lithe; supple. **2.** Capable of moving with ease; limber; nimble. [Variant of LITHESOME.] —**lis·some·ly** *adv.* —**lis·some·ness** *n.*

list¹ (lĭst) *n.* An item-by-item printed or written entry of persons or things, often arranged in a particular order, and usually of a specified nature or category: *a guest list; a shopping list.* ~*v.* **listed, listing, lists.** —*tr.* **1.** To make a list of; itemize. **2.** To enter in a list or register, especially: **a.** To register (a security) as officially approved for trading on the stock exchange. **b.** *British.* To classify as a listed building. **3.** *Archaic.* To enlist. —*intr. Archaic.* To enlist in the armed forces. [Old French *liste,* band, border, strip of paper, list, from Old Italian *lista,* from Germanic.]

list² *n.* **1.** A border or selvage of cloth, usually of a different material from the cloth it is bordering. **2.** A stripe or band of color. **3.** *Obsolete.* A boundary; a border. **4.** **lists. a.** An arena for tournaments or other contests. **b.** Any scene of combat. **5.** A ridge thrown up between two furrows in ploughing. [Middle English *liste,* border, edge, strip, Old English *līste.*]

list³ *n.* An inclination to one side, as of a ship; a tilt.

~*v.* **listed, listing, lists.** *Nautical.* —*intr.* To lean or tilt to the side. —*tr.* To cause (a ship) to list. [Origin unknown.]

list⁴ *v.* **listed, listing, lists.** *Poetic.* —*tr.* To listen to. —*intr.* To listen. [Middle English *listen, lusten,* Old English *hlystan.*]

list⁵ *v.* **listed, listing, lists.** *Archaic.* —*tr.* To be pleasing to; satisfy; please. —*intr.* To be disposed; choose. ~*n. Archaic.* A desire or inclination. [Middle English *listen,* Old English *lystan.*]

list·ed building (lĭs′təd) *n. British.* A building designated as being of particular historical or architectural interest and therefore subject to restrictions regarding its alteration or demolition.

lis·tel (lĭs′təl) *n. Architecture.* A narrow border, molding, or fillet. [Old French, from Old Italian *listello,* diminutive of *lista,* band, border, LIST.]

EASY-TO-READ FACES FOR CLOCKS AND CALCULATORS
How a well-known theory of bending light was put to practical use

Liquid crystal displays (LCDs) are used for showing the numbers on pocket calculators and digital watches and clocks. The numbers show up dark against a light background. Although the unusual properties of liquid crystals were known almost a century ago, it was not until the 1960's that anyone thought of using them for display panels.

A liquid crystal is one of a range of complex chemicals that share certain properties of a crystal—the molecules, for example, are arranged in an ordered, repeating pattern. But they also share a property of liquids—their molecular arrangement can easily change. A liquid crystal rearranges its molecules when an electric voltage is applied to it.

When a minute amount of power is applied to certain parts of an LCD, the liquid crystals in those parts change formation and alter the path of light passing through them. The parts no longer reflect light and their sections of the display panel appear dark.

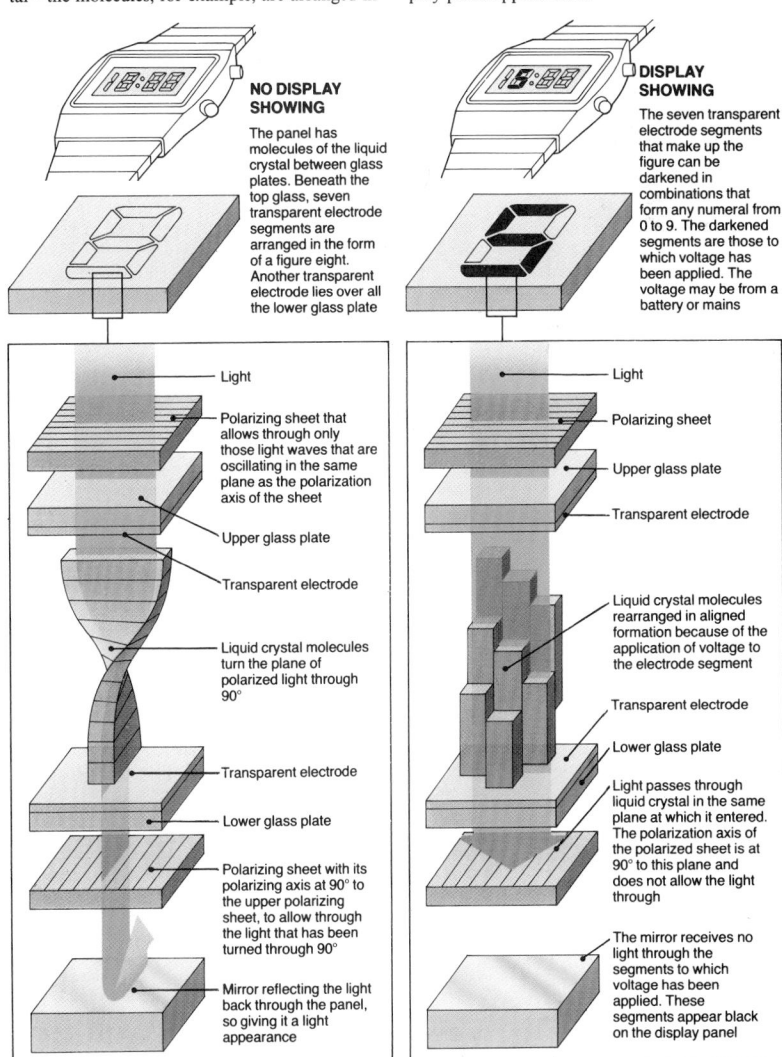

NO DISPLAY SHOWING
The panel has molecules of the liquid crystal between glass plates. Beneath the top glass, seven transparent electrode segments are arranged in the form of a figure eight. Another transparent electrode lies over all the lower glass plate

DISPLAY SHOWING
The seven transparent electrode segments that make up the figure can be darkened in combinations that form any numeral from 0 to 9. The darkened segments are those to which voltage has been applied. The voltage may be from a battery or mains

Light
Polarizing sheet that allows through only those light waves that are oscillating in the same plane as the polarization axis of the sheet
Upper glass plate
Transparent electrode
Liquid crystal molecules turn the plane of polarized light through 90°
Transparent electrode
Lower glass plate
Polarizing sheet with its polarizing axis at 90° to the upper polarizing sheet, to allow through the light that has been turned through 90°
Mirror reflecting the light back through the panel, so giving it a light appearance

Light
Polarizing sheet
Upper glass plate
Transparent electrode
Liquid crystal molecules rearranged in aligned formation because of the application of voltage to the electrode segment
Transparent electrode
Lower glass plate
Light passes through liquid crystal in the same plane at which it entered. The polarization axis of the polarized light is at 90° to this plane and does not allow the light through
The mirror receives no light through the segments to which voltage has been applied. These segments appear black on the display panel

HOW A WATCH USES LIQUID CRYSTALS *In a digital watch, a liquid crystal display shows the time in dark numbers. Each numeral is made up from seven electrode segments, which darken in many combinations to show any numeral required. The segments are activated by electrodes controlled by oscillations of the watch's quartz crystal.*

lis·ten (lĭs′ən) *intr.v.* **-tened, -tening, -tens. 1.** To apply oneself to hearing something. **2.** To take notice; heed: *begged her to reconsider, but she wouldn't listen.* **3.** To be alert so as to hear. Used with *for.* **—listen in. 1.** To tune in and listen to a broadcast. **2.** To listen to a conversation, sometimes surreptitiously. [Middle English *listnen,* Old English *hlysnan.*] **—lis·ten·er** *n.*

listening post *n.* A strategic spot for gathering information.

Lis·ter (lĭs′tər), **Joseph, 1st Baron** (1827–1912). British surgeon. He demonstrated in 1865 that carbolic acid was an effective antiseptic agent, showing that hygiene could save lives during surgery.

list·ing (lĭs′tĭng) *n.* **1.** An entry in a list. **2.** A list. **3.** *Computer Science.* A series of records on a file.

list·less (lĭst′lĭs) *adj.* Marked by a lack of energy or enthusiasm; disinclined toward any effort; indifferent; languid. [Middle English *listles* : *list,* desire, from *listen,* to be pleasing, to LIST + -LESS.] **—list·less·ly** *adv.* **—list·less·ness** *n.*

list price *n.* A basic published or advertised price, often subject to discount.

Liszt (lĭst), **Franz** (1811–86). Hungarian composer. In his lifetime he was more famous for his virtuoso piano playing than his compositions. His popular works include 20 *Hungarian Rhapsodies,* 6 Paganini *Études,* and 2 piano concertos.

lit[1]**. 1.** Alternate past tense and past participle of **light** (to illuminate). **2.** Alternate past tense and past participle of **light** (to descend).

lit[2]**. 1.** literal; literally. **2.** literary; literature.

lit·a·ny (lĭt′n-ē) *n., pl.* **-nies. 1.** A liturgical prayer consisting of phrases recited by a leader alternating with responses by the congregation. **2. Litany.** The set of prayers in this form in the Book of Common Prayer. **3.** Any repetitive or incantatory recital. [Middle English *letanie,* from Old French, from Late Latin *litanīa,* from Greek *litaneia,* entreaty, from *litanuein,* to entreat, from *litanos,* entreating, from *litē*†, supplication.]

li·tchi, li·chee, ly·chee (lē′chē) *n.* **1.** A Chinese tree, *Litchi chinesis,* bearing edible fruit. **2.** The small, round fruit of this tree, consisting of a thin, brown, scaly shell enclosing a white, fleshy interior with a seed at the center. In this sense also called "litchi nut." [Cantonese *lai chi,* corresponding to Mandarin Chinese *li*[4] *chih*[1].]

litchi *The warty-skinned fruits of the lychee tree,* Nephelium chinensis, *contain pale, jellylike edible flesh. The tree is native to southern China but is now grown commercially in warm regions around the world.*

-lite *suffix.* Indicates stone. Used in names of minerals; for example, **cryolite, actinolite.** [French *-lite* and German *-lit,* variants of *-lithe* and *-lith,* from Greek *lithos,* stone.]

li·ter (lē′tər) *n.* Also *chiefly British* **li·tre.** *Abbr.* **l** A metric unit of volume equal to a cubic decimeter, approximately 1.056 liquid quart or 0.908 dry quart. [French *litre,* from obsolete *litron,* old measure of capacity, from Medieval Latin *lītra,* from Greek *litra,* a unit of weight, a pound, a silver coin of Sicily.]

lit·er·a·cy (lĭt′ər-ə-sē) *n.* **1.** The condition or quality of being literate; especially, the ability to read, write, and use language. **2.** A basic understanding of or ability in a specified discipline.

lit·er·al (lĭt′ər-əl) *adj. Abbr.* **lit. 1.** In accordance with, conforming to, or upholding the explicit or primary meaning of a word or the words of a text. **2.** Word for word; verbatim: *a literal translation.* **3.** Matter-of-fact; prosaic: *a literal mind.* **4.** Avoiding exaggeration, metaphor, or embellishment; plain: *a literal statement.* **5.** Consisting of, using, or expressed by letters: *literal notation.* [Middle English *lit(t)eral,* of letters, written, from Old French *literal,* from Late Latin *litterālis,* from Latin *littera,* letter.] **—lit·er·al·ness** *n.*

lit·er·al·ism (lĭt′ər-ə-lĭz′əm) *n.* **1.** Adherence to the explicit sense of a given text or doctrine. **2.** Literal portrayal; realism. **—lit·er·al·ist** *n.* **—lit·er·al·is·tic** *adj.*

lit·er·al·ize (lĭt′ər-ə-līz′) *tr.v.* **-ized, -izing, -izes.** To make literal.

lit·er·al·ly (lĭt′ər-ə-lē) *adv. Abbr.* **lit. 1.** In a literal or strict sense. **2.** Really; actually: *"There are people in the world who literally do not know how to boil water"* (Craig Claiborne).

lit·er·ar·y (lĭt′ə-rĕr′ē) *adj. Abbr.* **lit. 1.** Of, pertaining to, or dealing with literature. **2. a.** Found in or appropriate to literature: *a new literary style.* **b.** Employed chiefly in writing rather than speaking: *a literary language.* **3.** Versed in or fond of literature or learning: *a literary woman.* **4.** Of or pertaining to writers or the profession of literature: *literary circles.* [French *littéraire,* from Latin *litterārius,* of writing, from *litterae,* epistle, writing, plural of *littera,* letter.] **—lit·er·ar·i·ly** *adv.* **—lit·er·ar·i·ness** *n.*

literary agent *n.* A person who handles an author's business affairs, especially in dealing with publishers. **—literary agency** *n.*

lit·er·ate (lĭt′ər-ĭt) *adj.* **1. a.** Able to read and write. **b.** Able to write well. **2.** Knowledgeable; educated. **3.** Familiar with literature; literary.
~*n.* **1.** A literate person. **2.** A well-informed, educated person. [Middle English *litterate,* from Latin *lit(t)erātus,* acquainted with writings, learned, from *litterae,* epistle, writing, plural of *littera,* letter.]

lit·e·ra·ti (lĭt′ə-rä′tē) *pl.n.* The literary intelligentsia. [Italian, from Latin *litterātī,* plural of *litterātus,* LITERATE.]

lit·e·ra·tim (lĭt′ə-rā′tĭm, -rä′tĭm) *adv.* Literally; letter for letter. [Medieval Latin, from *lit(t)era,* letter.]

lit·er·a·ture (lĭt′ər-ə-cho͝or′) *n. Abbr.* **lit. 1.** A body of writings in prose or verse. **2.** Writings of particular excellence or artistic value. **3.** The art or occupation of a writer of artistic or critical works. **4.** The body of written work produced by scholars or researchers in a given field: *medical literature.* **5.** Printed material of any kind, as for a political or publicity campaign. **6.** *Music.* The aggregate of compositions, especially for a specific instrument or ensemble. [Middle English *litterature,* from Old French, from Latin *litterātūra,* writing, learning, from *litterātus,* learned, LITERATE.]

-lith *suffix.* Indicates stone or rock; for example, **monolith, paleolith.** [Greek *lithos,* stone.]

lith. lithograph; lithographic; lithography.

lith·arge (lĭth′ärj′, lĭ-thärj′) *n.* A yellow lead oxide, PbO, used in storage batteries, glass, and as a pigment. Also called "lead monoxide." Compare **massicot.** [Middle English *lit(h)arge,* from Old French, from Latin *lithargyrus,* from Greek *litharguros,* "silver stone" : LITH(O)- + *arguros,* silver.]

lithe (līth) *adj.* **1.** Supple; limber. **2.** Marked by effortless grace. [Middle English *lith(e), lythe,* meek, mild, flexible, Old English *līthe.*] **—lithe·ly** *adv.* **—lithe·ness** *n.*

lithe·some (līth′səm) *adj.* Lithe; lissom.

lith·i·a (lĭth′ē-ə) *n.* **Lithium oxide** *(see).* [New Latin, from Greek *lithos,* stone.]

li·thi·a·sis (lĭ-thī′ə-sĭs) *n. Pathology.* The formation of stones in the body. [New Latin, from Greek : LITH(O)- + -IASIS.]

lithia water *n.* Mineral water containing some lithium salts.

lith·ic (lĭth′ĭk) *adj.* **1.** Pertaining to stone. **2.** Pertaining to lithium. [Greek *lithikos,* from *lithos,* stone.] **—lith·ic·al·ly** *adv.*

-lithic *suffix.* Indicates the use of stone; for example, **Neolithic.**

lith·i·um (lĭth′ē-əm) *n. Symbol* **Li** A soft, silvery, highly reactive metallic element that is used as a heat-transfer medium, in thermonuclear weapons, and in various alloys, ceramics, and optical forms of glass. Atomic number 3, atomic weight 6.939, melting point 179°C, boiling point 1,317°C, specific gravity 0.534, valence 1. [New Latin : LITH(O)- (from its mineral origin) + -IUM.]

lithium carbonate *n.* A white crystalline solid, Li_2CO_3, used in the ceramic and glass industries and as a drug in the treatment and prevention of schizophrenia and some depressive conditions.

lithium oxide *n.* A strongly alkaline white powder, Li_2O, used in ceramics and glass. Also called "lithia."

litho–, lith– *prefix.* Indicates stone; for example, **lithosphere, lithia.** [Latin, from Greek, from *lithos*†, stone.]

litho., lithog. lithograph; lithographic; lithography.

lith·o·graph (lĭth′ə-grăf′, -gräf′) *n. Abbr.* **lith., litho., lithog.** A print produced by lithography.
~*tr.v.* **lithographed, -graphing, -graphs.** To produce by lithography. [Back-formation from LITHOGRAPHY.] **—li·thog·raph·er** (lĭ-thŏg′rə-fər) *n.* **—lith·o·graph·ic, lith·o·graph·i·cal** *adj.* **—lith·o·graph·i·cal·ly** *adv.*

li·thog·ra·phy (lĭ-thŏg′rə-fē) *n. Abbr.* **lith., litho., lithog.** A printing process in which the image to be printed is rendered on a flat surface, as on stone or now chiefly on sheet zinc or aluminum, and treated so that it will retain ink while the nonimage areas are treated to repel ink. [German *Lithographie* : LITHO- + -GRAPHY.]

li·thol·o·gy (lĭ-thŏl′ə-jē) *n.* **1.** The physical character of a rock or rock formation. **2.** The study, description, and classification of rock, generally in handheld specimens and outcrops. [New Latin *lithologia* : LITHO- + -LOGY.] **—lith·o·log·ic, lith·o·log·i·cal** *adj.* **—lith·o·log·i·cal·ly** *adv.* **—li·thol·o·gist** *n.*

lith·o·marge (lĭth′ə-märj′) *n.* A white, reddish, or mottled clay, having a greasy feel. [New Latin *lithomarga* : LITHO- + *marge,* marl.]

lith·o·phyte (lĭth′ə-fīt′) *n.* **1.** *Botany.* A plant that grows on a rocky surface. **2.** An organism, such as coral, having a stony structure. [French : LITHO- + -PHYTE.] **—lith·o·phyt·ic** (lĭth′ə-fĭt′ĭk) *adj.*

lith·o·pone (lĭth′ə-pōn′) *n.* A white pigment consisting of a mixture of zinc sulfide, zinc oxide, and barium sulfate. [LITHO- + Greek *ponos,* artifact, product.]

lith·o·sphere (lĭth′ə-sfîr′) *n.* The solid outer layer of the earth. It lies above the semifluid asthenosphere and includes the crust and the solid upper part of the mantle down to about 75 kilometers (47 miles).

lith·o·stra·tig·ra·phy (lĭth′ō-strə-tĭg′rə-fē) *n.* **1.** Stratigraphy based on the physical and petrographic properties of rocks. **2.** The interpretation of the physical characters of sedimentary rocks. **—lith·o·strat·i·graph·ic** (lĭth′ō-străt′ĭ-grăf′ĭk) *adj.*

li·thot·o·my (lĭ-thŏt′ə-mē) *n., pl.* **-mies.** A surgical operation to remove stones from the urinary tract. [Late Latin *lithotomia,* from Greek : LITHO- + -TOMY.]

li·thot·ri·ty (lĭ-thŏt′rə-tē) *n., pl.* **-ties.** A surgical operation to pulverize stones in the bladder or urethra. [Irregularly from Greek *lithōn thrutika,* "stone-crushing (drug)" : *lithōn,* genitive plural of *lithos,* stone + *thrutikos,* crushing, from *thruptein,* to crush.]

Lith·u·a·ni·an (lĭth′o͞o-ā′nē-ən) *adj.* Of or pertaining to Lithuania, its people, or their language.
~*n.* **1.** An inhabitant or native of Lithuania. **2.** The Baltic language of the Lithuanian S.S.R.

Lithuanian Soviet Socialist Republic. Also **Lith·u·a·ni·a** (-nē-ə). One of the U.S.S.R.'s 15 republics, bordering on the Baltic Sea. Once a flourishing state, Lithuania was a province of Russia after 1795, but became an independent republic in 1918. It was incorporated into the U.S.S.R. in 1940. Vilnius is the capital.

lit·i·ga·ble (lĭt′ĭ-gə-bəl) *adj.* Capable of being litigated.

lit·i·gant (lĭt′ĭ-gənt) *n.* One who is engaged in a lawsuit.
~*adj.* Engaged in a lawsuit. [Latin *lītigāns* (stem *lītigant-*), present participle of *lītigāre,* LITIGATE.]

lit·i·gate (lĭt′ĭ-gāt′) *v.* **-gated, -gating, -gates.** —*tr.* To subject (something) to legal proceedings. —*intr.* To engage in legal proceedings. [Latin *lītigāre,* to dispute, quarrel, sue : *līs*† (stem *līt-*), lawsuit + *agere,* to drive, lead, act.] **—lit·i·ga·tor** (lĭt′ĭ-gā′tər) *n.*

PRONUNCIATION KEY

ă, pat; ā, pay; âr, care; ä, father, are; b, **bib**; ch, **church**; d, **deed**; ĕ, pet; ē, be; f, **fife**; g, **gag**; h, **hat**; hw, **which**; ĭ, pit; ī, pie; îr, pier; j, **judge**; k, **kick**; l, lid, needle; m, **mum**; n, no, sudden; ng, thing; ŏ, pot; ō, toe; ô, **paw**, for; oi, noise; ou, **out**; o͝o, **book**; o͞o, **boot**; p, **pop**; r, roar; s, sauce; sh, **ship**, **dish**; t, tight; th, **thin**, **path**; *th*, this, bathe; ŭ, cut; ûr, **fur**; v, valve; w, **with**; y, yes; z, zebra, size; zh, vision; ə, about, item, edible, gallop, circus, peaceful

IN FOREIGN WORDS:

à, *Fr.* ami; œ, *Fr.* **feu**, *Ger.* schön; ü, *Fr.* **tu**, *Ger.* **über**; KH, *Ger.* **ich**, *Scot.* loch; N, *Fr.* bon; y′, *Fr.* Compiègne

STRESS MARKS:

Primary stress: ′ **in·cite′** (ĭn-sīt′)
Secondary stress: ′ **in′sight′** (ĭn′sīt′)

lit·i·ga·tion (lĭt′ĭ-gā′shən) *n.* Legal action or process.
li·ti·gious (lĭ-tĭj′əs) *adj.* **1.** Given to or fond of litigation. **2.** Disputable at law; litigable. **—li·ti·gious·ly** *adv.* **—li·ti·gious·ness** *n.*
lit·mus (lĭt′məs) *n.* A blue, amorphous powder derived from certain lichens, that takes on a red color in acid solutions and a blue in alkaline solutions. [Perhaps from Old Norse *litmosi,* "dye moss" : *litr,* a dye, color + *mosi,* moss.]
litmus paper *n.* An unsized white paper impregnated with litmus and used as an acid-base indicator.
litmus test *n.* **1.** A test to determine alkalinity or acidity using litmus paper. **2.** Any decisive test: *The strike will be a litmus test of the government's industrial relations policy.*
li·to·tes (lī′tə-tēz′, lĭt′ə-, lī-tō′tēz′) *n.* A figure of speech consisting of an understatement in which an affirmative is expressed by the negation of its opposite, as in *This is no small problem.* [Greek *litotēs,* from *lītos,* simple, plain, unadorned.]
litre. *Chiefly British.* Variant of **liter.**
Litt. B., Lit. B. Bachelor of Letters. [Latin *Litterarum Baccalaureus*]
Litt.D., Lit.D. Doctor of Letters. [Latin *Litterarum Doctor*]
lit·ter (lĭt′ər) *n.* **1.** A disorderly accumulation of objects; especially, carelessly discarded rubbish, paper, and the like. **2.** The young produced at one birth by a multiparous mammal. **3. a.** Straw or other material used as bedding for livestock. **b.** Granules of a porous material kept in a tray so that pets may excrete indoors. **4.** A conveyance carried by people or animals, typically consisting of an enclosed couch mounted on shafts. **5.** A stretcher for the sick or wounded. **6.** The uppermost layer of a forest floor, consisting chiefly of decaying leaves.
~v. **littered, -tering, -ters.** *—tr.* **1.** To give birth to (young). **2. a.** To make untidy by discarding rubbish carelessly. **b.** To lie scattered untidily about (a place): *discarded cans and bottles littering the streets.* **3.** To scatter about. **4. a.** To supply (animals) with litter for bedding. *—intr.* **1.** To give birth to a litter. **2.** To scatter litter. [Middle English *litere,* bed, offspring at birth, from Norman French, variant of Old French *litiere,* from Medieval Latin *lectāria,* from Latin *lectus,* bed.]
lit·té·ra·teur, lit·ter·a·teur (lĭt′ər-ə-tûr′; *French* lē-tā-rà-tœr′) *n.* A literary person, especially a writer. [French, from Latin *litterātor,* elementary teacher, grammarian, from *littera,* LETTER.]
lit·ter·bug (lĭt′ər-bŭg′) *n. Informal.* One who litters public areas with discarded rubbish.
lit·tle (lĭt′l) *adj.* **littler** or **less** (lĕs) (especially for senses 2, 3, 4), **littlest** or **least** (lēst) (especially for senses 2, 3, 4). **1.** Small, or smaller by comparison. **2.** Short in extent or duration; brief: *in a little while.* **3. a.** Small in quantity or degree; not as much as needed or desired: *little hope of a recovery; speaks little English.* **b.** Small, but not too small, in quantity or degree. Preceded by *a*: *speaks a little English; Would you like a little sugar?* **4.** Unimportant; trivial; insignificant: *life's little troubles.* **5.** Without much force; weak. **6.** Narrow; petty. **7.** Without much power or influence; of minor status. **8. a.** Being at an early stage of growth. Said of children and animals. **b.** Younger: *my little sister.* **c.** Smaller or smallest of a set: *little toe.* **9.** Operating on a relatively small scale: *the little shop that fixes radios.* **10.** Resembling the specified person, place, or thing, but on a smaller scale: *Little Venice.* **11.** Appealing; endearing: *the little rascal; a pretty little cottage.* —See Synonyms at **small.**
~adv. **less, least. 1.** Not much; scarcely: *He sleeps little.* Often used in combination: *little-known; little-loved.* **2.** Rarely: *I see her very little.* **3.** Not at all; not in the least. Used before a verb: *I little thought I'd see you here; little did she know.*
~n. **1.** A small quantity: *Give me a little.* **2.** An insignificant amount. **3.** A short distance or time: *a little down the road; a little past four o'clock.* **—in little.** On a small scale. **—little by little.** By small degrees or increments; gradually. **—make little of.** To regard or treat as not very important; dismiss. **—think little of. 1.** To have no hesitation about (some course of action). **2.** To think of as relatively unimportant or valueless. [Middle English *litel, lutel,* Old English *lȳtel.*] **—lit·tle·ness** *n.*
Little A·mer·i·ca (ə-mĕr′ĭ-kə). A U.S. exploration base in western Antarctica, on the Ross Ice Shelf. Richard Byrd established the base in 1929.
little auk *n.* A small, short-billed, stout-bodied diving bird, *Plautus alle,* with a black and white plumage. It is found in northern oceans. Also called "dovekie."
Little Bear *n.* A constellation, **Ursa Minor** *(see).*
Little Big·horn (bĭg′hôrn′). River, *c.* 145 kilometers (90 miles) long, of northern and southern Wyoming. On the banks of the river Sioux and Cheyenne warriors defeated and killed Gen. George A. Custer and most of his troops (June 25–26, 1876). The battle is known as "Custer's Last Stand."
Little Col·o·ra·do (kŏl′ə-rä′dō, -răd′ō). A river rising in the mountains near the border of Arizona and New Mexico. It flows *c.* 507 kilometers (315 miles) to the Colorado River just above the Grand Canyon.
Little Dipper *n.* A constellation, **Ursa Minor** *(see).*
little end *n. Mechanics.* **1.** The smaller end of a connecting rod. **2.** The bearing between this and the gudgeon pin.
little finger *n.* The smallest finger on the hand, the fifth and last as counted from the thumb.
little grebe *n.* A small Old World grebe, *Podiceps ruficollis,* having a chestnut throat.
little hours *pl.n. Roman Catholic Church.* The canonical hours of prime, terce, sext, and nones, and sometimes including vespers and compline.
little magazine *n.* A literary magazine specializing in experimental writings and appealing to a limited readership.
Little Mis·sou·ri (mĭ-zo͝or′ē). River, *c.* 900 kilometers (560 miles) long, rising in northeastern Wyoming and flowing northeastward to the Missouri River in western North Dakota.
lit·tle·neck (lĭt′l-nĕk′) *n.* A clam, the quahog, when small and suitable for eating raw. [From *Littleneck* Bay, Long Island.]
Little Ouse. See **Ouse** (Suffolk).
little owl *n.* A small Old World owl, *Athene noctua,* having speckled brownish plumage.
little people *pl.n. Chiefly Irish.* Fairies, pixies, and the like; especially, leprechauns.
Little Rock (rŏk). Capital of Arkansas, in the central part of the state, on the Arkansas River. It is a river port and a commercial, transportation, and cultural center for the surrounding area.
Little Russian *n.* Ukrainian *(see).*
little slam *n.* See **slam** (bridge).
Little St. Bernard Pass. See **St. Bernard Pass.**
little theater *n.* A small theater usually for a community, collegiate, or experimental drama group.
lit·to·ral (lĭt′ər-əl) *adj.* Of or existing on a shore.
~n. A shore or coastal region, especially the zone between the high- and low-tide marks of spring tides. [Latin *littorālis, lītorālis,* from *lītus* (stem *lītor-*), shore.]
li·tur·gics (lĭ-tûr′jĭks) *n. Used with a singular verb.* The study of liturgies. Also called "liturgiology."
lit·ur·gist (lĭt′ər-jĭst) *n.* **1.** One who uses or advocates the use of liturgical forms. **2.** A scholar in liturgics.
lit·ur·gy (lĭt′ər-jē) *n., pl.* **-gies. 1.** The rite of the Eucharist. **2. a.** A system of public worship in the Christian church. **b.** The Book of Common Prayer. [Late Latin *lītūrgia,* from Greek *leitourgia,* public service, service of a priest, from *leitourgos,* public servant, minister, priest : *leōs* (stem *leit-*), variant of *laos,* people, multitude + *ergon,* work.] **—li·tur·gi·cal** (lĭ-tûr′jĭ-kəl) *adj.* **—li·tur·gi·cal·ly** *adv.*
Lit·vi·nov (lĭt-vē′nôf′, -nôv′), **Maxim Maximovich** (1876–1951). Soviet politician. He was Soviet foreign minister (1930–39) and ambassador to the United States (1941–43).
Liu Shao-qi or **Liu Shao-ch'i** (lyo͞o′ shou′chē′) (*c.* 1898–1973). Chinese Communist leader. He was chairman of the People's Republic of China from 1959 until he was purged in 1966 during the Cultural Revolution. He was officially rehabilitated in 1980.
liv·a·ble, live·a·ble (lĭv′ə-bəl) *adj.* **1.** Fit to live in; habitable. **2.** Worth living.
live¹ (lĭv) *v.* **lived, living, lives.** *—intr.* **1.** To exhibit the characteristic signs of life. **2.** To continue to remain alive: *lived to a great age.* **3.** To subsist; be maintained: *living on rice and fish; lived on inherited income.* **4.** To have one's usual dwelling in a particular place; reside. **5.** To conduct one's existence in a particular manner: *lived by the old code of personal honor; lives for her work.* **6.** To enjoy life and experience it to the full: *They really know how to live.* **7. a.** To remain in human memory: *She lives in the minds of us all.* Often used with *on.* **b.** To remain in existence; escape destruction. Often used with *on*: *Despite persecution, the faith lived on.* *—tr.* **1.** To go through (a particular form of existence or experience): *lived a nightmare.* **2.** To embody in one's manner of existence: *We lived our beliefs.* **—live and let live.** To be tolerant. **—live down.** *Informal.* To live sufficiently long, or sufficiently blamelessly, to overcome the effects of (a scandal, for example). **—live it up.** *Informal.* To have fun, especially in an extravagant way. **—live out. 1.** To reside away from the place where one works or studies. **2.** To live through (a period); live beyond (a time limit): *The injured butterfly lived out the day.* **—live together.** To reside together, especially in sexual intimacy. **—live up to. 1.** To succeed in guiding one's life by: *live up to religious ideals.* **2.** To show oneself to be as good as: *live up to a great reputation.* **—live with. 1.** To reside with, especially in sexual intimacy. **2.** To put up with (a continuing adverse factor). [Middle English *liven,* Old English *libban, lifian.*]
live² (līv) *adj.* **1.** Having life. **2.** Characteristic of life. **3.** Of current interest: *a live topic.* **4.** Actual, as opposed to pretended or imitation: *a real live princess.* **5.** Glowing; burning: *a live coal.* **6.** Brilliant; vivid. **7. a.** Capable of exploding: *a live bomb.* **b.** Charged with a bullet or shell; not blank: *live ammunition.* **8.** *Electricity.* Carrying current or electric potential. **9.** Native; not mined or quarried. Said of rocks and ores. **10. a.** Designating or participating in a program broadcast at the time of filming rather than recorded in advance. **b.** Involving actual performers rather than recorded material: *a party with live music.* **11.** *Printing.* **a.** Not yet set into type: *live copy.* **b.** Set and still in use. Said of type. **12.** *Sports.* Being or capable of being in play: *a live ball.*
~adv. As, participating in, or during a live broadcast, performance, or the like: *a rock band playing live.* [Shortened from ALIVE.]
live-bear·er (līv′bâr′ər) *n.* An ovoviviparous fish, such as a guppy. **—live-bear·ing** *adj.*
live-for·ev·er (lĭv′fər-ĕv′ər) *n.* A plant, the **orpine** *(see).*
live in *intr.v.* To reside in the place where one works or studies.
live-in (lĭv′ĭn′) *adj.* **1.** Living in the place where one works: *a live-in baby sitter.* **2.** Living with another person without being married: *her live-in companion.*
live·li·hood (līv′lē-ho͝od′) *n.* Means of support; subsistence. [Variant (influenced by LIVELY and -HOOD) of Middle English *liv(e)lode,*

little auk *The little auk (above), which lives around the Arctic Ocean, is a member of the auk family of seabirds. The family also includes razorbills, guillemots, and puffins.*

course of life, sustenance, Old English *līflād* : *līf*, LIFE + *lād*, course.]

Synonyms: *keep, living, maintenance, subsistence.*

live load (līv) *n.* A moving, variable weight added to the dead load or intrinsic weight of a structure or vehicle. Compare **dead load.**

live·long (lĭv′lông′, -lŏng′) *adj.* **1.** Long or seemingly long in passing. **2.** Complete; whole. Used chiefly in the phrase *the livelong day.* ∼*n. British.* A plant, the **orpine** (see). [Middle English *lefe longe,* "dear long" : *lef,* "dear" (here used as an intensive), Old English *lēof* + LONG.]

live·ly (līv′lē) *adj.* **-lier, -liest. 1.** Full of life; vigorous; energetic. **2.** Full of activity, interest, or excitement. **3.** Exhibiting or characterized by intense intellectual or emotional activity; keen: *a lively debate.* **4.** Exhibiting or inspiring liveliness; gay; cheerful. **5.** Effervescent; sparkling. **6.** Invigorating; brisk. **7.** Bouncing readily upon impact; resilient, as a ball is. **8.** *Nautical.* Buoyant; rising lightly with the sea swell. **9.** Lifelike. —See Synonyms at **active.** ∼*adv.* In a vigorous, energetic, or spirited manner. —**look lively.** To hurry up; make haste. Usually used in the imperative. [Middle English *lifliche,* Old English *līflic,* living, vital, from *līf,* life.] —**live·li·ly** *adv.* —**live·li·ness** *n.*

li·ven (lī′vən) *v.* **-vened, -vening, -vens.** —*tr.* To cause to become lively. Often used with *up.* —*intr.* To become lively. Often used with *up.*

live oak (līv) *n.* Any of several evergreen North American oaks, such as *Quercus virginiana,* of the southeastern United States, or *Q. agrifolia,* of southwestern North America.

liv·er¹ (lĭv′ər) *n.* **1.** *Anatomy.* A large, reddish-brown, multilobed, vertebrate gland situated in the top right hand part of the abdominal cavity. It secretes bile and acts in the formation of blood and in the metabolism of carbohydrates, fats, proteins, minerals, and vitamins. **2.** A similar invertebrate organ. **3.** The liver of an animal, used as food. [Middle English *liver,* Old English *lifer.*]

liv·er² *n.* One who lives in a specified manner: *a high liver.*

liver extract *n.* A dry, brownish powder containing vitamin B_{12}, which is prepared from mammalian livers and is capable of increasing the number of healthy red blood corpuscles in persons suffering from pernicious anemia.

liver fluke *n.* **1.** Any of several parasitic trematode worms, such as *Fasciola hepatica* or *Opisthorchis sinensis* (or *Clonorchis sinensis*), that infest the liver of various animals, including human beings. **2.** Infestation with such parasites. Also called "liver rot."

liv·er·ied (lĭv′ə-rēd) *adj.* Wearing livery, especially as a servant.

liv·er·ish (lĭv′ər-ĭsh) *adj.* **1.** Resembling liver, particularly in color. **2.** Having a liver disorder; bilious. **3.** Having a disagreeable disposition; irritable.

Liv·er·pool (lĭv′ər-pool′). City and port on the Mersey River in Merseyside, England, Britain's second-largest port after London. The city's Anglican cathedral, begun in 1904 and completed in 1978, is the largest Anglican cathedral in the world. Liverpool's industries include chemicals and engineering.

Liv·er·pud·li·an (lĭv′ər-pŭd′lē-ən) *n.* A native or inhabitant of Liverpool. ∼*adj.* Of or pertaining to Liverpool, its inhabitants, or their characteristic speech. [From *Liverpool,* with humorous substitution of *puddle* for *pool.*]

liver salts *pl.n. British.* A mixture of mineral salts taken to relieve indigestion or biliousness.

liver spot *n.* A localized brown discoloration of the skin occurring especially in old age; a lentigo.

liver starch *n.* A carbohydrate, **glycogen** (see).

liv·er·wort (lĭv′ər-wûrt′, -wôrt′) *n.* Any of numerous green nonflowering plants of the class Hepaticae within the division Bryophyta, found in moist habitats and lacking true roots. Also called "hepatic." [Referring to its liver-shaped leaves.]

liv·er·wurst (lĭv′ər-wûrst′) *n.* A type of sausage made with or containing chopped liver.

liv·er·y (lĭv′ə-rē) *n., pl.* **-ies. 1.** The distinctive uniform or insignia worn by a person's servants or retainers. **2.** The distinctive dress or garb worn by the members of a particular organization or group. **3.** Any distinctive dress or outward marking. **4.** Persons collectively who wear such costumes or uniforms, such as the members of a livery company. **5. a.** The provision of food or clothing to servants. **b.** The boarding and care of horses for a fee. **6.** A livery stable. **7.** *Law.* The official transfer of property, especially land, to a new owner. [Middle English *livere, liverye,* from Norman French *livere,* variant of Old French *livree,* "something delivered or given," allowance (later clothes) granted to servants, from the feminine past participle of *livrer,* to deliver, relieve, from Latin *līberāre,* to set free, from *līber,* free.]

livery company *n.* Any of various associations in the City of London that originated from the early trade guilds. Their members are no longer necessarily connected with the trades after which the companies are named, but they retain considerable influence over the election of the Lord Mayor and other City officers.

liv·er·y·man (lĭv′ə-rē-mən) *n., pl.* **-men** (-mĭn). **1.** A keeper or employee of a livery stable. **2.** A member of a livery company.

livery stable *n.* A stable that boards horses and keeps horses and carriages for hire.

lives. Plural of **life.**

live steam (līv) *n.* Steam coming from a boiler at full pressure.

live·stock (līv′stŏk′) *n.* Used *with a singular or plural verb.* Domestic

---

liver

THE VITAL WORK OF THE LIVER
The body's complex chemical factory

The liver is the largest organ in the body—a wedge-shaped gland weighing about 1.4 kilograms (3 pounds). In the liver, millions of cells process, store, and distribute the products of digestion that have been absorbed by the blood. They transform some into forms that the body can use; they break down poisons, such as alcohol, for removal as waste; and they build up and store the sugars that are needed for short-term energy. The liver also removes worn-out cells from the blood and reprocesses their red pigment hemoglobin. Another function of the liver is to secrete bile—a bitter liquid that facilitates digestion of food in the duodenum.

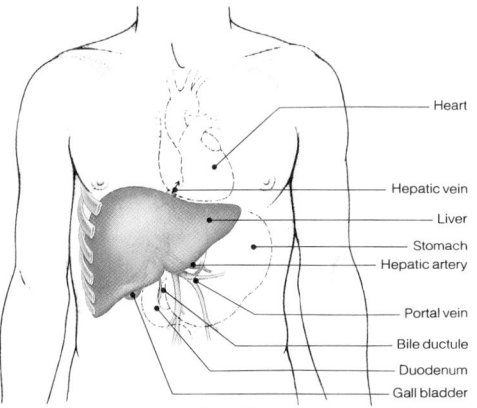

THE LIVER'S ROLE *Chemicals, such as sugars, amino acids, and vitamins, enter the bloodstream during digestion. The blood then passes from the stomach and intestines to the liver through a portal vein. When it has been filtered, the hepatic vein returns it to the heart. The bile ductule takes bile to the gallbladder, from where it passes to the duodenum. The hepatic artery supplies the liver with oxygenated blood.*

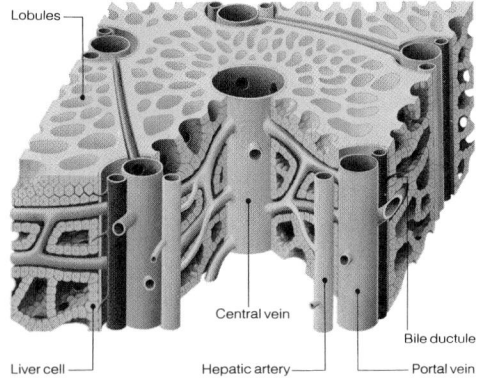

ANATOMY OF THE LIVER *Blood enters the liver and diffuses through thousands of minute lobules where the liver cells process the products of digestion.*

animals, such as cattle, sheep, or goats, raised for home use or for profit, especially on a farm.

live wire (līv) *n.* **1.** A wire carrying electric current. **2.** *Slang.* An extremely vivacious, alert, or energetic person.

liv·id (lĭv′ĭd) *adj.* **1.** Having a bluish discoloration of the skin, as from a bruise. **2.** Ashen or pallid, as with illness or rage. **3.** Extremely angry; furious. [French *livide,* from Latin *līvidus,* from *līvēre,* to be bluish.] —**li·vid·i·ty, liv·id·ness** *n.* —**liv·id·ly** *adv.*

liv·ing (lĭv′ĭng) *adj.* **1.** Possessing life; alive. **2. a.** Still alive; not yet dead. **b.** In active function or use. **c.** Still in existence as a species; extant. **3.** Of or pertaining to persons who are alive. **4. a.** Of, pertaining to, or characteristic of daily life: *living standards.* **b.** Of or pertaining to the maintenance of existence: *living costs.* **5.** True to life; real: *the living image of her mother.* **6.** Experienced while still alive: *a living hell.* ∼*n.* **1.** The state or condition of being alive. **2.** A manner or style of life: *plain living.* **3.** A manner or means of maintaining life; a

livelihood. **4.** *British.* A church benefice, including the revenue attached to it. —See Synonyms at **livelihood.**
Synonyms: *alive, extant.*

living fossil *n.* An extant organism, such as a coelacanth, that belongs to a taxonomic group whose other members are extinct.

living memory *n.* The collective experience or memory of all those currently alive: *the worst winter in living memory.*

living room *n.* A room in a private residence intended for the general use of the members of the household and for the reception and entertainment of guests.

Liv·ing·ston (lĭv′ĭng-stən), **Robert R.** (1746–1813). U.S. Revolutionary leader and diplomat. A member of the Continental Congress (1775–81), U.S. congressman (1784–85), chancellor of New York (1777–1801), and minister to France (1801–04), he helped draft the Declaration of Independence, administered the presidential oath to George Washington, and, with James Madison, purchased the Louisiana Territory (1803).

Livingstone. See **Maramba.**

Liv·ing·stone (lĭv′ĭng-stən), **David** (1813–73). Scottish missionary and explorer. He discovered the Zambezi River in 1851 and Victoria Falls in 1855. While searching for the source of the Nile (after 1866), he discovered Lake Mweru and Lake Bangweulu. Sickness forced him to return to Ujiji, on Lake Tanganyika, where Henry M. Stanley found him in 1871.

living wage *n.* A wage sufficient to provide minimally satisfactory living conditions.

Li·vo·ni·a (lĭ-vō′nē-ə). Region of the Soviet Union comprising southern Latvia and northern Estonia. It borders on the Baltic Sea and two of its arms, the gulfs of Riga and Finland. Control of Livonia was contested by Poland, Russia, and Sweden until 1772, when the region finally passed to Russia.

Li·vor·no (lē-vôr′nō). *English* **Leg·horn** (lĕg′hôrn′). Seaport and capital of Livorno province, Tuscany, Italy.

li·vre (lē′vər; *French* lē′vr′) *n. Abbr.* **lv.** A former French unit of account originally worth a pound of silver. [French, from Latin *lībra,* a pound.]

Liv·y (lĭv′ē). Latin name Titus Livius (*c.* 59 B.C.–A.D. 17). Roman historian, born in Padua. His history of Rome originally consisted of 142 books, of which only 35 survive.

lix·iv·i·ate (lĭk-sĭv′ē-āt′) *tr.v.* **-ated, -ating, -ates.** To wash or percolate the soluble matter from. [Late Latin *lixīvium,* lye, from the neuter of Latin *lixīvius,* of lye, from *lixa,* lye.] —**lix·iv·i·al** *adj.* —**lix·iv·i·a·tion** *n.*

lix·iv·i·um (lĭk-sĭv′ē-əm) *n., pl.* **-ums** or **-ia** (-ē-ə). A solution obtained by lixiviation; especially, the lye obtained by leaching wood ash. [Late Latin, from *lixivius,* of lye, from *lix,* lye.]

liz·ard (lĭz′ərd) *n.* **1.** Any of numerous reptiles of the suborder Sauria (or Lacertilia), characteristically having an elongated, scaly body, four legs, and a tapering tail. **2.** Broadly, any reptile or amphibian resembling a lizard. **3.** Leather made from the skin of a lizard. [Middle English *liserd, lesard(e),* from Old French *lesard, laisarde,* from Latin *lacertus, lacerta*†.]

lizard fish *n.* Any of various bottom-dwelling fishes of the family Synodontidae, of warm seas, having a lizardlike head.

ll. lines.

lla·ma (lä′mə) *n.* **1.** A South American ruminant mammal, *Lama peruana* (or *L. glana*), domesticated as a beast of burden and for its soft, fleecy wool. **2.** Any other animal of the genus *Lama,* such as the guanaco. [Spanish, from Quechua.]

lla·no (lăn′ō, lä′nō) *n., pl.* **-nos.** A large, grassy, almost treeless plain, as in Latin America; savannah. [Spanish, from Latin *plānum,* a plain, from the neuter of *plānus,* level.]

LLa·no Es·ta·ca·do (lăn′ō ĕs′tə-kä′dō, lä′nō). A southern section of the Great Plains, extending over southeastern New Mexico and northwestern Texas. [Spanish, "staked plain."]

LL.B. Bachelor of Laws. [Latin *Legum Baccalaureus*]

LL.D. Doctor of Laws. [Latin *Legum Doctor*]

Llew·el·lyn (lo͞o-ĕl′ĭn), **Richard,** pen name of Richard Dafydd Vivian Llewellyn Lloyd (1906–83). British novelist, born in Wales. He wrote *How Green Was My Valley* (1939), a portrait of life in a southern Wales mining village.

LL.M. Master of Laws. [Latin *Legum Magister*]

Lloyd, Harold (1894–1971). U.S. comedian of the silent screen. His stunts included hanging from a clock face high above a street in *Safety Last* (1923).

Lloyd George (jôrj), **David, 1st Earl of Dwyfor** (1863–1945). British prime minister (1916–22). He was elected a Liberal M.P. in 1890 and as Chancellor of the Exchequer (1908–15) initiated the welfare state, introducing old-age pensions, unemployment benefit, and national health insurance. In 1916 he succeeded Herbert Asquith as prime minister. His postwar coalition government set up the Irish Free State, but lost power in 1922. Lloyd George remained Liberal Party leader until 1931, but never held office again.

Lloyd's (loidz) *n.* An association of underwriters founded in London in 1688, originally specializing in marine insurance and shipping information and now noted for the variety of insurance dealt with. [After *Lloyd's* Coffee House in London, a gathering place of marine underwriters.]

Lloyd's List *n.* A daily news sheet concerned with shipping matters, published by Lloyd's.

Lloyd's Register *n.* A compilation of data about oceangoing vessels of all nations, published annually by Lloyd's.

lm lumen.

ln natural logarithm.

lo (lō) *interj.* Used to attract attention or to show surprise. Now archaic except in the phrase *lo and behold.* [Middle English *lo, la,* Old English *lā.*]

loach (lōch) *n.* Any of various Eurasian and African freshwater fishes of the family Cobitidae, having barbels around the mouth. [Middle English *loch(e),* from Old French *loche*†.]

load (lōd) *n. Abbr.* **ld.** **1. a.** A supported weight or mass. **b.** The overall force to which a structure is subjected in supporting a weight or mass, or in resisting externally applied forces. **2. a.** Anything that is transported by a motor vehicle, ship, or aircraft, or carried by a person or pack animal. **b.** The quantity so transported or capable of being so transported: *a full load.* Often used in combination: *a busload of football supporters.* **3. a.** The share of work allocated to or required of an individual, machine, group, or organization: *has a fairly light teaching load.* **b.** The demand for services or performance made on a machine or system. **4.** The amount that can be loaded into a machine or device at one time. **5.** A single charge of ammunition for a firearm. **6.** A source of stress or anxiety, regarded as a depressing weight on the mind; a burden. **7.** The external mechanical resistance against which a machine acts. **8. a.** The power output of a generator or power plant. **b.** A device, or the resistance of a device, to which power is delivered. **9.** *Geology.* Material carried by a river, stream, sea, glacier, or wind during the process of denudation. **10.** *Usually* **loads.** *Informal.* Any large amount or quantity. —**get a load of.** *Slang.* To look at or pay attention to: *Get a load of that!*
—*v.* **loaded, loading, loads.** —*tr.* **1.** To put or place (a load) in or on a structure, device, or conveyance. **2.** To put or place in or on (a structure, device, or conveyance). **3.** To provide with an abundant or excessive supply. **4.** To weigh down; burden; oppress. **5.** To charge (a firearm) with ammunition. **6. a.** To insert (film or tape, for example) into a holder or magazine. **b.** To insert film or tape, for example, into (a magazine, camera, or similar device). **7.** To tamper with; especially, to make (dice) heavier on one side by adding weight. **8. a.** To twist or bias (evidence). **b.** To charge (a question) with broader implications that may not be immediately obvious, especially so as to trap the person being questioned. **9.** To dilute, adulterate, or doctor. **10.** To increase (an insurance premium) by adding a loading. **11.** *Electricity.* **a.** To raise the power demand in (a circuit), as by adding resistance. **b.** To draw power from (a generator). **12.** To raise the power output of (an engine). **13.** *Physics.* To add a material such as barium to (concrete, for example) in order to increase radiation-shielding efficiency. —*intr.* **1.** To receive a load; take on cargo. **2.** To be charged with ammunition. **3.** To insert ammunition, film, or tape, for example. [Middle English *lode* (influenced in sense by Middle English *laden,* to load, LADE), Old English *lād,* way, course, conveyance.]
Usage: The past tense and past participle of this verb are both *loaded: We loaded the goods; The goods were loaded. Laden* is an adjective, generally used after the verb unless premodified itself: *The table was laden with good things to eat; a heavily laden table.* In contexts where either word could be used, there is usually a difference in meaning: *The ship was loaded with ammunition* (i.e., ammunition was put on board by someone or something), but *The ship was laden with ammunition* (it was weighed down with ammunition).

load displacement *n. Nautical.* The displacement of a fully loaded ship.

load·ed (lō′dĭd) *adj.* **1.** Having a load. **2.** Filled with ammunition, film, tape, or the like. **3.** Weighted or tampered with, as fraudulent dice. **4.** Meant to trick or trap: *a loaded question.* **5.** *Slang.* Extremely wealthy. **6.** *Slang.* Drunk. **7.** *Slang.* Drugged.

load·er (lō′dər) *n.* **1.** One that loads. **2.** *Computer Science.* A program that transfers data from an off-line memory to an on-line memory by means of an input or storage device. **3.** An apparatus, such as a washing machine or firearm, that is loaded in a specified way. Used in combination: *top-loader; breechloader.*

load factor *n.* **1.** A measure of the load on an electrical supply system, equal to the ratio of average load to peak load. **2. a.** The ratio of the load of an aircraft to its unloaded weight. **b.** The ratio of the load carried by an aircraft to its maximum load, often expressed as a percentage.

load·ing (lō′dĭng) *n. Abbr.* **ldg.** **1.** A weight, stress, or burden. **2.** The act of supplying a load. **3.** A substance added to something; a filler. **4.** An addition to an insurance premium taking account of special circumstances: *an extra loading for those with hazardous occupations.* **5.** *Electricity.* The addition of inductance to a transmission line to improve its transmission characteristics. **6.** *Aeronautics.* The ratio of the weight of an aircraft to its power (the *power loading*), to its wing span (the *span loading*), or to its wing area (the *wing loading*). **7.** *Psychology.* The correlation or degree of correlation between a specific factor or variable, such as a test score, and a broad condition or constant, such as a personality trait. **8.** A contractually agreed bonus or extra payment added to basic wages or salary in certain conditions; a weighting.

loading program *n. Computer Science.* A sequence of computer instructions that starts the processing of a program entered by means of an automatic input device.

load line *n. Nautical.* A **Plimsoll line** *(see).*

load shedding *n.* Temporary reduction of the electric power supply in an area to avoid overloading the generators.

loadstar. Variant of **lodestar.**

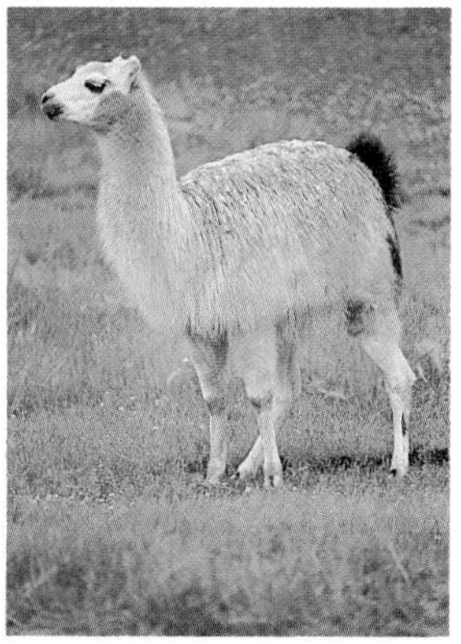

llama *The llama, which is a member of the camel family, is one of the few animals apart from dogs to have been domesticated in the New World prior to 1492. (Horses, cattle, and sheep were unknown until the Spanish Conquest.) Indian peoples in the Andes rely upon the llama still as a pack animal and for its meat, milk, and fleece. Its droppings also are dried and burned to provide heat in the mountains. The vicuña, alpaca, and guanaco (wild llama) are close relatives.*

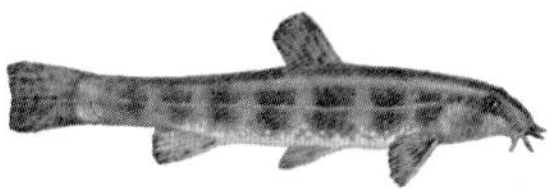

loach *There are over 200 species of loach, a bony freshwater fish that is found chiefly in Asia and Europe. It lives and feeds on muddy riverbeds. The stone loach (above) lives in fast-flowing streams.*

loadstone. Variant of **lodestone.**

loaf¹ (lōf) n., pl. **loaves** (lōvz). **1.** A shaped mass of bread baked in one piece. **2.** Any shaped, typically oblong mass of food: nut loaf. **3.** British Slang. The head; the brains: Use your loaf. [Middle English lo(o)f, laf, Old English hlāf, loaf, bread, from Germanic hlaibaz (unattested). See also **lord, lady.** Sense 3, rhyming slang, loaf of bread, head.]

loaf² v. **loafed, loafing, loafs.** —intr. **1.** To spend time lazily or aimlessly. Used with around or about. **2.** To waste time on a job; dawdle. —tr. To spend (time) lazily or idly. Usually used with away. [Probably back-formation from LOAFER.] —**loaf·er** n.

Loaf·er (lō'fər) n. A trademark for a low leather step-in shoe with an upper resembling a moccasin but with a broad, flat heel.

loam (lōm) n. **1.** Fertile soil consisting of sand, clay, silt, and organic matter. **2.** A mixture of moist clay and sand, together with straw, used principally in making bricks and foundry molds. [Middle English lome, lame, Old English lām.] —**loam·y** adj.

loan¹ (lōn) n. **1.** A sum of money lent at interest. **2.** Anything lent for temporary use. **3.** An act of lending or permission to borrow: gave me the loan of her bike. **4.** A loanword. —**on loan. 1.** Borrowed: She has my coat on loan. **2.** Transferred temporarily to some duty or place away from a regular position or location.
~tr.v. **loaned, loaning, loans.** To lend; grant a loan of. [Middle English lone, lane, from Old Norse lān.]
   Usage: Loan has long been established as a verb, especially in business usage, though some hold that lend is the preferred form, in general as well as formal writing. Many writers prefer lend in these examples: If you lend (not loan) money to a friend, he may cease to be your friend. When I refused to lend (not loan) him my pen, he became very angry. Many phrases and figurative uses require lend: lend an ear; a moneylender. Distance lends enchantment.

loan² n. Also **loan·ing** (lō'nĭng). Chiefly Scottish. **1.** A lane. **2.** An open space where cows are milked. [Middle English, variant of LANE.]

loan shark n. Slang. A usurer, especially one who is financed and supported by gangsters.

loan·shark·ing (lōn'shär'kĭng) n. Informal. The practice of lending money at usurious and often illegal interest rates.

loan translation n. The process or an instance of verbal borrowing from one language to another, whereby the semantic components or morphemes of a given term are literally translated into their equivalents in the borrowing language; for example, superman is a loan translation of the German Übermensch (über, over = super-; Mensch, man = man). Also called "calque."

loan-word, loan·word (lōn'wûrd') n. A word adopted from another language that has become at least partly naturalized; for example, angst, hors d'oeuvre.

loath, loth (lōth, lōth) adj. Unwilling; reluctant; disinclined. Usually used with an infinitive: loath to go. —**nothing loath.** Willing; willingly. [Middle English loth(e), lath, Old English lāth, hateful, loathsome.]

loathe (lōth) tr.v. **loathed, loathing, loathes.** To detest greatly; abhor. [Middle English lothen, Old English lāthian.] —**loath·er** n. —**loath·ing·ly** adv.

loath·ing (lō'thĭng) n. Abhorrence.

loath·ly (lōth'lē, lōth'-) adj. Loathsome. [Middle English lothly, Old English lāthlic : lāth, loathsome (see loath) + -LY.]

loath·some (lōth'səm, lōth'-) adj. Repulsive; disgusting. [Middle English lothsum : loth, hatred, Old English lāth, from adjective (see loath) + -SOME.] —**loath·some·ly** adv.

loaves. Plural of **loaf.**

lob (lŏb) v. **lobbed, lobbing, lobs.** —tr. **1.** To hit, toss, or propel slowly in or as if in a high arc. **2.** Informal. To throw casually; toss. —intr. To hit a ball in a high arc.
~n. **1.** A ball hit, bowled, or thrown in a high arc. **2.** An act of lobbing a ball. [Probably of Low German origin, akin to Low German lubbe, awkward person, Flemish lobbe, fool, Middle Low German lobbe†, hanging lip, thus extended to anything clumsy, pendulous, or slow.]

Lo·ba·chev·ski (lō'bə-chĕf'skē, -chĕv'skē), **Nikolai Ivanovich** (1793–1856). Russian mathematician. His revolutionary system of geometry, published in 1829, challenged the accepted Euclidean theory.

lo·bar (lō'bər, -bär') adj. Of or pertaining to a lobe, such as one of those in the lungs: lobar pneumonia.

lo·bate (lō'bāt') adj. Also **lo·bat·ed** (-bā'tĭd). **1.** Having lobes. **2.** Resembling a lobe. **3.** Having separate toes, each bordered with a weblike lobe. Said of certain birds. —**lo·bate·ly** adv.

lo·ba·tion (lō-bā'shən) n. **1.** The state of being lobed. **2.** A lobe or part resembling a lobe.

lob·by (lŏb'ē) n., pl. **-bies. 1. a.** An entrance hall or corridor. **b.** A foyer, waiting room, or reception area in a hotel, theater, or other public building. **2. a.** A public room next to the assembly chamber of a legislative body, where legislators and members of the public can meet. **b.** Any of three anterooms in the British Houses of Parliament, the members' lobby for members of the House of Commons, the peers' lobby for members of the House of Lords, and the central lobby for all members of Parliament and members of the public. **3.** Chiefly British. Either of the two corridors attached to a legislative chamber to which the members go to register their votes. In this sense, also called "division lobby." **4.** A group of people, usually representing a particular interest, who seek to influence legislation: the environmental lobby. **5.** Often **Lobby.** A group of British

political journalists having access to cabinet ministers and senior civil servants, from whom they acquire confidential information on lobby terms, allowing the information to be reported without the source being identified.
~v. **lobbied, -bying, -bies.** —intr. To seek to influence legislators in favor of some special interest. —tr. **1.** To seek to influence or gain the support of (legislators or public opinion, for example). **2.** To seek to influence legislators to pass (legislation). [Medieval Latin lobium, lobia, laubia, a monastic cloister, from Germanic.] —**lob·bi·er, lob·by·er** n.

lob·by·ist (lŏb'ē-ĭst) n. One employed to influence legislators to introduce or vote for measures favorable to the interest he represents. —**lob·by·ism** n.

lobe (lōb) n. **1.** A rounded projection; especially, a rounded, projecting anatomical part such as the **ear lobe** (see). **2.** A subdivision of an organ or part bounded by fissures, connective tissue, or other structural boundaries. **3.** A loop forming part of a curve or graph. [Late Latin lobus, from Greek lobos, lobe (of the ear or liver).]

lo·bec·to·my (lō-bĕk'tə-mē) n., pl. **-mies.** A surgical operation for the excision of a lobe. [LOB(E) + -ECTOMY.]

lobed (lōbd) adj. Having lobes: lobed leaves.

lobe·fin (lōb'fĭn') n. Any of various mostly extinct bony fishes of the subclass Sarcopterygii, of which the coelacanth is a living representative.

lo·be·li·a (lō-bē'lē-ə, -bēl'yə) n. Any of numerous plants of the genus Lobelia, having terminal clusters of variously colored, often blue, flowers. It is widely grown as an ornamental border plant. [New Latin, after Matthias de Lobel (1538–1616), Flemish botanist.]

lob·lol·ly (lŏb'lŏl'ē) n., pl. **-lies.** Regional. **1.** A mudhole; a mire. **2.** A lout. [Originally, "a thick gruel": perhaps dialectal lob†, to bubble, boil + lolly†, broth.]

loblolly pine n. A pine, Pinus taeda, of the southeastern United States, having strong wood used as lumber or for paper pulp.

lo·bo (lō'bō) n., pl. **-bos.** The gray or timber wolf, Canis lupus. [Spanish, from Latin lupus, wolf.]

lo·bo·la (lō'bə-lə) n. Also **lo·bo·lo** (-lō). South African. **1.** A wedding gift, comparable to a dowry, among black African peoples, consisting of a payment in cash or cattle made by the bridegroom or his family to the family of his prospective wife. **2.** The amount involved in such a transaction; the bride price. [Zulu.]

lo·bot·o·my (lō-bŏt'ə-mē, lə-) n., pl. **-mies. 1.** A surgical division of one or more cerebral nerve tracts in the frontal lobe of the brain. **2.** Surgical incision into a lobe. [LOB(E) + -TOMY.]

lob·scouse (lŏb'skous') n. A seaman's stew made of meat, vegetables, and hardtack. [Perhaps dialectal lob, to bubble, boil + scouse†, broth.]

lob·ster (lŏb'stər) n., pl. **-sters** or collectively **lobster. 1.** Any of several relatively large marine crustaceans of the genus Homarus, having five pairs of legs, the first pair modified into large claws. **2.** Any of several related crustaceans, such as the **spiny lobster** (see). **3.** The flesh of any of these crustaceans, used as food. **4.** A bright orange-red, the color of cooked lobster. [Middle English lobster, lopster, Old English loppestre, lopystre, from Latin locusta, locust, lobster (influenced by Old English loppe, spider).] —**lob·ster** adj.

lobster pot n. A slatted cage with an opening covered by a funnel-shaped net, used for trapping lobsters underwater. Also called "lobster trap."

lobster ther·mi·dor (thûr'mə-dôr') n. A dish consisting of cooked lobster meat mixed with a cream sauce and then returned to its shell, sprinkled with cheese, and browned.

lob·u·late (lŏb'yə-lĭt, -lāt') adj. Also **lob·u·lat·ed** (-lā'tĭd). Having or consisting of lobules. —**lob·u·la·tion** n.

lob·ule (lŏb'yōōl) n. **1.** A small lobe. **2.** A section or subdivision of a lobe. [French, from New Latin lobulus, diminutive of Late Latin lobus, LOBE.] —**lob·u·lar** (lŏb'yə-lər), **lob·u·lose** adj. —**lob·u·lar·ly** adv.

lob·worm (lŏb'wûrm') n. A lugworm (see). [LOB (obsolete sense "lump") + WORM.]

lo·cal (lō'kəl) adj. **1.** Of or pertaining to a place. **2.** Pertaining to, existing in, of interest to, peculiar to, or serving a certain locality: local government. **3.** Not broad or general; confined: a little local difficulty. **4.** Medicine. Of or affecting a limited part of the body; not systemic: a local disease. **5.** Making many stops; not express: a local train.
~n. **1.** A local person; a native inhabitant. **2.** A public conveyance that makes all possible or scheduled stops. **3.** A local branch of an organization, especially of a labor union. **4.** Informal. A local anesthetic. **5.** British Informal. A pub close to one's work or home. [Middle English, from Old French, from Late Latin locālis, from Latin locus, place, LOCUS.]

local anesthetic n. Medicine. An injected or topically applied anesthetic that induces loss of sensation in a particular region of the body. Compare **general anesthetic.**

local area network n. Abbr. **LAN** A network of word processors or computers connected together, for example in an office building, so that information can be transferred from one to another or accessed from a main store.

local authority n. British. A local council and its officials, responsible for administering the services of an area; the organ of local government.

local color n. The atmosphere or flavor of a locality imparted by the presentation, as in a novel, of the customs and sights peculiar to that locality.

lo·cale (lō-kăl′, -käl′) *n.* **1.** A locality, with reference to some event. **2.** The scene or setting, as of a novel. [French *local,* locality, from Old French, LOCAL.]

lo·cal·ism (lō′kə-lĭz′əm) *n.* **1.** An idiom, mannerism, custom, or the like peculiar to a locality. **2.** Provincialism.

lo·cal·i·ty (lō-kăl′ə-tē) *n., pl.* **-ties. 1.** A neighborhood, place, or district. **2.** A site, as of an event. **3.** The fact or quality of having position in space. —See Synonyms at **area.** [French *localité,* from Late Latin *locālitās* (stem *locālitāt-*), from *locālis,* LOCAL.]

lo·cal·ize (lō′kə-līz′) *v.* **-ized, -izing, -izes. 1.** To make local. **2.** To confine or restrict to a particular area or part. **3.** To assign to a locality or determine more precisely the origin or source of: *localize a dialect.* **—lo·cal·i·za·tion** *n.*

lo·cal·ly (lō′kə-lē) *adv.* At or near a particular location: *lives locally.*

local option *n.* An option granted usually by a central or regional government to a community or a local government, allowing it discretion, sometimes subject to a referendum, in such issues as whether to keep stores open on Sundays or to sell liquor.

local solar time *n.* Local time.

local time *n.* The time of day at any point on earth indicated by the apparent movement of the sun, as shown on a sundial. Also called "apparent time," "local solar time." Compare **mean solar time.**

Lo·car·no (lō-kär′nō). Resort on Lake Maggiore in the south of Ticino canton, Switzerland. In 1925 representatives of Belgium, Czechoslovakia, France, Germany, Great Britain, Italy, and Poland drew up the Locarno Pact here. Among other things, the pact resolved the status of the Rhineland and guaranteed the French-German and Belgian-German borders.

lo·cate (lō′kāt′, lō-kāt′) *v.* **-cated, -cating, -cates.** —*tr.* **1.** To determine or specify the position and boundaries of: *locate Timbuktu on the map.* **2.** To find by searching, examining, or experimenting: *locate the source of error.* **3.** To station, situate, or place: *locate an agent in Chicago.* —*intr.* To become established in some spot; settle. [Latin *locāre,* to place, from *locus,* place, LOCUS.]

lo·ca·tion (lō-kā′shən) *n.* **1.** The act or process of locating. **2.** The fact of being located or settled. **3.** A place or position where something is or might be located. **4.** In television or motion-picture production, a site away from the studio grounds, where a scene is shot: *That safari film was made on location.* [Latin *locātio* (stem *locātiōn-*), a placing, from *locāre,* to place, LOCATE.]

loc·a·tive (lŏk′ə-tĭv) *n. Grammar.* **1.** The noun case in certain Indo-European languages, such as Sanskrit or Old Church Slavonic, that denotes the place where. **2.** A form or construction in this case. ~*adj.* Designating, pertaining to, or inflected in the locative. [French *locatif,* from Old French, from Latin *locāre,* to LOCATE.]

lo·ca·tor (lō′kā′tər) *n.* One that locates, as a person who fixes the boundaries of a mining claim or other land.

loc. cit., in loc. cit. *adv.* In the place cited. [Latin *locō citātō.*]

loch (lŏKH, lŏk) *n. Scottish.* **1.** A lake. **2.** A sea loch. [Middle English (Scottish) *louch,* from Scottish Gaelic *loch,* probably from Old Irish.]

lo·chi·a (lō′kē-ə, lŏk′ē-ə) *pl.n.* The normal discharge of blood, tissue, and mucus from the vagina after childbirth. [New Latin, from Greek *lokhia,* from neuter plural of *lokhios,* of childbirth, from *lokhos,* childbirth.] **—lo·chi·al** *adj.*

lo·ci. Plural of **locus.**

lock[1] (lŏk) *n.* **1.** A device used to provide restraint; especially, a key- or combination-operated mechanism used to fasten shut a door, lid, or the like. **2.** Such a device used to prevent unauthorized operation of a machine: *a telephone lock.* **3.** A section of a canal closed off by gates, within which a vessel may be raised or lowered by the raising or lowering of the section's water level. **4.** A mechanism in a firearm for exploding its charge of ammunition. Usually used in combination: *a flintlock.* **5.** A jamming or locking together of elements or parts. **6.** Any of several holds in wrestling. **7.** *Rugby.* **a.** Either of the two forwards who form the second row of the scrum. **b.** The position of such a player. In both senses, also called "lock forward." **8.** *British.* The degree of turn of which a motor vehicle is capable; the turning base. **9.** A gas bubble or pocket preventing the flow of liquid through a pipe. **—lock, stock, and barrel.** Completely; totally. **—under lock and key.** In complete security or safety.
~*v.* **locked, locking, locks.** —*tr.* **1.** To fasten with a lock, as: **a.** To secure against passage or entry: *lock a door.* **b.** To secure against loss or theft: *lock a bicycle.* **2.** To confine or safeguard by putting behind a lock. Used with *in* or *up*: *lock the dog in for the night.* **3.** To engage and fix together securely; intertwine. **4.** To clasp or embrace tightly. **5.** To entangle in struggle or battle. **6.** To jam or force together so as to make unmovable. **7.** To pass (a vessel) through a lock. **8.** To provide or section off (a waterway) with locks. —*intr.* **1. a.** To become fastened by or as if by a lock. **b.** To admit of being locked: *Does this drawer lock?* **2.** To become entangled; interlock. **3.** To become rigid or unmovable. **4.** To pass or flow through a lock. **5.** To find, fasten onto, and automatically follow a target, especially with radar. Used with *on* or *onto.* [Middle English *lo(c)k,* Old English *loc.*] **—lock·a·ble** *adj.*

lock[2] *n.* **1.** A strand or curl of hair; a tress. **2. locks.** The hair of the head. **3.** A small wisp or tuft, as of wool or cotton. [Middle English *lock, lok(k),* Old English *locc.*]

lock·age (lŏk′ĭj) *n. Nautical.* **1.** The passage of a vessel through a lock by operation of the lock. **2.** The toll for the use of a lock. **3. a.** A system of locks. **b.** The works of a lock. **4.** The amount of the rise and fall effected by a lock or system of locks.

Locke (lŏk), **John** (1632–1704). English empiricist philosopher, author of *An Essay Concerning Human Understanding* (1690). His *Two Treatises of Government* (1690) justified the English Revolution of 1688, opposing the notion of the divine right of kings.

lock·er (lŏk′ər) *n.* **1.** One that locks. **2.** A small metal cupboard or enclosure that may be locked; especially, one of many provided at a gymnasium or school for the safekeeping of clothing and valuables. **3.** A flat storage trunk. **4.** A heavily insulated refrigerated cabinet, compartment, or room for storing frozen foods for extended periods.

locker room *n.* **1.** A room in a gymnasium, school, clubhouse, or the like, furnished with rows of lockers. **2.** A room for changing one's clothes, as at a public swimming pool.

lock·et (lŏk′ĭt) *n.* A small ornamental metal case for a picture or keepsake, such as a lock of hair, usually worn as a pendant. [Old French *locquet,* latch, small lock, diminutive of *loc,* lock, probably from Old English *loc,* lock.]

lock·jaw (lŏk′jô′) *n. Pathology.* **1. Tetanus** *(see).* **2.** A symptom of tetanus, in which the jaws are clamped shut because of a tonic spasm of the muscles of mastication. Also called "trismus."

lock·nut (lŏk′nŭt′) *n.* **1.** A usually thin nut screwed down on a primary nut to keep the latter from loosening. **2.** A self-locking nut.

lock out *tr.v.* **1.** To bar or shut out by locking a door. **2.** To refuse work to (employees) during a dispute.

lock·out (lŏk′out′) *n.* The closing down of a place of employment by an employer to coerce the workers into meeting his terms or modifying theirs. Also called "shutout."

lock·smith (lŏk′smĭth′) *n.* One who makes or repairs locks.

lock step *n.* A marching technique in which the marchers follow each other as closely as possible.

lock stitch *n.* A stitch made on a sewing machine by the interlocking of the upper thread and the bobbin thread.

lock up *tr.v.* **1.** To shut and make secure by fastening all locks: *lock up a house.* **2.** To put in jail or some other place of confinement. **3.** *Printing.* **a.** To secure (letterpress type) in a chase or press bed by tightening the quoins. **b.** To fasten (a curved plate) to the cylinder of a rotary press. **4.** To invest (funds) in such a way that they cannot easily be converted back into cash.
~*intr.v.* To shut and make secure a house or other premises, as when going out in the evening.

lock·up (lŏk′ŭp′) *n.* **1.** An act of locking up or the state of being locked up. **2.** *Informal.* A jail, especially a local one in which offenders are held while awaiting a court hearing. **3.** *British.* A small shop or other business premises where the manager or proprietor does not live. Also used adjectivally: *a lockup shop.* **4.** *British.* A garage or row of garages, often at some distance from the owner's home or place of work.

lo·co[1] (lō′kō) *n. British Informal.* A railroad train or engine. [Shortened from LOCOMOTIVE.]

loco[2] *adj. Slang.* Mad; insane. [Spanish *loco*†, crazy, insane.]

loco disease *n.* A disease of livestock caused by locoweed poisoning, and characterized by dullness, lack of coordination, and partial paralysis. Also called "locoweed disease," "locoism."

lo·co·mo·tion (lō′kə-mō′shən) *n.* **1.** The act of moving or ability to move from place to place. **2.** Movement from place to place; travel. [Latin *locō,* ablative of *locus,* place, LOCUS + MOTION.]

lo·co·mo·tive (lō′kə-mō′tĭv) *n.* A self-propelled engine, now usually electric or diesel-powered, that pulls or pushes trains along railroad tracks.
~*adj.* **1.** Of or involved in locomotion. **2.** Able to move independently from place to place. **3.** Of or pertaining to travel. [Latin *locō* (see **locomotion**) + MOTIVE.]

lo·co·mo·tor (lō′kə-mō′tər) *adj.* Locomotive. [Latin *locō* (see **locomotion**) + *mōtor,* mover, MOTOR.]

locomotor ataxia *n. Pathology.* **Tabes dorsalis** *(see).*

lo·co·weed (lō′kō-wēd′) *n.* Any of several plants of the genera *Oxytropis* and *Astragalus,* of the western and central United States, causing severe poisoning when eaten by livestock. [Mexican Spanish *loco,* locoweed, from Spanish, LOCO (referring to the effects of the poison, which seems to drive livestock mad).]

loc·u·lar (lŏk′yə-lər) *adj.* Also **loc·u·late** (-lāt′, -lĭt), **loc·u·lat·ed** (-lā′tĭd). *Biology.* Having, formed of, or divided into small cells or cavities. **—loc·u·la·tion** *n.*

loc·ule (lŏk′yo͞ol) *n.* Also **loc·u·lus** (-yə-ləs) *pl.* **-li** (-lī′). A small cavity or compartment within an organ or part, such as any of the cavities within a plant ovary. [Latin, diminutive of *locus,* place, LOCUS.]

lo·cum (lō′kəm) *n. Chiefly British.* A clergyman or, especially, a doctor, temporarily replacing another. Also called "locum tenens." [Medieval Latin *locum tenēns,* "(one) holding the place."]

lo·cus (lō′kəs) *n., pl.* **-ci** (-sī′). **1.** A place, especially when considered as the site of a particular activity. **2.** *Mathematics.* The set or configuration of all points satisfying given conditions. **3.** *Genetics.* The position that a gene occupies on a chromosome. [Latin *locus*†, place.]

locus clas·si·cus (klăs′ĭ-kəs) *n., pl.* **loci classici** (klăs′ĭ-sī′). A passage from a classic or standard work that is often cited as an authoritative illustration or instance. [Latin, "classical place."]

locus stan·di (stăn′dī) *n.* **1.** *Law.* The right of a party to be heard in court. **2.** Any recognized right or official status, such as the right to participate in meetings. [Latin, "place of standing."]

lo·cust[1] (lō′kəst) *n.* **1.** Any of numerous grasshoppers of the family Locustidae, often traveling in swarms and devouring vegetation in huge quantities. **2.** A cicada such as the **seventeen-year locust**

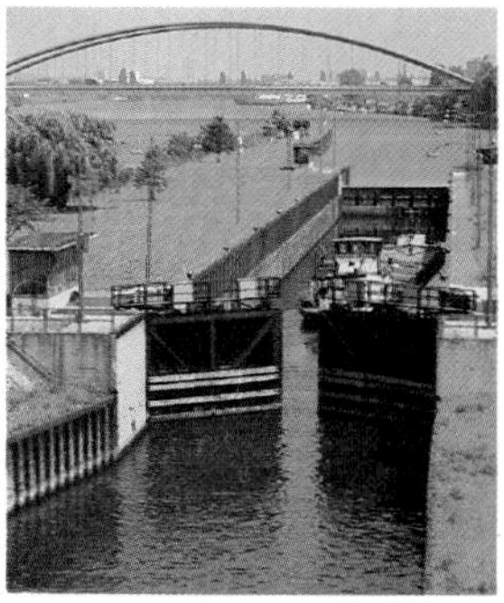

lock *Locks have been built on navigable waterways for at least 2,000 years. This one is at Offenbach in West Germany, on the Main River.*

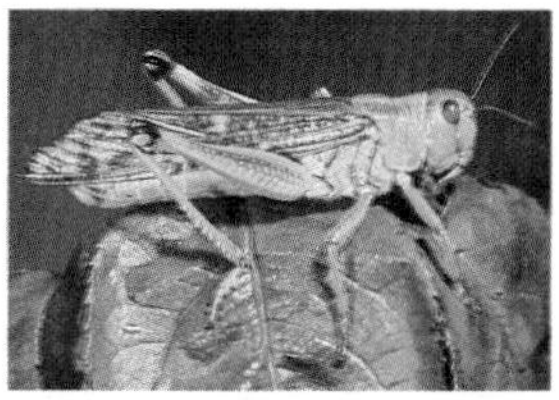

locust *These large flying grasshoppers migrate periodically—sometimes over hundreds of miles—when the population outgrows its food supplies; they can devastate crops along the way.*

(see). [Middle English, from Old French *locuste,* from Latin *lōcusta,* locust, lobster.]

locust² *n.* **1.** A North American tree, *Robinia pseudo-acacia,* having compound leaves, drooping clusters of fragrant white flowers, and hard, durable wood. Also called "false acacia." **2.** *British.* A tree, the **carob** *(see).* [From the locust-shaped pods of some species.]

locust bird *n.* Any of the African pratincoles, such as *Glareola pratincola,* that feed on swarms of locusts.

lo·cu·tion (lō-kyo͞o'shən) *n.* **1.** A particular word, phrase, or expression considered from the point of view of style. **2.** Style of speaking; phraseology. [Middle English *locucion,* from Latin *locūtiō* (stem *locūtiōn-*), speech, utterance, from *loquī* (past participle *locūtus*), to speak.]

Lod (lŏd). Also **Lyd·da** (lĭd'ə). Ancient Hebrew city, southeast of Tel Aviv, Israel, the site of Israel's main international airport.

lode (lōd) *n.* **1.** A mineral deposit contained in hard rock, usually in the form of a group of veins. **2.** A rich source or supply. [Middle English *lode, lade,* course, way, Old English *lād.*]

lo·den (lō'dən) *n.* **1.** A thick, waterproof, woolen fabric used in making coats. **2.** A dark green color. [German, from Old High German *lodo,* heavy cloth.]

lode·star, load·star (lōd'stär') *n.* **1.** A star that is used as a point of reference; especially, the North Star. **2.** A guiding principle, interest, or ambition: *Nuclear disarmament was her constant lodestar.* [Middle English *lo(o)de sterre,* "guiding star" : *lode, lade,* course, guidance (see **lode**) + STAR.]

lode·stone, load·stone (lōd'stōn') *n.* **1.** A magnetized piece of magnetite. **2.** One that attracts or magnetizes. [From its former use by sailors as a compass to guide their course.]

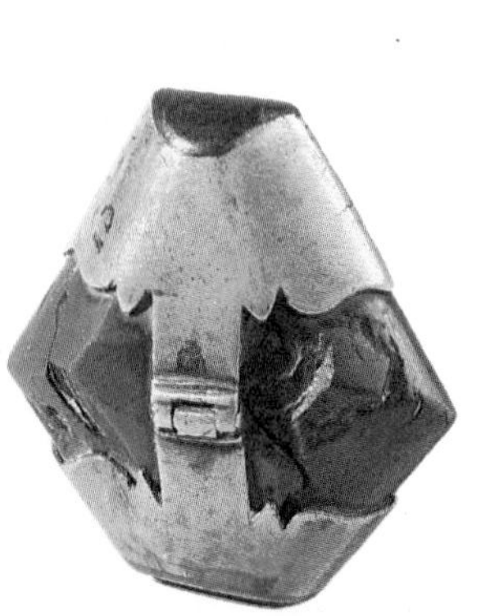

lodestone *The Chinese discovered the magnetic properties of lodestone—a naturally occurring type of iron oxide known as magnetite—about 2,500 years ago. However, the discovery was not applied to direction finding until the invention of the compass in about the 11th century* A.D. *This brassbound lodestone, dating from the 17th century, was used to magnetize iron compass needles.*

lodge (lŏj) *n.* **1.** A small house on the grounds of an estate or park for a caretaker, gatekeeper, or the like. **2.** A cottage or hut, often located in an isolated place, used as temporary accommodation or shelter by huntsmen, climbers, or the like: *a ski lodge.* **3.** An inn. **4. a.** A local chapter of certain fraternal organizations. **b.** The members of such a chapter considered collectively. **c.** The meeting hall of such a society. **5.** The den of certain animals, such as otters. **6.** The central building in a camping ground or national park. **7. a.** A North American Indian living unit such as a hogan, wigwam, or long house. **b.** The group living in such a unit.
~*v.* **lodged, lodging, lodges.** —*tr.* **1.** To provide with temporary quarters. **2.** To rent a room or rooms to; take in as a paying guest. **3.** To place or establish in quarters: *lodge children with relatives.* **4.** To serve as a depository for; harbor. **5.** To place, leave, or deposit for safety. **6.** To fix, embed, or implant. **7.** To register (a charge) in court or with an appropriate authority or official: *lodge a complaint.* **8.** To vest (authority or power, for example). Used with *in* or *with.* **9.** *Archaic.* To beat down (crops). Used of wind or rain: *"If rye or wheat be lodged, cut it though it be not ripe"* (Robert Browning). —*intr.* **1.** To reside temporarily. **2.** To rent living accommodations; be a lodger. **3.** To be or become embedded. [Middle English *log(g)e,* from Old French *loge,* shed, small house, from Frankish *laubja* (unattested).]

Lodge (lŏj), **Henry Cabot** (1850–1924). U.S. politician and author. As U.S. congressman (1887–93) and senator (1893–1924), he contributed to the Sherman Anti-Trust Act (1890) and advocated bold military action during World War I. He wrote several notable biographies, including *Alexander Hamilton* (1882) and *George Washington* (1889).

Lodge, Henry Cabot, Jr. (1902–85). U.S. politician and diplomat. A U.S. senator (1937–44, 1947–52) and Richard Nixon's running mate in the 1960 presidential election, he also served as ambassador to South Vietnam (1963–67) and West Germany (1967–69) and represented the U.S. in the Paris peace talks on Vietnam (1969).

lodge·pole pine (lŏj'pōl') *n.* A pine, *Pinus contorta,* of western North America, having light wood used in construction.

lodg·er (lŏj'ər) *n.* A person who rents and lives in a furnished room or rooms in the landlord's home.

lodg·ing (lŏj'ĭng) *n.* **1. lodgings.** Rented rooms. **2.** *Often* **lodgings.** Sleeping accommodations.

lodg·ment, lodge·ment (lŏj'mənt) *n.* **1. a.** The act of lodging. **b.** The state of being lodged. **2.** A place for lodging. **3.** An accumulation or deposit. **4.** *Military.* A foothold, beachhead, or salient gained in enemy or neutral territory.

lod·i·cule (lŏd'ĭ-kyo͞ol') *n. Botany.* Any of the small scales at the base of the ovary in grasses. [Late Latin *lōdīcula,* diminutive of *lōdīx* (stem *lōdīc-*), covering, perhaps from Celtic.]

Łódź (lo͞oj). Second-largest city in Poland, renowned for its textiles.

lo·ess, löss (lō'ĕs, lĕs, lŭs) *n.* A fine-grained, friable, porous, yellowish to gray silt or dust, generally thought to have been initially worn away and then deposited by the wind. [German *Löss,* from Swiss German *Lösch,* from *lösch,* loose.]

Loewe (lō), **Frederick** (1904–). U.S. composer, born in Austria. When he was 15 years old, one million copies of the music for his song "Katrina" were sold. He moved to the United States (1924) and collaborated with Jay Lerner on several highly successful musicals, including *My Fair Lady* (1956) and *Camelot* (1960).

Loe·wy (lō'ē), **Raymond Fernand** (1903–86) U.S. industrial designer, born in France. His adherence to the principle that form follows function is evident in his highly practical yet pleasing designs of modern manufactures, including a 1934 Sears refrigerator and the interiors of NASA spacecraft.

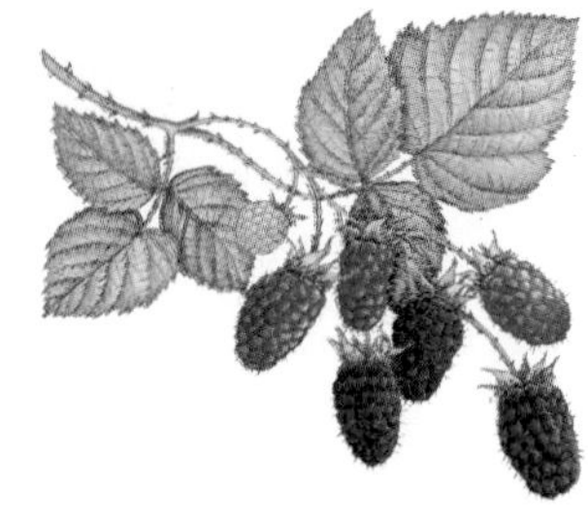

loganberry *The hybrid loganberry is said to have been created in California by the accidental crossing of a blackberry and a raspberry.*

loft (lôft, lŏft) *n.* **1.** An open space under a roof; an attic or atticlike space. **2.** A gallery or balcony, as in a church. **3.** The top floor, usually unpartitioned, as of a factory or warehouse. **4.** A **hayloft** *(see).* **5. a.** A coop in which pigeons are kept. **b.** A flock of pigeons kept in such a coop. **6.** *Golf.* **a.** The backward slant of the face of a club head, designed to drive the ball in a high arc. **b.** A stroke that lofts the ball. **c.** The upward course of a lofted ball.
~*v.* **lofted, lofting, lofts.** —*tr.* **1.** To put, store, or keep in a loft. **2.** To send (a ball) in a high arc. **3.** To give a loft to (a golf club). —*intr.* To loft a golf ball. [Middle English *lofte,* upper room, sky, Old English *loft,* sky, air, from Old Norse *lopt,* air, attic.]

loft·er (lôf'tər, lŏf'-) *n.* A golf club designed to loft the ball. Also called "lofting iron."

loft·y (lôf'tē, lŏf'-) *adj.* **-ier, -iest. 1.** Of imposing height; towering. **2.** Elevated in character; exalted; noble. **3.** High-flown; affecting grandness; pompous. **4.** Arrogant; haughty. —See Synonyms at **high.** [Middle English, from *lofte,* raised, elevated, from *lofte,* sky, LOFT.] **—loft·i·ly** *adv.* **—loft·i·ness** *n.*

log¹ (lôg, lŏg) *n.* **1. a.** The trunk of a large fallen or felled tree. **b.** A thick section of trimmed but unhewn timber. **2.** *Nautical.* A device trailed from a ship to determine its speed through the water. **3. a.** A record of a ship's speed, progress, and shipboard events of navigational importance. **b.** The book in which this record is kept. Also called "logbook." **c.** Any record of performance, such as the flight record of an aircraft. **d.** Any record of events or experiences, such as the journal of an expedition. **4.** A record of radio transmissions, frequencies, and the like. **—sleep like a log.** To sleep soundly.
~*v.* **logged, logging, logs.** —*tr.* **1. a.** To cut down the timber of (a section of land). **b.** To cut (trees) into logs. **2.** To achieve and record (a specified time, distance, or speed, for example) in a ship's or other log. **3.** *Informal.* To achieve: *She's logged 25 years with her company.* —*intr.* To cut down, trim, and haul timber. **—log on.** To register, especially with a computer as an authorized user. [Middle English *logge*†.]

log² *n. Informal.* **1.** A logarithm. **2. logs.** Logarithmic tables.

Lo·gan, Mount (lō'gən). Canada's highest peak, 6,050 meters (19,850 feet). It is in the St. Elias Mts. in southwest Yukon Territory and was first climbed in 1925.

lo·gan·ber·ry (lō'gən-bĕr'ē) *n., pl.* **-ries. 1.** A trailing, prickly plant, *Rubus loganobaccus,* cultivated for its raspberrylike edible fruit. **2.** The dark red fruit of this plant. [First grown by James H. *Logan* (1841–1928), U.S. judge and horticulturist.]

log·a·oe·dic (lŏg'ə-ē'dĭk) *adj.* Of, pertaining to, or designating a form of verse in which different metrical units occur within a single line.
~*n.* A line of such verse. [Late Latin, from Greek *logaoidikos,* (of verse) like natural (prose) speech : *logos,* speech + *aoidē,* poetry.]

log·a·rithm (lô'gə-rĭth'əm, lŏg'ə-) *n.* The exponent indicating the power to which a fixed number, the base, must be raised to produce a given number. For example, if $n^x = a$, the logarithm of *a,* with *n* as the base, is *x;* symbolically, $\log_n a = x$. See **common logarithm, natural logarithm.** [New Latin *logarithmus* : Greek *logos,* reckoning, reason, ratio + *arithmos,* number.]

log·a·rith·mic (lô'gə-rĭth'mĭk) *adj.* **1.** Of or pertaining to logarithms. **2.** Involving a logarithmic function. Said of a scale in which successive distances are proportional to logarithms, as in certain measuring instruments, slide rules, and graph paper, for example. **—log·a·rith·mi·cal** *adj.* **—log·a·rith·mi·cal·ly** *adv.*

logarithmic function *n. Mathematics.* A function containing an expression of the form log *x.*

log·book (lôg'bo͝ok', lŏg'-) *n.* **1.** The official record book of a ship, aircraft, or expedition, for example. **2.** *British.* Formerly, the identifying document of a motor vehicle, listing its specifications, registration number, and owner.

loge (lōzh) *n.* **1.** A small compartment; especially, a box in a theater. **2.** The front rows of the upper block of seating in a theater, especially in Europe or the United States. [French, from Old French, shed, small house. See **lodge.**]

log·ger (lô'gər, lŏg'ər) *n.* **1.** A lumberjack. **2.** A tractor, crane, or other machine used for hauling or loading logs.

log·ger·head (lô'gər-hĕd', lŏg'ər-) *n.* **1.** A marine turtle, *Caretta caretta,* having a large, beaked head. **2.** An iron tool consisting of a long handle with a bulbous end, used when heated to melt tar or to warm liquids. **3.** *Nautical.* A post on a whaleboat used to help secure a rope holding a harpooned whale. **4.** *Archaic & Regional.* **a.** A blockhead; a dolt. **b.** A disproportionately large head. **5.** A loggerhead shrike. **—at loggerheads.** Engaged in a dispute. [Dialectal *logger,* wooden block, from LOG + HEAD.]

loggerhead shrike *n.* A North American bird, *Lanius ludovicianus,* having gray and white plumage and a hooked beak. Also called "loggerhead."

log·gi·a (lô'jē-ə, lŏj'ē-ə; *Italian* lôd'jä) *n., pl.* **-gias. 1.** A roofed but open gallery or arcade along the front or side of a building, often at an upper level. **2.** An open balcony in a theater. [Italian, from French *loge,* LOGE.]

log·ging (lô'gĭng, lŏg'ĭng) *n.* The work or business of felling and trimming trees and transporting the logs to a mill.

log·ic (lŏj'ĭk) *n.* **1.** *Philosophy.* The study of the principles of reasoning, especially of the structure of propositions as distinguished from their content and of method and validity in deductive reasoning. **2. a.** A system of reasoning. **b.** A mode of reasoning. **c.** The formal, guiding principles of a discipline, school, or science. **3.** Valid reasoning as distinguished from invalid or irrational argument. **4.** The relationship of elements to one another and to the whole in a set of objects, individuals, principles, or events. **5.** *Computer Science.* The way in which signals are combined in a circuit to perform logical operations. **6.** The apparently irresistible force which brings about or holds together a sequence of events: *the logic of circumstances.* **7.** *Informal.* Reasonableness; good sense: *What's the logic of trying to do it before you're ready?* [Middle English *logik,* from Old French *logique,* from Late Latin *logica,* from Greek *logikē (tekhnē),* "(art) of reasoning," from the feminine of *logikos,* of speech, of reasoning, from *logos,* speech, reason.]

log·i·cal (lŏj'ĭ-kəl) *adj.* **1.** Pertaining to, in accordance with, or of the nature of logic. **2.** Showing consistency of reasoning. **3.** Reasonable on the basis of earlier statements or events: *a logical development; a logical choice.* **4.** Able to reason clearly: *a logical thinker.* **—log·i·cal·i·ty, log·i·cal·ness** *n.* **—log·i·cal·ly** *adv.*

logical positivism *n. Philosophy.* A doctrine, developed in the 20th century, asserting the primacy of observation in assessing the truth of statements of fact and holding that metaphysical and subjective arguments not based on observable data are meaningless, meaningful statements being either a priori and analytic or a posteriori and synthetic.

logic gate *n. Computer Science.* An electronic gate that gives an output signal for certain combinations of two or more input signals, used for performing logical operations. Also called "logic circuit."

lo·gi·cian (lō-jĭsh'ən) *n.* A person who is trained in or expert at logic.

lo·gi·on (lō'gē-ŏn') *n., pl.* **-gia** (-gē-ä'). Any of the sayings of Jesus not recorded in the Gospels but supposed to have belonged to the source material from which they were compiled. [Greek, "saying."]

lo·gis·tic (lō-jĭs'tĭk) *adj.* Also **lo·gis·tic·al** (for sense 1). **1.** Of or pertaining to logistics. In this sense, also "logistical." **2.** *Rare.* Of or skilled in arithmetical calculation. [French *logistique,* from Late Latin *logisticus,* of reason, from Greek *logistikos,* skilled in calculation, from *logistēs,* calculator, from *logizein,* to calculate, from *logos,* reckoning.] **—lo·gis·tic·al·ly** *adv.* **—lo·gis·ti·cian** (lō'jĭ-stĭsh'ən) *n.*

lo·gis·tics (lō-jĭs'tĭks) *n.* **1.** *Used with a singular verb. Military.* The science or study of the procurement, distribution, maintenance, and replacement of equipment and personnel. **2.** *Used with a plural verb.* The planning and control of any complex operation, as for example in finance or transport.

log jam *n.* **1.** A mass of floating logs crowded immovably together. **2.** *Informal.* A deadlock in the progress of negotiations, debates, or the like.

log·log (lôg'lôg', lŏg'lŏg') *n.* The logarithm of a logarithm. Also used adjectivally: *a loglog scale.*

lo·go (lō'gō', lô'gō', lŏg'ō') *n., pl.* **-gos.** A logotype.

logo– *prefix.* Indicates word or speech; for example, **logogram.** [Greek, from *logos,* speech, word, reason, account.]

log·o·gram (lô'gə-grăm', lŏg'ə-) *n.* A symbol or letter representing an entire word, such as $ for dollars or *e* for energy (in physics). [LOGO- + -GRAM.] **—log·o·gram·mat·ic** (lô'gə-grə-măt'ĭk) *adj.* **—log·o·gram·mat·i·cal·ly** *adv.*

log·o·graph (lô'gə-grăf', -gräf') *n.* A logogram. [LOGO- + -GRAPH.]

log·o·graph·ic (lôg'ə-grăf'ĭk, lŏg'-) *adj.* Of or pertaining to logography or logograms. **—log·o·graph·i·cal·ly** *adv.*

lo·gog·ra·phy (lō-gŏg'rə-fē) *n.* The use of logotypes in design and printing. Also called "logotypy." [LOGO- + -GRAPHY.]

log·o·griph (lô'gə-grĭf', lŏg'ə-) *n.* A word puzzle, such as an anagram or one in which clues are given in a set of verses. [French *logogriphe* : LOGO- + Greek *griphos*†, fishing basket.]

lo·gom·a·chy (lō-gŏm'ə-kē) *n.* **1.** An argument about words or their meanings. **2.** An argument apparently about something substantial but in fact turning merely on different definitions of the terms involved. [Greek *logomakhia* : LOGO- + -MACHY.]

log·o·pe·dics (lôg'ə-pē'dĭks, lŏg'-) *n. Usually used with a singular verb.* **Speech therapy** *(see).* [LOGO- + Greek *paideia,* education (see **pedo-**) + -ICS.]

log·or·rhe·a (lôg'ə-rē'ə, lŏg'-) *n.* A compulsive tendency to talk, often incoherently, as in mental illness; excessive talkativeness. [LOGO- + -RRHEA.]

Log·os (lŏg'ŏs', lō'gŏs') *n.* **1.** *Often* **logos. a.** Cosmic reason, regarded in ancient Greek philosophy as the source of world order and intelligibility. **b.** Reason or an expression of reason in words or things. **2.** The self-revealing thought and will of God, as set forth in the Gospel of St. John, often associated with the second person of the Trinity. In this sense, also called the "Word." [Greek *logos,* speech, word, reason.]

lo·go·type (lô'gə-tīp', lŏg'ə-) *n. Printing.* **1.** A single piece of type bearing two or more usually separate elements. **2. a.** The name, trademark, or, especially, the identifying symbol of an organization or publication. In this sense, also called "logo." **b.** A piece of type bearing this. [LOGO- + TYPE.]

log·roll (lôg'rōl', lŏg'-) *v.* **-rolled, -rolling, -rolls.** *—tr.* To work toward the passage of (legislation) by logrolling. *—intr.* To engage in political logrolling.

log·roll·ing (lôg'rō'lĭng, lŏg'-) *n.* **1. Birling** *(see).* **2.** The transportation of logs by water. **3.** The exchanging of political favors; especially, the swapping of influence or votes between legislators to their mutual advantage. **—log·roll·er** *n.*

-logue, -log *suffix.* Indicates speech, discourse, recitation, or description; for example, **monologue, travelogue.** [Greek *-logos,* from *legein,* to speak.]

log·wood (lôg'wo͝od', lŏg'-) *n.* **1.** A tropical American tree, *Haematoxylon campechianum,* having dark heartwood from which a dyestuff is obtained. **2.** The wood of this tree. **3.** The blackish or brownish dye, hematoxylin, obtained from this wood.

-logy *suffix.* Indicates: **1.** Discourse or expression; for example, **phraseology. 2.** The science, theory, or study of; for example, **paleontology.** [Middle English *-logie,* from Old French, from Latin *-logia,* from Greek, from *logos,* word, speech.]

Lo·hen·grin (lō'ən-grĭn'). In Germanic legend, a son of Parsifal and knight of the Holy Grail.

loin (loin) *n.* **1.** *Usually* **loins.** *Anatomy.* The part of the side and back between the ribs and the pelvis. **2.** A cut of meat taken from this part of an animal. **3. loins. a.** The pelvic region, including the thighs and groin. **b.** *Literary.* The reproductive organs. **—gird up one's loins.** To prepare oneself for strenuous effort. [Middle English *loyne,* from Old French *loigne,* dialectal form for *longe,* from Vulgar Latin *lumbia* (unattested), from feminine of *lumbeus* (unattested), of the loin, from Latin *lumbus,* loin.]

loin·cloth (loin'klôth', -klŏth') *n., pl.* **-cloths** (-klôths', -klô*thz*', -klŏths', -klŏ*thz*'). A strip of cloth worn around the loins.

Loire (lwär). France's longest river. It flows some 1,015 kilometers (630 miles) from the Cévennes Mts. in the southeast roughly northward to Orléans and then westward through Tours and Nantes to the Bay of Biscay at St. Nazaire. The middle and lower Loire Valley is noted for its fine chateaux.

loi·ter (loi'tər) *intr. v.* **-tered, -tering, -ters. 1. a.** To stand idly about; linger aimlessly. **b.** To linger or wait somewhere with the intention of committing a crime. **2.** To proceed slowly or with many stops. **3.** To dawdle: *loiter over a job.* [Middle English *loyteren,* perhaps from Middle Dutch *loteren,* to shake, totter.] **—loi·ter·er** *n.*

Lo·ki (lō'kē). *Norse Mythology.* The god who creates discord, especially among his fellow gods. [Old Norse, probably related to *logi,* flame, fire.]

loll (lŏl) *v.* **lolled, lolling, lolls.** *—intr.* **1.** To move, stand, or recline in an indolent or relaxed manner. **2.** To hang or droop loosely. *—tr.* To allow to hang or droop loosely.
∼n. Archaic. An act or attitude of lolling. [Middle English *lollen,* probably of Low German origin, akin to Middle Dutch *lollen,* to lull to sleep.] **—loll·er** *n.* **—loll·ing·ly** *adv.*

lol·la·pa·loo·za (lŏl'ə-pə-lo͞o'zə) *n. Slang.* Something outstanding of its kind. [Origin unknown.]

Lol·lard (lŏl'ərd) *n.* A member of a sect of reformers who were followers of John Wycliffe in the 14th, 15th, and 16th centuries. [Middle English, from Middle Dutch *lollaerd,* "mumbler (of prayers)," from *lollen,* to mutter.] **—Lol·lard·ism, Lol·lard·ry** *n.*

lol·li·pop, lol·ly·pop (lŏl'ē-pŏp') *n.* A piece of hard candy attached to a narrow stick. [Perhaps northern English dialect *lolly,* the tongue, from LOLL, to hang out (the tongue) + POP.]

lol·lop (lŏl'əp) *intr.v.* **-loped, -loping, -lops.** *British.* **1.** *Informal.* To walk or run in an ungainly way. **2.** *Regional.* To loll. [From LOLL + *-op,* perhaps from GALLOP.]

lol·ly (lŏl'ē) *n., pl.* **-lies.** *British.* **1.** *Informal.* A lollipop. **2.** *Slang.* Money.

lol·ly·gag (lŏl'ĭ-găg') *intr.v.* **-gagged, -gagging, -gags.** *Slang.* To waste time by fooling around; dawdle. [Origin unknown.]

Lo·lo (lō'lō) *n.* **1.** A member of a Tibeto-Burman people living in the mountains between Sichuan and Yunnan provinces, southwest China. **2.** The language of this people. **—Lo·lo** *adj.*

Lom·bard (lŏm'bərd, -bärd', lŭm'-) *n.* **1.** A member of a Germanic people that invaded northern Italy in A.D. 568 and established a kingdom in the Po Valley. Also called "Langobard," "Longobard." **2.** A native of Lombardy. **3.** *Archaic.* A banker or pawnbroker.
∼adj. Also **Lom·bar·dic** (lŏm-bär'dĭk, lŭm-). Of or pertaining to the Lombards or to Lombardy.

Lom·bar·di (lŏm-bär'dē), **Vincent Thomas,** known as "Vince" (1913–70). U.S. football coach. He is best known as the coach (1958–68) of the Green Bay Packers, whom he led to six conference titles and five national championships.

Lom·bar·do (lŏm-bär'dō, lŭm-), **Guy Albert** (1902–77). U.S. bandleader, born in Canada. His band, the Royal Canadians, became perhaps the most popular dance band of the 1930's and 1940's. Lombardo's New Year's Eve performance at the Waldorf-Astoria Hotel in New York City was long an American tradition.

Lombard Street *n.* The British banking and financial world. [After the moneychangers and bankers from LOMBARDY who once occupied this street in the City of London.]

Lom·bar·dy (lŏm'bər-dē, lŭm'-). Region in north Italy bounded by the Alps and the Po River. It is the most densely populated region in Italy. The Po Valley is a rich agricultural area, while Milan, the capital, lies at the center of an industrial region.

Lombardy poplar *n.* A tree, *Populus nigra italica,* having upward-pointing branches that form a slender, columnar outline.

Lo·mé (lō-mā'). Capital of Togo, West Africa. Its deep-water port exports phosphates, cocoa, and coffee.

lo·ment (lō'mĕnt') *n.* A pod, as of the tick trefoil or similar leguminous plants, having constrictions separating the individual seeds, such that it divides into one-seeded portions when ripe. [New Latin *lomentum,* from Latin *lōmentum, lōvimentum,* a bean meal used by Roman women as a wash or cosmetic, from *lavāre,* to wash.]

Lo·mond, Loch (lō'mənd). Largest natural freshwater lake in Britain, 39 kilometers (24 miles) long and 8 kilometers (5 miles) wide at its broadest, in Strathclyde Region, Scotland.

Lon·don (lŭn'dən). Capital of the United Kingdom and one of the largest cities in the world, covering 1,580 square kilometers (610 square miles) north and south of the Thames River. The City of London, occupying the site of a Roman settlement, is surrounded

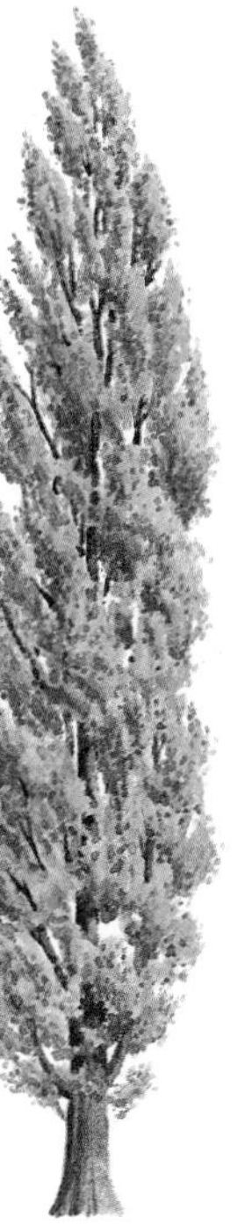

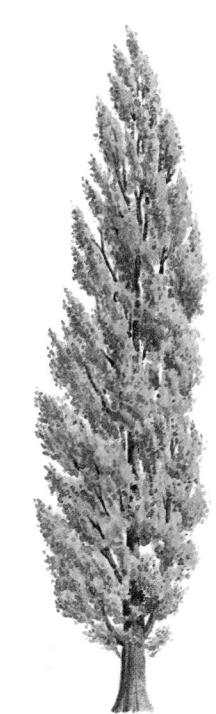

Lombardy poplar *This tree, now thought to be a native of Asia, acquired its common English name after cuttings were introduced into Britain from Lombardy in northern Italy during the 18th century.*

PRONUNCIATION KEY

ă, pat; ā, pay; âr, care;
ä, father, are; b, bib;
ch, church; d, deed; ĕ, pet;
ē, be; f, fife; g, gag; h, hat;
hw, which; ĭ, pit; ī, pie;
îr, pier; j, judge; k, kick;
l, lid, needle; m, mum;
n, no, sudden; ng, thing;
ŏ, pot; ō, toe; ô, paw, for;
oi, noise; ou, out; o͝o, book;
o͞o, boot; p, pop; r, roar;
s, sauce; sh, ship, dish;
t, tight; th, thin, path;
th, this, bathe; ŭ, cut; ûr, fur;
v, valve; w, with; y, yes;
z, zebra, size; zh, vision;
ə, about, item, edible,
gallop, circus, peaceful

IN FOREIGN WORDS:

à, *Fr.* ami; œ, *Fr.* feu, *Ger.* schön; ü, *Fr.* tu, *Ger.* über; KH, *Ger.* ich, *Scot.* loch; N, *Fr.* bon; y', *Fr.* Compiègne

STRESS MARKS:

Primary stress: '
in·cite' (ĭn-sīt')
Secondary stress: '
in'sight' (ĭn'sīt')

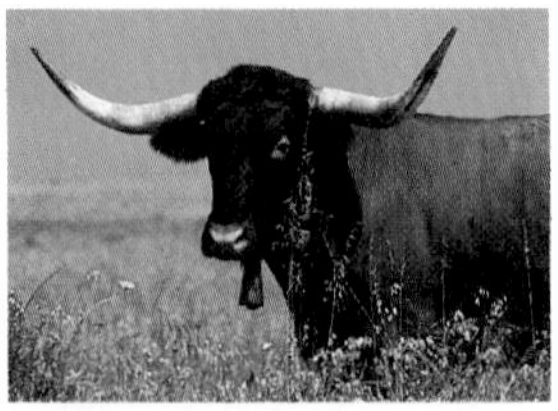

longhorn *This distinctive breed of cattle played a major role in the history of Texas and the economic development of the American West.*

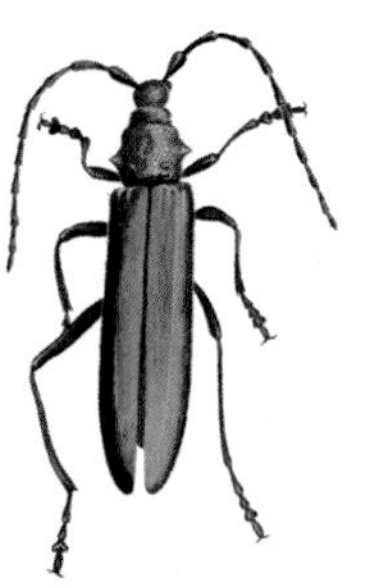

long-horned beetle *This beetle is a shiny green insect with long curved antennae. Found in woodlands, it has a pleasant musklike scent.*

PRONUNCIATION KEY

ă, pat; ā, pay; âr, care;
ä, father, are; b, bib;
ch, church; d, deed; ĕ, pet;
ē, be; f, fife; g, gag; h, hat;
hw, which; ĭ, pit; ī, pie;
îr, pier; j, judge; k, kick;
l, lid, needle; m, mum;
n, no, sudden; ng, thing;
ŏ, pot; ō, toe; ô, paw, for;
oi, noise; ou, out; o͝o, book;
o͞o, boot; p, pop; r, roar;
s, sauce; sh, ship, dish;
t, tight; th, thin, path;
th, this, bathe; ŭ, cut; ûr, fur;
v, valve; w, with; y, yes;
z, zebra, size; zh, vision;
ə, about, item, edible,
gallop, circus, peaceful

IN FOREIGN WORDS:

à, *Fr.* ami; œ, *Fr.* feu, *Ger.*
schön; ü, *Fr.* tu, *Ger.* über;
KH, *Ger.* ich, *Scot.* loch;
N, *Fr.* bon; y', *Fr.* Compiègne

STRESS MARKS:

Primary stress: ′
in·cite′ (ĭn-sīt′)
Secondary stress: ′
in′sight′ (ĭn′sīt′)

by Greater London, which consists of 32 boroughs. One of these, the City of Westminster, contains the Houses of Parliament, Westminster Abbey, government ministries, and Buckingham Palace. Much of the City of London was destroyed by the Great Fire of 1666, after which Sir Christopher Wren rebuilt St. Paul's Cathedral and many other buildings. London is one of the world's most important banking and insurance centers and Britain's largest port. It is also a major industrial area, its products ranging from machinery, chemicals, and motor vehicles to motion pictures, clothing, and luxury goods.

London, Jack, pen name of John Griffith London (1876–1916). U.S. writer. He was a tramp and a prospector in the Klondike Gold Rush (1897). His tales include *The Call of the Wild* (1903) and *The People of the Abyss* (1903).

London Bridge. First recorded bridge to span the Thames River in London, England. The first London Bridge of stone, which replaced a wooden one, was completed in 1209 and was lined with houses and a chapel. It was demolished after a new bridge, designed by John Rennie, was built to its west in 1824–31. In 1973 a 32-meter (105-foot) wide bridge replaced the Rennie bridge, which was re-erected at the resort of Lake Havasu City, in Arizona.

London broil *n.* Broiled flank steak, cut into thin slices.

Lon·don·der·ry[1] (lŭn′dən-dĕr′ē). Also **Der·ry** (dĕr′ē). Hilly county in Northern Ireland. It is mostly agricultural, with coastal and inland fishing and some light industries. In the 17th century much of the land was confiscated from its Irish owners (the O'Neill family) and granted to City Companies of London.

Londonderry[2]**.** Also **Derry.** Second-largest city of Northern Ireland, on the Foyle River, County Londonderry. Derry dates from 546 when St. Columba founded a monastery here. In 1613 the city was granted to the Corporation of the City of London (hence the name Londonderry).

Lon·don·er (lŭn′dən-ər) *n.* A native or inhabitant of London.

London plane *n.* A hybrid plane tree, *Platanus hybrida,* often planted in cities, having a bark which flakes off, making it resistant to smoke and fumes.

London pride *n.* An alpine garden plant that is a hybrid between *Saxifraga spathularis* and *S. umbrosa.* It has a basal rosette of leaves and a cluster of small pink flowers borne on a long stem.

lone (lōn) *adj.* **1.** Single; solitary: *a lone spectator.* **2.** Isolated; set apart: *a lone cottage.* **3.** *Poetic.* Lonely. **4.** *Rare.* Unmarried or widowed. [Shortened from ALONE (*a-* being taken for the indefinite article).]

lone hand *n.* **1.** In some card games, a hand played without help from a partner's hand. **2.** A cardplayer without a partner.

lone·ly (lōn′lē) *adj.* **-lier, -liest. 1. a.** Without companions; lone. **b.** Characterized by aloneness; solitary: *a lonely existence.* **2.** Unfrequented; empty of people; desolate: *a lonely crossroads.* **3. a.** Dejected by the awareness of being alone. **b.** Producing such dejection: *the loneliest night of the week.* [From LONE.] **—lone·li·ly** *adv.* **—lone·li·ness** *n.*

lonely hearts *pl.n.* People who are distressed by lack of emotional companionship, especially those who seek it through advertisements in newspapers or periodicals. **—lone·ly-hearts** *adj.*

lon·er (lō′nər) *n. Informal.* One who prefers to be or work alone.

lone·some (lōn′səm) *adj.* **1.** Dejected by being lonely. **2.** Inducing the sense of loneliness: *a lonesome trip.* **3.** Deserted; unfrequented: *a lonesome valley.* **4.** Lone: *a lonesome pine.*
~n. Informal. Self: *He ate all by his lonesome.*

lone wolf *n.* A person who likes to live or work alone.

long[1] (lông, lŏng) *adj.* **longer, longest. 1. a.** Having great length. **b.** *Rare.* Tall. **2.** Of relatively great duration: *a long time.* **3. a.** Of a specified linear extent or duration; in length: *a mile long; an hour long.* **b.** Lengthwise: *two inches long and one inch wide.* **4.** Extending beyond an average or a standard: *a long game; a long memory.* **5.** Tediously protracted; lengthy: *a long speech.* **6.** Concerned with distant issues; far-reaching: *the long view.* **7.** Risky; chancy: *long odds.* **8.** Having an abundance or an excess of. Used with *on: long on hope.* **9.** *Finance.* Having an unsold holding of a security or commodity in expectation of a rise in price: *long in steel.* **10.** *Phonetics.* Having a comparatively protracted sound: *a long vowel.* **11.** In verse: **a.** Designating a vowel sound of relatively great duration, as *feed* compared with *feet.* **b.** Bearing stress: *a long syllable.* **—in the long run.** Ultimately; eventually.
~adv. **1.** During or for an extended period of time: *The promotion was long due.* Often used in combination: *long-lasting; long-lost.* **2.** Far: *He read long into the night.* **3.** For or throughout a specified period: *They talked all night long.* **4.** At a point of time distant from that referred to: *long before we were born.* **—as** (or **so**) **long as. 1.** Since; inasmuch as. **2.** During or only during the time that. **3.** Provided that; on condition that. **—no longer.** Not now as formerly; no more: *He no longer smokes.*
~n. **1.** A long time. **2.** A relatively long sound, such as a vowel or a signal in Morse code. **3.** *Finance.* **a.** One who acquires large holdings of a security expecting a rise in price or commodity. **b. longs.** Long-dated gilt-edged securities. **4.** A clothing size for a tall person. **—before long.** Soon. **—the long and the short of it.** The essential details; the substance: *The long and the short of it is they won.* [Middle English *long, lang,* Old English *long, lang.*]

long[2] *intr.v.* **longed, longing, longs.** To yearn; wish earnestly; desire greatly: *He longed to go home.* —See Synonyms at **yearn.** [Middle English *longen,* Old English *langian,* "to seem long (to some)," to yearn for.]

long. longitude.

Long (lông, lŏng), **Huey Pierce** (1893–1935). U.S. politician. With the campaign slogan "Every Man a King," he gained the support of Louisiana's rural poor and developed tremendous political power in his home state. He served as governor (1928–32) and U.S. senator (1930–35). Long was assassinated by a local political enemy.

lon·gan (lông′gən, lŏng′-) *n.* **1.** A Chinese tree, *Euphoria longana.* **2.** The edible fruit of this tree, which is similar to but smaller than a litchi. [Chinese *lóng yăn,* dragon's eye.]

long-and-short work (lông′ən-shôrt′, lŏng′-) *n. Architecture.* The alternation of vertical and horizontal stone slabs at the corner of an Anglo-Saxon or Early English building.

lon·ga·nim·i·ty (lŏng′gə-nĭm′ə-tē) *n.* Equanimity in the face of suffering and adversity; forbearance. [Middle English *longanimyte,* from Late Latin *longanimitās,* from *longanimis,* "long-souled," patient : Latin *longus,* long + *animus,* soul, mind.]

Long Beach. Coastal resort south of Los Angeles, California. It has a large harbor, naval shipyard, dry dock, and refineries for oil, which was discovered nearby in the 1920's.

long·boat (lông′bōt′, lŏng′-) *n.* **1.** The longest boat carried by a sailing ship. **2.** A **longship** *(see).*

long·bow (lông′bō′, lŏng′-) *n.* **1.** A wooden bow roughly 1.5 to 1.8 meters (five to six feet) long. **2.** A powerful hand-drawn bow, sometimes as much as two meters (over six feet) in length, much used in medieval England.

long·case clock (lông′kās′, lŏng′-) *n.* A **grandfather clock** *(see).*

long-chain (lông′chān′, lŏng′-) *adj.* Designating a molecule whose constituent atoms are arranged in an extended chainlike structure.

long-dat·ed (lông′dā′tĭd, lŏng′-) *adj. Finance.* Designating gilt-edged securities redeemable after a time more than 15 years away. Compare **medium-dated, short-dated.**

long-day (lông′dā′, lŏng′-) *adj.* Of or designating plants that will flower only when exposed to periods of daylight in excess of ten hours. Compare **short-day.**

long distance *n.* **1.** An operator or system that places long-distance telephone calls. **2.** A long-distance telephone call.

long-dis·tance (lông′dĭs′təns, lŏng′-) *adj.* **1.** Located or from far away. **2.** Covering a long distance. **3.** Of or designating telephone communications to a distant place. **—long-distance** *adv.*

long division *n.* A process of division in arithmetic, usually used when the divisor has more than one digit, in which the remainders leading to succeeding steps of the procedure are recorded in a determinate pattern.

long dozen *n.* Thirteen; a baker's dozen.

long-drawn-out (lông′drôn′out, lŏng′-) *adj.* Unduly prolonged.

lon·ge·ron (lŏn′jər-ən) *n.* A structural member that runs from front to rear of an aircraft's fuselage. [French, from *longer,* to pass along, extend along, from Late Latin *longāre,* to lengthen, from Latin *longus,* long.]

longeur. Variant of **longueur.**

lon·gev·i·ty (lŏn-jĕv′ə-tē) *n.* **1.** A long duration of life. **2.** Long duration, as in an occupation or political office. [Late Latin *longevitās* (stem *longevitāt-),* from Latin *longaevus,* living to a great age : *longus,* long + *aevum,* age.] **—lon·ge·vous** (lŏn-jē′vəs) *adj.*

long face *n.* A discontented or sullen facial expression.

Long·fel·low (lông′fĕl′ō, lŏng′-), **Henry Wadsworth** (1807–82). U.S. poet. He wrote *The Wreck of the Hesperus* (1841), *Paul Revere's Ride* (1863), and *The Song of Hiawatha* (1855), an epic of Indian life written in the metrical pattern of a Norse saga.

Long·ford (lông′fərd, lŏng′-). Inland county in Leinster province, Republic of Ireland. The rearing of beef cattle and buttermaking are its main industries.

long green *n. Slang.* Paper money.

long·hair (lông′hâr′, lŏng′-) *n.* **1.** A person with long hair, especially a male whose hair length symbolizes alienation from or protest against the values of conventional society. **2. a.** One dedicated to the arts and especially to classical music. **b.** One whose taste in the arts is held to be overrefined. **—long·hair, long·haired** *adj.*

long·hand (lông′hănd′, lŏng′-) *n.* Handwriting as distinct from shorthand, typing, or printing.
~adj. Handwritten. **—long·hand** *adv.*

long haul *n.* **1.** A journey covering a great distance or taking a long time. **2.** Any task or project that takes a long time to carry out.

long-haul (lông′hôl′, lŏng′-) *adj.* Designating flights or other journeys over a long distance.

long·head·ed (lông′hĕd′ĭd, lŏng′-) *adj.* **1.** Dolichocephalic. **2.** Possessing foresight; shrewd; astute; cunning.

long·horn (lông′hôrn′, lŏng′-) *n.* A member of any of several breeds of beef cattle having long horns.

long-horned beetle (lông′hôrnd′, lŏng′-) *n.* Any of numerous beetles of the family Cerambycidae, having long legs and long antennae. Also called "longicorn," "longicorn beetle."

long house *n.* A long, often communal wooden dwelling used especially by the Iroquois.

long hundredweight *n.* See **hundredweight** (sense 2).

longi– *prefix.* Indicates long; for example, **longicorn.** [Latin, from *longus,* long.]

lon·gi·corn (lŏn′jĭ-kôrn′) *adj.* **1.** Having long antennae. **2.** Of or belonging to the family Cerambycidae, which includes the long-horned beetles.
~n. A long-horned beetle. Also called "longicorn beetle." [New Latin *Longicornia* (former classification) : LONGI- + Latin *cornū,* horn.]

long·ing (lông′ĭng, lŏng′-) *n.* A persistent, unfulfilled yearning or desire.
~*adj.* Affected by or expressing such a yearning: *look with longing eyes.* **—long·ing·ly** *adv.*

Lon·gi·nus (lŏn-jī′nəs), **Dionysius Cassius** (*c.* A.D. 210–73). Greek philosopher. He served as political adviser to Zenobia and as tutor to her children. He was a renowned scholar and critic and possibly wrote the famous essay *On the Sublime.* Longinus was beheaded by Emperor Aurelian after Zenobia's fall from power.

long·ish (lông′ĭsh, lŏng′-) *adj.* Fairly long.

Long Island. Island in New York State, separated from Connecticut by Long Island Sound and including part of New York City.

lon·gi·tude (lŏn′jə-to͞od′, -tyo͞od′) *n. Abbr.* **long. 1.** The angular distance east or west of the prime meridian at Greenwich, England, to the point on the earth's surface for which the longitude is being ascertained, expressed either in degrees or in hours, minutes, and seconds. **2.** *Astronomy.* The angular distance, measured in degrees eastward along the ecliptic from the vernal equinox to the great circle passing through the pole of the ecliptic and the celestial point being measured. Also called "celestial longitude." [Middle English, from Latin *longitūdō,* from *longus,* LONG.]

lon·gi·tu·di·nal (lŏn′jə-to͞od′n-əl, -tyo͞od′n-əl) *adj.* **1.** Of or pertaining to length. **2.** Placed or running lengthwise. **3.** Pertaining to longitude. **—lon·gi·tu·di·nal·ly** *adv.*

longitudinal wave *n.* A wave propagated in the same direction as the displacement of the transmitting medium. Compare **transverse wave.**

long johns *pl.n. Informal.* Long, warm underwear.

long jump *n. Sports.* In track-and-field events, a jump for distance rather than for height, made either from a stationary position or a running start. Also called "broad jump."

long·leaf pine (lông′lēf′, lŏng′-) *n.* An evergreen coniferous tree, *Pinus australis* (or *P. palustris*), of the southeastern United States, having long needles and heavy, tough, resinous wood valued as timber and as a source of turpentine.

long-lived (lông′līvd′, -lĭvd′, lŏng′-) *adj.* **1.** Having a long life. **2.** Persistent: *a long-lived rumor.* **—long-lived·ness** *n.*

Long March. The hazardous journey to safety undertaken (1934–35) by an army of about 100,000 Communist Chinese soldiers and officials, of whom a third at most survived. Their route led northwest across China from Jiangxi to Shaanxi, a distance of about 10,000 kilometers (6,000 miles).

long measure *n.* **Linear measure** *(see).*

long multiplication *n.* A method for obtaining the product of two numbers, especially when both numbers consist of several digits. The multiplicand is multiplied by each digit of the multiplier in turn, the partial products so obtained being set out in an array that takes account of the position of their decimal points; the final product is the sum of the partial products.

Lon·go·bard (lŏng′gō-bärd′) *n., pl.* **-bards** or **-bardi** (-bär′dē). An early **Lombard** *(see).* **—Lon·go·bar·di·an, Lon·go·bar·dic** *adj.*

Long Parliament *n.* The English Parliament that was convened by Charles I in 1640, dismissed by Oliver Cromwell in 1653, and reconvened in 1659–1660. See **Rump Parliament.**

long pig *n.* A human being used for meat by cannibals.

long-play·ing (lông′plā′ĭng, lŏng′-) *adj. Abbr.* **LP** Pertaining to or designating a microgroove phonograph record, especially one turning at 33¹/₃ revolutions per minute.

long-range (lông′rānj′, lŏng′-) *adj.* **1.** Requiring or involving a span of years; not immediate: *long-range planning.* **2.** Of, suitable for, or equipped to travel long distances: *long-range aircraft.*

long·ship (lông′shĭp′, lŏng′-) *n.* A narrow uncovered vessel powered by oars and sail, used by the Vikings and other peoples in Europe during the early Middle Ages. Also called "longboat."

long·shore (lông′shôr′, -shōr′, lŏng′-) *adj.* Occurring, living, or working along a seacoast. [Short for ALONGSHORE.]

long·shore·man (lông′shôr′mən, -shōr′mən, lŏng′-), *n., pl.* **-men** (-mĭn). A dock worker who loads and unloads ships.

long shot *n.* **1. a.** An entry, as in a horse race, with only a slight chance of winning. **b.** A bet made at and against great odds. **2. a.** A risky venture that will pay off handsomely if successful. **b.** An attempt or guess that has only a slight chance of proving successful. **3.** A film scene shot at some distance from the subject. **—by a long shot.** By a great extent or amount.

long-sight·ed (lông′sī′tĭd, lŏng′-) *adj.* **1.** Suffering from **hyperopia** *(see);* able to see only distant objects clearly. **2.** Possessing foresight; planning for the future.

long-sight·ed·ness (lông′sī′tĭd-nĭs, lŏng′-) *n.* **Hyperopia** *(see).*

long·spur (lông′spûr′, lŏng′-) *n.* Any of several birds of the genera *Calcarius* and *Rhyncophanes,* of northern regions, having brownish plumage and long-clawed hind toes.

long-stand·ing (lông′stăn′dĭng, lŏng′-) Having been in existence or force for a long time.

Long·street (lông′strēt′, lŏng′-), **James** (1821–1904). U.S. Confederate general in the Civil War. He helped lead Confederate forces at Bull Run (1861 and 1862), Antietam (1862), and Fredericksburg (1862), but was criticized for delaying when he personally disagreed with the strategy, a trait that contributed to the Confederate defeat at Gettysburg (1863).

long-suf·fer·ing (lông′sŭf′ər-ĭng, lŏng′-) *adj.* Patiently enduring wrongs or difficulties.
~*n.* Also **long-suf·fer·ance** (-əns). Patient endurance. **—long-suf·fer·ing·ly** *adv.*

long suit *n.* **1.** In card games, a suit containing more cards than any of the other suits in a hand. **2.** *Informal.* The personal quality or talent that is one's strongest asset.

long-tailed tit (lông′tāld′, lŏng′-) *n.* A small Eurasian songbird, *Aegisthalos caudatus,* with black, pink, and white plumage and a long, black and white tail.

long-term (lông′tûrm′, lŏng′-) *adj.* In effect for, involving, or maturing after a number of years: *a long-term investment.*

long-time (lông′tīm′, lŏng′-) *adj.* Having existed or persisted for a long time: *a long-time acquaintance.*

long tom *n. Sometimes* **Long Tom. 1.** A long pivoted cannon formerly used on warships. **2.** A similar long-range gun used on land. **3.** A trough in which gold-bearing sand is washed.

long ton *n.* See **ton** (sense 1a).

lon·gueur, lon·geur (lôN-gœr′) *n. Often* **longueurs. 1.** A boring or tedious period of time. **2.** A tedious, overlong passage, as in a book or film. [French, "length."]

long-waisted (lông′wā′stĭd, lŏng′-) *adj.* Having or being of more than average length between shoulders and waist.

long wave *n.* A radio waveband in which the wavelength exceeds 1,000 meters (frequency less than 300 kilohertz).

long-wind·ed (long′wĭn′dĭd, lŏng′-) *adj.* **1.** Wearisomely verbose: *a long-winded bore.* **2.** Not subject to quick loss of breath. **—long-wind·ed·ly** *adv.* **—long-wind·ed·ness** *n.*

long·wise (lông′wīz′, lŏng′-) *adv.* Lengthwise.

Long·worth (lông′wûrth′, lŏng′-), **Alice Roosevelt** (1884–1980). U.S. socialite and wit. The daughter of Theodore Roosevelt, her headstrong rebelliousness and madcap antics were a favorite with the national press during her father's presidency. She remained in Washington, D.C., until her death and was known for her sharp wit and biting comments on the political and social scene.

loo¹ (lo͞o) *n., pl.* **loos.** *British Informal.* A toilet; lavatory. [Perhaps from French *lieux (d'aisances),* privy.]

loo² *n., pl.* **loos.** A card game in which each player contributes stakes to a pool. [Shortened from *lanterloo,* from French *lanturlu,* originally the refrain of a popular song.]

loo·by (lo͞o′bē) *n., pl.* **-bies.** *Informal.* A stupid or clumsy person. [Middle English *loby,* probably of Low German origin, akin to Middle Low German *lobbe,* loose-hanging lip, bumpkin. See **lob.**]

loo·fa, loo·fah (lo͞o′fə) *n.* Also **luf·fa** (lŭf′ə). **1.** The dried, fibrous, spongelike interior of the fruit of the dishcloth gourd, used as a washing sponge or as a filter. Also called "vegetable sponge." **2.** The **dishcloth gourd** *(see).* [New Latin *Luffa,* from Arabic *lūf, lūfah.*]

look (lo͝ok) *v.* **looked, looking, looks.** —*intr.* **1.** To employ one's eyes in seeing. **2. a.** To turn one's glance. **b.** To turn one's attention. Often used with *at.* **3.** To seem or appear to be: *look morose.* **4.** To face in a specified direction. Often used with *onto* or *out onto*: *The cottage looks onto the river.* **5.** *Informal.* To hope or expect. Used with an infinitive: *He looked to hear from her.* —*tr.* **1.** To turn one's eyes on. **2.** To express by one's appearance: *She looked her joy.* **3.** To have an appearance in conformity with: *look one's age.* **—look after.** To take care of. **—look as if.** To seem likely that. **—look back.** To reflect on the past; remember. **—look down on** (or **upon**). To regard with contempt or condescension. **—look for. 1.** To search for. **2.** To expect. **—look forward to.** To anticipate eagerly. **—look into.** To investigate. **—look like.** To indicate as a likely possibility: *It looks like war.* **—look on. 1.** To be a spectator. **2.** To consider; regard: *look on the accident as a stroke of luck.* **—look over.** To inspect; especially, to inspect casually. **—look sharp** (or **lively**). To hurry up, or respond quickly. Usually used as an imperative. **—look through. 1.** To inspect briefly: *look through a report.* **2.** To pretend to be unacquainted with (a person); ignore; snub. **—look to. 1.** To expect. **2.** To attend to. **3.** To rely upon. **4.** To resort to: *If you won't help, I will look to others for support.* **—look toward.** To be a pointer to; herald; prefigure: *His poetry looks toward the modernist revolution.* **—look up. 1.** To search for and find, as in a reference book. **2.** To locate and call upon; visit. **3.** *Informal.* To improve: *Things are looking up.* **—look up and down. 1.** To inspect critically, coldly, or disdainfully. **2.** To search everywhere. **—look up to.** To admire. **—never look back.** To make uninterrupted progress. **—not look at.** To refuse to have anything to do with: *He won't look at Spanish wines.*
~*n.* **1.** The action or an instance of looking; a gaze or glance. **2.** An appearance or aspect. **3. looks.** Physical appearance, especially when pleasing. **—by the look of.** Taking appearances as a guide or indication: *by the look of her, she's ill.*
~*interj.* Used to request attention, preface an objection, or express impatience or insistence. [Middle English *loken,* to look, have the appearance, Old English *lōcian,* to look, from West Germanic *lokōn* (unattested).]

look·a·like (lo͝ok′ə-līk′) *n.* One that closely ʳ sembles another; especially, one bearing a close resemblance to a celebrity. **—look·a·like** *adj.*

look·down (lo͝ok′doun′) *n.* A marine fish, *Selene vomer,* of Atlantic waters, having a steep frontal profile.

look·er (lo͝ok′ər) *n.* **1.** One that looks. **2.** *Informal.* A very attractive person.

look·er-on (lo͝ok′ər-ŏn′, -ôn′) *n., pl.* **lookers-on.** A spectator.

look in *intr.v.* To drop in; make a brief visit. Often used with *on.*

look-in (lo͝ok′ĭn′) *n.* **1.** A short visit. **2.** A quick glance.

looking glass *n.* A mirror.

look·ing-glass (lo͝ok′ĭng-glăs′) *adj.* Topsy-turvy; disconcertingly

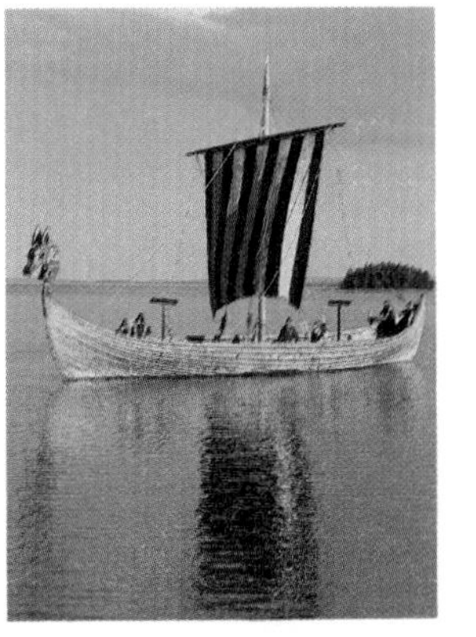

longship *Viking longships were used to attack coastal villages all over northern Europe during the early Middle Ages. This is a modern Norwegian replica.*

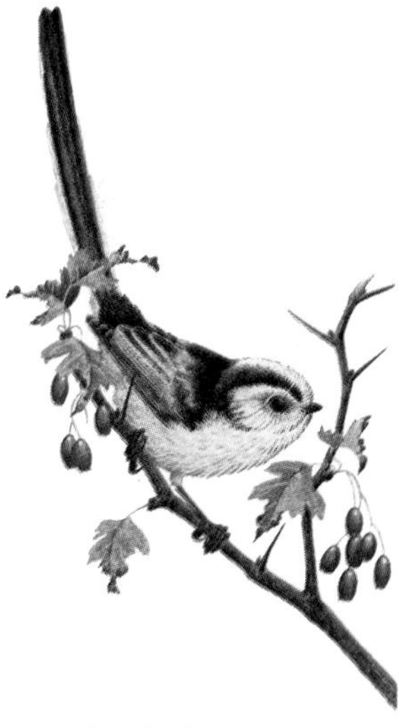

long-tailed tit *This insect eater uses lichen, animal hair, and cobwebs to build a complex domed nest. It is found throughout Europe and across Asia to China and Japan.*

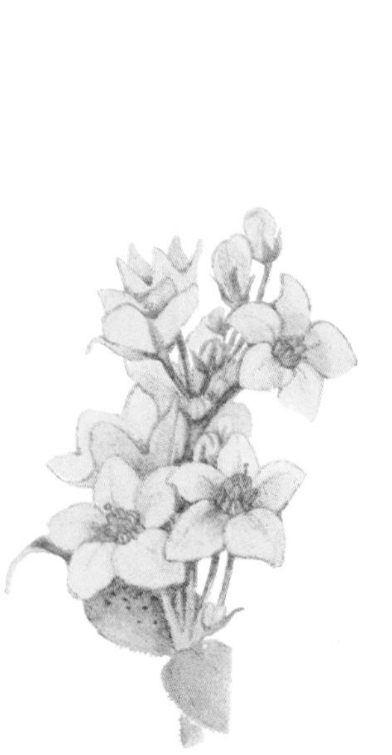

loosestrife *Yellow loosestrife used to be tied in bunches around the necks of draft animals to keep away irritating flies and insects and to keep the animals calm. A tea made from the whole plant serves as an astringent wash and gargle.*

unfamiliar: *Traveling in the East, she felt herself to be in a looking-glass world.* [After the fantastic logic of Lewis Carroll's *Through the Looking-Glass.*]

look out *intr.v.* **1.** To be careful or protective: *looking out for one's interests.* **2.** To be careful to notice some hazard: *Look out for the step!* **3.** To watch in the hope of finding something: *looking out for bargains.*

look·out (lo͝ok′out′) *n.* **1.** The act of observing or keeping watch. **2.** A high place or structure commanding a wide view for observation. **3.** One who keeps watch. **4.** An outlook; prospects. **5.** *Informal.* An unfortunate prospect; a problem: *If they don't work, that's their lookout!* **—on the lookout.** Watching out, as for a hazard or something needed.

look-see (lo͝ok′sē′) *n. Informal.* A quick survey or glance.

look-up (lo͝ok′ŭp′) *n. Computer Science.* A procedure in which a table of values stored in a computer is searched for a specified value.

loom¹ (lo͞om) *intr.v.* **loomed, looming, looms. 1.** To come into view as a massive, distorted, or indistinct image. **2.** To appear to the mind in a magnified and threatening form. **3.** To seem imminent; impend. **4.** To tower above; overhang. Used with *over*: *The crag looms over the house.* **—loom large. 1.** To be a preoccupation. **2.** To be a significant element: *Beethoven's influence looms large in the composer's earlier works.*
~*n.* A distorted, threatening appearance of something, as through fog or darkness. [Probably of Low German origin; akin to East Frisian *lōmen,* to move slowly, *lōm,* lame, crippled.]

loom² *n.* **1.** A machine or device from which a textile is produced by interweaving thread or yarn at right angles. **2.** *Nautical.* The shaft of an oar. [Middle English *lome,* Old English *gelōma,* utensil, tool : *ge-* (collective prefix) + *-lōma,* akin to Middle Dutch *allame*†, tool.]

loon¹ (lo͞on) *n.* Any of several northern diving birds of the genus *Gavia,* having a laughlike cry. Also called "diver." [Probably from Old Norse *lomr.*]

loon² *n. Informal.* A simple-minded or mad person. [Middle English *loun, lownt*†.]

loon·y, loon·ey (lo͞o′nē) *adj.* **-ier, -iest.** *Informal.* **1.** So odd as to appear demented; mad; crazy. **2.** Foolish; senseless.
~*n., pl.* **loonies.** *Informal.* A loony person.

loony bin *n. Slang.* A mental hospital. Often considered offensive.

loop¹ (lo͞op) *n.* **1.** A length of line, as of wire, thread, rope, or ribbon, that is folded over and joined at the ends. **2.** The opening formed by such a doubled line. **3.** Any roughly oval, closed, or nearly closed turn or figure. **4.** Something having such a turn or figure. **5.** *Electricity.* A closed circuit. **6.** A flight maneuver in which an aircraft flies a circular path in a vertical plane with the lateral axis of the aircraft remaining horizontal. **7.** The commonest of the basic patterns of ridges making up the human fingerprint. Compare **arch, whorl. 8.** *Anatomy.* A bend in a tubular organ, such as *Henle's loop* in a kidney tubule. **9.** An intrauterine contraceptive consisting of a small device in the shape of a loop. **10.** *Mathematics.* A closed curve on a graph. **11.** *Computer Science.* A series of program instructions that are performed repeatedly until one specific condition is fulfilled. **12.** A loop aerial. **13.** A loopline. **14.** A **tape-loop** *(see).* **15.** A figure executed by an ice-skater by describing a figure eight on one edge and doubling back into and out of the eight at the top and bottom.
~*v.* **looped, looping, loops.** —*tr.* **1.** To form (thread, for example) into a loop or loops. **2.** To fasten, join, or encircle with a loop or loops. **3.** To fly (an aircraft) in a loop. **4.** *Electricity.* To join (conductors) so as to complete a circuit. —*intr.* **1.** To form a loop or loops. **2.** In aviation, to make a loop or loops. **3.** To progress by looping the body. Used of measuring worms. **—loop the loop.** To make a vertical loop or loops in the air. Used of an aircraft. [Middle English *loupe*†.]

loop² *n. Archaic.* A small opening in a wall; a loophole. [Middle English *loupe*†.]

Loop. The central business district of Chicago, Illinois.

loop aerial *n.* A radio aerial consisting of one or more coils of wire wound on a frame. Also called "frame aerial," "loop."

loop·er (lo͞o′pər) *n.* **1.** One that makes loops. **2.** The caterpillar of a geometrid moth, a **measuring worm** *(see).*

loop·hole (lo͞op′hōl′) *n.* **1.** A small hole or slit in a wall, especially one through which small arms may be fired. **2.** A way of escaping a difficulty; especially, an omission or an ambiguity, as in the wording of a contract or law, that provides a means of evasion. [LOOP (opening) + HOLE.]

loop·line (lo͞op′līn′) *n.* A railroad line that leaves and later rejoins a main line.

loop·y (lo͞o′pē) *adj.* **1.** Containing, resembling, or pertaining to loops: curly. **2.** *Informal.* Eccentric; crazy.

Loos (lo͞os), **Anita** (*c.* 1893–1981). U.S. author. A screenwriter for more than 60 silent movies, including *A Virtuous Vamp* (1919) and *The Perfect Woman* (1920), she earned international fame with her novel *Gentlemen Prefer Blondes* (1925).

loose (lo͞os) *adj.* **looser, loosest. 1. a.** Not fastened or restrained; unbound. **b.** Not tightly anchored or secured: *a loose tooth.* **2.** Not taut or drawn up tightly; slack. **3.** Free from confinement or imprisonment; unfettered. **4.** Not tight-fitting or tightly fitted. **5.** Allowing some latitude; not rigidly arranged: *a loose association.* **6.** Not bound, bundled, packed, stapled, or gathered together. **7.** Not compact or dense. **8.** Not fast: *a loose dye.* **9.** Lacking a sense of restraint or responsibility; idle: *loose talk.* **10.** Licentious; unchaste; immoral. **11.** Not precise or exact: *a loose translation.* **12.** Not strict or totally correct: *a loose use of the term.* **13.** Readily available; not committed: *loose cash.* **14.** *Informal.* Calm; unruffled. **15.** Designating bowels that empty easily or overactively. **16.** Designating a cough that produces or results from an excess of phlegm in the throat. **—at loose ends.** Without plans or direction. **—on the loose.** *Informal.* **1.** At large; free from confinement. **2.** Acting in an uninhibited or licentious fashion.
~*adv.* In a loose manner.
~*v.* **loosed, loosing, looses.** —*tr.* **1.** To let loose; set free; release. **2.** To undo, untie, or unwrap. **3.** To release pressure on; make less tight, firm, or compact. **4.** To relax (rules or regulations); make less strict. **5.** To let fly (a projectile). —*intr.* **1.** To become loose. **2.** To discharge a projectile; fire. [Middle English *lous(e), lo(o)s,* from Old Norse *lauss, louss.*] **—loose·ly** *adv.* **—loose·ness** *n.*

loose cover *n.* A fitted, removable cover of cloth or other material for a piece of upholstered furniture.

loose-joint·ed (lo͞os′join′tĭd) *adj.* **1.** Having freely articulated joints. **2.** Supple in movement. **—loose-joint·ed·ness** *n.*

loose-leaf (lo͞os′lēf′) *adj.* Designating a binder or folder that allows the insertion and removal of pages.

loose-limbed (lo͞os′lĭmd′) *adj.* Having supple limbs.

loos·en (lo͞o′sən) *v.* **-ened, -ening, -ens.** —*tr.* **1.** To make looser. **2.** To untie. **3.** To free from restraint, pressure, or strictness. **4.** To free (the bowels) from constipation. —*intr.* To become loose or looser. [Middle English *lo(o)snen,* from *lo(o)s,* LOOSE.]

loose·strife (lo͞os′strīf′) *n.* **1.** Any of various plants of the genus *Lysimachia,* having typically yellow flowers. **2.** Any of various plants of the genus *Lythrum.* See **purple loosestrife. 3.** Any of various related or similar plants. [LOOSE + STRIFE (literal translation of Latin *lysimachia,* from Greek *lusimakheion.*]

loot (lo͞ot) *n.* **1.** Valuables that have been looted; spoils. **2.** *Informal.* Goods illicitly obtained, as by theft or bribery. **3.** *Informal.* Money.
~*v.* **looted, looting, loots.** —*tr.* **1.** To steal from in the process of war or civil disturbance. **2.** To take as spoils. —*intr.* To loot property. —See Synonyms at **rob.** [Hindi *lūṭ,* from Sanskrit *lō(p)tra,* booty.]

lop¹ (lŏp) *tr.v.* **lopped, lopping, lops. 1.** To cut off branches or twigs from; trim. **2.** To cut off (branches) from a tree or shrub. **3.** To cut off (a part), especially with a single swift blow. Usually used with *off.* **4.** To eliminate or excise as superfluous. Used with *off.*
~*n.* **1.** The trimmings of a felled tree; twigs and branches. **2.** Anything lopped off. [Middle English, Old English *loppian* (unattested), to prune.] **—lop·per** *n.*

lop² *v.* **lopped, lopping, lops.** —*intr.* **1.** To hang loosely; droop. **2.** To slouch; dawdle; loiter. **3.** To lope. —*tr.* To allow or cause to hang loosely. [Akin to LOB.]

lope (lōp) *intr.v.* **loped, loping, lopes.** To run or ride with a steady, easy gait.
~*n.* A steady, easy stride or movement. [Middle English *lo(u)pen,* from Old Norse *hlaupa,* to leap.] **—lop·er** *n.*

lop-eared (lŏp′îrd′) *adj.* Having bent or drooping ears. Said of certain animals: *lop-eared beagles.*

Lope de Vega. See **Vega, Lope Felix de.**

lopho- *prefix.* Indicates a crested or tufted part; for example, **lophobranch.** [From Greek *lophos,* crest.]

lo·pho·branch (lŏf′ə-brăngk′) *n.* Any fish of the suborder Lophobranchii, having gills arranged in tufts, and including the sea horses. [LOPHO- + -BRANCH.] **—lo·pho·branch** *adj.*

lo·pho·phore (lŏf′ə-fôr′, -fōr′) *n.* The filter-feeding organ of certain small, aquatic, invertebrate animals, such as brachiopods, consisting of a circular or horseshoe-shaped ring of tentacles around the mouth. [LOPHO- + -PHORE.] **—lo·pho·phor·ate** *adj.*

Lop Nor or **Lop Nur** (lôp′ nôr′). Largely dried-up salt lake in the Tarim basin, Xinjiang Uigur Zizhiqu, western China. Since 1964 it has been the country's nuclear research and testing site.

lop·o·lith (lŏp′ə-lĭth′) *n.* A saucer-shaped body of intrusive igneous rock. [Greek *lopos,* shell + -LITH.]

lop·py (lŏp′ē) *adj.* **-pier, -piest.** Hanging limp; pendulous.

lop·sid·ed (lŏp′sī′dĭd) *adj.* **1.** Heavier, larger, or higher on one side than on the other; not symmetrical. **2.** Sagging or leaning to one side. **3.** Not showing proper balance. **—lop·sid·ed·ly** *adv.* **—lop·sid·ed·ness** *n.*

loq. loquitur.

lo·qua·cious (lō-kwā′shəs) *adj.* Very talkative; garrulous. —See Synonyms at **talkative.** [Latin *loquāx* (stem *loquāc-*), from *loquī,* to speak.] **—lo·qua·cious·ly** *adv.* **—lo·qua·cious·ness, lo·quac·i·ty** (lō-kwăs′ə-tē) *n.*

lo·quat (lō′kwŏt′, -kwăt′) *n.* **1.** A small tree, *Eriobotrya japonica,* native to eastern Asia, with white flowers and yellow pear-shaped fruit. **2.** The edible fruit of this tree. [Cantonese *lō kwat, lō kat.*]

lo·qui·tur (lō′kwə-to͝or′, lŏk′wə-tər) *Abbr.* **loq.** He or she speaks or begins to speak. Used as a stage direction. [Latin.]

lo·ran (lôr′ăn′, lōr′-) *n.* A long-range navigational system based on pulsed radio signals from two or more pairs of ground stations of known position, with which a navigator can establish his own position by an analysis involving the time intervals between pulses. [*Lo*ng-*ra*nge *n*avigation.]

Lor·ca (lôr′kə), **Federico García** (*c.* 1899–1936). Spanish poet and playwright. His work, notably *Gipsy Ballads* (1928), draws on Andalusian culture. He was shot by Falangists in the Civil War.

lord (lôrd) *n.* **1.** A man of high rank in a feudal society or in one that retains feudal forms and institutions, as: **a.** A king. **b.** A territorial

PRONUNCIATION KEY

ă, pat; ā, pay; âr, care;
ä, father, are; b, bib;
ch, church; d, deed; ĕ, pet;
ē, be; f, fife; g, gag; h, hat;
hw, which; ĭ, pit; ī, pie;
îr, pier; j, judge; k, kick;
l, lid, needle; m, mum;
n, no, sudden; ng, thing;
ŏ, pot; ō, toe; ô, paw, for;
oi, noise; ou, out; o͝o, book;
o͞o, boot; p, pop; r, roar;
s, sauce; sh, ship, dish;
t, tight; th, thin, path;
th, this, bathe; ŭ, cut; ûr, fur;
v, valve; w, with; y, yes;
z, zebra, size; zh, vision;
ə, about, item, edible,
gallop, circus, peaceful

IN FOREIGN WORDS:

à, *Fr.* ami; œ, *Fr.* feu, *Ger.* schön; ü, *Fr.* tu, *Ger.* über; KH, *Ger.* ich, *Scot.* loch; N, *Fr.* bon; y′, *Fr.* Compiègne

STRESS MARKS:

Primary stress: ′
in·cite′ (ĭn-sīt′)
Secondary stress: ′
in′sight′ (ĭn′sīt′)

magnate. **c.** The proprietor of a manor. **2. Lord.** *British. Abbr.* **Ld.** The general masculine title of nobility and other rank, used: **a.** Semiformally for any peer other than a duke: *Lord Cardigan* (the Earl of Cardigan). **b.** As the usual style for a baron: *Lord Morrison* (titularly, Baron Morrison of Lambeth). **c.** As a courtesy title for a younger son of a duke or marquis: *Lord Randolph Churchill* (third son of the Duke of Marlborough). **d.** As part of the titles of certain high officials and dignitaries, as *the Lord Mayor of London, the Lord Chancellor, the Lords of the Admiralty.* **e.** As a nominal title for a bishop. ***Note:*** In direct address, *my lord* and *your lordship* are deferential appellations for any of the above. *My lord,* usually pronounced (mə-lŭd′), is also used in addressing a British judge in court. In direct address and in informal reference, **c** may be shortened to *Lord Randolph,* but it may never be given as *Lord Churchill,* while **a** and **b** may never be used with Christian names. With **b** and **c**, the formal usage (as in addressing a letter) is *The Lord Morrison.* **3. a. Lord.** God or Jesus. **b.** *Archaic.* The head of a household. **c.** A husband. **d.** A man of renowned power. **e.** A man who has mastery in some field or activity. **—the Lords.** The House of Lords.
~*interj.* Used to express surprise, distress, and the like. Often used in phrases such as *Lord knows!* and *Good Lord!*
~*intr.v.* **lorded, lording, lords.** To play the lord; domineer. Used with *over* and often with *it*: *lording it over the newcomers.* [Middle English *lord, loverd,* Old English *hlāford, hlāfweard,* "keeper of the bread" : *hlāf,* LOAF + *weard,* WARD.]

Lord Chancellor *n., pl.* **Lords Chancellor.** The presiding officer and speaker of the House of Lords, Keeper of the Great Seal, Head of the judiciary in England and Wales, and usually a senior cabinet minister. Also called "Lord High Chancellor."

lord·ing (lôr′dĭng) *n. Archaic & Poetic.* Lord; sir. Used chiefly as a form of address.

lord·ling (lôrd′lĭng) *n.* A young or unimportant lord.

lord·ly (lôrd′lē) *adj.* **-lier, -liest. 1.** Of or pertaining to a lord. **2.** Dignified; noble. **3.** Arrogant; overbearing; haughty.
~*adv. Archaic.* In a lordly fashion. **—lord·li·ness** *n.*

Lord Mayor *n.* The mayor in certain cities such as London.

Lord of Hosts *n.* Jehovah; God.

Lord of Misrule *n.* The master of traditional Christmas revelry in England during the 15th and 16th centuries.

lor·do·sis (lôr-dō′sĭs) *n. Pathology.* An abnormal forward curvature of the spine in the lumbar region. [New Latin, from Greek *lordōsis* : *lordos,* bent backward + -OSIS.] **—lor·dot·ic** (lôr-dŏt′ĭk) *adj.*

lords-and-la·dies (lôrdz′ən-lā′dēz) *n. Used with a singular verb.* A plant, the **cuckoopint** *(see).* [From its dark (for lords) and light (for ladies) spadices.]

Lord's Day, Lord's day *n.* The Christian Sabbath; Sunday.

lord·ship (lôrd′shĭp′) *n.* **1.** *Usually* **Lordship.** A title of or form of address for a British nobleman, judge, or bishop. Used with *Your, His,* or *Their.* See Note at **lord. 2.** The position or authority of a lord. **3.** The territorial fief of a feudal lord.

Lord's Prayer *n.* The prayer taught by Jesus to his disciples. Matthew 6:9–13. Also called "Our Father," "paternoster."

Lord's Supper *n.* **1.** The **Last Supper** *(see).* **2.** The Eucharist.

Lord's Table *n.* The Communion table.

lore[1] (lôr, lōr) *n.* **1.** Accumulated fact, tradition, or belief about a particular subject: *country lore.* **2.** Knowledge acquired through education or experience. —See Synonyms at **knowledge.** [Middle English *lore,* Old English *lār.*]

lore[2] *n.* The area between a bird's eye and the base of the bill. [New Latin *lorum,* from Latin *lōrum*†, thong.]

Lo·re·lei (lôr′ə-lī′, lō′rə-lī′). *Germanic Mythology.* A siren of the Rhine whose singing lures sailors to shipwreck.

Lo·ren (lôr′ən, lə-rĕn′), **Sophia,** born Sophia Scicoloni (1934–). Italian film actress. Her films include *Two Women* (1961), for which she won an Academy Award, *Yesterday, Today, and Tomorrow* (1963), and *Man of La Mancha* (1972). In 1957 she married the film producer Carlo Ponti (1913–).

Lo·rentz (lō′rĕnts′), **Hendrik Antoon** (1853–1928). Dutch physicist. His studies of the influence of magnetism on radiation won him and his pupil, Pieter Zeeman, the 1902 Nobel Prize in physics.

Lorentz contraction *n.* The contraction in length of a moving body, as measured by an observer at rest with respect to the body, by the factor $(1-v^2/c^2)$ 1/2, where v is the relative speed of the moving body and c the speed of light. Also called "Lorentz-Fitzgerald contraction." [After Hendrik LORENTZ.]

Lo·renz (lō′rĕnts′), **Konrad Zacharias** (1903–). Austrian zoologist. He was the first to describe imprinting, the learning process that occurs during the first hours of life. His book *On Aggression* (1963) describes the ritualization of aggressive impulses in animals. He was awarded a Nobel Prize in physiology and medicine (1973) jointly with Karl von Frisch and Nikolaas Tinbergen (1907–).

lor·gnette (lôrn-yĕt′) *n.* A pair of spectacles or opera glasses with a short handle. Also called "lorgnon." [French, from *lorgner,* to leer at, from Old French, from *lorgne*†, squinting.]

lo·ri·ca (lô-rī′kə, lō-) *n., pl.* **-cae** (-sē′). **1.** *Zoology.* A protective external shell or case, as of a rotifer. **2.** A cuirass or body armor, usually of leather and metal, worn by soldiers in ancient Rome. [Latin *lōrīca,* leather cuirass, from *lōrum,* thong.] **—lor·i·cate** (lôr′ĭ-kāt′, lŏr′-), **lor·i·ca·ted** (lôr′ĭ-kā′tĭd) *adj.*

lor·i·keet (lôr′ĭ-kēt′, lŏr′-) *n.* Any of several small Australasian parrots of the subfamily Loriinae; a small lory. [LOR(Y) + (PARA)-KEET.]

lor·i·mer (lôr′ə-mər) *n.* One who made spurs, bits, and similar metal accessories for horse riders in former times. [Middle English, from Old French *loremier, lorenier,* from *lorain,* harness strap, from Vulgar Latin *loranum* (unattested), from Latin *lōrum,* thong, strap.]

lo·ris (lôr′ĭs, lōr′-) *n., pl.* **lorises** or collectively **loris.** Any of several slow-moving, nocturnal, arboreal, prosimian primates of the genera *Loris* and *Nycticebus,* of tropical Asia, having dense, woolly fur, large eyes, and a vestigial tail. [French, probably from obsolete Dutch *loeris*†, simpleton, clown.]

lorn (lôrn) *adj. Poetic.* Forlorn; desolate. [Middle English *lorn, loren,* lost, Old English *-loren,* past participle of *-lēosan,* to lose.]

Lorrain, Claude. See **Claude Lorrain.**

Lor·raine (lô-rān′, lō-). *German* **Loth·ring·en** (lō′trĭng-ən). Former province in northeast France, now comprising the departments of Vosges, Moselle, Meurthe-et-Moselle, and Meuse. It was originally part of the kingdom of Lotharingia, belonging to Charlemagne's grandson Lothair I. Lorraine, with its neighbor Alsace—disputed between France and Germany for many years—was returned to France after World War I. The area contains deposits of iron ore. The main industrial towns are Metz and Nancy.

Lor·re (lôr′ē), **Peter** (1904–64). U.S. actor, born in Czechoslovakia. In the classic German film *M* (1931) he portrayed a psychotic killer, establishing his trademark role, the sinister, diminutive miscreant. His many other films include *Crime and Punishment* (1931), *The Maltese Falcon* (1941), and *Casablanca* (1942).

lor·ry (lôr′ē, lŏr′ē) *n., pl.* **-ries. 1.** A low, horse-drawn, four-wheeled wagon. **2.** *Chiefly British.* A motor truck. **3.** Any of various flat carts or vehicles that run on rails and are used for carrying goods. [Origin obscure.]

lo·ry (lôr′ē, lōr′ē) *n., pl.* **-ries.** Any of various brightly colored Australasian parrots of the subfamily Loriinae, having a tongue with a brushlike tip for feeding on pollen and nectar. [Malay *luri, nuri.*]

Los Al·a·mos (lôs ăl′ə-mōs′). A town of north-central New Mexico. The U.S. government chose the site in 1942 for atomic research, and the first atomic bombs were produced here and tested nearby. The town was run by the Atomic Energy Commission from 1947 to 1962, when it became a self-governing community.

Los An·ge·les (lŏs ăn′jə-ləs, -lēz′). Commercial, industrial, and tourist city in southern California. It is the third-largest city in the United States, and its greater metropolitan area, including independent cities such as Long Beach, Santa Monica, and Beverly Hills, stretches 80 kilometers (50 miles). Los Angeles harbor handles oil and petroleum, and the city's main industries include the manufacture of cars, planes, textiles, and electrical equipment. It also produces motion pictures and television programs in Hollywood, now a suburb of the city.

lose (lo͞oz) *v.* **lost** (lôst, lŏst) **losing, loses.** *—tr.* **1.** To experience the disappearance of (a possession, for example); be unable to find; mislay. **2. a.** To be unable to maintain, sustain, or keep: *lose one's balance.* **b.** To cease to feel: *lose hope.* **3. a.** To be deprived of: *lose a friend.* **b.** To be deprived of through death. **4.** To fail to win: *lose the game.* **5.** To fail to use or take advantage of: *lose a chance.* **6.** To fail to hear, see, or understand: *lose the thread of an argument.* **7.** To remove (oneself), as from everyday reality into a fantasy world; engross. Often used in the passive: *lost in thought.* **8.** To rid oneself of: *lose ten pounds.* **9.** To stray or wander from: *lose one's way.* **10.** To allow to disappear or fade from view: *We lost him in the crowd.* **11.** To elude or outdistance: *lose one's pursuers.* **12.** To cause or result in the loss of: *Failure to reply lost her a job.* **13.** To cause to die or be destroyed. Used in the passive: *Both planes were lost in the crash.* **14.** To fail to keep alive or resuscitate: *The surgeon lost his patient on the operating table.* **15.** To fail to give birth to (a living baby), as through miscarriage. *—intr.* **1.** To suffer loss. **2.** To be defeated. **3.** To run slow. Used of a timepiece. **4.** To suffer a reduction in impact or value: *The play lost slightly in translation.* **—lose out.** To be defeated. **—lose out on.** To fail to benefit from: *lose out on the sponsorship scheme.* [*Lose, lost, lost*; Middle English *losen, lost, loste,* Old English *lōsian, lōsode, gelōsod,* from *los,* loss, perdition, destruction.]

lo·sel (lō′zəl, lo͞o′-, lŏz′əl) *n. Archaic.* One that is worthless. [Middle English, profligate, "lost one," from *losen,* alternate past participle of *losen,* to lose, Old English *-lēosan.*]

los·er (lo͞o′zər) *n.* **1.** One that loses or seems fated to lose. **2.** One who accepts defeat in a specified way: *a good loser.* **3.** One who fails repeatedly, or is always being taken advantage of: *a born loser.*

los·ing (lo͞o′zĭng) *adj.* **1.** Unprofitable: *sell off the losing parts of the company.* **2.** Being defeated: *the losing team.*

loss (lôs, lŏs) *n.* **1.** The act or an instance of losing. **2.** Something or someone that is lost. **3.** The harm or suffering caused by losing or by being lost. **4. losses.** The number of people killed in war or an accident. **5.** *Electricity.* The power decrease in a circuit, circuit element, or device caused by resistance. **6. a.** A failure to make a profit on a commercial transaction. **b.** The amount of money lost on an unprofitable transaction. **c. losses.** The amount by which a business enterprise's spending exceeds its income. **7.** *Insurance.* **a.** An instance of theft, damage by fire, or the like, as a result of which a policyholder may make a claim. **b.** The amount of such a claim by an insured. **—at a loss.** Reduced to a state of helplessness or perplexity: *at a loss for words.* **—cut one's losses.** To withdraw from a situation so that losses or damage are kept to a minimum. [Middle English *los,* probably back-formation from *loste,* past participle of *losen,* to lose, Old English *lōsian,* to perish, be destroyed or ruined, from *los,* destruction, loss.]

löss. Variant of **loess.**

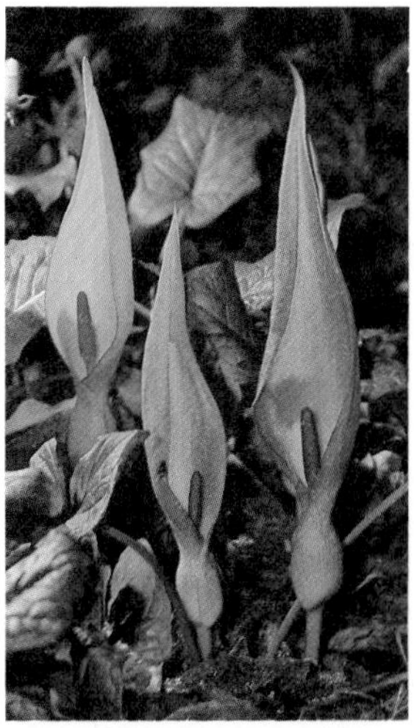

lords-and-ladies *The roots of lords-and-ladies,* Arum maculatum *(above), have a very high starch content and were used in Elizabethan Britain for stiffening the high pleated linen ruffs that were then fashionable. Arum grows throughout the Northern Hemisphere and is better known as cuckoopint in North America.*

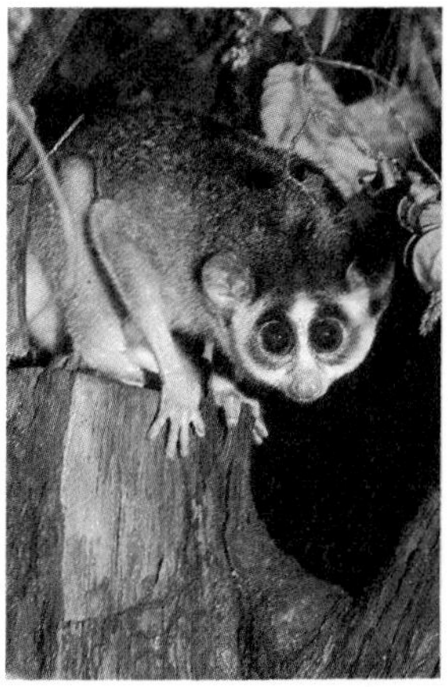

loris *The thumbs and big toes of these tree-dwelling primates are set at right angles to their other fingers and toes so that they can grip branches. Lorises, which are native to Asia, are meat eaters and hunt at night.*

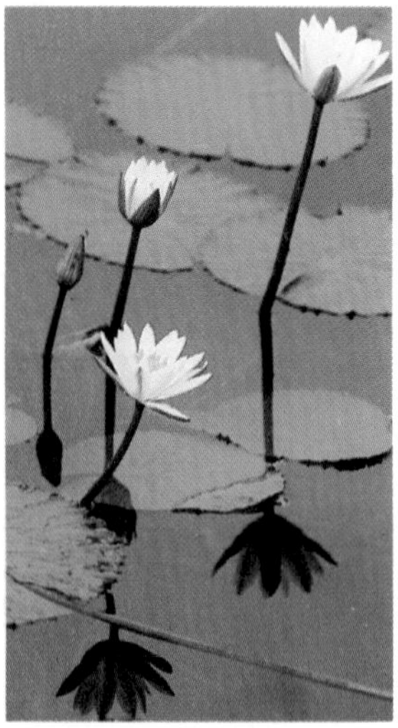

lotus *Several aquatic plants are known as lotuses. This is a Sri Lankan species that is related to the white water lily of Europe.*

loss leader *n.* An item of merchandise offered by a retailer at cost price or less to attract customers.

loss ratio *n.* The ratio between the premiums paid to an insurance company and the claims settled by the company.

los·sy (lô′sē, lŏs′ē) *adj.* Designating a transmission line, dielectric material, or the like that has a high attenuation. [From LOSS.]

lost (lôst, lŏst) *adj.* **1.** Strayed; unable to find one's way. **2.** Misplaced; missing. **3.** Gone in time; passed away: *lost youth.* **4.** Gone morally astray; fallen. **5.** Bewildered or bemused. **6.** No longer possessed or practiced: *a lost art.* **7.** Not appreciated or made use of. Used with *on*: *His hints were lost on her.* **8.** Dead or destroyed: *his lost comrades.* **9.** Unavailable; forfeited: *That opportunity is now lost to you.* **10.** Unconscious; not susceptible. Used with *to*: *lost to reason.* **11.** Absorbed; engrossed: *lost in her book.* **12.** Damned: *lost souls.* **—get lost.** *Informal.* To go away. Usually used in the imperative. [From the past participle of LOSE.]

lost cause *n.* A cause that seems hopeless or bound for failure.

Lost Generation *n.* The generation of promising young men who died as soldiers in World War I.

lost wax process *n.* A technique of casting bronze, in which a wax model is used to form a mold and is then melted and drained off. Also called "cire perdue." [Translation of French *cire perdue.*]

lot (lŏt) *n.* **1.** Any of a group of nearly identical objects used in making a determination or choice by chance. **2.** The use of such objects for selection. **3.** The selections made. **4.** That which befalls an individual as a result of such a selection. **5. a.** A share; an allotted portion. **b.** One's fortune in life; one's fate. **6.** A number or group of people or things: *Let's get rid of that lot.* **7.** Kind, type, or sort: *him and his lot.* **8. a.** A **job lot** *(see).* **b.** An item or group of items sold at an auction. **9.** *Sometimes* **lots.** A large amount or number. **10. a.** A piece of land: *a parking lot.* **b.** A piece of land having fixed boundaries. **c.** A motion-picture studio. **—a lot.** A great deal: *I like him a lot.* **—draw** (or **cast**) **lots.** To arrive at a decision or selection by means of lots. **—the lot.** All of a specific collection, quantity, or group. **—throw** (or **cast**) **in one's lot with.** To join with voluntarily.

~*v.* **lotted, lotting, lots.** —*tr.* **1.** To apportion by lots; allot. **2.** To draw lots for. **3.** To divide (land) into lots. —*intr.* To draw lots. [Middle English *lot(te),* Old English *hlot.*]

Lot[1] (lŏt). Abraham's nephew, whose wife was turned into a pillar of salt when she looked back as they fled from Sodom. Genesis 19:1–26. [Hebrew *lōṭ,* "covering."]

Lot[2] (lôt). River of France, rising in the southeast in the Cévennes Mts. and flowing *c.* 485 kilometers (300 miles) west to the Garonne River. The limestone plateaus through which it flows are noted for fertile valleys and vineyards.

loth. Variant of **loath.**

Lo·thar·i·o (lō-thâr′ē-ō) *n., pl.* **-os.** A seducer; a sexually promiscuous man. [Name of a seducer in *The Fair Penitent* (1703) by Nicholas Rowe (1674–1718).]

Lo·thi·an (lō′*th*ē-ən). Region in southeastern Scotland, stretching along the south shore of the Firth of Forth. It comprises the former counties of East Lothian, Midlothian, and West Lothian. Edinburgh is the administrative center.

Lothringen. See **Lorraine.**

lo·ti (lō′tē) *n., pl.* **maloti** (mə-lō′tē). The basic monetary unit of Lesotho, equal to 100 lisente. See feature at **currency.**

lo·tic (lō′tĭk) *adj.* Of, pertaining to, or designating ecological communities living in fast-flowing rivers or streams. Compare **lentic.** [Latin *lotus,* past participle of *lavāre,* to wash.]

lo·tion (lō′shən) *n.* **1.** A medicated liquid for external application, especially one containing a substance in suspension, having a soothing or antiseptic effect. **2.** Any of various externally applied cosmetic liquids. [Middle English *loscion,* from Old French *lotion,* from Latin *lōtiō* (stem *lōtiōn-*), washing, from *lavere* (past participle *lautus, lōtus*), to wash.]

lots (lŏts) *adv. Informal.* A great deal; very much: *She's lots prettier than she used to be.*

lot·ter·y (lŏt′ə-rē) *n., pl.* **-ies. 1.** A game of chance offering money or prizes in which tickets are distributed or sold, the winning ticket or tickets being secretly predetermined or ultimately selected in a chance drawing. **2.** An activity or event regarded as having an outcome depending on fate. [Old French *loterie,* from Middle Dutch *loterije,* from *lot,* lot.]

lot·to (lŏt′ō) *n.* A game of chance resembling bingo, played mainly by children. [French *loto,* from Italian *lotto,* from Old French *lot,* lot, from Frankish *lot* (unattested).]

lo·tus, lo·tos (lō′təs) *n.* **1. a.** An aquatic plant, *Nelumbo nucifera,* native to southern Asia and widely regarded as sacred there, having large leaves, fragrant, pinkish flowers, and a broad, rounded, perforated seed pod. **b.** Any of several similar or related plants, such as certain water lilies of the genus *Nymphaea*; especially, *N. lotus,* a white-flowered species regarded as sacred in ancient Egypt. **2.** A representation of such a plant in sculpture, architecture, and art. **3.** Any of several leguminous plants of the genus *Lotus.* **4. a.** A plant in Greek legend whose fruit was eaten by the lotus-eaters. **b.** The fruit of this tree. [Latin *lōtus,* from Greek *lōtos,* fruit eaten by the lotus-eaters, of Semitic origin; akin to Hebrew *lōṭ,* myrrh.]

lo·tus-eat·er (lō′təs-ē′tər) *n.* **1.** A member of a North African people described in the *Odyssey* who lived on the lotus, in a drugged, indolent state. **2.** One who defers the tasks of life in favor of self-indulgent pleasure; an indolent sybarite.

lotus position *n.* A sitting position in which the legs are crossed with the feet resting on opposite thighs and the hands resting on the knees, used in yoga and meditation.

louche (lo͞osh) *adj.* Dubious; appearing disreputable. [French, "squinting."]

loud (loud) *adj.* **louder, loudest. 1.** Characterized by high volume and intensity of sound: *a loud crash.* **2.** Producing or capable of producing a sound of high volume and intensity. **3.** Clamorous and insistent: *loud denials.* **4. a.** Having offensively bright colors: *a loud tie.* **b.** Brash and vulgar in manner.

~*adv.* **louder, loudest.** In a loud manner. **—out loud.** Audibly. [Middle English *l(o)ud, lowde,* Old English *hlūd.*] **—loud·ly** *adv.* **—loud·ness** *n.*

Usage: *Loud* (adverb) and *loudly* are often used interchangeably after certain common verbs, such as *laugh, play, roar, say, scream, shout, sing,* and *talk. Loudly* occurs more frequently in formal usage, especially in writing. *Loudly* is the idiomatic form after verbs such as *boast, brag, insist,* and *proclaim.*

loud·en (loud′n) *v.* **-ened, -ening, -ens.** —*tr.* To make louder. —*intr.* To become louder.

loud·hail·er (loud′hā′lər) *n.* A **bullhorn** *(see).*

loud·mouth (loud′mouth′) *n.* One whose speech is loud and irritating or indiscreet. **—loud·mouthed** (loud′mou*th*d′, -moutht′) *adj.*

loud pedal *n. Music.* A **sustaining pedal** *(see).*

loud·speak·er (loud′spē′kər) *n.* A device that converts electric signals to audible sound. Also called "speaker."

lough (lŏKH, lŏk) *n. Irish.* **1.** A lake. **2.** A bay or inlet of the sea. [Middle English *lough, lowe,* perhaps from Old English *luh,* from Old Irish *loch.*]

Lou·is IX (lo͞o′ē, lo͞o′ĭs), known as "Saint Louis" (1214–70). King of France (1226–70). Crowned before his 13th birthday, he became a just and highly popular sovereign. He led the Seventh Crusade (1248–50) and died in a subsequent crusade to Tunisia. He was canonized by the Roman Catholic Church in 1297.

Louis XIII (1601–43). King of France (1610–43). Relying heavily on his political adviser Cardinal Richelieu, he overcame familial insurgence and war with Spain and the Hapsburgs to establish France as a major European power. His son became Louis XIV.

Louis XIV, also known as the "Sun King" (1638–1715). King of France (1643–1715), the greatest of the Bourbon monarchs. After the death of Cardinal Mazarin in 1661, Louis asserted his authority, insisting on the divine right of kings. He waged three major wars: the Dutch War (1672–78), the War of the Grand Alliance (1688–97), and the War of the Spanish Succession (1701–14). Louis presided over a brilliant court at Versailles, but the unity of France that he sought was foiled by his persecution of the Huguenots after his revocation of the Edict of Nantes (1685).

Louis XV (1710–74). King of France (1715–74). Louis was a weak ruler much influenced by his mistresses, Madame de Pompadour and Madame du Barry. He led France into the War of the Austrian Succession (1740–48) and the Seven Years' War (1756–63), which led to the loss of the French territories in India, Canada, and the West Indies.

Louis XVI (1754–93). King of France (1774–92), whose reign ended in the turmoil of the French Revolution. In the French economic crisis following the American Revolution, Louis summoned the States-General (1789), but was reluctant to grant the wide-ranging reforms demanded. Revolution followed. Louis and his queen Marie Antoinette fled, but were arrested at Varennes (1791) and brought back to Paris. In 1792 the monarchy was abolished. Louis was guillotined the following year.

Louis XVIII (1755–1824). King of France (1814–24). He declared himself king (1795) after the execution of Louis XVI (his brother) and Marie Antoinette and the death of their son, Louis XVII. He did not truly rule until 1814, when he entered Paris with the promise of a French constitution. His reign was interrupted by Napoleon during the Hundred Days (1815).

Lou·is (lo͞o′ĭs), **Joe,** born Joseph Louis Barrow (1914–81). U.S. boxer, known as "the Brown Bomber." He held the world heavyweight title for nearly 12 years (1937–49), successfully defending it for a record 25 times.

Lou·is·burg or **Lou·is·bourg** (lo͞o′ĭs-bûrg′). Town on eastern Cape Breton Island in Nova Scotia, Canada. It is near the site of the great fortress of Louisbourg, built from 1720 to 1740 by the French. In 1758 the fortress fell to the British, who reduced it to ruins in the attack. The site is now a national historical park, and many buildings have been reconstructed.

lou·is d'or (lo͞o′ē-dôr′) *n., pl.* **louis d'or** *(pronounced as singular).* **1.** A gold coin of France from 1640 until the Revolution. **2.** A 20-franc gold coin of post-Revolutionary France. Also called "louis." [French, "gold Louis," first minted in the reign of Louis XIII.]

Lou·ise, Lake (lo͞o-ēz′). Lake, 2.4 kilometers (1.5 miles), long, in southwestern Alberta, Canada, in Banff National Park at an altitude of 1,732 meters (5,680 feet). Noted for its scenic beauty, it is surrounded by high peaks, glaciers, and snow fields of the Rocky Mts. It is a popular year-round tourist center.

Lou·i·si·an·a (lo͞o-ē′zē-ăn′ə). *Abbr.* **La.** State in the southern United States, on the Gulf of Mexico. It is dominated by the marshy valley of the Mississippi River. Louisiana is a primary source of salt and sulfur, and a major producer of oil and natural gas, cotton, sugar cane, and rice. It was part of a French province, named after Louis XIV, and was sold to the United States (1803). It became a state in 1812. Baton Rouge is the capital, and New Orleans the largest city.

Louisiana French *n.* French as spoken by descendants of the original French settlers of Louisiana.

Louisiana Purchase. The purchase in 1803 by the United States from France of a vast area of land between the Mississippi and the Rocky Mts. This area, extending over some 2,144,500 square kilometers (*c.* 828,000 square miles), doubled the national territory of the United States at a cost of $15 million.

Lou·is Phi·lippe (lo͞o′ē fĭ-lēp′), known as "the Citizen King" (1773–1850). King of France (1830–48). When the Bourbons were overthrown in the July Revolution (1830), Louis succeeded to the throne. He abdicated during the Revolution of 1848 and retired to England.

Louis Qua·torze (lo͞o′ē kă-tôrz′) *adj.* Pertaining to the baroque style in architecture, furniture, and decoration of the reign of Louis XIV. [French, "Louis XIV."]

Louis Quinze (lo͞o′ē kăNz′) *adj.* Pertaining to the rococo style in architecture, furniture, and decoration of the reign of Louis XV. [French, "Louis XV."]

Louis Seize (lo͞o′ē sĕz′) *adj.* Pertaining to the neoclassical style in architecture, furniture, and decoration of the reign of Louis XVI. [French, "Louis XVI."]

Louis Treize (lo͞o′ē trĕz′) *adj.* Pertaining to the heavy late-Renaissance style in architecture, furniture, and decoration of the reign of Louis XIII. [French, "Louis XIII."]

Lou·is·ville (lo͞o′ē-vĭl′). Industrial city and port on the Ohio River in Kentucky. Its manufactures include cars, electrical equipment, and whiskey.

lounge (lounj) *v.* **lounged, lounging, lounges.** —*intr.* **1.** To stand, lean, sit, or lie in a lazy, relaxed way; loll. **2.** To walk in a leisurely way. **3.** To pass time idly. —*tr.* To pass (time) in lounging.
~*n.* **1.** The act of lounging. **2.** A period of lounging. **3.** A lounging walk or gait. **4.** A public waiting room with seats, as in a hotel or air terminal, often having smoking or lavatory facilities. **5. a.** A living room in a house. **b.** A lobby. **6.** A long couch, especially one having no back and a headrest at one end. [16th century : origin obscure.] —**loung·er** *n.*

lounge chair *n.* A deep, comfortable chair.

lounge lizard *n. Informal.* A man who does nothing but frequent social gatherings; a hanger-on in fashionable society.

loupe (lo͞op) *n.* A small magnifying glass usually set in an eyepiece and used chiefly by watchmakers and jewelers. [French, from Old French *loupe*†, imperfect gem.]

loup-ga·rou (lo͞o′gə-ro͞o′, -gä-) *n., pl.* **loups-garous** (lo͞o′-gə-). A werewolf. [French, from Old French *leu garoul* : *leu,* wolf, from Latin *lupus* + *garoul, garulf,* werewolf, from Frankish *werwulf* (unattested), "man wolf."]

loup·ing ill (lou′pĭng, lō′-) *n.* A disease of sheep caused by a virus and transmitted by ticks, characterized by partial paralysis and twitching. Also called "trembles." [From earlier *loup,* to leap, Middle English *loupen,* to LOPE.]

lour. Variant of **lower** (scowl).

Lourdes (lo͝ord, lo͝ordz). Town at the foot of the Pyrenees in Hautes-Pyrénées department, France. The Virgin Mary is said to have appeared in a grotto here to a peasant girl, Marie Bernarde Soubirous (St. Bernadette), several times in 1858. Since that time pilgrims have flocked here, many seeking cures.

Lourenço Marques. See **Maputo.**

louse (lous) *n., pl.* **lice** (līs) or **louses** (for sense 4). **1.** Any of numerous small, flat-bodied, wingless, bloodsucking insects of the order Anoplura, many of which are external parasites on various animals, including man. Common species are the head louse, *Pediculus capitis,* and the body louse, *Pediculus corporis.* **2.** Any of numerous small, wingless, biting insects of the order Mallophaga, which are external parasites on birds. In this sense, also called "bird louse." **3.** Any of various similar insects, such as the book louse. **4.** *Slang.* A mean or despicable person.
~*tr.v.* **loused, lousing, louses. 1.** *Slang.* To bungle. Often used with *up*: *louse up a deal.* **2.** To remove lice from; delouse. [Louse, lice; Middle English *lous, lys,* Old English *lūs, lȳs.*]

louse·wort (lous′wûrt′, -wôrt′) *n.* Any of numerous plants of the genus *Pedicularis,* having clusters of irregular, variously colored flowers. Also called "wood betony." [Sheep feeding on it were believed to be subject to vermin.]

lous·y (lou′zē) *adj.* **-ier, -iest. 1.** Infested with lice. **2.** *Slang.* Mean; nasty; contemptible: *a lousy trick.* **3.** *Slang.* **a.** Painful; unpleasant: *a lousy headache.* **b.** Unwell; sick: *feel lousy.* **c.** Paltry; mere: *gave a lousy quarter.* **4.** *Slang.* Inferior; worthless. **5.** *Slang.* Abundantly supplied; having a surfeit of. Used with *with*: *lousy with money.* —**lous·i·ly** *adv.* —**lous·i·ness** *n.*

lout¹ (lout) *n.* An awkward or ill-mannered man or youth; a boor. [Perhaps ultimately from Old Norse *lūtr,* bent low, from *lūta,* to bend down, bow.] —**lout·ish** *adj.*

lout² *intr.v.* **louted, louting, louts.** *Archaic.* **1.** To bow or curtsy. **2.** To bend or stoop. [Middle English *l(o)uten,* Old English *lūtan,* to bend down, bow.]

Louth (louth). Smallest county in the Republic of Ireland, on the northeastern coast. Cattle rearing, fishing, crop raising, brewing, food processing, and textile manufacturing are its main industries. Dundalk is the county town.

Lou·vain (lo͞o-văN′). City in northern Brabant, Belgium. It is a commercial, industrial, and cultural center, with a 15th-century university.

lou·var (lo͞o′vär′) *n.* A widely distributed, silvery whalelike fish, *Louvaris imperialis,* that feeds on plankton. [Italian (Calabrian and Sicilian dialect) *luvaru,* perhaps akin to Latin *ruber,* red.]

L'Ouverture, Toussaint. See **Toussaint L'Ouverture.**

lou·ver, lou·vre (lo͞o′vər) *n.* **1. a.** A framed opening, as in a wall, fitted with fixed or movable slanted slats. **b.** Such a slatted frame. **c.** A structure, such as a door or window, incorporating a slatted frame. **2.** Any of the slats used in a louver. **3.** *Architecture.* A lantern-shaped cupola on the roof of many medieval buildings to admit air and provide for the escape of smoke. **4.** Any slatted ventilating opening. [Middle English *luver, lover,* from Old French *lov(i)er*†.] —**lou·vered** *adj.*

lov·a·ble, love·a·ble (lŭv′ə-bəl) *adj.* Having characteristics that attract love or affection; endearing. —**lov·a·bil·i·ty, lov·a·ble·ness** *n.* —**lov·a·bly** *adv.*

lov·age (lŭv′ĭj) *n.* **1.** A European plant, *Levisticum officinale,* having small, aromatic seeds used as seasoning. **2.** A similar and related plant, *L. scoticum.* [Middle English *lov(e)ache,* from Old French *luvesche, levesche,* from Late Latin *levisticum (apium),* "Ligurian (parsley)," variant of *ligusticum,* neuter of *ligusticus,* of LIGURIA.]

love (lŭv) *n.* **1.** An intense affectionate concern for another person. **2.** An intense sexual desire and overwhelming affection for another person. **3.** A beloved person. Often used as a term of endearment. **4.** A strong fondness or enthusiasm for something: *a love of the woods.* **5. a. Love.** Eros or Cupid, the god of sexual love in classical mythology. **b.** Sexual love as a force, as a literary subject or personified. **6.** *Theology.* **a.** God's benevolence and mercy toward man. **b.** Man's devotion to or adoration of God. **c.** The benevolence, kindness, or brotherhood that human beings should rightfully feel toward others. **7. Love.** *Christian Science.* God. **8.** An expression of one's warm feelings: *Give them my love.* **9.** One that is liked or thought of as sweet and endearing: *He's a love.* **10.** *British Informal.* Used as a term of address, especially in northern England. **11.** A zero score in tennis. —**fall in love.** To become enamored of or feel strong affection and sexual desire for someone. —**for love.** As a favor; out of fondness; without payment. —**for love or money.** Under any circumstances. Usually used in the negative: *He would not do that for love or money.* —**for the love of. 1.** For the sake of. **2.** Used in expressions of impatience or surprise: *for the love of Mike!* —**in love.** Feeling love for someone or something; enamored. —**make love. 1.** To have sexual intercourse. **2.** To embrace and caress. **3.** *Archaic.* To court; pay amorous attention to a person.
~*v.* **loved, loving, loves.** —*tr.* **1.** To feel love for. **2.** To make love to. **3.** To like or desire enthusiastically; delight in. **4.** To thrive on: *The cactus loves hot, dry air.* —*intr.* **1.** To experience loving tenderness for another. **2.** To be in love. —See Synonyms at **like.** [Middle English *love,* Old English *lufu.*]
Synonyms: *affection, devotion, fondness, infatuation.*

love affair *n.* **1.** An intimate sexual episode between lovers. **2.** An episode characterized by an enthusiastic liking or desire.

love apple *n. Archaic.* A tomato.

love·bird (lŭv′bûrd′) *n.* **1.** Any of various small African parrots, chiefly of the genus *Agapornis,* often kept as a cage bird. **2. lovebirds.** *Informal.* Sweethearts; lovers.

love child *n.* An illegitimate child.

love feast *n.* **1.** Among early Christians, a meal eaten with others as a symbol of love. **2.** A similar symbolic meal among certain modern Christians. **3.** A gathering intended to promote goodwill among the participants.

love game *n.* In tennis, a game in which the winner loses no points.

love-hate (lŭv′hāt′) *adj.* Characterized by alternating feelings of love and hatred or approval and disapproval: *a love-hate relationship.*

love-in-a-mist (lŭv′ĭn-ə-mĭst′) *n.* A plant, *Nigella damascena,* native to Europe, having blue or whitish flowers surrounded by numerous threadlike bracts.

love-in-i·dle·ness (lŭv′ĭn-īd′l-nĭs) *n. Archaic.* A plant, **heartsease** *(see).*

love knot *n.* A stylized knot, generally in the form of a bow, regarded as a symbol of the constancy of two lovers or as an emblem of love. Also called "true lover's knot."

Love·lace (lŭv′lās′), **Richard** (1618–58). English poet. He supported the Royalists during the English Civil War and was twice imprisoned. He wrote "To Althea, from Prison" (1642).

love·less (lŭv′lĭs) *adj.* **1.** Characterized by an absence of love. **2.** Feeling no love; unloving. **3.** Receiving no love; unloved.

love-lies-bleed·ing (lŭv′līz-blē′dĭng) *n.* A tropical plant, *Amaranthus caudatus,* having clusters of small red flowers.

love·lock (lŭv′lŏk′) *n.* **1.** A lock of hair, often curled and tied with ribbon, worn over the shoulder by men of fashion during the 17th and 18th centuries. **2.** A lock of hair curled over the forehead.

love·lorn (lŭv′lôrn′) *adj.* Suffering because of love; feeling unrequited love or bereft of love or one's lover.

love·ly (lŭv′lē) *adj.* **-lier, -liest. 1. a.** Having pleasing or attractive qualities: *a lovely landscape.* **b.** Beautiful; graceful: *a lovely girl.* **2.** Enjoyable; delightful: *a lovely party.* **3.** Inspiring love or affection. **4.** *Rare.* Full of love; loving. —See Synonyms at **beautiful.**
~*n., pl.* **lovelies.** *Informal.* **1.** A beautiful person, especially a woman. **2.** A lovely object. —**love·li·ness** *n.* —**love·ly** *adv.*

love·mak·ing (lŭv′mā′kĭng) *n.* **1.** Sexual activity between lovers; especially, sexual intercourse. **2.** *Archaic.* Courtship.

love match *n.* A marriage based on love, rather than on financial, dynastic, or other considerations.

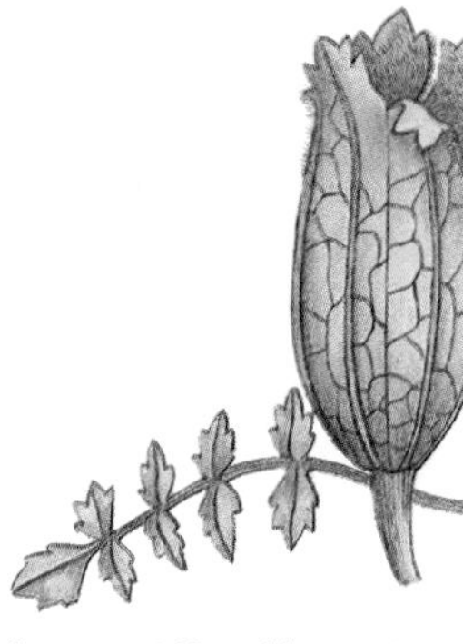

lousewort *Named because it was once thought to infest sheep with lice, lousewort probably does transmit the parasitic liver fluke. Sheep infested with liver fluke almost always have lice, hence the mistaken belief. The species shown here is the common lousewort,* Pedicularis sylvatica.

PRONUNCIATION KEY

ă, pat; ā, pay; âr, care;
ä, father, are; b, bib;
ch, church; d, deed; ĕ, pet;
ē, be; f, fife; g, gag; h, hat;
hw, which; ĭ, pit; ī, pie;
îr, pier; j, judge; k, kick;
l, lid, needle; m, mum;
n, no, sudden; ng, thing;
ŏ, pot; ō, toe; ô, paw, for;
oi, noise; ou, out; o͝o, book;
o͞o, boot; p, pop; r, roar;
s, sauce; sh, ship, dish;
t, tight; th, thin, path;
th, this, bathe; ŭ, cut; ûr, fur;
v, valve; w, with; y, yes;
z, zebra, size; zh, vision;
ə, about, item, edible, gallop, circus, peaceful

IN FOREIGN WORDS:

à, *Fr.* ami; œ, *Fr.* feu, *Ger.* schön; ü, *Fr.* tu, *Ger.* über; KH, *Ger.* ich, *Scot.* loch; N, *Fr.* bon; y′, *Fr.* Compiègne

STRESS MARKS:

Primary stress: ′
in·cite′ (ĭn-sīt′)
Secondary stress: ′
in′sight′ (ĭn′sīt′)

love nest *n.* A place used by lovers, especially in an illicit love affair. Often used euphemistically.

lov·er (lŭv′ər) *n.* **1.** Someone who loves another; especially, a man in love with a woman. **2. lovers.** A couple having a love affair. **3. a.** Someone engaged in an extramarital love affair. **b.** A sexual partner. **4.** One who is fond of or devoted to something. Usually used in combination: *a dog-lover.* —**lov·er·ly** *adj. & adv.*

love seat *n.* A small sofa or double chair that seats two people.

love set *n. Tennis.* A set in which the winner loses no games.

love·sick (lŭv′sĭk′) *adj.* **1.** Stricken, as if with illness, by love. **2.** Exhibiting unhappiness because of love. —**love·sick·ness** *n.*

lov·ey (lŭv′ē) *n. British Informal.* Used as an affectionate form of address.

lov·ey-dov·ey (lŭv′ē-dŭv′ē) *adj. Informal.* Exhibiting excessive sentimentality and affection toward a loved one.

lov·ing (lŭv′ĭng) *adj.* **1.** Feeling love; affectionate; tenderly devoted. **2.** Indicative of or exhibiting love.

loving cup *n.* **1.** A large, ornamental wine vessel, usually made of silver and having two or more handles, from which each person drinks in turn, as at a ceremonial banquet. **2.** A similar cup given as an award in modern sporting events and similar contests.

lov·ing-kind·ness (lŭv′ĭng-kīnd′nĭs) *n.* Affection or tenderness stemming from sincere love for someone.

low¹ (lō) *adj.* **lower, lowest. 1. a.** Having little relative height; not tall. **b.** Rising only slightly above surrounding surfaces: *a low hill.* **c.** Situated or placed below normal height: *a low lighting fixture.* **d.** Situated below the surrounding surfaces, especially below sea level: *water standing in low spots.* **e.** Dead or prostrate. **f.** Cut to show the wearer's chest, back, and neck; décolleté. **2.** Near or at the horizon: *The sun is low in the sky.* **3.** *Phonetics.* Sounded with all or part of the tongue depressed. Said of a vowel, for example (ä) in *large.* **4.** Of less than usual or average depth; shallow: *The river is low.* **5. a.** Of inferior quality or character: *low intelligence.* **b.** Of relatively simple structure in the scale of living organisms. **c.** Inferior in rank or scale: *a low priority.* **6. a.** Morally base. **b.** Having inferior social, moral, or cultural status. **c.** Vulgar; coarse: *low jokes.* **7. a.** Wanting vigor; weak. **b.** Emotionally or mentally depressed. **c.** Giving little nourishment. **8. a.** Below average in quantity, degree, or intensity: *a low temperature.* **b.** Below an average or standard figure: *low wages.* **c.** Pertaining to or designating latitudes nearest to the equator. **d.** Of relatively small price: *The cost is low.* **e.** Involving or having a small amount: *low in fat.* **9. a.** *Music.* Being a sound produced by a relatively small frequency of vibrations: *a low note.* **b.** Hushed; not loud: *a low voice.* **10.** Being almost without money: *low in funds.* **11.** Not well supplied with; not adequately provided with or equipped for. **12.** Of small value or quality; depreciatory; disparaging: *a low opinion of his qualities.* **13.** Brought down or reduced in health or wealth. **14.** Overthrown; defeated. **15.** Designating a gear designed to produce power and slow speed. **16.** *Often* **Low.** Low-Church. —See Synonyms at **mean** (ignoble).

~*adv.* **1. a.** In a low position, level, or space. **b.** In a low condition or rank; humbly: *You value yourself too low.* **2.** In or to a reduced, humbled, or degraded condition: *"A woman too brought Parnell low"* (James Joyce). **3.** Softly; quietly: *speak low.* **4.** With a deep pitch. **5.** At a small price: *bought low, sold high.* **6.** In hiding; biding one's time: *keep low; lie low.*

~*n.* **1.** A low level, position, or degree: *The stock market fell to a new low.* **2.** *Meteorology.* A **depression** (see). **3.** The gear configuration or setting that produces the lowest range of output speeds, as in the transmission of a motor vehicle. **4.** In some card games, the lowest trump. **5.** In some other games, the lowest score. [Middle English *low(e), lah,* from Old Norse *lāgr.*] —**low·ness** *n.*

low² *n.* The characteristic sound uttered by cattle; a moo.

~*v.* **lowed, lowing, lows.** —*intr.* To emit a low. —*tr.* To utter by means of a low. [Middle English *loowen,* Old English *hlōwan.*]

Low (lō), **Sir David Alexander Cecil** (1891-1963). British cartoonist, born in New Zealand. He created a character called Colonel Blimp, a pompous and die-hard reactionary.

Low, Juliette Magill Kinzie Gordon (1860-1927). U.S. founder of the Girl Scouts. Impressed with the Girl Guides, the sister organization of the English Boy Scouts, she founded an American chapter in 1912. When other groups formed and consolidated under the name "Girl Scouts" (1915), they elected her president of the growing organization.

low-born (lō′bôrn′) *adj. Rare.* Of humble birth.

low-boy (lō′boi′) *n.* A low, tablelike chest of drawers.

low-bred (lō′brĕd′) *adj.* **1.** Lowborn. **2.** Coarse; vulgar.

low-brow (lō′brou′) *n. Informal.* One having uncultivated tastes. Compare **highbrow, middlebrow.** —**low-brow, low-browed** *adj.*

Low Church *n.* A movement or faction in the Anglican Church that is opposed to excessive ritualism and favors a more evangelical doctrine. Compare **Broad Church, High Church.** —**Low-Church** (lō′chûrch′) *adj.* —**Low-Church·man** *n.*

low comedy *n.* Comedy characterized by slapstick, and by visual and physical humor.

Low Countries. Region in northwest Europe comprising Belgium, the Netherlands, and Luxembourg.

low-down (lō′doun′) *n. Informal.* All the facts; the relevant information from an informed source. Preceded by *the.*

low-down (lō′doun′) *adj.* Mean; unfair; despicable.

Low Dutch *n.* The language of the Netherlands, **Dutch** (see).

Low·ell (lō′əl), **Amy** (1874-1925). U.S. poet. She was a leading im-

agist writer. Her works include *Men, Women, and Ghosts* (1916).

Lowell, James Russell (1819-91). U.S. editor, poet, and diplomat. His poetry, social and literary criticism, and wide-ranging essays established him as a versatile man of letters. He taught at Harvard (1855-86), edited the *Atlantic Monthly* (1857-61), and served as U.S. minister to Spain (1877-80) and Britain (1880-85).

Lowell, Robert Traill Spence (1917-77). U.S. poet. He was imprisoned as a conscientious objector in World War II. His works include *Lord Weary's Castle* (1946) and *For the Union Dead* (1964).

low·er¹ (lou′ər) *intr.v.* **-ered, -ering, -ers.** Also **lour, loured, louring, lours. 1.** To look angry, sullen, or threatening; scowl. **2.** To appear dark or threatening. Said especially of the sky or weather.

~*n.* Also **lour. 1.** A threatening, sullen, or angry look. **2.** A dark and ominous look. [Middle English *l(o)uren†.*] —**low·er·ing·ly** *adv.*

low·er² (lō′ər) *adj.* Comparative of **low.**

~*adj.* **1.** Below someone or something in rank, position, or authority. **2.** Below a similar or comparable thing: *a lower shelf.* **3. Lower.** *Geology & Archaeology.* Being an earlier division of.

~*n.* One that is beneath another; especially, a lower berth.

~*v.* **lowered, -ering, -ers.** —*tr.* **1.** To let, bring, or move something down to a lower level. **2.** To reduce in value, degree, intensity, or quality. **3.** To weaken; undermine: *lower one's energy.* **4.** To reduce in standing or respect. —*intr.* To diminish; become less.

Lower Aus·tri·a (ôs′trē-ə). State in northeast Austria. It is a largely agricultural region, crossed by the Danube. Vienna is the capital.

Lower Avon. See **Avon** (Gloucestershire).

lower bound *n. Mathematics.* A number that is not greater than any number in a set.

Lower Cal·i·for·nia (kăl′ə-fôrn′yə, -fôr′nē-ə). *Spanish* **Ba·ja Cal·i·for·nia** (bä′hä). Mountainous peninsula in western Mexico separated from the mainland by the Gulf of California. It is mainly desert with limited agriculture. However, it has pearl and deep-sea fisheries and considerable mineral resources, including gold, silver, copper, and iron.

Lower Can·a·da (kăn′ə-də). Name given (1791-1841) to the chiefly French-speaking southern portion of the province of Quebec.

lower case *n. Abbr.* **l.c. 1.** Small letters, as opposed to capitals. **2.** The case of printing type containing the small letters.

low·er-case (lō′ər-kās′) *adj. Abbr.* **l.c.** *Printing.* Pertaining to or designating small letters as distinguished from capitals: *a, b, and c are lower-case letters.*

~*tr.v.* **lower-cased, -casing, -cases.** To print in lower-case letters.

lower class *n. Often* **lower classes.** The class of lower than middle rank in a society. —**low·er-class** *adj.*

low·er-class·man (lō′ər-klăs′mən, -kläs′mən) *n., pl.* **-men** (-mĭn). An **underclassman** (see).

lower criticism *n.* Textual criticism and verbal examination of Biblical texts. Compare **higher criticism.**

lower deck *n.* **1.** The deck of a ship immediately above the hold. **2.** *Informal.* The petty officers and seamen of a navy, or of a ship, collectively.

Lower E·gypt (ē′jəpt). Name traditionally given to the section of northern Egypt comprising the Nile delta. It was united with Upper Egypt in *c.* 3100 B.C.

Lower House *n.* The branch of a bicameral legislative body that is larger and more representative of the population, such as the House of Commons in the British Parliament. Also called "Lower Chamber." Compare **Upper House.**

low·er·most (lō′ər-mōst′) *adj.* Lowest.

Lower Peninsula. The section of Michigan lying south of the Straits of Mackinac and between Lakes Michigan and Huron.

Lower Sax·o·ny (săk′sə-nē). State in northern West Germany comprising the former province of Hanover and the states of Brunswick, Oldenburg, and Schaumburg-Lippe. It is mainly agricultural, but has several manufacturing centers, including Brunswick and Hanover, its capital.

lower world *n.* **1.** The realm of the dead, considered in ancient times to be beneath the surface of the earth; hell. Also called "lower regions." **2.** The earth.

low·er·y (lou′ə-rē) *adj.* Overcast; threatening: *a lowery sky.*

lowest common denominator *n. Abbr.* **l.c.d., L.C.D. 1.** The least common multiple of the denominators of a set of fractions. Also called "least common denominator." **2. a.** The most basic, least sophisticated level of taste, sensibility, or opinion among a group of people. **b.** A group reacting at such a level.

lowest common multiple *n. Abbr.* **l.c.m., L.C.M.** The least quantity that is exactly divisible by each of two or more specified quantities; for example, 12 is the lowest common multiple of 2, 3, 4, and 6. Also called "least common multiple."

lowest terms *pl.n.* The numerator and denominator of a fraction that have had all common factors but 1 factored out and canceled.

low explosive *n.* An explosive, as used in firearms, that has relatively low power.

low frequency *n. Abbr.* **lf** A **radio frequency** *(see)* in the range from 30 to 300 kilohertz.

Low German *n. Abbr.* **LG, L.G. 1.** Any of several German dialects spoken in northern Germany. **2.** All of the West Germanic languages except High German. See **High German.**

low-key (lō′kē′) *adj.* **1.** Having low intensity; restrained, as in style or quality. **2.** In photography, having or producing uniformly dark tones with little contrast.

low-keyed (lō′kēd′) *adj.* Restrained; low-key.

low·land (lō'lənd) n. 1. Low-lying ground. b. **lowlands.** A flat low-lying region of a country.
~adj. Pertaining to or characteristic of low, usually level, land.
Low·land (lō'lənd) n. The English dialect of the Scottish Lowlands; Lallans.
~adj. Of or from the Scottish Lowlands.
low·land·er (lō'lənd-ər) n. 1. A native or inhabitant of a lowland. 2. Lowlander. An inhabitant of the Scottish Lowlands.
Low·lands, the (lō'ləndz). Scotland south of the Highlands.
Low Latin n. Loosely, late or medieval Latin.
low-level (lō'lĕv'əl) adj. 1. Pertaining to or being of low rank or importance. 2. Situated in or occurring at a low level.
low-level language n. Computer Science. A computer language that bears more resemblance to a machine language than to human language. Compare **high-level language.**
low life n. Life among the less respectable sections of society. —**low-life** adj.
low·ly (lō'lē) adj. -lier, -liest. 1. Having or suited for a low rank or position. 2. Humble; meek. 3. Plain; simple; undistinguished.
~adv. 1. In a low manner, condition, or position. 2. Humbly; meekly. —**low·li·ness** n.
Low Mass n. A Mass without singing or ceremonial.
low-mind·ed (lō'mīn'dĭd) adj. Exhibiting a coarse, vulgar character. —**low-mind·ed·ly** adv. —**low-mind·ed·ness** n.
low-necked (lō'nĕkt') adj. Also **low-neck** (-nĕk'). Having a low-cut neckline; décolleté.
low-pass filter (lō'păs') n. An electronic filter that allows frequencies below a specific value to pass but substantially attenuates frequencies above this value.
low-pitched (lō'pĭcht') adj. 1. Low in tone or tonal range. 2. Having a moderate slope: a low-pitched roof.
low-pres·sure (lō'prĕsh'ər) adj. 1. Having, working under, or exerting little pressure. 2. Relaxed; calm; easy-going.
low profile n. An unobtrusive, restrained behavior or stance; especially, an avoidance of militancy, publicity, or intervention.
low relief n. Bas-relief (see). [Translation of French bas-relief.]
low-rise (lō'rīz') adj. Of or designating a building or buildings having few stories: a low-rise apartment building. Compare **high-rise.**
Low·ry (lou'rē), **(Clarence) Malcolm** (1909–57). British novelist. His best-known work is Under the Volcano (1947), a partly autobiographical novel about an alcoholic ex-consul in Mexico.
low-spir·it·ed (lō'spĭr'ə-tĭd) adj. In low spirits; depressed.
Low Sunday n. The Sunday following Easter.
low-ten·sion (lō'tĕn'shən) adj. Abbr. **LT** Having, carrying, or operating at a low voltage.
low-test (lō'tĕst') adj. Having low volatility and a high boiling point. Said of gasoline.
low tide n. 1. The tide at its lowest ebb. 2. The time of this ebb.
low water n. Abbr. **L.W.** 1. Low tide. 2. The lowest level of water in a body of water, such as a river, lake, or reservoir.
low-wa·ter mark (lō'wô'tər) n. 1. A mark that indicates the lowest level reached by a river or sea water at low tide or on some other regular occasion. 2. The lowest point in something, when there seems the least prospect of success: the low-water mark in her acting career.
lox¹ (lŏks) n. Smoked salmon. [Yiddish laks, from Middle High German lahs, salmon, from Old High German.]
lox² n. Liquid oxygen (see).
lox·o·drome n. See rhumb line (sense 1). Also called "loxodromic curve."
lox·o·drom·ic (lŏk'sə-drŏm'ĭk) adj. Also **lox·o·drom·i·cal** (-ĭ-kəl). Nautical. Pertaining to sailing on a rhumb line. [Greek loxos†, slanting + dromos, a running, course.] —**lox·o·drom·i·cal·ly** adv.
loy·al (loi'əl) adj. 1. Steadfast in support and devotion to and never betraying the interests of one's homeland, government, or sovereign. 2. Faithful to a person, ideal, or custom; constantly supporting or following. 3. Of or professing loyalty. —See Synonyms at **faithful.** [French, from Old French loyal, loial, leial, faithful to obligations, legal, from Latin lēgālis, legal, from lēx (stem lēg-), law.] —**loy·al·ism** n. —**loy·al·ly** adv.
loy·al·ist (loi'ə-lĭst) n. 1. One who maintains loyalty to a lawful government, political party, or sovereign, especially during war or revolutionary change. 2. Loyalist. A Northern Irish Protestant wishing to keep Northern Ireland as part of the United Kingdom and strongly opposed to the unification of Ireland. 3. Loyalist. One who supported the lawful government of Spain during the Spanish Civil War.
loy·al·ty (loi'əl-tē) n., pl. -ties. 1. The state or quality of being loyal. 2. loyalties. Feelings of devoted attachment, affection, or duty: divided loyalties. —See Synonyms at **fidelity.**
Loyalty Islands. Group of coral islands in the southwest Pacific Ocean, forming part of the French Overseas Territory of New Caledonia. The group comprises Maré, Lifou, Uvéa, and numerous islets and exports copra and rubber.
Lo-yang. See Luoyang.
Loyola, Saint Ignatius. See Saint Ignatius Loyola.
loz·enge (lŏz'ĭnj) n. 1. a. A four-sided planar figure with a diamondlike shape; a rhombus that is not a square. b. Something with this shape, especially a heraldic device. 2. A medicated drop that dissolves slowly in the mouth for local medication of the mouth or throat. [Middle English losenge, from Old French, originally a diamond-shaped figure in heraldic design, from Gaulish lausa (unattested), flat stone.]

LP adj. Long-playing.
~n., pl. **LP's** or **LPs.** A long-playing phonograph record.
LPG liquefied petroleum gas.
LPN, L.P.N. licensed practical nurse.
Lr The symbol for the element lawrencium.
L.S. the place of the seal. [Latin locus sigilli.]
LSD (ĕl'ĕs-dē') n. Lysergic acid diethylamide (see).
LSS lifesaving service.
lt. light.
Lt. lieutenant.
l.t. local time.
LT low tension.
Lt. Col. lieutenant colonel.
Lt. Comdr. lieutenant commander.
ltd, ltd., Ltd. limited.
Lt. Gen. lieutenant general.
Lt. Gov. lieutenant governor.
Lu The symbol for the element lutetium.
Lu·an·da (loo-än'də). Capital and port of Angola, on the Atlantic coast of Africa. It was founded by the Portuguese in 1575. The city has a fine natural harbor, an oil refinery, and chemical, cement, and textile industries.
lu·au (loo'ou') n. An elaborate Hawaiian feast. [Hawaiian lu'au.]
lub. lubricant; lubrication.
Lu·ba (loo'bə) n., pl. **Luba.** 1. A member of a Negroid people of the southeastern Congo. 2. The language of this people. —**Lu·ba** adj.
lub·ber (lŭb'ər) n. 1. A clumsy fellow. 2. An inexperienced sailor; a landlubber. [Middle English lobur, lobre†.] —**lub·ber·ly** adj. & adv.
lubber line n. Also **lubber's line.** A line or mark on a compass or cathode-ray indicator that represents the heading of a ship or aircraft.
lubber's hole n. A hole through the platform surrounding the upper part of a ship's mast, through which one may climb to go aloft.
Lub·bock (lŭb'ək). City in northwest Texas. It is the major distribution center for a cotton, grain, and oil region.
Lü·beck (loo'bĕk). Commercial city and river port in Schleswig-Holstein, West Germany. A major Baltic port and industrial center, it has foundries and shipyards and is connected to the Elbe River by canal. The present city, dating from 1143, was the leading town of the Hanseatic League. It remained a free city until 1937, when it was included in Schleswig-Holstein, a province of the Prussian state.
Lu·bitsch (loo'bĭch), **Ernst** (1892–1947). U.S. film director, born in Germany. His Hollywood productions include Design For Living (1933), Ninotchka (1939), and Heaven Can Wait (1943).
Lub·lin (loo'blĭn, -blĕn') Russian **Lyu·blin** (lyoo'blĭn). Industrial and agricultural marketing city of central Poland. It is also a regional capital and cultural center. A council of workers and peasants proclaimed Poland's independence from Russia here in 1918. A Soviet-sponsored liberation group declared itself the provisional government of Poland here in December 1944, and this was recognized by the Allies at the Potsdam Conference (August 1945).
lu·bri·cant (loo'brĭ-kənt) n. Abbr. **lub.** 1. Any of various usually oily liquids or solids, such as grease, machine oil, or graphite, that reduce friction, heat, and wear when applied as a surface coating to moving parts. 2. Informal. Something or someone that helps to reduce difficulty or conflict. [Latin lūbricāns (stem lūbricant-), present participle of lūbricāre, to LUBRICATE.] —**lu·bri·cant** adj.
lu·bri·cate (loo'brĭ-kāt') v. -cated, -cating, -cates. —tr. 1. To apply a lubricant to. 2. To make slippery. 3. Informal. To reduce friction or difficulty in. —intr. To act as a lubricant. [Latin lūbricāre, from lūbricus, slippery.] —**lu·bri·ca·tion** n. —**lu·bri·ca·tive** adj.
lu·bri·ca·tor (loo'brĭ-kā'tər) n. 1. One who lubricates. 2. A lubricant. 3. A device for applying a lubricant.
lu·bri·cious (loo-brĭsh'əs) adj. Also **lu·bri·cous** (loo'brĭ-kəs). 1. Having a slippery or smooth quality. 2. a. Marked by lewdness; wanton. b. Sexually stimulating; salacious. 3. Marked by shiftiness or trickery. [Latin lubricus, slippery.] —**lu·bri·cious·ly** adv. —**lu·bri·cious·ness** n.
lu·bric·i·ty (loo-brĭs'ə-tē) n. The quality or condition of being lubricious. [Late Latin lūbricitās (stem lūbricitāt-), slipperiness, from Latin lūbricus, slippery.]
Lu·bum·ba·shi (loo'boom-bä'shē). Formerly **E·lis·a·beth·ville** (ĭ-lĭz'ə-bəth-vĭl'). Capital of Shaba province, southern Zaire. It is a copper mining and smelting center, and also a marketing point. The city was the capital of the secessionist state of Katanga (the former name of Shaba province) in Zaire's civil war (1960–63).
Lu·can¹ (loo'kən) (A.D. 39–65). Roman poet. Author of the historic epic Bellum civile, he attracted the envy of Nero, who then banned all public readings of his work. Embittered, he led a conspiracy to assassinate Nero. When the plot failed, Lucan was forced to commit suicide.
Lucan² adj. Pertaining to those parts of the New Testament attributed to St. Luke. [Ecclesiastical Latin Lucas, from Greek Loukas, Luke.]
lu·carne (loo-kärn') n. A dormer window. [Variant (influenced by French lucarne) of earlier lucane, Old French lucanne, from Frankish lukinna (unattested), from lūk (unattested), something that closes.]
luce (loos) n. A pike, especially when full-grown. [Middle English, from Old French lus(is), from Latin lūcius.]
Luce (loos), **Clare Boothe** (1903–). U.S. editor, author, politician, and diplomat. An editor of Vogue (1930) and Vanity Fair (1930–34),

she also wrote plays, such as *The Woman* (1936), and books, including *Stuffed Shirts* (1931). She served as U.S. congresswoman (1943-47) and ambassador to Italy (1953-56).

lu·cent (lōō'sənt) *adj. Literary.* **1.** Giving off light; luminous. **2.** Translucent. [Latin *lūcēns* (stem *lūcent-*), present participle of *lūcēre*, to shine.] —**lu·cen·cy** *n.* —**lu·cent·ly** *adv.*

lu·cerne (lōō-sûrn') *n. Chiefly British.* A plant, **alfalfa** *(see)*. [French *luzerne*, from Provençal *luzerno*, special use of *luzerno*, glowworm (from its shiny seeds), perhaps from Latin *lucerna*, lamp.]

Lu·cerne (lōō-sûrn'). German **Lu·zern** (lōō-tsĕrn'). Canton in central Switzerland, noted for dairy and forest products. The city of Lucerne, on Lake Lucerne, is the capital and one of Switzerland's leading resorts.

Lucerne, Lake. Resort lake in central Switzerland. Surrounded by mountains, the lake is noted for its scenic beauty.

Lu·cian (lōō'shən) (*fl.* 2nd century A.D.). Greek satirist and rhetorician. His many works of critical and satiric commentary, including *Dialogues of the Gods* and *Banquet of Philosophers*, contributed to his reputation as one of the most brilliant authors of Greek literature during the Roman Empire.

lu·cid (lōō'sĭd) *adj.* **1.** Easily understood; clear: *a lucid speech.* **2.** Sane; rational: *a lucid moment.* **3.** *Poetic.* Shining. [French *lucide* and Italian *lucido*, from Latin *lūcidus*, from *lūcēre*, to shine.] —**lu·cid·i·ty, lu·cid·ness** *n.* —**lu·cid·ly** *adv.*

lu·ci·fer (lōō'sə-fər) *n.* A friction match. Not in current usage. [After LUCIFER.]

Lu·ci·fer¹ (lōō'sə-fər) *n.* The archangel cast from Heaven for leading a revolt of the angels; Satan. [Middle English *Lucifer*, Old English *Lucifer*, from Latin *Lūcifer*, "light-bearer" : *lūx* (stem *lūc-*), light + *-FER.*]

Lucifer² *n.* The planet Venus in its appearance as the morning star.

lu·cif·er·ase (lōō-sĭf'ə-rās') *n.* An enzyme that catalyzes the oxidation of luciferin. [LUCIFER(IN) + -ASE.]

lu·cif·er·in (lōō-sĭf'ər-ən) *n.* A pigment in bioluminescent animals, such as fireflies or certain marine crustaceans, that produces an almost heatless, bluish-green light when oxidized. [Latin *lūcifer*, "light-bearer." See **Lucifer.**]

luck (lŭk) *n.* **1.** The fortuitous happening of fortunate or adverse events; fortune. **2.** One's (often specified) fate or lot. **3.** Good fortune; prosperity or success that comes by chance: *I wish you luck.* —**down on one's luck.** Afflicted by misfortune. —**in luck.** Fortunate; enjoying success. —**out of luck.** Unsuccessful; not having good fortune. —**push one's luck.** To take a risk, often by acting overconfidently and relying on luck. —**try one's luck.** To attempt something without knowing if one will be successful. [Middle English *lucke*, perhaps from Low German *luk* or Middle Dutch *luc*, akin to Middle High German *gelücke†*.]

luck·i·ly (lŭk'ə-lē) *adv.* With or by favorable chance.

luck·less (lŭk'lĭs) *adj.* Unlucky; having poor luck.

Luck·now (lŭk'nou). Capital city and rail center of Uttar Pradesh, northern India, once the capital of the kings of Oudh (1775-1856). The city was besieged for five months during the Indian Mutiny (1857).

luck·y (lŭk'ē) *adj.* **-ier, -iest. 1.** Having or resulting in good luck. **2.** Occurring by fortunate chance. **3.** Believed to bring good luck: *a lucky number.* —**luck·i·ness** *n.*

lu·cra·tive (lōō'krə-tĭv) *adj.* Producing wealth; profitable. [Middle English *lucratif*, from Old French, from Latin *lucrātīvus*, from *lucrārī*, to profit, from *lucrum*, gain, LUCRE.]

lu·cre (lōō'kər) *n.* Money; profits. [Middle English, from Latin *lucrum*, gain, profit.]

Lu·cre·ti·us (lōō-krē'shəs), Latin name Titus Lucretius Carus (*c.* 95-*c.* 55 B.C.). Roman poet. He wrote *De Rerum Natura*, a philosophical poem on the teachings of Democritus and Epicurus, which tried to explain the universe without a divinity.

lu·cu·brate (lōō'kyōō-brāt') *intr.v.* **-brated, -brating, -brates.** To write in a scholarly fashion. [Latin *lūcubrāre*, to work at night by lamplight.]

lu·cu·bra·tion (lōō'kyōō-brā'shən) *n.* **1. a.** Laborious study or writing. **b.** A product of such study, such as a treatise. **2.** Pedantry in speech or writing.

lu·cu·lent (lōō'kyōō-lənt) *adj. Archaic.* Easily understood; clear; lucid. [Middle English, full of light, clear, from Latin *lūculentus*, from *lūx* (stem *lūc-*), light.]

Lu·cul·lan (lōō-kŭl'ən) *adj.* Lavish; luxurious. [After Lucius *Lucullus*, first-century B.C. Roman general noted for his luxurious banquets.]

Lü·da or **Lü·ta** (lōō'dä'). Also **Dai·ren** (dī-rĕn') or **Ta·lien** (dä'lyĕn'). Industrial conurbation and rail terminus in southern Liaoning province, northeast China. It now includes the city of Lü-shun (Port Arthur), northeast China's chief port and major naval station.

Lud·dite (lŭd'īt') *n.* **1.** Any of a group of British workmen who, between 1811 and 1816, rioted and destroyed textile machinery in the belief that mechanization would diminish employment. **2.** One who aggressively opposes technical or technological progress. [Probably after Ned *Lud(d)*, an insane person who destroyed some stocking frames about 1779.]

Lu·den·dorff (lōō'dn-dôrf'), **Erich** (1865-1937). German general and politician. He was Hindenburg's chief of staff in the east during World War I and won the Battle of Tannenberg (1916). He was defeated as a Nazi candidate for the presidency in 1925.

lu·dic (lōō'dĭk) *adj.* Pertaining to play. [Latin *lūdus*, game, and *lūdere*, to play.]

lu·di·crous (lōō'dĭ-krəs) *adj.* Laughable or hilarious through obvious absurdity or incongruity. —See Synonyms at **foolish.** [Latin *lūdicrus*, done playfully, from *lūdus*, game.] —**lu·di·crous·ly** *adv.* —**lu·di·crous·ness** *n.*

lu·do (lōō'dō) *n.* A children's board game played with counters that are moved according to the throw of a dice. [Latin, "I play."]

lu·es (lōō'ēz) *n., pl.* **lues.** *Pathology.* **1.** Syphilis. **2.** A plague; pestilence. [New Latin, from Latin *luēs*, plague.] —**lu·et·ic** (lōō-ĕt'ĭk) *adj.* —**lu·et·i·cal·ly** *adv.*

luff (lŭf) *n.* **1.** The forward side of a fore-and-aft sail. **2.** The fullest part of the bow of a ship.
~*v.* **luffed, luffing, luffs.** —*intr.* **1.** To steer a sailing vessel nearer into the wind, especially with the sails flapping. **2.** To flap while losing wind. Used of a sail. **3.** To sail closer to the wind than, or to come between the wind and, an opponent's yacht during a race. **4.** To move the jib of a crane or the boom of a derrick. —*tr.* To cause (a ship, for example) to sail closer to the wind. [Earlier *loufe*, Middle English *luff, lof*, from Old French *lof*, perhaps from Middle Dutch *loef* (unattested).]

luffa. Variant of **loofah.**

Luft·waf·fe (lōōft'väf'ə) *n.* The German air force before and during World War II. [German, "air weapon."]

lug¹ (lŭg) *n.* **1.** An earlike handle or projection on a vessel or machine, used as a hold or support. **2.** In machinery, a nut, especially one that is closed at one end to serve as a cap. **3.** A loop, usually of leather, at the side of the saddle of a harness rig through which one of the shafts of a cart or other conveyance passes. **4.** A projection from a battery plate to which an electrical connection can be made. **5.** *Chiefly Scottish.* An ear. **6.** A lugsail. [Middle English (Scottish) *lugge*, flap, ear, perhaps from *luggen*, to LUG (to pull, as the ear).]

lug² *v.* **lugged, lugging, lugs.** —*tr.* **1.** To drag or haul (something) laboriously. **2.** To introduce or include (something irrelevant) in a forced manner. —*intr.* To pull with difficulty; tug.
~*n.* **1.** The act or an instance of lugging. **2.** Something that is lugged. [Middle English *luggen*, to pull, perhaps from Scandinavian, akin to Swedish *lugga†*, to pull one's hair.]

lug³ *n.* The lugworm.

Lu·gan·da (lōō-gän'də) *n.* The Bantu language of the Ganda, a people of Uganda. —**Lu·gan·da** *adj.*

luge (lōōzh) *n.* A light, short toboggan for one person.
~*intr.v.* **luged, luging, luges.** To ride or travel on a luge. [French.]

Lu·ger (lōō'gər) *n.* A trademark for a German automatic pistol.

lug·gage (lŭg'ĭj) *n.* The suitcases, trunks, bags, and the like of a traveler; baggage. [Probably LUG (to drag) + (BAG)GAGE.]

lug·ger (lŭg'ər) *n.* A small boat used for fishing, sailing, or coasting and having two or three masts, each with a lugsail, and two or three jibs set on the bowsprit. [From LUG(SAIL).]

Lu·go·si (lōō-gō'sē), **Bela** (1884-1956). U.S. actor, born in Hungary. He first played the vampire in *Dracula* on stage in 1927, recreating that role on screen in 1931. In subsequent films he played a variety of sinister characters and fanciful monsters.

lug·sail (lŭg'səl) *n.* A quadrilateral sail lacking a boom and having the foot larger than the head, bent to a yard hanging obliquely on the mast. Also called "lug." [Perhaps from LUG "ear."]

lu·gu·bri·ous (lōō-gōō'brē-əs, lōō-gyōō'-) *adj.* Mournful or doleful, especially to an excessive degree. [Latin *lūgubris*, mournful, from *lūgēre*, to mourn.] —**lu·gu·bri·ous·ly** *adv.* —**lu·gu·bri·ous·ness** *n.*

lug·worm (lŭg'wûrm') *n.* Any of various segmented, burrowing marine worms of the genus *Arenicola*; especially, *A. marina*, often used as fishing bait. Also called "lug," "lobworm." [17th century : origin obscure.]

Luik. See **Liège.**

Luke (lōōk) *n.* A book of the New Testament, the third Gospel, attributed to St. Luke.

Luke, Saint *n.* A companion of the Apostle Paul, traditionally regarded as author of the third Gospel and the Acts of the Apostles.

luke·warm (lōōk'wôrm') *adj.* **1.** Mildly warm; tepid. **2.** Lacking in enthusiasm; indifferent. [Middle English : *luke*, perhaps from *lew*, tepid, Old English *hlēow*, warm + WARM.] —**luke·warm·ly** *adv.* —**luke·warm·ness** *n.*

lull (lŭl) *v.* **lulled, lulling, lulls.** —*tr.* **1.** To cause to sleep or rest; soothe; calm. **2.** To dispel or quiet (fears or suspicions). **3.** To deceive into trustfulness. —*intr.* To become calm.
~*n.* **1.** A relatively calm interval in a storm or other turbulence. **2.** An interval of lessened activity: *a lull in sales.* [Middle English *lullen*, perhaps of German origin; akin to Middle Low German *lollen.*]

lull·a·by (lŭl'ə-bī') *n., pl.* **-bies.** A soothing song with which to lull a child to sleep.
~*tr.v.* **lullabied, -bying, -bies.** To quiet with or as if with a lullaby. [Perhaps LULL + good*bye.*]

Lul·ly (lōō-lē'), **Jean Baptiste,** born Giovanni Battista Lulli (1632-87). Italian-born French composer. He was court composer to Louis XIV of France, founding French opera and producing court ballets for Molière's plays.

lu·lu (lōō'lōō) *n. Slang.* An object, action, or idea that is remarkable. [Perhaps from *Lulu*, pet form of the name *Louise.*]

lum·ba·go (lŭm-bā'gō) *n.* Pain in the region of the lower back, resulting from various causes. [Latin *lumbāgo*, from *lumbus*, loin.]

lum·bar (lŭm'bər, -bär') *adj.* Of, near, or situated in the part of the back and sides between the lowest ribs and the pelvis. [New Latin *lumbaris*, from Latin *lumbus*, loin.]

lumbar puncture *n.* The insertion of a hollow needle into the lumbar region of the spinal cord in order to withdraw cerebrospinal fluid for diagnostic examination or inject drugs.

lum·ber¹ (lŭm′bər) n. **1.** Timber sawed into boards, planks, or structural members of standard or specified length. **2.** *Chiefly British.* Miscellaneous stored articles. **3.** Anything useless or cumbersome. ~v. **lumbered, -bering, -bers.** —*tr.* **1. a.** To cut or saw into timber. **b.** To cut down the timber of. **2.** *Chiefly British.* To clutter with or as if with unused articles. —*intr.* To cut and prepare timber for the market. [Perhaps from LUMBER (to move clumsily, hence something clumsy).] —**lum·ber** adj. —**lum·ber·er, lum·ber·man** n.

lum·ber² intr.v. **-bered, -bering, -bers. 1.** To walk or move with heavy clumsiness. **2.** To move with a rumbling noise. [Middle English *lomeren*, perhaps from Scandinavian; akin to Swedish dialectal *loma*, to move heavily.]

lum·ber·jack (lŭm′bər-jăk′) n. One who fells trees and transports the timber to a mill; a logger. [LUMBER (wood) + JACK (man).]

lum·ber·jack·et (lŭm′bər-jăk′ĭt) n. A heavy, waist-length jacket worn especially by outdoor workers.

lum·ber·yard (lŭm′bər-yärd′) n. An establishment that sells lumber and other building materials from a yard.

lum·bri·coid (lŭm′brĭ-koĭd′) adj. Resembling or pertaining to an earthworm. ~n. A parasitic roundworm, *Ascaris lumbricoides,* that infests the human intestine. [New Latin *lumbricoides* : Latin *lumbrīcus,* earthworm + -OID.]

lu·men (lōō′mən) n., pl. **-mens** or **-mina** (-mə-nə). **1.** *Anatomy.* The inner open space of a tubular organ, as of a blood vessel or an intestine. **2.** *Botany.* The space enclosed by the cell walls of a plant cell that has lost its living contents. **3.** *Abbr.* **lm** *Physics.* The SI unit of luminous flux, equal to the luminous flux emitted in a solid angle of one steradian by a uniform point source having an intensity of one candela. [New Latin, from Latin *lūmen,* light, eye, opening.] —**lu·men·al, lu·min·al** adj.

Lu·met (lōō-mět′), **Sidney** (1924–). U.S. film director. With a critical, naturalistic style and a deep interest in human conflict, he has directed several motion pictures adapted from plays and novels, including *Twelve Angry Men* (1957), *Long Day's Journey Into Night* (1962), and *The Seagull* (1968).

Lu·mière (lōō-myěr′), **Auguste** (1862–1954). French photographer. Auguste and his brother **Louis Jean Lumière** (1864–1948) gave the first public showing of a projected cinematic film in Paris (1895).

lu·mi·nance (lōō′mə-nəns) n. **1.** The condition or quality of being luminous. **2.** *Physics.* The luminous intensity in a given direction of a small element of surface area divided by the orthogonal projection of this area onto a plane at right angles to the direction. Formerly called "brightness." [Latin *lūmen* (stem *lūmin-*), light + -ANCE.]

lu·mi·nar·y (lōō′mə-něr′ē) n., pl. **-ies. 1.** An object, as a celestial body, that gives light. **2.** A source of intellectual or spiritual enlightenment. **3.** A notable person in a given field. [Middle English *luminarye,* from Old French *luminarie,* from Late Latin *lūmināre,* lamp, heavenly body, from Latin *lūmen* (stem *lūmin-*), light.] —**lu·mi·nar·y** adj.

lu·mi·nesce (lōō′mə-něs′) intr.v. **-nesced, -nescing, -nesces.** To be or become luminescent. [Back-formation from LUMINESCENT.]

lu·mi·nes·cence (lōō′mə-něs′əns) n. **1.** The emission of light, as in phosphorescence, fluorescence, and bioluminescence, by processes that derive energy from essentially nonthermal sources such as chemical, biochemical, or crystallographic changes, the motion of subatomic particles, or the excitation of an atomic system by radiation; especially, such emission distinguished from incandescence. **2.** The light so emitted.

lu·mi·nes·cent (lōō′mə-něs′ənt) adj. Capable of, exhibiting, or suitable for the emission of luminescence. [Latin *lūmen* (stem *lūmin-*), light + -ESCENT.]

lu·mi·nif·er·ous (lōō′mə-nĭf′ər-əs) adj. Generating, yielding, or transmitting light. [Latin *lūmen* (stem *lūmin-*), light (see **luminous**) + -FEROUS.]

lu·mi·nos·i·ty (lōō′mə-nŏs′ə-tē) n. **1.** The condition or quality of being luminous. **2.** Something luminous. **3.** The attribute of an object or color that allows the observation of the extent to which an object emits light. **4.** *Astronomy.* A measure of the absolute brightness of a star, equal to the total power radiated.

lu·mi·nous (lōō′mə-nəs) adj. **1.** Emitting light; especially, emitting self-generated light. **2.** Full of light; illuminated. **3.** Designating a photometric physical quantity that is evaluated on the basis of the visual sensation it produces in the observer. Compare **radiant. 4.** Intelligible; clear. —See Synonyms at **bright.** [Middle English, from Old French *lumineux,* from Latin *lūminōsus,* full of light, from *lūmen* (stem *lūmin-*), light.] —**lu·mi·nous·ly** adv. —**lu·min·ous·ness** n.

luminous efficacy n. **1.** The ratio of the total luminous flux to the total radiant flux of an emitting source. **2.** The ratio of the luminous flux emitted by a source of radiation to the power it consumes, usually expressed in lumens per watt.

luminous efficiency n. The efficiency of polychromatic radiation in producing a visual sensation measured as the ratio of the radiant flux, weighed according to the spectral luminous efficiencies of its constituent wavelengths, to the corresponding radiant flux.

luminous energy n. Energy in the form of light, expressed as luminous flux multiplied by its duration and measured in lumen seconds.

luminous exitance n. The ability of a surface to emit light, equal to the luminous flux per unit area at a specific position on the surface.

luminous flux n. The rate of flow of luminous energy evaluated on the basis of its ability to produce a visual sensation. For monochromatic light it is the radiant flux multiplied by the spectral luminous efficiency and is measured in lumens.

luminous intensity n. The amount of light radiated by a point source in a given direction expressed as the luminous flux in that direction per unit of solid angle. It is measured in candelas.

luminous paint n. A paint containing a phosphorescent or fluorescent substance that makes it glow in the dark.

lum·mox (lŭm′əks) n. An oaf; lout. [Origin unknown.]

lump¹ (lŭmp) n. **1.** An irregularly shaped mass or piece. **2.** A small cube or cuboid of sugar. Also used adjectively: *lump sugar.* **3.** *Pathology.* A swelling or small, palpable tumor. **4.** An aggregate; collection; totality. **5.** An ungainly, heavy, or lazy person. **6.** A piece of coal or coke suitable for use in a stove or fireplace. **7. lumps. a.** Punishment in the form of beatings. **b.** One's just deserts. —**a lump in the throat.** A feeling of constriction in the throat caused by emotion. ~v. **lumped, lumping, lumps.** —*tr.* **1.** To put together or amass in a single group or pile. **2.** To treat as a single group; fail to differentiate. Often used with *together.* **3.** To make lumpy. —*intr.* **1.** To become lumpy. **2.** To move heavily. [Middle English, perhaps of Low German origin; Low German *lump,* coarse.]

lump² tr.v. **lumped, lumping, lumps.** *Informal.* To tolerate (what must be endured): *like it or lump it.* [16th century : origin obscure.]

lump·ec·to·my (lŭmp-ĕk′tə-mē) n., pl. **-mies.** A surgical operation for the removal of a tumor from the breast. [LUMP + -ECTOMY.]

lump·en (lŭm′pən) adj. Ignorant or stupid. Used derogatorily or humorously. [German *Lumpen,* rag, vagabond.]

lum·pen·pro·le·tar·i·at (lŭm′pən-prō′lə-târ′ē-ət) n. **1.** According to Marxist analysis, a social grouping consisting of outcasts such as tramps and thieves, considered to be below the proletariat. **2.** The unthinking, ignorant lower classes, uninterested in advancement or social change. Used derogatorily. [German, "ragged proletariat."]

lump·er (lŭm′pər) n. A laborer employed to load and unload ships; stevedore. [From LUMP ("to put together," "load").]

lump·fish (lŭmp′fĭsh′) n., pl. **-fishes** or collectively **lumpfish.** Any of various fishes of the family Cyclopteridae; especially, *Cyclopterus lumpus,* of Atlantic waters, having a body covered with tuberous excrescences, a ventral sucker formed from fused pelvic fins, and an edible roe resembling caviar. Also called "lumpsucker." [Obsolete *lump,* lumpfish, from Middle Dutch *lumpe* + FISH.]

lump·ish (lŭm′pĭsh) adj. **1.** Stupid; dull. **2.** Clumsy; heavy; cumbersome. —**lump·ish·ly** adv. —**lump·ish·ness** n.

lump sum n. A sum of money as an inclusive payment.

lump·y (lŭm′pē) adj. **-ier, -iest. 1.** Covered with lumps. **2.** Full of lumps. **3.** Thickset or cumbersome in appearance. **4.** Characterized by short, choppy waves. Said of a windblown sea.

lumpy jaw n. *Pathology.* Actinomycosis (see).

Lu·mum·ba (lōō-mōōm′bə), **Patrice** (1925-61). First prime minister (1960-61) of the Congo (now Zaire). He fought to form a united Congo, but was ousted in 1961 and murdered by secessionists.

lu·na (lōō′nə) n. In alchemy, silver. [Middle English, from Medieval Latin *lūna,* from Latin, moon (from its color).]

Lu·na (lōō′nə). The Roman goddess of the moon. [Latin.]

lu·na·cy (lōō′nə-sē) n., pl. **-cies. 1.** Insanity. Not in technical usage. **2.** Foolish and irresponsible conduct. **3.** *Archaic.* Mental derangement associated with certain phases of the moon. —See Synonyms at **insanity.** [From LUNATIC.]

luna moth n. A large, pale-green North American moth, *Actias luna,* having a long projection on each hind wing. [Latin *lūna,* moon (from the yellow rings on its wings).]

lu·nar (lōō′nər) adj. **1.** Of, involving, caused by, or affecting the moon. **2.** Measured by or based on the revolution of the moon: *a lunar month; a lunar calendar.* **3.** Of or pertaining to silver. [Latin *lūnāris,* from *lūna,* moon.]

lunar caustic n. Silver nitrate in the form of sticks, formerly used in cauterization.

lunar excursion module n. *Abbr.* **LEM** A spacecraft designed to transport astronauts from a command module orbiting the moon to the lunar surface and back. Also called "lunar module."

lunar month n. See **month** (sense 4).

lunar year n. An interval of 12 lunar months.

lu·nate (lōō′nāt′) adj. Also **lu·nat·ed** (-nā′tĭd). Crescent-shaped. [Latin *lūnātus,* from *lūnāre,* to form into a crescent, from *lūna,* moon.]

lunate bone n. The second of three bones forming the upper row of bones in the wrist. Also called "semilunar bone."

lu·na·tic (lōō′nə-tĭk) adj. **1.** Suffering from lunacy; insane. Not in technical usage. **2.** Of or for the insane: *a lunatic asylum.* Not in technical usage. **3.** Wildly or absurdly foolish: *a lunatic decision.* [Middle English *lunatik,* from Old French *lunatique,* from Latin *lūnāticus,* "moonstruck," crazy, from *lūna,* moon.] —**lu·na·tic** n.

lunatic fringe n. The fanatical, extreme, or irrational members of a society or group.

lu·na·tion (lōō-nā′shən) n. See **month** (sense 4). [Middle English *lunacioun,* from Medieval Latin *lūnātiō* (stem *lūnātiōn-*), from Latin *lūna,* moon.]

lunch (lŭnch) n. **1.** A meal eaten at midday. **2.** The food provided for this meal. —**out to lunch.** *Slang.* Crazy; mad. ~intr.v. **lunched, lunching, lunches.** To have one's lunch. [Shortened from LUNCHEON.] —**lunch·er** n.

lunch·eon (lŭn′chən) n. **1.** A lunch, especially a formal one. **2.** An

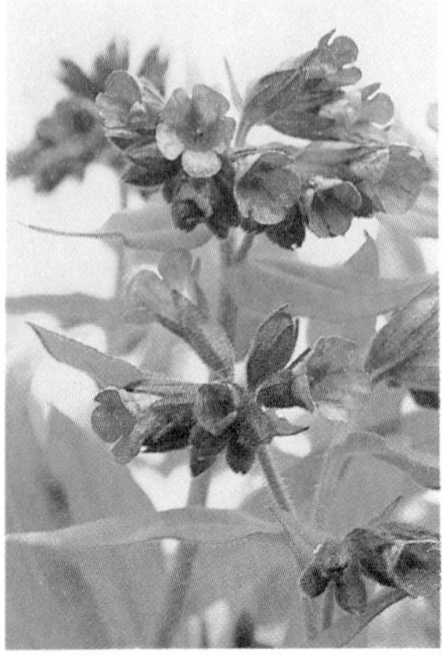

lungwort *Lungworts—a group of spring-flowering European plants with coarse leaves—were so named because they were once thought to be a cure for lung diseases. This species is* Pulmonaria officinalis.

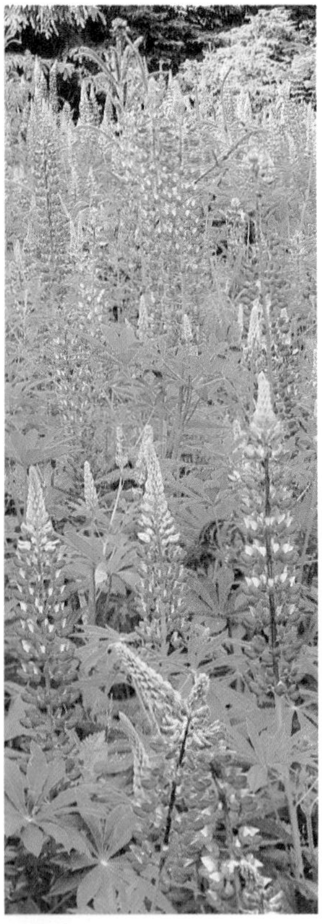

lupine *There are about 200 species of lupine, a plant native to the Americas and the Mediterranean. Most garden varieties—like the ones shown here —are hybrids of the North American species* Lupinus polyphyllus *and are commonly known as Russell lupines after one of the breeders who developed the strain.*

early afternoon party at which a light meal is served. [17th century : origin obscure.]

lunch•eon•ette (lŭn′chə-nĕt′) *n.* A small restaurant that serves simple meals, especially lunches.

luncheon meat *n.* Meat, often pork, processed and pressed into a small loaf shape and usually canned.

lunch•room (lŭnch′ro͞om′, -ro͝om′) *n.* **1.** A luncheonette. **2.** A room, as in a school, in which lunches may be purchased or those brought from home may be eaten.

Lund (lŭnd). A market and industrial city north of Malmö, Sweden. It was the largest town in Scandinavia during the Middle Ages, and is now an educational center with a university (founded in 1666) and technical institute (1961).

Lun•dy (lŭn′dē), **Benjamin** (1789–1839). U.S. abolitionist and editor. Convinced of the inherent evil of slavery, he founded the Union Humane Society (1815) and urged the consolidation of antislavery organizations. He edited two abolitionist newspapers and wrote *The War in Texas* (1836), about the annexation of Texas as a slave state.

lune (lo͞on) *n.* A portion of a sphere enclosed between two semicircles having their common end points at opposite poles. [Latin *lūna,* moon.]

Lü•ne•burg (lo͞o′nə-bûrg′). City and river port in Lower Saxony, West Germany. It is also a spa. Johann Sebastian Bach studied music at Lüneburg's Michaelis Kirche.

lu•nette (lo͞o-nĕt′) *n.* **1.** *Architecture.* **a.** A small, circular or crescent-shaped opening in a vaulted roof. **b.** A crescent-shaped or semicircular space, usually over a door or window, that may contain another window, a sculpture, or a mural. **2.** *Military.* A type of fieldwork fortification that has two projecting faces and two parallel flanks. **3.** A flattened, glass covering for a watch. **4.** *Roman Catholic Church.* A flat, round case with a hinged glass lid used for holding the consecrated host in a monstrance. [French, diminutive of *lune,* from Latin *lūna,* moon.]

lung (lŭng) *n.* **1.** Either of two spongy, saclike respiratory organs in air-breathing vertebrates, occupying the chest cavity together with the heart, and functioning to remove carbon dioxide from the blood and provide it with oxygen. **2.** A comparable invertebrate structure. [Middle English *lunge,* from Old English *lungen.*]

lunge¹ (lŭnj) *n.* **1.** A sudden thrust or pass, as with a sword or rapier. **2.** Any sudden forward movement or plunge.
~v. **lunged, lunging, lunges.** *—intr.* **1.** To make a thrust or pass. **2.** To move with a lunge. *—tr.* To thrust forward suddenly. [Earlier *allonge, elonge,* from French *allonger, alongier,* to lengthen, extend, from Vulgar Latin *allongāre* (unattested) : Latin *ad-* (toward) + *longus,* long.] **—lung•er** *n.*

lunge² *n.* A long rope or leather rein used for schooling or exercising a horse by someone on foot. Also called "lunging rein."
~tr.v. **lunged, lunging, lunges.** To school or exercise (a horse) by means of a lunge. [French *longe,* "long (rein)," from Latin *longus,* long.]

lung•fish (lŭng′fĭsh′) *n., pl.* **-fishes** or collectively **lungfish.** Any of several elongated tropical freshwater fishes of the order Dipnoi (or Dipneusti), having lungs as well as gills, and in certain species constructing a mucus-lined mud covering in which to withstand an extended drought.

lun•gi, lun•gee (lo͝ong′gē) *n.* **1.** A loincloth, turban, or scarf, as worn by Indian men. **2.** The long piece of fabric used to form this. [Hindi, from Persian *lungi*†.]

lung•worm (lŭng′wûrm′) *n.* Any of various parasitic nematode worms that are parasites of the lungs of mammals, such as any of the family Metastrongylidae.

lung•wort (lŭng′wûrt′, -wôrt′) *n.* **1.** Any of several plants of the genus *Pulmonaria,* native to Europe, with long-stalked leaves and coiled clusters of blue or purple flowers. **2.** Any of various plants of the genus *Mertensia,* having drooping clusters of tubular, usually blue flowers. [Formerly used to treat lung diseases.]

lu•ni•so•lar (lo͞o′nĭ-sō′lər) *adj.* Of, caused, or measured by both the sun and the moon. [Latin *lūna,* moon + SOLAR.]

lu•ni•ti•dal (lo͞o′nĭ-tīd′l) *adj.* Of or pertaining to tidal phenomena caused by the moon. [Latin *lūna,* moon + TIDAL.]

lunitidal interval *n.* The time elapsing between the moon's transit at a place and the next high tide there.

lunk•er (lŭng′kər) *n. Informal.* Something unusually large of its kind, especially a large game fish. [Origin unknown.]

lunk•head (lŭngk′hĕd′) *n. Slang.* A stupid person. [Probably formed from LUMP and HEAD.] **—lunk•head•ed** *adj.*

Lunt (lŭnt), **Alfred** (1893–1977). U.S. actor. He debuted in Boston in *The Gingerbread Man* (1913) and in 1917 first saw Lynn Fontanne perform in New York. They were married in 1922, creating one of America's premier husband-and-wife acting teams. *Pygmalion* (1926), *The Sea Gull* (1938), and *The Visit* (1958) are a few of their many credits.

lu•nu•la (lo͞on′yə-lə) *n., pl.* **-lae** (-lē′). Also **lu•nule** (-yo͞ol). A small crescent-shaped structure or marking; especially, the white crescent-shaped area at the base of a fingernail. [Latin *lūnula,* crescent-shaped ornament, "little moon," from *lūna,* moon.]

lu•nu•lar (lo͞on′yə-lər) *adj.* Crescent-shaped.

lu•nu•late (lo͞on′yə-lāt′, -lĭt) *adj.* Also **lu•nu•lat•ed** (-lā′tĭd). **1.** Small and lunular. **2.** Having lunular markings.

Luo•yang or **Lo-yang** (lwō′yăng′). Formerly **Ho•nan** or **Ho-nan** (hō′năn′). Industrial city in Henan province, north-central China. It is the market center of an agricultural and coal-mining region. An ancient city, it was a Chinese capital under the Han, Tang, and Song dynasties.

Lu•per•ca•li•a (lo͞o′pər-kā′lē-ə) *n.* A fertility festival in ancient Rome, celebrated on February 15 in honor of the pastoral god Lupercus. **—Lu•per•ca•li•an** *adj.*

lu•pine¹, lu•pin (lo͞o′pən) *n.* Any of various plants of the genus *Lupinus,* having tall spikes of brightly colored flowers. [Middle English, from Latin *lupīnum,* from *lupīnus,* LUPINE (wolflike), from the ancient belief that it destroyed the soil.]

lu•pine² (lo͞o′pīn′) *adj.* **1.** Wolflike. **2.** Rapacious; ravenous. [Latin *lupīnus,* from *lupus,* wolf.]

lu•pu•lin (lo͞op′yə-lĭn) *n.* Minute yellowish-brown hairs from the female flowers of the hop plant, formerly used as a sedative. [New Latin *lupulus,* hop plant, diminutive of Latin *lupus,* wolf, hop plant + -IN.]

lu•pus (lo͞o′pəs) *n.* Any of several diseases of the skin and mucous membranes, many causing disfiguring lesions, especially: **1.** *Lupus vulgaris,* tuberculosis of the skin characterized by ulcerating, nodular facial lesions, especially around the nose and ears. **2.** *Lupus erythematosus,* a chronic inflammatory disease affecting the skin and internal organs characterized by a scaly red rash on the face. [New Latin, from Latin, wolf.]

Lupus *n.* A constellation in the Southern Hemisphere near Centaurus and Scorpius. [Latin *lupus,* wolf.]

lurch¹ (lûrch) *intr.v.* **lurched, lurching, lurches. 1.** To stagger. **2.** To roll or pitch suddenly or erratically, as a ship during a storm.
~n. **1.** A staggering or tottering movement or gait. **2.** An abrupt rolling or pitching. [From *lee-lurch,* variant of *lee-latch,* drifting to leeward.]

lurch² *n.* **1.** A position of difficulty or discomfort. Now used only in the phrase *to leave (someone) in the lurch.* **2.** In the game of cribbage, the losing position of a player who scores 30 points or less to the winner's 61. [French *lourche,* a game resembling backgammon, also a defeat or bad score in this game, probably from Middle High German *lurz,* left, wrong, "defeat."]

lurch•er (lûr′chər) *n.* **1.** *Archaic.* A lurker; a sneak thief. **2.** *Chiefly British.* A crossbred hunting dog, especially one formerly used by poachers. [From obsolete *lurch,* to lurk, Middle English *lorchen,* variant of *lurken,* to LURK.]

lure (lo͝or) *n.* **1. a.** Anything that entices, tempts, or attracts with the promise of gaining a pleasure or reward. **b.** An attraction or appeal. **2.** Any decoy used in catching animals; especially, an artificial bait used in catching fish. **3.** A bunch of feathers attached to a long cord, used in falconry to recall the hawk.
~tr.v. **lured, luring, lures. 1.** To attract by wiles or temptation; entice. **2.** To recall (a falcon) with a lure. [Middle English, from Old French *loirre,* bait, from Germanic *lōthr* (unattested).]
Synonyms: *beguile, decoy, entice, inveigle, seduce, tempt.*

lu•rid (lo͝or′ĭd) *adj.* **1.** Causing shock or horror. **2.** Vivid; glaring; unnaturally bright. **3.** Glowing or glaring through a haze. **4.** *Rare.* Sallow in color; pallid. —See Synonyms at **ghastly.** [Latin *lūridus,* pallid, ghastly, from *lūror*†, pale yellow, ghastliness.] **—lu•rid•ly** *adv.* **—lu•rid•ness** *n.*

lurk (lûrk) *intr.v.* **lurked, lurking, lurks. 1.** To lie in wait, as in ambush or for some other evil purpose. **2.** To move furtively; sneak; slink. **3.** To exist unobserved or unsuspected. [Middle English *lurken,* probably frequentative of *luren,* LOWER (to frown).]

lurk•ing (lûr′kĭng) *adj.* Concealed; hitherto unacknowledged or unsuspected: *a lurking suspicion.*

Lu•sa•ka (lo͞o-sä′kə). Capital city and industrial center of Zambia, central Africa. It replaced Livingstone (Maramba) as the capital of the then British colony of Northern Rhodesia in 1935.

Lu•sa•tia (lo͞o-sā′shə). Home of the Sorbs, an ancient Slavic people. The area, successively part of Brandenburg, Bohemia, Saxony, and Prussia, is now confined between the Elbe and Oder rivers in East Germany.

Lu•sa•tian (lo͞o-sā′shən) *n.* **1.** A native of Lusatia. **2.** A language, **Wendish** *(see).* **—Lu•sa•tian** *adj.*

lus•cious (lŭsh′əs) *adj.* **1.** Sweet and pleasant to taste or smell; delicious: *a luscious melon.* **2.** Having strong sensory appeal; voluptuous. **3.** *Archaic.* Excessively rich or sweet; cloying. [Perhaps from Middle English *lucius, licius,* possibly shortened from DELICIOUS.]

lush¹ (lŭsh) *adj.* **lusher, lushest. 1.** Having or characterized by luxuriant growth or vegetation. **2.** Luxurious; opulent: *lush carpets.* **3.** Succulent; juicy. [Middle English *lusch,* lax, soft, perhaps variant of *lasche,* soft, watery, from Old French, lax, slack, from Latin *laxus,* spacious, loose.]

lush² *n. Slang.* **1.** A drunkard. **2.** Intoxicating drink. [18th century : perhaps humorous use of LUSH, opulent, delicious.]

Lü-shun. See **Lüda.**

Lusitania. See **Portugal.**

lust (lŭst) *n.* **1.** Sexual desire, especially excessive or unrestrained. **2.** Any overwhelming desire or craving: *a lust for power.*
~intr.v. **lusted, lusting, lusts.** To have or feel lust. Usually used with *after* or *for.* [Middle English *lust,* Old English *lust.*]

lus•ter (lŭs′tər) *n.* Also *chiefly British* **lus•tre. 1.** Soft reflected light; sheen; gloss. **2.** Brilliance or radiance of light; brightness. **3. a.** Brilliant or radiant quality. **b.** Glory; distinction. **4.** A glass pendant, especially on a chandelier. **5.** A decorative object, such as a chandelier, having glass pendants. **6.** Any of various substances, such as wax, used to give an object a gloss or polish. **7.** An opalescent, shiny glaze on pottery and porcelain. **8.** *Mineralogy.* The appearance of a mineral surface judged by its brilliance and ability to

lung

THE BREATH OF LIFE FOR HUMAN BEINGS
How the lungs provide the body with oxygen to burn its fuel

Just as the furnace of a boiler needs air to burn its fuel and produce heat and power, so every living animal needs constant supplies of oxygen to burn up its intake of food and produce energy from it. In human beings these oxygen needs are supplied by the lungs, two spongy organs in the chest that contain air sacs

called alveoli. It is in the alveoli that carbon dioxide, the exhaust gas of the body's energy system, is exchanged for oxygen drawn from the air. The human body has some 750 million alveoli; laid out flat they would cover more than 40 square meters (50 square yards).

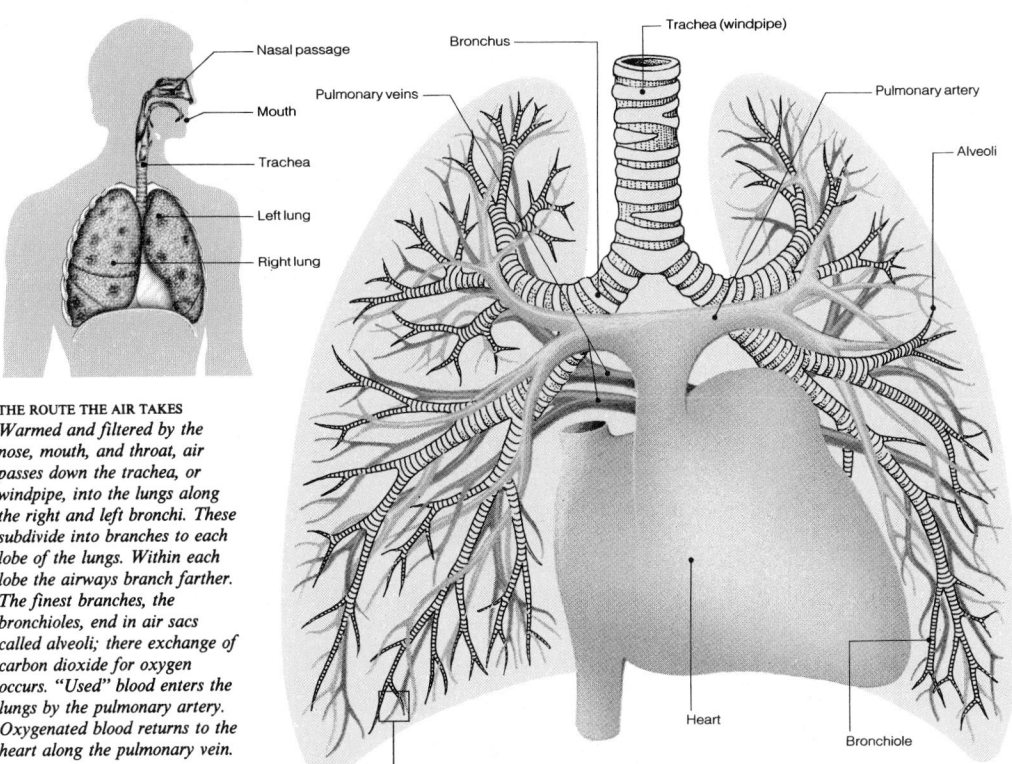

THE ROUTE THE AIR TAKES
Warmed and filtered by the nose, mouth, and throat, air passes down the trachea, or windpipe, into the lungs along the right and left bronchi. These subdivide into branches to each lobe of the lungs. Within each lobe the airways branch farther. The finest branches, the bronchioles, end in air sacs called alveoli; there exchange of carbon dioxide for oxygen occurs. "Used" blood enters the lungs by the pulmonary artery. Oxygenated blood returns to the heart along the pulmonary vein.

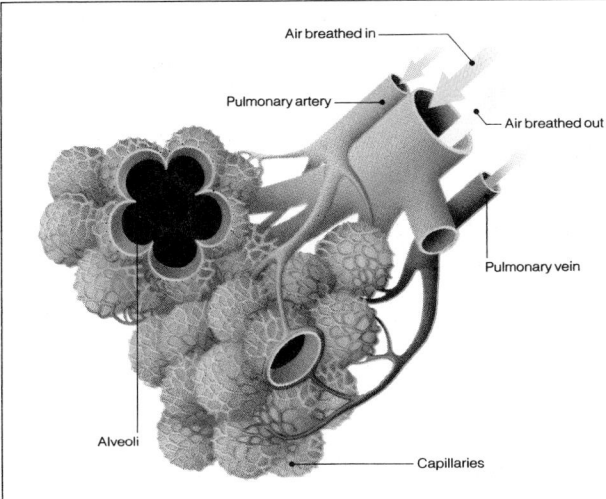

The airways of the lungs, branching and ever-branching, end in some 750 million alveoli, or air sacs, each surrounded by a network of minute, thin-walled blood vessels called capillaries. Carbon dioxide, a waste product of bodily processes, is carried to the alveoli in the bloodstream. It passes through the walls of the capillaries to be breathed out from the lungs. Molecules of hemoglobin capture oxygen from the air in the alveoli, and freshly oxygenated blood is returned to the heart, to be pumped on another circuit of the body. The entire exchange takes less than a second. The lungs can hold 4–5.5 liters (7–10 pints) of air, but someone at rest may take in only 0.4 liter (³/₄ pint) at a time and breathe in and out less than 6 liters (10¹/₂ pints) in a minute. During strenuous exercise, when the body needs more oxygen, this can increase nearly 25-fold to more than 140 liters (250 pints) a minute. Respiratory systems of other animals are similar.

reflect light in comparison with metals, glasses, diamonds, and other materials regarded as standards.
~*v.* **lustered, -tering, -ters.** Also *chiefly British* **lustre, -tred, -tring, -tres.** —*tr.* To give a gloss or sheen to. —*intr.* To become or be lustrous. [French *lustre,* from Italian *lustro,* from *lustrare,* to brighten, from Latin *lūstrāre,* to purify, make bright, from *lūstrum,* purification.]
lus·ter·ware (lŭs´tər-wâr´) *n.* Pottery having a metallic sheen.
lust·ful (lŭst´fəl) *adj.* **1.** Excited by lust. **2.** *Archaic.* Vigorous.
lus·tral (lŭs´trəl) *adj.* **1.** Of, pertaining to, or used in a rite of purification. **2.** Pertaining to a lustrum. [Latin *lustrālis,* from LUSTRUM.]
lus·trate (lŭs´trāt´) *tr.v.* **-trated, -trating, -trates.** To purify ceremoni-

ally. [Latin *lustrāre,* to purify, from LUSTRUM.] —**lus·tra·tion** *n.* —**lus·tra·tive** (lŭs´trə-tĭv) *adj.*
lus·trous (lŭs´trəs) *adj.* **1.** Having a sheen. **2.** Radiant; bright: *a lustrous gaze.* —See Synonyms at **bright.** —**lus·trous·ly** *adv.* —**lus·trous·ness** *n.*
lus·trum (lŭs´trəm) *n., pl.* **-trums** or **-tra. 1.** A ceremonial purification of the entire ancient Roman population after the census every five years. **2.** A period of five years. [Latin.]
lust·y (lŭs´tē) *adj.* **-ier, -iest. 1.** Full of vigor; robust. **2.** Powerful; strong: *a lusty drink.* **3.** Lustful. **4.** *Archaic.* Merry; joyous. —**lust·i·ly** *adv.* —**lust·i·ness** *n.*

lu·sus na·tu·rae (lōō′səs nə-tōōr′ē, -tyōōr′ē) *n.* A freak of nature. [Latin *lūsus nātūrae,* "a joke of nature."]

Lüta. See **Lüda.**

lu·ta·nist, lu·te·nist (lōōt′n-ĭst) *n.* A lute player. [Medieval Latin *lūtānista,* from *lūtāna,* from Old French *lut,* LUTE.]

lute¹ (lōōt) *n.* A musical stringed instrument having a body shaped like a pear halved lengthwise and usually a bent neck with a fretted fingerboard with pegs for tuning it. [Middle English, from Old French *lut,* earlier *leut,* from Arabic *al-'ud,* "the wood."]

lute² *n.* A substance, such as dried clay or cement, used to pack and seal joints and other connections or seal a porous surface. ~*tr.v.* **luted, luting, lutes. 1.** To apply lute to. **2.** To seal with lute. [Middle English, from Old French *lut,* from Latin *lutum,* mud, clay.]

lute-, luteo- *prefix.* Indicates corpus luteum; for example, **luteal.** [New Latin (corpus) *luteum,* from Latin, neuter of *luteus,* yellow.]

lu·te·al (lōō′tē-əl) *adj.* Of or pertaining to the **corpus luteum** (*see*) or to the phase of the estrous cycle during which it develops.

lu·te·in (lōō′tē-ən) *n.* **1.** A yellow pigment isolated from the corpus luteum and found in body fats and egg yolk. **2.** A photosynthetic pigment found in green leaves and certain algae. [LUTEO- + -IN.]

lu·te·in·iz·ing hormone (lōō′tē-ə-nīz′ĭng) *n. Abbr.* **LH** A hormone, secreted by the anterior lobe of the pituitary gland, that stimulates ovulation and corpus luteum formation in female mammals and androgen synthesis by the interstitial cells of the testis in male mammals. Also called "interstitial-cell-stimulating hormone."

lu·te·o·tro·phic hormone (lōō′tē-ə-trō′fĭk, -trŏf′ĭk) *n.* **Prolactin** (*see*). [LUTEO- + -TROPHIC.]

lu·te·ous (lōō′tē-əs) *adj.* Of a light or moderate greenish yellow. [Latin *lūteus,* yellow, from *lūtum†,* yellow weed.]

lu·te·ti·um, lu·te·ci·um (lōō-tē′shē-əm) *n. Symbol* **Lu** A silvery-white rare-earth element that is exceptionally difficult to separate from the other rare-earth elements, used in nuclear technology. Atomic number 71, atomic weight 174.97, melting point 1,652°C, boiling point 3,327°C, specific gravity 9.872, valence 3. [New Latin, from *Lūtētia,* Latin name for Paris, native city of its discoverer, Georges Urbains (1872–1938), French chemist.]

Lu·ther (lōō′thər), **Martin** (1483–1546). German leader of the Reformation. Luther, an Augustinian monk, visited Rome in 1510–11 and was shocked by the wealth and corruption of the papacy. In 1517 he nailed to the chapel door at Wittenberg castle 95 theses attacking the sale of papal indulgences. In 1520 Luther launched the Protestant Reformation, publicly burning a papal bull of condemnation against him, and was excommunicated in 1521. He refused to recant at the Diet of Worms (1521) and was sheltered by the Elector of Saxony. He translated the New Testament into German and married in 1525, breaking the rule of celibacy. Luther confirmed the Augsburg Confession (1530), which effectively established the Lutheran churches.

Lu·ther·an (lōō′thər-ən) *adj.* **1.** Of or pertaining to Martin Luther or his religious teachings and especially to the doctrine of justification by faith alone. **2.** Of, pertaining to, or designating the branch of the Protestant Church adhering to the views of Martin Luther. ~*n.* A member of the Lutheran Church. **—Lu·ther·an·ism** *n.*

Lutheran Church *n.* The Protestant denomination founded in Germany in the 16th century by Martin Luther.

lu·tist (lōō′tĭst) *n.* **1.** A maker of lutes. **2.** A lute player.

Lu·tyens (lōō′chənz), **Sir Edwin Landseer** (1869–1944). British architect. He combined traditional and modern influences in his work, which includes the Whitehall Cenotaph. He was chief architect of New Delhi (1912–30).

lutz (lōōts) *n., pl.* **lutzes.** A jump by an ice-skater, performed by taking off from the back off one blade, making a complete spin in the air, and landing on the rear of the other blade. [Probably after Gustave *Lussi* (born 1898), Swiss figure skater.]

lux (lŭks) *n., pl.* **lux.** *Abbr.* **lx** The SI unit of illumination, equal to one lumen per square meter. [Latin *lūx,* light.]

lux·ate (lŭk′sāt′) *tr.v.* **-ated, -ating, -ates.** To put out of joint; dislocate. [Latin *luxāre,* from *luxus,* dislocated.] **—lux·a·tion** *n.*

luxe *n.* See **de luxe.**

Lux·em·bourg¹ (lŭk′səm-bûrg′). *German* **Lux·em·burg** (lōōk′-səm-bōōrk′). Capital of Luxembourg, on the Alzette River. The city has several offices of the European Economic Community, the European Court of Justice, and the European Parliament and a commercial radio station transmitting in six languages.

Luxembourg². Small independent state in northwest Europe. The north is part of the Ardennes, the south being a continuation of Lorraine. From 1443 to 1839 it was ruled in turn by Burgundians, Spaniards, Austrians, French, and Dutch. Its neutrality was guaranteed in 1867. Luxembourg joined with Belgium and the Netherlands in the Benelux Customs Union in 1948. Area, 2,586 square kilometers (998 square miles). Population, 360,000. Capital, Luxembourg. See map at **Belgium.**

Lux·em·burg (lŭk′səm-bûrg′), **Rosa** (*c.* 1870–1919). German socialist leader, born in Poland. She took part in the revolution of 1905 while in Russian Poland. With Karl Liebknecht she led the antiwar Spartacus Party (1916), which became the German Communist Party after the war. She was arrested and killed by soldiers during the Spartacist revolt in Berlin.

Lux·or (lŭk′sôr, lōōk′-). Town on the east bank of the Nile River in central Egypt. It covers part of the site of the ancient city of Thebes, with the great Temple of Luxor.

lux·u·ri·ant (lŭg-zhōōr′ē-ənt, lŭk-shōōr′-) *adj.* **1.** Growing abundantly, vigorously, or lushly. **2.** Exuberantly elaborate; ornate;

florid. **3.** Abundantly fertile or productive. [Latin *luxuriāns (stem luxuriant-),* present participle of *luxuriāre,* to grow profusely, LUXURIATE.] **—lux·u·ri·ance** *n.* **—lux·u·ri·ant·ly** *adv.*

lux·u·ri·ate (lŭg-zhōōr′ē-āt′, lŭk-shōōr′-) *intr.v.* **-ated, -ating, -ates. 1.** To take luxurious pleasure; indulge oneself. Used with *in.* **2.** To proliferate. **3.** To grow profusely. [Latin *luxuriāre,* to grow profusely, from *luxuria,* excess, LUXURY.]

lux·u·ri·ous (lŭg-zhōōr′ē-əs, lŭk-shōōr′-) *adj.* **1.** Sensuously comfortable: *a luxurious hot bath.* **2.** Characterized by or contributing to luxury. **3.** Fond of or given to luxury. —See Synonyms at **sensuous.** **—lux·u·ri·ous·ly** *adv.* **—lux·u·ri·ous·ness** *n.*

lux·u·ry (lŭg′zhə-rē, lŭk′shə-) *n., pl.* **-ries. 1.** Rich or sumptuous comfort. **2.** An item or activity that is expensive, pleasurable, and unnecessary: *I can't afford luxuries.* **3.** Anything conducive to physical comfort. **4.** The enjoyment of sumptuous living. ~*adj.* **1.** Providing sumptuous comfort: *a luxury hotel.* **2.** Of high quality, and usually expensive: *luxury goods.* [Middle English *luxurie,* from Old French, from Latin *luxuria,* excess, rankness, from *luxus,* excess, extravagance.]

Luzern. See **Lucerne.**

Lu·zon (lōō-zŏn′). Main island of the Philippines. It has fertile volcanic soils and many fine natural harbors, including Manila Bay, on which the country's capital, Manila, is located.

lv. 1. leave. **2.** livre.

LVN, L.V.N. licensed vocational nurse.

Lvov (lə-vôf′, -vŏv′). *German* **Lem·berg** (lĕm′bûrg′, -bōōrk′). Capital of the Lvov region of the Ukraine, U.S.S.R. It is a center of communications, learning, trade, and industry. The city was founded by Ukrainians in the 13th century and captured by the Poles a century later. From 1772 it was the capital of Galicia, an Austrian province. The Poles regained the city in 1919, but formally ceded it to the U.S.S.R. in 1945.

Lw The former symbol for the element lawrencium (now Lr).

L.W. low water.

lwei (lwā) *n., pl.* **lwei** or **lweis.** A unit of currency equal to ¹/₁₀₀ of the kwanza of Angola. See feature at **currency.**

Lwoff (lwôf), **André Michel** (1902–). French microbiologist. In the 1920's he worked on the morphogenesis of protozoa and in 1941 published *L'evolution Physiologique,* which developed the thesis of biochemical evolution by progressive losses of biosynthetic capacity. He shared the Nobel Prize for physiology and medicine (1965).

lx lux.

LXX Septuagint.

-ly¹ *suffix.* Indicates: **1.** Having the characteristics of or resembling; for example, **sisterly. 2.** Appearing or occurring at specified intervals; for example, **weekly, monthly.** [Middle English *-li, -lich,* Old English *-lic,* "having the form of."]

-ly² *suffix.* Indicates: **1.** In a specified manner or degree; for example, **gradually, partly. 2.** From a specified point of view; for example, **politically. 3.** At every specified interval; for example; **hourly, daily. 4.** The event or statement in question is viewed as specified; for example, **regrettably, ironically. 5.** Speaking in a specified way; for example, **frankly, honestly.** [Middle English *-li, -liche,* Old English *-lice,* from *-lic,* -LY (adjectival suffix).]

ly·ase (lī′ās′) *n.* Any of a group of enzymes that catalyze the formation of double bonds or the addition of groups to double bonds. [LYO- + -ASE.]

ly·can·thrope (lī′kən-thrōp′, lī-kăn′-) *n.* **1.** A werewolf. **2.** A person suffering from lycanthropy. [New Latin *lycanthropus,* from Greek *lukanthrōpos,* werewolf : *lukos,* wolf + *anthrōpos,* man.]

ly·can·thro·py (lī-kăn′thrə-pē) *n.* **1.** The mythical, supernatural ability to assume the form and characteristics of a wolf. **2.** A psychological illness in which someone believes himself to be a wolf.

ly·cée (lē-sā′) *n., pl.* **lycées.** A state secondary school in France or a French-speaking country. [French, "lyceum."]

ly·ce·um (lī-sē′əm) *n.* A large public building or hall. Now used chiefly in place names. [Latin *Lyceum,* garden near temple of Apollo where Aristotle taught, from Greek *Lukeion,* neuter of *Lukeios* (epithet of Apollo).]

lychee. Variant of **litchi.**

lych gate. Variant of **lich gate.**

lych·nis (lĭk′nĭs) *n.* Any of various plants of the genus *Lychnis,* which includes the campions and ragged robin. [New Latin *Lychnis,* from Latin, a kind of rose of fiery color, from Greek *lukhnis,* from *lukhnos,* lamp.]

Lyc·i·a (lĭsh′ē-ə). Ancient country and later a Roman province on the southwestern coast of Asia Minor.

Lyc·i·an (lĭsh′ē-ən, lĭsh′ən) *n.* **1.** An inhabitant of ancient Lycia. **2.** The Anatolian language of the Lycians. **—Lyc·i·an** *adj.*

ly·co·pod (lī′kə-pŏd′) *n.* Any pteridophyte plant of the order Lycopodiales; especially, any of the genus *Lycopodium.*

ly·co·po·di·um (lī′kə-pō′dē-əm) *n.* **1.** Any plant of the genus *Lycopodium;* a **club moss** (*see*). **2.** The yellowish powdery spores of certain club mosses, especially *Lycopodium clavatum,* used in fireworks and explosives, and as a covering for pills. [New Latin *Lycopodium,* "wolf foot" (from its claw-shaped roots) : Greek *lukos,* wolf + *pous* (stem *pod-*), foot.]

Ly·cur·gus (lī-kûr′gəs) (*c.* 9th century B.C.). Spartan lawmaker. He is traditionally considered the founder of the Spartan constitution, although nothing is known of his life. The earliest mention of the name is in Herodotus.

Lydda. See **Lod.**

lyd·dite (lĭd′īt′) *n.* An explosive consisting chiefly of picric acid.

[From *Lydd,* town in Kent where it was first tested.]

Lyd·i·a (lĭd′ē-ə). Ancient country that in 546 B.C. covered all Asia Minor west of the Halys River, excluding Lycia. The Lydians probably coined the first money.

Lyd·i·an (lĭd′ē-ən) *n.* **1.** A member of a people of ancient Lydia. **2.** The Anatolian language of this people. —**Lyd·i·an** *adj.*

Lydian mode *n. Music.* A church mode with F as final and C as dominant. [After an ancient Greek mode associated with Lydia.]

lye (lī) *n.* **1.** The alkaline liquid containing potassium hydroxide obtained by leaching wood ashes. **2. Potassium hydroxide** *(see).* **3. Sodium hydroxide** *(see).* [Middle English *lye, ley(e),* Old English *lēag.*]

Ly·ell (lī′əl), **Sir Charles** (1797–1875). British geologist. His *Principles of Geology* (1830–33) made him the most influential geologist of the 19th century.

ly·ing (lī′ĭng) *adj.* Untruthful; false. —See Synonyms at **dishonest.**

ly·ing-in (lī′ĭng-ĭn′) *n., pl.* **lyings-in** or **lying-ins.** The confinement of a woman in childbirth.

lyme grass (līm) *n.* A perennial grass, *Elymus arenarius,* with bluish-green leaves, that grows on sand dunes in north temperate regions. [Perhaps from LIME (respelling influenced by genus name, *Elymus*), alluding to its binding effect (as lime in mortar).]

lymph (lĭmf) *n.* **1.** A clear, transparent, watery, sometimes faintly yellowish liquid, derived from body tissues, that contains mainly white blood cells and travels through the lymphatic system to return to the venous bloodstream through the thoracic duct. It acts to remove bacteria and certain proteins from the tissues, to transport fat from the intestines, and to supply lymphocytes to the blood. **2.** *Archaic.* A spring or stream of pure, clear water. [Latin *lympha,* earlier *lumpa, limpa,* water.]

lym·phad·e·ni·tis (lĭm-făd′n-ī′tĭs, lĭm′fə-də-nī′-) *n.* Inflammation of the lymph nodes. [New Latin : *lympha,* LYMPH + Greek *adēn,* gland + -ITIS.]

lym·phan·gi·tis (lĭm′fən-jī′tĭs) *n.* Inflammation of the lymphatic vessels, most commonly occurring during a streptococcal infection. [LYMPH + ANGIO- + -ITIS.]

lym·phat·ic (lĭm-făt′ĭk) *adj.* **1.** Of or pertaining to lymph, a lymph vessel, or a lymph node. **2.** Sluggish; indifferent; phlegmatic. ~*n.* A vessel that conveys lymph. [New Latin *lymphaticus,* from *lympha,* LYMPH.]

lymphatic system *n.* The interconnected system of spaces and vessels between tissues and organs by which lymph is circulated throughout the body and returned to the venous system.

lym·pha·tism (lĭm′fə-tĭz′əm) *n.* A pathological condition of infancy and childhood characterized by overgrowth of the lymphatic structures, spleen, and bone marrow.

lym·pha·ti·tis (lĭm′fə-tī′tĭs) *n.* Inflammation of lymph nodes or vessels. [LYMPHAT(IC) + -ITIS.]

lymph follicle *n.* Any of the round masses of lymphocytes in the cortex of a lymph node.

lymph node *n.* Any of numerous oval or round bodies, located along the lymphatic vessels, that supply lymphocytes to the circulatory system and remove bacteria and foreign particles from the lymph. Also called "lymph gland."

lymph nodule *n.* A lymph follicle.

lympho–, lymph– *prefix.* Indicates lymph or lymphatic system; for example, **lymphocyte, lymphoma.** [From LYMPH.]

lym·pho·blast (lĭm′fə-blăst′) *n.* An abnormal cell found in the blood in a type of leukemia, formerly believed to be an immature lymphocyte. [LYMPHO- + -BLAST.] —**lym·pho·blas·tic** *adj.*

lym·pho·cyte (lĭm′fə-sīt′) *n.* A white blood cell formed in lymphoid tissue, as in the lymph nodes, spleen, thymus, and tonsils, and constituting between 22 to 28 percent of all leucocytes in the normal adult human's blood. Also called "lymph cell." [LYMPHO- + -CYTE.] —**lym·pho·cyt·ic** (lĭm′fə-sĭt′ĭk) *adj.*

lym·pho·cy·to·sis (lĭm′fō-sī-tō′sĭs) *n. Pathology.* A form of leucocytosis in which lymphocytes are greatly increased in number. —**lym·pho·cy·tot·ic** (lĭm′fō-sī-tŏt′ĭk) *adj.*

lym·phoid (lĭm′foid′) *adj.* Of or pertaining to lymph or the lymphatic system. [LYMPH(O)- + -OID.]

lymphoid tissue *n.* Tissue responsible for the production of lymphocytes, which includes the lymph nodes, tonsils, thymus, and spleen.

lym·pho·ma (lĭm-fō′mə) *n., pl.* **-mata** (-mə-tə) or **-mas.** Any of various malignant tumors of lymph nodes or lymphoid tissue. —**lym·pho·ma·toid, lym·phom·a·tous** (lĭm-fŏm′ə-təs) *adj.*

lym·pho·poi·e·sis (lĭm′fō-poi-ē′sĭs) *n., pl.* **-ses** (-sēz′). The formation of lymphocytes. [New Latin : LYMPHO- + -POIESIS.] —**lym·pho·poi·et·ic** (lĭm′fō-poi-ĕt′ĭk) *adj.*

lyn·ce·an (lĭn-sē′ən) *adj.* **1.** Of or resembling a lynx. **2.** *Rare.* Sharp-sighted. [Latin *lynceus,* from Greek *Lunkeios,* pertaining to Lynceus (an Argonaut noted for his keenness of sight), from *Lunkeos,* Lynceus.]

lynch (lĭnch) *tr.v.* **lynched, lynching, lynches.** To kill (a person suspected of a crime), especially by hanging, without due process of law. [Probably after William LYNCH.]

Lynch, William (d. 1820). U.S. captain and vigilante. A Virginian concerned with the problem of crime in his remote town, he wrote a compact that called for vigilante justice (1780). Criminals who were sentenced to death by the townspeople were usually hanged, which perhaps gave the name *lynch* to this process of justice.

Lynch·burg (lĭnch′bûrg′). City of central Virginia, on the James

lymphatic system

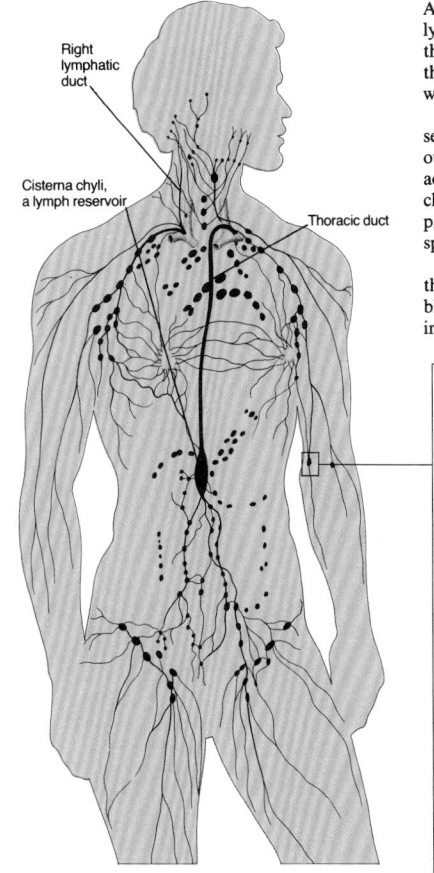

THE FLUID THAT FIGHTS DISEASE
How the body strikes back at bacteria

Right lymphatic duct

Cisterna chyli, a lymph reservoir

Thoracic duct

A painful, swollen throat is a sign that your lymphatic system is doing its job of protecting the body against infection. For the swelling is the result of a "battle" between bacteria and white blood cells in the lymph nodes.

These white cells, known as lymphocytes, seek out, surround, and ingest bacteria and other foreign proteins. The lymph nodes also act as filters against bacteria and foreign particles, such as tiny bits of dead tissue; and they produce antibodies that give immunity against specific diseases.

Lymph is a colorless fluid that flows through a network of vessels and joins the bloodstream where the lymph system drains into veins at the base of the neck.

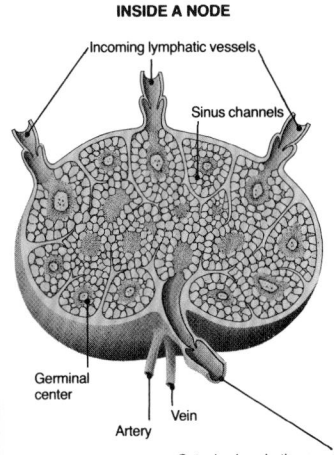

INSIDE A NODE

Incoming lymphatic vessels

Sinus channels

Germinal center

Artery

Vein

Outgoing lymphatic vessel

NETWORK OF PROTECTION *Bean-sized lymph glands, or nodes, are situated throughout the body, with concentrations in the neck, armpits, chest, abdomen, and groin.*

Infection-fighting white blood cells, the lymphocytes, are produced in the germinal centers. Sinus channels filter out bacteria and foreign particles.

River. It is a trade center and tobacco market in the foothills of the Blue Ridge Mts.

lynch law *n.* The punishment of persons suspected of crime without due process of law.

lynch mob *n.* A group or crowd of people wishing to kill or succeeding in killing a person they suspect of a crime.

lynchpin. Variant of **linchpin.**

Lynd (lĭnd), **Robert Staughton** (1892–1970) and **Helen Merrell** (1897–1982). U.S. sociologists. Together they made a pioneering sociological study of Muncie, Indiana, published in 1929 as *Middletown: A Study in Contemporary American Culture.*

lynx (lĭngks) *n.* Any of several wild cats of the genus *Lynx;* especially, *L. lynx* (or *canadensis*), of Eurasia and northern North America, having thick, soft fur, a short tail, and tufted ears. [Latin, from Greek *lunx.*]

Lynx (lĭngks) *n.* A constellation in the Northern Hemisphere near Ursa Major and Auriga.

lynx-eyed (lĭngks′īd′) *adj.* Keen of vision; sharp-sighted.

lyo– *prefix.* Indicates dispersion or dissolution; for example, **lyophilic.** [Greek *luein,* to loosen, dissolve.]

Lyon (lē-ôN′). English **Ly·ons** (-ōNz′). Administrative center of Rhône department in east-central France and the country's second-largest metropolis after Paris. A communications, cultural, and financial center, the city grew after Italians introduced silk manufacturing in the 15th century. It now specializes in artificial fibers, and also makes cars, clothing, chemicals, and machinery.

Ly·on (lī′ən), **Mary Mason** (1797–1849). U.S. educator. Dedicated to creating excellent educational opportunities for women, she established Mount Holyoke College, originally called Mount Holyoke Female Seminary, the first American institution of higher learning for women (1837).

ly·on·naise (lī′ə-nāz′, lē-′) *adj.* Cooked, usually fried, with onions: *potatoes lyonnaise.* [French *à la Lyonnaise,* in the manner of LYON.]

ly·o·phil·ic (lī′ə-fĭl′ĭk) *adj. Chemistry.* Of, pertaining to, or exhibit-

lynx *A short-tailed wildcat found in the coniferous forests of North America, Europe, and Asia, the lynx lives alone or in small groups and hunts at night. It is a good climber and strong jumper and generally feeds on small mammals.*

ing a strong affinity between the dispersed phase and the dispersing medium of a colloid. [LYO- + -PHILIC.]

ly·oph·i·liz·er (lī-ŏf′ə-lī′zər) *n.* A device for freeze-drying. [LYO-PHIL(IC) + -IZE.]

ly·o·pho·bic (lī′ə-fō′bĭk) *adj. Chemistry.* Of, pertaining to, or exhibiting a lack of strong affinity between the dispersed phase and the dispersing medium of a colloid. [LYO- + PHOBIC.]

Ly·ra (lī′rə) *n.* A constellation in the Northern Hemisphere near Cygnus and Hercules containing the star Vega. [Latin *lyra,* LYRE.]

ly·rate (lī′rāt′, -rĭt) *adj.* 1. Having a form or curvature suggestive of a lyre. 2. Designating leaves having a large terminal lobe and smaller lateral lobes. [New Latin *lyratus,* from Latin *lyra,* LYRE.]

lyre (līr) *n.* A stringed instrument of the harp family used to accompany a singer or reader of poetry, especially in ancient Greece. [Middle English *lire,* Old French, from Latin *lyra,* from Greek *lura†*.]

lyre-bird (līr′bûrd′) *n.* Either of two Australian birds, *Menura superba* (or *M. novaehollandae*) or *M. alberti,* the male of which has a long tail spread during courtship in a lyre-shaped display.

lyr·ic (lĭr′ĭk) *adj.* 1. a. Of or pertaining to a category of poetry or verse that is distinguished from the narrative and dramatic, is typically lucid and simple or direct, with smooth, regular rhythms, and is often considered representational of music in its sound patterns. b. Writing this type of verse. 2. a. Of or pertaining to the lyre or harp. b. Appropriate for accompaniment by the lyre. 3. *Music.* a. Having a singing voice of a light, rather than dramatic quality. b. Pertaining to or designating opera or musical drama, especially of the lighter kind.
~*n.* 1. A lyric poem. 2. *Often* **lyrics.** The words of a song, especially a popular song. [Old French *lyrique,* of a lyre, from Latin *lyricus,* from Greek *lurikos,* from *lura,* LYRE.]

lyr·i·cal (lĭr′ĭ-kəl) *adj.* 1. Highly enthusiastic or emotional; exuberant. 2. Romantic and poetic. 3. Lyric.

lyr·i·cism (lĭr′ĭ-sĭz′əm) *n.* 1. The character or quality of subjectivism and sensuality of expression, especially in the arts. 2. An intense outpouring of exuberant emotion.

lyr·i·cist (lĭr′ĭ-sĭst) *n.* A writer of song lyrics.

lyr·ism (lĭr′ĭz-əm) *n.* Lyricism. [French *lyrisme,* from Greek *lurismos,* played on the lyre, from *lura,* LYRE.]

lyr·ist (lĭr′ĭst *for sense 1;* līr′ĭst *for sense 2) n.* 1. *Rare.* A lyricist. 2. One who plays a lyre. [Latin *lyristēs,* one who plays a lyre, from Greek *luristēs,* from *lura,* LYRE.]

Ly·san·der (lī-săn′dər) (d. 395 B.C.). Spartan military leader. As an admiral, he led the Spartan forces in the Battle of Aegospotami (405), in which the Athenians' fleet was destroyed and their grain route was closed, forcing them to surrender to the Spartans and thus ending the Peloponnesian War (404).

lyse (līs) *v.* **lysed, lysing, lyses.** —*tr.* To cause (something) to undergo lysis. —*intr.* To undergo lysis. [From LYSIS.]

Ly·sen·ko (lĭ-sĕng′kō), **Trofim Denisovich** (1898–1976). Soviet biologist. Stalin backed his belief that acquired characteristics could be inherited. This seriously hampered Soviet research into chromosomes and the mechanics of inheritance.

Ly·sen·ko·ism (lĭ-sĕng′kō-ĭz′əm) *n.* The biological doctrine of Trofim Lysenko that maintains the possibility of inheriting environmentally acquired characteristics.

ly·ser·gic acid (lĭ-sûr′jĭk, lī-) *n.* A crystalline alkaloid, $C_{16}H_{16}N_2O_2$, derived from ergot and used in medical research. [From LYS(O)- + ERG(OT) + -IC.]

lysergic acid di·eth·yl·am·ide (dī′ĕth-əl-ăm′īd′) *n.* A crystalline compound, $C_{20}H_{25}N_3O$, prepared from lysergic acid and used illegally as a hallucenogenic drug. Also called "acid," "LSD."

ly·sin (lī′sĭn) *n.* A specific antibody that acts to destroy blood cells, tissues, or microorganisms. [LYS(O)- + -IN.]

ly·sine (lī′sēn) *n.* An essential, crystalline amino acid, $C_6H_{14}N_2O_2$, used in nutrition studies, in culture media, and to fortify foods and feeds. [LYS(O)- + -INE.]

Ly·sip·pus (lī-sĭp′əs) (*fl.* 4th century B.C.). Greek sculptor. Particularly active during the reign of Alexander the Great, he created figures that were more lifelike than the traditional forms. *Apoxyomenos* (*c.* 310) is the best existing example of his work.

ly·sis (lī′sĭs) *n.* 1. *Biochemistry.* The dissolution or destruction of red blood cells, bacteria, or other antigens by a specific lysin. 2. *Medicine.* The gradual subsiding of the symptoms of an acute disease. [New Latin, from Greek *lusis,* a loosening, deliverance, from *luein,* to loosen, unbind.]

–lysis *suffix.* Indicates dissolving or decomposition; for example, **hydrolysis.** [New Latin, from Greek *lusis.* See **lysis.**]

lyso-, lys– *prefix.* Indicates loosening, dissolving, or freeing; for example, **lysin, lysogenesis.** [Greek *lusis,* a loosening. See **lysis.**]

ly·so·gen·e·sis (lī′sō-jĕn′ə-sĭs) *n.* The production of lysins. [New Latin : LYSO- + -GENESIS.]

Ly·sol (lī′sôl′, -sŏl′, -sōl′) A trademark for a liquid antiseptic and disinfectant. [LYS(O)- + -OL (phenol).]

ly·so·some (lī′sə-sōm′) *n.* Any of a number of particles in the cytoplasm of cells that contain enzymes capable of breaking down substances in the cell. [LYSO- + -SOME (body).]

ly·so·zyme (lī′sə-zīm′) *n.* An enzyme occurring naturally in tears, capable of destroying the cell walls of certain bacteria, thereby acting as a mild antiseptic. [LYSO- + -ZYME.]

–lyte *suffix.* Indicates a substance that can be decomposed by a specified process; for example, **electrolyte.** [Greek *lutos,* soluble, from *luein,* to loosen.]

lyt·ic (lĭt′ĭk) *adj.* 1. Of, pertaining to, or causing lysis. 2. Of or pertaining to a lysin. [Greek *lutikos,* able to loosen, laxative, from *lutos,* capable of being untied, from *luein,* to untie, loosen. See **lysis.**]

–lytic *suffix.* Indicates a loosening or dissolving; for example, **hydrolytic.** [Greek *lutikos,* able to loose. See **lytic.**]

lyt·ta (lĭt′ə) *n., pl.* **lyttae** (lĭt′ē′). A thin cartilaginous strip on the underside of the tongue of certain carnivorous mammals, such as dogs. [Latin, "worm under a dog's tongue" (believed to cause madness), from Greek *lutta, lussa,* madness, frenzy.]

Lyt·ton (lĭt′n), **Edward George Earle Bulwer-Lytton, 1st Baron,** known as "Owen Meredith" (1803–73). British novelist. He wrote *Pelham* (1828) and *The Last Days of Pompeii* (1834), a historical romance. He sat as a Liberal, then a Tory, M.P. and was secretary for the Colonies (1858–59).

Lyublin. See Lublin.

–lyze *suffix.* Indicates the causing of chemical decomposition; for example, **pyrolyze.** [From -LYSIS.]

M

m, M (ĕm) *n., pl.* **m's** or **M's. 1.** The 13th letter of the modern English alphabet. See feature at **alphabet. 2.** Any of the speech sounds represented by this letter. **3.** Roman numeral for 1,000. [Latin *mille*] **4.** The 13th in a series; 12th when *J* is omitted.

m, M, m-, M. *Note:* As an abbreviation or symbol, *m* may be a small or a capital letter, with or without a period. Established forms or those generally preferred precede the definition. When no form is given, all four forms are in general use in that sense. **1.** m, M *Printing.* em. **2.** M *Physics.* Mach number. **3.** M. majesty (in titles). **4.** male; masculine. **5.** M. mark (currency). **6.** m, M *Physics.* mass. **7.** M. master (in titles). **8.** M. medieval. **9.** medium. **10.** M mega-. **11.** M. member (in titles). **12.** m., M. meridian. **13.** M *Chemistry.* metal. **14.** m meter (measure). **15.** M *Logic.* middle term of a syllogism. **16.** m. mile. **17.** m milli-. **18.** M. minim (liquid measure). **19.** m, M *Physics.* modulus. **20.** M *Chemistry.* molar. **21.** M *Physics.* moment. **22.** M. Monday. **23.** M. Monsieur. **24.** month. **25.** M *Physics.* mutual inductance. **26.** m., M. noon. [Latin *meridies*]

ma (mä, mô) *n. Informal.* Mother. [Shortened form of MAMA.]

mA milliampere.

MA 1. Maritime Administration. **2.** Massachusetts (with Zip Code). **3.** mental age.

M.A. 1. Master of Arts. [Latin *Magister Artium*] **2.** mental age.

Ma'am (măm). Contraction of *Madam.*

maar (mär) *n.* A flat-bottomed, roughly circular volcanic crater of explosive origin, often filled with water. [Dialectal North German *maar,* from Middle Low German *mare,* lake.]

Maas. See **Meuse.**

Maas·tricht or **Maes·tricht** (mä'strĭкнt'). Industrial city in southeast Netherlands, capital of Limburg province. Its cathedral of St. Servatius, founded in the 6th century, is the country's oldest church.

Mab·i·no·gi·on (măb'ĭ-nō'gē-ən) *n.* A collection of medieval Welsh folk tales. [Welsh, plural of *mabinogi,* "tales of youth," from *mab,* youth, son, from Old Welsh *map,* from Common Celtic *makwos* (unattested), son.]

mac, mack (măk) *n. Chiefly British Informal.* A mackintosh.

Mac (măk) *n. Informal.* A fellow; guy. Used to address a man whose name is unknown: *Hey, Mac, can you tell me how to get to town?* [Probably from MAC-.]

Mac-, M'-, Mc- *prefix.* Indicates son of. Used in surnames. [Gaelic *Mac-,* from Common Celtic *makkos* (unattested), son.]

Mac. Maccabees (books of the Apocrypha).

ma·ca·bre (mə-kä'brə, -bər) *adj.* **1.** Suggesting the horror of death and decay; gruesome; ghastly. **2.** Associated with or suggestive of the danse macabre, in which an allegorical figure of death summons those about him to dance with him to their deaths. —See Synonyms at **ghastly.** [French, ghastly, from Old French *danse macabre,* dance of death, probably originally *danse Macabé,* "Maccabean dance," translation of Medieval Latin *Chorea Maccabaeorum,* probably referring to a representation of the slaughter of the Maccabees in a miracle play.] —**ma·ca·bre·ly** *adv.*

ma·ca·co (mə-kä'kō) *n. pl.* **-cos.** Any of various lemurs; especially, the species *Lemur macaco.* [French *mococo†.*]

mac·ad·am (mə-kăd'əm) *n.* **1.** A surface, especially of a road, made of layers of compacted small stones, now usually bound with tar or asphalt. **2.** The material used to make this surface. [After John L. McADAM.]

mac·a·da·mi·a (măk'ə-dā'mē-ə) *n.* Any of five trees of the genus *Macadamia,* native to eastern Australia; especially, *M. ternifolia,* now cultivated in Hawaii for its nutlike seeds. [New Latin, after John *Macadam* (1827–65), Australian chemist.]

macadamia nut *n.* The round, hard-shelled nut of the macadamia tree.

mac·ad·am·ize (mə-kăd'ə-mīz') *tr.v.* **-ized, -izing, -izes.** To construct or pave (a road) with macadam. —**mac·ad·am·i·za·tion** *n.* —**mac·ad·am·iz·er** *n.*

Ma·cao (mə-kou'). *Portuguese* **Ma·cau.** Portuguese overseas province in southeastern China. The Portuguese founded a trading post between the Xi Jiang and Zhuiang (Pearl River) estuaries in 1557 and paid China tribute for it until 1849, when it became a free port.

In 1887 China formally leased Macao to Portugal, but the colony declined following the rise of Hong Kong. It is now a gambling, tourist, and transit trade center. Area, 16 square kilometers (6 square miles). Capital, Macao.

ma·caque (mə-kăk', -käk') *n.* Any of several short-tailed monkeys of the genus *Macaca,* of Southeast Asia, Japan, Gibraltar, and northern Africa. See **Barbary ape, rhesus monkey.** [French, from Portuguese *macaco,* from Fiot *makaku,* "some monkeys" : *ma,* numerical sign + *kaku,* monkey.]

mac·a·ro·ni, mac·ca·ro·ni (măk'ə-rō'nē) *n., pl.* **macaroni** or **maccaroni** (for senses 1 and 2), **-nis** or **-nies** (for sense 3). **1.** A pasta of wheat flour in the form of hollow tubes or other shapes that is dried and prepared for eating by boiling. **2.** A dish containing or consisting of macaroni. **3.** A fashionable fop of the 18th century. [Italian (Neapolitan dialect), plural of *maccarone,* from Late Greek *makaria,* food made from barley.]

mac·a·ron·ic (măk'ə-rŏn'ĭk) *adj.* **1.** Of or pertaining to a literary composition containing a mixture of vernacular words with Latin words or with non-Latin words that are humorously given Latin endings: *macaronic verse.* **2.** Of or involving a mixture of two or more languages.

~*n.* *Usually* **macaronics.** A macaronic composition. [New Latin *macaronicus,* "like macaroni" (i.e., a crude rustic mixture), from Italian *maccaroni,* MACARONI.]

macaroni and cheese *n.* A dish consisting of cooked macaroni baked in a cheese sauce.

mac·a·roon (măk'ə-rōōn') *n.* A chewy cooky made with sugar, egg whites, and ground almonds or coconut. [French *macaron,* from Italian *maccarone,* MACARONI.]

Mac·Ar·thur (mə-kär'thər), **Douglas** (1880–1964). U.S. general. Much decorated in World War I, he rose to become U.S. chief of staff (1930–37). He was recalled from retirement by the Army in 1941, but failed to prevent the invasion of the Philippines by the Japanese. He regained the Philippines (1944–45), and with the surrender of Japan became supreme commander of the Allied Forces in Japan (1945–51). He was commander (1950–51) of the United Nations Forces in the Korean War, until President Harry Truman relieved him of his command for insubordination.

Ma·cas·sar oil (mə-kăs'ər) *n.* A perfumed oil used, especially in the 19th century, as a dressing for the hair. [After *Macassar* (Makassar), port and region in Celebes (Sulawesi), Indonesia, which was claimed to be the source of the ingredients.]

Macau. See **Macao.**

Ma·cau·lay (mə-kô'lē), **Thomas Babington, 1st Baron** (1800–59). English historian, politician, and poet. He was elected an M.P. (1830), then, after a period in India, became secretary for war (1839–41). He was made a peer in 1857. Besides his essays for the *Edinburgh Review,* he wrote the uncompleted *History of England* (1848–61) and *Lays of Ancient Rome* (1842).

ma·caw (mə-kô') *n.* Any of various tropical and subtropical American parrots of the genera *Ara* and *Anodorhynchus,* including the largest parrots, characterized by long saber-shaped tails, powerful curved bills, and usually brilliant plumage. [Portuguese *macaú,* perhaps from *macaúba,* a kind of palm (on whose fruit the parrot feeds), from Tupi *macahuba, macahiba* : probably *maca-,* thorn (of African origin) + *-yba,* tree.]

Mac·beth (mək-bĕth') (died 1057). King of Scotland (1040–57). In pursuit of a tenuous claim to the throne, he killed Duncan in battle (1040) to become king. He was later killed by Malcolm, son of Duncan. Shakespeare loosely based *Macbeth* on his life.

Macc. Maccabees (books of the Apocrypha).

Mac·ca·be·an (măk'ə-bē'ən) *adj.* Of or pertaining to Judas Maccabeus or to the Maccabees.

Mac·ca·bees[1] (măk'ə-bēz'). A Jewish dynasty of patriots, high priests, and kings of the 2nd and 1st centuries B.C. SEE **Judas Maccabeus.**

Maccabees[2] *pl.n. Abbr.* **Mac., Macc.** Four books in the Old Testament Apocrypha, the first two of which tell about the feats of the Maccabees. In the Protestant churches, all four books are apocry-

macaque Macaca mulatta, *the Indian rhesus monkey (above), is one of a dozen species of this Asian primate. It is widely used in medical research because of its biological similarity to humans.*

macaw *The macaw parrot probably gets its name because it feeds chiefly on the large nuts of the macaw palm, cracking them open with its large hooked beak. The blue and yellow macaw (above) is native to South America.*

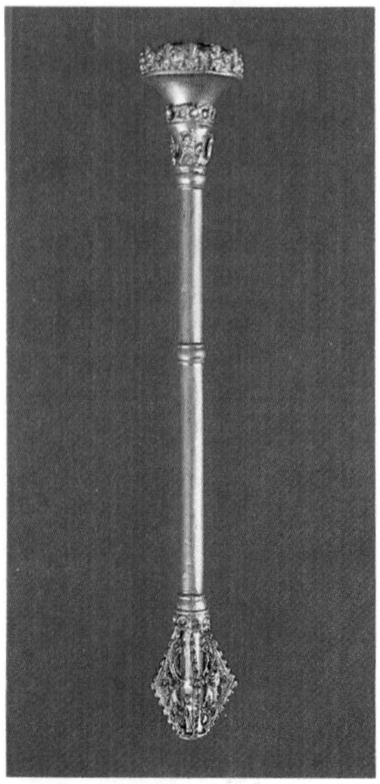

mace *These heavy metal clubs, often fearsomely spiked, were developed as weapons in the Middle Ages after the adoption of plate armor made knights almost invulnerable to sword thrusts. This ceremonial mace was probably made in the 15th century; it is now a symbol of office carried on formal occasions by town officials in Great Britain and Europe.*

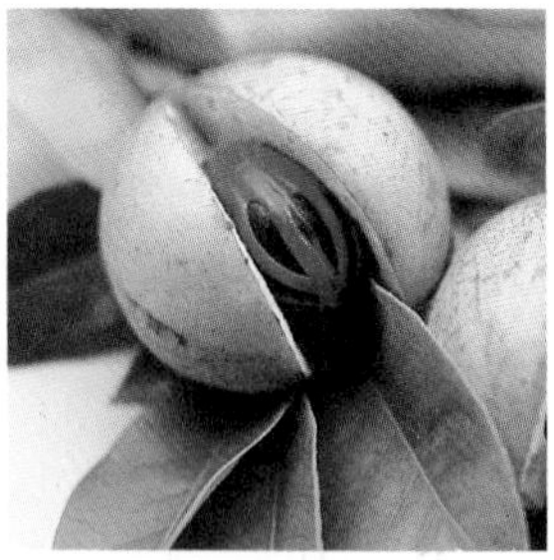

mace *The waxy red coating on the seed of the nutmeg tree (above) is dried and powdered to produce mace, which is used as a spice in cooking as well as a scent in perfumes and soaps.*

phal; in the Roman Catholic and Eastern Orthodox churches, the first two are canonical. Also called in the Douay Bible "Machabees."

Mac·ca·be·us (măk′ə-bē′əs), **Judas** (died 160 B.C.). Jewish patriot, most famous of the Maccabees; leader of a Jewish revolt against Syria in 166. His rededication of the Temple at Jerusalem (164) is commemorated by the Feast of Chanukah.

mac·ca·boy (măk′ə-boi′) *n.* A perfumed snuff made in Martinique. [French *macouba,* after *Macouba,* district of Martinique.]

maccaroni. Variant of **macaroni.**

Mac·Diar·mid (mək-dûr′mĭd), **Hugh,** born Christopher Murray Grieve (1892–1978). Scottish poet, Marxist, and a founder of the Scottish Nationalist Party. He wrote in Scots dialect, his early work including *Sangschaw* (1925) and *Penny Wheep* (1926). *A Drunk Man Looks at the Thistle* (1926), giving his views on Scottish independence, was a landmark in modern Scots poetry.

Mac·don·ald (mək-dŏn′əld), **Sir John Alexander** (1815–91). Scottish-born Canadian politician, the first prime minister (1867–73, 1878–91) of the Dominion of Canada. He was a powerful advocate of the movement that led to Canadian confederation in 1867.

Mac·Don·ald (mək-dŏn′əld), **Flora** (1722–90). Scottish Jacobite heroine. On the Isle of Benbecula she met Prince Charles Edward Stuart, the Young Pretender, who was in hiding after the Battle of Culloden Moor (1746). She took him, disguised as a maid, to Skye, and he escaped to France. She was imprisoned briefly in the Tower of London.

MacDonald, (James) Ramsay (1866–1937). Britain's first Labour prime minister, born in Scotland. He became an M.P. (1906) and prime minister and Secretary of State for foreign affairs (1924). MacDonald was out of parliament (1924–29), but returned as prime minister of a minority government until he lost the support of his own party (1931). He then formed a coalition government made up mainly of Conservatives and resigned in 1935.

Mac·Dow·ell (mək-dou′əl), **Edward Alexander** (1861–1908). U.S. composer. America's first internationally admired composer, he studied music in Europe (1876–88) and then returned to the U.S., where he continued composing, performed with the Boston Symphony Orchestra, and was Columbia University's first professor of music (1896–1904).

mace[1] (mās) *n.* **1.** A heavy medieval war club, usually with a spiked or flanged metal head, used to crush armor. **2.** A ceremonial staff borne or displayed as the symbol of authority of a legislative body. **3.** A macebearer. [Middle English, from Old French *mace, masse,* from Vulgar Latin *matteat*† (unattested), club.]

mace[2] *n.* An aromatic spice made from the dried, waxy, scarlet or yellowish covering that partly encloses the kernel of the nutmeg. [Middle English, formed as singular of *macis* (wrongly taken to be plural), from Medieval Latin, misreading of Latin *macir,* from Greek *makir,* an Indian spice.]

Mace (mās) *n.* **Chemical Mace** *(see).*
~*tr.v.* **Maced, Macing, Maces** or **maced, macing, maces.** To spray by attacking with Chemical Mace.

mace·bear·er (mās′bâr′ər) *n.* An official who carries a mace of office. Also called "mace," "macer."

Maced. Macedonia; Macedonian.

mac·é·doine (măs′ə-dwän′) *n.* **1.** A mixture of finely cut or diced vegetables or fruits, sometimes jellied, served as a salad, dessert, or appetizer. **2.** A mixture; medley. [French *macédoine,* "Macedonian" (the population of Macedonia is a mixture of various peoples).]

Mac·e·do·ni·a (măs′ə-dō′nē-ə). *Abbr.* **Maced.** Region in the Balkans, in southeastern Europe. Largely mountainous, it was peopled by Slavs in the 6th century A.D. and is now divided between Bulgaria, Greece, and Yugoslavia. A powerful empire under Philip II and his son Alexander the Great (4th century B.C.), Macedonia was later ruled by the Romans, Byzantine Greeks, Bulgars, Serbs, and Turks. The present division resulted largely from the Second Balkan War (1913).

Mac·e·do·ni·an (măs′ə-dō′nē-ən) *adj. Abbr.* **Maced.** Of or pertaining to ancient or modern Macedonia, or the people or languages of these regions.
~*n. Abbr.* **Maced. 1.** A native or inhabitant of ancient or modern Macedonia. **2.** The language of ancient Macedonia, which is of uncertain linguistic affiliation but has features that are considered to be Indo-European. **3.** The Slavic language of modern Macedonia.

mac·er (mā′sər) *n.* **1.** A macebearer. **2.** A Scottish usher in a law court.

mac·er·ate (măs′ə-rāt′) *v.* **-ated, -ating, -ates.** —*tr.* **1.** To soften (a solid substance) by soaking or steeping in a liquid, sometimes using heat. **2.** To separate (a solid substance) into constituents by soaking. **3.** To cause to become lean; emaciate, usually by starvation. —*intr.* To become macerated; undergo macerating. [Latin *mācerāre,* to soften.] **—mac·er·a·tion** *n.* **—mac·er·a·tor, mac·er·at·er** *n.*

Mac·Fad·den (mək-făd′n), **Bernarr** (1868–1955). U.S. physical-culture advocate and publisher. He popularized physical culture, a healing method based on health food and fasting that once attracted a large following. He also published several newspapers and pulp magazines, including *True Stories,* established in 1919.

Mac·gil·li·cud·dy's Reeks (mə-gĭl′ə-kŭd′ēz rēks′). Mountain range in County Kerry, Republic of Ireland. It lies between the lakes of Killarney and Lough Caragh and rises to 1,041 meters (3,414 feet) at Carrantuohill, the highest mountain in Ireland.

Mach, mach (mäk) *n.* **Mach number** *(see).*

Mach (mäk. mäKH), **Ernst** (1838–1916). Austrian physicist and philosopher. He gave his name to the Mach number, and contributed to the philosophy of scientific positivism.

mach. machine; machinery; machinist.

Mach·a·bees (măk′ə-bēz′). In the Douay Bible, **Maccabees** *(see).*

mach·air (măKH′ər) *n.* **1.** A whitish, almost entirely calcareous sand forming undulating lowlands along the coasts of western Scotland and the Hebrides and providing light, arable soils. **2.** A coastal lowland formed from machair. [Gaelic *machair(e).*]

ma·chet·e (mə-shĕt′ē, -chĕt′ē) *n.* Also **match·et** (măch′ĭt). A large, heavy knife with a broad blade, used for cutting vegetation and as a weapon. [American Spanish, from Spanish, diminutive of *macho,* ax, club, hammer, from Late Latin *marcus*†, hammer.]

Mach·i·a·vel·li (măk′ē-ə-vĕl′ē), **Niccolò** (1469–1527). Italian statesman and writer. As a diplomat and statesman, he served the Florentine Republic (1498–1512). His book, *The Prince* (1513), describes the achievement and maintenance of power by a determined ruler indifferent to moral considerations.

Mach·i·a·vel·li·an (măk′ē-ə-vĕl′ē-ən, -vĕl′yən) *adj.* **1.** Of or pertaining to Niccolò Machiavelli. **2.** Of or pertaining to Machiavellianism. **3.** Suggestive of or characterized by the principles of expediency, deceit, and cunning attributed to Machiavelli; devious.
~*n.* One who believes in or practices Machiavellianism.

Mach·i·a·vel·li·an·ism (măk′ē-ə-vĕl′ē-ə-nĭz′əm) *n.* Also **Mach·i·a·vel·lism** (-vĕl′ĭz′m). The political doctrine of Machiavelli, which denies the relevance of morality in political affairs and holds that craft and deceit are justified in pursuing and maintaining political power; political opportunism.

ma·chic·o·late (mə-chĭk′ə-lāt′) *tr.v.* **-lated, -lating, -lates.** To build or furnish with machicolations. [Old French *machicoler,* from Medieval Latin *machicollāre,* from Provençal *machacol* : *macar,* to crush + *col,* neck, from Latin *collum.*] **—ma·chic·o·la·ted** *adj.*

ma·chic·o·la·tion (mə-chĭk′ə-lā′shən) *n.* **1. a.** A projecting gallery at the top of a castle wall or above an entrance, supported by a row of corbeled arches, having openings in the floor through which stones and boiling liquids could be dropped on attackers. **b.** Any of these openings. **c.** Any of these corbeled arches. **2.** A row of small corbeled arches used as an ornamental architectural feature.

mach·i·nate (măk′ə-nāt′, măsh′-) *v.* **-nated, -nating, -nates.** —*tr.* To devise (a plot). —*intr.* To plot. [Latin *māchinārī,* from *māchina,* contrivance, MACHINE.] **—mach·i·na·tor** *n.*

mach·i·na·tion (măk′ə-nā′shən, măsh′-) *n.* **1.** The act of plotting. **2.** *Often* **machinations.** A crafty plot or cunning action that is usually intended to achieve an evil purpose.

ma·chine (mə-shēn′) *n. Abbr.* **mach. 1. a.** A system or device formed and connected to alter, transmit, and direct applied forces in a predetermined manner to accomplish a specific objective, such as the performance of useful work. **b.** Any of a number of simple devices, such as the lever, the pulley, the wedge, the screw, or the inclined plane, that alter the magnitude or direction, or both, of an applied force. In this sense, also called "simple machine." **2.** A machine such as an automobile, an aircraft, or a jackhammer together with its power source and auxiliary equipment. **3. a.** A system or device, such as an electronic computer, that performs or assists in the performance of a human task. **b.** An automated device such as a slot machine. **4. a.** An intricate natural system or organism, such as the human body. **b.** A functional unit of such a system, as the heart or kidney. **5.** A person who acts in a rigid, mechanical, or unfeeling manner. **6. a.** A complex system, organization, or agency of people that functions in what appears to be an inexorable manner: *the military machine; a propaganda machine.* **b.** An organized group of persons whose members are under the control of one or more political leaders: *the party machine.* **7.** A **deus ex machina** *(see).*
~*v.* **machined, -chining, -chines.** —*tr.* To cut, shape, or finish by machine. —*intr.* To be cut, shaped, or finished by machine. [French, from Old French, from Latin *māchina,* engine, contrivance, from Doric Greek *makhana,* from *makhos,* contrivance, means.] **—ma·chin·a·ble** *adj.*

machine bolt *n.* A bolt with a square or hexagonal head.

machine code *n.* Machine language.

machine finish *n.* A finish on paper surfaces, **mill finish** *(see).*

machine gun *n.* An automatic gun that fires rapidly and repeatedly. **—machine gunner** *n.*

ma·chine-gun (mə-shēn′gŭn′) *tr.v.* **-gunned, -gunning, -guns.** To fire at or kill with a machine gun.
~*adj.* Fast and staccato.

machine language *n.* Any of various systems of symbols used to code information that is to be fed into a computer. Also called "machine code."

ma·chine-read·a·ble (mə-shēn′rē′də-bəl) *adj.* Capable of being fed directly into a computer. Said of data stored magnetically or on punched cards or punched tape.

ma·chin·er·y (mə-shē′nə-rē, -shēn′rē) *n., pl.* **-ies.** *Abbr.* **mach. 1.** Machines or machine parts collectively. **2.** The working parts of a particular machine. **3. a.** An organized, highly interdependent system that often exerts power: *bureaucratic machinery; the machinery of government.* **b.** A system of related elements that operates in a definable manner: *"Many languages are burdened with unnecessary machinery, such as grammatical gender"* (E.H. Sturtevant). **4.** A

machine gun

"THE DEVIL'S SPRINKLER"
How sustained firing comes from "waste" energy

A machine gun will fire a continuous stream of bullets as long as the trigger is pressed and ammunition fed in by belt or magazine. The automatic mechanism for cartridge ejection and reloading is powered by the gun's "waste" energy—the force of the recoil or the gas generated by the explosion of the cartridge. Because of its deadly firepower, the weapon became known as "The Devil's Sprinkler."

The earliest machine guns had multiple barrels; the first practical one was the hand-cranked Gatling gun invented by an American, Richard Gatling, in 1862 but it had to be mounted on a field carriage. The first automatic machine gun was the recoil-operated Maxim gun produced in 1884 by another American, Hiram Maxim (who was later knighted in Britain). It

was single-barreled and weighed about 27 kilograms (60 pounds). The British Army used it in the Sudan in 1896, and it was used throughout World War I by both sides. Development trends were toward lighter weapons, and the gas-operated Lewis light machine gun, with a weight of about 12 kilograms (26 pounds), was also extensively used beginning in 1915.

The Bren gun (the name comes from *Br*no, Czechoslovakia, where the gun was developed, and *En*field, where it was made in England) was the standard British light machine gun of World War II. A shoulder weapon weighing 9.5 kilograms (21 pounds), the Bren could fire 500 rounds per minute. The BAR (Browning Automatic Rifle) was a similar U.S. weapon, developed from designs patented by John M. Browning

early in the century. Browning is perhaps better known for the heavier machine guns that bear his name. The .30-caliber and especially the .50-caliber Brownings proved ideal for use in aircraft and in armored vehicles.

Lighter but less powerful were the submachine guns, fired from hip or shoulder. Best known were the British Sten gun and the U.S. Thompson (Tommy), the latter invented in the 1920's by J.T. Thompson, a retired U.S. ordnance officer.

After World War II fully automatic rifles increasingly became standard-issue combat weapons. Chief among them were the U.S. M-16 and the Soviet AK-47. The lightweight Israeli Uzi submachine gun was also widely used.

GATLING *The Gatling gun, invented in 1862 and adopted by the U.S. Army in 1866, had up to ten barrels around a central axis cranked by hand. Each barrel was mechanically loaded from a cartridge box at the top of its circuit, and fired when it reached the bottom.*

MAXIM *Hiram Maxim, above, observes as the Prince of Wales (England's future King Edward VII) test-fires one of his machine guns. Although born in the United States, Maxim moved to England in the 1880's and it was there that he invented the revolutionary weapon bearing his name. He became a British citizen in 1900 and received a knighthood the following year.*

AT THE FRONT *By the time of World War I the Maxim gun, capable of firing up to 600 rounds per minute of .303 caliber ammunition, was used by armies on both sides of the conflict. Above, a tripod-mounted model is operated by an American unit in the Argonne forest in October 1918.*

generally unsubtle device in literature, as the introduction of a new character or an unlikely event, for bringing about a calculated effect such as a happy ending. See **deus ex machina.**

machine screw *n.* A screw with a thread along the whole length of its shank.

machine shop *n.* A workshop where power-driven tools are used for making, finishing, or repairing machines or machine parts.

machine tool *n.* A power-driven tool for machining, as a lathe or milling machine.

machine translation *n.* Automatic translation, as by computer, from one language to another.

ma·chine-wash (mə-shēn′wŏsh′, -wôsh′) *v.* **-washed, -washing, -washes.** *—tr.* To wash (clothing, for example) in a washing machine. *—intr.* To undergo washing in a washing machine. **—ma·chine-wash·a·ble** *adj.*

ma·chin·ist (mə-shē′nĭst) *n. Abbr.* **mach. 1.** One who makes, operates, or repairs machines. **2.** One skilled in operating machine tools. **3.** A warrant officer who assists the engineering officer in the machine room of a naval vessel. **4.** *Archaic.* A person in charge of stage machinery.

ma·chis·mo (mä-chēz′mō, -kēz′mō, -kĭz′mō, -chĭz′mō, mə-) *n.* An exaggerated sense of masculinity stressing such attributes as physical courage, virility, domination of women, and aggressiveness or violence. [Spanish : MACHO + *-ismo,* -ISM.]

Mach·me·ter (mäk′mē′tər) *n.* An aircraft instrument that indicates speed in Mach numbers.

Mach number *n. Abbr.* **M** The ratio of the speed of an object to the speed of sound in the surrounding medium. For example, an aircraft moving twice as fast as sound is said to be traveling at Mach 2. [After Ernst MACH.]

ma·cho (mä′chō′) *adj.* Characterized by machismo; exaggeratedly masculine. *—n., pl.* **machos. 1.** Machismo. **2.** A macho man. [Spanish, male, virile, from Latin *masculus,* MALE.]

ma·chree (mə-krē′) *n. Irish.* My dear. Used as a term of endearment. [Irish *mo chroidhe,* "my heart."]

Mach's principle *n. Physics.* The principle that inertia is not an intrinsic property of a body but results from the presence of other matter in the universe. [After Ernst MACH.]

Ma·chu Pic·chu (mä′chōō pēk′chōō). Inca city northwest of Cuzco, Peru. Built on a mountain overlooking the Urubamba River, it lay forgotten after the Spanish conquest in the 16th century until it was discovered almost intact in 1911.

mach·zor, mah·zor (mäKH-zôr′, mäKH′zər) *n., pl.* **machzorim, mahzorim** (mäKH′zô-rēm′) or **-zors.** A Jewish prayer book containing rituals prescribed for holidays and festivals. Compare **siddur.** [Hebrew, "cycle."]

macintosh. Variant of **mackintosh.**

mack¹. Variant of **mac** (mackintosh).

mack² (măk) *n. Slang.* A procurer of clients for a prostitute; pimp. [Shortening of *mackerel,* from Old French *maquerel,* from Middle Dutch *makelaer,* broker.]

Mack (măk), **Connie** (1862–1956). U.S. baseball player and manager. As manager and part owner of the Philadelphia Athletics (1901–51) in the newly formed American League, he used his patient and respectful managing style to lead his team to nine pennants and five world championships between 1902 and 1930.

Mack·ay (măk′ē), **Clarence Hungerford** (1874–1938). U.S. businessman. As head of the Commercial Cable-Postal Telegraph empire, inherited from his father, he completed the first transpacific cable (1903). He was also a generous patron of the arts.

Mac·ken·zie¹ (mə-kĕn′zē). District in Canada's Northwest Territories. It is rich in gold, oil, zinc, and uranium, and is peopled mainly by Eskimos and North American Indians. Yellowknife is the capital.

Mackenzie². River in Northwest Territories, Canada. It flows from Great Slave Lake to the Arctic Ocean and is navigable from June to October. The Finlay-Peace-Mackenzie system is Canada's longest river (4,212 kilometers; 2,635 miles).

Mackenzie, Sir Alexander¹ (1764–1820). Canadian fur trader and explorer, born in Scotland. He charted the Mackenzie River (1789) and was the first man to cross the North American continent north of Mexico.

Mackenzie, Alexander² (1822–92). First Liberal prime minister (1873–78) of Canada. He left Scotland to settle in Canada in 1842 and was elected to the Canada assembly in 1861.

mack·er·el (măk′ər-əl, măk′rəl) *n., pl.* **-els** or collectively **mackerel.** 1. Any of several marine fishes of the family Scombridae, found worldwide. Some species are important food fishes, especially the Atlantic mackerel, *Scomber scombrus,* which has dark, wavy bars on the back and a silvery belly. 2. Any of the smaller fishes of the suborder Scombroidea, such as the **Spanish mackerel** *(see).* 3. Any of various fishes resembling mackerel. [Middle English *makerel,* from Norman French, from Old French *maquerel†.*]

mackerel shark *n.* The **porbeagle** *(see).*

mackerel sky *n.* A striped formation of high, white cirrocumulus or altocumulus clouds suggesting the bars on a mackerel's back.

Mack·i·nac (măk′ĭ-nô′). Island of Michigan, on the Lake Huron side of the Straits of Mackinac, a channel between Michigan's Upper and Lower peninsulas. The area was long an important Indian gathering place. Today the straits are a crucial link in the Great Lakes–St. Lawrence waterway.

mack·i·naw (măk′ə-nô′) *n.* 1. A short, double-breasted coat of heavy, usually plaid woolen material. 2. The cloth from which a mackinaw coat is made, usually of wool, often with a heavy nap. 3. A flat-bottomed boat with a pointed bow and a square stern that was formerly used on the upper Great Lakes. [After MACKINAC Island.]

Mackinaw blanket *n.* A thick blanket in solid colors or stripes that was formerly used in northern and western North America by Indian, traders, and trappers.

Mackinaw trout *n.* The **lake trout** *(see).*

mack·in·tosh, mac·in·tosh (măk′ĭn-tŏsh′) *n. Chiefly British.* 1. A raincoat, especially one made of a patented rubberized cotton. Also informally called "mac," "mack." 2. A lightweight waterproof fabric used to make mackintoshes. [After Charles *Macintosh* (1766–1843), Scottish chemist.]

mack·le (măk′əl) *n.* Also **mac·ule** (măk′yōol). *Printing.* A spot, especially a blurred or double impression caused by a slipping of the type or a wrinkle in the paper.
~*v.* **mackled, -ling, -les.** Also **mac·ule, -uled, -uling, -ules.** —*tr.* To blur or double (a printed impression). —*intr.* To become blurred. [French *macule,* from Latin *macula,* spot.]

Mac·lau·rin series (mə-klôr′ĭn) *n. Mathematics.* An infinite series by which a function can be expressed in terms of the values of its derivatives when the independent variable is zero. It has the form $f(x) = f(0) + f'(0)/1! + f''(0)/2! + f'''(0)/3! + \ldots$. [After Colin *Maclaurin* (1698–1746), Scottish doctor and mathematician.]

mac·le (măk′əl) *n.* 1. A mineral, **chiastolite** *(see).* 2. A crystalline form, **twin** *(see).* 3. A spot or discoloration in a mineral. [French, double crystal, from Old French *macle,* heraldic term for a voided lozenge (one diamond shape within another), originally a stylized mesh of a net, from Latin *macula,* mesh, hole in a net, spot.]

Mac·leish (mə-klēsh′), **Archibald** (1892–1982). U.S. poet and playwright. He was Librarian of Congress (1939–44). His works include *Streets in the Moon* (1926), and he won Pulitzer Prizes for *Conquistador* (1932), *Collected Poems 1917–52* (1952), and *J.B.* (1958).

Mac·Mil·lan (mək-mĭl′ən), **(Maurice) Harold** (1894–). British prime minister (1957–63). He became an M.P. in 1924, and during the 1930's he backed Churchill in condemning British appeasement of Hitler. From 1955 to 1957 he was Chancellor of the Exchequer.

MacMillan, Kenneth (1929–). British choreographer. Beginning as a ballet dancer, he turned to choreography in 1953, directing the Royal Ballet, Covent Garden (1970–77), and becoming its principal choreographer (1977). His many creations include *Romeo and Juliet, Song of the Earth, Manon,* and *Isadora.*

Mac·Neice (mək-nēs′), **(Frederick) Louis** (1907–63). British poet and playwright, born in Northern Ireland. He wrote satirical poetry in colloquial style in a literary group with Christopher Isherwood, Cecil Day Lewis, and W.H. Auden. His works include *Blind Fire-works* (1929), *Autumn Journal* (1939), *Holes in the Sky* (1948), and *The Strings are False* (published 1965).

Ma·con (mā′kən), **Nathaniel** (1758–1837). U.S. legislator. Although he opposed ratification of the U.S. Constitution, he served as congressman from North Carolina (1791–1815), Speaker of the House (1801–07), and senator (1815–28). His reactionary views reflected his fear of an expansive federal government and his aversion to government spending.

Mâ·con¹ (mä-kôN′). French town, capital of Saône-et-Loire department, on the Saône River. It is noted for its fine Burgundy wines.

Mâ·con² (mä-kôN′) *n.* A red or white Burgundy wine produced in the area around Mâcon, France. [After MÂCON.]

Mac·pher·son (mək-fûr′sən), **James** (1736–96). Scottish poet. He claimed to have translated the works of Ossian, a 3rd-century Gaelic poet and warrior. Although the authenticity of the original works was contested, Macpherson's translations, published between 1760 and 1763, widely influenced writers of the period.

Mac·quar·ie (mə-kwôr′ē). River of New South Wales, Australia, flowing 950 kilometers (590 miles) from the Blue Mts. to the Darling River.

macr–. Variant of **macro-.**

mac·ra·mé (măk′rə-mā′) *n.* 1. Coarse ornamental lacework made by weaving and knotting cords, especially string, into a pattern. 2. The art of weaving and knotting cords into a pattern. 3. Cord, as string, to be used or suitable for use in macramé. [French, from Italian *macramè,* from Turkish *makrama,* napkin, towel, from Arabic *miqramah,* striped cloth.]

mac·ren·ceph·a·ly (măk′rĕn-sĕf′ə-lē) *n.* Also **mac·ren·ce·pha·li·a** (-sə-fā′lē-ə, -fāl′yə). *Pathology.* Abnormal enlargement of the brain. [MACR(O)- + ENCEPHAL(O)- + -Y.]

mac·ro (măk′rō′) *n., pl.* **-ros.** *Computer Science.* An instruction in assembly language that is implemented by a sequence of instructions in machine language. [Short for MACROINSTRUCTION.]

macro–, macr– *prefix.* Indicates: 1. Largeness in extent, duration, or size; for example, **macrocosm.** 2. Abnormal largeness or overdevelopment, especially in a particular part; for example, **macrencephaly.** Compare **micro-.** [Greek *makros,* large, long.]

mac·ro·bi·o·sis (măk′rō-bī-ō′sĭs) *n.* Longevity. [Late Greek *makrobiōsis* : MACRO- + -BIOSIS.]

mac·ro·bi·o·ta (măk′rō-bī-ō′tə) *n.* The macroscopic plant and animal life of a particular region. [New Latin : MACRO- + Greek *biotos,* life.]

mac·ro·bi·ot·ics (măk′rō-bī-ŏt′ĭks) *n. Used with a singular verb.* 1. The theory or practice of promoting longevity. 2. A method that purports to promote longevity, principally by means of a diet consisting chiefly of unprocessed cereals and vegetables grown without chemical additives. [Greek *makrobiotos,* long-lived : MACRO- + *biotos,* life + -ICS.] —**mac·ro·bi·ot·ic** (măk′rō-bī-ŏt′ĭk) *adj.*

mac·ro·ceph·a·ly (măk′rō-sĕf′ə-lē) *n.* Also **mac·ro·ce·pha·li·a** (-sə-fā′lē-ə, -fāl′yə). *Pathology.* Abnormally large cranial capacity, often observed in the mentally handicapped. Also called "megacephaly," "megalocephaly." [French *macrocéphalie,* from *macrocéphale,* having a long head, from Greek *makrokephalos* : MACRO- + -CEPHALOUS.] —**mac·ro·ce·phal·ic** (măk′rō-sə-fāl′ĭk), **mac·ro·ceph·a·lous** (-sĕf′ə-ləs) *adj.*

mac·ro·chem·is·try (măk′rō-kĕm′ĭ-strē) *n.* Chemistry requiring neither microscopy nor microanalysis. Compare **microchemistry.** —**mac·ro·chem·i·cal** (măk′rō-kĕm′ĭ-kəl) *adj.*

mac·ro·cli·mate (măk′rō-klī′mĭt) *n. Meteorology.* The climate of a large geographic area. Compare **microclimate.** —**mac·ro·cli·mat·ic** (măk′rō-klī-măt′ĭk) *adj.*

mac·ro·code (măk′rə-kōd′) *n.* 1. A coding system that assembles sets of computer instructions. 2. A single code representing a set of computer instructions.

ma·cro·con·sum·er (măk′rō-kən-sōō′mər) *n.* An organism in an ecological community that feeds on other organisms or organic matter.

mac·ro·cosm (măk′rə-kŏz′əm) *n.* 1. a. The entire world; universe. b. The concept of universe. 2. A system reflecting on a large scale one component of its subsystems or parts. Compare **microcosm.** [French *macrocosme,* from Medieval Latin *macrocosmus,* from Late Greek *makros kosmos,* the great world : MACRO- + *kosmos,* world.] —**mac·ro·cos·mic** (măk′rə-kŏz′mĭk) *adj.* —**mac·ro·cos·mi·cal·ly** *adv.*

mac·ro·cyte (măk′rō-sīt′) *n. Pathology.* An abnormally large red blood cell associated with some forms of anemia. [MACRO- + (ERYTHRO)CYTE.] —**mac·ro·cyt·ic** (măk′rō-sĭt′ĭk) *adj.*

mac·ro·cy·to·sis (măk′rō-sī-tō′sĭs) *n. Pathology.* A condition in which the blood contains macrocytes. —**mac·ro·cy·tot·ic** (măk′rō-sī-tŏt′ĭk) *adj.*

mac·ro·ec·o·nom·ics (măk′rō-ĕk′ə-nŏm′ĭks, -ē′kə-nŏm′ĭks) *n. Used with a singular verb.* The study of the economics of large-scale systems; especially, the study of the overall aspects and workings of a national economy, including income, output, and the interrelationship among diverse economic sectors. Compare **microeconomics.** —**mac·ro·ec·o·nom·ic** *adj.*

mac·ro·ev·o·lu·tion (măk′rō-ĕv′ə-lōō′shən, -ē′və-lōō′shən) *n.* Evolution involving whole species or large groups of organisms. —**mac·ro·ev·o·lu·tion·ar·y** *adj.*

mac·ro·ga·mete (măk′rō-gə-mēt′, -găm′ēt′) *n. Biology.* The larger of two conjugating cells, usually female, in protozoans. Also called "megagamete." Compare **microgamete.**

mac·ro·glob·u·lin (măk′rō-glŏb′yə-lĭn) *n.* A plasma globulin that has an unusually large molecular weight.

mac·ro·glob·u·lin·e·mi·a (măk′rō-glŏb′yə-lə-nē′mē-ə) *n.* The presence in the blood of an abnormal form of macroglobulin.

mac·ro·graph (măk′rə-grăf′, -gräf′) *n.* A representation of an object that is at least as large as the object. [MACRO- + -GRAPH.]

ma·crog·ra·phy (mə-krŏg′rə-fē) *n.* **1.** Examination of objects with the unaided eye. Compare **micrography. 2.** Abnormally large handwriting, sometimes indicating a nervous disorder. [MACRO- + -GRAPHY.] **—mac·ro·graph·ic** (măk′rə-grăf′ĭk) *adj.*

mac·ro·in·struc·tion (măk′rō-ĭn-strŭk′shən) *n.* A macro.

mac·ro·mol·e·cule (măk′rō-mŏl′ə-kyōōl′) *n.* **1.** A very large molecule, especially in a natural or synthetic polymer, such as a protein or synthetic resin. **2.** A covalent or ionic crystal, such as diamond or salt, in which individual atoms or molecules cannot be distinguished. **—mac·ro·mo·lec·u·lar** (măk′rō-mə-lĕk′yə-lər) *adj.*

ma·cron (mā′krŏn′, -krən, măk′rŏn′, -rən) *n.* **1.** A diacritical mark placed above a vowel to indicate that it has a long sound, as the (ō) in the word *pole.* Compare **breve. 2.** A horizontal mark (—) used to indicate a stressed or long syllable in a foot of verse. [Greek *makron,* neuter of *makros,* long.]

mac·ro·nu·cle·us (măk′rō-nōō′klē-əs, -nyōō′klē-əs) *n., pl.* **-clei** (-klē-ī′). The larger of the two nuclei in ciliate protozoans, which is involved in the nonreproductive functions of the cell. Compare **micronucleus.**

mac·ro·nu·tri·ent (măk′rō-nōō′trē-ənt, -nyōō′trē-ənt) *n.* An element, such as carbon, hydrogen, oxygen, or nitrogen, required in relatively large proportion for growth and development.

mac·ro·phage (măk′rə-fāj′) *n.* A large phagocytic cell present in connective tissue, bone marrow, lymph nodes, and the like. [MACRO- + -PHAGE.] **—mac·ro·phag·ic** (măk′rə-fāj′ĭk) *adj.*

mac·ro·phys·ics (măk′rō-fĭz′ĭks) *n. Used with a singular verb.* The physics of macroscopic phenomena.

ma·crop·ter·ous (mə-krŏp′tər-əs) *adj. Zoology.* Having unusually large wings. [Greek *makropteros* : MACRO- + -PTEROUS.]

mac·ro·scop·ic (măk′rə-skŏp′ĭk) *adj.* Also **mac·ro·scop·i·cal** (-ĭ-kəl). **1.** Large enough to be perceived or examined without instruments, especially by the unaided eye. **2.** Pertaining to observations made without magnifying instruments, especially by the unaided eye; megascopic. **3.** *Physics.* Of or pertaining to systems or properties that depend on large numbers of atoms rather than individual atoms or molecules. **4.** Of, pertaining to, or concerned with large units or wide issues; large-scale. [MACRO- + -SCOP(Y) + -IC.] **—mac·ro·scop·i·cal·ly** *adv.*

mac·ro·spo·ran·gi·um (măk′rō-spə-răn′jē-əm) *n., pl.* **-gia** (-jē-ə). *Botany.* A **megasporangium** (see).

mac·ro·spore (măk′rə-spôr′, -spōr′) *n. Botany.* A **megaspore** (see).

mac·u·la (măk′yə-lə) *n., pl.* **-lae** (-lē′). Also **mac·ule** (măk′yōōl) (for sense 2). **1.** A spot, stain, blemish, or pit; especially, a discoloration of the skin caused by excess or lack of pigment. **2.** *Anatomy.* A small area distinguishable from surrounding tissue, as the macula lutea. **3.** A sunspot. [Latin *macula,* spot, blemish.] **—mac·u·lar** *adj.*

macula lu·te·a (lōō′tē-ə) *n., pl.* **maculae luteae** (lōō′tē-ē′). *Anatomy.* An area in the eye near the center of the retina at which visual perception is most acute. [New Latin, "yellow spot."]

mac·u·late (măk′yə-lāt′) *tr.v.* **-lated, -lating, -lates.** To spot, blemish, or pollute.
~adj. (-lĭt). **1.** Spotted or blotched. **2.** Stained; impure. [Middle English *maculaten,* to stain, from Latin *maculāre,* from *macula,* spot, blemish.]

mac·u·la·tion (măk′yə-lā′shən) *n.* **1.** The act of spotting or staining. **2.** A spotted or stained condition. **3.** The spotted markings of a plant or animal, as the spots of the leopard.

mac·ule (măk′yōōl) *v.* **-uled, -uling, -ules.** Variant of **mackle.**
~n. **1.** *Printing.* Variant of **mackle. 2.** *Anatomy.* Variant of **macula.** [Middle English, from Old French, from Latin *macula,* spot, blemish.]

mad (măd) *adj.* **madder, maddest. 1.** Suffering from a disorder of the mind; insane. **2.** Temporarily or apparently deranged by violent sensations, emotions, or ideas: *mad with pain; mad with love.* **3.** *Informal.* Feeling or showing strong liking or enthusiasm: *mad about golf.* Sometimes used in combination: *golf-mad.* **4.** *Informal.* Angry; resentful. **5.** Lacking restraint or reason; foolish: *I'd have to be mad to go back to that restaurant.* **6.** Marked by extreme excitement, confusion, or agitation; frantic: *a mad scramble to catch the bus.* **7.** Boisterously gay; hilarious: *had a mad time.* **8.** Affected by rabies; rabid. **—have a mad on.** To be angry and sulk. **—like mad.** *Slang.* Wildly; impetuously: *He drove like mad.*
~v. **madded, madding, mads.** *Archaic.* **—tr.** To make mad; madden. **—intr.** To act, be, or become mad. [Middle English *madd,* Old English *gemǣdd,* past participle of *gemǣdan,* to madden, from *gemǣd,* mad.]

Mad. Madagascar.

Mad·a·gas·car (măd′ə-găs′kər). Formerly **Mal·a·gas·y Republic** (măl′ə-găs′ē). Island republic off southeastern Africa. Its coastal plains in the east and west rise to a central plateau. Rice growing and livestock rearing are the main occupations, and exports include chrome ore, coffee, vanilla, cloves, and meat. Made a French colony in 1896, it was granted self-rule as the Malagasy Republic in 1958 and full independence in 1960. It became a democratic republic in 1975. The island separated from Africa 150 million years ago and is noted for its unique wildlife. Area, 587,041 square kilometers

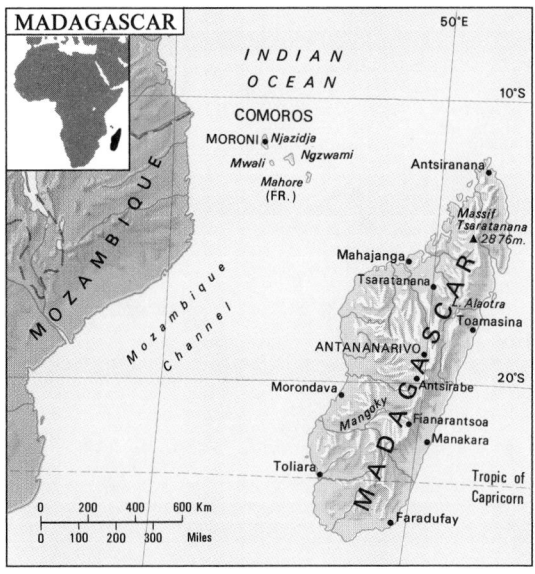

(226,658 square miles). Population, 8,700,000. Capital, Antananarivo. **—Mad·a·gas·can** *n. & adj.*

Madagascar periwinkle *n.* A plant, *Catharanthus roseus* (or *Vinca rosea*), native to Madagascar, that has pink or white flowers and is a source of various alkaloids used in treating cancer.

mad·am (măd′əm) *n., pl.* **mesdames** (mā-däm′, -dăm′) (for sense 1) or **madams** (for senses 2 and 3). **1. a.** A title of courtesy used in addressing a woman. **b.** A conventional form of address used instead of a woman's name at the opening of a letter. **c.** A respectful form of address formerly used before a woman's given name but now used only before a surname or a title indicating rank or office: *Madam Ambassador.* **2.** The mistress of a household. **3.** A woman who manages a brothel. [Middle English, from MADAME.]

Ma·dame (mə-dăm′, măd′əm) *n., pl.* **Mesdames** (mā-däm′, -dăm′). *Abbr.* **Mme. 1.** The French title of courtesy for a married woman, equivalent to the English *Mrs.*; sometimes used of older unmarried women. **2.** A title of courtesy prefixed to the surname of certain foreign women, especially heads of state or the wives of heads of state and performing artists, as in the opera or ballet. [Middle English, from Old French *ma dame,* my lady.]

mad·cap (măd′kăp′) *n.* A rash or impulsive person.
~adj. Rash; impulsive; wild. [MAD + CAP (head).]

mad·den (măd′n) *v.* **-dened, -dening, -dens. —tr. 1.** To make mad; drive insane. **2.** To make angry; excite or irritate. **—intr.** To become infuriated.

mad·den·ing (măd′n-ĭng) *adj.* **1.** Tending to drive mad. **2.** Tending to anger or irritate; infuriating: *a maddening delay before the plane took off.* **—mad·den·ing·ly** *adv.*

mad·der¹ (măd′ər) *n.* **1. a.** Any of various plants of the genus *Rubia*; especially, a Eurasian species, *R. tinctoria,* having small, yellow flowers and a red, fleshy root. **b.** The root of this plant, formerly an important source of dye. **2.** A red dye obtained from the madder root. **3.** A medium to strong red or reddish orange. [Middle English *mader,* Old English *mædere.*]

madder². Comparative of **mad.**

mad·ding (măd′ĭng) *adj. Archaic.* Acting as if mad; frenzied.

mad·dish (măd′ĭsh) *adj.* Somewhat mad.

mad-dog skullcap (măd′dôg′, -dŏg′) *n.* A North American plant, *Scutellaria lateriflora,* having one-sided clusters of two-lipped blue or white flowers.

made (mād). The past tense and past participle of **make.**
~adj. **1.** Produced or manufactured by constructing, shaping, or forming. Used in combination: *handmade chocolate.* **2.** Produced or created artificially; not found naturally. **3.** Invented; contrived. **4.** Assured of success or fortune: *a made man.* **—have it made.** *Informal.* To be assured of success. **—made for.** Perfectly suited for: *made for each other.*

Ma·dei·ra¹ (mə-dîr′ə, -dâr′ə) *n.* **1.** A fortified white dessert wine from the island of Madeira. **2.** A wine similar to Madeira but made elsewhere.

Madeira². River in Brazil, the most important tributary of the Amazon. It forms on the Bolivian border and flows 3,315 kilometers (2,060 miles) to the Amazon below Manáus.

Madeira Islands. Archipelago off northwestern Africa, forming the Funchal overseas district of Portugal. Only two of the volcanic islands are inhabited, Madeira, the larger, and Port Santo. The main industries are tourism, fishing, agriculture, and the production of Madeira wine. See map at **Atlantic Ocean. —Ma·dei·ran** (mə-dîr′ən, -dâr′ən) *adj. & n.*

mad·e·leine (măd′l-ən, măd′l-ĕn′) *n.* A small, rich cake baked in a shell-shaped mold. [French, perhaps after *Madeleine* Paulmier, 19th-century French pastry cook.]

mad·e·moi·selle (măd′ə-mə-zĕl′, măd′əm-wə-) *n., pl.* **mad·e·moi·selles** (-zĕlz′) or **mesdemoiselles** (mā′də-mə-zĕl′, mād′mwä-zĕl′). *Abbr.* **Mlle. 1.** The French title of courtesy for a young girl or an unmarried woman, equivalent to the English *Miss.* It may be used separately or prefixed to either a first or last name. **2.** A French governess or teacher. [French, from Old French *ma demoiselle : ma*, my, from Latin *mea + demoiselle*, young lady, from Gallo-Roman *dom(i)nicella* (unattested), diminutive of Latin *domina*, lady, feminine of *dominus*, lord.]

made-to-meas·ure (măd′tə-mĕzh′ər) *adj.* **1.** Made to fit particular measurements, as of a person. **2.** Made-to-order.

made-to-or·der (măd′tōō-ôr′dər) *adj.* **1.** Made in accordance with particular instructions to fill the requirements of a customer. Compare **ready-made. 2.** Highly appropriate; just right.

made-up (măd′ŭp′) *adj.* **1.** Fabricated; fictitious; imaginary; invented: *a made-up story.* **2.** Wearing cosmetics or make-up: *a made-up actress.* **3. a.** Complete; finished: *a made-up package.* **b.** Put together; assembled; arranged: *a made-up page of type.*

mad·house (măd′hous′) *n.* **1.** An asylum for the mentally ill. **2.** A place of confusion or great disorder.

Mad·i·son (măd′ĭ-sən). Capital of Wisconsin, in the south-central part of the state. It is a trading and manufacturing center in a fertile agricultural region. The main campus of the University of Wisconsin is here.

Madison, Dolley Payne Todd (1768–1849). U.S. hostess and first lady. The genial White House hostess (1801–17) during the presidency of the widowed Thomas Jefferson and the two terms of her husband James Madison, she heroically carried important government papers and a portrait of George Washington to safety during the British invasion of Washington (1814).

Madison, James (1751–1836). Fourth president of the United States (1809–17). As a member of the Constitutional Convention (1787) he helped frame that document and the Bill of Rights. The War of 1812 was fought during his administration.

Madison Avenue *n.* **1.** A street in Manhattan, New York City, the center of the American advertising business. **2.** The principles, attitudes, ideas, and methods of advertising and mass communications. Often used derogatorily.

mad·ly (măd′lē) *adv.* **1.** Insanely. **2.** Wildly; furiously; frantically. **3.** Foolishly; rashly. **4.** *Informal.* To an extreme or excessive degree; very much: *madly in love.*

mad·man (măd′măn′, -mən) *n., pl.* **-men** (-mĕn′, -mĭn). A man who is or seems to be mentally ill: *drives like a madman.*

mad money *n. Slang.* **1.** Carfare carried by a girl on a date to pay her way home in the event of a quarrel with her escort. **2.** A small sum of money kept by a woman for unlikely contingencies.

mad·ness (măd′nĭs) *n.* **1.** Insanity. **2.** Great folly. **3.** Fury; rage. **4.** Wild enthusiasm; excitement. —See Synonyms at **insanity.**

ma·don·na (mə-dŏn′ə) *n.* **1.** Madonna. **a.** The Virgin Mary. **b.** An artistic representation of the Virgin Mary. **2.** A woman having qualities of purity, serenity, gentleness, or steadfast love that suggest the Madonna. **3.** *Obsolete.* A married woman in Italy. [Italian : *ma*, my, from Latin *mea + donna*, lady, from Latin *domina*, feminine of *dominus*, lord.]

Madonna lily *n.* A plant, *Lilium candidum*, native to Eurasia and widely cultivated for its white, trumpet-shaped flowers. Also called "Annunciation lily."

mad·ras (măd′rəs, mə-drăs′, -dräs′) *n.* **1.** A fine cotton cloth, usually with a plaid, striped, or checked pattern. **2.** A light cloth, usually of cotton, used for curtains. **3.** A large kerchief of brightly colored silk or cotton that is often worn as a turban. [Originally produced in MADRAS.]

Ma·dras (mə-drăs′, -dräs′). **1.** Indian seaport and capital of Tamil Nadu state, regarded as the traditional burial place of St. Thomas. It was founded as Fort St. George by the British East India Company in 1639. Its chief manufacturing products are bicycles, cars, cement, textiles, and leather products. **2.** See Tamil Nadu.

mad·re·pore (măd′rə-pôr′, -pōr′) *n.* Any of various corals of the genus *Madrepora*, including the reef builders of tropical seas. [French, from Italian *madrepora*, "mother-stone," referring to the manner in which polyps produce coral : *madre*, mother, from Latin *māter* + Latin *pōrus*, tufa, from Greek *pōros*†.] —**mad·re·por·ic** (măd′rə-pôr′ĭk, -pōr′ĭk) *adj.*

mad·re·por·ite (măd′rə-pôr′īt′, -pōr′īt′) *n.* A sievelike structure that forms the inlet of the water-vascular system in echinoderms. [MADREPOR(E) + -ITE.]

Ma·drid (mə-drĭd′). Capital of Spain and of Madrid province. Built on the Castile plateau overlooking the Manzanares River, it is a cultural, commercial, and industrial center, producing leather, textiles, and chemicals. Begun on the site of a Moorish fortress in the 10th century, it became capital under Philip II in 1561 and was a Republican stronghold during the Spanish Civil War (1936–39). Its fine buildings include the Prado Museum.

mad·ri·gal (măd′rĭ-gəl) *n.* **1.** An unaccompanied vocal composition for two or three voices in simple harmony, following a strict poetic form, developed in Italy in the early 14th century. **2.** A contrapuntal part song, typically unaccompanied and with parts for five or six voices, using a secular text. This form was developed in Italy in the 16th century, and was popular in England in the 16th and early 17th centuries. **3.** A lyric poem with a pastoral, idyllic, or amatory subject, developed from the lyrics of the 14th-century Italian madrigal. **4.** A part song. [Italian *madrigale*, earlier *madriale*, "(piece) without accompaniment," probably from Medieval Latin *mātrīcālis*,

"of the womb," newly sprung from the womb, simple, from *mātrix*, womb, from *māter*, mother.] —**mad·ri·gal·ist** *n.*

ma·dri·lène, ma·dri·lene (măd′rĭ-lĕn′, -län′) *n.* A consommé flavored with tomato, generally served chilled. [French (*consommé*) *madrilène*, from Spanish *madrileño*, of MADRID.]

ma·dro·ña (mə-drō′nyə) *n.* Also **ma·dro·ño** (mə-drō′nyō), **ma·dro·ne** (mə-drō′nə). A tree, *Arbutus Menziesi*, of western North America, having glossy, evergreen leaves, white flowers, and red-orange fruit. [Spanish *madroño*†.]

mad tom *n.* Any of several small freshwater North American catfishes of the genus *Noturus*, common in the east-central United States, having poisonous spines. [MAD + TOM (cat).]

Ma·du·rai (mä′də-rī′). Formerly **Ma·thu·rai** (mä′thə-rī′). City on the Vaigai River in Tamil Nadu state, southern India. Known as the city of festivals and temples, it is a center of Hindu pilgrimage, with the great temple complex of Sundareswara and Meenakshi, which has 1,000 exquisitely carved columns. The city is a cultural, craft, and market center. It was the capital of the Pandya kingdom (5th century B.C. to 11th century A.D.) and part of the Hindu Vijayanagar kingdom (1378 to c. 1550).

Mad·u·rese (măd′yə-rēz′, -rēs′) *n., pl.* **Madurese. 1.** A member of a Malayan people inhabiting the Indonesian island of Madura. **2.** The Austronesian language of the Malayans of Madura and eastern Java. —**Mad·u·rese** *adj.*

ma·du·ro (mə-dōōr′ō) *n., pl.* **-ros.** A strong-flavored cigar with a dark wrapper. [Spanish, MATURE.] —**ma·du·ro** *adj.*

mad·wom·an (măd′wōōm′ən) *n., pl.* **-women** (-wĭm′ĭn). A woman who is or seems to be mentally ill.

mad·wort (măd′wûrt′, -wôrt′) *n.* **1.** A low-growing plant, *Asperugo procumbens*, native to Eurasia, having rough stems and small blue flowers. **2.** Any of several plants of the genus *Alyssum.* [Formerly believed to cure madness.]

Mae·an·der (mē-ăn′dər). Turkish river, flowing c. 400 kilometers (250 miles) from the west of Afyonkarahisar province into the Aegean Sea.

Mae·ce·nas (mĭ-sē′nəs, mī-) *n.* A patron, especially one generous to artists. [After Gaius *Maecenas*, 1st century B.C. Roman statesman, patron of Horace and Virgil.]

mael·strom (māl′strəm) *n.* **1.** A whirlpool of extraordinary size or violence. **2.** A strong eddy in a tidal current in a restricted, irregular channel. **3.** A state of great confusion or turbulence that resembles a whirlpool in violence or power to engulf. [Early Modern Dutch *maelstrom*, "whirlstream" : *malen*, to whirl, grind + *stroom*, stream.]

Mael·strom (māl′strəm). A notoriously dangerous tidewater whirlpool, between the Lofoten Islands off the northwest coast of Norway.

mae·nad (mē′năd′) *n., pl.* **-nads** or **maenades** (mĕn′ə-dēz′). **1.** *Greek Mythology.* A woman member of the orgiastic cult of Dionysus. **2.** A frenzied woman. [Latin *maenas* (stem *maenad*-), from Greek *mainas*, "she who is mad," from *mainesthai*, to be mad.] —**mae·nad·ic** (mē-năd′ĭk) *adj.*

maes·to·so (mī-stō′sō, -zō) *adv. Music.* In a majestic and stately manner. Used as a direction. [Italian, majestic, from *maestà*, majesty, from Latin *mājestās*.] —**maes·to·so** *adj. & n.*

Maestricht. See **Maastricht.**

maes·tro (mī′strō) *n., pl.* **-tros** or **-tri** (-trē). A master in any art, especially a composer, conductor, or teacher of music. Often used as a term of address. [Italian, from Latin *magister*, master.]

Mae·ter·linck (mā′tər-lĭngk′), Count Maurice (1862–1949). Belgian poet and playwright, and a leading member of the symbolist movement. Among his plays were *Pelléas et Mélisande* (1892), on which Debussy based his opera (1902), and *The Blue Bird* (1909). He received the Nobel Prize for literature (1911).

Mae West (mā′ wĕst′) *n.* An inflatable life preserver. [After *Mae* WEST, whose generous figure it was thought to be reminiscent of.]

Ma·fi·a, Maf·fi·a (mä′fē-ə) *n.* **1.** An alleged international criminal organization active, especially in Italy and the United States, since the late 19th century. Compare **Black Hand, Camorra, Cosa Nostra. 2.** A secret terrorist organization in Sicily, operating since the early 19th century in opposition to legal authority. **3.** An organization using terrorist methods to control an activity. **4.** An exclusive group or clique, especially an influential one. [Italian (Sicilian dialect) *mafia*, boldness, "boasting," from Arabic *mahyah*, boasting.]

Maf·i·keng (măf′ə-kĕng′, -kĭng′). Formerly **Maf·e·king** (-kĭng′). A town in the Republic of Bophuthatswana, formerly included in the Cape Province of South Africa. The 217-day siege and relief of the city (October 1899–May 1900) was one of the celebrated events of the Boer War.

Ma·fi·o·so (mä′fē-ō′sō, -zō) *n., pl.* **-si** (-sē, -zē). A member of the Mafia. [Italian.]

mag (măg) *n. Slang.* A magazine.

mag. 1. magazine. **2.** magnetism. **3.** magnitude.

mag·a·zine (măg′ə-zēn′, măg′ə-zēn′) *n. Abbr.* **mag. 1. a.** A place where goods are stored; especially, a building, as in a fort, or storeroom, as on a warship, where ammunition is stored. **b.** The contents of a storehouse, especially a stock of ammunition. **2.** A publication appearing at regular intervals, containing articles, stories, photographs, or other features. **3. a.** A compartment in some types of firearms, often a small, detachable box, in which cartridges are held to be fed into the firing chamber. **b.** A compartment in a camera in which rolls or cartridges of film are held for feeding through the exposure mechanism. **c.** Any of various other compartments attached to machines for storing or supplying necessary material. [Old French *magazin*, storehouse, from Italian *magazzino*, from Arabic *makhāzin*, plural of *makhzan*, storehouse, from *khazana*, to store up.]

mag·da·len (măg′də-lən) *n.* Also **mag·da·lene** (-lēn′). **1.** A reformed prostitute. **2.** A reformatory for prostitutes. [From MARY MAGDALENE.]

Mag·da·le·ni·an (măg′də-lē′ne-ən) *adj. Archaeology.* Of, belonging to, or designating the last upper Paleolithic culture of Europe, characterized by cave art and decorative work in bone and ivory. [French *magdalénien*, from *La Madeleine*, village in Dordogne, France, near which artifacts were found.]

Mag·de·burg (măg′də-bûrg′, măg′də-bŏŏrg′). Capital of Magdeburg district in East Germany, on the Elbe River. It became self-governing (13th century) and was a leader of the Hanseatic League. It is a major river port and rail and canal center and makes steel and metal goods, petroleum products, sugar, textiles, and chemicals.

mage (māj) *n. Archaic.* **1.** A magician. **2.** One of the Magi. [Middle English, from Latin *magus*, sorcerer. See **Magi**.]

Ma·gel·lan (mə-jĕl′ən), **Ferdinand** (c. 1480–1521). Portuguese navigator. He was financed by Charles V of Spain (1519) to find a westward route to the Moluccas. Magellan crossed the Atlantic without charts and was blown by storms into the strait that carries his name (1520). He crossed the ocean, which he named the Pacific, reaching the Marianas and the Philippines, where he was killed fighting for the king of Cebu. One of his ships arrived back in Spain (1522), completing the world's first circumnavigation.

Magellan, Strait of. A passage between the Atlantic and Pacific oceans, between mainland South America and Tierra del Fuego. It is some 530 kilometers (330 miles) long and a maximum of only 24 kilometers (15 miles) wide. Magellan discovered it in 1520.

Mag·el·lan·ic cloud (măj′ə-lăn′ĭk) *n.* Either of two small companion galaxies of the Milky Way, faintly visible near the south celestial pole. They are the *Large Magellanic Cloud* (Nubecula Major) and the *Small Magellanic Cloud* (Nubecula Minor). [After Ferdinand MAGELLAN.]

Ma·gen Da·vid, Mo·gen Da·vid (mô′gən dô′vĭd) *n.* The **Star of David** (see). [Hebrew *māgēn Dāwid*, shield of (King) David.]

ma·gen·ta (mə-jĕn′tə) *n.* **1.** A coal-tar dye, **fuchsin** (see). **2.** A moderate to vivid purplish red or strong reddish purple. See **primary color**. [After *Magenta*, Italy.]

mag·gie (măg′ē) *n. Australian Informal.* A magpie.

Mag·gio·re, Lake (mə-jôr′ē, -jōr′ē). Italy's second-largest lake, on the Swiss border. Lying in the Alpine foothills, it is a tourist area with resorts such as Locarno and Stresa.

mag·got (măg′ət) *n.* **1.** The legless, soft-bodied larva of any of various insects of the order Diptera, especially of the housefly and the bluebottle, usually found in decaying matter or as a parasite. **2.** An extravagant notion; a whim. [Middle English *magot, maked*, earlier *maddock, madhek*, from Old Norse *mathkr*.]

mag·got·y (măg′ə-tē) *adj.* **1.** Infested with maggots. **2.** Full of extravagant notions. **3.** *Australian Informal.* Angry.

Ma·ghreb or **Ma·ghrib** (măg′rəb, mä′grĭb). Region of northwestern Africa comprising the coastlands and Atlas Mts. of Algeria, Morocco, and Tunisia. Its Arabic name means "the western island," the island of land between the Sahara and the Mediterranean.

Ma·gi (mā′jī′) *pl.n. Singular* **Ma·gus** (mā′gəs). **1. magi.** The members of the Zoroastrian priestly caste of the Medes and Persians. **2.** The three wise men from the East, who traveled to Bethlehem to pay homage to the infant Jesus. Matthew 2:1-12. According to St. Augustine their names were Balthazar, Caspar, and Melchior. [Middle English, from Latin, plural of *magus*, sorcerer, from Greek *magos*, from Old Persian *maguš*.] —**Ma·gi·an** (mā′jē-ən) *adj. & n.*

mag·ic (măj′ĭk) *n.* **1.** The art that purports to control or forecast natural events, effects, or forces by invoking the supernatural. **2.** The practice of using charms, spells, or rituals to attempt to produce supernatural effects or to control events in nature. **3.** The exercise of sleight of hand or conjuring for entertainment; the use of deception to produce baffling effects. **4.** A mysterious and overpowering quality that lends singular distinction and enchantment. ~*adj.* **1.** Of or pertaining to magic, the practice of magic, or the supernatural. **2.** Possessing distinctive qualities that produce unaccountable or baffling effects: *a magic wand.* **3.** *British Slang.* Wonderful; marvelous: *His new car is really magic.*

~*tr.v.* **magicked, -icking, -ics.** To produce or make by or as if by magic. [Middle English, from Old French *magique*, from Late Latin *magica*, from Greek *magikē (tekhnē)*, the sorcerer's art, from *magikos*, pertaining to sorcery, from *magos*, sorcerer, from Old Persian *maguš*.]

Synonyms: alchemy, black magic, necromancy, sorcery, voodoo, witchcraft.

mag·i·cal (măj′ĭ-kəl) *adj.* **1.** Of, pertaining to, or produced by or as if by magic. **2.** Having a mysteriously captivating quality. —**mag·i·cal·ly** *adv.*

magic carpet *n.* A legendary carpet possessing magical powers that enable it to transport a person to any desired destination.

magic eye *n.* A **photoelectric cell** (see).

ma·gi·cian (mə-jĭsh′ən) *n.* **1.** A sorcerer; a wizard. **2.** A person who performs magic for entertainment or diversion. **3.** One whose skill or art seems to be magical: *a magician with words.*

magic lantern *n.* An early type of slide projector used to project the enlarged image of a picture. Also called "lantern," "stereopticon."

magic mushroom *n.* A hallucinogenic mushroom, *Psilocybe semilanceata*, having a conical pileus with a sharply pointed umbo. Also called "liberty cap."

magic number *n. Physics.* Any of the numbers 2, 6, 8, 14, 20, 28, 50, 82, 126, that represent the number of neutrons or protons in strongly bound, exceptionally stable, and abundant atomic nuclei.

magic square *n.* A square arrangement of numbers such that the numbers in any row, column, or diagonal all add up to the same sum.

magilp. Variant of **megilp.**

Ma·gi·not Line (măzh′ĭ-nō′) *n.* A 320-kilometer (200-mile) line of fortifications built by France along its border with Germany before World War II. It was thought to be impregnable, but fell to the Germans in 1940 after they had by-passed it through Belgium. [After André *Maginot* (1877–1932), French minister of war.]

mag·is·te·ri·al (măj′ĭ-stîr′ē-əl) *adj.* **1.** Of or pertaining to a person in a position of authority, as a master or teacher. **2. a.** Characteristic of a master; authoritative. **b.** Dogmatic; overbearing: *offended by his magisterial manner of giving advice.* **3.** Of or pertaining to a magistrate or his official functions. [Latin *magisterius*, from *magister*, master.] —**mag·is·te·ri·al·ly** *adv.*

mag·is·te·ri·um (măj′ĭ-stîr′ē-əm) *n.* The teaching authority of the Roman Catholic Church. [Late Latin, from Latin *magister*, teacher, MASTER.]

mag·is·ter·y (măj′ĭ-stĕr′ē) *n., pl.* **-ies.** Also **ma·gis·ter** (mə-jĭs′tər). A substance or power in nature supposed by alchemists to be capable of effecting transmutation, as the philosopher's stone. [Medieval Latin *magisterium*, from Latin, position of a master, from *magister*, MASTER.]

mag·is·tra·cy (măj′ĭ-strə-sē) *n., pl.* **-cies.** **1.** The position, function, or term of office of a magistrate. **2.** A body of magistrates. **3.** The district under the jurisdiction of a magistrate.

mag·is·tral (măj′ĭ-strəl, mə-jĭs′trəl) *adj.* **1.** Magisterial. **2.** Prepared as specified by a physician's prescription. Said of medicine. Compare **officinal.** [Latin *magistrālis*, masterful, from *magister*, MASTER.]

mag·is·trate (măj′ĭ-strāt′, -strĭt) *n.* **1.** A civil officer with power to administer and enforce law. **2.** A minor official, as a justice of the peace or the judge of a police court, with limited judicial authority. [Latin *magistrātus*, magistracy, magistrate, from *magister*, MASTER.]

magistrate's court *n.* A minor court in England that is presided over by a minimum of two magistrates and that deals with minor crimes and holds preliminary criminal hearings.

mag·is·tra·ture (măj′ĭ-strā′chər, -strə-chŏŏr′) *n.* A magistracy.

Ma·gle·mo·si·an (mä′glə-mō′zē-ən) *adj. Archaeology.* Of, designating, or pertaining to an early Mesolithic forest culture of northern Europe, characterized by woodworking tools and dugout canoes. [After *Maglemose*, Denmark, where evidence was found.]

mag·ma (măg′mə, măg′-) *n., pl.* **magmata** (măg-mä′tə, măg-) or **-mas.** **1.** A mixture of finely divided solids with enough liquid to produce a pasty mass. **2.** *Geology.* The molten matter under the earth's crust from which igneous rock is formed by cooling. **3.** In pharmacology, a suspension of particles in a liquid. [Middle English, dregs of a liquid, from Latin, sediment, from Greek *magma*, unguent.] —**mag·mat·ic** (măg-măt′ĭk) *adj.*

Mag·na Car·ta, Mag·na Char·ta (măg′nə kär′tə) *n.* **1.** The great charter of English political and civil liberties granted by King John at Runnymede on June 15, 1215. **2.** A document or piece of legislation that serves as a guarantee of basic rights. [Medieval Latin, "Great Charter."]

mag·na cum lau·de (măg′nə kŏŏm lou′də, măg′nə kŭm lô′dē) *adv.* With high honors. Used on university and college diplomas to designate the second-highest degree of academic distinction. Compare **cum laude, summa cum laude.** [Latin.]

Mag·na Grae·ci·a (măg′nə grē′shē-ə, -shə). The colonies of ancient Greece in southern Italy and Sicily in the 8th to 4th centuries B.C. [Latin, "Great Greece."]

mag·nan·i·mous (măg-năn′ə-məs) *adj.* Noble of mind and heart; generous in forgiving and above revenge or resentment. [Latin *magnanimus*, "great-souled" : *magnus*, great + *animus*, soul.] —**mag·na·nim·i·ty** (măg′nə-nĭm′ə-tē), **mag·nan·i·mous·ness** *n.* —**mag·nan·i·mous·ly** *adv.*

mag·na o·per·a. Plural of **magnum opus.**

mag·nate (măg′nāt′, -nĭt) *n.* A powerful or influential person, especially in business or industry: *a steel magnate.* [Middle English *magnates* (plural only), from Late Latin *magnātēs*, plural of *magnās*, "great man," from Latin *magnus*, great.]

mag·ne·sia (măg-nē′zhə, -shə) *n.* **Magnesium oxide** (see), especially when processed for purity. [Middle English, from Medieval Latin, from Late Greek *magnēsia*, name of various minerals, from *Magnēsia*, name of a metalliferous region of Thessaly.] —**mag·ne·sian** (măg-nē′zhən, -shən) *adj.*

magnesian limestone *n. Geology.* **Dolomite** (see).

mag·ne·site (măg′nə-sīt′) *n.* **1.** A white, yellowish, or brown mineral composed of magnesium carbonate, $MgCO_3$. It is used in the manufacture of refractory bricks. **2.** Any of several grades of magnesium oxide obtained from this material. [MAGNES(IUM) + -ITE.]

mag·ne·si·um (măg-nē′zē-əm, -zhəm) *n. Symbol* **Mg** A light, silvery, moderately hard metallic element that in ribbon or powder form burns with a brilliant white flame. It is used in structural alloys, pyrotechnics, flash photography, and incendiary bombs. Atomic number 12, atomic weight 24.312, melting point 651°C, boiling point 1,107°C, specific gravity 1.74, valence 2. [New Latin, from MAGNESIA.]

magnesium carbonate *n.* A very light, odorless, white powdery compound, $MgCO_3$, used in a wide variety of manufactured products including inks, glass, dentifrices, and cosmetics.

magnesium hydroxide *n.* A white powder, $Mg(OH)_2$, used as an antacid and laxative, especially in milk of magnesia.

magnesium oxide *n.* A white, powdery compound, MgO, having a high melting point (2,800°C) and used in high-temperature refractories, electric insulation, and semiconductor devices and in medicine as a mild antacid and laxative. Also called "magnesia."

magnesium sulfate *n.* A colorless crystalline compound, $MgSO_4$, used in fireproofing, ceramics, matches, explosives, and fertilizers. The hydrate, $MgSO_4 \cdot 7H_2O$, is **Epsom salts** *(see).*

mag·net (măg′nĭt) *n.* **1.** A body that attracts iron and certain other materials by virtue of a surrounding field of force produced by the motion of its atomic electrons and the alignment of its atoms. **2.** An **electromagnet** *(see).* **3.** A person, place, object, or situation that exerts attraction, especially irresistible attraction. [Middle English *magnete,* from Old French, from Latin *magnēs* (stem *magnēt-*), from Greek *magnēs,* short for *Magnēs lithos,* "the Magnesian stone," from *Magnēs,* pertaining to *Magnēsia.* See **magnesia.**]

mag·net·ic (măg-nĕt′ĭk) *adj.* **1.** Of or relating to magnetism or magnets. **2.** Having the properties of a magnet; exhibiting magnetism. **3.** Relating to the magnetic poles of the earth: *a magnetic compass bearing.* **4.** Capable of being magnetized or of being attracted by a magnet. **5.** Operating by means of magnetism: *a magnetic recorder.* **6.** Exerting great powers of attraction: *a magnetic personality.* **—mag·net·i·cal·ly** *adv.*

magnetic bearing *n.* The angular direction from magnetic north.

magnetic bottle *n.* An arrangement of magnetic fields used to confine the plasma in a controlled thermonuclear reaction.

magnetic bubble *n.* A small, nonvolatile, cylindrical region of magnetization in a thin film of material that can be manipulated by an external magnetic field and used to represent data in the memory of a computer.

magnetic character recognition *n.* A method of introducing printed or written information into a computer. The information is printed using magnetic ink and the resulting text is scanned with a *magnetic character reader,* which recognizes each character by its magnetic outline.

magnetic circuit *n.* A closed path through which a magnetic flux can pass, analogous to a circuit through which a current flows.

magnetic compass *n.* An instrument using a **magnetic needle** *(see)* to show direction relative to the earth's magnetic field.

magnetic constant *n.* The permeability of free space. It has the value $4\pi \times 10^{-7}$ henry per meter. Also called "absolute permeability."

magnetic core *n. Computer Science.* A **core** *(see).*

magnetic declination *n.* The angle between the geographic meridian and the local magnetic meridian, in navigation indicated as degrees plus (+) to the east or degrees minus (–) to the west of the geographic meridian. Also called "declination," "magnetic variation."

magnetic dip *n.* The angle that the earth's magnetic field makes with the horizontal plane at any specific location. Also called "dip," "inclination," "magnetic inclination."

magnetic dipole moment *n.* A **magnetic moment** *(see).*

magnetic disk *n.* A computer storage device consisting of a stack of plates coated with a magnetic layer arranged so that they can be rotated at high speed as one unit. A read-write head can move radially on concentric tracks to enter or remove data from the device. **2.** A floppy disk *(see).*

magnetic domain *n. Physics.* A **domain** *(see).*

magnetic drum *n.* A computer storage device consisting of a rotating cylinder covered with magnetic material.

magnetic equator *n.* A line connecting all points on the earth's surface at which there is no magnetic dip. Also called "aclinic line." Compare **geomagnetic equator.**

magnetic field *n.* A condition in a region of space established by the presence of a magnet or of an electric current and characterized by the existence of a detectable magnetic force at every point in the region.

magnetic field strength *n.* **1.** Magnetic intensity. **2.** Magnetic induction.

magnetic flux *n.* The total number of magnetic lines of force passing through a bounded area in a magnetic field.

magnetic flux density *n.* Magnetic induction.

magnetic force *n.* **1.** The force on a **magnetic pole** *(see)* in a magnetic field. **2.** The force on an electrically charged particle or on an electric current in a magnetic field.

magnetic head *n.* A device, as in a tape recorder, that converts electric impulses into variations in the magnetism of a surface for storage and subsequent retrieval. See **magnetic recording.**

magnetic hysteresis *n.* The failure of the **magnetization** *(see)* in a body to return to its original value when the external field is reduced.

magnetic inclination *n.* **Magnetic dip** *(see).*

magnetic induction *n.* **1.** A vector quantity that specifies the direction and magnitude of magnetic force at every point in a magnetic field. Also called "magnetic field strength," "magnetic flux density." **2.** The temporary conversion of a piece of iron or of certain other materials into a magnet by a magnetic field.

magnetic ink *n.* Ink that contains particles of a magnetic material to enable it to be used in **magnetic character recognition** *(see).*

magnetic intensity *n.* That part of a magnetic field related solely to external currents as a cause, without reference to the presence of matter. Also called "magnetic field strength."

magnetic lens *n.* An arrangement of magnets, usually electromagnets, used to focus a beam of particles in such devices as an electron microscope or particle accelerator.

magnetic line of force *n.* A curve whose tangent at any point is along the direction of magnetic force at that point. The number of lines of force per unit area in the neighborhood of a point is proportional to the magnetic induction at that point.

magnetic meridian *n.* A meridian passing through the earth's magnetic poles.

magnetic mine *n.* A marine mine detonated by a mechanism that responds to magnetic material, such as the steel hull of a ship.

magnetic mirror *n.* An arrangement of magnetic fields that can reflect charged particles, used to contain the plasma in thermonuclear reactors.

magnetic moment *n.* A measure of the strength of a magnet or coil expressed as the torque produced when the magnet or coil is set with its axis perpendicular to the unit magnetic field. Also called "magnetic dipole moment."

magnetic mon·o·pole (mŏn′ə-pōl′) *n.* A hypothetical elementary particle that has a single north or south magnetic pole, predicted theoretically but so far undiscovered.

magnetic needle *n.* A needle-shaped bar magnet usually suspended on a low-friction mounting and used in various instruments, especially in the magnetic compass, to indicate the alignment of a local magnetic field.

magnetic north *n.* The direction of the earth's magnetic pole to which the north-seeking pole of a magnetic needle points when free from local magnetic influence. See **magnetic declination.**

magnetic permeability *n.* A characteristic of a medium in a magnetic field that is equal to the ratio of magnetic induction to magnetic intensity. Also called "permeability."

magnetic pickup *n.* A type of phonograph pickup that utilizes a coil in a magnetic field to receive vibrations from the stylus and convert them into electric impulses. Compare **crystal pickup.**

magnetic pole *n.* **1.** Either of two limited regions in a magnet at which the magnet's field is most intense, each of which is designated by the approximate geographic direction to which it is attracted: *a north or north-seeking pole; a south or south-seeking pole.* **2.** Either of two variable points on the earth close to but not coinciding with the North and South poles that correspond to the poles of the earth's magnetic field.

magnetic pole strength *n.* A measure of the effectiveness of a magnet, equal to the magnetic moment divided by the magnetic induction.

magnetic pyrites *n.* A mineral, **pyrrhotite** *(see).*

magnetic recording *n.* **1.** A recording of a signal, such as sound or computer instructions, in the form of a magnetic pattern on a magnetizable surface for storage and subsequent retrieval. **2.** A surface containing a magnetic recording. **—magnetic recorder** *n.*

magnetic storm *n.* A severe but short-lived disturbance in the earth's magnetic field believed to be produced by currents of charged particles and gamma rays and resulting from abnormal solar activity.

magnetic susceptibility *n.* The ratio of the magnetic permeability of a medium to that of a vacuum, minus one. It is positive for a paramagnetic or ferromagnetic medium and negative for a diamagnetic medium. Also called "susceptibility."

magnetic tape *n.* A plastic tape coated with a magnetizable material such as iron oxide for use in magnetic recording.

magnetic variation *n.* **Magnetic declination** *(see).*

mag·net·ism (măg′nə-tĭz′əm) *n. Abbr.* **mag.** **1.** The class of phenomena exhibited by the field of force produced by a magnet or by an electric current. **2.** The study of magnets and their effects. **3.** The force exerted by a magnetic field. **4.** Unusual power to attract, fascinate, or influence: *the magnetism of money.* **5.** Animal magnetism *(see).*

mag·net·ite (măg′nə-tīt′) *n.* A black mineral of iron oxide, Fe_3O_4, that often occurs with titanium or magnesium and is an important ore of iron. A magnetically polarized piece of this mineral is called a **lodestone** *(see).*

mag·net·i·za·tion (măg′nə-tĭ-zā′shən) *n.* **1.** The process of making a substance temporarily or permanently magnetic. **2.** The magnetic moment per unit volume induced in a body by an external field. **3.** The property of being magnetic.

mag·net·ize (măg′nə-tīz′) *tr.v.* **-ized, -izing, -izes. 1.** To make magnetic. **2. a.** To exert a strong influence on. **b.** To attract strongly. **—mag·net·iz·a·ble** *adj.* **—mag·net·iz·er** *n.*

mag·ne·to (măg-nē′tō) *n., pl.* **-tos.** A small generator of alternating current with permanent magnets that is used in the ignition systems of some internal-combustion engines. [Short for *magnetoelectric machine.*]

magneto– *prefix.* Indicates magnetic properties; for example, **magnetometer, magnetohydrodynamics.** [From MAGNET.]

mag·ne·to·chem·is·try (măg-nē′tō-kĕm′ĭ-strē) *n.* The study of the interrelation of magnetic and chemical phenomena. **—mag·ne·to·chem·i·cal** *adj.*

mag·ne·to·e·lec·tric (măg-nē′tō-ĭ-lĕk′trĭk) *adj.* Pertaining to both magnetism and electricity, especially to electricity produced by magnetic means. **—mag·ne·to·e·lec·tric·i·ty** *n.*

mag·ne·to·graph (măg-nē′tə-grăf′, -gräf′) *n.* A magnetometer with three variometers that are equipped for recording three perpendicular components of a magnetic field. [MAGNETO- + -GRAPH.]

mag·ne·to·hy·dro·dy·nam·ics (măg-nē′tō-hī′drō-dī-năm′ĭks) *n.* *Abbr.* **MHD** *Used with a singular verb.* **1.** The study of electrically conducting fluids, such as molten metal or plasma, in electric and magnetic fields. **2.** A method of generating electricity by subjecting a plasma to a magnetic field so that the flow of free electrons constitutes a current. Also called "hydromagnetics," "magnetoplasmadynamics." **—mag·ne·to·hy·dro·dy·nam·ic** *adj.*

mag·ne·tom·e·ter (măg′nə-tŏm′ĭ-tər) *n.* An instrument for comparing the magnitude and direction of magnetic fields. [MAGNETO- + -METER.]

mag·ne·to·mo·tive force (măg-nē′tō-mō′tĭv, măg-nĕt′ō-) *n.* *Abbr.* **mmf, m.m.f.** **1.** The agency that produces **magnetic flux** *(see)* in a magnetic circuit. **2.** The strength of such an agency, equal to the work required to carry a hypothetical isolated magnetic pole of unit strength completely around the circuit.

mag·ne·ton (măg′nə-tŏn′) *n.* A unit of magnetic moment applied to atoms, molecules, and subatomic particles, equal to $eh/4\pi mc$, where e is the particle's electric charge, m its mass, h Planck's constant, and c the speed of light; especially: **1.** The *Bohr magneton,* calculated using the mass and charge of the electron. **2.** The *nuclear magneton,* calculated using the mass of the nucleon. [French *magnéton* : MAGNET + -ON.]

mag·ne·to·plas·ma·dy·nam·ics (măg-nē′tō-plăz′mə-dī-năm′ĭks, măg-nĕt′ō-) *n.* *Used with a singular verb.* Magnetohydrodynamics. **—mag·ne·to·plas·ma·dy·nam·ic** *adj.*

mag·ne·to·sphere (măg-nē′tə-sfîr′, măg-nĕt′ə-) *n.* An asymmetric region surrounding the earth, extending from about 400 to several thousand miles above the surface, in which charged particles are trapped and their behavior dominated by the earth's magnetic field. [MAGNETO- + -SPHERE.]

mag·ne·to·stric·tion (măg-nē′tō-strĭk′shən, măg-nĕt′ō-) *n.* The deformation of a ferromagnetic material subjected to a magnetic field. **—mag·ne·to·stric·tive** *adj.*

mag·ne·tron (măg′nə-trŏn′) *n.* A thermionic tube in which the electron beam is controlled by electromagnetic fields and generates high-power microwaves. [MAGNE(T) + -TRON.]

mag·nif·ic (măg-nĭf′ĭk) *adj.* Also **mag·nif·i·cal** (-ĭ-kəl). Magnificent; grand. [Middle English *magnifyque,* from Old French *magnifique,* from Latin *magnificus,* "great in deeds" : *magnus,* great + -FIC.] **—mag·nif·i·cal·ly** *adv.*

Mag·nif·i·cat (măg-nĭf′ĭ-kăt′, -kät′) *n.* **1. a.** The canticle beginning *Magnificat anima mea Dominum* ("My soul doth magnify the Lord"). The text is Luke 1:46-55. **b.** A musical setting of this text. **2. magnificat.** A hymn or song of praise. [Latin, "it magnifies."]

mag·ni·fi·ca·tion (măg′nə-fĭ-kā′shən) *n.* **1. a.** The act of magnifying or the state of being magnified. **b.** The process of enlarging the size of something, such as an optical image. **c.** Something that has been magnified; an enlarged representation, image, or model. **d.** The degree to which something is magnified. **2.** In optics, the ratio of image size to object size.

mag·nif·i·cence (măg-nĭf′ĭ-səns) *n.* **1.** Greatness or lavishness of surroundings or ornament; splendor; sumptuousness. **2.** Grand or imposing beauty: *the magnificence of the scenery.*

mag·nif·i·cent (măg-nĭf′ĭ-sənt) *adj.* **1. a.** Splendid; stately; grand. **b.** Lavishly decorated; sumptuous. **2.** Grand or imposing to the mind; marked by nobility of thought or deed; exalted. **3.** Outstanding of its kind; superlative: *a magnificent sunset.* —See Synonyms at **grand.** [Latin *magnificent-,* variant stem of *magnificus,* MAGNIFIC.] **—mag·nif·i·cent·ly** *adv.*

mag·nif·i·co (măg-nĭf′ĭ-kō′) *n., pl.* **-coes.** **1.** A person of distinguished rank, importance, or appearance. **2.** A nobleman of the Venetian Republic. [Italian, from *magnifico,* magnificent, from Latin *magnificus,* MAGNIFIC.]

mag·ni·fi·er (măg′nə-fī′ər) *n.* **1. a.** A magnifying glass. **b.** Any system of optical components, as lenses, that magnifies. **2.** A person who magnifies.

mag·ni·fy (măg′nə-fī′) *v.* **-fied, -fying, -fies.** *—tr.* **1.** To make greater in size; enlarge, amplify, or intensify: *Our problems are magnified by lack of time.* **2.** To cause to appear greater or seem more important; exaggerate. **3.** To increase the apparent size of, especially by means of a lens. **4.** To glorify or praise. *—intr.* To increase or have the power to increase the size or volume of an image or sound. —See Synonyms at **increase.** [Middle English *magnifien,* from Old French *magnifier,* from Latin *magnificāre,* to make great, from *magnificus,* MAGNIFIC.]

magnifying glass *n.* A converging lens that enlarges the image of an object. Also called "magnifier."

mag·nil·o·quent (măg-nĭl′ə-kwənt) *adj.* Lofty and extravagant in speech; grandiloquent. [Latin *magniloquus* : *magnus,* great + *loquī,* to speak.] **—mag·nil·o·quence** *n.* **—mag·nil·o·quent·ly** *adv.*

mag·ni·tude (măg′nĭ-to͞od′, -tyo͞od′) *n.* *Abbr.* **mag.** **1. a.** Greatness of rank or position. **b.** Greatness in size or extent. **c.** Greatness in significance or influence: *the magnitude of the achievement.* **2.** *Astronomy.* The relative brightness of a celestial body designated on a numerical scale, originally integers from 1 (brightest) to 6 (faintest visible), now extended to include negative integers, integers above 6, and decimals, with the scale rule that a decrease of 1 unit represents an increase in apparent brightness by a factor of 2.512. Also called "apparent magnitude." **3.** *Mathematics.* A property that can be quantitatively described, such as the volume of a sphere or the length of a vector. **4.** The force of an earthquake as measured on the Richter scale. [Middle English, from Latin *magnitūdō,* greatness, from *magnus,* great.]

mag·no·lia (măg-nōl′yə) *n.* **1.** Any of various evergreen or deciduous trees and shrubs of the genus *Magnolia,* of the Western Hemisphere and Asia, many of which are cultivated for their showy white, pink, purple, or yellow flowers. **2.** The flower of any of these trees or shrubs. **3.** A creamy white tinged with pink. [New Latin, after Pierre *Magnol* (1638–1715), French botanist.]

mag·num (măg′nəm) *n.* **1.** A bottle for wine or liquor that holds about two fifths of a gallon. **2.** The amount of liquid contained in a magnum. **3.** An extremely powerful .44-caliber handgun. [Latin, "a big one," neuter of *magnus,* great.]

mag·num o·pus (măg′nəm ō′pəs) *n., pl.* **magna opera** (măg′nə ō′pər-ə, ŏp′ər-ə). **1.** A great work; especially, a literary or artistic masterpiece. **2.** The greatest single work of an artist, writer, or composer. [Latin, "great work."]

mag·nus hitch (măg′nəs) *n.* A clove hitch with one extra turn. [Probably from Latin *magnus,* "large."]

Magog. See **Gog and Magog.**

ma·got (mă-gō′, măg′ət) *n.* **1.** A fanciful, often grotesque figure in the Chinese or Japanese style. **2.** The **Barbary ape** *(see).* [French *magot, magog,* a monstrous figure, after the Biblical giant Magog.]

mag·pie (măg′pī′) *n.* **1.** Any of various birds of the family Corridae, found worldwide, having a long, graduated tail and noted for their chattering call. The species *Pica,* the black-billed magpie, is widespread in the Northern Hemisphere. **2.** Any of various birds resembling the magpie. **3.** Any of several piping crows and bell magpies of the family Cracticidae, of Australia. **4.** A person who chatters. **5.** *British.* A person who compulsively collects miscellaneous small objects. [*Mag,* a nickname for *Margaret* + PIE (magpie).]

magpie lark *n.* A distinctively marked black and white bird, *Grallina cyanoleuca,* found throughout Australia and parts of New Zealand. Also called "mudlark."

Ma·gritte (mə-grēt′, mä-), **René** (1898–1967). Belgian surrealist painter. He produced dreamlike paintings showing ordinary objects in impossible situations.

ma·guey (mə-gā′) *n.* **1. a.** Any of various plants of the genus *Agave,* native to tropical America; especially, one yielding a fiber or beverage. Also called "mescal." **b.** A plant of the related genus *Furcraea.* **2.** The fiber obtained from maguey. [Spanish, from Taino.]

Ma·gus (mā′gəs) *n., pl.* **-gi** (-jī′). **1. magus.** A member of the Zoroastrian priestly caste of the Medes and Persians. **2. magus.** A wizard or sorcerer. **3.** One of the three **Magi** *(see).*

Mag·yar (măg′yär′, mäg′-, mŭd′-) *n.* **1.** A member of the principal ethnic group of Hungary. **2.** The Finno-Ugric language of the Magyars that is the official language of Hungary; Hungarian.
∼adj. Of or pertaining to the Magyars or their language; Hungarian. [Hungarian *Magyar*†.]

Magyarország. See **Hungary.**

ma·ha·ra·jah, ma·ha·ra·ja (mä′hə-rä′jə, -zhə) *n.* A king or prince in India, especially the sovereign of any of the former States. [Hindi *mahārājā,* from Sanskrit : *mahā,* great + *rājā,* king.]

ma·ha·ra·ni, ma·ha·ra·nee (mä′hə-rä′nē) *n.* **1.** The wife of a maharajah. **2.** A princess in India ranking above a rani, especially the sovereign ruler of any of the former States. [Hindi *mahārānī,* from Sanskrit *mahārājñī* : *mahā,* great + *rājñī,* queen.]

Ma·ha·rash·tra (mä′hə-räsh′trə). State of western India bordering the Arabian Sea. Its rice-producing coastlands rise to the Western Ghats, beyond which lies the Deccan plateau, where cotton is grown. Mostly peopled by Marathas, the state was created when the former Bombay state was divided between its Marathi and Gujarati inhabitants. Bombay is the capital.

ma·ha·ri·shi (mä′ə-rē′shē, mə-här′ə-shē) *n.* *Hinduism.* **1.** A great sage or spiritual leader. **2. Maharishi.** A title of or form of address for a guru or spiritual leader, preceding the person's name. [Sanskrit *māha,* great + *rishi,* sage.]

ma·hat·ma (mə-hät′mə, -hăt′mə) *n.* **1.** In India and Tibet, any of a class of persons venerated for great knowledge and love of humanity. **2. Mahatma.** A Hindu title of respect for a man renowned for spirituality and high-mindedness. [Sanskrit *mahātman* : *mahā,* great + *ātman,* soul.]

Ma·ha·ya·na (mä′hə-yä′nə) *n.* One of the major schools of Buddhism, active in Japan, Korea, Nepal, Tibet, Mongolia, and China, that teaches social concern and universal salvation. [Sanskrit *mahāyāna,* "the great vehicle" : *mahā,* great + *yāna,* vehicle.]

Mah·di (mä′dē) *n.* **1.** The Islamic messiah who, it is believed, will appear at the end of the world and establish a reign of peace and righteousness. **2.** An Islamic leader who assumes the role of a messiah; especially, Muhammad Ahmed (*c.* 1843–85), Sudanese leader of a religious war against the British and Egyptians. [Arabic *mahdīy,* "rightly guided (one)," past participle of *madā,* to lead rightly.] **—Mah·dism** (mä′dĭz′əm) *n.* **—Mah·dist** (-dĭst) *adj.* & *n.*

Ma·hé (mä-hā′). Chief island of the Seychelles, in the Indian Ocean northeast of Madagascar.

Ma·hi·can (mə-hē′kən) *n., pl.* **-cans** or collectively **Mahican.** Also **Mo·hi·can** (mō-hē′kən, mə-). **1.** A member of a group or confederacy of Algonquian-speaking North American Indians that formerly lived between the upper Hudson River Valley and Lake Champlain. **2.** The Algonquian language of the Mahican.

mah·jong, mah·jongg (mä′zhŏng′, -zhông′) *n.* A game of Chinese

magnolia *There are about 80 species of* Magnolia. *All are trees and shrubs native to North and Central America and Asia.*

origin usually played by four persons. Tiles bearing various designs are drawn and discarded until one player wins with a hand of four combinations of three tiles each and a pair of matching tiles. [Chinese *má jiàng*, possibly from *máquè*, sparrow (from the figure of a sparrow on a leading piece of one of the suits).]

Mah·ler (mä′lər), **Gustav** (1860–1911). Austrian composer and conductor. He was conductor at the Vienna State Opera House (1897–1907). He completed nine symphonies and a number of song cycles, including *Das Lied von der Erde* (1908) and *Kindertotenlieder* (1902).

mahlstick. Variant of **maulstick.**

ma·hoe (mə-hō′) *n.* A New Zealand tree, *Melicytus ramiflorus*, yielding a useful fiber and a wood from which charcoal is produced. [Maori.]

ma·hog·a·ny (mə-hŏg′ə-nē) *n., pl.* **-nies. 1. a.** Any of various tropical American trees of the genus *Swietenia*, valued for their hard, reddish-brown wood. **b.** The wood of any of these trees, especially that of *S. mahogani*, much used for making furniture. **2. a.** Any of several trees having wood resembling true mahogany. **b.** The wood of any of these trees. See **African mahogany, Philippine mahogany. 3.** A moderate reddish brown. [17th century : origin obscure.]

Mahomet. See **Muhammad.**

Mahometan. Variant of **Muhammadan.**

Mahometanism. Variant of **Muhammadanism.**

ma·ho·ni·a (mə-hō′nē-ə) *n.* An evergreen plant of the genus *Mahonia*, certain of which are cultivated as ornamental shrubs. [New Latin, after Bernard *McMahon* (1775–1816), U.S. botanist.]

Ma·hore (mə-hôr′, -hōr′). Formerly **Ma·yotte** (mə-yôt′). An island in the Indian Ocean, the southeasternmost of the Comoros group. When the Comoros government declared its independence from France in 1975, the Mayottes refused to join them and the following year voted overwhelmingly (80 percent) to become an overseas department of France. Dzaoudzi is the capital.

ma·hout (mə-hout′) *n.* The keeper and driver of an elephant. [Hindi *mahāut, mahāwat*, from Sanskrit *mahāmātra*, "of great measure," originally an honorific title : *mahā*, great + *mātra*, measure.]

Mahrati, Mahratti. Variants of **Marathi.**

Mahratta. Variant of **Maratha.**

Mähren. See **Moravia.**

mah·seer (mä′sîr′) *n., pl.* **mahseer.** Any of several large Indian freshwater fishes of the carp family, such as *Barbus tor*. [Hindi, probably from Sanskrit *mahāciras*, "big-head."]

mahzor. Variant of **machzor.**

Mai·a¹ (mā′ə, mī′ə). *Greek Mythology.* A goddess, the eldest of the **Pleiades** *(see).* [Greek, from *maia*, mother, nurse.]

Maia² *n.* The brightest star in the **Pleiades** *(see).*

maid (mād) *n.* **1.** A female servant. **2. a.** A girl or unmarried woman. **b.** A virgin. [Middle English *maide*, shortening of MAIDEN.]

mai·dan (mī-dän′) *n.* In India and Southeast Asia, an open space in or near a town, used especially for parades or sports events. [Urdu, from Arabic.]

maid·en (mād′n) *n.* **1. a.** An unmarried girl or woman. **b.** A virgin. **2.** A machine resembling the guillotine that was used to behead criminals in the 16th and 17th centuries in Scotland. **3.** A racehorse that has never won a race. ~*adj.* **1.** Of, pertaining to, or befitting a maiden: *maiden beauty*. **2.** Being an unmarried woman: *a maiden aunt*. **3.** Inexperienced; untried. Said especially of a soldier or weapons. **4.** Designating a racehorse that has never won a race. **5.** First or earliest: *a maiden voyage*. **6.** Designating territory that has never been explored or captured. [Middle English *maiden*, Old English *mægden*, diminutive of *mægeth*, maid, from Germanic.]

maid·en·hair (mād′n-hâr′) *n.* Any of various ferns of the genus *Adiantum*, having dark stems and light green, feathery fronds with fan-shaped leaflets. Also called "maidenhair fern." [From the fineness of the stems.]

maidenhair tree *n.* The ginkgo *(see).*

maid·en·head (mād′n-hĕd′) *n.* **1.** The condition or quality of being a virgin; virginity. **2.** The hymen.

maid·en·hood (mād′n-hood′) *n.* The condition or time of being a maiden.

maid·en·ly (mād′n-lē) *adj.* Pertaining to or suitable for a maiden. **—maid·en·li·ness** *n.*

maiden name *n.* A woman's family name before marriage.

maid in waiting *n., pl.* **maids in waiting.** An unmarried woman attending a queen or princess.

Maid Mar·i·an (mâr′ē-ən, mär′-) *n.* The Queen of the May in morris dances and May Day games.

maid of honor *n., pl.* **maids of honor. 1.** An unmarried noblewoman attendant upon a queen or princess. **2.** The chief unmarried female attendant of a bride. Compare **bridesmaid, matron of honor. 3.** *British.* An almond-flavored custard tart.

Maid of Orléans. See **Joan of Arc.**

maid·ser·vant (mād′sûr′vənt) *n.* A female servant.

Maid·stone (mād′stən, -stōn′). County town of Kent, southeastern England, on the Medway River. Its main industries are papermaking and brewing, and it is a major market for hops and grain.

mai·eu·tic (mā-yōo′tĭk, mī-) *adj.* Also **mai·eu·ti·cal** (-tĭ-kəl). Pertaining to the Socratic method of bringing forth latent ideas through a logical sequence of questions and answers. [Greek *maieutikos*, obstetric, "bringing ideas to birth," from *maieuesthai*, to act as midwife, from *maia*, midwife, nurse.]

mai·gre (mā′grə, -gər) *adj.* **1.** Not containing meat or its juices: *a maigre diet*. **2.** *Roman Catholic Church.* Of or designating a day of abstinence on which only maigre food is permitted. [French, thin, from Old French, from Latin *macer*, thin.]

mail¹ (māl) *n.* **1. a.** Letters, packages, and other material handled in a postal system. **b.** Postal material for a specific person or organization: *I received my mail today*. **c.** Material collected or processed for distribution from a post office at a specified time: *the morning mail*. **2.** A system by which postal materials, such as letters and packages, are transported. **3.** A vehicle, as a train, ship, or aircraft, by which mail is transported. ~*adj.* Of, pertaining to, carrying, or used in the handling of mail: *mail delivery*. ~*tr.v.* **mailed, mailing, mails.** To send by mail; post. [Middle English *male*, mailbag, from Old French *male*, pouch, bag, from Old High German *malha*.] **—mail·a·ble** *adj.*

mail² *n.* **1.** Flexible body armor composed of small overlapping metal rings, interlocking loops of chain, or scales. See **chain mail, coat of mail. 2.** The protective shell or covering of certain animals, such as the turtle. ~*tr.v.* **mailed, mailing, mails.** To cover or armor with mail. [Middle English *maille*, from Old French, from Latin *macula*, spot, mesh.]

mail·bag (māl′băg′) *n.* **1.** A large canvas sack used for transporting mail. **2.** A leather or canvas bag suspended from the shoulder and used by letter carriers for carrying mail.

mail·box (māl′bŏks′) *n.* **1.** A public container for the deposit of outgoing mail. **2.** A private box for incoming mail.

mail call *n.* Distribution of mail to the members of a military unit.

mail carrier *n.* A mailman.

mail drop *n.* **1.** A receptacle for mail at the address of delivery. **2.** A slot for the insertion of mail. **3.** An address at which a person receives mail but does not reside.

mailed (māld) *adj.* **1.** Covered with or made of plates of mail. **2.** Having a hard covering of scales, spines, or horny plate, as an armadillo or lobster.

mailed fist *n.* The threat of the use of force, as between nations.

mail·er (mā′lər) *n.* **1.** One who mails. **2.** A container, such as a cardboard tube, used to hold material to be mailed. **3.** An advertising leaflet included with a letter.

Mail·er (mā′lər), **Norman** (1923–). U.S. author. Concerned with political, moral, and social questions, he rose to prominence with a World War II novel, *The Naked and the Dead* (1948). His other books include *The Armies of the Night* (1968), which won a Pulitzer Prize, and *The Executioner's Song* (1979).

Mail·gram (māl′grăm′). A trademark for a telegram delivered by the postal service.

mail·ing (mā′lĭng) *n.* A batch of mail dispatched at one time by a sender.

mailing machine *n.* Any of various machines that stamp, address, or seal material for mailing.

mail·lot (mī-ō′, mä-yō′) *n.* **1.** A coarsely knitted, stretchable jersey fabric. **2. a.** A pair of tights or a leotard made of maillot and worn for ballet or gymnastics. **b.** A bathing suit, usually of one piece, made of maillot. [French, tight garment, originally a child's swaddling bands, from Old French, from *maille*, band of cloth, mail, from Latin *macula*, spot, mesh.]

mail·man (māl′măn′) *n., pl.* **-men** (-mĕn′). One who carries and delivers mail.

mail order *n.* *Abbr.* **m.o., M.O.** A request for goods or services that is received and usually filled through the mail.

mail-or·der house (māl′ôr′dər) *n.* A business establishment that is primarily organized to promote, receive, and fill requests for goods or services through the mail.

maim (mām) *tr.v.* **maimed, maiming, maims. 1.** To disable or disfigure, usually by depriving of the use of a limb or bodily part. **2.** To make imperfect or defective; impair. [Middle English *maymen*, to wound, from Old French *mahaignier†*.]

Mai·mon·i·des (mī-mŏn′ə-dēz′), **Moses ben Maimon** (1135–1204). Doctor, rabbi, and philosopher. He codified Jewish laws and philosophy in such works as *The Mishnah Torah* and *The Guide of the Perplexed*.

main¹ (mān) *adj.* **1.** Most important; principal: *The library is in the main building*. **2.** Exerted to the utmost; sheer: *succeeded by main strength*. **3.** *Obsolete.* Of or pertaining to a continuous area or stretch, as of land or water. **4.** *Archaic.* **a.** Very great or considerable of its kind; remarkable: *"I am a main bungler at a long story"* (R.B. Sheridan). **b.** Highly important; momentous: *"by the main accident of time"* (Bacon). **5.** *Grammar.* Designating the principal clause, verb, or phrase referring to the subject in a complex sentence. **6.** *Nautical.* Connected to or located near the mainmast: *a main skysail.* —See Synonyms at **chief.** ~*n.* **1.** The principal, most important, or largest part or point: *In the main his latest symphonies are difficult to listen to. "The main of life is composed of small incidents"* (Samuel Johnson). **2.** The principal pipe or conduit in a system for conveying a utility, as water, gas, or oil. **3.** Physical strength. Used chiefly in the phrase *might and main.* **4.** The mainland as distinguished from islands. **5.** The open ocean. **6.** *Nautical.* **a.** A mainsail *(see).* **b.** A mainmast *(see).* [Middle English, from Old English *mægen*, strength, and *mægn-* (used in compounds), strong, great.]

main² *n.* **1.** A number greater than four but not exceeding nine that is called by the caster before throwing the dice in the game of hazard. **2.** A series of cockfights consisting of an odd number of matches. [16th century : perhaps from the phrase MAIN CHANCE.]

Main (mān, mĭn). River rising in eastern West Germany and flowing *c.* 500 kilometers (310 miles) generally west through a heavily industrialized area. It joins the Rhine River at Mainz.

main brace *n.* A rope that controls the movement of the main yard on a sailing ship.

main chance *n.* One's most advantageous opportunity.

main clause *n. Grammar.* A clause in a complex sentence, containing a subject, verb and sometimes an object and modifiers, that is capable of standing alone syntactically as a complete sentence. Also called "independent clause."

main drag *n. Slang.* The principal street of a city or town.

Maine[1] (mān). *Abbr.* **Me.** Largest state in New England. The north and west are mountainous, the east hilly with a fragmented coast. There are more than 2,200 lakes. Maine is four-fifths forested. Tourism, timber, dairying, market gardening, fishing, and the making of paper and wood products are its chief industries. It has considerable mineral wealth. Augusta is the capital.

Maine[2] (mān, mĕn). Former province of northwestern France, largely corresponding with the departments of Mayenne and Sarthe. Le Mans was its capital. The region is noted for its cattle.

main·frame (mān'frām') *n.* **1.** A high-speed computer with a large memory bank. Compare **minicomputer.** **2.** The central processing unit of a computer exclusive of peripheral and remote devices.

main·land (mān'lănd', -lənd) *n.* The principal land mass of a continent as distinguished from an island or peninsula.

Main·land[1] (mān'lənd). Also **Po·mo·na** (pə-mō'nə). Largest of the 65 Orkney Islands. It has Stone Age and other prehistoric remains. The main town is Kirkwall.

Mainland[2]. Largest of the Shetland Islands. The main town is Lerwick.

main·line (mān'lĭn') *v.* **-lined, -lining, -lines.** *Slang.* —*tr.* To inject (narcotics) directly into a major vein. —*intr.* To take narcotics by mainlining. —**main·lin·er** *n.*

main line *n.* **1.** A principal section of a railroad line. **2.** *Slang.* A principal and easily accessible vein, usually in the arm or leg, into which narcotics can be injected.

Main Line. Fashionable suburbs west of Philadelphia, Pennsylvania, along a commuter line to Paoli.

main·ly (mān'lē) *adv.* For the most part; chiefly.

main·mast (mān'məst, -măst', -mäst') *n.* **1.** The principal mast of a vessel. **2.** The taller mast, whether forward or aft, of a two-masted sailing vessel. **3.** The second mast aft of a sailing ship with three or more masts.

main roy·al·mast (roi'əl-məst, -măst', -mäst') *n.* The section of the mainmast of a square-rigged vessel above the main topgallantmast.

main·sail (mān'səl, -sāl') *n.* **1.** The principal sail of a vessel. **2.** A quadrilateral or triangular sail set from the after part of the mainmast on a fore-and-aft rigged vessel. **3.** A square sail set from the main yard on a square-rigged vessel.

main sequence *n.* A major grouping of stars, containing the sun and 90 percent of the known stars, characterized by an approximately uniform average increase of luminosity with surface temperature as represented by a single band on the **Hertzsprung-Russell diagram** *(see).*

main·sheet (mān'shēt') *n.* The rope that controls the angle at which a mainsail is adjusted to take advantage of the wind.

main·spring (mān'sprĭng') *n.* **1.** The principal spring in a mechanical device, especially in a watch or clock, that drives the mechanism by uncoiling. **2.** A motivating force; an impelling cause: *He was the mainspring of the reform movement.*

main·stay (mān'stā') *n.* **1.** A strong rope that serves to steady and support the mainmast of a sailing vessel. **2.** A principal support: *Agriculture is a mainstay of the economy.*

main stem *n.* **1.** The principal street in a city or town. **2.** The main line of a railroad.

main·stream (mān'strēm') *n.* The prevailing current or direction of a movement, activity, or influence: *writers in the mainstream of 18th-century thought.*

~*adj.* Having, influenced by, or harmonizing with the prevalent attitudes and values of a society or group: *mainstream jazz.*

~*tr.v.* **mainstreamed, -streaming, -streams.** To place (a handicapped student) in regular school classes.

main street *n.* **1.** The principal street of an American small town or city. **2. Main Street.** The culture of smug, materialistic, and provincial small towns. [Sense 2, influenced by *Main Street* (1920), novel by Sinclair LEWIS.]

main·tain (mān-tān') *tr.v.* **-tained, -taining, -tains.** **1.** To continue; carry on; keep up: *maintain good relations; maintain a custom.* **2.** To preserve or retain: *tried to maintain her composure.* **3.** To keep in a condition of good repair or efficiency: *maintain public roads.* **4. a.** To provide for; bear the expenses of: *maintain a family.* **b.** To keep in existence; sustain: *food to maintain life.* **5.** To defend, as against danger or attack. **6. a.** To declare to be true; defend against dispute: *The defendant maintains his innocence.* **b.** To assert in or as if in an argument; state; declare: *He maintained that he was innocent.* —See Synonyms at **keep, support.** [Middle English *mainteine,* from Old French *maintenir,* from Medieval Latin *manūtenēre,* from Latin *manū tenēre,* "to hold in the hand," support, know : *manū,* ablative of *manus,* hand + *tenēre,* to hold.] —**main·tain·a·ble** *adj.* —**main·tain·er** *n.*

maintained school *n.* In Britain, a school maintained by public funds rather than by private money.

main·te·nance (mān'tə-nəns) *n.* **1.** The action of maintaining or the state of being maintained: *the maintenance of tribal custom.* **2.** *Law.* An unlawful interference in a lawsuit by someone who is a disinterested party. **3.** The act or work of keeping something in proper condition. Also used adjectively: *a maintenance man.* **4. a.** The provision or means of support or livelihood: *maintenance of serfs by a feudal lord.* **b.** *Law.* Financial support ordered by a court to be given by one person to another, as in the case of a divorced couple; alimony. —See Synonyms at **livelihood.** [Middle English *maintenaunce,* from Old French *maintenance,* from *maintenir,* to MAINTAIN.]

Main·te·non (măn'tə-nôn', mănt-nôn'), **Marquise de,** born Françoise d'Aubigné (1635–1719). Second wife of Louis XIV. Her first husband, Paul Scarron, died in 1660. She married Louis in secret in 1685 after the death of Queen Marie Thérèse.

main·top (mān'tŏp') *n.* A platform at the head of the mainmast on a square-rigged vessel.

main topgallant *n.* A sail or yard set from the topgallant section of a mainmast.

main top·gal·lant·mast (tə-găl'ənt-məst, tŏp-) *n.* The section of the mainmast immediately above the main topmast on a square-rigged vessel.

main topmast *n.* The section of the mainmast on a square-rigged sailing vessel between the lower mast and the main topgallantmast.

main topsail *n.* The sail that is set above the mainsail.

main yard *n.* The lower yard on a mainmast.

Mainz (mīnts). *French* **Ma·yence** (mä-yäNs'). River port and capital of Rhineland-Palatinate, West Germany. At the confluence of the Rhine and Main rivers, it grew on an early Roman campsite (*c.* 13 B.C.), was the seat of the first German archbishopric (8th century), and was made Europe's first printing center by Johann Gutenberg (15th century). An industrial and communications center, it is also important in the wine trade.

maiolica. Variant of **majolica.**

mai·son·ette, mai·son·nette (mā'zə-nĕt', mā'sə-) *n.* A self-contained unit of living accommodation, especially one occupying two or more floors of a larger building and having its own outside front door. [Diminutive of French *maison,* house.]

maî·tre d' (mā'trə dĕ', mā'tər) *n., pl.* **maî·tre d's** (dēz'). *Informal.* A maître d'hôtel.

maî·tre d'hô·tel (mā'trə dō-tĕl') *n., pl.* **maîtres d'hôtel** (pronounced as singular). **1.** A major-domo *(see).* **2.** A headwaiter *(see).* **3.** A sauce of melted butter, chopped parsley, lemon juice, salt, and pepper. [French, "master of hotel."]

maize (māz) *n.* **1.** A New World grain, **corn** *(see).* **2.** A light yellow to moderate orange yellow. [Spanish *maíz* or French *maïs,* probably from Taino *mahiz.*] —**maize** *adj.*

Maj. major.

ma·jes·tic (mə-jĕs'tĭk) *adj.* Also **ma·jes·ti·cal** (-tĭ-kəl). Having or exhibiting stateliness or great dignity; royal; dignified: *a majestic gesture.* —See Synonyms at **grand.** —**ma·jes·ti·cal·ly** *adv.*

maj·es·ty (măj'ĭ-stē) *n., pl.* **-ties. 1. a.** The greatness and dignity of a sovereign. **b.** The sovereignty and power of God. **2. a.** A royal personage. **b. Majesty.** *Abbr.* **M.** A title or form of address for a sovereign monarch. Used with *His, Her,* or *Your: His Majesty's wish; Your Majesty.* **3. a.** Royal dignity of bearing or aspect; grandeur. **b.** Stateliness, splendor, or magnificence, as of appearance, style, or character; imposing quality. **4.** Supreme authority or power: *the majesty of the law.* [Middle English *maieste, mageste,* from Old French *majeste,* from Latin *mājestās* (stem *mājestāt-*), authority, grandeur.]

Maj. Gen. major general.

ma·jol·i·ca (mə-jŏl'ĭ-kə, mə-yŏl'-) *n.* Also **mai·ol·i·ca** (mə-yŏl'-). **1.** A type of richly colored and decorated pottery that is enameled and glazed, especially as produced in Italy in the 16th century. **2.** A type of pottery made, especially in the 19th century, in imitation of majolica. [Old Italian *maiolica,* from *Majolica,* MALLORCA.]

ma·jor (mā'jər) *adj.* **1.** Greater in importance, rank, or stature: *a major writer; a major scientific discovery.* **2.** Requiring great attention or concern; serious or dangerous: *major difficulties; a major illness.* **3.** *Law.* Having attained full legal age. **4.** Designating the senior or older of two pupils with the same surname. Used especially in some British schools. **5.** Designating or pertaining to the principal field of academic specialization chosen by students in a college or university. **6.** *Logic.* More inclusive in scope; broader, as are the **major premise** and **major term** *(both of which see).* **7.** *Music.* **a.** Designating a scale or mode having half steps between the third and fourth and the seventh and eighth degrees. **b.** Equivalent to the distance between the tonic tone and the second or third or sixth or seventh degrees of a major scale or mode: *a major interval.* **c.** Based on a major scale: *a major key.* Compare **minor.**

~*n.* **1.** *Abbr.* **Maj.** *Military.* **a.** An officer in the U.S. Army, Air Force, or Marine Corps ranking above a captain and below a lieutenant colonel. **b.** An officer of similar rank in other military or paramilitary organizations. **2.** *Law.* One who has reached full legal age. **3. a.** The principal field of academic specialization of a student in a college or university: *His major is chemistry.* **b.** A student specializing in such a field: *a history major.* **4.** A **major premise** or **major term** *(both of which see).* **5.** *Music.* A major scale, key, interval, or mode. **6. majors.** *Sports.* The major leagues.

~*intr.v.* **majored, -joring, -jors.** To pursue academic studies in a

majolica *A tin-glazed earthenware plate painted by Alfonso Patanazzi near the end of the 16th century. The plate is entitled* Latona Changing Peasants into Frogs.

PRONUNCIATION KEY

ă, pat; ā, pay; âr, care;
ä, father, are; b, bib;
ch, church; d, deed; ĕ, pet;
ē, be; f, fife; g, gag; h, hat;
hw, which; ĭ, pit; ī, pie;
îr, pier; j, judge; k, kick;
l, lid, needle; m, mum;
n, no, sudden; ng, thing;
ŏ, pot; ō, toe; ô, paw, for;
oi, noise; ou, out; o͝o, book;
o͞o, boot; p, pop; r, roar;
s, sauce; sh, ship, dish;
t, tight; th, thin, path;
th, this, bathe; ŭ, cut; ûr, fur;
v, valve; w, with; y, yes;
z, zebra, size; zh, vision;
ə, about, item, edible, gallop, circus, peaceful

IN FOREIGN WORDS:

à, *Fr.* ami; œ, *Fr.* feu, *Ger.* schön; ü, *Fr.* tu, *Ger.* über; KH, *Ger.* ich, *Scot.* loch; N, *Fr.* bon; y', *Fr.* Compiègne

STRESS MARKS:

Primary stress: ′
in·cite′ (ĭn-sīt′)
Secondary stress: ′
in′sight′ (ĭn′sīt′)

major field. Used with *in.* [As adjective, Middle English, from Latin *mājor,* greater. As noun (in military sense), from French, shortened from SERGEANT MAJOR.]

major axis *n.* In geometry: **1.** The line intersecting an ellipse and passing through both its focuses. **2.** The longest axis of an ellipsoid.

Majorca. See **Mallorca.** **—Ma·jor·can** (mə-jôr′kən, -yôr′-) *adj. & n.*

ma·jor-do·mo (mā′jər-dō′mō) *n., pl.* **-mos. 1.** The head steward or butler in the household of a sovereign or great nobleman. Also called "maître d'hôtel." **2.** A steward or butler. [Italian *maggiordomo* and Spanish *mayordomo,* from Medieval Latin *mājor domūs,* "head of the house," "mayor of the palace" : *mājor,* noun use of Latin *mājor,* greater + *domūs,* genitive of *domus,* house.]

ma·jor·ette (mā′jə-rĕt′) *n.* A **drum majorette** *(see).*

major general *n. Abbr.* **Maj. Gen.** *Military.* An officer in the U.S. Army, Air Force, or Marine Corps who ranks above a brigadier general and below a lieutenant general. [French *major-général* : MAJOR (officer) + *général* (adjective), "of general rank."] **—major generalcy, major generalship** *n.*

ma·jor·i·ty (mə-jôr′ĭ-tē, mə-jŏr′-) *n., pl.* **-ties. 1.** The greater number or part: *the majority of the consumers.* See Usage note below. **2. a.** A number more than half of the total number of a given group. Compare **minority. b.** The number of votes cast in an election above the total number of all other votes cast. Compare **plurality. 3.** The political party, group, or faction having the most power by virtue of its larger representation or electoral strength. **4.** The status of legal age when full civil and personal rights may be exercised legally. **5.** The military rank, commission, or office of a major. **6.** *Obsolete.* The fact or state of being greater; superiority. [French *majorité,* from Medieval Latin *mājōritās* (stem *mājōritāt-*), the state of being greater, greater number, from Latin *mājor,* greater.]

Usage: When *majority* refers to a particular number of votes, it takes a singular verb: *Her majority was five votes. His majority has been growing by 5 percent every year.* When it refers to a group of persons or things that are in the majority, it may take either a singular or plural verb, depending on whether the group is considered as a whole or as a set of people functioning individually. So we say *the majority elects* (not *elect*) *the candidate it wants* (not *they want*), since the election is accomplished by the group as a whole; but *the majority of the voters live* (not *lives*) *in the city,* since living in the city is something that each voter does individually. • *Majority* is often preceded by *great* (but not by *greater*) in expressing, emphatically, the sense of "most of": *The great majority approved. Greater majority* is appropriate only when considering two majorities: *He won by a greater majority in this election than in the last.*

majority carrier *n. Electronics.* The electrons in n-type semiconductors and the holes in p-type semiconductors that carry the majority of the current. Compare **minority carrier.**

majority leader *n.* The leader of the majority party in a legislative body, as the U.S. Senate or House of Representatives. Compare **minority leader.**

majority rule *n.* A political doctrine and practice by which a numerical majority of the voters holds the power to make decisions binding on all the voters.

major league *n.* **1.** Either of the two principal groups of professional baseball teams in the United States. **2.** A league of principal importance in other professional sports, such as basketball or football.

ma·jor-league (mā′jər-lēg′) *adj.* **1.** Of or pertaining to a major league. **2.** Being in a leading or significant position: *Car rental is now a major-league business.*

major orders *pl.n.* See **holy orders.**

major planet *n.* Any of the four planets, Jupiter, Saturn, Uranus, or Neptune, that are larger than Earth. Compare **terrestrial planet.**

major premise *n. Logic.* The premise containing the major term in a syllogism.

Major Prophets *pl.n.* **1.** The Hebrew prophets Isaiah, Jeremiah, and Ezekiel. **2.** In the Old Testament, the books of the Major Prophets.

major scale *n. Music.* A diatonic scale having half steps between the third and fourth and the seventh and eighth tones. Compare **minor scale.**

major suit *n.* In the game of bridge, a suit, either spades or hearts, of superior scoring value.

major term *n. Logic.* A term of a syllogism that forms the predicate of the conclusion and the subject or predicate of the major premise.

ma·jus·cule (mə-jŭs′kyo͞ol, măj′ə-skyo͞ol′) *n.* A large letter, either capital or uncial, used in writing or printing. Compare **minuscule.** *~adj.* **1.** Of or pertaining to a majuscule. **2.** Written in majuscules. [French *majuscule,* from Medieval Latin *(littera) mājuscula,* largish (script), from *mājusculus,* somewhat larger, diminutive of *mājor,* larger.] **—ma·jus·cu·lar** (mə-jŭs′kyə-lər) *adj.*

Mak·a·lu (mŭk′ə-lo͞o′). The world's fifth-highest mountain, in the Himalayas of Nepal. Its higher peak, rising to 8,481 meters (27,825 feet), was first climbed in 1955.

Ma·kar·i·os III (mə-kăr′ē-əs, -ōs′), **Archbishop,** born Mikhail Christodoulou Mouskos (1913–77). Primate of the Orthodox Church of Cyprus. He was deported by the British (1956) for alleged support of the EOKA terrorists. He returned in 1959 to become president. He fled in 1974 after a coup by Greek extremists and a subsequent invasion by Turkey, but returned later that year to resume his presidency.

make (māk) *v.* **made** (mād), **making, makes.** *—tr.* **1. a.** To cause to exist or happen; create. **b.** To bring into existence by forming or modifying materials; construct: *make a coat.* **2.** To give a new form or use to: *make a stone into a weapon.* **3.** To cause to become: *That'll make him sorry.* **4.** To cause to acquire a specified characteristic or property: *make a stone sharp.* **5. a.** To cause to behave in a specified manner: *Heat makes a gas expand.* **b.** To compel: *make him obey.* **6.** To use or adopt for a specified purpose: *made the city his home.* **7.** To bring about; cause: *make trouble; make a noise.* **8.** To engage in: *make war.* **9.** To perform: *make a phone call.* **10.** To arrive at; come around to: *make a decision.* **11.** To gain through behavior or effort; acquire: *make a friend.* **12. a.** To score; achieve: *make a run in baseball; make two tricks in bridge.* **b.** To earn: *make money.* **c.** To manage to come within reach of; attain: *couldn't make my quota.* **13.** To confer rank upon: *made him president.* **14. a.** To put into condition for use; set in order: *make the bed.* **b.** To cook or prepare: *making chicken for dinner.* **15.** To prepare and start: *make a fire.* **16.** To regard as the nature or meaning: *What do you make of his behavior?* **17.** To allow provision for; provide: *make room.* **18.** To be suitable for; serve as: *Oak makes a good building material.* **19. a.** To constitute: *Twenty members make a quorum.* **b.** To add up to: *One and one makes two.* **c.** To amount to: *It makes no difference.* **20.** To be the completion or satisfaction of: *That makes my day.* **21.** To succeed in becoming a member of: *He didn't make the debating team.* **22.** To calculate as being; estimate: *We make the distance 20 miles.* **23.** To reach or arrive at: *made Washington by sunset; made the train in time.* **24.** To develop into: *She will make a fine doctor.* **25.** To cause to be or seem: *The beard makes him quite distinguished.* **26.** To close (an electrical circuit). **27.** *Slang.* To induce to have sexual intercourse. **28.** In some card games: **a.** To name (the trump). **b.** To win a trick with (a card). **c.** To shuffle (the cards). *—intr.* **1. a.** To begin or appear to begin an action: *She made as if to shake my hand.* **b.** To behave or act in a specified manner: *make merry.* **2.** To have a particular effect: *little details that make for comfort.* **—make after.** To chase or pursue. **—make away with. 1.** To make off with. **2.** To use up; consume. **—make do.** To manage to get along with the means available: *had to make do on a small salary.* **—make ends meet.** To manage so that one's means are sufficient for one's needs. **—make fun of.** To treat with ridicule; mock. **—make good. 1.** To carry out successfully: *make good her plans.* **2.** To repay; indemnify: *made good their debts.* **3.** To succeed: *made good in the big city.* **—make it. 1.** *Informal.* To become successful: *made it as a dancer.* **2.** *Slang.* To have sexual intercourse. **—make off. 1.** To leave in a hurry. **2.** To snatch; steal: *made off with the profits.* **—make out. 1. a.** To discern or see, especially with difficulty. **b.** To decipher: *I can't make out her handwriting.* **2.** To understand or comprehend: *I can't make out what he is saying.* **3. a.** To write out or draw up: *She made out the invoices.* **b.** To fill in by writing: *make out an application.* **4.** To attempt to prove, show, or imply: *He makes me out to be a liar.* **5.** To get along; manage: *How is he making out in his new job?* **—make over. 1.** To change or redo; renovate: *We made over the cellar into a playroom.* **2.** To change or transfer the ownership of, usually by means of a legal document: *He made over the property to his son.* **—make with.** *Slang.* To perform; produce: *Start making with the hard work.*

~n. **1.** The act or process of making. **2.** The style or manner in which a thing is made: *I dislike the make of this coat.* **3. a.** A manufacturing style. **b.** A specific line of manufactured goods, identified by the maker's name or the registered trademark: *a famous make of shirt.* **4.** The physical or moral nature of a person: *Let's see what make of man you are.* **5.** The amount produced; the yield or output, especially of a factory. **6.** In cards: **a.** The act of naming trumps. **b.** The act of shuffling the cards. **—on the make. 1.** Applying oneself eagerly and often brashly to social or financial advancement. **2.** *Slang.* Sexually adventurous or aggressive. [Make (infinitive), made (past tense), made (past participle); Middle English *maken, mad, mad,* Old English *macian, macode, macod,* from Germanic.]

make believe *tr.v.* To feign; pretend: *Let's make believe we're movie stars.* *—intr.v.* To feign an action or character, as in a play: *She's just making believe.*

make-be·lieve (māk′bə-lēv′) *n.* Playful or fanciful pretense, as in the conscious suspension of reality in a child's game. **—make-be·lieve** *adj.*

make-or-break (māk′ər-brāk′) *adj.* Liable to end in either complete success or complete failure: *a make-or-break policy.*

mak·er (mā′kər) *n.* **1.** One that makes. **2.** *Law.* An individual who signs a promissory note. **3. Maker.** God. Usually used with a possessive pronoun: *our Maker.* **4.** A manufacturer: *a maker of computer components.* **5.** *Archaic.* A poet.

make-read·y (māk′rĕd′ē) *n. Printing.* The operation of preparing a form for printing by adjusting and leveling the plates to ensure a clear impression.

make·shift (māk′shĭft′) *adj.* Used or assembled as a temporary or expedient substitute. **—make·shift** *n.*

make up *tr.v.* **1.** To create or put together by assembling parts or ingredients: *make up a prescription.* **2.** To take (an examination, for example) again or at a later time because of a previous absence or failure. **3.** To apply cosmetics to (the face). **4.** To devise as a fiction or falsehood; invent: *make up an excuse.* **5.** *Printing.* To arrange material into (columns or pages) ready for printing. **6. a.** To add up to or constitute. **b.** To make complete: *make up a foursome at golf.* **7. a.** To make good (a deficit or lack): *make up the difference.* **b.** To resolve (a personal difference or quarrel). *—intr.v.* **1. a.** To apply cosmetics to the face. **b.** To apply theatrical make-up. **2.** To be reconciled after a personal difference: *Let's kiss and make up.* —**make up for.** To compensate for: *make up for lost time.* —**make up to. 1.** To act in a friendly or ingratiating manner toward. **2.** To make amorous overtures to.

make-up (māk'ŭp') *n.* **1.** The way in which something is composed or arranged; construction. **2.** *Printing.* The arrangement or composition, as of type or illustrations, on a page or in a book. **3.** The qualities or temperament that constitute a personality; disposition: *Lying is not in her make-up.* **4.** Cosmetics applied especially to the face. **5.** The cosmetics that an actor uses in playing a role. **6.** A special examination for a student who has been absent from or has failed a previous examination.

make·weight (māk'wāt') *n.* **1.** Something added on a scale in order to meet a required weight. **2.** A counterweight; counterbalance.

make·work (māk'wûrk') *n.* Work of little or no value done only to keep someone busy.

mak·ing (mā'kĭng) *n.* **1. a.** The act of one that makes. **b.** The process of being made: *Watch out for trouble in the making.* **2.** A means of gaining success or realizing potential: *The job will be the making of him.* **3. a.** Something made. **b.** The amount or quantity of something made at one time. **4.** *Often* **makings.** The materials or substances necessary for making or achieving something: *I bought the makings for new slipcovers. We have the makings of a fine team.* **5. makings.** *Slang.* The paper and tobacco for rolling a cigarette.

ma·ko (mä'kō) *n., pl.* **-kos.** Either of two sharks of the genus *Isurus,* characterized by a large, heavy body and a nearly symmetrical tail. [Maori.]

ma·ko-ma·ko (mä'kō-mä'kō) *n., pl.* **-kos.** A small evergreen tree, *Aristotelia serrata,* native to New Zealand, having large racemes of reddish flowers. [Maori.]

ma·ku·ta Plural of **likuta.**

mal– *prefix.* Indicates bad, badly, not, or wrongly; for example, **maladminister, malodorous.** [Middle English, from Old French *mal-* (prefix) and *mal* (adverb and adjective), from Latin *mal-, male-* (prefix), *male* (adverb), ill, and *malus* (adjective), bad.]

Mal. 1. Malachi (Old Testament). **2.** Malay; Malayan.

Mal·a·bar Coast (māl'ə-bär'). The southwestern coast of India. It stretches from Goa in the north to Cape Comorin and produces coconuts, rice, spices, and hardwoods.

Mal·a·bo (mäl'ə-bō', mə-lä'-). Formerly **San·ta Is·a·bel** (săn'tə ĭz'ə-bĕl'). Capital of Equatorial Guinea and the chief town of the island of Bioko.

Ma·lac·ca¹, Me·lak·a (mə-lăk'ə). Seaport of peninsular Malaysia and capital of Malacca state. Founded on the Strait of Malacca in *c.* 1400, the city became one of the chief trading centers of the Far East. It was later colonized in turn by the Portuguese, Dutch, and British (1824). Its commercial importance declined with the expansion of Singapore.

Malacca² *n.* The stem of the rattan palm of Asia, used for walking sticks. [After MALACCA.]

Malacca, Strait of. Sea channel in Southeast Asia, between Sumatra and the Malay Peninsula. It is a major world shipping route and has been claimed by both Indonesia and Malaysia.

Mal·a·chi¹ (māl'ə-kī'). A Hebrew prophet of the 5th century B.C., the last of the Minor Prophets.

Malachi² *n. Abbr.* **Mal.** A prophetic book of the Old Testament attributed to Malachi.

mal·a·chite (māl'ə-kīt') *n.* A green to nearly black mineral carbonate of copper, $CuCO_3·Cu(OH)_2$, used as a source of copper and for ornamental stoneware. [French, from Old French *melochite,* from Latin *molochītēs,* from Greek *molokhitis,* malachite, "the mallow-green stone," from *molokhē,* variant of *malakhē,* mallow.]

Mal·a·chy (māl'ə-kē), **Saint** (1095-1148). Irish churchman. He became bishop of Connor (1124) and archbishop of Armagh (1134-37) and founded the first Cistercian abbey in Ireland (1142).

mal·a·col·o·gy (māl'ə-kŏl'ə-jē) *n.* The scientific study of mollusks. [French *malacologie,* shortening of *malacozoologie,* from New Latin *Malacozoa,* mollusks : Greek *malakos,* soft + -ZOA + -LOGY.] —**mal·a·col·o·gist** *n.*

mal·a·cop·te·ryg·i·an (māl'ə-kŏp'tə-rĭj'ē-ən) *adj.* Of or pertaining to the Malacopterygii, a group of soft-finned fishes including the herring and salmon.
~*n.* A malacopterygian fish. Compare **acanthopterygian.** [Greek *malakos,* soft + *pterux* (stem *pterug-*), wing, fin + -IAN.]

mal·ad·just·ment (māl'ə-jŭst'mənt) *n.* **1.** Faulty adjustment, as in a machine. **2.** *Psychology.* Inability to adjust personality needs to the demands of the social environment. —**mal·ad·just·ed** *adj.*

mal·ad·min·is·ter (māl'əd-mĭn'ĭ-stər) *tr.v.* **-tered, -tering, -ters.** To administer or manage inefficiently or dishonestly. —**mal·ad·min·is·tra·tion** *n.* —**mal·ad·min·is·tra·tor** *n.*

mal·a·droit (māl'ə-droit') *adj.* Lacking dexterity; clumsy; awkward. —See Synonyms at **awkward.** [French, from Old French : MAL- + ADROIT.] —**mal·a·droit·ly** *adv.* —**mal·a·droit·ness** *n.*

mal·a·dy (māl'ə-dē) *n., pl.* **-dies.** A disease, disorder, or ailment. **2.** An unwholesome condition: *the malady of widespread unemployment.* [Middle English *maladie,* from Old French, from *malade,* sick, from Latin *male habitus,* "ill-kept," "in poor condition" : *male,* ill, from *malus,* bad + *habitus,* past participle of *habēre,* to have, keep.]

ma·la fi·de (māl'ə fī'dē) *adv.* In bad faith. Compare **bona fide.** [Latin.] —**ma·la fi·de** *adj.*

Mal·a·ga (māl'ə-gə) *n.* A sweet white wine originally from Málaga.

Mál·a·ga (māl'ə-gə, mä'lə-gä'). Seaport and capital of Málaga prov-

ince, Spain. Founded in the 12th century B.C. by the Phoenicians on the coast of Andalusia, it became a Moorish city (711-1487) and is now a major resort of the Costa del Sol. It exports wine, almonds, dried fruits, and olives. Pablo Picasso was born here.

Mal·a·gas·y (māl'ə-găs'ē) *n., pl.* **-gasies** or collectively **Malagasy. 1.** A native of Madagascar (formerly Malagasy Republic). **2.** The Austronesian language of the Malagasy. —**Mal·a·gas·y** *adj.*

Malagasy Republic. See **Madagascar.**

ma·la·gue·ña (mä'lə-gān'yə) *n.* **1.** A dance native to Málaga, Spain, that is a variety of the fandango. **2.** The music for the malagueña. [Spanish, feminine of *malagueño,* of MÁLAGA.]

mal·aise (mă-lāz', -lĕz') *n.* **1.** A feeling of illness or depression. **2.** A vague feeling of unease. **3.** An unwholesome or undesirable condition or state of affairs: *Violence is a symptom of a malaise in society.* [French, from Old French : MAL- + *aise,* EASE.]

mal·a·mute, mal·e·mute (māl'ə-myōōt') *n.* A powerful dog of a breed developed in Alaska as a sled dog, having a thick gray, black, or white coat. Also called "Alaskan malamute." [Inuit Eskimo *Mahlemut,* name of the Alaskan tribe that bred the dog.]

Mal·a·mud (māl'ə-məd), **Bernard** (1914-86). U.S. author. A Pulitzer Prize winner (1967) and two-time National Book Award recipient (1959 and 1967), he often wrote about Jewish characters coping with a lonely and seemingly unfair world. *The Magic Barrel* (1958) and *The Fixer* (1966) are among his many works.

mal·a·pert (māl'ə-pûrt') *adj.* Impudent in speech or manner; saucy; bold.
~*n.* An impudent, saucy person. [Middle English, from Old French : MAL- + *apert,* clever, from Latin *apertus,* open, from the past participle of *aperīre,* to open.] —**mal·a·pert·ly** *adv.* —**mal·a·pert·ness** *n.*

mal·a·prop·ism (māl'ə-prŏp'ĭz'əm) *n.* A humorous misuse of a word, especially by confusion with one of similar sound: *"A shrewd awakening" instead of "a rude awakening" is a malapropism.* [After Mrs. Malaprop in Sheridan's play *The Rivals* (1775), from MALAPROPOS.] —**mal·a·prop·i·an** (māl'ə-prŏp'ē-ən) *adj.*

mal·a·pro·pos (māl-ăp'rə-pō') *adj.* Inappropriate; out of place.
~*adv.* In an inappropriate or inopportune manner. [French *mal à propos,* "not to the purpose."]

ma·lar (mā'lər, -lär') *adj. Anatomy.* Of or pertaining to the cheekbone or the cheek.
~*n. Anatomy.* The cheekbone, the **zygomatic bone** (*see*). [Latin *mālāris,* from *māla†,* cheekbone, upper jaw. See **maxilla.**]

ma·lar·i·a (mə-lâr'ē-ə) *n.* **1.** An infectious disease characterized by cycles of chills, fever, and sweating, transmitted by the bite of a female anopheles mosquito infected with a protozoan parasite of the genus *Plasmodium.* Also called "paludism," "swamp fever." **2.** *Archaic.* Bad or foul air. [Italian *mal'aria,* foul air: *mal(a),* bad + *aria,* air.] —**ma·lar·i·al, ma·lar·i·an, ma·lar·i·ous** *adj.*

ma·lar·i·ol·o·gy (mə-lâr'ē-ŏl'ə-jē) *n.* The medical study and treatment of malaria. —**ma·lar·i·ol·o·gist** *n.*

ma·lar·key, ma·lar·ky (mə-lär'kē) *n. Slang.* Exaggerated or meaningless talk; nonsense. [20th century : origin obscure.]

mal·as·sim·i·la·tion (māl'ə-sĭm'ə-lā'shən) *n. Pathology.* Incomplete assimilation of food.

mal·ate (māl'āt', māl'āt') *n.* A salt or an ester of malic acid. [MAL(IC ACID) + -ATE.]

Mal·a·thi·on (māl'ə-thī'ŏn') *n.* A trademark for an organic compound, $C_{10}H_{19}O_6PS_2$, similar to but less toxic than parathion and used as a garden insecticide.

Ma·la·wi (mə-lä'wē). Formerly **Ny·as·a·land** (nī-ăs'ə-lănd'). Small, landlocked country in east-central Africa. It depends on agriculture, exporting sugar, tobacco, tea, and groundnuts. However, it has untapped deposits of bauxite and coal and considerable hydroelectric potential. A British protectorate after 1891, the country joined Northern and Southern Rhodesia (now Zambia and Zimbabwe) in a federation (1953-63). It became independent as Malawi in 1964 and a republic in 1966. Area, 118,484 square kilometers (45,747 square miles). Population, 6,000,000. Capital, Lilongwe. See map, next page.

Malawi, Lake. Also **Lake Ny·as·a** (nī-ăs'ə). Lake of east-central Africa, at the southern end of the Great Rift Valley. With an area of *c.* 30,040 square kilometers (11,600 square miles), it is the third largest of Africa's lakes and drains southward via the Shiré River to the Zambezi. David Livingstone reached the lake in 1859.

Ma·lay (mā'lā', mə-lā') *n. Abbr.* **Mal. 1. a.** A member of a people inhabiting much of Malaysia and Indonesia and some adjacent areas. **b.** The Austronesian language of this people. **2.** One of a breed of fowl with red and black plumage domesticated in Asia.
~*adj.* **1.** Of or pertaining to the Malays or their language. **2.** Of or pertaining to Malaya or Malaysia. —**Ma·lay·an** (mə-lā'ən) *adj. & n.*

Ma·lay·a (mə-lā'ə). **1.** Also **Peninsular Malaysia.** Former state in Southeast Asia. The British established trading centers on Penang (now Pinang) Island (1786) and Singapore (1819). In 1824 they formally acquired Malacca from the Dutch. The three territories were joined as the Straits Settlements (1926). By 1930 the British controlled the entire Malay Peninsula, and the independent Federation of Malaya was formed in 1957. See also **Malaysia. 2.** See **Malay Peninsula.**

Mal·a·ya·lam (māl'ə-yä'ləm) *n.* A Dravidian language of the Malabar Coast in southwestern India.

Malay Archipelago. Chain of islands off Southeast Asia separating the Indian and Pacific oceans. Extending *c.* 6,100 kilometers (3,800 miles) from Sumatra to Timor, it includes the Indonesian, Malay-

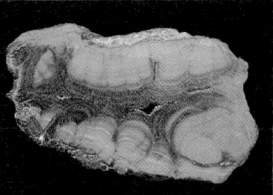

malachite *A naturally occurring copper carbonate. The vivid green pigment produced from powdered malachite was used by the ancient Egyptians for eye make-up.*

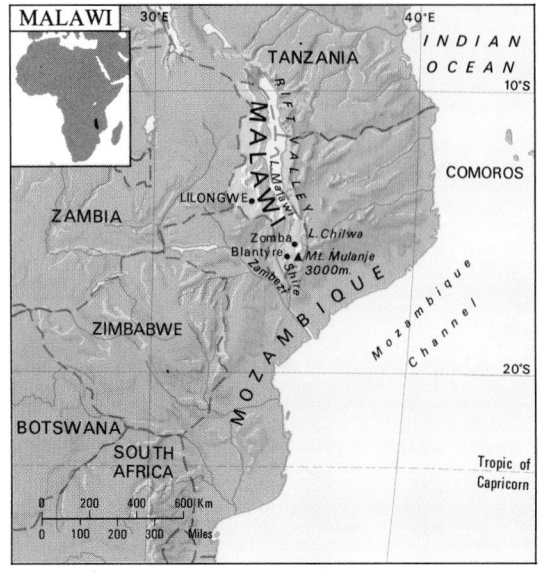

sian, and Philippine islands. The island of New Guinea (without the Bismarck Archipelago) is sometimes included.

Ma·lay·o·Pol·y·ne·sian (mə-lā′ō-pŏl′ə-nē′zhən, -shən) *n.* **Austronesian** *(see).* **—Ma·lay·o·Pol·y·ne·sian** *adj.*

Malay Peninsula. Also **Malaya.** Peninsula of Southeast Asia. Extending south between the Andaman Sea and the South China Sea, it includes part of Thailand in the north, Peninsular Malaysia in the south, and the island of Singapore.

Ma·lay·sia (mə-lā′zhə, -shə). Country in Southeast Asia. Formed in 1963, it comprises West Malaysia (formerly the Federation of Malaya and now called Peninsular Malaysia) and East Malaysia, the former British colonies of Sabah (North Borneo) and Sarawak on the northwestern coast of Borneo, now called by their original names. Singapore seceded in 1965. Generally mountainous, with much tropical rain forest, Malaysia is the world's leading producer of tin and natural rubber, and Sabah and Sarawak have valuable oil fields. Tension between the Malay (44 percent) and Chinese (36 percent) populations has contributed to a history of political unrest. Area, 329,749 square kilometers (127,317 square miles). Population, 13,500,000. Capital, Kuala Lumpur. **—Ma·lay·sian** *adj. & n.*

Mal·colm III (măl′kəm), also known as Malcolm Canmore (1031–93). King of Scotland (1057–93). He was the son of Duncan and became king on the death of Macbeth (1057). He was killed at Alnwick while raiding England.

Malcolm X, born Malcolm Little (1925–65). U.S. black militant leader. Joining the Black Muslims (1952), he preached that Western society was inherently racist and that black people must create a separate society, by violence if necessary. Suspended from the Black Muslims (1963), he founded the Organization of Afro-American Unity (1964) and was assassinated in New York while addressing a rally.

mal·con·tent (măl′kən-tĕnt′) *adj.* Discontented with or in rebellion against established conditions.

~*n.* A discontented or rebellious person. [French : MAL- + CONTENT.]

mal de mer (măl′ də mâr′) *n.* Seasickness. [French.]

mal·dis·tri·bu·tion (măl-dĭs′trə-byōō′shən) *n.* Faulty distribution or apportionment over an area or among a group.

Mal·dives (môl′dīvz′, -dēvz′, măl′-). Formerly **Mal·dive Islands** (-dīv′, -dēv′). South Asian country comprising a group of *c.* 2,000 coral islands in the Indian Ocean, 220 of which are inhabited. It was a sultanate (1100–1965) and after 1887 was under British protection. The sultanate gained full independence in 1965 and became a republic in 1968. Fishing and coconuts are the mainstay of the

economy. Area, 298 square kilometers (115 square miles). Population, 143,000. Capital, Malé. See map at **Indian Ocean**. **—Mal·div·i·an** (môl-dĭv′ē-ən, măl-) *adj. & n.*

male (māl) *adj. Abbr.* **m, M, m., M. 1.** Of, pertaining to, or designating the sex that has organs to produce spermatozoa for fertilizing ova. **2.** Of, pertaining to, or characteristic of the male sex; masculine: *enjoyed male companionship.* **3.** Virile; manly. **4.** Composed of men or boys or both: *a male choir.* **5.** *Botany.* Bearing stamens but not pistils; staminate: *male flowers.* **6.** Of, pertaining to, or being an object, as an electric plug, designed for insertion into a corresponding hollow part or socket.

~*n. Abbr.* **m, M, m., M. 1.** A male human or animal. **2.** A plant having only staminate flowers. [Middle English, from Old French *male, masle,* from Latin *masculus,* diminutive of *mas,* male.] **—male·ness** *n.*

ma·le·ate (mā′lē-āt′, -ət) *n.* A salt or an ester of maleic acid. [MA-LE(IC) + -ATE.]

Male·branche (mäl-bränsh′), Nicolas de (1638–1715). French philosopher. He attempted to reconcile the philosophy of Descartes with religion.

male chauvinist *n.* A man who regards women as being innately inferior to men. **—male chauvinism** *n.*

mal·e·dict (măl′ə-dĭkt′) *adj.* Accursed.

~*tr.v.* **maledicted, -dicting, -dicts.** To pronounce a curse against. [Middle English, from Latin *maledictus,* past participle of *maledicere,* to speak ill of, curse : *male,* ill, from *malus,* bad + *dicere,* to say.]

mal·e·dic·tion (măl′ə-dĭk′shən) *n.* **1. a.** The utterance of a curse. **b.** A curse. **2.** Slander. **—mal·e·dic·to·ry** (măl′ə-dĭk′tə-rē) *adj.*

mal·e·fac·tor (măl′ə-făk′tər) *n.* **1.** One who has committed a crime; a criminal. **2.** An evildoer. [Middle English, from Latin *malefactor,* from *malefacere,* to do wrong : *male,* ill, from *malus,* bad + *facere,* to do.] **—mal·e·fac·tion** (măl′ə-făk′shən) *n.*

male fern *n.* A fern, *Dryopteris filix-mas,* that yields the drug used to treat tapeworm infestation.

ma·lef·ic (mə-lĕf′ĭk) *adj.* Producing or causing evil or disaster: *malefic arts.* [Latin *maleficus,* doing wrong : *male,* ill, from *malus,* bad + -FIC.]

ma·lef·i·cence (mə-lĕf′ə-səns) *n.* **1.** Evil or harm; mischief. **2.** Harmful or evil nature or quality. [Latin *maleficentia,* from *maleficus,* MALEFIC.] **—ma·lef·i·cent** *adj.*

ma·le·ic acid (mə-lē′ĭk, -lā′ĭk) *n.* A colorless crystalline acid, HOOCCH:CHCOOH, used in the synthesis of resins and as an oil and fat preservative. [French *maléique,* variant of *malique,* MALIC (ACID).]

malemute. Variant of **malamute.**

Ma·len·kov (mä′lĕn-kôf′), Georgi Maximilianovich (1902–). Soviet Communist leader. He became a trusted aide of Stalin and deputy premier (1946), succeeding him as premier in 1953. He was also briefly first secretary of the Communist Party. He resigned in 1955 because of the failure of the government's agricultural policy.

mal·en·ten·du (măl-ŏn′tŏn-dōō′) *n.* A misunderstanding. [French, from *mal entendu,* misunderstood.]

ma·lev·o·lent (mə-lĕv′ə-lənt) *adj.* **1.** Having or exhibiting ill will; wishing harm to others; malicious. **2.** Having an evil influence: *malevolent stars.* [Latin *malevolēns* (stem *malevolent-*) : *male,* ill, from *malus,* bad + *volēns,* present participle of *velle,* to will, wish.] **—ma·lev·o·lence** *n.* **—ma·lev·o·lent·ly** *adv.*

mal·fea·sance (măl-fē′zəns) *n. Law.* Misconduct or wrongdoing; especially, wrongdoing that is committed by one who has official obligations. Compare **misfeasance, nonfeasance.** [MAL- + Old French *faisance,* doing, from Medieval Latin *faciēntia,* from Latin *facere,* to do.] **—mal·fea·sant** *adj. & n.*

mal·for·ma·tion (măl′fôr-mā′shən) *n.* **1.** The condition of being malformed. **2.** An abnormal structure or form, especially a deformity present at birth.

mal·formed (măl-fôrmd′) *adj.* Abnormally or faultily formed.

mal·func·tion (măl-fŭngk′shən) *intr.v.* **-tioned, -tioning, -tions. 1.** To fail to function. **2.** To function abnormally; perform imperfectly.

~*n.* The act or an instance of malfunctioning.

Mal·herbe (mä-lĕrb′), François de (1555–1628). French poet. He helped formulate the French classical style.

Ma·li (mä′lē). Formerly **French Su·dan** (sōō-dăn′). A landlocked West African country. The Sahara covers the north and savanna the south. The country's agricultural economy has been ravaged by drought, and its exports of cotton and groundnuts have to be supplemented by foreign aid, especially from France. The seat of several ancient empires, Mali was conquered by the French (1893) and became part of French West Africa. In 1959 it joined Senegal in the Mali Federation but broke away to full independence the next year. Area, 1,240,000 square kilometers (478,767 square miles). Population, 7,000,000. Capital, Bamako.

mal·ic acid (măl′ĭk, mā′lĭk) *n.* A colorless crystalline compound, COOHCH₂CH(OH)COOH, that occurs naturally in a wide variety of unripe fruit, including apples, cherries, and tomatoes, and is used as a flavoring and to aid in aging wine. [French *acide malique,* from Latin *mālum,* apple, from Doric Greek *malon,* variant of Attic *mēlon.*]

mal·ice (măl′ĭs) *n.* **1.** The desire to harm others or to see others suffer; ill will or spite: *Her eyes glittered with malice.* **2.** *Law.* The intent, without just cause or reason, to commit an unlawful act that will result in harm to another or others. Often used in the phrases

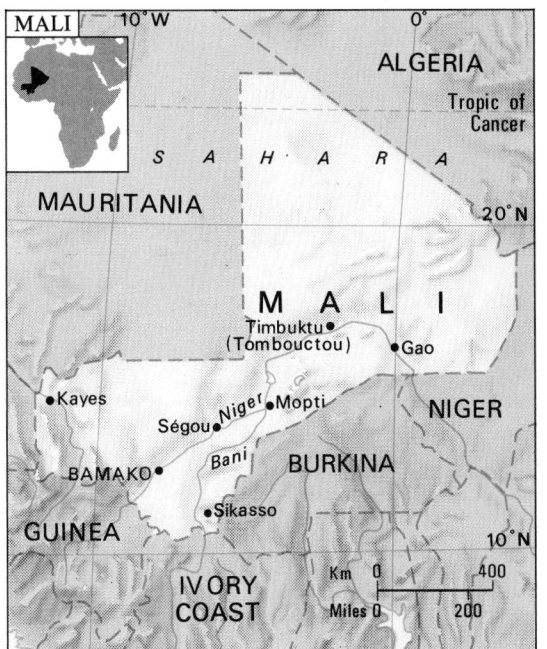

MALI

ALGERIA

Tropic of Cancer

MAURITANIA

20°N

S A H A R A

M A L I

Timbuktu (Tombouctou)

• Gao

• Kayes

Niger

• Mopti

NIGER

Ségou

Bani

BURKINA

BAMAKO

• Sikasso

GUINEA

10°N

IVORY COAST

Km 0 400
Miles 0 200

founder with Paul Verlaine of the symbolist school. He developed a deliberately obscure style, using allegory and unconventional construction and vocabulary. His works include *L'Après-midi d'un Faune* (1876), which inspired Debussy, and *Un Coup de Dés Jamais N'abolira le Hasard* (1897).

mal·le·a·ble (măl'ē-ə-bəl) *adj.* **1.** Capable of being shaped or formed, as by hammering or pressure: *a malleable metal.* **2.** Capable of being altered or influenced; tractable: *the malleable mind of the pragmatist.* [Middle English *malliable,* from Old French *malleable,* from Medieval Latin *malleābilis,* from *malleāre,* to hammer, from *malleus,* a hammer.] **—mal·le·a·bil·i·ty, mal·le·a·ble·ness** *n.* **—mal·le·a·bly** *adv.*

mal·lee (măl'ē) *n.* **1.** Any of several low, scrubby evergreen trees of the genus *Eucalyptus,* of western Australia. **2.** A thicket or growth of mallee. [Native Australian name.]

mal·le·muck (măl'ə-mŭk') *n.* Any of several sea birds, such as the fulmar, the petrel, or the shearwater. [Dutch *mallemok,* fulmar : Middle Dutch *mal,* silly + *mocke,* thing.]

mal·le·o·lus (mə-lē'ə-ləs) *n., pl.* **-li** (-lī'). *Anatomy.* Either of the two rounded protuberances on each side of the ankle, formed by a projection of the tibia or fibula. [New Latin, diminutive of Latin *malleus,* hammer (from the resemblance to a hammerhead).]

mal·let (măl'ĭt) *n.* **1. a.** A short-handled hammer, usually with a wooden head, used chiefly to drive a chisel or wedge. **b.** A tool with a large head used to strike a surface without damaging it. **2.** A long-handled implement used to strike a ball, as in croquet and polo. **3.** A light hammer with a spherical, often padded head used to play instruments such as the vibraphone or xylophone. [Middle English *maillet,* from Old French, from *mailler,* to hammer, from *mail,* a hammer, from Latin *malleus,* hammer.]

mal·le·us (măl'ē-əs) *n., pl.* **mallei** (măl'ē-ī'). The largest of three small bones in the middle ear. Also called "hammer." Compare **incus, stapes.** See **ear.** [Latin, hammer.]

Mal·lon (măl'ən), **Mary,** known as "Typhoid Mary" (c. 1870–1938). U.S. disease carrier. An immune typhoid carrier, she was a professional cook, and while moving from job to job she infected more than 50 people with typhoid fever. After health officials found her, she was institutionalized for much of the rest of her life.

Mal·lor·ca (mə-yôr'kə, məl-yôr'-). English **Ma·jor·ca** (mə-jôr'kə, -yôr'kə). Largest of the Balearic Islands, Baleares province, Spain. Its northern mountains give it a mild climate, and tourism is the economy's mainstay, together with agriculture, fishing, and mining. Palma is the capital and chief port. **—Mal·lor·can** *adj. & n.*

mal·low (măl'ō) *n.* **1.** Any plant of the widely distributed genus *Malva,* typically having pink flowers. **2.** Any of various related plants, such as the marsh mallow or musk mallow. [Middle English *malwe,* Old English *mealuwe, mealwe,* from Latin *malva.*]

malm (mäm) *n.* **1. a.** A soft, easily crumbled limestone. **b.** Loam formed by the disintegration of such limestone. **2.** A mixture of clay and chalk used in making bricks. [Middle English *malme,* Old English *mealm-* (only in compounds).]

Mal·mö (măl'mō', măl'mœ'). Seaport in Sweden, on the Oresund opposite Copenhagen. It is a naval port and a shipbuilding and textile center.

malm·sey (mäm'zē) *n., pl.* **-seys.** A sweet fortified white wine originally made in Greece but now also produced in Madeira, the Canary Islands, the Azores, and Spain. [Middle English, from Medieval Latin *Malmasia,* alteration of Greek *Monembasia,* Greek seaport from which it was shipped.]

mal·nour·ished (măl-nûr'ĭsht) *adj.* Suffering from improper nutrition or insufficient food.

mal·nu·tri·tion (măl'nōō-trĭsh'ən, măl'nyōō-) *n.* A lack of or condition resulting from a lack of adequate nutrition. It is caused by an insufficient or ill-balanced diet or by defective digestion or utilization of food.

mal·oc·clu·sion (măl'ə-klōō'zhən) *n.* Failure of the upper and lower teeth to meet when the mouth is closed.

mal·o·dor·ous (măl-ō'dər-əs) *adj.* Having a bad odor; ill-smelling. **—mal·o·dor·ous·ly** *adv.* **—mal·o·dor·ous·ness** *n.*

ma·lon·ic acid (mə-lō'nĭk, -lŏn'ĭk') *n.* A colorless crystalline acid, $C_3H_4O_4$, derived from malic acid and used in making barbiturates. [French *acide malonique,* alteration of *acide malique,* MALIC ACID.]

Mal·o·ry (măl'ə-rē), **Sir Thomas** (died 1471). English writer. He was the author of *Le Morte d'Arthur* (published by William Caxton, 1485), a collection of Arthurian romances adapted from French sources.

Mal·pi·ghi (măl-pē'gē), **Marcello** (1628–94). Italian physiologist. He was the first to use a microscope in the study of anatomy. He became physician to Pope Innocent XII (1691).

Mal·pigh·i·an corpuscle (măl-pĭg'ē-ən, -pē'gē-ən) *n. Anatomy.* A mass of arterial capillaries enveloped in a capsule and attached to a tubule in the kidney. Also called "Malpighian body." [Discovered by Marcello MALPIGHI.]

Malpighian layer *n. Anatomy.* The deepest layer of the epidermis, from which the outer layers develop.

Malpighian tubule *n.* Any of the excretory tubes leading into the rear part of the gut of arthropods. Also called "Malpighian tube."

mal·po·si·tion (măl'pə-zĭsh'ən) *n.* An abnormal position, especially of a fetus or of a bodily part.

mal·prac·tice (măl-prăk'tĭs) *n.* **1.** Improper or negligent treatment of a patient by a physician, resulting in damage or injury. **2.** Improper or unethical conduct by the holder of an official or profes-

malice aforethought and *malice prepense.* [Middle English, from Old French, from Latin *malitia,* from *malus,* bad.]

ma·li·cious (mə-lĭsh'əs) *adj.* **1.** Resulting from or having the nature of malice: *malicious rumors.* **2.** *Law.* Motivated by or experiencing malice. **—ma·li·cious·ly** *adv.* **—ma·li·cious·ness** *n.*

ma·lign (mə-līn') *tr.v.* **-ligned, -ligning, -ligns.** To speak evil of; slander; defame.

~*adj.* **1.** Evil in nature or intent. **2.** Evil in influence; injurious; baleful. [Middle English *maligne,* evil, from Old French, from Latin *malignus,* from *malus,* bad.] **—ma·lign·er** *n.* **—ma·lign·ly** *adv.*

> **Synonyms:** *calumniate, defame, libel, revile, slander, vilify, vituperate.*

ma·lig·nan·cy (mə-lĭg'nən-sē) *n., pl.* **-cies.** Also **ma·lig·nance** (-nəns). **1.** The state or quality of being malignant. **2.** A malignant tumor.

ma·lig·nant (mə-lĭg'nənt) *adj.* **1.** Showing great malevolence; actively evil in nature. **2.** Highly injurious; pernicious. **3.** *Pathology.* **a.** Designating an abnormal growth that tends to metastasize. Compare **benign. b.** Threatening to life or health; virulent: *a malignant disease.* **—ma·lig·nant·ly** *adv.*

ma·lig·ni·ty (mə-lĭg'nə-tē) *n., pl.* **-ties. 1. a.** Intense ill will or hatred; great malice. **b.** An act or feeling of great malice. **2.** The condition or quality of being highly dangerous or injurious; deadliness.

ma·li·hi·ni (mä'lĭ-hē'nē) *n.* A newcomer, foreigner, or stranger among the natives of Hawaii. [Hawaiian.]

ma·lines, ma·line (mə-lēn') *n., pl.* **malines. 1.** A thin, stiff, gauzy material woven in a hexagonal pattern. **2.** A fine lace, **Mechlin** *(see).* [French, from *Malines* (MECHELEN), Belgium, where the lace was made.]

Malines. See **Mechelen.**

ma·lin·ger (mə-lĭng'gər) *intr.v.* **-gered, -gering, -gers.** To pretend to be ill or injured in order to avoid duty or work. [French *malingre,* sickly, from Old French *malingre†* : perhaps MAL- + *haingre,* weak.] **—ma·lin·ger·er** *n.*

Ma·lin·ke (mə-lĭng'kē) *n., pl.* **-kes** or collectively **Malinke. 1.** A member of a people of west Africa related to the Mandingos. **2.** The language of the Malinke.

Ma·li·now·ski (mä'lə-nôf'skē, măl'ə-), **Bronislaw Kasper** (1884–1942). Polish-born English anthropologist. He believed that customs and beliefs have specific social functions. His works, based on his research in New Guinea, include *Crime and Custom in Savage Society* (1926) and *The Sexual Life of Savages in Northwestern Melanesia* (1929).

mal·i·son (măl'ə-sən, -zən) *n. Archaic.* A curse. [Middle English *malisoun,* from Old French *maleison,* from Latin *maledictiō* (stem *maledictiōn-),* from *maledicere,* to MALEDICT.]

mall (môl, măl) *n.* **1.** A shady public walk or promenade. **2. a.** A street lined with shops and closed to vehicles. **b.** A shopping center. **c.** A large building or complex of buildings containing various shops, businesses, and restaurants that are usually accessible by common passageways. **3.** A median strip dividing a road or highway. [After The *Mall* in London, England, originally a pall-mall walk, shortened from PALL-MALL.]

mal·lard (măl'ərd) *n., pl.* **-lards** or collectively **mallard.** A wild duck, *Anas platyrhynchos,* the male of which has a green head and neck. It is the ancestor of most domestic ducks. [Middle English, from Old French *mallart,* probably from *maslart* (unattested) : *masle,* MALE + *-art,* -ARD.]

Mal·lar·mé (măl'är-mā'), **Stéphane** (1842–98). French poet,

mallard *Found throughout the Northern Hemisphere, the mallard is the ancestor of most domestic duck breeds.*

sional position. **3.** An act or instance of improper practice.
—mal·prac·ti·tion·er (măl′prăk-tĭsh′ə-nər) *n.*

Mal·raux (măl-rō′), **André** (1901–76). French writer and political figure. Under De Gaulle's Fifth Republic he served as minister of information (1945–46) and minister for culture (1959–69). His books include *La Condition Humaine* (1933), *Le Temps du Mépris* (1935), and an autobiography, *Antimémoires* (1967).

malt (môlt) *n.* **1.** Grain, usually barley, that has been allowed to sprout, used chiefly in brewing and distilling. **2.** An alcoholic beverage brewed from malt. **3.** A beverage made with malted milk. ~*v.* **malted, malting, malts.** —*tr.* **1.** To process (grain) into malt. **2.** To treat or mix with malt or a malt extract. —*intr.* To become malt. [Middle English, from Old English *mealt.*] —**malt′y** *adj.*

Mal·ta (môl′tə). Mediterranean republic comprising the islands of Malta, Gozo, and Comino and two uninhabited islets. Its strategic value led to a series of foreign invasions, starting with that of the Phoenicians before 1000 B.C., and it became a British colony (1814). Malta became an independent Commonwealth republic in 1974. The economy depends on shipping, tourism, and light industries. Area, 316 square kilometers (122 square miles). Population, 344,000. Capital, Valletta.

Malta fever *n.* **Brucellosis** *(see).*

mal·tase (môl′tās′, -tāz′) *n.* An enzyme that hydrolyzes maltose to glucose.

malted milk *n.* **1.** A soluble powder made of dried milk, malted barley, and wheat flour. **2.** A beverage made by mixing milk with malted milk powder and often adding ice cream and flavoring. In this sense, also called "malt."

Mal·tese (môl-tēz′, -tēs′) *adj.* Of or pertaining to Malta or its inhabitants or to the language spoken in Malta. ~*n., pl.* **Maltese. 1.** A native or inhabitant of Malta. **2.** The language spoken in Malta, a dialect of North Arabic with elements of Italian. **3.** One of a breed of toy dogs, probably originating in Malta, having a long, silky white coat, a black nose, short legs, and a tail arched over the back. **4.** A Maltese cat.

Maltese cat *n.* A North American domestic cat with short, silky, bluish-gray fur.

Maltese cross *n.* A cross having the form of four triangles, often with the outer edges indented, placed with their points toward the center of a circle.

mal·tha (măl′thə) *n.* **1.** A black, viscous natural bitumen. **2.** Any of certain mineral waxes composed of mixtures of hydrocarbons. [Latin, from Greek *maltha,* a mixture of wax and pitch.]

malt·house (môlt′hous′) *n.* A building where malt is made or stored.

Mal·thus (măl′thəs), **Thomas Robert** (1766–1834). British economist. He wrote *An Essay on the Principle of Population* (1798), arguing that a population without planning increased faster than food production. His ideas were used to justify birth control. —**Mal·thu·sian** (măl-thōō′zhən, môl′-) *n. & adj.* —**Mal·thu·sian·ism** *n.*

malt liquor *n.* An alcoholic drink, such as beer, brewed from malt.

mal·tose (môl′tōs′, -tōz′) *n.* A sugar, $C_{12}H_{22}O_{11}$, formed during the digestion of starch and also occurring in germinating cereal grains. Also called "malt sugar."

mal·treat (măl-trēt′) *tr.v.* **-treated, -treating, -treats.** To treat cruelly; handle roughly. —See Synonyms at **abuse.** [French *maltraiter* : MAL- + *traiter,* to TREAT.] —**mal·treat·ment** *n.*

malt·ster (môlt′stər) *n.* One who makes malt. [Middle English : MALT + -STER.]

malt sugar *n.* Maltose.

mal·va·ceous (măl-vā′shəs) *adj.* Of or pertaining to the Malvaceae, a family of flowering plants that includes the mallow, cotton, and hollyhock. [Latin *malvaceus,* from *malva,* MALLOW.]

mal·va·si·a (măl′və-zē′ə, -sē′ə) *n.* **1.** A grape from which malmsey wine is made. **2.** Malmsey wine. [Italian, from Medieval Greek *Monemvasia,* MALMSEY.] —**mal·va·si·an** *adj.*

mal·ver·sa·tion (măl′vər-sā′shən) *n.* Misconduct committed while in public office. [Old French, from *malverser,* to misbehave, from Latin *male versārī* : *male,* ill, from *malus,* bad + *versārī,* to behave.]

Malvinas, Islas. See **Falkland Islands.**

mal·voi·sie (măl′vwə-zē′) *n.* **1.** Malmsey wine. **2.** A type of grape from which malmsey wine is made. [Middle English *malvesie,* from Old French, from Medieval Greek *Monemvasia,* MALVASIA.]

mam (măm) *n. British Regional.* Mother. Used familiarly, especially by children.

ma·ma, mam·ma (mä′mə; *also* mə-mä′ *for sense 1*) *n.* **1.** Mother. Used familiarly, as by children. **2.** *Slang.* **a.** A woman. **b.** A wife. [Of baby-talk origin.]

mam·ba (mäm′bə, măm′-) *n.* Any of several venomous arboreal snakes of the genus *Dendraspis,* found in equatorial and southern Africa; especially, *D. angusticeps,* a green or black tree snake. [Zulu *im-amba.*]

mam·bo (mäm′bō) *n., pl.* **-bos. 1.** A dance of Latin-American origin that resembles the rumba. **2.** The syncopated music for the mambo, in ⁴/₄ time. ~*intr.v.* **mamboed, -boing, -bos.** To dance the mambo. [American Spanish, from Haitian Creole *mambo,* a voodoo priestess.]

mam·e·lon (măm′ə-lən) *n.* A small, rounded hill. [French, "nipple," from *mamelle,* breast. See **mammilla.**]

Mam·e·luke (măm′ə-lōōk′) *n.* A member of a former military caste, originally composed of slaves from Turkey, that held the Egyptian throne from about 1250 until 1517 and remained powerful until 1811. [Arabic *mamlūk,* slave.]

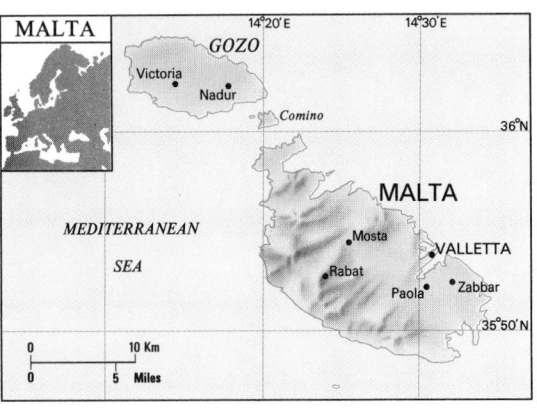

MALTA

mam·ma¹. Variant of **mama.**

mam·ma² (măm′ə) *n., pl.* **mammae** (măm′ē). An organ of female mammals that contains milk-producing glands; a breast or udder. [Latin.] —**mam·mate** (măm′āt′) *adj.*

mam·mal (măm′əl) *n.* A member of the class Mammalia. [From MAMMALIA.] —**mam·ma·li·an** (mə-mā′lē-ən, -măl′yən) *adj. & n.*

Mam·ma·li·a (mə-mā′lē-ə, -măl′yə) *pl.n.* A class of vertebrate animals of more than 15,000 species, including humans, distinguished by self-regulating body temperature, separation of oxygenated and deoxygenated blood in the heart, and, in the females, milk-producing mammae. [New Latin, from Latin *mammalis,* of the breast, from *mamma,* breast.]

mam·mal·o·gy (mə-măl′ə-jē, mə-mŏl′-) *n.* The branch of zoology dealing with the study of the Mammalia. [MAMMAL + -LOGY.] —**mam·ma·log·i·cal** (măm′ə-lŏj′ĭ-kəl) *adj.* —**mam·mal·o·gist** (mə-măl′ə-jĭst, mə-mŏl′-) *n.*

mam·ma·plas·ty (măm′ə-plăs′tē) *n., pl.* **-ties.** The altering of the shape or size of the breast by plastic surgery. [MAMMA (breast) + -PLASTY.]

mam·ma·ry (măm′ə-rē) *adj.* Of or pertaining to a breast or mamma.

mammary gland *n.* A milk-producing organ in female mammals that consists of clusters of alveoli or small cavities with ducts terminating in a nipple or teat.

mam·mee (mă-mē′) *n.* **1.** A tropical American tree, *Mammea americana,* bearing large, edible fruits. **2.** The large, red-rinded fruit of the mammee, having a yellow, pulpy center. In this sense, also called "mammee apple." [Spanish *mamey, mamei,* from Haitian.]

mam·mif·er·ous (mə-mĭf′ər-əs) *adj.* Having mammary glands. [French *mammifère* : MAMMA (breast) + -FEROUS.]

mam·mil·la (mə-mĭl′ə) *n., pl.* **-millae** (-mĭl′ē). **1.** A nipple or teat. **2.** A nipple-shaped protuberance. [Latin, diminutive of *mamma,* breast.] —**mam·il·lar·y** (măm′ə-lĕr′ē, mə-mĭl′ə-rē) *adj.*

mam·mil·late (măm′ə-lāt′) *adj.* Also **mam·mil·lat·ed** (-lā′tĭd). **1.** Having nipples or mammillae. **2.** Shaped like a nipple or mammilla. —**mam·mil·la·tion** *n.*

mam·mo·gram (măm′ə-grăm′) *n.* An x-ray photograph or radiograph of the breast. [MAMMA (breast) + -GRAM.]

mam·mog·ra·phy (mə-mŏg′rə-fē) *n.* Examination of the breast by x-rays, used for the early detection of abnormal growths. [MAMMA (breast) + -GRAPHY.]

Mam·mon (măm′ən) *n.* **1.** In the New Testament, riches, avarice, and worldly gain personified as a false god. Matthew 6:24; Luke 16:9,11,13. **2.** *Often* **mammon.** Riches regarded as a worldly goal or an evil influence. [Middle English *Mammona,* from Medieval Latin *mammōna,* from Greek *mamōnas,* from Aramaic *māmōnā,* riches.] —**mam·mon·ism** *n.* —**mam·mon·ist** *n.*

mam·moth (măm′əth) *n.* **1.** An extinct elephant of the genus *Mammuthus,* once found throughout the Northern Hemisphere. The best-known species is the woolly mammoth, *M. primigenius,* of northern Eurasia and North America. **2.** Something of great size. ~*adj.* Of enormous size, scale, or importance; gigantic. —See Synonyms at **enormous.** [Obsolete Russian *mammot,* from Tartar *mamont,* "earth" (because the first mammoth remains were dug out of the earth in Siberia).]

Mammoth Cave National Park. A park (20,799 hectares; 51,534 acres) in southern Kentucky. It contains Mammoth Cave, one of the largest in the world, consisting of five levels of subterranean chambers and narrow passages, with limestone formations and underground lakes and rivers. Its full extent is still unknown. Kentucky pioneers first visited the cave, long an Indian habitation site, in 1799.

mam·my (măm′ē) *n., pl.* **-mies. 1.** Mother. Used familiarly, especially by children. **2.** A black nurse for white children, especially formerly in the southern United States. [Baby talk, variant of MAMA.]

man (măn) *n., pl.* **men** (mĕn). **1.** An adult male human being as distinguished from a female: *Statistics show that women live longer than men.* Sometimes used in combination: *a real he-man.* **2.** A human being as distinguished from an animal or deity; a member of the human race; a person: *A man could drop from the heat.* Sometimes used in combination: *draftsman; workmanlike; man-day.* —See Usage note at **-person. 3.** The human race; mankind: *Man is* a *selfish creature.* **4.** *Zoology.* A member of the genus *Homo,* family Hominidae, order Primates, class Mammalia, characterized by erect posture and an opposable thumb; especially, a member of the only extant species, *Homo sapiens,* distinguished by the ability to communicate by means of organized speech and to record information in a variety of symbolic systems. **5.** A male human being endowed with such qualities as courage, strength, and fortitude, considered characteristic of manhood: *Stop sniveling and be a man!* **6.** *Informal.* **a.** A husband. **b.** A lover, sweetheart, or boyfriend. **7.** *men.* **a.** Enlisted servicemen of the armed forces: *Officers and men alike attended the party.* **b.** Workers or subordinates as opposed to management. **8.** A male servant, especially a valet. **9.** *Informal.* Fellow. Used as a term of address: *Look here, my good man!* **10.** One who swore allegiance to a lord in the Middle Ages; a liegeman; a vassal. **11.** Any of the pieces used in a board game, as chess, checkers, or backgammon. **12.** *Nautical.* A ship. Used in combination: *merchantman; man-of-war.* **13.** A representative, as of a government or large company, in a specified town or country: *our man in Paris.* **14.** *Often* **Man.** *Slang.* **a.** A policeman. **b.** White men as a group; white society: *feared the Man.* **—as one man.** With complete assent or agreement; unanimously: *They answered him as one man.* **—man and boy.** From boyhood on: *Man and boy, I've lived here 40 years.* **—one's own man.** Independent in judgment and action. **—to a man.** Including everyone; without exception. **—See Usage note at **gentleman.**

~*tr.v.* **manned, manning, mans.** **1.** To supply or furnish with men for defense, support, or service: *manning a ship.* **2.** To be stationed at in order to defend, care for, or operate: *man the guns.*

~*interj.* *Slang.* Used as an expletive to indicate strong feeling or to draw attention: *Man, it's hot in here!* [Middle English *man* (plural *men*), Old English *mann* (plural *menn*), from Germanic *mann-* (unattested).]

Man (măn), **Isle of.** Island in the Irish Sea, an autonomous possession of the British Crown. Its parliament, the Court of Tynwald, is one of the oldest legislative assemblies in the world. The island depends on tourism, agriculture, sheep raising, and fishing. Douglas is the capital. See map at **United Kingdom.**

Man. Manitoba.

ma·na (mä′nə) *n.* **1.** An impersonal supernatural force thought to be inherent in a person, god, or sacred object. **2.** Power, prestige, or influence; authority. [Maori.]

man-a·bout-town (măn′ə-bout′toun′) *n., pl.* **men-a·bout-town** (mĕn′-). A worldly and sophisticated man, especially one who frequents fashionable places.

man·a·cle (măn′ə-kəl) *n.* **1.** A device for confining the hands, usually consisting of two metal rings that are fastened about the wrists and joined by a metal chain. **2.** Something that confines or restrains.

~*tr.v.* **manacled, -cling, -cles.** **1.** To restrain with manacles. **2.** To confine or restrain as if with manacles; shackle; fetter. [Middle English *manicle,* from Old French, from Latin *manicula,* little hand, handle, diminutive of *manus,* hand.]

man·age (măn′ĭj) *v.* **-aged, -aging, -ages.** —*tr.* **1.** To direct or control the use of; handle, wield, or use (a tool, machine, or weapon, for example). **2.** To exert control over; make submissive to one's authority, discipline, or persuasion: *She can't manage her children.* **3.** To direct or administer the affairs of (an organization or estate, for example): *He manages a football team.* **4. a.** To contrive or arrange; succeed in doing or accomplishing, especially with difficulty: *I'll manage to come on Friday.* **b.** To deal or cope with: *She couldn't manage any more food.* —*intr.* **1.** To direct, supervise, or carry on business affairs; especially, to perform the duties of a manager. **2.** To carry on or get along, as in financial matters: *They can't manage without her.* **—See Synonyms at conduct.** [Italian *maneggiare,* to handle (a horse), probably from Vulgar Latin *manidiāre* (unattested), to handle, from Latin *manus,* hand.] **—man·age·a·bil·i·ty, man·age·a·ble·ness** *n.* **—man·age·a·ble** *adj.* **—man·age·a·bly** *adv.*

managed currency *n.* A monetary system in which the money supply and its buying power are controlled by a governmental agency or a central bank rather than being automatically regulated by the gold standard.

man·age·ment (măn′ĭj-mənt) *n.* **1.** The act, manner, or practice of managing, handling, or controlling something. **2.** The person or persons who manage a business establishment, organization, or institution. **3.** Skill in managing; executive ability.

man·ag·er (măn′ĭ-jər) *n. Abbr.* **mgr., Mgr. 1.** A person who manages a business or enterprise. **2.** A person who is in charge of the business affairs of an entertainer or group of entertainers. **3.** *Sports.* **a.** A person in charge of the training and performance of an athlete or team. **b.** A student in charge of the equipment and records of a school or college team. **4.** In Britain, any of a number of members of either of the Houses of Parliament appointed to arrange business matters in which both Houses are involved. **5.** *Law.* One who is appointed by a court to run a business while it is in the hands of a receiver. **—man·ag·er·ship** *n.*

man·ag·er·ess (măn′ĭ-jər-ĭs) *n.* A woman who is a manager, as of a restaurant.

man·a·ge·ri·al (măn′ə-jîr′ē-əl) *adj.* Of, pertaining to, or characteristic of a manager or management. **—man·a·ge·ri·al·ly** *adv.*

managing editor *n.* An editor with administrative and executive control over all editorial work of a publication.

Ma·na·gua (mə-nä′gwə). Capital of Nicaragua since 1855. It lies on the south shore of Lake Managua and is a center for industry, trade,

and administration. It was badly damaged by earthquakes (1931 and 1972) and in the civil war (1979).

man·a·kin (măn′ə-kĭn) *n.* **1.** Any of various small, colorful birds of the family Pipridae, found in forests of Central and South America. **2.** Variant of **manikin.** [Alteration of MANIKIN.]

Ma·na·ma, Ma·na·mah (mə-nä′mə, -näm′ə). *Arabic* **Al Ma·na·mah** (äl′ mə-nä′mə). Capital of Bahrain since 1971. It was formerly a pearl-fishing center; its newer activities include oil refining, fishing, petrochemicals, and marine industries. It is also the free transit port for the southern Persian Gulf.

ma·ña·na (män-yä′nə) *adv.* **1.** Tomorrow. **2.** At some unspecified future time.

~*n.* Some indefinite time in the future. [Spanish, tomorrow, from Vulgar Latin *(cras) māneāna* (unattested), "early tomorrow" : *crās,* tomorrow (see **procrastinate**) + *māneāna,* early, from Latin *māne,* in the morning.]

Manáos. See **Manaus.**

Ma·nas·sas (mə-năs′əs). Town in northern Virginia, in a farming area. During the Civil War it was a key railroad junction. The Battles of Bull Run (known in the South as the Battles of Manassas) were fought nearby in 1861 and 1862.

Ma·nas·seh¹ (mə-năs′ə). The elder son of Joseph. Genesis 41:51.

Manasseh². A king of Judah in the 7th century B.C. II Kings 21:1–18.

Manasseh³ *n.* A tribe of Israel descended from Manasseh, son of Joseph.

man-at-arms (măn′ət-ärmz′) *n., pl.* **men-at-arms** (mĕn′-). A soldier; especially, a medieval cavalryman supplied with heavy arms.

man·a·tee (măn′ə-tē′) *n.* A whalelike mammal of the genus *Trichechus,* found in Atlantic coastal waters of the tropical Americas and Africa. It has paddlelike forelimbs and a horizontally flattened tail. [Spanish *manati,* from Carib *manattouï.*]

Ma·naus, Ma·náos (mə-nous′). Capital of Amazonas state, Brazil. On the Río Negro, near the Amazon, it is a free port accessible to oceangoing ships and the commercial center for the upper Amazon basin. Around 1900 it was the center of a rubber boom. With the opening up of Amazonas and the discovery of oil nearby, it is booming again.

Mancha, La. See **La Mancha.**

Man·ches·ter (măn′chĕs′tər, -chĭ-stər). City in the metropolitan county of Greater Manchester in northwestern England. It began as a Roman camp, Mancunium, and its people are still known as Mancunians. A medieval wool town, it became the country's main cotton center during the Industrial Revolution. England's first passenger railway linked it with Liverpool in 1830, and with the completion of the Manchester Ship Canal (1894) the city became a major port and financial center.

Manchester terrier *n.* A short-haired, black-and-tan dog of a breed that originated in Manchester, England. Formerly called "black-and-tan terrier."

man·chi·neel (măn′chĭ-nēl′) *n.* A tropical American tree, *Hippomane mancinella,* having poisonous sap and fruit. [French *mancenille,* from Spanish *manzanilla,* "small apple," MANZANILLA.]

Man·chu (măn′chōō, măn-chōō′) *n., pl.* **-chus** or collectively **Manchu. 1.** A member of a nomadic Mongoloid people, native to Manchuria, who conquered China in 1644 and established a dynasty that was overthrown by revolution in 1911. **2.** The Tungusic language of the Manchu.

~*adj.* **1.** Of or pertaining to the Manchu, their dynasty, language, or culture. **2.** Of or pertaining to Manchuria. [Manchu, "pure."]

Man·chu·guo, Man·chu·kuo (măn′chōō′gwō′, -kwō′). A former state of eastern Asia (1932–46), established by the Japanese and comprising Manchuria and the former province of Jehol, now mostly in the Inner Mongolian Autonomous Region.

Man·chu·ri·a (măn-chōōr′ē-ə). Region of northeastern China composed of the modern provinces of Heilongjiang, Jilin, and Liaoning. It was the home of the Manchu conquerors of China in the 17th century. Of great strategic value, it was subsequently seized by the Russians, then the Japanese, who in 1932 set up their protégé state of Manchuguo. **—Man·chu·ri·an** *adj. & n.*

man·ci·ple (măn′sə-pəl) *n.* In Britain, a steward responsible for purchasing provisions, especially for a monastery or college. [Middle English, from Norman French, from Latin *mancipium,* purchase : *manus,* hand + *cip-,* from *capere,* to take.]

Man·cu·ni·an (măn-kyōō′nē-ən) *n.* A native or inhabitant of Manchester, England. [Medieval Latin *Mancunium,* MANCHESTER.] **—Man·cu·ni·an** *adj.*

-mancy *suffix.* Indicates divination by a specified means or in a specified manner; for example, **chiromancy, necromancy.** [Middle English, from Old French *-mancie,* from Late Latin *-mantīa,* from Greek *manteia,* divination, from *manteuesthai,* to prophesy, from *mantis,* a prophet.]

Mandaean. Variant of **Mandean.**

man·da·la (mŭn′də-lə) *n.* In Oriental art and religion, any of various usually circular designs symbolic of the universe. [Sanskrit *maṇḍala,* circle, probably from Tamil *muṭalai.*]

Man·da·lay (măn′də-lā′). Last capital of the Burman kingdom, annexed by the British in 1885. On the Irrawaddy River, it is a major port and commercial center.

man·da·mus (măn-dā′məs) *n., pl.* **-muses.** *Law.* An order issued by a higher court ordering a public official or body or a lower court to perform a specified duty.

~*tr.v.* **mandamused, -musing, -muses.** *Law.* To serve with a man-

mandala *This symbolic map of the Buddhist universe was painted in the 19th century. The mandala's central circle contains an eight-armed figure of Avalokitesvara, the Bodhisattva of Infinite Compassion.*

mandarin duck *The damp woodlands of China are the natural habitat of the mandarin duck, but it is also kept as an ornamental bird in the West. Mandarin ducks usually nest in holes in trees.*

mandrill *This member of the baboon family is found in the coastal forests of West Africa. It lives mainly on the ground in small groups led by a male and feeds on insects and plants.*

damus. [Latin *mandāmus,* "we order," from *mandāre,* to order.]

man·da·rin (măn′də-rĭn) *n.* **1.** In imperial China, a member of any of the nine ranks of high public officials. **2. a.** A high civil servant thought to exercise wide undefined powers outside political control. **b.** A person of influence or high status, especially in intellectual or political circles. **3. Mandarin. Mandarin Chinese** *(see).* **4.** The dialect used by mandarins and other officials in imperial China. **5. a.** The mandarin orange. **b.** The fruit of the mandarin orange. —*adj.* **1.** Of or resembling a mandarin. **2.** Marked by elaborate and intricate language or literary style. [Portuguese, from Malay *mĕntĕri,* from Hindi *mantrī,* from Sanskrit *mantrin,* counselor, from *mantra,* counsel.]

Mandarin Chinese *n. Chinese* **Kuo·yü** (kŏŏ′yŏŏ′), **Guo·yü** (gwô′-yŏŏ′). The national language of the People's Republic of China and of Taiwan, based on the principal dialect spoken in the area around Beijing (Peking). Also called "Mandarin."

mandarin collar *n.* A narrow, stiff collar that stands up around the neck and is usually divided in front.

mandarin duck *n.* A waterfowl, *Aix galericulata,* of Asia, having brightly colored plumage and a crested head in the male.

mandarin orange *n.* **1.** A small Chinese orange tree, *Citrus reticulata,* cultivated for its edible fruit. **2.** The small, loose-skinned fruit of the mandarin orange. Also called "mandarin." [French *mandarine,* perhaps from MANDARIN (Chinese public official), comparing the color of the fruit to the yellow robes worn by mandarins.]

man·da·tar·y (măn′də-tĕr′ē) *n., pl.* **-ies.** A person or nation that receives a mandate. [Late Latin *mandātārius* : MANDATE + -ARY.]

man·date (măn′dāt′) *n.* **1.** An authoritative command or instruction. **2.** An instruction or authorization to a government to follow a particular policy, expressed by a political electorate in election results. **3. a.** A commission from the League of Nations authorizing a nation to administer a territory. **b.** A region under such administration. Compare **trusteeship, trust territory. 4.** *Law.* **a.** An order issued by a superior court to a lower court. **b.** A contract by which an individual agrees to perform services for another without payment.

—*tr.v.* **mandated, -dating, -dates. 1.** To assign (a colony or territory) to a specified nation under a mandate. **2.** To make mandatory; require: *mandated desegregation of public schools.* [Latin *mandātum,* a command, from *mandāre,* to command.]

man·da·tor (măn′dā′tər) *n.* One who gives a mandate.

man·da·to·ry (măn′də-tôr′ē, -tōr′ē) *adj.* **1.** Of, pertaining to, having the nature of, or containing a mandate. **2.** Required as if by mandate; obligatory. **3.** Holding a mandate over a region. Said of a nation.

—*n., pl.* **mandatories.** One receiving a mandate; mandatary.

man-day (măn′dā′) *n., pl.* **man-days.** The work performed by one person during one day.

Man·de (män′dā′, măn-dā′) *n., pl.* **-des** or collectively **Mande. 1.** A Mandingo. **2.** A branch of the Niger-Congo language family spoken chiefly in Mali, Liberia, and Sierra Leone. [Mandingo : *ma-,* "mother" + *-nde,* diminutive suffix. See **Mandingo.**]

Man·de·an, Man·dae·an (măn-dē′ən) *n.* **1.** A member of an ancient Gnostic sect of Mesopotamia. **2.** A form of Aramaic used by the Mandeans. [Mandean *mandaya,* having knowledge, from *manda,* knowledge.] **—Man·de·an** *adj.*

Man·de·la (măn-dĕl′ə), **Nelson Rolihlahla** (1918–). South African black political leader. While a practicing lawyer in Johannesburg, he became the national organizer of the banned African National Congress. He was tried for treason and acquitted (1956–61), retried (1963–64), and sentenced to life imprisonment. His publications include *No Easy Walk to Freedom* (1965).

Man·de·ville (măn′də-vĭl′), **Sir John** (*fl.* mid-14th century). English compiler of travel tales. Drawing heavily from literature, he created colorful descriptions of his extensive but possibly fictitious journeys. A collection of his tales, *The Voyage and Travels of Sir John Mandeville, Knight,* was published between 1357 and 1371.

man·di·ble (măn′də-bəl) *n.* A jaw, especially: **1.** The lower jaw in vertebrates. **2.** Either the upper or lower part of the beak in birds. **3.** Any of various mouth parts in insects. [Middle English, from Old French, from Latin *mandibula,* from *mandere,* to chew.] **—man·dib·u·lar** (măn-dĭb′yə-lər) *adj.*

man·dib·u·late (măn-dĭb′yə-lĭt, -lāt′) *n.* An animal having mandibles. **—man·dib·u·late** *adj.*

Man·din·go (măn-dĭng′gō) *n., pl.* **-gos** or **-goes** or collectively **Mandingo. 1.** A member of any of various Negroid peoples inhabiting the region of the upper Niger river valley of western Africa. **2.** Any of the languages of the Mandingo. [Mandingo : *ma-,* "mother" + *-ndi, -nde,* diminutive suffix + *-ngo,* variant of *-ko,* suffix of nationality or tribe.] **—Man·din·go** *adj.*

man·do·la (măn-dō′lə) *n.* An early lute that was the precursor of the mandolin. [Italian.]

man·do·lin (măn′də-lĭn′, măn′də-lĭn′) *n.* Also **man·do·line** (măn′-də-lēn′). **1.** A musical instrument with a usually pear-shaped wooden body and a fretted neck over which several pairs of metal strings are stretched. **2.** A utensil for slicing and shredding that consists of a wooden board fitted with an adjustable metal blade. [French *mandoline,* from Italian *mandolino,* diminutive of *mandola, mandora,* lute, from Greek *pandoura.*] **—man·do·lin·ist** *n.*

man·dor·la (măn-dôr′lə) *n.* An oval aureole used especially in medieval painting and sculpture. [Italian, almond.]

man·drag·o·ra (măn-drăg′ər-ə) *n.* The mandrake. [Old English. See **mandrake.**]

man·drake (măn′drāk′) *n.* **1. a.** A Eurasian plant, *Mandragora officinarum,* having purplish flowers and a branched root thought to resemble the human body. **b.** The root of the mandrake, from which a narcotic drug was formerly prepared. **2.** A North American plant, the **May apple** *(see).* [Middle English *mandragge, mandrake* (probably influenced by DRAKE, dragon), from Middle Dutch *mandragre* and Old English *mandragora,* both from Latin *mandragoras,* from Greek *mandragoras*†.]

man·drel, man·dril (măn′drəl) *n.* **1.** A spindle or axle used to secure or support material being machined or milled. **2.** A metal core around which wood and other materials may be shaped. **3.** A shaft on which a working tool is mounted, as in a dental drill. [16th century : perhaps akin to French *madrin,* lathe.]

man·drill (măn′drəl) *n.* A large, fierce baboon, *Mandrillus sphinx,* of western Africa, having a beard, a crest, and a mane, with brilliant blue, purple, and scarlet markings on the face and scarlet markings on the hindquarters in the adult male. [MAN + DRILL (baboon).]

mane (mān) *n.* **1. a.** The long hair along the top and sides of the neck of such mammals as the horse and the male lion. **b.** The feathers on the back of the neck and head of some pigeons. **2.** A long, thick growth of hair on a person's head. [Middle English, from Old English *manu.*] **—maned** *adj.*

man-eat·er (măn′ē′tər) *n.* **1.** An animal that eats or is reputed to eat human flesh. **2.** A cannibal.

ma·nège, ma·nege (mă-nĕzh′, -nāzh′) *n.* **1.** The art and practice of training a horse in the stylized and difficult exercises of classical riding. **2.** A riding academy. [French *manège,* from Italian *maneggio,* from *maneggiare,* to MANAGE.]

ma·nes, Ma·nes (mā′nēz′, mä′nās′) *pl.n.* In ancient Rome: **1.** The spirits of the dead, especially ancestors, deified as minor gods. **2.** A revered spirit of one who has died. [Latin *mānēs,* probably "the good ones," from *mānis,* good.]

Ma·nes (mā′nēz′), Also **Ma·ni** (mä′nē) (*c.* A.D. 216–76). Persian prophet. The founder of Manichaeism, he professed that the world is a union of spirit and matter, a fusion of the equal but opposite forces of good and evil. He was allowed to preach in Persia, but was jailed by Zoroastrian priests and died in prison.

Ma·net (mə-nā′), **Edouard** (1832–83). French painter. His *Déjeuner sur l'Herbe* (1863), showing a nude woman at a picnic, was rejected by the Paris Salon and caused a scandal. He had a considerable influence on the impressionists.

ma·neu·ver (mə-nōō′vər, mə-nyōō′-) *n.* Also *chiefly British* **ma·noeu·vre. 1. a.** A strategic or tactical military movement. **b.** *Often* **maneuvers.** A large-scale military training exercise simulating combat. **2. a.** A physical movement or way of doing something generally requiring skill and dexterity. **b.** A controlled change in the flight path of an aircraft, rocket, or space vehicle. **3.** A calculated and skillful act or stratagem: *devious political maneuvers.* —See Synonyms at **artifice.**

—*v.* **maneuvered, -vering, -vers.** Also *chiefly British* **ma·noeu·vre, -vred, -vring, -vres.** —*intr.* **1.** To perform or carry out a military maneuver. **2.** To make a change or a series of changes in position or direction for a desired end. **3.** To change tactics, as in negotiation: *The opposition had no room in which to maneuver.* **4.** To attempt to bring about something by planning or scheming. —*tr.* **1.** To alter the tactical placement of (troops or warships, for example). **2.** To move into a desired position. **3.** To manipulate (people, for example) for one's own ends: *maneuvered her into signing the contract.* [French *manoeuvre,* from Medieval Latin *man(u)operārī,* from Latin *manus,* hand + *operārī,* to work.] **—ma·neu·ver·a·bil·i·ty** *n.* **—ma·neu·ver·a·ble** *adj.* **—ma·neu·ver·er** *n.*

man Friday *n.* A devoted male servant, aide, or employee, especially one having a high degree of responsibility. [After *Friday,* the devoted native servant in Defoe's novel *Robinson Crusoe* (1719).]

man·ful (măn′fəl) *adj.* Having or displaying qualities thought to befit a man; manly. **—man·ful·ly** *adv.* **—man·ful·ness** *n.*

man·ga·bey (măng′gə-bā′, -bē′) *n., pl.* **-beys.** A monkey of the genus *Cercocebus,* of equatorial Africa, having a long tail and a relatively long muzzle. [After *Mangaby,* a region of Madagascar.]

man·ga·nate (măng′gə-nāt′) *n.* Any salt containing manganese in its anion, especially a salt containing the MnO_4^{2-} ion. [MANGA-N(ESE) + -ATE (salt).]

man·ga·nese (măng′gə-nēz′, -nēs′) *n. Symbol* **Mn** A gray-white or silvery brittle metallic element that is found worldwide, especially in the ore pyrolusite. Manganese is alloyed with steel to increase hardness and resistance and with other metals to form highly ferromagnetic materials. Atomic number 25, atomic weight 54.9380, melting point 1,244°C, boiling point 2,097°C, specific gravity 7.21 to 7.44, valences 2, 3, 4, 6, 7. [French *manganèse,* from Italian *manganese,* probably alteration of Medieval Latin *magnēsia,* manganese, magnesia, from Late Greek *magnēsia.* See **magnesia.**]

manganese dioxide *n.* A black crystalline compound, MnO_2, used as a depolarizer for dry-cell batteries and in textile dyeing.

manganese spar *n.* A mineral, **rhodonite** *(see).*

man·gan·ic (măn-găn′ĭk, măng-) *adj.* Pertaining to or containing manganese. Used especially to designate compounds of manganese with a valence of 3 or 6. [MANGAN(ESE) + -IC.]

man·ga·nite (măng′gə-nīt′) *n.* A steel-gray to black mineral form of manganese oxide, $MnO(OH)$, found in North America and Europe. It is an important ore of manganese. [MANGAN(ESE) + -ITE.]

man·ga·nous (măng′gə-nəs) *adj.* Pertaining to or containing manganese. Used especially to designate compounds of manganese with a valence of 2. [MANGAN(ESE) + -OUS.]

mange (mānj) *n.* A contagious skin disease of many mammals, occasionally affecting humans, that is caused by parasitic mites and characterized by itching and loss of hair. [Middle English *maniewe,* from Old French *manjue,* "eating," itch, from *mangier,* to eat, from Latin *mandūcāre,* to eat, chew, from *mandūcō,* glutton, from *mandere,* to chew.]

man•gel-wur•zel (măng'gəl-wûr'zəl) *n.* A variety of the common beet having a large yellowish root, used chiefly as cattle feed. [German, (properly) *Mangold-wurzel,* "beetroot" : *Mangold,* beet, from Old High German *mānegolt*† + *Wurzel,* root, from Old High German *wurzala.*]

man•ger (mān'jər) *n.* **1.** A trough or open box in which feed for horses or cattle is placed. **2.** *Nautical.* A small basinlike device in the bows of a ship for catching any water entering through the hawseholes. [Middle English *maniure, ma(w)nger,* from Old French *mangeoire, manjeure,* from Vulgar Latin *mandūcātōria* (unattested), feeding place, from *mandūcāre,* to chew. See **mange.**]

man•gle[1] (măng'gəl) *tr.v.* **-gled, -gling, -gles. 1.** To mutilate or disfigure by battering, hacking, cutting, or tearing. **2.** To ruin or spoil through ineptitude or ignorance: *mangle a speech.* [Middle English *manglen,* from Norman French *mangler, mahangler,* probably frequentative of Old French *mahaignier,* to MAIM.] **—man•gler** *n.*

mangle[2] *n.* **1.** A laundry machine for pressing fabrics. **2.** *Chiefly British.* A clothes wringer.

~tr.v. **mangled, -gling, -gles.** To press with a mangle. [Dutch *mangel,* from German, diminutive of Middle High German *mange,* mangle, from Late Latin *manganum,* MANGONEL.]

man•go (măng'gō) *n., pl.* **-goes** or **-gos. 1. a.** A tropical evergreen tree, *Mangifera indica,* native to Asia, cultivated for its edible fruit. **b.** The ovoid fruit of this tree, having a smooth rind and sweet, juicy, yellow-orange flesh. **2.** Any of various types of pickle. [Portuguese *manga,* from Malay *mangā,* from Tamil *mānkāy* : *mān,* mango tree + *kāy,* fruit.]

man•go•nel (măng'gə-nĕl') *n.* A military machine used during the Middle Ages for hurling stones and other missiles. [Middle English, from Old French, from Medieval Latin *mangonellus, manganellus,* diminutive of Late Latin *manganum,* mangonel, from Greek *manganon,* enchantment, contrivance, war machine.]

man•go•steen (măng'gə-stēn') *n.* **1.** A tropical tree, *Garcinia mangostana,* having thick, leathery leaves and edible fruit. **2.** The fruit of this tree, having a hard rind and segmented, sweet, juicy pulp. [From obsolete Malay *manggustan.*]

man•grove (măn'grōv', măng'-) *n.* **1.** Any of various tropical evergreen trees or shrubs of the genus *Rhizophora,* having stiltlike aerial roots and forming dense thickets along tidal shores. **2.** Any of various similar shrubs or trees, especially one of the genus *Avicennia.* [Portuguese *mangue* (influenced by GROVE), from Taino *mangle.*]

mang•y (mān'jē) *adj.* **-ier, -iest. 1.** Having, resembling, or caused by mange. **2.** Having many bare spots; shabby: *a mangy old mink coat.* **3.** Having a squalid appearance; wretched: *mangy tenements.* **—mang•i•ly** *adv.* **—mang•i•ness** *n.*

man•han•dle (măn'hăn'dəl) *tr.v.* **-dled, -dling, -dles. 1.** To handle roughly. **2.** To move by manpower, without machinery.

Man•hat•tan[1] (măn-hăt'n, mən-). Borough of New York City. Most of it lies on Manhattan Island, the original nucleus of the city, bounded by the Hudson, East, and Harlem rivers and New York Bay. The financial, business, and cultural heart of the city, it includes Broadway, Wall Street, and Greenwich Village.

Manhattan[2] *n.* A cocktail made from vermouth, whiskey, and angostura bitters. [After MANHATTAN.]

Manhattan District *n.* In World War II, the name given to a unit of the U.S. Army Corps of Engineers established in 1942 to administer the nuclear energy project that produced the atomic bomb. Also unofficially called "Manhattan Project."

man•hole (măn'hōl') *n.* A hole through which a person may enter a boiler, pipe, conduit, or drain.

man•hood (măn'ho͝od') *n.* **1.** The state or condition of being an adult male as distinguished from being a boy or a woman: *Boys grow to manhood.* **2.** The composite of qualities, such as courage, determination, and vigor, considered desirable in an adult male. **3.** Men collectively. **4.** The state or condition of being part of or endowed with humanity.

man-hour (măn'our') *n., pl.* **man-hours.** An industrial unit of production equal to the work a person can produce in one hour.

man•hunt (măn'hŭnt') *n., pl.* **manhunts.** An organized and extensive search for a person, usually a fugitive criminal.

Mani. See **Manes.**

ma•ni•a (mā'nē-ə, mān'yə) *n.* **1.** *Psychology.* A state of mind characterized by profuse and rapidly changing ideas, exaggerated gaiety that may quickly change to irritability or violence, and physical overactivity. **2.** *Informal.* An inordinately intense desire or enthusiasm for something; a craze. **3.** Violent abnormal behavior. [Middle English, madness, from Late Latin, from Greek.]

-mania *suffix.* Indicates an exaggerated desire for, pleasure in, or pathological excitement induced by something; for example, **monomania, pyromania.** [From MANIA.]

ma•ni•ac (mā'nē-ăk') *n.* **1.** An insane person; a lunatic. **2.** *Informal.* A person who has an excessive enthusiasm or desire for something: *a bridge maniac.* **3.** A person who behaves in a wild, irresponsible way: *Look out for maniacs on the highway.*

~adj. Variant of **maniacal.** [From Late Latin *maniacus,* maniacal, from Greek *maniakos,* from *mania,* madness.]

ma•ni•a•cal (mə-nī'ə-kəl) *adj.* Also **ma•ni•ac** (mā'nē-ăk'). **1.** Insane: *a maniacal killer.* **2.** Characterized by excessive enthusiasm: *a maniacal fondness for gambling.* **—ma•ni•a•cal•ly** *adv.*

man•ic (măn'ĭk) *adj.* **1.** Of, pertaining to, or afflicted with mania. **2.** Insane or apparently insane, especially in a frenetic way: *manic humor.*

~n. A person afflicted with mania. [MAN(IA) + -IC.]

man•ic-de•pres•sive (măn'ĭk-dĭ-prĕs'ĭv) *adj. Psychiatry.* Designating, displaying, or suffering from a psychosis in which periods of manic excitation alternate with melancholic depressions.

~n. Psychiatry. A person suffering from a manic-depressive psychosis. **—man•ic-de•pres•sion** *n.*

Man•i•chae•an, Man•i•che•an (măn'ĭ-kē'ən) *n.* Also **Man•i•chee** (măn'ĭ-kē'). A believer in Manichaeism.

~adj. Of or pertaining to Manichaeism. [Middle English, from Medieval Latin *Manichaeus,* from Late Greek *Manikhaios,* a follower of *Manikhaios* or *Manes,* the Persian founder of the sect.]

Man•i•chae•ism, Man•i•che•ism (măn'ĭ-kē'ĭz'əm) *n.* Also **Man•i•chae•an•ism, Man•i•che•an•ism** (-kē'ə-nĭz'əm). **1.** The syncretic dualistic religious philosophy taught by the Persian prophet Manes about the 3rd century A.D., according to which God and Satan reigned as equals. It combined elements of Zoroastrian, Christian, and Gnostic thought. **2.** A dualistic philosophy similar to Manichaeism, especially one considered a heresy by the Roman Catholic Church.

man•i•cot•ti (măn'ĭ-kŏt'ē) *n.* A dish of Italian origin that consists of pasta with a filling of chopped meat or ricotta cheese, often served hot with a tomato sauce. [Italian, "sleeves," plural of *manicotto,* augmentative of *manica,* sleeve, from Latin *manica,* from *manus,* hand.]

man•i•cure (măn'ĭ-kyo͝or') *n.* A cosmetic treatment of the hands and fingernails, including shaping, cleaning, and polishing of the nails. Also used adjectivally: *a manicure set.*

~tr.v. **manicured, -curing, -cures. 1.** To care for (the hands and fingernails) by shaping, cleaning, and polishing. **2.** To clip or trim evenly and closely: *manicured hedges.* [French *manicure,* "hand-care" : Latin *manus,* hand + *cūra,* care.]

man•i•cur•ist (măn'ĭ-kyo͝or'ĭst) *n.* One who gives manicures.

man•i•fest (măn'ə-fĕst') *adj.* **1.** Clearly apparent to the sight or understanding; obvious. **2.** *Psychology.* Of or pertaining to impulses that appear to be conscious but that may hide unconscious ones. —See Synonyms at **evident.**

~v. **manifested, -festing, -fests.** *—tr.* **1.** To show or demonstrate plainly; reveal. **2.** To be evidence of; prove. **3. a.** To record or list in a ship's manifest. **b.** To display or present a manifest of (cargo). *—intr.* To appear. Used of a ghost or spirit.

~n. **1. a.** A list of cargo or passengers, especially one for use by customs officials. **b.** A list of railroad cars according to owner and location. **2.** A fast freight train, usually one that carries perishable goods. [Middle English, from Latin *manifestus, manufestus,* palpable, "grasped by hand" : *manus,* hand + *-festus,* "gripped."] **—man•i•fest•ly** *adv.*

man•i•fes•tant (măn'ə-fĕs'tənt) *n.* A participant in a manifestation or a public demonstration.

man•i•fes•ta•tion (măn'ə-fĕ-stā'shən) *n.* **1. a.** The act of manifesting or the state of being manifested. **b.** The demonstration of the existence, reality, or presence of a person, object, or quality: *a manifestation of ill will.* **c.** Any of the forms in which someone or something, such as an individual, a divine being, or an idea, is revealed. **2.** A public demonstration, usually of a political nature.

Manifest Destiny. The 19th-century doctrine that the United States had the right and duty to expand throughout the North American continent.

man•i•fes•to (măn'ə-fĕs'tō) *n., pl.* **-toes** or **-tos.** A public declaration of principles, policies, or intentions, especially of a political nature.

~intr.v. **manifestoed, -toing, -toes.** To issue a manifesto. [Italian, "manifestation," from adjective, manifest, from Latin *manifestus,* MANIFEST.]

man•i•fold (măn'ə-fōld') *adj.* **1.** Of many kinds; varied; multiple: *our manifold failings.* **2.** Having many features or forms: *manifold intelligence.* **3.** Consisting of or operating several of one kind.

~n. **1.** A whole composed of diverse elements. **2.** One of many copies. **3.** A pipe so fitted that it has several apertures for making multiple connections. **4.** *Mathematics.* A set of elements sharing a number of properties, usually of a topologic nature, such as orientability, differentiability, and dimensionality.

~adv. By a large amount: *increased her happiness manifold.*

~tr.v. **manifolded, -folding, -folds. 1.** To make several copies of. **2.** To make manifold; multiply. [Middle English, from Old English *manig-feald* : MANY + -FOLD.] **—man•i•fold•ly** *adv.* **—man•i•fold•ness** *n.*

man•i•fold•er (măn'ə-fōl'dər) *n.* A machine for making manifold copies, as of documents.

man•i•kin, man•ni•kin (măn'ĭ-kĭn) *n.* Also **man•a•kin** (măn'ə-) (for sense 1). **1. a.** A dwarf or pixie. **b.** A little boy. **2.** An anatomical model of the human body, used primarily for study in art and medical schools. **3.** A mannequin. [Middle Dutch *mannekīn,* diminutive of *man,* MAN.]

ma•nil•a, ma•nil•la (mə-nĭl'ə) *n. Often* **Manila** or **Manilla. 1.** A cigar or cheroot of a type made in Manila. **2.** Manila hemp. **3.** Manila paper. **4.** A light yellowish brown.

Ma•nil•a (mə-nĭl'ə). Capital and main seaport of the Philippines, on Luzon Island. It was founded (1571) by the Spanish on Manila Bay,

mangrove *Rhizophora mangle, a mangrove species that grows in Florida. The trunk grows above ground, supported by roots anchored in the mud below. The wood is so dense that it sinks in water.*

PRONUNCIATION KEY

ă, pat; ā, pay; âr, care;
ä, father, are; b, bib;
ch, church; d, deed; ĕ, pet;
ē, be; f, fife; g, gag; h, hat;
hw, which; ĭ, pit; ī, pie;
îr, pier; j, judge; k, kick;
l, lid, needle; m, mum;
n, no, sudden; ng, thing;
ŏ, pot; ō, toe; ô, paw, for;
oi, noise; ou, out; o͝o, book;
o͞o, boot; p, pop; r, roar;
s, sauce; sh, ship, dish;
t, tight; th, thin, path;
th, this, bathe; ŭ, cut; ûr, fur;
v, valve; w, with; y, yes;
z, zebra, size; zh, vision;
ə, about, item, edible,
gallop, circus, peaceful

IN FOREIGN WORDS:

à, *Fr.* ami; œ, *Fr.* feu, *Ger.* schön; ü, *Fr.* tu, *Ger.* über;
KH, *Ger.* ich, *Scot.* loch;
N, *Fr.* bon; y', *Fr.* Compiègne

STRESS MARKS:

Primary stress: '
in•cite' (ĭn-sīt')
Secondary stress: '
in'sight' (ĭn'sīt')

one of the finest natural harbors in the world, and is the country's industrial center.

Manila hemp *n.* The fiber of the abaca used for making rope, cordage, and paper. Also called "Manila."

Manila paper *n.* Strong paper or thin cardboard with a smooth finish, usually buff in color, made from Manila hemp or wood fibers similar to it. Also called "manila."

ma·nil·la¹ (mə-nĕl′ə, -nĕl′yə) *n.* A metal bracelet worn by certain western African peoples that was formerly used as currency. [Spanish, bracelet, probably diminutive of *mano,* hand.]

manilla² Variant of **manila.**

ma·nille (mə-nĭl′) *n.* The second-best trump in the card games quadrille and ombre. [French, from Spanish *malilla,* diminutive of *mala,* bad.]

man in the moon *n.* The face or shape of a man in the light and dark areas of the moon's surface that is apparently visible from the earth.

man in the street *n.* The ordinary citizen; the common man: *The man in the street is opposed to higher taxes.*

man·i·oc (măn′ē-ŏk′) *n.* Also **man·i·o·ca** (măn′ē-ō′kə). A tropical plant, the **cassava** *(see).* [French, from Tupi *mandioca.*]

man·i·ple (măn′ə-pəl) *n.* **1.** An ornamental silk band hung as an ecclesiastical vestment on the left arm near the wrist. **2.** A subdivision of an ancient Roman legion, containing 60 or 120 men. [Sense 1, Middle English, from Old French, handkerchief, from Latin *manipulus,* handful. Sense 2, direct from Latin *manipulus,* handful, hence, a bundle of hay on a pole used as a standard, hence a detachment of troops : *manus,* hand + *-pulus†.*]

ma·nip·u·lar (mə-nĭp′yə-lər) *adj.* **1.** Of or pertaining to an ancient Roman maniple. **2.** Of or pertaining to manipulation. ~*n.* A Roman soldier in a maniple.

ma·nip·u·late (mə-nĭp′yə-lāt′) *tr.v.* **-lated, -lating, -lates. 1.** To operate or control by skilled use of the hands; handle: *manipulated the lights to get exactly the effect he wanted.* **2. a.** To influence or manage shrewdly or deviously: *She manipulated public opinion in her favor.* **b.** To control the will or emotions of (another person) by exploiting feelings such as guilt or affection to one's own ends: *His parents quite openly manipulate him.* **3.** To tamper with or falsify (financial records) for personal gain. **4.** To handle and move (a limb, for example) in an examination or for therapeutic purposes, as a chiropractor does. —See Usage note at **handle.** [Back-formation from MANIPULATION.] **—ma·nip·u·la·bil·i·ty** *n.* **—ma·nip·u·la·ble** *adj.* **—ma·nip·u·la·tive** (mə-nĭp′yə-lā′tĭv, -lə-tĭv), **ma·nip·u·la·to·ry** (-lə-tôr′ē, -tōr′ē) *adj.* **—ma·nip·u·la·tor** *n.*

ma·nip·u·la·tion (mə-nĭp′yə-lā′shən) *n.* **1.** The act of manipulating. **2.** The state of being manipulated. **3.** Shrewd or devious effort to manage or influence for one's own purposes: *manipulation of popular feeling.* **4.** The therapeutic handling of body parts such as bones, as by an osteopath or physiotherapist, to restore normal action. [Latin *manipulus,* handful. See **maniple.**]

man·i·pu·ri (măn′ə-pŏor′ē) *n., pl.* **-ris.** One of the four classical Hindu dance forms, presenting episodes from the life of the god Krishna. [After *Manipur,* region of India where the dance originated.]

Man·i·to·ba (măn′ĭ-tō′bə). *Abbr.* **Man.** Province of central Canada, the most easterly of the Prairie Provinces. The southwest produces vast amounts of wheat, and the northern tundra, furs. There are large reserves of timber, oil, and metal ores. Winnipeg is the capital. **—Man·i·to·ban** *adj. & n.*

man·i·tou, man·i·tu (măn′ĭ-tōō′) *n.* Also **man·i·to** (-tō′). **1.** A spirit or force of nature, either good or bad, deified in the religion of the Algonquian Indians. **2.** A representation or image of a manitou. [French, from Ojibwa *manitu,* "he has surpassed."]

man jack *n. Informal.* A single one; individual: *Every man jack should do his duty.* [MAN + JACK (fellow, chap).]

man·kind (măn′kīnd′, -kīnd′ *for sense 1;* măn′kīnd′ *for sense 2*) *n.* **1.** The human race. **2.** Men as distinguished from women.

mank·y (măng′kē) *adj.* **-ier, -iest. 1.** *Scottish.* Decaying and dirty. **2.** *British Regional.* Spoiled; naughty. [From obsolete (Scottish) *mank,* maimed, defective, from Old French *manc,* from Latin *mancus,* maimed; current sense perhaps influenced by French *manqué,* failed, missed, miscarried.]

Man·ley (măn′lē), **Michael Norman** (1923–). Jamaican socialist politician. He worked as a journalist before entering politics, leading the People's National Party in opposition (1969–72) and as prime minister (1972–80).

man·like (măn′līk′) *adj.* **1.** Resembling a man. **2.** Belonging to or befitting a man.

man·ly (măn′lē) *adj.* **-lier, -liest. 1.** Having qualities generally considered desirable in a man: *manly courage.* **2.** Suited to or befitting a man; masculine: *manly clothes.* ~*adv.* In a manly manner. **—man·li·ness** *n.*

man-made (măn′mād′) *adj.* Made by human beings; not of natural origin.

Mann (măn), **Horace** (1796–1859). U.S. educator. As president of the Massachusetts senate, he signed an epoch-making education bill (1837) and then became the first secretary of the state's new board of education. Between 1837 and 1848 he almost completely transformed the public school system, adding new high schools and teachers' institutes, revamping curricula and methods, and establishing a six-month minimum school year.

Mann (măn, män), **Thomas** (1875–1955). German novelist. He was concerned with the artist's role in society in his works, including

Death in Venice (1912), *The Magic Mountain* (1924), and *Dr. Faustus* (1947). He was awarded the Nobel Prize in 1929. He became a naturalized U.S. citizen in the 1940's.

man·na (măn′ə) *n.* **1.** The food miraculously provided for the Israelites in the wilderness during their flight from Egypt. Exodus 16:14–36. **2.** Spiritual nourishment of divine origin, especially the Eucharist. **3.** Something of value that a person receives unexpectedly when in need. **4.** The dried exudate of certain plants, especially that of a Eurasian ash tree, *Fraxinus ornus,* formerly used as a laxative. [Aramaic *mannā,* from Hebrew *mān.*]

man·nan (măn′ăn′, -ən) *n.* Any of a group of polysaccharides that are polymers of mannose. [MANN(OSE) + -AN.]

manned (mănd) *adj.* Transporting or operated by a human being: *a manned space capsule.*

man·ne·quin (măn′ĭ-kĭn) *n.* Also **manikin, mannikin** (for sense 1). **1.** A life-size full or partial representation of the human body used for the fitting or displaying of clothes; a dummy. **2.** A **lay figure** *(see).* **3.** A person who models clothes; a model. [French, from Middle Dutch *mannekīn,* MANIKIN.]

man·ner (măn′ər) *n.* **1.** A way of doing something or the way in which a thing is done or happens: *boasting in their usual manner.* **2.** A way of acting; a person's bearing or behavior: *a very flirtatious manner.* **3. manners. a.** The socially correct way of acting; etiquette: *tried to teach the children manners.* **b.** The prevailing systems or modes of social conduct of a specific society, period, or group, especially as the subject of a literary work. **4.** Practice, style, execution, or method in the arts: *This fresco is typical of the painter's early manner.* **5.** Exaggerated style; a mannerism. **6.** Kind or sort: *What manner of man is that?* —See Synonyms at **bearing, method.** **—by all manner of means.** Of course; surely. **—in a manner of speaking.** In a way; so to speak. **—not by any manner of means.** In no way whatever. **—to the manner born. 1.** *Obsolete.* Born to follow or obey a particular practice or custom. **2. a.** Fitted by birth, education, or experience to occupy a specific position, usually one of leadership. **b.** Accustomed by family background to a particular, usually lavish lifestyle. [Middle English *manere,* from Norman French, from Old French *maniere,* from Vulgar Latin *manuāria* (unattested), "way of handling," manner, from Latin *manuārius,* of the hand, from *manus,* hand.]

man·nered (măn′ərd) *adj.* **1.** Having a manner or manners of a specified kind. Often used in combination: *ill-mannered.* **2.** Artificial or affected: *His mannered speech irks me.* **3.** Of, pertaining to, or exhibiting mannerisms. Said especially of art or literature.

Man·ner·heim (mä′nər-hām′, -hīm′, măn′ər-), **Baron Carl Gustaf Emil von** (1867–1951). Finnish soldier and statesman. After fortifying the Finnish-Soviet border (1931–39), he commanded a valiant defense during the Soviet offensive of 1939. He was president of Finland (1944–46) and signed an armistice with the Soviets (1944).

man·ner·ism (măn′ə-rĭz′əm) *n.* **1.** A distinctive behavioral trait; an idiosyncrasy. **2.** An exaggerated or affected style or habit, as in dress, speech, or art. **3. Mannerism.** An artistic style of the late 16th century characterized by distortion of such elements as scale and perspective. **—man·ner·ist** *n.*

man·ner·ly (măn′ər-lē) *adj.* Having good manners; polite. ~*adv.* With good manners; politely. **—man·ner·li·ness** *n.*

Mann·heim (măn′hīm′, män′-). City of Baden-Württemberg, central West Germany, at the junction of the Rhine and Neckar rivers. It is a major river port and industrial center. In the late 18th century Mozart and Schiller contributed to its cultural brilliance.

mannikin. Variant of **manikin.**

Man·ning (măn′ĭng), **Henry Edward, Cardinal** (1808–92). British cardinal. An adherent of the Oxford movement, he entered the Anglican ministry and became archdeacon of Chichester (1841) before his conversion to Roman Catholicism (1851).

man·nish (măn′ĭsh) *adj.* **1.** Of or befitting a man. **2.** Resembling a man in appearance or bearing. Said of a woman. **—man·nish·ly** *adv.* **—man·nish·ness** *n.*

man·nite (măn′īt′) *n.* Mannitol. [French, from *manna,* manna, from Late Latin.]

man·ni·tol (măn′ĭ-tôl′, -tōl′) *n.* An alcohol, C₆H₈(OH)₆, used as a nutrient, as a dietary supplement, and as the basis of dietetic sweets. [MANN(A) + -IT(E) + -OL.]

man·nose (măn′ōs′, -ōz′) *n.* A sugar, C₆H₁₂O₆, occurring in various polysaccharides. [MANN(A) + -OSE.]

manoeuvre. *Chiefly British.* Variant of **maneuver.**

man of God *n.* **1.** A man who is notably holy. **2.** A clergyman.

man of letters *n.* A man who is engaged in literary or scholarly pursuit; author or scholar.

man of straw *n.* A **straw man** *(see).*

man of the cloth *n.* A clergyman.

man of the house *n.* The principal male of a household.

man of the world *n.* A sophisticated or worldly-wise man.

man-of-war *n., pl.* **men-of-war** (mĕn′-). **1.** A warship. **2.** A jellyfish, the **Portuguese man-of-war** *(see).*

Ma·no·le·te (mä′nō-lā′tā), born Manuel Laureano Rodríguez y Sánchez (1917–47). Spanish bullfighter. Probably the best-known bullfighter of his time, he began his professional career at the age of 17. He was gored to death in the ring at Linares, Spain.

ma·nom·e·ter (mə-nŏm′ə-tər) *n.* **1.** Any of various instruments for measuring the pressure of liquids and gases. **2.** An instrument for measuring blood pressure, a **sphygmomanometer** *(see).* [French *manomètre* : Greek *manos,* sparse (here used of gaseous conditions) + -METER.] **—man·o·met·ric** (măn′ə-mĕt′rĭk), **man·o·met·ri·cal**

(-rĭ·kəl) *adj.* —**man·o·met·ri·cal·ly** *adv.* —**ma·nom·e·try** (mə-nŏm′-ə-trē) *n.*

man·or (măn′ər) *n.* **1. a.** The district over which a lord had domain in medieval western Europe. **b.** The lord's residence in such a district. **2.** A landed estate. **3.** The main house on an estate; a mansion. **4.** In certain North American colonies, a tract of land with hereditary rights granted to the proprietor by royal charter. **5.** *British Slang.* **a.** A police district. **b.** The area of operations of a criminal or gang. [Middle English *maner,* from Norman French *manere,* Old French *maneir,* "dwelling place," from *maneir,* to dwell, from Latin *manēre,* to dwell, remain.] —**ma·no·ri·al** (mə-nôr′ē-əl, -nōr′ē-əl) *adj.*

man-o'-war bird (măn′ə-wôr′) *n.* The **frigate bird** (*see*).

man·pow·er (măn′pou′ər) *n.* **1.** The power of human physical strength. **2.** Power in terms of the workers available to a particular group or required for a particular task.

man·qué (măn-kā′) *adj.* Unsuccessful or frustrated; unfulfilled. Used after the noun: *an artist manqué.* [French, from *manquer,* to fail, lack, from Italian *mancare,* from *manco,* lacking, defective, from Latin *mancus,* maimed.]

man·rope (măn′rōp′) *n. Nautical.* A rope rigged as a handrail on a gangplank or ladder.

man·sard (măn′särd, -sərd) *n.* **1.** A roof having two slopes on all four sides, with the lower slope almost vertical and the upper almost horizontal. Also called "mansard roof." **2.** The upper story formed by the lower slope of a mansard. [French *(toit en) mansarde,* "mansard (roof)"; originally designed by François MANSART.]

Man·sart (măn′särt′, măn-sär′), **François** (1598–1666). French classical architect. He adapted the baroque style and developed the mansard roof for the Château de Blois (1635–38).

manse (măns) *n.* **1. a.** *Chiefly Scottish.* A Church of Scotland clergyman's house and land. **b.** A Methodist or Nonconformist clergyman's house. **2.** *Archaic.* A mansion. [Medieval Latin *mansa, mansus, mansum,* dwelling place, from Latin *manēre,* to dwell, remain.]

man·ser·vant (măn′sûr′vənt) *n., pl.* **menservants** (měn′sûr′vənts). A male servant, especially a valet.

Mans·field (măns′fēld′), **Katherine,** born Kathleen Mansfield Beauchamp (1888–1923). New Zealand short-story writer. Educated in London, she settled in Europe (1908) and wrote chiefly short stories in a style reminiscent of Chekhov's. Her works include *Bliss* (1920) and *The Garden Party* (1922).

Mansfield, Mount. The highest peak (1,340 meters; 4,393 feet) of the Green Mts. in Vermont.

-manship *suffix.* Indicates: **1.** Skill in a specified field; for example, **horsemanship. 2.** The act of maneuvering to gain advantage; for example, **gamesmanship.** [Abstracted from terms such as *workmanship (workman* + *-ship)* and used to create new terms such as *one-upmanship (one up* + *-manship).*]

man·sion (măn′shən) *n.* **1.** A large, stately house. **2.** A manor house. **3.** *Archaic.* A dwelling; an abode. **4. a.** *Astrology.* A **house** (*see*). **b.** Any one of the 28 divisions of the moon's monthly path. [Middle English, house, from Old French, from Latin *mānsiō* (stem *mānsiōn-*), dwelling, from *manēre,* to dwell, remain.]

man-sized (măn′sīzd′) *adj.* Also **man-size** (-sīz′). *Informal.* Large enough for a man; hefty: *a man-sized piece of cheese.*

man·slaugh·ter (măn′slô′tər) *n.* **1.** The taking of human life without premeditation. **2.** *Law.* The unlawful killing of one human being by another without express or implied intent to do injury. Compare **murder.**

man·slay·er (măn′slā′ər) *n.* A person or animal that slays a human being.

man·sue·tude (măn′swĭ-tōōd′, -tyōōd′) *n.* Gentleness of manner; mildness. [Middle English, from Latin *mānsuētūdō,* from *mānsuēscere,* to tame, "to accustom to the hand" : *manus,* hand + *suēscere,* to accustom.]

man·ta (măn′tə) *n.* **1.** A rough-textured cotton fabric or blanket made and used in Latin America and the southwestern United States. **2.** Any of several fishes of the family Mobulidae, having large, flattened bodies with winglike pectoral fins. Also called "devilfish," "manta ray." [Spanish, cape, blanket, hence (in American Spanish) fish trap shaped like a blanket, manta ray (caught with such a trap), from Vulgar Latin *manta* (unattested), cloak, variant of Latin *mantus,* shortened from *mantellum*†, MANTLE.]

manta ray *n.* A fish, the **manta** (*see*).

man·teau (măn-tō′) *n., pl.* **-teaus** (-tōz′) or **-teaux** (-tō′). A loose cloak or mantle. [French, from Old French *mantel,* from Latin *mantellum*†, MANTLE.]

Man·te·gna (män-tān′yə), **Andrea** (c. 1431–1506). Italian painter and engraver. Influenced by Donatello, his works reflect an interest in the classical period and include a Pietà and the *Triumph of Caesar,* a series of nine paintings.

man·tel, man·tle (măn′təl) *n.* **1.** An ornamental facing around a fireplace. **2.** The protruding shelf over a fireplace. Also called "mantelpiece." [Middle English *mantel,* cloak, covering, from Old French, from Latin *mantellum*†, MANTLE.]

man·tel·et (măn′tə-lĕt′, mănt′lĭt) *n.* Also **mant·let** (mănt′lĭt) (for sense 2). **1.** A short cape worn by women in the mid-19th century. **2.** A mobile screen or shield formerly used to protect soldiers. [Middle English, from Old French, diminutive of *mantel,* mantle, from Latin *mantellum*†, MANTLE.]

man·tel·let·ta (măn′tə-lĕt′ə) *n.* A knee-length, sleeveless vestment worn by Roman Catholic prelates. [Italian, from Old French *mantelet,* MANTELET.]

man·tel·piece or **man·tle·piece** (măn′təl-pēs′) *n.* See **mantel** (sense 2).

man·tel·tree (măn′təl-trē′) *n.* A beam, stone, or arch that functions as a lintel over a fireplace, supporting the masonry above. [Middle English : MANTEL + TREE (beam).]

man·tic (măn′tĭk) *adj.* Of, pertaining to, or having the power of divination; prophetic. [Greek *mantikos,* from *mantis,* prophet.]

man·ti·core (măn′tĭ-kôr′, -kōr′) *n.* A fabulous monster having the head of a man, the body of a lion, and the tail of a dragon or scorpion. [Middle English, from Latin *mantichōra,* from Greek *mantikhōras,* a misreading of *martikhoras,* a fabulous Oriental beast.]

man·til·la (măn-tē′yə, -tĭl′ə) *n.* **1.** A scarf, usually of lace, worn over the head and shoulders, often over a high comb, by women in Spain and Latin America. **2.** A shawl or a short veil, as one worn by Roman Catholic women in church. [Spanish, diminutive of *manta,* cape, MANTA.]

man·tis (măn′tĭs) *n., pl.* **-tises** or **-tes** (-tēz′). Any of various carnivorous insects of the family Mantidae, primarily tropical but including a few Temperate Zone species. They are usually pale green and have two pairs of walking legs and powerful forelimbs that are often folded in a praying position. See **praying mantis.** [New Latin, from Greek *mantis,* prophet, diviner, hence (from its praying appearance) mantis.]

man·tis·sa (măn-tĭs′ə) *n. Mathematics.* The decimal part of a common logarithm when the logarithm is written as the sum of an integer and a decimal. In 1.7041 the mantissa is .7041. [Latin, makeweight, probably from Etruscan.]

mantis shrimp *n.* A burrowing crustacean, the **squilla** (*see*).

man·tle (măn′təl) *n.* **1.** A loose, sleeveless coat worn over outer garments; cloak. **2.** Something that covers, envelops, or conceals: *a mantle of ivy.* **3.** Variant of **mantel. 4.** A zone of hot gases around a flame. **5.** A device in gas lamps consisting of a sheath of gauze, impregnated with certain salts, that gives off brilliant illumination when heated by the flame. **6.** *Anatomy.* The outer part of the brain, the **cerebral cortex** (*see*). **7.** *Geology.* The layer of the earth between the crust and the core. See **Mohorovičić discontinuity. 8.** *Zoology.* The wings, shoulder feathers, and back of a bird when differently colored from the rest of the body. **9.** *Zoology.* In mollusks and brachiopods, a membrane that covers most of the body and secretes the substance forming the shell. **10.** The outer wall and casing of a blast furnace above the hearth.
~*v.* **mantled, -tling, -tles.** —*tr.* To cover with or as if with a mantle; cloak and conceal: *mountains mantled in snow.* —*intr.* **1.** To spread or become extended over a surface. **2.** To become covered with a coating, such as scum or froth on the surface of a liquid. **3.** To be or become covered or overspread by blushes or colors: *Her face mantled with joy.* **4.** To spread the wings over food. Used of hawks. [Middle English, from Old French, from Latin *mantellum*†, cloak.]

Man·tle (măn′təl), **Mickey Charles** (1931–). U.S. baseball player. Known as one of the greatest sluggers of the game, Mantle played center field for the New York Yankees from 1958 to 1968, establishing a lifetime batting average of .298 and scoring 536 home runs. He is a member of the Baseball Hall of Fame.

mantle rock *n. Geology.* **Regolith** (*see*).

mantlet. Variant of **mantelet.**

man-to-man (măn′tə-măn′) *adj.* **1.** Characterized by forthrightness and candor: *We had a man-to-man discussion.* **2.** *Sports.* Of, pertaining to, or being a strategy in which a defending player deals with one particular player on the offensive team, as in basketball.

Man·toux test (măn′tōō′, măn-tōō′) *n.* A test to determine whether a person has developed an immunity to tuberculosis. Some tuberculin is injected below the skin, and the appearance of inflammation during the next 24 hours indicates a certain degree of immunity. Also called "tuberculin test." [After Charles *Mantoux* (1877–1947), French physician.]

man·tra (măn′trə, mŭn′-) *n.* **1.** *Hinduism.* A sacred formula believed to embody the divinity invoked and to possess magical power. It is used in prayer and incantation. **2.** A formula or word similar to a mantra that is repeated, often in one's head, to induce a contemplative state in some techniques of meditation. **3.** A Vedic psalm of praise. [Sanskrit, "prayer," "hymn."]

man·tu·a (măn′chōō-ə, -tōō-ə) *n.* A loose gown, worn open in front to reveal an underskirt, worn in the 17th and 18th centuries. [French *manteau,* mantle (influenced by MANTUA, formerly famous for silks), from Old French *mantel,* from Latin *mantellum,* MANTLE.]

Man·tu·a (măn′tōō-ə, -chōō-ə, măn′-). *Italian* **Man·to·va** (män′tō-və, män′-). City on the Mincio River, Lombardy, Italy. It is the capital of Mantova province and is a tourist, manufacturing, and agricultural center. —**Man·tu·an** *adj. & n.*

man·u·al (măn′yōō-əl) *adj.* **1. a.** Of, pertaining to, or done by the hands. **b.** Used by or operated with the hands, as a weapon, tool, or simple machine may be: *a manual typewriter.* **c.** Employing human rather than mechanical energy: *manual labor.* **d.** Engaged in work done with the hands as opposed to clerical or administrative work: *manual workers.* **2.** Of, pertaining to, or resembling a manual or guidebook.
~*n.* **1.** A small reference book, especially one giving instructions; a guidebook or handbook. **2.** A manual keyboard, especially one of the keyboards of an organ. **3.** *Military.* A set of prescribed move-

mantis *There are about 1,800 species of mantis—all members of the insect family Mantidae and often known as praying mantises. They feed on live insects, including others of their own kind. The female often eats the male after they mate; the young nymphs often eat each other.*

maple

THE FIERY FOLIAGE OF THE MAPLE FAMILY

Trees used for garden ornament, building timber—and sweet syrup

Maple wood was used to make spears in prehistoric times—hence its botanical name *Acer,* the Latin for "sharp." In the past 2,000 years, maple wood has been used in cabinetwork and to make musical instruments—for example, the sycamore is also called the fiddleback maple.

The giant maples from the temperate regions of Europe and North America, which grow to more than 33 meters (100 feet), are the most valued for timber.

Most forest species, such as America's red maple, have brilliant autumn foliage, and some, such as the Chinese paperbark maple, have decorative bark. The Norway maple also bears flowers in spring, which is unusual for a forest tree. The delicate Japanese maples are the most highly prized as garden trees.

Among the maple family's 200 or more members at least one is edible. The extraction of the sugar maple's rich sap, and its preservation as syrup or sugar, was a secret given the 18th-century settlers of Canada by native Indians.

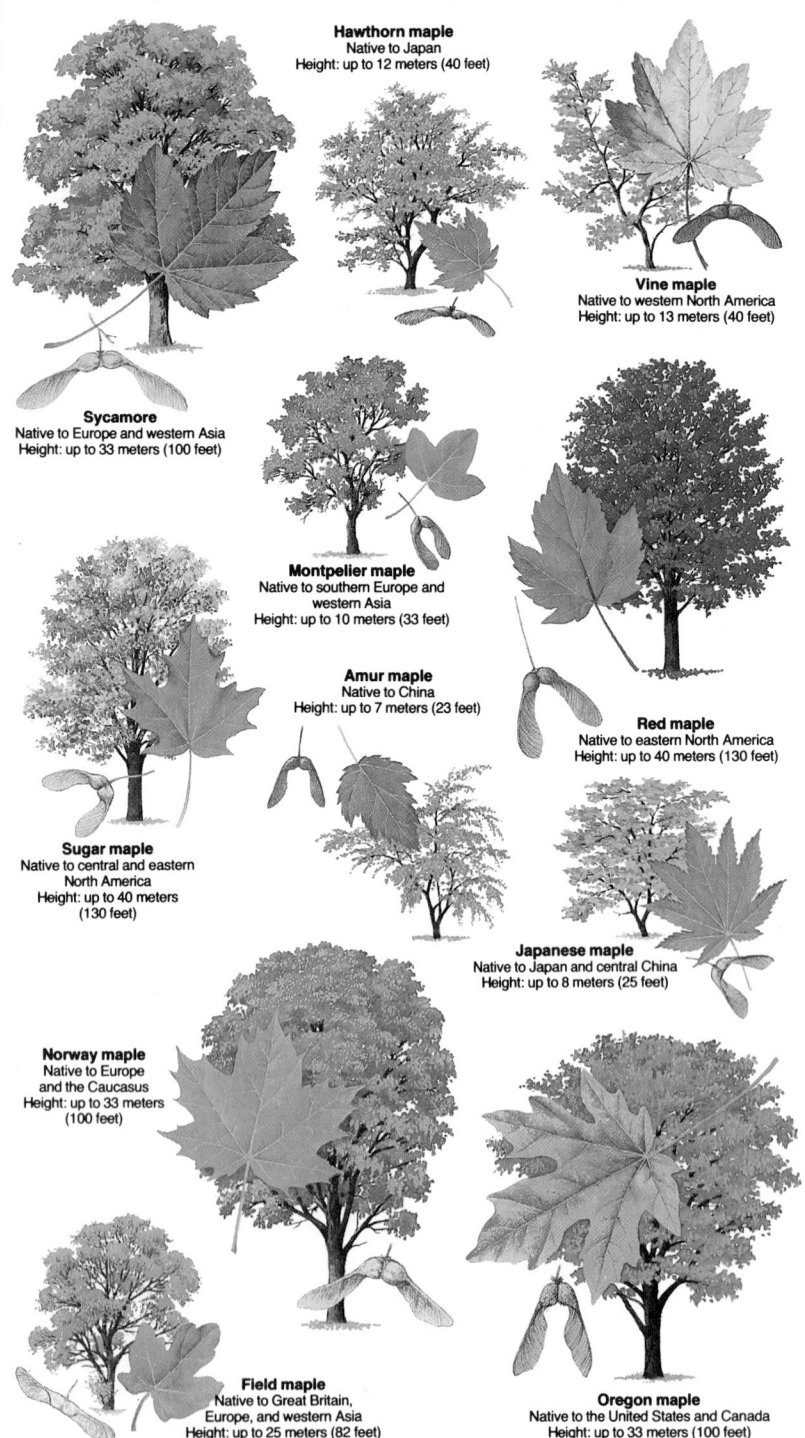

Hawthorn maple
Native to Japan
Height: up to 12 meters (40 feet)

Vine maple
Native to western North America
Height: up to 13 meters (40 feet)

Sycamore
Native to Europe and western Asia
Height: up to 33 meters (100 feet)

Montpelier maple
Native to southern Europe and western Asia
Height: up to 10 meters (33 feet)

Amur maple
Native to China
Height: up to 7 meters (23 feet)

Red maple
Native to eastern North America
Height: up to 40 meters (130 feet)

Sugar maple
Native to central and eastern North America
Height: up to 40 meters (130 feet)

Japanese maple
Native to Japan and central China
Height: up to 8 meters (25 feet)

Norway maple
Native to Europe and the Caucasus
Height: up to 33 meters (100 feet)

Field maple
Native to Great Britain, Europe, and western Asia
Height: up to 25 meters (82 feet)

Oregon maple
Native to the United States and Canada
Height: up to 33 meters (100 feet)

---

ments in the handling of a weapon, especially a rifle. **4.** Manual control: *switched the machine to manual.* [Middle English *manuel,* from Old French, from Latin *manuālis,* of the hand, from *manus,* hand.] —**man·u·al·ly** *adv.*

manual alphabet *n.* An alphabet of hand signals used for communication with or among deaf-mutes.

manual training *n.* A course of training to develop dexterity in practical arts, as carpentry.

ma·nu·bri·um (mə-nōō′brē-əm, mə-nyōō′-) *n., pl.* **-bria** (-brē-ə). *Anatomy.* **1.** The upper part of the breastbone. **2.** The handle-shaped projection of the malleus in the ear. [New Latin, from Latin *manubrium,* handle, from *manus,* hand.]

Ma·nu·el I (măn′yōō-ĕl′, -əl), known as "Manuel the Great" (1469–1521). King of Portugal (1495–1521). He presided over the golden age of Portugal's overseas exploration, including the discovery of the sea route to India by Vasco da Gama.

man·u·fac·to·ry (măn′yə-făk′tə-rē, măn′ə-) *n., pl.* **-ries.** A factory. [MANUFACT(URE) + (FACT)ORY.]

man·u·fac·ture (măn′yə-făk′chər, măn′ə-) *v.* **-tured, -turing, -tures.** —*tr.* **1. a.** To make or process (a raw material) into a finished product, especially by means of a large-scale industrial operation. **b.** To make or process (a product), especially by industrial machines. **2.** To create, produce, or turn out in a mechanical manner: *a street artist manufacturing portraits to order.* **3.** To concoct or invent; fabricate. —*intr.* To make or process goods, especially in large quantities and by means of industrial machines.

~*n. Abbr.* **manuf., manufac., mfg., mfr. 1.** The act, craft, or process of manufacturing. **2.** A product that is manufactured. **3.** An industry that uses industrial machines. [French, a making by hand, handiwork, from Late Latin *manūfactus,* handmade : Latin *manus,* hand + *factus,* from *facere,* to make.] —**man·u·fac·tur·a·ble** *adj.*

manufactured gas *n.* A gaseous fuel made from various petroleum products or from soft coal.

man·u·fac·tur·er (măn′yə-făk′chər-ər, măn′ə-) *n. Abbr.* **mfr.** A person, entity, or enterprise that manufactures; especially, the owner or operator of a factory.

ma·nu·ka (mä′nə-kə) *n.* An ornamental tree or shrub, *Leptospermum scoparium,* native to New Zealand, with aromatic leaves and hard timber. [Maori.]

man·u·mit (măn′yə-mĭt′) *tr.v.* **-mitted, -mitting, -mits.** To free from slavery or bondage; emancipate. [Middle English *manumitten,* from Old French *manumitter,* from Latin *manumittere,* from *manū ēmittere,* to liberate, release from one's hand : *manū,* ablative of *manus,* hand + *ēmittere,* to EMIT.] —**man·u·mis·sion** (măn′yə-mĭsh′ən) *n.* —**man·u·mit·ter** *n.*

ma·nure (mə-nōōr′, -nyōōr′) *n.* Material such as animal dung or compost used to fertilize soil.

~*tr.v.* **manured, -nuring, -nures.** To apply manure to. [Middle English *manour,* cultivation of soil, from *manouren,* to till, from Norman French *mainoverer,* from Old French *manoeuvrer,* to till, "work by hand," from Medieval Latin *manuoperārī* : Latin *manus,* hand + *operārī,* to work.] —**ma·nur·er** *n.*

ma·nus (mā′nəs, mä′-) *n., pl.* **manus.** **1.** *Zoology.* The end of the forelimb in vertebrates, as the hand, claw, or hoof. **2.** In Roman law, the authority of a husband over his wife. [Latin, hand.]

man·u·script (măn′yə-skrĭpt′) *n. Abbr.* **ms, MS, ms., MS. 1.** A book, document, or other composition written by hand. **2.** A typewritten or handwritten version of a book, article, document, or other work, prepared and submitted for publication in print. **3.** Handwriting as opposed to printing.

~*adj.* Handwritten or typewritten. [Medieval Latin *manūscrīptus,* handwritten : Latin *manus,* hand + *scrīptus,* from *scrībere,* to write.]

Ma·nu·ti·us (mə-nōō′shē-əs, -shəs, mə-nyōō′-), **Aldus,** born Aldo Manucci (1450–1515). Italian printer. He established the Aldine Press in Venice (*c.* 1498) to publish Greek and Latin classics. His son **Paulus** (1512–74) and grandson **Aldus the Younger** (1547–97) directed the papal press.

Manx (măngks) *adj.* Of or pertaining to the Isle of Man or the Manx language.

~*n., pl.* **Manx. 1.** A native or resident of the Isle of Man. **2.** The nearly extinct Goidelic Celtic language spoken on the Isle of Man. **3.** A Manx cat.

Manx cat, manx cat *n.* A domestic cat of a breed having short hair and an internal vestigial tail. Also called "Manx."

Manx shearwater *n.* A small European oceanic bird, *Puffinus puffinus,* that shows remarkably accurate homing ability.

man·y (mĕn′ē) *adj.* **more, most. 1.** Amounting to or consisting of a large, indefinite number: *many friends; as many eggs as you can eat.* **2.** Being one of a large, indefinite number of persons or things: *many a woman; many another day.*

~*n.* Used with a plural verb. **1.** A large, indefinite number of persons or things: *Many of the children were ill.* **2.** The great body of the people; the masses: *"The many fail; the one succeeds"* (Alfred, Lord Tennyson).

~*pron.* Used with a plural verb. A large number of persons or things: *"Many are called, but few are chosen"* (Matthew 22:14). —**as many.** The same number of: *had six cars in as many years.* [Middle English, from Old English *manig, mænig.*]

man·y·fold (mĕn′ē-fōld′) *adv.* By many times: *The state's population has increased manyfold.*

man·y·plies (mĕn′ĭ-plīz′) *n.* The third stomach of a cud-chewing mammal, the **omasum** *(see).* [MANY + *plies,* plural of PLY (modeled by analogy on *manifolds*).]

man·y-sid·ed (mĕn′ē-sī′dĭd) *adj.* Having a variety of aspects or qualities: *a many-sided book.* **—man·y-sid·ed·ness** *n.*

man·za·ni·lla (măn′zə-nē′yə, -nĭl′ə) *n.* A pale dry sherry from Spain. [Spanish, small apple, hence (from its aromatic bouquet) manzanilla sherry, diminutive of *manzana,* apple, from Old Spanish, from Latin *(māla) Matiāna,* "(apples) of *Matius,*" a particular kind of apple, probably named after Caius *Matius* Calvena, Roman author of a cookbook (1st century B.C.).]

man·za·ni·ta (măn′zə-nē′tə) *n.* Any of several evergreen shrubs of the genus *Arcostaphylos,* of the Pacific coast of North America; especially, *A. manzanita,* bearing white or pink flowers in clusters. [American Spanish, diminutive of Spanish *manzana,* apple. See **manzanilla.**]

Man·zo·ni (män-zō′nē), **Alessandro** (1785–1873). Italian novelist and poet. He was the leader of the Italian romantic school and is best known for his romantic-historical novel *I Promessi Sposi* (*The Betrothed,* 1825–27). The refined Florentine dialect that he used as a literary language set the standard for modern Italian prose.

MAO monoamine oxidase.

Mao·ism (mou′ĭz′əm) *n.* The Communist political philosophy and practice developed in China chiefly by Mao Ze-dong and emphasizing the peasantry's role in a revolution. **—Mao·ist** *n. & adj.*

Mao·ri (mou′rē) *n., pl.* **-ris** or collectively **Maori. 1.** A member of the aboriginal people of New Zealand, of Polynesian-Melanesian descent. **2.** The Austronesian language of this people. **—Mao·ri** *adj.*

mao-tai (mou′tī′, -dī′) *n.* A potent colorless Chinese alcoholic drink distilled from a mixture of Chinese sorghum and millet. [Chinese, after *Maotai,* town in southwestern China where it is produced.]

Mao Ze-dong or **Mao Tse-t'ung** (mou′ dzŭ′do͝ong′), known as "Chairman Mao" (1893–1976). Chinese Communist leader. In 1921 he helped form the Chinese Communist Party, and with its split from the Guomindang Nationalist Party (1927) he became a leader of the Chinese Soviet Republic in southeastern China (1931). He led the Long March (1934–35) to Yan'an, where after the collapse of the Japanese he defeated the Nationalists and proclaimed the People's Republic of China (1949). As chairman of the People's Republic (1949–59), he instituted the Great Leap Forward and the founding of the communes. He continued as party chairman after 1959 and instituted the Cultural Revolution (1966–69) to re-establish the revolutionary spirit. His writings have had great influence on revolutionary thinking throughout the world.

map (măp) *n.* **1. a.** A representation, usually on a plane surface, of a region of the earth. **b.** A similar representation of heavenly bodies, as stars and planets. **2.** Something suggesting a map, as in comprehensiveness or clarity of representation. **3.** *Mathematics.* A mapping. **4.** *Slang.* The face. **5.** The arrangement of genes on a chromosome. **—put on the map.** To make famous or known. **—wipe off the map.** To destroy completely; annihilate.
∼*tr.v.* **mapped, mapping, maps. 1.** To make a map of. **2.** To explore or make a survey of (a region) for the purpose of making a map. **3.** To plan or delineate, especially in detail; arrange. Often used with *out: mapping out holiday plans.* **4.** *Mathematics.* To establish a mapping of (a set or aggregate). **5.** To locate (a gene) on a chromosome. [Medieval Latin *mappa (mundī),* map (of the world), from *mappa,* napkin, sheet, cloth.] **—map·per** *n.*

ma·ple (mā′pəl) *n.* **1.** A tree or shrub of the genus *Acer,* found in the North Temperate Zone. Most are deciduous trees with lobed leaves and winged seeds borne in pairs. **2.** The wood of a maple, especially the hard, close-grained wood of the sugar maple, much used for furniture and flooring. **3.** The flavor of the concentrated sap of the sugar maple. [Middle English, Old English *mapel(treow),* maple (tree).]

maple sugar *n.* A sugar made by boiling down maple syrup.

maple syrup *n.* **1.** A sweet syrup made from the sap of the sugar maple. **2.** Syrup made from various sugars and flavored with maple syrup or artificial maple flavoring.

map·mak·er (măp′mā′kər) *n.* A person who makes maps; a cartographer.

map·ping (măp′ĭng) *n.* *Mathematics.* A rule of correspondence established between two sets that associates each member of the first set with one or more members of the second; a function. Also called "map."

map projection *n.* A representation of the earth's parallels of latitude and meridians of longitude as a network, or graticule, on a plane surface. See feature, next page.

Ma·pu·to (mə-po͞o′tō). Formerly **Lou·ren·ço Mar·ques** (lə-rĕn′sō mär′kĕs′, lô-rĕn′so͞o mär′kĕsh′). Capital of Mozambique, on Maputo Bay. It is a resort and a major seaport, exporting metal ores and coal from southern Africa.

ma·quette (mă-kĕt′) *n.* A preliminary model or sketch made by a sculptor. [French, from Italian *machietta,* diminutive of *macchia,* spot, ultimately from Latin *macula,* spot.]

ma·quil·lage (mä′kē-äzh′, -kē-yäzh′) *n.* **1.** Cosmetics; make-up. **2.** The application of cosmetics. [French, from *maquiller,* to make up, from Old French *masquiller,* to stain.]

ma·quis (mă-kē′, mä-) *n., pl.* **maquis. 1.** In the Mediterranean area, a dense growth of mainly evergreen small trees and bushes. **2.** *Often* **Maquis. a.** The French underground organization that fought against German occupation forces during World War II; the resistance. **b.** A member of this organization. [French (via Corsica), from Italian *macchia,* thicket, "spot," from Latin *macula,* spot.]

mar (mär) *tr.v.* **marred, marring, mars. 1.** To damage or deface. **2.** To spoil the quality of: *"Mend your speech lest it mar your fortunes"* (Shakespeare). —See Synonyms at **injure.**
∼*n.* A mark that disfigures; a blemish. [Middle English *marren, merran,* Old English *merran, mierran.*]

mar. maritime.

Mar. March.

mar·a·bou, mar·a·bout (măr′ə-bo͞o′) *n.* **1.** Any of several large Old World storks of the genus *Leptoptilus,* having a soft down used to trim women's garments. Also called "adjutant," "adjutant stork." **2.** A neckpiece, hat, dress, or coat trimmed with the down of the marabou. **3. a.** A raw silk that can be dyed without being separated from the gum. **b.** A fabric or an article of clothing made from such silk. [French *marabout,* from Portuguese *marabuto,* from Arabic *murābit,* holy man, hermit, hence stork (the stork is a sacred bird in Islam). See **marabout.**]

mar·a·bout[1] (măr′ə-bo͞o′, -bo͞ot′) *n.* **1.** A Muslim hermit or saint, especially in northern Africa. **2.** The tomb of a marabout or a shrine to his memory. [French, from Portuguese *marabuto,* from Arabic *murābit,* hermit, holy man, "(one) stationed (at a frontier post)," from *ribāt,* frontier post (those stationed there fought against infidels and were thus considered holy).]

marabout[2]. Variant of **marabou.**

ma·ra·ca (mə-rä′kə, -răk′ə) *n.* A percussion instrument consisting of a hollow gourd rattle containing pebbles or beans. Maracas are often played in pairs. [Brazilian Portuguese *maracá,* from Tupi.]

Mar·a·cai·bo (măr′ə-kī′bō, mä′rə-). City of northwestern Venezuela, a commercial and industrial center and the hub of a rich oil-producing area. It is at the outlet of Lake Maracaibo, the largest lake in South America. A dredged channel gives oceangoing vessels access to the lake.

mar·ag·ing (mä′rā′jĭng) *n.* *Metallurgy.* The process of heating a martensite steel at around 500°C and cooling it in air without quenching. It is used to modify the martensite structure and produce strong low-carbon steels. [MAR(TENSITE) + AGING.]

Ma·ram·ba (mə-răm′bə, -räm′bə). Formerly **Liv·ing·stone** (lĭv′-ĭng-stən). City of southern Zambia, situated on the Zambezi River. Founded in 1905 and named at first after the explorer David Livingstone, it was the capital of Northern Rhodesia from 1911 to 1935, when Lusaka replaced it.

ma·ran·ta (mə-răn′tə) *n.* **1.** Any plant of the tropical American genus *Maranta,* one species of which, *M. arundinacea,* yields arrowroot. Several species are cultivated for their ornamental foliage. **2.** A starch made from arrowroot. [New Latin, after Bartolomeo *Maranta,* 16th-century Italian herbalist.]

ma·ras·ca (mə-răs′kə) *n.* A European cherry tree, *Prunus cerasus marasca,* bearing bitter red fruit from which maraschino is made. [Italian, shortened from *amarasca (ciliegia),* bitter (cherry), from *amaro,* bitter, from Latin *amārus,* bitter.]

mar·a·schi·no (măr′ə-skē′nō, -shē′nō) *n.* A liqueur made from the fermented juice and crushed kernels of the marasca cherry. [Italian, from MARASCA.]

maraschino cherry *n.* A maraschino-flavored preserved cherry.

ma·ras·mus (mə-răz′məs) *n.* *Pathology.* A wasting away of the body, especially of infants, associated with inadequate or inadequately assimilated food. [Late Latin, from Greek *marasmos,* from *marainein,* to waste away.] **—ma·ras·mic** *adj.*

Ma·rat (mä-rä′), **Jean Paul** (1743–93). French journalist and Revolutionary politician. He was trained as a doctor and wrote scientific works before founding (1789) and editing *L'Ami du Peuple,* which supported the French Revolution. Hero of the working classes, he was elected to the National Convention (1792) and struggled against the Girondins, one of whose supporters, Charlotte Corday, murdered him in his bath.

Ma·ra·tha, Mah·rat·ta (mə-rä′tə) *n., pl.* **-thas** or **-tas** or collectively **Maratha** or **Mahratta.** A member of a Scytho-Dravidian people of southwestern India.

Ma·ra·thi, Mah·ra·ti, Mah·rat·ti (mə-rä′tē) *adj.* Of or pertaining to the state of Maharashtra, India.
∼*n.* The major Indic language in Maharashtra.

mar·a·thon (măr′ə-thŏn′) *n.* **1.** A cross-country footrace of 26 miles 385 yards (42.195 kilometers). It is an event in the Olympic games. **2.** A long-distance race: *a swimming marathon.* **3.** A contest of endurance: *a dance marathon.* **4.** A task or action that requires endurance: *a letter-writing marathon.* [Named in commemoration of the messenger who ran to Athens to report the news of the Greek victory at MARATHON .] **—mar·a·thon** *adj.*

Mar·a·thon (măr′ə-thŏn′). Village and plain of ancient Greece, northeast of Athens. It was the site of a Greek victory, led by Miltiades, over the Persians in 490 B.C.

ma·raud (mə-rôd′) *v.* **-rauded, -rauding, -rauds.** —*intr.* To rove in search of booty; raid for plunder. —*tr.* To invade for loot; raid or pillage.
∼*n.* *Archaic.* A raid. [French *marauder,* from *maraud,* vagabond, rogue, perhaps from dialectal *maraud,* tomcat (imitative of purring).] **—ma·raud·er** *n.*

mar·ble (mär′bəl) *n.* **1.** A metamorphic rock, chiefly calcium carbonate, $CaCO_3$, often irregularly colored by impurities. It is used for architectural and ornamental purposes. **2.** A piece of marble. **3.** A sculpture of marble: *the Elgin marbles.* **4. a.** A small hard ball, usually made of glass, used in children's games. **b. marbles.** *Used with a singular verb.* Any of various children's games played with marbles, the object being especially to hit a marble or group of marbles belonging to one's opponent or to knock the greatest possi-

Manx cat *A tailless cat probably first bred on the Isle of Man in Great Britain. Its long hind legs give it a curious hopping gait.*

marabou *The African adjutant stork, or marabou, is the world's largest species of stork, growing to a height of 1.5 meters (5 feet). Native to central and parts of southern Africa, it feeds on fish, frogs, and carrion.*

PRONUNCIATION KEY

ă, pat; ā, pay; âr, care;
ä, father, are; b, bib;
ch, church; d, deed; ĕ, pet;
ē, be; f, fife; g, gag; h, hat;
hw, which; ĭ, pit; ī, pie;
îr, pier; j, judge; k, kick;
l, lid, needle; m, mum;
n, no, sudden; ng, thing;
ŏ, pot; ō, toe; ô, paw, for;
oi, noise; ou, out; o͝o, book;
o͞o, boot; p, pop; r, roar;
s, sauce; sh, ship, dish;
t, tight; th, thin, path;
th, this, bathe; ŭ, cut; ûr, fur;
v, valve; w, with; y, yes;
z, zebra, size; zh, vision;
ə, about, item, edible, gallop, circus, peaceful

IN FOREIGN WORDS:

à, *Fr.* ami; œ, *Fr.* feu, *Ger.* schön; ü, *Fr.* tu, *Ger.* über; KH, *Ger.* ich, *Scot.* loch; N, *Fr.* bon; y', *Fr.* Compiègne

STRESS MARKS:

Primary stress: ′
in·cite′ (ĭn-sīt′)
Secondary stress: ′
in′sight′ (ĭn′sīt′)

MAPPING THE WORLD

Every type of map projection distorts the world in some way

The Age of Discovery, when European mariners explored the world in the late 15th and 16th centuries, saw the work of the first great modern mapmaker, Gerardus Mercator (1512–94).

As maps became more accurate and as it became widely understood that the earth was round, it proved apparent that no large-scale map could be drawn on a flat surface without being distorted in some way—whether in areas, angles, or distances. Since then many methods of map projection have been devised, but it is possible only to minimize distortion. More accuracy in one way will mean that there will be distortion in the others.

Mercator's projection is probably the most familiar. It is based on an imaginary cylinder of paper wrapped around the earth and touching it at the equator. An imaginary light from inside the earth "projects" the continents onto the cylinder. When the cylinder is flattened out, the lines of latitude and longitude are straight, but the length along them is greatly exaggerated. The land areas near the Poles, such as Greenland and Antarctica, are greatly exaggerated, but the angles are correct. In marine navigation, this allows a course to be plotted by drawing a straight line from point to point.

For aircraft navigation, however, different problems arise. The shortest distance between London and Tokyo is not a straight line across Europe and Asia, as the map projection suggests, but a route across the North Pole. A special map is produced for each airport, using a zenithal projection. On it any route from that airport is shown as a straight line, with lines of latitude and longitude curved.

Another type of map, called a conical projection, involves an imaginary cone placed over the earth so that a line parallel with the equator is touched by the cone. The tip of the cone is directly over the North (or South) Pole. By varying the size of the cone, almost any spot on a hemisphere can be made to touch it. An imaginary light from the center of the earth would show up the projection on the cone. If the area to be mapped is small, the distortion is negligible.

Numerous types of map projection have been devised mathematically, and atlases usually carry the name of the projection under each map.

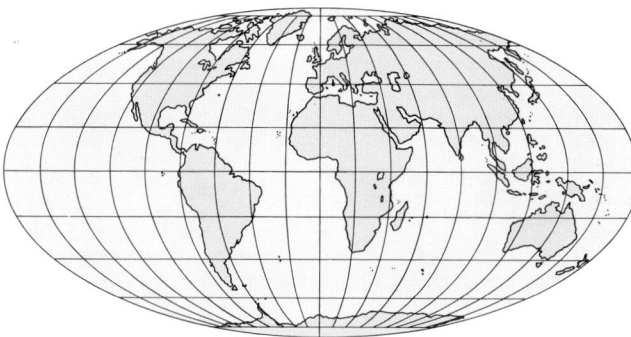

MOLLWEIDE'S HOMOLOGRAPHIC PROJECTION *An equal-area projection on which each land mass corresponds to the real one in relative size. However, angles are distorted and navigation would have to be plotted on curved lines.*

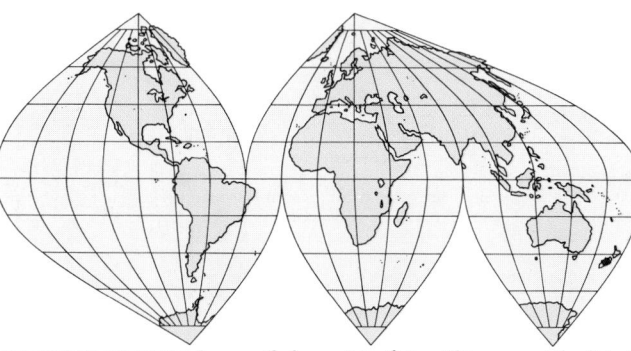

INTERRUPTED PROJECTION *A map with three points of view. This evens out the distortion of angles across the map and represents shapes fairly accurately. Despite its appearance, it could not be cut out and wrapped around a sphere.*

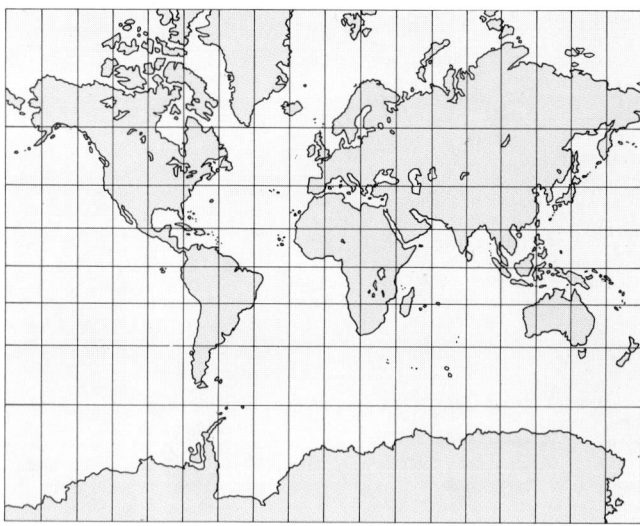

MERCATOR PROJECTION *A correct-angle projection, suitable for marine navigation. The lines of longitude run parallel rather than converging. Consequently Antarctica and Greenland are shown about ten times their relative size.*

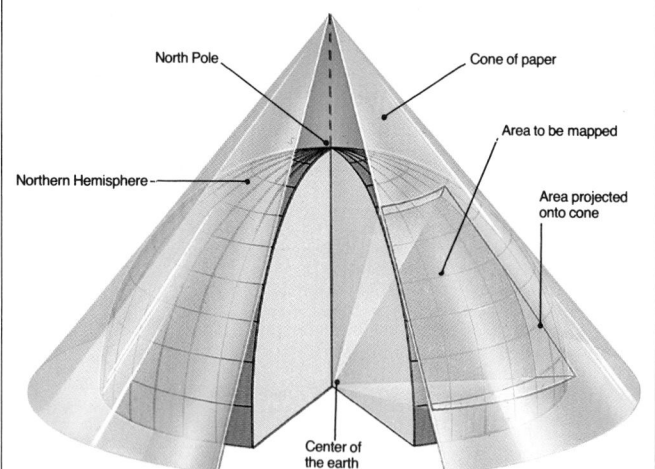

CONICAL PROJECTION *Suitable for small areas as well as for much of a hemisphere. An imaginary cone is placed over the earth so that it touches the area to be mapped. The point of projection is the center of the earth, the tip of the cone is above a Pole.*

ble number of marbles out of a ring. **5. marbles.** *Slang.* Common sense or sanity: *She still has all her marbles.*
~*tr.v.* **marbled, -bling, -bles. 1.** To mottle and streak with colors and veins in imitation of marble: *marbled paper.* **2.** To intermix with flecks or thin strips of fat: *a well-aged and well-marbled steak.*
~*adj.* **1.** Consisting of or constructed with marble: *marble halls.* **2.** Resembling marble in consistency, texture, venation, color, or coldness: *a marble heart.* [Middle English *marbel,* from Old French *marbre,* from Latin *marmor,* from Greek *marmaros†,* marble, originally any hard stone.] **—mar·bly** *adj.*
marble cake *n.* A sponge cake with a marbled appearance, made by swirling together light and dark batter.
Mar·ble·head (mär′bəl-hĕd′, mär′bəl-hĕd′). A resort town in northeastern Massachusetts, on the Atlantic Ocean. The town, founded

in the 17th century and noted today for its fine harbor for pleasure boats, has many old houses.
mar·ble·ize (mär′bə-līz′) *tr.v.* **-ized, -izing, -izes.** To give a veined or mottled appearance to.
mar·bling (mär′blĭng) *n.* **1.** A mottling or streaking that resembles marble. **2.** The process or operation of giving something the surface appearance of marble. **3.** The decorative imitation of marble patterns printed on page edges and endpapers of books. **4.** Flecks or thin strips of fat evenly distributed in a cut of meat of good quality.
Mar·burg (mär′bûrg′, -bŏŏrg′). City in Hesse, West Germany. It is the site of Germany's first Protestant university (1527) and the 13th- to 14th-century castle where Luther and Zwingli held their famous religious debate (1529). It produces precision machinery, pharmaceuticals, and pottery.
Mar·burg disease (mär′bûrg′) *n.* A fatal virus disease that is trans-

mitted to humans from the vervet or green monkey by contact with infected tissue in a laboratory. Also called "green monkey disease." [After MARBURG, West Germany.]

marc (märk) *n.* **1.** The pulpy residue left after the juice has been pressed from grapes, apples, or other fruit. **2.** Brandy distilled from grape residue. [French, from Old French *marcher,* to trample (grapes), MARCH.]

Mar·can (mär′kən) *adj.* Pertaining to or designating St. Mark's Gospel. [Latin *Marcus,* Mark + -AN.]

mar·ca·site (mär′kə-sīt′, -zīt′) *n.* **1.** A mineral form of iron disulfide, FeS₂, having the same composition as pyrite but differing in crystalline structure. Also called "white iron pyrites." **2.** An ornament of pyrite, polished steel, or white metal. **3.** Any of several minerals resembling iron disulfide. [Middle English *marchasite,* from Medieval Latin *marcasīta,* from Arabic *marqashīṭā,* probably from Persian.]

Mar·ceau (mär-sō′), **Marcel** (1923-). French mime, trained as a conventional actor. His most famous character is the clown-harlequin Bip. His films include *Un Jardin Public* (1955).

mar·cel (mär-sĕl′) *n.* A formerly fashionable hairstyle characterized by deep, regular waves made by a heated curling iron. Also called "marcel wave." —*tr.v.* **marcelled, -celling, -cels.** To style (the hair) in a marcel. [After *Marcel* Grateau (1852-1936), French hairdresser.]

marcel wave *n.* A marcel.

mar·ces·cence (mär-sĕs′əns) *n.* The state or quality of being marcescent.

mar·ces·cent (mär-sĕs′ənt) *adj. Botany.* Withering but not falling off. Said especially of a blossom that persists on a twig after flowering. [Latin *marcēscēns* (stem *marcēscent*-), present participle of *marcēscere,* inceptive of *marcēre,* to wither.]

march¹ (märch) *v.* **marched, marching, marches.** —*intr.* **1. a.** To walk in a formal military manner with measured steps at a steady rate. **b.** To begin to move in such a manner: *The troops will march at dawn.* **2.** To advance in an assertive or determined manner: *marched up to the shop assistant to make a complaint.* **3.** To proceed steadily: *Time marches on.* —*tr.* **1.** To cause to march: *soldiers being marched into battle.* **2.** To traverse by marching: *They marched the route in a day.* —*n.* **1. a.** The act of marching. **b.** The steady forward movement of a body of troops. **2.** A long tiring journey on foot. **3.** Forward movement; progression: *the march of time.* **4.** A regulated pace: *quick march.* **5.** The distance covered by marching: *a week's march away.* **6.** A procession held as a form of public demonstration. **7.** *Music.* A musical composition in regularly accented, usually duple meter with a rhythm suitable for accompanying marching. —**on the march.** Advancing steadily; progressing: *Science is on the march.* —**steal a march on.** To get ahead of, especially by quiet enterprise. [French *marcher,* to walk, tramp, trample, from Frankish *markôn* (unattested), to mark out with footprints.] —**march·er** *n.*

march² *n.* **1.** The border or boundary of a country or area of land; frontier. **2.** A tract of land bordering on two countries and claimed by both. —*intr.v.* **marched, marching, marches.** To have a common boundary, border, or frontier: *England marches with Scotland.* [Middle English *marche,* from Old French *marche, marc,* borderland, from Germanic.]

March (märch) *n. Abbr.* **Mar.** The third month of the Gregorian calendar. March has 31 days. See feature at **calendar.** [Middle English, from Old French *Marche, Marz,* from Latin *Mārtius (mēnsis),* (month) of Mars, from *Mārs* (stem *Mārt*-), MARS (god).]

March. marchioness.

Mar·che (mär′kā′). Also **the March·es** (mär′chĭz). Coastal region of central Italy, covered largely by Apennine ranges and foothills. It produces cereals, fruit, wine, tobacco, cattle, and fish. It is so called because it was on the southern border (or march) of the Holy Roman Empire. Ancona is the capital.

Mär·chen (mâr′KHən) *n., pl.* **Märchen.** A folk tale or fairy story. [German.]

March·es, the (mär′chĭz). **1.** The areas along the English-Welsh and English-Scottish borders. In medieval times the lords of these areas were given wide-ranging powers to defend the borders. **2.** See **Marche.**

mar·che·sa (mär-kā′zə) *n., pl.* **-se** (-zā). A wife or widow of a marchese. [Italian, feminine of MARCHESE.]

mar·che·se (mär-kā′zā) *n., pl.* **-si** (-zē). An Italian nobleman ranking between a prince and a count. [Italian, from Late Latin *marcēnsis,* "ruler of a march," from *marca,* borderland, MARCH.]

Mar·chesh·van (mär-KHĕsh′vən) *n.* **Heshvan** (see).

marching orders *pl.n.* **1. a.** Orders to begin a march. **b.** Official instructions to proceed. **2.** A notice that one is no longer wanted; dismissal: *was given her marching orders by her lover.*

mar·chio·ness (mär′shə-nĭs, mär′shə-nĕs′) *n. Abbr.* **March. 1.** The wife or widow of a marquis. **2.** A peeress of the rank of marquis in her own right. In certain countries, also called "marquise." [Medieval Latin *marchionissa,* feminine of *marchiō,* marquis, "ruler of the march," from *marca,* borderland, MARCH.]

march·land (märch′lănd′) *n.* A borderland; a march.

march·pane (märch′pān′) *n.* Marzipan.

march·past (märch′păst′, -päst′) *n.* A ceremonial marching, as of troops, past a reviewing stand.

Mar·cion·ism (mär′shə-nĭz′əm) *n.* A Gnostic movement of the 2nd and 3rd centuries A.D. that rejected the Old Testament and emphasized the teachings of St. Paul. [After *Marcion* of Sinope (c. 100-160), who founded the sect.]

Mar·co·ni (mär-kō′nē), **Marchese Guglielmo** (1874-1937). Italian physicist and electrical engineer. He developed the equipment for converting radio waves into electrical signals; in 1895 he successfully transmitted long-wave radio signals and in 1901 sent signals across the Atlantic. He shared the Nobel Prize for physics (1909).

Marconi rig *n.* A Bermuda rig (see). [After Guglielmo MARCONI.]

Mar·cos (mär′kōs, -kəs), **Ferdinand Edralin** (1917-). President of the Philippines (1965-86). He declared martial law (1972) and suppressed political opposition. He fled the country in 1986 after a hard-fought and highly disputed election against Corazon Aquino.

Mar·cus Au·re·li·us An·to·ni·nus (mär′kəs ô-rē′lē-əs ăn′tə-nī′nəs), born Marcus Annius Verus (121-180 A.D.). Roman emperor (161-180) and Stoic philosopher. An active emperor, he ruled with Lucius Verus until 169 A.D., afterward ruling alone. Sometimes called the Philosopher Emperor, he wrote the *Meditations,* 12 volumes of aphorisms, illustrating his Stoic ideals.

Mar·di gras (mär′dē grä′) *n.* Shrove Tuesday, the last day before Lent. It is celebrated in some places, such as New Orleans, by carnivals, masquerade balls, and parades of costumed merrymakers. [French, "fat Tuesday."]

Mar·duk (mär′dŏŏk′). The chief god of ancient Babylon.

mar·dy (mär′dē) *adj. British Regional.* **1.** Spoiled. **2.** Naughty; sulky. Said of a child. [From *marred,* past participle of MAR.]

mare¹ (mâr) *n.* A female horse or the female of other equine species. [Middle English *mare, mere,* Old English *mēre* (unattested).]

ma·re² (mä′rā) *n., pl.* **-ria** (-rē-ə). *Astronomy.* Any of the large dark areas on the moon or Mars, originally thought to be seas. [New Latin, from Latin, sea.]

ma·re clau·sum (mä′rā klou′səm, klô′-) *n. Law.* A navigable body of water, as a sea, that is under the jurisdiction of one nation and closed to all others. [Latin, "closed sea."]

ma·re li·be·rum (mä′rā lē′bə-rŏŏm′) *n. Law.* A navigable body of water, as a sea, that is open to navigation by all nations. [Latin, "free sea."]

ma·rem·ma (mə-rĕm′ə) *n.* Low, unhealthy coastal marshland, especially in Italy. [Italian, from Latin *maritima.* See **maritime.**]

Ma·ren·go (mə-rĕng′gō) *adj.* Browned in oil and sautéed in a sauce of tomatoes, mushrooms, garlic or onion, and white wine. Used after the noun: *veal Marengo.* [After *Marengo,* Italy, probably from the chicken dish served to Napoleon after his victory here in 1800 over the Austrians.]

ma·re nos·trum (mä′rā nō′strəm) *n. Law.* A navigable body of water, as a sea, that is under the jurisdiction of one nation or is shared by two or more nations. [Latin, "our sea."]

mare's nest *n., pl.* **mare's nests** or **mares' nests. 1.** A hoax or fraud. **2.** An extraordinarily complicated situation. [From the proverbial expression "to find a mare's nest" (that is, an impossible fantasy).]

mare's-tail (mârz′tāl′) *n., pl.* **mare's-tails** or **mares'-tails. 1.** An aquatic plant, *Hippuris vulgaris,* of the North Temperate Zone, having minute flowers and whorls of tapering leaves. **2.** A drawn out, wispy cirrus cloud.

Mar·ga·ret Rose (mär′gə-rĭt rōz′, mär′grĭt), **Princess,** Countess of Snowdon (1930-). A princess of the United Kingdom, the younger daughter of George VI and the sister of Queen Elizabeth II. She was married (1960-78) to Anthony Armstrong-Jones, later Lord Snowdon.

Margaret of An·jou (ăn′jōō, äN-zhōō′) (1430-82). Queen of England. Daughter of René of Anjou, she was married to Henry VI of England (1445) in an attempt to establish peace between France and England. The incompetent rule of Henry led to the Wars of the Roses (1455-85), during which Margaret led the Lancastrian faction, hoping to secure the succession of her son Edward (1453-71). Defeated and captured at the Battle of Tewkesbury (1471), she was ransomed to France (1476), where she died in poverty.

Margaret of Val·ois (văl-wä′) (1553-1615). Queen of Navarre and France. She was the daughter of Henry II of France and Catherine de Medici. Her marriage to Henry of Navarre (later Henry IV of France) in 1572 was annulled in 1599. Remembered for her *Mémoires,* she formed a literary circle during her stay at Usson (1587-1605).

mar·gar·ic (mär-găr′ĭk) *adj.* Also **mar·ga·rit·ic** (mär′gə-rĭt′ĭk). Resembling pearl; pearly. [French *margarique,* from Greek *margaron,* pearl.]

margaric acid *n.* A synthetic crystalline fatty acid, $C_{16}H_{33}COOH$. Also called "heptadecanoic acid." [French *margarique,* "pearly" (referring to its color), from Greek *margaron,* pearl.]

mar·ga·rine (mär′jər-ĭn, -jə-rēn′) *n.* A fatty solid consisting of a blend of hydrogenated vegetable or animal oils mixed with emulsifiers, vitamins, coloring matter, and other ingredients. It is used as a butter substitute. Also called "oleomargarine." [French, from *margarique,* MARGARIC (ACID).]

mar·ga·ri·ta (mär′gə-rē′tə) *n.* A cocktail made with tequila and lemon or lime juice, usually served with salt encrusted on the rim of the glass. [Mexican Spanish, probably from *Margarita,* a feminine name.]

mar·ga·rite¹ (mär′gə-rīt′) *n.* A mineral, $CaAl_2(Si_2Al_2)O_{10}(OH)_2$, with a pearly, translucent luster, that is formed in sheets of monoclinic crystals and is related to mica. [From German *Margarit,* from Greek *margarītēs,* pearl, from *margaron.*]

Marduk *A detail from a boundary stone with the serpent symbol of the ancient Babylonian god Marduk. The stone was carved in about 1120 B.C.*

mare *A female horse, or mare, normally has a single foal at a time after a gestation period of 11 months.*

marionette *Strings attached to the marionette's limbs, and operated from above, make it possible to reproduce even complicated movements such as dancing. A simple marionette may have nine strings, but others can have three times as many.*

margarite² *n.* **1.** *Archaic.* A pearl. **2.** A rock formation that resembles beads. [Middle English, from Old French, from Latin *margarita,* from Greek *margaritēs,* from *margaron.*]

mar·gay (mär′gā′, mär-gā′) *n.* A spotted wildcat, *Felis weidii,* resembling a small, long-tailed ocelot and found from Texas to Brazil. [Spanish (South America), from Tupi *marakaya.*]

marge (märj) *n. Archaic.* A margin.

mar·gin (mär′jĭn) *n.* **1.** An edge and the area immediately adjacent to it; a border, rim, or verge. **2. a.** The blank space bordering the written or printed area on a page. **b.** A vertical line, drawn usually on the left-hand side of a page, marking off such a blank space. **3.** A limit of a state or process: *the margins of reality.* **4.** An amount allowed beyond what is strictly necessary; a surplus measure or amount: *a margin of safety.* **5.** A measure, quantity, or degree of difference: *a margin of 500 votes.* **6.** *Economics.* **a.** The minimum return that an enterprise may earn and still pay for itself. **b.** The difference between the cost and the selling price of securities or commodities. **c.** The difference between the market value of collateral and the face value of a loan. **7.** *Finance.* An amount in money, or represented by securities, deposited by a customer with a broker as a provision against loss on transactions made on account. **8.** *Australian.* An additional or bonus payment made to an employee, especially for extra responsibilities. **9.** *Botany.* The border of a leaf. **10.** *Zoology.* The boundary area of an insect's wing. —See Synonyms at **border.**
~*tr.v.* **margined, -gining, -gins. 1.** To provide with a margin. **2.** To be a margin to; border. **3.** To inscribe or enter in the margin of a page. **4.** *Finance.* **a.** To add margin to: *margin up a brokerage account.* **b.** To deposit for margin: *margin a transaction.* **c.** To buy or hold (securities) by depositing or adding to a margin. [Middle English, from Latin *margō* (stem *margin-*).]

mar·gin·al (mär′jə-nəl) *adj.* **1.** Of, pertaining to, or constituting a margin: *the marginal strip of beach.* **2.** Geographically adjacent: *counties marginal to the state line.* **3.** Written or printed in the margin of a book: *marginal notes.* **4. a.** Barely within a lower standard or limit of quality: *marginal writing ability.* **b.** Amounting to mere subsistence: *a marginal existence.* **c.** Barely noticeable; very small: *a marginal difference.* **5.** *Economics.* **a.** Designating enterprises that produce goods or are capable of producing goods at a rate that barely covers production costs. **b.** Pertaining to commodities thus manufactured and sold. **6.** *Psychology.* Pertaining to or located at the fringe of consciousness. **7.** Lying next to more fertile agricultural land and yielding only a small crop. **8.** Only loosely associated with a main body; fringe: *marginal social groups.* **9.** *British.* Designating an electoral district where the majority of the elected councilor or member of Parliament is so small that it may easily be won by an opposing candidate at a subsequent election. [Medieval Latin *marginālis,* from Latin *margō* (stem *margin-*), margin.] —**mar·gin·al·i·ty** (mär′jə-năl′ə-tē) *n.* —**mar·gin·al·ly** *adv.*

mar·gi·na·li·a (mär′jə-nā′lē-ə) *pl.n.* Notes in the margin of a book or other printed matter. [New Latin, neuter plural of Medieval Latin *marginālis,* MARGINAL.]

mar·gin·ate (mär′jə-nāt′) *tr.v.* **-ated, -ating, -ates.** To provide with margins or a margin.
~*adj.* (-nĭt, -nāt′). Also **mar·gin·at·ed** (-nā′tĭd). *Biology.* Having a border or edge of distinctive color or pattern. —**mar·gin·a·tion** *n.*

mar·grave (mär′grāv′) *n.* **1.** The lord or military governor of a medieval German border province. **2.** A hereditary title of certain princes in the Holy Roman Empire. [Middle Dutch *markgrave,* "count of the march" : *mark,* border, MARCH + *grave,* count.]

mar·gra·vi·ate (mär-grā′vē-ĭt, -āt′) *n.* Also **mar·gra·vate** (mär′grə-vāt′). The territory governed by a margrave.

mar·gra·vine (mär′grə-vēn′) *n.* The wife or widow of a margrave. [Middle Dutch *markgravin,* feminine of *markgrave,* MARGRAVE.]

Mar·gre·the II (mär-grā′tə) (1940–). Queen of Denmark. She inherited the throne from her father, Frederick IX (1972), after alterations to the constitution permitted the accession of women.

mar·gue·rite (mär′gə-rēt′, mär′gyə-) *n.* **1.** A garden plant, *Chrysanthemum frutescens,* native to the Canary Islands, having white or pale yellow flowers that resemble those of the common American daisy. **2.** Any of several plants similar or related to the marguerite and having daisylike flowers. [French, from Old French *margarite,* daisy, from Latin *margarīta,* pearl, from Greek *margaritēs,* pearl.]

Ma·ri (mär′ē). Ancient Amorite city of Mesopotamia (now Tel Hariri, Syria), on the Euphrates River. Excavations began in 1933, and the royal palace yielded over 20,000 cuneiform tablets, mostly letters and historical accounts.

ma·ri·a. Plural of **mare** (dark area on the moon).

ma·ri·a·chi (mä′rē-ä′chē) *n.* **1.** A street band in Mexico. **2. a.** The music performed by a mariachi. **b.** A musician belonging to a mariachi. [Mexican Spanish.]

Mar·i·an (mâr′ē-ən, măr′-) *n.* **1.** A devotee of the Virgin Mary. **2. a.** A supporter of Queen Mary I of England. **b.** A supporter of Mary, Queen of Scots.
~*adj.* Of or pertaining to the Virgin Mary, Queen Mary I of England, or Mary, Queen of Scots.

Mar·i·an·as (măr′ē-ăn′əz). Also **Mar·i·an·a Islands** (-ăn′ə), **Northern Marianas.** A commonwealth of the United States in the northwestern Pacific. The Mariana Islands, after 1947 part of the United Nations Trust Territory of the Pacific Islands, administered by the United States, voted for their present status in 1978, with the exception of Guam. They rely heavily on tourism and exports of copra. Saipan is the largest island, with the most inhabitants. Area, 471 square kilometers (182 square miles). Capital, Saipan. See map at **Pacific Ocean.**

Marianas Trench. Ocean trench just east of the Marianas in the northwestern Pacific. It includes Challenger Deep, the deepest point of any ocean in the world (11,033 meters; 36,197 feet).

Ma·ri·a The·re·sa (mə-rē′ə tə-rā′zə, -sə) (1717–80). Archduchess of Austria and queen of Hungary and Bohemia (1740–80). Her reign was marked by the War of the Austrian Succession (1740–48) and the Seven Years' War (1756–63), which curtailed Austria's power. She was the wife of Holy Roman Emperor Francis I and the mother of Marie Antoinette of France.

Ma·ri Autonomous Soviet Socialist Republic (mär′ē). Republic in R.S.F.S.R., U.S.S.R, on the east bank of the Volga between Gorky and Kazan. About half is forested, and most industries are timber-related. Grain, flax, and potatoes are grown. The Mari people, who now make up some 40 percent of the population, were conquered by Ivan the Terrible in 1552.

mar·i·cul·ture (măr′ĭ-kŭl′chər) *n.* The cultivation of marine organisms in their natural habitat. [Latin *mare, mari-,* sea + CULTURE.] —**mar·i·cul·tur·ist** (măr′ĭ-kŭl′chər-ĭst) *n.*

Ma·rie An·toi·nette (mə-rē′ ăn′twə-nĕt′) (1755–93). Austrian princess and wife of Louis XVI of France. Her origins, extravagances, and political intrigue made her highly unpopular. She attempted to influence French policy in favor of Austria and resisted the post-revolutionary settlement for the monarchy proposed by Mirabeau. She was tried for treason by the Revolutionary Tribunal and guillotined.

Marie de Mé·di·cis (də mā′dē-sēs′) (1573–1642). Queen of France. Married to Henry IV of France from 1600 to 1610, she was regent, after his murder, for her son Louis XIII (1610–17). She was banished by Louis (1617), but they were reconciled in 1622. She encouraged the rise of Richelieu to chief minister but then lost all influence. She fled to the Netherlands (1631) and died in poverty.

mar·i·gold (măr′ə-gōld′, mâr′-) *n.* **1.** Any of various plants of the genus *Tagetes,* native to tropical America. Several species are widely cultivated for their showy yellow or orange flowers. **2.** Any of several plants having similar flowers, such as the **corn marigold** and the **marsh marigold** *(both of which see).* [Middle English *marygould* : *Mary* (with some reference to the Virgin Mary) + dialectal *gold,* a marigold, Old English *gold,* probably from GOLD.]

mar·i·jua·na, mar·i·hua·na (măr′ə-wä′nə, -hwä′nə) *n.* The dried flower clusters and leaves of the hemp plant, especially when taken as a drug to induce euphoria. Slang equivalents include "grass," "pot," "weed," and as a cigarette, "joint," "reefer." See **hashish.** [Mexican Spanish *mariguana, marihuana*†.]

ma·rim·ba (mə-rĭm′bə) *n.* Any of various xylophones with resonators. [Bantu : *ma-,* plural prefix + *rimba, limba,* musical note.]

ma·ri·na (mə-rē′nə) *n.* A boat basin that has docks, moorings, supplies, and other facilities for small boats. [Italian, feminine of *marino,* MARINE.]

mar·i·nade (măr′ə-nād′) *n.* A pickling liquid of vinegar or wine and oil, with various spices and herbs, in which meat, fish, or vegetables are soaked before cooking.
~*tr.v.* **marinaded, -nading, -nades.** To marinate. [French, from Spanish *marinada,* from *marinar,* to marinate, from *marino,* "briny," MARINE.]

mar·i·nar·a (măr′ə-nâr′ə, mä′rə-nä′rä) *adj.* Being or served with a sauce made of tomatoes, onions, garlic, and spices: *spaghetti marinara.* [Italian *(alla) marinara,* in sailor style, from *marinaro,* of sailors, from *marino,* marine, from Latin *marīnus.*]

mar·i·nate (măr′ə-nāt′) *tr.v.* **-nated, -nating, -nates.** To soak (food, as meat or fish) in a marinade. [French *mariner* or Italian *marinare* + -ATE.]

ma·rine (mə-rēn′) *adj.* **1. a.** Of or pertaining to the sea: *marine exploration.* **b.** Native to or formed by the sea: *marine plant life.* **2.** Of or pertaining to shipping or maritime affairs: *marine insurance.* **3.** Of or pertaining to sea navigation; nautical: *a marine chart.* **4.** Designating or pertaining to troops that serve at sea as well as on land.
~*n.* **1.** The mercantile or naval ships or shipping fleet of a country. **2. a.** A soldier serving on a ship or at a naval installation. **b. Marine.** A member of the U.S. Marine Corps. **3.** In some nations, the governmental department in charge of naval affairs. **4.** A painting or photograph of the sea. —**tell it to the marines.** *Informal.* Used to express skepticism. [Middle English, from Old French *marin,* from Latin *marīnus,* from *mare,* sea.]

Marine Corps *n. Abbr.* **MC, USMC, U.S.M.C.** A branch of the U.S. Armed Forces composed chiefly of amphibious troops under the authority of the Secretary of the Navy. Also officially called "United States Marine Corps."

mar·i·ner (măr′ə-nər) *n.* A person who navigates or serves on a ship; a sailor or seaman. [Middle English, from Old French *marinier,* from *marin,* MARINE.]

Mar·i·ol·a·try (măr′ē-ŏl′ə-trē) *n.* Excessive or idolatrous worship of the Virgin Mary. [Latin *Maria,* Mary + -LATRY (by analogy with *idolatry*).]

Mar·i·ol·o·gy, Mar·y·ol·o·gy (măr′ē-ŏl′ə-jē) *n.* The body of belief pertaining to the Virgin Mary. [MARY + -LOGY.]

Mar·i·on (măr′ē-ən, mâr′-), **Francis,** known as "the Swamp Fox" (*c.* (1732–95). U.S. Revolutionary soldier. He commanded militia troops in South Carolina, harassing British forces and disrupting their communications with his guerrilla tactics. He earned his nickname because he often escaped by fleeing into the swamps and forests.

mar·i·o·nette (măr′ē-ə-nĕt′) n. A jointed puppet manipulated by strings or wires attached to its limbs. [French, diminutive of the feminine name *Marion*.]

mar·i·po·sa lily (măr′ə-pō′zə, -sə) n. Any of several bulbous plants of the genus *Calochortus*, of the southwestern United States and Mexico, having variously colored, tuliplike flowers. Sometimes called "mariposa tulip." [Spanish *mariposa*, butterfly : probably *Maria*, Mary + *posar*, to perch, alight.]

mar·ish (măr′ĭsh) adj. Archaic. Marshy.
~ n. Archaic. A marsh. [Middle English *mareis*, Old English *merisc*, ultimately from West Germanic *marisk-* (unattested), MARSH.]

Mar·ist (măr′ĭst, mär′-) n. 1. A member of the Society of Mary, a congregation of Roman Catholic missionary priests founded in 1824. 2. A member of the Little Brothers of Mary, a Roman Catholic teaching order founded in 1817. —**Mar·ist** adj.

Ma·ri·tain (mä′rē-tăn′), **Jacques** (1882–1973). French Catholic philosopher. He abandoned the philosophy of Henri Bergson to become a neo-Thomist, applying the medieval techniques of St. Thomas Aquinas to modern social problems. His works include *Les Degrés du Savoir* (1932) and *La Philosophie Morale* (1960).

mar·i·tal (măr′ə-təl) adj. 1. Of, pertaining to, or required by marriage. 2. Of or pertaining to a husband. [Latin *marītālis*, from *marītus*, married, husband.] —**mar·i·tal·ly** adv.

mar·i·time (măr′ə-tīm′) adj. Abbr. **mar.** 1. Located on or near the sea. 2. Of or concerned with shipping or navigation. 3. Designating a climate characteristic of coastal areas, with relatively small seasonal and daily temperature changes. [French, from Latin *maritimus*, from *mare*, sea.]

Maritime Alps (ălpz). A branch of the western Alps along the French-Italian border, extending to the Mediterranean. They give their name to the French department of Alpes Maritimes, whose resorts include Cannes, Nice, and Grasse. Punta Argentera (3,297 meters; 10,817 feet) is the highest peak.

maritime pine n. A tree, the **pinaster** (see).

Maritime Provinces. Atlantic region of Canada, comprising the provinces of New Brunswick, Nova Scotia, and Prince Edward Island. It covers most of the area of the former region of Acadia in French Canada (1605–1713).

Mar·i·us (mâr′ē-əs, măr′-), **Gaius** (c. 155–86 B.C.). Roman general and politician. A brave and skillful soldier, he used his popularity with his troops to win election as consul seven times. However, his failure to gain the acceptance of the aristocracy embittered him and may have caused his cruelly vindictive treatment of his political and personal enemies.

Ma·ri·vaux (mä′rē-vō′), **Pierre Carlet de Chamblain de** (1688–1763). French dramatist, a writer of sophisticated romantic comedies. His works include *Le Jeu de l'Amour et du Hasard* (1730) and the unfinished *La Vie de Marianne* (1731–41).

mar·jo·ram (mär′jər-əm) n. 1. An aromatic plant, *Marjorana hortensis*, having small purplish or white flowers and leaves used as seasoning. Also called "sweet marjoram." 2. A plant, *Origanum vulgare*, similar to the marjoram, having spikes of pinkish flowers and leaves used in cooking. Also called "pot marjoram," "wild marjoram." [Middle English *majorane*, from Old French, from Medieval Latin *majorāna†*.]

mark¹ (märk) n. Abbr. **mk.** 1. A visible trace or impression on something, as a spot, dent, or line. 2. A cross or other sign made in lieu of a signature by an illiterate person. 3. **a.** A written or printed symbol used for punctuation; a punctuation mark. **b.** A written or printed symbol used to give information or instructions: *proofreaders' marks.* 4. **a.** A number, letter, or symbol used to indicate the quality of academic work: *high marks in history.* **b.** An indication of how strongly one approves or disapproves of a person's actions; appraisal: *I give her high marks for initiative.* 5. **a.** A name, stamp, label, seal, or inscription placed on an article to signify ownership, quality, manufacture, or origin. See **trademark, hallmark. b.** A notch in an animal's ear or hide indicating ownership. 6. *Nautical.* A knot or piece of material placed at various measured lengths on a lead line to indicate the depth of the water. 7. Something that indicates a position; a marker. 8. **a.** A sign or indication of a quality, property, or feature: *bore all the marks of dejection; tipped my hat as a mark of my respect.* **b.** A visible sign or symbol, such as a badge or brand adopted by or imposed on a person: *Trouble had set its mark on her.* **c. Mark.** A particular type or version of a product, especially of machines or vehicles under development: *This automobile is the Mark 3 model.* 9. Quality, note, or importance: *"A fellow of no mark nor likelihood"* (Shakespeare). 10. Notice; attention: *Little worthy of mark happened.* 11. Something aimed at; target: *The arrow hit the mark.* 12. Something that one wishes to achieve; a goal. 13. An object or point that serves as a guide. 14. *Slang.* A person who is an easy target for a swindler; a dupe. 15. The place from which competitors in a race begin and sometimes end their contest: *on your mark.* 16. A point reached or gained: *the halfway mark in the race.* 17. A strike or spare in bowling. 18. The best performance known, as in a sport; record: *set a new mark in the long jump.* 19. A boundary between countries. 20. In medieval England and Germany, a tract of land held in common by a community. 21. *Statistics.* A **class mark** (see). —See Synonyms at **sign.** —**beside the mark.** Beside the point; irrelevant. —**make one's mark.** To achieve recognition; be successful.
~ v. **marked, marking, marks.** —tr. 1. To make a visible impres-

sion on, as with a spot, line, or dent. 2. To form, make, or depict by making a visible impression, as with a spot, line, or dent: *She marked a square on the board.* 3. **a.** To distinguish or indicate by making a visible impression: *She marked the spot where the treasure is buried.* **b.** To distinguish, indicate, or characterize: *This year marks their tenth anniversary.* **c.** To show (an emotion, for example): *marked her anger by leaving the room.* 4. **a.** To set off by or separate as if by a mark. **b.** To limit or demarcate (a boundary, for example), as on a label. 5. **a.** To attach price tags, maker's labels, or other identification to (articles for sale). **b.** To write or print (a price, for example), as on a label. 6. To correct and assess (scholastic work) by evaluating it according to a scale of letters or numbers. 7. **a.** To give attention to; notice: *"Mark what radiant state she spreads"* (Milton). **b.** To take note of in writing; write down. 8. To consider; study; observe: *Mark my word.* 9. To keep (score) in various games. —intr. 1. To make a visible impression: *This pen will mark under water.* 2. To receive a visible impression: *The floor marks easily.* 3. To pay attention; notice: *"Pray you, mark"* (Shakespeare). 4. To keep score. Used of various games. 5. To determine scholastic grades: *Our teacher marks strictly.* —**mark time.** 1. To move the feet alternately in the rhythm of a marching step without advancing. 2. To suspend progress for the time being; wait in readiness. 3. To work in a halfhearted or unproductive manner. [Middle English, Old English *mearc*, boundary, hence landmark, sign, trace, from Germanic *markō* (unattested), boundary.]

mark² n. Abbr. **M.** 1. A former English and Scottish monetary unit equal to 13 shillings and 4 pence. 2. **a.** A former German monetary unit, the **Reichsmark** (see). **b.** The **Deutsche Mark** (see). **c.** The basic monetary unit of East Germany, divided into 100 pfennigs. Formerly called "ostmark." 3. Any of several former European units of weight equal to about 225 grams (8 ounces), used especially for weighing gold and silver. 4. A Finnish monetary unit, a **markka** (see). [Sense 1, Middle English *mark*, Old English *marc.* Sense 2, German *Mark*, from Middle High German *marke.* The word exists in all Germanic and Romance languages; the source is probably identical with that of MARK (sign), in a sense such as "a mark on a bar of metal."] See feature at **currency.**

Mark¹ (märk). In Arthurian legend, a king of Cornwall who was the husband of Iseult and the uncle of Tristan.

Mark² n. A book of the New Testament, the second Gospel, attributed to St. Mark.

Mark, Saint. A disciple of St. Peter, reputedly the author of the second Gospel of the New Testament.

Mark An·to·ny (ăn′tə-nē) or **An·tho·ny** (-thə-nē). Latin **Mar·cus An·to·ni·us** (mär′kəs ăn-tō′nē-əs) (c. 83–30 B.C.). Roman soldier and statesman. Dissolute in his youth, he fought under Julius Caesar in Gaul (54–50 B.C.) and after Caesar's assassination (44 B.C.) formed a triumvirate with Octavius and Lepidus, which defeated Cassius and Brutus at Philippi (42 B.C.). He met and fell in love with Cleopatra (41 B.C.) while in Egypt, gaining her territory in his division of the empire. When the senate declared war on Egypt, Antony was defeated at the naval battle of Actium (31 B.C.) and committed suicide, as did Cleopatra.

mark down tr.v. To reduce (goods) in price: *There was little demand for fountain pens, so the proprietor of the store marked them all down.*

mark-down (märk′doun′) n. 1. A reduction in price. 2. The amount by which a price is reduced.

marked (märkt) adj. 1. Having a mark or marks. 2. Having a noticeable character or trait; clearly defined: *"certain strongly marked variations, which no one would rank as mere individual differences"* (Charles Darwin). 3. Singled out, especially for an exceptional fate: *a marked man.* 4. *Linguistics.* Of, pertaining to, or being that one of a closely connected pair of linguistic units, as words, that has a feature held to distinguish it from the other more neutral or general form; for example, in the pairs *dog/dogs* and *dog/bitch, dogs* and *bitch* are the marked forms. —**mark·ed·ly** (mär′kĭd-lē) adv. —**mark·ed·ness** n.

marked cheque n. *Chiefly British.* A certified check.

mark·er (mär′kər) n. 1. Something that marks or distinguishes, as a bookmark, tombstone, milestone, or buoy. 2. A person who marks objects, especially for industrial purposes. 3. A person who grades examination papers. 4. *Sports.* A line, stake, flag, or other device on a playing field that shows the playing or scoring position. 5. **a.** A person or device that keeps score in various games. **b.** A score in a game. 6. A pen or other writing instrument used for making marks on objects, as for identification or pricing. 7. *Slang.* A written, signed promissory note; an IOU.

mar·ket (mär′kĭt) n. Abbr. **mkt.** 1. A public gathering held at regular intervals for buying and selling merchandise. 2. A place or building where goods are offered for sale. Also called "marketplace." 3. A store or shop that sells a particular type of merchandise: *a meat market.* 4. **a.** The business of buying and selling a specified commodity. **b.** A market price. **c.** Commercial activity; trading: *a brisk market.* **d.** A subdivision of a population considered as buyers or potential buyers: *cosmetics for the teenage market.* 5. **a.** The opportunity to buy or sell; demand for or availability of merchandise. **b.** An area in which sales may be made: *one of our biggest export markets.* 6. **a.** An exchange for buying and selling stocks or commodities: *securities sold on the New York market.* **b.** The entire enterprise of buying and selling commodities and securities. —**at the market.** At the price prevailing when a customer's order to buy or sell is placed. —**in the market for.** Interested in acquiring or buying: *I'm in the market for a new car.* —**on the market.** Up for sale;

Their apartment is on the market. **—play the market.** To speculate on the stock exchange. **—price out of the market.** To price so high as to remove demand.

~v. marketed, -keting, -kets. —*tr.* **1.** To offer for sale. **2.** To sell. **3.** To promote the sale of (a product) by means of marketing techniques. —*intr.* **1.** To deal in a market. **2.** To buy household supplies: *He marketed for Sunday dinner.* [Middle English, Old English, from Vulgar Latin *marcātus* (unattested), variant of Latin *mercātus,* from the past participle of *mercārī,* to trade, from *merx,* merchandise.] **—mar·ket·er** *n.*

mar·ket·a·ble (mär′kĭ-tə-bəl) *adj.* **1.** Fit to be offered for sale. **2.** Capable of being sold; salable: *a marketable product; a marketable skill.* **3.** Pertaining to selling or buying. **—mar·ket·a·bil·i·ty** *n.*

market basket *n.* **1.** A grocery cart. **2.** A selection of goods needed for a statistical household of 3.2 persons or for a family of four, considered in terms of its fluctuating cost.

market economy *n.* An economy in which the principles of free enterprise apply and there is no government intervention.

market forces *pl.n. Economics.* The effects on an economy of supply and demand unmodified by government intervention.

market garden *n. Chiefly British.* A truck farm. **—market gardener** *n.* **—market gardening** *n.*

mar·ket·ing (mär′kĭ-tĭng) *n.* **1.** The act or process of buying and selling in a market. **2.** The act or business of promoting sales of a product, as by market research, advertising, and packaging. **3.** The commercial functions involved in transferring goods from producer to consumer.

market order *n.* An order to buy or sell stocks or commodities at the prevailing market price.

mar·ket·place, market place (mär′kĭt-plās′) *n.* **1.** A place in which a market is set up. **2.** The processes of buying and selling goods or services: *prices determined by the marketplace.* **3.** The world of business and commerce: *After finishing college she went out in the marketplace to work.* **4.** A figurative place of assembly where views, opinions, ideas, and information can be debated and exchanged.

market price *n.* The prevailing price at which merchandise, securities, or commodities are sold. Also called "market."

market research *n.* The study of how a product or service is likely to sell or is already selling, usually carried out by asking questions of a cross section of the population in order to determine consumers' reactions.

market value *n.* The amount that a seller may expect to obtain for merchandise, services, or securities in the open market.

Mark·ham (mär′kəm), **(Charles) Edwin** (1852–1940). U.S. poet. His most famous poem was "The Man with the Hoe" (1899). Inspired by Millet's painting, the poem was a protest against the exploitation of labor. Markham's only other famous poem was "Lincoln, the Man of the People" (1901).

mar·khor (mär′kôr′, -kōr′) *n., pl.* **-khors** or collectively **markhor.** A Himalayan goat, *Capra falconeri,* having a red-brown coat and large, spirally curved horns. [Persian, "snake-eater" : *mār,* snake + *-khōr,* -eating.]

mark·ing (mär′kĭng) *n.* **1.** The act of making a mark or marks. **2.** A mark or marks. **3.** The characteristic arrangement or pattern of coloration of a plant or animal.

mark·ka (mär′kä′) *n., pl.* **-kaa** (-kä′). *Abbr.* **mk.** The basic monetary unit of Finland, equal to 100 penniä. Also called "mark." See feature at **currency.** [Finnish, from Swedish *mark.* See mark (money).]

Mar·ko·va (mär′kə-və, mär-kō′və), **Dame Alicia,** born Lilian Alicia Marks (1910–). British ballet dancer. She studied with Pavlova and worked with Diaghilev's company; she was noted for her delicacy and gracefulness in works that included *Swan Lake* and *Giselle.*

Mar·kov chain (mär′kôf′) *n. Statistics.* A sequence of events in which the probability of each event's taking place depends on the event immediately preceding it. [After Andrei *Markov* (1856–1922), Russian mathematician.]

marks·man (märks′mən) *n., pl.* **-men** (-mĭn). A person skilled at shooting a weapon, as a gun. [*Mark's man,* from MARK (target).] **—marks·man·ship** *n.*

marks·wom·an (märks′wŏom′ən) *n., pl.* **-women** (-wĭm′ĭn). A woman skilled at shooting a weapon, as a gun.

mark up *tr.v.* To raise the price of.

mark·up (märk′ŭp′) *n.* **1.** An increase in price. **2.** An amount added to a cost price in calculating a selling price, especially an amount that takes overhead and profit into account.

marl¹ (märl) *n.* **1.** A fine-grained mixture of clay, calcium carbonate (including shell fragments), and magnesium carbonate, forming a loam used as a fertilizer. **2.** A friable clay soil. **~tr.v. marled, marling, marls.** To fertilize with marl. [Middle English, Old English *marle,* from Late Latin *margila,* diminutive of *marga†.*]

marl² *tr.v.* **marled, marling, marls.** To bind with a marline. [Back-formation from MARLINE.]

Marl·bor·ough (märl′bər-ə, môl′-), **John Churchill, 1st Duke of** (1650–1722). English soldier and statesman. He served under James II at the defeat of Monmouth but supported William of Orange against James in the Revolution of 1688. In the War of the Spanish Succession he led the English to victories at Blenheim (1704), Ramillies (1706), Oudenaarde (1708), and Malplaquet (1709). Dismissed for alleged corruption in 1711, he fled to Holland, returning to England in 1714.

mar·lin (mär′lĭn) *n.* Any of several large game fish of the genus *Makaira,* of the Atlantic and Pacific oceans, having a long upper

jaw. Also called "spearfish." [Short for MARLINESPIKE (from the pointed shape of the snout).]

mar·line, mar·lin (mär′lĭn) *n.* Also **mar·ling** (-lĭng). *Nautical.* A light rope made of two loosely twisted strands. [Middle English, from Middle Dutch *marlijn,* "tie-line" : *marren,* to tie + *lijn,* LINE.]

mar·line·spike, mar·lin·spike (mär′lĭn-spīk′) *n.* Also **mar·ling·spike** (mär′lĭng-). *Nautical.* A pointed metal spike used to separate strands of rope in splicing.

mar·lite (mär′līt′) *n.* A marl containing 25 to 75 percent clay, the remainder being calcium carbonate, that is resistant to decomposition in air. Also called "marlstone." [MARL (loam) + -ITE.] **—mar·lit·ic** (mär-lĭt′ĭk) *adj.*

Mar·lowe (mär′lō), **Christopher** (1564–93). English playwright and poet. His development of blank verse influenced Shakespeare. Among his plays are *Tamburlaine the Great* (c. 1587), *Dr. Faustus* (c. 1588), and *Edward II* (1592). While awaiting trial for atheism he was killed in a tavern brawl.

marl·stone (märl′stōn′) *n.* Marlite.

mar·ma·lade (mär′mə-lād′) *n.* A preserve made from the pulp and rind of fruits, especially citrus fruits. [French *marmelade,* from Portuguese *marmelada,* "quince jam," from *marmelo,* quince, from Latin *melimēlum,* from Greek *melimēlon,* "honey-apple," the fruit of an apple tree grafted on a quince : *meli,* honey + *mēlon,* apple, fruit.]

marmalade box *n.* A tree, the genipap *(see).*

Mar·ma·ra, Sea of (mär′mər-ə). Small sea in northwestern Turkey between Asia and Europe. It is connected to the Aegean Sea by the Dardanelles and to the Black Sea by the Bosporus.

mar·mite (mär-mēt′, mär′mĭt′) *n.* **1. a.** A large covered pot, usually made of earthenware or metal. **b.** A small covered earthenware casserole designed to hold an individual serving. **2.** Broth made or served in a marmite. [French, kettle, pot.]

mar·mo·re·al (mär-môr′ē-əl, -mōr′ē-əl) *adj.* Also **mar·mo·re·an** (-ē-ən). **1.** Of or pertaining to marble. **2.** Resembling marble, as in being cold, smooth, white, or hard: *a complexion of marmoreal luster.* [Latin *marmoreus,* from *marmor,* MARBLE.]

mar·mo·set (mär′mə-sĕt′, -zĕt′) *n.* Any of various small monkeys of the genera *Callithrix, Cebuella, Saguinus,* and *Leontideus,* found in tropical forests of the Americas. They have soft, dense fur, tufted ears, and long tails. [Middle English, from Old French *marmoset†,* grotesque figure.]

mar·mot (mär′mət) *n.* Any of various stocky, coarse-furred rodents of the genus *Marmota,* having short legs and bushy tails, found throughout the Northern Hemisphere. [French *marmotte,* from earlier *marmottaine,* from Medieval Latin *mormotāna,* "mountain mouse" : Latin *mūs* (stem *mūr-*), mouse + *montānus,* mountain.]

Marne (märn). River of northern France. Flowing 525 kilometers (326 miles) from the Plateau de Langres to the Seine at Paris, it forms, with the Marne-Rhine and the Marne-Saône canals, a major inland waterway network. The two Battles of the Marne (1914, 1918) ended in decisive victories for the Allies.

mar·o·cain (mär′ə-kān′) *n.* **1.** A crepe dress fabric, especially one made of silk. **2.** A garment made of marocain. [French, "Moroccan," from *Maroc,* Morocco.]

Mar·o·nite (mär′ə-nīt′) *n.* A member of a Christian sect established in Syria in the 5th century and now found mainly in Lebanon. [Medieval Latin *Marōnīta,* from *Maro,* 5th-century Syrian monk and founder of the sect.] **—Mar·o·nite** *adj.*

ma·roon¹ (mə-rōon′) *tr.v.* **-rooned, -rooning, -roons. 1.** To put (a person) ashore on a deserted island or coast. **2.** To abandon or isolate (a person) with little hope of rescue or escape.

~n. 1. a. A fugitive black slave in the West Indies in the 17th and 18th centuries. **b.** A descendant of such a slave. **2.** A person who is marooned. [French *marron,* alteration of American Spanish *cimarrón,* fugitive slave, originally "living on the mountaintops," possibly from *cima,* summit, from Latin *cȳma,* sprout, from Greek *kuma.*]

ma·roon² *n.* A dark reddish brown to dark purplish red. [Originally "chestnut," from French *marron†.*] **—ma·roon** *adj.*

mar·plot (mär′plŏt′) *n.* A stupid and officious meddler whose interference compromises the success of an undertaking. [After *Marplot* ("to spoil plots"), character in *The Busybody* (1709), a comic play by Susanna Centlivre (c. 1667–1723), English author.]

Mar·quand (mär-kwŏnd′), **John Phillips** (1893–1960). U.S. author. He first won popularity for his tales about Mr. Moto, a Japanese sleuth. Later he produced comedies of manners, gently satirizing the life of the rich and socially prominent families of New England. His works include *The Late George Apley* (1937), which won a Pulitzer Prize, and *H.M. Pulham, Esq.* (1941).

marque (märk) *n.* A make of a product, as a car. [French, mark.]

mar·quee (mär-kē′) *n.* **1.** A large tent, often with open sides, used chiefly for outdoor entertainment or for serving refreshments. **2.** A rooflike structure, often made of canvas and bearing a signboard, projecting over an entrance to a building. In this sense, also called "marquise." [French *marquise* (taken as a plural), a linen tent pitched over an officer's tent to distinguish it from others, from *marquis,* MARQUIS.]

Már·ques (mär′kĕs), **Gabriel García** (1928–). Colombian novelist and short-story writer. His most famous work is the novel *One Hundred Years of Solitude* (1967). He was awarded the Nobel Prize (1982).

Mar·que·san (mär-kā′zən, -sən) *n.* **1.** An inhabitant of the Marquesas Islands. **2.** The Austronesian language of the Marquesans.

marmot *There are about 16 species of this ground-dwelling burrowing squirrel, found in North America, the European Alps, and in mountainous parts of Asia. This is* Marmota flaviventus, *the yellow-bellied marmot, which is native to the western United States and Canada.*

~adj. Of or pertaining to the Marquesas Islands, their inhabitants, or their language.

Mar·que·sas Islands (mär-kā′zəs, -səs). Group of 11 volcanic islands in the eastern Pacific, part of French Polynesia. They were annexed by France in 1842 and now export copra, vanilla, cotton, and tobacco. Gauguin is buried on Hiva Oa, near the capital, Atuona. See map at **Pacific Ocean.**

mar·que·try, mar·que·terie (mär′kə-trē) n. Inlaid work, as in wood or ivory, used chiefly in decorating furniture. [French *marqueterie*, from *marqueter*, to checker, from MARQUE.]

Mar·quette (mär-kĕt′), **Père Jacques** (1637–75). French Jesuit missionary and explorer. He was sent to New France in 1666 and in 1673 traveled down the Mississippi with Louis Joliet to its juncture with the Arkansas River, thus establishing the existence of a water highway from the St. Lawrence to the Gulf of Mexico.

mar·quis (mär′kwĭs, mär-kē′) n., pl. **marquis** or **-quises.** Also chiefly British **mar·quess** (mär′kwĭs). A nobleman ranking below a duke and above an earl or count. [Middle English *marchis, markis,* from Old French *marquis, marchis,* "count of the march," from *marche,* MARCH (frontier).]

Mar·quis (mär′kwĭs), **Donald Robert Perry,** known as "Don" (1878–1937). U.S. journalist. He is best known for his columns and books featuring archy, a literary cockroach who can't manipulate the typewriter shift key, and archy's friend mehitabel the cat. The creatures and their antics provided a medium for Marquis's satirical view of the contemporary scene.

mar·quis·ate (mär′kwĭ-zĭt, -sĭt) n. The rank or territory of a marquis.

mar·quise (mär-kēz′) n. **1.** A marchioness (see). **2.** A marquee (see). **3. a.** A finger ring set with a pointed oval stone or cluster of pointed oval stones. **b.** A pointed oval shape of a gem, as a diamond. [French, feminine of *marquis,* MARQUIS.]

mar·qui·sette (mär′kĭ-zĕt′, mär′kwĭ-) n. A sheer fabric of cotton, rayon, silk, or nylon, used for clothing, curtains, and mosquito nets. [(MARQUIS)E + -ETTE.]

Marquis of Queensberry Rules pl.n. See **Queensberry Rules.**

Mar·ra·kesh, Mar·ra·kech (mär′ə-kĕsh′). Former capital of Morocco. A major Islamic, commercial, and tourist center, it is best known for its leatherwork.

mar·ram (măr′əm) n. **1.** A beach grass, *Ammophila arenaria,* widely planted to stabilize shifting dunes. **2.** Any of several other grasses of the genus *Ammophila.* Also called "marram grass." [East Anglian dialect, from Old Norse *maralmr : marr,* sea + *halmr,* grass.]

mar·riage (măr′ĭj) n. **1. a.** The state of being wife and husband; wedlock. **b.** The legal union of a woman and man as wife and husband. **2.** The act of marrying or the ceremony of being married; a wedding. **3.** Any close union: *a true marriage of minds.* **4.** In some card games, such as pinochle, the combination of the king and queen of the same suit. [Middle English *mariage,* from Old French, from *marier,* to MARRY.]

Synonyms: matrimony, nuptials, wedding, wedlock.

mar·riage·a·ble (măr′ĭ-jə-bəl) adj. Suitable or ready for marriage. **—mar·riage·a·bil·i·ty, mar·riage·a·ble·ness** n.

marriage of convenience n. A marriage or joint undertaking arranged for political, economic, or social benefit rather than from personal attachment.

mar·ried (măr′ēd) adj. **1. a.** Having a spouse: *a married man.* **b.** United in matrimony: *a married couple.* **2.** Of or pertaining to the state of marriage: *married bliss.* **~n.** A married person: *young marrieds.*

mar·ron (mă-rôN′) n. A tree, the **Spanish chestnut** (see) or its fruit. [French. See **maroon** (color).]

mar·rons gla·cés (mă-rôN′ glă-sā′) pl.n. Chestnuts preserved in or glazed with sugar or syrup. [French.]

mar·row (măr′ō) n. **1.** The soft material that fills bone cavities, consisting, in varying proportions, of fat cells and maturing blood cells, together with supporting connective tissue and numerous blood vessels. **2.** Spinal marrow; the spinal cord. **3.** Chiefly British. A squash, **vegetable marrow** (see). **4. a.** The inmost, choicest, or essential part; pith: *chilled to the marrow.* **b.** Strength or vigor; vitality. [Middle English *marowe, margh,* Old English *mærg, mærh.*]

mar·row·bone (măr′ō-bōn′) n. A bone containing marrow, used especially for flavoring soup.

mar·row·fat (măr′ō-făt′) n. **1.** Any of several varieties of pea that produce large seeds. **2.** The seed of a marrowfat.

mar·ry¹ (măr′ē) v. **-ried, -rying, -ries. —tr. 1. a.** To become united with in matrimony: *They married each other in June.* **b.** To take as a husband or wife: *She married her sweetheart.* **c.** To give in marriage: *married her son to a doctor's daughter.* **2.** To obtain by marriage: *marry wealth.* **3.** To join (a couple) together in marriage. **4.** To join together or unite closely: *a woman in whom wisdom and love were married.* **5.** To maneuver into a matching or locking position: *married up the two edges before gluing them.* **6.** Nautical. To join (two ropes) end to end by interweaving their strands. **—intr. 1.** To take a wife or husband; wed: *The couple married too young.* **2. a.** To match; join easily. **b.** To enter into a close relationship; unite: *Peaches and cream seem to marry perfectly.* **—marry into. 1.** To become a member of (a family) by marriage. **2.** To obtain or become involved in through marriage: *married into trouble.* [Middle English *marien,* from Old French *marier,* from Latin *marītāre,* from *marītus,* husband.]

marry² interj. Archaic. Used to express surprise, indignation, or emphasis. [Middle English *Marie,* "Mary!" (the Virgin).]

Mar·ry·at (măr′ē-ət), **Captain Frederick** (1792–1848). British naval officer and author. He used the experiences of his naval career (1806–30) as a source for novels such as *Mr. Midshipman Easy* (1834–36). His children's books include *The Children of the New Forest* (1847) and *Masterman Ready* (1841).

Mars¹ (märz). Roman Mythology. The god of war; identified with the Greek god Ares.

Mars² n. The fourth planet from the sun, having a sidereal period of revolution around the sun of 687 days at a mean distance of 227.9 million kilometers (141.6 million miles), a mean radius of approximately 3,393 kilometers (2,108 miles), and a mass approximately 0.11 that of Earth. See feature, next page.

Mar·sa·la¹ (mär-sä′lə). Seaport and major fishing center in western Sicily, Italy. Founded by the Carthaginians (397 B.C.), it exports Marsala wine, salt, and grain. Garibaldi landed here in 1860 for his campaign against the Kingdom of the Two Sicilies.

Marsala² n. A pale brown dry to sweet wine. [After MARSALA.]

mar·seille (mär-sāl′) n. Also **mar·seilles** (-sālz′). A heavy cotton fabric with a raised pattern of stripes or figures, used for bedspreads, curtains, or the like. [Shortened from *Marseille quilting,* originally made in MARSEILLE, France.]

Mar·seille (mär-sā′). Also **Mar·seilles** (-sā′, -sālz′). Principal seaport of France and capital of Bouches-du-Rhône department, founded on the Mediterranean by the Greeks (c. 600 B.C.). It is linked to the Rhône by canal, and its industries include oil refining, ore smelting, chemicals, shipbuilding, and food processing.

marsh (märsh) n. **1.** An area of temporarily flooded, often silty land beside a river or lake, characterized by the presence of plants such as reeds. **2.** An area of low-lying wet land; a fen, swamp, or bog. **3.** A salt marsh (see). [Middle English *mersh,* Old English *mersc, merisc.*]

Marsh (märsh), **Dame Ngaio Edith** (1899–1982). New Zealand author. She wrote many detective novels, including *A Man Lay Dead* (1934), *Death in a White Tie* (1938), and *Last Ditch* (1977).

mar·shal (mär′shəl) n. **1.** In some countries, a military officer of the highest rank. See **field marshal. 2.** In the United States: **a.** A federal officer who carries out court orders. **b.** A city officer who carries out court orders. **c.** The head of a police or fire department. **3.** A person in charge of arranging for and directing a ceremony, as a parade. **4.** Formerly in England, a high official in the royal court, especially one aiding the sovereign in judicial matters. Also called "knight marshal." **5.** In England, a clerical assistant accompanying a judge on circuit. **~v. marshaled** or **-shalled, -shaling** or **-shalling, -shals. —tr. 1.** To arrange or place (soldiers, for example) in line for a parade, maneuver, or review. **2.** To arrange, place, or set in methodical order: *marshaled facts; marshaled her thoughts.* **3.** To enlist and organize: *"our interests in marshalling the French colonies against Germany"* (Winston Churchill). **4.** To guide (a person) ceremoniously; conduct or usher. **5.** Heraldry. To join together (two or more coats of arms) on one shield. **—intr.** To take form or order; especially, to take up positions in or as if in a military formation. **—See** Synonyms at **gather.** [Middle English *mareschal,* from Old French, from Late Latin *mariscalcus,* from Germanic *marhas kalkaz* (unattested), "keeper of the horses" : *marhaz,* horse + *skalkaz,* servant.] **—mar·shal·cy** (mär′shəl-sē), **mar·shal·ship** (-shĭp′) n.

Mar·shall (mär′shəl), **George Catlett** (1880–1959). U.S. soldier and statesman. While secretary of state (1947–49) he initiated the European Recovery Program, known as the Marshall Plan, which gave economic aid to Europe. He served briefly as secretary of defense (1950–51) and received the Nobel Peace Prize (1953).

Marshall, John (1755–1835). U.S. jurist; chief justice of the Supreme Court (1801–35). In his years on the bench he dominated the court, elevating it from an anomalous position in the federal system to a powerful and prestigious branch of government. He was the first chief justice to proclaim that the Constitution, while a precise document setting forth specific powers, could also be a living document that should be broadly interpreted to give the federal government the means to act effectively.

Marshall, Thurgood (1908–). U.S. jurist. As legal chief of the NAACP (after 1938), he was active in civil-rights litigation, including the landmark *Brown v. Board of Education* decision (1954). In 1965 he was appointed to the Supreme Court, the first black to sit on the high court.

Marshall Islands. State in the central Pacific Ocean, comprising some 1,259 islets and atolls. The economy depends on exports of copra and U.S. payments for a military base. Fishing is also important. Germany bought the islands from Spain (1899), and they became a Japanese mandate (1920). From 1947 they were part of the U.S. Trust Territory of the Pacific Islands, but became self-governing in 1979. Area, 118 square kilometers (70 square miles). Population, 12,000. Capital, Majuro. See map at **Pacific Ocean.**

Marshall Plan n. See **European Recovery Program.**

marsh andromeda n. A plant, **bog rosemary** (see).

marsh crocodile n. A crocodile, the **mugger** (see).

marsh elder n. Any of several shrubs of the genus *Iva,* of eastern and central North America, often growing in salt marshes.

marsh gas n. Methane produced by rotting vegetation in marshes.

marsh harrier n. A Eurasian hawk, *Circus aeruginosus,* that frequents beds of reeds and marshes. It has a dark brown plumage with paler markings.

marsh hawk n. A hawk, *Circus cyaneus,* found in marshy areas of North America and Eurasia. Also called "hen harrier."

Mars

MARS: A BARREN PLANET WITH AN ACTIVE PAST

Pink skies overhang an icy, windswept, rock-strewn terrain

Mars is smaller than the earth, only about half the diameter, and is roughly 1½ times as far from the Sun. In some ways it is more earthlike than any other planet, with a day that lasts 24 hours 37 minutes and 23 seconds, and similar seasons to those on Earth—although they are much longer because Mars takes 687 days to orbit the Sun.

Viewed from Earth, Mars shows white polar caps, dark patches, and red areas usually called deserts. The Mariner and Viking spacecraft probes of the 1960's and 1970's have shown that the dark areas are not, as once thought, old seabeds filled with vegetation. Some are plateaus, differing from the deserts in color only.

The Martian landscape is harsh—cratered and rock-strewn and subject to violent dust storms. There are giant volcanoes—Olympus

Mons is three times as high as Everest—and gigantic canyons such as Valles Marineris, four times as deep as the Grand Canyon. Mars has no oceans, but the islands around some craters were formed by massive floods. Because of the freezing temperatures and thin atmosphere, there are icy fogs and clouds that vaporize in the day's heat and freeze again toward night.

As recently as the mid-20th century, it was believed that Mars might support advanced forms of life. Some astronomers even believed there were irrigation canals. But the 1976 Viking spacecraft programmed to search for life found no evidence of it.

Two dwarf satellites, Phobos and Deimos, orbit Mars. Each is less than 30 kilometers (19 miles) across, and unlikely to light up the Martian night.

APPROACH TO MARS *The spacecraft camera reveals the planet's craters, massive volcanoes (including Olympus Mons), ground frost or fog (bottom left), and thin white cloud patches.*

RED DESERT *The red-colored landscape around Viking Lander 2 justifies Mars's ancient nickname: the Red Planet. The salty whiteness on the soil is a thin coating of ice.*

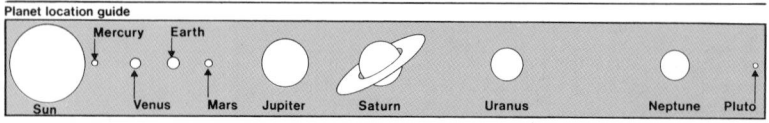

Planet location guide

marsh hen *n.* Any of various marsh birds of the family Rallidae, which includes the gallinules, coots, and rails.

marsh·land (märsh′lănd′) *n.* A marshy tract of land.

marsh·mal·low (märsh′mĕl′ō, -măl′ō) *n.* **1.** A confection of sweetened paste formerly made from the root of the marsh mallow. **2.** A soft confection made of corn syrup, gelatin, sugar, and starch and dusted with powdered sugar. [From MARSH MALLOW.] —marsh·mal·low *adj.*

marsh mallow *n.* A plant, *Althaea officinalis,* native to Europe, having showy pink flowers and a mucilaginous root used as a demulcent and in confectionery. [Middle English *mershmalwe,* from Old English *merscmealwe : mersc,* marsh + *mealwe,* mallow.]

marsh marigold *n.* Any plant of the genus *Caltha;* especially, *C. palustris,* growing in swampy places and having bright yellow flowers. Also called "king-cup."

marsh tit *n.* A small European songbird, *Parus palustris,* having a grayish body and a black head.

marsh·y (mär′shē) *adj.* **-ier, -iest.** Of, like, or characterized by marshes; boggy. —marsh·i·ness *n.*

Mar·ston Moor (mär′stən). The site in Yorkshire of the first decisive battle of the English Civil War (July 2, 1644), won by the Parliamentarians.

mar·su·pi·al (mär-sōō′pē-əl) *n.* Any mammal of the order Marsupialia, including kangaroos, opossums, bandicoots, and wombats, found principally in the Australian region and South and Central America. The female of most species lacks a placenta and possesses a marsupium.
~*adj.* **1.** Of or pertaining to the Marsupialia. **2.** Of or pertaining to a marsupium. [New Latin *marsupialis,* from MARSUPIUM.]

mar·su·pi·um (mär-sōō′pē-əm) *n., pl.* **-pia** (-pē-ə). **1.** An external abdominal pouch in female marsupials that contains mammary glands and that shelters the young. **2.** A temporary egg pouch in various animals. [Latin *marsupium,* pouch, from Greek *marsupion, marsipion,* diminutive of *marsipos,* purse, probably from Avestan *maršu†,* belly.]

mart (märt) *n.* **1.** A market; a trading or auction center. **2.** *Archaic.* A fair. [Middle English, shortened from MARKET.]

mar·ta·gon (mär′tə-gən) *n.* A Eurasian lily, *Lilium martagon,* having pinkish-purple, spotted flowers. [Middle English, from Old French, from Old Spanish, from Turkish *martagăn,* a kind of turban.]

Martel, Charles. See **Charles Martel.**

Mar·tel·lo tower (mär-tĕl′ō) *n.* A small circular fort formerly used in Europe for coastal defense. [Alteration of (Cape) *Mortella,* Corsica.]

mar·ten (märt′n) *n., pl.* **-tens** or collectively **marten. 1.** A carnivore of the genus *Martes,* similar to the weasel and found in northern wooded areas. **2.** The fur of the marten. [Middle English *martren,* marten, marten's fur, from Old French *martrine,* marten's fur, from *martre,* marten, from Germanic *marthuz* (unattested).]

mar·ten·site (märt′n-zīt′) *n.* A solid solution of iron and up to one percent of carbon, the chief constituent of hardened carbon tool steels. [After Adolf *Marten* (1914–), German metallurgist.]

Mar·tha (mär′thə). In the New Testament, a sister of Lazarus and Mary and friend of Jesus.

Mar·tha's Vine·yard (mär′thəz vīn′yərd). Resort island, *c.* 260 square kilometers (100 square miles), off the southeastern coast of Massachusetts. It was settled in 1642 and became an important whaling and fishing center in the 18th and early 19th centuries.

Mar·tí (mär-tē′), **José Julian** (1853–95). Cuban author and revolutionary leader. Through his poems and essays he fired the cause of Cuban independence from Spain. Living in exile for most of the years after 1871, he returned to Cuba in April 1895 as the leader of an invasion force and was killed in battle a month later.

mar·tial (mär′shəl) *adj.* **1.** Of, pertaining to, or suggesting war. **2.** Of or pertaining to the armed forces or the military profession. **3.** Resembling, characteristic of, or befitting a warrior: *a martial roar of indignation.* [Middle English, from Latin *mărtiălis,* from *Mărs* (stem *Mărt-*), MARS.] —mar·tial·ly *adv.*

Mar·tial (mär′shəl), born Marcus Valerius Martialis (A.D. 40–104). Latin poet. Spanish-born, he went to Rome (A.D. 64), gaining patronage from the Senecas. His 12 books of epigrams are keen, witty observations of contemporary Roman life.

martial art *n.* Any of several methods of fighting or self-defense, such as judo or karate, originating in the East.

martial law *n.* Rule by military authorities imposed upon a civilian population in time of war or when civil authority is unable to maintain public safety.

Mar·tian (mär′shən) *adj.* Of or pertaining to the planet Mars.
~*n.* A hypothetical inhabitant of the planet Mars, especially as a stock fictional character. [Middle English, from Latin *mărtius,* from *Mărs* (stem *Mărt-*), MARS.]

mar·tin (märt′n) *n.* Any of several birds resembling and closely related to the swallows, such as the **house martin** (see). [Old French, probably from the name *Martin,* Martin.]

Mar·tin (märt′n), **Glenn Luther** (1886–1955). U.S. airplane manufacturer. He established one of the earliest airplane factories in the country (1909) and received the first government order for aircraft (1913). Martin also designed and built clipper airplanes used in transpacific flights.

Martin, Mary (1913–). U.S. actress and singer. In her first Broadway role she scored a major success singing Cole Porter's risqué hit "My Heart Belongs to Daddy." Since then she has starred in countless Broadway hits, including *One Touch of Venus, South Pacific, Peter Pan,* and *The Sound of Music.*

Mar·ti·neau (mär′tə-nō′), **Harriet** (1802–76). British writer. Her work dealt with economic and religious themes based on the ideas of Ricardo and Mill. Her works include *Illustrations of Political Economy* (1832–34) and the children's story *The Play Fellow* (1841).

mar·ti·net (märt′n-ĕt′) *n.* **1.** A rigid military disciplinarian. **2.** A person who demands absolute adherence to standards or rules. [After Jean *Martinet,* 17th-century French general.]

mar·tin·gale (märt′n-gāl′) *n.* Also **mar·tin·gal** (-găl′). **1.** A part of a harness designed to prevent a horse from throwing back its head. **2.** *Nautical.* Any of several parts of standing rigging strengthening the bowsprit and jib boom against the force of the head stays. **3.** A method of gambling in which one doubles the stakes after each loss. [16th century : from French *martingale†.*]

mar·ti·ni (mär-tē′nē) *n., pl.* **-nis.** A cocktail made of gin or vodka with dry vermouth. [Origin unknown.]

Mar·ti·nique (mär′tə-nēk′). Overseas department of France in the Caribbean, settled by the French in 1635. The small volcanic island is dominated by Mt. Pelée, which erupted in 1902, killing more than 30,000 people and destroying the town of Saint Pierre. The economy depends on bananas, sugar, pineapple canning, and rum. Fort-de-France is the capital. See map at **Latin America.**

Mar·tin·mas (märt′n-məs) *n.* A Christian festival celebrated annually on St. Martin's Day, November 11. [Middle English *martinmesse : Martin,* Martin + *messe,* Mass.]

mart·let (märt′lĭt) *n.* **1.** The martin. **2.** *Heraldry.* A representation of a bird without feet, used as a crest or bearing to indicate a fourth son. [French *martelet,* probably an alteration of *martinet,* diminutive of MARTIN.]

mar·tyr (mär′tər) *n.* **1.** One who chooses to suffer death rather than renounce religious or political principles. **2.** One who makes great sacrifices or suffers much in order to further a belief, cause, or principle. **3.** A person who endures great suffering: *a martyr to migraine.* **4.** A person who makes a great show of suffering in order to arouse sympathy.
~*tr.v.* **martyred, -tyring, -tyrs. 1.** To make a martyr of (a person). **2.** To inflict great pain upon; torment: *martyred by toothache.* [Middle English *martir,* Old English *martyr,* from Late Latin *martyr,* from Greek *martus†* (stem *martur-*), witness (of Christ).]

mar·tyr·dom (mär′tər-dəm) *n.* **1.** The state of being a martyr; the suffering of death by a martyr. **2.** Extreme suffering.

mar·tyr·ize (mär′tə-rīz′) *tr.v.* **-ized, -izing, -izes.** To martyr.

mar·tyr·ol·o·gy (mär′tə-rŏl′ə-jē) *n., pl.* **-gies. 1.** A list or catalogue of saints and martyrs. **2.** The history of religious martyrs, especially Christian martyrs.

mar·tyr·y (mär′tə-rē) *n., pl.* **-ies.** A monument, such as a shrine or chapel, erected in honor of a martyr. [Middle English, from Medieval Latin *martyrium,* from Greek *marturion,* martyrdom.]

mar·vel (mär′vəl) *n.* **1.** Something that evokes surprise, admiration, or wonder. **2.** A sense of wonder or astonishment.
~*v.* **marveled, -veling, -vels.** Also *chiefly British* **-velled, -velling, -vels.** —*intr.* To be or become filled with wonder or astonishment. —*tr.* To wonder at or about. [Middle English *marveile,* from Old French *merveille,* from Vulgar Latin *mīrābilia* (unattested), marvel, originally "wonderful things," Latin neuter plural of *mīrābilis,* wonderful, from *mīrārī,* to wonder, from *mīrus,* wonderful.]

Mar·vell (mär′vəl), **Andrew** (1621–78). English metaphysical poet. His frequently satirical work includes the poems *To His Coy Mistress* and *The Definition of Love* and pamphlets attacking the monarchy and political corruption.

mar·vel·ous, mar·vel·lous (mär′və-ləs) *adj.* **1.** Causing wonder or astonishment: *a marvelous cure.* **2.** Of the highest or best kind or quality: *a marvelous recipe.* **3.** Miraculous; supernatural. —**mar·vel·ous·ly** *adv.* —**mar·vel·ous·ness** *n.*

mar·vel-of-Pe·ru (mär′vəl-əv-pə-rōō′) *n.* A plant, the **four-o'clock** *(see).* [Originally found in Peru.]

Marx (märks), **Karl** (1818–83). German journalist and philosopher. He edited the *Rheinische Zeitung* (1842–43) before working with Friedrich Engels, producing the *Communist Manifesto* in 1847. Expelled from Prussia (1849), he settled in London. He adapted Hegel's ideas to produce a theory of social change, dialectical materialism, and believed that violent revolution by the proletariat is necessary to create a classless society. *Das Kapital* (1867) greatly influenced subsequent socialism and communism.

Marx Brothers. U.S. family of comedians. Touring from early childhood in vaudeville, they later starred in films full of irreverent and anarchic humor, both verbal and visual, including *Duck Soup* (1933), *A Night at the Opera* (1935), and *A Day at the Races* (1937). **Julius** (Groucho) (1895–1977), with his comic mustache, cigar, and biting sarcasm, **Arthur** (Harpo) (1893–1964), the dumb clown and harpist, and **Leonard** (Chico) (1891–1961), the piano-playing confidence trickster, contrasted with **Herbert** (Zeppo) (1901–79), who played the straight man before retiring from films. **Milton** (Gummo) (1894–1977) followed his own career.

Marx·i·an (märk′sē-ən) *n.* One who studies or makes use of Karl Marx's philosophical or other concepts as a method of analysis and interpretation, as in political economy or in literary or historical criticism. —**Marx·i·an** *adj.* —**Marx·i·an·ism** *n.*

Marx·ism (märk′sĭz′əm) *n.* The political and economic ideas of Karl Marx and Friedrich Engels; specifically, a system of thought in which the concept of class struggle plays a primary role both in analyzing Western society in general and in understanding its alleg-

edly inevitable development from bourgeois oppression under capitalism to a socialist society and thence to Communism.

Marx·ism-Len·in·ism (märk′sĭz′əm-lĕn′ə-nĭz′əm) *n.* Marxism as developed to include Lenin's concept of imperialism as the final form of capitalism and a shift in the focus of struggle from the developed to the underdeveloped countries. —**Marx·ist-Len·in·ist** *n. & adj.*

Marx·ist (märk′sĭst) *n.* One who believes in or follows the ideas of Marx and Engels; especially, a militant Communist.
~*adj.* Of or pertaining to Marxism.

Mar·y (mâr′ē), also known as "the Virgin Mary," "Our Lady." The mother of Jesus. Matthew 1:18–25.

Mary I, also known as "Mary Tudor" (1516–58). Queen of England (1553–58). Daughter of Henry VIII and Catherine of Aragon, she came to the throne on the death of her half-brother, Edward VI. She married Philip II of Spain (1554) and restored papal supremacy in England; the persecution of the Protestants followed, including the burning of bishops Thomas Cranmer, Hugh Latimer, and Nicholas Ridley, earning her the nickname Bloody Mary.

Mary II (1662–94). Queen of England, Scotland, and Ireland (1689–94). Daughter of James II, she married her cousin William of Orange (1677), ruling jointly with him after the Glorious Revolution (1688) that forced her father's abdication.

Mary, Queen of Scots, also known as "Mary Stuart" (1542–87). Queen of Scotland (1542–67). The daughter of James V and Mary of Guise, she was brought up as a Catholic in France, where she married the dauphin (later Francis II). She returned to Scotland after the death of her husband (1561). She married her cousin the Earl of Darnley (1565), by whom she had a son, later to be James VI of Scotland and James I of England. Darnley was murdered by the Earl of Bothwell (1567), whom she married three months later. Forced to abdicate by the nobles in favor of her son, she fled to England (1568) and was imprisoned by Elizabeth I. Catholic supporters plotted to place her on the throne of England, and this resulted in her trial and execution.

Mary Jane (jān) *n. Slang.* Marijuana. [By folk etymology from MARIJUANA.]

Mar·y·land (mâr′ə-lənd). *Abbr.* **Md.** Atlantic state of the United States. One of the original 13 states, it was founded (1634) by Lord Baltimore as a refuge for English Roman Catholics. Its Atlantic plain, divided by Chesapeake Bay, rises in the northwest to the Blue Ridge Mts. in the Appalachians. Although livestock, cereal, and tobacco farming are important, the economy rests mainly on manufacturing, particularly of steel, metal products, and machinery. Annapolis is the capital.

Mary Mag·da·lene (măg′də-lēn′, -lən) Also **Mary Mag·da·len** (-lən). A woman in the New Testament (Luke 8:2) whom Jesus cured of evil spirits. She is usually considered identical with the repentant prostitute in Luke 7:36–50.

Maryology. Variant of **Mariology.**

mar·zi·pan (mär′zə-pän′, märt′sə-pän′) *n.* A confection in the form of a paste made of ground almonds, egg whites, and sugar, often molded into decorative forms. [German *Marzipan,* from Italian *marzapane,* fine box for confections, originally a box containing a tenth of a load, from Venetian *matapan,* coin bearing a seated Christ figure, originally, a 10 percent tax, from Arabic *mawthabān,* "seated king," name given to similar coins in circulation since the Crusades.]

-mas *suffix.* Indicates a Christian festival; for example, **Christmas.** [Middle English *masse,* MASS.]

Ma·sac·cio (mə-zä′chō, -chē-ō′), born Tommaso di Giovanni di Simone Guidi (1401–28). Early Italian Renaissance painter. His revolutionary use of linear perspective and mastery of light and shade are illustrated in his fresco series in the Brancacci Chapel at Santa Maria del Carmine, Florence.

Ma·sa·da (mə-sä′də). Mountain fortress in the Judaean Desert, Israel, overlooking the Dead Sea. In A.D. 73, after a two-year siege, the Zealots, a Jewish sect who were defending the fortress, committed mass suicide rather than surrender to the Romans.

Ma·sai (mä-sī′) *n., pl.* **-sais** or collectively **Masai. 1.** A member of a nomadic people of Kenya and parts of Tanzania. **2.** The Nilotic language of this people. —**Ma·sai** *adj.*

Mas·a·ryk (măs′ə-rĭk′, mä′sə-), **Tomáš Garrigue** (1850–1937). Czech statesman. He became first president of the independent Czech Republic, retiring in 1935. His son **Jan** (1886–1948) entered the Czech diplomatic service (1918), was minister to Britain (1925–38), and foreign minister in the exiled Czech government in London (1940–45) and in Czechoslovakia (1945–48). After the Communist takeover, he is alleged to have committed suicide.

masc. masculine.

mascalonge. Variant of **muskellunge.**

mas·car·a (mă-skăr′ə, -skä′rə) *n.* A cosmetic applied to darken or thicken the eyelashes. [Italian *mascara, maschera,* MASK, probably from Arabic *maskharah,* "buffoon."]

mas·cle (măs′kəl, mä′skəl) *n. Heraldry.* A charge consisting of a lozenge with the inner area also shaped like a lozenge. [Middle English, from Norman French, from Medieval Latin *mascula,* from Latin *macula,* spot.]

mas·con (măs′kŏn′) *n.* Any of several areas of high-density mass below the surface of the moon causing an exceptionally high gravitational attraction. [From *mas*s *con*centration.]

mas·cot (măs′kŏt′, -kət) *n.* A person, animal, or object believed to bring good luck, especially one kept as the symbol of an organiza-

marten *These tree-dwelling members of the weasel family live in the forests of the Northern Hemisphere, feeding largely on rodents and small birds. This is the pine marten,* Martes martes.

FACES TRANSFIGURED IN CEREMONY, ENTERTAINMENT, AND DEATH

Masks vary in style as much as the cultures that produced them

Masks—which disguise, transform, or define the beings behind them—have been vital in primitive rituals and in drama for many hundreds, even thousands, of years.

They are used by tribes the world over to impersonate supernatural beings or animals, for numerous reasons. A mask may be a totem to represent a protective spirit, like the 6-meter (20-foot) masks of the Papuans in New Guinea.

In many places, shamans (or medicine men) don grotesque demon masks to scare off evil spirits, a task also performed by the so-called False Face society of the Iroquois Indians, whose long-haired, grimacing masks were used to exorcise demons. The golden masks of Andean tribes were sometimes purely formal (for burial) or practical (for ceremonial use) or both.

In Greek theater, masks were worn to represent fixed characteristics, like grief or rage. The tradition was preserved in Roman theater and inherited much later, in the 16th century, by the Italian commedia dell'arte, masked comedies with stock characters that found their way into modern pantomime, Punch and Judy, and clowning traditions.

Masks are integral as well to Japanese and Chinese theatrical traditions. The Japanese No plays of the 14th century and onward use in rigidly formal terms no less than 125 types of wooden masks, each with its own fixed role.

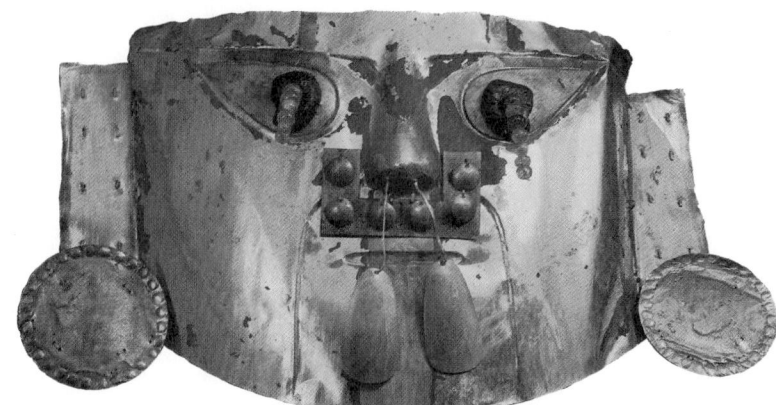

BURIAL MASK *Made in the 12th–13th centuries by the Chimu of Peru, this mask has emerald eyes, red paint, and large ear spools that indicate the high status of its wearer.*

DEMONIC MASK *Ornate masks, like this demonic wooden one from the Baron tribe of Indonesia, are—with shields and baskets—important forms of artistic expression among many Indonesian peoples.*

BADGE OF SECRECY *In Liberia masks are worn by members of the Poro secret society, which regulates male behavior.*

PROTECTIVE TOTEM *Papuan tribesmen make wood and barkcloth masks, some of them enormously large, as totems to protect members of a tribe.*

---

tion, as an athletic team. [French *mascotte,* from Provençal *mascotto,* diminutive of *masco,* sorcerer, from Late Latin *masca,* witch, from Langobard.]

mas·cu·line (măs′kyə-lĭn) *adj.* *Abbr.* **m, M, m., M., masc.** **1.** Of or pertaining to men or boys; male. **2.** Suggestive or characteristic of a man; mannish. **3.** *Grammar.* Of, pertaining to, or being a category of words or grammatical forms denoting or referring normally to males: *a masculine suffix.*
~*n.* *Abbr.* **m, M, m., M., masc.** **1.** The masculine gender. **2.** A word or word form of the masculine gender. [Middle English *masculin,* from Old French, from Latin *masculīnus,* from *masculus,* male, diminutive of *mas,* male.] —**mas·cu·line·ly** *adv.* —**mas·cu·lin·i·ty** (măs′kyə-lĭn′ə-tē), **mas·cu·line·ness** *n.*

masculine ending *n.* The ending of a line of verse with a stressed final syllable. Compare **feminine ending.**

masculine rhyme *n.* A rhyme of only a single syllable, terminal and stressed, as in *cat, hat.* Compare **feminine rhyme.**

mas·cu·lin·ize (măs′kyə-lə-nīz′) *tr.v.* **-ized, -izing, -izes.** **1.** To give a masculine appearance or character to. **2.** To cause to assume masculine characteristics, as through hormonal imbalance or male hormone therapy. —**mas·cu·lin·i·za·tion** *n.*

Mase·field (mās′fēld), **John Edward** (1878–1967). British poet and novelist. His poetry includes the colloquial *Everlasting Mercy* (1911), *Dauber* (1913), and the Chaucerian *Reynard the Fox* (1919), while his novels include *Sard Harker* (1924) and *Basilissa* (1940). He became poet laureate in 1930.

ma·ser (mā′zər) *n.* *Physics.* Any of several devices that convert inci-

dent electromagnetic radiation from a wide range of frequencies to one or more discrete frequencies of highly amplified and coherent microwave radiation. Compare **laser.** [*M*icrowave *a*mplification by *s*timulated *e*mission of *r*adiation.]

Mas·er·u (măz′ə-rōō′). Capital of Lesotho, in the west near the border with South Africa.

mash (măsh) *n.* **1.** Any fermentable, starchy mixture from which alcohol or spirits can be distilled. **2.** A mixture of ground grain and nutrients fed to livestock and poultry. **3. a.** Any soft, pulpy mixture or mass. **b.** *British Informal.* Mashed potatoes.
~*tr.v.* **mashed, mashing, mashes.** **1.** To convert (malt or grain) into mash. **2.** To convert (something) into a soft, pulpy mixture resembling mash: *mash potatoes.* **3.** To crush or grind. **4.** *Slang.* To flirt with. [Middle English, from Old English *māsc.*]

mash·er (măsh′ər) *n.* **1.** A kitchen utensil for mashing vegetables or fruit. **2.** *Slang.* A man who attempts to force his sexual attentions upon a woman.

Mash·had, Me·shed (mə-shĕd′). Ancient city of northeastern Iran at the junction of major caravan routes. It is a provincial capital and center of a rich agricultural region.

mash·ie, mash·y (măsh′ē) *n., pl.* **-ies.** A golf club of medium loft. [Perhaps from French *massue,* club.]

Mashona. Variant of **Shona.**

mas·jid (mŭs′jĭd) *n.* A **mosque** (*see*). [Arabic.]

mask (măsk, mäsk) *n.* **1.** A covering worn on the face to conceal one's identity, especially: **a.** A cloth, plastic, or paper covering that has openings for the eyes, entirely or partly conceals the face, and is

worn especially at a masquerade ball, fancy-dress dance, or the like. **b.** A representation of a grotesque face: *a horror mask.* **c.** A facial covering worn for a parade, carnival, ritual, or the like. **d.** A complete facial covering and headdress, usually made of plaster or wood, worn by actors in Greek and Roman drama to emphasize a single character trait. **2. a.** A protective covering for the face or head, as worn in fencing and some other sports. **b.** A facial covering worn to prevent infection, especially during surgery. **3. a.** A gas mask *(see).* **b.** A device fitting over the mouth and nose through which oxygen or an anesthetic gas may be supplied. **4.** A representation of a face or head, as: **a.** A death mask *(see).* **b.** An often grotesque representation of a head and face, used for ornamentation. **5.** The face or facial markings of certain animals, such as a fox or dog. **6.** A face having a blank, fixed, or enigmatic expression: *She displayed an impenetrable mask to the world.* **7.** Something, often a trait, that disguises or conceals: *hid his shyness under a mask of confidence.* **8.** A natural or artificial feature of terrain that conceals and protects military forces or installations. **9. a.** An opaque border or pattern placed between a source of light and a photosensitive surface to prevent exposure of specific portions of the surface. **b.** The translucent border framing a television picture tube and screen. **10.** See **face pack. 11.** A **masque** *(see).* **12.** *Archaic.* A person wearing a mask. **13.** *Electronics.* A thin sheet of material with a pattern cut into it to enable a semiconducting chip to be made into an integrated circuit.
~*tr.v.* **masked, masking, masks. 1.** To cover (the face, for example) with a decorative or protective mask. **2.** To disguise; especially, to make indistinct or blurred to the senses: *The spice masks the strong flavor of the meat.* **3.** To cover up for concealment or protection: *They masked their guns with branches.* **4.** To block the view of: *Undergrowth masked the entrance.* **5.** To cover (a part of a photographic film) by the application of an opaque border. **6.** To apply masking paper or masking tape to (an area not to be painted). **7.** *Chemistry.* To inhibit (a compound or radical) with a reagent more active in a specific reaction. [French *masque,* from Italian *maschera,* perhaps from Arabic *maskharah,* "buffoon."]
maskalonge. Variant of **muskellunge.**
masked (măskt, măskt) *adj.* **1.** Wearing a mask. **2.** Disguised; concealed: *masked intentions.* **3.** Latent or hidden, as a symptom or disease may be. **4.** *Botany.* Resembling a mask; personate. **5.** *Zoology.* Having masklike markings on the head or face.
maskeg. Variant of **muskeg.**
mask·er, masqu·er (măs′kər, mä′skər) *n.* A participant in a masquerade or masque.
mask·ing (măs′kĭng, mä′skĭng) *n.* **1.** The concealment or screening of one sensory process by another. **2.** A piece of theatrical scenery used to conceal a part of the stage from the audience.
masking paper *n.* Paper used to cover and protect a surface that is not to be painted.
masking tape *n.* An adhesive tape used to cover and protect a surface that is not to be painted.
mas·o·chism (măs′ə-kĭz′əm) *n.* **1.** The deriving of pleasure, especially sexual arousal, from having physical or emotional pain inflicted on one. **2.** Loosely, the practice of deliberately undergoing unpleasant experiences, usually in the pursuit of some higher satisfaction: *the sheer masochism of entering a marathon.* [After Leopold von Sacher-*Masoch* (1836-95), Austrian novelist who wrote on the theme of sexual masochism.] —**mas·o·chist** *n.* —**mas·o·chis·tic** *adj.* —**mas·o·chis·ti·cal·ly** *adv.*
ma·son (mā′sən) *n.* **1. a.** A person who builds with stone. **b.** A person who cuts or carves stone. **c.** A bricklayer. **2. Mason.** See **Freemason** (sense 2).
~*tr.v.* **masoned, -soning, -sons.** To build or strengthen with masonry. [Middle English *masoun, machoun,* from Norman French *machun,* from Old French *masson,* from Frankish *makjo* (unattested), from *makōn,* to make (unattested).]
mason bee *n.* Any of various solitary bees of the family Megachilidae, found worldwide, that build nests of sand or clay.
Ma·son-Dix·on Line (mā′sən-dĭk′sən) *n.* Former political boundary between Pennsylvania and Maryland, drawn up (1763-67) by the astronomers Charles Mason (1730-87) and Jeremiah Dixon (*fl.* 1763-67). It was considered to be the division between the free and slave states before the Civil War.
Ma·son·ic (mə-sŏn′ĭk) *adj.* Of or pertaining to Freemasons or Freemasonry.
Mason jar *n.* A wide-mouthed glass jar with a screw top, used widely for home canning and preserving. [Patented by John L. *Mason* (1832-1902), American inventor.]
ma·son·ry (mā′sən-rē) *n., pl.* **-ries. 1.** The trade of a mason. **2.** The work done by a mason. **3.** Stonework or brickwork. **4. Masonry.** See **Freemasonry** (sense 2).
masonry cement *n.* A kind of cement especially prepared to be used in the mortar of block and brick masonry.
Ma·so·ra, Ma·so·rah (mə-sôr′ə, -sōr′ə) *n.* **1.** The body of tradition pertaining to correct textual reading of the Old Testament. **2.** The critical notes in which this tradition is embodied, made by Jewish scholars before the 10th century A.D. [Middle Hebrew *māsōrāh,* "tradition," from Hebrew *māsar,* root of *limsor,* to hand over, transmit.] —**Mas·o·ret·ic** (măs′ə-rĕt′ĭk) *adj.*
masque, mask (măsk, mäsk) *n.* **1.** A dramatic entertainment, usually based on a mythological or allegorical theme, popular in England in the 16th and early 17th centuries. **2.** A dramatic verse

composition written for a masque production. **3.** A masquerade. [Variant of MASK.]
masquer. Variant of **masker.**
mas·quer·ade (măs′kə-rād′) *n.* **1.** A costume ball or party at which masks are worn; a masked ball. Also called "masque." **2.** The costume for such a party or ball. **3.** Any disguise or false outward show; a pretense: *a masquerade of humility.*
~*intr.v.* **masqueraded, -ading, -ades. 1.** To wear a mask or disguise, as at a masquerade: *She masqueraded as a shepherdess.* **2.** To pretend to be something one is not: *He masqueraded as the ship's surgeon.* [French *mascarade,* from Italian *mascherata* or Spanish *mascarada,* from Italian *maschera,* MASK.] —**mas·quer·ad·er** *n.*
mass (măs) *n.* **1.** A unified body of matter with no specific shape. **2.** A grouping of individual parts or elements that compose a unified body of unspecified size or quantity: *A mass of people poured into the streets.* **3.** Any large but nonspecific amount or number: *a mass of bruises.* **4.** The major part of something; majority. **5.** The bulk of a solid body. **6.** *Physics. Abbr.* **m, M** The measure of a body's resistance to acceleration. The mass of a body is different from but proportional to its **weight** *(see),* is independent of the body's position but dependent on its velocity relative to other bodies, and may be expressed in mass units, such as kilograms or slugs, or corresponding energy units, by means of the mass-energy relationship of the special theory of relativity. **7.** In painting, an area of unified light, shade, or color. **8.** In pharmacology, a thick, pasty mixture of drugs used to form pills. **9.** In mining, a mineral deposit with no specific shape. Compare **bed, vein. 10.** *Usually* **masses.** The body of common people as distinguished from the elite; proletariat. —**in the mass.** Considered as a whole.
~*v.* **massed, massing, masses.** —*tr.* To gather or form into a mass. —*intr.* To assemble in a mass.
~*adj.* **1.** Of, pertaining to, characteristic of, or involving a large number of people: *mass education; mass destruction.* **2.** Done on a large scale; involving great numbers or large amounts: *mass production.* [Middle English, from Old French *masse,* from Latin *massa,* from Greek *maza,* barley cake, lump, mass.]
Mass (măs) *n. Sometimes* **mass. 1.** In the Roman Catholic and some Protestant churches, such as the Lutheran, the celebration of the Eucharist. See **High Mass, Low Mass. 2.** A musical setting of certain parts of the Mass, especially the Kyrie, Gloria, Credo, Sanctus, Benedictus, and Agnus Dei. [Middle English *masse,* Old English *mæsse, messe,* from Late Latin *missa,* eucharist, perhaps deriving from the final words, *Ite, missa est,* "Go, it is the dismissal," from *mittere* (past participial stem *miss-*), to send away.]
Mass. Massachusetts.
Mas·sa·chu·set, Mas·sa·chu·sett (măs′ə-chōō′sĭt, -zĭt) *n., pl.* **-sets** or collectively **Massachuset, -setts** or collectively **Massachusett. 1.** A member of an Algonquian-speaking Indian people who lived on or near Massachusetts Bay. **2.** The Algonquian language of these Indians.
Mas·sa·chu·setts (măs′ə-chōō′sĭts, -zĭts). *Abbr.* **Mass.** New England state of the United States. It was the destination of the *Mayflower* (1620) and became one of the 13 original states. Massachusetts is largely a manufacturing state with shipping, machinery, paper, printing, textile, and leather industries. Boston is the capital.
mas·sa·cre (măs′ə-kər) *n.* **1.** An act of savage and indiscriminate killing, especially of large numbers of people. **2.** *Informal.* A severe defeat, as in a sports event. **3.** *Informal.* An act of wanton destruction: *the massacre of our hopes.*
~*tr.v.* **massacred** (-kərd), **-cring** (-krĭng, -kər-ĭng), **-cres. 1.** To kill indiscriminately and wantonly; slaughter. **2.** *Informal.* To defeat decisively, as in a sports event. [French, from Old French *maçacre†, slaughterhouse.] —**mas·sa·crer** (măs′ə-kər-ər, -krər) *n.*
mas·sage (mə-säzh′, -säj′) *n.* The rubbing or kneading of parts of the body, as to aid circulation or relax the muscles.
~*tr.v.* **massaged, -saging, -sages. 1.** To give a massage to. **2.** To treat by or as if by means of a massage: *massaged her ego.* **3.** *Informal.* To mold or adjust to suit a preconceived interpretation: *massage statistics.* [French, from *masser,* to massage, probably from Portuguese *amassar,* to knead, from *massa,* dough, MASS.]
mas·sa·sau·ga (măs′ə-sô′gə) *n.* A brown and white venomous rattlesnake, *Sistrurus catenatus,* of North America. [After the *Missisauga* River, Ontario, Canada.]
Mas·sa·soit (măs′ə-soit′) (c. 1580-1661). Chief of the Wampanoag Indians. One of the most powerful native rulers of New England, he signed a peace treaty with the Pilgrims of Plymouth Colony (1621). He also befriended Roger Williams.
mass defect *n. Physics.* The amount by which the mass of an atomic nucleus is less than the sum of the masses of its constituent particles. It is equivalent to the **binding energy** *(see)* of the nucleus. Also called "mass deficiency."
mas·sé (mă-sā′) *n.* In billiards, a stroke made by hitting the cue ball on its side with the cue held nearly perpendicular to the table, such that the cue ball will curve around a ball that is immediately obstructing it. [French, from *masser,* to cue, from *masse,* cue, MACE.]
mass-en·er·gy equivalence (măs′ĕn′ər-jē) *n. Physics.* The principle that a measured quantity of energy is equivalent to a measured quantity of mass. The equivalence is expressed by Einstein's equation, $E = mc^2$, where E represents energy, m the equivalent mass, and c the speed of light.
Mas·se·net (măs′ə-nā′), **Jules Émile Frédéric** (1842-1912). French composer. Both a student and a professor at the Paris Con-

servatoire, he composed over 20 operas, including *Manon Lescaut* (1884) and *Thaïs* (1894).

mas·se·ter (mə-sē′tər, mă-) *n.* A large muscle in the cheek that acts to close the jaws and is therefore important in chewing. [Greek *masētēr,* one who chews, from *masasthai,* to chew.] —**mas·se·ter·ic** (măs′ə-tĕr′ĭk) *adj.*

mas·seur (mă-sûr′, mə-) *n.* A man who gives massages professionally. [French, from *masser,* TO MASSAGE.]

mas·seuse (mă-sœz′, mə-) *n.* A woman who gives massages professionally. [French, feminine of *masseur.*]

mas·si·cot (măs′ə-kŏt′, -kō′) *n.* **1.** A rare mineral, the yellow crystalline mineral form of lead monoxide, PbO. Compare **litharge. 2.** A yellow pigment, lead monoxide. [Middle English *masticot,* from Old French, akin to Italian *marzacotto,* ointment.]

mas·sif (mă-sēf′) *n.* **1.** A large plateaulike region with marked edges, often formed by faults. **2.** A compact group of connected mountains forming a distinct portion of a mountain range. [French, from *massif,* MASSIVE.]

Mas·sif Cen·tral (mă-sēf′ sĕn-träl′, mä-sēf′ säɴ-träl′). The central upland of France, covering nearly a sixth of the country. It is a mountainous plateau, rising to Puy de Sancy (1,886 meters; 6,186 feet). Stock rearing and dairying are the chief occupations, but coal and kaolin deposits support industrial centers such as Limoges and Clermont-Ferrand.

Mas·sine (mă-sēn′), **Léonide** (1896–1979). Russian ballet dancer and choreographer. He worked with Diaghilev's Ballets Russes. He created the first cubist ballet, *Parade* (1917), *La Boutique Fantasque* (1919), and *Les Présages* (1933).

mas·sive (măs′ĭv) *adj.* **1.** Consisting of or making up a large mass; bulky; heavy; solid: *a massive piece of furniture.* **2.** Unusually large or imposing: *a massive head.* **3.** Large or impressive in quantity, scope, or scale: *a massive work of the finest scholarship.* **4.** *Medicine.* Large in comparison with the usual amount. Said of dosage. **5.** *Pathology.* Affecting a large area of bodily tissue; widespread and severe: *massive gangrene.* **6.** *Physics.* Having mass: *a massive particle.* **7.** *Geology.* Lacking obvious layering, banding, or foliation, or having very thick layers. Said of rock or rocks. **8.** *Mineralogy.* Lacking externally observable crystalline form. —See Synonyms at **heavy.** [Middle English, from Old French *massif,* from Vulgar Latin *massīceus* (unattested), from Latin *massa,* MASS (amount).] —**mas·sive·ly** *adv.* —**mas·sive·ness** *n.*

mass·less (măs′lĭs) *adj.* Having no mass: *a massless particle.* —**mass·less·ness** *n.*

mass media *pl.n. Singular* **mass medium.** A means of public communication, such as television, radio, or sometimes newspapers, that can reach large numbers of people over a widespread area in a relatively short time.

mass noun *n.* A **noncountable** *(see)* noun. Compare **count noun.**

mass number *n.* The total number of neutrons and protons in an atomic nucleus. Also called "nucleon number." See **atomic number, atomic mass.**

mass production *n.* The manufacture of goods in large quantities, using assembly-line techniques. —**mass-pro·duce** (măs′prə-dōōs′, -dyōōs′) *v.* —**mass-pro·duced** *adj.*

mass ratio *n.* The mass of a rocket loaded with fuel at liftoff divided by the mass of the rocket without fuel.

mass spectrograph *n. Physics.* An instrument used to separate charged particles in a prepared beam by means of an electromagnetic field and to photograph the resulting distribution or spectrum of masses.

mass spectrometer *n.* An instrument used to separate charged particles in a prepared beam by means of an electromagnetic field according to their charge to mass ratio. An electrical detector moves across the beam, recording the relative amounts of the various types of ion present.

mass spectrum *n.* The record produced by a mass spectrometer or mass spectrograph, characteristic of the compound analyzed.

mass·y (măs′ē) *adj.* **-ier, -iest.** *Archaic.* Massive; solid; having great mass or bulk. [Middle English, perhaps from Old French *massiz,* variant of *massif,* MASSIVE.] —**mass·i·ness** *n.*

mast[1] (măst, mäst) *n.* **1.** A tall vertical spar, sometimes sectioned, that rises from the keel of a sailing vessel to support the sails and running rigging. **2.** Any tall, narrow pole or structure. —**before the mast.** Serving as an ordinary seaman.
~*tr.v.* **masted, masting, masts.** To fit out (a ship) with masts. [Middle English *maste,* Old English *mæst.*]

mast[2] *n.* The nuts of forest trees, such as beech and oak, accumulated on the ground, used especially as food for pigs. [Middle English *maste,* Old English *mæst.*]

mas·ta·ba, mas·ta·bah (măs′tə-bə) *n.* An ancient Egyptian tomb with a rectangular base and sloping sides. [Arabic *maṣṭabah,* stone bench.]

mast cell *n.* A cell present in connective tissue that releases histamine and other chemicals during inflammatory conditions. [Partial translation of German *Mastzelle* : *Mast,* food + *Zelle,* cell.]

mas·tec·to·my (mă-stĕk′tə-mē) *n., pl.* **-mies.** Surgical removal of a breast, usually as a treatment for cancer. [MAST(O)- + -ECTOMY.]

mas·ter (măs′tər, mä′stər) *n.* **1.** A man having control over the action of another or others. **2.** The captain of a merchant ship. Also called "master mariner." **3.** An employer. **4.** The owner of a slave or an animal. **5.** The male head of a household: *Who is the master of the house?* **6. a.** One who has complete mastery over something requiring skill, such as the playing of a game or a musical instru-

ment: *a master of the backhand pass.* **b.** One who has the ability to control or deal with something: *master of his emotions; master of the situation.* **7.** One who defeats another; a victor. **8.** A male teacher; a schoolmaster. **9. a.** A person whose teachings or doctrines are accepted by followers. **b. Master.** Jesus. Preceded by *our* or *the.* **10.** A person holding a master's degree such as a Master of Arts or Master of Science. **11.** A skilled craftsman, especially one qualified to teach apprentices. Also used adjectively: *a master engraver.* **12.** An **old master** *(see).* **13.** A former title for a naval officer just below a lieutenant and in charge of navigation on a warship. **14.** The title of the head or presiding officer of certain societies, clubs, orders, colleges, or other institutions. **15.** *Chiefly British.* The title of any of various law court officers, such as the chief clerks in Chancery. **16.** A master of foxhounds. **17. Master.** *Abbr.* **M.** A title prefixed to the name of a boy or youth not considered old enough to be addressed as Mr. **18.** An **International Master** *(see).* **19. a.** An original from which copies can be made. Also called "master copy." **b.** The machine playing a videotape master from which **slave** *(see)* machines can copy.
~*adj.* **1.** Of, pertaining to, or characteristic of a master. **2.** Chief; principal: *the master bedroom.* **3.** Highly skilled; masterful: *a master thief.* **4.** Being a part of a mechanism that controls all other parts: *a master switch.* **5.** Being an original from which copies are made.
~*tr.v.* **mastered, -tering, -ters. 1.** To make oneself a master of (an art, craft, or science). **2.** To overcome or defeat: *mastered the tyranny of gambling.* **3.** To reduce to subjugation; break or tame (a person or animal). [Middle English, from Old English *mægister, magister,* and Old French *maistre,* both from Latin *magister.*] —**mas·ter·dom** *n.* —**mas·ter·hood** *n.* —**mas·ter·ship** *n.*

mas·ter-at-arms (măs′tər-ət-ärmz′, mä′stər-) *n., pl.* **masters-at-arms.** A naval petty officer assigned to maintain discipline.

master cylinder *n.* A large cylinder in a hydraulic system in which a fluid is compressed by a piston so that the compressed fluid will operate the pistons in smaller slave cylinders.

mas·ter·ful (măs′tər-fəl, mä′stər-) *adj.* **1.** Revealing an inclination to play the master; imperious; domineering. **2.** Revealing mastery; expert; skillful: *a masterful rendition of Othello.* —See Usage note below. —**mas·ter·ful·ly** *adv.* —**mas·ter·ful·ness** *n.*

Usage: *Masterful* generally means "domineering or powerful"; *masterly* means "showing the knowledge or skill of a master." Thus one would expect *a masterful man* but *a masterly argument.* Occasionally *masterful* is used in contexts where *masterly* would normally be expected *(masterful Spanish; a masterful speech),* but this use has been criticized and is best avoided.

master key *n.* A key that opens several locks whose keys are usually different. Also called "passkey."

mas·ter·ly (măs′tər-lē, mä′stər-) *adj.* Like a master; indicating the knowledge or skill of a master. —See Usage note at **masterful.**
~*adv.* With the skill of a master. —**mas·ter·li·ness** *n.*

master mason *n.* **1.** An expert mason. **2. Master Mason.** One who has achieved the third degree of Freemasonry.

mas·ter·mind (măs′tər-mīnd′, mä′stər-) *n.* **1.** A highly intelligent person. **2.** Such a person who plans and directs a project.
~*tr.v.* **masterminded, -minding, -minds.** To direct, plan, or supervise (a project, often one of a criminal nature).

Master of Arts *n. Abbr.* **M.A. 1.** A degree granted by a university or other institution of higher education, normally to a person who has completed at least one year of postgraduate study, especially in the liberal arts. **2.** A person holding such a degree. Compare **Bachelor of Arts, Doctor of Philosophy.**

master of ceremonies *n. Abbr.* **m.c., M.C. 1.** A person who acts as host at a formal event, making the welcoming speech and introducing other speakers. **2.** A performer who acts as the host of a variety show. Also called "emcee."

master of foxhounds *n. Abbr.* **M.F.H.** The chief officer of a hunt, who is responsible for the hounds and for organizing the hunting program. Also called "master."

Master of Science *n. Abbr.* **M.Sc. 1.** A degree granted by a university or other institution of higher education to a person who has completed at least one year of postgraduate study in the sciences. **2.** A person holding such a degree. Compare **Bachelor of Science, Doctor of Philosophy.**

mas·ter·piece (măs′tər-pēs′, mä′stər-) *n.* **1. a.** An outstanding work of art or craft. **b.** An artist's greatest work: *"Paradise Lost"* was Milton's masterpiece. **2.** Any superlative achievement: *a masterpiece of public speaking.* [Probably translation of Dutch *meesterstuk* or German *Meisterstück,* the piece of work presented to a guild by a craftsman for admission to the rank of master.]

master race *n.* A people who consider themselves endowed with the right to dominate and exploit other supposedly inferior peoples; especially, the German nation viewed as a master race in the ideology of German imperialism (c. 1890–1945). Also called "Herrenvolk."

Mas·ters (măs′tərz), **Edgar Lee** (1869–1950). U.S. poet and biographer. A successful lawyer in Chicago, Masters began writing as an avocation. His *Spoon River Anthology* (1915), a collection of free verse epitaphs of the citizens of a small Midwestern town, was acclaimed for its directness and simplicity. He continued to write but never again achieved the popularity of his first book.

master sergeant *n. Abbr.* **MSgt, M. Sgt.** A noncommissioned officer of the next-to-highest rating in the U.S. Army, Air Force, and Marine Corps.

mas·ter·sing·er (măs′tər-sĭng′ər, mä′stər-) *n.* A **Meistersinger** (*see*).

Mas·ter·son (măs′tər-sən), **William Barclay**, known as "Bat" (1853–1921). U.S. journalist. A sports writer for the New York *Morning Telegraph* (1902–21), Masterson is better known for his colorful earlier life as an Indian fighter, army scout, gambler, and sheriff or marshal in such towns as Dodge City, Deadwood, and Tombstone.

mas·ter·stroke (măs′tər-strōk′, mä′stər-) *n.* A masterly achievement or maneuver: *a masterstroke of statesmanship.*

mas·ter·work (măs′tər-wûrk′, mä′stər-) *n.* A masterpiece.

mas·ter·y (măs′tə-rē, mä′stə-) *n., pl.* **-ies. 1.** Possession of consummate skill: *displayed mastery in handling the situation.* **2.** The state or condition of having power or control: *mastery of the seas.* **3.** Full command of a subject of study: *a poet's mastery of the language.*

mast·head (măst′hĕd′, mäst′-) *n.* **1.** The top of a ship's mast. **2.** The listing in a newspaper, magazine, or other publication of information about its staff and operation.

mas·tic (măs′tĭk) *n.* **1.** The aromatic resin of the mastic tree, used in varnishes and lacquers and as an astringent. **2.** A pastelike cement, especially one made with powdered lime or brick and tar. [Middle English *mastyk,* from Old French *mastic,* from Late Latin *mastichum,* variant of *mastichē,* from Greek *mastikhē,* mastic, "chewing gum," from *mastikhān,* to grind the teeth.]

mas·ti·cate (măs′tĭ-kāt′) *tr.v.* **-cated, -cating, -cates. 1.** To chew. **2.** To grind and knead. [Late Latin *masticāre,* from Greek *mastikhān,* to grind the teeth.] **—mas·ti·ca′tion** *n.* **—mas′ti·ca′tor** *n.*

mas·ti·ca·to·ry (măs′tĭ-kə-tôr′ē, -tōr′ē) *adj.* **1.** Of, pertaining to, or used in mastication. **2.** Being adapted for chewing. *~n., pl.* **masticatories.** A substance chewed to increase salivation.

mastic tree *n.* A small evergreen tree, *Pistacia lentiscus,* of the Mediterranean region, that yields mastic. Also called "lentisk."

mas·tiff (măs′tĭf) *n.* A large dog of an ancient breed, probably originating in Asia, having a short fawn-colored coat. [Middle English *mastif,* from Old French *mastin,* from Vulgar Latin *mānsuētīnus* (unattested), "tame," from Latin *mānsuētus,* tamed, "accustomed to the hand" : *manus,* hand + *suēscere,* to accustom.]

mastiff bat *n.* Any of various bats of the family Molossidae, found in the tropics, having narrow wings and brown, gray, or black fur.

mas·ti·goph·o·ran (măs′tĭ-gŏf′ər-ən) *n.* Also **mas·tig·o·phore** (mă-stĭg′ə-fôr′, -fōr′). Any member of the class Mastigophora, which includes protozoans with one or more flagella. [New Latin *Mastigophora,* "whip bearers" : Greek *mastix†* (stem *mastig-*), whip, lash + *-phora,* -PHORE.] **—mas′ti·goph′o·ran** *adj.*

mas·ti·tis (mă-stī′tĭs) *n.* Inflammation of the breast or udder. [MAST(O)- + -ITIS.]

masto-, mast- *prefix.* Indicates the breast or protuberances resembling a breast or nipple; for example, **mastitis, mastodon.** [New Latin, from Greek *mastos†,* breast.]

mas·to·don (măs′tə-dŏn′) *n.* Any of several extinct mammals of the genus *Mammut* (sometimes called *Mastodon*), resembling the elephant. [New Latin, "breast-tooth" : MAST(O)- + -ODON; from the nipple-shaped protuberances on the teeth.] **—mas′to·don′tic** *adj.*

mas·toid (măs′toid′) *n.* The mastoid process. *~adj.* Pertaining to the mastoid process. [New Latin *mastoides,* "breast-shaped" : MAST(O)- + -OID.]

mastoid cell *n.* One of the small, air-filled spaces in the mastoid process.

mas·toid·ec·to·my (măs′toi-dĕk′tə-mē) *n., pl.* **-mies.** Surgical removal of part or all of the mastoid process.

mas·toid·i·tis (măs′toi-dī′tĭs) *n. Pathology.* Inflammation of part or all of the mastoid process.

mastoid process *n. Anatomy.* The nipple-shaped rear portion of the temporal bone on each side of the head behind the ear in humans and many other vertebrates. Also called "mastoid," "mastoid bone."

mas·tur·bate (măs′tər-bāt′) *v.* **-bated, -bating, -bates.** *—intr.* To perform an act of masturbation. *—tr.* To perform an act of masturbation on. [Latin *masturbārī†.*]

mas·tur·ba·tion (măs′tər-bā′shən) *n.* Excitation of the genital organs, usually to orgasm, by means other than sexual intercourse. **—mas·tur·ba′tion·al, mas·tur·ba·to·ry** (măs′tər-bə-tôr′ē, -tōr′ē) *adj.* **—mas′tur·ba′tor** *n.*

ma·su·ri·um (mə-zoor′ē-əm, mə-soor′-) *n.* A chemical element, technetium (*see*). Not in current technical usage. [New Latin, after *Masuria,* region of northeastern Poland, where it was discovered.]

mat¹ (măt) *n.* **1.** A flat piece of fabric or other material used for wiping one's shoes or feet or as a floor covering. **2.** A small, flat piece of decorated material, such as cloth or cork, placed under a lamp, dish of food, or other object to protect a surface or for ornament. **3.** A thick floor pad to protect athletes, as in wrestling and gymnastics. **4.** Any densely woven or thickly tangled mass: *a mat of hair.* **5.** A heavy, woven net of rope or wire cable placed over a blasting site to keep debris from scattering. *~v.* **matted, matting, mats.** *—tr.* **1.** To cover, protect, or decorate with a mat or mats. **2.** To interweave into or cover with a thick mass: *A heavy growth of vines matted the tree.* *—intr.* To be interwoven into a thick mass; become entangled. [Middle English, Old English *matt(e),* from Late Latin *matta†,* mat.]

mat² *n.* **1.** A decorative border of cardboard or similar material placed around a picture to serve as a frame or act as a contrast between the picture and the frame. **2.** Variant of **matt.** *~tr.v.* **matted, matting, mats. 1.** To put a mat around (a picture). **2.** Variant of **matt.**

~adj. Variant of **matt.** [French, Old French, "dead." See **checkmate.**]

mat³ *n. Printing.* See **matrix** (sense 10b).

mat. matinee.

Mat·a·be·le (măt′ə-bē′lē) *n., pl.* **-les** or collectively **Matabele. 1.** An Ndebele (*see*). **2.** A language, Ndebele (*see*). [Sotho, from *letebele,* "the disappearing ones"; so called because the warriors of this people would sink down (*teba*) behind their huge shields during battle.]

mat·a·dor (măt′ə-dôr′) *n.* **1.** A bullfighter who performs the final passes and kills the bull. **2.** One of the highest trumps in certain card games, such as ombre. [Spanish, "killer," from *matar,* to kill, from Latin *mactāre,* to sacrifice, from *mactus,* sacred.]

Ma·ta Ha·ri (mä′tə hä′rē), born Margaretha Geertruida Zelle (1876–1917). Dutch spy. Married to a Dutch army officer, she became a professional dancer in Paris (1905) and adopted her stage name. During World War I she worked for both the French and the Germans and was finally shot by the French for espionage.

Mat·a·mo·ros (măt′ə-môr′əs, -mōr′əs). Seaport of northeastern Mexico, near the mouth of the Rio Grande opposite Brownsville, Texas. Fishing, trade, and tourism are important to its economy.

match¹ (măch) *n.* **1. a.** A person or thing that is exactly like another; counterpart. **b.** A person or thing that is similar to another in some specified quality: *He is John's match for bravery.* **2. a.** A person or thing that closely resembles or harmonizes with another. **b.** A pair made up of two things or persons that resemble or harmonize with each other: *The colors were a close match.* **3.** A person or thing equal in qualities or able to compete with another of the same class or type: *The boxer had met his match.* **4. a.** An organized athletic contest or game in which individuals or teams oppose and compete with each other: *a boxing match; a football match.* **b.** A tennis contest decided on the basis of victory in a certain number of sets, usually two out of three or three out of five. **5. a.** A marriage or an arrangement of marriage: *Her parents tried to arrange a match for her.* **b.** A person viewed as a prospective marriage partner. *~v.* **matched, matching, matches.** *—tr.* **1. a.** To be exactly like; correspond exactly to. **b.** To be equal or comparable to (another) with respect to some specified quality: *The new model doesn't match the old one for speed.* **c.** To equal; rival: *beauty that could never be matched.* **2.** To resemble or harmonize with: *The coat matches the dress.* **3.** To adapt or suit so that a balanced or harmonious result is achieved; cause to correspond: *matching skill with speed.* **4.** To fit together or cause to fit together. **5.** To join or give in marriage; find a suitable match for. **6.** To place in opposition or competition with; pit: *The only way to ensure peace is to match strength with strength.* **7.** To provide with an adversary or competitor, especially one of equivalent worth: *well-matched contestants.* **8.** To couple (electric circuits) by means of a transformer. *—intr.* To be a close counterpart; correspond. [Middle English *macche,* match, mate, from Old English *gemæcca,* mate.] **—match′a·ble** *adj.* **—match′er** *n.*

match² *n.* **1.** A narrow strip of wood, cardboard, or wax coated on one end with a compound that ignites easily by friction. See **safety match. 2.** An easily ignited cord or wick formerly used for detonating powder charges or firing cannons and muzzle-loading firearms. [Middle English *macche, mecche,* lamp wick, candle, from Old French *meiche,* from Medieval Latin *myxa,* lamp wick, from Latin, nozzle of a lamp.]

match·board (măch′bôrd′, -bōrd′) *n.* A board cut with a tongue on one side and a matching groove on the other to fit with other boards of identical cut.

match·book (măch′book′) *n.* A small cardboard folder containing rows of detachable matches and a rough strip for striking them against.

match·box (măch′bŏks′) *n.* A box for holding matches, edged on one or two sides with a rough strip or treated paper for striking the matches against.

matchet. Variant of **machete.**

match·less (măch′lĭs) *adj.* Having no match or equal; peerless; unsurpassed: *matchless beauty.* **—match·less·ly** *adv.* **—match·less·ness** *n.*

match·lock (măch′lŏk′) *n.* **1.** A gunlock in which powder is ignited by a match. **2.** A musket having such a gunlock.

match·mak·er (măch′mā′kər) *n.* One who attempts to arrange marriages by bringing unmarried people together, either for personal satisfaction or, in some societies, as a profession. **—match·mak·ing** *n. & adj.*

match·mark (măch′märk′) *n.* Any of several marks made on the mating components of a machine or engine to ensure that the components are assembled in the correct relative positions. *~tr.v.* **-marked, -marking, -marks.** To stamp such marks on (components).

match play *n.* The form of competition in golf in which the basis of the score is the number of holes won by each side rather than the number of strokes taken. Compare **medal play.**

match point *n.* The final point needed to win a sports match, especially in tennis.

match·wood (măch′wood′) *n.* **1.** Wood in small pieces or splinters suitable especially for making matches. **2.** Splinters.

mate¹ (māt) *n.* **1. a.** Either of a conjugal pair of animals or birds. **b.** Either of a pair of animals brought together for breeding. **2.** A spouse. **3.** A person with whom one is in close association. Often used in combination. **4.** Either of a matched pair: *the mate to this glove.* **5.** *Chiefly British.* **a.** *Slang.* A friend. **b.** An informal form of address used to men. **6.** A deck officer on a merchant ship ranking

"A PAINTING ON A WALL SHOULD BE LIKE A BOUQUET OF FLOWERS"

The artist whose use of color and simple shapes influenced the course of 20th-century art

Matisse's use of pure color and simple shapes, and his exquisite sense of design, made him a dominant influence on 20th-century art. He believed that color should parallel light in nature. A painting on a wall, he said, should be like a bouquet of flowers in an interior.

With André Derain he led the Fauvist movement (1905–8), from whose bold use of colors he developed his characteristic simplified style in which figures, objects, and background all form part of a flat, brightly colored, decorative pattern. In his *Notes of a Painter*

(1908), he wrote that he was seeking an art of balance, purity, and serenity "devoid of troubling or depressing subject matter."

Matisse's style evolved from the contrast of patterns in *Odalisque with Raised Hand* (1920), through simplified interiors with plants and women, to its final extreme of large colored-paper collage works, the most notable of which are *Jazz: Cavalier and Clown* (1947) and *The Snail* (1953).

Among his other works are *Open Window, Collioure*

(Fauvist period, 1905), *Bonheur de Vivre* (1906), *Bathers with a Turtle* (1908), *The Dance* (1909), and the *Red Room* (1948). In 1949 he designed the stained-glass windows and murals for the Dominican Chapel of the Rosary in Vence, a work that he considered to be the summation of his career as an artist. But he will be chiefly remembered for his brilliant use of color and line drawings of the human figure, which he perfected by shifting the emphasis from powerful muscles to the body's pure outlines.

THE DANCE *In these murals (1930–32), which are now in the Museum of Modern Art, Paris, Matisse refined his art until reduced to its simplest and purest state.*

below the master. **7.** In some professions, an assistant: *a plumber's mate.*
~*v.* **mated, mating, mates.** —*tr.* **1.** To pair (animals) for breeding. **2.** To unite in marriage. **3.** To join closely; pair; couple. **4.** To connect (gear wheels, machine parts, or the like) together so that parts interlock. —*intr.* **1.** To pair for reproduction; breed. **2.** To become mated; join together. **3.** To become joined in marriage. **4.** To fit or interlock exactly. Used of gears, machine parts, and the like. [Middle English, from Middle Low German *mate, gemate,* companion.]
mate² *n. Chess.* A checkmate *(see).*
~*v.* **mated, mating, mates.** *Chess.* —*tr.* To checkmate. —*intr.* To achieve a checkmate: *White mated in 20 moves.* [Middle English *mat,* from Old French, short for *eschec mat,* CHECKMATE.]
ma·té (mä′tā′) *n.* **1.** An evergreen tree, *Ilex paraguayensis,* of South America, where it is widely cultivated. **2.** A mildly stimulant beverage, popular in South America, made from the dried leaves of this tree. Also called "Paraguay tea," "yerba maté." [American Spanish *maté,* alteration (influenced by *té,* tea) of Quechua *mate,* beverage.]
mate·lot (măt′lō) *n. Chiefly British Slang.* A sailor. [French.]
mat·e·lote (măt′l-ōt′) *n.* **1.** A wine sauce for fish. **2.** Fish stewed in such a sauce. [French *(sauce) matelote,* "sailor (sauce)."]
ma·ter (mā′tər) *n. British Slang.* Mother. Now used only humorously. [Latin *māter.*]
ma·ter·fa·mil·i·as (mā′tər-fə-mĭl′ē-əs) *n., pl.* **matresfamilias** (mā′trēz-). The mother of a family. [Latin : *māter,* mother + *familias,* archaic genitive of *familia,* FAMILY.]
ma·te·ri·al (mə-tîr′ē-əl) *n.* **1.** The substance or substances out of which a thing is or may be constructed: *raw material; building material.* **2.** The basic elements, such as factual data, plans, and ideas, to be refined and made or incorporated into a finished effort: *material for a novel.* **3. materials.** Tools or apparatus for the performance of a given task: *writing materials.* **4.** Fabric or cloth. **5.** A person having sufficient qualities for a specified job or level of achievement: *a competent athlete but not world-record material.*
~*adj.* **1.** Composed of or pertaining to physical substances; relating to matter; corporeal. **2.** Of, pertaining to, or affecting the enjoyment of physical well-being: *material comfort.* **3.** Of or concerned with the physical as distinct from the intellectual or spiritual. **4.** Of substantial or crucial importance: *a material part of the plan.* **5.** *Law.* Relevant to or having significant bearing upon the case: *a material witness.* **6.** *Philosophy.* Of or pertaining to the matter of reasoning rather than the form. —See Synonyms at **relevant.** [Middle English, from Old French *materiel,* from Late Latin *māteriālis,* from *māteria,* matter.] —**ma·te·ri·al·ness** *n.*
ma·te·ri·al·ism (mə-tîr′ē-ə-lĭz′əm) *n.* **1.** *Philosophy.* **a.** The theory or doctrine that physical matter in its movements and modifications is the only reality and that everything in the universe, including thought, feeling, mind, and will, can be explained in terms of physical laws. Compare **idealism.** **b.** The theory or doctrine that physical well-being constitutes the greatest good and highest value in

life. **2.** An excessive devotion to worldly rather than spiritual concerns and especially to the acquisition of material possessions. —**ma·te·ri·al·ist** *adj. & n.* —**ma·te·ri·al·is·tic** (mə-tîr′ē-ə-lĭs′tĭk) *adj.* —**ma·te·ri·al·is·ti·cal·ly** *adv.*
ma·te·ri·al·i·ty (mə-tîr′ē-ăl′ə-tē) *n., pl.* **-ties. 1.** The state or quality of being material. **2.** Matter; physical substance.
ma·te·ri·al·ize (mə-tîr′ē-ə-līz′) *v.* **-ized, -izing, -izes.** —*tr.* **1.** To invest with material or physical characteristics; cause to become real or actual: *By building the house he materialized his dream.* **2.** To cause to adopt materialistic values. —*intr.* **1.** To assume material or effective form: *The promised reinforcements did not materialize.* **2.** To take form or shape. **3.** To take bodily form or shape. Used of a ghost, spirit, or the like. —**ma·te·ri·al·i·za·tion** *n.* —**ma·te·ri·al·iz·er** *n.*

Usage: Materialize as an intransitive verb has the primary sense "to assume material form" or, more generally, "to take effective shape": *If our plans materialize, we will be independent for life.* Though it is well established in the sense "appear" or "happen," as in *Three more witnesses testified, but no new evidence materialized,* such a usage is not acceptable to most traditionalists. See also Usage note at **transpire.**
ma·te·ri·al·ly (mə-tîr′ē-ə-lē) *adv.* **1.** *Philosophy.* With regard to matter as distinguished from form. **2.** To a significant extent or degree; importantly. **3.** With regard to the physical world.
ma·te·ri·a med·i·ca (mə-tîr′ē-ə mĕd′ĭ-kə) *n. Medicine.* **1.** The study of medicinal drugs and their sources, preparation, and use. **2.** A substance used in preparing medicines or as a medicine. [Latin, "medical material."]
ma·te·ri·el, ma·té·ri·el (mə-tîr′ē-ĕl′) *n.* **1.** The equipment, apparatus, and supplies, such as guns and ammunition, of a military force. **2.** The equipment, apparatus, and supplies of any organization. [French, from *matériel,* MATERIAL (adjective).]
ma·ter·nal (mə-tûr′nəl) *adj.* **1.** Pertaining to or characteristic of a mother or motherhood; motherly: *maternal instinct.* **2.** Received or inherited from one's mother: *a maternal trait.* **3.** Related through one's mother: *my maternal uncle.* [Middle English, from Old French *maternel,* from Latin *māternus,* from *māter,* mother.] —**ma·ter·nal·ly** *adv.*
ma·ter·ni·ty (mə-tûr′nə-tē) *n.* **1.** The state of being a mother; motherhood. **2.** The feelings or characteristics associated with being a mother; motherliness.
~*adj.* Associated with or adapted for pregnancy and childbirth: *a maternity dress.* [French *maternité,* from Medieval Latin *māternitās* (stem *māternitāt-*), from *māternus,* MATERNAL.]
mat·ey (mā′tē) *adj. Chiefly British Informal.* Sociable; friendly. —**mat·ey·ness, mat·i·ness** *n.* —**mat·i·ly** *adv.*
math (măth) *n.* Mathematics.
math·e·mat·i·cal (măth′ə-măt′ĭ-kəl) *adj.* Also **math·e·mat·ic** (-măt′ĭk). **1.** Of or pertaining to mathematics. **2.** Precise; rigorous; exact. [Old French *mathematique,* from Latin *mathēmaticus,* from Greek

mathēmatikos, from *mathēma,* science, from *manthanein* (stem *math*-), to learn.] —**math·e·mat·i·cal·ly** *adv.*

mathematical induction *n.* A principle and method of proof in mathematics. See **induction.**

mathematical logic *n.* **Symbolic logic** *(see).*

math·e·ma·ti·cian (măth'ə-mə-tĭsh'ən). *n.* A person skilled or learned in mathematics.

math·e·mat·ics (măth'ə-măt'ĭks) *n.* **1.** *Used with a singular verb.* The study of number, form, arrangement, and associated relationships, using rigorously defined literal, numerical, and operational symbols. **2.** *Used with a plural verb.* The application of mathematics to a calculation or problem. [Probably from French *(les) mathématiques,* from Latin *mathēmatica* (neuter plural), from Greek *(ta) mathēmatika.* See **mathematical.**]

Math·er (măth'ər), **Increase** (1639-1723). Puritan clergyman and author. He and his son, **Cotton** (1663-1728), wielded enormous theological and political influence in Boston and the colony of Massachusetts. Both were staunch upholders of the old Puritan theocracy and of the established order in church and state. The Mathers have often been accused of inciting the hysteria that surrounded the Salem witchcraft trials, but Cotton played only a small role in the episode and Increase wrote the first outspoken attack against the practices of the witchcraft court.

Ma·thi·as (mə-thī'əs), **Robert Bruce,** known as "Bob" (1930-). U.S. athlete. He was the Olympics decathlon champion in both 1948 and 1952, the first person to win the gold medal in that grueling event in successive games.

maths (măths) *n. Chiefly British.* Mathematics.

Ma·thu·ra (mŭt'ər-ə). Also **Mut·tra** (mŭt'rə). City in Uttar Pradesh, northern India. On the Jumna River, it is the region's commercial center and, as the traditional birthplace of Krishna, a place of pilgrimage for Hindus. The Mathura school of Indian art flourished here (2nd to 5th century A.D.).

Mathurai. See **Madurai.**

ma·til·da (mə-tĭl'də) *n. Australian Informal.* A bushman's pack or bundle. [From *Matilda,* woman's name.]

Ma·til·da (mə-tĭl'də), also known as "Empress Maud" (1102-67). Queen of England (1141-53). The daughter of Henry I, she married Emperor Henry V (1114) and, after his death, Geoffrey of Anjou (1128), by whom she bore Henry II. When her cousin Stephen was elected king, she waged civil war against him and was crowned queen in 1141.

ma·til·i·ja poppy (mə-tĭl'ē-hä') *n.* A shrubby plant, *Romneya coulteri,* of California and Mexico, having very large, solitary white flowers. [From *Matilija* Canyon, California.]

mat·in (măt'n) *adj.* Also **mat·in·al** (măt'n-əl). **1.** Of or pertaining to matins. **2.** Of or pertaining to the early morning. [From MATINS.]

mat·i·nee, mat·i·née (măt'n-ā') *n. Abbr.* **mat.** A concert, theatrical performance, or showing of a film given in the daytime, usually in the afternoon. [French *matinée,* "morning," early performance, from Old French *matinee,* from *matin,* morning, from Latin *(tempus) mātūtīnum,* morning (time), from *mātūtīnus,* of the morning, from *Mātūta,* goddess of dawn.]

mat·ins (măt'nz) *n.* Also *chiefly British* **mat·tins.** *Used with a singular or plural verb.* **1.** In the Roman Catholic Church, the office that together with lauds constitutes the first of the seven **canonical hours** *(see).* **2.** In the Anglican Church, **Morning Prayer** *(see).* **3.** *Poetic.* The morning song of a bird. [Middle English *matines,* from Old French, from Medieval Latin *(vigiliae) mātūtīnae,* morning (watches, vigils).] See **matinee.**]

Ma·tisse (mä-tēs'), **Henri** (1869-1954). French painter and sculptor. After studying under Gustave Moreau (1862-98), he led the artistic group of fauves after 1905, with colorful, strongly patterned, and often distorted portraits, still lifes, and nudes. He was also influenced by impressionist, cubist, and Islamic art. His works include *The Pink Nude* and *Woman with the Hat.*

Ma·to Gros·so (măt'ə grō'sō). A state in west-central Brazil. Its name means "thick forest," but the forest is largely confined to its river valleys, with extensive wooded savannas between. The state is being opened up, with new roads, development of a beef industry, and exploitation of its rich mineral deposits. Cuiabá is the capital.

mat·rass, mat·trass (măt'rəs) *n.* A glass vessel with a long neck, formerly used in chemistry for distilling. [French *matras*†.]

ma·tres·fa·mil·i·as. Plural of **materfamilias.**

matri- *prefix.* Indicates mother; for example, **matriclinous.** [Latin *māter,* mother.]

ma·tri·arch (mā'trē-ärk') *n.* **1.** A woman who rules a family, clan, or tribe. **2.** A woman who dominates any group or activity. [MATRI- + -ARCH.] —**ma·tri·ar·chal** (mā'trē-är'kəl), **ma·tri·ar·chic** (mā'trē-är'kĭk) *adj.* —**ma·tri·ar·chism** *n.*

ma·tri·ar·chate (mā'trē-är'kĭt, -kāt') *n.* **1.** A matriarchy. **2.** A hypothetical stage in the evolution of primitive society in which authority is held by matriarchs.

ma·tri·ar·chy (mā'trē-är'kē) *n., pl.* **-chies.** A social system in which women are dominant and descent is traced through the mother of the family.

mat·ri·cide (măt'rə-sīd') *n.* **1.** The act of killing one's mother. **2.** One who kills his mother. [Latin *mātricīda* (person) and *mātricīdium* (act) : MATRI- + -CIDE.] —**mat·ri·cid·al** (măt'rə-sīd'l) *adj.*

mat·ri·cli·nous (măt'rə-klī'nəs) *adj.* Having predominantly maternal hereditary traits. Said of plants and animals. Compare **patriclinous.** [MATRI- + -clinous, from Greek -klinēs, "leaning," from klinein, to lean.]

ma·tric·u·lant (mə-trĭk'yə-lənt) *n.* A person who matriculates or is a candidate for matriculation.

ma·tric·u·late (mə-trĭk'yə-lāt') *v.* **-lated, -lating, -lates.** —*tr.* To admit formally to membership of a college, university, or the like. —*intr.* To be so admitted.
~*n.* One who has matriculated. [Medieval Latin *mātriculāre,* to enroll, from *mātricula,* list, roll, from *mātrīx,* list, originally, womb, source. See **matrix.**]

ma·tric·u·la·tion (mə-trĭk'yə-lā'shən) *n.* **1.** The act or process of matriculating. **2.** The qualification acquired by matriculating.

mat·ri·lin·e·al (măt'rə-lĭn'ē-əl) *adj.* Pertaining to, based upon, or tracing ancestral descent through the maternal line rather than through the paternal. Compare **patrilineal.**

mat·ri·lo·cal (măt'rə-lō'kəl) *adj. Anthropology.* Designating or following a system of marriage in primitive societies whereby the couple goes to live in the home territory of the wife's kin group or clan. Compare **patrilocal.** —**mat·ri·lo·cal·ly** *adv.*

mat·ri·mo·ny (măt'rə-mō'nē) *n., pl.* **-nies.** **1.** The state of being married. **2.** The sacrament or rite of marriage. **3. a.** A card game in which the combination of a king and queen is needed to win. **b.** Such a winning combination. —See Synonyms at **marriage.** [Middle English, from Norman French *matrimonie,* from Latin *mātrimōnium,* marriage, "motherhood" : MATRI- + -mōnium, abstract noun suffix.] —**mat·ri·mo·ni·al** (măt'rə-mō'nē-əl) *adj.* —**mat·ri·mo·ni·al·ly** *adv.*

matrimony vine *n.* Any of various often thorny shrubs of the genus *Lycium,* some species of which are cultivated for their purplish flowers and brightly colored berries. Also called "boxthorn."

ma·trix (mā'trĭks) *n., pl.* **matrices** (mā'trə-sēz', măt'rə-) or **-trixes.** **1.** The environment or surrounding substance within which something originates, develops, or is contained: *contented children nurtured in the matrix of parental love.* **2.** The womb. No longer in technical usage. **3.** *Anatomy.* **a.** The formative cells of a tooth, fingernail, or toenail. **b.** The substance between the cells of animal or plant tissue. **4.** *Geology.* The fine-grained rock material in which a fossil or crystal is embedded. **5.** A mold or die. **6.** The principal metal in an alloy, such as the iron in steel. **7.** A binding substance, such as cement in concrete. **8.** *Mathematics.* A rectangular array of numerical or algebraic quantities treated as an algebraic entity. **9.** The network of intersections between input and output leads in a computer, functioning as an encoder or decoder. **10.** *Printing.* **a.** A metal plate used for casting type faces. **b.** A mold used in stereotyping and designed to receive positive impressions of type or illustrations from which metal plates can be cast. In this sense, also called "mat." [Latin *mātrix,* womb, originally, pregnant animal, from *māter,* mother.]

matrix mechanics *n. Physics. Used with a singular verb.* A formulation of quantum mechanics developed by Heisenberg using matrix algebra to determine the behavior of physical systems, mathematically equivalent to **wave mechanics** *(see).* Physical quantities are represented by operators in matrix element form.

ma·tron (mā'trən) *n.* **1.** A married woman; especially, a mother of mature age with established dignity and social position. **2.** A woman who acts as a supervisor or monitor in a public institution, as a school, hospital, or prison. [Middle English, from Old French *matrone,* from Latin *mātrōna,* matron, wife, from *māter,* mother.] —**ma·tron·al** *adj.* —**ma·tron·li·ness** *n.* —**ma·tron·ly** *adj. & adv.*

matron of honor *n., pl.* **matrons of honor** *n.* A married woman serving as chief attendant of the bride at a wedding. Compare **bridesmaid, maid of honor.**

matronymic. Variant of **metronymic.**

Mat·su (măt'sōō', mät'-). Island in the East China Sea, part of Taiwan. It is *c.* 19 kilometers (12 miles) off the southeastern coast of mainland China.

matt, mat, matte (măt) *n.* A dull, often rough finish, as on glass, metal, or paper.
—*tr.v.* **matted, matting, matts.** To produce a dull finish on.
~*adj.* Having a dull surface; not shiny. [French *mat,* "dead." See **checkmate.**]

Matt. Matthew (New Testament).

matte¹ (măt) *n. Metallurgy.* A mixture of a metal with its oxides and sulfides, produced by smelting certain sulfide ores. Also called "regulus." [French, from dialectal *mate*†, a lump.]

matte². Variant of **matt.**

mat·ted (măt'ĭd) *adj.* **1.** Covered with or made from mats. **2.** Tangled in a dense mass: *matted hair.* —**mat·ted·ly** *adv.*

mat·ter (măt'ər) *n.* **1. a.** Something that occupies space, can be perceived by one or more senses, and constitutes a physical body or the universe as a whole; something corporeal as distinguished from something spiritual or intellectual. **b.** *Physics.* An entity displaying gravitation and inertia when at rest as well as when in motion. **2.** A specified type of substance: *inorganic matter.* **3.** Discharge or waste from a living organism, as pus or feces. **4.** The actual substance of thought or expression; the theme of what is expressed as distinguished from the manner in which it is stated or conveyed. **5.** *Philosophy.* In Aristotelian and scholastic use, that which is in itself undifferentiated and formless and which, as the subject of change and development, receives form and becomes substance and experience. **6.** *Law.* **a.** Something that must be proved or is the subject of litigation. **b.** Statements, allegations, or the like brought before the court. **7.** Something that is the subject of consideration or attention; a concern or affair, especially of a specified kind: *a personal matter. In matters of finance his advice is usually reliable.* **8. a.** A

circumstance tending to evoke a specified response: *a matter for regret.* **b.** Something largely dependent on or likely to be determined by a specified factor: *a matter of luck.* **c.** A situation presenting a choice that depends on the application of a specified faculty: *a matter of conscience; a matter of opinion.* **9.** A particular factor adversely affecting a person or thing; a trouble or difficulty: *What's the matter with the car?* **10.** An indefinite or approximate quantity, amount, or extent: *a matter of a few hours.* **11.** Something that is printed or otherwise set down in writing: *reading matter.* **12.** *Printing.* **a.** Composed type. **b.** Material to be set in type. **—for that matter.** With regard to that: *For that matter, we didn't know when to come.* **—no matter.** Irrespective or regardless of: *No matter what the time is, come!*
~*intr.v.* **mattered, -tering, -ters. 1.** To be of importance: *It matters very much.* **2.** To suppurate. [Middle English *matere,* from Norman French, from Latin *mātēria,* matter.]

Mat·ter·horn (măt'ər-hôrn'). Mountain (4,477 meters; 14,688 feet) in the Pennine Alps, on the Swiss-Italian border near Zermatt. Its distinctive pyramidal crest was first climbed (1865) by the Englishman Edward Whymper (1840–1911).

matter of course *n.* An expected, natural, or logical outcome. **—mat·ter-of-course** (măt'ər-əv-kôrs', -kōrs') *adj.*

matter of fact *n.* That which pertains to fact as opposed to opinion; especially, the establishing of the truth of certain alleged facts in the course of a judicial inquiry.

mat·ter-of-fact (măt'ər-əv-făkt') *adj.* Adhering to or solely concerned with facts; prosaic, unemotional, or unimaginative: *discussed her divorce in a very matter-of-fact way.* **—mat·ter-of-fact·ly** *adv.* **—mat·ter-of-fact·ness** *n.*

Mat·the·an (mă-thē'ən, mə-) *adj.* Of, pertaining to, or designating the Gospel of Saint Matthew. [MATTHE(W) + -AN.]

Mat·thew (măth'yōō) *n. Abbr.* **Matt.** A book of the New Testament, the first Gospel, attributed to Saint Matthew.

Matthew, Saint. One of the Apostles of Christ and traditionally the author of the first Gospel.

Matthew Paris. See Matthew **Paris.**

Mat·thi·as (mə-thī'əs), **Saint.** One of the Apostles of Jesus, chosen by lot to take the place of Judas Iscariot. Acts 1:23–26.

mat·ting[1] (măt'ĭng) *n.* **1.** A coarsely woven fabric used for covering floors and similar purposes. **2.** Mat-making.

matting[2] *n.* **1.** A dull surface or finish. **2.** A border or mat used for framing a picture.

mattins *Chiefly British.* Variant of **matins.**

mat·tock (măt'ək) *n.* A digging tool with a blade set at right angles to the handle and used with a downward motion. [Middle English *mattok,* Old English *mattuc†.*]

mat·tress (măt'rĭs) *n.* **1.** A rectangular pad of heavy cloth enclosing soft material, such as foam rubber, and sometimes coiled springs, used as or on a bed. **2.** A closely woven mat of brush and poles used to protect an embankment, dike, or dam from erosion. **3.** A raft or slab made of concrete or metal, used as a foundation. **4.** A network of reinforcing rods or expanded metal forming the basis of reinforced concrete. [Middle English *materas,* from Old French, from Italian *materasso,* from Arabic *maṭraḥ,* place where something is thrown, from *ṭaraḥa,* to throw, fling.]

mat·u·rate (măch'ōō-rāt') *v.* **-rated, -rating, -rates.** —*intr.* **1.** To mature, ripen, or develop. **2.** To suppurate. —*tr.* To cause to maturate. [Latin *mātūrāre,* to mature, from *mātūrus,* MATURE.] **—mat·u·ra·tive** *adj.*

mat·u·ra·tion (măch'ōō-rā'shən) *n.* **1.** The process of becoming mature; development or ripening: *the maturation of the personality.* **2.** *Biology.* **a.** Formation of a sex cell, **gametogenesis** *(see).* **b.** The final differentiation processes in biological systems, such as the final ripening of a seed. **3.** Discharge of pus, **suppuration** *(see).*

ma·ture (mə-tyŏŏr', -tŏŏr', -chŏŏr') *adj.* **-turer, -turest. 1. a.** Complete and finished in natural growth or development: *a mature cell.* **b.** Fully developed; ripe: *a mature cheese.* **c.** Fully established: *a mature garden.* **2. a.** Having reached a stage of intellectual and emotional development usually associated with adulthood: *mature for her age.* **b.** Characteristic of one who has reached such a stage. **3.** Worked out fully by the mind; carefully considered: *a mature piece of criticism.* **4.** *Finance.* At the limit of its time; payable; due: *a mature bond.* **5.** *Geology.* Designating a landscape in which hills and valleys predominate over flat areas as a result of erosion.
~*v.* **matured, -turing, -tures.** —*tr.* **1.** To bring to full development; ripen. **2.** To work out fully in the mind: *was able to mature his thoughts.* —*intr.* **1.** To evolve toward or attain full development: *Judgment matures with age.* **2.** *Finance.* To become due. Used of notes, bonds, or the like. [Middle English, from Latin *mātūrus,* timely.] **—ma·ture·ly** *adv.* **—ma·ture·ness** *n.*

ma·tur·i·ty (mə-tyŏŏr'ə-tē, -tŏŏr'ə-tē, -chŏŏr'ə-tē) *n., pl.* **-ties. 1.** The state or quality of being fully grown or fully developed. **2. a.** The time at which a note, bill, or bond is due. **b.** The state of a note, bill, or bond being due. **3.** *Geology.* The state of being mature. [Middle English *maturite,* from Latin *mātūritās* (stem *mātūritāt-*), from *mātūrus,* MATURE.]

ma·tu·ti·nal (mə-tōōt'n-əl, -tyōōt'n-əl, măch'ōō-tī'nəl) *adj.* Of pertaining to, or occurring in the morning; early. [Late Latin *mātūtīnālis,* from Latin *mātūtīnus,* from *Mātūta,* goddess of dawn.] **—ma·tu·ti·nal·ly** *adv.*

mat·zo (măt'sə) *n., pl.* **-zoth** (-sōth', -sōt', -sōs') or **-zos** (-səz, -səs, -sōz') or **-zot** (-sōt'). A brittle, flat piece of unleavened bread, eaten

Matterhorn *Perhaps the most spectacular of the Alps, this pyramidal peak on the Swiss-Italian border was first climbed by the British mountaineer Edward Whymper in 1865.*

especially during the Passover. [Yiddish *matse,* from Hebrew *maṣṣah.*]

maud·lin (môd'lĭn) *adj.* **1.** Effusively sentimental. **2.** Tearfully emotional, especially because of drunkenness. [Alteration of Mary *Magdalene,* who was frequently depicted as a weeping penitent.] **—maud·lin·ly** *adv.*

Maugham (môm), **(William) Somerset** (1874–1965). British novelist and dramatist. Born in Paris and trained as a doctor, he wrote such realistic novels as *Liza of Lambeth* (1897), *Of Human Bondage* (1915), and *Cakes and Ale* (1930). He was also a popular dramatist and is perhaps most famous for his short stories.

mau·gre (mô'gər) *prep. Archaic.* In spite of; notwithstanding. [Middle English, in spite of, "to the displeasure of," from noun, "ill will," from Old French *maugré* (whence French *malgré*) : *mal,* bad, from Latin *malus* + *gré,* pleasure, from Latin *grātus,* pleasing.]

Mau·i (mou'ē). Second-largest island of Hawaii, between Molokai and the island of Hawaii. Maui consists of two mountainous masses. Its economy is based mainly on sugar cane and pineapples.

maul (môl) *n.* A heavy, long-handled hammer used to drive stakes, piles, or wedges.
~*tr.v.* **mauled, mauling, mauls. 1.** To handle roughly; bruise or mangle: *a hunter mauled by a bear.* **2.** To injure by or as if by beating: *badly mauled by his critics.* [Middle English *meall, mal,* from Old French *mail,* from Latin *malleus,* hammer.] **—maul·er** *n.*

Maul·din (môl'dĭn), **William Henry,** known as "Bill" (1921–81). U.S. cartoonist. He became famous in World War II for his realistic, bitterly comic drawings of front-line soldiers. After the Korean War, he became a political cartoonist for a Chicago newspaper. His drawings won him two Pulitzer Prizes (1944 and 1958).

maul·stick, mahl·stick (môl'stĭk') *n.* A long wooden stick used by painters to support the hand that holds the brush. [Partial translation and alteration of Dutch *maalstok* : *maalen,* to paint, from Middle Dutch *malen* + *stok,* STICK.]

Mau Mau (mou' mou') *n., pl.* **Mau Maus** or collectively **Mau Mau. 1.** A secret organization of Kikuyu tribesmen in Kenya that used terrorism during the 1950's with the aim of driving out white settlers and ending colonial rule. **2.** A member of this organization. [Origin obscure.]

Mau·na Ke·a (mou'nə kā'ə). Volcano, 4,208 meters (13,796 feet) high, in the south-central part of the island of Hawaii. It is the highest peak of the Hawaiian Islands.

Mauna Lo·a (lō'ə). Volcano in Hawaii Volcanoes National Park on the island of Hawaii. It is the world's largest volcano, rising to 4,170 meters (13,681 feet).

maund (mônd) *n.* Any of several Asian units of weight of varying amounts; especially, the official maund in India, equivalent to about 37 kilograms (82 pounds). [Hindi *mān,* from Persian, from Akkadian *manū,* designating a unit of weight. See **mina.**]

maun·der (môn'dər, môn'-) *intr.v.* **-dered, -dering, -ders. 1.** To talk incoherently or aimlessly. **2.** To move or act aimlessly or vaguely; wander. [Perhaps from obsolete *maunder†,* to beg.] **—maun·der·er** *n.* **—maun·der·ing·ly** *adv.*

Maun·dy (môn'dē) *n. Sometimes* **maundy.** In the Roman Catholic Church, the ceremony of washing the feet of twelve people on Maundy Thursday in commemoration of Jesus' washing of his apostles' feet at the Last Supper. [Middle English, from Old French *mandé,* a thing commanded, from Medieval Latin *mandātum,* the ceremony, "command," from the words of Christ in the first antiphon of Maundy Thursday, *Mandātum novum dō vōbis,* "A new commandment give I unto you" (John 13).]

Maundy Thursday *n.* The Thursday before Easter, commemorating Jesus' Last Supper. Also called "Holy Thursday."

Mau·pas·sant (mō′pä-säN′), **(Henri René Albert) Guy de** (1850–93). French novelist and short-story writer. While a civil servant, he was encouraged to write by Flaubert and produced his first success with *Boule de Suif* (1880). His works, mainly realistic short stories, examine hypocrisy, madness, the social world of Paris, and peasant life in Normandy.

Mau·re·ta·ni·a (môr′ə-tā′nē-ə, mōr′-). North African district of the Roman Empire, comprising the Atlas Mts. of Morocco and western Algeria and land to the north. Settled before 2000 B.C. by Maures (Moors), a Berber people, it fell to Rome *c.* 100 B.C. Arabs overran the area in the 7th century A.D., and by 1000 the Moors had spread into Spain and southwestward in Africa.

Mau·riac (môr-yäk′, môr′ē-äk′), **François** (1885–1970). French novelist. His works include *Le Baiser au Lépreux* (1922), *Le Noeud de Vipères* (1932), and his play *Asmodée* (1938). He was awarded the Nobel Prize for literature (1952).

Mau·ri·ta·ni·a (môr′ĭ-tā′nē-ə, mōr′-). A large, sparsely populated, mostly desert Islamic republic of northwestern Africa. Its only major fertile area is along the Senegal River, and most people live by stock rearing. The country, badly hit by the droughts of the 1970's, depends on exports of iron ore. Fish is also exported. The area was settled by Berbers from the north in about *c.* A.D. 1000, and their Arab-Berber descendants, the Moors, make up 75 percent of the population. The rest, mostly in the south, are black Africans. European traders plied the coast from the 15th century. The French took over the country (1860–1903) and governed it until it became fully independent in 1960. In 1964 it became a one-party state, and has been under military rule since 1979, the same year in which it renounced its claim to southern Western Sahara. Area, 1,030,700 square kilometers (397,956 square miles). Population, 1,600,000. Capital, Nouakchott. —**Mau·ri·ta·ni·an** *adj. & n.*

Mau·ri·tius (mô-rĭsh′əs, -ē-əs). Country in the Indian Ocean, comprising the mountainous island of Mauritius and several tiny dependencies. The economy rests on the growing and processing of sugar cane, but tea and tobacco growing, small-scale manufacturing, fishing, and tourism are increasingly important. The first European settlers were Dutch (1598–1710). During French occupation (1715–1810), black African slaves were imported to work the sugar plantations. Creoles (of French-African descent) now make up about one third of the population. The British captured the islands (1810), abolished slavery, and brought in Indian contract laborers, whose descendants now account for some two thirds of Mauritians. Tension between the two groups and high unemployment are major problems for the country, independent within the Commonwealth since 1968. Area, 2,045 square kilometers (790 square miles). Population, 1,000,000. Capital, Port Louis. —**Mau·ri·tian** *n. & adj.*

Mau·rois (môr-wä′), **André**, born Émile Herzog (1885–1967). French biographer and novelist. Having served with the British army during World War I, he produced two perceptive portrayals of the British character with *Les Silences du Colonel Bramble* (1918) and *Les Discours du Docteur O'Grady* (1921).

Mau·ser (mou′zər) *n.* A trademark for a repeating rifle or pistol. [After Paul (1838–1914) and Wilhelm (1834–82) *Mauser*, German arms manufacturers, who invented it.]

mau·so·le·um (mô′sə-lē′əm, mô′zə-) *n., pl.* **-leums** or **-lea** (-lē′ə). A large and stately tomb or a building housing such a tomb or tombs. [Latin *mausōlēum*, from Greek *mausōleion*, originally the tomb of *Mausolos*, satrap of Caria (377–353 B.C.), at Halicarnassus.] —**mau·so·le·an** *adj.*

mauve (mōv) *n.* **1.** Brilliant violet to strong or brilliant purple to moderate reddish purple. **2. a.** A mauve dye. **b.** Mauveine. [French *mauve*, "mallow(-colored)," from Latin *malva*, mallow.] —**mauve** *adj.*

mauv·eine (mō′vēn′, -vĭn) *n.* A purple dye made from aniline; the first synthetic dye. Also called "mauve," "Perkin's mauve." [MAUVE + -INE.]

ma·ven, ma·vin (mā′vən) *n.* A person who has special knowledge or experience; expert. [Yiddish *meyvn*, from Hebrew *mēbhīn*.]

mav·er·ick (măv′ər-ĭk, măv′rĭk) *n.* **1.** An unbranded calf or colt that has strayed from the herd, traditionally considered the property of the first person who brands it. **2. a.** One who refuses to abide by the dictates of his group; a dissenter. **b.** One who resists adherence to or affiliation with any single organized group or faction; an independent. Often used adjectively: *maverick politicians.* [After Samuel A. *Maverick* (1803–70), Texas cattleman who did not brand his calves.]

ma·vis (mā′vĭs) *n.* A bird, the **song thrush** *(see).* [Middle English *mavys*, from Old French *mauvis†*.]

ma·vour·neen, ma·vour·nin (mə-vŏŏr′nēn′) *n. Irish.* My darling. [Irish *mo mhuirnín* : *mo*, my + *muirnín*, darling, diminutive of *muirn*, delight, from Old Irish, revels, banquet, tumult.]

maw (mô) *n.* **1.** The stomach, mouth, jaws, or gullet of a voracious carnivore. **2.** Something suggestive of a gaping opening or the appetite of a voracious animal. [Middle English *mawe*, Old English *maga.*]

mawk·ish (mô′kĭsh) *adj.* **1.** Excessively and objectionably sentimental: *a mawkish farewell performance.* **2.** Sickening or insipid in taste. [From Middle English *mawke*, variant of *magot*, MAGGOT.] —**mawk·ish·ly** *adv.* —**mawk·ish·ness** *n.*

max. maximum.

max·i (măk′sē) *n.* **1.** An ankle- or floor-length skirt or coat. **2.** Something larger or longer than other members of its class. Often used adjectively and in combination: *a maxicoat.* [Short for MAXIMUM.]

max·il·la (măk-sĭl′ə) *n., pl.* **-lae** (-sĭl′ē) or **-las. 1.** *Anatomy.* Either of a pair of bones forming part of the upper jaw. See **skull. 2.** *Zoology.* Either of two laterally moving appendages behind the mandibles in insects and most other arthropods, used in feeding. [Latin, "lower jaw," akin to *māla†*, upper jaw. See also **malar.**] —**max·il·lar** (măk′sə-lər, măk-sĭl′ər), **max·il·lar·y** (măk′sə-lĕr′ē) *adj.*

max·il·li·ped (măk-sĭl′ə-pĕd′) *n.* The first pair or first three pairs of appendages in crustaceans, situated behind the maxillae and used for feeding. [MAXILL(A) + -PED.]

max·im (măk′sĭm) *n.* A succinct formulation of some fundamental principle or rule of conduct. —See Synonyms at **saying.** [Middle English, from Old French *maxime*, from Medieval Latin (*prōpositiō) maxima*, "greatest proposition," philosophical term for a fundamental axiom, from *maximus*, greatest.]

max·i·mal (măk′sə-məl) *adj.* **1.** Of, pertaining to, or consisting of a maximum. **2.** Being the greatest or highest possible. **3.** *Mathematics.* Designating an element in an ordered set that is followed by no other.
~*n. Mathematics.* A maximal element. —**max·i·mal·ly** *adv.*

max·i·mal·ist (măk′sə-mə-lĭst) *n.* **1.** *Sometimes* **Maximalist.** One who advocates direct revolutionary action to secure social and political gains. **2.** One who rejects all compromise and insists on all his demands being met. [French *maximaliste*, probably from English MAXIMAL.]

Max·im gun (măk′sĭm) *n.* The first automatic repeating gun. [After Sir Hiram *Maxim* (1840–1916), British engineer who invented it.]

Max·i·mil·ian (măk′sə-mĭl′yən), **(Ferdinand Joseph)** (1832–67). Emperor of Mexico (1864–67). The younger brother of Francis Joseph I of Austria, he accepted the title Emperor of Mexico from the French, who had recently captured the country. Lacking popular support, he was captured and shot by the republicans when the French withdrew under American pressure.

max·i·min (măk′sē-mĭn′) *n.* **1.** *Mathematics.* The highest of a set of minimum values. **2.** In games theory, the selection of a strategy for a member of the group that gives the maximum value for the member's minimum gains. Compare **minimax.** [*Maxi*mum + *mini*mum.]

max·i·mize (măk′sə-mīz′) *tr.v.* **-mized, -mizing, -mizes. 1.** To make as great as possible; increase to a maximum. **2.** To represent as having the greatest degree of importance or value; magnify. **3.** *Mathematics.* To find a maximum value of (a function). —**max·i·mi·za·tion** *n.* —**max·i·miz·er** *n.*

max·i·mum (măk′sə-məm) *n., pl.* **-mums** or **-ma** (-mə). *Abbr.* **max. 1. a.** The greatest possible quantity, degree, or number. **b.** The time or period during which the highest point or degree is attained. **2.** An upper limit stipulated by law or otherwise fixed or agreed upon: *a price maximum; a wage increase maximum.* **3.** *Astronomy.* **a.** The moment when a variable star is most brilliant. **b.** The magnitude of the star at such a moment. **4.** *Mathematics.* **a.** The value of a function that is not exceeded by neighboring values. **b.** The greatest value assumed by a function within some subset of its domain of definition. **c.** The largest number in a set.
~*adj. Abbr.* **max. 1.** Having, being, or showing the greatest quantity or the highest degree that has been or can be attained: *maximum temperature.* **2.** Of, pertaining to, or making up a maximum or maximums: *a maximum number in a series.* [Latin *maximum*, "greatest (quantity)," neuter of *maximus*, greatest.]

maximum permissible dose. *Physics.* See **dose** (sense 5).

ma·xixe (mə-shēsh′, mə-shē′shə) *n.* A Brazilian dance similar to the two-step. [Brazilian Portuguese *maxixe†.*]

max·well (măks′wĕl′, -wəl) *n. Abbr.* **Mx** A unit of magnetic flux in the centimeter-gram-second electromagnetic system, equal to the flux perpendicularly intersecting an area of one square centimeter in a region where the magnetic induction is one gauss. [After James Clerk MAXWELL.]

Max·well (măks′wĕl′, -wəl), **Elsa** (1883–1963). U.S. columnist and professional party-giver. Her parties were known not only for the glittering guests she managed to attract but also for the gimmicks and novelties she planned to keep the "prejet set" amused. Among these gimmicks was the scavenger hunt game.

Maxwell, James Clerk (1831–79). British physicist. Educated at Edinburgh and Cambridge, he published in 1873 the *Treatise on Electricity and Magnetism*, expounding a set of four equations that were applicable to electricity, magnetism, and light. He predicted the existence of radio waves and worked on the kinetic theory of gases and the study of color perception.

may¹ (mā) *v.* Past **might** (mīt), present **may** or *archaic* **mayest** (mā′-ĭst) or **mayst** (māst) (for second person singular). Used as an auxiliary, followed by an infinitive without *to* or with the infinitive understood, to indicate: **1.** A requesting or granting of permission: *May I take a swim? You may.* **2.** Possibility: *It may rain this afternoon.* **3.** Ability or capacity, with the force of *can: if I may be of service.* **4.** Obligation or function, with the force of *must* or *shall*, in statutes, deeds, and other legal documents. **5.** Desire or fervent wish. Used chiefly in exclamatory phrases: *Long may he live!* **6.** Purpose or result in clauses introduced by *so that: express ing ideas so that the average person may understand.* **7.** Contingent or conditional: *Whatever you may think, I still believe he's innocent.* **8.** Less abrupt or pointed questioning: *How old may this little girl*

Maya

LOST CITIES IN THE CENTRAL AMERICAN JUNGLE

A civilization that excelled in mathematics, astronomy, and architecture

Nineteenth-century explorers in the lowland jungles of Mexico and Guatemala were amazed to find massive stone ruins swamped by vegetation. They were remains of the Maya civilization, which began to emerge about 2000 B.C. and reached a peak in the period A.D. 300–900.

The three million Maya, living in hamlets surrounding the large temple-cities, were ruled by hereditary chiefs and priests skilled in the arts, astronomy, and mathematics. Their mathematics—not equaled by Europe for several centuries—was based on a unit of 20 and incorporated the concept of zero, unknown to the Greeks and Romans. They calculated the solar year and lunar months accurately enough to predict eclipses. Their written literature began to be deciphered in the late 20th century.

Despite the Maya's failure to invent the true arch, their stone cities, with pyramids 60 meters (200 feet) high and huge palaces, were masterpieces of architecture. They also built great courts, some more than 80 meters (over 250 feet) long, used for a ritual ball game, *pok-ta-pok*.

In line with then-prevailing standards of beauty, Maya artists gave the figures in wall paintings and sculptures a cross-eyed look. Some figures have flattened, egg-shaped heads with receding chins and teeth filed down flat. Some have nose plugs and decorative fillings in the teeth.

In about 900, perhaps as a result of peasant revolts, the old cities were abandoned. The center of civilization moved north to the Yucatán and Chichén Itzá was made the capital. In the 16th and 17th centuries, parts of Maya lands were conquered by the Spanish, but the Maya remained unsubdued and today number about two million. Many of their old traditions are mixed with Christianity taught them by Spanish missionaries.

DIFFERENT CONSTRUCTION *Like all Maya buildings, the Pyramid of the Soothsayer at Uxmal (above) had mortar used in its construction—unique on that continent then.*

MAYA WRITING *The symbols around the pictures in the codex, or folding-screen book (at left), are hieroglyphics, and the subject matter of this page is astrological.*

be? **—be that as it may.** Nevertheless; despite that. **—come what may.** Whatever happens. **—may as well.** To have no compelling reason not to. **—may well.** To be very likely. [Middle English *may*, past *mighte*, *moghte*, Old English *maeg* (first and third person singular), past *mighte*, *moghte*, infinitive *magan*, to be strong, be able, have permission.]

Usage: *May* and *might* are basically alike in meaning in the senses of possibility and permission; they differ principally in intensity, not in time. (This is because in modern usage these words are treated as subjunctive verbs, each capable of expressing present and future time, although *might* is, grammatically, the past tense of *may*.) *May* is stronger than *might* in both senses: *He may leave* suggests greater likelihood than *He might leave,* and *May I go?* is more forceful than the less importunate *Might I go? Might* is also used to signify obligation in statements containing a mild reproof: *You might show some gratitude.* In the past perfect *might* sometimes signifies a condition opposed to fact: *He might have succeeded if he had tried harder.* See also Usage note at **can.**

may² *n. British.* The **hawthorn** (see). Also called "may tree." [From **May.**]

May (mā) *n.* **1.** The fifth month of the year according to the Gregorian calendar. May has 31 days. See feature at **calendar. 2.** *Poetic.* The springtime of life; youth. **3.** The festivities of May Day. [Middle English, from Old French *Mai*, from Latin *Maius (mēnsis),* (the month) of *Maia*, Italic goddess.]

May, Cape. Peninsula in southern New Jersey, between Delaware Bay and the Atlantic Ocean. The cape is bisected by a canal that is part of the Delaware Intracoastal Waterway.

ma·ya (mä′yə) *n. Hinduism.* Illusion; especially, the visible material world conceived of as being purely illusory. [Sanskrit *māyā*†.]

Ma·ya (mä′yə) *n., pl.* **Mayas** or collectively **Maya. 1.** A member of an Indian people of southern Mexico and Central America whose civi-

lization reached its height in about A.D. 300–900. **2.** The language spoken by the Maya; Mayan. **—Ma·ya** *adj.*

Ma·ya·kov·sky (mī′ə-kôf′skē), **Vladimir** (1893–1930). Soviet poet and playwright. He combined experimental poetic techniques with Bolshevik propaganda and was a leading member of the futurist movement. His works include the poems *150 Million* (1920) and *Mystery Bouffe* (1918).

Ma·yan (mä′yən) *adj.* Of or pertaining to the Maya, their culture, or their language or the language group to which it belongs. ~*n.* **1.** A Maya. **2.** A linguistic stock of Central America that includes the language of the Maya.

Ma·ya·pán (mī′ə-pän′). Village in Yucatán, southeastern Mexico. It is on the site of the ruined capital of the Mayan Empire.

May apple *n.* **1.** A North American plant, *Podophyllum peltatum,* having a single, nodding white flower and oval edible fruit. **2.** The fruit of this plant.

may·be (mā′bē) *adv.* Perhaps; possibly.

May beetle *n.* The **June beetle** (see).

May bug *n.* The **cockchafer** (see).

May Day *n.* **1.** The first day of May, traditionally marked by the celebration of spring. **2.** May 1, or the first working day of May, widely observed as a public holiday in honor of labor organizations.

may·day (mā′dā′) *n.* An international radio-telephone signal word used by aircraft and ships in distress. [Phonetic rendering of French *m'aidez*, help me.]

Mayence. See **Mainz.**

May·er (mā′ər), **Louis Burt,** known as "L.B." (1885–1957). U.S. motion-picture producer. He began his career in 1907 as the operator of a single theater; by the mid-1920's he was in charge of Metro-Goldwyn-Mayer, a giant and enormously successful movie studio. One of the most powerful film tycoons of his time, Mayer was known for his strict paternalistic management of his studio and stars.

May·fair (mā′fâr′). A district of the City of Westminster, Greater London, England. A wealthy residential, recreational, and commercial area of London's West End, it takes its name from the annual fair held there until the end of the 18th century.

may·flow·er (mā′flou′ər) n. 1. Any of a wide variety of plants that bloom in May, such as the hawthorn and cowslip. 2. The **trailing arbutus** (see).

May·flow·er (mā′flou′ər) n. The name of the ship on which the Pilgrims sailed to America in 1620.

may·fly (mā′flī′) n., pl. **-flies.** Any of various fragile, winged insects of the order Ephemeroptera that develop from aquatic nymphs and live in the adult stage for a few days at most. Also called "dayfly." [So named because it swarms in May.]

may·hap (mā′hăp′, mā-hăp′) adv. Archaic. Perhaps; perchance. [From the phrase it may hap.]

may·hem (mā′hĕm′, mā′əm) n. 1. The infliction of violent injury upon a person or thing; wanton destruction: children committing mayhem in the flower beds. 2. A state of violent disorder or riotous confusion; havoc. 3. Law. The offense of willfully maiming or crippling a person. [Middle English, from Norman French maihem, mahaym, injury, from Old French mahaignier, to MAIM.]

May·hew (mā′hyōō′), **Henry** (1812–87). English journalist and sociologist. He pioneered a study of London's poor, London Labour and the London Poor, published in four volumes (1851–64).

may·ing (mā′ĭng) n. The celebration of or participation in traditional May Day festivities. [From MAY.]

may·n't (mā′ənt, mānt). Contraction of may not.

May·o¹ (mā′ō). Family of U.S. physicians and surgeons. **William Worrall** (1819–1911), born in England, came to the United States in 1845 and concentrated on gynecological surgery. A clinic he started in Rochester, Minnesota, grew into the renowned Mayo Clinic under the supervision of his sons, **William James** (1861–1939) and **Charles Horace** (1865–1939).

Mayo². Atlantic county in Connacht province, in the western part of the Republic of Ireland. It is mountainous and barren in the west, but more fertile in the east, producing oats, potatoes, and livestock. It has many lakes and a fragmented coastline. The county town is Castlebar.

may·on·naise (mā′ə-nāz′, mā′ə-nāz′) n. 1. A creamy dressing made of beaten raw egg yolk, oil, vinegar or lemon juice, and seasonings. 2. A dish prepared with mayonnaise: salmon mayonnaise. [French.]

may·or (mā′ər, mâr) n. The chief officer of a city, town, borough, or municipal corporation. [Middle English mair, from Old French maire, from Medieval Latin mājor, title of various officials, from Latin mājor, "greater."] —**may·or·al** adj. —**may·or·ship** n.

may·or·al·ty (mā′ər-əl-tē, mâr′əl-) n., pl. **-ties.** 1. The office of a mayor. 2. The term of office of a mayor. [Middle English, from Old French mairalté, from maire, MAYOR.]

may·or·ess (mā′ər-ĭs, mâr′ĭs) n. 1. A woman holding the office of mayor. 2. The wife of a mayor.

Mayotte. See Mahore.

May·pole (mā′pōl′) n. Sometimes **maypole.** A pole decorated with streamers that May Day celebrants hold while dancing.

May queen n. A young woman or girl who is crowned with a ring of flowers and presides over the traditional May Day celebrations.

Mays (māz), **Willie Howard Jr.** (1931–). U.S. baseball player. He joined the New York Giants in 1951 and led them in 1954 to their first world championship in 21 years. A superb outfielder, base stealer, and hitter, he retired in 1973 with a career batting average of .302 and a total of 660 home runs.

may tree n. British. The hawthorn (see).

may·weed (mā′wēd′) n. A widespread weed, Anthemis cotula, having unpleasant-smelling leaves and white flowers. Also called "dog fennel," "stinking mayweed."

Maz·a·rin (măz′ər-ĭn, mä′zä-răN′), **Jules**, born Giulio Mazarini (1602–61). French statesman, born in Italy. He became adviser to Louis XIII's chief minister, Richelieu. After the death of Louis (1643), he was the chief minister of the regent, Anne of Austria, and after 1653 was all-powerful in the French government. He was never ordained a priest, but was made a cardinal on the recommendation of Louis XIII in 1641.

Ma·zat·lán (mä′sät-län′). Seaport of western Mexico, on the Pacific Ocean. Its beautiful setting has made it a popular resort.

Maz·da·ism (măz′də-ĭz′əm) n. A religion, **Zoroastrianism** (see). [Avestan mazda, the good principle in Zoroastrianism + -ISM.]

maze (māz) n. 1. **a.** An intricate, usually confusing network of walled or hedged pathways; labyrinth. **b.** Any physical situation resembling such a network, in which it is easy to get lost. **c.** Any elaborate, confusing, or impenetrable network: a maze of regulations. 2. A puzzle consisting of a graphic representation of a maze. 3. A state of confusion or perplexity. ~tr.v. **mazed, mazing, mazes.** Archaic. To daze, bewilder, or perplex. [Middle English mase, maze, confusion, from mazen, to bewilder, amaze. See amaze.] —**maz·y** adj.

ma·zer (mā′zər) n. A large, often elaborately ornamented drinking bowl made of hard wood or metal. [Middle English mazer, originally "an outgrowth of maple wood" (from which a mazer was made), from Germanic.]

ma·zu·ma (mə-zōō′mə) n. Slang. Money; cash. [Yiddish mazumen, from Hebrew mzumān, fixed.]

ma·zur·ka, ma·zour·ka (mə-zûr′kə, -zōōr′kə) n. 1. A lively Polish dance resembling the polka. 2. A piece of music for such a dance.

[French, from Polish Mazurka, oblique form of mazurek, diminutive of mazur, one from Mazovia province.]

maz·zard (măz′ərd) n. A wild sweet cherry, Prunus avium, often used as grafting stock. [Perhaps akin to MAZER.]

Maz·zi·ni (mät-sē′nē), **Giuseppe** (1805–72). Italian revolutionary nationalist. He was exiled in 1830 for joining a secret society, the Carbonari, and lived mainly in London after 1837. In 1849 he was a leader of the Roman Republic, and after its fall he organized an unsuccessful uprising in Milan (1853). In 1858, in London, he began the revolutionary paper Thought and Action, stirring Italian nationalist opinion.

M.B.A. Master of Business Administration.

Mba·bane (əm-bä-bän′). Capital of Swaziland, in the Mdimba Mts. It is also a commercial center.

M·bo·ya (əm-boi′ə), **Thomas Joseph,** (1930–69). Kenyan politician. In 1958 he was elected president of the All-African People's Conference at Accra. After Kenya's independence in 1963 he served in Jomo Kenyatta's government as minister of justice (1963–64) and minister of economic planning (1964–69).

MC Marine Corps.

m.c. master of ceremonies.

M.C. 1. Master of Ceremonies. 2. Member of Congress.

Mc·Ad·am (mə-kăd′əm), **John Loudon** (1756–1836). British engineer. He developed the technique of improving roads by raising their level and covering them with graded stones.

Mc·Au·liffe (mə-kô′lĭf), **Anthony Clement** (1898–1975). U.S. army officer. He is noted for his staunch defense of U.S. positions at Bastogne, Belgium, during the Battle of the Bulge (1944–45). When the Germans demanded that he surrender, his succinct reply was "Nuts!"

Mc·Car·thy (mə-kär′thē), **Joseph Raymond,** known as "Joe" (1908–57). U.S. politician. He was elected to the U.S. Senate (1947). As chairman of the permanent subcommittee on investigations, he began public hearings, accusing army officials, media employees, and public personalities of communism. His charges were never proved, and he was censured by the Senate (1954).

McCarthy, Mary Therese (1912–). U.S. writer. She has satirized urban American life in novels such as The Company She Keeps (1942), The Group (1963), and Birds of America (1971).

Mc·Car·thy·ism (mə-kär′thē-ĭz′əm) n. 1. A political stance, especially prevalent in the United States in the 1950's, of intense anticommunism, characterized by the practice of driving suspected communists from government office by means of well-publicized but often unsubstantiated allegations. 2. The use of underhand methods or unsupported allegations in order to suppress opposition. [Coined by opponents of Joseph R. McCARTHY.] —**Mc·Car·thy·ist, Mc·Car·thy·ite** n. & adj.

Mc·Cart·ney (mə-kärt′nē), **(James) Paul** (1942–). British rock musician and composer. As a member of the Beatles (1960–71), he wrote with John Lennon many memorable songs, including She Loves You and Yesterday. He has since worked as a solo artist and with the group Wings.

Mc·Cau·ley (mə-kô′lē), **Mary Ludwig Hays,** known as "Molly Pitcher" (1754–1832). U.S. Revolutionary heroine. She earned her nickname at the Battle of Monmouth (June 28, 1778) when she carried water to the hot and thirsty soldiers. During the same battle her husband was overcome by the heat, and she took over his gun for the remainder of the fighting.

Mc·Clel·lan (mə-klĕl′ən), **George Brinton** (1826–85). U.S. army officer and politician. He fought in the Mexican War and led the Union Army for a year during the Civil War. His overcautiousness irked Lincoln, who replaced him as commander at Antietam in November 1862. McClellan ran unsuccessfully for president in 1864.

Mc·Cor·mack (mə-kôr′mək, -mĭk), **John** (1884–1945). U.S. tenor, born in Ireland. He made his debut in London in 1907 and moved to the United States in 1909. Among his notable roles were Rodolpho in La Bohème and Lt. F.B. Pinkerton in Madame Butterfly.

Mc·Cor·mick (mə-kôr′mĭk), **Cyrus Hall** (1809–84). U.S. inventor and manufacturer. He first demonstrated his mechanical harvesting device in 1831 but did not patent it until 1834, when a competitor announced the invention of a similar machine. In 1847 McCormick began to manufacture his machine on a large scale.

McCormick, Joseph Medill (1877–1925) and **Robert Rutherford** (1880–1955). U.S. newspaper publishers. The brothers worked on the family-owned newspaper, the Chicago Tribune, with first Joseph, then Robert in charge. Joseph entered politics in 1912, serving in the Illinois legislature and both houses of Congress. Robert became sole owner of the paper after World War I and rapidly extended his journalistic holdings, soon dominating the Midwestern newspaper world. Under his control the Tribune consistently maintained a right-wing and isolationist position.

Mc·Coy (mə-koi′) n. Slang. The authentic thing or quality; something that is not an imitation or substitute. Used in the phrase the real McCoy. [After Kid McCoy, professional name of Norman Selby (1873–1940), American boxer.]

Mc·Crae (mə-krā′), **John** (1872–1918). Canadian physician and poet. His famous poem "In Flanders Field," written under fire in World War I, was first published anonymously in Punch in 1915 and later in a posthumous volume of his poems. He died of pneumonia during the war.

Mc·Cul·lers (mə-kŭl′ərz), **Carson Smith** (1917–67). U.S. novelist. Her books, set in the South, are compassionate studies of the maca-

mayfly In their nymph stage, mayflies live in ponds and streams for a period of from several months to three years. Then the nymphs molt to become a subimago and a second time to become a true adult (above)—the only insects to undergo this two-stage transformation. Adult mayflies do not eat; they live for only a few hours, just long enough to mate and lay eggs.

bre and grotesque. They include *The Heart is a Lonely Hunter* (1940) and *The Member of the Wedding* (1946).

Mc·Gov·ern (mə-gŭv′ərn), **George Stanley** (1922–). U.S. politician. He was elected to the U.S. Senate in 1962. In 1972 he was chosen as the Democratic candidate for president, but his grass-roots and antiwar campaign was troubled by charges of radicalism and his handling of the resignation of his running mate, Thomas F. Eagleton (1929–). McGovern was soundly defeated by Richard M. Nixon.

Mc·Guf·fey (mə-gŭf′ē), **William Holmes** (1800–73). U.S. educator. He is remembered chiefly as the compiler of the *McGuffey Eclectic Readers* (six volumes, 1836–57), schoolbooks that combined reading lessons with traditionally moralistic teachings. An estimated 122 million copies of the books were sold.

Mc·In·tosh (măk′ĭn-tŏsh′) *n.* A variety of red eating apple grown commercially in the northern United States. [After John *McIntosh* (*fl.* 1796), its first cultivator.]

Mc·Kin·ley, Mount (mə-kĭn′lē). The highest mountain in North America. It is in Mount McKinley National Park in the Alaska Range, and rises to 6,194 meters (20,322 feet).

McKinley, William (1843–1901). 25th president of the United States (1897–1901). He was elected to Congress as a Republican in 1876; he introduced the protectionist McKinley Tariff Act (1890). His presidency was expansionist, with the additon of Duba after the Spanish-American War (1898) and the annexation of the Philippines. He was shot by an assassin.

Mc·Lu·han (mə-klo͞o′ən), **(Herbert) Marshall** (1911–81). Canadian literary critic and communications sociologist. He argued that the media, such as print or television, affect or overshadow the message they convey. His books include *The Medium is the Message* (1967).

Mc·Mil·lan (mək-mĭl′ən), **Edwin Mattison** (1907–). U.S. physicist. He discovered neptunium in 1940 by bombarding uranium with neutrons. He was awarded the Nobel Prize for chemistry (1951).

Mc·Na·mar·a (măk′nə-măr′ə), **Robert Strange** (1916–). U.S. businessman. He was an executive of the Ford Motor Company (1946–60) and U.S. secretary of defense (1961–68).

Md The symbol for the element mendelevium.

Md. Maryland.

MD Maryland (with Zip Code).

M.D. Doctor of Medicine [Latin *Medicinae Doctor*].

M.D.S. Master of Dental Surgery.

mdse. merchandise.

me (mē) *pron.* The objective case of the first person pronoun *I.* It is used: **1.** As the direct object of a verb: *He assisted me.* **2.** As the indirect object of a verb: *They offered me a lift.* **3.** As the object of a preposition: *This letter is addressed to me.* **4.** After *than* or *as* in comparisons in which the first term is in the objective case: *The judges praised you more than me.* **5.** *Informal.* In place of the reflexive pronoun *myself* as the indirect object of a verb: *I'm going to get me a gun.* **6.** In various elliptical, absolute, or interjectional phrases in which it is neither subject nor object: *Goodness me! Unlucky me. Who, me?*

∼*n.* The speaker's image or personality: *This dress isn't really me.* [Middle English, Old English *mē, mĕ.*]

Usage: Until about thirty years ago grammarians taught that the correct answer to the question *"Who is there?"* is *"It is I,"* not *"It's me."* They pointed out that the verb *be* has no object, so that any pronoun following it should be in the subjective form. Today, however, *It is I* sounds overcareful to the point of being pedantic, and objective forms of the pronouns *(me, him, her, us, them)* are acceptable even in formal contexts unless there is a following construction: *It was he who told the vicar.* In such cases formal speech requires the subjective form, informal speech the objective. Similarly, following *than* or *as,* subjective forms of the pronoun are used in formal writing (*John is bigger than I*), objective forms in other styles. If the construction continues, the subjective form must be used in standard English whether written or spoken, formal or informal: *John is bigger than I am.* The choice of an objective as opposed to a possessive form of these pronouns is an issue when an *-ing* form of a verb follows. Purists insist on the possessive form in such sentences as *I remember your doing that.* But the objective form has become normal in informal usage and is often heard in all but the most formal contexts. Sometimes a subtle distinction of meaning is involved: *I remember you acting in "Macbeth"* means "I remember the fact that you acted in that play," whereas *I remember your acting in "Macbeth"* may additionally mean "I remember the quality of your acting."

Me methyl group (CH_3–).

ME **1.** Maine (with Zip Code). **2.** Middle English.

M.E. **1.** mechanical engineer; mechanical engineering. **2.** Middle English. **3.** mining engineer.

me·a cul·pa (mā′ə kŭl′pə, mē′ə) *n.* An admission of fault or error. Often used interjectionally. [Latin, "though my fault."]

mead¹ (mēd) *n.* An alcoholic drink made from fermented honey and water. [Middle English *mede,* Old English *medu, meodu.*]

mead² *n. Archaic.* A meadow. [Middle English *mede,* Old English *mǣd.*]

Mead (mēd), **Margaret** (1901–78). U.S. anthropologist. She was a curator of ethnology at the American Museum of Natural History in New York (1926–69). She wrote *Coming of Age in Samoa* (1928) and *Growing Up in New Guinea* (1930).

Meade (mēd), **George Gordon** (1815–72). U.S. army officer. He served in the Mexican War and as a Union general in the Civil War, distinguishing himself at the battles of Bull Run, Antietam, Fredericksburg, and Chancellorsville. His greatest triumph was at Gettysburg (July 1863), though he was criticized for his failure to take advantage of his victory.

meadowlark *A female greater red-breasted meadowlark of South America. The species gets its name from the coloring of the male bird. All meadowlarks are songbirds, living in fields and meadows in South, Central, and North America.*

mead·ow (mĕd′ō) *n.* **1.** A tract of grassland, either in its natural state or used as pasture or for growing hay. **2.** A **water meadow** *(see).* [Middle English *medwe,* Old English *mǣdwe,* oblique case of *mǣd,* MEAD.] **—mead·ow·y** *adj.*

meadow beauty *n.* Any plant of the genus *Rhexia,* of eastern North America, growing in wet ground and having showy purple flowers.

meadow fescue *n.* A grass, *Festuca pratensis* (or *eliator*), native to Eurasia and introduced in North America.

meadow grass *n.* A perennial grass, *Poa pratensis,* widely distributed in meadows and fields in northern temperate regions.

mead·ow·land (mĕd′ō-lănd′) *n.* Land having the characteristics of or used as a meadow.

mead·ow·lark (mĕd′ō-lärk′) *n.* **1.** Either of two North American songbirds, *Sturnella magna* or *S. neglecta,* related to the Baltimore oriole. **2.** Any of various other birds of the genus *Sturnella,* of North, Central, and South America.

meadow mouse *n.* The **field mouse** *(see).*

meadow mushroom *n.* A **field mushroom** *(see).*

meadow pipit *n.* A European songbird, *Anthus pratensis,* with brown and white speckled plumage.

meadow pipit *This small songbird, which grows to about 145 millimeters (5¾ inches), is something of a victim among birds. It is the chief prey of the merlin and a favorite host for the cuckoo, whose fostered young grow so large that the meadow pipit sometimes stands on the nestling's back to feed it. Meadow pipits nest in open country—often on the edge of meadows—in northern Europe and migrate in winter to southwestern Europe and around the Mediterranean.*

meadow rue *n.* Any of various plants of the genus *Thalictrum,* having clusters of small white, yellowish, or purplish flowers.

meadow saffron *n.* A plant, the **autumn crocus** *(see).*

mead·ow·sweet (mĕd′ō-swēt′) *n.* Any of several plants of the genus *Spiraea*; especially, *S. alba* or *S. latifolia,* of eastern North America, having pyramidal clusters of flowers.

mea·ger, mea·gre (mē′gər) *adj.* **1.** Having little flesh; thin; lean. **2.** Markedly deficient in quantity, fullness, or extent; scanty. **3.** Markedly deficient in richness, fertility, or vigor; barren or feeble. [Middle English *megre,* from Norman French *megre* and Old French *maigre,* from Latin *macer* (stem *macr-*), thin.] **—mea·ger·ly** *adv.* **—mea·ger·ness** *n.*

Synonyms: *scant, scanty, skimpy, spare, sparse.*

meal¹ (mēl) *n.* **1.** The edible seed or other edible part of a pulse or grain, usually excluding wheat, coarsely ground. **2.** *Scottish.* Oatmeal. **3.** Any granular substance produced by grinding. [Middle English *mele,* Old English *melu,* flour.]

meal² *n.* **1.** An amount of food served and eaten, often as several courses, in one sitting. **2.** A customary time or occasion of eating food. [Middle English *meel,* Old English *mǣl,* "mark," "measure," fixed time, mealtime.]

meal·ie (mē′lē) *n. South African.* **1.** An ear of corn. **2. mealies.** Corn; maize. [Afrikaans *mielie,* from Portuguese *milho,* millet, from Latin *milium.*]

meals on wheels *n. Used with a singular verb.* A service, usually funded by a local authority, providing hot meals to elderly or disabled people in their own homes.

meal ticket *n.* **1.** A card or ticket entitling the holder to a meal or meals. **2.** *Slang.* A person or thing depended on as a source of financial support.

meal·time (mēl′tīm′) *n.* The usual time for eating a meal.

meal·worm (mēl′wûrm′) *n.* The larva of any of several beetles of the genus *Tenebrio.* Mealworms infest flour and other grain products and are raised for bird feed.

meal·y (mē′lē) *adj.* **-ier, -iest. 1.** Resembling meal in texture or consistency; granular: *mealy potatoes.* **2. a.** Made of or containing meal. **b.** Sprinkled or covered with meal or a similar granular substance. **3.** Flecked with spots; mottled. **4.** Unhealthily pale. Said of the complexion. **5.** Mealy-mouthed. **—meal·i·ness** *n.*

meal·y·bug (mē′lē-bŭg′) *n.* Any insect of the genus *Pseudococcus* and related genera. Some species, such as *P. citri,* are destructive to plants, especially citrus trees. [So named because they are covered with a white powdery substance.]

meal·y-mouthed (mē′lē-mou*thd*′, -moutht′) *adj.* Unwilling to state facts or opinions simply and directly.

mean¹ (mēn) *v.* **meant** (mĕnt), **meaning, means.** *—tr.* **1. a.** To be defined or described as; refer to; denote: *The word "dog" means a certain species of mammal.* **b.** To convey the same sense as; refer to the same thing as: *The French word "chien" means "dog."* **c.** To act as a symbol of; represent. **d.** To signify; serve as a sign. Used with a clause: *The flashing light means that you can cross.* **2. a.** To intend to convey or indicate: *What do you mean by that look?* **b.** To have in mind as one's true meaning or intention: *said Thursday but meant Friday; said she would resign and meant it.* **3.** To have as a purpose, aim, or intention; want: *I mean to get to the bottom of this.* **4.** To design or intend for a certain purpose, person, or end: *a building meant for storage. Was this letter meant for me?* **5.** To have as a consequence; entail; imply: *This decision means higher rates.* **6.** To have as a full implication or true character: *He doesn't know what hard work means.* **7.** To require or oblige. Used in the passive: *You're meant to knock before you go into his office.* *—intr.* **1.** To be of a specified importance or significance; matter: *The opinions of critics meant little to him.* **2.** To have intentions of a specified kind; be disposed. Followed by *well* or *ill: She means well, despite her blunders.* [Middle English *menen,* Old English *mǣnan,* to intend, tell, signify.]

Synonyms: *denote, import, purport, represent, signify.*

mean² *adj.* **meaner, meanest. 1.** Ignoble; small-minded; petty: *a mean motive.* **2.** Lacking elevating human qualities, such as kind-

ness or generosity, as: **a.** Reluctant to help or oblige; selfish. **b.** Cruel; malicious; spiteful. **c.** Reluctant to give; stingy. **3.** Low in quality or grade; inferior. **4.** Low in social status; of humble origin or rank. **5.** Common or poor in appearance; shabby. **6.** Ill-tempered. Said often of animals. **7.** *Informal.* In poor health; out of sorts; ill. **8.** *Slang.* Skillful; hard to beat: *She plays a mean game of bridge.* —See Synonyms at **stingy.** —**no mean.** Very good: *He's no mean cook.* [Middle English *mene, imene,* Old English *gemǣne,* "common."] —**mean·ly** *adv.* —**mean·ness** *n.*
Synonyms: *abject, base, ignoble, infamous, low.*

mean³ *n.* **1.** That which lies between two extremes; a middle point, condition, quality, or course of action. See **golden mean. 2.** *Mathematics.* **a.** A number that represents a set of numbers in any of several ways determined by a rule involving all members of the set; an average. **b.** The **arithmetic mean** *(see).* Compare **geometric mean. 3.** *Logic.* The middle term in a syllogism. **4. means.** A method, instrument, or course of action by which some act or end can be accomplished: *The fastest means of communication is the telephone.* **5.** Material resources; income, wealth, or property: *a person of means.* —**by all means.** Without fail; certainly. —**by means of.** With the use of; owing to: *They succeeded by means of patience and sacrifice.* In no sense; certainly not: *by no means an easy opponent.*
~*adj.* **1.** Occupying a middle or intermediate position between two extremes. **2.** Intermediate in size, extent, quality, time, or degree; medium. **3.** Constituting a mean; average. [Middle English *mene,* from Norman French *meen* and Old French *meien,* from Latin *mediānus,* median, from *medius,* middle.]
Usage: *Means* in the sense "resources" (money or property, for example) takes a plural verb: *His means are sufficient to keep him alive. Means* in the sense "way to an end" takes either a singular or a plural verb, depending on the type of construction in which it occurs. Used with *a, any, each,* and so on, it takes a singular verb: *A means of transport is essential.* Used with *all, several, such,* and the like, it takes a plural verb: *Several means of transport are available.* Used with *the,* it takes a verb that may be singular or plural, depending on whether or not a collective sense of the noun is intended: *The means of transport is for you to decide* (collective), but *The means of transport are many and various* (individualized).

me·an·der (mē-ăn′dər) *intr.v.* **-dered, -dering, -ders. 1.** To follow a winding and turning course: *Streams tend to meander through level land.* **2.** To wander aimlessly and idly without fixed direction: *vagabonds meandering through life.* —See Synonyms at **wander.**
~*n.* **1. meanders.** Circuitous, sinuous windings, as of a stream or path. **2.** A circuitous journey or excursion; a ramble. **3.** An ornamental pattern of intertwining lines used in art and architecture; a fret. [Originally as a noun, from Latin *maeander,* from Greek *maiandros,* from *Maiandros,* the river MAEANDER, noted for its windings.] —**me·an·der·er** *n.* —**me·an·der·ing·ly** *adv.* —**me·an·drous** (mē-ăn′drəs) *adj.*

mean deviation *n. Statistics.* The arithmetic mean of the absolute values of deviations from the arithmetic mean, or from the median, in a statistical distribution.

mean distance *n.* The average distance between two bodies; especially, the average of the greatest and the least distances between an orbiting body and the body about which it is orbiting.

mean free path *n.* The average distance covered by a particle, molecule, ion, or the like between collisions.

mean free time *n.* The average time that elapses between collisions of a particle, molecule, ion, or the like.

meanie. Variant of **meany.**

mean·ing (mē′nĭng) *n.* **1.** That which is signified or denoted by a linguistic expression such as a word or phrase; sense; semantic content: *a word with several different meanings.* **2.** That which one wishes to convey by words or actions; import: *I listened carefully to grasp his meaning.* **3.** The full implications or true character of something: *doesn't know the meaning of pain.* **4.** That which is felt to be the inner significance of something: *the meaning of dreams.* **5.** Functional value; efficacy; significance.
~*adj.* **1.** Full of meaning; expressive: *a meaning look.* **2.** Intentioned or disposed in a specified manner. Used in the combinations *ill-meaning* and *well-meaning.*
Synonyms: *import, purport, sense, significance, signification.*

mean·ing·ful (mē′nĭng-fəl) *adj.* Having meaning, function, value, or purpose; significant. —**mean·ing·ful·ly** *adv.*

mean·ing·less (mē′nĭng-lĭs) *adj.* Having no meaning or significance; senseless. —**mean·ing·less·ly** *adv.*

mean life *n.* The average time for which an unstable or reactive particle, ion, or the like can exist.

mean sea level *n.* The average level of the sea, used in geography as a basis from which to measure height.

mean solar day *n.* The average period between successive transits of the sun, equal to 24 hours, and now measured from midnight to midnight. It is used because the apparent solar day, the actual period between successive transits of the sun, varies. Also called "civil day."

mean solar time *n.* Time based on the mean solar day. Also called "civil time," "mean time."

mean square *n. Mathematics.* The arithmetic mean of the squares of a set of numbers.

means test *n.* An official examination of a person's material resources to establish eligibility for benefits such as social security.

mean sun *n.* A hypothetical sun defined as moving at a uniform rate along the celestial equator so that it completes its orbit in the same period as the apparent sun. It is used in computing the mean solar day.

meant. Past tense and past participle of **mean** (to denote).

mean time *n.* Mean solar time.

mean·time (mēn′tīm) *n.* **1.** The time between one occurrence and another; an interval.
~*adv.* During a period of intervening time; meanwhile.
Usage: *Meantime* is used principally as a noun, usually in the phrase *in the meantime. Meanwhile* is used principally as an adverb: *Meanwhile we were waiting in the shop.*

mean·tone system (mēn′tōn′) *n. Music.* A former system for tuning keyboard instruments. It has now been replaced by **equal temperament** *(see).*

mean·while (mēn′hwīl′) *adv.* **1.** During or in the intervening time: *Meanwhile life goes on.* **2.** At the same time: *The court is deliberating; meanwhile he must be patient.*
~*n.* The intervening time. —See Usage note at **meantime.**

mean·y, mean·ie (mē′nē) *n., pl.* **-ies.** *Informal.* **1.** A miserly, ungenerous person. **2.** A malicious, spiteful person.

Mea·ny (mē′nē), **George** (1894–1980). U.S. labor leader. An able lobbyist for the concerns of labor, he was president of the New York State Federation of Labor and secretary, then president of the American Federation of Labor. When the AFL and the Congress of Industrial Organizations (CIO) merged in 1955, Meany became the first president of the new federation.

meas. measurable; measure.

mea·sles (mē′zəlz) *n. Used with a singular verb.* **1.** An acute, contagious virus disease, usually occurring in childhood. Its symptoms include those of the common cold and the eruption of red spots. Also called "morbilli," "rubeola." See **German measles. 2.** A disease of cattle and pigs, caused by tapeworm larvae. **3.** A plant disease, usually caused by fungi and producing minute spots on leaves and stems. [Middle English *maseles,* plural of *masel,* from Middle Dutch *māsel,* blemish.]

mea·sly (mēz′lē) *adj.* **-slier, -sliest. 1.** Infected or spotted with measles. **2.** Infected with larval tapeworms. Said of meat. **3.** *Slang.* Contemptibly small; meager: *a measly tip.*

meas·ur·a·ble (mĕzh′ər-ə-bəl) *adj. Abbr.* **meas. 1.** Capable of being measured. **2.** Important; significant: *a measurable feat.*

meas·ure (mĕzh′ər) *n. Abbr.* **meas. 1.** The dimensions, quantity, or capacity of anything as ascertained by measuring: *Length, area, volume, and mass are basic measures of material properties.* **2.** A reference standard or sample used for the quantitative comparison of properties: *The standard kilogram is maintained as a measure of mass.* **3.** A unit specified by a scale, such as an inch, or by variable conditions, such as a day's march. **4.** A system of measurement, such as the metric system. **5.** A device, such as a marked tape or a graduated container, used for measuring. **6.** An act of measurement. **7.** A basis for evaluation or comparison: *the measure of an achievement.* **8.** An amount taken or prescribed as a standard: *a good measure of oats; short measure.* **9.** A specified extent, degree, or amount: *achieved some measure of success; hasn't yet grasped the full measure of the calamity.* **10.** An implied extent, degree, or amount, such as: **a.** A fitting amount: *a measure of recognition.* **b.** A limited amount: *a measure of happiness.* **11.** Limit; bounds: *a generosity knowing no measure.* **12.** Appropriate restraint; moderation: *criticism in measure.* **13.** An action taken as a means to an end; an expedient: *desperate measures.* **14.** A legislative bill or enactment: *"I have opposed measures, not men"* (Lord Chesterfield). **15. a.** Poetic meter. **b.** Poetic rhythm or cadence. **16. a.** A dance. **b.** A tune. **17.** *Music.* **a.** The characteristic beat of musical rhythm; time. **b.** The metric unit between two bars on the staff; a **bar** *(see).* **18.** *Printing.* The width of a page or column of type. —**for good measure.** In addition to the required amount.
~*v.* **measured, -uring, -ures.** —*tr.* **1.** To ascertain the dimensions, quantity, or capacity of. **2.** To mark, lay out, or establish dimensions for by measuring. Often followed by *off: measure off an area.* **3.** To evaluate, especially by comparison with something else: *an encouraging result when measured against last year's figures.* **4.** To bring into opposition: *She measured her power with that of a dangerous adversary.* **5.** To serve as a measure of: *The inch measures length.* **6.** To mark off or separate, usually with reference to some unit of measurement. Often followed by *out: measure out a pint of milk.* **7.** To allot or distribute as if by measuring; mete. Often followed by *out: The revolutionary tribunal measured out harsh justice.* **8.** To consider or choose with care; weigh: *She measures her words with pedantic caution.* **9.** *Archaic.* To travel over or through. —*intr.* **1.** To take measurements; work out the dimensions of something. **2.** To have a particular measurement: *The room measures 10 by 12 meters.* —**measure up.** To have the right qualifications. —**measure up to.** To match (expectations, standards, or the like). [Middle English *mesure,* from Old French *mesure,* from Latin *mēnsūra,* a measure, from *mētīrī* (past participial stem *mēns-*), to measure.] —**meas·ur·er** *n.*

meas·ured (mĕzh′ərd) *adj.* **1.** Regular in rhythm. **2.** Carefully weighed; calculated; deliberate: *with measured irony.* **3.** Written in meter. —**meas·ured·ly** *adv.* —**meas·ured·ness** *n.*

meas·ure·less (mĕzh′ər-lĭs) *adj.* Limitless; immeasurable; infinite: *"Through caverns measureless to man"* (S.T. Coleridge). —See Synonyms at **infinite.** —**meas·ure·less·ly** *adv.*

measurement

TWO SYSTEMS OF WEIGHTS AND MEASURES

How the customary and metric forms of measurement were established

By an order of Elizabeth I in 1588 the pound weight and the yard were defined by a bronze weight and a bronze bar. "Pound" came from the Latin *pondo,* "by weight." A yard was made up of three feet, and a foot was the length of a man's foot. It was divided into 12 inches—from the Latin *uncia,* "a twelfth."

In 1824 Parliament set up the "imperial" system. A new standard yard and pound weight were stored in the House of Commons but were destroyed with the building in 1834.

New standards were made and authorized in 1855. They were designed to be affected as little as possible by variations in atmosphere, temperature, air pressure, and humidity. The yard was defined as the distance between lines engraved in gold studs set into a gun-metal bar. The pound was defined as the weight of a cylinder of platinum-iridium alloy, 1.15 inches in diameter and 1.35 inches high. The standards were stipulated to be correct at 62°F and an atmospheric pressure of 30 inches of mercury.

The metric system was devised in France in the 1790's and named after its basic unit of length, the meter—from the Greek for "measure." The meter was defined as one ten-millionth of the distance from the North Pole to the equator. Latin and Greek prefixes were given to divisions and multiples of the meter: "centimeter" for one-hundredth of a meter; "millimeter" for one-thousandth; "kilometer" for 1,000 meters, and so on. The new unit of weight was the gram, the weight of one cubic centimeter of water at 4°C, when at its densest. The unit of capacity was the liter, defined as 100 cubic centimeters.

The metric system was gradually expanded to incorporate units of electricity, magnetism, temperature, and other quantities. In 1960 all these units were formalized in a single worldwide system called the *Système International.*

U.S. CUSTOMARY UNITS

LENGTH		Metric equivalent
	1 inch	2.54 centimeters
12 inches	1 foot	30.48 centimeters
3 feet	1 yard	0.9144 meters
1,760 yards	1 mile	1.609 kilometers
AREA		
	1 square inch	6.4516 sq. centimeters
144 square inches	1 square foot	929.030 sq. centimeters
9 square feet	1 square yard	0.836 sq. meters
4,840 sq. yards	1 acre	4,047 square meters
640 acres	1 square mile	2.590 sq. kilometers
VOLUME		
	1 cubic inch	16.387 cu. centimeters
1,728 cubic inches	1 cubic foot	0.028 cu. meters
27 cubic feet	1 cubic yard	0.7645 cu. meters
16 fluid ounces	1 pint	0.473 liters
2 pints	1 quart	0.946 liters
4 quarts	1 gallon	3.785 liters
WEIGHT		
	1 ounce	28.350 grams
16 ounces	1 pound	0.4536 kilograms
14 pounds	1 stone	6.35 kilograms
1 hundredweight	100 pounds	45.359 kilograms
2,000 pounds	1 (short) ton	0.907 metric tons

HOW TO CONVERT FROM U.S. CUSTOMARY TO METRIC

To convert	into	multiply by
LENGTH		
inches	millimeters	25.4
inches	centimeters	2.54
feet	meters	0.3048
yards	meters	0.9144
miles	kilometers	1.6093
AREA		
square inches	sq. centimeters	6.4516
square feet	square meters	0.093
square yards	square meters	0.836
acres	hectares	0.4047
square miles	square kilometers	2.590
VOLUME		
cubic inches	cubic centimeters	16.387
cubic feet	cubic meters	0.0283
cubic yards	cubic meters	0.765
fluid ounces	milliliters	29.573
pints	liters	0.473
gallons	liters	3.785
WEIGHT		
ounces	grams	28.35
pounds	kilograms	0.4536
tons (short)	metric tons	0.907

METRIC UNITS

LENGTH		U.S equivalent
	1 millimeter	0.03937 inches
10 millimeters	1 centimeter	0.3937 inches
10 centimeters	1 decimeter	3.9370 inches
100 centimeters	1 meter	39.37 inches
1,000 meters	1 kilometer	0.62 miles
AREA		
	1 sq. millimeter	0.00155 sq. inches
	1 sq. centimeter	0.155 sq. inches
100 sq. centimeters	1 sq. decimeter	15.50 sq. inches
10,000 square cm.	1 square meter	10.7639 square feet
10,000 sq. meters	1 hectare	2.47 acres
VOLUME		
	1 cubic centimeter	0.061 cubic inch
1,000 cu. centimeters	1 cubic decimeter	61.024 cu. inches
1,000 cu. decimeters	1 cubic meter	35.31467 cubic feet
		or 1.308 cu. yards
	1 liter	1.0567 quarts
100 liters	1 hectoliter	26.417 gallons
WEIGHT		
	1 gram	0.035 ounces
1,000 grams	1 kilogram	2.2046 pounds
1,000 kilograms	1 metric ton	1.10231 short tons

HOW TO CONVERT METRIC TO U.S. CUSTOMARY UNITS

To convert	into	multiply by
LENGTH		
millimeters	inches	0.0394
centimeters	inches	0.3937
meters	feet	3.2808
meters	yards	1.0936
kilometers	miles	0.6214
AREA		
sq. centimeters	square inches	0.155
square meters	square feet	10.764
square meters	square yards	1.196
hectares	acres	2.471
square kilometers	square miles	0.386
VOLUME		
cubic centimeters	cubic inches	0.061
cubic meters	cubic feet	35.315
cubic meters	cubic yards	1.308
liters	quarts	1.0567
liters	gallons	0.2642
WEIGHT		
grams	ounces	0.0353
kilograms	pounds	2.2046
metric tons	(short) tons	1.1023

sq. = square   cu. = cubic   cm. = centimeter

meas·ure·ment (mĕzh′ər-mənt) *n.* **1.** The act of measuring or the process of being measured. **2.** A system of measuring: *measurement in miles.* **3.** The dimensions, quantity, or capacity determined by measuring: *room measurements.*

measuring cup *n.* A cup marked with a graduated scale and used in cooking to measure dry or liquid ingredients.

measuring worm *n.* A geometrid caterpillar that moves in alternate contractions and expansions suggestive of measuring. Also called "inchworm," "looper," "spanner," "spanworm."

meat (mēt) *n.* **1.** The edible flesh of mammals as distinguished from that of fish or poultry. **2.** Edible flesh including poultry and some fish and shellfish: *crab meat.* **3.** The edible portions of eggs, fruits, or nuts. **4. a.** The essence or principal part of something: *the meat of the editorial.* **b.** Valuable or significant content; substance: *a witty book but without much meat in it.* **5.** *Slang.* Something one enjoys or excels in; forte: *Tennis is her meat.* **6.** Food in general, especially solid food: *meat and drink.* [Middle English *mete,* "food," meat, Old English *mete,* food.]

meat·ball (mēt′bôl′) *n.* **1.** A small ball of ground meat variously prepared and cooked. **2.** *Slang.* A stupid person.

Meath (mēth, mē*th*). County in Leinster province, Republic of Ireland, on the Irish Sea. It is mainly agricultural, producing grain, potatoes, cattle, and horses. Trim is the county town.

meat·less (mēt′lĭs) *adj.* **1.** Lacking meat or food. **2.** Being or relating to a time when meat is not to be eaten: *meatless days.*

meat loaf *n.* A dish of meat and other ingredients shaped into a loaf and usually baked.

me·a·tus (mē-ā′təs) *n., pl.* **-tuses** or **meatus.** A body canal or opening, such as the opening of the ear or the urethral canal. [Latin *meātus,* passage, from *meāre* (past participial stem *meāt-*), to pass.]

meat·y (mē′tē) *adj.* **-ier, -iest.** Of, resembling, or full of meat. **2.** Supplying ample food for thought; substantial: *a meaty theme for study and debate.* **—meat′i·ness** *n.*

mec·a·myl·a·mine (mĕk′ə-mĭl′ə-mēn′) *n.* A drug, $C_{11}H_{21}N \cdot HCL$, taken orally to treat high blood pressure. [Originally a trademark.]

mec·ca (mĕk′ə) *n.* **1.** A place that is the center of an activity or the goal to which adherents of a faith or practice aspire. **2.** A place visited by many people. [After MECCA.]

Mec·ca (mĕk′ə). Holiest city of Islam. Capital of Hejaz province, western Saudi Arabia, it is circled by hills. The birthplace of Muhammad (c. A.D. 570), Mecca is a pilgrimage center that all Muslims hope to visit at least once in their lives.

mech. 1. mechanical; mechanics. **2.** mechanism.

me·chan·ic (mĭ-kăn′ĭk) *n.* **1.** A worker skilled in making, using, or repairing machines and tools. **2.** *Archaic.* A craftsman; an artisan. [Earlier form of MECHANICAL.] **—me·chan·ic** *adj.*

me·chan·i·cal (mĭ-kăn′ĭ-kəl) *adj. Abbr.* **mech. 1.** Of or pertaining to machines or tools. **2.** Operated or produced by a machine. **3.** Of or pertaining to mechanics. **4.** Acting like a machine or performed as if by a machine; automatic: *The speaker's delivery was mechanical.* **5.** Pertaining to, produced by, or dominated by physical forces. **6.** Interpreting and explaining the phenomena of the universe by reference to causally determined material forces; mechanistic. **7.** *Archaic.* Of or pertaining to manual labor, its tools, and its skills. *~n. Printing.* A layout consisting of type proofs, artwork, or both, exactly positioned and prepared for making an offset or other printing plate. Also called "paste-up." [Middle English, pertaining to manual labor, earlier *mechanic,* from Latin *mēchanicus,* from Greek *mēkhanikos,* from *mēkhanē,* MACHINE.] **—me·chan·i·cal·ly** *adv.* **—me·chan·i·cal·ness** *n.*

mechanical advantage *n.* The ratio of the output force of a machine to the input force.

mechanical drawing *n.* **1. Drafting** *(see).* **2. a.** A drawing, as an architect's plans or a scale drawing of a machine or engine that enables measurements to be interpreted. **b.** The art or skill of producing such drawings; draftsmanship.

mechanical engineering *n. Abbr.* **M.E.** The branch of engineering that encompasses the generation and application of heat and mechanical power and the design, production, and use of machines and tools. **—mechanical engineer** *n.*

me·chan·ics (mĭ-kăn′ĭks) *n. Abbr.* **mech. 1.** *Used with a singular verb.* The analysis of the action of forces on matter or material systems. See **dynamics, statics, quantum mechanics, statistical mechanics. 2.** *Used with a singular verb.* The design, construction, operation, and application of machinery or mechanical structures. **3.** *Used with a plural verb.* The process by or way in which something operates, is constructed, or is carried out; the technical or procedural aspects of something: *grasps the mechanics of music but has no feel for it; the mechanics of getting a bill through Congress.*

mech·a·nism (mĕk′ə-nĭz′əm) *n.* **1.** *Abbr.* **mech. a.** A machine or mechanical appliance. **b.** The arrangement of connected parts in a machine. **2.** Any system of parts that operate or interact like those of a machine: *the mechanism of the solar system.* **3.** An instrument or process, physical or mental, by which something is done or comes into being: *The mechanism of learning includes studying.* **4. a.** *Psychology.* The automatic and consistent response of an organism to various stimuli. **b.** *Psychoanalysis.* A usually unconscious mental and emotional pattern that influences behavior: *a defense mechanism.* **5.** *Philosophy.* The doctrine that all natural phenomena are explicable by material causes and mechanical principles. [Late Latin *mēchanisma,* from Greek *mēkhanē,* machine.]

mech·a·nist (mĕk′ə-nĭst) *n.* One who subscribes to the philosophical doctrine of mechanism.

mech·a·nis·tic (mĕk′ə-nĭs′tĭk) *adj.* **1.** Of or pertaining to mechanics as a branch of physics. **2.** Of or pertaining to the philosophy of mechanism; specifically, tending to explain phenomena only by reference to physical or biological causes. **—mech·a·nis·ti·cal·ly** *adv.*

mech·a·nize (mĕk′ə-nīz′) *tr.v.* **-nized, -nizing, -nizes. 1.** To equip with or perform by means of machinery: *mechanize a factory; mechanized farming.* **2.** To equip (a military unit) with motor vehicles, such as tanks and trucks. **3.** To make (something) mechanical, automatic, or unspontaneous. [MECHAN(ICAL) + -IZE.] **—mech·a·ni·za·tion** *n.*

mech·a·no·chem·i·cal coupling (mĕk′ə-nō-kĕm′ĭ-kəl) *n. Biochemistry.* The reversible conversion of chemical energy into mechanical work, as in the control of muscle contraction and relaxation by ATP.

mech·a·no·ther·a·py (mĕk′ə-nō-thĕr′ə-pē) *n.* Physiotherapy using mechanical methods to improve the functioning of joints and muscles by producing repeated movements.

Me·che·len (mĕKH′ə-lən). *French* **Ma·lines** (mä-lēn′). Also **Mech·lin** (mĕk′lĭn). City on the Dijle River, Antwerp province, north-central Belgium. Once a famous lace-making center, it is now an important commercial and industrial city.

Mech·lin (mĕk′lĭn) *n.* A delicate lace in which the pattern details are defined by a flat thread. Also called "malines." [After MECHELEN, where it was made.]

M. Econ. Master of Economics.

me·co·ni·um (mĭ-kō′nē-əm) *n.* Excrement in the fetal intestinal tract that is discharged after birth. [New Latin, from Latin, from Greek *mēkōnion,* "poppy juice," from *mēkōn,* poppy; from a fancied resemblance.]

med. 1. medical; medicine. **2.** medieval. **3.** medium.

M. Ed. Master of Education.

med·al (mĕd′l) *n.* A piece of metal stamped with a design or inscription commemorating an event or person, often given as an award. *~tr.v.* **medaled, -aling, -als.** Also *chiefly British* **-alled, -alling.** To honor or decorate with a medal. [French *médaille,* from Italian *medaglia,* from Common Romance *medallia* (unattested), from Vulgar Latin *metallea* (unattested), from Latin *metallum,* METAL.]

med·al·ist (mĕd′l-ĭst) *n.* Also *chiefly British* **med·al·list. 1.** One who designs, makes, or collects medals. **2.** One who receives a medal.

me·dal·lion (mə-dăl′yən) *n.* **1.** A large medal. **2.** Something resembling a large medal, such as an oval or circular panel or tablet bearing a design or portrait. [French *médaillon,* from Italian *medaglione,* augmentative of *medaglia,* MEDAL.]

Medal of Freedom *n.* A decoration awarded by the United States to civilians for outstanding achievement in various fields of endeavor.

Medal of Honor *n. Abbr.* **MH** The highest U.S. military decoration, awarded for bravery beyond the call of duty in action against an enemy. Also called "Congressional Medal of Honor."

medal play *n.* A form of competition in golf in which the total number of strokes taken is the basis of the score. Also called "stroke play." Compare **match play.**

Med·a·war (mĕd′ə-wər), **Sir Peter Brian** (1915–). British zoologist and anatomist. He developed techniques of joining the ends of severed nerves. He shared the Nobel Prize in physiology and medicine (1960) for work on tissue transplants.

med·dle (mĕd′l) *intr.v.* **-dled, -dling, -dles. 1.** To intrude in other people's affairs or business; interfere. Used with *in* or *with.* **2.** To handle something idly or ignorantly; tamper. Used with *with.* —See Synonyms at **interfere.** [Middle English *medlen,* "to mix," meddle, from Old French *medler,* variant of *mesler,* from Vulgar Latin *misculāre* (unattested), frequentative of Latin *miscēre,* to mix.] **—med·dler** (mĕd′lər, mĕd′l-ər) *n.*

med·dle·some (mĕd′l-səm) *adj.* Inclined to meddle or interfere. **—med·dle·some·ly** *adv.* **—med·dle·some·ness** *n.*

Mede (mēd) *n.* A native or inhabitant of ancient Media.

Me·de·a (mĭ-dē′ə). *Greek Mythology.* A princess and sorceress of Colchis who helped Jason to obtain the Golden Fleece, lived as his consort, and killed their children as revenge for his infidelity.

me·di·a¹ (mē′dē-ə) *n., pl.* **-diae** (-dē-ē′). **1.** The middle layer of the wall of an artery or vein. **2.** The middle layer of various other parts or organs. **3.** Any of the main veins in an insect's wing. [Latin, feminine of *medius,* middle.]

media² Alternate plural of **medium.** —See Usage note at **medium.**

Me·di·a (mē′dē-ə). Ancient country of western Asia, in what is now northern Iran. **—Me·di·an** *adj. & n.*

me·di·a·cy (mē′dē-ə-sē) *n.* The state or quality of being mediate.

mediaeval. Variant of **medieval.**

mediaevalism. Variant of **medievalism.**

me·di·al (mē′dē-əl) *adj.* **1.** Pertaining to, situated in, or extending toward the middle; median. **2.** *Phonetics.* Designating a sound, syllable, or letter occurring between the initial and final positions in a word or morpheme. **3.** Designating or pertaining to a mathematical average or mean. **4.** Of average or ordinary size. [Late Latin *mediālis,* from Latin *medius,* middle.] **—me·di·al·ly** *adv.*

me·di·an (mē′dē-ən) *adj.* **1.** Pertaining to, located in, or directed toward the middle; medial. **2.** *Anatomy & Zoology.* Of, pertaining to, or lying in the plane that divides a bilaterally symmetrical animal into right and left halves; mesial. **3.** *Statistics.* Pertaining to or constituting the middle value in a distribution. *~n.* **1.** A median point, plane, line, or part. **2.** *Statistics.* The middle value in a distribution, above and below which lie an equal number of values. **3.** In geometry: **a.** The line that joins a vertex of

medicine man *This North American Indian medicine man was painted by John White, a 16th-century artist who is thought to be the same John White who was governor of the lost colony at Roanoke, Virginia, in 1587-88. (White survived, because he had gone back to England to represent the colonists' interests.)*

PRONUNCIATION KEY

ă, pat; ā, pay; âr, care; ä, father, are; b, bib; ch, church; d, deed; ĕ, pet; ē, be; f, fife; g, gag; h, hat; hw, which; ĭ, pit; ī, pie; îr, pier; j, judge; k, kick; l, lid, needle; m, mum; n, no, sudden; ng, thing; ŏ, pot; ō, toe; ô, paw, for; oi, noise; ou, out; o͝o, book; o͞o, boot; p, pop; r, roar; s, sauce; sh, ship, dish; t, tight; th, thin, path; *th*, this, bathe; ŭ, cut; ûr, fur; v, valve; w, with; y, yes; z, zebra, size; zh, vision; ə, about, item, edible, gallop, circus, peaceful

IN FOREIGN WORDS:

à, *Fr.* ami; œ, *Fr.* feu, *Ger.* schön; ü, *Fr.* tu, *Ger.* über; KH, *Ger.* ich, *Scot.* loch; N, *Fr.* bon; y', *Fr.* Compiègne

STRESS MARKS:

Primary stress: ′
in·cite′ (ĭn-sīt′)
Secondary stress: ′
in′sight′ (ĭn′sīt′)

a triangle to the midpoint of the opposite side. **b.** The line that joins the midpoints of the nonparallel sides of a trapezoid. [Latin *mediānus,* from *medius,* middle.] **—me·di·an·ly** *adv.*

median plane *n.* A plane dividing a bilaterally symmetrical animal into right and left halves.

median point *n.* The intersection of the medians of a triangle.

me·di·ant (mē′dē-ənt) *n.* The third tone in a diatonic musical scale between the tonic and the dominant, traditionally related harmonically to them.

me·di·as·ti·num (mē′dē-ə-stī′nəm) *n., pl.* **-na** (-nə). **1.** The space between the pleural sacs in mammals, containing all the thoracic viscera except the lungs. **2.** A membrane between two parts of a cavity or organ. [New Latin, from neuter of Latin *mediastīnus,* median, from *medius,* middle.] **—me·di·as·ti·nal** *adj.*

me·di·ate (mē′dē-āt′) *v.* **-ated, -ating, -ates.** *—tr.* **1.** To resolve or settle (differences) by acting as an intermediary agent between two or more conflicting parties. **2.** To bring about (a settlement, agreement, or compromise) by action as an intermediary. **3.** To serve as a vehicle for bringing about (a result) or for transmitting (information, for example) to others. *—intr.* **1.** To occupy an intermediate or middle position. **2.** To intervene between parties in a dispute in order to effect an agreement, settlement, or compromise.
~adj. (mē′dē-ĭt). Acting through, involving, or dependent upon some intervening agency. [Latin *mediāre,* to be in the middle, from *medius,* middle.] **—me·di·ate·ly** (mē′dē-ĭt-lē) *adv.* **—me·di·a·tive** (-ā′tĭv) *adj.*

me·di·a·tion (mē′dē-ā′shən) *n.* **1.** The act of mediating; intervention. **2.** The intervention of a neutral power in an attempt to bring about a peaceful settlement between disputing nations.
Synonyms: *arbitration, conciliation.*

me·di·a·tize (mē′dē-ə-tīz′) *tr.v.* **-tized, -tizing, -tizes.** To annex (a small state) to a large one, leaving the ruler of the smaller power with his title and a share of authority. [German *mediatisieren,* from *mediat,* mediate, from Latin *mediāre,* to be in the middle, MEDIATE.] **—me·di·a·ti·za·tion** *n.*

me·di·a·tor (mē′dē-ā′tər) *n.* One that mediates; especially, a person who serves as an intermediary to reconcile differences. **—me·di·a·to·ry** (mē′dē-ə-tôr′ē, -tōr′ē) *adj.*

med·ic[1], med·ick (mĕd′ĭk) *n.* Any of several plants of the genus *Medicago,* native to the Old World and having clusters of small, usually yellow flowers and compound leaves with three leaflets. [Middle English *medike,* from Latin *Mēdica,* from Greek *Mēdikē (poa),* Median (grass), from *Mēdikos,* Median, from *Mēdos,* MEDE.]

medic[2] *n. Informal.* **1.** A physician or surgeon. **2.** A medical student or intern. **3.** A military medical corpsman. [Latin *medicus,* doctor.]

medic–. Variant of **medico-.**

med·i·ca·ble (mĕd′ĭ-kə-bəl) *adj.* Potentially responsive to treatment with medicine; curable.

Med·i·caid, med·i·caid (mĕd′ĭ-kād′) *n.* A publicly funded program providing medical aid for people who fall below a certain income level. [MEDIC(AL) + AID.]

med·i·cal (mĕd′ĭ-kəl) *adj. Abbr.* **med. 1.** Of or pertaining to the study or practice of medicine. **2.** Requiring or concerned with treatment by medicine as distinct from surgery. **3.** Medicinal; curative.
~n. Informal. A thorough physical examination. [French *médical,* from Medieval Latin *medicālis,* from Latin *medicus,* doctor, from *medērī,* to heal.]

medical certificate *n.* A certificate given by a medical practitioner after a medical examination, stating a person's fitness or unfitness, as for work, military service, or the like.

medical examiner *n.* A public official responsible for determining the cause of death in cases of death by crime or violence.

medical jurisprudence *n.* **Forensic medicine** *(see).*

medical law *n.* A branch of law concerned with the legal regulation of medicine and medical practice.

me·dic·a·ment (mĭ-dĭk′ə-mənt, mĕd′ĭ-kə-mənt) *n.* An agent that promotes recovery from injury or ailment; a medicine. [Latin *medicāmentum,* from *medicārī,* to MEDICATE.]

Med·i·care, med·i·care (mĕd′ĭ-kâr′) *n.* A program under the Social Security Administration that provides medical care for the aged. [MEDI(CAL) + CARE.]

med·i·cate (mĕd′ĭ-kāt′) *tr.v.* **-cated, -cating, -cates. 1.** To treat medicinally. **2.** To tincture or permeate with a medicinal substance. [Latin *medicārī,* from *medicus,* a doctor, from *medērī,* to heal.] **—med·i·ca·tive** *adj.*

med·i·ca·tion (mĕd′ĭ-kā′shən) *n.* **1.** A medicine. **2.** The act or process of being medicated. **3.** The administration of medicine.

Med·i·ci (mĕd′ə-chē). Italian noble and banking family that produced three popes (Leo X, Clement VII, and Leo XI) and two queens of France (Catherine de Medici and Marie de Médicis). The family's lavish patronage of the arts helped to make Florence one of the richest storehouses of European culture. The first of the family to rule Florence was **Cosimo** (1389–1464). The most outstanding patron of learning and the arts was **Lorenzo** "the Magnificent" (1449–92), whose artists included Michelangelo and Botticelli. The line ended with **Gian Gastone's,** who died in 1737.

me·dic·i·nal (mə-dĭs′ə-nəl) *adj.* Pertaining to or having the properties of medicine; healing; curative.
~n. A medicinal substance. **—me·dic·i·nal·ly** *adv.*

med·i·cine (mĕd′ə-sĭn) *n.* **1.** *Abbr.* **med.** The science of diagnosing, treating, alleviating, or preventing disease and other damage to the body or mind. **2.** The branch of this science encompassing treatment by drugs, diet, exercise, and other nonsurgical means. **3.** The practice of medicine. **4.** Any drug or other agent used to treat disease or injury. **5.** Among various tribal peoples, something believed to control natural or supernatural powers and to serve as a preventive or remedy. **—take one's medicine.** To endure deserved punishment. [Middle English, from Old French, from Latin *medicīna,* the art of a physician, from *medicus,* doctor, from *medērī,* to heal.]

medicine ball *n.* A large, heavy ball used for exercise.

medicine chest *n.* A cabinet, chest, or cupboard containing medicines, bandages, and the like.

medicine dance *n.* A ritual dance performed by some Plains Indians of North America to obtain supernatural assistance.

medicine lodge *n.* A large wooden structure used by some North American Indian peoples for various ritualistic ceremonies.

medicine man *n.* **1.** A person believed, especially among North American Indians, to possess supernatural powers for healing, invoking spirits, and other purposes; sorcerer; shaman. **2.** A hawker of brews and potions among the audience in a medicine show.

medicine show *n.* A traveling show, popular especially in 19th-century America, that offered varied entertainment between the acts of which medicines were peddled.

medick. Variant of **medic[1].**

med·i·co (mĕd′ĭ-kō′) *n., pl.* **-cos.** *Informal.* A doctor or medical student. [Italian and Spanish, from Latin *medicus,* doctor, from *medērī,* to heal.]

medico–, medic– *prefix.* Indicates medical and; for example, **medicolegal.** [Latin *medicus,* doctor.]

med·i·co·le·gal (mĕd′ĭ-kō-lē′gəl) *adj.* Of or pertaining to both medicine and law. [MEDICO- + LEGAL.]

me·di·e·val, me·di·ae·val (mē′dē-ē′vəl, mĕ-dē′vəl) *adj. Abbr.* **M., med. 1.** Of, pertaining to, or characteristic of the Middle Ages. **2.** *Informal.* Old-fashioned or out-of-date. [New Latin *Medium Aevum,* the Middle Age : Latin *medium,* neuter of *medius,* middle + *aevum,* age.] **—me·di·e·val·ly** *adv.*

Medieval Greek *n. Abbr.* **Med. Gr.** Greek as used from about A.D. 700 to 1500. Also called "Middle Greek."

me·di·e·val·ism, me·di·ae·val·ism (mē′dē-ē′və-lĭz′əm, mĕ-dē′-) *n.* **1.** The spirit, beliefs, or practices of the Middle Ages. **2.** Devotion to or acceptance of the ideas of the Middle Ages. **3.** Scholarly study of the Middle Ages. **—me·di·e·val·ist** *n.*

Medieval Latin *n. Abbr.* **ML, M.L.** Latin as used throughout Europe in the Middle Ages, from about A.D. 700 to 1500.

me·di·na (mə-dē′nə) *n.* The ancient native quarter of various North African towns. [Native name in North Africa.]

Me·di·na (mə-dē′nə). *Arabic* **Al Ma·di·nah** (ăl′ mə-dī′nə). Second-holiest city of Islam, in western Saudi Arabia, in a fertile date-producing oasis some 355 kilometers (220 miles) north of Mecca. Muhammad lived in the city after fleeing from Mecca (A.D. 622) and died here. The Mosque of the Prophet contains his tomb.

me·di·o·cre (mē′dē-ō′kər) *adj.* Neither good nor very bad; lacking in commendable qualities; very ordinary. —See Synonyms at **average.** [Latin *mediocris,* "halfway up the mountain," in a middle state : *medius,* middle + *ocris,* mountain, peak.]

me·di·oc·ri·ty (mē′dē-ŏk′rə-tē) *n., pl.* **-ties. 1.** The state or quality of being mediocre. **2.** Mediocre ability, achievement, or performance. **3.** A person who displays mediocre qualities.

med·i·tate (mĕd′ə-tāt′) *v.* **-tated, -tating, -tates.** *—tr.* **1.** To plan or intend in the mind: *He meditated revenge.* **2.** To reflect upon; ponder; contemplate. *—intr.* **1.** To direct one's thoughts; reflect. Used with *on* or *upon*: *He meditated upon his loss.* **2.** To engage in deep, contemplative thought or concentrate on one thing or nothing, having emptied the mind of all thoughts, especially as a religious exercise or a means of achieving spiritual enlightenment. [Latin *meditārī.*] **—med·i·ta·tor** *n.*

med·i·ta·tion (mĕd′ə-tā′shən) *n.* **1. a.** The act of meditating. **b.** A devotional exercise of contemplation. **2.** A contemplative discourse, usually on a religious or philosophical subject. —See **transcendental meditation.**

med·i·ta·tive (mĕd′ə-tā′tĭv) *adj.* Devoted to, characterized by, or expressing meditation. —See Usage note at **pensive. —med·i·ta·tive·ly** *adv.* **—med·i·ta·tive·ness** *n.*

Med·i·ter·ra·ne·an (mĕd′ə-tə-rā′nē-ən, -rān′yən) *adj.* **1.** Designating a subgroup of the Caucasian race characterized by dark hair and complexion and relatively short stature. **2.** Of, pertaining to, or characteristic of the Mediterranean Sea or the countries bordering it and their inhabitants. **3.** *Meteorology.* Having or pertaining to a type of climate with hot, dry summers and warm, wet winters. **4. mediterranean.** Surrounded or almost surrounded by land. Said of large bodies of water.
~n. **1.** The Mediterranean Sea. **2.** A member of the Mediterranean racial subgroup. **3.** A native or inhabitant of the Mediterranean region. [Latin *mediterrāneus* : *medius,* middle + *terra,* land.]

Mediterranean fever *n.* A disease, **brucellosis** *(see).*

Mediterranean fruit fly *n.* A black and white, two-winged fly, *Ceratitis capitata,* that is found in most subtropical countries and that attacks citrus and other fruits.

Mediterranean Sea. Almost landlocked body of water between Europe, North Africa, and Asia. It connects with the Atlantic through the Strait of Gibraltar, with the Black Sea through the Dardanelles, the Sea of Marmara, and the Bosporus, and with the Red Sea through the Suez Canal. Its larger islands include Crete, Cyprus, Sardinia, Corsica, and Sicily, and its shores have cradled many civilizations. Commercial developments have caused severe pollution that is aggravated by the sea's nearly tideless nature; nevertheless, tourism is important.

me·di·um (mē′dē-əm) *n., pl.* **-dia** (-dē-ə) or **-ums** (the only form for sense 5). *Abbr.* **m, M, m., M., med. 1.** Something occupying a position or having a condition midway between extremes; a mean; a compromise. **2.** *Physics.* An intervening substance through which something is transmitted or carried, such as an agency for transmitting energy. **3.** An agency, such as a person, object, or quality, by means of which something is accomplished, conveyed, or transferred: *Money is used as a medium of exchange.* **4.** A means of mass communication, such as newspapers, magazines, or television. See Usage note below. **5.** A person thought to have powers of communicating with the spirits of the dead. **6.** A surrounding environment in which something functions and thrives, especially: **a.** The substance in which a specific organism lives and thrives. **b.** A substance in which microorganisms are cultivated for scientific purposes; a culture medium. **7. a.** A specific type of artistic technique or means of expression as determined by the materials used or the creative methods involved. **b.** The materials used. **8.** Any solvent with which paint is thinned to the proper consistency. **9.** *Chemistry.* A filtering substance, such as filter paper. **10.** A size of paper, usually 46 × 58 centimeters (18 × 23 inches).
~*adj. Abbr.* **m, M, m., M., med. 1.** Occurring or being between two degrees, positions, amounts, or quantities; intermediate: *a medium steak.* **2.** Average; mean: *a medium-grade ore.* —See Synonyms at **average.** [Latin *medium,* the middle, from *medius,* middle.]
Usage: In the sense "means of mass communication," *media* is a plural noun, derived from *medium.* The incorrect use of *media* as a singular is sometimes heard: *Television is an unpredictable media* (should be *medium*). A new plural form is sometimes used *(medias),* but it is still considered unacceptable.

me·di·um-dat·ed (mē′dē-əm-dā′tĭd) *adj. Finance.* Of, pertaining to, or being gilt-edged securities that are redeemable at any time between 5 and 15 years after the date of purchase. Compare **long-dated, short-dated.**

medium frequency *n. Abbr.* **MF, M.F.** A radio frequency or radio-frequency band in the range 3,000 to 300 kilohertz.

medium of exchange *n.* Anything that is commonly used in a specific area or among a certain group of people as money. See **circulating medium, money.**

medium wave *n. Abbr.* **MW, M.W.** A radio wave or band of radio waves with wavelengths between 100 and 1,000 meters.

med·lar (mĕd′lər) *n.* **1.** A tree, *Mespilus germanica,* cultivated for its fruit. **2.** The fruit of this tree, similar in appearance to a crab apple but eaten when soft. [Middle English, from Old French *medler,* from *medle* (unattested), variant of *mesle,* a medlar fruit, from Latin *mespila,* from Greek *mespilē* †.]

med·ley (mĕd′lē) *n., pl.* **-leys. 1.** A jumbled assortment; a mixture: *a medley of grating noises.* **2.** A musical arrangement made up of a series of melodies from various sources. **3.** A swimming race in which each participant swims lengths using various different, prescribed strokes (in individual races) or in which each member of a team swims using a different stroke (in relay races).
~*adj.* **1.** Made up of a jumbled mixture of elements. **2.** Of or pertaining to a swimming medley: *a medley relay.* [Middle English *medlee,* from Old French, variant of *meslee,* from Vulgar Latin *misculāta* (unattested), from Late Latin *misculāre,* to mix up, frequentative of *miscēre,* to mix.]

Mé·doc[1] (mā-dôk′). A region of southwestern France, north of Bordeaux, between the Gironde estuary and the Bay of Biscay. It is particularly famous for its red wines.

Médoc[2] *n.* A red Bordeaux wine. [After MÉDOC.]

me·dul·la (mə-dŭl′ə) *n., pl.* **-las** or **-lae** (-lē). **1.** *Anatomy.* The inner core of certain animal body structures, as bone marrow, where this differs in form or function from the outer zone. **2.** The medulla oblongata. **3.** *Botany.* The **pith** *(see)* or central tissue in stems of certain plants. [Latin *medulla,* marrow.] **—me·dul·lar** (mə-dŭl′ər), **med·ul·lar·y** (mĕd′ə-lĕr′ē, mə-dŭl′ə-rē) *adj.*

medulla ob·lon·ga·ta (ŏb′lông-gä′tə) *n., pl.* **medulla oblongatas** or **medullae oblongatae** (-gä′tē). The nervous tissue at the bottom of the brain that controls respiration, circulation, and certain other bodily functions. [New Latin, "elongated marrow."]

medullary ray *n. Botany.* The undifferentiated tissue between the vascular bundles in young plants and in plants not undergoing secondary thickening.

medullary sheath *n.* **1.** *Anatomy.* See **myelin** (sense 1). **2.** *Botany.* A layer of thick-walled cells surrounding the pith in the stems of various plants.

med·ul·lat·ed (mĕd′ə-lā′tĭd) *adj.* **1.** *Anatomy.* Myelinated. **2.** Having a medulla. [Late Latin *medullātus,* having a marrow, from Latin *medulla,* MEDULLA.] **—med·ul·la·tion** *n.*

med·ul·li·za·tion (mĕd′ə-lə-zā′shən, mĕj′ə-) *n.* Replacement of bone tissue by marrow, as in inflammatory bone disease.

me·du·sa (mə-dōō′sə, -zə, mə-dyōō′-) *n., pl.* **-sas** or **-sae** (-sē, -zē). The tentacled, free-swimming sexual stage in the life cycle of a coelenterate of the class Scyphozoa or Hydrozoa; a jellyfish. Compare **polyp.** [New Latin.] **—me·du·san** *adj.*

Me·du·sa (mə-dōō′sə, -zə, mə-dyōō′-). *Greek Mythology.* One of the three Gorgons, slain by Perseus.

me·du·soid (mə-dōō′soid′, -zoid′, mə-dyōō′-) *n.* A jellyfish or a shape resembling a jellyfish. **—me·du·soid** *adj.*

meed (mēd) *n. Archaic.* A merited gift or reward. [Middle English *mede,* Old English *mēd.*]

meek (mēk) *adj.* **meeker, meekest. 1. a.** Showing patience and humility; gentle. **b.** Easily imposed upon; submissive. **2.** *Archaic.* Kind; merciful: *"that I am meek and gentle with these butchers"* (Shakespeare). —See Synonyms at **humble.** [Middle English *mēk, mēoc,* from Old Norse *mjūkr,* gentle, soft.] **—meek·ly** *adv.* **—meek·ness** *n.*

meer·kat (mîr′kăt′) *n.* Any of several small South African mammals similar to the mongoose; especially, *Suricata suricatta.* [Afrikaans, from Dutch, "sea-cat," originally a type of monkey, so called because imported from overseas.]

meer·schaum (mîr′shəm, -shôm′) *n.* **1.** A compact, usually white mineral of hydrous magnesium silicate, $Mg_4[Si_6O_{15}](OH)_2 \cdot 6H_2O$, found chiefly in the Mediterranean area and used in fashioning tobacco pipes and as a building stone. Also called "sepiolite." **2.** A tobacco pipe with a bowl of meerschaum. [German, "sea-foam," translation of Persian *kef-i-daryā,* referring to its frothy appearance.]

meet[1] (mēt) *v.* **met** (mĕt), **meeting, meets.** —*tr.* **1.** To come into the presence or company of by chance or by arrangement: *met her on the stairs.* **2.** To come into the presence or company of for the purpose of conferring: *meeting the directors at noon.* **3.** To be present at the arrival of: *I plan to meet the train.* **4.** To be introduced to; make the acquaintance of: *We'd like to meet your sister.* **5.** To come into association or conjunction with; join: *where the sea meets the sky.* **6.** To come to the notice of (the senses): *more than meets the eye.* **7.** To experience; undergo; suffer: *met his fate with courage.* **8.** To encounter in conflict or competition; oppose: *"We have met the enemy and they are ours"* (Oliver Hazard Perry). **9.** To cope or contend effectively with: *met every accusation with a satisfactory explanation.* **10.** To come into conformity with the views, wishes, or opinions of: *The firm must meet us on that point.* **11.** To satisfy (a demand, obligation, or the like); fulfill: *meet a need.* **12.** To pay; settle: *enough money to meet the expenses.* —*intr.* **1.** To come together by chance or by arrangement. Often used with *up* or *up with: met up with an old friend. Let's meet for a drink.* **2.** To come into conjunction or contact; be joined: *"East is East, and West is West, and never the twain shall meet"* (Rudyard Kipling). **3.** To come together as opponents; contend. **4.** To be introduced or become acquainted. **5.** To assemble, as for a meeting. **—meet someone halfway.** To compromise. **—meet with. 1.** To experience or encounter: *The housing bill met with approval.* **2.** To suffer or undergo: *meet with an accident.*
~*n.* **1.** A meeting or contest, especially an athletic competition. **2.** The gathering of hounds and riders for a hunt. [Middle English *meten,* Old English *mētan.*]

meet[2] *adj. Archaic.* Fitting; proper; suitable. [Middle English *mete, y-mete,* Old English *gemǣte.*] **—meet·ly** *adv.*

meet·ing (mē′tĭng) *n. Abbr.* **mtg. 1. a.** A coming together of people for a common purpose; an assembly. **b.** The persons so assembled. **2.** A place or point where things meet; a conjunction. **3.** A hostile or competitive encounter. **4.** A program of horse racing or dog racing at a particular racetrack. **—meeting of the minds.** Agreement; concord.

meet·ing·house (mē′tĭng-hous′) *n.* A place of worship, especially one used by Quakers.

meet·ing-point (mē′tĭng-point′) *n.* **1.** A place of assembly. **2.** An area where different cultures, ideas, or the like converge: *a meeting-point between East and West.*

mega– *prefix.* Indicates: **1.** *Abbr.* **M** One million (10^6); for example, **megahertz. 2. a.** Large; for example, **megalith. b.** Large in comparison with others of its kind; for example, **megatanker. 3.** *Informal.* Great or exaggeratedly large; for example **megastar, megahype.** [Greek, from *megas,* great.]

meg·a·buck (mĕg′ə-bŭk′) *n. Slang.* One million dollars.

meg·a·ceph·a·ly (mĕg′ə-sĕf′ə-lē) *n.* Enlargement of the head, **macrocephaly** *(see).* [MEGA- + -CEPHALY.] **—meg·a·ce·phal·ic** (mĕg′-ə-sə-făl′ĭk), **meg·a·ceph·a·lous** (mĕg′ə-sĕf′ə-ləs) *adj.*

meg·a·cy·cle (mĕg′ə-sī′kəl) *n. Physics.* One million cycles per second; a megahertz. Not in current technical usage.

meg·a·death (mĕg′ə-dĕth′) *n.* The death of one million people or a very large number of people, especially as the result of nuclear warfare.

Me·gae·ra (mə-jîr′ə). *Greek Mythology.* One of the **Furies** *(see).*

meg·a·ga·mete (mĕg′ə-gə-mēt′, -găm′ēt′) *n.* A **macrogamete** *(see).*

meg·a·hertz (mĕg′ə-hûrtz′) *n., pl.* **megahertz.** *Abbr.* **MHz** *Physics.* One million cycles per second, used especially as a radio-frequency unit. Also called "megacycle."

meg·a·lith (mĕg′ə-lĭth′) *n.* A very large stone used in various prehistoric architectures or monumental styles, notably in western Europe during the second millennium B.C. See **dolmen, menhir.** [MEGA- + -LITH.] **—meg·a·lith·ic** (mĕg′ə-lĭth′ĭk) *adj.*

megalo–, megal– *prefix.* Indicates largeness, greatness, or exaggerated size; for example, **megalocephaly, megalomania.** [Greek, from *megas* (extended stem *megal-*), great.]

meg·a·lo·blast (mĕg′ə-lō-blăst′, -bläst′) *n.* A large blood cell that is an abnormal form of a red-blood-cell precursor. It occurs in certain types of anemia *(megaloblastic anemias).* [MEGALO- + -BLAST.] **—meg·a·lo·blas·tic** (mĕg′ə-lō-blăs′tĭk) *adj.*

meg·a·lo·car·di·a (mĕg′ə-lō-kär′dē-ə) *n. Pathology.* Enlargement of the heart. Also called "cardiomegaly." [MEGALO- + Greek *kardia,* heart.]

meg·a·lo·ceph·a·ly (mĕg′ə-lō-sĕf′ə-lē) *n.* Enlargement of the head, **macrocephaly** *(see).* [MEGALO- + -CEPHALY.] **—meg·a·lo·ce·phal·**

Medusa *In Greek mythology, anyone who looked at the face of this snake-haired monster was turned to stone. Medusa was killed eventually by the hero Perseus, who avoided looking at her directly by watching her reflection in his polished shield. This representation of her is on the handle of a krater—a vessel used for diluting wine—and dates from about 520* B.C.

megalith *A prehistoric standing stone, or megalith, in Brittany, France. Megaliths, which were usually of undressed stone, are thought to have had religious significance for their builders, and this one has been converted into a Christian shrine.*

ic (mĕg′ə-lō-sə-făl′ĭk), **meg·a·lo·ceph·a·lous** (-sĕf′ə-ləs) *adj.*

meg·a·lo·ma·ni·a (mĕg′ə-lō-mā′nē-ə, -mān′yə) *n.* A psychopathological condition involving fantasies of wealth or power. —**meg·a·lo·ma·ni·ac** (mĕg′ə-lō-mā′nē-ăk′) *adj. & n.* —**meg·a·lo·ma·ni·a·cal** (-mə-nī′ə-kəl) *adj.*

meg·a·lop·o·lis (mĕg′ə-lŏp′ə-lĭs) *n.* A region made up of several large cities and their surrounding areas in sufficiently close proximity to be considered a single urban complex. [MEGALO- + Greek *polis,* city.] —**meg·a·lo·pol·i·tan** (mĕg′ə-lə-pŏl′ĭ-tən) *adj.*

meg·a·lo·saur (mĕg′ə-lə-sôr′) *n.* Also **meg·a·lo·sau·rus** (mĕg′-ə-lə-sôr′əs). An extinct gigantic carnivorous dinosaur, genus *Megalosaurus,* of the Jurassic period. [New Latin *Megalosaurus* : MEGALO- + -SAURUS.] —**meg·a·lo·sau·ri·an** *n. & adj.*

meg·a·phone (mĕg′ə-fōn′) *n.* A funnel-shaped device used to direct and amplify the voice. Compare **bullhorn.** —**meg·a·phon·ic** (mĕg′-ə-fŏn′ĭk) *adj.* —**meg·a·phon·i·cal·ly** *adv.*

meg·a·pode (mĕg′ə-pōd′) *n.* Any bird of the family Megapodiidae, found in Australia and many South Pacific islands, that incubates its eggs by natural heat from mounds of rotting vegetation, sand, and the like. Also called "mound-builder," "scrub fowl." [New Latin *Megapodius* : MEGA- + -PODE.]

Még·a·ra (mĕg′ər-ə). The capital of Mégaris, a small Dorian state. It was a wealthy center of sea trade (8th–5th century B.C.), and its people founded many colonies, including Byzantium.

meg·a·ron (mĕg′ə-rŏn′) *n., pl.* **-ara** (-ər-ə). The main hall or central room of an ancient Greek house, having a hearth. [Greek, from *megas,* large.]

meg·a·scop·ic (mĕg′ə-skŏp′ĭk) *adj.* Visible to the naked eye; macroscopic. —**meg·a·scop·i·cal·ly** *adv.*

meg·a·spo·ran·gi·um (mĕg′ə-spə-răn′jē-əm) *n., pl.* **-gia** (-jē-ə). *Botany.* A structure that encloses a megaspore. Sometimes called "macrosporangium."

meg·a·spore (mĕg′ə-spôr′, -spōr′) *n. Botany.* **1.** The larger of two types of spores formed by heterosporous plants, such as certain ferns, giving rise to the female gametophyte. Compare **microspore.** **2.** A spore that forms the embryo sac in seed plants. Sometimes called "macrospore." —**meg·a·spor·ic** *adj.*

meg·a·spo·ro·phyll (mĕg′ə-spôr′ə-fĭl′, -spōr′ə-fĭl′) *n. Botany.* A leaflike structure that bears megasporangia.

meg·a·there (mĕg′ə-thîr′) *n.* A member of the extinct family Megatheriidae, composed of large ground sloths of the Miocene and Pleistocene epochs. [New Latin *Megatherium* : MEGA- + -THERE.] —**meg·a·the·ri·an** (mĕg′ə-thîr′ē-ən) *adj.*

meg·a·ton (mĕg′ə-tŭn′) *n.* A unit of explosive force equal to one million tons of TNT. —**meg·a·ton·nage** *n.*

meg·a·watt (mĕg′ə-wŏt′) *n. Abbr.* **MW, M.W.** One million watts.

Me·gid·do (mə-gĭd′ō). Ancient fortress town of northern Israel. Strategically situated in the valley of Esdraelon, on the route between Mesopotamia and Egypt, it was the site of many battles, and it may be the Armageddon of the Bible (Revelation 16:16), where the last battle on earth will be fought.

Me·gil·lah (mə-gĭl′ə) *n.* **1.** The Judaic scroll containing the Biblical narrative of the Book of Esther, traditionally read in synagogues to celebrate the festival of Purim. **2.** **megillah.** *Informal.* A prolix, tediously detailed narrative or explanation. [Hebrew *məgillāh,* "scroll," from *gālal,* to roll.]

me·gilp, ma·gilp (mə-gĭlp′) *n.* A base used for oil colors, usually linseed oil and mastic varnish. [18th century : origin obscure.]

meg·ohm (mĕg′ōm′) *n. Symbol* MΩ. One million ohms. [MEGA- + OHM.]

me·grim (mē′grĭm) *n.* **1.** A migraine headache. **2.** *Often* megrims. A caprice or fancy: *"Can't one work for sober truth as well as for megrims?"* (George Eliot). **3.** megrims. Depression or unhappiness: *"If these megrims are the effect of Love, thank Heaven, I never knew what it was"* (Samuel Richardson). **4.** megrims. A disease of cattle and horses. In this sense, also called "blind staggers." [Middle English *mygreyn,* from Old French, MIGRAINE.]

Me·hem·et A·li (mə-hĕm′ĭt ä-lē′), Also **Mo·ham·med A·li** (mō-hăm′ĭd ä-lē′) (*c.* 1769–1849). Turkish soldier, pasha of Egypt (1805–49). He rose from common soldier to command the Turkish army in Egypt and became pasha of Egypt, then an Ottoman province. In the late 1830's he attacked Turkey. The European powers forced a peace that made Mehemet's line hereditary in Egypt.

Mei·ji (mā′jē′), also **Mu·tsu·hi·to** (mōō′tsōō-hē′tō) (1852–1912). Emperor of Japan (1867–1912). Aged 15, he took the throne in the Meiji Restoration of 1867 and presided over the transformation of Japan from a feudal state into a modern constitutional one. His name means "enlightened government."

mei·o·sis (mī-ō′sĭs) *n., pl.* **-ses** (-sēz′). **1.** *Biology.* The cell division in sexually reproducing organisms that reduces the number of chromosomes in reproductive cells to half that found in the somatic cells, leading to the production of gametes in animals and spores in plants. Also called "reduction division." Compare **mitosis.** **2.** Rhetorical understatement; litotes. [New Latin, from Greek *meiōsis,* diminution, from *meioun,* to diminish, from *meiōn,* less.] —**mei·ot·ic** (mī-ŏt′ĭk) *adj.* —**mei·ot·i·cal·ly** *adv.*

Me·ir (mī′ər, mä-îr′), **Golda,** born Golda Mabovitch (1898–1978). Russian-born Israeli stateswoman, prime minister of Israel (1969–74). She lived in the United States from 1906 and settled in Palestine in 1921. After Israel was created (1948) she became minister of labor (1949–56) and foreign minister (1956–66). In 1969 she became prime minister. She resigned in April 1974.

Meis·sen (mī′sən). City in Dresden district, East Germany, on the

Elbe River. It is famous for its porcelain, known as Meissen ware or Dresden china, made from local kaolin. Production of the porcelain began in 1710.

Meissen ware *n.* A delicate porcelain ware made in Meissen, East Germany. Also called "Dresden china."

Meis·ter·sing·er (mī′stər-sĭng′ər) *n., pl.* **-ers** or **Meistersinger.** A member of any of the guilds organized in the principal cities of Germany in the 14th, 15th, and 16th centuries for the purpose of establishing competitive standards for the composition and performance of music and poetry. Also called "mastersinger." [German, "master singer."]

Meit·ner (mīt′nər), **Lise** (1878–1968). Austrian-born physicist. She worked in Berlin with Otto Hahn, and in 1918 they discovered the element protactinium. Her analysis of Hahn's experiments on uranium nuclei marks the discovery of nuclear fission (1939).

Mek·nès (mĕk-nĕs′). A city of north-central Morocco. The city was founded *c.* 1672 and was known as the Versailles of Morocco because of its palatial buildings constructed by Sultan Ismail (*c.* 1670's).

Me·kong (mā′kŏng′, -kōng′). *Chinese* **Lan·cang Ji·ang** or **Lan·ts'ang Chi·ang** (läng′säng′ jē-äng′). Major river of Southeast Asia, 4,184 kilometers (2,600 miles) long. Rising in Tibet, China, it flows mainly south through China, Laos, Kampuchea, and Vietnam to the South China Sea. Its delta is a major rice-growing area, and its last 550 kilometers (340 miles) can take moderate-sized ships.

mel (mĕl) *n.* A constituent of certain pharmaceutical preparations, consisting of a pure form of honey. [Latin, "honey".]

Melaka. See **Malacca.**

mel·a·mine resin (mĕl′ə-mēn′) *n.* A thermosetting resin produced from melamine, $C_3H_6N_6$, used for molded products, adhesives, and surface coatings. [German *Melamin* : *Melam* (arbitrary term for distillate of ammonium thiocyanate) + AMINE.]

mel·an·cho·li·a (mĕl′ən-kō′lē-ə) *n.* A mental disorder characterized by feelings of dejection and usually by withdrawal. It is often a phase of manic-depressive psychosis. [New Latin, MELANCHOLY.] —**mel·an·cho·li·ac** (mĕl′ən-kō′lē-ăk′) *adj. & n.*

mel·an·chol·ic (mĕl′ən-kŏl′ĭk) *adj.* **1.** Suffering from or subject to melancholy; depressed. **2.** Pertaining to, subject to, or suffering from melancholia. —**mel·an·chol·ic** *n.* —**mel·an·chol·i·cal·ly** *adv.*

mel·an·chol·y (mĕl′ən-kŏl′ē) *n.* **1.** Sadness or depression of the spirits; gloom. **2.** Pensive reflection or contemplation. **3.** *Archaic.* **a.** Black bile, one of the four humors of ancient or medieval physiology. **b.** An emotional state characterized by sullenness and outbreaks of violent anger, believed to arise from the bile.

~*adj.* **1.** Sad; depressed; gloomy. **2. a.** Tending to cause sadness or gloom. **b.** Expressive of gloom or sadness: *a melancholy sigh.* **3.** Pensive; thoughtful: *"He had a pleasing face and a melancholy air"* (Jane Austen). —See Synonyms at **sad.** [Middle English *melencolie, melancholye,* from Old French *melancolie,* from Late Latin *melancholia,* from Greek *melankholia,* sadness, "(an excess of) black bile" : *melas* (stem *melan-*), black + *kholē,* bile.] —**mel·an·chol·i·ly** *adv.* —**mel·an·chol·i·ness** *n.*

Me·lanch·thon (mə-lăngk′thən), **Philip,** born Philipp Schwarzert (1497–1560). German theologian and a leader of the German Reformation. He was a friend of Luther, and wrote *Loci Communes* (1521), outlining Lutheran doctrine.

Mel·a·ne·sia (mĕl′ə-nē′zhə, -shə). A division of the Pacific islands, including Papua New Guinea, the Solomons, Vanuatu, New Caledonia, the Bismarck Archipelago, Fiji, and other islands in the southwest. The name comes from the Greek word *melas* (black), referring to the dark skin of the dominant race of inhabitants. See also **Micronesia, Polynesia.** See map at **Pacific Ocean.**

Mel·a·ne·sian (mĕl′ə-nē′zhən, -shən) *adj.* Of or pertaining to Melanesia, its people, or their languages.

~*n.* **1.** An indigenous inhabitant of Melanesia. **2.** A subfamily of Austronesian languages spoken in Melanesia.

mé·lange, me·lange (mā-länzh′) *n.* **1.** A mixture. **2.** *Geology.* A mixture of different rock types of diverse origin and age. [French, from Old French, from *mesler,* to mix, from Vulgar Latin *misculāre* (unattested), from Latin *miscēre,* to mix.]

mel·an·ic (mə-lăn′ĭk) *adj.* **1.** Of, pertaining to, or exhibiting melanism. **2.** Suffering from melanosis.

mel·a·nin (mĕl′ə-nĭn) *n.* A dark pigment found in the skin, retina, and hair. [MELAN(O)- + -IN.]

mel·a·nism (mĕl′ə-nĭz′əm) *n.* **1.** Dark coloration of the skin, hair, fur, or feathers due to excessive production of melanin. It occurs, for example, among populations of moths in regions blackened by pollution *(industrial melanism),* where dark coloration provides camouflage. **2.** *Pathology.* Melanosis. [MELAN(O)- + -ISM.] —**mel·a·nist** *n.* —**mel·a·nis·tic** (mĕl′ə-nĭs′tĭk) *adj.*

mel·a·nite (mĕl′ə-nīt′) *n.* A black variety of garnet. [German *Melanit* : MELAN(O)- + -ITE.] —**mel·a·nit·ic** (mĕl′ə-nĭt′ĭk) *adj.*

melano-, melan- *prefix.* Indicates blackness or darkness; for example, **melanocyte, melanoma.** [New Latin, from Greek, from *melas* (stem *melan-*), black.]

mel·a·noch·ro·i (mĕl′ə-nŏk′rō-ī′, -nŏk′roi′) *pl.n.* The members of a subdivision of Caucasians having dark hair and light skin. [New Latin, "the dark-pale (people)" : MELAN(O)- + Greek *ōkhroi,* plural of *ōkhros,* pale.] —**mel·a·noch·roid** (mĕl′ə-nŏk′roid′) *adj.*

mel·a·no·cyte (mĕl′ə-nō-sīt′) *n. Biology.* An epidermal cell capable of synthesizing the black pigment melanin, and responsible for color variations in the skin of many animals including humans. [MELANO- + -CYTE.]

mel·a·noid (mĕl′ə-noid′) *adj.* **1.** Black-pigmented; dark in color. **2.** Suffering from or resembling melanosis. [Greek *melanoeidēs,* black-looking : MELAN(O)- + -OID.] —**mel·a·noid** *n.*

mel·a·no·ma (mĕl′ə-nō′mə) *n., pl.* **-mas** or **-ma·ta** (-mə-tə). A dark-pigmented malignant tumor. [New Latin : MELAN(O)- + -OMA.]

mel·a·no·sis (mĕl′ə-nō′sĭs) *n. Pathology.* Abnormally dark pigmentation of the skin or other tissues, resulting from sunburn and various dermatoses. Also called "melanism." [New Latin : MELAN(O)- + -OSIS.] —**mel·a·not·ic** (mĕl′ə-nŏt′ĭk) *adj.*

mel·a·nous (mĕl′ə-nəs) *adj.* Having a swarthy or black complexion and black hair. Compare **xanthous.** [MELAN(O)- + -OUS.] —**mel·a·nos·i·ty** (mĕl′ə-nŏs′ə-tē) *n.*

mel·a·to·nin (mĕl′ə-tō′nĭn) *n.* A hormone secreted by the pineal gland that causes lightening of the skin in certain animals. [*Mel*anocyte + *seroto*nin (referring to its ability to lighten melanocytes).]

Mel·ba (mĕl′bə), **Dame Nellie,** stage name of Helen Porter Mitchell (1859–1931). Australian soprano. She made her debut in Brussels (1887) and sang regularly at Covent Garden (1888–1926) and the Metropolitan Opera (1893–1910).

Melba toast *n.* Very thin crisp toast. [After Dame Nellie MELBA.]

Mel·bourne (mĕl′bərn). Capital of Victoria, southeastern Australia, and the country's second-largest city. It was founded (1835) at the mouth of the Yarra River on Port Phillip Bay, and after the gold rush of 1851 it developed into a financial and market center. Its industries include engineering, vehicle and textile production, and food processing. Melbourne was the national capital (1901–27) and the site of the 1956 Olympic Games.

Melbourne, William Lamb, 2nd Viscount (1779–1848). British prime minister (1834 and 1835–41). He was home secretary in Lord Grey's government (1830–34) and succeeded Grey as prime minister.

Mel·chi·or (mĕl′kē-ôr′) *n.* One of the three **Magi** *(see)* who traveled to see the infant Jesus.

Melchior, Lauritz Lebrecht Hommel (1890–1973). U.S. operatic tenor, born in Denmark. He made his debut in Copenhagen in *I Pagliacci.* From 1926 to 1950 he was the leading Wagnerian tenor at the Metropolitan Opera in New York, singing in more than 1,000 performances.

Mel·chite (mĕl′kīt′) *n.* A member of the Uniat Greek Catholic Church, concentrated in the Middle East. [Medieval Latin *Melchita,* from Greek *Melkhitēs,* "royalist," from Syriac *malkā,* king.] —**Mel·chite** *adj.*

Mel·chiz·e·dek (mĕl-kĭz′ə-dĕk′). The king of Salem and high priest who blessed Abraham. Genesis 14:18.

meld¹ (mĕld) *v.* **melded, melding, melds.** —*tr.* To declare or display (a card or combination of cards) for inclusion in one's score in a game such as canasta or rummy. —*intr.* To present a meld. —*n.* **1.** An act of melding. **2.** A combination of cards to be declared for a score. [German *melden,* to declare, from Old High German *meldōn.*]

meld² *v.* **melded, melding, melds.** —*tr.* To cause to unite, blend, or combine. —*intr.* To become blended or combined. [Perhaps MELT + WELD.]

me·lee (mā′lā′, mā-lā′) *n.* Also **mê·lée** (mĕ-lā′). **1. a.** Confused hand-to-hand fighting in a pitched battle. **b.** A violent free-for-all. **2.** A confused and tumultuous mingling, as of a crowd: *the rush-hour melee.* —Synonyms at **conflict.** [French *mêlée,* a mixture, from Old French *meslee,* MEDLEY.]

mel·ic (mĕl′ĭk) *adj.* Designating poetry intended to be sung, especially ancient Greek lyric poems. [Latin *melicus,* from Greek *melikos,* from *melos,* song.]

mel·i·lot (mĕl′ə-lŏt′) *n.* Any of several plants of the genus *Melilotus,* native to the Old World, having compound leaves and narrow clusters of small, fragrant, white or yellow flowers. Also called "sweet clover." [Middle English *mellilot,* from French *melilot,* from Latin *melilōtus,* from Greek *melilōtos,* sweet clover, "honey-lotus" : *meli,* honey + *lōtos,* LOTUS.]

mel·i·nite (mĕl′ə-nīt′) *n.* A high explosive made with picric acid. [French *mélinite,* from Greek *melinos,* quince-yellow, pertaining to quinces or apples, from *melon,* fruit, apple.]

me·lio·rate (mĕl′yə-rāt′, mē′lē-ə-) *v.* **-rated, -rating, -rates.** —*tr.* To make better; improve. —*intr.* To grow better; especially, to evolve toward higher forms. [Latin *meliorāre,* from *melior,* better.] —**me·lio·ra·ble** (mĕl′yər-ə-bəl, mē′lē-ər-) *adj.* —**me·lio·ra·tive** *adj. & n.* —**me·lio·ra·tor** *n.*

me·lio·ra·tion (mĕl′yə-rā′shən, mē′lē-ə-) *n.* **1. a.** The act or process of improving something or the state of being improved. **b.** A specific instance of this; an improvement. **2.** *Linguistics.* **Amelioration** *(see).*

me·lio·rism (mĕl′yə-rĭz′əm, mē′lē-ə-) *n.* The belief that society has an innate tendency toward improvement and that this tendency may be furthered through deliberate human effort. [Latin *melior,* better.] —**me·lio·rist** *adj. & n.* —**me·lio·ris·tic** (mĕl′yə-rĭs′tĭk, mē′lē-ə-) *adj.*

me·lis·ma (mə-lĭz′mə, -lĭs′mə) *n., pl.* **-mas** or **-ma·ta** (-mə-tə). *Music.* **1.** A passage of several notes sung to one syllable of text, as in Gregorian chant. **2.** Any elaborate vocal passage. [Greek, from *melizein,* to sing, from *melos,* song.] —**mel·is·mat·ic** (mĕl′ĭz-măt′ĭk) *adj.*

mel·lif·er·ous (mə-lĭf′ər-əs) *adj.* Also **mel·lif·ic** (mə-lĭf′ĭk). Forming or bearing honey. [Latin *mellifer* : *mel,* honey + -FER.]

mel·lif·lu·ous (mə-lĭf′lōō-əs) *adj.* Also **mel·lif·lu·ent** (-ənt). **1.** Flow-

ing with honey or sweetness. **2.** Smooth and sweet; rich and harmonious. Said especially of sounds and utterances. [Latin *mellifluus* : *mel,* honey + *-fluus,* flowing.] —**mel·lif·lu·ous·ly** *adv.* —**mel·lif·lu·ous·ness** *n.*

Mel·lon (mĕl′ən), **Andrew William** (1855–1937). U.S. financier, industrialist, and public official. He amassed a huge fortune financing oil, steel, aluminum, and electrical enterprises and served as secretary of the treasury (1921–32). His vast art collection was the foundation of the National Gallery of Art in Washington, D.C.

mel·lo·phone (mĕl′ō-fōn′) *n.* A brass musical wind instrument sometimes used as a substitute for the French horn, which it resembles in tone. [MELLO(W) + -PHONE.]

mel·lo·tron (mĕl′ə-trŏn′) *n.* An electronic keyboard instrument that uses prerecorded tape loops to imitate the individual sounds of an orchestra. [*Mellow* + *electro*nic.]

mel·low (mĕl′ō) *adj.* **-lower, -lowest.** **1. a.** Soft, sweet, juicy, and full-flavored because of ripeness. Said of fruit. **b.** Suggesting any of these qualities. **2.** Rich and soft in quality; not harsh: *a mellow sound.* **3.** Having the gentleness, wisdom, or dignity often characteristic of maturity. **4.** Relaxed and at ease; genial. **5.** Slightly and pleasantly intoxicated. **6.** Moist, rich, soft, and loamy. Said of soil. **7.** Fully matured and free from acidity. Said of wine.
~*v.* **mellowed, -lowing, -lows.** —*tr.* To bring to maturity; ripen. —*intr.* **1.** To become ripe; mature. **2.** To become gentle and sympathetic: *He mellowed as he aged.* [Middle English *mel(o)we,* probably from an attributive use of Old English *melu,* meal, "soft and rich, like meal."] —**mel·low·ly** *adv.* —**mel·low·ness** *n.*

me·lo·de·on (mə-lō′dē-ən) *n.* A small reed organ similar to the harmonium. [Alteration of earlier *melodium,* from MELODY (by analogy with HARMONIUM).]

me·lod·ic (mə-lŏd′ĭk) *adj.* Pertaining to or containing melody. —**me·lod·i·cal·ly** *adv.*

me·lod·i·ca (mə-lŏd′ĭ-kə) *n.* A small instrument like a harmonica but with a small keyboard on top that is played with the fingers. [*Melode*on + harmonic*a.*]

melodic minor scale *n. Music.* A minor scale in which the sixth and seventh tones are sharpened in its ascending form and natural in its descending form. Compare **harmonic minor scale.**

me·lo·di·ous (mə-lō′dē-əs) *adj.* **1.** Containing or pertaining to a pleasing succession of sounds; tuneful. **2.** Agreeable or pleasant to the ear. —**me·lo·di·ous·ly** *adv.* —**me·lo·di·ous·ness** *n.*

mel·o·dize (mĕl′ə-dīz′) *v.* **-dized, -dizing, -dizes.** —*tr.* **1.** To write a melody for (a song lyric). **2.** To make melodious. —*intr.* **1.** To compose a melody. **2.** To mingle or blend: *"To murmur through the . . . groves, and melodize with man's blest nature there"* (P.B. Shelley). —**mel·o·diz·er, mel·o·dist** *n.*

mel·o·dra·ma (mĕl′ə-drä′mə, -dräm′ə) *n.* **1.** A dramatic presentation characterized by the heavy use of suspense, sensational episodes, romantic sentiment, and usually a happy ending. **2.** The dramatic genre characterized by this treatment. **3.** Behavior or occurrences having melodramatic characteristics. **4.** *Music.* A dramatic composition in which the spoken part is accompanied by music. [French *mélodrame,* originally "musical drama" : Greek *melos,* song + French *drame,* DRAMA.]

mel·o·dra·mat·ic (mĕl′ə-drə-măt′ĭk) *adj.* **1.** Having the excitement and emotional appeal of melodrama: *a melodramatic account of her arrest by the police.* **2.** Exaggeratedly sensational, emotional, or sentimental; histrionic.
~*n.* **melodramatics.** Melodramatic behavior. —**mel·o·dra·mat·i·cal·ly** *adv.*

mel·o·dra·ma·tize (mĕl′ə-drä′mə-tīz′, -dräm′ə-tīz′) *tr.v.* **-tized, -tizing, -tizes.** To create a melodrama out of; make melodramatic. —**mel·o·dra·ma·ti·za·tion** *n.*

mel·o·dy (mĕl′ə-dē) *n., pl.* **-dies.** **1.** A pleasing succession or arrangement of sounds. **2.** Musical quality: *the melody of verse.* **3.** *Music.* **a.** A rhythmically organized sequence of single tones so related to one another as to make up a particular musical phrase or idea; a tune. **b.** The structure of music with respect to the arrangement of single tones in succession. Together with harmony and rhythm, melody is one of the three basic elements of traditional Western music. **c.** The leading part or the air in a harmonic composition. [Middle English *melodie,* from Old French, from Late Latin *melōdia,* from Greek *melōidia,* choral song : *melos,* tune + *-ōidia,* "singing," from *aoidein,* to sing.]

mel·oid (mĕl′oid′, mĕl′ō-ĭd) *n.* Any beetle of the family Meloidae, which includes the oil beetles and blister beetles.
~*adj.* Of or pertaining to such beetles. [New Latin *meloidae* (family), from *Meloe*† (genus name).]

mel·on (mĕl′ən) *n.* **1.** Any of several varieties of two related vines, *Cucumis melo* or *Citrullus vulgaris,* widely cultivated for their edible fruit. **2.** The fruit of any of these vines, characteristically having a hard rind and juicy flesh. See **cantaloupe, honeydew melon, muskmelon, watermelon.** [Middle English, from Old French, from Late Latin *mēlo* (stem *mēlōn-*), shortening of Latin *mēlopepōn,* from Greek, melon, "apple-gourd," from *mēlon,* apple.]

Me·los (mē′lŏs). Greek **Mi·los** (mē′lŏs). Greek island in the Cyclades group in the Aegean Sea. It was a thriving center of early Aegean civilization, but later declined and was conquered by the Athenians (416 B.C.). Excavations on the island have unearthed many treasures, including (1820) the Venus de Milo, a marble statue of the 2nd or 1st century B.C., now in the Louvre, Paris.

Mel·pom·e·ne (mĕl-pŏm′ə-nē). *Greek Mythology.* The Muse of tragedy. [Latin *Melpomenē,* from Greek, "the singing one," from the

melon *A member of the Cucurbitaceae family, which includes gourds, cucumbers, and pumpkins. This is a tiger melon, a type of cantaloupe.*

feminine present participle of *melpesthai*, to sing, sing of, from *melpein†*, to sing.]

melt (mělt) *v.* **melted, melted** or *archaic* **molten** (mōl′tən), **melting, melts.** —*intr.* **1.** To be changed from a solid to a liquid state, as by the application of heat. **2.** To become liquid; dissolve: *Icing melts in the mouth.* **3.** To disappear or vanish gradually as if by melting. Often used with *away: The crowd melted away.* **4.** To pass or merge imperceptibly into something else; blend gradually. Used with *into: Sea melted into sky.* **5.** To become softened in feeling, as by compassion; be made gentle: *Her heart melted at the child's tears.* **6.** *Informal.* To be extremely hot; perspire from heat. —*tr.* **1. a.** To reduce from a solid to a liquid state, as by the application of heat. **b.** To reduce (manufactured metal articles) to the state of raw material, usually for making other metal articles. Used with *down: They melted everything down, from statues to spoons, for shell casings.* **2.** To dissolve: *She melted some honey in hot milk.* **3.** To cause to disappear gradually; disperse: *The sun melted the fog.* **4.** To cause to pass or merge imperceptibly; blend (colors or outlines, for example): *"This effect is produced by melting . . . the shadows in a ground still darker"* (Sir Joshua Reynolds). **5.** To soften (someone's feelings); make gentle or tender: *"O ye critics! will nothing melt you?"* (Laurence Sterne). —*n.* **1. a.** A melted solid. **b.** A blended or fused mass. **2.** The state of being melted. **3. a.** The act or operation of melting. **b.** The quantity melted in one period or operation. [Melt (infinitive), molten (past participle); Middle English *melten, molten,* Old English *meltan, gemolten,* from Germanic *maltjan* (unattested), to dissolve.] —**melt·a·bil·i·ty** *n.* —**melt·a·ble** *adj.* —**melt·er** *n.*

Synonyms: *deliquesce, dissolve, liquefy, thaw.*

Usage: The standard past tense form is *melted: The sun melted the ice. Molten* can be used only as an adjective; it differs from the adjectival use of *melted* in that it refers only to substances that melt at a very high temperature. Thus one may refer to *molten rock,* but to *melted ice cream.*

melt·age (mĕl′tĭj) *n.* **1.** The quantity or substance produced by a melting process. **2.** The process or act of melting.

melt·down (mĕlt′doun′) *n.* Severe overheating of the core of a nuclear reactor causing melting of the core and supporting base, so that molten radioactive material flows into the space below the reactor.

melting point *n. Abbr.* **mp, m.p. 1.** The temperature at which a solid becomes a liquid at standard atmospheric pressure. **2.** The temperature at which a solid and its liquid are in equilibrium, at any fixed pressure.

melting pot *n.* **1.** A container in which a substance is melted or fused. **2.** A place where much change or mixing occurs, as of people, ideas, or cultures.

mel·ton (mĕl′tən) *n.* A heavy, woolen cloth used chiefly for making overcoats and hunting jackets. [After *Melton* Mowbray, town in Leicestershire, England.]

melt·wa·ter (mĕlt′wô′tər, -wŏt′ər) *n.* Water produced by the melting of snow or ice.

Mel·ville (mĕl′vĭl′), **Herman** (1819–91). U.S. novelist. Many of his works, such as his allegorical masterpiece *Moby Dick* (1851), draw on his experiences as a crewman on a whaler. He also wrote *Redburn* (1849) and *Billy Budd* (published 1924).

mem (mĕm) *n.* The thirteenth letter of the Hebrew alphabet. See feature at **alphabet.** [Hebrew, perhaps from *mayim,* water.]

mem. 1. member. **2.** memoir. **3.** memorandum. **4.** memorial.

mem·ber (mĕm′bər) *n.* **1.** *Abbr.* **M., mem.** An individual belonging to a group or organization. **2.** *Abbr.* **M., mem.** *Often* **Member.** One who serves on or is elected to a political body such as Congress. **3.** A distinct part of a whole, such as an architectural support in a building or a proposition of a syllogism. **4.** A part or organ of a human or animal body, especially: **a.** A limb, such as an arm or leg. **b.** The penis. **5.** A part of a plant. **6.** *Biology.* Any individual organism belonging to a taxonomic group. **7.** *Mathematics.* **a.** The expression on either side of an equality sign. **b.** An element of a set. [Middle English, from Old French *membre,* from Latin *membrum.*]

mem·ber·ship (mĕm′bər-shĭp′) *n.* **1.** The state of being a member. **2.** The total number of members of a group or organization.

mem·brane (mĕm′brān′) *n.* **1.** *Biology.* A thin, pliable layer of tissue covering surfaces or separating or connecting regions, structures, or organs of an animal or plant. **2.** A piece of parchment. **3.** *Chemistry.* A thin sheet of natural or synthetic material that is permeable to substances in solution. **4.** A thin piece of skin or plastic stretched over the end of a drum. [Latin *membrāna,* membrane, "skin covering an organ or member of the body," from *membrum,* member.]

membrane bone *n.* A bone formed directly in the connective tissue, as some cranial bones are. Compare **cartilage bone.**

mem·bra·nous (mĕm′brə-nəs) *adj.* Also **mem·bra·na·ceous** (mĕm′brə-nā′shəs). Made of or similar to a membrane.

membranous labyrinth *n.* The sensory structures of the inner ear.

Memel. See **Klaipeda.**

me·men·to (mə-mĕn′tō) *n., pl.* **-tos** or **-toes.** Any reminder of the past; a keepsake, souvenir, or relic. [Middle English, from Latin *mementō,* "remember," imperative of *meminisse,* to remember.]

memento mo·ri (môr′ē, mōr′ī′) *n.* Any reminder of death or mortality, such as a skull or an ornament bearing symbols of death. [Latin, "remember that you must die."]

Mem·ling (mĕm′lĭng), **Hans** (c. 1430–95). Flemish painter of religious works and portraits, born in Germany. Among his paintings

are *Tommaso Portinari and His Wife* (c. 1468) and the *Diptych of Martin van Nieuwenhoven* (1487).

Mem·non¹ (mĕm′nŏn′). *Greek Mythology.* An Ethiopian king killed by Achilles in the Trojan War and made immortal by Zeus.

Memnon² *n.* A huge statue of the Egyptian Pharaoh Amenhotep III at Thebes.

mem·o (mĕm′ō) *n., pl.* **-os.** A memorandum.

mem·oir (mĕm′wär′, -wôr′) *n. Abbr.* **mem. 1. a.** A narrative of one's experiences or a historical account based on personal experience. **b.** *Usually* **memoirs.** An autobiography. **c.** A biography or biographical sketch. **2.** A monograph: *a memoir on anthills.* **3.** **memoirs.** The report or a collection of reports of the proceedings of a learned society. [French *mémoire,* MEMORY.]

mem·o·ra·bil·i·a (mĕm′ər-ə-bĭl′ē-ə, -bĭl′yə) *pl.n.* Things worthy of remembrance. [Latin *memorābilia,* from *memorābilis,* MEMORABLE.]

mem·o·ra·ble (mĕm′ər-ə-bəl) *adj.* Worth being remembered; notable. [Middle English, from Latin *memorābilis,* from *memorāre,* to remember, from *memor,* mindful.] —**mem·o·ra·bil·i·ty, mem·o·ra·ble·ness** *n.* —**mem·o·ra·bly** *adv.*

mem·o·ran·dum (mĕm′ə-rǎn′dəm) *n., pl.* **-dums** or **-da** (-də). *Abbr.* **mem. 1.** A short note written as a reminder. **2.** A written record or communication, as in a business office. **3.** *Law.* A short, written statement outlining the terms of an agreement, transaction, or contract. **4.** A brief, unsigned diplomatic communication. [Middle English, from Latin, "let it be remembered," neuter singular gerundive of *memorāre,* to remember, from *memor,* mindful.]

me·mo·ri·al (mə-môr′ē-əl, mə-mōr′-) *n. Abbr.* **mem. 1.** Something, such as a monument or a public holiday, designed or established to serve as a remembrance of a person or an event. **2.** A written statement of facts or a petition presented to a legislative body or an executive. —*adj.* **1.** Serving as a remembrance of a person or event; commemorative. **2.** Of, pertaining to, or in memory. [Middle English, from Latin *memoriālis,* belonging to memory, from *memoria,* MEMORY.] —**me·mo·ri·al·ly** *adv.*

Memorial Day *n.* May 30, a U.S. holiday officially celebrated on the last Monday in May in honor of members of the armed forces killed in war.

me·mo·ri·al·ist (mə-môr′ē-ə-lĭst, mə-mōr′-) *n.* **1.** A person who writes memoirs. **2.** A person who writes or signs a memorial.

me·mo·ri·al·ize (mə-môr′ē-ə-līz′, mə-mōr′-) *tr.v.* **-ized, -izing, -izes. 1.** To commemorate. **2.** To present a memorial to; petition. —**me·mo·ri·al·i·za·tion** *n.* —**me·mo·ri·al·iz·er** *n.*

me·mo·ri·a tech·ni·ca (mə-môr′ē-ə tĕk′nĭ-kə, mə-mōr′-) *n.* A device or system that is used to aid the memory, as a mnemonic. [New Latin, artificial memory.]

mem·o·rize (mĕm′ə-rīz′) *tr.v.* **-rized, -rizing, -rizes.** To commit to memory; learn by heart. —**mem·o·riz·a·ble** *adj.* —**mem·o·ri·za·tion** *n.* —**mem·o·riz·er** *n.*

mem·o·ry (mĕm′ə-rē) *n., pl.* **-ries. 1.** The mental faculty of retaining and recalling past experience; the ability to remember. **2.** An act or instance of remembering; recollection: *pleasant memories of his childhood.* **3.** All that a person can remember or all that is retained in the mind. **4.** Something remembered of a person, thing, or event: *He has no memory of that occasion.* **5. a.** The fact of being remembered, as after death. **b.** Remembrance: *in memory of our loved ones.* **6.** The period of time covered by the remembrance or recollection of a person or group of persons: *within the memory of man.* **7.** *Physics.* The property of a substance or system that depends on past treatment or states of the substance or system. **8. a.** A unit, such as one in or attachable to a computer, calculator, or word processor, that preserves data for retrieval. Also called "memory store," "store." **b.** The capacity of such a unit. **9.** *Statistics.* The set of past events affecting a given event in a stochastic process. [Middle English *memorie,* from Old French, from Latin *memoria,* from *memor,* mindful.]

Synonyms: *recollection, remembrance, reminiscence.*

memory engram *n.* An engram (see).

memory span *n.* The length of time that a person is able to retain something in his short-term memory.

memory trace *n.* A hypothetical change to a brain cell or to structures of brain cells as a result of learning.

Mem·phis¹ (mĕm′fĭs). Ruined city on the Nile River 18 kilometers (12 miles) south of Cairo, Egypt. Reputedly founded by the pharaoh Menes, it was the capital of the Old Kingdom (c. 3100–c. 2258 B.C.), the first united Egyptian state, and was the center for the worship of Ptah. The city declined with the rise of Thebes, but temporarily revived under the Persians, Ptolemies, and Romans. Its remains include the temple of Ptah.

Memphis². City of southwestern Tennessee, at the confluence of the Mississippi and Wolf rivers. It is an important river port and rail center.

mem·sa·hib (mĕm′sä′ĭb) *n.* Formerly, a title of respect or form of address for a European woman in India. [MA'AM + SAHIB.]

men. Plural of **man.**

men·ace (mĕn′ĭs) *n.* **1. a.** A threat: *the menace of nuclear war.* **b.** The act of threatening. **2.** A dangerous or potentially dangerous person or thing. **3.** *Informal.* A troublesome or annoying person: *She has become a menace with her gossip.* —*v.* **menaced, -acing, -aces.** —*tr.* **1.** To threaten in a hostile or nasty manner. **2.** To constitute a threat to. —*intr.* To make threats; indicate danger or coming harm. —See Synonyms at **threaten.** [Middle English *manace,* from Old French, from Latin *minācia,* menace, originally "threatening things," neuter plural of *minax* (stem *minac-*), threatening, from *minārī,* to threaten, from *minae,* threats.] **—men·ac·er** *n.* **—men·ac·ing·ly** *adv.*

men·a·di·one (mĕn′ə-dī′ōn′) *n.* A yellow crystalline powder, $C_{11}H_8O_2$, having physiological effects similar to vitamin K. It is used as a medicine and as a fungicide. [*me*thyl + *na*phtha + DI- + -ONE.]

mé·nage, me·nage (mā-näzh′) *n.* **1.** A group of people living together as a unit; a household. **2.** The management of a household. [French, from Old French *menage,* from Vulgar Latin *mansiōnāticum* (unattested), household, from *mansiō* (stem *mansiōn-*), house, dwelling, from *manēre,* to dwell.]

ménage à trois (ä trwä) *n., pl.* **ménages à trois** (*(pronounced as singular)*. A sexual relationship involving three people, as a married couple and the lover of one of them, who live together. [French, "household of three."]

me·nag·er·ie (mə-năj′ə-rē, mə-năzh′-) *n.* **1.** A collection of live wild animals on exhibition. **2.** The enclosure in which such animals are kept. [French *ménagerie,* originally "the management of domestic animals," from *ménage,* MÉNAGE.]

Men·ai Strait (mĕn′ī′). Channel of the Irish Sea separating the island of Anglesey from the mainland, in Gwynedd, Wales. It is 23 kilometers (14 miles) long.

Me·nan·der (mə-năn′dər) (*c.* 342–290 B.C.). Greek dramatist who wrote tangled love plays. Only one, *The Curmudgeon,* discovered at Cairo in 1957, survives intact.

men·a·qui·none (mĕn′ə-kwī-nōn′) *n.* A form of **vitamin K** *(see).* [*me*thyl*na*phtho*quinone.*]

me·nar·che (mə-när′kē) *n.* The first occurrence of menstruation in young women. [New Latin : Greek *mēn,* month + *arkhē,* beginning.] **—me·nar·che·al** *adj.*

Men·ci·us (mĕn′shē-əs) (*c.* 372–289 B.C.). Chinese Confucian philosopher. He traveled from place to place throughout China, teaching that man is by nature good and that his innate nature can be developed by cultivation or perverted by an unfavorable environment.

Menck·en (mĕng′kən), **Henry Louis** (1880–1956). U.S. journalist and literary critic. He founded the magazine *American Mercury* with George Jean Nathan in 1924. His essays are collected in the six-volume work *Prejudices* (1919–27). He also wrote the four-volume work *The American Language* (1918).

mend (mĕnd) *v.* **mended, mending, mends.** *—tr.* **1.** To make right or correct; repair. **2.** To reform or improve. Used chiefly in the phrases *mend one's ways* or *manners.* *—intr.* **1.** To undergo a moral improvement; reform. **2. a.** To improve in health: *He is mending well.* **b.** To heal: *The bone mended in a month.*
∼n. **1.** The act of mending. **2.** A part or place mended or repaired after breaking or coming apart. **3.** A place on a piece of material that has been mended, as by a patch or darning. **—on the mend.** Improving, especially in health; recuperating. [Middle English *menden,* shortening of *amenden,* to AMEND.] **—mend·a·ble** *adj.* **—mend·er** *n.*

men·da·cious (mĕn-dā′shəs) *adj.* **1.** Lying; untruthful: *a mendacious child.* **2.** False; untrue: *a mendacious statement.* —See Synonyms at **dishonest.** [Latin *mendāx* (stem *mendāc-*), mendacious.] **—men·da·cious·ly** *adv.* **—men·dac·i·ty** (mĕn-dăs′ə-tē) *n.*

Men·del (mĕn′dəl), **Gregor Johann** (1822–84). Moravian monk and founder of the science of genetics. He entered the Augustinian monastery at Brno in 1843 and for 25 years experimented with plants, chiefly garden peas. He discovered the principle of the inheritance of characteristics through the combination of genes from parent cells. His conclusions, published in 1866 and ignored during his lifetime, form the basis of scientific genetics.

men·de·le·vi·um (mĕn′də-lē′vē-əm) *n. Symbol* **Md** A radioactive transuranic element of the actinide series. Atomic number 101, half-life of the most stable isotope (Md^{258}) 60 days. Also called "unnilunium." [New Latin, after Dmitri MENDELEYEV.]

Men·de·le·yev (mĕn′də-lā′əf), **Dmitri Ivanovich** (1834–1907). Russian chemist. He formulated the periodic table of the elements, noting the regular recurrence of their chemical and physical properties when they are arranged by their atomic numbers. Other scientists, notably Lothar Meyer (1830–95), independently reached the same conclusions, but Mendeleyev was the first to draw attention to gaps in the periodic arrangement and to postulate the existence of undiscovered elements to fill them.

Men·de·li·an (mĕn-dē′lē-ən, -dēl′yən) *adj.* Of or pertaining to Gregor Mendel or his theories of genetics.

Men·del·ism (mĕn′də-lĭz′əm) *n.* Also **Men·de·li·an·ism** (mĕn-dē′lē-ə-nĭz′əm). The theoretical principles of heredity formulated by Gregor Mendel. See **Mendel's laws.**

Mendel's laws *pl.n.* The principles of heredity of sexually reproducing organisms formulated by Gregor Mendel, now usually summarized in three laws: **1.** *Law of Segregation:* Certain paired characteristics, one from each parent, do not blend with or alter each other in the offspring, thus accounting for contrasting traits in successive generations. **2.** *Law of Independent Assortment:* The genes determining such pairs of traits combine in the offspring according to the laws of chance. **3.** *Law of Dominance:* If one of a pair of genes is dominant and the other recessive, the recessive trait may appear in an offspring only if both genes of its pair are recessive.

Men·dels·sohn (mĕn′dəl-sən), **Felix,** born Jacob Ludwig Felix Mendelssohn-Bartholdy (1809–47). German composer. Mendelssohn was a child prodigy; his overture to *A Midsummer Night's Dream* and his *Octet* for strings were both written by the time he was 17. Among his other works are five symphonies, the oratorios *St. Paul* (1836) and *Elijah* (1846), the violin concerto in E minor (1844), and six string quartets.

Men·dès-France (mäN′dĕs-fräNs′), **Pierre** (1907–82). French prime minister (1954–55). He was economic minister in De Gaulle's government (1944–45). As prime minister he negotiated France's withdrawal from Indochina, but he resigned when his liberal policies on the North African colonies were rejected. He led the Radical Socialist Party until 1957.

men·di·cant (mĕn′dĭ-kənt) *adj.* **1.** Depending upon alms for a living; practicing begging. **2.** Characteristic of a beggar or begging. *∼n.* **1.** A beggar. **2.** A member of a mendicant order of friars. [Latin *mendīcāns* (stem *mendīcānt-*), present participle of *mendīcāre,* to beg, from *mendīcus,* beggar, poor man, originally "injured," from *mendum,* physical defect.] **—men·di·can·cy, men·dic·i·ty** (mĕn-dĭs′ə-tē) *n.*

mend·ing (mĕn′dĭng) *n.* Articles, especially clothes, that are to be or have been mended.

Men·dip Hills (mĕn′dĭp′). Limestone range in Somerset, southwestern England. The range runs northwest from the Frome valley, reaching 325 meters (1,068 feet) at Blackdown.

Men·e·la·us (mĕn′ə-lā′əs). *Greek Mythology.* The king of Sparta, brother of Agamemnon, and husband of Helen whose abduction gave rise to the Trojan War.

men·folk (mĕn′fōk′) *pl.n.* **1.** Men collectively. **2.** A particular group of men, as in a family: *They lost their menfolk in the war.*

men·ha·den (mĕn-hād′n) *n., pl.* **-dens** or collectively **menhaden.** An abundant inedible fish, *Brevoortia tyrannus,* of American Atlantic and Gulf waters, used as a source of fish oil, fish meal, fertilizer, and bait. Also called "mossbunker," "oldwife." [Algonquian; akin to Natick *munnohquohteau,* "he fertilizes" (menhaden were used by the Algonquins as fertilizer for corn).]

men·hir (mĕn′hîr′) *n.* A prehistoric monument of a class found chiefly in the British Isles and northern France, consisting of a single tall, upright megalith. Compare **dolmen.** [French, from Breton *men hir,* "long stone" : *men,* stone + *hir,* long.]

me·ni·al (mē′nē-əl, mēn′yəl) *adj.* **1.** Of, pertaining to, or appropriate for a servant. **2.** Of or pertaining to work or a job regarded as servile or degrading. **3.** Of, pertaining to, or involving work, such as cleaning, that is routine, boring, and requires little skill.
∼n. **1.** A servant, especially a domestic servant. **2.** A person who has a servile or low nature. [Middle English *meynial,* from Norman French *menial,* Old French *meinie, mesne,* servant, from Vulgar Latin *mānsiōnatā* (unattested), household, from *mānsiō,* house, dwelling. See **mansion.**] **—me·ni·al·ly** *adv.*

Mé·nière's disease (mən-yârz′, mĕn′yərz) *n.* A disorder of the inner ear involving progressive deafness, loss of balance, ringing in the ear, and nausea. Also called "Ménière's syndrome." [After Prosper *Ménière* (1799–1862), French physician.]

me·nin·ge·al (mə-nĭn′jē-əl) *adj.* Of, pertaining to, or concerned with a meninx or meninges.

men·in·gi·tis (mĕn′ĭn-jī′tĭs) *n. Pathology.* Inflammation of any or all of the meninges of the brain and the spinal cord, usually caused by a bacterial infection. Also called "brain fever." [New Latin : *meninges* + -ITIS.] **—men·in·git·ic** (mĕn′ĭn-jĭt′ĭk) *adj.*

me·ninx (mē′nĭngks) *n., pl.* **meninges** (mə-nĭn′jēz). Any of the three membranes enclosing the brain and spinal cord in vertebrates. [New Latin, from Greek *mēninx* (stem *mēning-*), membrane.]

me·nis·cus (mə-nĭs′kəs) *n., pl.* **-cuses** or **menisci** (-nĭs′ī′). **1.** A crescent-shaped body. **2.** A concavo-convex lens. **3.** The curved upper surface of a stationary liquid in a container. It is concave if the liquid wets the container walls and convex if it does not. **4.** *Anatomy.* A cartilage disk that cushions the ends of bones in a joint. [New Latin, from Greek *mēniskos,* crescent, diminutive of *mēnē,* moon.] **—me·nis·cal** (mə-nĭs′kəl), **me·nis·cate** (-nĭs′kāt′), **me·nis·coid** (-nĭs′koid′), **men·is·coi·dal** (mĕn′ĭ-skoid′l) *adj.*

Men·ning·er (mĕn′ĭn-jər). Family of U.S. psychiatrists, including **Charles Frederick** (1862–1953) and his sons **Karl Augustus** (1893–1966) and **William Claire** (1899–1966). The family established the Menninger Clinic in Topeka, Kansas, in 1920 and the Menninger Foundation in 1941. Both are dedicated to treatment, research, training, and public education in psychiatry.

Men·non·ite (mĕn′ə-nīt′) *n.* A member of a Protestant Christian sect opposed to baptism, taking oaths, holding public office, or performing military service. [German *Mennonit,* after *Menno* Simons (1492–1559), religious reformer.]

me·nol·o·gy (mə-nŏl′ə-jē) *n., pl.* **-gies.** **1.** An ecclesiastical calendar of the months with important religious events recorded. **2.** In the Eastern Orthodox Church, a collection of short biographies of the lives of the saints arranged in the form of a calendar. [Medieval Greek *mēnologion,* "list of months" : Greek *mēn,* month + -LOGY.]

me·no mos·so (mā′nō mô′sō) *adv. Music.* With less speed. Used as a direction. [Italian, "less rapid."]

Men·on (mĕn′ən), **(Vengalil Krishnan) Krishna** (1897–1974). Indian politician. In 1952 he headed the Indian delegation to the United Nations, and in 1957 he became defense minister. He resigned in 1962, after China attacked India's border.

men·o·pause (mĕn′ə-pôz′) *n.* The period of cessation of menstruation, occurring typically between the ages of 45 and 50. Also called "change of life," "climacteric." [New Latin *menopausis* : *meno-,* from Greek *mēn,* month + *pausis,* PAUSE.] **—men·o·paus·al** (mĕn′ə-pô′zəl) *adj.*

PRONUNCIATION KEY

ă, pat; ā, pay; âr, care;
ä, father, are; b, bib;
ch, church; d, deed; ĕ, pet;
ē, be; f, fife; g, gag; h, hat;
hw, which; ĭ, pit; ī, pie;
îr, pier; j, judge; k, kick;
l, lid, needle; m, mum;
n, no, sudden; ng, thing;
ŏ, pot; ō, toe; ô, paw, for;
oi, noise; ou, out; o͝o, book;
o͞o, boot; p, pop; r, roar;
s, sauce; sh, ship, dish;
t, tight; th, thin, path;
th, this, bathe; ŭ, cut; ûr, fur;
v, valve; w, with; y, yes;
z, zebra, size; zh, vision;
ə, about, item, edible,
gallop, circus, peaceful

IN FOREIGN WORDS:

à, *Fr.* ami; œ, *Fr.* feu, *Ger.* schön; ü, *Fr.* tu, *Ger.* über; KH, *Ger.* ich, *Scot.* loch; N, *Fr.* bon; y′, *Fr.* Compiègne

STRESS MARKS:

Primary stress: ′
in·cite′ (ĭn-sīt′)
Secondary stress: ′
in′sight′ (ĭn′sīt′)

me·no·rah (mə-nôr′ə, -nōr′ə) *n.* **1.** A ceremonial seven-branched candelabrum of the Jewish Temple symbolizing the seven days of the Creation. Exodus 37:17-24. **2.** A nine-branched candelabrum used in the celebration of Chanukah. [Hebrew *mənorāh,* candlestick.]

Me·nor·ca (mə-nôr′kə). *English* **Mi·nor·ca** (mĭ-). Second largest of the Balearic Islands, Spain. Situated in the Mediterranean Sea, it is predominantly low-lying; agriculture, fishing, and tourism are its main industries. Mahón is the chief town and port. **—Me·nor·can** *adj. & n.*

men·or·rha·gi·a (mĕn′ə-rā′jē-ə) *n. Pathology.* Abnormally heavy menstrual flow. [New Latin : Greek *mēn,* month + -RRHAGIA.]

Me·not·ti (mə-nŏt′ē), **Gian-Carlo** (1911-). Italian composer who has lived chiefly in the United States since 1927. He has written his own English librettos for most of his operas, which include *The Medium* (1946) and *The Consul* (1950).

Men·sa¹ (mĕn′sə) *n.* A southern constellation between Hydrus and Carina. [Latin *mēnsa†,* table.]

Mensa² *n.* An international society established in 1946 for the stimulation of and exchange of ideas among its members. Membership is restricted to those with an I.Q. in the top two percent in each member country.

men·sal¹ (mĕn′səl) *adj.* Belonging to or used at the table. [Late Latin *mēnsālis,* from *mēnsa†,* table.]

mensal² *adj.* Monthly. [Latin *mēnsis,* month.]

mensch (mĕnsh) *n. Informal.* A person having admirable characteristics, such as fortitude and firmness of purpose. [Yiddish *mens(c)h,* from Middle High German *mensch,* man, from Old High German *mennisco.*]

men·ses (mĕn′sēz′) *pl.n.* **1.** *Physiology.* Blood and dead cell debris that is discharged from the uterus through the vagina by nonpregnant adolescent girls and women at approximately monthly intervals between puberty and menopause. **2.** Menstruation. [Latin *mēnsēs,* months, hence also "monthly periods," plural of *mēnsis,* month.]

Men·she·vik (mĕn′shə-vĭk′) *n., pl.* **-viks** or **Mensheviki** (mĕn′shə-vē′kē). **1. a.** A member of the liberal minority faction of the Russian Social Democratic Party that struggled against the Bolsheviks from 1903 until the Russian Revolution in 1917. Also called "Minimalist." **b.** A member of a liberal socialist group established after the Russian Revolution to oppose the Bolshevik Party. **2.** A person having views in accord with the Menshevik faction. Compare **Bolshevik.** [Russian *men'shevik,* a member of the smaller (faction), from *men'she,* less, from Old Church Slavonic *mǐnǐshǐ,* less.] **—Men·she·vism** *n.* **—Men·she·vist** *adj. & n.*

mens re·a (mĕnz′ rē′ə) *n. Law.* Criminal intent. [Latin, "guilty mind."]

men's room *n.* A restroom for men.

men·stru·al (mĕn′strōō-əl) *adj.* Also **men·stru·ous** (mĕn′strōō-əs). Pertaining to menstruation. [Middle English *menstruall,* from Latin *mēnstruālis,* from *mēnstruus,* menstrual, monthly, from *mēnsis,* month.]

men·stru·ate (mĕn′strōō-āt′) *intr.v.* **-ated, -ating, -ates.** To undergo menstruation. [Latin *mēnstruāre,* from *mēnstruus,* MENSTRUAL.]

men·stru·a·tion (mĕn′strōō-ā′shən) *n.* **1.** *Physiology.* The process or an instance of discharging the menses. **2.** The period of time during which this occurs. Also called "menses."

men·stru·um (mĕn′strōō-əm) *n., pl.* **-ums** or **-strua** (-strōō-ə). A solvent, especially one used in extracting and preparing drugs. [Middle English, from Medieval Latin *mēnstruum,* solvent, originally "menstrual blood" (alchemists regarded the gold-transmuting solvent as similar to menstrual blood, which they believed transformed sperm in the womb into an embryo), from Latin *mēnstruus,* MENSTRUAL.]

men·su·ra·ble (mĕn′sər-ə-bəl, mĕn′shər-ə-) *adj.* **1.** Capable of being measured. **2.** Having fixed rhythm and measure, as in music; mensural. **—men·su·ra·bil·i·ty** *n.*

men·su·ral (mĕn′sər-əl, mĕn′shər-) *adj.* **1.** Of or pertaining to measure. **2.** *Music.* Of, pertaining to, or designating music having notes of fixed rhythmic value. [Latin *mēnsūrālis,* from *mēnsūra,* MEASURE.]

men·su·ra·tion (mĕn′sə-rā′shən, mĕn′shə-) *n.* **1.** The process, act, or art of measuring. **2.** The measurement of geometric quantities. **—men·su·ra·tive** (mĕn′sə-rā′tĭv) *adj.*

mens·wear (mĕnz′wâr′) *n.* Clothing and accessories for men.

-ment *suffix.* Indicates: **1.** Product or result; for example, **pavement, statement. 2.** Means, action, or process; for example, **appeasement, measurement. 3.** State or condition; for example, **amazement, merriment.** [Middle English, from Old French, from Latin *-mentum,* abstract noun suffix originally added only to verbs.]

men·tal¹ (mĕn′təl) *adj.* **1.** Of or pertaining to the mind, as: **a.** Intellectual rather than emotional or physical. **b.** Occurring in the mind; inner: *mental turmoil.* **2.** Done or performed by the mind; existing in the mind: *a mental image; mental arithmetic.* **3.** Concerning, involving, or dealing with disorders of the mind: *mental illness; mental institutions.* **4.** Suffering from a disorder or illness of the mind: *a mental patient.* **5.** Of or relating to mind reading or telepathy. [Middle English, from Old French, from Latin *mentālis,* from *mēns* (stem *ment-*), mind.] **—men·tal·ly** *adv.*

mental² *adj.* Of or pertaining to the chin. [French, from Latin *mentum,* chin.]

mental age *n. Abbr.* **MA, M.A.** A measure of mental development as determined by intelligence tests, generally restricted to children and

expressed as the age at which the level achieved is considered to be average.

mental block *n.* A temporary inability to think, remember, or concentrate.

mental cruelty *n.* Cruel behavior toward or ill-treatment of another person that causes emotional and psychological distress but does not involve physical violence. It is sometimes cited as grounds for divorce.

mental deficiency *n.* Subnormal intellectual development, either congenital or induced by brain injury or disease, characterized broadly by deficiencies ranging in severity from impaired learning ability through social and vocational inadequacy to inability to learn connected speech or guard against common dangers. Also called "amentia," "mental retardation," "subnormality."

mental hospital *n.* A hospital or institution that provides care and treatment for the mentally ill. Also called "mental institution."

men·tal·ism (mĕn′tə-lĭz′əm) *n.* **1.** *Philosophy.* The doctrine that the mind is the only true reality and that the material world exists only on a subjective level as aspects of the individual's mind. **2.** *Philosophy.* The doctrine that mental processes exist independently of and can account for their manifestations in observable behavior. **—men·tal·ist** *n.* **—men·tal·is·tic** (mĕn′tə-lĭs′tĭk *adj.*

men·tal·i·ty (mĕn-tăl′ə-tē) *n., pl.* **-ties. 1.** The sum of a person's intellectual capabilities or endowments; mental capacity; intelligence. **2.** Cast or turn of mind; mental make-up or inclination: *She has a very conservative mentality.* —See Synonyms at **mind.**

mental retardation *n.* Mental deficiency.

mental telepathy *n.* Telepathy *(see).*

men·thol (mĕn′thôl′) *n.* A white, crystalline, organic compound, $C_{10}H_{20}O$, that is obtained from peppermint oil or synthesized. It is used in perfumes, as a mild anesthetic, and as a flavoring. [German *Menthol* : Latin *mentha,* MINT + -OL.] **—men·tho·lat·ed** (mĕn′thə-lā′tĭd) *adj.*

men·tion (mĕn′shən) *tr.v.* **-tioned, -tioning, -tions. 1.** To cite or refer to incidentally. **2.** To refer to by name, especially as an acknowledgment or to show appreciation. **—don't mention it.** A formula of courtesy used as a self-deprecating reply to proffered thanks or apologies.

~*n.* **1. a.** The act of briefly or casually referring to something. **b.** An incidental reference or allusion. **2.** A reference to a person by name, especially in order to acknowledge or honor him. [Middle English *mencioun,* from Old French *mention,* from Latin *mentiō* (stem *mentiōn-*), remembrance, mention.] **—men·tion·a·ble** *adj.* **—men·tion·er** *n.*

men·tor (mĕn′tôr′, -tər) *n.* A wise and trusted counselor or teacher. [French, after *Mentor,* a character in Fénelon's *Télémaque* (1699), based on Homer's MENTOR.]

Men·tor (mĕn′tôr′, -tər). *Greek Mythology.* Odysseus' trusted counselor who became the guardian and teacher of Telemachus. [Greek *Mentōr,* name probably meaning "adviser," "wise man," from *men-* (unattested), to think.]

men·u (mĕn′yōō, mān′yōō) *n.* **1.** A list of the dishes that are served or that can be ordered, as in a restaurant. **2.** The dishes served or available. **3.** *Computer Science.* A list of available options, usually displayed on a screen, from which a user can select and access a particular program, function, or file. [French, menu, list, from *menu,* detailed, small, from Latin *minūtus,* minute, diminished, past participle of *minuere,* to diminish.]

Men·u·hin (mĕn′yōō-ĭn), **Yehudi** (1916-). U.S. violinist. He made his professional debut in San Francisco in 1924. Bartók's sonata for solo violin (1945) was written for him. Resident in England since 1959, he was director of the Bath music festival (1959-68) and in 1963 founded a school for musically gifted children.

Men·zies (mĕn′zēz), **Sir Robert Gordon** (1894-1978). Australian prime minister (1939-41 and 1949-66). His second period as prime minister was as the head of a Liberal/Country Party coalition.

me·ow (mē-ou′) *n.* **1.** The characteristic high-pitched crying sound of a cat. **2.** A sound similar to a meow. **3.** A malicious, spiteful comment.

~*v.* **meowed, -owing, -ows.** —*intr.* To emit a meow. —*tr.* To express by means of a meow. [Imitative.]

mep, m.e.p. mean effective pressure.

mep·a·crine (mĕp′ə-krīn′) *n. Chiefly British.* **Quinacrine hydrochloride** *(see).*

me·per·i·dine hydrochloride (mə-pĕr′ə-dēn′) *n.* An organic compound, $C_{15}H_{21}NO_2 \cdot HCl$, used as an analgesic and sedative. Also called "meperidine." [ME(THYL) + (PI)PERIDINE.]

meph·i·stoph·e·les (mĕf′ə-stŏf′ə-lēz′) *n.* **1.** The part of a beard directly below the lower lip. **2.** A beard consisting solely of the hairs between the lower lip and the chin, often waxed and shaped in an upward curve. [19th century : after MEPHISTOPHELES, represented in medieval and Renaissance painting as having a pronounced beard or part of a beard of this type.]

Meph·i·stoph·e·les (mĕf′ə-stŏf′ə-lēz′). The devil in the Faust legend to whom Faust sold his soul. **—Me·phis·to·phe·le·an, Me·phis·to·phe·li·an** (mə-fĭs′tō-fē′lē-ən, -fēl′yən, mĕf′ə-stə-) *adj.*

me·phi·tis (mə-fī′tĭs) *n.* **1.** An offensive smell; stench. **2.** A poisonous or foul-smelling gas emitted from the earth. [Latin *mefitis†,* stench.] **—me·phit·ic** (mə-fīt′ĭk), **me·phit·i·cal** *adj.* **—me·phit·i·cal·ly** *adv.*

mep·ro·bam·ate (mĕp′rō-băm′āt′, mə-prō′bə-māt′) *n.* A bitter white powder, $CH_3(C_3H_7)C(CH_2OOCNH_2)_2$, used as a tranquilizer. [methyl + propyl + dicar*bamate.*]

mer. meridian.

–mer. Variant of -mere.

mer·bro·min (mər-brō'mĭn) *n.* A green, crystalline, organic compound, $C_{20}H_8Br_2HgNa_2O_6$, that forms a red aqueous solution. It is used as a germicide and antiseptic. [*mercuric* + d*i*bromofl*u*oresce*in*.]

mer·can·tile (mûr'kən-tēl', -tīl', -tĭl) *adj.* **1.** Of or pertaining to merchants, trade, or commerce. **2.** Of or pertaining to mercantilism. [French, from Italian, from *mercante*, MERCHANT.]

mer·can·til·ism (mûr'kən-tē-lĭz'əm, -tĭ-lĭz'əm) *n.* **1.** The theory and system of political economy prevailing in Europe after the decline of feudalism, based on national policies of accumulating bullion, establishing colonies and a merchant navy, and developing industry and mining to attain a favorable balance of trade. Also called "mercantile system." **2.** Commercialism. [French *mercantilisme*, from MERCANTILE.] —**mer·can·til·ist** *n. & adj.*

mer·cap·tan (mər-kăp'tăn') *n.* Any sulfur-containing organic compound with the general formula RSH, R being any radical; for example, ethyl mercaptan, C_2H_5SH. Also called "thiol." [German, from Danish, from Medieval Latin *(corpus) mercurium captans*, "(substance) seizing mercury" : *mercurium*, MERCURY + *captāns*, present participle of *captāre*, frequentative of *capere*, to take.]

mer·cap·tide (mər-kăp'tīd') *n.* A salt of a mercaptan containing the ion RS-, where R is an alkyl or aryl group. [MERCAPT(AN) + -IDE.]

Mer·ca·tor (mər-kā'tər), **Gerardus**, born Gerhard Kremer (1512–94). Flemish inventor of the map projection (1568) that bears his name. He produced his first world map in 1538 and his first globe in 1541. His great atlas, begun in 1585, was completed in 1594 by his son.

Mercator projection *n.* Also **Mercator's projection.** A map projection in which the globe is projected onto a cylinder, the meridians and parallels appearing as straight lines crossing at right angles. Lines of constant direction are straight lines, so it is used widely for navigation, despite increasing expansion and distortion of areas the farther they are from the equator.

mer·ce·nar·y (mûr'sə-nĕr'ē) *adj.* **1. a.** Motivated solely by a desire for monetary or material gain. **b.** Greedy; venal. **2.** Hired for service in a foreign army.
~*n., pl.* **mercenaries. 1.** A professional soldier who is hired by a foreign country or organization. **2.** A person who serves or works merely for monetary gain; a hireling. [Middle English *mercenarie*, from Latin *mercēnārius*, from *mercēs*, pay.] —**mer·ce·nar·i·ly** (mûr'sə-nâr'ə-lē) *adv.* —**mer·ce·nar·i·ness** *n.*

mer·cer (mûr'sər) *n. British.* A dealer in textiles, especially in expensive fabrics such as silks. [Middle English, from Old French *mercier*, trader, from Vulgar Latin *merciārius* (unattested), from Latin *merx* (stem *merc*-), merchandise.]

mer·cer·ize (mûr'sə-rīz') *tr.v.* **-ized, -izing, -izes.** To treat (cotton thread) with sodium hydroxide in order to shrink the fiber and increase its color absorption and luster. [After John *Mercer* (1791–1866), English textile maker.] —**mer·cer·i·za·tion** *n.*

mer·chan·dise (mûr'chən-dīz', -dīs') *n. Abbr.* **mdse.** Commodities of commerce; goods that may be bought or sold.
~*v.* (-dīz') **merchandised, -dising, -dises.** —*tr.* **1.** To buy and sell (commodities). **2.** To promote the sale of, as by advertising or display. —*intr.* To trade commercially. [Middle English, from Old French, from *marcheant*, MERCHANT.] —**mer·chan·dis·er** *n.*

mer·chant (mûr'chənt) *n.* **1.** A person whose occupation is the wholesale purchase and retail sale of goods for profit; trader. **2.** A person who runs a retail business; shopkeeper. **3.** Someone fond of or involved with something specified that is generally thought undesirable: *a speed merchant.*
~*adj.* **1.** Of or pertaining to a merchant, merchandise, or commercial trade; dealing in commerce: *a merchant guild.* **2.** Of or pertaining to the merchant marine. [Middle English, from Old French *marcheant*, trader, from Vulgar Latin *mercātāns* (unattested), present participle of *mercātāre* (unattested), to trade, from Latin *mercārī*, to trade, from *merx* (stem *merc*-), merchandise.]

mer·chant·a·ble (mûr'chən-tə-bəl) *adj.* Suitable for buying and selling; marketable.

merchant bank *n. British.* An institution engaged in a number of financial activities, such as accepting foreign bills of exchange, dealing in loans and securities, and supervising the issue of new securities. —**merchant banker** *n.* —**merchant banking** *n.*

mer·chant·man (mûr'chənt-mən) *n., pl.* **-men** (-mĭn). **1.** A ship used in commerce. **2.** *Archaic.* A merchant.

merchant marine *n.* **1.** A nation's ships that are engaged in commerce. **2.** The personnel of such ships.

Mer·ci·a (mûr'shē-ə, -shə). Anglo-Saxon kingdom of England, roughly corresponding with the Midlands. It became a major power under Penda (c. 632–54), overlord of all England south of the Humber: East Anglia, Kent, Mercia, Sussex, and Wessex. Offa (757–96) extended this power, controlling Northumberland too. Mercia came under Wessex overlordship (825), and the east was incorporated into the Danelaw (886).

Mer·ci·an (mûr'shē-ən, -shən) *n.* **1.** A native or inhabitant of Mercia. **2.** The dialect of Old English used in Mercia. —**Mer·ci·an** *adj.*

mer·ci·ful (mûr'sĭ-fəl) *adj.* Full of mercy; compassionate; lenient. —**mer·ci·ful·ness** *n.*

mer·ci·ful·ly (mûr'sĭ-fə-lē, -sĭ-flē) *adv.* **1.** In a merciful manner. **2.** As a mercy: *The climber fell but mercifully landed in a tree.*

mer·ci·less (mûr'sĭ-lĭs) *adj.* Having no mercy; pitiless; cruel. —**mer·ci·less·ly** *adv.* —**mer·ci·less·ness** *n.*

Mer·cou·ri (mər-koor'ē), **Melina** (1925–). Greek film actress. She starred in *Never on Sunday* (1959). In 1981 she was elected to the Greek parliament and appointed minister of culture and sciences.

mer·cu·rate (mûr'kyə-rāt') *tr.v.* **-rated, -rating, -rates.** To treat or mix with mercury. —**mer·cu·ra·tion** *n.*

mer·cu·ri·al (mər-kyoor'ē-əl) *n.* A medical or chemical preparation containing mercury.
~*adj.* **1.** *Usually* **Mercurial.** Of or pertaining to the Roman god Mercury or the planet Mercury. **2.** Having the characteristics of eloquence, shrewdness, swiftness, and thievishness attributed to the god Mercury in Roman mythology. **3.** Containing or caused by the action of the element mercury. **4.** Being quick and changeable in character: *a mercurial temperament.* [Latin *mercuriālis*, from *Mercurius*, the god MERCURY.] —**mer·cu·ri·al·ly** *adv.*

mer·cu·ri·al·ism (mər-kyoor'ē-ə-lĭz'əm) *n.* Poisoning that is caused by mercury or its compounds. Also called "hydrargyria," "hydrargyrism."

mer·cu·ric (mər-kyoor'ĭk) *adj. Chemistry.* Pertaining to or containing bivalent mercury.

mercuric chloride *n.* A poisonous white crystalline compound, $HgCl_2$, used as an antiseptic and disinfectant and in insecticides, preservatives, and batteries, and in metallurgy and photography. Also called "corrosive sublimate."

mercuric oxide *n.* A mercuric compound, HgO, existing as red and yellow crystals and used as a pigment.

mercuric sulfide *n.* A poisonous compound, HgS, having two forms: **1.** *Black mercuric sulfide*, a black powder obtained from mercury salts or by the reaction of mercury with sulfur, used as a pigment. Also called "metacinnabar." **2.** *Red mercuric sulfide*, a bright scarlet powder derived from heating mercury with sulfur, used as a pigment. In this form, also called "artificial cinnabar," "vermilion."

mer·cu·ro·chrome (mər-kyoor'ə-krōm') *n.* A solution of **merbromin** *(see)*, used as an antiseptic. [Formerly a trademark.]

mer·cu·rous (mər-kyoor'əs, mûr'kyər-əs) *adj. Chemistry.* Pertaining to or containing monovalent mercury.

mercurous chloride *n.* A white powder, Hg_2Cl_2, used as a fungicide and formerly used in medicine as a cathartic.

mer·cu·ry (mûr'kyə-rē) *n., pl.* **-ries. 1.** Symbol **Hg** A silvery-white poisonous metallic element, liquid at room temperature. It is used in thermometers, barometers, vapor lamps, and batteries, and in the preparation of chemical pesticides. Atomic number 80, atomic weight 200.59, melting point –38.87°C, boiling point 356.58°C, specific gravity 13.546, valences 1, 2. Also called "quicksilver." **2.** Temperature. **3.** Any of several weedy plants of the genera *Mercurialis* or *Acalypha.* See **dog's mercury. 4.** *Archaic.* A messenger or guide. Now used only in the titles of some newspapers. [Middle English *Mercurie*, god, planet, metal, and plant (after Greek *Hermou poa*, "herb of Hermes"), from Latin *Mercurius*, MERCURY.]

Mer·cu·ry¹ (mûr'kyə-rē). *Roman Mythology.* A god, often identified with the Greek god **Hermes**, serving as messenger to the other gods and being the god of commerce, travel, and thievery.

Mercury² *n.* The smallest of the planets (with the possible exception of Pluto) and the one nearest the sun. It has a sidereal period of revolution around the sun of 88 days at a mean distance of 58 million kilometers (36 million miles), a mean radius of approximately 2,420 kilometers (1,500 miles), and a mass approximately 0.05 that of Earth. [Latin *Mercurius*, the god, the planet.] See feature, next page.

mercury arc *n.* A bluish discharge containing some ultraviolet radiation produced by passing a high current through ionized mercury vapor.

mercury barometer *n.* A type of **barometer** *(see)* in which pressure is measured by the height of a column of mercury.

mer·cu·ry-va·por lamp (mûr'kyə-rē-vā'pər) *n.* A lamp in which ultraviolet and yellowish-green to blue visible light is produced by an electric discharge through mercury vapor. It is used as a source of ultraviolet light and for outdoor lighting.

mer·cy (mûr'sē) *n., pl.* **-cies. 1.** Kind and compassionate treatment of an offender, enemy, prisoner, or other person under one's power who might deserve harsh treatment; clemency. Also used ironically in the phrase *tender mercies: He was left to the tender mercies of the Inquisition.* **2.** A possible disposition to be kind and forgiving: *I threw myself on her mercy.* **3.** Something for which to be thankful; a fortunate occurrence: *It's a mercy he survived the crash.* **4.** Alleviation of distress; relief: *Her death was a mercy.* —**at the mercy of.** Totally in the power of. [Middle English *merci*, from Old French, compassion, forbearance (to someone in one's power), from Late Latin *mercēs*, reward, God's gratuitous compassion, from Latin, pay, reward.]
Synonyms: clemency, forbearance, leniency.

mercy killing *n.* Euthanasia *(see).*

mercy seat *n.* **1.** The golden covering of the ark of the covenant regarded as the resting place of God. Exodus 25:12–22. Also called "propitiatory." **2.** The throne of God.

mere¹ (mîr) *adj.* Superlative **merest. 1.** Being nothing more than what is specified: *The fee was a mere ten dollars.* **2.** *Archaic.* Pure; unadulterated. [Latin *merus*, clear, pure, unmixed.]

mere² *n.* A small, usually circular lake or pond. [Middle English, Old English, sea, lake.]

mere³ *n. Archaic.* A boundary. [Middle English, Old English *mǣre, gemǣre*, boundary.]

–mere, –mer *suffix. Zoology.* Indicates a part or segment; for example, **blastomere, elastomer.** [French, from Greek *meros*, a part.]

Mercury

A SCORCHED (AND FROZEN) WORLD
Mercury, the Sun's neighbor, scarred by ancient craters

Mercury, the closest planet to the Sun, is an arid, airless world with a cratered surface baked above 350°C (about 662°F) at midday and cooled to −150°C (about −240°F) at night. Mercury orbits at about 58 million kilometers (about 36 million miles) from the Sun and takes 88 Earth days to complete an orbit.

It is difficult to observe Mercury from Earth. For one thing, it is small—only 1½ times as large as the Moon; for another, the Sun's glare washes out almost all detail.

For almost a century, astronomers believed that Mercury kept one face permanently pointed toward the Sun. Not until 1965 did radar waves reflected from the surface reveal that the planet rotates on its axis, with a rotation period that is a fraction under 59 Earth days.

In 1974–75, the U.S. spacecraft Mariner 10 flew past Mercury three times, and the obscure little planet suddenly became very well known. Mariner's photographs revealed a lunarlike surface scarred with ancient craters made by meteorites early in the history of the Solar System. Although Mercury looks like the Moon, and is as lifeless, it lacks the Moon's large "seas" of volcanic basalt; Mercury appears to have been geologically inactive for more than 4 billion years.

The planet has two unique types of feature. Massive scarps hundreds of miles long slice across its surface. And on one side there is an area of strangely jumbled rock. A huge crater, the Caloris Basin, lies on the opposite side of the planet. Possibly the impact that made the crater produced shock waves that met precisely on the opposite side of the planet, throwing the ground into convulsions.

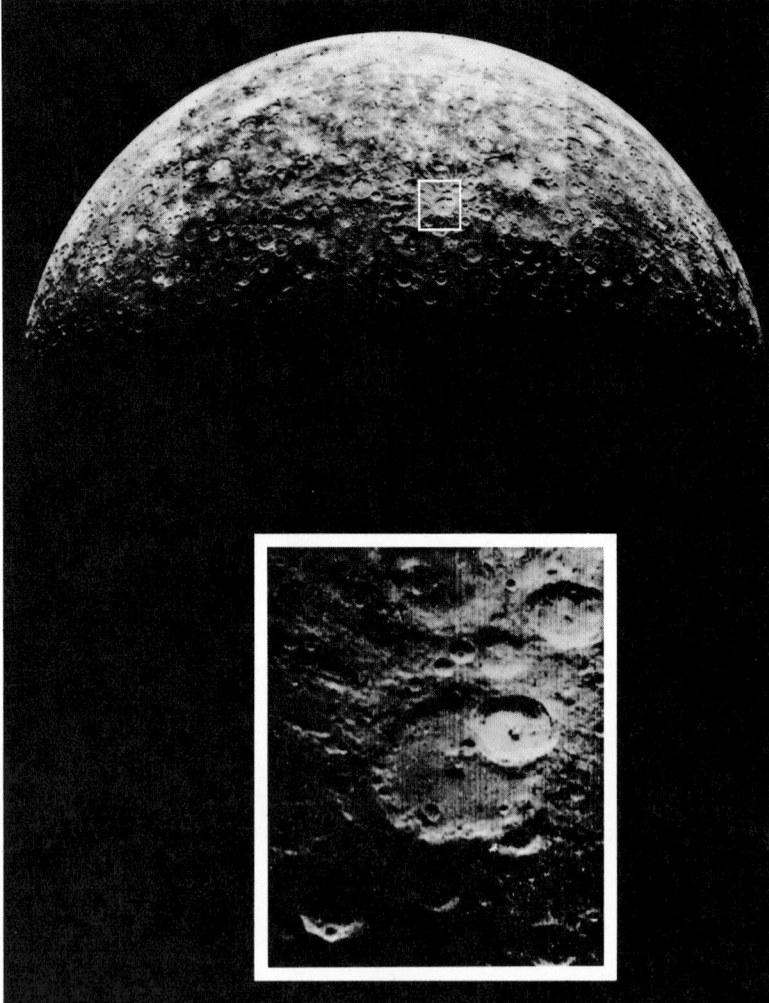

FEWER METEORITE STRIKES *This crescent of Mercury, with north at the right, is a photomosaic built up from Mariner 10 pictures. The inset shows a bright, small crater, Kuiper, 40 kilometers (25 miles) across, formed on the wall of a more ancient crater, Murasaki. After its formation, Murasaki was partly eroded by minor meteorite strikes, but Kuiper was not, evidence that the level of bombardment fell with time.*

Planet location guide

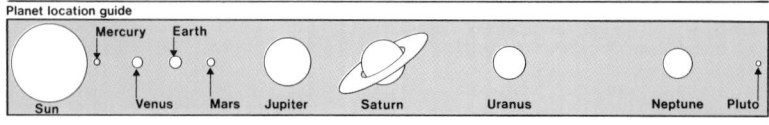

Mer·e·dith (mĕr′ə-dĭth), **George** (1828–1909). British novelist and poet. His novels include *The Ordeal of Richard Feverel* (1859), *The Adventures of Harry Richmond* (1871), *The Egoist* (1879), and *Diana of the Crossways* (1885).

mere·ly (mîr′lē) *adv.* **1.** Nothing more than what is specified; only: *"Although he seem.. so firm to us / He is merely flesh and blood"* (T.S. Eliot). **2.** *Obsolete.* Absolutely; completely.

mer·e·tri·cious (mĕr′ə-trĭsh′əs) *adj.* **1. a.** Superficially attractive. **b.** Attracting attention in a vulgar manner: *meretricious ornamentation.* **2.** Lacking sincerity: *a meretricious argument.* **3.** Pertaining to or resembling a prostitute. [Latin *meritricius,* from *meretrix,* a prostitute, from *merere,* to earn pay.] —**mer·e·tri·cious·ly** *adv.* —**mer·e·tri·cious·ness** *n.*

mer·gan·ser (mər-găn′sər) *n., pl.* **-sers** or collectively **merganser**. Any marine fish-eating duck of the genus *Mergus,* having a slim, hooked, serrated bill. Also called "sawbill." [New Latin, "divergoose" : Latin *mergus,* diver (bird) + *anser,* goose.]

merge (mûrj) *v.* **merged, merging, merges.** —*tr.* To cause to blend, fuse, or be absorbed so as to lose identity. —*intr.* To blend together so as to lose identity. —See Synonyms at **mix.** [Latin *mergere,* to dive, plunge.] —**mer·gence** *n.*

merg·er (mûr′jər) *n.* **1.** The union of two or more commercial interests or companies. **2.** *Law.* The absorption of a lesser estate, liability, right, action, or offense into a greater one.

me·rid·i·an (mə-rĭd′ē-ən) *n. Abbr.* **m., M., mer. 1.** *Geography.* **a.** Half of any of the imaginary great circles on the earth's surface passing through both geographic poles. **b.** A representation of such a half-circle; a line of longitude on a map. **2.** *Astronomy.* A great circle passing through the two poles of the celestial sphere and the observer's zenith; the celestial meridian. **3.** *Mathematics.* **a.** A curve on a surface of revolution, formed by the intersection of a plane containing the axis of revolution with the surface. **b.** A plane section of a surface of revolution containing the axis of revolution. **4.** The highest point or stage of development of anything; zenith: *"Men come to their meridian at various periods of their lives"* (J.H. Newman). **5.** *Archaic.* Noon. [Middle English *meridien,* noon, meridian circle, from Old French, from Latin *merīdiānus,* from *merīdiēs,* midday, dissimulated variant of *medidiēs* : *medius,* middle + *diēs,* day.] —**me·rid·i·an** *adj.*

meridian circle *n.* **1.** *Geography.* Any of the imaginary great circles on the earth's surface passing through both geographic poles and consisting of a meridian and its complementary meridian, as 0° and 180°. **2.** An astronomical instrument consisting of a telescope mounted on a graduated circle, used to determine the declination and right ascension of stars.

me·rid·i·o·nal (mə-rĭd′ē-ə-nəl) *adj.* **1.** Of or pertaining to a meridian. **2.** Characteristic of southern areas or people. **3.** Located in the south; southerly.
~*n.* An inhabitant of a southern region, especially of France. [Middle English, from Old French *meridionel,* from Late Latin *merīdionālis,* variant extension of Latin *merīdiānus,* MERIDIAN.]

Mé·ri·mée (mĕr′ə-mā′, mā′rē-mā′), **Prosper** (1803–70). French writer. His work includes *The Chronicle of the Reign of Charles IX* (1829), a historical novel, and *Carmen* (1845), on which Bizet's opera is based.

me·ringue (mə-răng′) *n.* **1.** Beaten egg whites mixed with sugar and baked, used as a topping for puddings or pies. **2.** A small, crisp shell or cake made of meringue, often eaten with whipped cream. [French *méringue*†.] —**me·ringue** *adj.*

me·ri·no (mə-rē′nō) *n., pl.* **-nos. 1. a.** A sheep of a breed originally from Spain. **b.** The fine wool of this sheep. **2.** A soft, lightweight fabric made originally of merino wool but now of any fine wool. **3. a.** A type of fine wool and cotton yarn used for knitting underwear, hosiery, and other articles of clothing. **b.** A knitted fabric made from merino yarn.
~*adj.* Made of merino wool, yarn, or cloth. [Spanish, perhaps from Berber *Benī Merīn,* a people that developed the breed.]

Mer·i·on·eth·shire (mĕr′ē-ŏn′ĭth-shĭr′, -shər). Former county of Wales, since 1974 part of Gwynedd and Clwyd counties. It borders Cardigan Bay, and its fine mountain scenery attracts many tourists.

mer·i·stem (mĕr′ĭ-stĕm′) *n. Botany.* The growing point or area of rapidly dividing cells in the cambium or at the tip of a stem, root, or branch. [Greek *meristos,* divided, divisible, from *merizein,* to divide, from *meris,* a division, part + *-em,* by analogy with *xylem.*] —**mer·i·ste·mat·ic** (mĕr′ĭ-stə-măt′ĭk) *adj.*

me·ris·tic (mə-rĭs′tĭk) *adj. Biology.* **1.** Made up of segments, as some worms are. **2.** Modified by changes in the number or placement of entire body parts, as contrasted with modification by gradual change of the entire organism. [Greek *meristos,* divided, divisible. See meristem.]

mer·it (mĕr′ĭt) *n.* **1.** Value, excellence, or superior quality: *a play of some merit.* **2.** An aspect of a person's character or behavior deserving approval or disapproval: *to each according to his merits.* **3.** *Theology.* Spiritual credit granted for good works. **4. merits.** *Law.* **a.** A party's strict legal rights, excluding jurisdictional or technical aspects. **b.** The factual substance of a case as distinguished from its form and procedural aspects. **5. merits. a.** The intrinsic right or wrong of any matter. **b.** The actual facts of a matter.
~*tr.v.* **merited, -iting, -its.** To earn; deserve; warrant: *"How can the unknown merit reverence?"* (Harold Pinter). [Middle English, from Old French *merite,* that which is deserved, from Latin *meritum,* recompense, desert, from *merēre* (past participle *meritus*), to earn, deserve.] —**mer·it·ed·ly** *adv.*

mer·i·toc·ra·cy (mĕr′ə-tŏk′rə-sē) *n.*, *pl.* **-cies.** **1.** A system in which advancement is based on ability or achievement. **2. a.** An elite composed of talented people who have achieved success through their own efforts. **b.** Leadership by such an elite. [MERIT + -CRACY.] —**mer·i·to·crat** (mĕr′ə-tə-krăt′) *n.* —**mer·it·o·crat·ic** *adj.*

mer·i·to·ri·ous (mĕr′ə-tôr′ē-əs, -tōr′ē-əs) *adj.* Deserving reward or praise; having merit. [Latin *meritōrius*, earning money, from *merēre* (past participle *meritus*), to earn, MERIT.] —**mer·i·to·ri·ous·ly** *adv.*

merit system *n.* A system of appointing and promoting civil service personnel on the basis of merit, determined by competitive examinations. Compare **spoils system.**

merle, merl (mûrl) *n.* The European blackbird, *Turdus merula.* See **blackbird.** [Middle English, from Old French, from Latin *merulus, merula,* blackbird.]

mer·lin (mûr′lĭn) *n.* A small falcon, *Falco columbarius,* that has dark plumage and a black-striped tail. [Middle English *meriloun,* from Norman French *merilun,* from Old French *esmerillon, esmeril,* merlin, from Frankish *smeril†* (unattested).]

Mer·lin (mûr′lĭn) *n.* In Arthurian legend, a wizard and prophet serving as mentor and counselor to King Arthur.

mer·lon (mûr′lən) *n.* The solid portion of a crenellated wall between two open spaces. [French, from Italian *merlone,* from *merlo,* blackbird, battlement (probably from ranks of blackbirds perched on castle walls), from Latin *merulus, merula,* blackbird.]

mer·maid (mûr′mād′) *n.* A fabled creature of the sea with the head and upper body of a woman and the tail of a fish. [Middle English : MERE (sea) + MAID.]

mermaid's purse *n.* A flat, rectangular envelope containing fertilized eggs, produced by certain sharks and skates such as the dogfish. Also called "sea purse."

mer·man (mûr′măn′, -mən) *n.*, *pl.* **-men** (-mĕn′, -mĭn). A fabled creature of the sea with the head and upper body of a man and the tail of a fish. [By analogy with MERMAID.]

Mer·man (mûr′mən), **Ethel,** born Ethel Zimmerman (1908–84). U.S. actress and singer. She made her debut in *Girl Crazy* (1930). After that she appeared in such hits as *Anything Goes* (1934), *Annie Get Your Gun* (1946), *Call Me Madam* (1950), and *Gypsy* (1959). She was known for her booming "wake 'em up in the last row" voice.

mero– *prefix.* Indicates parts or segments; for example, **meroblastic, merocrine.** [New Latin, from Greek *meros,* part, division.]

mer·o·blas·tic (mĕr′ə-blăs′tĭk) *adj.* *Biology.* Undergoing partial cleavage. Said of an egg with a large yolk. Compare **holoblastic.** [MERO- + -BLAST + -IC.] —**mer·o·blas·ti·cal·ly** *adv.*

mer·o·crine (mĕr′ə-krĭn, -krīn′, -krēn′) *adj.* Of or pertaining to a gland the cells of which remain intact during secretion; eccrine. Compare **holocrine.** [Literally, "partly separating" (referring to the cells) : MERO- + Greek *krinein,* to separate.]

Meroë. See **Merowe.**

Mer·o·pe[1] (mĕr′ə-pē′). *Greek Mythology.* One of the **Pleiades** *(see),* who, after marrying a mortal, hid her face in shame.

Merope[2] *n.* The seventh star in the Pleiades cluster and the only one not visible to the naked eye. [After MEROPE.]

me·ro·pi·a (mə-rō′pē-ə) *n.* Partial blindness. [New Latin : MER(O)- + -OPIA.] —**me·ro·pic** (mə-rō′pĭk, -rŏp′ĭk) *adj.*

–merous *suffix.* *Biology.* Having a specified number or kind of parts; for example, **pentamerous.** [New Latin *-merus,* from Greek *-meres,* from *meros,* a part.]

Mer·o·vin·gi·an (mĕr′ə-vĭn′jē-ən, -jən) *adj.* Of or pertaining to the first dynasty of Frankish kings that ruled over Gaul from about A.D. 500 until 751.

~*n.* A member of this dynasty. [French *mérovingien,* from Medieval Latin *Merovingī,* "the descendants of Merovaeus," from Frankish *Merowig,* the eponymous ancestor.]

Mer·o·we, Me·ro·ë (mĕr′ō-ē′). Ruined capital of Cush (ancient Ethiopia) on the Nile River north of Khartoum, Sudan.

mer·o·zo·ite (mĕr′ə-zō′īt′) *n.* A cell produced by fission of a sporozoan. [MERO- + ZO(O)- + -ITE.]

Mer·rick (mĕr′ĭk), **David** (1912–). U.S. producer. He has produced countless Broadway hits, including *The Matchmaker, Look Back in Anger,* and *Rosencrantz and Guildenstern Are Dead.* Merrick is best known for his lavish musicals, such as *Gypsy, Oliver!,* and *Hello Dolly!,* for which he won a Tony Award.

Mer·ri·mack (mĕr′ə-măk′). River, *c.* 175 kilometers (110 miles) long, rising in south-central New Hampshire and flowing south past Concord and Manchester into northeastern Massachusetts. It then flows northeastward past Lowell and Lawrence to the Atlantic Ocean.

mer·ri·ment (mĕr′ĭ-mənt) *n.* Gay conviviality; hilarity. —See Synonyms at **mirth.**

mer·ry (mĕr′ē) *adj.* **-rier, -riest.** **1.** Full of spirited gaiety; jolly. **2.** Marked by or offering humor and fun; festive. **3.** *Informal.* Slightly drunk. —See Synonyms at **jolly.** [Middle English *merie,* Old English *mirige,* pleasant.] —**mer·ri·ly** *adv.* —**mer·ri·ness** *n.*

mer·ry-an·drew (mĕr′ē-ăn′drōō) *n.* A prankster, jester, or clown. [MERRY + the name *Andrew.*]

mer·ry-go-round (mĕr′ē-gō-round′) *n.* **1. a.** A circular platform fitted with seats, often in the form of wooden animals, revolved mechanically, usually to music, and ridden for amusement. **b.** A piece of playground equipment consisting of a small circular platform that revolves when pushed or pedaled. In both senses, also called "roundabout." **2.** Any whirl or swift round: *a merry-go-round of parties.*

mer·ry·mak·ing (mĕr′ē-mā′kĭng) *n.* **1.** Participation in a party or revel. **2.** A festivity; revelry. —**mer·ry·mak·er** *n.*

mer·ry·thought (mĕr′ē-thôt′) *n.* *Archaic.* A wishbone.

Mer·sey (mûr′zē). River of northwestern England. Formed by the confluence of the Tame and Goyt rivers, it flows 113 kilometers (70 miles) from Stockport to the Irish Sea, where its estuary, 26 kilometers (16 miles) long, can be used by oceangoing ships. The river connects with the Manchester Ship Canal.

Mer·sey·side (mûr′zē-sīd′). County of northwestern England, created in 1974 from northwestern Cheshire and southwestern Lancashire. It includes Liverpool, the administrative capital, its suburbs, the coast northward to Southport, St. Helens, and the Wirral.

mes–. Variant of **meso-.**

me·sa (mā′sə) *n.* A flat-topped elevation with one or more clifflike sides, common in the southwestern United States. [Spanish, from Old Spanish, from Latin *mēnsa†,* table.]

Me·sa (mā′sə). City of south-central Arizona, in the fertile Salt River valley. Its manufactures include electronic components, aircraft, and machine tools. It is one of the fastest-growing cities in Arizona.

Me·sa·bi Range (mə-sä′bē). Range of low hills in northeastern Minnesota, noted for its extensive iron ore deposits. The ore was first discovered in 1887. Reserves of the higher-grade hematite ore are nearly depleted, and taconite deposits are now being worked.

mé·sal·li·ance (mā′zăl-yäns′, mā-zăl′ē-əns) *n.* A marriage with a person of inferior social position. [French : *més-,* MIS + *alliance,* ALLIANCE.]

Mesa Verde National Park (vûrd, vûr′dē). Area, 21,090 hectares (52,074 acres), in southwestern Colorado. It includes well-preserved cliff dwellings and relics spanning four archaeological periods.

mes·cal (mĕ-skăl′) *n.* **1.** A spineless, globe-shaped cactus, *Lophophora williamsii,* of Mexico and the southwestern United States, having buttonlike tubercles (*mescal buttons*) that are dried and chewed as a drug. Also called "peyote." See **mescaline.** **2.** A Mexican alcoholic drink distilled from the fermented juice of certain species of **agave** *(see).* **3.** A plant, the **maguey** *(see).* [Spanish *mescal, mezcal, mexcal,* from Nahuatl *mexcalli.*]

mes·ca·line, mes·ca·lin (mĕs′kə-lēn′, -lĭn) *n.* An alkaloid drug, $(CH_3O)_3C_6H_2(CH_2CH_2NH_2)$, that produces hallucinations and other psychedelic effects.

Mes·dames. *Abbr.* **Mmes.** Plural of **Madame** or **Madam** or **Mrs.**

Mes·de·moi·selles. *Abbr.* **Mlles.** Plural of **Mademoiselle.**

mes·en·ceph·a·lon (mĕz′ən-sĕf′ə-lŏn′, mĕs′-) *n.* Also **mes·o·ceph·a·lon** (mĕz′ō-, mĕs′ō-). The region of the brain that develops from the middle section of the embryonic brain. Also called "midbrain." See **brain.** [New Latin : MES(O)- + ENCEPHALON.] —**mes·en·ce·phal·ic** (mĕz′ən-sə-făl′ĭk, mĕs′-) *adj.*

mes·en·chyme (mĕz′ən-kīm′, mĕs′-) *n.* Also **mes·en·chy·ma** (mĕz-ĕng′kĭ-mə, mĕs-). The part of the embryonic mesoderm from which develop connective tissue, cartilage, and the circulatory and lymphatic systems. [German *Mesenchym* : MES(O)- + ENCHYMA.] —**mes·en·chy·mal** (mĕz-ĕng′kĭ-məl, mĕs-), **mes·en·chym·a·tous** (mĕz′ən-kĭm′ə-təs, mĕs′-) *adj.*

mes·en·ter·i·tis (mĕz-ĕn′tə-rī′tĭs, mĕs-) *n.* Inflammation of the mesentery. [New Latin : *mesenterium,* MESENTERY + -ITIS.]

mes·en·ter·on (mĕz-ĕn′tə-rŏn′, mĕs-) *n.* *Biology.* **1.** The middle part of the digestive tract, the **midgut** *(see).* **2.** The middle part of the gastrovascular cavity in sea anemones and corals. [New Latin : MES(O)- + ENTERON.] —**mes·en·ter·on·ic** *adj.*

mes·en·ter·y (mĕz′ən-tĕr′ē, mĕs′-) *n.*, *pl.* **-ies.** Also **mes·en·te·ri·um** (mĕz′ən-tîr′ē-əm, mĕs′-) *pl.* **-ia** (-ē-ə). Any of several peritoneal folds that connect the intestines to the dorsal abdominal wall. [New Latin *mesenterium* : MES(O)- + ENTERON.] —**mes·en·ter·ic** *adj.*

mesh (mĕsh) *n.* **1.** Any of the open spaces in a cord, thread, or wire network. **2.** *Often* **meshes.** The cords, threads, or wires surrounding these spaces. **3.** A net or network. **4.** Either of two measures of the fineness of a net, according to the frequency of strands or the distance between strands. **5.** Something that snares or entraps: *entangled in the meshes of politics.* **6.** The engagement of gear teeth. ~*v.* **meshed, meshing, meshes.** —*tr.* **1.** To entangle or ensnare. **2.** To cause (gear teeth) to become engaged. **3.** To cause to work closely or harmoniously together. —*intr.* **1.** To be or become entangled. **2.** To be or become engaged or interlocked, as gear teeth might. **3. a.** To coordinate or fit harmoniously and effectively: *mesh with the boss's idiosyncratic methods.* **b.** To accord with another; harmonize. [Earlier *meash, mash,* from Middle Dutch *masche, maesche.*] —**mesh·y** *adj.*

Me·shach (mē′shăk′). A Hebrew captive who, with Shadrach and Abednego, miraculously escaped death in Nebuchadnezzar's fiery furnace. Daniel 3.

Meshed. See **Mashhad.**

me·shug·ga, me·shug·ga (mə-shoog′ə) *adj.* *Slang.* Mad; crazy. [Yiddish, from Hebrew.]

mesh·work (mĕsh′wûrk′) *n.* Meshes; network.

me·si·al (mē′zē-əl, mĕz′ē-, mĕzh′əl) *adj.* Of, in, near, or toward the middle; medial. [MES(O)- + -IAL.] —**me·si·al·ly** *adv.*

me·si·tes (mə-sī′tēz) *n.* A flightless, raillike bird, *Monias benschi,* found in the forests and brushlands of Madagascar. [New Latin, from Greek *mesitēs,* mediator.]

me·sit·y·lene (mə-sĭt′l-ēn′) *n.* A hydrocarbon, $(CH_3)_3C_6H_3$, occurring in coal and petroleum tar and synthesized from acetone; 1,3,5-trimethylbenzene. [MESITYL (OXIDE) + -ENE.]

mes·i·tyl oxide (mĕs′ə-tĭl) *n.* An oily liquid, $(CH_3)_2C{:}CHCOCH_3$,

merlin *The merlin, which is a small falcon, little larger than a thrush, flies fast and low to catch small birds in flight. The male takes its prey to a "plucking post," a rock outcrop or stone wall, where it plucks the kill before presenting the carcass to its mate.*

Mesopotamia *A king of southern Mesopotamia relaxes on his throne with a drink in a detail from a mosaic known as the* Standard of Ur, *made in about 2500* B.C. *Ur—a city that is identified with the biblical Ur of the Chaldeans and is reputed to have been the early home of Abraham—was one of the principal city-states of ancient Mesopotamia, now part of Iraq. Founded on the banks of the Euphrates some time before 3000* B.C., *Ur was abandoned in about 316* B.C. *after the river changed its course.*

obtained from acetones and used as a solvent and insect repellent. [Greek *mesitēs,* mediator, from *mesos,* middle + -YL.]

Mes•mer (mĕz′mər, mĕs′-), **Franz** or **Friedrich Anton** (1734–1815). German medical practitioner who pioneered hypnotism and psychoanalysis in medicine. He first used magnets in treatment, then treated patients by psychological suggestion. He settled in Paris in 1778, and although they were denounced by the French Academy of Medicine, his methods, known as mesmerism, led to the development of therapeutic hypnotism.

mes•mer•ism (mĕz′mə-rĭz′əm, mĕs′-) *n.* **1.** Hypnotism or a theory concerning it. See **animal magnetism. 2.** Hypnotic appeal. [After Franz Anton MESMER.] **—mes•mer•ic** (mĕz-mĕr′ĭk, mĕs-) *adj.* **—mes•mer•i•cal•ly** *adv.* **—mes•mer•ist** *n.*

mes•mer•ize (mĕz′mə-rīz′, mĕs′-) *tr.v.* **-ized, -izing, -izes. 1.** To hypnotize. **2.** To enthrall: *She mesmerized the audience.*

mesne (mēn) *adj. Law.* Intermediate; intervening. [Middle English, from Norman French *mesne, meen,* from Old French *meien,* from Latin *mediānus,* median, from *medius,* middle.]

mesne lord *n.* A feudal lord intermediate between a superior lord and his own vassals or tenants.

meso–, mes– *prefix.* Indicates center or intermediate; for example, **mesoblast, mesoderm.** [Greek, from *mesos,* middle.]

mes•o•blast (mĕz′ə-blăst′, mĕs′-) *n.* The middle germinal layer of the embryo; the mesoderm in its early stage of development. [MESO- + -BLAST.] **—mes•o•blas•tic** *adj.*

mes•o•carp (mĕz′ə-kärp′, mĕs′-) *n. Botany.* The middle, usually fleshy layer of a **pericarp** *(see).* [MESO- + -CARP.]

mes•o•ce•phal•ic (mĕz′ō-sə-făl′ĭk, mĕs′-) *adj.* Having a head form intermediate between **brachycephalic** and **dolichocephalic** *(both of which see).* [MESO- + -CEPHALIC.]

mesocephalon. Variant of **mesencephalon.**

mes•o•derm (mĕz′ə-dûrm′, mĕs′-) *n.* The embryonic germ layer, lying between the ectoderm and the endoderm, from which develop connective tissue, muscles, and the urogenital and vascular systems. [MESO- + -DERM.] **—mes•o•der•mal** (mĕz′ə-dûr′məl, mĕs′-), **mes•o•der•mic** (-mĭk) *adj.*

mes•o•gle•a, mes•o•gloe•a (mĕz′ə-glē′ə, mĕs′-) *n.* The layer of jellylike material that separates the inner and outer cell layers in coelenterates. [New Latin : MESO- + Greek *gloia,* glue.]

Mes•o•lith•ic (mĕz′ə-lĭth′ĭk, mĕs′-) *adj. Archaeology.* Designating the cultural period between the Paleolithic and Neolithic Ages, marked by the appearance of microlithic cutting tools and the introduction of boats and fishing.
~*n. Archaeology.* The Mesolithic Age. Preceded by *the.* Also called "Middle Stone Age." [MESO- + -LITHIC.]

Mesolóngion. See **Missolonghi.**

mes•o•morph (mĕz′ə-môrf′, mĕs′-) *n.* A human build characterized by powerful musculature and a predominantly bony framework. Compare **ectomorph, endomorph.** [MESO- + -MORPH.]

mes•o•mor•phic (mĕz′ə-môr′fĭk, mĕs′-) *adj.* Also **mes•o•mor•phous** (-fəs) (for sense 1). **1.** *Chemistry.* Of, pertaining to, or existing in a state of matter intermediate between liquid and crystal. **2.** *Anatomy.* Of or pertaining to a mesomorph. **—mes•o•mor•phism** (mĕz′ə-môr′fĭz′əm, mĕs′-) **—mes•o•mor•phy** (mĕz′ə-môr′fē, mĕs′-) *n.*

mes•on (mĕz′ŏn′, mē′zŏn′, mĕs′ŏn′, mē′sŏn′) *n. Physics.* Any of several elementary particles having integral spins and masses generally intermediate between those of leptons and baryons. Formerly called "mesotron." [MES(O)- + -ON.] **—me•son•ic** (mĕ-zŏn′ĭk, -sŏn′ĭk, mē-) *adj.*

mes•o•neph•ros (mĕz′ə-nĕf′rəs, -rŏs′, mĕs′-) *n.* The middle part of the embryonic excretory system in vertebrates that becomes the functioning kidney in fish and amphibians and the epididymis in reptiles, birds, and mammals. Also called "Wolffian body." [New Latin : MESO- + Greek *nephros,* kidney.] **—mes•o•neph•ric** *adj.*

mes•o•pause (mĕz′ə-pôz′, mĕs′-) *n.* The atmospheric zone, about 80 kilometers (50 miles) above the earth, forming the upper limit of the mesosphere.

mes•o•phil•ic (mĕz′ə-fĭl′ĭk, mĕs′-) *adj.* Pertaining to or designating an organism, usually a bacterium, thriving at moderate temperatures, between 20°C and 40°C. Compare **psychrophilic, thermophilic.** [MESO- + -PHIL(E) + -IC.]

mes•o•phyll (mĕz′ə-fĭl′, mĕs′-) *n.* The soft tissue of a leaf, between the upper and lower epidermis, that contains the chloroplasts and is involved in photosynthesis. [New Latin *mesophyllum* : MESO- + -PHYLL.] **—mes•o•phyl•lic, mes•o•phyl•lous** *adj.*

mes•o•phyte (mĕz′ə-fīt′, mĕs′-) *n.* A land plant that grows in a temperate environment having a moderate amount of moisture. Compare **xerophyte, hydrophyte.** [MESO- + -PHYTE.] **—mes•o•phyt•ic** (mĕz′ə-fĭt′ĭk, mĕs′-) *adj.*

Mes•o•po•ta•mi•a (mĕs′ə-pə-tā′mē-ə). Ancient region of southwestern Asia, between the Euphrates and Tigris rivers. Its name is derived from the Greek for "between rivers." Most of it lies in modern Iraq. The site of some of the earliest human settlements, such as Jarmo (*c.* 7000 B.C.), it saw the rise of early civilizations: Sumer (*c.* 3100 B.C.), Akkad (*c.* 2340 B.C.), and Babylon (*c.* 1800 B.C.).

mes•o•some (mĕz′ə-sōm′, mĕs′-) *n.* A convoluted invagination of the cytoplasmic membrane in some bacterial cells.

mes•o•sphere (mĕz′ə-sfîr′, mĕs′-) *n.* **1.** The portion of the atmosphere from about 50 to 80 kilometers (30 to 50 miles) above the earth, characterized by a temperature range that decreases from 10°C to -90°C with increasing altitude. See **atmosphere. 2.** The solid part of the earth's mantle, lying between the semifluid asthenosphere and the fluid outer core. [MESO- + -SPHERE.] **—mes•o•spher•ic** (mĕz′ə-sfîr′ĭk, -sfĕr′ĭk, mĕs′-) *adj.*

mes•o•spo•ri•um (mĕz′ə-spôr′ē-əm, -spōr′-ē-əm, mĕs′-) *n. Botany.* The **exointine** *(see).*

mes•o•the•li•um (mĕz′ə-thē′lē-əm, mĕs′-) *n., pl.* **-lia** (-lē-ə). A layer of squamous cells of the epithelium lining the peritoneum, pericardium, and pleura, derived from the mesoderm. [New Latin : MESO- + (EPI)THELIUM.] **—mes•o•the•li•al** *adj.*

mes•o•tho•rax (mĕz′ə-thôr′ăks′, -thōr′ăks′, mĕs′-) *n., pl.* **-raxes** or **-races** (-thôr′ə-sēz′, -thōr′ə-sēz′). The middle section of an insect's thoracic region, bearing the middle legs and the front wings.

mes•o•tho•ri•um (mĕz′ə-thôr′ē-əm, -thōr′ē-əm, mĕs′-) *n. Abbr.* **Ms-Th.** Either of two decay products of thorium: **1.** Mesothorium I, now called radium-228. **2.** Mesothorium II, now called actinium-228. Not in technical usage.

mes•o•tron (mĕz′ə-trŏn′, mĕs′-) *n. Physics.* A **meson** *(see).* No longer in technical usage. [MESO- + (ELEC)TRON.]

Mes•o•zo•ic (mĕz′ə-zō′ĭk, mĕs′-) *adj.* Of, belonging to, or designating the third era of geologic time, which includes the Cretaceous, Jurassic, and Triassic periods and is characterized by the predominance of reptilian life forms.
~*n.* The Mesozoic era. Preceded by *the.* [MESO- + -ZOIC.]

mes•quite, mes•quit (mĕ-skēt′, mə-skēt′) *n.* Any of several shrubs or small trees of the genus *Prosopis*; especially, *P. juliflora,* of the southwestern United States and Mexico. Its pods are used as forage. Also called "algarroba," "honey locust." [Spanish *mezquite,* from Nahuatl *mizquitl.*]

mess (mĕs) *n.* **1.** A disorderly accumulation of items. **2. a.** A cluttered, untidy, usually dirty state or condition. **b.** An untidy or dirty person or thing. **3. a.** A disturbing, confusing, and troublesome state of affairs; muddle. **b.** *Informal.* A confused, muddled, or disturbed person or thing. **4.** *Archaic.* An amount of food for a meal, course, or dish: *"at their savoury dinner set / Of herbs, and other country messes"* (John Milton). **5.** A serving of soft, semiliquid food. **6.** A distasteful and unappetizing concoction. **7.** An amount or number acquired, usually of something edible: *a mess of fish.* **8. a.** A group of persons, usually in the military, who regularly eat meals together. **b.** A meal eaten in such a group. **c.** The place where such meals are served and, in the armed forces, where there are facilities for recreation, entertainment, and accommodation: *the officers' mess.* **—make a mess of.** To bungle or ruin.
~*v.* **messed, messing, messes.** *—tr.* **1.** To make disorderly and soiled; clutter. Often used with *up: messed up the kitchen with pots and pans.* **2.** To bungle, mismanage, or botch. Usually used with *up: She messed up the test.* **3.** *Slang.* To be rough with; manhandle. Usually used with *up: a mugger messing up his victim. —intr.* **1.** To take a meal in a military mess. **2.** To cause or make a mess. **3.** To interfere; meddle. Usually used with *with.* **—mess around** (or **about**). *Informal.* **1.** To occupy time by puttering or tinkering; work aimlessly: *"there is nothing . . . half so much worth doing as simply messing about in boats"* (Kenneth Grahame). **2.** To waste time; idle. **3.** To keep company; associate. [Middle English *mes,* course of a meal, dish of food, group of messmates, from Old French, from Latin *missus,* "placement," course of a meal, from *mittere* (past participle *missus*), to send, place, put.]

mes•sage (mĕs′ĭj) *n. Abbr.* **msg. 1.** A communication transmitted by spoken or written words, by signals, or by other means from one person or group to another. **2.** A formal diplomatic communication. **3.** A statement made or read before a gathering: *a farewell message.* **4.** An apparent communication from God, delivered by a prophet. **5.** A moral or religious point or theme. **6.** The basic theme, inspiration, or significance of something: *"the life of Britain, her message, and her glory"* (Winston Churchill). **—get the message.** *Informal.* To understand; learn the truth. [Middle English, from Old French, from Vulgar Latin *missāticum* (unattested), "something sent," communication, from Latin *mittere* (past participle *missus*), to send.]

Mes•sa•li•na (mĕs′ə-lī′nə, -lē′nə), **Valeria** (died 48 A.D.). Roman empress. She was the third wife of Claudius I. Noted for her greed, profligacy, and political intriguing, she was executed after Claudius discovered she had publicly married her favorite lover during the emperor's absence from Rome.

mes•sa•line (mĕs′ə-lēn′) *n.* A lightweight, soft, shiny silk cloth with a twilled or satin weave. [French *messaline*†.]

Mes•sei•gneurs. Plural of **Monseigneur.**

mes•sen•ger (mĕs′ən-jər) *n.* **1.** One charged with transmitting messages or performing errands, especially: **a.** One employed to carry telegrams, letters, or parcels. **b.** A military or official dispatch bearer; courier. **2.** A bearer of news. Also used in the titles of some newspapers. **3.** *Archaic.* A forerunner or prophet; harbinger. **4.** *Nautical.* A chain or rope used for hauling in a cable. [Middle English *messager, messanger,* from Old French *messagier,* from MESSAGE.]

messenger RNA *n. Abbr.* **mRNA** A **ribonucleic acid** *(see)* that carries the genetic information required for protein synthesis in cells from DNA to the ribosomes. Also called "messenger ribonucleic acid."

Mes•ser•schmitt (mĕs′ər-schmĭt′), **Wilhelm,** known as "Willy" (1898–1978). German aircraft designer. He designed the Messerschmitt 109 (1937), which set a world speed record; the Messerschmitt 163 Komet, the first aircraft to be powered by a liquid-fuel rocket; and the Messerschmitt 262, the first jet airplane used in combat (1944).

Mes·si·ah (mə-sī′ə) *n.* Also **Mes·si·as** (mə-sī′əs) (for sense 1).
1. a. *Judaism.* The anticipated deliverer and king of the Jews.
b. Jesus Christ. **2. messiah.** An expected or supposed deliverer or
liberator. [Middle English, from Old French *Messie,* from Late
Latin, from Greek *Messias,* from Aramaic *məshīḥa,* Hebrew *mā-
shiaḥ,* "the anointed," the Messiah.]

mes·si·an·ic (mĕs′ē-ăn′ĭk) *adj.* Of or pertaining to a messiah or the
salvation and ideal state he is expected to produce.

Mes·sieurs. *Abbr.* **Messrs., MM.** Plural of **Monsieur.**

Mes·si·na (mə-sē′nə). Port of northeastern Sicily, Italy, on the
Strait of Messina. It exports wine, fruit, and olive oil and manufactures chemicals and pasta. The city was founded by the Greeks (late
8th century B.C.). Its many occupiers included the Carthaginians,
Romans, and Spaniards. It was destroyed by earthquakes in 1783
and 1908.

Messina, Strait of. Channel of the Mediterranean Sea between Sicily and mainland Italy. Linking the Ionian and Tyrrhenian seas, it is
32 kilometers (20 miles) long and at its narrowest 3 kilometers (2
miles) wide. Its rocks, currents, and whirlpools may have given rise
to the legend of Scylla and Charybdis.

mess jacket *n.* A man's fitted, waist-length jacket worn especially
as part of a dress uniform. Also called "monkey jacket."

mess kit *n.* Special cooking and eating utensils for soldiers in the
field.

mess·mate (mĕs′māt′) *n.* A person with whom one eats regularly,
as in a military or naval mess.

Messrs. **1.** Messieurs. **2.** Plural of **Mr.**

mes·suage (mĕs′wĭj) *n. Law.* A dwelling house with its outbuildings and adjoining lands. [Middle English, from Norman French,
household, probably based on a misreading of Old French *me(s)-
nage,* MÉNAGE.]

mess·y (mĕs′ē) *adj.* **-ier, -iest.** Resembling, being in, or causing a
mess; untidy; dirty; disordered. **—mess·i·ly** *adv.* **—mess·i·ness** *n.*

Mes·ta (mĕs′tə), **Perle,** known as "the hostess with the mostest"
(1889–1975). U.S. socialite and diplomat. She was a noted hostess
in Washington, D.C., and was appointed as the first ambassador to
Luxembourg in 1949. The Broadway hit *Call Me Madam,* written
by Irving Berlin, was based on her career.

Meš·tro·vić (mĕsh′trə-vĭch′, mĕs′-), **Ivan** (1883–1962). Yugoslavian
sculptor. His sculptures include religious, mythological, and Slavic
folklore subjects. He came to the United States in 1946 and taught
at Syracuse University and Notre Dame.

mes·ti·zo (mĕ-stē′zō) *n., pl.* **-zos** or **-zoes.** *Feminine* **mes·ti·za**
(mĕ-stē′zə). In Latin America, a person of mixed European and
American Indian ancestry. [Spanish, from *mestizo,* mixed, from
Old Spanish, from Vulgar Latin *mixtīcius* (unattested), of mixed
race, from Latin *mixtus,* from the past participle of *miscēre,* to mix.]

mes·tra·nol (mĕs′trə-nôl′, -nōl′) *n.* A synthetic estrogen, C₂₁H₂₆O₂,
used as an oral contraceptive in combination with progestogens.
[*Methyl estrogen pregnane* + -OL.]

met. Past tense and past participle of **meet** (to come upon).

met. **1.** metaphor. **2.** metaphysics. **3.** meteorological; meteorology.
4. metropolitan.

met·a (mĕt′ə) *adj. Chemistry.* **1.** Of, pertaining to, or designating
positions in a benzene ring separated by one carbon atom. Used in
combination: *metadichlorobenzene.* Compare **ortho, para, pyro.**
2. Of, pertaining to, or designating the least hydrated form of an
acid. Used in combination: *metaphosphoric acid.* **3.** Of, pertaining
to, or designating a polymer of an organic compound. Used in
combination: *metaldehyde.* [From META-.]

meta-, met– *prefix.* Indicates: **1.** *Anatomy.* Situated behind; for
example, **metacarpus. 2.** Occurring later; for example, **metazoan.**
3. a. Going beyond or transcending; for example, **metalanguage.**
b. A discipline concerned with the analysis of a specified and related discipline; for example, **metalinguistics. 4.** Changed or involving change; for example, **metachromatism. 5.** Alternating; for
example, **metagenesis. 6.** *Geology.* Having undergone metamorphic change. [In borrowed Greek compounds, *meta-* indicates: 1.
Between, as in **metope.** 2. After, following, as in **method.** 3. Behind,
backward, hence reversed, changed, as in **metathesis, metamorphosis. 4.** Intensified action, as in **meteor.** *Meta-* is the preverbal form
of the preposition *meta,* between, with, beside, after.]

met·a·bol·ic (mĕt′ə-bŏl′ĭk) *adj. Biology.* Of, pertaining to, or exhibiting metabolism. [Greek *metabolikos,* changeable, from *metabolē,*
change. See **metabolism.**] **—met·a·bol·i·cal·ly** *adv.*

metabolic pathway *n.* Any of the chains or cycles of reactions
occurring in living cells during which materials are broken down or
built up with accompanying release or expenditure of energy.

me·tab·o·lism (mə-tăb′ə-lĭz′əm) *n. Biology.* **1. a.** The complex of
physical and chemical processes involved in the maintenance of life.
See **anabolism, catabolism. b.** The rate at which such processes
function: *a slow metabolism.* **2.** The functioning of any specified
substance within the living body: *water metabolism; iodine metabolism.* [Greek *metabolē,* change, from *metaballein,* to change : *meta*
(denoting change) + *ballein,* to throw.]

me·tab·o·lite (mə-tăb′ə-līt′) *n.* Any of various organic compounds
produced by or taking part in metabolism. [METABOL(ISM) + -ITE.]

me·tab·o·lize (mə-tăb′ə-līz′) *v.* **-lized, -lizing, -lizes.** *—tr.* To subject (a substance) to metabolism or produce (a substance) by metabolism. *—intr.* To undergo metabolism.

met·a·car·pal (mĕt′ə-kär′pəl) *adj. Anatomy.* Pertaining to the metacarpus.
~n. Anatomy. Any of the bones of the metacarpus.

met·a·car·pus (mĕt′ə-kär′pəs) *n. Anatomy.* The part of the hand or
forefoot in mammals that includes the five bones between the fingers and the wrist. [New Latin : META- + CARPUS.]

met·a·cen·ter (mĕt′ə-sĕn′tər) *n.* Also *chiefly British* **met·a·cen·tre.**
The intersection of the verticals through the center of buoyancy of
a floating body when in equilibrium and when tilted. This point
must be above the center of gravity for stability. **—met·a·cen·tric**
(mĕt′ə-sĕn′trĭk) *adj.*

met·a·chro·mat·ic (mĕt′ə-krō-măt′ĭk) *adj.* **1.** Changing to a different color from that of the dye used for staining. Said of cells and
tissues stained for microscopic examination. **2.** Designating a dye
that is able to stain cells or tissues a different color from its own.
3. Characteristic of or pertaining to metachromatism.

met·a·chro·ma·tism (mĕt′ə-krō′mə-tĭz′əm) *n.* A change in color
caused by variation of the physical conditions to which a body is
subjected, as in heating. [META- (denoting change) + CHROMAT(O)-
+ -ISM.]

met·a·cin·na·bar (mĕt′ə-sĭn′ə-bär′) *n.* The black form of **mercuric
sulfide** (see).

met·a·gal·ax·y (mĕt′ə-găl′ək-sē) *n., pl.* **-ies.** The entire collection of
all galaxies considered as the total physical universe.

met·age (mē′tĭj) *n.* **1.** The official measurement of weight or contents, as of trucks using state roads. **2.** The fee charged for metage.
[From METE (to measure).]

met·a·gen·e·sis (mĕt′ə-jĕn′ə-sĭs) *n. Biology.* **Alternation of generations** (see). **—met·a·ge·net·ic** (mĕt′ə-jə-nĕt′ĭk) *adj.* **—met·a·ge·net·
i·cal·ly** *adv.*

me·tag·na·thous (mə-tăg′nə-thəs) *adj.* Having a beak in which the
tips of the mandibles cross. Said of birds. [META- + -GNATHOUS.]
—me·tag·na·thism *n.*

met·al (mĕt′l) *n. Symbol* **M** Any of a category of electropositive
elements that are usually silvery-white, lustrous, good conductors of
electricity and heat, and, in the transition metals, typically ductile
and malleable with high tensile strength. Typical metals form salts
with nonmetals, basic oxides with oxygen, and alloys with one another. **2.** An alloy of two or more metallic elements. **3.** An object
made of metal. **4.** Basic character; mettle. **5.** *British.* Broken stones
used to form the surface of a macadamized road. In this sense, also
called "road metal." **6.** Molten glass, especially when used in glassmaking. **7.** Molten cast iron. **8.** *Printing.* Type made of metal.
9. The total weight, number, or power of a warship's guns. **10.** *Heraldry.* Either of the tinctures *or* (gold) and *argent* (silver), as distinguished from the colors and the furs.
~tr.v. **metaled, -aling, -als.** Also *chiefly British* **-alled, -alling.**
1. To cover or equip with metal. **2.** *British.* To make (a road) with
broken stones. [Middle English, from Old French, from Latin *metallum,* from Greek *metallon†,* a mine, mineral, metal.]

metal. metallurgical; metallurgy.

met·a·lan·guage (mĕt′ə-lăng′gwĭj) *n.* A natural language, formal
language, or logical system used to discuss or analyze another language.

met·a·lin·guis·tics (mĕt′ə-lĭng-gwĭs′tĭks) *n. Used with a singular
verb.* The study of the interrelationship between language and other
cultural or behavioral phenomena. **—met·a·lin·guis·tic** *adj.*

met·al·ist (mĕt′l-ĭst′) *n.* **1.** One who works with metals; especially, a
craftsman producing fine metal objects. **2.** One who has an expert
knowledge of metals.

met·al·ize (mĕt′l-īz′) *tr.v.* **-ized, -izing, -izes.** To make metallic; treat
or coat with metal. **—met·al·i·za·tion** *n.*

metall. metallurgical; metallurgy.

me·tal·lic (mə-tăl′ĭk) *adj.* **1.** Of, pertaining to, or having the characteristics of a metal. **2.** Containing a metal: *a metallic compound.*
3. Having a quality characteristic of metal: *a metallic tinkle.*
[French *métallique,* from Latin, from Greek *metallikos.* See **metal.**]
—me·tal·li·cal·ly *adv.*

metallic bond *n.* The chemical bond characteristic of metals, produced by the sharing of valence electrons between atoms in a usually stable crystalline structure.

metallic soap *n.* A soft, waxlike organic compound composed of a
metal and a fatty acid, used as a drier or lubricant.

met·al·lif·er·ous (mĕt′l-ĭf′ər-əs) *adj.* Containing metal. [Latin *met-
allifer : metallum,* METAL + -FEROUS.]

met·al·line (mĕt′l-īn′, -ēn′) *adj.* **1.** Of, resembling, or having the properties of a metal. **2.** Containing metal ions. [METAL + -INE.]

met·al·log·ra·phy (mĕt′l-ŏg′rə-fē) *n.* **1.** The study of the structure of
metals and their compounds, especially with a microscope. **2.** A
printing process, **lithography** (see), in which metal plates are used.
[METAL + -GRAPHY.] **—met·al·log·ra·pher** *n.* **—me·tal·lo·graph·ic**
(mə-tăl′ə-grăf′ĭk) *adj.* **—me·tal·lo·graph·i·cal·ly** *adv.*

met·al·loid (mĕt′l-oid′) *n.* A nonmetallic element, such as arsenic,
that has some of the chemical properties of a metal, or one, such as
carbon, that can form an alloy with metals.
~adj. Also **met·al·loid·al** (mĕt′l-oid′l). **1.** Pertaining to or having
the properties of a metalloid. **2.** Having the appearance of a metal.
[METAL + -OID.]

met·al·lo·phone (mə-tăl′ə-fōn′) *n.* **1.** Any of various musical instruments resembling the xylophone but having metal bars. **2.** A musical instrument resembling a piano but having metal bars rather
than strings. [METAL + -PHONE.]

me·tal·lo·ther·a·py (mə-tăl′ō-thĕr′ə-pē) *n. Medicine.* The use of
metals or metal compounds in the treatment of disease.

met·al·lur·gy (mĕt′l-ûr′jē) *n. Abbr.* **metal., metall. 1.** The science or
procedures of extracting metals from their ores, of purifying metals,

and of creating useful objects from metals. **2.** The knowledge and study of metals and their properties in bulk and at the atomic level. [New Latin *metallurgia,* from Greek *metallourgos,* a miner : *metallon†,* a mine + *-ourgos,* agent suffix of *ergon,* work.] —**met·al·lur·gic** (mĕt'l-ûr'jĭk), **met·al·lur·gi·cal** (-jĭ-kəl) *adj.* —**met·al·lur·gi·cal·ly** *adv.* —**met·al·lur·gist** (mĕt'l-ûr'jĭst) *n.*

met·al·work (mĕt'l-wûrk') *n.* **1.** The craft of working in or making objects from metal. **2.** Articles of or work done in metal.

met·al·work·ing (mĕt'l-wûr'kĭng) *n.* **1.** The craft or process of shaping things out of metal. **2.** The processing of metal to prepare it for industrial use, as by rolling or flattening it. —**met·al·work·er** *n.*

met·a·math·e·mat·ics (mĕt'ə-măth'ə-măt'ĭks) *n.* The study of the principles, conceptual elements, consistency, and other aspects of logical systems, especially of mathematical systems. —**met·a·math·e·mat·i·cal** *adj.* —**met·a·math·e·ma·ti·cian** (mĕt'ə-măth'ə-mə-tĭsh'ən) *n.*

met·a·mer (mĕt'ə-mər) *n.* Any pair or larger group of isomeric compounds that exhibit metamerism. [META- + -MER.]

met·a·mere (mĕt'ə-mîr') *n.* Any of a series of similar body segments, as in worms and lobsters. Also called "somite." [META- + -MERE.]

met·a·mer·ic (mĕt'ə-mĕr'ĭk, -mîr'ĭk) *adj.* **1.** *Zoology.* Of, pertaining to, or having metameres. **2.** *Chemistry.* Of, pertaining to, or exhibiting metamerism. —**met·a·mer·i·cal·ly** *adv.*

metameric segmentation *n.* The repetition of similar body segments along the length of an animal, as seen in the earthworm. In most animals such segmentation is confined to embryonic stages. Also called "metamerism," "segmentation."

me·tam·er·ism (mə-tăm'ə-rĭz'əm) *n.* **1.** *Chemistry.* A form of isomerism in which different organic radicals form compounds (metamers) by attachment to the same central atom or group. **2.** *Zoology.* Metameric segmentation.

met·a·mor·phic (mĕt'ə-môr'fĭk) *adj.* Also **met·a·mor·phous** (mĕt'ə-môr'fəs). **1.** Of or pertaining to metamorphosis. **2.** *Geology.* Characteristic of, pertaining to, or changed by metamorphism. [From METAMORPHOSIS.]

met·a·mor·phism (mĕt'ə-môr'fĭz'əm) *n.* **1.** *Geology.* Any alteration in composition, texture, or structure of rock masses, caused by great heat or pressure or both. **2.** Metamorphosis, as of an insect or amphibian. [METAMORPH(OSIS) + -ISM.]

met·a·mor·phose (mĕt'ə-môr'fōz', -fōs') *v.* **-phosed, -phosing, -phoses.** —*tr.* **1.** To transform, as by sorcery: *"His eyes turned bloodshot, and he was metamorphosed into a raging fiend"* (Jack London). **2.** To cause to change in form, structure, or character; subject to metamorphosis or metamorphism. —*intr.* To be changed or transformed by or as if by metamorphosis or metamorphism. [French *metamorphoser,* from *metamorphose,* transformation, from METAMORPHOSIS.]

met·a·mor·pho·sis (mĕt'ə-môr'fə-sĭs) *n., pl.* **-ses** (-sēz'). **1.** A transformation, as by magic or sorcery. **2.** A marked change in appearance, character, condition, or function. **3.** One that has been transformed or changed in this way. **4.** *Biology.* Change in the structure and habits of an animal during normal growth, usually in the postembryonic stage. Metamorphosis includes in insects the emerging of an adult fly from a maggot or of a butterfly from a caterpillar and in amphibians the changing of a tadpole into a frog. **5.** *Physiology.* Transformation of one kind of tissue into another; especially, degeneration; metaplasia. [Latin *metamorphōsis,* from Greek : *meta-* (involving change) + MORPHOSIS.]

met·a·neph·ros (mĕt'ə-nĕf'rŏs') *n.* The section of the embryonic kidney that is the third and last stage to be formed in reptiles, birds, and mammals. It develops into the adult kidney. [New Latin : META- + Greek *nephros,* kidney.]

metaph. **1.** metaphor; metaphorical. **2.** metaphysics.

met·a·phase (mĕt'ə-fāz') *n. Biology.* The stage of mitosis or meiosis during which the chromosomes are aligned along the equator of the nuclear spindle.

met·a·phor (mĕt'ə-fôr', -fər) *n.* **1.** *Abbr.* **met., metaph.** A figure of speech in which a term is transferred from the object it ordinarily designates to an object it may designate only by implicit comparison or analogy, as in the phrase *evening of life.* Compare **simile.** **2.** Figurative language: *the effective use of metaphor in her poetry.* [Old French *metaphore,* from Latin *metaphora,* from Greek, transference, from *metapherein,* to transfer : *meta-* (involving change) + *pherein,* to bear.] —**met·a·phor·ic** (mĕt'ə-fôr'ĭk, -fŏr'ĭk), **met·a·phor·i·cal** *adj.* —**met·a·phor·i·cal·ly** *adv.*

met·a·phos·phate (mĕt'ə-fŏs'fāt') *n.* The inorganic anion PO₃⁻, or a compound containing it.

met·a·phos·phor·ic acid (mĕt'ə-fŏs-fôr'ĭk, -fŏr'ĭk) *n.* A polymeric inorganic compound, (HPO₃)ₙ, used as a dehydrating agent and in dental cements.

met·a·phrase (mĕt'ə-frāz') *n.* A word-for-word translation. —*tr.v.* **metaphrased, -phrasing, -phrases.** **1.** To manipulate the wording of (a text), especially as a means of subtly altering the sense. **2.** To make a word-for-word translation of. [New Latin *metaphrasis,* from Greek, from *metaphrazein,* to translate : *meta-* (involving change) + *phrazein,* to relate, tell.] —**met·a·phras·tic** (mĕt'ə-frăs'tĭk) *adj.*

met·a·phrast (mĕt'ə-frăst') *n.* One who changes a text into a different form, as by recasting prose into verse. [Middle Greek *metaphrastēs,* from Greek, from *metaphrazein,* to METAPHRASE.]

met·a·phys·i·cal (mĕt'ə-fĭz'ĭ-kəl) *adj.* **1.** Of or pertaining to metaphysics. **2.** Based on speculative or abstract reasoning. **3.** Too ab-

stract; excessively subtle: *Those are metaphysical speculations.* **4. a.** Immaterial; incorporeal. **b.** Supernatural. **5.** *Usually* **Metaphysical.** Of or designating a group of 17th-century English poets, such as John Donne, whose verse is characterized by scholarly imagery and elaborate metaphors.
~*n. Usually* **Metaphysical.** Any of the Metaphysical poets or their imitators. [Middle English, from Medieval Latin *metaphysicālis,* from *metaphysica,* METAPHYSICS.] —**met·a·phys·i·cal·ly** *adv.*

met·a·phy·si·cian (mĕt'ə-fə-zĭsh'ən) *n.* One who specializes or is skilled in metaphysics.

met·a·phys·ics (mĕt'ə-fĭz'ĭks) *n. Used with a singular verb.* **1.** *Abbr.* **met., metaph.** The branch of philosophy that systematically investigates the nature of first principles and problems of ultimate reality. Metaphysics includes the study of being (ontology) and often the study of the structure of the universe (cosmology). See **epistemology.** **2.** Speculative or critical philosophy in general. **3.** Excessively subtle, abstract, or speculative reasoning. Used derogatorily. [Medieval Latin *metaphysica,* metaphysics, from Greek *Ta meta ta phusika,* "the (works) after the *Physics,*" Aristotle's treatise on transcendental philosophy, so called because it followed his work on physics.]

met·a·pla·sia (mĕt'ə-plā'zhə, -zhē-ə) *n.* The change of cells from a normal to an abnormal state. [New Latin : META- + -PLASIA.]

met·a·plasm (mĕt'ə-plăz'əm) *n.* **1.** *Biology.* Inert material in the protoplasm of a cell, such as the yolk of an egg. **2.** *Grammar.* **a.** Alteration of a word by adding, subtracting, or transposing letters or syllables. **b.** Alteration of the word order of a sentence. [Sense 1, META- + PLASM; sense 2, Latin *metaplasmus,* transformation, from Greek *metaplasmos,* from *metaplassein,* to remold : *meta-* (change) + *plassein,* to mold.] —**met·a·plas·mic** (mĕt'ə-plăz'mĭk) *adj.*

met·a·pro·tein (mĕt'ə-prō'tēn', -prō'tē-ĭn) *n.* Any of various organic compounds resulting from a reaction between an acid or alkali and a protein. Metaproteins are soluble in weak acids or alkalis and insoluble in neutral solutions.

met·a·psy·chol·o·gy (mĕt'ə-sī-kŏl'ə-jē) *n.* **1.** Philosophical speculation on the origin, structure, and function of the mind, and on the relationship between the mind and objective reality. **2.** The philosophical analysis of the foundations or laws of psychology. —**met·a·psy·cho·log·i·cal** (mĕt'ə-sī'kə-lŏj'ĭ-kəl) *adj.*

met·a·so·ma·tism (mĕt'ə-sō'mə-tĭz'əm) *n.* Also **met·a·so·ma·to·sis** (mĕt'ə-sō'mə-tō'sĭs). *Geology.* Metamorphism in which chemical as well as physical changes occur as a result of reaction with external material. [META- + SOMAT(O)- + -ISM.]

met·a·sta·ble (mĕt'ə-stā'bəl) *adj.* Designating a relatively unstable, transient, but significant state or condition of a chemical or physical system, as of a supersaturated solution or an energetically excited atom. —**met·a·sta·bil·i·ty** (mĕt'ə-stə-bĭl'ə-tē) *n.*

me·tas·ta·sis (mə-tăs'tə-sĭs) *n., pl.* **-ses** (-sēz'). **1.** *Pathology.* Transmission of disease from an original site to one or more sites elsewhere in the body, as in tuberculosis or cancer. **2.** *Rhetoric.* A sudden transition from one point to another. **3.** A geological process, **paramorphism** *(see).* [New Latin, from Late Latin, transition, from Greek, from *methistanai,* to change : *meta-* (involving change) + *histanai,* to cause to stand.] —**met·a·stat·ic** (mĕt'ə-stăt'ĭk) *adj.*

me·tas·ta·size (mə-tăs'tə-sīz') *intr.v.* **-sized, -sizing, -sizes.** To be transmitted, transferred, or transformed by metastasis.

met·a·tar·sal (mĕt'ə-tär'səl) *adj.* Of or pertaining to the metatarsus.
~*n.* Any of the bones of the metatarsus.

met·a·tar·sus (mĕt'ə-tär'səs) *n., pl.* **-si** (-sī'). **1.** The middle part of the foot in humans, composed of the five bones between the toes and the tarsus, that forms the instep. **2.** A corresponding part of the hind foot in four-legged animals or of the foot in birds.

met·a·the·ri·an (mĕt'ə-thîr'ē-ən) *adj.* Of or pertaining to the Metatheria, a group of mammals consisting of the marsupials.
~*n.* A metatherian mammal; a marsupial.

me·tath·e·sis (mə-tăth'ə-sĭs) *n., pl.* **-ses** (-sēz'). **1.** Transposition within a word of letters, sounds, or syllables, as in the change from Old English *brid* to modern English *bird* or in the confusion of *revelant* for *relevant.* **2.** *Chemistry.* **Double decomposition** *(see).* [Late Latin, from Greek, from *metatithenai,* to transpose : *meta-* (involving change) + *tithenai,* to place.] —**met·a·thet·ic** (mĕt'ə-thĕt'ĭk), **met·a·thet·i·cal** *adj.*

me·tath·e·size (mə-tăth'ə-sīz') *v.* **-sized, -sizing, -sizes.** —*tr.* To subject to metathesis. —*intr.* To undergo metathesis.

met·a·tho·rax (mĕt'ə-thôr'ăks', -thōr'ăks') *n., pl.* **-raxes** or **-thoraces** (-thôr'ə-sēz', -thōr'ə-sēz'). The hindmost of the three thoracic segments of an insect, which bears the third pair of legs and the hind wings.

Me·tax·as (mə-tăk'səs), **Joannes** (1871-1941). Greek general and politician. Chief of staff of the Greek army, he was exiled in 1917, returned to Greece in 1920, and was exiled again (1923-24). He became premier in 1936 and established a reactionary dictatorship that lasted until his death.

met·a·xy·lem (mĕt'ə-zī'ləm) *n. Botany.* Xylem that is differentiated after the protoxylem is distinguished by wider vessels and thickening of supporting cells. Compare **protoxylem.**

met·a·zo·an (mĕt'ə-zō'ən) *n.* A member of a division of the animal kingdom, the Metazoa, which includes all animals more complex than protozoans and sponges. [New Latin *Metazoa* : META- + -ZOA.] —**met·a·zo·al, met·a·zo·an, met·a·zo·ic** *adj.*

mete¹ (mēt) *tr.v.* **meted, meting, metes.** **1.** To distribute by or as if by measure; deal out; allot. Often used with *out: a judge meting out justice.* **2.** *Archaic.* To measure.

~ *n. Archaic.* A measure. [Middle English *meten*, Old English *metan*.]

mete² *n.* A boundary line or limit. Used chiefly in the phrase *metes and bounds.* [Middle English, from Old French, from Latin *meta*, boundary.]

me·tem·psy·cho·sis (mə-těm'sĭ-kō'sĭs, mět'əm-sī-kō'sĭs) *n., pl.* **-ses** (-sēz'). The passing of a soul into another body or form of existence after bodily death; the transmigration of souls. [Greek *metempsukhōsis*, from *metempsukhousthai*, to transmigrate : *meta-* (transfer) + *empsukhos*, animate : *en-*, in + *psukhē*, soul.]

met·en·ceph·a·lon (mět'ěn-sěf'ə-lŏn', -lən) *n., pl.* **-la** (-lə). The part of the embryonic hindbrain from which the cerebellum and the pons develop. [New Latin : MET(A)- + ENCEPHALON.] —**met·en·ce·phal·ic** (mět'ěn-sə-făl'ĭk) *adj.*

me·te·or (mē'tē-ər, -ôr') *n.* **1.** The luminous trail or streak that appears in the sky when a meteoroid, usually no larger than a grain of sand, is made incandescent by friction with the earth's atmosphere. Also called "shooting star." **2.** A meteoroid. **3.** An atmospheric phenomenon, such as a rainbow or lightning. [Middle English, from Old French *meteore*, from Medieval Latin *meteōrum*, from Greek *meteōron*, astronomical phenomenon, from *meteōros*, high in the air : *meta-* (intensifier) + *aeirein*, to raise.]

meteor. meteorological; meteorology.

me·te·or·ic (mē'tē-ôr'ĭk, -ŏr'ĭk) *adj.* **1.** Of, pertaining to, or formed by a meteor or meteors. **2.** Resembling a meteor in speed and brilliance: *a meteoric rise to fame.* **3.** Of or pertaining to the earth's atmosphere. —**me·te·or·i·cal·ly** *adv.*

me·te·or·ite (mē'tē-ə-rīt') *n.* The stony or metallic object consisting of the material of a meteoroid that is large enough to survive the passage through the atmosphere and reach the earth's surface. —**me·te·or·it·ic** (mē'tē-ə-rĭt'ĭk) *adj.*

me·te·or·o·graph (mē'tē-ôr'ə-grăf', -gräf', -ôr'ə-grăf', -gräf') *n.* An instrument that records simultaneously several meteorological conditions, such as temperature, barometric pressure, and moisture. [French *météorographe* : METEOR + -GRAPH.]

me·te·or·oid (mē'tē-ə-roid') *n.* Any of numerous celestial bodies, ranging in size from specks of dust to asteroids weighing thousands of tons, that appear as meteors when entering the earth's atmosphere.

me·te·or·ol·o·gy (mē'tē-ə-rŏl'ə-jē) *n. Abbr.* **met., meteor., meteorol.** The science dealing with the phenomena of the atmosphere, especially weather and weather conditions. [Greek *meteōrologia*, discussion of astronomical phenomena : *meteōron*, METEOR + -LOGY.] —**me·te·or·o·log·i·cal** (mē'tē-ər-ə-lŏj'ĭ-kəl), **me·te·or·o·log·ic** *adj.* —**me·te·or·o·log·i·cal·ly** *adv.* —**me·te·or·ol·o·gist** *n.*

meteor shower *n.* Any group of meteors that appear together and have an apparent common origin.

me·ter¹ (mē'tər) *n.* Any of various devices designed to measure time, distance, speed, or intensity, or to indicate and record or regulate the amount or volume of something, such as a flow of fluid or an electric current, or the passage of time, as in a coin-operated parking meter.

~ *tr.v.* **metered, -tering, -ters.** **1.** To measure or regulate with a metering device. **2.** To imprint with postage or other revenue stamps by means of a postage meter or similar device: *metered mail.* [From -METER.]

meter² *n.* Also *chiefly British* **me·tre.** **1. a.** The measured rhythm characteristic of verse. **b.** A specified rhythmic pattern of verse, usually determined by the number and kinds of metric units in a typical line. See **foot** (sense 7). **2. a.** The division of music into measures or bars. **b.** A specific musical rhythm determined by the number of beats and the time value assigned to each note in a measure. —See Synonyms at **rhythm.** [Middle English *meter, metre*, from Old English *meter* and Old French *metre*, from Latin *metrum*, measure, from Greek *metron*.]

meter³ *n.* Also *chiefly British* **me·tre.** *Abbr.* **m** The fundamental unit of length, equivalent to 39.37 inches, in the metric system. It was defined in 1790 as one ten-millionth (10⁻⁷) of the earth's quadrant passing through Paris, but was redefined in 1960 as the length equal to 1,650,763.73 wavelengths in a vacuum of the orange-red radiation of krypton 86. [French *metre*, from Greek *metron*, measure.]

-meter *suffix.* Indicates: **1.** A measuring device; for example, **barometer, speedometer. 2.** A line of verse having a specified number of feet; for example, **hexameter.** [New Latin *-metrum* or French *-mètre*, both from Greek *metron*, meter, measure.]

me·ter-kil·o·gram-sec·ond-am·pere system (mē'tər-kĭl'ə-grăm-sĕk'ənd-ăm'pîr') *n. Abbr.* **MKSA.** A coherent system of units for mechanics, electricity, and magnetism, using the meter, the kilogram, the second, and the ampere as basic units for length, mass, time, and current intensity. See **SI unit.**

me·ter-kil·o·gram-sec·ond system (mē'tər-kĭl'ə-grăm-sĕk'ənd) *n. Abbr.* **mks.** A coherent system of units for mechanics, using the meter, the kilogram, and the second as basic units of length, mass, and time. See **centimeter-gram-second system.**

meter maid *n.* A woman who is a member of a police traffic department and who is assigned the duty of writing parking tickets.

met·es·trus (mē-těs'trəs) *n.* The period of sexual inactivity that follows estrus in the female of most mammals apart from higher primates and humans. [META- (after) + ESTRUS.]

Meth. Methodist.

meth- *prefix.* Indicates chemical compounds containing methyl; for example, **methacrylate.** [From METHYL.]

meth·ac·ry·late (měth-ăk'rə-lāt') *n.* **1.** An ester of methacrylic acid,

CH₂:C(CH₃)COOR, R being an organic radical. It is used in the manufacture of plastics. **2.** A resin derived from methacrylic acid. [METH- + ACRYL(IC) + -ATE.]

meth·a·cryl·ic acid (měth'ə-krĭl'ĭk) *n.* A colorless liquid, CH₂:C(CH₃)COOH, used in the manufacture of resins and plastics.

meth·a·done hydrochloride (měth'ə-dōn') *n.* A synthetic organic compound, C₂₁H₂₇NO·HCl, used as an analgesic and in treating morphine addiction. [*di*methyl + *a*mino + *di*phenyl + heptan*one*.]

meth·ane (měth'ān') *n.* An odorless, colorless, flammable gas, CH₄, that is the major constituent of natural gas. It is used as a fuel and is an important source of hydrogen and a wide variety of organic compounds. See **marsh gas.** [METH- + -ANE.]

methane series *n.* The **paraffin series** (see).

meth·a·nol (měth'ə-nôl', -nŏl') *n.* A colorless, flammable, poisonous liquid, CH₃OH, used as an antifreeze, general solvent, fuel, and denaturant for ethanol. Also called "methyl alcohol," "wood alcohol," "wood spirit." [METHAN(E) + -OL.]

meth·a·qua·lone (měth'ə-kwā'lōn') *n.* A drug, C₁₆H₁₄N₂O, that is a habit-forming sedative and hypnotic. [Blend of METH- and *quinazoline*, a derivative of quinoline.]

me·theg·lin (mə-thěg'lĭn) *n.* A kind of spiced mead. [Welsh *meddyglyn* : *meddyg*, medicinal, from Latin *medicus*, MEDICAL + *llyn*, alcoholic liquor.]

met·he·mo·glo·bin (mět-hē'mə-glō'bĭn, -hěm'ə-glō'bĭn) *n.* A brownish-red, crystalline, organic compound formed by oxidation of hemoglobin and found in the blood after poisoning by chlorates, nitrates, ferricyanides, or after ingestion of oxidizing drugs. [MET(A)- + HEMOGLOBIN.]

me·the·na·mine (mə-thē'nə-mēn', -mĭn) *n. Chemistry.* **Hexamine** (see). [METH- + -EN(E) + AMINE.]

me·thinks (mĭ-thĭngks') *v.* Past tense **me·thought** (mĭ-thôt'). *Archaic.* It seems to me. [Middle English *me thinketh*, Old English *mē thyncth* (impersonal) : *mē*, ME + *thyncth*, third person singular present of *thyncan*, to seem.]

me·thi·o·nine (mə-thī'ə-nēn') *n.* An essential amino acid, C₅H₁₁NO₂S, used as a dietary supplement and in pharmaceuticals. [METH- + THION- + -INE.]

meth·od (měth'əd) *n.* **1.** A means or manner of procedure; especially, a regular and systematic way of accomplishing something. **2.** Orderly and systematic arrangement; orderliness. **3.** The procedures and techniques characteristic of a particular discipline or field of knowledge: *the scientific method.* **4. Method.** A system of acting in which the actor recalls emotion and reactions from his past experience and utilizes them in the role he is playing. Also used adjectivally: *a Method actor.* [French *méthode*, from Latin *methodus*, from Greek *methodos*, "a going after," pursuit (as of knowledge) : *met(a)-*, after + *hodos*, road, journey.]

  Synonyms: manner, mode, routine, system, way.

me·thod·i·cal (mə-thŏd'ĭ-kəl) *adj.* Also **me·thod·ic** (-ĭk). **1.** Arranged or proceeding in regular, systematic order. **2.** Characterized by ordered and systematic habits or behavior. —See Synonyms at **orderly.** —**me·thod·i·cal·ly** *adv.* —**me·thod·i·cal·ness** *n.*

Meth·od·ism (měth'ə-dĭz'əm) *n.* The beliefs, worship, and system of organization of the Methodists.

Meth·od·ist (měth'ə-dĭst) *n. Abbr.* **Meth.** A member of any of various Nonconformist Protestant Christian denominations having an evangelistic theology based on the teachings of John and Charles Wesley and others in the early 18th century and characterized by an emphasis on the doctrines of free grace and individual responsibility. See **United Methodist Church.** [From METHOD.] —**Meth·od·ist, Meth·od·is·tic** (měth'ə-dĭs'tĭk), **Meth·od·is·ti·cal** *adj.*

meth·od·ize (měth'ə-dīz') *tr.v.* **-ized, -izing, -izes.** To reduce to or organize according to a method; systematize. —**meth·od·i·za·tion** *n.* —**meth·od·iz·er** *n.*

meth·od·ol·o·gy (měth'ə-dŏl'ə-jē) *n., pl.* **-gies. 1.** The system of principles, practices, and procedures applied to any specific branch of knowledge. **2.** The philosophical study of scientific method; the branch of logic dealing with the general principles of the formation of knowledge. —**meth·od·o·log·i·cal** (měth'ə-də-lŏj'ĭ-kəl) *adj.* —**meth·od·o·log·i·cal·ly** *adv.*

methought. Past tense of **methinks.**

meth·ox·ide (měth-ŏk'sīd') *n.* A methylate.

me·thox·y·chlor (mě-thŏk'sĭ-klôr', -klōr') *n.* A white crystalline compound, C₁₆Cl₃H₁₅O₂, used as an insecticide. [METH- + OXY- + (TRI)CHLOR(ETHANE).]

meths (měths) *n. British Informal.* Methylated spirits.

me·thu·se·lah (mə-thōō'zə-lə) *n.* **1.** A champagne bottle holding the equivalent of eight standard bottles. **2.** An extremely old man. [After METHUSELAH.]

Me·thu·se·lah (mə-thōō'zə-lə). A Biblical patriarch said to have lived for 969 years. Genesis 5:27.

meth·yl (měth'əl) *n.* The univalent organic radical CH₃, derived from methane and occurring in many important organic compounds. [French *méthyle*, back-formation from *méthylène*, METHYLENE.] —**me·thyl·ic** (mə-thĭl'ĭk) *adj.*

methyl acetate *n.* An organic compound, CH₃COOCH₃, used as a paint remover, general solvent, and in the manufacture of perfumes.

meth·yl·al (měth'ə-lăl') *n.* A colorless flammable liquid, CH₂(OCH₃)₂, used in the manufacture of perfumes, adhesives, and protective coatings.

methyl alcohol *n.* **Methanol** (see).

meth·yl·a·mine (měth'ə-lə-mēn', -lăm'ēn', mə-thĭl'ə-mēn') *n.* A flammable gas, CH₃NH₂, produced by the decomposition of organic matter and synthesized for use as a solvent and in the manufacture of many products, such as dyes and insecticides.

meth·yl·ate (mĕth'ə-lāt') n. An organic compound in which the hydrogen of the hydroxyl group (OH) of methanol is replaced by a metal. Also called "methoxide." ~tr.v. **methylated, -lating, -lates. 1.** To mix or combine with methanol. **2.** To combine with the methyl radical. —**meth·yl·a·tion** n. —**meth·yl·a·tor** n.

methylated spirits pl.n. Sometimes **methylated spirit.** A denatured form of ethanol containing methanol and pyridine.

methyl chloride n. An explosive gas, CH_3Cl, used in organic synthesis and polymerization, as a refrigerant, and as an anesthetic.

meth·yl·ene (mĕth'ə-lēn') n. A bivalent organic radical, CH_2, a component of unsaturated hydrocarbons. [French méthylène : Greek methu, wine, mead + hulē, wood + -ENE.]

methylene blue n. An organic compound, $C_{16}H_{18}N_3SCl·3H_2O$, the dark-green crystals or powder of which forms a deep-blue solution when dissolved in water. It is used to treat the accumulation of methemoglobin induced by drugs and as a bacteriological stain.

methyl ethyl ketone n. Chemistry. **Butanone** (see).

methyl methacrylate n. A colorless liquid, $CH_2:C(CH_3)COOCH_3$, that is used as a monomer in plastics.

meth·yl·naph·tha·lene (mĕth'əl-năf'thə-lēn', -năp'thə-lēn') n. An organic compound, $C_{10}H_7CH_3$, obtained from coal tar in two isomeric forms, one a liquid, the other a solid. The liquid is used to standardize diesel fuels, the solid for insecticides, and both are used in organic synthesis.

me·thyl·pro·pane (mĕth'əl-prō'pān') n. A gaseous hydrocarbon, $CH_3C_3H_7$; an isomer of **butane** (see).

met·ic (mĕt'ĭk) n. In ancient Greece, an alien enjoying certain rights of citizenship in the city where he resided. [Greek metoikos : META- + oikos, house.]

met·i·cal (mĕt'ĭ-kəl) n. The basic monetary unit of Mozambique. See feature at **currency.**

me·tic·u·lous (mə-tĭk'yə-ləs) adj. **1.** Extremely careful and precise. **2.** Excessively concerned with details; overscrupulous. [Latin meticulōsus, overconcerned, fearful : metus†, fear + (per)īculōsus, perilous, from perīculum, PERIL.] —**me·tic·u·los·i·ty** (mə-tĭk'yə-lŏs'ə-tē) n. —**me·tic·u·lous·ness** n. —**me·tic·u·lous·ly** adv.

Synonyms: conscientious, fastidious, punctilious, scrupulous.

mé·tier (mā-tyā') n. **1.** An occupation, trade, or profession; especially, the work for which one is especially suited. **2.** One's special interest, talent, or strong point; specialty. [French, from Old French mestier, from Vulgar Latin misterium (unattested), from Latin ministerium, trade, service.]

mé·tis (mā-tēs') n., pl. **métis** (pronounced as singular). Feminine **mé·tisse** (mā-tēs'). **1.** A person of mixed American Indian and French-Canadian ancestry. **2.** Any person of mixed descent. [Canadian French, from Old French metis, mongrel, from Vulgar Latin mixtīcius (unattested). See **mestizo.**]

Me·tol (mē'tôl', -tōl') n. A trademark for a colorless substance, $CH_3(NH_2)C_6H_3OH$, used in photographic developers.

Me·ton·ic cycle (mə-tŏn'ĭk) n. A period of 235 lunar months or about 19 Julian years, at the end of which the phases of the moon recur in the same order and on the same days as in the preceding cycle. [Discovered by Meton, Athenian astronomer of the 5th century B.C.]

met·o·nym (mĕt'ə-nĭm') n. A word or phrase used in metonymy. [Back-formation from METONYMY.]

me·ton·y·my (mə-tŏn'ə-mē) n., pl. **-mies.** A figure of speech in which an attribute or commonly associated feature is used to name something, as in "The pen is mightier than the sword." [Late Latin metōnymia, from Greek metōnumia, "substitute naming" : meta- (involving transfer) + onoma, name.] —**met·o·nym·ic** (mĕt'ə-nĭm'ĭk), **met·o·nym·i·cal** adj.

me-too (mē'tōō') adj. Informal. Advocating principles or practices copied from and closely similar to those of a rival. —**me-too·er** n. —**me-too·ism** n.

met·o·pe (mĕt'ə-pē, mĕt'ōp') n. Architecture. The space between any two triglyphs on a Doric frieze. [Latin metopa, from Greek metopē, area between two beam ends : meta, between + opē, opening.]

me·top·ic (mə-tŏp'ĭk) adj. Anatomy. Of or pertaining to the forehead. [Greek metōpikos, from metōpon, forehead.]

metre. Chiefly British. **1.** Variant of **meter** (rhythm). **2.** Variant of **meter** (unit of length).

met·o·pon hydrochloride (mĕt'ə-pŏn') n. A narcotic drug, $C_{18}H_{21}NO_3·HCl$, derived from morphine. [English metopon, a morphine derivative + HYDROCHLORIDE.]

met·ric¹ (mĕt'rĭk) adj. Designating, pertaining to, or using the metric system. [French métrique, from mèter, METER (unit of length).]

metric² n. **1.** A standard of measurement. **2.** In geometry, a function defined for a coordinate system such that the distance between any two points in that system may be determined from their coordinates.

met·ri·cal (mĕt'rĭ-kəl) adj. **1.** Of, pertaining to, or composed in rhythmic meter. **2.** Of or pertaining to measurement. [From Latin metricus, from Greek metrikos, from metron, measure, meter.] —**met·ri·cal·ly** adv.

met·ri·cate (mĕt'rĭ-kāt') v. **-cated, -cating, -cates.** —tr. To convert to the metric system. —intr. To adopt the metric system.

met·ri·ca·tion (mĕt'rĭ-kā'shən) n. Conversion to the metric system of weights and measures; metrification.

metric centner n. A unit of mass equal to 100 kilograms.

metric grain n. A unit of weight, a grain (see).

metric hundredweight n. A unit of mass equal to 50 kilograms.

met·rics (mĕt'rĭks) n. Used with a singular verb. The branch of prosody dealing with measure and metrical structures; the use of poetic meter: Greek metrics.

-metrics suffix. The application of statistics and mathematical analysis to a specified field of study; for example, **econometrics.**

metric system n. A decimal system of weights and measures based on the meter as a unit length and the kilogram as a unit mass. Derived units include the liter for liquid volume, the stere for solid volume, and the are for area. See **SI unit.**

metric ton n. Abbr. **m.t., M.T.** A unit of mass equal to 1,000 kilograms.

met·ri·fi·ca·tion (mĕt'rə-fĭ-kā'shən) n. Metrication.

met·ri·fy (mĕt'rə-fī') tr. & intr.v. **-fied, -fying, -fies. 1.** To put into or compose in rhythmic meters. **2.** To convert to or adopt the metric system. [Old French metrifier, from Medieval Latin metrificare : Latin metrum, measure (from Greek metron) + Latin facere, to make.]

me·tri·tis (mə-trī'tĭs) n. Inflammation of the uterus. [New Latin : METR(O)- + -ITIS.]

met·ro (mĕt'rō) n., pl. **-ros.** A subway system. [French, short for (chemin de fer) métropolitain, "metropolitan (railway)."]

metro-, metr– prefix. Indicates the uterus or things pertaining to the uterus; for example, **metritis.** [New Latin, from Greek metro-, metr-, from metra, womb, uterus, from mētēr, mother.]

me·trol·o·gy (mē-trŏl'ə-jē) n., pl. **-gies. 1.** The science that deals with measurement. **2.** A system of measurement. [French métrologie, from Greek metrologia, theory of measurements : metron, measure + -LOGY.]

met·ro·nome (mĕt'rə-nōm') n. A device to mark time at a steady beat in adjustable intervals, used especially as an aid to keeping time when practicing music. [Greek metron, measure + nomos, rule, law.] —**met·ro·nom·ic** (mĕt'rə-nŏm'ĭk) adj.

me·tro·nym·ic (mĕ'trə-nĭm'ĭk) n. Also **mat·ro·nym·ic** (măt'-). A name derived from the name of one's mother or a female ancestor. [Medieval Greek mētronumikos : Greek mētēr, mother + onoma, name + -LOGY.]

me·trop·o·lis (mə-trŏp'ə-lĭs) n., pl. **-lises. 1.** A major city; especially, the capital, largest, or most important city of a particular country, state, or region. **2.** A large urban center of culture, trade, or other activity. **3.** The chief see of a metropolitan bishop; especially, the main diocese of a specific ecclesiastical province. **4.** The mother city of a state or colony in ancient Greece. **5.** Zoology. A region or area where a particular kind of organism lives and thrives. **6.** British Informal. London. [Late Latin metropolis, from Greek : mētēr, mother + polis, city.]

met·ro·pol·i·tan (mĕt'rə-pŏl'ə-tən) adj. Abbr. **met. 1. a.** Of, pertaining to, or characteristic of a metropolis. **b.** Making up a metropolis. **2.** Pertaining to or constituting the home territory of a sovereign state as distinguished from its dependencies, protectorates, or overseas territories and provinces: metropolitan France. **3.** Of or pertaining to a metropolitan. ~n. **1.** In the Roman Catholic and other episcopal churches, an archbishop who has authority over bishops. **2.** In the Eastern Orthodox Church, a bishop ranking just below the patriarch who serves as the head of an ecclesiastical province. **3.** One who resides in a metropolis, especially one who displays big-city characteristics, attitudes, and values. [Middle English, from Late Latin metropolītānus, from Greek mētropolītēs, a citizen of a METROPOLIS.]

me·tror·rha·gi·a (mē'trə-rā'jē-ə, -jə, mĕt'rə-) n. An abnormal hemorrhage of the uterus, especially between menstrual flows. [New Latin : METRO- + -RHAGIA.]

-metry suffix. Indicates the science or process of measuring; for example, **calorimetry, photometry.** [Middle English -metrie, from Old French, from Latin -metria, from Greek, from metron, meter, measure.]

Met·ter·nich (mĕt'ər-nĭKH'), **Klemens Wenzel Nepomuk Lothar, Prince von** (1773–1859). Austrian statesman. In 1809 he became the Austrian foreign minister and helped form the Quadruple Alliance that ultimately defeated Napoleon. For the next 30 years he upheld Austrian rule in Italy.

met·tle (mĕt'l) n. **1.** Inherent quality of character and temperament. **2.** Courage and fortitude; spirit: show one's mettle in combat. —Synonyms at **courage.** —**on one's mettle.** Ready to put one's spirit, courage, or energy to the test. [Middle English metel, fortitude, metal, variant of metal, METAL.]

met·tled (mĕt'əld) adj. Mettlesome; full of mettle.

met·tle·some (mĕt'l-səm) adj. Full of mettle; high-spirited; plucky. —See Synonyms at **brave.**

Metz (mĕts). Capital of Moselle department, northeastern France. On the Moselle River, it is a cultural and market center in a fertile agricultural and wine-producing area at the heart of the Lorraine iron and steel region.

meu·nière (mən-yâr', mœn-yâr') adj. Designating a fish dish or a style of cooking fish, in which the fish is lightly coated with flour, fried in butter, and served with melted butter, lemon juice, and parsley: sole meunière. [French (à la) meunière, (in the manner of the) miller's wife.]

Meuse (myōōz, mœz). Dutch **Maas** (mäs). River of western Europe. Rising in the Plateau de Langres, northeastern France, it flows through Belgium and the Netherlands, entering the North Sea by the Rhine delta.

MeV mega electronvolts.

mew¹ (myōō) n. 1. A cage for hawks, especially when molting. 2. A secret place; hideaway.
~v. **mewed, mewing, mews.** —tr. To confine in or as if in a cage. Often followed by up. —intr. To molt. Used of a hawk. [Middle English mewe, hawk cage, from Old French mue, a molting, from muer, to molt, from Latin mūtāre, to change.]

mew² n. 1. The crying sound of a cat; a meow. 2. Any similar sound.
~v. **mewed, mewing, mews.** —intr. To emit a mew. —tr. To express by means of a mew. [Middle English mewen (imitative).]

mew³ n. A sea bird, Larus canus, one of the gulls. It is found in northern Eurasia and western North America. [Middle English mew, Old English mǣw, from Germanic mai(g)wiz (unattested).]

mewl (myōōl) n. A whimper or weak cry.
~v. **mewled, mewling, mewls.** —intr. To cry weakly; emit a mewl. —tr. To express by means of a mewl. [Imitative.]

mews (myōōz) n. Used with a singular verb. 1. A small street behind a residential street, formerly containing private stables for town houses, now mostly converted into small houses and apartments. 2. Such a house or apartment, or a row of them. [After the Mews at Charing Cross, London, England, medieval royal stables built on a site previously used for hawk cages, plural of MEW (cage).]

Mex. Mexican; Mexico.

Mex·i·can (měk′sĭ-kən) n. A native or inhabitant of Mexico.
~adj. Abbr. **Mex.** Of or pertaining to Mexico or to its inhabitants, their language, or their culture.

Mexican bean beetle n. A spotted beetle, Epilachna varivestis, found in the southern United States and Mexico. It causes serious damage to bean crops.

Mexican hairless n. A small dog of a breed of unknown origin, found in Mexico, having a smooth, almost hairless body.

Mexican Spanish n. The Spanish language as used in Mexico.

Mexican War. A war between the United States and Mexico (1846–48), settled by the Treaty of Guadalupe Hidalgo.

Mex·i·co (měks′ĭ-kō′). Abbr. **Mex.** Central American republic. Three quarters of it lies above 500 meters (1,640 feet), the Sierra Madre ranges flanking a central plateau. Half the land is too dry for crops, but farming is the chief occupation, with corn the main crop. Tourism and fishing are also important. Large mineral deposits, including iron ore, oil, natural gas, and some coal, give Mexico great industrial potential, and it has established iron and steel, vehicle, engineering, textile, and fertilizer plants. In 1979 crude oil, cotton, sugar, coffee, shrimp, zinc, lead, and copper were the chief exports, but the country has been badly hit by the slump in world demand for oil. Mexico's Indian civilizations included the Maya, Toltec, and finally the Aztec, conquered by Hernán Cortés (1521). Mexico, the nucleus of New Spain, achieved independence only after a struggle (1810–21). It lost its territory north of the Rio Grande to the United States after the war of 1846–48. Internal strife finally erupted in revolution (1910–17). Since 1930 the republic has been one of Latin America's most stable countries. Area, 1,972,547 square kilometers (761,605 square miles). Population, 67,400,000. Capital, Mexico City.

Mexico City. The capital and largest city of Mexico. It lies on the southern edge of the earthquake-prone central plateau at c. 2,380 meters (7,800 feet), on the site of the Aztec city of Tenochtitlán, destroyed by Cortés (1521). It is a center of commerce, finance, and industry. A cultural center, with Spanish colonial and modern architecture and the national university (founded 1551), the city is a major tourist attraction. The 1968 Olympic Games were held here.

Mey·er·beer (mī′ər-bîr′, -bâr′), **Giacomo,** born Jakob Liebmann Beer (1791–1864). German composer. He worked mainly in France and wrote operas such as Les Huguenots (1836).

me·ze·re·on (mə-zîr′ē-ən) n. 1. A shrub, Daphne mezereum, native to Eurasia, having fragrant lilac-purple flowers and small scarlet fruit. 2. Mezereum. [Middle English mizerion, from Medieval Latin mezereon, from Arabic māzaryūn.]

me·ze·re·um (mə-zîr′ē-əm) n. 1. The mezereon. 2. The dried bark of certain shrubs of the genus Daphne, once used externally as a vesicant (blistering agent) and internally for arthritis. [New Latin, variant of Medieval Latin mezereon, MEZEREON.]

me·zu·zah, me·zu·za (mə-zōōz′ə, -zōō′zə) n., pl. **mezuzoth** (mə-zōōz′ōth′, -zōō′zōth′) or **-zahs.** Judaism. A small piece of parchment inscribed with the Biblical passages Deuteronomy 6:4–9 and 11:13–21 and marked with the word "Shaddai," a name for God. The parchment is rolled up in a container and affixed to a door frame as a sign that a Jewish family lives within. It may also be carried as an amulet. [Hebrew məzūzāh, "doorpost."]

mez·za·nine (měz′ə-nēn′, měz′ə-nēn′) n. 1. A partial story situated between two main stories of a building, especially one between the first and second floors. 2. British. A floor beneath a theater stage. 3. The lowest balcony in a theater or its first few rows. [French, from Italian mezzanino, from mezzano, middle, from Latin mediānus, MEDIAN.]

mez·zo (mět′sō, měd′zō, měz′ō) n., pl. **-zos.** A mezzo-soprano.

mez·zo·re·lie·vo (mět′sō-rĭ-lē′vō, -rēl-yā′vō, měd′zō-, měz′ō-) n., pl. **-vos.** Sculptural relief in which the modeled forms project about halfway from the background. Also called "demirelief," "half relief." [Italian mezzorilievo : mezzo, half + rilievo, relief, from rilevare, to raise.]

mez·zo·so·pran·o (mět′sō-sə-prăn′ō, -prä′nō, měd′zō-, měz′ō-) n., pl. **-os** or **-prani** (-prä′nē). 1. A voice or voice part having a range

between soprano and contralto. 2. A woman having such a voice. [Italian : mezzo, half + SOPRANO.]

mez·zo·tint (mět′sō-tĭnt′, měd′zō-, měz′ō-) n. 1. A method of engraving a copper plate by scraping and burnishing areas to produce effects of light and shadow. 2. A print made from a plate so treated.
~tr.v. **mezzotinted, -tinting, -tints.** To engrave (a metal plate) using the method of mezzotint. [Italian mezzotinto : mezzo, half + tinto, tint, from Latin tingere (past participle stem tinctus), to TINT.]

mF millifarad.

MF, M.F. medium frequency.

mfg. manufacture; manufactured; manufacturing.

MFH Master of Foxhounds.

mfr. manufacture; manufacturer.

mg milligram.

Mg The symbol for the element magnesium.

M.G. Major General.

mgr. manager.

Mgr. 1. manager. 2. Monseigneur; Monsignor.

mH millihenry.

MH Medal of Honor.

MHD magnetohydrodynamics.

MHG Middle High German.

mho (mō) n., pl. **mhos.** Electricity. A unit of conductance, a **siemens** (see). [Backward spelling of OHM.]

MHz megahertz.

mi (mē) n. Music. The third tone of the diatonic scale in solmization. [Medieval Latin, from Latin mīra, "wonders," a word sung to this note in a hymn to St. John the Baptist (see **gamut**), from Latin mīrārī, to be amazed at, from mīrus, wonderful.]

MI 1. Michigan (with Zip Code). 2. Military Intelligence.

MIA (ĕm′ī-ā′) n. A serviceman who is reported missing following a combat mission and whose death can neither be confirmed nor denied. [M(ISSING) I(N) A(CTION).]

mi. 1. mile. 2. mill (monetary unit).

Mi·am·i¹ (mī-ăm′ē, -ăm′ə) n., pl. **-is** or collectively **Miami.** A member of an Algonquian North American Indian people who lived in what is now Ohio, Indiana, Illinois, and Wisconsin. —**Mi·am·i** adj.

Miami². A city and port in southeastern Florida. It grew during the 1920's land boom and is now a famous holiday resort and cruise center for the Caribbean.

Miami Beach. City of southeastern Florida, on an island between Biscayne Bay and the Atlantic Ocean. It is connected to Miami by causeways. Miami Beach is a popular year-round resort, with its "gold coast" strip of hotels, palatial estates, and recreational facilities.

mi·as·ma (mī-ăz′mə, mē-) n., pl. **-mas** or **-mata** (-mə-tə). 1. **a.** A poisonous atmosphere formerly thought to rise from swamps and putrid matter and cause disease. **b.** A thick, vaporous atmosphere: a miasma around the factory. 2. Any noxious atmosphere or influence: a miasma of evil. [New Latin, from Greek, from miainein, to pollute.] —**mi·as·mal, mi·as·mat·ic** (mī′əz-măt′ĭk), **mi·as·mic** adj.

Mic. Micah (Old Testament).

mi·ca (mī′kə) n. Any of a group of chemically and physically related complex mineral silicates, common in igneous and metamorphic rocks, occurring as thin flaky sheets. The two main members of the group are muscovite and biotite. [New Latin (meaning influenced

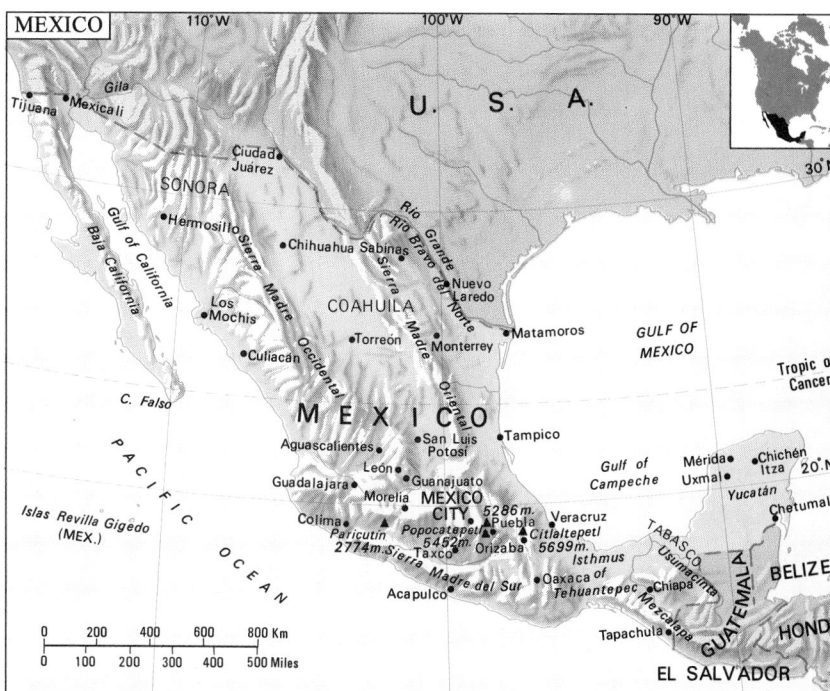

MEXICO

Michelangelo

CREATOR OF THE SISTINE CHAPEL'S MASTERPIECE

Michelangelo endowed his works with a unique spiritual quality

Although he regarded himself chiefly as a sculptor, Michelangelo (1475–1564) was an artist of many talents—painter, sculptor, architect, and poet. He studied under Ghirlandaio and Bertoldo in Florence, then went to Rome (1496), establishing a reputation as a sculptor (1499) with his magnificent pietà in St. Peter's, Rome. Returning to Florence, he carved another great masterpiece, the 4.8-meter (16-foot)-high statue of *David,* and also completed (1504) one of his best-known paintings, *The Holy Family.*

In 1505 he was called to Rome by Pope Julius II to design the Pope's tomb, which he finished in 1545, in a much reduced form from the original intention; the tomb is in San Pietro in Vincoli, with the statue of *Moses* as the main element. In 1508 he began the ceiling of the Sistine Chapel, which he painted, virtually unaided, in four years. This masterpiece, one of the greatest achievements in the history of art, consists of a profusion of Biblical scenes, from the Creation to the aftermath of the Flood.

From 1520 to 1534, Michelangelo worked in Florence as architect and sculptor on the Medici Chapel, where his impressive sculptures include the figures of *Dawn, Evening, Night, and Day.* He returned once more to Rome (1534) and was commissioned (1536) by Pope Paul III to paint the vast fresco of the *Last Judgment* behind the high altar of the Sistine Chapel, which he finished in 1541.

In his declining years, Michelangelo carved another pietà for his own tomb; at present it is in Florence's cathedral museum. He also finished the Palazzo Farnese, laid out the plan of the Capitoline Hill, designed the dome of St. Peter's, Rome, painted frescoes for the Cappella Paolina in the Vatican, and began his final, unfinished, pietà (in the Castello, Milan). His literary works include letters and some 200 poems, mostly sonnets.

A master of the human form, Michelangelo endowed his works with a spiritual quality never before achieved by an artist.

MASTERPIECE IN MARBLE *After Michelangelo had finished the pietà in St. Peter's, Rome, critics commented that the Virgin Mary appeared too young in relation to Christ's age. Michelangelo replied to the effect that a chaste woman long retains her youth and beauty.*

by Latin *micāre,* to shine), from Latin *mīca,* grain.] —**mi·ca·ceous** (mī-kā′shəs) *adj.*

Mi·cah¹ (mī′kə). Also **Mi·che·as** (mī-kē′əs). A Hebrew prophet of the 8th century B.C.

Micah² *n.* Also **Micheas.** *Abbr.* **Mic.** The sixth of the Old Testament books of the Minor Prophets.

mi·caw·ber (mə-kô′bər) *n.* An improvident person who, despite constant adversity, remains doggedly optimistic about a change in his luck. [After Wilkins *Micawber,* a character in Charles Dickens's novel *David Copperfield* (1849–50).] —**mi·caw·ber·ish** *adj.*

mice. Plural of **mouse.**

mi·celle, mi·cell (mī-sĕl′) *n.* Also **mi·cel·la** (mī-sĕl′ə), *pl.* -**cellae** (-sĕl′ē). 1. A submicroscopic aggregation of molecules such as a

droplet in a colloidal system. 2. A coherent strand or structure in natural or synthetic fibers. 3. A submicroscopic structural unit of protoplasm. [New Latin *micella,* from Latin *mīca,* grain, MICA.] —**mi·cel·lar** (mī-sĕl′ər) *adj.*

Mich. Michigan.

Mi·chael¹ (mī′kəl). The guardian archangel of the Jews in the Old Testament. Daniel 10:13; Revelation 12:7–9.

Michael², born Mikhail Fyodorovich Romanov (1596–1645). Czar of Russia (1613–45) and founder of the Romanov dynasty.

Michael I (1921–). King of Romania (1927–30 and 1940–47). He became king on the death of his grandfather, King Ferdinand, but was reduced to crown prince when his father, Carol II, returned from exile in 1930. On his father's abdication, he became king again in 1940. He was forced into exile by the communist government.

Mich·ael·mas (mĭk′əl-məs) *n.* A church festival celebrated on September 29 in honor of the archangel Michael. [Middle English *mychelmesse,* Old English *Michaeles mæsse* : *Michaeles,* genitive of *Michael* + *mæsse,* MASS.]

Michaelmas daisy *n.* Any of several hybrid asters derived primarily from North American species such as *A. novi-belgii,* having clusters of small, variously colored, daisylike flowers.

Micheas. 1. Variant of **Micah** (prophet). 2. Variant of **Micah** (book of Bible).

Mi·chel·an·ge·lo Buo·nar·ro·ti (mī′kə-lăn′jə-lō′ bwô′nə-rô′tē, mĭk′-ə-) (1475–1564). Italian sculptor, painter, and architect. He created some of the greatest masterpieces of world art: the marble sculpture *David,* commissioned in 1501 by the council of Florence; the paintings that decorate the ceiling of the Sistine Chapel (1508–12); and the plans for much of St. Peter's, Rome.

Mi·che·let (mē′shə-lā′), **Jules** (1798–1874). French historian. His multivolume *Histoire de France* (1833–67) is a masterful study of the history of a people. Michelet deliberately immersed himself in his narrative, believing that it is the historian's duty personally to resurrect the past.

Mi·chel·son (mī′kəl-sən), **Albert Abraham** (1852–1931). U.S. physicist, born in Prussia. He accurately measured the speed of light and was awarded the Nobel Prize for physics (1907).

Mi·chel·son-Mor·ley experiment (mī′kəl-sən-môr′lē) *n.* An experiment performed (1887) in an attempt to detect the motion of the earth through the ether by measuring the difference in velocity of two perpendicular beams of light; no such difference was detected. This important result led to disbelief in the existence of the ether and was later explained by the theory of relativity. [After Albert Abraham MICHELSON and Edward Williams MORLEY (1838–1923), U.S. chemist.]

Mich·e·ner (mĭch′ə-nər), **James Albert** (1907–). U.S. author. He is known for his sweeping historical novels, many of them set in the Far East, such as *The Bridges at Toko-ri* (1953), *Sayonara* (1954), and *Hawaii* (1959). His Pulitzer Prize winning *Tales of the South Pacific* (1947) was adapted as a Broadway musical by Rodgers and Hammerstein. He also wrote *Centennial* (1974) and *Space* (1982).

Mich·i·gan (mĭsh′ĭ-gən). *Abbr.* **Mich.** Midwestern state of the United States, comprising two peninsulas divided by Lake Michigan and linked by a bridge across the Straits of Mackinac since 1957. The state is predominantly industrial, with automobile manufacturing the chief industry. Other products include iron ore and oil and gas. French explorers reached the area in the early 17th century. It was occupied by the British (1763–96), became a territory (1805), and was admitted to the Union (1837). Lansing is the capital. —**Mich·i·gan·der** (mĭsh′ĭ-găn′dər) *n.* —**Mich·i·gan·ite** (mĭsh′-ĭ-gə-nīt′) *n.*

Michigan, Lake. The largest freshwater lake in the United States, with an area of 57,757 square kilometers (22,300 square miles). It is the largest of the Great Lakes and the only one of them wholly within the country. Lake Michigan is a major trade artery, linked via the Illinois Waterway with the Mississippi and Gulf of Mexico. Oceangoing ships from the Atlantic reach it via the St. Lawrence Seaway. The ports of Gary, Chicago, and Milwaukee constitute a major industrial region.

Mick·ey Finn (mĭk′ē fĭn′) *n. Slang.* An alcoholic drink that is surreptitiously drugged to stupefy, render unconscious, or otherwise incapacitate the drinker. [20th century : origin unknown.]

mick·ey mouse (mĭk′ē) *adj. Slang.* 1. Not serious; childish. 2. Of little importance; insignificant: *mickey mouse rules.* [After *Mickey Mouse,* a character in the cartoons of Walt Disney.]

Mic·kie·wicz (mĕts-kyā′vĭch), **Adam** (1798–1855). Polish poet and playwright. His verse expressed a romantic view of the soul, often employing Polish folk themes. *Pan Tadeusz* (1834), his masterpiece, is an epic treatment of the life of the Polish gentry.

mick·le (mĭk′əl) *adj.* Also **muck·le** (mŭk′əl). *Scottish.* Great. ~*adv.* Also **muck·le.** *Scottish.* Greatly. ~*n. Chiefly Scottish.* Also **muck·le** (for sense 2). 1. A small amount. Used chiefly in the proverb *Many a mickle makes a muckle.* 2. A large amount: *Many a pickle makes a mickle.* [Middle English *mikell,* from Old Norse *mikill,* replacing Old English *micel,* MUCH.]

Mic·mac (mĭk′măk′) *n., pl.* -**macs** or collectively **Micmac.** 1. A member of an Algonquian North American Indian people formerly inhabiting the areas that are now Nova Scotia and New Brunswick. 2. The Algonquian language of this people.

mi·cra. Alternate plural of **micron.**

micro– *prefix.* Indicates: 1. The smaller, inner, or more detailed of two contrasting things; for example, **microcosm.** Compare **macro–.** 2. An instrument or technique for working with small quantities;

for example, **microchemistry. 3.** Use of a microscope and related tools; for example, **microscopy. 4.** Abnormally small size; for example, **microcephaly. 5.** Amplification or enlargement; for example, **microphone. 6.** *Symbol* **μ** One-millionth (10⁻⁶) part of a unit in the metric or related measurement systems; for example, **microampere.** *Note:* Many compounds other than those entered here may be formed with *micro-.* In forming compounds, *micro-* is normally joined to the following word or element without space or hyphen: *micrometer.* However, if the second element begins with a capital letter, it is separated with a hyphen: *micro-America.* If the second element begins with *o,* a hyphen is normally used, but as the compound grows widely familiar the hyphen may be dropped. An example is the word *microorganism,* which the usage of scientists has established in that form. [Middle English, from Latin *mīcro-,* from Greek *mikro-, mikr-,* from *mikros,* small.]

mi·cro·a·nal·y·sis (mī′krō-ə-năl′ə-sĭs) *n. Chemistry.* The analysis of quantities weighing one milligram or less. —**mi·cro·an·a·lyst** (mī′-krō-ăn′ə-lĭst) *n.* —**mi·cro·an·a·lyt·ic** (mī′krō-ăn′ə-lĭt′ĭk), **mi·cro·an·a·lyt·i·cal** *adj.*

mi·cro·a·nat·o·my (mī′krō-ə-năt′ə-mē) *n. Histology.* —**mi·cro·an·a·tom·i·cal** (mī′krō-ăn′ə-tŏm′ĭ-kəl) *adj.*

mi·cro·bal·ance (mī′krō-băl′əns) *n.* A very accurate balance capable of weighing quantities of between a milligram and a microgram.

mi·crobe (mī′krōb′) *n.* A minute life form; a microorganism, especially one that causes disease. Not in technical usage. —See Usage note at **germ.** [MICRO- + Greek *bios,* life.] —**mi·cro·bi·al** (mī-krō′bē-əl), **mi·cro·bic** (mī-krō′bĭk) *adj.*

mi·cro·bi·ol·o·gy (mī′krō-bī-ŏl′ə-jē) *n.* The science that deals with microorganisms and especially with their effects on other forms of life. —**mi·cro·bi·o·log·i·cal** (mī′krō-bī′ə-lŏj′ĭ-kəl) *adj.* —**mi·cro·bi·o·log·i·cal·ly** *adv.* —**mi·cro·bi·ol·o·gist** *n.*

mi·cro·ceph·a·ly (mī′krō-sĕf′ə-lē) *n.* Abnormal smallness of the head, often associated with pathological mental conditions. [Greek *mikrokephalos,* small-headed : MICRO- + -CEPHALOUS.] —**mi·cro·ce·phal·ic** (mī′krō-sə-făl′ĭk) *n. & adj.* —**mi·cro·ceph·a·lous** (mī′-krō-sĕf′ə-ləs) *adj.*

mi·cro·chem·is·try (mī′krō-kĕm′ĭ-strē) *n.* Chemistry that deals with minute quantities of materials, weighing one milligram or less. Compare **macrochemistry.** —**mi·cro·chem·i·cal** *adj.*

mi·cro·chip (mī′krō-chĭp′) *n.* A chip of semiconductor material carrying integrated circuits, especially one having logic circuits for computers. —**mi·cro·chipped** *adj.*

mi·cro·cir·cuit (mī′krō-sûr′kĭt) *n.* A very small electronic circuit, especially one using small integrated circuits on semiconductor chips. —**mi·cro·cir·cuit·ry** (mī′krō-sûr′kĭ-trē) *n.*

mi·cro·cli·mate (mī′krō-klī′mĭt) *n.* The climate of a specific place within an area rather than that of the area as a whole. Compare **macroclimate.** —**mi·cro·cli·mat·ic** (mī′krō-klī-măt′ĭk) *adj.*

mi·cro·cli·ma·tol·o·gy (mī′krō-klī′mə-tŏl′ə-jē) *n.* The scientific study of microclimates. —**mi·cro·cli·ma·to·log·ic** (mī′krō-klī′mə-tə-lŏj′ĭk), **mi·cro·cli·ma·to·log·i·cal** *adj.*

mi·cro·cline (mī′krō-klīn′) *n.* A mineral of the feldspar group, potassium aluminum silicate, KAlSi₃O₈, used in making pottery. [German *Mikroklin* : MICRO- + CLINE.]

mi·cro·coc·cus (mī′krō-kŏk′əs) *n., pl.* **-cocci** (-kŏk′sī′, -kŏk′ī′). A bacterium of any of several species of the genus *Micrococcus,* containing Gram-positive spherical cells that occur in irregular clusters.

mi·cro·com·put·er (mī′krō-kəm-pyōō′tər) *n.* A small computer consisting of a microprocessor and input and output devices such as a visual display unit, usually with external memory.

mi·cro·cop·y (mī′krō-kŏp′ē) *n., pl.* **-ies.** A greatly reduced photographic copy, usually reproduced by projection.

mi·cro·cosm (mī′krə-kŏz′əm) *n.* **1.** A diminutive, representative system more or less analogous to a much larger system in constitution, configuration, or development: *The town meeting is a microcosm of American democracy.* **2.** The human race or any specific person, community, or the like regarded as the epitome of the universe. Compare **macrocosm.** [Middle English *microcosme,* from Medieval Latin *mĭcro(s)cosmus,* from Greek *mikros kosmos,* small world : MICRO- + COSMOS.] —**mi·cro·cos·mic** (mī′krə-kŏz′mĭk), **mi·cro·cos·mi·cal** *adj.*

microcosmic salt *n.* A white solid, ammonium sodium hydrogen phosphate, obtained from human urine and used in bead tests on metal oxides.

mi·cro·crys·tal·line (mī′krō-krĭs′tə-lĭn) *adj.* Designating a solid substance that consists of microscopic crystals.

mi·cro·cyte (mī′krə-sīt′) *n.* An abnormally small red blood cell, less than five microns in diameter. [MICRO- + (ERYTHRO)CYTE.]

mi·cro·dot (mī′krō-dŏt′) *n.* A piece of text reduced in size to a small dot, typically used for secret messages.

mi·cro·ec·o·nom·ics (mī′krō-ĕk′ə-nŏm′ĭks, -ē′kə-nŏm′ĭks) *n. Used with a singular verb.* The study of the economics of small-scale systems such as families, companies, and the production and selling of particular commodities. Compare **macroeconomics.**

mi·cro·e·lec·tron·ics (mī′krō-ĭ-lĕk-trŏn′ĭks) *n. Used with a singular verb.* The branch of electronics that deals with components of miniature size. —**mi·cro·e·lec·tron·ic** *adj.*

mi·cro·fiche (mī′krō-fēsh′) *n., pl.* **microfiche** or **-fiches.** A sheet of microfilm, usually measuring 10 by 15 centimeters (4 by 6 inches), capable of accommodating and preserving a considerable number of book pages in reduced form. Also called "fiche." ~*tr.v.* **microfiched, -fiching, -fiches.** To record on microfiche. [French : MICRO- + *fiche,* slip of paper.]

mi·cro·fi·lar·i·a (mī′krə-fə-lâr′ē-ə) *n., pl.* **-lariae** (-lâr′ē-ē′). A slender larval form of a filaria, often found in the blood of people infected with filariae.

mi·cro·film (mī′krə-fĭlm′) *n.* **1.** A film upon which documents are photographed greatly reduced in size. **2.** A reproduction on microfilm. ~*tr.v.* **microfilmed, -filming, -films.** To reproduce (documents or other materials) on microfilm. See feature, next page.

mi·cro·form (mī′krə-fôrm′) *n.* Any arrangement of images reduced in size, as on microfilm or microfiche.

mi·cro·ga·mete (mī′krō-gə-mēt′, -găm′ēt′) *n. Biology.* The smaller of a pair of conjugating gametes in protozoans; the male gamete. Compare **macrogamete.**

mi·cro·ga·me·to·cyte (mī′krō-gə-mē′tə-sīt′) *n.* A cell that divides to produce microgametes in protozoa.

mi·cro·graph (mī′krə-grăf′, -gräf′) *n.* **1.** A photograph or drawing of an object enlarged by a microscope. **2.** A device for producing very small writing or engraving. [MICRO- + -GRAPH.]

mi·crog·ra·phy (mī-krŏg′rə-fē) *n.* **1.** The representation, study, or description of microscopic objects. **2.** The writing or engraving of very small characters. Compare **macrography.** [MICRO- + -GRAPHY.] —**mi·cro·graph·ic** (mī′krə-grăf′ĭk) *adj.*

mi·cro·groove (mī′krō-grōōv′) *n.* A narrow groove of the type used on long-playing records.

mi·cro·hab·i·tat (mī′krō-hăb′ə-tăt′) *n.* The smallest unit of a habitat, as in a clump of grass or a space between rocks.

mi·cro·light (mī′krō-līt′) *n.* A light motorized aircraft consisting essentially of a wing structure similar to that of a hang glider with a suspended frame to carry one or two people.

mi·cro·lith (mī′krō-lĭth′) *n. Archaeology.* A small flint that is the remnant of a Stone Age tool or weapon. [MICRO- + -LITH.]

mi·cro·ma·nip·u·la·tion (mī′krō-mə-nĭp′yə-lā′shən) *n.* The manipulation of minute instruments under a microscope, as in microsurgery. —**mi·cro·ma·nip·u·la·tor** (mī′krō-mə-nĭp′yə-lā′tər) *n.*

mi·cro·me·te·or·ite (mī′krō-mē′tē-ə-rīt′) *n.* A very small meteorite, typically having a diameter of a few micrometers.

mi·cro·me·te·or·ol·o·gy (mī′krō-mē′tē-ə-rŏl′ə-jē) *n.* The study of meteorological conditions in a small region, usually a shallow layer up to about 100 meters (110 yards) above ground in which temperature and humidity extremes are found. —**mi·cro·me·te·or·o·log·i·cal** (mī′krō-mē′tē-ôr′ə-lŏj′ĭ-kəl, -ər-ə-lŏj′ĭ-kəl) *adj.* —**mi·cro·me·te·or·ol·o·gist** *n.*

mi·crom·e·ter¹ (mī-krŏm′ə-tər) *n.* A device for measuring minute distances, especially an instrument (*micrometer gauge*) based on the rotation of a finely threaded screw. [French *micromètre* : MICRO- + -METER.]

mi·cro·me·ter² (mī′krō-mē′tər) *n.* A unit of length equal to one-millionth (10⁻⁶) of a meter. Also called "micron."

micrometer screw *n.* A screw that has a fine, accurately cut thread, used in a micrometer.

mi·crom·e·try (mī-krŏm′ə-trē) *n.* Measurement with a micrometer. —**mi·cro·met·ric** (mī′krō-mĕt′rĭk), **mi·cro·met·ri·cal** *adj.* —**mi·cro·met·ri·cal·ly** *adv.*

mi·cro·min·i·a·tur·ize (mī′krō-mĭn′ē-ə-chə-rīz′) *tr.v.* **-ized, -izing, -izes.** To construct or produce (very small electronic circuits) using integrated circuits. —**mi·cro·min·i·a·tur·i·za·tion** *n.*

mi·cron, mi·kron (mī′krŏn′) *n., pl.* **-crons** or **-cra** (-krə) also **-krons** or **-kra.** *Symbol* **μ** A micrometer. In technical usage *micrometer* is preferred. [New Latin, from Greek, from *mikros,* small.]

Mi·cro·ne·sia¹ (mī′krō-nē′zhə, -shə) *n.* A division of the Pacific islands including Kiribati, the Caroline, Marianas, and Marshall groups, and other islands. See also **Melanesia, Polynesia.** See map at **Pacific Ocean.**

Micronesia². A country of the western Pacific comprising the Caroline Islands excluding Belau. The federation's 600 or so coral or volcanic islands export copra, fish products, and handicrafts, and tourism is increasing. However, most islanders, of Australoid and Polynesian origin, are subsistence farmers. The Spaniards discovered the islands (16th century). They were seized by Japan (1914) and were part of the UN Trust Territory of the Pacific Islands administered by the United States (1947–81). The federation is self-governing at home and in foreign affairs, but the United States is responsible for its defense and has rights to military facilities until 1996. Area, 701 square kilometers (271 square miles). Population, 81,700. Capital, Kolonia (on Ponape). See map at **Pacific Ocean.**

Mi·cro·ne·sian (mī′krō-nē′zhən, -shən) *adj.* Of or pertaining to Micronesia, its inhabitants, their languages, or their culture. ~*n.* **1.** A native or inhabitant of Micronesia. **2.** A subfamily of Austronesian languages spoken in Micronesia.

mi·cro·nu·cle·us (mī′krō-nōō′klē-əs, -nyōō′klē-əs) *n., pl.* **-clei** (-klē-ī′) or **-uses.** The smaller nuclear mass in protozoans as distinguished from the macronucleus in such animals, functioning in sexual reproduction. Compare **macronucleus.**

mi·cro·nu·tri·ent (mī′krō-nōō′trē-ənt, -nyōō′trē-ənt) *n.* A substance, such as a vitamin, that in minute amounts is essential to life.

mi·cro·or·gan·ism, mi·cro·or·gan·ism (mī′krō-ôr′gə-nĭz′əm) *n.* An animal or plant of microscopic size, especially a bacterium or a protozoan.

mi·cro·pa·le·on·tol·o·gy (mī′krō-pā′lē-ŏn-tŏl′ə-jē, -ən-tŏl′ə-jē) *n.* The scientific study of microscopic fossils. —**mi·cro·pa·le·on·to·log·ic** (mī′krō-pā′lē-ŏn′tə-lŏj′ĭk), **mi·cro·pa·le·on·to·log·i·cal** *adj.* —**mi·cro·pa·le·on·tol·o·gist** *n.*

microfilm

SAVING SPACE WITH PHOTOGRAPHIC FILES OF DOCUMENTS AND PUBLICATIONS
The process that fitted Queen Victoria's family into a finger ring

The principles and practice of microfilming are almost as old as photography itself. In the 1850's an Englishman, John Dancer, produced minute film slides. One series was of Queen Victoria's family mounted in a ring with a built-in magnifying glass. The first commercial process, Kodak's Recordak, used for reducing checks onto 16-millimeter film, was launched in 1928, and in ensuing decades reductions ranging from 10 to 60 times were stored on film or on cards (microfiches). Techniques have since been refined with the advent of the microchip; but microfilm remains in wide use for storage of records and documents.

SIZE BEFORE REDUCTION *Printed above at their actual size, three headline letters from the magazine on the right occupy about the same space as ten pages reduced onto microfilm.*

FILES IN MINIATURE *A 98-page magazine, such as* Business Week *shown here, can be recorded on a single microfilm card about 140 × 90 millimeters (5¹/₂ × 3¹/₂ inches)—about the same size as a postcard.*

---

mi·cro·pas·cal (mī′krō-pă-skăl′, -pä-skăl′) *n. Symbol* **mPa** A unit of pressure equal to one thousandth of a pascal.

mi·cro·phage (mī′krə-fāj′) *n.* A small phagocyte.

mi·cro·phone (mī′krə-fōn′) *n.* An instrument that converts sound waves into an electric current or voltage, usually fed into an amplifier, recorder, or broadcast transmitter. [MICRO- + -PHONE.] —**mi·cro·phon·ic** (mī′krə-fŏn′ĭk) *adj.*

mi·cro·pho·to·graph (mī′krō-fō′tə-grăf′, -gräf′) *n.* **1.** A photograph requiring magnification for viewing. **2.** A photograph on microfilm. **3.** A photomicrograph. —**mi·cro·pho·to·graph·ic** (mī′krō-fō′tə-grăf′ĭk) *adj.* —**mi·cro·pho·tog·ra·phy** (mī′krō-fə-tŏg′rə-fē) *n.*

mi·cro·phys·ics (mī′krō-fĭz′ĭks) *n. Used with a singular verb.* The physics of molecular, atomic, nuclear, and subnuclear systems. —**mi·cro·phys·i·cal** *adj.*

mi·cro·phyte (mī′krə-fīt′) *n.* Any plant of microscopic size. [MICRO- + -PHYTE.] —**mi·cro·phyt·ic** (mī′krə-fīt′ĭk) *adj.*

mi·cro·print (mī′krə-prĭnt′) *n.* The printed or positive reproduction of a microphotograph.

mi·cro·proc·es·sor (mī′krō-prŏs′ĕs′ər, -prō′sĕs′ər) *n.* A small integrated circuit used as the processor in a minicomputer or microcomputer.

mi·cro·pyle (mī′krə-pīl′) *n.* **1.** *Botany.* A minute opening in the ovule of a plant through which the pollen tube usually enters. **2.** *Zoology.* A pore in the membrane of the ova of some animals through which the spermatozoon enters. [MICRO- + Greek *pulē*, gate.] —**mi·cro·py·lar** (mī′krə-pī′lər) *adj.*

mi·cro·read·er (mī′krō-rē′dər) *n.* An optical device for producing an enlarged image of microfilm, microfiche, or the like.

mi·cro·scope (mī′krə-skōp′) *n.* An optical instrument that uses a combination of lenses to produce magnified images of small objects, especially of objects too small to be seen by the unaided eye. See **simple microscope, compound microscope, electron microscope, x-ray microscope.** [New Latin *microscopium* : MICRO- + -SCOPE.]

mi·cro·scop·ic (mī′krə-skŏp′ĭk) *adj.* Also **mi·cro·scop·i·cal** (-ĭ-kəl). **1.** Too small to be seen by the unaided eye but large enough to be studied under a microscope. **2.** Exceedingly small; minute. **3.** Characterized by or done with extreme attention to detail: *conducted a microscopic investigation.* **4.** Of, pertaining to, or concerned with a microscope. **5.** Like or resembling a microscope; having the ability to observe very small objects. **6.** *Physics.* Involving or per-taining to the properties of individual atoms or molecules rather than collections of atoms. In this sense, compare **macroscopic.** —**mi·cro·scop·i·cal·ly** *adv.*

Mi·cro·sco·pi·um (mī′krə-skō′pē-əm) *n.* A constellation in the Southern Hemisphere. [New Latin, MICROSCOPE.]

mi·cros·co·py (mī-krŏs′kə-pē) *n.* **1.** Investigation employing a microscope. **2.** The study or use of microscopes. —**mi·cros·co·pist** *n.*

mi·cro·seism (mī′krə-sī′zəm) *n.* A faint, recurrent tremor of the earth's crust. —**mi·cro·seis·mic** (mī′krə-sīz′mĭk, -sīs′mĭk), **mi·cro·seis·mi·cal** *adj.*

mi·cro·some (mī′krə-sōm′) *n.* A cell particle of the smallest size, typically consisting of a piece of endoplasmic reticulum to which ribosomes are attached. [German *Mikrosom* : MICRO- + -SOME.] —**mi·cro·so·mal** (mī′krə-sō′məl), **mi·cro·so·mic** (mī′krə-sō′mĭk) *adj.*

mi·cro·spo·ran·gi·um (mī′krō-spə-răn′jē-əm) *n., pl.* **-gia** (-jē-ə). A structure or receptacle in which microspores are formed.

mi·cro·spore (mī′krə-spôr′, -spōr′) *n. Botany.* **1.** The smaller of two types of spores produced by heterosporous plants, such as ferns, giving rise to the male gametophyte. Compare **megaspore.** **2.** A pollen grain. —**mi·cro·spo·ric** (mī′krə-spôr′ĭk, -spōr′ĭk), **mi·cro·spo·rous** (mī′krə-spôr′əs, -spōr′əs, mī-krŏs′pər-əs) *adj.*

mi·cro·spo·ro·phyll (mī′krə-spôr′ə-fĭl′, -spōr′ə-fĭl′) *n.* The structure in ferns and similar plants that bear microsporangia.

mi·cro·state (mī′krō-stāt′) *n.* An independent country that is very small in area and population.

mi·cro·struc·ture (mī′krō-strŭk′chər) *n.* Microscopic structure; especially, the structure of a material as viewed under a microscope.

mi·cro·sur·ger·y (mī′krō-sûr′jə-rē) *n.* Surgery involving intricate operations on relatively inaccessible parts of the body, performed through a microscope using minute instruments. —**mi·cro·sur·geon** *n.* —**mi·cro·sur·gi·cal** *adj.*

mi·cro·tome (mī′krə-tōm′) *n.* An instrument used to cut samples into very thin sections for microscopic examination.

mi·crot·o·my (mī-krŏt′ə-mē) *n.* The preparation of specimens by use of a microtome. —**mi·cro·tom·ic** (mī′krə-tŏm′ĭk) *adj.*

mi·cro·tone (mī′krə-tōn′) *n. Music.* An interval smaller than a half tone.

mi·cro·vil·lus (mī′krō-vĭl′əs) *n., pl.* **-villi** (-vĭl′ī′). Any of the minute, hairlike structures that project from the surface of absorptive or secretory epithelial cells, such as those of the intestinal tract.

mi·cro·wave (mī′krə-wāv′) *n.* **1.** Electromagnetic radiation having a

microscope

SEEING FURTHER INTO MINIATURE WORLDS DURING 400 YEARS OF IMPROVING MICROSCOPES
How combinations of lenses reveal the minute structure of materials

Without the microscope, there could have been no proper understanding of the nature of living things. Mankind would still be largely ignorant of (among other things) the nature of germs, chromosomes and the mechanisms of heredity, the manner in which muscles contract, and how malaria is transmitted.

The first compound microscope was pioneered (*c.* 1590) by Dutch eyeglass makers Zacharias and Hans Janssen. It is called "compound" because it has more than one lens—an objective lens, which magnifies the object, and an eyepiece lens, which enlarges the magnified image. Since then, microscopes have been progressively refined: magnifications have been increased and distortions eliminated by adding extra lenses. By the 1880's, magnifications of 2,000 times had been achieved, the limit for compound microscopes dictated by the nature of light itself.

The first electron microscope was made in Germany in 1931. It uses electron beams instead of light rays to reveal detail. Today electron microscopes can magnify specimens by up to 1,000,000 times. They have extended our ability to view matter to the level of the infinitesimal molecule.

Microscopes have proved invaluable not only in medicine and biology but also in metallurgy, geology, forensic science, and other specialties interested in the minute structure of materials.

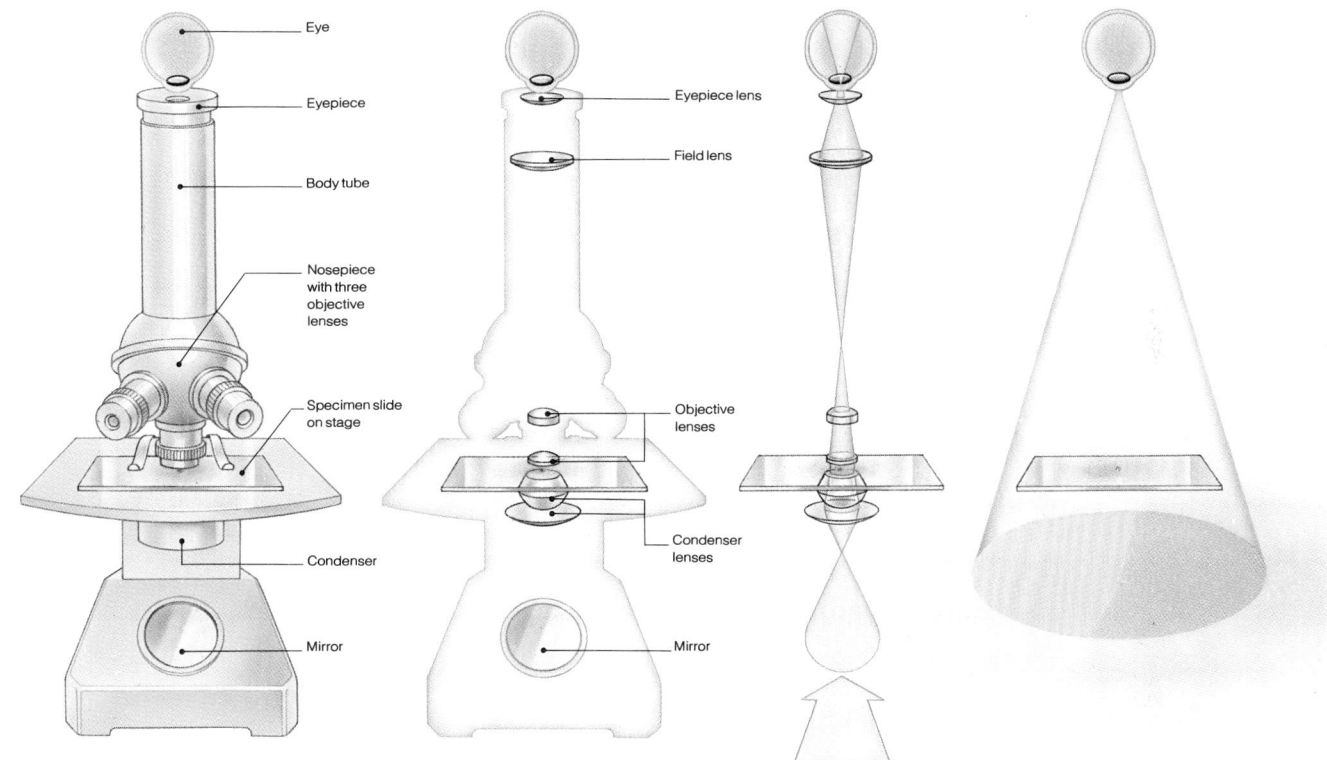

THE STRUCTURE *The slide is seen under a basic compound microscope, which has a single body tube. The eye sees an image formed by one of three objective lenses of different powers in the rotating nosepiece. The image is magnified by lenses in the eyepiece. The whole microscope can be tilted for convenience, the slide moving with the body tube and nosepiece to keep the objective lens that is in use in the same plane as the slide.*

THE LENSES *To form the image, three systems of lenses are used. Under the stage is the condenser, made of two or three separate lenses. Above the stage is the objective lens, made of up to 18 separate lenses. At the top of the microscope is the eyepiece, consisting of a field lens and an eye lens. If a high-powered objective lens is lowered into a drop of oil on the glass that covers the specimen, magnification up to ×2,000 can be obtained.*

FORMING THE IMAGE *Artificial light reaches the eye of the observer through the three lens systems. The light, generated by a lamp, is reflected by a mirror through the condenser, which concentrates light on the specimen on the stage. The objective lenses and the eyepiece lenses together form a reversed image of the specimen. This is what is seen by an observer looking into the microscope.*

MAGNIFICATION *The eye sees an image of part of the specimen in fine detail. Careful lens design and manufacture correct distortion in the image, giving it clarity and sharpness—called high resolution. To help to achieve this, the lenses are made of two kinds of glass—crown and flint—and sometimes of a transparent mineral, fluorite, which is necessary for the very best image. Objective and eyepiece lenses of different magnifications give a range of powers, usually between ×40 and ×1,500.*

---

wavelength in the approximate range from one millimeter to one meter, the region between infrared and short-wave radio wavelengths. Also used adjectivally: *microwave radiation.* **2.** A **microwave oven** (see).
microwave background *n.* Background microwave radiation throughout the universe, corresponding to blackbody radiation at a temperature of 2.7K and thought to be a remnant of the big-bang origin of the universe. Also called "cosmic background."
microwave oven *n.* An oven that heats and cooks food by means of microwaves. Food is heated as water molecules dissipate the energy they have absorbed from the microwaves. Also called "microwave."
mic·tu·rate (mĭk′chə-rāt′, mĭk′tə-) *intr.v.* **-rated, -rating, -rates.** To urinate. [Latin *micturīre,* from *mingere* (past participial stem *mict-*), to urinate.] **—mic·tu·ri·tion** (mĭk′chə-rĭsh′ən, mĭk′tə-) *n.*
mid¹ (mĭd) *adj.* **1.** Middle; central. **2.** Being the part in the middle or center: *in the mid Pacific.* **3.** *Phonetics.* Pronounced with the tongue approximately intermediate between high and low, as in the (u) in *cut* or the (e) in *pet.* Said of vowel sounds.

~*n. Archaic.* The middle. [Middle English *mid, midde,* Old English *midd.*]
mid² *prep.* Amid: *mid smoke and flame.*
mid– *prefix.* Indicates a middle part, time, or location; for example, **midship, midway.** *Note:* Many compounds other than those entered here may be formed with *mid-.* In forming compounds, *mid-* is normally joined to the following word or element without space or hyphen: *midday.* However, many editors prefer the hyphenated form, especially in less standardized compounds: *mid-season.* If the second element begins with a capital letter, it is always separated with a hyphen: *mid-May.* It is always acceptable to separate the elements with a hyphen to prevent possible confusion with another form, as to distinguish *mid-den* (the middle of a den) as distinct from the word *midden.* Note that the adjective **mid** above is a separate word, though, as with any adjective, it may be joined to another word with a hyphen when used as a unit modifier: *in the mid Pacific,* but *a mid-Pacific island.* [From MID (middle).]

mid. middle.

mid·air (mĭd′âr′) *n.* A point or region in the middle of the air; space: *floating in midair.*

Mi·das (mī′dəs). The legendary king of Phrygia to whom Dionysus gave the power of turning to gold all that he touched.

Mid-At·lan·tic Ridge (mĭd′ăt-lăn′tĭk). Mountain range on the floor of the Atlantic Ocean, stretching from Iceland to the Antarctic Circle. Some of its peaks rise above sea level, forming islands such as the Azores group, Ascension, Iceland, and Tristan da Cunha.

mid·brain (mĭd′brān′) *n.* **1.** The middle region of the embryonic vertebrate brain, the **mesencephalon** *(see).* **2.** The parts that develop from this region.

mid·course (mĭd′kôrs′, -kōrs′) *n.* The part of a missile's or spacecraft's flight between burnout and the point where final connective maneuvers are made.

mid·day (mĭd′dā′) *n.* The middle of the day; noon.
~*adj.* Of, pertaining to, or occurring in the middle of the day or at noon: *a midday snack.* [Middle English *midday,* Old English *middæg* : MID (middle) + *dæg,* DAY.]

mid·den (mĭd′n) *n.* **1.** A dunghill or refuse heap, especially one near a dwelling. **2.** A **kitchen midden** *(see).* [Middle English *myddung,* from Old Norse *myki-dyngja* (unattested) : *myki-,* muck + *dyngja,* heap (see dung).]

mid·dle (mĭd′l) *adj. Abbr.* **mid.** **1. a.** Equally distant from extremes or limits; central; mean: *the middle point on a line.* **b.** Approximately halfway between two limits: *the middle ground.* **2.** Intermediate; in between: *the middle piece of cake.* **3.** Medium; moderate: *"He was about the middle height"* (Charles Dickens). **4.** Intervening between an earlier and later period of time; being part of a sequence or series: *the middle years.* **5.** Middle. Designating a stage in the development of a language or literature between earlier and later stages: *Middle English.* **6.** *Logic.* Designating a term that appears in both premises of a syllogism but not in the conclusion. **7.** *Grammar.* Intermediate between the active and the passive voice. Said of verb forms in Sanskrit and Greek in which the subject is represented as acting on, for, or with reference to itself.
~*n.* **1.** An area or point equidistant between extremes; the center: *the middle of a circle.* **2.** Something intermediate between extremes; a mean. **3.** The interior portion: *the middle of the chain.* **4.** The middle part of the human body; the waist. **5.** *Logic.* The **middle term** *(see).*
~*tr.v.* **middled, -dling, -dles. 1.** To place in the middle. **2.** *Nautical.* To fold in the middle: *middle the sail.* [Old English *middel.*]

middle age *n.* The time of human life between youth and old age, usually reckoned as the years between 40 and 60.

mid·dle-aged (mĭd′l-ājd′) *adj.* Of or pertaining to middle age.

Middle Ages *pl.n.* **1.** The period in European history between Antiquity and the Renaissance, often dated from A.D. 476, when the last emperor of the Western Roman Empire was deposed, to A.D. 1453, when Constantinople was conquered by the Turks. **2.** The period from about A.D. 1000 to A.D. 1400. Compare **Dark Ages.**

mid·dle-age spread (mĭd′l-āj′) *n.* Also **mid·dle-aged spread** (-ājd′). Thickening of the waistline and a general gain in weight that often takes place in middle age.

Middle America *n.* **1.** That part of the U.S. middle class thought of as being average in income and education and conservative in values and attitudes. **2.** The American heartland thought of as being made up of small towns, small cities, and suburbs. **3.** Mexico, Central America, and sometimes the West Indies. **—Middle American** *adj.*

Middle Atlantic States. Those states of the United States having Atlantic Ocean ports and lying between New England and Virginia. They are New York, Pennsylvania, New Jersey, Delaware, and Maryland.

mid·dle·brow (mĭd′l-brou′) *n. Informal.* A person of some education and culture, but whose interests may be considered artistically and intellectually limited and conventional. Compare **highbrow, lowbrow. —mid·dle·brow** *adj.*

middle C *n. Music.* The musical note represented by the first ledger line below the treble clef or the first ledger line above the bass clef. It is near the middle of a piano keyboard.

middle class *n. Often* **middle classes.** The members of society occupying an intermediate social and economic position between the working classes and those who are wealthy in money or land.

mid·dle-class (mĭd′l-klăs′, -kläs′) *adj.* Of, pertaining to, or characteristic of the middle class.

middle distance *n.* **1.** The area between the foreground and background in a painting, drawing, or photograph. Also called "middle ground." **2.** In athletics, a division of competition in racing with events usually ranging from 440 yards to 1 mile or from 800 meters to 1500 meters. **—mid·dle-dis·tance** (mĭd′l-dĭs′təns) *adj.*

Middle Dutch *n.* Dutch from the mid-12th century through the 15th century.

middle ear *n.* The space between the tympanic membrane and the internal ear. It contains the auditory ossicles that convey vibrations to the internal ear. Also called "tympanic cavity," "tympanum." See **ear.**

Middle East. Also **Mid·east** (mĭd′ēst′). The western subcontinent of Asia. It includes only 5 percent of the world's land and 4 percent of its people. The region's northern mountains, enclosing high plateaus, are part of the Alpine-Himalayan system, subject to frequent earthquakes. The stabler tablelands of Arabia and Egypt are slashed by the Great Rift Valley. The Middle East is the driest of the world's major regions by far. More than 75 percent of it has less than 250 millimeters (c. 10 inches) of rain a year and is covered by desert, semidesert, or mountain steppe, yet some 60 percent of its inhabitants rely on farming for a living. Economically, oil dominates the region, which has half the world's known reserves. It produces more than 30 percent of the world's crude oil. The oil states are using their vast wealth to industrialize and diversify their economies against the day when the oil wells run dry. They spend much on irrigation, welfare, and education schemes, interregional aid, and aid to other Third World countries. **—Middle Eastern** *adj.* **—Middle Easterner** *n.*

Middle Empire. The Middle Kingdom of Egypt.

Middle English *n. Abbr.* **M.E., ME., ME** English from about 1100 to about 1500. The five main dialects of Middle English were Kentish (southeastern), Southern (southwestern), East Midland, West Midland, and Northern. See **Midland.**

Middle French *n.* French from the mid-15th century to the mid-16th.

Middle Greek *n.* **Medieval Greek** *(see).*

middle ground *n.* **1.** See **middle distance** (sense 1). **2.** A point of view midway between extremes.

Middle High German *n. Abbr.* **MHG** High German from the 11th century to the 16th.

Middle Irish *n.* Irish Gaelic from the 10th century to the 15th.

Middle Island. See **South Island.**

Middle Kingdom. 1. A kingdom of ancient Egypt lasting from *c.* 2100 to *c.* 1600 B.C. Its capitals were Heracleopolis and later Thebes. Also called "Middle Empire." **2.** The former Chinese empire, considered by its inhabitants to be the center of the world.

Middle Low German *n.* Low German from the middle of the 13th century to the 16th.

mid·dle·man (mĭd′l-măn′) *n., pl.* **-men** (-mĕn′). **1.** A trader who buys from producers and sells to retailers or consumers. **2.** An intermediary or go-between.

middle management *n.* Middle-ranking executives responsible for the day-to-day running of a department.

mid·dle·most (mĭd′l-mōst′) *adj.* Midmost. [Middle English *middelmast* : *middel,* MIDDLE + *-mast,* -MOST.]

middle name *n.* **1.** A name that comes between a person's first or Christian name and surname. **2.** *Informal.* A person's most significant character trait: *Carefulness is his middle name.*

mid·dle-of-the-road (mĭd′l-əv-thə-rōd′) *adj. Abbr.* **MOR 1.** Moderate; not extreme, as in tastes or views. **2.** Of, pertaining to, or being a type of popular music that is conventional and usually melodic and has wide popular appeal.

middle passage *n.* The passage of slave ships from Africa to the West Indies and America during the 16th to the 19th centuries.

Middle Persian *n.* The language of the Sassanians, from the 3rd century A.D. to the 7th.

middle school *n.* A school that usually includes grades five through eight.

Mid·dle·sex (mĭd′l-sĕks′). Former county of southeastern England. It was absorbed mainly by Greater London in 1965, with small areas passing to Surrey and Hertfordshire.

Middle South A·sia (ā′zhə, ā′shə). The subcontinent of India. It covers only 3 percent of the world's land, but has 20 percent of its people and is the world's most densely peopled region of comparable size. Its fertile Indus and Ganges plains comprise a vast alluvium-filled trough. To the south the stable tableland of the Deccan has fertile volcanic soils, but generally soils are poor. The rising fold mountains of Baluchistan and the Himalayas have the highest peaks in the world—more than 30 of them higher than 8,600 meters (28,200 feet). The region is dominated by its monsoon climate, all but parts of the western half having a wet season from June to October. Rainfall varies greatly from year to year, much of the region having periodic floods and droughts. Even so, farming is still the main occupation. Rice is the major food crop, the region producing (and consuming) 25 percent of the world's output. Important commercial crops include tea, cotton, hemp, and jute. Although less than 7 percent of the region remains forested, it provides 10 percent of the world's hardwoods. The subcontinent has rich mineral resources, including iron ore, bauxite, mica, and chrome, but they are mostly in peninsular India. Pakistan and Bangladesh have sizable gas deposits, and Pakistan also has oil. However, Middle South Asia will be hard pressed to sustain its population, which could reach nearly 1,400 million by the year 2000. Already the region has some of the world's largest cities—more than 15 with well over a million inhabitants.

Middle Stone Age *n.* The **Mesolithic Age** *(see).*

Middle Temple *n.* One of the four legal societies forming the **Inns of Court** *(see)* in England.

middle term *n. Logic. Abbr.* **M** The term in a syllogism presented in both premises but not appearing in the conclusion.

Mid·dle·ton (mĭd′l-tən), **Thomas** (*c.* 1570-1627). English playwright. His comedies, written between 1604 and 1611, include *A Chaste Maid in Cheapside,* a mirror of contemporary corruption.

mid·dle·weight (mĭd′l-wāt′) *n.* **1.** A professional boxer weighing between 147 and 160 pounds (66.8 and 72.6 kilograms). **2.** An amateur boxer weighing between 157 and 165 pounds (71 and 75 kilograms).

Middle West. See **Midwest. —Middle Western** *adj.* **—Middle Westerner** *n.*

mid·dling (mĭd′lĭng, -lĭn) *adj.* Of medium size, quality, or state; mediocre; ordinary. **—See Synonyms at average.**

~*adv. Informal.* Fairly; moderately. [Middle English (Scottish) *mydlyn* : *midde*, MID (middle) + -LING (small).] —**mid·dling·ly** *adv.*
mid·dlings (mĭd′lĭngz) *pl.n.* **1.** Products that are intermediate in quality, size, price, or grade. **2.** Coarsely ground wheat mixed with flour. **3.** *Chiefly Southeastern U.S.* Pork or bacon cut from between the ham and shoulder of a pig.
mid·dy (mĭd′ē) *n., pl.* -**dies. 1.** *Informal.* A midshipman. **2.** A middy blouse.
middy blouse *n.* A woman's or child's loose blouse with a sailor collar. Also called "middy."
Mideast. See **Middle East.** —**Mideast, Mideastern** *adj.* —**Mideasterner** *n.*
mid·field (mĭd′fēld′) *n.* **1.** The section of a football, soccer, or other playing field midway between goals. **2.** Players on a team whose usual position is in the midfield. —**mid·field·er** *n.*
Mid·gard (mĭd′gärd′). Also **Mid·garth** (mĭd′gärth′), **Mith·gar·thr** (mĭth′gär′thər). *Norse Mythology.* The part of the world inhabited by men, imagined as a fortress encircled by a huge serpent, built by the gods around the middle region of the universe. [Old Norse *Midhgardhr.* See **mid, yard.**]
midge (mĭj) *n.* **1.** Any of various widely distributed gnatlike flies of the family Chironomidae, particularly common near water, where they form large swarms. **2.** Any of various similar insects, such as any member of the family Ceratopogonidae *(biting midges),* which suck the blood of mammals and birds. **3.** *Informal.* Any small person. [Middle English *migge,* Old English *mycg.*]
midg·et (mĭj′ĭt) *n.* **1.** An extremely small person who is otherwise normally proportioned. **2.** A small or miniature version of something. **3.** A class of small objects, such as a class of very small sailboats or racing automobiles.
~*adj.* **1.** Miniature; diminutive; dwarfed. **2.** Belonging to a type or class much smaller than what is considered standard: *a midget poodle.* [Diminutive of MIDGE.]
Mid Gla·mor·gan (mĭd′ glə-môr′gən). County of southern Wales, comprising the central region of the former county of Glamorganshire plus the Rhymney valley, formerly in Monmouthshire, and a few villages from south Breconshire. The new county (1974) has mines and industries concentrated in its deep valleys, including the Rhondda. The steel industry is being replaced by light industries, with Aberdare, Bridgend, and Merthyr Tydfil the main centers. Its administrative center is Cardiff.
mid·gut (mĭd′gŭt′) *n.* The middle section of a digestive tract; especially, the middle section of the digestive tract in the vertebrate embryo, from which the ileum and the jejunum develop. Also called "mesenteron."
mid·i (mĭd′ē) *n.* A dress, skirt, or coat of mid-calf length. [From MIDDLE.] —**mid·i** *adj.*
Mi·di (mē-dē′). The south of France.
Mid·i·an·ite (mĭd′ē-ə-nīt′) *n.* A member of an ancient Arabian tribe claiming descent from Midian, a son of Abraham. Exodus 2:15–22; Judges 6–8. —**Mid·i·an·ite** *adj.*
mid·i·ron (mĭd′ī′ərn) *n.* An iron golf club that has more loft than a driver and less than a mashie, used for medium fairway shots and long approach shots.
mid·land (mĭd′lənd) *n.* The middle or interior part of a country or region. —**mid·land** *adj.*
Mid·land (mĭd′lənd) *n.* The dialect of Middle English spoken in the Midlands of England, which formed the basis of Modern English.
Mid·lands (mĭd′ləndz). A region of central England. Imprecisely defined, it roughly corresponds with the Anglo-Saxon kingdom of Mercia, which originally included the present counties of Derbyshire, Nottinghamshire, Staffordshire, West Midlands, northern Leicestershire, and northern Warwickshire. Mercia expanded to include all of Leicestershire, Warwickshire, and Northamptonshire and eastern Hereford and Worcester. In the broadest sense, the Midlands include Shropshire, all of Hereford and Worcester, and parts of Bedfordshire, Buckinghamshire, and Oxfordshire.
mid·life crisis (mĭd′līf′) *n.* A stage in a person's life when the realization of the approach of middle or old age may lead to anxiety and stress.
mid·line (mĭd′līn′) *n.* A medial line, especially the medial line or plane of the body.
Mid·lo·thi·an (mĭd-lō′thē-ən). Former county of southeastern Scotland, now part of Lothian region. It was south of the Firth of Forth and the county town was Edinburgh.
mid·most (mĭd′mōst′) *adj.* **1.** Situated in the exact middle; middlemost. **2.** Situated nearest the middle.
~*adv.* In the middle. [Middle English *midmest,* Old English *midmest* : *midd,* MID + -*mest,* -MOST.]
mid·night (mĭd′nīt′) *n.* **1.** The middle of the night; specifically, twelve o'clock at night. **2. a.** Intense darkness or gloom. **b.** A period of darkness and gloom.
~*adj.* **1.** Of or at the hour of midnight: *a midnight swim.* **2.** Of or pertaining to the middle of the night. **3.** Resembling the middle of the night; dark; gloomy; dreary. —**burn the midnight oil.** To work or study very late at night. [Middle English *midnight,* Old English *midniht* : *midd,* MID + *niht,* NIGHT.]
midnight blue *n.* A very deep blue.
midnight sun *n.* The sun as seen at midnight during the summer within the Arctic or Antarctic Circle.
mid·point (mĭd′point′) *n.* **1.** The point of a line segment or curvilinear arc that divides it into two parts of the same length. **2.** A position midway between two extremes.

Mid·rash (mĭd′räsh′) *n., pl.* **Midrashim** (mĭd-rä′shĭm), **Midrashoth** (mĭd-rä′shōth′). Any of a group of Jewish commentaries on the Hebrew Scriptures written between A.D. 400 and 1200. [Late Hebrew *midhrāsh,* commentary.] —**Mid·rash·ic** (mĭd-rä′shĭk) *adj.*
mid·rib (mĭd′rĭb′) *n.* The central or principal vein of a leaf.
mid·riff (mĭd′rĭf′) *n.* **1.** A muscular partition between the abdominal and thoracic cavities, the **diaphragm** *(see).* **2.** The middle outer portion of the front of the human body, extending roughly from just below the breast to the waistline. [Middle English *midrif,* Old English *midhrif* : *midd,* MID + *hrif,* belly.]
mid·ship (mĭd′shĭp′) *adj.* Pertaining to the middle of a ship.
mid·ship·man (mĭd′shĭp′mən) *n., pl.* -**men** (-mĭn). **1.** Formerly, a naval cadet on British ships of war whose battle station was amidships or abreast of the mainmast. **2.** A noncommissioned officer ranking below sublieutenant in the Royal and British Commonwealth navies. **3.** A student training to be commissioned as an officer in the U.S. Navy or Coast Guard. **4.** Any of various American fishes of the genus *Porichthys,* having several rows of light-producing organs along their bodies. [From earlier *midshipsman* : MIDSHIPS + MAN.]
mid·ships (mĭd′shĭps′) *adv. Nautical.* **1.** Amidships. **2.** In the center position. Said of the helm.
~*n.* The middle part of a ship.
midst (mĭdst, mĭtst) *n.* **1.** The middle position or part; center: *in the midst of the desert.* **2.** A position of proximity to other individuals or members: *a stranger in our midst.* **3.** The condition of being surrounded by or beset by something: *in the midst of all our problems.* **4.** A time period about the middle of a continuing condition or act: *in the midst of the war.*
~*prep.* Among. [Middle English *middest,* alteration of *middes,* from *midde,* in the middle, from Old English, middle.]
mid·stream (mĭd′strēm′) *n.* The middle of a stream or river.
mid·sum·mer (mĭd′sŭm′ər) *n.* **1.** The middle of the summer. **2.** The summer solstice. —**mid·sum·mer** *adj.*
Midsummer's Day *n.* Also **Midsummer Day.** June 24, the feast of Saint John the Baptist.
mid·term (mĭd′tûrm′) *n.* **1.** The middle of an academic term, a political term of office, or a pregnancy. **2. a.** An examination given at the middle of an academic term. **b. midterms.** A series of such examinations. —**mid·term** *adj.*
mid·Vic·to·ri·an (mĭd′vĭk-tôr′ē-ən, -tōr′ē-ən) *adj.* Pertaining to, occurring in, or characteristic of the middle period of the reign of Queen Victoria in Great Britain (1837–1901), a period known for rigid social standards.
~*n.* **1.** A person living in the mid-Victorian period. **2.** A person having mid-Victorian ideas.
mid·way (mĭd′wā′) *n.* **1.** The area of any fair, carnival, circus, or exposition where side shows and other amusements are located. **2.** *Obsolete.* **a.** The middle of a way or distance. **b.** A middle way or course of action or thought.
~*adv.* (mĭd′wā′, mĭd′wā′). **1.** In the middle of a way or distance; halfway. **2.** In an intermediate position: *midway between thrift and stinginess.* —**mid·way** *adj.*
Midway Islands. Two small islands surrounded by an atoll in the North Pacific, annexed by the United States in 1867. There is no indigenous population, but some 2,200 people maintain the U.S. military base here. In the Battle of Midway during World War II (June 1942) U.S. forces won a decisive victory over the Japanese; this marked the turning point of the war in the Pacific.
mid·week (mĭd′wēk′) *n.* The middle of the week.
~*adj.* Happening in the middle of the week. —**mid·week** *adv.* —**mid·week·ly** *adj. & adv.*
Mid·west (mĭd′wĕst′) *n.* Also **Middle West.** A region of north-central United States, around the Great Lakes and upper Mississippi valley. Although its limits are ill defined, it is generally considered to include the states of Indiana, Iowa, Ohio, Illinois, Michigan, Minnesota, Missouri, Wisconsin, and Nebraska. Kansas is usually included, and sometimes the Ontario peninsula of Canada. It is a rich farming region, and its chief products are corn and pigs. —**Mid·west, Mid·west·ern** *adj.* —**Mid·west·ern·er** *n.*
mid·wife (mĭd′wīf′) *n., pl.* -**wives** (-wīvz′). One qualified to assist women in childbirth. [Middle English *midwif* : *mid,* with, Old English *mid* + *wif,* WIFE.]
mid·wife·ry (mĭd′wīf′rē, -wī′fə-rē, mĭd-wĭf′ə-rē) *n.* The techniques and practice of a midwife.
midwife toad *n.* A European toad, *Alytes obstetricans,* the male of which carries the fertilized eggs on its hind legs until they hatch.
mid·win·ter (mĭd′wĭn′tər) *n.* **1.** The middle of the winter. **2.** The winter **solstice** *(see).*
mid·year (mĭd′yĭr′) *n.* **1.** The middle of the calendar or academic year. **2. a.** An examination in the middle of the academic year. **b. midyears.** A series of such examinations. —**mid·year** *adj.*
mien (mēn) *n.* **1.** One's bearing or manner; expression: *a person of noble mien.* **2.** An appearance or aspect: *of fearsome mien.* —See Synonyms at **bearing.** [From earlier *meane, mine* (influenced by French *mine,* appearance), short for DEMEAN.]
Mies van der Ro·he (mēs′ văn dər rō′ə), **Ludwig** (1886–1969). German-born U.S. architect. His steel-frame and glass buildings include the Seagram Building, New York (1956–59), and the Chicago Federal Center (1963–68).
miff (mĭf) *n. Informal.* **1.** A petulant, bad-tempered mood; a huff. **2.** A petty quarrel or argument; a tiff.
~*tr.v.* **miffed, miffing, miffs.** To cause (a person) to become of-

fended or annoyed. [Perhaps imitative of an expression of disgust.]

mif·fy (mĭf′ē) *adj.* **-fier, -fiest. 1.** *Informal.* Easily offended; oversensitive. **2.** Difficult to raise except under perfect conditions. Said of certain plants. **—mif·fi·ness** *n.*

might¹ (mīt) *n.* **1. a.** Tremendous power held by an individual or group: *"defend the island against the whole might of the German Air Force"* (Winston Churchill). **b.** Supreme power attributed to a divine being: *the might of God.* **2.** Physical or bodily strength. —See Synonyms at **strength. —with might and main.** With all one's strength; with the utmost effort. [Middle English *might*, Old English *miht*.]

might². Past tense of **may.**

might·i·ly (mīt′l-ē) *adv.* **1.** In a mighty manner; forcefully; powerfully. **2.** To a great degree; greatly.

might·y (mī′tē) *adj.* **-ier, -iest. 1. a.** Having might; powerful; strong. **b.** Having great emotional or intellectual power: *a mighty intelligence.* **2. a.** Exerting great force; violent: *a mighty blow of his ax.* **b.** Very strong or urgent: *a mighty clamor.* **3.** Awesomely huge: *"the city stood on a mighty hill"* (John Bunyan). ~*adv. Informal.* In a great degree; very; extremely: *mighty fine pie.* **—might·i·ness** *n.*

mi·gnon·ette (mĭn′yə-nĕt′) *n.* **1.** A plant of the genus *Reseda;* especially, *R. odorata,* native to the Mediterranean region and widely cultivated for its clusters of fragrant but inconspicuous greenish flowers. **2.** A light, fine pillow lace. [French, feminine of obsolete *mignonnet,* diminutive of *mignon,* dainty, small, MINION.]

mi·graine (mī′grān′) *n.* **1.** Severe, recurrent headache, usually affecting only one side of the head, characterized by sharp pain and often accompanied by nausea. **2.** An attack of such headache. [French, from Old French, from Late Latin *hēmicrānia,* pain in half of the head, from Greek *hēmikrania* : HEMI- + *kranion,* CRANIUM.] **—mi·grain·oid** (mī′grā-noid′), **mi·grain·ous** (mī′grā-nəs) *adj.*

mi·grant (mī′grənt) *n.* **1.** A person, animal, bird, or fish that moves from one region to another by chance, instinct, or plan. **2.** An itinerant worker who travels from one area to another in search of work. **3.** *Australian.* An immigrant. ~*adj.* Moving from one place to another; migratory. [Latin *migrāns* (stem *migrant-*), present participle of *migrāre,* to MIGRATE.]

mi·grate (mī′grāt′) *intr.v.* **-grated, -grating, -grates. 1.** To move from one country or region and settle in another. **2.** To change location periodically; move seasonally from one region to another. Used of such animals as birds and fish: *"The birds that fish the cold sea for a living must either migrate or starve"* (Rachel Carson). **3.** *Physics & Chemistry.* To move from one position to another. Used of atoms, molecules, ions, or groups of atoms. [Latin *migrāre.*]

Usage: *Migrate* is used with reference both to the place of departure and the destination and can be followed by *from* or *to.* It is said of persons, animals, and birds, and sometimes implies lack of permanent settlement (notably seasonal movement). *Emigrate* pertains to a single move by persons and implies permanence. It has specific reference to the place of departure, emphasizes movement from that place, and is usually followed by *from. Immigrate* specifies a single move by persons and implies permanence. But it refers to the destination, emphasizes movement there, and is appropriately followed by *to.*

mi·gra·tion (mī-grā′shən) *n.* **1.** The action or an act of migrating. **2.** A group migrating together. **—mi·gra·tion·al** *adj.*

mi·gra·to·ry (mī′grə-tôr′ē, -tōr′ē) *adj.* **1.** Characterized by migration; migrating periodically: *migratory birds.* **2.** Of or relating to a migration. **3.** Roving; nomadic.

mih·rab (mē′räb′, mē′räb′) *n. Islam.* A chamber or niche in a mosque showing the direction of Mecca. [Arabic.]

mi·ka·do (mĭ-kä′dō) *n., pl.* **-dos.** *Often* **Mikado.** The emperor of Japan. The title is not used by Japanese people, who use "Tenno." [Japanese, "exalted gate" : *mi,* honorific prefix + *kado,* gate.]

mike¹ (mīk) *n. Informal.* A microphone. ~*v.* **miked, miking, mikes.** *Informal.* **1.** To amplify the sound of by means of a microphone. **2.** To attach a microphone to. In both senses, often used with *up.*

mike² *intr.v.* **miked, miking, mikes.** *British Slang.* To avoid work; shirk. [19th century : origin obscure.]

Mikonos. See Mykonos.

Mi·koy·an (mē′kō-yän′), **Anastas Ivanovich** (1895–1978). Soviet leader. He joined the Communist Party in 1915 and rapidly rose through the ranks, becoming, finally, chairman of the Presidium of the Supreme Soviet (1964–65). He subsequently lost power and was not accorded the traditional honor of interment in the Kremlin wall.

mikron. Variant of **micron.**

mil¹ (mĭl) *n.* **1.** A unit of length equal to one-thousandth (10⁻³) of an inch. Used chiefly to specify the diameter of wire. **2.** A milliliter. **3.** A unit of angular measurement used in artillery and equal to 1/6400 of a complete revolution. [Short for Latin *mīllēsimus,* thousandth, from *mīlle,* thousand.]

mil². A monetary unit equal to 1/1000 of the pound of Cyprus. See feature at **currency.** [Latin *mīlle,* thousand.]

mil. military; militia.

mi·la·dy, mi·la·di (mĭ-lā′dē) *n., pl.* **-dies** or **-dis. 1.** My lady. A title or form of address formerly used in Europe of an English noblewoman or gentlewoman. **2.** A chic or fashionable woman. [French, from English *my lady.*]

milage. Variant of **mileage.**

Mi·lan (mĭ-lăn′, -län′). *Italian* **Mi·la·no** (mĭ-lä′nō). Capital of Milan province and of Lombardy region, northern Italy. At a strategic crossing of the Olona River, it has been a market, industrial, financial, and cultural center since medieval times. It is now Italy's second-largest city and chief manufacturing center, producing textiles, motor vehicles, machinery, aircraft, and clothing. Printing and publishing are also important. The city has three universities and numerous historic buildings including the cathedral (1386–1813) and La Scala opera house (1778).

Mil·an·ese (mĭl′ə-nēz′, -nēs′) *n., pl.* **Milanese. 1.** A native or inhabitant of Milan. **2.** The Italian dialect spoken in Milan. **3.** A fine fabric of silk or rayon. ~*adj.* **1.** Of or pertaining to Milan or its people, dialect, culture, or products. **2.** Coated with bread crumbs or flour and fried in oil or butter.

milch (mĭlch) *adj.* Giving milk: *a milch goat.* [Middle English *milche,* Old English *-milce.*]

milch cow *n.* **1.** A cow that produces milk for human consumption. **2.** A source of advantage or gain, especially one that can be taken for granted: *treated his family as a milch cow.*

mild (mīld) *adj.* **milder, mildest. 1.** Gentle or kind in disposition, manners, or behavior: *a strong but mild man.* **2.** Moderate in type, degree, effect, or force: *a mild punishment.* **3.** Not very harmful; light: *a mild fever.* **4.** Having no extremes in temperature; temperate: *a mild climate.* **5.** Not sharp, bitter, or strong in taste or smell: *a mild cheese; mild tobacco.* **6.** Rather easily molded, shaped, or worked; malleable: *a mild alloy.* ~*n. British.* A dark beer with a low hop content. [Middle English *mild,* Old English *milde.*] **—mild·ly** *adv.* **—mild·ness** *n.*

mil·dew (mĭl′dōō′, -dyōō′) *n.* **1.** Any of various plant diseases in which a fungus forms a superficial growth on the plant. See **downy mildew, powdery mildew. 2.** A superficial coating or discoloring of organic materials, such as paint, paper, cloth, leather, and the like, caused by fungi, especially under damp conditions. Compare **mold.** ~*v.* **mildewed, -dewing, -dews.** —*tr.* To affect with mildew. —*intr.* To become affected with mildew: *Ceilings in a bathroom will often mildew.* [Middle English *mildew,* Old English *mildēaw,* from Germanic *melith* (unattested), honey + *dawwaz* (unattested), DEW.] **—mil·dew·y** *adj.*

mild steel *n.* A type of steel containing a low amount of carbon (up to 0.25 percent).

mile (mīl) *n. Abbr.* **m., mi. 1.** A unit of length equal to 5,280 feet, 1,760 yards, or 1.60934 kilometers, used in most English-speaking countries. Also called "statute mile." **2.** A **nautical mile** *(see).* **3.** An **air mile** *(see).* **4.** A race of a mile. **5.** *Informal.* **a.** A relatively great distance: *Your guess was a mile off.* **b. miles.** By a great amount or to a great extent. Used as an intensive: *She's miles better at golf than I am.* **—by a mile.** By a wide margin: *He won by a mile.* [Middle English *mile,* Old English *mīl,* from West Germanic *mīlja* (unattested), from Latin *mīlia, mīllia,* plural of *mīle, mīlle,* thousand.]

mile·age, mil·age (mī′lĭj) *n.* **1.** Total length, extent, or distance measured or expressed in miles. **2.** Total miles covered or traveled in a given time. **3.** The amount of service, use, or wear estimated by miles used or traveled: *This tire will give very good mileage.* **4.** The number of miles traveled by a motor vehicle on a certain quantity, usually a gallon, of fuel: *Lighter cars give better mileage.* **5.** *Informal.* The amount of service something has yielded or may yield in the future; usefulness; benefit; advantage: *get full mileage out of a typewriter.* **6.** An allowance for travel expenses established at a specified rate per mile. **7.** Expense per mile, as for the use of a car: *We paid a mileage fee for the rental car.*

mile·om·e·ter (mī-lŏm′ə-tər) *n.* A device for indicating the number of miles traveled by a vehicle.

mile·post (mīl′pōst′) *n.* **1.** A post set up to indicate distance in miles, as along a road. **2.** An important point in a course of progress or development.

mil·er (mī′lər) *n.* One specializing in mile races.

mi·les glo·ri·o·sus (mē′lās glôr′ē-ō′səs, glōr′ē-) *n., pl.* **milites gloriosi** (mē′lə-tās glôr′ē-ō′sē, glōr′ē-). A bragging, swaggering soldier, especially as a stock comic character. [After *Miles Gloriosus* ("The Boastful Soldier"), a comedy (c. 206 B.C.) by Plautus.]

Mi·le·sian¹ (mī-lē′zhən, -shən) *adj.* Of or pertaining to Miletus or its inhabitants. ~*n.* A native or inhabitant of Miletus.

Milesian² *n.* A native of Ireland; an Irishman. ~*adj.* Of or pertaining to Ireland or its people; Irish. [After *Milesius,* legendary Spanish king whose sons were supposed to have conquered Ireland in about 1300 B.C.]

mile·stone (mīl′stōn′) *n.* **1.** A stone marker set up on a roadside to indicate the distance in miles to or from a given point. **2.** An important event or turning point in a person's history or career. **3.** An important point in a course of development.

Mi·le·tus (mī-lē′təs). Ancient Greek seaport of Ionia, western Asia Minor (now Turkey). A center of learning, Miletus produced the philosophers Thales (c. 634–546 B.C.) and Anaximander (c. 611–547 B.C.). St. Paul visited it twice (Acts 20:15; 2 Timothy 4:20).

mil·foil (mĭl′foil′) *n.* **1.** A plant, the **yarrow** *(see).* **2.** The **water milfoil** *(see).* [Middle English, from Old French, from Latin *millefolium,* "thousand-leafed" (from the fine divisions of the leaves) : *mille,* thousand + *folium,* leaf.]

Mil·haud (mē-yō′), **Darius** (1892–1974). French composer. He composed chiefly ballet scores and chamber works, including *Le Pauvre Matelot* and *Le Boeuf sur le Toit*.

mil·i·ar·i·a (mĭl′ē-âr′ē-ə) *n. Pathology.* A skin disease caused by an inflammation of the sweat glands and characterized by blebs, redness, and a prickling or burning sensation. Also called "prickly heat," "heat rash." [New Latin *(febris) miliaria,* "miliary (fever)," from Latin *mīliārius,* MILIARY.]

mil·i·ar·y (mĭl′ē-ĕr′ē) *adj.* **1.** Designating a lesion or growth that is about one-eighth inch in diameter. **2.** Designating a disease marked by small skin lesions that look like millet seeds. [Latin *mīliārius,* of millet, like millet seeds (as lesions may be), from *milium,* MILLET.]

miliary tuberculosis *n.* An acute form of tuberculosis characterized by very small tubercles in various body organs, caused by the spread of tubercle bacilli through the bloodstream.

mi·lieu (mēl-yœ′) *n., pl.* **-lieus** or **-lieux.** Environment or surroundings. [French, environment, midst, from Old French, midst, center : *mi,* middle, from Latin *medius* + *lieu,* place, from Latin *locus,* place, LOCUS.]

mil·i·tant (mĭl′ə-tənt) *adj.* **1.** Fighting or warring. **2.** Aggressive or combative: *a militant mood.* **3.** Vigorously pursuing some cause, especially through a course of confrontation: *militant labor unions.* ~*n.* A militant person; especially, a political activist. [Middle English, from Old French, from Latin *militāns* (stem *militānt-*), present participle of *militāre,* to MILITATE.] —**mil·i·tan·cy** *n.* —**mil·i·tant·ly** *adv.*

mil·i·tar·i·a (mĭl′ə-târ′ē-ə) *pl.n.* Items of military equipment and uniform considered as antiques or collectors' pieces. [Latin, neuter plural of *mīlitāris,* MILITARY.]

mil·i·ta·rism (mĭl′ə-tə-rĭz′əm) *n.* **1.** The glorification of the ideals of a professional military class. **2.** Predominance of the armed forces in the administration or policy of a nation.

mil·i·ta·rist (mĭl′ə-tə-rĭst) *n.* **1.** One who supports or advocates militarism or warlike policies. **2.** *Archaic.* One who studies or is skilled in military science. —**mil·i·ta·ris·tic** (mĭl′ə-tə-rĭs′tĭk) *adj.* —**mil·i·ta·ris·ti·cal·ly** *adv.*

mil·i·ta·rize (mĭl′ə-tə-rīz′) *tr.v.* **-rized, -rizing, -rizes.** **1.** To make military; equip or train for war. **2.** To imbue with militarism. —**mil·i·ta·ri·za·tion** *n.*

mil·i·tar·y (mĭl′ə-tĕr′ē) *adj. Abbr.* **mil. 1.** Of, pertaining to, characteristic of, or performed by a soldier or soldiers; soldierly: *military installations; military attire.* **2.** Characteristic of or befitting the armed forces: *military precision.* **3.** Of or pertaining to war. ~*n., pl.* **military** or **-ies.** *Abbr.* **mil.** The armed forces. Preceded by *the: ruled by the military.* [French *militaire,* from Latin *mīlitāris,* from *mīles†* (stem *mīlit-*), soldier.] —**mil·i·tar·i·ly** (mĭl′ə-târ′ə-lē) *adv.*

military academy *n.* **1.** A school where army officers are trained. **2.** A boys' school where the students wear uniforms and engage in military drill.

military attaché *n.* An army officer on the official staff of an ambassador, consul general, or minister to a foreign country.

military honors *pl.n.* The ceremonial procedures performed by soldiers on such occasions as state funerals.

military intelligence *n.* **1.** Any information important for its military value. **2.** The branch of the military that procures, analyzes, and uses information of military value.

military law *n.* Regulations and rules pertaining to the discipline and administration of the armed forces.

military police *n. Abbr.* **MP, M.P.** Members of the armed forces assigned to perform police duties. —**military policeman** *n.*

mil·i·tate (mĭl′ə-tāt′) *intr.v.* **-tated, -tating, -tates. 1.** To have force as evidence: *The facts available to us militate against this interpretation.* **2.** To have weight or influence: *factors militating against industrial recovery.* [Latin *mīlitāre,* to serve as a soldier, from *mīles†,* soldier.]

Usage: Militate and mitigate are not interchangeable in standard English. Militate means to provide forceful evidence: *The findings militate against the view that he is innocent.* Mitigate means to lessen in force or intensity: *His apology should mitigate the President's anger.* Care should be taken not to confuse the words.

mi·li·tia (mə-lĭsh′ə) *n. Abbr.* **mil. 1. a.** A citizen army as distinct from a body of professional soldiers. **b.** The armed citizenry as distinct from the regular army. **2.** The able-bodied male citizens in a state who are not members of the regular armed forces but who are called to military service in cases of emergency. **3.** The whole body of physically fit male civilians eligible by law for military service. [Original sense, "military organization," from Latin *mīlitia,* warfare, from *mīles†,* soldier.] —**mi·li·tia·man** *n.*

mil·i·um (mĭl′ē-əm) *n., pl.* **-ia** (-ē-ə). *Pathology.* A small, hard, white or yellowish mass just below the surface of the skin, caused by blockage of the secretion of a sebaceous gland. [Middle English, from Latin, millet (the lesions resemble millet seeds).]

milk (mĭlk) *n.* **1. a.** A whitish liquid that is produced by the mammary glands of all mature female mammals after they have given birth and is used for feeding their young until weaned. **b.** The milk of cows, goats, or other animals, used as food by man, or as the principal ingredient of other foods such as butter and cheese. **2.** Any liquid similar to milk in appearance, such as coconut milk, milkweed sap, or plant latex. **3.** Any of various medicinal emulsions or suspensions. —**cry over spilt milk.** To lament what is already past and beyond remedying. ~*v.* **milked, milking, milks.** —*tr.* **1.** To draw milk from the teat or udder of (a female mammal). **2.** To press out, drain off, or remove by or as if by milking: *He milked information from the prisoner.*

Milky Way

EARTH'S OWN GALAXY
A band of hazy light stretching across the night sky

The hazy belt of stars stretching across the night sky is known as the Milky Way. It goes from horizon to horizon, passing within about 30° of the Pole Star and through the constellations of Perseus, Cassiopeia, Scorpio, Sagittarius, and the Southern Cross in the Southern Hemisphere. The hazy appearance of the Milky Way results from the combined light of stars too far away to be seen by the naked eye.

In the Milky Way there are 100 billion stars that make up the Galaxy to which our Solar System belongs. The Galaxy is just one of millions of galaxies that make up the universe. It is a disk-shaped collection of stars with Earth about a third of the way out from the center. An observer looking at the Milky Way from Earth is actually looking edge on into the Galaxy.

The Galaxy, which started to form more than 14 billion years ago, is about 100,000 light-years in diameter. It is called a spiral galaxy because it has a dense central region with several arms coiling around it in the same plane.

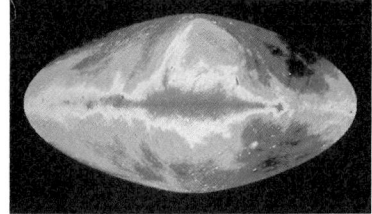

RADIO REVELATION *Seen by the naked eye or through an ordinary telescope, the Milky Way (above) appears to be shaped like a flattish box, with the stars concentrated more in one section—the center—than anywhere else. But studies made with radio telescopes show that it is shaped like a disk with a central bulge (as seen in the radio map, left). When we look up at the sky at night, we are observing at right angles to the disk. We see far fewer stars than there really are, as our eyes cannot penetrate the Galaxy as radio can.*

3. To draw out or extract something from as if by milking: *milk the snake of its venom.* **4.** To obtain money or benefits from for personal gain; exploit: *corrupt officials milking the company's treasury.* —*intr.* **1.** To yield or supply milk. **2.** To draw milk from a female mammal. [Middle English *milk,* Old English *milc, meolc,* from Germanic *meluks* (unattested).] —**milk·er** *n.*

milk adder *n.* The **milk snake** (see).

milk-and-wa·ter (mĭlk′ən-wô′tər, -wŏt′ər) *adj.* Lacking forcefulness; insipid; feeble.

milk bar *n.* A café, or a counter in a café, serving ice cream, nonalcoholic drinks, and light snacks.

milk chocolate *n.* Sweetened chocolate made with milk and other ingredients to give it a creamy taste or appearance.

milk fever *n.* **1.** A mild fever, usually occurring at the beginning of lactation, associated with infection following childbirth. **2.** A disease affecting dairy cows and occasionally sheep or goats, especially soon after giving birth.

milk·fish (mĭlk′fĭsh′) *n., pl.* **-fishes** or collectively **milkfish.** A large fish, *Chanos chanos,* of the South Pacific and Indian oceans, widely used for food. [From its milky color.]

milk glass *n.* An opaque or translucent whitish glass.

milking machine *n.* An apparatus fitted with suction devices used for milking cows mechanically.

milking stool *n.* A low stool with three legs.

milk leg *n. Pathology.* A painful swelling of the leg occurring in

milk vetch *Goats that ate* Astragalus glycyphyllos *were thought to give more milk: hence its common name. It is sometimes difficult to identify because the creamy green flowers blend with surrounding foliage.*

PRONUNCIATION KEY

ă, pat; ā, pay; âr, care;
ä, father, are; b, bib;
ch, church; d, deed; ĕ, pet;
ē, be; f, fife; g, gag; h, hat;
hw, which; ĭ, pit; ī, pie;
îr, pier; j, judge; k, kick;
l, lid, needle; m, mum;
n, no, sudden; ng, thing;
ŏ, pot; ō, toe; ô, paw, for;
oi, noise; ou, out; o͝o, book;
o͞o, boot; p, pop; r, roar;
s, sauce; sh, ship, dish;
t, tight; th, thin, path;
th, this, bathe; ŭ, cut; ûr, fur;
v, valve; w, with; y, yes;
z, zebra, size; zh, vision;
ə, about, item, edible,
gallop, circus, peaceful

IN FOREIGN WORDS:

à, *Fr.* ami; œ, *Fr.* feu, *Ger.* schön; ü, *Fr.* tu, *Ger.* über; KH, *Ger.* ich, *Scot.* loch; N, *Fr.* bon; y', *Fr.* Compiègne

STRESS MARKS:

Primary stress: ′
in·cite′ (ĭn-sīt′)
Secondary stress: ′
in′sight′ (ĭn′sīt′)

women after childbirth as a result of clotting and inflammation in the femoral veins. Also called "white leg."

milk·maid (mĭlk′mād′) *n.* A girl or woman who milks cows.

milk·man (mĭlk′măn′) *n., pl.* **-men** (-mĕn′). A man who sells or delivers milk to customers.

milk of magnesia *n.* A liquid suspension of magnesium hydroxide, $Mg(OH)_2$, used as an antacid and laxative.

milk pudding *n.* A pudding prepared by cooking rice, semolina, or other grains in sweetened milk.

milk run *n. Slang.* A military aerial mission that is either of short duration or lacking in danger. [From the suggestion that it is as monotonous as the daily delivery of milk.]

milk shake *n.* A beverage made of milk, flavoring, and usually ice cream, shaken or beaten until frothy.

milk snake *n.* A nonvenomous grayish or tan snake, *Lampropeltis doliata* (or *L. triangulum*), of the northeastern United States. It grows to 30 inches in length, has black-rimmed brown splotches, and feeds on frogs and mice. Also called "milk adder," "house snake."

milk·sop (mĭlk′sŏp′) *n.* A boy or man lacking in courage and manliness; a weakling. [Middle English, sop dipped in milk, hence child fed on this, weakling.] —**milk·sop·py, milk·sop·ping** *adj.*

milk sugar *n.* A constituent of milk, **lactose** *(see).*

milk thistle *n.* An annual or biennial herb, *Silybum marianum,* native to southern Europe and widely naturalized, that has an erect grooved stem and red or purple flowers.

milk tooth *n.* Any of the temporary first teeth of a young mammal. Also called "baby tooth."

milk vetch *n.* Any of various plants of the genus *Astragalus,* having compound leaves and clusters of purple, white, or yellowish flowers. [From its supposed ability to increase a goat's yield of milk.]

milk·weed (mĭlk′wēd′) *n.* **1.** Any plant of the chiefly North American genus *Asclepias,* most of which have milky juice and pointed pods that split open to release seeds with downy tufts. **2.** Loosely, any of various other plants having milklike juice.

milkweed butterfly *n.* A butterfly, the **monarch** *(see).*

milk·wort (mĭlk′wûrt′, -wôrt′) *n.* A plant of the genus *Polygala,* having variously colored, usually small flowers. [From its supposed ability to increase human lactation.]

milk·y (mĭl′kē) *adj.* **-ier, -iest. 1.** Like milk in color or consistency; opaque-white: *milky glass.* **2.** Filled with, consisting of, or yielding milk or a fluid resembling milk: *a milky kernel of corn.* **3.** Timorous; apprehensive. —**milk·i·ness** *n.*

Milky Way *n.* **1.** The faint luminous band sometimes observed across the sky, consisting of very large numbers of faint stars visible when the observer looks toward the center of our galaxy. **2.** Our galaxy itself, a spiral containing *c.* 100 billion stars. Also called "Galaxy," "Milky Way Galaxy." [Middle English, translation of Latin *Via lactea.*] See feature, page 1077.

mill[1] (mĭl) *n.* **1.** A building or establishment equipped with machinery for grinding grain into flour or meal. **2.** A device or mechanism, such as rotating millstones, that grinds grain. **3.** A mechanical appliance or machine that reduces a solid or coarse substance into a pulp or minute grains by crushing, grinding, or pressing: *a pepper mill.* **4.** A machine that releases the juice of fruits and vegetables by pressing or grinding: *a cider mill.* **5. a.** Any machine that produces something by the repetition of a simple process, such as a machine for stamping coins. **b.** Any of various machines for shaping, cutting, polishing, or dressing metal surfaces. **6. a.** A building or group of buildings equipped with machinery for processing materials such as wood, hay, textile fibers, and iron ore into finished products, such as paper, fodder, cloth, and steel: *a textile mill.* **b.** Any building or collection of buildings that has machinery for manufacture; a factory. **7.** An agency, institution, or process that operates in a routine way or turns out products in the manner of a factory: *Don't treat the university like a diploma mill.* **8.** A slow or laborious process: *It took three years for the bill to get through the legislative mill.* **9.** A difficult experience that marks the personality or character: *These combat veterans had clearly been through the mill.* **10.** A steel roller bearing a raised design, such as one used for making a die or a printing plate by pressure. **11.** *Slang.* A fistfight.
~*v.* **milled, milling, mills.** —*tr.* **1.** To grind, pulverize, or break down into smaller particles in a mill. **2.** To transform or process mechanically in a mill. **3.** To shape, polish, dress, or finish in a mill or with a milling tool. **4. a.** To produce a ridge around the edge of (a coin, for example). **b.** To groove or flute the rim of (a coin, for example). **5.** To agitate or stir until foamy. —*intr.* **1.** To move around in churning confusion: *A crowd milled around the stage door.* **2.** *Slang.* To fight with the fists; box. **3.** To undergo milling. [Middle English *mille,* Old English *mylen,* from West Germanic *mulīna* (unattested), from Late Latin *molīna,* from *molīnus,* of a mill, from Latin *mola,* millstone.]

mill[2] *n. Abbr.* **M., mi.** A monetary unit that is equal to $1/1000$ of the U.S. dollar or to $1/10$ of the cent. [Short for Latin *millēsimus,* thousandth.]

Mill (mĭl), **John Stuart** (1806–73). British philosopher. He wrote *A System of Logic* (1843) and *Principles of Political Economy* (1848). He expressed his utilitarian views in *On Liberty* (1859) and *Utilitarianism* (1863). Mill was a Liberal M.P. (1865–68).

Mil·lais (mĭ-lā′), **Sir John Everett** (1829–96). English painter and a founder of the Pre-Raphaelite Brotherhood (1848). His work includes *Christ in the Carpenter's Shop* (1850) and *Order of Release* (1853).

Mil·lay (mĭ-lā′), **Edna St. Vincent** (1892–1950). U.S. poet. Her first volume of verse was *Renascence* (1917). *The Ballad of the Harp Weaver* won her the Pulitzer Prize (1923).

mill·board (mĭl′bôrd′, -bōrd′) *n.* A stiff, heavy pasteboard used mainly for book covers. [Alteration of *milled board.*]

mill·dam (mĭl′dăm′) *n.* A dam constructed across a stream to raise the water level so the overflow will turn a mill wheel.

milled (mĭld) *adj.* **1.** Processed or manufactured in a mill. **2.** Fluted or grooved around the edge, as certain coins are.

mille·feuille (mēl-fœ′yə) *n.* A small rectangular pastry consisting of layers of puff pastry filled with custard or whipped cream; napoleon. [French, "thousand-leaf."]

mil·le·nar·i·an (mĭl′ə-nâr′ē-ən) *adj.* **1.** Of or pertaining to a thousand, especially to a thousand years. **2.** Of, pertaining to, or believing in millenarianism.
~*n.* One who believes the millennium will occur; an adherent of millenarianism. [Late Latin *millēnārius,* MILLENARY.]

mil·le·nar·i·an·ism (mĭl′ə-nâr′ē-ə-nĭz′əm) *n.* **1.** In Christianity, the belief in the holy millennium. **2.** Any belief in, doctrine of, or movement aimed at a perfect period or society in the future.

mil·le·nar·y (mĭl′ə-nĕr′ē, mə-lĕn′ə-rē) *adj.* **1.** Of or pertaining to a thousand; millenarian. **2.** Of or pertaining to millenarianism or the millenarians.
~*n., pl.* **millenaries. 1. a.** A sum or total of one thousand, especially a thousand years. **b.** A thousandth anniversary. **2.** A millenarian. [Late Latin *millēnārius,* of a thousand, from Latin *millēnī,* a thousand each, from *mille,* thousand.]

mil·len·ni·um (mə-lĕn′ē-əm) *n., pl.* **-ums** or **-lennia** (-lĕn′ē-ə). **1. a.** A span of one thousand years; a millenary. **b.** A thousandth anniversary. **2.** A thousand-year period of holiness either following or preceding the Second Coming of Christ. Revelation 20:1–5. **3.** A hoped-for period of joy, prosperity, and justice. [New Latin (influenced by BIENNIUM) : Latin *mille,* thousand + *annus,* year.] —**mil·len·ni·al** *adj.* —**mil·len·ni·al·ist** *n.* —**mil·len·ni·al·ly** *adv.*

milleped, millepede. Variants of **millipede.**

mil·le·pore (mĭl′ə-pôr′, -pōr′) *n.* Any of various reef-building hydrocorals of the genus *Millepora,* of tropical marine waters, forming white or yellowish calcareous formations, and resembling the true corals of the class Anthozoa. [New Latin *Millepora* (genus), "thousand-pored" : Latin *mille,* thousand + *porus,* PORE.]

mill·er (mĭl′ər) *n.* **1.** One who works in, operates, or owns a mill for grinding grain. **2.** A **milling machine** *(see).* **3.** Any of various moths having wings and bodies covered with a powdery substance.

Mil·ler (mĭl′ər), **Arthur** (1915–). U.S. playwright. *Death of a Salesman* won the Pulitzer Prize (1949). Other works include *A View from the Bridge* (1955), *The Crucible* (1953), and *After the Fall* (1964).

Miller, Glenn (1909–44). U.S. band leader. He began playing the trombone in dance bands as early as 1920 and by 1938 had launched his own band. After many popular hits and successful tours, he disbanded the orchestra in 1942 to join the army. He was lost on a flight from England to France on December 15, 1944.

Miller, Henry (1891–1980). U.S. novelist. His two early novels, *Tropic of Cancer* (1931) and *Tropic of Capricorn* (1935), were published in Paris but banned from the United States until the 1960's because of their frank sexual themes. He also wrote *The Colossus of Maroussi* (1941) and a trilogy, *The Rosy Crucifixion* (1949–60).

Miller, William (1782–1849). U.S. religious leader. He was convinced from his reading of the Bible that the Second Coming of Christ was at hand and in 1831 began preaching his apocalyptic gospel to enthralled audiences. When the appointed year, 1843, passed without incident, Miller set a new final date, October 22, 1844. This was known as the "Great Disappointment" and effectively ended the movement.

mil·ler·ite (mĭl′ə-rīt′) *n.* A mineral, nickel sulfide, NiS, usually occurring in long slender crystals, and used as a nickel ore. [German *Millerit,* after William *Miller* (1801–80), British mineralogist.]

miller's thumb *n., pl.* **miller's thumbs.** Any of several freshwater fishes of the genus *Cottus,* found in Europe and North America. They have spiny heads and fins and are mainly bottom dwellers. Also called "bullhead." [Middle English *millarys thowmbe.*]

mil·les·i·mal (mə-lĕs′ə-məl) *adj.* **1.** Thousandth. **2.** Consisting of a thousandth. **3.** Pertaining to thousandths.
~*n.* A thousandth. [From Latin *millēsimus,* from *mille,* thousand.]

mil·let (mĭl′ĭt) *n.* **1.** A grass, *Panicum miliaceum,* cultivated in Asia and Africa for its seed and in Europe and North America for hay. **2.** The white seeds of this plant, widely used as a food grain in Africa and Asia. **3.** Any of several milletlike grasses, such as *Setaria italica,* Italian millet, or their seeds. [Middle English *milet,* from Old French, from *mil,* millet, from Latin *milium.*]

Mil·let (mĭ-lā′), **Jean François** (1814–75). French painter whose pictures concentrated on scenes of peasant life, as in *The Gleaners* (1857) and *The Angelus* (1859).

mill finish *n.* A smooth surface made by machine on various papers. Also called "machine finish."

milli– *prefix. Abbr.* **m** Indicates one-thousandth (10^{-3}) of a unit; for example, **millibar, millimeter.** [French, from Latin *milli-,* from *mille,* thousand.]

mil·liard (mĭl′yərd, -yärd′, mĭl′ē-ärd′) *n. British.* One thousand million; a billion. [French, from Old French *miliart,* from *milion,* MILLION.]

mil·li·ar·y (mĭl′ē-ĕr′ē) *adj.* Pertaining to or marking the distance of an ancient Roman mile, which equaled 1,000 paces. [Latin *milliār-*

ius, consisting of a thousand, one mile long, from *mīlle,* thousand.]

mil·li·bar (mĭl′ə-bär′) *n. Abbr.* **mb.** A unit of pressure, used especially for measuring the pressure of the atmosphere, equal to one thousandth of a bar or 100 newtons per square meter.

mil·lième (mēl-yĕm′, mē-yĕm′) *n., pl.* **millièmes** (-yĕm′, -yĕmz′). **1.** A monetary unit equal to 1/1000 of the pound of Egypt. **2.** A monetary unit equal to 1/1000 of the pound of Sudan. See feature at **currency.** [French, "thousandth," from *mille,* thousand, from Old French, from Latin *mīlle,* thousand.]

mil·li·gram (mĭl′ə-grăm′) *n.* Also *chiefly British* **mil·li·gramme.** *Abbr.* **mg.** A unit of mass equal to one thousandth of a gram.

Mil·li·kan (mĭl′ĭ-kən), **Robert Andrews** (1868–1953). U.S. physicist. He was awarded the Nobel Prize in physics (1923) for his measurement of the charge of the electron.

mil·li·li·ter (mĭl′ə-lē′tər) *n. Abbr.* **ml.** A unit of volume equal to one thousandth of a liter, or one cubic centimeter (0.001 liquid quart or 0.0009 dry quart).

mil·lime (mə-lēm′) *n.* A coin equal to 1/1000 of the dinar of Tunisia. See feature at **currency.** [Perhaps from MILLIÈME.]

mil·li·me·ter (mĭl′ə-mē′tər) *n. Abbr.* **mm** A unit of length equal to one thousandth (10^{-3}) of a meter, or 0.0394 inch.

mil·li·ner (mĭl′ə-nər) *n.* **1.** A person who makes, trims, designs, or sells women's hats. **2.** *Obsolete.* A seller of ribbons, laces, and other trimmings. [Variant of obsolete *Milaner,* importer of goods, such as women's finery, from MILAN.]

mil·li·ner·y (mĭl′ə-nĕr′ē) *n.* **1.** Articles, especially women's hats, sold by a milliner. **2.** The profession, business, or shop of a milliner.

mill·ing (mĭl′ĭng) *n.* **1.** The act or process of grinding, especially of grinding grain into flour or meal. **2.** The operation of cutting, shaping, finishing, or working metal, cloth, or any other product manufactured in a mill. **3.** The ridges cut on the edges of coins.

milling machine *n.* A machine tool with a rotating cutter acting on a metal workpiece held on a movable table. Also called "miller."

mil·lion (mĭl′yən) *n., pl.* **million** or **-lions.** **1.** The cardinal number written 1,000,000 or 10^6. **2.** A million monetary units, as of dollars: *She made a million on the stock market.* **3.** *Often* **millions.** An indefinitely large number: *millions of ants.* **4. millions.** The masses; the common people. [Middle English *milioun,* from Old French *milion,* from Italian *milione,* augmentative of *mille,* thousand, from Latin *mīlle.*] **—mil·lion** *adj.*

mil·lion·aire (mĭl′yə-nâr′) *n.* A person whose wealth amounts to a million or more dollars or its equivalent in another currency. [French *millionnaire,* from MILLION.]

mil·lion·air·ess (mĭl′yə-nâr′ĭs) *n.* A female millionaire.

mil·lionth (mĭl′yənth) *n.* **1.** The ordinal number one million in a series. **2.** Any of a million equal parts. **—mil·lionth** *adj. & adv.*

mil·li·pede, mil·le·pede (mĭl′ə-pēd′) *n.* Also **mil·li·ped, mil·le·ped** (mĭl′ə-pĕd′). Any crawling, herbivorous arthropod of the class Diplopoda, found throughout the world. They have wormlike bodies with two pairs of legs on each body segment. Compare **centipede.** [Latin *mīllepeda,* woodlouse, "thousand-feet" : *mīlle,* thousand + *pēs* (stem *ped-*), foot.]

mil·li·sec·ond (mĭl′ə-sĕk′ənd) *n. Abbr.* **ms.** A unit of time equal to one thousandth of a second.

mill·pond (mĭl′pŏnd′) *n.* **1.** The pond or dam from which water is channeled to drive a mill. **2.** Any still stretch of water.

mill·race (mĭl′rās′) *n.* The fast-moving stream of water that drives a millwheel. Also called "millrun."

mill·run (mĭl′rŭn′) *n.* **1.** A millrace. **2.** The output of a sawmill. **3. a.** A test of the mineral quality or content of a rock or ore by the process of milling. **b.** The mineral yielded by this test.

Mills (mĭlz), **Sir John,** born Lewis Ernest Watts (1908–). British actor. He has had a distinguished career in the theater, besides giving many noted screen performances, as in *Tunes of Glory* (1960) and *Ryan's Daughter* (1971), which won him an Academy Award.

mill·stone (mĭl′stōn′) *n.* **1.** Either of a pair of cylindrical stones used in a mill for grinding grain. **2.** A heavy weight; a burden, especially a mental burden, such as a responsibility or debt.

mill·stream (mĭl′strēm′) *n.* **1.** The water flowing in a millrace. **2.** A stream whose flow is used to run a mill.

mill·wheel (mĭl′hwēl′) *n.* A large wheel, especially one turned by a stream of water, used to work a mill.

mill·wright (mĭl′rīt′) *n.* A person who designs, builds, or repairs mills or mill machinery.

Milne (mĭln), **A(lan) A(lexander)** (1882–1956). British writer. He wrote for the magazine *Punch* before turning to children's books. His tales of Christopher Robin and his animal friends are told in *Winnie-the-Pooh* (1926) and *The House at Pooh Corner* (1928).

mi·lo (mī′lō) *n., pl.* **-los.** An early-growing grain sorghum. Some varieties are drought-resistant. Compare **durra, feterita, kaffircorn.** [Sotho *maili.*]

mi·lord (mĭ-lôrd′) *n.* My lord. A title or form of address formerly used in Europe of an English nobleman or gentleman. [French, from English *my lord.*]

Mílos. See **Melos.**

milque·toast (mĭlk′tōst′) *n.* A person with a meek, timid, and retiring nature. [After Caspar *Milquetoast,* a character in the newspaper cartoon *The Timid Soul,* by H(arold) T(ucker) Webster (1885–1952), from *milk toast,* a bland dish of hot buttered toast in warm milk, often associated with frail persons.]

mil·reis (mĭl′rās′) *n., pl.* **milreis.** A former coin and monetary unit of Portugal and Brazil, worth 1,000 reis. [Portuguese *milréis* : *mil,* thousand, from Latin *mīlle* + *réis,* plural of *real,* royal, from Latin *rēgālis,* REGAL.]

milt (mĭlt) *n.* **1.** Fish sperm, including the seminal fluid. **2.** The reproductive glands of male fishes when filled with this fluid. **3.** *Zoology.* The **spleen** *(see)* of certain vertebrates.
~*tr.v.* **milted, milting, milts.** To fertilize (fish roe) with milt. [Sense 1: probably from Middle Dutch *milte,* milt, spleen. Sense 3: Middle English *milte,* Old English *milte.* Both from Germanic *miltjaz* (unattested).]

milt·er (mĭl′tər) *n.* A male fish that is ready to breed.

Mil·ti·a·des (mĭl-tī′ə-dēz′) (*c.* 540–489 B.C.). Athenian general. He defeated the Persians at Marathon (490) by a pincer movement that drove the Persians into retreat on their ships, then rushed back to Athens with his army to defend the unprotected city against the seaborne enemy.

Mil·ton (mĭl′tən), **John** (1608–74). English poet. In the Civil War he supported Parliament and wrote *Areopagitica* (1644) in defense of a free press. The essay *The Tenure of Kings and Magistrates* (1649), in defense of the regicides, gained him a post as Cromwell's secretary for foreign affairs. Shortly afterward he became totally blind. The epic poem *Paradise Lost* was published in 10 books in 1667 and in 12-book form in 1674. *Paradise Regained* and *Samson Agonistes* were published in 1671. **—Mil·ton·ic** (mĭl-tŏn′ĭk), **Mil·to·ni·an** (mĭl-tō′nē-ən) *adj.*

Mil·wau·kee (mĭl-wô′kē). Port and largest city of Wisconsin, on Lake Michigan. It exports coal and grain from the Midwest via the St. Lawrence Seaway and produces heavy machinery, electrical equipment, tractors, engines, beer, and canned meat.

mim (mĭm) *adj. British Regional.* Old-fashioned in appearance or behavior; prim. [Perhaps imitative of pursing of the lips.]

mim·bar (mĭm′bär′) *n.* A pulpit in a mosque with steps on which the preacher stands. [Arabic *minbar.*]

mime (mīm) *n.* **1. a.** A performing art in which characters are mimicked or ideas and moods conveyed by means of facial expressions, gestures, and the like, without the use of words. **b.** A performance or act of mime. **c.** A performer of mime. **2.** An actor or comedian who specializes in comic mimicry; a buffoon or clown. **3. a.** A form of ancient Greek and Roman drama in which realistic characters and situations were farcically portrayed and actual persons were mimicked on the stage. **b.** A performance of or dialogue for such a comic drama. **c.** An actor in such a drama.
~*v.* **mimed, miming, mimes.** *—tr.* **1.** To portray in mime; act out with gestures and facial expressions. **2.** To ridicule by imitation; mimic. *—intr.* **1.** To act as a mimic. **2.** To portray characters and situations by wordless gesture, facial expression, and body movement. [Latin *mīmus,* from Greek *mimos,* imitator.] **—mim·er** *n.*

mim·e·o·graph (mĭm′ē-ə-grăf′, -gräf′) *n.* **1.** A duplicating machine that makes copies of written, drawn, or typed material from a stencil that is fitted around an inked drum. **2.** A copy made by such a machine.
~*v.* **mimeographed, -graphing, -graphs.** *—tr.* **1.** To make copies of (a stencil or text) on a mimeograph. **2.** To make (copies) on a mimeograph. *—intr.* To use a mimeograph. [Originally a trademark : from Greek *mimeomai,* first person singular of *mimeisthai,* to imitate + -GRAPH.]

mi·me·sis (mĭ-mē′sĭs, mī-) *n.* **1. a.** The imitation or representation of nature or human nature, especially in art and literature. **b.** An instance of such imitation or representation. **2.** *Biology.* Mimicry. **3.** *Medicine.* The appearance, often due to hysteria, of symptoms of a disease not actually present. [Greek *mimēsis,* from *mimeisthai,* to imitate, from *mimos,* imitator.]

mi·met·ic (mĭ-mĕt′ĭk, mī-) *adj.* **1.** Pertaining to, characteristic of, or showing mimicry. **2. a.** Of or pertaining to an imitation; imitative. **b.** Using imitative means of representation: *a mimetic dance*; *mimetic gesture.* [Greek *mimētikos,* from *mimeisthai,* to imitate.] **—mi·met·i·cal·ly** *adv.*

mim·ic (mĭm′ĭk) *tr.v.* **-icked, -icking, -ics.** **1.** To copy or imitate closely, especially by reproducing external characteristics such as speech, expression, and gesture; ape. **2.** To copy or imitate so as to ridicule; mock. **3.** To resemble closely; simulate: *an insect mimicking a twig.* —See Synonyms at **imitate.**
~*n.* **1.** One who imitates, as: **a.** A performer skilled in mimicking. **b.** A person or trained animal that copies or mimics others, especially for entertainment. **c.** An animal that resembles another. **2.** A copy or imitation of some person or object.
~*adj.* **1.** Pertaining to, acting as, resembling, or characteristic of a mimic or of mimicry; imitative. **2.** Imitating a person or object, often for amusement; make-believe: *"to devise mimic and fabulous worlds of their own"* (Bacon). [Latin *mīmicus,* imitative, from Greek *mimikos,* from *mimos,* imitator.] **—mim·ick·er** *n.*

mim·ic·ry (mĭm′ĭ-krē) *n., pl.* **-ries.** **1. a.** The act, practice, or art of mimicking. **b.** An instance of mimicking. **2.** *Biology.* The resemblance, through natural selection, of one organism to another or to a natural object, as a natural aid in concealment. Also called "mimesis."

Mi·mir (mē′mîr′). *Norse Mythology.* A giant who dwelled by the roots of Yggdrasil, where he guarded the well of wisdom.

mi·mo·sa (mĭ-mō′sə, -zə) *n.* **1.** Any of various mostly tropical plants, shrubs, and trees of the genus *Mimosa,* having ball-like clusters of small flowers and compound leaves that are often sensitive to touch or light. See **sensitive plant.** **2.** Loosely, any of several similar or related plants or trees, such as species of acacia used by

milkweed *Floss from the seedpods of this native American genus has been used as a stuffing in life jackets and upholstery. The milkweed species shown here is* Asclepias speciosa.

minaret *Two minarets flank the entrance to a mosque at Mahan, in Iran. In the seventh century the Prophet Muhammad said that the call to prayer five times a day should be made from the highest roof near a mosque. Minarets were eventually added to the mosques themselves.*

florists. [New Latin, from Latin *mīmus,* MIME, from its imitation of animal sensitivity.]
min minute (unit of time).
min. **1.** mineralogical; mineralogy. **2.** minimum. **3.** mining.
Min. Minister; Ministry.
mi·na¹ (mī′nə) *n., pl.* **-nas** or **-nae** (-nē). A varying unit of weight or money used in ancient Greece and Asia Minor. [Latin, from Greek *mna,* from Akkadian *manû,* designating a unit of weight, from Sumerian *mana.*]
mina². Variant of **myna**.
mi·na·cious (mĭ-nā′shəs) *adj.* Of a menacing or threatening nature. [Latin *minăx* (stem *minăc-*), from *minārī,* to menace, from *minae,* threats.] **—mi·na·cious·ness, mi·nac·i·ty** (mĭ-năs′ə-tē) *n.*
Mi·na·mo·to (mē′nə-mō′tō), **Yoritomo** (1148–99). Japanese warrior landlord, the founder of the shogunate, or *bakufu,* the feudal system by which Japan was ruled until 1867. In 1185 he put down a rebellion against the emperor, then set up a rival government. In 1192 he assumed supreme authority as shogun, with his capital at Kamakura.
min·a·ret (mĭn′ə-rĕt′) *n.* A tall, slender tower on a mosque, with one or more projecting balconies from which a muezzin summons the people to prayer. [French, from Spanish *minarete,* from Turkish *minārat,* from Arabic *manārat,* lamp.]
min·a·to·ry (mĭn′ə-tôr′ē, -tōr′ē) *adj.* Also **min·a·to·ri·al** (mĭn′ə-tôr′ē-əl, -tōr′ē-əl). Menacing; threatening. [French *minatoire,* from Late Latin *minātōrius,* from Latin *minārī,* to menace. See **minacious.**] **—min·a·to·ri·ly** (mĭn′ə-tôr′ə-lē, -tōr′ə-lē) *adv.*
mince (mĭns) *v.* **minced, mincing, minces.** *—tr.* **1.** To cut or chop into very small pieces. **2.** To pronounce in an affected way, as with forced elegance and refinement: *He minced his phrases in the presence of his employer.* **3.** To moderate or restrain for the sake of politeness and decorum: *She spoke frankly and didn't mince words.* *—intr.* **1.** To walk with very short steps or with excessive primness. **2.** To speak in an affected way, as with forced refinement.
∼n. Food, especially meat, that is finely chopped; mincemeat. [Middle English *mincen,* from Old French *mincier,* to diminish, from Vulgar Latin *minūtiāre* (unattested), from Late Latin *minūtia,* minutia, from Latin *minuere,* to diminish.] **—minc·er** *n.*
mince·meat (mĭns′mēt′) *n.* **1.** Finely chopped meat. **2.** A mixture of finely chopped dried fruit, spices, and other ingredients, used especially as a pie filling. **—make mincemeat of.** *Slang.* To defeat or destroy utterly as if by cutting into little pieces.
mince pie *n.* A sweet pie filled with mincemeat.
minc·ing (mĭn′sĭng) *adj.* Affectedly refined. **—minc·ing·ly** *adv.*
mind (mīnd) *n.* **1.** Consciousness considered as residing in the human brain, manifested especially in thought, perception, feeling, will, memory, and imagination. **2.** The totality of conscious and unconscious processes of the brain and central nervous system that directs mental and physical activity. **3. a.** In some philosophical systems, a principle of intelligence or consciousness held to pervade reality. **b.** Intelligence or the nonmaterial aspect of being in contrast to the material: *mind over matter.* **4.** A person's ability to reason as distinguished from emotion or will: *Follow your mind, not your heart.* **5. a.** Intellectual power or ability. **b.** A person considered with reference to intellect: *the greatest mind of the century.* **6. a.** A person's awareness of and attitude to the external world as shaped by remembered experience: *To my mind, it's impossible.* **b.** Collective memory or attitudes: *the British mind.* **7.** An attitude or emotional state: *left him in a very different mind.* **8.** Opinion or sentiment: *I may change my mind when I hear the facts.* **9.** A desire or purpose. Often used with *good*: *I have a good mind to leave.* **10. a.** Focus of thought; attention; concentration. **b.** Processes of thought and feeling: *preying on her mind.* **11.** Mental balance; sanity: *losing one's mind.* **—blow one's mind.** *Slang.* To affect with intense emotion, as amazement, excitement, or shock. **—bring** (or **call) to mind.** **1.** To remember; recollect. **2.** To produce the memory or thought of (a past experience, for example). **—in one's mind's eye.** Visualized within one's imagination. **—in** (or **of**) **two minds.** Unable to choose; undecided. **—make up one's mind.** To decide between alternatives; come to a definite decision or opinion. **—on one's mind.** In one's thoughts; especially, worrying one. **—piece of one's mind.** *Informal.* One's bluntly expressed opinion; especially, a strongly worded rebuke or condemnation. **—put one in mind.** *Informal.* To fill one with memories; remind one: *The novel put her in mind of her youth.* **—put** (or **set**) **someone's mind at rest.** To reassure someone. **—speak one's mind.** To speak frankly and in a forthright way.
∼v. **minded, minding, minds.** *—tr.* **1. a.** To object to; dislike: *Of course I mind your smoking.* **b.** Used in the negative to express willingness or desire: *We don't mind sleeping on the floor.* **c.** Used to express polite requests: *Would you mind asking her?* **2.** To care or be concerned about: *I don't mind who wins.* **3.** To pay attention to the advice or instructions of: *The children minded their mother.* **4.** To make sure: *"And before you let the sun in, mind it wipes its shoes"* (Dylan Thomas). **5. a.** To attend to; heed: *Mind closely what I tell you.* **b.** Used in negative commands to express reassurance: *Don't mind his shouting.* **6.** To be careful about; take heed of or watch out for. **7.** To take care or take charge of; look after. **8.** *Regional.* **a.** To remember or reflect on. **b.** To cause (a person) to remember or reflect on. *—intr.* **1.** To find something objectionable: *Do you mind if I leave now?* **2.** To be concerned or troubled; care: *Nobody minds about what happens to him.* **3.** To be cautious or careful: *Mind as you go down the stairs.* **4.** To get out of the way; shift one's position so as to cease being an obstruction. Usually used in the imperative. **—mind out.** *Regional.* To be careful; pay attention. Usually used in the imperative. **—mind you.** Come to think of it; on the other hand. Used as a mild qualification of a statement: *He seems suitable for the job. Mind you, he's had very little experience.* **—never mind.** *Informal.* Disregard it; it doesn't matter. [Middle English *minde,* Old English *gemynd,* memory, mind, from Germanic *gamundhiz* (unattested).]
Synonyms: *brains, intellect, intelligence, mentality, reason, sense, wits.*
Min·da·na·o (mĭn′də-nä′ō, -nou′). Second-largest island of the Philippines, separated from the Visayan Islands by the Mindanao Sea. Its volcanic, heavily forested mountains include Mt. Apo, an active volcano and the country's highest point (2,954 meters; 9,692 feet). The rich volcanic soils produce pineapples, hemp, coffee, rice, and timber. Iron, gold, and coal are mined. Davao is the island's chief port and city.
Mindanao Trench. Ocean depth, *c.* 10, 675 meters (35,000 feet), off the northeastern coast of Mindanao, in the Philippine Sea. It is one of the deepest known ocean trenches.
mind-blow·ing (mīnd′blō′ĭng) *adj. Slang.* **1.** Hallucinogenic. **2.** Extremely surprising or exciting.
mind-bog·gling (mīnd′bŏg′lĭng) *adj. Informal.* Overwhelming.
mind·ed (mīn′dĭd) *adj.* **1.** Having an intention; disposed; inclined: *I am not minded to answer any of your questions.* **2.** Having a specified kind of mind or tendency. Often used in combination: *evil-minded.* **3.** Having an interest in a specified field. Often used in combination: *arts-minded; ecologically minded.*
mind·er (mīn′dər) *n. British.* A baby sitter.
mind-ex·pand·ing (mīnd′ĭk-spăn′dĭng) *adj.* Producing intensified or distorted perceptions; psychedelic; hallucinogenic. Said especially of drugs.
mind·ful (mīnd′fəl) *adj.* Attentive; heedful. Used with *of*: *mindful of her responsibilities.* **—mind·ful·ly** *adv.* **—mind·ful·ness** *n.*
mind·less (mīnd′lĭs) *adj.* **1. a.** Lacking intelligence or good sense; foolish. **b.** Without the need of much mental effort: *a mindless job.* **c.** Without intelligent purpose, meaning, or direction: *mindless violence.* **2.** Giving or showing little attention or care; heedless. Usually used with *of*: *They proceeded, mindless of the dangers.* **—mind·less·ly** *adv.* **—mind·less·ness** *n.*
mind reading *n.* **1.** The act of guessing what someone is thinking by observing facial expressions and other signs. **2.** The supposed faculty of discerning another's thoughts through extrasensory means of communication; telepathy. **—mind reader** *n.*
Mind·szen·ty (mĭnd′sĕn′tē), **József** (1892–1975). Hungarian prelate who became primate of Hungary after World War II. In 1946 he was made a cardinal. He opposed the Communist regime and in 1948 was jailed for life on a charge of treason. He was freed in 1955, but after suppression of the 1956 uprising he took refuge in the American legation in Budapest. In 1971, the Hungarian government allowed him to go to the Vatican.
mine¹ (mīn) *n.* **1. a.** An excavation in the earth for the purpose of extracting free metals, coal, salt, or other minerals. **b.** The site of such an excavation, with its surface buildings, shafts, and equipment. **2.** Any deposit of ore or minerals in the earth or on its surface. **3.** An abundant supply or source of something valuable: *a mine of information.* **4.** *Military.* **a.** A tunnel dug under an enemy emplacement to gain an avenue of attack or to lay explosives. **b.** An explosive device used to destroy enemy personnel, ships, vehicles, or equipment, usually placed just beneath the surface of the ground or sea and designed to be detonated by contact or by a time fuse. **5.** A burrow, tunnel, or gallery made by an insect.
∼v. **mined, mining, mines.** *—tr.* **1. a.** To extract (ores or minerals) from the earth. **b.** To dig a mine or mines in (the earth) to obtain ores or minerals. **2. a.** To dig under (the earth or a surface feature); tunnel under. **b.** To make (a tunnel) by digging. **3.** *Military.* To lay explosive mines in or under. **4.** To attack, damage, or destroy by underhand means; undermine; subvert. **5.** To delve into and make use of; exploit: *mine the archives for information.* *—intr.* **1.** To excavate the earth for the purpose of extracting minerals or ores; work in a mine. **2.** To dig a tunnel or tunnels under the earth; especially, to dig under an enemy emplacement or fortification. **3.** *Military.* To lay explosive mines. [Middle English, from Old French, from Vulgar Latin *mina* (unattested), perhaps from Celtic *meini-*† (unattested), ore.] **—min·a·ble, mine·a·ble** *adj.*
mine² *pron. Used with a singular or plural verb.* Absolute form of *my.* **1.** Belonging to me; my own. Used after a verb: *The green boots are mine.* **2.** The one or ones belonging or pertaining to me: *Mine is the one in the corner.* **3.** *Archaic.* Used to modify: **a.** A following noun beginning with a vowel or *h*: *mine host.* **b.** A preceding noun: *mother mine.* **—of mine.** Belonging or pertaining to me: *a friend of mine.* [Middle English *min,* Old English *mīn.*]
mine detector *n.* Any of various electromagnetic devices used to locate explosive mines. **—mine detection** *n.*
mine·field (mīn′fēld′) *n.* **1.** An area in which explosive mines have been anchored or sunk in water or buried on land. **2.** Something that is full of hidden dangers: *These negotiations are a minefield.*
mine·lay·er (mīn′lā′ər) *n.* A ship or aircraft equipped for laying explosive underwater mines.
min·er (mī′nər) *n.* **1. a.** One who works in a mine. **b.** One who makes his living from extracting minerals from the earth. **2.** A machine for the automatic extraction of minerals, especially of coal. **3.** A member of a military unit engaged in laying explosive mines.

PRONUNCIATION KEY

ă, pat; ā, pay; âr, care;
ä, father, are; b, bib;
ch, church; d, deed; ĕ, pet;
ē, be; f, fife; g, gag; h, hat;
hw, which; ĭ, pit; ī, pie;
îr, pier; j, judge; k, kick;
l, lid, needle; m, mum;
n, no, sudden; ng, thing;
ŏ, pot; ō, toe; ô, paw, for;
oi, noise; ou, out; ŏŏ, book;
ōō, boot; p, pop; r, roar;
s, sauce; sh, ship, dish;
t, tight; th, thin, path;
th, this, bathe; ŭ, cut; ûr, fur;
v, valve; w, with; y, yes;
z, zebra, size; zh, vision;
ə, about, item, edible, gallop, circus, peaceful

IN FOREIGN WORDS:

à, *Fr.* ami; œ, *Fr.* feu, *Ger.* schön; ü, *Fr.* tu, *Ger.* über; KH, *Ger.* ich, *Scot.* loch; N, *Fr.* bon; y′, *Fr.* Compiègne

STRESS MARKS:

Primary stress: ′
in·cite′ (ĭn-sīt′)
Secondary stress: ′
in′sight′ (ĭn′sīt′)

4. Any of various insects that burrow in leaves; a **leaf miner** (see).

min·er·al (mĭn′ər-əl) n. **1.** Any naturally occurring, homogeneous inorganic substance having a definite chemical composition and characteristic crystalline structure, color, and hardness. **2.** Any of various natural substances, as: **a.** An element, such as gold or silver. **b.** A mixture of inorganic compounds, such as bauxite. **c.** An organic derivative, such as coal or petroleum. **3.** Any substance that is neither animal nor vegetable; inorganic matter. **4.** An ore. **5.** British Informal. **a.** Often **minerals.** Mineral water. **b.** A nonalcoholic carbonated drink, usually with a sweet flavoring. ~adj. **1.** Of or pertaining to minerals: a mineral deposit; mineral salts. **2.** Impregnated with minerals: mineral water. [Middle English, from Medieval Latin minerāle (noun), from minerālis (adjective), from Old French miniere, from mine, MINE.]

min·er·al·ize (mĭn′ər-ə-līz′) v. -ized, -izing, -izes. —tr. **1.** To convert to a mineral substance; petrify. **2.** To transform (a metal) into a mineral by oxidation. **3.** To impregnate with minerals. —intr. To develop or hasten mineral formation. —**min·er·al·i·za·tion** n. —**min·er·al·iz·er** n.

mineral jelly n. Petrolatum (see).

mineral kingdom n. The group of objects and substances that are composed only of inorganic matter. Compare **animal kingdom, plant kingdom.**

min·er·al·o·cor·ti·coid (mĭn′ər-ə-lō-kôr′tĭ-koid′) n. Any corticosteroid hormone that regulates ionic balance and, indirectly, fluid absorption. The main mineralocorticoid is **aldosterone** (see).

min·er·al·o·gy (mĭn′ə-rŏl′ə-jē, -rŏl′ə-jē) n. Abbr. **min.** The study of minerals, including their distribution, identification, and properties. [MINERA(L) + -LOGY.] —**min·er·a·log·i·cal** (mĭn′ər-ə-lŏj′ĭ-kəl) adj. —**min·er·a·log·i·cal·ly** adv. —**min·er·al·o·gist** n.

mineral oil n. **1.** Any of various light hydrocarbon oils, especially a distillate of petroleum. **2.** A clear oily liquid obtained by distillation of petroleum and used medicinally as a laxative.

mineral pitch n. A bituminous material, **asphalt** (see).

mineral tar n. A form of bitumen, **maltha** (see).

mineral water n. Naturally occurring or prepared water that contains dissolved minerals or gases, often used therapeutically.

mineral wax n. A hydrocarbon wax, **ozocerite** (see).

mineral wool n. Any inorganic fibrous material produced by steam blasting and cooling molten silicate or a similar substance. It is used chiefly as an insulator.

Mi·ner·va (mĭ-nûr′və). Roman Mythology. The goddess of wisdom, invention, the arts, and martial prowess, identified with the Greek Athena. [Latin.]

min·e·stro·ne (mĭn′ə-strō′nē) n. A soup of Italian origin containing assorted vegetables, vermicelli, and herbs in a meat or vegetable broth. [Italian, augmentative of minestra, from minestrare, to serve, dish out, from Latin ministrāre, to serve.]

mine·sweep·er (mīn′swē′pər) n. A ship equipped for destroying, removing, or neutralizing explosive marine mines.

Ming n. A dynasty that ruled China from 1368 until the Manchu conquest of 1644. It was founded by a rebel Buddhist monk, Zhu Yuan-zhang, who proclaimed himself emperor in 1368. By 1382 he had unified most of China. The arts flourished and periods of foreign trade made the distinctive blue and white porcelain famous abroad. [Mandarin Chinese míng, "luminous," "enlightened."] —**Ming** adj.

min·gle (mĭng′gəl) v. -gled, -gling, -gles. —tr. **1.** To mix or bring together (two or more different elements) in close association; combine. **2.** To mix (things) so that the components become united; merge: "I desired my dust to be mingled with yours" (Ezra Pound). —intr. **1.** To be or become mixed or united. **2.** To move freely about in social contact; associate: Servants mingled with guests. —See Synonyms at **mix.** [Middle English menglen, frequentative of mengen, to mix, from Old English mengan.] —**min·gler** n.

Min·gus (mĭng′gəs), **Charles** (1922–79). U.S. jazz musician, composer, and band leader. Although a virtuoso on the string bass, he was more influential as a composer. His many compositions include Conversation (1957) and Folk Forms No. 1 (c. 1959).

min·gy (mĭn′jē) adj. -gier, -giest. Informal. **1.** Miserly, stingy; mean: a mingy old man. **2.** Paltry; inadequate: a mingy helping of dessert. [Perhaps a blend of MEAN and STINGY.]

Minho. See **Miño.**

min·i (mĭn′ē) n. Informal. Something distinctively smaller or shorter than other members of its class, especially: **1.** A miniskirt. **2.** A very small automobile. —**min·i** adj.

mini– prefix. Indicates something distinctively smaller or shorter than other members of its class; for example, **minibus, miniskirt.** [Shortening of MINIATURE.]

min·i·a·ture (mĭn′ē-ə-chŏŏr′, -chər, mĭn′ə-chŏŏr′, -chər) n. **1.** A copy or model that represents or reproduces something in a greatly reduced size. **2. a.** A small painting executed with great detail, often on a surface of ivory or vellum. **b.** A small portrait, picture, or decorative letter on an illuminated manuscript. **c.** The art of making such paintings, portraits, or letters. **3.** Any extremely small representative or example of a class: These goldfish are miniatures. —**in miniature.** On a small scale: The classroom is the real world in miniature. ~adj. On a small or greatly reduced scale: miniature furniture. [Italian miniatura, painting (especially the miniature illuminations in medieval manuscripts), from miniare, to illuminate, from Latin miniāre, to color with red lead, from minium, MINIUM.]

miniature golf n. A simplified form of golf played on a miniature course.

min·i·a·tur·ist (mĭn′ē-ə-chər-ĭst, mĭn′ə-chər-ĭst) n. An artist who paints miniatures.

min·i·a·tur·ize (mĭn′ē-ə-chə-rīz′, mĭn′ē-chə-rīz′) tr.v. -ized, -izing, -izes. To plan or make on a greatly reduced scale; especially, to make (compact electronic equipment) by using integrated circuits. —**min·i·a·tur·i·za·tion** n.

min·i·bike (mĭn′ē-bīk′) n. A small motorbike having a low frame, small wheels, and elevated handlebars.

min·i·bus (mĭn′ē-bŭs′) n. A small bus.

min·i·cab (mĭn′ē-kăb′) n. Chiefly British. A small automobile used as a taxi.

min·i·car (mĭn′ē-kär′) n. A very small automobile.

min·i·com·put·er (mĭn′ē-kəm-pyōō′tər) n. A relatively small digital computer. Compare **mainframe.**

Minicoy Island. See **Lakshadweep.**

min·ié ball (mĭn′ē, mĭn′ē-ā′) n. Often **Minié ball.** A conical rifle bullet made in the 19th century and designed with a hollow base that expands when fired to fit the spiral grooves of the bore. [After Captain Claude Minié (1814–79), French army officer who invented it.]

min·i·fy (mĭn′ə-fī′) tr.v. -fied, -fying, -fies. To make smaller or less significant; reduce. [MIN(IMUM + (MAGN)IFY.] —**min·i·fi·ca·tion** n. —**min·i·fi·er** n.

min·i·kin (mĭn′ĭ-kĭn) n. Archaic. A very small or delicate creature. ~adj. **1.** Diminutive. **2.** Archaic. Dainty. [Middle Dutch minneken, darling, diminutive of minne, love.]

min·im (mĭn′ĭm) n. **1.** Abbr. **M.** A unit of fluid measure: **a.** In the United States, 1/60 of a fluid dram or 0.00376 cubic inch. **b.** In Great Britain, 1/20 of a scruple or 0.00361 cubic inch. **2.** Music. A half note (see). **3.** An insignificantly small portion, thing, or person. **4.** A downward vertical stroke in handwriting. [In music, Middle English mynym, from Medieval Latin minimus, from Latin, least; other senses, from Latin minimus, least. See **minimum.**]

min·i·mal (mĭn′ə-məl) adj. **1.** Smallest in amount or degree. **2.** Of, pertaining to, or being minimal art. ~n. Mathematics. In an ordered set, a member that precedes all others. —**min·i·mal·ly** adv.

minimal art n. A style of abstract painting and sculpture that seeks to obtain an effect of impersonality and restraint by the use of simple geometric shapes and primary colors.

min·i·mal·ist (mĭn′ə-mə-lĭst) n. **1.** A person who champions or produces minimal art. **2.** A person who advocates restraint in or the least possible use of something, as ornamentation in art, melodic or rhythmic variation in music, or policing in society. **3. Minimalist. a.** A member of a revolutionary group in Russia during the early 20th century whose policy was the immediate implementation of democracy. **b.** A **Menshevik** (see). —**min·i·mal·ism** n. —**min·i·mal·ist** adj.

minimal pair n. Linguistics. A pair of words or sounds, as bin and pin, differing in only one respect and thereby serving to isolate minimum distinctive units, as phonemes and morphemes.

min·i·max (mĭn′ə-măks′) adj. Mathematics. Of or pertaining to the strategic principle in game theory by which a player selects the strategy to minimize an opponent's greatest possible gain and maximize his own. Compare **maximin.** [minimum + maximum.]

min·i·mize (mĭn′ə-mīz′) tr.v. -mized, -mizing, -mizes. **1.** To reduce to the smallest possible amount, extent, size, or degree. **2.** To represent as having the least degree of importance, value, or size; depreciate. [From MINIMUM.] —**min·i·mi·za·tion** n. —**min·i·miz·er** n.

Usage: Because the traditional senses of this verb relate to an absolute value (the least possible, or lowest), the use of qualifiers such as greatly, somewhat, and very much is criticized. When a qualification needs to be made, another verb, such as reduce or lessen, is preferred.

min·i·mum (mĭn′ə-məm) n., pl. -mums or -ma (-mə). Abbr. **min.** **1.** The least possible quantity or degree. **2.** The lowest quantity, degree, or number reached or recorded; the lower limit of variation. **3.** Mathematics. **a.** A number not greater than any other in a set of numbers. **b.** A value of a function that is exceeded for any sufficiently small increase or decrease in the function's variables. ~adj. Abbr. **min.** Of, consisting of, or representing the lowest possible amount or degree permissible or attainable. [Latin, from minimus, least, superlative of minor, minor.]

minimum wage n. The lowest wage, determined by law or contract, that an employer may pay an employee.

min·ing (mī′nĭng) n. Abbr. **min.** **1.** The process or business of extracting coal, minerals, or ore from a mine. **2.** The process of laying explosive mines.

min·ion (mĭn′yən) n. **1.** One who is especially esteemed; a favorite. **2. a.** An obsequious follower or dependent; a sycophant. **b.** A subordinate of an individual or organization: the devil and his minions. **3.** Printing. A size of type, 7-point. ~adj. Archaic. Endearingly dainty; delicate. [French mignon, darling, from Old French mignot, from Gaulish; akin to Old High German minna, love.]

min·i·ser·ies (mĭn′ē-sîr′ēz) n. A televised dramatic production presented in several parts, often on consecutive evenings.

min·i·skirt (mĭn′ē-skûrt′) n. A short skirt with a hem reaching several inches above the knees. —**min·i·skirt·ed** adj.

min·is·ter (mĭn′ĭ-stər) n. **1.** A person serving as an agent for another by carrying out specified orders or functions. **2. a.** A person autho-

miniature A watercolor portrait of a young man, by the English artist Nicholas Hilliard (1547–1619). The painting is only 13.5 centimeters (5³/₈ inches) high and 7 centimeters (2³/₄ inches) wide.

minnow *These inconspicuous fish rarely grow to more than 80 millimeters (about 3 inches) long. They are particularly common in upland streams with gravel bottoms but are also found in ponds and lakes.*

Minotaur *Minos, a legendary ruler of Crete, demanded periodic sacrifices of Athenian youths and girls to the bull-headed Minotaur. This Athenian black-figure vase, from the sixth century* B.C.*, depicts the monster's death at the hands of the Greek hero Theseus.*

rized to perform religious functions in a church, especially in a Protestant church; a clergyman. **b.** A clergyman officiating at a religious service. **3.** A member of a government: *the British foreign minister.* **4.** In some countries, a person authorized to represent a government in diplomatic dealings with other governments, usually ranking next below an ambassador.
~v. **ministered, -tering, -ters.** *—intr.* **1.** To attend to the wants and needs of others. Usually followed by *to: Volunteers ministered to the injured.* **2.** To exercise clerical functions. *—tr.* **1.** To administer or dispense: *ministered the Sacrament.* **2.** *Archaic.* To furnish or provide. [Middle English *ministre,* from Old French, from Latin *minister,* attendant, servant, from *minus,* less.]

min·is·te·ri·al (mĭn'ĭ-stîr'ē-əl) *adj.* **1.** Of, pertaining to, or characteristic of a minister of religion or of the ministry. **2. a.** Of or pertaining to a government minister or department. **b.** Of, pertaining to, or representing a parliamentary government when challenged by the opposition. **3.** *Law.* Of or designating a mandatory act or delegated duty admitting of no personal discretion or judgment or requiring no special expertise in its performance. Compare **judicial. 4.** Acting or serving as an agent; instrumental. **—min·is·te·ri·al·ly** *adv.*

minister of state *n.* **1.** A government minister who is not head of a department and usually not in the cabinet and who works as an assistant to a senior minister. **2.** Any government minister.

Minister of the Crown *n.* Any of the senior British government ministers, usually but not necessarily in the cabinet, appointed by the Crown on the recommendation of the Prime Minister.

minister plenipotentiary *n.* A diplomatic representative with full authority to speak and act for his government, though lower in rank than an ambassador; a plenipotentiary.

minister resident *n.* A diplomatic agent ranking below a minister plenipotentiary.

min·is·trant (mĭn'ĭ-strənt) *adj.* Serving as a minister.
~n. One who ministers. [Latin *ministrāns* (stem *ministrant-*), present participle of *ministrāre,* to serve, from *minister,* MINISTER.]

min·is·tra·tion (mĭn'ĭ-strā'shən) *n.* **1.** An act or process of serving or aiding. **2.** The act of performing the duties of a minister of religion. [Latin *ministrātiō* (stem *ministrātiōn-*), from *ministrāre,* to serve, from *minister,* MINISTER.] **—min·is·tra·tive** (mĭn'ĭ-strā'tĭv) *adj.*

min·is·try (mĭn'ĭ-strē) *n., pl.* **-tries. 1.** The act of serving; ministration. **2. a.** The profession, duties, and services of a minister of religion. **b.** Ministers of religion as a group; the clergy. **c.** The period of service of a minister of religion. **3. a.** A government department presided over by a minister. **b.** The building in which such a department is housed. **c.** The duties, functions, or term of a government minister and staff. **d.** *Often* **Ministry.** Government ministers as a group. [Middle English *ministerie,* from Latin *ministerium,* functions of a MINISTER.]

min·i·track (mĭn'ē-trăk') *n.* An electronic measuring system designed to follow the course of satellites and rockets and to correlate radio signals received by a network of ground stations.

min·i·um (mĭn'ē-əm) *n. Chemistry.* A lead oxide, **red lead** *(see).* [Middle English, from Latin, cinnabar, red lead, probably of Iberian origin; akin to Basque *arminea,* cinnabar.]

min·i·ver (mĭn'ə-vər) *n.* **1.** A white or light-gray fur of uncertain origin, used as a rich trim on medieval robes. **2.** The ermine used in the ceremonial robes of peers. [Middle English, from Norman French *menuver,* Old French *menu vair,* small vair : *menu,* small, from Latin *minūtus,* small, MINUTE + *vair,* VAIR.]

min·i·vet (mĭn'ə-vĕt') *n.* Any tropical Asian songbird of the genus *Pericrocotus,* related to the cuckoo shrikes and having brightly colored plumage. [19th century : origin obscure.]

mink (mĭngk) *n., pl.* **minks** or collectively **mink. 1.** Any of various semiaquatic carnivores of the genus *Mustela,* especially *M. vison* of North America, resembling the weasel and having short ears, a pointed snout, short legs, and partly webbed toes. **2.** The soft, thick, lustrous fur of the mink. **3.** A coat, jacket, or stole made of mink. [Middle English *mynk,* from Scandinavian; akin to Danish *mink*†.]

Minn. Minnesota.

Min·ne·ap·o·lis (mĭn'ē-ăp'ə-lĭs). A city of southeastern Minnesota, at the head of navigation on the Mississippi River. Adjacent to St. Paul, it is in a rich agricultural area. Meat packaging and flour milling are its main industries.

Min·nel·li (mə-nĕl'ē), **Liza** (1946–). U.S. singer and actress. Daughter of Judy Garland, Hollywood film actress, and Vincente Minnelli (1910–86), film director. She has been hailed for her performances in the films *Cabaret* (1972) and *New York, New York* (1977).

min·ne·sing·er (mĭn'ĭ-sĭng'ər, mĭn'ə-zĭng'ər) *n.* Any of the German lyric poets and singers in the troubadour tradition who flourished from the 12th to the 14th centuries. [German, "love singer."]

Min·ne·so·ta (mĭn'ĭ-sō'tə). *Abbr.* **Minn.** Northernmost state of the continental United States. Its southern two thirds are prairieland, producing dairy products, meat, and grain. To the north lie reforested hills, the basis of the state's timber industry. In the eastern mountains beside Lake Superior exploitation of nickel and copper reserves has superseded the mining of iron ore. Manufacturing is the state's chief activity, yielding processed foods, paper products, machinery, and electronic equipment. With more than 11,000 lakes, tourism is also important. St. Paul is the capital. **—Min·ne·so·tan** *adj. & n.*

min·now (mĭn'ō) *n., pl.* **-nows** or collectively **minnow. 1.** Any of a large number of small, freshwater fishes of the family Cyprinidae, widely used as live bait. **2.** Any other small, silver-colored fish. **3.** A small or unimpressive person. [Middle English *menow,* Old English *mynwe* (unattested).]

Mi·ño, Mi·nho (mēn'yō). A river of the Iberian Peninsula. Rising in Galicia in northwestern Spain, it flows generally southwest to the Atlantic. Its lower course forms Portugal's northern boundary with Spain.

Mi·no·an (mĭ-nō'ən) *adj.* **1.** Of, pertaining to, or designating the advanced Bronze Age culture that flourished in Crete from about 3000 to 1100 B.C. **2.** Of, pertaining to, or designating either of two writing systems, **Linear A** and **Linear B** *(both of which see).*
~n. A person living in this Bronze Age culture. [From Greek *Minōs,* MINOS.]

mi·nor (mī'nər) *adj.* **1.** Lesser or smaller in amount, extent, quantity, or size. **2.** Lesser or relatively low in importance, rank, or stature: *a minor essayist.* **3.** Lesser or relatively small in seriousness or danger; requiring comparatively little attention or concern: *minor difficulties; a minor injury.* **4.** *Law.* Under legal age; not yet a legal adult. **5.** Designating the junior or younger of two pupils, especially brothers, with the same surname. Used especially in British public schools. **6.** Designating or pertaining to a field of academic specialization requiring fewer class hours or credits than a major field. **7.** *Logic.* Dealing with a more restricted category; narrower in scope. **8.** *Music.* **a.** Designating a **minor scale** *(see).* **b.** Less in distance by a half tone than the corresponding major interval. **c.** Based on a minor scale: *a minor key.* **9.** Of or pertaining to the minority.
~n. **1.** A person or thing that is lesser in comparison with others of the same class. **2.** *Law.* One who has not reached full legal age (21 years in most U.S. states). **3. a.** An area of specialized study of a degree candidate in a college or university that requires fewer class hours or credits than the student's major. **b.** One studying a minor: *a chemistry minor.* **4.** *Logic.* A **minor premise** or **minor term** *(both of which see).* **5.** *Music.* A minor key, scale, or interval. **6.** In bell ringing, a change rung on six bells. **7.** *Sports.* **a.** A **minor league** *(see).* **b. minors.** The minor leagues of a sport as a group. **8. Minor.** A Minorite.
~intr.v. **minored, -noring, -nors.** To pursue academic studies in a minor subject. Used with *in.* [Middle English, from Latin *minor,* less.]

Mi·nor·ca[1] (mĭ-nôr'kə). See **Menorca. —Minorcan** *adj. & n.*

Minorca[2] *n.* A domestic fowl of a breed originating in the Mediterranean region, having white or black plumage. [After MINORCA.]

Mi·nor·ite (mī'nə-rīt') *n.* Also **Mi·nor·ist** (mī'nər-ĭst). A Franciscan friar. [From *Friars Minor* (Medieval Latin *Frātrēs Minōrēs*), name given to the order by its founder, Saint Francis of Assisi, as a title of humility.]

mi·nor·i·ty (mə-nôr'ə-tē, -nŏr'ə-tē, mī-) *n., pl.* **-ties. 1.** The smaller in number of two groups that together form a whole; a group of persons or things numbering less than half of a total. Compare **majority. 2. a.** A racial, religious, political, national, or other group regarded as different from the larger group of which it is part. Also used adjectivally: *minority parties.* **b.** A member of such a group. **3.** The state or period of being under legal age: *an heir still in his minority.* [French *minorité,* from Medieval Latin *minōritās* (stem *minōritāt-*), from Latin *minor,* MINOR.]

minority carrier *n. Electronics.* The carrier that transports the smaller fraction of the current in a semiconductor. Compare **majority carrier.**

minority leader *n.* The head of the minority party in a legislative body. Compare **majority leader.**

minor league *n.* A league of professional sports clubs, especially baseball clubs, not belonging to the major leagues.

mi·nor-league (mī'nər-lēg') *adj.* **1.** Pertaining or belonging to a minor sports league. **2.** Being of subordinate position or secondary importance: *a minor-league politician.* **—mi·nor-leagu·er** *n.*

minor orders *pl.n. Roman Catholic Church.* The former orders of acolyte, exorcist, reader or lector, and doorkeeper.

minor planet *n.* An **asteroid** *(see).*

minor premise *n. Logic.* The premise in a syllogism containing the minor term, which will form the subject of the conclusion.

Minor Prophets *pl.n.* **1.** The Hebrew prophets Hosea, Joel, Amos, Obadiah, Jonah, Micah, Nahum, Habakkuk, Zephaniah, Haggai, Zechariah, and Malachi. **2.** The group of books of the Old Testament containing their prophecies.

minor scale *n. Music.* A diatonic scale having a minor third between the first and third tones. It has several forms with different intervals above the fifth. Compare **major scale.**

minor suit *n.* In bridge, the suit of clubs or of diamonds. [So called because of their lower scoring value.]

minor term *n. Logic.* The term in a syllogism that is stated in the minor premise and forms the subject of the conclusion.

Mi·nos (mī'nəs, -nŏs'). *Greek Mythology.* A king of Crete, the son of Zeus and Europa, who ordered the building of the Labyrinth.

Mi·no·taur (mī'nə-tôr', mĭn'ə-). *Greek Mythology.* The son of Pasiphaë by a sacred bull, having a man's body and a bull's head, slain by Theseus in the Labyrinth. [Middle English, ultimately from Greek *Minōtauros* : MINOS (husband of Pasiphaë) + *tauros,* bull.]

Minsk (mĭnsk). The capital of Belorussian S.S.R., U.S.S.R. It is a communications, market, and cultural and industrial center. Its substantial Jewish population (40 percent) was virtually exterminated by the Germans in World War II.

min·ster (mĭn′stər) *n. British.* **1.** A monastery church. **2.** Any of certain abbeys or cathedrals, such as those of Beverley or York. [Middle English *minster,* Old English *mynster,* from Vulgar Latin *monisterium* (unattested), variant of Late Latin *monastērium,* MONASTERY.]

min·strel (mĭn′strəl) *n.* **1.** A medieval musician who traveled from place to place singing and reciting poetry. **2. a.** A lyric poet. **b.** A musician. **3. a.** A performer in a minstrel show. **b.** A performance of a minstrel show. [Middle English *ministral,* from Old French *menestral,* entertainer, servant, from Late Latin *ministeriālis,* household officer, from Latin *ministerium,* MINISTRY.]

minstrel show *n.* A variety show, formerly popular in the United States, in which performers, some with blackened faces, sing, dance, and tell jokes.

min·strel·sy (mĭn′strəl-sē) *n., pl.* **-sies. 1.** The art or profession of a minstrel. **2.** A troupe of minstrels. **3.** A group of ballads and lyrics sung by minstrels.

mint¹ (mĭnt) *n.* **1.** A place where the coins of a country are manufactured by authority of the government. **2.** An abundant amount or repository, especially of money: *He is worth a mint.* **3.** Anything that can be exploited as a source of money or ideas: *She proved to be a mint of useful ideas.*
~*tr.v.* **minted, minting, mints. 1.** To produce (money) by stamping metal; coin. **2.** To invent or fabricate (a word, for example).
~*adj.* Undamaged as if freshly minted: *in mint condition.* [Middle English *mynt,* Old English *mynet,* money, from West Germanic *munita* (unattested), from Latin *monēta,* money, mint, after the temple of Juno *Monēta* in Rome, where money was minted.]

mint² *n.* **1.** Any of various plants of the genus *Mentha,* characteristically having aromatic foliage and spiked flowers. Many species are cultivated for their leaves, used for flavoring. See **peppermint, spearmint. 2.** Any of various similar or related plants. **3.** A candy flavored with mint. [Middle English *minte,* Old English *minte,* from West Germanic *minta* (unattested), from Latin *menta, mentha,* from Greek *minthē,* of Mediterranean origin.] —**mint′y** *adj.*

mint·age (mĭn′tĭj) *n.* **1.** The act or process of minting coins. **2.** Money manufactured in a mint. **3.** The fee paid to a mint by the government. **4.** The impression stamped on a coin.

mint jelly *n.* A clear green jelly, usually made with apples or crab apples, chopped mint, and green vegetable coloring.

mint julep *n.* A tall, frosted drink made of bourbon, sugar, crushed mint leaves, and shaved ice. Also called "julep."

mint sauce *n.* A sauce, traditionally served with roast lamb, made of chopped mint leaves with vinegar and sugar.

min·u·end (mĭn′yŏŏ-ĕnd′) *n.* The quantity or number from which another, the subtrahend, is to be subtracted. [Latin *minuendum,* something to be diminished, neuter gerundive of *minuere,* to lessen.]

min·u·et (mĭn′yŏŏ-ĕt′) *n.* **1.** A slow, stately pattern dance for groups of couples that originated in 17th-century France. **2.** A piece of music for or in the rhythm of this dance, in 3/4 time. [French, from obsolete *menuet,* dainty, small, from Old French *menu,* small, from Latin *minūtus,* small, MINUTE.]

Min·u·it (mĭn′yŏŏ-ĭt′), **Peter** (1580–1638). Dutch colonial administrator. Sent by the Dutch West Indian Company to be director general of New Netherland, he arrived in Manhattan in 1626 and subsequently purchased the island from the Indians for the equivalent of $24. Minuit was a stubborn man who lacked diplomacy and was recalled in 1631. He later founded the colony of New Sweden.

mi·nus (mī′nəs) *prep.* **1.** *Mathematics.* Reduced by the subtraction of; less: *Seven minus four equals three.* **2.** *Informal.* Lacking; without: *arrived minus her gloves.*
~*adj.* **1.** Negative or on the negative part of a scale: *a minus value; minus five degrees.* **2.** Designating one subdivision of a grade less than; slightly less than: *a mark of B minus.* **3.** Of, pertaining to, or involving a loss, deficiency, or disadvantage: *a minus consideration.* **4.** Having a negative electric charge.
~*n.* **1.** A minus sign (-). **2.** A negative quantity. **3.** A loss, deficiency, or disadvantage. **4.** A negative electric charge. [Middle English *mynus,* from Latin *minus,* less, from *minor,* less, minor.]

min·us·cule (mĭn′ə-skyōōl′, mĭ-nŭs′kyōōl) *n.* **1.** A small, cursive script developed from uncial between the 7th and 9th centuries A.D. and used in medieval manuscripts. **2.** A letter written in this script. **3.** A lower-case letter. Compare **majuscule.**
~*adj.* **1. a.** Of, pertaining to, or written in minuscule. **b.** Of, pertaining to, or written in lower-case letters. **2.** Lower-case. Said of letters of the alphabet. **3.** Very small; tiny; minute. —See Synonyms at **small.** [French, from Latin *minuscula (littera),* minuscule (letter), from *minusculus,* diminutive of *minor* (stem *minus-*), less, minor.] —**mi·nus·cu·lar** (mĭ-nŭs′kyə-lər) *adj.*

minus sign *n. Mathematics.* The symbol (-), as in 4 - 2 = 2. It is used to indicate subtraction or a negative quantity. Also called "minus." Compare **plus sign.**

min·ute¹ (mĭn′ĭt) *n.* **1.** *Abbr.* **min** *Symbol* ′ **a.** A unit or period of time equal to one-sixtieth of an hour, or to 60 seconds. **b.** A unit of angular measurement equal to one-sixtieth of a degree, or to 60 seconds. Also called "minute of arc." **2.** Any short interval of time; a moment. **3.** A specific point in time. **4.** *Informal.* The distance that can be covered in a minute: *ten minutes from here.* **5.** A note or summary covering points to be remembered; a memorandum. **6. minutes.** An official record of proceedings at the meeting of an

organization. —See Synonyms at **moment.**
~*tr.v.* **minuted, -uting, -utes. 1.** To record exactly with the precise time: *minuted the arrival of each contestant.* **2.** To record in a memorandum or other notation. **3.** To send a minute to (a person). **4.** To record in the minutes of a meeting. [Middle English, from Old French, from Medieval Latin *minūta,* minute, small note, from Late Latin, from *minūtus,* small, MINUTE.]

mi·nute² (mī-nōōt′, -nyōōt′, mĭ-) *adj.* **1.** Exceptionally small; tiny: *minute spores carried by the wind.* **2.** Beneath notice; insignificant; trifling. **3.** Characterized by careful scrutiny and close examination: *her minute and accurate research.* —See Synonyms at **small.** [Latin *minūtus,* small, from the past participle of *minuere,* to lessen.] —**mi·nute′ness** *n.*

minute hand (mĭn′ĭt) *n.* The long hand on a clock or watch that indicates the minutes.

min·ute·ly¹ (mĭn′ĭt-lē) *adj.* At intervals of one minute.
~*adv.* Every minute.

mi·nute·ly² (mī-nōōt′lē, -nyōōt′lē, mĭ-) *adv.* **1.** With attention to minutiae. **2.** On a very small scale.

min·ute·man (mĭn′ĭt-măn′) *n., pl.* **-men** (-mĕn′). **1.** An American militiaman or armed civilian pledged during the Revolutionary War to be ready to fight at a minute's notice. **2.** A type of U.S. intercontinental ballistic missile.

minute mark *n.* The symbol ′, used to indicate feet and also minutes of arc.

minute of arc *n.* A minute (unit of angular measurement).

minute steak *n.* A small, thin steak that can be cooked quickly.

mi·nu·ti·a (mĭ-nōō′shē-ə, -nyōō′shē-ə, -shə) *n., pl.* **-tiae** (-shē-ē′). A small, exact, or trivial detail: *"all the particulars of past sad scenes, all the minutia of distress upon distress"* (Jane Austen). [Latin *minūtia,* smallness, from *minūtus,* small, MINUTE.]

minx (mĭngks) *n., pl.* **minxes. 1.** A pert, impudent, or flirtatious woman or girl. **2.** *Archaic.* A prostitute or promiscuous woman. [16th century : origin obscure.]

min·yan (mĭn′yən) *n., pl.* **-yans** or **minyanim** (mĭn′yə-nēm′). The quorum of ten male Jews aged 13 or older required according to orthodox Jewish law before a religious service can take place. [Hebrew, "number."]

Mi·o·cene (mī′ə-sēn′) *adj. Geology.* Of, belonging to, or characteristic of the geological time and rock series of the fourth epoch of the Tertiary period, characterized by the appearance of primitive apes, whales, and grazing animals.
~*n. Geology.* **1.** The Miocene epoch. Preceded by *the.* **2.** The deposits of this epoch. [Greek *meiōn,* less + -CENE.]

mi·o·sis, my·o·sis (mī-ō′sĭs) *n., pl.* **-ses** (-sēz′). *Pathology.* An excessive contraction of the pupil of the eye, often due to the action of drugs. [New Latin : Greek *muein,* to close the eyes + -OSIS.]

mi·ot·ic (mī-ŏt′ĭk) *n.* An agent that causes contraction of the pupil of the eye. [From MIOSIS.] —**mi·ot·ic** *adj.*

Miquelon. See St. Pierre and Miquelon.

mir (mîr) *n.* A prerevolutionary Russian peasant commune. [Russian, commune, peace, world, from Old Church Slavonic *mirŭ,* joy, peace.]

Mi·ra·beau (mîr′ə-bō′, mē′rä-bō′), **Honoré Gabriel Riqueti, Comte de** (1749–91). French revolutionary leader. In 1789 he was a delegate to the States-General, where his oratory made him spokesman for the Third Estate. His policy of a constitutional monarchy weakened his influence, and in 1790 he entered into secret negotiations with the court.

mi·ra·bi·le dic·tu (mī-rä′bĭ-lā dĭk′tōō) *adv.* Wonderful to relate. [Latin.]

mi·ra·cid·i·um (mîr′ə-sĭd′ē-əm, mī′rə-) *n., pl.* **-ia** (-ē-ə). A ciliated larva of a parasitic fluke in the form in which it hatches from the egg. [New Latin, from Late Latin *miracidion,* diminutive of Greek *meirax* (stem *meirac-*), offspring.]

mir·a·cle (mîr′ə-kəl) *n.* **1.** An event that appears unexplainable by the laws of nature and so is held to be supernatural in origin or an act of God. **2.** Broadly, any event that seems exceptionally fortunate: *It was a miracle she escaped unhurt.* **3.** A person, thing, or event that excites admiring awe. **4.** A miracle play. [Middle English, from Old French, from Latin *mīrāculum,* from *mīrārī,* to wonder at, from *mīrus,* wonderful.]

miracle play *n.* A form of religious drama of the Middle Ages in which scenes and events of the Bible or the lives of saints and martyrs were represented. Compare **mystery play.**

mi·rac·u·lous (mī-răk′yə-ləs) *adj.* **1.** Of the nature of a miracle. **2.** Caused by or as if by a miracle: *a miraculous cure.* **3.** Having the power to work miracles. [French *miraculeux,* from Medieval Latin *mīrāculōsus,* from Latin *mīrāculum,* MIRACLE.] —**mi·rac·u·lous·ly** *adv.* —**mi·rac·u·lous·ness** *n.*

mir·a·dor (mîr′ə-dôr′) *n.* A balcony, window, or turret affording a wide view. [Spanish, from *mirar,* to look.]

mi·rage (mĭ-räzh′) *n.* **1.** An optical phenomenon in which an image, often inverted, is produced as a result of refraction of light by layers of air with differing densities. The commonest form involves an image of the sky, producing the illusion of water. **2.** Something that is illusory or insubstantial like a mirage. [French, from *mirer,* to look at, from Latin *mīrārī,* to wonder at, from *mīrus,* wonder.]

mire (mīr) *n.* **1.** An area of wet, soggy, and muddy ground; a bog. **2.** Deep, slimy soil or mud. **3.** A difficult or unpleasant position. ~*v.* **mired, miring, mires.** —*tr.* **1.** To cause to sink or become stuck in mire. **2.** To soil with mud. **3.** To trap or entangle as if in mire. —*intr.* To sink or become stuck in mire. [Middle English,

minstrel *Strolling players portrayed in a 15th-century Flemish book of hours.*

from Old Norse *mȳrr*, a bog, from Germanic; akin to MOSS.] —**mir·i·ness** *n.* —**mir·y** *adj.*

mire·poix (mîr-pwä′) *n., pl.* **mirepoix.** A mixture of finely diced vegetables used especially under meat being braised. [French, probably in honor of C.P.G.F. de Lévis, Duc de *Mirepoix*, 18th-century French general.]

Mir·i·am (mîr′ē-əm). The sister of Moses. Exodus 15:20.

mirk. Variant of **murk.**

mirky. Variant of **murky.**

Mi·ró (mē-rō′), **Joan** (1893–1983). Spanish surrealist painter, born in Catalonia. His style is distinguished by naive, free-floating forms. He donated much of his work to the Joan Miró museum of contemporary art in Barcelona.

mir·ror (mîr′ər) *n.* **1.** Any surface capable of reflecting sufficient undiffused light to form an image of an object placed in front of it; especially, one of coated glass or polished metal, often mounted in a frame. **2.** Anything that faithfully reflects or gives a true picture of something else: *The novel is a mirror of society.* **3.** A speculum *(see)* on a bird's wing. ~*tr.v.* **mirrored, -roring, -rors.** To reflect in or as if in a mirror: *"Under the October twilight the water Mirrors a still sky"* (Yeats). [Middle English *mirour*, from Old French *miroir, mirour*, from *mirer*, to look at, from Latin *mīrārī*, to wonder at, from *mīrus*, wonderful.]

mirror carp *n.* A variety of the common carp that has a smooth, shiny body.

mirror image *n.* **1.** An image in or as if in a mirror, showing left and right reversed but otherwise identical to the original. **2.** Something that has the same constituent parts as something else but has them in reverse order or with inverted values: *Is fascism the mirror image of communism?*

mirror plane *n.* A plane that divides an object or system into two halves that are mirror images of each other.

mirror symmetry *n.* Symmetry such that one half of an object or system is identical to the mirror image of the other half.

mirror writing *n.* Writing in which both letters and words are reversed, appearing normal when seen reflected in a mirror.

mirth (mûrth) *n.* Merriment, gaiety, or enjoyment, especially when expressed in laughter. [Middle English *mirthe*, Old English *myrgth*. See **merry, -th.**] —**mirth·ful** *adj.* —**mirth·less** *adj.*

     Synonyms: *glee, hilarity, merriment.*

MIRV (mûrv) *n.* **1.** An offensive ballistic-missile system in which a number of warheads aimed at independent targets can be launched by a single booster rocket. **2.** Any of the warheads of a MIRV. [*Mul*tiple *I*ndependently targeted *R*e-entry *V*ehicles.]

mir·za (mîr′zə) *n.* **1.** In Iran, a respectful title used: **1.** After the name of a prince. **2.** Before the name of a hero, scholar, or high official. [Persian *mīrzā*, short for *mīrzād*, "son of a lord" : *mīr*, prince, from Arabic *amīr*, prince, EMIR + *zād*, born, from *zādan*, to be born.]

mis-¹ *prefix.* Indicates: **1.** Error or wrongness; for example, **misspell.** **2.** Badness or impropriety; for example, **misbehave, misdeed. 3.** Unsuitableness; for example, **misalliance. 4.** Opposite or lack of; for example, **mistrust. 5.** Failure; for example, **misfire.** [There are two separate developments of *mis-* that became confused in Modern English: 1. Middle English *mis-*, wrong, Old English *mis-*, from Germanic *missa-* (unattested), amiss, divergent, mutual. 2. Middle English *mes-*, bad, wrong, from Old French, from Vulgar Latin *minus-* (unattested), from Latin *minus*, MINUS.]

mis-² Variant of **miso-.**

mis·ad·ven·ture (mĭs′əd-vĕn′chər) *n.* **1.** An instance of great misfortune; a disaster. **2.** *Law.* Death as a result of an accident rather than negligence or crime. —See Synonyms at **misfortune.** [Middle English *misaventure*, from Old French *mesaventure*, from *mesavenir*, to result in misfortune : *mes-*, badly, MIS- + *avenir*, to turn out, from Latin *advenīre*, to come to : *ad*, to + *venīre*, to come.]

mis·ad·vise (mĭs′əd-vīz′) *tr.v.* **-vised, -vising, -vises.** To advise wrongly.

mis·al·li·ance (mĭs′ə-lī′əns) *n.* An unsuitable alliance, especially in marriage. [French *mésalliance* : *més-*, improper, MIS- + ALLIANCE.]

mis·al·ly (mĭs′ə-lī′) *tr.v.* **-lied, -lying, -lies.** To ally or unite badly.

mis·an·dry (mĭs′ăn′drē, mĭ-săn′drē) *n.* Hatred of or hostility toward men. [MIS(O)- + -*andry*, from Greek *anēr* (stem *andr-*), man.] —**mis·an·drist** *n. & adj.*

mis·an·thrope (mĭs′ən-thrōp′, mĭz′-) *n.* Also **mis·an·thro·pist** (mĭ-săn′thrə-pĭst, mĭ-zăn′-). A person who hates or distrusts humankind. [French, from Greek *misanthrōpos*, hating humankind : *misein*, to hate + *anthrōpos*, man.] —**mis·an·throp·ic** (mĭs′ən-thrŏp′ĭk, mĭz′-) *adj.* —**mis·an·throp·i·cal·ly** *adv.* —**mis·an·thro·py** (mĭ-săn′thrə-pē, mĭ-zăn′-) *n.*

mis·ap·ply (mĭs′ə-plī′) *tr.v.* **-plied, -plying, -plies. 1.** To apply wrongly. **2.** To make wrong use of; especially, to misappropriate (funds). —**mis·ap·pli·ca·tion** (mĭs-ăp′lĭ-kā′shən) *n.*

mis·ap·pre·hend (mĭs-ăp′rĭ-hĕnd′) *tr.v.* **-hended, -hending, -hends.** To fail to interpret correctly; misunderstand. —**mis·ap·pre·hen·sion** (mĭs-ăp′rĭ-hĕn′shən) *n.*

mis·ap·pro·pri·ate (mĭs′ə-prō′prē-āt′) *tr.v.* **-ated, -ating, -ates. 1.** To appropriate (money, funds, or the like) wrongly or dishonestly, especially for one's own use. **2.** To use illegally or wrongly.

mis·be·come (mĭs′bĭ-kŭm′) *tr.v.* **-came** (-kām′), **-come, -coming, -comes.** To be unsuitable or inappropriate for: *"what I have done that misbecame my place"* (Shakespeare).

mis·be·got·ten (mĭs′bĭ-gŏt′n) *adj.* Also **mis·be·got** (-bĭ-gŏt′). Begotten in an illegal or disreputable way; especially, illegitimate.

mis·be·have (mĭs′bĭ-hāv′) *v.* **-haved, -having, -haves.** —*intr.* To behave badly. —*tr.* To conduct (oneself) badly.

mis·be·hav·ior (mĭs′bĭ-hāv′yər) *n.* Also *chiefly British* **mis·be·hav·iour.** Improper or rude behavior.

mis·be·lief (mĭs′bĭ-lēf′) *n.* **1.** A wrong or faulty belief; an erroneous opinion. **2.** A heretical or unorthodox religious belief.

mis·be·lieve (mĭs′bĭ-lēv′) *intr.v.* **-lieved, -lieving, -lieves.** *Obsolete.* To believe wrongly; hold a false or erroneous opinion.

misc. miscellaneous.

mis·cal·cu·late (mĭs-kăl′kyə-lāt′) *v.* **-lated, -lating, -lates.** —*tr.* To calculate wrongly; make a wrong estimate of. —*intr.* To make an error in calculation or judgment. —**mis·cal·cu·la·tion** *n.*

mis·call (mĭs-kôl′) *tr.v.* **-called, -calling, -calls. 1.** To call by a wrong or inappropriate name. **2.** *Regional.* To call by a bad name; revile.

mis·car·riage (mĭs-kăr′ĭj, mĭs′kăr′-) *n.* **1. a.** Mismanagement; bad administration: *a miscarriage of justice.* **b.** Failure to attain the right or desired end: *the miscarriage of a hope; a miscarriage of a cargo.* **2.** Premature expulsion of a nonviable fetus from the uterus. In this sense, also called "spontaneous abortion."

mis·car·ry (mĭs-kăr′ē) *intr.v.* **-ried, -rying, -ries. 1.** To go astray; be lost in transit: *The freight miscarried.* **2.** To go wrong; fail: *a good idea that miscarried.* **3.** To bring forth a nonviable fetus prematurely; abort.

mis·cast (mĭs-kăst′, -kăst′) *tr.v.* **-cast, -casting, -casts. 1.** To cast in an unsuitable role. **2.** To cast (a role or a theatrical production) inappropriately.

mis·ce·ge·na·tion (mĭs′ĭ-jə-nā′shən, mĭ-sĕj′ə-nā′shən) *n.* Intermarriage or interbreeding between different races; especially, marriage between white and nonwhite persons. [Latin *miscēre*, to mix + *genus*, race.] —**mis·ce·ge·net·ic** (mĭs′ĭ-jə-nĕt′ĭk, mĭ-sĕj′ə-) *adj.*

mis·cel·la·ne·a (mĭs′ə-lā′nē-ə) *pl.n.* A conglomeration of various items; especially, a collection of diverse literary works. [Latin *miscellānea*, from the neuter plural of *miscellāneus*, MISCELLANEOUS.]

mis·cel·la·ne·ous (mĭs′ə-lā′nē-əs) *adj.* *Abbr.* **misc. 1.** Made up of a variety of parts or ingredients: *a miscellaneous collection.* **2.** Having a variety of characteristics, abilities, or appearances: *miscellaneous opinions.* **3.** Concerned with diverse subjects or aspects: *"various miscellaneous objections . . . against my views"* (Charles Darwin). [Latin *miscellāneus*, from *miscellus*, mixed, from *miscēre*, to mix.] —**mis·cel·la·ne·ous·ly** *adv.* —**mis·cel·la·ne·ous·ness** *n.*

     Synonyms: *assorted, heterogeneous, mixed, motley, varied.*

mis·cel·la·nist (mĭs′ə-lā′nĭst, mĭ-sĕl′ə-nĭst) *n.* *Chiefly British.* One who compiles, writes, or edits a miscellany.

mis·cel·la·ny (mĭs′ə-lā′nē; *British* mĭ-sĕl′ə-nē) *n., pl.* **-nies. 1.** A collection of various items, parts, or ingredients, especially one composed of diverse literary works. **2.** *Often* **miscellanies.** A book or other publication containing writings of differing types or on different subjects. [Latin *miscellānea*, MISCELLANEA.]

mis·chance (mĭs-chăns′, -chănz′) *n.* **1.** An unfortunate occurrence; an unlucky incident. **2.** Bad luck. —See Synonyms at **misfortune.** [Middle English *mischaunce*, from Old French *mescheaunce* : *mes-*, ill, MIS- + *cheaunce*, CHANCE.]

mis·chief (mĭs′chĭf) *n.* **1.** Behavior that causes discomfiture or annoyance in another. **2.** An inclination or tendency to play pranks or cause embarrassment: *full of mischief.* **3.** One that causes minor trouble or a disturbance: *The child was a mischief in school.* **4.** Damage, destruction, or injury caused by a specified person or thing: *Wind wreaked untold mischief upon the crops.* **5.** The state or quality of being mischievous: *a little girl with mischief in her eyes.* [Middle English *meschief*, from Old French *mischief, meschef*, from *meschever*, to meet with misfortune : *mes-*, amiss, ill, MIS- + *chever*, "to come to a head," happen, ultimately from Latin *caput*, head.]

mis·chie·vous (mĭs′chə-vəs) *adj.* **1.** Causing mischief. **2.** Playfully naughty; teasing: *a mischievous smile.* **3.** Troublesome; irritating: *a mischievous prank.* **4.** Causing harm, injury, or damage: *mischievous lies.* —See Synonyms at **playful.** [MISCHIEF + -OUS.] —**mis·chie·vous·ly** *adv.* —**mis·chie·vous·ness** *n.*

misch metal (mĭsh) *n.* An alloy of cerium and several rare-earth elements. It produces sparks when struck and is used in lighter flints. [Partial translation of German *Mischmetall*, from *mischen*, to mix.]

mis·ci·ble (mĭs′ə-bəl) *adj.* *Chemistry.* Capable of being mixed in all proportions. Said especially of liquids. [Medieval Latin *miscĭbilis*, from Latin *miscēre*, to mix.] —**mis·ci·bil·i·ty** (mĭs′ə-bĭl′ə-tē) *n.*

mis·con·ceive (mĭs′kən-sēv′) *tr.v.* **-ceived, -ceiving, -ceives.** To interpret in the wrong way; misunderstand. —**mis·con·ceiv·er** *n.*

mis·con·ceived (mĭs′kən-sēvd′) *adj.* Based on a false understanding; badly thought out.

mis·con·cep·tion (mĭs′kən-sĕp′shən) *n.* An incorrect interpretation or understanding; a delusion.

mis·con·duct (mĭs-kŏn′dŭkt) *n.* **1.** Behavior not conforming to prevailing standards or laws; impropriety: *professional misconduct.* **2.** Dishonest or bad management, especially by persons entrusted to act on another's behalf; malfeasance. ~*tr.v.* (mĭs′kən-dŭkt′) **misconducted, -ducting, -ducts. 1.** To behave (oneself) improperly. **2.** To administer or manage poorly or dishonestly.

mis·con·struc·tion (mĭs′kən-strŭk′shən) *n.* **1.** An inaccurate explanation, interpretation, or report; a misunderstanding. **2.** A faulty construction, especially of a sentence or clause.

mis·con·strue (mĭs′kən-strōō′) *tr.v.* **-strued, -struing, -strues.** To mistake the meaning of; misinterpret; misunderstand.

mis·count (mĭs-kount') v. **-counted, -counting, -counts.** —*tr.* To count or estimate incorrectly; miscalculate. —*intr.* To err in counting.
~n. (mĭs'kount'). An inaccurate count.

mis·cre·ant (mĭs'krē-ənt) n. **1.** An evildoer or villain. **2.** An infidel or heretic. [Middle English *miscreaunt,* heretical, unbelieving, from Old French *mescreant,* present participle of *mescroire,* to disbelieve : *mes-,* MIS- + *croire,* to believe, from Latin *crēdere.*] —**mis·cre·ant** *adj.*

mis·cre·ate (mĭs'krē-āt') tr.v. **-ated, -ating, -ates.** To make or shape badly.
~adj. (mĭs'krē-ĭt, -āt'). *Rare.* Formed unnaturally; deformed. —**mis·cre·a·tion** n.

mis·cue (mĭs-kyōō') n. **1.** In billiards, a stroke that misses or just brushes the ball due to a slip of the cue. **2.** A blunder or mistake. ~intr.v. **miscued, -cuing, -cues. 1.** To make a miscue. **2.** In acting, to miss one's own cue or mistake someone else's cue for one's own.

mis·date (mĭs-dāt') tr.v. **-dated, -dating, -dates.** To date wrongly or incorrectly.

mis·deal (mĭs-dēl') v. **-dealt** (-dĕlt') **-dealing, -deals.** —*tr.* To deal (playing cards) in the wrong order or incorrectly. —*intr.* To deal cards incorrectly. —**mis·deal'** (-dēl') n. —**mis·deal·er** n.

mis·deed (mĭs-dēd') n. A wicked, immoral, or illegal deed.

mis·de·mean·ant (mĭs'dĭ-mē'nənt) n. One who is guilty of or has been convicted and sentenced for a misdemeanor.

mis·de·mean·or (mĭs'dĭ-mē'nər) n. Also *chiefly British* **mis·de·mean·our. 1.** A wrong action; a misdeed. **2.** *Law.* An offense of lesser gravity than a felony, for which punishment is likely to be a fine or a brief imprisonment. Compare **crime, felony.**

mis·di·ag·nose (mĭs-dī'əg-nōs', -nōz') tr.v. **-nosed, -nosing, -noses.** To diagnose incorrectly. —**mis·di·ag·no·sis** n.

mis·di·al (mĭs-dī'əl) tr.v. **-aled, -aling, -als** or *chiefly British* **-alled, -alling.** To dial (a telephone number) incorrectly.

mis·di·rect (mĭs'dĭ-rĕkt', -dī-rĕkt') tr.v. **-rected, -recting, -rects. 1.** To instruct incorrectly: *The judge misdirected the jury.* **2. a.** To put a wrong address on. **b.** To give incorrect directions to (someone seeking a location or address). **3.** To direct (energy or an emotion) mistakenly or misguidedly. —**mis·di·rec·tion** n.

mis·do (mĭs-dōō') v. **-did** (-dĭd') **-done** (-dŭn') **-doing, -does** (-dŭz'). —*tr.* To do wrongly or awkwardly; botch. —*intr. Obsolete.* To do wrong or harm. —**mis·do·er** n.

mis·doubt (mĭs-dout') v. **-doubted, -doubting, -doubts.** —*tr.* To feel wary of; suspect. —*intr.* To have doubts or be fearful.

mis·em·ploy (mĭs'ĕm-ploi') tr.v. **-ployed, -ploying, -ploys.** To put to a wrong use; employ improperly. —**mis·em·ploy·ment** n.

mise en scène (mēz' äN sĕn') n. **1. a.** The properties and scenery used to stage a play or a scene in a play. **b.** The arrangement of the performers and of such properties. **2.** An environment; surroundings. [French, "placing on stage."]

mi·ser (mī'zər) n. **1.** One who deprives himself of all but the barest essentials in order to hoard money. **2.** A greedy, stingy, or avaricious person. [Originally, "wretch," from Latin *miser,* wretched.]

mis·er·a·ble (mĭz'ər-ə-bəl, mĭz'rə-bəl) adj. **1.** Very unhappy; wretched. **2.** Causing or accompanied by wretchedness or other discomfort: *a miserable climate.* **3.** Mean; shameful: *a miserable trick.* **4.** Of poor quality; inferior. **5.** Wretchedly inadequate: *miserable rations.* —See Synonyms at **sad.** [Middle English, from Old French *miserable,* from Latin *miserābilis,* pitiable, from *miserārī,* to have pity, from *miser,* wretched, unfortunate.] —**mis·er·a·ble·ness** n. —**mis·er·a·bly** adv.

mis·e·re·re (mĭz'ə-rârē, -rîr'ē) n. **1.** Part of a church seat, a **misericord** (*see*). **2.** A prayer for mercy. [From MISERERE.]

Mis·e·re·re (mĭz'ə-rârē, -rîr'ē) n. **1.** The 51st Psalm, which opens with *"Miserere mei Deus"* (Have mercy upon me, O God). **2.** A musical setting of this psalm. [Latin, imperative of *miserērī,* to have pity, from *miser,* wretched.]

mis·er·i·cord, mis·er·i·corde (mĭz'ər-ĭ-kôrd', mĭ-zĕr'ĭ-kôrd') n. **1. a.** The relaxation of a monastic rule, such as a dispensation from fasting. **b.** A room used by monks granted such a dispensation. **2.** A bracket, sometimes in the form of a carved figure, attached to the underside of a hinged seat in a church stall, against which a standing person may lean. Also called "miserere." **3.** A narrow dagger used in medieval times to deliver the death stroke to one who was seriously wounded, especially a knight. [Middle English, pity, mercy, dagger, from Old French, from Latin *misericordia,* from *misericors,* pitiful : *miserērī,* to have pity + *cors* (stem *cord-*), heart.]

mi·ser·ly (mī'zər-lē) adj. Characteristic of a miser; tending to hoard money or possessions; extremely mean: *too miserly to leave a tip.* —See Synonyms at **stingy.** —**mi·ser·li·ness** n.

mis·er·y (mĭz'ə-rē) n., pl. **-ies. 1.** Prolonged or extreme suffering; a state of great mental, emotional, or physical pain; wretchedness. **2.** A cause or source of suffering or pain, such as an affliction or deprivation. **3.** *British Informal.* One who is constantly depressed or gloomy. [Middle English *miserie,* from Norman French, from Latin *miseria,* from *miser,* wretched.]

mis·es·teem (mĭs'ə-stēm') tr.v. **-teemed, -teeming, -teems.** To fail to regard with deserved esteem; disrespect.

mis·es·ti·mate (mĭs-ĕs'tə-māt') tr.v. **-mated, -mating, -mates.** To estimate or appraise inaccurately or wrongly.
~n. (mĭs-ĕs'tə-mĭt). An inaccurate estimate or appraisal.

mis·fea·sance (mĭs-fē'zəns) n. *Law.* The improper and unlawful execution of some act that in itself is lawful and proper. Compare **malfeasance, nonfeasance.** [Old French *mesfaisance,* from *mesfaire,* to misdo : *mes-,* wrongly, MIS- + *faire,* to do, from Latin *facere.*]

mis·fea·sor (mĭs-fē'zər) n. *Law.* One guilty of misfeasance.

mis·fire (mĭs-fīr') intr.v. **-fired, -firing, -fires. 1.** To fail to explode or ignite when expected, as a gun or internal-combustion engine may. **2.** To fail to achieve the anticipated result: *a scheme that misfired.* —**mis·fire'** (-fīr') n.

mis·fit (mĭs'fĭt, mĭs-fĭt') n. **1.** Something of the wrong size or shape for its purpose. **2.** A person who is maladjusted or finds it difficult to fit in with people or the immediate environment.
~v. (mĭs-fĭt') **misfitted, -fitting, -fits.** *Rare.* —*tr.* To fit poorly. —*intr.* To be of the wrong size or shape.

mis·for·tune (mĭs-fôr'chən) n. **1.** Bad fortune or ill luck. **2.** An instance of this; unfortunate occurrence.
Synonyms: adversity, misadventure, mischance, mishap.

mis·give (mĭs-gĭv') v. **-gave** (-gāv') **-given** (-gĭv'ən), **-giving, -gives.** —*tr.* To arouse suspicion or apprehension in. —*intr.* To be suspicious, apprehensive, or doubtful. [Originally, to suggest doubt (used of the mind) : MIS- (wrongly) + GIVE (in the Middle English sense "to suggest").]

mis·giv·ing (mĭs-gĭv'ĭng) n. *Often* **misgivings.** A feeling of uncertainty or apprehension: *approached the empty house with some misgivings.* —See Synonyms at **apprehension, qualm.**

mis·gov·ern (mĭs-gŭv'ərn) tr.v. **-erned, -erning, -erns.** To govern or administrate inefficiently or badly. —**mis·gov·ern·ment** n. —**mis·gov·er·nor** n.

mis·guide (mĭs-gīd') tr.v. **-guided, -guiding, -guides.** To give wrong or misleading directions to; lead astray; misdirect. —**mis·guid·ance** n. —**mis·guid·er** n.

mis·guid·ed (mĭs-gī'dĭd) adj. Confused or erring in thought or action; foolish: *a misguided decision.* —**mis·guid·ed·ly** adv.

mis·han·dle (mĭs-hăn'dəl) tr.v. **-dled, -dling, -dles.** To treat or deal with clumsily or inefficiently.

mis·hap (mĭs'hăp', mĭs-hăp') n. **1.** Bad luck or misfortune. **2.** An unfortunate accident. —See Synonyms at **misfortune.**

mis·hear (mĭs-hîr') tr.v. **-heard** (-hûrd'), **-hearing, -hears.** To hear wrongly or badly.

Mi·shi·ma (mĭ-shē'mə), **Yukio,** born Kimitake Hiraoka (1925–70). Japanese writer. His stories are often evocations of the imperial past. His novels include *Confessions of a Mask* (1949) and *The Sailor Who Fell from Grace with the Sea* (1963).

mis·hit (mĭs'hĭt') n. In certain games, such as tennis or squash, a faulty or bad hit: *mishits that come off the handle and not the strings.* ~tr.v. (mĭs-hĭt') **mishit, -hitting, -hits.** To hit (a ball) faultily or badly.

mish·mash (mĭsh'măsh', -mäsh') n. A collection or mixture of unrelated things; a hodgepodge. [Reduplication of MASH.]

Mish·nah, Mish·na (mĭsh'nə) n., pl. **Mish·na·yoth** (mĭsh'nə-yōth', -yōt'). **1.** The first section of the Talmud, consisting of a collection of early oral interpretations of the scriptures as compiled about A.D. 200. **2.** A paragraph from this collection. [Rabbinical Hebrew *mishnāh,* repetition, instruction, from *shānāh,* to repeat.] —**Mish·na·ic** (mĭsh-nā'ĭk), **Mish·nic** (mĭsh'nĭk), **Mish·ni·cal** adj.

mis·in·form (mĭs'ĭn-fôrm') tr.v. **-formed, -forming, -forms.** To give wrong or inaccurate information to. —**mis·in·form·ant** (mĭs'ĭn-fôr'mənt), **mis·in·form·er** n. —**mis·in·for·ma·tion** n.

mis·in·ter·pret (mĭs'ĭn-tûr'prĭt) tr.v. **-preted, -preting, -prets. 1.** To explain inaccurately. **2.** To understand incorrectly. —**mis·in·ter·pre·ta·tion** n. —**mis·in·ter·pret·er** n.

mis·join·der (mĭs-join'dər) n. *Law.* Improper joining of different causes of action or different parties in a suit. Compare **nonjoinder.**

mis·judge (mĭs-jŭj') v. **-judged, -judging, -judges.** —*tr.* To make a mistake in one's judgment of. —*intr.* To be wrong in judging. —**mis·judg·ment** n.

Miskito. Variant of **Mosquito.**

mis·lay (mĭs-lā') tr.v. **-laid** (-lād') **-laying, -lays. 1.** To put in a place that is afterward forgotten; lose. **2.** To place or put down incorrectly: *mislay linoleum.* —**mis·lay·er** n.

mis·lead (mĭs-lēd') tr.v. **-led** (-lĕd') **-leading, -leads. 1.** To lead or guide in the wrong direction. **2.** To lead into error or wrongdoing, whether by accident or design. —See Synonyms at **deceive.**

mis·lead·ing (mĭs-lē'dĭng) adj. Tending to mislead; deceptive. —**mis·lead·ing·ly** adv.

mis·like (mĭs-līk') tr.v. **-liked, -liking, -likes. 1.** To disapprove of; dislike. **2.** *Archaic.* To be displeasing to.
~n. Dislike; disapproval. [Middle English *misliken,* Old English *mislīcian* : *mis-,* ill + *līcian,* to LIKE.]

mis·man·age (mĭs-măn'ĭj) tr.v. **-aged, -aging, -ages.** To manage badly or carelessly. —**mis·man·age·ment** n.

mis·match (mĭs-măch') tr.v. **-matched, -matching, -matches.** To match unsuitably or inaccurately, especially in marriage. —**mis·match'** (mĭs'măch') n.

mis·mate (mĭs-māt') tr.v. **-mated, -mating, -mates.** To mate or match unsuitably: *Those two are mismated.*

mis·name (mĭs-nām') tr.v. **-named, -naming, -names.** To call by a wrong or inappropriate name.

mis·no·mer (mĭs-nō'mər) n. **1.** An error in naming a person or place. **2.** A name wrongly or unsuitably applied to a person or object. [Middle English, from Norman French, from Old French *mesnommer,* to misname : *mes-,* wrongly, MIS- + *nommer,* to name, from Latin *nōmināre,* from *nōmen,* name.]

miso–, **mis–** *prefix.* Indicates hating, hatred, or hostility; for example, **misogyny, misandry.** [Greek, from *misein,* to hate, and *misos†,* hatred.]

mi·sog·a·my (mĭ-sŏg′ə-mē) *n.* Hatred of marriage. [MISO- + -GAMY.] **—mi·sog·a·mist** *n. & adj.*

mi·sog·y·ny (mĭ-sŏj′ə-nē) *n.* Hatred of or hostility toward women. [Greek *misogunia* : MISO- + -GYNY.] **—mi·sog·y·nist** *n. & adj.* **—mi·sog·y·nis·tic** (mĭ-sŏj′ə-nĭs′tĭk), **mi·sog·y·nous** (mĭ-sŏj′ə-nəs) *adj.*

mi·sol·o·gy (mĭ-sŏl′ə-jē) *n.* Hatred of reason, argument, or enlightenment. [Greek *misologia* : MISO- + -LOGY.] **—mi·sol·o·gist** *n.*

mis·o·ne·ism (mĭs′ə-nē′ĭz′əm) *n.* Hatred of change or innovation. [Italian *misoneismo* : MISO- + Greek *neos,* new.] **—mis·o·ne·ist** *n. & adj.*

mis·pick·el (mĭs′pĭk′əl) *n.* A mineral, **arsenopyrite** *(see).* [German, variant of earlier *Mispŭtl, Mispilt†.*]

mis·place (mĭs-plās′) *tr.v.* **-placed, -placing, -places.** **1. a.** To put in a wrong place. **b.** To lose; mislay. **2.** To bestow (faith, affection, or confidence, for example) wrongly, as on an improper, unsuitable, or unworthy person or idea: *Your loyalty to that firm is quite misplaced.* **—mis·place·ment** *n.*

mis·play (mĭs-plā′) *n.* A mistaken action in a game. ~*tr.v.* (mĭs-plā′) **misplayed, -playing, -plays.** To make a misplay of: *The outfielder misplayed the fly ball.*

mis·plead·ing (mĭs-plē′dĭng) *n. Law.* An error in pleading.

mis·print (mĭs-prĭnt′) *tr.v.* **-printed, -printing, -prints.** To print incorrectly. ~*n.* (mĭs′prĭnt′). An error in printing.

mis·pri·sion (mĭs-prĭzh′ən) *n. Law.* **1.** Maladministration of public office. **2.** Neglect in reporting a crime: *misprision of treason.* [Middle English, from Norman French *mesprisioun,* from *mesprendre* : *mes-,* wrongly, MIS- + *prendre,* to take, from Latin *praehendere,* to grasp, seize.]

mis·prize (mĭs-prīz′) *tr.v.* **-prized, -prizing, -prizes.** To undervalue; disparage.

mis·pro·nounce (mĭs′prə-nouns′) *tr.v.* **-nounced, -nouncing, -nounces.** To pronounce badly or incorrectly. **—mis·pro·nun·ci·a·tion** (mĭs′prə-nŭn′sē-ā′shən) *n.*

mis·quote (mĭs-kwōt′) *tr.v.* **-quoted, -quoting, -quotes.** To quote incorrectly. **—mis·quo·ta·tion** (mĭs′kwō-tā′shən) *n.*

mis·read (mĭs-rēd′) *tr.v.* **-read** (-rĕd′), **-reading, -reads.** **1.** To read inaccurately. **2.** To misinterpret: *misread her intentions.*

mis·re·mem·ber (mĭs′rĭ-mĕm′bər) *tr.v.* **-bered, -bering, -bers.** **1.** To recollect incorrectly. **2.** *Regional.* To forget.

mis·re·port (mĭs′rĭ-pôrt′) *tr.v.* **-ported, -porting, -ports.** To report mistakenly or falsely. ~*n.* An inaccurate or wrong report. **—mis·re·port·er** *n.*

mis·rep·re·sent (mĭs′rĕp′rĭ-zĕnt′) *tr.v.* **-sented, -senting, -sents.** **1.** To give an incorrect or misleading representation of: *misrepresented the facts of the case.* **2.** To serve incorrectly or dishonestly as an official representative of. **—mis·rep·re·sen·ta·tion** *n.* **—mis·rep·re·sen·ta·tive** *adj.* **—mis·rep·re·sent·er** *n.*

mis·rule (mĭs-rōōl′) *tr.v.* **-ruled, -ruling, -rules.** To rule wrongly, unjustly, or unwisely; misgovern. ~*n.* **1.** Misgovernment. **2.** Disorder or lawless confusion.

miss¹ (mĭs) *v.* **missed, missing, misses.** —*tr.* **1.** To fail to hit, reach, attain, catch, meet, or otherwise make contact with: *miss the target; missed the bus.* **2.** To fail to perceive, understand, or otherwise experience: *missed the subtlety of the argument.* **3.** To fail to accomplish or achieve: *You missed catching her by ten minutes.* **4.** To fail to be present for or perform: *We don't want to miss a day of work.* **5. a.** To leave out or omit: *My heart missed a beat. You missed a name in typing the list.* **b.** To overlook or let go by; let slip: *miss a chance.* **6.** To escape or avoid: *missed death by inches.* **7. a.** To discover the absence or loss of: *I was halfway home before I missed my gloves.* **b.** To feel the lack or loss of; yearn for (what is past or absent): *I miss the good old days.* —*intr.* **1.** To fail to hit or otherwise make contact with something: *She fired her final shot and missed again.* **2.** To be unsuccessful; fail. **3.** To misfire. **—miss out.** To fail to benefit from or achieve something desirable. Often used with *on: She missed out on getting a promotion.* ~*n.* A failure to hit, succeed, or find. [Middle English *missen,* Old English *missan,* from Germanic *missjan* (unattested); akin to MIS-.]

miss² *n., pl.* **misses. 1. Miss.** A title or form of address used when speaking to or of an unmarried woman or girl, used before her name. **2.** A title used in speaking to a woman, especially a young woman, used without her name: *I beg your pardon, miss.* **3.** An unmarried woman or girl. **4. Miss.** A title given to a young woman representing a town, country, institution, or the like at certain events, especially beauty contests: *Miss Sweden.* [Short for MISTRESS.]

Usage: In recent years criticism has been directed at the twofold titular classification of women into *Miss* and *Mrs.* — a distinction that, unlike the male *Master* and *Mr.,* is not restricted in terms of age. As the title of respect for a woman without regard for her marital status, *Ms.* is the equivalent of *Mr.,* the courtesy title for a man: *Ms. Smith; Ms. Judith Smith. Ms.* should not be used when a woman is addressed by her husband's given name and surname: *Ms. Green,* but not *Ms. Paul Green.* But *Ms.* is the appropriate courtesy title to use when a woman keeps her own name after marriage. If Kathleen Brown marries Roger Smith but does not change her name to Smith, she can be addressed as *Ms. Brown,* but *Mrs. Brown* is incorrect. Some women who keep their maiden name for

professional purposes use the title *Miss* in that context, while others use *Ms.* Though *Ms.* was controversial when it was first introduced, it has come to be widely used in business and professional situations, on forms, and in many social contexts. While many women consider it both important and convenient to use this title in social as well as business contexts, others prefer *Miss* or *Mrs.*

Miss. Mississippi (state).

mis·sal (mĭs′əl) *n.* **1.** A book containing all the prayers and responses necessary for celebrating the Roman Catholic Mass throughout the year. **2.** Any prayer book. [Middle English *messel,* from Medieval Latin *missāle,* from *missālis,* pertaining to the mass, from Late Latin *missa,* MASS.]

missel thrush. Variant of **mistle thrush.**

mis·shape (mĭs-shāp′) *tr.v.* **-shaped, -shaped** or **-shapen** (-shā′pən) **-shaping, -shapes.** To shape badly; deform.

mis·sile (mĭs′əl, mĭs′īl′) *n.* **1.** Any object or weapon that is fired, thrown, dropped, or otherwise projected at a target; a projectile. **2.** A **guided missile** *(see).* **3.** A **ballistic missile** *(see).* [Latin *missilis,* from *mittere* (past participle *missus*), to let go, send.]

mis·sile·ry, mis·sil·ry (mĭs′əl-rē) *n.* **1.** The science of making and using guided or ballistic missiles. **2.** Missiles collectively.

miss·ing (mĭs′ĭng) *adj.* **1.** Not present; absent; lost; lacking. **2.** *Military.* Unaccounted for after combat or maneuvers and possibly killed or injured.

missing link *n.* **1.** A theoretical primate postulated to bridge the evolutionary gap between the anthropoid apes and humans. **2.** Something needed to complete a series or solve a mystery.

mis·sion (mĭsh′ən) *n.* **1. a.** A body of persons sent to a foreign country, especially to conduct negotiations or establish relations. **b.** The business with which such a body of persons is charged. **2. a.** A body of persons sent to do missionary work in a foreign land. **b.** An establishment of missionaries abroad. **c.** The district assigned to a missionary. **d.** Missionary duty or work. **e.** A missionary building or compound. **f.** An organization for carrying on missionary work in any territory. **3.** A permanent diplomatic office in a foreign country. **4. a.** A journey undertaken to perform an assigned task, such as espionage or exploration. **b.** *Military.* A combat operation assigned to an individual or unit; especially, an air operation against an enemy. **5.** A church welfare establishment, especially in a large city: *a seaman's mission.* **6.** A church or congregation, especially of a Protestant church, without a resident minister. **7.** A series of special religious services to deepen or spread religious faith. **8.** An impelling task or duty; a vocation: *a woman with a mission.* ~*adj.* **1.** Of or pertaining to a mission. **2.** In the style of early Spanish missions of the southwestern United States: *mission furniture.* ~*v.* **missioned, -sioning, -sions.** —*tr.* **1.** To send on a mission. **2.** To organize or establish a mission among (a people) or in (a territory). —*intr.* To conduct a religious mission. [French, from Latin *missiō* (stem *missiōn-*), from *mittere* (past participle *missus*), to let go, send.] **—mis·sion·er** *n.*

mis·sion·ar·y (mĭsh′ə-nĕr′ē) *n., pl.* **-ies.** One who is sent on a mission; especially, a person sent to do religious or charitable work in some territory or foreign country. ~*adj.* **1.** Of or pertaining to missions or missionaries. **2.** Engaged in the activities of a mission or missionary. **3.** Acting with or characterized by zealous devotion to a cause.

Missionary Ridge. Ridge extending from southern Tennessee to northern Georgia. A section of the ridge near Chattanooga was the site of a Union victory in the Civil War (November 25, 1863).

missis. Variant of **missus.**

Mis·sis·sip·pi¹ (mĭs′ə-sĭp′ē). *Abbr.* **Miss.** State of the southern United States, on the Gulf of Mexico, bounded by the Mississippi River in the west. Mississippi is the leading state in cotton production, and soya beans, rice, corn, and hay are also important. The state has vast reserves of oil and natural gas, and its manufactures include wood products, clothing, processed foods (including seafood), and chemicals. The first settlers were French (1699), and the area became part of Louisiana. It was controlled by the British (1763-79), then by the Spanish until it was ceded to the United States (1783). Jackson is the capital and largest city.

Mississippi². Chief river of the United States. Rising in the lake region of northern Minnesota, it flows 3,780 kilometers (2,348 miles) to the Gulf of Mexico through a delta in southern Louisiana. Its many tributaries include the Missouri, Ohio, Arkansas, and Red rivers. The Mississippi-Missouri system, 6,212 kilometers (3,860 miles) long, is the world's third-longest river after the Nile and Amazon. Its vast basin stretches into Canada and includes or touches 31 states.

Mis·sis·sip·pi·an (mĭs′ə-sĭp′ē-ən) *adj.* **1.** *Geology.* Of, belonging to, or designating the geologic time, system of rocks, and sedimentary deposits of the fifth period of the Paleozoic era, characterized by the submergence of extensive land areas under shallow seas. **2.** Of or pertaining to the state of Mississippi. ~*n.* **1.** *Geology.* The Mississippian period. Preceded by *the.* **2.** A native or inhabitant of Mississippi.

mis·sive (mĭs′ĭv) *n.* A letter or message, especially a formal or official one. Sometimes used humorously. [Noun, Middle English phrase *letter missive,* letter sent by superior authority, from Medieval Latin *litterae missīvae* (plural); adjective, Medieval Latin *missīvus,* from Latin *mittere* (past participle *missus*), to let go, send.]

Mis·so·lon·ghi (mĭs′ə-lông′gē). *Greek* **Me·so·lón·gi·on** (mĕs′ə-lông′gē-ôn′). Port of west-central Greece. On the north shore of the Gulf of Patras, it withstood two sieges by the Turks during the Greek War of Independence (1822–23 and 1825–26).

Mis·sou·ri[1] (mĭ-zo͝or′ē, -zo͝or′ə). *Abbr.* **Mo.** State of the central United States, bounded in the east by the Mississippi River. Prairies lie north of the Missouri, with the Great Plains to the west, the rolling hills of the Ozark Plateau in the south, and the Mississippi cotton lands to the southeast. The state produces lead, zinc, coal, iron ore, cattle, pigs, corn, soya beans, wheat, and cotton, but is a predominantly manufacturing state, with major transport equipment and food-processing industries. The area was under Spanish control (1762–1800) and passed to the United States with the Louisiana Purchase (1803). Jefferson City is its capital.

Missouri[2]. Longest river of the United States. It rises in the Rocky Mts. of Montana and flows 4,130 kilometers (2,565 miles) across the Great Plains to join the Mississippi near St. Louis. French explorers reached the river in the late 17th century.

mis·spell (mĭs-spĕl′) *tr.v.* **-spelled** or **-spelt** (-spĕlt′), **-spelling, -spells.** To spell incorrectly. **—mis·spell·ing** *n.*

mis·spend (mĭs-spĕnd′) *tr.v.* **-spent** (-spĕnt′), **-spending, -spends.** To spend improperly or extravagantly; squander.

mis·state (mĭs-stāt′) *tr.v.* **-stated, -stating, -states.** To state wrongly or falsely. **—mis·state·ment** *n.*

mis·step (mĭs-stĕp′) *n.* **1.** A misplaced or awkward step. **2.** An instance of wrong or improper conduct.

mis·sus, mis·sis (mĭs′ĭz, mĭs′ĭs) *n. Informal.* **1.** The mistress of a household. Usually preceded by *the.* **2.** One's wife. Usually preceded by *the.*

miss·y (mĭs′ē) *n., pl.* **-ies.** *Often* **Missy.** A familiar form of address to a young girl, especially a pert one.

mist (mĭst) *n.* **1.** A mass of fine droplets of water in the atmosphere, impairing visibility near the ground. **2.** Water vapor condensed on and clouding the appearance of a surface. **3.** Fine drops of any liquid, such as perfume, sprayed into the air. **4.** A colloidal suspension of a liquid in a gas. **5.** Something that dims or conceals sight or judgment. **6.** Something that produces or gives the impression of dimness or obscurity: *lost in the mists of time.*
~*v.* **misted, misting, mists.** *—intr.* To be or become obscured or misty; be blurred or concealed by or as if by a mist. Often used with *up.* *—tr.* To conceal or veil as if with a mist. [Middle English, Old English *mist,* from Germanic.]

mis·tak·a·ble (mĭ-stā′kə-bəl) *adj.* Capable of being mistaken or misunderstood. **—mis·tak·a·bly** *adv.*

mis·take (mĭ-stāk′) *n.* **1.** An error or fault. **2.** A misconception or misunderstanding.
~*v.* **mistook** (-sto͝ok′), **-taken** (-stā′kən), **-taking, -takes.** *—tr.* **1.** To understand wrongly; misinterpret: *"Aziz overrated hospitality, mistaking it for intimacy"* (E.M. Forster). **2.** To recognize or identify incorrectly: *We mistook her for her sister.* **3.** To judge incorrectly: *mistook her own talent.* *—intr.* To make a mistake. [Middle English *mistaken,* from Old Norse *mistaka,* to take in error : *miss-,* wrongly + *taka,* to TAKE.]

mis·tak·en (mĭ-stā′kən) *adj.* **1.** Wrong or incorrect in opinion, understanding, or perception. **2.** Based on error; wrong: *a mistaken view of the situation.* **—mis·tak·en·ly** *adv.* **—mis·tak·en·ness** *n.*

Mis·ter (mĭs′tər) *n.* **1.** *Abbr.* **Mr.** A title or form of address used when speaking to or of a man. It is usually written in its abbreviated form and placed before a man's surname: *Mr. Jones.* **2.** *Abbr.* **Mr.** A form of address used before a man's title of office: *Mr. Speaker.* **3.** The official term of address for certain military and naval personnel, as: **a.** A warrant officer. **b.** A flight officer. **c.** Any naval officer below the rank of commander. **d.** A cadet at a service academy. **4. mister.** *Informal.* A form of address used without a name when speaking to a man. [Alteration of MASTER.]

mist·flow·er (mĭst′flou′ər) *n.* A plant, *Eupatorium coelestinum,* of southeastern North America, having clusters of small, blue flowers.

mis·time (mĭs-tīm′) *tr.v.* **-timed, -timing, -times.** To time (a remark, for example) wrongly or inappropriately.

Mis·tin·guett (mĭs′tăN-gĕt′), stage name of Jeanne Bourgeois (1875–1956). French comedienne. She took her name from Miss Tinguett in the musical comedy *Miss Helyett.*

mis·tle thrush, mis·sel thrush (mĭs′əl) *n.* A European thrush, *Turdus viscivorus,* with a spotted breast. [Referring to its feeding on mistletoe berries.]

mis·tle·toe (mĭs′əl-tō′) *n.* **1.** A Eurasian parasitic shrub, *Viscum album,* having leathery evergreen leaves and waxy white berries. **2.** A mistletoe sprig, used as a Christmas decoration, under which kissing is traditionally permitted. [Middle English *mistilto,* Old English *misteltān* : *mistel,* mistletoe + *tān,* twig, from Germanic *tainaz* (unattested).]

mis·took. Past tense of **mistake.**

mis·tral (mĭs′trəl, mĭ-sträl′) *n.* A dry, cold, northerly wind that blows in squalls through the Rhône Valley and nearby areas toward the Mediterranean coast of southern France. [French, from Provençal, from Latin *magistrālis (ventus),* "master (wind)," from *magistrālis,* MAGISTRAL.]

mis·trans·late (mĭs′trăns-lāt′, mĭs′trănz-) *tr.v.* **-lated, -lating, -lates.** To translate (material, especially in a foreign language) wrongly. **—mis·trans·la·tion** *n.*

mis·treat (mĭs-trēt′) *tr.v.* **-treated, -treating, -treats.** To handle or treat roughly or wrongly; abuse. —See Synonyms at **abuse.** **—mis·treat·ment** *n.*

mis·tress (mĭs′trĭs) *n.* **1.** A woman in a position of authority, as the head of a college, household, or estate: *"Thirteen years had seen her mistress of Kellynch Hall"* (Jane Austen). **2.** A woman owning an animal or, formerly, a slave. **3.** A woman who has ultimate control over something: *mistress of the situation.* **4.** An entity personified as a woman having control or authority over something: *Britain was once mistress of the seas.* **5.** A woman who has mastered a skill: *a mistress of mechanical engineering.* **6. a.** A woman who has a continuing sexual relationship with a man to whom she is not married, especially one who receives financial support from the man. **b.** *Archaic.* A woman loved by a man. **7. Mistress.** A title or form of address used with a woman's name. Now archaic except in parts of Scotland. **8.** *Chiefly British.* A female schoolteacher. [Middle English, from Old French *maistresse,* from *maistre,* MASTER.]

mis·tri·al (mĭs-trī′əl, -trīl′) *n. Law.* **1.** A trial that becomes invalid because of a basic error in procedure. **2.** An inconclusive trial, such as one in which the jurors fail to agree on a verdict.

mis·trust (mĭs-trŭst′) *n.* Lack of trust; suspicion; doubt.
~*v.* **mistrusted, -trusting, -trusts.** *—tr.* To regard without confidence; be wary or suspicious of. *—intr.* To be wary or doubtful. —See Synonyms at **uncertainty.** **—mis·trust·ful** *adj.* **—mis·trust·ing·ly** *adv.*

mist·y (mĭs′tē) *adj.* **-ier, -iest.** **1.** Consisting of or resembling mist: *a misty rain.* **2.** Obscured or clouded by or as if by mist. **3.** Lacking in clarity; vague: *misty ideas.* **—mist·i·ly** *adv.* **—mist·i·ness** *n.*

mis·un·der·stand (mĭs-ŭn′dər-stănd′) *tr.v.* **-stood** (-sto͝od′), **-standing, -stands.** To understand incorrectly; misinterpret.

mis·un·der·stand·ing (mĭs-ŭn′dər-stăn′dĭng) *n.* **1.** A failure to understand correctly. **2.** A disagreement or quarrel.

mis·un·der·stood (mĭs-ŭn′dər-sto͝od′) *adj.* **1.** Understood wrongly or incorrectly. **2.** Not appreciated or given sympathetic understanding: *Is she a misunderstood genius or merely a crank?*

mis·use (mĭs-yo͞os′) *n.* Also **mis·us·age** (-yo͞o′sĭj). Improper or wrong use; misapplication.
~*tr.v.* (mĭs-yo͞oz′) **-used, -using, -uses.** **1.** To use wrongly or incorrectly. **2.** To mistreat or abuse. —See Synonyms at **abuse.** **—mis·us·er** *n.*

mis·val·ue (mĭs-văl′yo͞o) *tr.v.* **-ued, -uing, -ues.** To value or estimate incorrectly.

mis·word (mĭs-wûrd′) *tr.v.* **-worded, -wording, -words.** To express incorrectly; word inaccurately.

M.I.T. Massachusetts Institute of Technology.

Mitch·ell (mĭch′əl), **John** (1870–1919). U.S. labor leader. He became a miner at the age of 12 and first led a successful strike of miners in 1897. From 1898 to 1908 he was president of the United Mine Workers. The anthracite coal miners' strike of 1902 brought him national recognition as an effective labor leader.

Mitchell, Margaret (1900–49). U.S. writer. Her only novel, *Gone with the Wind* (1936), won the Pulitzer Prize (1937). The film of the same name, a Hollywood epic, was released in 1939.

Mitchell, William, known as "Billy" (1879–1936). U.S. army officer. He served as commander of the U.S. air forces in World War I. Afterward he embarked on a campaign urging the strategic importance of a strong military air force. His public criticism of senior officers reluctant to adopt his ideas led to his court-martial, demotion, and resignation (1926). He was posthumously elevated to the rank of major general (1942) after the early days of World War II had proved correct his theories about air power.

mite[1] (mīt) *n.* Any of various small arachnids of the order Acarina (or Acari), some of which are parasitic. They may infest foods and carry disease. [Middle English *mite,* Old English *mīte,* from Germanic *mītōn* (unattested).]

mite[2] *n.* **1. a.** A very small amount of money or contribution. **b.** A **widow's mite** *(see).* **2.** A coin of very small value, especially a former Flemish coin. **3.** The smallest bit or slightest thing: *not a mite of sympathy.* **4.** Any very small object or creature. [Middle English (originally in the phrase "not worth a mite"), from Middle Dutch *mīte,* probably of the same origin as MITE (arachnid).]

mi·ter (mī′tər) *n.* Also *chiefly British* **mi·tre.** **1.** A tall, pointed hat with peaks in front and back, worn by bishops and certain other ecclesiastics. **2. a.** A thong for binding the hair, worn by women in ancient Greece. **b.** The ceremonial headdress worn by ancient Jewish high priests. **3.** A covering or top of a chimney that keeps out rain and debris while permitting the release of smoke. **4. a.** A **miter joint** *(see).* **b.** The edge of a piece of material that has been prepared for making a miter joint. **c.** A **miter square** *(see).*
~*v.* **mitered, -tering, ters.** Also *chiefly British* **mitre, -tred, -tring, -tres.** *—tr.* **1.** To bestow a miter upon. **2.** To join with a miter joint. *—intr.* To meet in a miter joint. [Middle English, from Old French, from Latin *mitra,* from Greek, headband, priest's headdress.]

miter box *n.* **1.** A box open at the ends with sides slotted to guide a saw in cutting miter joints. **2.** A device for handsaws that may be set to guide cuts at various degrees.

miter joint *n.* A joint made by beveling each of two surfaces to be joined, usually at a 45° angle, to form a 90° corner.

miter square *n.* A carpenter's square with a blade set at 45° or at an adjustable angle.

Mithgarthr. Variant of **Midgard.**

Mith·ra·ism (mĭth′rə-ĭz′əm, mĭth′rā-) *n.* A Persian religious cult that flourished in the late Roman Empire, in the first three centuries A.D., rivaling Christianity. See **Mithras.** **—Mith·ra·ic** (mĭ-thrā′ĭk) *adj.* **—Mith·ra·ist** (mĭth′rə-ĭst, mĭth′rā-, mĭ-thrā′ĭst) *n.* & *adj.*

mistletoe *Viscum album (above) is one of several species of this parasitic plant that grows on trees. The berries are poisonous to humans but are eaten safely by birds. The seeds—in the center of the fruit—are spread to new trees through the birds' droppings. The mistletoe was foremost among the magical plants of Europe from prehistoric times; it has been identified as the "golden bough" mentioned in Virgil's* Aeneid.

miter *A miter worn by St. Maurice in a painting by the 16th-century German artist Matthias Grünewald. Miters, which first came into use in the 11th century, were modeled originally on the papal crown.*

mith·ra·my·cin (mĭth′rə-mī′sĭn) *n.* An antibiotic that prevents the growth of cancer cells and is used mainly in the treatment of cancer of the testicle. [From Medieval Latin *mithridatum* (see **mithridate**) + (STREPTO)MYCIN.]

Mith·ras (mĭth′rəs). Also **Mith·ra** (-rə). *Persian Mythology.* The god of light and guardian against evil, often identified with the sun. [Latin, from Greek, from Old Persian *mithra-*, from Sanskrit *Mitra*, Vedic god.]

mith·ri·date (mĭth′rə-dāt′) *n.* A substance thought to be an antidote against poison. [Medieval Latin *mithridatum*, from Late Latin, antidote, from Latin, dogtooth violet (used as an antidote). See **mithridatism**.] —**mith·ri·dat·ic** (mĭth′rə-dăt′ĭk) *adj.*

mith·ri·da·tism (mĭth′rə-dā′tĭz′əm) *n.* Tolerance for a poison acquired by taking gradually larger doses of it. [After *Mithridates* VI, king of Pontus (132–63 B.C.), said to have acquired tolerance for poison.]

mit·i·cide (mĭt′ĭ-sīd′) *n.* An agent that kills mites. —**mit·i·cid·al** (mĭt′ĭ-sīd′l) *adj.* [MIT(E) (arachnid) + -CIDE.]

mit·i·gate (mĭt′ĭ-gāt′) *tr.v.* **-gated, -gating, -gates.** —*tr.* **1.** To moderate (a quality or condition) in force or intensity; alleviate: *mitigate anger; mitigate heat.* **2.** To serve to lessen the gravity of (an offense); extenuate: *mitigating circumstances.* —See Synonyms at **relieve.** —See Usage note at **militate.** [Middle English *mitigaten*, from Latin *mītigāre*, from *mītis*, gentle, mild.] —**mit·i·ga·ble** (mĭt′ĭ-gə-bəl) *adj.* —**mit·i·ga·tion** (mĭt′ĭ-gā′shən) *n.* —**mit·i·ga·tive** (mĭt′ĭ-gā′tĭv), **mit·i·ga·to·ry** (mĭt′ĭ-gə-tôr′ē, -tōr′ē) *adj.* —**mit·i·ga·tor** *n.*

Mitilíni. See **Mytilene.**

mi·to·chon·dri·on (mī′tə-kŏn′drē-ən) *n., pl.* **-dria** (-drē-ə). *Biology.* A microscopic body or organelle found in the cytoplasm of eukaryotic cells, consisting of two sets of membranes. The inner membrane is invaginated, and is the site of energy production by the process of cellular respiration. Also called "chondriosome." [New Latin : Greek *mitos*, thread + *khondrion*, small grain, diminutive of *khondros*.] —**mi·to·chon·dri·al** *adj.*

mi·to·gen (mī′tə-jən) *n.* An agent that induces mitosis in cells. [MITO(SIS) + -GEN.] —**mi·to·gen·ic** (mīt′ə-jĕn′ĭk) *adj.* —**mi·to·ge·nic·i·ty** (mīt′ə-jə-nĭs′ĭ-tē) *n.*

mi·to·sis (mī-tō′sĭs) *n. Biology.* A type of cell division in which the nucleus divides to produce two daughter cells, each with the same number of chromosomes as the parent cell. Also called "karyokinesis." Compare **meiosis.** See **anaphase, metaphase, prophase, telophase.** [New Latin : Greek *mitos*, a thread + -OSIS.] —**mi·tot·ic** (mī-tŏt′ĭk) *adj.* —**mi·tot·i·cal·ly** *adv.*

mi·tral (mī′trəl) *adj.* **1.** Of or resembling a miter. **2.** Pertaining to a mitral valve. [New Latin *mitrālis*, from Latin *mitra*, MITER.]

mitral valve *n.* The heart valve between the left atrium and the left ventricle that regulates blood flow from the atrium to the ventricle.

mitre. *Chiefly British.* Variant of **miter.**

mitt (mĭt) *n.* **1.** A type of glove that extends over the hand but only partially covers the fingers. **2.** A mitten. **3.** A large leather padded glove worn by baseball catchers and first basemen. **4.** *Slang.* The hand. [Short for MITTEN.]

mit·ten (mĭt′n) *n.* A covering for the hand that encases the thumb separately and the four fingers together. Also called "mitt." [Middle English *mytayne*, from Old French *mitaine*, from Vulgar Latin *medietāna* (unattested), "skin-lined glove cut off at the middle," from Latin *medietās*, half, from *medius*, middle.]

Mit·ter·rand (mē′tä-räN′), **François Maurice Marie** (1916–). French president (1981–). A World War II Resistance fighter, he lost the presidential election to Charles De Gaulle in 1965. He lost again to Giscard d'Estaing in 1974 and was finally elected in 1981.

mit·ti·mus (mĭt′ə-məs) *n., pl.* **-muses. 1.** *Law.* A writ committing a person to prison. **2.** *British Archaic.* A dismissal. [Latin, "we send," the first word of such a writ, from *mittere*, to send.]

mitz·vah (mĭts′və) *n., pl.* **mitzvoth** (mĭts′vōth′, -vōt′) or **-vahs.** *Judaism.* **1.** A command enjoined by the Scriptures. **2.** A meritorious act. [Hebrew *miṣwāh*, "(divine) commandment," from *ṣiwwāh*, to command.]

mix (mĭks) *v.* **mixed, mixing, mixes.** —*tr.* **1. a.** To combine or blend (ingredients or elements) into one mass or mixture so that the constituent parts are indistinguishable: *mix sugar and egg yolks.* **b.** To create or form by adding ingredients together: *mix a cake; mixing purple from red and blue.* **c.** To add (an ingredient or element) to another: *mix flour into the batter.* **2.** To combine; bring together: *mix business and pleasure.* **3.** To consume (different types of drink or food) in succession: *mixed gin and wine and was sick.* **4.** To crossbreed. **5.** To combine (two or more sounds) for broadcasting or recording. —*intr.* **1. a.** To become mixed or blended together. **b.** To be capable of being blended together: *Oil and water do not mix.* **2. a.** To join in socially or get along easily with others: *She does not mix well at parties.* **b.** To associate oneself with a group of people: *mixed with the jet set.* **3.** To be crossbred. ~*n.* **1.** An act of mixing. **2. a.** A product of mixing; a mixture: *a good mix of people at the party.* **b.** A mixture of ingredients packaged and sold commercially: *a cake mix.* [Back-formation from *mixed, mixt,* from Middle English, from Old French *mixte,* from Latin *miscēre* (past participle *mixtus*), to mix.] —**mix·a·ble** *adj.*

> **Synonyms:** amalgamate, blend, coalesce, combine, compound, fuse, merge, mingle.

Mix (mĭks), **Thomas Edwin,** known as "Tom" (1880–1940). U.S. actor. He began working as a cowboy in Oklahoma in 1906 and soon afterward started appearing in Wild West shows and silent motion pictures. Before his retirement in 1928, he appeared in some 100 feature films, always wearing a white suit, black boots, and a ten-gallon hat.

mixed (mĭkst) *adj.* **1.** Composed of or involving a variety of differing, sometimes conflicting entities or elements: *mixed feelings; got a mixed reception from the critics; mixed-ability classes.* **2.** Composed of or involving people of different sex, race, or social class: *a joke not fit for mixed company.* —See Synonyms at **miscellaneous.**

mixed bag *n. Informal.* An assortment or collection of diverse elements.

mixed blessing *n.* An event or situation that has disadvantages as well as its more obvious advantages.

mixed crystal *n. Chemistry.* A crystalline material composed of two or more compounds that have crystallized in a single lattice but have retained their chemical identity.

mixed doubles *pl.n.* A doubles game, as in tennis or badminton, with each team consisting of a male and a female.

mixed farming *n.* The farming of both crops and livestock on the same farm.

mixed grill *n.* A dish consisting of a variety of broiled meats, such as lamb chops and bacon.

mixed marriage *n.* A marriage between persons of different races or religions.

mixed metaphor *n.* A succession of metaphors that produce an incongruous or ludicrous effect, as: *Her mounting ambition was soon bridled by a wave of opposition.*

mixed nerve *n.* A nerve containing both sensory and motor nerve fibers.

mixed number *n.* A number, such as 7¼, made up of an integer and a fraction.

mixed-up (mĭkst′ŭp′) *adj. Informal.* Emotionally confused: *a mixed-up kid.*

mix·er (mĭk′sər) *n.* **1.** One that mixes. **2.** A sociable person: *She was a good mixer with people of all ages.* **3.** A device, especially a mechanical or electrical device, that blends or mixes substances or ingredients. **4.** A beverage, such as soda water or ginger ale, used in diluting alcoholic drinks. **5.** *Electronics.* A circuit or device for combining two or more signals or sounds into a single output. **6.** An informal dance or party arranged to give members of a group an opportunity to get acquainted.

mix·o·lyd·i·an (mĭk′sə-lĭd′ē-ən) *adj. Music.* Of or designating a Greek mode represented on the white keys of the piano keyboard by a descending diatonic scale from G to G. [Greek *mixoludios,* half-Lydian : *mixo-,* half + *ludios,* Lydian.]

Mix·tec (mēs-tĕk′, mēsh-) *n., pl.* **-tecs** or collectively **Mixtec. 1.** A member of an American Indian people inhabiting Mexico. **2.** The language of this people. —**Mixtec** *adj.*

mix·ture (mĭks′chər) *n.* **1.** Something produced by mixing. **2.** Anything consisting of diverse elements. **3.** A fabric made of different kinds of thread or yarn. **4.** The act or process of mixing or of being mixed. **5.** *Chemistry.* Any composition of two or more substances that are not chemically bound to each other. **6.** A liquid medicine containing a combination of different drugs, such as a suspension of a solid in a liquid. [French, from Latin *mixtūra,* from *miscēre* (past participle *mixtus*), to mix.]

mix up *tr.v.* **1.** To confuse: *I always mix her up with her sister.* **2.** To put into disorder. **3.** To associate with a group or activity of a usually undesirable nature: *He got mixed up with a bad crowd.*

mix-up (mĭks′ŭp′) *n.* **1.** A state of confusion; a muddle. **2.** *Informal.* A fight or melee.

Mi·zar (mī′zär′) *n.* The star at the crook of the handle of the Big Dipper. [Arabic *mi'zar,* veil, cloak.]

miz·zen, miz·en (mĭz′ən) *n.* **1.** A fore-and-aft sail set on the mizzenmast. **2.** A mizzenmast. [Middle English *mesan, meseyn,* from Old French *misaine,* from Italian *mezzana,* mizzen sail, from *mezzano,* middle, from Latin *mediānus,* MEDIAN.] —**miz·zen** *adj.*

miz·zen·mast (mĭz′ən-məst, -măst′, -mäst′) *n.* **1.** The third mast aft on sailing ships carrying three or more masts. **2.** A **jigger mast** (see).

miz·zle¹ (mĭz′əl) *intr.v.* **-zled, -zling, -zles.** To rain in fine, mistlike droplets; drizzle. [Late Middle English *misellen,* perhaps from Middle Dutch *miezelen,* to mist.] —**miz·zle** *n.*

miz·zle² *intr.v.* **-zled, -zling, -zles.** *British Slang.* To leave suddenly; vanish; decamp. [18th century : origin obscure.]

mk. 1. mark. **2.** markka.

mks meter-kilogram-second (system of units).

mksA meter-kilogram-second-ampere (system of units).

mkt. market.

ml milliliter.

ML, M.L. Medieval Latin.

MLD minimum lethal dose.

M.Litt. Master of letters. [Latin *Magister Litterarum.*]

Mlle. Mademoiselle.

Mlles. Mesdemoiselles.

M.L.S. Master of Library Science.

MLW mean low water.

mm millimeter; millimeters.

MM. Messieurs.

m.m. with the necessary changes having been made. [Latin *mutatis mutandis.*]

Mme. Madame.

Mmes. Mesdames.

mmf, m.m.f. magnetomotive force.

mmHg millimeter of mercury (unit of pressure).

M.Mus. Master of Music.
Mn The symbol for the element manganese.
MN Minnesota (with Zip Code).
M.N. Merchant Navy (in Britain).
mne·mon·ic (nĭ-mŏn′ĭk) *adj.* Pertaining to, assisting, or designed to assist the memory.
~*n.* A device, such as a formula or rhyme, used as an aid in remembering. [Medieval Latin *mnēmonicus,* from Greek *mnēmonikos,* from *mnēmōn,* mindful.] **—mne·mon·i·cal·ly** *adv.*
mne·mon·ics (nĭ-mŏn′ĭks) *n. Used with a singular verb.* A system for improving or developing the memory.
Mne·mos·y·ne (nĭ-mŏs′ə-nē, nĭ-mŏz′-). *Greek Mythology.* The goddess of memory, mother of the Muses. [Latin, from Greek *mnēmosunē,* memory, from *mnasthai,* to remember.]
Mngr. Monseigneur; Monsignor.
-mo *suffix.* Indicates the specified number of leaves formed by folding a larger sheet of paper; used after numerals or the names of numerals; for example, **duodecimo,** which is generally written "12 mo" and called by printers "twelvemo." [Latin ablative ending of ordinals, after the preposition *in,* in, as in *duodecimo,* from *duodecimus,* twelfth.]
Mo The symbol for the element molybdenum.
MO Missouri (with Zip Code).
MΩ megohm.
mo. month.
m.o., M.O. **1.** mail order. **2.** medical officer. **3.** money order.
Mo. Missouri.
mo·a (mō′ə) *n.* Any of various large, long-necked, flightless birds of the family Dinorthidae, native to New Zealand and now extinct for over a century. [Maori.]
Mo·ab (mō′ăb′). Ancient kingdom east of the Dead Sea, in an area that is now part of Jordan.
Mo·ab·ite (mō′ə-bīt′) *n.* **1.** A descendant of Moab, the son of Lot. Genesis 19:37. **2.** A native of Moab. **—Mo·ab·ite** *adj.*
moan (mōn) *n.* **1.** A low, sustained, mournful sound, usually indicative of sorrow or pain. **2.** Any similar sound: *the moan of the wind.* **3.** *Informal.* A complaint or grievance.
~*v.* **moaned, moaning, moans.** *—intr.* **1.** To utter a moan or moans. **2.** To make a sound resembling a moan: *The wind moaned through the trees.* **3.** To lament, grieve, or complain: *moaned about his problems.* *—tr.* **1.** To complain; bewail: *She moaned that she had been cheated.* **2.** To utter with a moan or moans. **—See Synonyms at cry.** [Middle English *mone,* complaint, from Old English *mān* (unattested), complaint, from Germanic.]
moat (mōt) *n.* **1.** A wide, deep ditch, usually filled with water, surrounding a medieval town, fortress, or castle as a protection against assault. **2.** A ditch similar to a moat, as one surrounding an area where animals in a zoo are confined.
~*tr.v.* **moated, moating, moats.** To surround with or as if with a moat. [Middle English *mote,* originally, "mound," "embankment," from Old French *mote, motte,* clod, hill, mound, probably from (unattested) Gaulish *mutt(a)†.*]
mob (mŏb) *n.* **1.** A large, disorderly crowd or throng; a rabble. **2.** The common people, regarded as ignorant, brutish, or fickle; the masses. Preceded by *the.* **3.** *Informal.* An organized gang of criminals. **4.** *Informal.* Any indiscriminate or loosely associated group of persons or things. **5.** *Australian.* A flock or herd of animals.
~*tr.v.* **mobbed, mobbing, mobs.** **1.** To crowd around and jostle or annoy, especially in anger or excessive enthusiasm: *The fans mobbed the singer.* **2.** To crowd into (a place): *Crowds mobbed the fairgrounds.* **3. a.** To attack violently, usually in a crowd or mob. **b.** To surround and attack (a wounded member of one's own species or a member of another species). Used especially of birds. [Shortening of earlier *mobile,* from Latin *mōbile (vulgus),* "the fickle (crowd)," neuter of *mōbilis,* MOBILE.]
mob·cap (mŏb′kăp′) *n.* A large, high cap trimmed with frills and ribbons, worn indoors by women in the 18th and early 19th centuries. [From earlier *mob,* "negligee," "informal attire," earlier, "slattern," variant of *mab,* short for the name *Mabel.*]
mo·bile (mō′bəl, -bēl′, -bīl′) *adj.* **1.** Capable of moving or of being moved from place to place. **—See Usage note at movable. 2.** Moving quickly from one state to another: *a mobile face.* **3.** Changing or capable of changing from one social class or level to another: *an upwardly mobile generation.* **4.** Flowing freely; not viscous: *a mobile liquid.* **5. a.** *Military.* Equipped with transport and capable of rapid deployment: *a mobile unit.* **b.** *Informal.* Having one's own means of transport: *no longer mobile since she lost her license.* **c.** Incorporated in a vehicle and therefore capable of being driven from place to place: *a mobile library.*
~*n.* (mō′bēl′). An ornament or type of sculpture that is suspended and consists of parts that move, especially in response to air currents. [Old French *mobile,* from Latin *mōbilis,* from the root of *movēre,* to move.] **—mo·bil·i·ty** (mō-bĭl′ə-tē) *n.*
Mo·bile (mō-bēl′, mō′bēl′). A city in southwestern Alabama, at the head of Mobile Bay, an arm of the Gulf of Mexico. A major port, Mobile is an important shipbuilding center.
-mobile *suffix.* Indicates a specialized kind of vehicle; for example, **snowmobile.** [From AUTOMOBILE.]
mobile home *n.* A house trailer that is used as a permanent home and is usually hooked up to utilities.
mo·bi·lize (mō′bə-līz′) *v.* **-lized, -lizing, -lizes.** *—tr.* **1. a.** To make mobile or capable of movement. **b.** To put into circulation. **2.** To assemble, prepare, or put into operation for war or a similar emer-

gency: *mobilize troops.* **3.** To organize or gather together for a purpose. *—intr.* To become prepared for war or a similar emergency. [French *mobiliser.*] **—mo·bi·li·za·tion** *n.*
Mö·bi·us strip (mœ′bē-əs) *n.* A one-sided surface that can be formed from a rectangular strip by rotating one end 180° and attaching it to the other end. Also called "Möbius band." Compare **Klein bottle.** [After its inventor, August *Möbius* (1790–1868), German mathematician.]
mob·oc·ra·cy (mŏb-ŏk′rə-sē) *n., pl.* **-cies.** Political control by a mob. **—mob·o·crat** (mŏb′ə-krăt′) *n.* **—mob·o·crat·ic** (mŏb′ə-krăt′ĭk), **mob·o·crat·i·cal** *adj.*
mob·ster (mŏb′stər) *n.* A gangster.
Mo·bu·tu (mō-bōō′tōō), **Joseph Désiré** (1930–). President of Zaire. In September 1960, he took control of the Congo in a coup supported by the army. In 1967 he became president of the Congo (now Zaire).
Mobutu Lake. Formerly **Lake Al·bert** (ăl′bərt). A shallow body of water 160 kilometers (100 miles) long and 30 kilometers (18 miles) wide, lying above sea level in the Great Rift Valley on the border between Zaire and Uganda. Its high salinity is caused by rapid evaporation.
moc·ca·sin (mŏk′ə-sĭn) *n.* **1.** A soft flat-soled leather slipper worn by American Indians. **2.** A shoe or slipper resembling an Indian moccasin. **3.** A snake, the **water moccasin** *(see).* [Natick *mohkussin,* from Proto-Algonquian *maxkeseni* (unattested).]
moccasin flower *n.* Any of several orchids of the genus *Cypripedium.* See **lady's-slipper.**
mo·cha (mō′kə) *n.* **1.** A rich, pungent Arabian coffee. **2.** Coffee of high quality. **3.** A flavoring made of coffee often mixed with chocolate. **4.** A soft, thin glove leather made from goatskin or sheepskin. **5.** Dark olive brown. [Originally exported from *Mocha,* a port of Yemen.] **—mo·cha** *adj.*
mock (mŏk) *v.* **mocked, mocking, mocks.** *—tr.* **1.** To treat with scorn, ridicule, or contempt; deride. **2. a.** To mimic, as when teasing or in derision. **b.** To imitate; counterfeit. **3.** To frustrate the hopes of; disappoint. **4.** To challenge; defy: *To disregard the doctor's warning would be to mock fate.* *—intr.* To express scorn or ridicule. Often used with *at: They mocked at the idea.* **—See Synonyms at ridicule.**
~*n.* **1.** An act of mocking: *"Fools make a mock at sin"* (Proverbs 14:9). **b.** Mockery; derision. **2.** Something deserving of derision. **3.** Something simulated; an imitation or counterfeit.
~*adj.* Simulated; false; imitation: *a mock battle; mock cream.*
~*adv.* In an insincere or sham manner: *mock-sorrowful.* [Middle English *mokken, mocquen,* from Old French *mocquer,* to deride, from Vulgar Latin *moccāre* (unattested), probably from a root *mok-,* imitative of laughter.] **—mock·ing·ly** *adv.*
mock·er (mŏk′ər) *n.* **1.** One that mocks. **2.** *Informal.* A mockingbird.
mock·er·y (mŏk′ə-rē) *n., pl.* **-ies.** **1.** Scornful contempt; ridicule; derision. **2.** A derisive or contemptuous act or remark. **3.** An object of scorn or ridicule. **4.** A contemptible, shameful, or impudent imitation; a travesty: *The trial was a mockery of justice.* **5.** Something that is ludicrously futile or unsuitable: *His dishonesty made a mockery of our principles.*
mock-he·ro·ic (mŏk′hĭ-rō′ĭk) *n., pl.* **mock-heroics.** A satirical imitation or burlesque of the heroic manner or style. **—mock-he·ro·ic** *adj.* **—mock-he·ro·i·cal·ly** *adv.*
mock·ing·bird (mŏk′ĭng-bûrd′) *n.* Any of several New World birds of the family Mimidae that are noted for their ability to mimic other birds; especially, *Mimus polyglottus,* of the southern and eastern United States, a gray bird with white patches on the wings and tail.
mock moon *n.* A paraselene *(see).*
mock orange *n.* **1.** Any of several deciduous shrubs of the genus *Philadelphus,* having white, usually fragrant flowers. Also called "philadelphus," "syringa." **2.** Any of various other shrubs or trees having flowers or fruit resembling those of the orange.
mock sun *n.* A parhelion *(see).*
mock turtle soup *n.* Soup made from calf's head or veal and spiced to taste like real turtle soup.
mock up *tr.v.* To make a mockup of.
mock·up, mock-up (mŏk′ŭp′) *n.* **1.** A usually full-sized model of a building, machine, or structure, used for demonstration, study, or testing. **2.** A layout of printed matter.
Moctezuma. See **Montezuma II.**
mod¹ (mŏd) *n.* **1.** A fashionable style of dress that originated in England in the 1960's. **2.** A person who dresses in this or in a similar style.
~*adj.* **1.** In or characteristic of this style of dress. **2.** Stylishly up-to-date, especially in dress. [From *the Mods,* name of a style-conscious group of English youths, shortening of MODERN.]
mod² *n. Sometimes* **Mod.** An annual Gaelic meeting for the holding of literary and musical competitions. [Gaelic *mòd,* assembly, from Old Norse; akin to MOOT.]
mod³ *Mathematics.* modulus.
MOD, MoD Ministry of Defence (in Britain).
mod. **1.** moderate. **2.** *Music.* moderato. **3.** modern.
mo·dal (mōd′l) *adj.* **1.** Of, pertaining to, or characteristic of a mode. **2.** *Grammar.* Of, pertaining to, or expressing the mood of a verb. **3.** *Music.* Of, pertaining to, characteristic of, or composed in a mode, especially any of the modes typical of medieval church music. **4.** *Philosophy.* Of or pertaining to mode or form as opposed to

moccasin *There are two varieties of this poisonous pit viper: the water moccasin and the Mexican moccasin. The Mexican one shown here, of the species Agkistrodon bilineatus, is young; the yellow tip on the tail disappears in the adult.*

mockingbird *The mockingbird is so called because of its habit of imitating the calls of other birds. It is found throughout North and South America and feeds on fruit and insects.*

substance or attributes. **5.** *Logic.* Expressing or characterized by modality. **6.** *Statistics.* Of or pertaining to a statistical mode; most frequent, common, or typical.
~*n.* A modal auxiliary. [Medieval Latin *modālis,* from Latin *modus,* measure, mode.] **—mo•dal•ly** *adv.*

modal auxiliary *n. Grammar.* Any of a set of English verbs, including *can, may, must, ought, shall, should, will,* and *would,* that are characteristically used with other verbs to express mood or tense. Also called "modal verb."

mo•dal•i•ty (mō-dăl′ə-tē) *n., pl.* **-ties. 1.** The fact, state, or quality of being modal. **2.** A modal quality or attribute of something; a mode. **3.** *Logic.* The classification of propositions on the basis of whether they assert or deny the possibility, impossibility, contingency, or necessity of their content. **4.** *Medicine.* **a.** A method of therapy, usually physical, such as massage. **b.** An apparatus for such a therapy. **5.** Any of the five senses, such as smell or hearing.

modal logic *n.* The logical study of the formal properties of concepts such as necessity, contingency, possibility, or impossibility and the study of the modality of propositions.

mode (mōd) *n.* **1. a.** Manner, way, or method of doing or acting: *"The modern mode of travelling cannot compare with the old mail-coach system in grandeur and power"* (Thomas De Quincey). **b.** A particular form, variety, or manner: *a mode of communication.* **c.** A condition in which a specified operation can be performed: *switched the tape machine to the record mode.* **2.** The current or customary fashion or style. **3.** *Music.* **a.** Any of certain arrangements of the diatonic tones of an octave. The two chief modes in Western music have been the **major** and **minor** *(both of which see).* **b.** Any of several patterned arrangements characteristic of classical Greek and medieval church music. **4.** *Philosophy.* The particular form or manner in which an underlying substance, or some permanent aspect or attribute of it, is manifested. **5.** *Logic.* **a.** The arrangement or order of the propositions in a syllogism according to both quality and quantity. **b.** The modality of a proposition. **6.** *Statistics.* The value or item occurring most frequently in a series of observations or set of statistical data. Also called "norm." **7.** *Geology.* The mineral composition of a specific sample of igneous rock expressed in percentages of weight. **8.** *Physics.* Any of numerous patterns of vibration or wave motion, as of acoustic or electromagnetic waves, corresponding to resonant frequencies of physical systems. —See Synonyms at **fashion, method.** [French *mode,* fashion, from Latin *modus,* measure, manner, size, harmony, melody.]

mod•el (mŏd′l) *n.* **1.** A representation, usually smaller but built to scale, of a building or other structure. **2.** A preliminary pattern or representation of an item not yet constructed, serving as the plan from which the finished work, usually larger, will be produced. **3.** A tentative description of a system that accounts for its known properties and helps one to visualize or conceive of the system and to study it further: *Conflicting models of light depict it as consisting of waves and of particles.* **4.** A style or design of a product, especially one of a series: *Her car is last year's model.* **5. a.** A person or quality regarded as an example to be imitated or compared: *"in her temper, manners, mind, a model of female excellence"* (Jane Austen). **b.** A pattern, design, or arrangement serving as a basis for imitation: *a constitution on the American model.* **6.** A person or object serving as the subject for an artist or photographer. **7.** A person employed to display clothing, cosmetics, or the like for prospective buyers or in advertisements. **8.** A figure or object made in a malleable material, as clay or wax, especially one used by a sculptor as a preliminary work to be copied in a more durable or precious material, such as marble or bronze. —See Synonyms at **ideal.**
~*v.* **modeled, -eling, -els.** Also *chiefly British* **-elled, -elling.** —*tr.* **1.** To make or construct a model of. **2.** To plan, form, or construct according to a particular model or standard. **3. a.** To manipulate or work (a plastic substance): *model clay.* **b.** To make by shaping a plastic substance: *modeled animals in clay.* **4.** To display by wearing or posing with. **5.** In painting and drawing, to give a three-dimensional appearance to, as by shading. —*intr.* **1.** To make a model. **2.** To work as a model: *He models for a living.*
~*adj.* **1.** Serving as or used as a model. **2.** Serving as a standard of excellence; worthy of imitation: *a model husband.* [Obsolete French *modelle,* from Italian *modello,* from Vulgar Latin *modellus* (unattested), from Latin *modulus,* little measure, diminutive of *modus,* measure, rhythm, harmony.] **—mod•el•er** *n.*

Model T *n.* A trademark for Ford automobiles of 1908–28. Referred to formerly as a symbol of simplicity, economy, and dependability and later as a symbol of the old-fashioned. Also *slang* "tin lizzie."

mo•dem (mō′dĕm′) *n.* A device used in transmitting data between computers along a telephone line. It converts signals from a computer into audio signals and vice versa. [From *mo*dulator + *de*modulator.]

Mo•de•na (mō-dā′nə, mô′də-nə, -nä′). Capital of Modena province, Emilia-Romagna, northern Italy. It is a commercial and industrial center in a rich agricultural region. Motor vehicles, agricultural machinery, and shoes are made in Modena. An Etruscan town, colonized by the Romans (2nd century B.C.), who called it Mutina, it was ruled by the Este family from 1288 to 1859 and has many fine buildings.

mod•er•ate (mŏd′ər-ĭt) *adj. Abbr.* **mod. 1.** Keeping or kept within reasonable limits; not excessive or extreme: *moderate drinking.* **2.** Not violent; mild; calm: *a moderate climate.* **3. a.** Of medium or average quantity, quality, or extent: *a moderate increase in living standards.* **b.** Of relatively low or below average quantity, quality, or extent: *very moderate prices.* **4.** Opposed to radical or extreme views or measures, especially in politics.
~*n.* One who holds moderate opinions, especially in politics.
~*v.* (mŏd′ə-rāt′) **moderated, -ating, -ates.** —*tr.* **1.** To make less violent, severe, or extreme. **2.** *Physics.* To reduce the energy of (neutrons), especially by use of a moderator. —*intr.* **1.** To become less violent, severe, or extreme; abate. **2.** To act as a moderator. [Latin *moderātus,* past participle of *moderārī, moderāre,* to reduce, regulate, control; akin to *modus,* MODE.] **—mod•er•ate•ly** *adv.* **—mod•er•ate•ness** *n.* **—mod•er•at•ism** (mŏd′ər-ə-tĭz′əm) *n.*

moderate breeze *n.* A wind whose speed is 13 to 18 miles per hour (5.5 to 7.9 meters per second); force 4 on the Beaufort scale.

moderate gale *n.* A wind whose speed is 32 to 38 miles per hour (13.9 to 17.1 meters per second); force 7 on the Beaufort scale.

mod•er•a•tion (mŏd′ə-rā′shən) *n.* **1. a.** An act or instance of moderating. **b.** The state or quality of being moderate. **2.** Freedom from excess or extremes; temperance. **—in moderation.** In moderate amounts or degrees; within reasonable limits.

mod•e•ra•to (mŏd′ə-rä′tō) *adv. Abbr.* **mod.** *Music.* At a moderate tempo; slower than allegretto but faster than andante. Used as a direction. [Italian, from Latin *moderātus,* MODERATE.] **—mod•e•ra•to** *adj. & n.*

mod•er•a•tor (mŏd′ə-rā′tər) *n.* **1. a.** An arbitrator or mediator. **b.** One who presides over a meeting, assembly, or discussion group. **2.** The officer who presides over a synod or general assembly of the Presbyterian Church. **3.** *Physics.* A substance, such as water or graphite, that is used in a nuclear reactor to decrease the speed of fast neutrons, increase the likelihood of fission, and sustain a chain reaction.

mod•ern (mŏd′ərn) *adj. Abbr.* **mod. 1.** Of, pertaining to, or characteristic of recent times or the present: *modern science; modern dress.* **2.** Up-to-date; modish: *a very modern apartment with white walls and high-tech furniture.* **3.** Designating the period of history from about 1450 until the present day. **4.** Of, pertaining to, or characteristic of contemporary art, music, or drama; especially, avant-garde or experimental. **5. Modern.** Designating the form of a language that is in current use.
~*n.* **1.** One who lives in modern times. **2.** One who has modern ideas, standards, or beliefs; especially, an artist or writer who works in an avant-garde or experimental style. **3.** *Printing.* Any of various typefaces characterized by strongly contrasted heavy and thin parts. [French *moderne,* from Late Latin *modernus,* from *modō,* "just now," originally "to the measure," from *modus,* measure.] **—mo•dern•i•ty** (mə-dûr′nə-tē) *n.* **—mod•ern•ly** *adv.*

modern dance *n.* A style of contemporary dance based on ballet but using much freer and often more expressive bodily movements.

Modern English *n.* English since the early 16th century.

Modern Greek *n.* Greek since the early 16th century, divided into **Dhimotiki** and **Katharevusa** *(both of which see).*

Modern Hebrew *n.* The form of Hebrew, revived from ancient Hebrew, that is now in current use in Israel.

mod•ern•ism (mŏd′ər-nĭz′əm) *n.* **1. a.** Modern thought, character, or practice. **b.** Sympathy with modern ideas, practices, or standards. **2.** Something, such as a peculiarity of usage or style, that is characteristic of modern times. **3.** *Often* **Modernism.** In Christian Churches, any of various movements that attempt to adapt church teachings to take account of modern scientific and philosophical thought; especially, such a movement in the Roman Catholic Church in the late 19th and early 20th centuries. **4.** The theory or practice of modern art or literature. **—mod•ern•ist** *n. & adj.* **—mod•ern•ist•ic** (mŏd′ər-nĭs′tĭk) *adj.*

mod•ern•ize (mŏd′ər-nīz′) *v.* **-ized, -izing, -izes.** —*tr.* To make modern; bring up to date in technology, appearance, style, or character. —*intr.* To accept or adopt modern ways, views, procedures, or styles. **—mod•ern•i•za•tion** *n.* **—mod•ern•iz•er** *n.*

modern pentathlon *n.* A **pentathlon** *(see).*

mod•est (mŏd′ĭst) *adj.* **1.** Having or showing a moderate estimation of one's own talents, abilities, and value. **2.** Having a shy and retiring nature; reserved. **3.** Having a regard for decencies of behavior or dress. **4.** Quiet and humble in appearance; unpretentious: *a modest house.* **5.** Moderate; not extreme or excessive: *a modest charge.* —See Synonyms at **humble, shy.** [French *modeste,* from Latin *modestus,* "keeping due measure"; akin to *modus,* MODE.] **—mod•est•ly** *adv.*

mod•es•ty (mŏd′ĭ-stē) *n., pl.* **-ties.** The state or quality of being modest, especially: **1.** Lack of vanity or pretentiousness. **2.** Reserve or propriety in speech, dress, or behavior.

mod•i•cum (mŏd′ĭ-kəm) *n., pl.* **-cums** or **-ca** (-kə). A small or moderate amount or quantity. [Latin, short way, short time, from *modicus,* moderate, from *modus,* (due) measure.]

mod•i•fi•ca•tion (mŏd′ə-fĭ-kā′shən) *n.* **1.** The act of modifying or the condition of being modified. **2.** The result of modifying; a modified form. **3.** A small alteration, adjustment, or limitation: *a modification in the terms of the contract.* **4.** *Biology.* A physical change in an organism due to environment or activity that is not transmitted to the organism's descendants. **—mod•i•fi•ca•tive** (mŏd′ə-fĭ-kā′tĭv), **mod•i•fi•ca•to•ry** (mŏd′ə-fĭ-kə-tôr′ē, -tōr′ē, mŏd′ə-fĭk′ə-, mŏd′ə-fĭ-kā′tər-ē) *adj.* **—mod•i•fi•ca•tor** (mŏd′ə-fĭ-kā′tər) *n.*

mod•i•fi•er (mŏd′ə-fī′ər) *n.* **1.** One that modifies. **2.** *Grammar.* A word, phrase, or clause that limits or qualifies the sense of another word, phrase, or clause. Also called "qualifier."

mod•i•fy (mŏd′ə-fī′) *v.* **-fied, -fying, -fies.** —*tr.* **1.** To change in form or character, usually without fundamental transformation: *"the first* tools must have been natural objects only slightly modified" (V. Gordon Childe). **2.** To make less extreme, severe, or strong: *cannot be persuaded to modify her position in any way.* **3.** *Grammar.* To qualify or limit the meaning of. For example, *"wet"* modifies *"day"* in the phrase *a wet day.* **4.** *Linguistics.* To change (a vowel) by umlaut. —*intr.* To be or become modified. —See Synonyms at **change.** [Middle English *modifien,* to limit, moderate, from Old French *modifier,* from Latin *modificāre* : *modus,* a measure + *facere,* to do, make.] —**mod·i·fi·a·ble** (mŏd′ə-fī′ə-bəl) *adj.*

Mo·di·glia·ni (mō′dēl-yä′nē), **Amedeo** (1884–1920). Italian painter and sculptor who settled in Paris (1906), where he concentrated on chiseling heads in stone and painting portraits, mostly of women, in a characteristic elongated style.

mo·dil·lion (mō-dĭl′yən) *n. Architecture.* An ornamental bracket used in series under the cornice of the Corinthian, Composite, or Roman Ionic orders. [French *modillon,* from Italian *modiglione,* from Vulgar Latin *mutellio* (stem *mutellion-*), from *mutellus* (unattested), alteration of Latin *mutulus,* projecting block under cornice (Doric order).]

mo·di·o·lus (mō-dī′ə-ləs) *n., pl.* **-li** (-lī′). *Anatomy.* The central, conical, bony shaft of the cochlea. [New Latin, from Latin, hub of a wheel, bucket of a water wheel, diminutive of *modius,* a measure for grain.]

mod·ish (mō′dĭsh) *adj.* Being in or conforming to the prevailing or current fashion; stylish. [From MODE (fashion).] —**mod·ish·ly** *adv.* —**mod·ish·ness** *n.*

mo·diste (mō-dēst′) *n.* One who produces, designs, or deals in ladies' fashions. [French, from *mode,* MODE (fashion).]

Mo·dred (mō′drĭd). Also **Mor·dred** (môr′drĭd). In Arthurian legend, a knight of the Round Table who led a rebellion against his uncle, King Arthur, and fatally wounded him.

mod·u·lar (mŏj′ŏō-lər, mŏd′yə-) *adj.* **1.** Pertaining to, based on, or made up of modules: *a modular training scheme; modular furniture.* **2.** Of or pertaining to a modulus.

mod·u·late (mŏj′ŏō-lāt′, mŏd′yə-) *v.* **-lated, -lating, -lates.** —*tr.* **1.** To adjust or adapt to a certain measure or proportion; regulate; temper. **2.** To change or vary the pitch, intensity, or tone of: *modulated his voice to a confidential murmur.* **3.** *Electronics.* To vary the frequency, amplitude, phase, or some other characteristic of (a carrier wave). —*intr.* **1.** *Music.* To pass from one key or pitch to another by means of a regular melodic or chord progression. **2.** *Electronics.* To alter the frequency, amplitude, phase, or some other characteristic of a carrier wave. See **modulation.** [Latin *modulārī,* to measure off, set to a measure, play music, from *modulus,* diminutive of *modus,* measure, rhythm.] —**mod·u·la·tive** (mŏj′ŏō-lā′tĭv), **mod·u·la·to·ry** (mŏj′ŏō-lə-tôr′ē, -tōr′ē) *adj.*

mod·u·la·tion (mŏj′ŏō-lā′shən, mŏd′yə-) *n.* **1.** The act or process of modulating. **2.** *Music.* A passing from one key to another by means of a regular melodic or chord progression. **3. a.** A change in pitch or loudness of the voice; an inflection of the voice. **b.** The use of a particular intonation or inflection of the voice to convey meaning. **4.** *Electronics.* The variation of a property of an electromagnetic wave or signal, such as its amplitude, frequency, or phase, in a manner determined by another wave or signal, especially for the purpose of transferring information from an audible signal, such as the human voice, to a carrier wave suitable for radio or telephonic transmission.

mod·u·la·tor (mŏj′ŏō-lā′tər, mŏd′yə-) *n.* **1.** One that modulates. **2.** *Electronics.* A device or electric circuit used to modulate a carrier wave. See **modulation.** **3.** *Anatomy.* A receptive sensory end organ, found in light-adapted eyes, that is thought to be related to the discrimination of color.

mod·ule (mŏj′ŏōl, mŏd′yŏōl) *n.* **1.** A standard or unit of measurement. **2. a.** *Architecture.* The part of a construction used as a standard to which the rest is proportioned. **b.** A standardized structural component used as a unit in a building or item of furniture. **3.** *Electronics.* A self-contained assembly of electronic components and circuitry. **4.** Any of the self-contained, often separable units that make up a spacecraft. **5.** Any of a set of distinct learning units that make up a course of education or training. [Latin *modulus,* MODULUS.]

mod·u·lus (mŏj′ŏō-ləs, mŏd′yə-) *n., pl.* **-li** (-lī′). *Abbr.* **m, M** **1.** *Physics.* A constant or coefficient that expresses the degree to which a substance possesses some property; especially, a ratio of the stress on a solid to the strain produced, measuring the elastic properties of the material. See **bulk modulus, rigidity modulus, Young's modulus.** **2.** *Mathematics.* **a.** The absolute value *(see)* of a complex number, a negative quantity, or a vector. **b.** *Abbr.* **mod** A number or quantity that produces the same remainder when divided into each of two quantities. **c.** The number by which a logarithm in one system must be multiplied to obtain the corresponding logarithm in another system. [New Latin, from Latin, diminutive of *modus,* measure.]

mo·dus op·er·an·di (mō′dəs ŏp′ə-rän′dē, -dī′) *n., pl.* **modi operandi** (mō′dē). **1.** The manner in which something operates. **2.** A person's manner of working. [Latin.]

mo·dus vi·ven·di (mō′dəs vĭ-vĕn′dē, -vĕn′dī′) *n., pl.* **modi vivendi** (mō′dē). **1.** A way of living. **2.** A practical compromise enabling contending parties to coexist peacefully, either indefinitely or pending a final settlement of their differences. [Latin.]

Moe·so·goth (mē′sə-gŏth′, mē′zə-) *n.* A Goth of Moesia, an ancient region corresponding approximately to modern Bulgaria and Serbia. —**Moe·so·goth·ic** (mē′sə-gŏth′ĭk, mē′zə-) *adj.*

mo·fette (mō-fĕt′) *n.* **1.** An opening in the earth from which carbon dioxide and other gases escape, usually marking the last stage of volcanic activity. **2.** The gases escaping from such a fissure. [French, "fetid exhalation," from Italian (Neapolitan dialect) *mofetta,* from *muffa,* mustiness, probably of imitative origin.]

Mog·a·dish·u (mŏg′ə-dĭsh′ŏō). Capital and main port of Somalia, on the Indian Ocean. A commercial and financial center, it exports fruit, livestock, hides, and skins. Founded by the Arabs in the 9th or 10th century, it was taken by the sultan of Zanzibar (1871), was sold to Italy (1905), and became the capital of Italian Somaliland.

Mogen David. Variant of **Magen David.**

mo·gul[1] (mō′gəl) *n.* A small mound on a ski slope. [Probably of Scandinavian origin.]

mogul[2] *n.* **1.** A very rich or powerful person: *an oil mogul.* **2.** A kind of heavy steam locomotive. [From MONGOL.]

Mo·gul (mō′gəl, mō-gŭl′) *n.* Also **Mo·ghul, Mu·ghal** (mŏō-gŭl′) (for sense 1). **1. a.** One of the followers of Baber, who conquered India in 1526 and founded a Muslim empire that lasted formally until 1857. See **Great Mogul. b.** A descendant of a follower of Baber. **2.** A Mongol or Mongolian. [Persian and Arabic *mugūl,* MONGOL.] —**Mo·gul** *adj.*

Mo·hács (mō′häch′). Small industrial town and important Danube port in southern Hungary near the Yugoslav border. The annihilation of a Hungarian army by the Ottoman Turks (1526) resulted in their domination of Hungary for more than 150 years and paved the way for the Turkish sieges of Vienna. The retreating Turks were defeated at the Second Battle of Mohács (1687).

mo·hair (mō′hâr′) *n.* **1.** The hair of the Angora goat. **2.** A shiny, heavy, shaggy yarn or fabric made of this hair, often with a mixture of cotton or wool. **3.** An upholstery fabric with mohair pile. [Variant (influenced by HAIR) of earlier *moochary, mocayare,* from Italian *moccaiaro,* from Arabic *mukhayyar,* "select," "choice," cloth of goat's hair, from *khayyara,* to choose.] —**mo·hair** *adj.*

Mohammed. See **Muhammad.**

Mohammed Ali. See **Mehemet Ali.**

Mohammedan. Variant of **Muhammadan.**

Moharram. Variant of **Muharram.**

Mo·ha·ve, Mo·ja·ve (mō-hä′vē) *n., pl.* **-ves** or collectively **Mohave** or **Mojave.** A member of a Yuman-speaking North American Indian people formerly living along the Gila and Colorado rivers. —**Mo·ha·ve** *adj.*

Mohave Desert. See **Mojave Desert.**

Mo·hawk[1] (mō′hôk′) *n., pl.* **-hawks** or collectively **Mohawk.** **1.** A member of the Iroquoian-speaking North American Indian people that occupied the territory from the Mohawk River to the St. Lawrence. **2.** The language of this people. —**Mo·hawk** *adj.*

Mohawk[2]. River, *c.* 225 kilometers (140 miles) long, of central New York State, flowing to the Hudson River. Its fertile valley was the scene of many battles in the French and Indian Wars and the American Revolution and was long an important gateway to the West.

Mo·he·gan (mō-hē′gən) *n., pl.* **-gans** or collectively **Mohegan.** A member of an Algonquian-speaking North American Indian people formerly living in Connecticut. —**Mo·he·gan** *adj.*

Mo·hen·jo-Da·ro (mō-hĕn′jō-där′ō). Ruined ancient city on the Indus River in the Sind province of Pakistan, dating from *c.* 2500 to 1500 B.C.

Mohican. Variant of **Mahican.**

Mo·ho (mō′hō′) *n.* The **Mohorovičić discontinuity** *(see).*

Mo·hock (mō′hŏk′) *n.* A member of a band of young aristocrats who terrorized London, England, in the early 18th century. [Variant of MOHAWK.]

Mo·holy-Nagy (mō′hoi-nŏd′yə), **Laszlo** (1895–1946). Hungarian painter and photographer. He made "photograms" and "space modulators" out of plastic at the Bauhaus in the 1920's. In 1937 he settled in the United States, where his ideas influenced commercial and industrial design.

Mo·ho·ro·vi·čić discontinuity (mō′hə-rō′və-chĭch′) *n.* The boundary between the earth's crust and mantle, ranging in depth from about 3 miles (5 kilometers) under ocean basins to 19 to 22 miles (30 to 35 kilometers) under continents. Also called "Moho." [After Andrija *Mohorovičić* (1857–1936), Yugoslav geophysicist.]

Mohs scale (mōz) *n.* A scale for determining the relative hardness of a mineral according to its resistance to scratching by one of the following minerals, arranged in order of increasing hardness: 1. talc; 2. gypsum; 3. calcite; 4. fluorite; 5. apatite; 6. orthoclase; 7. quartz; 8. topaz; 9. corundum; 10. diamond. [After Friedrich *Mohs* (1773–1839), German mineralogist who devised it.]

mo·hur (mō′ər, mə-hŏōr′) *n.* **1.** A monetary unit equal to ½ of the rupee of Nepal. See feature at **currency.** **2.** A gold coin, formerly used in India, equal to 15 rupees. [Hindi *muhur, muhr,* from Persian *muhr,* a seal.]

moi·dore (moi′dôr′, -dōr′, moi-dôr′, -dōr′) *n.* A former Portuguese gold coin. [Earlier *moyodore,* from Portuguese *moeda d'ouro,* "coin of gold" : *moeda,* from Latin *monēta,* MONEY + *d'ouro,* "of gold."]

moi·e·ty (moi′ə-tē) *n., pl.* **-ties. 1.** A half. **2.** A part, portion, or share of indefinite size. **3.** *Anthropology.* Either of two basic social divisions that make up a people on the basis of unilateral descent. [Middle English *moite, moitie,* from Old French *moite,* from Latin *medietās* (stem *medietāt-*), half, from *medius,* middle.]

moil (moil) *intr.v.* **moiled, moiling, moils. 1.** To toil or slave. Used chiefly in the phrase *toil and moil.* **2.** To churn about. —*n.* **1.** Toil; drudgery. **2.** Confusion; turmoil. [Middle English *moillen,* to moisten, smear, from Old French *moillier,* to moisten, paddle in mud, from Vulgar Latin *molliāre* (unattested), from Latin *mollis,* soft.]

Moi·rae (moi′rī′) *pl.n. Greek & Roman Mythology.* The **Fates** *(see).* [Greek.]

moi·ré (mwä-rā′) *n.* Also **moire** (mwär). **1.** Cloth, especially silk, that has a watered or wavy pattern. **2.** A watered pattern produced on cloth by engraved rollers. [French, from *moire, mouaire,* from MOHAIR (the fabric originally used for this pattern).] —**moi·ré** *adj.*

moiré pattern *n.* A pattern produced by superimposing a repetitive design, such as a grid, on a slightly displaced design, either the same or different, to produce a pattern distinct from its components.

moist (moist) *adj.* **moister, moistest. 1.** Slightly wet or damp. **2.** Filled with moisture. **3.** Humid. —See Synonyms at **wet.** [Middle English, from Old French *moiste,* probably from Vulgar Latin *muscidus* (unattested), moldy, wet, alteration of Latin *mūcidus,* from *mūcus,* mucus.] —**moist·ly** *adv.* —**moist·ness** *n.*

mois·ten (mois′ən) *v.* **-tened, -tening, -tens.** —*tr.* To make moist. —*intr.* To become moist. —**mois·ten·er** *n.*

mois·ture (mois′chər) *n.* Diffuse wetness that can be felt as vapor in the atmosphere or as condensed liquid on the surfaces of objects; dampness. [Middle English, from Old French *moistour,* from *moiste,* MOIST.]

mois·tur·ize (mois′chə-rīz′) *tr.v.* **-ized, -izing, -izes.** To add moisture to (the skin, for example).

mois·tur·iz·er (mois′chə-rī′zər) *n.* A cosmetic lotion or cream applied to the skin to soften it and counter dryness.

Mojave. Variant of **Mohave.**

Mo·ja·ve Desert or **Mo·ha·ve Desert** (mō-hä′vē). Arid region of southern California. Part of the Great Basin, it has low mountains and broad valleys. Its mineral reserves include iron, potash, gold, and silver. Death Valley National Monument is included in the region.

moke (mōk) *n. Slang.* **1.** *British.* A donkey. **2.** A dull or boring person. **3.** *Australian & New Zealand.* An old, broken-down horse. [19th century : origin obscure.]

mo·ko (mō′kō) *n., pl.* **-kos.** A Maori pattern of tattoos. [Maori.]

mol *Chemistry.* The symbol for **mole** (basic unit).

mol. molecular; molecule.

mo·lal (mō′ləl) *adj. Chemistry.* Of or designating a solution containing one mole of solute in 1,000 grams of solvent, usually water. Compare **molar.** [From MOLE (chemistry) + -AL.]

mo·lal·i·ty (mō-lăl′ə-tē) *n., pl.* **-ties.** *Chemistry.* The molal concentration of a solute, usually expressed as the number of moles of solute per 1,000 grams of solvent. See **molal.**

mo·lar[1] (mō′lər) *adj. Abbr.* **M** *Chemistry.* **1.** Designating a physical property that is measured for unit amount of substance, usually for one mole: *molar enthalpy.* **2.** Of or designating a solution that contains one mole of solute per liter of solution. Compare **molal.** [From MOLE (quantity).]

molar[2] *n.* A tooth with a broad crown for grinding food, located behind the premolars. A human being has twelve molars, three on each side of the upper and lower jaws.
—*adj.* **1.** Of or pertaining to the molar teeth. **2.** Capable of grinding. [Latin *molāris* (adjective), from *mola,* millstone.]

mo·lar·i·ty (mō-lăr′ə-tē) *n., pl.* **-ties.** *Chemistry.* The molar concentration of a solute, usually expressed as the number of moles of solute per liter of solution. See **molar.**

mo·las·ses (mə-lăs′īz) *n., pl.* **molasses.** A thick dark syrup produced in refining sugar. [Earlier *melasus, malassos,* from Portuguese *melaço,* from Late Latin *mellāceum,* must, from Latin *mel,* honey.]

mold[1] (mōld) *n.* Also *chiefly British* **mould. 1.** A hollow form or matrix for shaping a fluid or plastic substance: *a jelly mold.* **2.** A frame or model around or on which something is formed or shaped. **3.** Something that is made in or shaped on a mold. **4.** The pattern of a mold. **5.** General shape or form: *the oval mold of her face.* **6.** Distinctive shape, character, or type: *in the mold of her ancestors.* **7.** *Architecture.* A molding.
—*tr.v.* **molded, molding, molds.** Also *chiefly British* **mould, moulded, moulding, moulds. 1.** To shape in or on a mold. **2.** To form into a desired shape. **3.** To guide or determine the growth or development of; influence: *mold public opinion.* **4.** To make a mold of or from (sand, for example) prior to casting metal. [Middle English, probably from Old French *modle,* from Latin *modulus,* MODULE.] —**mold·a·bil·i·ty** *n.* —**mold·a·ble** *adj.*

mold[2] *n.* Also *chiefly British* **mould. 1.** A rough, variously colored coating that forms on organic matter, as food, owing to the action of saprophytic fungi. **2.** A fungus that causes mold. Compare **mildew.**
—*v.* **molded, molding, molds.** Also *chiefly British* **mould, moulded, moulding, moulds.** —*intr.* To become moldy. —*tr.* To cause to become moldy. [From Northern English dialectal *mouled,* moldy, from the past participle of *moul,* to become moldy, probably from Old Danish *mul,* mold, from Old Norse *mugla, mygla,* mold.]

mold[3] *n.* Also *chiefly British* **mould. 1.** Loose, friable soil that is rich in humus. **2.** *British Regional.* **a.** The earth; the ground. **b.** The earth of the grave. **c.** The grave. [Middle English, Old English *molde,* from Germanic *moldō* (unattested); akin to MEAL.]

Mol·da·vi·a (mōl-dā′vē-ə). The major grain-producing province of Romania, between the Prut River and the Carpathian Mts. Founded as a principality in the 14th century, it included Bukovina and Bessarabia but lost the former to Austria (1775) and the latter

---

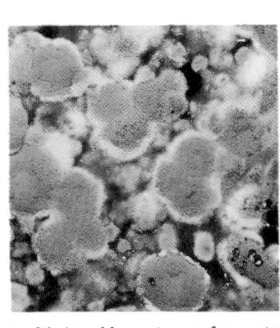

mold *A mold growing on fermenting elderberry wine.*

---

mollusk

WIDE DIVERSITY, UNDERLYING UNITY
Ancient and successful life forms

Mollusks include creatures as superficially different as slugs, snails, periwinkles, oysters, and squids. They do, however, have several features in common; they have soft, unsegmented bodies consisting of a head, muscular foot, and humped back—all covered by a tentlike mantle of skin. In most species this mantle secretes a shell. Mollusks, which inhabit watery environments from deep oceans to moist places on land, are one of the most ancient life forms. Some 35,000 extinct species are known, dating back nearly 600 million years.

Living mollusks can be divided into three main classes: gastropods, bivalves, and cephalopods. Gastropods, or "belly-footed" mollusks, such as slugs and snails, have sensory tentacles and generally a coiled shell, but in some the shell is reduced or absent. Bivalves, such as cockles, mussels, and oysters, have a shell in two hinged halves, or valves. Cephalopods, or "head-footed" mollusks, include squids and octopuses. These are the most highly evolved mollusks, with a well-developed nervous system.

There are also three lesser classes of mollusk: amphineura—some with crossbands of shell, some wormlike and without shells; monoplacophora—with one-piece, capshaped shells; and scaphopods—tiny, burrowing, tubular-shelled creatures.

SNAIL *The thousands of species of snail are typical gastropods, with a conical shell, eyes on stalks, and a large foot on which they move.*

OCTOPUS *The common octopus grows to a width of almost 10 feet. Other cephalopods range from about 2 inches across to* *about 30 feet in the case of the Pacific giant octopus. All have strong beaks and sharp eyes.*

MUSSEL *Bivalves, which include the mussel, feed and breathe by filtering some 10 gallons of water a day. Most bivalves move by extending a foot outside the hinged shell.*

---

to Russia (1812). Following the Crimean War, it united with Walachia (1859) to form modern Romania.

Mol·da·vi·an (mōl-dā′vē-ən, -dāv′yən) *n.* **1.** A native or inhabitant of Moldavia or the Moldavian S.S.R. **2.** The language of Moldavia, a form of Romanian. —**Mol·da·vi·an** *adj.*

Moldavian Soviet Socialist Republic. Landlocked republic of the southwest U.S.S.R. between the Prut and Dniester rivers. It was created (1940) from the Moldavian A.S.S.R. in the Ukraine and part of Bessarabia, the Moldavian territory gained by Russia in 1812 and held by Romania (1918–40). Its economy rests on sturgeon fisheries. Kishinev is the capital.

mold·board (mōld′bôrd′, -bōrd′) *n.* Also *chiefly British* **mould·board.** The curved plate of a plow that turns over the furrow. [MOLD (soil) + BOARD.]

mold·er (mōl′dər) *v.* **-ered, -ering, -ers.** Also *chiefly British* **mould·er.** —*intr.* To become dust gradually, by natural decay; crumble. Often used with *away.* —*tr.* To cause to decay or crumble. Often used with *away.* —See Synonyms at **decay.** [Perhaps from MOLD (soil).]

mold·ing (mōl′dĭng) *n.* Also *chiefly British* **mould·ing. 1.** *Architecture.* A decorative strip, as of stone, wood, or plaster, used as an embellishment on a surface, as a wall. Also called "mold." **2.** An object that has been molded.

mold·y (mōl′dē) *adj.* **-ier, -iest.** Also *chiefly British* **mould·y. 1.** Covered with or containing mold: *moldy bread.* **2.** Musty or stale, as from age or decay. **—mold·i·ness** *n.*

mole[1] (mōl) *n.* A small, pigmented growth on the human skin, usually slightly raised and brown, and sometimes hairy. It is a type of **nevus** *(see).* [Middle English *mool, mole,* Old English *māl.*]

mole[2] *n.* **1.** Any of various small, insectivorous, burrowing mammals of the family Talpidae, having thickset bodies with silky light brown to dark gray fur, rudimentary eyes, tough muzzles, and strong forefeet for digging. Most live underground. See **desman, shrew mole. 2.** The pelt of the mole, **moleskin** *(see).* **3.** A spy, especially a double agent. [Middle English *molle, mulle, mole,* from Middle Dutch *mol* and Medieval Latin *mulus,* both from an unknown Germanic source.]

mole[3] *n.* **1.** A massive stone wall used as a breakwater or jetty. **2.** The harbor enclosed by such a barrier. [French *môle,* from Medieval Greek *mōlos,* from Latin *mōlēs,* pier, dam, massive structure, mass.]

mole[4] *n.* A mass or tumor in the uterus, caused by the degeneration or abortive development of an ovum. [French *môle,* from Latin *mola,* "millstone" (since it is a hardened mass), MOLE (wall).]

mole[5] *n. Chemistry. Symbol* **mol** The amount of a substance that has a weight in grams numerically equal to the molecular weight of the substance. [German *Mol,* short for *Molekulargewicht,* molecular weight.]

mole cricket *n.* Any of various burrowing crickets with short wings and front legs well adapted for digging and shearing.

mo·lec·u·lar (mə-lĕk′yə-lər) *adj. Abbr.* **mol.** Pertaining to, consisting of, caused by, or existing between molecules.

molecular beam *n. Physics.* A parallel stream of atoms or molecules, having a low pressure such that the number of collisions between molecules within the beam is negligible. It is used to study atomic and nuclear properties and chemical reactions.

molecular biology *n.* The field of biology in which the structure and development of biological systems are analyzed in terms of the physics and chemistry of their molecular constituents. **—molecular biologist** *n.*

molecular film *n.* A surface film of thickness comparable to that of a single molecule.

molecular formula *n.* A type of chemical formula that indicates the number of each type of atom in each molecule of a compound. Compare **empirical formula, structural formula.**

molecular weight *n. Abbr.* **mol. wt.** *Chemistry.* The sum of the atomic weights of a molecule's constituent atoms. Also called "formula weight."

mol·e·cule (mŏl′ə-kyo͞ol′) *n. Abbr.* **mol. 1.** A stable configuration of atomic nuclei and electrons bound together by electrostatic and electromagnetic forces. It is the simplest structural unit that displays the characteristic physical and chemical properties of a compound. **2.** A small particle; a very tiny bit. [French *molécule,* from New Latin *molecula,* diminutive of Latin *mōlēs,* mass, bulk.]

mole·hill (mōl′hĭl′) *n.* A small mound of loose earth thrown up by a burrowing mole. **—make a mountain out of a molehill.** To exaggerate a minor problem.

mole-rat (mōl′răt′) *n.* A rodent, the **bandicoot** *(see).*

mole·skin (mōl′skĭn′) *n.* **1.** The short, soft, silky, dark gray fur of the mole. Also called "mole." **2. a.** A heavy-napped cotton twill fabric. **b. moleskins.** Clothing, especially trousers, of this fabric.

mo·lest (mə-lĕst′) *tr.v.* **-lested, -lesting, -lests. 1.** To disturb, torment, or annoy. **2.** To accost and harass sexually. [Middle English *molesten,* to vex, molest, from Old French *molester,* from Latin *molestāre,* to annoy, from *molestus,* troublesome.] **—mo·les·ta·tion** (mō′lĕ-stā′shən) *n.* **—mo·lest·er** *n.*

Mo·lière (mōl-yâr′), born Jean Baptiste Poquelin (1622–73). French dramatist. His plays include *Les Précieuses Ridicules* (1659), *Tartuffe* (1664), *Le Misanthrope* (1666), *L'Avare* (1668), *Le Bourgeois Gentilhomme* (1670), and his last play, *Le Malade Imaginaire* (1673).

moll (mŏl) *n. Slang.* **1.** A female companion of a thief or gangster. **2.** A prostitute. [From *Moll,* nickname for the name *Mary.*]

mol·li·fy (mŏl′ə-fī′) *tr.v.* **-fied, -fying, -fies. 1.** To allay the anger of; placate; calm. **2.** To make gentler; soften or ease: *"with a countenance greatly mollified by the softening influence of tobacco"* (Charles Dickens). —See Synonyms at **pacify.** [Middle English *mollifien,* from Old French *mollifier,* from Latin *mollificāre,* to make soft : *mollis,* soft + *facere,* to make, do.] **—mol·li·fi·a·ble** *adj.* **—mol·li·fi·ca·tion** *n.* **—mol·li·fi·er** *n.* **—mol·li·fy·ing·ly** *adv.*

mol·lus·can, mol·lus·kan (mə-lŭs′kən) *adj.* Of or pertaining to the mollusks.
~*n.* A mollusk.

mol·lusk, mol·lusc (mŏl′əsk) *n.* Any invertebrate animal of the phylum Mollusca, having a soft body typically, protected by a shell. The group includes the snails and slugs, the clams and other bivalves, and the octopuses and squids. [French *mollusque,* from New Latin *Mollusca,* "the soft ones," from Latin *molluscus,* extension of *mollis,* soft.] **—mol·lus·cous** (mə-lŭs′kəs) *adj.*

Moll·wei·de projection (môl′vī′də, mōl′-) *n.* An equal-area map projection using an ellipsoidal shape and having straight lines for parallels of latitude and for the central meridian, other meridians being curved. It is used for representing the whole earth and often split into sections, with continental areas having their own central meridians. [After Karl *Mollweide* (died 1825), German mathematician and astronomer.]

mol·ly, mol·lie (mŏl′ē) *n., pl.* **-lies.** Any of several tropical and subtropical fishes of the genus *Mollienesia.* The males of some species have saillike dorsal fins and are bred in aquariums. [New Latin *Mollienesia,* after Comte François N. *Mollien* (1758–1850), French statesman.]

mol·ly·cod·dle (mŏl′ē-kŏd′l) *n.* A person of weak character who seeks to be pampered and protected.
~*tr.v.* **mollycoddled, -dling, -dles.** To be overprotective and indulgent toward. —See Synonyms at **pamper.** [British slang *molly,* milksop, from the name *Molly* + CODDLE.] **—mol·ly·cod·dler** *n.*

Mol·ly Ma·guire (mŏl′ē mə-gwīr′) *n.* **1.** A member of a secret society in Ireland that terrorized law officers attempting to evict tenants in the 1840's. **2.** A member of a secret society of Pennsylvania miners who terrorized mine owners from about 1865 to 1877 in order to secure better working conditions and better pay. [The name refers to the female disguise adopted by members.]

Mo·loch (mō′lŏk′, mŏl′ək) *n.* **1.** In the Old Testament, a god of the Ammonites and Phoenicians to whom children were sacrificed by burning. **2.** Anything regarded as demanding a terrible sacrifice. [Late Latin *Moloch,* from Greek *Molokh,* from Hebrew *Molekh.*]

Mo·lo·kai (mō′lə-kī′, mŏl′ə-). Island of Hawaii, between Oahu and Maui. The island is generally mountainous. On the northern coast is the site of a leper colony established (1860) by Father Damien.

Mol·o·tov (mŏl′ə-tôf′), **Vyacheslav Mikhailovich,** born Vyacheslav Mikhailovich Skriabin (1890–). Soviet politician. He joined the Bolsheviks in 1906 and took the surname Molotov, meaning "the hammer." He helped found *Pravda* in 1912 and became its acting editor. In 1939 he was made foreign secretary and cosigned, with Ribbentrop, the Hitler-Stalin pact. He remained foreign minister until 1949 and held the office again from 1953 to 1956.

Molotov cocktail *n.* A makeshift incendiary bomb made of a breakable container filled with inflammable liquid and provided with a rag wick. [After V.M. MOLOTOV.]

molt (mōlt) *v.* **molted, molting.** Also *chiefly British* **moult, moulted, moulting, moults.** *—intr.* To shed part or all of an outer covering, such as feathers, fur, or skin, that is replaced periodically by a new growth. *—tr.* To shed or cast off by molting.
~*n.* Also *chiefly British* **moult. 1.** The process of molting, which occurs in certain mammals, birds, and reptiles. See **ecdysis, exuviae. 2.** The material cast off during molting. [Middle English *moute,* Old English *mutian* (unattested), ultimately from Latin *mutāre,* to change.] **—molt·er** *n.*

mol·ten (mōl′tən). Archaic past participle of **melt.**
~*adj.* **1.** Made liquid by heat; melted. Said chiefly of substances, such as metal or rock, that melt at extremely high temperatures. **2.** Brilliantly glowing.

Molt·ke (mōlt′kə), **Helmuth Karl Bernhard, Count von** (1800–91). Prussian field marshal. He reorganized the Prussian army, and his brilliant tactics led to victories in the Danish War (1864), Austro-Prussian War (1866), and Franco-Prussian War (1870–71).

mol·to (mŏl′tō) *adv. Music.* Very; much. Used with directions: *molto sostenuto.* [Italian, from Latin *multum,* much (adverb), from *multus,* much (adjective).]

Mo·luc·cas (mə-lŭk′əz, mō-). Formerly **Spice Islands** (spīs). Group of islands in eastern Indonesia. They are hot, humid, and fertile, and their cloves, nutmeg, and other spices attracted traders and colonizers in the 16th and 17th centuries. They gained independence from the Dutch (1949) as a province of Indonesia. Ambon is the capital. **—Mo·luc·can** *n. & adj.*

mol. wt. molecular weight.

mo·ly (mō′lē) *n., pl.* **-lies. 1.** A mythical magic herb with black roots and white flowers, given to Odysseus to nullify the spells of Circe. **2.** A plant, the **lily leek** *(see).* [Latin *mōly,* from Greek *mōlu,* akin to Sanskrit *mūlam,* root.]

mo·lyb·de·nite (mə-lĭb′də-nīt′) *n.* A mineral form of molybdenum sulfide, MoS_2, that is the principal ore of molybdenum. [MOLYBDEN(UM) + -ITE.]

mo·lyb·de·num (mə-lĭb′də-nəm) *n. Symbol* **Mo** A hard, gray metallic element used in steel and tungsten alloys, fertilizers, dyes, enamels, and reagents. Atomic number 42, atomic weight 95.94, melting point 2,620°C, boiling point 4,800°C, specific gravity 10.2, valences 2, 3, 4, 5. [New Latin, from obsolete *molybdena,* from Latin *molybdaena,* galena, from Greek *molubdaina,* a lead (of a plumb line), from *molubdos,* lead.]

mo·lyb·dic (mə-lĭb′dĭk) *adj.* Of or containing molybdenum, especially in its higher valences.

mo·lyb·dous (mə-lĭb′dəs) *adj.* Of or containing molybdenum, especially in its lower valences.

mom (mŏm) *n. Informal.* Mother. [Short for MOMMA.]

mom-and-pop (mŏm′ən-pŏp′) *adj. Informal.* Of or designating a small business that is run by the owners: *a mom-and-pop grocery store.*

Mom·ba·sa (mŏm-bä′sə). Seaport and industrial center of southeastern Kenya. It is the country's chief port and also handles trade for Uganda and Tanzania.

mo·ment (mō′mənt) *n.* **1.** A brief, indefinite interval of time: *She'll join you in a moment.* **2. a.** A specific point in time: *at that moment.* **b.** The present time: *out at the moment.* **3.** The appropriate or right point in time: *This is the moment to act.* **4.** A particular period or event of importance or excellence: *"Swinburne's entry was for me a great moment"* (Max Beerbohm). **5.** Outstanding significance or value; importance: *matters of no great moment.* **6.** *Philosophy.* A phase or aspect of a logically developing process; a momentum.

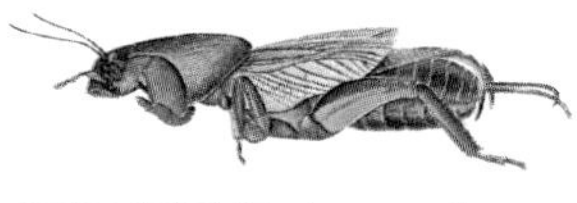

mole cricket *The brown mole cricket, which grows to more than 6 centimeters (about 2½ inches) long, spends most of its life in underground burrows. The male's burrow has a double entrance that acts like a loudspeaker. When the cricket "sings"—by rubbing its forewings together—the horn-shaped entrances amplify the sound so that it can be heard more readily by any passing females.*

mole-rat *Animals from several different families of rodents are given the name mole-rat because of their resemblance to the mole and their similar burrowing habits. This is an African mole-rat, a member of the family Bathyergidae, which lives and feeds almost entirely underground in the dry earth of the African plains.*

PRONUNCIATION KEY

ă, pat; ā, pay; âr, care;
ä, father, are; b, bib;
ch, church; d, deed; ĕ, pet;
ē, be; f, fife; g, gag; h, hat;
hw, which; ĭ, pit; ī, pie;
îr, pier; j, judge; k, kick;
l, lid, needle; m, mum;
n, no, sudden; ng, thing;
ŏ, pot; ō, toe; ô, paw, for;
oi, noise; ou, out; o͝o, book;
o͞o, boot; p, pop; r, roar;
s, sauce; sh, ship, dish;
t, tight; th, thin, path;
th, this, bathe; ŭ, cut; ûr, fur;
v, valve; w, with; y, yes;
z, zebra, size; zh, vision;
ə, about, item, edible, gallop, circus, peaceful

IN FOREIGN WORDS:

à, *Fr.* ami; œ, *Fr.* feu, *Ger.* schön; ü, *Fr.* tu, *Ger.* über; KH, *Ger.* ich, *Scot.* loch; N, *Fr.* bon; y′, *Fr.* Compiègne

STRESS MARKS:

Primary stress: ′ **in·cite′** (ĭn-sīt′)
Secondary stress: ′ **in′sight′** (ĭn′sīt′)

money spider Linyphia triangularis, *shown here about 1½ times life size, is one of many species called money spiders, from old popular beliefs associating them with wealth. On warm mornings following cool nights, they spin long gossamer threads that they use as parachutes. Rising warm air currents carry threads and spiders aloft. Cooler air brings them down again, sometimes hundreds of miles from their starting point.*

7. *Physics. Abbr.* **M a.** The product of a quantity, especially a force, and its perpendicular distance from a reference point. **b.** The rotation produced in a body when a force is applied; torque. See **moment of inertia. 8.** *Statistics.* The expected value of a positive integral power of a random variable. The first moment is the mean of the distribution. —See Synonyms at **importance.** [Middle English, from Old French, from Latin *mōmentum,* movement, MOMENTUM.]

Synonyms: *flash, instant, jiffy, minute, second, trice.*

mo·men·tar·i·ly (mō′mən-târ′ə-lē) *adv.* **1.** For only a moment. **2.** From moment to moment. **3.** Very soon.

mo·men·tar·y (mō′mən-tĕr′ē) *adj.* **1.** Lasting only a brief time. **2.** Occurring at every moment: *in momentary fear.* **3.** Short-lived; ephemeral. —See Synonyms at **transient.** [Latin *mōmentārius,* from *mōmentum,* MOMENT.] **—mo·men·tar·i·ness** *n.*

mo·ment·ly (mō′mənt-lē) *adv.* **1.** Every moment; from moment to moment: *"The throng momently increased"* (Edgar Allan Poe). **2.** For a moment. **3.** At any moment.

moment of inertia *n. Physics.* **1.** A measure of a body's resistance to angular acceleration, equal to: **a.** The product of the mass of a particle and the square of its distance from a reference point or line. **b.** The sum of the products of each mass element of a body multiplied by the square of its distance from an axis. **2.** The sum of the products of each element of an area multiplied by the square of its distance from a coplanar axis.

moment of momentum *n.* **Angular momentum** *(see).*

moment of truth *n.* **1.** The final kill in a bullfight. **2.** A decisive time on which much depends.

mo·men·tous (mō-mĕn′təs) *adj.* Of utmost importance or outstanding significance; having grave implications or consequences: *a momentous decision affecting our future.* **—mo·men·tous·ly** *adv.* **—mo·men·tous·ness** *n.*

mo·men·tum (mō-mĕn′təm) *n., pl.* **-ta** (-tə) or **-tums. 1.** *Physics. Symbol* **p a.** The product of a body's mass and linear velocity. Also called "linear momentum." **b.** See **angular momentum. 2.** The force associated with a moving body; impetus. **3.** Impetus or force gained through movement or progression: *the campaign's momentum.* **4.** *Philosophy.* A moment. [Latin *mōmentum,* motion, movement, from *movimentum* (unattested), from *movēre,* to move.]

mom·ma (mŏm′ə) *n.* Also **mom·mie, mom·my** (mŏm′ē), *pl.* **-mies.** *Informal.* A mother. [Variant of MAMA.]

Momm·sen (mŏm′zən), **Theodor** (1817–1903). German historian. His most noted work is his *History of Rome,* a re-creation of Roman society and culture based largely on his study of ancient coins, inscriptions, and literature. He was awarded the Nobel Prize for literature (1902).

mo·mus (mō′məs) *n., pl.* **-muses** or **-mi** (-mī′). One who finds fault; a critic of petty details. [After MOMUS.]

Mo·mus (mō′məs). *Greek Mythology.* The god of blame and ridicule. [Greek *Mōmos,* from *mōmos,* blame.]

Mon (mōn) *n., pl.* **Mons** or collectively **Mon. 1.** A member of the principal native people of the Pegu region in Burma. **2.** The Mon-Khmer language of this people. **—Mon** *adj.*

mon. 1. monastery. **2.** monetary.

Mon. Monday.

mon–. Variant of **mono–.**

mo·na (mō′nə) *n.* An African monkey, *Cercopithecus monas,* with a dark back and pale underparts. It is a type of guenon. [Portuguese or Spanish, monkey.]

mon·a·chism (mŏn′ə-kĭz′əm) *n.* Monasticism. [Middle English, from Medieval Latin *monachismus,* from Late Greek *monakhismos,* from *monakhos,* MONK.] **—mon·a·chal** (mŏn′ə-kəl) *adj.*

monacid, monacidic. Variants of **monoacid.**

Mon·a·co (mŏn′ə-kō′, mə-nä′kō). Small, independent principality on France's southern coast. Business interests, centered at La Condamine, gambling at the casino at Monte Carlo, and tourism are the main sources of revenue and spare the Monégasques (who are excluded from the gambling tables) taxation. The Genoese family of Grimaldi have ruled the principality since 1297. Monaco was at various times under the protection of Spain, Sardinia, and France, but its sovereignty was restored in 1861. Area, 1 square kilometer (.4 square miles). Population, 25,000. Capital, Monaco-Ville. See map at **France. —Mon·a·can** *adj. & n.*

mo·nad (mō′năd′, mŏn′ăd′) *n.* **1.** An independent, indivisible, and impenetrable unit of substance viewed as the basic constituent element of physical reality in the philosophy of Leibnitz. **2.** *Biology.* Any single-celled microscopic organism, especially a flagellate protozoan. Also called "monas." **3.** *Chemistry.* An atom or radical with a valence of 1. [Late Latin *monas* (stem *monad-*), unit, from Greek, from *monos,* single.]

mon·a·del·phous (mŏn′ə-dĕl′fəs, mō′nə-) *adj. Botany.* **1.** United by the filaments into a single tubelike group. Said of stamens. **2.** Having stamens thus united. Compare **diadelphous.** [MON(O)- + -ADELPHOUS.]

mo·nad·ic (mə-năd′ĭk) *adj.* Also **mo·nad·i·cal** (-ĭ-kəl). **1.** Considered or dealt with singly, not comparatively. **2.** *Biology & Chemistry.* Of or pertaining to a monad. **—mo·nad·i·cal·ly** *adv.*

mo·nad·ism (mō′nə-dĭz′əm, mŏn′ə-) *n. Philosophy.* The doctrine, as in the philosophy of Leibnitz, that monads are the basic constituent elements of physical reality.

mo·nad·nock (mə-năd′nŏk′) *n.* A mountain or rocky mass that has resisted erosion and stands isolated in a plain or peneplain. [After Mt. *Monadnock,* southern New Hampshire.]

Mon·a·ghan (mŏn′ə-gən, -hăn′). County in the Republic of Ireland. It is in the ancient province of Ulster and is largely agricultural, producing beef and dairy cattle. The county town, Monaghan, produces footwear.

mo·nan·drous (mə-năn′drəs) *adj.* **1.** *Botany.* Of, pertaining to, or characterized by monandry. **2. a.** Designating flowers having a single stamen. **b.** Having flowers bearing a single stamen. **3.** Of or pertaining to the custom of monandry. [MON(O)- + -ANDROUS.]

mo·nan·dry (mə-năn′drē) *n.* **1.** The custom of having one husband at a time. Compare **polyandry. 2.** *Botany.* The condition of being monandrous. [MON(O)- + -ANDRY.]

mo·nan·thous (mə-năn′thəs) *adj. Botany.* Bearing a single flower. [MON(O)- + Greek *anthos,* flower.]

mon·arch (mŏn′ərk, -ärk′) *n.* **1.** A person, such as a king or emperor, who is a head of state, usually by hereditary right and for life, and whose powers vary from those of an absolute ruler to the constitutionally limited powers of a figurehead. **2.** One that surpasses others in power or pre-eminence: *"Mont Blanc is the monarch of the mountains"* (Byron). **3.** A large orange and black butterfly, *Danaus plexippus,* having a wingspread of up to 4 inches. Also called "milkweed butterfly." [Late Latin *monarcha,* from Greek *monarkhēs* : *mono-,* sole + *-arkhes,* -ARCH.] **—mo·nar·chal** (mə-när′kəl), **mo·nar·chi·al** (mə-när′kē-əl), **mon·ar·chic** (mə-när′kĭk), **mon·ar·chi·cal** *adj.* **—mo·nar·chal·ly, mon·ar·chi·cal·ly** *adv.*

mo·nar·chi·an·ism (mə-när′kē-ə-nĭz′əm) *n.* A Christian heresy of the 2nd and 3rd centuries that denied the doctrine of the Trinity. [Late Latin *monarchiānī,* "the monarchians," from *monarchia,* MONARCHY.] **—mo·nar·chi·an** *n. & adj.*

mon·ar·chism (mŏn′ər-kĭz′əm) *n.* **1.** The principles of monarchy. **2.** Belief in or advocacy of monarchy. **—mon·ar·chist** (mŏn′ər-kĭst′) *n. & adj.* **—mon·ar·chis·tic** (mŏn′ər-kĭs′tĭk) *adj.*

mon·ar·chy (mŏn′ər-kē) *n., pl.* **-chies. 1.** Government by a monarch. **2.** A state that is ruled by or has a monarch. [Middle English *monarchie,* from Old French, from Late Latin *monarchia,* from Greek *monarkhia,* from *monarkhēs,* MONARCH.]

mo·nas (mō′năs′, mŏn′ăs′) *n., pl.* **monades** (mŏn′ə-dēz′). *Biology.* A **monad** *(see).* [Late Latin *monas* (stem *monad-*), MONAD.]

mon·as·ter·y (mŏn′ə-stĕr′ē) *n., pl.* **-ies.** *Abbr.* **mon.** The residence of a community of persons, especially monks, living under religious vows and usually in seclusion. [Middle English *monasterie,* from Late Latin *monastērium,* from Late Greek *monastērion,* from Greek *monazein,* to live alone, from *monos,* alone.] **—mon·as·te·ri·al** (mŏn′ə-stîr′ē-əl, -stĕr′ē-əl) *adj.*

mo·nas·tic (mə-năs′tĭk) *adj.* Also **mo·nas·ti·cal** (mə-năs′tĭ-kəl). **1.** Pertaining to or characteristic of monasteries or persons living in religious or contemplative seclusion. **2.** Loosely, leading an ascetic or celibate life.

~*n.* A person who lives a monastic life; especially, a monk. [Late Latin *monasticus,* from Late Greek *monastikos,* from Greek *monazein,* to live alone. See **monastery.**] **—mo·nas·ti·cal·ly** *adv.*

mo·nas·ti·cism (mə-năs′tə-sĭz′əm) *n.* The monastic life or system.

mon·a·tom·ic (mŏn′ə-tŏm′ĭk) *adj.* **1.** Occurring as single atoms, as helium. **2.** Having one replaceable atom or radical. **3.** Univalent. [MON(O)- + ATOMIC.]

mon·au·ral (mŏn-ôr′əl) *adj.* **1.** Designating sound reception by one ear. **2.** *Electronics.* Monophonic. [MON(O)- + AURAL.] **—mon·au·ral·ly** *adv.*

mon·ax·i·al (mŏn-ăk′sē-əl) *adj.* Having one axis; uniaxial.

mon·a·zite (mŏn′ə-zīt′) *n.* A pale yellow to reddish-brown mineral phosphate of rare-earth metals, chiefly cerium, yttrium, and lanthanum, usually together with thorium. [German *Monazit,* from Greek *monazein,* to live alone (because it is rare). See **monastery.**]

Monck or **Monk** (mŭngk), **George, 1st Duke of Albemarle** (1608–70). English military commander. Having earlier fought for Charles I, he was commissioned by Cromwell to put down rebellions in Ireland and Scotland in 1652, but in 1660 he led his forces successfully in support of the Royalist cause.

Mon·dale (mŏn′dāl′), **Walter Frederick,** known as "Fritz" (1928–) U.S. politician. A protégé of Hubert Humphrey, he was appointed to Humphrey's vacated Senate seat in 1964 and served there until 1976, when he was chosen as the running mate of Jimmy Carter. He held the office of vice president from 1977 to 1981.

Mon·day (mŭn′dē, -dā′) *n. Abbr.* **M., Mon.** The day of the week following Sunday; the first day of the working week. [Middle English *monday,* Old English *mōnan dæg,* moon's day (translation of Late Latin *lūnae diēs*) : *mōna,* MOON + *dæg,* DAY.]

mon·di·al (mŏn′dē-əl) *adj.* Of, pertaining to, or involving the whole world. [French, from ecclesiastical Latin *mundiālis,* from *mundus,* world.]

Mond process (mŏnd) *n.* An industrial process for producing nickel by heating the ore in carbon monoxide and decomposing, at a higher temperature, the nickel carbonyl vapor that is produced. [After Ludwig *Mond* (1839–1909), German-born British chemist and industrialist who developed the process.]

Mon·dri·an (môn′drē-än′), **Piet** (1872–1944). Dutch painter, influenced by cubism in Paris after 1910. He painted compositions in primary colors of space enclosed by lines and rectangles. He outlined his theories in his book *Neo-Plasticism* (1920).

monecious. Variant of **monoecious.**

Mo·né·gasque (mŏn′ə-găsk′, mô′nā-găsk′) *n.* A citizen of Monaco; a Monacan. [French, from Provençal *Mounegasc,* from *Mounegue,* MONACO.] **—Mo·né·gasque** *adj.*

PRONUNCIATION KEY

ă, pat; ā, pay; âr, care;
ä, father, are; b, bib;
ch, church; d, deed; ĕ, pet;
ē, be; f, fife; g, gag; h, hat;
hw, which; ĭ, pit; ī, pie;
îr, pier; j, judge; k, kick;
l, lid, needle; m, mum;
n, no, sudden; ng, thing;
ŏ, pot; ō, toe; ô, paw, for;
oi, noise; ou, out; o͝o, book;
o͞o, boot; p, pop; r, roar;
s, sauce; sh, ship, dish;
t, tight; th, thin, path;
th, this, bathe; ŭ, cut; ûr, fur;
v, valve; w, with; y, yes;
z, zebra, size; zh, vision;
ə, about, item, edible, gallop, circus, peaceful

IN FOREIGN WORDS:

à, *Fr.* ami; œ, *Fr.* feu, *Ger.* schön; ü, *Fr.* tu, *Ger.* über; KH, *Ger.* ich, *Scot.* loch; N, *Fr.* bon; y′, *Fr.* Compiègne

STRESS MARKS:

Primary stress: ′
in·cite′ (ĭn-sīt′)
Secondary stress: ′
in′sight′ (ĭn′sīt′)

Mo·nel (mō-nĕl′) *n.* A trademark for a corrosion-resistant alloy of nickel, copper, iron, and manganese. [After Ambrose *Monel*, president of International Nickel Co. (1873-1921).]

Mo·net (mō-nā′), **Claude** (1840-1926). French painter and a founder of impressionism. He began to experiment with depicting variations of light and atmosphere from the outset of his career. It was his painting *Impression: Sunrise* (1872) that gave the impressionists their name.

mon·es·trous (mŏn-ĕs′trəs) *adj.* Having one estrous cycle per year.

mon·e·tar·ist (mŏn′ə-tə-rĭst, mŭn′-) *n.* One who advocates the regulation of the money supply as a method of controlling and stabilizing the economy. —**mon·e·tar·ism** *n.* —**mon·e·tar·ist** *adj.*

mon·e·tar·y (mŏn′ə-tĕr′ē, mŭn′-) *adj. Abbr.* **mon. 1.** Of or pertaining to money. **2.** Of or pertaining to a nation's money supply, interest rates, or the like. —See Synonyms at **financial.** [Late Latin *monētārius,* from Latin *monēta,* MONEY.] —**mon·e·tar·i·ly** (mŏn′ə-târ′ə-lē, mŭn′-) *adv.*

mon·e·tize (mŏn′ə-tīz′, mŭn′-) *tr.v.* **-tized, -tizing, -tizes. 1.** To establish as legal tender. **2.** To make into money; mint. [Latin *monēta,* MONEY.] —**mon·e·ti·za·tion** *n.*

mon·ey (mŭn′ē) *n., pl.* **-eys** or **-ies. 1.** A commodity such as gold or silver that is legally established as an exchangeable equivalent of all other commodities and is used as a measure of their comparative values on the market. **2.** The official currency, as coins and negotiable paper notes, issued by a government. **3. a.** Assets and property that may be converted into actual currency; wealth: *She made her money in the property boom of the 1970's.* **b.** *Informal.* Opportunities to acquire wealth: *There's no money in writing.* **c.** Those who own wealth: *married into money.* **4.** An unspecified amount of money: *put a lot of money into the business. The company is still losing money.* **5.** *Often* **monies.** Sums of money: *sued for the return of all monies paid into the firm.* —**for one's money.** According to one's choice or way of thinking. —**in the money. 1.** Taking first, second, or third place in a dog or horse race. **2.** *Slang.* Having plenty of money; rich. —**on the money.** *Slang.* On target; exactly right. —**put money on. 1.** To place a bet on. **2.** *Informal.* To place one's confidence in. [Middle English *moneye,* from Old French *moneie,* from Latin *monēta,* money, mint, from *Monēta,* epithet of Juno, whose temple in Rome housed the mint.]

mon·ey·bags (mŭn′ē-băgz′) *n. Used with a singular verb. Slang.* A rich or miserly person.

mon·ey·chang·er (mŭn′ē-chān′jər) *n.* **1.** A person who exchanges money, as from one currency to another. **2.** A machine that holds and dispenses coins.

money cowry *n.* A small shell used as money in certain parts of Africa and the South Pacific. See **cowry.**

mon·eyed, mon·ied (mŭn′ēd) *adj.* **1.** Having a great deal of money. **2.** Representing or arising from the possession of money: *the triumph of moneyed interests over landed interests.*

mon·ey·er (mŭn′ē-ər) *n.* Formerly, a person authorized to coin or mint money. [Middle English *monyer,* from Old French *monier,* from Late Latin *monētārius,* minter, from *monēta,* MONEY.]

mon·ey·grub·ber (mŭn′ē-grŭb′ər) *n. Slang.* A person who is intent on accumulating money at every opportunity. —**mon·ey·grub·bing** *adj.*

mon·ey·lend·er (mŭn′ē-lĕn′dər) *n.* One whose business is lending money at an interest rate. —**mon·ey·lend·ing** *n.*

mon·ey·mak·er (mŭn′ē-mā′kər) *n.* **1.** One who accumulates wealth. **2.** An enterprise or product that is actually or potentially profitable. —**mon·ey·mak·ing** *n. & adj.*

money market *n.* The sphere of the financial market dealing in short-term securities and loans, gold, and foreign exchange.

money of account *n.* Any of various monetary units in which accounts are kept, which may or may not correspond to actual current denominations. Also called "unit of account."

money order *n. Abbr.* **m.o., M.O.** An order for the payment of a specific amount of money, usually issued and payable at a bank or post office.

money spider *n.* Any of various spiders of the family Linyphiidae, having a small reddish or black body. [From the belief that the tiny spider brings good luck.]

money spinner *n. British Informal.* A moneymaker. [Originally a name for the money spider, extended to promising or profitable businesses.]

money supply *n. Economics.* The total amount of money held by individuals and organizations in a country at a given time as measured by any of several indicators.

mon·ey·wort (mŭn′ē-wûrt′, -wôrt′) *n.* Any of several plants with rounded, coinlike leaves; especially, a creeping perennial, *Lysimachia hummularia,* of Europe and eastern North America, having opposite leaves and yellow flowers. Also called "creeping Jenny." [From the coinlike shape of its leaves.]

mon·ger (mŭng′gər, mŏng′-) *n.* **1.** A dealer in a specified commodity. Usually used in combination: *ironmonger.* **2.** A person promoting something specified and usually undesirable. Used in combination: *scandalmonger; warmonger.* ~*tr.v.* **mongered, -gering, -gers.** To peddle or deal in. [Middle English *mongere,* Old English *mangere,* from *mangian,* to traffic, from Germanic *mangōjan* (unattested), from Latin *mangō,* (fraudulent) dealer.]

mon·go (mŏng′gō) *n., pl.* **mongo.** A Mongolian monetary unit equal to ¹/₁₀₀ of the tugrik. See feature at **currency.** [Mongolian.]

---

money

THE MEANS OF BUYING AND SELLING
From internal bartering to international credit cards

Ancient civilizations such as the Egyptians and Babylonians traded by barter—a farmer, for instance, would trade livestock for its equivalent in other goods. This was a clumsy way of doing business. Transactions speeded up when the first coins appeared in Asia Minor in about 700 B.C., and their use later spread throughout the Mediterranean world, the Greeks minting large numbers of coins bearing artistic designs. The Chinese were using a form of coin (a miniature of a knife or spade with the exchange value of the real thing) by the 7th century B.C.

Although paper money had been used in China in the 7th century A.D., it was not until the 11th century that it was issued in bulk—when the Mongol emperor Kublai Khan paid his soldiers in paper currency. In 1661 the first European banknotes were issued in Stockholm, and the first Bank of England notes—redeemable in gold—appeared in London in the 1690's.

Today coins have little intrinsic value and banknotes can no longer be converted into gold. Even this "token" money has been partly replaced by the use of checks for large payments. The check, in turn, is being replaced by the credit card.

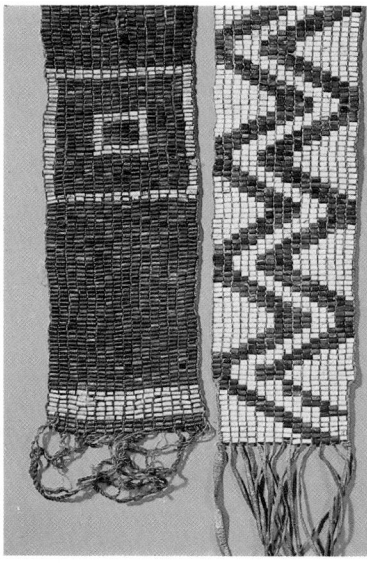

SHELL MONEY *Early settlers in North America commonly used as money Indian wampum—tubular white and mauve shells threaded into strings or belts. Wampum was made legal tender in Massachusetts in 1641.*

SILVER DOWRY *A bride of a hill tribe in North Vietnam wears silver coins in her bridal headdress. The headdress and silver necklets are part of her dowry, which is handed down from generation to generation.*

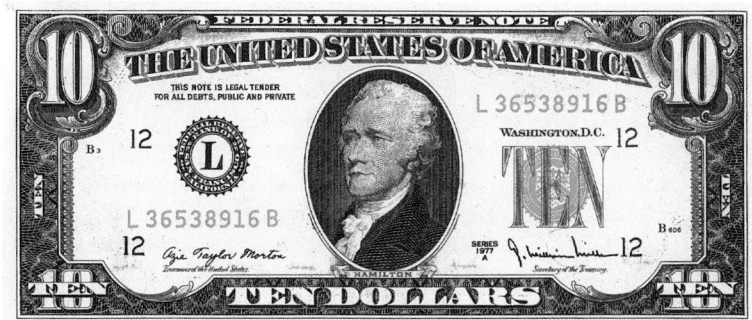

U.S. BANKNOTE *The world's first decimal currency, with 100 cents to the dollar, appeared in the American colonies in 1729. Present-day United States banknotes are authorized by the U.S. Treasury.*

---

mon·gol (mŏng′gəl, -gōl′) *n.* A person affected with **Down's syndrome** (see). —See Usage note at **mongolism.**

Mon·gol (mŏng′gəl, -gōl′) *n.* **1. a.** A member of one of the nomadic peoples of Mongolia. **b.** A native of Mongolia. **2.** A member of the Mongoloid ethnic group. **3.** The language of Mongolia. **4.** Loosely, the Yuan dynasty of China. [Mongol *Mongol,* perhaps from *mong,* brave.] —**Mon·gol** *adj.*

Mon·go·li·a (mŏng-gō′lē-ə, -gōl′yə, mŏn-). **1.** Ancient region inhabited by the Mongols and now comprising the Mongolian People's Republic and the Inner Mongolian Autonomous Region of China. In the 13th century the Mongols under Genghis Khan built one of the world's greatest empires, stretching from China to the Danube and into Persia. **2.** See **Mongolian People's Republic.**

Mongolia, Inner. See **Inner Mongolian Autonomous Region.**

Mon·go·li·an (mŏng-gō'lē-ən, -gōl'yən, mŏn-) *n.* **1.** A Mongol. **2.** The Mongolic language of Mongolia. —**Mon·go·li·an** *adj.*

Mongolian People's Republic. Also **Mongolia, Outer Mongolia.** Republic of east-central Asia. It consists of a high plateau, with mountains in the center, west, and north and the Gobi Desert in the south and east. Much of the terrain is used for pasture; livestock herding (now largely collectivized) is the principal occupation of the seminomadic people. Once the center of the Mongol Empire (1206), it was a province of China (1691-1911 and 1919-21) and then an independent republic under the protection of the U.S.S.R. Area, 1,565,000 square kilometers (604,250 square miles). Population, 1,600,000. Capital, Ulan Bator. See map at **China.**

Mon·gol·ic (mŏng-gŏl'ĭk, mŏn-) *n.* The Altaic subfamily that includes Mongolian and Kalmuck. —**Mon·gol·ic** *adj.*

mon·gol·ism, Mon·gol·ism (mŏng'gə-lĭz'əm, mŏn'-) *n.* A congenital condition, **Down's syndrome** *(see).* [From the supposed resemblance of the features of an affected person to those of ethnic Mongols.]

Usage: The terms *mongolism* and *mongol* have been replaced in medical usage by *Down's syndrome* and *Down's baby* (or *child*), respectively, and should be avoided, as they may give offense.

mon·gol·oid (mŏng'gə-loid', mŏn'-) *adj.* Characterized by or pertaining to **Down's syndrome** *(see).* —**mon·gol·oid** *n.*

Mon·gol·oid (mŏng'gə-loid', mŏn'-) *adj. Anthropology.* **1.** Of, pertaining to, or designating a major ethnic division of the human species whose members are characterized by yellowish-brown to white skin pigmentation, coarse straight black hair, dark eyes with pronounced epicanthic folds, and prominent cheekbones. This division is considered to include the Chinese, Japanese, Malayans, Mongolians, Siberians, Eskimos, and American Indians. **2.** Characteristic of or like a Mongol.
~*n.* A member of the Mongoloid ethnic division of the human species.

mon·goose (mŏng'gōōs', mŏn'-) *n., pl.* **-gooses.** Any of various Old World carnivorous mammals of the genus *Herpestes* and related genera, having a slender body and a long tail and notable for the ability to kill poisonous snakes. [Marathi *mangūs,* from Dravidian, akin to Telugu *mangisu.*]

mon·grel (mŭng'grəl, mŏng'-) *n.* **1.** An animal or plant resulting from various interbreedings; especially, a dog of mixed breed or no definable breed. **2.** A person of mixed racial stock. Used derogatorily or facetiously. **3.** A cross between one thing and another. Also used adjectively: *a mongrel language, half English, half Spanish.* [Probably diminutive of Middle English *mong,* Old English *gemang,* mixture.] —**mon·grel·ism** *n.* —**mon·grel·ly** *adj.*

mon·grel·ize (mŭng'grə-līz', mŏng'-) *tr.v.* **-ized, -izing, -izes.** To make mongrel in race, nature, or character. Usually used derogatorily when applied to human beings.

monied. Variant of **moneyed.**

mon·ies. Alternate plural of **money.**

mon·i·ker, mon·ick·er (mŏn'ĭ-kər) *n. Slang.* A personal name or nickname: *"No one but Pinky and Sister Heavenly knew his straight monicker"* (Chester Himes). [19th century : origin obscure.]

mo·ni·li·a·sis (mō'nə-lī'ə-sĭs, mŏn'ə-) *n.* **Candidiasis** *(see).* [New Latin : *Monilia* (genus), from Latin *monīle,* necklace (referring to the chain of spores) + -IASIS.]

mo·nil·i·form (mō-nĭl'ə-fôrm') *adj. Biology.* Resembling a string of beads, as do various fungi, the antennae of certain insects, and the nuclei of some members of the Ciliata. [Latin *monīle,* necklace + -FORM.]

mon·ish (mŏn'ĭsh) *tr.v.* **-ished, -ishing, -ishes.** *Archaic.* To admonish. [Middle English *monisshen,* variant of *monesten,* from Old French *monester,* from Vulgar Latin *monestāre* (unattested), extension of Latin *monēre,* to warn.]

mo·nism (mō'nĭz'əm, mŏn'ĭz'əm) *n. Philosophy.* A metaphysical theory according to which reality is conceived as consisting of only one basic substance. Compare **dualism, pluralism.** [German *Monismus* : MON(O)- + -ISM.] —**mo·nist** *n. & adj.* —**mo·nis·tic** (mō-nĭs'tĭk, mə-) *adj.* —**mo·nis·ti·cal·ly** *adv.*

mo·ni·tion (mō-nĭsh'ən, mə-) *n.* **1.** A warning or intimation of some impending danger. **2. a.** Admonition. **b.** A piece of advice. **3.** A formal order from a bishop or ecclesiastical court to refrain from some particular offense. [Middle English *monicioun,* from Old French *monition,* from Latin *monitiō* (stem *monitiōn-*), from *monēre,* to warn.]

mon·i·tor (mŏn'ə-tər) *n.* **1.** One that admonishes, cautions, or reminds. **2. a.** A pupil who assists a teacher in routine duties. **b.** A senior pupil with various responsibilities such as keeping order in class. **3. a.** Any device used to record, check, or control a process. **b.** A television set in a studio showing images for transmission. **4.** An articulated device holding the rotating nozzle of a water jet, used in mining and firefighting. **5.** A heavily ironclad warship of the 19th century with a low, flat deck and one or more gun turrets. **6.** Any carnivorous lizard of the family Varanidae, of tropical and subtropical regions, ranging in length from about 8 inches to 10 feet. See **Komodo dragon.**
~*v.* **monitored, -toring, -tors.** —*tr.* **1.** To check (the transmission quality of a signal) by means of a receiver or monitor. **2.** To test (a surface) for radiation intensity. **3.** To keep track of by means of an electronic device. **4.** To check by means of a receiver for significant content: *monitor foreign radio broadcasts.* **5.** To scrutinize or check systematically: *carefully monitored the experiment at every stage.*

6. To keep watch over; supervise: *monitor an examination.* **7.** To direct as a monitor. —*intr.* To act as a monitor. [Latin, one who warns, from *monēre,* to warn.] —**mon·i·to·ri·al** (mŏn'ə-tôr'ē-əl, -tōr'ē-əl) *adj.* —**mon·i·tress** (mŏn'ə-trĭs) *n.*

mon·i·to·ry (mŏn'ə-tôr'ē, -tōr'ē) *adj.* Conveying an admonition or warning: *a monitory glance.*
~*n., pl.* **monitories.** A letter containing the admonition of a bishop or ecclesiastical court. [Latin *monitōrius,* from *monitor,* MONITOR.]

monk (mŭngk) *n.* A member of a religious brotherhood living in a monastery, bound by vows such as those of poverty, chastity, and obedience, and devoted to a discipline prescribed by a religious order. [Middle English *munk,* Old English *munuc,* from Late Latin *monachus,* from Late Greek *monakhos,* solitary, monk, from Greek *monos,* alone.]

Monk, George. See **Monck.**

Monk (mŭngk), **Thelonious Sphere** (1917–82). U.S. jazz pianist and composer. His spare piano style and unusual harmonic sense made him one of the most influential of modern jazz musicians. His notable compositions include *Round About Midnight* (c. 1947).

monk·er·y (mŭng'kə-rē) *n., pl.* **-ies.** **1.** Monastic life or practices. **2.** A monastery. **3.** Monks collectively.

mon·key (mŭng'kē) *n., pl.* **-keys.** **1. a.** Any long-tailed primate, including the Old and New World monkeys and the marmosets, but excluding the anthropoid apes and the lemurs, lorises, tree shrews, and tarsiers. **b.** Loosely, any member of the order Primates, apart from the human race. **2.** A mischievous, playful child or young person. **3.** The iron block or ram of a pile driver. **4.** A narrow passageway in a coal mine. **5.** *Slang.* A person who is mocked, duped, or made to appear a fool. Used chiefly in the phrase *make a monkey out of.* **6.** *Slang.* Drug addiction, regarded as a burdensome affliction: *have a monkey on one's back.*
~*v.* **monkeyed, -keying, -keys.** —*intr. Informal.* To play or fiddle with something idly: *Don't monkey around with my watch.* —*tr.* To imitate or mimic; ape. [Probably of Low German origin.]

monkey bread *n.* The fruit of the **baobab** *(see).*

monkey business *n. Slang.* Mischievous or deceitful behavior.

mon·key-flow·er (mŭng'kē-flou'ər) *n.* Any of various plants of the genus *Mimulus,* especially *M. luteus,* which has yellow, two-lipped flowers, and is widely cultivated. [From the supposed resemblance of the flower to a monkey's face.]

monkey jacket *n.* **1.** A short, tight-fitting jacket, formerly worn by sailors. **2.** A **mess jacket** *(see).* [From its similarity to the jackets worn by performing monkeys.]

monkey pot *n.* **1.** The large, urn-shaped lidded pod of tropical trees of the genus *Lecythis.* **2.** Any tree bearing this type of pod.

monkey puzzle *n.* A coniferous tree, *Araucaria araucana,* native to Chile, having intricately ramifying branches covered with broad, stiff, prickle-tipped leaves. [Because its branches supposedly make it difficult for a monkey to climb.]

mon·key·shine (mŭng'kē-shīn') *n. Slang.* A playful, mischievous trick. [MONKEY + SHINE (prank).]

monkey suit *n. Slang.* A man's formal dress suit or a full-dress military uniform.

monkey wrench *n.* A large wrench with adjustable jaws for turning nuts of varying sizes.

monk·fish (mŭngk'fĭsh') *n., pl.* **-fishes** or collectively **monkfish.** The **goosefish** *(see).* [From the cowled appearance of the head.]

Mon-Khmer (mōn'kmâr') *n.* A family of languages, including Khmer, spoken in Southeast Asia. —**Mon-Khmer** *adj.*

monk·hood (mŭngk'hŏŏd') *n.* **1.** The state or profession of a monk; monasticism. **2.** Monks collectively.

monk·ish (mŭng'kĭsh) *adj.* Of, pertaining to, or characteristic of monks or monasticism.

monk's cloth *n.* A heavy cotton cloth in a coarse basket weave. [Originally for the habits of monks.]

monk seal *n.* A seal of the nearly extinct genus *Monachus,* formerly much hunted in Mediterranean and Caribbean waters for its fur, which may be gray or yellow with black spots or uniformly brown. [From the cowled appearance of its head.]

monks·hood (mŭngks'hŏŏd') *n.* Any of various plants of the genus *Aconitum,* having hooded flowers; especially, *A. napellus,* with purplish flowers. Most species are poisonous. Also called "aconite," "wolfsbane."

Mon·mouth (mŏn'məth). Locality in east-central New Jersey, site of the Revolutionary War Battle of Monmouth Court House (June 28, 1778) in which the Continental Army beat off repeated attacks by the British forces.

Mon·mouth (mŏn'məth, mŭn'-), **James Scott, 1st Duke of** (1649–85). English pretender to the throne, illegitimate son of Charles II by Lucy Walter. After 1662 he lived at court, and Charles acknowledged him as his son, creating him duke in 1663. When the Catholic James II succeeded (1685), Monmouth led a rebellion. He was defeated at Sedgemoor, captured, and beheaded.

Mon·mouth·shire (mŏn'məth-shîr', -shər, mŭn'-). Former county of western England, for some purposes, such as censuses, included in Wales. Most of it is now incorporated in the Welsh county of Gwent, the far west now being in Mid Glamorgan and South Glamorgan.

Mon·net (mō-nā', mô-ně'), **Jean Omer Marie Gabriel** (1888–1979). French statesman, called "father of Europe." He was the first president (1952–55) of the European Coal and Steel Community and laid the plans for the European Economic Community.

monkey puzzle Araucaria araucana, *which is native to Chile and Argentina, is thought to be the most ancient and primitive conifer in the world. It acquired its common name because its branches were said to be so tangled that they would baffle a monkey wanting to climb it.*

mon·o¹ (mŏn′ō) *adj. Electronics.* Monophonic.
~*n., pl.* **monos.** Monophonic sound reproduction.
mono² *n.* See **mononucleosis** (sense 2).
mono-, mon- *prefix.* Indicates: **1.** One; single; alone; for example, **monogamy. 2.** The presence of a single atom, radical, or group in a compound; for example, **monohydric.** [Middle English, from Old French, from Latin, from Greek, from *monos,* single, sole, alone.]
mon·o·ac·id (mŏn′ō-ăs′ĭd) *adj.* Also **mon·o·a·cid·ic** (mŏn′ō-ə-sĭd′ĭk), **mon·a·cid·ic** (mŏn-ăs′ĭd), **mon·a·cid·ic** (mŏn′ə-sĭd′ĭk). *Chemistry.* Having only one hydroxyl group to react with acids. Said of bases.
mon·o·am·ine (mŏn′ō-ăm′ēn′, -ə-mēn′) *n. Chemistry.* An amine that has only one functional (-NH₂) group per molecule.
monoamine oxidase *n. Abbr.* **MAO** An enzyme that catalyzes the oxidation of epinephrine and other monoamines. Drugs that inhibit its action are used in the treatment of depression.
mon·o·ba·sic (mŏn′ə-bā′sĭk) *adj. Chemistry.* **1.** Monoprotic. **2.** Having only one metal ion or positive radical.
mon·o·carp (mŏn′ə-kärp′) *n. Botany.* A monocarpic plant. [MONO- + -CARP.]
mon·o·car·pel·lar·y (mŏn′ə-kär′pə-lĕr′ē) *adj. Botany.* Consisting of or having only one carpel.
mon·o·car·pic (mŏn′ə-kär′pĭk) *adj.* Also **mon·o·car·pous** (-kär′pəs). *Botany.* Flowering and bearing fruit only once.
mon·o·cha·si·um (mŏn′ə-kā′zē-əm, -zhē-əm) *n., pl.* **-sia** (-zē-ə, -zhē-ə). *Botany.* A cyme *(see)* in which each flowering branch gives rise to one other branch only. Compare **dichasium.** [MONO- + (DI)CHASIUM.] —**mon·o·cha·si·al** *adj.*
mon·o·chord (mŏn′ə-kôrd′) *n.* A musical instrument consisting of a sounding box with one string and a movable bridge, used to study musical tones and intervals. [Middle English *monocorde,* from Old French, from Medieval Latin *monochordum,* from Greek *monokhordon* : MONO- + *khordē,* CHORD.]
mon·o·chro·mat (mŏn′ə-krō′măt′) *n.* A person who is completely colorblind, perceiving all colors as a single hue. [Back-formation from MONOCHROMATIC.] —**mon·o·chro·ma·tism** (mŏn′ə-krō′mə-tĭz′əm) *n.*
mon·o·chro·mat·ic (mŏn′ə-krō-măt′ĭk) *adj.* Also **mon·o·chro·ic** (mŏn′ə-krō′ĭk). **1.** Having or being in only one color or shades of one color. **2.** Having or producing electromagnetic radiation of only one wavelength. **3.** Having a single kinetic energy. Said of a beam of particles. [Greek *monokhrōmatos* : MONO- + *khrōma,* -CHROME.] —**mon·o·chro·mat·i·cal·ly** *adv.*
mon·o·chrome (mŏn′ə-krōm′) *n.* **1.** A painting done in different shades of one color. **2.** The technique of executing such paintings. **3.** A black-and-white photograph. Also called "monotint." ~*adj.* **1.** Black-and-white. **2.** Having or being in only one color or shades of one color. [Medieval Latin *monochrōma,* from Greek *monokhrōmos,* of one color : MONO- + *khrōma,* -CHROME.] —**mon·o·chro·mic** (mŏn′ə-krō′mĭk) *adj.*
mon·o·cle (mŏn′ə-kəl) *n.* A single lens correcting the vision for one eye. [French, from Late Latin *monoculus,* one-eyed : MONO- + *oculus,* eye.] —**mon·o·cled** *adj.*
mon·o·cline (mŏn′ə-klīn′) *n.* A geologic formation in which all strata are inclined in the same direction. Compare **isocline.** —**mon·o·cli·nal** (mŏn′ə-klī′nəl) *adj.*
mon·o·clin·ic (mŏn′ə-klĭn′ĭk) *adj. Crystallography.* Having three unequal axes, two of which intersect obliquely and are perpendicular to the third. Said of crystals. [MONO- + Greek *-klinēs,* leaning, from *klinein,* to lean.]
mon·o·cli·nous (mŏn′ə-klī′nəs) *adj. Botany.* Having pistils and stamens in the same flower. [New Latin *monoclinus,* monoclinous, "hermaphroditic" : MONO- + Greek *klinē,* couch.]
mon·o·coque (mŏn′ə-kŏk′, -kōk′) *n.* A metal structure, as of an aircraft or racing car, in which the covering absorbs a large part of the stresses to which the body is subjected. [French : MONO- + *coque,* shell, from Latin *coccum,* berry.]
mon·o·cot·y·le·don (mŏn′ə-kŏt′l-ēd′n) *n.* Also **mon·o·cot** (mŏn′-ə-kŏt′). *Botany.* Any plant of the Monocotyledonae, one of the two major divisions of angiosperms, characterized by a single embryonic seed leaf that appears at germination. Included among the monocotyledons are such plants as grasses, orchids, and lilies. Compare **dicotyledon.** —**mon·o·cot·y·le·don·ous** *adj.*
mo·noc·ra·cy (mŏ-nŏk′rə-sē) *n.* Government or rule by a single person; autocracy. [MONO- + -CRACY.]
mon·o·crat (mŏn′ə-krăt′) *n.* One who favors monocracy, autocracy, or monarchy. —**mon·o·crat·ic** (mŏn′ə-krăt′ĭk) *adj.* —**mon·o·crat·i·cal·ly** *adv.*
mo·noc·u·lar (mŏ-nŏk′yə-lər, mə-) *adj.* **1.** Having or pertaining to one eye. **2.** Adapted for the use of only one eye. [Late Latin *monoculus,* one-eyed. See **monocle.**]
mon·o·cy·cle (mŏn′ə-sī′kəl) *n.* A unicycle *(see).*
mon·o·cyte (mŏn′ə-sīt′) *n.* A large white blood cell having an oval nucleus. It engulfs foreign particles, such as bacteria. [MONO- + -CYTE.] —**mon·o·cyt·ic** (mŏn′ə-sĭt′ĭk), **mon·o·cy·toid** (mŏn′ə-sī′toid′) *adj.*
Mo·nod (mô-nō′), **Jacques** (1910–76). French molecular biologist, director of the Pasteur Institute in Paris after 1971. He described the process of synthesis of protein in cells, for which he and his collaborators were awarded the Nobel Prize in medicine and physiology (1965).
mon·o·dac·tyl (mŏn′ə-dăk′təl) *n.* An animal having only one claw on each limb. [French *monodactyle,* from Greek *monodaktulos,* one-

toed, one-fingered : MONO- + *daktulos,* DACTYL.] —**mon·o·dac·ty·lous** (mŏn′ə-dăk′tə-ləs) *adj.*
mon·o·dra·ma (mŏn′ə-drä′mə, -drăm′ə) *n.* A dramatic composition for one performer. —**mon·o·dra·mat·ic** (mŏn′ə-drə-măt′ĭk) *adj.*
mon·o·dy (mŏn′ə-dē) *n., pl.* **-dies. 1.** In Greek tragedy, an ode for one voice or actor. **2.** An elegiac verse expressing personal lament. **3.** *Music.* **a.** A style of composition in which one vocal part or melodic line predominates. **b.** A composition in this style. [Late Latin *monōdia,* from Greek *monōidia* : MONO- + *ōidē,* song.] —**mo·nod·ic** (mə-nŏd′ĭk), **mo·nod·i·cal** *adj.* —**mon·o·dist** (mŏn′ə-dĭst) *n.*
mon·oe·cious, mo·ne·cious (mə-nē′shəs) *adj.* Also **mo·noi·cous** (mə-noi′kəs). **1.** *Botany.* Having male and female reproductive organs in separate flowers on a single plant. Compare **dioecious. 2.** *Zoology.* Hermaphroditic. [New Latin *Monoecia* : MONO- + Greek *oikia,* dwelling, from *oikos,* house.] —**mo·noe·cious·ly** *adv.*
mon·o·fil·a·ment (mŏn′ō-fĭl′ə-mənt) *n.* A single filament, as of yarn or plastic. Also called "monofil."
mo·nog·a·my (mə-nŏg′ə-mē) *n.* **1. a.** The custom or condition of being married to or having a sexual relationship with only one person at a time. **b.** The practice of marrying only once during one's lifetime. **2.** *Zoology.* The habit of having only one mate. [French *monogamie,* from Late Latin *monogamia,* from Greek : MONO- + -GAMY.] —**mo·nog·a·mist** *n.* —**mo·nog·a·mous** *adj.* —**mo·nog·a·mous·ly** *adv.*
mon·o·gen·e·sis (mŏn′ə-jĕn′ə-sĭs) *n.* **1.** The theory that all living organisms are descended from a single cell. Compare **polygenesis. 2.** Asexual reproduction, as by sporulation. **3.** The development of an ovum into an organism resembling the parent, without metamorphosis. [New Latin : MONO- + -GENESIS.] —**mo·nog·e·nous** (mə-nŏj′ə-nəs) *adj.* —**mo·nog·e·nous·ly** *adv.*
mon·o·ge·net·ic (mŏn′ō-jə-nĕt′ĭk) *adj.* **1.** Pertaining to or showing monogenesis. **2.** Asexual. **3.** *Geology.* Formed by a single process or from a single source: *a monogenetic range.*
mon·o·gen·ic (mŏn′ə-jĕn′ĭk) *adj.* **1.** Of or regulated by one gene or one of a pair of allelic genes. **2.** Producing offspring mostly of one sex. **3.** Of or pertaining to monogenism. [MONO- + -GENIC.] —**mon·o·gen·i·cal·ly** *adv.*
mo·nog·e·nism (mə-nŏj′ə-nĭz′əm) *n.* The theory that humankind has descended from a single pair of ancestors. [MONO- + -GEN + -ISM.] —**mo·nog·e·nist** *n.* —**mo·no·ge·nis·tic** (mə-nŏj′ə-nĭs′tĭk) *adj.*
mon·o·glot (mŏn′ə-glŏt′) *adj.* Monolingual. —**mon·o·glot** *n.*
mon·o·gram (mŏn′ə-grăm′) *n.* A design composed of one or more letters, usually the initials of a name. ~*tr.v.* **monogrammed** or **-gramed, -gramming** or **-graming, -grams.** To mark with a monogram. [Late Latin *monogramma* : MONO- + -GRAM.] —**mon·o·gram·mat·ic** (mŏn′ə-grə-măt′ĭk) *adj.*
mon·o·graph (mŏn′ə-grăf′, -gräf′) *n.* A scholarly book, article, or pamphlet on a specific and usually narrowly limited subject. ~*tr.v.* **monographed, -graphing, -graphs.** To write a monograph on. [MONO- + -GRAPH.] —**mo·nog·ra·pher** (mə-nŏg′rə-fər) *n.* —**mon·o·graph·ic** (mŏn′ə-grăf′ĭk) *adj.* —**mon·o·graph·i·cal·ly** *adv.*
mo·nog·y·ny (mə-nŏj′ə-nē) *n.* The practice or condition of having only one wife at a time. [MONO- + -GYNY.] —**mo·nog·y·nist** *n. & adj.* —**mo·nog·y·nous** *adj.*
mon·o·hy·brid (mŏn′ō-hī′brĭd) *n.* Hybrid offspring of parents differing in a single characteristic or genetic factor.
mon·o·hy·drate (mŏn′ō-hī′drāt′) *n. Chemistry.* A compound, especially a crystalline salt, that contains one molecule of water per molecule of compound. —**mon·o·hy·drat·ed** *adj.*
mon·o·hy·dric (mŏn′ō-hī′drĭk) *adj. Chemistry.* Containing one hydroxyl radical. [MONO- + HYDR(O)- + -IC.]
monoicous. Variant of **monoecious.**
mon·o·ki·ni (mŏn′ō-kē′nē) *n.* A woman's topless swimsuit. [MONO- + (BI)KINI.]
mo·nol·a·try (mə-nŏl′ə-trē) *n.* The worship of one god to the exclusion of but without denying the existence of others. [MONO- + -LATRY.] —**mo·nol·a·trous** *adj.*
mon·o·lay·er (mŏn′ō-lā′ər) *n.* **1.** A film of a compound one molecule thick; a monomolecular layer. **2.** A layer one atom thick; a monatomic layer.
mon·o·lin·gual (mŏn′ə-lĭng′gwəl) *adj.* Speaking, knowing, using, or expressed in only one language. —**mon·o·lin·gual** *n.*
mon·o·lith (mŏn′ə-lĭth′) *n.* **1.** A large block of stone, especially a natural rock buttress or one used in architecture or sculpture. **2.** A column, monument, or the like made from one large block of stone. **3.** Something resembling or suggestive of a monolith, especially in being large, uniform, impersonal, or immovable. [French *monolithe,* from Greek *monolithos* : MONO- + -LITH.]
mon·o·lith·ic (mŏn′ə-lĭth′ĭk) *adj.* **1.** Consisting of a monolith or monoliths. **2.** Like a monolith; massive, solid, impersonal, or uniform: *a monolithic bureaucracy.* —**mon·o·lith·i·cal·ly** *adv.*
monolithic circuit *n. Electronics.* A type of integrated circuit in which all the components are formed in the surface of the chip, with no added connections. Compare **hybrid circuit.**
mon·o·logue, mon·o·log (mŏn′ə-lôg′, -lŏg′) *n.* **1.** A long speech or talk made by one person, often monopolizing a conversation. **2. a.** A long speech delivered by an actor; a soliloquy. **b.** Any literary composition in the form of a soliloquy: *dramatic monologue.* **3.** A continuous series of comic stories or jokes delivered by a comedian. [French : MONO- + (DIA)LOGUE.] —**mon·o·log·ic** (mŏn′-ə-lŏj′ĭk), **mon·o·log·i·cal** *adj.* —**mo·nol·o·gist** (mə-nŏl′ə-jĭst, mŏn′ə-lô′gĭst, -lŏg′ĭst) *n.*

monolith *A prehistoric monolith at Carnac, in Brittany, France.*

mon·o·ma·ni·a (mŏn′ō-mā′nē-ə, -mān′yə) n. **1.** Pathological obsession with one idea. Not in technical usage. See **paranoia. 2.** Intent concentration on or exaggerated enthusiasm for a subject or an idea. [New Latin : MONO- + -MANIA.] —**mon·o·ma·ni·ac** (mŏn′-ō-mā′nē-ăk′) n. —**mon·o·ma·ni·a·cal** (mŏn′ō-mə-nī′ə-kəl) adj.

mon·o·mer (mŏn′ə-mər) n. Any molecule, usually of a simple structure and of low molecular weight, that can be chemically bound as a unit of a polymer (see). [MONO- + Greek meros, part.] —**mon·o·mer·ic** (mŏn′ə-mĕr′ĭk) adj.

mon·o·me·tal·lic (mŏn′ō-mə-tăl′ĭk) adj. **1.** Consisting of or containing one metal. **2.** Pertaining to monometallism.

mon·o·met·al·lism (mŏn′ō-mĕt′l-ĭz′əm) n. **1.** The use of only one metal, usually gold or silver, as a standard of money. **2.** The economic theory supporting the use of one metallic monetary standard. —**mon·o·met·al·list** n.

mon·o·me·ter (mə-nŏm′ə-tər) n. A line of verse that consists of only one metrical foot. —**mon·o·met·ric** (mŏn′ə-mĕt′rĭk), **mon·o·met·ri·cal** adj.

mon·o·mi·al (mŏ-nō′mē-əl, mŏ-, mə-) n. **1.** Algebra. An expression consisting of only one term. **2.** Biology. A taxonomic name consisting of a single word. [MON(O)- + (BIN)OMIAL.] —**mo·no·mi·al** adj.

Mo·non·ga·he·la (mə-nŏn′gə-hē′lə). River, 206 kilometers (128 miles) long, flowing north from northern West Virginia into southwestern Pennsylvania. It joins the Allegheny River at Pittsburgh to form the Ohio River.

mon·o·mo·lec·u·lar (mŏn′ō-mə-lĕk′yə-lər) adj. **1.** Of or pertaining to a single molecule. **2.** Of or consisting of a layer one molecule thick.

mon·o·mor·phic (mŏn′ə-môr′fĭk) adj. Also **mon·o·mor·phous** (-fəs). Zoology. Having a basic structure remaining unchanged through a series of developmental changes. —**mon·o·mor·phism** n.

mon·o·mor·phous (mŏn′ə-môr′fəs) adj. **1.** Chemistry. Existing in only one crystalline form. **2.** Variant of **monomorphic.**

mon·o·nu·cle·ar (mŏn′ō-nōō′klē-ər, -nyōō′klē-ər) adj. Having only one nucleus. Said of cells.

mon·o·nu·cle·o·sis (mŏn′ō-nōō′klē-ō′sĭs, -nyōō′klē-ō′sĭs) n. **1.** The presence of an abnormally large number of monocytes in the bloodstream. **2.** Pathology. An infectious disease mainly affecting adolescents and young adults, causing an abnormally large number of monocytes in the bloodstream and characterized by fever, headache, and loss of energy. In this sense, also called "glandular fever," "infectious mononucleosis," "mono." [New Latin : MONO- + NUCLE(US) + -OSIS.]

mon·o·nu·cle·o·tide (mŏn′ō-nōō′klē-ə-tīd′, -nyōō′klē-ə-tīd′) n. Biochemistry. A compound consisting of one molecule each of a pentose sugar, phosphoric acid, and a purine or pyrimidine base.

mon·o·pet·al·ous (mŏn′ə-pĕt′l-əs) adj. Having petals united to form one corolla; gamopetalous.

mo·noph·a·gous (mə-nŏf′ə-gəs) adj. Eating only one kind of food. Said especially of insects. [MONO- + -PHAGOUS.]

mon·o·pho·bi·a (mŏn′ō-fō′bē-ə) n. Excessive fear of solitude. [New Latin : MONO- + -PHOBIA.] —**mon·o·pho·bic** (mŏn′ō-fō′bĭk) adj.

mon·o·phon·ic (mŏn′ə-fŏn′ĭk) adj. **1.** Music. Of the nature of monophony; having a single melodic line; monodic. **2.** Electronics. Designating a system of transmitting, recording, or reproducing sound that uses only one channel to carry or reproduce the sound; monaural. —**mon·o·phon·i·cal·ly** adv.

mo·noph·o·ny (mə-nŏf′ə-nē) n. Music consisting of a single melodic line, as in plainsong. Compare **homophony, polyphony.** [MONO- + -PHONY.]

mon·oph·thong (mŏn′əf-thŏng′, -thŏng′) n. **1.** A single vowel sound made while the supraglottal speech organs are in a fixed position. **2.** Two written letters representing a single vowel sound; for example, ea in plead is a monophthong. [Late Greek monophthongos : MONO- + phthongos†, vowel.] —**mon·oph·thon·gal** (mŏn′əf-thŏng′-əl, -thŏng′gəl, -thŏng′əl, -thŏng′gəl) adj.

mon·oph·thong·ize (mŏn′əf-thŏng′īz′, -thŏng′gīz′, -thŏng′īz′, -thŏng′gīz′) v. **-ized, -izing, -izes.** —tr. To make into a monophthong. —intr. To become a monophthong. —**mon·oph·thong·i·za·tion** n.

mon·o·phy·let·ic (mŏn′ō-fī-lĕt′ĭk) adj. **1.** Of or descended from a single ancestral group of plants or animals. **2.** Belonging to one stock.

Mo·noph·y·site (mə-nŏf′ə-sīt′) n. Theology. An adherent of the doctrine, held by Coptic and Syrian Christians, that in the person of Christ there was only one single, divine nature. [Medieval Latin monophysīta, from Medieval Greek monophusitēs : MONO- + phusis, nature.] —**Mo·noph·y·sit·ic** (mə-nŏf′ə-sīt′ĭk) adj. —**Mo·noph·y·sit·ism** n.

mon·o·plane (mŏn′ə-plān′) n. An aircraft with only one pair of wings. Compare **biplane.**

mon·o·ple·gi·a (mŏn′ə-plē′jē-ə, -plē′jə) n. Paralysis of a single limb or part of the body, such as one side of the face. [MONO- + -PLEGIA.] —**mon·o·ple·gic** (mŏn′ə-plē′jĭk) adj. & n.

mon·o·ploid (mŏn′ə-ploid′) adj. Having a single set of chromosomes; haploid. —n. A monoploid individual or cell. [MONO- + -ploid, as in HAPLOID.]

mon·o·pod (mŏn′ə-pŏd′) n. An adjustable single-legged support for a camera, used in situations where a tripod would be too cumbersome. [MONO- + -POD.]

mon·o·po·di·um (mŏn′ə-pō′dē-əm) n., pl. **-dia** (-dē-ə). Also **mon·o·pode** (mŏn′ə-pōd′). Botany. A main axis of a plant, such as the trunk of certain conifers, that maintains a single line of growth, giving off lateral branches. Compare **sympodium.** [New Latin, from Late Latin monopodius, one-footed, from Greek monopous (stem monopod-) : MONO- + pous, foot.] —**mon·o·po·di·al** adj.

mo·nop·o·lis·tic competition (mə-nŏp′ə-lĭs′tĭk) n. Economics. A situation in commerce that exists when a large number of competitive firms produce products that are similar but are not perfect substitutes, so that one firm can afford to raise its prices relative to the others without necessarily jeopardizing its sales. Also called "imperfect competition."

mo·nop·o·lize (mə-nŏp′ə-līz′) tr.v. **-lized, -lizing, -lizes. 1.** To acquire or maintain a monopoly of. **2.** To dominate or take complete possession of to the exclusion of others. —**mo·nop·o·li·za·tion** (mə-nŏp′ə-lĭ-zā′shən) n. —**mo·nop·o·liz·er** n.

mo·nop·o·ly (mə-nŏp′ə-lē) n., pl. **-lies. 1.** Economics. **a.** Exclusive control by one person, group, or company of the means of producing or selling a commodity or service. Compare **oligopoly. b.** Such control that is not exclusive but is sufficient to allow the person or company to control prices. **2.** Law. A right granted by a government, giving exclusive control over a specified commercial activity to a single party. **3. a.** A company or group having exclusive control over a commercial activity. **b.** A commodity or service controlled exclusively by one company or group. **4.** Exclusive possession of or control over anything: You haven't got a monopoly on hardship, you know. [Latin monopōlium, from Greek monopōlion, sole selling rights : MONO- + pōlein, to sell.] —**mo·nop·o·lism** n. —**mo·nop·o·list** n. & adj. —**mo·nop·o·lis·tic** adj.

Mo·nop·o·ly (mə-nŏp′ə-lē) n. A trademark for a board game in which two to six players advance by throws of dice and attempt to acquire the property marked on the board and put the other players out of business.

mon·o·pro·pel·lant (mŏn′ō-prə-pĕl′ənt) n. A rocket propellant in which fuel and oxidizer, such as a mixture of hydrogen peroxide and alcohol, are combined prior to combustion.

mon·o·pro·tic (mŏn′ō-prō′tĭk) adj. Chemistry. Having only one hydrogen ion to donate to a base in an acid-base reaction; monobasic. [MONO- + PROT(ON) + -IC.]

mo·nop·so·ny (mə-nŏp′sə-nē) n., pl. **-nies.** A situation in commerce in which the product or service of several sellers is sought by only one buyer. Compare **oligopsony.** [MON(O)- + Greek opsōnia, buying, from opsōnein, to buy food (see **opsonin**).]

mon·o·rail (mŏn′ə-rāl′) n. **1.** A railway system in which trains run on a single rail, often an elevated one from which they are suspended. **2.** The track used in such a system.

mon·o·sac·cha·ride (mŏn′ə-săk′ə-rīd′, -rĭd) n. A simple sugar, such as glucose or fructose, that cannot be decomposed by hydrolysis, having the general formula $C_nH_{2n}O_n$. Also called "simple sugar."

mon·o·sep·al·ous (mŏn′ə-sĕp′ə-ləs) adj. Botany. Having sepals united to form a single calyx; gamosepalous.

mon·o·so·di·um glu·ta·mate (mŏn′ə-sō′dē-əm glōō′tə-māt′) n. Abbr. **MSG** A white crystalline salt, $NaC_5H_8O_4$, with a meatlike taste, used extensively as a food additive. Also called "glutamate," "sodium glutamate."

mon·o·some (mŏn′ə-sōm′) n. An unpaired chromosome, particularly an X chromosome, in an otherwise diploid cell or organism. [MONO- + -SOME (body).] —**mon·o·so·mic** (mŏn′ə-sō′mĭk) adj. —**mon·o·so·my** (mŏn′ə-sō′mē) n.

mon·o·sper·mous (mŏn′ə-spûr′məs) adj. Also **mon·o·sper·mal** (mŏn′ə-spûr′məl). Having a single seed. Said of certain plants. [MONO- + -SPERMOUS.]

mon·o·stome (mŏn′ə-stōm′) adj. Also **mo·nos·to·mous** (mə-nŏs′tə-məs). **1.** Having one oral sucker only, as do certain flatworms. **2.** Having one mouth or similar opening. [Greek monostomos, having one mouth : MONO- + stoma, -STOME.]

mon·o·strophe (mŏn′ə-strōf′) n. A poem in which all the stanzas or strophes have the same metrical form. —**mon·o·stroph·ic** (mŏn′-ə-strŏf′ĭk, -strō′fĭk) adj.

mon·o·sty·lous (mŏn′ə-stī′ləs) adj. Botany. Having one style.

mon·o·syl·lab·ic (mŏn′ə-sī-lăb′ĭk) adj. **1.** Having only one syllable. **2.** Characterized by or consisting of monosyllables; terse or laconic. —**mon·o·syl·lab·i·cal·ly** adv.

mon·o·syl·la·ble (mŏn′ə-sĭl′ə-bəl) n. A word or utterance of one syllable. [Late Latin monosyllabum, from Greek monosullabon : MONO- + sullabē, SYLLABLE.]

mon·o·the·ism (mŏn′ə-thē-ĭz′əm) n. The doctrine or belief that there is only one God. Compare **henotheism.** —**mon·o·the·ist** n. & adj. —**mon·o·the·is·tic** (mŏn′ə-thē-ĭs′tĭk) adj. —**mon·o·the·is·ti·cal·ly** adv.

mon·o·tint (mŏn′ə-tĭnt′) n. A picture, a **monochrome** (see).

mon·o·tone (mŏn′ə-tōn′) n. **1.** A succession of sounds or words uttered without changing the pitch of the voice. **2.** Music. **a.** A single tone that is continuously repeated with different words or time values, as in plainsong. **b.** A chant on a single tone. **3.** Sameness, dull repetition, or lack of variety in sound, style, manner, or color. —adj. Also **mon·o·ton·ic** (mŏn′ə-tŏn′ĭk) (for sense 2). **1.** Of, pertaining to, or characteristic of sounds emitted at a single pitch. **2.** Mathematics. Designating sequences of which the successive members either consistently increase or decrease but do not oscillate in relative value. Each member of a monotone increasing sequence is greater than or equal to the preceding member; each member of a monotone decreasing sequence is less than or equal to the preceding member. See **sequence.** [Greek monotonos, having one tone : MONO-, single + tonos, TONE.] —**mon·o·ton·i·cal·ly** adv.

monorail The monorail train at Disneyland in California. The car rides on a single rail of concrete and is supported by rubber wheels on top and at the sides.

mo·not·o·nous (mə-nŏt′n-əs) *adj.* **1.** Unvarying in vocal inflection or pitch; sounded in one persistent tone: *a monotonous drone.* **2.** Without variation or variety; boringly dull: *monotonous work.* —See Synonyms at **boring.** [Greek *monotonos* : MONO-, single + *tonos,* TONE.] —**mo·not·o·nous·ly** *adv.* —**mo·not·o·nous·ness** *n.*

mo·not·o·ny (mə-nŏt′n-ē) *n.* **1.** Uniformity or lack of variation in pitch, intonation, or inflection. **2.** Wearisome sameness; lack of variety. [Greek *monotonia,* from *monotonos,* MONOTONOUS.]

mon·o·treme (mŏn′ə-trēm′) *n.* A member of the Monotremata, an order of egg-laying mammals restricted to Australia and New Guinea, and including the platypus and the echidna. [New Latin *Monotremata* : MONO- + Greek *trēma* (stem *trēmat*-), hole.] —**mon·o·tre·ma·tous** (mŏn′ə-trē′mə-təs, -trĕm′ə-təs) *adj.*

mo·not·ri·chous (mə-nŏt′rĭ-kəs) *adj.* Also **mon·o·trich·ic** (mŏn′-ə-trĭk′ĭk). Having one flagellum at only one pole or end. Said of certain bacteria. [MONO- + TRICH(O)- + -OUS.]

mon·o·troph·ic (mŏn′ə-trŏf′ĭk, -trō′fĭk) *adj.* Requiring only one kind of food; monophagous.

mon·o·type (mŏn′ə-tīp′) *n.* **1.** *Printing.* A single impression from a metal or glass plate of a design or picture. **2.** *Biology.* The sole member of its group, such as a species that also constitutes a genus. —**mon·o·typ·ic** (mŏn′ə-tĭp′ĭk) *adj.*

Mon·o·type (mŏn′ə-tīp′) *n.* A trademark for a typesetting machine operated from a keyboard that activates a unit that casts individual letters from matrices and assembles them.

mon·o·va·lent (mŏn′ə-vā′lənt) *adj. Chemistry.* Possessing a valence of one; univalent. —**mon·o·va·lence, mon·o·va·len·cy** *n.*

mon·ox·ide (mŏ-nŏk′sīd′, mə-) *n.* A compound having only one atom of oxygen. [MON(O)- + OXIDE.]

mon·o·zy·got·ic twin (mŏn′ō-zī-gŏt′ĭk) *n.* An **identical twin** *(see).*

Mon·roe (mən-rō′), **James** (1758–1831). Fifth U.S. president (1817–25), after whom the Monroe Doctrine is named.

Monroe, Marilyn, born Norma Jean Mortenson, also known as "Norma Jean Baker" (1926–62). U.S. film star. She first came to attention in *The Asphalt Jungle* (1950) and revealed her talent for comedy in *Gentlemen Prefer Blondes* (1953) and *How to Marry a Millionaire* (1953). Her other most notable films were *The Seven Year Itch* (1955), *Bus Stop* (1956), *Some Like It Hot* (1959), and her last film, *The Misfits* (1961), written by her husband Arthur Miller. She died from an overdose of sleeping pills.

Monroe Doctrine *n.* The U.S. policy of opposition to outside interference by Europe in the Americas. [After a foreign-policy statement (1823) by President James MONROE.]

Mon·ro·vi·a (mən-rō′vē-ə). Capital of Liberia. The country's chief port and industrial center, it was founded (1822) as a settlement for freed U.S. slaves and was named after President James Monroe.

mons (mŏnz) *n., pl.* **montes** (mŏn′tēz). A protuberance of the human body; especially, the mons pubis or mons veneris, situated over the junctions of the pubic bones at the front of the body. [New Latin, from Latin *mōns* (stem *mont*-), mountain.]

Mons (mōNS). *Flemish* **Ber·gen** (bâr′кнən, -кнə). Capital of Hainaut province, Belgium. British forces fought their first major action of World War I here (1914).

Mon·sar·rat (mŏn-sə-rät′), **Nicholas John Turney** (1910–79). English novelist. He served in the Royal Navy (1940–46) on convoy runs in the Atlantic and wrote *The Cruel Sea* (1951), a best-selling book based on his experiences.

Mon·sei·gneur (môn′sĕn-yœr′) *n., pl.* **Messeigneurs** (mā′sĕn-yœr′). *Abbr.* **Mgr., Mngr., Msgr.** A title of honor and form of address for princes and prelates. [French, "my lord."]

Mon·sieur (mə-syœ′) *n., pl.* **Messieurs** (mĕs′ərz, mā-syœ′). *Abbr.* **M.** **1.** A title of of honor courtesy prefixed to the name or title of a Frenchman, equivalent to the English "Mister," "Sir," or "my Lord," according to the rank of the man. **2.** A respectful form of address for a Frenchman, used instead of the man's name. [French, "my lord."]

Mon·si·gnor (mŏn-sēn′yər) *n., pl.* **-gnors.** *Italian* **Mon·si·gno·re** (mŏn′sēn-yō′rā) *pl.* **-ri** (-rē). *Abbr.* **Mgr., Mngr., Monsig., Msgr.** A title and form of address for certain officials of the Roman Catholic Church. [Italian, from French *monseigneur,* MONSEIGNEUR.]

mon·soon (mŏn-sōōn′) *n.* **1.** A pressure and wind system that influences large climatic regions and reverses seasonally; specifically, the Asiatic monsoon that produces dry and wet seasons in southern and southeastern Asia. **2.** The rain brought by such a system. [Obsolete Dutch *monssoen,* from Portuguese *monção,* from Arabic *mausim,* season, monsoon season.]

mons pu·bis (pyōō′bĭs) *n.* The male mons.

mon·ster (mŏn′stər) *n.* **1.** An imaginary being, such as a cyclops or dragon, made up of elements from various human or animal forms. **2.** An animal or plant having structural defects or deformities. **3.** *Pathology.* A fetus or infant that is grotesquely abnormal. **4.** Any very large animal, plant, or object. **5.** One who inspires horror or disgust: *a monster of wickedness.* ~*adj.* Gigantic; huge. [Middle English *monstre,* from Old French, from Latin *mōnstrum,* prodigy, portent, from *monēre,* to warn.]

mon·ster·a (mŏn′stĕr-ə) *n.* Any plant of the tropical American genus *Monstera,* often cultivated for its glossy foliage. [New Latin, perhaps irregularly from Latin *mōnstrum,* MONSTER.]

mon·strance (mŏn′strəns) *n. Roman Catholic Church.* A receptacle in which the Host is held and exhibited to the congregation. [Middle English, from Old French, from Medieval Latin *mōnstrantia,* from Latin *mōnstrāre,* to show.]

mon·stros·i·ty (mŏn-strŏs′ə-tē) *n., pl.* **-ties.** **1.** One that is monstrous. **2.** The quality or character of being monstrous.

mon·strous (mŏn′strəs) *adj.* **1.** Deviating excessively from the norm in appearance or structure; grotesquely unnatural. **2.** Exceptionally large; enormous: *"Just then flew down a monstrous crow"* (Lewis Carroll). **3.** Hideous; shocking; loathsome: *a monstrous crime.* **4.** Outrageous; disgraceful; indefensible: *a monstrous waste of money.* **5.** Of, pertaining to, or like a fabulous monster: *"Harpies and Hydras, or all the monstrous forms / 'Twixt Africa and Ind"* (Milton). [Middle English from Old French *monstruex,* from Latin *mōnstruōsus,* from *mōnstrum,* MONSTER.] —**mon·strous·ly** *adv.* —**mon·strous·ness** *n.*

mons ven·er·is (vĕn′ər-ĭs) *n.* The female mons.

Mont. Montana.

mon·tage (mŏn-täzh′, môN-) *n.* **1. a.** The art, style, or process of making one pictorial composition from many pictures or designs closely arranged or superimposed upon each other. **b.** A picture so made. **2.** In motion pictures: **a.** The technique of producing a rapid sequence of thematically related short scenes or images exhibiting different aspects of the same idea or situation. **b.** A sequence using this effect. **3.** A mixture of images. [French, "mounting," from *monter,* to MOUNT.]

Mon·ta·gu (mŏn′tə-gyōō′), **Lady Mary Wortley** (1689–1762). English author. She is best known for her lively and amusing letters, first published in *Turkish Letters* (1763). Lady Mary is often considered one of the first advocates of women's rights.

Mon·taigne (môn-tān′, môN-tĕn′yə), **Michel Eyquem, Seigneur de** (1533–92). French essayist. His essays, skeptical, discursive, witty, and lively, are held to be the highest expression of 16th-century French prose.

Mon·ta·le (mŏn-tä′lə), **Eugenio** (1896–1981). Italian poet and critic. His works include *Ossi de Seppia* (1925), *Le Occasioni* (1940), and *La Poesia non Esiste* (1971). He was awarded the Nobel Prize for literature (1975).

Mon·tan·a (mŏn-tăn′ə). *Abbr.* **Mont.** The fourth-largest state of the United States, in the northwestern part of the country. The Rockies rely on forestry, tourism, and mining, while the Great Plains to the east produce cattle, oil, gas, and coal. Part of the Louisiana Purchase (1803), Montana was admitted to the Union in 1889. The capital is Helena. —**Mon·tan·an** *adj. & n.*

mon·tane (mŏn′tān′) *adj.* Of, growing in, or inhabiting mountain areas. [Latin *montānus,* from *mōns.* See **mons.**]

mon·tan wax (mŏn′tən, -tän′) *n.* A hard, white wax obtained from lignite and used in the manufacture of polishes, candles, and insulators. [Latin *montānus,* MONTANE.]

Mon·tauk Point (mŏn′tôk′). The easternmost extremity of Long Island, in southeastern New York State. It is a popular tourist and vacation spot.

Mont Blanc (môN blän′). Mountain in France, near the French-Italian border. It is the highest peak (4,807 meters; 15,771 feet) in Europe outside the U.S.S.R. Beneath it runs a road tunnel (12 kilometers; 7.5 miles) opened in 1965.

Mont·calm de Saint-Vé·ran (mŏnt-käm′ də săn′vā-rän′, môN-kälm′), **Louis Joseph de, Marquis** (1712–59). French general. Sent to Canada to command the French forces in the French and Indian War (1756), he defended Fort Ticonderoga (1758) and held Quebec (1759) until the Battle of the Plains of Abraham, in which the British were victorious, but both he and the English general, James Wolfe, were killed.

mon·te (mŏn′tē) *n.* A game in which each player bets that one of two cards will be matched by the dealer before the other one. Also called "monte bank." [Spanish, "mountain," referring to the pile of unplayed cards, from Latin *mōns* (stem *mont*-), mountain.]

Mon·te Al·bán (mŏn′tä äl-bän′). A ruined Zapotec city in southwestern Mexico.

Mon·te Car·lo (mŏn′tē kär′lō). Seaside resort of Monaco, famous for its casinos, its annual automobile rally, and the Monaco Grand Prix race.

Monte Cas·si·no (kə-sē′nō). A hill overlooking the town of Cassino, central Italy. Its monastery, which was founded (*c.* 529) by St. Benedict, was used in World War II by the Nazis as a fortress and was destroyed by the Allies. It has since been restored and rededicated (1964).

Mon·te·ne·gro (mŏn′tə-nē′grō). The smallest constituent republic of Yugoslavia. Lying on the Adriatic, it is predominantly mountainous and agricultural, but does have considerable mineral resources. An ancient state of the Balkans, it was an independent kingdom from 1910 until 1918, when it joined the new Kingdom of Serbs, Croats, and Slovenes, which became Yugoslavia in 1929.

Mon·te·rey (mŏn′tə-rā′). A city of western California, on Monterey Bay, an inlet of the Pacific. It is a commercial and manufacturing center for the fertile Salinas River valley. The Monterey peninsula is a noted scenic resort region that includes Big Sur and Carmel.

mon·te·ro (mŏn-târ′ō) *n., pl.* **-ros.** A huntsman's cap with side flaps. [Spanish, "hunter," from *monte,* forest region, mountain. See **monte.**]

Mon·ter·rey (mŏn′tə-rā′). Capital of Nuevo León state, northeastern Mexico. The country's third-largest city, it is an important industrial center with iron, steel, and lead works and textile, glass, and chemical industries. It is also a resort with hot springs.

mon·tes. Plural of **mons.**

Mon·tes·quieu (mŏn′tə-skyōō′, môN′tĕs-kyœ′), **Charles Louis de Secondat, Baron de la Brède et de** (1689–1755). French jurist and political philosopher, one of the oustanding figures of the early

monstera *A genus of plants cultivated for their ornamental leaves. This is the fruit of* Monstera tuberculata.

Moon

A DEAD AND BATTERED WORLD
Over craters large and small lies a blanket of dust

The Moon is Earth's only natural satellite, and is exceptionally large compared to satellites of other planets. Its obvious features have long been known—that it creates tides, that its phases mark its monthly orbit, that it is scarred with craters and dark areas known as "seas" (maria), and that it keeps one side permanently toward Earth.

It is no longer believed that the Earth and the Moon were originally one body. The Moon has always been separate from the Earth and is about as old. The Moon was formed 4.6 billion years ago. Many astronomers believe that its craters were formed by meteorite impacts more than 3 billion years ago. Very large strikes caused molten rock to flow and form the maria. However, other astronomers consider that volcanic activity has played a major role in the molding of the lunar surface. A rain of tiny particles has eroded the surface into a thin layer of dust. Space research between 1960 and 1975 revealed much detail about the Moon.

METEORITE-MADE "SEAS" *The Moon's disk as seen from an approaching spacecraft clearly reveals the huge, dark maria and also shows their roughly circular shapes. They may be the result of massive meteorite impacts in the early stages of the formation of the Earth, Moon, and Solar System. One such feature is the Mare Imbrium, about 676 kilometers (420 miles) across and produced by the impact of a meteorite 128 kilometers (80 miles) across. It scattered rocks for over 1,600 kilometers (1,000 miles). The basins were filled with dark lava welling up from the Moon's interior. The lava was later pitted with secondary impacts. Generally, the larger the crater, the older it is. Apparently, larger meteorites ceased to exist soon after the Solar System formed.*

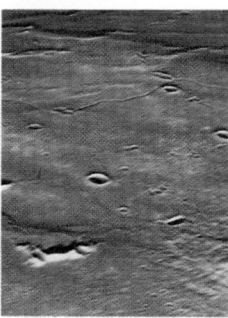

MEN ON THE MOON *The site where Apollo 11, the first manned mission to the Moon, landed was here, in the Sea of Tranquillity. It is typical of the floors of the maria—a smooth lava base that filled in the impact crater, a scattering of younger smaller craters, and a light covering of dust formed by the rain of micrometeorites. It was on July 21, 1969, that Neil Armstrong took what he called "one small step for a man, one giant leap for mankind" as he stepped onto the Moon.*

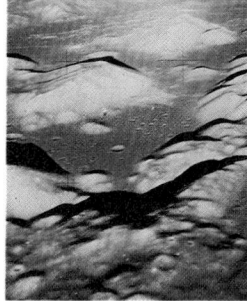

GLASS AT HIS FEET *Apollo 17, the last of the U.S. lunar missions, landed on this rough area on the edge of the Sea of Serenity in December 1972. One of the crew was geologist Harrison Schmitt, the first scientist on the moon. Lunar soil and rocks had been returned to earth on previous missions, but Schmitt caused excitement when he kicked up some "orange soil" —tiny glass beads formed by intense heat. This type of information made the Apollo missions very valuable to science.*

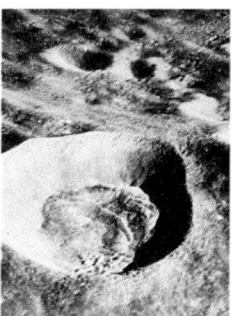

A YOUNG CRATER *A steep, crisply outlined young crater overlapping the heavily eroded ridge of a much older crater clearly shows its meteoric origins. Although some craters on the Moon may be the result of volcanic activity, this one is not. The floor of the crater is below that of the surrounding rock, whereas in a volcano the crater is created on the top of a mound of ejected lava. The nearly circular rim is the result of the explosion of compressed hot rock that took place at impact.*

French Enlightenment. He is famous chiefly for two books, the *Persian Letters* (1721), a veiled attack on the monarchy and institutions of the ancien régime, and *The Spirit of the Laws* (1748), a lengthy disquisition on the forms of government.

Mon·tes·so·ri method (mŏn′tə-sôr′ē, -sōr′ē-) *n.* A method of educating young children that stresses development of a child's own initiative and natural abilities, especially through practical play. Also called "Montessori system." [After Maria *Montessori* (1870–1952), Italian educator.]

Mon·te·ver·di (mŏn′tə-vâr′dē), **Claudio Giovanni Antonio** (1567–1643). Italian composer. Throughout his life he wrote madrigals and sacred music, but his great importance is as one of the founders of opera. His operas include *Orfeo* (1607), *Il Ritorno di Ulisse in Patria* (1641), and *L'Incoronazione di Poppea* (1642).

Mon·te·vi·de·o (mŏn′tə-vĭ-dā′ō). Capital of Uruguay since 1828. An important seaport, fishing center, resort, and railway junction, it was founded (1726) by the Spanish on the Río de la Plata. The country's only important industrial city, it has footwear, textiles, soap, and food-processing and tanning industries.

Mon·tez (mŏn-tĕz′), **Lola,** born Marie Dolores Eliza Rosanna Gilbert (c. 1818–61). Irish dancer famous for her beauty. She adopted the name Lola Montez when she began to dance, claiming Spanish descent. She had affairs with Liszt and Dumas *père* and also, most notoriously, with Ludwig I, king of Bavaria, from 1846 to 1848.

Mon·te·zu·ma II (mŏn′tə-zōō′mə), also **Moc·te·zu·ma** (mŏk′tə-zōō′-mə) (c. 1480–1520). Aztec emperor (c. 1502–20). The Spanish explorer Cortés tried to govern through him, but during an Aztec insurrection Montezuma was killed, though whether by the Spanish or the Aztecs it is not certain.

Montezuma's revenge *n.* An attack of diarrhea experienced by a tourist visiting a tropical country. Used humorously.

Mont·fort (mŏnt′fərt), **Simon de, Earl of Leicester** (c. 1208–65). English baron, born in France, leader of the baronial opposition to Henry III. He and other barons forced Henry to sign the Provisions of Oxford (1258), and after his victory over the king at Lewes (1264) he was the effective ruler of England. He called a parliament in 1265 that included representatives from the boroughs and is often regarded as the first modern parliament.

Mont·gol·fi·er (mŏnt-gŏl′fē-ər, môn′gôl-fyā′), **Joseph Michel** (1740–1810) and **Jacques Étienne** (1745–99). French brothers who invented the hot-air balloon in which the first manned flight took place in November 1783.

Mont·gom·er·y (mŏnt-gŭm′ə-rē, -gŭm′rē). Capital of Alabama, in the central part of the state. It is a market and industrial center on the Alabama River. It became the first capital of the Confederate States of America (1861). In the 1950's and 1960's it was the center of the civil rights movement.

Montgomery of Al·a·mein (ăl′ə-mān′), **1st Viscount,** born Bernard Law Montgomery (1887–1976). British soldier. He served in both India and World War I. In 1939 he commanded the Third Division in France; he was made leader of the Fifth Corps after Dunkirk and at the end of 1941 was given command of the South Eastern Army in England. In command of the Eighth Army in North Africa, he halted Rommel's Africa Corps at Alam el-Haifa in August 1942 and in October won victory at El Alamein. Promoted to general, he led the Allied assault through Normandy in 1944, and in 1945 he became a field marshal and commander in chief of the British Army in Germany.

Mont·gom·er·y·shire (mənt-gŭm′rē-shîr′, -shər). Former county of central Wales, since 1974 part of Powys.

month (mŭnth) *n. Abbr.* m, M, m., M., mo. **1.** Any of the 12 divisions of a year as determined by the Gregorian calendar. Also called "calendar month." **2.** Any period extending from a date in one calendar month to the corresponding date in the following month. **3.** The average period of revolution of the moon around the earth determined by using a fixed star as a reference point and equal to 27 days 7 hours 43 minutes 12 seconds. Also called "sidereal month." **4.** The average time between successive new or full moons, equal to 29 days 12 hours 44 minutes. Also called "lunar month," "synodic month," "lunation." **5.** One twelfth of a tropical year, totaling 27 days 7 hours 43 minutes 5 seconds. Also called "solar month." **—month of Sundays.** *Informal.* An indefinitely long period of time. [Middle English *moneth,* Old English *mōnath,* from Germanic; akin to MOON.]

month·ly (mŭnth′lē) *adj.* **1.** Occurring, appearing, or coming due every month. **2.** Continuing or lasting for a month.
—*adv.* Once a month; by the month; every month.
—*n., pl.* **monthlies. 1.** A periodical publication appearing once each month. **2.** *Informal.* A menstrual period.

Mon·ti·cel·lo (mŏn′tĭ-chĕl′ō, -sĕl′ō). Home and estate of Thomas Jefferson, in central Virginia near Charlottesville. Designed by Jefferson, it dates from 1770. Sold by his daughter after Jefferson's death, it was transferred (1923) from private hands to the Thomas Jefferson Memorial Foundation. Restored to its original beauty, Monticello has been open to the public since 1954.

mon·ti·cule (mŏn′tĭ-kyōōl′) *n.* **1.** A small hill. **2.** A small mound produced by volcanic action. [French, from Late Latin *monticulus,* diminutive of Latin *mōns* (stem *mont-*), mountain.]

Mont·mar·tre (môn-mär′trə). A district in northern Paris, noted for its cafes and nightclubs.

Mont·par·nasse (môn′pär-näs′). A district of southern Paris, on the left bank of the Seine, noted as a gathering place for intellectuals and artists.

Mont·pel·ier (mŏnt-pēl′yər). Capital of Vermont, in the central part of the state. It is the trading center of a lumber, granite-quarrying, and winter resort area. The state government is important to its economy.

Mont·pel·lier (môn′pĕl-yā′). Capital of Hérault department, southern France. It is a center of the wine trade and famous for its university (1289), incorporating a 10th-century medical school.

Mon·tre·al (mŏn′trē-ôl′). *French* **Mont·ré·al** (môn′rā-äl′). City in Quebec, southeastern Canada. On Montreal Island at the confluence of the St. Lawrence and Ottawa rivers, it was founded (1642) as the French settlement of Ville Marie de Montréal, at the foot of Mount Royal. Today it is Canada's largest city and most important port (it lies on the St. Lawrence Seaway), the world's second-largest French-speaking city, and an important communications, industrial, trade, and cultural center.

Mon·treux (môN-trœ′). Town in Vaud canton, Switzerland, at the eastern end of Lake Geneva. An important tourist center, it has an annual television festival. The 13th-century Château de Chillon nearby figures in Byron's *Prisoner of Chillon.*

Mont·ser·rat (mŏnt′sə-răt′). British island colony, in the Caribbean Sea. It was discovered by Columbus (1493) and settled by the British. Tourism and agriculture are important, and exports include cotton and bananas. Plymouth is the capital.

Mont St. Mi·chel (môN′săN mē-shĕl′). Rocky islet in Manche department, northwestern France. Its principal feature is a Benedictine abbey (708–9), used as a prison from the French Revolution until 1863. It is connected to the mainland by a causeway.

mon·u·ment (mŏn′yə-mənt) *n.* **1.** A structure, such as a building, tower, or sculpture, erected as a memorial. **2.** An inscribed stone or other marker placed at a grave or tomb; a tombstone. **3.** A site or building of special historical or archaeological importance, preserved by the government. See **national monument.** **4.** A written legal document. **5.** An outstanding and enduring achievement viewed as a model for later generations and worthy of lasting fame. **6.** Something that commemorates by association: *"Although Henry Hudson himself was gone, his bay, his strait and his river remained as monuments to his life"* (Virginia S. Eifert). **7.** An exceptional example of something: *"Thousands of them wrote texts, some of them monuments of dullness"* (Robert L. Heilbroner). [Middle English, from Latin *monumentum,* from *monēre,* to remind, warn.]

mon·u·men·tal (mŏn′yə-mĕn′tәl) *adj.* **1.** Of, resembling, or serving as a monument. **2.** Impressively large, sturdy, and enduring. **3.** Of outstanding and lasting significance: *her monumental contribution to the theater.* **4.** Enormous and astounding: *her monumental stupidity.* **5.** *Fine Arts.* Larger than life-size. **—mon·u·men·tal·ly** *adv.*

mon·u·men·tal·ize (mŏn′yə-mĕn′tə-līz′) *tr.v.* **-ized, -izing, -izes.** To memorialize with a monument.

mon·zo·nite (mŏn-zō′nīt′, mŏn′zə-nīt′) *n.* A coarse-grained igneous rock composed chiefly of plagioclase and orthoclase in approximately equal proportions, with small amounts of other minerals. [French, after Mount *Monzoni* in northeastern Italy, where it was discovered.]

moo (mo͞o) *n., pl.* **moos. 1.** The characteristic deep, bellowing sound made by a cow. **2.** Any similar sound.
~*intr.v.* **mooed, mooing, moos.** To make a moo. [Imitative.]

mooch (mo͞och) *v.* **mooched, mooching, mooches.** Also *chiefly British* **mouch** (mo͞och). *Slang.* —*tr.* **1.** To obtain by cajolery or begging. **2.** To steal or filch. —*intr.* **1.** To dawdle or loiter aimlessly. Often used with *along.* **2.** To lurk or skulk about. [Middle English *mowche,* from Old French *muchier,* to hide.] **—mooch·er** *n.*

mood[1] (mo͞od) *n.* **1.** A temporary state of mind or feeling, as evidenced by one's behavior or the tendency of one's thoughts: *a gloomy mood.* **2.** A prevailing spirit, disposition, or set of attitudes: *The book captures the mood of the Edwardian period.* **3.** A pervading impression on the feelings of an observer: *the somber mood of the painting.* **4.** A spell of sulking or morose behavior: *He's in one of his moods.* **—in the mood.** Inclined; disposed. [Middle English *mod,* Old English *mōd,* mind, thought, from Germanic.]
Synonyms: *humor, temper.*

mood[2] *n.* **1.** *Grammar.* A class of verb forms used to indicate the speaker's attitude toward the utterance or the person addressed or toward the factuality or likelihood of the action or condition expressed. In English, the indicative mood is usually used for factual statements, the subjunctive mood to indicate doubt, unlikelihood, or wish, and the imperative mood to express a command. Compare **aspect. 2.** *Logic.* Any of the various ways in which a proposition may be constructed. [Alteration of MODE, influenced by MOOD (state of mind).]

mood·y (mo͞o′dē) *adj.* **-ier, -iest. 1.** Given to changeable emotional states; temperamental. **2.** Gloomy; glum; grumpy: *a moody silence.* **—mood·i·ly** *adv.* **—mood·i·ness** *n.*

Moo·dy (mo͞o′dē), **Dwight Lyman** (1837–99). U.S. evangelist. Never ordained, he was a noted fundamentalist preacher whose simple, colorful, and direct style stressed God's love and mercy. He founded a number of educational institutions.

moo goo gai pan (mo͞o′ go͞o′ gī′ păn′) *n.* A Cantonese dish of chicken, mushrooms, vegetables, and spices, steamed together. [Cantonese, corresponding to Mandarin *mu*[2] *gu*[2] *ji*[1] *pian*[1] : *mu*[2] *gu*[2], mushroom + *ji*[1], chicken + *pian*[1], slice.]

Moog synthesizer (mōg, mo͞og) *n.* A trademark for an electronic keyboard instrument that is capable of generating a large variety of sounds. Also called "Moog," "synthesizer." [After R.A. *Moog,* U.S. engineer who invented it.]

moo·la, moo·lah (mo͞o′lə) *n. Slang.* Money. [Origin unknown.]

mool·vi, mool·vie (mo͞ol′vē) *n.* A Muslim who is very learned or a doctor of the law. Used especially in India as a title of respect. [Urdu *Mulvī,* from Arabic *mawlawīyah,* judicial.]

moon (mo͞on) *n.* **1. Moon.** *Astronomy.* The natural satellite of the earth, visible by reflection of sunlight, having a slightly elliptical orbit, approximately 356,500 kilometers (221,600 miles) distant at perigee and 407,000 kilometers (252,900 miles) at apogee. Its mean diameter is 3,475 kilometers (2,160 miles), its mass approximately one eightieth that of the earth, and its average period of revolution around the earth 29 days 12 hours 44 minutes calculated with respect to the sun. **2.** A natural satellite orbiting a planet. **3.** The moon as it appears at a particular time in its cycle of phases: *the full moon; a half moon.* **4.** A month, especially a lunar month. **5.** A disk, globe, or crescent resembling the moon. **6.** Moonlight. **—crying for the moon.** Striving or yearning for something unattainable. **—once in a blue moon.** Never or hardly ever.
~*v.* **mooned, mooning, moons.** —*intr.* **1.** To wander about or pass time languidly and aimlessly. **2.** To exhibit infatuation, especially by being inattentive or listless: *mooning over a lost girlfriend.* —*tr.* To pass (time) idly. Used with *away.* [Middle English *moone, mon,* Old English *mōna,* from Germanic; akin to MONTH.]

moon·beam (mo͞on′bēm′) *n.* A ray of moonlight.

moon blindness *n.* Recurrent inflammation of horses' eyes, often resulting in blindness. Also called "mooneye."

moon·calf (mo͞on′kăf′, -käf′) *n.* **1.** A fool from birth; a stupid creature. **2.** An inattentive, daydreaming person. **3.** *Archaic.* A freak. [From the supposed maleficent influence of the moon on the unborn.]

moon dog *n.* A bright spot on a lunar halo, a **paraselene** *(see).*

moon·eye (mo͞on′ī′) *n.* **1.** A silvery freshwater fish, *Hiodon tergisus,* of northern North America. **2.** Moon blindness.

moon-faced (mo͞on′fāst′) *adj.* Having a round face.

moon·fish (mo͞on′fĭsh′) *n., pl.* **-fishes** or collectively **moonfish. 1.** Any of various fishes of the family Carangidae, having rounded bodies that are silver to yellowish in color. Also called "dollarfish." **2.** A large marine fish, the **opah** *(see).*

moon·flow·er (mo͞on′flou′ər) *n.* Any of various white-flowered, often night-blooming plants, such as *Ipomaea alba,* a morning glory.

moon·light (mo͞on′līt′) *n.* The light reflected from the surface of the moon, principally that originating at the sun.
~*adj.* **1.** Of moonlight. **2.** Under moonlight.
~*intr.v.* **moonlighted, -lighting, -lights.** *Informal.* To work at a second job, often at night, in addition to one's full-time job. **—moon·light·er** *n.* **—moon·light·ing** *n.*

moon·lit (mo͞on′lĭt′) *adj.* Illuminated by the moon.

moon rat *n.* A large, ratlike, nocturnal, insectivorous mammal, *Echinosorex gymnurus,* of Southeast Asia, having grayish fur and a long snout.

moon·scape (mo͞on′skāp′) *n.* **1.** A view or picture of the surface of the moon. **2.** A desolate landscape. [MOON + -SCAPE.]

moon·seed (mo͞on′sēd′) *n.* Any of several climbing vines of the genus *Menispermum* or related genera, having red or blackish fruit with crescent-shaped or ring-shaped seeds.

moon shell *n.* Any of various marine gastropod mollusks of the family Naticidae, having smooth spherical shells.

moon·shine (mo͞on′shīn′) *n.* **1.** Moonlight. **2.** *Informal.* Foolish or nonsensical talk, thought, or action. **3.** *Slang.* Illegally distilled whiskey.
~*v.* **moonshined, -shining, -shines.** —*tr.* To distill (alcoholic liquor) illegally. —*intr.* To operate an illegal still. **—moon·shine** *adj.* **—moon·shin·er** *n.*

moon·shot (mo͞on′shŏt′) *n.* A launching of a spacecraft or rocket to the moon.

moon·stone (mo͞on′stōn′) *n.* A feldspar valued as a gem for its pearly translucence; especially, **albite, labradorite,** or **orthoclase** *(all of which see).* It is found worldwide.

moon·struck (mo͞on′strŭk′) *adj.* **1.** Dazed or distracted with romantic sentiment; lovelorn. **2.** Afflicted with insanity; crazed; deranged. [From the belief that moonlight inspires romantic love and causes insanity.]

Moon type (mo͞on) *n.* A system of printing for the blind that uses embossed letters instead of the raised dots of Braille, requiring less sensitivity of the fingers. [After William *Moon* (1819–94), British inventor.]

moon·wort (mo͞on′wûrt′, -wôrt′) *n.* The **grape fern** *(see).* [The leaflets are shaped like the crescent moon.]

moon·y (mo͞o′nē) *adj.* **-ier, -iest. 1. a.** Of or resembling the moon. **b.** Resembling moonlight. **c.** Moonlit. **2.** Dreamy in mood or nature; absent-minded. **—moon·i·ly** *adj.*

moor[1] (mo͝or) *v.* **moored, mooring, moors.** —*tr.* **1.** To secure or make fast (a boat, for example) by means of cables, anchors, or other contrivances. **2.** To fix in place; secure. —*intr.* **1.** To secure a vessel or aircraft. **2.** To be secured, as is a vessel or hot-air balloon. [Middle English *moren,* from Middle Low German *mōren.*]

moor[2] *n.* A broad tract of open land, often high but poorly drained, with patches of heath and peat bogs. [Middle English *mor,* Old English *mōr,* from Germanic.]

Moor (mo͝or) *n.* **1.** A member of a Muslim people of mixed Berber and Arab descent, now living chiefly in northern Africa. **2.** Any of the Muslims who invaded Spain in the 8th century A.D. and established a civilization there that lasted until 1492. [Middle English *More,* from Old French, from Latin *Maurus,* from Greek *Mauros,* probably of North African origin.]

moor·age (mo͝or′ĭj) *n.* **1.** A place where a vessel can be moored. **2.** The act of mooring or state of being moored. **3.** A charge for the use of mooring facilities.

moor·cock (mo͝or′kŏk′) *n.* A male red grouse.

Moore (mo͝or), **Clement Clarke** (1779–1863). U.S. educator and poet. He was a professor of Oriental and Greek literature at Columbia University, but is best remembered as the author of "A Visit from St. Nicholas" (1823), the classic Christmas poem.

Montezuma II *The Aztec emperor Montezuma is carried in state on his way to meet Cortés (detail of a painting on mother-of-pearl by Miguel Gonzales in the Museo de America, Madrid).*

moonstone *This semiprecious stone, found in Sri Lanka and India, appears to shimmer like moonlight when it is cut "en cabochon"—with a domed top and flat bottom. In folklore, it is said to have magic properties that change with the phases of the moon: during a waxing moon it is a love charm; during a waning moon it is an aid to clairvoyance.*

Henry Moore

SCULPTURES WHOSE BEAUTY IS THEIR VITALITY

The natural forms of bones, shells, and rocks inspire Britain's most original sculptor

Born the seventh son of a Yorkshire coal miner in 1898, Henry Moore began his working life at 18 as a schoolteacher in his hometown of Castleford. After serving in the latter part of World War I, he studied sculpture in Leeds and London and became attracted by Egyptian, African, Etruscan, and Mexican art forms. They had a profound influence on his future work.

Moore exhibited his first concrete sculptures—of reclining female figures—in 1926 in London. He obtained his first public commission in 1928; it was for a relief carving, *North Wind,* to be placed on the façade of the new London Underground station, St. James's Park.

During the 1930's he concentrated on stone and wood carvings, both figurative and abstract. In September 1940 during the German blitz on London, he made an evocative set of drawings of people sheltering in the Underground from the bombs and became an official war artist. He made a series of drawings of miners working at the coal face at Castleford, then in 1942 resumed his sculpture.

In sculpting human forms, he strove to make the spaces they contained as meaningful as the figures themselves. He rejected traditional ideas of beauty in sculpture. "A work of art must have a vitality of its own," he stated. "When a work has this powerful vitality we do not connect the word 'beauty' with it."

After his early work, Moore's sculptures became less abstract. He examined bones, shells, rocks, and hills to find what he called "nature's principles of form and rhythm," and he tried to use these natural forms, rather than geometric shapes, in his work. He separated the shapes that make up the human body, but they remained powerful human figures, expressing intense emotions.

In 1943–44 Moore carved a tender *Madonna and Child* for St. Matthew's Church, Northampton, England. His later works include forms for outdoor settings—among them the striking, two-piece reclining figure set in a pool at New York's Lincoln Center (1963–64).

Henry Moore has been internationally hailed as Britain's most original sculptor and was awarded the Order of Merit in 1963. In New York in May 1982, an elmwood figure carved by him fetched a price higher than any previously paid at auction for a work by a living artist: $1,265,000.

FAMILY GROUP *Moore became a father in 1946 when he was 47. He celebrated the birth of his only child, Mary, with this casting in bronze, now at Barclay School, Stevenage, Hertfordshire, England.*

Moore, George Edward (1873–1958). English philosopher. From 1925 to 1939 he was professor of philosophy at Cambridge University. His *Principia Ethica* (1903) laid the foundations of much of 20th-century epistemology and linguistic analysis.

Moore, Henry (1898–1986). English sculptor. He established his international reputation with a one-man retrospective show at the Museum of Modern Art, New York, in 1946. Moore carves abstract figures in many media.

Moore, Marianne Craig (1887–1972). U.S. poet. She worked as a librarian and editor of the *Dial* in New York City. Her poetry, mosaiclike in form, features wit, irony, and deep moral feelings. She won a Pulitzer Prize for her *Collected Poems* (1951).

Moore, Thomas (1779–1852). Irish-born poet. His lyrics include *Believe Me If All Those Endearing Young Charms.*

moor·fowl (mŏŏr'foul') *n.* The **red grouse** (see).

moor·hen (mŏŏr'hĕn') *n.* **1.** A common, widely distributed water bird, *Gallinula chloropus,* having dark plumage, a red bill and found in ponds and marshes. **2.** A female red grouse.

moor·ing (mŏŏr'ĭng) *n.* **1. a.** *Usually* **moorings.** Equipment, such as anchors, chains, or lines, for holding fast a vessel. **b.** A permanent anchor for mooring a vessel, with a buoy attached. **2.** A place at which a vessel can be moored. **3.** *Usually* **moorings.** An element providing stability or security: *lost her emotional moorings.*

Moor·ish (mŏŏr'ĭsh) *adj.* **1.** Of or pertaining to the Moors or their culture. **2.** Designating a style of Spanish architecture of the 13th to 16th centuries, characterized by the horseshoe arch and ornate decoration.

Moorish idol *n.* A tropical marine fish, *Zanclus canescens,* with a deeply compressed body marked with black and yellow stripes, a beaklike mouth, and an enlarged dorsal fin.

moor·land (mŏŏr'lănd, -lənd') *n. British.* A tract of moors.

moor·wort (mŏŏr'wûrt', -wôrt') *n.* A plant, the **bog rosemary** (see). [MOOR + WORT.]

moose (mŏŏs) *n., pl.* **moose.** A hoofed mammal, *Alces alces* (or *A. americana*), of the deer family, found in forests of northern North America and in Eurasia. It has a broad, pendulous muzzle, and the male has large, flat antlers. [Natick *moos,* from Proto-Algonquian *mooswa* (unattested).]

moose·wood (mŏŏs'wŏŏd') *n.* A slender maple, *Acer pennsylvanicum,* of eastern North America, having smooth bark with vertical whitish or greenish stripes.

moot (mŏŏt) *n.* **1.** In early medieval England, a meeting; especially, a representative meeting of the freemen of a shire. **2.** A hypothetical case argued by law students as an exercise. *~tr.v.* **mooted, mooting, moots. 1. a.** To offer as a subject for debate; bring up for discussion. **b.** To discuss or debate. **2.** To plead or argue (a case) in a moot court. *~adj.* **1.** Subject to debate; arguable; unresolved: *a moot point.* **2. a.** *Law.* Without legal significance through having been previously decided or settled. **b.** Of no practical importance. [Middle English *mot, moot,* from Old English *mōt,* moot, assembly, from Germanic; akin to MEET.]

moot court *n.* A mock court where hypothetical cases are tried for the training of law students.

mop¹ (mŏp) *n.* **1.** A household implement made of absorbent material attached to a handle and used especially for cleaning or drying floors. **2.** Any loosely tangled bunch or mass: *a mop of hair.* *~tr.v.* **mopped, mopping, mops.** To wash, scrub, or wipe with or as if with a mop. Often used with *up: mopped floors; mopped up the spilled water.* [Middle English *mappe,* perhaps from *mappel,* from Medieval Latin *mappula,* towel, cloth, diminutive of Latin *mappa,* cloth.]

mop² *intr.v.* **mopped, mopping, mops.** *Archaic.* To grimace. *~n. Archaic.* A grimace. [Perhaps imitative of a pout.]

mop·board (mŏp'bôrd', -bōrd') *n.* The baseboard around a room next to the floor.

mope (mōp) *intr.v.* **moped, moping, mopes. 1.** To be gloomy or dejected. **2.** To give oneself up to brooding or sulking. *~n.* **1.** A person given to gloomy or dejected moods. **2. mopes.** Low spirits; the blues. [Originally, to move as in a daze, perhaps from Middle Dutch *mopen.*] **—mop·er** *n.* **—mop·ing·ly** *adv.* **—mop·ish** *adj.* **—mop·ish·ly** *adv.*

mo·ped (mō'pĕd') *n.* A light motorbike that can be pedaled and has a low-powered motor. [Swedish *mo*(tor) *ped*(aler), motor pedals.]

mo·poke (mō'pōk') *n.* Also **more·pork** (môr'pôrk', mōr'pōrk'). A small owl, *Ninox novaeseelandiae,* of Australia and New Zealand, having spotted plumage. [Imitative of the bird's song.]

mop·pet (mŏp'ĭt) *n.* A young child; especially, a little girl. [Diminutive of obsolete *moppe,* child, fool, probably of Low German origin, akin to Low German *mops,* fool.]

mop up *tr.v.* **1. a.** To destroy (remaining enemy resistance) after an initial victory. **b.** To clear (an area) of remaining enemy troops after a victory. **2.** *Informal.* To acquire or achieve; garner: *a film that mopped up all the Academy Awards.* *—intr.v.* To complete a task or action; finish: *Now that we're done, you go home—I'll mop up.*

mop-up (mŏp'ŭp') *n.* A finishing action.

mo·quette (mō-kĕt') *n.* **1.** A heavy fabric with a thick nap, used for upholstery. **2.** A type of carpet with a deep, tufted pile. [French, variant of obsolete *moucade†.*]

MOR middle-of-the-road.

mor. morocco (leather).

Mor. Morocco.

mo·ra (môr′ə, mōr′ə) *n., pl.* **morae** (môr′ē, mōr′ē) or **-ras.** **1.** In quantitative verse, the unit of metrical time equal to the short syllable. **2.** A phonological unit equal to one short-voweled syllable or half of a long-voweled syllable. [Latin, "pause."]

mo·raine (mə-rān′) *n.* An accumulation of rocks, stones, or other debris carried and deposited by a glacier or ice sheet. *A ground moraine* is taken up by the base of the ice and deposited over wide areas. *A terminal moraine* is material carried forward by the ice and deposited as a ridge at the tip or edge. A *lateral moraine*, carried on the side of a valley glacier, is mostly derived from the valley wall and is deposited at the sides. A *medial moraine* is the combined adjacent lateral moraines of two valley glaciers below their confluence. [French, from Italian dialectal *morena*†.] **—mo·rain·al, mo·rain·ic** *adj.*

mor·al (môr′əl, mŏr′-) *adj.* **1.** Of or concerned with the judgment of the goodness or badness of human action and character; pertaining to the discernment of good and evil: *the moral point of view of a novel.* **2.** Designed to teach goodness or correctness of character and behavior; instructive of what is good and bad: *a moral lesson; moral advice.* **3.** Being or acting in accordance with standards and precepts of goodness or with established codes of behavior, especially with regard to sexual conduct. **4.** Arising from conscience or the sense of right and wrong: *a moral obligation.* **5.** Having psychological rather than physical or tangible effects; concerning morale: *moral support.* **6.** Based upon strong likelihood or firm conviction rather than upon the actual evidence or demonstration: *a moral certainty.*
∼n. **1. a.** The lesson or principle contained in or taught by a fable, story, or event. **b.** This lesson as encapsulated in the concluding sentence of a fable: *Moral: Look before you leap.* **2.** A concisely expressed precept or general truth; a maxim. **3. morals.** Rules or habits of conduct, especially sexual conduct, with reference to standards of right and wrong: *loose morals.* [Middle English, from Old French, from Latin *mōrālis,* from *mōs* (stem *mōr-*), custom.]
Synonyms: *ethical, righteous, virtuous.*
Usage: *Moral* and *morale* are sometimes confused in their noun uses. *Moral* has the sense "lesson, precept" and has a plural form referring to "rules of proper conduct." *Morale* refers to the degree of confidence or optimism of a person or group, as shown in their behavior; it has no plural form.

mo·rale (mə-răl′) *n.* The state of the spirits of an individual or group as shown in willingness to perform assigned tasks, confidence, cheerfulness, and discipline. —See Usage note at **moral.** [French, feminine of *moral,* moral, from Old French, MORAL.]

moral hazard *n. Insurance.* A risk to an insurer resulting from uncertainty about an insured's honesty or discretion.

mor·al·ism (môr′ə-lĭz′əm, mŏr′-) *n.* **1.** A conventional moral maxim or attitude. **2.** The act or practice of moralizing. **3.** The practice of or belief in a system of principles governing conduct as distinct from a religion. **3.** An often undue concern with morality.

mor·al·ist (môr′ə-lĭst, mŏr′-) *n.* **1.** A teacher or student of ethics. **2.** A person who follows a system of moral principles as distinct from an established religion. **3.** One who is unduly concerned with the morals of others.

mor·al·is·tic (môr′ə-lĭs′tĭk, mŏr′-) *adj.* **1.** Characterized by or given to moralizing, especially in a priggish way. **2.** Marked by narrow-minded morality. **—mor·al·is·ti·cal·ly** *adv.*

mo·ral·i·ty (mə-răl′ə-tē, mô-) *n., pl.* **-ties.** **1.** The quality of being moral. **2.** The evaluation of or a means of evaluating human conduct, especially: **a.** A set of ideas of right and wrong: *Christian morality.* **b.** A set of customs of a given society, class, or social group that regulate personal and social relationships and prescribe modes of behavior to facilitate the group's existence or ensure its survival: *middle-class morality.* **3.** Virtuous conduct, especially conduct in compliance with approved codes for sexual behavior. **4.** A rule or lesson in moral conduct; a moral. **5.** A morality play.

morality play *n.* A play in a genre of the 15th and 16th centuries in which moral instruction is conveyed by allegorically personifying virtues and vices in stories drawn from popular legend.

mor·al·ize (môr′ə-līz′, mŏr′-) *v.* **-ized, -izing, -izes.** *—tr.* **1.** To derive a moral lesson from (a story, for example); explain in moral terms. **2.** To improve the morals of; reform. *—intr.* **1.** To think about or discuss moral or ethical issues. **2.** To make moral judgments or statements, often in a priggish way. **—mor·al·i·za·tion** *n.* **—mor·al·iz·er** *n.*

mor·al·ly (môr′ə-lē, mŏr′-) *adv.* **1.** In accordance with accepted rules of conduct; virtuously. **2.** With reference to moral law; ethically. **3.** In all probability; virtually: *morally certain.*

moral philosophy *n.* See **ethics** (sense 1a).

Moral Rearmament *n. Abbr.* **M.R.A., MRA** An international movement advocating spiritual revival and the consolidation of morality on conservative Christian principles. It was established in 1938 by Frank Buchman. Also called "Buchmanism," "Oxford Group."

mo·rass (mə-răs′, mô-) *n.* **1.** An area of low-lying, soggy ground; a bog or marsh. **2.** A difficult or perplexing situation from which it is difficult to escape. [Dutch *moeras,* variant (influenced by *moer,* moorland) of Middle Dutch *marasch,* from Old French *marasc,* from Germanic; akin to MARSH.]

mor·a·to·ri·um (môr′ə-tôr′ē-əm, -tōr′ē-əm, mŏr′-) *n., pl.* **-ums** or **-toria** (-tôr′ē-ə, -tōr′ē-ə). **1.** *Law.* An authorization to a debtor, such as a bank or nation, permitting temporary suspension of payments. **2.** A deferment or delay of any action; temporary suspension. [New Latin, from Late Latin *morātōrius,* MORATORY.]

mor·a·to·ry (môr′ə-tôr′ē, -tōr′ē, mŏr′-) *adj.* Authorizing delay in payment; postponing: *a moratory contract.* [French *moratoire,* from Late Latin *morātōrius,* from Latin *morārī,* to delay, from *mora,* delay.]

Mo·ra·vi·a (mə-rā′vē-ə). *Czech* **Mo·ra·va** (mô′rä-vä). *German* **Mähr·en** (mâr′ən). Region of central Czechoslovakia. It is a fertile agricultural area with major mineral resources and industries. A great Slavic empire in the 9th century, Moravia eventually passed to the Hapsburgs of Austria (1526), under whom most of its towns became German-speaking. It became part of Czechoslovakia in 1918. In 1938, because of its high proportion of Germans, Hitler annexed parts of Moravia, later making the whole a German protectorate. After World War II most of its German-speaking people were expelled. Brno is the chief town.

Mo·ra·vi·a (mō-rä′vē-ə), **Alberto,** born Alberto Pincherle (1907–). Italian novelist. His first novel, *The Indifferent Ones* (1929), introduced the continuing theme of his works, the despair and alienation of contemporary human life. His best-known works are *The Woman of Rome* (1947), *The Conformist* (1951), and *Two Women* (1957).

Mo·ra·vi·an (mə-rā′vē-ən) *n.* **1.** A native or inhabitant of Moravia. **2.** The Czech dialects spoken in Moravia. **3.** A member of the Moravian Church, a Protestant denomination founded in Saxony in 1722 by Hussite emigrants from Moravia. **—Mo·ra·vi·an** *adj.*

mo·ray (môr′ā, mōr′ā, mə-rā′) *n.* Any of various often voracious, brightly colored marine eels of the family Muraenidae, of chiefly tropical coastal waters. Also called "moray eel." [Portuguese *moreia,* from Latin *mūrēna,* from Greek *muraina*†.]

Mor·ay (mûr′ē). Also **Mor·ay·shire** (-shîr′, -shər). Former county of northeastern Scotland, divided between the Highland and Grampian regions (1975). Elgin was the county town.

Moray, James Stewart or **Stuart, Earl of** (*c.* 1531–70). Regent of Scotland (1567–70), illegitimate son of King James V, one of the first Scottish noblemen to embrace Protestantism. When Mary married Darnley in 1565, he opposed the marriage and fled to England; in 1566 he returned to Scotland and after Mary's overthrow was appointed regent for James VI.

Moray Firth. An arm of the North Sea between the Highland and Grampian regions of eastern Scotland, containing valuable oil fields. Inverness lies at its head.

mor·bid (môr′bĭd) *adj.* **1. a.** Of, pertaining to, or caused by disease. **b.** Psychologically unhealthy: *a morbid fear of dogs.* **2.** Susceptible to or characterized by preoccupation with unwholesome matters: *a morbid imagination.* **3.** Gruesome; grisly. **4.** *Informal.* Sad; melancholy. [Latin *morbidus,* diseased, from *morbus,* disease.] **—mor·bid·ly** *adv.* **—mor·bid·ness** *n.*

morbid anatomy *n.* The branch of medicine concerned with the anatomy of diseased organs and tissues.

mor·bi·dez·za (môr′bē-dĕt′sə) *n. Art.* Great delicacy, especially in the painting of flesh tints. [Italian, from *morbido,* delicate, tender. See **morbid.**]

mor·bid·i·ty (môr-bĭd′ə-tē) *n., pl.* **-ties.** **1.** The state or quality of being morbid. **2.** The number of cases of a particular disease occurring in a given number of a population. In this sense, also called "morbidity rate." **3.** A concern with morbid matters.

mor·bif·ic (môr-bĭf′ĭk) *adj.* Causing or producing disease; pathogenic. [New Latin *morbificus* : Latin *morbus,* disease + *-ficus,* -FIC.]

mor·bil·li (môr-bĭl′ī) *n.* A disease, **measles** *(see).* [Latin, plural of *morbillus,* pustule, from *morbus,* disease.]

mor·ceau (môr-sō′) *n., pl.* **-ceaux** *(pronounced as singular).* A short literary or musical composition. [French, from Old French *morsel,* morsel.]

mor·da·cious (môr-dā′shəs) *adj.* **1.** Given to biting; biting. **2.** Caustic; sarcastic. [Latin *mordāx* (stem *mordāc-*), caustic, biting, from *mordēre,* to bite.] **—mor·da·cious·ly** *adv.* **—mor·dac·i·ty** (môr-dăs′ə-tē) *n.*

mor·dant (môr′dənt) *adj.* **1. a.** Bitingly sarcastic. **b.** Incisive and trenchant. **2.** Bitingly painful. **3.** Serving to fix colors in dyeing.
∼n. **1.** A reagent, such as alumina or tannic acid, used to fix coloring matter in textiles, leather, or other materials. **2.** A corrosive substance, such as an acid, used to etch treated areas on a metal or other surface, especially a printing plate. —See Synonyms at **incisive.**
∼tr.v. **mordanted, -danting, -dants.** To treat with a mordant. [French, from Old French, from the present participle of *mordre,* to bite, from Latin *mordēre.*] **—mor·dan·cy** *n.* **—mor·dant·ly** *adv.*

mor·dent (môr′dənt, môr-dĕnt′) *n. Music.* A melodic ornament in which a principal note is rapidly alternated with a note a half or full step above *(upper mordent)* or below *(lower mordent).* [German, from Italian *mordente,* a grace note, from *mordere,* to bite (in allusion to the sharpness of attack with which it is executed), from Latin *mordēre.*]

Mordred. Variant of **Modred.**

more (môr, mōr). **1.** Comparative of **many.** **2.** Comparative of **much.**
∼adj. **1. a.** Greater in number. **b.** Greater in size, amount, extent, or degree. **2.** Additional; extra: *They need more food.*
∼n. **1.** A greater or additional quantity, number, degree, or amount. Used with *of* and a plural verb: *More of them are coming.* **2.** Something that exceeds or surpasses expectation: *Ten is more than necessary.*
∼adv. **1. a.** To a greater extent or degree: *His insults upset her more than his blows did.* **b.** Used to form the comparative of many adjectives and adverbs, especially those of two or more syllables: *more*

moose *The moose of North America and the elk of Europe and Asia are the same species,* Alces alces. *The largest of the deer family, growing to 2 meters (6½ feet) tall, they use their mobile lips to gather water plants and browse on trees and bushes.*

PRONUNCIATION KEY

ă, pat; ā, pay; âr, care;
ä, father, are; b, bib;
ch, church; d, deed; ĕ, pet;
ē, be; f, fife; g, gag; h, hat;
hw, which; ĭ, pit; ī, pie;
îr, pier; j, judge; k, kick;
l, lid, needle; m, mum;
n, no, sudden; ng, thing;
ŏ, pot; ō, toe; ô, paw, for;
oi, noise; ou, out; ŏŏ, book;
ōō, boot; p, pop; r, roar;
s, sauce; sh, ship, dish;
t, tight; th, thin, path;
th, this, bathe; ŭ, cut; ûr, fur;
v, valve; w, with; y, yes;
z, zebra, size; zh, vision;
ə, about, item, edible,
gallop, circus, peaceful

IN FOREIGN WORDS:

à, *Fr.* ami; œ, *Fr.* feu, *Ger.* schön; ü, *Fr.* tu, *Ger.* über;
KH, *Ger.* ich, *Scot.* loch;
N, *Fr.* bon; y′, *Fr.* Compiègne

STRESS MARKS:

Primary stress: ′
in·cite′ (ĭn-sīt′)
Secondary stress: ′
in′sight′ (ĭn′sīt′)

difficult; more intelligently. **2.** In addition; besides; further; again; longer: *I can't eat a mouthful more.* **—more and more.** To an increasing extent or degree: *She sees him more and more.* **—more or less. 1.** About; approximately. **2.** To an undetermined degree: *The glue should be more or less dry by now.* [Middle English *more,* Old English *māra* (adjective), *māre* (adverb and noun).]

More (môr, mōr), **Sir Thomas** (1478–1535). English statesman, humanist scholar, writer, and saint. His essay *Utopia* (1516) described an ideal communal state. He was knighted (1521) and made Lord Chancellor by Henry VIII (1529). After resigning (1532), he refused to subscribe to the Act of Supremacy, which made Henry, not the pope, head of the English Church. He was imprisoned in the Tower and beheaded.

mo·reen (mə-rēn′, mô-) *n.* A sturdy ribbed fabric of wool or cotton, often with an embossed finish, used for clothing and upholstery. [Perhaps from MOIRÉ.]

mo·rel¹ (mə-rĕl′, mô-) *n.* Any of various edible mushrooms of the genus *Morchella* and related genera, characterized by a brownish, spongelike cap. Also called "sponge mushroom." [French *morille,* from Dutch *morilje†.*]

morel² *n.* A nightshade; especially, the **black nightshade** *(see).* [Middle English, from Old French *morele,* feminine noun from *morel,* dark brown, from Vulgar Latin *maurellus* (unattested), from Latin *Maurus,* MOOR.]

mo·rel·lo (mə-rĕl′ō) *n., pl.* **-los.** A variety of the sour cherry, *Prunus cerasus austera,* having fruit with dark red skin. Also called "morello cherry." [Probably from Italian *amarello,* from Medieval Latin *amarellum,* diminutive of Latin *amarus,* bitter.]

more·o·ver (môr-ō′vər, mōr-, môr′ō′vər, mōr′-) *adv.* Beyond what has been stated; furthermore; besides. **—See Synonyms at** *also.*

morepork. Variant of **mopoke.**

mo·res (môr′āz, -ēz, mōr′-) *pl.n.* **1.** The accepted traditional customs and usages of a particular social group that come to be regarded as essential to its survival and welfare. Through general observance mores often become part of a formalized legal code. **2.** Manners; ways. [Latin *mōrēs,* plural of *mōs,* custom.]

Moresco. Variant of **Morisco.**

Mo·resque (mô-rĕsk′, mə-) *adj.* Moorish. Said of decoration and architecture.
~*n.* An ornament or decoration in Moorish style. [French, from Spanish *Morisco,* MORISCO.]

Mor·gan (môr′gən) *n.* A saddle horse or trotting horse of an American breed. [After Justin *Morgan* (1747-98), owner of the stallion from which the breed is descended.]

Morgan, Sir Henry (c.1635–88). Welsh buccaneer and colonial administrator. As commander of the British pirates in the Caribbean, he sacked Portobello (1688) and captured Maracaibo (1669) and Panama (1671). In 1672 he was sent to England as a prisoner for his acts of piracy, but was received as a hero and knighted (1673). He went back to Jamaica as governor.

Morgan, John Pierpont, known as "J.P. Morgan" (1837–1913). U.S. industrialist and financier. He founded (1901) the U.S. Steel Corporation, the first billion-dollar corporation in the world.

Morgan, Lewis Henry (1818–81). U.S. anthropologist. In 1847 he became an adopted member of the Seneca, and in 1851 he published his first book on the tribes of upstate New York. His *Ancient Society* (1877) classified society into progressive stages—savagery, barbarism, and civilization—and was claimed by the Marxists as a confirmation of their theories of cultural evolution.

mor·ga·nat·ic (môr′gə-năt′ĭk) *adj.* Of, pertaining to, or designating a legal marriage between a woman or man of royal or noble birth and a partner of lower rank, in which an agreement is made that any titles or estates of the royal or noble partner will not be shared by the commoner or by any of their offspring. [French or German, from Medieval Latin *matrimonium ad morganaticam,* "marriage for (no dowry but) the morning-gift" (i.e., the husband's token gift to the wife on the morning after the wedding night), from Old High German *morgan,* morning.] **—mor·ga·nat·i·cal·ly** *adv.*

mor·gan·ite (môr′gə-nīt′) *n.* A rosy-pink variety of beryl valued as a semiprecious gem. [Named in honor of J.P. MORGAN.]

Mor·gan le Fay (môr′gən lə fā′). In Arthurian legend, a sorceress, sister, and enemy of King Arthur.

mor·gen (môr′gən) *n., pl.* **morgen** or **-gens. 1.** A former Dutch and South African unit of land area equal to 0.86 hectare (2.116 acres). **2.** A unit of land area formerly used in Norway, Denmark, and Prussia, equal to about two thirds of an acre. [Dutch, from Middle Dutch *morghen,* morning, "a morning's plowing."]

morgue (môrg) *n.* **1.** A place in which the bodies of persons found dead are kept until identified and claimed or until arrangements for burial have been made. **2.** A reference file or storage room containing old newspapers, clippings, notebooks, and the like in a newspaper or magazine office. [French, from *le Morgue†,* the mortuary building in Paris.]

mor·i·bund (môr′ə-bŭnd′, mōr′-) *adj.* **1.** At the point of death; about to die. **2.** Approaching an end; obsolescent: *moribund ideas.* [Latin *moribundus,* from *morī,* to die.] **—mor·i·bun·di·ty** (môr′ə-bŭn′də-tē, mōr′-) *n.* **—mor·i·bund·ly** *adv.*

mo·ri·on¹ (môr′ē-ŏn′, mōr′-) *n.* A crested metal helmet with curved peaks in front and behind, worn by soldiers in the 16th and 17th centuries. [French, from Spanish *morrion,* from *morro,* crown of the head, from Vulgar Latin *murrum†* (unattested), round thing.]

morion² *n.* A variety of smoky quartz, often nearly black. [Manuscript error for *mormorion†.*]

Mo·ris·co (mə-rĭs′kō) *n., pl.* **-cos** or **-coes.** Also **Mo·res·co** (mə-rĕs′kō) *pl.* **-cos** or **-coes.** A Spanish Moor.
~*adj.* Also **Mo·res·co.** Moorish. Said of a style of architecture. [Spanish, from *Moro,* Moor, from Latin *Maurus,* MOOR.]

Mor·i·son (môr′ĭ-sən) *n.,* **Samuel Eliot** (1887–1976). U.S. naval officer and historian. He produced scholarly and readable works such as *Builders of the Bay Colony* (1930), *By Land and Sea* (1953), and *One Boy's Boston* (1962). Two of his books, *Admiral of the Ocean Sea* (1942) and *John Paul Jones* (1959), won the Pulitzer Prize.

Mo·ri·sot (mō′rē-zō′), **Berthe** (1841–95). French impressionist painter. A student of Corot, she is most admired for her graceful paintings of women and children.

Mor·mon¹ (môr′mən). In the Mormon Church, an American prophet, warrior, and historian of the 4th century A.D. who was revealed to Joseph Smith as the author of a sacred history of the Americas, which Smith translated as the Book of Mormon.

Mormon² *n.* **1.** A member of the Church of Jesus Christ of Latter-day Saints, founded by Joseph Smith in 1830. **2.** A member of any of various sects deriving from Smith's original church that accept the Book of Mormon as the word of God.
~*adj.* Of or pertaining to the Mormons, their religion, or their church. **—Mor·mon·ism** *n.* **—Mor·mon·ist** *adj.*

morn (môrn) *n.* **1.** *Poetic.* The morning. **2.** *Scottish.* Tomorrow. [Middle English *morwen, morn,* Old English *morgen.*]

Mor·nay (môr-nā′, môr′nā′) *n.* A white cream sauce flavored with grated cheese.
~*adj.* Designating a dish prepared with Mornay sauce: *eggs Mornay.* [20th century : origin obscure.]

morn·ing (môr′nĭng) *n.* **1.** The first or early part of the day, lasting from midnight to noon or from sunrise to noon. **2.** The hour from daybreak to sunrise; dawn. **3.** The first or early part of anything. [Middle English *morwening,* from *morwen,* MORN (by analogy with EVENING).] **—morn·ing** *adj.*

morn·ing-af·ter pill (môr′nĭng-ăf′tər, -äf′tər) *n.* An oral contraceptive that prevents the implantation of a fertilized egg in the uterus.

morn·ing-glo·ry (môr′nĭng-glôr′ē, -glōr′ē) *n., pl.* **-ries.** Any of various usually twining vines of the genus *Ipomoea,* having funnel-shaped, variously colored flowers that close late in the day.

Morning Prayer *n.* In the Anglican Church, the service of morning worship. Also called "matins."

morn·ings (môr′nĭngz) *adv. Informal.* In the mornings; every morning.

morning sickness *n.* Nausea and vomiting upon rising in the morning, often one of the early symptoms of pregnancy.

morning star *n.* A planet visible in the east just before sunrise, especially Venus. Compare **evening star.**

morning suit *n.* A suit for a man, worn on formal occasions during the day, as at weddings, and consisting of a tailcoat *(morning coat)* and gray striped trousers, worn with a top hat.

Mo·ro (môr′ō, mōr′ō) *n., pl.* **-ros** or collectively **Moro. 1.** A member of any of various Muslim Malay tribes of the southern Philippines. **2.** Any of the Austronesian languages spoken by the Moro. [Spanish, from Latin *Maurus,* MOOR.] **—Mo·ro** *adj.*

mo·roc·co (mə-rŏk′ō) *n., pl.* **-cos.** *Abbr.* **mor. 1.** A soft, fine leather of goatskin tanned with sumac, made originally in Morocco. It is used chiefly for bookbindings and shoes. **2.** Any imitation of this. Also called "morocco leather."

Mo·roc·co (mə-rŏk′ō). *Abbr.* **Mor.** Country of northwestern Africa comprising the Atlas Mts., a fertile plain along the Atlantic, and the Sahara to the southeast. Most of the people are Arabic-speaking Muslims, but a third are Muslim Berbers. European penetration

morel *Morchella esculenta is one of about 15 edible species of this genus of fungus; it is found in temperate climates, often growing on rotting wood.*

MOROCCO

10° W
PORT.
SPAIN
ATLANTIC
OCEAN
Tanger
(Tangier)
Ceuta (SP)
Tetuan
Rif
Moulouya
Kenitra
Sebou
Taza
Oujda
RABAT
Fès (Fez)
Dar el Beida
(Casablanca)
Meknès
Safi
Atlas
Marrakesh
MOROCCO
Essaouira
High
Toubkal
4165m.
Sous
Anti Atlas
30° N
Lanzarote
Canary Is
(SPAIN)
Fuerteventura
S A H A R A
ALGERIA
Bu Graa
Km   0   400
MAURITANIA
Miles 0   200

begun by Portugal and Spain in the 15th century increased in the 19th century, and by 1912 virtually all of Morocco was administered by France or Spain, with an international zone at Tangier. Independence came in 1956. In 1976 Morocco occupied the northern two thirds of the phosphate-rich Spanish Sahara and in 1979 the rest. A border dispute with Algeria from 1963 and from 1976 war against the Polisario Front, fighting for an independent Sahara, drained Morocco's resources. The economy now relies on agriculture and mining, especially of phosphates, with fishing and tourism. Its area is *c.* 659,970 square kilometers (254,748 square miles), but the southern borders are not defined. Population, 20,200,000. Capital, Rabat. —**Mo·roc·can** *adj. & n.*

mo·ron (môr'ŏn', mōr'-) *n.* **1.** *Informal.* A remarkably stupid or oafish person. **2.** A mentally retarded person having a mental age between 7 and 12 years or an intelligence quotient between 50 and 75. Not in current technical usage. [Greek *mōron,* neuter of *mōros,* foolish.] —**mo·ron·ic** (mə-rŏn'ĭk) *adj.* —**mo·ron·i·cal·ly** *adv.* —**mo·ron·ism, mo·ron·i·ty** (mə-rŏn'ə-tē) *n.*

mo·rose (mə-rōs', mō-) *adj.* Sullenly melancholy; gloomy; illhumored. —See Synonyms at **glum.** [Latin *mōrōsus,* captious, fretful, from *mōs* (stem *mōr-*), custom, manner, humor, caprice.] —**mo·rose·ly** *adv.* —**mo·rose·ness** *n.*

morph (môrf) *n. Linguistics.* **1.** An allomorph. **2.** A phoneme or sequence of phonemes that is assumed to be an allomorph although its alignment to a particular morpheme has not been established. [Back-formation from MORPHEME.]

morph., morphol. morphological; morphology.

morph–. Variant of **morpho–.**

–morph *suffix.* Indicates: **1.** A specified form, shape, or structure; for example, **endomorph.** **2.** A morpheme; for example, **allomorph.** [Greek *-morphos,* from *morphē,* shape, form.]

morph·ac·tin (môr-făk'tĭn) *n.* Any of a group of substances that regulate plant growth, usually by inhibiting elongation of shoots.

mor·phal·lax·is (môr'fə-lăk'sĭs) *n., pl.* **-laxes** (-lăk'sēz'). *Biology.* The regeneration of a part by means of structural reorganization of existing cells with only limited production of new cells, a process observed primarily in invertebrate organisms, such as certain lobsters. [New Latin, "structure exchange" : MORPH(O)- + Greek *allaxis,* exchange, from *allassein,* to exchange, from *allos,* other.]

mor·pheme (môr'fēm') *n.* A linguistic unit of relatively stable meaning that cannot be divided into smaller meaningful parts, as words such as *god,* word elements such as *-ly* in *godly,* or grammatical inflections such as the plural ending *-s* in *gods.* [French *morphème,* from Greek *morphē,* form (by analogy with PHONEME).] —**mor·phe·mic** (môr-fē'mĭk) *adj.* —**mor·phe·mi·cal·ly** *adv.*

mor·phe·mics (môr-fē'mĭks) *n. Used with a singular verb. Linguistics.* The study of morphemes, their forms, and their functions.

Mor·phe·us (môr'fē-əs, -fyōōs'). The god or personification of sleep: *in the arms of Morpheus.* —**Mor·phe·an** *adj.*

mor·phi·a (môr'fē-ə) *n.* Morphine. Not in current technical usage. [New Latin : obsolete *morphium,* from MORPHEUS + -IA.]

mor·phic (môr'fĭk) *adj.* Pertaining to form; morphological. [MORPH(O)- + -IC.] —**mor·phi·cal·ly** *adv.*

–morphic, –morphous *suffix.* Indicates possession of a specified shape or form; for example, **polymorphic, amorphous.** [From -MORPH.]

mor·phine (môr'fēn') *n.* A narcotic drug, $C_{17}H_{19}NO_3$, extracted from opium, the soluble salts of which are used in medicine to relieve severe and persistent pain. Repeated dosage causes addiction. [French, from *Morphée,* MORPHEUS.]

mor·phin·ism (môr'fē-nĭz'əm, môr'fə-) *n.* **1.** Morphine addiction. **2.** A chronic condition of poisoning caused by sustained or immoderate dosage of morphine.

morpho–, morph– *prefix.* Indicates: **1.** A shape, form, or structure; for example, **morphogenesis, morphology. 2.** A morpheme; for example, **morphophonemics.** [German, from Greek, from *morphē,* shape.]

mor·pho·gen·e·sis (môr'fə-jĕn'ə-sĭs) *n.* **1.** Evolutionary development of the structure of an organism or part. **2.** Embryological development of the structure of an organism or part. —**mor·pho·ge·net·ic** (môr'fə-jə-nĕt'ĭk), **mor·pho·gen·ic** (môr'fə-jĕn'ĭk) *adj.*

mor·phol·o·gy (môr-fŏl'ə-jē) *n. Abbr.* **morph., morphol. 1.** The biological study of the form and structure of living organisms. **2.** The structure and form of an organism, excluding its functions. **3.** *Linguistics.* **a.** The form and structure of words in any given language; especially, the consistent and classifiable forms and changes of inflections and derivations. **b.** The study of such form and structure. **4.** *Geology.* The study of the structure of earth features, **geomorphology** *(see).* [German *Morphologie* : MORPHO- + -LOGY.] —**mor·pho·log·ic** (môr'fə-lŏj'ĭk), **mor·pho·log·i·cal** *adj.* —**mor·pho·log·i·cal·ly** *adv.* —**mor·phol·o·gist** (môr-fŏl'ə-jĭst) *n.*

mor·pho·pho·neme (môr'fō-fō'nēm') *n. Linguistics.* A phonological unit consisting of a set of phonemes that occur but do not contrast in the allomorphs of a given morpheme. For example, the plural morpheme *s* occurs as (s) in *cats* but as (z) in *dogs.*

mor·pho·pho·ne·mics (môr'fō-fə-nē'mĭks) *n. Used with a singular verb. Linguistics.* The study of phonological variations within allomorphs of the same morpheme; the study of morphophonemes. Also called "morphophonology." —**mor·pho·pho·ne·mic** *adj.*

mor·pho·sis (môr-fō'sĭs) *n., pl.* **-ses** (-sēz') The manner in which an organism or one of its parts changes form or the manner or order of its development. [New Latin, from Greek *morphōsis,* formation, from *morphoun,* to form, from *morphē,* form.]

Mor·ris (môr'ĭs, mŏr'-), **Gouverneur** (1752–1816). U.S. politician and diplomat. He was an influential member of the Continental Congress and the Constitutional Convention, contributing a strong knowledge of fiscal matters and a centralist view of government. He served as minister to France from 1792 to 1794.

Morris, Robert, known as "the financier of the American Revolution" (1734–1806). U.S. merchant, born in England. Although he voted against the original motion for independence in July 1776, he signed the Declaration in August. By the early 1790's he was reputedly the richest man in America, but he overspeculated with his funds and spent three years in debtors' prison (1798–1801).

Morris, William (1834–96). British craftsman, poet, painter, and political activist. He first made his name in the 1850's as a painter attached to the Pre-Raphaelites and as a poet, with *The Defence of Guenevere and Other Poems,* which appeared in 1858. In 1861 he founded a firm of decorators dedicated to combating the mass-produced art of the industrial system by producing handmade goods. In 1884 he helped found the Socialist League.

Morris chair *n.* A large armchair with an adjustable back and removable cushions. [Designed by William MORRIS.]

morris dance *n.* An English country dance traditionally performed by men *(morris men)* wearing bright costumes, handkerchiefs, and bells, and often representing a folk tale. Also called "morris." [Middle English *Moreys,* Moorish, from *More,* MOOR.]

mor·row (môr'ō, mŏr'ō) *n.* **1.** The day following some particular day. Preceded by *the.* **2.** The time immediately subsequent to some particular event. **3.** *Archaic.* The morning: *Good morrow!* [Middle English *morwe,* Old English *morgen.*]

morse (môrs) *n.* The clasp or fastening, often of gold or silver, on a cope. [Middle English, from Old French *mors,* from Latin *morsus,* bite, clasp, from *mordēre* (past participial stem *mors-*), to bite.]

Morse (môrs), **Samuel Finley Breese** (1791–1872). U.S. painter and inventor. He is most famous for his refinement of the electric telegraph and earlier telegraph codes (1838).

Morse code *n.* A system of communication in which letters of the alphabet and numbers are represented by patterns of short and long signals, which may be conveyed as sounds, flashes of light, written dots and dashes, or the waving of flags. Also called "Morse," "Morse alphabet." [Invented by Samuel MORSE.] See feature, next page.

mor·sel (môr'səl) *n.* **1.** A small piece or bite of food. **2.** A light meal; a snack. **3.** A small piece or amount of anything. [Middle English, from Old French *mors,* a bite, from Latin *morsum,* past participle of *mordēre,* to bite.]

mort[1] (môrt) *n.* The note sounded on a hunting horn to announce the death of the hunted animal. [Middle English, from Old French, from Latin *mors* (stem *mort-*), death.]

mort[2] *n.* A great number or quantity: *a mort of money.* [Perhaps from MORTAL, "extremely."]

mort[3] *n.* A salmon two to three years old. [16th century : origin obscure.]

mor·tal (môrt'l) *adj.* **1.** Liable or subject to death: *All living beings are mortal.* **2.** Of or pertaining to humans as beings who must die: *The coffin contained his mortal remains.* **3.** Of, pertaining to, or accompanying death: *mortal throes.* **4.** Causing death; deadly: *a mortal wound.* **5.** Fought to the death: "*with victorious Germany and Italy engaged in mortal attack upon us*" (Winston Churchill). **6.** Unrelenting; implacable: *one's mortal enemy.* **7.** Of or like the fear of death; dire: *in mortal terror.* **8.** *Roman Catholic Church.* Entailing or causing spiritual death. Said of sins, crimes, or transgressions. **9.** *Chiefly Regional.* Very great; extreme: "*I go there a mortal sight of times*" (Charles Dickens). **10.** Conceivable; earthly: *There is no mortal reason for us to go.* **11.** Used as an intensifier: *The bore spoke for six mortal hours.* —See Synonyms at **fatal.** —*n.* A human being. —*adv. Regional.* Extremely; very: *mortal angry.* [Middle English, from Old French *mortal, mortel,* from Latin *mortālis,* from *mors* (stem *mort-*), death.] —**mor·tal·ly** *adv.*

mor·tal·i·ty (môr-tăl'ə-tē) *n., pl.* **-ties. 1.** The condition of being subject to death. **2. a.** *Archaic.* Death. **b.** The loss of a great many lives: *high mortality during a plague epidemic.* **3.** The frequency of deaths in proportion to a population; **death rate** *(see).* **4.** Deadliness. **5.** The quality of being mortal. Said of a sin. **6.** The human race; humankind.

mortality rate *n.* See **death rate** (sense 1).

mortality table *n. Insurance.* An actuarial table that lists the life expectancies of people according to their age, sex, occupation, and other considerations.

mortal sin *n.* **1.** *Theology.* A sin that totally estranges the soul from the grace of God. Compare **venial sin. 2.** *Informal.* Any major miscalculation or common error.

mor·tar (môr'tər) *n.* **1.** A receptacle made of a hard material in which substances are crushed or ground with a pestle. **2.** Any machine in which materials are ground and blended or crushed. **3.** *Military.* A muzzle-loading cannon used to fire shells at low velocities, short ranges, and great angular elevation. Also called "trench mortar." **4.** Any of several similar devices used for various purposes, such as shooting lifelines across a stretch of water. **5.** A mixture of cement or lime with sand and water that is used in building. —*v.* **mortared, -taring, -tars.** —*tr.* **1.** To plaster or join with mortar. **2.** To bombard with a mortar; hit with mortar shells. —*intr.* To fire mortars. [Middle English *morter,* partly from Old English *mor-*

Morse code

SAMUEL MORSE'S SIMPLE SYSTEM

Dots and dashes to be flashed, bleeped, or written

Samuel Morse invented his code, in which letters are represented by combinations of long and short signals, in about 1838. It simplified the transmission of telegraphic messages and required only a single-wire machine. The code can also be written in dots and dashes or signaled with flashlights or radio bleeps. In 1912 the easily memorized letters SOS were chosen to be the international distress signal. "*Save Our Souls*" was a catchphrase devised later.

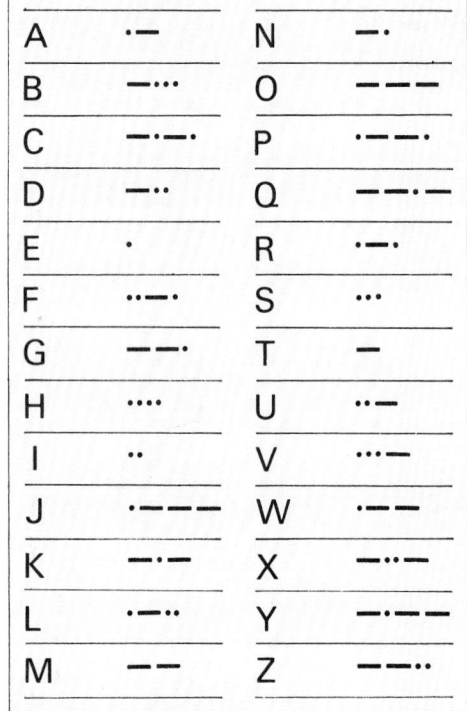

A	·—	N	—·
B	—···	O	———
C	—·—·	P	·——·
D	—··	Q	——·—
E	·	R	·—·
F	··—·	S	···
G	——·	T	—
H	····	U	··—
I	··	V	···—
J	·———	W	·——
K	—·—	X	—··—
L	·—··	Y	—·——
M	——	Z	——··

SIMPLIFIED VERSION *The International Morse code is a form of Morse's original code, simplified for use in radio telegraphy. It differs from the American Morse adaptation in 11 letters and in all numerals except 4.*

mosaic *A fish portrayed in a Roman mosaic from North Africa.*

tere and partly from Old French *mortier,* both from Latin *mortārium,* a mortar and the substance made in it.]

mor·tar·board (môr′tər-bôrd′, -bōrd′) *n.* **1.** A square board with a handle, for holding and carrying mortar. **2.** An academic cap topped by a flat square covered with cloth, usually black and having a tassel on top.

Morte d'Ar·thur, Le (lə môrt′ där′thər) *n.* A collection of Arthurian stories compiled and translated from Old French by Sir Thomas Malory and printed by William Caxton in 1485.

mort·gage (môr′gĭj) *n. Abbr.* **mtg., mtge.** *Law.* **1.** A temporary and conditional pledge or conveyance of property to a creditor as security against a debt. **2.** A contract or deed specifying the terms of such a conveyance. **3.** The claim that the mortgagee or creditor has upon property pledged in this manner. ~*tr.v.* **mortgaged, -gaging, -gages. 1.** To pledge (property) by mortgage. **2.** To pledge or stake against future success or failure; place an advance liability upon: *By living so dangerously, he mortgaged his own future and his family's.* [Middle English *morgage,* from Old French *mortgage,* "dead pledge" : *mort,* dead, from Latin *mortuus,* from *mors* (stem *mort-*), death + *gage,* GAGE (pledge).]

mort·ga·gee (môr′gĭ-jē′) *n.* The holder of a mortgage, usually as security against a loan.

mort·ga·gor (môr′gĭ-jôr′, môr′gĭ-jər) *n.* Also **mort·gag·er** (môr′gĭ-jər). A person who mortgages his property.

mor·ti·cian (môr-tĭsh′ən) *n.* A funeral director; an undertaker. [MORT(UARY) + -ICIAN.]

mor·ti·fi·ca·tion (môr′tə-fĭ-kā′shən) *n.* **1.** A feeling of shame, humiliation, or wounded pride. **2.** The cause of such a feeling: *Confessing in public was a mortification to her.* **3.** The mortifying of the body and appetites. **4.** The death or decay of one part of a living body; necrosis; gangrene.

mor·ti·fy (môr′tĭ-fī′) *v.* **-fied, -fying, -fies.** —*tr.* **1.** To cause to experience shame, humiliation, or wounded pride; humiliate. **2.** To dis-cipline (one's body and appetites) by self-denial and austerity: *mortify the flesh.* **3.** To cause (a bodily part) to die, as by gangrene. —*intr.* **1.** To practice ascetic discipline or punishment of the body. **2.** To become gangrenous or necrosed, as a part of the body might. —See Synonyms at **degrade.** [Middle English *mortifien,* from Old French *mortifier,* from Late Latin *mortificāre,* to cause to die : *mors* (stem *mort-*), death + *facere,* -FY.] —**mor·ti·fy·ing·ly** *adv.*

mor·tise, mor·tice (môr′tĭs) *n.* **1.** A cavity, usually rectangular, in a piece of wood, stone, or other material, cut to receive a similarly shaped projection or **tenon** *(see)* of another piece to hold the two together. **2.** *Printing.* A hole cut in a plate for the insertion of type. ~*tr.v.* **mortised** or **morticed, -tising** or **-ticing, -tises** or **-tices. 1.** To join or fasten securely, as with a mortise and tenon. **2.** To cut or make a mortise in. **3.** *Printing.* **a.** To cut a hole in (a plate) for the insertion of type. **b.** To cut such a hole and insert (type). [Middle English *mortays,* from Old French *mortoise,* from Arabic *murtazz,* fixed in.]

mortise lock *n.* A lock fixed into a mortise in the edge of a door, such that the body of the lock is enclosed. Compare **deadlock, Yale lock.**

mort·main (môrt′mān′) *n.* **1.** *Law.* Perpetual ownership of land by institutions such as churches that cannot transfer or sell them. Also called "dead hand." **2.** The often oppressive influence of the past upon the present. [Middle English *mortemayne,* from Old French *mortemain,* "dead hand" (that is, institutional possession) : *morte,* feminine of *mort,* dead, from Latin *mortuus,* from *mors* (stem *mort-*), death + *main,* hand, from Latin *manus.*]

Mor·ton (môrt′n), **Jelly Roll,** born Ferdinand Joseph La Menthe Morton (1885–1941). U.S. jazz musician and composer. He began as a ragtime piano player in the Storyville district of New Orleans and later wrote numerous jazz classics that often reflected his Creole background.

mor·tu·ar·y (môr′chōō-ĕr′ē) *n., pl.* **-ies. 1.** A place, especially in a funeral home, where dead bodies are prepared or kept prior to burial or cremation. **2.** A funeral home. ~*adj.* Of or pertaining to death or to the burial of the dead. [Middle English *mortuarie,* from Norman French, from Late Latin *mortuārium,* from *mortuārius,* of burial, from Latin *mortuus,* dead, from *mors* (stem *mort-*), death.]

mor·u·la (môr′yə-lə, môr′ə-) *n., pl.* **-lae** (-lē′) or **-las.** *Biology.* **1.** The spherical mass of embryonic cells formed by cleavage of a fertilized ovum before blastulation. Compare **gastrula. 2.** A spherical mass of developing male gametes occurring especially in certain annelid worms. [New Latin, diminutive of Latin *mōrum,* mulberry.] —**mor·u·lar** (môr′yə-lə, môr′ə-) *adj.*

mor·wong (môr′wŏng′) *n.* An Australasian food fish of the family Cheilodactylidae. [From a native Australian language.]

mos. months.

mo·sa·ic (mō-zā′ĭk) *n.* **1. a.** A picture or decorative design made by setting small colored pieces of glass, stone, or tile in mortar. **b.** The art or process of making such designs. **2.** Anything that resembles a piece of mosaic work: *The stained-glass windows cast light in a mosaic on the church floor.* **3.** Any of several virus diseases of plants resulting in light and dark areas in the leaves, which often become shriveled and dwarfed. **4.** A set of overlapping photographs, usually aerial, assembled into a composite picture. **5.** A photosensitive surface in a television camera, consisting of a large number of small sensitive patches on an insulating base. **6.** *Genetics.* An organism containing genetically different types of tissue; a chimera. ~*adj.* **1.** Of, pertaining to, resembling, or being mosaic: *a mosaic pattern.* **2.** Marked by mosaicism. ~*tr.v.* **mosaicked, -icking, -ics. 1.** To make by or as if by mosaic. **2.** To adorn with or as if with mosaic. [Middle English, from Old French *mosaique,* from Italian *mosaico,* from Medieval Latin *mosaicus, musaicus,* irregularly from Late Greek *mouseion,* a mosaic, from *mouseios,* belonging to the Muses, from *Mousa,* Muse.] —**mo·sa·i·cal·ly** *adv.* —**mo·sa·i·cist** (mō-zā′ə-sĭst) *n.*

Mo·sa·ic (mō-zā′ĭk) *adj.* Also **Mo·sa·i·cal** (mō-zā′ĭ-kəl). Of or pertaining to Moses or the laws and writings attributed to him. [New Latin *Mosaicus,* from MOSES.]

mosaic gold *n.* An alloy resembling gold, **ormolu** *(see).*

mo·sa·i·cism (mō-za′ĭ-sĭz′əm) *n. Genetics.* The condition in which tissues of genetically different types occur in the same organism. [From MOSAIC.]

Mosaic Law *n.* The ancient law of the Hebrews, traditionally attributed to Moses and contained mainly in the Pentateuch. Also called "Law of Moses."

mo·sa·saur (mō′zə-sôr′) *n.* Any of various extinct marine lizards of the genus *Mosasaurus* and related genera, which attained a very large size and had paddlelike limbs. [New Latin : *Mosa,* Meuse River (near which fossil remains were found) + *-saurus,* -SAUR.]

mos·cha·tel (mŏs′kə-tĕl′, mŏs′kə-tĕl′) *n.* A plant, *Adoxa moschatellina,* of northern regions, having greenish-white, musk-scented flowers. [French *moscatelle,* from Italian *moscatella,* from *moscato,* MUSK.]

Mos·cow (mŏs′kou′, -kō). *Russian* **Mos·kva** (mŏsk-vä′). Capital of the U.S.S.R. and of the R.S.F.S.R., on the Moscow River. It is the communications, economic, and cultural center of the country and accounts for a sixth of the national industrial output, with metalworking, oil-refining, aircraft, publishing, vehicle, chemical, textile, and clothing plants. Founded in the 12th century, the minor principality of Moscow gradually assumed sovereignty over its neighbors by virtue of its strategic importance at the crossing of major trade

mosque

THE MUSLIM PLACE OF WORSHIP
Ancient desert building traditions embodied in the monuments of Islam

The Muslim enclosure for prayer, the mosque (from the Arabic word *masjid,* "place of worship"), was the first Islamic architectural form. The earliest mosque to have survived intact, the Great Mosque built in Damascus in 707, is roofed and domed, but many early mosques consisted of a large rectangular open courtyard surrounded by roofed or vaulted colonnades. Typical of the building traditions of the desert, they were featureless from the outside like fortified desert villages built around their wells. During the 13th century cruciform mosques were introduced into Egypt by Suleiman, an Ottoman ruler from Turkey.

Every mosque has a niche called the *mihrab* built into the wall facing Mecca to indicate the direction for worshipers to face when praying. There may be a space in front of it, enclosed by a screen, for the caliph, sultan, or governor. Nearby is a raised pulpit, often canopied, called the *minbar.* Most mosques have at least one high minaret, from which the muezzin, or crier, calls the faithful to prayer five times a day. Most have running water for ritual ablution—often a fountain or well set in the center of the colonnaded courtyard.

Walls, gates, minarets, roofs, and domes may be ornately decorated with abstract designs and inscriptions from the Koran. The *Haddith,* the Islamic Traditions, forbid the representation of living human figures in art, because man is a work of God. Decoration may take the form of patterned brickwork (often found in Turkish mosques); of painted and gilded stucco (seen in early Egyptian mosques); of marbles or mosaics (used in Syria and other areas once part of the Byzantine Empire); or of ceramic tiles (found in many Persian mosques).

A proverb that is familiar throughout the Islamic world, "prayer is better than sleep," reflects the special emphasis placed on prayer in Muslim tradition. Above, a muezzin calls to the faithful from a minaret of the Darwishiya Mosque in Damascus. Minaret comes from an Arabic word meaning "candlestick, lighthouse, lamp, minaret."
The Blue Mosque of Istanbul, above right, was constructed in the 17th century as the centerpiece of a complex that included a hospital, a school, and other buildings. At right, the ornate marble- and mosaic-lined interior of the Umayyad (or Great Mosque) of Damascus.

routes and as a bulwark against the Tatars. By the 15th century it was the capital of the Russian state, and Grand Duke Ivan IV took the title of czar in 1547. The capital was transferred to St. Petersburg in 1712 but returned to Moscow in 1918, after the revolution. It is the site of the Kremlin with its many cathedrals and Red Square with the Lenin Mausoleum and 16th-century cathedral of St. Basil. Many times destroyed by fire, as during the French occupation (1812), and rebuilt, the city was heroically defended against the Nazis in World War II (1941). It was the site of the 1980 Summer Olympics.

Mose·ley (mōz′lē), **Henry Gwyn-Jeffreys** (1887–1915). English physicist. His research on radioactivity demonstrated the relationship betwen x-ray spectra and the atomic number of an element and enabled him to formulate (1913) the law that established the atomic number of elements.

Mo·selle¹ (mō-zĕl′). *German* **Mo·sel** (mō′zəl). River of northwestern Europe, flowing 547 kilometers (340 miles) from the Vosges in France to join the Rhine at Koblenz in West Germany.

Moselle² *n.* A light, dry white wine produced in the valley of the Moselle River.

Mo·ses (mō′zĭz, -zĭs). The Hebrew prophet and lawgiver who led the Israelites out of Egypt.

Moses, Grandma, born Anna Mary Robertson Moses (1860–1961). U.S. artist. She was self-taught and began to paint when she was in her seventies. Her paintings—colorful, straightforward, and primitive in style—were immensely popular and have been widely sold as lithographs and greeting cards.

mo·sey (mō′zē) *intr.v.* **-seyed, -seying, -seys.** *Informal.* **1.** To walk in a leisurely manner; stroll. **2.** To get going; move along. [19th century : origin obscure.]

mo·shav (mō-shäv′) *n., pl.* **moshavim** (mō′shə-vēm′). An Israeli cooperative settlement consisting of small farms. [Hebrew *moshāb,* "dwelling."]

Moskva. See **Moscow.**

Moslem. Variant of **Muslim.** —See Usage note at **Muslim.**

Mos·ley (mōz′lē), **Sir Oswald Ernald** (1896–1980). English politician. He entered the House of Commons as a Conservative in 1918 and switched to the Labour Party in 1924. In 1932 he founded the New Party, and a year later the British Union of Fascists. He married his second wife, Diana Mitford, then Diana Guinness, in 1936 and they were both interned (1940–43) during World War II.

Mo·so·tho (mŏŏ-sŏŏ′tŏŏ) *n., pl.* **-thos** or collectively **Mosotho.** A member of the Sotho people of southern Africa or a citizen of **Lesotho** *(see).* Also called "Basotho," formerly "Basuto."

mosque (mŏsk) *n.* A Muslim house of worship. Also called "masjid," "musjid." [French *mosquée,* from Italian *moschea,* from Arabic *masjid,* a place of worship, from *sajada,* to worship.]

mos·qui·to (mə-skē′tō) *n., pl.* **-toes** or **-tos.** Any of various winged insects of the family Culicidae, in which the female of most species is distinguished by a long proboscis for sucking blood. Some species are vectors of diseases such as malaria and yellow fever. [Spanish, diminutive of *mosca,* fly, from Latin *musca.*]

Mos·qui·to (mə-skē′tō) *n., pl.* **-tos** or collectively **Mosquito.** Also **Mis·ki·to** (mĭ-) *pl.* **-tos** or collectively **Misquito. 1.** A member of a Central American people of mixed native Indian and Negro descent, living on the Mosquito Coast. **2.** The language of this people. —**Mos·qui·to** *adj.*

PRONUNCIATION KEY

ă, pat; ā, pay; âr, care;
ä, father, are; b, bib;
ch, church; d, deed; ĕ, pet;
ē, be; f, fife; g, gag; h, hat;
hw, which; ĭ, pit; ī, pie;
îr, pier; j, judge; k, kick;
l, lid, needle; m, mum;
n, no, sudden; ng, thing;
ŏ, pot; ō, toe; ô, paw, for;
oi, noise; ou, out; ŏŏ, book;
ōō, boot; p, pop; r, roar;
s, sauce; sh, ship, dish;
t, tight; th, thin, path;
th, this, bathe; ŭ, cut; ûr, fur;
v, valve; w, with; y, yes;
z, zebra, size; zh, vision;
ə, about, item, edible,
gallop, circus, peaceful

IN FOREIGN WORDS:

à, *Fr.* ami; œ, *Fr.* feu, *Ger.*
schön; ü, *Fr.* tu, *Ger.* über;
KH, *Ger.* ich, *Scot.* loch;
N, *Fr.* bon; y′, *Fr.* Compiègne

STRESS MARKS:

Primary stress: ′
in·cite′ (ĭn-sīt′)
Secondary stress: ′
in′sight′ (ĭn′sīt′)

mosquito boat *n.* *Chiefly British.* A **PT** boat *(see).* [Referring to its speed and small size.]

Mosquito Coast. Sparsely populated banana-growing plain on the Caribbean coast of Nicaragua and Honduras, named after its indigenous Indians. It was discovered (1502) by Columbus and later became a British protectorate (1678–1860).

mosquito hawk *n.* See **nighthawk** (sense 1).

mosquito net *n.* A fine net used for covering windows and beds to keep out mosquitoes.

moss (môs, mŏs) *n.* **1.** Any of various green, usually small bryophytic plants of the class Musci, typically growing in clumps on moist ground or trees. **2.** A patch or covering of such plants. **3.** Any of various other plants that are similar in appearance or manner of growth, such as **club moss,** **Irish moss,** or **Spanish moss** *(all of which see).* **4.** *Chiefly Scottish.* A peat bog or moor. [Middle English *moss, mos,* Old English *mos.*]

Moss (môs, mŏs), **Stirling** (1929–). British racing driver. He was the British champion in 1955 and became the number-one driver on the Maserati team in 1954. He won 33 Grand Prix races during his career (1947–62).

moss agate *n.* A semiprecious stone with greenish-brown markings. It is a type of chalcedony.

moss·back (môs′băk′, mŏs′-) *n.* **1.** An old shellfish or turtle with a growth of algae on its back. **2.** *Slang.* An extremely old-fashioned or conservative person. **—moss·backed** *adj.*

Möss·bau·er effect (mŏs′bou′ər, mŏs′-) *n.* *Physics.* The emission of gamma rays by excited nuclei in some solids such that the recoil momentum is taken up by the whole lattice rather than by the emitting atom. The resulting gamma rays have a very narrow frequency range and can be used in studying the corresponding gamma-ray absorption in a sample material *(Mössbauer spectroscopy),* giving information about the energies of nuclei and the molecular structure of the sample. [After Rudolf *Mössbauer* (born 1929), German physicist.]

moss·bunk·er (môs′bŭng′kər, mŏs′-) *n.* Also **moss·bank·er** (môs′băng′kər, mŏs′-). A fish, the **menhaden** *(see).* [Dutch *marsbanker†*.]

moss campion *n.* A low-growing plant, *Silene acaulis,* of cool regions, having purplish-red flowers and forming dense, cushionlike mats.

moss green *n.* A moderate yellowish to grayish green. **—moss-green** (môs′grēn′, mŏs′-) *adj.*

moss·grown (môs′grōn′, mŏs′-) *adj.* **1.** Overgrown with moss. **2.** Old-fashioned; antiquated.

moss·hag, moss·hagg (môs′hăg′, mŏs′-) *n.* *Scottish.* **1.** Ground from which peat has been removed. **2.** A pit in a bog. [MOSS + dialectal and Scottish *hag,* gap, pit, from Scandinavian; akin to Old Norse *hogg,* gap, cut, from *hoggva,* to strike, hack, HEW.]

mos·so (mô′sō) *adv.* *Music.* With motion or animation. Used as a direction. [Italian, from the past participle of *muovere,* to move, from Latin *movēre.*]

moss pink *n.* A low-growing plant, *Phlox subulata,* forming dense, mosslike mats. It is widely cultivated for its profuse pink or white flowers. Also called "ground pink."

moss rose *n.* A variety of rose, *Rosa centifolia muscosa,* having fragrant pink flowers with a mossy flower stalk and calyx.

moss stitch *n.* A pattern or stitch in knitting consisting of alternate plain and purl stitches on one row and alternate purl and plain stitches on the next row, giving a minutely checkered fabric with the nubbly texture of moss.

moss·troop·er (môs′trōō′pər, mŏs′-) *n.* **1.** A member of a band of raiders operating in the marshy lands on the borders of England and Scotland during the 17th century. **2.** A raider or marauder.

moss·y (mô′sē, mŏs′ē) *adj.* **-ier, -iest. 1.** Covered with moss or anything resembling moss. **2.** Resembling moss. **3.** Old-fashioned; antiquated. **—moss·i·ness** *n.*

most (mōst). **1.** Superlative of **many. 2.** Superlative of **much.**

~adj. **1.** Greatest in number or quantity. **2.** Largest or greatest in amount, size, or degree. **3.** In the greatest number of instances: *Most fish have fins.*

~n. **1.** The greatest amount, quantity, or degree; the largest part: *Most of the land was fertile.* **2.** *Used with a plural verb.* The greatest number of a group or classification; the majority: *Most of her novels have been well received.* **—at (the) most.** Not over; at the absolute limit: *It's four miles at most.* **—make the most of.** To use as advantageously as possible: *making the most of one's talents.* **—the most.** *Slang.* A person or thing that produces great excitement or satisfaction.

~adv. **1.** In the highest degree, quantity, or extent. Used with many adjectives and adverbs to form the superlative degree: *most honest; most impatiently.* **2.** Very: *a most impressive piece of writing.* **3.** *Informal & Regional.* Almost: *Most everyone agrees.* [Middle English *most, mest, mast,* Old English *mǣst.*]

-most *suffix.* Indicates the superlative degree; for example, **foremost, innermost.** [Middle English *-most, -mast,* Old English *-mǣst, -mest,* originally an independent superlative suffix, later erroneously regarded as being from the adverb *mǣst,* most.]

most·ly (mōst′lē) *adv.* **1.** For the most part; almost entirely. **2.** Usually; as a rule.

> *Usage: Mostly* is used at all levels of style to refer to the largest number of a group: *The trees are mostly evergreens. They arrested mostly adolescents.* In speech and informal writing it is used also to mean "in the greatest degree" or "for the most part," but this usage is best avoided in formal writing: *Those most (not mostly) affected are farmers. For the most part (not mostly) we eat out.*

mot (mō) *n.* A witty, incisive, or clever remark. [French, from Old French, from Vulgar Latin *mottum* (unattested), from Latin *muttum,* grunt, from *muttīre,* to mutter.]

mote¹ (mōt) *n.* A speck, especially of dust. [Middle English *mot, moot,* Old English *mot.*]

mote² *intr.v.* *Archaic.* May; might. [Middle English *moten,* Old English *mōtan,* to be allowed.]

mo·tel (mō-těl′) *n.* A hotel for motorists, usually with rooms opening directly onto a parking area. Also called "motor court." [Blend of *motor* + *hotel.*]

mo·tet (mō-tět′) *n.* A polyphonic musical composition based on a text of a sacred nature and usually sung without accompaniment. [Middle English, from Old French, from *mot,* phrase, word, MOT.]

moth (môth, mŏth) *n., pl.* **moths** (môthz, mŏthz, môths, mŏths). **1.** Any of numerous insects of the order Lepidoptera, generally distinguished from butterflies by their nocturnal activity, hairlike or feathery antennae, and stout bodies. **2.** The **clothes moth** *(see).* [Middle English *motthe,* Old English *moththe.*]

moth·ball (môth′bôl′, mŏth′-) *n.* **1.** A marble-sized ball, originally of camphor but now of naphthalene, stored with clothes to repel moths. **2. mothballs.** A condition of long storage: *After the war, the fleet was put into mothballs.*

~tr.v. **mothballed, -balling, -balls. 1.** To preserve with or as if with mothballs. **2.** To remove from active service or use and put into storage: *mothball a battleship.* **3.** To defer (a project) indefinitely; shelve.

moth-eat·en (môth′ēt′n, mŏth′-) *adj.* **1.** Eaten away by moths. **2.** Old and decayed; timeworn: *a moth-eaten phrase.* **3.** In shabby condition.

moth·er¹ (mŭth′ər) *n.* **1.** A female that has borne offspring. **2.** One's own female parent. Often used as a term of address. **3.** A female who has adopted a child or otherwise established a maternal relationship with another person. **4.** A pregnant woman: *When a fetus quickens, the mother begins to feel its movements.* **5.** A woman having some of the responsibilities of a mother: *a house mother; a cub-scout den mother.* **6.** Qualities attributed to a mother, such as the capacity to love selflessly: *a man who appealed to the mother in her.* **7.** *Archaic.* An affectionate or familiar form of address for an elderly woman. **8.** *Sometimes* **Mother.** A title of or form of address for certain senior nuns: *Mother Abbess.* **9.** A creative source; progenitor: *Necessity is the mother of invention.*

~adj. **1.** Being or resembling a mother: *a mother duck.* **2.** Characteristic of a mother: *mother love.* **3.** Having a maternal relationship: *the mother church.* **4.** Derived from or as if from one's mother; native: *one's mother language.*

~tr.v. **mothered, -ering, -ers. 1.** To give birth to; be the mother of. **2.** To create and care for; instigate and carry through. **3.** To watch over, nourish, and protect. **4.** *Informal.* To behave in an overprotective manner toward; coddle: *Stop mothering me—I'm a grown woman.* [Middle English *moder,* Old English *mōdor.*] **—moth·er·less** *adj.* **—moth·er·less·ness** *n.*

mother² *n.* A stringy slime composed of yeast cells and bacteria that forms on the surface of fermenting liquids. It is added to wine or cider to start the production of vinegar. Also called "mother of vinegar." [Possibly from MOTHER.]

Mother Car·ey's chicken (kâr′ēz) *n.* Any of various petrels, especially the **storm petrel** *(see).* [Perhaps from Latin *Mater Cara,* "Dear Mother," title of the Virgin Mary as patroness of seamen.]

mother cell *n.* A cell that gives rise to other cells.

mother country *n.* The country from which the settlers or colonists, or their forebears, of a distant territory or dominion originally came and for which they still feel an attachment.

Mother Goose *n.* The imaginary storyteller of *Mother Goose's Tales,* a traditional collection of the main bulk of English nursery rhymes, first published in the 18th century.

mother hen *n.* A person, especially a woman, who is fussy and overprotective.

moth·er·hood (mŭth′ər-hŏŏd′) *n.* **1.** The state or condition of being a mother. **2.** The feelings or qualities considered characteristic of a mother. **3.** Mothers collectively.

moth·er·house (mŭth′ər-hous′) *n.* **1.** The convent in which the mother superior of a religious community lives. **2.** The original convent of a religious community.

Mother Hub·bard (hŭb′ərd) *n.* A woman's loose, unbelted dress. [After a character in a nursery rhyme.]

moth·er-in-law (mŭth′ər-ĭn-lô′) *n., pl.* **mothers-in-law.** The mother of one's wife or husband.

mother-in-law's tongue *n.* A plant, **sansevieria** *(see).*

moth·er·land (mŭth′ər-lănd′) *n.* **1.** The land or country of one's birth. **2.** The native land of one's ancestors. **3.** The country of origin, as of a movement.

mother liquor *n.* *Chemistry.* The liquid remaining after crystals have separated out of a solution.

mother lode *n.* The main lode in a source of ore.

moth·er·ly (mŭth′ər-lē) *adj.* Of, befitting, resembling, or characteristic of a mother; maternal. **—moth·er·li·ness** *n.*

moth·er·na·ked (mŭth′ər-nā′kĭd) *adj.* Completely naked.

Mother of Parliaments *n.* The British Parliament, which initiated and provided the model for a number of other national parliaments.

moth·er-of-pearl (mŭth′ər-əv-pûrl′) *n.* The pearly, iridescent internal layer of certain mollusk shells, used to make decorative objects.

Also called "nacre." —**moth·er·of·pearl** *adj.*

moth·er-of-thou·sands (mŭ*th*′ər-əv-thou′zəndz) *n.* A European perennial plant, *Helxine soleirolii,* forming dense evergreen mats, as on walls. Also called "mother-of-millions."

Mother's Day *n.* An annual day of commemoration of mothers and motherhood observed on the second Sunday in May.

mother superior *n., pl.* **mothers superior** or **mother superiors.** A woman in charge of a female religious community.

mother tongue *n.* **1.** One's native language. **2.** The language from which another has developed.

Moth·er·well (mŭ*th*′ər-wĕl′), **Robert** (1915-). U.S. artist, a noted exponent of abstract expressionism. His paintings are characterized by large, amorphous shapes painted in brilliant colors. He is especially known for his series *Elegy for the Spanish Republic.*

mother wit *n.* Innate intelligence; common sense.

moth·er·wort (mŭ*th*′ər-wûrt′, -wôrt′) *n.* Any of several plants of the genus *Leonurus;* especially, *L. cardiaca,* a weed having clusters of small purple or pink flowers. [Middle English *moderwort* : MOTHER (from its once reputed power to cure diseases of the uterus) + WORT.]

moth mullein *n.* A plant, *Verbascum blattaria,* native to Eurasia, having spikelike clusters of yellow or white flowers.

moth·proof (môth′prōōf′, mŏth′-) *adj.* Resistant to damage by moths.
~*tr.v.* **mothproofed, -proofing, -proofs.** To make resistant to damage by moths.

moth·y (mô′thē, mŏth′ē) *adj.* **-ier, -iest. 1.** Infested with moths. **2.** Shabby or moth-eaten.

mo·tif (mō-tēf′) *n.* Also **mo·tive** (mō′tĭv, mō-tēv′). **1.** A recurrent thematic element used in the development of an artistic or literary work. **2.** A short significant phrase in a musical composition. **3.** A repeated figure or design in architecture or decoration. **4.** A dominant theme. [French, from Old French, MOTIVE.]

mo·tile (mōt′l, mō′tīl′) *adj.* Moving or having the power to move spontaneously, as certain spores and microorganisms do.
~*n. Psychology.* A person whose mental imagery chiefly consists of his own bodily motion. [Latin *motus,* motion + -ILE.] —**mo·til·i·ty** (mō-tĭl′ə-tē) *n.*

mo·tion (mō′shən) *n.* **1.** The action or process of changing position. **2.** A meaningful or expressive change in the position of the body or a part of the body; a gesture. **3.** The way in which a body moves. **4.** The ability or power to move. **5.** A prompting from within; an impulse. **6.** *Music.* Melodic ascent or descent of pitch. **7.** *Law.* An application to a court for a ruling. **8.** A formal proposal put to the vote under parliamentary procedures, as at a meeting or conference. **9.** *Chiefly British.* **a.** The act or process of evacuating the bowels. **b.** Feces. **10. a.** A mechanical device or piece of machinery that moves or causes motion, as in a watch. **b.** The movement or action of such a device. —**go through the motions.** To perform an action or engage in a course of action in a perfunctory manner and without serious effort.
~*v.* **motioned, -tioning, -tions.** —*tr.* To signal to or direct by making a gesture. —*intr.* To make a gesture signifying something: *The clerk motioned for me to step forward.* [Middle English *mocioun,* from Old French *motion,* from Latin *mōtiō* (stem *mōtiōn-*), from *movēre,* to move.]

mo·tion·less (mō′shən-lĭs) *adj.* Not moving. —**mo·tion·less·ly** *adv.* —**mo·tion·less·ness** *n.*

motion picture *n.* **1.** A series of photographic images to be projected onto a screen, creating the impression of a continuously moving subject, often accompanied by a sound track. **2.** A story or other representation depicted in such a series of images. Also called "cinema," "film," "moving picture," and informally "movie." **3.** **motion pictures.** Such works collectively as an industry, entertainment, or art form.

motion sickness *n.* Sickness induced by motion, as in travel by automobile, ship, or airplane, and characterized by nausea, vomiting, and often dizziness. Also called "travel sickness."

motion study *n.* A **time and motion study** *(see).*

mo·tion·work (mō′shən-wûrk′) *n.* The mechanism for moving the hands of a watch or clock.

mo·ti·vate (mō′tə-vāt′) *tr.v.* **-vated, -vating, -vates.** To stimulate to action; provide with an incentive. [From MOTIVE.]

mo·ti·va·tion (mō′tə-vā′shən) *n.* **1.** The act or process of motivating. **2.** Something that motivates; incentive, inducement, or motive. **3.** *Psychology.* The mental process, function, or instinct that produces and sustains incentive or drive in human and animal behavior. —**mo·ti·va·tion·al** *adj.*

motivational research *n.* The use of certain techniques borrowed from psychology and sociology, especially by advertisers and marketers, to assess consumer attitudes toward products and services. Also called "motivation research."

mo·tive (mō′tĭv; *also* mō-tēv′ *for sense 2*) *n.* **1.** An emotion, desire, physiological need, or similar impulse acting as an incitement to action: *The motive for the crime was revenge.* **2.** A **motif** *(see).*
~*adj.* **1.** Causing or able to cause motion: *motive power.* **2.** Of, pertaining to, or constituting a motive.
~*tr.v.* **motived, -tiving, -tives.** To provide with an incentive; motivate. [Middle English, from Old French *motif,* from adjective, "causing to move," from Late Latin *mōtivus,* from Latin *movēre* (past participle *mōtus*), to move.] —**mo·tiv·i·ty** (mō-tĭv′ə-tē) *n.*

mot juste (mō zhüst′) *n., pl.* **mots justes** (*pronounced as singular*). The most suitable word or expression. [French, "exact word."]

mot·ley (mŏt′lē) *adj.* **1.** Having components of great variety; heterogeneous: *"I didn't realize how motley are the qualities that go to make up a human being."* (W. Somerset Maugham). **2.** Exhibiting or having many colors; multicolored. —See Synonyms at **miscellaneous.**
~*n.* **1.** The particolored professional attire of a court jester. **2.** A heterogeneous mixture or assemblage. **3.** A professional jester; clown. —**wear motley. 1.** To play the fool; jest in a frivolous manner. **2.** To be a fool. [Middle English *motteley,* perhaps from Norman French *motelé* (unattested), from MOTE (speck).]

mot·mot (mŏt′mŏt′) *n.* Any of several tropical American birds of the family Momotidae, usually having green and blue plumage. [American Spanish *mot-mot.*]

mo·to·cross (mō′tō-krôs′, -krŏs′) *n.* **1.** Motorcycle racing over a hazardous cross-country course. **2.** A motorcycle race over such a course. [Alteration of *motor* + *cross-country.*]

mo·to·neu·ron (mō′tə-nōōr′ŏn′, -nyōōr′ŏn′) *n. Anatomy.* A neuron that stimulates motion; motor nerve cell. [*Motor* + *neuron.*]

mo·tor (mō′tər) *n.* **1.** Something that imparts or produces motion, such as a machine or engine. **2.** A device that converts any form of energy into mechanical energy, especially an **internal-combustion engine** *(see)* or an arrangement of coils and magnets that converts electrical energy into mechanical power. **3.** A motorized conveyance; especially, an automobile.
~*adj.* **1.** Causing or producing motion: *motor power.* **2.** Driven by or having a motor: *a motor scooter.* **3.** Of, pertaining to, or for motor vehicles: *motor oil.* **4.** *Physiology.* **a.** Of, pertaining to, or designating nerves carrying impulses from the nerve centers to the muscles. **b.** Of or pertaining to movements of the muscles: *motor coordination.*
~*v.* **motored, -toring, -tors.** —*intr.* To drive or travel in a motor vehicle. —*tr.* To carry by motor vehicle. [Latin *mōtor,* agent noun of *movēre* (past participle *mōtus*), to move.]

mo·tor·bike (mō′tər-bīk′) *n.* **1.** A lightweight motorcycle. **2.** A pedal bicycle that has an attached motor.

mo·tor·boat (mō′tər-bōt′) *n.* A boat with a propeller driven by an internal-combustion engine.

mo·tor·bus (mō′tər-bŭs′) *n., pl.* **-buses** or **-busses.** A passenger bus, especially one that is powered by an internal-combustion engine. Also called "motor coach."

mo·tor·cade (mō′tər-kād′) *n.* A procession of cars or other motor vehicles. [*Motor* + caval*cade.*]

mo·tor·car, motor car (mō′tər-kär′) *n.* An automobile.

motor caravan *n. Chiefly British.* A house trailer or mobile home.

motor court *n.* A **motel** *(see).*

mo·tor·cy·cle (mō′tər-sī′kəl) *n.* A vehicle with two wheels in tandem propelled by an internal-combustion engine.
~*intr.v.* **motorcycled, -cycling, -cycles.** To ride on or drive a motorcycle. —**mo·tor·cy·clist** *n.*

motor drive *n.* A system consisting of an electric motor and accessory parts, used to power machinery.

motor home *n.* A motor vehicle built on a truck or bus chassis and designed to serve as self-contained living quarters for recreational travel.

motor inn *n.* Also **motor hotel.** An urban motel usually having several stories and facilities for guest parking.

mo·tor·ist (mō′tər-ĭst) *n.* One who drives an automobile.

mo·tor·ize (mō′tə-rīz′) *tr.v.* **-ized, -izing, -izes. 1.** To equip with a motor or motors: *Buses were motorized at the turn of the century.* **2.** To supply with motor-driven vehicles in substitution for ones drawn by horses or other animals. **3.** To provide motor-vehicle transport for. —**mo·tor·i·za·tion** *n.*

mo·tor·man (mō′tər-mən) *n., pl.* **-men** (-mĭn). One who drives an electrically powered streetcar, locomotive, or subway train.

motor neuron *n.* **1.** A **motoneuron** *(see).* **2.** A disease that causes progressive spinal muscular atrophy.

motor pool *n.* A centrally managed group of motor vehicles intended for the use of personnel, as of a governmental agency or military installation.

motor scooter *n.* A two-wheeled vehicle with small wheels and a low-powered gasoline engine geared to the rear wheel.

motor vehicle *n.* Any self-propelled, wheeled conveyance that does not run on rails, especially one driven by an internal-combustion engine.

mo·tor·way (mō′tər-wā′) *n. Chiefly British.* A main road designed for fast-moving traffic; expressway.

motte[1], **mott** (mŏt) *n. Western U.S.* A small stand of shrubs or trees on a prairie. [Mexican Spanish *mata,* from Spanish, shrub, probably from Late Latin *matta,* MAT.]

motte[2] (mŏt) *n.* A mound on which a castle or fortification is sited. [Middle English, from Old French *mote,* mound, MOAT.]

mot·tle (mŏt′l) *tr.v.* **-tled, -tling, -tles.** To cover (a surface) with spots or streaks of different shades or colors.
~*n.* **1.** A spot of color or shading contrasting with the rest of the surface on which it is found. **2.** A variegated pattern, as on marble. [Probably back-formation from MOTLEY.]

mottled enamel *n.* Discolored tooth enamel, usually caused by excessive amounts of fluorides in drinking water.

mot·to (mŏt′ō) *n., pl.* **-toes** or **-tos. 1.** A brief sentence, phrase, or single word used to express a principle, goal, or ideal, especially when accompanying a coat of arms *"E pluribus unum" (one out of many) is the motto on the Great Seal of the United States.* **2.** A maxim adopted as a guide to one's conduct. **3.** A quotation prefacing a book or chapter. **4.** A briefly stated sentiment of appropriate

mountain

HOW MOUNTAINS ARE MADE

The growth of mountains shows that the earth's surface is mobile

Mountains are made in four main ways: by volcanoes, faulting, folding, and doming. Folding generally also involves one or more of the other three methods.

Folding is a by-product of the forces of continental drift. In the last two decades, the earth's surface has come to be seen as a collection of plates of lightweight rock resting on denser material that moves in response to heat in the earth's interior. The plates, some of which bear the continents, move about the earth's surface at the rate of about an inch a year. The edges at which they meet crumple, forming mountain ranges. Mountains are continuously eroded. Old ranges like the Urals, remnants of an ancient clash between Europe and Asia, are worn down almost flat, but younger ranges like the Alps retain their youthful ruggedness.

VOLCANIC *Volcanoes form mountains by erupting lava, which creates several different shapes, from conical stratovolcanoes like Mt. Fuji to low-shield volcanoes like Hawaii's Mauna Loa.*

FAULTING *The upthrust edge of a deep fault—caused by subterranean forces cracking the earth's crust—is weathered to form a block mountain. Streams may carve out peaks.*

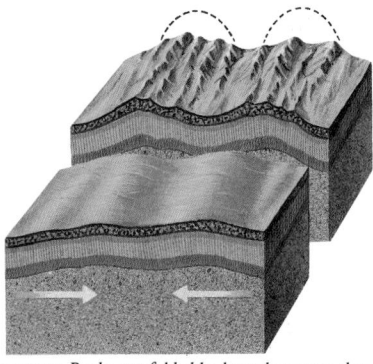

FOLDING *Rocks are folded by lateral pressure that compresses the strata. Often the folding is made more complex by other layers of rock thrusting underneath the raised area.*

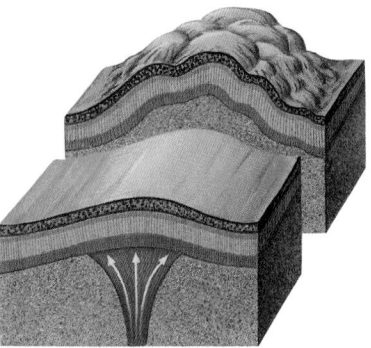

DOMING *A dome mountain is formed when an upsurge of molten rock from below does not break the earth's surface, but instead causes it to swell like a giant blister.*

character inscribed on or attached to an object. **5.** *Music.* A recurring theme or motif. —See Synonyms at **saying.** [Italian, "a word," from Gallo-Roman *mottum* (unattested), a sound uttered, from Latin *muttum,* a mutter, grunt, from *muttīre,* to mutter.]

mo·tu pro·pri·o (mō′tŏō prō′prē-ō′) *n., pl.* **motu proprios.** An administrative papal bull. [Latin, of (our) own accord.]

mouch. *Chiefly British.* Variant of **mooch.**

moue (mōō) *n.* A sulky or disdainful expression; a pout. [French, from Old French, from Germanic, akin to Middle Dutch *mouwe,* pouting lip.]

mou·flon, mouf·flon (mōōf′lŏn′) *n., pl.* **-flons** or collectively **mouflon** or **moufflon.** A wild sheep, *Ovis musimon,* of Sardinia and Corsica. [French, from dialectal Italian *muvrone,* from Vulgar Latin *mufro†,* sheep.]

mouil·lé (mōō-yā′) *adj. Phonetics.* Pronounced palatally; palatalized. [French, past participle of *mouiller,* to moisten, palatalize, from Old French *moullier,* to soften by soaking, from Vulgar Latin *molliāre* (unattested), from Latin *mollis,* soft.]

moujik. Variant of **muzhik.**

mou·lage (mōō-läzh′) *n.* **1.** The making of a mold from a mark, such as a footprint, especially for identification. **2.** A mold of this kind. [French, from Old French, from *mouler,* to mold, from *moule, modle,* a mold, from Latin *modulus,* diminutive of *modus,* a measure, manner.]

mould. *Chiefly British.* Variant of **mold.**

mouldboard. *Chiefly British.* Variant of **moldboard.**

moulder. *Chiefly British.* Variant of **molder.**

moulding. *Chiefly British.* Variant of **molding.**

mouldy. *Chiefly British.* Variant of **moldy.**

mou·lin (mōō-lăn′) *n.* A vertical shaft in a glacier, kept open by falling water and rock debris. [French, "mill," from Old French, from Late Latin *molīnum,* from Latin *molīnus,* of a mill, from *mola,* mill, millstone.]

moult. *Chiefly British.* Variant of **molt.**

mound¹ (mound) *n.* **1.** A pile of earth, gravel, sand, rocks, or debris heaped for protection or concealment. **2.** A natural elevation, such as a small hill. **3.** Any raised mass, as of hay. **4.** *Archaeology.* A **barrow** *(see).* **5.** In baseball, the small elevation where the pitcher stands when pitching. ~*tr.v.* **mounded, mounding, mounds. 1.** To fortify or conceal with a mound. **2.** To heap in a mound. [Originally "enclosing hedge or fence," perhaps from Dutch *mond,* protection, or Old Norse *mund.*]

mound² *n. Heraldry.* An orb or ball of gold representing the earth. [Middle English, from Old French *monde,* from Latin *mundus,* world.]

Mound Builder *n.* A member of one of the prehistoric North American Indian peoples who built burial and effigy mounds, mainly in the Mississippi valley.

mound-build·er (mound′bĭl′dər) *n.* A bird, the **megapode** *(see).*

mount¹ (mount) *v.* **mounted, mounting, mounts.** —*tr.* **1.** To climb or ascend. **2.** To get up on; place oneself upon: *mount a horse.* **3.** To get up on in order to copulate. Used of male animals. **4.** To provide with a horse or horses for riding: *The stable mounted all the riders.* **5.** To prepare, place, or fix on or in an appropriate or convenient setting, as for display, study, or use: *mount pictures on cardboard.* **6.** To prepare for display, production, or public viewing: *mount a theatrical performance.* **7.** To place (a specimen) on a microscope slide in preparation for microscopic examination. **8.** *Military.* **a.** To set (guns) in position. **b.** To put in readiness and start to carry out: *mount an attack.* **c.** To be furnished with or carry: *The warship mounted ten guns.* **d.** To post (a guard): *mount sentries.* —*intr.v.* **1.** To go or move upward. **2.** To get or climb up on a horse or vehicle. **3.** To increase, as in amount, degree, extent, intensity, or number: *The temperature mounts rapidly in desert regions. Reinforcements were sent as casualties mounted up.* —See Synonyms at **rise.** ~*n.* **1. a.** A horse, other animal, or vehicle on which to ride. **b.** The opportunity to ride a horse, especially in a race. **2.** An object to which another is affixed, such as a piece of cardboard, or on which another is placed for accessibility, display, or use, such as a stamp hinge. **3.** A glass slide on which specimens are placed for microscopy. **4.** A setting for a jewel. **5.** An undercarriage or stand on which a device rests while in use: *a gun mount.* [Middle English *mounten,* from Old French *monter,* from Vulgar Latin *montāre* (unattested), "to climb a mountain," from Latin *mōns* (stem *mont-*), mountain.] —**mount·a·ble** *adj.* —**mount·er** *n.*

mount² *n.* **1.** *Abbr.* **mt., Mt.** A mountain or hill. Used chiefly as part of a proper name or in poetry. **2.** In palmistry, any of the seven fleshy cushions around the edges of the palm of the hand. [Middle English *mont, munt,* from Old French *mont* and Old English *munt,* both from Latin *mōns* (stem *mont-*), mountain.]

moun·tain (moun′tən) *n. Abbr.* **mt., Mt., mtn. 1.** A natural elevation of the earth's surface having considerable mass, generally steep sides, and a height greater than that of a hill. **2. a.** A large heap: *a mountain of ironing.* **b.** A huge quantity. **3. Mountain.** The extreme revolutionary party of the French Revolution, so called because its members occupied the uppermost seats in the National Convention Hall in 1793. Preceded by *the.* [Middle English *mountaine,* from Old French *montaigne,* from Vulgar Latin *montānea* (unattested), from Latin *montānus,* mountainous, from *mōns* (stem *mont-*), mountain.] —**moun·tain** *adj.*

mountain ash *n.* **1.** Any of various deciduous trees of the genus *Sorbus,* especially: **a.** *S. americana,* of eastern North America, having clusters of small white flowers and bright orange-red berries. **b.** *S. aucuparia,* the European mountain ash, having similar flowers and berries. Both species are also called "rowan." **2.** Any of several Australian eucalyptus trees.

mountain cat *n.* The mountain lion.

mountain dew *n. Slang.* Illegally distilled corn liquor.

moun·tain·eer (moun′tə-nîr′) *n.* **1.** One who climbs mountains as a sport or hobby. **2.** An inhabitant of a mountainous area. ~*intr.v.* **mountaineered, -eering, -eers.** To climb mountains as a hobby or sport. —**moun·tain·eer·ing** *n.*

mountain goat *n.* A hoofed mammal, *Oreamnos americanus,* of northwestern North American mountains, having short, curved black horns and yellowish-white hair and beard. Also called "Rocky Mountain goat."

mountain laurel *n.* An evergreen shrub, *Kalmia latifolia,* of eastern North America, having leathery, poisonous leaves and clusters of pink or white flowers. Also called "calico bush."

mountain lion *n.* A large, powerful wild cat, *Felis concolor,* of mountainous regions of the Western Hemisphere, having an unmarked tawny body. Also called "catamount," "cougar," "mountain cat," "panther," and "puma."

moun·tain·ous (moun′tə-nəs) *adj.* **1.** Of, pertaining to, or designating a region having many mountains. **2.** Of impressive size or height.

mountain range *n.* An extensive series or cluster of mountains alike in form, direction, and origin.

mountain ringlet *n.* Any of several brown butterflies of the genus *Erebia,* found in mountains and northern regions of Eurasia and North America.
mountain sheep *n.* **1.** The **bighorn** *(see).* **2.** Any wild sheep native to a mountainous area.
mountain sickness *n.* **Altitude sickness** *(see).*
moun·tain·side (moun'tən-sīd') *n.* Any of the sloping sides of a mountain.
Mountain Standard Time *n. Abbr.* **MST, M.S.T.** Local time in one of the standard time zones of North America, based on the 105th meridian west of Greenwich, England, seven hours behind Greenwich Mean Time.
moun·tain·top (moun'tən-tŏp') *n.* The summit of a mountain.
Mount·bat·ten, Louis Alexander (mount-băt'n), born Prince Louis Alexander of Battenberg; also known as 1st Marquis of Milford Haven (1854–1921). British admiral and first sea lord (1912–14). He became a naturalized British subject when he joined the Royal Navy (1868), and married a granddaughter of Queen Victoria (1884). He subsequently gave up his German titles, changed his surname, and was created a marquis by George V.
Mountbatten of Burma, Louis, 1st Earl (1900–79). English naval officer, great-grandson of Queen Victoria. In 1943 he was appointed Supreme Allied Commander in Southeast Asia. He was made a viscount in 1946 and an earl in 1947 when he was appointed viceroy of India, presiding over the transfer of power to independent India in that year. He stayed in India as governor general until 1948. He was killed by the I.R.A. when a bomb detonated by remote control exploded on his yacht.
Mount Des·ert (dĕz'ərt). Island, *c.* 260 square kilometers (100 square miles), off the coast of Maine. The island has numerous lakes and streams and a chain of rounded granite peaks. The peaks were named *Mont Desert,* "wilderness mountains," by the French explorers who landed here in 1604. The island is a famous resort area.
moun·te·bank (moun'tə-băngk') *n.* **1.** A hawker of quack medicines and nostrums who attracts customers with stories, jokes, or tricks. **2.** Any charlatan or trickster. [Italian *montambanco, montimbanco,* "one who climbs on a bench" : *montare,* to mount (see **mount**[1]) + *in,* in, on, from Latin + *banco, banca,* bench.]
mount·ed (moun'tĭd) *adj.* **1.** Seated upon or riding on a horse, bicycle, or other means of conveyance. **2.** Serving on horseback or equipped with a horse or horses: *a mounted policeman.* **3.** Fitted into or set in a backing or support: *mounted photographs.*
Mount·ie, Mount·y (moun'tē) *n., pl.* **-ies.** *Informal.* A Royal Canadian Mounted Policeman.
mount·ing (moun'tĭng) *n.* Something that provides a backing, support, or appropriate setting for something else: *a telescope mounting; a mounting for a gem.*
mounting block *n.* A block of stone used as an aid in mounting a horse.
Mount Mc·Kin·ley National Park (mə-kĭn'lē). Area of 785,495 hectares (1,939,493 acres) in the Alaska Range of south-central Alaska, containing spectular mountain scenery.
Mount Rai·nier National Park (rā-nîr'). Area of 98,007 hectares (241, 992 acres) in the Cascade Range of southwestern Washington, including Mt. Rainier and 26 glaciers.
Mount Rushmore National Memorial. See **Rushmore, Mount.**
Mount Ver·non (vûr'nən). Home and estate of George Washington, on the Potomac in northeastern Virginia near Washington, D.C. The house was built in 1743 by Lawrence Washington, George's half brother. George Washington lived here from 1747 until his death in 1799. The beautiful restored Georgian mansion contains much original furniture and family memorabilia and is open to the public.
mourn (môrn, mōrn) *v.* **mourned, mourning, mourns.** *—intr.* **1.** To express or feel grief or sorrow, especially for someone who has died. **2.** To express public grief for a death by conventional signs; be in mourning. *—tr.* **1. a.** To feel grief for (a dead person, for example). **b.** To show public signs of grief for (a dead person, for example). **2.** To feel or express regret over; lament: *mourned the abolition of the death penalty.* [Middle English *mournen,* Old English *murnan.*]
mourn·er (môr'nər, mōr'nər) *n.* One who mourns, especially: **1.** A person attending a funeral out of grief or respect. **2.** Formerly, a person hired to attend a funeral.
mourn·ful (môrn'fəl, mōrn'-) *adj.* **1.** Feeling or expressing sorrow or grief. **2.** Arousing or suggesting sorrow or grief: *the mournful sound of the train whistle.* —See Synonyms at **glum.** **—mourn·ful·ly** *adv.* **—mourn·ful·ness** *n.*
mourn·ing (môr'nĭng, mōr'-) *n.* **1.** The actions or expressions of one who has suffered a bereavement. **2.** The symbols or conventional outward signs of grief for the dead. **3.** The period during which a death is mourned. **—in mourning. 1.** Wearing clothes conventionally expressive of mourning, as a black tie or armband or black clothes. **2.** Abiding by appropriate conduct during a period of mourning: *I can't remarry yet—I'm still in mourning for my husband.* **—mourn·ing·ly** *adv.*
mourning cloak *n.* A butterfly, *Nymphalis antiopa,* of Europe and North America, having purplish-brown wings with a broad yellow border. Also called "Camberwell beauty."
mourning dove *n.* A buff-colored wild dove, *Zenaidura macroura,* of North America, noted for its plaintive call and its ability to survive in deserts.
mourning warbler *n.* A warbler, *Oporornis philadelphia,* that breeds chiefly in southern Canada and is olive above and yellow below, with a gray hood that suggests mourning.
mouse (mous) *n., pl.* **mice** (mīs). **1. a.** Any of numerous small rodents of the families Muridae and Cricetidae, such as the **house mouse** or the **harvest mouse** *(both of which see),* characteristically having a long, naked or almost hairless tail. **b.** Any of various similar or related animals, such as the **jumping mouse** or the **pocket mouse** *(both of which see).* **2.** *Informal.* **a.** A cowardly or timid person. **b.** An affectionate term for a little girl or young woman. **3.** *Slang.* A black eye. **4.** *Nautical.* A mousing on a hook.
~*intr.v.* (mouz) **moused, mousing, mouses. 1.** To hunt, stalk, or catch mice. **2.** To search furtively for something; prowl. Often used with *about.* [Mouse, mice; Middle English *mous, mys,* Old English *mūs, mȳs.*]
mouse deer *n.* A **chevrotain** *(see).*
mouse-ear (mous'îr') *n.* Any of various weedy plants of the genus *Cerastium,* having small white flowers. Also called "mouse-ear chickweed."
mous·er (mou'zər) *n.* An animal that catches mice, especially a cat.
mouse-tail (mous'tāl') *n.* Any plant of the genus *Myosurus,* especially *M. minimus,* having a taillike flower spike.
mouse·trap (mous'trăp') *n.* **1.** A trap for catching mice. **2.** A tempting trap; lure.
mous·ing (mou'zĭng) *n. Nautical.* **1.** A binding around the point and shank of a hook to prevent it from slipping from an eye. **2.** A metal shackle used for the same purpose. [From its mouselike shape.]
mous·sa·ka, mous·a·ka (mōō-sä'kə, mōō'sä-kä') *n.* A Greek dish consisting of layers of ground lamb or beef and sliced eggplant topped with a cheese sauce. [Modern Greek *moussakas.*]
mousse (mōōs) *n.* **1.** Any of various chilled desserts made with sweetened whipped cream or whipped egg whites, gelatin, and flavoring. **2.** A molded dish made from a purée of meat, fish, or shellfish with whipped cream: *lobster mousse.* **3.** A preparation with the consistency of mousse that is used to give the hair body and hold it in place. [French *mousse*†, "froth."]
mousse·line (mōō-slēn') *n.* A fine cotton or silk fabric originally made in Mosul, Iraq. [French, MUSLIN.]
Moussorgsky. See **Mussorgsky.**
moustache. *Chiefly British.* Variant of **mustache.**
Mous·te·ri·an, Mous·tie·ri·an (mōō-stîr'ē-ən) *adj. Archaeology.* Designating or belonging to a Middle Paleolithic culture following the Acheulian, characterized by the use of flint implements. [French *moustérien, moustiérien,* from *Le Moustier,* village in southwestern France near which archaeological specimens were found.]
mous·y, mous·ey (mou'sē, -zē) *adj.* **-ier, -iest. 1.** Of a dull, pale brown color. Said of hair. **2.** Resembling a mouse in appearance: *a mousy face.* **3.** Shy; retiring; unassertive. **—mous·i·ness** *n.*
mouth (mouth) *n., pl.* **mouths** (mou*th*z). **1.** *Anatomy.* **a.** The body opening through which an animal takes in food; the oral cavity. **b.** The system of related organs including the lips, teeth, tongue, and associated parts with which food is chewed and swallowed and sounds and speech are articulated. **2.** The part of the lips visible on the human face. **3.** A person viewed as a consumer of food: *I've got three mouths to feed at home.* **4.** A pout, grimace, or similar expression. **5. a.** The capacity for speech or propensity for speaking: *"A fool's mouth is his destruction"* (Proverbs 18:7). **b.** A manner of speech, especially when considered as inappropriate: *a foul mouth.* **c.** *Slang.* Impudent or vulgar talk: *Watch your mouth.* **6.** The part of the inner lip of an animal such as a horse or donkey on which the bit presses and which varies in sensitivity to the bit: *a hard mouth.* **7.** A natural opening, such as the part of a stream or river that empties into a larger body of water or the entrance to a harbor, canyon, valley, or cave. **8.** The opening through which a container is filled or emptied. **9.** An opening in tools and devices whose function is to hold or grip. **10. a.** An opening in the pipe of an organ. **b.** The opening in the mouthpiece of a flute across which the player blows. **—down in** (or **at**) **the mouth.** *Informal.* Crestfallen; unhappy. **—shoot one's mouth off.** To speak freely and often in an insulting manner without regard to the consequences or effect on others. **—shut one's mouth.** *Informal.* To desist from speaking.
~*v.* (mou*th*) **mouthed, mouthing, mouths.** *—tr.* **1. a.** To utter in a declamatory manner or mechanically and without conviction: *mouthing empty compliments.* **b.** To form or articulate soundlessly: *mouthed Hamlet's soliloquy in time with the actor.* **2.** To put, take, or move around in the mouth. **3.** To train the mouth of (a horse). *—intr.* **1.** To orate affectedly; declaim: *"the mouthing of a man whose praise would be as insolent as his slander is impotent"* (Oscar Wilde). **2.** To grimace. **—mouth off.** *Slang.* To complain, criticize, or brag loudly and indiscreetly. [Middle English *mouth,* Old English *mūth.*]
mouth·breed·er (mouth'brē'dər) *n.* Also **mouth·brood·er** (mouth'-brōō'dər). Any of various African cichlid fishes that carry their eggs and young in the mouth.
mouth·ful (mouth'fōōl') *n., pl.* **mouthfuls. 1.** The amount of food or other material that can be placed or held in the mouth at one time. **2.** A small amount to be tasted or eaten. **3.** *Informal.* An utterance, such as a long name, that is complicated or difficult to pronounce. **—say a mouthful.** *Slang.* To utter an important or especially perceptive remark or observation.
mouth organ *n.* Either of two musical instruments, a **harmonica** or **panpipes** *(both of which see).*
mouth·part, mouth-part (mouth'pärt') *n.* Any of the appendages,

mountaineer *A modern mountaineer wearing an oxygen mask, used on high-altitude climbs.*

mountain ringlet *A brown European butterfly that lives in rough, often boggy moorland and among fir trees at altitudes of between 500 meters (1,650 feet) and 2,600 meters (8,000 feet). The illustrations show the top and the underside of its wings.*

Mount Rushmore National Memorial *These rock portraits of four American presidents—from the left, Washington, Jefferson, Theodore Roosevelt, and Lincoln—are about 28 meters (60 feet) high and can be seen for nearly 100 kilometers (60 miles). Their sculptor, Gutzon Borglum, died in 1941 when they were nearly complete, and his son finished them.*

as the maxillae and mandibles, situated around the mouth in arthropods and adapted for feeding.

mouth·piece (mouth'pēs') *n.* **1.** A part, as of a musical instrument or a telephone, that functions in or near the mouth. **2.** A protective rubber device worn over the teeth by boxers; a gumshield. **3.** *Informal.* One through whom views are expressed, such as a spokesman or newspaper. **4.** *Slang.* A defense lawyer.

mouth-to-mouth (mouth'tə-mouth') *adj.* Designating a method of artificial respiration in which air is blown forcefully into the lungs of the patient by one whose mouth is placed firmly over the patient's mouth: *mouth-to-mouth resuscitation.*

mouth·wash (mouth'wŏsh', -wôsh') *n.* An aqueous solution containing an antiseptic or astringent, used for gargling and for cleansing the mouth and teeth.

mouth·wa·ter·ing (mouth'wô'tər-ĭng, -wŏt'ər-ĭng) *adj.* Appetizing; delicious.

mouth·y (mou'thē, -thē) *adj.* **-ier, -iest.** Given to ranting; grandiloquent; bombastic. **—mouth·i·ly** *adv.* **—mouth·i·ness** *n.*

mou·ton (mōō'tŏn') *n.* Sheepskin sheared and processed to resemble beaver or seal and used for garments. [French, "sheep," from Old French *mo(u)ton,* MUTTON.]

mou·ton·née (mōōt'n-ā') *adj.* Also **mou·ton·néed** (mōōt'n-ād'). *Geology.* Rounded by glacial action to a shape likened to a sheep's back. Said of a rock formation. [Short for French *roche moutonnée* : *roche,* rock + *moutonnée,* fleecy.]

mov·a·ble, move·a·ble (mōō'və-bəl) *adj.* **1.** Capable of being moved. **2.** Varying in date from year to year: *a movable holiday.* **3.** *Law.* Of or pertaining to personal property that can be moved as opposed to real property such as land. **4.** *Printing.* Cast with each character on a separate piece of type.
~n. **1.** *Usually* **movables.** Something that can be moved, especially as opposed to permanent fixtures. **2.** *Law.* Personal property as distinguished from real property such as land. **—mov·a·bil·i·ty** (mōō'və-bĭl'ə-tē), **mov·a·ble·ness** *n.* **—mov·a·bly** *adv.*
   Usage: Something is *movable* if it can be moved at all (*movable furniture; a movable wall*); it is *mobile* if it is designed for easy transportation (*a mobile home*) or if it moves frequently (*a mobile staff headquarters*). • The expression *movable feast* is used of a religious holiday, like Easter, that falls on different calendar days in different years.

movable feast *n.* A religious feast, such as Easter, that varies in date from year to year.

move (mōōv) *v.* **moved, moving, moves.** **—intr.** **1.** To change in position from one point to another. **2.** To march, as an army or procession does. **3.** To progress in sequence, as in the development of a literary or musical composition. **4.** To follow some specified course: *The earth moves in orbit around the sun.* **5. a.** To be transferred from one position to another in a board game. **b.** To transfer a piece in a board game. **6.** To change to or settle in a new place of residence or business. Often used with *in, out,* or *away.* **7.** To be disposed of commercially: *Furs move slowly in summer.* **8.** To change posture or position; stir. **9.** To be disturbed or displaced: *The foliage moved in the breeze. When you pressed it, the key moved down.* **10.** To be put into motion or to turn according to a prescribed motion. Used of machinery. **11.** To hum with activity; be busy. **12.** To initiate some action: *Wait for the election results before we move.* **13. a.** To behave, progress, or proceed as specified: *move toward a solution.* **b.** To change: *The situation hasn't moved.* **14.** To live or be active in a specified environment: *move in diplomatic circles.* **15.** To make a legal submission or a formal motion in parliamentary procedure: *move for an adjournment.* **16.** To stir the emotions: *a painting that delights and moves.* **17.** To be evacuated; void. Used of the bowels. **—tr.** **1. a.** To change the place of; shift; remove; displace. **b.** To change the position of: *move one's head.* **c.** To cause to change position: *moved the spectators on.* **d.** To change the course of: *moved the discussion on to more general topics.* **2.** To dislodge from a fixed point of view, especially by persuasion. **3.** To prompt (someone) to some action; actuate: *She was moved to intercede on his behalf.* **4.** To set or maintain in motion. **5.** To set astir; agitate; shake: *The wind moved the blossoms.* **6.** To excite or provoke to the expression of some feeling: *moved to tears.* **7.** To affect, arouse, or stir the emotions of: *Her sad story moved him deeply.* **8.** To propose or request in formal parliamentary procedure: *move an adjournment.* **9.** To cause to change hands commercially: *had trouble moving the big cars.* **10.** To cause (the bowels) to evacuate. **—See Synonyms at affect.**
~n. **1.** An act of moving: *Nobody dared make a move.* **2.** A change of residence or place of business. **3.** In board games: **a.** An act of transferring a piece from one position to another. **b.** The prescribed manner in which a piece may be maneuvered. **c.** A player's turn to maneuver a piece. **4.** One of a series of calculated actions undertaken to achieve some end. **—See Synonyms at affect. —get a move on.** *Informal.* To get started; get going. **—on the move. 1.** In the process of moving about. **2.** Making progress; advancing. [Middle English *moven,* from Norman French *mover,* variant of Old French *moveir,* from Latin *movēre,* to move.]

move·ment (mōōv'mənt) *n.* **1. a.** The act or an instance of moving; a change in position. **b.** *Military.* A change in the location of troops, ships, or aircraft for tactical or strategic purposes; a maneuver. **2. a.** The activities of a group of people to achieve a specific goal: *the peace movement.* **b.** A group of people associated through some common aim: *an early leader of the labor movement.* **c.** A tendency or trend. **3.** Activity, especially: **a.** Commercial trading.

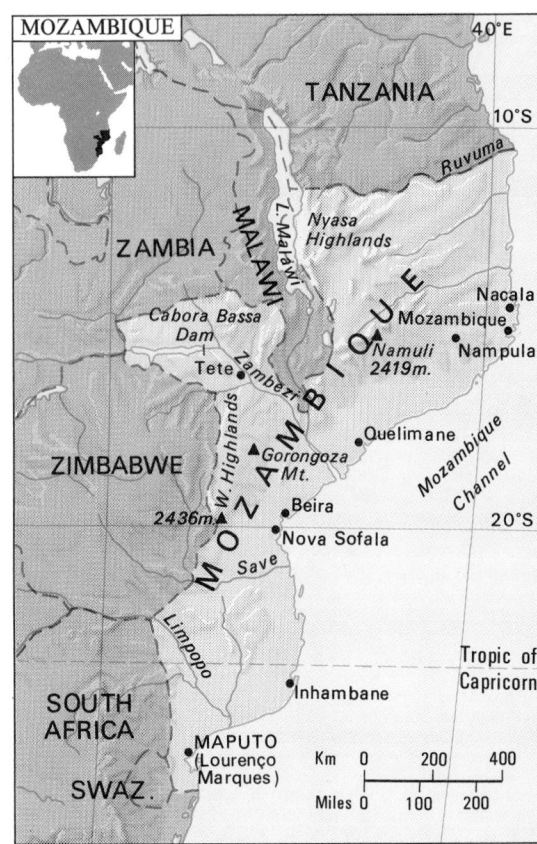

MOZAMBIQUE

b. A change in price of a security or commodity. **4. a.** An evacuation of the bowels. **b.** The feces evacuated. **5.** *Fine Arts.* The impression or illusion of motion. **6.** The progression of events in the development of a literary plot. **7.** The rhythmical or metrical structure of a poetic composition. **8.** *Music.* A self-contained component section of a composition. **9.** A mechanism that produces or transmits motion, as do the works of a watch. [Middle English, from Old French, from Medieval Latin *movimentum,* from Latin *movēre,* to move.]

mov·er (mōō'vər) *n.* **1.** One that moves. **2.** One who proposes a motion in a debate. **3.** One whose occupation is transporting household or office goods from one location to another.

mov·ie (mōō'vē) *n.* *Informal.* **1.** A motion picture *(see).* **2.** A theater that shows motion pictures. **3. movies. a.** A showing of a motion picture. Preceded by *the.* **b.** The motion picture industry. [Shortened from MOVING PICTURE.]

mov·ing (mōō'vĭng) *adj.* **1.** Changing or capable of changing position. **2.** Causing or producing motion. **3.** Of, pertaining to, or used for transporting household or office goods from one location to another: *moving day.* **4.** Affecting the emotions, especially those of sympathy and sorrow: *a moving tale.* **—mov·ing·ly** *adv.* **—mov·ing·ness** *n.*
   Synonyms: *affecting, pathetic, poignant, stirring, touching.*

moving average *n.* A form of statistical average obtained by replacing one item in the numerator but keeping the denominator unchanged. It therefore has several successive values.

moving pavement *n.* A flat surface on a horizontal continuously circulating belt for conveying people, as passengers at an airport, from one area to another.

moving picture *n.* A motion picture *(see).*

moving staircase *n.* An escalator *(see).*

mow[1] (mō) *v.* **mowed, mowed** *or* **mown** (mōn), **mowing, mows.** **—tr.** **1.** To cut down (crops, grass, or similar growth) with a scythe or a mechanical device such as a lawn mower or mowing machine. **2.** To cut such growth from: *mow the lawn.* **—intr.** To mow growth such as crops or grass. **—mow down.** To fell in great numbers, as in battle: *mowed down by the enemy's guns.* [Mow, mown; Middle English *mowen, mowen,* Old English *māwan, māwen,* from Germanic.] **—mow·er** *n.*

mow[2] (mou) *n.* **1.** A place for storing hay or crops. **2.** Feed so stored. [Middle English *mough, mow,* stack of hay, Old English *mūga, mūha, mūwa,* from Scandinavian; akin to Old Norse *mūgi,* crowd.]

mow[3] (mou, mō) *n. Archaic.* A grimace.
~intr.v. **mowed, mowing, mows.** *Archaic.* To grimace. Used chiefly in the phrase *mop and mow.* [Middle English *mouwe,* from Old French. See **moue.**]

mowing machine *n.* A machine for cutting hay, grass, or crops.

mox·i·bus·tion (mŏk'sə-bŭs'chən) *n.* An Asian method of treating skin irritation and various other disorders by placing down from the leaves of *Artemisia moxa* on the skin and igniting it. [Blend of (*Artemisia*) *moxa* + *combustion*.]

mox·ie (mŏk′sē) *n. Slang.* **1.** The ability to face difficulty with spirit; pluck. **2.** Energy or pep. [From *Moxie,* a trademark for a soft drink.]

Mo·zam·bique (mō′zăm-bēk′). Formerly **Por·tu·guese East Af·ri·ca** (pôr′chə-gēz′, pōr′-; ăf′rĭ-kə). Country of southeastern Africa, consisting in the center and south of a broad coastal plain crossed by the Zambezi, Save, and Limpopo rivers and of plateaus and highlands elsewhere. Some 80 percent of the people are subsistence farmers producing cassava and corn, but the country is the world's leading exporter of cashew nuts. Shipping is a vital economic factor, since Mozambique acts as a port for South Africa and Zaire and landlocked Swaziland, Zambia, Malawi, and Zimbabwe. Portuguese colonization began in 1505. After World War II African nationalists demanded independence and set up the Mozambique Liberation Front (Frelimo), which began guerrilla activity in 1964. Led by Samora Machel, it achieved independence as a Marxist one-party state in 1975. Area, 783,030 square kilometers (302,330 square miles). Population, 12,130,000. Capital, Maputo. —**Mo·zam·bi·qu·an** *adj. & n.*

Mozambique Current *n.* A warm ocean current flowing southward down the east coast of southern Africa.

Moz·ar·ab (mō-zăr′əb) *n.* A member of a group of Spanish Christians who practiced a modified form of their religion under the Muslims. [Spanish *Mozárabe,* from Arabic *Musta'rib,* "a would-be Arab," from *'arab,* ARAB.] —**Moz·ar·a·bic** (mō-zăr′ə-bĭk) *adj.*

Mo·zart (mōt′särt′), **Wolfgang Amadeus** (1756–91). Austrian composer, one of the most highly gifted and prolific composers in history. Although he began as a child prodigy, both as a performer and a composer, he had irregular patronage and was often destitute. He wrote most of his greatest works in the last five years of his short life, including his last three symphonies (1788) and the operas *Don Giovanni* (1787) and *Die Zauberflöte* ("The Magic Flute") (1791). —**Mo·zart·i·an, Mo·zart·e·an** (mōt-sär′tē-ən) *adj. & n.*

mo·zet·ta, moz·zet·ta (mō-zĕt′ə, mōt-sĕt′ə) *n. Roman Catholic Church.* A short, hooded cape worn by bishops. [Italian, short for *almozzetta,* irregular diminutive formed from Medieval Latin *almūtia,* ALMUCE.]

moz·za·rel·la (mōt′sə-rĕl′ə, mōt′-) *n.* A soft, white Italian curd cheese, formerly made from buffalo milk and often used melted in cookery. [Italian, diminutive of *mozza,* "slice," (sliced) cheese, from *mozzare,* to cut off, perhaps from Vulgar Latin *mutiāre* (unattested), from Latin *mutilāre,* to mutilate, cut up, from *mutilus,* cut short.]

mp, m.p. melting point.

MP military police; military policeman.

M.P. **1.** Member of Parliament. **2.** Metropolitan Police. **3.** military police; military policeman. **4.** mounted police; mounted policeman.

mpg, m.p.g. miles per gallon.

mph, m.p.h. miles per hour.

M.Phil, M.Ph. Master of Philosophy.

M.P.S. Member of the Pharmaceutical Society.

Mr. (mĭs′tər) *n., pl.* **Messrs.** The abbreviated form of the title **Mister,** placed before a man's last name.

M.R. **1.** Master of the Rolls. **2.** motivational research.

M.R.A., MRA Moral Rearmament.

M.R.C. Medical Research Council.

mRNA messenger RNA.

Mrs. (mĭs′ĭz) *n., pl.* **Mmes.** A title of courtesy used in speaking to or of a married woman, preceding the woman's surname or office. —See Usage note at **miss.** [Abbreviation of MISTRESS.]

ms **1.** manuscript. **2.** millisecond.

MS **1.** manuscript. **2.** Mississippi (state). **3.** multiple sclerosis.

ms., MS. manuscript.

Ms, Ms. (mĭz, ĕm′ĕs′) *n., pl.* **Mses** or **Mss.** A title of courtesy used before a woman's surname or before her first name and surname, without regard to her marital status. —See Usage note at **Miss.** [Blend of MISS and MRS.]

M.S. **1.** Master of Science [Latin *Magister Scientiae*]. **2.** memorial sacrum.

M.Sc. Master of Science.

MSG monosodium glutamate.

msg. message.

m.s.l., M.S.L. mean sea level.

mss, MSS, mss., MSS. manuscripts.

MST, M.S.T. Mountain Standard Time.

MSW Master of Social Work.

MT Montana (with Zip Code).

mt., Mt. mount; mountain.

m.t., M.T. metric ton.

mtg. **1.** meeting. **2.** mortgage.

mtge. mortgage.

mtn. mountain.

mu (myōō, mōō) *n.* The 12th letter in the Greek alphabet, written M, μ. Transliterated in English as *M, m.* See feature at **alphabet.** [Greek, of Phoenician origin; akin to Hebrew *mēm.*]

muc–. Variant of **muco–.**

much (mŭch) *adj.* **more, most.** Great in quantity, degree, or extent: *Was there much rain?* —**a bit much.** *Informal.* Difficult to accept. ~*pron.* **1.** A large quantity or amount. **2.** Anything remarkable or important: *As a leader, she is not much.* —**make much of.** To pay great attention to. —**think much of.** To esteem highly. ~*adv.* **more, most.** **1.** To a great degree; to a large extent: *much*

impressed. See Usage note at **very.** **2.** Often. Used especially in negative sentences: *She doesn't visit us much these days.* **3.** Just about; almost: *much the same.* —**as much.** What is indicated or implied: *I expected as much.* —**much as.** However much: *Much as I regret it, I'm going to have to refuse.* [Middle English *muche, miche,* shortened from *muchel, michel,* Old English *mycel, micel,* great, large, greatly, much.]

much·ness (mŭch′nĭs) *n.* **1.** Magnitude; bulk. **2.** Greatness in quantity, number, or degree.

mu·cic acid (myōō′sĭk) *n.* An organic acid, $HOOC(CHOH)_4$-COOH, often derived from milk sugar. [From MUCUS.]

mu·ci·lage (myōō′sə-lĭj) *n.* **1.** A sticky substance used as an adhesive. **2.** A gummy substance obtained from certain plants. [Middle English *muscilage,* from Old French *mucilage,* from Late Latin *mūcilāgō,* musty juice, from Latin *mūcus,* MUCUS.] —**mu·ci·lag·i·nous** (myōō′sə-lăj′ə-nəs) *adj.*

mu·cin (myōō′sĭn) *n.* Any of a group of glycoproteins produced by mucous membranes. [MUC(O)- + -IN.]

muck (mŭk) *n.* **1.** A moist, sticky mixture, especially of mud or filth. **2.** Moist animal dung, especially when mixed with decayed vegetable matter and used as a fertilizer; manure. **3.** Dark, fertile soil containing putrid vegetable matter. **4.** Anything regarded as inferior, filthy, or disgusting. **5.** Earth, rocks, or clay excavated in mining. —**make a muck of.** *Informal.* To botch or mismanage. ~*tr.v.* **mucked, mucking, mucks.** **1.** To fertilize with manure or compost. **2.** *Informal.* To soil or make dirty with or as if with muck. **3. a.** To remove muck or dirt from (a mine or site). **b.** To remove muck from (a stable, for example). Used with *out.* —**muck about.** *Chiefly British Informal.* **1.** To behave badly or in a silly way. **2.** To spend time idly; do nothing in particular. —**muck up.** *Informal.* **1.** To make dirty or untidy. **2.** To mismanage or interfere with (a plan or project); bungle. [Middle English *muk,* from Old Norse *mykr.*] —**muck·i·ly** *adv.* —**muck·y** *adj.*

muck·a·muck (mŭk′ə-mŭk′) *n.* Also **muck·e·ty·muck** (mŭk′ə-tē-mŭk′). *Slang.* An important and often self-important person. Also called "high muckamuck." [Originally *high muckamuck,* from Chinook jargon *hiu muckamuck.*]

muckle. Variant of **mickle.**

muck·rake (mŭk′rāk′) *intr.v.* **-raked, -raking, -rakes.** To search for and expose scandalous conduct, especially personal, political, or commercial misconduct in public affairs. ~*n.* A rake used for gathering and spreading muck. [Backformation from *muckraker,* used in 1906 by Theodore Roosevelt in allusion to the "man with a Muck-rake" in Bunyan's *Pilgrim's Progress.*] —**muck·rak·er** *n.*

muck·worm (mŭk′wûrm′) *n.* Any worm or larva found in mud and animal droppings.

muco–, muc– *prefix.* Indicates mucus or something pertaining to the mucous membrane; for example, **mucoprotein, mucin.** [Latin *mūcus.*]

mu·co·cu·ta·ne·ous (myōō′kō-kyōō-tā′nē-əs) *adj.* Of or involving both the skin and the mucous membrane.

mu·coid (myōō′koid′) *n.* Any of a group of glycoproteins similar to the mucins and found in connective tissue. [MUC(O)- + -OID.] —**mu·coid, mu·coi·dal** (myōō-koid′l) *adj.*

mu·co·pol·y·sac·cha·ride (myōō′kō-pŏl′ē-săk′ə-rīd′) *n.* Any of the polysaccharides that form chemical bonds with water to produce mucilaginous and lubricating fluids and that contain sugar derivatives such as amino acids.

mu·co·pro·tein (myōō′kō-prō′tēn′, -prō′tē-ĭn) *n.* Any of a group of organic compounds, such as the mucins, that contain proteins and mucopolysaccharides.

mu·co·sa (myōō-kō′sə, -zə) *n., pl.* **-sae** (-sē, -zē) or **-sas.** A mucous membrane. [New Latin *mūcōsa (membrana),* from *mūcōsus,* MUCOUS.] —**mu·co·sal** *adj.*

mu·cous (myōō′kəs) *adj.* Also **mu·cose** (myōō′kōs′). **1.** Producing or secreting mucus. **2.** Pertaining to, consisting of, or resembling mucus. [Latin *mūcōsus,* from *mūcus,* MUCUS.]

mucous membrane *n.* The membrane lining all bodily channels that communicate with the air, such as the respiratory and alimentary tracts, the glands of which secrete mucus.

mu·cro (myōō′krō) *n., pl.* **mucrones** (myōō-krō′nēz). *Biology.* A sharp tip of certain plant and animal organs. [New Latin, from Latin *mucrō†,* a sharp point, sword's point.]

mu·cro·nate (myōō′krə-nāt′) *adj. Biology.* Having a mucro. [Latin *mucronātus,* from *mucrō,* a point, MUCRO.] —**mu·cro·na·tion** (myōō′krə-nā′shən) *n.*

mu·cus (myōō′kəs) *n.* The viscous suspension of mucin, water, cells, and inorganic salts secreted as a protective lubricant coating by glands in the mucous membrane or by the external body surface of many animals. [Latin *mūcus, muccus.*]

mud (mŭd) *n.* **1.** Wet, sticky, soft earth. **2.** *Informal.* Slanderous or defamatory charges: *threw mud at her opponents.* **3. a.** The lowest, severest, or worst place or part; depths: *My name was dragged in the mud.* **b.** *Informal.* Something contemptible or disreputable: *Her name was mud.* ~*tr.v.* **mudded, mudding, muds.** To soil or bury with or as if with mud. [Middle English *mudde, mode†.*]

mud bath *n.* **1.** A therapeutic immersion in heated mud. **2.** A muddy event or experience.

mud cat *n.* Any of several large catfish of southeastern U.S. streams.

mud dauber *n.* Any of several wasps, including those of the genus

mulberry *There are about 15 species of this ornamental fruit-bearing tree, native to Asia and North America.* Morus alba, *the Asian species shown here, is now grown widely around the world.*

mule *A cross between a donkey and a horse, a mule is larger and stronger than a donkey and more sure-footed on rough ground than a horse. Every generation of mules has to be bred afresh from the parent animals because the hybrid is always sterile.*

mullein *The flowers of mullein plants—the white mullein is shown here—were once used to make a medicine for the relief of coughs and chills.*

Sceliphron, having long hind legs and a slender abdomen terminating in a bulb. The female lays eggs in paralyzed insect larvae, which are placed in a nest of mud.

mud•dle (mŭd′l) *v.* **-dled, -dling, -dles.** —*tr.* **1.** To mix confusedly; jumble: *muddled the two names.* **2.** To mix up (the mind), as with alcohol; confuse or befuddle. **3.** To mismanage or bungle. **4.** To make turbid; muddy. **5.** To stir or mix (a drink) gently. —*intr.* **1.** To act or think in a confused manner. **2.** To progress in an ineffective or disorganized way. Used with *on* or *along.* **—muddle through.** To push on to a successful conclusion in a disorganized way.
∼*n.* A confusion, jumble, or mess: *"Endless confusion results from the semantic muddle in which we find ourselves today"* (E.F. Schumacher). [Perhaps from Middle Dutch *moddelen,* to make muddy, from *modde*†, mud.] **—mud•dler** *n.*

mud•dle-head•ed (mŭd′l-hĕd′ĭd) *adj.* **1.** Mentally confused. **2.** Stupid or inept. **—mud•dle-head•ed•ness** *n.*

mud•dy (mŭd′ē) *adj.* **-dier, -diest. 1.** Covered in, full of, or spattered with mud. **2. a.** Not bright or pure: *muddy blue.* **b.** Not clear; cloudy: *This beer is rather muddy.* **3.** Confused, vague, or obscure, as in expression or meaning: *a muddy style of writing.*
∼*tr.v.* **muddied, -dying, -dies. 1.** To make muddy or dirty. **2.** To make dull or cloudy. **3.** To make obscure or confused. **—mud•di•ly** *adv.* **—mud•di•ness** *n.*

Mu•dé•jar, mu•dé•jar (mo͞o-thĕ′här′) *n., pl.* **-jares** (-hä-rās). Any of the Christianized Moors permitted to remain in Spain after it had been restored to Christian control in the Middle Ages.
∼*adj.* Of or pertaining to a type of Moorish architecture of the Middle Ages. [Spanish, from Arabic *mudajjan,* permitted to stay.]

mud•fish (mŭd′fĭsh′) *n., pl.* **-fishes** or collectively **mudfish.** Any of various fishes found in muddy water, such as the **bowfin** *(see).*

mud flat *n.* Land covered at high tide and exposed at low tide.

mud•guard (mŭd′gärd′) *n.* A shield over a bicycle's or other vehicle's wheel; fender.

mud•lark (mŭd′lärk′) *n.* **1.** A bird, the **magpie lark** *(see).* **2.** *British Slang.* A street urchin.

mud•pack (mŭd′păk′) *n.* A paste made from a type of mud, spread thickly, especially over the face, for cosmetic purposes.

mud puppy *n.* Any of various aquatic salamanders of the genus *Necturus,* especially *N. maculosus,* of North America, having conspicuous clusters of external gills.

mu•dra (mə-drä′) *n.* In Hindu classical dancing, a series of body postures and hand movements enacting a narrative. [Hindi.]

mud•skip•per (mŭd′skĭp′ər) *n.* Any of several species of fishes of the family Gobiidae that are found along the coast of tropical Africa and in the Indo-Pacific region and are noted for their ability to maneuver on land and withstand drought.

mud•sling•er (mŭd′slĭng′ər) *n.* One who makes malicious charges against an opponent. **—mud•sling•ing** *n.*

mud•stone (mŭd′stōn′) *n.* A fine-grained, nonfissile rock similar to shale that decomposes into mud when exposed to moisture.

mud•wort (mŭd′wûrt′, -wôrt′) *n.* Any of various waterweeds of the genus *Limosella,* having creeping runners and small flowers.

Muen•ster, Mun•ster (mo͞on′stər, mŭn′-) *n.* A semisoft, creamy yellow fermented Alsatian cheese of mild flavor. [After *Munster,* city in northeastern France where it was originally made.]

mues•li (myo͞oz′lē, müs′lē, müz′-) *n.* A food consisting of a mixture of nuts, cereal, dried fruit, honey, and the like, often eaten with milk. [Swiss German.]

mu•ez•zin (myo͞o-ĕz′ĭn, mo͞o-) *n. Islam.* The crier who calls the faithful to prayer five times a day, usually from a minaret. [Arabic *mu'adhdhin,* active participle of *adhana,* to cause to listen, from *adhina,* to listen.]

muff[1] (mŭf) *tr.v.* **muffed, muffing, muffs.** *Informal.* **1.** To perform (an act) clumsily; bungle: *muffed the job.* **2.** *Sports.* To fail to execute (a kick, catch, or the like).
∼*n. Informal.* **1.** A clumsy or bungling person. **2.** A clumsy or bungled act. [19th century : origin obscure.]

muff[2] *n.* A small cylindrical fur or cloth cover, open at both ends, in which the hands are placed to keep them warm. [Dutch *mof,* from Middle Dutch *moffel,* from Medieval Latin *muffula*†.]

muf•fin (mŭf′ĭn) *n.* A small, cup-shaped bread, often sweetened and usually served hot. [Probably from Low German *muffen,* plural of *muffe*†, cake.]

muf•fle[1] (mŭf′əl) *tr.v.* **-fled, -fling, -fles. 1.** To wrap up in a blanket, shawl, or scarf for warmth, protection, or secrecy. **2.** To wrap or pad in order to deaden a sound: *muffled drums.* **3.** To deaden (a sound): *Their hoofbeats were muffled by the sand.* **4.** To make vague or obscure: *a message muffled by excess of detail.*
∼*n.* **1.** Anything that muffles. **2.** A kiln or part of a kiln in which pottery can be fired without being exposed to direct flame. [Middle English *muflen,* from Old French *enmoufler,* "to put on a muff or mittens," from *moufle,* mitten, from Medieval Latin *muffula*†.]

muffle[2] *n.* The hairless snout of ruminants and rodents. [French *mufle*†.]

muf•fler (mŭf′lər) *n.* **1.** A heavy scarf worn around the neck for warmth. **2.** A device that absorbs noise, especially one used with an internal-combustion engine.

muf•ti[1] (mŭf′tē, mo͝of′-) *n., pl.* **-tis.** A judge who interprets Muslim religious law. [Arabic *muftī,* "one who decides," from *aftā,* to decide (by legal opinion).]

muf•ti[2] (mŭf′tē) *n.* Civilian dress, especially when worn by one whose regular clothing is a military or other uniform. [Probably from MUFTI (judge).]

mug[1] (mŭg) *n.* **1.** A cylindrical drinking vessel, usually having a handle. **2.** The liquid contained in such a vessel. **3.** The quantity that such a vessel can contain. [Probably from Scandinavian.]

mug[2] *n. Slang.* **1.** The face of a person. **2.** The area of the mouth, chin, and jaw. **3.** A mugshot. **4.** A grimace. **5.** *British.* A person who is easily deceived or duped. **6.** A hoodlum; thug. **—a mug's game.** *British Slang.* A foolish and unprofitable activity.
∼*v.* **mugged, mugging, mugs.** *Slang.* —*tr.* **1.** To waylay and sometimes beat severely, usually with intent to rob. **2.** To photograph (a person's face) for police files. —*intr.* **1.** To grimace. **2.** To overact as a performer by means of exaggerated facial expressions. [Probably from MUG (vessel), from tankards shaped like grotesque human faces. Sense of "attack" from noun sense "hoodlum."]

Mu•ga•be (mo͞o-gä′bē), **Robert Gabriel** (1924–). Zimbabwean politician. He entered black nationalist politics in Rhodesia (1960) and helped found the Zimbabwe African National Union (ZANU) in 1963. In 1976 he became president of ZANU and a leader of the Patriotic Front that waged war against the ruling white minority in Rhodesia. He became prime minister in April 1980 after the first elections under the new constitution.

mug•ger[1] (mŭg′ər) *n.* One who commits a mugging.

mug•ger[2]**, mug•gar, mug•gur** (mŭg′ər) *n.* A large crocodile, *Crocodylus palustris,* of southwestern Asia, having an exceptionally broad, wrinkled snout. Also called "marsh crocodile." [Hindi *magar,* from Sanskrit *makara,* a crocodile, from Dravidian.]

mug•ging (mŭg′ĭng) *n. Informal.* An aggravated assault, usually by surprise and with intent to rob.

mug•gins (mŭg′ĭnz) *n. British Slang.* A fool or simpleton. [Perhaps from the surname *Muggins.*]

mug•gy (mŭg′ē) *adj.* **-gier, -giest.** Warm and extremely humid. [From dialectal *mug,* fine rain, from Middle English *muggen,* to drizzle, from Old Norse *mugga.*] **—mug•gi•ness** *n.*

Mughal. Variant of **Mogul.**

mug•shot (mŭg′shŏt′) *n.* A photograph of a person's face, especially one of a criminal used for purposes of identification.

mug•wort (mŭg′wûrt′, -wôrt′) *n.* Any of several plants of the genus *Artemisia*; especially, *A. vulgaris,* native to Eurasia, having clusters of small yellowish-brown flowers. [Middle English *mugwort,* Old English *mucgwyrt* : *mucg-,* a midge, fly + *wyrt,* WORT.]

mug•wump (mŭg′wŭmp′) *n.* **1.** *Often* **Mugwump.** A Republican who bolted his party in 1884, refusing to support presidential candidate James A. Blaine. **2.** *Slang.* A person who acts independently or neutrally, especially in politics. [Natick *mugquomp, mugwomp,* "captain."] **—mug•wump•er•y** *n.*

Mu•ham•mad (mo͞o-hăm′ĭd), also **Mo•ham•med** (mō-, mə-) or **Ma•hom•et** (mə-hŏm′ĭt) (*c.* 570–632). Prophet and the founder of Islam. He was a rich merchant who had a vision in the cave of Mt. Hira telling him to preach true religion. In 622 he fled from Mecca, where he had made few converts, and set up a theocracy at Yathrib, which was renamed Medina, meaning "city of the prophet." In 630 Muhammad conquered Mecca without a struggle and began to convert Arabia to Islam. His teachings are recorded in the Koran.

Mu•ham•ma•dan (mo͞o-hăm′ə-dən) *adj.* Also **Mo•ham•me•dan** (mō-, mə-), **Ma•hom•e•tan** (mə-hŏm′ə-tən). Of or pertaining to Muhammad or Islam; Muslim.
∼*n.* A follower of Muhammad or believer in Islam; a Muslim.

Mu•ham•ma•dan•ism (mo͞o-hăm′ə-də-nĭz′əm) *n.* Also **Mo•ham•me•dan•ism** (mō-, mə-), **Ma•hom•e•tan•ism** (mə-hŏm′ə-tə-nĭz′əm). The Muhammadan religion, **Islam** *(see).*

Muhammad Re•za Pah•la•vi (rä′zə pä′lə-vē) (1919–80). Shah of Iran (1941–79). His attempts to modernize Iranian society, together with the growth of corruption and the activities of the secret police under his regime, provoked the Islamic reaction culminating in the revolution of 1979, by which he was overthrown.

Mu•har•ram, Mu•har•rum (mo͞o-hăr′əm) *n.* Also **Mo•har•ram** (mō-). **1.** The first month of the Muslim calendar. See feature at **calendar. 2.** A festival held during the first ten days of Muharram. [Arabic *muḥarram,* past participle of *ḥarrama,* "he forbade."]

Müh•len•berg (myo͞o′lən-bûrg′), **Henry Melchior** (1711–87). U.S. religious leader, born in Germany. He arrived (1742) in Philadelphia to serve as pastor of several congregations in the area but soon became the leader of all the Lutheran groups in the colonies. Mühlenberg organized the first Lutheran synod in the country (1748).

Muir (myo͝or), **John** (1838–1914). U.S. naturalist, born in Scotland. He arrived in the United States in 1849 and settled in California in 1868. A strong crusader for conservation and national parks and reservations, he made extended trips throughout the country, often on foot.

Muir Woods National Monument. Area occupying 170 hectares (424 acres) in western California, north of San Francisco. It preserves a magnificent grove of towering redwood trees.

Muj•i•bur Rah•man (mo͞oj′ə-bo͝or rä′mən), also known as "Sheik Mujib" (1920–75). Bengali politician, the first president of Bangladesh. After winning the provincial election of 1970, he proclaimed East Pakistan's independence and was arrested and convicted of treason in 1971. When Indian intervention gained Bangladesh its independence, he became prime minister (1972). He was killed in a coup in 1975, soon after naming himself president with dictatorial powers.

mujik. Variant of **muzhik.**

Mukden. See **Shenyang.**

muk·luk (mŭk′lŭk′) *n.* **1.** A soft Eskimo boot made of reindeer skin or sealskin. **2.** A boot resembling this. [Eskimo *muklok,* "large seal."]

mu·lat·to (moo-lăt′ō, -lä′tō, myoo-) *n., pl.* **-tos** or **-toes. 1.** A person having one white and one black parent. **2.** Any person of mixed Caucasian and Negro ancestry. [Spanish *mulato,* young mule, mulatto, from *mulo,* mule, from Latin *mūlus,* MULE.] **—mu·lat·to** *adj.*

mul·ber·ry (mŭl′bĕr′ē, -bə-rē) *n., pl.* **-ries. 1.** Any of several trees of the genus *Morus,* especially the black mulberry, *M. nigra,* having edible fruit and leaves that are used to feed silkworms. **2.** The sweet, berrylike fruit of any of these trees. **3.** Any of several related or similar trees, such as the **paper mulberry** (*see*). **4.** A grayish to dark purple. [Middle English *mulberrie, murberie,* Old English *mōr-berie* : *mōr-,* a Germanic borrowing, from Latin *mōrum,* mulberry + Old English *berie,* BERRY.] **—mul·ber·ry** *adj.*

mulch (mŭlch) *n.* A mixture of straw, earth, leaves, peat, and the like, placed around plants to prevent evaporation of moisture and freezing of roots and to fertilize the soil.
~*tr.v.* **mulched, mulching, mulches.** To cover with a mulch. [Originally "rotten hay," probably extended use of Middle English *mulsh,* soft, yielding, variant of *melsh,* Old English *mel(i)sc, mylsc,* mild, mellow.]

mulct (mŭlkt) *n.* A fine or similar penalty.
~*tr.v.* **mulcted, mulcting, mulcts. 1.** To penalize by fining or demanding forfeiture. **2.** To cheat or swindle. [Latin *mulcta, multa,* a fine, of Italic origin.]

mule¹ (myool) *n.* **1.** A sterile hybrid of a male donkey and a female horse. Compare **hinny. 2.** Any sterile hybrid, as between a canary and other finches. **3.** *Informal.* A stubborn person. **4.** A type of spinning machine that makes thread or yarn from fibers. Also called "spinning mule." [Middle English *mul,* from Old English *mūl* and Old French *mul,* both from Latin *mūlus,* mule, probably from Mediterranean; akin to Albanian *mušk,* mule.]

mule² *n.* A slipper that has no counter or strap to fit around the heel of the foot. [French, from Latin *mulleus (calceus),* "red (shoe)."]

mule deer *n.* A hoofed mammal, *Odocoileus hemionus,* of western North America. It has long ears and two-pronged antlers and is brownish gray. Also called "black-tailed deer."

mule·skin·ner (myool′skĭn′ər) *n. Informal.* A driver of mules.

mu·le·ta (moo-lā′tə, -lĕt′ə, myoo-) *n.* A short red cape, suspended from a hollow staff, that is used by the matador during the final stage of a bullfight. [Spanish, crutch, support, "small mule," from *mula,* "she-mule," from Latin *mūla,* feminine of *mūlus,* MULE.]

mu·le·teer (myoo′lə-tîr′) *n.* A mule driver. [French *muletier,* from *mulet,* diminutive of Old French *mul,* MULE.]

mu·ley (myoo′lē, moo′lē, moo′lē) *adj.* Hornless. Said of cattle.
~*n., pl.* **muleys.** A hornless animal. [Variant of dialectal *moiley,* from *moil,* hornless, a hornless cow, from Irish *maol,* from Old Irish *máel,* bald, hornless.]

Mul·ha·cén (mool′lä-sän′). Peak, 3,485 meters (11,424 feet), in southern Spain, in the Sierra Nevada. It is the highest point in the country.

mu·li·eb·ri·ty (myoo′lē-ĕb′rə-tē) *n.* **1.** The state of being a woman. **2.** The qualities characteristic of women. [Late Latin *muliebritās,* from Latin *muliebris,* womanly, from *mulier†,* a woman.]

mul·ish (myoo′lĭsh) *adj.* Characteristic of a mule; stubborn. —See Synonyms at **obstinate. —mul·ish·ly** *adv.* **—mul·ish·ness** *n.*

mull¹ (mŭl) *tr.v.* **mulled, mulling, mulls.** To heat and spice (an alcoholic drink such as wine or ale). [17th century : origin obscure.]

mull² *v.* **mulled, mulling, mulls.** To reflect on or consider (a problem, for example) deeply; deliberate. —*intr.* To engage in contemplation; ponder: *mull over a plan.* [Middle English *mullen,* to grind, pulverize, from *mul,* dust, from Middle Dutch *mol, mul.*]

mull³ *n.* A soft, thin muslin used in dresses and for trimmings. [Short for *mulmull,* from Hindi *malmal,* from Persian *malmal†.*]

mull⁴ *n.* A moist type of humus that is formed under nonacid conditions and found mingled with mineral soil rather than as a distinct layer. [German, from Danish *muld.*]

Mull (mŭl). The largest of the Inner Hebrides, western Scotland, and since 1975 part of Strathclyde Region. The island is mountainous, rising to 966 meters (3,169 feet) at Ben More.

mul·lah, mul·la (mŭl′ə, mool′ə) *n.* A Muslim religious teacher or leader. Sometimes used as a title. [Turkish *mulla* and Persian *mullā,* from Arabic *mawlā,* "master."]

mul·lein (mŭl′ən) *n.* Any plant of the genus *Verbascum,* having leaves covered with white, woolly down, and yellow flowers. See **Aaron's rod.** [Middle English *moleyne,* from Old French *moleine,* from Gaulish *melena* (unattested).]

mul·ler (mŭl′ər) *n.* **1.** Any of several manual or mechanical devices used for grinding. **2.** A device with a stone or other hard base, used manually or mechanically to grind paints or drugs. [Middle English *molour,* probably from *mullen,* to grind, pulverize. See **mull².**]

mul·let¹ (mŭl′ĭt) *n., pl.* **-lets** or collectively **mullet.** Any of various edible fishes of the families Mugilidae or Mullidae, found worldwide in tropical and temperate coastal waters and some freshwater streams; especially the gray mullets of the genus *Mugil.* [Middle English *molet,* from Old French *mulet,* from Latin *mullus,* red mullet, from Greek *mollos.*]

mullet² *n. Heraldry.* A star having five straight points. [Old French *molette,* rowel on a spur.]

mul·li·gan (mŭl′ĭ-gən) *n.* A stew of various meats and vegetables. Also called "mulligan stew." [Probably from the Irish surname *Mulligan.*]

mul·li·ga·taw·ny (mŭl′ĭ-gə-tô′nē) *n.* An East Indian meat soup that is strongly flavored with curry. [Tamil *miḷagutaṇṇī(r),* "pepper-water."]

mul·li·grubs (mŭl′ĭ-grŭbz′) *pl.n. Informal.* **1.** A griping of the intestines; stomachache or colic. **2.** Ill temper or depression. [Alteration of earlier *mulligrums,* perhaps alteration of MEGRIM.]

mul·lion (mŭl′yən) *n.* A vertical strip dividing the panes of a window. [Perhaps variant of Middle English *monial,* from Old French *moinel,* from *moien,* MEAN.] **—mul·lioned** *adj.*

mul·lo·way (mŭl′ə-wā′) *n.* A large Australian marine food fish, *Sciaena antarctica.* Also called "jewfish." [19th century : origin obscure.]

mullion *Wooden mullions divide the windowpanes in the 15th-century Little Hall, at Lavenham, in Suffolk, England.*

multi– *prefix.* Indicates: **1.** Many or much; for example, **multicolored. 2.** More than one; for example, **multiparous. Note:** Many compounds other than those entered here may be formed with *multi-.* In this dictionary, in forming compounds, *multi-* is normally joined to the following word or element without space or hyphen: *multiangular.* However, if the second element begins with *i,* it is separated with a hyphen: *multi-infection.* [Middle English, from Latin, from *multus,* much.]

mul·ti·ad·dress (mŭl′tē-ăd′rĕs′) *adj. Computer Science.* Designating a storage system of data-processing computers in which it is possible to store instructions or quantities in more than one position.

mul·ti·cel·lu·lar (mŭl′tē-sĕl′yə-lər) *adj.* Consisting of more than one cell. Said chiefly of metazoans.

mul·ti·col·ored (mŭl′tĭ-kŭl′ərd) *adj.* Having many colors.

mul·ti·cul·tur·al (mŭl′tē-kŭl′chər-əl) *adj.* Of, relating to, or intended for several different cultures: *a multicultural city.*

mul·ti·di·men·sion·al (mŭl′tē-dĭ-mĕn′shə-nəl) *adj.* Of, relating to, or having several dimensions. **—mul·ti·di·men·sion·al·i·ty** (mŭl′tē-də-mĕn′shə-năl′ə-tē) *n.*

mul·ti·dis·ci·pli·nar·y (mŭl′tē-dĭs′ə-plə-nĕr′ē) *adj.* Embracing or involving contributions from several distinct academic or other disciplines: *a multidisciplinary approach.*

mul·ti·eth·nic (mŭl′tē-ĕth′nĭk) *adj.* Of, relating to, or including a variety of ethnic groups: *a multiethnic city.*

mul·ti·fac·et·ed (mŭl′tē-făs′ĭ-tĭd) *adj.* Having many different facets.

mul·ti·fac·to·ri·al (mŭl′tē-făk-tôr′ē-əl, -tōr′ē-əl) *adj. Genetics.* Designating inheritance or a characteristic, such as height, that is controlled by two or more genes. See **multiple factor.**

mul·ti·far·i·ous (mŭl′tə-fâr′ē-əs) *adj.* Having great variety; made up of many parts or kinds. [Latin *multifārius* : MULTI- + *-fārius,* doing.] **—mul·ti·far·i·ous·ly** *adv.* **—mul·ti·far·i·ous·ness** *n.*

mul·ti·fid (mŭl′tə-fĭd′) *adj. Biology.* Having many clefts forming lobes: *multifid leaves.* [Latin *multifidus* : MULTI- + -FID.]

mul·ti·flo·ra rose (mŭl′tə-flôr′ə, -flōr′ə) *n.* A climbing or sprawling shrub, *Rosa multiflora,* native to Asia, having clusters of small, fragrant flowers. It is the origin of many horticultural varieties. [New Latin *Rosa multiflōra,* "many-flowered rose."]

mul·ti·foil (mŭl′tə-foil′) *adj. Architecture.* Having many foils.
~*n.* Any design or object having many foils or scalloped edges.

mul·ti·fold (mŭl′tə-fōld′) *adj.* Many times doubled; manifold.

mul·ti·form (mŭl′tə-fôrm′) *adj.* Occurring in or having many forms, shapes, or appearances. [Latin *multiformis* : MULTI- + -FORM.] **—mul·ti·for·mi·ty** (mŭl′tə-fôr′mə-tē) *n.*

mul·ti·grav·i·da (mŭl′tə-grăv′ə-də) *n., pl.* **-dae** (-dē). A pregnant woman who has had at least two previous pregnancies. [New Latin : MULTI- + *gravida,* pregnant woman. See **gravid.**]

mul·ti·lat·er·al (mŭl′tə-lăt′ər-əl) *adj.* **1.** Having many sides. **2.** Involving more than two nations or groups: *multilateral disarmament.* **—mul·ti·lat·er·al·ly** *adv.*

mul·ti·lat·er·al·ist (mŭl′tə-lăt′ər-ə-lĭst) *n.* One who favors multilateral action, especially multilateral nuclear disarmament. Compare **unilateralist. —mul·ti·lat·er·al·ist** *adj.*

mul·ti·lin·gual (mŭl′tə-lĭng′gwəl) *adj.* **1.** Capable of speaking or writing in many languages. **2.** Written in many languages. **3.** Designating a society composed of various different language groups.

mul·ti·me·di·a (mŭl′tə-mē′dē-ə) *adj.* Including or involving the use of several media of communication, such as motion pictures, still photographs, and records, for the purpose of education or entertainment.

mul·ti·mil·lion·aire (mŭl′tə-mĭl′yə-nâr′) *n.* A person whose financial assets equal many millions of dollars or other currency.

mul·ti·na·tion·al (mŭl′tē-năsh′ə-nəl, -năsh′nəl) *adj.* **1.** Having operations, subsidiaries, or investments in more than one country: *a multinational corporation.* **2.** Of, in, or involving several or many countries.
~*n.* A multinational company or corporation.

mul·ti·no·mi·al (mŭl′tə-nō′mē-əl) *n. Mathematics.* A polynomial (*see*). [MULTI- + binomial.] **—mul·ti·no·mi·al** *adj.*

multinomial theorem *n. Mathematics.* The theorem that establishes the rule for forming the terms of a polynomial expansion. See **binomial theorem, expansion, polynomial.**

mul·tip·a·ra (mŭl-tĭp′ər-ə) *n., pl.* **-arae** (-ə-rē). A pregnant woman who has borne at least one child; especially, one who is in labor for the second time. [New Latin, feminine of *multiparus,* MULTIPAROUS.]

mul·tip·a·rous (mŭl-tĭp′ər-əs) *adj.* **1.** Having borne more than one child. **2.** Giving birth to more than one offspring at one time. [New Latin *multiparus* : MULTI- + -PAROUS.]

mul·ti·par·tite (mŭl′tə-pär′tīt′) *adj.* **1.** Having many parts. **2.** Multilateral. [Latin *multipartītus* : MULTI- + PARTITE.]

mul·ti·ple (mŭl′tə-pəl) *adj.* Having, pertaining to, or consisting of

more than one individual, element, part, or other component; manifold; multiplicate.
~*n. Mathematics.* A quantity into which another quantity may be divided with zero remainder: *4, 6, and 12 are multiples of 2. A common multiple* is a quantity into which each of two or more other quantities may be divided with zero remainder: *6, 12, and 24 are common multiples of 2 and 3.* A *lowest common multiple* is the least quantity into which two or more other quantities may be divided with zero remainder: *6 is the lowest common multiple of all common multiples of 2 and 3.* [Old French, from Late Latin *multiplus* : MULTI- + *-plus*, -fold.] —**mul·ti·ply** *adv.*

multiple allele *n. Genetics.* A set of three or more alternative forms of a gene at a single locus. Also called "multiple allelomorph."

mul·ti·ple-choice (mŭl′tə-pəl-chois′) *adj.* Offering a number of solutions from which one correct one is to be chosen: *multiple-choice exam questions.*

multiple factor *n. Genetics.* A combination of genes having a joint or cumulative effect.

multiple fruit *n.* A fruit, such as a pineapple or mulberry, in which the fruits of several flowers are combined into a single structure. Also called "collective fruit." Compare **aggregate fruit.**

multiple root *n. Mathematics.* A root *a* of the polynomial equation $f(x) = 0$ in which $(x - a)$ occurs at least twice as a factor of $f(x)$. Also called "root."

multiple sclerosis *n. Abbr.* **MS** A degenerative disease of the central nervous system in which the sheaths surrounding individual nerve cells of the brain or spinal cord or both are damaged, causing disorders of speech, vision, and muscle coordination and partial paralysis.

multiple star *n.* Three or more stars, usually with a common gravitational center, that appear as one to the naked eye.

multiple store *n. Chiefly British.* A chain store.

mul·ti·plet (mŭl′tə-plĕt′, -plĭt) *n. Physics.* **1.** A spectral line having more than one component representing slight variations in energy states characteristic of the atom. **2.** Any of several classes or groupings of subatomic particles, such as the nucleon, each member of which has the same set of **quantum numbers** *(see)* except for electric charge. [From MULTIPLE.]

mul·ti·plex (mŭl′tə-plĕks′) *adj.* **1.** Multiple; manifold. **2.** Designating a simultaneous communication of two or more messages on the same wire or radio channel. Compare **duplex, simplex. 3.** Designating a method of making topographic maps with three cameras arranged to employ stereoscopic principles.
~*v.* **multiplexed, -plexing, -plexes.** —*intr.* To send messages or signals in a multiplex system. —*tr.* To send (more than one signal) simultaneously using one radio frequency. [Latin : MULTI- + *-plex*, -fold.] —**mul·ti·plex·er** *n.*

mul·ti·pli·a·ble (mŭl′tə-plī′ə-bəl) *adj.* Also **mul·ti·pli·ca·ble** (mŭl′tə-plĭk′ə-bəl). Capable of being multiplied.

mul·ti·pli·cand (mŭl′tə-plĭ-kănd′) *n.* The number that is or is to be multiplied by another. [Latin *multiplicandum*, neuter of *multiplicandus*, gerundive of *multiplicāre*, to MULTIPLY.]

mul·tip·li·cate (mŭl-tĭp′lĭ-kĭt) *adj.* **1.** Having more than one layer or fold, as some shells or leaves. **2.** Manifold; multiple. [Middle English, from Latin *multiplicātus*, past participle of *multiplicāre*, to MULTIPLY.]

mul·ti·pli·ca·tion (mŭl′tə-plĭ-kā′shən) *n.* **1.** The act of multiplying or the process of being multiplied. **2.** The propagation of plants and animals. **3.** *Mathematics.* **a.** An operation in which an integer, the multiplicand, is added to itself a specific integral number of times. **b.** The extension of this process to the combination of two real numbers by using laws valid for integers. **c.** Any of certain analogous operations combining expressions other than real numbers. Compare **division. 4.** An increase or build-up achieved by adding. —**mul·ti·pli·ca·tion·al** *adj.*

multiplication sign *n. Mathematics.* The sign $\times$ placed between multiplicand and multiplier or operand and operator, as in $a \times b$.

multiplication table *n.* A table listing the products of certain numbers multiplied together, usually the numbers 1 to 12.

mul·ti·pli·ca·tive (mŭl′tə-plĭ-kā′tĭv, mŭl′tə-plĭk′ə-tĭv) *adj.* **1.** Tending to multiply or capable of multiplying or increasing. **2.** Pertaining to multiplication. —**mul·ti·pli·ca·tive·ly** *adv.*

mul·ti·plic·i·ty (mŭl′tə-plĭs′ə-tē) *n., pl.* **-ties. 1.** The state of being various or manifold. **2.** A large number: *a multiplicity of ideas.* **3.** *Physics.* **a.** The number of subatomic particles in a **multiplet** *(see).* **b.** The number of levels into which the energy of an atom, molecule, nucleus, or the like can split as a result of coupling between spin angular momentum and orbital angular momentum. [French *multiplicité*, from Latin *multiplicitās*, from *multiplex* (stem *multiplic-*), having many folds, MULTIPLEX.]

mul·ti·pli·er (mŭl′tə-plī′ər) *n.* **1.** One that multiplies. **2.** *Mathematics.* The number by which the multiplicand is multiplied. If 3 is multiplied by 2, 3 is the multiplicand, 2 is the multiplier, and 6 is the product. **3.** *Physics.* Any device, such as a phototube, used to enhance or increase an effect. **4.** *Economics.* The ratio between an initial increase in investment expenditure and the total income amassed from that first expenditure.

mul·ti·ply (mŭl′tə-plī′) *v.* **-plied, -plying, -plies.** —*tr.* **1.** To increase the amount, number, or degree of; make more numerous. **2.** *Mathematics.* To perform multiplication on. —*intr.* **1.** To become more in number, amount, or degree. **2.** To breed; propagate. **3.** *Mathematics.* To perform multiplication. [Middle English *multiplien*, from Old French *multiplier*, from Latin *multiplicāre*, from *multiplex* (stem

multiplic-), having many folds, MULTIPLEX.]

mul·ti·pur·pose (mŭl′tē-pûr′pəs) *adj.* Having several different purposes: *a multipurpose machine.*

mul·ti·ra·cial (mŭl′tē-rā′shəl) *adj.* Of, pertaining to, or composed of people of different races: *a multiracial community.*

mul·ti·sense (mŭl′tĭ-sĕns′) *adj.* Having multiple meanings: *"Make" is a multisense word.*

mul·ti·se·ri·ate (mŭl′tē-sîr′ē-āt′, -ĭt) *adj. Botany.* Borne in many whorls or rows. Said of flower parts.

mul·ti·stage (mŭl′tĭ-stāj′) *adj.* **1.** Functioning by stages. **2.** Designating a device, such as a turbine, compressor, or supercharger, that has more than one rotating section.

multistage rocket *n.* A rocket composed of two or more stages, each stage firing in succession. Also called "step rocket."

mul·ti·sto·ry (mŭl′tĭ-stôr′ē, -stōr′ē) *adj.* Of or designating a building that has several stories: *a multistory motel.*

mul·ti·tude (mŭl′tĭ-tōōd′, -tyōōd′) *n.* **1.** The condition or quality of being numerous. **2. a.** A great, indefinite number: *"there certainly were a dreadful multitude of ugly women in Bath"* (Jane Austen). **b.** A huge gathering of people. **3.** The masses; the populace. Preceded by *the.* [Middle English, from Old French, from Latin *multitūdō*, a great number, from *multus*, many.]
   Synonyms: army, array, host, legion.

mul·ti·tu·di·nous (mŭl′tĭ-tōōd′n-əs, -tyōōd′n-əs) *adj.* **1.** Very numerous; existing in great numbers. **2.** Consisting of many parts. **3.** Crowded. —**mul·ti·tu·di·nous·ly** *adv.*

mul·ti·va·lent (mŭl′tə-vā′lənt, mŭl-tĭv′ə-lənt) *adj.* **1.** *Chemistry.* Polyvalent. **2.** *Biology.* Of or pertaining to homologous chromosomes during meiosis. **3.** Having various meanings or values. —**mul·ti·va·lence** *n.*

mul·tum in par·vo (mōōl′tōōm ĭn pär′vō) *n.* A large amount within a small space or range. [Latin, literally "much in little."]

mul·ture (mŭl′chər) *n.* A fee, usually in the form of a quantity of flour, paid to a miller for grinding grain at a mill. [Middle English, from Old French *mo(u)lture*, from Medieval Latin *molitura*, from *molere* (past participial stem *molit-*), to grind.]

mum¹ (mŭm) *adj.* Not talking; silent: *Keep mum about my mistake.* —**mum's the word.** Used to enjoin or promise silence: *Remember our secret—mum's the word!* [Middle English *mum, mom*, probably from Low German.]

mum² *n. Chiefly British Informal.* A mother.

mum³ *intr.v.* **mummed, mumming, mums. 1.** To act or play in a pantomime. **2.** To go merrymaking in a mask or disguise, especially during a festival. [Middle English *mummen, mommen*, from Old French *mum.*]

mum⁴ *n. Informal.* A crysanthemum.

mum·ble (mŭm′bəl) *v.* **-bled, -bling, -bles.** —*tr.* **1.** To utter indistinctly by lowering the voice or partially closing the mouth. **2.** To chew (food) slowly or painfully without or as if without teeth. —*intr.* **1.** To speak indistinctly, as by lowering the voice or partially closing the mouth. **2.** To chew food slowly or painfully, as if without teeth. —See Synonyms at **mutter.**
~*n.* A low, indistinct sound or speech. [Middle English *momelen*, frequentative of *mom*, inarticulate sound, MUM¹.] —**mum·bler** *n.*

mum·ble·ty-peg (mŭm′bəl-tē-pĕg′, mŭm′blē-pĕg′) *n.* Also **mum·ble-the-peg** (mŭm′bəl-*th*ə-pĕg′). A children's game in which the players flip a knife from various positions with the object of having the blade stick firmly in the ground. [From the phrase *mumble the peg*, from the fact that originally the loser's penalty was to pull up with his teeth a peg driven into the ground.]

mum·bo jum·bo (mŭm′bō jŭm′bō) *n.* **1.** Confusing or meaningless words or actions. **2.** Unintelligible or obscure ritual. **3.** An object believed to have supernatural powers; a fetish. [Perhaps from the name of a Mandingo idol.]

mu meson *n. Physics.* A particle, the **muon** *(see).* Not in current technical usage.

Mum·ford (mŭm′fərd), **Lewis** (1895-). U.S. sociologist and critic. He has written numerous books on social philosophy, architecture, and city planning and taught at such universities as Stanford and MIT. Mumford believes that humanity's only hope lies in a return to human sensitivities and moral values.

mum·mer (mŭm′ər) *n.* **1.** One who acts or plays in a pantomime or traditional masque. **2.** An actor. **3.** A masked merrymaker. [Middle English *mummar*, from Middle Dutch *mommer*, from Old French *mommeur*, from *momer*, to MUM³.]

mum·mer·y (mŭm′ə-rē) *n., pl.* **-ies. 1.** A performance by mummers. **2.** A pretentious or hypocritical show or ceremony.

mum·mi·fy (mŭm′ə-fī′) *v.* **-fied, -fying, -fies.** —*tr.* **1.** To make into a mummy by embalming and drying. **2.** To cause to shrivel or dry up. **3.** To invest with the appearance or qualities of a mummy: *mummified ideas.* —*intr.* To shrivel or dry up like a mummy. —**mum·mi·fi·ca·tion** (mŭm′ə-fĭ-kā′shən) *n.*

mum·my¹ (mŭm′ē) *n., pl.* **-mies. 1.** The body of a human being or animal embalmed after death, as found in ancient Egyptian tombs. **2.** A withered or shrunken body, living or dead, that resembles a preserved mummy. [Middle English *mummie*, from Old French *momie*, embalming ointment, mummy, from Medieval Latin *mumia*, from Arabic *mūmiyā*, mummy, bitumen, from *mūm*, wax.]

mummy² *n., pl.* **-mies.** *Informal.* Mother. [Alteration of MAMMY.]

mump (mŭmp) *v.* **mumped, mumping, mumps.** *Archaic.* —*intr.* To beg. —*tr.* To get by begging. [Perhaps from obsolete Dutch *mompen*, to cheat.]

mumps (mŭmps) *n. Used with a singular or plural verb.* An acute,

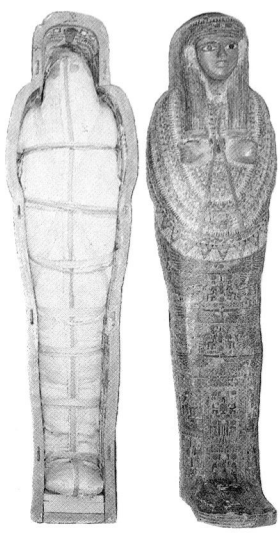

mummy *The mummy and case of an ancient Egyptian priestess from Thebes, who died in the 11th century* B.C.

contagious viral infection of the salivary glands, especially the parotids, that may spread to the pancreas, brain, or testicles. It is common in children and is characterized by swelling of the area under the lower jaw. [From the plural of dialectal *mump,* grimace.]

munch (mŭnch) *v.* **munched, munching, munches.** *—tr.* **1.** To chew (food) steadily with a crunching sound. **2.** *Slang.* To eat. *—intr.* **1.** To chew steadily. Sometimes used with *away, at,* or *on.* **2.** *Slang.* To eat. [Middle English *monchen* (imitative).]

Munch (mo͝ongk), **Edvard** (1863–1944). Norwegian painter, etcher, and lithographer. In the 1890's he painted the best known of his works, the cycle called *Frieze of Life,* which included what has become by far his most famous painting (also produced as a woodcut and a lithograph), *The Scream.*

Münch·hau·sen (münKH'hou'zən, mŭn'chou'-, mŭnch'hou'-), **Karl Friedrich Hieronymus, Baron von** (1720–97). German soldier and storyteller. He was known as a raconteur of extraordinary tales about his life as a soldier, hunter, and sportsman. A collection of his stories appeared in 1781–83.

mun·dane (mŭn-dān', mŭn'dān') *adj.* **1.** Of this world; bodily or worldly: *Mundane pleasures undermined those of the spirit.* **2.** Typical of or concerned with the ordinary; banal: *lived a dull, mundane existence.* —See Usage note at **earthly.** [Middle English *mondeyne,* from Old French *mondain,* from Late Latin *mundānus,* from Latin *mundus,* the world.] **—mun·dane·ly** *adv.* **—mun·dane·ness, mun·dan·i·ty** (mŭn-dăn'ə-tē) *n.*

mung bean (mŭng) *n.* A bean, *Phaseolus aureus,* of eastern Asia. It is the source of bean sprouts. [*Mung,* shortened form *mungo,* from Tamil *mūngu,* from Sanskrit *mudga.*]

mun·go (mŭng'gō) *n.* **1.** Recycled wool used for cheap cloth. **2.** The cloth produced from such wool. See **shoddy.** [Perhaps from Yorkshire dialect *mong†,* mixture.]

Mu·nich (myo͞o'nĭk). *German* **Mün·chen** (mün'KHən). Capital of Bavaria, West Germany. It is the cultural, industrial, and commercial focus of southern Germany and a major tourist center. Its products include machinery, chemicals, instruments, and beer. Founded on the Isar River (1158), Munich became the home of the Wittelsbach family (1255). They made it their capital (1506), from which they ruled Bavaria until 1918, from 1806 as kings. Hitler founded the National Socialist (Nazi) movement in Munich (*c.* 1919). He attempted his "beer-hall putsch" (1923) and signed the Munich Agreement (1938) here. The city was the site of the 1972 summer Olympic Games. Munich's Oktoberfest, an annual beer festival, is world famous.

mu·nic·i·pal (myo͞o-nĭs'ə-pəl) *adj. Abbr.* **mun. 1. a.** Of or pertaining to a city or its government. **b.** Having local self-government: *a municipal borough.* **2.** Of or pertaining to the internal affairs of a nation as distinguished from its international affairs. [Latin *mūnicipālis,* from *mūnicipium,* a franchised city, from *mūniceps,* citizen of a *mūnicipium* (who could perform public offices but not hold magistracies) : *mūnus,* public office + *-ceps,* "-taker," from *capere,* to take.] **—mu·nic·i·pal·ly** *adv.*

mu·nic·i·pal·i·ty (myo͞o-nĭs'ə-păl'ə-tē) *n., pl.* **-ties.** *Abbr.* **mun. 1.** A city, town, village, borough, or other district having local self-government. **2.** A body of officials appointed or elected to manage the affairs of such a community.

mu·nic·i·pal·ize (myo͞o-nĭs'ə-pə-līz') *tr.v.* **-ized, -izing, -izes. 1.** To place under municipal ownership. **2.** To make a municipality of. **—mu·nic·i·pal·i·za·tion** *n.*

mu·nif·i·cence (myo͞o-nĭf'ə-səns) *n.* **1.** A disposition to bestow lavish benefits; a generous nature. **2.** The lavish bestowal of gifts, entertainment, hospitality, or other benefits.

mu·nif·i·cent (myo͞o-nĭf'ə-sənt) *adj.* **1.** Extremely liberal in giving; very generous. **2.** Showing great generosity: *a munificent gift.* [Latin *mūnificens* (stem *mūnificent-*), from *mūnificus,* "present-making," generous, bountiful : *mūnus,* office, duty, gift + *-ficus,* -FIC.] **—mu·nif·i·cent·ly** *adv.*

mu·ni·ment (myo͞o'nə-mənt) *n.* **1. muniments.** *Law.* Documentary evidence of ownership; written proof by which a person can defend a title to a claim to property or rights. **2.** *Archaic.* A means of defense or protection. [Middle English, from Old French, from Medieval Latin *mūnīmentum,* from Latin, defense, from *mūnīre,* to defend.]

mu·ni·tion (myo͞o-nĭsh'ən) *n. Often* **munitions.** War materiel, especially weapons and ammunition.
~tr.v. **munitioned, -tioning, -tions.** To supply with munitions. [Originally, "fortification," from French, from Latin *mūnītiō* (stem *mūnītiōn-*), from *mūnīre,* to defend, fortify.] **—mu·ni·tion·er** *n.*

Mu·ñoz Ma·rín (mo͞o-nyōs' mä-rēn'), **Luis** (1898–1980). Puerto Rican journalist and statesman. Educated in the United States, Muñoz Marín returned to Puerto Rico in 1926 and entered politics, serving in the senate (1932–48) and as the first elected governor of Puerto Rico (1948–64).

Mun·ro (mŭn-rō'), **Hector Hugh,** known as "Saki" (1870–1916). English short-story writer, born in Burma. His highly original short stories are written in a mordant, witty style and are often bitter in tone. The first collection of these, *Reginald,* appeared in 1904. It was followed by *Reginald in Russia* (1910), *The Chronicles of Clovis* (1911), and *Beasts and Super-Beasts* (1914).

Mun·sell scale (mŭn'səl) *n.* A scale used in specifying color, based on equal changes in visual hue. [After Albert Henry *Munsell* (1858–1918), U.S. painter and inventor.]

Mun·ster[1] (mŭn'stər). Province in the southwest of the Republic of Ireland. A former kingdom, it is the largest Irish province, covering the counties of Clare, Cork, Kerry, Limerick, Tipperary, and Waterford.

Munster[2]. Variant of **Muenster.**

munt·jac, munt·jak (mŭnt'jăk') *n.* Any of several small deer of the genus *Muntiacus,* of southeastern Asia and the East Indies. *M. muntjak* is now widespread in the woods of south-central England. Also called "barking deer." [Malay *menjangan,* deer.]

muntjac *Even when fully grown, this small deer is only about 50 centimeters (20 inches) tall. It is native to the forests of India, southern China, and Southeast Asia, but has also been introduced into European woods.*

Muntz metal (mŭnts) *n.* A form of brass, used for extrusions, that consists of three parts copper and two parts zinc. [After G.F. *Muntz* (died 1857), English manufacturer.]

mu·on (myo͞o'ŏn') *n. Symbol* μ *Physics.* A subatomic particle in the lepton family, having a mass 207 times that of the electron, a negative electric charge, and a mean lifetime of 2.2×10^{-6} second. Formerly called "mu meson." [From *mu* (Greek letter) + -ON.] **—mu·on·ic** (myo͞o-ŏn'ĭk) *adj.*

mu·o·ni·um (myo͞o-ō'nē-əm) *n. Physics.* A short-lived entity formed by a muon and its antiparticle attracted together and revolving about a common center.

mu·rage (myo͝or'ĭj) *n.* Formerly, a tax levied to finance the building or repairing of city walls. [Middle English, from Old French, from *mur,* from Latin *murus,* wall.]

mu·ral (myo͝or'əl) *n.* A picture or decoration, usually a very large one, applied directly to a wall or ceiling.
~adj. **1.** Of, pertaining to, or resembling a wall. **2.** On or affixed to a wall: *a mural painting.* [Old French, from Latin *mūrālis,* from *mūrus,* a wall.] **—mu·ral·ist** *n.*

Mu·ra·sa·ki (mo͞o'rä-sä'kē), **Baroness,** known as "Lady Murasaki" (*c.* 978–1031). Japanese novelist. She is celebrated as the author of *The Tale of Genji,* one of the first great works of fiction written in Japanese. Her story of Prince Genji and his descendants is a subtle examination of a complex society.

mur·der (mûr'dər) *n.* Also *obsolete* **mur·ther** (mûr'*th*ər). **1.** The unlawful, usually premeditated killing of one human being by another. Compare **homicide, manslaughter. 2.** *Slang.* Something that is very difficult or hazardous or that causes extreme discomfort: *This heat is murder.* **—get away with murder.** *Informal.* To escape punishment for or detection of a blameworthy act.
~v. **murdered, -dering, -ders.** Also *obsolete* **mur·ther, -thered, -thering, -thers.** *—tr.* **1.** To kill (a human being) unlawfully. **2.** To kill (one or more human beings) brutally or inhumanly. **3.** To destroy or put an end to. **4.** To mar or spoil by ineptness: *murdering the English language.* **5.** *Slang.* To defeat decisively; trounce: *The new magazine was murdering the competition.* **6.** *British Slang.* To consume ravenously: *I could murder a pint.* *—intr.* To commit murder. [Middle English *murther, mordre,* Old English *morthor.*] **—mur·der·er** *n.* **—mur·der·ess** (mûr'dər-ĭs) *n.*

mur·der·ous (mûr'dər-əs) *adj.* **1.** Capable of, guilty of, or intending murder: *a murderous rage.* **2.** Characteristic of or involving murder: *a murderous ambush.* **3.** *Informal.* Very difficult or dangerous: *a murderous exam.* **—mur·der·ous·ly** *adv.* **—mur·der·ous·ness** *n.*

Mur·doch (mûr'dŏk'), **(Jean) Iris** (1919–). Irish-born British novelist. She was trained as a philosopher and in 1948 was appointed lecturer in philosophy at Oxford University. Her first novel, *Under the Net,* was published in 1954. Among the most popular of her later novels are *The Flight from the Enchanter* (1955), *A Severed Head* (1961), *The Unicorn* (1963), and *The Sea, the Sea* (1978).

mure (myo͝or) *tr.v.* **mured, muring, mures.** *Rare.* To immure; confine; wall in. [Middle English *muren,* from Old French *murer,* from Late Latin *mūrāre,* to wall in, from Latin *mūrus,* a wall.]

mu·rex (myo͝or'ĕks') *n., pl.* **murices** (myo͝or'ə-sēz') or **-rexes.** Any of various marine gastropods of the genus *Murex,* with rough, spiny shells, common in warm seas. One species, *M. trunculus,* was the source of the royal dye, Tyrian purple. [New Latin, from Latin *mūrex,* of Mediterranean origin.]

mu·ri·ate (myo͝or'ē-ət, -āt') *n.* A **chloride** *(see).* Not in current technical usage. [Latin *muria,* brine.]

mu·ri·at·ic acid (myo͝or'ē-ăt'ĭk) *n.* **Hydrochloric acid** *(see).* Not in current technical usage. [Latin *muriāticus,* from *muria,* brine.]

mu·ri·cate (myo͝or'ə-kāt') *adj.* Also **mu·ri·cat·ed** (-kā'tĭd). Having a roughened surface because of many short spines. [Latin *mūricātus,* murex-shaped, pointed, from MUREX.]

Mu·ril·lo (myo͞o-rĭl'ō, myo͞o-rēl'yō), **Bartolomé Esteban** (1617–82). Spanish painter. He painted chiefly religious subjects, genre paintings, and portraits. In 1660 he helped found the academy of painting and drawing at Seville.

Murillo painting *Murillo's* The Immaculate Conception, *in the Prado, Madrid, is one of several versions of the same subject by the artist.*

mu·rine (myo͝or'īn') *adj.* **1.** Of or pertaining to a member of the rodent family Muridae, including rats and mice. **2.** Caused, transmitted, or affected by rodents of the family Muridae: *a murine plague.* **3.** Resembling a rat or mouse.
~n. A murine rodent. [Latin *mūrinus,* from *mūs* (stem *mūr-*), mouse.]

murk, mirk (mûrk) *n.* Darkness; gloom.
~adj. Archaic. Dark; gloomy. [Middle English *mirke,* from an oblique case of Old English *mirce,* darkness.]

murk·y, mirk·y (mûr'kē) *adj.* **-ier, -iest. 1.** Dark or gloomy: *"Haste to Pluto's murky abode."* (Cowper). **2.** Heavy and thick with or as if with smoke, fog, or mist. —See Usage note at **dark. —murk·i·ly** *adv.* **—murk·i·ness** *n.*

Mur·mansk (mo͝or-mänsk', -mănsk'). City of northwestern European U.S.S.R., on the Kola Gulf of the Barents Sea. It is a leading freight and fishing port and a naval base. The largest city north of the Arctic Circle, Murmansk is ice-free year-round.

mur·mur (mûr'mər) *n.* **1.** A low, indistinct, and continuous sound or

SERVANTS OF THE BRAIN

How body movement is controlled by contracting tissues

A muscle is tissue that moves by contracting and relaxing. Most muscles work in pairs—one contracts to move a bone or organ at the same time as its paired muscle relaxes. To reverse the movement, the second muscle contracts and the first relaxes.

There are about 640 muscles in the body and they are of three different types: striated, smooth, and cardiac. Striated (or striped, or skeletal) muscles are made up of parallel bundles of fibers attached to bones by connective tissue known as tendons. Many of them move under the conscious control of the brain and are known as voluntary muscles.

Smooth (or visceral) muscles are found in the walls of the tubes and cavities of the body, such as the intestines, the stomach, and the blood vessels. One type of smooth muscle, found in the digestive tract, produces slow waves of contraction (a process called peristalsis) that propel food along. Another type of smooth muscle moves rapidly; it is found in the iris and internal muscles of the eye.

Because the nerves stimulating the visceral muscles are part of the autonomic nervous system, these muscles work without conscious effort and are therefore known as involuntary muscles. There is no sensation of movement as they work.

Some organs of the body have a mixture of muscle types. For example, the top of the esophagus, or gullet, is operated by voluntary muscle, but the lower part is moved by involuntary muscle. When food is swallowed, sensation of its passage ends as it reaches the lower end of the esophagus. The bladder also has a combination of voluntary and involuntary muscles.

Cardiac muscle is found only in the heart. It resembles skeletal muscle in its structure, but it is not under conscious control.

Muscles need two types of nerve—sensory nerves to carry information from the muscles to the brain and motor nerves to carry from the brain to the muscles the impulses that make them move.

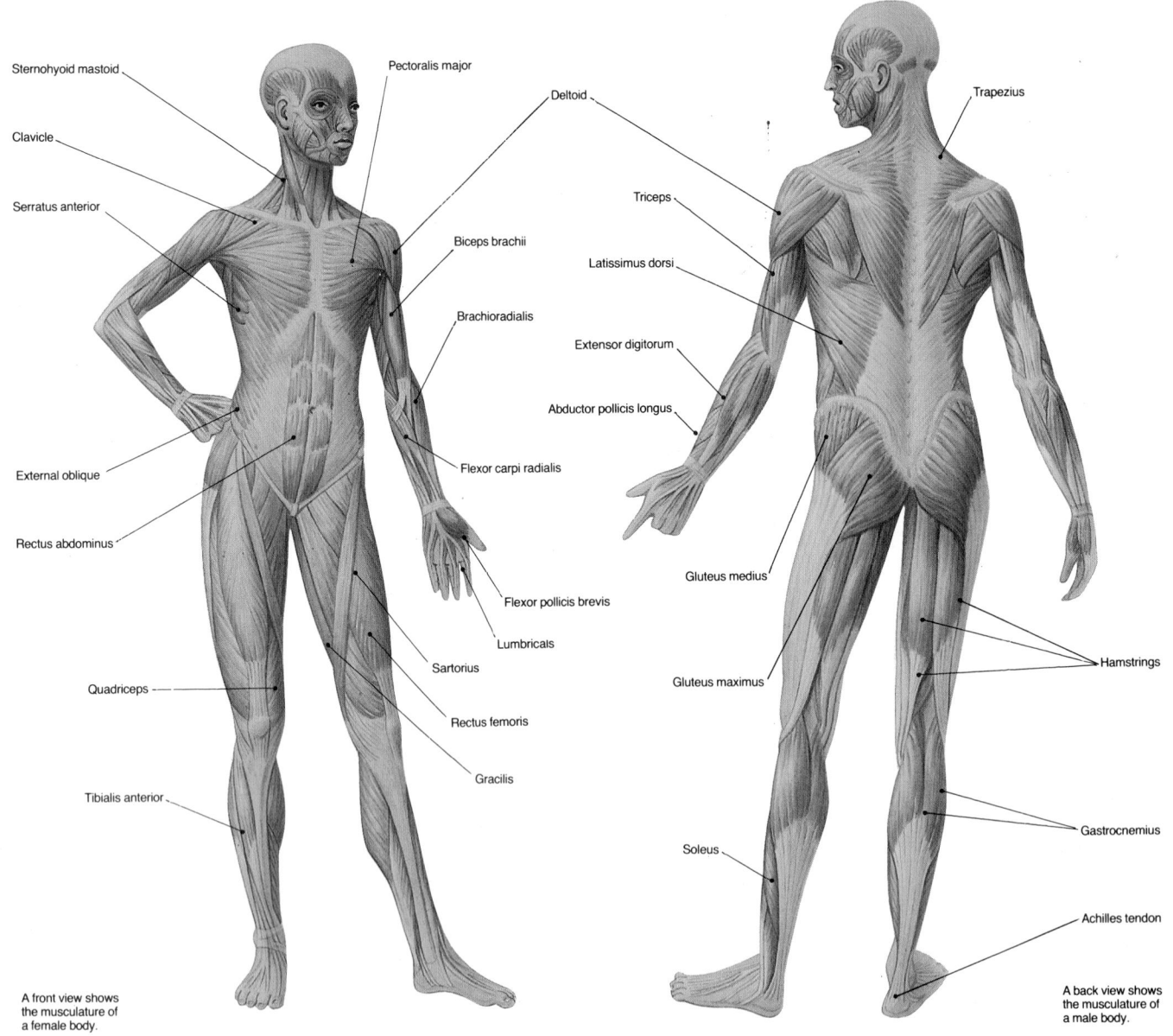

Sternohyoid mastoid

Clavicle

Serratus anterior

External oblique

Rectus abdominus

Quadriceps

Tibialis anterior

A front view shows the musculature of a female body.

Pectoralis major

Deltoid

Biceps brachii

Brachioradialis

Flexor carpi radialis

Flexor pollicis brevis

Lumbricals

Sartorius

Rectus femoris

Gracilis

Triceps

Latissimus dorsi

Extensor digitorum

Abductor pollicis longus

Gluteus medius

Gluteus maximus

Soleus

Trapezius

Hamstrings

Gastrocnemius

Achilles tendon

A back view shows the musculature of a male body.

BODY SHAPERS WORKING IN PAIRS *The shape of the body is defined largely by the striated muscles, which form by far the greatest part of the body's muscle tissue. These muscles, of which the major ones are shown above, vary greatly in size—from the* gluteus maximus, *or buttock muscle, which extends the thigh, to the tiny* stapedius, *1.27 millimeters (¹/₂₀ inch) long, which controls the stirrup bone of the inner ear. Muscles consume four or five times as much energy as they produce. Their efficiency can increase with training. Because muscles cannot push—they can work only by contraction—most striated muscles are in pairs to move arms, legs, spine, and head. In the upper arm, for example, the biceps contracts to raise the forearm, then relaxes while the triceps contracts to lower the forearm again.*

succession of sounds: *the murmur of the waves.* **2.** An indistinct or muttered complaint. **3.** A low utterance: *a murmur of approval.* **4.** *Medicine.* An abnormal sound, usually in the thoracic cavity, originating from the heart or lungs and detectable by the ear or a device such as a stethoscope.
∼*v.* **murmured, -muring, -murs.** —*intr.* **1.** To make a low, continuous, and indistinct sound or succession of sounds. **2.** To complain in low mumbling tones; grumble. —*tr.* To say in a low indistinct voice; utter indistinctly. —See Synonyms at **mutter.** [Middle English *murmure,* from Old French, from Latin *murmur,* rumble, murmur.] —**mur·mur·er** *n.* —**mur·mur·ing·ly** *adv.* —**mur·mur·ous** (mûr′mər-əs) *adj.* —**mur·mur·ous·ly** *adv.*

mur·phy (mûr′fē) *n., pl.* **-phies.** *Slang.* A potato. [From the Irish surname *Murphy* (the potato was a staple Irish food).]

Mur·phy bed (mûr′fē) *n.* A bed that folds or swings into a closet for concealment. [Designed by William L. *Murphy* (1878–1959), U.S. inventor.]

Murphy's Law *n.* An axiom of engineers and scientists: "If anything can go wrong, it will." [20th century : origin obscure.]

mur·ra, mur·rah (mûr′ə) *n.* A precious substance, variously conjectured to have been jade, fluorite, or porcelain, obtained by the Romans from Parthia to make cups and bowls. [Latin *murr(h)a,* from Late Greek *morria*†.]

mur·rain (mûr′ĭn) *n.* **1.** Any highly infectious and malignant disease of cattle, such as anthrax. **2.** *Archaic.* Any pestilence or dire disease. [Middle English *moreyne,* from Old French *morine,* from *morir,* to die, from Vulgar Latin *morīre* (unattested), variant of Latin *morī,* to die.]

Mur·ray (mûr′ē). River of southeastern Australia. Flowing from the Australian Alps to Lake Alexandrina, it forms, with its tributaries, the country's main river system.

Murray, Sir James Augustus Henry (1837–1915). British philologist and lexicographer. He established his reputation by his article on the English language for the *Encyclopaedia Britannica.* His most important work was establishing the general framework of the *Oxford English Dictionary,* of which he was appointed editor in 1879.

mur·rey (mûr′ē) *n.* The color mulberry. [Middle English *morreye,* from Old French *more,* from Medieval Latin *morātum,* from *morātus,* mulberry-colored, from Latin *morum,* mulberry.] —**mur·rey** *adj.*

mur·rhine glass, mur·rine glass (mûr′ĭn, -īn′) *n.* **1.** Glassware believed to resemble ancient Roman vessels of murra. **2.** Glassware embedded with precious stones or with colored metals and glass. [Latin *murr(h)inus,* from *murr(h)a,* MURRA.]

Mur·row (mûr′ō), **Edward Roscoe** (1908–65). U.S. broadcast journalist. As a CBS war correspondent (1939–45), Murrow was noted for his broadcasts from London, which brought a dramatic and factual description of the Battle of Britain into the homes of Americans. He later produced and broadcast the popular television programs *See It Now* and *Person to Person.*

murther. *Obsolete.* Variant of **murder.**

mus. 1. museum. **2.** music; musical; musician.

Mus. B., Mus. Bac. Bachelor of Music. [Latin *Musicae Baccalaureus.*]

Mus·ca (mŭs′kə) *n.* A constellation in the polar region of the Southern Hemisphere near Apus and Carina. [Latin, "fly."]

Mus·ca·det (mŭs′kə-dā′) *n.* A dry white wine of French origin. [French, from Provençal, muscadet grape, from *musc,* musk odor.]

mus·ca·dine (mŭs′kə-dīn′, -dĭn) *n.* A musky grape used to make wine. Also called "scuppernong." [Variant of MUSCATEL.]

mus·cae vo·li·tan·tes (mŭs′ē vŏl′ĭ-tăn′tēz′) *pl.n.* Small motes and threads that seem to move about the field of vision, due to the presence of cell fragments or other defects in the vitreous humor and the lens of the eye. [Latin, "fluttering flies."]

mus·ca·rine (mŭs′kə-rēn′, -rĭn) *n.* A highly toxic organic compound, $C_8H_{19}O_3N$, related to the cholines and derived from the mushroom *Amanita muscaria.* [New Latin *(Amanita) muscaria,* from Latin *muscārius,* of a fly, from *musca,* a fly.]

mus·cat (mŭs′kăt′, -kət) *n.* **1.** Any of various sweet white grapes used for making wine or raisins. **2.** Muscatel. [French, from Provençal *muscat,* "musky" (flavor), from *musc,* MUSK.]

Mus·cat (mŭs′kăt′). Capital of Oman. It was an important port, but it has lately been eclipsed by neighboring Matrah. Exports include dates, mother-of-pearl, and dried fish, and it has an oil terminal.

Muscat and Oman. See **Oman.**

mus·ca·tel (mŭs′kə-tĕl′) *n.* Also **mus·ca·del** (mŭs′kə-dĕl′). **1.** A rich, sweet wine made from muscat grapes. **2.** A muscat grape or raisin. [Middle English *muscadelle,* from Old French *muscadel,* diminutive of MUSCAT.]

mus·cle (mŭs′əl) *n.* **1.** A tissue composed of fibers capable of contracting and relaxing to effect bodily movement. The principal types are **striated muscle** and **smooth muscle,** with **cardiac muscle** *(all of which see)* intermediate between them. **2.** A contractile organ consisting of muscle tissue. **3.** Strength, power, or authority: *Her credentials added muscle to her argument.*
∼*v.* **muscled, -cling, -cles.** —*intr.* To force one's way into a place or situation where one is not wanted. Usually used with *in.* —*tr.* To push (one's way) into a crowded or restricted place or situation: *She muscled her way into the crowded hall.* [French, from Latin *mūsculus,* "little mouse," muscle (from the shape of certain muscles, as the biceps), from *mūs,* mouse.]

mus·cle-bound (mŭs′əl-bound′) *adj.* **1.** Having stiff, overdeveloped muscles, usually as the result of excessive exercise. **2.** Unable to act flexibly; rigid: *an army too muscle-bound to be effective in a crisis.*

muscle fiber *n.* An elongated, contractile cell having highly striated cytoplasm.

mus·cle·man (mŭs′əl-măn′) *n., pl.* **-men** (-mĕn′). A man with large, highly developed muscles; especially, an aggressive, powerful, or intimidating man.

mus·co·va·do, mus·ca·va·do (mŭs′kə-vä′dō) *n.* Unrefined sugar obtained from the juice of sugar cane by evaporation and extraction of the molasses. [Portuguese *(açúcar) mascavado,* unrefined or low quality (sugar), from *mascavar,* to adulterate, depreciate, from Vulgar Latin *minuscapāre* (unattested) : *minus,* less, from *minor,* smaller + *capāre* (unattested), "to bring to a head," cause, from Latin *caput,* head.]

mus·co·vite (mŭs′kə-vīt′) *n.* A mineral, the most common form of mica, consisting essentially of hydrous potassium aluminum silicate with hydroxyl and fluorine, $KAl_2(AlSi_3O_{10})(OH,F)_2$. It ranges from colorless or pale yellow to gray and brown, has a pearly luster, and is used as an insulator. Also called "isinglass," "white mica." [From *Muscovy glass,* its former name.]

Mus·co·vite (mŭs′kə-vīt′) *n.* A native or resident of Moscow or of Muscovy. —**Mus·co·vite** *adj.*

Mus·co·vy (mŭs′kə-vē). **1.** The principality of Moscow (12th–16th centuries). **2.** A former name for Russia.

Muscovy duck *n.* A waterfowl, *Cairina moschata,* found wild from Mexico to Brazil but domesticated around the world for its succulent flesh. It is greenish black with heavy red wattles. Also called "musk duck." [By folk etymology from *musk duck* (by mistaken association with MUSCOVY).]

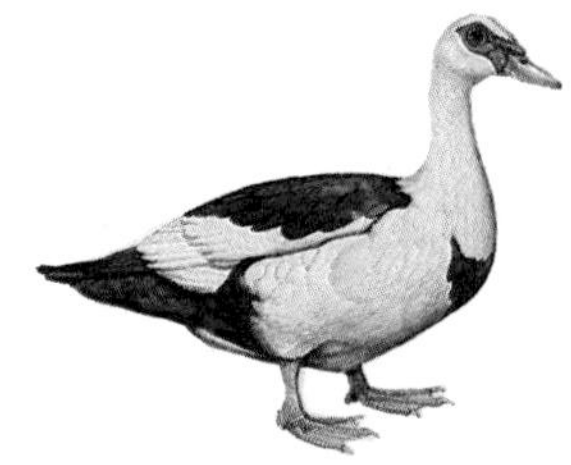

Muscovy *Wild flocks of Muscovy ducks flourish along the inland waterways of Brazil. Muscovies are also common ducks in the farmyards and on the tables of Europe.*

mus·cu·lar (mŭs′kyə-lər) *adj.* **1.** Pertaining to or consisting of muscle or muscles. **2.** Accomplished with or involving the use of muscle or muscles: *muscular effort.* **3.** Having strong muscles. [Latin *mūsculus,* MUSCLE.] —**mus·cu·lar·i·ty** (mŭs′kyə-lăr′ə-tē) *n.* —**mus·cu·lar·ly** *adv.*

muscular dystrophy *n.* A chronic noncontagious congenital disease in which complete incapacitation follows gradual but irreversible muscular deterioration.

mus·cu·la·ture (mŭs′kyə-lə-cho͝or′, -chər) *n.* The system of muscles of an animal or a body part. [French, from Latin *mūsculus,* MUSCLE.]

Mus. D., Mus. Doc. Doctor of Music. [Latin *Musicae Doctor.*]

muse (myo͞oz) *v.* **mused, musing, muses.** —*intr.* To ponder or meditate, usually in silence; consider or deliberate at length. Often followed by *over, on,* or *upon*: *She gazed into the distance, musing on what had been said.* —*tr.* **1.** To meditate on; consider reflectively: *muse the problem.* **2.** To wonder: *"The maiden paused, musing what this might mean."* (S.T. Coleridge).
∼*n.* A state of musing or deep meditation. [Middle English *musen,* from Old French *muser,* to muse, dawdle, "sniff around," from *mus,* snout, from Medieval Latin *mūsum.*] —**muse·ful** *adj.* —**muse·ful·ly** *adv.*

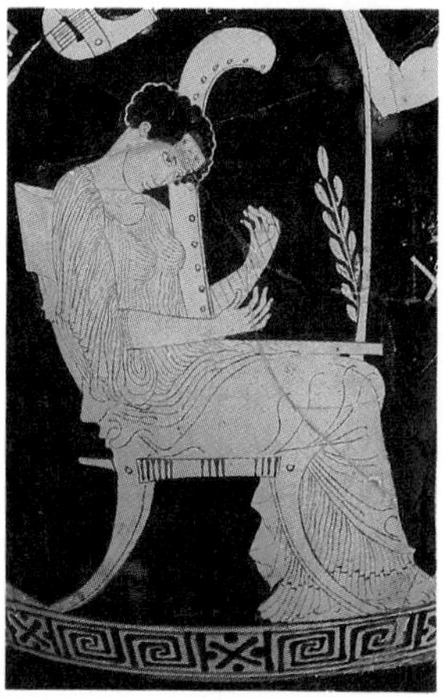

Muse *In classical mythology, the Muses were deities who gave inspiration to poets, artists, and philosophers. Terpsichore, the Muse of dance and choral singing, is shown here on a Greek red-figure vase dating from about 440 B.C.*

Muse (myo͞oz) *n.* **1.** *Greek Mythology.* Any of the nine daughters of Mnemosyne and Zeus, each of whom presided over a different art or science. The Muses are Calliope, Clio, Erato, Euterpe, Melpomene, Polyhymnia, Terpsichore, Thalia, and Urania. **2. muse.** The spirit or power regarded as inspiring poets, musicians, and artists; a source of inspiration. Often preceded by *the.* [Middle English, from Old French, from Latin *Mūsa,* from Greek *Mousa.*]

mu·sette (myo͞o-zĕt′) *n.* **1.** A small French bagpipe with a soft sound. **2.** A soft pastoral tune that imitates the sound of a bagpipe. **3.** A kind of dance performed to such a tune. **4.** A small canvas bag worn over the shoulder or on the back, especially by soldiers. Also called "musette bag." [Middle English, from Old French, from *muser,* to MUSE, dawdle, play the musette.]

mu·se·um (myo͞o-zē′əm) *n. Abbr.* **mus.** A place or building in which works of artistic, historical, and scientific value are cared for and exhibited. [Latin *mūsēum,* library, study, museum, from Greek *mouseion,* "place of the Muses," from *mouseios,* of the Muses, from *Mousa,* a Muse.]

museum piece *n.* **1.** An object of sufficient artistic or historical interest to warrant its inclusion in a museum. **2.** *Informal.* Someone or something considered to be old-fashioned.

mush¹ (mŭsh) *n.* **1.** Boiled cornmeal. **2.** Anything thick, soft, and pulpy in texture. **3.** *Informal.* Maudlin sentimentality. [Probably alteration of MASH.]

mush² (mŭsh, mo͝osh) *interj.* Used as a command to a team of sled dogs to start or to go faster.
∼*intr.v.* **mushed, mushing, mushes.** To travel with a dog sled.
∼*n.* A journey by dog sled. [Canadian French *mouche!,* "run," from *moucher,* to fly, hasten, from French *mouche,* a fly, from Latin *musca.*] —**mush·er** *n.*

mush·room (mŭsh′ro͞om′, -ro͝om′) *n.* **1.** Any of various fleshy fruiting bodies produced by fungi of the class Basidiomycetes, characteristically having an umbrella-shaped cap borne on a stalk; especially, any of the edible varieties. **2.** Any of the fungi producing such structures. **3.** Something resembling a mushroom in shape.
∼*intr.v.* **mushroomed, -rooming, -rooms. 1.** To multiply, grow, or expand rapidly: *The demonstration mushroomed into a riot.* **2.** To spread out, flatten, or swell into a mushroomlike shape. **3.** To search for and gather mushrooms. [Middle English *musseroun, muscheron,* from Old French *mousseron, moisseron,* from Gallo-Roman *mussirọ*† (unattested), agaric.]

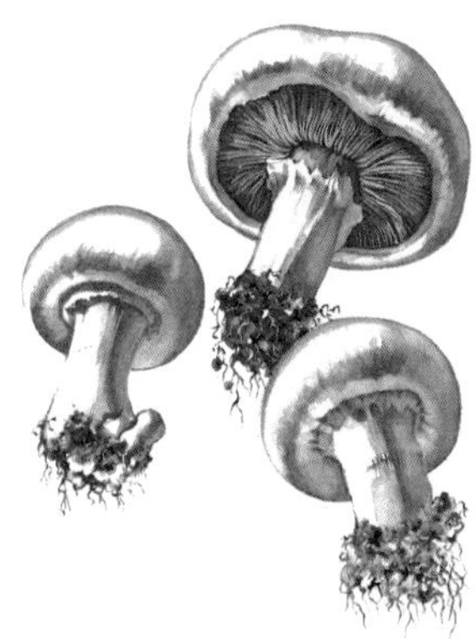

mushroom *The common name for a number of types of wild, edible fungi. They are often abundant in pastures where cattle or horses have grazed. This species is the common field mushroom,* Agaricus campestris.

mush·y (mŭsh′ē) *adj.* **-ier, -iest. 1.** Like mush; soft and pulpy. **2.** *Informal.* Excessively sentimental. —**mush·i·ly** *adv.* —**mush·i·ness** *n.*

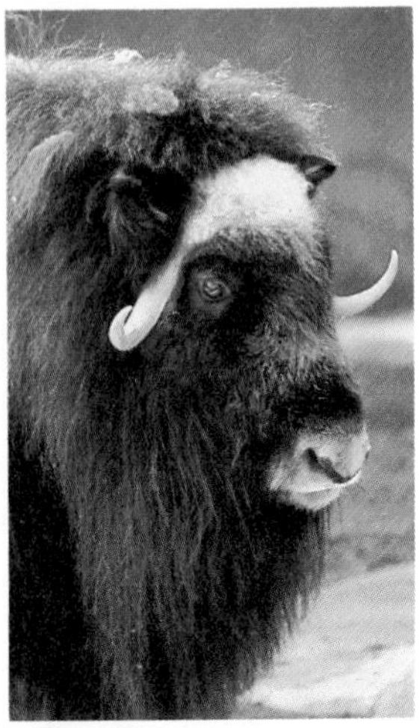

musk ox *Herds of musk oxen roam the northern regions of Canada and Greenland. Both sexes have horns, and when the herd is attacked—by wolves, for example—the adults bunch together in a ring around the calves, forming a defensive barricade with their horns. Musk oxen are so called because they have a musky scent; the musk used in perfumes, however, comes from the musk deer.*

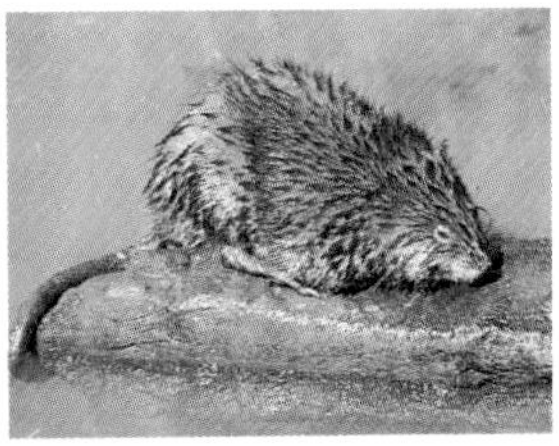

muskrat *This North American rodent lives in marshes, streams, and shallow lakes. Its partially webbed hind feet and its flattened rudderlike tail make it a strong swimmer, and it can remain submerged for up to ten minutes to avoid danger.*

Mu·si·al (myo͞o′zē-əl), **Stanley Frank,** known as "Stan the Man" (1920–). U.S. baseball player. He joined the St. Louis Cardinals in 1941. Known as one of the greatest hitters of all time, Musial retired in 1963 with a lifetime batting average of .331 and a record of 475 home runs and 3,630 base hits.

mu·sic (myo͞o′zĭk) *n. Abbr.* **mus. 1.** An art or art form consisting of organized tones in a coherent sequence of sounds intended to elicit an aesthetic response in a listener. **2.** Vocal or instrumental sounds having some degree of rhythm, melody, and harmony. **3. a.** A musical composition. **b.** A body of such compositions: *the music of Béla Bartók; French music.* **c.** The written or printed score for a musical composition. **d.** Such scores collectively. **e.** A particular category or kind of music: *program music; country music.* **4.** A musical accompaniment. **5.** The study of musicology. **6.** An aesthetically pleasing or harmonious sound or combination of sounds: *the music of your voice; the music of the wind in the trees.* **—face the music.** *Informal.* To accept the consequences, especially of one's own actions. [Middle English *musik,* from Old French *musique,* from Latin *mūsica,* from Greek *mousikē (tekhnē),* (art) of the Muses, from *mousikos,* of the Muses, from *Mousa,* Muse.]

mu·si·cal (myo͞o′zĭ-kəl) *adj. Abbr.* **mus. 1.** Of, pertaining to, or capable of producing music: *a musical instrument.* **2.** Characteristic of or resembling music; melodious: *a musical tone of voice.* **3.** Set to or accompanied by music: *a musical revue.* **4.** Devoted to or skilled in music.
~n. A musical comedy. **—mu·si·cal·ly** *adv.*

musical chairs *n. Used with a singular verb.* **1.** A game in which the players walk to music around a row of chairs containing one chair fewer than the number of players. When the music stops, the players rush to sit down, and the one left without a chair is ruled out of the game. **2.** *Informal.* A rearrangement, as of the elements of a situation, having little practical influence or significance.

musical comedy *n.* **1.** A play or motion picture in which dialogue is interspersed with songs and dances, usually based upon a rather sketchy plot. **2.** Such plays or films collectively.

mu·si·cale (myo͞o′zĭ-kăl′) *n.* A program of music performed at a party or social gathering. [French *(soirée) musicale,* "musical (evening)," from *musical,* musical, from Old French, from *musique,* MUSIC.]

mu·si·cal·i·ty (myo͞o′zĭ-kăl′ə-tē) *n.* **1.** Musical quality. **2.** Skill in the performance of, ability to respond to, or talent for music.

music box *n.* A box containing a device, activated by clockwork, that reproduces tunes mechanically.

music drama *n.* **1.** An opera in which the musical and dramatic continuity is sustained, without being interrupted by arias, recitatives, or ensembles, while its text is set to continuously expressive music often based extensively on leitmotifs. **2.** Such operas collectively. See **opera.**

music hall *n.* **1.** An auditorium for musical performances. **2.** *Chiefly British.* **a.** A vaudeville theater. **b.** Vaudeville.

mu·si·cian (myo͞o-zĭsh′ən) *n. Abbr.* **mus.** A person skilled in composing or performing music, especially professionally. [Middle English *musicien,* from Old French, from Latin *mūsica,* MUSIC.] **—mu·si·cian·ly** *adj.*

mu·si·cian·ship (myo͞o-zĭsh′ən-shĭp′) *n.* Skill, taste, and artistry in performing or composing music.

music of the spheres *n.* An inaudible harmony thought by Pythagoras to be produced by the movements of celestial bodies.

mu·si·col·o·gy (myo͞o′zĭ-kŏl′ə-jē) *n.* The historical and scientific study of music. **—mu·si·co·log·i·cal** (myo͞o′zĭ-kə-lŏj′ĭ-kəl) *adj.* **—mu·si·co·log·i·cal·ly** *adv.* **—mu·si·col·o·gist** (myo͞o′zĭ-kŏl′ə-jĭst) *n.*

music paper *n.* Paper printed with staves on which music can be written.

music roll *n.* A roll of paper that is perforated and used in certain mechanical keyboard instruments, such as the player piano.

music stand *n.* A stand that can be raised or lowered, used for holding a musical score.

mus·jid (mŭs′jĭd) *n.* A **mosque** *(see).*

musk (mŭsk) *n.* **1.** A greasy secretion with a powerful odor, produced in a glandular sac beneath the skin of the abdomen of the male musk deer. It is used in perfumes. **2.** Any similar secretion of certain other vertebrates, such as the otter or civet. **3.** Any synthetic chemical resembling natural musk in odor or use. **4.** The odor of musk or an odor resembling it. **5.** The **musk deer** *(see).* **6.** A plant, *Mimulus moschatus,* formerly cultivated for its musky scent. [Middle English *muske,* from Old French *musc,* from Late Latin *muscus,* from Greek *moskhos,* from Persian *mushk,* probably from Sanskrit *muṣka,* testicle, scrotum (from the scrotum-shaped musk bag of a musk deer), "little mouse," from *mūṣ,* mouse.] **—musk·i·ness** *n.* **—musk·y** *adj.*

musk deer *n.* A small, hornless deer, *Moschus moschiferus,* of central and northeastern Asia. The male secretes musk.

musk duck *n.* **1.** A waterfowl, the **Muscovy duck** *(see).* **2.** A waterfowl, *Biziura lobata,* of Australia. The male has a leathery chin lobe and emits a musky odor during the breeding season.

mus·keg (mŭs′kĕg′) *n.* Also **mas·keg** (măs′kĕg′). A swamp or bog formed by an accumulation of sphagnum moss, leaves, and decayed matter resembling peat. [Cree *maskeek,* from Proto-Algonquian *maškyeekwi* (unattested), swamp.]

mus·kel·lunge (mŭs′kə-lŭnj′) *n., pl.* **-lunges** or collectively **muskellunge.** Also **mas·ka·longe** (măs′kə-lŏnj′), **mas·ca·nonge** (măs′kə-nŏnj′). A large game fish, *Esox masquinongy,* similar to the pike, found in the cooler fresh waters of North America. Also informally called "muskie." [Of Algonquian origin; akin to Algonquian *maskinonge,* "big pike."]

mus·ket (mŭs′kĭt) *n.* A smoothbore shoulder gun used from the late 16th to the 18th century. [French *mousquet,* from Italian *moschetto,* crossbolt, later musket, diminutive of *mosca,* a fly, from Latin *musca.*]

mus·ket·eer (mŭs′kĭ-tîr′) *n.* A soldier armed with a musket; specifically, a member of the French royal household bodyguard in the 17th and 18th centuries. [French *mousquetaire,* from *mousquet,* MUSKET.]

mus·ket·ry (mŭs′kĭ-trē) *n.* **1.** Muskets collectively. **2.** Musketeers collectively. **3.** The technique of using small arms.

Mus·kho·ge·an, Mus·ko·ge·an (mŭ-skō′gē-ən) *n.* A North American Indian language family including Chickasaw, Choctaw, Creek, and Seminole. **—Mus·kho·ge·an, Mus·ko·ge·an** *adj.*

Mus·kie (mŭs′kē), **Edmund Sixtus** (1914–). U.S. politician. Muskie was the first Democrat elected governor of Maine (1954) since the 1930's and the first Democrat ever elected to the U.S. Senate (1958) by Maine voters. He served in the Senate until 1980, was secretary of state (1980–81), and ran unsuccessfully for vice president with presidential candidate Hubert Humphrey (1968).

musk mallow *n.* **1.** A plant, *Malva moschata,* native to Europe, having finely divided leaves and pink flowers with a faint scent of musk. **2.** A plant, the **abelmosk** *(see).*

musk·mel·on (mŭsk′mĕl′ən) *n.* **1.** Any of several varieties of the melon *Cucumis melo,* such as the cantaloupe, having fruit characterized by a netted rind and flesh with a musky aroma. **2.** The fruit of any of these plants.

musk ox *n.* A large, hoofed mammal, *Ovibos moschatus,* of northern Canada and Greenland, that emits a musky odor. It has a long, dark, shaggy coat and downward-curving horns.

musk·rat (mŭsk′răt′) *n., pl.* **-rats** or collectively **muskrat. 1.** An aquatic rodent, *Ondatra zibethica,* native to North America, having a brown coat that is widely used as a fur. It has partly webbed hind feet and musk glands under a broad, flat tail. Also called "musquash." **2.** The fur of this rodent. [MUSK + RAT (possibly influenced by Algonquian (Natick) *musquash,* MUSQUASH).]

musk rose *n.* A prickly shrub, *Rosa moschata,* native to the Mediterranean region, having musk-scented white flowers.

musk thistle *n.* A plant, *Carduus nutans,* that has nodding purple brushlike flowers that emit a musky fragrance.

Mus·lim (mŭz′ləm, mo͝os′-, mo͞oz′-) *n.* Also **Mos·lem** (mŏz′ləm, mŏs′-). **1.** A believer in or adherent of Islam. **2.** A member of the **Nation of Islam** *(see).*
~adj. **1.** Of or pertaining to Islam, its adherents, or their culture. **2.** Pertaining or belonging to the Nation of Islam. [Arabic *muslim,* "one who surrenders (to God)," active participle of *salama,* to surrender.]

Usage: *Moslem* is the form generally preferred in popular journalism and in popular usage. *Muslim* is preferred by scholars and by English-speaking adherents of Islam. It is considered the only correct form by members of the Nation of Islam (Black Muslims). *Mohammedan* is offensive to many Muslims because of the implication of worship of the Prophet, which is forbidden by Islam.

Muslim calendar *n.* The lunar calendar used in Muslim countries, reckoning time from July 16, A.D. 622, the day after the Hegira, and based on a cycle of 30 years, 19 of which have 354 days each and 11 of which are leap years having 355 days each. See feature at **calendar.**

mus·lin (mŭz′lĭn) *n.* **1.** Any of various sturdy, plain-weave cotton fabrics, used especially for sheets. **2.** A model, as of a garment, to be used as a pattern. [French *mousseline,* from Italian *mussolina,* "cloth of Mosul," from Arabic *mūṣlin,* originally made in *Al-Mawsil,* in Iraq.]

Mus. M. Master of Music. [Latin *Magister Musicae.*]

mus·quash (mŭs′kwŏsh′, -kwôsh′) *n.* The **muskrat** *(see).* [Algonquian (Natick).]

muss (mŭs) *tr.v.* **mussed, mussing, musses.** To make messy or untidy; rumple. Often used with *up.*
~n. A state of disorder; a mess. [Perhaps variant of MESS.] **—muss·i·ly** *adv.* **—muss·y** *adj.*

mus·sel (mŭs′əl) *n.* **1. a.** Any of several marine bivalve mollusks, especially *Mytilus edulis,* having a blue-black shell. **b.** The edible flesh of any of these mollusks. **2.** Any of several freshwater bivalve mollusks of the genera *Anodonta* and *Unio,* whose shells provide mother-of-pearl. [Middle English, Old English *mus(c)le,* from West Germanic *muskul,* from Latin *mūsculus,* "little mouse," muscle, mussel (from its mouselike shape), from *mūs,* mouse.]

Mus·set (mü-sā′), **(Louis Charles) Alfred de** (1810–57). French poet and dramatist, one of the leading poets of the French romantic movement. He is most famous for the four poems *Les Nuits* (1835–37) and for his plays, such as *On ne Badine pas avec l'Amour* and *Lorenzaccio* (1834).

Mus·so·li·ni (mo͞o′sə-lē′nē), **Benito,** known as "Il Duce" (1883–1945). Italian politician, founder of the Fascist movement and prime minister and dictator of Italy (1922–45). He founded the first *fascio di combattimento* at Milan (1919), and two years later, when he was elected to parliament, the National Fascist party was formally established. He was invited by King Victor Emmanuel III to form a government in October, 1922. Opposition parties were suppressed and parliamentary government ended by 1928. In the 1930's Mussolini conducted an expansionist foreign policy, invading Ethiopia (1935) and annexing Albania (1939). The Rome-Berlin Axis forged during the Spanish Civil War was confirmed by a formal alliance (1939). He brought Italy into World War II on the side of the Axis powers in June 1940. He was dismissed by the king and arrested in July 1943, but he escaped and headed a puppet Nazi government in northern Italy until April 1945, when he was captured and executed by Italian partisans.

Mus·sorg·sky or **Mous·sorg·sky** (mə-zôrg′skē, mo͞o-sôrg′skē), **Modest Petrovich** (1839–81). Russian composer. His works include the opera *Boris Godunov* (first produced in 1874), the piano suite *Pictures at an Exhibition* (1874), and many songs.

Mus·sul·man (mŭs′əl-mən) *n., pl.* **-men** (-mĭn) or **-mans.** *Archaic.* A Muslim. [Turkish *musulmān,* probably from Arabic *mushmūn,* plural of *muslim,* MUSLIM.]

must[1] (mŭst) *v.* Used as an auxiliary followed by an infinitive without *to,* or, in reply to a question or suggestion, with the infinitive understood. It can indicate: **1.** Compulsion or obligation: *When duty calls, you must answer.* **2.** Requirement or prerequisite: *You must register in order to vote.* **3.** Probability, expectation, or supposition: *It must be nearly midnight.* **4.** Inevitability or certainty: *To each of us, death must come.* **5. a.** In the first person, insistence or fixed resolve: *I must finish this tonight.* **b.** In the second and third persons, insistence imputed by the speaker to others: *Have another drink if you must.* **6.** Unpleasant inevitability. Used as a past or historical present: *The rain was coming down, and now I must lose my umbrella!*
∼*n.* **1.** A requirement or necessity: *In teaching, patience is a must.* **2.** Something that should without fail be done, seen, or otherwise acted upon: *If you visit Rome, the Vatican is a must.* [Middle English *moste* (past tense), Old English *mōste,* past tense of *mōtan,* to be allowed, from Germanic.]

must[2] *n.* Mold; mustiness. [Back-formation from MUSTY.]

must[3] *n.* The unfermented or fermenting juice being processed for wine; new wine. [Middle English *must,* Old English *must, moste,* from Latin *mustum,* neuter of *mustus,* new, newborn.]

must[4]**.** Variant of **musth.**

mus·tache (mŭs′tăsh′, mə-stăsh′) *n.* Also *chiefly British* **mous·tache. 1.** *Sometimes* **mustaches.** The hair growing on the upper lip, especially when it is cultivated and groomed. **2.** Something similar to a mustache in appearance and position, especially: **a.** A group of bristles or hairs around the mouth of an animal. **b.** Distinctive coloring or feathers near the bill of a bird. [French, from Italian *mostaccio,* from Greek *mustax* (stem *mustak-*).]

mus·ta·chio (mə-stăsh′ō, -stăsh′ē-ō′, -stä′shō, -stä′shē-ō′) *n., pl.* **-chios.** *Often* **mustachios.** A mustache, especially a luxuriant one. [Spanish *mostaccho* and Italian *mustaccio,* MUSTACHE.] **—mus·ta·chioed** *adj.*

mus·tang (mŭs′tăng′) *n.* A wild horse of the North American plains, descended from Spanish stock. [Mexican Spanish *mesten(g)o,* from Spanish, stray (animal), from *mesta,* meeting of owners of stray animals, from Medieval Latin *(animalia) mixta,* wild or stray animals that mixed with and became attached to a grazier's herd, "mixed animals," from Latin *mixtus,* past participle of *miscēre,* to mix.]

mus·tard (mŭs′tərd) *n.* **1.** Any of various plants of the genus *Brassica,* native to Eurasia, having four-petaled yellow flowers and slender pods. Some species, especially *B. nigra* and *B. alba,* are cultivated for their pungent seeds, and others for their edible leaves and stems. **2.** Any of various other plants of the family Cruciferae (or Brassicaceae), such as garlic mustard. **3. a.** Powdered mustard seeds used medicinally, as in mustard plasters. **b.** A condiment consisting of a paste made from powdered mustard seeds mixed with wine, vinegar, or water and various spices, such as turmeric. **3.** Dark yellow to light olive brown. [Middle English *mustarde,* condiment, later also plant, from Old French *mo(u)starde,* from Common Romance *mosto,* from Latin *mustum,* MUST, "new wine" (because mustard paste was originally made by mixing grape juice with mustard powder).] **—mus·tard** *adj.*

mustard gas *n.* An oily, volatile liquid, $(ClCH_2CH_2)_2S$, used in warfare as a gaseous blistering agent. [From its mustardlike odor.]

mustard oil *n.* Any oil obtained from mustard seeds.

mustard plaster *n.* A pastelike mixture of powdered mustard, flour, and water spread on cloth or paper and applied in poultice as a counterirritant. Also called "plaster."

mus·ter (mŭs′tər) *v.* **-tered, -tering, -ters.** —*tr.* **1.** To summon or assemble (troops, for example). **2.** To collect or gather. Sometimes used with *up: muster your arguments; muster up courage.* —*intr.* To assemble or gather: *mustering for inspection.*
∼*n.* **1. a.** A gathering, especially of troops, for service, inspection, review, or roll call. **b.** The persons assembled for such a gathering. **2.** The official roll of personnel in a military or naval unit. Also called "muster roll." **3.** Any gathering or collection. **4.** A flock of peacocks. **—pass muster.** To be acceptable. [Middle English *mostren,* from Old French *mo(u)strer,* from Latin *monstrāre,* to show, indicate (originally by an omen), from *mōnstrum,* an omen, prodigy, probably from *monēre,* to warn.]

musth, must (mŭst) *n.* A condition of frenzied sexual excitement occurring in the males of certain mammals such as the elephant and camel.
∼*adj.* Designating a mammal in musth. [Urdu, from Persian *mast,* drunk.]

must·n't (mŭs′ənt). Contraction of *must not.*

must·y (mŭs′tē) *adj.* **-ier, -iest. 1.** Having a stale or moldy odor or taste. **2.** Hackneyed; dull; antiquated; stale: *musty views on life.* [Variant (influenced by MUST, juice) of obsolete *moisty,* from MOIST.] **—must·i·ly** *adv.* **—must·i·ness** *n.*

mu·ta·ble (myo͞o′tə-bəl) *adj.* **1.** Subject to change or alteration. **2.** Prone to frequent change; inconstant; fickle. [Latin *mūtābilis,* from *mūtāre,* to change, MUTATE.] **—mu·ta·bil·i·ty** (myo͞o′tə-bĭl′ə-tē), **mu·ta·ble·ness** *n.* **—mu·ta·bly** *adv.*

mu·ta·gen (myo͞o′tə-jən, -jĕn′) *n.* Any agent, including radioactive elements, ultraviolet radiation, and certain chemicals, that causes biological mutation. [MUTA(TION) + -GEN.] **—mu·ta·gen·ic** (myo͞o′tə-jĕn′ĭk) *adj.* **—mu·ta·gen·i·cal·ly** *adv.*

mu·tant (myo͞o′tənt) *n. Biology.* **1.** An individual or organism differing from the parental strain or strains as a result of mutation. **2.** A gene that has undergone mutation. [Latin *mūtans* (stem *mūtant-*), changing, present participle of *mūtāre,* to change, MUTATE.] **—mu·tant** *adj.*

mu·tate (myo͞o′tāt′, myo͞o-tāt′) *v.* **-tated, -tating, -tates.** —*tr.* To cause to undergo alteration, especially by mutation. —*intr.* To undergo change by mutation. [Latin *mūtāre* (past stem *mutat-*).] **—mu·ta·tive** (myo͞o′tā′tĭv, myo͞o′tə-) *adj.*

mu·ta·tion (myo͞o-tā′shən) *n.* **1.** The act or process of being altered or changed. **2.** An alteration or change, as in nature, form, or quality. **3.** *Biology.* **a.** Any heritable alteration of the genes or chromosomes of an organism. **b.** A mutant. **4.** *Linguistics.* **a.** The change that is caused in the sound of one vowel by its assimilation to another vowel; especially, **umlaut** *(see).* **b.** In Celtic languages, a change in the initial consonant of a word or morpheme based upon the phonetic nature of the word preceding it or upon its gender or syntactic function. [Middle English *mutacioun,* from Old French *mutation,* from Latin *mūtātiō* (stem *mūtātiōn-*), from *mūtāre,* to change, MUTATE.] **—mu·ta·tion·al** *adj.* **—mu·ta·tion·al·ly** *adv.*

mu·ta·tis mu·tan·dis (mo͞o-tä′tēs mo͞o-tän′dēs, myo͞o-tā′tĭs myo͞o-tăn′dĭs) *adv. Abbr.* **m.m.** The necessary changes having been made; substituting new terms. [Latin.]

mutch (mŭch) *n.* In Scotland, a linen cap worn by children or women. [Middle English, from Middle Dutch *mutse,* from Medieval Latin *almucia,* AMICE.]

mutch·kin (mŭch′kĭn) *n. Scottish.* A unit of liquid measure equal to approximately one pint. [Middle English (Scottish) *muchekyn,* from obsolete Dutch *mudseken,* diminutive of *mudde,* bushel, from Latin *modius.*]

mute[1] (myo͞ot) *adj.* **muter, mutest. 1. a.** Refraining from producing speech or vocal sound. **b.** Not expressed in speech or vocal sound: *a mute agreement.* **2. a.** Unable to speak; dumb. **b.** Unable to vocalize, as certain animals are. **3.** *Law.* Refusing, as a defendant, to plead either guilty or not guilty when under arraignment. Used chiefly in the phrase *stand mute.* **4.** *Phonetics.* Not pronounced; silent, as is the *e* in *house.* —See Synonyms at **dumb.**
∼*n.* **1.** A person incapable of speech; especially, one both deaf and mute. **2.** *Law.* A defendant who refuses to plead either guilty or not guilty when under arraignment. **3.** *Music.* Any of various devices used to muffle or soften the tone of a musical instrument. **4.** *Phonetics.* **a.** A silent or unpronounced letter. **b.** A plosive; a stop. **5.** One who acts in a dumb show. **6.** Formerly, a hired mourner.
∼*tr.v.* **muted, muting, mutes. 1.** To muffle or soften the sound of (a musical instrument, for example). **2.** To soften the tone, color, shade, or hue of. **3.** To lessen the intensity of: *muted criticism.* [Middle English *muet,* from Old French, diminutive of *mu,* mute, from Latin *mūtus,* silent, dumb.] **—mute·ly** *adv.* **—mute·ness** *n.*

mute[2] *v.* **muted, muting, mutes.** —*tr.* To discharge (feces). Used of a bird. —*intr.* To discharge feces. Used of a bird. [Middle English, from Old French *meutir, esmeutir,* from Frankish *smeltjan* (unattested), to SMELT.]

mute swan *n.* A white Eurasian swan, *Cygnus olor,* with an orange bill and a curved neck.

mu·ti·late (myo͞ot′l-āt′) *tr.v.* **-lated, -lating, -lates. 1.** To deprive (a person or animal) of a limb or other essential part. **2.** To render imperfect by damaging or excising a part: *mutilated books.* [Latin *mutilāre,* to cut off, from *mutilus,* maimed.] **—mu·ti·la·tion** (myo͞ot′l-ā′shən) *n.* **—mu·ti·la·tive** (myo͞ot′l-ā′tĭv) *adj.* **—mu·ti·la·tor** *n.*

mu·ti·neer (myo͞ot′n-îr′) *n.* A person, especially a soldier or sailor, who takes part in a mutiny. [Obsolete French *mutinier,* from Old French *mutin,* MUTINY.]

mu·ti·nous (myo͞ot′n-əs) *adj.* **1.** Pertaining to, engaged in, or disposed toward mutiny. **2.** Rebellious; unruly; disaffected. —See Usage note at **insubordinate.** [From obsolete *mutine,* MUTINY.] **—mu·ti·nous·ly** *adv.* **—mu·ti·nous·ness** *n.*

mu·ti·ny (myo͞ot′n-ē) *n., pl.* **-nies.** Open rebellion against constituted authority; especially, rebellion of sailors or soldiers against superior officers. —See Synonyms at **rebellion.**
∼*intr.v.* **mutinied, -nying, -nies.** To rebel by engaging in or as if in a mutiny. [From obsolete *mutine,* mutiny, from Old French *mutin,* rebellious, rebellion, from *muete,* revolt, "movement," from Vulgar Latin *movita* (unattested), from Latin *movēre,* to move.]

mut·ism (myo͞o′tĭz′əm) *n.* **1.** The condition of being unable to speak. **2.** *Psychology.* A condition resulting in a refusal to speak.

Mutsuhito. See **Meiji.**

mutt (mŭt) *n. Slang.* **1.** A mongrel dog. **2.** A fool. [Shortened from MUTTONHEAD.]

mut·ter (mŭt′ər) *v.* **-tered, -tering, -ters.** —*intr.* **1.** To speak indistinctly in low tones. **2.** To complain or grumble morosely. —*tr.* To utter or say in low, indistinct tones.
∼*n.* A low, indistinct uttering or utterance, often of discontent.

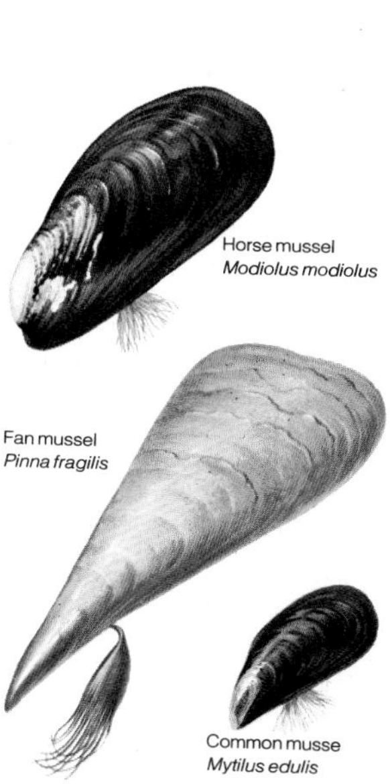
Horse mussel
Modiolus modiolus
Fan mussel
Pinna fragilis
Common musse
Mytilus edulis

mussel *The common mussel (bottom) is found along the shores and estuaries of the northern Atlantic. It may grow as long as 100 millimeters (4 inches). Mussels are usually edible but may be unsafe in polluted areas because chemicals can build up in their bodies as they filter food particles from the water. The horse mussel (top) and the fan mussel (center) are found in deeper waters of the northern Atlantic and are larger than the common type.*

PRONUNCIATION KEY

ă, pat; ā, pay; âr, care; ä, father, are; b, bib; ch, church; d, deed; ĕ, pet; ē, be; f, fife; g, gag; h, hat; hw, which; ĭ, pit; ī, pie; îr, pier; j, judge; k, kick; l, lid, needle; m, mum; n, no, sudden; ng, thing; ŏ, pot; ō, toe; ô, paw, for; oi, noise; ou, out; o͝o, book; o͞o, boot; p, pop; r, roar; s, sauce; sh, ship, dish; t, tight; th, thin, path; *th*, this, bathe; ŭ, cut; ûr, fur; v, valve; w, with; y, yes; z, zebra, size; zh, vision; ə, about, item, edible, gallop, circus, peaceful

IN FOREIGN WORDS:

à, *Fr.* ami; œ, *Fr.* feu, *Ger.* schön; ü, *Fr.* tu, *Ger.* über; KH, *Ger.* ich, *Scot.* loch; N, *Fr.* bon; y′, *Fr.* Compiègne

STRESS MARKS:

Primary stress: ′
in·cite′ (ĭn-sīt′)
Secondary stress: ′
in′sight′ (ĭn′sīt′)

[Middle English *muteren*, akin to Old Norse *mudhla*.] —**mut·ter·er** *n.* —**mut·ter·ing·ly** *adv.*
    Synonyms: *mumble, murmur.*

mut·ton (mŭt′n) *n.* The flesh of fully grown sheep. [Middle English *moto(u)n*, from Old French *moton*, sheep, from Medieval Latin *multō* (stem *multōn-*).]

mutton chop *n.* **1.** A thick chop cut from the loin section of mutton. **2. mutton chops.** Side whiskers shaped like chops of meat. Also called "mutton-chop whiskers."

mut·ton·head (mŭt′n-hĕd′) *n. Slang.* A stupid person. [From the stupidity of sheep.] —**mut·ton·head·ed** *adj.*

Muttra. See Mathura.

mu·tu·al (myōō′chōō-əl) *adj.* **1.** Having the same relationship each to the other: *mutual well-wishers.* **2.** Directed and received in equal amount: *our mutual esteem.* **3.** Possessed in common: *mutual interests.* [Middle English *mutuall*, from Old French *mutuel*, from Latin *mūtuus*, exchanged, reciprocal, mutual.] —**mu·tu·al·i·ty** (myōō′-chōō-ăl′ə-tē) *n.* —**mu·tu·al·ly** *adv.*

    Usage: Mutual is often used in the general sense of "common" (*We all had a mutual interest in getting a decision made*), but this usage is criticized by purists, who feel that the word should be restricted to what only two people do, feel, or represent to each other. Thus, when two people have a *mutual distrust,* each distrusts the other in like manner. As a consequence, in strict usage a phrase such as *a mutual distrust of each other* is felt to be repetitive.

mutual fund *n.* An investment company without fixed capitalization that purchases shares in numerous enterprises and issues its own shares for public sale. Also called "open-end investment company," *British* "unit trust."

mutual inductance *n. Abbr.* M *Physics.* **1.** The ratio expressed by the flux linking one circuit with a neighboring circuit divided by the current in the neighboring circuit. **2.** The ratio expressed by the electromotive force induced in a circuit by a neighboring circuit divided by the corresponding change of current in the neighboring circuit. See **inductance.**

mutual induction *n. Physics.* Electromagnetic induction in which electromotive force in one circuit is produced by a changing current in a neighboring circuit.

mutual insurance *n.* An insurance system in which the insured persons become company members, each paying specific amounts into a common fund from which members are entitled to protection and compensation in case of loss.

mu·tu·al·ism (myōō′chōō-ə-lĭz′əm) *n. Biology.* Any association between two or more organisms in which all benefit. See **symbiosis.**

mu·tu·al·ize (myōō′chōō-ə-līz′) *tr.v.* **-ized, -izing, -izes. 1.** To make mutual. **2.** To set up or reorganize (a business) as a cooperative.

muu·muu (mōō′mōō′) *n.* A long, loose dress that hangs free from the shoulders. [Hawaiian *mu'u mu'u.*]

Muy·bridge (mī′brĭj′), **Eadweard,** born Edward James Muggeridge (1830–1904). English photographer. His reputation rests on his experiments in photographing moving objects, especially horses. His *zoöpraxiscope,* patented in 1881, projected animated figures onto a screen and was the forerunner of cinematic photography.

Mu·zak (myōō′zăk′) *n.* A trademark for a system of recorded music transmitted by wire and played as a background, as in factories, shops, and airports, on a subscription basis.

mu·zhik, mou·jik, mu·jik (mōō-zhēk′, -zhĭk′) *n.* A peasant in czarist Russia. [Russian *muzhik,* a peasant, diminutive of *muzh,* man, from Old Church Slavonic *mǫzhi.*]

muz·zle (mŭz′əl) *n.* **1.** The forward, projecting part of the head, including the jaws and nose, of certain animals. **2.** A leather or wire device fitted over an animal's snout to prevent biting and eating. **3.** Something that prevents free movement or expression. **4.** The forward, discharging end of the barrel of a firearm.
    —*tr.v.* **muzzled, -zling, -zles. 1.** To put a muzzle on (an animal). **2. a.** To restrain (a person) from expressing opinions. **b.** To prevent (views, for example) from being expressed. [Middle English *mosel, musell,* from Old French *musel,* from Gallo-Roman *mūsellum* (unattested), diminutive of Late Latin *mūsum,* snout.] —**muz·zler** *n.*

muz·zle·load·er (mŭz′əl-lō′dər) *n.* A firearm loaded through the muzzle. —**muz·zle·load·ing** *adj.*

muz·zy (mŭz′ē) *adj.* **-zier, -ziest.** *Informal.* **1.** Muddled; confused. **2.** Blurred; indistinct. [18th century : origin obscure.] —**muz·zi·ly** *adv.* —**muz·zi·ness** *n.*

mV millivolt.

MV 1. megavolt. **2.** motor vessel.

M.V. 1. motor vessel. **2.** muzzle velocity.

MVD, M.V.D. (ĕm′vē-dē′) *n.* A former administrative branch of the Soviet government (1946-1960) whose secret police functions were taken over by the KGB in 1954. [Russian *Ministyerstvo Vnutryennikh Dyel,* ministry of internal affairs.]

mW milliwatt.

MW, M.W. 1. medium wave. **2.** megawatt.

Mx *Physics.* maxwell.

my (mī). The possessive form of the pronoun *I.* **1.** Used attributively to indicate possession, agency, or reception of an action by the speaker: *my wallet; pursuing my tasks; suffered my first rebuff.* —See Usage note at **me. 2.** Used preceding various forms of polite, affectionate, or familiar address: *my lady; my dear Dr. Mitchell; my good man.* **3.** Used in various interjectional phrases: *My word!*
    —*interj.* Used as an exclamation of surprise, pleasure, or dismay. [Middle English *my, mi, min,* Old English *mīn.*]

my-. Variant of **myo-.**

my·al·gi·a (mī-ăl′jē-ə, -jə) *n. Pathology.* Muscular pain. [New Latin : MY(O)- + -ALGIA.]

my·all[1] (mī′ôl′) *n.* Any of various Australian acacias with hard wood used for fences. [From *maiāl,* native Australian name.]

myall[2] *n. Australian.* An aborigine living in a traditional way outside white civilization. [From a native Australian language.]

myasis. Variant of **myiasis.**

my·as·the·ni·a (mī′əs-thē′nē-ə) *n.* Abnormal muscular weakness or fatigue. [New Latin : MY(O)- + ASTHENIA.] —**my·as·then·ic** (mī′-əs-thĕn′ĭk) *adj.*

myc. mycological; mycology.

my·ce·li·um (mī-sē′lē-əm) *n., pl.* **-lia** (-lē-ə). The vegetative part of a fungus, consisting of a mass of branching, threadlike filaments called hyphae. [New Latin, from Greek *mukēs,* fungus + -*elium,* as in *epithelium.*] —**my·ce·li·al, my·ce·li·oid** (mī-sē′lē-oid′) *adj.*

My·ce·nae (mī-sē′nē). City of ancient Greece, in the northeastern Peloponnese. It flourished from *c.* 1600 to 1200 B.C. as a center of Mycenaean civilization and was the seat of King Agamemnon. Excavations begun by Heinrich Schliemann in the late 19th century revealed the noted Lion Gate and treasure-filled tombs.

My·ce·nae·an (mī′sə-nē′ən) *adj.* Of, pertaining to, or designating the Aegean civilization that spread its influence from Mycenae to many parts of the Mediterranean region from about 1400 B.C. to 1150 B.C. —**My·ce·nae·an** *n.*

Mycenaean Greek *n.* The early East Greek dialect of the Mycenaeans, attested in documents in Linear B script.

-mycete *suffix.* Indicates a member of a specified class of fungi; for example, **basidiomycete.** [New Latin *-mycetes* (class), from Greek *mukētes,* plural of *mukēs,* fungus.]

my·ce·to·ma (mī′sə-tō′mə) *n., pl.* **-mas** or **-mata** (-mə-tə). **1.** A chronic fungous infection usually affecting the foot, characterized by nodules that discharge oily pus. **2.** A mycetoma nodule. [New Latin : Greek *mukētes,* fungi (see -**mycete**) + -OMA.] —**my·ce·tom·a·tous** (mī′sə-tŏm′ə-təs, -tō′mə-təs) *adj.*

my·ce·to·zo·an (mī-sē′tə-zō′ən) *n.* A slime mold *(see).*
    —*adj.* Of or pertaining to slime molds. [New Latin *Mycetozoa,* "fungus-animals" (formerly classed in the animal kingdom) : Greek *mukētes,* fungi (see -**mycete**) + -ZOA.]

-mycin *suffix.* Indicates derivation of a substance from bacteria or fungi; for example, **streptomycin.** [MYC(O)- + -IN.]

myco-, myc- *prefix.* Indicates fungus; for example, **mycelium, mycology.** [New Latin, from Greek *mukēs,* fungus.]

my·co·bac·te·ri·um (mī′kō-băk-tîr′ē-əm) *n., pl.* **-teria** (-tîr′ē-ə). Any slender, rod-shaped bacterium of the genus *Mycobacterium,* which includes the bacterium that causes tuberculosis.

mycol. mycological; mycology.

my·col·o·gy (mī-kŏl′ə-jē) *n. Abbr.* **myc., mycol. 1.** The branch of botany that deals with fungi. **2.** The fungi native to a region. [New Latin *mycologia* : MYCO- + -LOGY.] —**my·co·log·ic** (mī′kə-lŏj′ĭk), **my·co·log·i·cal** *adj.* —**my·col·o·gist** (mī-kŏl′ə-jĭst) *n.*

my·cor·rhi·za, my·co·rhi·za (mī′kə-rī′zə) *n., pl.* **-zae** (-zē) or **-zas.** *Botany.* The symbiotic association of the mycelium of a fungus with the roots of certain plants, such as conifers or orchids. [New Latin : MYCO- + Greek *rhiza,* a root.] —**my·cor·rhi·zal** *adj.*

my·co·sis (mī-kō′sĭs) *n., pl.* **-ses** (-sēz′). **1.** A fungous growth in the body. **2.** A disease caused by a fungous growth. [New Latin : MYC(O)- + -OSIS.]

my·co·tox·in (mī′kō-tŏk′sĭn) *n.* Any poisonous substance produced by a fungus.

my·dri·a·sis (mī-drī′ə-sĭs, mī-) *n.* Prolonged and abnormal dilatation of the pupil of the eye as a result of disease or a drug. [Latin, from Greek *mudriasis†.*]

myd·ri·at·ic (mī′drē-ăt′ĭk) *n.* A drug that produces dilatation of the pupils of the eye. [From MYDRIASIS.] —**myd·ri·at·ic** *adj.*

myel-, myelo- *prefix.* Indicates the spinal cord or bone marrow; for example, **myelencephalon, myelitis.** [New Latin, from Greek *muelos,* marrow, from *mus,* muscle.]

my·e·len·ceph·a·lon (mī′ə-lĕn-sĕf′ə-lŏn′) *n.* The rear part of the embryonic hindbrain from which the medulla oblongata develops. —**my·e·len·ce·phal·ic** (mī′ə-lĕn′sə-făl′ĭk) *adj.*

my·e·lin (mī′ə-lĭn) *n.* Also **my·e·line** (mī′ə-lĭn, -lēn′). **1.** A white, fatty material encasing some nerve fibers. Also called "medullary sheath." **2.** One of several fatlike substances found in body tissues. [MYEL- + -IN.] —**my·e·lin·ic** (mī′ə-lĭn′ĭk) *adj.*

my·e·li·nat·ed (mī′ə-lī-nā′tĭd) *adj.* Having a myelin sheath; medullated. Said of nerves.

my·e·li·tis (mī′ə-lī′tĭs) *n.* Inflammation of the spinal column or bone marrow. [New Latin : MYEL- + -ITIS.]

my·e·loid (mī′ə-loid′) *adj.* **1.** Of, related to, or derived from bone marrow. **2.** Of or pertaining to the spinal cord. [MYEL- + -OID.]

my·e·lo·ma (mī′ə-lō′mə) *n., pl.* **-mas** or **-mata** (-mə-tə). A malignant tumor of the bone marrow. [New Latin : MYEL- + -OMA.] —**my·e·lo·ma·toid** (mī′ə-lō′mə-toid′) *adj.*

my·i·a·sis (mī′ə-sĭs, mī-ī′ə-sĭs) *n.* Also **my·a·sis** (mī′ə-sĭs). *Pathology.* Infestation of human tissue by fly maggots or a disease resulting from it. [New Latin : Greek *muia, mua,* fly + -IASIS.]

Myk·o·nos (mĭk′ə-nŏs′). *Greek* **Mi·ko·nos** (mē′kô-nôs′). Mountainous Greek island in the Aegean Sea. One of the Cyclades, it is a popular resort.

My·lar (mī′lär′) *n.* A trademark for a thin, strong polyester film.

my·lo·nite (mī′lə-nīt′) *n.* A fine-grained laminated rock formed along zones of extensive crustal dislocation. [Greek *mulōn,* mill, from *mulē, mulos,* mill, millstone + -ITE.]

my·na, my·nah, mi·na (mī′nə) n. Any of various birds of the family Sturnidae, of southeastern Asia. They are blue-black to dark brown with yellow bills. Certain species can mimic human speech. Also called "myna bird." [Hindi mainā, from Sanskrit madana.]

myn·heer (mīn-hâr′, -hîr′) n. 1. Often **Mynheer**. The Dutch title of courtesy and respect equivalent to the English sir or Mr. 2. Informal. A Dutchman. [Dutch mynheer, obsolete variant of mijnheer, "my lord" : mijn, my, from Middle Dutch mijni + heer, lord, sir, master, from Middle Dutch.]

myo–, my– prefix. Indicates muscle; for example, **myograph, myasthenia**. [New Latin, from Greek mus, muscle.]

my·o·car·di·al infarction (mī′ō-kär′dē-əl) n. Death of a section of heart muscle that occurs when its blood supply is obstructed by coronary thrombosis, characterized by severe pain in the chest.

my·o·car·di·o·graph (mī′ō-kär′dē-ə-grăf′, -gräf′) n. An instrument for recording graphically the movement of the heart muscle.

my·o·car·di·tis (mī′ō-kär-dī′tĭs) n. Inflammation of the myocardium. [MYOCARD(IUM) + -ITIS.]

my·o·car·di·um (mī′ō-kär′dē-əm) n. The muscle tissue of the heart. [New Latin : MYO- + Greek kardia, heart.] —**my·o·car′di·al** adj.

my·o·gen·ic (mī′ə-jĕn′ĭk) adj. Also **my·o·ge·net·ic** (mī′ō-jə-nĕt′ĭk). 1. Giving rise to muscle tissue. 2. Of muscular origin. [MYO- + -GENIC.]

my·o·glo·bin (mī′ə-glō′bĭn) n. The form of hemoglobin found in muscle fibers, having a greater affinity for oxygen than blood hemoglobin.

my·o·graph (mī′ə-grăf′, -gräf′) n. An instrument that records muscular contractions by means of tracings. [MYO- + -GRAPH.]

my·ol·o·gy (mī-ŏl′ə-jē) n. The scientific study of muscles. —**my·o·log·ic** (mī′ə-lŏj′ĭk) adj. —**my·ol·o·gist** (mī-ŏl′ə-jĭst) n.

my·o·ma (mī-ō′mə) n., pl. **-mas** or **-mata** (-mə-tə). A benign tumor composed of muscle tissue. [MY(O)- + -OMA.] —**my·om·a·tous** (mī-ŏm′ə-təs, -ō′mə-təs) adj.

my·ope (mī′ōp′) n. One who has myopia. [French, from Late Latin myops, myopic, from Greek muōps. See **myopia**.]

my·o·pi·a (mī-ō′pē-ə) n. 1. Pathology. A visual defect in which distant objects appear blurred because their images are focused in front of the retina rather than on it; nearsightedness. Compare **hyperopia**. 2. Mental shortsightedness or lack of discernment in thinking or planning. [New Latin, from Greek muōpia, from muōps, myopic, "closing or contracting the eyes" : muein, to close + ops, eye.] —**my·op·ic** (mī-ŏp′ĭk, -ō′pĭk) adj. —**my·op′i·cal·ly** adv.

my·o·sin (mī′ə-sĭn) n. A common protein in muscle; with **actin** it forms **actomyosin** (both of which see). [Greek muos, genitive of mus, muscle + -IN.]

myosis. Variant of **miosis**.

my·o·so·tis (mī′ə-sō′tĭs) n. Any plant of the genus Myosotis, such as the forget-me-not. [New Latin, from Latin myosotis, from Greek muosōtis, "mouse-ear" (from its furry leaves) : muos, genitive of mus, mouse + ous (stem ōt-), ear.]

my·o·to·ni·a (mī′ə-tō′nē-ə) n. Pathology. Tonic spasm or temporary muscular rigidity. [MYO- + -TONIA.] —**my·o·ton·ic** (mī′ə-tŏn′ĭk) adj.

Myr·dal (mür′däl′, mûr′-), **(Karl) Gunnar** (1898–). Swedish economist and sociologist. He is chiefly famous for Rich Lands and Poor Lands (1957), Asian Drama (1968), and The Challenge of World Poverty (1970). He was awarded the Nobel Prize in economics in 1974.

myria– prefix. Indicates a very large or countless number; for example, **myriapod**. [Greek murios, countless, and its plural murioi, ten thousand.]

myr·i·ad (mîr′ē-əd) adj. 1. Amounting to a very large, indefinite number. 2. Highly varied. ~n. 1. Archaic. Ten thousand. 2. A vast number; a great multitude. [Late Latin mȳrias (stem mȳriad-), from Greek murias, from murios, countless, and its plural murioi, ten thousand.]

myr·i·a·pod (mîr′ē-ə-pŏd′) n. Any of a class of arthropods, such as the centipedes, having a distinct head, one pair of antennae, and many segments bearing legs. [New Latin myriapoda : MYRIA- -POD.] —**myr·i·ap·o·dan** (mîr′ē-ăp′ə-dən) adj. & n. —**myr·i·ap·o·dous** (mîr′ē-ăp′ə-dəs) adj.

my·ris·tic acid (mə-rĭs′tĭk, mī-) n. An organic compound, $CH_3(CH_2)_{12}COOH$, occurring in animal and vegetable fats. It is used in cosmetics and flavorings. [Greek muristikos, fragrant, from muron, perfume.]

myrmeco– prefix. Indicates ant; for example, **myrmecophile**. [Greek, from murmēx, ant.]

myr·me·col·o·gy (mûr′mĭ-kŏl′ə-jē) n. The study of ants. [MYRMECO- + -LOGY.] —**myr·me·co·log·i·cal** (mûr′mĭ-kə-lŏj′ĭ-kəl) adj. —**myr·me·col·o·gist** (mûr′mĭ-kŏl′ə-jĭst) n.

myr·me·coph·a·gous (mûr′mĭ-kŏf′ə-gəs) adj. 1. Feeding on ants. 2. Adapted for feeding on ants. Said especially of jaws. [MYRMECO- + -PHAGOUS.]

myr·me·co·phile (mûr′mĭ-kə-fīl′) n. Any organism that habitually shares the nest of an ant colony. [MYRMECO- + -PHILE.] —**myr·me·coph·i·lous** (mûr′mĭ-kŏf′ə-ləs) adj. —**myr·me·coph·i·ly** (mûr′mĭ-kŏf′ə-lē) n.

myr·mi·don (mûr′mə-dŏn′, -dən) n. A faithful follower who carries out orders without question. [After MYRMIDON.]

Myr·mi·don (mûr′mə-dŏn′, -dən) n. One of a legendary Greek warrior people of ancient Thessaly who followed their king, Achilles, on the expedition against Troy.

my·rob·a·lan (mī-rŏb′ə-lən, mə-) n. 1. A tree, Prunus cerasifera, native to Asia, bearing edible red or yellow fruit. Also called "cherry plum." 2. A tree, the **Indian almond** (see). 3. The fruit of either of these trees. [Old French mirobolan, from Latin, from Greek murobalanos : muron, perfume, unguent + balanos, acorn, date.]

My·ron (mī′rən) (fl. 5th century B.C.). Greek sculptor. He worked in bronze, sculpting animals and athletes in action. His works, however, have disappeared and are known only through descriptions by ancient writers and two marble copies made during Roman times. His Discus Thrower is an especially powerful work.

myrrh (mûr) n. 1. An aromatic gum resin obtained from several trees and shrubs of the genus Commiphora, of India, Arabia, and eastern Africa. It is used in perfume and incense and was one of the gifts of the Magi to the infant Jesus. 2. Any shrub or tree that exudes such a gum resin. 3. A plant, **sweet cicely** (see). [Middle English myrre, Old English myrrha, from Common Germanic murra (unattested), from Latin myrrha, from Greek murrha, perhaps from Semitic, akin to Hebrew murr.]

myr·tle (mûr′tl) n. 1. Any of several evergreen shrubs or trees of the genus Myrtus; especially, M. communis, an aromatic shrub native to the Mediterranean region. 2. Any of various other plants or shrubs, such as the **crape myrtle** and the **bog myrtle** (both of which see). 3. A plant, the **periwinkle** (see). [Middle English mirtille, from Old French, from Medieval Latin myrtillus, diminutive of Latin myrtus, from Greek murtos†.]

my·self (mī-sĕlf′) pron. A specialized form of the first person singular pronoun. It is used: 1. As a reflexive pronoun, forming the direct or indirect object of a verb or the object of a preposition: hurt myself; give myself time; talk to myself. 2. For emphasis after I: I myself wasn't certain. 3. As an emphasizing substitute: Myself in debt, I could offer her no assistance. 4. Used as an indication of one's real, normal, or healthy condition or identity: I have not been myself lately. [Middle English miself, alteration of meself, Old English mē selfum (dative), mē selfne (accusative) : mē, me + selfum, selfne, dative and accusative of self, SELF.]

Usage: Myself is often heard in everyday speech as part of a compound subject or object, especially in some regional speech: She asked Jane and myself to go to the meeting. But the usage has attracted criticism, and in formal speech and in writing the basic form of the pronoun should be used: She asked Jane and me to go to the meeting.

my·so·pho·bi·a (mī′sō-fō′bē-ə) n. A pathological fear of dirt, contamination, or feces. [New Latin : Greek musos, uncleanness, defilement + -PHOBIA.] —**my·so·pho·bic** adj.

Mysore. See **Karnataka**.

mys·ta·gogue (mĭs′tə-gôg′, -gŏg′) n. 1. In Mediterranean mystery religions, one who prepared candidates for initiation into the mysteries. 2. A teacher of religious mysteries; a hierophant. 3. One who holds or spreads mystical doctrines. [Old French, from Latin mystagogus, from Greek mustagōgos : mustēs, an initiate (see **mystery**) + agōgos, leader, from agein, to lead.] —**mys·ta·gog·ic** (mĭs′tə-gŏj′ĭk) adj. —**mys·ta·go·gy** (mĭs′tə-gō′jē) n.

mys·te·ri·ous (mĭ-stîr′ē-əs) adj. 1. Full of mystery; difficult to explain or account for; of obscure origin: a mysterious light in the sky. 2. Beyond human understanding. Used especially in religious contexts: the mysterious love of God. 3. Implying a mystery. 4. Enigmatic in manner: She was given to mysterious silences. [Old French mystérieux, from mystère, mystery, from Latin mystērium, MYSTERY (riddle).] —**mys·te·ri·ous·ly** adv. —**mys·te·ri·ous·ness** n.

mys·ter·y¹ (mĭs′tə-rē) n., pl. **-ies.** 1. Anything that arouses curiosity because it is unexplained, inexplicable, or secret. 2. The quality or air of being unexplained, secret, or unknown. 3. A piece of fiction dealing with a mystery, especially a puzzling crime. 4. The behavior of someone given to secrecy and intrigue: "He professed to despise all mystery . . . either in a prince or a minister" (Jonathan Swift). 5. Theology. A religious truth divinely revealed and unknowable through reason. 6. a. A Christian rite, such as the Eucharist. b. Often **mysteries**. The elements of the Eucharist. 7. Any of 15 incidents in the lives of Christ and the Virgin Mary as commemorated in the 15 divisions of the rosary and considered as subjects of meditation. 8. A mystery play. 9. Often **mysteries**. a. Among some ancient Mediterranean peoples, any of certain cults and secret rites to which only initiates were admitted. b. The secrets of Freemasonry. [Middle English misterie, mysterie, from Latin mystērium, from Greek mustērion, "secret rites," from mustēs, one initiated into secret rites, from muein, to initiate, from muein, to close the eyes or mouth, hence to keep secret (as in religious initiation).]

mystery² n., pl. **-ies.** Archaic. A trade or occupation: "The invention of man has been sharpening and improving the mystery of murder" (Edmund Burke). [Middle English mysterie, misterie, from Late Latin misterium, variant (by association with mystērium, secret rites, mystery) of Latin ministerium, service, work, occupation, from minister, servant.]

mystery play n. A medieval drama based on episodes in the life of Christ. Compare **miracle play**. [Old French mistere, mystere, from Latin mystērium, religious symbol, MYSTERY.]

mystery tour n. Chiefly British. A pleasurable excursion, such as a bus trip or train journey, to an unknown destination.

mys·tic (mĭs′tĭk) adj. 1. Of or pertaining to the religious mysteries of Greece and Rome or to other occult rites. 2. Mysteriously symbolic; inspiring a sense of mystery and wonder. 3. Mystical. ~n. One who practices or believes in mysticism or a specified form of mysticism. [Middle English mistik, from Latin mysticus, from

Greek *mustikos*, from *mustēs*, an initiated person. See **mystery**[1].]

mys·ti·cal (mĭs′tĭ-kəl) *adj.* **1.** Characteristic of mystics or of the nature of mysticism. **2.** Believing in or practicing mysticism. **3.** Mysterious; enigmatic; symbolic. **4.** *Theology.* **a.** Of a nature or import that by virtue of its divinity surpasses understanding: *the mystical vision of God.* **b.** Spiritually symbolic: *a mystical emblem of the Trinity.* —**mys·ti·cal·ly** *adv.* —**mys·ti·cal·ness** *n.*

mys·ti·cete (mĭs′tə-sēt′) *n.* The **whalebone whale** *(see).* [New Latin *mysticetus,* from Greek *mustikētos,* some kind of whale, supposedly a corruption of *ho mus to kētos,* "the mouse, the whale," "that whale (that is called) the mouse" (the semantic development is obscure) : *mus,* mouse + *kētos,* whale (see **cetacean**).]

mys·ti·cism (mĭs′tə-sĭz′əm) *n.* **1. a.** A spiritual discipline aiming at union with the divine through deep meditation or trancelike contemplation. **b.** The experience of such communion as described by mystics. **2.** Any belief in the existence of realities beyond perceptual or intellectual apprehension but central to being and directly accessible by intuition. —**mys·ti·cist** *n. & adj.*

mys·ti·fi·ca·tion (mĭs′tə-fĭ-kā′shən) *n.* **1.** The act or an instance of deliberately or willfully making something obscure or mysterious. **2.** The fact or condition of being mystified; bafflement.

mys·ti·fy (mĭs′tə-fī′) *tr.v.* **-fied, -fying, -fies. 1.** To awe or perplex; bewilder. **2.** To make obscure or difficult to comprehend. —See Synonyms at **puzzle.** [French *mystifier,* irregularly from *mystère,* mystery, from Latin *mystērium,* MYSTERY.] —**mys·ti·fi·er** *n.* —**mys·ti·fy·ing·ly** *adv.*

mys·tique (mĭ-stēk′) *n.* **1.** An attitude of mystical veneration conferring upon an occupation, person, or thing an awesome and mythical status; the special cult of anything: *the mystique of the cowboy.* **2.** A mystical or philosophical conception used as a guide, especially for a doctrine or cult: *Hegelian mystique.* **3.** A rarefied quality that sets a person or thing apart and apparently beyond the understanding of an outsider. [French, from adjective, "mystic," from Latin *mysticus,* MYSTIC.]

myth (mĭth) *n.* **1. a.** A traditional story originating in a preliterate society, dealing with supernatural beings, ancestors, or heroes that serve as primordial types in a primitive view of the world. **b.** A body of such stories told among a given people; a mythology: *in Norse myth.* **c.** All such stories collectively. **2.** Any real or fictional story, recurring theme, or character type that appeals to the consciousness of a people by embodying its cultural ideals or by expressing commonly felt emotions: *the Oedipal myth; the myth of the golden age.* **3.** An allegorical story. **4.** Any of the fictions or half-truths forming part of the ideology of a society; a notion based more on tradition or convenience than on fact: *the myth of male superiority.* **5.** Any fictitious or imaginary story, explanation, person, or thing. [New Latin *mythus,* from Late Latin *mythos,* tale, myth, from Greek *muthos*†.]

myth. mythological; mythology.

myth·i·cal (mĭth′ĭ-kəl) *adj.* Also **myth·ic** (mĭth′ĭk). **1.** Having the nature of a myth. **2.** Existing only in myth: *the mythical unicorn.* **3.** Imaginary; fictitious; fancied. —**myth·i·cal·ly** *adv.*

myth·i·cize (mĭth′ə-sīz′) *tr.v.* **-cized, -cizing, -cizes. 1.** To turn (a person or event) into myth. **2.** To interpret as a myth. —**myth·i·cism** *n.* —**myth·i·ciz·er, myth·i·cist** *n.*

myth·mak·er (mĭth′mā′kər) *n.* **1.** One who creates a myth. **2.** One who produces false stories or doctrines, especially as propaganda: *combating the inventions of the mythmakers.* —**myth·mak·ing** *n. & adj.*

my·thog·ra·pher (mĭ-thŏg′rə-fər) *n.* A recorder or narrator of myths. [Greek *muthographos* : MYTH + -GRAPHER.]

my·thoi. Plural of **mythos.**

mythol. mythological; mythology.

myth·o·log·i·cal (mĭth′ə-lŏj′ĭ-kəl) *adj.* Also **myth·o·log·ic** (-lŏj′ĭk). *Abbr.* **myth., mythol. 1.** Of, pertaining to, or celebrated in mythology. **2.** Fabulous; imaginary; mythical. **3.** Mythmaking. —**myth·o·log·i·cal·ly** *adv.*

my·thol·o·gist (mĭ-thŏl′ə-jĭst) *n.* **1.** A student of mythology. **2.** A writer of myths.

my·thol·o·gize (mĭ-thŏl′ə-jīz′) *v.* **-gized, -gizing, -gizes.** —*tr.* To convert into myth; mythicize. —*intr.* **1.** To construct or relate a myth. **2.** To interpret or write about myths or mythology. —**my·thol·o·giz·er** *n.*

my·thol·o·gy (mĭ-thŏl′ə-jē) *n., pl.* **-gies.** *Abbr.* **myth., mythol. 1. a.** A collection of myths, especially about the origin and history of a people and their deities, ancestors, and heroes. **b.** A body of myths, especially mistaken beliefs, concerning some individual, event, or institution. **2.** The field of scholarship dealing with the collection and study of myths. [French *mythologie,* from Late Latin *mythologia,* from Greek *muthologia* : *muthos,* MYTH + *-logia,* -LOGY.]

myth·o·ma·ni·a (mĭth′ə-mā′nē-ə, -mān′yə) *n.* A compulsion to embroider the truth, exaggerate, or tell lies. [MYTH + -MANIA.] —**myth·o·ma·ni·ac** (mĭth′ə-mā′nē-ăk′) *n. & adj.*

myth·o·pe·ic, myth·o·pe·ic (mĭth′ə-pē′ĭk) *adj.* Productive of or creating myths; mythmaking. [Greek *muthopoios,* mythmaker, from *muthopoiein,* to make a myth : *muthos,* MYTH + *poiein,* to make, create.] —**myth·o·poe·ia** (mĭth′ə-pē′ə), **myth·o·po·e·sis** (mĭth′ə-pō-ē′sĭs) *n.*

my·thos (mī′thŏs′, mĭth′ŏs′) *n., pl.* **mythoi** (mī′thoi′, mĭth′oi′). **1.** Myth. **2.** Mythology. **3.** The pattern of basic values and historical experiences of a people, characteristically transmitted through the arts. **4.** A deliberately fostered cult; a mystique. [Greek *muthos*†, MYTH.]

Myt·i·le·ne (mĭt′ə-lē′nē). *Modern Greek* **Mit·i·li·ni.** Ancient port on the island of Lesbos in Greece.

myx·e·de·ma, myx·oe·de·ma (mĭk′sə-dē′mə) *n.* A disease caused by decreased activity of the thyroid gland in adults and characterized by dry skin, swellings around the lips and nose, mental deterioration, and a subnormal basal metabolic rate. [MYX(O) + EDEMA.] —**myx·e·dem·a·tous** (mĭk′sə-dĕm′ə-təs, -dē′mə-təs), **myx·e·dem·ic** (-dĕm′ĭk, -dē′mĭk) *adj.*

myxo-, myx– *prefix.* Indicates mucus or mucuslike material; for example, *myxomycete, myxoma, myxocyte.* [New Latin, from Greek *muxa,* mucus, slime.]

myx·o·cyte (mĭk′sə-sīt′) *n.* A cell found in mucous tissue. [MYXO- + -CYTE.]

myx·o·ma (mĭk-sō′mə) *n., pl.* **-mas** or **-mata** (-mə-tə). A benign tumor composed of connective tissue and mucous elements. [New Latin : MYX(O)- + -OMA.] —**myx·om·a·tous** (mĭk-sŏm′ə-təs, -sō′mə-təs) *adj.*

myx·o·ma·to·sis (mĭk-sō′mə-tō′sĭs) *n., pl.* **-ses** (-sēz′). A highly infectious, usually fatal viral disease of rabbits characterized by many skin tumors similar to myxomas. [New Latin : MYXOMA + -OSIS.]

myx·o·my·cete (mĭk′sō-mī-sēt′, -mī′sēt′) *n.* A **slime mold** *(see).* [New Latin *Myxomycetes* (class) : MYXO- + -MYCETE.]

myx·o·vi·rus (mĭk′sō-vī′rəs) *n.* Any of a group of RNA-containing viruses that cause such diseases as influenza and mumps. [MYXO- + VIRUS.]

n, N (ĕn) *n., pl.* **n's** or **N's. 1.** The 14th letter of the modern English alphabet. See feature at **alphabet. 2.** Any of the speech sounds represented by this letter. **3.** The 14th in a series; 13th when *J* is omitted.

n, N, n., N. *Note:* As an abbreviation or symbol, *n* may be a small or a capital letter, with or without a period. Established forms or those generally preferred precede the definition. When no form is given, all four forms are in general use in that sense. **1. N** Avogadro number. **2. n.** born. [Latin *nātus*] **3. n, N** *Printing.* en. **4. n** nano-. **5. n., N.** *Grammar.* neuter. **6. n.** neutron. **7. N** neutron number. **8. N** newton. **9. N** The symbol for the element nitrogen. **10. n, N, n-** *Chemistry.* normal; normality. **11.** north; northern. **12. n.** note. **13. n.** noun. **14. N.** November. **15. n.** number. **16. n** *Mathematics.* The symbol for an indefinite number. **17. n.** *Commerce.* net. **18. N** *Chess.* knight.

Na The symbol for the element sodium. [Latin *natrium*.]

N.A. North America.

NAACP, N.A.A.C.P. National Association for the Advancement of Colored People.

nab (năb) *tr.v.* **nabbed, nabbing, nabs.** *Slang.* **1.** To catch in the act of wrongdoing; arrest. **2.** To grab; snatch. [Variant of dialectal *nap*, to seize, probably from Scandinavian; akin to KIDNAP.]

Nab·a·tae·an, Nab·a·te·an (năb'ə-tē'ən) *n.* **1.** A member of a northwestern Arab people whose kingdom, centered on Petra, flourished from the 4th century B.C. to the 1st century A.D. **2.** The Aramaic dialect of this people. **—Nab·a·tae·an** *adj.*

nab·la (năb'lə) *n. Mathematics.* Del *(see).*

na·bob (nā'bŏb') *n.* **1.** A governor in India under the Mogul Empire. **2.** In the 18th century, an Englishman who returned from India having acquired a fortune. **3.** A man of wealth and prominence. [Portuguese *nababo*, from Urdu, NAWAB.] **—na·bob·er·y, na·bob·ism** *n.*

Na·bo·kov (nə-bô'kəf, nä'bə-kôf'), **Vladimir** (1899–1977). Russian-born U.S. novelist. He is best known for his novel *Lolita* (1958). His later novels include *Pale Fire* (1962) and *Ada* (1969).

na·celle (nə-sĕl') *n.* A separate streamlined enclosure on some aircraft for sheltering the crew or cargo or housing an engine. [French, "small boat," from Late Latin *nāvicella*, diminutive of *nāvis*, ship.]

na·cho (nä'chō') *n.* A small, often triangular piece of tortilla topped with cheese or chili-pepper sauce and broiled. [Possibly from Spanish, flat-nosed.]

na·cre (nā'kər) *n.* Mother-of-pearl *(see).* [French, from Old Italian *naccara*, mother-of-pearl, from Arabic *naqqārah*, shell.]

na·cre·ous (nā'krē-əs) *adj.* **1.** Consisting of mother-of-pearl. **2.** Like mother-of-pearl; pearly.

NAD *n. Biochemistry.* A coenzyme that carries hydrogen atoms in electron-transfer reactions. [Nicotinamide *a*denine *d*inucleotide.]

Na·dar (nä-där'), pseudonym of Gaspard Félix Tournachon (1820–1910). French photographer. Known during his lifetime as a novelist and caricaturist, he is best remembered as a pioneer of photography. He took aerial photographs (1858) from a balloon.

Na-De·ne, Na-Déné (nä-dā'nĕ) *n.* A phylum of North American Indian languages that includes Athapascan, Haida, and Tlingit. [Coined by E. Sapir : Haida *na*, "to dwell," "house" + Athapascan *dene* (unattested), "people."]

Na·der (nā'dər), **Ralph** (1934–). U.S. lawyer. A pioneer in the field of consumer protection, he founded the Center for the Study of Responsive Law (1969).

NADH *n. Biochemistry.* NAD chemically reduced by the addition of hydrogen.

na·dir (nā'dər, nā'dîr') *n.* **1.** A point on the celestial sphere diametrically opposite the zenith. **2.** The point or time of deepest depression, greatest misfortune, or the like; the lowest point. [Middle English, from Old French, from Arabic *nazīr as-samt* : *nazīr*, opposite + *as-samt*, the ZENITH.]

NADP *n. Biochemistry.* A coenzyme similar in action to NAD. [Nicotinamide *a*denine *d*inucleotide *p*hosphate.]

nae (nā) *adj. Scottish.* No.
~*adv. Scottish.* Not.

naevus. Variant of **nevus.**

nag¹ (năg) *v.* **nagged, nagging, nags.** —*tr.* **1.** To pester or annoy by constant scolding, complaining, or urging. **2.** To torment with anxiety, discomfort, or doubt: *nagged by worries.* —*intr.* **1.** To scold, complain, or find fault constantly. **2.** To be a continuing source of discomfort, anxiety, or annoyance. Often followed by *at: The problem nagged at his mind.* —See Synonyms at **scold.**
~*n.* A person who habitually nags. [British (chiefly Northern) dialectal *nag, naeg,* to bite, worry at, nag, from Old Norse *gnaga,* to bite.] **—nag·ger** *n.* **—nag·ging·ly** *adv.*

nag² *n.* **1. a.** An old or worn-out horse. **b.** *Slang.* Any horse, especially a racehorse, regarded with contempt. **2.** *Archaic.* A small saddle horse or pony. [Middle English *nagge†.*]

na·ga·na, n'ga·na (nə-gä'nə) *n.* An often fatal disease of African livestock transmitted by the bite of the tsetse or other flies. [Zulu *u-nakane.*]

Na·ga·sa·ki (nä'gə-sä'kē). A port in western Kyushu, Japan. The city was devastated (August 1945) by an atomic bomb at the end of World War II. Rebuilt, it is now a shipbuilding and steel-making center.

na·gor (nä'gôr') *n.* The **reedbuck** *(see).* [French, name arbitrarily invented by Buffon, based on earlier *nanguer.*]

Nagy (nŏj), **Imre** (1896–1958). Hungarian politician. Taken prisoner in World War I by the Russians, he later became a Soviet citizen, and when Hungary was overrun by the U.S.S.R., he was installed as a member of the new government. While prime minister (1953–55), he implemented agrarian reforms. In the uprising of 1956 he was seized by Russian troops and later executed.

Na·hua·tl (nä'wät'l) *n., pl.* **-tls** or collectively **Nahuatl. 1.** A member of a group of Mexican and Central American Indian tribes, including the Aztecs. **2.** The Uto-Aztecan language of the Nahuatl. [Spanish, from Nahuatl, singular of *Nahua,* the Nahuatl people.] **—Na·hua·tl** *adj.*

Na·hum¹ (nā'həm, nā'əm). A Hebrew prophet of the 7th century B.C. who predicted the fall of Nineveh.

Nahum² *n.* The book of the Old Testament containing the prophecies of Nahum.

nai·ad (nā'əd, -ăd', nī'-) *n., pl.* **-ades** (-ə-dēz') or **-ads. 1.** *Greek Mythology.* Any of the nymphs living in and presiding over brooks, springs, and fountains. **2.** The aquatic nymph of certain insects, such as the mayfly. **3.** An aquatic plant of the genus *Naias.* [Greek *Naias* (stem *Naiad-*), from *naein,* to flow.]

naif, naïf. Variants of **naive.**

nail (nāl) *n.* **1.** A slim piece of metal, pointed at one end and usually having a flat head at the other, hammered into wood or other materials as a fastener. **2. a.** A fingernail or toenail. **b.** A claw or talon. **3.** Anything resembling a nail in shape, sharpness, or use. **4.** A former measure of length for cloth, equal to 2¼ inches. **—hard as nails. 1.** Callous; harsh; pitiless. **2.** In rugged physical condition; tough. **—hit the nail on the head.** To express the sense of something exactly and concisely. **—on the nail.** *Informal.* Immediately; without any delay: *paid cash on the nail.*
~*tr.v.* **nailed, nailing, nails. 1.** To fasten, join, or attach with or as if with nails. **2.** To cover or shut by fastening with nails. Often used with *down* or *up: nail up a window.* **3.** To keep fixed, motionless, or intent: *Fear nailed him to his seat; eyes nailed to the stage.* **4.** To secure or make sure of, especially by prompt action or concentrated effort; clinch. Often used with *down: nail down the facts.* **5.** To bind to an agreement, promise, or the like. Often used with *down: tried to nail her down to a date.* **6.** *Informal.* To detect and expose; trap: *nailed him in a lie.* **7.** *Informal.* To strike or bring down, especially with something shot or hurled: *nail a bird in flight.* **8.** *Informal.* To stop and seize; catch: *The police nailed him.* [Middle English *nail,* Old English *nægl.*] **—nail·er** *n.*

nail-bit·ing (nāl'bī'tĭng) *n.* Biting of the fingernails, usually as a sign of nervousness or as a habit.
~*adj.* Causing anxiety or a feeling of suspense: *a nail-biting climax.*

nail·brush (nāl'brŭsh') *n.* A small brush with short, stiff bristles for cleaning the fingernails.

nail file *n.* A small, flat metal file, or piece of emery board, used for shaping the fingernails.

nail fold *n.* A keratinous material overlapping the base of a fingernail or toenail as a circular fold; a cuticle.

nail·head (nāl′hĕd′) *n.* **1.** The broadened or flattened, often circular, end of a nail opposite the point. **2.** An ornamental device resembling the head of a nail.

nail polish *n.* A clear or colored cosmetic lacquer applied to the fingernails or toenails. Also called "nail enamel."

nail scissors *pl.n.* Small scissors with short, curved blades for trimming and shaping fingernails or toenails.

nail set *n.* A tool for driving a nail so that its head is below or flush with the surface. Also called "nail punch."

nain·sook (nān′sŏok′) *n.* A soft, light cotton material, often with a woven stripe. [Hindi *nainsukh,* "pleasure to the eye" : *nain,* eye + *sukh,* pleasure.]

Nai·paul (nī′pôl), **Vidiadhar Surajprasad** (1932-). West Indian novelist. His novels and reportage concentrate on the subtly destructive effects of Western culture on the Third World, as in *A Bend in the River* (1979).

nai·ra (nī′rə) *n., pl.* **naira.** The basic monetary unit of Nigeria, equal to 100 kobo. See feature at **currency.** [Alteration of NIGERIA.]

Nairn (nârn). Also **Nairn·shire** (-shîr′, -shər). Former county in northeastern Scotland, since 1975 part of Highland Region. Nairn was its county town.

Nai·ro·bi (nī-rō′bē). The capital of Kenya. Founded (1899) on the Mombasa-Uganda railway, it lies in Kenya's eastern highlands. Nairobi is a major industrial and commercial center and is also one of Africa's chief tourist centers, attracting visitors to the Nairobi National Park, a wildlife preserve on the city's outskirts.

na·ive, na·ïve (nä-ēv′) *adj.* Also **na·if, na·ïf** (nä-ēf′). **1. a.** Lacking worldliness and sophistication; artless; inexperienced. **b.** Simple and credulous as a child; ingenuous. **2.** Lacking critical ability or analytical insight; not subtle or learned: *"This extravagance of metaphors, with its naïve bombast"* (H.L. Mencken). **3.** Using unsophisticated or primitive techniques, especially in art; untrained. **4.** Not previously exposed to particular experiences, conditions, or information. Said, for example, of a subject in a psychology experiment who has not taken part in one before.
~*n.* Also **na·if, na·ïf.** A naive person. [French, feminine of *naif,* from Old French, ingenuous, natural, from Latin *nātīvus,* NATIVE.]
—**na·ive·ly** *adv.* —**na·ive·ness** *n.*
    Synonyms: *artless, guileless, ingenuous, innocent, natural, simple, unaffected, unsophisticated.*

na·ive·té, na·ïve·té (nä′ēv-tā′) *n.* Also **na·ive·ty, na·ïve·ty** (nä-ēv′tē), *pl.* **-ties. 1.** The quality of being naive; natural simplicity or artlessness; ingenuousness. **2.** A naive statement or action. [French, ingenuousness, from *naif,* NAIVE.]

na·ked (nā′kĭd) *adj.* **1.** Without clothing or covering on the body; nude. **2.** Without covering; especially, without the usual covering: *a naked flame; a naked sword.* **3.** Devoid of vegetation, trees, or foliage: *"Beneath them the earth was naked of grass"* (William Styron). **4.** Without addition, concealment, disguise, or embellishment: *the naked truth; naked aggression.* **5.** Stripped or bare of something specified; destitute. Used with *of: a room naked of furniture.* **6.** Inadequately armed or protected; defenseless; vulnerable: *naked before his enemies.* **7.** *Botany.* **a.** Not encased in ovaries. Said of seeds. **b.** Unprotected by scales. Said of buds. **c.** Lacking a perianth. Said of flowers. **d.** Without leaves or pubescence. Said of branches or stalks. **8.** Lacking protective covering such as scales, fur, feathers, or a shell. **9.** *Physics.* Designating a quark flavor, especially charm or bottom, which is present in an elementary particle unaccompanied by its antiparticle. **10.** Unsupported or uncorroborated by authority, evidence, or proof. Chiefly used in legal contexts. [Middle English *naked,* Old English *nacod,* from Germanic.] —**na·ked·ly** *adv.* —**na·ked·ness** *n.*

naked eye *n.* The eye unassisted by an optical instrument.

naked option *n.* A securities option sold by a trader who does not own the optioned stock.

naked singularity *n.* *Astronomy.* A **singularity** (*see*) that is not surrounded by an event horizon, regarded as a point at which matter may be created and ejected.

na·led (nā′lĕd′) *n.* A nonpersistent chemical, $C_4H_7O_4PBr_2Cl_2$, used as an insecticide against crop pests and mosquitoes. [Origin unknown.]

nal·ox·one (năl′ək-sōn′) *n.* A drug, $C_{19}H_{21}NO_{4,}$ used in the form of its hydrochloride as an antagonist to narcotic drugs, such as morphine. [N-AL(LYL) + (HYDR)OX(Y) + -ONE.]

Na·ma·qua·land (nə-mä′kwə-lănd′). Large, relatively arid northwestern district of South Africa, noted for its spectacular display of spring wildflowers following the winter rains.

Na·math (nā′məth), **Joseph William,** known as **"Joe"** (1943-). U.S. football player. He led the New York Jets, formerly a mediocre AFL team, to a brilliant Super Bowl victory in 1969.

nam·by-pam·by (năm′bē-păm′bē) *adj.* **1.** Weakly sentimental; insipidly affected. **2.** Lacking vigor or decisiveness; spineless.
~*n., pl.* **namby-pambies. 1.** Insipid, mawkish language or style. **2.** A namby-pamby person. [From *Namby-Pamby,* a satire on the sentimental pastorals of Ambrose Philips (c. 1675-1749), by Henry Carey (died 1743).]

name (nām) *n.* **1.** A word or words by which any person or thing is designated and distinguished from others. **2.** A word or words used to describe or evaluate, often disparagingly: *Names will never hurt*

me. **3.** Verbal representation or repute as opposed to effective reality: *a democracy in name, a police state in fact.* **4. a.** General reputation: *a bad name.* **b.** A distinguished reputation; renown. **5.** *Informal.* A famous or outstanding person: *a name in state politics.* —**in the name of. 1.** On behalf of; for the sake of. **2.** By the authority of: *in the name of the law.* —**know someone by name.** To have heard of someone but not met him or her. —**name names.** To reveal the identity of people involved in criminal or otherwise dubious activities. —**the name of the game.** The essential or indispensable part or quality of some activity: *If you're job-hunting, persistence is the name of the game.* —**to one's name.** Belonging to one: *not a penny to his name.* —**under the name of.** Using as a name.
~*tr.v.* **named, naming, names. 1.** To give a name to: *They named the baby James.* **2.** To identify by name; call by the right name: *name the Stuart kings of England.* **3.** To mention, specify, or cite by name: *He was named in the report.* **4.** To call by some epithet: *He named them all cowards.* **5.** To nominate or appoint to some duty, office, or honor. **6.** To specify or fix: *name a price.* **7.** *British.* To indicate that (a Member of Parliament) has behaved in an unacceptable way and is required to leave the chamber. Used of the Speaker of the House of Commons. —**name the day.** To arrange to get married and, usually, specify a date for the ceremony. —**you name it.** *Informal.* Whatever you can think, say, or imagine: *Writing, acting, selling encyclopedias —you name it, he's done it.*
~*adj. Informal.* Well-known by name: *a name brand of baby food.* [Middle English *name,* Old English *nama.*] —**nam·a·ble, name·a·ble** *adj.*

name-call·ing (nām′kô′lĭng) *n.* Verbal abuse; insulting language. —**name-call·er** *n.*

name day *n.* *Roman Catholic Church.* The feast day of the saint after whom one is named.

name-drop (nām′drŏp′) *intr.v.* **-dropped, -dropping, -drops.** To show off by implying that one is on friendly terms with famous people, especially by mentioning their names in a familiar fashion. —**name-drop·per** *n.* —**name-drop·ping** *n.*

name·less (nām′lĭs) *adj.* **1.** Having or bearing no name: *nameless stars.* **2.** Unknown by name; obscure: *the nameless dead.* **3. a.** Not designated by name; anonymous: *a nameless benefactor.* **b.** Intentionally left unnamed: *a certain person who shall be nameless.* **4.** Inexpressible; indescribable: *nameless horror.* —**name·less·ly** *adv.* —**name·less·ness** *n.*

name·ly (nām′lē) *adv.* That is to say; to wit; specifically.

name·plate (nām′plāt′) *n.* A small sign, such as a brass plate, fastened to a door or wall of an office or building and showing the occupant's name and sometimes profession.

name·sake (nām′sāk′) *n.* A person having the same name as another, especially one named after another. [From *for the name's sake.*]

name·tape (nām′tāp′) *n.* A small strip of cloth sewn or glued to a garment and showing the owner's name.

Na·mib Desert (nä′mĭb′). Extremely dry region running along the coast of Namibia, considered by some authorities to be the oldest of the world's present desert regions. It is noted for its population of plant and animal species adapted to survive in desert conditions.

Na·mib·i·a (nə-mĭb′ē-ə). Formerly **South-West Af·ri·ca** (ăf′rĭ-kə). Country of southwestern Africa. Rich in minerals, including diamonds, uranium, and copper, it is sparsely populated and mostly too dry for crops. The Namib Desert along the Atlantic is one of the harshest in the world, and the Kalahari Desert covers much of

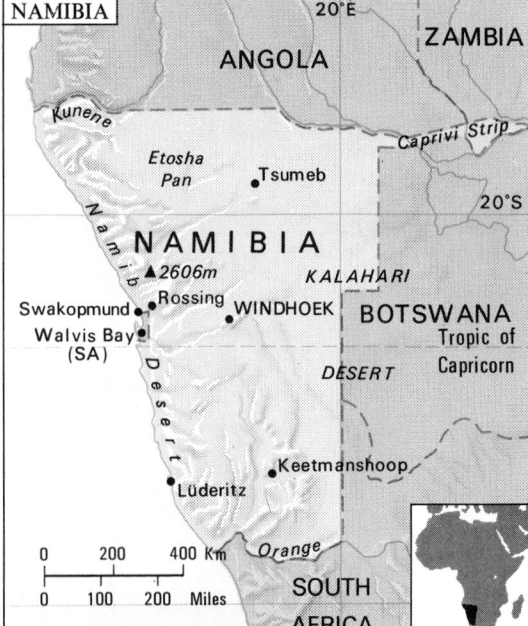

the northeast. A German protectorate after 1884, it was occupied by South Africa (1915), which governed it under a League of Nations mandate (1920–46), but refused to accept the U.N. trusteeship that replaced it. In 1971 the International Court of Justice ruled South Africa's presence in Namibia to be illegal. The South-West African People's Organization (SWAPO), recognized by the U.N. as the lawful representative of the Namibian people, began guerrilla activity in 1966. Area, 826,269 square kilometers (318,252 square miles). Population, 1,200,000. Capital, Windhoek. —**Na·mib·i·an** *adj. & n.*

Na·mur (nə-mŏŏr'). *Flemish* **Na·men** (nä'mən). The capital of Namur province, south-central Belgium. Because of its strategic position at the confluence of the Sambre and Meuse rivers, it has been fought over many times. It was severely damaged in World Wars I and II.

nan·a (năn'ə) *n.* **1.** A nurse or nursemaid. **2.** A grandmother. [From baby talk.]

Na·nak (nä'nək) (1469–1538). Indian spiritual teacher and first Sikh guru. Under Islamic influence he broke away from orthodox Hinduism to preach a monotheistic faith.

nance (năns) *n.* An effeminate man, especially a homosexual. Used derogatorily. [From *Nancy* (woman's name).]

Nan·cy (năn'sē, nän-sē'). The capital of Meurthe-et-Moselle department, northeastern France. The former seat of the dukes of Lorraine, it passed to France in 1766. The city is still the economic and cultural focus of Lorraine. Its products include iron and steel, machinery, and textiles.

NAND gate (nănd) *n. Computer Science.* A logic gate in which the output signal is high if any one or more of the input signals is low, and low if all the input signals are high. Also called "NAND circuit." [N(OT) + AND (that is, the reverse of an AND GATE).]

nan·din (năn'dĭn) *n.* An evergreen Asiatic shrub, *Nandina domestica*, having compound leaves, small white flowers that grow in a branching cluster, and bright-red berries. [New Latin *Nandina* (genus name), from Japanese *nanten*, "southern sky."]

Nan·jing or **Nan·ching** (năn'jĭng'). Also **Nan·king** (năn'kĭng'). The capital of Jiangsu province, eastern China. On the Chang Jiang (Yangtze River), it is a former national capital (1368–1421, 1928–37). The Japanese took the city in 1937, and it was here that they formally surrendered to the Chinese (1945). It is an important cultural and industrial center.

nan·keen (năn-kēn') *n.* Also **nan·kin** (năn-kēn', -kĭn'). **1.** A sturdy yellow or buff cotton cloth. **2.** A yellow or buff color. **3. nankeens.** Trousers made of nankeen cloth, worn especially in the 19th century. **4. Nankeen.** A kind of Chinese porcelain with a blue-and-white pattern. [Originally imported from NANJING.]

nan·ny (năn'ē) *n., pl.* **-nies.** *Chiefly British.* A woman employed to look after a child or children in a family; a children's nurse. [Alteration of NANA.]

nanny goat *n., pl.* **nanny goats.** A female goat. Compare **billy goat.** [From *Nanny*, pet form for *Ann*.]

nano– *prefix. Abbr.* **n** Indicates: **1.** Extreme smallness; for example, **nanoplankton.** **2.** One-billionth of a specified unit; for example, **nanosecond.** [Latin *nānus*, dwarf, from Greek *nan(n)os.*]

nan·o·gram (năn'ə-grăm') *n.* One-billionth (10⁻⁹) of a gram.

nan·o·me·ter (năn'ə-mē'tər) *n.* One billionth (10⁻⁹) of a meter.

nan·o·plank·ton, nan·no·plank·ton (năn'ō-plăngk'tən) *n.* Aquatic animal and plant organisms of microscopic size comprising the smallest of the **plankton** *(see).*

nan·o·sec·ond (năn'ə-sĕk'ənd) *n.* One billionth (10⁻⁹) of a second.

Nan·sen (năn'sən, nän'-), **Fridtjof** (1861–1930). Norwegian explorer and politician. He helped negotiate Norwegian independence (1905) and was awarded the Nobel Peace Prize (1922) for his League of Nations work for refugees and Russian famine relief. He took part in polar and North Atlantic expeditions (1882–1914).

Nansen bottle *n.* An ocean-water sampling bottle with spring-loaded valves at both ends that are closed at an appropriate depth by a messenger device sent down the wire connecting the bottle to the surface. [After Fridtjof NANSEN.]

Nansen passport *n.* A passport issued after World War I by the League of Nations to individuals who were stateless. [After Fridtjof NANSEN who, as High Commissioner for Refugees, introduced it.]

Nantes (nănts; *French* näNt). City and capital of Loire-Atlantique department, in western France on the Loire River. It is an important industrial and shipping center.

Nantes, Edict of *n.* A decree issued in 1598 by Henry IV of France, granting restricted religious and civil liberties to Huguenots; revoked in 1685 by Louis XIV.

Nan·tuck·et (năn-tŭk'ĭt). A resort island off southeastern Massachusetts. It was settled in 1659 and was an Atlantic whaling center until the 1850's.

Naoi·se (nē'sē). *Irish Mythology.* The husband of **Deirdre** *(see).*

Na·o·mi (nā-ō'mē). The mother-in-law of Ruth. Ruth 1:1–4.

nap¹ (năp) *n.* A brief period of sleep, especially during the day. ~*intr.v.* **napped, napping, naps.** **1.** To doze or sleep for a brief period, especially during the day. **2.** *Informal.* To be unaware of imminent danger or trouble; be off guard. Used chiefly in such phrases as *to be caught napping.* [Middle English *nappen*, to doze, Old English *hnappian.*]

nap² *n.* A dense, soft or fuzzy surface on certain textiles or leathers, usually formed by raising fibers from the underlying material. Compare **pile.** ~*tr.v.* **napped, napping, naps.** To form or raise a nap on (fabric or leather). [Middle English *noppe*, from Middle Dutch *noppe.*]

nap³ *n.* **1.** A card game played for money and resembling whist. Also called "napoleon." **2.** A bid in this game, announcing the intention to win the maximum number (five) of tricks in a hand.

na·palm (nā'päm') *n.* **1.** An aluminum soap of various fatty acids that when mixed with gasoline makes a firm jelly used in flame throwers and incendiary bombs. **2.** The jelly so used. **3.** A similar incendiary mixture of polystyrene, benzene, and gasoline. Also called "napalm-B." ~*tr.v.* **napalmed, -palming, -palms.** To bombard with napalm. [*Naphthenic* (see **naphthene**) + *palmitic acid.*]

Na·pa Valley (năp'ə). Area of western California, in a mountainous region crossed by the Napa River. It has been a major wine-producing region since the 1850's.

nape (nāp) *n.* The back of the neck. [Middle English, probably akin to Old Frisian *(hals)knapt*, nape.]

Naph·ta·li¹ (năf'tə-lī'). A son of Jacob. Genesis 30:7, 8.

Naphtali² *n.* A tribe of Israel descended from Naphtali. Numbers 1:15, 43.

naph·tha (năf'thə, năp'-) *n.* **1.** A colorless flammable liquid obtained from crude petroleum and used as a solvent and cleaning fluid and as a raw material for gasoline. **2.** Any of several volatile hydrocarbon liquids derived from coal tar and other materials and used as solvents. **3.** Petroleum. In this sense, not in current technical usage. [Greek *naphtha†.*]

naph·tha·lene (năf'thə-lēn', năp'-) *n.* A white crystalline compound, $C_{10}H_8$, derived from coal tar or petroleum and used to manufacture dyes, moth repellents, explosives, and solvents. [NAPHTHA + *alcohol* + -ENE.]

naph·thene (năf'thĕn', năp'-) *n.* Any of several cycloalkanes and their alkyl derivatives having the general formula C_nH_{2n}, found in various petroleums. [*Naphtha* + -ENE.]

naph·thol (năf'thôl', -thōl', năp'-) *n.* An organic compound, $C_{10}H_7OH$, occurring in two isomeric forms: **1. a.** *alpha-naphthol*, colorless or yellow prisms or powder, used in dyes, organic synthesis, and perfumes. **b.** *beta-naphthol*, white lustrous leaflets or powder, used in dyes, insecticides, and in the manufacture of rubber. [*Naphthalene* + -OL (hydroxyl group).]

naph·thyl (năf'thĭl, năp'-) *n.* Either of two forms of the univalent organic radical $C_{10}H_7$-, derived from naphthalene. [*Naphtha* + -YL.]

Na·pi·er (nā'pē-ər), **John** (1550–1617). Scottish mathematician. He is best known for his discovery of natural logarithms (published 1614) and his work on spherical trigonometry.

Na·pier·i·an logarithm (nə-pîr'ē-ən, nā-) *n.* A **natural logarithm** *(see).*

Na·pier's bones (nā'pē-ərz) *n.* A device consisting of a set of graduated rods formerly used for multiplication and division. [After John NAPIER, who invented the method on which it is based.]

na·pi·form (nā'pə-fôrm') *adj.* Shaped like a turnip. Said of a root. [Latin *nāpus*, turnip (probably of Mediterranean origin) + -FORM.]

nap·kin (năp'kĭn) *n.* **1.** A piece of cloth or absorbent paper, used at table to protect clothes or wipe the lips and fingers. Also called "table napkin." **2.** Any similar cloth or towel. **3.** *Chiefly British.* A diaper. **4.** A **sanitary napkin** *(see).* [Middle English *nappekin*, diminutive of *nappe*, tablecloth, from Old French, from Latin *mappa*, napkin, towel.]

Na·ples (nā'pəlz). *Italian* **Na·po·li** (nä'pō-lē). The capital of Campania, south-central Italy. Founded by Greeks in the 6th century B.C. below Mt. Vesuvius on the Bay of Naples, it became the capital of the kingdom of Naples (1270–1860). Naples is now a major seaport and a cultural, tourist, and industrial center. It suffered severe earthquake damage in 1980.

Naples yellow *n.* **1.** A permanent yellow pigment consisting of lead antimonate. **2.** A similar pigment consisting of zinc oxide mixed with a yellow coloring matter. **3.** The color of either of these pigments. [After NAPLES, where it was originally manufactured.]

na·po·le·on (nə-pō'lē-ən, -pōl'yən) *n.* **1.** A rectangular piece of pastry, iced on top, with crisp, flaky layers filled with custard cream. **2.** A former 20-franc gold coin of France. **3.** A card game, **nap** *(see).* [After NAPOLEON I.]

Na·po·le·on I (nə-pō'lē-ən, -pōl'yən), born Napoléon Bonaparte or Buonaparte (1769–1821). Emperor of the French and king of Italy. His victories as French Revolutionary commander in his time (1796–97) established him as the most brilliant general of his time and as a skilled politician. Following an abortive attempt to conquer Egypt (1798–99), he deposed the Directory and proclaimed himself first consul (1799) and later emperor (1804). His military ascendancy in Europe over the next decade was insufficient to combat the commercial and maritime power of Britain despite his attempted trade embargo, known as the Continental System. After the disastrous Russian campaign (1812–13) an alliance of hostile powers forced him to abdicate (1814). After a brief exile on the island of Elba, he regained power (1815), but was finally defeated at Waterloo and exiled to St. Helena. His grasp of military technique remains unsurpassed, and his codification of laws, the Code Napoléon, still forms the basis of French civil law. —**Na·po·le·on·ic** (nə-pō'lē-ŏn'ĭk) *adj.*

Napoleon III, born Louis Napoléon Bonaparte (1808–73). Emperor of the French (1852–70). The nephew of Napoleon I, he led Bonapartist opposition to Louis Philippe, became president of the Second Republic (1848), and later (1852) proclaimed himself emperor. He instituted reforms and rebuilt Paris. His imperialist adventures in the Crimea (1854–56) and Italy (1859) were successful, but his lack of judgment was shown in the Mexican campaign (1861–67) and culminated in the disastrous Franco-Prussian War and his abdication (1870).

nappe (năp) n. **1.** A sheet of water flowing over a dam or similar structure. **2.** *Geology.* A folded sheetlike formation that has been moved from its site of origin by tectonic forces that caused the folding. **3.** *Geometry.* Either of the two parts into which a cone is divided by the vertex. [French *nappe (d'eau),* sheet (of water), from Old French *nappe,* tablecloth, from Latin *mappa,* napkin, towel.]

nap·py¹ (năp′ē) n., pl. **-pies.** *Chiefly British.* A diaper. [From NAP-KIN.]

nappy² adj. **-pier, -piest.** Having a nap; shaggy; fuzzy.

Na·ra (nä′rä). City of southern Honshu, Japan. The first permanent capital of Japan (710–84), it is a cultural and religious center. Nearby is Mt. Kasuga, the traditional home of the gods.

Nar·bonne (när-bôn′). City of southern France. The first Roman colony in Transalpine Gaul, it was later a port until its harbor silted up in the 14th century. It is the commercial center for a wine-producing area.

narc, nark (närk) n. *Slang.* A law-enforcement officer who deals with crimes concerning illegal drugs; a narcotics agent.

nar·ce·ine (när′sē-ēn′, -ĭn) n. Also **nar·ce·in** (-ĭn). A white crystalline narcotic, $C_{23}H_{27}O_8N\cdot3H_2O$, obtained from opium. [French *narcéine* : Greek *narkē,* numbness + -INE.]

nar·cis·sism (när′sə-sĭz′əm) n. Also **nar·cism** (när′sĭz′əm). **1.** Excessive admiration of oneself. **2.** *Psychoanalysis.* An arresting of development at, or a regression to, the infantile stage of development in which one's own body is the object of erotic interest. [After NARCISSUS.] —**nar·cis·sist** n. —**nar·cis·sis·tic** adj.

nar·cis·sus (när-sĭs′əs) n., pl. **-cissuses** or **-cissi** (-sĭs′ī′, -sĭs′ē). **1.** Any of several widely cultivated plants of the genus *Narcissus,* having narrow, grasslike leaves and usually white or yellow flowers characterized by a cup-shaped or trumpet-shaped central crown. See **daffodil, jonquil, Chinese sacred lily** *(see).* **2. Pheasant's eye** *(see).* [Latin, from Greek *narkissos,* probably of Mediterranean origin.]

Nar·cis·sus (när-sĭs′əs). *Greek Mythology.* A youth who, having spurned the love of Echo, pined away in love for his own reflection in a pool of water and was transformed into the flower that bears his name.

narco- prefix. Indicates: **1.** Numbness, sluggishness, or stupor; for example, **narcolepsy.** **2.** A narcotic drug; for example, **narcotine.** [Greek *narko-,* from *narkoun,* to benumb, from *narkē,* numbness.]

nar·co·a·nal·y·sis (när′kō-ə-năl′ə-sĭs) n. Psychoanalysis conducted while the patient is in a drug-induced drowsy state.

nar·co·lep·sy (när′kə-lĕp′sē) n. *Pathology.* A condition characterized by sudden and uncontrollable attacks of deep sleep for brief periods. [NARCO- + -LEPSY.] —**nar·co·lep·tic** adj. & n.

nar·co·sis (när-kō′sĭs) n. A state of diminished consciousness or complete unconsciousness produced by a drug. Also called "narcotism." [Greek *narkōsis,* a numbing, from *narkoun,* to make numb, from *narkē,* numbness.]

nar·co·syn·the·sis (när′kō-sĭn′thə-sĭs) n. Narcoanalysis directed toward making the patient recall suppressed memories and emotional traumas for later interpretation.

nar·cot·ic (när-kŏt′ĭk) n. **1. a.** Any drug that dulls the senses, induces sleep, and with prolonged use becomes addictive. **b.** Broadly, any illegal drug. **2.** Something that numbs, soothes, or induces a dreamlike or insensitive state.
~adj. **1.** Inducing sleep or stupor. **2.** Of or pertaining to narcotics, their effects, or their use. **3.** Of or pertaining to one addicted to a narcotic drug. [Middle English *narkotike,* from Old French *narcotique* (originally an adjective), from Medieval Latin *narcōticus,* from Greek *narkōtikos,* numbing, narcotic, from *narkoun,* to make numb, from *narkē,* numbness.] —**nar·cot·i·cal·ly** adv.

nar·co·tine (när′kə-tēn′) n. An alkaloid, $C_{22}H_{23}NO_7$, obtained from opium and used to relieve coughing, fever, and spasms. [French : *narcotique,* NARCOT(IC) + -INE.]

nar·co·tism (när′kə-tĭz′əm) n. **1.** Addiction to narcotics such as opium, heroin, or morphine. **2.** A drugged state; narcosis. [French *narcotisme,* from *narcotique,* NARCOTIC.]

nar·co·tize (när′kə-tīz′) tr.v. **-tized, -tizing, -tizes. 1.** To place under the influence of a narcotic. **2.** To lull or induce sleep in. **3.** To dull; deaden. —**nar·co·ti·za·tion** n.

nard (närd) n. **1.** A plant, **spikenard** *(see).* **2.** A balm made from spikenard. **3.** Any of several plants of the genus *Valeriana* or related plants whose aromatic roots have been used in medicine. [Middle English *narde,* from Old French *narde,* from Latin *nardus,* from Greek *nardos,* from Semitic.]

nar·doo (när′dōō) n. An Australian cloverlike fern, *Marsilea drummondii,* found growing in swamps. [From a native language.]

nar·es (nâr′ēz) pl.n. Singular **naris** (nâr′ĭs). The openings in the nasal cavities of vertebrates; nostrils. [Latin *nārēs,* plural of *nāris,* nostril.] —**nar·i·al** (nâr′ē-əl) adj.

nar·ghi·le, nar·gi·le (när′gə-lě′, -lě′) n. An Oriental tobacco pipe, **hookah** *(see).* [French *narguilé,* from Persian *nārgīleh,* a pipe (whose bowl was originally made of coconut shell), from *nārgīl,* coconut, from Sanskrit *nārikela†,* coconut.]

nark¹ (närk) n. *British Slang.* An informer, especially to the police; stool pigeon. [Thieves' slang, from Romany *nāk,* nose.]

nark². Variant of **narc.**

Nar·ra·gan·set, Nar·ra·gan·sett (năr′ə-găn′sĭt) n., pl. **-sets** or collectively **Narraganset, -setts** or collectively **Narragansett. 1.** A

member of an Algonquian-speaking North American Indian people that formerly lived in the area of Rhode Island. **2.** The language of this tribe. —**Nar·ra·gan·set** adj.

Narragansett Bay. An inlet of the Atlantic Ocean in Rhode Island. It is known for its resorts and fishing centers.

nar·rate (năr′āt′, nă-rāt′) v. **-rated, -rating, -rates.** —tr. To give an oral or written account of; tell (a story). —intr. To give an account or description; especially, to supply a running commentary for a film, television program, or the like. [Latin *narrāre,* from *gnārus,* knowing.] —**nar·ra·tor, nar·rat·er** n.

nar·ra·tion (nă-rā′shən) n. **1.** The act or an instance of narrating. **2.** Something narrated; a narrative.

nar·ra·tive (năr′ə-tĭv) n. **1.** A story or description of actual or fictional events; a narrated account. **2.** The part of a piece of writing that is concerned with the narration of events. **3.** The act, technique, or process of narrating.
~adj. **1.** Consisting of or characterized by the telling of a story or the description of events without analysis: *narrative poetry.* **2.** Of or pertaining to narration: *narrative skill.* —**nar·ra·tive·ly** adv.

nar·row (năr′ō) adj. **-rower, -rowest. 1.** Of small or limited width, especially in comparison with length: *a narrow corridor.* **2. a.** Limited in area; cramped; confined. **b.** Limited in scope; restricted: *the inquiry's narrow terms of reference.* **3.** Lacking flexibility; rigid in adherence to an idea or way: *narrow principles; a narrow outlook.* **4.** Straitened; pinched: *narrow circumstances.* **5.** Barely sufficient or successful; precarious: *a narrow margin of victory.* **6.** Painstakingly thorough or attentive: *a narrow scrutiny.* **7.** *Regional.* Miserly; stingy. **8.** *Phonetics.* Tense.
~v. **narrowed, -rowing, -rows.** —tr. **1.** To make narrow or narrower; reduce in width or extent. **2.** To limit or restrict. Often used with *down: That narrowed down the possibilities.* —intr. To grow less in width or extent; contract.
~n. **1.** A narrow place or part, such as a pass through mountains or a valley. **2. narrows.** A narrow body of water, especially one that connects two larger ones. [Middle English *nearwe, narow,* Old English *nearu,* from Germanic.] —**nar·row·ly** adv. —**nar·row·ness** n.

narrow gauge n. A distance between the rails of a railroad track that is less than the standard width of 56½ inches. —**nar·row-gauge** adj.

nar·row-mind·ed (năr′ō-mīn′dĭd) adj. Lacking breadth of view, tolerance, or sympathy; bigoted; prejudiced. —**nar·row-mind·ed·ly** adv. —**nar·row-mind·ed·ness** n.

Nar·rows, the (năr′ōz). Strait of southeastern New York State, between Brooklyn and Staten Island. It connects Upper and Lower New York Bay.

nar·thex (när′thĕks′) n. **1.** A portico or lobby of an early Christian church or basilica, separated from the nave by a railing or screen. **2.** Any church entrance hall leading to the nave. [Medieval Greek *narthēx,* "enclosure," originally "casket," "box" (made of hollow stems of giant fennel), from Greek *narthēx,* giant fennel.]

Nar·vik (när′vĭk). Ice-free port and tourist center in northern Norway, within the Arctic Circle.

nar·whal (när′wəl) n. An arctic aquatic mammal, *Monodon monoceros,* having a spotted pelt and (in the male) a spiral tusk several feet long. It is hunted for ivory and oil. [Dutch *narwal,* from Danish *narhval,* from Old Norse *nāhvalr,* "corpse-whale" (so called because with its whitish color it resembles a floating corpse) : *nār,* corpse + *hvalr,* whale.]

nar·y (nâr′ē) adj. *Regional.* Not one; no. Usually followed by *a* or *an: Nary a person remained.* [From *ne'er a,* "never a."]

NASA (năs′ə) National Aeronautics and Space Administration.

na·sal (nā′zəl) adj. **1.** Of or pertaining to the nose. **2.** *Phonetics.* Formed by lowering the soft palate so that most of the air is exhaled through the nose rather than the mouth, as in sounding *m, n,* and *ng* in English or *un, on,* or *en* in French. **3.** Characterized by or resembling sounds so formed: *a nasal whine.*
~n. **1.** *Phonetics.* A nasal sound. **2.** A nasal part or bone. **3.** The nosepiece of a helmet. [French, from New Latin *nāsālis,* from Latin *nāsus,* nose.] —**na·sal·i·ty** (nā-zăl′ə-tē) n. —**na·sal·ly** adv.

nasal index n. The ratio of the width to the length of the nose, multiplied by 100. It is used in anthropological measurements.

na·sal·ize (nā′zəl-īz′) v. **-ized, -izing, -izes.** —tr. To render nasal. —intr. To produce nasal sounds. —**na·sal·i·za·tion** n.

nas·cent (năs′ənt, nā′sənt) adj. **1.** Coming into existence; in the process of emerging. **2.** *Chemistry.* Designating or pertaining to a substance that is produced in a highly active form in the reaction mixture: *nascent hydrogen.* [Latin *nāscēns* (stem *nāscent-*), present participle of *nāscī,* to be born.] —**nas·cence, nas·cen·cy** n.

nase·ber·ry (nāz′bĕr′ē, -bə-rē) n., pl. **-ries.** A tropical tree, the **sapodilla** *(see),* or its fruit. [Spanish *néspera* (influenced by BERRY), from Latin *mespila,* MEDLAR.]

Nash (năsh), **John** (1752–1835). English architect. He designed much of the area around Regent's Park, as well as Regent Street and Brighton Pavilion, and remodeled Buckingham Palace. He is also responsible for many of England's finest country houses.

Nash, Ogden (1902–71). U.S. humorist. A regular contributor to the *New Yorker,* he is best known for his epigrammatic verse.

Nashe (năsh), **Thomas** (1567–1601). English writer. His witty, colorful works include several anti-Puritan pamphlets, a lost dramatic collaboration with Ben Jonson, *The Isle of Dogs* (1597), for which he was imprisoned, and possibly the best of all Elizabethan narrative works, *The Unfortunate Traveller* (1594).

Nash·ville (năsh′vĭl′). The capital of Tennessee, on the Cumberland

River. It is an important communications, industrial, and commercial center, with publishing and music industries, and is the home of country-and-western music.

na·si·on (nā′zē-ŏn′) *n.* The point at the top of the nose marking the boundary between the nasal bone and the frontal bone of the forehead. [French, from Latin *nāsus,* nose.]

naso– *prefix.* Indicates nose; for example, **nasofrontal.** [New Latin, from Latin *nāsus,* nose.]

na·so·fron·tal (nā′zō-frŭn′təl) *adj.* Of or pertaining to the nasal and frontal bones.

na·so·phar·ynx (nā′zō-făr′ĭngks) *n., pl.* **-pharynges** (-fə-rĭn′jēz) or **-ynxes.** The portion of the pharynx directly behind the nasal cavity and above the soft palate. **—na·so·pha·ryn·ge·al** (nā′zō-fə-rĭn′jē-əl, -jəl, -făr′ĭn-jē′əl) *adj.*

Nas·sau¹ (năs′ô′). The capital of the Bahamas, on New Providence Island. Tourism, fundamental to the country's economy, is centered here.

Nas·sau² (năs′ô′, nä′sou′). Former duchy in West Germany, now incorporated in Hesse and Rhineland Palatinate. Its capital was Wiesbaden. The area is fertile and known for its wines and mineral springs. Branches of the house of Nassau still rule the Netherlands and Luxembourg.

Nas·ser (nä′sər, năs′ər), **Gamal Abdul** (1918–70). Egyptian soldier and statesman. He was president of Egypt (1956–58) and of the United Arab Republic (1958–70). After the war with Israel (1948–49), he led the revolt (1952) under Gen. Muhammad Neguib that deposed King Farouk. In 1954 Nasser supplanted Neguib as premier. His nationalization of the Suez Canal (1956) provoked Anglo-French intervention and precipitated an international crisis. He subsequently formed close ties with the U.S.S.R. Despite unsuccessful attempts to form an Arab federation, he did much for Egyptian prosperity.

Nast (năst), **Thomas** (1840–1902). U.S. cartoonist and illustrator. His acidly brilliant caricatures in *Harper's Weekly* led to the downfall of the Tweed Ring in New York City. Nast established the donkey and elephant as symbols for the Democratic and Republican parties. He also drew a classic image of Santa Claus for Clement Clarke Moore's poem "A Visit from St. Nicholas."

nas·tic (năs′tĭk) *adj.* Of, pertaining to, or characterized by a tendency in plants to move in a direction determined by an internal stimulus, such as growth movement, rather than an external stimulus. [From Greek *nastos,* pressed down, from *nassein†,* to press.]

na·stur·tium (nə-stûr′shəm, nă-) *n.* Any of various trailing plants of the genus *Tropaeolum,* having flowers with five broad petals that are usually yellow, orange, or red. Their round pungent leaves and seeds are sometimes used as seasoning. [Latin *nāsturtium,* a kind of cress, originally *nāsitortium* (unattested), "nose-pain" (so called because cress plants such as mustard when eaten cause burning sensations in the nose) : *nāsus,* nose + *tort-,* past stem of *torquēre,* to twist, torture.]

nas·ty (năs′tē) *adj.* **-tier, -tiest. 1.** Disgusting to see, smell, or touch; filthy; foul. **2.** Morally offensive; indecent. **3.** Malicious; spiteful; mean: *said nasty things about us.* **4.** Causing discomfort or annoyance; unpleasant; disagreeable: *nasty weather.* **5.** Painful or dangerous; grave: *a nasty accident.* [Middle English, *nasty, naxty,* probably akin to Dutch *nestig,* earlier *nistich,* perhaps meaning "fouled like a dirty bird's nest," from *nest,* nest.] **—nas·ti·ly** *adv.* **—nas·ti·ness** *n.*

-nasty *suffix.* Indicates a specified kind of nastic response or change; for example, **epinasty.** [From NASTIC.]

nat. 1. national. **2.** native. **3.** natural.

na·tal (nāt′l) *adj.* **1.** Of or relating to birth; accompanying birth: *natal injuries.* **2.** Of or pertaining to the time or place of one's birth: *a natal star.* [Middle English, from Latin *nātālis,* from *nāscī* (past participle *nātus),* to be born.]

Na·tal (nə-tăl′, -täl′). The smallest province of South Africa. Inland uplands rise to the Drakensberg Mts. Industries, dominated by sugar refining, are concentrated around Durban and the capital, Pietermaritzburg. A Boer republic (1838), Natal was annexed by the British (1843). It absorbed Zululand in 1897.

na·tal·i·ty (nā-tăl′ə-tē, nə-) *n., pl.* **-ties.** Birthrate (*see*).

Natal plum *n.* A South African shrub, *Carissa grandiflora,* having forked spines, white flowers, and an edible scarlet berry. [From NATAL, South Africa.]

na·tant (nā′tənt) *adj.* Swimming or floating; especially, floating on the surface. Said, for example, of an aquatic plant. [Latin *natāns* (stem *natant-),* from *natāre,* to swim.]

na·ta·tion (nā-tā′shən, nə-) *n.* The action or art of swimming. [Latin *natātiō* (stem *natātiōn-),* from *natāre,* to swim.]

na·ta·to·ry (nā′tə-tôr′ē-əl, -tōr′ē) *adj.* Also **na·ta·to·ry** (-tôr′ē, -tōr′ē). Of, pertaining to, or adapted for swimming. [Late Latin *natātōrius,* from *natāre,* to swim.]

na·ta·to·ri·um (nā′tə-tôr′ē-əm, -tōr′-, năt′ə-) *n., pl.* **-toriums** or **-toria** (-tôr′ē-ə, -tōr′-). An indoor swimming pool. [Late Latin, from Latin *natāre,* to swim.]

natch (năch) *adv. Slang.* Of course; naturally. [Shortening and alteration of NATURALLY.]

Natch·ez¹ (năch′ĭz) *n., pl.* **Natchez. 1.** A member of a Muskhogean-speaking North American Indian people that formerly lived in the area of Mississippi. **2.** The language of this tribe. **—Natch·ez** *adj.*

Natchez². City of southwestern Mississippi, on bluffs above the Mississippi River. It is the trade, shipping, and processing center for a cotton, livestock, and timber region. Oil and natural gas are found in the area.

na·tes (nā′tēz) *pl.n. Anatomy.* The buttocks. [Latin *natēs,* plural of *natis,* buttock.]

Na·than (nā′thən). A prophet during the reigns of David and Solomon. II Samuel 12:1–15.

Nathan, George Jean (1882–1958). U.S. editor and drama critic. With H.L. Mencken, he founded the *American Mercury* in 1924. During his long career, Nathan was perhaps the most widely read drama critic in the United States.

Na·than·ael (nə-thăn′yəl). One of the 12 Apostles, usually identified as **Bartholomew** (*see*).

nathe·less (nāth′lĭs, năth′-) *adv.* Also **nath·less** (năth′-). *Archaic.* Nevertheless; notwithstanding. [Middle English *nathles,* Old English *nā thē lǣs,* "not less by that" : *nā,* NO + *thē,* by that, instrumental case of *sē,* that + *lǣs,* LESS.]

Na·tick (nā′tĭk) *n.* A dialect based on English and the language of the Massachuset tribe. [Origin unknown.]

na·tion (nā′shən) *n.* **1.** A people, usually the inhabitants of a specific territory, who share common customs, origins, history, and frequently language or related languages. **2. a.** An aggregation of people organized under a single government; a country. **b.** The entire people of a country, as distinct from any of the various groups and classes composing it. Preceded by *the: The nation responded in a wonderful show of solidarity.* **3.** The government of a sovereign state: *The Western nations have reacted favorably to the proposal.* **4. a.** A federation or tribe, as of North American Indians. **b.** The territory occupied by such a federation or tribe. **—the nations.** In Biblical use, the gentile or heathen peoples: "*And the Lord shall scatter you among the nations*" (Deuteronomy 4:27). [Middle English *nacioun,* from Old French *nacion,* from Latin *nātiō* (stem *nātiōn-),* "race," "breed," from *nāscī* (past participle *nātus),* to be born.]

Usage: nation, state, country, people, race. Nation primarily signifies a political body rather than a physical territory—the citizens united under one independent government, without close regard for their origins. *State* even more specifically indicates political organization, generally on a sovereign basis and pertaining to a well-defined area. *Country,* in strict usage, is a geographical term signifying the territory of one nation, but it is often used in the extended sense of *nation. People,* in this context, signifies a group united over a long period by common cultural and social ties, although not necessarily by racial and national bonds. *Race* refers to those recognizable physical traits, stemming from common ancestry, that succeeding generations have in common.

Na·tion (nā′shən), **Carry** or **Carrie Amelia Moore** (1846–1911). U.S. social reformer. A fanatic believer in the temperance movement, she began in the 1890's a series of hatchet-wielding attacks against saloons in Kansas and later in large cities across the country. She often paid her fines for disturbing the peace by selling souvenir hatchets.

na·tion·al (năsh′ən-əl, năsh′nəl) *adj. Abbr.* **nat., natl. 1.** Of, pertaining to, or belonging to a nation as an organized whole. **2.** Characteristic of or peculiar to the people of a nation: *a national trait.* **3.** Occurring, distributed, or recognized nationwide: *a national figure.* **4.** Of or maintained by the government of a nation: *a national park.* **5.** Devoted to one's own nation or its interests; patriotic. **~***n.* **1.** A citizen of a particular nation. **2.** *Usually* **nationals.** A competition involving participants from all parts of a nation. **—na·tion·al·ly** *adv.*

national anthem *n.* A hymn or song adopted by a nation and sung or played as an expression of national pride and unity, as on state occasions.

National Assembly *n.* A national legislative body in various countries; especially, the first of the Revolutionary assemblies in France (1789–91).

national bank *n.* **1.** A bank associated with national finances and usually owned or controlled by a government. **2.** In the United States, any in a system of federally chartered, privately owned banks, each required by law to be an investing member of its district Federal Reserve Bank and to be insured by the Federal Deposit Insurance Corporation.

national debt *n.* The total amount of money borrowed by a national government.

national forest *n.* A large expanse of forest that is protected by a government and that may be harvested only under controlled conditions.

National Front *n. Abbr.* **N.F.** In Britain, an extreme right-wing political party known for its racist policies.

National Guard *n.* The military reserve units controlled by each state of the United States, equipped by the federal government and subject to the call of either the federal or the state government.

National Health Service *n. Abbr.* **NHS.** A comprehensive service providing medical care in the United Kingdom, financed by national insurance and from taxation, in operation since 1948.

national income *n.* The total net value of all goods and services produced within a nation over a specific period of time, usually a year, and representing the sum of wages, profits, rents, interest, and pension payments to residents of the nation. Compare **gross national product.**

national insurance *n.* In the United Kingdom, the insurance system used to help finance state welfare provisions such as pensions and medical care through regular contributions required from employers and employees.

na·tion·al·ism (năsh′ən-əl-ĭz′əm, năsh′nəl-) *n.* **1.** Pride in and devotion to one's own nation and its interests, especially when excessive. **2.** A strong sense of national identity, often associated with aspirations for national independence or separatism. **—na·tion·al·ist** *n.* **—na·tion·al·is·tic** *adj.* **—na·tion·al·is·ti·cal·ly** *adv.*

na·tion·al·i·ty (năsh′ə-năl′ə-tē) *n., pl.* **-ties. 1.** The status of belonging to a particular nation by origin, birth, or naturalization. **2.** A people having common origins or traditions and constituting or being considered to constitute a nation. **3.** Existence as a politically autonomous entity; the status of a nation. **4.** National character. **5.** A nation or country: *people of different nationalities.*

na·tion·al·ize (năsh′ən-əl-īz′, năsh′nəl-) *tr.v.* **-ized, -izing, -izes. 1.** To convert (a sector of industry, agriculture, commerce, or public service, together with associated means of production) from private to governmental ownership and control. **2.** To make national in character. **3.** To accept as a citizen or national; naturalize. **—na·tion·al·i·za·tion** *n.*

national monument *n.* A natural landmark or a structure or site of historic interest set aside by a national government and maintained for enjoyment or study by the public.

national park *n.* A tract of land declared public property and administered by a government-appointed body to preserve its natural character and wildlife.

national seashore *n.* A seacoast recreational area that is protected and maintained by the federal government.

national service *n.* In various countries, compulsory military service for a limited period of time.

National Socialism *n.* **Nazism** *(see).*

na·tion·hood (nā′shən-ho͝od′) *n.* The condition of being a nation.

Nation of Islam *n.* An organization of black Americans who follow the religious practices of Islam and propose segregation of blacks and whites with a view to the establishment of a new black nation. Members are known as Black Muslims.

na·tion-state (nā′shən-stāt′) *n.* A state whose people have a sense of national identity based on a common cultural heritage.

na·tion·wide (nā′shən-wīd′) *adj.* Throughout a whole nation. **—na·tion·wide** *adv.*

na·tive (nā′tĭv) *adj. Abbr.* **nat. 1.** Belonging to one by nature; inborn; innate: *native ability.* **2.** Belonging by birth or origin to a specified country or place: *a native Englishman.* **3.** One's own because of the place or circumstances of one's birth: *our native land.* **4.** Originating, growing, or produced in a certain place; indigenous as opposed to exotic or foreign: *native products.* **5.** Belonging to or characteristic of the original inhabitants of a particular place, especially those of primitive culture: *native customs of Borneo.* **6.** Occurring in nature pure or uncombined with other substances. Said of metallic or other solid elements: *native copper.* **7.** In a natural state; unaffected by artificial influences: *native beauty.* **8.** *Archaic.* Closely related, as by birth or race.

~*n. Abbr.* **nat. 1.** One who is connected with a place by birth or origin. **2.** An established local resident, as distinguished from a visitor or newcomer. **3.** One who is an original inhabitant of a place; especially, one belonging to a people of primitive culture originally occupying a country, as distinguished from an invader or settler. **4.** Something, especially an animal or a plant, that originated in a particular place. [Middle English *natif,* from Old French, from Latin *nātīvus,* born, native, from *nāscī* (past participle *nātus*), to be born.] **—na·tive·ly** *adv.* **—na·tive·ness** *n.*

Native American *n.* An American Indian.

Usage: The term *Indian* has always been a misnomer for the first inhabitants of the Western Hemisphere. Many now prefer the designation *Native American,* but usage varies according to tribe and region. In Canada and Alaska, in particular, *American Indian* is still preferred as suggesting a useful distinction from Eskimos. *Native American* has also been used to refer to Hawaiians of Polynesian descent.

na·tive-born (nā′tĭv-bôrn′) *adj.* Belonging to a place by birth.

native speaker *n.* One who speaks a particular language as a first language.

na·tiv·ism (nā′tĭv-ĭz′əm) *n.* **1.** A sociopolitical policy, especially in the United States in the 19th century, favoring the interests of native inhabitants over those of immigrants. **2.** *Philosophy.* The doctrine that the mind produces ideas that are not derived from external sources; the doctrine of innate ideas. **3.** The reestablishment or perpetuation of native cultural traits, especially in opposition to acculturation. **—na·tiv·ist** *n.* **—na·tiv·is·tic** *adj.*

na·tiv·i·ty (nə-tĭv′ə-tē, nā-) *n., pl.* **-ties. 1.** Birth, especially the place, conditions, or circumstances of one's birth. **2. Nativity. a.** The birth of Jesus. **b.** A representation, such as a painting or a play, of this. **c.** Christmas. **3.** *Astrology.* A horoscope based on the time of one's birth. [Middle English *nativite,* from Old French, from Latin *nātīvitās,* from *nātīvus,* born, NATIVE.]

nativity play *n.* A play, especially a short one performed by schoolchildren, based on the gospel accounts of the birth of Christ.

natl. national.

NATO (nā′tō) North Atlantic Treaty Organization.

na·tro·lite (nā′trə-līt′) *n.* A white zeolite mineral, $Na_2(Al_2Si_3O_{10})\cdot 2H_2O$. [German *Natrolith* : NATRO(N) + -LITE.]

na·tron (nā′trŏn′, -trən) *n.* A mineral form of hydrous sodium carbonate, $Na_2CO_3\cdot 10H_2O$, often found crystallized with other salts. [French, from Spanish *natrón,* from Arabic *naṭrūn,* from Greek *nitron,* NITER.]

nat·ter (năt′ər) *intr.v.* **-tered, -tering, -ters.** *Chiefly British.* To talk idly about trivial subjects; chatter; gossip. [19th century (Scottish): imitative.]

nat·ter·jack (năt′ər-jăk′) *n.* A European toad, *Bufo calamita,* with short legs and a yellow stripe down its back. It inflates its body when alarmed. [Perhaps from NATTER (referring to its loud croak) + JACK (chap).]

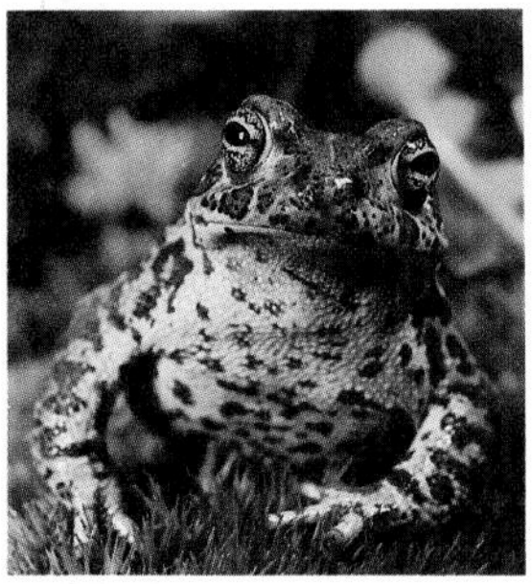

natterjack *The natterjack toad,* Bufo calamita, *a native of western Europe, adopts a peculiar stance when threatened, with its body inflated, front legs tucked under, and hind legs extended on tiptoe.*

nat·ty (năt′ē) *adj.* **-tier, -tiest.** Neat, trim, and smart; spruce; dapper. [Perhaps variant of obsolete *netty,* from Middle English *net,* trim, neat, from Old French *net,* NEAT (tidy).]

nat·u·ral (năch′ər-əl, năch′rəl) *adj. Abbr.* **nat. 1.** Present in or produced by nature; not artificial or man-made: *a natural reservoir; natural dyes.* **2.** Pertaining to or concerning physical reality, as opposed to a spiritual, intellectual, or imagined reality: *natural science.* **3.** Pertaining to or produced solely by nature or the expected order of things: *a natural event; died of natural causes.* **4. a.** Pertaining to or resulting from inherent nature; not acquired empirically: *Self-preservation is an instinct natural to man.* **b.** Distinguished by innate qualities or aptitudes: *a natural leader; a natural athlete.* **5.** Free from affectation or artificiality; spontaneous: *Despite her fame, she retains a natural manner.* **6.** Not altered, treated, or disguised: *natural coloring; a natural landscape.* **7.** Consonant with particular circumstances; expected and accepted: *She saw children as a natural consequence of marriage.* **8.** Based on or in accordance with a supposedly innate sense of what is right and fair: *natural justice.* **9.** Faithfully representing nature or life. **10.** In a primitive, unenlightened, or unregenerate state. **11. a.** Illegitimate: *The king had two natural sons.* **b.** Related by blood, as distinguished from adoption: *They were his natural parents.* **12.** *Music.* **a.** Neither sharp nor flat: *a natural note.* **b.** Having no sharps or flats: *a natural key.* —See Synonyms at **naive, normal, sincere.**

~*n.* **1.** One seeming to have the qualifications necessary for success or likely to be especially suited by reason of talent or abilities: *a natural for the job; a baseball natural.* **2.** *Music.* **a.** The sign (♮) placed before a note to cancel a preceding sharp or flat. **b.** A note so affected. **3.** In certain card and dice games, a combination that wins immediately, as seven or eleven on the first cast in craps. [Middle English, from Old French, from Latin *nātūrālis,* from *nātūra,* NATURE.] **—nat·u·ral·ness** *n.*

Usage: There are two ways of forming the opposite of *natural.* The general antonym is *unnatural,* which has a range of applications all to do with being "outside the expected order of things." *Supernatural* and *preternatural* are restricted to contexts where the contrast is between this world and some other miraculous one.

natural childbirth *n.* An approach to childbirth that seeks to avoid the use of anesthesia and surgical intervention and to ensure the psychological and physiological well-being of the mother through preparatory training and education.

natural classification *n.* Classification of animals and plants according to similarities based on supposed descent from a common ancestor.

natural food *n.* Food that contains no additives, such as preservatives or artificial coloring or flavoring.

natural frequency *n. Physics.* The frequency at which a given system will vibrate or oscillate freely.

natural gas *n.* A mixture of hydrocarbon gases found within the earth, often with petroleum deposits, principally methane together with varying quantities of ethane, propane, butane, and other gases. It is used as a fuel and in the manufacture of organic compounds.

natural gender *n.* Gender based upon the actual sex or absence of sex (for neuter) of the referent of a noun. Compare **common gender, grammatical gender.**

natural history *n.* **1.** The study of natural objects and organisms, their origins, evolution, interrelationships, and description. **2.** The natural phenomena of a particular region or time.

nat·u·ral·ism (năch′ər-ə-lĭz′əm, năch′rə-) *n.* **1.** Conformity to nature; factual or realistic representation, especially: **a.** In literature, the practice of and belief in presenting a detailed and lifelike account of the circumstances of human life, rather than a conventionalized, fantastic, or symbolic account. **b.** In the visual arts, the practice of and belief in reproducing subjects as exactly as possible. **c.** A movement or school advocating such a practice or belief. **2.** *Philosophy.* The system of thought holding that all phenomena can be explained in terms of natural causes and laws, without attributing moral, spiritual, or supernatural significance to them. **3.** *Theology.* The doctrine that all religious truths are derived from nature and natural causes and not from revelation. **4.** Conduct or thought prompted by natural desires or instincts.

nat·u·ral·ist (năch′ər-ə-lĭst, năch′rə-) *n.* **1.** One versed in natural history, especially in zoology or botany. **2.** One who believes in and follows the tenets of naturalism.

nat·u·ral·is·tic (năch′ər-ə-lĭs′tĭk, năch′rə-) *adj.* **1.** Imitating or producing the effect or appearance of nature. **2.** Of, pertaining to, or in accordance with the doctrines of naturalism. **3.** Of or pertaining to natural history.

nat·u·ral·ize (năch′ər-ə-līz′, năch′rə-) *v.* **-ized, -izing, -izes.** —*tr.* **1.** To grant full citizenship to (one of foreign birth). **2.** To adopt (something foreign, such as a word or custom) into general use. **3.** To adapt (a plant or animal) to life in a new environment. **4.** To cause to conform to nature; make natural or lifelike. **5.** To explain or account for (a phenomenon) in terms of natural, rather than supernatural, causes. —*intr.* To become naturalized or acclimatized; adapt. —**nat·u·ral·i·za·tion** *n.*

natural language *n.* A human written or spoken language as opposed to a machine language.

natural law *n.* **1.** A law of morality thought to derive from an instinctive sense of right and wrong rather than from the legislation of society. **2.** A law of science that ascribes order and regularity to natural phenomena such as tides.

natural logarithm *n.* *Symbol* **ln** *Mathematics.* A logarithm to the base e (= 2.71828 . . .). For example, in 10 = log$_e$ 10 = 2.30258. Also called "Napierian logarithm."

nat·u·ral·ly (năch′ər-ə-lē, năch′rə-) *adv.* **1.** In a natural manner. **2.** By nature; inherently. **3. a.** As might be expected in the circumstances. **b.** Without a doubt; of course.

natural number *n. Mathematics.* One of the set of positive whole numbers; a positive integer.

natural philosophy *n.* The study of nature and the physical universe, especially studies that led historically to the modern science of physics.

natural resources *pl.n.* Material sources of wealth that occur in a natural state, such as forests or minerals.

natural science *n.* **1.** A science, such as biology, chemistry, or physics, based on the study of the physical world and its phenomena. **2.** These sciences collectively.

natural selection *n.* The phenomenon that individuals possessing characteristics advantageous for survival in a specific environment constitute an increasing proportion of the population in that environment with each succeeding generation. See **Darwinism.**

natural theology *n.* A theology in which knowledge of God is based on reasoning from natural phenomena rather than on divine revelation.

natural varnish *n.* See **varnish** (sense 1c).

natural virtues *pl.n.* The **cardinal virtues** *(see).*

na·ture (nā′chər) *n.* **1.** The intrinsic characteristics and qualities of a person or thing: *the essential nature of poetry.* **2.** The order, disposition, and essence of all entities composing the physical universe. **3.** The physical world, usually the outdoors, including all living things and natural phenomena such as fire, snow, and thunder. **4.** Natural scenery: *gaze upon nature.* **5.** *Often* **Nature.** The forces or processes of the physical world, sometimes personified as a female being: *leave it to Mother Nature.* **6.** The primitive state of existence, untouched and uninfluenced by civilization or artificiality. **7.** *Theology.* Man's natural state, as distinguished from the state of grace. **8.** Kind; type: *something of that nature.* **9.** The aggregate of a person's instincts and preferences. **10. a.** A particular kind of individual character or disposition; temperament: *a sweet nature.* **b.** A person or thing characterized by some particular disposition: *"Strange natures made a brotherhood of ill"* (P.B. Shelley). **11.** The natural or real aspect of a person, place, or thing: *her true nature.* **12.** Generally accepted standards of morality or conduct: *thought homosexuality to be against nature.* **13.** Bodily processes and functions, such as urination. Often used euphemistically in the phrase *a call of nature.* —See Synonyms at **disposition, type.** —**by nature.** Because of natural qualities; inherently: *She is by nature a loving sister.* —**in** (or **of**) **the nature of.** Belonging to the type or category of: *in the nature of an insult.* [Middle English, from Old French, from Latin *nātūra,* nature, "birth," from *nāscī* (past participle *nātus*), to be born.]

nature study *n.* The observation and study of plants, animals, and natural phenomena, usually nontechnical and informal.

nature trail *n.* A trail, as through the woods or along a seashore, usually having the natural features labeled for study.

na·tur·ism (nā′chə-rĭz′əm) *n.* **Nudism** *(see).*

na·tur·op·a·thy (nā′chə-rŏp′ə-thē) *n.* A system of therapy that relies exclusively on natural remedies, such as sunlight, organically grown foods, fresh air, and massage, to treat the sick. [From NATURE + -PATHY] —**na·tur·o·path** (nā′chər-ə-păth′, nə-chŏŏr′-) *n.* —**na·tur·o·path·ic** *adj.*

Nau·cra·tis (nô′krə-tĭs′). Ancient city of Egypt, on the Nile southeast of Alexandria. It was probably the first Greek settlement in Egypt (*c.* 7th century B.C.). The rise of Alexandria and the shifting of the Nile's course led to its decline.

Nau·ga·hyde (nô′gə-hīd′) *n.* A trademark for fabrics coated with vinyl.

naught, nought (nôt) *n.* **1.** Nothing: *All her work was for naught.* **2.** The figure 0; cipher; zero. —**set at naught.** To consider as being of little importance.
~*adj.* Worthless; of no value. [Middle English *nauht,* Old English *nāwiht:* nā, NO + *wiht,* creature, thing.]

naugh·ty (nô′tē) *adj.* **-tier, -tiest. 1.** Disobedient; mischievous. Usually said of a child or a child's misdeeds. **2.** Indecent or suggestive of indecency: *a naughty wink.* **3.** *Archaic.* Wicked; evil. [Middle English *nauhty,* from *nauht,* "worthless," NAUGHT.] —**naugh·ti·ly** *adv.* —**naugh·ti·ness** *n.*

Nau·pli·a (nô′plē-ə). *Greek* **Náv·pli·on** (näf′plē-ŏn′). A seaport and capital of Argolís prefecture, Peloponnese, southeastern Greece. It was the first capital of independent Greece (1830–34).

nau·pli·us (nô′plē-əs) *n., pl.* **-pli·i** (-plē-ī′). *Zoology.* The microscopic, free-swimming larva of certain crustaceans, having an oval body and three pairs of limbs. [Latin, from Greek *nauplios,* sailor, perhaps variant of *nautilos,* sailor, NAUTILUS.]

Na·u·ru (nä-ŏŏ′rŏŏ). Formerly **Pleas·ant Island** (plĕz′ənt). A republic of the central Pacific. Consisting of one coral island, its sole

product is phosphates, reserves of which will run out in *c.* 2000. Area, 21 square kilometers (8 square miles). Population, 7,000. Capital, Yaren. See map at **Pacific Ocean.**

nau·se·a (nô′zē-ə, -zhə, -sē-ə, -shə) *n.* **1.** A stomach disturbance characterized by a feeling of the need to vomit. **2.** Strong aversion; repugnance; disgust. [Latin, from Greek *nausia,* seasickness, from *naus,* ship.]

nau·se·ate (nô′zē-āt′, -zhē-āt′, -sē-āt′, -shē-āt′) *v.* **-ated, -ating, -ates.** —*tr.* **1.** To cause to feel nausea; make queasy. **2.** To cause to feel loathing or disgust; sicken. —*intr.* To feel nausea or queasiness; be queasy. [Latin *nauseāre,* from *nausea,* NAUSEA.] —**nau·se·at·ing·ly** *adv.* —**nau·se·a·tion** *n.*

nau·seous (nô′shəs, nô′zē-əs) *adj.* **1.** Causing nausea; sickening. **2.** Repulsive to the mind or senses; very offensive. **3.** Suffering nausea; nauseated. —**nau·seous·ly** *adv.* —**nau·seous·ness** *n.*

naut. nautical.

nautch (nôch) *n.* A dance form of northern India for girl dancers accompanied by several musicians and sometimes by a singer. [Hindi *nāc,* from Prakrit *nacca,* dance, from Sanskrit *nr̥tya,* from *nr̥tyati,* he dances.] —**nautch** *adj.*

nau·ti·cal (nô′tĭ-kəl) *adj.* *Abbr.* **naut.** Of, pertaining to, or characteristic of ships, shipping, seamen, or navigation. [From Latin *nauticus,* from Greek *nautikos,* from *nautēs,* seaman, from *naus,* ship.] —**nau·ti·cal·ly** *adv.*

Usage: Nautical is a general term pertaining to sailors, ships, and navigation, as in *nautical miles.* Naval now pertains specifically to the personnel and ships of a navy or a military sea force.

nautical mile *n.* *Abbr.* **nm, n.m.** A unit of length used in sea and air navigation: **1.** An international and U.S. unit equal to 1,852 meters (6,076.103 feet). In this sense, also called "air mile." **2.** A British unit equal to 6,080 feet (1,853 meters). In this sense, formerly called "geographic mile." Compare **sea mile.**

nau·ti·loid (nô′tə-loid′) *n.* A mollusk of the subclass Nautiloidea, which includes the nautiluses and numerous extinct species known only as fossils. [From New Latin *Nautiloidea* : NAUTIL(US) + -oidea, from Latin *-oīdēs,* -OID.] —**nau·ti·loid** *adj.*

nau·ti·lus (nô′tə-ləs) *n., pl.* **-luses** or **-li** (-lī′). **1.** Any cephalopod mollusk of the genus *Nautilus,* found in the Indian and Pacific oceans, and having a spiral shell with a series of air-filled chambers. See **chambered nautilus. 2.** The **paper nautilus** *(see).* [Latin, from Greek *nautilos,* sailor, from *naus,* ship.]

nav. 1. naval. **2.** navigable. **3.** navigation.

Nav·a·jo, Nav·a·ho (năv′ə-hō′, nä′və-) *n., pl.* **-jos** or collectively **Navajo, -hos** or collectively **Navaho. 1.** A member of a group of Athapascan-speaking North American Indians occupying an extensive reservation in parts of New Mexico, Arizona, and Utah. **2.** The language of this group. [From Spanish, pueblo.] —**Nav·a·ho** *adj.*

na·val (nā′vəl) *adj.* *Abbr.* **nav. 1.** Of or pertaining to the equipment, operations, personnel, or customs of a navy: *a naval officer.* **2.** Having a navy: *a great naval power.* —See Usage note at **nautical.** [Latin *nāvālis,* from *nāvis,* ship.]

naval architect *n.* One who designs ships. —**naval architecture** *n.*

naval stores *pl.n.* Products such as turpentine or pitch, originally used to caulk the seams of wooden ships.

nav·ar (năv′är′) *n.* A method of air navigation in which traffic in a pilot's vicinity is observed by ground radar and relayed to the pilot's radarscope. [N*avigational* + rad*ar.*]

Na·varre (nə-vär′). *Spanish* **Na·var·ra** (nä-vär′ä). Former kingdom in the Pyrenees in southwestern Europe. Ruled by a Basque dynasty (9th–13th century), it was absorbed by Spain and France (1589). Today, much of it forms the Spanish province of Navarra.

nave[1] (nāv) *n.* The central part of a church, extending from the narthex to the chancel and flanked by aisles. [Medieval Latin *nāvis,* "ship" (referring to the general shape), from Latin.]

nave[2] *n.* The hub of a wheel. [Middle English *nave,* Old English *nafu.*]

na·vel (nā′vəl) *n.* **1.** The mark on the abdomen of mammals where the umbilical cord was attached during gestation; the umbilicus. **2.** A central point; the middle. —**contemplate one's navel.** To indulge in introspection. Used humorously. [Middle English *navel,* Old English *nafela.*]

navel orange *n.* A sweet, usually seedless orange having at its apex a navellike formation enclosing an underdeveloped fruit.

na·vel·wort (nā′vəl-wûrt′) *n.* **1.** A plant, **pennywort** *(see).* **2.** Any plant of the genus *Omphalodes,* having one-sided clusters of usually blue flowers. [From the navellike depression on its leaves.]

na·vic·u·lar (nə-vĭk′yə-lər) *n.* *Anatomy.* **1.** A comma-shaped bone of the wrist. **2.** The concave bone in front of the anklebone on the instep of the foot. Also called "scaphoid."
~*adj.* Shaped like a boat. [Late Latin *nāviculāris,* "boat-shaped," from Latin *nāvicula,* boat, diminutive of *nāvis,* ship.]

nav·i·ga·ble (năv′ə-gə-bəl) *adj.* *Abbr.* **nav. 1.** Sufficiently deep or wide to provide passage for ships or boats: *a navigable river.* **2.** Capable of being steered or guided. Said of vessels, aircraft, or missiles. —**nav·i·ga·bil·i·ty, nav·i·ga·ble·ness** *n.* —**nav·i·ga·bly** *adv.*

nav·i·gate (năv′ə-gāt′) *v.* **-gated, -gating, -gates.** —*tr.* **1.** To plan, record, and control the course and position of (a ship or aircraft). **2.** To follow a planned course on, across, or through: *navigate a stream.* **3.** *Informal.* To direct the course of (someone or something) toward some destination. —*intr.* **1.** To control the course of a ship or aircraft. **2.** To voyage over water in a boat or ship; sail. **3.** *Informal.* **a.** To make one's way. **b.** To walk: *too unsteady on his legs to*

Neanderthal man *An artist's impression shows how archaeologists visualize Neanderthal man, a Stone Age hunter who lived in Europe 35–70,000 years ago. The hunters were named after the site where their skeletal remains were first discovered: the Neander Valley near Düsseldorf in West Germany.*

navigate. [Latin *nāvigāre,* to manage a ship : *nāvis,* ship + *agere,* to drive, conduct.]

nav·i·ga·tion (năv′ə-gā'shən) *n. Abbr.* **nav.** 1. The theory and skill of navigating, especially the charting of a course for a ship or aircraft. 2. The act or practice of navigating. 3. Travel or traffic by vessels, especially commercial shipping. **—nav·i·ga'tion·al** *adj.*

nav·i·ga·tor (năv′ə-gā'tər) *n.* 1. One who navigates, especially: **a.** One who explores by ship. **b.** A crew member who plots the course of a ship or aircraft. 2. A device that directs the course of an aircraft or missile.

Náv·plion. See **Nauplia.**

Nav·ra·ti·lo·va (năv′rə-tə-lō′və), **Martina** (1956–). U.S. tennis player, born in Czechoslovakia. She defected to the United States in 1975. She was the U.S. Open champion in 1983 and 1984 and Wimbledon singles champion in 1978, 1979, 1982, 1983, 1984, 1985, and 1986.

nav·vy (năv′ē) *n., pl.* **-vies.** *British Informal.* A laborer, especially one employed in construction or excavation projects. [Slang shortening of NAVIGATOR, humorously applied to laborers who built the navigation canals of England in the 18th and 19th centuries.]

na·vy (nā′vē) *n., pl.* **-vies.** 1. All of a nation's warships. 2. *Often* **Navy.** A nation's entire military organization for sea warfare and defense, including vessels, personnel, and shore establishments. 3. *Archaic.* A group of ships; a fleet. 4. Navy blue. [Middle English *navie,* from Old French, from Vulgar Latin *nāvia* (unattested), fleet, from Latin *nāvis,* ship.] **—na·vy** *adj.*

navy bean *n.* A variety of kidney bean grown for its nutritious white seeds. [From its former use as a standard provision of the U.S. Navy.]

navy blue *n.* A dark grayish blue. [From the color of the British naval uniform.] **—na·vy-blue** *adj.*

Navy Cross *n.* A decoration awarded by the U.S. Navy for exceptional heroism in action.

navy yard *n.* A dockyard for the construction, repair, equipping, or docking of naval ships.

na·wab (nə-wôb′) *n.* 1. A governor or ruler in India under the Mogul empire. 2. A title given to eminent Muslims in India. [Urdu *nawwāb,* from Arabic *nuwwāb,* originally plural of *nā'ib,* deputy.]

Nax·os (năk′sŏs′, -sôs). The largest island of the Cyclades, in the Aegean Sea, Greece. It was associated, through its wine trade, with Dionysiac cults in ancient times.

nay (nā) *adv.* 1. No. Now archaic or regional except in recording or expressing a vote. 2. And moreover. Used to introduce a further, more precise or emphatic expression: *He was ugly, nay, hideous.* *—n.* 1. A denial or refusal. 2. A negative or dissenting vote or voter. **—say someone nay.** To deny, refuse, or forbid someone. [Middle English *nay, nei,* from Old Norse *nei* : *ne,* not + *ei,* ever.]

na·ya pai·sa (nə-yä′ pī-sä′) *n., pl.* **naye paise** (nə-yä′ pī-sä′). A monetary unit of India, the *paisa* (see). [Hindi *nayā paisā,* "new pice."]

Naz·a·rene (năz′ə-rēn′, năz′ə-rēn′) *n.* 1. **a.** A native or inhabitant of Nazareth. **b.** Jesus. Preceded by *the.* 2. A member of a sect of early Christians of Jewish origin who retained many of the prescribed Jewish observances. 3. A member of an American Protestant denomination, the Church of the Nazarene, that follows many of the doctrines of early Methodism. [Middle English *Nazaren,* from Late Latin *Nazarēnus,* from Greek *Nazarēnos,* from *Nazarat,* NAZARETH.] **—Naz·a·rene** *adj.*

Naz·a·reth (năz′ə-rĭth). Market town in Galilee, northern Israel. It is a place of pilgrimage for both Christians and Muslims.

Na·zi (nät′sē, nät′-) *n., pl.* **-zis.** 1. A member of the National Socialist German Workers' Party, founded in Germany in 1919 and brought to power in 1933 under Adolf Hitler. 2. *Often* **nazi.** An adherent or advocate of policies characteristic of this party; a fascist. [German, phonetic shortening of *Nationalsozialist* National Socialist.] **—Na·zi** *adj.* **—Na·zi·fy** *v.*

Naz·i·rite, Naz·a·rite (năz′ə-rīt′) *n.* In Biblical times, a person, usually a man, who had made a vow to God and was bound to abstain from strong drink and ritual defilement. [From Late Latin *Nazaraeus,* from Hebrew *nāzir,* from *nāzar,* to consecrate oneself.]

Na·zism (nät′sĭz′əm, nät′-) *n.* Also **Na·zi·ism** (nät′sē-ĭz′əm, nät′-). The ideology and practice of the Nazis; especially, the policy of state control of the economy, racist nationalism, and national expansion. Also called "National Socialism."

Nb The symbol for the element niobium.

n.b. nota bene.

N.B. 1. New Brunswick. 2. nota bene.

NBA, N.B.A. 1. National Basketball Association. 2. National Boxing Association.

N.B.C. National Broadcasting Corporation.

NbE north by east.

n-bu·tane (ĕn′byōō'tān′) *n.* A gaseous hydrocarbon, **butane** (see).

NbW north by west.

NC North Carolina (used with a Zip Code).

N.C. North Carolina.

NCO, N.C.O. noncommissioned officer.

Nd The symbol for the element neodymium.

ND North Dakota (used with a Zip Code).

n.d. No date.

N.Dak. North Dakota.

Nde·be·le (ən-də-bē′lē) *n., pl.* **-les** or collectively **Ndebele.** 1. A member of a Bantu-speaking Zulu people of southern Africa, now living chiefly in northern Transvaal and Matabeleland. 2. The language of this people. Also called "Matabele." [See **Matabele.**] **—Nde·be·le** *adj.*

N'dja·me·na (ən-jä′mə-nə). Formerly **Fort-La·my** (fôr′lə-mē′). The capital of Chad. At the confluence of the Chari and Longone rivers, it is a port city on a main caravan route.

né (nā) *adj.* Born. Used after a man's name to indicate an original name: *John Smith, né Johann Schmidt.* [French, masculine past participle of *naître,* be born.]

Ne The symbol for the element neon.

NE 1. Nebraska (used with a Zip Code). 2. northeast; northeastern.

N.E. 1. New England. 2. northeast; northeastern.

Neagh, Lough (nā). Lake in Northern Ireland. With an area of 396 square kilometers (153 square miles), it is the largest freshwater lake in the British Isles.

Ne·an·der·thal (nē-ăn′dər-thôl′, -tôl′, nä-än′dər-täl′) *adj.* 1. Of or pertaining to Neanderthal man. 2. *Informal.* Crude or reactionary: *a Neanderthal mentality.* **—Ne·an·der·thal** *n.*

Neanderthal man An extinct species or race of man, *Homo sapiens neanderthalensis,* living during the late Pleistocene age in the Old World, and associated with Middle Paleolithic tools. [After *Neanderthal,* valley near Düsseldorf, West Germany, where remains were found.]

ne·an·throp·ic (nē′ən-thrŏp′ĭk) *adj.* Of or pertaining to members of the extant species *Homo sapiens* as compared with other, now extinct species of *Homo.* [NE(O)- + ANTHROP(O)- + -IC.]

neap (nēp) *adj.* Of or pertaining to a neap tide. *~n.* A neap tide. [Old English *nēp-†,* as in *nēpflōd,* "neap flood."]

Ne·a·pol·i·tan (nē′ə-pŏl′ə-tən) *adj.* Of, belonging to, or characteristic of Naples. *~n.* A native or resident of Naples.

Neapolitan ice cream *n.* Ice cream in brick form, with layers of different colors and flavors.

neap tide *n.* A tide of lowest range, occurring when the sun and moon are in quadrature. Compare **spring tide.**

near (nîr) *adv.* **nearer, nearest.** 1. To, at, or within a short distance or interval in space or time: *The day was drawing near.* 2. Almost; nearly; all but: *The freezing cold near killed him. He arrived near exhausted.* 3. With or in a close relationship. *~adj.* **nearer, nearest.** 1. Close in time, space, position, or degree: *near neighbors; near equals; the near future.* 2. Closely related by kinship or association; intimate: *near and dear friends.* 3. **a.** Accomplished by a small margin; close; narrow: *a near escape.* **b.** Missed or avoided by a small margin: *a near disaster.* 4. Closely corresponding to or resembling an original: *a near likeness.* 5. **a.** Closer of two or more: *the near side.* **b.** On the left side, as of a vehicle, animal, or draft team: *the near front wheel; the near hind leg.* 6. Short and direct: *the near route to town.* 7. *Archaic.* Strictly economical; stingy; parsimonious. *~prep. Abbr.* **nr.** Close to; within a short distance or time of: *an inn near London.* *~v.* **neared, nearing, nears.** *—tr.* To come close or closer to. *—intr.* To draw near or nearer. [Middle English *nere,* Old English *nēar,* comparative adverb of *nēah,* "near."] **—near·ness** *n.*

near beer *n.* A malt liquor that does not contain enough alcohol to be considered an alcoholic beverage.

near·by (nîr′bī′) *adj.* Located a short distance away; close at hand; adjacent. **—near·by** *adv.*

Ne·arc·tic (nē-ärk′tĭk, -är′tĭk) *adj.* Of or designating the zoogeographical region that includes the arctic and temperate areas of North America and also includes Greenland. Compare **Palearctic.** [NE(O)- + ARCTIC.]

Near East. 1. A region that includes the countries of the eastern Mediterranean, the Arabian Peninsula, and, sometimes, northeastern Africa. 2. Formerly, the Balkan Peninsula and Turkey. **—Near-East·ern** *adj.*

near·ly (nîr′lē) *adv.* 1. Almost but not quite. 2. Closely; intimately: *a matter nearly affecting our interests.* **—not nearly.** Deficient by a long way: *not nearly good enough.*

near point *n.* The closest point to the eye at which an object can be focused without strain. The distance of this point increases with age; for the normal eye it is about 10 inches.

near·sight·ed (nîr′sī′tĭd) *adj.* Afflicted with **myopia** (see); shortsighted. **—near·sight·ed·ly** *adv.* **—near·sight·ed·ness** *n.*

neat[1] (nēt) *adj.* 1. In good order or clean condition; tidy. 2. Orderly and precise in appearance or procedure; not careless or messy. 3. Skillfully executed; deft; adroit: *a neat turn of phrase.* 4. Simply, precisely, or cleverly worked out or arranged: *a neat solution to the problem.* 5. Not diluted or mixed with other substances; straight. Said of liquor. 6. Obtained after all deductions; net: *neat profit.* 7. *Slang.* Great; terrific: *What a neat idea!* [Old French *net,* from Latin *nitidus,* elegant, shiny, from *nitēre,* to shine.] **—neat·ly** *adv.* **—neat·ness** *n.*

neat[2] *n., pl.* **neat.** *Archaic.* A domestic bovine animal. [Middle English *nete,* Old English *nēat.*]

neat·en (nēt′n) *tr.v.* **-ened, -ening, -ens.** To put in order; make neat.

neath, 'neath (nēth) *prep. Poetic.* Beneath.

neat·herd (nēt′hûrd′) *n. Archaic.* A cowherd.

neat's-foot oil (nēts′fŏŏt′) *n.* A light, yellow oil obtained from the feet and shinbones of cattle, used chiefly to dress leather.

neb (nĕb) *n. Chiefly Scottish.* 1. **a.** A beak of a bird. **b.** A nose or snout. 2. A projecting part, especially a nib. [Middle English *neb(b),* Old English *neb(b).*]

N.E.B. New English Bible.

neb·bish (nĕb'ĭsh, -ĭкн) *n.* A weak-willed and timid person. [Yiddish *nebech*.]

Ne·bras·ka (nə-brăs'kə). *Abbr.* **Nebr.** State in the central United States. Rising from the Missouri prairie lands in the east to the Great Plains and foothills of the Rocky Mts. in the west, it is predominantly agricultural, producing cattle, corn, pigs, and wheat. The state also has large oil reserves. Part of the Louisiana Purchase, it was admitted to the Union in 1867. Lincoln is the capital. —**Ne·bras·kan** *adj. & n.*

Neb·u·chad·nez·zar (nĕb'ə-kəd-nĕz'ər, nĕb'yŏŏ-) *n.* An extremely large wine bottle, equivalent in capacity to 20 standard bottles. [After NEBUCHADNEZZAR II (from the custom of naming very large wine bottles after Old Testament characters).]

Nebuchadnezzar II (*c.* 630–562 B.C.). Chaldean King of Babylon. He extended Chaldean power throughout the old Assyrian empire. After sacking Jerusalem in 586 B.C., he deported its inhabitants to Babylon.

neb·u·la (nĕb'yə-lə) *n., pl.* **-lae** (-lē') or **-las. 1.** *Astronomy.* **a.** Any diffuse mass of interstellar dust, gas, or both, visible as luminous patches or areas of darkness depending on the way the mass absorbs, scatters, or emits electromagnetic radiation. There are two types: bright nebulae, which include emission and reflection nebulae, and dark nebulae, which are also called absorption nebulae. **b.** A galactic nebula. **2.** *Pathology.* **a.** A cloudy spot on the cornea. **b.** Cloudiness in the urine. **3.** *Medicine.* A liquid medication applied by spraying. [New Latin, from Latin, cloud.] —**neb·u·lar** (nĕb'yə-lər) *adj.*

nebular hypothesis *n.* A hypothesis put forward by Laplace in 1796 to account for the origin of the solar system, according to which a rotating nebula cooled and contracted, throwing off rings of matter that contracted into the planets and their moons, while the greater mass of the condensing nebula became the sun. Compare **planetesimal hypothesis, presolar nebular hypothesis.**

neb·u·lize (nĕb'yə-līz') *tr.v.* **-lized, -lizing, -lizes. 1.** To convert (a liquid) to a fine spray; atomize. **2.** To treat with a medicated spray. [From NEBULA.] —**neb·u·li·za·tion** *n.* —**neb·u·liz·er** *n.*

neb·u·los·i·ty (nĕb'yə-lŏs'ə-tē) *n., pl.* **-ties. 1.** The quality or condition of being nebulous. **2.** A nebula or a mass of material constituting a nebula.

neb·u·lous (nĕb'yə-ləs) *adj.* **1.** Cloudy, misty, or hazy. **2.** Lacking definite form or limits; unclearly identified or established; vague: *gave an evasive, nebulous answer.* **3.** Of or characteristic of a nebula. [Latin *nebulōsus*, from *nebula*, cloud, NEBULA.] —**neb·u·lous·ly** *adv.* —**neb·u·lous·ness** *n.*

nec·es·sar·i·ly (nĕs'ə-sĕr'ə-lē) *adv.* **1.** As dictated by necessity; of necessity. **2.** As a necessary or logical consequence: *His silence does not necessarily mean he's angry.*

nec·es·sar·y (nĕs'ə-sĕr'ē) *adj.* **1.** Needed for the continuing existence or functioning of something; essential; indispensable: *Oxygen is necessary to most living organisms.* **2.** Needed to achieve a certain result or effect; requisite: *the necessary tools.* **3.** Following unavoidably from conditions, circumstances, or premises; inevitable: *the necessary results of overindulgence.* **4.** Required by obligation, compulsion, or convention: *making the necessary apologies.* **5.** *Logic.* **a.** Designating a proposition whose denial would be a self-contradiction. **b.** Designating an argument or inference whose denial would lead to a contradiction. ~*n., pl.* **necessaries. 1.** *Often* **necessaries.** That which is needed; especially, money or provisions: *the necessaries for the trip.* **2.** **necessaries.** *Law.* Whatever is needed for the maintenance of a dependent, in keeping with his or her economic and social status. [Middle English *necessarie*, from Latin *necessārius*, extension of *necesse*, necessary.]

Synonyms: essential, indispensable, prerequisite, required, requisite, vital.

necessary condition *n. Logic.* A condition for the truth of a proposition or state of affairs that must hold if the proposition is true, but that does not guarantee its truth. For example, it is a necessary condition for a car to start that it has not run out of gasoline: it is not a **sufficient condition** *(see)* since many other things may be wrong with the car.

ne·ces·si·tar·i·an·ism (nə-sĕs'ə-târ'ē-ə-nĭz'əm) *n. Also* **nec·es·sar·i·an·ism** (nĕs'ə-sâr'ē-ə-nĭz'əm). The doctrine that events are inevitably determined by preceding causes. —**ne·ces·si·tar·i·an** *adj. & n.*

ne·ces·si·tate (nə-sĕs'ə-tāt') *tr.v.* **-tated, -tating, -tates. 1.** To make necessary or unavoidable: *The emergency necessitated a change in plans.* **2.** To require or compel. —See Synonyms at **force.** [Medieval Latin *necessitāre* (past participle *necessitātus*), from Latin *necessitās*, NECESSITY.] —**ne·ces·si·ta·tion** *n.*

ne·ces·si·tous (nə-sĕs'ə-təs) *adj.* Needy; destitute; indigent. [French *nécessiteux*, from Old French *necessite*, NECESSITY.] —**ne·ces·si·tous·ly** *adv.*

ne·ces·si·ty (nə-sĕs'ə-tē) *n., pl.* **-ties. 1.** An essential requirement for the existence, effectiveness, or success of something. **2.** Something that must inevitably exist or occur, as: **a.** That which is dictated by invariable physical laws or strict social requirements. **b.** That which is dictated by constraining circumstances: *the grim necessities of war.* **3.** The state or fact of being indispensable or unavoidable. **4.** Pressing or urgent need, such as that arising from poverty, misfortune, or emergency: *Necessity drove him to desperation.* —**of necessity.** As an inevitable consequence; necessarily. [Middle English *necessite*, from Old French, from Latin *necessitas* (stem *necessitāt-*), from *necesse*, to be NECESSARY.]

CLOUDS OF STARDUST AND GAS
The birthplace of the stars

Nebulae are huge, wispy patches of dust and gas (mainly hydrogen) and are the material from which new stars are produced. A nebula starts to form into stars when it becomes dense enough to collapse under the inward pull of its own gravity. As the nebula collapses, it separates into clumps, each of which will form a star. Eventually the pressure and temperature at the center of the clump rise sufficiently for nuclear reactions to begin, and the star is born.

When stars form in the nebula their light makes the gas in the surrounding cloud glow, creating a bright (or emission) nebula. Some, however, do not emit light but reflect it from nearby stars (reflection nebulae).

Dark (or absorption) nebulae have not yet begun to create stars, and form a dark cloud in space, obscuring other stars beyond them.

The Crab Nebula in the constellation Taurus is not a nebula but a remnant of a supernova (a huge stellar explosion) in which a massive star blew itself to pieces. It left a gas cloud within which is a small, dense pulsar (a flashing object made up of particles called neutrons).

TRIFID NEBULA *Dark clefts in the cloud mass seem to split the Trifid Nebula in Sagittarius into three. A bright (emission) nebula, it was discovered in the 18th century by the French astronomer Legentil de la Galaisière but named in the 19th century by British astronomer Sir John Herschel.*

neck (nĕk) *n.* **1.** The part of the body joining the head to the trunk. **2. a.** The part of a garment around or near the neck of the wearer. **b.** The neckline of a dress, blouse, or other garment. **3.** *Anatomy.* Any relatively narrow portion of a structure, as of a bone or organ, that joins its parts. **4.** The part of a tooth between the crown and the root. **5.** Any relatively narrow elongation, projection, or connecting part, as: **a.** A peninsula. **b.** A strait. **c.** A pass. **d.** The narrow top part of a bottle, jug, or the like. **6.** *Music.* The narrow part along which the strings of a stringed instrument extend to the pegs. **7.** *Architecture.* The narrow, upper part of a column, just below the capital. **8.** *Geology.* Solidified lava filling the vent of an extinct volcano. **9.** *Botany.* The upper, tubular section of an archegonium. **10.** The siphon of a bivalve mollusk, such as a clam. **11. a.** The length of the head and neck of a horse: *won the race by a neck.* **b.** A narrow margin by which a competition is won or lost. **12.** *Informal.* One's life or personal safety: *risked her neck by dashing out in traffic.* —**break one's neck.** *Informal.* To make a great effort to accomplish something. —**get it in the neck.** *Informal.* To undergo severe punishment, rebuke, or penalty. —**neck and neck.** Even in a race or contest. —**save one's neck.** *Slang.* To get out of a situation that threatens one's life or security. —**stick one's neck out.** *Informal.* To act boldly, despite the risk of criticism, trouble, or danger. ~*intr.v.* **necked, necking, necks.** *Slang.* To kiss and caress. [Middle English *necke,* Old English *hnecca.*]

Neck·ar (nĕk'ər). River, rising in the Black Forest, southern West Germany. It flows 367 kilometers (228 miles) generally north and west to join the Rhine at Mannheim.

necked (nĕkt) *adj.* Having a neck or neckline of a specified kind. Used in combination: *a low-necked dress.*

Neck·er (nĕk′ər, nā-kĕr′), **Jacques** (1732–1804). French financier and politician. As a director of the French East India Company (1768) and director of general finance (1777), he introduced reforms and fought corruption. He resigned (1781), was reappointed (1788), and was then dismissed and imprisoned.

neck·er·chief (nĕk′ər-chĭf, -chēf′) *n.* A kerchief worn around the neck.

neck·ing (nĕk′ĭng) *n. Architecture.* A molding or moldings between the upper part of the shaft of a column and the projecting part of the capital.

neck·lace (nĕk′lĭs) *n.* An ornament, such as a string of beads or a flexible metal chain or band, worn around the neck.

neck·let (nĕk′lĭt) *n.* **1.** A close-fitting necklace. **2.** Something worn about the neck for ornamentation, such as a fur piece.

neck·line (nĕk′līn′) *n.* The line formed by the edge of a garment at or near the neck: *a plunging neckline.*

neck of the woods *n. Informal.* Region; neighborhood.

neck·tie (nĕk′tī′) *n.* A long, narrow band of fabric worn around the neck and tied in front with the ends left hanging down the shirt front.

neck·wear (nĕk′wâr′) *n.* Articles of dress worn around the neck, such as neckties, scarves, and collars.

necro–, necr– *prefix.* Indicates: **1.** Death or the dead; for example, **necrology. 2.** A dead body or dead tissue; for example, **necrobiosis, necropsy.** [New Latin, from Greek *nekros,* corpse.]

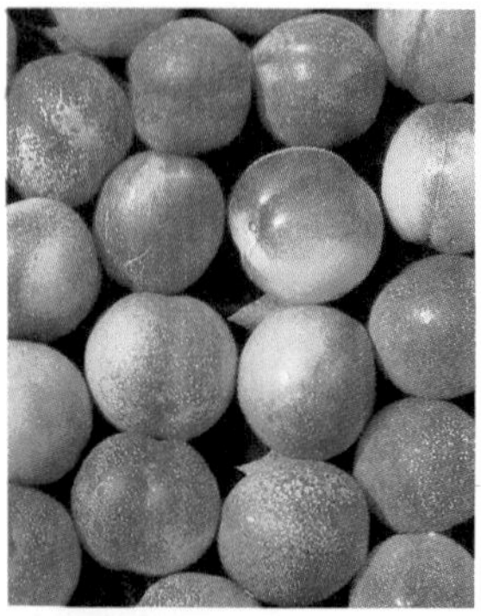

nectarine *These fruit resemble plums with their smooth skin, but they are, in fact, a type of peach.*

nec·ro·bi·o·sis (nĕk′rō-bī-ō′sĭs) *n.* The natural degeneration and death of cells and tissues, as opposed to death from injury or disease and distinguished from death of the entire organism. Compare **gangrene, necrosis.** [New Latin : NECRO- + -BIOSIS.] **—nec·ro·bi·ot·ic** (nĕk′rō-bī-ŏt′ĭk) *adj.*

ne·crol·a·try (nə-krŏl′ə-trē, nĕ-) *n.* Worship of the dead. [NECRO- + -LATRY.]

ne·crol·o·gy (nə-krŏl′ə-jē, nĕ-) *n., pl.* **-gies. 1.** A list or record of people who have died, especially in the recent past. **2.** An obituary. [New Latin *necrologium* : NECRO- + -LOGY.] **—nec·ro·log·i·cal** (nĕk′rə-lŏj′ĭ-kəl) *adj.* **—ne·crol·o·gist** *n.*

nec·ro·man·cy (nĕk′rə-măn′sē) *n.* **1.** The art that professes to conjure up the spirits of the dead and commune with them in order to predict the future. **2.** Magic, especially black magic or sorcery. —See Synonyms at **magic.** [Confusion of: **a.** Late Latin *necromantīa,* from Greek *nekromanteia,* divination by corpses : NECRO- + -MANCY; **b.** Middle English *nigromancie,* from Old French, from Medieval Latin *nigromantia,* black magic : *niger,* black + -MANCY.] **—nec·ro·man·cer** *n.* **—nec·ro·man·tic** *adj.*

ne·croph·a·gous (nə-krŏf′ə-gəs, nĕ-) *adj.* Feeding on carrion or corpses. [Greek *nekrophagos* : NECRO- + -PHAGOUS.]

nec·ro·phil·i·a (nĕk′rə-fĭl′ē-ə) *n.* Also **ne·croph·i·lism** (nə-krŏf′ə-lĭz′əm, nĕ-). Sexual attraction to corpses. [NECRO- + -PHILIA.] **—nec·ro·phil·i·ac** (nĕk′rə-fĭl′ē-ăk′), **nec·ro·phile** (nĕk′rə-fīl′) *n.* **—nec·ro·phil·ic** (nĕk′rə-fĭl′ĭk) *adj.*

nec·ro·pho·bi·a (nĕk′rə-fō′bē-ə) *n.* **1.** A morbid fear of death. **2.** A morbid horror of corpses. [New Latin : NECRO- + -PHOBIA.] **—nec·ro·pho·bic** *adj.*

ne·crop·o·lis (nə-krŏp′ə-lĭs, nĕ-) *n., pl.* **-lises** or **-leis** (-lās′). A cemetery, especially a large and elaborate one belonging to an ancient city. [Greek *nekropolis* : NECRO- + *polis,* city.]

nec·rop·sy (nĕk′rŏp′sē) *n., pl.* **-sies.** Also **ne·cros·co·py** (nə-krŏs′kə-pē, nĕ-) *pl.* **-pies.** An **autopsy** *(see).* [NECR(O)- + -OPSY.]

ne·crose (nĕ-krōs′, nĕk′rōs′) *v.* **-crosed, -crosing, -croses.** Also **nec·ro·tize** (nĕk′rə-tīz′), **-tized, -tizing, -tizes.** *—intr.* To be affected with necrosis. *—tr.* To affect with necrosis. [Back-formation from NECROSIS.]

ne·cro·sis (nə-krō′sĭs, nĕ-) *n., pl.* **-ses** (-sēz′). **1.** The death of living tissue due to disease, injury, or interruption of the blood supply. **2.** The death of plant tissue due to injury, frost, or the like. Compare **necrobiosis.** [Late Latin *necrōsis,* from Greek *nekrōsis,* mortification, from *nekroun,* to mortify, from *nekros,* corpse.] **—ne·crot·ic** (nə-krŏt′ĭk, nĕ-) *adj.*

ne·crot·o·my (nə-krŏt′ə-mē, nĕ-) *n., pl.* **-mies. 1.** The dissection of a dead body. **2.** Surgical removal of a piece of dead tissue, especially bone. [NECRO- + -TOMY.]

nec·tar (nĕk′tər) *n.* **1.** A sweet liquid secreted by flowers of various plants and gathered by bees for making honey. **2.** *Greek & Roman Mythology.* The drink of the gods. Compare **ambrosia. 3.** Any delicious or invigorating drink. **4.** The undiluted juice of a fruit. [Latin, from Greek *nektar.*] **—nec·tar·ous** *adj.*

nec·tar·ine (nĕk′tə-rēn′) *n.* A variety of peach, *Prunus persica nectarina,* having a smooth, waxy skin. [Short for *nectarine peach,* from obsolete *nectarine,* "sweet as nectar," from NECTAR.]

nec·ta·ry (nĕk′tə-rē) *n., pl.* **-ries. 1.** *Botany.* **a.** A glandlike organ, usually at the base of a flower, that secretes nectar. **b.** The part of a flower in which such an organ is contained. **2.** *Entomology.* A **siphuncle** *(see).* Not in current technical usage. [New Latin *nectarium,* from NECTAR.] **—nec·tar·i·al** (nĕk-târ′ē-əl) *adj.*

NED, N.E.D. New English Dictionary (Oxford English Dictionary).

Nederland. See **Netherlands.**

née, nee (nā) *adj.* Born. Used when identifying a married woman by her maiden name: *Mrs. Brown née Jones.* [French, feminine past participle of *naître,* to be born.]

need (nēd) *n.* **1.** A condition or situation in which something necessary or desirable is required or wanted: *in need of water.* **2.** A wish or strong desire for something that is lacking: *a need for affection.* **3.** Necessity; obligation: *There is no need for you to go.* **4.** Something required or wanted; a requisite: *Our needs are modest.* **5.** A condition of poverty or misfortune: *in dire need.*
~v. **needed, needing, needs.** Used as an uninflected auxiliary verb followed by an infinitive without *to,* or as an inflected auxiliary followed by an infinitive with *to,* meaning "to be under the necessity of, be obliged, or have to": *He need not come. Need you have been so rude? —tr.* To have need of; require: *This plant needs water. —intr.* **1.** To be in need or want. **2.** *Archaic.* To be necessary. —See Synonyms at **lack.** [Middle English *nede,* Old English *nēd, nēod,* necessity, distress.]

Usage: When combined with another verb, *need* has two forms, one regular and one irregular. The regular form is marked for person and is followed by the infinitive with *to: She needs to go. Does she need to go?* The irregular form occurs only in questions, negations, and *if* clauses. Like the modal verbs (*must, can,* and the like), it is not marked for person and is followed by a bare verb with no *to*; moreover, its negated and questioned forms are not formed with *do.* Thus, we say *he need not go,* not *he doesn't need go, he need not to go,* or *he needs not go.* Similarly, the questioned form with the irregular *need* would be *Need it be done in a hurry?* rather than *Does it need be done?* or *Need it to be done?* • The two forms of *need* are subtly different in meaning. The irregular form is roughly equivalent to "to be obliged to" and is generally reserved for situations in which there is some question as to whether its subject is under an externally imposed obligation to perform the action named by the accompanying verb. Thus, *you needn't come* means "you are under no obligation to come." Where the subject is under no external compulsion to perform the action of the accompanying verb, the regular form of *need* is used. Thus, we would say: *Since I was there at the game, I don't need to read the newspaper accounts* (not *needn't read,* since the decision not to read the newspaper is entirely the subject's own). But a teacher might say, *If you have already done all the homework assignments, you needn't take the final* (not *don't need to take,* since it is the students' obligations and not their interests that are at issue).

need·ful (nēd′fəl) *adj.* **1.** Necessary; required. **2.** *Archaic.* In want; needy.
~n. Whatever is needed, especially money. Preceded by *the: Have you got the needful?* **—need·ful·ly** *adv.* **—need·ful·ness** *n.*

nee·dle (nēd′l) *n.* **1.** A small, slender sewing implement, now usually of polished steel, pointed at one end, and having an eye at the other through which a length of thread is passed and held. **2.** Any of various implements similar in appearance and use: **a.** A short, sharp instrument with an eye near the pointed end, used in sewing machines. **b.** A slender, pointed rod used in knitting. **c.** A similar implement, usually shorter, and with a hook at one end, used in crocheting. **3.** A small, pointed stylus used to transmit vibrations from the grooves of a phonograph record. **4. a.** Any slender pointer or indicator on a dial, scale, or similar part of a mechanical device. **b.** A **magnetic needle** *(see).* **5.** *Medicine.* **a.** A **hypodermic needle** *(see).* **b.** A slender, sharp-pointed instrument used in suturing tissues during surgery. **6.** A stiff, narrow leaf, as on a conifer. **7.** Any fine, sharp projection, such as a spine of a sea urchin or a needlelike crystal. **8.** A sharp, pointed instrument used in engraving. **9.** A beam passed through or under a wall to serve as a temporary support. **10.** *Informal.* A teasing or goading remark. **—give someone the needle.** *Informal.* To tease or goad so as to provoke.
~v. **needled, -dling, -dles.** *—tr.* **1.** To prick, pierce, or stitch with or as if with a needle. **2.** *Informal.* To goad, provoke, or tease. *—intr.* To sew or do similar work with a needle. [Middle English *nedle,* Old English *nǣdl,* from Germanic.]

nee·dle·fish (nēd′l-fĭsh′) *n., pl.* **-fishes** or collectively **needlefish. 1.** Any of several marine carnivorous fishes of the family Belonidae, having slender bodies and narrow jaws with sharp teeth. **2.** Any of various fishes with projecting jaws, such as the **pipefish** *(see).*

nee·dle·point (nēd′l-point′) *n.* **1.** Decorative needlework on canvas, usually in a diagonal stitch covering the entire surface of the material. See **gros point, petit point. 2.** A type of lace worked on paper patterns with a needle, as distinguished from bobbin lace. Also called "point lace." **—nee·dle·point** *adj.*

need·less (nēd′lĭs) *adj.* Not needed or wished for; unnecessary. **—need·less·ly** *adv.* **—need·less·ness** *n.*

needle valve *n.* A valve having a slender point fitting into a conical seat, for accurately regulating the flow of a liquid or gas.

nee·dle·wom·an (nēd′l-wo͝om′ən) *n., pl.* **-women** (-wĭm′ĭn). A woman who does needlework, especially a seamstress.

nee·dle·wood (nēd′l-wo͝od′) *n.* An Australian tree, *Hakea leucoptera,* with needlelike leaves and soft wood used mainly for veneers.

nee·dle·work (nēd′l-wûrk′) *n.* Work done with a needle, such as sewing or embroidery. **—nee·dle·work·er** *n.*

need·n't (nēd′nt). Contraction of *need not.*

needs (nēdz) *adv.* Of necessity; necessarily. Used following *must* and preceding a simple infinitive: *He must needs go;* or preceding *must,* with an infinitive understood: *"She shall go, if needs must"* (Robert Browning). [Middle English *nedes,* Old English *nēdes,* "of need," genitive of *nēd,* NEED.]

need·y (nē′dē) *adj.* **-ier, -iest.** Being in need; impoverished: *needy families.* **—need·i·ness** *n.*

Né·el temperature (nā-ĕl′) *n. Physics.* The characteristic temperature above which a given material changes from an antiferromagnetic state to a ferromagnetic state. Also called "Néel point." [After Louis E. F. Néel (born 1904), French physicist.]

ne'er (nâr). *Poetic.* Contraction of **never.**

ne'er-do-well (nâr'dŏō-wĕl') *n.* A worthless, good-for-nothing person; especially, an irresponsible person who never succeeds in any enterprise. —**ne'er-do-well** *adj.*

ne·far·i·ous (nĭ-fâr'ē-əs) *adj.* Extremely wicked; evil: *a nefarious plot.* [Latin *nefārius,* from *nefās,* sin : *ne-,* not + *fās,* divine law, right.] —**ne·far·i·ous·ly** *adv.* —**ne·far·i·ous·ness** *n.*

Nef·er·ti·ti (nĕf'ər-tē'tē) (c. 1372–50 B.C.). Queen of Egypt. She was the chief wife of Akhenaton. The exquisite limestone bust of Nefertiti (now in the Berlin Museum) has given rise to the tradition that she was one of the most beautiful women in antiquity.

neg. negative.

ne·gate (nĭ-gāt') *tr.v.* **-gated, -gating, -gates. 1.** To render ineffective or invalid; nullify: *Later experiments tended to negate his findings.* **2.** To rule out; deny the existence of. —See Synonyms at **neutralize, nullify.** [Latin *negāre,* to deny.]

ne·ga·tion (nĭ-gā'shən) *n.* **1.** The act or process of negating. **2.** A denial, contradiction, or negative statement. **3.** The opposite or absence of something regarded as actual, positive, or affirmative: *"Death is nothing more than the negation of life"* (Henry Fielding).

neg·a·tive (nĕg'ə-tĭv) *adj. Abbr.* **neg. 1.** Expressing, containing, or consisting of a negation, refusal, or denial: *a negative answer.* **2. a.** Lacking the quality of being positive or affirmative: *negative indications of their guilt.* **b.** Being of an opposite nature to that expected or intended: *a negative return on my investments.* **3.** Indicating opposition, indifference, or resistance: *a negative response to an advertising campaign.* **4.** Tending to oppose or disagree with that which is considered positive or constructive: *a negative attitude.* **5.** *Medicine.* Not indicative of the presence of microorganisms, disease, or a specific condition. **6.** *Logic.* Denying agreement between the subject and its predicate. Said of a proposition. **7.** *Mathematics.* Pertaining to or designating: **a.** A quantity less than zero. **b.** The sign (-). **c.** A quantity to be subtracted from another. **d.** A quantity, number, angle, velocity, or direction, in a sense opposite to another of the same magnitude indicated or understood to be positive. **8.** *Physics.* Pertaining to or designating: **a.** Electric charge of the same sign as that of an electron, designated by the symbol (-). **b.** Any body having an excess of electrons. **9.** *Chemistry.* Pertaining to or designating an ion, the anion, that is attracted to a positive electrode. **10.** *Biology.* Indicating resistance to, opposition to, or motion away from a stimulus: *a negative tropism.* **11.** *Optics.* Producing divergent rays. Said of a lens. **12.** Of or pertaining to a photographic negative. Compare **positive.**
~*n.* **1.** A statement or act indicating or expressing a contradiction, denial, or refusal. **2.** A thing or concept considered to be the counterpart or negation of something positive. **3.** *Grammar.* A word or part of a word, such as *no, not,* or *non-,* that indicates negation. **4.** The side in a debate that contradicts or opposes the question being debated. **5.** In photography: **a.** An image in which the light areas of the object rendered appear dark and the dark areas appear light. **b.** A film, plate, or other photographic material containing such an image. **6.** *Mathematics.* A negative quantity. **7.** *Archaic.* A right of veto. —**in the negative.** In a sense or manner indicating a refusal or denial: *answer in the negative.*
~*interj.* Used, especially in a military context, to express negation or refusal. Compare **affirmative.**
~*tr.v.* **negatived, -tiving, -tives. 1.** To refuse to approve or accept; veto or reject. **2. a.** To deny; contradict. **b.** To give a negative sense to. **3.** To demonstrate to be false. **4.** To counteract or neutralize. —See Usage note at **affirmative.** [Late Latin *negātīvus,* from Latin *negāre,* to NEGATE.] —**neg·a·tive·ly** *adv.* —**neg·a·tive·ness, neg·a·tiv·i·ty** *n.*

negative feedback *n.* **1.** A type of **feedback** (*see*) in which an increase in output causes a decrease in input. **2.** Critical or discouraging reactions.

negative income tax *n.* A system of government payments to those whose income is below a specified level, proposed as an alternative to welfare.

negative transfer *n.* Interference with current learning or performance as a result of the transfer of previously learned responses.

negative prescription *n. Law.* Prescription (*see*).

neg·a·tiv·ism (nĕg'ə-tĭv-ĭz'əm) *n.* **1.** A system of thought marked by the questioning or denial of traditional beliefs with no attempt to propose alternatives. **2.** A habitual attitude of skepticism or resistance to the ideas of others. **3.** *Psychology.* Behavior characterized by stubborn and unfounded resistance to suggestions, orders, or instructions of others. —**neg·a·tiv·ist** *n. & adj.* —**neg·a·tiv·is·tic** *adj.*

ne·ga·tor (nĭ-gā'tər) *n. Computer Science.* A **NOT** gate (*see*).

neg·a·tron (nĕg'ə-trŏn') *n.* An electron. [NEGA(TIVE) + (ELEC)TRON.]

Neg·ev (nĕg'ĕv'). Also **Neg·eb** (-ĕb'). A desert covering the southern half of Israel, bounded in the north by the hills of Judaea. Irrigation projects support numerous agricultural settlements. There are valuable deposits of natural gas and phosphates.

ne·glect (nĭ-glĕkt') *tr.v.* **-glected, -glecting, -glects. 1.** To ignore or pay no attention to; disregard: *They neglected his warning.* **2.** To fail to care for or give proper attention to: *She neglected her appearance.* **3.** To fail to do or carry out through carelessness or oversight: *He neglected to make his point.*
~*n.* **1.** The act or an instance of neglecting something; disregard.

2. The state of being neglected; negligence. **3.** Habitual lack of care. [Latin *negligere, neglegere* (past participle stem *neglect-*), "not to choose," not to heed : *neg-,* not + *legere,* to choose.] —**ne·glect·er, ne·glec·tor** *n.*

ne·glect·ful (nĭ-glĕkt'fəl) *adj.* Tending to neglect; careless; heedless. Often followed by *of: neglectful of responsibilities.* —**ne·glect·ful·ly** *adv.* —**ne·glect·ful·ness** *n.*

neg·li·gee, neg·li·gée, neg·li·gé (nĕg'lĭ-zhā', nĕg'lĭ-zhā') *n.* **1.** A woman's loose dressing gown, often of soft, delicate fabric. **2.** Loosely, any informal or skimpy attire. [French, "casual," "neglected," from *négliger,* to neglect, from Latin *negligere,* NEGLECT.]

neg·li·gence (nĕg'lĭ-jəns) *n.* **1.** The state or quality of being negligent. **2.** Any negligent act or failure to act. **3.** *Law.* The omission or neglect of any reasonable precaution, care, or action, resulting in accident, injury, or loss.

neg·li·gent (nĕg'lĭ-jənt) *adj.* **1.** Habitually guilty of neglect; lacking in due care or concern. **2.** Careless, especially in a nonchalant or easygoing way. —See Synonyms at **careless.** [Middle English, from Old French, from Latin *negligens* (stem *negligent-*), present participle of *negligere,* to NEGLECT.] —**neg·li·gent·ly** *adv.*

neg·li·gi·ble (nĕg'lĭ-jə-bəl) *adj.* Not worth considering; trifling: *a negligible amount.* [From Latin *negligere,* to NEGLECT.] —**neg·li·gi·bil·i·ty, neg·li·gi·ble·ness** *n.* —**neg·li·gi·bly** *adv.*

ne·go·tia·ble (nĭ-gō'shə-bəl, -shē-ə-bəl) *adj.* **1.** Capable of being negotiated. **2.** Capable of being legally transferred from one person to another, sometimes after endorsement: *a negotiable document.* —**ne·go·tia·bil·i·ty** *n.*

ne·go·ti·ant (nĭ-gō'shē-ənt, -shənt) *n.* One that negotiates.

ne·go·ti·ate (nĭ-gō'shē-āt') *v.* **-ated, -ating, -ates.** —*intr.* To confer with another or others in order to come to terms or reach an agreement: *The mayor refused to negotiate.* —*tr.* **1.** To arrange, settle, or bring about by conferring or discussing: *negotiate a contract.* **2.** *Finance.* **a.** To transfer title to or ownership of (notes, funds, documents, or similar property) to another person or party in return for value received. **b.** To sell or discount (assets or securities, for example). **3.** To succeed in passing over, accomplishing, or coping with: *negotiate a sharp curve.* [Latin *negōtiārī,* to transact business, from *negōtium,* business, "lack of leisure" : *neg-,* not + *ōtium†,* leisure.] —**ne·go·ti·a·tor** *n.*

ne·go·ti·a·tion (nĭ-gō'shē-ā'shən, -sē-) *n.* The act or process of negotiating.

Ne·gril·lo (nĭ-grĭl'ō, -grē'yō) *n., pl.* **-los** or **-loes.** A member of a group of Negroid peoples of short stature living in Africa, including the Bushmen and the Pygmies. Also called "Negrito." [Spanish, diminutive of NEGRO.]

Ne·gri·to (nĭ-grē'tō) *n., pl.* **-tos** or **-toes. 1.** A Negrillo. **2.** Any of various groups of Negroid people of short stature inhabiting parts of Malaysia, the Philippines, and southeastern Asia. [Spanish, diminutive of NEGRO.]

ne·gri·tude (nē'grə-tōōd', -tyōōd', nĕg'rə-) *n.* An aesthetic and ideological concept affirming the independent validity of black culture. [French *négritude* (coined by Léopold SENGHOR), from *nègre,* NEGRO.]

Ne·gro (nē'grō) *n., pl.* **-groes. 1.** A member of the Negroid ethnic division of the human species, especially any of various peoples of central and southern Africa. —See Usage note at **black. 2.** A descendant of these or other Negroid peoples. [Spanish and Portuguese *negro,* black, from Latin *niger,* black.] —**Ne·gro** *adj.*

Ne·gro, Río (rē'ō nā'grō). River of South America. Rising in eastern Colombia (where it is known as the Guainía), it flows some 2,250 kilometers (1,400 miles) across Brazil to join the Amazon River near Manáus.

Ne·groid (nē'groid') *adj. Anthropology.* Of, pertaining to, or designating a major ethnic division of the human species whose members are generally characterized by brown to black pigmentation, and often by tightly curled hair, broad flat nose, and thick lips. This division includes the Negro and other peoples, such as the **Andamanese** and **Melanesian** (*both of which see*). [NEGR(O)- + -OID.] —**Ne·groid** *n.*

ne·gus (nē'gəs) *n.* A beverage made of wine, hot water, lemon juice, sugar, and nutmeg. [After Col. Francis *Negus* (died 1732), English soldier who invented it.]

Ne·gus (nē'gəs) *n.* The title of the emperor of Ethiopia. [Amharic *negūs,* king.]

Neh. Nehemiah.

Ne·he·mi·ah¹ (nē'hə-mī'ə, nē'ə-). A Jewish leader and governor of Judah during the Babylonian Captivity (5th century B.C.).

Nehemiah² *n. Abbr.* **Neh.** A book of the Old Testament describing the moral, political, and religious reforms of Nehemiah, and the rebuilding of Jerusalem under his leadership. Also called "Esdras."

Neh·ru (nā'rōō), **Jawaharlal** (1889–1964). Indian politician. Succeeding his father, Pandit Motilal Nehru, as president of the Indian Congress (1929), he took part in the campaign for independence from Britain and was frequently imprisoned. He became India's first prime minister (1947). The political dynasty was continued by his daughter, Indira Gandhi.

neigh (nā) *intr.v.* **neighed, neighing, neighs.** To utter the cry of a horse; whinny.
~*n.* The cry of a horse. [Middle English *neien,* Old English *hnǣgan,* from Germanic (imitative).]

neigh·bor (nā'bər) *n. Also chiefly British* **neigh·bour. 1.** One who lives near or next to another. **2.** A person or thing adjacent to or

located near another. **3.** A person like oneself; a fellow human being.
~*adj.* Living or situated near another.
~*v.* **neighbored, -boring, -bors.** Also *chiefly British* **neigh·bour.** —*tr.* To lie close to; border upon; adjoin. —*intr.* To live or be situated close by. [Middle English *neigh(e)bor,* Old English *nēahgebūr* : *nēah,* near + *gebūr,* dweller.]

neigh·bor·hood (nā′bər-ho͝od′) *n.* **1.** A district, especially one constituting a distinct community in a town or city, considered in regard to its inhabitants or distinctive characteristics: *a fashionable neighborhood.* **2.** The people who live in a particular vicinity: *The noise disturbed the entire neighborhood.* **3.** A range of numbers, prices, or other quantities: *in the neighborhood of a million dollars.* **4.** *Mathematics.* The set of points surrounding a given point, each of which is at a distance from the given point less than an arbitrary bound.

neigh·bor·ing (nā′bər-ĭng) *adj.* Living or situated close by.

neigh·bor·ly (nā′bər-lē) *adj.* Appropriate to, characteristic of, or showing the feelings of a friendly neighbor. —**neigh·bor·li·ness** *n.*

neighbour. *Chiefly British.* Variant of **neighbor.**

Neis·se (nī′sə). *Polish* **Ny·sa** (nĭs′ə). River of eastern Europe. Rising in Czechoslovakia, it flows 225 kilometers (140 miles) northward to the Oder River, forming part of the Polish-German border. It is known as the Lusatian Neisse to distinguish it from the Glatzer Neisse, another Oder tributary to the east.

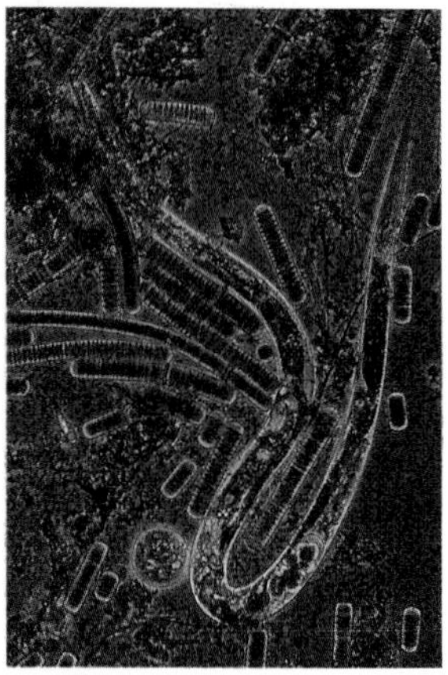

nematode *The intestinal parasites known as pinworms and roundworms that live in the digestive tracts of humans are both nematodes—a group of threadlike worms that range in length from 1 to 200 millimeters (0.04 to 8 inches). Here the lighter outline of a nematode curls through a logjam of smaller organisms.*

nei·ther (nē′*th*ər, nī′-) *adj.* Not either; not one and not the other: *Neither shoe fits comfortably.*
~*pron.* Not either one; not the one nor the other: *Neither of them fits.*
~*conj.* **1.** Not either; not in either case. Used with the correlative conjunction *nor: Neither we nor they want it.* **2.** Also not; nor yet: *John couldn't understand it, and neither could I. "They toil not, neither do they spin"* (Matthew 6:28).
~*adv.* **1.** Similarly not: *Just as you would not, so neither would they.* **2.** *Nonstandard.* In any case; either. Forms a double negative when used for *either* following a negative statement: *I don't like it, neither.* —**neither here nor there.** Of no immediate concern; immaterial: *Your objections are neither here nor there.* [Middle English *neither, nauther,* Old English *nāhwæther, nōhwæther* : *nā,* no, not + *hwæther,* which of two.]

Usage: According to the traditional rule, *neither* should be construed as singular when it occurs as the subject of a sentence: *Neither of the houses is* (not *are*) *finished.* Accordingly, a pronoun with *neither* as an antecedent must also be singular: *Neither of the doctors is likely to reveal her* (not *their*) *identity.* • As a conjunction, *neither* is supposed to be followed by *nor,* not *or: Neither prayer nor curses brought relief* (not *or curses*). When *neither . . . nor* connects two singular elements, the following verb is singular, as in *Neither Marge nor Chris is coming.* When both elements are plural, the verb is plural: *Neither the students nor the teachers have read the report.* When one element is singular and the other is plural, many have suggested that the verb should agree with the element closest to it. Thus, we would write *neither the students nor the teacher has read the report,* but *neither the teacher nor the students have read the report.* Other grammarians, however, have insisted that these sentences must be avoided entirely and that one must instead seek a paraphrase in which the problem does not arise, such as *The students have not read the report, and neither has the teacher.* • When *neither . . . nor* is used as an adverb, it should be placed in such a way that each of its elements is followed by a construction of the same type. Instead of *the report neither specified time nor place,* one should write *the report specified neither time nor place.* Instead of *he was neither told that the meeting was canceled nor that the bank was closed,* one should write *he was told neither that the meeting was canceled nor that the bank was closed.*

nek (nĕk) *n. South African.* A narrow ridge connecting two mountains. [Dutch, "neck."]

nek·ton (nĕk′tən, -tŏn′) *n.* The total population of actively swimming aquatic animals in a sea or lake, including fish, turtles, and whales. Compare **plankton.** [German, from Greek *nēkton,* "swimming thing," neuter of *nēktos,* swimming, from *nēkhein,* to swim.] —**nek·ton·ic** (nĕk-tŏn′ĭk) *adj.*

nel·son (nĕl′sən) *n.* In wrestling, any of a variety of holds in which the user places an arm under the opponent's arm and applies pressure with the palm of the hand against the opponent's neck. See also **full nelson, half nelson.** [Probably from surname *Nelson.*]

Nel·son (nĕl′sən). River in central Manitoba, Canada, flowing 640 kilometers (400 miles) from Lake Winnipeg into Hudson Bay.

Nelson, Horatio, 1st Viscount (1758–1805). British admiral. Despite the loss of an eye at Calvi (1794) and an arm at Santa Cruz (1797), he was the most successful naval commander of his age. He fought with distinction at Cape St. Vincent (1797) and Copenhagen (1801) and destroyed French power in the eastern Mediterranean at the Battle of the Nile (1798). His destruction of the French fleet, with its Spanish allies, at Trafalgar (1805) secured Britain from invasion.

ne·lum·bo (nə-lŭm′bō) *n., pl.* **-bos.** An aquatic plant of the genus *Nelumbo,* having large, variously colored flowers. See **lotus.** [New Latin, from Sinhalese *nelumbu,* lotus, probably of Dravidian origin.]

Nem·an (nĕm′ən). *Polish* **Nie·men** (nyĕ′mən). River of the western U.S.S.R. It was formerly the western border of the Russian empire.

ne·mat·ic (nĭ-măt′ĭk) *adj. Chemistry.* Pertaining to one of the two types of anisotropic melts characteristic of a liquid crystal in which the molecules are linearly oriented but are not in a planar arrangement. Compare **smectic.** [NEMATO- (referring to the threadlike chains of molecules) + -IC.]

nemato- *prefix.* Indicates threadlike form; for example, **nematocyst.** [New Latin, from Greek *nēma* (stem *nēmat-*), thread.]

nem·a·to·cyst (nĕm′ə-tō-sĭst′, nĭ-măt′ə-) *n. Zoology.* A stinging organ in various coelenterates, such as jellyfish, which when stimulated puts out a coiled tube that injects the victim with a paralyzing poison. [NEMAT(O)- + CYST.] —**nem·a·to·cys·tic** (nĕm′ə-tō-sĭs′tĭk, nĭ-măt′ə-) *adj.*

nem·a·tode (nĕm′ə-tōd′) *n.* Any worm of the phylum Nematoda, having unsegmented, threadlike bodies, many of which, including the hookworm, are parasitic. Also called "nematode worm," "roundworm." [New Latin *Nematoda,* "the threadlike ones" : NEMAT(O)- + -ODE (like).]

Nem·bu·tal (nĕm′byə-tôl′) *n.* A trademark for the drug **pentobarbital sodium** *(see).*

nem con (nĕm kŏn′) *adv.* Unanimously; without any opposition: *The proposal was adopted nem con.* [Abbreviation of Latin *nemine contradicente,* with no one opposing.]

ne·mer·te·an, ne·mer·ti·an (nĭ-mûr′tē-ən) *adj.* Also **nem·er·tine** (nĕm′ər-tīn′). Of, pertaining to, or belonging to the phylum Nemertea (or Nemertina), consisting chiefly of marine worms having soft, cylindrical or flattened bodies, usually brightly colored.
~*n.* A worm of this phylum. Also called "ribbon worm." [New Latin *Nemertea,* "the Nemertes group," from *Nemertēs,* name of one of the genera in the group, from Greek *Nēmertēs,* name of a Nereid.]

ne·me·sia (nĭ-mē′zhə) *n.* Any plant of the genus *Nemesia,* native to southern Africa, several species of which are cultivated as ornamental garden plants for their brightly colored flowers. [New Latin, from Greek *nemesion,* name of a plant resembling nemesia.]

nem·e·sis (nĕm′ə-sĭs) *n., pl.* **-ses** (-sēz′). **1.** One that inflicts relentless vengeance or destruction. **2.** Retributive justice in its execution or outcome: *to invite nemesis.* **3.** An unbeatable rival, as in sports: *The team met its nemesis.* **4.** A source of harm or ruin: *Gambling was his nemesis.* [From NEMESIS.]

Nem·e·sis (nĕm′ə-sĭs). *Greek Mythology.* The goddess of retributive justice or vengeance. [Greek, "retribution," from *nemein,* to allot.]

ne·ne (nā′nā) *n.* A goose, *Branta sandvicensis,* of the Hawaiian Islands, now very rare. [Hawaiian *nēnē.*]

nen·u·phar (nĕn′yə-fär′) *n.* A water lily. [From Medieval Latin, from Arabic and Persian *nīnūfar, nīlūfar,* from Sanskrit *nīlōtpala* : *nīla,* blue + *utpala,* lotus.]

neo- *prefix.* Indicates: **1.** A new, revived, or recent form, development, or type; for example, **neologism, neomycin. 2.** A recent formation, modification, or abnormal change; for example, **neoplasm. 3.** The most recent subdivision of a series of geological periods; for example, **Neolithic.** ***Note:*** Many compounds other than those entered here may be formed with *neo-.* In forming compounds, *neo-* is normally joined to the following word without space or hyphen: *neocolonialism.* However, if the second element begins with a capital letter, it is separated with a hyphen and the *N* of *Neo-* is also capitalized: *Neo-Platonism.* (The *N* may be capitalized in other words too: *Neolithic.*) If the second element begins with *o,* it is again separated by a hyphen: *neo-orthodoxy.* [Greek, from *neos,* new.]

ne·o·ars·phen·a·mine (nē′ō-ärs-fĕn′ə-mēn′) *n. Medicine.* A yellow powder, $C_{13}H_{13}As_2N_2NaO_4S$, containing arsenic, formerly used in the treatment of syphilis and yaws.

Ne·o·cene (nē′ə-sēn′) *n.* A division of the Tertiary period comprising the Miocene and Pliocene. Not in current technical use. [NEO- + -CENE.] —**Ne·o·cene** *adj.*

ne·o·clas·si·cism (nē′ō-klăs′ə-sĭz′əm) *n.* **1.** A revival of classical aesthetics and forms in art, architecture, music, and literature. **2.** *Usually* **Neoclassicism. a.** Such a revival that occurred in the 18th and 19th centuries in architecture and art, especially the decorative arts, characterized by order, symmetry, and simplicity of style. **b.** A similar revival that occurred in literature in the late 17th and 18th centuries, characterized by a regard for the classical ideals of reason, form, and restraint. **c.** A movement in music of the late 19th and early 20th centuries that sought to avoid subjective emotionalism and return to the style of the pre-Romantic composers. —**ne·o·clas·sic, ne·o·clas·si·cal** *adj.* —**ne·o·clas·si·cist** *n.*

ne·o·co·lo·ni·al·ism (nē′ō-kə-lō′nē-əl-ĭz′əm) *n.* The use by a major power of economic constraints as a means of perpetuating or extending its effective control over a less powerful nation, especially a former colony. —**ne·o·co·lo·ni·al** *adj.* —**ne·o·co·lo·ni·al·ist** *n. & adj.*

ne·o·cor·tex (nē′ō-kôr′tĕks′) *n.* The **neopallium** *(see).*

Ne·o-Dar·win·ism (nē′ō-där′wĭn-ĭz′əm) *n.* The theory that incorporates Darwin's theory of evolution by **natural selection** *(see)* with subsequent discoveries concerning the inheritance and source of genetic variation. See **Darwinism.** Compare **Neo-Lamarckism.** —**Ne·o-Dar·win·i·an** (nē′ō-där-wĭn′ē-ən) *adj. & n.*

ne·o·dym·i·um (nē′ō-dĭm′ē-əm) *n. Symbol* **Nd** A bright, silvery, rare-earth metal element of the lanthanide group found in the minerals monazite and bastnaesite, and used for coloring glass and for doping some glass lasers. Atomic number 60, atomic weight 144.24, melting point 1,024°C, boiling point 3,027°C, specific gravity 6.80 or 7.004 (depending on allotropic form), valence 3. [New Latin : NEO- + (DI)DYMIUM.]

Ne·o-Freud·i·an (nē′ō-froi′dē-ən) *adj. Psychoanalysis.* Of or relating to a theory based on Freudian philosophy but emphasizing the sig-

THE ROMANTIC REVIVAL OF NEOCLASSICISM

A rebirth of ancient Greek and Roman art in 18th- and 19th-century Europe

Neoclassicism was developed by European artists in the 18th and 19th centuries as a reaction against the extravagance of the rococo style. The neoclassical movement was an attempt to revive the artistic rules and values of ancient Greece and Rome and came about after the discovery and excavation of classical sites in Italy, Greece, and Asia Minor. The style is characterized by its principles of order, simplicity, and dignity. Leading exponents included the French painter Jacques-Louis David (1748–1825), whose paintings were inspired by Roman history, and the Italian sculptor Antonio Canova (1757–1822).

The architectural movement was often self-conscious and pedantic. During the second half of the 18th century, however, designs by Scottish architect Robert Adam (1728–92) dominated British architecture because he was able to combine precision with skillful delicacy.

The term neoclassicism can be used in a general sense; it is used to describe the style of 17th- and 18th-century writers such as Dryden, Johnson, La Fontaine, and Racine. In music it has been used to describe, for example, the reaction against excessive romanticism that led Stravinsky to adopt a simpler, purer style in such works as the opera-oratorio *Oedipus Rex* (1927) and the ballet *Apollon musagète* (1928).

DEATH OF SOCRATES *A favorite subject of neoclassical artists, the death of the famous Greek philosopher was painted by Jacques-Louis David in 1787. Socrates, who lived in the last part of the 5th century B.C., was accused of impiety— corruption of the young and neglect of the gods—because of his teachings and condemned to drink a bowl of the deadly poison hemlock.*

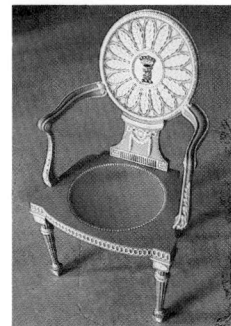

BEECHWOOD CHAIR *One of a set of decorative chairs made by Thomas Chippendale for the Adam-designed Harewood House, Yorkshire, England.*

WEDGWOOD JASPERWARE *John Flaxman designed a relief showing Apollo and the Nine Muses for this neoclassical vase.*

GREEK GODDESS *In Greek mythology Hebe is the goddess of eternal youth. This statue of her carved by Thorvaldsen in 1806 shows the neoclassical ideals of purity, proportion, and repose.*

nificance of social and cultural influences on personality development. **—Ne·o·Freud·i·an** *n.*

Ne·o·gae·a (nē′ə-jē′ə) *n.* Also **Ne·o·ge·a.** An area that is coextensive with the Neotropical region and is considered one of the primary zoogeographic regions. See **Neotropical.** [New Latin : NEO- + Greek *gaia*, earth.] **—Ne·o·gae·an** *adj.*

ne·o·gen·e·sis (nē′ō-jĕn′ə-sĭs) *n. Medicine.* The regeneration of tissue. **—ne·o·ge·net·ic** (nē′ō-jə-nĕt′ĭk) *adj.*

ne·o·im·pres·sion·ism, Ne·o·Im·pres·sion·ism (nē′ō-ĭm-prĕsh′ən-ĭz′əm) *n.* A movement in 19th-century painting that was led by Georges Seurat and characterized by strict and formal composition and meticulous execution using **pointillism** *(see).* **—ne·o·im·pres·sion·ist** *n. & adj.*

Ne·o·La·marck·ism (nē′ō-lə-mär′kĭz′əm) *n.* The theory that acquired characteristics can be inherited, but that natural selection is also a valid evolutionary principle. See **Lamarckism.** Compare **Neo-Darwinism. —Ne·o·La·marck·i·an** (nē′ō-lə-mär′kē-ən) *adj. & adj.*

ne·o·lith (nē′ə-lĭth′) *n.* A stone implement of the Neolithic Age. [Back-formation from NEOLITHIC.]

Ne·o·lith·ic (nē′ə-lĭth′ĭk) *adj. Sometimes* **neolithic.** *Archaeology.* Of or designating the cultural period beginning around 10,000 B.C. in the Middle East and later elsewhere, and characterized by the development of farming and the making of technically advanced, polished stone implements.

~n. Archaeology. The Neolithic period. Preceded by *the.* [NEO- + -LITHIC.]

ne·ol·o·gism (nē-ŏl′ə-jĭz′əm) *n.* **1.** A newly coined word, phrase, or expression, or a new meaning for an old word. **2.** The use or formation of new words, phrases, or expressions or of new meanings for old words. [French *néologisme* : NEO- + LOG(O)- + -ISM.] **—ne·ol·o·gist** *n.* **—ne·o·lo·gis·tic, ne·o·lo·gis·ti·cal** *adj.*

ne·ol·o·gize (nē-ŏl′ə-jīz′) *intr.v.* **-gized, -gizing, -gizes.** To coin or use neologisms.

ne·ol·o·gy (nē-ŏl′ə-jē) *n., pl.* **-gies.** Neologism or an instance of it. [French *néologie* : NEO- + -LOGY.] **—ne·o·log·i·cal** (nē′ə-lŏj′ĭ-kəl) *adj.* **—ne·o·log·i·cal·ly** *adv.*

ne·o·morph (nē′ə-môrf′) *n.* A biological structure that has not evolved from a similar structure in an ancestor. [NEO- + -MORPH.] **—ne·o·morph·ic** *adj.*

ne·o·my·cin (nē′ō-mī′sĭn) *n.* An antibiotic drug, $C_{12}H_{26}N_4O_6$, used to treat a wide range of infections, especially those affecting the skin and eyes. [NEO- + -MYCIN.]

ne·on (nē′ŏn′) *n. Symbol* **Ne** A rare, inert, gaseous element occurring in the atmosphere to the extent of 18 parts per million and obtained by fractional distillation of liquid air. It is colorless but glows reddish-orange in an electrical discharge and is used in fluorescent tubes. Atomic number 10, atomic weight 20.183, melting point –248.67°C, boiling point –245.95°C, valence 0.

~*adj.* Illuminated by a tube with neon in it: *a neon sign.* [Greek, "the new (gas)," neuter of *neos*, new.]

ne·o·nate (nē′ə-nāt′) *n.* A newborn child. [New Latin *neonātus* : NEO- + Latin *nātus*, born, from *nascī*, to be born.] —**ne·o·na·tal** (nē′ō-nāt′l) *adj.*

neon tetra *n.* A small tropical American freshwater fish, *Hyphessobrycon innesi*, having blue and red markings.

ne·o·or·tho·dox·y (nē′ō-ôr′thə-dŏk′sē) *n.* A Protestant movement of the 20th century that aims to revive adherence to certain Reformation doctrines. —**ne·o·or·tho·dox** *adj.*

ne·o·pal·li·um (nē′ō-pǎl′ē-əm) *n.* The tissue that makes up most of the cerebral cortex in the brain. Also called "neocortex."

ne·o·phyte (nē′ə-fīt′) *n.* **1.** A recent convert to a religion. **2. a.** A newly ordained Roman Catholic priest. **b.** A novice of a religious order. **3.** A beginner or novice. [Late Latin *neophytus*, from New Testament Greek *neophutos*, "newly planted" : NEO- + *phutos*, "grown," from *phuein*, to bring forth, produce.]

ne·o·plasm (nē′ə-plǎz′əm) *n.* Any abnormal new growth of tissue in animals or plants; a benign or malignant tumor. [NEO- + -PLASM.] —**ne·o·plas·tic** (nē′ə-plǎs′tĭk) *adj.*

Ne·o·Pla·to·nism, Ne·o·pla·to·nism (nē′ō-plāt′n-ĭz′əm) *n.* **1.** A philosophical and religious system developed in Alexandria in the 3rd century A.D., based on the doctrines of Plato and other Greek philosophers, and modified with elements of Oriental mysticism and some Judaic and Christian concepts. **2.** A revival of this system, as in the Middle Ages and Renaissance. —**Ne·o·Pla·ton·ic** (nē′ō-plə-tŏn′ĭk) *adj.* —**Ne·o·Pla·to·nist** *n.*

ne·o·prene (nē′ə-prēn′) *n.* A synthetic rubber produced by polymerization of chloroprene and used in waterproof products, adhesives, paints, and rocket fuels. [NEO- + PR(OPYL) + -ENE.]

Ne·o·scho·las·ti·cism (nē′ō-skə-lǎs′tə-sĭz′əm) *n.* A movement to revive the scholasticism of Aquinas by infusing it with modern concepts. —**Ne·o·scho·las·tic** *adj.*

ne·ot·e·ny (nē-ŏt′n-ē, nē′ə-tē′nē) *n.* The retention of larval features in the adult form of an animal. It occurs, for example, in the axolotl, which retains the external gills of the larva. [From German *Neotenie* : NEO- + Greek *teinein*, to extend.]

ne·o·ter·ic (nē′ə-tĕr′ĭk) *adj.* Of recent origin; new; modern. ~*n.* A modern writer or philosopher. [Late Latin *neōtericus*, from Greek *neōterikos*, "youthful," modern, from *neōteros*, younger, comparative of *neos*, new.]

Ne·o·trop·i·cal (nē′ō-trŏp′ĭ-kəl) *adj.* Of or designating the zoogeographic region stretching southward from the tropic of Cancer and including southern Mexico, Central and South America, and the West Indies. ~*n.* The Neotropical region.

ne·o·type (nē′ə-tīp′) *n.* A plant or animal specimen selected to replace an original holotype that has been lost or destroyed.

Ne·o·zo·ic (nē′ə-zō′ĭk) *adj.* Of or formed in any geological period after the end of the Mesozoic era.

Ne·pal (nə-pôl′, -päl′). Kingdom of south-central Asia. Lying in the Himalayas, it is a predominantly agricultural country, exporting jute and rice. With massive foreign aid, roads, hydroelectric power, and light industry are being developed. Tourism is important. It is ruled by a hereditary Hindu monarchy. Area, 140,797 square kilometers (54,348 square miles). Population, 14,200,000. Capital, Kathmandu. See map at **India.** —**Nep·al·ese** (nĕp′ə-lēz′) *adj. & n.*

Ne·pal·i (nə-pô′lē, -pä′lē, -pä′lē) *n., pl.* **-lis** or collectively **Nepali. 1.** A native or inhabitant of Nepal. **2.** The central Indic language of Nepal. —**Ne·pal·i** *adj.*

ne·pen·the (nĭ-pĕn′thē) *n.* **1.** A drug, perhaps opium, mentioned in the *Odyssey* as a remedy for grief. **2.** Anything that induces oblivion of sorrow or eases pain. [Greek *nēpenthes (pharmakon)*, "grief-banishing (drug)" : *nē-*, not + *penthos*, grief.] —**ne·pen·the·an** (nĭ-pĕn′thē-ən) *adj.*

ne·per (nē′pər, nā′-) *n. Symbol* **Np** A unit used for comparing quantities, used especially for telecommunication signal amplitudes. The natural logarithm of the ratio of the quantities is the value in nepers.

neph·e·line (nĕf′ə-lēn′, -lĭn) *n.* Also **neph·e·lite** (-līt′). A sodium or potassium aluminum silicate mineral, occurring worldwide in igneous rocks and used in the manufacture of ceramics and enamels. [French *néphéline*, from Greek *nephelē*, cloud (because it becomes cloudy when placed in acid).]

neph·e·lin·ite (nĕf′ə-lĭn-īt′) *n.* An igneous rock consisting chiefly of pyroxene and nepheline.

neph·e·lom·e·ter (nĕf′ə-lŏm′ə-tər) *n.* An apparatus used to measure the size or concentration of particles in a suspension by the amount of light scattered by the particles. [Greek *nephelē*, cloud + -METER.] —**neph·e·lo·met·ric** (nĕf′ə-lō-mĕt′rĭk) *adj.* —**neph·e·lom·e·try** *n.*

neph·ew (nĕf′yōō; *chiefly British* nĕv′yōō) *n.* The son of one's brother or sister, or of one's spouse's brother or sister. [Middle English *neveu*, nephew, grandson, from Old French *neveu*, from Latin *nepōs*, nephew, grandson.]

neph·o·graph (nĕf′ə-grǎf′, -gräf′) *n. Meteorology.* A device used for producing photographic records *(nephograms)* of clouds.

ne·phol·o·gy (nĭ-fŏl′ə-jē) *n.* The science of clouds. [Greek *nephos*, cloud + -LOGY.] —**neph·o·log·i·cal** (nĕf′ə-lŏj′ĭ-kəl) *adj.* —**ne·phol·o·gist** *n.*

neph·o·scope (nĕf′ə-skōp′) *n. Meteorology.* An instrument for observing clouds and measuring their height, speed, and direction of movement.

ne·phral·gi·a (nə-frăl′jē-ə, -jə) *n.* Pain in the kidney, caused by any

Neptune A 17th-century work by the Italian sculptor Bernini depicts the Roman god of the sea, Neptune, and Triton, the Greek demigod who was half man, half fish.

of various kidney disorders. —**ne·phral·gic** *adj.*

ne·phrec·to·my (nə-frĕk′tə-mē) *n., pl.* **-mies.** The surgical removal of a kidney. [NEPHR(O)- + -ECTOMY.]

ne·phrid·i·um (nə-frĭd′ē-əm) *n., pl.* **-ia** (-ē-ə). An excretory organ in many invertebrates, consisting basically of a tube through which waste products pass to the exterior. [New Latin : NEPHR(O)- + -IDIUM.] —**ne·phrid·i·al** *adj.*

neph·rite (nĕf′rīt′) *n.* A white to dark green variety of jade. [German *Nephrit*, "kidney mineral" (from its supposed power to cure kidney diseases) : NEPHR(O)- + -ITE.]

ne·phrit·ic (nə-frĭt′ĭk) *adj.* **1.** Pertaining to the kidneys. **2.** *Pathology.* Of, pertaining to, or affected by nephritis.

ne·phri·tis (nə-frī′tĭs) *n. Pathology.* Acute or chronic inflammation of the kidneys, as in Bright's disease. [Late Latin, from Greek : NEPHR(O)- + -ITIS.]

nephro-, nephr- *prefix.* Indicates the kidney; for example, **nephrogenous, nephritis.** [Greek, from *nephros*, kidney.]

ne·phrog·e·nous (nə-frŏj′ə-nəs) *adj.* Also **neph·ro·gen·ic** (nĕf′rə-jĕn′ĭk). Originating in the kidney. [NEPHRO- + -GENOUS.]

neph·ron (nĕf′rŏn′) *n.* Any of the excretory units of the kidney, consisting of a tiny, coiled tubule into which urine is filtered from the blood. [German *Nephron*, from Greek *nephros*, kidney.]

ne·phro·sis (nə-frō′sĭs) *n.* Any disease of the kidneys, especially when marked by degenerative changes in the renal tubules, as opposed to the inflammation characteristic of nephritis. [New Latin : NEPHR(O)- + -OSIS.] —**ne·phrot·ic** (nə-frŏt′ĭk) *adj.*

ne·phros·to·my (nə-frŏs′tə-mē) *n., pl.* **-mies.** A surgical operation in which a tube is inserted into a kidney so that the urine drains to the outside. [NEPHRO- + -STOMY.]

ne·phrot·o·my (nə-frŏt′ə-mē) *n., pl.* **-mies.** Surgical incision into the kidney. [New Latin *nephrotomia* : NEPHRO- + -TOMY.]

ne plus ul·tra (nē plŭs ŭl′trə; nä plōōs ōōl′trä) *n.* The extreme or utmost point; especially, the point of highest achievement. [Latin, "(sail) no more beyond (this point)," a warning to mariners allegedly inscribed on the Pillars of Hercules.]

nep·o·tism (nĕp′ə-tĭz′əm) *n.* Favoritism shown or patronage granted by persons in high office to relatives. [French *népotisme*, from Italian *nepotismo*, "favoring of nephews" (by 16th-century prelates), from *nepote*, nephew, from Latin *nepōs.*] —**nep·o·tist** *n.* —**nep·o·tis·ti·cal** *adj.*

Nep·tune¹ (nĕp′tōōn′, -tyōōn′). *Roman Mythology.* The god of the sea, corresponding to the Greek Poseidon. [Latin *Neptūnus†.*]

Neptune² *n. Poetic.* The ocean or sea.

Neptune³ *n.* The eighth planet from the sun, having a sidereal period of revolution around the sun of 164.8 years at a mean distance of 2.8 billion (2.8 × 10⁹) miles, a mean radius of 14,000 miles, and a density 17.2 times that of earth. —**Nep·tu·ni·an** (nĕp-tōō′nē-ən, -tyōō′-) *adj.*

nep·tu·ni·um (nĕp-tōō′nē-əm, -tyōō′-) *n. Symbol* **Np** A silvery, metallic, naturally radioactive element, atomic number 93, the first of the transuranium elements, having a number of isotopes with mass numbers from 231 to 241 and half-lives ranging from 7.3 minutes to 2.2 million years. It is found in trace quantities in uranium ores and is produced synthetically by nuclear reactions. [After *Neptune* (planet), since neptunium follows uranium in the periodic table, as Neptune is the next planet after Uranus.]

ne·ral (nîr′ăl, nē′răl) *n.* An isomeric form of citral that is used in perfumes and flavorings.

nerd (nûrd) *n. Slang.* A socially inept, foolish, or very unattractive person. [Perhaps from earlier *nert*, alteration of *nut.*]

Ne·re·id¹ (nîr′ē-ĭd) *n. Greek Mythology.* Any of the 50 daughters of Nereus; a sea nymph. [Greek *Nēreis*, from *Nēreus*, NEREUS.]

Nereid² *n.* The smaller of the two satellites of the planet Neptune. [From NEREID (nymph); the Nereids were attendants on Neptune.]

ne·re·is (nîr′ē-ĭs) *n., pl.* **nereides** (nə-rē′ə-dēz′). Any of several marine worms of the genus *Nereis*, having a long, flat, segmented body and a pair of paddles on each segment. See **ragworm.** [New Latin, from Latin *Nēreis*, NEREID.]

Ne·re·us (nîr′ē-əs). *Greek Mythology.* A sea god, father of the Nereids.

ne·rit·ic (nə-rĭt′ĭk) *adj.* Pertaining to or designating the waters and deposits of a shoreline. See **continental shelf.** [Probably from Latin *nērīta*, sea snail, from Greek *nēritēs*, from *Nēreus*, NEREUS.]

Nernst (nĕrnst), **Walther Hermann** (1864–1941). German physicist. Best known for his discovery of the third law of thermodynamics, he also carried out important research into free radicals. He received a Nobel Prize for chemistry (1920).

Nernst heat theorem *n.* The principle in thermodynamics that changes in entropy tend to zero as the temperature tends to absolute zero. It was an earlier form of the third law of thermodynamics.

Ne·ro (nîr′ō), **Claudius Caesar**, born Lucius Domitius Ahenobarbus (A.D. 37–68). Roman emperor (54–68). He was adopted by the emperor Claudius, but his early reign was dominated by his mother, Agrippina. He murdered his mother and wife and was rumored to have started the Great Fire of Rome (64), for which the Christians were blamed. His cruelty and irresponsibility provoked revolts throughout the empire that led to his suicide.

ner·o·li (nĕr′ə-lē) *n.* An essential oil distilled from orange flowers and used in perfumery. Also called "neroli oil," "orange flower oil." [Perhaps after Anna Maria de la Trémoille, princess of Neroli, who is said to have introduced it into France.]

Ne·ro·ni·an (nĭ-rō′nē-ən) *adj.* **1.** Marked by the cruelty, tyranny, or depravity characteristic of the emperor Nero. **2.** Of or pertaining to Nero or his times.

Ne·ru·da (nə-rōō′də), **Pablo,** pen name of Neftalí Ricardo Reyes (1904–73). Chilean poet and diplomat. Though his early works were nihilistic, his later poems reflected the socialist commitment of the Allende government, which he served as ambassador. He was awarded a Nobel Prize for literature (1971).

ner·vate (nûr′vāt′) *adj. Botany.* Having veins. Said of leaves.

ner·va·tion (nûr-vā′shən) *n.* A pattern of veins or nerves; venation.

nerve (nûrv) *n.* **1.** Any of the bundles of fibers interconnecting the central nervous system and the organs or parts of the body, capable of transmitting both sensory stimuli and motor impulses from one part of the body to another. **2.** A tendon or muscle. Now rare except in the phrase *to strain every nerve.* **3.** The source from which feeling, energy, or dynamic action emanates. **4.** A sensitive point or subject: *His criticism of her writing hit a nerve.* **5.** The sensitive tissue in the pulp of a tooth. **6. a.** Forcefulness; stamina. **b.** Courage and composure; firm self-control: *lost his nerve at the last minute.* **c.** *Informal.* Brazenness; effrontery: *What a nerve!* **7. nerves.** An agitated condition induced by anxiety; nervousness: *an attack of nerves.* **8.** *Biology.* A vein in an insect's wing. **9.** *Botany.* The midrib or any of the larger veins in a leaf. **—See Synonyms at temerity. —get on someone's nerves.** To exasperate or irritate someone. **~**tr.v. **nerved, nerving, nerves.** To give strength or courage to. [Latin *nervus,* sinew, nerve.]

nerve block *n.* A method of anesthetizing a part of the body by injecting a local anesthetic into another part of the body where it will block the passage of pain impulses along a nerve.

nerve cell *n.* Any of the cells of nerve tissue, consisting of a nucleated cell body and cytoplasmic extensions (the dendrites and axons). Also called "neuron."

nerve center *n.* **1.** A group of nerve cells that perform a specific function. **2.** A source or focus of power or control.

nerve fiber *n.* A threadlike process that is part of a nerve cell; an axon or dendrite.

nerve gas *n.* Any gas used in chemical warfare that affects the normal functioning of nerves and thereby paralyzes the muscles they supply.

nerve impulse *n.* The wavelike progression of electrical activity that marks the transmission of information along a stimulated nerve fiber.

nerve·less (nûrv′lĭs) *adj.* **1.** Lacking courage or energy; listless; spiritless. **2.** Undisturbed by danger or upsetting circumstances; confident, courageous, and self-controlled. **—nerve·less·ly** *adv.* **—nerve·less·ness** *n.*

nerve·rack·ing, nerve·wrack·ing (nûrv′răk′ĭng) *adj.* Intensely distressing, irritating, or exhausting.

Ner·vi (nĕr′vē), **Pier Luigi** (1891–1979). Italian architect. His public buildings, such as the UNESCO building in Paris (1953–57), pioneered the decorative use of reinforced concrete.

nerv·ine (nûr′vēn′) *adj.* Affecting the nerves; especially, calming nervous excitement.
~n. A tonic for nervous disorders.

nerv·ous (nûr′vəs) *adj.* **1. a.** Agitated, or liable to become agitated, as a result of anxiety; jittery. **b.** Indicating an anxious or agitated condition: *a nervous stammer.* **2.** Spirited or vigorous, especially in

---

nervous system

THE CONTROLLER OF THE BODY

How the brain receives information and organizes movement

The central nervous system consists of the brain and the spinal cord. Major peripheral nerves branch out from the cord to serve every organ and part of the body. By sending and receiving impulses along the nerves, the brain exercises voluntary control over muscular movements.

Sensation begins in specialized nerve endings, called receptors. There are light-sensitive receptors in the eye and others in the ear that respond to vibrations caused by sound as well as others in the skin that convey the senses of touch, pain, and temperature. Impulses from the receptors travel along the nerves to the brain carrying their information.

To control movement the brain transmits commands along motor nerves to the muscles, which are then stimulated into response. These commands may be a reaction to information received from the receptors or they may be originated independently within the brain, which can store memory and generate emotions such as fear, anger, shame, or delight.

Besides sending and receiving impulses, the brain exerts a ceaseless automatic control by means of a self-regulating nervous system that is known as the autonomic system. Through these nerves the brain can alter the pace of the heart, influence the rate of breathing, and control the processes of digestion and excretion.

The nerves themselves, which provide this web of communication through the body, are made of specialized tissue through which tiny impulses can pass back and forth. They consist of long nerve fibers, or neurons, bound by connective tissue and each capable of transmitting 1,000 separate impulses a second.

A typical neuron consists of a central body, a long threadlike extension called an axon, and a number of shorter branches called dendrites. There are millions of neurons in the body, all of which are formed before birth. This huge number provides a safety margin and the nervous system still functions very efficiently even if some neurons are diseased or destroyed.

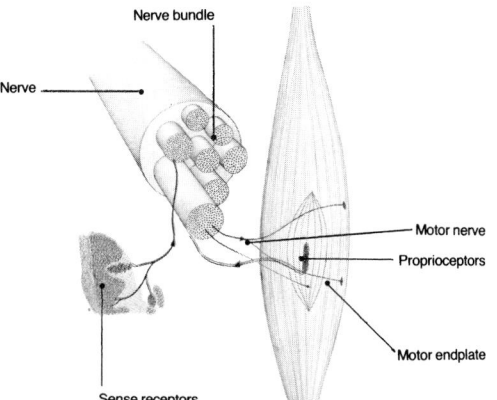

- Cerebrum
- Cerebellum
- Brainstem
- Cervical nerves
- Thoracic nerves
- Lumbar nerves
- Sacral and coccygeal nerves

Nerve bundle
Nerve
Motor nerve
Proprioceptors
Motor endplate
Sense receptors

THE SPINAL CORD *Part of the central nervous system, the spinal cord is a column of nervous tissue that extends two-thirds of the way down the backbone and provides a pathway to the brain. Both the spinal cord and the brain are based on one kind of cell—the neuron. The brain contains the greatest number of neurons, with most of them in the outer part—called the cerebrum. The entire nervous system is the controller of the body.*

A NERVE *Thousands of nerve fibers are bound together in bundles. Each bundle has sensory fibers and motor fibers. The sensory fibers carry information to the brain from sense receptors and the nerve endings known as proprioceptors, which provide information about the changes in muscle tone. Motor nerves carry instructions from the brain to the muscles. Nerve impulses are generated by tiny chemical changes that produce electrical pulses that pass along the bigger nerves at 100 meters (110 yards) a second and along the smallest at about 0.3 meter (1 foot) a second. When the impulse reaches the end of the nerve, it releases a chemical that passes the "message" across a junction, or synapse, to another nerve; or, when the nerve ends at a motor endplate in a muscle, the released chemical will generate a response from that muscle causing it to contract or relax.*

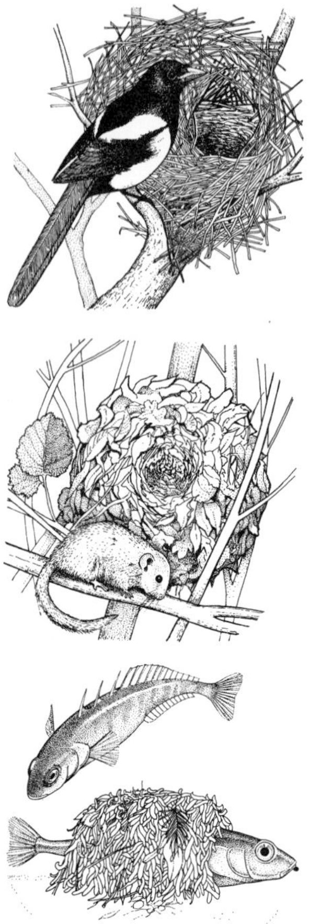

nest *Many creatures build nests, either as a place to rear their young or as a protective home. Seen here are a magpie's nest (top) built of twigs, the nest of a dormouse (center) built of leaves and moss, and a nest of weeds where the stickleback lays its eggs.*

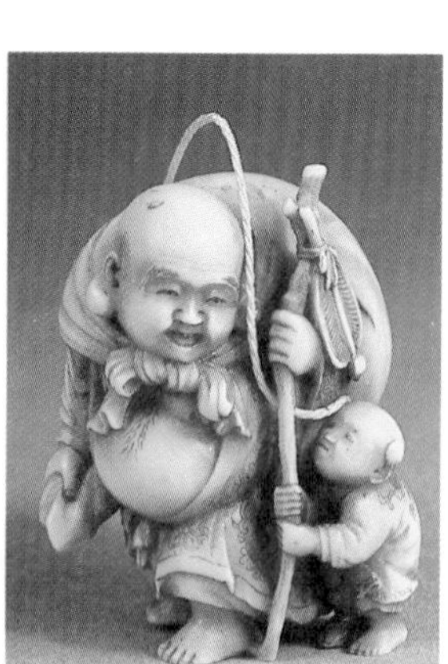

netsuke *Between the 17th and 19th centuries these ornamental toggles, usually made of wood or ivory, and used to secure the silk cord of a purse, became miniature works of art. This one depicts Hotei, one of the seven gods of luck in Japanese mythology.*

style, feeling, or thought: *a nervous, vibrant prose.* **3.** Strung with nerves; containing many delicate nerves. **4. a.** Of or pertaining to the nerves or nervous system. **b.** Stemming from or affecting the nerves or nervous system: *a nervous disorder.* **5. a.** Anxious or afraid: *nervous of heights.* **b.** Producing anxiety; uneasy: *the nervous moments before takeoff.* [Middle English, from Latin *nervōsus,* from *nervus,* sinew, NERVE.] **—nerv·ous·ly** *adv.* **—nerv·ous·ness** *n.*

nervous breakdown *n.* **1. Neurasthenia** *(see).* **2.** Any severe or incapacitating emotional disorder.

nervous exhaustion *n.* **Neurasthenia** *(see).*

nervous prostration *n.* **Neurasthenia** *(see).*

nervous system *n. Anatomy.* A coordinating mechanism in all multicellular animals, except sponges, that regulates internal body functions and responses to external stimuli. In vertebrates it consists of the brain, spinal cord, nerves, ganglia, and parts of receptor and effector organs. See **autonomic nervous system, central nervous system, peripheral nervous system.** See feature, page 1139.

ner·vure (nûr′vyo͝or) *n.* **1.** *Botany.* Any of the vascular ridges that form the framework of a leaf. **2.** *Biology.* Any of the thickened ribs of tissue that form the framework of an insect's wing. [French, from Latin *nervus,* NERVE.]

nerv·y (nûr′vē) *adj.* **-ier, -iest. 1.** *Informal.* Impudently confident; brazen; rude. **2.** Showing or requiring fortitude, energy, or endurance. **3.** *Chiefly British.* Jumpy; nervous. **4.** *Archaic.* Full of muscular force; sinewy.

nes·cience (nĕsh′əns, nĕsh′ē-əns, nĕs′ē-əns) *n.* **1.** Absence of knowledge or awareness; ignorance. **2.** Agnosticism. [Late Latin *nesciēntia,* from *nesciens* (stem *nescient-*), ignorant, from *nescīre,* to be ignorant : *ne-,* not + *scīre,* to know.] **—nes·cient** *adj.* & *n.*

-ness *suffix.* Indicates: **1.** State, quality, or condition of being; for example, **quietness. 2.** An instance or example of a state, quality, or condition; for example, **kindness.** [Middle English, from Old English *-ness, -niss,* of Germanic origin.]

Ness, Loch (nĕs). A lake of northern Scotland. It is on the Caledonian Canal between Lochend and Fort Augustus. Its depths are supposed to contain the Loch Ness Monster.

Nes·sel·rode (nĕs′əl-rōd′) *n.* A frozen dessert, often rum-flavored, made with chestnuts, preserved oranges, cherries, dried fruits, and cream. [After Count Karl NESSELRODE, whose chef invented it.]

Nesselrode, Karl Robert, Count (1780–1862). Russian foreign minister (from 1816). He pursued a belligerent policy in the Balkans and signed the treaty concluding the Crimean War (1853–56).

nest (nĕst) *n.* **1. a.** The structure made by a bird for holding its eggs and young. **b.** The structure or place in which fishes or insects deposit eggs or shelter their young. **c.** Any place where young are reared; a lair. **d.** A number of insects, birds, or other animals occupying such a place; a swarm, brood, or colony: *a nest of hornets.* **2.** A place affording snug seclusion or lodging. **3. a.** A place or environment favoring rapid growth or development of something bad or dangerous; a hotbed: *a nest of rebellion.* **b.** The persons occupying or frequenting such a place. **4.** A set of objects, such as small tables, of graduated size, that can be stacked together, each fitting within the one immediately larger. **5.** A group of weapons in a prepared position: *a nest of missiles.* **—feather one's nest.** To exploit one's position for personal gain.
~*v.* **nested, nesting, nests.** *—intr.* **1.** To build or occupy a nest. **2.** To hunt for birds' nests, especially in order to collect the eggs. **3.** To fit together in a stack. *—tr.* **1.** To place in or as if in a nest. **2.** To place within or arrange into a hierarchy, as of mathematical operations. [Middle English *nest,* Old English *nest.*]

nest egg *n.* **1.** An artificial or natural egg placed in a nest to induce a bird to lay. **2.** A sum of money put by as a reserve.

nes·tle (nĕs′əl) *v.* **-tled, -tling, -tles.** *—intr.* **1. a.** To settle snugly and comfortably: *The kittens nestled lazily among the cushions.* **b.** To lie or be situated in a sheltered or snug position: *The cottage nestled in the wood.* **2.** To draw or press close, especially in an affectionate manner. Often used with *up: She nestled up to him.* **3.** *Archaic.* To nest. *—tr.* **1.** To place or settle as if in a nest: *nestled the baby in my arms.* **2.** To snuggle or press affectionately or contentedly: *nestled his head against her shoulder.* [Middle English *nestlen,* Old English *nestlian,* to make a nest.] **—nes·tler** *n.*

nest·ling (nĕst′lĭng) *n.* **1.** A bird too young and frail to leave its nest. **2.** A young child.

Nes·tor (nĕs′tər, -tôr′) *n.* **1.** In the Homeric poems, a hero celebrated for his age and wisdom. **2.** *Often* **nestor.** A venerable and wise old man.

Nes·to·ri·an (nĕ-stôr′ē-ən) *adj.* Of or designating a church of the East that adheres to the doctrines of Nestorius, a 5th-century Patriarch of Constantinople, asserting that Christ had two distinct natures, divine and human, and that the Virgin Mary should not be called the Mother of God.
~*n.* A member of this church. **—Nes·to·ri·an·ism** *n.*

net[1] (nĕt) *n.* **1. a.** An openwork material of fibers, cords, wire, or the like, with the threads woven, knotted, or twisted together at regular intervals, forming meshes of varying sizes. **b.** A light mesh fabric, used especially as a curtain or dress material. **2.** Something made of net: **a.** A device for capturing birds, fish, butterflies, or other animals. **b.** A device for excluding birds or insects, especially a **mosquito net** *(see).* **c.** A mesh for holding the hair in place. **3.** *Sports.* **a.** In games such as tennis and volleyball, a barrier of meshwork cord or rope strung between two posts to divide the playing area in half. **b.** A ball that is hit into such a net. Also called "net ball." **c.** Either of the goals in soccer, hockey, and lacrosse. **4.** A meshed network of lines, figures, or fibers. **5.** A situation or circumstance that entraps or is intended to trap.
~*tr.v.* **netted, netting, nets. 1.** To catch or entangle in or as if in a net. **2.** To cover, protect, or surround with or as if with a net. **3.** To hit (a ball) into a net. [Middle English, Old English *net(t).*]

net[2] *adj.* **1.** *Abbr.* **n. a.** Remaining after all necessary deductions have been made or all losses accounted for: *net profit.* Compare **gross. b.** Designating the weight remaining after tare is deducted. **2.** Ultimate; final: *net result; net conclusion.*
~*n. Abbr.* **n.** Total gain; the net amount, as of profit, income, price, or weight.
~*tr.v.* **netted, netting, nets.** To bring in as profit or as a final total. [Middle English *net,* neat, clear, plain, from Old French *net,* neat, elegant, from Latin *nitidus,* bright, clear, from *nitēre,* to shine.]

net·ball (nĕt′bôl′) *n. British.* A team game, usually played by women, similar to basketball but in which a player is not allowed to move while holding the ball or to let it touch the ground.

neth·er (nĕth′ər) *adj.* Located beneath or below. [Middle English *nether,* Old English *nithera,* lower, from *nither,* down, downward.]

Neth·er·lands (nĕth′ər-ləndz). *Dutch* **Ne·der·land** (nā′dər-länt′). Often called **Hol·land** (hŏl′ənd). A kingdom of northwestern Europe. A low-lying area, much of it reclaimed from the sea, with 40 percent of the land below sea level, it is a heavily agricultural state, but its economy has come to depend increasingly on industry and commerce. Dominated throughout its history by various European powers, it was in the 16th century a leader in European culture, commerce, and colonialism. The Hague is the seat of government. Area, 33,812 square kilometers (13,055 square miles). Population, 14,200,000. Capital, Amsterdam.

Netherlands An·til·les (ăn-tĭl′ēz). Formerly **Dutch West Indies.** Dutch-administered islands in the Caribbean, in two groups of islands more than 800 kilometers (500 miles) apart. The main group comprises Curaçao, Aruba, and Bonaire, off the coast of Venezuela; to the northeast are Saba, St. Eustatius, and the southern half of St. Martin (the northern half is French-owned). The islands' chief economic activity is the refining of petroleum from Venezuela. Area, 996 square kilometers (385 square miles). Population, 246,000. Capital, Willemstad (on Curaçao).

neth·er·most (nĕth′ər-mōst′) *adj.* Farthest down; deepest.

nether world *n.* **1.** The world of the dead; Hades. **2.** Hell. **3.** A place or situation likened to hell. Also called "nether regions."

net·su·ke (nĕt′sə-kē) *n.* A small toggle of wood or ivory, usually elaborately carved, used in Japan to fasten a small container or other article to a kimono sash. [Japanese.]

net·ting (nĕt′ĭng) *n.* **1.** Any openwork fabric or structure of string, wire, or the like. **2.** A piece of this fabric.

net·tle (nĕt′l) *n.* **1.** Any plant of the genus *Urtica,* such as *U. dioica,* the stinging nettle, having toothed leaves often covered with hairs that secrete a stinging fluid that affects the skin on contact. **2.** Any of various other stinging or prickly plants.
~*tr.v.* **nettled, -tling, -tles. 1.** To sting with or as if with a nettle. **2.** To irritate; vex. [Middle English *nettle,* Old English *netle, netel(e),* from Germanic.]

nettle rash *n.* **Urticaria** *(see).*

net ton *n.* See **ton** (sense 1b).

net·work (nĕt′wûrk′) *n.* **1.** An openwork fabric or other structure in which rope, thread, wires, or other materials cross at regular intervals. **2.** Something resembling a net in concept or form, such as: **a.** A system of lines or routes that cross or interconnect: *a network of railroads.* **b.** Any complex, interconnected group or system: *an espionage network.* **3.** A chain of interconnected radio or television broadcasting stations. **4.** A group or system of electrical components and connecting circuitry designed to function as a unit.
~*tr.v.* **networked, -working, -works.** To broadcast over a radio or television network.

net·work·ing (nĕt′wûr′kĭng) *n.* Establishment and use of a system of professional contacts in business and industry for such purposes as mutual guidance and exchange of information about jobs.

Neu·châ·tel (nœ′shə-tĕl′). A city in northwestern Switzerland, capital of the canton of the same name, on the north shore of Lake Neuchâtel. The town is noted for its manufacture of watches, jewelry, and chocolate.

Neu·mann (noi′män′), **Johannes von,** known as "John" (1903–57). Hungarian-born U.S. mathematician, naturalized in 1937. He developed the game theory and contributed to the mathematical analysis of quantum physics.

neumes, neums (no͞omz, nyo͞omz) *pl.n.* The signs used in the notation of plainsong during the Middle Ages, surviving today in transcriptions of Gregorian chant. [Middle English, musical phrase sung to a single syllable, from Old French, from Medieval Latin *neuma, neupma,* from Greek *pneuma,* breath.] **—neu·mat·ic** (no͞o-măt′ĭk, nyo͞o-) *adj.*

neur. neurological; neurology.

neu·ral (no͝or′əl, nyo͝or′-) *adj.* **1.** Of or pertaining to the nerves or nervous system. **2.** Of, pertaining to, or located on the same side of the body as the spinal cord; dorsal. [NEUR(O)- + -AL.]

neu·ral·gia (no͞o-răl′jə, nyo͞o-) *n.* Paroxysmal pain along a nerve. [New Latin : NEUR(O)- + -ALGIA.] **—neu·ral·gic** *adj.*

neu·ras·the·ni·a (no͝or′əs-thē′nē-ə, nyo͝or′-) *n.* A condition marked by abnormal fatigue, loss of energy and memory, and feelings of inadequacy, once thought to result from exhaustion of the nervous system. Also called "nervous breakdown," "nervous exhaustion," "nervous prostration." [NEUR(O)- + ASTHENIA.] **—neu·ras·then·ic** (nŏŏr'əs-thĕn'ĭk, nyŏŏr-) *adj.* **—neu·ras·then·i·cal·ly** *adv.*

neu·rax·on (nŏŏ-răk'sŏn', nyŏŏ-) *n.* A part of a nerve cell, the **axon** (see). [New Latin : NEUR(O)- + AXON.]

neu·rec·to·my (nŏŏ-rĕk'tə-mē, nyŏŏ-) *n., pl.* **-mies.** Surgical removal of a nerve or part of a nerve. [NEUR(O)- + -ECTOMY.]

neu·ri·lem·ma (nŏŏr'ə-lĕm'ə, nyŏŏr'-) *n.* The outer covering of a nerve fiber. [New Latin : NEUR(O)- + Greek *eilēma*, veil, covering, from *eilein*, to wind.] **—neu·ri·lem·mal, neu·ri·lem·ma·tous** (nŏŏr'-ə-lĕm'ə-təs, nyŏŏr'-) *adj.*

neu·ris·tor (nŏŏ-rĭs'tər, nyŏŏ-) *n.* An electronic device that is capable of relaying a signal without attenuation in velocity. [NEUR(ON) + (TRANS)ISTOR.]

neu·ri·tis (nŏŏ-rī'tĭs, nyŏŏ-) *n.* Inflammation of a nerve, causing pain, loss of reflexes, and muscular atrophy. [New Latin : NEUR(O)- + -ITIS.] **—neu·rit·ic** (nŏŏ-rĭt'ĭk, nyŏŏ-) *adj.*

neuro-, neur– *prefix.* Indicates nerve or nervous system; for example, **neuroblast, neurectomy.** [New Latin, from Greek *neuron*, tendon, nerve.]

neu·ro·blast (nŏŏr'ə-blăst', nyŏŏr'-) *n.* An embryonic cell from which a nerve cell develops. [NEURO- + -BLAST.]

neu·ro·cyte (nŏŏr'ə-sīt', nyŏŏr'-) *n.* A nerve cell.

neu·ro·en·do·crine system (nŏŏr'ō-ĕn'də-krĭn, -krēn', -krīn', nyŏŏr'-) *n.* The system of nerves and hormones that function together to control certain activities of the body.

neu·ro·fi·bril (nŏŏr'ō-fī'brəl, nyŏŏr'-) *n.* Any of the cytoplasmic threads in the cell body of a neuron, extending into the axon in peripheral nerves.

neu·ro·gen·ic (nŏŏr'ə-jĕn'ĭk, nyŏŏr'-) *adj.* **1.** Originating in the nervous system. **2.** Caused by stimulation of the nerves. **3.** Caused by disease of the nervous system. **—neu·ro·gen·i·cal·ly** *adv.*

neu·rog·li·a (nŏŏ-rŏg'lē-ə, nyŏŏ-) *n.* The network of branched cells and fibers that supports the nerve cells of the central nervous system. Also called "glia." [New Latin : NEURO- + Medieval Greek *glia*, "glue," tissue.] **—neu·rog·li·al** *adj.*

neu·ro·gram (nŏŏr'ə-grăm', nyŏŏr'-) *n.* An **engram** (see). [NEURO- + -GRAM.]

neu·ro·hor·mone (nŏŏr'ō-hôr'mōn', nyŏŏr'-) *n.* A hormone that is produced within nervous tissue and secreted by specialized nerve cells. An example is oxytocin, produced in the hypothalamus and secreted by the pituitary gland.

neu·ro·hy·poph·y·sis (nŏŏr'ō-hī-pŏf'ə-sĭs, nyŏŏr'-) *n.* The posterior part of the pituitary gland. Compare **adenohypophysis.**

neurol. neurological; neurology.

neu·rol·o·gy (nŏŏ-rŏl'ə-jē, nyŏŏ-) *n. Abbr.* **neur., neurol.** The branch of medical science concerned with the nervous system and its disorders. [New Latin *neurologia* : NEURO- + -LOGY.] **—neu·ro·log·i·cal** (nŏŏr'ə-lŏj'ĭ-kəl, nyŏŏr'-) *adj.* **—neu·rol·o·gist** *n.*

neu·ro·ma (nŏŏ-rō'mə, nyŏŏ-) *n., pl.* **-mata** (-mə-tə). A tumor made of nerve tissue. [New Latin : NEUR(O)- + -OMA.]

neu·ro·mus·cu·lar (nŏŏr'ō-mŭs'kyə-lər, nyŏŏr'-) *adj.* Of, pertaining to, or affecting both nerves and muscles.

neu·ron (nŏŏr'ŏn', nyŏŏr'-) *n.* Also **neu·rone** (nŏŏr'ōn', nyŏŏr'-). A **nerve cell** (see). [Greek *neuron*, sinew, nerve.] **—neu·ron·ic** (nŏŏ-rŏn'ĭk, nyŏŏ-) *adj.* **—neu·ron·i·cal·ly** *adv.*

neu·ro·path (nŏŏr'ə-păth', nyŏŏr'-) *n.* One suffering from or having a hereditary tendency toward nervous disorders or neurosis. **—neu·ro·path·ic, neu·ro·path·i·cal** *adj.* **—neu·ro·path·i·cal·ly** *adv.*

neu·ro·pa·thol·o·gy (nŏŏr'ō-pə-thŏl'ə-jē, nyŏŏr'-) *n.* The medical study of diseases of the nervous system. **—neu·ro·path·o·log·i·cal** (nŏŏr'ō-păth'ə-lŏj'ĭ-kəl, nyŏŏr'-) *adj.* **—neu·ro·pa·thol·o·gist** *n.*

neu·rop·a·thy (nŏŏ-rŏp'ə-thē, nyŏŏ-) *n.* Any disease or abnormality of the nervous system. [NEURO- + -PATHY.]

neu·ro·phys·i·ol·o·gy (nŏŏr'ō-fĭz'ē-ŏl'ə-jē, nyŏŏr'-) *n.* The study of the physical and chemical changes associated with the functioning of the nervous system. **—neu·ro·phys·i·o·log·i·cal** (nŏŏr'ō-fĭz'-ē-ə-lŏj'ĭ-kəl, nyŏŏr'-) *adj.* **—neu·ro·phys·i·ol·o·gist** *n.*

neu·ro·psy·chi·a·try (nŏŏr'ō-sī-kī'ə-trē, nyŏŏr'-) *n. Abbr.* **NP** The integrated medical study of both neurological and psychiatric disorders. **—neu·ro·psy·chi·at·ric** (nŏŏr'ō-sī'kē-ăt'rĭk, nyŏŏr'-) *adj.* **—neu·ro·psy·chi·a·trist** *n.*

neu·rop·ter·an (nŏŏ-rŏp'tər-ən, nyŏŏ-) Any insect of the order Neuroptera, having four net-veined wings, such as the ant lion and lacewing. *—adj.* Of or belonging to the Neuroptera. [New Latin *Neuroptera*, "nerve-winged" : NEURO- + -PTER-.] **—neu·rop·ter·ous** *adj.*

neu·ro·sis (nŏŏ-rō'sĭs, nyŏŏ-) *n., pl.* **-ses** (-sēz'). Any of various illnesses affecting the mind or emotions, without obvious organic lesion or change, and involving anxiety, depression, phobia, hysteria, or other abnormal patterns of behavior. Also called "psychoneurosis." Compare **psychosis.** [New Latin : NEUR(O)- + -OSIS.]

neu·ro·sur·ger·y (nŏŏr'ō-sûr'jər-ē, nyŏŏr'-) *n.* Surgery of any part of the nervous system. **—neu·ro·sur·geon** *n.* **—neu·ro·sur·gi·cal** *adj.*

neu·rot·ic (nŏŏ-rŏt'ĭk, nyŏŏ-) *adj.* **1.** Of or pertaining to a neurosis: *a neurotic disorder.* **2.** Suffering from neurosis: *a neurotic patient.* **3.** *Informal.* Overly anxious; obsessive: *neurotic about germs.* *—n.* A person suffering from a neurosis. **—neu·rot·i·cal·ly** *adv.*

neu·rot·i·cism (nŏŏ-rŏt'ə-sĭz'əm, nyŏŏ-) *n.* A neurotic personality or trait.

neu·rot·o·my (nŏŏ-rŏt'ə-mē, nyŏŏ-) *n., pl.* **-mies.** The surgical cut-

ting or stretching of a nerve, usually to relieve pain. [NEURO- + -TOMY.]

neu·ro·trans·mit·ter (nŏŏr'ō-trăns'mĭt-ər, -trănz'-, nyŏŏr'-) *n.* A chemical substance, such as acetylcholine, released from nerve endings and transmitting impulses across a synapse to nerve, muscle, or other cells. Also called "transmitter."

Neus·tri·a (nŏŏs'trē-ə, nyŏŏs'-). The western part of the Frankish kingdom during the Merovingian period (6th to 8th century). It consisted of the areas adjoining the Loire and Seine rivers and land farther to the north. **—Neus·tri·an** *n. & adj.*

neut. **1.** neuter. **2.** neutral.

neu·ter (nŏŏ'tər, nyŏŏ'-) *adj. Abbr.* **neut. 1.** *Grammar.* Neither masculine nor feminine in gender. **2.** Lacking sexual organs or having only nonfunctional ones; specifically: **a.** *Botany.* Having no pistils or stamens; asexual. **b.** *Zoology.* Sexually undeveloped. **3.** Taking no side; neutral. *—n.* **1.** *Grammar.* **a.** The neuter gender. **b.** A neuter word. **2. a.** A castrated animal. **b.** A sexually undeveloped or imperfectly developed female insect; a worker. **c.** A plant without stamens or pistils. **3.** A neutral person. *—tr.v.* **neutered, -tering, -ters.** To castrate (an animal). [Middle English *neutre*, from Old French, from Latin *neuter*, neither : *ne-*, not + *uter*, either of two.]

neu·tral (nŏŏ'trəl, nyŏŏ'-) *adj. Abbr.* **neut. 1.** Not inclining toward or actively taking either side, as in a war or other dispute. **2.** Belonging to neither side or party: *on neutral ground.* **3.** Occupying a middle position; not one thing or the other; indifferent. **4.** Of no sex; sexless; neuter. **5.** *Chemistry.* Of or designating a compound that is neither acidic nor alkaline. **6.** *Physics.* **a.** Of or designating a particle, object, or system that has neither positive nor negative electric charge. **b.** Of or designating a particle, object, or system that has a net electric charge of zero. **7.** Of or pertaining to the state of a mechanical system in which gears are not engaged for transmission of power. **8.** Achromatic (see). **9.** *Phonetics.* Designating a vowel that is pronounced with the tongue in a relaxed, middle position, such as the *a* in *around.* *—n.* **1.** One who takes no side in a dispute. **2. a.** A neutral nation. **b.** A citizen of a neutral nation. **3.** An achromatic color. **4.** The position of gears in a power system when power cannot be transmitted: *The car is in neutral.* [Latin *neutrālis*, neuter (grammatically), from NEUTER.] **—neu·tral·ly** *adv.*

neu·tral·ism (nŏŏ'trə-lĭz'əm, nyŏŏ'-) *n.* A political attitude of nonalignment or noninvolvement with conflicting alliances. **—neu·tral·ist** *adj. & n.*

neu·tral·i·ty (nŏŏ-trăl'ə-tē, nyŏŏ-) *n.* The state or policy of being neutral; especially, nonparticipation in war.

neu·tral·i·za·tion (nŏŏ'trə-lə-zā'shən, nyŏŏ-) *n.* **1.** The act of neu-

NETHERLANDS

NORTH SEA

West Frisian Islands — Schiermonnikoog · Ameland · Terschelling · Vlieland · Texel · Den Helder

Waddenzee · IJsselmeer (Zuiderzee) · Ems · Delfzijl · GRONINGEN · Groningen · Slochteren · FRIESLAND · Leeuwarden · Assen · DRENTE · Emmen · N.E. Polder

NORTH HOLLAND · Alkmaar · Noordzee Kanaal · Haarlem · Markerwaard · East Flevoland · South Flevoland · AMSTERDAM · Edam · Zwolle · IJssel · OVERIJSSEL · Hilversum · Apeldoorn · Deventer · Hengelo · Enschede · Leiden · NETHERLANDS · Amersfoort · GELDERLAND · 's-Gravenhage (The Hague) · SOUTH · Utrecht · UTRECHT · Hook of Holland · Delft · Gouda · Lek · Arnhem · Europoort · Rotterdam · Kinderdijk · Waal · Rhine · HOLLAND · Dordrecht · Gorinchem · Nijmegen · Maas · 's-Hertogenbosch · Schouwen · NORTH BRABANT · Walcheren · E. Schelde · Breda · Roosendaal · Tilburg · Middelburg · ZEELAND · Bergen op Zoom · Eindhoven · Vlissingen (Flushing) · W. Schelde

BELGIUM

GERMAN FEDERAL REPUBLIC

LIMBURG · Roermond · Heerlen · Maastricht

0 — 50 — 100 Km
0 — 25 — 50 Miles

6°E · 52°N

tralizing. **2.** *Chemistry.* A reaction between an acid and a base that yields a salt and water.

neu·tral·ize (nōō′trə-līz′, nyōō′-) *v.* **-ized, -izing, -izes.** —*tr.* **1.** To make neutral. **2.** To counterbalance or counteract and so render ineffective. **3.** To prohibit warfare in (an area) by signed agreement. **4.** *Chemistry.* **a.** To make (a solution) chemically neutral. **b.** To cause (an acid or base) to undergo neutralization. —*intr.* To become neutral. —**neu·tral·iz·er** *n.*
    Synonyms: *counteract, negate, nullify.*

neutral spirits *pl.n.* Ethyl alcohol distilled at or above 190 proof and used frequently in alcoholic beverage blends.

neu·tri·no (nōō-trē′nō, nyōō-) *n., pl.* **-nos.** *Physics.* Any of various electrically neutral particles, thought to be massless, belonging to the lepton family. Each is associated with a specific massive lepton; for example, the *electron-type neutrino* or the *muon-type neutrino.* [Italian, diminutive of *neutrone,* neutron, from English NEUTRON.]

neu·tron (nōō′trŏn′, nyōō′-) *n. Symbol* **n** *Physics.* An elementary particle of the baryon family, having almost the same mass as the proton but no electric charge. It is stable when bound in an atomic nucleus, but has a mean lifetime of approximately 15.5 minutes as a free particle. It is present in any atomic nucleus with mass number greater than one. [NEUTR(AL) + -ON.]

neutron bomb *n.* A nuclear weapon that produces a large number of high-energy neutrons but relatively little blast or long-term radioactivity. It is designed to kill people without causing excessive damage or contamination in the target area. Also called "enhanced radiation bomb."

neutron number *n. Symbol* **N** The number of neutrons in the nucleus of a given isotope.

neutron star *n.* A celestial body of great density, formed by the collapse of a star under its own gravity and consisting almost entirely of neutrons. A neutron star has a mass of between 1.5 and 3 times that of the sun, but may have a radius as small as 62 miles.

neu·tro·phil (nōō′trə-fĭl′, nyōō′-) *adj.* Also **neu·tro·phile** (-fīl′). Easily stained by neutral dyes. Said of such cells as leucocytes.
    ~*n.* A phagocytic leucocyte of a type having a lobed nucleus and granular cytoplasm that stains with neutral dyes. [NEUTR(AL) + -PHIL(E).]

Nev. Nevada.

Ne·va (nē′və). Navigable river, 74 kilometers (46 miles) long, of northwestern European U.S.S.R., connecting Lake Ladoga with the Gulf of Finland, an arm of the Baltic Sea.

Ne·va·da (nə-văd′ə, -vä′də). *Abbr.* **Nev.** State in the western United States, between California on the west and Utah on the east. Most of the state is within the desert region known as the Great Basin. Carson City is the capital, but the largest city is Las Vegas. Nevada is a leading supplier of copper, gold, iron ore, and mercury, and oil was discovered here in 1954. —**Ne·va·dan** *adj. & n.*

né·vé (nā-vā′) *n.* **1.** The upper part of a glacier, where the snow turns into ice. **2.** A field of snow at the head of a glacier. **3.** The granular snow typically found in such a field. See **firn.** [French (Swiss dialect), from Latin *nix* (stem *niv-*), snow.]

Nev·el·son (nĕv′əl-sən), **Louise** (1899-). U.S. sculptor, born in Russia. Her massive sculptures, often made of wood, cast metal, and found objects, are noted for their complex and rhythmic abstract shapes.

nev·er (nĕv′ər) *adv.* **1. a.** Not ever; on no occasion; at no time: *We have never met before. I waited but he never arrived.* **b.** Absolutely not; under no circumstances whatsoever. Used emphatically: *Do such a thing? Never!* **2.** Not at all; in no way: *Never fear.* [Middle English *never,* Old English *nǣfre* : *ne,* not + *ǣfre,* ever.]

nev·er·more (nĕv′ər-môr′, -mōr′) *adv.* Never again.

nev·er-nev·er land (nĕv′ər-nĕv′ər) *n.* An imaginary and wonderful place; a fantasy land. [After the country in J.M. Barrie's play *Peter Pan* (1904).]

nev·er·the·less (nĕv′ər-thə-lĕs′) *adv.* None the less; however.

Nevis. See **St. Kitts-Nevis.**

ne·vus, nae·vus (nē′vəs) *n., pl.* **-vi** (-vī′). Any congenital growth or mark on the skin, such as a birthmark or mole. [Latin, birthmark; akin to (*g*)*natus,* born.]

new (nōō, nyōō) *adj.* **newer, newest. 1.** Of recent origin; having existed only a short time; lately made, produced, or grown: *a new television series.* **2. a.** Not yet old; fresh; recent. **b.** Used for the first time; not secondhand. **3. a.** Previously existing but recognized, discovered, or encountered lately for the first time: *a new galaxy.* **b.** Not belonging to one's own previous experience: *visiting new places.* **4.** Freshly introduced; unfamiliar; unaccustomed. Used with *to* or *at: I'm new at it.* **5.** Being the latest in a sequence: *the new edition.* **6. a.** Newly entered into a state or position; being so for the first time: *the new rich.* **b.** Changed for the better; refreshed; rejuvenated: *A nap made a new man of him.* **7.** Different and distinct from a former one of the same type: *new neighbors.* **8. a.** Modern; current; fashionable: *a new dance.* **b.** In the most recent form, period, or development of something: *New Latin.* **9.** Novel; unconventional: *a new concept in bathroom accessories.* **10.** Designating crops that are harvested early: *new potatoes.* **11.** Additional; more: *send him some new work.*
    ~*adv.* Freshly; recently. Used in combination: *new-cut grass.* [Middle English *newe,* Old English *nēowe, nīwe.*] —**new·ness** *n.*
    Usage: *new, novel, original. New* is a general term referring to both time and condition. *Novel,* which emphasizes condition, is applied to that which is both new and strikingly unusual: *His symphony is not only new* (chronologically), *but novel in its treatment of*

folk songs. Original also emphasizes state rather than time and is said of that which is the first of its kind.

New Am·ster·dam (ăm′stər-dăm′). Dutch settlement established (1624) on the Hudson River at the southern end of Manhattan Island. It was the capital of New Netherland (1626–64) until it was captured by the British and renamed New York.

New·ark (nōō′ərk, nyōō′-). City of northeastern New Jersey, on the Passaic River and Newark Bay. It is a major industrial and commercial center.

New Bed·ford (bĕd′fərd). City of southeastern Massachusetts, on Buzzards Bay. It is a fishing and scalloping port and an industrial center. New Bedford was settled in 1640 and was once a major whaling port.

new·born (nōō′bôrn′, nyōō′-) *adj.* **1.** Very recently born: *a newborn baby.* **2.** Born anew: *newborn courage.*

New Brit·ain (brĭt′n). Volcanic island in the southwest Pacific Ocean, belonging to Papua New Guinea. It is the largest island in the Bismarck Archipelago. The chief town and port is Rabaul. The island is mountainous, with many active volcanoes and hot springs. See map at **Pacific Ocean.**

New Bruns·wick (brŭnz′wĭk). *Abbr.* **N.B.** Province in eastern Canada, south of Quebec and east of Maine. The capital is Fredericton; the two largest cities are Saint John and Moncton. Three quarters of the province is forested, and timber is the chief industry. About 40 percent of the population is French-speaking.

New·burg (nōō′bûrg′, nyōō′-) *adj.* Served in a sauce made from cream, egg yolks, butter, and wine: *lobster Newburg.* [Alteration of *Wenburg,* name of patron for whom sauce was created.]

New Cal·e·do·ni·a (kăl′ə-dō′nē-ə, -dōn′yə). Large island in the southwestern Pacific Ocean, lying *c.* 1,200 kilometers (750 miles) east of Australia. It has a number of smaller islands as dependencies and is itself an overseas territory belonging to France. Coffee is the main crop, but the economic value of the island lies in its rich mineral deposits. It was annexed by France in 1853. See map at **Pacific Ocean.**

New·cas·tle (nōō′kăs′əl, nyōō′-). Coastal city and port of New South Wales, in southeastern Australia, at the mouth of the Hunter River. It is a leading steel-manufacturing center.

Newcastle disease *n.* A severe and often fatal viral disease of poultry. [After NEWCASTLE-UPON-TYNE, where there was an outbreak in 1926.]

Newcastle-upon-Tyne (tīn). City in the metropolitan county of Tyne and Wear, northeastern England, on the north bank of the Tyne River. It is the hub of an industrial region known as Tyneside and one of the world's largest shipbuilding centers.

New Church *n.* The **New Jerusalem Church** (see).

New·combe (nōō′kəm, nyōō′-), **John** (1944-). Australian tennis player. He won the U.S. Open singles title in 1967 and 1973 and the doubles title in 1967, 1971, and 1973. He was also Wimbledon singles champion (1967, 1970, and 1971) and six times doubles champion (between 1965 and 1974).

new·com·er (nōō′kŭm′ər, nyōō′-) *n.* One who has lately come to a place or situation.

New Criticism *n.* A form of literary criticism developed in the early 1940's that stresses detailed analysis of the language, structure, imagery, and thematic tensions of the text and rejects biographical and historical considerations surrounding its composition as irrelevant. —**New Critic** *n.*

New Deal *n.* **1.** The programs and policies for economic recovery and reform, relief, and social security introduced during the 1930's by President Franklin D. Roosevelt and his administration. **2.** The period between 1933 and 1940 during which these programs and policies were developed.

New Delhi. See **Delhi.**

New Economic Policy *n.* The program in the U.S.S.R. between 1921 and 1928 whereby concessions were made to capitalism in small industry, the retail trade, and agriculture.

new·el (nōō′əl, nyōō′-) *n.* **1.** The vertical support at the center of a winding staircase. **2.** Any of the posts supporting a handrail at the bottom or on the landings of a staircase. Also called "newel post." [Middle English *nowell,* from Old French *nouel,* "kernel," newel, from Latin *nucālis,* nut-shaped, from *nux,* nut.]

New England. The extreme northeastern states of the United States: Maine, New Hampshire, Vermont, Massachusetts, Rhode Island, and Connecticut. —**New Englander** *n.*

New English Bible *n. Abbr.* **N.E.B.** A Modern English translation of the Bible and Apocrypha, prepared by a British interdenominational panel and published in full in 1970.

new·fan·gled (nōō′făng′gəld, nyōō′-) *adj.* **1.** Excessively or needlessly novel: *newfangled ideas.* **2.** *Archaic.* Excessively fond of novelty. Used derogatorily in both senses. [Middle English *newe fangled,* alteration of *newefangel,* fond of new things : NEW + *-fangel,* from Old English *fangol* (unattested), "ready to seize," from *fangen,* past participle of *fōn,* to seize.]

new-fash·ioned (nōō′făsh′ənd, nyōō′-) *adj.* Made according to or following a current fashion.

New·found·land¹ (nōō′fən-lənd, -lănd′, nyōō′-) *Abbr.* **Newf., N.F., Nfld.** Province in eastern Canada, comprising the island of Newfoundland (north of the Gulf of St. Lawrence) and the mainland region of Labrador. The capital and largest city is St. John's. For centuries the island has been important for fishing, but mining is now the leading industry. Newfoundland is Canada's largest supplier of iron.

newel *A central stone newel supports the steps of a spiral stairway at Dover Castle, in Dover, England, built in the 12th century.*

New·found·land² (nōō'fən-lənd, nyōō'-) n. A dog of a large breed, with a broad head and square muzzle, a powerful body, and a dense, usually black coat. [Believed bred in NEWFOUNDLAND, Canada.]

New France. The French possessions in Canada in the Colonial era. The name derived from the fur-trading Company of New France, but the region was formally proclaimed the royal province of New France by Louis XIV in 1663. Although French rule in Canada ended with the Treaty of Paris in 1763, the seigneurial system instituted in the province by the French monarchy was not abolished formally until 1854.

New·gate (nōō'gāt', -gĭt, nyōō'-). A famous prison in London, demolished in 1902.

New Greek n. Abbr. **NGk., N.Gr.** Modern Greek (see).

New Guin·ea (gĭn'ē). Island, c. 885,780 square kilometers (342,000 square miles), in the southwest Pacific Ocean. The second-largest island in the world, it is divided between the countries of Indonesia and Papua New Guinea.

New Hamp·shire (hămp'shər, -shîr', hăm'-). Abbr. **N.H.** State in the northeast United States, between Vermont and Maine. The capital is Concord; the largest cities are Manchester and Nashua. The northern part of the state is noted for the scenic beauty of its lakes and mountains. The industrial centers to the south make the state one of the most heavily industrialized in the United States.

New Har·mo·ny (här'mə-nē). Town of southwestern Indiana, on the Wabash River. It was founded (1814) by the Harmony Society and was the site (1825–28) of a utopian community established by Robert Owen. Many of the original buildings have been restored.

New Ha·ven (hā'vən). City and port in southern Connecticut. It is the site of Yale University (since 1716).

New Hebrides. See Vanuatu.

New High German n. Abbr. **N.H.G.** High German since the 16th century.

new·ish (nōō'ĭsh, nyōō'-) adj. Of fairly recent origin; fairly new.

New Jer·sey (jûr'zē). Abbr. **N.J.** State in the northeastern United States, on the Atlantic coast south of New York State and east of Pennsylvania. The capital is Trenton; the largest city is Newark. It is one of the most heavily populated and industrialized states. New Jersey was one of the original 13 colonies. **—New Jer·sey·ite** n.

New Je·ru·sa·lem (jə-rōō'sə-ləm, -zə-) n. The celestial city; heaven. [From the Apocalypse (Revelation), chapter 21.]

New Jerusalem Church n. The church, founded in 1787, based on the philosophy and teachings of Swedenborg. Also called "New Church." See **Swedenborgianism.**

New Journalism n. Journalism that is characterized by the reporter's subjective interpretations and personal involvement and that often features fictional dramatized elements to emphasize that involvement. **—New Journalist** n.

new krona n. The krona (see) of Iceland.

New Latin n. Abbr. **NL, NL., N.L.** The form of Latin in use, especially for scientific nomenclature, since the early Renaissance.

New Learning n. The revived study of the Bible and Greek and Latin classics that occurred in the 15th and 16th centuries in Renaissance Europe.

New Left n. A political movement originating in the United States in the 1960's, especially among college students, marked by active advocacy of radical changes in government, politics, and society. **—New Leftist** n.

New Lon·don (lŭn'dən). City of southeastern Connecticut, on the Thames River near its mouth on Long Island Sound. Laid out in 1646, it was a pirates' rendezvous during the Revolution and later a noted whaling and sealing port.

New Look n. **1.** A fashion in women's clothing of the late 1940's characterized by long, full skirts. **2. new look.** Any up-to-date fashion.

new·ly (nōō'lē, nyōō'-) adv. **1.** Lately; recently: newly baked bread. **2.** In a new or different way: an old idea newly phrased. **3.** Once more; anew: a newly painted room.

new·ly·wed (nōō'lē-wĕd', nyōō'-) n. A person recently married.

New·man (nōō'mən, nyōō'-), **John Henry** (1801–90). English poet and priest. As an Anglican he helped found the Oxford Movement (1833); he later joined the Roman Catholic Church (1845) and was made a cardinal (1879). His best-known works are Apologia pro Vita Sua (1864) and The Dream of Gerontius (1866).

Newman, Paul (1925–). U.S. film actor. Among his many successful films are Butch Cassidy and the Sundance Kid (1969) and The Sting (1973). He has also produced and directed films of his own.

New·mar·ket¹ (nōō'mär'kĭt, nyōō'-) n. Sometimes newmarket. A long, close-fitting coat for men and women, worn in England in the late 19th century. [After NEWMARKET, Suffolk.]

Newmarket². Town in Suffolk, in eastern England. It has been a famous racing town since the reign of James I.

new mathematics n. Mathematics taught in elementary and secondary schools that constructs mathematical relationships from set theory. Also called "new math."

New Mex·i·co (mĕk'sĭ-kō'). Abbr. **N.Mex.** State in the southwestern United States, south of Colorado and east of Arizona. The capital is Santa Fe; the largest city is Albuquerque. Most of the state consists of arid desert and forested mountain wilderness. New Mexico is the United States' leading supplier of uranium ore and a major supplier of manganese, potash, salt, and copper. Strong traces of Spanish culture remain: about a third of the population is of mixed Spanish

---

new mathematics

SETS AND THEIR SYMBOLS

A new language to help children understand relationships

Set theory explains the logical relationship between sets of objects and is the cornerstone of the new mathematics. A set is a collection of distinct objects, which may be concrete (for example, playing cards) or abstract (for example, numbers). A range of traditional and new mathematical symbols is used to express the concept mathematically; Venn diagrams use geometrical figures such as squares and circles to represent sets and the relations between them. Set theory notation is a useful language for expressing complex mathematical ideas.

NOTATION	MEANING	EXAMPLE	VENN DIAGRAM
$=$	is equal to	$2+2=4$	
$\neq$	is not equal to	$2+3\neq4$	
$<$	is less than	$2+1<4$	
$>$	is greater than	$2+3>4$	
$S=\{1,3,5\}$	the set of numbers 1, 3, 5 (a listed set).	If $S=$ the suits in a pack of cards, then: $S=\{♣ ♦ ♥ ♠\}$	or
S is $\{x: x \text{ is odd and } x<7\}$	the set of numbers x such that x is odd and is less than 7 (a defined set).		
ε	is a member of	If $S=$ the suits in a pack of cards, then: $♣ \varepsilon S$	or
$\mathscr{E}$ or U	the universal set	The set of aces is contained in $\mathscr{E}$, the universal set of a pack of cards	
$\varnothing$	the empty set: a set having no members (see $A \cap B = \varnothing$ below)	The set of black hearts and diamonds is the empty set, which is contained in every set $S = \varnothing$ (there are no black hearts and diamonds)	
$A \subset B$	A is a subset of B	The set of vowels is a subset of the set of the letters of the alphabet Vowels $\subset$ Alphabet $= \{a, e, i, o, u\}$	
$A \cup B$	union of sets A and B	$A=\{3,4,6,8\}$ $B=\{6,8,12,16\}$ $A \cup B=\{3,4,6,8,12,16\}$	
$A \cap B$	intersection of sets A and B	$A \cap B = \{6,8\}$	
$A \cap B = \varnothing$	A and B are disjoint; they have no members in common and their intersection is therefore empty	$A=$ even numbers $= \{2,4,8,16\}$ $B=$ odd numbers $= \{3,5,7,9\}$	or $A \cap B$ (empty)
A'	complement of A	if $\mathscr{E}=\{1,2,3,4,5,6,7,8,9\}$ and $A=\{$all numbers that 6 can be divided evenly by$\}$ then $A=\{1,2,3,6\}$ and $A'=\{4,5,7,8,9\}$ The complement of set A is everything not in A	

---

descent, and Spanish is still the dominant language in many parts. **—New Mex·i·can** n. & adj.

new moon n. **1.** The phase of the moon occurring when it passes between the earth and the sun and is invisible, or visible only as a narrow crescent at sunset. **2.** The crescent moon.

New Neth·er·land (nĕth'ər-lənd). Land in the Hudson River valley granted by Holland to the Dutch West India Company in 1621. The area included New Amsterdam, founded in 1624 on Manhattan Island (later New York City). The region was seized by England in 1664 and divided into the colonies of New York and New Jersey.

New Or·le·ans (ôr'lē-ənz, ôr'lənz, ôr-lēnz'). City in Louisiana, on the banks of the Mississippi River. It is the largest city in Louisiana and a major port. New Orleans is famous for the surviving French flavor of its buildings and night life, for its annual Mardi Gras carnival, and for its jazz and blues tradition, dating from the late 19th century. Andrew Jackson's forces defeated the British at the Battle of New Orleans in 1815.

New Orleans jazz *n.* A style of jazz developed in New Orleans from 1900 to 1925, characterized by collective improvisation on simple harmonies by a front line of clarinet, trumpet, and trombone.

New Ply·mouth (plĭm'əth). City on the west coast of North Island, New Zealand. It was founded by the New Plymouth Company in 1841 and for some years served as the landing point for settlers to New Zealand. It is now a busy commercial port and the distributing center for a surrounding dairy-farming region.

New·port[1] (nōō'pôrt', -pōrt', nyōō'-). Town on the Isle of Wight, off the coast of southern England. Situated at the navigable head of the Medina River, it is the island's administrative center.

Newport[2]. Port city and resort of southeastern Rhode Island. Settled in 1639, Newport quickly gained prominence and prosperity as a trading and shipbuilding center. It is noted for its historic restorations and "cottages," mansions such as the Breakers and Marble House that were built in the late 19th and early 20th centuries.

Newport[3]. City in Gwent, southeastern Wales, on the Bristol Channel at the mouth of the Usk River. Long an important port serving the west Monmouthshire coal field, it is now a leading center for the manufacture of steel.

Newport News. City in southeastern Virginia, at the mouth of the James River. It is one of the world's largest shipbuilding and ship-repairing centers.

news (nōōz, nyōōz) *n. Used with a singular verb.* **1. a.** Information about recent events of general interest, especially as reported by the mass media. Often used in combination: *newscast.* **b.** A presentation or broadcast of such information. Also used adjectivally: *news bulletin.* **2.** New information about a subject: *What's the news about John's operation?* **3. a.** A person, event, or thing that is a source of interest or provides scope for conversation. **b.** A subject that is given a great deal of coverage by the press, radio, and television: *The government's policies are still news after two years.*

news agency *n.* An organization that provides news coverage to subscribers, as to newspapers and periodicals. Also called "press agency," "press association."

news·a·gent (nōōz'ā'jənt, nyōōz'-) *n. British.* A newsdealer.

news·boy (nōōz'boi', nyōōz'-) *n.* A boy who sells or delivers newspapers.

news·break (nōōz'brāk', nyōōz'-) *n.* A newsworthy event.

news·cast (nōōz'kăst', -käst', nyōōz'-) *n.* A radio or television broadcast, often with commentary, of events in the news. [NEWS + (BROAD)CAST.] —**news·cast·er** *n.* —**news·cast·ing** *n.*

New Scotland Yard *n.* The official name for **Scotland Yard** (see).

news·deal·er (nōōz'dē'lər, nyōōz'-) *n.* A dealer who sells newspapers and magazines.

news·flash (nōōz'flăsh', nyōōz'-) *n.* A brief, usually unscheduled announcement of important news.

news·let·ter (nōōz'lĕt'ər, nyōōz'-) *n.* A printed periodical report giving news or information of interest to a special group.

news·man (nōōz'măn', nyōōz'-) *n., pl.* **-men** (-mĕn'). A person who gathers, reports, or edits news, as for a newspaper.

news·mong·er (nōōz'mŭng'gər, -mŏng'-, nyōōz'-) *n.* A person who spreads news, especially a gossip.

New South Wales (wālz). *Abbr.* **N.S.W.** State in southeastern Australia, bounded on the east by the Pacific Ocean. The capital and largest city is Sydney. The state is economically the most important in Australia; the leading product is steel.

New Spain (spān). The former Spanish possessions governed from Mexico City, including islands in the West Indies, Central America north of Panama, Mexico, the southwestern United States, and the Philippine Islands.

news·pa·per (nōōz'pā'pər, nyōōz'-) *n.* **1.** A publication, typically issued daily or weekly, printed on folded sheets of paper, and containing news and opinion of current events, feature articles, and usually advertising. Also called "paper." **2.** A newspaper-publishing company. **3.** The paper on which a newspaper has been printed: *wrapped in newspaper.*

news·pa·per·man (nōōz'pā'pər-măn', nyōōz'-) *n., pl.* **-men** (-mĕn'). **1.** The owner or publisher of a newspaper. **2.** A journalist or editor employed by a newspaper.

news·pa·per·wom·an (nōōz'pā'pər-wōōm'ən, nyōōz'-) *n., pl.* **-women** (-wĭm'ĭn). A woman who owns, publishes, or works for a newspaper.

new·speak (nōō'spēk', nyōō'-) *n.* Ambiguous and contradictory language full of jargon and propaganda, especially as used by politicians or bureaucrats. [After the bureaucratic language in George Orwell's novel, *1984.*]

news·print (nōōz'prĭnt', nyōōz'-) *n.* A cheap paper made from wood pulp and used chiefly for printing newspapers.

news·reel (nōōz'rēl', nyōōz'-) *n.* A short motion picture dealing with recent events.

news·room (nōōz'rōōm', -rŏom', nyōōz'-) *n.* A room in a newspaper office or radio or television station where news stories are researched, written, and edited.

news·stand (nōōz'stănd', nyōōz'-) *n.* An open booth or stand at which newspapers are sold.

New Style *n. Abbr.* **N.S.** The current method of reckoning the months and days of the year according to the Gregorian calendar,

as distinct from the former style of reckoning according to the Julian calendar.

news vendor *n.* A person who sells newspapers, especially at a newsstand.

New Sweden. Swedish colony (1638–55) in North America, on the Delaware River. It included parts of what are now Pennsylvania, New Jersey, and Delaware. Peter Stuyvesant and his Dutch forces took control of the colony in 1655.

news·wom·an (nōōz'wōōm'ən, nyōōz'-) *n., pl.* **-women** (-wĭm'ĭn). A woman who gathers, reports, or edits news.

news·wor·thy (nōōz'wûr'thē, nyōōz'-) *adj.* Of sufficient interest or importance to be reported as news.

news·y (nōō'zē, nyōō'-) *adj.* **-ier, -iest.** *Informal.* Full of news; informative.

newt (nōōt, nyōōt) *n.* Any small amphibian of the genus *Triturus* or related genera, having a long, slender body and tail and short legs. [Middle English, from the phrase *a newt(e),* originally *an ewt(e) : an* (indefinite article) + *ewt(e), evete,* EFT.]

new technology *n.* Technology and technological products developed during and since the 1970's and chiefly characterized by the use of microprocessors.

New Territories. The portion of Hong Kong colony leased by Great Britain from China in 1898 for 99 years. The area includes most of the colony's islands and the greater part of its mainland north of Kowloon.

New Test. New Testament.

New Testament *n. Abbr.* **NT, N.T., New Test.** The Gospels, Acts, Pauline and other Epistles, and the Book of Revelation, which together have been viewed by Christians as forming the record of the new dispensation belonging to the Church, as distinct from the Old Testament dispensation shared with Judaism. Together with the Old Testament it makes up the Christian Bible. [Translation of Latin *Novum Testāmentum,* translation of Greek *Kainē Diathēkē,* "new dispensation, covenant, or testament" (Mark 14:24).]

New Thought *n.* A modern religious movement that emphasizes spiritual healing and the creative power of positive thought.

new·ton (nōōt'n, nyōōt'n) *n. Abbr.* **N** *Physics.* The SI unit of force, equal to the force required to accelerate a mass of one kilogram one meter per second per second. It is equal to 100,000 dynes. [After Sir Isaac NEWTON.]

New·ton (nōōt'n, nyōōt'n), **Sir Isaac** (1642–1727). English mathematician and physicist. He devised calculus independently of Leibnitz and made important discoveries about light. His greatest work is his treatise on gravitation (supposedly inspired by the sight of a falling apple), *Principia Mathematica* (1687).

New·to·ni·an (nōō-tō'nē-ən, nyōō-) *adj.* Pertaining to or in accordance with the work of Newton, especially that in mechanics and gravitation: *Newtonian physics; a Newtonian explanation.*

Newtonian frame *n.* An inertial frame (see).

Newtonian telescope *n.* A type of telescope in which light from a distant object is reflected by a large concave mirror onto an angled plane mirror, which directs the light into an eyepiece.

Newton's law of gravitation *n.* The principle that two bodies attract each other with a force that is directly proportional to the product of the masses and inversely proportional to the square of their distance apart. It is often written in the form $F = G\, m_1 m_2/d^2$, where G is the gravitational constant.

Newton's laws of motion *pl.n.* Three laws describing motion, used as the basis for Newtonian mechanics. They are: a body continues in a state of rest or of uniform motion in a straight line unless it is acted on by external forces; the rate of change of momentum of a body is proportional to the external force; any force (*action*) on a system gives rise to an equal and opposite force (*reaction*).

new town *n.* A planned urban community designed for self-sufficiency and comprising housing, industrial, commercial, and recreational facilities.

new wave *n. Often* **New Wave.** **1.** A movement in the French cinema in the 1960's, led by such directors as Jean-Luc Godard and Alain Resnais, that abandoned traditional narrative techniques in favor of greater use of symbolism and abstraction. Also called "nouvelle vague." **2.** A form of rock music developed from punk rock in the late 1970's, showing a more sophisticated and commercial approach. **3.** Any cultural movement that is considered to be avant-garde or in reaction against traditional methods, styles, or techniques. [Translation of French *nouvelle vague.*]

New World. The countries of the Western Hemisphere: North and South America and adjacent islands.

new year *n.* **1.** The year about to begin or just begun. **2. New Year.** The first day or days of the calendar year. **3.** Rosh Hashanah (see).

New Year's Day *n.* The first day of the year, as reckoned according to the Gregorian calendar; January 1.

New Year's Eve *n.* The eve of New Year's Day; December 31.

New York[1] (yôrk). *Abbr.* **N.Y.** State in the northeastern United States, bordering on Canada to the west and north and on Pennsylvania and New Jersey to the south. The capital is Albany; the largest city is New York. The other major cities, Buffalo, Rochester, and Syracuse, are near the New York State Barge Canal, which crosses the central region of the state from east to west. In the regions between New York's many industrial and commercial towns and cities there is rich mixed farming land. The state's origins can be traced to 1664, when England seized from the Dutch the land around the Hudson River known as New Netherland and divided it into the colonies of New York and New Jersey. New York

newt *These lizardlike amphibians are a type of salamander; they are widely distributed. Like all amphibians, they need a wet environment, absorbing water through their skin. Triturus alpestris (above) is found mostly in central and eastern Europe.*

was one of the original 13 colonies. —**New York·er** n.

New York². Largest city in the United States, on the northeastern coast at the mouth of the Hudson River on New York Bay. It consists of five boroughs: Manhattan (an island), Queens and Brooklyn (both on Long Island), Richmond (on Staten Island), and the Bronx (on the mainland). The metropolitan area of the city spills over into New Jersey and Connecticut. New York is one of the world's busiest ports. Since the end of World War II the city has gradually replaced London as the world's financial center and is the artistic and publishing center of the United States. Many of its streets, such as Wall Street (finance), Broadway (the theater), Madison Avenue (advertising), and Fifth Avenue (shopping), have become world famous. New York's population, including large numbers of blacks, Puerto Ricans, and European immigrants, is the most ethnically varied of any American city. It dates from the establishment of New Amsterdam on Manhattan Island in 1624. —**New York·er** n.

New Zea·land (zē′lənd). *Abbr.* **N.Z.** *Maori* **A·o·te·a·ro·a** (ä′ō-tē′ə-rō′-ə). Independent dominion within the Commonwealth, consisting of two main islands, North Island and South Island, and some smaller islands, in the southwest Pacific Ocean southeast of Australia. The islands are poor in natural resources, and the mainstay of the country's economy is the export of agricultural products, especially meat and dairy products. The population is predominantly of British stock; the indigenous Maoris make up less than 10 percent of the total. The islands were first settled by Polynesians in the 9th or 10th century. New Zealand became a British colony in 1840, received a large measure of self-government in 1852, and was granted dominion status in 1907. Area, 269,057 square kilometers (167,192 square miles). Population, 3,200,000. Capital, Wellington. —**New Zea·land·er** n.

New Zealand flax n. See **phormium.**

next (někst) *adj.* **1.** Nearest in space; adjacent: *the next room.* **2.** Coming directly after in time or sequence; immediately succeeding: *next Monday; the next person on the list.* —*adv.* **1.** In the time, order, or place immediately following: *What comes next?* **2.** On the first subsequent occasion: *when next I write.* —**next to. 1.** Adjacent to; in the closest place to: *the car next to yours.* **2.** Following in order or degree: *Next to skiing he likes hiking best.* **3.** Almost; practically: *next to impossible.* —*prep.* Next to: *I like the feel of cotton next my skin.* —*n.* The next person or thing: *The next will be better.* [Middle English *nexte,* Old English *nēahst, nēhst,* superlative of *nēah,* near.]

Usage: *Next* and *nearest* are sometimes interchangeable, but not always. *Next* always indicates direct succession in a series. *Nearest,* which does not necessarily imply a sequence, is employed more generally to indicate the closest proximity, as in time, space, or kinship.

next door *adv.* To or in the adjacent house or building. —**next-door** (někst′dôr′, -dōr′) *adj.*

next friend n. *Law.* One who is admitted to court to sue as the representative of a minor or other person under legal disability.

next of kin n., pl. **next of kin. 1.** The person most nearly related to one by blood. **2.** *Law.* **a.** The closest relative of a deceased person. **b.** *Used with a plural verb.* Those relatives entitled to the estate of a deceased person in accordance with the statutes of distribution.

nex·us (něk′səs) n., pl. **nexus** or **-uses. 1.** The bond, link, or tie existing between members of a group or series; a means of connection between things. **2.** A connected series or group. **3.** *Anatomy.* A connection or link. [Latin, from *nectere* (past participle *nexus*), to bind, connect.]

Ney (nā), **Michel, Duc d'Elchingen et Prince de la Moskova** (1769–1815). French marshal. His command of the rear guard in the retreat from Moscow (1812) saved Napoleon's army from annihilation. He deserted Louis XVIII to rejoin Napoleon in the Waterloo campaign. Ney was shot for treason by the restored monarchy.

Nez Perce (něz′ pûrs′) n., pl. **Nez Perces** (pûr′sĭz) or collectively **Nez Perce. 1.** A member of an American Indian people formerly occupying much of the Pacific Northwest. **2.** The language of this people, of the Sahaptin family of languages. [Canadian French *Nez Percé,* "pierced nose," either translation of Salish *Chopunnish,* "Nez Perce," or from the pierced nose sign whereby the tribe was designated in Salishan sign language, presumably with reference to the custom of wearing ornamental seashells on pierced noses.]

N.F. 1. Newfoundland. **2.** Norman French.

NFL National Football League.

Nfld. Newfoundland.

N.G. National Guard.

ngai·o (nī′ō) n. A small tree, *Myoporum laetum,* of New Zealand, producing a useful wood. [Maori.]

n'gana. Variant of **nagana.**

NGk., N.Gr. New Greek.

NGO n., pl. **NGOs.** An organization not under direct government control that is concerned with human welfare in such fields as health, the environment, or economics. [*N*ongovernmental *o*rganization.]

ngul·trum (əng-gŭl′trəm) n. The monetary unit of Bhutan, introduced in 1974, equivalent in value to an Indian rupee and equal to 100 tikchungs or chetrum. See feature at **currency.** [Bhutanese.]

Ngu·ni (əng-gōō′nē) n. A group of languages of the Bantu family, including Swazi, Xhosa, and Zulu, spoken chiefly in southern Africa.

ngwee (əng-gwā′) n. A coin equal to 1/100 of the kwacha of Zambia.

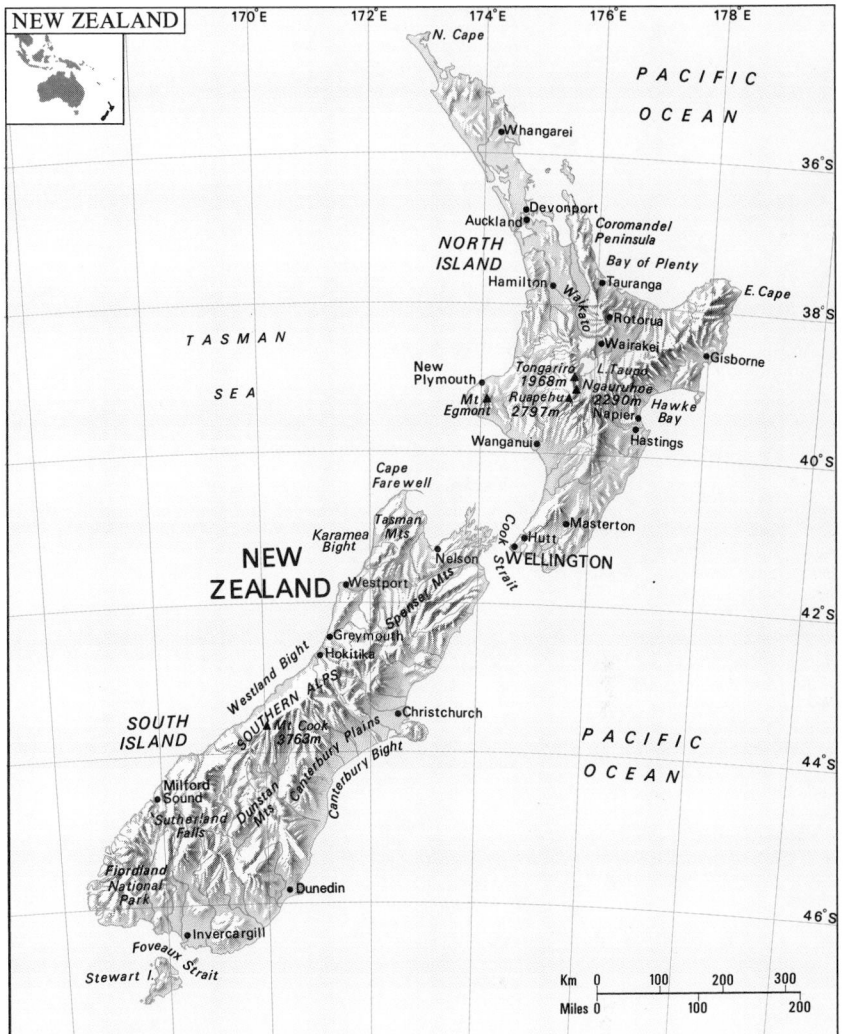

See feature at **currency.** [Chibemba, "bright."]

NH New Hampshire (used with a Zip Code).

N.H. New Hampshire.

N.H.G. New High German.

NHL National Hockey League.

NHS National Health Service (in Britain).

Ni The symbol for the element nickel.

N.I. 1. National Insurance (in Britain). **2.** Northern Ireland.

ni·a·cin (nī′ə-sĭn) n. One of the B vitamins, **nicotinic acid** *(see).* [NI(COTINIC) AC(ID) + -IN.]

Ni·ag·a·ra Falls (nī-ăg′rə, -ər-ə). Spectacular cataract on the border between Canada and the United States, on the Niagara River between Lake Erie and Lake Ontario. The cataract consists of two main falls, the American Falls (51 meters; 167 feet) in New York State and the Canadian or Horseshoe Falls (48 meters; 158 feet) in the province of Ontario. The falls are a popular tourist attraction and a major supplier of hydroelectric energy.

Nia·mey (nyä-mā′). Capital of Niger, on the Niger River in the southwest of the country. It is Niger's largest city and chief port. It has been the capital since 1926.

nib (nĭb) n. **1. a.** The point of a quill pen, especially when sharpened. **b.** A tapered penpoint designed to be inserted into a penholder or fountain pen. **2.** A beak or bill, as of a bird; a neb. **3.** Any small, sharp, projecting point or tip. [Probably of Low German origin, variant of NEB.]

nib·ble (nĭb′əl) v. **-bled, -bling, -bles.** —*tr.* **1.** To bite at gently and repeatedly. **2. a.** To eat with small, quick bites, in the manner of a mouse or other small creature. **b.** To eat in small morsels: *nibble a biscuit.* —*intr.* **1.** To take small or hesitant bites: *The fish nibbled at the bait.* **2.** To raise petty objections or criticisms; carp. Used with *at.* **3.** To show cautious interest. Used with *at.* —*n.* **1.** A very small quantity, especially of food; a bite; a morsel. **2.** An act or instance of nibbling. **3.** *Computer Science.* Half a **byte** *(see).* [Probably from Low German *nibbeln, knibbeln,* to gnaw, nibble.]

Ni·be·lung (nē′bə-lŏng′) n., pl. **-lungs** or **-lungen** (-lŏng′ən). *Germanic Mythology.* **1.** Any of a race of subterranean dwarfs who possessed a hoard of riches and a magic ring, taken from them by Siegfried. **2.** Any of the followers of Siegfried. **3.** Any of the Burgundian kings in the *Nibelungenlied.* [German, from Middle High

niche *A niche in the tomb of Pope Julius II, at the church of St. Peter in Chains (San Pietro in Vincoli), in Rome. The niche contains a statue of Leah, attributed to Michelangelo. He was commissioned by Julius to build the tomb, which was to have had 40 statues, but in the end Michelangelo sculpted only a statue of Moses, and possibly Leah and Rachel flanking Moses in their niches.*

PRONUNCIATION KEY

ă, pat; ā, pay; âr, care;
ä, father, are; b, bib;
ch, church; d, deed; ĕ, pet;
ē, be; f, fife; g, gag; h, hat;
hw, which; ĭ, pit; ī, pie;
îr, pier; j, judge; k, kick;
l, lid, needle; m, mum;
n, no, sudden; ng, thing;
ŏ, pot; ō, toe; ô, paw, for;
oi, noise; ou, out; o͝o, book;
o͞o, boot; p, pop; r, roar;
s, sauce; sh, ship, dish;
t, tight; th, thin, path;
th, this, bathe; ŭ, cut; ûr, fur;
v, valve; w, with; y, yes;
z, zebra, size; zh, vision;
ə, about, item, edible, gallop, circus, peaceful

IN FOREIGN WORDS:

à, *Fr.* ami; œ, *Fr.* feu, *Ger.* schön; ü, *Fr.* tu, *Ger.* über; KH, *Ger.* ich, *Scot.* loch; N, *Fr.* bon; y', *Fr.* Compiègne

STRESS MARKS:

Primary stress: ′
in·cite′ (ĭn-sīt′)
Secondary stress: ′
in′sight′ (ĭn′sīt′)

German *Nibelungen,* probably corresponding to a tribal name *Nebulones,* perhaps from Old High German *nĕbul,* mist.]

Ni·be·lung·en·lied (nē′bə-lo͝ong′ən-lēt′) *n.* A Middle High German epic poem written in the early 13th century by an unknown author, based on the legends of Siegfried and the Burgundian kings.

nib·lick (nĭb′lĭk) *n.* A golf club, a **nine iron** *(see).* [19th century : origin obscure.]

nibs (nĭbz) *n. Informal. Used with a singular verb.* A person who is in authority or who is self-important. Used humorously in the expression *his nibs.* [19th century : akin to earlier (cant) *nabs*† (as in *his nabs,* himself).]

Nic·a·ra·gua (nĭk′ə-rä′gwə). Largest republic on the Central American mainland. It is sparsely populated, and the mainstay of the economy is agriculture—cotton, coffee, rice, sugar, and tobacco. Nicaragua was a Spanish possession until it gained its independence in 1821. Area, 130,000 square kilometers (50,193 square miles). Population, 2,700,000. Capital, Managua. See map at **Central American States.** **—Nic·a·ra·guan** *adj. & n.*

Nicaragua, Lake. Largest lake in Central America, in southern Nicaragua. It is a freshwater lake, but supports some saltwater fish, especially tuna and sharks, that have adapted to its water.

nic·co·lite (nĭk′ə-līt′) *n.* A nickel ore, essentially nickel arsenide, NiAs, found in America and Europe. Also called "arsenical nickel," "copper nickel." [New Latin *niccolum,* nickel, probably from Swedish *nickel,* NICKEL + -ITE.]

nice (nīs) *adj.* **nicer, nicest. 1.** Pleasing to the mind or the senses; attractive; appealing: *a nice dress.* **2.** Kind; considerate; well-mannered: *a nice person.* Sometimes used ironically: *That's a nice thing to say!* **3.** Morally upright; virtuous: *a nice girl, careful of her reputation.* **4.** Showing refinement or delicacy; proper; seemly: *a nice way of putting it.* Sometimes used ironically: *You have some nice friends!* **5.** *Archaic.* Difficult to please; fastidious; exacting: *"Good company requires only birth, education, and manners, and with regard to education is not very nice"* (Jane Austen). **6. a.** Showing or requiring sensitive critical discernment; subtle: *a nice distinction.* **b.** Done with precision and skill; deft: *a nice bit of craftsmanship.* **7.** *Obsolete.* **a.** Wanton; profligate. **b.** Affectedly modest; coy. **c.** Silly. **—nice and.** Pleasingly: *nice and cozy.* [Middle English, foolish, wanton, shy, from Old French, silly, from Latin *nescius,* ignorant, from *nescīre,* to be ignorant : *ne-,* not + *scīre,* to know.] **—nice·ness** *n.*

Nice (nēs). Capital of the department of Alpes-Maritimes, France, on the Mediterranean Sea. It is a famous tourist resort and important as a commercial port and industrial city.

nice·ly (nīs′lē) *adv.* **1.** In a pleasing manner: *She sings nicely.* **2.** With precision; exactly: *nicely balanced.* **3.** Satisfactorily; acceptably: *That'll do nicely.*

Ni·cene Creed (nī′sēn′) *n.* **1.** A formal statement of the tenets of Christian faith, and chiefly of the doctrine of the Trinity, set forth by the Council of Nicaea in A.D. 325. **2.** Any of several modifications of this statement, now used in the services of various Christian churches.

ni·ce·ty (nī′sə-tē) *n., pl.* **-ties. 1.** The quality of showing or requiring careful and precise treatment; delicacy; subtlety: *the nicety of a diplomatic exchange.* **2.** Delicacy of character or feeling; scrupulousness; fastidiousness. **3.** *Usually* **niceties.** A subtle point, detail, or distinction: *He left the niceties of spelling to his secretary.* **4.** *Usually* **niceties.** An elegant or refined characteristic or feature; an amenity: *the niceties of civilized life.* **—to a nicety.** With the utmost care and precision; exactly. [Middle English *nicete,* nicety, foolishness, from Old French *nicete,* foolishness, from *nice,* silly, NICE.]

niche (nĭch) *n.* **1.** A recess in a wall for holding a statue or other ornament. **2.** Any steep, shallow recess or concavity, as in a rock or hill. **3.** A situation or activity specially suited to a person's abilities or character. **4.** *Ecology.* **a.** The role and status of an organism within the community it occupies. **b.** The area within a habitat occupied by an organism.
~tr.v. **niched, niching, niches.** To place in a niche. [French, from Old French *niche,* "nest," from *nichier,* to nest, from Vulgar Latin *nīdicāre* (unattested), from Latin *nīdus,* nest.]

Nich·o·las I (nĭk′ə-ləs) (1796–1855). Russian czar (1825–55). A reactionary, he suppressed the reformist Decembrist movement and strengthened the autocracy with the aid of censorship and the secret police. His willingness to assist Turkey's Christians against the sultan involved him in the Crimean War (1853–56). The outstanding achievement of his reign was the codification of all existing laws.

Nicholas II (1868–1918). The last Russian czar (1894–1917). He pursued a policy of expansionism in the Balkans and Asia. This culminated in Russia's defeat in the Russo-Japanese War (1904–05) and the 1905 Revolution. Internal difficulties, reverses during World War I, the unpopularity of the court under Rasputin and the czarina, and governmental incompetence all helped precipitate the 1917 Revolution. Forced to abdicate, he and his family were shot by Bolsheviks at Ekaterinburg (Sverdlovsk).

Nicholas, Saint (4th century A.D.). Patron saint of children, sailors, and Russia. Believed to have been bishop of Myra, he is attributed with charitable works and miracles; the practice of giving presents on his feast day (December 6) has been transferred to Christmas. He has passed into folklore as Father Christmas or Santa Claus.

Nich·ols (nĭk′əlz), **Mike** (1931–). U.S. comedian and director, born in Germany. He first won critical acclaim as an improvisational comedian paired with Elaine May. He has since won Tony Awards for his direction of the Broadway productions *Barefoot in the Park, The Odd Couple, Luv,* and *The Real Thing.*

Nich·ol·son (nĭk′əl-sən), **Jack** (1937–). U.S. actor. His films include *Chinatown* (1974) and *One Flew Over the Cuckoo's Nest* (1976), for which he won an Academy Award.

Ni·chrome (nī′krōm′) *n.* A trademark for an alloy of nickel, iron, and chromium. It has a high resistance and is used in electrical heating elements.

nick (nĭk) *n.* **1.** A shallow notch, cut, or indentation on a surface: *nicks in the table; a razor nick in his chin.* **2.** *Printing.* A groove down the side of a piece of type used to ensure that it is correctly placed. **3.** *British Slang.* A prison or police station. **—in the nick of time.** Just at the critical moment; just in time: *The police arrived in the nick of time.*
~v. **nicked, nicking, nicks.** *—tr.* **1.** To cut a nick or notch in. **2.** To graze and wound slightly: *A sliver of glass nicked his hand.* **3.** To cut short; check: *He nicked his impulse.* **4.** *Slang.* To cheat, especially by overcharging. **5.** *British Slang.* **a.** To steal. **b.** To arrest. *—intr.* To mingle or mate together successfully. Used of breeding stock. [Middle English *nyke*† (noun).]

nick·el (nĭk′əl) *n.* **1.** *Symbol* **Ni** A silvery, hard, ductile, ferromagnetic metallic element. It is used in alloys, in corrosion-resistant surfaces and batteries, and for electroplating. Atomic number 28, atomic weight 58.71, melting point 1,455°C, boiling point 2,900°C, specific gravity 8.902, principal valence 2. **2.** A U.S. coin worth five cents, made of a nickel and copper alloy.
~tr.v. **nickeled** or **-elled, -eling** or **-elling, -els.** To coat with nickel. [Shortened from German *Kupfernickel,* "copper-demon," an old mining term for niccolite, from which nickel was first extracted (so called because it appeared to contain copper but did not) : *Kupfer,* copper, from Old High German *kupfar,* from Late Latin *cuprum, cyprum,* COPPER + *nickel,* demon, dwarf, from *Nickel,* familiar form of the name *Nikolaus,* NICHOLAS (probably by association with *Nix,* sprite, NIX).]

nickel bloom *n.* A rare mineral, **annabergite** *(see).*

nick·el·ic (nĭ-kĕl′ĭk) *adj.* Of or containing nickel. Said especially of compounds containing nickel with a valence of 3.

nick·el·if·er·ous (nĭk′ə-lĭf′ər-əs) *adj.* Bearing or containing nickel. Said of ores.

nick·el·o·de·on (nĭk′ə-lō′dē-ən) *n.* **1.** In the early 20th century, a movie theater that charged an admission price of five cents. **2.** A juke box or player piano. [NICKEL + (MEL)ODEON.]

nick·el·ous (nĭk′ə-ləs) *adj.* Of or containing nickel. Said especially of compounds containing nickel with a valence of 2.

nickel plate *n.* **1.** A thin layer of nickel on a metal surface, usually formed by electrolysis. **2.** Material or articles with such a layer.

nick·el-plate (nĭk′əl-plāt′) *tr.v.* **-plated, -plating, -plates.** To deposit a thin, even layer of nickel on (a surface of metal or other conducting material), as by the electrolysis of a solution containing nickel.

nickel silver *n.* A silvery, hard, corrosion-resistant, malleable alloy of copper, zinc, and nickel, used in tableware. It contains no silver. Also formerly called "German silver."

nick·er¹ (nĭk′ər) *intr.v.* **-ered, -ering, -ers.** To neigh softly. [Perhaps from NEIGH.] **—nick·er** *n.*

nicker² *n. British Slang.* One pound sterling. [20th century : origin obscure.]

Nick·laus (nĭk′ləs), **Jack William** (1940–). U.S. golfer. He has won 17 major international titles, including 6 Masters' championships.

nick·nack. Variant of **knick-knack.**

nick·name (nĭk′nām′) *n.* **1.** A name added to or replacing the actual name of a person, place, or thing, often used humorously or affectionately and referring to some notable characteristic. **2.** A familiar or shortened form of a proper name.
~tr.v. **nicknamed, -naming, -names. 1.** To give a nickname to; call by a nickname. **2.** To call by an incorrect name; misname. [Middle English *a nekename,* originally *an ekename,* an additional name : *eke,* an addition, Old English *ēaca* + NAME.]

Nicobar Islands. See **Andaman and Nicobar Islands.**

Nic·o·de·mus (nĭk′ə-dē′məs). A Pharisee and member of the Sanhedrin who was a secret disciple of Christ and provided his tomb.

Ni·co·let (nĭk′ə-lā′), **Jean** (1598–1642). French explorer in North America. He accompanied Samuel de Champlain to New France (1618) and later lived among the Indians on the upper Ottawa River. Nicolet was the first European to explore Lake Michigan and northern Wisconsin.

Nic·ol prism (nĭk′əl) *n. Physics.* A device for producing or analyzing plane-polarized light, consisting of a piece of calcite cut at suitable angles and cemented with Canada balsam. It is used especially in microscopes to identify minerals within a thin slice of rock. Also called "polarizer," "polaroid." [After William *Nicol* (1768–1851), Scottish physicist who invented it.]

Nic·ol·son (nĭk′əl-sən), **Sir Harold George** (1886–1968). British diplomat, critic, and biographer. An M.P. (1935–45), he published studies of poets, a biography of George V, and volumes of his diaries and letters. He married the novelist Vita Sackville-West.

Nic·o·si·a (nĭk′ə-sē′ə). Capital city of Cyprus, in the north-central part of the island on the flat, arid Mesaoria Plain. It is the country's largest city and its chief trading center. Since the Turkish invasion of 1974, its northern half has been in Turkish hands.

ni·co·ti·an·a (nĭ-kō′shē-ăn′ə, -ä′nə, -ā′nə) *n.* Any of various flowering plants of the genus *Nicotiana,* native to the Americas and including ornamental species with fragrant flowers as well as the tobacco plant. [New Latin *herba nicotiana,* "herb of Nicot," after

Jean *Nicot*, French ambassador at Lisbon, who in 1560 sent some tobacco to Catherine de Médici.]

nic·o·tin·a·mide (nĭk′ə-tĭn′ə-mīd′, -tē′nə-) *n.* The amide of nicotinic acid, having similar vitamin activity. [NICOTIN(E) + AMIDE.]

nicotinamide adenine dinucleotide *n.* **NAD** *(see).*

nicotinamide adenine dinucleotide phosphate *n.* **NADP** *(see).*

nic·o·tine (nĭk′ə-tēn′) *n.* A poisonous alkaloid, $C_5H_4NC_4H_7NCH_3$, derived from the tobacco plant and used as an insecticide. [French, earlier *nicotiane,* from NICOTIANA.]

nic·o·tin·ic (nĭk′ə-tĭn′ĭk) *adj.* **1.** Of or pertaining to nicotine. **2.** Of or pertaining to nicotinic acid.

nicotinic acid *n.* A member of the vitamin B complex, C_5H_4NCOOH, essential for growth and synthesized for use in treating pellagra. Dietary sources include milk, yeast, and liver. Also called "niacin." [Often obtained by the oxidation of NICOTINE.]

nic·o·tin·ism (nĭk′ə-tēn-ĭz′əm) *n.* Nicotine poisoning.

nic·ti·tate (nĭk′tə-tāt′) *intr.v.* **-tated, -tating, -tates.** Also **nic·tate** (nĭk′tāt′). To wink. —**nic·ti·ta·tion** *n.*

nictitating membrane *n.* Also **nictating membrane.** An inner eyelid in birds, reptiles, and some mammals that helps to keep the eye clean.

Nidaros. See Trondheim.

nid·der·ing, nid·er·ing (nĭd′ər-ĭng) *n. Archaic.* A cowardly person; a wretch. ~*adj. Archaic.* Base; cowardly; vile. [Earlier *nidering,* 16th-century misreading of Middle English *nithing,* Old English *nīthing,* wretch, coward, villain, from Old Norse *nīdhingr,* from *nīdh,* scorn.]

nide (nīd) *n.* A nest or brood of pheasants. [Latin *nīdus,* nest.]

ni·dic·o·lous (nī-dĭk′ə-ləs) *adj.* Requiring a relatively long stay in the nest after hatching. Said of birds that are born blind and helpless. [Latin *nīdus,* nest + *colere,* to inhabit.]

ni·dif·u·gous (nī-dĭf′yə-gəs) *adj.* Able to leave the nest soon after hatching. Said of birds that are born well developed. [Latin *nīdus,* nest + *fugere,* to leave, flee.]

nid·i·fy (nĭd′ə-fī′) *intr.v.* **-fied, -fying, -fies.** Also **nid·i·fi·cate** (nĭd′ə-fĭ-kāt′) **-cated, -cating, -cates.** To build a nest. [Latin *nīdificāre* : *nīdus,* nest + *facere,* to make.] —**nid·i·fi·cant** (nĭd′ə-fĭ-kənt) *adj.* —**nid·i·fi·ca·tion** (nĭd′ə-fĭ-kā′shən) *n.*

ni·dus (nī′dəs) *n., pl.* **-duses** or **-di** (-dī′). **1.** A nest; especially, one for the eggs of insects or spiders. **2.** A cavity where spores develop. **3.** *Pathology.* The seat of bacterial growth in a living organism; a focus of infection. [Latin *nīdus,* nest.]

Nie·buhr (nē′boŏr), **Reinhold** (1892–1971). U.S. theologian. He was a professor at Union Theological Seminary in New York City from 1928 to 1960. His works include *Moral Man and Immoral Society* (1932), *The Nature and Destiny of Man* (two volumes, 1941–43), and *Faith and History* (1949).

niece (nēs) *n.* The daughter of one's brother or sister, or of one's spouse's brother or sister. [Middle English *nece,* from Norman French, Old French *niece,* from Vulgar Latin *neptia* (unattested), from Latin *neptis,* granddaughter, niece.]

ni·el·lo (nē-ĕl′ō) *n., pl.* **-elli** (-ĕl′ē) or **-los. 1.** Any of several black compounds of sulfur with copper, silver, or lead, used to fill an incised design on the surface of another metal. **2.** A surface or object decorated with niello. **3.** The art or process of ornamenting metal surfaces with niello. ~*tr.v.* **nielloed, -loing, -los.** To decorate or inlay with niello. [Italian, from Medieval Latin *nigellum,* from Latin *nigellus,* blackish, diminutive of *niger,* black.] —**ni·el·list** *n.*

Niemen. See Neman.

Nie·mey·er (nē-mī′ər), **Oscar** (1907–). Brazilian architect. He has had a major influence on South American architecture. His work can be seen in Rio de Janeiro and Brasília.

Nie·möl·ler (nē′mœl′ər), **Martin** (1892–1984). German churchman. A U-boat captain in World War I, he became a Lutheran pastor (1924) and was later sent to a concentration camp (1937) for denouncing Nazism.

Nier·stein·er (nēr′shtī′nər) *n.* A white Rhine wine. [After *Nierstein,* city in central West Germany.]

Nie·tzsche (nē′chə, -chē), **Friedrich Wilhelm** (1844–1900). German philosopher. Rejecting the slave morality and values of Christianity in works such as *Also Sprach Zarathustra* (1883–91), he proposed a philosophy asserting the self and the will to power.

Nie·tzsche·an·ism (nē′chē-ə-nĭz′əm) *n.* Also **Nie·tzsche·ism** (nē′chē-ĭz′əm). **1.** The philosophy of Nietzsche, based upon a distinction between thought and emotion, and emphasizing the value of intense emotion in art and life. **2.** Nietzsche's doctrine of the **superman** *(see).* —**Nie·tzsche·an** *adj.* & *n.*

nieve (nēv) *n. Scottish.* A fist. [Middle English, from Old Norse *hnefi*†.]

niff (nĭf) *n. British Slang.* A nasty or distasteful smell. ~*intr.v.* **niffed, niffing, niffs.** *British Slang.* To have an unpleasant smell; stink. [Of dialectal origin; perhaps akin to SNIFF.] —**niff·y** *adj.*

Nif·l·heim, Nif·el·heim (nĭv′əl-hām′) *n. Norse Mythology.* The realm of the dead. [Old Norse *niflheimr,* "home of mist" : *nifl,* mist + *heimr,* home.]

nif·ty (nĭf′tē) *adj.* **-tier, -tiest.** *Informal.* **1.** Stylish; pleasing; first-rate. **2.** *British.* Nimble; agile. [Perhaps from MAGNIFICENT.]

Ni·ger¹ (nī′jər). African republic. The largest nation in West Africa, it is landlocked. Its economy is based on livestock breeding and the export of cotton and groundnuts. Formerly a French possession, it became an independent republic in 1960. Area, 1,267,000 square

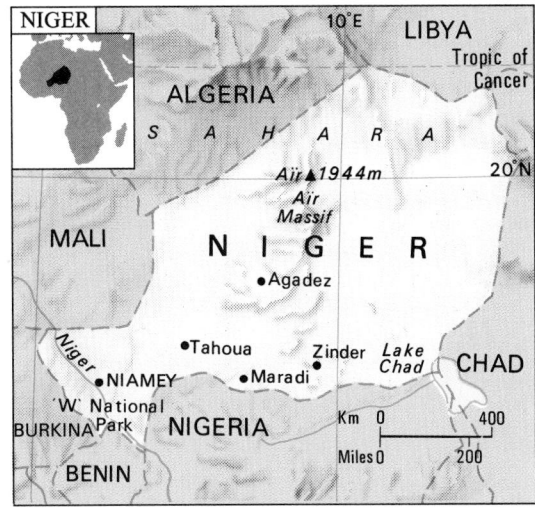

kilometers (489,191 square miles). Population, 5,100,000. Capital, Niamey.

Niger². Third-longest river in Africa (4,180 kilometers; 2,600 miles), rising in southwestern Guinea on the Fouta Djallon plateau. It follows a roughly semicircular course through Mali, Niger, and Nigeria to the Gulf of Guinea. In Mali it forms a huge inland delta, comprising hundreds of channels and shallow lakes used for irrigation, especially for rice production. The delta at its mouth, which is the largest in Africa, is an important source of petroleum and palm oil. Most of the Niger is navigable year-round.

Ni·ger-Con·go (nī′jər-kŏng′gō) *n.* A large language family of Africa that includes the Mande, Gur, Kwa, and Bantu languages.

Ni·ge·ri·a (nī-jîr′ē-ə). Republic in West Africa, by size the 14th largest, but by population the largest, country in Africa. The capital is Lagos, but a new capital district is being developed near Abuja in the central region of the country. Nigeria is self-sufficient in food and is also Africa's leading petroleum producer. Nigeria gained its independence from Great Britain in 1960. Area, 923,768 square kilometers (356,669 square miles). Population, 82,600,000. —**Ni·ge·ri·an** *adj.* & *n.*

Niger seed *n.* The seed of the African plant **ramtil** *(see),* used as birdseed and yielding a valuable oil. [Probably first found near the NIGER River.]

nig·gard (nĭg′ərd) *n.* A stingy, grasping person; a miser. ~*adj.* Parsimonious; niggardly. [Middle English *nigart, niggard,* earlier *nigon,* from *nig,* a miser, from Scandinavian; akin to Swedish dialect *nygg,* from Old Norse *hnöggr,* miserly.]

nig·gard·ly (nĭg′ərd-lē) *adj.* **1.** Unwilling to part with anything; reluctant to give or spend; stingy: *"Nature has been rather niggardly with Japan in mineral resources"* (Edwin Reischauer). **2.** Meager;

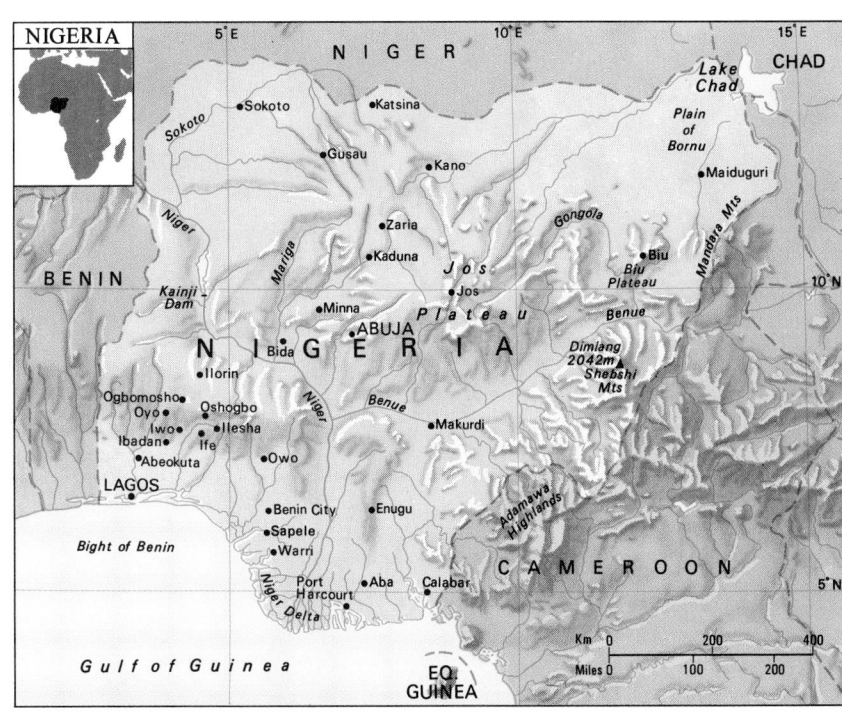

night heron *The black-crowned night heron,* Nycticorax nycticorax, *is one of three species in this genus that is found worldwide near lakes, streams, and rivers. Night herons feed by night on fish and spend the day in thick cover.*

insufficient: *left a niggardly tip.* —See Synonyms at **stingy.** —**nig·gard·li·ness** *n.* —**nig·gard·ly** *adv.*

nig·gle (nĭg′əl) *v.* **-gled, -gling, -gles.** —*intr.v.* **1.** To be preoccupied with trifles; worry over petty details; fret. **2.** To keep finding fault; complain trivially; carp. —*tr.v.* To annoy or irritate. [Probably from Scandinavian and akin to NIGGARD.] —**nig·gler** *n.*

nig·gling (nĭg′lĭng) *adj.* **1.** Excessively concerned with details; fussy. **2.** Persistently nagging; petty. **3.** Showing or requiring close attention to details; exacting: *niggling paperwork.* —**nig·gling** *n.* —**nig·gling·ly** *adv.*

nigh (nī) *adj.* **nigher, nighest** or **next.** *Archaic & Regional.* **1.** Close at hand; near. **2.** Short; direct: *the nighest route.* **3.** Being on the left side: *the nigh horse.*
∼*adv. Archaic & Regional.* **1.** Near in time or location: *Night is drawing nigh.* **2.** Nearly; almost. Used with *on* or *onto: nigh on two hours.*
∼*prep. Archaic & Regional.* Not far from; near to. [Middle English *neigh,* Old English *nēah.*]

night (nīt) *n.* **1. a.** The period between sunset and sunrise; especially, the hours of darkness. **b.** This period considered as a unit of time: *two nights running.* **c.** This period considered from the viewpoint of its conditions or events: *a starry night.* **2. a.** The period between evening and bedtime: *Tuesday night.* **b.** This period considered from the viewpoint of its activities or events: *a night at the opera.* **c.** This period set aside for a specific purpose or occasion: *Bridge Night at the club.* **3. a.** The period between bedtime and morning: *spent the night at a friend's.* **b.** One's sleep during this period: *had a bad night.* **4. a.** Darkness: *vanished into the night.* **b.** The onset of darkness. **5.** Any time or condition of gloom, obscurity, ignorance, or sorrow: *"In a real dark night of the soul it is always three o'clock in the morning"* (F. Scott Fitzgerald). —**make a night of it.** To spend the evening or most of a night celebrating or in festivity. —**night and day.** Continuously; without stopping.
∼*adj.* **1.** Pertaining to the night. **2.** Intended for use at night: *a night key.* **3.** Working or occurring during the night: *night shift; night porter.* [Middle English *niht, night,* Old English *niht, neaht.*]

night blindness *n.* Poor vision in the dark, **nyctalopia** *(see).* —**night-blind** (nīt′blīnd′) *adj.*

night-bloom·ing ce·re·us (nīt′blo͞o′mĭng sîr′ē-əs) *n.* Any of several flowering cacti of the genus *Salenicereus* and related genera, having large, fragrant flowers that open at night.

night·cap (nīt′kăp′) *n.* **1.** A cloth head-covering worn especially in bed. **2.** A drink, usually alcoholic, taken just before bedtime. **3.** *Sports.* The last event in a day's competition; especially, the final game in a baseball double-header.

night·clothes (nīt′klōz′, -klō*thz*′) *pl.n.* Clothes, such as pajamas or a nightgown, worn in bed.

night·club (nīt′klŭb′) *n.* An establishment that stays open late at night and usually provides food, drink, entertainment, and music for dancing.

night·dress (nīt′drĕs′) *n.* **1.** A nightgown. **2.** Nightclothes.

night·fall (nīt′fôl′) *n.* The approach of darkness; close of day.

night·gown (nīt′goun′) *n.* **1.** A loose gown, often long, worn in bed by women and children. **2.** A man's nightshirt.

night·hawk (nīt′hôk′) *n.* **1.** Any of several mainly nocturnal birds of the genus *Chordeiles,* having buff to black mottled feathers; especially, *C. minor,* of North America. Also called "bullbat," "mosquito hawk." **2.** A related European bird, the **nightjar** *(see).* **3.** *Informal.* A night owl.

night heron *n.* Any of several nocturnal herons of the genus *Nycticorax*; especially, *N. nycticorax,* the black-crowned heron, which has black and white plumage and short legs, neck, and bill.

night·ie, night·y (nī′tē) *n., pl.* **-ies.** *Informal.* A nightgown.

night·in·gale (nīt′n-gāl′, nī′tĭng-) *n.* **1.** A European songbird, *Luscinia megarhyncha,* with brownish plumage, noted for its nocturnal song. **2.** Any of various nocturnal songbirds. [Middle English *nihtyngale,* Old English *nihtegale,* "night-singer" : *niht,* NIGHT + *galan,* to sing.]

Night·in·gale (nīt′n-gāl′, nī′tĭng-), **Florence,** (1820–1910). British nurse. Although nursing was not an accepted occupation for upper-class women of her day, she became superintendent of a London hospital (1853). In 1854 she attached herself to the army in the Crimea and, despite strong opposition, reformed the medical services. On her return to England, she became a leading figure in the campaign for improved nursing care.

night·jar (nīt′jär′) *n.* Any of various nocturnal birds of the family Caprimulgidae; especially, the common European nightjar, *Caprimulgus europaeus,* having a dull-colored, mottled plumage. Sometimes called "nighthawk." [NIGHT + JAR (make a harsh sound).]

night jasmine *n.* **1.** A shrub, *Nyctanthes arbortristis,* cultivated for its small, white, fragrant flowers. **2.** A West Indian shrub, *Cestrum nocturnum,* having small, greenish-white flowers that are very fragrant at night.

night latch *n.* A spring lock that may be opened from the inside by turning a knob, but from the outside only with a key.

night letter *n.* A telegram sent at night at a reduced rate.

night·life (nīt′līf′) *n.* The entertainment or social activities to be found at night, as in nightclubs.

night·light (nīt′līt′) *n.* A dim light that is left on all night.

night·long (nīt′lông′, -lŏng′) *adj.* Lasting through the whole night. ∼*adv.* Through the night; all night.

night·ly (nīt′lē) *adj.* **1.** Of or occurring during the night; nocturnal: *nightly prowlings.* **2.** Happening or done every night: *nightly rounds.* ∼*adv.* Every night: *He visited her nightly.*

night·mare (nīt′mâr′) *n.* **1.** A dream arousing feelings of acute fear, dread, or anguish. **2.** An event or condition that evokes feelings of acute anguish or dread: *the nightmare of urban loneliness.* **3.** A demon or spirit formerly thought to plague sleeping people.
∼*adj.* Like something in a nightmare; appalling: *a nightmare journey into the unknown.* [Middle English *nihtmare,* female incubus : NIGHT + *mare,* incubus, Old English *mare, mære,* goblin.] —**night·mar·ish** *adj.* —**night·mar·ish·ly** *adv.* —**night·mar·ish·ness** *n.*

night owl *n.* A person who habitually stays up late and is active at night.

night·rid·er (nīt′rī′dər) *n.* Any of a band of mounted and usually masked white men who engaged in nocturnal terrorism for revenge or intimidation in the southern United States after the Civil War. —**night·rid·ing** *n.*

nights (nīts) *adv. Informal.* At night: *He works nights.* [Middle English *nightes,* Old English *nihtes,* adverbial genitive of *niht,* NIGHT.]

night-scent·ed stock (nīt′sĕn′tĭd) *n.* A plant, **evening stock** *(see).*

night school *n.* A school that offers classes, especially of a vocational nature, in the evening.

night·shade (nīt′shād′) *n.* Any of several plants of the family Solanaceae, many of them having a poisonous juice; especially, the **deadly nightshade** and the **bittersweet** *(both of which see).* See also **enchanter's nightshade.** [Middle English *nighteschede,* Old English *nihtscada* : probably NIGHT + SHADE (since it was used in folk medicine as a soporific).]

night·shirt (nīt′shûrt′) *n.* A long, loose shirt worn in bed, especially by men.

night soil *n.* Human feces collected for use as fertilizer.

night·spot (nīt′spŏt′) *n. Informal.* A nightclub.

night·stick (nīt′stĭk′) *n.* A club carried by a policeman.

night table *n.* A small table or stand placed at a bedside.

night·tide (nīt′tīd′) *n. Chiefly Poetic.* Night-time.

night·time (nīt′tīm′) *n.* The time between sunset and sunrise.

night watch *n.* **1.** A guard or watch kept during the night, as on a ship or at an encampment. **2.** A person who keeps watch at night. **3.** Any of the periods of a watch kept at night.

night watchman *n.* One who acts as guard during the night.

nighty. Variant of **nightie.**

ni·gres·cence (nī-grĕs′əns) *n.* **1.** The process of becoming black or dark. **2.** Blackness or darkness of hair, eyes, or skin. [Latin *nigrescens* (stem *nigrescent-*), from *nigrescere,* to become black, from *niger,* black.] —**ni·gres·cent** *adj.*

nig·ri·fy (nĭg′rə-fī′) *tr.v.* **-fied, -fying, -fies.** To make black; blacken. [Late Latin *nigrificāre* : *niger,* black + *facere,* to make.]

nig·ri·tude (nĭg′rə-to͞od′, -tyo͞od′) *n.* Blackness. [Late Latin *nigritūdō,* from *niger,* black.]

ni·gro·sine (nī′grə-sēn′) *n.* Also **ni·gro·sin** (-sĭn). Any of a class of dyes, varying from blue to black, used in the manufacture of inks and for dyeing leather, wood, and textiles. [Latin *niger,* black + -OS(E) + -INE.]

ni·hil (nī′hĭl, nē′hĭl) *n.* **1.** Nothing. **2.** A thing of no value. [Latin, shortened from *nihilum,* nothing.]

ni·hil·ism (nī′əl-ĭz′əm, nī′həl-, nē′-) *n.* **1.** A metaphysical doctrine that nothing exists, is knowable, or can be communicated. **2.** *Philosophy.* The rejection of all distinctions in moral value and a willingness to repudiate all previous theories of morality. **3.** The belief that destruction of existing political or social institutions is necessary to ensure future improvement. **4.** A doctrine among the Russian intelligentsia of the 1860's and 1870's, advocating terrorism and denying all authority in favor of individualism. [Latin *nihil,* nothing.] —**ni·hil·ist** *n.* —**ni·hil·is·tic** *adj.*

ni·hil·i·ty (nī-hĭl′ə-tē, nē-) *n.* Nonexistence; nothingness. [French *nihilité,* from Old French, from Medieval Latin *nihilitās* (stem *nihilitāt-*), from *nihil,* nothing.]

nihil ob·stat (ŏb′stăt′) *n.* **1.** An attestation by a Roman Catholic censor that a book contains nothing damaging to faith or morals. **2.** Official approval, especially of an artistic work. [Latin, "nothing hinders."]

Nihon. See **Japan.** [Japanese, "Land of the Rising Sun" : *ni,* the sun + *hon,* source, origin.]

Ni·jin·sky (nĭ-jĭn′skē, -zhĭn′-), **Vaslav** (1890–1950). Russian ballet dancer. Starting his career with the Imperial Ballet School in St. Petersburg, he later joined Diaghilev's company in Paris, where he performed in such works as *Petrushka* (1911) and choreographed many ballets, including *Le Sacre du Printemps* (*The Rite of Spring*) (1913). Schizophrenia forced him to retire (1919).

Nij·me·gen (nī′mā′gən). City in the eastern Netherlands, on the Waal River near the border with West Germany. One of the oldest cities in the Netherlands, it was founded by the Romans.

-nik *suffix. Informal.* Indicates: **1.** A person involved with or characterized by something specified; for example, **beatnik. 2.** A person who has undergone a specified experience; for example, **refusenik. 3.** A person promoting a specified aim or cause; for example, **peacenik.** [Russian *-nik* (as in SPUTNIK) and Yiddish *-nik* (agent suffix).]

Ni·ke (nī′kē). *Greek Mythology.* The goddess of victory. [Greek *Nikē.*]

nil (nĭl) *n.* Nothing; zero. [Latin, contraction of NIHIL.]

Nile (nīl). River in northeastern Africa, the longest in the world, *c.* 6,700 kilometers (4,150 miles) from its source in the highlands south of the equator to its outlet on the Mediterranean Sea. It drains an area of *c.* 2,850,000 square kilometers (1,000,000 square miles), or about one tenth of Africa. The trunk stream of the Nile is formed at Khartoum by the confluence of the Blue Nile and the White Nile. Only after Aswan, Egypt, site of the last of the river's cataracts, does the flood plain begin to widen. Since 4000 B.C., when the river spawned the rise of the early Egyptian civilization, the waters of the Nile have supported, by irrigation, almost all of Egypt's agriculture and much of Sudan's.

Nile blue *n.* Light greenish blue.

Nile green *n.* Light bluish green.

nil·gai (nĭl'gī') *n.* A large Indian antelope, *Boselaphus tragocamelus,* the male of which has a blue-gray coat with white underparts and short horns. The female is tawny brown and lacks horns. [Hindi *nīlgāi,* "blue cow" : Sanskrit *nīla,* blue + *gāi,* go, cow.]

nill (nĭl) *v.* **nilled, nilling, nills.** *Archaic.* —*tr.* To refuse. —*intr.* To be unwilling; will not: *will he, nill he.* [Middle English *nilen,* Old English *nyllan : ne,* not + *wyllan,* to wish.]

Ni·lo-Ham·ite (nī'lō-hăm'īt') *n.* A member of a group of Negroid peoples of eastern Africa.

Ni·lo-Ham·it·ic (nī'lō-hă-mĭt'ĭk) *n.* A former designation for a number of languages that are now considered part of the Nilotic group.

Ni·lo-Sa·har·an (nī'lō-sə-hâr'ən, -hä'rən) *n.* A large language family of Africa, including Chari-Nile and a number of smaller groups. —**Ni·lo-Sa·har·an** *adj.*

Ni·lot·ic (nī-lŏt'ĭk) *adj.* **1.** Belonging to the Nile or the Nile Valley. **2.** Pertaining to a group of peoples in eastern Africa who constitute a distinctive Negroid race, characterized especially by their extreme height. **3.** Pertaining to the languages of these peoples. ~*n.* A group of languages, including Dinka and Masai, considered as a family or as a branch of the Chari-Nile family. [Latin *Nīlōticus,* from Greek *Neilōtikos,* from *Neilos,* the NILE.]

Nils·son (nĭl'sən), **Birgit** (1918–). Swedish soprano. She is particularly noted for her performances in Wagnerian operas. In 1969 Nilsson debuted as Isolde at the Metropolitan Opera in New York City. She announced her retirement in 1986.

nim¹ (nĭm) *v.* **nimmed, nimming, nims.** *Archaic.* —*tr.* **1.** To take. **2.** To steal; filch. —*intr.* To steal; rob. [Middle English *nimen,* Old English *niman.*]

nim² *n.* A game in which two players alternately remove small objects from a collection, usually matchsticks arranged in rows, and attempt to take, or avoid taking, the last one. [20th century : probably special use of archaic NIM.]

nim·ble (nĭm'bəl) *adj.* **-bler, -blest. 1.** Quick and agile in movement or action; deft: *nimble fingers.* **2. a.** Quick at devising or understanding: *a nimble mind.* **b.** Cleverly contrived: *a nimble trick.* —See Synonyms at **dexterous.** [Middle English *nemel, nym-(b)yl,* agile, Old English *nǣmel,* quick to seize or understand, quick-witted, and *numol,* seizing.] —**nim·ble·ness** *n.* —**nim·bly** *adv.*

    Synonyms: agile, brisk, quick, sprightly, spry.

nim·bo·stra·tus (nĭm'bō-strā'təs, -străt'əs) *n.* A low, gray cloud, often dark, that precipitates rain, snow, or sleet. [NIMB(US) + STRATUS.]

nim·bus (nĭm'bəs) *n., pl.* **-bi** (-bī') or **-bus·es. 1.** In art: **a.** A cloudy luminescence surrounding a classical deity when depicted visiting mortals. **b.** Any of various pictorial devices symbolizing sanctity, usually a radiance or a bright circle, appearing behind or above the heads of saints and of the Deity. **2.** A favorable or splendid aura about someone or something. **3.** A rain cloud, a nimbostratus. [Latin *nimbus,* heavy rain, rain cloud.]

Nîmes (nēm). Town in southern France, capital of Gard department. An ancient Roman town, it was a Huguenot center before the revocation of the Edict of Nantes (1685). It is notable for its Roman remains, including a temple, the Pont du Gard, and an arena that is still in use.

ni·mi·e·ty (nĭ-mī'ə-tē) *n., pl.* **-ties. 1.** Excess; redundancy. **2.** An instance of this. [Late Latin *nimietās* (stem *nimietāt-*), from Latin *nimius,* excessive, from *nimis,* excessively.]

nim·i·ny-pim·i·ny (nĭm'ə-nē-pĭm'ə-nē) *adj.* Affectedly delicate or refined; mincing. [Perhaps variant of NAMBY-PAMBY.]

Nim·itz (nĭm'ĭts), **Chester William** (1885–1966). U.S. fleet admiral. Appointed commander in chief of the Pacific fleet after the Japanese attack on Pearl Harbor (1941), he stopped the expansion of the Japanese and eventually destroyed their battle fleets. His success owed much to his appreciation of aircraft carrier strategy.

Nim·rod¹ (nĭm'rŏd'). A mighty hunter and king. Genesis 10:8–9.

Nimrod² *n. Sometimes* **nimrod.** A skilled hunter.

nin·com·poop (nĭn'kəm-pōop', nĭng'-) *n.* A fool; a blockhead. [17th century *nicompoop* : origin obscure.] —**nin·com·poop·er·y** *n.*

nine (nīn) *n.* **1. a.** The cardinal number that is one more than eight. **b.** A symbol representing this, such as 9 or IX. **2.** A set made up of nine persons or things. **3. a.** The ninth in a series. **b.** A playing card marked with nine pips. **4.** Nine parts; the components of a whole that has been divided into nine. **5.** A size, as in clothing, designated as nine. **6.** Nine hours after midnight or midday. —**dressed (up) to the nines.** Dressed in one's most formal clothes or very elaborately. [Middle English *ni(gh)en, nyne,* Old English *nigon.*] —**nine** *adj. & pron.* —**nine·fold** (nīn'fōld') *adj. & adv.*

nine days' wonder *n.* Something that creates great interest or excitement for a brief period.

nine iron *n.* An iron-headed golf club with a face slanted at a greater angle than any other iron. Also called "niblick."

nine·pin (nīn'pĭn') *n.* A wooden pin used in the game of ninepins.

nine·pins (nīn'pĭnz') *n. Used with a singular verb.* A bowling game in which nine wooden pins are the target.

nine·teen (nīn'tēn') *n.* **1. a.** The cardinal number that is one more than 18. **b.** A symbol representing this, such as 19 or XIX. **2.** A set made up of 19 persons or things. **3.** The 19th in a series. —**talk nineteen to the dozen.** To talk very quickly and at length; babble. —**nine·teen** *adj. & pron.*

1984, nineteen eighty-four *n.* A totalitarian society in which government propaganda and control suppress free speech and create a dehumanized and regimented state. [From George Orwell's novel *1984,* which depicts a hypothetical totalitarian state.]

nine·teenth (nīn'tēnth') *n.* **1.** The ordinal number 19 in a series. **2.** Any of 19 equal parts. —**nine·teenth** *adj. & adv.*

nineteenth hole *n.* A place, especially the club bar, where golfers gather for relaxation after a game. Used humorously.

nine·ti·eth (nīn'tē-ĭth) *n.* **1.** The ordinal number 90 in a series. **2.** Any of 90 equal parts. —**nine·ti·eth** *adj. & adv.*

nine to five *n.* Usual office hours; working hours. —**nine-to-five** (nīn'tə fīv') *adj. & adv.*

nine·ty (nīn'tē) *n., pl.* **-ties. 1. a.** The cardinal number that is 10 more than 80. **b.** A symbol representing this, such as 90 or XC. **2.** A set made up of 90 persons or things. **3.** The 90th in a series. **4. nineties. a.** The range of numbers from 90 to 99, considered as a range of age, price, temperature, or the like. **b.** *Often* **Nineties.** The years numbered 90 to 99 in a century. Also used adjectivally: *nineties fashions.* —**nine·ty** *adj. & pron.*

nine·ty-day wonder (nīn'tē-dā') *n.* An officer commissioned in the armed forces after a short training period.

Nin·e·veh (nĭn'ə-və). Capital of the ancient empire of the Assyrians, on the eastern bank of the Tigris River, opposite the modern Iraqi town of Mosul. It was at its glory during the reigns of Sennacherib (704–681 B.C.) and Assurbanipal (699–626 B.C.). It fell to the combined forces of the Babylonians, Medes, and Scythians in 612 B.C. Excavation has uncovered magnificent remains.

nin·ny (nĭn'ē) *n., pl.* **-nies.** A fool; a simpleton. [Perhaps from *innocent* (simple, foolish), on analogy with *Ninny,* familiar form for the Christian name *Innocent.*]

ni·non (nē'nŏn'; *French* nē-nôN') *n.* A sheer fabric of silk, rayon, or nylon made in a variety of tight, smooth weaves or open lacy patterns. [Probably from French *Ninon,* a nickname for *Anne.*]

ninth (nīnth) *n.* **1.** The ordinal number nine in a series. **2.** Any of nine equal parts. **3.** *Music.* **a.** A harmonic or melodic interval of an octave and a second. **b.** The note at the upper limit of such an interval. **c.** A chord consisting of a triad and its seventh and ninth. [Middle English *nynthe,* Old English *nigotha,* from *nigon,* NINE.] —**ninth** *adj. & adv.*

Ni·o·be (nī'ō-bē). *Greek Mythology.* The daughter of Tantalus and wife of Amphion of Thebes; she was turned to stone by Zeus while bewailing the loss of her children.

ni·o·bic (nī-ō'bĭk) *adj. Chemistry.* Of or containing niobium. Said especially of compounds that contain niobium with a valence of 5.

ni·o·bi·um (nī-ō'bē-əm) *n. Symbol* **Nb** A silvery, soft, ductile, metallic element. It occurs chiefly in columbite-tantalite and is used in steel alloys, arc welding, and superconductivity research. Atomic number 41, atomic weight 92.906, melting point 2,468°C, boiling point 4,927°C, specific gravity 8.57, valences 2, 3, and 5. Formerly called "columbium." [New Latin, after NIOBE (because obtained from tantalite, which is named after Tantalus, father of Niobe).]

ni·o·bous (nī-ō'bəs) *adj. Chemistry.* Of or containing niobium. Said especially of compounds that contain niobium with a valence of 3.

nip¹ (nĭp) *v.* **nipped, nipping, nips.** —*tr.* **1. a.** To catch, pinch, or press between two surfaces or points, such as the fingers. **b.** To give a small, sharp bite to. Used of animals. **2.** To remove or sever by pinching, biting, or snipping. Usually used with *off.* **3.** To have a stinging or biting effect on: *nipped by the cold.* **4.** To check in growth or cut off the development of: *nip the scandal before it spreads.* **5.** *Slang.* To snatch; steal. —*intr.* **1.** To give small, sharp bites. Used of animals. **2.** *British Informal.* To go or move quickly and nimbly: *nipped out to the shops.*
~*n.* **1.** The act of catching, pressing, or pinching between two surfaces; a bite or pinch. **2. a.** A pinch or snip that cuts off or removes a part: *He gave a nip to each corner.* **b.** The small piece removed in this manner. **3. a.** A sharp, stinging quality, as of frosty air. **b.** Severely sharp cold or frost. **4.** A cutting or stinging remark; a taunt. **5.** A pungent or sharp flavor; a tang: *the nip of Mexican cooking.* —**nip and tuck.** Very close; neck and neck. [Middle English *nippen, nīpen,* perhaps from Old Norse *hnippa.*]

nip² *n.* A small quantity or sip of liquor: *an occasional nip.*
~*v.* **nipped, nipping, nips.** —*tr.* To drink (liquor) in small doses: *He had been nipping brandy.* —*intr.* To take a nip or sip of liquor. [Short for *nipperkin,* probably from Dutch *nippertje,* a dram, from *nippen,* to sip.] —**nip·per** *n.*

ni·pa (nē'pə) *n.* **1.** A large, distinctive palm, *Nipa fruticans,* of the Philippines and Australia, having long leaves much used for thatching and basketry. Also called "nipa palm." **2.** An alcoholic beverage made from the sap of this palm. [Spanish and Portuguese, from Malay *nipah.*]

nip·per (nĭp'ər) *n.* **1.** One that nips. **2. nippers.** Any of various devices for squeezing or snipping, such as pliers or pincers. **3.** The large claw of a crustacean. **4.** *Chiefly British Informal.* A young child, especially a small boy.

nip·ping (nĭp'ĭng) *adj.* **1.** Sharp and biting, as the cold. **2.** Sarcastic. —**nip·ping·ly** *adv.*

nitrogen cycle

AN ELEMENT ESSENTIAL TO LIFE
How nitrogen circulates through nature

All life on earth needs nitrogen because it is an essential ingredient of every protein. Plants and animals cannot, however, absorb nitrogen directly from the air. The element circulates in nature through various organisms whose life processes depend on it, a progression known as the nitrogen cycle.

Some atmospheric nitrogen is fixed, or combined, by the action of bacteria in the roots of leguminous plants, such as clover, and by the action of atmospheric electricity. Fertilizers and other inorganic nitrogen compounds in the soil are used by plants, which combine them with other elements to form nucleic acids and proteins. These proteins are part of the food used by grazing animals. The decay of plant and animal matter (by microorganisms that include bacteria) releases nitrogen into the soil as ammonium compounds, which are converted by other bacteria into nitrogen salts usable by plants, and nitrogen gas. Some combined nitrogen is also set free by denitrifying bacteria.

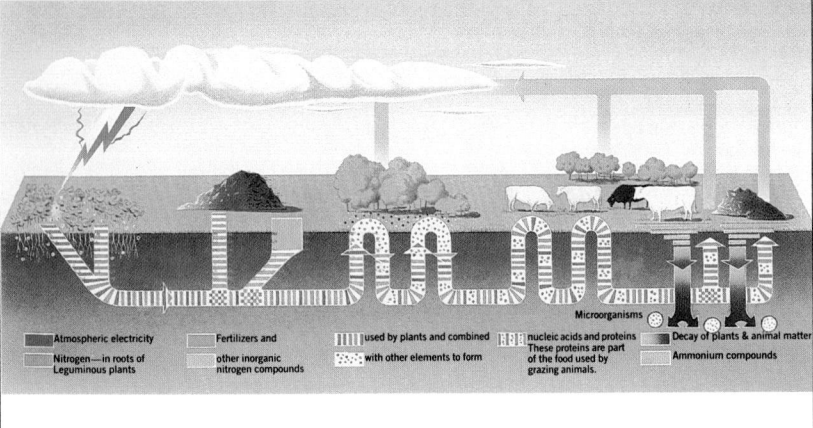

Atmospheric electricity
Nitrogen—in roots of Leguminous plants
Fertilizers and other inorganic nitrogen compounds
used by plants and combined with other elements to form
nucleic acids and proteins These proteins are part of the food used by grazing animals.
Microorganisms
Decay of plants & animal matter
Ammonium compounds

nip·ple (nĭp′əl) *n.* **1. a.** The small conical protuberance near the center of the mammary gland containing the outlets of the milk ducts. Also called "mammilla." **b.** A corresponding vestigial protuberance on the male chest. **2. a.** The rubber cap on a nursing bottle. **b.** A pacifier for an infant. **3.** Any of various devices resembling a nipple in appearance or function: **a.** A regulated opening for discharging a liquid, as in a small stopcock. **b.** A pipe coupling threaded at both ends. **c.** A short extension of pipe to which a nozzle can be attached. **4.** A small projection through which grease can be forced into a bearing from a grease gun. **5.** Any natural or geographic body or projection resembling a nipple, such as a mountain crest. [From earlier *neble, nible,* perhaps diminutives of *neb, nib,* a point, beak, NEB.]

nip·ple·wort (nĭp′əl-wûrt′) *n.* A plant, *Lapsana communis,* having a milky juice and small, yellow flower heads. [Formerly used in folk medicine to treat breast tumors.]

Nippon. See Japan. [Short for *Nippon-koku,* "land of the origin of the sun."] —**Nip·pon·ese** *adj. & n.*

nip·py (nĭp′ē) *adj.* **-pier, -piest. 1.** Sharp or biting; nipping. **2.** *British Informal.* **a.** Active; vigorous; sharp; quick. **b.** Small but having a relatively powerful engine. Said of a motor vehicle. —**nip·pi·ly** *adv.* —**nip·pi·ness** *n.*

nip-up (nĭp′ŭp′) *n.* An acrobatic spring from a supine to an upright position.

nir·va·na (nîr-vä′nə, nər-) *n.* **1.** *Often* **Nirvana. a.** *Buddhism.* The state of absolute blessedness, characterized by release from the cycle of reincarnations and attained through the extinction of the self. **b.** *Hinduism.* A similar state in which reunion with Brahma is attained through the suppression of individual existence. **2.** Freedom from the pain and care of the external world; bliss. [Sanskrit *nirvāna,* "extinction (of individual existence)," from *nirvā,* to be extinguished, be blown out : *nir-, nis-†,* out + *vātī,* he blows.]

Ni·san, Nis·san (nĭs′ən, nē-sän′) *n.* In the Hebrew calendar, the seventh month of the civil year and the first of the religious year. Formerly called "Abib." See feature at **calendar.** [Hebrew *Nīsān,* from Akkadian *Nissanu,* "the first month."]

ni·si (nī′sī′) *adj. Law.* Taking effect at a specified date unless cause is shown for modification or nullification: *a decree nisi.* [Latin *nisi,* unless.]

nisi pri·us (prī′əs) *n. Abbr.* **n.p.** *Law.* **1. a.** The court in which a civil action is tried before a judge and jury, as distinguished from an appellate court. Also called **nisi prius court. b.** The trial of a civil action before such a court: *cause of nisi prius.* **2.** *British.* **a.** A trial of a civil cause before a single judge and a jury in Crown Court. **b.** Formerly, a trial before an assize court. [Medieval Latin, "unless before" (originally the first two words of a writ ordering a sheriff to provide a jury at the Westminster court on a fixed day, *unless* the judges of assize come to the county *before* this day).]

Nis·sen hut (nĭs′ən) *n.* A prefabricated building of corrugated steel in the shape of half a cylinder, used as a military shelter. [After

Peter N. *Nissen* (1871–1930), British mining engineer.]

ni·sus (nī′səs) *n., pl.* **nisus.** Effort; endeavor; exertion; impulse. [Latin *nīsus,* from the past participle of *nītī,* to strive, endeavor.]

nit¹ (nĭt) *n.* **1.** The egg of a parasitic insect, such as that of a head louse or body louse. **2.** The young insect. [Middle English *nite,* Old English *hnitu,* louse egg.] —**nit·ty** *adj.*

nit² *n. Chiefly British Informal.* A nitwit.

nit³ *n.* A unit of luminance equal to 1 candela per square meter. [Latin *nitor,* brightness.]

nit⁴ *n. Computer Science.* A unit of information equal to 1.44 bits. [From Napierian dig*it.*]

ni·ter (nī′tər) *n. Also chiefly British* **ni·tre. 1. Potassium nitrate** *(see).* **2. Sodium nitrate** *(see).* [Middle English, from Old French, from Latin *nitrum,* from Greek *nitron,* of Semitic origin.]

nit-pick (nĭt′pĭk′) *intr.v. Informal.* To find fault or argue over insignificant details. —**nit-pick·er** *n.* —**nit-pick·ing** *adj. & n.*

ni·tra·mine (nī′trə-mĕn′) *n.* **Tetryl** *(see).* [NITRO- + AMINE.]

ni·trate (nī′trāt′) *n.* **1.** The radical NO_3^- or any compound containing it, as a salt or ester of nitric acid. **2.** Fertilizer consisting of sodium nitrate or potassium nitrate. ~*tr.v.* **nitrated, -trating, -trates.** To treat or combine with nitric acid or with a nitrate, usually to change an organic compound into a nitrate. [French : NITR(O)- + -ATE.] —**ni·tra·tion** (nī-trā′shən) *n.*

ni·traz·e·pam (nī-trăz′ə-păm′) *n.* A hypnotic drug used in the form of pills to induce sleep.

nitre. *Chiefly British.* Variant of **niter.**

ni·tric (nī′trĭk) *adj.* Of, derived from, or containing nitrogen, especially in a valence state higher than that in a comparable nitrous compound. [French *nitrique* : NITR(O)- + -IC.]

nitric acid *n.* A transparent, colorless to yellowish, fuming, corrosive liquid, HNO_3, a highly reactive oxidizing agent, used in the production of fertilizers, explosives, and rocket fuels, and in a wide variety of industrial metallurgical processes. Formerly called "aqua fortis."

nitric oxide *n.* A colorless, poisonous gas, NO, produced as an intermediate during the manufacture of nitric acid from ammonia or atmospheric nitrogen.

ni·tride (nī′trīd′) *n.* A compound containing nitrogen with another, more electropositive element. [NITR(O)- + -IDE.]

ni·trid·ing (nī′trī′dĭng) *n. Metallurgy.* The case-hardening of a ferrous alloy, such as steel, by heating it in ammonia.

ni·tri·fi·ca·tion (nī′trə-fə-kā′shən) *n.* **1.** The attachment of a nitro group to an organic compound either as an addition or substitution. **2.** The oxidation of ammonium compounds in the soil by nitrifying bacteria, which convert them into nitrates and nitrites.

ni·tri·fy (nī′trə-fī′) *tr.v.* **-fied, -fying, -fies. 1.** To oxidize into nitric acid, nitrous acid, or any nitrate or nitrite, as by the action of nitrifying bacteria. **2.** To treat or combine with nitrogen or compounds containing nitrogen. [French *nitrifier* : NITR(O)- + -FY.] —**ni·tri·fi·er** *n.*

ni·tri·fy·ing bacteria (nī′trə-fī′ĭng) *pl.n. Also* **ni·tro·bac·te·ri·a** (nī′trō-băk-tîr′ē-ə). Any of various soil bacteria, such as *Nitrosomonas* and *Nitrobacter,* that oxidize ammonium compounds to nitrite or nitrite to nitrate.

ni·trile (nī′trəl, -trĭl′) *n. Also* **ni·tril** (-trəl). Any compound containing trivalent nitrogen, N^{-3}, in a cyanogen group. [NITR(O)- + -ILE.]

ni·trite (nī′trīt′) *n.* Any salt or ester of nitrous acid. [NITR(O)- + -ITE.]

nitro-, nitr– *prefix.* Indicates a compound containing the univalent group NO_2; for example, **nitrobenzene, nitride.** [New Latin, from Latin *nitrum,* from Greek *nitron,* NITER.]

ni·tro·ben·zene (nī′trō-bĕn′zēn′, -bĕn-zēn′) *n.* A poisonous organic compound, $C_6H_5NO_2$, occurring either as bright-yellow crystals or as an oily liquid, having the odor of almonds and used in the manufacture of aniline, insulating compounds, and polishes.

ni·tro·cel·lu·lose (nī′trō-sĕl′yə-lōs′) *n.* A pulpy or cottonlike polymer derived from cellulose treated with sulfuric and nitric acids and used in the manufacture of explosives, collodion, plastics, and solid monopropellants. Also called " cellulose nitrate," "guncotton."

ni·tro·chlo·ro·form (nī′trō-klôr′ə-fôrm′, -klōr′-) *n.* A poison gas, **chloropicrin** *(see).*

ni·tro·gen (nī′trə-jən) *n. Symbol* **N** A nonmetallic element constituting nearly four-fifths of the air by volume, occurring as a colorless, odorless, almost inert diatomic gas, N_2, in various minerals and in all proteins. It is used in the manufacture of a wide variety of important compounds, including ammonia, nitric acid, TNT, and fertilizers. Atomic number 7, atomic weight 14.0067, melting point −209.86°C, boiling point −195°C, valences 3, 5. [French *nitrogène* : NITR(O)- + -GEN.] —**ni·trog·e·nous** (nī-trŏj′ə-nəs) *adj.*

ni·trog·e·nase (nī-trŏj′ə-nās′, -năz′) *n.* An enzyme that takes part in the fixation of atmospheric nitrogen.

nitrogen balance *n.* The difference between the amounts of nitrogen taken into and lost by the body or the soil.

nitrogen cycle *n.* **1.** The cyclic progression of natural chemical reactions to atmospheric nitrogen: the nitrogen either forms organic compounds in rainwater or is fixed by nitrogen-fixing bacteria; it is then assimilated and metabolized by plants and animals and returned by decomposition to the soil; here some is recycled as organic compounds by bacteria and fungi, and the remainder is returned to the atmosphere. **2.** The **carbon-nitrogen cycle** *(see).*

nitrogen dioxide *n.* A mildly poisonous brown gas, NO_2, often found in smog and internal-combustion engine exhaust fumes and synthesized for use as a nitrating agent, catalyst, and oxidizing agent. Also called "nitrogen peroxide."

nitrogen fixation *n.* **1.** The conversion of atmospheric nitrogen into nitrogenous compounds by natural agencies or by various industrial processes. **2.** The conversion by certain fungi and soil bacteria of atmospheric nitrogen or inorganic nitrogen compounds into organic compounds assimilable by plants. —**ni·tro·gen-fix·ing** (nī′trə-jən-fĭk′sĭng) *adj.*

ni·trog·en·ize (nī-trŏj′ə-nīz′, nī′trə-jə-nīz′) *tr.v.* **-ized, -izing, -izes.** To combine or treat with nitrogen.

nitrogen mustard *n.* Any of a group of toxic, blistering compounds resembling mustard gas but containing nitrogen instead of sulfur and having the general formula, RN (CH₂CH₂CL)₂, where R is an organic group. They are used in the chemotherapy of cancer.

nitrogen peroxide *n.* **1.** Nitrogen dioxide. **2.** The equilibrium mixture of nitrogen dioxide and nitrogen tetroxide.

nitrogen tetroxide *n.* A brown liquid, N_2O_4, formed by freezing or pressurizing nitrogen dioxide and used as an oxidizing, nitrating, and bleaching agent. Also called "dinitrogen tetroxide."

ni·tro·glyc·er·in, ni·tro·glyc·er·ine (nī′trō-glĭs′ər-ĭn) *n.* A thick, pale yellow liquid, $CH_2NO_3CHNO_3CH_2NO_3$, explosive on concussion or exposure to sudden heat. It is used in the production of dynamite and blasting gelatin, and as a vasodilator in medicine. Also called "trinitroglycerin."

nitro group *n. Chemistry.* The group of atoms $-NO_2$, present in certain types of organic compounds *(nitro compounds).*

ni·tro·hy·dro·chlo·ric acid (nī′trō-hī′drə-klôr′ĭk, -klôr′-) *n.* A mixture of acids, aqua regia *(see).*

ni·trom·e·ter (nī-trŏm′ə-tər) *n.* Any device or instrument for measuring the amount of nitrogen in a substance. [NITRO- + METER.]

ni·tro·meth·ane (nī′trō-mĕth′ān′) *n.* An oily, colorless liquid, CH_3NO_2, used in making dyes and resins, in organic synthesis, and as a rocket propellant.

ni·tro·par·af·fin (nī′trō-păr′ə-fĭn) *n.* Any of a group of organic compounds formed by replacing one or more of the hydrogen atoms of a paraffin hydrocarbon with the nitro group, NO_2^-, as in nitromethane, CH_3NO_2.

ni·tro·sa·mine (nī-trō′sə-mēn′) *n.* Any of a group of oily, yellow compounds that contain the divalent group –NNO. [Latin *nitrōsus,* full of niter + AMINE.]

ni·tro·so (nī-trō′sō) *adj.* Designating an organic compound that contains the monovalent group –NO. Compare **nitrosyl.** [Latin *nitrōsus,* full of niter.]

ni·tro·syl (nī′trə-sĭl) *adj.* Designating an inorganic compound that contains the monovalent group –NO. Compare **nitroso.** [Latin *nitrōsus* (see **nitroso**) + -YL.]

ni·trous (nī′trəs) *adj.* Of, derived from, or containing nitrogen, especially in a valence state lower than that in a comparable nitric compound. [New Latin *nitrosus,* from Latin *nitrōsus,* full of niter, from *nitrum,* from Greek *nitron,* NITER.]

nitrous acid *n.* An unstable inorganic acid, HNO_2, existing in solution only.

nitrous oxide *n.* A colorless inorganic gas, N_2O, used as a mild anesthetic. Also called "laughing gas."

nit·ty-grit·ty (nĭt′ē-grĭt′ē) *n. Slang.* The core of a matter; the specific or practical details: *Let's get down to the nitty-gritty.* [Probably based on a reduplication of *grit* in various senses.]

nit·wit (nĭt′wĭt′) *n. Informal.* A stupid or silly person. [Perhaps NIT + WIT.]

ni·val (nī′vəl) *adj. Botany.* Of or growing in or under snow. [Latin *nivālis,* from *nix* (stem *niv-*), snow.]

ni·va·tion (nī-vā′shən) *n.* The weathering of rocks as a result of the alternate freezing and thawing of surrounding snow. [Latin *nix* (stem *niv-*), snow.]

Niv·en (nĭv′ən), **(James) David Graham** (1910-83). British actor, known chiefly for his portrayals of easygoing, upper-class Englishmen. His racy, anecdotal volumes of autobiography, beginning with *The Moon's a Balloon* (1971), have been popular best sellers.

niv·e·ous (nĭv′ē-əs) *adj.* Like snow; snow-white. [Latin *niveus,* from *nix* (stem *niv-*), snow.]

nix¹ (nĭks) *n. Germanic Mythology.* A water sprite, usually in human form or half-human and half-fish. [German *Nix,* from Middle High German *nickes,* from Old High German *nihhus.*]

nix² *n. Slang.* Nothing.
~*adv. Slang.* No.
~*interj. Slang.* Stop! Watch out!
~*tr.v.* **nixed, nixing, nixes.** *Slang.* To forbid; veto; deny: *Congress nixed the tax hike.* [German, dialect and colloquial variant of *nichts,* nothing, from Old High German *niwiht,* nothing : *ni, ne,* no + *wiht,* thing, man.]

Nix·ie tube (nĭk′sē) *n.* A trademark for a **digitron** *(see).*

Nix·on (nĭk′sən), **Richard Milhous** (1913-). U.S. politician and 37th president. Vice president from 1953 to 1960, he served as Republican president from 1969 to 1974, during which term he established close ties with China and a measure of détente with the U.S.S.R. Although he increased U.S. commitment in Southeast Asia, he was responsible for the eventual withdrawal of U.S. forces from the area. He became the first U.S. president to resign, when the Watergate scandal linked him with electoral malpractices.

ni·zam (nī-zăm′, -zăm′, nī-) *n., pl.* **nizam.** A Turkish soldier, especially in the 19th century. [Turkish, from Arabic *niẓām,* government, NIZAM.]

Ni·zam (nī-zăm′, -zăm′, nī-) *n.* The title of the former rulers of Hyderabad, India. [Hindi *nizām(-al-mulk),* "governor (of the empire)," from Arabic *niẓām,* government.]

Ni·zer (nī′zər), **Louis** (1902-). U.S. lawyer and author, born in England. He represented many show business personalities, including Charlie Chaplin and Mae West. His books about his celebrated cases include *My Life in Court* (1962) and *The Jury Returns* (1966).

Nizhny Novgorod. See **Gorky.**

NJ New Jersey (used with a Zip Code).

N.J. New Jersey.

Nkru·mah (əng-krōō′mə), **Kwame** (1909-72). Ghanaian statesman. His country's first premier (1952-60), he was instrumental in achieving Ghana's independence from the United Kingdom (1957). He became president (1960), but was deposed and exiled after a military coup (1966).

NKVD, N.K.V.D. *n.* A former administrative branch of the Soviet government corresponding to the later **KGB** *(see).* [Russian *Narodny Kommissariat Vnutryennikh Dyel,* "People's Commissariat for Internal Affairs."]

NL, NL., N.L. New Latin.

N.L.F. National Liberation Front.

NLRB, N.L.R.B. National Labor Relations Board.

n.m., nm 1. nanometer. **2.** nautical mile.

NM New Mexico (used with a Zip Code).

N.Mex. New Mexico.

NMR nuclear magnetic resonance.

NNE, N.N.E. north-northeast.

NNW, N.N.W. north-northwest.

no¹ (nō) *adv.* **1.** Not so; opposed to "yes." Used in expressing refusal, denial, disagreement, or disbelief. **2.** Not at all; not by any degree. Used with the comparative: *no better; no more.* **3.** *Archaic.* Not: *whether or no.*
~*n., pl.* **noes. 1.** A negative response; a denial or refusal: *The proposal produced only noes.* **2.** A negative vote or voter. [Middle English *no, na,* Old English *nā : ne,* not + *ā,* ever.]

no² *adj.* **1.** Not any; not one; not a: *No biscuits are left.* Also used in the imperative: *No smoking.* **2.** Not at all; not close to being: *He is no child.* **3.** Hardly any: *got there in no time.* [Middle English *no, na,* Old English *nā,* reduced form of *nān,* NONE.]

No The symbol for the element nobelium.

Nō. Variant of **Noh.**

no. number.

No. 1. northern. **2.** number.

no-ac·count (nō′ə-kount′) *adj.* Also **no-count** (nō′kount′). *Regional.* Worthless; good-for-nothing: *a no-account fellow.* —**no-ac·count** *n.*

No·a·chi·an (nō-ā′kē-ən) *adj.* Also **No·ach·ic** (no-ăk′ĭk, -ā′kĭk). Of or relating to Noah or his time: *the Noachian flood.*

No·ah (nō′ə). The patriarch chosen by God to build the ark in which he, his family, and many animals were saved from the Flood. Genesis 5-9. [Hebrew *Nōah,* "rest."]

nob¹ (nŏb) *n. Slang.* **1.** The head. **2.** In cribbage, the jack of the suit turned up by the dealer, scoring one point for the holder: *one for his nob.* [Slang variant of KNOB.]

nob² *n. Chiefly British Slang.* A person of wealth or social standing. [18th century (Scottish *knabb, nab*) : origin obscure.] —**nob·bi·ly** *adv.* —**nob·by** *adj.*

no-ball (nō′bôl′) *n. Cricket.* A ball rendered invalid, for which the batting side receives one run.

nob·ble (nŏb′əl) *tr.v.* **-bled, -bling, -bles.** *British Slang.* **1.** To disable (a racehorse), especially with drugs. **2.** To win over, outdo, or get the better of by devious means. **3.** To filch or steal. **4.** To kidnap. [Perhaps from dialect *knobble,* to knock, beat : KNOB + -LE.] —**nob·bler** *n.*

nob·by (nŏb′ē) *adj.* **-bier, -biest.** *British Slang.* Fashionable; chic.

No·bel (nō-bĕl′), **Alfred Bernhard** (1833-96). Swedish chemist, entrepreneur, and philanthropist. The inventor of dynamite and developer of nitroglycerin as a high explosive, he was so appalled at the use of explosives in war that he bequeathed the considerable fortune he had amassed to institute the Nobel Prizes.

No·bel·ist (nō-bĕl′ĭst) *n.* One who receives a Nobel Prize.

no·bel·i·um (nō-bĕl′ē-əm) *n.* Symbol **No** A radioactive transuranic element in the actinide series, artificially produced in trace amounts. Atomic number 102, isotopic masses 251-259, of which 259 has the longest half-life. Also called "unnilbium." [After the *Nobel* Institute at Stockholm, where it was discovered.]

Nobel Prize *n.* Any of the six prizes awarded annually (since 1901) by the Nobel Foundation for outstanding achievements in the fields of physics, chemistry, physiology or medicine, literature, and (since 1969) economics and for the promotion of world peace.

No·bi·le (nō-bē′lē), **Umberto** (1885-1978). Italian aeronautical engineer and explorer. He designed several airships, including the semirigid dirigibles, *Roma, Italia,* and *Norge,* in the last of which he flew over the North Pole with Roald Amundsen (1926).

no·bil·i·ar·y (nō-bĭl′ē-ĕr′ē, -yər-ē) *adj.* Of or pertaining to the nobility. [French *nobiliaire,* from Latin *nōbilis,* NOBLE.]

nobiliary particle *n.* A preposition occurring as a mark of noble rank before a title or surname; for example, the German *von* and French *de* in *Ulrich von Bertele* and *Guy de Maupassant.*

no·bil·i·ty (nō-bĭl′ĭ-tē) *n., pl.* **-ties. 1. a.** The class comprising nobles, which in Britain consists of dukes, marquesses, earls, viscounts, and barons, together with their female counterparts. **b.** The state of being a noble. **2.** The state or quality of being exalted in character or being morally noble. [Middle English *nobilite,* from Old French, from Latin *nōbilitās* (stem *nōbilitāt-*), from *nōbilis,* NOBLE.]

noctule *A large European bat,* Nyctalus noctula *(above), has a 38-centimeter (15-inch) wingspan. It usually roosts in hollow trees, emerging at daybreak and dusk to hunt insects that it catches on the wing.*

no·ble (nō′bəl) *adj.* **-bler, -blest. 1.** Possessing hereditary rank in a political system or social class usually derived directly or indirectly from a feudalistic stage of a country's development. **2. a.** Lofty and exalted in character: *a noble spirit.* **b.** Proceeding from such a character; showing greatness and magnanimity: *a noble deed.* **3.** Grand, stately, and magnificent in appearance: *noble mountain peaks.* **4.** Of superior quality. **5.** Designating an especially corrosion-resistant metal, such as gold.
~*n.* **1.** A person of high birth, rank, or title; a nobleman. **2.** A former English gold coin. [Middle English, from Old French, from Latin *nōbilis,* knowable, known, famous, noble.] **—no·ble·ness** *n.* **—no·bly** *adv.*

noble gas *n. Chemistry.* An **inert gas** *(see).*

no·ble·man (nō′bəl-mən) *n., pl.* **-men** (-mĭn). A man of noble rank.

noble rot *n.* A fungus, *Botrytis cinerea,* that coats the skins of grapes, resulting in a grape of increased sweetness that is used for making Sauternes and certain Rhine wines. [Translation of German *Edelfäule.*]

noble savage *n.* Primitive man portrayed in Romantic literature as uncorrupted by civilization.

no·blesse (nō-blĕs′) *n.* **1.** Noble birth or condition. **2.** The nobility; the aristocracy. [Middle English *noblesce, noblesse,* from Old French *noblesse,* from *noble,* NOBLE.]

noblesse o·blige (ō-blēzh′) *n.* Benevolent and honorable behavior considered to be the responsibility of persons of high birth or rank. [French, "nobility obliges."]

no·ble·wom·an (nō′bəl-wo͝om′ən) *n., pl.* **-women** (-wĭm′ĭn). A woman of noble rank.

no·bod·y (nō′bŏd′ē, -bə-dē) *pron.* No person; no one: *Nobody told him what to do.*
~*n., pl.* **nobodies.** A person of no importance, influence, or social position.

Usage: *Nobody* and *no one* take singular verbs and pronominal forms: *Nobody has arrived yet; No one likes his or her time to be wasted.* Plural pronominal forms are quite often heard in casual speech, but a sentence such as *No one likes their time to be wasted* presents an inappropriate contrast between singular *likes* and plural *their.* However, when short questions (so-called "tag questions") are added to sentences containing *nobody* or *no one,* the use of plural forms is hard to avoid: *Nobody's left me a message, have they?*

no·cent (nō′sənt) *adj.* **1.** Causing injury; harmful. **2.** *Archaic.* Guilty of a crime. [Middle English, from Latin *nocēns* (stem *nocent-*), from the present participle of *nocēre,* to harm.]

no·ci·cep·tive (nō′sĭ-sĕp′tĭv) *adj.* Concerned with or causing pain.

nock (nŏk) *n.* **1.** The groove at either end of a bow for holding the bowstring. **2.** The notch in the end of an arrow that fits on the bowstring.
~*tr.v.* **nocked, nocking, nocks. 1.** To put a notch in (a bow or arrow). **2.** To fit (an arrow) to a bowstring. [Middle English *nocke, nokke,* from Middle Dutch *nocke.*]

no-count. *Regional.* Variant of **no-account.**

noc·tam·bu·lism (nŏk-tăm′byə-lĭz′əm) *n.* Also **noc·tam·bu·la·tion** (nŏk-tăm′byə-lā′shən). The condition or practice of **sleepwalking** *(see).* [NOCT(I)- + AMBULATION.] **—noc·tam·bu·list** *n.*

nocti–, noct– *prefix.* Indicates night; for example, **noctambulism.** [New Latin, from Latin *nox* (stem *noct-*), night.]

noc·ti·lu·ca (nŏk′tə-lo͞o′kə) *n., pl.* **-cae** (-sē′). Any of various plantlike, bioluminescent marine organisms of the genus *Noctiluca* that when grouped in large numbers, make the seas phosphorescent. [New Latin, from Latin *noctilūca,* moon, lantern : NOCTI- + *lūcere,* to shine.]

noc·ti·lu·cent (nŏk′tə-lo͞o′sənt) *adj.* Luminous at night. Said especially of certain high clouds. **—noc·ti·lu·cence** *n.*

noc·tu·id (nŏk′cho͞o-ĭd) *n.* Any night-flying moth of the family Noctuidae, the larvae of which are destructive pests. [New Latin *Noctuidae* (family name) : *Noctua,* generic name, from Latin *noctua,* night owl + -IDAE.] **—noc·tu·id** *adj.*

noc·tule (nŏk′cho͞ol) *n.* Any large, reddish-brown, insectivorous bat of the genus *Nyctalus,* found in Eurasia, Indonesia, and the Philippines. Also called "noctule bat." [French, from Italian *nottola,* from Late Latin *noctula,* diminutive of Latin *noctua,* night owl.]

noc·turn (nŏk′tûrn′) *n. Roman Catholic Church.* Any of the three canonical divisions of the office of **matins** *(see).* [Middle English *nocturne,* from Old French, from Medieval Latin *nocturna,* from the feminine of Latin *nocturnus,* NOCTURNAL.]

noc·tur·nal (nŏk-tûr′nəl) *adj.* **1.** Of, suitable to, or occurring at night. **2.** *Botany.* Having flowers that open during the night. **3.** *Zoology.* Active by night, as certain animals are. Compare **diurnal.** [Late Latin *nocturnālis,* from Latin *nocturnus,* of night, at night, from *nox* (stem *noct-*), night.] **—noc·tur·nal·i·ty** (nŏk′tər-năl′ə-tē) *n.* **—noc·tur·nal·ly** *adv.*

nocturnal emission *n.* An emission of semen during an erotic dream at night.

noc·turne (nŏk′tûrn′) *n.* **1.** *Music.* A romantic composition intended to embody sentiments appropriate to the evening or night; a pensive melody. **2.** A painting of a night scene. [French, "nocturnal," from Latin *nocturnus,* NOCTURNAL.]

noc·u·ous (nŏk′yo͞o-əs) *adj.* Harmful; noxious. [Latin *nocuus,* from *nocēre,* to harm.]

nod (nŏd) *v.* **nodded, nodding, nods.** —*intr.* **1.** To lower and raise the head quickly in a gesture of agreement or acknowledgment. **2.** To let the head fall forward when sleepy; doze momentarily. Often used with *off.* **3.** To be careless or momentarily inattentive as if sleepy; lapse: *Even Homer nods.* **4.** To sway, move up and down, or bend, as flowers do in the wind. —*tr.* **1.** To lower and raise (the head) quickly in agreement or acknowledgment. **2.** To express (greetings or approval, for example) by lowering and raising the head: *He nodded his agreement.* **3.** To summon, guide, send, or the like by nodding the head: *He nodded her into the room.*
~*n.* **1.** A forward or up-and-down inclination of the head, usually expressive of affirmation or drowsiness. **2.** The nodding motion of anything. **—give** (or **get**) **the nod.** *Informal.* To give (or receive) approval or assent: *Her performance got the nod from the critics.* **—on the nod.** *British Informal.* **1.** Without formal deliberation. **2.** On credit. [Middle English *nodden,* perhaps of Low German origin; akin to Middle High German *notten.*] **—nod·der** *n.*

Nod, Land of. See **Land of Nod.**

no·dal (nōd′l) *adj.* Of, resembling, or located at a node. **—no·dal·i·ty** (nō-dăl′ə-tē) *n.*

nod·ding (nŏd′ĭng) *adj. Botany.* Designating flowers that droop from their stalks, as in the bluebell.

nodding acquaintance *n.* A slight acquaintance with a person or subject.

nod·dle¹ (nŏd′l) *n. Informal.* The head. Used humorously: *not an idea in his noddle.* [Middle English *nodle*†, back of the head.]

noddle² *v.* **-dled, -dling, -dles.** —*intr.* To nod frequently. —*tr.* To nod (the head) briefly. [Frequentative of NOD (verb).]

nod·dy (nŏd′ē) *n., pl.* **-dies. 1.** A dunce or fool; a simpleton. **2.** Any of several dark brown, white-headed terns of the genus *Anous,* found in tropical waters. [From obsolete adjective *noddy,* foolish, "sleepy," "drowsy," probably from NOD (verb). The tern is so named because it is fearless of man and therefore seems stupid.]

node (nōd) *n.* **1.** A knob, knot, protuberance, or swelling: *a lymph node.* **2.** *Botany.* The often enlarged point on a stem where a leaf, bud, or other organ diverges from the stem to which it is attached; a joint. **3.** *Physics.* A point or region of minimum or zero amplitude in a periodic system. Compare **antinode. 4. a.** *Mathematics.* The point at which a continuous curve crosses itself. **b.** The point where lines branch or intersect. **5.** *Astronomy.* **a.** Either of two diametrically opposite points at which the orbit of a planet intersects the ecliptic. The *ascending node* is the point at which the planet moves from the south of the ecliptic to the north, the opposite point being the *descending node.* **b.** Either of two points at which the orbit of a satellite intersects the orbital plane of a planet. **6.** Any central point. [Latin *nōdus,* a knob, knot.]

node of Ran·vi·er (rän-vē-ā′) *n.* Any of the regions of exposed axon that occur along a myelinated nerve fiber at regular intervals. [After Louis Antoine *Ranvier* (1835–1922), French histologist.]

no·di·cal (nō′dĭ-kəl, nŏd′ĭ-) *adj. Astronomy.* Of or pertaining to the nodes of a heavenly body. [NOD(E) + -ICAL.]

no·dose (nō′dōs′) *adj.* Also **no·dous** (nō′dəs). Having nodes or knots: *a nodose branch.* [Latin *nodōsus,* from *nodus,* NODE.] **—no·dos·i·ty** (nō-dŏs′ə-tē) *n.*

nod·ule (nŏj′o͞ol) *n.* **1.** A small, knotlike protuberance; a node. **2.** *Pathology.* A small tumorous growth or localized swelling. **3.** *Botany.* A small, knoblike outgrowth, such as any of those found on the roots of most leguminous plants. **4.** A small lump of a mineral. [Latin *nōdulus,* diminutive of *nōdus,* a knob, NODE.] **—nod·u·lar** (nŏj′o͞o-lər), **nod·u·lose** (nŏj′o͞o-lōs′), **nod·u·lous** (nŏj′o͞o-ləs) *adj.*

no·dus (nō′dəs) *n., pl.* **-di** (-dī′). A knotty situation, problem, or point; a complication. [Latin *nōdus,* "knot," NODE.]

No·ël (nō-ĕl′) *n.* **1.** Christmas. **2. noël.** A Christmas carol. [French, from Old French *no(u)el, nael,* from Latin *nātālis (dies),* "birth(day of Christ)," from *nātālis,* of birth, from *nāscī* (past participle *nātus*), to be born.]

no·e·sis (nō-ē′sĭs) *n.* **1.** *Psychology.* The cognitive process; the mental process by which knowledge is gained. **2.** *Philosophy.* The highest knowledge, as of universal forms. [Greek *noēsis,* intelligence, understanding, from *noein,* to perceive, from *nous,* the mind.]

no·et·ic (nō-ĕt′ĭk) *adj.* **1.** Of, pertaining to, originating in, or comprehended by the intellect. **2.** Of cognition or rational thought that is comprehended by the intellect alone. [Greek *noētikos,* from *noēsis,* NOESIS.]

no-fault (nō′fôlt′) *adj.* **1.** Of or designating a type of divorce in which blame is not assigned to either party for the breakup of the marriage. **2.** Of or designating a system of motor vehicle insurance in which accident victims are compensated by their own insurance companies regardless of who caused the accident.

nog¹ (nŏg) *n.* **1.** A wooden block built into a masonry wall to hold nails that support joinery structures. **2.** A wooden peg or pin. [17th century : origin obscure.]

nog² *n.* **1. Eggnog** *(see).* **2.** *British Regional.* A strong beer of a type brewed in East Anglia. [17th century : origin obscure.]

nog·gin (nŏg′ĭn) *n.* **1.** A small mug or cup. **2.** A unit of liquid measure equal to one quarter of a pint. **3.** *Informal.* The head. [17th century : origin obscure.]

nog·ging (nŏg′ĭng) *n.* **1.** Brickwork used to fill in the boards of a wooden framework. **2.** A short horizontal wooden beam used to strengthen upright posts in the framework of a wall. Also called "nogging piece." [From NOG (wooden block, peg).]

no-go (nō′gō′) *adj. Slang.* Not in a suitable condition for proceeding or functioning properly: *The space launch was no-go because of the weather.*

no-good (nō′go͝od′) *adj. Slang.* Good-for-nothing; contemptible.

No·gu·chi (nō-go͞o′chē), **Isamu** (1904–). U.S. sculptor. He studied sculpture with Gutzon Borglum and Constantin Brancusi and had his first successful show of bronze sculptures in 1930. Noguchi later extended his art into the environment, using stone and terra cotta and incorporating the shapes of plants, animals, and geologic formations into his constructions.

Noh, Nō (nō) *n. Sometimes* **noh, nō.** The classical drama of Japan, performed with music and dancing in a highly stylized manner by elaborately dressed actors on an almost bare stage. [Japanese *nō,* "talent," "ability," from Chinese *néng.*]

no·hit (nō′hĭt′) *adj. Baseball.* Of, pertaining to, or being a game in which one pitcher allows the opposing team no base hits.

no·hit·ter (nō′hĭt′ər) *n. Baseball.* A no-hit game.

no·hop·er (nō′hō′pər) *n. British Informal.* **1.** A person who appears doomed to failure; a loser. **2.** Anything that appears extremely unpromising, such as a bet, plan, or racehorse.

no·how (nō′hou′) *adv.* In no way; not at all.

noil (noil) *n.* A short fiber combed from the long fibers during the preparation of textile yarns. [Probably from Old French *noel,* "small knot (of wool)," from Medieval Latin *nōdellus,* diminutive of Latin *nōdus,* knot, NODE.]

noise (noiz) *n.* **1.** A sound of any kind, especially when loud, confused, indistinct, or disagreeable. **2.** An outcry or clamor: *the noise of the mob.* **3.** General interest or commotion; a stir: *"the notorious beauty who made so much noise in her own day"* (Henry B. Wheatley). **4.** *Physics.* Any electrical disturbance, especially a random and persistent one, that obscures or reduces the clarity or quality of a signal. **5.** *Computer Science.* Irrelevant or meaningless data generated by a computer along with desired data. **6. noises.** Superficial remarks conveying a specified impression: *made approving noises.* —*v.* **noised, nois·ing, nois·es.** —*tr.* To spread the rumor or report of. Usually used with *about* or *abroad.* —*intr.* **1.** To talk much or volubly. **2.** To make a noise. [Middle English, from Old French *noise, noyse,* from Latin *nausea,* seasickness (with extended senses in popular use, such as "unpleasant situation," "noisy confusion"), from Greek *nausia,* from *naus,* a ship.]

    Synonyms: babel, clamor, din, hubbub, hullabaloo, pandemonium, racket, uproar.

noise·less (noiz′lĭs) *adj.* Creating no noise; silent; quiet. —See Synonyms at **still.** —**noise·less·ly** *adv.* —**noise·less·ness** *n.*

noise·mak·er (noiz′mā′kər) *n.* One that makes noise, especially a device such as a horn or rattle used in celebrating. —**noise·mak·ing** *n. & adj.*

noise pollution *n.* Environmental noise of sufficient loudness to be annoying, distracting, or physically harmful.

noi·sette (nwä-zĕt′) *n.* A small round piece of meat, especially loin or fillet of lamb, veal, or pork. —*adj.* Made or flavored with hazelnuts. [French, diminutive of *noix,* nut.]

noi·some (noi′səm) *adj.* **1.** Offensive to the point of arousing disgust; foul and filthy: *a noisome smell.* **2.** Harmful or dangerous; noxious: *noisome fumes.* [Middle English *noyesum* : (a)*noy,* vexation, annoyance, from *anoien,* ANNOY + -SOME.] —**noi·some·ly** *adv.* —**noi·some·ness** *n.*

nois·y (noi′zē) *adj.* **-i·er, -i·est. 1.** Making noise: *a noisy dog.* **2.** Full of or characterized by noise: *a noisy classroom.* —**nois·i·ly** *adv.* —**nois·i·ness** *n.*

No·lan (nō′lən), **Sir Sidney Robert** (1917–). Australian painter. He began his career as an abstract painter, but it was through his landscapes of the Australian outback and figures from Australia's history that he achieved recognition.

no·lens vo·lens (nō′lənz vō′lənz) *adv. Latin.* Whether willing or not; willy-nilly.

no·li-me-tan·ge·re (nō′lē-mē-tăn′jə-rē′) *n.* **1.** A warning or prohibition against meddling, touching, or interfering. **2.** A picture representing Christ appearing to Mary Magdalene after the Resurrection. [Latin, "do not touch me," Christ's warning to Mary Magdalene (Vulgate, John 20:17).]

nol·le pros·e·qui (nŏl′ē prŏs′ə-kwī′) *n. Abbr.* **nol. pros.** *Law.* A declaration entered in court records that the plaintiff in a civil case or the prosecutor in a criminal case will drop prosecution of all or part of a suit or indictment. [Latin, "to be unwilling to pursue."]

no·load (nō′lōd′) *adj.* Free of sales commission charges: *a no-load mutual fund.*

no·lo con·ten·de·re (nō′lō kən-tĕn′də-rē′) *n. Law.* A plea made by the defendant in a criminal action that is equivalent to an admission of guilt and subjects him to punishment but does not prevent him from denying the alleged facts in other proceedings. [Latin, "I do not wish to contend."]

nom. nominative.

no·ma (nō′mə) *n.* A severe, often gangrenous inflammation of the mouth, occurring especially in a young child after a debilitating disease. [Latin *nomē,* "eating ulcer," from Greek *nomē,* spreading ulcer, "a feeding," "a pasturage."]

no·mad (nō′măd′) *n.* **1.** Any of a group of pastoral people having no fixed abode and usually moving from place to place in a search for food and water. **2.** One who has no permanent domicile; a wanderer. —*adj.* Nomadic. [French *nomade,* from Latin *nomas* (stem *nomad-*), from Greek *nomas,* one that wanders about for pasture; related to *nemein,* to feed or pasture animals.] —**no·mad·ism** *n.*

no·mad·ic (nō-măd′ĭk) *adj.* Also **no·mad·i·cal.** Leading the life of a nomad; wandering; roving. —**no·mad·i·cal·ly** *adv.*

no·man's-land (nō′mănz′lănd′) *n.* **1.** Land under dispute by two opposing parties; especially, the field of battle between two oppos-

ing entrenched armies. **2.** An unclaimed or unowned piece of land. **3.** Any area of indefiniteness or ambiguity.

nom·arch (nŏm′ärk′) *n.* A governor, especially of a nome or nomarchy. [Greek *nomarkhēs* : NOME + -ARCH.]

nom·ar·chy (nŏm′är′kē) *n., pl.* **-ies.** Any of the administrative provinces of modern Greece. [Greek *nomarkhia* : NOME + -ARCHY.]

nom·bril (nŏm′brəl) *n. Heraldry.* The point on an escutcheon between the fess point and the base point; the midpoint in the lower half of an escutcheon. [Old French *nombril,* navel, probably alteration of *l'ombril,* the navel.]

nom de guerre (nŏm′ də gâr′) *n.* A fictitious name adopted for a particular course of action; a pseudonym. [French, "war name."]

nom de plume (nŏm′ də ploom′) *n.* A pseudonym adopted by a writer. [French, "pen name."]

nome (nōm) *n.* **1.** A province of ancient Egypt. **2.** A nomarchy. [Greek *nomos,* division, district.]

Nome (nōm). City of western Alaska, on the southern side of Seward Peninsula. It was founded *c.* 1898 when gold was discovered in the area and was a boom town from 1899 to 1903. Today its economy depends on tourism, fishing, and fur trapping.

no·men (nō′mən) *n., pl.* **nom·i·na** (nŏm′ə-nə). The second name of a citizen of ancient Rome, designating gens or patrilinear clan. Compare **cognomen, praenomen.** [Latin, name.]

no·men·cla·tor (nō′mən-klā′tər) *n.* One who assigns names, as in scientific classification. [Latin *nōmenclātor,* "namecaller," a slave who accompanied his master to tell him the names of people he met : *nōmen,* name + -*clātor,* caller, from *calāre,* to call.]

no·men·cla·ture (nō′mən-klā′chər, nō-mĕn′klə-) *n.* A system of names or terms; a systematic naming in any art, science, or area of activity. [Latin *nōmenclātūra,* from *nōmenclātor,* NOMENCLATOR.] —**no·men·cla·tur·al** (nō′mən-klā′chər-əl) *adj.*

nom·i·nal (nŏm′ə-nəl) *adj.* **1. a.** Of, like, or consisting of a name or names. **b.** Bearing a person's name: *nominal shares.* **2.** Existing in name only; not real or actual; theoretical: *the nominal head of the firm.* **3.** Minimal in comparison to the real value: *a nominal sum.* **4.** *Grammar.* Of, like, or functioning as a noun or nouns. —*n.* A word or phrase that functions as a noun. [Latin *nōminālis,* from *nōmen* (stem *nōmin-*), name.] —**nom·i·nal·ly** *adv.*

nom·i·nal·ism (nŏm′ə-nəl-ĭz′əm) *n. Philosophy.* The doctrine that abstract concepts, general terms, or universals have no objective reference but exist only as names. Compare **realism.** —**nom·i·nal·ist** *adj. & n.* —**nom·i·nal·is·tic** *adj.*

nominal value *n.* The stated or par value of a share certificate or bond, as opposed to the actual or market value.

nom·i·nate (nŏm′ə-nāt′) *tr.v.* **-nat·ed, -nat·ing, -nates. 1.** To propose by name as a candidate. **2.** To designate or appoint to some office, responsibility, or honor. **3.** To designate; name. —*adj.* (nŏm′ə-nĭt). Having a particular name. [Latin *nōmināre,* to name, from *nōmen* (stem *nōmin-*), name.] —**nom·i·na·tor** *n.*

nom·i·na·tion (nŏm′ə-nā′shən) *n.* **1.** The act or an instance of nominating. **2.** The state of being nominated.

nom·i·na·tive (nŏm′ə-nə-tĭv *for sense 1;* nŏm′ə-nā′tĭv, nŏm′ə-nə-tĭv *for senses 2 and 3*) *adj. Abbr.* **nom. 1.** *Grammar.* Of or designating the case of the subject of a finite verb (as *We* in *We awoke at dawn*) and of words identified with the subject, such as *women* in *These are the women.* **2.** Having or bearing a person's name. **3. a.** Appointed to office. **b.** Nominated as a candidate to office. —*n.* (nŏm′ə-nə-tĭv). *Abbr.* **nom.** *Grammar.* The nominative case. **2.** A form or construction in this case. [Noun, Middle English *nominatif (case),* from Old French *(cas) nominatif,* from Latin *nōminātīvus (cāsus),* from *nōmināre,* to NOMINATE.]

nom·i·nee (nŏm′ə-nē′) *n.* One who is nominated to an office or as a candidate. [NOMIN(ATE) + -EE.]

nomo– *prefix.* Indicates law, usage, or custom; for example, **nomology.** [Greek *nomos,* usage, law.]

nom·o·gram (nŏm′ə-grăm′, nō′mə-) *n.* Also **nom·o·graph** (-grăf′, -grāf′). A graph consisting of three coplanar curves, usually parallel straight lines, each graduated for a different variable so that a straight line connecting all three curves intersects the related values of each variable. It is used to represent an equation containing three variables. Also called "alignment chart." [NOMO- + -GRAM.]

no·mog·ra·phy (nō-mŏg′rə-fē) *n.* The science of constructing nomograms.

no·mol·o·gy (nō-mŏl′ə-jē) *n.* The science of physical and logical laws. [NOMO- + -LOGY.] —**no·mo·log·i·cal** (nō′mə-lŏj′ĭ-kəl, nŏm′ə-) *adj.* —**no·mol·o·gist** *n.*

nom·o·thet·ic (nŏm′ə-thĕt′ĭk, nō′mə-) *adj.* Also **nom·o·thet·i·cal** (-ĭ-kəl). **1.** Lawmaking; legislative. **2.** Of or concerned with the formulation of general or scientific laws. [From obsolete *nomothete,* from Greek *nomothetēs,* legislator : *nomos,* law + *tithēnai,* to put.]

–nomy *suffix.* Indicates the systematization of knowledge about, or laws governing, a specified field; for example, **astronomy.** [Latin *-nomia,* from Greek; either from agent nouns or adjectives in *-nomos,* from *nemein,* to distribute, manage, or from *nomos,* distribution, law.]

non– *prefix.* Indicates: **1.** Failure or lack; for example, **noncompliance. 2.** Absence of the qualities or characteristics typically associated with; for example, **nonperson. 3.** Not; for example, **nonviable.** *Note:* Many compounds other than those entered here may be formed with *non-.* In forming compounds, *non-* is normally joined with the following element without space or hyphen: *nonnutritive.* However, if the second element begins with a capital letter, it is separated with a hyphen: *non-French.* See also **un-.** [Middle Eng-

Nolan painting The Dog and Duck Hotel—*a heat-laden Australian scene, typical of the manner that made Sidney Nolan famous.*

lish *non-*, from Old French *non-*, from Latin *nōn,* not.]

   Usage: Non- is generally restricted in meaning to simple negation; it adds the sense of *not* and implies nothing further. It is usually less forceful than the following prefixes used in negation: *un-, in-, il-, im-, ir-,* and *a-.* Unlike *non-,* these generally either emphasize negation strongly or add a sense in direct opposition to that of the words to which they are joined. *Non-American* specifies only a limitation; *un-American* implies active opposition. *Nonreligious* and *nonhuman* are not directly opposed to religious and human in the sense that *irreligious and inhuman* are. See Usage note at **un-.**

nona– *prefix.* Indicates nine or ninth; for example, **nonagon.** [From Latin *nōnus,* ninth.]

non·ad·di·tive (nŏn-ăd′ə-tĭv) *adj. Mathematics.* Having a numerical value that is not equal to the sum of its component parts. **—non·ad·di·tiv·i·ty** (nŏn′ăd-ə-tĭv′ə-tē) *n.*

non·age (nŏn′ĭj, nō′nĭj) *n.* **1.** The period during which one is legally underage. **2.** A stage of immaturity: *"the bravest achievements were always accomplished in the nonage of a nation"* (Thomas Paine). [Middle English, from Old French : NON- + *age, aage,* AGE.]

non·a·ge·nar·i·an (nŏn′ə-jə-nâr′ē-ən, nō′nə-) *adj.* **1.** Being ninety years old or between ninety and one hundred years old. **2.** Of or like someone of this age.
   ~*n.* A person of ninety or between ninety and one hundred years of age. [Latin *nōnāgēnārius,* from *nōnāgēnī,* ninety each, from *nōnāginta,* ninety : *novem,* nine + *-gintā,* ten times.]

non·ag·gres·sion (nŏn′ə-grĕsh′ən) *n.* The avoidance of aggression or hostilities, as between nations. Also used adjectivally: *a nonaggression pact.*

non·a·gon (nŏn′ə-gŏn′, nō′nə-) *n.* A polygon having nine sides and nine angles. [NONA- + -GON.]

non·ag·o·nal (nŏn-ăg′ə-nəl) *adj.* **1.** Having nine sides and nine angles. **2.** Of, pertaining to, or formed in nonagons.

non·al·co·hol·ic (nŏn′ăl-kə-hôl′ĭk, -hŏl′ĭk) *adj.* Containing no alcohol.

non·a·ligned (nŏn′ə-līnd′) *adj.* Not in alliance with any power bloc; neutral: *a nonaligned nation.* **—non·a·lign·ment** *n.*

non·al·ler·gen·ic (nŏn′ăl-ər-jĕn′ĭk) *adj.* Not causing an allergic reaction.

non·a·no·ic acid (nŏn′ə-nō′ĭk) *n.* A chemical, **pelargonic acid** *(see).* [From *nonane,* a paraffin : NONA- + -ANE (because it is the ninth in the methane series).]

non·ap·pear·ance (nŏn′ə-pîr′əns) *n.* Failure to appear, as in a court of law.

non·bel·lig·er·ent (nŏn′bə-lĭj′ər-ənt) *n.* A person or a country that takes no part in a war. **—non·bel·lig·er·ent** *adj.*

nonce¹ (nŏns) *n.* The present or particular time or occasion. Used in the phrase *for the nonce: "her tendency to discover a touch of sadness had for the nonce disappeared"* (Theodore Dreiser). [Middle English *for the nones, for the nanes,* originally *for then anes,* "for the one (purpose or occasion)" : FOR + *then,* dative singular neuter of THE + *anes,* ONCE.]

nonce² *n. British Slang.* An imprisoned sex offender. [20th century : origin obscure.]

nonce word *n.* A word invented and used only once, to meet a particular requirement; an example is the word *mileconsuming* in *"the wagon beginning to fall into its slow and mileconsuming clatter"* (William Faulkner).

non·cha·lance (nŏn′shə-läns′) *n.* Debonair lack of concern.

non·cha·lant (nŏn′shə-länt′) *adj.* Appearing casually unconcerned; coolly indifferent. **—**See Synonyms at **cool.** [French, from Old French, from *nonchaloir,* to be unconcerned : NON- + *chaloir,* to be interested or concerned, from Latin *calēre,* to be warm.] **—non·cha·lant·ly** *adv.*

non·com (nŏn′kŏm′) *n. Informal.* A noncommissioned officer.

non·com·bat·ant (nŏn′kəm-băt′nt, nŏn-kŏm′bə-tənt) *n.* **1.** A person connected with the armed forces whose duties are other than fighting, such as a chaplain. **2.** A civilian in wartime.

non·com·mis·sioned officer (nŏn′kə-mĭsh′ənd) *n. Abbr.* **NCO, N.C.O.** A member of the armed forces, as a sergeant or corporal, appointed to a rank conferring leadership over other enlisted personnel but not holding a commission. Compare **commissioned officer, warrant officer.**

non·com·mit·tal (nŏn′kə-mĭt′l) *adj.* Refusing commitment to any particular course of action or opinion; revealing no preference or purpose. **—non·com·mit·tal·ly** *adv.*

non·com·pli·ance (nŏn′kəm-plī′əns) *n.* Failure or refusal to comply with something. **—non·com·pli·ant** *adj. & n.*

non com·pos men·tis (nŏn kŏm′pəs mĕn′tĭs) *adj.* Not of sound mind, and hence not legally responsible. [Latin, "not having control of the mind."]

non·con·duc·tor (nŏn′kən-dŭk′tər) *n.* A substance that conducts little or no electricity or heat. **—non·con·duct·ing** *adj.*

non·con·form·ist (nŏn′kən-fôr′mĭst) *n.* **1.** One who refuses to be bound by the accepted rules, beliefs, or practices of a group. **2. Nonconformist.** A member of a Protestant church that dissents from the Church of England. **—non·con·form·ism** *n.* **—non·con·form·ist** *adj.*

non·con·form·i·ty (nŏn′kən-fôr′mə-tē) *n.* **1.** Refusal or failure to conform to accepted customs, beliefs, or practices. **2. Often Non·conformity.** Refusal to accept or conform to the doctrines of the Church of England.

non·con·trib·u·to·ry (nŏn′kən-trĭb′yə-tôr′ē, -tōr′ē) *adj.* **1.** Not re-

quiring contributions, as a pension plan funded by the employer. **2.** Not contributing.

non·co·op·er·a·tion (nŏn′kō-ŏp′ə-rā′shən) *n.* **1.** Failure or refusal to cooperate. **2.** Resistance to government through civil disobedience or refusal to perform civil duties, such as paying taxes. **—non·co·op·er·a·tion·ist** *n. & adj.* **—non·co·op·er·a·tive** *adj.* **—non·co·op·er·a·tor** *n.*

non·count·a·ble (nŏn-koun′tə-bəl) *adj. Grammar.* Designating a noun that refers to an object lacking clearly standardized or defined limits and that is not preceded by the indefinite article or a number; for example, *earth* and *soil* are noncountable nouns, whereas *pebble* and *boulder* are not. Some nouns, such as *speed* or *fear,* have both countable and noncountable senses. A noncountable noun is also called a "mass noun." Compare **countable.**

non·de·nom·i·na·tion·al (nŏn′dĭ-nŏm′ə-nā′shən-əl) *adj.* Not restricted to or associated with a particular religious denomination.

non·de·script (nŏn′dĭ-skrĭpt′) *adj.* Lacking in distinctive qualities; without any individual character or form.
   ~*n.* A person or thing with no outstanding or distinguishing features. [NON- + Latin *dēscrīptus,* past participle of *dēscrībere,* DESCRIBE.]

non·dis·junc·tion (nŏn′dĭs-jŭngk′shən) *n. Biology.* Failure of homologous chromosomes to separate during meiosis.

non·dis·tinc·tive (nŏn′dĭs-tĭngk′tĭv) *adj.* **1.** Not distinctive. **2.** *Linguistics.* Not helping to distinguish meaning: *The vowel sound in the words "hit" and "slip" is nondistinctive; only the consonant sounds are differentiated.*

none (nŭn) *pron.* **1.** No one; not one; nobody: *None dared to do it.* **2.** Not any; no persons or things of a specified group: *None of my cardigans will go with this new dress.* **3.** No part; not any: *none of my business; none of his concern.*
   ~*adj. Archaic.* Not any; no. Now used only before vowels: *There is none other available.*
   ~*adv.* In no way; not at all: *We were none the wiser.* [Middle English *nan, none,* Old English *nān : ne,* no + *ān,* one.]

   Usage: None may be used with either a singular or a plural verb, depending on the construction in which it appears. Thus when *none* precedes or refers back to a singular noun, the verb is also in the singular: *None of the laundry is clean; Where's the orange juice?* — *There is none* (which is a more formal version of *There isn't any*). A singular verb is also used when *none* can be interpreted as "not one" or "no one": *None of us is to blame.* A plural verb is used when *none* refers back to a plural noun: *Where are the sugar lumps?* — *There are none.* The plural verb is also generally used when the meaning of *none* is "not any of a group of persons or things": *None have been more in need of a pay raise than the nurses.* Problems of usage arise when *none* can be interpreted as either singular or plural: *None of these books is* (or *are*) *helpful.* Purists insist on the singular form in such contexts, but the plural is often used in all styles, when no individualizing sense is intended. In every case the verb and related personal pronouns and pronominal adjectives must agree in number: *none has his* (or *none have theirs*). See also **neither.**

non·e·go (nŏn-ē′gō, -ĕg′ō) *n., pl.* **-gos.** *Philosophy.* All that is not part of the ego or the conscious self.

non·e·lec·tro·lyte (nŏn′ĭ-lĕk′trə-līt′) *n.* A substance that does not ionize in solution or in liquid form and therefore forms solutions or liquids of low conductivity.

non·emp·ty (nŏn-ĕmp′tē) *adj. Mathematics.* Designating a set that has at least one member.

non·en·ti·ty (nŏn-ĕn′tə-tē) *n., pl.* **-ties. 1.** An insignificant person or thing. **2.** Nonexistence. **3.** Something that does not exist or that exists only in the imagination.

nones (nōnz) *pl.n.* **1.** In the ancient Roman calendar, the ninth day before the ides of a month; the seventh of March, May, July, or October and the fifth day of the other months. **2.** *Ecclesiastical.* **a.** The fifth of the seven **canonical hours** *(see).* **b.** The time of day set aside for this prayer, usually the ninth hour after sunrise. [In sense 1, Middle English *nonys, nonas,* from Old French *nones,* from Latin *nōnae,* feminine plural of *nōnus,* ninth. In sense 2, plural of *none,* from Old French *none,* from Late Latin *nōna (hōra),* the ninth hour, from the feminine of Latin *nōnus,* ninth.]

non·es·sen·tial (nŏn′ĭ-sĕn′shəl) *adj.* **1.** Not essential. **2.** *Biochemistry.* Designating amino acids that a particular organism is able to synthesize and that are therefore not essential to its diet.

none·such, non·such (nŭn′sŭch′) *n.* **1.** A person or thing without equal: *a nonesuch among athletes.* **2.** A plant, the **black medick** *(see).* **—none·such** *adj.*

no·net (nō-nĕt′) *n. Music.* **1.** A composition for nine instruments or voices. **2.** A group of nine musicians or performers. [Italian *nonetto,* from *nono,* ninth, from Latin *nōnus.*]

none·the·less (nŭn′thə-lĕs′) *adv.* Nevertheless; however.

non-Eu·clid·e·an (nŏn′yoō-klĭd′ē-ən) *adj.* Designating any of several modern geometries that change or discard one or more of the axioms of Euclid.

non·e·vent (nŏn′ĭ-vĕnt′) *n.* An anticipated event that fails to take place or to live up to expectations.

non·ex·ist·ence (nŏn′ĭg-zĭs′təns) *n.* **1.** The condition of not existing. **2.** A thing that does not exist. **—non·ex·ist·ent** *adj.*

non·fat (nŏn′făt′) *adj.* Lacking fat solids or having the fat content removed: *nonfat milk.*

non·fea·sance (nŏn-fē′zəns) *n. Law.* Failure to perform some act that is either an official duty or a legal requirement. Compare **mal-**

feasance, misfeasance. [NON- + obsolete *feasance,* a doing, from Old French *faisance* (see **malfeasance**).]
non·fer·rous (nŏn-fĕr'əs) *adj.* **1.** Not composed of or containing iron. **2.** Of or pertaining to metals other than iron.
non·fic·tion (nŏn-fĭk'shən) *n.* Prose works other than fiction. **—non·fic·tion·al** *adj.*
non·flam·ma·ble (nŏn-flăm'ə-bəl) *adj.* Not flammable; not easily set alight. —See Usage note at **flammable.**
non·gov·ern·men·tal organization (nŏn'gŭv-ərn-mĕn'təl) *n.* See **NGO.**
non·har·mo·nic (nŏn'här-mŏn'ĭk) *adj.* Of or designating a note, such as a grace note, that is not part of the chord with which it is played.
non·i·den·ti·cal (nŏn'ī-dĕn'tĭ-kəl) *adj.* **1.** Not the same; different. **2.** Fraternal (sense 3).
no·nil·lion (nō-nĭl'yən) *n.* **1.** In the United States and France, the cardinal number represented by the figure 1 followed by 30 zeros; usually written 10^{30}. Also *British* "quintillion." **2.** In Great Britain and Germany, the cardinal number represented by the figure 1 followed by 54 zeros; usually written 10^{54}. [French, from Old French, "the ninth power of a million" : *non-,* nine, ninth + *(m)ilion, (m)illion,* (M)ILLION.] **—no·nil·lion** *adj.*
no·nil·lionth (nō-nĭl'yənth) *n.* **1.** The ordinal number nonillion in a series. **2.** Any of a nonillion equal parts. **—no·nil·lionth** *adj.*
non·in·duc·tive (nŏn'ĭn-dŭk'tĭv) *adj. Electricity.* Having low inductance.
non·in·ter·ven·tion (nŏn'ĭn-tər-vĕn'shən) *n.* Failure or refusal to interfere or intervene in the affairs of another; especially, a deliberate refusal of one nation to intervene in the affairs of another nation or one of its own subdivisions. **—non·in·ter·ven·tion·ist** *n.* & *adj.*
non·i·ron (nŏn-ī'ərn) *adj. Chiefly British.* Requiring little or no ironing. Said of garments or fabrics.
non·join·der (nŏn-join'dər) *n. Law.* The omission of a party, plaintiff, defendant, or cause of action that should have been included as a necessary part of an action or suit. Compare **misjoinder.**
non·ju·ror (nŏn-jo͝or'ər, -jo͝or'ôr') *n.* **1.** One who refuses to take an oath, as of allegiance. **2. Nonjuror.** An Anglican clergyman who refused to swear allegiance to William and Mary in 1689.
non li·cet (nŏn lī'sĭt) *adj. Law.* Not allowed; unlawful. [Latin.]
non·lin·e·ar (nŏn-lĭn'ē-ər) *adj.* **1.** Not in a straight line. **2.** *Mathematics.* Occurring as a result of a nonadditive operation. **—non·lin·e·ar·i·ty** (nŏn'lĭn-ē-ăr'ə-tē) *n.*
non li·quet (nŏn lī'kwĭt) *adj. Law.* Unclear. Said of evidence. [Latin.]
non·lit·er·ate (nŏn-lĭt'ər-ĭt) *adj.* Having no written language: *a nonliterate people.*
non·met·al (nŏn-mĕt'l) *n. Chemistry.* Any of a number of elements, such as oxygen or sulfur, that generally occur as negatively charged ions or radicals, form oxides that produce acids, and are poor conductors of heat and of electricity when solid.
non·me·tal·lic (nŏn'mə-tăl'ĭk) *adj.* **1.** Not of metal. **2.** *Chemistry.* Of or pertaining to a nonmetal.
non·mor·al (nŏn-môr'əl, -mŏr'əl) *adj.* Unrelated to morals or to ethical considerations; neither moral nor immoral.
non-New·ton·i·an fluid (nŏn'no͞o-tō'nē-ən, -nyo͞o-) *n.* A fluid with a flow behavior such that the rate of shear is not proportional to the corresponding stress.
non·nu·cle·ar (nŏn-no͞o'klē-ər, -nyo͞o'-) *adj.* **1.** Not possessing, producing, or involving nuclear weapons. **2.** Not powered by nuclear energy.
no-no (nō'nō') *n., pl.* **-noes.** *Slang.* Something that is forbidden or unacceptable.
non·ob·jec·tive (nŏn'əb-jĕk'tĭv) *adj.* Designating a style of art that does not represent objects; abstract.
non ob·stan·te (nŏn ŏb-stăn'tē, nōn ōb-stän'tā) *prep. Abbr.* **non obs., non obst.** *Latin.* Notwithstanding.
no-non·sense (nō-nŏn'sĕns', -səns) *adj.* **1.** Not tolerating extremes of behavior or taste. **2.** Practical; down-to-earth.
non·pa·reil (nŏn'pə-rĕl') *adj.* Without rival; matchless; peerless; unequaled.
~n. **1.** A person or thing that is unmatched or unequaled; a paragon. **2.** *Printing.* A size of type, 6-point type. **3.** A small, flat chocolate drop covered with white pellets of sugar. **4.** A bird, the **painted bunting** *(see).* [Middle English *nonparaille,* from Old French *nonpareil* : NON- + *pareil,* equal, like, from Vulgar Latin *pariculus* (unattested), diminutive of Latin *pār,* equal.]
non·par·tic·i·pat·ing (nŏn'pär-tĭs'ə-pā'tĭng) *adj.* **1.** Not participating. **2.** *Insurance.* Not giving the right to participate in the profits of a company. **—non·par·tic·i·pat·or** *n.*
non·par·ti·san (nŏn-pär'tə-zən) *adj.* **1.** Not partisan. **2.** Not influenced by, affiliated with, or supporting the interests or policies of any one political party.
non·per·son (nŏn-pûr'sən) *n.* An **unperson** *(see).*
non pla·cet (nŏn plā'sĭt) *n.* A negative vote. [Latin, "it is not pleasing."]
non·plus (nŏn'plŭs') *n.* A state of perplexity or bafflement preventing action, speech, or thought: *never at a nonplus; reduced to a perfect nonplus.*
~tr.v. **nonplused, -plusing, -pluses.** Also *chiefly British* **-plussed, -plussing, -plusses.** To perplex; baffle. [Latin *nōn plūs,* "no more (can be said)" : *nōn,* not + *plūs,* more.]
non pos·su·mus (nŏn pŏs'ə-məs, nōn) *n.* A statement indicating an inability to take action on a matter. [Latin, "we cannot."]
non·pro·duc·tive (nŏn'prə-dŭk'tĭv) *adj.* **1.** Of or belonging to that part of the labor force that does not directly produce goods, such as clerical personnel. **2.** Not yielding what was expected; unproductive. **—non·pro·duc·tive·ly** *adv.* **—non·pro·duc·tive·ness** *n.*
non·prof·it (nŏn-prŏf'ĭt) *adj.* Not set up with the aim of making a profit: *a nonprofit organization.*
non·pro·lif·e·ra·tion (nŏn'prə-lĭf'ə-rā'shən) *n.* Limitation of the production or spread of something, especially nuclear weapons. Also used adjectivally: *a nonproliferation agreement.*
non·pros (nŏn'prŏs') *tr.v.* **-prossed, -prossing, -prosses.** *Law.* To enter a judgment of non prosequitur against (a plaintiff).
non pro·se·qui·tur (nŏn prō-sĕk'wĭ-to͝or') *n. Abbr.* **non pros.** *Law.* The judgment entered against a plaintiff who fails to appear in court to prosecute a suit. [Latin, "he does not prosecute."]
non·re·new·a·ble (nŏn'rĭ-no͞o'ə-bəl, -nyo͞o'-) *adj.* **1.** Unable to be renewed or extended. **2.** Not replaceable once exhausted, as fossil fuels.
non·rep·re·sen·ta·tion·al (nŏn'rĕp-rē-zĕn-tā'shən-əl) *adj.* **1.** Not representational. **2.** In art, nonobjective.
non·res·i·dent (nŏn-rĕz'ə-dənt, -dĕnt') *adj.* **1.** Not living in a particular place. **2.** Not living in the place where one works. **—non·res·i·dence, non·res·i·den·cy** *n.* **—non·res·i·dent** *n.*
non·re·sis·tant (nŏn'rĭ-zĭs'tənt) *adj.* **1.** Not resistant; submissively obedient. **2.** Unable to resist illness or infection.
~n. **1.** One who believes in complete obedience to authority, even though it may be unjust or arbitrary. **2.** One who will not resort to force, even in self-defense. **—non·re·sis·tance** *n.*
non·re·stric·tive (nŏn'rĭ-strĭk'tĭv) *adj.* **1.** Not restrictive. **2.** *Grammar.* Designating a word, clause, or phrase that is descriptive of but does not limit the basic application of the element it modifies, as the nonrestrictive clause *who has brown hair* in the sentence *Anne, who has brown hair, is two years older than Laura.* Compare **restrictive.**
non·re·turn·a·ble (nŏn'rĭ-tûr'nə-bəl) *adj.* Not returnable, especially in exchange for a deposit: *nonreturnable bottles.*
non·rig·id (nŏn-rĭj'ĭd) *adj.* **1.** Not rigid. **2.** Designating a lighter-than-air aircraft that holds its shape by gas pressure.
non·sched·uled (nŏn-skĕj'o͞old) *adj.* **1.** Operating without fixed flying schedules: *a nonscheduled airline.* **2.** Not according to a schedule or plan: *a nonscheduled stop at Chicago.*
non·se·cre·tor (nŏn'sĭ-krē'tər) *n.* A person of blood type A or B in whose saliva and other body fluids the A or B antigens determining blood group cannot be detected. Compare **secretor.**
non·sec·tar·i·an (nŏn'sĕk-târ'ē-ən) *adj.* Not limited to or associated with any particular religious denomination.
non·sense (nŏn'sĕns', -səns) *n.* **1.** Something that does not make or have sense; especially, behavior or language that is meaningless or absurd. Also used adjectivally: *a nonsense poem.* **2.** Extravagant foolishness or frivolity. **3.** Things of little or no importance or usefulness; trifles: *ribbons, laces, and other nonsense.* **4.** *Genetics.* A sequence of DNA that is not used as a template for the synthesis of messenger RNA during transcription.
~interj. Used to express rejection or dismissal of an idea or statement. [NON- (not) + SENSE.] **—non·sen·si·cal** (nŏn-sĕn'sĭ-kəl) *adj.* **—non·sen·si·cal·ly** *adv.*
nonsense verse *n.* A form of verse dealing with illogical and absurd ideas or characters, and usually employing words invented for humorous effect.
non se·qui·tur (nŏn sĕk'wĭ-to͝or') *n. Abbr.* **non seq.** **1.** *Logic.* An inference or conclusion that does not follow from established premises or evidence. **2.** A statement that appears to have no relevance to what has just been said. [Latin, "it does not follow."]
non·sig·nif·i·cant (nŏn'sĭg-nĭf'ĭ-kənt) *adj.* **1.** Not significant; meaningless. **2.** Having, producing, or being a value obtained from a statistical test that lies within the limits assigned to random occurrence. **—non·sig·nif·i·cant·ly** *adv.*
non·skid (nŏn'skĭd') *adj.* Having a ridged tread or specially treated surface designed to prevent or inhibit skidding: *a nonskid tire.*
non·smok·er (nŏn-smō'kər) *n.* **1.** A person who does not smoke. **2.** A train compartment in which smoking is forbidden.
non·spe·cif·ic urethritis (nŏn'spĭ-sĭf'ĭk) *n. Abbr.* **NSU.** Inflammation of the urethra, a sexually transmitted infection not caused by gonococcal or other specific infectious agents.
non·stan·dard (nŏn-stăn'dərd) *adj.* **1.** Varying from or not adhering to a standard. **2.** *Linguistics.* Of or pertaining to usages or varieties of a language that do not conform to those characteristic of educated native users of the language.
non·start·er (nŏn-stär'tər) *n.* **1.** A horse, racing car, or the like that does not compete in a race for which it was entered. **2.** *Informal.* A person, idea, or project regarded as unlikely to succeed and hence not worthy of consideration.
non·stick (nŏn'stĭk') *adj.* Coated with a substance that keeps food from sticking during cooking: *a nonstick frying pan.*
non·stop (nŏn'stŏp') *adj.* **1.** Making or having made no stops: *a nonstop flight.* **2.** *Informal.* Not relieved by any pause; unceasing: *nonstop noise.* **—non·stop** *adv.*
non·stri·at·ed (nŏn-strī'ā'tĭd) *adj.* Having no striations. Said chiefly of certain muscle fibers.
nonsuch. Variant of **nonesuch.**
non·suit (nŏn-so͞ot') *n. Law.* A judgment given against a plaintiff for failure to prosecute his case or to introduce sufficient evidence.
~tr.v. **nonsuited, -suiting, -suits.** To dismiss the lawsuit of. [Mid-

PRONUNCIATION KEY

ă, pat; ā, pay; âr, care; ä, father, are; b, bib; ch, church; d, deed; ĕ, pet; ē, be; f, fife; g, gag; h, hat; hw, which; ĭ, pit; ī, pie; îr, pier; j, judge; k, kick; l, lid, needle; m, mum; n, no, sudden; ng, thing; ŏ, pot; ō, toe; ô, paw, for; oi, noise; ou, out; o͝o, book; o͞o, boot; p, pop; r, roar; s, sauce; sh, ship, dish; t, tight; th, thin, path; *th,* this, bathe; ŭ, cut; ûr, fur; v, valve; w, with; y, yes; z, zebra, size; zh, vision; ə, about, item, edible, gallop, circus, peaceful

IN FOREIGN WORDS:

å, *Fr.* ami; œ, *Fr.* feu, *Ger.* schön; ü, *Fr.* tu, *Ger.* über; KH, *Ger.* ich, *Scot.* loch; N, *Fr.* bon; y', *Fr.* Compiègne

STRESS MARKS:

Primary stress: ' in·cite' (ĭn-sīt')
Secondary stress: ' in'sight' (ĭn'sīt')

dle English, from Norman French *no(u)nsuyte* : NON- + Old French *suite, sieute,* SUIT.]

non·sup·port (nŏn′sə-pôrt′, -pōrt′) *n. Law.* Failure to provide for the maintenance of one's legal dependents.

non·triv·i·al (nŏn-trĭv′ē-əl) *adj.* **1.** Not trivial. **2.** *Mathematics.* Designating a relationship or expression in which at least one variable is not equal to zero.

non trop·po (nŏn trô′pō) *adv. Music.* Moderately. Used to modify a direction: *adagio non troppo.* [Italian, "not too much."]

non-U (nŏn′yōō′) *adj. British Informal.* Not belonging or appropriate to upper-class custom, especially in language. Compare **U.**

non·un·ion (nŏn-yōōn′yən) *adj.* **1. a.** Not belonging to a labor union. **b.** Not unionized: *a nonunion shop.* **2.** Not manufactured or serviced by union labor.
~*n. Medicine.* Failure of a bone fracture to heal.

non·u·ple (nŏn′yə-pəl) *adj.* **1.** Consisting of nine members; having nine parts or elements; ninefold. **2.** Multiplied by nine.
~*n.* A number or total that is nine times as great as another. [Old French *nonuple* : *non-,* nine + *-ple,* -fold, from Latin *-plus.*]

non·us·er (nŏn-yōō′zər) *n.* One who does not make use of or take something, especially narcotic drugs.

non·ver·bal (nŏn-vûr′bəl) *adj.* **1.** Being other than verbal: *nonverbal communication.* **2. a.** Involving little use of language: *a nonverbal intelligence test.* **b.** Measuring low on a scale of verbal ability.

non·vi·a·ble (nŏn-vī′ə-bəl) *adj.* **1.** Not capable of living or developing: *a nonviable fetus.* **2.** Not workable or practicable.

non·vi·o·lence (nŏn-vī′ə-ləns) *n.* Lack of violence; specifically, a social philosophy based on the rejection of violent means to gain objectives. —**non·vi·o·lent** *adj.* —**non·vi·o·lent·ly** *adv.*

non·vol·a·tile (nŏn-vŏl′ə-təl) *adj. Computer Science.* Designating or pertaining to a computer memory in which information is retained when the power is switched off.

non·vot·er (nŏn-vō′tər) *n.* A person who does not vote or who has no right to vote. —**non·vot·ing** *adj.*

non·white (nŏn-hwīt′, -wīt′) *n.* **1.** A person not of the white race. **2.** *South African.* A person not of European descent or not classified as white. —**nonwhite** *adj.*

noo·dle¹ (nōōd′l) *n.* A narrow, ribbonlike strip of dried dough, usually made of flour, eggs, and water. [German *Nudel*†.]

noodle² *n.* **1.** A fool; a simpleton. **2.** *Slang.* The head. [In sense 1, perhaps blend of NODDLE (head) and NOODLE (food).]

noodle³ *intr.v.* **-dled, -dling, -dles.** To improvise music on an instrument in an idle, haphazard fashion. [Origin unknown.]

nook (nōōk) *n.* **1.** A corner, especially in a room; a recess: *They searched for it in every nook and cranny.* **2.** A quiet, narrow, or secluded spot outdoors. [Middle English *noke, nok,* perhaps from Scandinavian; akin to Norwegian (dialectal) *nok,* hook.]

noon (nōōn) *n.* **1. a.** Twelve o'clock in the daytime; midday. **b.** The time or the point in the sun's path when it is on the local meridian. **2.** The highest point or zenith; the best or brightest part. **3.** *Archaic.* The midpoint: *the noon of night.* [Middle English *none, noon,* midday, the hour of the nones (originally 3 P.M.), Old English *nōn,* "the ninth hour (after sunrise)," from Late Latin *nōna (hōra),* from the feminine of Latin *nōnus,* ninth.] —**noon** *adj.*

noon·day (nōōn′dā′) *n.* Noon. —**noon·day** *adj.*

no one, no-one (nō′wŭn′) *pron.* No person; nobody. —See Usage note at **nobody.**

noon·tide (nōōn′tīd′) *n.* Noon. [Middle English *nonetyde,* Old English *nōntīd* : *nōn,* NOON + *tīd,* TIDE (time).] —**noon·tide** *adj.*

noon·time (nōōn′tīm′) *n.* Noon.

noose (nōōs) *n.* **1.** A loop secured in a rope or cord by means of a slipknot so that it tightens if pulled. **2.** A snare or trap.
~*tr.v.* **noosed, noosing, nooses. 1.** To capture or hold by or as if by a noose. **2.** To make a noose of or in. [Middle English *nose,* from Old French *nos, nous,* from Latin *nōdus,* a knot.]

Noot·ka (nōōt′kə) *n., pl.* **-kas** or collectively **Nootka. 1.** A member of a Wakashan-speaking North American Indian people living on Vancouver Island, British Columbia, and Cape Flattery, northwestern Washington. **2.** The language of this tribe.

no·pal (nō′pəl, nō-päl′, -päl′) *n.* **1.** Any cactus of the genus *Nopalea,* found chiefly in Mexico; especially, *N. coccinellifera,* having erect petals and scarlet flowers. **2.** A prickly pear of the genus *Opuntia,* having yellow or red flowers and purple fruit. [Spanish, from Nahuatl *nopalli.*]

no-par (nō′pär′) *adj.* Without face value; having no par value. Said of share certificates.

nope (nōp) *adv. Slang.* No. [Alteration of NO (adverb).]

nor¹ (nôr; *unstressed* nər) *conj.* **1.** And not; or not; likewise not; not either. Used: **a.** As a correlative to give continuing negative force: *She neither worked nor offered to help.* **b.** For rhetorical effect following a clause that is affirmative: *The day was bright, nor were there clouds above.* **2.** *Archaic.* Used in place of *neither,* as the first correlative of a negative pair: *Nor gray his beard, nor shambling his gait.* [Middle English *nor,* contraction of *nother, nauther,* NEITHER.]
Usage: *Neither* is followed by *nor,* not by *or.* When other negative forms are used early in a sentence, the continuation of the negative meaning requires *nor* when separate clauses are involved (*I have no experience of chemistry, nor does the subject interest me*). Or may be used when the constructions are within a single clause (*I have no experience or interest in chemistry*), or share one or more elements (such as she in *She will not permit the change, or even consider it*). This substitution, common in modern usage, is possible only when it is clear that the negative sense, stated once, is felt in

the succeeding element or elements without restatement.

nor² *conj. Regional.* Than. [Middle English *nor*†.]

nor- *prefix. Chemistry.* Indicates an unaltered parent compound; for example, **norepinephrine.** [From NORMAL.]

Nor. 1. Norman. **2.** north. **3.** Norway; Norwegian.

nor·a·dren·a·line, nor·a·dren·a·lin (nôr′ə-drĕn′ə-lĭn) *n.* A hormone, **norepinephrine** *(see).* [NOR- + ADRENALINE.]

Nord·hau·sen acid (nôrd′hou′zən) *n.* **Fuming sulfuric acid** *(see).* [After *Nordhausen,* a town in Prussian Saxony where it was made.]

Nor·dic (nôr′dĭk) *adj. Anthropology.* **1.** Of, pertaining, or belonging to a subdivision of the Caucasoid ethnic group most predominant in Scandinavia. The typical Nordic person is tall, long-headed, blond, and blue-eyed. **2.** Of or pertaining to cross-country skiing and ski-jumping. Compare **Alpine.**
~*n.* A member of a Nordic people. [French *nordique,* from Old French *nord,* north, from Old English *north.*]

nor·easter. Variant of **northeaster.**

Nor·ell (nô-rĕl′), **Normal** (1900-72). U.S. fashion designer. He was known for his dramatic and spectacular designs for women's clothing. Many of his distinctive styles became classics.

nor·ep·i·neph·rine (nôr′ĕp′ə-nĕf′rĭn) *n.* A hormone, $(OH)_2C_6H_3$·$CHOH$·CH_2·NH_2, secreted by the adrenal medulla and the endings of sympathetic nerves. It is a vasoconstrictor and acts as a transmitter of nerve impulses. Also called "noradrenaline." [NOR- + EPINEPHRINE.]

Nor·folk¹ (nôr′fək). County in eastern England, bordering on the North Sea. The county town is Norwich. It is a chiefly agricultural county. The eastern portion is notable for the series of shallow lakes and channels known as the Broads.

Norfolk². Largest city in Virginia, on the Elizabeth River. It is a major industrial and commercial port and an important military center.

Norfolk Island pine *n.* An evergreen tree, *Araucaria excelsa,* native to Norfolk Island in the South Pacific.

Norfolk jacket *n.* A single-breasted men's jacket with a belt, a pocket on each side, and two box pleats in front and back. [Formerly worn for duck hunting in NORFOLK, England.]

NOR gate (nôr) *n. Computer Science.* A logic gate having one output wire and two or more input wires in which there is an output signal only if all the input signals are low. Also called "NOR circuit." Compare **AND gate.** [From NOR, since the gate has a function comparable to the operation of the conjunction *nor* in logic.]

Norge. See **Norway.**

no·ri·a (nôr′ē-ə, nōr′-) *n.* A waterwheel with buckets attached to its rim that are used to raise water from a stream, especially for transferal to an irrigation trough. [Spanish, from Arabic *nā'ūrah,* "creaking device," from *na'ara,* to grunt, creak.]

nor·ite (nôr′īt′, nōr′-) *n.* A mineral, **gabbro** *(see).* [Norwegian *norit,* "Norwegian rock," from *Norge,* Norway.] —**nor·it·ic** (nô-rĭt′ĭk) *adj.*

nor·land (nôr′lənd) *n. Often* **Norland.** *Poetic.* Northland.

norm (nôrm) *n.* **1.** A standard, model, or pattern regarded as typical for a specific group. **2.** *Mathematics.* **a.** A **mode** *(see).* **b.** An average. **c.** The length of a vector. **3.** *Geology.* The theoretical composition of a standard igneous rock. [Latin *norma,* carpenter's square, pattern.]

norm. normal.

Nor·ma (nôr′mə) *n.* A constellation in the Southern Hemisphere within the Milky Way near Lupus and Ara.

nor·mal (nôr′məl) *adj.* **1.** Conforming, adhering to, or constituting a usual or typical pattern, standard, level, or type; usual; typical: *normal room temperature; normal weight.* **2.** *Abbr.* **norm.** *Biology.* **a.** Not affected, immunized, or changed by experimentation. **b.** Functioning or occurring in a natural way. **3.** *Chemistry.* **a.** *Abbr.* **n, N** Designating a solution having one gram equivalent weight of solute per liter of solution. **b.** *Abbr.* **n-** Designating an aliphatic hydrocarbon having a straight and unbranched chain of carbon atoms. **4.** *Abbr.* **norm.** *Geometry.* At right angles; perpendicular. **5.** *Abbr.* **norm.** *Psychology.* Considered average in intelligence, ability, emotional traits, or personality.
~*n. Abbr.* **norm. 1.** Anything that is normal; the standard. **2.** The usual or expected state, form, amount, or degree. **3. a.** Correspondence to a norm. **b.** An average. **4.** *Geometry.* A perpendicular; especially, a perpendicular to a line tangent to a plane curve or to a plane tangent to a space curve. [French, or Late Latin *normālis,* from Latin, made according to the carpenter's square, rectangular, from *norma,* NORM.] —**nor·mal·ly** *adv.*
Synonyms: *natural, regular, standard.*

nor·mal·cy (nôr′məl-sē) *n.* Normality.
Usage: This alternative to *normality* is now frequently encountered in formal speech and writing, especially of a technical or semi-technical kind; it continues to attract criticism when used in everyday contexts, where *normality* would be considered the more natural form.

normal decane *n.* A **decane** *(see).*

normal distribution *n. Statistics.* A theoretical frequency distribution for a set of variable data, represented by a bell-shaped curve symmetrical about the mean. Also called "Gaussian distribution."

nor·mal·i·ty (nôr-măl′ə-tē) *n.* **1.** The state or fact of being normal. —See Usage note at **normalcy. 2.** *Symbol* N *Chemistry.* An obsolescent measure of the concentration of a solution equal to the number of gram equivalents of the solute per liter of the solution.

nor·mal·ize (nôr′mə-līz′) *tr.v.* **-ized, -izing, -izes. 1.** To make normal; cause to conform to a standard or norm. **2.** *Metallurgy.* To remove strains and reduce coarse crystalline structures in (steel) by applying heat. **3.** *Mathematics.* To introduce a numerical factor into (an equation) in order to make the area under the graph of the function equal to one, as in quantum mechanics and probability calculations. **—nor·mal·i·za·tion** *n.* **—nor·mal·iz·er** *n.*

normal pentane *n.* A pentane *(see)*.

normal school *n.* A school that trains teachers, chiefly for the elementary grades. [Translation of French *école normale*, originally the name of a school founded as a model for other teacher-training colleges, from Late Latin *normālis*, NORMAL.]

Nor·man (nôr′mən) *n. Abbr.* **Nor.** **1.** A member of a Scandinavian people who conquered Normandy in the 10th century. **2.** A member of the Norman French people of Normandy who conquered England in 1066. **3.** A native or inhabitant of Normandy. **4.** A language, **Norman French** *(see).*
~*adj.* **1.** Of or pertaining to Normandy, the Normans, their culture, or their language. **2.** Designating a variety of Romanesque architecture that was introduced from Normandy into England before the Norman Conquest and flourished until about 1200. [Middle English from Old French *Normant,* from Old Norse *Northmathr* (stem *Northmann-*), Northman, Scandinavian.]

Norman Conquest *n.* The conquest of England by the Normans under William the Conqueror, beginning in 1066 with the Battle of Hastings.

Nor·man·dy (nôr′mən-dē). *French* **Nor·man·die** (nôr-mäN-dē′). Region and former province of northern France, on the English Channel. Industries include agriculture, cheesemaking (Camembert, Brie), iron ore (at Caen), textiles, shipbuilding, and oil refining. Its major ports are Cherbourg and Le Havre. Viking raids on Normandy began in the 9th century, and it was finally ceded to the Norsemen or Normans (911). After the Norman conquest, Normandy passed to England (1106), but was finally recognized to be French territory in 1450. The historic capital of the region is Rouen, where Joan of Arc was burned at the stake in 1431.

Norman French *n. Abbr.* **N.F.** **1.** The dialect of Old French used in medieval Normandy and England. **2.** The form of this dialect used in English court and legal circles from the Norman conquest until the 15th century, still surviving in some legal formulas. Also called "Anglo-French," "Anglo-Norman."

nor·ma·tive (nôr′mə-tĭv) *adj.* **1.** Based upon or prescribing a norm, especially one regarded as a standard of usage in speech and writing: *normative grammar.* **2.** Pertaining to, implying, or establishing a norm or standard: *normative laws.* [French *normatif,* from *norme,* NORM.] **—nor·ma·tive·ly** *adv.* **—nor·ma·tive·ness** *n.*

nor·mo·blast (nôr′mō-blăst′) *n.* An immature red blood cell, characterized by abundant hemoglobin and a small nucleus.

nor·mo·ten·sive (nôr′mō-tĕn′sĭv) *adj.* Having blood pressure that is within the normal range.

Norn (nôrn) *n., pl.* **Nornir** (nôr′nîr′) or **Norns.** *Norse Mythology.* Any of the Fates: Skuld (the Future), Verdandi (the Present), and Urd (the Past). [Old Norse.]

Nor·ris (nôr′ĭs, nŏr′-), **Benjamin Franklin,** known as "Frank" (1870–1902). U.S. author. He worked for a number of magazines and newspapers before writing *McTeague* (1899), the first of his naturalistic novels about greed and violence in the American world of commerce. His other books include *The Octopus* (1901) and *The Pit* (1903).

Norse (nôrs) *adj. Abbr.* **N.** **1.** Of or pertaining to ancient Scandinavia, its people, or their language. **2. a.** Of or pertaining to West Scandinavia (Norway, Iceland, and the Faeroe Islands) or the languages of its inhabitants. **b.** Of or pertaining to Norway, its people, or their language.
~*n., pl.* **Norse.** *Abbr.* **N.** **1.** *Used with a plural verb.* **a.** The people of Scandinavia; the Scandinavians. **b.** The people of West Scandinavia; especially, the Norwegians. **c.** The ancient Norwegians. **2.** The Scandinavian or North Germanic branch of Germanic languages; especially, Norwegian. **3.** Any of the West Scandinavian languages or dialects. [Dutch *noor(d)sch,* from *noord,* north, from Middle Dutch *nort.*]

Norse·man (nôrs′mən) *n., pl.* **-men** (-mĭn). Any of the ancient Scandinavians.

north (nôrth) *n. Abbr.* **n, N, n., N., No., Nor.** **1. a.** The direction along a meridian to the left of an observer facing in the direction of the earth's rotation; the direction to the left as one faces the rising sun. **b.** The cardinal point on the mariner's compass, located at 0°. **2.** Any area or region lying in this direction. **3.** *Often* **North. a.** The one of four positions at 90° intervals that lies in the north, points south, and stands at right angles to east and west. **b.** In games such as bridge or mah-jong, a player who occupies or is said to occupy this position. **4.** *Poetic.* The north wind. **—the North. 1.** The northern or arctic parts of the earth. **2.** The states north of Maryland, the Ohio River, and Missouri, including those that fought for the Union against the Confederacy (the South) in the Civil War.
~*adj.* **1.** To, toward, of, facing, or in the north. **2.** Coming from the north: *the north wind.* **3. North.** Officially or conventionally designating the northern part of a country, continent, or other geographical area: *North Korea.*
~*adv.* In, from, or toward the north. [Middle English *north,* Old English *north.*]

North America. *Abbr.* **N.A.** A continent of the northern Western Hemisphere extending north from the Colombia-Panama border through Central America, the United States, Canada, and the Arctic Archipelago to the northern tip of Greenland. **—North American** *adj. & n.* See maps, next page and **Central American States.**

North·amp·ton (nôr-thămp′tən, nôrth-hămp′-). County town of Northamptonshire, central England, on the Nene River. It has long been one of the country's shoemaking centers, and today there is also considerable manufacture of machinery.

North·amp·ton·shire (nôr-thămp′tən-shîr′, -shər, nôrth-hămp′-). County in central England. Most of it consists of gently rolling pasture and woods. Iron ore deposits, now largely worked out, led to the building of iron and steel works at Corby. The county town is Northampton.

North Atlantic Current. An ocean current or drift formed southeast of Newfoundland by the junction of the Gulf Stream and the Labrador Current and flowing generally northeast across the Atlantic. Also called "North Atlantic Drift."

North Atlantic Treaty Organization *n. Abbr.* **NATO.** An alliance for military and naval defense established on April 4, 1949, by countries located on or near the Atlantic Ocean. The original membership was Belgium, Canada, Denmark, France (withdrew from some military aspects in 1966 and now has an independent nuclear deterrent), Iceland, Italy, Luxembourg, the Netherlands, Norway, Portugal, the United Kingdom, and the United States. Greece and Turkey joined in 1952 and West Germany in 1955. The headquarters of the organization is in Brussels.

north·bound (nôrth′bound′) *adj.* Heading toward or leading toward the north.

north by east *n. Abbr.* **NbE** The direction, or point on a compass, halfway between due north and north-northeast. It is 11° 15′ east of due north. **—north by east** *adv. & adj.*

north by west *n. Abbr.* **NbW** The direction, or point on a compass, halfway between due north and north-northwest. It is 11° 15′ west of due north. **—north by west** *adv. & adj.*

North Ca·na·di·an (kə-nā′dē-ən). River, 1,223 kilometers (760 miles) long, rising in northeastern New Mexico and flowing generally east southeast to join the Canadian River in eastern Oklahoma.

North Car·o·li·na (kăr′ə-lī′nə). *Abbr.* **N.C.** State on the Atlantic coast of the eastern United States. Since colonial times it has been a tobacco-producing state, and it still leads the nation in the production of tobacco, as well as textiles and furniture. North Carolina joined the Union in 1789 as one of the original 13 states. The capital is Raleigh.

North Caucasia. See Ciscaucasia.

north celestial pole *n. Astronomy.* The North Pole *(see).*

North·cliffe (nôrth′klĭf′), **Alfred Charles William Harmsworth, 1st Viscount** (1865–1922). Irish-born British newspaper proprietor. A pioneer of popular journalism, he founded the *Daily Mail* (1896), the first daily paper to achieve a circulation of one million, and the *Daily Mirror* (1903).

North Country *n.* The north of England. Preceded by *the.* **—North·coun·try·man** (nôrth′kŭn′trē-mən) *n.*

North Da·ko·ta (də-kō′tə). *Abbr.* **N. Dak.** State in the north-central United States, on the border with Canada. One of the most rural states in the Union, its only industries of importance are connected with food processing. The leading products are wheat, cattle, oil, and natural gas. The capital is Bismarck.

North Downs. See Downs, North and South.

north·east (nôrth-ēst′; *nautical* nôr-ēst′) *n. Abbr.* **NE 1.** The direction, or point on a compass, halfway between north and east. It is 45° east of due north. **2.** Any area or region lying in this direction. **—the Northeast.** The area including New England, New York, and sometimes Pennsylvania and New Jersey.
~*adj.* **1.** Situated toward, facing, or in the northeast. **2.** Coming from the northeast: *a northeast wind.*
~*adv.* In, from, or toward the northeast. **—north·east·ern** *adj.* **—north·east·ern·er** *n.*

northeast by east *n. Abbr.* **NEbE** The direction, or point on a compass, halfway between northeast and east-northeast. It is 56° 15′ east of due north. **—northeast by east** *adv. & adj.*

northeast by north *n. Abbr.* **NEbN** The direction, or point on a compass, halfway between northeast and north-northeast. It is 33° 45′ east of due north. **—northeast by north** *adv. & adj.*

north·east·er (nôrth-ē′stər; *nautical* nôr-ē′stər) *n.* Also **nor'east·er** (nôr-ē′stər). A storm or gale from the northeast.

north·east·er·ly (nôrth-ē′stər-lē; *nautical* nôr-ē′stər-lē) *adj.* **1.** Situated in or toward the northeast. **2.** From the northeast.
~*n., pl.* **northeasterlies.** A storm or wind from the northeast. **—north·east·er·ly** *adv.*

Northeast Passage. Sea route between the Atlantic and Pacific oceans along the northern coast of Europe and Asia. It was first traversed (1878–79) by the Swedish explorer Nils Nordenskjöld (1832–1901). Since the establishment of the Northern Sea Route (a shipping lane) by the U.S.S.R. in the 1930's, the passage has largely been controlled by a fleet of Soviet icebreakers that keep the passage open from June to October.

north·east·ward (nôrth-ēst′wərd; *nautical* nôr-ēst′wərd) *adj.* Situated toward or facing the northeast.
~*n.* **1.** A direction or point toward the northeast. **2.** A region or part situated in or toward the northeast.
~*adv.* Also **northeastwards.** Toward the northeast. **—north·east·ward·ly** *adj. & adv.*

north·er (nôr′thər) *n.* A sudden, cold gale from the north, especially around the Gulf of Mexico. The norther may reach a speed of 60 miles per hour.

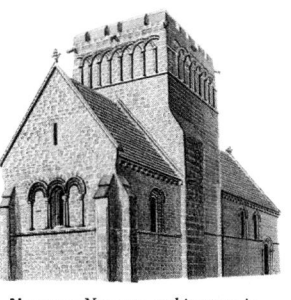

Norman *Norman architecture is characterized by round-arched doors and windows and heavy buttresses. Roofs are usually steeply pitched; towers are squat and square.*

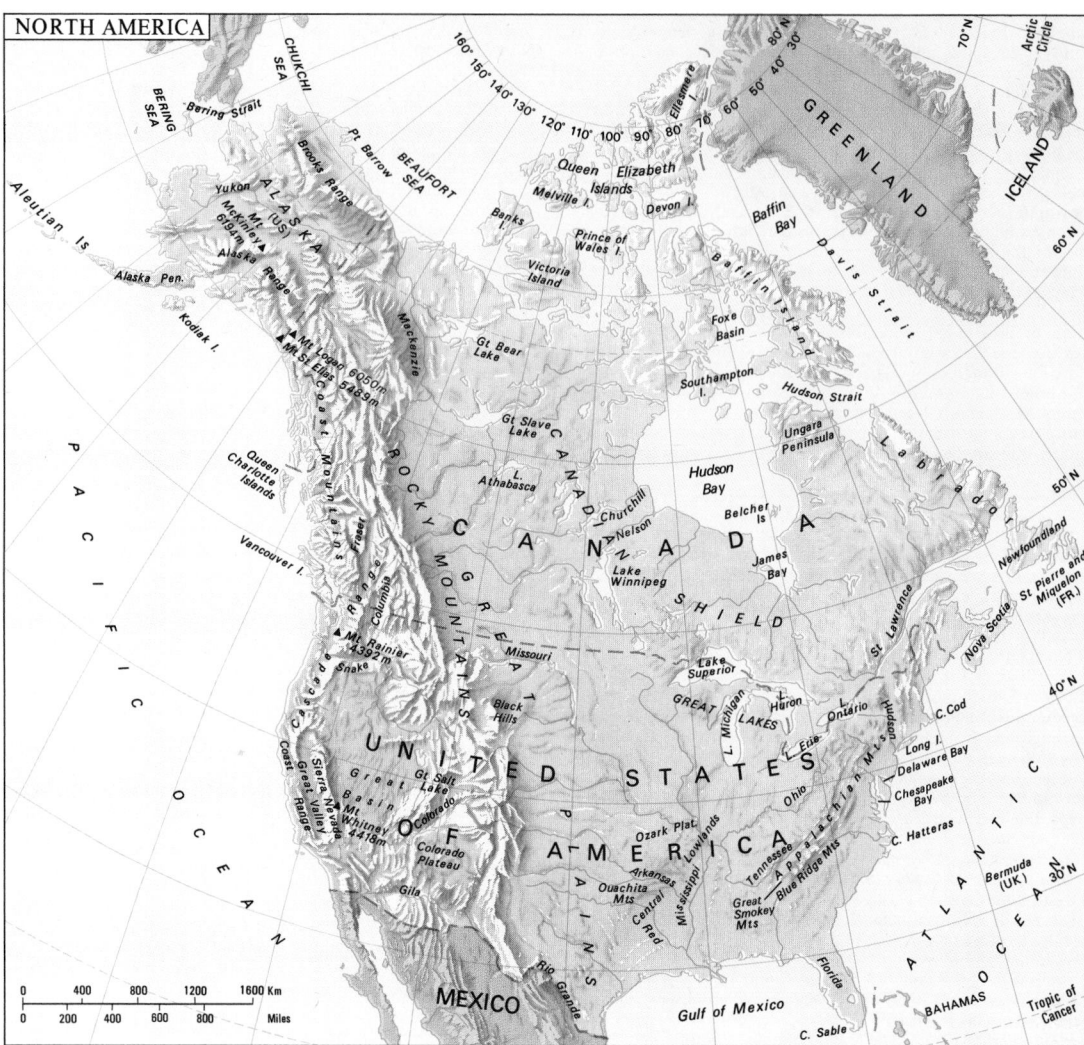

NORTH AMERICA

north·er·ly (nôr´thər-lē) adj. **1.** Situated in or toward the north. **2.** From the north: a northerly wind. —n., pl. **northerlies.** A storm or wind from the north. —**north·er·ly** adv.

north·ern (nôr´thərn) adj. Abbr. **n, n., N, N. 1.** Situated toward, in, or facing the north. **2.** Coming from the north: a northern wind. **3.** Growing in the north. **4.** Often **Northern.** Of, pertaining to, or characteristic of northern regions or the North. **5.** Astronomy. North of the celestial equator. [Middle English northerne, Old English northerne.]

Northern Cross n. A cross formed by six stars in the constellation **Cygnus** (see).

Northern Crown n. A constellation, **Corona Borealis** (see).

Northern Dvina. See **Dvina, Northern.**

north·ern·er (nôr´thər-nər) n. **1.** A native or inhabitant of the north. **2.** Often **Northerner.** A native or inhabitant of the northeastern United States.

Northern Hemisphere n. The half of the earth lying north of the equator.

Northern Ire·land (īr´lənd). Province of the United Kingdom consisting of 6 of the counties in the ancient Irish province of Ulster, by which name it is often inaccurately known. Mostly low-lying, it rises to the Sperrin Mts. in the northwest, and the Mourne Mts. in the southeast. Lough Neagh, Ireland's largest lake, is in the center of the province. Its traditional industries, shipbuilding and linen weaving, have been in decline since World War II. Attempts by successive British governments to revive its economy have been hampered by the state of near civil war that has existed since 1969 between Protestant and Roman Catholic extremists. Its unemployment rate is the highest in the United Kingdom. Until 1972, when all powers were transferred to Westminster, the province had its own semiautonomous parliament, which sat at Stormont near Belfast, the capital and chief port.

northern lights pl.n. The **aurora borealis** (see).

Northern Marianas. See **Marianas.**

north·ern·most (nôr´thərn-mōst´) adj. Farthest north.

Northern Spy n. A large, yellowish-red, late-ripening apple.

Northern Territory. Territory in north-central Australia, with a coastline along the Timor Sea, the Arafura Sea, and the Gulf of Carpentaria. The chief economic activity is stockbreeding, although

exploitation of the region's mineral resources—gold, uranium, bauxite, iron, lead, and zinc—is increasing. The territory was formerly part of New South Wales (1825–63) and South Australia (1863–1911), but since 1911 it has been ruled directly by the Commonwealth of Australia. The capital and largest town is Darwin.

North Frisians. See **Frisian Islands.**

North Germanic n. A branch of the Germanic group of languages, which includes Danish, Faroese, Icelandic, Norwegian, and Swedish. See **Germanic.** —**North Germanic** adj.

North Hol·land (hŏl´ənd). Province of the Netherlands, occupying the peninsula between the North Sea and the Isselmeer. It also includes a number of the West Frisian Islands. The capital is Haarlem, the largest city, Amsterdam. A region of low-lying marshland, it is now largely a manufacturing area.

north·ing (nôr´thĭng, -thĭng) n. **1.** In navigation: **a.** The difference in latitude between two positions as a result of a movement to the north. **b.** Progress toward the north. **2.** Astronomy. A north declination.

North Island. The northern of the two main islands that make up New Zealand. It is the smaller of the two, but the more heavily populated. The main cities are Wellington, the national capital, and Auckland. Most of New Zealand's dairy industry is here.

north·land (nôrth´lănd´, -lənd) n. **1.** Often **Northland.** A region in the north, such as the northern part of the earth or of a country. **2. Northland.** Norway and Sweden. —**north·land·er** n.

North·man (nôrth´mən), n., pl. **-men** (-mĭn). A Norseman.

north-north·east (nôrth´nôrth-ēst´; nautical nôr´nôr-ēst´) n. Abbr. **NNE** The direction, or point on a compass, halfway between due north and northeast. It is 22° 30´ east of due north. —adj. Situated toward, facing, or in this direction. —adv. In, from, or toward this direction.

north-north·west (nôrth´nôrth-wĕst´; nautical nôr´nôr-wĕst´) n. Abbr. **NNW** The direction, or point on a compass, halfway between due north and northwest. It is 22° 30´ west of due north. —adj. Situated toward, facing, or in this direction. —adv. In, from, or toward this direction.

North Pole n. **1.** The northern end of the earth's axis of rotation. **2.** The celestial zenith of this terrestrial point, slightly more than 1 degree from Polaris, the North Star. Also called "north celestial pole." **3. north pole.** The north-seeking **magnetic pole** *(see)* of a magnet.

North Rhine-West·pha·lia (rīn′wĕst-fāl′yə, -fā′lē-ə). State in western West Germany, in the lower Rhine basin. It is a densely populated and extensively industrialized state, the region known as the Ruhr district being the most highly concentrated industrial complex in western Europe. The state was created in 1946 by merging Westphalia, Lippe, and the northern part of the Rhine province. The capital is Düsseldorf.

North Sea. Arm of the Atlantic Ocean, between Great Britain and northwest Europe, connected to the English Channel by the Strait of Dover. Long the source of valuable fish, it gained a new economic importance in the late 1960's when large deposits of oil and natural gas were discovered under its sea bed.

North Star *n.* A star, **Polaris** *(see)*.

North·um·ber·land (nôr-thŭm′bər-lənd). County in northeastern England, bordering on Scotland and the North Sea. It is an almost entirely rural county, having lost Newcastle (formerly the county town) and Tynemouth to the new metropolitan county of Tyne and Wear in 1974. The county includes the Farne Islands, with their large bird sanctuary. Sheep farming is the main agricultural activity. The county is especially rich in remains of medieval military architecture, and the Roman wall is well preserved from Heddon-on-the-Wall to the Cumbria border.

Northumberland Strait. Arm of the Gulf of St. Lawrence, *c.* 320 kilometers (200 miles) long and from 15 to 49 kilometers (9–30 miles) wide. It separates Prince Edward Island from New Brunswick and Nova Scotia.

North·um·bri·a (nôr-thŭm′brē-ə). Kingdom of Anglo-Saxon England, extending from eastern Scotland to the East Riding of Yorkshire. It was settled by Angles early in the 6th century and originally consisted of two kingdoms, Bernicia and Deira, which were separated by the Tees River. The two kingdoms were united by Ethelfrith of Bernicia early in the 7th century, and shortly thereafter Northumbria became the most powerful kingdom in the country. During the late 7th century the power of Northumbria waned as that of Mercia grew.

North·um·bri·an (nôr-thŭm′brē-ən) *adj.* **1.** Of or pertaining to Northumbria or its dialect. **2.** Of or pertaining to Northumberland. —*n.* **1.** A native of Northumbria or Northumberland. **2. a.** The Old English dialect of Northumbria. **b.** The Modern English dialect of Northumberland.

north·ward (nôrth′wərd; *nautical* nôr′thərd) *adj.* Situated toward, facing, or in the north. —*n.* **1.** A direction or point toward the north. **2.** A region situated in or toward the north. —*adv.* Also **northwards.** Toward the north. —**north·ward·ly** *adj.* & *adv.*

north·west (nôrth-wĕst′; *nautical* nôr-wĕst′) *n. Abbr.* **NW 1.** The direction, or point on a compass, halfway between north and west. It is 45° west of due north. **2.** Any area or region lying in this direction. —**the Northwest. 1.** Formerly, the area west of the Mississippi and generally north of the Missouri. **2.** The present states of Washington, Oregon, and Idaho. —*adj.* **1.** To, toward, of, facing, or in the northwest. **2.** Coming from the northwest: *a northwest wind.* —*adv.* In, from, or toward the northwest. —**north·west·ern** *adj.* —**north·west·ern·er** *n.*

northwest by north *n. Abbr.* **NWbN** The direction, or point on a compass, halfway between northwest and north-northwest. It is 33° 45′ west of due north. —**northwest by north** *adv.* & *adj.*

northwest by west *n. Abbr.* **NWbW** The direction, or point on a compass, halfway between northwest and west-northwest. It is 56° 15′ west of due north. —**northwest by west** *adv.* & *adj.*

north·west·er (nôrth-wĕs′tər; *nautical* nôr-wĕs′tər) *n.* Also **nor'west·er** (nôr-wĕs′tər). A storm or gale from the northwest.

north·west·er·ly (nôrth-wĕs′tər-lē; *nautical* nôr-wĕs′tər-lē) *adj.* **1.** Toward or in the northwest. **2.** From the northwest. —*n., pl.* **northwesterlies.** A storm or wind from the northwest. —**north·west·er·ly** *adv.*

North-West Frontier Province. Province of northwest Pakistan, bordering on Afghanistan to the north and west. It is a largely mountainous area, with agriculture practiced in the fertile valleys. The chief product is wheat. Historically of great importance because of its proximity to the Khyber Pass, the region came under British control in 1849; it remained British until 1947 when the people of the province voted to become part of newly independent Pakistan. The capital is Peshawar.

Northwest Passage. Northern sea route joining the Atlantic and Pacific oceans, through the Canadian Arctic Archipelago and the waters north of Alaska. The first explorations were undertaken by Sir Martin Frobisher (1576–78); proof of the existence of the passage was obtained by the early 19th century, but the first expedition actually to navigate the whole of the route was led by Roald Amundsen (1903–06). The first commercial ship to cross the passage was a U.S. oil tanker, the S.S. *Manhattan* (1969).

Northwest Semitic *n.* A subgroup of the Semitic family of languages, consisting of Canaanite and Aramaic.

Northwest Territories. *Abbr.* **N.W.T.** Territory in northwestern Canada, lying between the Yukon to the west and Hudson Bay to the east and extending north from the borders of the Prairie Provinces to include the Arctic Archipelago. In all, the Territories occupy one third of Canada's area. Only the extreme south is outside the permafrost area, and the region is sparsely populated, mostly by Indians, Eskimos, and métis. Fur trading and fishing are the traditional economic activities of the region, but mining is now by far the most important source of wealth. The capital is Yellowknife.

Northwest Territory. A region extending from the Ohio and Mississippi rivers to the Great Lakes. It was awarded to the United States in 1783 by the Treaty of Paris. Organized by Congress in 1787, it included the present states of Illinois, Indiana, Michigan, Ohio, Wisconsin, and part of Minnesota.

north·west·ward (nôrth-wĕst′wərd; *nautical* nôr-wĕst′wərd) *adj.* Situated toward, facing, or in the northwest. —*n.* **1.** A direction or point toward the northwest. **2.** A region or part situated in or toward the northwest. —*adv.* Also **northwestwards.** Toward the northwest. —**north·west·ward·ly** *adj.* & *adv.*

North York·shire (yôrk′shîr′, -shər). County in northeastern England, created in 1974 from the rural parts of the North Riding of the former county of Yorkshire. It also includes some parts of the former East and West ridings. The major towns in the county are York, Harrogate, and Scarborough.

Norw. Norway; Norwegian.

Nor·way (nôr′wā′). *Abbr.* **Nor., Norw.** *Norwegian* **Nor·ge** (nôr′gə). Kingdom of northern Europe, occupying the western coastland of the Scandinavian peninsula. Most of the country consists of a mountainous plateau unsuited to agriculture; only *c.* 3 percent of the land is cultivated. Fishing, timber, and shipbuilding have traditionally been the mainstays of the economy. Now an industrial country, Norway relies on shipping and on exports of natural gas and petroleum (discovered in the North Sea in the 1960's), aluminum, iron and steel, chemicals, wood products, and fish. At various times united with Sweden and Denmark after the 14th century, Norway finally gained its independence in 1905. Area, 324,219 square kilometers (125,182 square miles). Population, 4,100,000. Capital, Oslo.

Norway maple *n.* A tall European maple, *Acer platanoides,* widely used as a shade tree in the United States.

Norway pout *n.* A small greenish fish, *Trisopterus esmarkii,* found

in the northeastern Atlantic. It is important in the diet of several food fish, such as cod and haddock. Also called "pout."

Norway rat *n.* The brown rat *(see).*

Norway spruce *n.* A tall evergreen tree, *Picea abies,* of northern regions, growing up to 150 feet in height and having long, dark green needles. It is commonly used as a Christmas tree.

Nor·we·gian (nôr-wē'jən) *n. Abbr.* **Nor., Norw. 1.** A native or inhabitant of Norway. **2.** The North Germanic language of the Norwegians. See **Bokmål, Nynorsk. —Nor·we·gian** *adj.*

Norwegian elkhound *n.* An elkhound *(see).*

Norwegian Sea. Part of the Atlantic Ocean, northwest of Norway, between the Greenland Sea and the North Sea. The warm Norway Current gives the sea generally ice-free conditions.

nor'west·er (nôr-wĕs'tər) *n.* **1.** Variant of **northwester. 2.** A drink of strong spirits. **3.** A waterproof hat, a **sou'wester** *(see).*

Nor·wich¹ (nôr'ĭj, -ĭch). County town of Norfolk, east-central England, on the Wensum River just above its confluence with the Yare. An important provincial center since the rise of the wool trade in the high Middle Ages, Norwich is now a market city.

Nor·wich² (nôr'wĭch). City of southeastern Connecticut, on the Thames River. Settled in 1659, it was one of the earliest centers of colonial industry.

nos., Nos. numbers.

nose (nōz) *n.* **1.** In humans and other primates, the part of the face bearing the nostrils and containing the organ of smell and the beginning of the respiratory tract. **2.** In many other animals, a similar feature or organ in the face, muzzle, snout, or front end. **3. a.** The sense of smell: *a dog with a good nose.* **b.** The ability to detect or discover, as if by smell: *a nose for a good story.* **4.** An aroma or bouquet, as of wine or tea. **5.** *Informal.* The nose as a symbol of prying: *Keep your nose out of my business.* **6.** Anything that resembles a nose because of shape or position, such as the forward part of an aircraft. **—by a nose.** In horse racing, by the length of a horse's nose, considered as a narrow margin of victory. **—follow one's nose. 1.** To go straight ahead. **2.** To be guided by instinct. **—keep one's nose clean.** *Informal.* To keep out of trouble. **—lead by the nose.** To control (someone) completely, often humiliatingly, without his perceiving it. **—look down one's nose at.** *Informal.* To treat haughtily. **—on the nose.** *Slang.* **1.** Designating a bet on a horse to win. **2.** Exactly; precisely. **—pay through the nose.** *Informal.* To pay an exorbitant price. **—put someone's nose out of joint.** To displease, as by thwarting. **—turn up one's nose at.** To treat with contempt.

~*v.* **nosed, nosing, noses.** *—tr.* **1.** To find out by or as if by smell.

nose

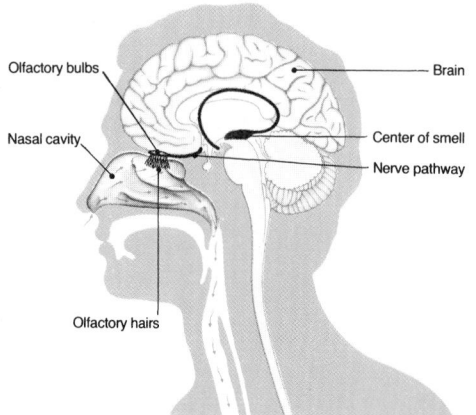

THE TWO FUNCTIONS OF THE NOSE
Protecting the lungs and picking up scents

The nose has a dual function. It is both the organ of smell and one of the entrances to the respiratory tract. Its purpose is to warm, moisten, and filter air passing through it in order to protect the lungs. Bones and cartilage form it and the septum, which divides it into two nostrils. In the skull behind the nose are a number of nasal cavities, or sinuses, which are linked and open into the nasal cavity. Like the nasal passages themselves, they are lined with a mucous membrane in which cells secrete mucus—a lubricating and moistening fluid.

Olfactory bulbs — — Brain

Nasal cavity — — Center of smell

— Nerve pathway

Olfactory hairs —

DETECTING SMELL *Sense of smell begins in a patch of tissue at the top of the nasal passage. Thousands of brush-shaped receptors are located there on olfactory bulbs. Nerve fibers lead directly from the olfactory bulbs, carrying the impulses about scent along a pathway to the center in the brain where they are interpreted as different odors.*

2. To touch or examine with the nose; nuzzle. **3.** To steer (a vehicle or one's way) with care to avoid a collision. *—intr.* **1.** To smell or sniff. **2.** *Informal.* To pry out of curiosity or in a meddlesome way. Followed by *around, about,* or *into.* **3.** To move forward slowly and carefully. **—nose out.** To defeat by a very narrow margin. [Middle English *nose,* Old English *nosu.*]

nose·bag (nōz'băg') *n.* A feedbag *(see).*

nose·band (nōz'bănd') *n.* The part of a bridle or halter that passes over the animal's nose. Also called "nosepiece."

nose·bleed (nōz'blēd') *n.* A nasal hemorrhage; bleeding from the nose. Also called "epistaxis."

nose cone *n.* The front, usually separable, section of a rocket or guided missile, shaped to offer minimum aerodynamic resistance and often bearing a heat shield.

nose dive *n.* **1.** A sudden plunge of an aircraft with its nose toward the earth. **2.** Any sudden, swift, downward plunge or drop.

nose-dive (nōz'dīv') *intr.v.* **-dived** or **-dove** (-dōv'), **-diving, -dives.** To perform a nose dive.

nose·gay (nōz'gā') *n.* A small bunch of flowers. [Middle English : NOSE (fragrance) + *gay,* toy, ornament, from GAY (adjective).]

nose·piece (nōz'pēs') *n.* **1.** A piece of armor forming part of a helmet and serving as a guard for the nose. **2.** The bridge of a pair of eyeglasses. **3.** Part of a bridle, a **noseband** *(see).* **4.** The part of a microscope, often rotatable, to which one or more objective lenses are attached.

nose·wheel (nōz'hwēl', -wēl') *n.* The landing wheel fitted below the nose of an aircraft.

nosh (nŏsh) *n. Informal.* A snack; tidbit.
~*intr.v.* **noshed, noshing, noshes.** *Informal.* To eat a snack. [Yiddish, from *nosherai,* tidbits, from Old High German *(h)nascōn,* to gnaw, nibble.]

no-show (nō'shō') *n. Slang.* A person who reserves a place, as on an aircraft, but neither claims it nor cancels the reservation.

nos·ing (nō'zĭng) *n.* **1.** The edge of a stair tread that projects over the riser. **2.** A shield covering this edge. **3.** A projecting edge of a molding.

noso– *prefix.* Indicates disease; for example, **nosology.** [Greek, from *nosos†,* a disease.]

no·so·co·mi·al (nō'sə-kō'mē-əl, nŏs'ə-) *adj.* Of or having to do with a hospital: *nosocomial infection.* [Greek *nosokomeion,* hospital, from *nosos,* disease + *komeion,* to take care of.]

no·sog·ra·phy (nō-sŏg'rə-fē) *n.* The written systematization and description of diseases. [New Latin *nosographia* : NOSO- + -GRAPHY.] **—no·sog·ra·pher** *n.* **—no·so·graph·ic** (nō'sə-grăf'ĭk, nŏs'ə-), **no·so·graph·i·cal** *adj.*

no·sol·o·gy (nō-sŏl'ə-jē) *n.* The branch of medicine that deals with the naming and classification of diseases. [New Latin *nosologia* : NOSO- + -LOGY.] **—no·so·log·i·cal** (nō'sə-lŏj'ĭ-kəl, nŏs'ə-) *adj.* **—no·so·log·i·cal·ly** *adv.* **—no·sol·o·gist** *n.*

nos·tal·gia (nŏ-stăl'jə, nə-) *n.* **1.** A wistful or sentimental longing for things, persons, or situations that are past and irrevocable. **2.** Homesickness. [New Latin (translation of German *Heimweh,* homesickness) : Greek *nostos,* a return + -ALGIA.] **—nos·tal·gic** *adj.* **—nos·tal·gi·cal·ly** *adv.*

nos·toc (nŏs'tŏk') *n.* Any freshwater blue-green alga of the genus *Nostoc,* forming colonies of filaments with a gelatinous covering. [New Latin; coined by Paracelsus as a name for algae that he believed were derived from starlight.]

Nos·tra·da·mus (nŏs'trə-dā'məs, -dä'-, nŏs'-), born Michel de Nostre-Dame (1503–66). French astrologer and physician. He was court physician to Charles IX but is best known for his book of prophecies, *Centuries* (1555), written in quatrains.

nos·tril (nŏs'trəl) *n.* Either of the external openings of the nose. [Middle English *nostrill,* Old English *nosthyrl* : *nosu,* NOSE + *thyrl, thyrel,* hole.]

nos·trum (nŏs'trəm) *n., pl.* **-trums. 1.** A patent medicine or one made of secret ingredients; especially, a quack remedy. **2.** A pet scheme for the solution of some problem. [New Latin *nostrum,* "our own" (that is, invented and made by the seller), from Latin, neuter of *noster,* ours.]

nos·y, nos·ey (nō'zē) *adj.* **-ier, -iest.** *Informal.* Prying; inquisitive. —See Usage note at **curious.** [From NOSE.] **—nos·i·ly** *adv.* **—nos·i·ness** *n.*

nosy parker *n. Informal.* A person who pries into other people's affairs. [Arbitrary use of surname *Parker.*]

not (nŏt) *adv.* In no way; to no degree. Used to express negation, denial, refusal, disbelief, or prohibition: *Definitely not. I will not go. You may not have any.* In informal speech and writing, *not* is often contracted and suffixed to auxiliary verbs, for example, *aren't, don't.* **—not at all.** You do not need to thank me. Used as a polite reply when one has been thanked. **—not that.** Although it is not to be supposed that: *She denies everything—not that I believe her.* [Middle English *not,* reduced form of *nought,* nothing, not, Old English *nōwiht, nāwiht* : *nō, nā,* no + *wiht,* a man, thing.]

not–. Variant of **noto–.**

no·ta be·ne (nō'tə bĕ'nē, bĕn'ē).) *Abbr.* **n.b., N.B.** *Latin.* Note well.

no·ta·bil·i·ty (nō'tə-bĭl'ə-tē) *n., pl.* **-ties. 1.** The state or quality of being notable. **2.** A notable or prominent person.

no·ta·ble (nō'tə-bəl; *also* nŏt'ə-bəl *for sense 3)* *adj.* **1.** Worthy of notice; remarkable: *a notable beauty.* **2.** Prominent; distinguished. **3.** *Archaic.* Diligent and capable, especially in household duties.
~*n.* **1.** A person of note or distinction. **2.** *Often* **Notable.** Any of a council of prominent persons, before the French Revolution, called

into assembly by the king at times of emergency. [Middle English, from Old French, from Latin *notābilis,* from *notāre,* to note, from *nota,* a NOTE.] **—no·ta·ble·ness** *n.* **—no·ta·bly** *adv.*

no·tar·i·al (nō-târ′ē-əl) *adj.* **1.** Of or pertaining to a notary public. **2.** Executed or drawn up by a notary public. **—no·tar·i·al·ly** *adv.*

no·ta·rize (nō′tə-rīz′) *tr.v.* **-rized, -rizing, -rizes.** To authenticate or attest as a notary public. [From NOTARY.] **—no·ta·ri·za·tion** *n.*

no·ta·ry (nō′tə-rē) *n., pl.* **-ries. 1.** A notary public. **2.** *Obsolete.* A clerk, especially one licensed to draft legal documents. [Middle English *notarie,* "clerk," from Latin *notārius,* "stenographer," from *notārius,* cipher, shorthand character, from *nota,* mark, NOTE.]

notary public *n., pl.* **notaries public.** *Abbr.* **N.P.** A public officer or other person legally empowered to witness and certify documents and to take affidavits and depositions.

no·tate (nō′tāt′) *tr.v.* **-tated, -tating, -tates.** To represent (for example, music) in notation. [Back-formation from NOTATION.]

no·ta·tion (nō-tā′shən) *n.* **1.** A system of figures or symbols used in specialized fields to represent numbers, quantities, or other facts or values: *musical notation.* **2.** The act or process of using such a system. **3.** A jotting or annotation; a note: *a notation in the margin.* [Latin *notātiō* (stem *notātiōn-*), from *notāre,* to note, from *nota,* a NOTE.] **—no·ta·tion·al** *adj.*

notch (nŏch) *n.* **1. a.** A V-shaped cut or indentation. **b.** A cut or slit used for keeping count. **2.** A narrow pass between mountains. **3.** *Informal.* A level or degree: *a notch better than the competition.* ~*tr.v.* **notched, notching, notches. 1.** To cut a notch or notches in. **2.** To record by or as if by making notches: *notched the score on a stick.* **3.** *Informal.* To score. Often used with *up*: *She notched up three wins in succession.* [Norman French *noche*†.]

note (nōt) *n. Abbr.* **n. 1.** *Often* **notes.** A brief record of something, written down to aid the memory. **2.** A brief written communication. **3.** A formal written diplomatic or official communication. **4.** A commentary to or explanation of a passage in a text, printed in the margin, at the foot of the page, or at the end of the text. **5. a.** A piece of paper currency. **b.** A certificate issued by a government or a bank and sometimes negotiable as money. **c.** A **promissory note** *(see).* **6.** *Music.* **a.** A musical tone of definite pitch. **b.** The symbol of such a tone in musical notation, indicating the pitch by its position on the staff and the duration by its shape. **c.** A key of a piano or similar instrument. **7. a.** The musical call of a bird. **b.** Any expressive vocal sound, such as the cry or call of an animal. **8.** A tone, sign, or suggestion that reveals or characterizes a quality, mood, or atmosphere; a mark: *He ended his speech on a note of optimism.* **9.** Importance or consequence: *Nothing of note happened.* **10.** Notice or observation: *Take note of the speed limit.* **11.** *Poetic.* A song, melody, or tune. **—compare notes.** To exchange ideas, views, or opinions.
~*tr.v.* **noted, noting, notes. 1.** To observe carefully; notice; perceive. **2.** To write down; make a note of. **3.** To show; indicate. **4.** To make particular mention of; remark. [Middle English *note,* from Old French, from Latin *nota,* mark, sign, cipher, shorthand character.] **—not·er** *n.*

note·book (nōt′bo͝ok′) *n.* A small book for writing notes in.

note·case (nōt′kās′) *n. Chiefly British.* A slim flat wallet designed to hold paper money.

not·ed (nō′tĭd) *adj.* Distinguished by reputation; notable; eminent: *a noted author.* **—not·ed·ly** *adv.* **—not·ed·ness** *n.*

note·less (nōt′lĭs) *adj.* Unnoticed; indistinguished.

note of hand *n.* A **promissory note** *(see).*

note·pa·per (nōt′pā′pər) *n.* Writing paper used for brief letters.

note·wor·thy (nōt′wûr′*th*ē) *adj.* Deserving recognition; worthy of notice; remarkable: *a noteworthy young talent.* **—note·wor·thi·ly** *adv.* **—note·wor·thi·ness** *n.*

NOT gate (nŏt) *n. Computer Science.* A logic gate that provides an output signal if the input signal is low and vice versa. Also called "inverter," "negator," "NOT circuit." [From NOT, since the gate's function is comparable to the operation of *not* in logic.]

noth·ing (nŭth′ĭng) *n.* **1.** No thing; not anything. **2.** No significant or notable thing: *There is nothing on television tonight.* **3.** No part; no portion: *Nothing remains of its former glory.* **4.** Insignificance; obscurity: *rising from nothing.* **5.** Absence of anything perceptible; nonexistence: *The sound faded into nothing.* **6.** That which has no qualitative value or positive effect: *amount to nothing.* **7.** A zero; a naught. **8.** A person or thing of no consequence or significance. **9. nothings.** An affectionate word or remark: *sweet nothings.* **—for nothing. 1.** Free of charge; gratis. **2.** To no avail; *all that trouble for nothing.* **—have (got) nothing on. 1.** To be naked. **2.** To have no social engagements or obligations. **3.** To be markedly inferior in comparison to. **—have (got) nothing on one.** To have no money on one's person. **—have (got) nothing on someone.** To have no incriminatory evidence against. **—look like nothing on earth.** To appear ugly or outlandish. **—make nothing of. 1.** To treat lightly. **2.** To be unable to understand or cope with: *I can make nothing of this jigsaw puzzle.* **—nothing but.** Only; no other than: *nothing but the truth.* **—nothing doing.** *Informal.* **1.** Certainly not. Used as an emphatic refusal. **2.** Nothing of interest happening; not a thing going on. **—nothing for it.** No other course of action is possible: *There is nothing for it but to sell the house.* **—nothing like. 1.** Not at all like: *She's nothing like her sister.* **2.** Not nearly: *The blizzard here was nothing like as heavy as it was up north.* **—nothing short of.** No less than; tantamount to: *His dealings with the enemy were nothing short of treason.* **—nothing to it.** It is quite straightforward.
~*adj. Slang.* Insignificant or unimportant: *a nothing job.*
~*adv.* In no way or degree; not at all: *nothing daunted.* [Middle English *nathing, nothing,* Old English *nāthing, nān thing* : *nān,* NONE + THING.]

noth·ing·ness (nŭth′ĭng-nĭs) *n.* **1.** The condition or quality of being nothing; nonexistence. **2.** Empty or featureless space; the void. **3.** Lack of consequence; insignificance. **4.** Something inconsequential or insignificant.

no·tice (nō′tĭs) *n.* **1.** The act of observing or regarding with the senses; perception; attention: *That detail escaped my notice.* **2.** Heed or attention paid to another person or thing; especially, respectful attention or consideration: *grateful for the notice you took; a play worthy of notice.* **3.** A formal written announcement, published or displayed for all to see: *a notice of sale.* **4. a.** A formal announcement of purpose, especially of intention to withdraw from an agreement, such as a lease, or leave a job: *She gave her boss two weeks' notice.* **b.** Notification of dismissal from a job. **5.** A printed critical review of a play, book, or other cultural work: *favorable notices.* **6.** Any announcement of some present or coming event.
~*tr.v.* **noticed, -ticing, -tices. 1.** To observe; perceive; be aware of: *She did not notice the child in the doorway.* **2.** To consider; take note of; mark: *notice the discrepancy.* **3.** To comment on; mention in passing: *She began her speech by noticing the size of the audience.* **4.** To treat with courteous attention. [Middle English *notyce,* from Old French *notice,* from Latin *nōtitia,* knowledge, acquaintance, from *nōtus,* known, from the past participle of *nōscere,* to get acquainted with.]

no·tice·a·ble (nō′tĭs-ə-bəl) *adj.* **1.** Readily observed or detected; evident. **2.** Worth noticing; significant. **—no·tice·a·bly** *adv.*

notice board *n. British.* A board on which notices, advertisements, and the like are displayed.

notifiable disease *n.* Any of certain infectious diseases, such as cholera, diphtheria, and tuberculosis, cases of which must be reported to the health authorities.

no·ti·fi·ca·tion (nō′tə-fĭ-kā′shən) *n.* **1.** The act or an instance of notifying. **2.** The sign, letter, or other form by which notice is given.

no·ti·fy (nō′tə-fī′) *tr.v.* **-fied, -fying, -fies. 1.** To give formal notice to; inform. **2.** *Chiefly British.* To give notice or information of (something); make known; proclaim. [Middle English *notifien,* from Old French *notifier,* from Latin *nōtificāre,* to make known : *nōtus,* known, from *nōscere,* to get acquainted with + *facere,* to make.] **—no·ti·fi·a·ble** *adj.* **—no·ti·fi·er** *n.*

no·tion (nō′shən) *n.* **1.** A general impression or idea. **2.** A belief or theory, especially if subjective or mistaken. **3.** An inclination or whim: *I have a notion to throw a party.* **4.** *Rare.* Intention: *"Men's notion was, not for abolishing punishments, but for making laws just"* (Thomas Carlyle). **5. notions.** Small items for household and clothing use, such as needles, buttons, thread, and ribbons. —See Synonyms at **caprice, idea.** [Latin *nōtiō* (stem *nōtiōn-*), "a becoming acquainted," from *nōscere* (past participle *nōtus*), to get acquainted.]

no·tion·al (nō′shən-əl) *adj.* **1.** Of, containing, or being a notion or notions. **2.** Speculative or theoretical rather than actual. **3.** Existing only in the mind; imaginary. **4.** *Linguistics.* **a.** Having full lexical meaning, as distinguished from relational meaning. In the phrase *we did the work,* the verb *did* refers to a real activity (*doing* work), and is therefore notional; in the phrase *we did not agree, did* serves merely as a grammatical marker and is therefore relational. **b.** Conveying an idea directly to the mind; nonsymbolic. **—no·tion·al·ly** *adv.*

noto-¹, not- *prefix.* Indicates south or southern; for example, **Notogaea.** [New Latin, from Greek *notos,* south, south wind.]

noto-², not- *prefix.* Indicates back or back part; for example, **notochord.** [Greek *nōton,* the back.]

no·to·chord (nō′tə-kôrd′) *n.* **1.** A flexible rodlike structure in some lower vertebrates that provides dorsal support; the primitive backbone. **2.** A similar structure in embryos of higher vertebrates, from which the spine develops. [Greek *nōtos,* back + CHORD (cord).]

No·to·gae·a (nō′tə-jē′ə) *n.* A zoogeographical region that includes Australia, New Zealand, and the southwestern Pacific islands. Compare **Arctogaea.** [New Latin, "south realm" : NOTO- + Greek *gaia,* land, earth.] **—No·to·gae·al, No·to·gae·an** *adj.*

no·to·ri·e·ty (nō′tə-rī′ə-tē) *n.* The quality or condition of being notorious. —See Synonyms at **fame.**

no·to·ri·ous (nō-tôr′ē-əs, -tōr′-) *adj.* **1.** Known widely and regarded unfavorably; infamous: *a notorious thief.* **2.** Generally known and discussed: *the notorious facts in the case.* [Medieval Latin *nōtōrius,* from Late Latin, causing to be known, from *nōtus,* known, from the past participle of *nōscere,* to get acquainted.] **—no·to·ri·ous·ly** *adv.* **—no·to·ri·ous·ness** *n.*

no·tor·nis (nō-tôr′nĭs) *n.* Any of several rare, flightless birds, of the genus *Notornis,* found in New Zealand. See **takahe.** [New Latin, "bird of the south" (that is, New Zealand) : NOT(O)- + Greek *ornis,* bird.]

no-trump (nō′trŭmp′) *n.* **1.** In bridge and other card games, a declaration to play a hand without a trump suit. **2.** A hand played without a trump suit. **—no-trump** *adj.*

Not·ting·ham (nŏt′ĭng-əm). County town and largest city of Nottinghamshire, central England, on the Trent River. It has long been a center for the manufacture of lace and hosiery.

Not·ting·ham·shire (nŏt′ĭng-əm-shîr′, -shər). County in central England. Most of the land is low-lying and fertile. The rich Nottinghamshire coal fields lie in the west. There are also small oilfields. The county town is Nottingham.

not·with·stand·ing (nŏt′wĭth-stăn′dĭng, -wĭ*th*-) *prep.* In spite of; re-

PRONUNCIATION KEY

ă, pat; ā, pay; âr, care; ä, father, are; b, **bib**; ch, **church**; d, **deed**; ĕ, pet; ē, be; f, **fife**; g, **gag**; h, hat; hw, **which**; ĭ, pit; ī, pie; îr, **pier**; j, **judge**; k, **kick**; l, lid, needle; m, **mum**; n, no, sudden; ng, thing; ŏ, pot; ō, **toe**; ô, **paw**, for; oi, **noise**; ou, **out**; o͝o, **book**; o͞o, **boot**; p, **pop**; r, roar; s, sauce; sh, **ship**, **dish**; t, **tight**; th, **thin**, path; *th*, **this**, bathe; ŭ, **cut**; ûr, **fur**; v, **valve**; w, **with**; y, yes; z, zebra, size; zh, vision; ə, about, item, edible, gallop, circus, peaceful

IN FOREIGN WORDS:

à, *Fr.* ami; œ, *Fr.* feu, *Ger.* schön; ü, *Fr.* tu, *Ger.* über; KH, *Ger.* ich, *Scot.* loch; N, *Fr.* bon; y′, *Fr.* Compiègne

STRESS MARKS:

Primary stress: ′ **in·cite′** (ĭn-sīt′)
Secondary stress: ′ **in′sight′** (ĭn′sīt′)

gardless of hindrance by: *She left notwithstanding her father's opposition. Her father's opposition notwithstanding, she left.*
~*adv.* All the same; nevertheless: *We proceeded, notwithstanding.*
~*conj.* In spite of the fact that; although: *Her books sold well, notwithstanding she had little talent.* [Middle English *notwithstonding* : NOT + present participle of *withstonden*, to WITHSTAND.]
Nouak·chott (nwäk'shŏt'). Capital of Mauritania, in the western part of the country near the Atlantic Ocean. It became the capital of the country in 1957.
nou·gat (nōō'gət) *n.* A confection made from a sweet sugar or honey paste into which almonds and cherries or other nuts and fruits are mixed. [French *nougat*, from Provençal, from Old Provençal *nogat*, confection of nuts, from Vulgar Latin *nucātum* (unattested), from Latin *nux* (stem *nuc-*), nut.]
nought. Variant of **naught.**
noughts and crosses *n. British.* **Ticktacktoe** *(see).*
Nou·mé·a (nōō-mā'ə). Capital of the French overseas territory of New Caledonia, in the South Pacific on New Caledonia Island.
nou·me·non (nōō'mə-nŏn') *n., pl.* **-na** (-nə). In the philosophy of Kant: **1.** An object of purely intellectual intuition, as opposed to an object perceived by the senses. **2.** A thing in itself, independent of sensory or intellectual perception of any kind. Compare **phenomenon.** [German *Noumenon*, from Greek *noumenon*, concept, thought, from *nouein*, to think, apprehend, from *nous*, mind.] —**nou·me·nal** *adj.* —**nou·me·nal·ism** *n.* —**nou·me·nal·ist** *n.* —**nou·me·nal·ly** *adv.*
noun (noun) *n. Abbr.* **n. 1.** A word used to denote or name a person, place, thing, quality, or act. **2. a.** The part of speech of a word that is used as the subject or object of a verb, as object of a preposition, as a predicate after a copula, or as an appositive. **b.** Any word, phrase, or clause used in this way. [Middle English *nowne*, from Norman French *noun*, Old French *non, nom*, from Latin *nōmen*, name.] —**noun, noun·al** *adj.* —**noun·al·ly** *adv.*
nour·ish (nûr'ĭsh) *tr.v.* **-ished, -ishing, -ishes. 1.** To provide with food or other substances necessary for life and growth. **2.** To foster the development of; promote and sustain: *Freedom nourishes self-respect.* [Middle English *nurishen, norishen*, from Old French *norrir* (stem *norriss-*), from Latin *nūtrīre*, to feed.] —**nour·ish·a·ble** *adj.* —**nour·ish·er** *n.* —**nour·ish·ing·ly** *adv.*
nour·ish·ment (nûr'ĭsh-mənt) *n.* **1. a.** The act of nourishing. **b.** The state of being nourished. **2.** That which supports life and growth in a living organism; food; sustenance. **3.** That which promotes the development or vitality of something.
nous (nōōs, nous) *n.* **1.** *Philosophy.* Mind; reason; specifically, the principle of divine reason. **2.** *Chiefly British.* Common sense. [Greek.]
nou·veau riche (nōō'vō rēsh') *n., pl.* **nouveaux riches** (*pronounced as singular*). One who has lately become rich, especially one who flaunts his wealth; a parvenu. [French, "new rich."]
nou·velle vague (nōō-vĕl' väg') *n.* The **new wave** *(see).* [French.]
Nov. November.
no·va (nō'və) *n., pl.* **-vas** or **-vae** (-vē). *Astronomy.* A variable star that suddenly increases in brightness to several times its normal magnitude and then returns to its original appearance in a few months or years. Compare **supernova.** [New Latin (*stella*) *nova*, "new (star)," from Latin *novus*, new.]
no·vac·u·lite (nō-văk'yə-līt') *n.* A very hard, dense, silica-bearing rock used in whetstones. [Latin *novācula*, razor + -ITE.]
No·va Sco·tia (nō'və skō'shə). *Abbr.* **N.S.** Easternmost province of mainland Canada, connected to New Brunswick by the Chignecto Isthmus. It also includes Cape Breton Island. Coal mining and fishing are the chief industries, but the Annapolis Valley is also famous for its apple orchards. It was one of the four original provinces in the Canadian confederation (1867). The capital and largest city is Halifax. —**No·va Sco·tian** *adj. & n.*
no·va·tion (nō-vā'shən) *n. Law.* The substitution of a new obligation for an old one; especially, the transference of a debt. [Late Latin *novātiō* (stem *novātiōn-*), a making new, from Latin *novāre*, to make new, from *novus*, new.]
No·va·ya Zem·lya (nō'və-yə zĕm-lyä'). Largest group of islands in the Eurasian Arctic, lying off the Arctic coast of the U.S.S.R. It consists mainly of two large islands, which are continuations of the Ural and Pai-Khoy mountain systems.
nov·el[1] (nŏv'əl) *n.* **1.** A fictional prose narrative of considerable length, typically having a plot that is unfolded by the actions, speech, and thoughts of the characters. **2.** The literary genre represented by this form of narrative: *"The novel . . . is a perpetual quest for reality"* (Lionel Trilling). [Italian (*storia*) *novella*, a short tale, "new story," from feminine of *novello*, new, from Latin *novellus*, NOVEL.]
nov·el[2] *adj.* Strikingly new, unusual, or different. —See Usage note at **new.** [Middle English *novel*, from Old French, from Latin *novellus*, from *novus*, new.]
nov·el·ette (nŏv'ə-lĕt') *n.* **1.** A short novel. **2.** A light romantic or trivial novel, usually short and of little literary merit. **3.** A short, lyrical instrumental piece.
nov·el·ist (nŏv'ə-lĭst) *n.* A writer of novels.
nov·el·is·tic (nŏv'ə-lĭs'tĭk) *adj.* Of, pertaining to, or characteristic of novels.
nov·el·ize (nŏv'ə-līz') *tr.v.* **-ized, -izing, -izes. 1.** To turn (facts or a film script, for example) into a novel. **2.** To make novel or new. —**nov·el·i·za·tion** *n.*
no·vel·la (nō-vĕl'ə) *n., pl.* **-vellas** or **-vellae** (-vĕl'ē). **1.** A short prose tale of the type developed by Boccaccio, characterized by epigram-

matic terseness. **2.** A short novel. [Italian. See **novel** (narrative).]
Nov·els (nŏv'əlz) *pl.n. Roman Law.* Amendments made to the Justinian Code by the Emperor Justinian and his successors. [New Latin *novella*, singular of Late Latin *novellae* (*constitutiōnēs*), "new (statutes)," from Latin *novellus*, new, from *novus*, new.]
nov·el·ty (nŏv'əl-tē) *n., pl.* **-ties. 1.** The quality of being novel; newness; originality. **2.** Something that is novel; a new or unusual thing; an innovation. **3. novelties.** Small mass-produced articles, such as toys or trinkets. [Middle English *noveltee*, from Old French *novelte*, from *novel*, new, NOVEL.]
No·vem·ber (nō-vĕm'bər) *n. Abbr.* **Nov., N.** The 11th month of the Gregorian calendar. November has 30 days. See feature at **calendar.** [Middle English *Novembre*, from Old French, from Latin *Novembris* (*mēnsis*), the ninth (month) (of the Roman calendar), from *novem*, nine.]
no·ve·na (nō-vē'nə) *n., pl.* **-nas** or **-nae** (-nē). *Roman Catholic Church.* A recitation of prayers and devotions over a period of time, usually nine consecutive days. [Medieval Latin *novēna*, from Latin *novēnus*, nine each, from *novem*, nine.]
no·ver·cal (nō-vûr'kəl) *adj.* Of, pertaining to, or characteristic of a stepmother. [Latin *novercālis*, from *noverca*, a stepmother.]
Nov·go·rod (nŏv'gə-rŏd'). City in the northwestern U.S.S.R., on the Volkhov River. It is one of the oldest Russian cities. During the Middle Ages it rose to commercial prosperity because of its position on one of the major trade routes of eastern Europe. The city's rich architectural heritage was largely destroyed by bombing in World War II, but much has since been restored.
nov·ice (nŏv'ĭs) *n.* **1.** A person new to any field or activity; a beginner. **2.** A person who has entered a religious order but who is on probation before taking final vows. Compare **postulant. 3.** *Sports.* **a.** A competitor who has not previously won a prize or reached a certain standard. **b.** A racehorse that has yet to win a certain number of races. [Middle English *novyce*, from Old French *novice*, from Medieval Latin *novīcius*, from Latin *novīcius*, extension of *novus*, new.]
no·vi·ti·ate (nō-vĭsh'ē-ĭt, -āt') *n.* **1.** *Ecclesiastical.* **a.** The period of time served by a novice. **b.** A place where novices live. **c.** A novice. **2.** The state or time of being a beginner. **3.** A beginner. [French *noviciat*, from Medieval Latin *novīciātus*, from *novīcius*, NOVICE.]
No·vo·cain (nō'və-kān') *n.* A trademark for the anesthetic **procaine hydrochloride** *(see).*
No·vo·cas·tri·an (nō'və-kăs'trē-ən) *n.* A native or inhabitant of Newcastle. —**No·vo·cas·tri·an** *adj.*
No·vo·si·birsk (nō'vō-sə-bîrsk'). City of south Siberian U.S.S.R., on the Ob River and the Trans-Siberian Railroad. It was founded in 1893 during the building of the railroad. Its proximity to the Kuznetsk Basin contributed greatly to its growth.
now (nou) *adv.* **1.** At the present time. **2.** At once; immediately: *Stop now.* **3.** In the immediate past; very recently. Often preceded by *just: She left just now.* **4.** In the immediate future; very soon. Often preceded by *just: They are going just now.* **5.** At this point in a series of events; then: *The ship was now listing to port.* **6.** Nowadays: *Now you rarely hear his name.* **7.** In these circumstances; as things are: *Now we won't be able to stay.* **8. a.** Used to introduce a statement or question: *Now, what do you think?* **b.** Used in commands to add emphasis: *Now be a good boy. Hurry up, now!* —**now and again** (or **then**). Occasionally.
~*conj.* Since. Often followed by *that: Now that we have eaten, let's get back to work.*
~*n.* The present time or moment: *He's been alone up to now.*
~*adj.* **1.** *Informal.* Of the present time; current: *the now generation.* **2.** *Slang.* In tune with the latest trends; with-it: *a now magazine.*
~*interj.* Used: **1.** To express mild rebuke. **2.** To soothe or placate. [Middle English *now*, from Old English *nū.*]
now·a·days (nou'ə-dāz') *adv.* In these days; at the present time. [Middle English *now a dayes*, "on this day" : NOW + *a dayes*, Old English *on dæges* (adverbial genitive) : ON + DAY.]
no·way (nō'wā') *adv.* Also **no·ways** (-wāz'). Nowise; certainly not.
no way *adv. Informal.* Not at all; absolutely not.
~*interj. Informal.* Used to express emphatic refusal.
no·where (nō'hwâr', -wâr') *adv.* Also *nonstandard* **no·wheres** (-wârz'). In, to, or at no place; not anywhere.
~*n.* **1.** No place; a nonexistent or insignificant place. **2.** An insignificant or obscure position: *came from nowhere to win the election.*
no·win (nō'wĭn') *adj.* Bound to end in failure or disappointment: *trapped in a no-win situation.*
no·wise (nō'wīz') *adv.* In no way, manner, or degree; not at all. [Middle English *nawyse* : NO + WISE (way).]
nowt (nowt, nŏt) *n. British Regional.* Nothing. [Variant of NOUGHT.]
nox·ious (nŏk'shəs) *adj.* Injurious or harmful to health or morals. [Latin *noxius*, from *noxa*, injury, damage.] —**nox·ious·ly** *adv.* —**nox·ious·ness** *n.*
no·yade (nwä-yäd') *n.* Execution by drowning, especially that carried out on a large scale at Nantes, France, in 1794 during the Reign of Terror. [French, from *noyer*, to drown, from Latin *necāre*, from *nex* (stem *nec-*), slaughter.]
noz·zle (nŏz'əl) *n.* A projecting, often adjustable, spout through which gas or liquid is discharged, such as the end of a hose or the pipe in a jet engine or rocket outlet. [Earlier *nosel, nosle*, diminutive of NOSE.]
Np 1. The symbol for the element neptunium. **2.** neper.
NP 1. neuropsychiatric; neuropsychiatry. **2.** noun phrase.

n.p. 1. new paragraph. 2. *Law.* nisi prius. 3. no place of publication.

N.P. notary public.

NPN, N.P.N. nonprotein nitrogen.

nr. near.

NRA National Recovery Administration.

N.R.C. Nuclear Regulatory Commission.

N.S. 1. New Style. 2. not satisfactory or sufficient. 3. not specified. 4. Nova Scotia. 5. nuclear ship.

NSF 1. National Science Foundation. 2. not sufficient funds.

N.S.P.C.A. National Society for the Prevention of Cruelty to Animals.

NSU nonspecific urethritis.

N.S.W. New South Wales.

NT, N.T. New Testament.

nth (ĕnth) *adj.* 1. Pertaining to an indefinitely large ordinal number: *ten to the nth power.* 2. Infinitely or indefinitely large; highest; utmost: *exaggerated to the nth degree.*

n.t.p., N.T.P. normal temperature and pressure (a temperature of 0°C and a pressure of 101.325 kPa).

n-type (ĕn'tīp') *adj. Electronics.* Of or designating a semiconductor or its type of conductivity, in which the bulk of the electric current is carried by electrons. Compare **p-type.** [*Negative type.*]

nu (nōō, nyōō) *n.* The thirteenth letter of the Greek alphabet (N, *ν*), corresponding to the English *N, n.* See feature at **alphabet.** [Greek *nu,* from a Phoenician word meaning "fish," from a Semitic root *nyn* meaning "to increase" or "to endure."]

nu·ance (nōō-äns', nyōō-, nōō'äns', nyōō'-) *n.* A subtle or slight variation, as in meaning, color, or quality; a gradation of meaning: *"I seem to grasp at certain moments the nuance that divides bad from worse"* (Samuel Beckett). [French *nuance,* from Old French, from *nuer,* to show shades of color (as in clouds), from *nue,* cloud, from Vulgar Latin *nūbe* (unattested), from Latin *nūbēs.*]

nub (nŭb) *n.* 1. A protuberance or knob. 2. A small lump or piece. 3. The gist or point: *the nub of a story.* [Variant of *knub,* from Middle Low German *knubbe,* knot on a tree, variant of *knobbe,* KNOB.]

Nu·ba (nōō'bə, nyōō'-) *n., pl.* **Nuba.** 1. A Nubian. 2. A member of any of several Nilotic peoples of southern Sudan. 3. The language spoken by these peoples. —**Nu·ba** *adj.*

nub·bin (nŭb'ĭn) *n.* 1. A small, stunted ear of corn. 2. Anything stunted or imperfectly developed. [Diminutive of NUB.]

nub·ble (nŭb'əl) *n.* A small protuberance or lump. [Diminutive of NUB.] —**nub·bly** *adj.*

Nu·bi·a (nōō'bē-ə, nyōō'-). Ancient state of northeastern Africa, extending at its height from Aswan to Khartoum. By the 20th century B.C. it had come completely under the sway of the Egyptians, although in the 8th and 7th centuries B.C. an independent kingdom of Nubia again asserted itself and Nubian kings conquered Egypt, establishing the XXV Dynasty in 712 B.C. In the 6th century A.D. Nubia was joined to Ethiopia, then a Christian kingdom. After Ethiopia fell to the Muslims in the 14th century, Nubia ceased to have a distinctive existence.

Nu·bi·an (nōō'bē-ən, nyōō'-) *n.* 1. A native or inhabitant of Nubia. 2. Any of the languages of Nubia. —**Nu·bi·an** *adj.*

Nubian Desert. An arid wilderness in northeastern Sudan, lying between the Nile River and the Red Sea and merging into the Arabian Desert of eastern Egypt. The desert is largely uninhabited.

nu·bile (nōō'bĭl, -bīl', nyōō'-) *adj.* 1. Young and physically attractive. Said of a girl or young woman: *a nubile young girl.* 2. Ready for marriage; of a marriageable age. Said of a woman. [French *nubile,* from Latin *nūbilis,* marriageable, from *nūbere,* to take a husband.] —**nu·bil·i·ty** (nōō-bĭl'ə-tē, nyōō-) *n.*

nu·cel·lus (nōō-sĕl'əs, nyōō-) *n., pl.* **-celli** (-sĕl'ī'). *Botany.* The center of the ovule of a plant, containing the embryo sac. [New Latin, irregularly from Latin *nucella,* diminutive of *nux* (stem *nuc-*), nut.] —**nu·cel·lar** *adj.*

nu·cha (nōō'kə, nyōō'-) *n.* The nape of the neck. [Middle English *nucha, nuca,* from Medieval Latin *nucha,* from Arabic *nukhā',* spinal marrow.] —**nu·chal** *adj.*

nucle-. Variant of **nucleo-.**

nu·cle·ar (nōō'klē-ər, nyōō'-) *adj.* 1. *Biology.* Of, pertaining to, or forming a nucleus: *a nuclear membrane.* 2. *Physics.* Of or concerning atomic nuclei: *nuclear physics.* 3. Using, armed with, or derived from the energy of atomic nuclei; atomic: *nuclear power plants.* 4. Of, involving, or possessing atomic or hydrogen bombs: *nuclear war; nuclear nations.* [From NUCLEUS.]

nuclear bomb *n.* 1. An explosive weapon of great destructive power derived from the rapid release of energy in the fission of heavy atomic nuclei, as of uranium-235. 2. Any bomb deriving its destructive power from the release of nuclear energy. Also called "A-bomb," "atom bomb," "atomic bomb." See **hydrogen bomb.** See feature, next page.

nuclear emulsion *n. Physics.* Any of several photographic emulsions used to detect and display the paths of charged elementary particles, especially of charged cosmic-ray particles.

nuclear energy *n. Physics.* 1. The energy released by a nuclear reaction, especially by fission, fusion, or radioactive decay. 2. This energy regarded as a source of industrial, commercial, or military power. Also called "atomic energy." See feature, page 1165.

nuclear family *n.* A self-contained family unit consisting of a mother and father and their children. Compare **extended family.**

nuclear fission *n. Physics.* See **fission.**

nu·cle·ar-free zone (nōō'klē-ər-frē', nyōō'-) *n.* An area in which the siting of nuclear reactors or missiles is banned.

nuclear fuel *n.* A fuel used to provide nuclear power in a nuclear reactor.

nuclear fusion *n. Physics.* See **fusion.**

nuclear isomer *n. Physics.* A type of **isomer** (see).

nuclear magnetic resonance *n. Abbr.* **NMR** A technique for measuring the nuclear **magnetic moment** (see) of a substance by exposing a sample to a strong magnetic field and high-frequency electromagnetic radiation. It is used, as in spectroscopy, for providing information on the molecular structure of the substance.

nuclear magneton *n. Physics. Symbol* μ_N A unit of the magnetic moment of the nucleon. See **magneton.**

nuclear physics *n. Used with a singular verb.* The scientific study of the forces, reactions, and internal structures of atomic nuclei.

nuclear power *n.* 1. The electric or motive power produced by a nuclear reactor. Also called "atomic power." 2. A state that possesses nuclear weapons. —**nu·cle·ar-pow·ered** *adj.*

nuclear reaction *n. Physics.* A reaction that alters the energy, composition, or structure of an atomic nucleus. Also called "reaction."

nuclear reactor *n.* Any of several devices in which a **chain reaction** (see) is initiated and controlled, with the consequent production of heat typically used for the generation of power, and of neutrons and fission products used for experimental and medical purposes. Also called "atomic pile," "atomic reactor," "pile," "reactor."

nu·cle·ase (nōō'klē-ās', -āz', nyōō'-) *n.* Any of several enzymes that hydrolize nucleic acids. [NUCLE(O)- + -ASE.]

nu·cle·ate (nōō'klē-āt', nyōō'-) *adj.* Also **nu·cle·at·ed** (-ā'tĭd). Having a nucleus or nuclei.
~*v.* (nōō'klē-āt', nyōō'-) **nucleated, -ating, -ates.** —*tr.* To bring together into a nucleus. —*intr.* To form a nucleus. [NUCLE(US) + -ATE.] —**nu·cle·a·tion** *n.*

nu·cle·i. Plural of **nucleus.**

nu·cle·ic acid (nōō-klē'ĭk, -klā'-, nyōō-) *n.* Any member of either of two groups of complex compounds found in all living cells, and composed of purines, pyrimidines, sugars, and phosphoric acid. See **DNA, RNA.** [NUCLE(O)- + -IC (because found in nucleoproteins).]

nucleo-, nucle- *prefix.* Indicates: 1. A nucleus; for example, **nucleon.** 2. Nucleic acid; for example, **nucleoprotein, nucleoside.** [From NUCLEUS.]

nu·cle·o·late (nōō'klē-ə-lāt', nyōō'-) *adj.* Also **nu·cle·o·lat·ed** (-lā'tĭd). Having a nucleolus or nucleoli. [NUCLEOL(US) + -ATE.]

nu·cle·o·lus (nōō-klē'ə-ləs, nyōō-) *n., pl.* **-li** (-lī'). Also **nu·cle·ole** (-ōl'). *Biology.* 1. A small, usually round body composed of protein and RNA in the nucleus of a cell. Also called "plasmosome." 2. Any discrete, cellular particle resembling a nucleolus, other than a chromosome. [New Latin, from Latin, diminutive of *nucleus,* a kernel, NUCLEUS.] —**nu·cle·o·lar** *adj.*

nu·cle·on (nōō'klē-ŏn', nyōō'-) *n.* A proton or a neutron, especially as part of an atomic nucleus. [NUCLE(O)- + -ON.] —**nu·cle·on·ic** *adj.*

nu·cle·on·ics (nōō'klē-ŏn'ĭks, nyōō'-) *n. Used with a singular verb.* The technology of nuclear energy. [From NUCLEON.]

nucleon number *n. Physics.* **Mass number** (see).

nu·cle·o·phile (nōō'klē-ə-fīl', nyōō'-) *n.* A substance whose atoms or molecules behave as an electron pair donor in combining with other atoms or molecules. [NUCLEO- + -PHILE.] —**nu·cle·o·phile, nu·cle·o·phil·ic** (nōō'klē-ə-fīl'ĭk, nyōō'-) *adj.*

nu·cle·o·plasm (nōō'klē-ə-plăz'əm, nyōō'-) *n.* The protoplasm of a cell nucleus. Also called "karyoplasm." [NUCLEO- + -PLASM.] —**nu·cle·o·plas·mat·ic** (nōō'klē-ō-plăz-măt'ĭk, nyōō'-), **nu·cle·o·plas·mic** *adj.*

nu·cle·o·pro·tein (nōō'klē-ō-prō'tēn', -prō'tē-ĭn, nyōō'-) *n.* Any of a group of substances found in all living cells and viruses, and composed of a protein and a nucleic acid.

nu·cle·o·side (nōō'klē-ə-sīd', nyōō'-) *n.* Any compound made of a sugar and a purine or pyrimidine base without a phosphate group. [NUCLE(O) + -OS(E) + -IDE.]

nu·cle·o·some (nōō'klē-ə-sōm', nyōō'-) *n.* Any of the basic globular subunits of chromatin consisting of DNA and histone. [NUCLEO- + -SOME.] —**nu·cle·o·som·al** *adj.*

nu·cle·o·tide (nōō'klē-ə-tīd', nyōō'-) *n.* Any of various organic compounds consisting of a nucleoside combined with phosphoric acid. [Irregularly from NUCLEO- + -IDE.]

nu·cle·us (nōō'klē-əs, nyōō'-) *n., pl.* **-clei** (-klē-ī') or **-cleuses.** 1. A central thing or part around which other things are grouped; a core: *the nucleus of a city.* 2. Anything regarded as a basis for future development and growth; a kernel: *the nucleus of a stamp collection.* 3. *Biology.* A complex, usually spherical, protoplasmic body within a living cell that contains the cell's hereditary material and that controls its metabolism, growth, and reproduction. 4. *Botany.* The central point of a starch granule. 5. *Anatomy.* A group of nerve cells or localized mass of gray matter in the brain, where nerve fibers interconnect. 6. *Physics.* The positively charged central region of an atom, composed of protons and neutrons, and containing almost all of the mass of the atom. See **atomic number, mass number.** 7. *Chemistry.* A group of atoms chemically bound in a structure resistant to alteration in chemical reactions. 8. *Astronomy.* a. The central portion of the head of a comet. b. The central or brightest part of a nebula or of a galaxy. 9. *Meteorology.* A minute solid particle upon which water vapor molecules accumulate to form a droplet or ice crystal. 10. *Phonetics.* The most sonorous part

HOW THE POWER OF THE ATOM BECAME A WEAPON OF WAR

The growth of nuclear weapons from the atomic bomb to the neutron bomb

There are two main kinds of bomb that release the energy of the atomic nucleus: those that split nuclei (atomic or fission bombs) and those that fuse nuclei (hydrogen or thermonuclear bombs). An atomic-bomb explosion is a vast release of energy caused by a chain reaction in which some two quintillion atoms (of uranium or plutonium) are split in a millionth of a second. The first plans for an atomic bomb were produced in England in 1940 by two refugee German scientists, Otto Frisch and Rudolph Peierls. Parallel research was going on in the United States, and in 1941 British and American scientists joined forces in the Manhattan Project led by Robert Oppenheimer.

The first atomic explosion took place on July 16, 1945, at Alamogordo, New Mexico. In August President Truman decided to use the world's only two atomic bombs against Japan. One was dropped on Hiroshima on August 6, the other on Nagasaki three days later. The Hiroshima bomb had an explosive force of 20 kilotons (equivalent to 20,000 tons of TNT) and killed 80,000 people outright.

The first hydrogen bomb, or H-bomb, was exploded by the United States on November 1, 1952, over Eniwetok Atoll in the Pacific. Its explosive force was about 10 megatons (10 million tons of TNT)—500 times that of the Hiroshima bomb. By 1982 six countries were known to possess nuclear bombs: the United States, Russia, Britain, France, China, and India. In 1982 the United States began stockpiling the neutron bomb, which is designed to destroy people rather than buildings. It has a limited blast range but a long radiation range. The present stock of such weapons could wipe out life on earth.

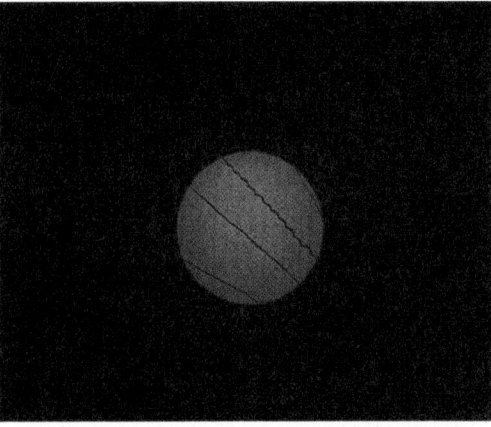

1

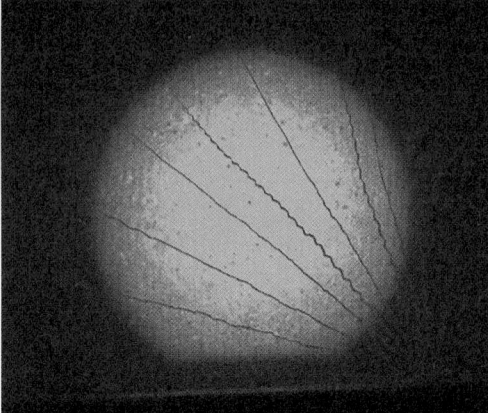

2

3

4

H-BOMB OVER THE PACIFIC *On November 1, 1952, the United States exploded the first hydrogen bomb 450 meters (1,476 feet) over Eniwetok Atoll in the Pacific Ocean. This color-film sequence shows stages of the thermonuclear explosion from shortly after detonation to the final "flourishing" of the fireball.* **1** *Vapor trails left by instrumentation rockets are silhouetted against the fireball.* **2** *The fireball's surface is dotted with light and dark spots. The exact nature of the spots is not known, but they are thought to be connected with the shock wave caused by the bomb.* **3** *The shock wave is reflected from the surface of the ocean and this flattens the bottom of the fireball.* **4** *The rising fireball starts to leave the vapor trails beneath it as it assumes the shape of a rotating doughnut.* **5** *The fireball takes the shape of a giant mushroom as it rises higher over the atoll. Brown metal oxides from the bomb debris gather on the fireball rim. The explosion formed a crater almost 1.5 kilometers (1 mile) across.*

Less than a year after the explosion at Eniwetok Atoll, the Russians tested a hydrogen bomb, and Britain followed in May 1956. The 1950's saw the start of a nuclear arms race as Russia, the United States, Britain, and France tested ever more powerful bombs and strove to outstrip one another in delivery systems.

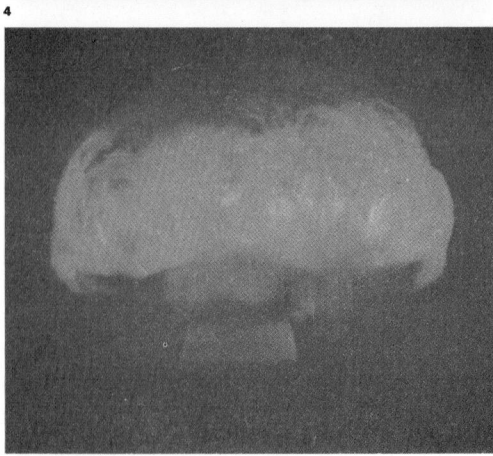

5

nuclear energy

MASTERING THE MIGHTY ATOM
How man controls nuclear energy

In 1942, an Italian physicist, Enrico Fermi, working at the University of Chicago, withdrew some cadmium rods from a pile he had built of graphite with uranium inserts and began a chain reaction in the uranium atoms that created a new and mighty power—nuclear energy. In so doing he controlled the reaction that occurs when the nucleus of an unstable atom, such as uranium, splits, or undergoes fission.

When fission occurs, enormous energy is released, together with several neutrons. These neutrons will be captured by other uranium nuclei that will become unstable and, in turn, undergo fission. This chain reaction, if unchecked, will in fractions of a second set off the gigantic explosion of a nuclear blast. When the reaction is controlled, energy can be released as a steady flow of heat, which can be used for generating electricity.

Fermi's experiment is the basis on which nuclear-powered electricity-generating stations work. The flow of heat is controlled by the cadmium rods.

The heat is extracted by water, gas, or sodium, and used to raise steam to drive the generator. Nuclear reactors pose problems. If they break down, they may release dangerous radioactivity, and their fuel, even when expended, remains radioactive probably for centuries (making it difficult to dispose of). The answer may lie in nuclear fusion—as yet unmastered. It is the harnessing of the energy created when two nuclei join, or fuse, together—a process that does not have such a great waste-disposal problem.

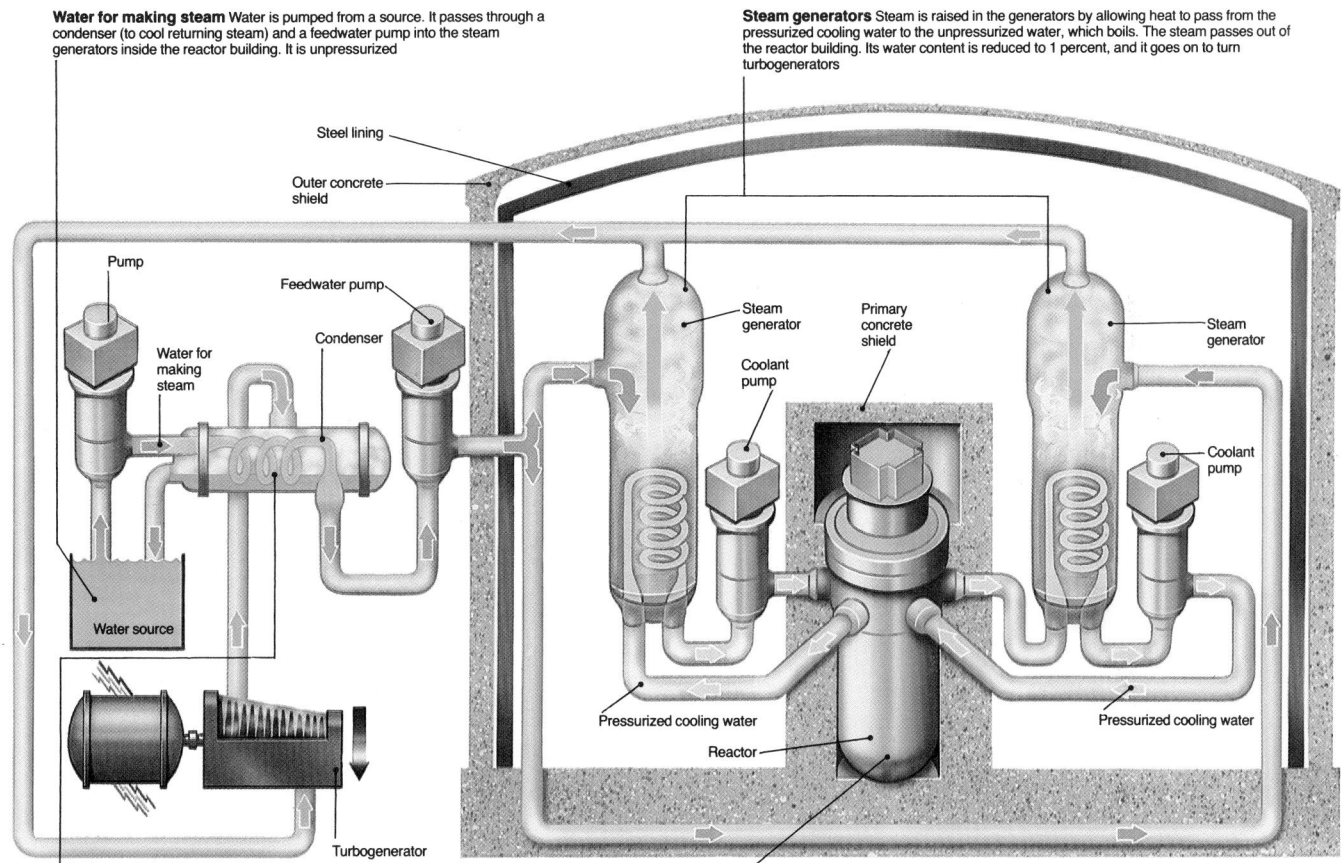

Water for making steam Water is pumped from a source. It passes through a condenser (to cool returning steam) and a feedwater pump into the steam generators inside the reactor building. It is unpressurized

Steam generators Steam is raised in the generators by allowing heat to pass from the pressurized cooling water to the unpressurized water, which boils. The steam passes out of the reactor building. Its water content is reduced to 1 percent, and it goes on to turn turbogenerators

Steel lining

Outer concrete shield

Pump

Feedwater pump

Condenser

Water for making steam

Steam generator

Coolant pump

Primary concrete shield

Steam generator

Coolant pump

Water source

Pressurized cooling water

Reactor

Pressurized cooling water

Turbogenerator

Condenser The steam passes on to the condenser, where it is turned back into water by the coldness of the water coming in from the source. It is then returned to the source

Reactor Water for cooling the reactor is maintained at a constant pressure to prevent it from boiling in the reactor. Impelled by coolant pumps, the cooling water circulates between the reactor core and the steam generators

POWER FROM A REACTOR *Pressurized cooling water is driven around the reactor core to draw off the heat. It is then passed through steam generators, where it turns other water into steam. The steam is siphoned off to drive a turbogenerator, which produces electric-ity. The steam is then cooled into water in a condenser and sent around the system to be used again. This type of pressurized water reactor is cheap and simple to build, but it uses fuel less economically than later gas-cooled reactors.*

---

of a syllable; especially, a vowel. [Latin, "a nut," "kernel," from *nux* (stem *nuc*-), a nut.]

nu·clide (nōō′klīd′, nyōō′-) *n. Physics.* Any atomic nucleus specified by its atomic number, atomic mass, and energy state. Compare **isotope.** [NUCLE(O)- + -IDE.] —**nu·clid·ic** (nōō-klĭd′ĭk, nyōō-) *adj.*

nude (nōōd, nyōōd) *adj.* **1. a.** Without clothing; naked. **b.** Without covering; exposed. **2.** *Law.* Lacking any of various legal requisites, such as evidence: *a nude contract.* —*n.* **1.** A nude human figure or a representation of it. **2.** The condition of being nude: *in the nude.* [Latin *nūdus,* nude, bare.] —**nude·ly** *adv.* —**nude·ness** *n.*

nudge (nŭj) *tr.v.* **nudged, nudging, nudges. 1.** To push or prod (a person) gently, especially with the elbow and in order to gain attention or give a signal. **2.** To push against (an object) lightly: *The car tire just nudged the pavement.* **3.** To come close to; near: *She's nudging 60 years of age.* **4.** To encourage or compel gradually: *Slowly they nudged her into joining the conspiracy.* —*n.* **1.** A gentle push. **2.** An encouragement or incentive. [Perhaps from a Scandinavian word akin to Norwegian dialectal *nugga, nyggja†,* to push, rub.]

nudi– *prefix.* Indicates nakedness or bareness; for example, **nudibranch, nudicaul.** [Latin *nūdus,* NUDE.]

nu·di·branch (nōō′də-brăngk′, nyōō′-) *n.* Any mollusk of the order Nudibranchia; the **sea slug** *(see).* [New Latin *Nudibranchia,* "ones having naked gills" : NUDI- + BRANCHIA.] —**nu·di·bran·chi·an** (nōō′də-brăng′kē-ən, nyōō′-) **nu·di·bran·chi·ate** (nōō′də-brăng′kē-ĭt, -āt′, nyōō′-) *adj. & n.*

nu·di·caul (nōō′də-kôl′, nyōō′-) *adj.* Also **nu·di·cau·lous** (nōō′-də-kô′ləs, nyōō′-). *Botany.* Having no leaves on the stem. [NUDI- + Latin *caulis,* stalk, stem.]

nud·ie (nōō′dē, nyōō′-) *n. Slang.* **1.** A **skin flick** *(see).* **2.** A magazine containing pornographic photographs of nudes. —*adj. Slang.* Characterized by or featuring pornographic nudity: *a nudie film.* [From NUDE.]

nud·ism (nōō′dĭz′əm, nyōō′-) *n.* The doctrine or practice of living in the nude. Also called "naturism." —**nud·ist** *adj. & n.*

nu·di·ty (nōō′də-tē, nyōō′-) *n., pl.* **-ties. 1.** The quality or state of being nude; bareness; nakedness. **2.** *Rare.* A nude figure as represented in painting or sculpture.

nud·nik, nud·nick (nōōd′nĭk) *n. Slang.* A boring or bothersome person; a pest. [Yiddish : Russian *nudny,* boring, wearisome + -NIK.]

nu·ée ar·dente (nōō-ā′ är-däNt′) *n.* A turbulent, incandescent cloud of gas, ash, and rock fragments that flows rapidly over the ground after a violent volcanic eruption, destroying all forms of life in its path within seconds. [French, "burning cloud."]

nuevo peso (nwā′vō pĕ′sō) *n.* The basic monetary unit of Uruguay, equal to 100 centesimos. See feature at **currency.**

nu·ga·to·ry (nōō′gə-tôr′ē, nyōō′-) *adj.* **1.** Of no value; worthless; trifling: *a nugatory objection.* **2.** Having no power; invalid; inoperative: *a nugatory statute.* [Latin *nūgātōrius,* trifling, from *nūgārī,* to jest, trifle, from *nūgae†,* jokes.]

nug·gar (nŭg′ər) *n.* A broad-beamed sailing boat used for carrying cargo on the upper Nile River. [Arabic *nukkār.*]

nug·get (nŭg′ĭt) *n.* **1.** A small lump, especially one of natural gold. **2.** A small but valuable portion or unit: *nuggets of information.* [Probably diminutive of dialect *nug†,* lump.] —**nug·get·y** *adj.*

nui·sance (nōō′səns, nyōō′-) *n.* **1.** A source of inconvenience, annoyance, or vexation; a bother. **2.** *Law.* A use of property or course of conduct that interferes with the legal rights of others by causing damage, annoyance, or inconvenience. [Middle English *nusaunce,* injury, harmful thing, from Old French *nuisance,* from *nuire* (stem *nuis-*), to harm, injure, from Latin *nocēre.*]

nuisance tax *n.* A tax levied in small amounts on separate purchases and collected directly from the consumer.

nuisance value *n.* The capacity to annoy or frustrate, considered as a useful asset.

Nuits-Saint-Georges (nwē-săN-zhôrzh′) *n.* A fine red Burgundy wine. [After the town of *Nuits-Saint-Georges,* France.]

nuke (nōōk, nyōōk) *n. Slang.* A nuclear bomb.
~*tr.v.* **nuked, nuking, nukes.** *Slang.* To attack or destroy with nuclear bombs.

Nu·ku·a·lo·fa (nōō′kə-wə-lō′fə). Capital of Tonga, on Tongatapu Island, in the South Pacific.

null (nŭl) *adj.* **1.** Having no legal force; invalid. Often used in the phrase *null and void.* **2. a.** Of no consequence, effect, or value; insignificant. **b.** Lacking distinctive personality; colorless: *a null face.* **3.** Amounting to nothing; lacking; absent; nonexistent. **4.** *Mathematics.* Of or pertaining to zero magnitude or to a set having no members.
~*n.* **1.** Zero. **2.** An instrumental reading of zero. **3.** A letter that has no meaning in a code or cipher. [French *nul, nulle,* "none," from Latin *nūllus : ne,* not + *ūllus,* any.]

nul·lah (nŭl′ə) *n.* In India, a ravine or watercourse. [Hindi *nālā,* rivulet, ravine, probably from Dravidian.]

nul·la-nul·la (nŭl′ə-nŭl′ə) *n. Australian.* A hardwood club used by Aborigines. [From a native Australian language.]

Null·ar·bor Plain (nŭl′ə-bôr′, nŭl-är′bər). Extensive plateau stretching along the Great Australian Bight in southern Australia from Ooldea to the lake district of Western Australia and extending north to the Great Victoria Desert. It is generally flat, with occasional peaks rising 400 meters above sea level.

null hypothesis *n. Statistics.* A hypothesis that is tested against another but is nullified in favor of the alternative, subject to a given level of error.

nul·li·fi·ca·tion (nŭl′ə-fĭ-kā′shən) *n.* **1.** The action of nullifying. **2.** The refusal or failure of a state to recognize or enforce within its boundaries a law of the United States: *"Where powers are assumed which have not been delegated, a nullification of the act is the rightful remedy"* (Jefferson). —**nul·li·fi·ca·tion·ist** *n. & adj.*

nul·li·fid·i·an (nŭl′ə-fĭd′ē-ən) *n.* A person having no beliefs, especially in religious matters; a skeptic.
~*adj.* Having or characterized by a lack of faith or belief. [Medieval Latin *nullifidius :* Latin *nullus,* no, none + *fidēs,* faith.]

nul·li·fy (nŭl′ə-fī′) *tr.v.* **-fied, -fying, -fies. 1.** To deprive of legal force; annul; make void: *The court nullified the contract.* **2.** To make ineffective or useless; reduce to nothing: *"Thus content was he to be nullified, that the Lord might be magnified"* (Cotton Mather). —See Synonyms at **neutralize.** [Late Latin *nūllificāre,* to make light of, despise : *nūllus,* none, NULL + *facere,* to make.] —**nul·li·fi·er** *n.*
Synonyms: abolish, abrogate, annul, cancel, repeal, rescind, revoke, void.

nul·lip·a·ra (nŭ-lĭp′ər-ə) *n.* A woman who has never given birth. [New Latin : Latin *nullus,* no, none + *-para,* from *parere,* to give birth.] —**nul·li·par·i·ty** (nŭl′ə-păr′ə-tē) *n.* —**nul·lip·a·rous** (nŭ-lĭp′ər-əs) *adj.*

nul·li·pore (nŭl′ə-pôr′, -pōr′) *n.* Any of several small red seaweeds that secrete calcium carbonate and form encrustations on rocks. [Latin *nullus,* no, none + PORE.]

nul·li·ty (nŭl′ə-tē) *n., pl.* **-ties. 1.** The state or quality of being null: *the nullity of third parties in a two-party system.* **2.** *Law.* **a.** The fact of being null and void. **b.** An act having no legal validity. **3.** A nonentity.

null set *n. Mathematics.* An **empty set** *(see).*

num. 1. number. **2.** numeral.

Num. Numbers (Old Testament).

numb (nŭm) *adj.* **number** (nŭm′ər), **numbest** (nŭm′ĭst). **1.** Deprived of the power to feel or move normally, as from excessive chill; benumbed: *toes numb with cold.* **2.** Stunned or paralyzed, as from shock or strong emotion: *numb with grief.* **3.** Insensitive or inept. **4.** Resembling or of the nature of loss of sensation: *a numb feeling.*
~*v.* **numbed, numbing, numbs.** —*tr.* To make numb; deaden. —*intr.* To become numb. [Middle English *nome(n),* originally "seized with palsy, paralyzed," past participle of *nimen,* to take, seize, Old English *niman.*] —**numb·ly** *adv.* —**numb·ness** *n.*

num·bat (nŭm′băt′) *n.* Either of two marsupial mammals, *Myrmecobius fasciatus* or *M. rufus,* native to southern Australia, having a long snout and an extensile tongue for catching termites. [From a native Australian language.]

num·ber (nŭm′bər) *n. Abbr.* **n., no., No., num. 1.** *Mathematics.* **a.** A member of the set of positive integers; a member of a series of symbols of unique meaning in a fixed order which may be derived by counting. See **cardinal number, ordinal number. b.** A member of any of the further sets of mathematical objects that may be derived from the positive integers by mathematical induction. See **induction.** Thus, given the positive integers and zero, the operation of addition makes it possible to define the negative integers (those which added to the positive integers produce zero). The integers together with the fractions (of the form m/n, where m and n are integers and n is not zero) form the set of *rational numbers.* The rational numbers together with the *irrational numbers* (those not expressible as quotients of integers, such as $\sqrt{2}$) form the set of *real numbers.* Numbers of the form $a + bi$, where a and b are real numbers and $i^2 = -1$, form the set of *complex numbers,* which is the broadest set commonly used in mathematics. Numbers, such as π (pi), that are not expressible as roots of any algebraic equation with rational coefficients, form the set of *transcendental numbers.* See **transfinite number. c.** A symbol used to represent a number; a numeral. **2. numbers.** The study or processes of arithmetic. **3. a.** A numeral or series of numerals assigned to or designating a specific person or thing: *a telephone number.* **b.** The person or thing thus designated: *You are next, number three.* **4.** A specific quantity composed of equal units: *The number of apples in the bowl is ten.* **5.** Quantity of units or individuals: *The crowd was small in number.* **6. numbers.** A large quantity or collection: *Numbers of people visited the fair.* **7.** One item in a group or series, as of a journal, considered to be in numerical order: *I saw her article in the latest*

---

number

WAYS OF REPRESENTING QUANTITY
Using position to extend a symbol's meaning

A number describes a quantity; it evaluates an amount from one to millions by a symbol or a group of symbols. The oldest-known writing, from Sumer in Mesopotamia, was an account— a 5,000-year-old record of supplies. Ancient Egyptians, Chinese, Greeks, Mayas, and Hindus all developed numbering systems—and all counted in tens, probably because they used their fingers. Some Brazilian Indians, however, use the joints of one finger, and thus all their counting is based on three numbers. The system most often used today is based on the original Hindu and was brought to Europe by Arab traders. Its place-value system, in which the position of a numeral determines its value, made it easier to work than the Roman system. Each move to the left makes the number's value ten times greater. Only a small range of symbols is needed no matter how large the number, and calculations are therefore less cumbersome.

Babylonian										
Egyptian										
Greek	A	B	Γ	Δ	E	F	Z	H	Θ	I
Roman	I	II	III	IV	V	VI	VII	VIII	IX	X
Ancient Chinese										
Maya										
Hindu										
Arabic/European 15th century										
Modern Arabic/European	1	2	3	4	5	6	7	8	9	10	0
Digits designed for computer printing										

number of the *Herald.* **8. a.** One of the separate offerings in a program of music: *A Chopin sonata was the second number.* **b.** A song or piece of instrumental music: *sang several popular numbers.* **c.** Any self-contained item within a larger piece of music, such as an aria in an opera. **d.** One of the separate performances in a show: *the dance number in the second act.* **9.** *Informal.* A person or thing singled out from a group for some characteristic; especially: **a.** A woman: *a cute little number.* **b.** An item of merchandise, especially of clothing: *These are the fall numbers.* **10.** *Informal.* A means or circumstance that allows one to gain profit or advantage: *has a nice little number with a generous expense account.* **11.** A usually exclusive group of people: *He is one of the president's number.* **12.** *Usually* **numbers.** Strength or superiority based on quantity: *There's safety in numbers.* **13.** *Grammar.* The indication, as by inflection, of the singularity, duality, or plurality of a linguistic form. **14. a.** **numbers.** Metrical periods or feet; verses: *the melodious numbers of our old poets.* **b.** Measured rhythm in verse. **15. numbers.** Musical periods or measures. **16. numbers.** A kind of lottery in which bets are made on an unpredictable number, such as a daily stock-exchange figure. **—a number of.** A considerable, indefinite quantity of. **—See** Usage note below. **—any number of.** A large, indefinite quantity of; numerous. **—by the numbers. 1.** *Military.* Step by step, as consecutive numbers are called out. **2.** In a mechanical or excessively regulated manner: *runs his department by the numbers.* **—get** (or **have**) **someone's number.** *Informal.* To determine or know someone's real character or motives. **—one's number is up.** *Informal.* One is, or is soon to be, in trouble, defeated, or dead. **—without** (or **beyond**) **number.** In a quantity too great to be counted: *worlds without number.* **~v. numbered, -bering, -bers.** *—tr.* **1.** To total in number or amount; add up to: *The class numbers 20 students.* **2.** To count or determine the number or amount of. **3.** To include in a group or category: *She was numbered among the lost.* **4.** To mention one by one; enumerate. **5.** To assign a number to. **6.** To limit or restrict in number: *The days of her life are numbered.* *—intr.* **1.** To count or call out numbers: *numbering to ten.* **2.** To constitute a group or number: *The applicants numbered in the thousands.* [Middle English *n(o)umbre,* from Old French *nombre,* from Latin *numerus.*] **—num·ber·er** *n.*

Usage: When preceded by *the,* **number** takes a singular verb: *The number of people in the area is small.* When preceded by *a,* it takes a plural verb: *A number of people have left the area.*
number crunching *n. Informal.* Complex arithmetical calculations, especially as done by computers.
num·ber·less (nŭm′bər-lĭs) *adj.* **1.** Innumerable; countless. **2.** Not consisting of or concerned with numbers; lacking a number. **—See** Synonyms at **infinite.**
number one *n. Informal.* **1.** One's own interests; oneself: *He looks out only for number one.* **2.** The first or most important: *Our team is number one.* **—number one** *adj.*
Num·bers (nŭm′bərz) *n. Used with a singular verb. Abbr.* **Num.** The fourth book of the Old Testament, containing the two censuses of the Israelites after the Exodus.
number theory *n. Mathematics.* The study of integers and the relationships between them.
numb·fish (nŭm′fĭsh′) *n., pl.* **-fishes** or collectively **numbfish.** A fish, the **electric ray** (*see*).
num·bles (nŭm′bəlz) *pl.n. Archaic.* Entrails, especially of a deer, used for food. Also called "umbles." [Middle English, from Old French *nomble(s),* thigh muscle of deer or other game, from Latin *lumbulus,* diminutive of *lumbus,* loin.]
numbskull. Variant of **numskull.**
num·dah (nŭm′də) *n.* Also **num·nah** (-nə). **1.** A coarse felt made in India. **2.** An article made from this felt, especially an embroidered rug. [Urdu *namdā,* from Persian *namad,* carpet.]
nu·men (nōō′mən, nyōō′-) *n., pl.* **numina** (nōō′mə-nə, nyōō′-). **1.** The presiding divinity or spirit of a place. **2.** The spirit believed by animists to inhabit certain natural objects. **3.** Creative energy regarded as a guiding genius or demon dwelling within one. [Latin *nūmen,* "a nod," hence "command," divine power, deity.]
nu·mer·a·ble (nōō′mər-ə-bəl, nyōō′-) *adj.* Capable of being counted; countable. [Latin *numerabilis,* from *numerāre,* to number, count, from *numerus,* NUMBER.]
nu·mer·a·cy (nōō′mər-ə-sē, nyōō′-) *n.* The condition or quality of being numerate. Compare **literacy.** [NUMER(ATE) + -CY.]
nu·mer·al (nōō′mər-əl, nyōō′-) *n. Abbr.* **num.** A symbol, such as a letter or figure used alone or in a group to represent a number. See **Arabic numeral, Roman numeral.**
~adj. **1.** Of, pertaining to, or expressing numbers. **2.** Consisting of numbers. [Old French *numeral,* from Latin *numerālis,* from Latin *numerus,* NUMBER.] **—nu′mer·al·ly** *adv.*
nu·mer·ar·y (nōō′mə-rĕr′ē, nyōō′-) *adj.* Of or pertaining to a number or numbers. [Medieval Latin *numerārius,* from Latin *numerus,* NUMBER.]
nu·mer·ate (nōō′mər-ĭt, nyōō′-) *adj.* Familiar with the basic principles of mathematics, especially arithmetic.
~tr.v. (nōō′mə-rāt′, nyōō′-) **numerated, -ating, -ates. 1.** To enumerate; number; reckon. **2.** To read (numerals). [Latin *numerāre,* to number, count, from *numerus,* NUMBER.]
nu·mer·a·tion (nōō′mə-rā′shən, nyōō′-) *n.* **1.** The act or process of counting by means of reading, writing, or naming numbers. **2.** A system of numbering or of reading numbers. **—nu·mer·a·tive** (nōō′-mə-rā′tĭv, -mər-ə-, nyōō′-) *adj.*

nu·mer·a·tor (nōō′mə-rā′tər, nyōō′-) *n.* **1.** *Mathematics.* **a.** The expression written above the line in a common fraction. Compare **denominator.** **b.** An expression to be divided by another; the dividend. **2.** One that numbers; an enumerator.
nu·mer·ic (nōō-mĕr′ĭk, nyōō-) *n.* A number or numeral.
~adj. Variant of **numerical.** [Medieval Latin *numericus,* from Latin *numerus,* NUMBER.]
nu·mer·i·cal (nōō-mĕr′ĭ-kəl, nyōō-) *adj.* Also **numeric. 1.** Of or pertaining to a number or series of numbers; *numerical order.* **2.** Designating number or a number: *a numerical symbol.* **3.** Expressed in numbers: *numerical strength.* **4.** Represented by a number or numbers rather than by letter or symbol. [Medieval Latin *numericus,* from Latin *numerus,* NUMBER.] **—nu·mer·i·cal·ly** *adv.*
numerical taxonomy *n.* The branch of taxonomy that assesses quantitatively the relationships between organisms.
numerical value *n. Mathematics.* The absolute value of a number, regardless of its sign. The numerical values of −9 and +9 are equal.
nu·mer·ol·o·gy (nōō′mə-rŏl′ə-jē, nyōō′-) *n.* The study of the occult meanings of numbers and of their supposed influence on human fate. [Latin *numerus,* NUMBER + -LOGY.] **—nu·mer·o·log·i·cal** (nōō′mər-ə-lŏj′ĭ-kəl, nyōō′-) *adj.* **—nu·mer·ol·o·gist** *n.*
nu·mer·ous (nōō′mər-əs, nyōō′-) *adj.* **1.** Consisting of many persons or things: *a numerous collection.* **2.** Many: *numerous books.* [Latin *numerōsus,* from *numerus,* NUMBER.] **—nu·mer·ous·ly** *adv.* **—nu·mer·ous·ness** *n.*
Nu·mid·i·a (nōō-mĭd′ē-ə, nyōō′-). Ancient country of northern Africa, roughly corresponding to modern Algeria. It was part of the Carthaginian empire before the Punic Wars, but with the peace of 201 B.C., Numidia emerged as a separate kingdom under the rule of Masinissa. Its independence lasted until Juba I sided with Pompey in the Roman civil war; after Julius Caesar's victory (46 B.C.), it was absorbed into the Roman empire. **—Nu·mid·i·an** *adj. & n.*
nu·mi·na. Plural of **numen.**
nu·mi·nous (nōō′mə-nəs, nyōō′-) *adj.* **1.** Of or pertaining to a numen. **2.** Spiritually elevated or elevating; mysterious and awe-inspiring.
~n. The presence or revelation of a numen. Used with *the.* [Latin *nūmen* (stem *nūmin-*), NUMEN.]
nu·mis·mat·ics (nōō′mĭz-măt′ĭks, -mĭs′, nyōō′-) *n. Used with a singular verb.* The study and collection of coins, paper money, and medals. Also called "numismatology." [From *numismatic* (adjective), from French *numismatique,* from Latin *numisma,* a coin, from Greek *nomisma,* usage, current coin, from *nomizein,* to have in use, from *nomos,* custom.] **—nu·mis·mat·ic** *adj.* **—nu·mis·ma·tist** (nōō-mĭz′mə-tĭst, -mĭs′-, -nyōō′-) *n.*
nu·mis·ma·tol·o·gy (nōō′mĭz′mə-tŏl′ə-jē, -mĭs′-, nyōō′-) *n.* Numismatics.
num·ma·ry (nŭm′ə-rē) *adj.* Of or pertaining to coins. [Latin *nummārius,* from *nummus,* coin.]
num·mu·lar (nŭm′yə-lər) *adj.* Shaped like a coin; circular. [French *nummulaire,* from Latin *nummulus,* diminutive of *nummus,* a coin, "currency," probably from Greek *nomimos,* customary, legal, from *nomos,* custom.]
num·mu·lite (nŭm′yə-līt′) *n.* Any extinct protozoan of the family Nummulitidae. They were chiefly marine foraminifers characterized by a coin-shaped shell closely coiled and divided into chambers. [New Latin *Nummulites* (genus name) : Latin *nummulus,* coin (see **nummular**) + -ites, -ITE.] **—num·mu·lit·ic** (nŭm′yə-lĭt′ĭk) *adj.*
numnah. Variant of **numdah.**
num·skull, numb·skull (nŭm′skŭl′) *n.* A stupid person; a blockhead. [NUMB + SKULL.]
nun¹ (nŭn) *n.* **1.** A woman who belongs to a religious order devoted to religious service or meditation, usually under vows of poverty, chastity, and obedience, as in the Roman Catholic, Anglican, and Orthodox churches. **2.** Any of various birds, especially one of a breed of pigeons having a tuft of feathers on its head. [Middle English *nunne, nun, nonne,* from Old English *nunne* and Old French *nonne,* both from Medieval Latin *nonna,* nun (originally a respectful form of address to old women).]
nun² (nōōn) *n.* **1.** The 14th letter of the Hebrew alphabet. **2.** The 25th letter of the Arabic alphabet. **3.** The consonant sound represented by either of these letters. See feature at **alphabet.** [Hebrew and Arabic *nūn,* akin to NU.]
nun·a·tak (nŭn′ə-tăk′) *n.* An isolated mountain peak or hill that projects through the surface of surrounding glacial ice or snow. [Eskimo.]
nun buoy (nŭn) *n.* A conical buoy, painted red, marking the right side of a channel leading into a harbor. [From obsolete *nun,* child's spinning top.]
Nunc Di·mit·tis (nŭngk′ dĭ-mĭt′ĭs, nōōngk′) *n.* **1.** The canticle of Simeon, beginning "*Nunc dimittis servum tuum*" ("Now lettest thou thy servant depart"). Luke 2:29-32. **2.** A musical setting of this. **3. nunc dimittis.** Permission to depart; a dismissal. [Latin.]
nun·ci·a·ture (nŭn′sē-ə-choor′, nōōn′-) *n.* The office or term of a nuncio. [Italian *nunciatura,* from *nuncio,* NUNCIO.]
nun·ci·o (nŭn′sē-ō, nōōn′-) *n., pl.* **-os.** An ambassador from the pope. [Italian, from Latin *nūntius,* messenger.]
nun·cle (nŭng′kəl) *n. Archaic & Regional.* An uncle. [From *an uncle.*]
nun·cu·pa·tive (nŭng′kyə-pā′tĭv, nŭng-kyōō′pə-tĭv) *adj. Law.* Designating a will delivered orally to witnesses rather than written. [Medieval Latin *nūncupātīvus,* from Latin *nūncupāre,* to call by name, name one's heirs : *nōmen,* name + *capere,* to take.]

nuthatch *Sitta europaea, the nuthatch, is one of the few birds that regularly climb down trees head first. It gets its name from its habit of wedging nuts in the bark of a tree and using its bill as a hatchet to split them open and get at the kernel.*

nutmeg *The aromatic spice used in cooking is made from the fruit of the nutmeg tree,* Myristica fragrans, *that is native to the Molucca Islands of Indonesia and also grown in the West Indies. The nutmeg is the kernel of the tree's red and black seeds, and the seeds are contained in the fleshy fruit that splits open naturally when ripe (above). The seeds' waxy red coating is dried to produce another spice, mace.*

Nun·ea·ton (nŭn-ēt′n). Manufacturing town in Warwickshire, central England. It was the birthplace of the novelist George Eliot. It derives its name from the local 12th-century nunnery.

nun·ner·y (nŭn′ə-rē) *n., pl.* **-ies.** A community of nuns or the building or buildings in which they live.

nup·tial (nŭp′shəl, -chəl) *adj.* **1.** Of or pertaining to marriage or the wedding ceremony. **2.** *Zoology.* Of or at the time of mating: *the nuptial flight of ants.*
~*n. Usually* **nuptials.** A wedding ceremony. —See Synonyms at **marriage.** [Latin *nuptiālis,* from *nuptiae,* wedding, from *nūbere* (past participle *nuptus*), to take a husband.] **—nup·tial·ly** *adv.*

Nu·rem·berg (no͝or′əm-bûrg′, nyo͝or′-). *German* **Nürn·berg** (no͝orn′-bĕrg′, nyo͝orn′-). City in Bavaria, southern West Germany, on the Pegnitz River. It dates from the 11th century. From 1933–38 the Nazis held their annual party congresses here, and in 1945–46 it was the site of the trials of the Nazi war criminals.

Nu·re·yev (no͞o-rā′ĕf, no͝or′ĭ-yĕv′), **Rudolf Hametovich** (1938–). Russian-born ballet dancer and choreographer. With the Kirov Ballet of Leningrad until his defection to the United Kingdom (1961), he joined the Royal Ballet and became the most celebrated male dancer of his generation. His association with Margot Fonteyn is remembered as one of the great partnerships of classical ballet. He became an Austrian citizen in 1982 and is now director of the Paris Opera Ballet Company.

nurse (nûrs) *n.* **1.** A person trained to care for the sick or disabled. See **registered nurse, licensed practical nurse. 2.** Especially formerly, a woman employed to take care of another's children; a nursemaid. **3.** A woman employed to suckle another's child; a wet nurse. **4.** The state of being nursed: *The baby was put out to nurse.* **5.** That which fosters some quality or condition: *Leisure is the nurse of culture.* **6.** A worker ant or bee that cares for the young in the insect colony. **7.** A mature tree that shields a younger or newly planted tree from the elements.
~*v.* **nursed, nursing, nurses.** *—tr.* **1.** To feed (a child) at the breast; suckle. **2.** To care for or tend (a child or invalid). **3.** To try to cure or treat: *to nurse a cough.* **4.** To take special care of; foster; cultivate: *She nursed her business through the depression.* **5.** To keep in touch and foster relations with for one's own advantage. **6.** To harbor or bear privately in the mind: *nursing a grudge.* **7.** To hold or clasp carefully or soothingly: *He nursed his bruised knee.* **8.** To sit near, as if taking care of (a fire). **9.** To use sparingly so as to conserve. **10.** To consume slowly: *nursed one drink all evening.* **11.** In billiards, to keep (the balls) together so as to make a series of cannons. *—intr.* **1.** To take nourishment from the breast; suckle. **2.** To feed a child from the breast. **3.** To serve as a nurse. [Middle English *norse, nurse,* from Old French *norrice,* from Late Latin *nūtrīcia,* from *nūtrīcius,* adjective of *nūtrix,* a nurse.] **—nurs·er** *n.*

nurse hound *n.* A type of **dogfish** *(see).*

nurseling. Variant of **nursling.**

nurse·maid (nûrs′mād′) *n.* Also **nurs·er·y·maid** (nûr′sər-ē-mād′, nûrs′rē-) A girl or woman employed to take care of children.

nurs·er·y (nûr′sə-rē, nûrs′rē) *n., pl.* **-ies. 1.** A building, room, or area set apart for the use of young children. **2.** A nursery school. **3.** A place where plants are grown for sale, transplanting, or experimentation. **4.** Any place in which something is produced or developed. **5.** In billiards, a series of cannons made when the three balls are adjacent to a cushion. In this sense, also called "nursery cannon." [Middle English *norserie,* from *norse,* NURSE.]

nurs·er·y·man (nûr′sə-rē-mən, nûrs′rē-) *n., pl.* **-men** (-mĭn). A man who owns or works in a nursery for plants.

nursery rhyme *n.* A short, traditional rhymed poem or song for children.

nursery school *n.* A school for children who are not old enough to attend kindergarten. Also called "nursery."

nursery slopes *pl.n.* The lower, gentle ski slopes used by those still learning to ski.

nursery stakes *pl.n. Used with a singular or plural verb.* A horse race for two-year-olds.

nurse shark *n.* Any of various large sharks of the family Orectolobidae, such as *Ginglymostoma cirratum,* a scavenging shark found in the Atlantic. [Middle English *nusse fisshe* (later altered through influence of *nurse*), perhaps from mistaken division of *a nuss* for *an huss* (fish), from *huss*†, shark, dogfish.]

nurs·ing home (nûr′sĭng) *n.* A private hospital for the care of the aged or chronically ill.

nursing mother *n.* A woman who is breastfeeding her child.

nurs·ling, nurse·ling (nûrs′lĭng) *n.* **1.** A nursing infant or young animal. **2.** A carefully nurtured person or thing.

nur·tur·ance (nûr′chər-əns) *n.* The providing of loving care and attention. **—nur·tur·ant** *adj.*

nur·ture (nûr′chər) *n.* **1.** Anything that nourishes; sustenance; food. **2.** The act of promoting development or growth; upbringing; training. **3.** *Biology.* The sum of environmental influences and conditions acting upon an organism and partly determining its structure or behavior.
~*tr.v.* **nurtured, -turing, -tures. 1.** To nourish; feed. **2.** To educate or train. **3.** To promote the growth or development of; foster. [Middle English *norture, nurture,* from Old French *nour(e)ture,* from Late Latin *nūtrītūra,* a feeding, from Latin *nūtrīre,* to feed.] **—nur·tur·er** *n.*

nut (nŭt) *n.* **1. a.** A hard-shelled, solid-textured, one-seeded fruit that does not split open, such as an acorn or a hazelnut. **b.** Any seed borne in a fruit having a hard shell, such as the peanut or almond. **c.** The kernel of any of these. **2.** *Informal.* Any difficult person, endeavor, or problem. Used chiefly in the phrase *a hard* or *tough nut to crack.* **3.** *Slang.* The head. **4.** *Slang.* An eccentric, fanciful, or deranged person. **5.** *Slang.* An enthusiast; a buff: *a chess nut.* **6. a.** A ridge of wood at the top of the fingerboard or neck of stringed instruments, over which the strings pass. **b.** A device at the lower end of the bow of a violin or similar instrument, used for adjusting the hairs. **7.** A small block of metal or wood having a central threaded hole, designed to fit around and secure a bolt or screw. **8.** Any small piece of a substance, as of coal or butter. **9.** Complete operating expenses, as of a theatrical production. **—off one's nut.** *Slang.* Crazy; mad. See **nuts.**
~*intr.v.* **nutted, nutting, nuts.** To gather or search for nuts. [Middle English *note, nute,* Old English *hnutu.*]

nu·tant (no͞ot′ənt, nyo͞o′-) *adj. Botany.* Pointing downward; drooping. Said of flowers. [Latin *nutāns* (stem *nutant-*), present participle of *nutāre,* to nod.]

nu·ta·tion (no͞o-tā′shən, nyo͞o-) *n.* **1.** A nodding of the head. **2.** *Astronomy.* A small periodic motion of the celestial pole of the earth with respect to the pole of the ecliptic. **3.** *Botany.* A spiral growth movement in the stems of certain plants, especially climbers, caused by differential growth rates in the stem. [Latin *nūtātiō* (stem *nūtātiōn-*), from *nūtāre,* frequentative of *nuere* (unattested), to nod.] **—nu·ta·tion·al** *adj.*

nut-brown (nŭt′broun′) *n.* A rich reddish brown color. **—nut-brown** *adj.*

nut·case (nŭt′kās′) *n. Slang.* A deranged or very stupid person.

nut·crack·er (nŭt′krăk′ər) *n.* **1.** An implement used to crack nuts, typically consisting of two hinged metal levers between which the nut is squeezed. **2. a.** A bird, *Nucifraga caryocatactes,* of northern Eurasia. **b.** A bird, *N. columbianus,* of western North America. **c.** A bird, the nuthatch.

nut·gall (nŭt′gôl′) *n.* A nutlike swelling produced on an oak or other tree by certain parasitic wasps. Also called "gallnut."

nut·hatch (nŭt′hăch′) *n.* Any of several small birds of the family Sittidae, having long, sharp bills and noted for their ability to maneuver on tree trunks and branches. Also called "nutcracker." [Middle English *notehache, nuthak,* "nut hatchet" (named from its habit of wedging nuts in bark and hacking them open) : *nute,* NUT + *hache,* ax, hatchet, from Old French, from Medieval Latin *hapia,* from Germanic *hapja* (unattested).]

nut·house (nŭt′hous′) *n. Slang.* A mental institution.

nut·let (nŭt′lĭt) *n.* **1.** A small nut. **2.** The stone in certain fruits, such as the peach or cherry. **3.** A hard, one-seeded portion of a schizocarpic fruit, such as the four parts making up fruits of the dead nettle family.

nut·meat (nŭt′mēt′) *n.* The edible kernel of a nut.

nut·meg (nŭt′mĕg′) *n.* **1.** An evergreen tree, *Myristica fragrans,* native to the East Indies and cultivated elsewhere in the tropics. **2.** The hard, aromatic seed of this tree, much used as a spice when grated or ground. See **mace. 3.** Grayish to moderate brown. [Middle English *notemugge, nutemuge,* from Old French *nois muscade,* from Vulgar Latin *nuce muscāta* (unattested), "musky nut" : Latin *nux,* nut + *muscus,* MUSK.] **—nut·meg** *adj.*

nut oil *n.* Oil obtained from nuts such as walnuts and hazelnuts and used in paints and varnishes.

nut·pick (nŭt′pĭk′) *n.* A small, sharp-pointed tool used for digging the meat from nuts.

nu·tri·a (no͞o′trē-ə, nyo͞o′-) *n.* **1.** A rodent, the **coypu** *(see).* **2.** The fur of the coypu, often dyed to resemble beaver. **3.** Olive gray. [Spanish *nutr(i)a,* nasalized variant of *lutra,* otter, from Latin *lutra.*] **—nu·tri·a** *adj.*

nu·tri·ent (no͞o′trē-ənt, nyo͞o′-) *n.* Something that nourishes; especially, a nourishing ingredient in a food, or the mineral substances absorbed by the roots of plants.
~*adj.* Having nutritive value; providing nourishment. [Latin *nūtriēns* (stem *nūtrient-*), present participle of *nūtrīre,* to nourish.]

nu·tri·ment (no͞o′trə-mənt, nyo͞o′-) *n.* **1.** Anything that nourishes; food. **2.** Anything that aids growth or development. [Latin *nūtrīmentum,* from *nūtrīre,* to nourish.] **—nu·tri·men·tal** (no͞o′trə-mĕn′-təl, nyo͞o′-) *adj.*

nu·tri·tion (no͞o-trĭsh′ən, nyo͞o-) *n.* **1.** The process of nourishing or being nourished; especially, the interrelated steps by which a living organism assimilates food and uses it for growth and for replacement of tissues. **2.** The study of the biochemistry and physiology of nutrient utilization in humans. [Old French, from Late Latin *nūtrītiō* (stem *nūtrītiōn-*), from Latin *nūtrīre,* to nourish.] **—nu·tri·tion·al** *adj.* **—nu·tri·tion·al·ly** *adv.*

nu·tri·tion·ist (no͞o-trĭsh′ən-ĭst, nyo͞o-) *n.* A person who specializes in the study of nutrition.

nu·tri·tious (no͞o-trĭsh′əs, nyo͞o-) *adj.* **1.** Providing nourishment; nourishing. **2.** Aiding the growth and development of a living organism. [Latin *nūtrītius,* from *nūtrix,* a nurse.] **—nu·tri·tious·ly** *adv.* **—nu·tri·tious·ness** *n.*

nu·tri·tive (no͞o′trə-tĭv, nyo͞o′-) *adj.* **1.** Promoting nutrition; nourishing. **2.** Of or pertaining to nutrition.
~*n.* A nutritious food. [Middle English *nutritif,* from Old French, from Late Latin *nūtrītīvus,* from Latin *nūtrīre,* to feed, nourish.] **—nu·tri·tive·ly** *adv.*

nuts (nŭts) *adj. Slang.* **1.** Crazy; insane. **2.** Extremely fond or enthusiastic: *She's nuts about opera.*
~*interj. Slang.* Used to express contempt, disappointment, defi-

ance, or emphatic refusal. [From NUT (in various senses).]

nuts and bolts *pl.n.* The basic working components or practical details.

nut·shell (nŭt′shĕl′) *n.* The shell enclosing the kernel of a nut. **—in a nutshell.** In concise or brief form; epitomized.

nut·ter[1] (nŭt′ər) *n.* A person who gathers nuts.

nutter[2] *n. British Slang.* A deranged or eccentric person. [From NUT (mad person).]

nut·ty (nŭt′ē) *adj.* **-tier, -tiest.** **1.** Containing or producing many nuts. **2.** Having a flavor or texture like that of nuts. **3.** *Slang.* Deranged; crazy. **4.** *Informal.* Ridiculous; silly: *a nutty idea.* **—nut·ti·ly** *adv.* **—nut·ti·ness** *n.*

Nuuk (nōōk). Formerly **Godt·håb** (gôt′hôb′, gŏt′-). Capital of Greenland, a port on the southwest coast of the country. Founded by the Danes (1721), it is a center for the fishing of cod and halibut.

nux vom·i·ca (nŭks′ vŏm′ĭ-kə) *n.* **1.** A tree, *Strychnos nux-vomica,* native to southeastern Asia, having poisonous seeds that are the source of strychnine, brucine, and a medicinal preparation. **2.** A seed of this tree. [Medieval Latin, "emetic nut" : Latin *nux,* nut + *vomica,* from Latin *vomere,* to VOMIT.]

nuz·zle (nŭz′əl) *v.* **-zled, -zling, -zles.** *—tr.* **1.** To rub or push against gently with or as if with the nose or snout. **2.** To uproot with the snout. *—intr.* **1.** To make rubbing or pressing motions with the nose or snout. **2.** To nestle or cuddle. [Earlier *nousle,* Middle English *noselen,* from *nose,* NOSE.]

NV Nevada (used with a Zip Code).

NW northwest; northwestern.

N.W. northwest; northwestern.

NWbN northwest by north.

NWbW northwest by west.

N.W.T. Northwest Territories.

NY New York (used with a Zip Code).

N.Y. New York.

N.Y.C. New York City.

nya·la (nyä′lə) *n., pl.* **-las** or collectively **nyala.** A large spiral-horned antelope, *Tragelaphus angasi,* native to southern Africa. Also called "inyala." [Venda, from Zulu *inxala.*]

Nyan·ja (nyăn′jə) *n., pl.* **-jas** or collectively **Nyanja.** **1.** A member of a central African people living mainly in Malawi. **2.** The Bantu language of this people, of the Niger-Congo family of languages. **—Nyan·ja** *adj.*

Nyasa, Lake. See **Lake Malawi.**

Nyasaland. See **Malawi.**

nyct-, nycti-, nycto- *prefix.* Indicates night or darkness; for example, **nyctophobia.**

nyc·ta·lo·pi·a (nĭk′tə-lō′pē-ə) *n.* **1.** Vision that is normal in daylight but abnormally weak when the light is dim. In this sense, also called "night blindness." Compare **hemeralopia.** **2.** The inability to see clearly except when the light is dim. Not in technical usage. [Late Latin *nyctalōpia,* from Latin *nyctalops,* night-blind, from Greek *nuktalōps* : *nux* (stem *nukt-*), night + *alaos*†, blind + *ōps,* eye.] **—nyc·ta·lo·pic** (nĭk′tə-lō′pĭk, -lŏp′ĭk) *adj.*

nyc·ti·nas·ty (nĭk′tə-năs′tē) *n.* The opening and closing of leaves and petals in response to changes of light and temperature. [Greek *nux* (stem *nukt-*), night + -NASTY.] **—nyc·ti·nas·tic** *adj.*

nyc·tit·ro·pism (nĭk-tĭt′rə-pĭz′əm) *n.* The tendency of the leaves or other parts of some plants to change their position at nightfall.

[Greek *nux* (stem *nukt-*), night + -TROPISM.] **—nyc·ti·tro·pic** (nĭk′tə-trō′pĭk, -trŏp′ĭk) *adj.*

nyc·to·pho·bi·a (nĭk′tə-fō′bē-ə) *n.* An abnormal fear of the dark or of night. **—nyc·to·pho·bic** *adj.*

Nye·re·re (nyĕ-râr′ē), **Dr. Julius Kambarage** (1922–). Tanzanian politician. After campaigning for Tanganyika's independence from the United Kingdom, he became its premier (1961) before taking office as president (1962) of the new independent republic. In 1964 he negotiated a union with Zanzibar to form the state of Tanzania.

ny·lon (nī′lŏn) *n.* **1.** Any of a family of high-strength, resilient, synthetic materials, the long-chain molecules of which contain the recurring amide group CONH. **2.** Cloth or thread made from nylon. **3. nylons.** Women's stockings made of nylon or a similar synthetic fabric. [Coined by the inventors, with *-on* by analogy with forms such as *rayon.*]

nymph (nĭmf) *n.* **1.** *Greek & Roman Mythology.* Any of numerous female nature spirits inhabiting and animistically representing features of nature, as woodlands, trees, and waters. **2.** *Poetic.* A beautiful young woman. **3.** *Zoology.* Any of the young of insects, such as the mayfly or dragonfly, that undergoes incomplete metamorphosis. Compare **pupa.** [Middle English *nimphe,* from Latin *nympha,* nymph, pupa, from Greek *numphē,* nymph, bride.] **—nymph·al** (nĭm′fəl), **nym·phe·an** (nĭm′fē-ən, nĭm-fē′ən) *adj.*

nym·phae (nĭm′fē) *pl.n. Singular* **nym·pha** (-fə). *Anatomy.* The **labia minora** *(see).* [New Latin, from Latin, NYMPH.]

nym·pha·lid (nĭm′fə-lĭd) *n.* Any of various medium to large butterflies of the family Nymphalidae, found worldwide and often brilliantly colored. The family includes the admirals, fritillaries, and tortoiseshells. [New Latin *Nymphalidae* (family) : *Nymphalis* (genus), from Latin *nymphālis,* "nymphal," from *nympha,* NYMPH + -IDAE.] **—nym·pha·lid** *adj.*

nym·phet (nĭm-fĕt′, nĭm′fĭt) *n.* **1.** A young nymph. **2.** A pubescent or prepubescent girl regarded as sexually desirable to adult men. [Old French *nymphette,* diminutive of *nymphe,* NYMPH.]

nym·pho (nĭm′fō) *n., pl.* **-phos.** *Slang.* A nymphomaniac.

nym·pho·lep·sy (nĭm′fə-lĕp′sē) *n., pl.* **-sies.** A frenzy induced by an obsession for something unattainable. [From NYMPHOLEPT.]

nym·pho·lept (nĭm′fə-lĕpt′) *n.* One in a state of nympholepsy. [Greek *numpholēptos,* "caught by nymphs" : *numphē,* NYMPH + *lēptos,* seized.] **—nym·pho·lept, nym·pho·lep·tic** *adj.*

nym·pho·ma·ni·a (nĭm′fə-mā′nē-ə) *n.* Abnormally strong sexual desire in a woman. Compare **satyriasis.** [New Latin : NYMPH + -MANIA.] **—nym·pho·ma·ni·ac** *n. & adj.* **—nym·pho·ma·ni·a·cal** (nĭm′fə-mə-nī′ə-kəl) *adj.*

Ny·norsk (nōō-nôrsk′) *n.* One of the two officially recognized and mutually intelligible forms of Norwegian, incorporating various dialects. Formerly called "Landsmål." Compare **Bokmål.** [Norwegian, "new Norwegian."]

NYP not yet published.

Nysa. See **Neisse.**

nys·tag·mus (nĭ-stăg′məs) *n. Pathology.* A rapid, involuntary movement of the eyeball. [New Latin, from Greek *nustagmos,* drowsiness, from *nustazein,* to be sleepy.] **—nys·tag·mic** *adj.*

nys·ta·tin (nĭs′tə-tĭn) *n.* An antibiotic derived from the bacterium *Streptomyces noursei,* used to treat various fungal infections, especially thrush. [From *New York State* (where it was developed) + -IN.]

N.Z. New Zealand.

PRONUNCIATION KEY

ă, pat; ā, pay; âr, care; ä, father, are; b, bib; ch, church; d, deed; ĕ, pet; ē, be; f, fife; g, gag; h, hat; hw, which; ĭ, pit; ī, pie; îr, pier; j, judge; k, kick; l, lid, needle; m, mum; n, no, sudden; ng, thing; ŏ, pot; ō, toe; ô, paw, for; oi, noise; ou, out; ŏŏ, book; ōō, boot; p, pop; r, roar; s, sauce; sh, ship, dish; t, tight; th, thin, path; *th*, this, bathe; ŭ, cut; ûr, fur; v, valve; w, with; y, yes; z, zebra, size; zh, vision; ə, about, item, edible, gallop, circus, peaceful

IN FOREIGN WORDS:

à, *Fr.* ami; œ, *Fr.* feu, *Ger.* schön; ü, *Fr.* tu, *Ger.* über; KH, *Ger.* ich, *Scot.* loch; N, *Fr.* bon; y′, *Fr.* Compiègne

STRESS MARKS:

Primary stress: ′
  in · cite′ (ĭn-sīt′)
Secondary stress: ′
  in′sight′ (ĭn′sīt′)

O

oasis *Palm trees and lush vegetation in an otherwise arid desert appear where underground water comes to the surface. Oases can be much larger than this one in Nigeria, and the water may be fed from hundreds of miles away.*

o, O (ō) *n., pl.* **o's** or **O's. 1.** The 15th letter of the modern English alphabet. See feature at **alphabet. 2.** Any of the speech sounds represented by this letter. **3.** A zero. **4.** Something shaped like the letter O. **5.** The 15th in a series; 14th when *J* is omitted. **6. O** A human blood type of the ABO group. See **ABO.**

o, O, o., O. *Note:* As an abbreviation or symbol, *o* may be a small or a capital letter, with or without a period. Established forms or those generally preferred precede the definition. When no form is given, all four forms are in general use in that sense. **1. O,** O. ocean. **2. o., O.** octavo. **3. O.** October (unofficial). **4. O.** Ohio (unofficial). **5. O, O.** old. **6. O, O.** order. **7. O** The symbol for the element oxygen. **8. o.** *Pharmacology.* pint [Latin *octarius*].

O (ō) *interj.* **1.** Used before the name of a person or thing being formally addressed: *O my people, what have I done unto thee?* (Micah 6:3). **2.** Used to express surprise or strong emotion: *O my goodness!*

> *Usage:* O and *oh* have separate functions. Except for infrequent use as a variant of *oh, O* is confined to direct address, in prayer and invocation, in literary and religious contexts *(O God on high! O mighty ocean!),* and to the exclamations *O dear!* and *O my!* In such use it is always dependent on the words that follow it; it is always capitalized and never followed directly by punctuation. The interjection *oh* is more independent. It can stand alone or as part of a sentence to express strong emotions or merely a reflective pause: *Oh! What a horse!* or *Oh, I see.* It is only capitalized when it is the first word of a sentence and is followed directly by a comma or, when the emphasis is strong, by an exclamation point.

o' (ə, ō) *prep.* A reduced form of the preposition *of.* Used especially in the phrase *o'clock* but also found in such terms as *will-o'-the-wisp* and *man-o'-war* and in numerous dialects.

O' (ō, ə) *prefix.* Indicates a descendant of. Used in various Irish surnames, such as *O'Connor, O'Malley, O'Reilly.* [Irish *ō,* grandson, descendant, from Old Irish *aue.*]

-o *suffix.* Used to form an informal, abbreviated, or slang variant or word; for example, **ammo, blotto, wino.** [Perhaps from *oh* (interjection).]

-o- *infix.* Used to connect word elements; for example, **acidophilic, meritocracy.** [Middle English, from Old French, from Latin, from Greek, thematic vowel of nouns and adjectives used in combination.]

oaf (ōf) *n.* **1.** A stupid or clumsy person. **2.** *Obsolete.* A deformed child supposedly substituted for a human one by elves; a changeling. [Earlier *ouph, aufe,* elf, goblin, from Old Norse *alfr.*] **—oaf·ish** *adj.* **—oaf·ish·ly** *adv.* **—oaf·ish·ness** *n.*

O·a·hu (ō-ä′hōō). Third-largest island of the state of Hawaii in the North Pacific. It is the most populous and highly developed of the islands, with an economy based on sugar and pineapple plantations and tourism. The important U.S. military installations on the island include Pearl Harbor, attacked by the Japanese (1941). Honolulu is the chief port and state capital.

oak (ōk) *n.* **1.** Any of various deciduous or evergreen trees or shrubs of the genus *Quercus,* having lobed leaves and bearing acorns as fruit. See **cork oak, durmast, holm oak. 2.** The durable wood of an oak tree. **3.** Any of various trees or shrubs resembling the oak, as the **poison oak** *(see).* **4.** Something, as furniture, made of oak wood. **5.** Any of various brown shades resembling that of oak wood. [Middle English *ok, ook,* Old English *āc,* from Germanic *aik-* (unattested).] **—oak** *adj.*

oak apple *n.* A harmless gall on oak trees, caused by the larva of a type of wasp. Also called "oak gall."

oak·en (ō′kən) *adj.* Made of oak wood.

oak fern *n.* Any of various ferns, especially *Dryopteris linnaeana,* having lobed fronds resembling oak leaves.

oak gall *n.* Oak apple.

Oak·land (ōk′lənd). City of western California, on the east side of San Francisco Bay. A port and rail terminus, it is connected with San Francisco by the San Francisco–Oakland Bay Bridge (completed 1936).

oak leaf cluster *n.* A decoration of bronze or silver oak leaves awarded to holders of various U.S. military medals in recognition of acts entitling them to a second decoration with the same medal.

Oak·ley (ōk′lē), **Annie,** born Phoebe Anne Oakley Mozee (1860-1926). U.S. sharpshooter. She was a star attraction of Buffalo Bill's Wild West Show.

Oak Ridge. City in eastern Tennessee. It was founded (1943) by the U.S. government around the plants set up to produce uranium and plutonium for nuclear bombs.

oa·kum (ō′kəm) *n.* Loose hemp or jute fiber, sometimes treated with tar, creosote, or asphalt. It is used for caulking seams in wooden ships and packing pipe joints. [Middle English *okum,* Old English *ācumba,* "off-combings" : *ā-,* off, away + *-cumba,* from *cemban,* to comb.]

oak wilt *n.* A disease of oak trees that is caused by a fungus, *Chalara quercina,* and that often results in wilting and dropping of leaves.

OAPC Office of Alien Property Custodian.

oar (ôr, ōr) *n.* **1.** A long, thin pole, usually wooden, with a blade at one end, used to row and, occasionally, to steer a boat. **2.** A person using an oar; oarsman. **3.** An implement for stirring, especially one used in brewing. **—put one's oar in.** To intrude impertinently; meddle. **—rest on one's oars.** To stop trying or working; take a rest.

~*v.* **oared, oaring, oars.** *—tr.* **1.** To propel with or as if with oars. **2.** To traverse with or as if with oars: *an hour to oar the strait.* *—intr.* To move forward by or as if by rowing. [Middle English *oor, or,* Old English *ār,* from Common Germanic *airo* (unattested).] **—oared** *adj.*

oar·fish (ôr′fĭsh′, ōr′-) *n., pl.* **-fishes** or collectively **oarfish.** A marine fish, *Regalecus glesne,* having a slender body up to 8 meters (26 feet) in length, a dorsal fin extending the entire body length, and red-tipped rays above the head.

oar·lock (ôr′lŏk′, ōr′-) *n.* A device, usually a U-shaped metal hoop on a swivel in the gunwale, that is used as a fulcrum to hold an oar in place during rowing.

oars·man (ôrz′mən, ōrz′-) *n., pl.* **-men** (-mĭn). A person who rows, especially an expert in rowing; a rower. [*Oar's,* possessive of OAR + MAN.]

oar·weed (ôr′wēd′, ōr′-) *n.* Any of various seaweeds of the family Laminariaceae, such as kelp. [From dialectal *oare, ore,* seaweed (from Middle English *ware,* Old English *wār*) + WEED.]

OAS Organization of American States.

o·a·sis (ō-ā′sĭs) *n., pl.* **-ses** (-sēz′). **1.** A fertile or green area in a desert, resulting from the presence of water. **2.** A place or situation preserved from surrounding unpleasantness; a refuge: *The library was an oasis of calm in the noisy building.* [Late Latin *oasis,* from Greek, probably from an Egyptian word akin to Coptic *ouahe,* oasis, "dwelling area."]

oast (ōst) *n.* **1.** A kiln for drying hops or malt or for drying and curing tobacco. **2.** An oasthouse. [Middle English *ost,* Old English *āst.*]

oast·house (ōst′hous′) *n.* A building containing hop-drying kilns and usually having a conical roof.

oat (ōt) *n.* **1.** *Often* **oats. a.** Any of several grasses of the genus *Avena;* especially, *A. sativa,* widely cultivated for its edible seeds. **b.** The seeds of the oat, used as a food and fodder. **2.** *Archaic.* A musical pipe made of an oat straw. **—feel one's oats.** *Informal.* **1.** To be joyous or frisky. **2.** To feel or act self-satisfied and important. **—sow one's oats.** To indulge in adventures and licentiousness during one's youth. [Old English *āte*† (plural *ātan*).] **—oat** *adj.*

oat·cake (ōt′kāk′) *n.* A flattened cake of baked oatmeal, eaten especially in Scotland and northern England.

oat·en (ōt′n) *adj.* Of, made of, or containing oats, oatmeal, or oat straw: *oaten fodder.*

Oates (ōts), **Joyce Carol** (1938–). U.S. novelist, short-story writer, and poet. Her third novel, *Them,* was awarded the National Book Award in 1969.

Oates, Titus (1649-1705). English clergyman and agitator. His allegations of a Roman Catholic conspiracy (the Popish Plot, 1678) to murder Charles II aroused public anti-Catholic hysteria and led to the arrest and execution of many Catholics and the passing of the 1678 Test Act excluding Catholics from Parliament. Oates was later discredited and imprisoned.

oat grass *n.* **1.** A grass of the genus *Arrhenatherum;* especially, *A. elatius,* common in meadows. **2.** Any of several oatlike grasses.

oath (ōth) *n., pl.* **oaths** (ōthz, ōths). **1. a.** A solemn, formal declaration or promise to fulfill a pledge, often calling upon God or a sacred object as witness. **b.** The words or formula of such a declaration or promise. **c.** Something that is promised or declared. **2.** An irreverent or blasphemous use of the name of God or something held sacred. **3.** An act or instance of cursing or swearing. —**on** (or **under**) **oath.** Bound by an oath. [Middle English *ooth,* Old English *āth,* from Germanic *aithaz* (unattested).]

oat·meal (ōt′mēl′) *n.* **1.** Meal made from oats; rolled or ground oats. **2.** A porridge made from rolled or ground oats. **3.** A grayish yellow to fawn. —**oat·meal** *adj.*

O.A.U. Organization of African Unity.

Oa·xa·ca (wə-hä′kə). City of southern Mexico, capital of Oaxaca state. It is a commercial and tourist center, with gardens and fine examples of colonial church architecture.

Ob (ŏb). River of Siberia, U.S.S.R., formed by the meeting of the Biya and Katun rivers, which rise in the Altai Mts. It flows north to the Arctic Ocean via the Gulf of Ob and Kara Sea.

ob– *prefix.* Indicates inverse shape or attachment; for example, **obcordate, obovate.** [In borrowed Latin compounds, *ob-* becomes *o-* before *m,* as in *omit, oc-* before *c,* as in *occlude, of-* before *f,* as in *offend, op-* before *p,* as in *oppose.* *Ob-* indicates: **1.** To, toward, as in **offer, obvert. 2.** Directed toward in a negative way, against, in opposition to, as in **opponent, obstacle. 3.** Opposite to, before, on, in front of, as in **obsess, obstetric. 4.** On account of, for, as in **obsecrate. 5.** In a certain direction, down, down upon, over, behind, as in **occasion, omit. 6.** Out of, away from, as in **obliterate. 7.** Intensified action, as in **obdurate, obtain.** Latin *ob-,* from the preposition *ob,* to, toward, in front of, on account of, against.]

ob. 1. incidentally [Latin *obiter*]. **2.** oboe. **3.** obstetric.

Obad. Obadiah (Old Testament).

O·ba·di·ah[1] (ō′bə-dī′ə). A Hebrew prophet.

Obadiah[2] *n.* **Abbr. Obad.** The book in the Old Testament written by Obadiah.

ob·bli·ga·to (ŏb′lĭ-gä′tō) *adj. Music.* Not to be left out; indispen-

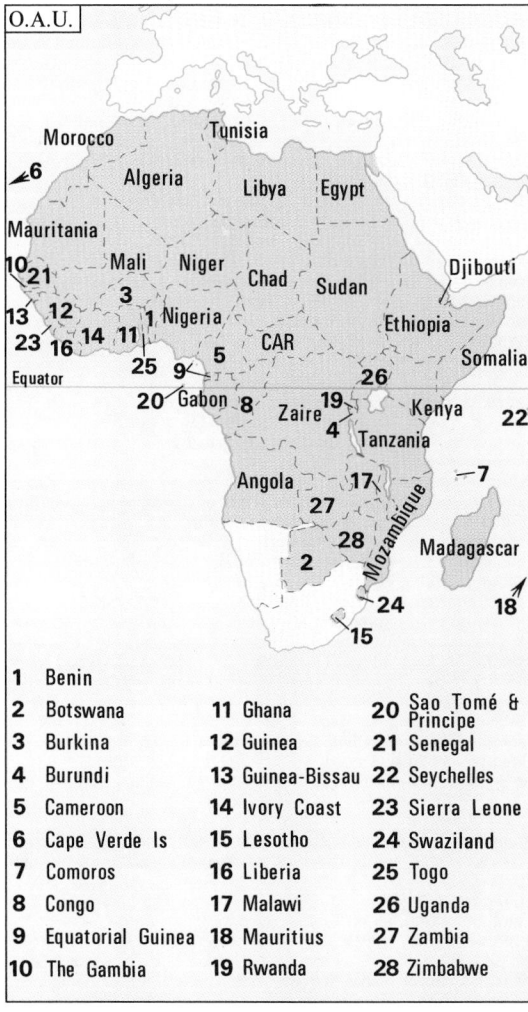

O.A.U.

Morocco
Tunisia
Algeria
Libya
Egypt
Mauritania
Mali
Niger
Chad
Sudan
Djibouti
Nigeria
CAR
Ethiopia
Somalia
Equator
Gabon
Zaire
Kenya
Tanzania
Mozambique
Angola
Malawi
Madagascar
Zambia

1	Benin				
2	Botswana	11	Ghana	20	Sao Tomé & Principe
3	Burkina	12	Guinea	21	Senegal
4	Burundi	13	Guinea-Bissau	22	Seychelles
5	Cameroon	14	Ivory Coast	23	Sierra Leone
6	Cape Verde Is	15	Lesotho	24	Swaziland
7	Comoros	16	Liberia	25	Togo
8	Congo	17	Malawi	26	Uganda
9	Equatorial Guinea	18	Mauritius	27	Zambia
10	The Gambia	19	Rwanda	28	Zimbabwe

sable. Said of an accompaniment that is an integral part of a piece. ~*n., pl.* **obbligatos** or **-ti** (-tē). *Music.* An obbligato musical accompaniment. [Italian, past participle of *obbligare,* to obligate, from Latin *obligāre,* to OBLIGE.]

ob·con·ic (ŏb-kŏn′ĭk) *adj. Botany.* Also **ob·con·i·cal** (-ĭ-kəl). Cone-shaped, with the tapering end at the point of attachment: *an obconic fruit.*

ob·cor·date (ŏb-kôr′dāt′) *adj. Botany.* Heart-shaped, with the tapering end at the point of attachment: *an obcordate leaf.*

ob·du·ra·cy (ŏb′dōō-rə-sē, ŏb′dyōō-) *n.* The state or quality of being obdurate.

ob·du·rate (ŏb′dōō-rĭt, ŏb′dyōō-) *adj.* **1.** Hardened against persuasion or feeling; intractable or hardhearted: *an obdurate judge.* **2.** Hardened against good or moral influence; stubbornly impenitent: *"obdurate conscience of the old sinner"* (Sir Walter Scott). —See Synonyms at **inflexible.** [Middle English *obdurat,* from Latin *obdūrātus,* past participle of *obdūrāre,* to harden : *ob-* (intensive) + *dūrāre,* to harden, from *dūrus,* hard.] —**ob·du·rate·ly** *adv.* —**ob·du·rate·ness** *n.*

O.B.E. 1. Officer (of the Order) of the British Empire. **2.** Order of the British Empire.

o·be·ah (ō′bē-ə) *n.* Also **o·bi** (ō′bē). **1.** A form of religious belief, probably of African origin, involving witchcraft or sorcery and practiced especially in the West Indies. **2.** A fetish or object used in the practice of obeah. [Of West African origin.]

o·be·di·ence (ō-bē′dē-əns) *n.* **1. a.** The quality or condition of being obedient. **b.** The act of obeying. **2. a.** A sphere of ecclesiastical authority. **b.** A group of persons under such authority. **3.** An office or duty in a convent or monastery.

o·be·di·ent (ō-bē′dē-ənt) *adj.* **1.** Obeying or carrying out a request, command, or instruction. **2.** Submissive to control; dutiful. [Middle English, from Old French, from Latin *oboediēns* (stem *oboedient-*), present participle of *oboedīre,* to OBEY.] —**o·be·di·ent·ly** *adv.*
    Synonyms: acquiescent, amenable, compliant, docile, dutiful, servile, tractable.

o·be·di·en·tia·ry (ō-bē′dē-ĕn′shə-rē) *n., pl.* **-ries.** A holder of an office subordinate to that of the superior in a convent or monastery. [Medieval Latin *obedientiarius,* from *obedient.* See **obedient, -ary.**]

o·bei·sance (ō-bā′səns, ō-bē′-) *n.* **1.** A gesture or movement of the body expressing reverence or respect, as a bow or curtsy. **2.** An attitude associated with this gesture, as deference or homage. [Middle English *obeisaunce,* from Old French *obeissance,* from *obeissant,* present participle of *obeir,* to OBEY.] —**o·bei·sant** *adj.*

ob·e·lisk (ŏb′ə-lĭsk′, ō′bə-) *n.* **1. a.** A tall, four-sided shaft of stone, usually monolithic and tapering, that rises to a pyramidal point. **b.** A monument in this shape, especially one in ancient Egypt. **2.** *Printing.* The dagger sign (†), used especially as a reference mark. In this dictionary it refers to an etymological footnote indicating that the word or form so marked is of obscure origin. In this sense, also called "obelus," "dagger." [Old French *obelisque,* from Latin *obeliscus,* from Greek *obeliskos,* diminutive of *obelos,* spit, OBELUS.] —**ob·e·lis·cal** (ŏb′ə-lĭs′kəl, ō′bə-) *adj.* —**ob·e·lis·koid** (ŏb′ə-lĭs′koid′) *adj.*

ob·e·lize (ŏb′ə-līz′) *tr.v.* **-lized, -lizing, -lizes.** To mark or annotate with an obelus. [Greek *obelizein,* from OBELUS.]

ob·e·lus (ŏb′ə-ləs) *n., pl.* **-li** (-lī′). **1.** A mark (— or ÷) used in ancient manuscripts to indicate a doubtful or spurious passage. **2.** *Printing.* An obelisk. [Late Latin *obelus,* from Greek *obelos†,* spit, obelisk.]

O·ber·am·mer·gau (ō′bər-ä″mər-gou′). Town in Bavaria, southwestern West Germany. It is the site of Passion plays, held every 10 years since 1634 in thanksgiving for deliverance from the Black Death (1633).

O·ber·on (ō′bə-rŏn′, ō′bər-ən). In medieval folklore, the king of the fairies, husband of Titania. [French, from Old French *Auberon,* of Frankish origin; akin to Old High German *Alberich.*]

o·bese (ō-bēs′) *adj.* Extremely fat; unpleasantly overweight. —See Synonyms at **fat.** [Latin *obēsus,* "grown fat by eating," from past participle of *obedere,* to eat away : *ob-,* away + *edere,* to eat.] —**o·be·si·ty** (ō-bē′sə-tē), **o·bese·ness** *n.*

o·bey (ō-bā′) *v.* **obeyed, obeying, obeys.** —*tr.* **1.** To carry out or fulfill the command, order, or instruction of. **2.** To carry out or comply with (a command or request). **3.** To act in accordance with (one's own instincts or feelings). —*intr.* To behave obediently: *Docile children obey.* [Middle English *obeien,* from Old French *obeir,* from Latin *oboedīre,* "to listen to" : *ob-,* to, toward + *audīre,* to hear.] —**o·bey·er** *n.*

ob·fus·cate (ŏb′fə-skāt′, ŏb-fŭs′kāt′) *tr.v.* **-cated, -cating, -cates.** **1.** To confuse or make obscure; cloud: *His emotions obfuscated his judgment.* **2.** To bewilder or stupefy. **3.** To render indistinct or dim; darken: *The fog obfuscated the shore.* [Late Latin *obfuscāre,* to darken : *ob-* (intensive) + Latin *fuscāre,* to darken, from *fuscus,* dark.] —**ob·fus·ca·tion** *n.*

o·bi[1] (ō′bē) *n.* A wide sash, fastened at the back with a large flat bow, worn by women in Japan as a part of the traditional dress. [Japanese, "belt," "band," "sash."]

obi[2]. Variant of **obeah.**

O·bie (ō′bē) *n.* An award given annually for exceptional achievement in off-Broadway theater. [From O.B., abbreviation for OFF-BROADWAY.]

o·bit (ō′bĭt, ō-bĭt′) *n.* **1.** *Informal.* An obituary. **2.** *Archaic.* A memorial service.

o·bi·ter dic·tum (ō′bĭ-tər dĭk′təm) *n., pl.* **obiter dic·ta** (dĭk′tə).

1. *Law.* An opinion voiced by a judge that has only incidental bearing on the case in question and is therefore not binding. **2.** An incidental remark or observation; a passing comment. [Latin, "a statement in passing."]

o·bit·u·ar·y (ō-bĭch′o͞o-ĕr′ē) *n., pl.* **-ies.** *Abbr.* **obit.** A notice of a death, usually with a brief biography of the deceased. [Medieval Latin *obituārius,* (report) of death, from Latin *obitus,* death, from the past participle of *obīre,* to fall, die : *ob-,* down + *īre,* to go.] **—o·bit·u·ar·y** *adj.*

obj. **1.** *Grammar.* object; objective. **2.** objection.

ob·ject[1] (əb-jĕkt′) *v.* **-jected, -jecting, -jects.** *—intr.* **1.** To present a dissenting or opposing argument; raise an objection. Usually followed by *to: object to the testimony of a witness.* **2.** To be averse to or express disapproval of something. Usually followed by *to: object to modern materialism.* *—tr.* To put forward in or as a reason for, opposition; offer as criticism: *They objected that discipline was lacking.* [Middle English *objecten,* from Latin *objicere, obicere* (past participle *objectus*), to throw against, oppose : *ob-,* toward + *jacere,* to throw.] **—ob·jec·tor** *n.*

Synonyms: *complain, demur, dissent, expostulate, protest, remonstrate.*

ob·ject[2] (ŏb′jĭkt, -jĕkt′) *n.* **1.** Something perceptible by one or more of the senses, especially something that can be seen or felt; a material thing. **2.** *Philosophy.* Something intelligible or perceptible by the mind. **3.** A person or thing serving as a focus of attention, curiosity, discussion, feeling, thought, or action; especially, one that evokes ridicule or pity: *an object of contempt.* **4.** The purpose, aim, or goal of a specific action or effort: *the object of the game.* **5.** *Abbr.* **obj.** *Grammar.* **a.** A noun, pronoun, or noun phrase that receives or is affected by the action of a verb within a sentence. In *Mary hit Julia, Julia* is the object of the verb *hit.* **b.** A noun, pronoun, or noun phrase governed by a preposition. In *on television,* the noun *television* is the object of the preposition *on.* —See Synonyms at **intention.** **—no object.** *Informal.* Not an obstacle or hindrance: *Cost is no object.* [Middle English, from Latin *objectus,* "something thrown before or presented to (the mind)," from the past participle of *obicere,* to throw before or against, OBJECT (verb).]

object ball *n.* In billiards and pool, the ball that the striker hits or intends to hit first with the cue ball.

object glass *n.* A lens in an optical instrument, an **objective** *(see).*

ob·jec·ti·fy (əb-jĕk′tə-fī′) *tr.v.* **-fied, -fying, -fies.** **1.** To present (someone) as an object; depersonalize: *Pornography objectifies women.* **2.** To impart reality to; externalize or make objective. [From OBJECT (noun).] **—ob·jec·ti·fi·ca·tion** *n.*

ob·jec·tion (əb-jĕk′shən) *n. Abbr.* **obj.** **1.** An act of objecting. **2.** A statement or other expression offered in opposition. **3.** A reason or cause for expressing opposition or disagreement.

ob·jec·tion·a·ble (əb-jĕk′shə-nə-bəl) *adj.* Arousing disapproval; offensive: *objectionable behavior.* —See Synonyms at **offensive.** **—ob·jec·tion·a·bil·i·ty** *n.* **—ob·jec·tion·a·bly** *adv.*

ob·jec·tive (əb-jĕk′tĭv) *adj.* **1.** Of or having to do with a material object as distinguished from a mental concept, idea, or belief. **2.** Having actual existence or reality. **3. a.** Not influenced by emotion, surmise, or personal prejudice: *an objective critic.* **b.** Based on observable phenomena; presented factually: *an objective appraisal.* **4.** *Medicine.* Designating a symptom or condition perceived as a sign of disease by someone other than the person afflicted. **5.** *Grammar.* **a.** Of, pertaining to, or being the case of a noun or pronoun serving as the object of a verb or preposition. **b.** Of, pertaining to, or being a noun or pronoun used in such a case. Compare **subjective.** —See Synonyms at **fair.**

~n. **1.** Something that actually exists as distinguished from something thought or felt to exist. **2.** Something worked toward or striven for; a goal. **3.** *Abbr.* **obj.** *Grammar.* **a.** The objective case. **b.** A noun or pronoun in the objective case. **4. a.** The lens or lens system in a microscope or telescope that is closest to the object being viewed. **b.** A lens or lens system in a camera or projector that forms the image of the object. Also called "object glass," "object lens." —See Synonyms at **intention.** [Medieval Latin *objectīvus,* from Latin *objectus,* an OBJECT.] **—ob·jec·tive·ly** *adv.* **—ob·jec·tive·ness** *n.*

objective case *n. Grammar.* The case of a noun or pronoun when it is the object of a verb or preposition.

objective complement *n. Grammar.* A noun, noun phrase, or adjective serving as a complement to a verb and qualifying its direct object, as *secretary* in *They elected me secretary.*

objective correlative *n.* A set of circumstances or situation that objectifies or symbolizes an emotion, often used as a literary device to elicit a particular emotional response in the reader.

ob·jec·tiv·ism (əb-jĕk′tə-vĭz′əm) *n.* **1.** *Philosophy.* Any of several doctrines holding that all reality is objective and external to the mind and that knowledge is reliably based on observed objects and events. Compare **solipsism.** **2.** In art and literature, an emphasis on objective themes or subjects. **—ob·jec·tiv·ist** *n.* **—ob·jec·tiv·is·tic** (əb-jĕk′tə-vĭs′tĭk) *adj.*

ob·jec·tiv·i·ty (ŏb′jĕk-tĭv′ə-tē) *n.* **1.** The state, condition, or quality of being objective. **2.** External or material reality.

object language *n.* **1.** A language that is under discussion or being analyzed, especially when being discussed in a metalanguage. **2.** A **target language** *(see).*

object lens *n.* A lens in an optical instrument, an **objective** *(see).*

object lesson *n.* **1.** A lesson taught by using a material object. **2.** A practical illustration of a moral or principle.

object program *n.* A computer program transcribed into machine language by the compiler or assembler from the equivalent source program.

ob·jet d'art (ôb′zhā där′) *n., pl.* **objets d'art** *(pronounced as singular).* A usually small artifact valued for its artistic merit. [French, "object of art."]

objet trou·vé (tro͞o-vā′) *n., pl.* **objets trouvés** *(pronounced as singular).* An ordinary or commonplace object considered or presented as a work of art. [French, "found object."]

ob·jur·gate (ŏb′jər-gāt′, ŏb-jûr′-) *tr.v.* **-gated, -gating, -gates.** To scold or rebuke sharply; berate. [Latin *objurgāre,* "to bring a lawsuit against," chide : *ob-,* against + *jurgāre,* "to bring a lawsuit," rebuke, from *jūs* (stem *jūr-*), law + *agere,* to act, perform.] **—ob·jur·ga·tion** *n.* **—ob·jur·ga·to·ri·ly** (ŏb-jûr′gə-tôr′ə-lē, -tōr′ə-lē) *adv.* **—ob·jur·ga·to·ry** (ŏb-jûr′gə-tôr′ē, -tōr′ē) *adj.*

obl. **1.** oblique. **2.** oblong.

ob·lan·ce·o·late (ŏb-lăn′sē-ə-lāt′) *adj. Botany.* Broader and rounded at the apex and tapering at the base: *an oblanceolate leaf.*

o·blast (ô′bləst, ô′blăst′, ô′bläst′) *n.* A local administrative division in the Soviet Union. [Russian *oblast′,* from Old Church Slavonic : *ob-,* on + *vlast′,* power, administration.]

ob·late[1] (ŏb′lāt′, ō-blāt′) *adj.* **1.** Having the shape of a sphere; spheroidal. **2.** Having an equatorial diameter greater than the distance between poles; compressed along or flattened at the poles: *The earth is an oblate solid.* Compare **prolate.** [New Latin *oblatus,* "carried toward," stretched, from Latin *oblātus* (past participle of *obferre,* to bring to, offer) : *ob,* to, toward + *-lātus,* "carried."] **—ob·late·ly** *adv.* **—ob·late·ness** *n.*

ob·late[2] (ŏb′lāt′) *n.* **1.** A person who is dedicated to a religious life, but who has not taken formal vows. **2. Oblate.** *Roman Catholic Church.* A member of any of various religious communities for men or women. [Medieval Latin *oblātus,* "one offered (to God)," from Latin, past participle of *obferre,* to offer. See **oblate** (spheroidal).] **—ob·late** *adj.*

ob·la·tion (ə-blā′shən, ō-blā′-) *n.* **1.** The act of offering something, such as worship or thanksgiving, to a deity. **2. Oblation. a.** The act of offering the bread and wine of the Eucharist. **b.** Something that is offered, especially the bread and wine of the Eucharist. **3.** A charitable offering or gift. [Middle English *oblacioun,* from Old French *oblation,* from Medieval Latin *oblātiō* (stem *oblātiōn-*), from *oblātus,* OBLATE (noun).] **—ob·la·tion·al, ob·la·to·ry** (ŏb′lə-tôr′ē, -tōr′ē) *adj.*

ob·li·gate (ŏb′lə-gāt′) *tr.v.* **-gated, -gating, -gates.** **1.** To bind, compel, or constrain by a legal, moral, or social tie. **2.** To cause to be grateful or indebted; oblige. **3.** To commit (money, for example) in order to fulfill an obligation.

~adj. (-gĭt, -gāt′). **1.** *Biology.* Able to survive in only one kind of environment; obligatory. Said of parasites that cannot live independently of their hosts. Compare **facultative.** **2.** Absolutely indispensable; essential. **3.** *Obsolete.* Bound or constrained; obliged. [Latin *obligāre,* to OBLIGE.] **—ob·li·ga·ble** (ŏb′lə-gə-bəl) *adj.* **—ob·li·ga·tor** *n.*

ob·li·ga·tion (ŏb′lə-gā′shən) *n.* **1.** The act of binding oneself or state of being bound by a legal, moral, or social tie. **2. a.** A duty, contract, promise, or other legal, moral, or social requirement that compels one to follow or avoid a certain course of action. **b.** A course of action imposed by law, society, or conscience by which one is bound or restricted. **3.** The constraining power of a law, promise, contract, or sense of duty. **4.** *Law.* **a.** A legal agreement stipulating a specified payment or action, especially if the agreement also specifies the penalty for failure to comply. **b.** The document containing the terms of such an agreement. **5. a.** Something owed as payment or in return for a special service or favor. **b.** The service or favor for which one is indebted to another. **6.** The state, fact, or feeling of being indebted to another for a special service or favor received.

o·blig·a·to·ry (ə-blĭg′ə-tôr′ē, -tōr′ē, ŏb′lĭ-gə-) *adj.* **1.** Legally or morally constraining; binding. **2.** Of the nature of an obligation; compulsory: *Attendance is obligatory.* **3.** Imposing or recording an obligation: *a bill obligatory.* **4.** *Biology.* Restricted to one mode of life; obligate. **—o·blig·a·to·ri·ly** (ə-blĭg′ə-tôr′ə-lē, -tōr′ə-lē) *adv.*

o·blige (ə-blīj′) *v.* **obliged, obliging, obliges.** *—tr.* **1.** To cause to do or refrain from doing something by physical, legal, social, or moral means or by the force of circumstances: *was obliged to find work.* **2.** To give cause for indebtedness or gratitude: *They were obliged to him for his hospitality.* **3.** To gratify the wishes of; do a service or favor for: *He obliged us by arriving early.* *—intr.* To do a service or favor or perform a courtesy: *The pianist will oblige with an encore.* —See Synonyms at **force.** [Middle English *obligen,* from Old French *obliger,* from Latin *obligāre,* to tie to : *ob-,* to + *ligāre,* to bind.] **—o·blig·er** *n.*

ob·li·gee (ŏb′lə-jē′) *n.* **1.** A person who is under obligation to another. **2.** *Law.* A person to whom another is bound by contract or legal agreement.

o·blig·ing (ə-blī′jĭng) *adj.* Ready to do favors for others; accommodating, helpful, and considerate. **—o·blig·ing·ly** *adv.* **—o·blig·ing·ness** *n.*

ob·li·gor (ŏb′lĭ-gôr′, -jôr′) *n. Law.* A person who binds himself to another by contract or legal agreement.

o·blique (ō-blēk′, ə-blēk′) *adj. Abbr.* **obl.** **1. a.** Having a slanting or sloping direction, course, or position; inclined. **b.** In geometry, designating lines or planes that are neither parallel nor perpendicular. **2.** Indirect or evasive in execution, meaning, or expression; not straightforward. **3.** Devious, misleading, or dishonest: *oblique answers.* **4.** Not direct in descent; collateral. **5.** *Botany.* Having sides of unequal length or form: *an oblique leaf.* **6.** *Anatomy.* Inclined at an angle; not perpendicular or horizontal: *oblique muscles.* **7.** *Grammar.* Designating any noun case except the nominative or the vocative.

~n. **1.** Something that is oblique, such as a line, direction, or muscle. **2.** *Nautical.* The act of changing course by less than 90°. **3.** A **virgule** *(see).*

~adv. (ō-blīk′, ə-blīk′). *Military.* At an angle of 45°: *Right oblique, march!* [Middle English *oblike,* from Latin *oblīquus*†.] **—o·blique·ly** *adv.* **—o·blique·ness** *n.*

oblique angle *n.* An angle that is not a right angle; an acute or obtuse angle.

oblique triangle *n.* A triangle having no right angle.

o·bliq·ui·ty (ō-blĭk′wə-tē, ə-blĭk′-) *n., pl.* **-ties. 1.** The state, quality, or condition of being oblique. **2. a.** A deviation from a vertical or horizontal line, plane, position, or direction. **b.** The angle or extent of such a deviation. **3. a.** A mental deviation or aberration. **b.** Immoral conduct. **4. a.** Obscurity or indirectness in conduct or verbal expression. **b.** An obscure, cloudy statement. **5.** *Symbol* ε *Astronomy.* The angle at which the earth's axis is tilted from the vertical, equal to the angle between the ecliptic and the celestial equator. It varies regularly between extreme values, and the average value also changes with time; at present it is about 23°27′. [Middle English *obliquitee,* from Old French *obliquite,* from Latin *oblīquitas,* from *oblīquus,* OBLIQUE.] **—o·bliq·ui·tous** (ō-blĭk′wə-təs, ə-blĭk′-) *adj.*

o·blit·er·ate (ə-blĭt′ə-rāt′, ō-blĭt′-) *tr.v.* **-ated, -ating, -ates. 1.** To do away with completely; destroy so as to leave no trace: *The forest was obliterated by the building of the new town.* **2.** To wipe out, rub off, or obscure (writing or other markings). [Latin *obliterāre,* "to strike out words," erase : *ob-,* away from + *littera,* letter.] **—o·blit·er·a·tion** *n.* **—o·blit·er·a·tive** (ə-blĭt′ər-ə-tĭv, -ə-rā′tĭv, ō-blĭt′-) *adj.* **—o·blit·er·a·tor** *n.*

o·bliv·i·on (ə-blĭv′ē-ən) *n.* **1.** The state or quality of being completely forgotten. **2.** An act or an instance of forgetting or overlooking. **3.** The state of being completely unaware of oneself or one's surroundings: *drank myself into oblivion.* **4.** *Law.* **a.** Official overlooking of offenses. **b.** The remission of punishment for offenses; amnesty. [Middle English, from Old French, from Latin *oblīviō* (stem *oblīviōn-*), from *oblīvīscī,* to forget.]

o·bliv·i·ous (ə-blĭv′ē-əs) *adj.* **1.** Lacking all memory of something; forgetful. **2.** Lacking conscious awareness; unmindful. —See Synonyms at **forgetful. —o·bliv·i·ous·ly** *adv.* **—o·bliv·i·ous·ness** *n.*

Usage: The usual preposition following this word is *of*: *oblivious of the people around her,* though *to* is sometimes used, especially with inanimate nouns: *oblivious to the difficulties.* Purists have objected to the use of *oblivious* to mean "unaware," but this sense is now both common and widely accepted.

ob·long (ŏb′lông′, -lŏng′) *adj. Abbr.* **obl. 1.** Having a long dimension, especially having one of two perpendicular dimensions, such as length or width, greater than the other; elongated. **2.** Having the shape of or resembling a rectangle or an ellipse. **3.** *Botany.* Having a somewhat elongated form with approximately parallel sides: *an oblong leaf.*

~n. An object or figure, such as a rectangle, with an elongated shape. [Middle English *oblonge,* from Latin *oblongus* : *ob-* (intensive) + *longus,* long.]

ob·lo·quy (ŏb′lə-kwē) *n., pl.* **-quies. 1.** Abusively detractive language or utterance; condemnation. **2.** Ill repute or discredit, as that suffered by one subjected to obloquy. —See Synonyms at **disgrace.** [Middle English *obloqui,* from Late Latin *obloquium,* from Latin *obloquī,* to speak against, contradict : *ob-,* against + *loquī,* to speak.]

ob·nox·ious (ŏb-nŏk′shəs, əb-) *adj.* **1.** Highly disagreeable or offensive; odious. **2.** Exposed to harm, injury, or evil. **3.** *Archaic.* Deserving of or liable to censure or punishment; reprehensible. —See Synonyms at **hateful.** [Latin *obnoxiōsus,* injurious, from *obnoxius,* subject to harm : *ob-,* to + *noxa,* a hurt.] **—ob·nox·ious·ly** *adv.* **—ob·nox·ious·ness** *n.*

ob·nu·bi·late (ŏb-no͞o′bə-lāt′, ŏb-nyo͞o′-) *tr.v.* **-lated, -lating, -lates.** To darken with or as if with clouds or fog; obscure. [Latin *obnūbilare,* from *ob-,* in the way + *nubilāre,* to be cloudy, from *nubilus,* cloudy, from *nubes,* cloud.] **—ob·nu·bi·la·tion** *n.*

o·boe (ō′bō) *n. Abbr.* **ob. 1.** A slender woodwind musical instrument with a conical bore and a double-reed mouthpiece. It has a range of three octaves and a penetrating, poignant sound. **2.** A reed stop in an organ that produces a sound similar to that of an oboe. [Italian, from French *hautbois,* HAUTBOY.] **—o·bo·ist** *n.*

ob·ol (ŏb′əl, ō′bəl) *n.* Also **ob·o·lus** (ŏb′ə-ləs) *pl.* **-li** (-lī′). **1.** A silver coin or unit of weight of ancient Greece equal to one sixth of a drachma. **2. a.** Any of various coins, mostly of small value, circulated in medieval Europe. **b.** A small coin. [Latin, from Greek *obolos,* variant of *obelos,* OBELUS.]

ob·o·vate (ŏb-ō′vāt′) *adj. Botany.* Egg-shaped in outline, with the narrow end attached to the stalk: *an obovate leaf.*

ob·o·void (ŏb-ō′void′) *adj. Botany.* Egg-shaped, with the narrow end attached to the stem: *an obovoid fruit.*

O'Bri·en (ō-brī′ən), **Conor Cruise** (1917–). Irish politician and journalist. He served as a Labour member of the Irish parliament from 1969 to 1977, when he became a senator (until 1979). From 1977 to 1981 he was editor of the *Observer* newspaper.

O'Brien, Edna (1936–). Irish novelist and short-story writer. Her first novel, *The Country Girls,* was published in 1960. Her other works include *A Pagan Place* (1970) and a play, *Virginia* (1979).

obs. 1. obscure. **2.** observation. **3.** observatory. **4.** obsolete. **5.** obstetric; obstetrician; obstetrics.

Obs. observatory.

ob·scene (ŏb-sēn′, əb-) *adj.* **1.** Offensive to accepted standards of decency or modesty. **2.** Intended to incite lustful feelings; indecent; lewd. **3.** *Law.* Liable to deprave or corrupt. Said especially of a publication. **4. a.** Morally repulsive: *an obscene lie.* **b.** Offensive or repulsive to the senses; loathsome: *an obscene odor of decay.* —See Synonyms at **coarse.** [French *obscène* or Latin *obscēnus, obscaenus*†, inauspicious, repulsive.] **—ob·scene·ly** *adv.*

ob·scen·i·ty (ŏb-sĕn′ə-tē, əb-) *n., pl.* **-ties. 1.** The quality or state of being obscene. **2.** Indecency, lewdness, or offensiveness in behavior, expression, or appearance. **3.** Something obscene, as a word, act, or expression.

ob·scur·ant (ŏb-skyo͝or′ənt, əb-) *n.* **1.** One who opposes intellectual advancement and political reform; an enemy of rationalism. **2.** An opponent of the Enlightenment in 18th-century Germany. **3.** One who deliberately obscures the truth or fails to give a full explanation.

~adj. **1.** Of, pertaining to, or characteristic of an obscurant or of obscurantism. **2.** Tending to obscure. [Latin *obscūrāns* (stem *obscūrant-*), present participle of *obscūrāre,* to darken, from *obscūrus,* dark, OBSCURE.]

ob·scur·ant·ism (ŏb-skyo͝or′ən-tĭz′əm, əb-, ŏb′skyo͝o-răn′tĭz′əm) *n.* **1.** The principles or practice of obscurants. **2.** A policy of withholding information from the public. **3. a.** A style in art and literature characterized by deliberate vagueness or obliqueness. **b.** An example of this style. **—ob·scur·ant·ist** *n. & adj.*

ob·scure (ŏb-skyo͝or′, əb-) *adj.* **-scurer, -scurest.** *Abbr.* **obs. 1.** Not clearly expressed; vague, ambiguous, or cryptic: *an obscure text.* **2.** Imperfectly known or understood: *the obscure workings of nature.* **3.** Of undistinguished or humble descent, status, or reputation: *an obscure poet.* **4.** Not readily noticed or seen; inconspicuous: *an obscure flaw in a mighty statue.* **5.** Out of sight; hidden: *an obscure retreat.* **6. a.** So faintly perceptible as to lack clear delineation; indistinct. **b.** Hardly audible; faint. **c.** *Phonetics.* Having an unstressed neutral sound as represented by the schwa (ə). Said of a vowel. **7. a.** Of somber hue; dark. **b.** Dingy; dull. **8.** Partially or wholly deficient in light; gloomy. **9.** *Archaic.* Belonging to or inhabiting darkness: *"The obscure bird clamored the livelong night"* (Shakespeare). —See Usage note at **dark.**

~tr.v. **obscured, -scuring, -scures. 1.** To cause to be dim, dark, or indistinct: *Smog obscured our view.* **2.** *Phonetics.* To reduce (a vowel) to the neutral unstressed sound represented by the schwa (ə). **3.** To conceal in obscurity; hide: *details obscured in a maze of legal jargon.*

~n. Something that is obscure; obscurity. [Middle English, from Old French *obscur,* from Latin *obscūrus.*] **—ob·scure·ly** *adv.* **—ob·scure·ness** *n.*

ob·scu·ri·ty (ŏb-skyo͝or′ə-tē, əb-) *n., pl.* **-ties. 1.** Deficiency or absence of light; darkness: *"We wait for light, but behold obscurity"* (Isaiah 59:9). **2. a.** The condition of being unknown: *from obscurity to fame.* **b.** An unknown person. **3. a.** The condition or quality of being imperfectly known or of being difficult to understand: *The origin of the race is lost in obscurity.* **b.** An instance of this. [Old French *obscurité,* from Latin *obscūritās,* from *obscūrus,* OBSCURE.]

ob·se·crate (ŏb′sə-krāt′) *tr.v.* **-crated, -crating, -crates.** *Archaic.* To beg for (something) solemnly. [Latin *obsecrāre* (past participle *obsecrātus*), "to entreat in the name of something sacred" : *ob-,* for the sake of + *sacer,* sacred.] **—ob·se·cra·tion** *n.*

ob·se·quent (ŏb′sə-kwənt) *adj.* Flowing into another (subsequent) river in the opposite direction from the original (consequent) river. Said of a stream or river. Compare **consequent, subsequent.** [Latin *obsequens* (stem *obsequent-*), present participle of *obsequī,* to yield to : *ob-,* toward, over + *sequī,* to follow.]

ob·se·qui·ous (ŏb-sē′kwē-əs, əb-) *adj.* **1.** Displaying ingratiating servility. **2.** *Archaic.* Submissive and obedient; dutiful. [Middle English, from Latin *obsequiōsus,* from *obsequium,* compliance, from *obsequī,* to comply with : *ob-,* to + *sequī,* to follow.] **—ob·se·qui·ous·ly** *adv.* **—ob·se·qui·ous·ness** *n.*

ob·se·quy (ŏb′sə-kwē) *n., pl.* **-quies.** *Often* **obsequies.** A funeral rite or ceremony. [Middle English *obsequy,* from Norman French *obsequie,* Old French *obseque,* from Medieval Latin *obsequiae* (influenced by *exsequiae,* exequies), from Latin *obsequia,* plural of *obsequium,* compliance, service. See **obsequious.**] **—ob·se·qui·al** (ŏb-sē′kwē-əl, əb-) *adj.*

ob·serv·a·ble (əb-zûr′və-bəl) *adj.* **1.** Capable of being observed; noticeable; discernible: *observable improvement.* **2.** Deserving or worthy of notice or mention; noteworthy. **3.** Requiring or deserving special notice or observance: *an observable religious holiday.*

~n. Physics. A physical property, such as mass or temperature, that can be observed or measured directly as distinguished from a quantity, such as work or entropy, that must be derived from observed quantities. **—ob·serv·a·ble·ness** *n.* **—ob·serv·a·bly** *adv.*

ob·ser·vance (əb-zûr′vəns) *n.* **1.** The act or practice of observing or complying with a law, custom, command, duty, or rule. **2.** The act or custom of keeping or celebrating a holiday or other ritual occasion. **3.** A customary rite or ceremony. **4.** The action of watching; observation: *"Consider how much intellect was needed in the architect, and how much observance of nature"* (John Ruskin). **5.** *Roman Catholic Church.* **a.** The rules governing the members of a religious

PRONUNCIATION KEY

ă, pat; ā, pay; âr, care;
ä, father, are; b, bib;
ch, church; d, deed; ĕ, pet;
ē, be; f, fife; g, gag; h, hat;
hw, which; ĭ, pit; ī, pie;
îr, pier; j, judge; k, kick;
l, lid, needle; m, mum;
n, no, sudden; ng, thing;
ŏ, pot; ō, toe; ô, paw, for;
oi, noise; ou, out; o͝o, book;
o͞o, boot; p, pop; r, roar;
s, sauce; sh, ship, dish;
t, tight; th, thin, path;
th, this, bathe; ŭ, cut; ûr, fur;
v, valve; w, with; y, yes;
z, zebra, size; zh, vision;
ə, about, item, edible,
gallop, circus, peaceful

IN FOREIGN WORDS:

à, *Fr.* ami; œ, *Fr.* feu, *Ger.* schön; ü, *Fr.* tu, *Ger.* über;
KH, *Ger.* ich, *Scot.* loch;
N, *Fr.* bon; y′, *Fr.* Compiègne

STRESS MARKS:

Primary stress: ′
in·cite′ (ĭn-sīt′)
Secondary stress: ′
in′sight′ (ĭn′sīt′)

PRONUNCIATION KEY

ă, pat; ā, pay; âr, care;
ä, father, are; b, bib;
ch, church; d, deed; ĕ, pet;
ē, be; f, fife; g, gag; h, hat;
hw, which; ĭ, pit; ī, pie;
îr, pier; j, judge; k, kick;
l, lid, needle; m, mum;
n, no, sudden; ng, thing;
ŏ, pot; ō, toe; ô, paw, for;
oi, noise; ou, out; o͝o, book;
o͞o, boot; p, pop; r, roar;
s, sauce; sh, ship, dish;
t, tight; th, thin, path;
th, this, bathe; ŭ, cut; ûr, fur;
v, valve; w, with; y, yes;
z, zebra, size; zh, vision;
ə, about, item, edible,
gallop, circus, peaceful

IN FOREIGN WORDS:

à, *Fr.* ami; œ, *Fr.* feu, *Ger.* schön; ü, *Fr.* tu, *Ger.* über; KH, *Ger.* ich, *Scot.* loch; N, *Fr.* bon; y', *Fr.* Compiègne

STRESS MARKS:

Primary stress: ′
in·cite′ (ĭn-sīt′)
Secondary stress: ′
in′sight′ (ĭn′sīt′)

order. **b.** The order itself. **6.** *Archaic.* Respectful attention: *"He compassed her with sweet observances and worship"* (Alfred, Lord Tennyson).

Usage: Both *observance* and *observation* derive from *observe. Observance* is the practice of paying attention to laws, customs, holidays, duties, or the like, whereas *observation* is the act of seeing or noticing something.

ob·ser·vant (əb-zûr′vənt) *adj.* **1.** Characterized by or demonstrating an ability to perceive or apprehend quickly and accurately; alert: *an observant audience.* **2.** Diligent in observing a law, duty, or principle: *observant of the speed limit.* [French, from Latin *observāns* (stem *observant-*), present participle of *observāre,* to OBSERVE.] **—ob·ser·vant·ly** *adv.*

ob·ser·va·tion (ŏb′zər-vā′shən) *n. Abbr.* **obs. 1. a.** The act or faculty of observing. **b.** The fact of being observed; notice. **2. a.** The act of noting a phenomenon, often with instruments, and recording it, especially for scientific purposes. **b.** The result or record of such an act: *a meteorological observation.* **3.** A comment or remark. **4.** An inference or judgment that is acquired from or based on observing. **5.** The act of observing a rite; observance. —See Usage note at **observance.** [Middle English, from Latin *observātiō* (stem *observātiōn-*), from *observāre,* to OBSERVE.] **—ob·ser·va·tion·al** *adj.* **—ob·ser·va·tion·al·ly** *adv.*

observation car *n.* A railroad car with large windows providing passengers with extensive views of the countryside.

observation post *n. Military.* A position from which enemy activities can be observed or guns fired.

ob·ser·va·to·ry (əb-zûr′və-tôr′ē, -tōr′ē) *n., pl.* **-ries.** *Abbr.* **obs., Obs. 1.** A building designed and equipped for making observations of astronomical, meteorological, or other natural phenomena. **2.** A structure overlooking an extensive view. [New Latin *observatorium,* from Latin *observāre,* to OBSERVE.]

ob·serve (əb-zûrv′) *v.* **-served, -serving, -serves.** *—tr.* **1.** To perceive; notice: *I observed that those who spent freely often ran short of money.* **2.** To watch attentively: *observe a child's behavior.* **3.** To make a systematic or scientific observation of: *observe the moon's orbit.* **4.** To say by way of comment or remark. **5.** To adhere to or abide by (a law, duty, custom, or decision, for example): *observe the terms of a contract.* **6.** To keep or celebrate (a holiday, custom, or rite, for example): *observe an anniversary.* *—intr.* **1.** To take notice. **2.** To say something; make a comment or remark. **3.** To watch or be present without participating actively: *I was invited to the conference to observe.* —See Synonyms at **see.** [Middle English *observen,* from Old French *observer,* from Latin *observāre,* to pay attention to, look to : *ob-,* to + *servāre,* to keep, watch, pay attention.] **—ob·serv·ing·ly** *adv.*

Synonyms: *celebrate, commemorate, keep, solemnize.*

ob·serv·er (əb-zûr′vər) *n.* **1.** One that observes. **2. a.** A delegate sent to observe and report on the proceedings of an assembly or meeting but not to vote or otherwise participate. **b.** One sent to observe and report on the military, political, or administrative conditions in a country or area: *UN observers monitored the cease-fire.* **3.** *Military.* **a.** An aircraft crew member who makes observations. **b.** A soldier watching and reporting from an observation post. **4.** *Physics.* One whose observations are made in or referred to a completely specified frame of reference.

ob·sess (əb-sĕs′, ŏb-) *tr.v.* **-sessed, -sessing, -sesses.** To preoccupy the mind of excessively or exclusively: *He was obsessed by the fear of failure.* [Latin *obsidēre* (past participle *obsessus*), to sit down before, besiege, beset : *ob-,* on + *sedēre,* to sit.]

ob·ses·sion (əb-sĕsh′ən, ŏb-) *n.* **1. a.** Compulsive preoccupation with a fixed idea or an unwanted feeling or emotion, often with symptoms of anxiety. **b.** A compulsive, often unreasonable idea or emotion causing such preoccupation. **2.** *Archaic.* The state of being beset or actuated by the devil or an evil spirit. **—ob·ses·sion·al** *adj.* **—ob·ses·sion·al·ly** *adv.*

ob·ses·sive (əb-sĕs′ĭv, ŏb-) *adj.* **1.** Of, pertaining to, or characteristic of an obsession: *couldn't control his obsessive gambling.* **2.** Tending to cause an obsession. **3.** Excessive in degree or nature: *an obsessive need to win.*
∼*n.* One suffering from an obsession. **—ob·ses·sive·ly** *adv.* **—ob·ses·sive·ness** *n.*

ob·sid·i·an (ŏb-sĭd′ē-ən) *n.* An acid-resistant, lustrous volcanic glass, usually black or banded and displaying curved, shiny surfaces when fractured. [Latin *obsidiānus,* manuscript error for *obsiānus,* from *Obsius,* mentioned by Pliny as the discoverer of a stone similar to obsidian.]

ob·so·lesce (ŏb′sə-lĕs′) *intr.v.* **-lesced, -lescing, -lesces.** To become gradually obsolete. [Back-formation from OBSOLESCENT.]

ob·so·les·cent (ŏb′sə-lĕs′ənt) *adj.* In the process of passing out of use or usefulness; becoming obsolete. [Latin *obsolēscēns* (stem *obsolēscent-*), present participle of *obsolēscere,* to grow old, from *obsolēre* (unattested), to be old or in disuse. See **obsolete.**] **—ob·so·les·cence** *n.* **—ob·so·les·cent·ly** *adv.*

ob·so·lete (ŏb′sə-lēt′, ŏb′sə-lēt′) *adj.* **1.** *Abbr.* **obs.** No longer in use or practice: *an obsolete word.* **2.** No longer used or useful because of outmoded design or construction or because of hard wear. **3.** *Biology.* Increasingly vestigial or disappearing in each succeeding generation. Said of plant or animal characteristics or organs. —See Synonyms at **old.** [Latin *obsolētus,* from *obsolēre* (unattested), to be old or in disuse : *ob-,* away from + *solēre*†, to use, be accustomed.] **—ob·so·lete·ly** *adv.* **—ob·so·lete·ness** *n.* **—ob·so·let·ism** *n.*

ob·sta·cle (ŏb′stə-kəl) *n.* A person or thing that opposes, stands in the way of, or holds up progress toward a goal. [Middle English, from Old French, from Latin *obstāculum,* from *obstāre,* to hinder : *ob-,* against + *stāre,* to stand.]

Synonyms: *bar, barrier, block, encumbrance, hindrance, impediment, snag.*

obstacle course *n.* **1.** A series of physical obstacles, such as ladders and water jumps, to be negotiated at speed by soldiers undergoing training or by participants in an obstacle race. **2.** A situation full of obstacles that must be overcome.

obstacle race *n.* A race in which the participants have to go through, under, or over a number of obstacles.

obstet. obstetric; obstetrics.

ob·stet·ric (ŏb-stĕt′rĭk, əb-) *adj.* Also **ob·stet·ri·cal** (-rĭ-kəl). *Abbr.* **ob., obs., obstet.** Of or pertaining to the profession of obstetrics or to the care of women during and after pregnancy. [New Latin *obstetricus,* from Latin *obstetrīcius,* from *obstetrīx,* midwife, "she who is present," from *obstāre,* to stand before : *ob-,* before + *stāre,* to stand.] **—ob·stet·ri·cal·ly** *adv.*

ob·ste·tri·cian (ŏb′stə-trĭsh′ən) *n. Abbr.* **obs.** A physician specializing in obstetrics.

ob·stet·rics (ŏb-stĕt′rĭks, əb-) *n. Used with a singular verb. Abbr.* **ob., obs., obstet.** The branch of medicine concerned with the care of women during pregnancy, childbirth, and the recuperative period following delivery.

ob·sti·na·cy (ŏb′stə-nə-sē) *n., pl.* **-cies. 1.** The state or quality of being obstinate. **2.** An act or instance of stubbornness.

ob·sti·nate (ŏb′stə-nĭt) *adj.* **1.** Inflexibly and immovably adhering to an attitude, opinion, or course of action; resistant to argument or entreaty. **2.** Difficult to manage, control, or subdue; refractory. **3.** Difficult to alleviate or cure: *an obstinate headache.* —See Synonyms at **contrary.** [Middle English *obstinat,* from Latin *obstinātus,* past participle of *obstināre,* to persist, from *stāre,* to stand.] **—ob·sti·nate·ly** *adv.* **—ob·sti·nate·ness** *n.*

Synonyms: *dogged, headstrong, mulish, pertinacious, pigheaded, stiff-necked, stubborn.*

ob·strep·er·ous (ŏb-strĕp′ər-əs, əb-) *adj.* **1.** Noisily and stubbornly defiant. **2.** Aggressively boisterous. [Latin *obstreperus,* from *obstrepere,* to make noise against : *ob-,* against + *strepere,* to make noise.] **—ob·strep·er·ous·ly** *adv.* **—ob·strep·er·ous·ness** *n.*

ob·struct (əb-strŭkt′, ŏb-) *tr.v.* **-structed, -structing, -structs. 1.** To block or fill (a way or passage) with obstacles; make impassable. **2.** To impede, retard, or interfere with. **3.** To hide from view. —See Synonyms at **hinder.** [Latin *obstruere* (past participle *obstructus*) : *ob-,* against + *struere,* to pile up.] **—ob·struc·tive** *adj.* **—ob·struc·tive·ly** *adv.* **—ob·struc·tive·ness** *n.* **—ob·struc·tor** *n.*

ob·struc·tion (əb-strŭk′shən, ŏb-) *n.* **1.** A person or thing that gets in the way; an obstacle. **2. a.** An act or instance of obstructing. **b.** The state of being obstructed. **3.** The causing of delay or an attempt to cause a delay in the conduct of business, especially in a legislative body. **4.** *Sports.* The act of impeding another player or competitor in a match or race. **5.** *Medicine.* A blockage in a bodily organ or passage, especially the intestine. —See Synonyms at **obstacle.**

ob·struc·tion·ist (əb-strŭk′shə-nĭst, ŏb-) *n.* One who systematically obstructs or interrupts a process; especially, one who impedes the passage of legislation by delaying tactics, such as making long speeches. **—ob·struc·tion·ism** *n.* **—ob·struc·tion·ist** *adj.*

ob·tain (əb-tān′, ŏb-) *v.* **-tained, -taining, -tains.** *—tr.* **1.** To succeed in gaining possession of (something) as the result of planning or endeavor; get or acquire. **2.** *Archaic.* To reach or arrive at: *"obtain the age of manhood"* (Sir Walter Scott). *—intr.* **1.** To be established, accepted, or customary: *Certain formal customs still obtain today.* **2.** *Archaic.* To win a victory; prevail or succeed: *"This, though it failed at present, yet afterwards obtained"* (Jonathan Swift). [Middle English *obteinen,* from Old French *obtenir,* from Latin *obtinēre,* to attain : *ob-* (intensive) + *tenēre,* to hold.] **—ob·tain·a·ble** *adj.* **—ob·tain·er** *n.*

ob·tect (ŏb-tĕkt′) *adj.* Also **ob·tect·ed** (-tĕk′tĭd). *Zoology.* Enclosed in or covered by a hardened secretion. Said especially of pupae having wings, antennae, and legs enclosed and sealed against the body surface in this way. [Latin *obtectus,* past participle of *obtegere,* to cover up, conceal : *ob-,* down upon, over + *tegere,* to cover.]

ob·test (ŏb-tĕst′) *v.* **-tested, -testing, -tests.** *—tr.* **1.** To supplicate; entreat. **2.** To call as a witness. **3.** To object to; protest. *—intr.* To protest. [Latin *obtestārī,* to call as a witness to, entreat : *ob-,* to + *testārī,* to call as a witness, from *testis,* witness.] **—ob·tes·ta·tion** (ŏb′tĕ-stā′shən) *n.*

ob·trude (ŏb-tro͞od′, əb-) *v.* **-truded, -truding, -trudes.** *—tr.* **1.** To force (oneself or one's ideas) upon others with undue insistence or without invitation. **2.** To thrust out; push forward. *—intr.* To force oneself upon others or upon their attention. —See Synonyms at **intrude.** [Latin *obtrūdere* : *ob-,* against + *trūdere,* to thrust.] **—ob·trud·er** *n.* **—ob·tru·sion** (ŏb-tro͞o′zhən, əb-) *n.*

ob·tru·sive (ŏb-tro͞o′sĭv, -zĭv, əb-) *adj.* **1.** Projecting; protruding: *an obtrusive rock formation.* **2.** Tending to push self-assertively forward; brash: *The obtrusive behavior of a spoiled child.* **3.** Undesirably noticeable: *an obtrusive scar.* [Latin *obtrūs-,* past participial stem of *obtrūdere,* to OBTRUDE.] **—ob·tru·sive·ly** *adv.* **—ob·tru·sive·ness** *n.*

ob·tund (ŏb-tŭnd′) *tr.v.* **-tunded, -tunding, -tunds.** To dull or deaden; make less intense. [Middle English *obtunden,* from Latin *obtundere,* to strike against, blunt : *ob-,* against + *tundere,* to beat.] **—ob·tund·ent** *adj. & n.*

ob·tu·rate (ŏb′tə-rāt′, ŏb′tyə-) *tr.v.* **-rated, -rating, -rates. 1.** To close by obstructing or stopping up. **2.** To seal (a gun breech) in order to prevent gas from escaping on firing. [Latin *obtūrāre*†.] **—ob·tu·ra·tion** *n.*

ob·tu·ra·tor (ŏb′tə-rā′tər, ŏb′tyə-) *n.* One that closes or obstructs, as: **a.** A prosthetic device that closes an opening in the body, especially a denture that closes a defect in the palate. **b.** A device for sealing a gun breech to prevent gas from escaping on firing.

ob·tuse (ŏb-to͞os′, -tyo͞os′, əb-) *adj.* **1.** Lacking astuteness or discernment; slow to understand or perceive. **2. a.** Not sharp, pointed, or acute in form; blunt. **b.** Not acute or intense; indistinctly perceived; dull: *an obtuse pain.* **3.** *Botany.* Having a blunt or rounded tip: *an obtuse leaf.* —See Synonyms at **stupid.** [Latin *obtūsus,* past participle of *obtundere,* to blunt, OBTUND.] **—ob·tuse·ly** *adv.* **—ob·tuse·ness** *n.*

obtuse angle *n.* An angle greater than 90° and less than 180°.

ob·verse (ŏb-vûrs′, əb-, ŏb′vûrs′) *adj.* **1.** Facing or turned toward the observer: *the obverse side of a statue.* **2.** *Botany.* Having a narrower base than top; inverse. Said of certain leaves. **3.** Serving as a counterpart or complement.

∼*n.* (ŏb′vûrs′, ŏb-vûrs′, əb-). **1.** The side of something such as a coin, medal, or badge that bears the principal stamp or design. Compare **reverse. 2.** A counterpart or complement. **3.** *Logic.* The counterpart of a proposition obtained by exchanging the affirmative for the negative quality of the whole proposition and then negating the predicate. The obverse of *every act is predictable* is *no act is unpredictable.* [Latin *obversus,* past participle of *obvertere,* to turn toward, OBVERT.] **—ob·verse·ly** *adv.*

ob·ver·sion (ŏb-vûr′zhən, -shən, əb-) *n.* **1. a.** The process of obverting. **b.** The condition of being obverted. **2.** *Logic.* Inference of the obverse of a proposition.

ob·vert (ŏb-vûrt′, əb-) *tr.v.* **-verted, -verting, -verts. 1.** To turn so as to present another side or aspect to view. **2.** *Logic.* To subject (a proposition) to obversion. [Latin *obvertere,* to turn toward : *ob-,* toward + *vertere,* to turn.]

ob·vi·ate (ŏb′vē-āt′) *tr.v.* **-ated, -ating, -ates.** To anticipate so as to prevent or render unnecessary: *Carrying an umbrella obviated the need to buy one when the storm began.* —See Synonyms at **prevent.** [Late Latin *obviāre,* "to meet in the way," prevent, from Latin *ob viam,* in the way. See **obvious.**] **—ob·vi·a·tion** *n.* **—ob·vi·a·tor** *n.*

ob·vi·ous (ŏb′vē-əs) *adj.* **1.** Easily perceived or understood; quite apparent. **2.** Easily seen through because of a lack of subtlety; transparent. **3.** *Archaic.* Standing in the way or in front. —See Synonyms at **evident.** [Latin *obvius,* from *ob viam,* in the way : *ob,* against + *viam,* accusative of *via,* way.] **—ob·vi·ous·ness** *n.*

ob·vi·ous·ly (ŏb′vē-əs-lē) *adv.* **1.** In an obvious manner. **2.** As is obvious: *He is obviously extremely stupid.*

ob·vo·lute (ŏb′və-lo͞ot′, ŏb′və-lo͞ot′) *adj. Botany.* Folded together with overlapping edges. Said of leaves and petals in a bud. [Latin *obvolutus,* past participle of *obvolvere,* to wrap around, surround : *ob-,* over + *volvere,* to roll, wrap.] **—ob·vo·lu·tion** *n.* **—ob·vo·lu·tive** *adj.*

OC Officer Commanding.

oc., Oc. ocean.

o.c. in the work cited [Latin *opere citato*].

O.C. 1. Officer Commanding. **2.** Old Catholic.

o/c overcharge.

oc·a·ri·na (ŏk′ə-rē′nə) *n. Music.* A small terra-cotta or plastic wind instrument with a mouthpiece, finger holes, and an elongated ovoid shape. [Italian, "little goose" (from its shape), diminutive of *oca,* goose, from Vulgar Latin *avica* (unattested), from Latin *avicula,* diminutive of *avis,* bird.]

O'Ca·sey (ō-kā′sē), **Sean** (1880–1964). Irish playwright. Drawing on a childhood spent in the slums of Dublin and on his experiences in the Irish fight for independence, he produced three early works: *The Shadow of a Gunman* (1923), *Juno and the Paycock* (1924), and *The Plough and the Stars* (1926). His six volumes of autobiography were published under the title *Mirror in My House* (1956).

occ. 1. occident; occidental. **2.** occupation.

Occam, William of. See **Ockham.**

Occam's razor. Variant of **Ockham's razor.**

occas. occasional; occasionally.

oc·ca·sion (ə-kā′zhən) *n.* **1. a.** An event or happening. **b.** The time at which an event or happening occurs. **2.** A significant or special event, happening, or celebration. **3.** An appropriate or favorable time; opportunity. **4.** Something that brings on or precipitates an action or event; the immediate cause. **5.** Something that provides a reason; ground. **6.** A need created by a particular circumstance; a necessity: *"He must buy what he has little occasion for"* (Laurence Sterne). **7. occasions.** *Archaic.* Personal requirements or necessities. **8. occasions.** *Archaic.* Personal affairs or business matters. —See Usage note at **cause. —on occasion.** From time to time; now and then.

∼*tr.v.* **occasioned, -sioning, -sions.** To provide occasion for; cause. [Middle English *occasioun,* from Old French *occasion,* from Latin *occāsiō* (stem *occāsiōn-*), "a falling down, happening," from *occīdere* (past participle *occāsus*), to fall down : *ob-,* down + *cadere,* to fall.]

Usage: *Occasion* is followed by different prepositions or particles depending on its sense. When it means "reason" or "ground," it is followed by *for* or *to*: *This is an occasion for rejoicing. You have no occasion to object.* When it means "opportunity," it is followed by *to*: *He took the occasion to ask me for advice.* When it means "time of occurrence," it is followed by *of*: *on the occasion of your visit.*

oc·ca·sion·al (ə-kā′zhə-nəl) *adj. Abbr.* **occas. 1. a.** Coming irregularly; occurring from time to time: *an occasional visit.* **b.** Infrequent; not habitual: *took an occasional drink.* **2.** Occurring on or created for a special occasion: *occasional verse.* **3.** Designating a cause that is secondary or incidental. **4.** Designed not as part of a set but for use as the occasion requires: *an occasional chair for unexpected guests.* —See Synonyms at **periodic.**

oc·ca·sion·al·ism (ə-kā′zhə-nə-lĭz′əm) *n. Philosophy.* The theory that the connection between mental and bodily processes is the result of divine agency. **—oc·ca·sion·al·ist** *adj. & n.*

oc·ca·sion·al·ly (ə-kā′zhə-nə-lē) *adv. Abbr.* **occas.** Now and then; from time to time.

oc·ci·dent (ŏk′sə-dənt, -dĕnt′) *n. Abbr.* **occ. 1.** The west; western lands or regions. **2. Occident. a.** The Western Hemisphere. **b.** The countries of Europe and the Western Hemisphere. Compare **Orient.** [Middle English, from Old French, from Latin *occīdēns* (stem *occīdent-*), "quarter of the setting sun," west, from present participle of *occīdere,* to fall down, set (used of the sun). See **occasion.**]

oc·ci·den·tal (ŏk′sə-dĕn′təl) *adj. Abbr.* **occ.** *Often* **Occidental.** Of or pertaining to the countries of the Occident, their peoples, or their culture; western.

∼*n. Often* **Occidental.** A native or inhabitant of a western country. **—oc·ci·den·tal·ly** *adv.*

Oc·ci·den·tal·ism (ŏk′sə-dĕn′tə-lĭz′əm) *n.* The characteristic traits or customs of occidental peoples.

oc·ci·den·tal·ize (ŏk′sə-dĕn′tə-līz′) *v.* **-ized, -izing, -izes.** *Often* **Occidentalize.** —*tr.* To make occidental in character, outlook, or way of life. —*intr.* To become occidental; adopt occidental ways. **—oc·ci·den·tal·i·za·tion** *n.*

oc·cip·i·tal (ŏk-sĭp′ə-təl) *adj.* Of or pertaining to the occiput or to the occipital bone: *an occipital fracture.*

∼*n.* The occipital bone. [Old French, from Medieval Latin *occipitālis,* from Latin *occiput* (stem *occipit-*), OCCIPUT.]

occipital bone *n.* A curved compound bone that forms the lower posterior part of the skull.

occipital lobe *n.* The posterior portion of each cerebral hemisphere, functional in the interpretation of sensory impulses from the eyes.

oc·ci·put (ŏk′sə-pŭt′, -pət) *n., pl.* **-puts** or **occipita** (ŏk-sĭp′ə-tə). The back of the skull, especially the occipital area. [Middle English, from Latin : *ob-,* back of + *caput,* head.]

oc·clude (ə-klo͞od′) *v.* **-cluded, -cluding, -cludes.** —*tr.* **1.** To cause to become closed; obstruct: *occlude an artery.* **2.** To prevent the passage of; shut in, out, or off: *occlude light.* **3.** *Chemistry.* To absorb or adsorb (a substance) in great quantity. **4.** *Meteorology.* To force (air) upward from the earth's surface, as when a cold front overtakes and undercuts a warm front. **5.** To bring together (the upper and lower teeth) in proper alignment for chewing. —*intr.* To close so that the cusps fit together. Used of the teeth of the upper and lower jaws. [Latin *occlūdere* : *ob-* (intensive) + *claudere,* to close.] **—oc·clud·ent** *adj.*

occluded front *n. Meteorology.* The air front established when a cold front occludes a warm front. Also called "occlusion."

oc·clu·sion (ə-klo͞o′zhən) *n.* **1. a.** An act or the process of occluding. **b.** The state of being occluded. **c.** Something that occludes or blocks. **2.** *Meteorology.* **a.** The process of occluding air masses. **b.** An occluded front. **3.** The fit of the teeth when brought together. **4.** *Phonetics.* **a.** The complete closure of the breath passage in a stop. **b.** The blocking of the mouth passage in a nasal consonant.

oc·clu·sive (ə-klo͞o′sĭv, -zĭv) *adj.* Occluding or tending to occlude.

∼*n. Phonetics.* **1.** A closing of the breath passage; a stop. **2.** A nasal consonant.

oc·cult (ə-kŭlt′, ŏ-kŭlt′, ŏk′ŭlt′) *adj.* **1.** Of, pertaining to, dealing with, or knowledgeable in supernatural influences, agencies, or phenomena. **2.** Beyond the realm of human comprehension; mysterious; inscrutable. **3.** Available only to the initiated; not divulged; secret: *occult lore.* **4.** Hidden from view; concealed. **5.** *Medicine.* Not immediately obvious.

∼*n.* Occult practices or techniques: *a student of the occult.*

∼*v.* (ə-kŭlt′, ŏ-kŭlt′) **occulted, -culting, -cults.** —*tr.* **1.** To conceal or cause to disappear from view. **2.** *Astronomy.* To conceal by occultation: *The moon occulted Mars.* —*intr.* To become concealed or extinguished at regular intervals: *a lighthouse beacon that occults every 45 seconds.* [Latin *occultus,* past participle of *occulere,* to conceal; akin to *celāre,* to hide.] **—oc·cult·ly** *adv.* **—oc·cult·ness** *n.*

oc·cul·ta·tion (ŏk′əl-tā′shən) *n.* **1.** *Astronomy.* **a.** The passage of a celestial body across a line between an observer and another celestial object, as when the moon moves between the earth and the sun in a solar eclipse. **b.** The disappearance of the farther celestial object or the progressive blocking of light, radio waves, or other radiation from a celestial source during such a passage. **c.** An observational technique for determining the position or radiant structure of a celestial source so occulted: *a lunar occultation of a quasar.* **2.** The act of occulting or the state of being occulted. [Middle English *occultacion,* concealment, from Latin *occultātiō* (stem *occultātiōn-*), from *occultāre,* frequentative of *occulere,* to conceal. See **occult.**]

oc·cult·ism (ə-kŭl′tĭz′əm, ŏ-kŭl′-, ŏk′əl-) *n.* **1.** The study of the supernatural. **2.** A belief in occult powers and the possibility of bringing them under human control. **—oc·cult·ist** *n. & adj.*

obverse *A golden aureus of the Roman emperor Septimius Severus (A.D. 146–211), showing his head (left) with that of his son Caracalla (A.D. 186–217).*

oc·cu·pan·cy (ŏk′yə-pən-sē) *n., pl.* **-cies.** **1. a.** The act of taking or holding possession; the act of occupying. **b.** The condition of being occupied. **2. a.** The period during which one owns, rents, or uses certain premises or land. **b.** The use to which something occupied is put: *a building for commercial occupancy only.* **3.** The state of being an occupant or tenant. **4.** *Law.* The act of taking possession of previously unowned property with the intent of obtaining the right to own it.

oc·cu·pant (ŏk′yə-pənt) *n.* **1.** One who holds a position or place. **2.** One who has certain legal rights to or control over the premises he occupies; a tenant or owner. **3.** *Law.* One who is the first to take possession of something previously unowned. [French, from the present participle of *occuper*, to OCCUPY.]

oc·cu·pa·tion (ŏk′yə-pā′shən) *n. Abbr.* **occ.** **1. a.** An activity that serves as one's regular source of livelihood, as a profession or a vocation. **b.** An activity engaged in especially as a means of passing time. **2. a.** The act or process of holding or possessing a place. **b.** The state of being held or possessed. **3. a.** The invasion, conquest, and control of a nation or territory by a foreign military force. **b.** The military government exercising such control. **c.** The

period during which such control is in force. [Middle English *occupacioun*, from Old French *occupation*, from Latin *occupātiō* (stem *occupātiōn*-), from *occupāre*, to OCCUPY.]

oc·cu·pa·tion·al (ŏk′yə-pā′shə-nəl) *adj.* Of, pertaining to, or caused by engagement in a particular occupation: *occupational disease.* **—oc·cu·pa·tion·al·ly** *adv.*

occupational psychology *n.* The study of human behavior in relation to work, including such aspects as stress and job satisfaction. **—occupational psychologist** *n.*

occupational therapy *n.* Therapy, as for the physically or mentally ill, in which the principal element is some form of productive or creative activity, such as pottery or basket weaving. **—occupational therapist** *n.*

oc·cu·pi·er (ŏk′yə-pī′ər) *n.* **1.** One that occupies. **2.** *British.* A person who occupies or has possession of a building or piece of land. Usually used in combination: *owner-occupier.*

oc·cu·py (ŏk′yə-pī′) *tr.v.* **-pied, -py·ing, -pies.** **1.** To seize possession of and maintain control over (a place or region) by or as if by military conquest. **2.** To fill up (time or space): *a lecture that occupied three hours.* **3.** To live in or on or be a tenant in or of (premises

---

ocean

THE ELEMENT THAT COVERS SEVEN-TENTHS OF THE EARTH'S CRUST

Mountains, valleys, and canyons of the ocean deeps

The earth is the only watery planet in our Solar System. Although its waters are divided by the continents into the Atlantic, Pacific, Indian, Arctic, and Antarctic oceans, they are all connected, forming a single world ocean that covers some 70 percent of the surface of the earth. (The remaining 10 percent is fresh water.)

The continental shelves are the oceans' shallows. These regions are richest in fish and other food resources and in gas and oil deposits. They slope down from the coasts to the 200-meter

(656-foot) depth contour, then slope down much more steeply to form the continental rises. Winding submarine canyons scored into the continental rises may have been worn away by underwater currents or gouged out by sediment-laden waters gushing from large estuaries.

The ocean bottoms level out at around 4,000 meters (13,123 feet) below the surface into vast, shallow basins with seamounts edging them and scattered over them. They are floored with abys-

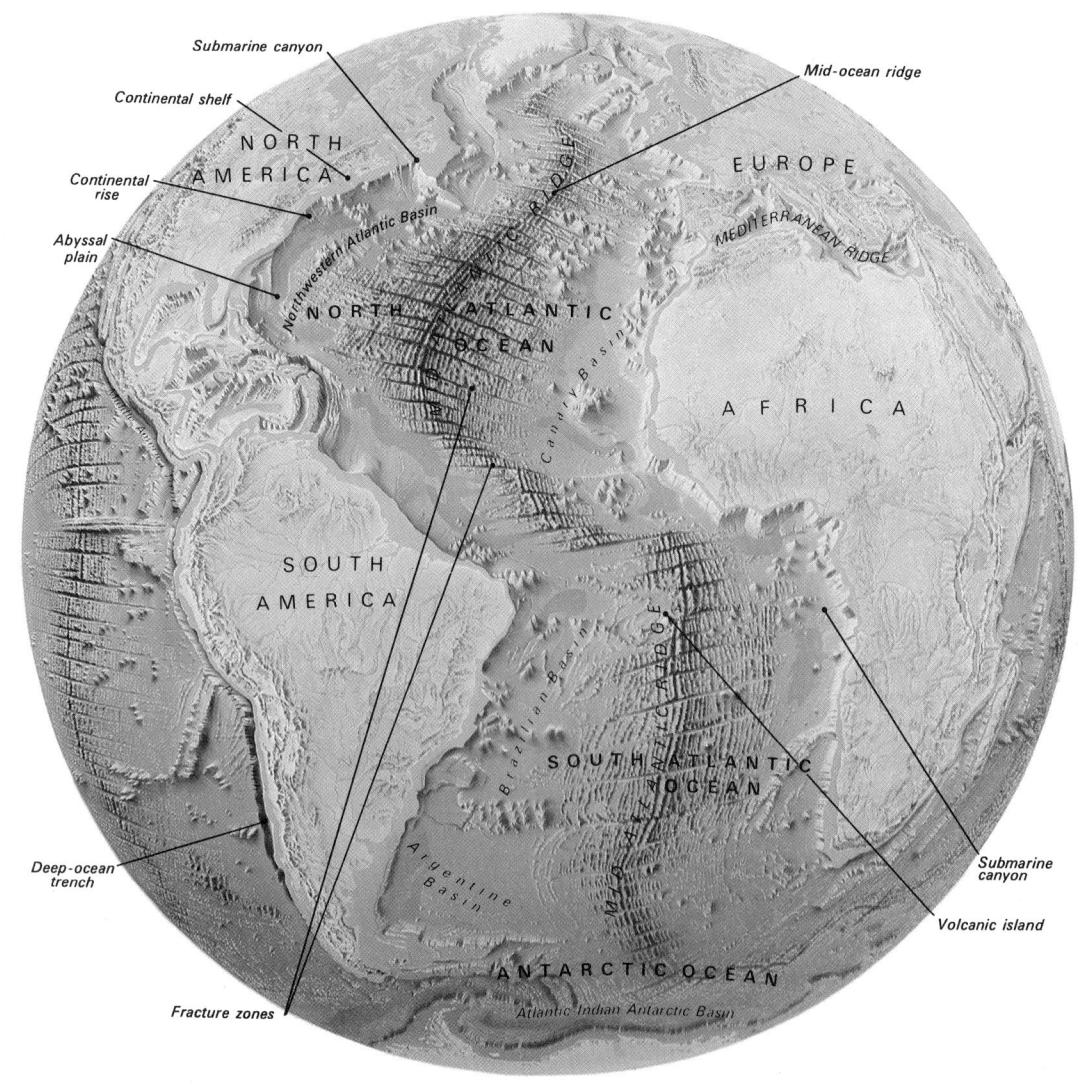

or land). **4.** To hold or fill (an office or position). **5.** To engage, employ, or busy: *occupied herself with a mystery story.* [Middle English *occupien,* from Old French *occuper,* from Latin *occupāre,* to seize : *ob-* (intensive) + *capere,* to take.]

oc·cur (ə-kûr′) *intr.v.* **-curred, -curring, -curs. 1.** To take place; come about. **2.** To be found to exist or appear: *Heavy rains occur during summer monsoons.* **3.** To come to mind: *The idea never occurred to me.* —See Synonyms at **happen.** [Latin *occurrere,* to run to meet : *ob-,* toward + *currere,* to run.]

oc·cur·rence (ə-kûr′əns) *n.* **1.** An act or instance of occurring. **2.** Something that takes place; an incident: *Their meeting was a dramatic occurrence.* —**oc·cur·rent** *adj.*

    Synonyms: circumstance, episode, event, happening, incident.

o·cean (ō′shən) *n. Abbr.* **O, O., oc., Oc. 1.** The entire body of salt water that covers about 72 percent of the earth's surface. **2.** *Often* **Ocean.** Any of the principal divisions of the ocean, including the Atlantic, Pacific, and Indian oceans, their southern extensions in Antarctica, and the Arctic Ocean. **3.** A great expanse or amount: *oceans of money.* **4.** In classical mythology, the sea encircling the earth. [Middle English *ocean,* from Old French, from Latin *ōceanus,* from Greek *ōkeanos,* OCEANUS.]

o·cean·ar·i·um (ō′shə-nâr′ē-əm) *n., pl.* **-iums** or **-ia** (-ē-ə). A large aquarium for the study or display of marine life.

ocean basin *n.* A basin (sense 6) *(see).*

O·ce·an·i·a (ō′shē-ăn′ē-ə, -ā′nē-ə). The islands of the central, western, and southern Pacific Ocean, customarily considered to include Australia and New Zealand. —**O·ce·an·i·an** *adj. & n.*

o·ce·an·ic (ō′shē-ăn′ĭk) *adj.* **1.** Of or pertaining to the ocean. **2.** Produced by or living in an ocean, especially in the open sea rather than in shallow coastal waters. **3.** Like an ocean in expanse; wide, huge, and sweeping.

O·ce·an·ic (ō′shē-ăn′ĭk) *adj.* **1.** Of or pertaining to a subfamily of the Austronesian language family comprising Melanesian and Polynesian. **2.** Of or pertaining to the cultures of the peoples speaking languages in the Oceanic subfamily. —**O·ce·an·ic** *n.*

O·ce·a·nid (ō-sē′ə-nĭd) *n., pl.* **-nids** or **Oceanides** (ō′sē-ăn′ə-dēz′). *Greek Mythology.* Any of the ocean nymphs held to be the daughters of Oceanus and Tethys. [Greek *ōkeanis* (stem *ōkeanid-*), from *Ōkeanos,* OCEANUS.]

---

sal plains, soft carpets of ooze formed from the perpetual rain of dead organisms from above and clayey debris washed down from the continents. Nodules of manganese, nickel, copper, and cobalt, looking like flintstones, accumulate on parts of the abyssal plains. The nodules take millennia to build up in concentric layers around fragments of shell.

    Underwater mountain ranges, the midocean ridges, run like spines down the centers of the oceans, often rising to within 1,000 meters (3,280 feet) of the surface. The highest peaks break the surface as islands. Geologists now accept that these ridges mark the paths of faults along which the continental plates are being forced apart by convection currents from deep within the earth's mantle. Volcanic material is constantly rising out of the mantle to the earth's surface and solidifying along the edges of the plates, causing the sea floors to spread. V-shaped trenches, cutting deep into the ocean floors, and arcs of volcanic islands mark the zones where the sea floor is being subducted, or thrust down, beneath the continental plates and absorbed back into the mantle. Such trenches almost encircle the Pacific. They are thousands of kilometers long, hundreds of kilometers wide, and the deepest, the Marianas Trench east of the Philippines, reaches 11,033 meters (36,197 feet) below sea level.

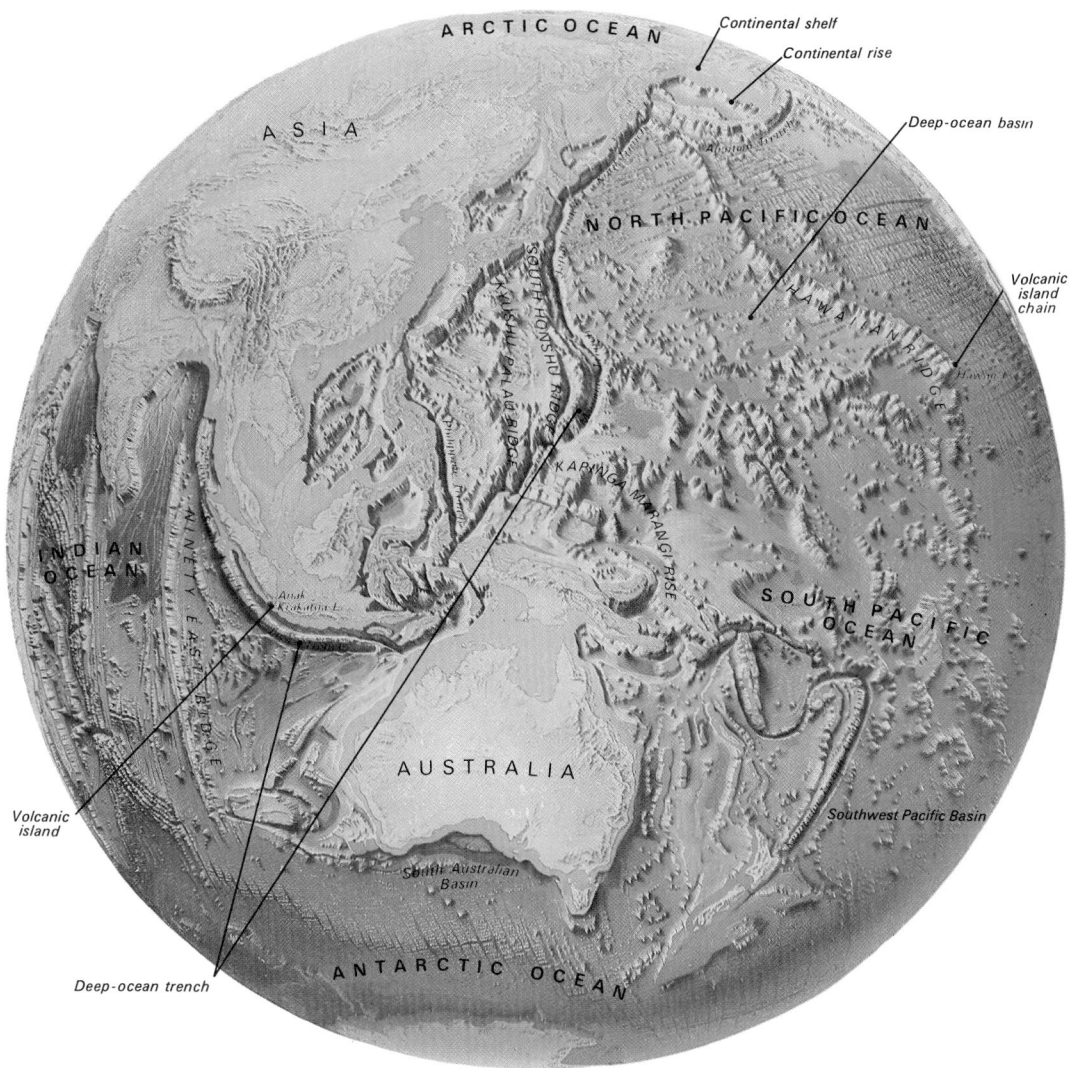

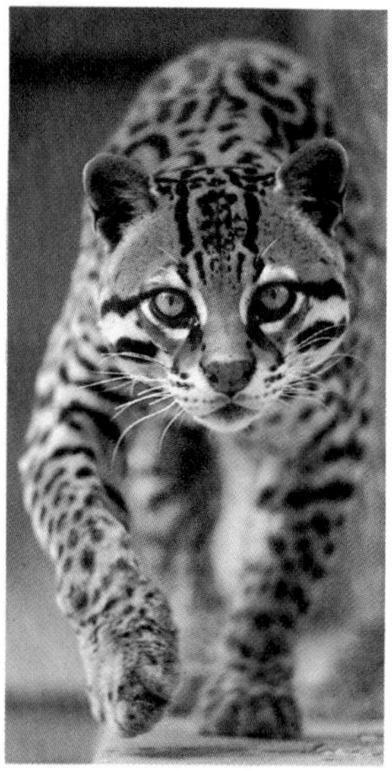

ocelot *Native to the forests of the southwestern United States and Central and South America, the ocelot is a large cat that feeds on reptiles and small mammals such as opossum and deer. It is a good climber and often sleeps in the branches of trees.*

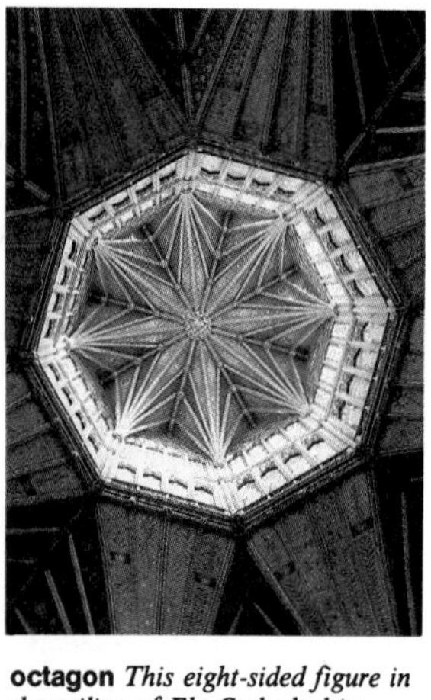

octagon *This eight-sided figure in the ceiling of Ely Cathedral in Cambridgeshire, England, is made of wood. It is 21 meters (70 feet) across and was finished in 1346.*

oceanog. oceanography.

o·cean·og·ra·phy (ō'shə-nŏg'rə-fē) *n. Abbr.* **oceanog.** The exploration and scientific study of the ocean and its phenomena. [OCEAN + -GRAPHY.] —**o·cean·og·ra·pher** *n.* —**o·cean·o·graph·ic** (ō'-shə-nə-grăf'ĭk), **o·cean·o·graph·i·cal** (-ĭ-kəl) *adj.*

o·cean·ol·o·gy (ō'shə-nŏl'ə-jē) *n.* Oceanography. —**o·cean·o·log·ic** (ō'shə-nə-lŏj'ĭk), **o·cean·o·log·i·cal** (-ĭ-kəl) *adj.* —**o·cean·o·log·i·cal·ly** *adv.* —**o·cean·ol·o·gist** (ō'shə-nŏl'ə-jĭst) *n.*

ocean sunfish *n.* See **sunfish** (sense 1).

O·ce·a·nus (ō-sē'ə-nəs). *Greek Mythology.* A Titan, the god of the outer sea encircling the earth and father of the Oceanids and of the river gods. [Greek *Ōkeanos.*]

oc·el·lat·ed (ŏs'ə-lā'tĭd, ō'sə-, ō-sĕl'ā'tĭd) *adj.* Also **oc·el·late** (ŏs'-ə-lāt', ō'sə-, ō-sĕl'āt'). **1.** Having an ocellus or ocelli. **2.** Resembling an ocellus. **3.** Marked with spots. [Latin *ocellātus,* having little eyes, from *ocellus,* little eye, OCELLUS.] —**oc·el·la·tion** *n.*

o·cel·lus (ō-sĕl'əs) *n., pl.* **ocelli** (ō-sĕl'ī') **1.** A small simple eye found in many invertebrates. **2.** A marking that resembles an eye. [New Latin, from Latin, diminutive of *oculus,* eye.] —**o·cel·lar** (ō-sĕl'ər) *adj.*

oc·e·lot (ŏs'ə-lŏt', ō'sə-) *n.* A brush- and forest-dwelling cat, *Felis pardalis,* of the southwestern United States and Central and South America, having a tawny-grayish or yellow coat with black-bordered brown spots. [French, from Nahuatl *ocelotl.*]

och (ŏKH) *interj. Scottish & Irish.* Used to express surprise, regret, or disagreement. [Gaelic, "oh."]

o·cher, o·chre (ō'kər) *n.* **1.** Any of several earthy mineral oxides of iron mingled with varying amounts of clay and sand, occurring in yellow, brown, or red and used either untreated or processed as pigments. **2.** A moderate orange yellow, from moderate or deep orange to moderate or strong yellow.
~*tr.v.* **ochered, ochering, ochers** also **ochred, ochring, ochres.** To color or mark with ocher. [Middle English *oker,* from Old French *ocre,* from Latin *lochra,* from Greek *ōkhra,* from *ōkhros*†, yellow, pale yellow.] —**o·cher** *adj.* —**o·cher·ous** (ō'kər-əs), **o·cher·y** (ō'-kə-rē, ō'krē) *adj.*

och·loc·ra·cy (ŏk-lŏk'rə-sē) *n., pl.* **-cies.** Government by the masses; mob rule. [French *ochlocratie,* from Greek *okhlokratia* : *okhlos,* mob + *-kratia,* -CRACY.] —**och·lo·crat** (ŏk'lə-krăt') *n.* —**och·lo·crat·ic** (ŏk'lə-krăt'ĭk), **och·lo·crat·i·cal** (-ĭ-kəl) *adj.* —**och·lo·crat·i·cal·ly** *adv.*

och·lo·pho·bi·a (ŏk'lə-fō'bē-ə) *n. Psychology.* Abnormal dread of crowds. [New Latin : Greek *okhlos,* crowd + -PHOBIA.] —**och·lo·pho·bic** *adj. & n.*

och·one (ŏ-KHōn') *interj. Scottish & Irish.* Used to express regret or grief. [Gaelic *ochóin,* "oh, alas."]

-ock *suffix.* Indicates smallness; for example, **hillock.** [Middle English *-oc,* Old English *-oc, -uc.*]

Ock·ham or **Oc·cam** (ŏk'əm), **William of** (*c.* 1300–49). English scholastic philosopher. He theorized that the real is always individual and that universals are only universal terms.

Ock·ham's razor, Oc·cam's razor (ŏk'əmz) *n.* A principle in science and philosophy urging the use of the most economical and least complex assumptions, terms, and theories and stating that an explanation for unknown phenomena should first be attempted in terms of what is already known. It is usually formulated as "Entities should not be multiplied unnecessarily." [After William of OCKHAM + RAZOR (as a sharp instrument for cutting away nonessentials).]

o'clock (ə-klŏk') *adv.* **1.** Of or according to the clock. Used to indicate the time: *three o'clock.* **2.** According to an imaginary clock dial with the observer at the center and 12 o'clock considered as straight ahead in horizontal position or straight up in vertical position. Used to indicate relative position: *enemy planes at 11 o'clock.* [Reduced from *of the clock.*]

O'Con·nor (ō-kŏn'ər), **Flannery** (1925–64). U.S. author. She is noted for her novels that feature bizarre imagination, strong Roman Catholic feelings, an uncompromising moral vision, and a unique literary style.

O'Connor, Sandra Day (1930–). U.S. jurist. After practicing law and serving as a jurist in Arizona, she was appointed (1981) as the first woman justice of the Supreme Court.

o·co·ti·llo (ō'kə-tē'yō) *n., pl.* **-llos.** A succulent, spiny shrub or tree, *Fouquieria splendens,* of Mexico and the southwestern United States, having clusters of tubular scarlet flowers. Also called "candlewood." [Mexican Spanish, diminutive of *ocote,* a Mexican pine, from Nahuatl *ocotl,* torch.]

OCR 1. optical character reader. **2.** optical character recognition.

oc·re·a, och·re·a (ŏk'rē-ə) *n., pl.* **-reae** (-rē-ē'). *Botany.* A sheath composed of one or more stipules that enclose the base of a leaf, as in some members of the Polygonaceae. [Latin *ocrea*†, greave, legging.] —**oc·re·ate** (ŏk'rē-ĭt, -āt') *adj.*

oct. octavo.

Oct. October.

octa–, oct–. Variants of **octo–.**

oc·ta·chord (ŏk'tə-kôrd') *n. Music.* **1.** An eight-stringed instrument. **2.** A sequence of eight notes, especially a scale. [Latin *octachordus,* from Greek *oktakhordos* : OCTA- + CHORD.]

oc·tad (ŏk'tăd') *n.* A group or series of eight. [Greek *oktas* (stem *oktad-*), number eight, from *oktō,* eight.] —**oc·tad·ic** (ŏk-tăd'ĭk) *adj.*

oc·ta·gon (ŏk-tə-gŏn') *n.* A polygon with eight sides and eight angles. [Latin *octagōnum,* from Greek *oktagōnon,* from neuter of *oktagōnos,* having eight angles : OCTO- + -GON.]

oc·tag·o·nal (ŏk-tăg'ə-nəl) *adj.* **1.** Having eight sides and eight angles. **2.** Of or formed in octagons. —**oc·tag·o·nal·ly** *adv.*

oc·ta·he·dral (ŏk'tə-hē'drəl) *adj.* **1.** Having eight plane surfaces. **2.** Of, relating to, or formed in octahedrons. —**oc·ta·he·dral·ly** *adv.*

oc·ta·he·drite (ŏk'tə-hē'drīt') *n.* A mineral, **anatase** *(see).* [French *octaédrite,* from *octaèdre,* octahedron (with reference to its octahedral crystals), from Greek *oktaedron,* OCTAHEDRON.]

oc·ta·he·dron (ŏk'tə-hē'drən) *n., pl.* **-drons** or **-dra** (-drə). A polyhedron with eight plane surfaces. [Greek *oktaedron* : OCTO- + -HEDRON.]

oc·tal (ŏk'təl) *adj.* Of, pertaining to, or being a number expressed in a numbering system of base eight. [OCTA- + -AL.] —**oc·tal** *n.*

oc·tam·er·ous (ŏk-tăm'ər-əs) *adj.* Also **oc·tom·er·ous** (ŏk-tŏm'-). *Biology.* Having or consisting of parts arranged in sets of eight. Said especially of flowers having sepals, petals, or other parts arranged in sets of eight. [Greek *oktamerēs* : OCTO- + -MEROUS.] —**oc·tam·er·ism** (ŏk-tăm'ə-rĭz'əm) *n.*

oc·tam·e·ter (ŏk-tăm'ə-tər) *n.* A line of verse consisting of eight metrical feet. [OCTO- + METER (after *hexameter*).] —**oc·tam·e·ter** *adj.*

oc·tan·dri·ous (ŏk-tăn'drē-əs) *adj. Botany.* Having eight stamens. [OCT(O)- + -ANDRY + -OUS.]

oc·tane (ŏk'tān') *n.* **1.** Any of various isomeric paraffin hydrocarbons with the formula C_8H_{18}. **2.** A colorless inflammable hydrocarbon, $CH_3(CH_2)_6CH_3$, found in petroleum and used as a solvent. **3.** Octane number. [OCT(O)- + -ANE.]

oc·tane·di·o·ic acid (ŏk'tān-dī-ō'ĭk) *n.* A colorless crystalline dicarboxylic derivative of octane, $HOOC(CH_2)_6COOH$, used in the manufacture of synthetic resins and occurring in castor oil and suberin. Also called "suberic acid."

octane number *n.* A numerical measure of the antiknock properties of motor fuel, based on the percentage by volume of isooctane in a standard reference fuel. For example, a gasoline that produces the same degree of knocking as a standard reference fuel containing 80 percent isooctane has an octane number of 80. Also called "octane," "octane rating." Compare **cetane number.**

octane rating *n.* Octane number.

oc·tan·gu·lar (ŏk-tăng'gyə-lər) *adj.* Octagonal.

Oc·tans (ŏk'tănz') *n.* The constellation that includes the south celestial pole. Also called "Octant." [New Latin, from Latin *octāns,* half-quadrant. See **octant.**]

oc·tant (ŏk'tənt) *n.* **1.** One eighth of a circle: **a.** A 45° arc. **b.** The area enclosed by two radii at a 45° angle and the intersected arc. **2.** An instrument based on the principle of the sextant but employing only a 45° angle, used as an aid in navigation. **3.** *Astronomy.* The position of a celestial body when it is separated from another by a 45° angle. **4.** One of eight parts into which three-dimensional space is divided by three usually perpendicular coordinate planes. **5. Octant.** Octans. [Latin *octans* (stem *octant-*), half-quadrant, from *octō,* eight.] —**oc·tan·tal** (ŏk-tăn'təl) *adj.*

octaroon. Variant of **octoroon.**

oc·ta·va·lent (ŏk'tə-vā'lənt) *adj. Chemistry.* Having a valence of eight.

oc·tave (ŏk'tĭv, -tāv') *n.* **1.** *Music.* **a.** The interval of eight diatonic degrees between two tones one of which has twice as many vibrations per second as the other. **b.** A tone that is eight full tones above or below another given tone. **c.** Two tones eight diatonic degrees apart that are sounded together. **d.** The consonance that results when two tones eight diatonic degrees apart are sounded. **e.** A series of tones included within this interval or the keys of an instrument that produce such a series. **f.** An organ stop that produces tones an octave above those usually produced by the keys played. **2.** *Ecclesiastical.* **a.** The eighth day after a feast day, counting the feast day as one. **b.** The entire period between a feast day and the eighth day following it. **3.** A group or series of eight. **4. a.** A stanza of eight lines in poetry. **b.** An octet in a sonnet. **5.** *Fencing.* A rotating parry.
~*adj.* **1.** Composed of eight elements or parts. **2.** *Music.* Producing tones at the octave, as an organ stop. [Middle English, the eighth day (after a festival), from Medieval Latin *octāva (diēs),* from Latin, feminine of *octāvus,* eighth, from *octō,* eight.] —**oc·ta·val** (ŏk-tā'vəl, ŏk'tə-vəl) *adj.*

octave coupler *n.* A mechanical device on an organ that automatically enables notes an octave apart to be played simultaneously by pressing the key or pedal for just one note.

Oc·ta·vi·a (ŏk-tā'vē-ə) (64–11 B.C.). Sister of the Roman emperor Augustus. At her brother's behest, she married (40 B.C.) Mark Antony. Though she raised an army for his Armenian campaign, he divorced her (32 B.C.) for Cleopatra.

Octavian. See **Augustus.**

oc·ta·vo (ŏk-tā'-vō, -tä'vō) *n., pl.* **-vos.** *Abbr.* **o., O., oct. 1.** The page size of a book composed of printer's sheets folded into eight leaves, originally printed on one side of each sheet. **2.** A book composed of pages of this size. Also called "eightvo." Also written *8vo, 8°.* [Latin *(in) octāvō,* "in eighth," ablative of *octāvus,* eighth. See **octave.**] —**oc·ta·vo** *adj.*

oc·ten·ni·al (ŏk-tĕn'ē-əl) *adj.* **1.** Happening or recurring every eight years. **2.** Lasting eight years. [Late Latin *octennium,* period of eight years : OCT(O)- + Latin *annus,* a year.] —**oc·ten·ni·al·ly** *adv.*

oc·tet (ŏk-tĕt') *n.* Also **oc·tette** (for senses 1, 2, 3, 5). **1.** A musical composition written for eight voices or eight instruments. **2.** A group of eight singers or eight instrumentalists. **3.** A group of eight. **4.** *Chemistry.* A group of eight electrons in the orbital shell of an

atom, necessary for stability in the formation of many molecules.
5. The first eight lines of an Italian sonnet. In this sense, also called "octave." Compare **sestet**. [Italian *ottetto* (influenced by *duet*), from *otto*, eight, from Latin *octō*.]

oc·til·lion (ŏk-tĭl′yən) *n*. **1**. In the United States, the cardinal number represented by the figure 1 followed by 27 zeros; usually written 10^{27}. **2**. In Great Britain, the cardinal number represented by the figure 1 followed by 48 zeros; usually written 10^{48}. [French : OCT(O)- + (M)ILLION.]

oc·til·lionth (ŏk-tĭl′yənth) *n*. **1**. The ordinal number octillion in a series. **2**. Any of an octillion equal parts. —**oc·til·lionth** *adj*.

octo–, octa–, oct– *prefix*. Indicates eight parts or elements; for example, **octopus, octameter, octane**. [Latin *octō-*, from *octō*, eight, and Greek *okta-*, from *oktō*, eight.]

Oc·to·ber (ŏk-tō′bər) *n*. *Abbr*. **Oct. 1**. The tenth month of the Gregorian calendar. October has 31 days. See feature at **calendar**. **2**. *British Archaic*. Ale brewed in October. [Middle English *octobre*, from Old French, from Latin *Octōber*, "eighth month," from *octō*, eight.]

October Revolution *n*. A part of the **Russian Revolution** *(see)*.

Oc·to·brist (ŏk-tō′brĭst) *n*. A member of a moderate Russian political party that accepted the reforms outlined in the Imperial Constitutional Manifesto issued by Nicholas II in October 1905. —**Oc·to·brist** *adj*.

oc·to·dec·i·mo (ŏk′tə-dĕs′ə-mō′) *n., pl.* **-mos. 1**. The page size of a book composed of printer's sheets folded into 18 leaves or 36 pages. **2**. A book composed of pages of this size. Also called "eighteenmo." Also written *18mo, 18°*. [Latin *octōdecimō*, ablative of *octōdecimus*, eighteenth, from *octōdecim*, eighteen: OCTO- + *decem*, ten.] —**oc·to·dec·i·mo** *adj*.

oc·to·ge·nar·i·an (ŏk′tə-jə-nâr′ē-ən) *adj*. Being eighty years old or between eighty and ninety years old.
~*n*. A person eighty years old or between eighty and ninety years old. [Latin *octōgēnārius*, containing eighty, from *octōgēnī*, eighty each, from *octōgintā*, eighty : *octō*, OCTO- + *-gintā*, "ten times."] —**octomerous**. Variant of **octamerous**.

oc·to·nar·y (ŏk′tə-nĕr′ē) *adj*. **1**. Of or pertaining to the number eight. **2**. Consisting of eight members or of groups containing eight.
~*n., pl.* **octonaries**. A group or set of eight. [Latin *octōnārius*, containing eight, from *octōnī*, eight at a time, from *octō*, eight.]

oc·to·ploid (ŏk′tə-ploid′) *adj*. *Genetics*. Having eight times the number of haploid chromosomes in a somatic cell nucleus. [OCTO- + -PLOID.] —**oc·to·ploid** *n*.

oc·to·pod (ŏk′tə-pŏd′) *n*. Any of various mollusks of the order Octopoda, such as an octopus, having eight arms and no internal shell. [New Latin *Octopoda*, from Greek *oktōpoda*, neuter plural of *oktōpous* (stem *oktōpod-*), OCTOPUS.]

oc·to·pus (ŏk′tə-pəs) *n., pl.* **-puses** or **octopi** (-pī′). **1**. Any of numerous carnivorous nocturnal marine mollusks of the genus *Octopus* or related genera, found worldwide. It has a rounded saclike body, eight tentacles, each bearing two rows of suckers, a large distinct head, and a strong beaklike mouth. Also called "devilfish." **2**. Something, such as a multinational corporation, that resembles an octopus in its many powerful centrally controlled branches. [New Latin, from Greek *oktōpous*, eight-footed : OCTO- + *pous*, foot.]

oc·to·roon, oc·ta·roon (ŏk′tə-rōōn′) *n*. A person who is the offspring of a white and a quadroon; one whose ancestry is one-eighth black. [OCTO- + (QUAD)ROON.]

oc·to·syl·la·ble (ŏk′tə-sĭl′ə-bəl) *n*. **1**. In poetry: **a**. A line of verse containing eight syllables. **b**. A verse with eight syllables in each line. **2**. A word of eight syllables. [Late Latin *octosyllabus*, having eight syllables : OCTO- + *syllaba*, SYLLABLE.] —**oc·to·syl·lab·ic** (ŏk′tə-sĭ-lăb′ĭk) *adj*.

oc·troi (ŏk′troi′, ŏk-trwä′) *n., pl.* **octrois** (ŏk′troiz′, ŏk-trwä′). **1**. A local tax levied on certain items brought into some European cities. **2**. The officials responsible for collecting this tax. **3**. The place where the tax is collected. [French, from Old French, a tax that a city is authorized to levy, from *octroyer*, to grant as a privilege, authorize, from Gallo-Roman *auctōricāre* (unattested), to authorize, from Latin *auctor*, author, originator, from *augēre*, to originate, increase.]

oc·tu·ple (ŏk′tə-pəl, ŏk-tōō′pəl, -tyōō′pəl) *adj*. **1**. Consisting of or having eight parts, members, or copies. **2**. Multiplied by eight; eight times as much, as many, or as large.
~*n*. An eightfold amount or number.
~*v*. **octupled, -pling, -ples.** —*tr*. To multiply or increase by eight. —*intr*. To be multiplied eightfold. [Latin *octuplus* : OCTO- + *-plus*, -fold.]

oc·u·lar (ŏk′yə-lər) *adj*. **1. a**. Of or pertaining to the eye: *ocular exercises*. **b**. Resembling the eye in form or function. **2**. Of or pertaining to the sense of sight: *an ocular aberration*. **3**. Seen by the eye; visual: *ocular proof*.
~*n*. The eyepiece of an optical instrument. [Late Latin *oculāris*, of the eyes, from Latin *oculus*, eye.]

oc·u·lar·ist (ŏk′yə-lər-ĭst) *n*. One who makes artificial eyes.

oc·u·list (ŏk′yə-lĭst) *n*. **1**. A physician who treats diseases of the eyes; an ophthalmologist. **2**. An optometrist. [French *oculiste*, from Latin *oculus*, eye.]

oc·u·lom·e·ter (ŏk′yə-lŏm′ĭ-tər) *n*. A device designed for measuring the direction, speed, and extent of eye movement. [Latin *oculus*, eye + -METER.]

oc·u·lo·mo·tor (ŏk′yə-lə-mō′tər) *adj*. **1**. Pertaining to movements of

the eyeball. **2**. Pertaining to the oculomotor nerve. [Latin *oculus*, eye + MOTOR.]

oculomotor nerve *n*. *Anatomy*. The third cranial nerve, which controls the muscles of the eyeballs.

Od, 'Od, Odd (ŏd) *interj*. *Archaic*. Used in oaths as a euphemism for God.

OD (ō′ dē′) *n*. *Slang*. An overdose of a narcotic drug.
~*intr.v.* **OD'd, OD'ing, OD's.** *Slang*. To take an overdose of a narcotic drug: *He OD'd on barbiturates.*

o.d. on demand.

O.D. 1. officer of the day. **2**. on demand. **3**. overdraft. **4**. overdrawn.

o·da·lisque, o·da·lisk (ō′də-lĭsk′) *n*. A female slave or concubine in a harem. [French, from Turkish *ōdalik*, chambermaid : *ōdah*, room + *-lik*, noun suffix.]

odd (ŏd) *adj*. **odder, oddest. 1**. Strange, unusual, or peculiar: *odd behavior*. **2. a**. Being a remainder; left over: *had some odd dollars in the account after paying the bill*. **b**. Greater than a specified number by a relatively small amount: *twenty-odd years ago*. **c**. Small in amount: *had only some odd change in his pocket*. **3. a**. Being one of an incomplete pair or set: *an odd shoe*. **b**. Remaining after others are paired or grouped: *odd man at the dinner party*. **4**. Occasional; irregular: *odd jobs*. **5**. Designating an integer not divisible by two: *1, 3, and 5 are odd numbers*. Compare **even**. —See Synonyms at **strange**. —**odd man out**. One who by the strangeness of his behavior or belief stands alone in a group. [Middle English *odde*, from Old Norse *oddi*, triangle, point, third, odd number.] —**odd·ly** *adv*. —**odd·ness** *n*.

   Usage: When *odd* is used to express an indefinite, usually small, amount in excess of a specified number, it should be used with a hyphen in order to prevent ambiguity: *thirty-odd guests*. *Odd* in this sense is used only with round numbers.

odd·ball (ŏd′bôl′) *n*. *Informal*. A person marked by eccentric behavior or attitudes. —**odd·ball** *adj*.

Odd Fellow *n*. A member of the Independent Order of Odd Fellows, a fraternal and benevolent secret society.

odd·ish (ŏd′ĭsh) *adj*. Somewhat odd; rather peculiar.

odd·i·ty (ŏd′ə-tē) *n., pl.* **-ties. 1**. A person or thing that is odd. **2**. An odd quality, trait, or characteristic; an eccentricity. **3**. The state or quality of being odd; strangeness.

odd-job·man (ŏd′jŏb′mən) *n., pl.* **-men** (-mĭn). *Chiefly British*. A man who does casual or occasional work, especially odd domestic jobs, for a living.

odd lot *n*. A quantity that differs from a standard trading unit, especially an amount of stock of fewer than 100 shares.

odd·ment (ŏd′mənt) *n*. **1. a**. Something left over. **b**. **oddments**. Odds and ends. **2**. An oddity.

odd-pin·nate (ŏd′pĭn′āt′) *adj*. *Botany*. Pinnate with a single unpaired leaflet at the end of the leafstalk.

odds (ŏdz) *pl.n*. **1**. A certain number of points given beforehand to a weaker side in a contest to equalize the chances of all participants. **2**. A ratio expressing the probability of an event or outcome. Used especially of sports contests: *The odds on the champion winning are three to two*. **3**. A ratio expressing the amount by which the stake of one bettor differs from that of his opposing bettor: *The bookmaker gave odds of ten to one*. **4**. The likelihood of one thing occurring rather than another in a contest or issue of indefinite outcome: *The odds are that she will get the leadership on the first ballot*. **5. a**. Favorable chance; advantage: *The odds are with me*. **b**. Unfavorable conditions; adversity: *overcame the odds*. **6**. *Chiefly British Informal*. Difference or significance. Used chiefly in phrases such as *it makes no odds* or *what's the odds?* —**at odds**. In disagreement; in conflict. —**by all odds**. In every possible way; unquestionably: *The film was by all odds the best of the year*. [Plural of ODD.]

odds and ends *pl.n*. Miscellaneous items, remnants, or pieces.

odds and sods *pl.n*. *Chiefly British Informal*. Miscellaneous items or people. [ODDS + SOD (person, thing).]

Odd's bodikins. Variant of **Od's bodikins**.

odds-on (ŏdz′ŏn′, -ôn′) *adj*. More likely to win than not; having a good chance of success.

ode (ōd) *n*. **1**. In classical literature, a poem intended to be sung by a chorus at a public festival or as part of a drama. **2**. A lengthy lyrical poem, usually rhymed, often addressed to a praised object, person, or quality and often characterized by a lofty style. See **Horatian ode, Pindaric ode**. [French, from Old French, from Late Latin *ōda, ōdē*, from Greek *ōidē, aoidē*, song.] —**od·ic** (ō′dĭk) *adj*.

-ode[1] *suffix*. Indicates a way or path; for example, **electrode**. [Greek *-odos*, from *hodos*, a way.]

-ode[2] *suffix*. Indicates resemblance or characteristic nature; for example, **nematode**. [Greek *-ōdēs*, from *eidos*, form, shape.]

O·der (ō′dər). Polish & Czechoslovakian **O·dra** (ō′drä). River in eastern Europe. Rising in the eastern Sudeten Mts., Czechoslovakia, it flows northward to the Baltic Sea near Szczecin. It is a major trading route, navigable from Ratibor. North of its confluence with the Neisse, it forms part of the German-Polish border.

O·der-Neis·se Line (ō′dər-nī′sə). The border between Poland and East Germany, running along the Oder and Neisse rivers. Adopted at the Potsdam Conference (August 1945), it was recognized by Poland and East Germany in 1950 and by West Germany in 1970.

O·des·sa (ō-dĕs′ə). Black Sea port in the Ukrainian S.S.R. It is a major administrative, industrial, cultural, and tourist center. Kept open all year by icebreakers, it has a major naval base and fishing and whaling fleets. Founded (14th century) as a Tatar fortress, it was claimed by Lithuanians and Turks and finally ceded to Russia.

O·dets (ō-dĕts'), **Clifford** (1906–63). U.S. playwright. He is perhaps the most noted American playwright of the Depression era of the 1930's. Among his plays are *Waiting for Lefty* (1935), *Golden Boy* (1937), and *The Country Girl* (1950), later made into an Academy Award-winning motion picture (1954).

o·de·um (ō-dē'əm, ō'dĕ-) *n., pl.* **odea** (ō-dē'ə, ō'dē-ə). Also **o·de·on** (ō'dē-ŏn'), *pl.* **-ons**. 1. A building of ancient Greece and Rome that was used for public performances of music and poetry. 2. A contemporary theater or concert hall. [Latin *ōdēum*, from Greek *ōideion*, from *ōidē*, song, ODE.]

O·din (ō'dĭn). *Norse Mythology*. The supreme deity and creator of the cosmos and humankind; the god of wisdom, war, art, culture, and the dead, often identified with the Teutonic god Woden. [Old Norse *Ōdhinn*.]

o·di·ous (ō'dē-əs) *adj*. Exciting or meriting hatred or repugnance; abhorrent: *an odious crime*. —See Synonyms at **hateful**. [Middle English, from Old French, from Latin *odiōsus*, from *odium*, ODIUM.] —**o·di·ous·ly** *adv*. —**o·di·ous·ness** *n*.

o·di·um (ō'dē-əm) *n*. 1. The state or quality of being odious. 2. Strong dislike; contempt or aversion. 3. Disgrace resulting from hateful conduct. —See Synonyms at **disgrace**. [Latin, hatred, from *ōdī*, I hate.]

o·do·graph (ō'də-grăf', -gräf') *n*. 1. A device for recording speed and distance traveled on foot. 2. An instrument for recording the distance and course traveled by a vehicle. [Greek *hodos*, road, journey + -GRAPH.]

o·dom·e·ter (ō-dŏm'ə-tər) *n*. An instrument that indicates distance traveled by a vehicle. [French *odomètre*, from Greek *hodometron* : *hodos*, road, journey + *metron*, measure, METER.] —**o·dom·e·try** (ō-dŏm'ə-trē) *n*.

-odon *suffix*. Indicates an animal having teeth of a specified type; for example, **mastodon**. [New Latin, from Greek *odous* (stem *odont-*), tooth.]

o·do·nate (ōd'n-āt', ō-dŏn'āt') *n*. Any of various predacious winged insects of the order Odonata, which includes the dragonflies and damselflies, characterized by two pairs of membranous wings and large compound eyes. [New Latin *Odonata*, order name, from Greek *odous*, *odont-*, tooth.]

-odont *suffix*. Indicates: 1. A tooth or teeth of a specified type; for example, **acrodont**. 2. Having a tooth or teeth of a specified type; for example, **diphyodont**. [Greek *odous* (stem *odont-*), tooth.]

-odontia *suffix*. Indicates the form of, condition of, or manner of treating the teeth; for example, **orthodontia**. [New Latin, from Greek *odous* (stem *odont-*), tooth.]

odonto- *prefix*. Indicates tooth or teeth; for example, **odontoblast**, **odontology**. [Greek, from *odous* (stem *odont-*), tooth.]

o·don·to·blast (ō-dŏn'tə-blăst') *n*. A tooth cell in the outer surface of dental pulp that produces dentine. [ODONTO- + -BLAST.] —**o·don·to·blas·tic** (ō-dŏn'tə-blăs'tĭk) *adj*.

o·don·to·glos·sum (ō-dŏn'tə-glŏs'əm) *n*. An orchid of the genus *Odontoglossum*, having large colorful flowers with a toothlike projection on the lip. [New Latin, "tooth-tongue" : ODONTO- + *glossum*, from Greek *glossa*, tongue.]

o·don·toid (ō-dŏn'toid') *adj*. 1. Resembling a tooth. 2. Of or pertaining to the odontoid process. [Greek *odontoeidēs* : ODONT(O)- + -OID.]

odontoid process *n. Anatomy*. A small, toothlike projection from the second vertebra of the neck around which the first vertebra rotates.

o·don·tol·o·gy (ō'dŏn-tŏl'ə-jē) *n*. The study of the anatomy, growth, and diseases of the teeth. [French *odontologie* : ODONTO- + -LOGY.] —**o·don·to·log·i·cal** (ō-dŏn'tə-lŏj'ĭ-kəl) *adj*. —**o·don·to·log·i·cal·ly** *adv*. —**o·don·tol·o·gist** (ō'dŏn-tŏl'ə-jĭst) *n*.

o·don·to·phore (ō-dŏn'tə-fôr', -fōr') *n*. A protrusile structure at the base of the mouth of most mollusks that supports the radula. [ODONTO- + -PHORE.] —**o·don·toph·o·ral** (ō'dŏn-tŏf'ər-əl), **o·don·toph·o·rine** (ō'dŏn-tŏf'ə-rīn', -ər-ĭn), **o·don·toph·o·rous** (-ər-əs) *adj*.

o·dor (ō'dər) *n*. Also *chiefly British* **o·dour**. 1. The property or quality of a thing that affects, stimulates, or is perceived by the sense of smell; scent. 2. A sensation, stimulation, or perception of the sense of smell: *the pleasant odor of a wood fire*. 3. A strong, pervasive quality; flavor: *An odor of corruption in the administration triggered an investigation*. 4. Judgment with respect to nature, quality, or character; repute: *a doctrine that is not currently in good odor*. —See Synonyms at **smell**. [Middle English, from Norman French *odour*, Old French *odor*, from Latin *odor*.]

o·dor·if·er·ous (ō'də-rĭf'ər-əs) *adj*. Having or giving off an odor. [Latin *odōrifer* : ODOR + -FER.] —**o·dor·if·er·ous·ly** *adv*. —**o·dor·if·er·ous·ness** *n*.

o·dor·less (ō'dər-lĭs) *adj*. Having no odor: *an odorless gas*. —**o·dor·less·ly** *adv*. —**o·dor·less·ness** *n*.

o·dor·im·e·ter (ō'də-rĭm'ə-tər) *n*. Also **o·dor·om·e·ter** (-rŏm'ə-tər). An instrument for measuring the intensity of odors. —**o·dor·im·e·try** (ō'də-rĭm'ə-trē) *n*.

o·dor·ous (ō'dər-əs) *adj*. Having a distinctive odor that is usually but not necessarily unpleasant. —**o·dor·ous·ly** *adv*. —**o·dor·ous·ness** *n*.

Odra. See **Oder**.

Od's bod·kins (ŏdz bŏd'kĭnz) *interj*. Also **Odd's bod·i·kins** (bŏd'ĭ-kĭnz). *Archaic*. Used as an oath. [Euphemism for *"(by) God's body."*]

O·dys·seus (ō-dĭs'yōōs', ō-dĭs'ē-əs). Latin name **U·lys·ses** (yōō-lĭs'ēz'). *Greek Mythology*. The cunning king of Ithaca, a leader of the Greeks in the Trojan War, whose return home was frustrated for ten years by the god Poseidon. [Greek *Odusseus*.]

od·ys·sey (ŏd'ə-sē) *n., pl.* **-seys**. 1. An extended adventurous wandering. 2. An intellectual or spiritual quest. [After the ODYSSEY.]

Od·ys·sey (ŏd'ə-sē) *n*. The second epic of Homer, recounting the wanderings and adventures of Odysseus after the fall of Troy and his eventual return home. [French *Odyssée*, from Latin *Odyssēa*, from Greek *Odusseia*, from *Odusseus*, ODYSSEUS.] —**Od·ys·sey·an** (ŏd'ə-sē'ən, -sā'ən) *adj*.

Oe oersted.

OE, OE., O.E. Old English.

OECD *n*. Organization for Economic Cooperation and Development.

OED, O.E.D. Oxford English Dictionary.

oedema. Variant of **edema**.

oed·i·pal (ĕd'ə-pəl, ē'də-) *adj*. Also **oed·i·pe·an** (ĕd'ə-pē'ən, ē'də-). Often **Oedipal**. Of, relating to, or characteristic of the Oedipus complex.

Oed·i·pus (ĕd'ə-pəs, ē'də-). *Greek Mythology*. A son of Laius and Jocasta who was abandoned at birth and who unwittingly killed his father and married his mother. [Greek *Oidipeus* : *oidan*, to swell + *pous*, foot.]

Oedipus complex *n. Psychoanalysis*. Libidinal feelings in a child, especially a male child, for the parent of the opposite sex, usually accompanied by hostility to the parent of the same sex and generally first manifesting itself between the ages of three and five. Compare **Electra complex**.

oeil-de-boeuf (ŭ'də-bŭf', ûr'də-bûrf', œ'ē-də-bœf') *n., pl.* **oeils-de-boeuf** *(pronounced as singular)*. A round or oval window. [French, "bull's eye."]

oe·nol·o·gy, e·nol·o·gy (ē-nŏl'ə-jē) *n*. Also **oi·nol·o·gy** (oi-nŏl'ə-jē). The study of wines. [Greek *oinos*, wine + -LOGY.] —**oe·no·log·i·cal** (ē'nə-lŏj'ĭ-kəl) *adj*. —**oe·nol·o·gist** (ē-nŏl'ə-jĭst) *n*.

oe·no·mel (ē'nə-mĕl') *n*. 1. A beverage of ancient Greece, consisting of wine and honey. 2. *Poetic*. A source of strength and sweetness. [Greek *oinomeli* : *oinos*, wine + *meli*, honey.]

o'er (ôr, ōr) *prep. & adv. Poetic*. Over.

oer·sted (ûr'stĕd') *n. Abbr*. **Oe** The centimeter-gram-second electromagnetic unit of magnetic field strength, equal to the magnetic field strength that would cause a unit magnetic pole to experience a force of one dyne in a vacuum. [After Hans Christian OERSTED.]

Oer·sted (ûr'stĕd'), **Hans Christian** (1777–1851). Danish physicist. Though his discoveries include metallic aluminum and the compressibility of water, he is best known for discovering the magnetic field generated by an electric current.

oesophagus. Variant of **esophagus**.

oestr-, oestro-. Variants of **estr-**.

oestradiol. Variant of **estradiol**.

oestriol. Variant of **estriol**.

oestrogen. Variant of **estrogen**.

oestrone. Variant of **estrone**.

oestrous. Variant of **estrous**.

oestrous cycle. Variant of **estrous cycle**.

oestrus. Variant of **estrus**.

oeu·vre (œ'vrə) *n., pl.* **oeuvres** *(pronounced as singular)*. 1. A work of art. 2. The sum of an artist's work. [French, from Latin *opus*, work.]

of (ŭv, ŏv; *unstressed* əv) *prep*. 1. Derived or coming from; originating at or from: *men of the north; a poet of humble birth*. 2. a. Caused by; resulting from: *of her own free will*. b. Owing to; through: *died of tuberculosis*. 3. Away from; at a distance from: *a mile east of here*. 4. Used to indicate: a. Lack or absence: *free of prejudice*. b. Separateness: *regardless of race*. c. Removal: *robbed of his dignity; cured of distemper*. 5. From the total or group comprising; from among: *give of one's time; two of his friends; most of the cases; the third week of March*. 6. Composed of or made from: *a dress of silk*. 7. Associated with or adhering to: *a man of your religion*. 8. Belonging or connected to: *the coughing of a smoker; the houses of my friends; the rungs of a ladder*. 9. Possessing; having: *a man of honor*. 10. Containing or carrying: *a field of three acres; a bag of groceries*. 11. a. That is: *the subject of philosophy*. b. Specified as; named or called: *a depth of ten feet; the Garden of Eden; the town of Cambridge*. 12. Centering upon; directed toward: *a love of horses; in search of the escaped prisoner*. 13. Produced by; issuing from: *the novels of Ernest Hemingway; products of the vine*. 14. Characterized or identified by: *a year of famine; a painter of distinction*. 15. Concerning; with reference to; about: *think highly of his proposals; speak of it later*. 16. Set aside for; having as a purpose; taken up by: *a hall of residence; a day of rest*. 17. a. Before; until. Used in telling the time: *five minutes of two*. b. Used in dates: *the third of May*. 18. During or at a specified time: *of recent years; of an evening*. 19. As specified: *smelling of lavender*. 20. By: *beloved of his family*. 21. Used after an adjective to express a personal judgment on the following noun or noun phrase: *How rude of him to leave!* 22. Used to indicate a particular relationship, as: a. Between an adjective and a noun or noun phrase, similar to that between a verb and its object: *sure of the facts; capable of stealing*. b. A verb and a noun or noun phrase: *She tired of waiting. I reminded him of the date*. c. A noun and a noun or noun phrase: *made a good job of it; a rogue of a lawyer*. d. An adverb and a noun or noun phrase:

upwind of the smoke. [Middle English *of,* Old English *of* (preposition and adverb).]

Usage: The normal use of *of* following a noun to express possession or close relationship is seen in such phrases as *the crew of the ship; a friend of my mother.* In certain circumstances it is also possible to use the possessive form of the noun following *of: a friend of my mother's.* However, the noun in the *of* phrase must be definite and human. One cannot say *a friend of a mother's* or *the crew of the ship's.* The noun before the *of* phrase is usually indefinite *(a friend . . .)*; one is unlikely to hear *the friend of my mother's,* though, in informal English, the use of a demonstrative such as *this* or *that* is common: *I was talking to that friend of my mother's.* The preposition *of* is also used after such verbs as *speak, inform,* and *talk* as a more formal literary variant of *about: I spoke of that to the committee.* After the verb *think,* however, two senses are involved: *think of* means "bring to mind," *think about* means "consider."

O'Fao·láin (ō-fāl'ən, ō-fă'lən), **Séan** (1900–). Irish author. He has written novels, short stories, plays, and biographies. His works often decry Irish provincialism and the effects of rigid Catholicism.

off (ôf; ŏf) *adv.* **1.** At or to a distance from a nearer place; so as to be away: *got in the car and drove off.* **2.** At a certain distance in space or time: *The station is a mile off. The party is a week off.* **3.** So as to be no longer on, attached, or connected: *He shaved his beard off. The electricity was cut off.* **4.** So as to be no longer continuing, operating, or functioning: *turn off the radio; shut off the lights.* **5. a.** So as to be completely removed: *Take your clothes off.* **b.** So as to finish, eliminate, or be rid of: *write off a report; kill off the mice.* **6.** So as to be smaller, fewer, or less: *Sales dropped off.* **7.** So as to be away from work or duty: *They took a day off. We took time off to go shopping.* **8.** Off-stage: *The actor bowed and went off left.* **9.** *British Informal.* So as no longer to like: *went right off her.* **—off and on.** With periodic interruptions; intermittently: *He slept off and on.* **—off with.** Remove, thrust aside, or depart. Used as an imperative interjection: *Off with his head! Off with all of you!*
~adj. **1.** Sour, rotten, bad, or stale. Said of food: *The eggs smell a little off.* **2.** Not on, attached, or connected; removed: *I walked around on the beach with my shoes off.* **3. a.** Not continuing, operating, or functioning: *The oven is off.* **b.** Effecting a disconnection: *the off switch.* **4.** No longer taking place or effective; canceled: *The wedding is off.* **5.** *British.* No longer available or on the menu: *Ham is off.* **6. a.** Not up to standard; below a normal or satisfactory level: *Your bowling is off today.* **b.** Characterized by mediocrity or low standards: *It was a poor concert; the artist must have been having an off day.* **7.** In a specified circumstance or condition: *You are better off staying home.* **8. a.** *British Informal.* Impolite or unfair; unacceptable: *Arriving so late is a bit off.* **b.** Inconsistent with accuracy or truth; in error: *My guess was slightly off.* **c.** Not completely sane; odd: *Everyone knows he's brilliant but a little off.* **9.** Started on the way; going: *The runners were off. I'm off to see a movie.* **10. a.** Absent or away from work or duty: *He's off every Tuesday.* **b.** Spent away from work or duty: *My wife plays golf on her off days.* **11.** More distant or removed; farther: *painted the off side of the barn.* **12. a.** Marked by reduced activity; sluggish: *Summer is an off season for tourism in the tropics.* **b.** Marked by a reduced level of trading or by lower prices: *The bond market is off.* **13.** In questionable taste; off-color. **14.** On the right-hand side of a vehicle, horse, or team of horses: *The off horse is lame.* **15.** *Nautical.* Farthest from the shore; seaward.
~prep. **1. a.** So as to be removed or distant from a position of rest or support: *The bird hopped off the branch.* **b.** Taken, detached, or subtracted from: *I cut a slice off the roast.* **2.** Away or relieved from: *They're off duty today.* **3. a.** By consuming: *living off locusts and honey.* **b.** With the means provided by: *She had difficulty living off her pension.* **c.** *Nonstandard.* From: *tried to get a loan off him.* **4. a.** Extending or branching out from: *an artery off the heart.* **b.** Near but not on; slightly away from: *The house is just off the central square.* **5. a.** Deviating from: *The ship is off course.* **b.** Not up to the standard of: *off my usual form.* **6.** Abstaining from: *He is off the booze.* **7.** To seaward of: *There's a lighthouse a mile off the coast.*
~v. **offed, offing, offs.** *—intr.* To go away; leave: *Off or I'll call the police.* *—tr. Slang.* To murder: *afraid the mob would off him if he didn't pay up.* [Middle English *of, off,* of, off, from Old English *of.*]

Usage: The use of *off* followed by *of* and sometimes by *from,* as in *He stepped off of the pavement and Leave off from doing that,* is unacceptable in formal speech and writing and open to criticism even in informal speech. The use of *off* for *from,* in indicating the notion of "source," should also be avoided: *He took the book from* (not *off*) *me.*

off. office; officer; official.

Of·fa (ô'fə) (died 796). Anglo-Saxon king of Mercia. Seizing power (757) from his cousin, he dominated much of England south of the Humber River. He issued the first Anglo-Saxon coins, established commercial and diplomatic links with the Frankish empire of Charlemagne, and accepted greater papal control of the English church. After repelling a Welsh invasion, he established the Welsh-Mercian border at the huge earthwork known as Offa's Dyke.

of·fal (ô'fəl, ŏf'əl) *n.* **1.** The edible internal organs, such as the heart, liver, or kidneys, of a butchered animal. **2.** Dead or decaying matter; putrid flesh. **3.** Refuse; rubbish. [Middle English *offal, ofall,* from Middle Dutch *afval,* "that which falls off," giblets, refuse : *af,* off + *vallen,* to fall.]

Of·fa·ly (ô'fə-lē, ŏf'ə-). County of the Republic of Ireland, the province of Leinster. Tullamore is the county town.

off-bal·ance (ôf'băl'əns, ŏf'-) *adj. & adv.* **1.** Not in balance. **2.** In or into a state of surprise or unpreparedness: *The remark caught her off-balance.*

off·beat (ôf'bēt', ŏf'-) *n.* An unaccented beat in a musical measure. *~adj.* (ôf'bēt', ŏf'-). *Slang.* Not conforming to an ordinary type or pattern; unconventional: *offbeat humor.*

off-Broad·way (ôf'brôd'wā', ŏf'-) *adj.* **1.** Designating or pertaining to theatrical activity, often experimental and low-cost, presented in theaters outside the Broadway entertainment district of New York City. **2.** Located outside of the Broadway entertainment district. *~n.* Off-Broadway theatrical productions. Compare **Broadway.**

off·cast (ôf'kăst', -käst', ŏf'-) *adj.* Cast off; rejected or discarded.

off-cen·ter (ôf'sĕn'tər, ŏf'-) *adj.* **1.** Not quite at the geometric center. **2.** Offbeat; eccentric. **—off-cen·ter** *adv.*

off chance *n.* A remote or slight chance; a hope: *I approached him on the off chance of a loan.*

off-col·or (ôf'kŭl'ər, ŏf'-) *adj.* **1.** Varying from the usual, expected, or required color. **2.** In bad taste; improper: *an off-color joke.* **3.** *Chiefly British.* Not in good health or spirits.

off-course (ôf'kôrs', -kōrs', ŏf'-) *adj. British.* Off-track.

off·cut (ôf'kŭt', ŏf'-) *n.* A piece of material, such as carpet or wood, that remains after larger pieces of the material have been cut off and sold.

Of·fen·bach (ô'fən-bäk'), **Jacques Levy** (1819–80). German-born French composer and cellist. He composed more than 90 pieces, including *Orpheus in the Underworld* (1858).

of·fend (ə-fĕnd') *v.* **-fended, -fending, -fends.** *—tr.* **1.** To create or excite anger, resentment, or annoyance in; affront: *Her brusqueness offends many people.* **2.** To be displeasing or disagreeable to: *Onions offend his sense of smell.* **3.** *Obsolete.* **a.** To transgress; violate: *"He hath offended the law"* (Shakespeare). **b.** To cause to sin: *"If thy right eye offend thee, pluck it out"* (Matthew 5:29). *—intr.* **1.** To cause displeasure. **2. a.** To break the law. **b.** To violate a moral or divine law; sin. [Middle English *offenden,* from Old French *offendre,* from Latin *offendere,* to strike against: *of-, ob-,* against + *fendere,* to strike.]

Synonyms: *affront, insult, outrage.*

of·fend·er (ə-fĕn'dər) *n.* **1.** A person who has broken a rule of conduct: *sent the offenders to bed early.* **2.** A person who has committed a crime: *a sex offender.* **3.** Something that causes vexation or harm: *The lights failed; a short circuit was the offender.*

of·fend·ing (ə-fĕn'dĭng) *adj.* **1.** Causing offense. **2.** Responsible for a fault or inconvenience: *removed the offending splinter.*

of·fense (ə-fĕns' *for senses 1, 2, 3;* ŏf'ĕns' *for senses 4, 5) n.* Also *chiefly British* **of·fence. 1.** The act of offending or causing anger, resentment, or displeasure. **2. a.** A violation or infraction of a moral or social code; a transgression or sin. **b.** A transgression of law; a crime. **3.** Something that offends. **4.** The act of attacking or assaulting. **5. a.** An athletic team in possession of the ball or puck. **b.** Scoring ability or potential. **—give offense.** To cause anger, displeasure, or resentment. **—no offense.** Used to excuse a possibly offensive remark. **—take offense.** To become angered, displeased, or resentful; feel hurt. [Middle English, from Old French, from Latin *offensa,* from the feminine past participle of *offendere,* to OFFEND.]

of·fen·sive (ə-fĕn'sĭv) *adj.* **1.** Disagreeable to the senses: *an offensive odor.* **2.** Causing anger, displeasure, resentment, or affront: *an offensive gesture.* **3. a.** Making an attack. **b.** Of, pertaining to, or designed for attack; aggressive: *offensive weapons.* **c.** Of, pertaining to, or being a team having possession of the ball or puck. —See Synonyms at **hateful.**
~n. **1.** An attitude of attack: *on the offensive.* **2.** An attack or assault, especially a military one. **3.** An aggressive campaign or initiative: *went on an offensive to stamp out crime.* **—of·fen·sive·ly** *adv.* **—of·fen·sive·ness** *n.*

Synonyms: *insulting, objectionable, obnoxious.*

of·fer (ô'fər, ŏf'ər) *v.* **-fered, -fering, -fers.** *—tr.* **1.** To present for acceptance or rejection; proffer. **2. a.** To put forward for consideration or examination; propose: *offer an opinion.* **b.** To present in order to meet a need or fulfill a requirement: *The applicant offered word processing as one of her skills.* **3.** To present for sale. **4.** To propose as payment; bid. **5.** To present as an act of worship: *offer up prayers.* **6.** To exhibit readiness or desire to do; volunteer: *offered to help me.* **7.** To put up; mount: *partisans who offered strong resistance to the invaders.* **8.** To threaten: *offered to hit him with a stick if he didn't stop.* **9.** To provide; furnish: *a hotel that offers conference facilities.* **10.** To produce or present (an artistic work) on the stage: *The repertory group is offering two new plays this season.* **11.** To present; reveal. *—intr.* **1.** To present an offering in worship or devotion. **2.** To make an offer or proposal; especially, to make an offer of marriage. **3.** To present itself: *"This plan was dropped, because of its risk, and because a better offered"* (T.E. Lawrence).
~n. **1.** The act of offering. **2. a.** Something offered, such as a suggestion, proposal, bid, or recommendation. **b.** A proposal of marriage: *She hadn't received any suitable offers.* **3.** *Law.* A proposal that if accepted constitutes a legally binding contract. **4.** The condition of being offered, especially for sale: *thousands of bushels of wheat on offer.* **5. a.** An attempt; try. **b.** Something, as a physical act, that indicates an intention: *made an offer of opening the door.* [Middle English *offeren, offren,* partly (in the sense "to sacrifice") from Old English *offrian* and partly (in other senses) from Old

French *offrir*; both from Latin *offerre* : *ob-*, to + *ferre*, to bring, carry.] —**of·fer·er, of·fer·or** *n.*

Synonyms: present, proffer, tender.

of·fer·ing (ô'fər-ĭng, ŏf'ər-) *n.* **1.** The act of making an offer. **2.** Something that is offered. **3.** A presentation made to a deity as an act of religious worship or sacrifice. **4.** A contribution or gift, especially one made at a religious service. [Middle English *offring*, Old English *offrung*, from *offrian*, to sacrifice, OFFER.]

of·fer·to·ry (ô'fər-tôr'ē, -tōr'ē, ŏf'ər-) *n., pl.* **-ries. 1.** *Often* **Offertory. a.** One of the principal parts of the Eucharistic liturgy at which bread and wine are offered to God by the celebrant. **b.** A musical setting of the Offertory. **2.** A collection of offerings at a religious service. [Old French *offertoire*, from Medieval Latin *offertōrium*, from Latin *offerre*, to OFFER.]

off·hand (ôf'hănd', ŏf'-) *adv.* Without preparation or forethought; extemporaneously.
~*adj.* Also **off·hand·ed** (-hăn'dĭd). Performed or expressed offhand: *She made an offhand remark that hurt my feelings.* —**off·hand·ed·ly** *adv.* —**off·hand·ed·ness** *n.*

off-hour (ôf'our', ŏf'-) *n.* A period of time that is not a rush hour: *Railroad tickets are often cheaper during off-hours.*

of·fice (ô'fĭs, ŏf'ĭs) *n. Abbr.* **off. 1. a.** A place, such as a building, room, or suite, in which business, clerical, or professional activities are conducted: *the manager's office; a booking office.* **b.** The administrative personnel, executives, or entire staff working in such a place. **2.** A duty or function assigned to or assumed by someone: *"the maternal office was supplied by my aunt"* (Edward Gibbon). **3.** A position of authority, duty, or trust given to a person, as in a government, business, or corporation: *the office of vice president.* **4. a.** Any of the branches of the federal government of the United States ranking just below the departments. **b.** A major executive division of the British government, often headed by a cabinet minister: *the Foreign Office.* **5.** A public position: *seeking office.* **6. of·fices.** *Chiefly British.* Formerly, the parts of a house, such as the laundry and kitchen and often outbuildings such as the barn, in which the servants carried out household work. **7.** *Often* **offices.** An act, usually beneficial, performed for another; a favor: *got the job through the offices of friends.* **8.** *Ecclesiastical.* A ceremony, rite, or service, usually prescribed by liturgy, especially: **a.** *Roman Catholic Church.* The canonical hours. **b.** *Anglican Church.* A prayer service, such as Morning or Evening Prayer. **c.** A ceremony or service for a special purpose; especially, a rite for the dead. —**in** (or **out of**) **office.** In (or out of) government; in (or out of) power. [Middle English, from Old French, from Latin *officium*, performance of duty, from *opificium* (unattested) : *opus*, work + *-ficium*, from *facere*, to do.]

office boy *n.* A boy or young man employed to do minor tasks and to run errands in a business office.

of·fice·hold·er (ô'fĭs-hōl'dər, ŏf'ĭs-) *n.* One who holds public office.

office hours *pl.n.* The usual period or periods of the day during which business is conducted or work performed in an office.

of·fi·cer (ô'fĭ-sər, ŏf'ĭ-) *n. Abbr.* **off. 1. a.** One who holds an office of authority or trust in a business, government, or other institution. **b.** A public or government official: *a medical officer; a customs officer.* **2.** One holding a commission in the armed forces. **3.** A person holding a license in the merchant marine as master, mate, chief engineer, or assistant engineer. **4.** A person performing police duties; policeman. **5. a.** One elected to an office in a society or club. **b.** A rank above the lowest rank in some honorary societies. **6.** *British.* A member of the Order of the British Empire with the grade below commander.
~*tr.v.* **officered, -cering, -cers. 1.** To provide with officers; allocate officers to. **2.** To direct or command; act as an officer over. [Middle English, from Norman French, from Old French *officier*, from Medieval Latin *officiārius*, "officeholder," from Latin *officium*, OFFICE.]

officer of arms *n. Heraldry.* A herald or pursuivant.

officer of the day *n. Abbr.* **O.D.** A military officer who for a given day assumes responsibility for security, order, and the performance of the guard.

officer of the deck *n.* A naval officer assigned to represent the commanding officer of a vessel or installation for a specified period during which he is superior to all officers below the executive officer.

of·fi·cial (ə-fĭsh'əl) *adj. Abbr.* **off. 1.** Of or pertaining to an office or post of authority: *official duties.* **2.** Authorized by a proper authority; authoritative: *official permission.* **3.** Holding office or serving in a public capacity; authorized to perform a special duty: *an official representative.* **4.** Characteristic of or befitting a person of authority: *an official manner.* **5.** Formal or ceremonial: *an official banquet.* **6.** Of, pertaining to, or being a drug that is authorized by or contained in the U.S. Pharmacopoeia or National Formulary.
~*n. Abbr.* **off. 1.** One who holds an office or position; especially, one who acts in a subordinate capacity for an institution such as a corporation or governmental agency. **2.** A referee or an umpire in various sports, as basketball. [Middle English, an authority, from Old French, from Late Latin *officiālis*, functionary, official, from Latin, of an office or duty, from *officium*, OFFICE.] —**of·fi·cial·ism** *n.* —**of·fi·cial·ly** *adv.*

of·fi·cial·dom (ə-fĭsh'əl-dəm) *n.* Officials or bureaucrats collectively.

of·fi·cial·ese (ə-fĭsh'ə-lēz', -lēs') *n.* Language characteristic of offi-

cial documents or statements, often considered obscure, pretentiously wordy, or formal in style.

of·fi·ci·ant (ə-fĭsh'ē-ənt) *n.* One who officiates at a religious service or ceremony; a celebrant.

of·fi·ci·ar·y (ə-fĭsh'ē-ĕr'ē) *n., pl.* **-ies. 1.** A body of officials or officers. **2.** *Rare.* An official or officer.
~*adj.* **1.** Attached to or resulting from an office held. Said of a title. **2.** Having a title resulting from the holding of an office. Said of a dignitary.

of·fi·ci·ate (ə-fĭsh'ē-āt') *intr.v.* **-ated, -ating, -ates. 1.** To perform the duties and functions of an office or position of authority. **2.** To serve as a priest or minister at a religious service. **3.** To take on a particular role and perform the duties and functions associated with that role, as at a special occasion or ceremony: *officiated as host.* **4.** To serve as a referee or an umpire in any of various sports. [Medieval Latin *officiāre*, to conduct a religious service, from Latin *officium*, OFFICE (in Late Latin, also "religious service").] —**of·fi·ci·a·tion** *n.* —**of·fi·ci·a·tor** *n.*

of·fic·i·nal (ə-fĭs'ə-nəl, ô'fĭ-sī'nəl, ŏf'ĭ-) *adj.* **1.** Designating a drug available without prescription. Compare **magistral. 2.** Designating a plant used in medicine.
~*n.* An officinal drug or plant. [Medieval Latin *officīnālis*, "used or kept in a workshop" (especially a medical laboratory), from Latin *officīna*, workshop, reduction of *opificīna*, workshop, from *opifex*, workman : *opus*, work + *facere*, to do.]

of·fi·cious (ə-fĭsh'əs) *adj.* **1.** Excessively forward in offering one's services or advice to others, especially when the services or advice are unnecessary and unwanted; intrusive. **2.** In diplomacy, of a casual nature; not official; unauthorized. **3.** *Archaic.* Eager to render services or to help others. [Latin *officiōsus*, eager to oblige, from *officium*, duty, service, OFFICE.] —**of·fi·cious·ly** *adv.* —**of·fi·cious·ness** *n.*

off·ing (ô'fĭng, ŏf'ĭng) *n.* **1.** The near or immediate future: *I think success is in the offing.* **2.** The part of the sea that is distant yet visible from the shore. **3.** A position at a distance from the shore. [Perhaps from OFF.]

off·ish (ô'fĭsh, ŏf'ĭsh) *adj.* Inclined to be distant and reserved in manner; aloof. —**off·ish·ly** *adv.* —**off·ish·ness** *n.*

off-key (ôf'kē', ŏf'-) *adj.* **1.** Being higher or lower in pitch than the correct notes of a melody. **2.** Being out of accord with what is considered normal or appropriate; irregular. —**off-key** *adv.*

off-li·cense (ôf'lī'səns, ŏf'-) *n. British.* **1.** An establishment selling alcoholic drinks for consumption off the premises. **2.** A license legally permitting such sales.

off-lim·its (ôf'lĭm'ĭts, ŏf'-) *adj.* Forbidden to a designated group: *a bar off-limits to military personnel.*

off-line (ôf'lĭn', ŏf'-) *adj.* **1.** Not in direct connection with a mainframe computer but controlled by a computer storage device. Said of part of a computer system or a peripheral device. **2.** Switched off. Said of a computer. Compare **on-line.**

off-load (ôf'lōd', ŏf'-) *tr.v.* **-loaded, -loading, -loads. 1.** *Aerospace.* To launch (a guided missile or rocket) with propellant tanks less than fully loaded in order to alter the center of gravity of the projectile. **2.** To unload (a vehicle, especially an aircraft). **3. a.** To shift or delegate (work, for example). **b.** To get rid of (something unwanted): *off-loaded her problems onto me.*

off-off-Broad·way (ôf'ôf-brŏd'wā', ŏf'ôf-) *n.* A theatrical movement in New York City that is involved in avant-garde experimental techniques and productions.

off-peak (ôf'pēk', ŏf'-) *adj.* **1.** Of, pertaining to, or being a period of time in which there is least demand for a facility, service, or the like. **2.** Of or pertaining to something offered or existing during off-peak periods: *off-peak prices.*

off-print (ôf'prĭnt', ŏf'-) *n.* A reproduction or excerpt of a printed article that was originally contained in a larger publication.
~*tr.v.* **offprinted, -printing, -prints.** To reproduce or reprint (an excerpt). [Translation of German *Abdruck*.]

off-put·ting (ôf'pŏot'ĭng, ŏf'-) *adj.* **1.** Unpleasant; unappealing. **2.** Disconcerting; discouraging.

off-sales (ôf'sālz', ŏf'-) *pl.n. British.* Sales of alcoholic drinks at an off-license.

off-scour·ing (ôf'skou'rĭng, ŏf'-) *n.* **1.** Something that is scoured off; refuse. **2.** A social outcast or misfit.

off-screen (ôf'skrēn', ŏf'-) *adj.* **1.** Out of sight of the viewer of a motion-picture or television screen: *an offscreen commentator.* **2.** In real life; away from the television or motion-picture screen: *offscreen romances between stars.* —**off-screen** *adv.*

off-sea·son (ôf'sē'zən, ŏf'-) *n.* A time of year when there is least demand for something, such as vacation accommodations. —**off-sea·son** *adj. & adv.*

off·set (ôf'sĕt', ŏf'-) *n.* **1.** Something that balances, counteracts, or compensates. **2.** Something deriving or originating but set off from something else. **3.** *Architecture.* A ledge or recess in a wall formed by a reduction in thickness above. Also called "setoff." **4.** *Botany.* A shoot that develops laterally at the base of a plant, often rooting to form a new plant. **5.** *Geology.* A spur of a range of mountains or hills. **6.** A bend in a pipe or bar to allow it to pass around an obstruction. **7.** *Mining.* A crosscut or drift from a main level. **8.** In surveying, a short distance measured perpendicularly from the main line, used to help in calculating the area of an irregular plot. **9.** *Printing.* **a.** A method of printing in which the impression or image to be printed is transferred from an inked plate to an intermediate surface, usually a rubber-covered cylinder, that transfers

the image onto paper. Also used adjectivally: *offset lithography.* **b.** The unintentional or faulty transfer of ink not yet dry from a printed sheet to a surface, such as the next sheet, that is laid over it.
~*v.* (ôf′sĕt′, ŏf′-, ôf-sĕt′, ŏf-) **offset, -setting, -sets.** —*tr.* **1.** To compensate or cause to compensate for: *offset the loss against tax.* **2.** *Printing.* **a.** To print by offset. **b.** To smear with an offset. **3.** To make or form an offset in (a wall, bar, or pipe). —*intr.* To develop as an offset. **—off•set** *adj.*

off•shoot (ôf′sho͞ot′, ŏf′-) *n.* **1.** Something that branches out or derives its existence or origin from a particular source: *an offshoot of the parent company.* **2.** A branch, descendant, or member of a family or social group. **3.** A lateral shoot from the main stem of a plant.

off•shore (ôf′shôr′, -shōr′, ŏf′-) *adj.* **1.** Moving or directed away from the shore: *an offshore wind.* **2.** Located or occurring at a distance from the shore: *an offshore oil rig.*
~*adv.* **1.** Away from the shore: *The storm moved offshore.* **2.** At a distance from the shore: *A boat moored offshore.*

off•side (ôf′sīd′, ŏf′-) *adj.* **1.** Illegally ahead of the ball or puck in the opponent's half of an attacking zone. Said of a player, team, or play in various games. **2.** *Chiefly British.* On the right-hand side of a vehicle, horse, or team of horses.
~*n.* **1.** A situation in a game in which a player is offside. **2.** *Chiefly British.* The right-hand side of a vehicle, horse, or team of horses.

off•spring (ôf′sprĭng′, ŏf′-) *n., pl.* **offspring. 1.** The progeny of a person, animal, or plant. **2.** A result; an outcome; a product. [Middle English *ofspring,* Old English *ofspring* : *of,* from + *springan,* to SPRING.]

off•stage (ôf′stāj′, ŏf′-) *adj.* Located or occurring in the area of a stage not visible to the audience.
~*adv.* **1.** Away from the area of a stage visible to the audience. **2. a.** In private life: *an actor known by another name off-stage.* **b.** Behind the scenes: *The meeting between the leaders took place off-stage.*

off-street (ôf′strēt′, ŏf′-) *adj.* Away from or not on the street: *off-street parking.*

off-the-cuff (ôf′*th*ə-kŭf′, ŏf′-) *adj.* Not planned in advance; impromptu. [Referring to notes written on a shirt cuff as reminders for someone delivering a speech.] **—off-the-cuff** *adv.*

off-the-peg (ôf′*th*ə-pĕg′, ŏf′-) *adj. British.* Ready-made: *an off-the-peg dress; off-the-peg ideas.*

off-the-rack (ôf′*th*ə-răk′, ŏf′-) *adj.* Ready-made.

off-the-rec•ord (ôf′*th*ə-rĕk′ərd, ŏf′-) *adj.* Not for publication or attribution. **—off-the-rec•ord** *adv.*

off-the-shelf (ôf′*th*ə-shĕlf′, ŏf′-) *adj.* Of or pertaining to merchandise carried in stock that is deliverable without alteration. **—off-the-shelf** *adv.*

off-the-wall (ôf′*th*ə-wôl′, ŏf′-) *adj. Informal.* Unusual, bizarre, or unconventional; crazy: *off-the-wall notions.* [Perhaps alluding to a ball off the wall in squash or handball, hence unexpected, surprising.] **—off-the-wall** *adv.*

off•track (ôf′trăk′, ŏf′-) *adj.* Of, pertaining to, or being gambling on horse races that is conducted away from a racetrack.

off-white (ôf′hwīt′, ŏf′-) *n.* A grayish or yellowish white. **—off-white** *adj.*

off year *n.* **1.** A year in which no major political elections occur. **2.** A year of reduced activity or production: *an off year for soybean crops.*

oft (ôft, ŏft) *adv. Poetic.* Often. Sometimes used in combination: *oft-repeated.* [Middle English, Old English *oft.*]

of•ten (ô′fən, ŏf′ən) *adv.* **1.** Many times; frequently, repeatedly, or customarily. **2.** Much of the time; in many instances. **—as often as. 1.** As many times as. **2.** Every time that. **—every so often.** Sometimes; fairly regularly. **—more often than not.** More than half the time; in most instances.
~*adj. Archaic.* Repeated; frequent. [Middle English *oftin, often,* variants (before vowels and *h*) of *ofte,* OFT.]

of•ten•times (ô′fən-tīmz′, ŏf′ən-) *adv.* Also **oft•times** (ôf′tīmz′, ŏf′-). Frequently; repeatedly.

OG, O.G. 1. officer of the guard. **2.** *Philately.* original gum.

Og•den (ŏg′dən), **Charles Kay** (1889–1957). British semanticist. From ideas presented in his book *The Meaning of Meaning* (1923), written in collaboration with I. A. Richards, he developed the concept of Basic English, an international language of 850 essential words and 150 scientific terms.

o•gee (ō′jē′) *n. Architecture.* **1.** A double curve with the shape of an elongated S. **2.** A molding having in profile an S-shaped curve. **3.** An arch of two curves meeting at a point. In this sense, also called "ogee arch." [Alteration of OGIVE.]

og•ham, o•gam (ŏg′əm, ō′əm) *n.* **1. a.** An alphabet used for writing Irish from the 4th or 5th century A.D. to the early 7th century. **b.** A character of this alphabet. **2. a.** An inscription in the ogham alphabet. **b.** A stone inscribed in the ogham alphabet. [Irish *ogham,* from Old Irish *ogom,* said to be named after its mythical inventor *Ogma*†.]

o•give (ō′jīv′) *n.* **1.** *Statistics.* **a.** The graphic representation of a frequency distribution in which every ordinate represents the sum of frequencies in preceding intervals. **b.** A frequency distribution. **2.** *Architecture.* **a.** A diagonal rib of a Gothic vault. **b.** A pointed arch. Also called "ogive curve." [Middle English, from Old French *augive*†.] **—o•gi•val** (ō-jī′vəl) *adj.*

o•gle (ō′gəl, ô′gəl) *v.* **ogled, ogling, ogles.** —*tr.* To stare at, especially impertinently, flirtatiously, or amorously. —*intr.* To stare impertinently, flirtatiously, or amorously. —See Synonyms at **gaze.**
~*n.* A stare, especially one that is impertinent, flirtatious, or amorous. [From Low German *oegeln,* frequentative of *oegen,* to eye, from *oog,* eye.] **—o•gler** *n.*

O•gle•thorpe (ō′gəl-thôrp′), **James Edward** (1696–1785). English soldier, philanthropist, and colonizer. In 1732 he secured a charter for the colony of Georgia as a refuge for unemployed debtors newly freed from prison. The first 120 settlers arrived in what is now Savannah in 1733.

OGPU, O.G.P.U. (ŏg′po͞o) *n.* A former security branch of the Soviet government functioning as a successor to the **Cheka** and corresponding in broad outline to the later **KGB** *(both of which see).* [Russian *Obyedinyonnoye Gosudarstvyennove Politicheskoye Upravlenie,* "unified government political administration."]

o•gre (ō′gər) *n.* **1.** A legendary man-eating giant or monster. **2.** Anyone who is especially cruel, brutish, or hideous. [French *ogre*† (first used by Perrault in *Contes de Ma Mère l'Oye,* 1697).] **—o•gre•ish** (ō′gər-ĭsh, ō′grĭsh) *adj.*

o•gress (ō′grĭs) *n.* A female ogre.

oh (ō) *interj.* **1.** Used to express strong emotion, such as surprise, fear, anger, or pain. **2.** Used in direct address: *Oh, sir, you forgot your change.* **3.** Used to indicate understanding or acknowledgment of a statement.
~*n., pl.* **oh's** or **ohs.** The exclamation *oh* or any occurrence of it. —See Usage note at **O.** [Middle English *o* (expressive formation). The spelling *oh* is not older than 1548.]

OH Ohio (used with a Zip Code).

O'Ha•ra (ō-hâr′ə, ō-hăr′ə), **John Henry** (1905–70). U.S. author. He wrote short stories for the *New Yorker,* novels such as *Appointment in Samarra* (1934) and *Butterfield 8* (1935), motion-picture scenarios and scripts, and plays.

ohc, o.h.c. overhead camshaft.

O. Henry. See William Sydney **Porter.**

OHG Old High German.

O'Hig•gins (ō-hĭg′ĭnz), **Bernardo,** known as "the Liberator of Chile" (1778–1842). Chilean politician and soldier. The illegitimate son of an Irish soldier, he was commander of the army that liberated Chile from Spain (1818). O'Higgins became president, but his social and economic reforms provoked unrest, and he was forced to resign (1823).

O•hi•o[1] (ō-hī′ō). State in the Great Lakes region of the Middle West. Rich in mineral resources, it is a major coal-producing area and an important industrial state. Agriculture is also extensive, and large amounts of corn, soybeans, wheat, and dairy goods are produced. Its capital is Columbus.

Ohio[2]**.** River of the east-central United States. Formed at Pittsburgh, Pennsylvania, by the confluence of the Monongahela and Allegheny rivers, it flows southwest to join the Mississippi at Cairo, Illinois. The river is important for the transportation of bulk cargoes such as coal and gravel.

Ohio buckeye *n.* A tree, *Aesculus glabra,* of the central United States, having compound leaves and yellowish-green flowers.

ohm (ōm) *n. Symbol* Ω A unit of electrical resistance equal to that of a conductor in which a current of one ampere is produced by a potential of one volt across its terminals. [After Georg Simon OHM.] **—ohm•ic** (ō′mĭk) *adj.*

Ohm (ōm), **Georg Simon** (1787–1854). German physicist. Though he made considerable contributions to mathematics and acoustics, he is best known for his work in the field of electrical resistance.

ohm•age (ō′mĭj) *n. Electricity.* Resistance expressed in ohms.

ohm•me•ter (ōm′mē′tər) *n. Electricity.* An instrument for the direct measurement of the resistance of a conductor in ohms.

OHMS, O.H.M.S. On His (or Her) Majesty's Service.

Ohm's law (ōmz) *n. Physics.* The law stating that the direct electric current flowing in a conductor is directly proportional to the potential difference between its ends. It is usually formulated as $V = IR$, where V is the applied voltage, I is the current, and R (the constant of proportionality) is the resistance of the conductor.

o•ho (ō-hō′) *interj.* Used especially to express ironic surprise or mock astonishment. [Middle English : O + HO.]

-oholic. Variant of **-holic.**

o.h.v., ohv overhead valve.

-oic *suffix.* Indicates the presence of a carboxyl group or a derivative of it; for example, **decanoic acid.** [Lengthening of -IC (denoting acids).]

oick (oik) *n. British Slang.* An uncultivated person. [Imitative of uncultivated speech.]

-oid *suffix.* Indicates: **1.** Likeness, resemblance, or similarity; for example, **anthropoid, crystalloid, planetoid. 2.** A spurious likeness; for example, **factoid.** [Latin *-oīdēs,* from Greek *-oeidēs,* of or having the shape or nature of, from *eidos,* form, shape.]

o•id•i•um (ō-ĭd′ē-əm) *n., pl.* **-ia** (-ē-ə). A spore produced by the fragmentation of a hypha in certain fungi. [New Latin, from Greek *ōion,* egg + *-idion,* diminutive suffix.]

oil (oil) *n.* **1.** Any of numerous mineral, vegetable, and synthetic substances and animal and vegetable fats, that are generally slippery, combustible, viscous, liquid or liquefiable at room temperatures, soluble in various organic solvents, such as ether, but not in water, and used in a great variety of products, especially lubricants and fuels. **2. a.** Petroleum. **b.** A petroleum derivative, such as a machine oil or lubricant. **3.** A substance with an oily consistency: *suntan oil; hair oil.* **4. a.** An **oil color** *(see).* **b.** An **oil paint** *(see).* **c.** An **oil painting** *(see).* **5.** *Informal.* Insincere flattery. **—burn the midnight oil.** To work hard or study late into the night: *When tax*

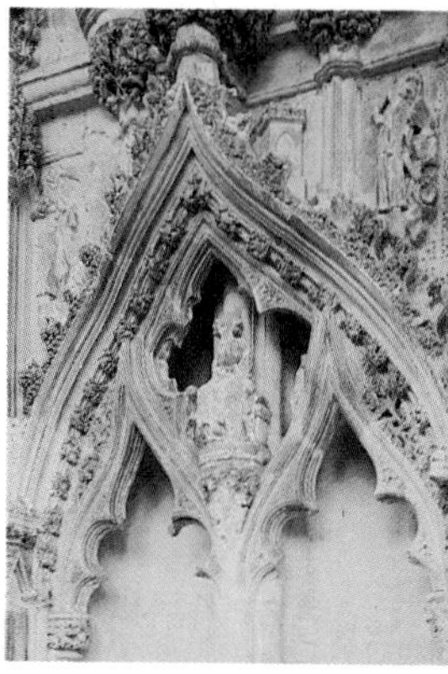

ogee *Each side of an ogee arch is formed from an S-shaped curve. This 14th-century example is at Ely Cathedral in Cambridgeshire, England.*

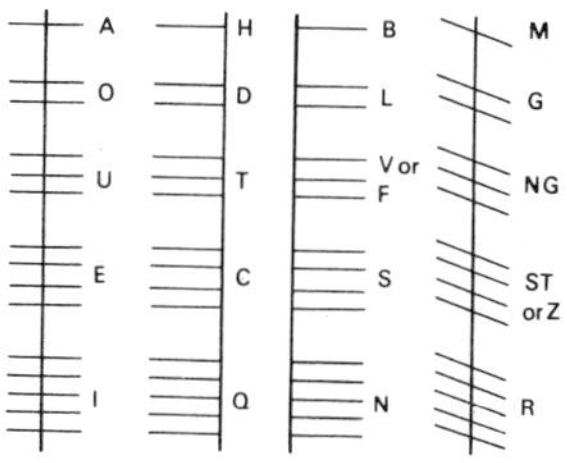

ogham *The five vowels and fifteen consonant sounds of this fourth-century Irish script were notched or drawn around the corners of objects such as stone monuments. Not many inscriptions have survived in legible form because of weathering of the objects.*

time came, *I had to burn the midnight oil.* —**pour oil on troubled waters.** To bring calm to a difficult situation. —**strike oil.** To gain sudden wealth or success. —**the good** (or **dinkum**) **oil.** *Australian & New Zealand Informal.* True and useful information.
~*v.* **oiled, oiling, oils.** —*tr.* To lubricate, supply, cover, or polish with oil: *oiled the moving parts of the sewing machine.* —*intr.* **1.** To load up with or take on fuel oil. **2. a.** To become oil by melting. **b.** To become oily in consistency. —**oil someone's hand** (or **palm**). *Informal.* **1.** To bribe. **2.** To give a tip to: *oiled the headwaiter's palm.* [Middle English *oli, oil(e),* (olive) oil, from Old French, from Latin *oleum,* from Greek *elaion,* from *elaia,* olive.] —**oil** *adj.*

oil beetle *n.* Any of various insects of the subfamily Meloinae that exude an oily yellow substance when disturbed.

oil·bird (oil′bûrd′) *n.* A nocturnal bird, *Steatornis caripensis,* native to tropical America, that navigates by echolocation and feeds on fruit detected by smell. The young have a layer of fat that yields an oil used in cooking and for lighting. Also called "guacharo."

oil burner *n.* **1.** A heating unit, furnace, or boiler that burns fuel oil. **2.** A device for spraying fine droplets of fuel oil into an oil burner prior to ignition.

oil cake *n.* The solid residue left after certain oilseeds, such as cottonseed and linseed, have been pressed free of their oil. It is used after grinding as cattle feed or fertilizer.

oil·can (oil′kăn′) *n.* A can for oil, especially a can with a spout that releases oil drop by drop, as for lubricating machinery.

oil·cloth (oil′klôth′, -klŏth′) *n.* A fabric treated with clay, oil, and pigments to make it waterproof. It is used as a cover for tables or shelving.

oil color *n.* A color consisting of pigment ground in oil.

oil·cup (oil′kŭp′) *n.* A small cup with a tube at the base that feeds oil continuously into a bearing.

oil drum *n.* A metal drum used to transport oil, oil products, or similar liquids.

oil·er (oi′lər) *n.* **1.** One that oils machinery and engines. **2.** An oil tanker. **3.** An oilcan. **4.** A well that produces oil. **5.** A ship that burns oil.

oil field *n.* An area with reserves of recoverable petroleum, especially one with several oil-producing wells.

oil gland *n.* **1.** Any gland that secretes oil. **2.** *Zoology.* The **uropygial gland** (*see*).

oil of cloves *n.* An oil derived from the flowers of the clove and used in microscopy, dentistry, and confectionery.

oil of turpentine *n.* Refined turpentine.

oil of vitriol *n. Chemistry.* **Sulfuric acid** (*see*).

oil paint *n.* A paint in which the vehicle is a drying oil, usually linseed.

oil painting *n.* **1.** A picture painted in oil colors. **2.** The art or practice of painting with oil colors.

oil palm *n.* **1.** A tall palm tree, *Elaeis guineensis,* native to tropical Africa, having nutlike fruits that yield a commercially valuable oil. **2.** Any of several other palms yielding oil.

oil pan *n.* The bottom of the crankcase of an internal-combustion engine that serves as an oil reservoir.

oil·pa·per (oil′pā′pər) *n.* Paper that is soaked in oil to make it transparent and water-resistant.

oil rig *n.* An installation on an oil well for drilling for and extracting oil and natural gas from the earth or the seabed.

oil sand *n. Geology.* **1.** Any stratum or rock formation containing oil. **2.** A stratum of porous sandstone from which petroleum can be extracted through drilled wells.

oil·seed (oil′sēd′) *n.* Any seed, such as linseed or rapeseed, from which oil can be extracted in commercially viable quantities.

oil shale *n. Geology.* A black or dark-brown shale containing hydrocarbons that yield petroleum by distillation.

oil·skin (oil′skĭn′) *n.* **1.** Cloth treated with oil so that it is waterproof. **2.** An outer garment made of oilskin.

oil slick *n.* A thin film of oil on water; especially, a large patch of oil on the surface of the sea that has leaked from or been discharged by a ship.

oil·stone (oil′stōn′) *n.* A smooth whetstone lubricated with oil, used for fine sharpening.

oil varnish *n.* See **varnish** (sense 1a).

oil well *n.* A hole dug or drilled in the earth or seabed from which petroleum flows or is pumped.

oil·y (oi′lē) *adj.* **-ier, -iest. 1.** Of or pertaining to oil. **2.** Impregnated or smeared with oil; greasy. **3.** Excessively suave in action or behavior; unctuous. —**oil·i·ly** *adv.* —**oil·i·ness** *n.*

oink (oingk) *n.* The natural grunting noise of a hog. [Imitative.]

oinology. Variant of **oenology.**

oint·ment (oint′mənt) *n.* Any of numerous viscous or semisolid substances used on the skin as a cosmetic, a soothing agent, or a medicament; an unguent; a salve. [Middle English, variant (influenced by obsolete *oint,* to anoint) of *oinement,* from Old French *oignement,* from Vulgar Latin *unguimentum* (unattested), from Latin *unguentum,* from *unguens* (stem *unguent-*), present participle of *unguere,* to anoint.]

Oise (wäz). River, rising in the Ardennes Mts. of southern Belgium and flowing 300 kilometers (186 miles) through northern France to join the Seine. It is an important transportation route.

O·jib·wa (ō-jĭb′wä′, -wə) *n., pl.* **-was** or collectively **Ojibwa.** Also **O·jib·way** (-wā′) *pl.* **-ways** or collectively **Ojibway. 1.** A member of an Algonquian-speaking North American Indian people inhabiting regions of the United States and Canada around Lake Superior. **2.** The Algonquian language spoken by this people. —**O·jib·wa** *adj.*

O·jos del Sa·la·do (ō′hōs dĕl sə-lä′dō). Peak in the Andes on the border between Argentina and Chile. It is thought to be higher than Mt. Aconcagua, long considered the highest peak in the Western Hemisphere.

OK Oklahoma (used with a Zip Code).

O.K., OK, o·kay (ō-kā′) *n., pl.* **O.K.'s** or **OK's** or **okays.** *Informal.* Approval; endorsement; agreement: *I need your okay before I make the reservations.*
~*tr.v.* **O.K.'d** or **OK'd** or **okayed, O.K.'ing** or **OK'ing** or **okaying, O.K.'s** or **OK's** or **okays.** *Informal.* To approve or endorse; agree to *She O.K'd* (or *okayed*) *the invoice.*
~*interj. Informal.* **1.** Used to express approval or agreement. **2.** Used to indicate that the speaker appreciates a point or objection made by another: *O.K., he's clever, but he's very slow.*
~*adj. Informal.* **1.** All right; satisfactory. **2.** In good condition or health. **3.** Very good; splendid: *an O.K. guy.* [Abbreviation of *oll korrect,* slang respelling of *all correct.* Popularized as a slogan of the O.K. Club, Democratic party political club of 1840; for *Old Kinder-*

oil

THE PRIMITIVE LIFE FORMS THAT PRODUCE "BLACK GOLD"

How oil is formed beneath the oceans

Oil, the lifeblood of industrialized society, is a mixture of chemicals derived from the smallest and most primitive life forms. Microorganisms called plankton, which inhabit the oceans, are thought to be the basis of crude oil.

Dead organisms, trapped in the mud and clay carried out to the continental shelves by rivers, are attacked by bacteria that break down the fatty and waxy organic debris into simpler chemical compounds. Under the high temperature resulting from gradual burial beneath new deposits, these are converted into a bituminous substance called kerogen. Further burial and increase of temperature converts this into oil and gas. Once formed, the oil migrates out of its bedrock and, being less dense, moves upward. If it meets a ceiling of impermeable rock it spreads out in a thin film beneath it, but where folding of the earth's crust has occurred, the oil and gas can accumulate in pockets.

Seepages to the surface, or "shows" of oil, such as those occurring in the Dead Sea and Mesopotamia, were exploited for caulking watercourses and ships and have been used as building materials for houses and roads since the dawn of civilization. The oil industry first developed in the 1850's in the United States, when oil discovered in brine wells was exploited for lighting. Oil could also be broken down, or refined, to produce gas, lubricating oil, and paraffin wax.

About 1910, with the development of the automobile, the oil industry began on a large scale, and during the 1920's and 1930's refining processes were devised to improve the yield of gasoline from oil. By-products could be converted into drugs, dyes, explosives, insecticides, plastics, detergents, and synthetic fibers. In little over a century the oil industry has become the world's biggest enterprise.

THE FORMATION OF AN OIL FIELD

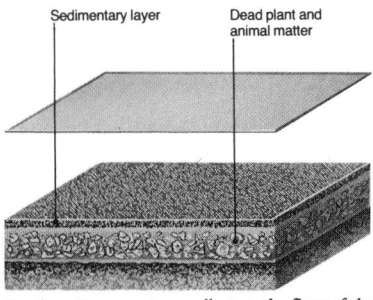

Dead marine organisms collect on the floor of the continental shelf and are broken down by bacteria. They are covered by muddy sediment washed down by the rivers.

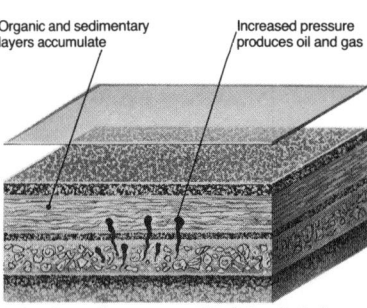

Oil and gas form as a result of chemical changes brought about by high temperatures to which the organic deposits are subjected beneath successive layers of sediment.

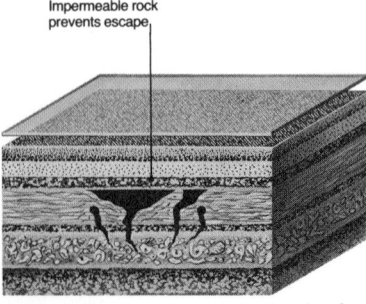

Helped perhaps by water pressure, the oil and gas move up from their bed of shale. Where flat impermeable rock above prevents their escape, they spread out in a thin layer.

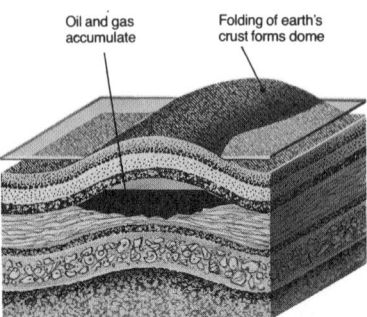

Where pressures in the earth's crust have caused an impermeable layer to rise in a dome shape, the oil and gas rise into it, and are trapped there, forming a potential oil field.

hook, nickname of President Martin Van Buren, born at *Kinderhook,* New York.] —**O.K.** *adv.*

Usage: This word, used as a noun or verb (*He gave his O.K. He okayed the agreement*), is restricted to informal speech and writing and to some forms of official correspondence, especially in business circles. The form *okay* is generally used when there is an inflectional ending, as in *okayed.*

o•ka•pi (ō-kä′pē) *n., pl.* **-pis** or collectively **okapi.** A ruminant forest mammal, *Okapia johnstoni,* related to the giraffe but smaller and having a short neck, found in the Congo region in Africa. [Central African name, from Mbuba.]

O•kee•cho•bee, Lake (ō′kē-chō′bē). Lake, *c.* 1,815 square kilometers (700 square miles) in southeastern Florida, north of the Everglades. It is part of the Cross-Florida Waterway, a shallow water passage from the Atlantic Ocean to Fort Myers on the Gulf of Mexico, used by small commercial and pleasure craft.

O'Keeffe (ō-kēf′), **Georgia** (1887–1986). U.S. artist. Her first one-woman show was in 1917. She is well known for her semiabstract paintings of flowers and desert landscapes.

O•ke•fe•no•kee Swamp (ō′kə-fə-nō′kē). A swamp on the Georgia-Florida border. It has rich and varied wildlife.

O•kie (ō′kē) *n. Informal.* An impoverished migrant farm worker; especially, one from Oklahoma forced to leave his farm during the depression of the 1930's. [From OKLAHOMA.]

O•ki•na•wa (ō′kĭ-nä′wə). An island of Japan. The main island of the Ryukyu group, it is 531 kilometers (330 miles) south of the main Japanese chain. Sugar cane, sweet potatoes, and rice are grown and fishing is important. It was occupied by the United States (1945–72).

Ok•la•ho•ma (ō′klə-hō′mə). *Abbr.* **Okla.** State of the south-central United States, drained by the Red and Arkansas rivers. Western Oklahoma is part of the Great Plains. The central and eastern regions are mostly prairie. Cotton was formerly the major crop, but has been superseded by wheat. It is a major oil- and gas-producing state. Explored by the Spanish, it was bought by the United States as part of the Louisiana Purchase (1803). Adverse weather conditions and overuse of the land combined to make northwestern Oklahoma part of the Dust Bowl of the 1930's. Its capital is Oklahoma City. —**Ok•la•ho•man** *adj. & n.*

Oklahoma City. Capital of Oklahoma, in the central part of the state, on the North Canadian River. It was founded (1889) during the Oklahoma Land Rush; it grew rapidly, becoming capital in 1910. An important livestock market, it has grain mills and meatpacking and cotton-processing plants. The city is the center of a vast oil and natural gas field. One of the nation's largest collections of Indian relics is here.

o•kra (ō′krə) *n.* **1.** A tall tropical and semitropical plant, *Hibiscus esculentus,* having edible mucilaginous green pods. **2.** The edible pods of the okra, used in soups and as a vegetable. **3.** A dish prepared with okra, **gumbo** *(see).* [West African native name *nkruma.*]

-ol *suffix. Chemistry.* Indicates alcohol or phenol; for example, **glycerol, naphthol.** [From ALCOHOL.]

Ok•to•ber•fest (ŏk-tō′bər-fĕst′) *n.* A festival held in autumn that usually features the consumption of beer. [German : *Oktober,* October + *Fest,* festival.]

O•laf I (ō′läf, ō′ləf), Also **O•lav** (ō′läv, ō′ləv), known as "Olaf Tryggvesson" (*c.* 969–1000). King of Norway. He was a Viking marauder of England until converted to Christianity. On his accession to the throne (995), he attempted to convert the people of Norway, causing disaffection. He died at the Battle of Svolder, leaping into the sea rather than surrender to the Danes.

Olaf II, Also **Olav, Saint,** known as "Olaf Haraldsson" (*c.* 995–1030). King and patron saint of Norway. On ascending the throne (1015), he continued Olaf I's conversion of Norway to Christianity. Driven from his kingdom (1028) by Canute, he died in battle at Stiklestad.

Olaf V, Also **Olav** (1903–). King of Norway. Grandson of Edward VII of the United Kingdom, he succeeded Haakon VII to the throne in 1957.

old (ōld) *adj.* **older, oldest. 1. a.** Having lived or existed for a relatively long time; far advanced in years or life. See Usage note at **elder. b.** Relatively advanced in age. **2. a.** Made long ago; in existence for many years; not new: *an old book.* **b.** No longer current or in use: *old magazines.* **c.** In existence long enough to lack freshness; stale: *the same old answers. This bread is a bit old.* **3.** Of or pertaining to a long life or to persons who have had a long life: *a ripe old age.* **4. a.** Having or exhibiting the physical characteristics of advanced life or an aged person: *She had an old face for her years.* **b.** Weak or infirm from or as if from age: *feeling very old.* **5.** Having or exhibiting the wisdom of age; mature; sensible: *That child is old for her years.* **6.** Having a specified age: *She was twelve years old.* **7. a.** Belonging to a remote or former period in history; ancient: *old fossils.* **b.** Belonging to or being of an earlier time: *his old classmates.* **c.** Previous; former: *his old job.* **8.** *Usually* **Old.** *Abbr.* **O, O.** Being the earlier or earliest of two or more related objects, stages, versions, or periods: *the Old Testament; Old High German.* **9.** *Geology.* **a.** Having become slower in flow and less vigorous in action. Said of rivers. **b.** Having become simpler in form and of lower relief. Said of land forms. **10.** Worn or dilapidated through age or use; worn-out: *an old coat.* **11.** Known through long acquaintance or use; long familiar: *an old friend; the old routine.* **12. a.** Dear or cherished, as through long acquaintance. Used as a term of affection or cordiality: *good old Harry.* **b.** *Chiefly British Informal.* Used with certain nouns as a form of address: *Sorry, old chap! Look here, old thing!* **c.** *Chiefly British Informal.* Used with no definite independent meaning to imply some humorous familiarity: *a touch of the old rheumatism.* **13.** Skilled or able through long experience; practiced: *an old campaigner.* **14.** *Informal.* Used as an intensive: *had a high old time; any old thing will do.*
~*n.* **1.** Former times; yore: *in days of old.* **2.** An individual of a specified age. Used in combination: *a five-year-old.* [Middle English *old, ald,* Old English *eald, ald,* from West Germanic *aldha* (unattested).] —**old•ish** *adj.* —**old•ness** *n.*

Synonyms: *aged, ancient, antiquated, antique, archaic, elder, elderly, obsolete, superannuated, venerable.*

old-age pension (ōld′āj′) *n.* A pension received by a person who has retired from his occupation. —**old-age pensioner** *n.*

Old Bai•ley (bā′lē). The popular name for the central criminal court of the Crown Court for the City of London, England. [So called because it stands in the thoroughfare called Old Bailey.]

old bird *n. British Informal.* One who is cunning, astute, or shrewd.

old boy *n.* **1.** A graduate or former pupil of a boys' school, especially a private one. **2.** *Informal.* **a.** An old man. **b.** A husband or senior male colleague. **c.** Used as a familiar term of address to a boy, man, or thing personified as a male.

old boy network *n.* An unofficial system of mutual help, especially in obtaining jobs, among men who have shared a usually privileged form of schooling, university background, or the like.

Old Bulgarian *n.* Old Church Slavonic.

Old Catholic *n. Abbr.* **O.C. 1.** A member of a Jansenist church originating in Utrecht, Holland, in the 18th century. **2.** A member of an independent religious organization formed by a group of German Roman Catholics who refused to accept the doctrine of papal infallibility proclaimed by the first Vatican Council of 1870.

Old Church Slavonic *n.* The literary Slavic language into which the Bible was translated in the 10th or early 11th century. It is still used as the liturgical language of several Eastern churches.

old country *n.* The native country of an immigrant.

Old Danish *n.* The Danish language from the beginning of the 12th to the end of the 14th century.

Old Dutch *n.* Dutch from the beginning of the 12th to the middle of the 13th century.

old•en (ōl′dən) *adj. Archaic & Poetic.* Old; ancient: *in olden times.* [Middle English, from *old,* OLD.]

Ol•den•burg (ōl′dən-bûrg′) **Claes Thure** (1929–). Swedish-born U.S. sculptor. A leading pop artist, he re-created "ordinary environments," as in *The Store* (1960–61), and "soft sculptures" of household objects made from stuffed vinyl and canvas.

Old English *n. Abbr.* **OE, OE., O.E. 1.** The English language from the middle of the 5th to the beginning of the 12th century. Also called "Anglo-Saxon." **2.** *Printing.* **Black letter** *(see).*

Old English sheepdog *n.* A large sturdy dog of a breed having a thick, shaggy bluish-gray and white coat and hair that hangs over the eyes.

oldest profession *n.* Prostitution.

old fashioned *n.* A cocktail made of whiskey, bitters, sugar, and fruit.

old-fash•ioned (ōld′făsh′ənd) *adj.* **1.** Of a style or method formerly in vogue; outdated: *used an old-fashioned manual typewriter.* **2.** Attached to or favoring methods, ideas, or customs of an earlier time: *an old-fashioned girl.*

old fogy, old fogey *n.* One who is tiresomely conservative or old-fashioned. [Scottish, from obsolete *old fogey,* an old and invalid soldier.] —**old•fo•gy•ish, old•fo•gey•ish** (ōld′fō′gē-ĭsh) *adj.*

Old French *n.* French from the 9th to the middle of the 16th century.

Old Frisian *n.* Frisian from the beginning of the 13th century to the end of the 15th century.

old girl *n.* **1.** A graduate or former pupil of a girls' school, especially a private one. **2.** *Informal.* **a.** An old woman. **b.** A wife, mother, or senior female colleague. **c.** Used as a familiar form of address to a girl, woman, or thing personified as a female.

Old Glory *n.* The flag of the United States.

old gold *n.* A dark yellow, from light olive or olive brown to deep or strong yellow. —**old-gold** (ōld′gōld′) *adj.*

old guard *n.* **1. Old Guard.** The imperial guard of Napoleon I of France. **2.** A group of defenders of an existing or formerly existing cause or principle. **3.** The conservative, often reactionary element of a given class, society, or political group. **4.** A group of people who are experienced in or veterans of a given field. [Translation of French *Vieille Garde.*]

old hand *n.* One who has had much practice or experience in a particular sphere of activity.

old hat *adj. Informal.* **1.** Behind the times; old-fashioned. **2.** Overused and commonplace; trite.

Old High German *n. Abbr.* **OHG** High German from the middle of the 9th to the end of the 11th century.

Old Icelandic *n.* Icelandic from the middle of the 12th to the middle of the 16th century. Also called "Old Norse."

old•ie (ōl′dē) *n. Informal.* Something that is old, especially a song that was popular in the past.

Old Iranian *n.* Any of the Iranian languages in use before the Christian era, the principal attested forms being Avestan and Old Persian.

Old Irish *n.* The Irish language from 725 to the mid-10th century.

oil beetle *This soft-bodied beetle has no hind wings and only short forewings, which leave most of its abdomen exposed. When molested, it exudes an evil-tasting oily secretion from its joints. The species shown here is native to Europe, but there are numerous related species all over Asia and the Americas.*

okapi *Native to the rain forests of central Africa, the okapi is a hoofed mammal related to the giraffe. It lives on leaves, twigs, and fruit and was unknown to science until 1900.*

okra *The gummy pods of this tropical and subtropical plant are used to thicken soups and stews. In the southern United States, the plant and the stew are known as gumbo.*

olive *A semitropical evergreen tree with leathery leaves and an edible fruit. Olive oil, derived from the crushed fruit, is used as a salad dressing, for cooking, and in the manufacture of soap.*

Old Italian *n.* The Italian language until the middle of the 16th century. —**Old Italian** *adj.*

old lady *n.* **1.** *Slang.* **a.** One's mother. **b.** One's wife. **c.** One's girlfriend. **2.** A moth, *Mormo maura,* having dark-brown patterned wings.

Old Latin *n.* Latin from the first texts, in the 6th century B.C., up to the 2nd century B.C.

old-line (ōld′līn′) *adj.* **1.** Adhering to conservative or reactionary principles. **2.** Long established; traditional. —**old-lin·er** *n.*

Old Low German *n.* Low German from the middle of the 9th to the middle of the 13th century. Also called "Old Saxon."

old maid *n.* **1.** *Informal.* A woman who is not married, especially an older woman; a spinster. **2.** *Informal.* A primly fastidious person. **3.** A card game in which the player who holds a designated card at the end is an "old maid." —**old-maid·ish** (ōld-mā′dĭsh) *adj.*

old man *n.* **1.** *Slang.* **a.** One's father. **b.** One's husband. **c.** One's boyfriend. **d.** A man in authority. **2.** A plant, the **southernwood** *(see).* **3.** *Australian.* An adult male kangaroo.

old-man-and-wom·an (ōld′măn′ənd-wo͝om′ən) *n.* A plant, the **houseleek** *(see).*

old-man cactus (ōld′măn′) *n.* A treelike cactus, *Cephalocereus senilis,* having tufts of long white hair on the tips of its branches.

old-man's-beard (ōld′mănz-bîrd′) *n.* Any of various plants, such as Spanish moss, having parts suggestive of a beard.

old master *n.* **1.** A distinguished European artist of the period from around 1500 to the early 1700's; especially, one of the great painters of this period. **2.** A work created by an old master.

old moon *n.* A phase of the waning moon; the last quarter.

Old Nick *n.* The devil; Satan.

Old Norse *n. Abbr.* **ON, O.N. 1.** The North Germanic language from which the modern Scandinavian languages are descended. **2.** This language as represented in either of two national literatures: **a. Old Icelandic** *(see).* **b. Old Norwegian** *(see).*

Old Norwegian *n.* Norwegian from the middle of the 12th to the end of the 14th century. Also called "Old Norse."

Old Persian *n.* An old Iranian language attested in cuneiform inscriptions dating from the 6th to the 5th century B.C.

Old Prussian *n.* The Baltic language of eastern Prussia that became extinct in the 18th century.

old rose *n.* A dark pink to grayish or moderate red.

Old Russian *n.* The Russian language as used in documents from the 11th to the end of the 16th century.

Old Saxon *n.* **Old Low German** *(see).*

old school *n.* **1.** A group committed to traditional ideas or practices. **2.** *British.* One's former school. —**old-school** (ōld′sko͞ol′) *adj.*

old-school tie *n.* **1.** A tie that bears the colors of a British public school, especially one that is prestigious. **2.** The solidarity and system of mutual assistance attributed to graduates of British public schools. **3.** A narrow, clannish attitude among members of a clique.

Old South *n.* The southern states of the original 13 American colonies, especially those that later joined the Confederate States of America: Virginia, North and South Carolina, and Georgia.

Old Spanish *n.* Spanish before the middle of the 16th century.

old squaw *n.* A marine duck, *Clangula hyemalis,* that has black and white plumage and long upward-pointing tail feathers and is found in Arctic and North Temperate regions. Also called "oldwife."

old stag·er (stā′jər) *n. British Informal.* A person with great experience; an old hand.

old·ster (ōld′stər) *n. Informal.* An old or elderly person.

Old Stone Age *n.* The Paleolithic age.

old style *n.* **1.** *Printing.* A style of type that originated in the 18th century and is characterized by slight contrast between light and heavy strokes and by slanting serifs. **2. Old Style.** *Abbr.* **O.S.** The method of reckoning dates according to the Julian calendar.

Old Testament *n. Abbr.* **OT, O.T. 1.** The first of the two main divisions of the Christian Bible, containing the Hebrew Scriptures. Compare **Hebrew Scriptures. 2.** The covenant of God with Israel as distinguished in Christianity from the dispensation of Christ constituting the New Testament. [Middle English, translation of Late Latin *Vetus Testāmentum,* translation of Greek *Palaia Diathēkē,* "Old Covenant," designation based on the Pauline distinction between the covenant with Israel and the new covenant of Christ.]

old-time (ōld′tīm′) *adj.* Of or pertaining to a time in the past: *old-time dancing; old-time music.*

old-tim·er (ōld′tī′mər) *n. Informal.* **1. a.** A veteran. **b.** An old man. **2.** Something that is very old or antiquated.

Old Turkic *n.* Turkic from the 7th century A.D. to the 10th century, attested in documents from various places in central Asia and divided into two principal dialects, Turkut and Old Uighur.

Old Uighur *n.* See **Old Turkic.**

Ol·du·vai Gorge (ōl′də-vī′). Gorge in northern Tanzania. It contains archaeological sites rich in fossils and Paleolithic implements. Detailed study of the site was begun in 1931 by Mary and Louis Leakey. One of their most famous discoveries was *Homo habilis. Homo erectus* remains have also been found.

Old Welsh *n.* Welsh before the 12th century.

old·wife (ōld′wīf′) *n., pl.* **-wives** (-wīvz′). **1.** A duck, the **old squaw** *(see).* **2.** Any of several fishes, such as the **alewife** and the **menhaden** *(both of which see).*

old wives' tale *n.* An example of superstitious folklore, usually claiming to explain natural or medical phenomena.

old woman *n.* **1.** *Slang.* A wife or mother. **2.** *Informal.* A nervous or fussy person, especially a male.

Old World *n.* The countries of the Eastern Hemisphere, including Eurasia and Africa and referring particularly to Europe.

old-world (ōld′wûrld′) *adj.* **1.** Antique; old-fashioned; quaint. **2.** *Often* **Old-World.** Of, pertaining to, or native to the Old World.

Old-World monkey *n.* Any monkey of the family Cercopithecidae, which is widespread throughout the warmer zones of the Eastern Hemisphere and includes the baboons, macaques, and rhesus and colobus monkeys.

Old Year's Night, Auld Year's Night *n. Scottish.* New Year's Eve.

o·lé (ō-lā′) *interj.* Used to express excited approval, especially in Spanish-speaking countries.
~*n.* A cry of olé. [Spanish.]

-ole[1] *suffix.* Indicates small, little; for example, **petiole.** [Latin *-olus, -ola, -olum,* diminutive suffixes.]

-ole[2]**.** Variant of **oleo-.**

o·le·a·ceous (ō′lē-ā′shəs) *adj.* Of or pertaining to the Oleaceae, a family of trees and shrubs including the olive, ash, and lilac.

o·le·ag·i·nous (ō′lē-ăj′ə-nəs) *adj.* **1.** Of or pertaining to oil. **2.** Oily; unctuous. [French *oléagineux,* from Latin *oleāginus,* belonging to the olive tree, from *olea,* olive, from Greek *elaia.*] —**o·le·ag·i·nous·ly** *adv.* —**o·le·ag·i·nous·ness** *n.*

o·le·an·der (ō′lē-ăn′dər, ō′lē-ăn′dər) *n.* Any poisonous evergreen shrub of the genus *Nerium,* found in warm climates, especially *N. oleander,* having fragrant white, pink, or red flowers. [Medieval Latin, alteration of *arodandrum, lorandrum,* perhaps from a Vulgar Latin deformation of Latin *rhododendron,* RHODODENDRON.]

o·le·an·do·my·cin (ō′lē-ăn′də-mī′sĭn) *n.* An antibiotic, $C_{35}H_{61}NO_{12}$, produced by *Streptomyces antibioticus,* mainly effective against Gram-positive microorganisms. [OLEAND(ER) + -MYCIN.]

o·le·as·ter (ō′lē-ăs′tər, ō′lē-ăs′tər) *n.* A small Eurasian tree, *Elaeagnus angustifolia,* having silvery leaves and flowers and olivelike fruit. Also called "wild olive." [Latin, wild olive tree : *olea,* olive tree, olive, from Greek *elaia* + *-aster,* diminutive suffix.]

o·le·ate (ō′lē-āt′) *n.* An ester or salt of oleic acid. [French *oléate* : OLE(O)- + -ATE.]

o·lec·ra·non (ō-lĕk′rə-nŏn′) *n. Anatomy.* The large point on the upper end of the ulna that projects behind the elbow joint and forms the point of the elbow. Also informally called "crazy bone," "funny bone." [New Latin, from Greek *ōlekranon,* "elbow-tip" : *ōlenē,* elbow + *kranion,* head, skull.] —**o·lec·ra·nal** (ō-lĕk′rə-nəl), **o·le·cra·ni·al** (ō′lə-krā′nē-əl), **o·le·cra·ni·an** (-krā′nē-ən) *adj.*

o·le·fin (ō′lə-fĭn) *n.* Any of a class of unsaturated hydrocarbons, such as ethylene, having the general formula C_nH_{2n} and characterized by relatively great chemical activity. [French *(gaz) oléfiant,* "oil-forming (gas)," ethylene (which forms an oily liquid with chlorine) : OLE(O)- + *-fiant,* making, from *-fier,* -FY + -IN.] —**o·le·fin·ic** (ō′lə-fĭn′ĭk) *adj.*

o·le·ic (ō-lē′ĭk) *adj.* Of or derived from oil.

oleic acid *n.* An oily liquid, $CH_3(CH_2)_7CH{:}CH(CH_2)_7COOH$, that occurs in animal and vegetable oils.

o·le·in (ō′lē-ĭn) *n.* Also **o·le·ine** (-ĭn, -ēn′). A yellow oily liquid, $(C_{17}H_{33}COO)_3C_3H_5$, occurring naturally in most fats and oils, including olive oil. It is used as a textile lubricant. Also called "triolein." [French *oléine* : OLE(O)- + -IN.]

o·le·o (ō′lē-ō′) *n.* Margarine.

oleo-, ole- *prefix.* Indicates oil or pertaining to oil; for example, **oleoresin, oleomargarine, oleic.** [French *olé-, oléo-,* from Latin *oleo-,* from *oleum,* (olive) oil, from Greek *elaion,* from *elaia,* olive.]

o·le·o·graph (ō′lē-ə-grăf′, -gräf′) *n.* **1.** A chromolithograph printed in imitation of an oil painting. **2.** The lacelike pattern formed by a drop of oil on the surface of water. [OLEO- + -GRAPH.] —**o·le·og·ra·pher** (ō′lē-ŏg′rə-fər) *n.* —**o·le·o·graph·ic** (ō′lē-ə-grăf′ĭk) *adj.* —**o·le·og·ra·phy** (ō′lē-ŏg′rə-fē) *n.*

o·le·o·mar·ga·rine (ō′lē-ō-mär′jər-ĭn, -jə-rēn′) *n.* **Margarine** *(see).*

oleo oil *n.* An oil obtained from beef fat and used in the manufacture of certain types of margarine.

o·le·o·res·in (ō′lē-ō-rĕz′ĭn) *n.* **1.** A naturally occurring mixture of an oil and resin, such as the exudate from pine trees. **2.** An oil-resin mixture extracted from plants. —**o·le·o·res·in·ous** *adj.*

o·le·um (ō′lē-əm) *n., pl.* **-lea** (-lē-ə) or **-ums.** A corrosive solution of sulfur trioxide in sulfuric acid. [Latin, OIL.]

ol·fac·tion (ŏl-făk′shən, ōl-) *n.* **1.** The sense of smell. **2.** The action of smelling. [Latin *olfacere,* to smell. See **olfactory.**]

ol·fac·tom·e·ter (ŏl′făk-tŏm′ĭ-tər, ōl′-) *n.* An instrument for measuring the acuity of the sense of smell. [OLFACT(ION) + -METER.] —**ol·fac·to·met·ric** (ŏl′făk-tə-mĕt′rĭk, ōl′-) *adj.* —**ol·fac·tom·e·try** *n.*

ol·fac·to·ry (ŏl-făk′tər-ē, -trē, ōl-) *adj.* Of, pertaining to, or contributing to the sense of smell.
~*n., pl.* **-ries.** A nerve or organ involved in the sense of smell. [Latin *olfactōrius* (unattested), from *olfacere,* to smell : *olēre,* to smell + *facere,* to make.]

olfactory lobe *n.* A projection of the lower anterior portion of each cerebral hemisphere.

olfactory nerve *n.* Either of two bundles of nerve fibers, one on each side of the nasal cavity, that conduct chemical indications of smell.

ol·fac·tron·ics (ŏl′făk-trŏn′ĭks, ōl′-) *n. Used with a singular verb.* The scientific study of the detection and identification of odors. [Blend of OLFACTION and ELECTRONICS.]

o·lib·a·num (ō-lĭb′ə-nəm) *n.* A gum resin, **frankincense** *(see).* [Middle English, from Medieval Latin, from Arabic *al-lubān,* "the frankincense," probably from Greek *libanos,* of Semitic origin, akin to Hebrew *lĕbōriā,* incense.]

ol·i·garch (ŏl′ə-gärk′) *n.* A member of an oligarchy. [Greek *oligarkhēs* : OLIG(O)- + -*arkhēs*, -ARCH.]

ol·i·gar·chy (ŏl′ə-gär′kē) *n., pl.* **-chies. 1. a.** Government by the few, especially by a small faction of persons or families. **b.** Those making up such a faction. **2.** A state governed by oligarchy. —**ol·i·gar·chal** (ŏl′ə-gär′kəl), **ol·i·gar·chic** (-kĭk), **ol·i·gar·chi·cal** (-kĭ-kəl) *adj.*

oligo-, olig- *prefix.* Indicates few; for example, **oligopoly, oligosaccharide.** [Greek, from *oligos,* few, little.]

Ol·i·go·cene (ŏl′ə-gō-sēn′, ō′lə-) *adj.* Of or designating the geologic time and deposits of the epoch in the Tertiary period of the Cenozoic era that extended from the Eocene to the Miocene. ∼*n.* **1.** The Oligocene epoch. Preceded by *the.* **2.** The deposits of this epoch. [OLIGO- + -CENE.]

ol·i·go·chaete (ŏl′ə-gō-kēt′, ō′lə-) *n.* Any of various worms of the class Oligochaeta, including the earthworms. [New Latin *Oligochaeta* : OLIGO- + CHAETA.] —**ol·i·go·chae·tous** (ŏl′ə-gō-kē′təs, ō′lə-) *adj.*

ol·i·go·clase (ŏl′ə-gō-klās′, -klāz′, ō′lə-) *n.* One of the plagioclase group of minerals. [German *Oligoklas* : OLIGO- + -CLASE.]

ol·i·go·cy·the·mi·a, ol·i·go·cy·thae·mi·a (ŏl′ĭ-gō-sī-thē′mē-ə, ō′lĭ-) *n.* Deficiency of the cellular elements of the blood, causing a form of anemia. [OLIGO- + CYT(O)- + -(H)EMIA.]

ol·i·go·gene (ŏl′ĭ-gō-jēn′, ō′lĭ-) *n.* A gene that determines major qualitative hereditary characteristics. —**ol·i·go·gen·ic** (ŏl′ĭ-gō-jĕn′ĭk, ō′lĭ-) *adj.*

o·lig·o·mer (ə-lĭg′ə-mər) *n.* A molecule consisting of only two, three, or four monomers that can combine with more monomers to form a polymer. [OLIGO- + -MER.]

ol·i·go·phre·ni·a (ŏl′ə-gō-frē′nē-ə, ō′lə-) *n.* Mental deficiency. [New Latin : OLIGO- + -PHRENIA.]

ol·i·gop·o·ly (ŏl′ə-gŏp′ə-lē, ō′lə-) *n., pl.* **-lies.** *Economics.* A market condition in which sellers are so few that the actions of any one of them will materially affect price and hence have a measurable impact upon competitors. Compare **monopoly.** [OLIGO- + (MONO)POLY.] —**ol·i·gop·o·lis·tic** (ŏl′ə-gŏp′ə-lĭs′tĭk, ō′lə-) *adj.*

ol·i·gop·so·ny (ŏl′ə-gŏp′sə-nē, ō′lə-) *n., pl.* **-nies.** *Economics.* A market condition in which purchasers are so few that the actions of any one of them can materially affect price and hence the costs that competitors must pay. Compare **monopsony.** [OLIG(O)- + (MON)OPSONY.] —**ol·i·gop·so·nis·tic** (ŏl′ə-gŏp′sə-nĭs′tĭk, ō′lə-) *adj.*

ol·i·go·sac·cha·ride (ŏl′ə-gō-săk′ə-rīd′, ō′lə-) *n.* Any carbohydrate in which a few monosaccharide units are joined together.

ol·i·go·tro·phic (ŏl′ə-gō-trō′fĭk, -trŏf′ĭk, ō′lə-) *adj.* Poor in plant nutrients and hence plant life but rich in oxygen. Said of lakes and similar habitats.

o·li·o (ō′lē-ō′) *n., pl.* **-os. 1.** A heavily spiced stew of meat, vegetables, and chickpeas. **2. a.** Any mixture or medley; a potpourri. **b.** A collection of various artistic or literary works or musical pieces; a miscellany. [Modification of Spanish *olla,* pot, OLLA.]

ol·i·va·ceous (ŏl′ə-vā′shəs) *adj.* Olive-green. [OLIV(E) + -ACEOUS.]

ol·i·var·y (ŏl′ə-vĕr′ē) *adj.* **1.** Shaped like an olive. **2.** *Anatomy.* Of or pertaining to one of the two oval bodies of nervous tissue found on either side of the medulla oblongata. [Latin *olīvārius,* from *olīva,* OLIVE.]

ol·ive (ŏl′ĭv) *n.* **1. a.** An Old World semitropical evergreen tree, *Olea europaea,* having an edible fruit, white flowers, and leathery leaves. **b.** The small ovoid fruit of this tree, an important food and a source of oil. **2.** The wood of the olive tree. **3.** A yellowish to brownish green. [Middle English, from Old French, from Latin *olīva,* from Greek *elaia.*] —**ol·ive** *adj.*

olive branch *n.* **1.** A branch of an olive tree regarded as an emblem of peace. **2.** An offer of peace.

olive drab *n.* **1.** A grayish olive to dark olive brown or olive gray. **2. a.** Cloth of this color. **b.** A military uniform made from such cloth.

olive green *n.* A greenish yellow.

o·liv·e·nite (ō-lĭv′ə-nīt′) *n.* A basic arsenate of copper, $Cu_3As_2O_8 \cdot Cu(OH)_2$, brown, olive green, or gray in color, found in copper deposits. [German *Olivenit* : OLIVE + -ITE.]

olive oil *n.* Oil pressed from olives, used in salad dressings, for cooking, as an ingredient of soaps, and as a skin softener.

Ol·ives, Mount of (ŏl′ĭvz). Hill in western Jordan, in east Jerusalem. It is the Biblical site of the Garden of Gethsemane.

O·liv·i·er (ə-lĭv′ē-ā′), **Laurence Kerr, Baron Olivier of Brighton** (1907–). British actor. He established himself as an international star of stage and films before World War II. He directed and starred in film adaptations of Shakespeare's *Henry V* (1944), *Hamlet* (1948), *Richard II* (1956), and *Othello* (1965) and is a character actor of international repute.

ol·i·vine (ŏl′ə-vēn′) *n.* **1.** Any of a group of mineral silicates, all members of which consist of compounds of iron silicate and magnesium silicate in various proportions. They occur in basic and ultrabasic igneous rocks and some metamorphic rocks. Also called "chrysolite." **2.** A transparent green variety valued as a gem. Also called "peridot." [German *Olivin,* chrysolite : OLIVE (because of its color) + -IN.]

ol·la (ŏl′ə, oi′lə) *n.* **1.** An earthenware pot or jar with a wide mouth. **2.** An olla podrida. [Spanish, from Old Spanish *olla,* variant of *aulla,* jar, pot.]

olla po·dri·da (pə-drē′də) *n.* **1.** A stew of highly seasoned meat and vegetables. **2.** Any assorted mixture or miscellany. [Spanish, "rotten pot" : OLLA + *podrida,* rotten, from Latin *putrida,* from *putrēre,* to rot, from *puter,* decaying, rotten.]

Olm·sted (ōm′stĕd′, -stĭd′, ŏm′-), **Frederick Law** (1822–1903). U.S. landscape architect. He was the chief architect of New York City's Central Park (1858–61) and later created parks and landscaped settings in Philadelphia, Boston, Brooklyn, Washington, D.C., and Montreal. His urban parks, many of which are being restored to his original designs, are a reflection of his love of greenery and space as a functional part of the city.

ol·o·gy (ŏl′ə-jē) *n., pl.* **-gies.** *Informal.* A branch of learning: *amphibology and other ologies.* [From -LOGY.]

o·lo·ro·so (ō′lə-rō′sō, -zō) *n.* A full-bodied, medium-sweet sherry. [Spanish, "fragrant."]

O·lym·pi·a¹ (ə-lĭm′pē-ə). City of ancient Greece, in the western Peloponnese. It was the scene of the Olympic games and the site of the Temple of Zeus, which contained the statue of Zeus by Phidias, one of the Seven Wonders of the World.

Olympia². The capital of Washington State, in the west on the southern end of Puget Sound.

O·lym·pi·ad (ə-lĭm′pē-ăd′) *n.* **1.** The interval of four years between celebrations of the Olympic games, by which the ancient Greeks reckoned dates. **2.** A celebration of the modern Olympic games. [Middle English *Olympiade,* from Latin *Olympias,* from Greek *Olumpias* (stem *Olympiad-*), from *Olumpia,* OLYMPIA, Greece.]

O·lym·pi·an (ō-lĭm′pē-ən) *adj.* **1.** Of or pertaining to the greater gods of the ancient Greek pantheon, whose abode was Mount Olympus. **2. a.** Majestic in manner. **b.** Superior to or aloof from mundane affairs. **3.** Of or pertaining to the Olympic games. ∼*n.* **1.** Any of the 12 major gods inhabiting Olympus. **2.** A contestant in the Olympic games.

O·lym·pic (ō-lĭm′pĭk) *adj.* Of or pertaining to the Olympic games.

Olympic games *pl.n.* **1.** In ancient Greece, a Pan-Hellenic festival of athletic games and contests of choral poetry and dance, first celebrated in 776 B.C. and held every four years until A.D. 393 on the plain of Olympia in honor of the Olympian Zeus. **2.** A modern international revival of athletic contests on the model of the Olympic games and held every four years. In this sense, also called "Olympics."

Olympic Mountains. Range on the Olympic Peninsula, a land mass between the Pacific Ocean and Puget Sound. The western part of the mountains is in the Olympic Rain Forest, with an annual rainfall of 330 centimeters (130 inches). The mountains have glaciers on their upper slopes. Most of the mountains are included in Olympic National Park, a resort area with alpine meadows, lakes and streams, and a scenic coastline on the Pacific Ocean.

O·lym·pus, Mount (ə-lĭm′pəs). The highest mountain of Greece (2,917 meters; 9,570 feet). In Greek mythology it was the home of the gods.

OM. ostmark.

-oma *suffix.* Indicates tumor; for example, **fibroma, myoma.** [New Latin, from Greek -*ōma,* abstract nominal ending formed from -*o-* stem verbs.]

O·ma·ha¹ (ō′mə-hô′, -hä′) *n., pl.* **-has** or collectively **Omaha. 1.** A tribe of Siouan-speaking Indians of northeastern Nebraska. **2.** A member of the Omaha. [Dhegia *umáhã.*] —**O·ma·ha** *adj.*

Omaha². City of eastern Nebraska, on the west bank of the Missouri River. It is a port of entry and a major transportation center for a farming and cattle-raising region. The city also has livestock markets and meat-processing plants.

O·man (ō-män′). Formerly **Mus·cat and O·man** (mŭs′kăt′). Sultanate in the southeast of the Arabian Peninsula. It is a fertile coastal plain backed by hill ranges and an interior desert region. Dates, limes, sugar cane, and cattle are the chief products. Oil is the major source of revenue. Area, 212,457 square kilometers (82,030 square miles). Population, 900,000. Capital, Muscat. —**O·man·i** *adj. & n.* See map, page 1188.

O·mar Khay·yám (ō′mär kī-äm′) (c. 1050–1123). Persian poet and mathematician. Though his astronomical observations were instrumental in the reform of the Islamic calendar, he is best known for his *Rubáiyát* of nearly 500 quatrains expressing wistful, agnostic hedonism, some of which were first translated into English (1859) by Edward Fitzgerald.

o·ma·sum (ō-mā′səm) *n., pl.* **-sa** (-sə). The third stomach of a ruminant animal, located between the **abomasum** and the **reticulum** (*both of which see*). Also called "manyplies," "psalterium." [Latin *omāsum,* pouch, bullock's tripe, probably from Gaulish.]

om·bre, om·ber (ŏm′bər) *n.* A card game, played by three players with 40 cards, that was popular in Europe during the 17th and 18th centuries. [Spanish *hombre,* "man" (name given to the player who attempts to win the pool), from Latin *homo.*]

om·buds·man (ŏm′bŭdz′mən, -bōōdz′mən) *n., pl.* **-men** (-mĭn). **1.** A government official, especially in Scandinavian countries, who investigates citizens' complaints of maladministration by government departments or functionaries. **2.** One that investigates complaints, as from consumers, reports findings, and assists in achieving fair settlements. [Swedish, from Old Norse *umbodhsmadhr,* "administration-man," king's representative" : *um,* about + *bodh,* command + *madhr,* (rarely) *mannr,* man.] —**om·buds·man·ship** *n.*

-ome *suffix. Biology.* Indicates mass, body, or group; for example, **biome, phyllome.** [Variant of -OMA.]

o·me·ga (ō-mēg′ə, ō-mē′gə, ō-mā′-) *n.* **1.** The 24th and final letter in the Greek alphabet, written Ω, ω. Transliterated in English as *o* or sometimes as *ō.* See feature at **alphabet. 2.** The end; last. **3.** *Symbol* Ω- *Physics.* A fundamental particle in the baryon family, having a mass 3,276 times that of the electron, a negative electric charge, and

olivine *The gemstone peridot (above) is a crystalline form of the mineral olivine. The mineral is also used to line the inside of furnaces because of its ability to withstand intense heat.*

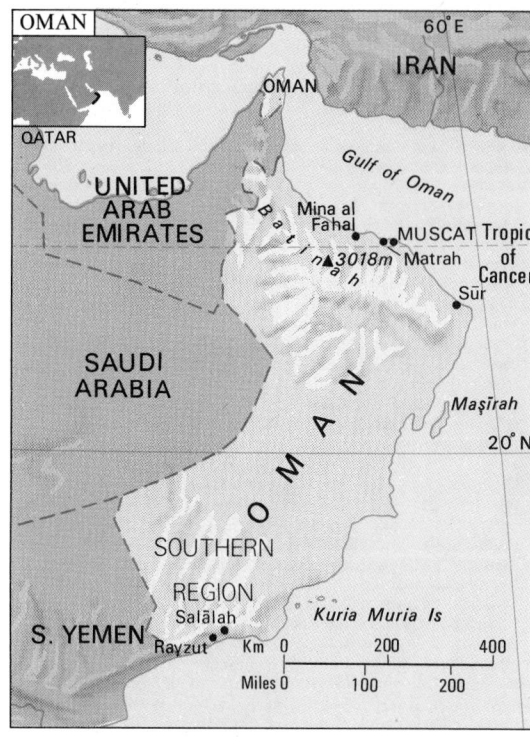

OMAN

a mean lifetime of 1.5×10^{-10} second. Also called "omega minus." See **particle.** [Greek *ō mega*, "large ō" : *ō* + *mega*, neuter of *megas*, large, great.]

om·e·let, om·e·lette (ŏm′ə-lĭt, ŏm′lĭt) *n.* A dish consisting of beaten eggs cooked until set and folded, often around a filling. [French *omelette*, from Old French *amelette*, "thin plate," alteration of *alumette*, variant of *alumelle*, from *lemelle*, from Latin *lāmella*, thin metal plate, diminutive of *lāmina*, plate, layer.]

o·men (ō′mən) *n.* 1. Any phenomenon supposed to portend good or evil; a prophetic sign. 2. Prognostication; portent. ~*tr.v.* **omened, omening, omens.** To be an omen of; portend; presage. [Latin *ōmen.*]

o·men·tum (ō-mĕn′təm) *n., pl.* **-ta** (-tə). *Anatomy.* Either of two pairs of peritoneal folds. The greater omentum consists of a double fold of peritoneum that covers the stomach and the intestine; the lesser omentum is doubled to link the stomach and duodenum to the liver. [Latin *ōmentum†.*] —**o·men·tal** *adj.*

om·i·cron (ŏm′ə-krŏn′, ō′mə-) *n.* The 15th letter in the Greek alphabet, written *O, o.* Transliterated in English as *o.* See feature at **alphabet.** [Greek *o mikron*, "small o" : *o* + *mikron*, neuter of *mikros*, small.]

om·i·nous (ŏm′ə-nəs) *adj.* 1. Menacing; threatening: *an ominous silence.* 2. Being or pertaining to an evil omen; portentous. [Latin *ōminōsus*, from *ōmen* (stem *ōmin-*), OMEN.] —**om·i·nous·ly** *adv.* —**om·i·nous·ness** *n.*

o·mis·sion (ō-mĭsh′ən) *n.* 1. The act or an instance of omitting. 2. The state of being omitted. 3. Something that is omitted or neglected. [Middle English *omissioun*, from Late Latin *omissiō* (stem *omissiōn-*), from Latin *omittere* (past participle *omissus-*), to OMIT.] —**o·mis·sive** (ō-mĭs′ĭv) *adj.*

o·mit (ō-mĭt′) *tr.v.* **omitted, omitting, omits.** 1. To leave out; fail to include: *a name omitted from the list.* 2. To pass over; neglect; fail to do: *omitted to tell her the message.* [Middle English *omitten*, from Latin *omittere*, from *ob-*, away + *mittere*, to send.] —**o·mis·si·ble** (ō-mĭs′ə-bəl) *adj.*

om·ma·tid·i·um (ŏm′ə-tĭd′ē-əm) *n., pl.* **-ia** (-ē-ə). *Zoology.* One of the elements, resembling a single simplified eye, that make up the compound eye of arthropods. [New Latin, "small eye" : Greek *omma* (stem *ommat-*), eye + -IDIUM.] —**om·ma·tid·i·al** *adj.*

om·mat·o·phore (ō-măt′ə-fôr′, -fōr′) *n. Zoology.* A movable stalk ending with an eye, as found in snails. [Greek *omma* (stem *ommat-*), eye + -PHORE.] —**om·ma·toph·o·rous** (ŏm′ə-tŏf′ər-əs) *adj.*

Ommiad. See **Umayyad.**

omni- *prefix.* Indicates all, everywhere; for example, **omnidirectional, omnirange.** [Latin, from *omnis*, all.]

om·ni·bus (ŏm′nə-bəs) *n., pl.* **-buses.** 1. A bus (*see*). 2. A printed anthology of the works of one author or of writings on a related subject. ~*adj.* Including or covering many things, classes, or situations at once. [French (*voiture*) *omnibus* "(vehicle) for all," and Latin *omnibus*, "for all," dative plural of *omnis*, all.]

om·ni·com·pe·tent (ŏm′nĭ-kŏm′pə-tənt) *adj.* Capable of judging or handling all matters. —**om·ni·com·pe·tence** *n.*

om·ni·di·rec·tion·al (ŏm′nē-dĭ-rĕk′shə-nəl, -dī-rĕk′shə-nəl) *adj.* Capable of transmitting or receiving signals in all directions.

omnidirectional radio range *n.* **Omnirange** (*see*).

om·ni·far·i·ous (ŏm′nə-fâr′ē-əs) *adj.* Of all sorts and kinds: *omnifarious knowledge.* [Late Latin *omnifarius* : OMNI- + *fārius*, "-doing"; akin to *facere*, to do.] —**om·ni·far·i·ous·ness** *n.*

om·nif·ic (ŏm-nĭf′ĭk) *adj.* Also **om·nif·i·cent** (-nĭf′ə-sənt). *Rare.* All-creating. [Medieval Latin *omnificus* : OMNI- + -FIC.]

om·nip·o·tent (ŏm-nĭp′ə-tənt) *adj.* Having unlimited or universal power, authority, force, or sway; all-powerful: *an omnipotent god.* ~*n.* **Omnipotent.** God. [Middle English, from Old French, from Latin *omnipotēns* : OMNI- + *potēns*, POTENT.] —**om·nip·o·tence** (ŏm-nĭp′ə-təns), **om·nip·o·ten·cy** *n.* —**om·nip·o·tent·ly** *adv.*

om·ni·pres·ence (ŏm′nĭ-prĕz′əns) *n.* The fact of being present everywhere. [Medieval Latin *omnipraesentia*, from *omnipraesēns* : OMNI- + *praesēns*, PRESENT.] —**om·ni·pres·ent** *adj.*

om·ni·range (ŏm′nĭ-rānj′, ŏm′nē-) *n.* A radio network that provides complete bearing information for aircraft. Also called "omnidirectional radio range."

om·nis·cient (ŏm-nĭsh′ənt) *adj.* 1. Having total knowledge; knowing everything. 2. Having great knowledge. ~*n.* **Omniscient.** God. [Latin *omnisciēns* : OMNI- + *sciēns* (stem *scient-*), present participle of *scīre*, to know.] —**om·nis·cience** (ŏm-nĭsh′əns) *n.* —**om·nis·cien·cy** (-ən-sē) *n.* —**om·nis·cient·ly** *adv.*

om·ni·um-gath·er·um (ŏm′nē-əm-găth′ər-əm) *n.* A miscellaneous collection; hodgepodge. [Mock Latin formation : Latin *omnium*, of all, genitive plural of *omnis*, all + GATHER.]

om·ni·vore (ŏm′nə-vôr′, -vōr′) *n.* An omnivorous animal. [Latin *omnivorus*, OMNIVOROUS.]

om·niv·o·rous (ŏm-nĭv′ər-əs) *adj.* 1. *Zoology.* Eating both animal and vegetable substances. 2. Eating all kinds of food: *Pigs are omnivorous creatures.* 3. Taking in everything available, as with the mind: *an omnivorous reader.* [Latin *omnivorus* : OMNI- + -VOROUS.] —**om·niv·o·rous·ly** *adv.* —**om·niv·o·rous·ness** *n.*

om·pha·los (ŏm′fə-lŏs′, -ləs) *n., pl.* **-li** (-lī′). 1. In ancient Greece, a stone at Delphi thought to mark the center of the earth. 2. The navel. 3. A center. [Greek.]

Omsk (ŏmsk). City of central U.S.S.R., founded (1716) at the confluence of the Om and Irtysh rivers. It is a major junction on the Trans-Siberian Railroad and an industrial center.

on (ŏn, ôn) *prep.* 1. Used to indicate: **a.** Position upon and above the surface of; position in contact with and supported by the surface of: *The vase is on the table.* **b.** Contact, as between two surfaces: *mud on his trousers; a ring on her finger.* **c.** Location at or along: *a house on the beach.* **d.** Proximity: *a town on the border; on the brink of extinction.* **e.** Attachment to or suspension from: *beads on a string.* 2. Used to indicate: **a.** Motion toward, against, or onto: *jump on the table; the march on Moscow.* **b.** Direction or tendency as regards: *had a crush on her; an attack on the press.* **c.** Affecting: *hard on her parents; backed out on us.* **d.** A comparison or point of reference: *an improvement on last time.* 3. Used to indicate: **a.** Occurrence during: *on the third of July.* **b.** The point of time of a specified action: *On entering the room, she saw me.* **c.** The exact moment or point of: *every hour on the hour.* **d.** After a specified process: *on reflection.* **e.** A current occupation: *on her rounds; on duty.* 4. Used to indicate a connection between an object and a perceptible agent or agency: *I cut my foot on the broken glass. Night fell on the town.* 5. Used to indicate: **a.** A means of support or a sustaining source or agency: *live on bread and water; survives on a small income.* **b.** A means of progress or transmission: *on foot; on the radio.* 6. Used to indicate: **a.** The state, condition, mode, or process of: *on record; on fire; on the increase.* **b.** The purpose of: *travel on business.* **c.** Availability by means of: *beer on tap; a nurse on call.* **d.** Association with; membership in: *a doctor on the hospital staff; on the board of directors.* **e.** The ground or basis for: *I refused it on principle.* **f.** Addition or repetition: *error on error; 10 percent on the bill.* 7. Concerning; about: *a book on astronomy.* 8. In one's possession; with: *I haven't got a penny on me.* 9. At the expense of: *drinks on the house.* 10. Indicates regular intake: *on drugs; back on the booze.* 11. Indicates way or manner. Preceded by *the: on the quiet; on the sly.* 12. Used preceded by an adjective indicating an attitude or characteristic: *keen on tennis; weak on dates.* 13. *British Informal.* Earning: *You must be on a small fortune in that job.* ~*adv.* 1. In or into a position of being attached to or covering something: *Put your clothes on.* 2. In or into a state or condition of receiving a source of energy, such as electricity: *put the kettle on; turn the radio on.* 3. **a.** In the direction of something visible: *looked on while the ship docked.* **b.** With a specified part forward or visible: *edge on.* 4. **a.** Toward or at a point lying ahead in space or time; forward: *moved on to the next town.* **b.** At or to a specified point in time or space: *I'll do it later on.* 5. In a continuous or persistent manner: *She worked on quietly.* 6. In or at the present position: *stay on; hang on.* —**and so on.** And like the preceding; and so forth. —**be on to.** *Informal.* To be aware of or have information about: *We're on to something big.* —**on and off.** Intermittently. —**on and on.** Without stopping; continuously. —**on at.** *British Informal.* Complaining to or nagging: *She's always on at me.* ~*adj.* 1. **a.** Operating; playing: *The radio is on.* **b.** Being supplied. Said especially of electricity, gas, and water. 2. Taking place or due to take place: *There's a conference on now.* 3. Onstage or about to go onstage: *You're on after the magician.* 4. Ready to join in some activity: *I'm on for a game.* 5. Planned; intended: *I have nothing on for this weekend.* —**not on.** *British Informal.* 1. Unable to be performed or accomplished: *a good idea, but it's not on.* 2. Violating accepted standards: *His behavior just wasn't on.* [Middle English *on,*

preposition and adverb, Old English *on, an,* from Germanic.]
   Usage: To indicate motion toward a position, both *on* and *onto* can be used: *The cat jumped on the table. The cat jumped onto the table. Onto* is more specific, however, in indicating that the motion was initiated from an outside point. *He wandered onto the battlefield* means that he began his wandering at some point off the battlefield. *He wandered on the battlefield* may mean that his wandering began on the battlefield. ● In constructions where *on* is an adverb attached to a verb, it should not be joined with *to* to form a single word *onto: move on to* (not *onto*) *new subjects; hold on to* (not *onto*) *our gains.* ● In their uses to indicate spatial relations, *on* and *upon* are often interchangeable: *It was resting on* (or *upon*) *two supports. She took it on* (or *upon*) *herself to finish the project. We saw a finch light on* (or *upon*) *a bough.* To indicate a relation between two things, however, instead of between an action and an end point, *upon* cannot always be used: *Hand me the book on* (not *upon*) *the table. It was the only town on* (not *upon*) *the main line.* Similarly, *upon* cannot always be used in place of *on* when the relation is not spatial: *He wrote a book on* (not *upon*) *alchemy. She will be here on* (not *upon*) *Tuesday.*
–on¹ *suffix.* Indicates subatomic particle, unit, or quantum; for example, **electron, photon.** [From (I)ON.]
–on² *suffix.* Indicates inert gas; for example, **radon.** [New Latin, from ARGON.]
on·a·ger (ŏn′ə-jər) *n.* **1.** A wild ass, *Equus hemionus onager,* of central Asia. **2.** An ancient and medieval stone-propelling siege engine. [Middle English, from Latin *onager,* from Greek *onagros : onos,* ass + *agros,* field.]
o·nan·ism (ō′nə-nĭz′əm) *n.* **1.** Masturbation. **2.** Coitus interruptus. [After *Onan,* son of Judah (Genesis 38:9).] —**o·nan·ist** *n.* —**o·nan·is·tic** (ō′nə-nĭs′tĭk) *adj.*
O·nas·sis (ō-năs′ĭs), **Aristotle Socrates** (1906–75). Greek entrepreneur. Owning one of the world's largest private commercial fleets, he pioneered the use of oil supertankers.
on-board (ŏn-bôrd′, -bōrd′, ŏn-) *adj.* Carried aboard a vehicle: *on-board computers.*
once (wŭns) *adv.* **1.** One time only: *once a day.* **2.** At one time in the past; formerly: *Once we were happy.* **3.** At any time; ever: *Once known, never forgotten.* **4.** By one degree of relationship: *She is my first cousin once removed.* —**once and for all.** Finally; conclusively: *I'm telling you once and for all that I'm not going.* ~*n.* A single occurrence; one time: *You can go this once.* —**all at once. 1.** All at the same time. **2.** Suddenly. —**at once. 1.** Without delay; immediately. **2.** All together; simultaneously. ~*conj.* As soon as; if ever; when: *Once he goes, I can clean up.* ~*adj.* Having been formerly; former: *The once capital of the nation.* [Middle English *ones, anes,* adverbial genitive of *on, an,* ONE.]
once-o·ver (wŭns′ō′vər) *n. Informal.* A quick but comprehensive glance or survey: *gave us the once-over when we came in.*
onc·er (wŭn′sər) *n. British Slang.* A one-pound note. [ONCE + -ER.]
onco– *prefix.* Indicates tumor; for example, **oncogenic, oncology.** [Greek *onkos,* mass.]
on·co·gen·e·sis (ŏn′kō-jĕn′ə-sĭs, ŏng′-) *n.* The formation and development of a tumor. [ONCO- + GENESIS.]
on·co·gen·ic (ŏn′kō-jĕn′ĭk, ŏng′-) *adj.* Tending to cause the formation of tumors. [ONCO- + -GENIC.]
on·col·o·gy (ŏn-kŏl′ə-jē, ŏng′-) *n.* The scientific study of tumors. [ONCO- + -LOGY.] —**on·co·log·i·cal** (ŏn′kə-lŏj′ĭ-kəl, ŏng′-), **on·co·log·ic** *adj.* —**on·col·o·gist** *n.*
on·com·ing (ŏn′kŭm′ĭng, ôn′-) *adj.* Coming nearer; approaching: *the oncoming storm.* ~*n.* An approach; an advance.
on·co·sphere (ŏn′kə-sfîr′, ông′-) *n.* The six-hooked larva of a tapeworm, which if ingested by an appropriate host penetrates the intestine wall and invades muscle tissue. Also called "hexacanth." [Greek *onkos,* barb + SPHERE.]
on-cost (ŏn′kôst′, ôn′-) *n. British.* An overhead cost.
ondes Mar·te·not (ônd′ mär′tə-nō′) *n.* A musical instrument that uses electronic vibrations to produce characteristically eerie tones. [French, "Martenot waves," after Maurice *Martenot* (born 1898), its inventor.]
on-dit (ôn-dē′) *n., pl.* **on-dits** (-dē′, -dēz′). A piece of gossip or hearsay. [French, "it is said."]
on·do·graph (ŏn′də-grăf′, -gräf′) *n.* An instrument that produces a graphic trace representing an alternating current by measuring the charge imparted to a capacitor at different points in the cycle. [French, from *onde,* wave + -GRAPH.]
on·dom·e·ter (ŏn-dŏm′ə-tər) *n.* An instrument that measures the frequency of electromagnetic waves, especially in the radio-frequency band. [French *onde,* wave + METER.]
one (wŭn) *adj.* **1.** Designating a single entity, unit, object, or being; single; individual: *one pencil.* Sometimes used in combination: *one-eyed.* **2.** Characterized by unity; of a single kind or nature; undivided: *with one accord; one with my colleagues.* **3.** Designating a person or thing that is contrasted with another or others: *from one end to the other.* **4.** Designating a specified but indefinite thing or time: *He will come one day.* **5. a.** Designating a certain person, especially a person not previously known or mentioned: *One Mr. Jones called for you.* **b.** Designating an indefinite time or occasion: *One Tuesday he returned.* **6.** A or an. Used informally as a substitute for the indefinite article for emphasis: *That is one fine dog.* **7.** Single in kind; alike or the same. **8.** Being unique of a specified or implied kind: *the one person she cared for.* ~*n.* **1. a.** The first cardinal number; the first positive whole num-

ber after zero. **b.** A symbol representing this, such as 1, I, or i. **2.** A size or thing designated as one. **3.** A single person or thing; a unit: *the one I saw on the street.* **4.** The first in a series. **5.** A one-dollar bill. **6.** One hour after midnight or noon: *We ate at one.* **7.** *British Informal.* A humorous or jocular person: *You are a one!* —**a right one.** *British Informal.* A fool or nuisance: *We've got a right one here!* ~*pron.* **1.** A certain person or thing; someone or something. **2.** Any person or thing; anyone or anything: *It's as good as one will get.* **3. a.** Any person representing the same, usually privileged social class as the speaker: *One does meet intelligent people at lectures.* **b.** The speaker: *One does so dislike package vacations.* **4.** A single person or thing among persons or things already known or mentioned: *one of the Elizabethans.* —**at one.** In accord or unity. —**in one.** At the first or in a single attempt: *got it in one; downed it in one.* —**one and all.** Everyone. —**one another.** Each other. Used to describe a reciprocal relation or action. —**one by one.** Individually and in succession. —**one up.** *Informal.* In a position of psychological superiority: *one up on the neighbors.* [Middle English *an, on,* Old English *ān.*]
   Usage: Constructions employing *one* often raise questions whether verbs should be singular or plural. One such construction is exemplified by this sentence: *One in every ten men was found deficient.* Although the plural *are* is sometimes used in such a sentence, many careful users of English feel that in formal writing a singular verb should be used, in agreement with the subject *one.* ● A more controversial construction involves *one of those who* or a variant: *He is one of those men who always complain about their wives. The defeat was one of the most costly blows that have been inflicted on our forces.* Many attentive writers or speakers feel that only the plural verbs (as used above) are possible, since the antecedents of *who* and *that* are plural nouns (*men* and *blows*). In other examples, however, *one* may be construed as the subject of the verb in the relative clause: *He is the only one of those men who has* (not *have*) *taken the test.* ● The construction *more than one* is always singular, despite the fact that logic would seem to require a plural verb: *More than one of the boys has failed the exam.* Conversely, *fewer than two* is always plural: *Fewer than two have failed.*
–one *suffix.* Indicates: **1.** An oxygen-containing or ketone compound; for example, **acetone. 2.** A chemical compound containing oxygen, especially in a carbonyl or similar group; for example, **lactone.** [Greek *-ōnē,* feminine patronymic suffix.]
one-armed bandit (wŭn′ärmd′) *n. Informal.* A slot machine, especially one with an armlike handle that is pulled to set it in motion.
one-base hit (wŭn′bās′) *n. Baseball.* A base hit by which a batter can reach first base safely. Also called "single."
one-di·men·sion·al (wŭn′dĭ-mĕn′shə-nəl, wŭn′dĭ-) *adj.* Having only one dimension; lacking depth.
O·ne·ga, Lake (ō-nĕg′ə). Lake of the northwest U.S.S.R. Europe's second-largest lake, it is drained by the Onega River northward to the White Sea and is connected by canal to the Baltic Sea and the Volga River.
one-hand·ed (wŭn′hăn′dĭd) *adj.* **1.** Having or using only one hand. **2.** Requiring or done by the use of only one hand.
one-horse (wŭn′hôrs′) *adj.* **1.** Drawn by or using only one horse: *a one-horse carriage.* **2.** Contemptibly small, limited, or insignificant: *a one-horse town.*
O·nei·da¹ (ō-nī′də) *n., pl.* **-das** or collectively **Oneida. 1.** A member of one of the five peoples belonging to the league of the Iroquois. **2.** The Iroquoian language of this people. —**O·nei·da** *adj.*
Oneida². City in central New York State. The Oneida Community was founded nearby in 1848 by John Humphrey Noyes (1811–86). Members of the community held all property in common and prospered by making steel traps and silverware. The community was reorganized as a joint-stock company in 1881.
Oneida Lake. Lake, *c.* 210 square kilometers (80 square miles), in central New York State, northeast of Syracuse. The Oneida River flows from the western end of the lake to the Oswego River.
O'Neill (ō-nēl′), **Eugene Gladstone** (1888–1953). U.S. playwright. His best-known works include *Mourning Becomes Electra* (1931), an adaptation of the trilogy of Aeschylus, and *Long Day's Journey into Night* (1956). He was awarded the Nobel Prize for literature (1936).
o·nei·ric (ō-nī′rĭk) *adj.* Of or pertaining to dreams. [Greek *oneiros,* dream.]
oneiro– *prefix.* Indicates dreams; for example, **oneirocritic.** [Greek *oneiros,* dream.]
o·nei·ro·crit·ic (ō-nī′rō-krĭt′ĭk) *n.* One who interprets dreams. [Greek *oneirokritikos : ONEIRO- + CRITIC.] —**o·nei·ro·crit·i·cal** *adj.* —**o·nei·ro·crit·i·cism** (ō-nī′rō-krĭt′ĭ-sĭz′əm) *n.*
o·nei·rol·o·gy (ō′nī-rŏl′ə-jē) *n.* The art of interpreting dreams. [ONEIRO- + -LOGY.]
o·nei·ro·man·cy (ō-nī′rō-măn′sē) *n.* Divination by dreams. [Greek *oneiros,* dream + -MANCY.] —**o·nei·ro·man·cer** *n.*
one-lin·er (wŭn′lī′nər) *n. Informal.* A short, pithy joke or comment.
one-man (wŭn′măn′) *adj.* **1.** Consisting of one individual: *a one-man team.* **2.** Featuring the work of one individual: *a one-man show.* **3.** Designed for or restricted to one individual: *a one-man toboggan.*
one-man band *n.* A performer who plays a number of instruments at once, as a drum, trumpet, and pair of cymbals that are fastened to each other and to his body.
one·ness (wŭn′nĭs) *n.* **1.** The quality or state of being one; singleness: *the infinite oneness of God.* **2.** Singularity; uniqueness. **3.** The state of being undivided; wholeness. **4.** Sameness of character or

onion *This vegetable has been cultivated since prehistoric times and is now unknown in the wild state. These are main crop onions, used mostly for cooking; smaller varieties are used for pickling.*

PRONUNCIATION KEY

ă, pat; ā, pay; âr, care; ä, father, are; b, bib; ch, church; d, deed; ĕ, pet; ē, be; f, fife; g, gag; h, hat; hw, which; ĭ, pit; ī, pie; îr, pier; j, judge; k, kick; l, lid, needle; m, mum; n, no, sudden; ng, thing; ŏ, pot; ō, toe; ô, paw, for; oi, noise; ou, out; o͝o, book; o͞o, boot; p, pop; r, roar; s, sauce; sh, ship, dish; t, tight; th, thin, path; *th*, this, bathe; ŭ, cut; ûr, fur; v, valve; w, with; y, yes; z, zebra, size; zh, vision; ə, about, item, edible, gallop, circus, peaceful

IN FOREIGN WORDS:

à, *Fr.* ami; œ, *Fr.* feu, *Ger.* schön; ü, *Fr.* tu, *Ger.* über; KH, *Ger.* ich, *Scot.* loch; N, *Fr.* bon; y', *Fr.* Compiègne

STRESS MARKS:

Primary stress: ′ in·cite′ (ĭn-sīt′)
Secondary stress: ′ in′sight′ (ĭn′sīt′)

nature: *the dull oneness of roadside landscapes.* **5.** Unison; agreement: *oneness of mind and purpose.*

one-night stand (wŭn′nīt′) *n.* **1.** A performance, as by a traveling musical or dramatic performer or group, in one place on one night only. **2.** *Informal.* **a.** A sexual encounter limited to only one occasion. **b.** One of the partners involved in such an encounter.

one-off (wŭn′ôf′, -ŏf′) *n. British.* One that is highly original or individual or is not intended to be copied or repeated. Also used adjectivally: *a one-off performance.*

one-piece (wŭn′pēs′) *adj.* Consisting of one piece: *a one-piece swimsuit.*

on·er·ous (ŏn′ər-əs, ō′nər-) *adj.* **1.** Troublesome or oppressive; burdensome. **2.** *Law.* Entailing obligations that exceed any advantage to the possessor. —See Synonyms at **burdensome.** [Middle English, from Old French *onereus,* from Latin *onerōsus,* from *onus* (stem *oner-*), burden.] **—on·er·ous·ly** *adv.* **—on·er·ous·ness** *n.*

one·self (wŭn-sĕlf′) *pron.* Also **one's self** (wŭn sĕlf′, wŭnz). A specialized form of the third person singular pronoun **one.** It is used: **1.** As a reflexive pronoun, forming the direct or indirect object of a verb or the object of a preposition: *faith in oneself.* **2.** For emphasis, after *one*: *One must take a certain amount of initiative oneself.* **3.** As an emphasizing substitute for *one*: *Oneself is usually to blame.* **4.** As an indication of one's real, normal, or healthy condition or identity: *come to oneself.*

one-sid·ed (wŭn′sī′dĭd) *adj.* **1. a.** Favoring one side or group; biased: *a one-sided view.* **b.** Placing obligation only on one party, as in a dispute: *a one-sided agreement.* **2.** Larger, stronger, or more developed on one side: *a one-sided pattern; a one-sided contest.* **3.** Existing or made on one side only: *a one-sided decision.* **—one-sid·ed·ly** *adv.* **—one-sid·ed·ness** *n.*

one-step (wŭn′stĕp′) *n.* **1.** A ballroom dance resembling the foxtrot and consisting of a series of unbroken rapid steps in 2/4 time. **2.** Music for such a dance.
~*intr.v.* **one-stepped, -stepping, -steps.** To dance the one-step.

one·time (wŭn′tīm′) *adj.* At or in some past time; former: *a onetime boxing champion.*

one-to-one (wŭn′tə-wŭn′) *adj.* **1.** Allowing the pairing of each member of a class uniquely with a member of another class. **2.** Characterized by pairing and equality between two individuals or groups: *one-to-one discussions.* **3.** *Mathematics.* Pertaining to a correspondence that assigns to each member of one set a unique member of another set. **4.** Characterized by proportional amounts on both sides. **—one-to-one** *adv.*

one-track (wŭn′trăk′) *adj.* Obsessively limited to a single idea or purpose: *a one-track mind.*

one-up·man·ship (wŭn-ŭp′mən-shĭp′) *n. Informal.* The technique of maintaining a psychological superiority over one's associates or keeping one step ahead of a competitor. [From the phrase *be one up (on),* after GAMESMANSHIP.]

one-way (wŭn′wā′) *adj.* **1.** Moving, operating, or permitting movement in one direction only: *a one-way street.* **2.** Providing for travel in one direction only: *a one-way ticket.*

one-wom·an (wŭn′wo͝om′ən) *adj.* Of, pertaining to, consisting of, or performed by one woman: *a one-woman show.*

on·go·ing (ŏn′gō′ĭng, ôn′-) *adj.* **1.** Currently taking place: *an ongoing exhibit.* **2.** Progressing or evolving.

ONI Office of Naval Intelligence.

on·ion (ŭn′yən) *n.* **1.** A bulbous plant, *Allium cepa,* cultivated worldwide as a vegetable. **2.** The rounded, edible bulb of the onion plant, composed of tight, concentric layers of succulent white leaf bases and having a pungent odor and taste. **3.** Any of several similar plants of the genus *Allium,* such as the **shallot** and the **chive** *(both of which see).* **—know one's onions.** *British Informal.* To have a thorough knowledge of an area or field of activity.
~*adj.* Of, pertaining to, tasting of, or resembling an onion: *onion flavor; an onion dome.* [Middle English *unyon, oyn(y)oun,* from Norman French, Old French *oignon,* from Latin *uniō* (stem *union-*), a dialectal word for a kind of onion, perhaps from *ūniō,* oneness, unity, from *ūnus,* one (perhaps referring to the concentric unity of the layers of an onion).] **—on·ion·y** *adj.*

on·ion·skin (ŭn′yən-skĭn′) *n.* A thin, strong, translucent paper.

on-line (ŏn′līn′, ôn′-) *adj.* **1.** Connected to and controlled by a mainframe computer. Said of a part of a computer system or a peripheral device. **2.** Switched on. Said of a computer. Compare **off-line.**

on·look·er (ŏn′lo͝ok′ər, ôn′-) *n.* One who looks on; a spectator. **—on·look·ing** *adj.* & *n.*

on·ly (ōn′lē) *adj.* **1. a.** Alone in kind or class; sole. **b.** Having no brothers or sisters. Said of a child. **2.** Standing alone by reason of superiority or excellence: *the only place to be.*
~*adv.* **1.** Without anyone or anything else; alone: *Only three survived.* **2. a.** No more than: *He left only an hour ago.* **b.** At least; just: *If you would only come home.* **c.** Merely: *I only work here.* **3.** Exclusively; solely: *facts known only to us.* **4.** With the final, often unexpected result: *They went, only to be turned away.* **—only too.** Extremely: *only too ready to laugh.*
~*conj.* Except that; but: *I would have called, only I couldn't remember the number.* [Middle English *only,* Old English *ānlīc* : *ān,* ONE + *-līc,* -LY.]

Usage: It is generally recommended that in written English *only* be placed before the words it limits: *I saw only Jane* (and no one else) rather than *I only saw Jane* (I did not speak to her). The tendency to use *only* apart from the limited word, putting it earlier in the sentence, usually before the verb, is widespread in speech: *I only saw Jane, not Jim.* Purists criticize this usage on logical grounds, maintaining that *only* should always go next to the word it limits, or else ambiguity will result. However, this construction is rarely ambiguous in speech, because the stress pattern of the sentence indicates clearly which word goes with which: *I* ONLY *saw* JANE (not Jim) as opposed to *I only* SAW *Jane* (I didn't speak to her). Even in the written language, context usually makes it clear which is the intended meaning, but the weight of grammatical tradition, together with the risk of ambiguity, is enough to foster widespread observance of the adjacency rule in formal written English. • The form *not only . . . but also* is a special instance of the general problem affecting the placement of *only.* The two components should be placed before the same word classes in the two parts of the construction: *They recognize not only the theoretical issues but also the practical consequences.* In a speech-influenced style, however, *They not only recognize . . .* will be used.

o.n.o. *British.* or near offer.

on·o·mas·tic (ŏn′ə-măs′tĭk) *adj.* **1.** Of or pertaining to a name or names. **2.** Of or being the signature of the nominal author of a document that is copied out in another's handwriting. [Greek *onomastikos,* from *onomazein,* to name, from *onoma,* a name.]

on·o·mas·tics (ŏn′ə-măs′tĭks) *n. Used with a singular verb.* The study of the origins of names, especially the proper names of people and places.

on·o·mat·o·poe·ia (ŏn′ə-măt′ə-pē′ə) *n.* **1. a.** The formation of a word, such as *buzz* or *cuckoo,* that sounds like what it denotes. **b.** A word so formed. **2.** The use, especially as a literary device, of words whose sounds suggest a sound referred to. [Late Latin, from Greek *onomatopoiia,* from *onomatopoiein,* to coin names : *onoma* (stem *onomat-*), name + *poiein,* to make.] **—on·o·mat·o·poe·ic** (ŏn′ə-măt′ə-pē′ĭk), **on·o·mat·o·po·et·ic** (-pō-ĕt′ĭk) *adj.* **—on·o·mat·o·poe·i·cal·ly, on·o·mat·o·po·et·i·cal·ly** *adv.*

On·on·da·ga (ŏn′ən-dô′gə, -dä′gə) *n., pl.* **-gas** or collectively **Onondaga. 1.** A member of a North American Iroquoian-speaking Indian people. **2.** The Iroquoian language of the Onondaga. **—On·on·da·gan** *adj.*

on·rush (ŏn′rŭsh′, ôn′-) *n.* A powerful forward rush or flow: *the onrush of events.* **—on·rush·ing** *adj.*

on·set (ŏn′sĕt′, ôn′-) *n.* **1.** An onslaught; an assault. **2.** A beginning; a start: *the onset of a cold.*

on·shore (ŏn′shôr′, -shōr′, ôn′-) *adj.* **1.** Toward the shore: *an onshore gale.* **2.** Located or operating on the shore: *an onshore patrol.*
~*adv.* Toward the shore: *The wind shifted onshore.*

on·slaught (ŏn′slôt′, ôn′-) *n.* A violent attack. [Earlier *anslaight* (influenced by obsolete English *slaught,* slaughter), from Middle Dutch *aenslag* : *aan,* on + *slag,* a striking.]

on·stage (ŏn′stāj′, ôn′-) *adj.* On the area of a stage that is visible to the audience: *onstage action.* **—on·stage** *adv.*

on·stream (ŏn′strēm′, ôn′-) *adj.* In operation or production. Said of industrial products, processes, or equipment.

On·tar·i·o (ŏn-târ′ē-ō). *Abbr.* **Ont.** Province of eastern Canada. Between the Great Lakes in the south and Hudson Bay and James Bay in the north, it is Canada's wealthiest and most populous province. Its industries include food processing, machinery, engineering, and timber. Hydroelectricity is exported to the United States. Ottawa and Toronto are the chief cities. Its capital is Toronto.

Ontario, Lake. The smallest of the Great Lakes. On the U.S.-Canadian border, it is the most easterly of the lakes and receives the entire drainage of the Great Lakes through the Niagara River; it is drained by the St. Lawrence. Its chief cities and ports include Toronto (in Canada) and Rochester (in the United States).

on-the-job (ŏn′*th*ə-jŏb′, ôn′-) *adj.* Of or pertaining to something learned, experienced, or done, often under supervision, while employed at a job: *on-the-job training.*

on·to (ŏn′to͞o′, -tə, ôn′-) *prep.* **1.** On top of; to a position on; upon: *The dog jumped onto the chair.* —See Usage note at **on. 2.** *Informal.* Aware or cognizant of; informed about: *I'm onto your schemes.*
~*adj. Mathematics.* Of, pertaining to, or being a mapping such that every element of the set referred to is the image of an element in another. [ON + TO.]

onto– *prefix.* Indicates being or existence; for example, **ontogeny.** [Greek, from *ōn* (stem *ont-*), present participle of *einai,* to be.]

on·tog·e·ny (ŏn-tŏj′ə-nē) *n., pl.* **-nies.** Also **on·to·gen·e·sis** (ŏn′tə-jĕn′ə-sĭs). The course of development of an individual organism. Compare **phylogeny.** [ONTO- + -GENY.] **—on·to·ge·net·ic** (ŏn′tə-jə-nĕt′ĭk) *adj.*

on·tol·o·gy (ŏn-tŏl′ə-jē) *n.* The branch of philosophy that deals with the nature of being. [New Latin *ontologia* : ONTO- + -LOGY.] **—on·to·log·i·cal** (ŏn′tə-lŏj′ĭ-kəl) *adj.* **—on·to·log·i·cal·ly** *adv.*

o·nus (ō′nəs) *n.* **1.** Anything that is burdensome, especially a responsibility or necessity. **2.** Loosely, stigma or blame. [Latin *onus,* burden.]

on·ward (ŏn′wərd, ôn′-) *adj.* Moving or tending forward.
~*adv.* Also **on·wards** (-wərdz). In a direction or toward a position that is ahead in space or time.

–onym *suffix.* Indicates word or name; for example, **acronym, tautonym.** [Latin *-onymum,* from Greek *-onumon,* from *onuma, onoma,* name.]

–onymy *suffix.* Indicates a set of names or the study of a kind of name; for example, **toponymy.** [Greek *-ōnumia,* from *-ōnumos,* having a (specific) name, from *onuma, onoma,* name.]

on·yx (ŏn′ĭks) *n.* **1.** A type of chalcedony that occurs in bands of different colors, usually white with gray or brown. It is used as a gemstone, especially in cameos and intaglios. **2.** Onyx marble. [Middle English *onix*, from Old French, from Latin *onyx*, from Greek *onux*, claw, fingernail, hence onyx (which sometimes has a vein of white on a pink background, like the lunula in a fingernail).]

onyx marble *n.* A banded form of calcite used as an ornamental stone. Also called "onyx," "oriental alabaster."

oo- *prefix.* Indicates egg or ovum; for example, **oogenesis, oology.** [Greek *ōio-,* from *ōion,* egg.]

o·o·cyst (ō′ə-sĭst′) *n.* An encysted form of the zygote that develops in certain sporozoan protozoans, such as the malaria parasite *(Plasmodium).*

o·o·cyte (ō′ə-sīt′) *n.* **1.** A cell of the animal ovary, derived from an oogonium, that undergoes meiosis and produces an ovum. **2.** A female gamete in certain protozoa. [OO- + -CYTE.]

oo·dles (ōōd′lz) *pl.n. Informal.* A great amount; a lot: *oodles of money.* [Origin unknown.]

o·og·a·mous (ō-ŏg′ə-məs) *adj.* **1.** Characterized by small male gametes and large, less mobile female gametes. **2.** Pertaining to reproduction by oogamy.

o·og·a·my (ō-ŏg′ə-mē) *n., pl.* **-mies.** Reproduction between oogamous gametes. [OO- + -GAMY.]

o·o·gen·e·sis (ō′ə-jĕn′ə-sĭs) *n. Biology.* The formation, development, and maturation of ova in the ovary from unspecialized precursor cells. [New Latin : OO- + -GENESIS.] —**o·o·ge·net·ic** (ō′ə-jə-nĕt′ĭk) *adj.*

o·o·go·ni·um (ō′ə-gō′nē-əm) *n., pl.* **-nia** (-nē-ə) or **-ums. 1.** *Biology.* Any of the cells of the animal ovary that develop into oocytes during ovum formation. **2.** *Botany.* A female reproductive structure in certain algae and fungi, containing oospores. [New Latin : OO- + -GONIUM.] —**o·o·go·ni·al** *adj.*

ooh (ōō) *interj.* Used to express a sudden thrill of excitement, pleasure, fear, or surprise.
~*intr v.* **oohed, oohing, oohs.** To utter "ooh": *All the guests oohed and ahed over the flower arrangements.*

o·o·lite (ō′ə-līt′) *n.* **1.** A sedimentary rock, usually a limestone, composed of tiny rounded grains embedded in a fine matrix. **2.** Any of the grains of which such rock is composed. [New Latin *oolites* (translation of German *Rogenstein,* "roe stone") : OO- + -LITE.] —**o·o·lit·ic** (ō′ə-lĭt′ĭk) *adj.*

o·ol·o·gy (ō-ŏl′ə-jē) *n.* The study of eggs, especially birds' eggs. [OO- + -LOGY.] —**o·o·log·i·cal** (ō′ə-lŏj′ĭ-kəl), **o·o·log·ic** *adj.* —**o·o·log·i·cal·ly** *adv.* —**o·ol·o·gist** *n.*

oo·long (ōō′lông′, -lŏng′) *n.* A dark Chinese tea that is partly fermented before drying. See **black tea.** [Mandarin Chinese *wū lóng,* black dragon.]

oomiak. Variant of **umiak.**

oom·pah (ōōm′pä′, ōōm′-) *n.* A sound made by a brass instrument, such as a tuba. [Imitative.]

oomph (ōōmf) *n. Slang.* **1.** Spirited vigor; enthusiasm. **2.** Sex appeal. [Expressive.]

o·o·pho·rec·to·my (ō′ə-fə-rĕk′tə-mē) *n., pl.* **-mies.** The surgical removal of one or both ovaries. [Greek *ōophoron,* ovary (*ōion,* egg + *-phoros,* bearing) + -ECTOMY.]

o·o·pho·ri·tis (ō′ə-fə-rī′tĭs) *n.* Inflammation of an ovary. Also called "ovaritis." [New Latin : Greek *ōophoron,* ovary + -ITIS.]

o·o·phyte (ō′ə-fīt′) *n. Botany.* The stage in the alternation of generations of lower plants when sexual organs are developed. [OO- + -PHYTE.] —**o·o·phyt·ic** (ō′ə-fĭt′ĭk) *adj.*

oops (ōōps, wōōps) *interj.* Used to express: **1.** Alarm or apology when dropping or breaking something. **2.** The sudden realization of a mistake or blunder. [Expressive.]

o·o·sperm (ō′ə-spûrm′) *n. Biology.* A fertilized ovum.

o·o·sphere (ō′ə-sfîr′) *n. Botany.* A nonmotile female gamete or egg formed in an oogonium and ready for fertilization. [OO- + -SPHERE.]

o·o·spore (ō′ə-spôr′, -spōr′) *n. Botany.* A thick-walled spore in certain algae and fungi, developed from a fertilized oosphere or by parthenogenesis. —**o·o·spor·ic** (ō′ə-spôr′ĭk, -spōr′ĭk), **o·os·po·rous** (ō-ŏs′pər-əs, ō′ə-spôr′əs, -spōr′əs) *adj.*

o·o·the·ca (ō′ə-thē′kə) *n., pl.* **-cae** (-sē) *Zoology.* The capsule or egg case of certain insects and mollusks. —**o·o·the·cal** *adj.*

ooze[1] (ōōz) *v.* **oozed, oozing, oozes.** —*intr.* **1.** To flow or leak out slowly, as through small openings. **2.** To disappear or ebb slowly: *His courage oozed away.* **3.** To emit or exude moisture. —*tr.* **1.** To give out; exude. **2.** To emit or radiate in pervasive abundance: *The waiter oozed charm.*
~*n.* **1.** The act of oozing; a gradual flow or leak. **2.** Something that oozes. **3.** An infusion of vegetable matter, as from oak bark, used in tanning. [Middle English *wosen,* from *wose,* juice, Old English *wōs;* akin to Old Norse *vás.*]

ooze[2] *n.* **1.** Soft, thin mud, especially that found at the bottom of rivers and lakes. **2.** The layer of mudlike sediment covering the floor of oceans and lakes, composed chiefly of remains of microscopic sea animals. **3.** Muddy, boggy ground. [Middle English *wose,* Old English *wāse;* akin to Old Norse *veisa,* puddle.]

ooz·y[1] (ōō′zē) *adj.* **-ier, -iest.** Slowly leaking; dripping. —**ooz·i·ly** *adv.* —**ooz·i·ness** *n.*

oozy[2] *adj.* **-ier, -iest.** Of, resembling, or containing ooze: *an oozy riverbed.* —**ooz·i·ness** *n.*

op. 1. operation. **2.** opposite. **3.** optical. **4.** opus. **5.** out of print.
Op. 1. operation. **2.** opus. **3.** out of print.
o.p. out of print.

O.P. Order of Preachers.

o·pac·i·ty (ō-păs′ə-tē) *n., pl.* **-ties. 1.** The quality or state of being opaque. **2.** Something that is opaque. **3.** *Physics.* The ratio of the amount of light or other radiation falling on a surface to the amount that passes through the surface. [French *opacité,* from Latin *opācitās* from *opācus,* OPAQUE.]

o·pah (ō′pə) *n.* A large, vividly colored marine fish, *Lampris regius,* found in all temperate and tropical seas. Also called "moonfish." [West African name; akin to Ibo * úbà.*]

o·pal (ō′pəl) *n.* A hydrated amorphous variety of silica, often used as a gem. See **fire opal.** [Latin *opalus,* from Greek *opallios,* from Sanskrit *úpala,* (precious) stone, from *úpara,* lower, comparative of *úpa,* under.]

o·pal·esce (ō′pə-lĕs′) *intr.v.* **-esced, -escing, -esces.** To emit or show an iridescent shimmer of colors. [Back-formation from OPALESCENT.]

o·pal·es·cent (ō′pə-lĕs′ənt) *adj.* Having or exhibiting a milky iridescence like that of an opal. [OPAL + -ESCENT.] —**o·pal·es·cence** *n.*

o·pal·ine (ō′pə-līn′, -lēn′) *adj.* Opalescent.
~*n.* A whitish opalescent or opaque glass.

o·paque (ō-pāk′) *adj.* **1. a.** Impenetrable by light; neither transparent nor translucent. **b.** Not reflecting light; without luster: *an opaque finish.* **2.** Impenetrable by a form of radiant energy other than visible light: *a chemical solution that is opaque to ultraviolet radiation.* **3. a.** So obscure as to be unintelligible: *an opaque remark.* **b.** Obtuse; dense. —See Usage note at **dark.**
~*n.* Something that is opaque; especially, an opaque pigment used to darken parts of a photographic print or negative. [Middle English *opake,* assimilated to French *opaque,* both from Latin *opācus†,* dark.] —**o·paque** *v.* —**o·paque·ly** *adv.* —**o·paque·ness** *n.*

op art (ŏp) *n.* A form of abstract art that features the use of geometric shapes, lines, or patterns, especially to create an optical illusion of movement. Also called "optical art." [*Op,* short for *optical.*]

op. cit. In the work cited. [Latin *opere citato.*]

OPEC (ō′pĕk′) *n.* The **Organization of Petroleum Exporting Countries** *(see).*

o·pen (ō′pən) *adj.* **1. a.** Affording unobstructed entrance and exit;

opal *The basic material of an opal is colorless—the vivid colors are produced by impurities or by light catching on minute cracks in the stone. Opals range in color from pearly white, through yellows and reds, to the most valuable black or blue gems.*

op art

THE ART OF ILLUSION
Paintings that deceive the eye

Op, or optical, art is a form of abstract art that became popular in the early 1960's. Based on geometric shapes, lines, stripes, or waves, it depends for its effects on deceiving the eye. The paintings create an illusion of movement. The French artist Victor Vasarély (1908–) and the British artist Bridget Riley (1931–) are well-known exponents.

MOVING PICTURE *A segment from* Fall, *which Bridget Riley painted in emulsion on board in 1963. The painting was constructed by using a template, or cutout shape, of undulating curves as a drawing guide some 240 times across the board. Every alternate space was filled in with black.*

not shut or closed: *an open door.* **b.** Affording unobstructed passage or view: *open waters; open countryside.* **2. a.** Having no protecting or concealing cover: *an open wound; an open sports car.* **b.** Unconcealed; blatant: *an open disregard for manners.* **3.** Not sealed, tied, or folded: *an open package; an open newspaper.* **4. a.** Having small holes; porous. **b.** Having interspersed gaps, spaces, or intervals: *open columns; an open weave.* **c.** Widely spaced or leaded. Said of printed matter. **d.** Having constituent elements separated by a space in printing or writing: *an open compound.* **5. a.** Accessible to all; unrestricted: *an open meeting.* **b.** Having no restrictions with regard to the status or age of a person: *an open competition.* **6. a.** Ready or willing to entertain or consider; susceptible. Used with *to*: *open to persuasion.* **b.** Unprotected; vulnerable: *open to attack.* **7. a.** Not yet filled; available: *The job is still open.* **b.** Available for use; active: *an open account.* **c.** Available as an option: *two courses open to us.* **8.** Ready to transact business; operating: *When is the zoo open?* **9.** To be considered further; without a definite conclusion: *an open question.* **10. a.** Characterized by lack of pretense; candid: *an open nature.* **b.** Free of prejudice; receptive to new ideas and arguments: *an open mind.* **11.** *Music.* **a.** Not stopped by a finger. Said of a string or hole of an instrument. **b.** Played without a mute: *an open wind instrument.* **c.** Produced by an unstopped string or hole or without the use of slides, valves, or keys: *an open note on a trumpet.* **12.** *Phonetics.* **a.** Articulated with the tongue in a low position: *The vowel sound in the word "far" is open.* **b.** Ending in a vowel or diphthong: *an open syllable.* **13. a.** Lacking effective regulation: *an open town.* **b.** Not legally controlled: *open drug trafficking.* **14.** *Mathematics.* **a.** Of, pertaining to, or being an interval that does not contain the end points. **b.** Of, pertaining to, or being a set in which each point has points in its neighborhood that also belong to the set. —See Synonyms at **frank.**
~*v.* **opened, opening, opens.** —*tr.* **1.** To cause to become open; release from a closed or fastened position. **2.** To remove obstructions from; clear. **3.** To make or force an opening in: *open an old wound.* **4.** To form spaces or gaps between; spread out: *soldiers opening ranks.* **5. a.** To remove the cover, cork, or lid from; expose: *Open the box.* **b.** To remove the wrapping from; undo: *opened the package.* **6.** To unfold so that the inner parts are displayed; spread out: *a newspaper opened at the sports page.* **7. a.** To begin; initiate; commence: *open a meeting.* **b.** To commence the operation of or start business in: *open an account; open a shop.* **c.** To begin (the action in a game of cards) by making the first bid, by placing a first bet, or by playing the first lead. **8. a.** To permit the use of; make available. **b.** To declare ceremonially to be ready for use or action: *The queen opened Parliament.* **9.** To make more responsive or understanding: *opened her heart to their pleas.* **10.** To reveal the secrets of; bare. —*intr.* **1.** To become open or unfastened. **2. a.** To draw apart; separate: *The wound opened under pressure.* **b.** To spread apart; separate. **3.** To extend; unfold: *The gardens opened out onto a stretch of woodland.* **4.** To come into view; become revealed: *The plain opened before us.* **5.** To become receptive or understanding. **6. a.** To begin; commence: *I opened with a bid.* **b.** To begin business or operation: *When does the shop open?* **c.** To give or have the first public performance: *The film opens in March.* **7.** To give access or view: *The door opens into a passage.* **8.** *Law.* To make preliminary statements in court. Used of an attorney. —**open up. 1.** *Informal.* To speak or act freely and unrestrainedly. **2.** To begin firing: *artillery opening up.* **3.** To accelerate. **4. a.** To make accessible: *The railroad opened up remoter regions.* **b.** To make available: *opened up new markets in other sections of the country.*
~*n.* **1. a.** An unobstructed area of land or water; an opening or clearing. **b.** The outdoors: *lived in the open.* **2.** An undisguised or unconcealed state: *The matter was brought out into the open.* **3.** A tournament or contest in which both professional and amateur players may participate. [Middle English *open,* Old English *open,* from Germanic *upanaz* (unattested).] —**o·pen·a·ble** *adj.* —**o·pen·ly** *adv.* —**o·pen·ness** *n.*

open admission *n.* Open enrollment.

o·pen-air (ō′pən-âr′) *adj.* Outdoor: *an open-air concert.*

o·pen-and-shut (ō′pən-ən-shŭt′) *adj.* Presenting no difficulties; easily settled: *an open-and-shut case.*

open book *n.* A person whose mind, motives, or character are easily understood.

open chain *n. Chemistry.* A linear arrangement of atoms in a molecule. Compare **closed chain.**

open circuit *n.* An electric circuit in which there is no continuous loop, so that no current can flow. Compare **closed circuit.** —**o·pen-cir·cuit** (ō′pən-sûr′kĭt) *adj.*

open city *n.* A city that is declared demilitarized during a war, thus under international law gaining immunity from attack.

open court *n.* A court session that is open to the public.

open door *n.* **1.** An unhindered opportunity for progress; free access. **2.** Admission to all on equal terms. **3.** A policy whereby a nation opens its foreign and internal trade to nationals of all other nations on equal terms. —**o·pen-door** (ō′pən-dôr′, -dōr′) *adj.*

o·pen-end (ō′pən-ĕnd′) *adj.* **1.** Having no definite limit of duration or amount: *an open-end contract.* **2.** Permitting the borrowing of additional funds under existing terms: *an open-end mortgage.*

o·pen-end·ed (ō′pən-ĕn′dĭd) *adj.* **1.** Not restrained by definite limits, restrictions, or structure. **2.** Open or adaptable to change. **3.** Inconclusive or indefinite. **4.** Allowing for a spontaneous, unstructured response: *an open-ended question.*

open-end investment company *n.* A **mutual fund** *(see).*

open enrollment *n.* A policy that permits enrollment of a student in a college or university without regard to academic qualifications.

o·pen·er (ō′pə-nər) *n.* **1.** One that opens, especially a device used to cut open cans or pry up bottle caps. **2. a.** The player who starts the betting in a card game. **b. openers.** Cards of sufficient value for the holder to open the betting legally in a card game. **3. a.** The first act in a theatrical variety show. **b.** The first game in a series. **4. openers.** A beginning; start: *For openers let's discuss the tax proposals.*

o·pen-eyed (ō′pən-īd′) *adj.* **1.** Having the eyes wide open as in surprise. **2.** Watchful and alert.

o·pen-faced (ō′pən-fāst′) *adj.* **1.** Having an undisguised or sincere face or expression. **2.** Having one side uncovered: *an open-faced sandwich.*

o·pen-hand·ed (ō′pən-hăn′dĭd) *adj.* Giving freely; generous. —**o·pen-hand·ed·ly** *adv.* —**o·pen-hand·ed·ness** *n.*

o·pen-heart (ō′pən-härt′) *adj.* Of, pertaining to, or designating surgery in which the heart is exposed while its normal functions in the circulatory system are assumed by external apparatus.

o·pen-heart·ed (ō′pən-här′tĭd) *adj.* **1.** Frank. **2.** Kindly. —**o·pen-heart·ed·ly** *adv.* —**o·pen-heart·ed·ness** *n.*

o·pen-hearth (ō′pən-härth′) *adj.* **1.** Of, pertaining to, or being a reverberatory furnace used in the production of high-quality steel. **2.** Of, pertaining to, or being steel produced in an open-hearth furnace.

open house *n.* **1.** Hospitality offered at one's home to friends who drop in. **2.** A social event at which hospitality is offered to all. **3.** An occasion when an institution, as a school, is open for visiting and inspection by the general public.

o·pen·ing (ō′pə-nĭng) *n.* **1.** The act or an instance of becoming open or being made to open. **2.** An open space serving as a passage or gap. **3.** A hole or aperture. **4.** The first period or stage: *The opening of the book was dull.* **5.** The first occasion for or performance of something, such as a play. **6.** A specific pattern or series of initial moves in certain games, especially chess. **7.** A favorable opportunity or chance. **8.** An unfilled job or position; a vacancy. **9.** *Law.* Preliminary remarks made by an attorney to a court or jury.

open letter *n.* A letter on a subject of general interest that is addressed to an individual but intended for general readership, as one published in a newspaper.

open loop *n. Computer Science.* A computer control system that is not self-correcting.

open market *n.* A market in which supply and demand determine prices and there is no external interference, as from a government.

open marriage *n.* A marriage in which both partners are free to pursue sexual relationships with others.

o·pen-mind·ed (ō′pən-mīn′dĭd) *adj.* Receptive to new ideas or to reason; free from prejudice or bias. —**o·pen-mind·ed·ly** *adv.* —**o·pen-mind·ed·ness** *n.*

o·pen-mouthed (ō′pən-mou*th*d′, -moutht′) *adj.* **1.** Having an open mouth. **2.** Affected with great amazement or wonder.

open order *n. Military.* A formation in which military or naval units are separated by open spaces; especially, in a ceremonial parade, a formation affording easier access between ranks of troops to an inspecting officer.

o·pen-plan (ō′pən-plăn′) *adj.* Having few or no walls or partitions.

open season *n.* **1.** A period during which hunting or fishing is permitted for a particular game animal or fish. **2.** *Informal.* A situation in which criticism is unrestrained: *After the exposé it was open season on government officials.*

open secret *n.* Something purporting to be a secret that is in fact widely known.

open ses·a·me (sĕs′ə-mē) *n.* A seemingly unfailing means of gaining admittance or attaining success. [From the formula used by Ali Baba in the *Arabian Nights* to open the door of the robbers' cave.]

open shop *n.* A business establishment or factory in which workers are employed without regard to union membership. Compare **closed shop, union shop.**

open university *n.* A university whose courses are designed especially for mature students and conducted by such means as television, radio, and correspondence.

o·pen·work (ō′pən-wûrk′) *n.* Ornamental or structural work, as of embroidery or metal, containing numerous openings, usually in set patterns. —**o·pen·work** *adj.*

op·er·a¹ (ŏp′ər-ə, ŏp′rə) *n.* **1. a.** A form of theatrical presentation in which a dramatic performance is set to music. See **grand opera, music drama, operetta. b.** A presentation of this kind. **c.** A work of this kind. **2.** A theater designed primarily for operas. [Italian, from Latin *opera,* works.]

opera². Alternate plural of **opus.**

op·er·a·ble (ŏp′ər-ə-bəl, ŏp′rə-) *adj.* **1.** Capable of being used or operated: *an outmoded but operable motor.* **2.** Capable of being put into practice; practicable: *an operable plan.* **3.** Capable of being treated by surgical operation: *an operable stage of cancer.* —**op·er·a·bil·i·ty** *n.* —**op·er·a·bly** *adv.*

opera buf·fa (bo͞o′fə) *n.* Also **o·pé·ra bouffe** (ō′pā-rä bo͞of′). **1.** A comic opera, especially one of the 18th century. **2.** A performance of an opera buffa. [Italian : OPERA + *buffa,* feminine of *buffo,* comic, BUFFO.]

o·pé·ra co·mique (ŏp′ər-ə kŏ-mēk′, ŏp′rə, ō-pā-rä kô-mēk′) *n., pl.* **opéras comiques** *(pronounced as singular).* Opera that in addition to musical solos and ensembles has dialogue that is spoken rather than sung. [French, "comic opera."]

opera glasses *pl.n.* Small, low-powered binoculars for use especially at a theatrical performance.

op·er·a·go·er (ŏp′ər-ə-gō′ər, ŏp′rə-) *n.* A person who attends operas, especially frequently or regularly.

opera hat *n.* A collapsible top hat.

opera house *n.* A theater designed chiefly for presenting operas.

op·er·and (ŏp′ər-ənd, -ə-rănd′) *n. Mathematics.* A quantity, variable, or function on which an operation is performed. For example, in d*y*/d*x*, *y* is the operand. See **operator.** [Latin *operandum,* something to be worked upon, neuter gerundive of *operārī,* to work.]

op·er·ant (ŏp′ər-ənt) *adj.* **1.** Operating to produce effects; effective. **2.** *Psychology.* Characterizing, pertaining to, or designating a response or behavior elicited, as from a rat, by an environment rather than by a specific stimulus and reinforced by rewarding consequences in the environment.
∼*n.* **1.** One that operates. **2.** *Psychology.* An instance of operant behavior. [Latin *operāns* (stem *operānt-*), present participle of *operārī,* to OPERATE.]

opera se·ri·a (sîr′ē-ə) *n.* Opera of a type popular especially in the 17th and 18th centuries that is characterized by serious themes and elaborate formal arias. [Italian.]

op·er·ate (ŏp′ə-rāt′) *v.* **-ated, -ating, -ates.** —*intr.* **1.** To function effectively; work: *The system is operating well.* **2. a.** To have an effect or influence. **b.** To bring about a desired or proper effect: *The medicine took some time to operate.* **3.** To perform surgery. **4.** To carry on a military or naval action or campaign. —*tr.* **1.** To run or control the functioning of: *operate a machine.* **2.** To conduct the affairs of; manage: *operate a business.* **3.** To bring about; effect. [Latin *operārī,* to work, from *opus* (stem *oper-*), a work.]

op·er·at·ic (ŏp′ə-răt′ĭk) *adj.* **1.** Of, pertaining to, or typical of the opera: *an operatic aria.* **2.** Histrionic or implausible in a way considered characteristic of grand opera. [From OPERA (influenced by DRAMATIC).] —**op·er·at·i·cal·ly** *adv.*

op·er·at·ics (ŏp′ə-răt′ĭks) *pl.n.* Histrionics.

operating system *n.* Computer software designed to complement the hardware of a specific data processing system.

op·er·a·tion (ŏp′ə-rā′shən) *n. Abbr.* **op., Op. 1.** The act, process, or way of operating. **2.** The state of being operative or functioning: *in operation.* **3.** A process or series of acts performed to effect a certain purpose or result. **4.** A process or method of productive activity: *the operation of preparing a meal for 20.* **5.** *Medicine.* A procedure for remedying an injury, ailment, or dysfunction in a living body, especially one performed with instruments. **6.** *Mathematics.* A process or action, such as addition, substitution, transposition, or differentiation, performed in a specified sequence and in accordance with specific rules of procedure. **7.** *Computer Science.* An action resulting from a single computer instruction. **8. a.** A military or naval action, campaign, or project. **b. operations.** The office at an airport or air base where pilots file flight plans and where flying from the field is controlled. **c. operations.** The agency of a business organization that carries out planning and operating functions on an executive level: *a vice president of operations.* [Middle English *operacioun,* from Old French *operation,* from Latin *operātiō* (stem *operātiōn-*), from *operārī,* to OPERATE.]

op·er·a·tion·al (ŏp′ə-rā′shə-nəl) *adj.* **1.** Of or pertaining to an operation or a series of operations. **2.** Of, for, or engaged in military operations. **3.** Serviced and declared fit for proper functioning: *an operational aircraft.* **4.** In use. —**op·er·a·tion·al·ly** *adv.*

op·er·a·tion·al·ism (ŏp′ə-rā′shə-nə-lĭz′əm) *n. Philosophy.* The doctrine that the meanings of many concepts are derived from or given by specific operations performed to investigate the phenomena to which the concepts allegedly refer. —**op·er·a·tion·al·ist** *n.*

operations research *n.* Mathematical or scientific analysis of the systematic efficiency and performance of manpower, machinery, equipment, and policies used in a government, military, or commercial operation, providing quantitative information that may be used in decision making.

op·er·a·tive (ŏp′ər-ə-tĭv, -ə-rā′tĭv, ŏp′rə-tĭv) *adj.* **1.** Exerting influence or force: *operative laws.* **2.** Functioning effectively; efficient. **3.** Significant; relevant. **4.** Engaged in, concerned with, or related to physical or mechanical activity. **5.** Of, pertaining to, or resulting from a surgical operation.
∼*n.* **1.** A skilled worker, especially in industry. **2. a.** A secret or trusted agent. **b.** A private detective. —**op·er·a·tive·ly** *adv.*

op·er·a·tor (ŏp′ə-rā′tər) *n.* **1.** A person who operates a mechanical device, especially one employed at a telephone exchange or switchboard to connect calls or assist callers. **2.** The owner or director of a business or industrial concern. **3.** A dealer in stocks or commodities. **4.** *Mathematics.* A symbol or symbols standing for a mathematical operation, as a plus sign representing addition or d/d*x* representing differentiation of the following term or function in an equation. See **operand. 5.** *Informal.* A shrewd and sometimes unscrupulous person who gets what he wants by devious means: *a smooth operator.* **6.** A chromosomal sequence that is the region of an operon responsible for regulation of structural genes.

o·per·cu·late (ō-pûr′kyə-lĭt) *adj.* Also **o·per·cu·lat·ed** (-lā′tĭd). Having an operculum.

o·per·cu·lum (ō-pûr′kyə-ləm) *n., pl.* **-la** (-lə) or **-lums. 1.** *Biology.* A lid or flap covering an aperture, as the gill cover in some fishes, the horny flap covering the shell opening in snails and other mollusks, or the lid of a moss capsule. **2. a.** *Anatomy.* A flap or lid, such as the layer of tissue over an erupting tooth. **b.** A plug of mucus that fills the opening of the uterus in a pregnant woman. [Latin, a lid, cover, diminutive formation from *operīre,* to cover.] —**o·per·cu·lar** *adj.* —**o·per·cu·lar·ly** *adv.*

op·er·et·ta (ŏp′ə-rĕt′ə) *n.* A theatrical production that has many of the musical elements of opera but is lighter and more popular in subject and style and contains spoken dialogue. Also called "light opera." [Italian, diminutive of OPERA.]

op·er·on (ŏp′ə-rŏn′) *n. Genetics.* A cluster of genes in physical proximity to one another that act together under the control of a regulator gene outside the operon to determine the production of a set of functionally related enzymes. [From OPERATE.]

op·er·ose (ŏp′ə-rōs′) *adj.* **1.** Involving great labor; laborious. **2.** Industrious; diligent. [Latin *operōsus,* from *opus* (stem *oper-*), work.] —**op·er·ose·ly** *adv.* —**op·er·ose·ness** *n.*

oph·i·cleide (ŏf′ĭ-klīd′, ō′fə-) *n.* A musical wind instrument consisting of a long, tapering brass tube bent double and having keys. [French *ophicléïde* : Greek *ophis,* snake (see **ophidian**) + *kleis* (stem *kleid-*), key.]

o·phid·i·an (ō-fĭd′ē-ən) *adj.* Of or pertaining to limbless reptiles or snakes; snakelike.
∼*n.* Any member of the suborder Ophidia or Serpentes; a snake; a serpent. [New Latin *Ophidia,* from Greek *ophis,* snake, serpent.]

oph·i·ol·o·gy (ŏf′ē-ŏl′ə-jē, ō′fē-) *n.* The scientific study of snakes. [Greek *ophis,* snake (see **ophidian**) + -LOGY.] —**oph·i·o·log·i·cal** (ŏf′ē-ə-lŏj′ĭ-kəl, ō′fē-) *adj.* —**oph·i·ol·o·gist** *n.*

o·phi·oph·a·gous (ō′fē-ŏf′ə-gəs) *adj.* Feeding on snakes. [Greek *ophiophagos,* from *ophis,* snake + *-phagos,* -PHAGOUS.]

oph·ite (ŏf′īt′, ō′fīt′) *n.* **1.** A mottled-green rock composed of diabase. **2.** Any of various green rocks, such as serpentine. [Latin *ophītes,* from Greek *ophitēs,* serpentine (stone), from *ophis,* serpent.]

o·phit·ic (ō-fĭt′ĭk, ō-fĭt′-) *adj. Mineralogy.* **1.** Of or pertaining to ophite. **2.** Having a structure composed of laths of plagioclase crystals occurring within an individual anhedral pyroxene crystal.

Oph·i·u·chus (ŏf′ē-yōō′kəs, ō′fē-) *n.* A constellation in the equatorial region near Hercules and Scorpius. [Latin *Ophiūchus,* from Greek *ophioukhos,* "serpent-holder" : *ophis,* snake + *ekhein,* to hold.]

oph·thal·mia (ŏf-thăl′mē-ə, ŏp-) *n.* Also **oph·thal·mi·tis** (ŏf′thăl-mī′tĭs, ŏf′thəl-, ŏp′-). Inflammation of the eye, especially of the conjunctiva. [Middle English *obtalmia,* from Late Latin *ophthalmia,* from Greek *ophthalmos,* eye.]

oph·thal·mic (ŏf-thăl′mĭk, ŏp-) *adj.* **1.** Of or pertaining to the eye or eyes; ocular. **2.** Affected by ophthalmia. [Greek *ophthalmikos,* from *ophthalmos,* eye.]

ophthalmo– *prefix.* Indicates the eye or eyeball; for example, **ophthalmology, ophthalmoscope.** [Greek, from *ophthalmos,* eye.]

oph·thal·mol·o·gist (ŏf′thăl-mŏl′ə-jĭst, ŏf′thəl-, ŏp′-) *n. Abbr.* **ophthal.** A physician who specializes in the treatment of diseases of the eye.

oph·thal·mol·o·gy (ŏf′thăl-mŏl′ə-jē, ŏf′thəl-, ŏp′-) *n. Abbr.* **ophthal.** The branch of medical science dealing with the anatomy, functions, pathology, and treatment of the eye. [OPHTHALMO- + -LOGY.] —**oph·thal·mo·log·i·cal** (ŏf-thăl′mə-lŏj′ĭ-kəl, ŏp-) *adj.* —**oph·thal·mo·log·i·cal·ly** *adv.*

oph·thal·mom·e·ter (ŏf′thăl-mŏm′ə-tər, ŏf′thəl-, ŏp′-) *n.* An optical instrument for measuring astigmatism. [OPHTHALMO- + -METER.] —**oph·thal·mo·met·ric** (ŏf-thăl′mə-mĕt′rĭk, ŏp-), **oph·thal·mo·met·ri·cal** (-rĭ-kəl) *adj.*

oph·thal·mo·scope (ŏf-thăl′mə-skōp′, ŏp-) *n.* An instrument consisting essentially of a mirror with a central hole and lenses of different strengths that is used to examine the interior of the eye through the pupil. [OPHTHALMO- + -SCOPE.] —**oph·thal·mo·scop·ic** (ŏf-thăl′mə-skŏp′ĭk, ŏp-) **oph·thal·mo·scop·i·cal** *adj.* —**oph·thal·mos·co·py** (ŏf′thăl-mŏs′kə-pē, ŏf′thəl-, ŏp′-) *n.*

–opia *suffix.* Indicates a specified visual condition or defect; for example, **diplopia, senopia.** [Greek *-ōpia,* from *ōps,* eye.]

o·pi·ate (ō′pē-ĭt, -āt′) *n.* **1.** Any of various sedative narcotics containing opium or one or more of its derivatives. **2.** Any sedative or narcotic drug. **3.** Anything that relaxes or induces sleep or torpor.
∼*adj.* **1.** Consisting of or containing opium. **2.** Causing or producing sleep or sedation.
∼*tr.v.* (ō′pē-āt′) **opiated, -ating, -ates. 1.** To subject to the action of an opiate. **2.** To dull or deaden as if with a narcotic drug. [Medieval Latin *opiātum,* an opiate, from *opiātus,* treated with opium, soporific, from Latin *opium,* OPIUM.]

o·pine (ō-pīn′) *tr.v.* **opined, opining, opines.** To hold or state as an opinion; think: *opined that we should work harder.* [Old French *opiner,* from Latin *opīnārī,* to think.]

o·pin·ion (ə-pĭn′yən) *n.* **1.** A belief or conclusion held with confidence but not substantiated by positive knowledge or proof. **2. a.** An evaluation or judgment based on special knowledge and given by an expert: *a medical opinion.* **b.** A formal statement given by a legal expert of his views on a particular case. **3.** A judgment or estimation of the worth or value of a person or thing: *In my opinion he is a fool.* **4.** The common, usual, or prevailing feeling or sentiment: *public opinion.* **5.** *Law.* A formal statement by a judge or jury of the legal reasons and principles for the conclusions of the court. —**be of the opinion.** To hold the view. [Middle English, from Old French, from Latin *opīniō* (stem *opīniōn-*), from *opīnārī,* to think.]
Synonyms: *belief, conviction, feeling, impression, judgment, persuasion, sentiment, view.*

o·pin·ion·at·ed (ə-pĭn′yə-nā′tĭd) *adj.* Holding stubbornly and often unreasonably to one's own opinions. —**o·pin·ion·at·ed·ly** *adv.* —**o·pin·ion·at·ed·ness** *n.*

PRONUNCIATION KEY

ă, pat; ā, pay; âr, care;
ä, father, are; b, bib;
ch, church; d, deed; ĕ, pet;
ē, be; f, fife; g, gag; h, hat;
hw, which; ĭ, pit; ī, pie;
îr, pier; j, judge; k, kick;
l, lid, needle; m, mum;
n, no, sudden; ng, thing;
ŏ, pot; ō, toe; ô, paw, for;
oi, noise; ou, out; ŏŏ, book;
ōō, boot; p, pop; r, roar;
s, sauce; sh, ship, dish;
t, tight; th, thin, path;
th, this, bathe; ŭ, cut; ûr, fur;
v, valve; w, with; y, yes;
z, zebra, size; zh, vision;
ə, about, item, edible,
gallop, circus, peaceful

IN FOREIGN WORDS:

ä, *Fr.* ami; œ, *Fr.* feu, *Ger.* schön; ü, *Fr.* tu, *Ger.* über; KH, *Ger.* ich, *Scot.* loch; N, *Fr.* bon; y′, *Fr.* Compiègne

STRESS MARKS:

Primary stress: ′
in·cite′ (ĭn-sīt′)
Secondary stress: ′
in′sight′ (ĭn′sīt′)

opium poppy *The seeds of this flower are used in cakes and bread and are crushed for oil. The drugs morphine, codeine, and heroin are derived from an Asian variety of the plant.*

opossum *There are more than 70 species of this marsupial in South America, but only one—the Virginia, or common, opossum pictured here—is found in North America as well. It hunts at night for insects and small animals, and when threatened, it feigns death—hence the term "playing possum."*

o·pin·ion·a·tive (ə-pĭn′yə-nā′tĭv) *adj.* **1.** Of, pertaining to, or of the nature of an opinion; based on opinion. **2.** Opinionated. **—o·pin·ion·a·tive·ly** *adv.*

opinion poll *n.* **1.** A canvassing of a selected sample group of persons to analyze public opinion on a particular question. **2.** The result of an opinion poll.

o·pis·tho·branch (ə-pĭs′thə-brăngk′) *n.* Any of various marine gastropod mollusks of the subclass Opisthobranchia, characterized by gills, a shell that is reduced or absent, and two pairs of tentacles. [New Latin *Opisthobranchia,* order name : from Greek *opisthen,* behind + -BRANCH.]

op·is·thog·na·thous (ŏp′ĭs-thŏg′nə-thəs) *adj.* Having receding jaws. [Greek *opisthen,* behind + -GNATHOUS.] **—op·is·thog·na·thism** *n.*

o·pi·um (ō′pē-əm) *n.* **1.** A bitter yellowish-brown drug prepared from the dried juice of unripe seed capsules of the opium poppy, containing many alkaloids such as morphine, narcotine, codeine, and papaverine. It may be chewed and smoked for its narcotic effects and is still used in medicine as an analgesic for severe pain. Habitual use induces strong addiction; excessive use is fatal. **2.** Something that numbs or stupefies. [Middle English, from Latin, from Greek *opion,* poppy juice, opium, diminutive of *opos,* juice.]

opium den *n.* A room or establishment where opium is sold and used.

opium poppy *n.* A poppy plant, *Papaver somniferum,* originally of Asia Minor, having grayish-green leaves and variously colored flowers. The juice of its unripe seed capsules is the original source of opium.

o·pos·sum (ə-pŏs′əm, pŏs′əm) *n., pl.* **-sums** or collectively **opossum. 1.** Any of various nocturnal, arboreal marsupials of the family Didelphidae, especially *Didelphis marsupialis,* of the Americas. **2.** Any of several Australian marsupials of the family Phalangeridae, some of which have valuable fur. In both senses, also called "possum." [Algonquian (Powhatan) *āpassūm,* from Proto-Algonquian *waap-a'themwa* (unattested), "white beast."]

opossum shrimp *n.* Any of various shrimplike crustaceans of the order Mysidacea, the females of which carry their eggs and young in a brood pouch.

opp. opposite.

Op·pen·hei·mer (ŏp′ən-hī′mər), **J(ulius) Robert** (1904–67). U.S. physicist. He led the Los Alamos bomb project (1942–45) and was responsible for the building of the first nuclear bomb. He opposed the development of the hydrogen bomb and was eventually dismissed (1953) by the Atomic Energy Commission as a security risk. He won the Fermi Award (1963) for his work on the peaceful application of nuclear energy.

op·po·nent (ə-pō′nənt) *n.* One that opposes another or others in a battle, contest, controversy, debate, or game.
∼*adj.* **1.** Acting against an antagonist or an opposing force. **2.** Opposite. **3.** *Anatomy.* Designating muscles that act to bring two parts into opposing positions. [Latin *oppōnēns* (stem *oppōnent-*), present participle of *oppōnere,* to OPPOSE.] **—op·po·nen·cy** *n.*

Synonyms: *adversary, antagonist, competitor, rival.*

op·por·tune (ŏp′ər-to͞on′, -tyo͞on′) *adj.* **1.** Suited or right for a particular purpose. **2.** Occurring at a time that is fitting or advantageous. [Middle English, from Old French *opportun,* from Latin *opportūnus,* seasonable, (originally of wind) "blowing toward the harbor" : *ob-,* to + *portus,* harbor.] **—op·por·tune·ly** *adv.* **—op·por·tune·ness** *n.*

op·por·tun·ist (ŏp′ər-to͞o′nĭst, -tyo͞o′nĭst) *n.* A person who takes advantage of any opportunity to achieve an end, usually with little or no regard for principles or consequences. [French *opportuniste,* from *opportunisme,* from Italian *opportunismo,* from *opportuno,* opportune, from Latin *opportūnus,* OPPORTUNE.] **—op·por·tun·ism** *n.* **—op·por·tun·ist, op·por·tun·is·tic** (ŏp′ər-to͞o-nĭs′tĭk, -tyo͞o-) *adj.*

op·por·tu·ni·ty (ŏp′ər-to͞o′nə-tē, -tyo͞o′nə-tē) *n., pl.* **-ties. 1.** A favorable or advantageous combination of circumstances; a suitable occasion or time. **2.** A chance for progress or advancement; prospect: *job opportunities.* [Middle English *opportunite,* from Old French, from Latin *opportūnitās* (stem *opportūnitāt-*), from *opportūnus,* OPPORTUNE.]

Usage: *Opportunity* may be followed by an infinitive form of the verb, introduced by *to* (*She has the opportunity to leave now*); a participial form of the verb, introduced by *of* or *for* (*You have a wonderful opportunity of* (or *for*) *getting back your job*); or a noun phrase, introduced by *for* (*an opportunity for new ideas*).

op·pos·a·ble (ə-pō′zə-bəl) *adj.* **1.** Capable of being opposed. **2.** Capable of being placed opposite or in opposition to something. Said especially of the thumb, which can be placed opposite the other digits. **—op·pos·a·bil·i·ty** *n.*

op·pose (ə-pōz′) *v.* **-posed, -posing, -poses.** —*tr.* **1.** To be in contention or conflict with; combat; resist: *oppose the enemy force.* **2.** To be hostile or resistant to: *oppose new ideas.* **3.** To place or be in opposition to; contrast or counterbalance by antithesis. **4.** To place so as to be opposite something else. —*intr.* To act or be in opposition to something. [French *opposer,* from Old French, from Latin *oppōnere* (past participial stem *opposit-*), to set against : *ob-,* against + *pōnere,* to put.] **—op·pos·er** *n.*

Synonyms: *combat, contest, resist, withstand.*

op·po·site (ŏp′ə-zĭt) *adj. Abbr.* **op., opp. 1.** Placed or located directly across from something else or from each other; lying in corresponding positions in relation to an intervening space or object: *The store and the bank are on opposite sides of the building.* **2.** Facing the other way; moving or tending away from each other: *They chatted for a while, then said good-by and walked in opposite directions.* **3.** Contrary or antithetical in nature or tendency; diametrically opposed; altogether different: *We have opposite opinions on that subject.* **4.** *Botany.* Growing in pairs on either side of a stem. Said especially of leaves. Compare **alternate.**
∼*n.* **1.** A person or thing that is opposite or contrary to another. **2.** A word that means the opposite of another; antonym. **3.** *Archaic.* An opponent or antagonist.
∼*adv.* In an opposite position or positions: *The two friends sat opposite at the table.*
∼*prep.* **1.** Across from or facing: *Park your car opposite the bank.* **2.** In a complementary dramatic role to: *He played opposite her in a recent movie.* [Middle English, from Old French, from Latin *oppositus,* from the past participle of *oppōnere,* to OPPOSE.] **—op·po·site·ly** *adv.* **—op·po·site·ness** *n.*

Synonyms: *antithetical, contradictory, contrary.*

opposite number *n.* A person who holds a position in an organization or system that corresponds to that of a specified person in another organization or system; counterpart.

op·po·si·tion (ŏp′ə-zĭsh′ən) *n.* **1.** The act of opposing or condition of being in conflict; resistance or antagonism. **2. a.** A position or location opposite to or facing another. **b.** Placement in such a position or location. **3.** Something that is or serves as an obstacle. **4. a.** *Often* **Opposition.** A political party or organized group opposed to the group, party, or government in power. **b.** A person or group hostile to the ideas of another. **5.** *Astronomy.* **a.** A geometric configuration in which the earth lies on a straight line between the sun and a planet. **b.** The position of the exterior planet in this configuration. **6.** *Logic.* The relation existing between two propositions having an identical subject and predicate but differing in quantity or quality or both. **7.** *Linguistics.* Contrast between two phonemes or other elements of a language that have a relationship such that the contrast is significant. [Middle English *opposicioun* (only in the astronomical sense), from Old French *opposition,* from Medieval Latin *oppositiō* (stem *oppositiōn-*), from Latin, act of opposing, from *oppōnere* (past participial stem *opposit-*), to OPPOSE.] **—op·po·si·tion·al** *adj.* **—op·po·si·tion·ist** *n.*

op·press (ə-prĕs′) *tr.v.* **-pressed, -pressing, -presses. 1.** To subjugate or persecute by unjust or tyrannical use of force or authority. **2.** To weigh heavily upon, especially so as to depress the mind or spirits: *Poverty oppressed me.* **3.** *Obsolete.* To overwhelm or crush. [Middle English *oppressen,* from Old French *oppresser,* from Medieval Latin *oppressāre,* frequentative of Latin *opprimere* (past participle *oppressus*), to press against : *ob-,* against + *premere,* to press.] **—op·pres·sor** *n.*

op·pres·sion (ə-prĕsh′ən) *n.* **1.** The act of oppressing or the state of being oppressed. **2.** Something that oppresses or burdens. **3.** A feeling of being heavily weighed down, either mentally or physically; depression or weariness.

op·pres·sive (ə-prĕs′ĭv) *adj.* **1.** Harsh; tyrannical. **2.** Causing a state of physical or mental discomfort or weariness: *an oppressive afternoon.* —See Synonyms at **burdensome.** [Medieval Latin *oppressīvus,* from Latin *opprimere,* to OPPRESS.] **—op·pres·sive·ly** *adv.* **—op·pres·sive·ness** *n.*

op·pro·bri·ous (ə-prō′brē-əs) *adj.* **1.** Expressing or carrying a sense of disgrace or contemptuous scorn: *opprobrious epithets.* **2.** Shameful; infamous. [Middle English, from Old French *opprobreus,* from Late Latin *opprobriōsus,* from Latin *opprobrium,* OPPROBRIUM.] **—op·pro·bri·ous·ly** *adv.*

op·pro·bri·um (ə-prō′brē-əm) *n.* **1.** Disgrace inherent in or arising from shameful conduct; ignominy. **2.** Scornful reproach or contempt: *a term of opprobrium.* **3.** A cause of shame or disgrace. —See Synonyms at **disgrace.** [Latin, "a reproach against," dishonor : *ob-,* against + *probrum,* reproach, infamy.]

op·pugn (ə-pyo͞on′) *tr.v.* **-pugned, -pugning, -pugns.** To oppose, contradict, or call into question. [Middle English *oppugnen,* from Latin *oppugnāre,* to fight against : *ob-,* against + *pugnāre,* to fight.] **—op·pugn·er** *n.*

op·sin (ŏp′sĭn) *n.* The protein constituent of **rhodopsin** *(see).*

-opsis *suffix.* Indicates view, appearance, or resemblance; for example, **coreopsis.** [Greek, from *opsis,* sight, appearance.]

op·son·ic (ŏp-sŏn′ĭk) *adj.* Of, pertaining to, or having the effect of opsonin. [OPSON(IN) + -IC.]

opsonic index *n.* The ratio of the number of bacteria per phagocyte in the blood of a test patient to the number in the blood of a normal individual. It is a measure of the power of a patient's serum to destroy invading bacteria.

op·son·i·fy (ŏp-sŏn′ə-fī′) *tr.v.* **-fied, -fying, -fies.** To make (invading bacteria) susceptible to phagocytosis by opsonic action; opsonize. [OPSON(IN) + -FY.] **—op·son·i·fi·ca·tion** *n.*

op·so·nin (ŏp′sə-nĭn) *n.* A substance naturally present in the blood that renders invading bacteria susceptible to phagocytosis. [Latin *opsōnium,* relish (opsonin being a "relish" enabling the body to "digest" bacteria), indirectly from Greek *opsōnein,* to buy food or delicacies, from *opson*†, relish, delicacy.]

op·so·nize (ŏp′sə-nīz′) *tr.v.* **-nized, -nizing, -nizes. 1.** To form opsonins in. **2.** To opsonify. [From OPSONIN.] **—op·so·ni·za·tion** *n.*

-opsy *suffix.* Indicates an examination; for example, **biopsy.** [New Latin *-opsia,* condition of the eyes, examination, from Greek, from *opsis,* sight, appearance.]

opt (ŏpt) *intr.v.* **opted, opting, opts. 1.** To make a choice: *I opted not to go.* **2.** To make a decision in favor of something: *He opted for early retirement.* **—opt out. 1.** To decide against participating in something: *opted out of the deal.* **2.** To refuse to conform with conventional society. [French *opter,* from Latin *optāre.*]

opt. **1.** optative. **2.** optical; optician; optics. **3.** optimum. **4.** optional.

op·ta·tive (ŏp′tə-tĭv) *adj.* **1.** Expressing a wish or choice. **2.** *Abbr.* **opt.** *Grammar.* **a.** Designating a mood of verbs in some languages, such as Greek, used to express a wish. **b.** Designating a statement using a verb in the subjunctive mood to indicate a wish or desire; for example, *Were I rich, I would do it.*
~*n. Abbr.* **opt.** *Grammar.* **1.** The optative mood. **2.** A verb or expression in this mood. [Middle English, from Old French *optatif,* from Late Latin *optātīvus,* from Latin *optāre,* to choose, wish.] **—op·ta·tive·ly** *adv.*

op·tic (ŏp′tĭk) *adj.* **1.** Of or pertaining to the eye or to vision. **2.** Of or pertaining to the science of optics.
~*n.* **1.** An eye. Not in technical usage. **2.** Any of the components of an optical instrument. [Old French *optique,* from Medieval Latin *opticus,* from Greek *optikos,* from *optos,* visible.]

op·ti·cal (ŏp′tĭ-kəl) *adj. Abbr.* **op., opt** **1.** Of or pertaining to sight: *an optical illusion.* **2.** Designed to assist sight: *optical instruments.* **3.** Of or pertaining to optics. **4.** Pertaining to or using light: *optical astronomy.* **5.** Using light-sensitive devices: *optical character recognition.* **—op·ti·cal·ly** *adv.*

optical activity *n. Chemistry.* A property of a substance that enables it to rotate the plane of transmitted polarized light.

optical art *n.* **Op art** *(see).*

optical bench *n.* An adjustable arrangement of lenses, mirrors, and other components for experiments on optical systems.

optical character reader *n. Abbr.* **OCR** A device for converting printed characters into digital form by optical character recognition. See **optical scanner.**

optical character recognition *n. Abbr.* **OCR** A method of scanning printed characters with an optical device and transforming them into electrical signals so that the data can be stored magnetically in a computer.

optical fiber *n.* A very thin, typically flexible optically transparent fiber, as of glass or plastic, through which light can be transmitted by successive internal reflections.

optical glass *n.* Any of various types of clear glass, such as flint and crown glass, having known reproducible optical properties and used in lenses, prisms, and the like.

optical isomer *n. Chemistry.* A type of **isomer** *(see).*

optical maser *n. Physics.* A laser, especially one that produces visible radiation.

optical rotation *n. Physics & Chemistry.* Rotation of the plane of polarization of polarized light by a substance that shows optical activity.

optical scanner *n.* A device for converting printed or illustrated matter into digital form. See **optical character reader.**

optic axis *n.* An optical path through a crystal along which a ray of light can pass without undergoing double refraction.

optic chiasma *n.* The X-shaped structure formed by the two optic nerves when they cross each other on the undersurface of the brain.

optic disk *n.* An area of the retina, the **blind spot** *(see).*

op·ti·cian (ŏp-tĭsh′ən) *n. Abbr.* **opt.** **1.** One who makes lenses and eyeglasses. **2.** One who sells lenses, glasses, and other optical instruments. Compare **optometrist.** [French *opticien,* from Medieval Latin *optica,* OPTICS.]

optic nerve *n.* A motor nerve that connects the retina of the eye with the brain.

op·tics (ŏp′tĭks) *n. Abbr.* **opt** *Used with a singular verb. Physics.* The scientific study of light and vision, chiefly of the generation, propagation, and detection of electromagnetic radiation having wavelengths greater than x-rays and shorter than microwaves. [Latin *optica,* from Greek *optika,* neuter plural of *optikos,* OPTIC.]

op·ti·mal (ŏp′tə-məl) *adj.* Most favorable or desirable; optimum. **—op·ti·mal·ly** *adv.*

op·ti·mism (ŏp′tə-mĭz′əm) *n.* **1.** A tendency or disposition to expect the best possible outcome or to dwell upon the most hopeful aspects of a situation. **2.** *Philosophy.* **a.** The doctrine, asserted by Leibnitz, that our world is the best of all possible worlds. **b.** The belief that the universe is improving and that good will ultimately triumph over evil. [French, from Latin *optimum,* best, OPTIMUM.]

op·ti·mist (ŏp′tə-mĭst) *n.* **1.** One who habitually or in a particular case expects a favorable outcome. **2.** A believer in philosophical optimism. **—op·ti·mis·tic** (ŏp′tə-mĭs′tĭk) *adj.* **—op·ti·mis·ti·cal·ly** *adv.*

op·ti·mize (ŏp′tə-mīz′) *tr.v.* **-mized, -mizing, -mizes.** **1.** To make as good or as effective as possible. **2.** To make the most effective use of. **—op·ti·mi·za·tion** *n.*

op·ti·mum (ŏp′tə-məm) *n., pl.* **-ma** (-mə) or **-mums.** *Abbr.* **opt** The best or most favorable condition, degree, or amount for a particular situation.
~*adj.* Most favorable or advantageous; best. [Latin, from neuter of *optimus,* best.]

op·tion (ŏp′shən) *n.* **1.** The act or an instance of choosing; a choice. **2.** The power or right of choosing; freedom to choose. **3. a.** The exclusive right, usually obtained for a fee, to buy or sell property within a stated time and at a stated price. **b.** A right to buy or sell specific securities or commodities at a stated price within a stated time. **c.** The privilege of demanding fulfillment of a contract during a specified future time. **d.** A clause in an insurance policy permitting the policyholder to specify the manner in which payments are to be made or credited to him. **4.** Something chosen or available as a choice. **—keep** (or **leave**) **one's options open.** To withhold one's decision; remain uncommitted. —See Synonyms at **choice.**
~*tr.v.* **optioned, -tioning, -tions.** **1. a.** To acquire an option on: *optioned the neighboring lot.* **b.** To grant an option on. **2.** To transfer (a baseball player) to a minor-league club with the option of recalling him within a specified period of time. [French, from Latin *optiō* (stem *optiōn-*), choice.]

op·tion·al (ŏp′shə-nəl) *adj. Abbr.* **opt.** Left to choice; not compulsory or automatic. **—op·tion·al·ly** *adv.*

op·tom·e·ter (ŏp-tŏm′ə-tər) *n.* An instrument used for measuring the refraction of the eye. [Greek *optos,* visible + METER.]

op·tom·e·trist (ŏp-tŏm′ə-trĭst) *n.* One who specializes in optometry. Compare **optician.**

op·tom·e·try (ŏp-tŏm′ə-trē) *n.* The techniques or profession of examining, measuring, and treating certain visual defects by means of corrective lenses or other methods that do not require license as a physician. [Greek *optos,* visible.] **—op·to·met·ric** (ŏp′tə-mĕt′rĭk), **op·to·met·ri·cal** (-rĭ-kəl) *adj.*

op·u·lent (ŏp′yə-lənt) *adj.* **1.** Having or characterized by great wealth; rich. **2.** Abundant; plentiful; lavish. [Latin *opulentus,* from *opēs,* wealth.] **—op·u·lence, op·u·len·cy** *n.* **—op·u·lent·ly** *adv.*

o·pun·ti·a (ō-pŭn′shē-ə, -shə) *n.* **1.** Any of various cacti of the genus *Opuntia.* **2.** The **prickly pear** *(see).* [New Latin, from Latin *(herba) Opuntia,* (herb) of Opus, an ancient city in Greece.]

opuntia *A genus of cacti that takes its name from the ancient Greek city of Opus, where it grew abundantly. The plants are sometimes grown for their juicy fruit, known as prickly pears.*

o·pus (ō′pəs) *n., pl.* **opuses** or **opera** (ō′pər-ə, ŏp′ər-ə). *Abbr.* **op., Op.** A creative work; especially, a musical composition numbered to designate the order of a composer's works. [Latin, work.]

o·pus·cule (ō-pŭs′kyo͞ol) *n.* A small and minor work. [French, from Latin *opusculum,* diminutive of *opus,* work, OPUS.]

or[1] (ôr; *unstressed* ər) *conj.* Used to indicate: **1. a.** An alternative, usually only before the last term of a series: *hot or cold; this, that, or the other.* **b.** The second of two alternatives, the first being preceded by *either* or *whether*: *Your answer is either ingenious or wrong. She didn't know whether to laugh or to cry.* **c.** *Archaic.* The first of two alternatives, with the force of *either* or *whether.* **2.** A synonymous or equivalent expression: *acrophobia, or fear of great heights.* **3.** Uncertainty or indefiniteness: *two or three.* [Middle English *or,* contraction of *other,* alteration (influenced by EITHER, WHETHER) of Old English *oththe,* from Common Germanic.]
Usage: When all of the elements connected by *or* are singular, the verb they govern must be singular: *Beer or wine is included in the price.* When all of the elements are plural, the verb is also plural: *Either the cars or the bikes are in need of recall.* When the elements are of different number, the verb generally agrees with the element closest to it: *Either the books or the newspaper is correct. Either the newspaper or the books are correct.* See also **either, neither, nor.**

or[2] *conj. Archaic.* Before. Followed by *ever* or *ere.*
~*prep. Archaic.* Before. [Middle English *ar, or,* Old English *ār,* early, before, from Old Norse.]

or[3] *n. Heraldry.* The metal gold, represented by a white field sprinkled with small dots.
~*adj. Heraldry.* Of gold. Used after the noun: *a bezant or.* [Old French, from Latin *aurum.*]

OR Oregon (used with a Zip Code).

-or[1] *suffix.* Indicates the person or thing performing the action expressed by the root verb; for example, **investor, percolator.** [Middle English *-our, -or,* from Norman French *-eour,* Old French *-eor, -eur,* partly from Latin *-or* and partly from Latin *-ātor* (past participial stem *-āt-* + *-or*).]

-or[2] *suffix.* Also *British* **-our.** Indicates a state, quality, or activity; for example, **behavior.** [Middle English *-or, -our,* from Old French *-eur,* from Latin *-or,* abstract suffix.]

o·ra. Plural of **os** (mouth).

or·ach, or·ache (ôr′ĭch, ŏr′-) *n.* Any of various plants of the genus *Atriplex*; especially, *A. hortensis,* whose edible leaves resemble spinach. [Middle English *arage, orage,* from Norman French *arasche,* modification of Vulgar Latin *atrapica* (unattested), variant of Latin *atriplex,* from Greek *atraphaxus*†.]

or·a·cle (ôr′ə-kəl, ŏr′-) *n.* **1. a.** A shrine consecrated to the worship and consultation of a prophetic god, as that of Apollo at Delphi. **b.** A person, as a priest, who transmits prophecies from a deity at such a shrine. **c.** A prophecy, often in the form of an enigmatic statement or allegory, made known at such a shrine. **2. a.** A person or agency considered to be a source of wise counsel or prophetic opinions; an infallible authority or judge. **b.** An authoritative statement or prediction from such a person or agency. **3.** *Theology.* A command or revelation from God. **4.** In the Old Testament, the sanctuary of the Temple; the holy of holies. I Kings 6:16, 19–23. [Middle English, from Old French, from Latin *ōrāculum,* from *ōrāre,* to speak.]

o·rac·u·lar (ô-răk′yə-lər, ō-răk′-) *adj.* **1.** Of or pertaining to an oracle. **2.** Resembling or characteristic of an oracle: **a.** Solemnly prophetic: *an oracular warning.* **b.** Brief and enigmatic; mysterious. [Latin *ōrāculum,* ORACLE.] **—o·rac·u·lar·ly** *adv.*

o·ral (ôr′əl, ŏr′-) *adj.* **1.** Spoken rather than written. **2. a.** Of or pertaining to the mouth: *oral hygiene.* **b.** Designating the surface of an invertebrate animal, such as a jellyfish, on which the mouth is situated. **3.** Used in or taken through the mouth: *an oral thermometer; oral vaccine.* **4.** Consisting of or using speech: *oral instruction.* **5.** *Phonetics.* Designating a speech sound emitted through the mouth only, with the nasal passages closed. **6.** *Psychoanalysis.* **a.** Of, pertaining to, or designating the first stage of psychosexual

PRONUNCIATION KEY

ă, pat; ā, pay; âr, care;
ä, father, are; b, bib;
ch, church; d, deed; ĕ, pet;
ē, be; f, fife; g, gag; h, hat;
hw, which; ĭ, pit; ī, pie;
îr, pier; j, judge; k, kick;
l, lid, needle; m, mum;
n, no, sudden; ng, thing;
ŏ, pot; ō, toe; ô, paw, for;
oi, noise; ou, out; o͝o, book;
o͞o, boot; p, pop; r, roar;
s, sauce; sh, ship, dish;
t, tight; th, thin, path;
th, this, bathe; ŭ, cut; ûr, fur;
v, valve; w, with; y, yes;
z, zebra, size; zh, vision;
ə, about, item, edible,
gallop, circus, peaceful

IN FOREIGN WORDS:

à, *Fr.* ami; œ, *Fr.* feu, *Ger.* schön; ü, *Fr.* tu, *Ger.* über;
KH, *Ger.* ich, *Scot.* loch;
N, *Fr.* bon; y′, *Fr.* Compiègne

STRESS MARKS:

Primary stress: ′
in·cite′ (ĭn-sīt′)
Secondary stress: ′
in′sight′ (ĭn′sīt′)

development of the infant, when sexual gratification is derived chiefly from stimulation of the mouth parts. **b.** Of, pertaining to, or designating a personality fixated at this stage, characterized by such traits as greediness and dependence. Compare **anal, genital.**
~*n. Often* **orals.** An academic examination in which the questions and answers are spoken rather than written. [Late Latin *orālis,* from Latin *ōs* (stem *ōr-*), the mouth.] **—o·ral·ly** *adv.*

oral contraceptive *n. Medicine.* Any of various hormone compounds in pill form, typically consisting of an estrogen and a progestogen, used in specific sequence to prevent ovulation and conception.

orangutan *Found in the tropical rain forests of Borneo and Sumatra, the orangutan has very long arms and is chiefly vegetarian. Its name comes from a Malay phrase meaning "man of the woods."*

oral history *n.* **1.** The practice or technique of gathering information by interviewing and usually tape-recording the interviews with eyewitnesses of or participants in historical events. **2.** Information gathered by means of oral history. **3.** A written account based on oral history. **—oral historian** *n.*

or·ange (ôr′ĭnj, ŏr′-) *n.* **1. a.** Any of several evergreen trees of the genus *Citrus,* cultivated in tropical and subtropical regions and having fragrant white flowers and round fruit with a yellowish-red rind and a sectioned, pulpy interior; especially, *C. sinensis,* the sweet orange, and *C. aurantium,* the Seville or sour orange. **b.** The fruit of these trees, having a sweetish, acid juice. **2.** Any of several plants or trees resembling the orange in some respect, as the **mock orange** *(see).* **3.** Any of a group of colors between red and yellow in hue, of medium lightness and moderate saturation. [Middle English, from Old French *orenge, orange,* from Arabic *nāranj,* from Persian *nārang,* from Sanskrit *nārangaḥ*†, orange, orange tree.] **—or·ange** *adj.* **—or·ange·y, or·ange·ish** *adj.*

Or·ange[1] (ôr′ĭnj) also **Or·ange-Nas·sau** (-năs′ô). A princely European family who have been rulers of the Netherlands since 1815.

Or·ange[2] (ô-räNzh′). Town in Vaucluse department, southeastern France. Founded by Charlemagne, it was the seat of the House of Orange.

Or·ange[3] (ôr′ĭnj). South African river, the longest in southern Africa. Rising in the Drakensberg Mts. of Lesotho, it flows 2,093 kilometers (1,300 miles) west to join the Atlantic at Alexander Bay.

or·ange·ade (ôr′ĭn-jād′, ŏr′-) *n.* A drink, often carbonated, of orange juice or orange flavoring, sugar, and water. [French : ORANGE + -ADE.]

orange flower oil *n.* An essential oil, **neroli** *(see).*

orange flower water *n.* A solution of neroli in water, used in pharmaceutical preparations and cooking.

Orange Free State. A province of South Africa, on the plateau of the Highveld. The economy is chiefly agricultural. Mineral resources include gold, uranium, and coal. Boer farmers settled in the territory during the 1820's, but it was annexed by Britain as the Orange River Sovereignty (1848). After conflicts with the Boers, Britain granted the territory independence as the Orange Free State (1854). The British again annexed the Free State as the Orange River Colony (1900), but it was granted self-government (1907) and became a founding province in the Union of South Africa (1910). Its capital is Bloemfontein.

orange hawkweed *n.* A plant, *Hieracium aurantiacum,* native to Europe, having hairy leaves and bearing clusters of orange-red flowers. Also called "devil's paintbrush."

Or·ange·man (ôr′ĭnj-mən, ŏr′-) *n., pl.* **-men** (-mĭn). **1.** A member of a secret society founded in Northern Ireland in 1795 to maintain the political and religious ascendancy of Protestantism. **2.** An Irish Protestant, especially of Northern Ireland. [After William, Prince of *Orange,* later King William III of England.]

orange milkweed *n.* **Butterfly flyweed** *(see).*

orange pekoe *n.* A grade of black tea consisting of the end buds and their surrounding small leaves.

or·ange·ry (ôr′ĭnj-rē, ŏr′-) *n., pl.* **-ries.** A place, especially a glass-walled enclosure or greenhouse, used for growing oranges in cool climates. [French *orangerie,* from *orange,* from Old French, ORANGE.]

orange stick *n.* A stick of orangewood with tapering ends, used to manicure the fingernails and cuticles.

orange tip *n.* A European butterfly, *Anthocharis cardamines,* having whitish wings tipped with orange.

or·ange·wood (ôr′ĭnj-wo͝od′, ŏr′-) *n.* The fine-grained wood of the orange tree, used in fine woodwork.

o·rang·u·tan (ō-răng′ə-tăn′, -ə-tăng′, ə-răng′-) *n.* Also **o·rang·ou·tang** (-tăng′). An arboreal anthropoid ape, *Pongo pygmaeus,* of Borneo and Sumatra, having a shaggy reddish-brown coat, small ears, very long arms, and no tail. [Malay *orang hutan* : *ōrang,* man + *hūtan,* forest.]

o·rate (ô-rāt′, ō-rāt′, ôr′āt′, ōr′-) *intr.v.* **orated, orating, orates.** **1.** To speak publicly in a pompous, oratorical manner. **2.** To deliver an oration. [Back-formation from ORATION.]

o·ra·tion (ô-rā′shən, ō-rā′-) *n.* **1.** A formal address or speech, especially one given on some special occasion such as an academic celebration or funeral. **2.** A speech written out and memorized, as for a school or college debating contest. **3.** A high-flown speech. [Latin *ōrātiō* (stem *ōrātiōn-*), from *ōrāre,* to speak.]

or·a·tor (ôr′ə-tər, ŏr′-) *n.* **1.** A person who delivers an oration. **2.** A person skilled in the art of public speaking. [Middle English *oratour,* from Old French *orateur,* from Latin *ōrātor,* from *ōrāre,* to speak.] **—or·a·tor·ship** *n.*

or·a·tor·i·cal (ôr′ə-tôr′ĭ-kəl, ŏr′ə-tŏr′-) *adj.* Of or pertaining to an orator or to oratory. **—or·a·tor·i·cal·ly** *adv.*

or·a·to·ri·o (ôr′ə-tôr′ē-ō′, -tōr′ē-ō′, ŏr′-) *n., pl.* **-os.** A musical composition for solo voices, choir, and orchestra that usually tells a sacred story but has no costumes, scenery, or dramatic action. [Italian, from *Oratorio,* the Oratory of St. Philip Neri at Rome, where famous musical services were held in the 16th century, from Late Latin *ōrātōrium,* ORATORY (chapel).]

or·a·to·ry[1] (ôr′ə-tôr′ē, -tōr′ē, ŏr′-) *n.* **1.** The art of public speaking; rhetoric. **2.** Rhetorical style or skill. **3.** Public speaking, especially when conventional or bombastic. [Old French *(art) oratoire,* from Latin *(ars) ōrātōria,* (the art) of public speaking, from *ōrātōrius,* of an orator, oratorical, from *ōrātor,* ORATOR.]

oratory[2] *n., pl.* **-ries.** **1.** A place for prayer, especially a small private chapel. **2. Oratory. a.** A Roman Catholic religious society founded in 1575 by St. Philip Neri (1515–95) and consisting of secular priests. **b.** A branch or church of this society. [Middle English *oratorie,* from Old French *oratori,* from Late Latin *ōrātōrium (templum),* (place) of prayer, from *ōrātōrius,* of praying, from Latin *ōrāre,* to pray, speak.]

orb (ôrb) *n.* **1.** A sphere or spherical object. **2.** An area of endeavor, influence, or activity; sphere or province. **3. a.** A heavenly body. **b.** *Archaic.* The earth. **4.** Any of a series of concentric transparent spheres thought by ancient and medieval astronomers to revolve about the earth and support the stars and planets. **5.** A jeweled globe surmounted by a cross that is part of the regalia of a sovereign and that symbolizes monarchial power and justice. **6.** An eye. **7.** *Archaic.* A circle or an object of circular form. **8.** The orbit of a planet or satellite.
~*v.* **orbed, orbing, orbs.** —*tr.* **1.** To shape into a circle or sphere. **2.** *Archaic.* To encircle; enclose. —*intr. Archaic.* To move in an orbit. [Old French *orbe,* from Latin *orbis*†, orb, disk.]

or·bic·u·lar (ôr-bĭk′yə-lər) *adj.* Also **or·bic·u·late** (-lĭt, -lāt′), **or·bic·u·lat·ed** (-lā′tĭd) **1.** Circular or spherical. **2.** *Botany.* Circular and flat. Said especially of leaves. **3.** Rounded out; complete: *"The household ruin was thus full and orbicular"* (Thomas De Quincey). [Middle English *orbiculer,* from Old French *orbiculaire,* from Late Latin *orbiculāris,* from Latin *orbiculus,* diminutive of *orbis,* ORB.] **—or·bic·u·lar·i·ty** (ôr-bĭk′yə-lăr′ə-tē) *n.* **—or·bic·u·lar·ly** *adv.*

or·bit (ôr′bĭt) *n.* **1. a.** The path of a celestial body or man-made satellite as it revolves around another body. **b.** One complete revolution of such a body. **2.** The path of a body in a field of force surrounding another body; for example, the movement of an atomic electron in relation to a nucleus. **3. a.** A range of activity, experience, or knowledge: *their social orbit.* **b.** A range of control or influence: *in the Democratic political orbit.* **4.** Either of two bony cavities in the skull containing an eye and its external structures; an eye socket.
~*v.* **orbited, -biting, -bits.** —*tr.* **1.** To put into or cause to move in an orbit: *The first manmade satellite was orbited in 1957.* **2.** To revolve around (a center of attraction). —*intr.* To revolve or move in an orbit. [Latin *orbita,* from *orbitus,* circular, from *orbis,* ORB.]

or·bit·al (ôr′bĭ-təl) *adj.* Of or pertaining to an orbit.
~*n. Chemistry.* A region around the nucleus of an atom *(atomic orbital)* or surrounding nuclei in a molecule *(molecular orbital)* containing one electron or a pair of electrons and characterized by a fixed energy. **—or·bit·al·ly** *adv.*

orbital decay *n.* The effect of atmospheric drag on an orbiting body, such as an earth-orbiting satellite, causing eventual re-entry.

orbital velocity *n.* The minimum velocity required to maintain a satellite in orbit around a celestial body.

orc (ôrk) *n.* **1.** Any of several whales; especially, the **killer whale** *(see).* **2.** Any of various mythical or fictional monsters. [Old French *orque,* from Latin *orca,* whale, probably from Greek *oruga,* accusative of *orux,* a pickax, hence (from its horn), narwhal, from *orussein,* to dig.]

Or·ca·di·an (ôr-kā′dē-ən) *n.* A native or inhabitant of the Orkney Islands. [Latin *Orcades,* Orkney Islands.] **—Or·ca·di·an** *adj.*

or·ce·in (ôr′sē-ĭn) *n.* A reddish dye made by oxidizing orcinol with hydrogen peroxide in the presence of ammonia and used as a biological stain and a mild antiseptic.

or·chard (ôr′chərd) *n.* **1.** An area of land devoted to the cultivation of fruit or nut trees. **2.** The trees cultivated in such an area. [Middle English *orchard,* Old English *ortceard, ortgeard* : Latin *hortus,* a garden + Old English *geard,* YARD.]

or·ches·tra (ôr′kĭ-strə, -kĕs′trə) *n. Abbr.* **orch.** **1. a.** A large group of musicians who play together on various musical instruments, usually including strings, woodwinds, brass instruments, and percussion instruments. **b.** The instruments played by such a group of musicians. **c.** A group of musicians all playing a specified instrument: *a gamelan orchestra.* **2.** An orchestra pit. **3. a.** The front section of seats nearest the stage in a theater. **b.** The entire main floor of a theater. Also called "parquet." **4.** In ancient Greek theaters, a semicircular space in front of the stage on which the chorus danced. [Latin *orchēstra,* from Greek *orkhēstra,* from *orkheisthai,* to dance.] **—or·ches·tral** (ôr-kĕs′trəl) *adj.* **—or·ches·tral·ly** *adv.*

orchestra pit *n.* In theaters and concert halls, the area where the musicians sit, immediately in front of and below the stage. Also called "orchestra," "pit."

or·ches·trate (ôr′kĭ-strāt′) *tr.v.* **-trated, -trating, -trates.** **1. a.** To compose or arrange (music) for performance by an orchestra. **b.** To provide a musical arrangement for. **2.** To arrange, put together, or organize so as to achieve a desired overall effect. [French *orchestrer,* from *orchestre,* orchestra, from Latin *orchēstra,* ORCHESTRA.] **—or·ches·tra·tor** *n.*

or·ches·tra·tion (ôr′kĭ-strā′shən) *n. Abbr.* **orch.** **1.** A musical com-

orchestra

MAKE-UP OF THE MODERN SYMPHONY ORCHESTRA
Striking a balance through the skill of the conductor

The typical modern symphony orchestra, with 90 to 120 players, has gradually evolved since the late 18th century. Before that, the composition of an orchestra was dependent on the instruments that were available and their technical limitations. Handel composed his *Water Music* in 1717 for two oboes, two horns, a bassoon, strings, and a harpsichord. Beethoven had to use trumpets with fixed pitch (as valves had not then been invented) and included trombones only in his later symphonies. During the 19th century, the orchestra settled into its familiar modern shape with balanced groups of instruments.

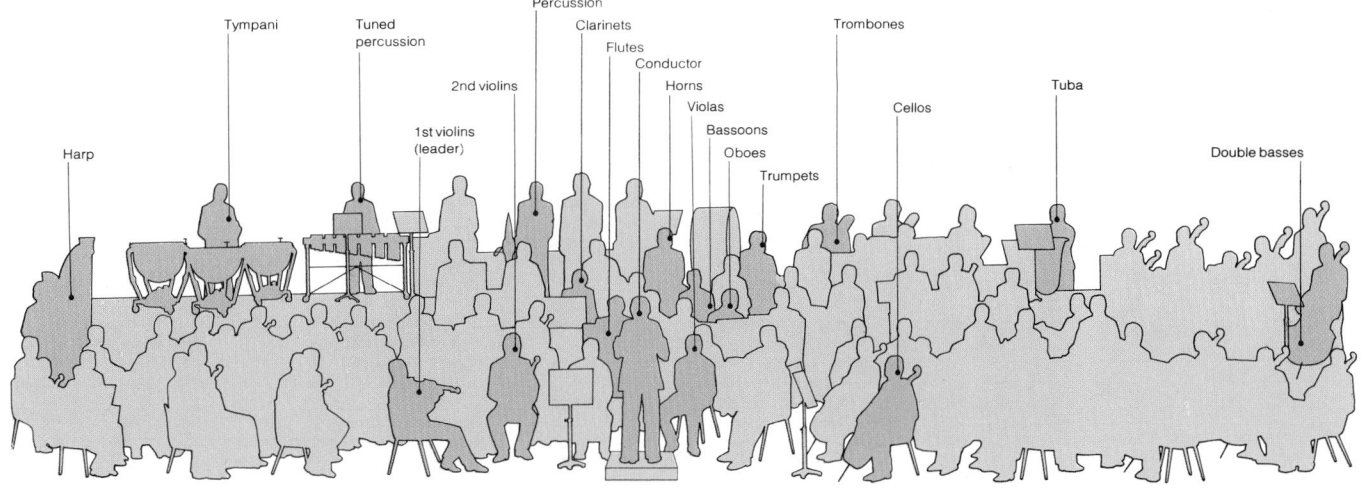

THE FOUR FAMILIES OF INSTRUMENT IN THE MODERN SYMPHONY ORCHESTRA

The woodwind section usually has two flutes, two oboes, two clarinets, two bassoons, and sometimes a piccolo. The percussion may include tympani, a xylophone, a glockenspiel, a marimba, chimes and gongs, drums, cymbals, tambourines, triangles, castanets, rattles, shakers, and clickers. The strings will have two groups of violins with the same number, usually 15, in each group. The other strings will be up to 12 violas, 10 cellos, and 8 double basses. The brass includes three trumpets, four French horns, and three trombones, and may include a bass tuba.

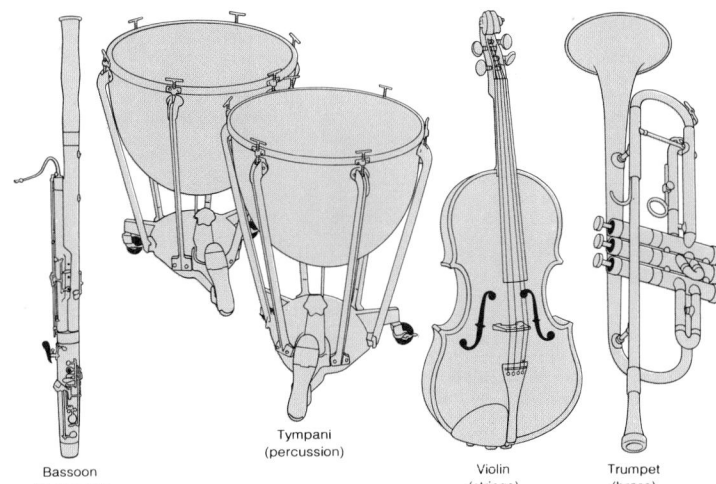

Bassoon (woodwind)

Tympani (percussion)

Violin (strings)

Trumpet (brass)

WHERE THE PLAYERS SIT *The conductor stands on a central rostrum, with the four groups of instruments—woodwind, percussion, brass, and strings—arranged in front of him.*

The principal first violinist—the "leader" of the orchestra—sits on the conductor's left. The other string players sit in groups to the left and right. The woodwind players sit in the center, with the percussion at the back on the left and the brass at the back on the right.

Extra instruments such as the piano or the harp, shown on the left of the picture, are added when needed for a particular musical work. (The figures in darker shading indicate the principal players of each instrument.)

Before the performance begins, one instrument, usually the oboe, plays a sustained "A" note to which all the other instruments are tuned. The conductor sets the tempo and indicates the beat with his baton. He cues in the players and controls the loudness or softness of the playing. He conducts the music from a full score that shows him what each individual instrument should play. He is the one responsible for the overall interpretation of the music.

---

position that has been orchestrated. **2.** Arrangement of music for performance by an orchestra.

or·ches·tri·on (ôr-kĕs′trē-ən) *n.* Also **or·ches·tri·na** (ôr′kĭ-strē′nə). A large mechanical musical instrument resembling a barrel organ and producing sound in imitation of an orchestra. [*Orchestra* + melod*ion*.]

or·chid (ôr′kĭd) *n.* **1. a.** Any of numerous epiphytic or terrestrial plants of the family Orchidaceae, found worldwide, though chiefly in the tropics, and often having brightly colored flowers of unusual shapes. **b.** The flower of any of these plants, especially one cultivated for ornament or personal adornment. **2.** A pale to light purple. [Latin *orchis* (stem *orchid-*), from Greek *orkhis*, testicle, hence (from the shape of its root) orchid.] —**or·chid** *adj.*

or·chi·da·ceous (ôr′kĭ-dā′shəs) *adj.* **1.** Of, pertaining to, or characteristic of the orchid family of plants. **2.** Suggesting ostentatious luxury; showy. [New Latin *Orchidaceae* (family); *orchis*, ORCHID + -ACEOUS.]

or·chi·dec·to·my (ôr′kĭ-dĕk′tə-mē) *n., pl.* **-mies.** Surgical removal of a testicle. [Greek *orkhis* (stem *orkhid-*), testicle + -ECTOMY.]

or·chil (ôr′kĭl, -chĭl) *n.* Also **ar·chil** (är′-). **1.** Any of several lichens from which a dye is obtained. **2.** The violet-colored dyestuff obtained from these lichens. Also called "cudbear." [Middle English, from Old French *orcheil*, perhaps ultimately from Latin *herba urceolāris*, plant used to polish pitchers, from *urceolus*, diminutive of *urceus*, pitcher.]

or·chis (ôr′kĭs) *n.* Any of various orchids of the genus *Orchis*, hav-ing magenta, white, or magenta-spotted flowers. See **fringed orchis.** [New Latin *Orchis*, from Latin, ORCHID.]

or·chi·tis (ôr-kī′tĭs) *n.* Inflammation of a testicle. [New Latin, from Greek *orkhis*, testicle + -ITIS.]

or·ci·nol (ôr′sə-nôl′, -nōl′) *n.* A white crystalline compound present in orchil and used as a source of the dye orcein.

OR circuit *n.* A computer logic gate, an **OR gate** (*see*).

Or·cus (ôr′kəs). *Roman Mythology.* **1.** The world of the dead; Hades. **2.** The underworld god Pluto. [Latin *Orcus†.*]

ord. 1. order. **2.** ordinal. **3.** ordinance. **4.** ordnance.

or·dain (ôr-dān′) *tr.v.* **-dained, -daining, -dains. 1. a.** To invest with ministerial or priestly authority; confer holy orders upon. **b.** To authorize as a rabbi. **2. a.** To order by virtue of superior authority. **b.** To decree as part of the order of nature or of the universe. **3.** To prearrange unalterably; predestine: *by fate ordained.* [Middle English *ordeinen*, from Norman French *ordeiner*, from Late Latin *ōrdināre*, from Latin, to arrange in order, from *ōrdō* (stem *ōrdin-*), order.] —**or·dain·er** *n.* —**or·dain·ment** *n.*

or·deal (ôr-dēl′, ôr′dēl′) *n.* **1. a.** A severely difficult or painful experience that tests character or endurance. **b.** A trying experience: *Going to the dentist can be a real ordeal.* **2.** A former method of legal trial in which the accused was subjected to physically painful or dangerous tests by way of determining guilt or innocence, the result being regarded as a divine judgment. [Middle English *ordal*, Old English *ordāl, ordēl*, from Germanic *uzdailjam* (unattested), "a dealing out," judgment, trial : *uz-* (unattested), out + *dailjan* (unattested), to DEAL.]

ordeal bark *n.* The poisonous bark of an African tree, *Erythrophloeum guineense.* [From its use in trials by ordeal.]

ordeal bean *n.* The **Calabar bean** *(see).*

or·der (ôr′dər) *n. Abbr.* **O, O., ord. 1.** A condition of logical or comprehensible arrangement among the separate elements of a group. **2. a.** A condition of methodical or prescribed arrangement among component parts such that proper functioning or appearance is achieved. **b.** The state, condition, or disposition of a thing: *in good order.* **3. a.** The structures of a given society and the relations defined among the individuals and classes constituting it: *"Every revolution exaggerates the evils of the old order"* (C. Wright Mills). **b.** The condition in which these structures and relations are maintained and preserved by the rule of law and the police power of the state: *Order was restored after the riot.* **c.** Discipline and good behavior in a group. **4.** A sequence or arrangement of successive things in time or space. **5.** The established sequence; the customary procedure: *the order of operations.* **6.** An authoritative indication to be obeyed; command or direction. **7.** *Military.* **a.** A command given by a superior officer requiring execution of a task or other obedience. **b. orders.** Formal written instructions to report for duty at a stated time and place: *He received his orders to fly to Japan.* **8. a.** A commission or instruction to buy, sell, or supply something. **b.** That which is supplied, bought, or sold. **9. a.** A request for a portion of food by a customer at a restaurant. **b.** The food requested. **10.** *Law.* A direction or command delivered by a court and entered into the court record but not included in the final judgment or verdict. **11. a.** Any of several grades of the Christian ministry: *the order of priesthood.* **b. orders.** The office and rank of an ordained minister or priest. **c. orders. Holy orders** *(see).* **12.** A prescribed form of religious service for various occasions. **13.** Any of the nine grades or choirs of angels. See **angel. 14.** An organization of people united by a common fraternal bond or social aim, especially: **a.** Any of various communities dedicated to a religious life, as through missionary work or monastic contemplation, and often bound by vows of poverty, chastity, and obedience: *the Order of St. Benedict.* **b.** An organization of knights similarly united: *the Order of the Knights of St. John of Jerusalem.* **15. a.** A group of persons upon whom a government or sovereign has formally conferred honor for unusual service or merit, entitling such persons to wear a special insignia: *the Order of Merit.* **b.** The insignia worn by such persons. **16.** *Often* **orders.** A social class: *the lower orders.* **17.** Degree of quality or importance; rank: *poetry of a high order.* **18.** *Architecture.* **a.** Any of several specific styles of classical architecture characterized by the type of column employed, as **Composite order, Corinthian order, Doric order, Ionic order, Tuscan order** *(all of which see).* **b.** A specific style of architecture: *a cathedral of the Gothic order.* **19.** *Biology.* A taxonomic category of plants and animals ranking above the family and below the class. See **taxonomy. 20.** *Mathematics.* **a.** An indicated number of successive differentiations that are to be performed on a function or that have been performed on a derivative. **b.** The number of elements in a finite group. **c.** The number of rows or columns in a determinant or square matrix. Compare **degree. 21.** A class that is defined by the common attribute or attributes possessed by all its members; kind. **—call to order. 1.** To request to be quiet and attentive. **2.** To begin (a meeting). **—in order.** Called for; appropriate: *I think a vacation is in order.* **—in order that.** So that: *We warned them of the danger in order that they might take precautions.* **—in order to.** For the purpose of; so that. **—in short order.** With no delay; quickly: *finished our dinner in short order.* **—keep order.** To ensure the continuation of order or discipline. **—on order.** Requested but not yet delivered. **—on the order of. 1.** In a fashion similar to; like: *a car on the order of the latest European sports models.* **2.** Approximately; about: *equipment costing on the order of a million dollars.* **—to order.** According to the buyer's specifications.
~*v.* **ordered, -dering, -ders.** —*tr.* **1.** To issue a command or instruction to. **2.** To give a command or instruction that (something be done): *The judge ordered a retrial.* **3.** To give an order for; request to be supplied with. **4.** To instruct or force to move to or from a specified locality: *She ordered me out of the house.* **5.** To put in a methodical and systematic arrangement. **6.** To prearrange unalterably; predestine. —*intr.* To give an order or orders; request that something be done or supplied: *Order now, before prices go up.* —See Synonyms at **command. —order around** (or **about**). To treat in a domineering way; bully. **—order up.** To summon (personnel) for active military duty: *ordered up the reservists.* [Middle English *ordre,* from Old French *ordre,* earlier *ord(e)ne,* from Latin *ōrdō.*] **—or·der·er** *n.*

or·der·ly (ôr′dər-lē) *adj.* **1.** Having a methodical and systematic arrangement; tidy: *an orderly room.* **2.** Without violence or disruption; peaceful: *an orderly transition of governments.* **3.** *Military.* Of or pertaining to the transmission of military orders.
~*n., pl.* **orderlies. 1.** An attendant who does unskilled work in a hospital. **2.** *Military.* A soldier assigned to attend a superior officer and carry orders or messages.
~*adv.* Systematically; regularly. **—or·der·li·ness** *n.*
Synonyms: *methodical, systematic.*

orderly room *n.* The office used for the administration of business in the barracks of a military unit.

order of business *n.* Something, such as a task, that must be addressed.

order of magnitude *n. Physics.* **1.** An estimate of size or magnitude expressed as a power of ten: *The earth's mass is of the order of magnitude of 10^{22} tons, that of the sun 10^{27} tons.* **2.** A range of values between a specified lower value and an upper value ten times as large: *The masses of the earth and the sun differ by five orders of magnitude.*

order of the day *n., pl.* **orders of the day. 1.** The set of commands or instructions issued by a commanding officer to his men. **2.** The list of business to be discussed by a legislative body on a given day. **3.** The prevailing trend or state of affairs. **4.** The most significant aspect or event: *Completing his income tax was the order of the day.*

order paper *n. British.* A list giving the order in which questions are to be raised by a legislative body, as the House of Commons.

or·di·nal (ôrd′n-əl) *adj. Abbr.* **ord. 1.** Having a specified position in a numbered series: *an ordinal rank of seventh.* **2.** Pertaining to a biological order.
~*n. Abbr.* **ord. 1.** An ordinal number. **2.** In the Christian Church: **a.** A book of instructions for daily services. **b.** A book of forms for ordination. [Late Latin *ōrdinālis,* from Latin *ōrdō* (stem *ōrdin-*), ORDER.]

ordinal number *n.* A number indicating position in a series or order. The ordinal numbers are first (1st), second (2nd), third (3rd), and so on. Compare **cardinal number.**

or·di·nance (ôrd′n-əns) *n. Abbr.* **ord. 1.** An authoritative command or order. **2.** A custom or practice established by long usage. **3.** A religious rite; especially, Holy Communion. **4.** A statute or regulation, especially one enacted by a city government. [Middle English *ordinaunce,* from Old French *ordenance,* "the art of arranging," from Medieval Latin *ōrdinantia,* from Latin *ōrdināns,* present participle of *ōrdināre,* to put in order, from *ōrdō* (stem *ōrdin-*), ORDER.]

or·di·nand (ôrd′n-ănd′) *n.* A prospective priest or minister; one about to be ordained. [Latin *ordinandus,* gerundive of *ordināre,* to ORDAIN.]

or·di·nar·i·ly (ôrd′n-âr′ə-lē, ôrd′n-ĕr′-) *adv.* **1.** As a general rule. **2.** In the regular or usual manner: *ordinarily dressed.* **3.** To the usual extent or degree: *ordinarily large profits.*

or·di·nar·y (ôrd′n-ĕr′ē) *adj.* **1.** Commonly encountered; usual: *"a man to be sought for on great emergencies, but ill adapted for ordinary services"* (Anthony Trollope). **2.** Occurring regularly or periodically; normal. **3. a.** Of no exceptional ability, degree, or quality; average or commonplace: *The ordinary person has difficulty reading insurance policies.* **b.** Of inferior quality; second-rate: *a very ordinary cup of coffee.* **4.** Having immediate rather than delegated jurisdiction, as a judge might. **5.** *Mathematics.* Designating a differential equation containing no more than two variables and derivatives of one with respect to the other. —See Synonyms at **common.**
~*n., pl.* **ordinaries. 1.** A person, object, or situation that is common, normal, or average. **2.** *Law.* A judge or other official with immediate rather than delegated jurisdiction. **3.** In some states of the United States, the judge of a probate court. **4.** *Usually* **Ordinary.** In the Christian Church: **a.** The part of the Mass that remains unchanged from day to day. Compare **proper. b.** A division of the Divine Office containing the unchangeable parts of the office other than the Psalms. **c.** A cleric, such as the residential bishop of a diocese, with ordinary jurisdiction. **5.** *Heraldry.* Any of the simplest and commonest charges, such as the bend or the cross. **6.** *British.* A priest or minister formerly assigned to visit condemned prisoners in jail. **—in ordinary.** *British.* Officially employed, especially by the monarchy; having regular rather than temporary or delegated responsibilities: *chaplain in ordinary to the sovereign.* **—out of the ordinary.** Extraordinary or exceptional; unusual: *Nothing out of the ordinary is likely to happen.* [Middle English *ordinarie,* from Latin *ōrdinārius,* from *ōrdō* (stem *ōrdin-*), ORDER.] **—or·di·nar·i·ness** *n.*

ordinary ray *n. Physics.* The ray of light in double refraction that obeys the ordinary laws of refraction. Compare **extraordinary ray.**

ordinary seaman *n. Abbr.* **O.S.** A seaman of the lowest grade in the merchant marine.

or·di·nate (ôrd′n-ĭt, -āt′) *adj.* Arranged in regular rows, as spots are on an insect's wings.
~*n. Symbol* **y** *Mathematics.* The plane Cartesian coordinate representing the distance from a given point to the *x*-axis, measured parallel to the *y*-axis. Compare **abscissa.** [Latin *ōrdināre,* to arrange in order, from *ōrdō* (stem *ōrdin-*), ORDER.]

or·di·na·tion (ôrd′n-ā′shən) *n.* **1.** The act of ordaining or state of being ordained. **2.** In the Christian Church: **a.** The ceremony during which a person is admitted to the ministry of a church. **b.** The admission itself. **3.** An arrangement or ordering.

ord·nance (ôrd′nəns) *n. Abbr.* **ord., ordn. 1. a.** Military weapons collectively, together with ammunition and the equipment to keep them in good repair. **b.** The branch of a military force that designs, develops, procures, stores, maintains, and issues weapons. **2.** Heavy guns; artillery. [Middle English *ordinaunce,* ORDINANCE.]

or·do (ôr′dō) *n., pl.* **-dines** (-də-nēz′). *Roman Catholic Church.* An annual calendar containing instructions for the Mass and office to be celebrated on each day of the year. [Medieval Latin *ōrdō,* from Latin, ORDER.]

or·don·nance (ôr′də-näNs′) *n.* **1.** The arrangement of elements in a literary or artistic composition or architectural plan. **2.** In French history: **a.** A royal decree or body of laws on a specific subject. **b.** An order of a criminal court. [French, variant (influenced by *ordonner,* to order) of Old French *ordenance,* ORDINANCE.]

Or·do·vi·cian (ôr′də-vĭsh′ən) *adj. Geology.* Of, pertaining to, formed

PRONUNCIATION KEY

ă, pat; ā, pay; âr, care;
ä, father, are; b, bib;
ch, church; d, deed; ĕ, pet;
ē, be; f, fife; g, gag; h, hat;
hw, which; ĭ, pit; ī, pie;
îr, pier; j, judge; k, kick;
l, lid, needle; m, mum;
n, no, sudden; ng, thing;
ŏ, pot; ō, toe; ô, paw, for;
oi, noise; ou, out; o͝o, book;
o͞o, boot; p, pop; r, roar;
s, sauce; sh, ship, dish;
t, tight; th, thin, path;
th, this, bathe; ŭ, cut; ûr, fur;
v, valve; w, with; y, yes;
z, zebra, size; zh, vision;
ə, about, item, edible,
gallop, circus, peaceful

IN FOREIGN WORDS:

à, *Fr.* ami; œ, *Fr.* feu, *Ger.* schön; ü, *Fr.* tu, *Ger.* über; KH, *Ger.* ich, *Scot.* loch; N, *Fr.* bon; y′, *Fr.* Compiègne

STRESS MARKS:

Primary stress: ′
in·cite′ (ĭn-sīt′)
Secondary stress: ′
in′sight′ (ĭn′sīt′)

in, or designating the second period of the Paleozoic era, characterized by the appearance of primitive types of fish.
~*n. Geology.* The Ordovician period. [After the *Ordovices,* an ancient Celtic tribe of North Wales, by analogy with SILURIAN.]
or·dure (ôr′jər) *n.* **1.** Excrement; dung. **2.** Something considered to be morally offensive. [Middle English, from Old French, from *ord,* dirty, "disgusting," from Latin *horridus,* horrid, from *horrēre,* to shudder.]
ore (ôr, ōr) *n.* A mineral or aggregate of minerals from which a valuable constituent, especially a metal, can be profitably mined or extracted. [Middle English *oor, or,* Old English *ār,* brass (in sense influenced by Old English *ora†,* unwrought metal, ore).]
ö·re (œ′rə) *n., pl.* **öre.** A coin equal to 1/100 of the krona of Sweden and the krone of Denmark and Norway. See feature at **currency.** [Danish and Norwegian *øre* and Swedish *öre,* from Latin *aureus,* gold coin, from *aurum,* gold.]
Ore. Oregon.
o·re·ad (ôr′ē-ăd′, ōr′-) *n. Greek Mythology.* A mountain nymph. [Greek *Oreias* (stem *Oreiad-*), from *oreios,* of a mountain, from *oros,* mountain. See **oro-.**]
o·rec·tic (ō-rĕk′tĭk, ə-rĕk′-) *adj.* Of or pertaining to the appetites or desires. [Greek *orektikos,* from *oregein,* to desire.]
o·reg·a·no (ə-rĕg′ə-nō′) *n.* An herb seasoning made from the dried leaves of a species of marjoram, *Origanum vulgare.* [Spanish, marjoram, from Latin *origanum,* Greek *origanon,* oregano, marjoram (probably from a North African language).]
Or·e·gon (ôr′ə-gən, -gŏn′, ŏr′-). *Abbr.* **Ore.** State of the northwest United States containing many areas of great natural beauty. The state is dominated by the Cascade Range, a rugged mountain chain running north to south some 160 kilometers (100 miles) inland. The region was jointly held by Britain and the United States (1818–46) and the Oregon Territory was then created (1848). It was admitted to the Union in 1859. Its capital is Salem.
Oregon fir *n.* The **Douglas fir** *(see).*
Oregon grape *n.* **1.** An evergreen shrub, *Mahonia aquifolium,* of northwestern North America, having fragrant yellow flowers and small, edible, bluish berries. **2.** The berry of this shrub.
Oregon myrtle *n.* A tree, the **California laurel** *(see).*
Oregon Trail. The main overland route to the Oregon country in the 1840's. It stretched over 3,200 kilometers (2,000 miles) from Independence, Missouri, to Astoria, at the mouth of the Columbia River. The first train of emigrants reached Oregon in 1842. Travel along the trail declined with the coming of the railroad, and it was abandoned in the 1870's.
oreide. Variant of **oroide.**
O·res·tes (ə-rĕs′tēz, ô-rĕs′-). *Greek Mythology.* The son of Agamemnon and Clytemnestra, who, with his sister Electra, avenged his murdered father by slaying his mother and her lover Aegisthus.
Ö·re·sund (œ′rə-sŭn′). Strait in northern Europe, between Sweden and the Danish island of Sjaelland. Connecting the Kattegat with the Baltic Sea, it is an important shipping route.
orfe (ôrf) *n.* A European freshwater fish, *Idus idus,* with a blue-gray back and a silvery belly. A reddish-gold variety, the golden orfe, is often kept in garden ponds and aquariums. [German and French; akin to Latin *orphus,* Greek *orphos,* sea perch.]
Orff (ôrf), **Carl** (1895–1982). German composer. The inventor of a system of percussion instruments, he is best known for *Carmina Burana* (1936), a lively setting of medieval poems.
orfray. Variant of **orphrey.**
org. 1. organic. **2.** organization; organized.
or·gan (ôr′gən) *n.* **1.** A musical instrument consisting of a keyboard and a number of pipes supplied with wind by means of bellows. Also called "pipe organ." **2.** Any of various instruments, such as the electronic organ, resembling the organ either in mechanism or in sound. **3.** *Biology.* A differentiated part of an organism adapted for a specific function. **4.** The penis. Used euphemistically. **5.** An organization that performs certain specified functions: *The FBI is an organ of the Department of Justice.* **6.** An instrument or vehicle of communication; especially, a periodical publication issued by a political party, business firm, or other group. [Middle English, from Old French *organe,* from Late Latin *organum,* church organ, from Latin, implement, instrument, from Greek *organon.*]
or·ga·na. 1. Alternate plural of **organon. 2.** Alternate plural of **organum.**
or·gan·dy, or·gan·die (ôr′gən-dē) *n., pl.* **-dies.** A transparent crisp fabric of cotton or silk, used for trimming, curtains, and light clothing. [French *organdi†.*] **—or·gan·dy** *adj.*
or·gan·elle (ôr′gə-nĕl′) *n. Biology.* A structure within a cell that is specialized for a particular function, as the nucleus and the mitochondria. [New Latin *organella,* diminutive of Latin *organum,* ORGAN.]
organ grinder *n.* A street musician who plays a hurdy-gurdy.
or·gan·ic (ôr-găn′ĭk) *adj. Abbr.* **org. 1.** Of, pertaining to, or affecting an organ of the body. **2.** Of, pertaining to, or derived from living organisms: *organic waste.* **3. a.** Using or grown with fertilizers and mulches consisting only of animal or vegetable matter, with no use of chemical fertilizers or pesticides: *organic gardening.* **b.** Free from chemical injections or additives: *organic foods.* **c.** Simple, basic, and close to nature: *an organic lifestyle.* **4.** Having properties associated with living organisms. **5.** Likened to an organism in organization or development; interconnected: *society as an organic whole.* **6. a.** Of or constituting an integral part of something; fundamental; structural. **b.** *Law.* Designating or pertaining to the fundamental or constitutional laws and precepts of a government or organization. **7.** *Chemistry.* Of or designating carbon compounds. Compare **inorganic.** [Old French *organique,* from Late Latin *organicus,* from Greek *organikos,* serving as an instrument, from *organon,* implement, ORGAN.] **—or·gan·i·cal·ly** *adv.*
organic chemistry *n.* The chemistry of carbon compounds. Compare **inorganic chemistry.**
organic disease *n.* A disease associated with changes in the structure of an organ or tissue. Compare **functional disease.**
or·gan·i·cism (ôr-găn′ĭ-sĭz′əm) *n.* **1.** The theory that the total organization of an organism, rather than the functioning of individual organs, is the principal or exclusive determinant of every life process; holism. **2.** The concept or doctrine that society is analogous to a biological organism, especially in its structure. **—or·gan·i·cist** *n. & adj.*
or·gan·ism (ôr′gə-nĭz′əm) *n.* **1.** A living individual; a plant or animal. **2.** A system regarded as analogous to a living body: *the social organism.* **—or·gan·is·mal** (ôr′gə-nĭz′məl), **or·gan·is·mic** (ôr′gə-nĭz′mĭk) *adj.*
or·gan·ist (ôr′gə-nĭst) *n.* One who plays the organ.
or·gan·i·za·tion (ôr′gə-nə-zā′shən) *n. Abbr.* **org. 1.** The act of organizing or the process of being organized. **2.** The state or manner of being organized: *a high degree of organization.* **3.** Something that has been organized or made into an ordered whole. **4.** Something comprising elements with varied functions that contribute to the whole and to collective functions; an organism. **5.** A number of persons or groups having specific responsibilities and united for a particular purpose or work. **6.** A corporate entity such as a business, charity, or international agency. **—or·gan·i·za·tion·al** *adj.* **—or·gan·i·za·tion·al·ly** *adv.*
Organization of African Unity *n. Abbr.* **O.A.U.** An association formed (1963) by most independent African states to promote mutual help and cooperation.
Organization of American States *n. Abbr.* **OAS** An association formed (1948) by the 21 American republics to promote mutual help and cooperation.
Organization of Petroleum Exporting States *n.* An association formed (1960) to advance its members' trade and development aims. The associated countries include Iran, Iraq, Kuwait, Saudi Arabia, and Venezuela (the founding members) and Algeria, Ecuador, Gabon, Indonesia, Libya, Nigeria, Qatar, and the United Arab Emirates. Also known as "OPEC."
or·gan·ize (ôr′gə-nīz′) *v.* **-ized, -izing, -izes.** *—tr.* **1.** To pull or put together into an orderly. functional, structured whole. **2. a.** To arrange in a coherent form; systematize: *organize one's thoughts before speaking.* **b.** To arrange or compose in a desired pattern or structure. **3.** To arrange systematically for harmonious or united action: *organize a strike.* **4.** To establish as an organization: *organize a club.* **5. a.** To cause (employees) to form or join a labor union. **b.** To induce the employees of (a business or industry) to form or join a union: *organize a factory.* *—intr.* **1.** To develop into or assume an organic structure. **2.** To join or form an activist group, especially a labor union. [Middle English *organysen,* from Old French *organiser,* from Medieval Latin *organizāre,* from Latin *organum,* instrument, ORGAN.]
or·gan·ized (ôr′gə-nīzd′) *adj. Abbr.* **org. 1.** Efficient and methodical. **2.** Of, pertaining to, or being an activity planned in the manner of a commercial business: *organized crime.*
or·gan·iz·er (ôr′gə-nī′zər) *n.* **1.** One who organizes or is skilled at organizing. **2.** A group of embryonic cells that releases a substance that stimulates differentiation in other embryonic cells.
organo– *prefix.* **1.** Indicates organ or organic; for example, **organology. 2.** Indicates carbon compounds; for example, **organometallic.** [Middle English, from Medieval Latin *organum,* organ of the body, from Latin, implement, ORGAN.]
organ of Cor·ti (kôr′tē) *n.* A sense organ situated on the inner surface of the cochlea in the inner ear that converts sound vibrations into nerve impulses that are then transmitted to the brain. [After Alfonso *Corti* (1822–88), Italian anatomist.]
or·gan·o·gen·e·sis (ôr′gə-nō-jĕn′ə-sĭs, ôr-găn′ə-) *n., pl.* **-ses** (-sēz′). The origin and development of biological organs. [New Latin : ORGANO- + -GENESIS.] **—or·gan·o·ge·net·ic** (ôr′gə-nō-jə-nĕt′ĭk, ôr-găn′ə-) *adj.* **—or·gan·o·ge·net·i·cal·ly** *adv.*
or·gan·og·ra·phy (ôr′gə-nŏg′rə-fē) *n.* The scientific description of the organs of animals and plants.
or·gan·o·lep·tic (ôr′gə-nō-lĕp′tĭk, ôr-găn′ə-) *adj.* Pertaining to, affecting, involving, or perceived by a sensory organ. [French *organoleptique* : ORGANO- + Greek *lēptikos,* receptive, from *lēptos,* to be apprehended (by the senses), from *lambanein,* to take, seize, apprehend.] **—or·gan·o·lep·ti·cal·ly** *adv.*
or·gan·ol·o·gy (ôr′gə-nŏl′ə-jē) *n.* The study of plant and animal organs and their functions. [ORGANO- + -LOGY.] **—or·gan·o·log·i·cal** (ôr′gə-nə-lŏj′ĭ-kəl) *adj.*
or·gan·o·me·tal·lic (ôr′gə-nō-mə-tăl′ĭk, ôr-găn′ō-) *adj.* Of, pertaining to, or designating an organic chemical compound that also contains metal atoms.
~*n.* An organometallic chemical compound.
or·ga·non (ôr′gə-nŏn′) *n., pl.* **-na** (-nə) or **-nons.** Also **or·ga·num** (-nəm) *pl.* **-na** (-nə) or **-nums.** *Philosophy.* A set of logical requirements used in scientific investigation or demonstration. [Greek, tool (used as the title of Aristotle's writings on logic).]
or·gan·o·ther·a·py (ôr′gə-nō-thĕr′ə-pē, ôr-găn′ō-) *n.* The treatment of disease with animal organs or extracts such as insulin and thy-

organ *The earliest organ of which there is any record was built in the third century* B.C. *A cathedral organ like this one at Ely Cathedral in Cambridgeshire, England, may have as many as 100 pipes for each note.*

oriel *An oriel window in a Tudor façade at St. Osyth's Priory in Essex, England. Oriels were usually built over gateways and arches.*

roxin. **—or·gan·o·ther·a·peu·tic** (ôr′gə-nō-thĕr′ə-pyo͞o′tĭk, ôr-găn′-ō-) *adj.*

or·gan·ot·ro·pism (ôr′gə-nŏt′rə-pĭz′əm) *n.* Also **or·gan·ot·ro·py** (-pē). *Medicine.* The attraction of certain chemical compounds or microorganisms to specific tissues or organs of the body. [ORGANO- + -TROPISM.] **—or·gan·o·trop·ic** (ôr′gə-nō-trŏp′ĭk, ôr-găn′ō-) *adj.* **—or·gan·o·trop·i·cal·ly** *adv.*

or·gan-pipe cactus (ôr′gən-pīp′) *n.* A tall, branching cactus, *Pachycereus marginatus,* of Mexico and the southwestern United States.

or·ga·num[1] (ôr′gə-nəm) *n., pl.* **-na** (-nə) or **-nums.** Any of several types of vocal polyphonic music, in two, three, or four parts, of the 9th to the early 13th century. [Medieval Latin, from Late Latin, ORGAN.]

organum[2]. Variant of **organon.**

or·gan·za (ôr-găn′zə) *n.* A sheer, stiff silk or synthetic fabric used for evening dresses or trimming. [Origin unknown.]

or·gan·zine (ôr′gən-zēn′) *n.* **1.** A thread of raw silk, usually used as a warp thread. **2.** A fabric made of this thread. [French *organsin,* from Italian *organzino*†.]

or·gasm (ôr′găz′əm) *n.* **1.** The climax of sexual excitement, marked by ejaculation of semen in the male and by the release of tumescence in erectile organs of both sexes. **2.** An onrush of intense excitement. [French *orgasme,* from Greek *orgasmos,* from *organ,* to swell (with lust), be excited.] **—or·gas·mic** (ôr-găz′mĭk), **or·gas·tic** (ôr-găs′tĭk) *adj.*

OR gate (ôr) *n. Computer Science.* A computer logic gate that has one output and two or more inputs and gives an output signal for any input signal or combination of input signals. Also called "OR circuit." [From its similarity to the function of the conjunction *or* in logic.]

or·geat (ôr′zhä′) *n.* **1.** A sweet flavoring of orange and almond used in cocktails and food. **2.** A drink containing this flavoring. [French, from Old French, from Old Provençal *orjat,* from *orge,* barley, from Latin *hordeum.*]

or·gi·as·tic (ôr′jē-ăs′tĭk) *adj.* Of, pertaining to, or characteristic of an orgy. [Greek *orgiastikos,* from *orgiazein,* to hold secret rites, from *orgia,* secret rites, ORGY.]

or·gy (ôr′jē) *n., pl.* **-gies.** **1.** A revel involving unrestrained indulgence, especially sexual excesses. **2.** Something like an orgy in lack of restraint; especially, excessive indulgence: *an orgy of reading.* **3.** A secret rite in the cults of ancient Greek or Roman deities, as Demeter or Dionysus, typically involving frenzied singing, dancing, drinking, and sexual activity. [Originally in the plural *orgies,* from Old French, from Latin *orgia,* from Greek.]

or·i·bi (ôr′ə-bē, ŏr′-) *n., pl.* **-bis** or collectively **oribi.** Any of several small, brownish African antelopes of the genus *Ourebia,* especially *O. ourebia,* the male of which has straight, ridged horns. [Afrikaans, said to be from a Hottentot word meaning "antelope."]

o·ri·el (ôr′ē-əl, ōr′-) *n.* A projecting bay window, usually in an upper story, supported from below with corbels or brackets. Also called "oriel window." [Middle English *oriole, oriel,* from Old French *oriol,* from Medieval Latin *oriolum*†, upper chamber.]

o·ri·ent (ôr′ē-ənt, -ĕnt′, ōr′-) *n.* **1.** The east; eastern lands or regions. **2. Orient. a.** The Eastern Hemisphere. **b.** The countries of Asia, especially of eastern Asia. Compare **Occident. c.** In ancient times, the lands and regions east of the Mediterranean. **3. a.** The luster characteristic of a pearl of high quality. **b.** A pearl having exceptional luster.
~*adj.* **1.** *Archaic.* Eastern; oriental. **2.** Having exceptional quality and luster. Said of pearls and gemstones. **3.** *Archaic.* Rising in the sky; ascending: *"The orient moon"* (P.B. Shelley).
~*v.* (-ĕnt′) **oriented, -enting, -ents.** *—tr.* **1.** To place or locate in a particular relation to the points of the compass: *orient the swimming pool north and south.* **2. a.** To locate or place so as to face the east. **b.** To build (a church) with the nave laid out west to east and the altar at the eastern end. **3.** To align or position with respect to: *They made every effort to orient their child to her future duties as a voter.* **4.** To determine the bearings of: *She oriented herself by finding a familiar landmark.* **5.** To cause to become familiar with or adjusted to facts, principles, or circumstances. *—intr.* **1.** To turn toward the east. **2.** To become adjusted or aligned. [Middle English, from Old French, from Latin *oriēns* (stem *orient-*), rising, rising sun, east, from *orīrī,* to rise.]

o·ri·en·tal (ôr′ē-ĕn′təl, ōr′-) *adj.* **1.** Eastern. **2.** *Usually* **Oriental.** Pertaining to the countries or regions of the Orient or to their peoples, languages, or culture. **3. Oriental.** *Ecology.* Of or designating the zoogeographic region that includes tropical Asia and the adjacent islands of the Malay Archipelago. **4.** Lustrous and valuable: *oriental pearls.* **5.** Pertaining to or designating precious varieties of corundum: *an oriental ruby.*
~*n. Usually* **Oriental.** A native of an Oriental country or tribe. **—o·ri·en·tal·ly** *adv.*

oriental alabaster *n.* A mineral, **onyx marble** *(see).*

oriental amethyst *n.* A type of **amethyst** *(see).*

O·ri·en·tal·ism, o·ri·en·tal·ism (ôr′ē-ĕn′tə-lĭz′əm, ōr′-) *n.* **1.** A quality, mannerism, or custom peculiar to or characteristic of the Orient. **2.** Scholarly knowledge of Eastern cultures, languages, and peoples. **—O·ri·en·tal·ist** *n. & adj.*

O·ri·en·tal·ize, o·ri·en·tal·ize (ôr′ē-ĕn′tə-līz′, ōr′-) *v.* **-ized, izing, izes.** *—tr.* To give an oriental character, lifestyle, or appearance to. *—intr.* To become oriental; adopt oriental qualities. **—o·ri·en·tal·i·za·tion** *n.*

Oriental poppy *n.* A plant, *Papaver orientale,* that is widely cultivated for its brilliant scarlet flowers.

Oriental rug *n.* Any of numerous types of rug made by hand in the Orient.

o·ri·en·tate (ôr′ē-ən-tāt′, ôr′ē-ĕn′-, ōr′-) *v.* **-tated, -tating, -tates.** *—tr.* To orient. *—intr.* To be or become oriented.

o·ri·en·ta·tion (ôr′ē-ən-tā′shən, ôr′ē-ĕn′, ōr′-) *n.* **1.** The act of orienting or the state of being oriented. **2.** Location or position relative to the points of the compass. **3.** *Architecture.* The location of a church so that its longitudinal axis is from west to east and its main altar at the eastern end. **4.** The line or direction followed in the course of a trend, movement, or development. **5.** An adjustment or adaptation to a new environment, situation, custom, or set of ideas. **6.** *Psychology.* Individual awareness of the outside world in its relation to the self. **7.** Introductory instruction concerning a new situation. [Probably ORIENT (verb) + -ATION.]

o·ri·en·teer·ing (ôr′ē-ən-tîr′ĭng, ôr′ē-ĕn-, ōr′-) *n.* A cross-country race in which the competitors have to work out the route by means of a compass and map and report to checkpoints on the way. [Swedish *orientering,* orientation.]

or·i·fice (ôr′ə-fĭs, ŏr′-) *n.* A mouth or vent; an aperture or cavity. [Old French, from Late Latin *ōrificium* : Latin *ōs* (stem *ōr-*), mouth + *facere,* to make.]

or·i·flamme (ôr′ə-flăm′, ŏr′-) *n.* **1.** The red flag of the Abbey of St. Denis, used as a standard by the early kings of France. **2.** Any inspiring standard or symbol. [Middle English *oriflamble,* from Old French *oriflambe,* from Medieval Latin *auriflamma* : Latin *aurum,* gold + *flamma,* FLAME.]

orig. original; originally.

o·ri·ga·mi (ôr′ĭ-gä′mē) *n.* **1.** The art or process, originating in Japan, of folding paper into shapes resembling flowers, birds, or other objects. **2.** A decorative object made in this way. Compare **kirigami.** [Japanese : *ori,* a folding + *-gami,* from *kami,* paper.]

o·rig·a·num (ə-rĭg′ə-nəm) *n.* A plant of the genus *Origanum;* especially, wild marjoram. [Middle English, from Old French, from Latin *origanum,* from Greek *origanon.*]

Or·i·gen (ôr′ə-jĭn, ŏr′-) (*c.* A.D. 185–254). Christian writer and teacher and one of the Greek Fathers of the Church. His many works include the *Hexapla* (interpretations of Old Testament texts) and *Contra Celsum,* a defense of Christianity against the attacks of the philosopher Celsus (2nd century A.D.).

or·i·gin (ôr′ə-jĭn, ŏr′-) *n.* **1.** The point at which something originates; source or cause. **2.** Parentage; ancestry: *"We cannot escape our origins, however hard we try"* (James Baldwin). **3.** A coming into being. **4.** *Anatomy.* **a.** The point of attachment of a muscle that remains fixed when the muscle contracts. **b.** The beginning of a nerve or blood vessel, especially when it arises from a larger nerve or blood vessel. **5.** *Mathematics.* The point of intersection of coordinate axes, from which measurements are made, as in the Cartesian coordinate system. [Middle English *origyne,* from Latin *orīgō* (stem *orīgin-*), from *orīrī,* to rise.]
Synonyms: *inception, root, source.*

o·rig·i·nal (ə-rĭj′ə-nəl) *adj. Abbr.* **orig. 1.** Of, pertaining to, or being the origin of something; first: *My original idea was to sell the house.* **2. a.** Not derived from something else; fresh and unusual: *The book reflects much original research.* **b.** Showing a marked departure from previous thinking or practice; new: *a truly original approach to solving the problem.* **3.** Productive of new things or new ideas; creative and inventive. **4.** Being the source from which a copy, reproduction, or translation is made. —See Usage note at **new.**
~*n. Abbr.* **orig. 1.** The primary form of something from which varieties arise or imitations are made: *Later models retained many features of the original.* **2.** An authentic work of art, such as a painting, as distinguished from a copy or reproduction. **3.** One that is the model for an artistic or literary work. **4.** One having an unusual turn of mind or pattern of behavior. **5.** A peculiar, odd, or eccentric person. [Middle English, from Old French, from Latin *orīginālis,* from *orīgō,* ORIGIN.]

o·rig·i·nal·i·ty (ə-rĭj′ə-năl′ə-tē) *n., pl.* **-ties. 1.** The quality of being original. **2.** The capacity to act or think independently. **3.** Something original.

o·rig·i·nal·ly (ə-rĭj′ə-nə-lē) *adv. Abbr.* **orig. 1.** With reference to origin. **2.** At first. **3.** In a highly distinctive manner.

original sin *n. Theology.* **1.** The tendency to evil inherent in human beings as a result of Adam's first act of disobedience. **2.** The state of deprivation from grace resulting from Adam's sinful disobedience.

o·rig·i·nate (ə-rĭj′ə-nāt′) *v.* **-nated, -nating, -nates.** *—tr.* To bring into being; create. *—intr.* To come into being; start. **—o·rig·i·na·tion** *n.* **—o·rig·i·na·tive** (ə-rĭj′ə-nā′tĭv, -nə-tĭv) *adj.* **—o·rig·i·na·tive·ly** *adv.* **—o·rig·i·na·tor** *n.*

o·ri·ole (ôr′ē-ōl′, ōr′-) *n.* **1.** Any of various Old World birds of the family Oriolidae, of which the males are characteristically bright yellow and black. **2.** Any of various New World birds of the family Icteridae, of which the males are black and orange or yellow. See **Baltimore oriole.** [French *oriol,* from Old French, from Medieval Latin *oriolus,* "golden (bird)," variant of Latin *aureolus,* diminutive of *aureus,* golden, from *aurum,* gold.]

O·ri·on[1] (ō-rī′ən). *Greek Mythology.* A giant hunter, pursuer of the Pleiades and lover of Eos, who was killed by Artemis.

Orion[2] *n.* A constellation in the celestial equator near Gemini and Taurus containing the stars Betelgeuse and Rigel. [Greek *Ōriōn.*]

or·i·son (ôr′ə-sən, -zən, ŏr′-) *n.* A prayer. [Middle English, from Old French, from Latin *ōrātiō* (stem *oration-*), ORATION.]

O·ris·sa (ō-rĭs′ə, ô-rĭs′ə). State of eastern India, on the Bay of Bengal. Its economy depends mainly on agriculture and fishing. Bhubaneswar is the capital.

O·ri·ya (ō-rē′ə) *n.* The Indic language of Orissa.

Ork·ney Islands (ôrk′nē). Group of 70 islands off northern Scotland. The islands belonged to Norway until 1471. Formerly a county, now constituting a region, the islands are used as a base for the North Sea oil industry. The principal islands are Mainland (Pomona), Hoy, and Sanday; Kirkwall is the chief town.

orle (ôrl) *n. Heraldry.* An inner border not quite touching the edge of a shield. [French *orle,* *ourle,* from *ourler,* to edge, hem, from Vulgar Latin *orulāre* (unattested), from *orula* (unattested), diminutive of Latin *ora,* edge, border.]

Or·le·an·ist (ôr′lē-ə-nĭst) *n.* A supporter of the Orléans branch of the French royal family, descended from the Duke of Orléans, younger brother of Louis XIV.

Or·lé·ans (ôr-lā-än′). City in north-central France. A royal residence since the 7th century, it is the capital of Loiret department. Joan of Arc raised the English siege here (1429) in the Hundred Years' War; its cathedral was destroyed (1568) by the Huguenots, who were themselves massacred here on St. Bartholomew's Day, 1572.

Orléans, Charles, Duc d' (1391-1465). French general and poet. Captured by the English at Agincourt (1415), he spent the next quarter of a century as a prisoner in England and devoted much of his time to writing poetry in English. His son became Louis XII of France.

Orléans, Louis Philippe Joseph, Duc d', known as "Philippe Égalité" (1747-93). French politician. He was a radical revolutionary despite being a member of the royal family. He voted for the execution of his cousin Louis XVI, but was himself executed for treason. His son, Louis Philippe, became king.

Or·lon (ôr′lŏn) *n.* A trademark for a synthetic acrylic fiber that is used alone or with other fibers in a variety of fabrics.

or·lop (ôr′lŏp′) *n. Nautical.* The lowest deck of a ship, especially a warship. Also called "orlop deck." [Middle English *overlop,* deck of a single-decker covering the hold, from Middle Low German *overlōp,* "a leaping over" : *over,* over + *lōpen,* to leap.]

Or·lov (ôr-lôf′), **Grigory Grigoryevich, Count** (1734-83). Russian politician. A lover of Catherine the Great, he engineered, with his brother Alexei (1737-1808), the coup (1762) that brought Catherine to power. As adviser to the empress, he unsuccessfully supported reforms such as emancipation of the serfs.

Or·man·dy (ôr′mən-dē), **Eugene** (1899-). U.S. musician and conductor, born in Hungary. A prodigy who began playing the violin before the age of four, he moved to the United States in 1921. He has conducted symphony orchestras in many cities and in 1938 became the musical director of the Philadelphia Orchestra.

Or·mazd, Or·muzd (ôr′məzd). The chief deity of Zoroastrianism, the creator of the world, the source of light, and the embodiment of good. Also called "Ahura Mazda." Compare **Ahriman.** [Persian *Ormazd,* from Avestan *Ahura-Mazda,* "wise spirit" : *ahura,* spirit + *mazdā,* wise.]

or·mer (ôr′mər) *n. British.* **1.** An edible abalone, *Haliotis tuberculata,* found chiefly in the Channel Islands. Also called "sea ear." **2.** The shell of the ormer. [Channel Islands French, from French *ormier,* short for *oreille-de-mer,* "sea-ear," from Latin *auris maris* : *auris,* ear + *maris,* genitive of *mare,* sea.]

or·mo·lu (ôr′mə-lōō′) *n.* **1.** Any of several copper and tin or zinc alloys resembling gold in appearance and used to decorate furniture, moldings, architectural ornamentations, and jewelry. Also called "mosaic gold." **2.** An imitation of gold. **3.** *Archaic.* Gold or gold leaf used for gilding. [French *or moulu,* "ground gold" : *or,* gold, from Latin *aurum* + *moulu,* past participle of *moudre,* to grind, from Latin *molere.*]

Ormuz. See **Hormuz.**

or·na·ment (ôr′nə-mənt) *n.* **1.** Something that decorates or adorns; an embellishment. **2.** Decorations or adornments collectively. **3.** A small object, such as a porcelain figure, used as decoration. **4.** A person considered as a source of pride, honor, or credit because of personality, talent, or skill: *He is an ornament to his profession.* **5.** *Music.* A note or group of notes that embellishes or decorates a melody.
~*tr.v.* (-mĕnt′) **ornamented, -menting, -ments. 1.** To furnish with ornaments. **2.** To be an ornament to. [Middle English, from Old French *ornement,* from Latin *ōrnāmentum,* from *ōrnāre,* to adorn.] —**or·na·ment·er** *n.*

or·na·men·tal (ôr′nə-mĕn′təl) *adj.* Of, pertaining to, or serving as an ornament; especially, decorative but inessential.
~*n.* Something that is ornamental; especially, a plant grown for its beauty. —**or·na·men·tal·ly** *adv.*

or·na·men·ta·tion (ôr′nə-mĕn-tā′shən) *n.* **1. a.** The act, process, or result of ornamenting. **b.** The state of being ornamented. **2.** That which ornaments. **3.** Ornaments collectively.

or·nate (ôr-nāt′) *adj.* **1.** Elaborately and heavily ornamented; excessively decorated. **2.** Showy or florid in style or manner; flowery. [Middle English *ornat,* from Latin *ōrnātus,* past participle of *ōrnāre,* to adorn.] —**or·nate·ly** *adv.* —**or·nate·ness** *n.*
Synonyms: flamboyant, florid, gaudy, lavish, ostentatious, showy.

or·ner·y (ôr′nə-rē) *adj.* **-ier, -iest.** Of a stubborn and mean-spirited nature; cantankerous. [Variant of ORDINARY.] —**or·ner·i·ness** *n.*

ornith. ornithological; ornithology.

or·nith·ic (ôr-nĭth′ĭk) *adj.* Of, pertaining to, or characteristic of birds. [Greek *ornithikos* : ORNITH(O)- + -ikos, -IC.]

or·ni·thine (ôr′nə-thēn′) *n.* An amino acid, $C_5H_{12}N_2O_{12}$, produced in the liver during the formation of urea. [ORNITH(O)- (representing *ornithuric acid,* secreted in the urine of birds and reptiles) + -INE.]

ornitho-, ornith- *prefix.* Indicates a bird or birds; for example, **ornithology.** [New Latin, from Greek, from *ornis* (stem *ornith-*), bird.]

or·ni·thol·o·gy (ôr′nə-thŏl′ə-jē) *n. Abbr.* **ornith., ornithol.** The scientific study of birds. [New Latin *ornithologia* : ORNITHO- + -LOGY.] —**or·ni·tho·log·i·cal** (ôr′nə-thə-lŏj′ĭ-kəl) *adj.* —**or·ni·tho·log·i·cal·ly** *adv.* —**or·ni·thol·o·gist** (ôr′nə-thŏl′ə-jĭst) *n.*

or·ni·thop·ter (ôr′nə-thŏp′tər) *n.* A hypothetical aircraft supported in the air and propelled by wing movements. Also called "orthopter." [ORNITHO- + -PTER.]

or·ni·tho·rhyn·chus (ôr′nə-thō-rĭng′kəs) *n.* The **duck-billed platypus** (*see*). [New Latin, from ORNITHO- + Greek *rhunkos,* bill.]

or·ni·tho·sis (ôr′nə-thō′sĭs) *n.* A contagious virus disease of the psittacosis group that infects domestic fowl and other birds and is transmissible to humans. [New Latin : ORNITH(O)- + -OSIS.] —**or·ni·thot·ic** (ôr′nə-thŏt′ĭk) *adj.*

oro- *prefix.* Indicates a mountain; for example, **orology.** [Greek *oros*†, mountain.]

o·rog·e·ny (ô-rŏj′ə-nē) *n.* Also **o·ro·gen·e·sis** (ôr′ə-jĕn′ə-sĭs, ōr′-). The process of mountain formation, especially by a folding and faulting of the earth's crust. [ORO- + -GENY.] —**or·o·gen·ic** (ôr′ə-jĕn′ĭk, ōr′-) *adj.* —**or·o·gen·i·cal·ly** *adv.*

o·rog·ra·phy (ô-rŏg′rə-fē) *n.* The study of the physical geography of mountains and mountain ranges. [ORO- + -GRAPHY.] —**or·o·graph·ic** (ôr′ə-grăf′ĭk, ōr′-), **or·o·graph·i·cal** (-ĭ-kəl) *adj.* —**or·o·graph·i·cal·ly** *adv.*

o·ro·ide (ôr′ō-īd′, ōr′-) *n.* Also **o·re·ide** (ôr′ē-īd′, ōr′-). An inexpensive alloy of copper, zinc, and tin used in imitation gold jewelry. [French *oréide* : *or,* gold, from Latin *aurum,* gold + -*éide,* -OID.] —**o·ro·ide, o·re·ide** *adj.*

o·rol·o·gy (ô-rŏl′ə-jē) *n.* The study of mountains. [ORO- + -LOGY.] —**o·ro·log·i·cal** (ôr′ə-lŏj′ĭ-kəl, ōr′-) *adj.* —**o·ro·log·i·cal·ly** *adv.* —**o·rol·o·gist** *n.*

o·rom·e·ter (ô-rŏm′ə-tər) *n.* An instrument that indicates height above sea level using barometric means. [ORO- + -METER.]

O·ron·tes (ô-rŏn′tēz). River of southwestern Asia. Rising in Lebanon, it flows 370 kilometers (230 miles) mainly northward through Syria and Turkey to join the Mediterranean. Though unnavigable, it is used extensively for irrigation.

o·ro·tund (ôr′ə-tŭnd′, ōr′-) *adj.* **1.** Full in sound; sonorous: *spoke in orotund tones.* **2.** Pompous and bombastic: *orotund talk.* [Latin *ōre rotundō,* "with round mouth" : *ōs* (stem *ōr-*), mouth + *rotundus,* rounded, ROTUND.]

O·roz·co (ō-rôs′kō), **José Clemente** (1883-1949). Mexican painter. He painted murals, often using a fresco technique, and also produced genre paintings and lithographs. His boldly executed works often dealt with social themes, particularly the conflict between man and machine.

or·phan (ôr′fən) *n.* A child whose parents are dead.
~*adj.* **1.** Being an orphan. **2.** For orphans: *an orphan home.*
~*tr.v.* **orphaned, -phaning, -phans.** To deprive (a child) by the death of one or both parents. [Late Latin *orphanus,* from Greek *orphanos,* orphaned.] —**or·phan·hood** (ôr′fən-hood′) *n.*

or·phan·age (ôr′fə-nĭj) *n.* **1.** An institution for the care and protection of orphans and abandoned children. **2.** The state or condition of being an orphan.

Or·phe·an (ôr-fē′ən, ôr′fē-) *adj.* **1.** Of or pertaining to Orpheus. **2.** Beautiful; entrancing. Said of sounds.

Or·phe·us (ôr′fē-əs, -fyōōs′). *Greek Mythology.* A poet and musician whose singing to the lyre had the power to move even inanimate objects and who nearly succeeded in rescuing his wife Eurydice from Hades.

Or·phic (ôr′fĭk) *adj.* **1.** Of or ascribed to Orpheus; Orphean: *the Orphic poems; Orphic mysteries.* **2.** Of, pertaining to, or characteristic of the dogmas, mysteries, and philosophical system set forth in the poems ascribed to Orpheus. **3.** *Sometimes* **orphic.** Mystic or occult in nature; esoteric. [Latin *Orphicus,* from Greek *Orphikos,* from ORPHEUS.] —**Or·phi·cal·ly** *adv.*

Or·phism (ôr′fĭz′əm) *n.* An ancient Greek mystic religion arising in the 6th century B.C. from a synthesis of pre-Hellenic beliefs with the cult of Zagreus. [French *orphisme,* from *Orphée,* from Greek *Orpheus,* ORPHEUS.] —**Or·phist** *n. & adj.*

or·phrey (ôr′frē) *n., pl.* **-phreys.** Also **or·fray** (-frā′) *pl.* **-frays. 1.** A band of elaborate embroidery decorating the front of certain ecclesiastical vestments. **2.** Elaborate embroidery, especially when worked in gold. [Middle English *orfrey, orphreis* (taken as plural), from Old French *orfreis,* from Medieval Latin *aurifrigium* : Latin *aurum,* gold + *Phrygium,* neuter of *Phrygius,* embroidered, PHRYGIAN.]

or·pi·ment (ôr′pə-mənt) *n.* A mineral, arsenic trisulfide, As_2S_3, used as a lemon-yellow pigment in tanning and linoleum manufacture. [Middle English, from Old French, from Latin *auripigmentum* : *aurum,* gold + *pigmentum,* PIGMENT.]

or·pine (ôr′pĭn) *n.* Any of several plants of the genus *Sedum;* especially, *S. telephium,* native to Eurasia, having clusters of reddish-purple flowers. Also called "live-forever," *British* "livelong." [Mid-

orrery *These mechanical planetariums are named after Charles Boyle, 4th Earl of Orrery, for whom the clockwork model shown here was made in 1716. When the model is operated, the earth and the moon (on the left) revolve around the central sun at the correct speed relative to each other.*

PRONUNCIATION KEY

ă, pat; ā, pay; âr, care; ä, father, are; b, **bib**; ch, **church**; d, **deed**; ĕ, pet; ē, be; f, **fife**; g, **gag**; h, **hat**; hw, **which**; ĭ, pit; ī, pie; îr, pier; j, **judge**; k, **kick**; l, **lid**, needle; m, **mum**; n, **no**, sudden; ng, **thing**; ŏ, pot; ō, toe; ô, paw, for; oi, noise; ou, out; o͝o, book; o͞o, boot; p, **pop**; r, **roar**; s, **sauce**; sh, **ship**, **dish**; t, **tight**; th, **thin**, **path**; *th*, **this**, **bathe**; ŭ, cut; ûr, fur; v, **valve**; w, **with**; y, **yes**; z, **zebra**, **size**; zh, **vision**; ə, about, item, edible, gallop, circus, peaceful

IN FOREIGN WORDS:

à, *Fr.* ami; œ, *Fr.* **feu**, *Ger.* **schön**; ü, *Fr.* **tu**, *Ger.* **über**; KH, *Ger.* **ich**, *Scot.* **loch**; N, *Fr.* **bon**; y', *Fr.* **Compiègne**

STRESS MARKS:

Primary stress: ′
in·cite′ (ĭn-sīt′)
Secondary stress: ′
in′sight′ (ĭn′sīt′)

dle English *orpin,* from Old French *orpine,* short for *orpiment,* ORPIMENT, probably after the yellow flowers of one species.]

Or·ping·ton (ôr′pĭng-tən) *n.* A domestic fowl of a breed having a large body, a single comb, and unfeathered legs. [After *Orpington,* England, where the breed originated.]

or·re·ry (ôr′ə-rē, ŏr′-) *n., pl.* **-ries.** A mechanical model of the solar system. [After Charles Boyle (1676–1731), 4th Earl of *Orrery,* for whom one was made.]

or·ris (ôr′ĭs, ŏr′-) *n.* **1.** Any of several species of iris having a fragrant rootstock; especially, *Iris florentina.* **2.** Orrisroot. [Probably variant of IRIS.]

or·ris·root (ôr′ĭs-ro͞ot′, -ro͝ot′, ŏr′-) *n.* The fragrant rootstock of the orris, used in perfumes and cosmetics.

Or·si·ni (ôr-sē′nē). An aristocratic family of medieval Italy. Originating in Rome, they supported the Papal (or Guelph) faction against the Imperial (or Ghibelline) faction. The family included two popes—Celestine III (reigned 1191–98) and Nicholas III (reigned 1277–80).

Or·te·ga y Gas·set (ôr-tā′gə ē gä-sĕt′), **José** (1883–1955). Spanish philosopher. He is best known for his neo-Kantian doctrines of individualism and willpower, as expounded in such works as *The Revolt of the Masses* (1929).

Or·te·li·us (ôr-tē′lē-əs), **Abraham** (1527–98). Flemish geographer. A careful scholar and extensive traveler, he published his *Theatrum Orbis Terrarum* in 1570, which appeared in 40 editions and is regarded as the first modern atlas.

orth. orthopedic; orthopedics.

or·thi·con (ôr′thĭ-kŏn′) *n.* A television camera pickup tube that uses a low-energy electron beam to scan a photoactive mosaic. Also called "image orthicon." [ORTH(O)- + ICON(OSCOPE).]

or·tho (ôr′thō) *adj.* **1.** *Chemistry.* **a.** Of, pertaining to, or designating adjacent positions in a benzene ring. **b.** Of, pertaining to, or designating the most fully hydrated form of an acid or of its salts. **2.** *Physics.* Of, pertaining to, or designating the form of a diatomic molecule in which the nuclear spins are parallel. [From ORTHO-.]

ortho-, orth- *prefix.* Indicates: **1.** Straight or upright; for example, **orthotropic. 2.** *Mathematics.* Perpendicular to or at right angles; for example, **orthorhombic. 3.** Correct or standard; for example, **orthography. 4.** *Medicine.* Correction of maladjustments or deformities; for example, **orthopedics.** [Middle English, from Old French, from Latin, from Greek *orthos,* straight, correct, right, upright.]

or·tho·bo·ric acid (ôr′thō-bôr′ĭk, -bōr′ĭk) *n.* **Boric acid** *(see).*

or·tho·cen·ter (ôr′thō-sĕn′tər) *n.* The point of intersection of the three altitudes of a triangle.

or·tho·ce·phal·ic (ôr′thō-sə-făl′ĭk) *adj.* Also **or·tho·ceph·a·lous** (-sĕf′ə-ləs). Having a ratio of skull height to skull length between 0.70 and 0.75. [ORTHO- + -CEPHALIC.] **—or·tho·ceph·a·ly** (ôr′thō-sĕf′ə-lē) *n.*

or·tho·chro·mat·ic (ôr′thō-krō-măt′ĭk) *adj.* **1.** Of, having, or reproducing accurately the colors of nature. **2.** Of or pertaining to a film, plate, or emulsion that renders all colors except red in tones of gray approximating the relative brilliance of these colors. Compare **panchromatic. —or·tho·chro·mat·i·cal·ly** *adv.* **—or·tho·chro·ma·tism** (ôr′thō-krō′mə-tĭz′əm) *n.*

or·tho·clase (ôr′thə-klās′, -klāz′) *n.* A **potassium feldspar** *(see),* essentially potassium aluminum silicate, $KAlSi_3O_8$, characterized by a monoclinic crystalline structure and found in igneous, metamorphic, and sedimentary rocks. [German *Orthoklas* : ORTHO- + -CLASE.]

or·tho·don·tia (ôr′thə-dŏn′shə) *n.* Orthodontics.

or·tho·don·tics (ôr′thə-dŏn′tĭks) *n. Used with a singular verb.* The dental specialty and practice of correcting abnormally aligned or positioned teeth. [ORTH(O)- + -ODONT + -ICS.] **—or·tho·don·tic** *adj.* **—or·tho·don·tist** *n.*

or·tho·dox (ôr′thə-dŏks′) *adj.* **1. a.** Adhering to a commonly accepted, customary, or traditional practice or belief. **b.** Conventional, as in outlook or behavior. **2.** Adhering to the accepted or traditional and established faith, especially in religion. Compare **heterodox. 3.** Adhering to the Christian faith as expressed in the early Christian ecumenical creeds. **4. Orthodox. a.** Of, pertaining to, or designating any of the churches of the Eastern Orthodox Church. **b.** Of, pertaining to, or designating Orthodox Judaism. ~*n.* **1.** One that is orthodox. **2. Orthodox.** A member of an Eastern Orthodox Church. [Old French *orthodoxe,* from Late Latin *orthodoxus,* from Greek *orthodoxos,* having the right opinion : ORTHO- + *doxa,* opinion, from *dokein,* to think.] **—or·tho·dox·ly** *adv.*

Orthodox Church *n.* The **Eastern Orthodox Church** *(see).*

Orthodox Judaism *n.* The branch of the Jewish faith that adheres to the Mosaic Law as interpreted in the Talmud, and considers it binding in modern as well as ancient times. Compare **Conservative Judaism, Reform Judaism.**

orthodox sleep *n.* The major part of sleep, during which no dreaming occurs and the body and brain are in a state of very low activity. Compare **paradoxical sleep.**

or·tho·dox·y (ôr′thə-dŏk′sē) *n., pl.* **-ies. 1.** The quality or state of being orthodox. **2.** Orthodox practice, custom, or belief. **3. Orthodoxy. a.** The practice and customs of the Eastern Orthodox Church. **b.** The practice and customs of Orthodox Judaism.

or·tho·e·py (ôr-thō′ə-pē, ôr′thō-ĕp′ē) *n.* **1.** The study of the pronunciation of words. **2.** The customary pronunciation of words. [New Latin *orthoepia,* from Greek *orthoepeia* : ORTHO- + *epos,* word.] **—or·tho·ep·ic** (ôr′thō-ĕp′ĭk), **or·tho·ep·i·cal** (-ĭ-kəl) *adj.* **—or·tho·e·pist** (ôr-thō′ə-pĭst, ôr′thō-ĕp′ĭst) *n.*

or·tho·gen·e·sis (ôr′thō-jĕn′ə-sĭs) *n.* **1.** *Biology.* The theory that evolutionary change is predetermined by the constitution of germ plasm and independent of external factors. **2.** *Anthropology.* The theory that all cultures pass through sequential periods in the same order. [New Latin : ORTHO- + -GENESIS.] **—or·tho·ge·net·ic** (ôr′thō-jə-nĕt′ĭk) *adj.* **—or·tho·ge·net·i·cal·ly** *adv.*

or·tho·gen·ic (ôr′thō-jĕn′ĭk) *adj.* **1.** In psychiatry, of or pertaining to the correction or treatment of mental and emotional abnormalities in children. **2.** Of or pertaining to orthogenesis. [ORTHO- + -GENIC.]

or·thog·na·thous (ôr-thŏg′nə-thəs) *adj.* Also **or·thog·nath·ic** (ôr′thŏg-năth′ĭk). Having the lower jaw correctly aligned with the upper so that it does not protrude or recede. [ORTHO- + -GNATHOUS.] **—or·thog·na·thism** (ôr-thŏg′nə-thĭz′əm), **or·thog·na·thy** (-thē) *n.*

or·thog·o·nal (ôr-thŏg′ə-nəl) *adj. Mathematics.* **1.** Pertaining to or composed of right angles. **2. a.** Having a defined scalar product of zero. Said of two vectors. **b.** Having a defined product of zero. Said of two functions. **c.** Of or designating a matrix that is equal to the inverse of its transpose. [Greek *orthogōnios* : ORTHO- + *gōnia,* angle.] **—or·thog·o·nal·ly** *adv.*

orthogonal projection *n.* The two-dimensional graphic representation of an object formed by the perpendicular intersections of lines drawn from points on the object to a plane of projection. Also called "orthographic projection."

or·tho·graph·ic (ôr′thə-grăf′ĭk) *adj.* Also **or·tho·graph·i·cal** (-ĭ-kəl). **1.** Of or pertaining to orthography. **2.** Spelled correctly. **3.** *Mathematics.* Having perpendicular lines. **—or·tho·graph·i·cal·ly** *adv.*

or·thog·ra·phy (ôr-thŏg′rə-fē) *n., pl.* **-phies. 1.** The art or study of correct spelling according to established usage. **2.** The aspect of language study concerned with letters and their sequences in words. **3.** Any method of representing the sounds of language by literal symbols. [Middle English *ortografie,* from Old French, from Latin *orthographia,* from Greek : ORTHO- + -GRAPHY.] **—or·thog·ra·pher, or·thog·ra·phist** *n.*

or·tho·hy·dro·gen (ôr′thō-hī′drə-jən) *n.* A form of hydrogen in which the two nuclei in each molecule have parallel spins; one of two possible forms of molecular hydrogen, constituting 75 percent of hydrogen at room temperature. Compare **parahydrogen.**

or·tho·pe·dics (ôr′thə-pē′dĭks) *n. Abbr.* **orth.** *Used with a singular verb.* The surgical or manipulative treatment of disorders of the skeletal system and associated muscles. [French *orthopédie* : ORTHO- + Greek *paideia,* education, from *pais* (stem *paid-*), child.] **—or·tho·pe·dic** *adj.* **—or·tho·pe·di·cal·ly** *adv.* **—or·tho·pe·dist** *n.*

or·tho·psy·chi·a·try (ôr′thō-sī-kī′ə-trē, -sĭ-kī′ə-trē) *n.* The prevention and early treatment of mental disorders, especially in the young. **—or·tho·psy·chi·at·ric** (ôr′thō-sī′kē-ăt′rĭk), **or·tho·psy·chi·at·ri·cal** *adj.* **—or·tho·psy·chi·a·trist** (ôr′thō-sī-kī′ə-trĭst, -sĭ-kī′ə-trĭst) *n.*

or·thop·ter (ôr′thŏp′tər) *n.* An aircraft, an **ornithopter** *(see).* [ORTHO- + -PTER.]

or·thop·ter·an (ôr-thŏp′tər-ən) *n.* Also **or·thop·ter·on** (-tə-rŏn′, -tər-ən). An insect of the order Orthoptera, characterized by membranous, folded hind wings covered by leathery, narrow forewings, and including the locusts, cockroaches, crickets, and grasshoppers. [New Latin *Orthoptera* (order), "straight-wings" : ORTHO- + *-ptera,* from *-pterus,* -PTEROUS.] **—or·thop·ter·al, or·thop·ter·an, or·thop·ter·ous** *adj.*

or·thop·tics (ôr-thŏp′tĭks) *n. Used with a singular verb.* The practice of using eye exercises and other nonsurgical methods to correct abnormalities of vision. [ORTH(O)- + OPTICS.] **—or·thop·tist** *n.*

or·tho·rhom·bic (ôr′thō-rŏm′bĭk) *adj.* Of, pertaining to, or designating a crystalline structure of three mutually perpendicular axes of different length.

or·tho·scope (ôr′thə-skōp′) *n.* An instrument for examining the eye through a layer of water that compensates for the curvature of the cornea. [ORTHO- + -SCOPE.]

or·tho·scop·ic (ôr′thə-skŏp′ĭk) *adj.* **1.** Of, pertaining to, or having normal vision. **2.** Of or pertaining to the use of the orthoscope. **3.** Giving an undistorted image.

or·thos·ti·chous (ôr-thŏs′tĭ-kəs) *adj. Biology.* Characterized by parallel arrangement in a vertical row. Said especially of leaves. [ORTHO- + Greek *stikhos,* a row.] **—or·thos·ti·chy** *n.*

or·thot·ics (ôr-thŏt′ĭks) *n. Used with a singular verb.* A branch of medicine concerned with the use of mechanical devices to support or correct weakened or deformed joints. [From *orthotic* : ORTH(O)- + -OTIC.] **—or·thot·ic** *adj.* **—or·thot·ist** (ôr-thŏt′ĭst, ôr′thə-tĭst) *n.*

or·tho·trop·ic (ôr′thə-trŏp′ĭk) *adj.* Tending to grow or form along a vertical axis. Said especially of plant parts. [ORTHO- + -TROPIC.] **—or·tho·trop·i·cal·ly** *adv.* **—or·thot·ro·pism** (ôr-thŏt′rə-pĭz′əm) *n.*

or·thot·ro·pous (ôr-thŏt′rə-pəs) *adj. Botany.* Growing straight, so that the micropyle is at the side opposite the stalk. Said of an ovule. [ORTHO- + -TROPOUS.]

or·to·lan (ôr′tə-lən) *n.* **1.** A small, brownish bird, *Emberiza hortulana,* of Europe and Asia, eaten as a delicacy. **2.** Any of several New World birds, such as the bobolink. [French, from Provençal, gardener, from Latin *hortolānus,* from *hortulus,* diminutive of *hortus,* garden.]

Or·vie·to[1] (ôr-vyâ′tō). Town of west-central Italy. Thought to be near the site of the Etruscan city of Volsinii, it has many Etruscan remains. Its most notable building is its cathedral.

Orvieto[2] *n.* A light, usually dry white Italian wine. [After ORVIETO, Italy.]

Or·well (ôr′wĕl′, -wəl), **George,** pen name of Eric Arthur Blair

(1903–50). British writer. Despite his prosperous background, he became a socialist and lived among low-paid workers and tramps, as recorded in *Down and Out in Paris and London* (1933). Disillusioned with communism while fighting the Nationalists in the Spanish Civil War, he attacked totalitarianism in novels such as *Animal Farm* (1946) and *1984* (1949). **—Or·well·i·an** *adj.*

-ory[1] *suffix.* Indicates: **1.** A place for; for example, **conservatory, observatory. 2.** Something used as; for example, **accessory, directory.** [Middle English *-orie,* from Norman French *-orie* or Old French *-orie, -oire,* from Latin *-ōrium, -ōria,* from *-ōrius,* adjective suffix.]

-ory[2] *suffix.* Indicates characterization by, possession of the nature of, or tendency toward; for example, **compensatory.** [Middle English *-orie,* from Old French *-oire, -orie,* from Latin *-ōrius,* adjective suffix.]

o·ryx (ôr′ĭks, ōr′-, ŏr′-) *n., pl.* **oryxes** or collectively **oryx.** Any of several antelopes of the genus *Oryx,* of Africa and Arabia, having long straight or arching horns. [Latin, from Greek *orux,* pickax, spike, hence (from the sharp horns) gazelle, perhaps from *orussein,* to dig.]

os[1] (ŏs) *n., pl.* **ora** (ôr′ə, ōr′ə). *Anatomy.* A mouth or opening. [Latin *ōs* (stem *ōr-*), mouth.]

os[2] (ŏs) *n., pl.* **ossa** (ŏs′ə). *Anatomy.* A bone. [Latin *os* (stem *oss-*), bone.]

os[3] (ōs) *n., pl.* **osar** (ō′sär′). *Geology.* An **esker** *(see).* [Swedish *ås,* ridge, from Old Norse *áss.*]

Os The symbol for the element osmium.

o.s., o/s out of stock.

O.S. 1. Old Style. **2.** ordinary seaman.

OSA, O.S.A. Order of St. Augustine.

O·sage (ō′sāj′, ō-sāj′) *n., pl.* **Osages** or collectively **Osage. 1.** A member of a Siouan-speaking North American Indian people, formerly inhabiting the region between the Missouri and Arkansas rivers. **2.** The Siouan language of this people. **—O·sage** *adj.*

O·sa·ka (ō-sä′kə). Port of southern Japan. On the Yodo delta, it is the center of the Osaka Bay conurbation of southwest Honshu and the country's second most important industrial and commercial city. Among its historic buildings are imperial palaces and Buddhist temples dating from the 4th century.

OSB, O.S.B. Order of St. Benedict.

Os·borne (ŏz′bərn, -bôrn′), **John James** (1929–). British playwright. His first major play, *Look Back in Anger* (1956), heralded a revolution in British postwar theater, with naturalistic, politically and socially conscious plays coming to dominate serious drama.

Os·can (ŏs′kən) *n.* **1.** A member of an ancient people of Campania. **2.** The Italic language of this people.
~*adj.* Of or pertaining to the Oscans or their language.

Os·car (ŏs′kər) *n.* A trademark for one of the statuettes given as an **Academy Award** *(see).*

Os·ce·o·la (ŏs′ē-ō′lə) (*c.* 1804–38). Seminole leader. He led the fight against the removal of the Seminole tribes from Florida in the 1830's. Osceola and his followers were tricked into coming out of hiding in the Everglades in October 1837, and Osceola was later imprisoned at Fort Moultrie, near Charleston, South Carolina, where he died under suspicious circumstances.

os·cil·late (ŏs′ə-lāt′) *v.* **-lated, -lating, -lates.** —*intr.* **1.** To swing back and forth with a steady uninterrupted rhythm. **2.** To waver between two or more thoughts or courses of action; vacillate. **3.** *Physics.* To move or change between alternate extremes, usually in a regular way with a definable period. Said of vibrating objects, systems, waves, and the like. —*tr.* To cause to oscillate. —See Synonyms at **swing.** [Latin *ōscillāre,* from *ōscillum,* a swing, originally a mask of Bacchus hung from a tree in a vineyard to swing in the wind (as a charm), diminutive of *ōs,* face, mouth.] **—os·cil·la·tor** *n.* **—os·cil·la·to·ry** (ŏs′ə-lə-tôr′ē, -tōr′ē) *adj.*

os·cil·la·tion (ŏs′ə-lā′shən) *n.* **1.** The state or act of oscillating. **2.** A single cycle in which a system changes to one extreme state, then to the other extreme and back to its original state; a period. **—os·cil·la·tion·al** *adj.*

os·cil·lo·gram (ō-sĭl′ə-grăm′, ə-sĭl′-) *n.* **1.** The graph traced by an oscillograph. **2.** An instantaneous oscilloscope trace or photograph of such a trace. [OSCILLO(GRAPH) + -GRAM.]

os·cil·lo·graph (ō-sĭl′ə-grăf′, -gräf′, ə-sĭl′-) *n.* A device that records oscillations as a continuous graph of variation in a quantity with time. [French *oscillographe* : OSCILL(ATION) + -GRAPH.] **—os·cil·log·ra·phy** (ŏs′ə-lŏg′rə-fē) *n.*

os·cil·lo·scope (ō-sĭl′ə-skōp′, ə-sĭl′-) *n.* An electronic instrument that produces an almost instantaneous graph of the change of some quantity with a variable such as time by deflection of a narrow beam of electrons focused onto a fluorescent screen. The varying quantity is converted into an electrical signal used to deflect the electrons in a vertical direction, with repeated scanning in the horizontal direction by a periodic deflecting potential, thus producing a trace on the screen. [OSCILL(ATION) + -SCOPE.] **—os·cil·lo·scop·ic** (ō-sĭl′ə-skŏp′ĭk, ə-sĭl′-) *adj.*

os·cine (ŏs′īn′) *adj.* Of or pertaining to the Oscines, a large suborder of the passerine birds that includes most songbirds. [New Latin *Oscines,* from Latin *oscinēs,* plural of *oscen,* a singing bird used for augury.] **—os·cine** *n.*

os·ci·tan·cy (ŏs′ə-tən-sē) *n., pl.* **-cies.** Also **os·ci·tance** (-təns). **1.** The act of yawning. **2.** The state of being drowsy or inattentive; dullness. [Latin *ōscitāns,* present participle of *ōscitāre,* to gape : *ōs,* mouth + *citāre,* to move.] **—os·ci·tant** *adj.*

Os·co-Um·bri·an (ŏs′kō-ŭm′brē-ən) *n.* A subdivision of the Italic languages, including Oscan and Umbrian.

os·cu·lant (ŏs′kyə-lənt) *adj. Biology.* **1.** Intermediate in characteristics between two similar or related taxonomic groups. **2.** Closely adhering or joined; embracing. [Latin *ōsculāns* (stem *ōsculant-*), present participle of *ōsculārī,* to OSCULATE.]

os·cu·late (ŏs′kyə-lāt′) *v.* **-lated, -lating, -lates.** —*tr.* To kiss. —*intr.* **1.** *Biology.* To have characteristics intermediate between those of two similar or related taxonomic groups. **2.** *Geometry.* To touch at a single point without crossing. Used of two curves or surfaces. [Latin *ōsculārī,* from *ōsculum,* kiss, OSCULUM.]

os·cu·la·tion (ŏs′kyə-lā′shən) *n.* **1. a.** The act of osculating. **b.** A kiss. **2.** *Geometry:* **a.** A point at which two figures touch. **b.** A **tacnode** *(see).* **—os·cu·la·to·ry** (ŏs′kyə-lə-tôr′ē, -tōr′ē) *adj.*

os·cu·lum (ŏs′kyə-ləm) *n., pl.* **-la** (-lə). Also **os·cule** (ŏs′kyo͞ol′). *Zoology.* An opening; especially, the opening in a sponge for expelling water. [New Latin, from Latin *ōsculum,* little mouth, kiss, diminutive of *ōs,* mouth.] **—os·cu·lar** *adj.*

-ose[1] *suffix.* Indicates possession of or similarity to; for example, **bellicose, grandiose.** [Middle English, from Latin *-ōsus.* See **-ous.**]

-ose[2] *suffix. Chemistry.* Indicates: **1.** A carbohydrate; for example, **fructose, lactose. 2.** A product of protein hydrolysis; for example, **proteose.** [From GLUCOSE.]

o·sier (ō′zhər) *n.* **1.** Any of several willows having long, rodlike twigs used in basketry; especially, *Salix viminalis* and *S. purpurea,* both native to Eurasia. **2.** A twig of such a willow. **3.** Any of various similar trees. [Middle English, from Old French, from Medieval Latin *ausēria*†, willow bed.]

O·si·ris (ō-sī′rĭs). *Egyptian Mythology.* The god who was ruler and judge in the underworld and the brother and consort of Isis. He is identified with the Nile, and his annual death and resurrection symbolized the self-renewing vitality and fertility of nature. **—O·si·ri·an** (ō-sī′rē-ən) *adj.*

-osis *suffix.* Indicates: **1.** A condition or process; for example, **metamorphosis, osmosis. 2.** A diseased or abnormal condition; for example, **tuberculosis, neurosis. 3.** An increase or formation of; for example, **sclerosis, leukocytosis.** [Middle English, from Latin, from Greek *-ōsis,* abstract noun suffix formed from *o*-stem verbs.]

Os·ler (ŏs′lər, ŏz′-), **Sir William** (1849–1919). Physician and educator. Born in Canada, he spent 16 years in the United States at Johns Hopkins University in Baltimore, establishing the university's new medical school as one of the foremost in the country. In 1905 Osler moved to Oxford University and helped found the Royal Society of Medicine (1907).

Os·lo (ŏz′lō, ŏs′-). Formerly **Chris·ti·an·i·a** (krĭs′che-ăn′ē-ə, -ä′nē-ə). Capital of Norway. An ice-free port at the head of Oslo Fjord, it was founded (1050) by Harold III and became the nation's capital in 1299. Following destruction by fire, it was rebuilt in 1624, when it was renamed Christiania, reverting to its former name in 1925.

Os·man I (ŏs-män′), also **Oth·man** (ŏth-). (1259–1326). Founder of the Ottoman dynasty that ruled Turkey after 1290. He raised a conquering army of Muslim Turks that held sway over most of northwestern Asia Minor.

Os·man·li (ŏz-măn′lē, ŏs-) *n., pl.* **-lis. 1.** An Ottoman Turk. **2. Ottoman Turkish** *(see).* **3.** The Turkish language when written in Arabic script, as it was until 1930.
~*adj.* Ottoman. [Turkish : *Osman,* Osman I + *-li,* adjectival suffix.]

os·mat·ic (ŏz-măt′ĭk) *adj.* Also **os·mic** (ŏz′mĭk). Having or characterized by a sense of smell. [Greek *osmē,* smell + -AT(E) + -IC.]

os·mic[1] (ŏz′mĭk) *adj.* Of, pertaining to, or containing osmium. Said especially of compounds containing osmium with a high valence. [From OSMIUM.]

osmic[2]. Variant of **osmatic.**

os·mi·rid·i·um (ŏz′mə-rĭd′ē-əm) *n.* A natural alloy of osmium and iridium, used in needles, electric-switch contacts, and other small items subject to wear. Also called "iridosmine." [German : OS-M(IUM) + IRIDIUM.]

os·mi·um (ŏz′mē-əm) *n. Symbol* **Os** A bluish-white, hard metallic element, found in small amounts in osmiridium and platinum ores. It has the highest measured density of any element. It is used as a platinum hardener, in making pen points and instrument pivots, and also as a catalyst in cortisone synthesis. Atomic number 76, atomic weight 190.2, melting point 3,000°C, boiling point 5,000°C, specific gravity 22.57, valences 2, 3, 4, 8. [New Latin, from Greek *osmē,* smell (from the smell of osmium tetroxide).]

os·mom·e·ter (ŏz-mŏm′ə-tər, ŏs-) *n.* Any of various instruments or pieces of apparatus used to measure osmotic pressures. [OSMO(SIS) + -METER.] **—os·mo·met·ric** (ŏz′mə-mĕt′rĭk, ŏs′-) *adj.* **—os·mo·met·ri·cal·ly** *adv.* **—os·mom·e·try** *n.*

os·mo·reg·u·la·tion (ŏz′mə-rĕg′yə-lā′shən, ŏs′-) *n.* The maintenance of the correct proportions of water and salts in the body of a living animal. [OSMO(SIS) + REGULATION.] **—os·mo·reg·u·la·to·ry** (ŏz′mə-rĕg′yə-lə-tôr′ē, -tōr′ē, ŏs′-) *adj.*

os·mose (ŏz′mōs′, ŏs′-) *v.* **-mosed, -mosing, -moses.** —*intr.* To undergo or diffuse by osmosis. —*tr.* To subject to osmosis. [From OSMOSIS, taken to be the common element of *exosmose* and *endosmose,* obsolete forms of EXOSMOSIS and ENDOSMOSIS.]

os·mo·sis (ŏz-mō′sĭs, ŏs-) *n.* **1. a.** The diffusion of fluid through a semipermeable membrane until there is an equal concentration of fluid on both sides of the membrane. **b.** The tendency of fluids to diffuse in such a manner. **2.** A gradual, often unconscious process

oryx *A long-horned antelope, the oryx is found in the deserts of Africa and Arabia. The points of its ringed horns are so sharp that they were once used by African peoples for the tips of spears. This is the Arabian oryx.*

Osiris *The ancient Egyptian god of the underworld, Osiris was also the god of fertility, responsible for the annual flooding of the Nile.*

of assimilation or absorption that resembles fluid osmosis: *learning a language by osmosis.* [Earlier *osmose,* from Greek *ōsmos,* action of pushing, from *ōthein,* to push.] **—os·mot·ic** (ŏz-mŏt′ĭk, ŏs-) *adj.* **—os·mot·i·cal·ly** *adv.*

osmotic pressure *n.* The pressure developed across a semipermeable membrane as a result of osmosis. For a given solution it is the pressure required to prevent osmosis from the solution to a pure solvent, such as water.

os·mous (ŏz′məs) *adj.* Also **os·mi·ous** (ŏz′mē-əs). Of, pertaining to, or containing osmium. Said especially of compounds containing osmium with a low valence.

os·mun·da (ŏz-mŭn′də) *n.* Also **os·mund** (ŏz′mənd). Any fern of the genus *Osmunda,* having erect compound fronds and in some species fibrous roots used as a potting medium for cultivated plants. [Middle English, from Old French *osmunde*†.]

osprey Pandion haliaetus, *the fish hawk, or osprey, feeds largely on fish, diving in a long, looping plunge onto lakes and rivers to pluck trout and even pike from the water with its talons.*

os·prey (ŏs′prē, -prā′) *n., pl.* **-preys. 1.** A fish-eating hawk, *Pandion haliaetus,* having plumage that is dark on the back and white below. Also called "fish eagle," "fish hawk," "ossifrage." **2.** A decorative feather formerly used to trim women's hats. [Middle English *ospray,* from Old French *ospreit* (unattested), from Vulgar Latin *avispreda* (unattested), from Latin *avis praedae,* "bird of prey" : *avis,* bird + *praeda,* prey. The Old French form and meaning are influenced by Old French *osfraie,* from Latin *ossifraga,* OSSIFRAGE.]

os·sa. Plural of **os** (bone).

os·se·in (ŏs′ē-ĭn) *n.* The protein residue of bone after acid dissolution, used in gelatin and glue. [OSSE(OUS) + -IN.]

os·se·ous (ŏs′ē-əs) *adj.* Composed of, containing, or resembling bone; bony. [Latin *osseus,* from *os,* bone.] **—os·se·ous·ly** *adv.*

Os·set (ŏs′ĭt, ŏ-sĕt′) *n.* Also **Os·sete** (ŏs′ēt′, ŏ-sēt′). A member of a people of Iranian origin living in Ossetia, a region in the southwestern U.S.S.R. that straddles the Caucasus Mountains. **—Os·se·tian** (ŏ-sē′shən) *n. & adj.*

Os·set·ic (ŏ-sĕt′ĭk) *n.* The Iranian language of the Ossets. *~adj.* Of or pertaining to the Ossets, their country, or their language.

os·si·a (ō-sē′ə) *conj. Music.* Or else. Used as a direction to the performer to indicate an alternative and often easier section or passage. [Italian, from *o sia,* "or let it be."]

Os·sian (ŏsh′ən, ŏs′ē-ən) (*c.* 3rd century A.D.). Legendary Irish warrior-poet. He occurs in the Fianna cycle of ballads under the name of Oisin.

os·si·cle (ŏs′ĭ-kəl) *n. Anatomy.* A small bone; especially, any of the three sound-conducting bones, the malleus, incus, and stapes, of the inner ear. [Latin *ossiculum,* diminutive of *os,* bone.] **—os·sic·u·lar** (ŏ-sĭk′yə-lər), **os·sic·u·late** (-lĭt, -lāt′) *adj.*

os·si·fi·ca·tion (ŏs′ə-fĭ-kā′shən) *n.* **1.** The natural process of bone formation. Also called "osteogenesis." **2. a.** The abnormal hardening or calcification of soft tissue into a bonelike material. **b.** A mass or deposit of such material. **3.** The process of becoming or state of being set in a rigidly conventional pattern, as of behavior, habits, or beliefs. **—os·sif·i·ca·to·ry** (ŏ-sĭf′ĭ-kə-tôr′ē, -tōr′ē) *adj.*

os·si·frage (ŏs′ə-frĭj, -frāj′) *n.* Either of two hawks, the **osprey** or the **lammergeier** *(both of which see).* [Latin *(avis) ossifraga,* "bone-breaking (bird)," lammergeier (which is said to drop its prey from a height to break the bones), from *ossifragus,* bone-breaking : *os* (stem *oss-*), bone + *frangere,* to break.]

os·si·fy (ŏs′ə-fī′) *v.* **-fied, -fying, -fies.** *—intr.* **1.** To change into bone; become bony. **2.** To become set in a rigidly conventional pattern, as of behavior or attitude. *—tr.* **1.** To make or form bone in or of; convert (a membrane or cartilage, for example) into bone. **2.** To mold into a rigidly conventional pattern, as of behavior or attitude. [Latin *os* (stem *oss-*), bone + -FY.] **—os·sif·ic** (ŏ-sĭf′ĭk) *adj.*

os·so bu·co (ō′sō bo͞o′kō, ŏs′ō) *n.* A dish of Italian origin that consists of shin of veal braised in white wine with tomatoes and spices. [Italian *ossobuco,* marrowbone.]

os·su·ar·y (ŏsh′o͞o-ĕr′ē, ŏs′yo͞o-) *n., pl.* **-ies.** A container or receptacle, such as an urn or vault, for holding the bones of the dead. [Late Latin *ossuārium,* from Latin, neuter of *ossuārius,* of bones, from *ossu,* variant of *os* (stem *oss-*), bone.]

os·te·al (ŏs′tē-əl) *adj.* **1.** Bony; osseous. **2.** Pertaining to bone or to the skeleton. [OSTE(O)- + -AL.]

os·te·ich·thy·es (ŏs′tē-ĭk′thē-ēz′) *n.* A class of fish having an endoskeleton made of bone, an air bladder or lungs, and gills covered by an operculum.

os·te·i·tis (ŏs′tē-ī′tĭs) *n.* Inflammation of bone or bony tissue. [New Latin : OSTE(O)- + -ITIS.]

Os·tend (ŏ-stĕnd′, ŏs′tĕnd′). Seaport of northwestern Belgium. In West Flanders province, it is the country's third-largest port, the base of its fishing fleet, and the terminal of a ferry service across the English Channel to Dover.

os·ten·si·ble (ŏ-stĕn′sə-bəl) *adj.* Represented or appearing as such but often falsely or misleadingly; seeming; apparent: *His ostensible purpose was charity, his real goal popularity.* [French, from Medieval Latin *ostensibilis,* from Latin *ostendere,* to show : *ob-,* before + *tendere,* to stretch.] **—os·ten·si·bly** *adv.*

os·ten·sive (ŏ-stĕn′sĭv) *adj.* **1. a.** Ostensible; apparent. **b.** Indicating meaning by a direct example of the term being defined. Said of a definition. **2.** Obviously or manifestly demonstrative. [Late Latin *ostensīvus,* from Latin *ostensus,* past participle of *ostendere,* to show. See **ostensible.**] **—os·ten·sive·ly** *adv.*

os·ten·so·ri·um (ŏs′tən-sôr′ē-əm, -sōr′ē-əm) *n., pl.* **-soria** (-sôr′ē-ə, -sōr′ē-ə). Also **os·ten·so·ry** (ŏ-stĕn′sə-rē), *pl.* **-ries.** *Roman Catholic Church.* A receptacle in which the Host is exposed for adoration; a monstrance. [Medieval Latin *ostensōrium,* from Latin *ostendere,* to show. See **ostensible.**]

os·ten·ta·tion (ŏs′tĕn-tā′shən, ŏs′tən-) *n.* **1.** Pretentious, gaudy, or showy display, often meant to impress others. **2.** *Archaic.* An act of showing; exhibition. [Middle English *ostentacioun,* from Old French *ostentation,* from Latin *ostentātiō* (stem *ostentātiōn-*), from *ostentāre,* frequentative of *ostendere,* to show. See **ostensible.**]

os·ten·ta·tious (ŏs′tĕn-tā′shəs, ŏs′tən-) *adj.* Characterized by or given to ostentation; pretentiously showy. —See Synonyms at **ornate.** **—os·ten·ta·tious·ly** *adv.* **—os·ten·ta·tious·ness** *n.*

osteo–, oste– *prefix.* Indicates bone or bones; for example, **osteomyelitis, osteoid.** [Greek, from *osteon,* bone.]

osteo. osteopath; osteopathy.

os·te·o·ar·thri·tis (ŏs′tē-ō-är-thrī′tĭs) *n.* Degenerative joint disease caused by destruction of joint cartilage and characterized by pain and impaired mobility of the affected joint.

os·te·o·blast (ŏs′tē-ə-blăst′) *n.* A cell from which bone develops. [OSTEO- + -BLAST.] **—os·te·o·blas·tic** (ŏs′tē-ə-blăs′tĭk) *adj.*

os·te·oc·la·sis (ŏs′tē-ŏk′lə-sĭs) *n.* **1.** The surgical fracture of a bone, performed to correct a deformity. **2.** The dissolution and resorption of bony tissue. [New Latin : OSTEO- + Greek *klasis,* breakage (see **-clase**).]

os·te·o·clast (ŏs′tē-ə-klăst′) *n.* **1.** An instrument used in surgical osteoclasis. **2.** A large multinuclear cell that resorbs bony tissue in osteoclasis. [OSTEO- + -CLAST.] **—os·te·o·clas·tic** *adj.*

os·te·o·cra·ni·um (ŏs′tē-ō-krā′nē-əm) *n.* The ossified embryonic cranium as distinguished from the **chondrocranium** *(see).* **—os·te·o·cra·ni·al** *adj.*

os·te·o·cyte (ŏs′tē-ə-sīt′) *n.* A bone cell. [OSTEO- + -CYTE.]

os·te·o·gen·e·sis (ŏs′tē-ō-jĕn′ə-sĭs) *n.* **Ossification** *(see).*

os·te·o·gen·ic sarcoma (ŏs′tē-ō-jĕn′ĭk) *n.* An **osteosarcoma** *(see).*

os·te·oid (ŏs′tē-oid′) *adj.* Resembling bone. [OSTE(O)- + -OID.]

os·te·ol·o·gy (ŏs′tē-ŏl′ə-jē) *n.* **1.** The anatomical study of bones. **2.** The bone structure or system of an animal. [Greek *osteologia* : OSTEO- + -LOGY.] **—os·te·o·log·i·cal** (ŏs′tē-ə-lŏj′ĭ-kəl) *adj.* **—os·te·ol·o·gist** *n.*

os·te·o·ma (ŏs′tē-ō′mə) *n., pl.* **-mas** or **-mata** (-mə-tə). A benign bony tumor. [OSTE(O)- + -OMA.]

os·te·o·ma·la·cia (ŏs′tē-ō-mə-lā′shə, -shē-ə) *n.* Softening of the bones because of a deficiency of vitamin D or of calcium. [New Latin : OSTEO- + *malacia,* softness, from Greek *malakia,* from *malakos,* soft.]

os·te·o·my·e·li·tis (ŏs′tē-ō-mī′ə-lī′tĭs) *n.* Inflammation of the bone marrow due to infection.

os·te·o·path (ŏs′tē-ə-păth′) *n.* Also **os·te·op·a·thist** (ŏs′tē-ŏp′ə-thĭst). *Abbr.* **osteo.** One who practices osteopathy.

os·te·op·a·thy (ŏs′tē-ŏp′ə-thē) *n. Abbr.* **osteo.** A medical therapy relying on manipulative techniques and based on the theory that many diseases are caused or exacerbated by the displacement of bones, especially those of the spine, from their correct positions. [OSTEO- + -PATHY.] **—os·te·o·path·ic** (ŏs′tē-ə-păth′ĭk) *adj.* **—os·te·o·path·i·cal·ly** *adv.*

os·te·o·phyte (ŏs′tē-ə-fīt′) *n.* A small abnormal bony outgrowth, as one occurring in osteoarthritis. [OSTEO- + -PHYTE.] **—os·te·o·phyt·ic** (ŏs′tē-ə-fĭt′ĭk) *adj.*

os·te·o·plas·tic (ŏs′tē-ə-plăs′tĭk) *adj.* **1.** *Medicine.* Of or pertaining to osteoplasty. **2.** *Physiology.* Pertaining to or functioning in bone formation.

os·te·o·plas·ty (ŏs′tē-ə-plăs′tē) *n., pl.* **-ties.** The surgical repair or alteration of bone. [OSTEO- + -PLASTY.]

os·te·o·po·ro·sis (ŏs′tē-ō-pə-rō′sĭs) *n.* Brittleness and porosity of the bones, resulting in a liability to fracture. **—os·te·o·po·rot·ic** (ŏs′tē-ō-pə-rŏt′ĭk) *adj.*

os·te·o·sar·co·ma (ŏs′tē-ō-sär-kō′mə) *n.* A malignant bone tumor.

os·te·ot·o·my (ŏs′tē-ŏt′ə-mē) *n., pl.* **-mies.** The surgical division or sectioning of bone. [OSTEO- + -TOMY.] **—os·te·ot·o·mist** *n.*

Österreich. See **Austria.**

Os·ti·a (ŏs′tē-ə). Ancient city of Italy, at the mouth of the Tiber River. It was founded (4th century B.C.) as a protection for Rome, then developed (from the 1st century B.C.) as a port. The city began to decline in the 3rd century A.D.

os·ti·ar·y (ŏs′tē-ĕr′ē) *n., pl.* **-ies.** A doorkeeper at a church. [Latin *ōstiārius,* doorkeeper, from *ōstium,* an opening, from *ōs,* mouth.]

os·ti·na·to (ŏs′tĭ-nä′tō) *n., pl.* **-tos.** *Music.* A short melody or phrase that is constantly repeated in the same pitch. [Italian, "stubborn," from Latin *obstinātus,* OBSTINATE.]

os·ti·ole (ŏs′tē-ōl′) *n. Biology.* A small opening or pore, such as that in the fruiting body of certain fungi. [Latin *ōstiolum,* diminutive of *ōstium,* OSTIUM.] **—os·ti·o·lar** (ŏs′tē-ō′lər) *adj.*

os·ti·um (ŏs′tē-əm) *n., pl.* **-tia** (-tē-ə). *Biology.* A small opening; ostiole. [Latin *ōstium,* river mouth, opening, from *ōs,* mouth.]

os·tler (ŏs′lər) *n.* Also **hos·tler** (hŏs′lər, ŏs′-) *n.* One who takes charge of horses, as at an inn; a stableman. [16th-century contraction of HOSTELER.]

ost·mark (ôst′märk′, ŏst′-) *n. Abbr.* **OM.** Former name of the East German **mark.**

os·tra·cism (ŏs′trə-sĭz′əm) *n.* **1.** Banishment or exclusion from a group; disgrace. **2.** In Athens and other city states of ancient Greece, the temporary banishment by popular vote of a citizen considered dangerous to the state. **3. a.** The act of ostracizing. **b.** The state or condition of being ostracized. [French *ostracisme,* from Greek *ostrakismos,* from *ostrakizein,* to OSTRACIZE.]

PRONUNCIATION KEY

ă, pat; ā, pay; âr, care;
ä, father, are; b, bib;
ch, church; d, deed; ĕ, pet;
ē, be; f, fife; g, gag; h, hat;
hw, which; ĭ, pit; ī, pie;
îr, pier; j, judge; k, kick;
l, lid, needle; m, mum;
n, no, sudden; ng, thing;
ŏ, pot; ō, toe; ô, paw, for;
oi, noise; ou, out; o͝o, book;
o͞o, boot; p, pop; r, roar;
s, sauce; sh, ship, dish;
t, tight; th, thin, path;
th, this, bathe; ŭ, cut; ûr, fur;
v, valve; w, with; y, yes;
z, zebra, size; zh, vision;
ə, about, item, edible,
gallop, circus, peaceful

IN FOREIGN WORDS:

à, *Fr.* ami; œ, *Fr.* feu, *Ger.* schön; ü, *Fr.* tu, *Ger.* über; KH, *Ger.* ich, *Scot.* loch; N, *Fr.* bon; y′, *Fr.* Compiègne

STRESS MARKS:

Primary stress: ′
in·cite′ (ĭn-sīt′)
Secondary stress: ′
in′sight′ (ĭn′sīt′)

os·tra·cize (ŏs′trə-sīz′) *tr.v.* **-cized, -cizing, -cizes. 1.** To banish or exclude from a group; shut out; shun. **2.** To banish by ostracism, as in ancient Greece. [Greek *ostrakizein,* from *ostrakon,* shell, shard (see **ostracon**).]

os·tra·cod (ŏs′trə-kŏd′) *n.* Any of various minute, chiefly freshwater crustaceans of the order Ostracoda, having a bivalve carapace. [New Latin *ostracoda,* from Greek *ostrakōdēs,* testaceous, from *ostrakon,* shell.]

os·tra·con (ŏs′trə-kŏn′) *n., pl.* **-ca** (-kə). A fragment of pottery used in ancient Athens when voting for the ostracism of a citizen. [Greek *ostrakon,* potsherd.]

os·trich (ŏs′trĭch, ô′strĭch) *n., pl.* **-triches** or collectively **ostrich. 1. a.** Any of various large, flightless African birds of the genus *Struthio,* especially *S. camelus,* characterized by a long, bare neck and legs, two-toed feet, and plumage often used for decoration and brushes. **b.** A similar bird, the **rhea** *(see).* **2.** A person who refuses to accept reality or tries to avoid disagreeable situations by refusing to confront them. [Middle English *ostriche,* from Old French *ostrusce,* from Vulgar Latin *avistrūthius* (unattested) : Latin *avis,* bird + Late Latin *strūthiō,* ostrich, from Greek *struthiōn* (see **struthious**).]

ostrich fern *n.* A fern, *Matteuccia struthiopteris,* of northern temperate regions, having long, plumelike fronds.

Os·tro·goth (ŏs′trə-gŏth′) *n.* A member of a tribe of eastern Goths that conquered and ruled Italy from A.D. 493 to 555. [Late Latin *Ostrogothis* : *ostro-,* eastward + *Gothus,* GOTH.] **—Os·tro·goth·ic** (ŏs′trə-gŏth′ĭk) *adj.*

Os·trov·sky (ō-strôf′skē), **Alexandr Nikolayevich** (1823–86). Russian dramatist. Often regarded in the U.S.S.R. as the greatest Russian playwright, he wrote more than 50 plays, of which the best known is *The Storm* (1860).

Os·ty·ak, Os·ti·ak (ŏs′tē-ăk′) *n.* **1.** A member of a Finno-Ugric people inhabiting western Siberia. **2.** The Ugric language spoken by this people. **—Os′ty·ak** *adj.*

OSU, O.S.U. Order of St. Ursula.

Os·wald (ŏz′wôld′), **Lee Harvey** (1939–63). Alleged assassin of President John F. Kennedy (November 22, 1963). Oswald was shot and killed two days later by Jack Ruby, a Dallas nightclub owner.

Oś·wię·cim (ôsh-vyĕn′sĕm). German *Ausch·witz* (oush′vĭts). Town of southern Poland. At the confluence of the Iola and Vistula rivers, it is near the site of the Auschwitz-Birkenau extermination camp, where, between 1942 and 1945, some 4,000,000 people, mostly German and East European Jews, were systematically put to death by the Nazis.

OT, O.T. Old Testament.

ot–. Variant of **oto-.**

o·tal·gia (ō-tăl′jə, -jē-ə) *n. Medicine.* Earache. [OT(O)- + -ALGIA.]

OTC, O.T.C. Officers' Training Corps.

oth·er (ŭth′ər) *adj.* **1. a.** Being or designating the remaining one of two or more: *the other ear.* **b.** Being or designating the remaining ones of several: *His other books are still in storage.* **2.** Different from that or those implied or specified: *Any other person would tell the truth. Call me some other time.* **3.** Of a different character or quality: *He has no friends other than classmates.* **4.** Of a different time or era either future or past: *other centuries; other generations.* **5.** Additional; extra: *I have no other shoes.* **6.** Opposite or contrary; reverse: *the other side.* **7.** Alternate; second: *every other day.* **8.** Recent but unspecified: *the other day; the other morning.*
—n. **1. a.** The remaining one of two or more: *One took a taxi, the other walked home.* **b. others.** The remaining ones of several: *After her departure the others resumed the discussion.* **2. a.** A different person or thing: *I don't want this toy, I want the other.* **b.** An additional person or thing: *How many others will come later?*
—pron. A different or another person or thing: *Others may disapprove, but who cares? He told me something or other, but I can't remember what it was.*
—adv. In another way; otherwise or differently: *She never performs other than perfectly. I felt a bit queasy, but other than that I was not carsick.* [Middle English *other,* Old English *ōther.*]

oth·er-di·rect·ed (ŭth′ər-dĭ-rĕk′tĭd, -dī-rĕk′tĭd) *adj.* Guided by the values of others, as one's peers or society at large, rather than by independent personal principles: *an other-directed personality.* Compare **inner-directed, tradition-directed. —oth·er·di·rect·ed·ness** *n.*

oth·er·ness (ŭth′ər-nĭs) *n.* The quality or condition of being different, distinct, or unusual.

oth·er·wise (ŭth′ər-wīz′) *adv.* **1.** In another way; differently: *She thought otherwise.* **2.** Under other circumstances: *Otherwise I might have helped.* **3.** In other respects: *an otherwise logical mind.*
—conj. If not: *Get going, otherwise they'll catch you.*
—adj. Other than supposed; different: *The evidence is otherwise.* [Middle English *otherwise,* Old English *(on) ōthre wīsan,* (in) another manner : *ōther,* OTHER + *wīse,* way, -WISE.]

oth·er·world (ŭth′ər-wûrld′) *n.* A world beyond earthly reality.

oth·er·world·ly (ŭth′ər-wûrld′lē) *adj.* **1.** Of, pertaining to, or characteristic of another world, especially a mystical or transcendental world. **2.** Devoted to the world of the mind; concerned with intellectual or imaginative things rather than with practical realities. **—oth·er·world·li·ness** *n.*

o·tic (ō′tĭk) *adj.* Of, pertaining to, or located near the ear; auricular. [Greek *ōtikos,* from *ous* (stem *ōt-*), ear.]

-otic *suffix.* Indicates: **1.** Affected with or by; for example, **sclerotic. 2.** Having a specific disease; for example, **epizootic. 3.** Producing or causing; for example, **narcotic.** [Old French *-otique* and

Latin *-ōticus,* from Greek *-ōtikos,* adjectival suffix formed from *-o-* stem verbs and *-ōt-* stem nouns.]

o·ti·ose (ō′shē-ōs′, ō′tē-) *adj.* **1.** Having no real use; purposeless. **2.** Ineffective; futile. **3.** Having a lazy nature; indolent. [Latin *ōtiōsus,* from *ōtium†,* leisure. See also **negotiate.**] **—o·ti·ose·ly** *adv.* **—o·ti·os·i·ty** (ō′shē-ŏs′ə-tē, ō′tē-) *n.*

O·tis (ō′tĭs), **Elisha Graves** (1811–61). U.S. inventor, best known for inventing the safety elevator (1852), which he demonstrated (1854) by severing the cable of an elevator in which he was riding.

Otis, James (1725–83). U.S. Revolutionary politician in Massachusetts. He was strongly in favor of the rights of the colonists, but did not believe in violence against the British or separation from Great Britain. His speeches and pamphlets were, however, influential in fueling the rising feeling against the British.

o·ti·tis (ō-tī′tĭs) *n.* Inflammation of the ear; especially, inflammation of the middle ear, causing pain and impaired hearing. [New Latin : OT(O)- + -ITIS.] **—o·tit·ic** (ō-tĭt′ĭk) *adj.*

oto–, ot– *prefix.* Indicates the ear; for example, **otology.** [New Latin, from Greek *ous* (stem *ōt-*), ear.]

o·to·cyst (ō′tə-sĭst′) *n.* **1.** The structure in the skull of a vertebrate embryo that develops into the inner ear. **2.** An organ of balance, the statocyst *(see).* **—o·to·cys·tic** (ō′tə-sĭs′tĭk) *adj.*

otol. otology.

o·to·lar·yn·gol·o·gy (ō′tō-lăr′ĭng-gŏl′ə-jē) *n.* The branch of medicine concerned with diseases of the ear and throat. [OTO- + LARYNGO- + -LOGY.] **—o·to·lar·yn·go·log·i·cal** (ō′tō-lə-rĭng′gə-lŏj′ĭ-kəl) *adj.* **—o·to·lar·yn·gol·o·gist** *n.*

o·to·lith (ō′tə-lĭth′) *n.* Any of many minute calcareous particles found in the inner ear of certain vertebrates and in the statocysts of numerous invertebrates. [French *otolithe* : OTO- + -LITH.]

o·tol·o·gy (ō-tŏl′ə-jē) *n. Abbr.* **otol.** The anatomy, physiology, and pathology of the ear. [OTO- + -LOGY.] **—o·to·log·i·cal** (ō′tə-lŏj′ĭ-kəl) *adj.* **—o·tol·o·gist** *n.*

o·to·rhi·no·lar·yn·gol·o·gy (ō′tō-rī′nō-lăr′ĭng-gŏl′ə-jē) *n.* The branch of medicine concerned with diseases of the ear, nose, and throat. [OTO- + RHINO- + LARYNGO- + -LOGY.] **—o·to·rhi·no·la·ryn·go·log·i·cal** (ō′tō-rī′nō-lə-rĭng′gə-lŏj′ĭ-kəl) *adj.* **—o·to·rhi·no·lar·yn·gol·o·gist** *n.*

o·to·scope (ō′tə-skōp′) *n.* An instrument for examining the eardrum and the passage in the outer ear leading to it. [OTO- + -SCOPE.] **—o·to·scop·ic** (ō′tə-skŏp′ĭk) *n.*

ottar. Variant of **attar.**

ot·ta·va (ō-tä′və) *adv. Music.* At an octave higher or lower than indicated. Used as a direction. [Italian.]

ottava ri·ma (rē′mə) *n.* A stanza form perfected by the poets Ariosto and Tasso that consists of eight lines of eleven syllables each in iambic pentameter and has a rhyme pattern *ababbcc.* [Italian, "eighth rhyme."]

Ot·ta·wa¹ (ŏt′ə-wə, -wä′, -wô′) *n., pl.* **-was** or collectively **Ottawa. 1.** A member of a North American Indian people, originally inhabiting the region of the Ottawa River in Ontario, Canada. **2.** The Ojibwa dialect of this people, of the Algonquian family of languages. **—Ot·ta·wa** *adj.*

Ottawa². Capital of Canada. Founded (1827) as Bytown on the Ottawa River, in the southeast of the country, it became the capital in 1867. The industrial development along the Ottawa valley, of which the city is the center, rests mainly on sawmilling and timber. One third of the population is French-speaking.

Ottawa³. River of eastern Canada. The principal tributary of the St. Lawrence, it rises in the Laurentian plateau of western Quebec and flows 1,120 kilometers (696 miles) west to join the St. Lawrence west of Montreal.

ot·ter (ŏt′ər) *n., pl.* **-ters** or collectively **otter. 1.** Any of various aquatic, carnivorous mammals of the family Mustelidae, such as *Lutra lutra,* the Eurasian otter, having webbed feet and dense, darkbrown fur. **2.** The fur of any of these animals. [Middle English *oter,* Old English *otor.*] **—ot·ter** *adj.*

ot·ter·hound (ŏt′ər-hound′) *n.* A dog of a British breed formerly used to hunt otters. It is a good swimmer and is strongly built, with a large head and long drooping ears.

otter shrew *n.* Any of various small, otterlike semiaquatic mammals of the family Potamogalidae, of western and central Africa.

otto. Variant of **attar.**

Ot·to I (ŏt′ō), also called "Otto the Great" (912–73). King of Germany (936–73); first Holy Roman Emperor (962–73).

Otto, Nikolaus August (1832–91). German engineer. His invention of the internal-combustion engine (1876) facilitated the development of the automobile.

Otto cycle *n.* A cycle of changes in a heat engine in which heat is produced and lost at constant volume, approximately applicable to a four-stroke gasoline engine. [After N.A. OTTO.]

ot·to·man (ŏt′ə-mən) *n., pl.* **-mans. 1. a.** An upholstered sofa or divan without arms or a back. **b.** An upholstered low seat or cushioned footstool. **2.** A heavy silk or rayon fabric with a corded texture, usually used for coats and trimmings. [French *ottomane,* feminine of OTTOMAN.]

Ot·to·man (ŏt′ə-mən) *n., pl.* **-mans.** A Turk, especially a Turk of the Ottoman Empire.
—adj. **1.** Of or pertaining to the Turks; Turkish. **2.** Of or pertaining to the Ottoman Empire and the dynasty founded by Osman I. [French, from Medieval Latin *Ottomānus,* from Arabic *Othmānī,* Turkish, from Turkish *Osman,* Osman I. See **Osmanli.**]

Ottoman Empire. An empire of the eastern Mediterranean. Span-

ostrich *The world's largest living bird cannot fly, but it can run up to 65 kilometers (40 miles) per hour. A male ostrich can be as much as 2.5 meters (8 feet) tall and can weigh up to 140 kilograms (300 pounds).*

ning over six hundred years (1300–1922), it started as a small enclave of Osmanli Turks, replaced the Byzantine Empire in Asia Minor, and during the 16th and 17th centuries included the Levant, Mesopotamia, much of North Africa, and southeastern Europe to the borders of Austria. By the end of World War I it had lost all its possessions outside Turkey, where it was finally overthrown by revolution.

Ottoman Turkish *n.* The form of Turkish used by the Ottoman Turks. Also called "Osmanli."

oua·ba·in (wä-bā′ĭn, wä′băn′) *n.* A white poisonous glucoside, $C_{29}H_{44}O_{12} \cdot 8H_2O$, extracted from the seeds of the African trees *Strophanthus gratus* and *Acokanthera ouabaio.* It is used as a heart stimulant and by some African peoples as a dart poison. [French *ouaba(io),* from Somali *wabayo.*]

Oua·ga·dou·gou (wä′gə-dōō′gōō). Capital of Upper Volta. Founded in the 11th century, in the heart of the country, it was once the center of a Mossi empire.

ou·bli·ette (ōō′blē-ĕt′) *n.* A dungeon with a trap door in the ceiling as its only means of entrance or exit. [French, from *oublier,* to forget, from Old French *oblier,* from Vulgar Latin *oblītāre* (unattested), from Latin *oblīviscī* (past participle *oblītus*), to forget.]

ouch¹ (ouch) *interj.* **1.** Used to express sudden pain. **2.** Used to express embarrassment, as on realizing an error one has made. **3.** Used to express pretended distaste, as on hearing a poor joke.

ouch² *n.* **1.** A setting for a precious stone. **2.** A brooch or ornament set with jewels. **3.** *Obsolete.* A clasp or brooch. [Middle English *ouche,* from the phrase *an ouche,* mistaken division of *a nouche,* from Old French *nouche,* brooch, from Frankish *nuskja.*]

oud (ōōd) *n.* A musical instrument of northern Africa and southwestern Asia resembling a lute. [Arabic *ūd,* "wood."]

Ou·de·naar·de (ōō′də-när′də). Town in East Flanders province, western Belgium. Here in 1708, during the War of the Spanish Succession, an allied army led by Eugene of Savoy and the Duke of Marlborough defeated the French.

ou·gui·ya (ōō-gē′ä) *n., pl.* **ouguiya.** The basic monetary unit of Mauritania. See feature at **currency.** [Native word in Mauritania.]

ought¹ (ôt) *v.* Used as an auxiliary followed by an infinitive with *to.* It can indicate: **1.** Obligation or duty: *You ought to work harder*

than that. **2.** Expediency or prudence: *You ought to wear a raincoat in this weather.* **3.** Desirability: *You ought to have been there; it was great fun.* **4.** Probability or likelihood: *She ought to have it finished by next week.* [Middle English *aghten, oughten,* to be obliged to, owe, from *aghte, oughte,* possessed, owned, Old English *āhte,* first and third singular past indicative of *āgan,* to possess.]

Usage: Sometimes the infinitive following *ought* is omitted if it is understood from the context: *Should we begin soon? We ought to. Ought,* used without *to,* is improper in such combinations as: *He ought and can come* (properly *can and ought to*); *He ought and could have come* (properly *could and ought to have*). *Ought* is not inflected. With a present infinitive, it expresses present time: *He ought to go.* Past time is indicated by the perfect infinitive: *He ought to have gone.* Negation is accomplished by using *not* immediately after *ought: ought not to have gone.* Auxiliary verbs such as *did, had, should,* and *could* are never used with *ought.* Thus, *He ought to write* (not *had ought*); *He ought not to complain* (not *hadn't ought* or *shouldn't ought*).

ought². *Regional.* Variant of **aught.**

ought³ *n. Obsolete.* Alternate past participle of **owe.**

Oui·ja (wē′jə, -jē) *n.* A trademark for a board with the alphabet and other symbols on it and a planchette that is thought, when touched with the fingers, especially by several people, to move in such a way as to spell out spiritualistic and telepathic messages on the board. [French *oui,* yes + German *ja,* yes.]

ounce¹ (ouns) *n. Abbr.* **os 1. a.** A unit of weight in the U.S. Customary System, an avoirdupois unit equal to 437.5 grains or 28.350 grams. **b.** A unit of apothecary weight equal to 480 grains or 31.103 grams. **2. a.** A unit of volume or capacity in the U.S. Customary System used in liquid measure and equal to 8 fluid drams or 29.573 milliliters. **b.** A unit of volume or capacity in the British Imperial System used in dry and liquid measure and equal to 1.734 cubic inches or 28.412 milliliters. **3.** A very small quantity or portion; bit. [Middle English *unce,* from Old French, from Latin *uncia,* a twelfth, ounce, from *ūnus,* unit, one.]

ounce² *n.* The **snow leopard** (*see*). [Middle English *once,* from Old French, variant of *lonce* (the *l* being taken as the definite article), from Latin *lynx* (stem *lync-*), lynx, from Greek *lunx.*]

our (our, är) *pron.* The possessive form of *we.* Used attributively to indicate possession or the recipient or agent of an action: *our house; our questioning of the witness; our defeat.* [Middle English *ure, oure,* Old English *ūre.*]

-our. *British.* Variant of **-or** (state, quality, or activity).

Our Father *n.* The **Lord's Prayer** (*see*).

Our Lady *n.* The Virgin Mary.

ours (ourz, ärz) *pron.* Possessive pronoun, absolute form of *our.* **1.** Belonging to us; for us; our own: *The house is ours.* **2.** The one or ones belonging or pertaining to us: *They couldn't find their hats so they took ours. Ours is the best.* **—of ours.** Belonging or pertaining to us: *a friend of ours.* [Middle English *ures, oures,* from *ure, oure,* OUR.]

our·self (our-sĕlf′, är-) *pron.* Myself or ourselves collectively. A specialized form corresponding to *ourselves* but used only in regal or formal proclamations or editorial comments with the formal *we* understood as singular.

our·selves (our-sĕlvz′, är-) *pron.* A specialized form of the first person plural pronoun. It is used: **1.** As a reflexive pronoun, forming the direct or indirect object of a verb or the object of a preposition: *We injured ourselves; gave ourselves time; talked among ourselves.* **2.** For emphasis after *we: We ourselves are excluded from the contract.* **3.** As an emphasizing substitute: *The Smiths and ourselves are in trouble. She invited only Tom and ourselves. Ourselves in debt, we couldn't help you.* **4.** As an indication of our normal, real, or healthy condition or identity: *We have not been ourselves lately.*

-ous *suffix.* Indicates: **1.** Possessing, having, or full of; for example, **cancerous, joyous.** **2.** *Chemistry.* Occurring with a valence that is lower than that in a comparable *-ic* system; for example, **ferrous, osmous.** Compare **-ic.** [Middle English, from Old French *-os, -us, -eus, -eux,* from Latin *-ōsus, -us,* adjectival suffixes.]

Ouse (ōōz). Any of four rivers of England: **1.** The **Great Ouse** (*see*). **2.** The **Yorkshire Ouse.** Formed by the Swale and Ure rivers, it flows 100 kilometers (60 miles) to join the Trent River, forming the Humber estuary on the northeast coast. **3.** The **Ouse.** Rising in the South Downs, it flows 48 kilometers (30 miles) across Sussex to enter the English Channel at Newhaven. **4.** The **Little Ouse.** Rising in the Gog Magog hills of Suffolk, it flows north and west across Norfolk to join the Great Ouse at the Cambridgeshire border.

ousel. Variant of **ouzel.**

oust (oust) *tr.v.* **ousted, ousting, ousts. 1.** To eject from a position or place; force out; displace. **2.** *Law.* To deprive of land or property. **3.** To take the place of, especially by force; supplant. [Norman French *ouster,* from Latin *obstāre,* to hinder : *ob-,* off, against + *stāre,* to stand.]

oust·er (ou′stər) *n.* **1.** One that ousts. **2.** *Law.* **a.** The act of forcing someone out of possession or occupancy of material property to which he is entitled. Also used adjectively: *an ouster injunction.* **b.** Illegal or wrongful dispossession. **3. a.** The act of ousting. **b.** The state of being ousted. [Norman French, substantive use of the infinitive *ouster,* to OUST.]

out (out) *adv.* **1.** Away or forth from inside: *go out of the office.* **2. a.** Away from the center or middle: *The troops fanned out.* **b.** Away from somewhere considered as central: *They live out in the country.* **3.** Away from a normal or usual place: *stepped out for a*

THE TURKISH EMPIRE THAT LASTED 700 YEARS

Constantinople, capital of Byzantium, fell to Islamic invaders

The Ottoman Empire, largest and longest surviving of all Islamic states, was founded about 1300 by Osman, leader of a race of Turks who had migrated into Asia Minor from central Asia.

The Ottomans captured Constantinople in 1453 and ended the 1,000-year-old Byzantine Empire. In the next 150 years they overran much of eastern Europe and the Arab world and most of North Africa.

The Ottoman Empire enlarged its civil service and its army by training and compulsorily converting to Islam Christian slaves from their subject races. The elite corps of troops called Janissaries was made up of Christians.

In the 16th century the Ottomans were unable to match the technological progress of the European nations and their empire went into a long, slow decline. It finally came to an end after World War I; the Republic of Turkey was set up in 1923.

OTTOMAN ART *This boldly colored miniature is in a 16th-century manuscript telling of the victories of Suleiman the Magnificent. It shows the capture of Rhodes in 1522. Figures were forbidden in Islamic art, but Ottoman artists interpreted the ban loosely; manuscripts were not for public show and contain many human scenes.*

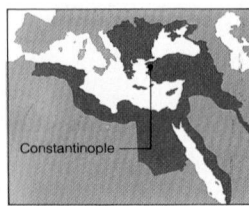

Constantinople—

EXTENT OF THE EMPIRE *The dark area shows the Ottoman Empire at its peak, soon after 1600.*

minute. **4.** Away from the coast: *The tide goes out at three o'clock.* **5.** From inside a building or shelter into the open air; outside: *The girl went out to play.* **6.** From within a container or source: *drain the water out.* **7. a.** To exhaustion or depletion: *The supplies have run out.* **b.** Into extinction or imperceptibility: *The fire has gone out.* **8. a.** To a finish or conclusion: *Hear me out.* **b.** Completely: *We fitted out the kitchen.* **9.** Into being or evident existence: *The new car models have come out.* **10.** Into view: *The moon came out.* **11.** Without inhibition; boldly: *Speak out.* **12.** Into the possession of another or others; into distribution: *giving out free passes.* **13.** Into disuse or an unfashionable status: *Knee-length hems have gone out.* **14.** So as to be unconscious or asleep: *went out like a light; knocked him out.* **15.** So as to embellish or complete a rough representation or version: *fill out the details.* **16.** So as to project: *stuck out her tongue.* **17.** From a state of harmony to one of discord: *I was very put out. The two friends fell out.* **18.** On strike: *The workers went out over pay and conditions.* **19.** *Informal.* Around; existing: *She's the best saxophone player out.* **20. a.** *Sports.* Incorrectly positioned or beyond a limit as defined by the rules: *He kept serving out.* **b.** *Baseball.* So as to be retired or counted as an out: *The batter grounded out to the shortstop.* **21.** So as to be part of or received into adult society, especially high society: *a debutante coming out the year after next.* **—out of. 1.** From among: *one out of thousands.* **2.** Past the boundaries or limits of: *The eagle soared out of sight.* **3.** With headquarters in: *She works out of the branch office.* **4.** From: *made out of wood.* **5.** Because of; owing to: *They did it out of malice.* **6.** Born of; foaled by. **7.** In or into a condition of no longer having: *We're out of coffee. She was tricked out of her savings.* **8.** Away from a usual place, state, or condition: *moving out of publishing; getting out of control.* **—out of it.** Not participating in an activity or belonging to a group; isolated.

∼adj. **1. a.** Outside: *She is out in the garden.* **b.** Not in the usual or expected place; absent: *She was out when I called.* **2.** Exhausted; depleted: *Our supplies are out.* **3.** Extinct or extinguished; imperceptible: *The fire is out.* **4.** Finished; concluded: *before the week is out.* **5. a.** In existence: *My new book is out.* **b.** In view; evident: *The daffodils are out.* **6.** No longer fashionable or in use: *Those hair styles are out.* **7.** Unconscious or asleep: *She's out for a good few hours.* **8.** Having left a courtroom to consider a verdict: *The jury is out.* **9.** On strike: *All our members are out.* **10. a.** *Sports.* Being in a correct position or beyond a limit as defined by the rules: *That last ball was out.* **b.** *Baseball.* Not allowed to continue to bat or run; retired. **11.** No longer in power or control: *After the election the conservatives were out.* **12.** *Informal.* Not allowed; prohibited: *Smoking here is out.* **13.** Not correct; inaccurate: *Your calculations were two millimeters out.* **14.** Having an outward destination; outgoing: *out mail.* **15.** Determined and desirous: *out to get you; out to win.* **16.** *Informal.* Without an amount possessed previously: *I am out ten dollars.* **17.** Not available for use or consideration: *Taking a taxi is out, because we haven't the money.* **18.** Bare or threadbare: *My jacket is out at the elbow.* **—out with it.** Used to demand that suppressed information be revealed. **—want out.** *Informal.* To wish to leave, escape, or be let out.

∼prep. Through; forth from: *I fell out the window.*

∼n. **1.** A means of escape: *The window was my only out.* **2.** *Baseball.* **a.** A play in which a batter or base runner is retired. **b.** The player retired in such a play. **3.** *Sports.* A serve or return that falls out of bounds in a court game, as tennis. **4.** A person or thing that is out; especially, one who is out of power. **5.** *Printing.* A word or other part of a manuscript omitted from the printed copy. **—on the outs** *Informal.* Not on friendly terms; disagreeing.

∼v. **outed, outing, outs.** *—intr.* To be disclosed or revealed; come out: *Truth will out.* *—tr.* **1.** To put (a person or thing) out. **2.** *British Slang.* To knock unconscious.

∼interj. **1.** Used to demand the departure of a person or animal, as from a room. **2.** Used by radio operators to indicate the end of transmission. **3.** Used in games such as tennis to declare a shot or ball out. [Middle English *out,* Old English *ūt.*]

out– *prefix.* Indicates: **1.** To a surpassing or greater degree; for example, **outplay, outshoot, outwork. 2.** Situated outside or externally; for example, **outboard, outhouse. 3.** Emerging or coming forth; for example, **outburst, outgrowth.** ***Note:*** Many compounds other than those entered here may be formed with *out-.* In forming compounds, *out-* is normally joined with the following element without space or hyphen: **outlive.** However, in formations (usually nonce words) in which the second element begins with a capital, the hyphen is used: *That jailbreaker could out-Houdini Houdini himself.* The separate word *out* also appears in a few phrases that are hyphenated. Those entered here are **out-and-out, out-group, out-of-bounds, out-of-date, out-of-door(s), out-of-phase, out-of-pocket, out-of-the-way, out-of-towner, and out-relief.**

out·age (ou'tĭj) *n.* **1.** A quantity or portion of something lacking after delivery or storage. **2.** A temporary suspension of operation, especially of electric power. [OUT + -AGE.]

out-and-out (out'n-out') *adj.* Complete; thoroughgoing: *an out-and-out swindler.* **—out-and-out** *adv.*

out·back (out'băk', -băk') *n.* The remote, rural, and underdeveloped area of a country; especially, the inland bush country of Australia or New Zealand. Also used adjectivally: *outback life.*

∼adv. In, to, or toward the outback. **—out·back·er** *n.*

out·bal·ance (out-băl'əns) *tr.v.* **-anced, -ancing, -ances.** To be more important than; outweigh.

out·bid (out-bĭd') *tr.v.* **-bid, -bidden** (-bĭd'n) or **-bid, -bidding, -bids.** To bid higher than: *She outbid her rivals at the auction.*

out·board (out'bôrd', -bōrd') *adj.* **1.** *Nautical.* **a.** Situated outside the hull of a vessel. **b.** Being away from the center line of the hull of a ship. **2.** *Aeronautics.* Situated toward or nearer the end of a wing.

∼n. **1.** An outboard motor. **2.** A boat with an outboard motor. **—out·board** *adv.*

outboard motor *n.* A detachable engine mounted on the stern of a boat or on outboard brackets.

out·bound (out'bound') *adj.* Outward bound; headed away: *The outbound train is always crowded during the rush hour.*

out·brave (out-brāv') *tr.v.* **-braved, -braving, -braves. 1.** To be braver than. **2.** To face or stand up to defiantly.

out·break (out'brāk') *n.* A sudden occurrence; an eruption: *an outbreak of arrests; an outbreak of measles.*

out·breed (out'brēd') *v.* **-bred** (-brĕd'), **-breeding, -breeds.** *—tr.* To subject to outbreeding. *—intr.* To produce offspring by outbreeding.

out·breed·ing (out'brē'dĭng) *n.* **1.** The breeding of distantly related or unrelated stocks of animals. **2.** *Anthropology.* The bearing of children by parents from different groups, often as a consequence of taboos against marriage within the group.

out·build·ing (out'bĭl'dĭng) *n.* An ancillary building detached from but associated with a main building.

out·burst (out'bûrst') *n.* A sudden, violent display, as of activity or passion; outpouring: *an outburst of spite.*

out·cast (out'kăst', -käst') *n.* One that has been excluded from a society or system; one that has been rejected. **—out·cast** *adj.*

out·caste (out'kăst', -käst') *n.* **1.** A Hindu who has been expelled from or has abandoned his caste. **2.** One who has no caste. **—out·caste** *adj.*

out·class (out-klăs', -kläs') *tr.v.* **-classed, -classing, -classes.** To surpass or defeat decisively, so as to appear of a higher class: *Her rival outclassed her in several categories, and she lost the championship.*

out·come (out'kŭm') *n.* A result or consequence. —See Synonyms at **effect.**

out·crop (out'krŏp') *n.* **1.** *Geology.* A portion of bedrock or other stratum protruding through the soil level. **2.** An emergence or outbreak: *an outcrop of labor unrest.*

∼intr.v. (out-krŏp') **outcropped, -cropping, -crops.** *Geology.* To protrude above the soil. Used of rock formations.

outcrop *Monument Valley, Utah, is rich in sandstone outcrops. This handlike formation is one of a pair of outcrops known as The Mittens.*

out·cross (out'krôs', -krŏs') *v.* **-crossed, -crossing, -crosses.** *—tr.* To breed (animals that belong to different strains of the same breed). *—intr.* To breed. Used of animals belonging to different strains of the same breed.

∼n. **1.** The process of outcrossing. **2.** An offspring produced by outcrossing.

out·cry (out'krī') *n., pl.* **-cries. 1.** A strong protest or objection: *public outcry over the government cuts.* **2.** A loud cry or clamor.

out·date (out-dāt') *tr.v.* **-dated, -dating, -dates.** To replace or make obsolete, antiquated, or old-fashioned.

out·dat·ed (out-dā'tĭd) *adj.* Out-of-date; antiquated.

out·dis·tance (out-dĭs'təns) *tr.v.* **-tanced, -tancing, -tances. 1.** To outrun, especially in a long-distance race. **2.** To surpass by a wide margin, especially through superior skill or endurance: *The veteran completely outdistanced the younger salesman.*

out·do (out-do͞o') *tr.v.* **-did** (-dĭd'), **-done** (-dŭn'), **-doing, -does** (-dŭz'). To exceed in performance; surpass. —See Synonyms at **excel.**

out·door (out'dôr', -dōr') *adj.* Also **out-of-door** (out'əv-dôr', -dōr'). Located in, done in, or suited to the open air.

out·doors (out-dôrz', -dōrz') *adv.* Also **out-of-doors** (out'əv-dôrz', -dōrz'). In or into the open; outside a house or shelter: *go outdoors for fresh air.*

∼n. Also **out-of-doors.** The open air; the area away from human habitation.

out·er (ou'tər) *adj.* **1.** Located on the outside; external. **2.** Farther from the center or middle.

outer ear *n.* The **external ear** *(see).*

Outer Hebrides. See **Hebrides.**

Outer Mongolia. See **Mongolian People's Republic.**

out·er·most (ou'tər-mōst') *adj.* Most distant from the center or inside; farthest out; outmost.

outer planet *n.* Any of the planets Jupiter, Saturn, Uranus, Neptune, or Pluto, whose orbit is beyond the asteroid belt. Compare **inner planet.**

outer space *n.* A region of space beyond limits determined with reference to the boundaries of a celestial body or system.

out·face (out-fās') *tr.v.* **-faced, -facing, -faces. 1.** To overcome with a bold or self-assured look; stare down. **2.** To defy; resist.

out·fall (out'fôl') *n.* The point where a sewer, drain, or stream discharges.

out·field (out'fēld') *n.* **1.** The grass-covered playing area extending outward from a baseball diamond and divided into right, center, and left fields. Compare **infield. 2.** The members of a baseball team playing in the outfield. **—out·field·er** *n.*

out·fit (out'fĭt') *n.* **1.** A set of tools or equipment for a specialized purpose: *a mountain-climber's outfit; a welder's outfit.* **2.** A set of clothing: *appear at the dance in an elegant outfit.* **3.** *Informal.* An association of persons, especially a military unit or a business organization. **4.** The act of equipping or fitting out.

∼v. **outfitted, -fitting, -fits.** *—tr.* To provide with an outfit: *This*

PRONUNCIATION KEY

ă, pat; ā, pay; âr, care; ä, father, are; b, bib; ch, church; d, deed; ĕ, pet; ē, be; f, fife; g, gag; h, hat; hw, which; ĭ, pit; ī, pie; îr, pier; j, judge; k, kick; l, lid, needle; m, mum; n, no, sudden; ng, thing; ŏ, pot; ō, toe; ô, paw, for; oi, noise; ou, out; o͝o, book; o͞o, boot; p, pop; r, roar; s, sauce; sh, ship, dish; t, tight; th, thin, path; *th,* this, bathe; ŭ, cut; ûr, fur; v, valve; w, with; y, yes; z, zebra, size; zh, vision; ə, about, item, edible, gallop, circus, peaceful

IN FOREIGN WORDS:

à, *Fr.* ami; œ, *Fr.* feu, *Ger.* schön; ü, *Fr.* tu, *Ger.* über; KH, *Ger.* ich, *Scot.* loch; N, *Fr.* bon; y', *Fr.* Compiègne

STRESS MARKS:

Primary stress: ' **in·cite'** (ĭn-sīt')
Secondary stress: ' **in'sight'** (ĭn'sīt')

shop outfits skiers. —*intr.* To acquire an outfit: *We outfitted for the expedition a week before departing.*

out·fit·ter (out′fĭt′ər) *n.* **1.** A shop that sells men's clothes; haberdasher. **2.** One who sells or provides outfits, as for camping expeditions.

out·flank (out-flăngk′) *tr.v.* **-flanked, -flanking, -flanks. 1.** To maneuver around and behind the flank of (an opposing force). **2.** To gain a tactical advantage over.

out·flow (out′flō′) *n.* **1.** The act of flowing out. **2.** Something that flows out. **3.** The amount flowing out.

out·fox (out-fŏks′) *tr.v.* **-foxed, -foxing, -foxes.** To be more cunning than; outwit.

out·gas (out′găs′, out-găs′) *v.* **-gassed, -gassing, -gasses.** *Physics.* —*tr.* To remove adsorbed gas from (a solid or liquid) by heating. —*intr.* To release gases.

out·go (out-gō′) *tr.v.* **-went** (-wĕnt′), **-gone** (-gôn′, -gŏn′), **-going, -goes** (-gōz′). To exceed; surpass.
~*n.* (out′gō′) *pl.* **outgoes. 1.** Something that goes out, especially expenditure or cost. **2.** The act of going out.

out·go·ing (out′gō′ĭng) *adj.* **1. a.** Going out; departing: *an outgoing steamship.* **b.** Retiring from or relinquishing a place, position, or office: *the outgoing president.* **2.** Friendly; sociable: *an outgoing personality.*

out·go·ings (out′gō′ĭngz) *pl.n.* Regular and unavoidable expenses, such as the payment of rent.

out·group (out′grŏŏp′) *n.* A group of people excluded from or not belonging to an in-group.

out·grow (out-grō′) *tr.v.* **-grew** (-grŏŏ′), **-grown** (-grōn′), **-growing, -grows. 1.** To grow too large for: *She outgrew her new suit.* **2.** To lose or discard in the course of maturation: *We outgrew our youthful idealism.* **3.** To surpass in growth: *He has outgrown his father.*

out·growth (out′grōth′) *n.* **1.** Something that grows out of something else; an offshoot: *an outgrowth of new buds on a branch.* **2.** The act or process of growing out. **3.** A result or consequence: *Inflation is an outgrowth of war.*

out·guess (out-gĕs′) *tr.v.* **-guessed, -guessing, -guesses. 1.** To anticipate correctly the actions of. **2.** To gain the advantage over by cleverness or forethought; outwit.

out·gun (out-gŭn′) *tr.v.* **-gunned, -gunning, -guns. 1.** To have more guns than. **2.** To outshoot. **3.** *Informal.* To outdo; surpass.

out·haul (out′hôl′) *n. Nautical.* A rope used to extend a sail along a spar or boom.

out·house (out′hous′) *n.* **1.** An outbuilding. **2.** An outdoor toilet housed in a small structure.

out·ing (ou′tĭng) *n.* **1.** An excursion or pleasure trip: *an outing to the zoo.* **2.** A walk outdoors; an airing. **3.** An appearance in a competition, such as a horse race.

outing flannel *n.* A soft, lightweight cotton fabric, usually with a short nap on both sides.

out·jock·ey (out-jŏk′ē) *tr.v.* **-eyed, -eying, -eys.** To get the better of, especially by trickery.

out·land (out′lănd′, -lənd) *n.* **1. outlands.** The outlying areas of a country; the provinces. **2.** A foreign land. [Middle English *outland,* Old English *ūtland : ūt,* OUT + *land,* LAND.] —**out·land** *adj.* —**out·land·er** *n.*

out·land·ish (out-lăn′dĭsh) *adj.* **1.** Conspicuously unconventional; bizarre or absurd. **2.** Strikingly foreign; unfamiliar. **3.** Geographically remote from the familiar world. **4.** *Archaic.* Of foreign origin; not native. —See Synonyms at **strange.** [Middle English *outlandish,* Old English *ūtlandisc :* OUTLAND + -ISH.] —**out·land·ish·ly** *adv.* —**out·land·ish·ness** *n.*

out·last (out-lăst′, -läst′) *tr.v.* **-lasted, -lasting, -lasts.** To endure or live longer than.

out·law (out′lô′) *n.* **1.** A habitual criminal. **2.** A fugitive from the law. **3.** A person excluded from normal legal protection and rights. **4.** A wild or vicious animal.
~*tr.v.* **outlawed, -lawing, -laws. 1.** To declare illegal. **2.** To ban. **3.** To deprive of the protection of the law. [Middle English *outlawe, outlage,* Old English *ūtlaga,* from Old Norse *ūtlagi,* from *ūtlagr,* outlawed : *ūt,* out + *lög,* law.]

out·law·ry (out′lô′rē) *n., pl.* **-ries. 1.** The act or process of outlawing. **2.** The state of being outlawed. **3.** Defiance of the law. [Middle English *outlagerie,* from Norman French *utlagerie,* from Middle English *outlage,* an OUTLAW.]

out·lay (out′lā′) *n.* **1.** The spending or disbursing of money. **2.** An amount spent. —See Synonyms at **price.**
~*tr.v.* (out-lā′) **outlaid** (-lād′), **-laying, -lays.** To spend (money).

out·let (out′lĕt′, -lĭt) *n.* **1.** A passage for escape or exit, such as a drain or river mouth; vent. **2. a.** A means of fulfilling potential or channeling energies or abilities: "*There is now scarcely any outlet for energy in this country except business*" (John Stuart Mill). **b.** A means of satisfying a drive, urge, or desire; emotional gratification. **c.** A means of achieving self-expression. **3. a.** A commercial market for goods or services. **b.** A store that sells the goods of a particular manufacturer or wholesaler. **4.** A receptacle, especially one mounted on a wall, that is connected to a power supply and equipped with a socket for a plug.

out·li·er (out′lī′ər) *n.* **1.** A portion of something that exists or lies apart from the main body or system to which it belongs. **2.** One whose home lies at some appreciable distance from his place of work. **3.** *Geology.* An area of stratified rock separated from a main formation by erosion.

out·line (out′līn′) *n.* **1. a.** A line described in the plane of vision by the outer boundary of an object or figure. **b.** The shape of an object or a figure. **2.** A drawing or style of drawing in which objects are delineated in contours without shading. **3. a.** A general description or schematic summary covering the main points of a subject: *an outline of English literature.* **b.** An abstract. **c.** A summary of a written work or speech, usually analyzed in headings and subheadings. **d.** A preliminary draft or plan. **4. outlines.** The salient characteristics or general principles of a subject under discussion; gist: *They agreed on the main outlines of the plan but quibbled over particulars.* —See Synonyms at **form.**
~*tr.v.* **outlined, -lining, -lines. 1.** To draw the outline of. **2.** To display or accentuate the outline of. **3.** To give the main points of; summarize.

out·live (out-lĭv′) *tr.v.* **-lived, -living, -lives. 1.** To live beyond or longer than; outlast. **2.** To live through; survive.

out·look (out′lŏŏk′) *n.* **1.** A point of view or attitude. **2.** Probable or expected outcome. **3.** The act of looking out. **4. a.** A place where something can be viewed. **b.** The view seen from such a place. —See Usage note at **prospect.**

out·ly·ing (out′lī′ĭng) *adj.* Comparatively distant or remote from a center or middle.

out·ma·neu·ver (out′mə-nōō′vər, -nyōō′vər) *tr.v.* **-vered, -vering, -vers.** To gain the advantage over by adroitness or skill.

out·mod·ed (out-mō′dĭd) *adj.* **1.** Not in fashion. **2.** No longer usable or practical; obsolete: *an outmoded technique.* —**out·mod·ed·ly** *adv.* —**out·mod·ed·ness** *n.*

out·most (out′mōst′) *adj.* Farthest out; outermost.

out·num·ber (out-nŭm′bər) *tr.v.* **-bered, -bering, -bers.** To exceed the number of; be more numerous than.

out-of-bounds (out′əv-boundz′) *adj.* Beyond prescribed limits or boundaries. —**out-of-bounds** *adv.*

out-of-date (out′əv-dāt′) *adj.* Outmoded; old-fashioned.

out-of-door. Variant of **outdoor.**

out-of-doors. Variant of **outdoors.**

out-of-phase (out′əv-fāz′) *adj.* Designating or pertaining to two or more waves, alternating signals, or other periodically varying quantities for which the maximum and minimum values of each quantity occur at different times.

out-of-pocket (out′əv-pŏk′ĭt) *adj.* Paid for or requiring payment in cash rather than being charged to an expense account or bought on credit: *out-of-pocket expenses.*

out-of-the-way (out′əv-thə-wā′) *adj.* **1.** Distant; remote; secluded. **2.** Out of the ordinary; unusual.

out-of-town·er (out′əv-tou′nər) *n.* A visitor from another town or city.

out·pa·tient (out′pā′shənt) *n.* A patient who receives treatment at a hospital or clinic without being hospitalized.

out·per·form (out′pər-fôrm′) *tr.v.* **-formed, -forming, -forms.** To surpass in performance.

out·play (out-plā′) *tr.v.* **-played, -playing, -plays.** To surpass (an opponent) in playing a game.

out·point (out-point′) *tr.v.* **-pointed, -pointing, -points. 1.** To score a greater number of points than. **2.** *Nautical.* To sail nearer to the direction of the wind than (another vessel).

out·post (out′pōst′) *n.* **1. a.** A detachment of troops stationed at a distance from a main unit of forces. **b.** The station occupied by such troops. **2.** An outlying settlement. **3.** Something likened to an outlying settlement; frontier: *The country club is the last outpost of 19th-century civilization.*

out·pour (out-pôr′, -pōr′) *tr.v.* **-poured, -pouring, -pours.** To pour out.
~*n.* (out′pôr′, -pōr′). A rapid outflow; an outpouring. —**out·pour·er** *n.*

out·pour·ing (out′pôr′ĭng, -pōr′ĭng) *n.* **1.** The act or an instance of pouring out: *an outpouring of love.* **2.** Something that pours out or is poured out; an outflow: *an outpouring of lava.*

out·put (out′pŏŏt′) *n.* **1.** The act of producing; production. **2.** The amount of something produced or manufactured, especially during a given span of time. **3.** The material or substance produced in a process. **4.** The power or energy delivered by a motor or machine. **5.** The energy, power, or work produced by a technical system. **6.** *Computer Science.* **a.** The data produced by a computer from a specific input. **b.** The form in which the data are delivered: *paper-tape output.* **c.** A device used in producing output. **7.** *Electronics.* **a.** The voltage or current produced by a component or circuit. **b.** The terminal or point in a circuit from which this voltage or current is taken.
~*tr.v.* **-putted** or **-put, -putting, -puts.** To produce or manufacture as output. Used especially of a factory, machine, or electronic device.

out·rage (out′rāj′) *n.* **1.** An act of extreme violence or viciousness. **2.** Any act grossly offensive to decency, morality, or good taste. **3.** A severe insult or offense to one's integrity or pride: "*I have only had insults and outrage from her*" (W.M. Thackeray). **4.** A strong feeling of resentful anger.
~*tr.v.* **outraged, -raging, -rages. 1.** To offend or enrage. **2.** To commit an outrage upon. **3.** To rape. —See Synonyms at **offend.** [Middle English, excess, from Old French, "excess," atrocity, from *outre,* beyond. See **outré**.]

out·ra·geous (out-rā′jəs) *adj.* **1. a.** Being an outrage; grossly offensive; heinous. **b.** Disgraceful; shameful. **2.** Having no regard for the conventions of morality, decency, or good taste; shocking. **3.** Extravagant; immoderate; extreme: *She spends an outrageous* *amount on clothes.* **4.** Violent or unrestrained in temperament or behavior. **—out·ra·geous·ly** *adv.* **—out·ra·geous·ness** *n.*

out·rank (out-răngk′) *tr.v.* **-ranked, -ranking, -ranks. 1.** To be of a higher rank than. **2.** To be more important than; take precedence over.

ou·tré (ōō-trā′) *adj.* Deviating from what is usual or proper; eccentric. [French, past participle of *outrer*, to pass beyond, go to excess, from *outre*, beyond, from Old French, from Latin *ultrā*, beyond, further.]

out·reach (out-rēch′) *v.* **-reached, -reaching, -reaches.** *—tr.* **1.** To reach or go beyond; surpass. **2.** To extend (something) outward. *—intr.* To reach out. *~n.* (out′rēch′). **1.** An act of reaching out. **2.** The extent of a reach. **3.** A systematic attempt to provide services beyond conventional limits, as to particular segments of a community.

out·re·lief (out′rĭ-lēf′) *n. British.* Financial assistance formerly given to the indigent not living in the poorhouse.

out·ride¹ (out-rīd′) *tr.v.* **-rode** (-rōd′), **-ridden** (-rĭd′n), **-riding, -rides.** To ride faster, farther, or better than; outstrip.

out·ride² (out′rīd′) *n.* In verse, an unstressed syllable or cluster of syllables within a given metrical unit that is omitted from the scansion pattern in sprung rhythm. [Coined by the poet Gerard Manley Hopkins.]

out·rid·er (out′rī′dər) *n.* **1.** A mounted attendant who rides in front of or beside a carriage. **2.** A person who precedes a procession or vehicle to clear the way and ensure easy progress. **3.** A person who patrols and reconnoiters ahead of a group, as of explorers or raiders; a scout. **4.** An escort. **5.** A cowboy supervising cattle, usually at some distance from a farmhouse or central camp.

out·rig·ger (out′rĭg′ər) *n.* **1. a.** In seagoing canoes, especially of the South Pacific and Indian oceans, a float attached to laterally projecting spars so as to ride parallel to the length of the craft on either side as a means of preventing it from capsizing. **b.** A vessel fitted with such a float. **2.** A frame extending laterally beyond the main structure of a vessel, vehicle, aircraft, building, or machine to stabilize the structure or support an extending part.

out·right (out′rīt′, out-rīt′) *adv.* **1.** Without reservation or qualification; openly: *Now he's laughing outright.* **2.** Entirely; wholly: *Legislators approved the tax bill outright.* **3.** Without delay; straightaway: *The couple was killed outright in the accident.* *~adj.* (out′rīt′). **1.** Without reservation; unqualified: *an outright gift.* **2. a.** Complete; total: *the outright cost.* **b.** Thoroughgoing; out-and-out: *outright cruelty.* **3.** Straightforward; forthright: *an outright speech.* **4.** *Archaic.* Directed straight on; moving straight onward: *"an even, outright, but imperceptible speed"* (R.L. Stevenson).

out·run (out-rŭn′) *tr.v.* **-ran** (-răn′), **-run, -running, -runs. 1.** To run faster than. **2.** To escape from: *outrun one's creditors.* **3.** To go beyond or exceed (some limit): *Her ingenuity outran her intelligence.*

out·sell (out-sĕl′) *tr.v.* **-sold** (-sōld′), **-selling, -sells. 1.** To surpass in amount sold. **2.** To outdo in selling.

out·set (out′sĕt′) *n.* **1.** The beginning; the start; the commencement. **2.** An initial stage, as of an activity.

out·shine (out-shīn′) *v.* **-shone** (-shōn′), **-shining, -shines.** *—tr.* **1.** To shine more brightly than. **2.** To surpass (a rival). *—intr.* To shine forth.

out·shoot (out-shōōt′) *v.* **-shot** (-shŏt′), **-shooting, -shoots.** *—tr.* **1.** To shoot better than. **2.** To extend beyond. *—intr.* To protrude or project. *~n.* (out′shōōt′). **1.** A protuberance, projection, or outgrowth. **2.** A flowing or gushing forth.

out·shout (out-shout′) *tr.v.* **-shouted, -shouting, -shouts.** To shout louder than.

out·side (out-sīd′, out′sīd′) *n.* **1.** The part or parts that face out; the outer surface; the exterior: *scrubbed the outside of the kitchen cabinets.* **2. a.** The part or side of an object that is presented to the viewer; the external aspect. **b.** A superficial or obvious aspect: *Benevolent on the outside, he was really quite unscrupulous.* **3.** The space beyond a boundary or limit. **4.** An outer or external position: *The car door opens only from the outside.* **5.** Society at large as opposed to an institution: *The former inmate had difficulty in adjusting to life on the outside.* **6.** The part of a playing field or area that is nearest the sidelines. **—at the outside.** At the utmost limit; at the most: *We'll be leaving in ten days at the outside.* *~adj.* **1.** Acting, occurring, originating, or existing at a place beyond certain limits; outer; foreign: *outside assistance.* **2.** Of, restricted to, or situated on the outside of an enclosure or boundary; external: *outside environs; an outside door lock.* **3.** Extreme; uttermost: *The cost exceeded even my outside estimate.* **4.** Slight; slim: *an outside possibility.* **5.** Not part of a group; not a member: *The trouble must have come from an outside source.* **6.** Originating, done, or made from the outside: *The forward made an outstanding outside jump shot.* **7.** Of, pertaining to, or being a curve that covers a greater distance than other concentric curves within it: *the outside track.* **8.** Not being a part of a person's regular responsibilities or work: *His outside activities include painting and music.* *~adv.* **1.** On or into the outside. **2.** *Outdoors.* **3.** *Slang.* Out of prison. **—outside of.** Outside: *She has few interests outside of her work.* *~prep.* **1.** On or to the outer side of. **2.** Beyond the limits of. **3.** With the exception of; except: *There was no information outside the figures given.*

out·sid·er (out-sī′dər) *n.* **1. a.** A person who is excluded from some particular party, association, or set. **b.** One who is isolated or de-

tached from the activities or concerns of the community in which he lives. **2.** A contestant in a race, especially a horse race, considered to have little chance of winning.

out·size (out′sīz′) *n.* **1.** An unusual size, especially a very large size. **2.** A garment designed to fit a very large person. **—out·size, out·sized** *adj.*

out·skirts (out′skûrts′) *pl.n.* The parts or regions remote from a central district; peripheral areas: *the outskirts of the city.*

out·smart (out-smärt′) *tr.v.* **-smarted, -smarting, -smarts.** To gain the advantage over by cunning; outwit.

out·span (out-spăn′) *v.* **-spanned, -spanning, -spans.** *South African.* *—intr.* To take off a yoke or harness from an animal. *—tr.* To unharness or unyoke (an animal). *~n.* (out′spăn′). *South African.* **1.** A time or a place set aside for outspanning. **2.** Grazing land. [Partial translation of Afrikaans *uitspan* : *uit*, OUT + *spannen*, to stretch, hitch.]

out·speak (out-spēk′) *tr.v.* **-spoke** (-spōk′), **-spoken** (-spō′kən), **-speaking, -speaks. 1.** To speak better or more cogently than. **2.** To say candidly and frankly.

out·spo·ken (out-spō′kən) *adj.* **1.** Spoken without reserve; candid. **2.** Frank and unsparing in speech. **—See Synonyms at frank.** **—out·spo·ken·ly** *adv.* **—out·spo·ken·ness** *n.*

out·spread (out-sprĕd′) *v.* **-spread, -spreading, -spreads.** *—intr.* To spread out; stretch. *—tr.* To cause to spread out. *~n.* (out′sprĕd′). **1.** The act of spreading out. **2.** Extent. *~adj.* Spread out; extended.

out·stand (out-stănd′) *intr.v.* **-stood** (-stōōd′), **-standing, -stands. 1.** To stand out plainly; be outstanding. **2.** *Nautical.* To set sail; put out to sea.

out·stand·ing (out-stăn′dĭng, out′stăn′-) *adj.* **1.** Standing out; projecting upward or outward. **2.** Standing out among others of its kind; prominent. **3.** Superior to others of its kind; distinguished; excellent. **4.** Still in existence; not settled or resolved: *outstanding debts; a long outstanding problem.*

out·stare (out-stâr′) *tr.v.* **-stared, -staring, -stares.** To defeat or overcome by or as if by staring; outface.

out·sta·tion (out′stā′shən) *n.* A remote station or post.

out·stay (out-stā′) *tr.v.* **-stayed, -staying, -stays. 1.** To stay longer than. **2.** To stay beyond (a certain limit); overstay: *We outstayed our welcome.* **3.** To have or show greater endurance than.

out·stretch (out-strĕch′) *tr.v.* **-stretched, -stretching, -stretches. 1.** To stretch out; extend. **2.** To stretch beyond.

out·strip (out-strĭp′) *tr.v.* **-stripped, -stripping, -strips. 1.** To run faster than and leave behind; outrun. **2.** To exceed in growth, skill, or achievement; surpass: *"Material development outstripped human development"* (Edith Hamilton). **—See Synonyms at excel.**

out·take (out′tāk′) *n.* A series of frames cut and discarded from the finished version of a film.

out·talk (out-tôk′) *tr.v.* **-talked, -talking, -talks. 1.** To outdo in talking. **2.** To outwit by talking.

out·turn (out′tûrn′) *n.* **1.** A total amount produced during a given period; output. **2.** *British.* Outcome: *"But whether the outturn would have been very different is quite another question"* (Manchester Guardian).

out·ward (out′wərd) *adj.* **1.** Of, pertaining to, located on, or moving toward the outside or exterior; outer. **2.** Pertaining to the physical self as distinguished from the mind or spirit: *Ascetics have no interest in the outward being.* **3.** Easily perceptible, especially to sight; evident: *Her outward manner remained composed.* **4.** Purely external; superficial. **5.** Toward or sailing toward a destination away from home or a home port. Said of a voyage or a ship. *~adv.* Also **out·wards** (-wərdz). **1.** Toward the outside; away from a central point. **2.** On the outside; externally. *~n.* **1.** The outside; the exterior. **2.** Outward appearance. [Middle English *outward*, Old English *ūtanweard* : *ūtan*, outside, from *ūt*, OUT + *-weard*, -WARD.] **—out·ward·ness** *n.*

out·ward·ly (out′wərd-lē) *adv.* **1.** According to external appearance, usually as distinct from the real state of affairs: *She remained outwardly composed at the news, but her mind was reeling.* **2.** From, to, or on the outside; externally.

out·wear (out-wâr′) *tr.v.* **-wore** (-wôr′, -wōr′), **-worn** (-wôrn′, -wōrn′), **-wearing, -wears. 1.** To wear out; exhaust by using. **2.** To last longer than; outlast. **3.** To outgrow or outlive: *ethics outworn by a changing society.*

out·weigh (out-wā′) *tr.v.* **-weighed, -weighing, -weighs. 1.** To weigh more than. **2. a.** To be more significant, important, or influential than. **b.** To be preferred to; prevail over.

out·wit (out-wĭt′) *tr.v.* **-witted, -witting, -wits. 1.** To surpass in cleverness or cunning; fool. **2.** *Archaic.* To surpass in intelligence. **—See Synonyms at deceive.**

out·with (out′wĭth′, -wĭth′) *prep. Scottish.* Outside.

out·work (out-wûrk′) *tr.v.* **-worked, -working, -works. 1.** To work better or faster than. **2.** To work out to a finish; complete. *~n.* (out′wûrk′). **1.** Work done outside a factory or shop. **2.** *Military.* A trench or fortification constructed beyond a main defensive position or fortification. **—out·work·er** *n.*

ou·zel, ou·sel (ōō′zəl) *n.* **1.** Any of various European birds of the genus *Turdies*, especially the **ring ouzel** (*see*). **2.** A blackbird. **3.** The water ouzel or **dipper** (*see*). [Middle English *ousel*, Old English *ōsle*.]

ou·zo (ōō′zō) *n., pl.* **-zos.** An aniseed-flavored Greek liqueur. [Modern Greek *ouzon*†.]

o·va. Plural of **ovum.**

ovenbird *The South American ovenbird* Funarius rufus *perches on the curious clay nest from which it gets its name.*

o·val (ō′vəl) *adj.* **1.** Resembling an ellipse in shape; ellipsoidal or elliptical. **2.** Resembling an egg in shape.
~*n.* **1.** An oval form or figure. **2.** An oval track, as for horse racing, or sports field, as for athletic events. [Medieval Latin *ōvālis,* from Latin *ōvum,* egg.] **—o·val·ly** *adv.* **—o·val·ness** *n.*

Oval Office *n.* President of the United States: *a statement from the Oval Office.* [From the President's oval-shaped office in the White House.]

O·vam·bo (ō-văm′bō) *n., pl.* **-bos** or collectively **Ovambo. 1.** A member of a southern African people of mixed Hottentot and Negroid descent, living chiefly in northern Namibia. **2.** The Bantu language of this people, of the Niger-Congo family of languages. **—O·vam·bo** *adj.*

o·var·i·ec·to·my (ō-vâr′ē-ĕk′tə-mē) *n., pl.* **-mies.** Surgical excision of an ovary. [OVAR(Y) + -ECTOMY.]

o·var·i·ot·o·my (ō-vâr′ē-ŏt′ə-mē) *n., pl.* **-mies. 1.** Ovariectomy. **2.** Surgical incision into an ovary, as to remove a tumor. [New Latin *ovariotomia* : OVAR(Y) + *-tomia,* -TOMY.]

o·va·ri·tis (ō′və-rī′tĭs) *n. Medicine.* **Oophoritis** *(see).* [New Latin : OVAR(Y) + -ITIS.]

o·va·ry (ō′və-rē) *n., pl.* **-ries. 1.** *Zoology.* Either of a pair of female reproductive glands that produce ova. **2.** *Botany.* The part of a pistil containing the ovules. [New Latin *ovarium,* from Latin *ōvum,* egg.] **—o·var·i·al** (ō-vâr′ē-əl), **o·var·i·an** (ō-vâr′ē-ən) *adj.*

o·vate (ō′vāt′) *adj.* **1.** Shaped like an egg; oval. **2.** *Botany.* Broad and rounded at the base and tapering toward the end: *an ovate leaf.* [Latin *ōvātus,* egg-shaped, from *ōvum,* egg.] **—o·vate·ly** *adv.*

o·va·tion (ō-vā′shən) *n.* **1.** Enthusiastic and prolonged applause. **2.** A show of public homage or welcome. **3.** An ancient Roman victory ceremony of lesser importance than a triumph. [Latin *ovātiō* (stem *ovātiōn-*), from *ovāre,* to rejoice, from imitative base *eu-.*]

ov·en (ŭv′ən) *n.* **1.** A chamber or enclosed compartment, as in a stove, in which food is heated, baked, or roasted. **2.** A device similar to an oven but usually refractory-lined in which ceramics are fired, metals treated with heat, or objects dried. [Middle English *oven,* Old English *ofen.*]

ov·en·bird (ŭv′ən-bûrd′) *n.* **1.** Any of various South American birds of the family Furnariidae that build intricate clay nests having a concealed entrance passage. **2.** A thrushlike North American warbler, *Seiurus aurocapillus,* having a shrill call and characteristically building a domed nest on the ground. [From its nest, shaped like a Dutch oven.]

ov·en·proof (ŭv′ən-pro͞of′) *adj.* Not harmed by heating in an oven; capable of withstanding the heat of an oven without cracking or shattering. Compare **flameproof.**

ov·en-read·y (ŭv′ən-rĕd′ē) *adj.* Ready for immediate roasting or cooking in an oven; especially, plucked, gutted, and trussed: *an oven-ready chicken.*

ov·en·ware (ŭv′ən-wâr′) *n.* Plates, dishes, and pots made of ovenproof material.

o·ver (ō′vər) *prep.* **1.** In or at a position above or higher than: *a sign over the door.* **2. a.** Above and across from one end or side to the other of: *a leap over the fence.* **b.** Down the side of or across and down the other side of: *jump over the cliff.* **3.** On the other side of: *a village over the border.* **4.** Upon the surface of: *a coat of varnish over the woodwork.* **5.** Covering all or various parts of; through the extent of: *The rash spread over her body.* **6.** So as to cover or close: *A rock slid over the cave entrance.* **7.** Up to or higher than the level or height of: *The water rose over their knees.* **8.** Through the period or duration of: *records maintained over two years.* **9.** Until or beyond the end of: *stay over the holidays.* **10.** More than in degree, quantity, or extent: *walked over ten miles.* **11.** In preference to: *One actor was respected over all others.* **12.** In a position to rule or control: *preside over the meeting.* **13.** Upon; directed toward: *The teacher has a good influence over the students.* **14.** While occupied with, engaged in, or partaking of: *a chat over coffee.* **15.** With reference to; concerning: *an argument over methods.* **16.** By means of; by the agency of: *Don't tell me over the phone.* **17.** Recovered from; past the effects of: *over the worst.* **—over a barrel.** At the mercy of others: *His competitors had him over a barrel.* **—over one's head.** Beyond one's comprehension or abilities.
~*adv.* **1.** Above the top or surface: *The flag flew directly over.* **2. a.** Across to another or opposite side. **b.** Across the edge or brim: *The water boiled over.* **3. a.** Across a distance in a particular direction or place: *We went over to Europe for our vacation.* **b.** To another specified place or position: *Move your chair over toward the fire.* **4.** Throughout an entire area or region: *Tourists were wandering all over.* **5.** To a different opinion or allegiance: *We won her over with superior reasons.* **6. a.** To a different person, condition, or title: *sign over land.* **b.** So as to be exchanged: *change over.* **7.** So as to be completely enclosed or covered: *The river froze over.* **8.** Through from beginning to end: *Think the problem over. Look this contract over before you sign it.* **9. a.** From an upright position: *The book fell over.* **b.** From an upward position to an inverted or reversed position: *turn the book over.* **10.** Another time; again: *Count your cards over.* **11.** In repetition: *ten times over.* **12.** In addition or excess; in surplus: *three pennies left over.* **13.** Beyond or until a specified time: *stay a day over.* **—over against. 1.** As opposed to; contrasted with. **2.** Opposite; in front of.
~*adj.* **1.** Completely finished; done; past: *The war is over.* **2.** Having gone across or to the other side. **3. a.** Upper; higher. **b.** External; outer. **4.** In excess or addition; in surplus: *My estimate was fifty dollars over.*
~*tr.v.* **overed, overing, overs.** To jump over.
~*interj.* Used in two-way radio conversations to mark the end of a transmission by one speaker and often to indicate that a reply is awaited. [Middle English *over,* Old English *ofer.*]

over– *prefix.* Indicates: **1.** Superiority of rank or power; for example, **overseer. 2.** Location above, outside, or across; for example, **overhead. 3.** Passage beyond or above a limit or boundary; for example, **overshoot. 4.** Movement or transference to a lower or inferior position; for example, **overturn. 5.** Quantity in excess of what is normal, agreed upon, or desirable; for example, **overheat.** ***Note:*** Many compounds other than those entered here may be formed with *over-.* In forming compounds, *over-* is joined with the following element without space or a hyphen: **overrule. —**See Usage note at **overly.** [Middle English *over-,* Old English *ofer-,* from *ofer,* OVER.]

o·ver·a·bun·dance (ō′vər-ə-bŭn′dəns) *n.* Prodigally lavish abundance; excessive profusion. **—o·ver·a·bun·dant** *adj.*

o·ver·a·chieve (ō′vər-ə-chēv′) *intr.v.* **-achieved, -achieving, -achieves.** To perform better than expected or justified. **—o·ver·a·chieve·ment** *n.* **—o·ver·a·chiev·er** *n.*

o·ver·act (ō′vər-ăkt′) *v.* **-acted, -acting, -acts.** —*tr.* To act (a part) with unnecessary exaggeration. —*intr.* To exaggerate a role; overact a dramatic part.

o·ver·ac·tive (ō′vər-ăk′tĭv) *adj.* Active to an excessive or abnormal degree.

o·ver·age[1] (ō′vər-ĭj) *n.* **1.** An amount, as of money or goods, actually on hand that exceeds the amount listed in records or books of account. **2.** A surplus or excess.

o·ver·age[2] (ō′vər-āj′) *adj.* Beyond the proper or required age.

o·ver·all, o·ver-all (ō′vər-ôl′, ō′vər-ôl′) *adj.* **1.** From one end to the other. **2.** Including everything; comprehensive.
~*adv.* (ō′vər-ôl′). **1.** From one end to the other: *The table measures six feet overall.* **2.** Generally; on the whole: *The rehearsal was adequate overall, and the performance should be excellent.*
~*n.* (ō′vər-ôl′) *Chiefly British.* A loose-fitting protective outer garment; a smock.

o·ver·alls (ō′vər-ôlz′) *pl.n.* Loose-fitting, coarse trousers with a bib front and shoulder straps, often worn over regular clothing as protection from dirt and wear.

o·ver·arch (ō′vər-ärch′) *tr.v.* **-arched, -arching, -arches. 1.** To form an arch over. **2.** To extend over or throughout.

o·ver·arm (ō′vər-ärm′) *adj. Sports.* Executed with the arm raised above the shoulder: *an overarm throw.* **—o·ver·arm** *adv.*

o·ver·awe (ō′vər-ô′) *tr.v.* **-awed, -awing, -awes.** To subdue by inspiring awe; overcome with awe.

o·ver·bal·ance (ō′vər-băl′əns) *v.* **-anced, -ancing, -ances.** —*tr.* **1.** To throw off balance. **2.** To have greater weight or importance than. —*intr.* To lose one's balance; tip over.
~*n.* (ō′vər-băl′əns). Something that overbalances; an excess of weight or quantity.

o·ver·bear (ō′vər-bâr′) *v.* **-bore** (-bôr′, -bōr′), **-borne** (-bôrn′, -bōrn′), **-bearing, -bears.** —*tr.* **1.** To crush or press down upon with physical force. **2.** To prevail over, as if by superior weight or force; dominate. —*intr.* To bear too much fruit or too many offspring.

o·ver·bear·ing (ō′vər-bâr′ĭng) *adj.* **1.** Domineering; arrogant: *"the overbearing character and insulting manners of the English people"* (Jawaharlal Nehru). **2.** Overwhelming in power or significance; predominant. **—**See Synonyms at **dictatorial. —o·ver·bear·ing·ly** *adv.*

o·ver·bid (ō′vər-bĭd′) *v.* **-bid, -bidden** (-bĭd′n) or **-bid, -bidding, -bids.** —*tr.* **1.** To outbid (a person) for something. **2.** To bid unjustifiably high for (something). —*intr.* **1.** To bid higher than the actual value of something. **2.** In bridge and similar card games, to bid higher than is warranted by the value of one's hand.
~*n.* (ō′vər-bĭd′). **1.** A bid that is higher than another bid. **2.** A bid that is too high.

o·ver·bite (ō′vər-bīt′) *n.* In dentistry, the condition in which the front upper incisor and canine teeth project over the lower.

o·ver·blouse (ō′vər-blous′, -blouz′) *n.* A blouse designed to be worn over a skirt or slacks, instead of tucked in.

o·ver·blow (ō′vər-blō′) *tr.v.* **-blew** (-blo͞o′), **-blown** (-blōn′), **-blowing, -blows.** To blow (a wind instrument) so as to produce a harmonic instead of a fundamental note.

o·ver·blown (ō′vər-blōn′) *adj.* **1.** Exaggerated; overdone. **2.** Pompous; conceited. **3.** Past the stage of full bloom. **4.** Blown past or over.

o·ver·board (ō′vər-bôrd′, -bōrd′) *adv.* Over the side of a boat or ship into the water. **—go overboard.** *Informal.* **1.** To show excessive enthusiasm. **2.** To react in an exaggerated or extreme way. **—throw overboard.** To get rid of; abandon.

o·ver·book (ō′vər-bo͝ok′) *v.* **-booked, -booking, -books.** —*tr.* To make more bookings for seats on or accommodation in (an airplane or hotel, for example) than there are places available. —*intr.* To overbook reservations, as in an airplane or hotel.

o·ver·build (ō′vər-bĭld′) *v.* **-built** (-bĭlt′), **-building, -builds.** —*tr.* **1.** To build over or on top of. **2.** To build more buildings in (an area) than is justified or necessary. **3.** To build with excessive size or elaboration. —*intr.* To build more buildings than needed or justified.

o·ver·bur·den (ō′vər-bûrd′n) *tr.v.* **-dened, -dening, -dens. 1.** To burden with too much weight. **2.** To burden with too much work, worry, or responsibility.
~*n.* (o′vər-bûrd′n). **1.** *Geology.* **a.** Material overlying a useful min-

eral deposit. **b.** Unconsolidated material covering solid rock or bedrock. **2.** *Archaeology.* A sterile stratum overlying a stratum bearing traces of the culture being studied.

o·ver·buy (ō'vər-bī') *v.* **-bought** (-bôt'), **-buying, -buys.** —*tr.* **1.** To buy in excessive amounts. **2.** *Finance.* To buy (stocks and shares) on margin in excess of one's ability to provide further security if prices drop. —*intr.* To buy goods beyond one's means or needs.

o·ver·call (ō'vər-kôl') *tr.v.* **-called, -calling, -calls. 1.** To overbid. **2.** In bridge, to bid higher than (one's opponent) when one's partner has not bid.
~*n.* (ō'vər-kôl'). **1.** An overbid. **2.** In bridge, an instance of overcalling.

o·ver·cap·i·tal·ize (ō'vər-kăp'ə-tə-līz') *tr.v.* **-ized, -izing, -izes. 1.** To provide an excess amount of capital for (a business enterprise). **2.** To estimate the value of (property) too highly. **3.** To place an unlawfully or unreasonably high value on the nominal capital of (a company). —**o·ver·cap·i·tal·i·za·tion** *n.*

o·ver·cast (ō'vər-kăst', -käst', ō'vər-kăst', -käst') *adj.* **1. a.** Covered or obscured, as with clouds. **b.** Clouded over: *overcast skies.* **2.** Gloomy; melancholy. **3.** Sewn with long, overlying stitches in order to prevent unraveling, as at the edges of fabric.
~*n.* (ō'vər-kăst', -käst'). **1.** A covering, as of clouds. **2.** In mining, an arch or support for a passage over another passage. **3.** A fishing cast falling beyond the point intended. **4.** An overcast stitch or seam.
~*tr.v.* (ō'vər-kăst', -käst', ō'vər-kăst', -käst') **-casted, -casting, -casts. 1.** To make cloudy or gloomy. **2.** In fishing, to cast beyond (the intended point). **3.** To sew with an overcast stitch.

o·ver·cast·ing (ō'vər-kăst'ĭng) *n.* An overcast stitch or seam.

o·ver·charge (ō'vər-chärj') *v.* **-charged, -charging, -charges.** —*tr.* **1.** To charge (a customer) too high a price for something. **2.** To fill too full; overload. **3.** To supply (a battery) with too much charge or too high a current, so as to damage the electrodes. **4.** To exaggerate. —*intr.* To charge too high a price.
~*n.* (ō'vər-chärj'). **1.** *Abbr.* **o/c** An excessive charge or price. **2.** A load or burden that is too full or heavy.

o·ver·cloud (ō'vər-kloud') *v.* **-clouded, -clouding, -clouds.** —*tr.* **1.** To cover with clouds. **2.** To make dark and gloomy. —*intr.* To become cloudy.

o·ver·coat (ō'vər-kōt') *n.* A heavy coat worn in cold weather.

o·ver·come (ō'vər-kŭm') *v.* **-came** (-kām'), **-come, -coming, -comes.** —*tr.* **1.** To defeat in competition or conflict; conquer. **2.** To surmount; prevail over. **3.** To overpower, as with emotion; affect deeply. —*intr.* To surmount opposition; be victorious. —See Synonyms at **defeat.** [Middle English *overcomen,* Old English *ofercuman* : *ofer,* OVER + *cuman,* to COME.]

o·ver·com·pen·sate (ō'vər-kŏm'pən-sāt') *v.* **-sated, -sating, -sates.** —*intr.* **1.** To make a greater effort than required to achieve compensation. **2.** To engage in overcompensation. —*tr.* To compensate excessively. —**o·ver·com·pen·sa·to·ry** (ō'vər-kəm-pĕn'sə-tôr'ē, -tōr'ē) *adj.*

o·ver·com·pen·sa·tion (ō'vər-kŏm'pən-sā'shən) *n.* The exertion of effort in excess of that needed to compensate for a physical or psychological characteristic or defect.

o·ver·crop (ō'vər-krŏp') *tr.v.* **-cropped, -cropping, -crops.** To exhaust the fertility of (land) by overcultivation.

o·ver·crowd (ō'vər-kroud') *tr.v.* **-crowded, -crowding, -crowds.** To put too much or too many in (one place).

o·ver·de·vel·op (ō'vər-dĭ-vĕl'əp) *tr.v.* **-oped, -oping, -ops. 1.** To develop to excess: *muscles overdeveloped by weightlifting.* **2.** In photography, to process (a plate or film) too long or in too concentrated a solution. —**o·ver·de·vel·op·ment** *n.*

o·ver·do (ō'vər-dōō') *v.* **-did** (-dĭd'), **-done** (-dŭn'), **-doing, -does** (-dŭz'). —*tr.* **1.** To do, use, or stress to excess; carry too far. **2.** To wear out the strength of; overtax. **3.** To cook too much or too long. —*intr.* To do something to excess.

o·ver·dose (ō'vər-dōs') *v.* **-dosed, -dosing, -doses.** —*intr.* To take an excessive or lethal dose of a drug. —*tr.* To administer too large a dose to.
~*n.* (ō'vər-dōs'). An excessive dose of a drug, especially a narcotic.

o·ver·draft (ō'vər-drăft', -dräft') *n.* Also **o·ver·draught** (for sense 2 only). **1. a.** The act of overdrawing an account. **b.** *Abbr.* **O.D.** The amount overdrawn. **2. a.** A current of air made to pass over the ignited fuel in a furnace. **b.** A series of flues in a brick kiln designed to force air down from the top. **c.** The air so forced.

o·ver·draw (ō'vər-drô') *v.* **-drew** (-drōō'), **-drawn** (-drôn'), **-drawing, -draws.** —*tr.* **1.** To draw on (a bank account) in excess of credit. **2.** To pull back too far: *overdraw a bow.* **3.** To spoil the effect of by exaggeration in telling or describing. —*intr.* To draw on a bank account in excess of credit. —**be overdrawn.** To have drawn money from a bank account in excess of credit.

o·ver·dress (ō'vər-drĕs') *intr.v.* **-dressed, -dressing, -dresses.** To dress in a more formal or elaborate manner than is desirable in a given situation.
~*n.* (ō'vər-drĕs'). A skirted garment, such as a pinafore, worn over other outer clothing.

o·ver·drive (ō'vər-drīv') *n.* A gearing mechanism in an automotive engine that reduces the power output required to maintain driving speed in a specific range by increasing the ratio of drive shaft to engine speed. —**go into overdrive.** To redouble one's energies or act with even greater speed or intensity, as if switching to the highest possible gear.
~*tr.v.* (ō-vər-drīv') **-drove** (-drōv'), **-driven** (-drĭv'ən), **-driving,**

-drives. 1. To drive (a vehicle) too far or too long. **2.** To push (oneself) too far; overwork.

o·ver·dub (ō'vər-dŭb') *tr.v.* **-dubbed, -dubbing, -dubs. 1.** To blend (recorded sound) with previously recorded sound in order to produce a multiple effect. **2.** To add in (new sounds) to a recording.
~*n.* (ō'vər-dŭb'). An act or instance of overdubbing sounds.

o·ver·due (ō'vər-dōō', -dyōō') *adj.* **1.** Being unpaid after becoming due. **2.** Past the due time of arrival; expected or required but not yet come. —See Synonyms at **tardy.**

o·ver·eat (ō'vər-ēt') *intr.v.* **-ate** (-āt'), **-eaten** (-ēt'n), **-eating, -eats.** To eat too much, especially habitually. —**o·ver·eat·er** *n.*

o·ver·es·ti·mate (ō'vər-ĕs'tə-māt') *tr.v.* **-mated, -mating, -mates. 1.** To estimate too highly. **2.** To esteem too greatly.
~*n.* (-mĭt). An estimate or estimation that is excessively high. —**o·ver·es·ti·ma·tion** *n.*

o·ver·ex·ert (ō'vər-ĭg-zûrt') *tr.v.* **-erted, -erting, -erts.** To exert too much; overtax; strain. —**o·ver·ex·er·tion** *n.*

o·ver·ex·pose (ō'vər-ĭk-spōz') *tr.v.* **-posed, -posing, -poses. 1.** To expose too long or too much. **2.** To expose (a photographic film or plate) too long or with too much light. —**o·ver·ex·po·sure** (ō'-vər-ĭk-spō'zhər) *n.*

o·ver·ex·tend (ō'vər-ĭk-stĕnd') *tr.v.* **-tended, -tending, -tends.** To expand or disperse (one's defenses or finances, for example) beyond a safe or reasonable limit. —**o·ver·ex·ten·sion** *n.*

o·ver·fa·tigue (ō'vər-fə-tēg') *n.* Extreme fatigue, often to a degree beyond an individual's power to recover.

o·ver·fish (ō'vər-fĭsh') *tr.v.* **-fished, -fishing, -fishes.** To fish (a body of water) to a degree that upsets the ecological balance or causes depletion of living organisms.

o·ver·flow (ō'vər-flō') *v.* **-flowed, -flowing, -flows.** —*intr.* **1.** To flow or run over the top, brim, or banks. **2.** To be filled beyond capacity, as a container or waterway may be. **3.** To have a boundless supply; be superabundant: *overflowing with gratitude.* —*tr.* **1.** To flow over the top, brim, or banks of. **2.** To spread over or cover; flood. **3.** To cause to fill beyond capacity.
~*n.* (ō'vər-flō'). **1.** The act of overflowing. **2. a.** Something that flows over. **b.** An amount that flows over. **3.** An outlet or vent through which excess liquid may escape.

o·ver·fly (ō'vər-flī') *tr.v.* **-flew** (-flōō'), **-flown** (-flōn'), **-flying, -flies. 1.** To fly over: *The helicopter accidentally overflew enemy territory.* **2.** To fly an aircraft beyond: *The pilot overflew the runway.* —**o·ver·flight** (ō'vər-flīt') *n.*

o·ver·gar·ment (ō'vər-gär'mənt) *n.* An outer garment.

o·ver·glaze (ō'vər-glāz') *n.* A second coat of glaze on pottery.
~*adj.* Applied to a glazed surface. Said especially of a color.
~*tr.v.* (ō'vər-glāz', ō'vər-glāz') **overglazed, -glazing, -glazes.** To apply an overglaze to.

o·ver·graze (ō'vər-grāz') *v.* **-grazed, -grazing, -grazes.** —*tr.* To destroy or seriously damage (grass cover or pastureland) by allowing animals to graze for too long a period. —*intr.* To overgraze grass cover or pastureland.

o·ver·grow (ō'vər-grō') *v.* **-grew** (-grōō'), **-grown** (-grōn'), **-growing, -grows.** —*tr.* **1.** To grow and spread across (an area): *The pathway was overgrown with weeds.* **2.** To grow too large for; outgrow. —*intr.* **1.** To grow beyond normal size. **2.** To become overgrown, as with vegetation.

o·ver·growth (ō'vər-grōth') *n.* **1.** A growth over or upon something. **2.** Excessively abundant or luxuriant growth.

o·ver·hand (ō'vər-hănd') *adj.* Also **o·ver·hand·ed** (ō'vər-hăn'dĭd). **1.** Sewn with stitches drawing two edges together, with each stitch passing over the seam formed by the edges. **2.** Thrown, struck, or executed with the hand above the level of the shoulder: *an overhand pitch.*
~*adv.* In an overhand manner.
~*n.* **1.** An overhand stitch or seam. **2.** An overhand throw, stroke, or delivery.
~*tr.v.* **overhanded, -handing, -hands.** To sew with an overhand seam or stitches.

overhand knot *n.* A knot formed by making a loop in a piece of cord and pulling one end through it. Also called "single knot."

o·ver·hang (ō'vər-hăng') *v.* **-hung** (-hŭng'), **-hanging, -hangs.** —*tr.* **1.** To project or extend beyond. **2.** To hang over or above. **3.** To threaten or menace; loom over. **4.** To ornament with hangings. —*intr.* To hang or project over something.
~*n.* (ō'vər-hăng'). **1.** A projecting part of something, such as an architectural structure or rock formation. **2.** The amount of projection: *an overhang of six inches.* **3.** The part of a ship's bow or stern that projects over the water.

o·ver·haul (ō'vər-hôl', ō'vər-hôl') *tr.v.* **-hauled, -hauling, -hauls. 1. a.** To examine or go over carefully, searching for defects to be repaired. **b.** To dismantle in order to make repairs. **c.** To make all needed repairs on; fix; renovate. **2.** *Nautical.* To slacken (a line) or release and separate the blocks of (a tackle). **3.** To catch up with; overtake.
~*n.* (ō'vər-hôl'). **1.** An act of overhauling. **2.** A comprehensive repair job; a renovation.

o·ver·head (ō'vər-hĕd') *adj.* **1.** Located, functioning, or performed above the level of the head: *an overhead light.* **2.** Of or pertaining to the operating expenses of a business concern.
~*n.* (ō'vər-hĕd'). **1.** The incidental operating expenses of a business, including the costs of rent, utilities, taxes, and interior decoration but excluding labor and materials. **2.** The top surface in an enclosed space of a ship.

~*adv.* (ō′vər-hĕd′). Over or above the level of the head: *look over-head.*

overhead camshaft *n. Abbr.* **ohc, o.h.c.** A camshaft in an internal-combustion engine that is situated above the valves and acts directly onto their stems or onto rocker arms.

overhead valve *n. Abbr.* **ohv, o.h.v.** An internal-combustion engine valve that is situated in the cylinder head above the piston. Compare **side-valve.**

o·ver·hear (ō′vər-hîr′) *tr.v.* **-heard** (-hûrd′), **-hearing, -hears.** To happen to hear (something spoken or someone speaking) without being addressed intentionally by the speaker. **—o·ver·hear·er** *n.*

o·ver·heat (ō′vər-hēt′) *v.* **-heated, -heating, -heats.** —*tr.* **1.** To heat too much. **2.** To cause to become angry or excited: *overheated by a sharp exchange of insults.* **3.** *Economics.* To overstimulate (the economy), particularly by generating a level of demand so high that it cannot be met by suppliers. —*intr.* To become overheated.

o·ver·in·dulge (ō′vər-ĭn-dŭlj′) *v.* **-dulged, -dulging, -dulges.** —*tr.* To indulge excessively; gratify too much or unwisely. —*intr.* To indulge in something to excess. **—o·ver·in·dul·gence** *n.* **—o·ver·in·dul·gent** *adj.* **—o·ver·in·dul·gent·ly** *adv.*

o·ver·is·sue (ō′vər-ĭsh′ōō) *tr.v.* **-sued, -suing, -sues.** To issue more than the necessary, sensible, or authorized number of (shares of stock, for example).
~*n.* An issue that exceeds what is necessary, sensible, or authorized.

o·ver·joyed (ō′vər-joid′) *adj.* Filled with joy; delighted.

o·ver·kill (ō′vər-kĭl′) *n.* **1.** Destructive capacity, especially that of nuclear weapons, exceeding the amount needed to defeat or destroy an enemy. **2.** A greatly excessive action or response: *government overkill in dealing with dissent.* **3.** Excessive killing.
~*tr.v.* **overkilled, -killing, -kills.** To destroy (an enemy target) with more nuclear force than is needed.

o·ver·land (ō′vər-lănd′, -lənd) *adj.* **1.** Proceeding over or across land: *an overland flight.* **2.** By land rather than by sea or air: *an overland journey.*
~*adv.* (ō′vər-lănd′, ō′vər-lănd′). Over, across, or by land.
~*v.* **overlanded, -landing, -lands.** *Australian.* —*tr.* To drive (livestock) overland for long distances. —*intr.* To overland livestock. **—o·ver·land·er** *n.*

o·ver·lap (ō′vər-lăp′) *v.* **-lapped, -lapping, -laps.** —*tr.* **1.** To lie or extend over and cover part of. **2.** To have an area, time span, interest, or other dimension or aspect in common with; coincide partly with. —*intr.* **1.** To lie over and partly cover something. **2.** To coincide partly: *Their duties overlap.*
~*n.* (ō′vər-lăp′). **1.** A part or portion that overlaps or is overlapped. **2.** An instance of overlapping.

o·ver·lay (ō′vər-lā′) *tr.v.* **-laid** (-lād′), **-laying, -lays.** **1.** To lay or spread over or upon. **2. a.** To cover or decorate the surface of: *overlay wood with silver.* **b.** To embellish superficially: *a simple tune overlaid with ornate harmonies.* **3.** *Printing.* To put an overlay upon.
~*n.* (ō′vər-lā′). **1.** Something that is laid over or covers something else. **2.** A layer of decoration, such as gold leaf or wood veneer, applied to a surface. **3.** *Printing.* A piece of paper or other material used on a press, cylinder, or plate to even out the pressure. **4.** A transparent sheet containing graphic matter, such as labels or colored areas, placed on illustrative matter to be incorporated into it.

Usage: Overlay and overlie have similar senses but are not usually interchangeable. *Overlay* applies mainly to the act of superimposing one thing on another, as when a carpenter *overlays* plywood with veneer. The past tense is *overlaid. Overlie* applies when one thing is seen to lie over or rest upon another, as when warm air *overlies* cold air. The past tense is *overlain.*

o·ver·leaf (ō′vər-lēf′) *adv.* On the other side of a page, as of a book.

o·ver·leap (ō′vər-lēp′) *tr.v.* **-leaped** or **-leapt** (-lĕpt′), **-leaping, -leaps.** **1.** To leap across or over. **2.** To pass over; omit or ignore. **3.** To thwart (oneself or one's purposes) by going too far.

o·ver·learn (ō′vər-lûrn′) *tr.v.* **-learned** or **-learnt** (-lûrnt′), **-learning, -learns.** To continue working at (a skill, for example) after becoming proficient.

o·ver·lie (ō′vər-lī′) *tr.v.* **-lay** (-lā′), **-lain** (-lān′), **-laying, -lies.** **1.** To lie over or upon. **2.** To kill (an infant, for example) by lying upon. —See Usage note at **overlay.**

o·ver·load (ō′vər-lōd′) *tr.v.* **-loaded, -loading, -loads.** To load too heavily.
~*n.* (ō′vər-lōd′). An excessive load.

o·ver·look (ō′vər-lŏŏk′) *tr.v.* **-looked, -looking, -looks.** **1.** To look over or at from a higher place. **2.** To rise above, especially so as to afford a view over: *The tower overlooks the sea.* **3.** To fail to notice or consider; miss. **4.** To ignore deliberately or indulgently; disregard. **5.** To look over; examine. **6.** To watch over; supervise; oversee. **7.** To cast a spell or the evil eye upon; bewitch.
~*n.* (ō′vər-lŏŏk′). **1.** An elevated place that affords an extensive view. **2.** An act or instance of overlooking something.

o·ver·lord (ō′vər-lôrd′) *n.* **1.** A lord having power or sway over other lords. **2.** One who is in a position of supremacy or domination over others: *science overlords.* **—o·ver·lord·ship** *n.*

o·ver·ly (ō′vər-lē) *adv.* To an excessive degree; too: *This hotel seems not to be overly clean.*

Usage: The use of this word as an intensifying adverb is common (*She has been overly cautious about the problem*), but it has attracted criticism as an unnecessary development, the same sense already being expressed by the prefix *over-* (as in *overcautious*).

o·ver·man (ō′vər-mən, -măn′ *for sense 1;* ō′vər-măn′ *for sense 2*) *n.,*

pl. **-men** (-mĭn, -mĕn′). **1.** A man having authority over others; especially, an overseer or foreman. **2.** The Nietzschean superman.
~*tr.v.* (ō′vər-măn′) **overmanned, -manning, -mans.** To provide with more personnel than are needed.

o·ver·mas·ter (ō′vər-măs′tər, -mäs′tər) *tr.v.* **-tered, -tering, -ters.** To overpower; overcome. **—o·ver·mas·ter·ing·ly** *adv.*

o·ver·match (ō′vər-măch′) *tr.v.* **-matched, -matching, -matches.** **1.** To be more than the match of; exceed. **2.** To match with a superior opponent.

o·ver·much (ō′vər-mŭch′) *adj.* Too much; excessive.
~*adv.* **1.** In too great a degree. **2.** Very much. Usually used in the negative: *I don't care for her overmuch.*
~*n.* (ō′vər-mŭch′, ō′vər-mŭch′). An excessive amount.

o·ver·night (ō′vər-nīt′) *adj.* **1.** Lasting for, extending over, or remaining during a night: *an overnight journey.* **2.** For use over a single night or for a short journey. **3.** Sudden; meteoric: *an overnight success.*
~*adv.* **1.** During or for the length of the night. **2.** In or as if in the course of one night; suddenly: *The situation changed overnight.* **3.** On the preceding night or evening.

overnight bag *n.* A small piece of luggage used to carry items needed for an overnight stay.

o·ver·pass (ō′vər-păs′, -päs′) *n.* A passage, bridge, or roadway that crosses above another path, roadway, or thoroughfare.
~*tr.v.* (ō′vər-păs′, -päs′) **overpassed, -passing, -passes. 1.** To pass over or across; traverse. **2.** To go beyond; exceed; surpass. **3.** To overlook; disregard.

o·ver·pay (ō′vər-pā′) *v.* **-paid** (-pād′), **-paying, -pays.** —*tr.* **1.** To pay (someone) too much. **2.** To pay an amount in excess of (a sum due). —*intr.* To pay too much. **—o·ver·pay·ment** *n.*

o·ver·per·suade (ō′vər-pər-swād′) *tr.v.* **-suaded, -suading, -suades.** To persuade or act contrary to one's wishes. **—o·ver·per·sua·sion** (ō′vər-pər-swā′zhən) *n.*

o·ver·play (ō′vər-plā′) *tr.v.* **-played, -playing, -plays. 1.** To play (a dramatic role) in an exaggerated manner; overact. **2.** To overestimate the strength of (one's holding or position) and thus contribute to one's own defeat. Used chiefly in the phrase *overplay one's hand.* **3.** To invest with too much importance; exaggerate. **4.** To hit a golf ball beyond (the green).

o·ver·plus (ō′vər-plŭs′) *n.* An amount in excess of need.

o·ver·pop·u·la·tion (ō′vər-pŏp′yə-lā′shən) *n.* Excessive population to the point of overcrowding, depletion of natural resources, or environmental deterioration. **—o·ver·pop·u·lat·ed** (ō′vər-pŏp′yə-lā′tĭd) *adj.*

o·ver·pow·er (ō′vər-pou′ər) *tr.v.* **-ered, -ering, -ers. 1.** To overcome or vanquish by superior force; subdue. **2.** To affect so strongly as to make helpless or ineffective; overwhelm: *Smoke from the fire overpowered the occupants of the house.* **3.** To furnish with excessive mechanical power. **—o·ver·pow·er·ing·ly** *adv.*

o·ver·price (ō′vər-prīs′) *tr.v.* **-priced, -pricing, -prices.** To put too high a price on.

o·ver·print (ō′vər-prĭnt′) *tr.v.* **-printed, -printing, -prints.** To imprint over something already printed; especially, to print over (printed images) with another color.
~*n.* (ō′vər-prĭnt′). **1.** A mark or impression made by overprinting. **2. a.** A mark or words printed over a postage stamp. **b.** A stamp so marked.

o·ver·pro·duce (ō′vər-prə-dōōs′, -dyōōs′) *v.* **-duced, -ducing, -duces.** —*tr.* To produce too much of; produce more than is needed or can be sold. —*intr.* To overproduce a commodity or article. **—o·ver·pro·duc·tion** (ō′vər-prə-dŭk′shən) *n.*

o·ver·proof (ō′vər-prōōf′) *adj.* Containing a greater proportion of alcohol than proof spirit.

o·ver·pro·tect (ō′vər-prə-tĕkt′) *tr.v.* **-tected, -tecting, -tects. 1.** To protect more than is necessary or advisable. **2.** To shelter (someone, especially a child) excessively from the hard physical and social realities of the world, thereby distorting or stunting emotional development. **—o·ver·pro·tec·tive** *adj.*

o·ver·qual·i·fied (ō′vər-kwŏl′ə-fīd′) *adj.* Having qualifications beyond what is necessary or desired.

o·ver·rate (ō′vər-rāt′) *tr.v.* **-rated, -rating, -rates. 1.** To rate or assess too highly. **2.** To overestimate the merits of.

o·ver·reach (ō′vər-rēch′) *v.* **-reached, -reaching, -reaches.** —*tr.* **1.** To reach or extend over or beyond. **2.** To miss by reaching too far or attempting too much: *overreach a goal.* **3.** To defeat (oneself) by going too far, doing or trying to gain too much, or being too cunning. **4.** To get the better of, especially by tricking; outwit. —*intr.* **1.** To reach or go too far. **2.** To outwit or cheat others. **3.** To strike the front part of a hind foot against the rear or side part of a forefoot or foreleg on the same side of the body. Used of horses. **—o·ver·reach·er** *n.*

o·ver·re·act (ō′vər-rē-ăkt′) *intr.v.* **-acted, -acting, -acts.** To react with excessive force or vehemence. **—o·ver·re·ac·tion** *n.*

o·ver·ride (ō′vər-rīd′) *tr.v.* **-rode** (-rōd′), **-ridden** (-rīd′n), **-riding, -rides. 1.** To declare null and void; set aside. **2.** To ride (a horse) too hard. **3.** To trample upon. **4.** To prevail over; conquer: *Budgetary concerns overrode all other considerations.* **5.** To ride across. **6.** To extend over or overlap.
~*n.* (ō′vər-rīd′). **1.** An act or instance of overriding. **2.** A sales commission collected by an executive in addition to the commission received by a subordinate salesman.

o·ver·ripe (ō′vər-rīp′) *adj.* **1.** More than ripe; too ripe. **2.** Jaded; decadent. **—o·ver·ripe·ness** *n.*

o·ver·rule (ō'vər-rōōl') *tr.v.* **-ruled, -ruling, -rules.** **1. a.** To disallow the arguments of (a person), especially by virtue of higher authority; rule against. **b.** To decide or rule against (an argument, action, or decision). **c.** To declare null and void; invalidate or reverse. **2.** To dominate by strong influence; prevail over so as to change the opinion or course of action.

o·ver·run (ō'vər-rŭn') *v.* **-ran** (-răn') **-run, -running, -runs.** *—tr.* **1.** To attack, defeat conclusively, and seize: *The troops overran the town.* **2.** To spread or swarm over destructively: *Locusts overran the prairie.* **3.** To spread swiftly throughout: *The new fashion overran the country.* **4.** To overflow: *The river overran its banks.* **5.** To run or extend beyond: *Her speech has overrun the time limit.* **6.** *Archaic.* To run faster than. **7.** *Printing.* **a.** To rearrange or move (set type or pictures) from one column, line, or page to another. **b.** To print (a job order) in a quantity larger than that ordered. *—intr.* **1.** To run over; overflow. **2.** To go beyond the normal or desired limit. *~n.* (ō'vər-rŭn'). **1.** An act or instance of overrunning. **2.** The amount by which something overruns. **3. a.** The act of exceeding estimated costs for work covered by a contract. **b.** The amount by which actual costs exceed estimates.

o·ver·score (ō'vər-skôr', -skōr') *tr.v.* **-scored, -scoring, -scores.** To cross out by drawing a line or lines over or through.

o·ver·sea (ō'vər-sē', ō'vər-sē') *adj. & adv.* Overseas.

o·ver·seas (ō'vər-sēz', ō'vər-sēz') *adv.* Beyond the sea; abroad. *~adj.* Of, pertaining to, originating in, or situated in areas across the sea: *overseas students; an overseas posting.* *~n. Informal.* Used with a singular verb. Overseas countries collectively.

overseas cap *n.* A garrison cap (*see*).

o·ver·see (ō'vər-sē') *tr.v.* **-saw** (-sô') **-seen** (-sēn') **-seeing, -sees.** **1.** To watch over and direct; supervise. **2.** *Archaic.* To scrutinize; inspect. —See Synonyms at **conduct.**

o·ver·se·er (ō'vər-sē'ər, -sîr') *n.* **1.** One who keeps watch over and directs the work of others, especially laborers. **2.** A supervisor or superintendent.

o·ver·sell (ō'vər-sĕl') *tr.v.* **-sold** (-sōld') **-selling, -sells.** **1.** To contract to sell more of (a commodity) than can be delivered within the terms of a contract. **2.** To be too aggressive in attempting to sell (someone) something. **3.** To present with excessive or unwarranted enthusiasm.

o·ver·sen·si·tive (ō'vər-sĕn'sĭ-tĭv) *adj.* Excessively sensitive.

o·ver·set (ō'vər-sĕt') *tr.v.* **-set, -setting, -sets.** **1.** To tip over; overturn. **2.** To throw into a confused or disturbed state; upset. **3.** *Printing.* To set too much (type) for a given space. *~n.* (ō'vər-sĕt'). **1.** *Printing.* An excess of set type. **2.** An upset.

o·ver·sew (ō'vər-sō') *tr.v.* **-sewed, -sewn** (-sōn') or **-sewed, -sewing, -sews.** To sew over (raw edges of fabric) to prevent fraying.

o·ver·sexed (ō'vər-sĕkst') *adj.* Having a sexual drive or interest that is judged to be excessive.

o·ver·shad·ow (ō'vər-shăd'ō) *tr.v.* **-owed, -owing, -ows.** **1. a.** To cast a shadow over. **b.** To cast gloom and despondency on. **2.** To make insignificant by comparison; dominate.

o·ver·shoe (ō'vər-shōō') *n.* An article of footwear worn over shoes as protection from water, snow, or cold.

o·ver·shoot (ō'vər-shōōt') *v.* **-shot** (-shŏt') **-shooting, -shoots.** *—tr.* **1.** To shoot or pass over or beyond. **2.** To miss by or as if by shooting, hitting, or propelling something too far. **3. a.** To fly beyond or past (a specific location): *The plane overshot the runway.* **b.** To fly (an aircraft) beyond or past a specific location. **4.** To go beyond; exceed. *—intr.* To shoot or go too far.

o·ver·shot (ō'vər-shŏt') *adj.* **1.** Having an upper part projecting beyond the lower: *an overshot jaw.* **2.** Of, pertaining to, or being a water wheel or mill in which the flowing water feeds and drives the wheel from the top.

o·ver·sight (ō'vər-sīt') *n.* **1.** An unintentional omission or mistake. **2.** Watchful care or management; supervision.

o·ver·sim·pli·fy (ō'vər-sĭm'plə-fī') *tr.v.* **-fied, -fying, -fies.** To distort by presenting in too simple a form. **—o·ver·sim·pli·fi·ca·tion** (ō'vər-sĭm'plə-fĭ-kā'shən) *n.*

o·ver·size (ō'vər-sīz') *adj.* Also **o·ver·sized** (-sīzd'). Larger in size than usual or necessary. *~n.* (ō'vər-sīz'). **1.** An unusually large size. **2.** An article made in an unusually large size.

o·ver·skirt (ō'vər-skûrt') *n.* An outer skirt, especially a shorter one worn draped over another skirt.

o·ver·sleep (ō'vər-slēp') *v.* **-slept** (-slĕpt') **-sleeping, -sleeps.** *—intr.* To sleep beyond one's usual or planned time for waking. *—tr.* To sleep beyond the time for: *overslept my appointment.*

o·ver·soul (ō'vər-sōl') *n.* In New England transcendentalism, a spiritual essence or vital force in the universe, in which all souls participate, and which therefore transcends individual consciousness.

o·ver·spend (ō'vər-spĕnd') *v.* **-spent** (-spĕnt') **-spending, -spends.** *—intr.* To spend more than is prudent or necessary. *—tr.* **1.** To spend in excess of: *overspend one's income.* **2.** To exhaust. Used chiefly in the past participle: *overspent with worry.*

o·ver·spill (ō'vər-spĭl') *n. British.* An overflow or excess; especially, an overflow of people from one area to another. Also used adjectivally: *an overspill estate.*

o·ver·state (ō'vər-stāt') *tr.v.* **-stated, -stating, -states.** To state in exaggerated terms. **—o·ver·state·ment** *n.*

o·ver·stay (ō'vər-stā') *tr.v.* **-stayed, -staying, -stays.** To stay beyond the set limits or expected duration of: *She overstayed her welcome.*

o·ver·steer (ō'vər-stîr') *n.* A tendency of a motor vehicle to turn more sharply than is usual or intended by the driver.

o·ver·step (ō'vər-stĕp') *tr.v.* **-stepped, -stepping, -steps.** To go beyond (a limit): *overstep the bounds of good taste.*

o·ver·stock (ō'vər-stŏk') *v.* **-stocked, -stocking, -stocks.** *—tr.* To supply with too much of (a commodity). *—intr.* To stock too much of a commodity. *~n.* (ō'vər-stŏk'). An excessive supply.

o·ver·strung (ō'vər-strŭng') *adj.* Tense and strained; highly strung.

o·ver·stuff (ō'vər-stŭf') *tr.v.* **-stuffed, -stuffing, -stuffs.** **1.** To stuff too much into. **2.** To upholster overall and thickly.

o·ver·sub·scribe (ō'vər-səb-skrīb') *tr.v.* **-scribed, -scribing, -scribes.** To subscribe for (something) in excess of available supply or accommodation: *The opera season was oversubscribed.* **—o·ver·sub·scrip·tion** (ō'vər-səb-skrĭp'shən) *n.*

o·ver·sup·ply (ō'vər-sə-plī') *n., pl.* **-plies.** A supply in excess of what is required. *~tr.v.* (ō'vər-sə-plī') **oversupplied, -plying, -plies.** To supply in excess.

o·vert (ō'vûrt, ō'vûrt') *adj.* Open and observable; not concealed or hidden. [Middle English, from Old French, from the past participle of *ovrir,* to open, from Vulgar Latin *operīre* (unattested), from Latin *aperīre.*] **—o·vert·ly** *adv.* **—o·vert·ness** *n.*

o·ver·take (ō'vər-tāk') *tr.v.* **-took** (-tōōk') **-taken** (-tā'kən) **-taking, -takes.** **1. a.** To move past and take up a position in front of. **b.** To pass or surpass after catching up with. **2.** To catch up with; draw even or level with. **3.** To come upon unexpectedly; take by surprise: *Night overtook us.*

o·ver·task (ō'vər-tăsk', -täsk') *tr.v.* **-tasked, -tasking, -tasks.** **1.** To give too demanding a task to. **2.** To be too demanding a task for; strain to exhaustion.

o·ver·tax (ō'vər-tăks') *tr.v.* **-taxed, -taxing, -taxes.** **1.** To impose an excessive tax or taxes on. **2.** To subject to an excessive burden or strain. **—o·ver·tax·a·tion** (ō'vər-tăk-sā'shən) *n.*

o·ver·the·count·er (ō'vər-thə-koun'tər) *adj.* **1.** Capable of being sold legally without a prescription. Said of certain drugs or medicines. **2.** Not listed or available on an officially recognized stock exchange but traded in direct negotiation between buyers and sellers. Said of securities. Compare **under-the-counter.** **3.** *Informal.* Legitimate; aboveboard.

o·ver·throw (ō'vər-thrō') *tr.v.* **-threw** (-thrōō') **-thrown** (-thrōn') **-throwing, -throws.** **1.** To throw over; overturn. **2.** To bring about the downfall or destruction of, especially by force or concerted action: *a plot to overthrow the government.* **3.** To throw something over and beyond (an intended mark): *The infielder overthrew first base.* *~n.* (ō'vər-thrō'). **1.** An instance of overthrowing. **2.** Downfall; destruction. **3.** The throwing of a ball over and beyond a target, especially in baseball.

o·ver·thrust (ō'vər-thrŭst') *n. Geology.* A fault caused by the movement of rocks on the upper surface of a gently inclined fault plane over the rocks on the lower surface. Compare **underthrust.**

o·ver·time (ō'vər-tīm') *n.* **1.** Time spent at a job in addition to regular working hours. Also used adjectively: *overtime payments.* **2.** Payment given for additional work done outside regular working hours. **3.** *Sports.* A period of playing time added after the expiration of the set time of an athletic contest. *~adv.* Beyond the established time limit, especially that of the normal working day: *The staff worked overtime.* *~tr.v.* (ō'vər-tīm') **overtimed, -timing, -times.** To exceed the desired time limit for: *overtime a photographic exposure.*

o·ver·tone (ō'vər-tōn') *n.* **1.** In music and acoustics, a **harmonic** (*see*). **2.** *Often* **overtones.** An implication or hint: *praise with overtones of envy.* [Translation of German *Oberton.*]

o·ver·top (ō'vər-tŏp') *tr.v.* **-topped, -topping, -tops.** **1.** To extend or rise over or beyond the top of; tower above. **2.** To be superior to; surpass in importance; override.

o·ver·trick (ō'vər-trĭk') *n.* In card games, a trick won in excess of contract or game.

o·ver·trump (ō'vər-trŭmp', ō'vər-trŭmp') *v.* **-trumped, -trumping, -trumps.** *—tr.* To trump with a higher trump card than any played on the same trick. *—intr.* To play a trump higher than one previously played on a trick.

o·ver·ture (ō'vər-chōōr', -chər) *n.* **1.** *Music.* **a.** An instrumental composition intended especially as an introduction to an opera, oratorio, or other extended musical work. **b.** A similar orchestral work, such as one written as introductory music to a play or as a concert piece. **2.** An introductory section or part, as of a poem. **3.** An act, offer, or proposal that indicates readiness to undertake a course of action or to open a relationship: *"I wanted revenge for her snub of my flirting overture"* (John Updike). **4.** *Presbyterian Church.* **a.** The submitting of a proposal by the highest church court to the presbyteries for their judgment on it preceding formal decision by the court. **b.** A proposal thus submitted. *~tr.v.* **overtured, -turing, -tures.** **1.** To present as an overture or proposal. **2.** To present or offer an overture to. **3.** To introduce with an overture or prelude. [Middle English, from Old French, from Vulgar Latin *opertūra* (unattested), from Latin *apertūra,* an opening, from *aperīre* (past participle *apertus*), to open.]

o·ver·turn (ō'vər-tûrn') *v.* **-turned, -turning, -turns.** *—tr.* **1.** To cause to turn over or capsize; upset. **2.** To overthrow; defeat. **3.** To negate; nullify: *overturn a decision.* *—intr.* To turn over or capsize: *The sailboat overturned in rough seas.* **—o·ver·turn** (ō'vər-tûrn') *n.*

owl *Sensitive sight and hearing enable owls to hunt at night, and their soft plumage allows them to swoop silently on their prey. The long-eared owl (above) is native to Europe, North America, and parts of Asia. It roosts in trees by day, when its speckled body merges with the twigs and branches.*

PRONUNCIATION KEY

ă, pat; ā, pay; âr, care;
ä, father, are; b, **bib**;
ch, **church**; d, **deed**; ĕ, pet;
ē, be; f, **fife**; g, **gag**; h, **hat**;
hw, **which**; ĭ, pit; ī, pie;
îr, **pier**; j, **judge**; k, **kick**;
l, **lid**, needle; m, **mum**;
n, no, sudden; ng, thing;
ŏ, pot; ō, toe; ô, paw, for;
oi, noise; ou, **out**; o͝o, book;
o͞o, boot; p, **pop**; r, **roar**;
s, sauce; sh, **ship**, **dish**;
t, **tight**; th, **thin**, **path**;
th, **this**, bathe; ŭ, cut; ûr, **fur**;
v, valve; w, **with**; y, **yes**;
z, zebra, size; zh, vision;
ə, about, item, edible, gallop, circus, peaceful

IN FOREIGN WORDS:

à, *Fr.* ami; œ, *Fr.* **feu**, *Ger.* schön; ü, *Fr.* **tu**, *Ger.* **über**; KH, *Ger.* **ich**, *Scot.* **loch**; N, *Fr.* bon; y', *Fr.* Compiègne

STRESS MARKS:

Primary stress: ′
in·cite′ (ĭn-sīt′)
Secondary stress: ′
in′sight′ (ĭn′sīt′)

o·ver·use (ō′vər-yo͞oz′) *tr.v.* **-used, -using, -uses.** To use to excess. ~*n.* (-yo͞os′). Excessive use.

o·ver·val·ue (ō′vər-văl′yo͞o) *tr.v.* **-ued, -uing, -ues.** To place too high a value on. **—o·ver·val·u·a·tion** *n.*

o·ver·view (ō′vər-vyo͞o′) *n.* **1.** A broad, comprehensive view; survey. **2.** A summary or review.

o·ver·ween·ing (ō′vər-wē′nĭng) *adj.* **1.** Presumptuously arrogant; overbearing. **2.** Excessive; immoderate: *overweening ambition.* [Middle English, "having an excessively high opinion of oneself" : OVER- + WEEN + -ING.] **—o·ver·ween·ing·ly** *adv.*

o·ver·weigh (ō′vər-wā′) *tr.v.* **-weighed, -weighing, -weighs. 1.** To weigh down excessively; overburden. **2.** To have more weight than; outweigh.

o·ver·weight (ō′vər-wāt′) *adj.* Weighing more than is normal, necessary, or allowed.
~*n.* (ō′vər-wāt′). **1.** More weight than is normal, necessary, or allowed. **2.** Greater weight or importance; preponderance.
~*tr.v.* (ō′vər-wāt′) **overweighted, -weighting, -weights. 1.** To weigh down too heavily; overload. **2.** To give too much emphasis, importance, or consideration to.

o·ver·whelm (ō′vər-hwĕlm′, -wĕlm′) *tr.v.* **-whelmed, -whelming, -whelms. 1.** To overcome completely physically or emotionally; overpower: *quite overwhelmed by all this praise.* **2.** To surge over and submerge; engulf. **3.** To turn over; upset.

o·ver·whelm·ing (ō′vər-hwĕl′mĭng, -wĕl′-) *adj.* Overpowering in effect or strength: *overwhelming news; an overwhelming majority.* **—o·ver·whelm·ing·ly** *adv.*

o·ver·wind (ō′vər-wīnd′) *tr.v.* **-wound** (-wound′), **-winding, -winds.** To wind (a watch, for example) too tightly.

o·ver·win·ter (ō′vər-wĭn′tər) *intr.v.* **-wintered, -wintering, -winters.** To survive the winter.
~*adj.* Occurring during the period of winter.

o·ver·work (ō′vər-wûrk′) *v.* **-worked, -working, -works.** *—tr.* **1.** To force to work too hard or long. **2.** To use or rework too often or to excess: *overwork a metaphor.* *—intr.* To work too hard or long. ~*n.* Work that is too hard or lasts too long.

o·ver·write (ō′vər-rīt′) *v.* **-wrote** (-rōt′), **-written** (-rĭt′n), **-writing, -writes.** *—tr.* **1. a.** To write (something) over other writing. **b.** To write something over (other writing). **2.** To write (a text) or write about (a subject) in an excessively flowery, mannered, or prolix style. *—intr.* **1.** To write at unnecessarily great length. **2.** To write in an inappropriately ornate or fulsome style.

o·ver·wrought (ō′vər-rôt′) *adj.* **1.** Excessively nervous or excited; agitated: *so overwrought that he fainted.* **2.** Extremely elaborate or ornate; overdone: *an overwrought prose style.*

ovi–, ovo– *prefix.* Indicates egg or ovum; for example, **ovoviviparous, oviduct.** [Latin *ōvi-, ōvo-,* from *ōvum,* egg.]

Ov·id (ŏv′ĭd), born Publius Ovidius Naso (43 B.C.–A.D. 18). Roman poet. His work includes *Metamorphoses,* an urbane treatment of several legends. He also wrote many love poems.

o·vi·duct (ō′və-dŭkt′) *n. Zoology.* A tube through which ova travel from an ovary. [New Latin *oviductus* : OVI- + DUCT.] **—o·vi·duc·tal** (ō′və-dŭk′təl) *adj.*

o·vif·er·ous (ō-vĭf′ər-əs) *adj.* Bearing or producing ova. [OVI- + -FEROUS.]

o·vi·form (ō′və-fôrm′) *adj.* Egg-shaped. [OVI- + -FORM.]

o·vine (ō′vīn′) *adj.* Of, pertaining to, or resembling a sheep; sheeplike.
~*n.* An ovine animal. [Late Latin *ovīnus,* from Latin *ovis,* sheep.]

o·vip·a·rous (ō-vĭp′ər-əs) *adj.* Producing eggs that hatch outside the body. Compare **ovoviviparous, viviparous.** [Latin *ōviparus* : OVI- + -PAROUS.] **—o·vi·par·i·ty** (ō′və-păr′ə-tē) *n.* **—o·vip·a·rous·ly** *adv.*

o·vi·pos·it (ō′və-pŏz′ĭt, ō′və-pŏz′-) *intr.v.* **-ited, -iting, -its.** To lay eggs, especially with an ovipositor. **—o·vi·po·si·tion** (ō′və-pə-zĭsh′ən) *n.*

o·vi·pos·i·tor (ō′və-pŏz′ə-tər) *n.* **1.** A tubular structure, consisting of a pair of valves extending near the rear of the abdomen, with which most insects lay eggs. **2.** An egg-laying organ in certain fish that is an extension of the edge of the genital opening.

o·vi·sac (ō′və-săk′) *n. Biology.* An egg-containing capsule, such as a Graafian follicle or an ootheca.

ovo–. Variant of **ovi-.**

o·void (ō′void′) *adj.* Also **o·voi·dal** (ō-void′l). **1.** Egg-shaped. **2.** *Botany.* Egg-shaped and having the broader end nearest the point of attachment. Said especially of leaves or fruits. [French *ovoide* : OV(I)- + -OID.] **—o·void** *n.*

o·vo·lo (ō′və-lō′) *n., pl.* **-li** (-lī′). *Architecture.* A rounded convex molding, often a quarter section of a circle or ellipse. Also called "thumb." [Italian, diminutive of *ovo,* egg, from Latin *ōvum.*]

o·von·ic (ō-vŏn′ĭk) *adj.* Of, pertaining to, or being a phenomenon or device based on the Ovshinsky effect.
~*n.* An Ovshinsky device. [Blend of *Ov*shinsky + electr*onic.*]

o·vo·tes·tis (ō′vō-tĕs′tĭs) *n., pl.* **-tes** (-tēz′). *Zoology.* The hermaphroditic reproductive organ of some gastropods.

o·vo·vi·vip·a·rous (ō′vō-vī-vĭp′ər-əs) *adj.* Producing eggs that hatch within the female's body, as do some fishes and reptiles. Compare **oviparous, viviparous.** [New Latin *ovoviviparus* : OVO- + *viviparus,* VIVIPAROUS.] **—o·vo·vi·vi·par·i·ty** (ō′vō-vī′və-păr′ə-tē), **o·vo·vi·vip·a·rous·ness** *n.* **—o·vo·vi·vip·a·rous·ly** *adv.*

Ov·shin·sky device (ŏv-shĭn′skē, ōv-) *n.* An electronic device using the Ovshinsky effect. Also called "ovonic."

Ovshinsky effect *n. Electronics.* An effect that occurs in certain glasses containing selenium and tellurium. When a suitable voltage is applied across a thin film of this material its resistance falls rapidly, enabling devices incorporating these glasses to be used as switches. [After Stanford R. *Ovshinsky* (born 1923).]

o·vu·late (ō′vyə-lāt′, ŏv′yə-) *intr.v.* **-lated, -lating, -lates.** *Biology.* **1.** To produce ova. **2.** To discharge ova. [New Latin *ovulum,* OVULE.] **—o·vu·la·tion** *n.*

o·vule (ō′vyo͞ol, ŏv′yo͞ol) *n.* **1.** *Botany.* A female reproductive structure consisting of the integuments, nucellus, and embryo sac that after fertilization becomes a seed. **2.** *Zoology.* An immature ovum. [French, from New Latin *ovulum,* diminutive of Latin *ōvum,* egg.] **—o·vu·lar** (ō′vyə-lər, ŏv′yə-), **o·vu·lar·y** (ō′vyə-lĕr′ē) *adj.*

o·vum (ō′vəm) *n., pl.* **ova** (ō′və). The female reproductive cell of animals; an egg cell. [New Latin, from Latin *ōvum, egg.*]

owe (ō) *v.* **owed** or *obsolete* **ought** (ôt), **owing, owes.** *—tr.* **1.** To be indebted to the amount of; have to pay or repay: *She owes me five dollars.* **2.** To have a moral obligation to render or offer: *I owe you an apology.* **3.** To be in debt to: *owe the department store for some merchandise.* **4. a.** To be indebted or obliged to: *I owe a lot to my friends.* **b.** To be indebted or obliged for the existence or origin of: *He owes his success to talent and luck.* **5.** To bear (a certain feeling) toward a person: *She owes them a grudge.* *—intr.* To be in debt: *She owes for everything she has.* [Middle English *owen,* to possess, own, owe, Old English *āgan,* to possess.]

Ow·en (ō′ĭn), **Robert** (1771–1858). Welsh philanthropist. After establishing the mill community of New Lanark (where he was manager and later owner) as a cooperative (1800), he started similar ventures in the United States and Ireland.

Owen, Wilfred (1893–1918). British poet, who served in World War I. His poems describe the nightmarish conditions in which soldiers lived and died; among his most famous poems is "Anthem for Doomed Youth." He was killed a week before the armistice.

Ow·ens (ō′ĭnz), **Jesse,** born James Cleveland Owens (1913–80). U.S. athlete. In 1935–36 he broke six world records in sprinting, hurdling, and the long jump; his records stood for 20 years. His greatest triumph came at the 1936 Olympics in Germany, when his success as a black athlete embarrassed the Nazi government.

ow·ing (ō′ĭng) *adj.* Still to be paid; due. **—owing to.** Because of; on account of. —See Usage note at **due.**

owl (oul) *n.* **1.** Any of various often nocturnal birds of prey of the order Strigiformes, having hooked and feathered talons, short necks, large heads with short, hooked beaks, and eyes set in a frontal facial plane. **2.** Any of various breeds of domestic pigeon resembling owls. **3.** A person who is like an owl, as in being solemn or wise-looking. [Middle English *owle,* Old English *ūle.*]

owl·et (ou′lĭt) *n.* A young owl.

owl·ish (ou′lĭsh) *adj.* Resembling an owl: *looked owlish in his horn-rimmed spectacles.* **—owl·ish·ly** *adv.* **—owl·ish·ness** *n.*

owl-light (oul′līt′) *n. Poetic.* Twilight; dusk.

own (ōn) *adj.* Of or belonging to oneself or itself; individual; particular. Used to intensify the fact of possession and usually preceded by a possessive pronoun: *my own book.* Sometimes used to indicate oneself as the sole agent of the action expressed by the verb: *She made her own bed while I made the rest.*
~*n.* That which belongs to one: *It is my own.* **—come into one's own. 1.** To obtain possession of what belongs to one. **2.** To reach one's deserved level; fulfill one's potential. **3.** To obtain rightful recognition. **—hold one's own.** To maintain one's place in spite of attack or criticism. **—of one's own.** Belonging completely to oneself alone. **—on one's own. 1.** Alone; without company; by oneself. **2.** Without help; through one's own unaided efforts. **3.** Completely independent; responsible for oneself.
~*v.* **owned, owning, owns.** *—tr.* **1.** To have or possess: *She owns the shop.* **2.** To acknowledge or admit: *"I own myself a debtor to the world for two items"* (Lawrence Sterne). *—intr.* To confess or acknowledge: *She owned to being annoyed.* —See Synonyms at **acknowledge. —own up.** To confess fully and openly. Sometimes used with *to.* [Middle English *owen,* Old English *āgen.*]

own·er (ō′nər) *n.* A person who owns something; especially, a person having legal ownership.

own·er·ship (ō′nər-shĭp′) *n.* **1.** The state or fact of being an owner. **2.** Legal right to the possession of something; proprietorship; dominion.

owt (ōt, ôt) *n. British Regional.* Anything.

ox (ŏks) *n., pl.* **oxen** (ŏk′sən). **1.** An adult castrated bull of the genus *Bos.* **2.** Any bovine mammal. [Middle English *ox,* Old English *oxa.*]

ox–. 1. Variant of **oxa-. 2.** Variant of **oxo-.**

oxa–, ox– *prefix. Chemistry.* Indicates the presence of oxygen atoms, especially when replacing carbon; for example, **oxalic acid.** [From OXYGEN.]

ox·a·cil·lin (ŏk′sə-sĭl′ĭn) *n.* A semisynthetic penicillin effective against penicillinase-producing staphylococci. [OX(O) + A(ZOLE) + (PENI)CILLIN.]

ox·a·late (ŏk′sə-lāt′) *n.* A salt or ester of oxalic acid.
~*tr.v.* **oxalated, -lating, -lates.** To treat (a specimen) with an oxalate or oxalic acid. [French : *oxalique,* OXALIC ACID + -ATE.]

ox·al·ic acid (ŏk-săl′ĭk) *n.* A poisonous, crystalline organic acid, $HOOCCOOH{\cdot}2H_2O$, used as a cleansing agent for motor-vehicle radiators and for metals in general, as a laundry bleach, and in textile finishing and cleaning. Also called "ethanedioic acid." [French *oxalique,* from Latin *oxalis,* wood sorrel, OXALIS.]

ox·a·lis (ŏk′sə-lĭs, ŏk-săl′ĭs) *n.* Any of various plants of the genus *Oxalis,* having cloverlike leaves and pink, yellow, or white flowers.

See **wood sorrel**. [New Latin, from Latin, from Greek, from *oxus*, "sharp," sour.]

ox·a·zine (ŏk'sə-zēn') *n.* A heterocyclic chemical compound, C_4H_5NO, that exists in 13 isomeric forms. [OXY- + AZINE.]

ox·blood red (ŏks'blŭd') *n.* A dark or deep red to medium reddish brown. Also called "oxblood."

ox·bow (ŏks'bō') *n.* **1.** A U-shaped piece of wood that fits under and around the neck of an ox, with its upper ends attached to the bar of the yoke. **2. a.** A U-shaped bend in a river. **b.** The land within such a bend of a river. **c.** A lake formed from a U-shaped bend in a river. In this sense, also called "oxbow lake." —**ox·bow** *adj.*

Ox·bridge (ŏks'brĭj') *n.* The universities of Oxford and Cambridge, especially considered as representing traditional academic and social excellence, privilege, and exclusiveness.
~*adj.* Of, pertaining to, or characteristic of Oxbridge: *Oxbridge philosophers; Oxbridge snobbery.* [*Ox*ford + Cam*bridge*.]

ox·er (ŏk'sər) *n.* An ox fence.

ox·eye (ŏks'ī') *n.* **1.** Any of various Eurasian plants of the genus *Buphthalmum,* having daisylike flowers with yellow rays and dark centers. **2.** Any of various North American plants of the genus *Heliopsis,* having flowers similar to those of the oxeye. **3.** A round or oval dormer window.

oxeye daisy *n.* A perennial plant, *Chrysanthemum leucanthemum,* having daisylike flowers with white rays and yellow centers.

ox fence *n.* A barrier for containing cattle that consists of a hedge, a railing, and usually a ditch. Also called "oxer."

ox·ford (ŏks'fərd) *n.* **1.** A stout, low shoe that laces over the instep. **2.** A cotton cloth of a tight basket weave, used primarily for shirts. **3.** Oxford. A sheep, **the Oxford Down** *(see).* [After OXFORD, England.]

Ox·ford (ŏks'fərd). City in south-central England. The county town of Oxfordshire, it is between the Thames River (known locally as the Isis) and its tributary, the Cherwell. Its university (1249) is one of the world's most important places of learning; its historic buildings dominate the city center.

Oxford bags *pl.n.* Trousers with extremely wide, baggy legs.

Oxford blue *n.* A dark, deep blue.

Oxford Down *n.* A large sheep of an English breed, having a dark brown face and legs and short wool. Also called "Oxford."

Oxford English *n.* A style of English pronunciation thought to be used at Oxford University and often considered to be affected.

Oxford frame *n.* A picture frame whose sides cross and project outward at the corners.

Oxford gray *n.* A dark gray.

Oxford Group *n.* **Moral Rearmament** *(see).*

Oxford movement *n.* A movement within the Church of England that originated at Oxford University in 1833. It sought to link the Anglican Church more closely to the Roman Catholic Church. See **Tractarianism.**

Ox·ford·shire (ŏks'fərd-shîr', -shər). *Abbr.* **Oxon.** County of south-central England. An agricultural valley rising to the Cotswolds in the west and the Chilterns in the south, it is drained by the Thames River. Dairy and sheep farming are important, and the major industrial center is Cowley. The county town is Oxford.

ox·i·dant (ŏk'sĭ-dənt) *n.* A chemical reagent that oxidizes.

ox·i·dase (ŏk'sə-dās', -dāz') *n.* Any of various plant or animal enzymes that act as oxidants. [OXID(ATION) + -ASE.] —**ox·i·da·sic** (ŏk'sə-dā'sĭk, -zīk) *adj.*

ox·i·da·tion (ŏk'sə-dā'shən) *n. Chemistry.* **1.** The process of oxidizing. **2.** A chemical reaction in which something is oxidized. Compare **reduction.** [French, from *oxyder,* to oxidize.] —**ox·i·da·tive** (ŏk'sə-dā'tĭv) *adj.* —**ox·i·da·tive·ly** *adv.*

ox·i·da·tion-re·duc·tion (ŏk'sə-dā'shən-rĭ-dŭk'shən) *n.* A chemical reaction in which an atom or molecule loses electrons to another atom or molecule. Also called "redox."

oxidative phosphorylation *n. Biochemistry.* A vital process of intracellular respiration occurring within the mitochondria of the cell and responsible for most ATP formation.

ox·ide (ŏk'sīd') *n.* A binary compound of an element or radical with oxygen. [French, from *oxygène,* OXYGEN.] —**ox·id·ic** (ŏk-sĭd'ĭk) *adj.*

ox·i·dim·e·try (ŏk'sə-dĭm'ə-trē) *n. Chemistry.* A form of volumetric analysis in which oxidizing agents are used in titrations. [*Oxid*ation + -METRY.]

ox·i·dize (ŏk'sə-dīz') *v.* **-dized, -dizing, -dizes.** Also **ox·i·date** (-dāt', -dated, -dating, -dates.** —*tr.* **1.** *Chemistry.* **a.** To add oxygen to (a compound), as in combustion reactions. **b.** To remove hydrogen from (a compound), as in dehydrogenation reactions. **c.** To remove electrons from (a compound, ion, or group), as in the change of ferrous ions (Fe^{2+}) to ferric ions (Fe^{3+}). **2.** To coat with oxide. —*intr.* **1.** *Chemistry.* To undergo oxidation; gain oxygen or lose hydrogen or electrons. Used of chemical compounds. **2.** To become coated with oxide. [From OXIDE.] —**ox·i·diz·a·ble** *adj.* —**ox·i·di·za·tion** *n.*

ox·i·diz·er (ŏk'sə-dī'zər) *n.* A substance that oxidizes or induces oxidization; especially, the oxidant in a rocket fuel.

oxidizing agent *n. Chemistry.* A substance, such as oxygen or hydrogen peroxide, that oxidizes another substance and is itself reduced in doing so. Compare **reducing agent.**

ox·i·do·re·duc·tase (ŏk'sĭ-dō-rĭ-dŭk'tās', -tāz') *n.* An enzyme that catalyzes an oxidation-reduction reaction. [OXID(ATION) + REDUC(TION) + -ASE.]

ox·ime (ŏk'sēm') *n.* Any of a group of chemical compounds used in chemical analysis that have the general formula RR'C:NOH. If R and R' are both organic groups the compound is called a *ketoxime;* if R' is an organic group and R is a hydrogen atom it is an *aldoxime.* [OXO- + -*ime* representing -IMIDE.]

ox·lip (ŏks'lĭp') *n.* **1.** A Eurasian plant, *Primula elatior,* very similar to the primrose, with flowers borne in clusters. **2.** A hybrid plant that is a cross between primroses and cowslips and has darker yellow flowers than the true oxlip. [Old English *oxanslyppe : oxan,* genitive of *oxa,* ox + *slyppe, slypa,* sticky substance, dung.]

oxo-, ox- *prefix. Chemistry.* Indicates a compound containing oxygen linked to another atom by a double bond; for example, **oxonium.** [From OXYGEN.]

Oxon. Oxfordshire.

Ox·o·ni·an (ŏk-sō'nē-ən) *adj.* Of, pertaining to, or characteristic of Oxford or Oxford University.
~*n.* **1.** A student, graduate, or member of Oxford University. **2.** A native or inhabitant of Oxford. [Medieval Latin *Oxōnia,* Oxford, from Old English *Ox(e)naford,* OXFORD.]

ox·o·ni·um (ŏk-sō'nē-əm) *n.* An ion with the general formula R_3O, where R is either a hydrogen atom or an organic group. Also used adjectively to designate a compound formed from this ion: *an oxonium salt.* [OXO- + -ON(E) + -IUM.]

ox·peck·er (ŏks'pĕk'ər) *n.* Either of two African birds, *Buphagus africanus* or *B. erythrorhynchus,* that feed upon ticks on the hides of animals. Also called "rhinoceros bird," "tick bird."

ox·tail (ŏks'tāl') *n.* The tail of an ox, as used in soups and stews.

ox·ter (ŏks'tər) *n. British Regional.* An armpit. [Old English *ōxta, ōhsta;* akin to Latin *axilla.*]

ox·tongue (ŏks'tŭng') *n.* **1.** The tongue of an ox used as food. **2.** Either of two plants, *Picris echioides* or *P. hieracioides,* having tongue-shaped, hairy leaves and yellow flowers.

Oxus. See **Amu Darya.**

ox·y (ŏk'sē) *adj.* **1.** Containing or mixed with oxygen. Often used in combination: *oxyhydrogen.* **2.** *Chemistry.* Combined with oxygen or containing oxygen in chemical combination. Used in combination: *oxyhemoglobin.* See **oxo-.**

oxy- *prefix.* Indicates something sharp; for example, **oxycephaly.** [Greek *oxus,* sharp.]

ox·y·a·cet·y·lene (ŏk'sē-ə-sĕt'l-ĭn, -ēn') *adj.* Containing a mixture of acetylene and oxygen, as commonly used in metal welding and cutting torches.

ox·y·ac·id (ŏk'sē-ăs'ĭd) *n.* An acid, such as sulfuric acid or nitric acid, that contains oxygen in its molecule.

ox·y·ceph·a·ly (ŏk'sē-sĕf'ə-lē) *n.* A congenital abnormality in which the skull has a conical shape. [OXY- (sharp) + *-cephaly,* from -CEPHALIC.] —**ox·y·ce·phal·ic** (ŏk'sē-sə-făl'ĭk), **ox·y·ceph·a·lous** *adj.*

ox·y·gen (ŏk'sĭ-jən) *n. Symbol* **O** A colorless, odorless, tasteless gaseous element constituting 21 percent of the earth's atmosphere by volume, from which the pure liquid form is obtained by fractional distillation. It combines with most elements, is essential for plant and animal respiration, and is required for nearly all combustion and combustive processes. Atomic number 8, atomic weight 15.9994, melting point –218.4°C, boiling point –183.0°C, gas density at 0°C 1.429 kilograms per cubic meter, valence 2. [French *oxygène,* "acid-former" : OXY-, sharp (here, "acid") + -GEN.] —**ox·y·gen·ic** (ŏk'sĭ-jĕn'ĭk), **ox·yg·e·nous** (ŏk-sĭj'ə-nəs) *adj.* —**ox·y·gen·i·cal·ly** *adv.*

oxygen acid *n.* An oxyacid.

ox·y·gen·ase (ŏk'sĭ-jə-nās', -nāz') *n.* An oxidoreductase that catalyzes the transfer of free oxygen to its substrate.

ox·y·gen·ate (ŏk'sĭ-jə-nāt') *tr.v.* **-ated, -ating, -ates.** Also **ox·y·gen·ize** (-nīz'), **-ized, -izing, -izes.** To treat, combine, or infuse with oxygen. —**ox·y·gen·a·tion** *n.*

oxygen debt *n.* The condition that exists in cells when insufficient oxygen is available for oxidation of foodstuffs to produce the energy required by the cells, as for strenuous exercise.

oxygen mask *n.* A device that covers the mouth and nose and supplies oxygen from a tank.

oxygen tent *n.* A canopy placed over the head and shoulders of a patient for administering oxygen to aid respiration.

ox·y·he·mo·glo·bin (ŏk'sē-hē'mə-glō'bĭn, -hĕm'ə-glō'bĭn) *n.* A bright-red chemical complex of hemoglobin and oxygen that transports oxygen from the lungs to the tissues through the bloodstream.

ox·y·hy·dro·gen blowpipe (ŏk'sē-hī'drə-jən) *n.* A torch that burns a mixture of hydrogen and oxygen for welding.

ox·y·mo·ron (ŏk'sē-môr'ŏn', -mōr'ŏn') *n., pl.* **-mora** (-môr'ə, -mōr'ə). A rhetorical figure in which an epigrammatic effect is created by the conjunction of incongruous or contradictory terms, as in "a deafening silence." [Greek *oxumōron,* a clever remark, more pointedly witty for seeming stupid, neuter of *oxumōros,* "sharp-foolish" : OXY-, sharp + *mōros,* stupid, foolish.]

ox·y·salt (ŏk'sē-sôlt') *n.* A salt of an oxyacid.

ox·y·sul·fide (ŏk'sē-sŭl'fīd') *n. Chemistry.* A compound consisting of sulfur and oxygen combined with a metal or positive radical in which part of the sulfur has been replaced by oxygen.

ox·y·tet·ra·cy·cline (ŏk'sē-tĕt'rə-sī'klĭn, -klēn') *n.* An antibiotic, $C_{22}H_{24}N_2O_9 \cdot 2H_2O$, derived from the mold *Streptomyces rimosus* and used to treat bacterial infection in humans and animals.

ox·y·to·cic (ŏk'sĭ-tō'sĭk) *adj.* Hastening the process of childbirth, especially by inducing contraction of the uterine muscle.
~*n.* An oxytocic drug or agent. [OXY-, sharp + Greek *tokos,* child-

oxeye daisy *A common flower found throughout the United States, the oxeye daisy grows wild in meadows and along roadsides.*

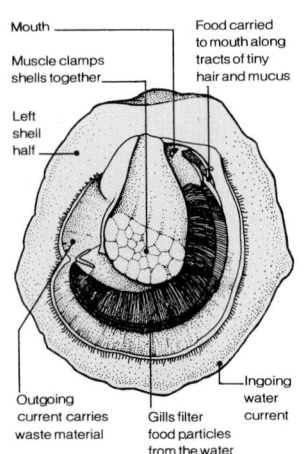

Mouth

Muscle clamps
shells together

Left
shell
half

Food carried
to mouth along
tracts of tiny
hair and mucus

Ingoing
water
current

Outgoing
current carries
waste material

Gills filter
food particles
from the water

oyster *Edible oysters belong to one genus (Ostrea), pearl oysters to another (Margaritifer). This common edible oyster, Ostrea edulis, traps minute food particles on its gills and passes them on a sheet of mucus to its mouth. Some species of oyster change sex several times in the course of their lives.*

birth, from *tiktein,* to bear + -IC.]

ox·y·to·cin (ŏk'sĭ-tō'sĭn) *n.* A pituitary hormone that increases contraction of the uterus during childbirth and stimulates the flow of milk. [See **oxytocic.**]

ox·y·tone (ŏk'sĭ-tōn') *adj.* Of, pertaining to, or being a Greek word that has an acute accent on the last syllable.

~*n.* An oxytone word. [Greek *oxutonos* : OXY-, sharp + *tonos,* TONE.] —**ox·y·ton·ic** (ŏk'sĭ-tŏn'ĭk) *adj.*

ox·y·u·ri·a·sis (ŏk'sē-yōō-rī'ə-sĭs) *n.* A disease, **enterobiasis** (*see*). [OXY- + URO- (urinary tract) + -IASIS.]

o·yez (ō'yĕs', ō'yĕz', ō-yā') *interj.* Also **o·yes** (ō'yĕs'). Used three times in succession to gain attention and silence, as by a public crier or to open a court of law.

~*n.* Also **o·yes,** *pl.* **oyesses** (ō-yĕs'ĭz). The cry "oyez": *"Fame with her loud'st Oyes cries 'This is he!'"* (Shakespeare). [Middle English *oyes!* from Norman French *oyez!* hear ye! imperative plural of *oyer,* Old French *oïr,* to hear, from Latin *audīre.*]

oys·ter (oi'stər) *n.* **1. a.** Any of several bivalve mollusks of the genus *Ostrea,* chiefly of shallow marine waters, having an irregularly shaped shell. **b.** The soft, edible flesh of such mollusks, valued as a delicacy. **c.** Any of various similar or related bivalve mollusks, such as the **pearl oyster** (*see*). **2.** An oval-shaped piece of muscle, regarded as a delicacy, found in the hollow of the pelvic bone of a fowl. **3. a.** A special delicacy. **b.** A source of complete fulfillment, affording every possible chance of personal advancement and satisfaction: *For the young the world is their oyster.* **4.** *Slang.* A close-mouthed, reserved person. **5.** Oyster white.

~*intr.v.* **oystered, -tering, -ters.** To gather, dredge for, or breed oysters. [Middle English *oistre,* from Old French, from Latin *ostrea,* from Greek *ostreon.*] —**oys·ter** *adj.*

oyster bed *n.* A place where oysters breed or are raised.

oys·ter-catch·er (oi'stər-kăch'ər) *n.* Any of several shore birds of the genus *Haematopus,* especially *H. ostralogus,* having black and white plumage and a long orange-red bill.

oyster crab *n.* A small crab, *Pinnotheres ostreum,* that lives inside the shells of living oysters.

oyster cracker *n.* A small, dry soda cracker.

oys·ter·man (oi'stər-mən) *n., pl.* **-men** (-mĭn). **1.** One who cultivates or sells oysters. **2.** An oyster-dredging vessel.

oyster mushroom *n.* A basidiomycete fungus, *Pleurotus ostreatus,* having a shell-shaped edible cap.

oyster plant *n.* **1.** A coastal plant, *Mertensia maritima,* having fleshy gray, oyster-flavored leaves and small blue flowers. **2.** A vegetable, **salsify** (*see*).

oyster white *n.* A pale yellowish green to light gray. Also called "oyster."

oz ounce; ounces.

Oz (ŏz) *n. Australian Slang.* Australia. [From the first syllable of *Australia.*]

O·zark Plateau (ō'zärk). Also **O·zark Mountains.** Highland of the south-central United States. It lies between the Arkansas River to the south and west, the Missouri to the north, and the Mississippi to the east.

o·zo·ce·rite (ō'zō-sîr'īt') *n.* Also **o·zo·ke·rite** (-kîr'īt'). A yellow-brown to black or green mineral hydrocarbon wax, used in making electrical insulation, lubricants, and inks. Also called "earth wax," "mineral wax." [German *Ozokerit* : Greek *ozein,* to smell + *kēros,* wax + -ITE.]

o·zone (ō'zōn') *n.* **1.** A blue gaseous allotrope of oxygen, O_3, derived or formed naturally from diatomic oxygen by electric discharge or exposure to ultraviolet radiation. It is an unstable, powerfully bleaching, poisonous oxidizing agent, with a pungent, irritating odor, used to purify and deodorize air, to sterilize water, and as a bleach. **2.** *Informal.* Fresh, pure, invigorating air, as that found at the seashore. [German *Ozon,* from Greek *ozōn,* present participle of *ozein,* to smell, reek.] —**o·zo·nic** (ō-zō'nĭk, ō-zŏn'ĭk), **o·zon·ous** (ō'zō'nəs) *adj.*

ozone layer *n.* The ozonosphere.

o·zo·nide (ō'zō-nīd') *n.* Any of various often explosive chemicals formed by attachment of ozone to the double bond of an unsaturated compound and used in analytical chemistry to locate such bonds.

o·zo·nize (ō'zō-nīz') *tr.v.* **-nized, -nizing, -nizes. 1.** To treat or impregnate with ozone. **2.** To convert (oxygen) to ozone. —**o·zon·i·za·tion** *n.* —**o·zon·iz·er** *n.*

o·zo·nol·y·sis (ō'zō-nŏl'ə-sĭs) *n. Chemistry.* A method of treating an organic compound with ozone to locate a double bond by the formation of an ozonide. [OZONE + -LYSIS.]

o·zo·no·sphere (ō-zō'nə-sfîr') *n.* **1.** A region of the upper atmosphere, between 10 and 20 miles (10 and 50 kilometers) in altitude, containing the greatest concentration of ozone, which absorbs solar ultraviolet radiation in a wavelength range not screened by other atmospheric components. **2.** A region of the atmosphere, between 6 and 30 miles (10 and 50 kilometers) in altitude, which contains a relatively high concentration of ozone. In both senses, also called "ozone layer." [OZON(E) + -SPHERE.] —**o·zo·no·spher·ic** (ō-zō'nə-sfîr'ĭk, -fĕr'ĭk), **o·zo·no·spher·i·cal** (-ĭ-kəl) *adj.*

p, P (pē) *n., pl.* **p's** or **P's.** **1.** The 16th letter of the modern English alphabet. **2.** Any of the speech sounds represented by this letter. **3.** The 16th in a series.

p, P, p., P. *Note:* As an abbreviation or symbol, *p* may be a small or a capital letter, with or without a period. Established forms or those generally preferred precede the definition. When no form is given, all four forms are in general use in that sense. **1.** p *Physics.* momentum. **2.** p. page. **3.** P *Physics.* parity. **4.** p. part. **5.** p. participle. **6.** p. past. **7.** P *Chess.* pawn. **8.** p. penny. **9.** p. per. **10.** p. peseta. **11.** p. peso. **12.** P The symbol for the element phosphorus. **13.** p, p. *Music.* piano (a direction). **14.** p *Physics.* pico-. **15.** p. pint. **16.** p. pipe. **17.** p. pole. **18.** p. population. **19.** p., P. president. **20.** P *Physics.* pressure. **21.** P. priest. **22.** p., P. prince. **23.** p. pro. **24.** p proton. **25.** p. purl. **26.** P The medieval Roman numeral for 400.

pa¹ (pä) *n. Informal.* Papa; father. [Short for PAPA.]

pa², pah *n.* **1.** A Maori village. **2.** A fortified Maori village. [Maori *pà.*]

Pa 1. The symbol for the element protactinium. **2.** pascal.

PA 1. Pennsylvania (with Zip Code). **2.** public-address system.

Pa. Pennsylvania.

p.a. per annum.

P.A. 1. power of attorney. **2.** press agent. **3.** prosecuting attorney.

P/A power of attorney.

pa·'an·ga (pä-äng'gə) *n.* The basic monetary unit of Tonga, equal to 100 seniti. See table at **currency.** [Tongan, "seed."]

PABA para-aminobenzoic acid.

pab·u·lum (păb'yə-ləm) *n., pl.* **-lums. 1.** Any substance that gives nourishment; food. **2.** Insipid intellectual nourishment. [Latin *pābulum,* food, fodder.]

pac, pack (păk) *n.* A type of moccasin or soft shoe designed to be worn inside a boot. [Delaware *paku.*]

Pac. Pacific.

pa·ca (pä'kə, păk'ə) *n.* A tailless, nocturnal tropical American rodent of the genus *Cuniculus;* especially, *C. paca,* having a large head and brown fur with three to five lines of white spots running down each side. [Portuguese and Spanish, from Tupi *páca.*]

pace¹ (pās) *n.* **1.** A step made in walking; a stride. **2.** The distance spanned by a step or stride, specifically: **a.** A unit of length equal to 30 inches (76 centimeters). **b.** Thirty inches (76 centimeters) at quick marching time or 36 inches (91.5 centimeters) at double time. Called in full "regulation pace." **c.** A length measured from the point at which the heel of one foot is raised to the point at which it is set down again after an intervening step by the other foot; about 1.5 meters or 5 feet. **3. a.** The rate of speed at which a person, animal, or group walks or runs. **b.** The rate of speed at which any activity or movement proceeds. **c.** Great speed or intensity of activity: *couldn't keep up with the pace.* **d.** *Cricket.* The fastest type of bowling. Also used adjectivally: *a pace bowler.* **4.** A manner of walking or running: *set out at a jaunty pace.* **5. a.** A gait of a horse in which both feet on one side leave and return to the ground together. **b.** Any of the gaits of a horse or other quadruped, such as the walk, trot, canter, or gallop. **—keep pace with.** To advance at the same speed as. **—put one through one's paces.** To test one's abilities; demand a demonstration of one's skills. **—set the pace. 1.** To go at a speed that other competitors attempt to match or surpass. **2.** To behave or perform in a way that others try to emulate. **—stand** (or **stay**) **the pace.** To be able to keep up with others. *~v.* **paced, pacing, paces.** *—tr.* **1.** To walk or stride back and forth across, as in agitation or distress. **2.** To measure by counting the number of steps needed to cover a distance. Often used with *off.* **3.** To set or regulate the rate of speed for. **4.** To train (a horse) in a particular gait, especially the pace. *—intr.* **1.** To walk with long, deliberate steps. **2.** To go at the pace. Used of a horse or rider. [Middle English *pas,* from Old French, from Latin *passus,* a step, "a stretch of the leg," from *pandere* (past participle *passus*), to stretch.]

pa·ce² (pä'sē) *prep.* With the permission of; with deference to. Used to express polite or ironically polite disagreement: *I have not, pace my detractors, entered into any deals.* [Latin *pāce,* ablative of *pāx,* peace.] **—pa·ce** *adv.*

pace·mak·er (pās'mā'kər) *n.* **1. a.** One who sets the pace in a race. **b.** A pacer. **2.** A leader in any field. **3. a.** *Physiology.* The **sinoatrial node** *(see).* **b.** *Medicine.* Any of several usually miniaturized and surgically implanted electronic devices used to regulate or to aid in the regulation of the heartbeat. **4.** *Biochemistry.* A substance that regulates a series of related actions. **—pace·mak·ing** *n.* & *adj.*

pac·er (pā'sər) *n.* **1.** A horse trained to pace. **2.** A pacemaker.

pace·set·ter (pās'sĕt'ər) *n.* A pacemaker (senses 1 and 2). **—pace·set·ting** *adj.*

pacha. Variant of **pasha.**

pa·chi·si (pə-chē'zē) *n.* **1.** An ancient game of India similar to backgammon but using cowry shells instead of dice. **2.** **Parcheesi** *(see).* [Hindi *pacīsī,* from *pacīs,* twenty-five (the highest throw) : Sanskrit *pañca,* five + *vimsati,* twenty.]

pachouli. Variant of **patchouli.**

pach·y·derm (păk'ĭ-dûrm') *n.* Any of various large, thick-skinned, hoofed mammals, such as the elephant or hippopotamus. [French *pachyderme,* from Greek *pakhudermos,* thick-skinned : *pakhus,* thick + *derma,* skin, -DERM.] **—pach·y·der·ma·tous** (păk'ĭ-dûr'mə-təs), **pach·y·der·mous** (păk'ĭ-dûr'məs) *adj.*

pach·y·san·dra (păk'ĭ-săn'drə) *n.* Any of several plants of the genus *Pachysandra;* especially, *P. terminalis,* native to Japan, having evergreen leaves and inconspicuous white flowers. This species is frequently cultivated as a ground cover and is also called "Japanese spurge." [New Latin, "with thick stamens" : Greek *pakhus,* thick + New Latin *-andra,* from -ANDROUS.]

pach·y·tene (păk'ĭ-tēn') *n. Biology.* The third stage of prophase in **meiosis** *(see)* during which the chromosomes coil up and shorten, the individual chromatids become visible, and crossing over may occur. [Greek *pakhus,* thick + *taina,* band.]

Pacif. Pacific.

pa·cif·ic (pə-sĭf'ĭk) *adj.* Also **pa·cif·i·cal** (-ĭ-kəl). **1.** Tending to diminish or put an end to conflict; appeasing; calming. **2.** Of a peaceful nature; tranquil; serene. [French *pacifique,* from Latin *pācificus* : *pāx* (stem *pāc-*), peace + *-ficus,* -FIC.] **—pa·cif·i·cal·ly** *adv.*

Pa·cif·ic (pə-sĭf'ĭk). *Abbr.* **Pac., Pacif.** The Pacific Ocean. **—Pa·cif·ic** *adj.*

pac·i·fi·ca·tion (păs'ə-fĭ-kā'shən) *n.* **1.** Placation; appeasement. **2.** The act or process of pacifying or bringing about a state of peace. **3.** *Often* **Pacification.** A peace treaty: *the Pacification of Ghent.* **4.** The reduction or elimination of insurgent or terrorist activity in an area. [French, from Latin *pācificātiō* (stem *pācificātiōn-*), "peace-making"; see **pacify.**] **—pa·cif·i·ca·tor** (pə-sĭf'ĭ-kā'tər) *n.* **—pa·cif·i·ca·to·ry** (pə-sĭf'ĭ-kə-tôr'ē, -tōr'ē) *adj.*

Pacific Islands, Trust Territory of the. Area of the northwestern Pacific Ocean including the Caroline, Marshall, and Marianas groups (excluding Guam), with more than 2,000 islands overall. Captured from Germany by Japan (1914), it was made a Japanese mandate by the Treaty of Versailles (1919). The United States captured the islands (1944), and they were under U.S. administration as a United Nations Trust Territory (1947–78). Separate constitutional governments were then set up. The Caroline Islands, excluding Palau, form the Federated States of Micronesia, a republic in "free association" with the United States. The Republic of Belau (the island of Palau) has the same status, while the Marshall Islands form another republic. The Northern Marianas (the Mariana Islands except Guam) form a commonwealth of the United States. Guam remains an unincorporated territory of the United States, administered by the Department of the Interior.

Pacific Northwest. Region of the northwestern United States, usually thought to include Washington and Oregon and sometimes southwestern British Columbia, Canada. It is a noted scenic resort area.

Pacific Ocean. Largest of the world's oceans, divided into the North Pacific and the South Pacific. It is larger than the world's entire land area and is deepest at Challenger Deep in the Marianas Trench (11,033 meters; 36,197 feet). To the south and west are coral and volcanic islands, while the ocean floor is scattered with volcanic mountains. See map, next page.

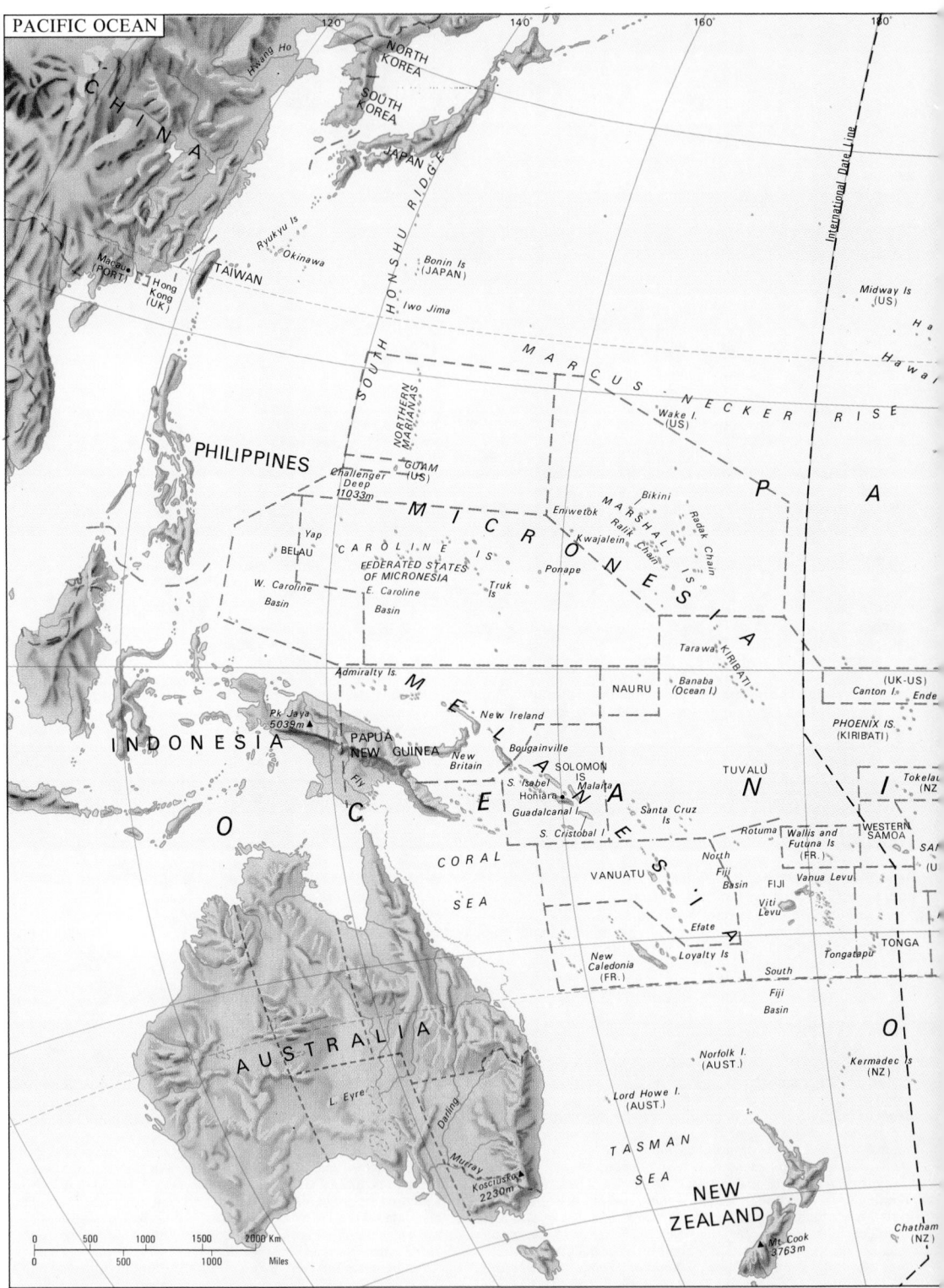

PACIFIC OCEAN

CHINA
NORTH KOREA
SOUTH KOREA
JAPAN
Hwang Ho
Ryukyu Is
Okinawa
TAIWAN
Macau (PORT.)
Hong Kong (UK)
SOUTH HONSHU RIDGE
Bonin Is (JAPAN)
Iwo Jima
MARCUS NECKER RISE
Midway (US)
Hawai
Wake I. (US)
PHILIPPINES
NORTHERN MARIANAS
GUAM (US)
Challenger Deep 11033m
MICRONESIA
Bikini
Eniwetok
Ralik Chain
Radak Chain
MARSHALL IS
Kwajalein
Yap
BELAU
CAROLINE IS
FEDERATED STATES OF MICRONESIA
Ponape
W. Caroline Basin
E. Caroline Basin
Truk Is
PA
Tarawa KIRIBATI
Admiralty Is.
MELANESIA
NAURU
Banaba (Ocean I.)
(UK-US)
Canton Is
Ende
INDONESIA
Pk. Jaya 5039m
PAPUA NEW GUINEA
New Ireland
Bougainville
New Britain
SOLOMON IS
S. Isabel
Honiara
Malaita
Guadalcanal I.
S. Cristobal I.
Santa Cruz Is
Rotuma
PHOENIX IS. (KIRIBATI)
TUVALU
North Fiji Basin
Wallis and Futuna Is (FR.)
Tokelau (NZ)
WESTERN SAMOA
SAI (U
Fiji
OCEA
CORAL SEA
VANUATU
Efate
FIJI
Viti Levu
Vanua Levu
New Caledonia (FR.)
Loyalty Is
South Fiji Basin
TONGA
Tongatapu
AUSTRALIA
L. Eyre
Darling
Murray
Kosciusko 2230m
Norfolk I. (AUST.)
Lord Howe I. (AUST.)
Kermadec Is (NZ)
TASMAN SEA
NEW ZEALAND
Mt. Cook 3763m
Chatham (NZ)

0   500   1000   1500   2000 Km
0   500   1000   Miles

Pacific Standard Time *n. Abbr.* **PST, P.s.t., P.S.T.** Time in one of the standard time zones of North America, equal to the local time at the 120th meridian west of Greenwich, England, eight hours behind Greenwich Mean Time. Also called "Pacific Time."

pac·i·fi·er (păs′ə-fī′ər) *n.* **1.** One that pacifies. **2.** A rubber or plastic nipple or teething ring for a baby to suck or chew on.

pac·i·fism (păs′ə-fĭz′əm) *n.* **1.** The belief that disputes between nations should and can be settled peacefully. **2. a.** Opposition to war or violence as a means of resolving disputes. **b.** Such opposition demonstrated by refusal to participate in military action. [French *pacificisme,* from *pacifique,* PACIFIC.]

pac·i·fist (păs′ə-fĭst) *n.* **1.** A person who supports or advocates pacifism. **2.** A person who refuses to do military service because of a belief in pacifism. **—pac·i·fist** *adj.* **—pac·i·fis·tic** (păs′ə-fĭs′tĭk) *adj.*

pac·i·fy (păs′ə-fī′) *tr.v.* **-fied, -fy·ing, -fies. 1.** To ease the anger or

agitation of; restore calm to; appease. **2.** To establish peace in; end war, fighting, or violence in. [Middle English *pacifien,* from Old French *pacifier,* from Latin *pācificāre* : *pāx* (stem *pāc-*), peace + *facere,* to make.]

Synonyms: *appease, conciliate, mollify, quiet, placate.*

pack¹ (păk) *n. Abbr.* **pk. 1.** A collection of items tied up or wrapped; a bundle. **2.** A container made to be carried on the back of a person or an animal, such as: **a.** A knapsack or rucksack. **b.** A parachute prepared for use. **3.** The amount of something, such as food, that is processed and packaged at one time or in one season. **4.** A small package containing a standard number of identical or similar items: *a pack of matches.* Also used in combination: *a six-pack.* **5. a.** A complete set of related items: *a pack of cards.* **b.** A large amount; a lot. Usually used derogatorily, chiefly in the phrase *a pack of lies.* **6. a.** A group of animals, such as dogs or wolves, that run and hunt together. **b.** A gang or band of people: *a pack of thugs.* **c.** A group

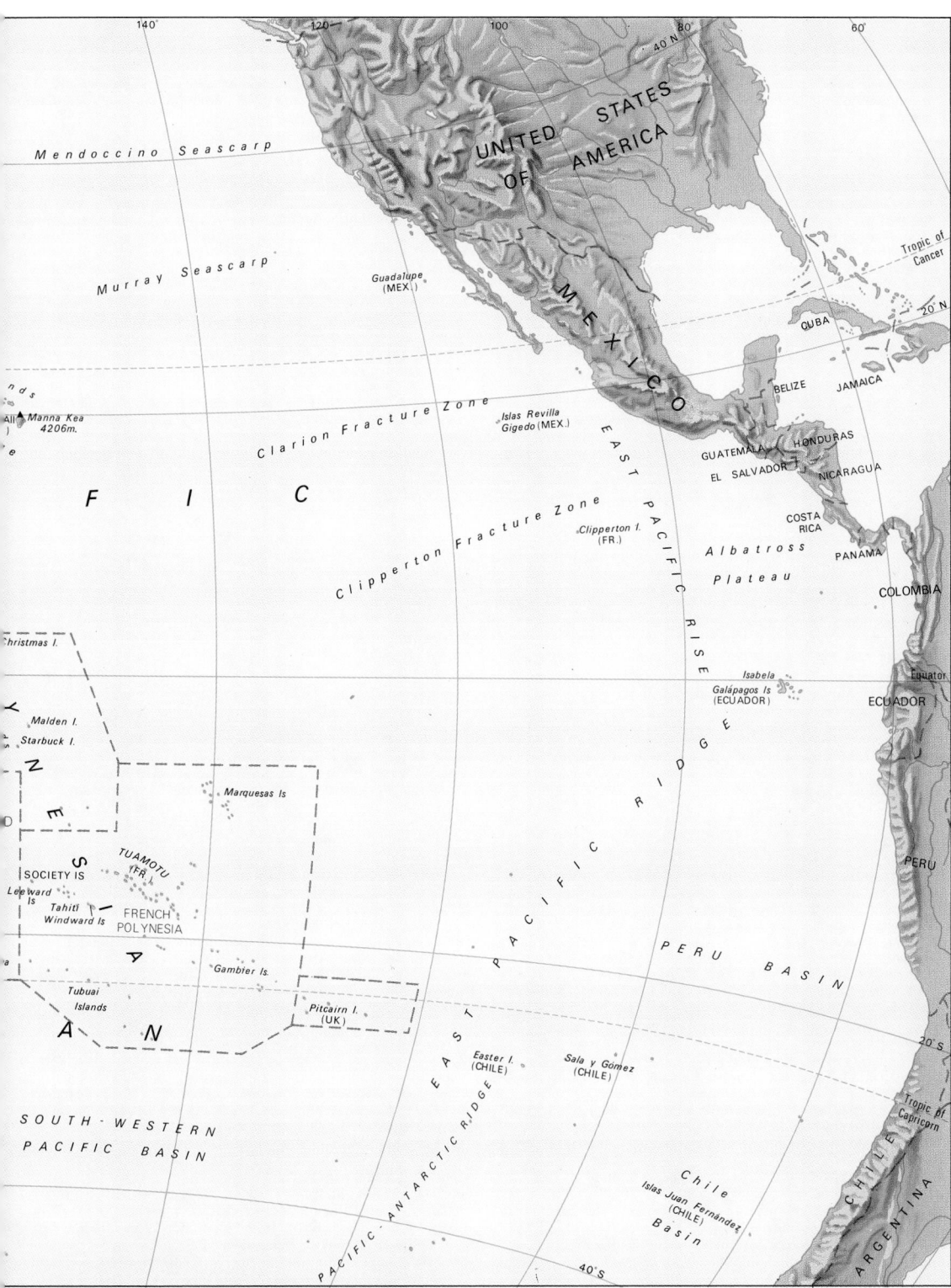

of aircraft, ships, or vehicles moving in or as if in formation. **d.** An organized local unit of Cub Scouts or Brownies. **7.** *Rugby.* The forwards in a team. **8.** *Medicine.* **a.** The swathing of a patient in hot, cold, wet, or dry sheets or blankets. **b.** The sheets or blankets so used. **c.** A material, such as gauze, therapeutically inserted into a body cavity or wound. **9.** An **ice pack** *(see).* **10.** A **face pack** *(see).* **11. Pack ice** *(see).*
~*v.* **packed, packing, packs.** —*tr.* **1.** To fold, roll, or combine into a bundle; wrap up. **2. a.** To put into a receptacle for transporting or storing: *pack one's belongings.* **b.** To fill up with items: *pack one's trunk.* **c.** To load (an animal) with a pack. **3.** To process and put into containers in order to preserve, transport, or sell. **4. a.** To bring together (persons or things) closely; crowd together. **b.** To fill up tight; cram: *The theater was packed.* **5.** *Medicine.* To wrap (a patient) in a pack. **6.** To wrap tightly for protection or insert packing into to prevent leakage: *pack a valve stem.* **7.** To press together;

compact firmly: *clay and straw packed into bricks.* **8.** *Informal.* **a.** To be capable of delivering: *pack a hard punch.* **b.** To carry: *pack a pistol.* **9.** To send away, especially peremptorily. Used with *off* or *away.* **10.** To rig (a voting panel) to be fraudulently favorable: *pack the jury.* —*intr.* **1.** To place one's belongings in boxes, suitcases, or the like for transporting or storing. **2.** To be susceptible of compact storage: *Dishes pack more easily than glasses.* **3.** To crowd together; cram. **4.** To become compacted; form lumps or masses: *Rain caused the loose soil to pack.* **5.** To depart abruptly. Sometimes used with *off* or *away.* —**pack down.** *Rugby.* To form a scrum. —**pack it in.** *Informal.* To stop doing or end an activity; call it quits. —**pack one's bags.** To prepare to depart. —**pack up.** *Informal.* To stop an activity; especially, to stop work. —**send packing.** To dismiss (a person) abruptly.
~*adj.* Used or suitable for carrying loads: *a pack animal.* [Middle

paddle wheel *A steamboat on the Mississippi River. The flat-bottomed boat is driven by the paddle wheel at its stern.*

paddy *The cultivation of rice began at least 5,000 years ago in India. Seedlings 25 to 50 days old are transplanted to fields called paddies, which are enclosed by levees and submerged about 5 to 10 centimeters (2 to 4 inches) underwater. These terraced paddy fields are on the Philippine island of Luzon.*

English *pak, pack,* from Middle Low German and Middle Dutch *pak*†.] **—pack·a·bil·i·ty** *n.* **—pack·a·ble** *adj.* **—pack·er** *n.*

pack[2]. Variant of **pac.**

pack·age (păk′ĭj) *n. Abbr.* **pkg. 1.** A wrapped or boxed object; a parcel or bundle containing one or more objects. **2.** A container in which something is packed for storage or transporting. **3.** A package deal. **4.** A comprehensive arrangement; especially, an undertaking to provide together all the various goods, products, and services required by a customer. **5.** *Computer Science.* A set of programs designed to operate a computer for some specified purpose: *a spreadsheet package.*
∼*tr.v.* **packaged, -aging, -ages. 1.** To place in a package; make a package of. **2.** To design or make wrappers or containers for (goods). **3.** To put together or produce in a comprehensive package. [PACK (bundle) + -AGE.]

package deal *n.* A proposition or offer made up of several items each of which must be accepted.

pack·ag·er (păk′ĭ-jər) *n.* **1.** A person who makes up packages. **2.** A person or company producing finished products, especially books or television programs, on another's behalf.

package store *n.* A store that sells sealed bottles of alcoholic beverages for consumption away from its premises.

pack·ag·ing (păk′ĭ-jĭng) *n.* **1.** The act, process, industry, art, or style of packing. **2.** Material used for making packages. **3.** The manner in which something, such as an idea or proposal, is presented. **4.** The occupation or activities of a packager.

packed cell volume *n.* The volume of erythrocytes in the blood, given as a fraction of the blood's total volume. Also called "hematocrit."

pack·et (păk′ĭt) *n.* **1.** *Abbr.* **pkt. a.** A small, thin container, as of cardboard or paper, with or without its contents: *a packet of granulated sugar.* **b.** A small package or bundle. **2.** *Slang.* A large sum of money: *It must have cost a packet.* **3.** A boat, usually a coastal or river steamer, that plies a regular route, carrying passengers, goods, and mail. In this sense, also called "packet boat." **—catch** (or **cop** or **get**) **a packet.** *British Slang.* To undergo an injury, punishment, or other unpleasant experience. [PACK (bundle) + -ET.]

pack·horse (păk′hôrs′) *n.* A horse used to carry loads.

pack ice *n.* Floating ice driven together into a single mass. Also called "pack."

pack·ing (păk′ĭng) *n.* **1.** The act or process of one that packs; especially, the processing and packaging of food products. **2.** Material used to cushion or fill gaps to protect fragile objects. **3.** A material used to prevent leakage or seepage, as around a pipe joint. **4. a.** The application of a medical pack. **b.** The material used to pack a wound.

packing box *n.* A **stuffing box** *(see).*

packing case *n.* A large wooden box or crate used for moving large objects or a large number of objects.

packing fraction *n. Physics.* The quotient of the algebraic difference between the isotopic mass and the mass number of a nuclide, divided by its mass number, often interpreted as a measure of stability. For most nuclides, a negative or small positive value indicates relatively high stability. [From the presumed manner in which neutrons and protons are packed in the atomic nucleus.]

packing house *n.* **1.** A firm that slaughters, processes, and packs livestock into meat and meat products. **2.** A firm that processes and packs food products other than meats.

pack·man (păk′măn′, -mən) *n., pl.* **-men** (-mĕn′, -mĭn). A **peddler** *(see).*

pack rat *n.* **1.** Any of various large western North American rodents of the genus *Neotoma* that collect in their nests a great variety of small objects. Also called "trade rat." **2.** *Western U.S. Slang.* A petty thief. **3.** *Slang.* An eccentric collector of miscellaneous objects.

pack·sack (păk′săk′) *n.* A canvas or leather traveling bag designed to be carried strapped to the shoulders.

pack·sad·dle (păk′săd′l) *n.* A saddle for a pack animal on which loads can be secured.

pack·thread (păk′thrĕd′) *n.* A strong two-ply or three-ply twine for sewing or tying up packages or bundles.

pack train *n.* A line of animals, such as horses or mules, loaded with supplies for an expedition.

pact (păkt) *n.* **1.** A formal agreement, as between nations; a treaty. **2.** A compact; a bargain. [Middle English, from Old French, from Latin *pactum,* from *pasciscī* (past participle *pactus*), to agree.]

pad[1] (păd) *n.* **1. a.** A thin, cushionlike mass of soft material used as filling, to give shape, or for protection against jarring, scraping, or other injury. **b.** A piece of soft but resilient material worn in certain sports to protect various parts of the body. **2.** A flexible saddle made without a frame. **3.** An **ink pad** *(see).* **4.** A number of sheets of paper of the same size stacked one on top of the other and glued together at one end, such as a notepad or writing pad. **5.** The broad, floating leaf of an aquatic plant, such as the water lily. **6. a.** The cushionlike flesh on the underpart of the toes and feet of many animals. **b.** The foot of any of these animals. **7.** The fleshy underside of the end of a finger or toe: *the pad of the thumb.* **8.** A **launching pad** *(see).* **9.** *Slang.* **a.** A home, apartment, or room. **b.** A bed.
∼*tr.v.* **padded, padding, pads. 1.** To line or stuff with soft material. **2.** To lengthen (something written or spoken) with extraneous material. Often used with *out.* [Dutch or Low German; akin to Flemish *pad* and probably to Lithuanian *pãdas,* "sole of the foot."]

pad[2] *v.* **padded, padding, pads.** —*intr.* **1.** To go about on foot, especially slowly. **2.** To move or walk about almost inaudibly: *padded barefoot over the rug.* —*tr.* To go along (a route) on foot, especially slowly and solemnly.
∼*n.* **1.** A muffled sound resembling that of soft footsteps. **2.** A horse with a plodding gait. [Probably from Middle Dutch *paden,* to walk along a path, from *pad,* path, road.]

pa·dauk (pə-dôk′) *n.* Also **pa·douk** (pə-do͞ok′). **1.** Any of various tropical trees of the genus *Pterocarpus,* having reddish wood with a mottled or striped grain. **2.** The wood of any of these trees, used for decorative cabinetwork. See **amboyna.** [Native Burmese name.]

pad·ding (păd′ĭng) *n.* **1.** Any soft material used to pad something. **2.** Matter added to a speech or written work to make it longer.

pad·dle[1] (păd′l) *n.* **1.** A wooden implement having a blade at one end, or sometimes at both ends, used without an oarlock to propel a canoe or small boat. **2.** Any of various implements resembling this, such as: **a.** An iron tool for stirring molten ore in a furnace. **b.** A tool with a shovellike blade used to mix materials in glassmaking. **c.** A pallet with which to mix and shape clay. **d.** A narrow board used to beat clothes when washing them by hand. **e.** A flattened board used to administer corporal punishment. **f.** A light wooden racket used in playing table tennis. **3.** A board of a paddle wheel. **4.** *Usually* **paddles.** A panel on the gate of a lock or on a sluice gate that controls the flow or level of water. **5.** A flipper or flattened appendage of certain animals. **6.** The act or an instance of paddling.
∼*v.* **paddled, -dling, -dles.** —*intr.* **1.** To propel a boat, canoe, or the like with a paddle. **2.** To row slowly and gently. **3.** To move through water by means of repeated short strokes of the limbs. —*tr.* **1.** To propel (a canoe, for example) with a paddle or paddles. **2.** To convey in a boat or canoe propelled by paddles: *paddle the supplies across.* **3.** To beat with a paddle. **4.** To stir or shape (material) with a paddle. [Middle English *padell*†.] **—pad·dler** *n.*

paddle[2] *intr.v.* **-dled, -dling, -dles. 1.** To wade or dabble about in shallow water, splashing gently with the hands or feet. **2.** To move with a waddling motion; toddle.
∼*n.* The act or an instance of paddling. [Of Dutch origin.]

paddle boat *n.* A steamship propelled through the water by paddle wheels on each side or by one paddle wheel astern.

pad·dle·fish (păd′l-fĭsh′) *n., pl.* **-fishes** or collectively **paddlefish.** Any of various large fishes of the family Polyodontidae, having an elongated, paddle-shaped snout. Also called "spoonbill."

paddle wheel *n.* A steam-driven wheel with boards or paddles affixed around its circumference, used to propel a ship.

pad·dock[1] (păd′ək) *n.* **1.** A fenced area, usually near a stable, used chiefly for grazing horses. **2. a.** An enclosure at a racetrack where the horses are assembled, saddled, and paraded before each race. **b.** In auto racing, an area near the racetrack where the cars assemble before a race. **3.** *Australian.* Any piece of fenced-in land.
∼*tr.v.* **paddocked, -docking, -docks.** To confine in a paddock. [Variant of dialectal *parrock,* Middle English *parrok,* Old English *pearruc,* from West Germanic *parruk* (unattested), perhaps from Medieval Latin *parricus*†. See also **park.**]

paddock[2] *n. Archaic.* A frog or toad. [Middle English *paddok,* from *pad, pade,* toad, from Old Norse *padda*†, toad.]

pad·dy (păd′ē) *n., pl.* **-dies. 1.** A specially irrigated or flooded field where rice is grown. Also called "paddy field." **2.** Rice, especially in the husk, whether gathered or still in the field. [Malay *pādi.*]

Pad·dy (păd′ē) *n. Informal.* An Irishman. Often considered offensive. [A nickname for *Patrick,* a common Irish name.]

paddy wagon *n. Slang.* A police van. [From PADDY.]

pad·dy·whack (păd′ē-hwăk′) *n.* **1.** *Informal.* A beating or spanking. **2.** *British Informal.* A rage or display of bad temper. [PADDY + WHACK.]

pad·e·mel·on, pad·dy·mel·on (păd′ē-mĕl′ən) *n.* A small Australian wallaby of the genus *Thylogale,* inhabiting scrub land. Also called "scrub wallaby." [From a native Australian language.]

Pad·e·rew·ski (păd′ə-rĕf′skē, -rĕv′skē), **Ignace Jan** (1860–1941). Polish pianist, composer, and politician. Famous for his interpretations of Chopin, he studied and taught at the Warsaw Conservatory and taught at the Strasbourg Conservatory before his performing debut in Vienna (1887). During World War I he organized the Polish Army in France and in 1919 became for 10 months the first prime minister of a newly independent Poland.

Pa·di·shah (pä′dĭ-shä′) *n.* **1.** Formerly, a title of a shah of Iran. **2.** Formerly, a title of the sultan of Turkey. [Persian *pādshāh,* from Middle Persian *pātakh-shāh* : *pati,* master + *shāh,* SHAH.]

pad·lock (păd′lŏk′) *n.* A detachable lock, usually with a U-shaped bar hinged at one end, designed to be passed through the staple of a hasp or a link in a chain, and then snapped shut.
∼*tr.v.* **padlocked, -locking, -locks.** To lock up with or as if with a padlock. [Middle English *padlok* : *pad*†, padlock + *lok,* LOCK.]

padouk. Variant of **padauk.**

pa·dre (pä′drā, -drē) *n.* **1.** Father. Used as a title of address for a priest in Italy, Spain, Portugal, and Latin America. **2.** *Informal.* A military chaplain. **3.** *Chiefly British Informal.* A clergyman. [Spanish, Portuguese, and Italian, father, from Latin *pater* (stem *patr-*).]

pa·dro·ne (pə-drō′nē, -nā; *Italian* pä-drō′nā) *n., pl.* **-nes** (-nēz, -nāz) or *Italian* **padroni** (pä-drō′nē). **1. a.** A master or patron. **b.** An owner or manager of an inn in Italy; proprietor. **2.** A person who exploits Italian immigrant labor in America. [Italian, from Latin *patrōnus,* protector, PATRON.] **—pa·dro·nism** *n.*

Pad·u·a (păj′o͞o-ə, păd′yo͞o-ə). *Italian* **Pa·do·va** (pä′dō-vä′). Capital of Padua province, Venetia region, northeastern Italy. On the Bacchiglione River, it became an important cultural center during the late Middle Ages. It has superb architectural and artistic works by Giotto and Donatello, while Galileo taught at the university (*c.* 1600).

pad·u·a·soy (păj′o͞o-ə-soi′) *n.* **1.** A rich, heavy silk fabric with a corded effect. **2.** A hanging or garment made of this fabric. [Variant (taken as *Padua say,* serge of Padua) of French *pou-de-soie,* from earlier *poult-de-soie*†.]

pae·an, pe·an (pē′ən) *n.* **1.** A song of joyful praise or exultation. **2.** Any fervent expression of joy or praise: *a paean to liberty.* **3.** An ancient Greek hymn of thanksgiving to a god, especially to Apollo. [Latin *paeān,* from Doric Greek *paian, paiōn,* war cry, hymn of praise to Apollo, from *Paian*†, title of Apollo as physician of the gods, ultimately from a cultic cry.]

paedo–, paed–. Variants of **pedo-, ped-** (child).

pae·do·gen·e·sis (pē′dō-jĕn′ə-sĭs) *n.* Reproduction of young during the larval or preadult stage, occurring chiefly in insects. [PAEDO- + GENESIS.] **—pae·do·ge·net·ic** (pē′dō-jə-nĕt′ĭk) *adj.*

pae·do·mor·pho·sis (pē′dō-môr′fə-sĭs) *n.* Evolutionary change in which primitive or embryonic structures appear in adult animals.

pa·e·lla (pä-ā′lyä, -ā′yä) *n.* A saffron-flavored Spanish dish made with varying combinations of rice, vegetables, chicken, and seafood. [Catalan, "frying pan," from Old French *paelle,* from Latin *patella,* diminutive of *patina,* pan, from Greek *patanē,* dish.]

pae·on (pē′ən, -ŏn′) *n. Greek & Latin Prosody.* A metrical foot having one long syllable and three short syllables occurring in random order. [Latin *paeōn,* from Greek *paiōn,* variant of PAEAN.]

Paes·tum (pĕs′təm). Ancient city of southern Italy. It was a colony of the Greek city of Sybaris (*c.* 600 B.C.) and flourished with the rest of Magna Graecia through the 6th century B.C. The ruins include some of the best-preserved Doric temples in the world.

pa·gan (pā′gən) *n.* **1.** A person who is not a Christian, Muslim, or Jew, although possibly having another faith; a heathen. **2.** One who has no religion. **3.** Formerly, any non-Christian.
∼*adj.* **1.** Of or pertaining to pagans. **2.** Not religious; heathen. [Middle English, from Late Latin *pāgānus,* civilian ("heathen" in patristic writers), from Latin *pāgānus,* country-dweller, from *pāgus,* village, country.] **—pa·gan·dom** (pā′gən-dəm) *n.* **—pa·gan·ish** *adj.* **—pa·gan·ism** *n.* **—pa·gan·ize** (pā′gə-nīz′) *v.*

Pa·gan (pə-gän′). Ruined city on the Irrawaddy River, central Burma. Founded in *c.* A.D. 849, it was the capital of the Pagan dynasty (11th–13th century). Many of their 5,000 Buddhist temples, pagodas, and monasteries still exist, despite capture of the city by the Mongols (1287), sacking by the Shans (1299), and a severe earthquake (1975). The city remains a center of pilgrimage and an important architectural site.

Pa·ga·ni·ni (păg′ə-nē′nē, pä′gə-), **Niccolò** (1782–1840). Italian violinist and composer. His works include six violin concertos and many other virtuoso violin pieces.

page[1] (pāj) *n.* **1.** In medieval times: **a.** A boy attending a knight as the first stage of training for knighthood. **b.** A youth in ceremonial employment to a person of rank or in attendance at court. **2.** A boy employed to run errands, carry messages, or act as a guide, as in a hotel or club. Also called "page boy." **3.** A boy who attends the bride at a wedding. Also called "page boy." **4.** A young person who acts as a messenger in Congress or certain other legislative bodies.
∼*tr.v.* **paged, paging, pages. 1.** To summon or call (a person) by name, especially over a public-address system or a signaling device. **2.** To attend as a page. [Middle English, from Old French, from Italian *paggio,* probably from Greek *paidion,* child, diminutive of *pais* (stem *paid-*), child, boy.]

page[2] *n. Abbr.* **p.,** *pl.* **pp. 1. a.** One side of a leaf of a book, letter, newspaper, manuscript, or the like. **b.** An entire leaf: *tear out a page.* **2.** The writing or printing on one side of a leaf. **3.** *Printing.* The type set for printing a page. **4.** A noteworthy or memorable event: *a new page in history.* **5. pages. a.** A source or record of knowledge: *in the pages of science.* **b.** An extract or passage: *pages from Johnson.* **6.** An amount of data displayed as a unit on a television or other screen. **7.** *Computer Science.* A unit of data in a computer memory that can be accessed or changed in a single operation.
∼*v.* **paged, paging, pages.** *—tr.* **1.** To number the pages of; paginate. **2.** *Computer Science.* To call and connect to (a terminal). **3.** To call up and display a page of (data) on a screen. *—intr.* To turn pages: *paged through the magazine.* [French, from Latin *pāgina,* page.]

pag·eant (păj′ənt) *n.* **1.** An elaborate public dramatic presentation, usually depicting some historical or traditional event. **2.** *Archaic.* **a.** A scene of a medieval mystery play. **b.** A portable platform on which mystery plays were presented. **3.** Any spectacular and colorful display or procession. **4.** Colorful display; pomp. [Middle English *pagyn,* from Medieval Latin *pāgina,* scene of a play, from Latin, PAGE.]

pag·eant·ry (păj′ən-trē) *n., pl.* **-ries. 1.** Pageants and their presentation. **2.** Grand display; pomp. **3.** Empty or flashy display.

page boy, page·boy (pāj′boi′) *n.* **1.** A boy who acts as a page. **2.** A woman's hairstyle with the ends curled under.

Pag·et's disease (păj′ĭts) *n.* **1.** A chronic disease affecting the elderly and characterized by thickening and deformation of the bones. **2.** An inflammatory condition of the nipple, associated with underlying cancer of the milk ducts. [After Sir James *Paget* (1814–99), British pathologist.]

pag·i·nal (păj′ə-nəl) *adj.* **1.** Of, pertaining to, or consisting of pages. **2.** Page for page: *paginal facsimile.* [Late Latin *pāginālis,* from Latin *pāgina,* PAGE.]

pag·i·nate (păj′ə-nāt′) *tr.v.* **-nated, -nating, -nates.** To number the pages of; page. Compare **foliate.** [Latin *pāgina,* PAGE.]

pag·i·na·tion (păj′ə-nā′shən) *n.* **1.** The system by which pages are numbered. **2.** The arrangement and number of pages in a book, as noted in a catalogue or bibliography.

pa·go·da (pə-gō′də) *n.* **1.** A religious building of the Far East, typically: **a.** An ornate pyramidal Hindu temple. **b.** A many-storied Buddhist tower, erected as a memorial or shrine. **2.** A structure, such as a garden pavilion, built in imitation of an Eastern pagoda. [Portuguese *pagode,* probably from Persian *butkada* : *but,* idol + *kada,* temple; altered by association with Prakrit *bhagodī,* holy.]

pagoda tree *n.* A Chinese deciduous tree, *Sophora japonica,* having pinnate leaves and clusters of white, pealike flowers. [Referring to its shape.]

Pa·go Pa·go (päng′gō päng′gō). Formerly **Pan·go Pan·go.** Harbor and town of Tutuila Island and the capital of American Samoa. It was a U.S. naval base (1878–1951) and was particularly important during World War II.

pah[1] (pä) *interj.* Used to express contempt.

pah[2]**.** Variant of **pa** (Maori village).

Pa·hang (pə-hăng′, -hŭng′). Longest river in Peninsular Malaysia. Navigable for most of its length (436 kilometers; 271 miles), it rises in the northwest, flows southward, and then turns eastward near Mengkarak through Pahang state to the South China Sea.

pah·la·vi (pä′lə-vē) *n., pl.* **-vis.** A gold coin of Iran, not part of the official currency of the country. [Persian *pahlawī,* after Muhammad Riza *Pahlavi* (1919–80), former shah of Iran.]

Pah·la·vi (pä′lə-vē) *n.* Also **Peh·le·vi** (pā′lə-vē). The Iranian language used in Persia from the 3rd to the 9th century. [Persian *pahlawī,* from *Pahlaw,* from Middle Persian, from Old Persian *Parthava,* PARTHIA.] **—Pah·la·vi** *adj.*

paid. Past tense and past participle of **pay.**

Paige (pāj), **Leroy Robert,** known as "Satchel" (1906–82). U.S. baseball player. He started pitching professionally in the mid-1920's and played for various black teams and in exhibition games until 1948, when he joined the Cleveland Indians. Paige was elected to the Baseball Hall of Fame in 1971.

pail (pāl) *n.* **1.** A bucket, especially one made of metal or wood. **2.** The amount contained in a pail. [Middle English *payle,* Old English *pægel*†, small measure, gill; Middle English form influenced by Old French *paelle,* pan; see **paella.**]

pail·lasse, pal·liasse (păl-yăs′, păl′yăs′) *n.* A thin mattress filled with straw, sawdust, or the like. [French, from *paille,* straw, from Latin *palea,* chaff, straw.]

pail·lette (pä-yĕt′, pā-, pă-lĕt′) *n.* **1.** A small piece of metal or foil used in enamel painting. **2.** A spangle used to ornament a dress or costume. [French, diminutive of *paille,* straw.]

pain (pān) *n.* **1.** An unpleasant sensation, occurring in varying degrees of severity, especially as a consequence of injury, disease, or emotional disorder. **2.** Suffering or distress. **3. pains.** The physical distress accompanying certain physiological processes such as labor or teething. **4. pains.** Great care or effort: *take pains with one's work.* **5.** *Informal.* An irritating or tiresome person or thing; a nuisance. In this sense, also called "pain in the neck." **—at pains.** Making great efforts: *at pains to be early.* **—on** (or **upon** or **under**) **pain of.** Subject to the penalty of (some specified punishment, such as death).
∼*v.* **pained, paining, pains.** *—tr.* **1.** To hurt or injure; cause pain to. **2.** To cause distress to or irritate. *—intr.* To hurt. [Middle English *paine,* from Old French *peine,* from Latin *poena,* penalty, from Greek *poinē,* penalty.]

Paine (pān), **Thomas** (1737–1809). British radical author. After his arrival in America (1774), he wrote the pamphlet *Common Sense* (1776), arguing for American independence from Britain. After the Revolutionary War he returned to Britain (1787) and published *The Rights of Man* (1791–92), defending the French Revolution. Accused of treason, he fled to France, but offended Robespierre and was imprisoned for 11 months (1793-94), during which time he continued writing his *Age of Reason,* a manifesto in favor of deism.

pain·ful (pān′fəl) *adj.* **1.** Causing pain; hurtful. **2.** Full of pain; distressing; hurting. **3.** Requiring care and labor; irksome: *a painful task.* **4.** *Informal.* Irritating; infuriating. **—pain·ful·ly** *adv.*

pain·kill·er (pān′kĭl′ər) *n.* Something, such as a drug, that relieves pain. **—pain·kill·ing** *adj.*

pain·less (pān′lĭs) *adj.* Free from pain, complication, or distress; not troublesome. **—pain·less·ly** *adv.* **—pain·less·ness** *n.*

pains·tak·ing (pānz′tā′kĭng) *adj.* Taking or involving great pains; careful and diligent. **—pains·tak·ing·ly** *adv.*

paint (pānt) *n.* **1. a.** A liquid mixture, usually of a solid pigment in a liquid vehicle such as oil or water, used as a decorative or protective coating. **b.** The thin dry film formed by such a mixture applied to a surface. **c.** The solid pigment before it is mixed with a liquid vehicle. **2. a.** A cosmetic, especially one that colors, such as rouge. **b. Grease paint** *(see).* **3.** *Medicine.* A liquid containing analgesics, antiseptics, or other healing agents, applied to the skin or mucous membranes. **4.** An act or instance of painting. **5.** A **pinto** *(see).*
∼*v.* **painted, painting, paints.** *—tr.* **1.** To make (a picture) with paints. **2. a.** To represent in a picture with paints. **b.** To portray vividly to the imagination, as with words or music. **3.** To coat or decorate with paint: *paint a house.* **4.** To apply cosmetics to. **5.** To

pagoda *Originally a religious building in the Far East, the pagoda became fashionable in the West in the mid-18th century as an ornament for parks and gardens.*

PRONUNCIATION KEY

ă, pat; ā, pay; âr, care;
ä, father, are; b, bib;
ch, church; d, deed; ĕ, pet;
ē, be; f, fife; g, gag; h, hat;
hw, which; ĭ, pit; ī, pie;
îr, pier; j, judge; k, kick;
l, lid, needle; m, mum;
n, no, sudden; ng, thing;
ŏ, pot; ō, toe; ô, paw, for;
oi, noise; ou, out; o͝o, book;
o͞o, boot; p, pop; r, roar;
s, sauce; sh, ship, dish;
t, tight; th, thin, path;
th, this, bathe; ŭ, cut; ûr, fur;
v, valve; w, with; y, yes;
z, zebra, size; zh, vision;
ə, about, item, edible,
gallop, circus, peaceful

IN FOREIGN WORDS:

à, *Fr.* ami; œ, *Fr.* feu, *Ger.* schön; ü, *Fr.* tu, *Ger.* über;
KH, *Ger.* ich, *Scot.* loch;
N, *Fr.* bon; y′, *Fr.* Compiègne

STRESS MARKS:

Primary stress: ′
in·cite′ (ĭn-sīt′)
Secondary stress: ′
in′sight′ (ĭn′sīt′)

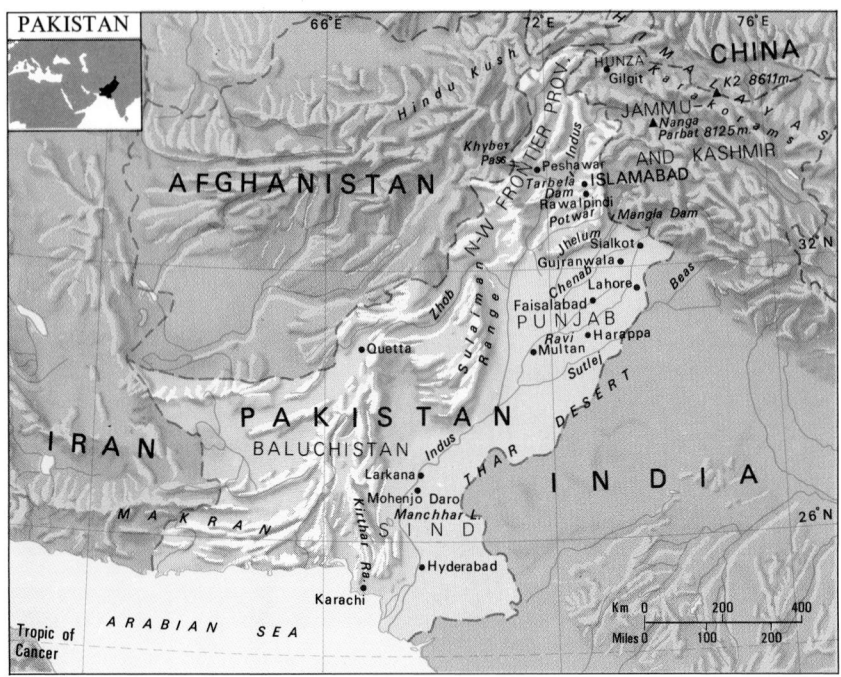

PAKISTAN

66°E   72°E   76°E
CHINA
HUNZA
Gilgit   K2 8611m
Hindu Kush   Nanga   JAMMU
Parbat 8125m   AND KASHMIR
Khyber   Peshawar   32°N
Pass   Tarbela   ISLAMABAD
AFGHANISTAN   Dam   Rawalpindi
Potwar   Mangla Dam
Jhelum   Sialkot
Gujranwala
Chenab   Lahore
Faisalabad   Beas
PUNJAB
•Quetta   Ravi   •Harappa
•Multan   Sutlej
IRAN   PAKISTAN   INDIA
BALUCHISTAN   Indus   THAR
Larkana   DESERT   26°N
Mohenjo Daro
Manchhar L.   SIND
MAKRAN   Kirthar Range
•Hyderabad
Karachi
Tropic of   ARABIAN   Km 0   200   400
Cancer   SEA   Miles 0   100   200

apply medicine to; swab: *paint a wound.* —*intr.* **1.** To practice the art of painting pictures. **2.** To cover something with paint. **3.** To serve as a surface to be coated with paint: *These nonporous surfaces paint badly with a brush and should be sprayed.* —**paint the town red.** *Slang.* To go on a bout of uproarious carousal. [Middle English *peynten,* to paint, from Old French *peindre* (past participle *peint*), from Latin *pingere.*]

paint·box (pānt′bŏks′) *n.* A box containing dry paints.

paint·brush (pānt′brŭsh′) *n.* A brush for applying paint.

paint·ed (pān′tĭd) *adj.* **1.** Represented in paint. **2.** Covered or adorned with paint. **3.** Excessively made up with cosmetics. **4.** Having no reality; false; pretended: *painted expressions.*

painted bunting *n.* A small bird, *Passerina ciris,* of the southern United States, having brilliant multicolored plumage. Also called "nonpareil."

painted cup *n.* A plant, the **Indian paintbrush** (see).

Painted Desert. Plateau in northeastern Arizona, on the banks of the Little Colorado River, stretching *c.* 320 kilometers (200 miles) from the Grand Canyon. Irregularly eroded layers of red and yellow sediment and clay have produced striking bands of color.

painted lady *n..* A widely distributed butterfly, *Vanessa cardui,* having brown, black, and orange markings.

paint·er[1] (pān′tər) *n.* A person who paints, either as an artist or as a workman.

paint·er[2] *n. Nautical.* A rope attached to the bow of a boat, used for tying up. [Middle English *paynter,* perhaps from Old French *pentoir,* clothesline, from *pendre,* to hang, from Latin *pendēre.*]

paint·er·ly (pān′tər-lē) *adj.* **1.** Of, pertaining to, or characteristic of a painter; artistic. **2. a.** Having qualities unique to the art of painting as distinguished from other visual arts. **b.** Designating a style of painting marked by openness of form, with shapes distinguished by variations of color rather than by outline or contour: *the painterly style of Titian.* Compare **linear.**

paint·ing (pān′tĭng) *n.* **1.** The process, art, or occupation of coating surfaces with paint, for either functional or artistic effect. **2.** An artistic composition, picture, or design done in paint.

pair (pâr) *n., pl.* **pairs** *or informal* **pair.** *Abbr.* **pr. 1.** Two corresponding persons or items, similar in form or function and matched or associated: *a pair of shoes.* **2.** One object composed of two joined, similar parts, dependent upon each other: *a pair of pliers.* **3. a.** Two persons joined together in marriage, engagement, or a similar relationship. **b.** Two persons having something in common and considered together: *a pair of dancers.* **c.** Two mated animals. **d.** Two animals joined together in work. **4.** Two playing cards of the same denomination. **5.** Two members of a deliberative body with opposing opinions on a given issue who agree to abstain from voting on the issue, thereby offsetting each other. **6.** A member of a pair: *lost the pair to this earring.* **7.** A pair-oar (see). **8.** *Chemistry.* An **electron pair** (see). —See Synonyms at **couple.**

~*v.* **paired, pairing, pairs.** —*tr.* **1.** To arrange in sets of two; couple. **2.** To join in a pair; mate. Sometimes followed by *off.* **3.** To provide a partner for. —*intr.* **1.** To form a pair or pairs. Often followed by *off.* **2.** To join in marriage; mate. **3.** To form a pair in a voting body. [Middle English *paire,* from Old French, from Latin *paria,* equal things, from the neuter plural of *pār,* equal.]

Usage: The noun *pair* can be followed by a verb in the singular or the plural depending on the intended meaning. The singular is used when *pair* emphasizes the unity of the components: *This pair*

of shoes *is not for sale.* The plural is used when the components are considered as individuals: *The pair are working together more harmoniously now.* When following a numeral other than *one,* the plural is standard (*six pairs of shoes*), though the singular is used informally. See also Usage note at **couple.**

pair bond *n.* The mutual attraction that binds a female and a male animal of the same species. It occurs particularly among birds and may last for one or more breeding seasons or for a lifetime. —**pair-bond·ed** (pâr′bŏn′dĭd) *adj.* —**pair bonding** *n.*

pair-oar (pâr′ôr′, -ōr′) *n.* A boat rowed by two people, each with one oar, sitting one behind the other. Also called "pair."

pair of compasses *n.* See **compass** (sense 2).

pair production *n. Physics.* The simultaneous creation of a positron and an electron from a high-energy gamma ray in a very strong electric field, especially in that of an atomic nucleus.

pai·sa (pī-sä′) *n., pl.* **paise** (pī-sä′) (for sense 1) or **paisa** (for sense 2). **1.** A coin equal to $^{1}/_{100}$ of the rupee of India. Also called "naya paisa." **2.** A coin equal to $^{1}/_{100}$ of the rupee of Pakistan or $^{1}/_{100}$ of the taka of Bangladesh. See feature at **currency.** [Hindi *paisā,* PICE.]

pai·sa·no (pī-zä′nō) *n., pl.* **-nos.** Also **pai·san** (pī-zän′). **1.** Countryman; compatriot. **2.** *Slang.* Friend; buddy; pal. [Spanish, from French *paysan,* from Old French *païsant,* PEASANT.]

pais·ley (pāz′lē) *adj.* *Sometimes* **Paisley. 1.** Made of a soft wool fabric with a colorful, intricate woven or printed pattern of abstract, curved shapes, ultimately derived from the palmette motif of Persian rugs. **2.** Marked with such a pattern.

~*n., pl.* **paisleys. 1.** A shawl or other article of clothing made of paisley fabric. **2.** A paisley pattern. [Originally popular in shawls made in PAISLEY.]

Pais·ley (pāz′lē). Industrial burgh and port of Strathclyde Region, Scotland. On the White Cart Water west-southwest of Glasgow, it became famous in the 19th century for its shawls based on Indian cashmere designs, to which it has given its name.

Paisley, Ian (1926–). Northern Irish politician. As a minister of the Free Presbyterian Church of Ulster since 1946 and as an M.P. both in the Northern Irish Parliament (1970-72) and in the House of Commons (since 1970) he has adopted a militant Protestant and Unionist position.

Pai·ute, Pi·ute (pī′yōōt′, pī-yōōt′) *n., pl.* **-utes** *or collectively* **Paiute** *or* **Piute. 1.** A member of either of two distinct North American Indian peoples, the Northern Paiute and the Southern Paiute, belonging to the Shoshonean subfamily of the Uto-Aztecan language family. They formerly lived in the southwestern United States. **2.** The language of either of these peoples. —**Pai·ute** *adj.*

pa·ja·mas (pə-jä′məz, -jăm′əz) *pl.n.* Also *chiefly British* **py·ja·mas. 1.** A loose-fitting garment consisting of trousers and a jacket, for sleeping or lounging. **2.** Loose-fitting trousers worn in the Orient by both sexes. [Hindi *pāejāma:* Persian *pāī,* leg, foot, from Middle Persian + *jāmah,* garment.]

pak choi (bäk′ choi′) *n.* A Chinese plant, *Brassica chinensis,* that is similar to the common cabbage and is used as a vegetable. Also called "Chinese cabbage." [Cantonese *paak ts'oi,* "white vegetable."]

Pak·i·stan (păk′ĭ-stăn′, pä′kĭ-stän′). Formerly **West Pakistan.** Country of southern Asia. It was originally created from Indian territory as a Muslim state (1947) by the efforts of Jinah and the Muslim League. It was formerly in two separate parts, but East Pakistan separated in 1971 to become Bangladesh. Pakistan has suffered with the loss of East Pakistan, a source of jute (formerly the country's chief export), and relations with India are generally poor. Pakistan remains chiefly agricultural, rice, leather, and cotton being the main exports. However, industry is expanding, and cotton (yarn and cloth) and carpets account for a third of exports. With considerable uranium reserves, Pakistan has an extensive nuclear program. Gen. Muhammad Zia al-Huq took power in a military coup (1977), deposing prime minister Zulfikar Ali Bhutto and tightening martial law. In 1982 stricter Muslim laws were introduced. Area, 803,943 square kilometers (310,322 square miles). Population, 83,800,000. Capital, Islamabad. —**Pak·i·stan·i** *adj. & n.*

pal (păl) *n. Informal.* A friend; a chum.

~*intr.v.* **palled, palling, pals.** *Informal.* To associate as pals: *palling around together.* [Romany (English) *pal, phal,* from *phrall* (continental), from Sanskrit *bhrātar-,* brother.] —**pal·ly** *adj.*

Pal. Palestine.

pal·ace (păl′ĭs) *n.* **1.** The official residence of royalty. **2.** The official residence of a high dignitary, such as a bishop or archbishop. **3. a.** Any large or splendid residence. **b.** Any large, often gaudy and ornate building used for entertainment, exhibitions, and the like. [Middle English *palais,* from Old French, from Latin *palātium,* from *Palātium,* the PALATINE Hill or the house built there by the emperor Augustus.]

palace revolution *n.* **1.** A usually peaceful overthrow of a sovereign or head of state effected by persons already in power. **2.** Any takeover of power or higher position in the hierarchy of an organization.

pal·a·din (păl′ə-dĭn) *n.* **1.** Any of the 12 peers of Charlemagne's court. **2.** A paragon of chivalry; a heroic champion. [French, from Italian *paladino,* from Latin *palātīnus,* PALATINE.]

palaeo–, palae–. Variants of **paleo–, pale–.**

palaestra. Variant of **palestra.**

pal·an·quin, pal·an·keen (păl′ən-kēn′) *n.* An east Asian covered litter, carried on poles on the shoulders of four men. [Portuguese *palanquim,* from Javanese *pĕlangki,* from Sanskrit *palyaṅka, paryaṅka,* bed : *pari,* around + *añcati,* he bends.]

painted lady *A common migratory butterfly that is found in North America, Europe, North Africa, and Asia.*

pal·at·a·ble (păl′ə-tə-bəl) *adj.* **1.** Acceptable to the taste; sufficiently agreeable in flavor to be eaten. **2.** Acceptable to the mind or sensibilities; agreeable: *a palatable suggestion.* [From PALATE.] —**pal·at·a·bil·i·ty, pal·at·a·ble·ness** *n.* —**pal·at·a·bly** *adv.*

pal·a·tal (păl′ə-təl) *adj.* **1.** Of or pertaining to the palate. **2.** *Phonetics.* **a.** Produced with the front of the tongue against the hard palate, as is the *y* in *young.* **b.** Produced with the blade of the tongue near the hard palate, as the *ch* in English *chin.* **c.** Produced with the front of the tongue in a forward position. Used of a vowel. —*n.* A palatal sound. —**pal·a·tal·ly** *adv.*

pal·a·tal·ize (păl′ə-tə-līz′) *v.* **-ized, -izing, -izes.** *Phonetics.* —*tr.* To pronounce with a palatal quality. —*intr.* To develop a palatal quality. Said especially of a phoneme considered diachronically. —**pal·a·tal·i·za·tion** *n.*

pal·ate (păl′ĭt) *n.* **1.** The roof of the mouth in vertebrates that separates the mouth from the nasal cavity and consists of a bony front, the *hard palate,* backed by the fleshy *soft palate.* **2.** The projection from the lower lip of a lipped flower. **3.** The sense of taste: *delicacies pleasing to the most refined palate.* [Middle English, from Latin *palātum,* perhaps from Etruscan.]

pa·la·tial (pə-lā′shəl) *adj.* **1.** Of or suitable for a palace: *the palatial gardens.* **2.** Of the nature of a palace; spacious and ornate. [Latin *palātium,* PALACE.] —**pa·la·tial·ly** *adv.*

pa·lat·i·nate (pə-lăt′n-āt′, -ĭt) *n.* The territory or jurisdiction of a palatine, especially: **1.** The **Palatinate** *(see).* **2.** Any of the English counties palatine (Durham, Lancaster, Chester, and Ely), whose lords in the Middle Ages had royal powers. **3.** Any of the American palatine colonies (Maine, Maryland, and Carolina), whose proprietors had royal prerogatives. [Medieval Latin *palātīnātus,* from *palātīnus,* a PALATINE.]

Pa·lat·i·nate (pə-lăt′n-āt′, -ĭt). Either of two former regions of West Germany. Lower (or Rhineland or Rhenish) Palatinate was in what are now Rheinland-Pfalz, Hesse, and Baden-Württemberg. Upper Palatinate was in what is now northeastern Bavaria. They were ruled by counts palatine, who became electors of the Holy Roman Emperor (1356) and were then known as electors palatine.

pal·a·tine¹ (păl′ə-tīn′) *n.* **1. a.** A soldier of the palace guard of the Roman emperors formed in the time of Diocletian. **b.** A soldier of a major division of the Roman army formed in the time of Constantine. **2.** Used as a title of various administrative officials of the late Roman and Byzantine empires. **3.** A count delegated with royal powers, as: **a.** An imperial minister or emissary in the Carolingian Empire. **b.** A minor imperial official in the late Holy Roman Empire. **c.** A ruler of either of the German **Palatinates** *(see);* an elector palatine. **d.** The lord of an English palatinate. **e.** The senior proprietor of a colonial American palatinate. —*adj.* **1.** Belonging to or fit for a palace. **2.** Pertaining to or designating a palatine or palatinate. [Latin *palātīnus,* from *palātium,* a PALACE.]

pal·a·tine² (păl′ə-tēn′) *n.* A fur cape and hood worn by women. [French; introduced about 1676 by Anne de Gonzague, Princess *Palatine.*]

pal·a·tine³ (păl′ə-tīn′) *adj.* **1.** Of or pertaining to the palate. **2.** Designating either of the two bones that make up the hard palate. —*n.* Either of the two bones that make up the hard palate.

Pal·a·tine¹ (păl′ə-tīn′) *adj.* Of or pertaining to the Palatinate. —*n.* **1.** A ruler of the Rhineland Palatinate; an elector palatine. **2.** A native or resident of the Palatinate.

Palatine². The most important of the seven hills of Rome. —*adj.* Designating this hill or situated on it.

Palau. See **Belau.**

pa·lav·er (pə-lăv′ər, -lä′vər) *n.* **1. a.** Idle chatter or fuss. **b.** Talk intended to charm or beguile. **2.** Formerly, a parley between European explorers and representatives of local populations, especially in Africa. —*v.* **palavered, -ering, -ers.** —*tr.* To flatter or cajole. —*intr.* To chatter idly. [Portuguese *palavra,* word, speech, from Late Latin *parabola,* speech, PARABLE.]

pale¹ (pāl) *n.* **1.** A stake or pointed stick; a picket. **2. a.** A boundary. **b.** *Archaic.* A fence enclosing an area. **3.** The area enclosed by a fence or boundary. **4.** *Heraldry.* A wide vertical stripe in the middle of a shield. —**beyond the pale.** Irrevocably unacceptable or unreasonable. —**the (English** or **Irish) Pale.** The medieval dominions of the English in Ireland. —*tr.v.* **paled, paling, pales.** To enclose with pales; fence in. [Middle English, pointed stake, boundary, from Old French *pal,* stake, from Latin *pālus.*]

pale² *adj.* **paler, palest. 1.** Whitish in complexion; pallid; wan. **2.** Of a low intensity of color; light. **3.** Designating a color having high lightness and low saturation. Compare **deep. 4.** Of a low intensity of light; dim; faint. **5.** Feeble; weak; inferior. —*v.* **paled, paling, pales.** —*tr.* To cause to turn pale. —*intr.* **1.** To become pale; blanch. **2.** To decrease in relative importance; be outshone; diminish. [Middle English, from Old French, from Latin *pallidus,* from *pallēre,* to be pale.] —**pale·ly** *adv.* —**pale·ness** *n.*

pa·le·a (pā′lē-ə) *n., pl.* **-leae** (-lē-ē′). *Botany.* A small, chafflike bract partly enclosing the flower of a grass spikelet. [New Latin, from Latin, chaff.]

Pa·le·arc·tic (pā′lē-ärk′tĭk, -är′tĭk) *adj.* Of or designating the zoogeographic region that covers the whole of Europe and Asia, Africa north of the Sahara, and the Himalayas. Compare **Nearctic.** [PALE(O)- + ARCTIC.]

pa·le·eth·nol·o·gy, pa·le·eth·nol·o·gy (pā′lē-ĕth-nŏl′ə-jē) *n.* The ethnology of early humankind. [PALE(O)- + ETHNOLOGY.] —**pa·le·eth·no·log·ic** (pā′lē-ĕth′nə-lŏj′ĭk), **pa·le·eth·no·log·i·cal** *adj.* —**pa·le·eth·nol·o·gist** *n.*

paleo-, pale- *prefix.* Also *chiefly British* **palaeo-, palae-.** Indicates ancient or prehistoric; for example, **paleography, pale-ethnology.** [Greek *palaio-,* from *palaios,* ancient, from *palai,* long ago.]

pa·le·o·an·thro·pol·o·gy (pā′lē-ō-ăn′thrə-pŏl′ə-jē) *n.* The study of humanlike creatures more primitive than *Homo sapiens.* —**pa·le·o·an·thro·po·log·ic** (pā′lē-ō-ăn′thrə-pə-lŏj′ĭk), **pa·le·o·an·thro·po·log·i·cal** *adj.* —**pa·le·o·an·thro·pol·o·gist** *n.*

pa·le·o·bot·a·ny (pā′lē-ō-bŏt′n-ē) *n.* The study of plant fossils and ancient vegetation. —**pa·le·o·bo·tan·ic** (pā′lē-ō-bə-tăn′ĭk), **pa·le·o·bo·tan·i·cal** *adj.* —**pa·le·o·bot·a·nist** *n.*

Pa·le·o·cene (pā′lē-ō-sēn′) *adj.* *Geology.* Of, belonging to, or designating the geologic time or rock series of the first epoch of the Tertiary period, preceding the Eocene and characterized by the appearance of placental mammals. —*n. Geology.* **1.** The Paleocene epoch. Preceded by *the.* **2.** The deposits of this epoch. Preceded by *the.* [PALEO- + -CENE.]

pa·le·og·ra·phy (pā′lē-ŏg′rə-fē) *n.* **1.** The study and scholarly interpretation of ancient written documents. Compare **epigraphy. 2.** The documents so studied. —**pa·le·og·ra·pher** *n.* —**pa·le·o·graph·ic** (pā′lē-ə-grăf′ĭk), **pa·le·o·graph·i·cal** *adj.*

pa·le·o·lith (pā′lē-ə-lĭth′) *n.* A stone implement of the Paleolithic period. [PALEO- + -LITH.]

Pa·le·o·lith·ic (pā′lē-ə-lĭth′ĭk) *adj. Archaeology.* Of, belonging to, or designating the cultural period beginning with the earliest chipped stone tools, about 2.5 to 3 million years ago, until the beginning of the Mesolithic, about 12,000 years ago. —*n. Archaeology.* The Paleolithic period. Preceded by *the.* Also called "Old Stone Age."

pa·le·o·mag·net·ism (pā′lē-ō-măg′nə-tĭz′əm) *n.* The study of the residual magnetism in rocks in order to try to reconstruct the configuration of the continents in the geologic past.

pa·le·on·tol·o·gy (pā′lē-ŏn-tŏl′ə-jē) *n.* **1.** The study of fossils and ancient life forms. **2.** Paleozoology. [PALE(O)- + ONTO- + -LOGY.] —**pa·le·on·to·log·ic** (pā′lē-ŏn′tə-lŏj′ĭk), **pa·le·on·to·log·i·cal** *adj.* —**pa·le·on·tol·o·gist** *n.*

Pa·le·o·zo·ic (pā′lē-ə-zō′ĭk) *adj. Geology.* Of, belonging to, or designating the era of geologic time between the Precambrian and Mesozoic eras, including the Cambrian, Ordovician, Silurian, Devonian, Carboniferous, and Permian periods, that is characterized by the appearance of marine invertebrates, primitive fishes, land plants, and primitive reptiles. —*n.* The Paleozoic period. Preceded by *the.* [PALEO- + -ZOIC.]

pa·le·o·zo·ol·o·gy (pā′lē-ō-zō-ŏl′ə-jē) *n.* The study of animal fossils and ancient animal life. —**pa·le·o·zo·o·log·i·cal** (pā′lē-ō-zō′ə-lŏj′ĭ-kəl) *adj.* —**pa·le·o·zo·ol·o·gist** *n.*

Pa·ler·mo (pə-lûr′mō, -lâr′mō). Capital of Sicily and Palermo province. On the Tyrrhenian Sea at the foot of Mount Pellegrino, it is the chief port of Sicily.

Pal·es·tine (păl′ĭ-stīn′). *Abbr.* **Pal.** Historic region of southwestern Asia, sometimes called the Holy Land. Situated on the eastern Mediterranean coast, it has at times included areas such as Bashan and Gilead to the east of the Jordan River, and now covers Israel and territories of Jordan and Egypt. Its many rulers have included the Hebrews, Egyptians, Romans, Byzantines, Arabs, and Turks. The area west of the Jordan was awarded to Britain under a League of Nations mandate (1920). Britain supported Jewish claims to a separate homeland, and in 1948 it was divided by the United Nations between two separate states, Israel and Jordan. However, the Arabs refused to recognize the newly created Israel and immediately attacked it. Arab-Israeli military conflict has been frequent ever since. Israel occupied Jordanian territory west of the Jordan (1967), and the Palestine Liberation Organization (formed in 1964) has continued to fight for the creation of a Palestinian homeland for Arabs and the destruction of Israel. —**Pal·es·tin·i·an** (păl′ə-stĭn′ē-ən) *adj.* & *n.*

pa·les·tra, pa·laes·tra (pə-lĕs′trə) *n., pl.* **-trae** (-trē) or **-tras.** In ancient Greece, a public place for training and practice in wrestling and other athletics. [Latin *palaestra,* from Greek *palaistra,* from *palaiein†,* to wrestle.] —**pa·les·tral** *adj.*

Pal·e·stri·na (păl′ĭ-strē′nə), **Giovanni Pierluigi da** (*c.* 1525-94). Italian composer. His works include more than 100 masses, 179 motets, and several magnificats, litanies, and madrigals. He was a master of polyphony and counterpoint.

pal·e·tot (păl′ə-tō′, păl′tō) *n.* **1.** Especially formerly, a loose cloak or coat. **2.** A 19th-century woman's fitted jacket. [French.]

pal·ette (păl′ĭt) *n.* **1.** A board, typically with a hole for the thumb, upon which an artist mixes colors. **2.** The range of colors used in a particular painting or by a particular artist: *a limited palette.* **3.** Variant of **pallette.** [French, from Old French, flat board, diminutive of *pale,* shovel, from Latin *pāla,* spade, shovel.]

palette knife. A knife with a thin, flexible blade used by artists for mixing, scraping, or applying paint.

Pa·ley (pā′lē), **William S.** (1901-). U.S. broadcasting executive. While working for his father's cigar business Paley became convinced that radio advertising had an important future. He bought a small radio network, renamed it the Columbia Broadcasting System in 1929, and turned it into a major radio and television network. He was president (1928-46) and chairman of the board (1946-82).

pal·frey (pôl′frē) *n., pl.* **-freys.** *Archaic.* A woman's saddle horse.

Palladian

Palladian

INSPIRATION FROM ITALY

Palladio's classical designs reborn in England

Palladian architecture takes its name from the work of Andrea Palladio, a 16th-century Italian architect whose symmetrical designs were modeled on the temples and baths of ancient Rome. He designed elegant palaces and villas in Vicenza and the surrounding northern Italian countryside, and two churches in Venice. The Villa Rotonda outside Vicenza is the most famous of his villas.

Inigo Jones introduced the Palladian style to Britain with the Queen's House at Greenwich in the early 17th century; it did not become fashionable until a century later, when it dominated English domestic architecture for decades.

The revival was inspired partly by the work of Lord Burlington and of Colen Campbell, whose book *Vitruvius Britannicus* (1715-21) was the most influential architectural work of the period. It was also partly due to Palladio's own *Quattro Libri dell'Architettura* (Four Books on Architecture) of 1570, translated into English in 1715. Textbook examples of the Palladian style are Mereworth Castle in Kent (1723)—almost an exact copy of Palladio's Rotonda; Chiswick House (1725, below); and Holkham Hall, Norfolk (1734). The city of Bath, planned from 1727 onward, remains a monument to the overwhelming impact of the style.

CHISWICK HOUSE *Lord Burlington designed the house, built to display his art collection, on the lines of Palladio's Villa Capra near Vicenza in Italy. Its symmetrical design, central dome, and pedimented portico with Corinthian columns are typical of the Palladian style.*

[Middle English, from Old French *palefrei,* from Medieval Latin *palafrēdus,* from Late Latin *paraverēdus,* extra post horse : Greek *para,* beside + Latin *verēdus,* post horse, of Gaulish origin.]

Pal·grave (păl′grāv′, pôl′-), **Francis Turner** (1827-97). British poet and anthologist. He was professor of poetry at Oxford University (1885-95). His best-known work is the anthology *The Golden Treasury of the Best Songs and Lyrical Poems in the English Language* (1861).

Pa·li (pä′lē) *n.* An ancient Indic language surviving in the scriptures of Theravada Buddhism. [Sanskrit *pāli-bhāsā* : *pāli,* canon (of scriptures) + *bhāsa,* language.] —**Pa·li** *adj.*

pal·i·kar (păl′ĭ-kär′) *n.* A Greek soldier in the struggle for Greece's independence from Turkey (1821-28). [Modern Greek *palikari,* youth, from Late Greek *pallikarion,* page, diminutive of Greek *pallēx†,* a youth.]

pal·imp·sest (păl′ĭmp-sĕst′) *n.* A manuscript, typically of vellum or parchment, that has been written upon several times, often with remnants of earlier, imperfectly erased writing still visible. Remnants of this kind are a major source for the recovery of lost literary works of classical antiquity. [Latin *palimpsēstus,* from Greek *palimpsēstos,* rubbed again : *palin,* again + *-psēstos,* "scraped," from *psēn,* to rub, scrape.] —**pal·imp·sest** *adj.*

pal·in·drome (păl′ĭn-drōm′) *n.* A word or sequence of words that reads the same backward or forward, as *A man, a plan, a canal, Panama!* [Greek *palindromos,* running back again : *palin,* again + *dromos,* a running.] —**pal·in·drom·ic** (păl′ĭn-drŏm′ĭk, -drō′mĭk) *adj.*

pal·ing (pā′lĭng) *n.* 1. Any of a row of upright, pointed sticks forming a fence; a pale; a picket. 2. Pointed sticks used in making fences; pales. 3. A fence made of pales or pickets.

pal·in·gen·e·sis (păl′ĭn-jĕn′ə-sĭs) *n., pl.* **-ses** (-sēz′). 1. The doctrine of transmigration of souls; metempsychosis. 2. *Biology.* Recapitulation *(see).* [Greek *palin,* again + GENESIS.] —**pal·in·ge·net·ic** (păl′ĭn-jə-nĕt′ĭk) *adj.* —**pal·in·ge·net·i·cal·ly** *adv.*

pal·i·node (păl′ə-nōd′) *n.* 1. A poem in which the poet recants something said in a previous poem. 2. Any formal statement of recantation. [Late Latin *palinōdia,* from Greek *palinōidia* : *palin,* again + *ōidē,* song.]

pal·i·sade (păl′ə-sād′) *n.* 1. A fence of pales forming a defense barrier or fortification. 2. Any of the pales of such a fence. 3. *Botany.* The upper part of the mesophyllic tissue of a leaf consisting of closely packed cylindrical cells and forming the main photosynthesizing area of the plant. 4. **palisades.** A line of lofty, steep cliffs, usually along a river.
~*tr.v.* **palisaded, -sading, -sades.** To equip or fortify with a palisade. [French *palissade,* from Provençal *palissada,* from *palissa,* a pale, from Vulgar Latin *pālicea,* from Latin *pālus,* stake.]

Pal·i·sades (păl′ə-sādz′). Row of cliffs along the west bank of the Hudson River in northeastern New Jersey and southeastern New York State. A large section of the most scenic part is included in Palisades Interstate Park, which has a chain of wooded recreational areas.

pall¹ (pôl) *n.* 1. A cover for a coffin, bier, or tomb, often made of black, purple, or white velvet. 2. A coffin, especially one being borne to a grave or tomb. 3. **a.** Any covering that darkens or obscures: *a pall of smoke over the city.* **b.** A gloomy or oppressive atmosphere: *Defeat cast a pall over the homecoming of the troops.* 4. *Ecclesiastical.* **a.** A linen cloth, or a square of cardboard faced with cloth, used to cover the chalice. **b.** A vestment, the **pallium** *(see).* 5. *Heraldry.* A Y-shaped charge on a shield.
~*tr.v.* **palled, palling, palls.** To cover with or as if with a pall. [Middle English *pal,* Old English *pæll,* from Latin *pallium,* a cover, cloak, PALLIUM.]

pall² *v.* **palled, palling, palls.** —*intr.* 1. To become insipid, boring, or wearisome. Often used with *on.* 2. To have a dulling, wearisome, or unpleasant effect. Often used with *on.* 3. To become cloyed or satiated. —*tr.* To cloy; satiate. [Middle English *pallen,* aphetic variant of *appallen,* to APPALL.]

Pal·la·di·an¹ (pə-lā′dē-ən) *adj.* 1. Of, pertaining to, or characteristic of Athena, the Greek goddess of wisdom. 2. Of, pertaining to, or characterized by wisdom or study. [Latin *palladius,* of Pallas, from Greek *palladios,* from *Pallas* (stem *Pallad-*), goddess of wisdom, PALLAS (Athena).]

Palladian² *adj. Architecture.* 1. In or designating the Renaissance style of Andrea Palladio. 2. In or designating a mid-18th-century style derived from that of Palladio, especially in Britain.

pal·lad·ic (pə-lăd′ĭk, -lā′dĭk) *adj. Chemistry.* Of or designating compounds containing trivalent or tetravalent palladium.

Pal·la·dio (pə-lā′dē-ō′), **Andrea,** born Andrea di Pietro (1508-80). Italian architect. The founder of modern Italian architecture, he developed a style based on the classical style of ancient Rome, breaking with the ornate Italian Renaissance style. His works include the Villa Rotonda and the Palazzo Chiericati in Venice.

pal·la·di·um¹ (pə-lā′dē-əm) *n. Symbol* **Pd** A soft, ductile, steelwhite, tarnish-resistant metallic element occurring naturally with platinum, especially in gold, nickel, and copper ores. It is used as a catalyst in hydrogenation and as a purification filter for hydrogen and is alloyed for use in electric contacts, jewelry, nonmagnetic watch parts, and surgical instruments. Atomic number 46, atomic weight 106.4, melting point 1,552°C, boiling point 2,927°C, specific gravity 12.02 (20°C), valences 2, 3, 4. [New Latin, from the asteroid PALLAS, discovered (1802) just before the element.]

palladium² *n., pl.* **-dia** (-dē-ə) or **-diums.** 1. A sacred object held to have the power to preserve a city or state possessing it. 2. A safeguard, especially one viewed as a guarantee of the integrity of social institutions: *the right to free speech, palladium of democracy.* [Latin, from Greek *Palladion,* the statue of Pallas Athena that assured the safety of Troy as long as it remained within the city, from *Pallas* (stem *Pallad-*), PALLAS (Athena).]

pal·la·dous (pə-lā′dəs, păl′ə-dəs) *adj. Chemistry.* Of, pertaining to, or containing palladium, especially bivalent palladium.

Pal·las (păl′əs) *n.* The second-largest asteroid of the solar system, approximately 450 kilometers (300 miles) in diameter. [Discovered by Peter S. Pallas (died 1811), German naturalist.]

Pallas Athena, Pallas Athene. The goddess **Athena** *(see).*

pall·bear·er (pôl′bâr′ər) *n.* Any of the persons carrying or attending the coffin at a funeral. Also called "bearer." [Originally, one who held up the corners of the pall covering the coffin.] —**pall·bear·ing** *n. & adj.*

pal·let¹ (păl′ĭt) *n.* 1. A machine part that converts reciprocating motion to rotary motion, or vice versa, such as a click or pawl for controlling the motion of a ratchet wheel in a watch escapement. 2. The lip or projection of a pawl for engaging the teeth on a ratchet wheel. 3. A wooden, paddlelike potter's tool for mixing and shaping clay. 4. A tool used for printing or gilding letters on book bindings or taking up and applying gold leaf. 5. A portable platform for storing or moving cargo or freight, especially by fork-lift truck. 6. A painter's palette. 7. A valve in the wind chest of an organ, connected to a key that when depressed admits air to a groove beneath the pipes corresponding to the key. [French PALETTE.]

pallet² *n.* A narrow, hard bed or straw-filled mattress. [Middle English *pailet,* from Norman French *paillete,* bundle of straw, from *paille,* straw, from Latin *palea,* chaff.]

pal·lette, pal·ette (pă-lĕt′) *n.* A plate that protects the armpit on a suit of armor. [Variant of PALETTE (thin board).]

palliasse. Variant of **paillasse.**

pal·li·ate (păl′ē-āt′) *tr.v.* **-ated, -ating, -ates.** 1. To make (an offense or crime) seem less serious; extenuate; excuse. 2. To make less severe without curing; reduce the pain or intensity of; mitigate; alleviate. [Late Latin *palliāre,* to cloak, from Latin *pallium,* cloak, PALLIUM.] —**pal·li·a·tion** *n.*

pal·li·a·tive (păl′ē-ā′tĭv, -ē-ə-tĭv) *adj.* Tending or serving to palliate. ~*n.* Something that palliates. **—pal·li·a·tive·ly** *adv.*

pal·lid (păl′ĭd) *adj.* **1.** Having an abnormally pale or wan complexion. **2.** Lacking color or brightness. **3.** Lacking in radiance or vitality; dull; lifeless: *a pallid performance.* [Latin *pallidus,* from *pallēre,* to be pale.] **—pal·lid·ly** *adv.* **—pal·lid·ness** *n.*

pal·li·um (păl′ē-əm) *n., pl.* **-liums** or **-lia** (-lē-ə). **1.** A large rectangular cloth worn as a cloak in ancient Rome. **2.** A woolen shoulder band with two pendants hanging from it at the front and back that is worn by the pope and conferred by him on archbishops and sometimes on bishops. Also called "pall." **3.** *Zoology.* An outer layer or covering, such as the mantle of a mollusk or the cerebral cortex. [Latin *pallium*†.]

pall-mall (pĕl′mĕl′, păl′măl′, pôl′môl′) *n.* **1.** A 17th-century game in which a boxwood ball was struck with a mallet to drive it through an iron ring suspended at the end of an alley. **2.** The alley in which this game was played. [Obsolete French *palle-maille,* from Italian *pallamaglio* : *palla, balla,* ball, from Middle High German *balle* + *maglio,* mallet, from Latin *malleus.*]

pal·lor (păl′ər) *n.* Extreme or unnatural paleness: *a ghostly pallor.* [Latin, from *pallēre,* to be pale.]

palm¹ (päm) *n.* **1.** The inner surface of the hand, extending from the wrist to the base of the fingers. **2.** The similar part of the forefoot of a quadruped. **3.** A unit of length equal to either the width, about 75 to 100 millimeters (3 to 4 inches), or the length, about 175 to 200 centimeters (7 to 10 inches) of the hand. **4.** The part of a glove or mitten that covers the palm of the hand. **5.** A metal shield worn by sailmakers over the palm of the hand and used to force a needle through heavy canvas. **6.** The blade of an oar or paddle. **7.** The flattened part of the antlers of certain animals, such as the moose. **—cross someone's palm.** To pay, tip, or bribe. **—grease someone's palm.** To bribe. **—in the palm of one's hand.** Completely subject to a person's will; ready to carry out a person's wishes. ~*tr.v.* **palmed, palming, palms. 1.** To conceal in the palm of the hand, as in cheating at dice or cards or in a sleight-of-hand trick. **2.** To pick up furtively. **—palm off. 1.** To dispose of or pass off by deception. **2.** To satisfy in a spurious or deceitful way: *tried to palm me off with some silly excuse.* **3.** To rid oneself of. Used with *on*: *palms off all his boring friends on her.* [Middle English *paume,* from Old French, from Latin *palma,* palm of the hand, palm tree.]

palm² *n.* **1.** Any of various chiefly tropical evergreen trees or shrubs of the family Palmae, characteristically having unbranched trunks with a crown of large pinnate or palmate leaves. **2.** A leaf or frond of a palm tree, carried as an emblem of victory, success, or joy. **3.** Triumph; victory. **4.** A small metallic representation of a palm leaf on certain military decorations indicating that they have been awarded a second time. **—bear** (or **carry**) **off the palm.** To win the prize in a given contest; be the victor. [Middle English *palme,* Old English *palm,* from Latin *palma,* PALM, hence (from the resemblance of its leaves to the outspread human hand) palm tree.]

Pal·ma (päl′mə). Capital and seaport of the Balearic Islands, Spain. Situated on the island of Mallorca, it exports wine and agricultural produce and has become an important tourist and commercial center.

pal·mar (păl′mər, päl′-, pä′mər) *adj.* Of, pertaining to, or corresponding to the palm of the hand or an animal's paw: *palmar folds.* [New Latin *palmaris,* from Latin *palma,* PALM (hand).]

pal·ma·ry (păl′mə-rē, päl′-, pä′mə-) *adj.* Worthy to receive the palm; outstanding; superior. [Latin *palmārius,* deserving of the palm of victory, from *palma,* PALM (tree).]

Palmas, Las. See **Las Palmas.**

pal·mate (păl′māt′, päl′-, pä′māt′) *adj.* Also **pal·mat·ed** (păl′mā′tĭd, päl′-, pä′mā′-). **1.** Resembling a hand with the fingers extended: *palmate antlers; palmate coral.* **2.** *Botany.* Having leaflets or lobes radiating or diverging from one point: *a palmate leaf.* **3.** *Zoology.* Having webbed toes, as the feet of many water birds. [Latin *palmātus,* from *palma,* PALM (hand).] **—pal·mate·ly** *adv.*

pal·ma·tion (păl-mā′shən, päl-, pä-mā′-) *n.* **1.** The state of being palmate. **2. a.** A palmate structure or form. **b.** A division or part of a palmate structure.

Palm Beach. Seaside resort of southeastern Florida, on a barrier beach between the Atlantic Ocean and Lake Worth.

palm civet *n.* Any of several arboreal mammals of the family Viverridae, of Africa and Asia, having long tails and gray or brown fur.

palm·er (pä′mər) *n.* In medieval Europe, a pilgrim who carried a palm branch as a token of having visited the Holy Land. [Middle English *palmere,* from Medieval Latin *palmārius,* from *palma,* PALM (branch).]

Palm·er (pä′mər), **Arnold** (1929–). U.S. golfer. After winning the U.S. amateur championship in 1954, he turned professional and became the first to win four Masters championships (1958, 1960, 1962, and 1964). He has always been one of the most popular golfers on the professional tour.

Palmer, Daniel David (1845–1913). U.S. founder of chiropractic, born in Canada. About 1895 he moved to Davenport, Iowa, and became interested in osteopathy. Gradually he evolved his own methods of treatment by mechanical adjustment of the skeleton, particularly the vertebrae.

Palm·er·ston (pä′mər-stən), **Henry John Temple, 3rd Viscount** (1784–1865). British Whig statesman. Entering Parliament as a Tory (1807), he was secretary of war (1809–28) before joining the Whigs. As foreign secretary (1830–34, 1835–41, and 1846–51) he helped secure Belgian independence and worked against the increase of Russian influence in the east. As prime minister (1855–58 and 1859–65), he nearly took Britain into the American Civil War on the side of the South, defeated the Sepoy revolt in the Indian Mutiny (1857–58), and spoke out for Italian nationalism. Popular with the people, he made many enemies among other ministers and abroad through his outspoken assertiveness.

palm·er·worm (pä′mər-wûrm′) *n.* Any of several caterpillars that injure fruit trees by feeding upon their leaves; especially, the small green caterpillar of a North American moth, *Dichomeris ligulella.*

pal·mette (păl-mĕt′) *n.* A stylized palm leaf used as a decorative element, notably in Persian rugs and in classical moldings, reliefs, frescoes, and vase paintings. [French, diminutive of *palme,* palm, from Latin *palma,* PALM.]

pal·met·to (păl-mĕt′ō) *n., pl.* **-tos** or **-toes.** Any of several small, mostly tropical palms having fan-shaped leaves; especially, *Sabal palmetto,* of the southern United States. This species is also called "cabbage palmetto." [Spanish *palmito,* diminutive of *palma,* palm, from Latin, PALM.]

palm·ist (pä′mĭst) *n.* Also **palm·i·ster** (pä′mĭ-stər). One who practices palmistry. [Back-formation from PALMISTRY.]

palm·is·try (pä′mĭ-strē) *n.* The practice or art of telling fortunes from the lines, marks, and patterns on the palms of the hands; chiromancy. [Middle English *pawmestrie* : *paume,* PALM + an obscure element not corresponding to *-ist* + *-ry.*]

pal·mi·tate (păl′mə-tāt′, päl′mə-, pä′mə-) *n. Chemistry.* An ester or salt of palmitic acid. [PALMIT(IN) + -ATE.]

pal·mit·ic acid (păl-mĭt′ĭk, päl-, pä-mĭt′-) A common saturated fatty acid, $CH_3(CH_2)_{14}COOH$, occurring in many natural oils and fats and used in making soaps. [From PALMITIN.]

pal·mi·tin (păl′mə-tĭn, päl′-, pä′mə-) *n.* The glyceryl ester, $C_3H_5(OOCC_{15}H_{31})_3$, of palmitic acid, found in palm oil and animal fats and used to manufacture soap. Also called "tripalmitin." [French *palmitine,* perhaps from *palmite,* pith of the palm tree, from *palme,* palm, from Latin *palma,* PALM.]

palm-ker·nel oil (päm′kûr′nəl) *n.* **1.** A hard, white oil obtained from the kernel of seeds of the West African palm, *Elaeis guineensis.* **2.** An oil extracted from the kernels of other palms.

palm oil *n.* **1.** A yellowish fatty oil obtained from the pericarp of the fruits of the West African palm, *Elaeis guineensis,* and used in the manufacture of margarine, cooking fats, chocolates, and cosmetics. **2.** Oil obtained from the pericarp of any other palm fruits.

Palm Springs. Resort in southern California, at the west end of the Coachella Valley.

palm sugar *n.* Sugar made from the sap of various palm trees.

Palm Sunday *n.* The Sunday before Easter, commemorating Christ's entry into Jerusalem, when palm branches were strewn before him.

palm·y (pä′mē) *adj.* **-ier, -iest. 1.** Of or pertaining to palm trees. **2.** Covered with palm trees. **3.** Prosperous; flourishing.

pal·my·ra (păl-mī′rə) *n.* A tall palm, *Borassus flabellifer,* of tropical Asia, having large, fanlike leaves used for matting. Also called "palmyra palm." [Variant of earlier *palmeira,* from Portuguese, palm tree, from *palma,* palm, from Latin, PALM.]

Pal·my·ra (păl-mī′rə). Biblical name **Tad·mor** (tăd′môr′). City of ancient Syria. On the trade route between the Roman and Parthian empires, in the 3rd century A.D. it was the capital of an empire that included Egypt, Syria, and Asia Minor. It was destroyed by the Romans (A.D. 273) and conquered by Muslims (A.D. 634).

pa·lo·lo worm (pə-lō′lō) *n.* Any of several edible polychaete worms of the families Eunicidae and Vereidae, living in reefs of the South Pacific, that come to the surface twice a year to reproduce. [Samoan and Tongan native name.]

Pal·o·mar, Mount (păl′ə-mär′). Peak in southwestern California. Rising to a height of 1,871 meters (6,140 feet), it is the site of an observatory having one of the world's largest reflecting telescopes, 508 centimeters (200 inches) in diameter.

pal·o·mi·no (păl′ə-mē′nō) *n., pl.* **-nos.** A horse of a type having a golden or tan coat and a white or cream-colored mane and tail. [American Spanish, from Spanish, dove-colored, from Latin *palumbīnus,* pertaining to ring doves, from *palumbes,* ring dove.]

pa·loo·ka (pə-lo͞o′kə) *n. Slang.* An incompetent or easily defeated person, especially a boxer. [Origin unknown.]

pal·o·ver·de (păl′ō-vûr′dē, -vûrd′) *n.* **1.** A spiny, nearly leafless shrub, *Cercidium torreyanum,* of southwestern North America, having showy yellow flowers. **2.** Any of several similar or related shrubs. [Mexican Spanish, "green tree" : Spanish *palo,* lumber, tree, from Latin *pālus,* stake + *verde,* green, from Latin *viridis.*]

palp (pălp) *n. Zoology.* **1.** Either of two elongated sensory organs, usually near the mouth, in invertebrate organisms such as crustaceans and insects. Also called "palpus." **2.** Either of two sensory organs extending from the heads of certain mollusks and annelids. **3.** A **pedipalp** *(see).* [French *palpe,* from Latin *palpus,* a touching.]

pal·pa·ble (păl′pə-bəl) *adj.* **1.** Capable of being handled, touched, or felt; tangible. **2.** Easily perceived; obvious: *a palpable fraud.* **3.** *Medicine.* Perceptible by palpation: *a palpable tumor.* —See Synonyms at **perceptible.** [Middle English, from Late Latin *palpābilis,* from Latin *palpāre,* to touch.] **—pal·pa·bil·i·ty** *n.* **—pal·pa·bly** *adv.*

pal·pate¹ (păl′pāt′) *tr.v.* **-pated, -pating, -pates.** *Medicine.* To examine or explore by touching (an organ or area of the body) as a diagnostic aid. [Latin *palpāre,* to touch.] **—pal·pa·tion** *n.* **—pal·pa·tor** *n.*

palpate² *adj. Zoology.* Having a palp or palps.

pal·pe·bral (păl′pə-brəl, păl-pē′brəl, -pĕb′rəl) *adj.* Of or pertaining

palmate *The hand-shaped, or palmate, leaf of the horse chestnut has seven leaflets stretching out like fingers.*

palomino *A golden-colored type of horse. Its name comes from a Spanish-American word, meaning "dovelike," used to describe its pale mane and tail.*

PRONUNCIATION KEY

ă, pat; ā, pay; âr, care;
ä, father, are; b, bib;
ch, church; d, deed; ĕ, pet;
ē, be; f, fife; g, gag, h, hat;
hw, which; ĭ, pit; ī, pie;
îr, pier; j, judge; k, kick;
l, lid, needle; m, mum;
n, no, sudden; ng, thing;
ŏ, pot; ō, toe; ô, paw, for;
oi, noise; ou, out; o͝o, book;
o͞o, boot; p, pop; r, roar;
s, sauce; sh, ship, dish;
t, tight; th, thin, path;
th, this, bathe; ŭ, cut; ûr, fur;
v, valve; w, with; y, yes;
z, zebra, size; zh, vision;
ə, about, item, edible, gallop, circus, peaceful

IN FOREIGN WORDS:

à, *Fr.* ami; œ, *Fr.* feu, *Ger.* schön; ü, *Fr.* tu, *Ger.* über; KH, *Ger.* ich, *Scot.* loch; N, *Fr.* bon; y′, *Fr.* Compiègne

STRESS MARKS:

Primary stress: ′
in·cite′ (ĭn-sīt′)
Secondary stress: ′
in′sight′ (ĭn′sīt′)

to the eyelids. [Late Latin *palpebrālis,* from Latin *palpebra,* eyelid.]

pal·pe·brate (păl'pə-brāt, păl-pē'brĭt, -pĕb'rĭt) *adj.* Having eyelids.

pal·pi·tant (păl'pə-tənt) *adj.* Palpitating; quivering. [Latin *palpitāns* (stem *palpitānt-*), present participle of *palpitāre,* to PALPITATE.]

pal·pi·tate (păl'pə-tāt') *intr.v.* **-tated, -tating, -tates.** 1. To shake; quiver; flutter. 2. To beat more quickly than normal; throb. Used especially of the heart. —See Synonyms at **pulsate.** [Latin *palpitāre,* to palpitate, frequentative of *palpāre,* to touch.] —**pal·pi·tat·ing·ly** *adv.*

pal·pi·ta·tion (păl'pə-tā'shən) *n.* 1. A trembling or shaking. 2. Irregular, rapid beating or pulsation of the heart.

pal·pus (păl'pəs) *n., pl.* **-pi** (-pī'). *Zoology.* A palp.

pals·grave (pôlz'grāv') *n.* A count palatine, especially one of the counts palatine of the Rhine or Electors Palatine. [Dutch *paltsgrave,* from Middle Dutch : *palts,* palatine, ultimately from Vulgar Latin *palāntius* (unattested), variant of *palātīnus,* PALATINE + *grave,* count, from Middle Dutch.]

pal·sied (pôl'zēd) *adj.* 1. *Medicine.* Afflicted with palsy. 2. Trembling; shaking.

pal·stave (pôl'stāv') *n. Archaeology.* A type of celt, resembling a chisel, usually made of bronze with a tongue that slots into a handle. [From Danish *paalstav,* from Old Norse *pálstavr : páll,* hoe, from Latin *palus,* stake + *stafr,* STAFF.]

pal·sy (pôl'zē) *n., pl.* **-sies.** 1. Paralysis. 2. A condition marked by loss of power to feel or to control movement in any part of the body. 3. **a.** A weakening or debilitating influence. **b.** An enfeebled condition or debilitated state thought to result from such an influence. 4. A fit of some strong emotion marked by an inability to act: *"a little palsy of indignation"* (Anthony Burgess).
~*tr.v.* **palsied, -sying, -sies.** 1. **a.** To paralyze. **b.** To deprive of strength: *palsied blows.* 2. To make helpless, as with fear. [Middle English *palesie,* from Old French *paralisie,* from Vulgar Latin *paralisia* (unattested), from Latin *paralysis,* PARALYSIS.]

pal·ter (pôl'tər) *intr.v.* **-tered, -tering, -ters.** 1. To talk or act insincerely; equivocate. 2. To be capricious; trifle. 3. To use trickery in bargaining. [16th century : origin obscure.]

pal·try (pôl'trē) *adj.* **-trier, -triest.** 1. Petty; trifling; insignificant. 2. Worthless; contemptible. —See Synonyms at **trivial.** [Dialectal *paltry,* feeble, from *palt, pelt†,* rags, rubbish.] —**pal·tri·ly** *adv.* —**pal·tri·ness** *n.*

pa·lu·dal (pə-lōōd'l, păl'yə-dəl) *adj.* 1. Of or pertaining to a swamp; marshy. 2. Malarial. [From Latin *palūs* (stem *palūd-*), marsh.]

pal·u·dism (păl'yə-dĭz'əm) *n.* A disease, **malaria** (see). [From Latin *palūs* (stem *palūd-*), marsh.]

pal·y¹ (pā'lē) *adj. Archaic.* Pale.

paly² *adj. Heraldry.* Designating a shield or heraldic charge that is vertically striped. [From Old French *palé,* from *pal,* PALE (stake).]

pal·y·nol·o·gy (păl'ə-nŏl'ə-jē) *n.* The scientific study of living and fossil spores and pollen. Also called "pollen analysis." [From Greek *palunein,* to sprinkle + -LOGY.]

pam (păm) *n.* The jack of clubs and highest trump in certain variations of the card game **loo** (see). [Probably from Greek *pamphilos,* "loved by all" : *pan,* all, PAN- + *philos,* beloved.]

pam. pamphlet.

Pa·mir (pə-mîr'). Also **Pa·mirs** (-mîrz'). Mountain complex lying mainly in Tadzhik S.S.R., U.S.S.R., but also reaching into China, Jammu and Kashmir, Pakistan, and Afghanistan.

Pam·li·co Sound (păm'lĭ-kō'). Lagoon, 129 kilometers (80 miles) long and 24 to 48 kilometers (15 to 30 miles) wide, of eastern North Carolina, separated from the Atlantic Ocean by a row of low, sandy barrier islands. Fish, oysters, and waterfowl abound in the area.

pam·pas (păm'pəz, -pəs) *pl.n. Singular* **-pa** (-pə). A nearly treeless grassland area of South America, chiefly in east-central Argentina and Uruguay. [Plural of American Spanish *pampa,* from Aymara and Quechua, plain.]

pam·pas grass (păm'pəs) *n.* Any of several tall grasses of the genus *Cortaderia,* native to South America; especially, *C. argentea,* which is widely cultivated for its creamy-white, long, fluffy panicles.

pam·pe·an (păm'pē-ən, păm-pē'ən) *adj.* Of or pertaining to the pampas or the Indian people who inhabit them.
~*n.* **Pampean.** An Indian of the pampas.

pam·per (păm'pər) *tr.v.* **-pered, -pering, -pers.** 1. To treat with excessive indulgence; spoil; coddle. 2. *Archaic.* To indulge with rich food; glut. [Middle English *pamperen,* frequentative of obsolete *pamp,* probably of Low German origin, akin to Flemish *pamperen.*] —**pam·per·er** *n.*
Synonyms: baby, coddle, indulge, mollycoddle, spoil.

pam·pe·ro (păm-pâr'ō, păm-) *n., pl.* **-ros.** A strong, cold southwest wind that blows across the pampas. [American Spanish, "pampean," from *pampa,* PAMPAS.]

pam·phlet (păm'flĭt) *n. Abbr.* **pam., pamph., pph.** 1. An unbound printed work, usually informative and with a paper cover. 2. A short essay or treatise, usually on a current topic, published without a binding. [Middle English *pamflet,* from *Pamflet,* familiar name of *Pamphilus,* a popular short amatory Latin poem of the 12th century.] —**pam·phlet·ar·y** (păm'flə-tĕr'ē) *adj.*

pam·phlet·eer (păm'flə-tîr') *n.* A writer of pamphlets or other short works that take a partisan stand on an issue.
~*intr.v.* **pamphleteered, -eering, -eers.** To write, issue, or publish pamphlets.

Pam·phyl·i·a (păm-fīl'ē-ə). An ancient region of southern Asia Minor that became a Roman province.

Pam·phyl·i·an (păm-fīl'ē-ən) *n.* The Ancient Greek dialect of Pamphylia, belonging to Arcado-Cyprian.

Pam·plo·na (păm-plō'nə). Capital of Navarra province, northern Spain. Situated in the Basque region at the foot of the Pyrenees, it is famous for the Fiesta de San Fermín, when bulls are let loose in the streets among crowds of revelers.

pan¹ (păn) *n.* 1. **a.** A shallow, wide, open container, usually of metal and often without a lid, used for holding liquids, cooking, and other domestic purposes: *a milk pan.* **b.** The quantity a pan will hold. 2. A vessel similar in form to a pan, as: **a.** An open metal dish used to separate gold or other metal from gravel, earth, or other waste by washing. **b.** Either of the receptacles on a balance or pair of scales. **c.** A vessel used for boiling and evaporating liquids. 3. See **dustpan.** 4. **a.** A basin or depression in the earth, often containing mud or water. **b.** A natural or artificial basin used to obtain salt by evaporating brine. 5. A piece of drift ice that has broken off a larger floe. 6. A **hardpan** (see). 7. In flintlocks, the small cavity in the lock used to hold powder. 8. *Slang.* The face.
~*v.* **panned, panning, pans.** —*tr.* 1. To wash (gravel, sand, or other sediments) in a pan for precious metal. 2. *Informal.* To criticize harshly. —*intr.* 1. To wash gravel, sand, or other sediments in a pan. 2. To yield gold as a result of washing in a pan. —**pan out.** *Informal.* To work out; turn out: *Let's see how things pan out.* [Middle English *panne,* Old English *panne,* from West Germanic *panna* (unattested), perhaps from Latin *patina,* from Greek *patanē,* pan, dish.]

pan² (păn) *n.* 1. The leaf of the betel palm. 2. A preparation of this leaf with betel nuts and lime, used for chewing in Asia. [Hindi *pān,* from Sanskrit *parṇá,* feather, leaf.]

pan³ (păn) *v.* **panned, panning, pans.** —*intr.* To move a motion-picture or television camera to follow a moving object or take in a larger scene. —*tr.* To move (a camera) in such a manner.
~*n.* An act or the process of panning with a camera. [Short for PANORAMA.]

Pan (păn). *Greek Mythology.* The god of woods, fields, and flocks, portrayed with a human torso with goat's legs, horns, and ears.

pan– *prefix.* Indicates: 1. All; entirely; for example, **panacea, panorama.** 2. **Pan-. a.** Of, involving, or comprising all; for example, **Pan-Arabism. b.** The aspiration for the political union of a specified group: **Pan-Africanism.** [Greek, from *pas* (neuter *pan*), all.]

pan·a·ce·a (păn'ə-sē'ə-) *n.* A remedy for all diseases, evils, or difficulties; a cure-all. [Latin *panacēa,* from Greek *panakeia,* from *panakēs,* all-healing : PAN- + *akos,* cure.] —**pan·a·ce·an** *adj.*

pa·nache (pə-năsh', -näsh') *n.* 1. A dashing or stylish manner: *leapt upon the platform with panache.* 2. A bunch of feathers or a plume, especially on a helmet. [French, from Italian *pennachio,* from Late Latin *pinnāculum,* diminutive of Latin *pinna,* feather.]

pa·na·da (pə-nä'də) *n.* A thick mixture of flour or bread crumbs combined with milk, stock, or water, used for soups, for thickening sauces, or as a base for soufflés. [Spanish, from *pan,* bread, from Latin *pānis,* bread.]

Pan·a·ma (păn'ə-mä', păn'ə-mä'). Republic of Central America. Situated in the Isthmus of Panama, it has central volcanic mountains and narrow coastal lowlands. Discovered by Columbus (1502), it was settled by the Spaniards, gaining independence from Spain as part of Colombia in 1819 and full independence in 1903. The Panama Canal, built in the Canal Zone by the United States, opened in 1914 and has dominated the country's economy. The country's chief source of foreign exchange is the canal, followed by petroleum products (made from imported oil), bananas, sugar, and shrimp. Area, 75,650 square kilometers (29,209 square miles). Population, 1,900,000. Capital, Panama City. See map at **Central American States.** —**Pan·a·ma·ni·an** (păn'ə-mā'nē-ən) *adj. & n.*

Panama, Isthmus of. Formerly **Isthmus of Dar·i·én** (dăr'ē-ĕn', dâr'ē-ĕn'). Strip of land that joins North and South America. Between the Pacific Ocean and the Caribbean Sea, it is *c.* 644 kilometers (400 miles) long and at its minimum is 50 kilometers (30 miles) wide.

Panama Canal. Canal crossing the Isthmus of Panama, joining the Caribbean Sea and the Pacific Ocean, 82 kilometers (51 miles) long. It was begun by the French in 1881 but later abandoned (1889). In 1903 the United States backed a successful Panamanian revolt against Colombian rule and gained construction rights for the canal, which opened in 1914. A treaty ratified in 1978 provided for U.S. administration of the canal until the end of 1999.

Panama Canal Zone. Land, *c.* 8 kilometers (5 miles) on each side of the Panama Canal, leased to the United States in 1903, when the canal was built. According to a treaty ratified in 1978, Panama assumed territorial jurisdiction in 1979.

Panama City. Capital of Panama. Situated on the Pacific coast, it was founded in 1519 and became the capital when Panama gained its independence (1903).

Panama hat *n.* A natural-colored, hand-plaited hat made from leaves of the jipijapa plant of South and Central America. Also called "Panama."

Pan-A·mer·i·can (păn'ə-mĕr'ĭ-kən) *adj.* Of or pertaining to North, South, and Central America collectively.

pan·a·tel·la, pan·a·tel·a (păn'ə-tĕl'ə) *n.* A long, slender cigar. [Spanish, from American Spanish, a long thin biscuit, from Italian *panatella,* from *panata,* PANADA.]

Pan·ath·e·nae·a (păn'ăth'ə-nē'ə) *n.* The main annual civic and religious festival of ancient Athens, held in honor of Athena. [New

Latin, from Greek *panathēnaia* : PAN- + *athēnaia,* from *Athēna,* Athena.] **—pan·ath·e·nae·ic** (păn′ăth′ə-nē′ĭk) *adj.*

pan-broil (păn′broil′) *tr.v.* **-broiled, -broiling, -broils.** To fry in a heavy pan using little or no fat.

pan·cake (păn′kāk′) *n.* A thin cake made of batter, poured on a hot, greased skillet and cooked on both sides until brown. Also called "griddle cake."
~*v.* **pancaked, -caking, -cakes.** —*intr.* To make a pancake landing. —*tr.* To cause to make a pancake landing.

pancake landing *n. Aviation.* An irregular or emergency landing in which an aircraft drops flat to the ground from a low altitude.

pan·chax (păn′chăks′) *n.* Any of various small, brightly colored Old World tropical fishes of the genus *Aplocheilus* and related genera, often kept in home aquariums. [New Latin *Panchax*†, former generic name.]

pan·cha·yat (pŭn-chä′yət) *n.* In India, a village council. [Hindi, from Sanskrit *pancha,* five (originally the number of members forming such a council).]

Pan·chen La·ma (pän′chən lä′mə) *n.* One of Tibet's two grand lamas, the other being the Dalai Lama. See **Lamaism.** [From the Tibetan title *Pan-chen-rin-po-che,* "great jewel (among the) scholars."]

pan·chro·mat·ic (păn′krō-măt′ĭk) *adj.* Sensitive to all colors: *panchromatic film.* **—pan·chro·ma·tism** (păn-krō′mə-tĭz′əm) *n.*

pan·cre·as (păng′krē-əs, păn′-) *n. Anatomy.* A long, soft, irregularly shaped gland lying near the stomach. It secretes pancreatic juice into the duodenum and contains the islets of Langerhans, which produce insulin. [Greek *pankreas,* "all-flesh," pancreas : PAN- + *kreas,* flesh.] **—pan·cre·at·ic** (păng′krē-ăt′ĭk, păn′krē-) *adj.*

pancreatic juice *n.* A clear, alkaline secretion of the pancreas containing enzymes that aid in the digestion of proteins, carbohydrates, and fats.

pan·cre·a·tin (păng′krē-ə-tĭn, păn′-, păn-krē′ə-tĭn) *n.* A mixture of enzymes extracted from the pancreases of cattle or pigs and used as a digestive aid. [From Greek *pankreas* (stem *pankreat-*), PANCREAS + -IN.]

pan·da (păn′də) *n.* **1.** A chiefly herbivorous, bearlike mammal, *Ailuropoda melanoleuca,* of the bamboo forests in the mountains of China and Tibet, having woolly fur with distinctive black and white markings. Also called "giant panda." **2.** A small, raccoonlike mammal, *Ailurus fulgens,* of Nepal and China, having reddish fur and a long, ringed tail. Also called "lesser panda." [French, perhaps from a native Nepalese word.]

pan·da·nus (păn-dā′nəs, -dăn′əs) *n.* Any of various palmlike trees and shrubs of the genus *Pandanus,* of southeastern Asia, having large buttress roots and a crown of narrow leaves. Also called "screw pine." [New Latin, from Malay *pandan.*] **—pan·da·na·ceous** (păn′də-nā′shəs) *adj.*

Pan·de·an pipe (păn-dē′ən). A panpipe *(see).* [From PAN.]

pan·dect (păn′dĕkt′) *n.* **1.** A comprehensive digest of or complete treatise on a subject. **2. pandects.** A complete body of laws; a legal code. **3. Pandects.** A digest of Roman civil law compiled for the emperor Justinian in the 6th century A.D. and part of the **Corpus Juris Civilis** *(see).* Also called "Digest." [Late Latin *Pandectēs,* the Corpus Juris Civilis, from Latin, book containing everything, from Greek *pandektēs,* all-receiving : PAN- + *dektēs,* receiver, from *dekheisthai,* to receive.]

pan·dem·ic (păn-dĕm′ĭk) *adj.* **1.** Widespread; general; universal. **2.** Epidemic over an especially wide geographic area.
~*n.* A pandemic disease. [From Late Latin *pandēmus,* from Greek *pandēmos,* of all the people : PAN- + *dēmos,* people.]

pan·de·mo·ni·um (păn′də-mō′nē-əm) *n.* **1.** A place characterized by great confusion, uproar, and noise. **2.** Wild uproar, noise, or chaos. —See Synonyms at **noise.** [From *Pandæmonium,* capital of Hell in Milton's *Paradise Lost* : PAN- + Greek *daimōn,* demon, spirit, deity.] **—pan·de·mo·ni·ac** (păn′də-mō′nē-ăk) *adj.*

pan·der (păn′dər) *n.* Also **pan·der·er** (păn′dər-ər). **1.** A go-between in sexual intrigues; a pimp; a procurer. **2.** One who caters to the lower tastes and desires of others or exploits their weaknesses.
~*v.* **pandered, -dering, -ders.** —*tr.* To act as a pander for. —*intr.* To act as a pander. Used with *to.* [From *Pandare,* character in Chaucer's *Troilus and Criseyde,* who procures Criseyde's love for Troilus; name taken from *Pandaro* (in Boccaccio's *Filostrata*), *Pandarus* (in the *Aeneid*), *Pandaros* (in the *Iliad*).] **—pan·der·ism** *n.*

pandit. Variant of **pundit.**

Pan·do·ra's box (păn-dôr′əz, -dōr′əz) *n.* **1.** *Greek Mythology.* The box that contained all the ills of mankind, opened by Pandora, the first woman, who was sent by Zeus as a punishment for Prometheus' theft of fire. **2.** Any source of great suffering or troubles, especially one that does not appear to be so at first.

pan·dore (păn′dôr′, -dōr′) *n.* An ancient musical instrument, a **bandore** *(see).* [From Italian *pandora,* from Late Latin, from Greek *pandoura,* three-stringed lute.]

pan·dow·dy (păn-dou′dē) *n., pl.* **-dies.** Sliced fruit baked with sugar and spices in a deep dish, with a thick crust on top. [19th century : origin obscure.]

pan·du·rate (păn-dŏŏr′ĭt, -dyŏŏr′ĭt) *adj.* Also **pan·du·ri·form** (păn-dŏŏr′ə-fôrm′, -dyŏŏr′ə-fôrm′). *Botany.* Resembling a violin in shape. Said of leaves. [New Latin *panduratus,* from Late Latin *pandūra,* three-stringed lute, PANDORE.]

pane (pān) *n.* **1.** Any of the divisions of a window or door, filled with glass. **2.** A single sheet of glass used in such a division. **3.** A panel of a door, wall, or other surface. **4.** Any of the flat surfaces or facets of an object, such as a bolt, having many sides. **5. a.** A rectangular division of a sheet of stamps. **b.** A sheet of stamps with such divisions. [Middle English *pane, pan,* piece of cloth, section, from Old French *pan,* from Latin *pannus,* rag.]

pan·e·gyr·ic (păn′ə-jîr′ĭk, -jī′rĭk) *n.* **1.** A formal eulogistic composition intended as a public compliment. **2.** Elaborate praise; an encomium. [French *panégyrique,* from Latin *panēgyricus,* from Greek *(logos) panēgurikos,* "(speech) for a public festival," from *panēguris,* general assembly, public festival : PAN- + *ēguris,* variant of *agora,* assembly.] **—pan·e·gyr·i·cal** *adj.* **—pan·e·gyr·i·cal·ly** *adv.*

pan·e·gy·rize (păn′ə-jə-rīz′) *v.* **-rized, -rizing, -rizes.** —*tr.* To eulogize. —*intr.* To compose or deliver a panegyric. [From Greek *panēgurizein;* see **panegyric, -ize.**] **—pan·e·gy·rist** (păn′ə-jîr′ĭst, -jī′rĭst) *n.*

pan·el (păn′əl) *n.* **1.** A flat, usually rectangular piece forming a part of a surface in which it is set and being raised, recessed, or framed. **2.** A distinct section of the body of a motor vehicle. **3.** A vertical section of fabric, as in a skirt; a gore. **4. a.** A thin wooden board used as a surface for oil painting. **b.** A painting on such a board. **5. a.** A board having switches to control parts of an electrical device. **b.** An **instrument panel** *(see).* **6.** A section of a telephone switchboard. **7. a.** The complete list of persons summoned for jury duty. **b.** Those persons selected from the list to compose a jury. **c.** A jury. **8. a.** A group of people gathered to plan or discuss an issue, answer questions, judge a contest, or act as a team on a radio or television quiz program. **b.** A discussion by such a group. **9.** *Law.* In Scotland, a person or persons standing trial.
~*tr.v.* **paneled, -eling, -els.** Also *chiefly British* **-elled, -elling.** **1.** To cover or furnish with panels. **2.** To decorate with panels. **3.** To separate into panels. **4.** To select or empanel (a jury). [Middle English, from Old French, piece of parchment on which names of a jury were written, from Vulgar Latin *panellus* (unattested), diminutive of Latin *pannus,* rag, cloth.]

panel heating *n.* A form of space heating in which heated panels are concealed in walls or ceilings. The panels are heated either by hot-water pipes or by electricity.

pan·el·ing (păn′ə-lĭng) *n.* **1.** A section of panels. **2.** A paneled wall. **3.** Panels collectively.

pan·el·ist (păn′ə-lĭst) *n.* A member of a panel, especially a radio or television panel.

panel truck *n.* A small delivery truck with a fully enclosed body.

pan·et·to·ne (păn′ə-tō′nē) *n., pl.* **-nes** or **-ni** (-nē). An Italian yeast cake made with candied fruit peels and raisins and eaten especially at Christmas. [Italian, from *panetto,* diminutive of *pane,* bread, from Latin *panis.*]

pang (păng) *n.* **1.** A sudden, sharp spasm of pain. **2.** A sudden, sharp feeling of emotional distress. [16th century : variant of earlier *prange,* of Germanic origin; akin to Middle Low German *prange,* a pinching.]

Pan·gae·a (păn-jē′ə). The single supercontinent into which all the world's landmass is thought to have been grouped before it began breaking up about 200 million years ago.

pan·gen·e·sis (păn-jĕn′ə-sĭs) *n. Biology.* The discredited hypothesis that every somatic cell generates self-representative hereditary materials that enter the bloodstream and eventually coalesce in reproductive cells, making possible the inheritance of hereditary characteristics. [PAN- + -GENESIS.] **—pan·ge·net·ic** (păn′jə-nĕt′ĭk) *adj.* **—pan·ge·net·i·cal·ly** *adv.*

Pan-Ger·man·ism (păn′jûr′mə-nĭz′əm) *n.* A political movement, prominent especially in the 19th century, advocating the union of all German-speaking peoples. [French *Pangermanisme* (translation of German *Alldeutschtum*) : PAN- + *Germanisme,* Germanism.] **—Pan-Ger·man·ist** *n.*

pan·go·lin (păng′gə-lĭn, păn′gə-) *n.* Any of several long-tailed, scale-covered mammals of the genus *Manis,* of tropical Africa and Asia, having a long snout and a sticky tongue with which it catches and eats ants. Also called "scaly anteater." [Malay *pĕngguling,* from *guling,* to roll (referring to its habit of rolling itself up).]

Pango Pango. See **Pago Pago.**

pan·han·dle¹ (păn′hănd′l) *v.* **-dled, -dling, -dles.** *Informal.* —*intr.* To beg, especially on the streets. —*tr.* **1.** To obtain from by panhandling. **2.** To beg from. [Back-formation from *panhandler,* beggar, from the resemblance of a beggar's outstretched arm to the handle of a pan.] **—pan·han·dler** *n.*

panhandle² *n.* **1.** The handle of a pan. **2.** *Often* **Panhandle.** A narrow strip of territory projecting from a larger, broader area to which it belongs in such a way that its borders as drawn on a map appear to outline the handle of a pan.

Pan-Hel·len·ic, Pan·hel·len·ic (păn′hə-lĕn′ĭk) *adj.* Of or pertaining to all Greek peoples or a movement to unify them.

pan·ic (păn′ĭk) *n.* **1.** A sudden, overpowering feeling of terror or anxiety. **2.** An outbreak of panic, often affecting many people at once. Also used adjectivally: *panic reactions.* **3.** Mass alarm concerning financial conditions, often resulting in an economic depression. **4.** *Slang.* One that is uproariously funny. —See Synonyms at **fear.** **—press** (or **push**) **the panic button.** *Informal.* To react to an emergency by taking hasty action.
~*v.* **panicked, -icking, -ics.** —*tr.* To affect with panic. —*intr.* To be affected with panic. —See Synonyms at **frighten.** [Originally adjectival, from French *panique,* from Greek *panikos,* of Pan (who would arouse terror in lonely places).] **—pan·ick·y** *adj.*

panic grass *n.* Any of numerous grasses of the genus *Panicum,*

panda *The giant panda, which is native to the mountains of China, feeds mainly on bamboo, but it also eats other plants, as well as small animals. It is very rare and notoriously hard to breed in captivity.*

pangolin *There are seven species of this scaly anteater, which is native to Africa and Southeast Asia and can grow to nearly 2 meters (6 feet) long. This is the Cape pangolin. When attacked, pangolins roll themselves into a tight ball.*

many of which are grown for grain and fodder. [Middle English *panyk*, from Latin *pānicum*†.]

pan·i·cle (păn'ĭ-kəl) *n. Botany.* **1.** A branched raceme in which each branch bears a further raceme. **2.** Loosely, any branched racemose inflorescence. [Latin *pānicula,* diminutive of *pānus,* tuft, from Greek *pēnos,* web.] —**pan·i·cled** *adj.*

pan·ic-strick·en (păn'ĭk-strĭk'ən) *adj.* Also **pan·ic-struck** (păn'-ĭk-strŭk'). Overcome by panic; terrified.

pa·nic·u·late (pə-nĭk'yə-lĭt, -lāt') *adj.* Also **pa·nic·u·lat·ed** (pə-nĭk'-yə-lā'tĭd). *Botany.* Growing or arranged in a panicle. [New Latin *paniculatus,* from Latin *pānicula,* PANICLE.] —**pa·nic·u·late·ly** *adv.*

Pa·ni·ni (pä'nē-nē, pä-nē'nē) (*fl.* 350 B.C.). Indian grammarian. His *Ashtadhyayi* is one of the earliest works of descriptive linguistics and is a classic treatise on Sanskrit. It also contains a wealth of historical, social, and geographic information.

Panjabi. Variant of **Punjabi.**

pan·jan·drum (păn-jăn'drəm) *n.* A pompous and pretentious person who has an exaggerated idea of his own importance. [After the Grand *Panjandrum,* character in a nonsense story by Samuel Foote (1720–77), English playwright.]

Pank·hurst (păngk'hûrst'), **Emmeline Goulden** (1858–1928). British suffragist. Founder of the Women's Social and Political Union (1903), she fought, with violence when she considered it necessary, for women's suffrage. Frequently imprisoned, she went on hunger strikes and was force-fed.

pan·mix·is (păn-mĭk'sĭs) *n. Genetics.* Random mating within an interbreeding population. [New Latin, from Greek : PAN- + *mixis,* act of mating.] —**pan·mic·tic** (păn-mĭk'tĭk) *adj.*

Pan·mun·jom (păn'mŏon'jŭm'). Village of South Korea, south of the 38th parallel, the demarcation line that partitions Korea. It was the site of the truce negotiations that ended the Korean War (1953).

pan·nage (păn'ĭj) *n.* **1.** Food or pasturage for pigs, especially in a forest. **2.** The right to pasture pigs in a forest or a fee paid to obtain this right. [Middle English, from Old French *pannage, pasnage,* from Medieval Latin *pastionaticum,* from Latin *pastiō* (stem *pastiōn-*), pasture, from *pascere,* to feed.]

panne (păn) *n.* A velvetlike fabric with a flattened pile and a very high luster. [French, from Old French, fur lining, from Latin *penna, pinna,* feather.]

pan·nier (păn'yər, păn'ē-ər) *n.* **1.** A large wicker basket, especially: **a.** Either of a pair of baskets carried on either side of a pack animal. **b.** A basket carried on a person's back. **2.** A container on the rear of a bicycle or motorcycle, often one of a pair. **3. a.** A framework of wire, bone, or other material formerly used to expand a woman's skirt at the hips. **b.** A part of a skirt or overskirt looped up around the hips so as to reveal the underskirt. [Middle English *panier,* from Old French, from Latin *pānārium,* breadbasket, from *pānis,* bread.] —**pan·niered** *adj.*

Pan·no·ni·a (pə-nō'nē-ə). An ancient Roman province in central Europe, occupying parts of modern Hungary and Yugoslavia.

pa·no·cha (pə-nō'chə) *n.* Also **pa·no·che** (pə-nō'chē). A coarse grade of Mexican sugar. [Mexican Spanish, diminutive of Spanish *pan,* bread, from Latin *pānis.*]

pan·o·ply (păn'ə-plē) *n., pl.* **-plies. 1.** The complete arms and armor of a warrior. **2.** An imposing array that covers or protects. [Greek *panoplia,* full suit of armor : PAN- + *hoplon*†, weapon.]

pan·op·tic (păn-ŏp'tĭk) *adj.* Also **pan·op·ti·cal** (-tĭ-kəl). Showing or seeing every part or aspect in one view. [From Greek *panoptēs,* all-seeing : PAN- + *optos,* visible.]

pan·o·ram·a (păn'ə-răm'ə, -rä'mə) *n.* **1.** An unlimited view of all visible objects over a wide area. **2.** A comprehensive picture of a chain of events or a specific subject: *a panorama of ancient history.* **3.** A picture or series of pictures exhibited a part at a time by being unrolled and passed before the spectator, thus representing a continuous scene. [PAN- + Greek *horāma,* sight, from *horān,* to see.] —**pan·o·ram·ic** *adj.* —**pan·o·ram·i·cal·ly** *adv.*

pan·pipe (păn'pīp') *n. Often* **panpipes.** A primitive wind instrument consisting of a series of pipes or reeds of graduated length bound together and played by blowing across the top open ends. Also called "mouth organ," "Pandean pipes," "Pan's pipes," "syrinx." [PAN + PIPE.]

pan·sy (păn'zē) *n., pl.* **-sies. 1.** Any plant of the genus *Viola,* especially *V. wittrockiana,* the garden pansy, having rounded, velvety petals of various colors. See **wild pansy. 2.** A deep to strong violet color. **3.** *Slang.* An effeminate man, especially a homosexual. [From French *pensée,* "thought," from the feminine past participle of *penser,* to think.]

pant (pănt) *v.* **panted, panting, pants.** —*intr.* **1.** To breathe rapidly in short gasps, as after exertion. **2.** To give off or emit smoke, steam, or the like in loud puffs. **3.** To pulsate rapidly; throb. **4.** To yearn frantically: *"my spirit began to burn and pant"* (R.D. Blackmore). —*tr.* To utter hurriedly or breathlessly.
—*n.* **1.** The act of panting. **2.** A short, labored breath; a gasp. **3.** A short, loud puff, as of steam from an engine. **4.** A throb; a pulsation. [Middle English *panten,* from Norman French *panter,* from Old French *pantaisier,* from Vulgar Latin *phantasiāre* (unattested), to fantasize, have nightmares, gasp with horror, from Latin *phantasia,* an apparition, fantasy, from Greek, from *phantazein,* to make visible, from *phainein,* to show.] —**pant·ing·ly** *adv.*

Pan·ta·gru·el·i·an (păn'tə-grŏo-ĕl'ē-ən) *adj.* Characteristic of or appropriate to Rabelais' character Pantagruel, noted for his ebullient, often coarse humor and huge appetite.

pan·ta·lets, pan·ta·lettes (păn'tə-lĕts') *pl.n.* **1.** Long underdrawers

trimmed at the bottom of the legs with ruffles and worn by women in the mid-19th century. **2.** A pair of frills attached to the legs of pantalets. [Diminutive of PANTALOON.]

pan·ta·loon (păn'tə-lōon') *n.* **1. pantaloons. a.** Men's wide breeches extending from waist to ankle, and worn in England during the reign of Charles II. **b.** Tight trousers extending from waist to ankle with straps passing under the instep, worn especially in the 19th century. **2. Pantaloon.** A character in the commedia dell'arte, portrayed as a foolish old man with slippers and tight trousers. [French *pantalon,* from Italian *pantalone,* originally a nickname for Venetian characters in Italian comedies, from *Pantaleone,* a saint once popular in Venice.]

pan·tech·ni·con (păn-tĕk'nĭ-kŏn', -kən) *n. British.* **1.** A large van, especially one used for moving furniture. **2.** A furniture warehouse. [Originally the name of a 19th-century bazaar in London where artistic things were sold : PAN- + Greek *tekhnikon,* neuter of *tekhnikos,* artistic, from *tekhnē,* art, skill.]

pan·the·ism (păn'thē-ĭz'əm) *n.* **1.** The doctrine that God is or is in everything and that the various forces and workings of nature are modes or manifestations of his existence. **2.** Belief in and worship of all gods. Compare **deism, theism.** —**pan·the·ist** *n.* —**pan·the·is·tic** (păn'thē-ĭs'tĭk), **pan·the·is·ti·cal** *adj.*

pan·the·on (păn'thē-ŏn', -ən) *n.* **1. Pantheon.** A circular temple in Rome, completed in 25 B.C., and dedicated to all the gods. **2.** Any temple dedicated to all gods. **3.** All the gods of a people. **4.** A public building commemorating and dedicated to the great or revered figures of a nation. **5.** The most eminent figures in the history of a particular field: *the philosophers' pantheon.* [Middle English *Panteon,* the Pantheon, from Latin *Panthēon,* from Greek *pantheion* : PAN- + *theos,* god.]

pan·ther (păn'thər) *n.* **1.** The leopard, *Panthera pardus,* especially in its black, unspotted form. **2.** Any of several similar or related animals, such as the mountain lion or jaguar. [Middle English *panter,* from Old French *pantere,* from Latin *panthēra,* from Greek *panthēr*†.]

pant·ies (păn'tēz) *pl.n. Informal.* Short underpants for women or children. [From PANTS.]

pan·tile (păn'tīl') *n.* An S-curved roofing tile, laid so the down curve of one tile overlaps the up curve of the next one. [PAN + TILE (i.e., "dish-tile," from the concave shape).]

pan·ti·soc·ra·cy (păn'tə-sŏk'rə-sē) *n.* A utopian society in which everyone is equal and everyone rules. [Greek *pas* (stem *pant-*), all + ISOCRACY.]

pan·tof·fle, pan·to·fle (păn-tŏf'əl, -tō'fəl, -tōo'fəl, păn'tə-fəl) *n.* A slipper. [Middle English *pantufle,* from Old French *pantoufle,* from Old Italian *pantofola,* perhaps from Medieval Greek *pantophellos,* "all cork" (of which medieval slippers were made) : *pas* (stem *pant-*), PAN- + *phellos*†, cork, cork oak.]

pan·to·graph (păn'tə-grăf', -gräf') *n.* **1.** An instrument for copying a picture or diagram to any desired scale, consisting of styluses for tracing and copying, mounted on four jointed rods in the form of a parallelogram with extended sides. **2.** Any similarly linked framework, used as an extensible support or contact, as on the framework that collects current from overhead cables in an electric locomotive. [French *pantographe* : PANTO- + -GRAPH.]

pan·to·mime (păn'tə-mīm') *n.* **1. a.** A genre of theatrical performance invented in Rome in the reign of Augustus, in which one actor played all the parts in mime, with music and singing in the background. **b.** The actor in this genre. **c.** Any of various revivals or derivatives of this genre. **2.** *British.* A kind of musical play performed at Christmas time, usually based on fairy stories, characterized by topical jokes and extravagant sets, and having specific conventions, especially farcical, deriving from the commedia dell'arte. **3.** Acting that consists mostly of gesture. **4.** Mime *(see).*
—*v.* **pantomimed, -miming, -mimes.** —*tr.* To represent by mime. —*intr.* To express oneself in mime. [Latin *pantomīmus,* "the complete mime" : Greek *pas* (stem *pant-*), PAN- + *mimos,* MIME.] —**pan·to·mim·ic** (păn'tə-mĭm'ĭk), **pan·to·mim·i·cal** *adj.* —**pan·to·mim·ist** (păn'tə-mī'mĭst) *n.*

pan·to·then·ic acid (păn'tə-thĕn'ĭk) *n.* A component of the vitamin B complex, $C_9H_{17}NO_5$, common in liver but found in all living tissue. [Greek *pantothen,* from all sides, from *pan,* all. See pan-.]

pan·toum (păn-tōom') *n.* A verse form consisting of quatrains in which the second and fourth lines are repeated as the first and third lines of the following quatrain, and in which the final line of the poem repeats the opening line. [French, from Malay *pantūn.*]

pan·try (păn'trē) *n., pl.* **-tries.** A small room or closet, usually off a kitchen, where food, china, and the like are stored. [Middle English *pantrie,* from Old French *paneterie,* bread closet, from *panetier,* servant in charge of the bread, from *pan,* bread, from Latin *pānis.*]

pants (pănts) *pl.n.* **1.** A pair of underpants. **2.** Trousers. —**with one's pants down.** Unprepared or in an awkward situation. [Short for *pantaloons,* plural of PANTALOON.]

pant·suit, pant suit (pănt'sōot') *n.* A woman's suit having trousers instead of a skirt.

pant·y·hose (păn'tē-hōz') *n., pl.* **pantyhose.** A garment consisting of stretchable stockings and underpants in one piece.

Pan·zer (păn'zər, pänt'sər) *adj.* Of, pertaining to, or designating the fast armored mechanical units of the German army, especially during World War II: *a Panzer division.*
—*n.* **1.** An armored tank in a Panzer unit. **2.** Panzer troops. [German *Panzer,* armor, from Middle High German *Panzier,* from Old

pantheon

A PLACE TO HONOR GODS AND HEROES

Style of a Roman temple and a French memorial

In Imperial Rome, many individual gods had temples dedicated exclusively to them. However, there were a number of pantheons—from the Greek words *pan* for "all" and *theos* for "god"—that were temples for the worship of all the Roman gods. The most famous of these temples, known today simply as the Pantheon, was begun in Rome about 27 B.C. by the statesman and general Marcus Vipsanius Agrippa. He intended it to be a temple in the classical style, but after a fire in the 2nd century A.D. the emperor Hadrian had it completely rebuilt as the present imposing circular building of elaborate brickwork.

It is noted for its massive dome, the largest Roman dome to survive intact. Until modern times, the Pantheon's dome was the largest in the world, with a diameter of some 43 meters (142 feet). The dome was mostly made of concrete containing pozzuolana, a volcanic earth that, when mixed with lime, became waterproof and extremely durable.

The Pantheon was consecrated as a Christian church in A.D. 609. It is now dedicated to Saint Maria Rotonda. With the rise in the belief of one God, the meaning of a pantheon changed. In France, the world's other remaining pantheon—the domed, cruciform Panthéon—was originally designed in 1759 as the Church of Sainte-Geneviève in Paris. But it was secularized in the 19th century and is now a civil temple of honor for the nation's heroes and famous men.

THE EYE OF THE PANTHEON *The central "eye," or oculus, in the dome of the Pantheon in Rome is 8 meters (27 feet) in diameter and allows a shaft of light to stream in.*

French *pancier,* body armor, from *panse,* body, from Vulgar Latin *pantica* (unattested), variant of Latin *pantex,* paunch.]

pap¹ (păp) *n.* **1.** *Regional.* A teat or nipple. **2.** Something resembling a nipple. [Middle English *pappe,* from Scandinavian (imitative of sucking).]

pap² *n.* **1.** Soft or semiliquid food, as for infants. **2.** Something lacking real value or substance; drivel. **3.** *Slang.* Money and favors given or obtained as political patronage. [Middle English *pape,* probably from Latin *pappa,* baby talk for food.]

pa·pa (pä′pə, pə-pä′) *n.* Also **pop·pa** (pŏp′ə). Father. [French, from Old French, from Late Latin, from Greek *pap(p)as.*]

pa·pa·cy (pā′pə-sē) *n., pl.* **-cies. 1.** The office and jurisdiction of a pope. **2.** The period of time during which a pope is in office. **3.** The system of church government headed by the pope. [Middle English *papacie,* from Medieval Latin *pāpātia,* from Late Latin *pāpa,* POPE.]

Pa·pa·do·pou·los (pä′pə-dô′pə-ləs), **Georgios** (1919–). Greek colonel and political leader. He seized power in a military coup (1967), abolished the monarchy (1973), and proclaimed himself president but was overthrown in a second military coup.

pa·pa·in (pə-pā′ĭn, -pī′ĭn) *n.* An enzyme capable of digesting protein, obtained from the unripe fruit of the papaya; it is used as a meat tenderizer and in medicine as a protein digestant. [From PAPAYA.]

pa·pal (pā′pəl) *adj.* **1.** Of, pertaining to, or issued by the pope: *a papal bull.* **2.** Of or pertaining to the papacy: *papal succession.* **3.** Of or pertaining to the Roman Catholic Church. [Middle English, from Old French, from Medieval Latin *pāpālis,* from Late Latin *pāpa,* POPE.] —**pa·pal·ly** *adv.*

Papal States. Former states of central Italy, under papal sovereignty (754–1870). They were originally given by Pepin the Short to Pope Stephen II and confirmed in this by Charlemagne (774). Varying in size over time owing to political struggles, the papal possessions were reduced after the Austro-Italian War (1859), and in 1870 Italian troops occupied Rome. The papacy did not recognize this loss of power until the Lateran Treaty (1929), when Vatican City was created as a separate state.

Pa·pan·dre·ou (pä′pən-drä′ōŏ), **Andreas George** (1919–). Greek statesman. Educated in the United States, he became a naturalized citizen in 1944 and taught economics at various universities. He returned to Greece in the 1960's and entered parliament. Jailed by the Papadopoulos government in 1967, he was freed later in the year and went into exile until 1974.

Pa·pa·ni·co·laou's test (pä′pə-nē′kə-louz′) *n.* A **Pap test** (see).

pa·pa·raz·zo (pä′pä-rät′sō) *n., pl.* **-razzi** (-rät′sē). A reporter or photographer, especially a free-lance one, who doggedly searches for sensational stories about or takes candid pictures of celebrities for magazines and newspapers. [After Signor *Paparazzo,* character in *La Dolce Vita,* a movie by Federico Fellini, from dialectal Italian *paparazzo,* a kind of buzzing insect.]

pa·pav·er·ine (pə-păv′ə-rēn′, -ər-ĭn) *n.* Also **pa·pav·er·in** (pə-păv′-ər-ĭn). A nonaddictive opium derivative, $C_{20}H_{21}NO_4$, used medicinally as an antispasmodic to treat such conditions as colic and asthma. [From New Latin *Papaver* (genus name), from Latin *papāver,* POPPY.]

pa·paw, paw·paw (pô′pô′) *n.* **1.** A tree, *Asimina triloba,* of central North America, having small, fleshy, edible fruit. **2.** The fruit of this tree. Also called "custard apple." **3.** The **papaya** (sense 2). [Probably from Spanish *papaya,* PAPAYA.]

pa·pa·ya (pə-pä′yə) *n.* **1.** An evergreen tropical American tree, *Carica papaya,* bearing large, yellow, edible fruit. **2.** The fruit of this tree. Also called "papaw." [Spanish, from Cariban.]

Pa·pe·e·te (pä′pē-ā′tē, pə-pä′tē, -pē′tē). Port on the island of Tahiti and capital of French Polynesia. It is a tourist center.

Pa·pen (pä′pən), **Franz von** (1879–1969). German politician. He served Hitler as vice chancellor (1933–34) and as a diplomat. Although acquitted at the Nuremberg Trials, he was imprisoned for three years to undergo denazification.

pa·per (pā′pər) *n.* **1.** A thin sheet material made of cellulose pulp, derived mainly from wood, rags, and certain grasses, processed into flexible leaves or rolls by deposit from an aqueous suspension, and used chiefly for writing, printing, drawing, wrapping, and covering walls. **2.** A single sheet or leaf of this material. **3.** One or more sheets of this material, bearing writing or printing, such as: **a.** An official document. **b.** An essay, treatise, or scholarly dissertation. **c.** An examination, report, essay, or similar exercise by a student. **d.** A newspaper. **3.** *Sometimes* **Paper.** *British.* Either of two documents issued by the government discussing potential legislation, a *Green Paper* or a *White Paper.* **4. papers.** A collection of letters, diaries, and other writings, especially those produced by one person. **5. papers.** Documents establishing the identity of the bearer. **6. papers. Ship's papers** (see). **7.** A negotiable document, such as a check or letter of credit. **8.** *Slang.* **a.** A free ticket to a theater. **b.** The audience admitted with free tickets. —**on paper. 1.** In writing or print. **2.** In theory as distinguished from actual performance or fact: *good on paper but poor in reality.*

~*tr.v.* **papered, -pering, -pers. 1.** To wrap or cover in paper. **2.** To supply with paper. **3.** To cover with wallpaper. **4.** *Slang.* To fill (a theater, for example) by issuing free passes: *paper the house.*

~*adj.* **1.** Made of or in the form of paper: *paper money.* **2.** Resembling paper in thinness or flimsiness. **3.** Existing only in printed or written form; notional; theoretical: *paper profits.* [Middle English *papir,* from Old French *papier,* from Latin *papȳrus,* paper, from Greek *papuros,* PAPYRUS.] —**pa·per·er** *n.* —**pa·per·y** *adj.*

pa·per·back (pā′pər-băk′) *n.* A book or edition having a flexible paper binding and selling relatively cheaply.

~*tr.v.* **paperbacked, -backing, -backs.** To publish in paperback form. —**pa·per·back, pa·per·backed** *adj.*

pa·per·bark tree (pā′pər-bärk′) *n.* Any of various Australian trees of the genus *Melaleuca,* having papery bark shed in thin layers.

paper birch *n.* A North American birch tree, *Betula papyrifera,* having paperlike white bark. Also called "white birch."

pa·per·board (pā′pər-bôrd′, -bōrd′) *n.* Cardboard; pasteboard.

pa·per·bound (pā′pər-bound′) *adj.* Bound in paper; paperback.

paper boy *n.* A boy who delivers newspapers.

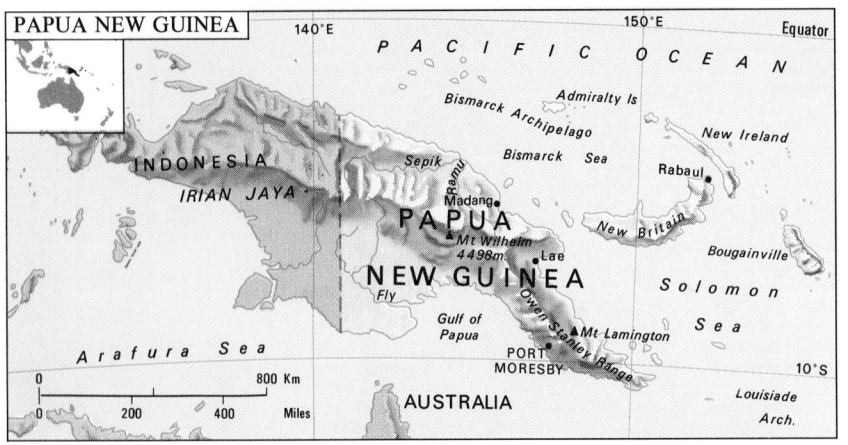

PAPUA NEW GUINEA

papyrus *About 5,500 years ago, the Egyptians discovered how to make a kind of paper from the papyrus plant by laying two thin sheets of its pith at right angles to each other and beating them into a sheet. The starch in the plant's juice formed a natural adhesive. This document on medicine, from the Egyptian Middle Kingdom, was written on papyrus in about 1700 B.C.*

parabola *The reflecting surface of this French solar furnace at Odeillo in the Pyrenees forms a parabola, with the furnace room at its focus. On a hillside opposite, thousands of mirrors can be moved to direct the sun's rays onto the parabola; the pollution-free furnace can reach 3500°C (6332°F).*

paper chase *n.* A cross-country run in which a trail of paper is left by one or more runners for the rest of the field to follow.

paper clip *n.* A clip, usually a piece of bent wire, for holding sheets of paper together.

paper girl *n.* A girl who delivers newspapers.

pa·per·hang·er (pā′pər-hăng′ər) *n.* One whose occupation is decorating walls with wallpaper. **—pa·per·hang·ing** *n.*

pa·per·knife (pā′pər-nīf′) *n., pl.* **-knives** (-nīvz′). A thin, blunt knife used for opening sealed envelopes, slitting uncut pages of books, and creasing paper.

pa·per·less (pā′pər-lĭs) *adj.* Using information technology, as in the form of computers and word processors, to the extent that documentation on paper is not necessary: *a paperless office.*

paper mulberry *n.* A tree, *Broussonetia papyrifera*, native to Asia, having bark that can be processed into a paperlike fabric. See **tapa**.

paper nautilus *n.* A marine cephalopod mollusk of the genus *Argonauta*, having a paper-thin spiral shell. Also called "argonaut."

paper tape *n.* Paper in a long narrow strip with rows of holes punched across it, different combinations of holes representing different characters. It is used in telex machines, computers, and similar devices in which information is represented digitally.

paper tiger *n.* A person, nation, or thing that appears strong, invincible, and threatening but is in fact weak and often ineffectual.

paper wasp *n.* Any wasp, such as a hornet, that builds paperlike nests.

pa·per·weight (pā′pər-wāt′) *n.* A small heavy object, often decorative, placed on top of loose papers to keep them in place.

pa·per·work (pā′pər-wûrk′) *n.* Work, such as clerical work, involving the handling of reports, letters, forms, and the like.

pap·e·terie (pāp′ə-trē, păp-trē′) *n.* A box used to hold paper and other writing materials. [French, stationery box, from *papier*, paper, from Old French, PAPER.]

Pa·pi·a·men·to (pā′pē-ə-mĕn′tō) *n.* The Spanish-based creole language of the Netherlands Antilles. [Spanish, from *papia*, talk.]

pa·pier-mâ·ché (pā′pər-mə-shā′, păp-yā′mä-shā′) *n.* A material made from paper pulp or shreds of paper mixed with glue or paste that can be molded into various shapes when wet and that becomes hard and suitable for varnishing when dry. [French, "chewed paper."] **—pa·pier-mâ·ché** *adj.*

pa·pil·la (pə-pĭl′ə) *n., pl.* **-pillae** (-pĭl′ē). Any small, nipplelike projection, such as a protuberance on the top of the tongue, at the root of a hair, or at the base of a developing tooth. [New Latin, from Latin, nipple, diminutive of *papula*, pimple.] **—pap·il·lar·y** (păp′-ə-lĕr′ē, pə-pĭl′ə-rē) *adj.* **—pap·il·late** (păp′ə-lāt′, pə-pĭl′ĭt), **pap·il·lose** (păp′ə-lōs′, pə-pĭl′ōs′) *adj.*

pap·il·lo·ma (păp′ə-lō′mə) *n., pl.* **-mata** (-mə-tə) or **-mas**. A small, benign epithelial tumor, usually occurring on the surface of a mucous membrane or the skin, such as a wart or corn. [PAPILL(A) + -OMA.] **—pap·il·lo·ma·tous** *adj.*

pap·il·lon (păp′ə-lŏn′, pā′pē-yôn′, păp′ē) *n.* A dog of a small breed with large, forward-facing ears and a long, fine coat that is white with colored patches. [French, "butterfly," ultimately from Latin *pāpiliō* (stem *pāpiliōn-*).]

pap·il·lote (pā′pē-yōt′, păp′ē-) *n.* **1.** A paper frill used to decorate the bone end of a cooked chop or cutlet. **2.** Oiled parchment in which some foods are baked. [French, from *papillon*, butterfly.]

pa·pist (pā′pĭst) *n.* A Roman Catholic. Usually used derogatorily. [French *papiste*, from *pape*, POPE.] **—pa·pis·tic** (pə-pĭs′tĭk), **pa·pis·ti·cal** *adj.* **—pa·pis·try** (pā′pĭ-strē) *n.*

pa·poose, pap·poose (pă-pōōs′, pə-) *n.* A North American Indian infant or young child. [Algonquian *papoos*.]

Papp (păp), **Joseph** (1921-). U.S. producer and director. He is best known for his determination to make the works of Shakespeare accessible to the public, both in the theater and outdoors, as in New York's Central Park.

pap·pus (păp′əs) *n., pl.* **pappi** (păp′ī). A tuft of bristles found on seeds of certain plants, such as dandelions and thistles, that aid dispersal. [Latin, from Greek *pappos*, grandfather.] **—pap·pose** (păp′ōs′), **pap·pous** (păp′əs) *adj.*

pap·py¹ (păp′ē) *adj.* **-pier, -piest**. Of or like pap; mushy; pulpy.

pap·py² *n., pl.* **-pies**. Father. [Diminutive of PAPA.]

pa·pri·ka (pă-prē′kə, pə-, păp′rĭ-kə) *n.* A mild, powdered seasoning made from sweet red peppers. [Hungarian, from Serbian, from *papar*, pepper, from Greek *peperi*, PEPPER.] **—pap·ri·ka** *adj.*

Pap test (păp) *n.* A test in which a smear of a bodily secretion, especially from the cervix or vagina, is fixed and examined for the presence of abnormal cells to detect cancer in an early stage. Also called "Pap smear," "Papanicolaou's test," "smear test." [Invented by George *Papanicolaou* (1883-1962), U.S. scientist.]

Pap·u·an (păp′yōō-ən) *n.* **1.** A native or inhabitant of Papua New Guinea. **2.** A member of a subgroup of an Oceanic Negroid people of Melanesia. **3.** Any of numerous languages of Papua New Guinea. **—Pap·u·an** *adj.*

Pap·u·a New Guin·ea (păp′yōō-ə nōō gĭn′ē, nyōō gĭn′ē). Country in the southwestern Pacific Ocean. It consists of the eastern part of New Guinea, the Bismarck Archipelago, Bougainville, and other islands. Formerly an Australian territory, it gained independence in 1975 and exports copper, coffee, cocoa, timber, and copra. Area, 461,691 square kilometers (178,259 square miles). Population, 3,000,000. Capital, Port Moresby.

pap·ule (păp′yōōl) *n.* Also **pap·u·la** (păp′yə-lə) *pl.* **-lae** (-lē′). A small, inflammatory, congested spot on the skin; a pimple. [Latin *papula*, pimple.] **—pap·u·lar, pap·u·lif·er·ous** (păp′yə-lĭf′ər-əs) *adj.*

pa·py·rus (pə-pī′rəs) *n., pl.* **-ri** (-rī′) or **-ruses**. **1.** A tall aquatic reedlike plant, *Cyperus papyrus*, of southern Europe and northern Africa. **2.** A kind of paper made from the pith stems of this plant, used by the ancient Egyptians, Greeks, and Romans as a writing material. **3.** A document written on this paper. [Middle English *papirus*, paper, from Latin *papyrus*, from Greek *papuros†*.]

par (pär) *n.* **1.** An accepted average; a normal standard: *up to par.* **2.** An equality of status, level, or value; an equal footing: *on a par.* **3.** *Finance.* **a.** The established face value of a monetary unit expressed in terms of a monetary unit of another country using the same metal standard. **b.** A condition of equality between the face value of a stock, bond, or other negotiable instrument and its current market value: *sell at par.* **4.** *Golf.* The number of strokes considered necessary to complete a hole in expert play.
~*tr.v.* **parred, parring, pars**. To score par on (a golf hole).
~*adj.* **1.** Equal to the standard; normal. **2.** *Finance.* Of or pertaining to face value. [Latin *par*, equal.]

par. **1.** paragraph. **2.** parallel. **3.** parenthesis. **4.** parish.

pa·ra¹ (pä-rä′, pä′rä) *n., pl.* **paras** or **para**. A monetary unit equal to $1/100$ of the dinar of Yugoslavia. See table at **currency**. [Serbo-Croatian, from Turkish, from Persian *parāh*, "piece."]

par·a² (păr′ə) *adj. Chemistry & Physics.* **1.** Of, pertaining to, or designating positions in a benzene ring separated by two carbon atoms. Used in combination: *para-dichlorobenzene.* Also written *p-*: *p-dichlorobenzene.* **2.** Of, pertaining to, or designating a polymer of a chemical compound. Used in combination: *paraformaldehyde.* **3.** Of, pertaining to, or designating a form of a diatomic molecule in which the nuclear spins are antiparallel. Used in combination: *parahydrogen.* Compare **ortho, meta.** [Independent use of PARA- (chemical prefix).]

Pará. See **Belém.**

para–¹, par– *prefix.* Indicates: **1.** Alongside; for example, **paragenesis. 2.** Near or beside; for example, **parathyroid gland. 3.** Beyond; over and above; for example, **paranormal. 4.** Incorrect; abnormal; for example, **paresthesia. 5.** Resembling or similar to; for example, **parablast, paratyphoid fever. 6.** Subsidiary or auxiliary to; for example, **paramedical. 7.** Isomeric to or polymeric to; for example, **paraldehyde.** [In borrowed Greek compounds, *para-* indicates: 1. Beside, to the side of, alongside, as in **paradigm, Paraclete.** 2. Beyond, as in **paradox.** 3. Wrongly, harmfully, unfavorably, as in **paralysis.** 4. Among, as in **parallax.** *Para-* is the preverbal form of the preposition *para*, beside, for.]

para–² *prefix.* Indicates something that protects or stops; for example, **parachute, parasol.** [French, from Italian, from *parare*, to defend, from Latin *parāre*, to make ready.]

par·a·a·min·o·ben·zo·ic acid (păr′ə-ə-mē′nō-bĕn-zō′ĭk, păr′ə-ăm′ə-nō-) *n.* A naturally occurring compound, $NH_2C_6H_4CO_2H$, used in the preparation of lotions and creams for preventing sunburn.

par·a·a·min·o·sal·i·cyl·ic acid (păr′ə-ə-mē′nō-săl′ə-sĭl′ĭk, păr′ə-ăm′ə-nō-) *n. Abbr.* **PAS, PASA** A drug, chemically similar to aspirin, used in the treatment of tuberculosis, usually in combination with isoniazid or streptomycin.

pa·rab·a·sis (pə-răb′ə-sĭs) *n., pl.* **-ses** (-sēz′). In ancient Greek comedies, an address by the chorus to the audience. [Greek, a stepping forward (to address the audience), from *parabainein*, to go forward : PARA- + *bainein*, to go.]

par·a·bi·o·sis (păr′ə-bī-ō′sĭs) *n. Biology.* The natural or artificial fusion of two organisms, as in the development of Siamese twins or the experimental joining of animals for research.

par·a·blast (păr′ə-blăst′, -blăst′) *n.* The food yolk of a meroblastic egg. [PARA- (resembling) + -BLAST.] **—par·a·blas·tic** *adj.*

par·a·ble (păr′ə-bəl) *n.* A simple story illustrating a moral or religious lesson, especially one told by Jesus in the Gospels. [Middle English, from Old French *parabole*, from Late Latin *parabola*, from Greek *parabolē*, juxtaposition, comparison, parable, from *paraballein*, to set beside : *para*, beside + *ballein*, to throw.]

pa·rab·o·la (pə-răb′ə-lə) *n. Geometry.* A plane curve formed by the locus of points equidistant from a fixed line and a fixed point not on the line. It is a conic section with an eccentricity of 1, formed by a plane intersecting a conical surface parallel to the axis of the cone.

[New Latin, from Greek *parabolē,* juxtaposition, parallelism (see **parable**); referring to the parallelism of the plane section containing the parabola and an element in the conical surface.]

par·a·bol·ic (păr′ə-bŏl′ĭk) *adj.* Also **par·a·bol·i·cal** (-ĭ-kəl). **1.** Of or like a parable. **2.** Of or having the form of a parabola. **3.** Of or having the form of a paraboloid; generated by a parabola: *a parabolic antenna.* —**par·a·bol·i·cal·ly** *adv.*

pa·rab·o·loid (pə-răb′ə-loid′) *n. Geometry.* A surface having sections that are parabolas; especially, one in which the sections parallel to two coordinate axes are parabolas, the sections parallel to the other axis being either an ellipse or circle (an *elliptic paraboloid*) or a hyperbola (a *hyperbolic paraboloid*). [PARABOL(A) + -OID.] —**pa·rab·o·loid·al** (pə-răb′ə-loid′l) *adj.*

paraboloid of revolution *n. Geometry.* An elliptic paraboloid formed by revolving a parabola about its own axis.

Par·a·cel·sus (păr′ə-sĕl′səs), **Philippus Aureolus,** born Theophrastus Bombastus von Hohenheim (*c.* 1493–1541). Swiss physician. He improved pharmacy, encouraged scientific experiments, and generally revolutionized European medicine.

par·a·ce·ta·mol (păr′ə-sē′tə-môl′, -mōl′) *n.* A drug that relieves pain and reduces fever, commonly used as an alternative to aspirin. [From *para-acetylaminophenol.*]

pa·rach·ro·nism (pă-răk′rə-nĭz′əm, pə-) *n.* An error made in a chronology, especially by giving too late a date. Compare **prochronism.** [PARA- (incorrect) + Greek *khronos,* time + -ISM, perhaps by analogy with *anachronism.*]

par·a·chute (păr′ə-sho͞ot′) *n.* **1.** An apparatus used to retard free fall from an aircraft, consisting of a canopy attached by cords to a harness and worn or stored folded until deployed in descent. **2.** Any of various similar unpowered devices for retarding free-speeding or free-falling motion, as on some jet aircraft. **3.** A membranous, winglike extension between the limbs of flying squirrels and certain lizards; a patagium.
~*v.* **parachuted, -chuting, -chutes.** —*tr.* To drop (supplies, for example) by means of a parachute. —*intr.* To descend by means of a parachute. [French : *para-,* "protecting against," "preventing," extracted from *parasol,* PARASOL + *chute,* fall, CHUTE.] —**par·a·chut·ist** *n.*

Par·a·clete (păr′ə-klēt′) *n.* **1.** The Holy Ghost as an advocate or counselor. **2. paraclete.** An advocate. [Middle English *Paraclit,* from Old French *Paraclet,* from Late Latin *Paraclētus,* from Greek *Paraklētos,* "the Comforter," advocate, "one called to help," from *parakalein,* to call to help : PARA- (alongside) + *kalein,* to call.]

pa·rade (pə-rād′) *n.* **1. a.** A public procession on some festive or ceremonial occasion. **b.** The occasion or action of making such a procession. **c.** The event itself, or the persons involved: *the Easter parade.* **2. a.** A ceremonial inspection of troops. **b.** The troops taking part in such an inspection. **c.** The place of assembly for an inspection of troops. Also called "parade ground." **3.** A continuous succession, as of persons or things on display or being reviewed: *a parade of fashions.* **4.** In fencing, a parry. **5.** An ostentatious show; a pompous display: *make a parade of humanitarian zeal.* **6.** A public square or a promenade. —**on parade. 1.** Being displayed or reviewed. **2.** Behaving ostentatiously.
~*v.* **paraded, -rading, -rades.** —*tr.* **1.** *Military.* **a.** To assemble (troops) for a formal display or inspection. **b.** To cause (troops, for example) to go on a ceremonial march. **2.** To march or walk through or around. **3.** To exhibit ostentatiously; flaunt. —*intr.* **1.** *Military.* To assemble for a formal inspection. **2.** To take part in a parade. **3.** To promenade in a public place. Used with *through* or *along.* —See Synonyms at **show.** [French, from Italian *parata,* from Vulgar Latin *parāta* (unattested), "a making ready," from Latin *parāre,* to prepare.] —**pa·rad·er** *n.*

par·a·digm (păr′ə-dīm′, -dĭm′) *n.* **1.** A list of all the inflectional forms of a word taken as an illustrative example of the conjugation or declension to which it belongs. **2.** Any example or model used as a standard. **3.** In the philosophy of science, the prevailing scientific framework of theories and concepts within which a scientist works. [Late Latin *paradīgma,* from Greek *paradeigma,* model, from *paradeiknunai,* to compare, exhibit : PARA- (alongside) + *deiknunai,* to show.] —**par·a·dig·mat·ic** (păr′ə-dĭg-măt′ĭk) *adj.*

par·a·dise (păr′ə-dīs′, -dīz′) *n.* **1.** *Often* **Paradise.** The Garden of Eden. **2.** *Theology.* **a.** Heaven, the abode of righteous souls after death. **b.** An intermediate resting place for righteous souls awaiting the Resurrection. **3.** The Muslim heaven, regarded as a garden of sensual delights and pleasures. **4.** Any place of ideal beauty or loveliness. **5.** A state of delight. [Middle English *paradis,* from Old French, from Late Latin *paradīsus,* from Greek *paradeisos,* garden, park, paradise, from Avestan *pairi-daēza,* circumvallation, walled-in park : *pairi,* around + *daēza,* wall.] —**par·a·di·si·a·cal** (păr′ə-dĭ-sī′ə-kəl, -zī′ə-kəl), **par·a·di·sa·i·cal** (păr′ə-dĭ-sā′ĭ-kəl, -zā′ĭ-kəl) *adj.* —**par·a·di·si·a·cal·ly, par·a·di·sa·i·cal·ly** *adv.*

par·a·dos (păr′ə-dŏs′, -dōs′, -dō′) *n.* A bank of earth, especially one backing a trench, that gives protection from the rear. [French : *para(sol)* + *dos,* back, from Latin *dorsum.*]

par·a·dox (păr′ə-dŏks′) *n., pl.* **-doxes. 1. a.** A seemingly contradictory statement that may nonetheless be true. **b.** A self-contradictory statement such as *I'm telling you the truth when I say I'm a liar.* **2.** A person, situation, or action exhibiting inexplicable or contradictory aspects. **3.** An assertion that is essentially self-contradictory, although perhaps based on a valid deduction from acceptable premises. **4.** A statement contrary to received opinion. [Latin *paradoxum,* from Greek *paradoxon,* from *paradoxos,* incredible, conflicting with expectation : PARA- (beyond) + *doxa,* opinion, from *dokein,* to think.] —**par·a·dox·i·cal** (păr′ə-dŏk′sĭ-kəl) *adj.* —**par·a·dox·i·cal·ly** *adv.* —**par·a·dox·i·cal·ness** *n.*

paradoxical sleep *n.* A stage of sleep characterized by **rapid eye movement** *(see)* and increased electrical activity of the brain. Compare **orthodox sleep.**

par·a·drop (păr′ə-drŏp′) *n. Military.* The delivery of supplies or personnel to a place by parachute.
~*tr.v.* **paradropped, -dropping, -drops.** To deliver (something) by parachute. [PARA(CHUTE) + DROP.]

paraesthesia. Variant of **paresthesia.**

par·af·fin (păr′ə-fĭn) *n.* **1.** *Chemistry.* A waxy, white or colorless, solid hydrocarbon mixture used to make candles, wax paper, lubricants, and sealing materials. Also called "paraffin wax." **2.** A member of the **paraffin series** *(see).* **3.** *British.* **Kerosene** *(see).*
~*tr.v.* **paraffined, -fining, -fins.** To saturate, impregnate, or coat with paraffin. [19th century : German, from Latin *parum,* (too) little + *affinis,* related, referring to its chemical inertia and lack of affinity to other substances.] —**par·af·fin·ic** (păr′ə-fĭn′ĭk) *adj.*

paraffin series *n. Chemistry.* A homologous group of saturated aliphatic hydrocarbons having the general formula C_nH_{2n+2}, the simplest and most abundant of which is methane. Also called "methane series," "alkane series."

par·a·for·mal·de·hyde (păr′ə-fôr-măl′də-hīd′) *n.* A white solid polymer of formaldehyde, $(HCHO)_n$, where *n* is at least 6, used as a disinfectant, a fumigant, and a fungicide. Also called "paraform."

par·a·gen·e·sis (păr′ə-jĕn′ə-sĭs) *n.* Also **par·a·ge·ne·sia** (păr′ə-jə-nē′zhə, -zhē-ə). *Geology.* The successive order in which a formation of associated minerals is generated. [PARA- (alongside) + -GENESIS.] —**par·a·ge·net·ic** (păr′ə-jə-nĕt′ĭk) *adj.*

par·a·go·ge (păr′ə-gō′jē) *n.* The addition of a sound or syllable to the end of a word, as the addition of *-st* to *again* to make *against.* [Late Latin, from Greek *paragōgē,* alteration, derivation, from *paragein,* to lead past, change : PARA- (beyond) + *agein,* to lead.] —**par·a·gog·ic** (păr′ə-gŏj′ĭk) *adj.*

par·a·gon (păr′ə-gŏn′, -gən) *n.* **1.** A model or pattern of excellence or perfection of a kind; a peerless example: *paragon of virtue.* **2. a.** An unflawed diamond weighing at least 100 carats. **b.** A very large spherical pearl. **3.** *Printing.* A type size of 20 points.
~*tr.v.* **paragoned, -goning, -gons. 1.** To compare. **2.** To match; equal. [Obsolete French, from Italian *paragone,* comparison, touchstone, from Medieval Greek *parakonē,* whetstone, from Greek *parakonan,* to sharpen against, to compare : *para,* alongside + *akonan,* to sharpen, from *akonē,* whetstone, from *akē,* point.]

par·a·graph (păr′ə-grăf′, -gräf′) *n. Abbr.* **par., para. 1.** A distinct division of a written work or composition that expresses some thought or point relevant to the whole but is complete in itself and usually marked by beginning on a separate, indented line. **2.** A mark (¶) used to indicate where a new paragraph should begin or to serve as a reference mark. **3.** A brief article, notice, or announcement, as in a newspaper.
~*tr.v.* **paragraphed, -graphing, -graphs.** *Abbr.* **par. 1.** To divide or arrange in paragraphs. **2.** To express or put in a paragraph. [Medieval Latin *paragraphus,* sign marking a new section of writing, from Greek *paragraphos,* line to mark exchange in dialogue, from *paragraphein,* to write beside : PARA- (beside) + *graphein,* to write.] —**par·a·graph·ic** (păr′ə-grăf′ĭk), **par·a·graph·i·cal** *adj.*

par·a·graph·i·a (păr′ə-grăf′ē-ə, -grä′fē-ə) *n. Psychiatry.* The writing of words or letters other than those intended, often resulting from certain brain disorders or injuries. [New Latin : PARA- (abnormal) + *-graphia,* "writing"; see **-graph.**]

Par·a·guay[1] (păr′ə-gwī′, -gwā′). Landlocked South American country. It is divided by the Paraguay River, with fertile lowlands and hills to the east and the infertile Gran Chaco region to the west. The eastern, more populous area produces cattle, oilseeds, sugar cane, and cotton. Area, 406,752 square kilometers (157,048 square miles). Population, 3,000,000. Capital, Asunción. —**Par·a·guay·an** (păr′ə-gwī′ən, -gwā′ən) *adj. & n.* See map, next page.

Paraguay[2]. South American river, 2,550 kilometers (1,585 miles) long. Rising in the Mato Grosso of Brazil, it flows south through Paraguay, joining the Paraná at the Argentine border.

Paraguay tea *n.* A tree, **maté** *(see),* or the beverage made from its leaves.

par·a·hy·dro·gen (păr′ə-hī′drə-jən) *n.* A form of hydrogen in which the two nuclei in each molecule have antiparallel spins; one of two possible forms of hydrogen, constituting 25 percent of the gas at room temperature. Compare **orthohydrogen.**

par·a·keet, par·ra·keet (păr′ə-kēt′) *n.* Also **par·a·quet** (-kĕt′). Any of various small parrots, usually having long, tapering tails and predominantly green plumage. [Old French *paroquet,* perhaps a nickname for *Pierre,* from Latin *Petrus* (the name Peter).]

par·al·de·hyde (pă-răl′də-hīd′) *n.* A colorless aromatic liquid polymer, $C_6H_{12}O_3$, of acetaldehyde, used as a solvent and as a sedative. [PAR(A)- + (ACET)ALDEHYDE.]

par·a·lin·guis·tic (păr′ə-lĭng-gwĭs′tĭk) *adj.* Of or pertaining to nonlinguistic features of verbal communication such as gestures or intonation.

par·a·lin·guis·tics (păr′ə-lĭng-gwĭs′tĭks) *n. Used with a singular verb.* The study of the paralinguistic features of verbal communication.

Par·a·li·pom·e·na (păr′ə-lĭ-pŏm′ə-nə) *pl.n.* The books of Chronicles in the Douay Bible. [Middle English, from Late Latin, from Greek, "things omitted" (that is, not covered in Kings), from *paraleipein,* to omit: PARA- (to one side) + *leipein,* to leave.]

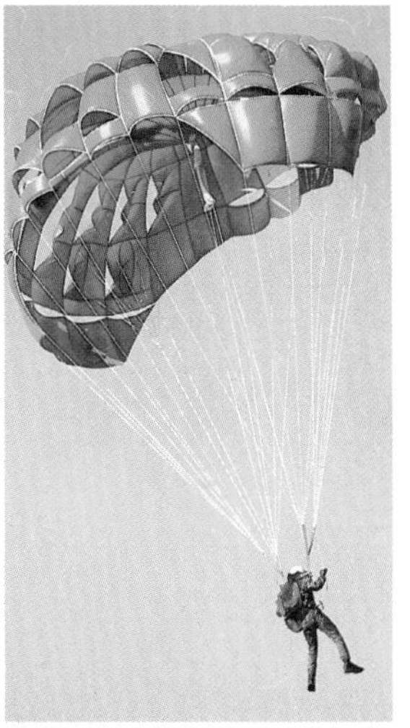

parachute *The earliest parachute—a large canvas umbrella stiffened with ribs—was used by a Frenchman, Louis Lenormand, in 1783. Modern parachutes are generally of synthetic material, and sporting versions, such as the one shown here, have vents that allow them to be steered.*

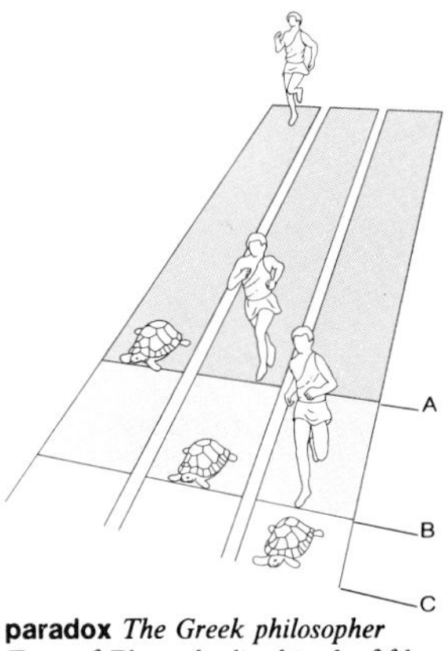

paradox *The Greek philosopher Zeno of Elea, who lived in the fifth century B.C., devised a number of mathematical paradoxes, of which the most celebrated is that of Achilles and the tortoise. If Achilles runs ten times as fast as the tortoise and the tortoise has a 100-yard start, the tortoise will have moved 10 yards by the time Achilles reaches its original position (A). But by the time Achilles reaches B, the tortoise will have moved another yard to C, and by the time he reaches C, it will have moved another tenth of a yard and so on. To catch the tortoise, the number of yards Achilles must travel is 100 + 10 + 1 + 1/10 + 1/100 + ... Since this series is open-ended, the paradox comes to the absurd conclusion that Achilles will never overtake the tortoise; always, during the time it takes him to reach its last position, the tortoise has edged a little forward. Only in the 19th century, after calculus was developed, were mathematicians able to resolve the paradox and prove that Achilles did catch up.*

PARAGUAY 60°W
BOLIVIA
BRAZIL
20°S
Gran Chaco
Paraguay
PARAGUAY
•Concepción
Tropic of Capricorn
Pilcomayo
•ASUNCIÓN
•Villarrica
Trinidad
Encarnación
Paraná
ARGENTINA
0   200   Km
0   200 Miles

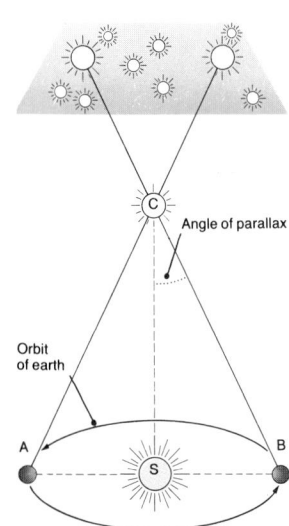

C
Angle of parallax
Orbit of earth
A   S   B

parallax *Up to a distance of about 100 light-years, the visual phenomenon of parallax can be used to calculate the distance of stars from the earth. From opposite points, A and B, on the earth's orbit around the sun, the relative position of star C is measured against the background of more distant stars. The greater the shift in the background, the greater the angle of parallax, and the closer the star is to the earth.*

par·a·lip·sis (păr′ə-lĭp′sĭs) *n., pl.* **-ses** (-sēz′). A rhetorical device in which one refers to something by saying that one will not speak of it, as in "to say nothing of her other achievements," "not to mention the latest revelations." [Late Latin, from Greek, "a leaving aside," from *paraleipein.* See **Paralipomena.**]

par·a·le·gal (păr′ə-lē′gəl) *adj.* Of, pertaining to, or being a person with specialized training who assists a lawyer. —**par·a·le·gal** *n.*

par·al·lax (păr′ə-lăks′) *n.* **1.** An apparent change in the position of an object when the observer changes position. **2.** *Astronomy.* **a.** Change in the observed position of a star or other celestial body resulting from motion of the earth. **b.** A measure of this effect. **c. Diurnal parallax, annual parallax,** or **secular parallax** (*all of which see*). [French *parallaxe,* from New Latin *parallaxis,* from Greek, change, from *parallassein,* to change, alternate : PARA- + *allassein,* to change, exchange, from *allos,* other.] —**par·al·lac·tic** (păr′ə-lăk′tĭk) *adj.*

par·al·lel (păr′ə-lĕl′) *adj.* *Abbr.* **par. 1.** Being an equal distance apart at every point. **2.** *Geometry.* **a.** Designating two or more equidistant coplanar lines that do not intersect. Compare **skew. b.** Designating two or more planes that do not intersect. **c.** Designating a line and a plane that do not intersect. **d.** Designating curves or surfaces that are everywhere equidistant. **e.** Designating two or more vectors that have parallel lines of action and act in the same direction. Compare **antiparallel. 3. a.** Having comparable parts, analogous aspects, or readily recognized similarities. **b.** Having the same tendency or direction. **4.** *Grammar.* Containing or characterized by corresponding syntactical forms or constructions. **5.** *Music.* Moving consistently by the same intervals. Said of two or more melodies. **6.** Designating or pertaining to a system of computer operation in which two or more users use the system at the same time by **time sharing** (*see*). Compare **serial. 7.** *Electricity.* Designating a circuit or part of a circuit connected in parallel.

~*adv. Abbr.* **par.** In a parallel relationship or manner.

~*n. Abbr.* **par. 1.** A surface or line that is equidistant from another. **2.** *Geometry.* One of a set of parallel geometric figures, usually lines. **3. a.** Anything that closely resembles or is analogous to something else. **b.** A comparison indicating likeness or analogy. **4.** The condition of being parallel; near similarity or exact agreement in particulars. **5.** *Geography.* Any of the imaginary lines joining places of equal latitude, encircling the earth parallel to the equator. **6.** *Printing.* A sign (‖), usually indicating material referred to in a note or reference. **7.** *Electricity.* A configuration of two or more two-terminal components connected between two points in a circuit with one terminal of each connected to each of the two points. Used chiefly in the phrase *in parallel.* See **series circuit.**

~*tr.v.* **paralleled, -leling, -lels.** Also *chiefly British* **-lelled, -lelling. 1.** To make or place parallel to. **2.** To be or extend parallel to. **3.** To be similar or analogous to. **4.** To be or provide an equal or match for. **5.** To show to be analogous; compare or liken. [Latin *parallēlus,* from Greek *parallēlos* : *para,* beside + *allēlōn,* of one another, from *allos,* other.]

parallel bars *pl.n.* A gymnastic apparatus consisting of two horizontal bars supported on posts, often at different heights.

par·al·lel·e·pi·ped, par·al·lel·o·pi·ped (păr′ə-lĕl′ə-pī′pĭd, -pĭp′ĭd) *n. Geometry.* A solid with six faces, each a parallelogram, having opposite pairs of faces congruent. [Greek *parallēlepipedon* : *parallēlos,* PARALLEL + *epipedon,* plane surface, from *epipedos,* level : *epi,* on + *pedon,* ground.]

par·al·lel·ism (păr′ə-lĕl-ĭz′əm) *n.* **1.** The state or position of being parallel; a parallel relationship. **2.** Likeness, correspondence, or similarity in aspect, course, or tendency. **3. a.** The use of corresponding syntactical forms or literary devices. **b.** An instance of this. **4.** *Philosophy.* The doctrine that to every mental change there

corresponds a concomitant but causally unconnected physical alteration.

par·al·lel·o·gram (păr′ə-lĕl′ə-grăm′) *n.* A four-sided plane figure with both pairs of opposite sides parallel. [Late Latin *parallēlogrammum,* from Greek *parallēlogrammon,* from *parallēlogrammos,* bounded by parallel lines : *parallēlos,* PARALLEL + *grammē,* line.]

parallelogram rule *n. Mathematics & Physics.* A rule for adding two vectors or vector quantities, such as forces or velocities, by forming a parallelogram in which two adjacent sides represent the vectors; their resultant is then indicated by the diagonal of the parallelogram through the point of intersection of the vectors.

parallel turn *n. Skiing.* A turn executed by shifting and dropping one's weight, keeping both skis parallel.

pa·ral·o·gism (pə-răl′ə-jĭz′əm) *n. Logic.* Fallacious or illogical reasoning; especially, a faulty argument of whose fallacy the reasoner is not aware. [French *paralogisme,* from Late Latin *paralogismus,* from Greek *paralogismos,* from *paralogos,* unexpected, beyond calculation : PARA- + *logos,* word.] —**pa·ral·o·gist** *n.* —**pa·ral·o·gis·tic** (pə-răl′ə-jĭs′tĭk) *adj.*

pa·ral·y·sis (pə-răl′ə-sĭs) *n., pl.* **-ses** (-sēz′). **1.** Loss or impairment of the ability to move or have sensation in a bodily part as a result of injury to or disease of its muscles or nerve supply. **2.** Partial or complete inability to move or function; stoppage or impairment of activity. [Latin, from Greek *paralusis,* from *paraluein,* to loosen, disable : *para,* "unfavorably" + *luein,* to release.]

paralysis ag·i·tans (ăj′ə-tănz′) *n.* **Parkinson's disease** (*see*). [New Latin, "shaking palsy."]

par·a·lyt·ic (păr′ə-lĭt′ĭk) *adj.* **1.** Affected with paralysis; paralyzed. **2.** Of or pertaining to paralysis. **3.** *British Slang.* Very drunk. ~*n.* A person suffering from paralysis. [Middle English, from Old French *paralytique,* from Latin *paralyticus,* from Greek *paralutikos,* from *paralusis,* PARALYSIS.] —**par·a·lyt·i·cal·ly** *adv.*

par·a·lyze (păr′ə-līz′) *tr.v.* **-lyzed, -lyzing, -lyzes. 1.** To affect with paralysis; cause to be paralytic. **2.** To make helpless or unable to move, as through emotion. **3.** To impair the progress or functioning of; make inoperative or powerless. [From French *paralyser,* from *paralysie,* paralysis.] —**par·a·ly·za·tion** *n.* —**par·a·lyz·er** *n.*

par·a·mag·net (păr′ə-măg′nĭt) *n.* A paramagnetic substance.

par·a·mag·net·ism (păr′ə-măg′nə-tĭz′əm) *n. Physics.* A type of magnetism occurring in substances with a positive magnetic susceptibility. It is caused by unpaired electron orbitals in the atoms, which result in each atom having a dipole moment. An applied magnetic field tends to align these dipoles in such a way that for small fields and high temperatures the induced field is proportional to the applied field. Below the Curie point certain paramagnetic materials exhibit ferromagnetism. —**par·a·mag·net·ic** (păr′ə-măg-nĕt′ĭk) *adj.* —**par·a·mag·net·i·cal·ly** *adv.*

Par·a·mar·i·bo (păr′ə-măr′ə-bō′). Capital of Surinam. It was founded by the French (1540), settled by the British (1630), and later taken over by the Dutch. Exports include bauxite and coffee.

paramatta. Variant of **parramatta.**

par·a·me·ci·um (păr′ə-mē′shē-əm, -sē-əm) *n., pl.* **-cia** (-shē-ə, -sē-ə) or **-ums.** Any of various ciliate protozoans of the genus *Paramecium,* usually oval and having an oral groove for feeding. [New Latin, from Greek *paramēkēs,* oblong : PARA- (alongside) + *mēkos,* length.]

par·a·med·ic (păr′ə-mĕd′ĭk) *n.* A person, as a laboratory technician, who assists a highly trained medical professional. —**par·a·med·i·cal** *adj.*

par·a·ment (păr′ə-mənt) *n., pl.* **-ments** or **-menta** (-mĕn′tə). An ecclesiastical vestment or hanging. [Middle English, from Medieval Latin *parāmentum,* from *parāre,* to decorate, prepare.]

pa·ram·e·ter (pə-răm′ə-tər) *n.* **1.** A variable or an arbitrary constant appearing in a mathematical expression, each value of which restricts or determines the specific form of the expression. **2.** *Informal.* **a.** A fixed limit or boundary; constant: *keep within the parameters of our budget.* **b.** A characteristic and defining feature or element; touchstone: *one of the parameters of democracy.* [New Latin : PARA- (alongside) + -METER.] —**par·a·met·ric** (păr′ə-mĕt′rĭk) *adj.* —**par·a·met·ri·cal·ly** *adv.*

Usage: Using *parameter* in its fairly recent nonmathematical sense ("a defining or limiting factor") has attracted criticism on the grounds that it sounds pretentious. In general it is better to use one of the older, simpler words, such as *limit* or *constraint.*

par·a·mil·i·tar·y (păr′ə-mĭl′ə-tĕr′ē) *adj.* **1.** Organized on a military pattern, especially as an auxiliary military force. **2.** Of or pertaining to paramilitary forces.

par·am·ne·sia (păr′am-nē′zhə) *n. Psychology.* A distortion of memory in which fantasy and experience are confused. [PAR(A)- (resembling) + AMNESIA.]

pa·ra·mo (păr′ə-mō′, păr′ə-) *n., pl.* **-mos.** A high, treeless plain of tropical South America. [American Spanish, from Spanish *paramo*†, a wasteland.]

par·a·morph (păr′ə-môrf′) *n.* A mineral crystal formed or affected by paramorphism. Also called "allomorph." [PARA- (subsidiary to) + -MORPH.]

par·a·mor·phism (păr′ə-môr′fĭz′əm) *n.* Structural alteration of a mineral without change of chemical composition. Also called "metastasis." —**par·a·mor·phic, par·a·mor·phous** *adj.*

par·a·mount (păr′ə-mount′) *adj.* **1.** Of chief concern or significance; primary; foremost: *of paramount importance.* **2.** Supreme in rank, power, or authority. —See Synonyms at **dominant.** ~*n.* A person of the highest power or authority; a supreme ruler.

[Norman French *paramont,* "superior" (used of feudal overlordship) : Old French *par,* by, from Latin *per* + *amont,* above : *a,* to, from Latin *ad* + *mont,* mountain, from Latin *mōns* (stem *mont-*).] **—par·a·mount·cy** *n.* **—par·a·mount·ly** *adv.*

par·a·mour (păr′ə-mo͝or′) *n.* **1.** A lover, of either sex; especially, the lover of someone who is married. **2.** *Archaic.* A sweetheart. [Middle English, originally an adverb, "by way of love," from Old French *par amour* : *par,* by, from Latin *per* + *amour,* love, from Latin *amor,* from *amāre,* to love.]

Pa·ra·ná (păr′ə-nä′). Second-largest river in South America. Formed by the confluence of the Grande and Paranaíba rivers in southeastern Brazil, it flows southwest for 2,900 kilometers (1,800 miles) through Paraguay to join the Uruguay River at the Río de la Plata estuary. It is important for navigation.

pa·rang (pä′răng′) *n.* A short, heavy, straight-edged knife used in Malaysia and Indonesia as a tool and weapon. [Malay.]

par·a·noi·a (păr′ə-noi′ə) *n.* **1.** A nondegenerative, limited, usually chronic psychosis characterized by delusions of persecution or of grandeur, defended by the afflicted with apparent logic and reason. **2.** Loosely, unwarranted fear or distrust of people or situations. [New Latin, from Greek, madness, from *paranoos,* demented : PARA- (beyond) + *nous,* mind.] **—par·a·noi·ac** (păr′ə-noi′ăk′, -noi′ĭk) *adj. & n.*

par·a·noid (păr′ə-noid′) *adj.* **1.** Pertaining to, characteristic of, or suffering from paranoia: *a paranoid delusion.* **2.** Suggestive of paranoia; showing unreasonable distrust, suspicion, or an exaggerated sense of one's own importance.
∼*n.* One afflicted with paranoia.

paranoid schizophrenia *n.* A type of schizophrenia resembling paranoia and characterized chiefly by delusions and hallucinations.

par·a·nor·mal (păr′ə-nôr′məl) *adj.* Not within the range of normal experience or scientifically explainable phenomena. **—par·a·nor·mal·ly** *adv.*

par·an·thro·pus (păr′ən-thrō′pəs, pă-răn′thrə-pəs) *n., pl.* **-puses.** An extinct anthropoid ape of the genus *Paranthropus* (later renamed as a species of *Australopithecus*), known from remains found in South Africa. [New Latin : PAR(A)- (resembling) + Greek *anthrōpos,* man.]

par·a·pet (păr′ə-pĭt, -pĕt′) *n.* **1.** A low, protective wall or railing along the edge of a roof, balcony, or similar structure. **2.** An earth or stone embankment protecting soldiers from enemy fire. —See Synonyms at **bulwark.** [French, from Italian *parapetto,* chest-high wall : PARA- (protecting) + *petto,* chest, from Latin *pectus.*] **—par·a·pet·ed** (păr′ə-pĕt′ĭd) *adj.*

par·aph (păr′əf, pə-răf′) *n.* A flourish made after or below a signature, originally to prevent forgery. [French *parafe, paraphe,* from Old French *paraffe,* from Medieval Latin *paraphus,* from *paragraphus,* PARAGRAPH.]

par·a·pher·na·lia (păr′ə-fər-nāl′yə, -fə-nāl′yə) *pl.n. Used with a singular or plural verb.* **1.** Personal belongings. **2.** The articles used in some activity; equipment or gear: *climbing paraphernalia.* **3.** *Common Law.* A married woman's personal property exclusive of her dowry. **4.** The problems or procedures accompanying a systematized activity: *all the paraphernalia of philosophical analysis.* [Medieval Latin *paraphernālia* (in sense 3), from Greek *parapherna* : PARA- (beyond) + *phernē,* dowry.]

par·a·phrase (păr′ə-frāz′) *n.* **1.** A restatement of a text or passage in another form or other words, often to clarify meaning. **2.** The making of paraphrases, often used as a teaching device.
∼*v.* **paraphrased, -phrasing, -phrases.** —*tr.* To express in a paraphrase. —*intr.* To compose a paraphrase. [French, from Latin *paraphrasis,* from Greek, from *paraphrazein,* to paraphrase : PARA- (alongside) + *phrazein,* to show.] **—par·a·phras·tic** (păr′ə-frăs′tĭk) *adj.*

pa·raph·y·sis (pə-răf′ə-sĭs) *n., pl.* **-ses** (-sēz′). Any of the sterile filaments found among the sexual organs of certain fungi, algae, and mosses. [PARA- (subsidiary to) + Greek *phusis,* nature.]

par·a·ple·gi·a (păr′ə-plē′jē-ə, -jə) *n.* Complete paralysis of the lower body, including both legs, caused by injury to or disease of the spinal cord. [New Latin, from Greek *paraplēgia,* a stroke on one side, from *paraplēssein,* to strike on one side : PARA- (alongside) + *plēssein,* to strike.] **—par·a·ple·gic** (păr′ə-plē′jĭk) *adj. & n.*

par·a·po·di·um (păr′ə-pō′dē-əm) *n., pl.* **-dia** (-dē-ə). Any of the lateral appendages of polychaete worms, which occur in pairs and are used in locomotion and respiration. [New Latin : PARA- + *-podium* (footlike part). See **podium.**]

par·a·psy·chol·o·gy (păr′ə-sī-kŏl′ə-jē) *n.* The study of phenomena such as telepathy, clairvoyance, and psychokinesis that are not explainable by known natural laws. **—par·a·psy·cho·log·i·cal** (păr′ə-sī′kə-lŏj′ĭ-kəl) *adj.* **—par·a·psy·chol·o·gist** (-sī-kŏl′ə-jĭst) *n.*

par·a·quat (păr′ə-kwŏt′) *n.* A poisonous, yellow water-soluble solid used as a herbicide. [PARA- + QUAT(ERNARY).]

paraquet. Variant of **parakeet.**

Pa·rá rubber (pə-rä′, păr′ə) *n.* Rubber obtained from various tropical South American trees of the genus *Hevea,* especially *H. brasiliensis.* [After *Pará,* a state in Brazil.]

par·a·sang (păr′ə-săng′) *n.* An ancient Persian unit of distance, usually estimated at about $5^{1}/_{2}$ kilometers ($3^{1}/_{2}$ miles). [Latin *parasanga,* from Greek *parasangēs,* from Iranian, akin to Persian *farsang*†.]

par·a·se·le·ne (păr′ə-sĭ-lē′nē) *n., pl.* **-nae** (-nē). A luminous spot on a lunar halo. Also called "mock moon," "moon dog." [New Latin : PARA- (resembling) + Greek *selēnē,* moon.] **—par·a·se·le·nic** (păr′ə-sĭ-lē′nĭk, -lĕn′ĭk) *adj.*

pa·ra·shah (pä′rə-shä′) *n., pl.* **parashoth** (pä′rə-shōt′, -shōth′). Any of the portions of the Torah read on the Sabbath and on festivals in the synagogue. [Hebrew, "explanation."]

Par·a·shu·ra·ma (păr′ə-sho͞o-rä′mə) *n. Hinduism.* See **Rama.**

par·a·site (păr′ə-sīt′) *n.* **1.** *Biology.* Any organism that grows, feeds, and is sheltered on or in a different organism while contributing nothing to the survival of its host. **2.** A person who habitually takes advantage of the generosity of others without making any useful return. **3.** In ancient Greece, one who was given free meals in return for his witty conversation. [Old French, from Latin *parasītus,* from Greek *parasitos,* originally "fellow guest," later "parasite" : PARA- (beside) + *sitos,* grain, food.]

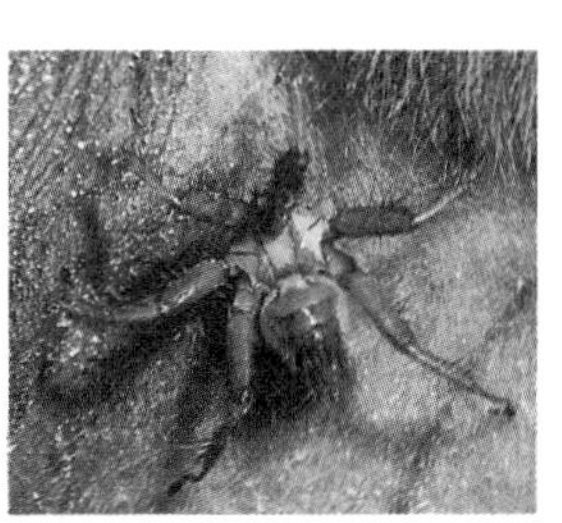

parasite *The bat fly, a member of the insect family* Nycteribiidae, *is a wingless parasite. It lives on the skin of bats.*

par·a·sit·ic (păr′ə-sĭt′ĭk) *adj.* Also **par·a·sit·i·cal** (-ĭ-kəl). **1.** Of, pertaining to, or characteristic of a parasite. **2.** Caused by a parasite, as certain diseases are. **—par·a·sit·i·cal·ly** *adv.*

par·a·sit·i·cide (păr′ə-sĭt′ə-sīd′) *n.* Something used to destroy parasites. [PARASIT(E) + -CIDE.] **—par·a·sit·i·cide, par·a·sit·i·cid·al** (păr′ə-sĭt′ə-sīd′l), **par·a·sit·i·cid·ic** (păr′ə-sĭt′ə-sīd′ĭk) *adj.* **—par·a·sit·i·cid·al·ly** *adv.*

par·a·sit·ism (păr′ə-sī-tĭz′əm, -sĭ-tĭz′əm) *n.* **1.** The characteristic behavior or mode of existence of a parasite. **2.** A diseased condition resulting from parasitic infestation.

par·a·sit·ize (păr′ə-sĭ-tīz′, -sī-tīz′) *tr.v.* **-ized, -izing, -izes.** To live on (a host) as a parasite.

par·a·si·tol·o·gy (păr′ə-sī-tŏl′ə-jē, -sĭ-tŏl′ə-jē) *n.* The scientific study of parasites. [PARASIT(E) + -LOGY.] **—par·a·si·to·log·i·cal** (păr′ə-sī′tə-lŏj′ĭ-kəl) *adj.* **—par·a·si·tol·o·gist** *n.*

par·a·sol (păr′ə-sôl′, -sŏl′) *n.* A light, usually small umbrella carried, especially by women, for protection from the sun. [French, from Italian *parasole* : PARA- (protecting) + *sole,* sun, from Latin *sōl.*]

par·a·sym·pa·thet·ic nervous system (păr′ə-sĭm′pə-thĕt′ĭk) *n.* The part of the autonomic nervous system originating in the central and back parts of the brain and in the lower part of the spinal cord that inhibits or opposes the physiological effects of the sympathetic nervous system, as in tending to stimulate digestive secretions, slowing the heart, and dilating blood vessels. Also called "craniosacral system."

par·a·syn·the·sis (păr′ə-sĭn′thə-sĭs) *n. Grammar.* The formation of words by a combination of compounding and adding an affix, as in the formation of the word *downhearted* from *down* plus *heart* plus *-ed,* rather than from *down* plus *hearted.* **—par·a·syn·thet·ic** (păr′ə-sĭn-thĕt′ĭk) *adj.*

par·a·tax·is (păr′ə-tăk′sĭs) *n.* The coordination of grammatical elements such as phrases or clauses without the use of coordinating elements such as conjunctions, as *It was cold; the snows came.* Compare **asyndeton, hypotaxis.** [Greek, from *paratassein,* to arrange side by side : PARA- (beside) + *tassein,* to arrange.] **—par·a·tac·tic** (păr′ə-tăk′tĭk), **par·a·tac·ti·cal** *adj.* **—par·a·tac·ti·cal·ly** *adv.*

par·a·thi·on (păr′ə-thī′ŏn′) *n.* A highly poisonous liquid insecticide, $(C_2H_5O)_2P(S)OC_6H_4NO_2$. [PARA- + *thio(phosphate)* + -ON.]

par·a·thor·mone (păr′ə-thôr′mōn′) *n.* **Parathyroid hormone** *(see).*

par·a·thy·roid (păr′ə-thī′roid′) *adj.* **1.** Situated close to the thyroid gland. **2.** Of pertaining to the parathyroid gland.
∼*n.* The parathyroid gland.

parathyroid gland *n.* Any of four small kidney-shaped glands that lie in pairs near or within the lateral lobes of the thyroid gland and secrete parathyroid hormone.

parathyroid hormone *n.* A hormone, synthesized and secreted by the parathyroid glands, that raises the level of calcium in the blood. Deficiency results in tetany. Also called "parathormone."

par·a·troop·er (păr′ə-tro͞o′pər) *n.* A member of the paratroops.

par·a·troops (păr′ə-tro͞ops′) *pl.n.* Infantry trained and equipped to carry out parachute missions. [PARA(CHUTE) + TROOPS.] **—par·a·troop** *adj.*

par·a·ty·phoid (păr′ə-tī′foid′) *adj.* **1.** Resembling typhoid fever. **2.** Of or pertaining to paratyphoid fever.
∼*n.* Paratyphoid fever.

paratyphoid fever *n.* An acute intestinal disease similar to typhoid fever but less severe and caused by any of three bacteria of the genus *Salmonella.* Also called "paratyphoid."

par·a·vane (păr′ə-vān′) *n. Nautical.* A device equipped with sharp teeth and towed alongside a ship to cut the mooring cables of submerged mines. [PARA- (alongside) + VANE.]

par a·vion (pär′ äv-yôN′) *adv.* By airplane. Used as a label or notation on letters or articles sent by air mail. [French.]

par·boil (pär′boil′) *tr.v.* **-boiled, -boiling, -boils. 1.** To cook partially by boiling for a brief period. **2.** To subject to intense, often uncomfortable heat. [Middle English *parboilen,* "to boil thoroughly," later (by influence of PART) to parboil, from Old French *parbo(u)illir,* from Late Latin *perbullīre* : Latin *per,* thoroughly + *bullīre,* to boil.]

par·buck·le (pär′bŭk′əl) *n.* **1.** A rope sling for rolling cylindrical objects up or down an inclined plane. **2.** A sling for raising or lowering a heavy object vertically.
∼*tr.v.* **parbuckled, -ling, -les.** To raise or lower with a parbuckle. [Alteration (influenced by BUCKLE) of earlier *parbunkle*†.]

Par·cae (pär′sē, pär′kī′) *pl.n.* The three **Fates** *(see).* [Latin.]

par·cel (pär′səl) *n.* **1.** Something wrapped up or packaged; a package. **2.** A portion or plot of land, usually a division of a larger area. **3.** A quantity of merchandise offered for sale. **4.** A group or company; a bunch. **5.** A distinct, often essential part of something. Used chiefly in the phrase *part and parcel.*

PRONUNCIATION KEY

ă, pat; ā, pay; âr, care;
ä, father, are; b, bib;
ch, church; d, deed; ĕ, pet;
ē, be; f, fife; g, gag; h, hat;
hw, which; ĭ, pit; ī, pie;
îr, pier; j, judge; k, kick;
l, lid, needle; m, mum;
n, no, sudden; ng, thing;
ŏ, pot; ō, toe; ô, paw, for;
oi, noise; ou, out; o͝o, book;
o͞o, boot; p, pop; r, roar;
s, sauce; sh, ship, dish;
t, tight; th, thin, path;
th, this, bathe; ŭ, cut; ûr, fur;
v, valve; w, with; y, yes;
z, zebra, size; zh, vision;
ə, about, item, edible,
gallop, circus, peaceful

IN FOREIGN WORDS:

à, *Fr.* ami; œ, *Fr.* feu, *Ger.* schön; ü, *Fr.* tu, *Ger.* über;
KH, *Ger.* ich, *Scot.* loch;
N, *Fr.* bon; y′, *Fr.* Compiègne

STRESS MARKS:

Primary stress: ′
in·cite′ (ĭn-sīt′)
Secondary stress: ′
in′sight′ (ĭn′sīt′)

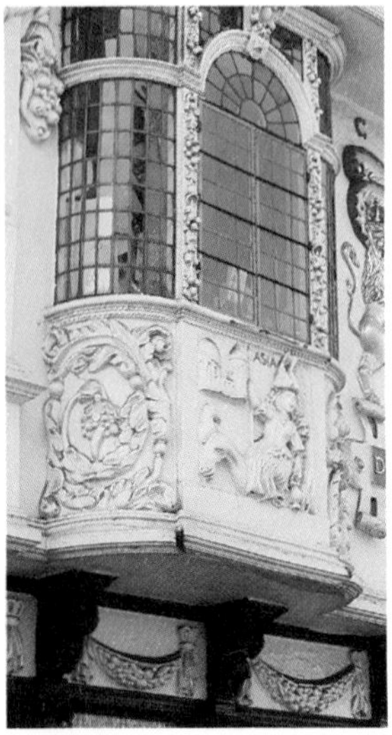

pargeting *Ornamental plasterwork seen here on a house built in 1567. This method of molding ornaments onto ceilings and walls was popular during the Tudor and Elizabethan periods.*

~*tr.v.* **parceled, -celing, -cels.** Also *chiefly British* **-celled, -celling. 1.** To divide into portions or allotments and distribute. Usually followed by *out.* **2.** To make into a parcel or parcels; wrap; package. Sometimes followed by *up.* **3.** *Nautical.* To wind protective strips of canvas round (rope). [Middle English *parcelle,* from Old French, from Vulgar Latin *particella* (unattested), from Latin *particula,* portion, particle, diminutive of *pars* (stem *part-*), part.]

parcel post *n. Abbr.* **p.p., P.P.** The branch of the postal service that handles and delivers parcels sent through the mail.

par·ce·nar·y (pär′sə-nĕr′ē) *n., pl.* **-ies.** *Law.* **Coparcenary** *(see).* [Norman French *parcenarie,* from Old French *parçonerie,* from *parçonier,* partner, PARCENER.]

par·ce·ner (pär′sə-nər) *n. Law.* A **coparcener** *(see).* [Norman French, from Old French *parçonier,* partner, from Vulgar Latin *partiōnārius* (unattested), from Latin *partītiō,* partition, from *partīre,* to divide, from *pars* (stem *part-*), part.]

parch (pärch) *v.* **parched, parching, parches.** —*tr.* **1.** To make very dry, especially by the action of heat. **2.** To make thirsty. Usually used in the passive: *I'm parched.* **3.** To dry or roast (corn, peas, or the like) by exposing to heat. —*intr.* **1.** To become very dry: *The fields will soon parch in this heat.* **2.** To become thirsty. —See Synonyms at **burn.** [Middle English *parchen*†.]

Par·chee·si (pär-chē′zē) *n.* A trademark for a board game based on the ancient game of **pachisi** *(see).*

parch·ment (pärch′mənt) *n.* **1.** The skin of a sheep or goat prepared for writing or painting upon. **2.** A written text or drawing on a sheet of this material. **3.** Stiff, durable paper made in imitation of this material. [Middle English *perchement, parchemin,* from Old French *parchemin, parcamin,* from Vulgar Latin *particamīnum* (unattested), blend of Latin *Parthica (pellis),* "Parthian (leather)," and *pergamīna,* parchment, from Greek *pergamēnē,* from *Pergamēnos,* of Pergamun, from *Pergamon,* Pergamum in western Turkey (where parchment was first used as a substitute for papyrus).]

par·close (pär′klōz′) *n.* A railing dividing a chapel or altar from the main body of a church. [Middle English, from Old French *parclos(e),* from the past participle of *parclore,* to close off. See **per-, close.**]

pard (pärd) *n. Archaic.* A leopard or other large cat. [Middle English *parde,* from Old French, from Latin *pardus,* from Greek *pardos,* from an Oriental source. See also **leopard.**]

par·da·lote (pär′də-lōt′) *n.* The **diamond bird** *(see).* [New Latin *pardalotus,* from Greek *pardalōtos,* having a leopard's spots, from *pardos* (stem *pardal-*), leopard.]

pard·ner (pärd′nər) *n. Regional.* A friend or partner. [Variant of PARTNER.]

par·don (pärd′n) *tr.v.* **-doned, -doning, -dons. 1.** To release (a person) from punishment; forgive. **2.** To pass over (an offense) without punishment. **3.** To make courteous allowance for; to excuse: *Pardon me, but I must go.* —See Synonyms at **forgive.**
~*n.* **1. a.** The act of forgiving. **b.** Forgiveness, as for a fault or offense. **2.** *Law.* **a.** The exemption of a convicted person from the penalties of an offense or crime by the power of the executor of the laws. **b.** The official document or warrant declaring such an exemption. **3.** A papal indulgence.
~*interj.* Used as a polite or conventional apology for causing inconvenience, or as a request for spoken words to be repeated. [Middle English *pardonen,* from Old French *pardoner,* to give, pardon, from Late Latin *perdōnāre,* to give wholeheartedly : *per,* thoroughly + *dōnāre,* to give, from *dōnum,* gift.] —**par·don·a·ble** *adj.* —**par·don·a·bly** *adv.*

par·don·er (pärd′n-ər) *n.* **1.** One who pardons. **2.** A medieval ecclesiastic authorized to raise money for religious works by granting papal indulgences to contributors.

pare (pâr) *tr.v.* **pared, paring, pares. 1.** To remove the outer covering or skin of (a fruit or vegetable) by peeling with a knife or similar instrument. **2.** To remove the edges of (toenails, for example). **3.** To remove by or as if by cutting, clipping, or shaving. Used with *off* or *away: paring off lemon rind.* **4.** To lessen or diminish bit by bit; whittle away. Often used with *off* or *down: paring expenditures down to a minimum.* [Middle English *paren,* from Old French *parer,* to prepare, from Latin *parāre.*]

Pa·ré (pä-rā′), **Ambroise** (*c.* 1510–90). French surgeon and pioneer of modern surgery. As an army surgeon he abandoned the practice of cauterizing amputated limbs with red-hot irons and boiling oil in favor of using ligatures to tie off arteries.

par·e·go·ric (păr′ə-gôr′ĭk, -gŏr′ĭk) *n.* Camphorated tincture of opium, taken internally for the relief of diarrhea and intestinal pain. [Late Latin *parēgoricus,* from Greek *parēgorikos,* from *parēgoros,* encouraging, soothing, addressing : PARA- (beside, alongside) + *agora,* assembly.]

pa·rei·ra (pə-râr′ə) *n.* A drug prepared from the root of a South American plant, *Chondrodendron tomentosum,* used as a diuretic and tonic. [From Portuguese *parreira brava,* "wild vine."]

paren. parenthesis.

pa·ren·chy·ma (pə-rĕng′kə-mə) *n.* **1.** *Anatomy.* The tissue characteristic of an organ as distinguished from connective tissue. **2.** *Botany.* Tissue composed of soft, unspecialized, thin-walled cells. **3.** *Zoology.* A loose connective tissue occurring in flatworms and related invertebrates. [New Latin, from Greek *parenkhuma,* visceral flesh, from *parenkhein,* to pour in beside (from the belief that the tissues of the organs were poured in by their blood vessels) : PARA- (beside) + *en,* in + *khein,* to pour.] —**pa·ren·chy·mal, par·en·chym·a·tous** (păr′ĕn-kĭm′ə-təs) *adj.* —**par·en·chym·a·tous·ly** *adv.*

par·ent (pâr′ənt) *n.* **1.** A father or mother. **2.** A forefather; an ancestor; a progenitor. **3.** Any organism that produces or generates another. **4.** A guardian; a protector. **5.** The source or cause of something; the origin. **6.** *Physics & Chemistry.* A nucleus, atom, ion, or molecule that breaks up or changes to give a different nucleus, atom, or the like. —*tr.v.* **parented, -enting, -ents.** To act or serve as the parent of. [Middle English, from Old French, from Latin *parēns* (stem *parent-*), from the present participle of *parere,* to give birth.] —**par·ent·hood** (pâr′ənt-ho͝od′) *n.*

par·ent·age (pâr′ən-tĭj) *n.* **1.** Descent or derivation from parents or ancestors; lineage; ancestry. **2.** Derivation from a source; origin or cause. **3.** The state or relationship of being a parent.

pa·ren·tal (pə-rĕnt′l) *adj.* **1.** Of, pertaining to, or characteristic of a parent. **2.** *Genetics.* Designating the generation from which a genetic experiment begins. Compare **filial.** —**pa·ren·tal·ly** *adv.*

par·en·ter·al (pă-rĕn′tər-əl) *adj.* **1.** Located outside the alimentary canal. **2.** Taken into the body or administered in a manner other than through the digestive tract, as by intravenous or intramuscular injection. [PAR(A)- + ENTER(O)- + -AL.]

pa·ren·the·sis (pə-rĕn′thə-sĭs) *n., pl.* **-ses** (-sēz′). *Abbr.* **par., paren. 1.** Either or both of the upright curved lines, (or), used to mark off explanatory or qualifying remarks in writing or printing. **2.** *Mathematics.* Such a mark used as one of a pair to enclose a sum, product, or other expression considered or treated as a collective entity in a mathematical operation. **3.** A qualifying or amplifying phrase occurring within a sentence in such a way as to form an interpolation independent of the surrounding syntactical structure; for example, in the sentence *It was the best film —and I go to a lot —I have seen in a long time,* the words *and I go to a lot* constitute a parenthesis. **4.** An interruption of continuity; an interval; an interlude. [Late Latin, from Greek, "a putting in beside," from *parentithenai,* to insert : PARA- + *en,* in + *tithenai,* to put.]

pa·ren·the·size (pə-rĕn′thə-sīz′) *tr.v.* **-sized, -sizing, -sizes. 1.** To insert as a parenthesis. **2.** To place between parentheses. **3.** To insert a parenthesis or parentheses into.

par·en·thet·i·cal (păr′ən-thĕt′ĭ-kəl) *adj.* Also **par·en·thet·ic** (-thĕt′ĭk). **1.** Contained in or as if in parentheses; qualifying or explanatory: *a parenthetical remark.* **2.** Using or containing parentheses. —**par·en·thet·i·cal·ly** *adv.*

par·ent·ing (pâr′ən-tĭng) *n.* The bringing up of children by or as if by a parent.

pa·rer·gon (pă-rûr′gŏn′) *n., pl.* **-ga** (-gə). Work done apart from one's main, primary, or professional work. [Latin, from Greek : PARA- + *ergon,* work.]

pa·re·sis (pə-rē′sĭs, păr′ə-sĭs) *n. Pathology.* **1.** Slight or partial paralysis. **2. General paresis** *(see).* [New Latin, from Greek, act of letting go, from *parienai,* to loose, let fall : PARA- (beside) + *hienai,* to throw.] —**pa·ret·ic** (pə-rĕt′ĭk) *n. & adj.* —**pa·ret·i·cal·ly** *adv.*

par·es·the·sia, par·aes·the·sia (păr′ĭs-thē′zhə) *n. Pathology.* An abnormal sensation of prickling, tingling, or itching of the skin. [Latin, from Greek : PARA- (incorrect) + *aisthēsia,* from *aisthēsis,* sensation.] —**par·es·thet·ic** (păr′ĭs-thĕt′ĭk) *adj.*

pa·re·u (pä′rā-o͞o′) *n.* A rectangular piece of cloth worn in Polynesia as a wraparound skirt or loincloth. [Tahitian.]

pa·re·ve (pä′rə-və) *adj.* Also **par·ve** (pär′və). *Judaism.* Designating or pertaining to foods that are prepared without meat, milk, or their derivatives, and that therefore may be eaten with meat or dairy dishes. [Yiddish *parev*†.]

par ex·cel·lence (pär ĕk′sə-läɴs′) *adv.* Pre-eminently.
~*adj.* Being the epitome of a kind; pre-eminent: *a conductor par excellence.* [French, "by (way of) pre-eminence."]

par·fait (pär-fā′) *n.* **1.** A dessert made of cream, eggs, sugar, and flavoring frozen together. **2.** A dessert made of several layers of different flavors of ice cream garnished and served in a tall glass. [French, from *parfait,* perfect, from Latin *perfectus,* PERFECT.]

par·get (pär′jĭt) *n.* **1.** Plaster, roughcast, or any similar mixture used to coat walls or line chimneys. **2.** Ornamental plasterwork. **3.** A cement mixture used to waterproof outer walls.
~*tr.v.* **pargeted, -geting, -gets.** Also *chiefly British* **-getted, -getting.** To cover or adorn with parget. [Middle English *pargetten,* from Old French *parjeter,* to throw onto a surface : *par,* onto, from Latin *per* + *jeter,* to throw. See **jet** (stream).] —**par·get·ing** *n.*

par·he·lic circle (pär-hē′lĭk) *n.* A type of halo consisting of a large circle of white light lying parallel to the horizon and passing through the sun. It is formed by reflection of the sun's rays off atmospheric ice crystals. Also called "parhelic ring." See **anthelion.**

par·he·li·on (pär-hē′lē-ən, -hēl′yən) *n., pl.* **-helia** (-hē′lē-ə, -hēl′yə). *Meteorology.* A bright spot sometimes appearing to either side of the sun, often on a luminous ring or halo. Also called "mock sun," "sundog." [Latin *parēlion,* from Greek : PARA- (beside, beyond) + *hēlios,* sun.] —**par·he·lic** (pär-hē′lĭk) *adj.*

pa·ri·ah (pə-rī′ə) *n.* **1.** A social outcast. **2.** A member of a low caste of agricultural and domestic workers in southern India and Burma. [Tamil *paṛaiyan,* drummer, from *paṛai,* drum (the pariahs having been originally a caste of drummers).]

pariah dog *n.* A **pye dog** *(see).*

Par·i·an (pâr′ē-ən) *adj.* **1.** Of or pertaining to the island of Paros or its inhabitants. **2.** Designating a type of white marble highly valued in ancient times for making statues. **3.** Designating a fine white porcelain.
~*n.* **1.** A native or inhabitant of Paros. **2.** Parian marble. **3.** Parian porcelain.

par·i·es (pâr′ē-ēz′) n., pl. **parietes** (pə-rī′ə-tēz′). Biology. The wall of an organ. [New Latin, from Latin pariēst, wall of a room.]

pa·ri·e·tal (pə-rī′ə-təl) adj. 1. Biology. Pertaining to or forming the wall of a hollow structure. 2. Anatomy. Of or pertaining to either of the parietal bones. 3. Botany. Attached to the ovary wall. Said of the ovules or placenta in certain plants. [French pariétal, from Late Latin parietālis, from Latin pariēs (stem pariet-), PARIES.]

parietal bone n. Anatomy. Either of two large, irregularly quadrilateral bones between the frontal and occipital bones that together form the sides and top of the skull.

parietal lobe n. Anatomy. The division of each hemisphere of the brain that lies beneath each parietal bone.

par·i·mu·tu·el (păr′ĭ-myōō′chōō-əl) n. 1. A system of betting on races whereby the winners divide the total amount bet, after deducting management expenses, in proportion to the sums they have wagered individually. 2. The machine that records bets under this system. Also called "totalizator." [French pari mutuel, mutual stake.]

par·i pas·su (păr′ē păs′ōō′) adj. With equal pace, speed, or progress; side by side: proceed pari passu. [Latin.]

Par·is¹ (păr′ĭs). Greek Mythology. The prince of Troy whose abduction of Helen provoked the Trojan War.

Par·is² (păr′ĭs, pä-rē′). Capital of France. On the Seine River in the north of the country, it is the administrative, cultural, and commercial center of France. Capital since 987, it has witnessed many revolutions, including the French Revolution of 1789, and was occupied by the Germans during World War II. Its architecture includes the churches of Nôtre Dame and Sacré Cœur, the Eiffel Tower, and the art galleries of the Louvre, the Jeu de Paume, and the Pompidou Center. —**Pa·ri·sian** (pə-rĭzh′ən, -rē′zhən) adj. & n.

Par·is (păr′ĭs), **Matthew** (c. 1200–59). English chronicler. He was a monk in the Benedictine monastery at St. Albans. His major work was the Chronica Majora, a history of the world from the Creation to 1259.

Paris, Treaty of. 1. A treaty (1763) between Great Britain, France, and Spain that ended their participation in the Seven Years' War. 2. A treaty (1783) between Great Britain and the United States that ended the American Revolution. 3. A treaty (1898) between the United States and Spain that ended the Spanish-American War.

Paris Commune n. 1. The revolutionary committee that governed Paris from 1789 to 1795. 2. The revolutionary government of Paris from March 18 to May 28, 1871. Also called "Commune."

Paris green n. A poisonous emerald-green powder, (CuO)₃As₂O₃·Cu(Cu₂H₃O₂)₂ used as a pigment, insecticide, and wood preservative. [After PARIS, where it was once made.]

par·ish (păr′ĭsh) n. Abbr. **par.** 1. In the Anglican, Roman Catholic, and some other churches, an administrative part of a diocese that has its own church. 2. In England, a political division of a county for local civil government, usually corresponding to the ecclesiastical parish. 3. A civil district in Louisiana corresponding to a county in other states. 4. Members of an ecclesiastical parish collectively; the community of parishioners. [Middle English paroche, parisshe, from Old French paroisse, from Late Latin parochia, from Late Greek paroikia, from paroikos, Christian, from Greek, "neighbor," "sojourner," "stranger" : para, near, beside + oikos, house.]

pa·rish·ion·er (pə-rĭsh′ə-nər) n. A member of a parish. [Middle English parisshoner, perhaps from Old French paroissien, from paroisse, PARISH.]

par·ish-pump (păr′ĭsh-pŭmp′) adj. Chiefly British. Of or designating an idea or outlook that is limited or parochial.

parish register n. The record of births, deaths, and marriages occurring in a parish.

par·i·son (păr′ə-sən) n. A roughly rounded mass of glass after removal from a furnace and prior to being blown or shaped. [From French paraison, from parer, to prepare.]

par·i·ty¹ (păr′ə-tē) n., pl. **-ties.** 1. Equality, as in amount, status, or value. 2. Equivalence, correspondence, or resemblance. 3. Finance. **a.** The equivalent in value of a sum of money expressed in terms of a different currency at a fixed official rate of exchange. **b.** The equivalence in value between coins of a different metal established at a fixed ratio. **c.** Equality of prices of goods or securities in two different markets. 4. Mathematics & Computer Science. The comparative odd-even relationship between two integers. If both are odd or both even, they are said to have the same parity; if one is odd and one even, they have different parity. Also used adjectivally: a parity error. 5. Symbol **P** Physics. **a.** An intrinsic symmetry property of elementary particles that is characterized by the behavior of the wave function of such particles under reflection through the origin of spatial coordinates. **b.** A quantum number, either +1 (even) or -1 (odd), that mathematically describes this property. [Latin paritās (stem paritāt-), from pār, equal.]

parity² n. 1. The condition of having borne offspring. 2. The number of children borne by one woman. [From -PAR(OUS) + -ITY.]

park (pärk) n. Abbr. **pk.** 1. A tract of land set aside for public use, such as: **a.** An expanse of enclosed grounds, sometimes landscaped, for recreational use within or adjoining a town or city. **b.** An enclosed area of land in which wild animals are kept: a deer park. **c.** An extensive tract of land kept in its natural state: a national park. 2. **a.** A stadium or enclosed playing field: a ball park. **b.** British Slang. A soccer pitch. 3. A country estate, especially when including extensive gardens, woods, or the like. 4. Military. **a.** An area where vehicles and artillery are stored and serviced. **b.** The materiel kept in such an area.

~v. **parked, parking, parks.** —tr. 1. To put or leave (a car or other vehicle) for a time in a certain location, such as a garage or at the side of the road. 2. Informal. To place, put, set, or leave somewhere: Park your coats on this chair. 3. Military. To assemble (artillery or other equipment) in order. —intr. To park a vehicle. [Middle English, from Old French parc, enclosure, from Medieval Latin parricust. See paddock.]

Park (pärk), **Mungo** (1771–1806). British explorer in Africa. He first explored the Niger River, traveling upstream some 483 kilometers (300 miles) to Bamako. On his second journey to the Niger, he was drowned when his party and their canoes were attacked by natives.

par·ka (pär′kə) n. 1. A hooded fur jacket worn as an outer garment by Eskimos. 2. A similar garment of warm cloth, worn for sports or outdoor work. [Aleutian, skin, from Russian, pelt of a reindeer, from Samoyed.]

Park Chung Hee (pärk′ chŭng′ hē′) (1917–79). President of South Korea (1963–79). After fighting as a general in the South Korean army, he came to power in a military coup (1961), became president, and later established martial law and assumed dictatorial powers (1972), ostensibly to resist invasion by North Korea. He was assassinated.

Par·ker (pär′kər), **Charlie** (1920–55). U.S. jazz musician. His brilliant technique as an alto saxophonist made him a legend and influenced the next generation of musicians.

Parker, Dorothy Rothschild (1893–1967). U.S. writer, poet, and critic. She was drama critic for Vanity Fair (1916–17) and book critic for the New Yorker (1927–33). She was noted for her satirical humor, as in her short stories Here Lies (1939).

Parker House roll n. A yeast-leavened roll, shaped by folding a flat round of dough in half. [Introduced by the Parker House, a hotel in Boston, Massachusetts.]

par·kin (pär′kĭn) n. A spicy ginger-flavored cake popular especially in Scotland and northern England. [Origin unknown.]

parking lot n. An area for parking motor vehicles.

parking meter n. A coin-operated meter monitoring the length of time purchased for the parking of a motor vehicle.

parking ticket n. A legal summons issued for a violation of parking regulations. Also called "ticket."

Par·kin·son's disease (pär′kĭn-sənz) n. A progressive neurological disease of the later years, characterized by muscular tremor, slowing of movement, partial facial paralysis, peculiarity of gait and posture, and weakness. Also called "parkinsonism," "paralysis agitans," "shaking palsy." [After James Parkinson (1755–1824), English surgeon.]

Parkinson's Law n. Any of several satirical observations propounded as economic laws, as "work expands to fill the time available for its completion." [After C. Northcote Parkinson (1909–), British historian.]

park·land (pärk′lănd′) n. 1. A stretch of land set aside for public use or enclosed as a park. 2. Such stretches of land collectively.

park·way (pärk′wā′) n. A wide highway, often having a middle strip planted with flowers or shrubs.

parl. parliamentary.

Parl. Parliament.

par·lance (pär′ləns) n. 1. A particular manner of speaking; a specified or personal language, style, or idiom: legal parlance. 2. Archaic. Conversation, especially a parley or debate. [Old French, from parler, to speak, from Medieval Latin parabolāre, to PARLEY.]

par·lan·do (pär-län′dō) adv. Also **par·lan·te** (pär-län′tā). Music. To be sung in a style suggestive of speech. Used as a direction. [Italian, from parlare, to speak, from Medieval Latin parabolāre, to PARLEY.] —**par·lan·do** adj.

par·lay (pär′lā, -lē) tr.v. **-layed, -laying, -lays.** 1. To bet (an original wager and its winnings) on a subsequent event, as in a race or contest. 2. To maneuver (an asset) to great advantage: She parlayed her physical attributes into a film career.

~n. A bet comprising the sum of an original wager plus its winnings, or a series of bets made in such a manner. Also British "accumulator." [French paroli, from dialectal Italian, plural of parolo, a set of dice, from paro, pair, from Latin pār, equal.]

par·ley (pär′lē) n., pl. **-leys.** A discussion or conference, especially between enemies over terms of truce or other matters.

~v. **parleyed, -leying, -leys.** —intr.v. To discuss, confer, or debate, as with an enemy or over a disagreement. —tr. To speak or converse in (a foreign language). Often used humorously. [French parlée, from the past participle of parler, to talk, from Old French, from Medieval Latin parabolāre, from Late Latin parabola, discourse, PARABLE.]

par·lia·ment (pär′lə-mənt) n. 1. A national representative body having supreme legislative powers within the state. 2. **Parliament. a.** Abbr. **Parl.** In Britain, the highest legislative body, made up of the sovereign, the **House of Lords,** and the **House of Commons** (both of which see). **b.** The people composing such a body at any one time. **c.** Any of various equivalent bodies in other countries. **d.** The lower house or chamber of such a body. [Middle English, from Old French parlement, from parler, to talk. See parley.]

par·lia·men·tar·i·an (pär′lə-mĕn-târ′ē-ən) n. 1. One who is expert in parliamentary procedures, rules, or debate. 2. **Parliamentarian.** A supporter of Parliament, as opposed to the king, during the English Civil War; a Roundhead. 3. Broadly, a member of a parliament.

~adj. **Parliamentarian.** Of or pertaining to the Long Parliament or to the Roundheads. —**par·lia·men·tar·i·an·ism** n.

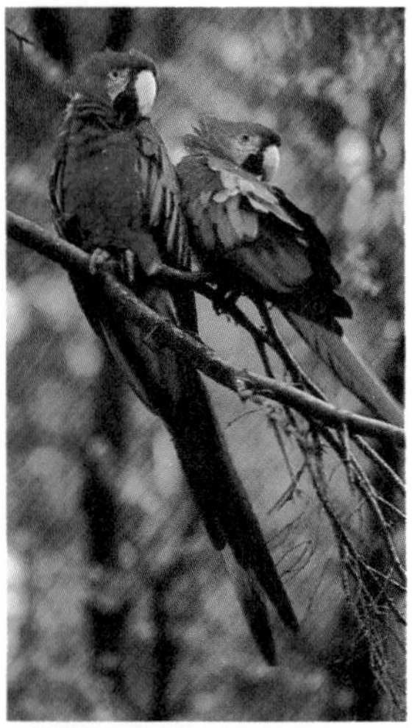

parrot *There are about 300 species of parrot—a family that includes macaws, cockatoos, and budgerigars—found worldwide in warm regions. They are brightly colored and normally live in trees, where they feed on fruit, nuts, and seeds. These are scarlet macaws from Central and South America.*

PRONUNCIATION KEY

ă, pat; ā, pay; âr, care;
ä, father, are; b, **bib**;
ch, **church**; d, **deed**; ĕ, pet;
ē, be; f, **fife**; g, **gag**; h, **hat**;
hw, **which**; ĭ, pit; ī, pie;
îr, pier; j, **judge**; k, **kick**;
l, lid, needle; m, **mum**;
n, no, sudden; ng, **thing**;
ŏ, pot; ō, toe; ô, paw, for;
oi, noise; ou, **out**; o͝o, **book**;
o͞o, **boot**; p, **pop**; r, roar;
s, sauce; sh, **ship**, **dish**;
t, **tight**; th, **thin**, **path**;
th, **this**, bathe; ŭ, cut; ûr, fur;
v, valve; w, **with**; y, yes;
z, zebra, size; zh, vision;
ə, about, item, edible, gallop, circus, peaceful

IN FOREIGN WORDS:

à, *Fr.* ami; œ, *Fr.* **feu**, *Ger.* schön; ü, *Fr.* **tu**, *Ger.* über; KH, *Ger.* **ich**, *Scot.* loch; N, *Fr.* bon; y', *Fr.* Compiègne

STRESS MARKS:

Primary stress: ′
in·cite′ (ĭn-sīt′)
Secondary stress: ′
in′sight′ (ĭn′sīt′)

par·lia·men·ta·ry (pär′lə-mĕn′tə-rē, -mĕn′trē) *adj. Abbr.* **parl.** *Often* **Parliamentary. 1.** Of, pertaining to, or resembling Parliament or a parliament. **2.** Proceeding from, passed, or decreed by Parliament or a parliament. **3.** In accordance with the rules and customs of Parliament or a parliament: *parliamentary procedure.* **4.** Having a parliament. **5.** Of or supporting Parliament during the English Civil War.

par·lor (pär′lər) *n.* Also *chiefly British* **par·lour. 1.** A room in a private home reserved for the entertainment of visitors. **2.** A small lounge or sitting room affording intimacy, as: **a.** In a hotel, club, or the like, a room reserved for guests who desire a greater degree of privacy than the public rooms provide. **b.** In a monastery or convent, a room for receiving visitors. **3.** A room equipped and furnished for a special function or business: *a beauty parlor.*
~adj. Designating one who puts forward ideas, often extreme or radical, from a position of safety, and who never takes any action to promote them: *a parlor socialist.* [Middle English *parlour,* from Old French *parleur,* room used for conversation, from *parler,* to talk. See **parley.**]

parlor car *n.* A railroad car for day travel fitted with individual reserved seats.

parlor game *n.* A game, especially one that involves words, played indoors.

par·lous (pär′ləs) *adj.* **1.** *Archaic.* Perilous; dangerous. **2.** *Obsolete.* Dangerously cunning.
~adv. Extremely; very. [Middle English, variant of *perilous,* from *peril,* PERIL.] **—par·lous·ly** *adv.*

Par·ma (pär′mə). City of Emilia-Romagna, capital of Parma province, northern Italy. On the Parma River near the Apennine Mts., it was a cultural center in the Middle Ages.

Parma violet *n.* A violet, *Viola odorata sempervirens,* cultivated for its fragrant lavender flowers. [After PARMA.]

Par·men·i·des (pär-mĕn′ĭ-dēz′) (*c.* 515–450 B.C.). Greek philosopher. The greatest of the Eleatic school, he believed that reality is unchanging, permanent, and part of the world of being, of which all that can be said is that it is. He greatly influenced Plato.

Par·me·san (pär′mə-zän′, -zăn′, -zən) *n.* A hard, dry Italian cheese made from skim milk and usually served grated as a garnish.
~adj. Of or from Parma. [French, from Italian *parmigiano,* of PARMA.]

Par·mi·gia·ni·no (pär′mĭ-jä-nē′nō) (1503–40). Italian painter and etcher. His work is characterized by elongation of form and includes the *Madonna of the Long Neck* and the *Vision of St. Jerome.*

par·mi·gia·na (pär′mə-jä′nə) *adj.* Prepared with Parmesan cheese: *veal parmigiana.* [Italian, feminine of *parmigiano,* PARMESAN.]

Par·nas·si·an¹ (pär-năs′ē-ən) *adj.* Of, pertaining to, or symbolically associated with Mount Parnassus or with the world of poetry.

Parnassian² *n.* A member of a school of late 19th-century French poets whose work is characterized by detachment and emphasis on metrical form. [*Le Parnasse contemporain* (1866) was the name of the group's first collection of poems.] **—Par·nas·si·an** *adj.*

Par·nas·sus, Mount (pär-năs′əs). *Greek* **Par·nas·sós** (pär′nä-sôs′). Greek mountain, 2,457 meters (8,061 feet). Situated to the north of the Gulf of Corinth, it was held sacred to Dionysus and Apollo in ancient times. The oracle of Delphi was located on its south side.

Par·nell (pär-nĕl′), **Charles Stewart** (1846–91). Irish politician and nationalist. He was president of the Irish National Land League (1879) and was imprisoned for his obstructive behavior in the House of Commons (1881). He fought for Irish Home Rule in Parliament and supported the unsuccessful Home Rule Bill of Gladstone.

pa·ro·chi·al (pə-rō′kē-əl) *adj.* **1.** Of, supported by, or located in a parish. **2.** Restricted to a narrow scope; provincial: *parochial views.* [Middle English *parochiel,* from Old French *parochial,* from Late Latin *parochiālis,* from *parochia,* PARISH.] **—pa·ro·chi·al·ism** *n.* **—pa·ro·chi·al·i·ty** (pə-rō′kē-ăl′ə-tē) *n.* **—pa·ro·chi·al·ly** *adv.*

par·o·dy (păr′ə-dē) *n., pl.* **-dies. 1. a.** A literary, musical, or artistic work that broadly mimics the characteristics of another work or style and holds it up to ridicule. **b.** The genre or composition of such works; satirical mimicry. **2.** Something so bad as to be equivalent to intentional mockery; travesty: *The trial was a parody of justice.* —See Synonyms at **caricature.**
~tr.v. **parodied, -dying, -dies.** To make a parody of. —See Synonyms at **imitate.** [Latin *parōdia,* from Greek *parōidia,* "mock-song," burlesque poem : PARA- (beside, "quasi-") + *ōidē,* song.] **—pa·rod·ic** (pə-rŏd′ĭk), **pa·rod·i·cal** *adj.* **—par·o·dist** *n.*

pa·rol (pə-rōl′) *n. Law.* An oral utterance; word of mouth. Now used only in the phrase *by parol.*
~adj. Law. Given by word of mouth; not written: *give parol evidence.* Compare **documentary.** [French *parole,* "word," from Old French, from Vulgar Latin *paraula* (unattested), variant of Late Latin *parabola,* discourse, PARABLE.]

pa·role (pə-rōl′) *n.* **1.** *Law.* **a.** The release of a prisoner before his term has expired on condition of continued good behavior. **b.** The duration of such conditional release. Used in the phrase *on parole.* **2.** A password used by a military officer of the day or an officer on guard. **3.** Word of honor; promise. **4.** *Linguistics.* Language as used or as realized in actual speech as opposed to **langue** *(see).* Compare **performance.**
~tr.v. **paroled, -roling, -roles.** To release (a prisoner) on parole. [French, word of honor, "word," PAROL.] **—pa·rol·ee** (pə-rō′lē′) *n.*

par·o·no·ma·sia (păr′ə-nō-mā′zhə, -zhē-ə) *n.* A play on words; especially, a **pun** *(see).* [Latin, from Greek, from *paronomazein,* to call by a different name, to name besides : PARA- + *onomazein,* to name, from *onoma,* name.] **—par·o·no·mas·tic** (păr′ə-nō-măs′tĭk) *adj.* **—par·o·no·mas·ti·cal·ly** *adv.*

par·o·nym (păr′ə-nĭm′) *n.* A paronymous word. [Greek *parōnumon,* from *parōnumos,* PARONYMOUS.] **—par·o·nym·ic** (păr′ə-nĭm′ĭk) *adj.*

pa·ron·y·mous (pə-rŏn′ə-məs) *adj.* Allied by derivation from the same root; having the same stem; cognate, as *beautiful* and *beauteous.* [Greek *parōnumos,* derivative : PARA- (beside) + *onuma, onoma,* name.] **—pa·ron·y·mous·ly** *adv.*

Par·os (pâr′ŏs′). Greek island in the Aegean Sea. In the Cyclades group to the south of the Greek mainland, it is famous for its translucent white marble, used in sculpture.

pa·rot·id gland (pə-rŏt′ĭd) *n.* Either of the largest of the paired salivary glands, located below and in front of each ear. Also called "parotid." [From Greek *parōtis* (stem *parotid-*), "(tumor) near the ear" : PARA- (beside) + *ōt-,* stem of *ous,* ear.]

par·o·ti·tis (păr′ə-tī′tĭs) *n.* Also **pa·rot·i·di·tis** (pə-rŏt′ĭ-dī′tĭs). Inflammation of the parotid glands, as in mumps. [PAROT(ID) + -ITIS.] **—par·o·tit·ic** (păr′ə-tĭt′ĭk) *adj.*

-parous *suffix.* Indicates giving birth to or bearing; for example, **multiparous.** [Latin *-parus,* from *parere,* to give birth to.]

Par·ou·si·a (pär′o͞o-sē′ə, pə-ro͞o′zē-ə) *n.* The **Second Coming** *(see).* [Greek, "presence" : PARA- + *ousia,* being, from *einai,* to be.]

par·ox·ysm (păr′ək-sĭz′əm) *n.* **1.** A sudden outburst of emotion or action: *a paroxysm of laughter.* **2.** *Pathology.* **a.** A crisis in or recurrent intensification of a disease. **b.** A spasm or fit; a convulsion. [French *paroxysme,* from Greek *paroxusmos,* irritation, exasperation, paroxysm, from *paroxunein,* to stimulate, irritate : PARA- (intensifier) + *oxunein,* to sharpen, goad, from *oxus,* sharp.] **—par·ox·ys·mal** (păr′ək-sĭz′məl) *adj.* **—par·ox·ys·mal·ly** *adv.*

par·ox·y·tone (pă-rŏk′sĭ-tōn′) *adj.* In ancient Greek grammar, of or designating a word that has an acute accent on the penultimate syllable.
~n. A paroxytone word. [Greek *paroxutonos* : PARA- (beside) + *oxutonos,* OXYTONE.]

par·quet (pär-kā′) *n.* **1. a.** Parquetry. **b.** A floor of parquetry. **2.** The main floor of a theater, the **orchestra** *(see).*
~tr.v. **parqueted** (-kād′), **-queting** (-kā′ĭng), **-quets** (-kāz′). **1.** To furnish (a room) with a floor of parquetry. **2.** To cover (a floor) with parquetry.
~adj. Made of parquetry: *a parquet floor.* [French, from Old French, small enclosure, diminutive of *parc,* enclosure, PARK.]

par·quet·ry (pär′kĭ-trē) *n., pl.* **-ries.** Wood, often of contrasting colors, worked into an inlaid mosaic, used especially for floors. [French *parqueterie,* from *parquet,* theater floor, PARQUET.]

parr (pär) *n., pl.* **parrs** or collectively **parr.** A young salmon during the first two years of its life when it lives in fresh water. [18th century : origin obscure.]

Parr (pär), **Catherine** (1512–48). Sixth wife of Henry VIII. She was the daughter of Sir Thomas Parr of Kendal; her marriage with Henry (1543) was her third and Henry's last.

parrakeet. Variant of **parakeet.**

par·ra·mat·ta, par·a·mat·ta (păr′ə-măt′ə) *n.* A light dress fabric made of a mixture of wool and cotton or silk. [After *Parramatta,* Australia, where it was first made.]

par·rel, par·ral (păr′əl) *n. Nautical.* A sliding loop of rope or chain to which a running yard or gaff is fastened, permitting movement of the yard up and down the mast. [Middle English *perell,* from *parail,* equipment, aphetic variant of APPAREL.]

par·ri·cide (păr′ə-sīd′) *n.* **1.** One who murders his father or mother or other near relative. **2.** The act of committing such a murder. [Latin *parricīda* (the perpetrator) and *parricīdium* (the crime) : *parri-*†, "kin" + -CIDE.] **—par·ri·cid·al** (păr′ə-sīd′l) *adj.*

Par·rish (păr′ĭsh), **Maxfield** (1870–1966). U.S. painter and illustrator. He is known for his colorful and highly decorative murals, posters, magazine covers, and book illustrations, including those for Washington Irving's *"Knickerbocker" History of New York.*

par·rot (păr′ət) *n.* **1.** Any of numerous tropical and semitropical birds of the order Psittaciformes, characterized by short, hooked bills, brightly colored plumage, and, in some species, the ability to mimic human speech or other sounds. **2.** One who mindlessly imitates the words or actions of another.
~tr.v. **parroted, -roting, -rots.** To repeat or imitate without meaning or understanding. [Dialectal French *perrot,* from Old French *perroquet,* variant of *paroquet,* PARAKEET.] **—par·rot·ry** *n.*

parrot fever *n.* A virus disease, **psittacosis** *(see).*

par·rot·fish (păr′ət-fĭsh′) *n., pl.* **-fishes** or collectively **parrotfish.** Any of various brightly colored tropical marine fishes of the family Scaridae, having jaws resembling a parrot's beak.

par·ry (păr′ē) *v.* **-ried, -rying, -ries.** *—tr.* **1.** To deflect or ward off (a fencing thrust or sword, for example). **2.** To avoid, counter, or turn aside: *parried her questions.* *—intr.* To deflect or ward off a blow.
~n., pl. **parries. 1.** An act of deflecting or warding off a blow, especially in fencing. **2.** An evasive answer or action; an evasion. [French *Parez,* "Parry!" (in fencing), imperative of *parer,* to defend, parry, from Italian *parare,* from Latin *parāre,* to prepare.]

Par·ry (păr′ē), **Sir William Edward** (1790–1855). British naval officer and Arctic explorer. He commanded three expeditions in search of the Northwest Passage (1819–20, 1821–23, and 1824–25). In 1827 he tried to reach the North Pole by sled but was forced to turn back because of the fatigue of his party.

Parry Islands. See **Queen Elizabeth Islands.**

parse (pärs) *v.* **parsed, parsing, parses.** *Grammar.* *—tr.* **1.** To break (a sentence) down into component parts of speech with an explanation of the form, function, and syntactical relationship of each part. **2.** To describe (a word) by stating part of speech, form, and syntactical relationships in a sentence. *—intr.* To admit of being parsed: *His sentences do not parse easily.* [From Latin *pars,* part (in the phrase *pars ōrātiōnis,* part of speech).]

par·sec (pär′sĕk′) *n. Symbol* **pc** A unit of length, used in astronomy, based on the distance from earth at which stellar parallax is one second of arc. It is equal to 3.2616 light years or 3.0857×10^{13} kilometers. [PAR(ALLAX) + SEC(OND).]

Par·see, Par·si (pär′sē, pär-sē′) *n.* A member of a Zoroastrian religious sect originally from Persia and now based mainly in western India. [Persian *Pārsī,* a Persian, from *Pārs,* Persia, from Old Persian *Pārsa,* PERSIA.] **—Par·see** *adj.* **—Par·see·ism** *n.*

Parsifal. Variant of **Percival.**

par·si·mo·ni·ous (pär′sə-mō′nē-əs) *adj.* Marked by parsimony. —See Synonyms at **stingy.** **—par·si·mo·ni·ous·ly** *adv.*

par·si·mo·ny (pär′sə-mō′nē) *n.* **1.** Unusual or excessive frugality, especially with regard to money; extreme economy. **2.** Meanness; stinginess. [Middle English *parcimony,* from Latin *parsimōnia,* from *parcere* (past participle *parsus*), to spare.]

pars·ley (pär′slē) *n.* **1.** A widely cultivated herb, *Petroselinum crispum,* native to the Mediterranean region, having much-divided, curled leaves that are used as a garnish and for seasoning. **2.** Any of various superficially similar plants, such as **cow parsley** *(see).* [Middle English *persely, peresil,* from Old English *petersilie* and Old French *persil, perresil,* both from Late Latin *petrosīlium,* from Latin *petroselīnum,* from Greek *petroselinon,* rock parsley : *petra,* rock + *selinon,* parsley, CELERY.]

pars·nip (pär′snĭp) *n.* **1.** A strong-scented plant, *Pastinaca sativa,* cultivated for its long, white, edible root. **2.** The root of this plant. [Middle English *pasnepe* (influenced by *nepe,* turnip), from Old French *pasnaie,* from Latin *pastināca,* parsnip, carrot, from *pastinum*†, a kind of two-pronged dibble.]

par·son (pär′sən) *n.* **1.** *Anglican Church.* A clergyman with full legal control of a parish under ecclesiastical law. **2.** Loosely, any clergyman. [Middle English *persone,* parish priest, from Old French, person, parson, from Medieval Latin *persōna (ecclēsiae),* "PERSON (of the church)."]

par·son·age (pär′sə-nĭj) *n.* The official residence of a parson.

parson bird *n.* The **tui** *(see).* [Referring to the white tuft at the throat, which resembles a clerical collar.]

Par·sons (pär′sənz), **Louella** (*c.* 1881–1972). U.S. newspaper columnist. In 1914 she began the first movie column in the country, and in 1922 she attracted the attention of William Randolph Hearst, who hired her for his *New York American.* She was Hearst's syndicated Hollywood columnist from 1925 to 1965, wielding tremendous power as a social and moral arbiter of the motion-picture community.

parson's nose *n.* The **pope's nose** *(see).*

part (pärt) *n. Abbr.* **p., pt. 1. a.** A portion, division, or segment of a whole; a piece: *a book in three parts.* **b.** An essential constituent; a vital element of the whole. **2.** Any of several equal portions or fractions into which a whole may be divided: *a drink of two parts gin and one part vermouth.* **3.** *Mathematics.* An aliquot part. **4. a.** An organ, member, or other division of an animal or plant. **b. parts.** The external genitals. **5.** A component that can be separated from a system: *a machine part.* **6. a.** A role given to an actor to play. **b.** The words of the role as spoken. **c.** These words written down. **7.** One's proper or expected share in responsibility or obligation; a duty: *It was not my part to give advice.* **8.** *Usually* **parts.** Ability; talent: *a man of many parts.* **9.** *Usually* **parts.** A region, land, or territory: *foreign parts.* **10.** The line where the hair on the head is parted. **11.** *Music.* **a.** Any of the melodic lines in concerted music or in harmony. **b.** The individual score for it. **—for one's part.** So far as one is concerned. **—for the most part.** To the greater extent; generally; mostly. **—in good part.** With good grace: *to take a joke in good part.* **—in part.** To some extent; partly. **—on the part of.** By, felt by, or done by. **—play a part. 1.** To act in a dissembling or deceitful manner. **2.** To be significant or of use. Used with *in: played a part in the revival of folk music.* **—take part.** To join in; participate. Usually used with *in: He took part in the celebration.* **—take someone's part.** To side with someone in a disagreement; support: *He took her part in the argument.*

~v. **parted, parting, parts.** *—tr.* **1.** To divide or break into separate pieces, portions, sections, or the like: *parted the bread.* **2.** To separate by or as if by coming between; put or keep apart: *parted the boxers.* **3.** To comb (the hair) away from a dividing line on the scalp. **4.** To break up or end (a relationship) by separating. Used chiefly in the expression *part company.* **5.** *Informal.* To cause to abandon or leave: *He won't be parted from the television.* *—intr.* **1.** To divide or break; come apart: *The curtain parted in the middle.* **2.** To go away from one another; separate: *parted as friends.* **3.** To separate into ways going in different directions: *The road parts in the forest.* **4.** To leave; depart. Usually used with *from.* **5.** To die. Used euphemistically. —See Synonyms at **separate. —part with.** To give up; relinquish.

~adv. Partially; in part: *part yellow, part green.*

~adj. Abbr. **p., pt.** Not full or complete; partial: *a part owner.* [Middle English, from Old French, from Latin *pars* (stem *part-*).]

part. 1. participle. **2.** particular.

par·take (pär-tāk′) *v.* **-took** (-to͝ok′), **-taken, -taking, -takes.** *—intr.* **1.** To take part or have a share; participate. Used with *in: partake in the festivities.* **2.** To take or be given part or portion. Usually used with *of: He partook of the cake.* **3.** To have some quality or characteristic; show evidence. Used with *of: a nature that partook of the ferocity of the lion.* *—tr.* To take or have part of; share. —See Synonyms at **share.** [Back-formation from *partaker,* from *part taker.*] **—par·tak·er** *n.*

part and parcel *n.* A basic part or essential function.

part·ed (pär′tĭd) *adj.* **1.** Separated or divided into parts; cleft. **2.** Kept apart; separated: *parted fingers.* **3.** *Botany.* Cleft almost to the base, so as to have distinct divisions or lobes; partite. **4.** *Archaic.* Deceased.

par·terre (pär-târ′) *n.* A flower garden having the beds and paths arranged to form a pattern. [French, from Old French, from *par terre,* on the ground : *par,* on, from Latin *per* + *terre,* ground, from Latin *terra.*]

par·the·no·car·py (pär′thə-nō-kär′pē) *n. Botany.* The production of fruit without fertilization or seed production. [Greek *parthenos*†, virgin + *karpos,* fruit.]

par·the·no·gen·e·sis (pär′thə-nō-jĕn′ĭ-sĭs) *n. Biology.* Reproduction of organisms in which an unfertilized egg cell develops into an individual genetically identical to the parent. [New Latin : Greek *parthenos*†, virgin + -GENESIS.] **—par·the·no·ge·net·ic** (pär′thə-nō-jə-nĕt′ĭk) *adj.* **—par·the·no·ge·net·i·cal·ly** *adv.*

Par·the·non (pär′thə-nŏn′) *n.* A temple dedicated to Athena on the Acropolis at Athens, built 447-432 B.C. The Elgin Marbles formed an outside frieze. See feature, next page.

Par·thi·a (pär′thē-ə). Ancient region south of the Caspian Sea. Roughly corresponding to Khorasan in northeastern Iran, it was part of the Persian Empire, but after 250 B.C. it established and expanded its own empire to control the area between the Euphrates and Indus rivers. It was eventually overthrown by the Sassanid Persians (A.D. 226).

Par·thi·an (pär′thē-ən) *adj.* **1.** Of or pertaining to Parthia, its inhabitants, or their culture. **2.** Delivered in or as if in retreat, like the Parthian archers who shot at the enemy while feigning flight.

~n. A native or inhabitant or Parthia.

par·tial (pär′shəl) *adj.* **1.** Of, pertaining to, or affecting only part; not total; incomplete: *a partial truth.* **2.** Favoring one person or side over another or others; biased; prejudiced. **3.** Having a particular liking for someone or something; especially fond. Usually used with *to: very partial to fat Turkish cigarettes and strawberries.* **4.** *Mathematics.* Of, designating, or pertaining to operations or sequences of operations, such as differentiation and integration, when applied to only one of several variables in a function at a time.

~n. **1.** In music and acoustics, a **harmonic** *(see).* **2.** *Mathematics.* A **partial derivative** *(see).* [Middle English *parcial,* from Old French *partial,* from Late Latin *partiālis,* from Latin *pars* (stem *part-*), PART.] **—par·tial·ness** *n.*

partial derivative *n. Mathematics.* The derivative with respect to a single variable of a function of two or more variables, regarding other variables as constants. Also called "partial."

partial eclipse *n.* An eclipse in which a celestial body is only partly obscured.

partial fraction *n.* Any of a set of fractions having an algebraic sum equal to a specified fraction, usually a ratio of polynomials.

par·ti·al·i·ty (pär′shē-ăl′ə-tē, pär-shăl′-) *n., pl.* **-ties. 1.** The state or condition of being partial. **2.** Favorable prejudice or bias. **3.** A special fondness; a predilection: *a partiality for antiques.*

par·tial·ly (pär′shə-lē) *adv.* **1.** In part; to a certain degree; partly. See Usage note at **partly. 2.** *Archaic.* **a.** In a prejudiced or biased manner. **b.** With special favor or fondness toward something or someone; with partiality.

partial pressure *n.* The individual pressure of one gas in a mixture of gases, equal to the pressure that the gas would exert if no other components were present. See **Dalton's Law.**

partial product *n. Mathematics.* A number formed in multiplication by multiplying one number by a digit of the multiplier.

partial tone *n.* In music and acoustics, a **harmonic** *(see).*

par·ti·ble (pär′tə-bəl) *adj.* Capable of being parted, divided, or separated; divisible. Said of estates or property. [Late Latin *partībilis,* from Latin *partīrī,* to divide, from *pars* (stem *part-*), PART.]

par·tic·i·pant (pär-tĭs′ə-pənt) *n.* One who participates or takes part in something.

~adj. Participating; taking part.

par·tic·i·pate (pär-tĭs′ə-pāt′) *intr.v.* **-pated, -pating, -pates.** To take part; join or share with others. Usually used with *in.* —See Synonyms at **share.** [Latin *participāre,* from *particeps,* a partaker : *pars* (stem *part-*), PART + *-ceps,* "-taking."] **—par·tic·i·pance** *n.* **—par·tic·i·pa·tor** (pär-tĭs′ə-pā′tər) *n.*

par·tic·i·pa·tion (pär-tĭs′ə-pā′shən) *n.* **1.** The act of participating: *participation in a game.* **2.** A taking part or sharing: *worker participation in the company's profits.*

par·ti·cip·i·al (pär′tə-sĭp′ē-əl) *adj.* Of, pertaining to, consisting of, or formed with a participle. [Latin *participālis,* from *participium,* PARTICIPLE.] **—par·ti·cip·i·al·ly** *adv.*

par·ti·ci·ple (pär′tə-sĭp′əl) *n. Abbr.* **p., part.** *Grammar.* A nonfinite form of a verb that is used with an auxiliary verb to indicate certain tenses, and that can also function independently as an adjective; for example, in the expressions *a glowing coal* and *a beaten dog, glowing* and *beaten* are participles. See **dangling participle, past participle, present participle** and Usage note at **gerund.** [Middle English, from Old French *participle, participe,* from Latin *participium,* from *particeps,* partaker (translation of Greek *metokhē*). See **participate.**]

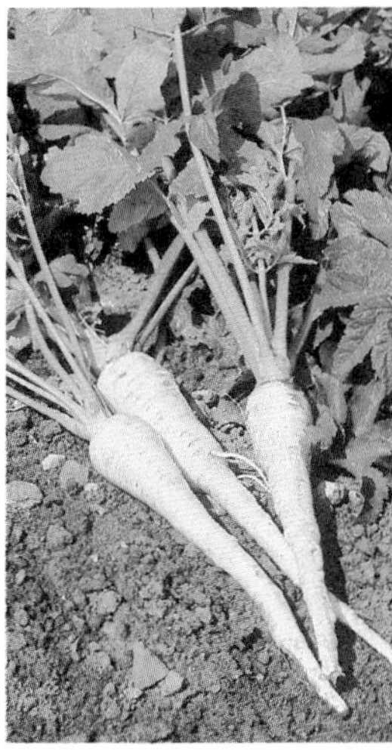

parsnip *A sweet-flavored root vegetable related to the carrot.*

Parthenon

ARCHITECTURAL MASTERPIECE OF ANCIENT GREECE
The Parthenon, the most perfect Doric temple

The Parthenon is the architectural triumph of ancient Greece, and even the time-ravaged remains that stand above Athens today express the power and grace so brilliantly combined by its builders. The temples on the Acropolis were built after the Persian wars at the inspiration of Pericles to glorify Athens. None does so more than the Parthenon. It was built between 447 and 432 B.C. by Ictinus, to the oldest Greek order of building, the Doric. The entablature above the chunky, fluted columns includes sculptured blocks (metopes) showing battles between centaurs and Lapiths—semilegendary people of ancient Thessaly.

par·ti·cle (pär′tĭ-kəl) *n.* **1.** A very small piece or part; a speck: *a particle of dust.* **2.** A very small amount, trace, or degree: *not a particle of doubt.* **3.** *Physics.* **a.** A body whose spatial extent and internal motion and structure, if any, are negligible. **b.** Any very small constituent of matter. **c.** An **elementary particle** *(see).* **4.** *Grammar.* **a.** In various languages, such as ancient Greek, any of a class of forms, such as prepositions or conjunctions, consisting of a single word that has no inflection. **b.** A suffix or prefix, such as *-ness* or *in-.* **5.** A small division or section of something written, such as a clause of a document. **6. a.** A small piece of a consecrated Host. **b.** Any of the smaller, individual Hosts. [Middle English, from Latin *particula,* diminutive of *pars* (stem *part-*), PART.]
particle accelerator *n. Physics.* An **accelerator** *(see).*
par·ti-col·ored (pär′tē-kŭl′ərd) *adj.* Having different parts or sections colored differently; pied. [Middle English *party,* particolored, from Old French *parti,* striped, from the past participle of *partir,* to divide, from Latin *partīre,* from *pars* (stem *part-*), PART.]
par·tic·u·lar (pər-tĭk′yə-lər) *adj.* Abbr. **part. 1.** Of, belonging to, or associated with a single person, group, thing, or category; not general or universal: *his particular beliefs.* **2.** Separate and distinct from others; specific: *I wanted a particular hat.* **3.** Worthy of note; exceptional; special: *of particular interest.* **4. a.** Especially or excessively attentive to or concerned with details or niceties; fussy: *particular about his dress.* **b.** Detailed; full: *a particular account of the events.* **5.** *Logic.* Encompassing some but not all of a class or group; restricted. Said of a proposition. *Some snakes are venomous* is a particular proposition. Compare **universal. 6.** *Mathematics.* Designating a solution of a differential equation that is distinguished from the general representation of the set of all solutions by virtue of not involving arbitrary constants.
~*n.* **1.** An individual item, fact, or detail: *correct in every particular.* **2. particulars.** Items or details of information or news: *Tell us the particulars of your trip to China.* **3.** *Logic.* A particular proposition. —**in particular.** Particularly; especially. [Middle English *particuler,* concerned with details, from Old French, from Late Latin *particulāris,* from Latin *particula,* detail, PARTICLE.]

par·tic·u·lar·ism (pər-tĭk′yə-lə-rĭz′əm) *n.* **1.** Exclusive adherence to or interest in one's own group, party, sect, or nation. **2.** A policy of allowing each state in a nation or federation to act independently. **3.** *Theology.* The belief that divine grace is reserved for a select group of people rather than for everyone. —**par·tic·u·lar·ist** *n.* —**par·tic·u·lar·is·tic** (pər-tĭk′yə-lə-rĭs′tĭk) *adj.*
par·tic·u·lar·i·ty (pər-tĭk′yə-lăr′ə-tē) *n., pl.* **-ties. 1.** The quality or state of being particular rather than general. **2.** Exactitude of detail, especially in description: *characters delineated with great particularity.* **3.** Attention to or concern with details; fastidiousness: *showed some particularity regarding his choice of friends.* **4.** A specific point or detail; a particular. **5.** An individual characteristic; a peculiarity.
par·tic·u·lar·ize (pər-tĭk′yə-lə-rīz′) *v.* **-ized, -izing, -izes.** —*tr.* **1.** To state or enumerate in detail; itemize. **2.** To mention or treat individually; specify; single out. —*intr.* To give particulars. —**par·tic·u·lar·i·za·tion** *n.* —**par·tic·u·lar·iz·er** *n.*
par·tic·u·lar·ly (pər-tĭk′yə-lər-lē) *adv.* **1.** To a great degree; especially: *I particularly wanted to go for a walk.* **2.** With particular reference or emphasis; specifically: *Any color will do, but I was thinking of blue particularly.* **3.** In a particular manner; severally; individually. **4.** With regard to particulars; in detail.
par·tic·u·late (pər-tĭk′yə-lĭt, -lāt′) *adj.* **1.** Of, pertaining to, or formed of separate particles. **2.** *Genetics.* Designating the type of inheritance proposed by Gregor Mendel, in which characteristics are determined by discrete particles. See **Mendel's laws.**
part·ing (pär′tĭng) *n.* **1.** The act or process of separating or dividing. **2.** A division or separation: *the parting of the ways.* **3.** A departure or leave-taking. **4.** *British.* A part (sense 10) *(see).* **5.** The act or time of a person's dying. Used euphemistically.
~*adj.* **1.** Given, received, or done at a departure or leave-taking: *a parting kiss.* **2.** Going away; departing.
par·ti pris (pär′tē prē) *n., pl.* **partis pris** *(pronounced as singular).* An opinion formed in advance; prejudice. [French, "side taken."]
par·ti·san¹, par·ti·zan (pär′tə-zən) *n.* **1.** A militant supporter of a party, cause, faction, person, or idea: *vociferous battle betwen partisans of the rival theories.* **2.** A member of a detached, often unofficially organized body of fighters who attack or harass an enemy within occupied territory; a guerrilla.
~*adj.* **1.** Of, pertaining to, or characteristic of a partisan or partisans. **2.** Favoring or supporting a single party or cause: *partisan politics.* [French, from Old Italian *partigiano,* from *parte,* part, from Latin *pars* (stem *part-*), PART.] —**par·ti·san·ship** *n.*
partisan², partizan *n.* A weapon, resembling a pike, having a long shaft surmounted by a blade with broad, projecting cutting edges, used chiefly in the 16th and 17th centuries. [Old French *partizane,* from Old Italian *partesana,* variant of *partigiano,* PARTISAN (supporter).]
par·ti·ta (pär-tē′tə) *n. Music.* A set of related instrumental pieces, such as a series of variations or a suite. [Italian, from the feminine past participle of *partire.* See **partite.**]
par·tite (pär′tīt′) *adj.* **1.** Divided into parts; parted. Often used in combination: *tripartite.* **2.** *Botany.* Parted. [Latin *partītus,* past participle of *partīre,* to divide, from *pars* (stem *part-*), PART.]
par·ti·tion (pär-tĭsh′ən) *n.* **1. a.** The act or process of dividing something into parts. **b.** The state of being so divided. **2.** Something that separates, such as a thin wall dividing a larger area. **3.** A part or section into which something has been divided. **4.** *Mathematics.* **a.** An expression of a positive integer as a sum of positive integers. **b.** The decomposition of a set into a family of mutually exclusive sets. **5.** *Logic.* The analysis of a class into its component parts. **6.** *Chemistry.* The distribution of a substance between two different phases, as between two solvents. **7.** *Law.* A division of real property among joint owners or tenants.
~*tr.v.* **partitioned, -tioning, -tions. 1. a.** To divide into parts, pieces, or sections: *The island was partitioned.* **b.** *Law.* To divide (property) among several owners. **2.** To divide or separate by means of a partition. Often used with *off: partition off an alcove.* [Middle English *particioun,* from Old French *partition,* from Latin *partītiō* (stem *partītiōn-*), from *partīre,* to divide. See **partite.**] —**par·ti·tion·er** *n.* —**par·ti·tion·ist** *n.* —**par·ti·tion·ment** *n.*
par·ti·tive (pär′tə-tĭv) *adj.* **1.** Serving to divide something into parts. **2.** *Grammar.* Indicating a part as distinct from a whole. The phrase *some of the coffee* is a partitive construction.
~*n. Grammar.* **1.** A partitive word, such as *many* or *less.* **2.** A partitive construction or case. [Medieval Latin *partītīvus,* from Latin, from *partīre,* to divide. See **partite.**] —**par·ti·tive·ly** *adv.*
part·let (pärt′lĭt) *n.* A woman's garment, worn especially in the 16th century, consisting of a covering for the neck and shoulders and having a band or ruffle at the neck. [Middle English *patelet,* from Old French *patelete,* band of cloth, diminutive of *patte,* paw, band. See **patten.**]
part·ly (pärt′lē) *adv.* In part; in some degree; not completely.
Usage: Partly and *partially* are not usually interchangeable. *Partly* has the wider application, being used primarily when the emphasis is on the part as opposed to the whole of a physical thing (*a partly finished jigsaw puzzle*) or when the meaning is "to some extent" (*He is partly to blame*). *Partially* indirectly emphasizes the whole of a condition or state and generally means "to a limited degree" (*The move was partially successful*).
part·ner (pärt′nər) *n.* **1.** A person associated with another or others in some activity of common interest, especially: **a.** A member of a business partnership. **b.** A spouse. **c.** Either of two persons dancing together. **d.** Either of a pair or a team in a game or sport, such

as bridge or tennis. **2.** *Usually* **partners.** *Nautical.* A wooden framework used to strengthen a ship's deck at the point where a mast or other structure passes through it.
~*tr.v.* **partnered, -nering, -ners. 1.** To make a partner of. **2.** To bring together as partners. **3.** To be the partner of. [Middle English *partener,* variant of *parcener,* from Norman French, PARCENER.]
Synonyms: *accomplice, ally, associate, colleague, confederate.*

part·ner·ship (pärt′nər-shĭp′) *n.* **1.** The state of being a partner; an association of partners. **2. a.** A contract entered into by two or more persons in which each agrees to share the labor and expenses in a joint business enterprise. **b.** The people involved in such a partnership. **c.** The relationship between these people.

part of speech *n. Grammar.* Any of a group of traditional classifications of words according to their functions in context. The chief ones are **noun, pronoun, verb, adjective, adverb, preposition, conjunction,** and **interjection** *(all of which see).* In addition, an **article** *(see)* is sometimes considered as belonging to this classification.

par·ton (pär′tŏn′) *n.* A hypothetical elementary particle, such as a quark, suggested as a constituent of nucleons. [PART + -ON.]

par·took. Past tense of **partake.**

par·tridge (pär′trĭj) *n., pl.* **-tridges** or collectively **partridge. 1.** Any of several plump-bodied Old World game birds, especially of the genera *Perdix* and *Alectoris.* **2.** Any of several similar or related birds such as the **ruffed grouse** or **bobwhite** *(both of which see).* [Middle English *partrich,* from Old French *perdriz,* from Latin *perdix,* from Greek.]

par·tridge·ber·ry (pär′trĭj-bĕr′ē) *n., pl.* **-ries. 1.** A creeping, woody evergreen plant, *Mitchella repens,* of eastern North America, having small white flowers and scarlet berries. Also called "twinberry." **2.** The fruit of this plant.

partridge wood *n.* The hard, durable, reddish-brown wood of a tropical American tree, *Andira inermis,* used for construction work and furniture. [Referring to its color and striping.]

part song *n.* A song for two or more voice parts; especially, a short, unaccompanied piece for a choir.

part-time (pärt′tīm′) *adj.* For or during less than the customary time: *a part-time job.* **—part-time** *adv.* **—part-tim·er** *n.*

par·tu·ri·ent (pär-tyo͝or′ē-ənt, pär-to͝or′-) *adj.* **1.** About to bring forth young; being in labor. **2.** Of or pertaining to giving birth. **3.** About to produce or come forth with something, such as an idea or discovery. [Latin *parturiēns* (stem *parturient-*), present participle of *parturīre,* to be in labor, from *parere* (future participle *parturus*), to bear.] **—par·tu·ri·en·cy** *n.*

par·tu·ri·tion (pär′tyo͝o-rĭsh′ən, pär′to͝o-, pär-cho͝o-) The act of giving birth; childbirth. [Late Latin *parturītiō* (stem *parturitiōn-*), from Latin *parturīre,* to be in labor. See **parturient.**]

par·ty (pär′tē) *n., pl.* **-ties. 1. a.** A social gathering for pleasure, amusement, or the like: *a cocktail party.* **b.** A group of persons gathered together to participate in some activity: *a sailing party.* **2.** *Sometimes* **Party.** A permanent political group organized to promote and support its principles and candidates for public office: *the Democratic Party.* **3.** *Law.* **a.** A person or group that has entered into a contract. **b.** A person or group involved in legal proceedings. **4.** A participant or accessory: *I won't be party to this corruption.* **5.** *Informal.* A person: *an amusing old party.*
~*adj.* **1.** Of or appropriate to a social gathering or party: *a party dress; the party spirit.* **2.** Of, pertaining to, or supporting a political party. **3.** *Heraldry.* Divided into two parts. Said of a shield.
~*intr.v.* **partied, -tying, -ties.** *Informal.* To have or attend a party. [Middle English *partie,* part, party, from Old French *partie,* from *partir,* to divide, from Latin *partīre.* See **partite.**]

party line *n.* **1.** A telephone line shared by two or more subscribers. **2.** The official policies, attitudes to particular issues, and principles of a political party to which loyal members are expected to adhere; especially, such policies, attitudes, and principles regarded as dogmatic. **—party liner** *n.*

party politics *n.* Politics conducted merely for the sake of one's political party rather than for a greater cause, such as the good of the country.

par·ty-poop·er (pär′tē-po͞o′pər) *n. Slang.* One who declines to participate enthusiastically at a social gathering.

party wall *n. Law.* A wall built on the boundary line of adjoining properties and shared by two owners or tenants.

pa·rure (pə-ro͝or′) *n.* A set of matched jewelry or other ornaments. [French, adornment, from Old French, from *parer,* to prepare, adorn, from Latin *parāre,* to prepare.]

par value *n.* The value imprinted on a stock certificate or bond that provides the basis for interest, dividend, or share of equity capital; face value.

parve. Variant of **pareve.**

par·ve·nu (pär′və-no͞o′, -nyo͞o′) *n.* A person who has risen above his socioeconomic class without the background or qualifications for his new status; upstart. [French, from the past participle of *parvenir,* to arrive, from Latin *parvenīre,* to come through : *per,* through + *venīre,* to come.] **—par·ve·nu** *adj.*

par·vis, par·vice (pär′vĭs) *n.* **1.** An enclosed courtyard or space in front of a palace or church. **2.** A portico or colonnade in front of a church. [Middle English *parvys,* from Old French *parvis,* from Late Latin *paradīsus,* enclosed garden, PARADISE.]

pas (pä) *n., pl.* **pas** (pä). **1.** A dance step or series of steps. **2.** A dance. **3.** The right to go before; precedence. [French, from Latin *passus,* step, from the past participle of *pandere,* to stretch out.]

PAS, PASA para-aminosalicyclic acid.

Pas·a·de·na (păs′ə-dē′nə). City of southern California, northeast of Los Angeles. It has a specialized electronics industry and is the site of the New Year's Day Rose Bowl parade and football game.

pas·cal (pă-skăl′, pä-skäl′) *n. Symbol* **Pa** A unit of pressure that is equal to a pressure of one newton per square meter. [After Blaise PASCAL.]

Pas·cal (pă-skăl′, pä-skäl′) *n.* A high-level computer language used for dealing with alphabetic data and widely used as a teaching language. [After Blaise PASCAL.]

Pascal, Blaise (1623–62). French mathematician, philosopher, and scientist. He invented a calculating machine, discovered that the pressure in a fluid is everywhere equal (leading to the invention of the hydraulic press and the barometer), and investigated the mathematical theory of probability and the differential calculus. After religious revelations (1654) he became a Jansenist; his posthumously published *Pensées* (1670) is a study of Christian beliefs, human nature, and the inadequacy of reason.

pas·cal celery, Pas·cal celery (păs′kəl) *n.* Any of several types of commercially grown celery having green, unblanched stalks. [Origin unknown.]

Pascal's triangle *n.* A triangular array of numbers in which each number is the sum of the two neighboring numbers in the row above. [After Blaise PASCAL, who devised it.]

pas·chal (păs′kəl) *adj.* Of or pertaining to the Passover or to Easter. [Middle English *paskal,* from Old French *pascal,* from Late Latin *paschālis,* from *pascha,* Passover, Easter, from Late Greek *paska,* from Hebrew *pesaḥ,* PESACH.]

paschal lamb *n.* **1.** A lamb eaten at the feast of the Passover. **2. Paschal Lamb.** Jesus Christ.

pas de deux (pä′ də dœ′) *n., pl.* **pas de deux.** A ballet figure or dance for two persons. [French, "step for two."]

pa·se (pä′sā) *n.* In bullfighting, a presentation and movement of the cape by the matador to attract, receive, and direct the charge of the bull. Also called "pass." [Spanish, "a passing," "pass," from *pasar,* to pass, from Vulgar Latin *passāre.* See **pass.**]

pasela. Variant of **bonsella.**

pa·sha, pa·cha (pä′shə, păsh′ə, pə-shä′, -shô′) *n.* **1.** Formerly, a high official, especially a provincial governor, in the Ottoman Empire and various Islamic kingdoms. **2. Pasha.** A mode of address for or title of such an official or a person considered worthy of equal respect. When used as a title, it is placed after the surname: *Glubb Pasha.* Also called "bashaw." [Turkish, probably from *baş,* chief.]

Pash·to (pŭsh′tō) *n.* **1.** An Iranian language, one of the two official languages of Afghanistan. **2.** A speaker of this language. Also called "Pushtu," "Afghan." [Persian *pashtu,* from Afghan *pashtó,* from Old Persian *parshtā-,* "one who asks."] **—Pash·to** *adj.*

Pa·siph·a·ë (pə-sĭf′ə-ē′). *Greek Mythology.* The wife of Minos and mother, by a white bull, of the Minotaur.

pa·so do·ble (pä′sō dō′blā) *n., pl.* **paso dobles. 1.** A Latin-American ballroom dance in duple time. **2.** A piece of music to which a paso doble is danced. [Spanish, "double step."]

Pa·so·li·ni (păs′ō-lē′nē), **Pier Paolo** (1922–75). Italian film director and writer. His films, frequently concerned with religion and Marxism, include *The Gospel According to St. Matthew* (1964). *Theorem* (1968), and the sordid *Salo or the 120 days of Sodom* (1975). His murder was never solved.

pasque·flow·er (păsk′flou′ər) *n.* Any of several plants of the genus *Anemone*; especially, the Eurasian species *A. pulsatilla,* having large purple or white flowers and plumed fruit. [Earlier *passeflower* (influenced by Old French *pasque,* Easter), from Old French *passefleur* : *passer,* to PASS (surpass) + *fleur, flor,* FLOWER.]

pas·qui·nade (păs′kwə-nād′) *n.* A lampoon; especially, one posted in a public place.
~*tr.v.* **pasquinaded, -nading, -nades.** To ridicule with a pasquinade. [French, from Italian *pasquinata,* from *Pasquino,* nickname of an ancient statue in Rome on which lampoons were posted in the 16th century.] **—pas·qui·nad·er** *n.*

pass (păs, päs) *v.* **passed, passing, passes.** —*intr.* **1.** To move on or ahead; proceed: *The path was too narrow for us to pass.* **2.** To run; extend: *The river passes through our land.* **3.** To carry on despite obstacles: *pass through difficult years.* **4.** To catch up with and move past; overtake: *The sports car passed on the right.* **5.** To move past in time; elapse: *The days passed quickly.* **6.** To be transferred from one to another; circulate: *The wine passed around the table.* **7.** To be communicated or exchanged: *Abusive language passed between the two candidates.* **8.** To be transferred or conveyed to another by a will, deed, or the like: *The title passed to the eldest son.* **9.** To undergo transition from one condition, form, quality, or characteristic to another: *Daylight passed into darkness. Joy passed into anger.* **10.** To come to an end; be terminated; subside: *His anger passed suddenly.* **11.** To cease to exist; die. Used euphemistically. **12.** To happen; take place: *What passed during the morning?* **13.** To be allowed to happen without notice or challenge: *Let their rude remarks pass.* **14.** To gain success in a test or examination by reaching the required standard: *Every pupil passed.* **15.** To be accepted as something different. Often used with *as* or *for: "would have his Noise and Laughter pass for Wit"* (William Wycherley). **16.** To be approved or adopted: *The motion to adjourn passed.* **17.** *Law.* **a.** To pronounce an opinion, judgment, or sentence. Used with *on* or *upon.* **b.** To sit in judicial or legal investigation. Used with *on* or *upon: A jury passed on that issue.* **c.** To pronounce an opinion, judgment, or sentence. Used with *on* or *upon.* **18.** *Sports.* To hit, throw,

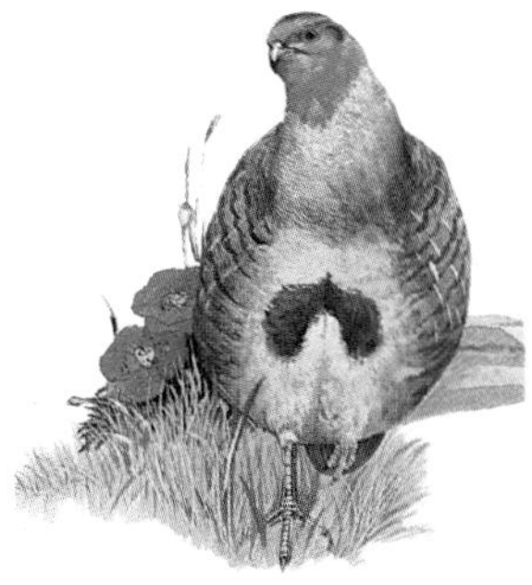

partridge *A plump game bird that lives mostly on the ground. It feeds largely on insects and plants and nests in a grass-lined scrape in the earth. Partridges are found in North America, Europe, and parts of western Asia. This is the common partridge,* Perdix perdix.

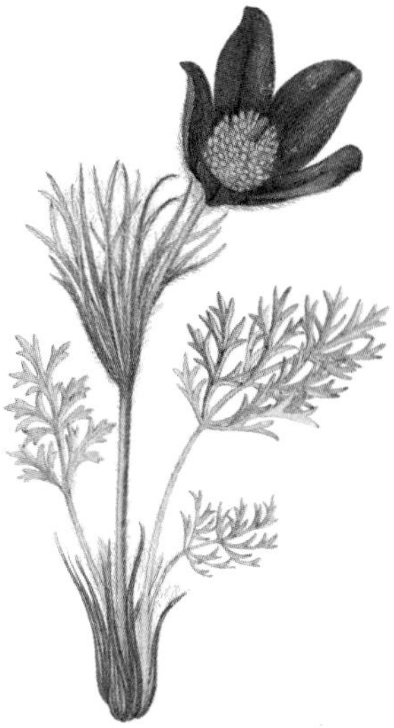

pasqueflower *The Eurasian pasqueflower,* Anemone pulsatilla*—also known as* Pulsatilla vulgaris*—is found among grasses on dry, chalky slopes. Some forms have reddish or whitish flowers instead of the violet one shown here.*

or kick a ball or puck to a teammate. **19.** *Fencing.* To thrust or lunge. **20. a.** *Card games.* To forgo one's turn to play or bid. **b.** In quizzes, board games, and similar contests, to miss a question or round of play by declining to attempt an answer or by opting to forgo one's turn. **21.** *Informal.* To decline an offer: *Who's for another beer? I'll pass.* —*tr.* **1.** To go by without stopping; leave behind: *passed him on the final bend.* **2. a.** To go by without paying attention to; let go unmentioned. **b.** To fail to pay (a dividend). **3.** To go beyond; exceed: *The returns passed all expectations.* **4.** To go across or through: *pass enemy lines.* **5. a.** To gain success in (a test or examination) by reaching the required standard: *He passed every quiz.* **b.** To cause or allow to pass a test, examination, or the like: *The instructor passed all the candidates.* **6. a.** To cause to move: *passed his hand over the fabric.* **b.** To cause to move into a specified position: *pass a cable around a cylinder.* **c.** To cause to move as part of a process: *pass liquid through a filter.* **7.** To cause to go by: *pass soldiers in review.* **8.** To allow to go by or elapse; spend: *passed the winter in Venice.* **9. a.** To cause to be transferred from one to another; circulate: *pass the news quickly.* **b.** To hand over to someone else: *pass the bread.* **c.** To circulate (money) fraudulently: *pass counterfeit banknotes.* **d.** *Law.* To transfer title or ownership of. **10.** *Sports.* To throw, hit, or kick (a ball, for example) to a teammate. **11.** To cross over; issue from: *No secrets pass her lips.* **12.** To discharge (bodily waste); void. **13. a.** To approve; adopt: *Congress passed the bill.* **b.** To be sanctioned, ratified, or approved by: *The bill passed the House of Representatives.* **14.** To pronounce; utter: *pass judgment.* **15.** To go past without noticing. Used with *by*: *passed them by.* —**bring to pass.** To cause to happen. —**come to pass.** To happen. —**pass away.** **1.** To go away in time; end; terminate. **2.** To die. Used euphemistically. **3.** To spend or while away (time). —**pass off.** **1.** To offer, sell, or put into circulation (an imitation of something) as genuine. **2.** To consider superficially: *passed off the remark.* —**pass on.** **1.** To transmit or convey. **2.** To move on. **3.** To die. Used euphemistically. —**pass out.** **1.** To distribute. **2.** To lose consciousness; faint. **3.** *British.* To finish a military course. —**pass over.** To leave out; overlook; disregard. —**pass up.** *Informal.* To reject; let go by: *pass up an opportunity.*

∼*n.* **1.** The act of passing; passage. **2.** A way through or on which one can move or travel; especially, one in the form of a narrow gap between mountain peaks. **3. a.** A permit, ticket, or authorization to come and go at will, as at restricted premises. **b.** A free ticket entitling one to use certain forms of public transport for a stated period of time. **c.** A ticket or card entitling one to admission to a usually specified place: *a backstage pass.* **d.** Written leave of absence from military duty. **e.** In South Africa, a **reference book** *(see).* **4.** A sweep or run by an aircraft over an area or target. **5.** A condition or situation, often critical in nature; a predicament: *This has come to a sorry pass.* **6.** *Informal.* A sexual invitation or overture: *He made passes at pretty girls.* **7.** A motion of the hand or the waving of a wand in conjuring. **8. a.** *Sports.* A transfer of a ball or puck between teammates. **b.** *Fencing.* A lunge or thrust. **c.** *Baseball.* A walk. **9. a.** *Card games.* A refusal to bid, draw, bet, or play. **b.** In quizzes, board games, and similar contests, a refusal to attempt an answer or play. **10.** A cape maneuver in bullfighting, **pase** *(see).* —See Synonyms at **way.**

∼*interj.* Used in card games, quizzes, and the like to indicate a refusal to bid, answer, attempt a play, or the like. [Middle English *passen,* to proceed, from Old French *passer,* from Vulgar Latin *passāre* (unattested), from Latin *passus,* step, pace, stride, from the past participle of *pandere,* to stretch out.]

Usage: The past tense and past participle of the verb *pass* is *passed: He passed/has passed the examination. Time had passed slowly. Past* is the corresponding adjective (*in centuries past*), adverb (*drove past*), and preposition (*past midnight*; *past the crisis*).

pass. **1.** passenger. **2.** passive (sense 5).

pass·a·ble (păs′ə-bəl, pä′sə-) *adj.* **1. a.** Capable of being passed: *a passable law.* **b.** Capable of being traversed or crossed, as a road or stream may be. **2.** Acceptable for general circulation: *passable currency.* **3.** Satisfactory but not outstanding. —**pass·a·ble·ness** *n.* —**pass·a·bly** *adv.*

pas·sa·ca·glia (pä′sə-käl′yə, păs′ə-kăl′yə) *n.* **1.** A 17th- and 18th-century musical form consisting of continuous variations on a ground bass in slow triple time. **2.** A dance to this music. Compare **chaconne.** [Italian, from Spanish *passacalle* : *pasar,* to pass, from Vulgar Latin *passāre* (unattested) (see **pass**) + *calle,* street, from Latin *callis*†, path.]

pas·sage (păs′ĭj) *n.* **1.** The act or process of passing, especially: **a.** A movement from one place to another; transit: *the passage of trains.* **b.** The process of elapsing: *the passage of time.* **c.** The process of passing from one state, condition, or stage to another; transition. **d.** The enactment into law of a legislative measure. **2.** A journey, especially one by air or water. **3. a.** The right to travel on something, especially a ship: *book a passage.* **b.** The price paid for this: *worked his passage.* **4.** The right, permission, or power to come and go freely. **5. a.** A channel or duct through, over, or along which something may pass: *the nasal passages.* **b.** A path, corridor, or the like. **6. a.** An exchange of words, arguments, or vows between two persons. **b.** An exchange of blows. Used in the phrase *passage at arms.* **7.** A segment of a literary work: *a passage from Gibbon.* **8.** *Music.* A segment of a composition, especially a section allowing virtuosity of performance: *a rapid scale passage.* **9.** *Medicine.* An emptying of the bowels. —See Synonyms at **way.** [Middle English, from Old French, from *passer,* to PASS.]

passage hawk *n.* A young falcon or hawk that is captured while it is migrating.

pas·sage·way (păs′ĭj-wā′) *n.* A corridor.

pas·sant (păs′ənt) *adj. Heraldry.* Designating a beast facing and walking toward the viewer's right with one front leg raised: *a lion passant.* [Middle English, from Old French, from the present participle of *passer,* to PASS.]

pass·book (păs′bo͝ok′, päs′-) *n. Abbr.* **P.B.** **1.** A **bankbook** *(see).* **2.** A book in which a merchant records credit sales. **3.** In South Africa, a **reference book** *(see).*

pas·sé (pă-sā′) *adj.* **1.** Out-of-date; no longer current or in fashion. **2.** Past the prime; faded; aged. [French, past participle of *passer,* to pass, from Old French, to PASS.]

passed ball *n. Baseball.* A pitch that a catcher should have been able to field but misses that allows a base runner to advance.

pas·sel (păs′əl) *n. Informal.* A large quantity or number: *They had a whole passel of children.* [Alteration of PARCEL.]

passe·men·terie (păs-mĕn′trē) *n.* Ornamental trimming for a garment, such as braid, lace, or metallic beads. [French, from *passement,* from *passer,* from Old French, to PASS.]

pas·sen·ger (păs′ən-jər) *n. Abbr.* **pass.** **1.** A person who travels in a train, airplane, ship, bus, or other conveyance without participating in its operation. **2.** *British Informal.* A member, as of a team, who fails to contribute sufficient effort toward the work or enterprise undertaken. **3.** A wayfarer or traveler.

∼*adj.* Of or for passengers rather than goods: *a passenger train.* [Middle English *passyngere, passager,* from Old French *passager,* (adjective), passing, from *passage,* PASSAGE.]

passenger pigeon *n.* An extinct migratory bird, *Ectopistes migratorius,* abundant in North America until the late 19th century.

passe-par·tout (păs′pär-to͞o′, päs′-). **1.** Something enabling one to pass or go everywhere; especially, a master key. **2. a.** A mounting for a picture in which colored tape forms the frame. **b.** The tape so used. **3.** A mat used in mounting a picture. [French, "pass everywhere."]

passe·pied (päs-pyā′) *n.* **1.** A dance, originating in France, that resembles but is faster than the minuet. **2.** A piece of music for the passepied. [French, "pass foot."]

pas·ser-by (păs′ər-bī′, pä′sər-) *n., pl.* **passers-by.** A person who passes by, often by chance and on foot.

pas·ser·ine (păs′ə-rīn′) *n.* A bird of the order Passeriformes, which includes perching birds and songbirds such as the jays, blackbirds, finches, warblers, and sparrows. More than half of all known birds belong to this order. [Latin *passerīnus,* from *passer*†, sparrow.] —**pas·ser·ine** *adj.*

pas seul (pä sœl′) *n.* A dance or ballet figure performed by one person. [French, "step by oneself."]

pas·si·ble (păs′ə-bəl) *adj.* Capable of suffering; sensitive. [Middle English, from Old French, from Medieval Latin *passibilis,* from Latin *patī* (past participle *passus*), to suffer.] —**pas·si·bil·i·ty** *n.*

pas·sim (păs′ĭm) *adv.* Throughout; frequently. Used in textual annotation to indicate that the word or passage occurs frequently in the work cited. [Latin *passim,* here and there, everywhere, scattered about, adverbial formation from *pandere,* to spread out, scatter.]

pass·ing (păs′ĭng, pä′sĭng) *adj.* **1.** Of brief duration; transitory: *a passing fancy.* **2.** Cursory; superficial; casual: *a passing glance.* **3.** Allowing one to pass an examination, test, course of study, or the like; satisfactory: *a passing mark on the test.* **4.** *Archaic.* Very; great: *"'Tis a passing shame"* (Shakespeare).

∼*adv. Archaic.* Very; surpassingly: *passing rich.*

∼*n.* **1.** The act of one that passes or the state of having passed. **2.** A place where or a means by which one can pass. **3.** Death. Used euphemistically. —**in passing.** Casually or briefly in the course of speaking about or doing something else: *mentioned in passing.*

passing bell *n.* A **death knell** *(see).*

passing note *n. Music.* A note that is not part of a particular chord but is placed between two chords to provide a smooth transition from one to the other.

passing shot *n.* In tennis, a shot that is hit beyond the reach of an opponent at the net.

pas·sion (păsh′ən) *n.* **1.** Any powerful emotion or appetite, such as love, joy, hatred, anger, or greed. **2. a.** Ardent adoring love. **b.** Strong sexual desire; lust. **c.** The object of such love or desire. **3. a.** Boundless enthusiasm: *a passion for traveling.* **b.** The object of such enthusiasm. **4.** An abandoned display of emotion, especially of anger: *a passion of remorse.* **5.** *Archaic.* Passivity as opposed to action. **6.** *Archaic.* Martyrdom. **7. Passion.** **a.** The sufferings of Christ in the period following the Last Supper and including the Crucifixion. **b.** A narrative of this, as in any of the Gospels, or a musical setting or serial pictorial representation of it. —See Synonyms below and at **feeling.** [Middle English, from Old French, from Late Latin *passiō* (stem *passiōn-*), (translation of Greek *pathos*), suffering, from Latin *patī* (past participle *passus*), to suffer.] —**pas·sion·less** *adj.* —**pas·sion·less·ly** *adv.*

Synonyms: *ardor, enthusiasm, fervor, zeal.*

pas·sion·al (păsh′ə-nəl) *adj.* Of or pertaining to passion.

∼*n.* A book relating the sufferings of saints and martyrs.

pas·sion·ate (păsh′ə-nĭt) *adj.* **1.** Capable of or having intense feelings. **2.** Easily angered; bad-tempered. **3.** Amorous; lustful. **4.** Showing or expressing strong emotion; ardent: *a passionate speech against injustice.* **5.** Arising from or marked by passion: *a passionate rage.* —**pas·sion·ate·ly** *adv.*

pas·sion·flow·er (păsh′ən-flou′ər) *n.* Any of various chiefly tropical

PRONUNCIATION KEY

ă, pat; ā, pay; âr, care;
ä, father, are; b, bib;
ch, church; d, deed; ĕ, pet;
ē, be; f, fife; g, gag; h, hat;
hw, which; ĭ, pit; ī, pie;
îr, pier; j, judge; k, kick;
l, lid, needle; m, mum;
n, no, sudden; ng, thing;
ŏ, pot; ō, toe; ô, paw, for;
oi, noise; ou, out; o͝o, book;
o͞o, boot; p, pop; r, roar;
s, sauce; sh, ship, dish;
t, tight; th, thin, path;
th, this, bathe; ŭ, cut; ûr, fur;
v, valve; w, with; y, yes;
z, zebra, size; zh, vision;
ə, about, item, edible,
gallop, circus, peaceful

IN FOREIGN WORDS:

à, *Fr.* ami; œ, *Fr.* feu, *Ger.* schön; ü, *Fr.* tu, *Ger.* über; KH, *Ger.* ich, *Scot.* loch; N, *Fr.* bon; y′, *Fr.* Compiègne

STRESS MARKS:

Primary stress: ′
in·cite′ (ĭn-sīt′)
Secondary stress: ′
in′sight′ (ĭn′sīt′)

American vines of the genus *Passiflora,* usually having large, showy flowers. Some species bear edible fruit. See **granadilla.** [From the resemblance of its parts to the instruments of the Passion.]

passion fruit *n.* The edible fruit of the passionflower. Also called "granadilla."

Passion play *n.* A play representing the Passion of Christ.

Passion Sunday *n.* The second Sunday before Easter.

Pas·sion·tide (păsh′ən-tīd′) *n.* The fortnight between Passion Sunday and Easter.

Passion Week *n.* **1.** The week between Passion Sunday and Palm Sunday. **2.** See **Holy Week.**

pas·sive (păs′ĭv) *adj.* **1.** Receiving or subjected to an action without responding or initiating an action in return. **2.** Accepting without objection or resistance; submissive; compliant: *passive obedience.* **3.** Not participating, acting, or operating; inert. **4.** *Finance.* Designating certain bonds or shares that do not bear interest. **5.** *Abbr.* **pass.** *Grammar.* Designating a verb form or voice used to indicate that the grammatical subject is the object of the action or the effect of the verb; for example, in the sentence *They were impressed by his manner,* the verb *were impressed* is in the passive voice. **6.** *Chemistry.* Rendered inactive. Said of metals that form a protective coating that prevents further reaction. **7.** *Electronics.* **a.** Having no source of power. **b.** Not amplifying or controlling a signal. **8.** Designating or relating to an aerial, satellite, or other device that receives or reflects radio waves without emitting them. Compare **active.** —See Synonyms at **inactive.**
~*n. Abbr.* **pass.** *Grammar.* **1.** The passive voice. **2.** A verb or construction in this voice. [Middle English, from Latin *passīvus,* capable of suffering, from *patī* (past participle *passus*), to suffer.] **—pas·sive·ly** *adv.* **—pas·sive·ness, pas·siv·i·ty** (pă-sĭv′ə-tē) *n.*

passive euthanasia *n.* Euthanasia effected by the withholding of treatment that would prolong the patient's life.

passive resistance *n.* Resistance to authority or law by nonviolent methods, such as refusal to comply or peaceful demonstrations.

passive smoking *n.* The inhalation of smoke from the cigarettes, cigars, or pipes of others, regarded as a health hazard.

pas·siv·ism (păs′ĭ-vĭz′əm) *n.* **1.** Passive character or behavior. **2.** The theory and practice of passive resistance. **—pas·siv·ist** *n.*

pass·key (păs′kē′, päs′-) *n.* Any of various kinds of keys, such as a **master key** or **skeleton key** *(both of which see).*

pass laws *pl.n.* In South Africa, the laws and by-laws regulating black people's rights of movement and domicile. See **reference book.**

Pass·o·ver (păs′ō′vər, päs′-) *n. Judaism.* A festival beginning on the evening of the 14th of Nisan and traditionally celebrated for eight days. It commemorates the escape of the Jews from Egypt. Exodus 12. Also called "Pesach," "Pesah." See **Seder.** [From the phrase *pass over,* translation of Hebrew *pesaḥ,* PESACH.]

pass·port (păs′pôrt′, -pōrt′, päs′-) *n.* **1.** An official document issued by a government that certifies the identity and citizenship of an individual and grants him or her permission to travel abroad. **2.** A permit issued by a foreign country allowing one to transport goods or to travel through that country. **3.** An official document issued to a ship, especially a neutral merchant ship in time of war, authorizing it to leave port or to enter certain waters freely. **4.** Something that enables one to be admitted or accepted: *His wit was his passport to success.* [French *passeport,* safe-conduct, permission to pass through a port : *passer,* to PASS + PORT.]

pas·sus (păs′əs) *n., pl.* **passus** or **-suses.** A section or division of a story, poem, or the like, especially in medieval literature. [Latin, a stretch, section, from the past participle of *pandere,* to stretch.]

pass·word (păs′wûrd′, päs′-) *n.* A secret word or phrase that certifies the speaker's identity, membership, or right to be admitted.

past (păst, päst) *adj.* **1.** No longer current; gone by; finished. **2.** Having existed in, occurred in, or belonged to an earlier time; bygone: *past events.* **3.** Just gone by or elapsed: *in the past month.* **4.** Having served formerly in some official capacity: *a past president.* **5.** *Grammar.* Of, pertaining to, or designating a verb tense or form used to express an action, event, or condition completed or begun prior to the time it is expressed.
~*n.* **1. a.** The time before the present. Preceded by *the*: *in the past.* **b.** That which has occurred in the past: *came to terms with the past.* **2. a.** Former background, career, experiences, and activities: *a distinguished past.* **b.** A former period of someone's life kept secret, especially so that his or her reputation may be maintained: *a man with a past.* **3.** *Grammar.* **a.** The past tense. **b.** A verb form in the past tense.
~*adv.* **1.** Earlier than the present time; ago: *forty years past.* **2.** So as to pass by or go beyond: *He waved as he walked past.*
~*prep.* **1.** Beyond in time; later than; after: *It is past midnight.* **2. a.** Beyond in position: *the lake past the meadow.* **b.** Moving beyond: *drove past the wreckage.* **3.** Beyond the power, scope, extent, or influence of: *The problem is past understanding.* **4.** Beyond the number or amount of: *The child couldn't count past 20.* —See Usage note at **passed.** **—would not put it past someone.** To regard (someone) as having such competence or as being of such a nature as to be capable of a particular action or achievement. [Middle English *passed, past,* from the past participle of *passen,* to PASS.]

pas·ta (pä′stə) *n.* **1.** Paste or dough made of flour and water, used dried, as in macaroni, or fresh, as in ravioli. **2.** A prepared dish of pasta. [Italian, from Late Latin, PASTE.]

paste¹ (pāst) *n.* **1.** A smooth viscous adhesive, such as flour and water or starch and water, used to join light materials, such as paper and cloth. **2.** Any similar soft, smooth, thick mixture. Often used in combination: *toothpaste.* **3.** A smooth dough of water, flour, and butter or other shortening, used in making pastry. **4.** A food that has been pounded until it is reduced to a smooth, creamy mass: *anchovy paste.* **5.** A sweet, doughy confection: *almond paste.* **6.** Moistened clay used in making porcelain or pottery. **7. a.** A hard, brilliant glass used in making artificial gems. **b.** A gem made of this glass. In this sense, also called "strass."
~*tr.v.* **pasted, pasting, pastes. 1.** To cause to adhere by applying paste. **2.** To cover with something to which paste has been applied: *He pasted the wall with posters.* [Middle English, from Old French, from Late Latin *pasta,* dough, paste, from Greek *pastē,* barley porridge, from *pastos,* sprinkled, from *passein,* to sprinkle.]

paste² *tr.v.* **pasted, pasting, pastes.** *Slang.* To punch, beat, or hit. [Alteration of BASTE (to beat).] **—paste** *n.*

paste·board (pāst′bôrd′, -bōrd′) *n.* **1.** A thin, firm board made of sheets of paper pasted together or of pressed paper pulp, used especially to make book covers. **2. a.** A ticket. **b.** A playing card. **c.** A visiting card.
~*adj.* **1.** Made of pasteboard. **2.** Weak and pliable; flimsy. **3.** Fake; counterfeit.

pas·tel (pă-stĕl′) *n.* **1. a.** A dried paste made of ground and mixed pigment, chalk, water, and gum, used to make crayons. **b.** A crayon of this material. **2.** A picture or sketch drawn with such a crayon. **3.** The art or process of drawing with such crayons. **4.** A soft, delicate hue; a light tint. **5.** A sketchy or brief prose work. [French, from Italian *pastello,* from Late Latin *pastellus,* woad dye, crayon, diminutive of *pasta,* PASTE (referring to the paste of decocted woad twigs).] **—pas·tel** *adj.* **—pas·tel·ist, pas·tel·list** *n.*

pas·tern (păs′tərn) *n.* **1.** The part of a horse's foot between the fetlock and hoof. **2.** The bone comprising this part. In this sense, also called "pastern bone." **3.** A comparable part of the leg of a dog or other quadruped. [Middle English *pastron,* a horse's hobble, hence the part of the leg to which it is attached, from Old French *pasturon,* variant of *pasture,* a hobble, from Late Latin *pāstōria,* a sheep's hobble, from *pāstor,* PASTOR.]

Pas·ter·nak (păs′tər-năk′), **Boris Leonidovich** (1890–1960). Russian author and translator. His *Doctor Zhivago* (1957), a novel of disillusionment with the Russian Revolution, was banned by the Soviet authorities. Expelled by the Soviet Writers' Union (1958), he was forced to refuse the Nobel Prize.

paste up *tr.v. Printing.* To prepare a mechanical of.

paste-up (pāst′ŭp′) *n.* **1.** Any composition of light, flat objects pasted on a sheet of paper or other backing; a collage. **2.** *Printing.* A **mechanical** *(see).*

Pas·teur (pă-stûr′), **Louis** (1822–95). French microbiologist and chemist. The founder of modern microbiology, he became professor at the Sorbonne (1867) and discovered that microorganisms in the air were responsible for fermentation in beer and milk. In investigating ways of excluding these organisms, he developed the process of pasteurization. He also developed vaccines for anthrax, rabies, and chicken cholera.

pas·teur·i·za·tion (păs′chər-ə-zā′shən, păs′tər-) *n.* The process of destroying most disease-producing microorganisms and limiting fermentation in milk, beer, and other liquids by application of heat. [After Louis PASTEUR.]

pas·teur·ize (păs′chə-rīz′, păs′tə-) *tr.v.* **-ized, -izing, -izes.** To subject (a liquid, especially milk) to pasteurization. **—pas·teur·iz·er** *n.*

Pasteur treatment *n.* A rabies treatment in which the growth of antibodies is stimulated during the incubation of the disease by increasingly strong inoculations of the attenuated rabies virus. Also called "pasteurism." [After Louis PASTEUR.]

pas·tic·cio (pă-stē′chō, -chē-ō′, pä-) *n., pl.* **-ci** (-chē). A work, especially of music, produced by borrowing fragments or motifs from various sources; potpourri. [Italian, from Medieval Latin *pastīcius,* pasty, from Late Latin *pasta,* PASTE.]

pas·tiche (pă-stēsh′, pä-) *n.* **1.** A dramatic, literary, or musical piece openly imitating the previous work of another artist, often with satirical intent. **2.** A hodgepodge; pasticcio. [French, from Italian *pasticcio,* PASTICCIO.]

pas·tille (pă-stēl′) *n.* Also **pas·til** (păs′tĭl). **1.** A small medicated or flavored tablet; a lozenge. **2.** A tablet containing aromatic substances, burned to fumigate or deodorize the air. **3.** A paste or pastel for making crayons. **4.** A pastel crayon. [French, from Latin *pāstillus,* roll, diminutive of *pānis,* bread.]

pas·time (păs′tīm′, päs′-) *n.* An activity that occupies one's time pleasantly; something that interests, amuses, or diverts.

pas·ti·na (pă-stē′nə) *n.* Tiny pieces of macaroni, usually cooked in soups or used as baby food. [Italian, diminutive of *pasta,* pasta, from Late Latin, PASTE.]

pas·tis (pă-stēs′) *n.* An alcoholic drink flavored with anise. [French *pastis*†.]

past master *n. Abbr.* **P.M. 1.** One who has formerly held the position of master in an organization such as a lodge or club. **2.** A person thoroughly experienced and skilled in a particular craft.

pas·tor (păs′tər, pä′stər) *n.* **1.** A Christian minister in the capacity of having spiritual charge over a congregation or other group. **2.** A shepherd. **3.** A starling, *Sturnus roseus,* of southern Europe and Asia, having pink and black plumage. In this sense, also called "rosy pastor." [Middle English *pastour,* from Old French, from Latin *pāstor,* shepherd, from *pāscere* (past participle *pāstus*), to graze, feed.]

pas·tor·al (păs′tər-əl, pä′stər-) *adj.* **1.** Of or pertaining to shepherds,

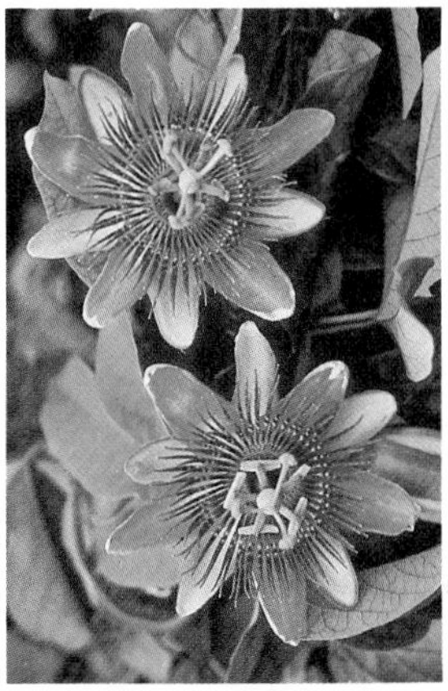

passionflower *This genus of flowering plants gets its name from its fancied association with the Passion of Christ. The bloom's spiny center is said to symbolize the crown of thorns, and the petals are said to represent ten of the twelve apostles. The two left out are Judas Iscariot—because he betrayed Christ—and Peter—because he denied Christ. This species is* Passiflora caerulea.

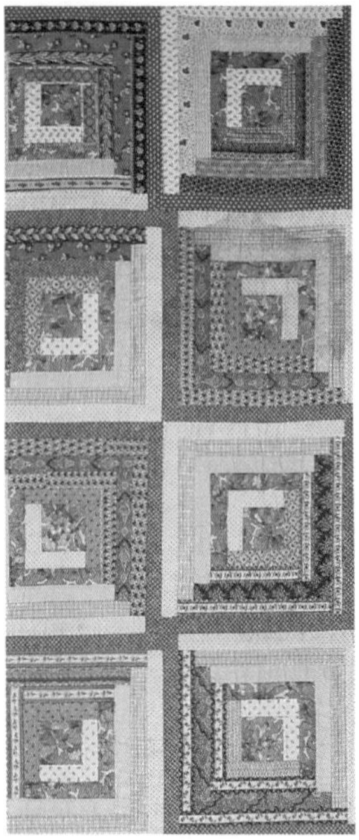

patchwork *An American patchwork quilt made around 1860. Patchwork was developed as a way of using up scraps of fabric.*

herdsmen, and others directly involved in animal husbandry. **2.** Used for pasture. Said of land. **3. a.** Of or pertaining to the country or country life; rural. **b.** Having the qualities of idealized country life, such as charming simplicity and a leisurely, carefree pace. **4.** Of or designating an artistic work that portrays country life in this way. **5.** Designating a branch of theology dealing with the relations between religious truth and spiritual needs or clerical duties. **6.** Of or pertaining to a pastor or his duties. —See Synonyms at **rural.**
~*n.* **1.** A literary or other artistic work that portrays rural life, usually in an idealized manner. **2.** A letter from a pastor, such as a bishop, to those in his care. **3.** *Music.* A pastorale. [Middle English, from Latin *pāstōrālis,* from *pāstor,* shepherd, PASTOR.] **—pas·tor·al·ism** *n.* **—pas·tor·al·ist** *n.* **—pas·tor·al·ly** *adv.*

pas·to·rale (păs′tə-räl′, -răl′, pä′stə-) *n. Music.* **1.** An opera or other vocal composition based on a rural theme or subject. **2.** An instrumental composition with a tender melody in a moderately slow rhythm, suggestive of idyllic rural life. Also called "pastoral." [Italian, from *pastorale,* pastoral, from Latin *pāstōrālis,* PASTORAL.]

pastoral staff *n.* A **crosier** *(see).*

pas·tor·ate (păs′tər-ĭt, pă′stər-) *n.* **1.** The office, rank, or jurisdiction of a pastor. **2.** A pastor's term of office with one congregation. **3.** A body of pastors; pastors collectively.

pas·to·ri·um (pă-stôr′ē-əm, -stōr′ē-əm, pä-) *n., pl.* **-ums.** *Southern U.S.* The residence of a pastor; a parsonage.

past participle *n. Abbr.* **pp., p.p.** A verb form indicating past or completed action or time. It is used as a verbal adjective in phrases such as *finished work, baked beans,* and with auxiliaries to form the passive voice or perfect and pluperfect tenses in constructions such as *The work was finished.* Also called "perfect participle."

past perfect *n.* **1.** The pluperfect tense. **2.** A verb in this tense.

pas·tra·mi (pə-strä′mē) *n.* A highly seasoned smoked beef, usually cut from the breast or shoulder. [Yiddish, from Romanian *pastramă,* from *păstra*†, to preserve.]

pas·try (pā′strē) *n., pl.* **-tries. 1.** A baked paste made from flour, water, and shortening and used for the crusts of pies, tarts, and the like. **2.** Baked foods, as pies or tarts, made with pastry. **3.** An individual piece of pastry. [From PASTE.]

past tense *n.* A verb tense used to express an action, event, or condition that occurred or began in the past. For example, in *While she was sewing he read aloud,* the verbs *was sewing* and *read* are in the past tense.

pas·tur·age (păs′chər-ĭj, päs′-) *n.* **1.** The grass or other vegetation eaten by grazing animals. **2. a.** Land covered with such grass or vegetation. **b.** A particular piece of such land. **c.** The right to graze cattle on such land. **3.** The business of grazing cattle.

pas·ture (păs′chər, päs′-) *n.* **1.** The grass or other vegetation eaten as food by grazing animals. **2. a.** Land on which such vegetation grows. **b.** A particular piece of such land.
~*v.* **pastured, -turing, -tures.** —*tr.* **1.** To herd (animals) into a pasture to graze. **2.** To provide (animals) with pasturage. Used of land. **3.** To feed on (vegetation). Used of animals. **4.** To use (land) for animals to graze on. —*intr.* To graze in a pasture. [Middle English, from Old French, from Late Latin *pāstūra,* from Latin *pāscere* (past participle *pāstus*), to pasture, feed.] **—pas·tur·a·ble** *adj.* **—pas·tur·er** *n.*

past·y[1] (pā′stē) *adj.* **-ier, -iest. 1.** Resembling paste in color or consistency. **2.** Pale and lifeless-looking. Said of the face or complexion. **—past·i·ness** *n.*

pas·ty[2] (păs′tē, pä′stē) *n., pl.* **-ties.** *Chiefly British.* A pie consisting of an envelope of pastry with a filling of seasoned meat and sometimes vegetables, or of jam or fruit. [Middle English *pastee,* from Old French *paste,* from noun, dough, PASTE.]

PA system (pē′ā′) *n.* A **public-address system** *(see).*

pat[1] (păt) *v.* **patted, patting, pats.** —*tr.* **1. a.** To tap gently with the open hand or with something flat. **b.** To tap or stroke lightly as a gesture of affection. **2.** To mold by tapping gently with the hands or a flat implement. —*intr.* **1.** To run or walk with a tapping sound. **2.** To hit something or against something gently or lightly.
~*n.* **1.** A light stroke or tap. **2.** The sound made by such a stroke or tap or by light footsteps. **3.** A small mass of something shaped by or as if by patting: *a pat of butter.* **—pat on the back.** *Informal.* A compliment, especially when intended as an encouragement. [Middle English *patte* (probably imitative).]

pat[2] *adj.* **1.** Timely; opportune; fitting: *a pat answer.* **2.** Needing no change; exactly right. **3.** Glib; somewhat insincere: *Her reply was too pat to be convincing.*
~*adv. Informal.* **1.** Without changing position; steadfastly. **2.** Perfectly; precisely; aptly. **—have down pat.** *Informal.* To know or have memorized completely. **—stand pat.** *Informal.* **1.** To refuse to change one's position or opinion. **2.** To decline to draw more cards to a poker hand. [Probably "with a hitting stroke," from PAT (to tap).] **—pat·ly** *adv.* **—pat·ness** *n.*

Pat (păt) *n. Informal.* An Irishman. [Short for *Patrick,* a very common Christian name in Ireland.]

pat. patent; patented.

pa·ta·gi·um (pə-tā′jē-əm) *n., pl.* **-gia** (-jē-ə). *Zoology.* **1.** A thin membrane extending between the fore and hind limb to form a wing or winglike extension, as in bats and flying squirrels. **2.** An expandable, membranous fold of skin between the wing and body of a bird. [New Latin, from Latin, gold edging on a woman's tunic, from Greek *patageion* (unattested), "clattering gold braid," from *patagos,* a clatter (imitative).]

Pat·a·go·ni·a (păt′ə-gō′nē-ə). Region of South America in Argentina and Chile. Extending southward from the Río Colorado to the Straits of Magellan, it is a cool, semiarid plateau at the foot of the Andes. The chief occupation is the raising of sheep, and its mineral wealth includes oil, iron ore, and coal. **—Pat·a·go·ni·an** *adj. & n.*

patch (păch) *n.* **1.** A small piece of material affixed to another, larger piece to conceal or reinforce a weakened or worn area. **2. a.** Any small piece of cloth used for patchwork. **b.** *Military.* A small cloth badge affixed to a sleeve or lapel to indicate the unit to which one belongs. **3.** A dressing or bandage applied to protect a wound or sore. **4.** A small pad or shield of cloth worn over an injured eye or to conceal a missing eye. **5.** A **beauty spot** *(see).* **6. a.** A small piece of land. **b.** The produce grown on such a piece of land: *a patch of beans.* **7.** A small part or section of a surface that differs from or contrasts with the whole: *The flowers made white patches against the grass.* **8.** A discolored area on the skin or mucous membrane. **9.** A small piece or part of anything: *"that little patch of blue which prisoners call the sky"* (Oscar Wilde).
~*tr.v.* **patched, patching, patches. 1. a.** To put a patch or patches on, especially when mending clothes. **b.** To be a patch for or on. Used of material. **2. a.** To make by sewing scraps of material together: *patch a quilt.* **b.** To make by piecing various elements together, especially hastily: *They patched together a plan.* **3.** To mend, repair, or put together, especially hastily, clumsily, or poorly: *patching old costumes for the tour.* **4.** *Electronics & Computer Science.* To join up (circuits) temporarily by a connected board into which plugs may be fitted. **—patch up.** To settle; make up: *They patched up their quarrel.* [Middle English *pacche,* perhaps variant of *peche,* from Old French *pece, pieche,* PIECE.] **—patch·a·ble** *adj.* **—patch·er** *n.*

Patch (păch), **Sam** (1807–29). U.S. daredevil. He was noted for leaping from bridges and great heights, including a jump into the Niagara River from Goat Island. Patch was killed in an attempt to leap from a height of 38 meters (125 feet) into the Genesee River at Rochester, New York.

patch board *n. Electronics.* A **plugboard** *(see).*

patch·ou·li, pach·oo·li (păch′o͝o-lē, pə-cho͞o′lē) *n., pl.* **-lis.** Also **patch·ou·ly** *pl.* **-lies. 1.** Any of several Asiatic trees of the genus *Pogostemon,* especially *P. patchouly* and *P. cablin,* having leaves that yield a fragrant oil used in the manufacture of perfumes. **2.** A perfume made from this oil. [Tamil *paccilai* : *paccu,* green + *ilai,* leaf.]

patch pocket *n.* A pocket consisting of a patch of material sewn onto the outside of a garment, as a shirt or a pair of jeans, rather than being set in through a slit in the fabric.

patch test *n.* A test for allergic sensitivity made by applying a suspected allergen to the skin on a small surgical pad.

patch·work (păch′wûrk′) *n.* **1.** Needlework consisting of various colored patches of material sewn together, as in a quilt. **2.** A collection of miscellaneous or incongruous parts; a jumble: *a patchwork of outmoded theories.*

patch·y (păch′ē) *adj.* **-ier, -iest. 1.** Made up of or marked by patches: *a patchy pair of trousers.* **2.** Uneven in quality or performance: *patchy work.* **—patch·i·ly** *adv.* **—patch·i·ness** *n.*

patd. patented.

pate (pāt) *n.* **1.** The head; especially, the top of the head: *a bald pate.* **2.** The brains; the intellect. [Middle English *pate*†.]

pâte (pät) *n.* Paste used in making porcelain and pottery. [French, patty, paste, from Old French *paste,* PASTE.]

pâ·té (pä-tā′) *n.* **1.** A firm meat paste often made with liver. **2.** A firm paste made of other ingredients, such as fish or vegetables. **3.** A small pastry filled with meat or fish. [French *paté(e),* from Old French *pasté(e),* from *paste,* PASTE.]

pâté de foie gras (də fwä grä′) *n.* A rich paste made from the livers of specially fattened geese, often with truffles added. Also called "foie gras." [French, "pâté of fat liver."]

pa·tel·la (pə-tĕl′ə) *n., pl.* **-tellae** (-tĕl′ē). **1. a.** A flat, triangular bone located at the front of the knee joint. Also called "kneecap." **b.** *Biology.* Any dish-shaped formation. **2.** An ancient Roman pan or dish. [Latin, diminutive of *patina,* plate. See **paten.**] **—pa·tel·lar, pa·tel·late** (pə-tĕl′ĭt, -āt′) *adj.*

pa·tel·li·form (pə-tĕl′ə-fôrm′) *adj.* Shaped like a pan, dish, or cup: *the patelliform shell of the limpet.* [New Latin *patelliformis* : PATELL(A) + -FORM.]

pat·en, pat·in (păt′n) *n.* Also **pa·tine** (pă-tēn′). **1.** A plate, especially one used to hold the Eucharistic bread. **2.** A thin disk of metal. Also called "patina." [Middle English *paten, pat(e)yn,* from Old French *patene,* from Latin *patina,* dish, pan, from Greek *patanē.*]

pa·ten·cy (pāt′n-sē) *n.* **1.** The state or quality of being obvious. **2.** The state of being open.

pat·ent (păt′ənt) *n. Abbr.* **pat. 1. a.** A grant made by a government to an inventor, assuring him the sole right to make, use, and sell his invention for a certain period of time. **b.** The official document certifying such a grant, **letters patent** *(see).* **c.** Something that is protected by such a grant. **2. a.** A grant made by a government to an individual, conveying to him fee-simple title to public lands. **b.** The official document of such a grant. **c.** The land so granted. **3.** An exclusive right, title, or claim: *He doesn't have a patent on honesty.*
~*adj.* (păt′ənt *for senses 1, 3, 4, 7;* pā′tənt *for senses 2, 5, 6, 8*). **1.** Open to general inspection; unsealed. Used chiefly in the phrase *letters patent.* **2.** Obvious; plain: *His insincerity was patent.* **3.** *Abbr.* **pat.** Protected by a patent. **4.** *Abbr.* **pat.** Of, pertaining to, or dealing in patents: *patent law.* **5.** *Biology.* Spreading open; expanded.

PRONUNCIATION KEY

ă, pat; ā, pay; âr, care;
ä, father, are; b, **bib;**
ch, **church;** d, **deed;** ĕ, pet;
ē, be; f, **fife;** g, **gag;** h, **hat;**
hw, **which;** ĭ, pit; ī, pie;
îr, pier; j, **judge;** k, **kick;**
l, lid, needle; m, **mum;**
n, no, sudden; ng, **thing;**
ŏ, pot; ō, toe; ô, paw, for;
oi, noise; ou, **out;** o͝o, **book;**
o͞o, **boot;** p, **pop;** r, **roar;**
s, sauce; sh, **ship, dish;**
t, **tight;** th, **thin, path;**
th, **this, bathe;** ŭ, cut; ûr, fur;
v, valve; w, with; y, yes;
z, zebra, size; zh, vision;
ə, about, item, edible,
gallop, circus, peaceful

IN FOREIGN WORDS:

à, *Fr.* ami; œ, *Fr.* **feu,** *Ger.* **schön;** ü, *Fr.* **tu,** *Ger.* **über;**
KH, *Ger.* **ich,** *Scot.* **loch;**
N, *Fr.* **bon;** y′, *Fr.* **Compiègne**

STRESS MARKS:

Primary stress: ′
in·cite′ (ĭn-sīt′)
Secondary stress: ′
in′sight′ (ĭn′sīt′)

6. *Anatomy.* Open; unobstructed. Said of vessels, ducts, and other hollow parts. 7. Of high quality. Said of flour. 8. *British.* Ground and polished on both sides of the glass.
~*tr.v.* **patented, -enting, -ents.** *Abbr.* **pat.** 1. To obtain a patent on. 2. To grant a patent to. [As noun, Middle English *(letters) patente,* letters patent, from Old French *(lettres) patentes,* from Medieval Latin *(litterae) patentes,* "open letters or documents," from *patentes,* plural of *patens,* open, from the present participle of *patēre,* to be open.] **—pat·ent·a·bil·i·ty** *n.* **—pat·ent·a·ble** *adj.*

pat·ent·ee (păt'n-tē') *n.* A person who has been granted a patent.

pat·ent leather (păt'ənt) *n.* 1. Black leather finished to a hard, glossy surface. 2. Any of several synthetic materials having a similar appearance. [Made by a once-patented process.]

pat·ent log (păt'ənt) *n. Nautical.* A torpedo-shaped instrument with rotary fins that is dragged from the stern of a vessel to measure the speed or distance traveled. Also called "screw log," "taffrail log."

pat·ent·ly (pāt'ənt-lē) *adv.* Obviously; clearly; plainly.

pat·ent medicine (păt'ənt) *n.* A drug or other medical preparation that is protected by a patent and can be bought without a prescription.

Patent Office *n.* A bureau of the U.S. Department of Commerce in which claims for patents are studied and patents are issued and recorded.

pat·en·tor (păt'n-tər, păt'n-tôr') *n.* One that grants a patent.

pat·ent right (păt'ənt) *n.* The right granted by a patent; especially, the right to have exclusive manufacture and sale of an invention.

pa·ter (pā'tər) *n. British.* Father. Usually used humorously. [Latin.]

Pa·ter (pā'tər) **Walter Horatio** (1839–94). British critic and essayist. His works include *Imaginary Portraits* (1887) and *Plato and Platonism* (1893).

pa·ter·fa·mil·i·as (pā'tər-fə-mĭl'ē-əs, pä'tər-) *n., pl.* **patresfamilias** (pā'trēz-fə-mĭl'ē-əs, pä'trēz-). The father of a family considered as the head of the household. [Latin : *pater,* father + *familiās,* archaic genitive of *familia,* FAMILY.]

pa·ter·nal (pə-tûr'nəl) *adj.* 1. Of, pertaining to, or characteristic of a father; fatherly. 2. Received or inherited from one's father. 3. Related through one's father. [Medieval Latin *paternālis,* from Latin *paternus,* fatherly, from *pater,* father.] **—pa·ter·nal·ly** *adv.*

pa·ter·nal·ism (pə-tûr'nə-lĭz'əm) *n.* A policy or practice of managing or governing people in a fatherly manner, especially by providing for their needs without giving them responsibility. **—pa·ter·nal·is·tic** (pə-tûr'nə-lĭs'tĭk) *adj.* **—pa·ter·nal·is·ti·cal·ly** *adv.*

pa·ter·ni·ty (pə-tûr'nə-tē) *n.* 1. The fact or condition of being a father; fatherhood. Also used adjectivally: *paternity leave; a paternity suit.* 2. Descent on a father's side; paternal descent. 3. Authorship; origin. [Old French *paternite,* from Late Latin *paternitās* (stem *paternitāt-*), from Latin *paternus,* fatherly, PATERNAL.]

pa·ter·nos·ter (pā'tər-nŏs'tər, pä'tər-, păt'ər-) *n.* 1. *Often* **Paternoster.** The **Lord's Prayer** *(see),* especially when recited in Latin. 2. Any of the large beads on a rosary on which the Lord's Prayer is said. 3. A sequence of words spoken as a prayer or as a magic formula. 4. *Chiefly British.* A type of elevator in which open compartments move continuously in a looped chain, passing each floor slowly enough for users to enter or alight. 5. A weighted fishing line having several jointed attachments for hooks connected by beadlike swivels. [Latin *pater noster,* "our father."]

path (păth, päth) *n., pl.* **paths** (păthz, päthz, păths, päths). 1. A trodden track or way. 2. Any surface track or way. 3. A way that allows forward movement: *clear a path through the forest.* 4. The route or course along which something moves: *the path of a hurricane.* 5. A course of action or conduct: *the path of righteousness.* —See Synonyms at **way.** [Middle English *path,* Old English *pæth.*] **—path·less** *adj.*

path. pathological; pathology.

-path *suffix.* Indicates: 1. One who practices a specified type of medicine; for example, **naturopath.** 2. One who suffers from a specified disease; for example, **psychopath.** [Back-formation from -PATHY.]

Pa·than (pə-tän') *n.* A member of a Pashto-speaking tribal people of Indo-Iranian stock and Muslim religion, living chiefly in northwestern Pakistan and Afghanistan. [Hindi *Paṭhan,* from Afghan *Pēṣtana,* plural of *Pēṣtūn,* an Afghan, from *pashtó,* the Afghan language. See **Pashto.**]

pa·thet·ic (pə-thĕt'ĭk) *adj.* 1. Of, pertaining to, expressing, or arousing pity, sympathy, or tenderness; full of pathos: *The ragged children made a pathetic sight.* 2. *Informal.* Inadequate: *a pathetic attempt.* 3. *Informal.* Of little interest or worth; feeble; useless. —See Synonyms at **moving.** [French *pathétique,* from Late Latin *pathēticus,* from Greek *pathētikos,* from *pathētos,* liable to suffer, from *pathos,* passion, suffering.] **—pa·thet·i·cal·ly** *adv.*
Synonyms: *lamentable, pitiful, regrettable.*

pathetic fallacy *n.* The attribution of human emotions or characteristics to inanimate things, as in romantic literature.

path·find·er (păth'fīn'dər, päth'-) *n.* 1. One who discovers a way through or into unexplored regions. 2. An aircraft pilot who finds a target area and marks it by flares or other signaling devices. 3. A radar system or radio beacon used for navigation or homing.

patho- *prefix.* Indicates disease or suffering; for example, **pathogen.** [New Latin, from Greek *pathos,* emotion, suffering.]

path·o·gen (păth'ə-jən) *n.* Also **path·o·gene** (păth'ə-jēn'). Any agent that causes disease, especially a microorganism such as a bacterium or fungus. [PATHO- + -GEN.]

path·o·gen·e·sis (păth'ə-jĕn'ə-sĭs) *n.* Also **pa·thog·e·ny** (pă-thŏj'ə-nē). The origin and development of a diseased or morbid condition. [New Latin : PATHO- + -GENESIS.]

path·o·gen·ic (păth'ə-jĕn'ĭk) *adj.* Also **path·o·ge·net·ic** (păth'ə-jə-nĕt'ĭk). Capable of causing disease: *pathogenic bacteria.* **—path·o·ge·nic·i·ty** (păth'ə-jə-nĭs'ə-tē) *n.*

pa·thog·no·mon·ic (pə-thŏg'nə-mŏn'ĭk) *adj.* Distinctive or characteristic of a particular disease. Said of signs and symptoms. [From Greek *pathognōmonikos,* "indicating a disease" : *pathos,* suffering + *gnōmonikos,* from *gnōmōn,* indicator, judge.]

pathol. pathological; pathology.

path·o·log·i·cal (păth'ə-lŏj'ĭ-kəl) *adj.* Also **path·o·log·ic** (păth'ə-lŏj'ĭk). *Abbr.* **path., pathol.** 1. Of or pertaining to pathology. 2. Pertaining to or caused by disease. 3. Unhealthy or compulsive in behavior: *a pathological liar.* **—path·o·log·i·cal·ly** *adv.*

pa·thol·o·gy (pă-thŏl'ə-jē) *n., pl.* **-gies.** *Abbr.* **path., pathol.** 1. The scientific study of the nature of disease and its causes, processes, development, and consequences. 2. The anatomic or functional manifestations of disease or of a particular disease, as changes in organs and tissues. [New Latin *pathologia* and Old French *pathologie,* from Greek *pathologia,* study of passions : PATHO- + -LOGY.] **—pa·thol·o·gist** *n.*

pa·thos (pā'thŏs', -thôs') *n.* 1. a. A quality in something or someone that arouses feelings of pity, sympathy, tenderness, or sorrow in another: *the pathos of their parting.* b. The evocation of such a quality in art or literature. 2. A feeling of sympathy or pity. [Greek, passion, suffering.]
Usage: *Pathos* and *pathetic* are general terms having to do with feelings of pity or sympathy. *Bathos* and *bathetic* are quite different in meaning and more restricted in application, referring to the sudden intrusion of something banal or ordinary in an elevated or high-flown context.

path·way (păth'wā', päth'-) *n.* 1. A path. 2. *Chemistry.* A particular chain of reactions leading to a given product.

-pathy *suffix.* Indicates: 1. Feeling; perception; for example, **telepathy.** 2. a. Disease; a diseased condition; for example, **neuropathy.** b. A system of treating disease; for example, **homeopathy.** [Latin *-pathia,* from Greek *-patheia,* from *pathos,* PATHOS.]

pa·tience (pā'shəns) *n.* 1. The capacity of calm, uncomplaining endurance or perseverance: *"This is the story of what a woman's patience can endure"* (Wilkie Collins). 2. Tolerant understanding: *had no patience with fools.* 3. The capacity to put up with delay and wait for the right moment. 4. *Chiefly British.* A game of solitaire.
Synonyms: *forbearance, resignation.*

pa·tient (pā'shənt) *adj.* 1. Capable of bearing affliction with calmness. 2. Tolerant; understanding. 3. Persevering; constant: *a patient worker.* 4. Capable of bearing delay; not hasty.
~*n.* 1. A person or animal receiving medical treatment. 2. One who is the recipient of an action. [Middle English *pacient,* from Old French *patient,* from Latin *patiēns* (stem *patient-*), from the present participle of *patī,* to suffer.] **—pa·tient·ly** *adv.*

patin. Variant of **paten.**

pat·i·na[1] (păt'n-ə) *n., pl.* **-nae** (-nē). A **paten** *(see).* [Medieval Latin, from Latin, a shallow dish, pan. See **paten.**]

pat·i·na[2] (păt'n-ə, pə-tē'nə) *n.* Also **pa·tine** (pă-tēn'). 1. A thin layer of corrosion, usually brown or green, that appears on copper or copper alloys, such as bronze, as a result of natural or artificial oxidation. Compare **verdigris.** 2. The sheen produced by age and use on a surface. 3. Any surface appearance. [Italian, originally "a mixture prepared in a bowl and used to coat calfskins," from Latin *patina,* shallow dish, plate. See **paten.**]

pa·tine (pă-tēn') *tr.v.* **-tined, -tining, -tines.** To coat with a patina.
~*n.* 1. Variant of **paten.** 2. Variant of **patina** (layer). [French *patine,* from Old French *patene,* from Latin PATINA.]

pat·i·o (păt'ē-ō', pä'tē-ō') *n., pl.* **-os.** 1. An inner, roofless courtyard. 2. A usually paved area for dining or relaxation adjacent to a house or apartment. [Spanish, courtyard.]

pa·tis·se·rie (pă'tēs-rē') *n.* 1. A bakery specializing in rich, fancy cakes and pastries. 2. Such cakes and pastries. [French *pâtisserie,* from Old French, "pastry," from *pâtissier,* pastry cook, from *pastitz* (unattested), pasty, from Vulgar Latin *pastīcium* (unattested), from Late Latin *pasta,* dough, PASTE.]

Pat·more (păt'môr', -mōr'), **Coventry Kersey Dighton** (1823–96). British poet and critic. His works include *The Angel in the House* (1854–63). Associated with the Pre-Raphaelite Brotherhood, he underwent conversion to Roman Catholicism (1864).

Pat·mos (păt'məs). *Greek* **Pát·mos** (pät'môs'). Greek island of the Dodecanese group, in the southeastern Aegean Sea. It is where St. John is reputed to have written the Book of Revelation.

Pat·na (pŭt'nə). Capital of Bihar state, India, on the Ganges. It is on the former site of Pataliputra, capital of the Maghda kingdom (5th century B.C.) and the Mauryan and Gupta empires. It is now the center of a rice-growing area.

Patna rice *n.* A type of rice having long grains. [After PATNA.]

pat·ois (păt'wä', pä-twä') *n., pl.* **patois** (păt'wäz', pä-twä'). 1. A regional French or Swiss dialect. 2. A West Indian French Creole, such as that spoken in St. Lucia. 3. An English Creole, especially Jamaican Creole. 4. A regional dialect. 5. Illiterate or substandard speech. 6. The special jargon of a group; cant. [French, perhaps from Old French *patoier,* to handle roughly, from *patte,* paw.]

Pat·on (pāt'n), **Alan** (1903–). South African novelist. He rose to international fame with *Cry, the Beloved Country* (1948), an indictment of South Africa's racial policies. His other books include *Debbie Go Home* (1961) and *The Long View* (1968).

Pat·ras (păt′rəs, pə-trăs′). Port of western Greece, situated on the east side of the Gulf of Patras, an inlet of the Ionian Sea, in the north Peloponnese. It was destroyed in the Greek War of Independence (1821).

pat·res·fa·mil·i·as. Plural of **paterfamilias.**

patri– *prefix.* Indicates father; for example, **patriclinous.** [Latin *pater,* father, and Greek *patēr,* father.]

pa·tri·al (pā′trē-əl) *n. British.* A citizen of the United Kingdom who has the right to British nationality by virtue of birth, adoption, naturalization, or registration in the United Kingdom. **—pa·tri·al·i·ty** (pā′trē-ăl′ə-tē) *n.*

pa·tri·arch (pā′trē-ärk′) *n.* **1.** The paternal leader of a family or tribe. Compare **matriarch. 2.** In the Old Testament: **a.** Any of the progenitors of the human race before the Flood, from Adam to Noah. **b.** Abraham, Isaac, Jacob, or any of Jacob's 12 sons, the eponymous progenitors of the 12 tribes of Israel: *"and Jacob begat the twelve patriarchs"* (Acts 7:8). **3.** In the early Christian church, any of the bishops of Rome, Constantinople, Jerusalem, Antioch, and Alexandria. **4.** *Roman Catholic Church.* A bishop who holds the highest episcopal rank after the pope. **5.** In the Eastern Orthodox Church: **a.** The bishop of Alexandria, Antioch, Constantinople, Jerusalem, Moscow, Serbia, or Romania. **b.** The bishop of Constantinople as leader of the Greek Orthodox Church. Also called "ecumenical patriarch." **6.** *Mormon Church.* A high dignitary of the priesthood empowered to invoke blessings. Also called "evangelist." **7.** A man regarded as the founder or original head of an enterprise, organization, or tradition. **8.** A very old and venerable man; an elder. **9.** The most venerable specimen in a group: *patriarch of the herd.* **10.** Loosely, any man holding a powerful or authoritative position in a conventional hierarchy who insists on being heard, respected, and obeyed. Often used derogatorily. [Middle English *patriarke,* from Old French *patriarche,* from Late Latin *patriarcha,* from Greek *patriarkhēs* : *patria,* lineage, family, from *patēr,* father + -ARCH.]

pa·tri·ar·chal (pā′trē-är′kəl) *adj.* Also **pa·tri·ar·chic** (-kĭk). **1.** Pertaining to or characteristic of a patriarch; venerable; dignified. **2.** Of or pertaining to a patriarchy: *a patriarchal social system.* **3.** Ruled by a patriarch: *a patriarchal see.* **—pa·tri·ar·chal·ism** *n.* **—pa·tri·ar·chal·ly** *adv.*

patriarchal cross *n.* A Latin cross having two horizontal bars of which the upper is the shorter.

pa·tri·ar·chate (pā′trē-är′kĭt, -kāt′) *n.* **1.** The territory, residence, rule, or rank of a patriarch. **2.** A patriarchy.

pa·tri·ar·chy (pā′trē-är′kē) *n., pl.* **-chies. 1.** A system of social organization in which descent and succession are traced through the male line. **2.** The rule of a people or family by men.

pa·tri·cian (pə-trĭsh′ən) *n.* **1.** A member of one of the noble families of the Roman Republic, which before the third century B.C. had exclusive rights to the Senate and the magistracies. Compare **plebeian. 2.** A dignity or title conferred by the Byzantine emperors. **3.** A member of the hereditary ruling class in the medieval free cities of Italy and Germany. **4.** A member of an aristocracy. **5.** A person of notably superior upbringing, manners, and tastes. [Middle English *patricion,* from Old French *patricien,* from Latin *patricius,* (nobleman) of senatorial rank, from *patres,* "fathers," senators, from *pater,* father.] **—pa·tri·cian** *adj.* **—pa·tri·cian·ly** *adv.*

pa·tri·ci·ate (pə-trĭsh′ē-ĭt, -āt′) *n.* **1.** The rank of patrician. **2.** Patricians as a class; nobility; aristocracy. [Latin *patriciātus,* from *patricius,* PATRICIAN.]

pat·ri·cide (păt′rə-sīd′) *n.* **1.** The act of murdering one's father. **2.** One who murders his father. [Late Latin *patricīdium* (crime) and Latin *patricīda* (killer) : PATRI- + -CIDE.] **—pat·ri·cid·al** (păt′rə-sīd′l) *adj.*

Pat·rick (păt′rĭk), **Saint** (*c.* A.D. 385–460). Patron saint of Ireland. Probably born in southern Wales, he was kidnapped by pirates and taken to Ireland, escaping after six years to France, where he was ordained as a bishop (*c.* 430). Returning to Ireland as a Christian missionary (*c.* 432), he established a see at Armagh and helped spread Christianity.

pat·ri·cli·nous, pat·ro·cli·nous (păt′rə-klī′nəs) *adj.* Mainly derived from the male line. Said of plants and animals. Compare **matriclinous.** [PATRI- + *-clinous,* from Greek *-klinēs,* leaning, from *klinein,* to lean.]

pat·ri·lin·e·al (păt′rə-lĭn′ē-əl) *adj.* Relating to, based on, or tracing descent through the male line. Compare **matrilineal.**

pat·ri·lo·cal (păt′rə-lō′kəl) *adj. Anthropology.* Pertaining to the custom in some primitive societies of living in the home territory of a husband's family or tribe. Compare **matrilocal.**

pat·ri·mo·ny (păt′rə-mō′nē) *n., pl.* **-nies. 1.** An inheritance from a father or other ancestor. **2.** A legacy; a heritage. **3.** An endowment or estate belonging to a church. [Middle English *patrimoine,* from Old French, from Latin *patrimōnium,* from *pater,* father.] **—pat·ri·mo·ni·al** (păt′rə-mō′nē-əl) *adj.* **—pat·ri·mo·ni·al·ly** *adv.*

pa·tri·ot (pā′trē-ət, -ŏt′) *n.* A person who loves, supports, and defends his country. [Old French *patriote,* compatriot, from Late Latin *patriōta,* from Greek *patriōtēs,* from *patris,* fatherland, from *patēr,* father.] **—pa·tri·ot·ic** (pā′trē-ŏt′ĭk) *adj.* **—pa·tri·ot·i·cal·ly** *adv.* **—pa·tri·ot·ism** (pā′trē-ə-tĭz′əm) *n.*

Patriots' Day *n.* April 19, the anniversary of the battles of Lexington and Concord in 1775, celebrated as a legal holiday in Maine and Massachusetts.

pa·tris·tic (pə-trĭs′tĭk) *adj.* Also **pa·tris·ti·cal** (-tĭ-kəl). **1.** Of or pertaining to patristics. **2.** *Biology.* Designating similarity between different types of plants or animals due to common ancestry. [PATR(I)- + -IST + -IC.] **—pa·tris·ti·cal·ly** *adv.*

pa·tris·tics (pə-trĭs′tĭks) *n. Used with a singular verb.* The study of the teachings and lives of the fathers of the early Christian church. Also called "patrology."

patroclinous. Variant of **patriclinous.**

pa·trol (pə-trōl′) *n.* **1.** The action of moving about an area for purposes of observation or security. **2.** A person or group of persons who carry out such an action. **3. a.** A military unit sent out on a reconnaissance mission. **b.** One or more vehicles, boats, ships, or aircraft assigned to guard or reconnoiter a given area. **4.** A small group, usually eight, of Boy Scouts or Girl Scouts, a division of a troop.
~*v.* **patrolled, -trolling, -trols.** *—tr.* To engage in a patrol of. *—intr.* To engage in a patrol. [French *patrouiller,* from Old French *patouiller,* to paw or paddle around in mud: *patte,* paw (see **patten**) + *-ouiller,* imitative verb suffix.] **—pa·trol·ler** *n.*

patrol car *n.* A **squad car** *(see).*

pa·trol·man (pə-trōl′mən) *n., pl.* **-men** (-mĭn). **1.** A policeman or guard who patrols an assigned area. **2.** *British.* A person employed by an automobile association to patrol a given area and go to the assistance of motorists who are in trouble.

pa·trol·o·gy (pə-trŏl′ə-jē) *n.* **1.** Patristics. **2.** A collection of the writings of the fathers of the early Christian church. [17th century : from Greek *patēr* (stem *patr-*), father + -LOGY.] **—pat·ro·log·i·cal** (păt′rə-lŏj′ĭ-kəl) *adj.* **—pa·trol·o·gist** *n.*

patrol torpedo boat *n.* A **PT boat** *(see).*

patrol wagon *n.* A police van used to convey prisoners.

pa·tron (pā′trən) *n.* **1.** Anyone who supports, protects, or champions; a benefactor: *a patron of the arts.* **2.** A regular customer. **3.** One who has the right to present a clergyman to an ecclesiastical benefice. **4.** In ancient Rome: **a.** The former owner of a freed slave who retained certain rights over him. **b.** The protector of a client. **5.** A **patron saint** *(see).* [Middle English *patroun,* from Old French *patron,* from Medieval Latin *patrōnus,* patron, patron saint, from Latin, defender, advocate, from *pater,* father.] **—pa·tron·al** (pā′trə-nəl) *adj.*

pa·tron·age (pā′trə-nĭj, păt′rə-) *n.* **1.** Support, encouragement, or championship from a patron. **2.** A patronizing manner. **3.** The trade given to a commercial establishment by its customers. **4.** Customers or patrons collectively; clientele. **5.** The power or action of distributing governmental or political positions. **6.** The positions so distributed. **7.** The right to present a clergyman to an ecclesiastical benefice.

pa·tron·ess (pā′trə-nĭs) *n.* A female patron.

pa·tron·ize (pā′trə-nīz′, păt′rə-) *tr.v.* **-ized, -izing, -izes. 1.** To act as a patron to; support. **2.** To go to regularly as a customer. **3.** To treat in an offensively condescending manner. **—pa·tron·iz·er** *n.* **—pa·tron·iz·ing·ly** *adv.*

patron saint *n.* The guardian saint of any nation, place, craft, activity, class, or person. Also called "patron."

pat·ro·nym·ic (păt′rə-nĭm′ĭk) *n.* A name derived from the first name of one's father or a paternal ancestor; especially, one formed by a suffix or prefix, as in *Johnson,* the son of John. In the Russian formula *Vladimir Ilyich Lenin, Ilyich* (son of Ilya) is a patronymic, while *Lenin* is a true surname. Compare **metronymic.** [Late Latin *patronymicum,* from *patrōnymicus,* "derived from the name of a father," from Greek *patrōnumia,* patronymic : PATR(I)- + *onuma,* name.] **—pat·ro·nym·i·cal** *adj.* **—pat·ro·nym·i·cal·ly** *adv.*

pa·troon (pə-tro͞on′) *n.* Formerly, a member of the Dutch West India Company who was granted proprietary and manorial rights in New York and New Jersey. [Dutch, from French *patron,* patron, from Old French, PATRON.]

pat·sy (păt′sē) *n., pl.* **-sies.** *Slang.* A person who is cheated, victimized, or made the butt of a joke. [20th century : origin obsure.]

pat·tée (pă-tā′, păt′ē) *adj.* Having triangular arms that become wider toward the ends. Said of a cross. Often used after the noun: *a cross pattée.* [French *patte,* paw.]

pat·ten (păt′n) *n.* A wooden sandal, shoe, or clog; especially, a wooden overshoe raised on a wooden or metal support. [Middle English *patin,* from Old French *patin,* from *patte,* a paw, hoof, from Vulgar Latin *patta*† (unattested).]

pat·ter¹ (păt′ər) *v.* **-tered, -tering, -ters.** *—intr.* **1.** To make a quick succession of light, soft taps: *Rain pattered on the roof.* **2.** To move with quick, light, soft steps. *—tr.* To cause to patter.
~*n.* A succession of quick, light, tapping sounds. [Frequentative of PAT (to tap lightly).]

patter² *v.* **-tered, -tering, -ters.** *—intr.* **1.** To chatter glibly and rapidly. **2.** To mumble prayers in a mechanical manner. *—tr.* To utter in a glib, rapid, or mechanical manner.
~*n.* **1.** Glib, rehearsed, rapid speech, as of an auctioneer, salesman, or comedian. **2.** The jargon of a particular group; cant. **3.** Meaningless talk; chatter. **4.** Rapid speech inserted into a song. [Middle English *patren, patern,* from Latin *pater(noster),* PATER(NOSTER), from the mechanical recitation of the prayer.] **—pat·ter·er** *n.*

pat·tern (păt′ərn) *n.* **1.** A plan, diagram, or model to be followed in making things: *a dress pattern.* **2.** A representative sample; a specimen. **3. a.** An archetype. **b.** An ideal worthy of imitation: *a pattern of womanly virtues.* **4. a.** Any artistic or decorative design: *a paisley pattern.* **b.** A design of natural or accidental origin: *the pattern of ice crystals on a windowpane.* **5.** A recurrent set of features or characteristics: *behavioral patterns.* **6.** Form and style in an artistic work or body of artistic works. **7. a.** The arrangement of identically

PRONUNCIATION KEY

ă, pat; ā, pay; âr, care;
ä, father, are; b, bib;
ch, church; d, deed; ĕ, pet;
ē, be; f, fife; g, gag; h, hat;
hw, which; ĭ, pit; ī, pie;
îr, pier; j, judge; k, kick;
l, lid, needle; m, mum;
n, no, sudden; ng, thing;
ŏ, pot; ō, toe; ô, paw, for;
oi, noise; ou, out; o͝o, book;
o͞o, boot; p, pop; r, roar;
s, sauce; sh, ship, dish;
t, tight; th, thin, path;
th, this, bathe; ŭ, cut; ûr, fur;
v, valve; w, with; y, yes;
z, zebra, size; zh, vision;
ə, about, item, edible,
gallop, circus, peaceful

IN FOREIGN WORDS:

à, *Fr.* ami; œ, *Fr.* feu, *Ger.* schön; ü, *Fr.* tu, *Ger.* über; KH, *Ger.* ich, *Scot.* loch; N, *Fr.* bon; y′, *Fr.* Compiègne

STRESS MARKS:

Primary stress: ′
in·cite′ (ĭn-sīt′)
Secondary stress: ′
in′sight′ (ĭn′sīt′)

aimed rifle shots upon a target. **b.** The distribution and spread of shot from a shotgun. **8.** A standardized diagram transmitted to test television picture quality. **9.** The ordered flight path of an aircraft about to land.
—tr.v. **patterned, -terning, -terns. 1.** To make, mold, or design by following a pattern. Usually used with *on, upon,* or *after.* **2.** To cover or ornament with a design or pattern. [Alteration of Middle English *patron,* from Old French, from Medieval Latin *patrōnus,* patron, (hence) "something to be imitated," pattern. See **patron.**]

Pat·ter·son (păt′ər-sən). Family of U.S. newspaper publishers and editors, including **Robert Wilson** (1850–1910), editor of the Chicago *Tribune* from 1899 until his death. His son **Joseph Medill** (1879–1946) was the founder of the New York *Daily News* (1919), the first successful tabloid publication in the country. Joseph's sister **Eleanor Medill,** known as "Cissy" (1881–1948), formed the Washington *Times-Herald* in 1939 and was known for her flamboyant personal and professional style. Joseph's daughter **Alicia** (1906–63) launched the Long Island tabloid *Newsday* with her husband Harry F. Guggenheim in 1940 and served as its publisher and editor until her death.

Patterson, Floyd (1935–) U.S. prizefighter. He won the Olympic middleweight championship in 1952, then turned professional, losing only one fight before he became, at the age of 21, the youngest man to win the heavyweight title (1956). Patterson held the title until 1959, regained it a year later, and remained champion until 1962.

Pat·ti (păt′ē, pä′tē), **Adelina** (1843–1919). Spanish-born Italian soprano. She had a voice remarkable for its range, timbre, and flexibility.

Pat·ton (păt′n), **George Smith Jr.** (1885–1945). U.S. general. A graduate of West Point (1909), during World War II he commanded the Seventh Army during the Sicilian campaign (1943) and led the Third Army in Europe, breaking through the German defenses in Normandy and crossing France (1944) to reach the Czech border (1945).

pat·ty (păt′ē) *n., pl.* **-ties. 1.** A small, oval, flattened cake of chopped or minced food. **2.** A candy shaped like a paty: *a peppermint patty.* **3.** A patty shell. [French *pâté,* from Old French *paste,* PASTE.]

patty shell *n.* A shell of baked puff pastry made to be filled with creamed meat, seafood, vegetables, or fruit.

pat·u·lous (păch′ōō-ləs) *adj.* Also **pat·u·lent** (-lənt). *Botany.* Spreading or expanded: *patulous branches.* [Latin *patulus,* from *patēre,* to be open.] —**pat·u·lous·ly** *adv.* —**pat·u·lous·ness** *n.*

Pau (pō). Town in southwestern France. Capital of the Pyrénées-Atlantiques department, it is a popular resort and produces textiles and leather. It was the seat of the kings of Navarre.

pau·a (pou′ə) *n.* A New Zealand abalone, *Haliotis iris,* having edible flesh and an ornamental shell used for decoration. [Maori.]

pau·ci·ty (pô′sə-tē) *n.* **1.** Smallness of number; fewness. **2.** Smallness of quantity; a scarcity. [Middle English *paucite,* from Old French, from Latin *paucitās* (stem *paucitāt-*), from *paucus,* few.]

Paul VI (pôl), born Giovanni Battista Montini (1897–1978). Italian pope (1963–78). He reconvened the Second Vatican Council, worked for reform within the Vatican, and reiterated the Church's teachings on contraception in the encyclical *Humanae Vitae* (1968).

Paul, Saint (*c.* A.D. 5–67), known as "Saul of Tarsus." Originally an anti-Christian, he had a vision on the road to Damascus that led to his conversion; his life and doctrines are set forth in the Acts of the Apostles and his epistles.

paul·dron (pôl′drən) *n.* Either of two metal plates in a suit of armor designed to protect the shoulder. [French *espauleron,* from Old French *espaule,* shoulder. See **epaulette.**]

Pau·li (pou′lē), **Wolfgang** (1900–58). Austrian-born U.S. physicist. He was educated at Munich and Copenhagen and in 1925 formulated his exclusion principle of quantum theory. He was awarded the Nobel Prize for physics (1945).

Pauli exclusion principle *n. Physics.* The **exclusion principle** *(see).* [After Wolfgang **Pauli.**]

Paul·ine (pô′lĭn′) *adj.* Of or pertaining to St. Paul, his writings, or his teachings and the theological doctrines derived from them. —**Paul·in·ism** (pô′lə-nĭz′əm) *n.* —**Paul·in·ist** (-nĭst) *n.*

Pau·ling (pô′lĭng), **Linus Carl** (1901–). U.S. biochemist. For his work on the nature of chemical bonding he received the Nobel Prize for chemistry (1954). For his views against nuclear weapons, detailed in *No More War* (1958), he received the Nobel Peace Prize (1962).

Paul Jones (jōnz) *n. British.* A dance in which partners are changed at a given signal. [After John Paul **Jones.**]

pau·low·ni·a (pô-lō′nē-ə) *n.* Any of several trees of the genus *Paulownia,* native to the Orient, having large, heart-shaped leaves and clusters of purplish or white flowers. [New Latin, after Anna *Paulovna* (died 1865), Russian princess.]

paunch (pônch, pänch) *n.* **1.** The belly; especially, a potbelly: *"His hands clasped themselves over his capacious paunch"* (Virginia Woolf).
—tr.v. **paunched, paunching, paunches.** To disembowel (an animal). [Middle English *paunche,* from Norman French, from Old French *pance,* from Latin *pantex†* (stem *pantic-*).] —**paunch·i·ness** *n.* —**paunch·y** *adj.*

pau·per (pô′pər) *n.* **1.** An extremely poor person. **2.** A person living on public charity. [Latin, poor.] —**pau·per·ism** *n.*

pau·per·ize (pô′pə-rīz′) *tr.v.* **-ized, -izing, -izes.** To make a pauper of; impoverish. —**pau·per·i·za·tion** *n.*

Pau·sa·ni·as (pô-sā′nē-əs) (*fl.* 2nd century A.D.). Greek traveler and geographer, probably born in Lydia. His *Description of Greece* is a wealth of information on the topography, monuments, and legends of ancient Greece.

pause (pôz) *intr.v.* **paused, pausing, pauses. 1.** To cease or suspend activity for a time: *She paused to listen.* **2.** To linger; tarry: *pausing for a while at the café.* **3.** To hesitate: *He paused before accepting the task.*
—n. **1.** A hiatus in action or activity; a temporary respite. **2.** A delay or suspended reaction, as from uncertainty; hesitation: *After a pause, the audience burst into cheers.* **3.** A break, stop, or rest in speaking or reading for a calculated purpose or effect: *a pause to let the words sink in.* **4.** *a. Music.* A sign indicating that a note or rest is to be held. **b.** *Prosody.* A measured break or rest; a caesura. **5.** A reason for hesitation. Usually used in the phrase *give one pause.* [Middle English, a pause, from Old French, from Latin *pausa,* from Greek *pausis,* a stopping, from *pauein,* to stop.]

pa·vane, pa·van (pə-vän′, -văn′) *n.* **1.** A slow, stately court dance of the 16th century. **2.** Music for the pavane. [Old French *pavane,* from Old Spanish *pavana,* from Old Italian *(danza) pavanna,* "(dance) of Padua," dialectal variant of *padovana,* feminine of *padovano,* of Padua, from *Padova,* PADUA.]

Pa·va·rot·ti (păv′ə-rŏt′ē, pä′və-), **Luciano** (1935–). Italian tenor. He sang in a local choir before winning a singing competition in Emilia-Romagna when aged 25. He made his debut at La Scala (1965) and now specializes in Verdi and Puccini.

pave (pāv) *tr.v.* **paved, paving, paves. 1.** To cover with any hard, smooth surface that will bear traffic. **2.** To cover uniformly as if with a pavement. **3.** To be or compose the pavement of. —**pave the way.** To make progress or development easier: *experiments that paved the way for future research.* [Middle English *paven,* from Old French *paver,* from Latin *pavīre,* to strike, stamp.] —**pav·er** *n.*

pa·vé (pă-vā′) *n.* **1.** A setting of precious stones placed together so closely that no metal shows: *diamonds in pavé.* **2.** A paved surface. [French, from the past participle of *paver,* to PAVE.]

pave·ment (pāv′mənt) *n.* **1.** A hard, paved surface, especially of a public area or thoroughfare. **2.** The material of which a pavement is made. **3.** *Chiefly British.* A sidewalk. **4.** A hard natural rock surface resulting from weathering, glacial action, or wind erosion.

pavement artist *n. British.* A **sidewalk artist** *(see).*

Pa·vi·a (pə-vē′ə). Capital of Pavia province, Lombardy, northern Italy, on the Ticino River. It was a center of Romanesque art in the 12th and 13th centuries. It is now an agricultural center.

pav·id (păv′ĭd) *adj.* Fearful; frightened; timid. [Latin *pavidus,* from *pavēre,* to fear.]

pa·vil·ion (pə-vĭl′yən) *n.* **1.** An ornate tent, especially of the kind used by knights in medieval Europe. **2.** *a.* A temporary, often open structure used at parks or fairs for amusement or shelter. **b.** A display stand at an exhibition. **3.** A building or other structure connected to a larger building; an annex. **4.** Any of a group of related buildings forming a complex, as of a hospital. **5.** A part of a building that is higher than the rest and usually ornate. **6.** The surface of a brilliant-cut gem that slants outward from girdle to culet. **7.** *British.* A building at the edge of a cricket pitch or other sports ground where players may change and rest.
—tr.v. **pavilioned, -ioning, -ions. 1.** To shelter in or as if in a pavilion. **2.** To provide with a pavilion or pavilions. [Middle English *pavilon,* from Old French *paveillon,* from Latin *pāpiliō†* (stem *pāpiliōn-*), butterfly, tent (from its resemblance to a butterfly's wings).]

pav·ing (pā′vĭng) *n.* **1.** A pavement. **2.** Material used to pave surfaces. Also used adjectivally: *a paving stone.*

pav·ior (pāv′yər) *n.* Also *chiefly British* **pav·iour. 1.** One that paves. **2.** Material or tools used for paving. [Middle English *pavier,* from *paven,* to PAVE.]

pav·is, pav·ise (păv′ĭs) *n.* A medieval shield large enough to protect the whole body. [Middle English, from Old French *pavais,* from Old Italian *pavese,* "of Pavia," from PAVIA, where pavises were first made.]

Pav·lov (păv′lôv′, păv′-), **Ivan Petrovich** (1849–1936). Russian physiologist and experimental psychologist. For his research on the nature of digestion he received the Nobel Prize for physiology and medicine (1904). He is best known for his work on conditioned reflexes in animals.

pav·lov·a (păv-lō′və, păv-) *n.* A meringue cake topped with fruit and whipped cream, popular especially in Australia and New Zealand. [After Anna PAVLOVA.]

Pav·lo·va (păv-lō′və, păv-), **Anna** (1881–1931). Russian ballerina. Making her debut in 1899, she worked with Diaghilev in 1909 and after 1914 toured the world with her own company. Her most famous roles were in *Swan Lake* and *Les Sylphides.*

Pav·lov·i·an (păv-lō′vē-ən, păv-) *adj.* **1.** Of or pertaining to Pavlov or his theories. **2.** Automatic; mechanical: *a Pavlovian response.*

Pa·vo (pā′vō) *n.* A constellation in the Southern Hemisphere near Apus and Indus. [Latin *pāvō,* peacock (probably imitative), obscurely related to Greek *taōs,* a peacock. See also **peacock.**]

pav·o·nine (păv′ə-nīn′) *adj.* **1.** Of or like a peacock. **2.** Resembling a peacock's tail in color, design, or iridescence. [Latin *pāvōnīnus,* from *pāvō,* peacock. See **peacock.**]

paw (pô) *n.* **1.** The nailed or clawed foot of an animal. **2.** *Informal.* A human hand, especially one that is large, clumsy, or dirty.
—v. **pawed, pawing, paws.** *—tr.* **1.** To strike with the paw or paws. **2.** To strike with a repeated scraping motion: *"His black charger pawed the straw"* (W.M. Thackeray). **3.** To handle clumsily, rudely,

or with too much familiarity; caress awkwardly. —*intr.* **1.** To scrape the ground with the forefeet: *The horse pawed restlessly.* **2.** To make clumsy, grasping motions with the hands. [Middle English *pawe, powe,* from Old French *poue,* from Germanic *pauta* (unattested).] —**paw·er** *n.*

pawl (pôl) *n.* A hinged or pivoted device adapted to fit into a notch of a ratchet wheel to impart forward or prevent backward motion. Also called "detent." [Dutch *pal,* possibly from Latin *pālus,* stake.]

pawn¹ (pôn) *n.* **1.** Something given as security for a loan; a pledge. **2.** The condition of being held as a pledge against the payment of a loan: *jewels in pawn.* **3.** A person serving as security; a hostage. **4.** The act of pawning.
~*tr.v.* **pawned, pawning, pawns. 1.** To give or deposit as security for the payment of money borrowed. **2.** To risk; hazard; stake: *pawn one's honor.* [Middle English *paun,* from Old French *pan, pand,* security, from West Germanic *panda* (unattested).] —**pawn·a·ble** *adj.* —**pawn·age** *n.* —**pawn·er, paw·nor** *n.*

pawn² *n.* **1.** *Abbr.* **P** A chessman of the lowest value, allowed to move one square at a time (or two squares for the first move) and capture on a one-space diagonal forward move. **2.** A person or thing used to further the purposes of another. [Middle English *poun, pawne,* from Old French *poon, peon,* from Medieval Latin *pedō* (stem *pedōn-*), a foot soldier, from Latin *pēs* (stem *ped-*), foot.]

pawn·bro·ker (pôn'brō'kər) *n.* One who lends money at interest in exchange for personal property left as security. —**pawn·bro·king** *n.*

Paw·nee (pô-nē') *n., pl.* **-nees** or collectively **Pawnee. 1.** A confederation of four North American Plains Indian peoples of Caddoan linguistic stock in the region of Kansas and Nebraska, now living on a reservation in Oklahoma. **2.** A member of this confederation. **3.** The language of this confederation.

pawn·shop (pôn'shŏp') *n.* The shop of a pawnbroker.

pawpaw. Variant of **papaw.**

Pax·ton (păk'stən), **Sir Joseph** (1801–65). British architect and landscape gardener. While working as chief gardener to the Duke of Devonshire he submitted the winning design for the Crystal Palace to house the Great Exhibition of 1851. He used a greenhouse he had designed as his model, producing one of the earliest examples of prefabricated construction, built of iron and glass.

pay¹ (pā) *v.* **paid** or **payed** (for sense 10), **paying, pays.** —*tr.* **1.** To remunerate or recompense for goods or services rendered. **2.** To give (money) in exchange for goods or services. Often used with *out.* **3.** To give the indicated amount of (money owed); discharge (a debt or obligation): *pay taxes.* **4.** To yield as recompense or return: *This job pays little.* **5.** To undergo; subject oneself to: *pay the penalty.* **6.** To bear the cost of: *He paid my way through college.* **7.** To afford an advantage to; profit: *It paid him to be generous.* **8.** To give or bestow: *pay compliments; pay attention.* **9.** To make (a visit or call). **10.** *Nautical.* To let out (a rope or cable) gradually. Used with *out.* —*intr.* **1.** To make payment. **2.** To discharge a debt or obligation. **3.** To be profitable or worthwhile. —**pay back. 1.** To return borrowed money to. **2.** To avenge oneself on; retaliate against: *paid him back for the unjust treatment he had received.* **3.** To make return to as deserved: *paid her back for her kindness.* —**pay down.** To pay as the first of a series of installment payments at the time of a purchase. —**pay one's dues.** To earn a right or position through hard work, long experience, or suffering. —**pay one's way.** To contribute one's own share; pay for oneself. —**pay the piper.** To bear the consequences of something. —**pay through the nose.** To pay excessively. —**pay up.** To pay the full amount due.
~*adj.* **1.** Requiring payment to operate: *a pay telephone.* **2.** Yielding valuable metal in mining: *a pay stratum.*
~*n.* **1.** The act of paying or state of being paid. **2.** Money given in return for work done; a salary; wages. **3.** Paid employment; hire: *the men in our pay.* **4. a.** Recompense or reward: *His thanks were pay enough.* **b.** Retribution or punishment. **5.** A person considered with regard to his credit or willingness to pay. [Middle English *payen,* from Old French *paier,* from Medieval Latin *pācāre,* to satisfy, pay, from Latin, to pacify, from *pāx* (stem *pāc-*), peace.]

pay² *tr.v.* **payed** or **paid, paying, pays.** *Nautical.* To coat or cover (seams of a ship, for example) with waterproof materials such as tar or asphalt. [Old French *peier,* from Latin *picāre,* to pitch, to tar, from *pix* (stem *pic-*), pitch.]

pay·a·ble (pā'ə-bəl) *adj.* **1.** Requiring payment on a certain date; due. **2.** That can or may be paid. **3.** Capable of producing profit: *a payable business venture.* —**pay·a·bly** *adv.*

pay·check (pā'chĕk') *n.* **1.** A check issued to an employee in payment of salary or wages. **2.** Salary or wages.

pay·day (pā'dā') *n.* The day on which wages are paid.

pay dirt *n.* **1.** Earth, ore, or gravel with enough metal content to make mining profitable. **2.** Something useful or profitable.

P.A.Y.E. 1. pay as you earn. **2.** pay as you enter.

payed. 1. Past tense and past participle of **pay** (to let out a rope). **2.** Alternate past tense and past participle of **pay** (to coat).

pay·ee (pā-ē') *n.* A person to whom money is paid.

pay·er (pā'ər) *n.* **1.** A person who pays. **2.** A person named as responsible for paying a bill or note.

paying guest *n. Abbr.* **P.G.** A lodger or boarder.

pay·load (pā'lōd') *n.* **1.** The revenue-producing part of a cargo. **2.** *Aerospace.* **a.** The passengers, mail, bombs, or cargo in an aircraft. **b.** The warhead of a missile. **c.** In rockets and satellites, the data-collecting and transmitting equipment. **d.** In manned spacecraft, the personnel, life-support system, and equipment necessary to accomplish missions.

pay·mas·ter (pā'măs'tər, -mä'stər) *n. Abbr.* **pm.** An official or employee in charge of paying wages and salaries.

pay·ment (pā'mənt) *n. Abbr.* **payt., pt. 1.** The act of paying or state of being paid. **2.** That which is paid; compensation; recompense. **3.** One's due, reward, or punishment; a requital.

Payne (pān), **John Howard** (1791–1852). U.S. actor, dramatist, and diplomat. He scored theatrical successes in New York, Boston, and Europe and was the first American to play *Hamlet* (1809 in Boston). He is best known for his song "Home, Sweet Home!" composed for his operetta *Clari* (1823).

pay·nim (pā'nĭm) *n. Archaic.* Any non-Christian, especially a Muslim. [Middle English *painim,* from Old French *paienime,* from Late Latin *pāgānismus,* heathendom, from *pāgānus,* PAGAN.]

pay off *tr.v.* **1.** To pay the full amount owed to (a debt). **b.** To get revenge on. **2.** To pay the wages due to and discharge (an employee). **3.** *Informal.* To bribe. —*intr.v.* **1.** To give full return; be profitable: *The effort pays off in the long run.* **2.** *Nautical.* To turn to leeward. Used of a vessel.

pay·off (pā'ôf', -ŏf') *n.* **1. a.** Full payment of a salary or wages. **b.** The time of payment. **2.** *Informal.* **a.** A final settlement or reckoning. **b.** The climax of a narrative, especially of a joke, or of a sequence of events. **3.** Final retribution or revenge. **4.** *Informal.* A bribe. **5.** *Mathematics.* In game theory, the amount gained or lost by a player.

pay·o·la (pā-ō'lə) *n. Slang.* **1.** Bribery; especially, the bribing of disc jockeys to promote records. **2.** Such a bribe. [PAY + (VICTR)OLA, originally of record payoffs.]

pay·roll (pā'rōl') *n.* **1.** A list of employees receiving wages, with the amounts due to each. **2.** The total sum of money to be paid out to employees at a given time.

pay·sage (pā'sĭj, pā'ē-zäzh') *n.* A representation of a rural scene in art; a landscape. [French, landscape, from *pays,* country, Old French *païs,* from Vulgar Latin *pagensis* (unattested), from Latin *pāgus,* rural district.] —**pay·sa·gist** (pā'sə-jĭst) *n.*

pay station *n.* A coin-operated telephone for public use.

payt. payment.

Pb The symbol for the element lead [Latin *plumbum*].

P.B. 1. passbook. **2.** prayer book.

PBX, P.B.X. private branch (telephone) exchange.

pc parsec.

pc. 1. piece. **2.** price.

p.c. 1. after meals. [Latin *post cibum.*] **2.** percent. **3.** petty cash. **4.** postcard.

P.C. 1. Past Commander. **2.** Police Constable. **3.** Post Commander. **4.** Privy Council; Privy Councilor.

p/c, P/C 1. petty cash. **2.** prices current.

pct. percent.

Pd The symbol for the element palladium.

pd. paid.

p.d. 1. per diem. **2.** potential difference.

P.D. 1. per diem. **2.** Police Department.

pe (pā) *n.* The 17th letter of the Hebrew alphabet. See feature at **alphabet.** [Hebrew *peh,* "mouth."]

PE 1. physical education. **2.** potential energy. **3.** printer's error. **4.** probable error.

pea (pē) *n.* **1.** A climbing annual vine, *Pisum sativum,* grown in all temperate zones, and having compound leaves, small white flowers, and edible seeds in a green, elongated pod. **2.** Any of the rounded green seeds of the pea, cooked and eaten as a vegetable. **3. peas.** The unopened pods of the pea plant. **4.** Any of several plants of the genus *Lathyrus,* such as the **sweet pea** or the **beach pea** (*both of which see*). See also **chickpea, cowpea. 5.** *Australian Informal.* One that seems likely to succeed or win. Preceded by *the.* [Taken as singular of earlier *pease,* Middle English *pese,* Old English *pise,* from Late Latin *pīsa,* from Latin, plural of *pīsum,* pea, from Greek *pisont,* a pea.]

Pea·bod·y (pē'bŏd'ē, -bə-dē), **Elizabeth Palmer** (1804–94). U.S. educator and reformer. She was a prominent member of the Transcendental Club and published works by Hawthorne and Margaret Fuller. In 1860 she established the first kindergarten in America.

peace (pēs) *n.* **1.** The absence of war or other hostilities. **2.** An agreement or treaty to end hostilities: *the Peace of Westphalia.* **3.** Freedom from quarrels and disagreement; harmonious relations: *They made peace with each other.* **4.** Public security; law and order: *disturbing the peace.* **5.** Calm; serenity: *peace of mind.* —**at peace. 1.** In a state of tranquillity; serene. **2.** Free from strife. —**hold** (or **keep**) **one's peace.** To be silent. —**keep the peace.** To maintain or observe law and order. —**make one's peace with.** To be reconciled with; renew friendly relations with. [Middle English *pes, pais,* from Old French, from Latin *pāx* (stem *pāc-*).]

Peace. River in British Columbia, Canada, flowing 1,520 kilometers (945 miles) from the Rocky Mts. through wheat-growing areas into the Slave River at Lake Athabaska.

peace·a·ble (pē'sə-bəl) *adj.* **1.** Inclined or disposed to peace; promoting calm: *They met in a peaceable spirit.* **2.** Peaceful; undisturbed. —**peace·a·ble·ness** *n.* —**peace·a·bly** *adv.*

Peace Corps *n.* A federal organization set up in 1961 that trains and sends volunteers abroad to work with people of developing countries on projects for technological, agricultural, and educational improvement.

peace·ful (pēs'fəl) *adj.* **1.** Undisturbed by strife, turmoil, or disagreement; tranquil. **2.** Opposed to strife; peaceable. **3.** Of or characteristic of a condition of peace. —See Synonyms at **calm.** **—peace·ful·ly** *adv.* **—peace·ful·ness** *n.*

peace·mak·er (pēs′mā′kər) *n.* One who makes peace, especially by settling the disputes of others. **—peace·mak·ing** *n.* & *adj.*

peace offering *n.* **1.** Any offering made to an adversary in the interests of peace or reconciliation. **2.** An offering made to God in thanksgiving; especially, a sacrificial offering as prescribed by Levitical law. Leviticus 3:2–6.

peace officer *n.* A law officer, such as a sheriff, responsible for maintaining civil peace.

peace pipe *n.* A **calumet** *(see).*

peace·time (pēs′tīm′) *n.* A time of absence of war. **—peace·time** *adj.*

peach[1] (pēch) *n.* **1.** A small tree, *Prunus persica,* native to China but widely cultivated throughout the temperate zones, having pink flowers and edible fruit. **2.** The soft, juicy, single-seeded fruit of this tree, having white or yellow flesh and downy, red-tinted, yellow skin. **3.** Yellowish pink to light orange. **4.** *Informal.* Any especially admirable or pleasing person or thing.
~*adj.* Of the color peach. [Middle English *peche,* from Old French, from Late Latin *persica,* from Latin, plural of *persicum (mālum),* "Persian (apple)," from *Persicus,* PERSIAN.]

peach[2] *v.* **peached, peaching, peaches.** *Slang.* —*intr.* To inform on someone. —*tr.* To inform against. [Middle English *pechen,* aphetic variant of *impechen,* to IMPEACH.]

peach·blow (pēch′blō′) *n.* A purplish-pink monochrome glaze used on Chinese porcelain. Also called "peachbloom."

peach Melba *n.* A dessert consisting of peach halves, ice cream, and raspberry sauce. [After Dame Nellie MELBA.]

peach·y (pē′chē) *adj.* **-ier, -iest. 1.** Like a peach, especially in color or texture. **2.** *Informal.* Splendid; fine. **—peach·i·ness** *n.*

pea coat *n.* A **pea jacket** *(see).*

pea·cock (pē′kŏk′) *n.* **1. a.** A male peafowl of the genus *Pavo,* distinguished by its crested head, brilliant blue or green feathers, and long tail feathers that are marked with eyelike, iridescent spots and can be spread in a fanlike form. **b.** Loosely, a female peafowl of the genus *Pavo.* **2.** A glossy, greenish-black peafowl, *Afropavo congensis,* from the forests of central Africa, having white plumes on the head. Also called "Congo peacock." **3.** A common butterfly, *Inachis* (or *Nymphalis*) *io,* with red, brown, and black wings each bearing a bright, bluish-purple eyespot. **4.** A vain person given to self-display; a dandy.
~*intr.v.* **peacocked, -cocking, -cocks.** To strut like a peacock; show off. [Middle English *pecok, pocok* : Old English *pēa,* peafowl, from Latin *pāvō,* peacock, obscurely related to Greek *taōs*†, peacock + *cok,* COCK.] **—pea·cock·ish, pea·cock·y** *adj.*

Pea·cock (pē′kŏk′), **Thomas Love** (1785–1866). British novelist and poet. In the service of the East India Company (1819–56), he wrote seven novels, most of them satirical, attacking intellectual fashions and caricaturing the poets of the romantic school, including his friend Shelley. His works include *Headlong Hall* (1816), *Crotchet Castle* (1831), and *Gryll Grange* (1860).

peacock blue *n.* A moderate to dark or strong greenish blue. **—pea·cock-blue** (pē′kŏk-blōō′) *adj.*

pea crab *n.* Any of various small, globular crabs of the genus *Pinnotheres,* the females of which live as commensals within the shells of oysters and similar mollusks.

pea·fowl (pē′foul′) *n., pl.* **-fowls** or collectively **peafowl.** Any of three large pheasants, *Pavo cristatus,* of India and Ceylon, *P. muticus,* of southeastern Asia, or *Afropavo congensis,* of central Africa. [*Peacock* + *fowl.*]

peag, peage (pēg) *n.* North American Indian money, **wampum** *(see).* [Narraganset *wampompeag,* WAMPUM.]

pea green *n.* A moderate, strong, or brilliant yellowish green. **—pea-green** (pē′grēn′) *adj.*

pea·hen (pē′hĕn′) *n.* The female peafowl.

pea jacket *n.* A short, double-breasted coat of heavy navy-blue wool, worn by sailors. Also called "pea coat." [Probably from Dutch *pijjakker* : *pij,* a kind of coarse cloth, from Middle Dutch *pīe*† + *jekker,* a jacket.]

peak[1] (pēk) *n. Abbr.* **pk. 1.** A tapering, projecting point; a pointed extremity: *peak of a cap; peak of a roof.* **2. a.** The pointed summit of a mountain. **b.** The mountain itself: *High Peak.* **3. a.** The point of a beard. **b.** A **widow's peak** *(see).* **4.** The point of greatest development, value, or intensity; height; maximum: *at the peak of her fame.* **5.** *Physics.* The highest value attained by a varying quantity: *a current peak.* **6.** *Nautical.* **a.** The narrow portion of a ship's hull at the bow or stern. **b.** The upper after corner of a fore-and-aft sail. **c.** The outermost end of a gaff. —See Synonyms at **summit.**
~*v.* **peaked, peaking, peaks.** —*tr.* **1.** *Nautical.* To raise (a gaff) above the horizontal. **2.** To raise (the blade of an oar) to a vertical position. **3.** To bring to a peak, head, or maximum. —*intr.* **1.** To be formed into a peak or peaks: *Beat the egg whites until they peak.* **2.** To achieve a maximum of development, value, or intensity.
~*adj.* Approaching or constituting the maximum: *peak efficiency.* [Perhaps back-formation from *peaked,* variant of dialectal *picked,* pointed, from PICK (tool).]

peak[2] *intr.v.* **peaked, peaking, peaks.** To become sickly, emaciated, or pale. [16th century : origin obscure.]

peaked[1] (pēkt, pē′kĭd) *adj.* Ending in a peak; pointed.

peak·ed[2] (pē′kĭd) *adj.* Having a sickly or pale appearance.

peal (pēl) *n.* **1.** A ringing of a set of bells; especially, a change or set of changes rung on bells. **2.** A set of bells tuned to each other; a chime; a carillon. **3.** A loud burst of noise or series of noises, as of laughter or thunder.
~*v.* **pealed, pealing, peals.** —*intr.* To sound in a peal; ring: *The bells pealed out.* —*tr.* To utter loudly and sonorously. [Middle English *pele,* summons to church by bell, short for *appel,* an appeal, from *appelen,* to APPEAL.]

Peale (pēl). Family of U.S. painters. **Charles Willson** (1741–1827) painted portraits, including the earliest known depiction of George Washington (1772). He was also a naturalist and an inventor. His brother **James** (1749–1831) also painted portraits, usually miniatures, including ones of George and Martha Washington. Of Charles Willson Peale's 17 children 4 became painters, perhaps prompted by their given names: **Raphael** (1774–1825), best known for his still lifes and miniatures; **Rembrandt** (1778–1860), a painter and lithographer who specialized in portraits and historical scenes; **Rubens** (1784–1865), a still-life artist; and **Titian** (1799–1885), a naturalist and explorer who painted animals. James's two daughters were also artists: **Anna Claypoole** (1791–1878), a miniaturist, and **Sarah Miriam** (1800–85), a portrait painter.

pean. Variant of **paean.**

pea·nut (pē′nŭt′) *n.* **1.** A vine, *Arachis hypogaea,* native to tropical America and widely cultivated in semitropical regions. It has yellow flowers on stalks that bend over and grow into the soil so that the seed pods ripen underground. **2.** The edible, nutlike, oily seed of this vine, used for food and as a source of oil. Also called "goober," "groundnut," "monkey nut." **3. peanuts.** *Slang.* A very small amount of money; a trifling sum: *Clothes were sold for peanuts at the sale.* **4.** *Slang.* A small or insignificant person.

peanut brittle. *n.* A hard candy containing peanuts.

peanut butter *n.* A paste made from roasted ground peanuts.

peanut oil *n.* The oil pressed from peanuts, used for cooking, in soaps, and as a pharmaceutical vehicle.

pear (pâr) *n.* **1.** A widely cultivated tree, *Pyrus communis,* having glossy leaves, white flowers, and edible fruit. **2.** The fleshy fruit of this tree, spherical at the apex and tapering toward the base. [Middle English *pere,* Old English *peru, pere,* from Latin *pirus,* pear tree, and *pirum,* pear; akin to Greek *apios,* pear tree.] See feature, next page.

pear haw *n.* A shrub or small tree, *Crataegus uniflora,* of southeastern North America, having white flowers and small, orange-red, pear-shaped fruit.

pearl[1] (pûrl) *n.* **1.** A smooth, lustrous, variously colored deposit, chiefly calcium carbonate, formed around a grain of sand or other foreign matter in the shells of certain mollusks and valued as a gem. **2.** Mother-of-pearl; nacre. **3.** A person or object likened to a pearl in beauty or value. **4.** *Printing.* A type size, 5 points. **5. pearls.** A string of pearls. **6.** A yellowish white.
~*v.* **pearled, pearling, pearls.** —*tr.* **1.** To decorate or cover with or as with pearls. **2.** To make into the shape or color of pearls. —*intr.* **1.** To dive or fish for pearls or pearl-bearing mollusks. **2.** To form beads resembling pearls.
~*adj.* **1.** Made of or containing pearl. **2.** Having the shape or color of pearls or mother-of-pearl. [Middle English *perle,* from Old French, from Vulgar Latin *per(nu)la* (unattested), diminutive of Latin *perna,* sea-mussel.]

pearl[2]. Variant of **purl** (embroidery).

pearl ash *n. Chemistry.* **Potassium carbonate** *(see).*

pearl barley *n.* Barley rubbed into small, rounded grains, used in stews and soups.

pearl diver *n.* A person who dives in search of mollusks containing pearls. Also called "pearler."

pearl·er (pûr′lər) *n.* **1.** A pearl diver. **2.** A boat engaged in searching for pearls. **3.** Variant of **purler.**

pearl·es·cent (pûr-lĕs′ənt) *adj.* Having a pearly shine or gloss. **—pearl·es·cence** *n.*

pearl·fish (pûrl′fĭsh′) *n., pl.* **-fishes** or collectively **pearlfish.** Any of various fishes of the family Carapidae, especially of the genus *Fierasfer,* that shelter inside sea cucumbers or occasionally pearl shells.

pearl gray *n.* A yellowish to light bluish gray. **—pearl-gray** (pûrl′grā′) *adj.*

Pearl Harbor. Inlet of the Pacific Ocean on Oahu Island, Hawaii. Site of a U.S. naval base, it was the object of a surprise attack by the Japanese Air Force on December 7, 1941, that precipitated the United States into World War II.

pearl·ite (pûr′līt′) *n.* **1.** A mixture of ferrite and cementite forming distinct layers or bands in slowly cooled carbon steels. **2.** Variant of **perlite.** [French *perlite,* from *perle,* a soft gelatinous capsule, from Old French, PEARL + -ITE.]

pearl·ized (pûr′līzd) *adj.* Having a pearlescent finish.

pearl millet *n.* A tropical grass, *Pennisetum typhoideum,* having long, bulrushlike flowering spikes and whitish seeds that are used as food in the Old World.

pearl oyster *n.* Any of several bivalve marine mollusks of the genus *Pinctada* and related genera, of tropical waters. *P. margaritifera* is a major commercial source of pearls.

pearl·wort (pûrl′wûrt′, -wôrt′) *n.* Any of various short, tufted plants of the genus *Sagina,* bearing tiny white or green flowers.

pearl·y (pûr′lē) *adj.* **-ier, -iest. 1.** Resembling pearls: *pearly teeth.* **2.** Covered or decorated with pearls or mother-of-pearl.

pearly everlasting *n.* A plant, *Anaphalis margaritacea,* having woolly, gray-green foliage and whitish, long-lasting flowers.

Pearly Gates *pl.n.* **1.** *Informal.* The gateway to heaven. **2. pearly gates.** *British Slang.* The teeth.

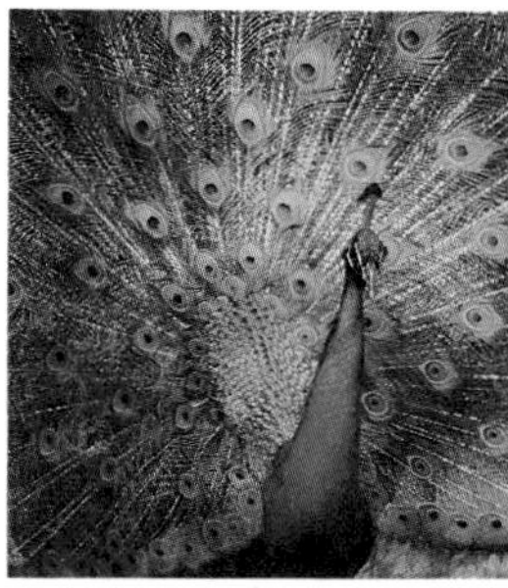

peacock *The eye-marked tail feathers of* Pavo cristatus, *the blue, or Indian, peacock (above), can grow up to 1.5 meters (5 feet) long. The train, which is lifted into a fan during courtship, is possessed only by the male. Each male may have a harem of up to five hens.*

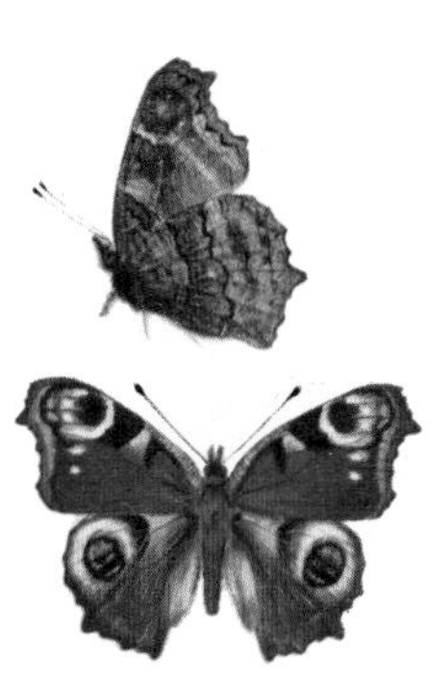

peacock butterfly Inachis io, *the peacock butterfly, is related to the tortoiseshell and red admiral. Adults hibernate in hollow trees or buildings, and the undersides of their wings are dull, looking like dead leaves when they are folded.*

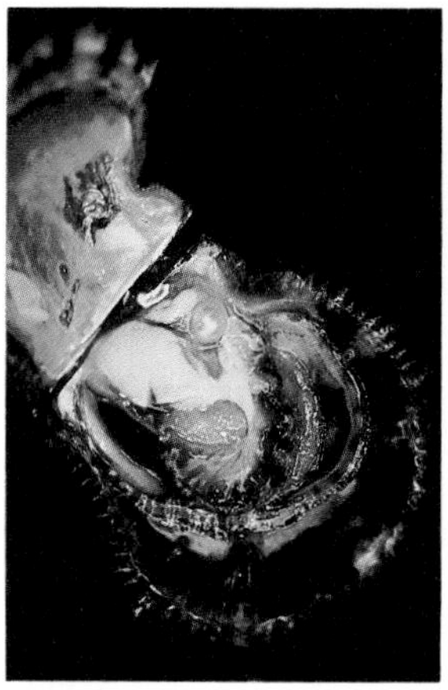

pearl *The pearl oyster—which belongs to the genus* Margaritifer*—has a shell lined with a smooth, iridescent substance known as nacre, or mother-of-pearl. If an irritant, such as a grain of sand, becomes trapped within its shell, the oyster gradually covers it with layers of nacre to reduce the friction, and this process forms the pearl. Cultured pearls, which take about four years to produce, are created by inserting an irritant artificially.*

pear

A SYMBOL OF LONGEVITY THAT BEARS FRUIT
The world's second most important fruit crop

The pear tree is a member of the rose family. As a fruit tree it is taller, straighter, and broader than most, and it lives longer—in China it is a symbol of longevity. Its wood is a warm, dark color and, because it is relatively free from warping, it has been popular for use in veneering and for making musical instruments and mathematical drawing instruments.

The wild pear tree is thorny, with bitter, gritty fruit, and is used as a rootstock onto which cultivated varieties are grafted. In continental Europe, the quince, for instance, is widely used as a rootstock for many varieties of pear, producing a smaller tree that fruits at an earlier age.

Worldwide, pears are the second most important fruit crop after apples, but in the United States they rank third after apples and peaches. Thousands of varieties have been produced since pre-Christian times in Europe alone, but they can be divided into three categories: sweet or dessert pears, cooking pears, and hard, bitter varieties for making perry, a ciderlike drink.

Although pears are cultivated in all countries that have temperate climates, the use of the crop varies. In North America and Australia, for example, half the production is preserved by canning, whereas in Europe most of the pear crop is eaten raw or freshly cooked.

Bartlett comes from 18th-century England.

Kieffer resists fire blight, a scourge of pears.

Seckel, a dessert pear, is small, sweet, and spicy.

Comice, a French pear, does best on the West Coast.

Anjou, a late pear, can be kept until January.

Moonglow pear was developed by U. S. government scientists.

Bosc, a pear from Belgium, reached the United States in 1832.

pearly nautilus *n.* The **chambered nautilus** *(see).*

pear·main (pâr′mān′) *n.* Any of several varieties of red-skinned apple. [Middle English *parmayn,* a kind of pear, from Old French *parmain,* from Vulgar Latin *parmānus* (unattested), of PARMA.]

pear oil *n.* A solvent, **amyl acetate** *(see).*

Pears (pîrz), **Sir Peter** (1910–86). British tenor. He joined Sadlers Wells (1943) and performed the title role in *Peter Grimes,* written by his friend and associate Benjamin Britten.

Pearse (pîrs), **Patrick Henry** (1879–1916). Irish nationalist, poet, and teacher. A leader of the Gaelic revival, particularly in schools, and of the Irish Republican Brotherhood, he commanded the rebels in the Easter Rising (1916), becoming president of the provisional government in an independent Irish republic. After the defeat of the insurgents, he was court-martialed and shot.

Pear·son (pîr′sən), **Lester Bowles** (1897–1972). Canadian Liberal prime minister (1963–68). He represented Canada at the United Nations, became chairman of NATO (1951), and received the Nobel Peace Prize (1957) for his key role in the negotiation of a solution to the Suez crisis (1956).

Pear·y (pîr′ē), **Robert Edwin** (1856–1920). U.S. rear admiral and explorer. He made a total of eight Arctic voyages and on his last expedition became the first man to reach the North Pole (1909).

Peary Land. Peninsula of northern Greenland. At its northernmost point, Cape Morris Jessup, it is 710 kilometers (440 miles) from the North Pole and is the world's most northerly point of land. A mountainous region, it was first explored by Robert Peary (1892).

peas·ant (pĕz′ənt) *n.* **1.** A member of the class comprising small farmers and tenants and laborers on the land where these constitute the main labor force in agriculture. **2.** A countryman; a rustic. **3.** An uncouth, crude, or ill-bred person; a boor. [Middle English *paissaunt,* from Old French *païsant,* from *païs,* country, from Medieval Latin *pāgēnsis,* "inhabitant of a district," rustic, peasant, from Latin *pāgus,* a district, canton, rural area.]

peas·ant·ry (pĕz′ən-trē) *n.* **1.** The social class constituted by peasants. **2. a.** The condition or rank of a peasant. **b.** Conduct or manners thought to be characteristic of peasants.

pease (pēz) *n., pl.* **pease** or **peasen** (pē′zən). *Obsolete.* A pea.

pease-cod, peas·cod (pēz′kŏd′) *n. Obsolete.* The pod of the pea. [Middle English *pesecod* : *pese,* PEA + COD (pod).]

pease pudding *n. Chiefly British.* A purée made from boiled dried peas. [*Pease,* Old English *pise* (plural *pisan*), PEA.]

pea-shoot·er (pē′shōō′tər) *n.* A toy consisting of a small tube through which dried peas or other pellets are blown at a target.

pea soup *n.* **1.** A purée or soup made of dried or fresh peas. **2.** *Slang.* Dense fog.

peat (pēt) *n.* Partially decomposed, compacted vegetable matter, usually mosses or sedges, found in bogs and fens, and used as fertilizer and fuel. [Middle English *pete,* from Medieval Latin *peta,* probably from Celtic, akin to Medieval Latin *pecia, petia,* PIECE.] —**peat·y** *adj.*

peat bog *n.* A **bog** *(see).*

peat moss *n.* **1.** Any moss, especially of the genus *Sphagnum,* growing in fens. **2.** The partly decomposed remains of such mosses, used as a mulch and plant food. Also called "bog moss."

peau de soie (pō′ də swä′) *n.* A smooth, satiny fabric of silk or rayon. [French, "skin of silk."]

pea·vey (pē′vē) *n., pl.* **-veys.** Also **pea·vy** *pl.* **-vies.** A wooden lever with a metal point and a hinged hook near the end, used by lumberjacks to handle logs. Compare **cant hook.** [After Joseph *Peavey,* American blacksmith, to whom its invention (about 1870) has been attributed.]

peb·ble (pĕb′əl) *n.* **1.** A small stone worn smooth by erosion. **2. a.** Clear, colorless quartz; rock crystal. **b.** A lens made of such quartz. **3.** A crinkled surface, as on leather or paper. **4.** *Australian Informal.* An obstinate or intractable person or animal.
—*adj.* Designating a spectacle lens that is thick and has high powers of magnification.
—*tr.v.* **pebbled, -bling, -bles. 1.** To pave or pelt with pebbles. **2.** To impart an irregularly rough, grainy surface to (leather or paper). [Middle English *pibbil, puble,* Old English *papol(stān)* : *papol-,* pebble (probably imitative) + *stān,* STONE.] —**peb·bly** *adj.*

peb·ble·dash (pĕb′əl-dăsh′) *n.* Mortar in which small pebbles are embedded, used as a finish for outside walls.
—*tr.v.* **pebbledashed, -dashing, -dashes.** To cover or coat with pebbledash.

pe·can (pĭ-kän′, -kăn′) *n.* **1.** A tree, *Carya illinoensis,* of the southern United States, having deeply furrowed bark and edible nuts. **2.** The smooth, thin-shelled, oval nut of the pecan. [Earlier *paccan,* from Algonquian, akin to Ojibwa *pagân,* Abnaki *pagann,* and Cree *pakan,* hard-shell nut.]

pec·ca·ble (pĕk′ə-bəl) *adj.* Liable to sin. [Old French, from Latin *peccāre,* to sin. See **peccant.**] —**pec·ca·bil·i·ty** *n.*

pec·ca·dil·lo (pĕk′ə-dĭl′ō) *n., pl.* **-loes** or **-los.** A small sin or fault. [Spanish *pecadillo,* diminutive of *pecado,* sin, from Latin *peccātum,* from *peccāre,* to sin. See **peccant.**]

pec·cant (pĕk′ənt) *adj.* **1.** Sinful; guilty. **2.** Violating a rule or accepted practice; erring; faulty. [Latin *peccāns* (stem *peccant-*), present participle of *peccāre,* to sin, stumble.] —**pec·can·cy** *n.* —**pec·cant·ly** *adv.*

pec·ca·ry (pĕk′ə-rē) *n., pl.* **-ries.** Either of two piglike, hoofed mammals, *Tayassu angulatus* or *T. pecari,* of southern North America, Central America, and South America, having dense, long, dark bristles. [Spanish *pecari,* from Carib *pakira.*]

pec·ca·vi (pĕ-kä′vī′, -kä′vē) *n., pl.* **-vis.** A confession of sin. [Latin, "I have sinned."]
Pe·chen·ga (pə-chĕn′gə, pĕch′ən-gə). Port on the Barents Sea, northwestern U.S.S.R. Ice-free, it has a large fishing fleet and is the center of a strategic mining region. The area was part of Finland from 1920 to 1944.
Pe·cho·ra (pə-chôr′ə, -chōr′ə). River of European U.S.S.R. It rises in the Ural Mts. and flows northward for 1,790 kilometers (1,112 miles) to the Barents Sea, passing through the important Pechora coal basin.
peck[1] (pĕk) *v.* **pecked, pecking, pecks.** —*tr.* **1.** To strike with a beak or some sharp-pointed instrument. **2.** To make (a hole, for example) by striking repeatedly with the beak or a pointed instrument. **3.** To grasp and pick up with the beak: *The bird pecked insects from the log.* **4.** *Informal.* To kiss briefly and casually: *He pecked her on the cheek.* —*intr.* **1.** To make strokes with the beak or something pointed like a beak: *the noise of birds pecking outside.* **2.** To eat in small, sparing bits; nibble. Used with *at*: *pecking at her food.* **3.** To criticize repeatedly; nag; carp. Used with *at.*
∼*n.* **1.** A stroke or light blow with the beak. **2.** A mark or hole made by such a stroke. **3.** *Informal.* A light, quick kiss. [Middle English *pecken,* probably from Middle Low German *pekken*†.]
peck[2] *n. Abbr.* **pk., pk 1. a.** A unit of volume or capacity in the U.S. System, used in dry measure, equal to 8 quarts or 537.605 cubic inches. **b.** A unit of volume or capacity in the British system, used in dry measure, equal to 554.84 cubic inches. **2.** A container holding or measuring this amount. **3.** *Informal.* A great deal: *a peck of troubles.* [Middle English, from Old French *pek*†.]
Peck (pĕk), **George Wilbur** (1840–1916). U.S. journalist, humorist, and politician. Best known for his Peck's Bad Boy stories, first published in book form in 1883, he was also mayor of Milwaukee and governor of Wisconsin (1890–95).
Peck, Gregory, born Eldred Gregory Peck (1916–). U.S. motion-picture actor. He made his first films in 1944 and soon became famous for his performances in films such as *Spellbound* (1945), *Duel in the Sun* (1946), *Twelve O'Clock High* (1949), and *The Gunfighter* (1950). He received an Academy Award for his performance in *To Kill a Mockingbird* (1962).
peck·er (pĕk′ər) *n.* **1.** One who or that which pecks. **2.** *British Slang.* Courage; pluck.
pecking order *n.* **1.** A hierarchy within certain flocks of birds, especially poultry, according to which each member submits to pecking and domination by the stronger or more aggressive members, and has the privilege of pecking and dominating the weaker members. Also called "peck order." **2.** A hierarchy in a human group. [Translation of German *Hackordnung.*]
Peck·in·pah (pĕk′ĭn-pä′), **(David) Sam(uel)** (1925–84). U.S. film director. He began by working for television on such serials as *Gunsmoke.* His often violent films, several of which are Westerns, include *The Wild Bunch* (1969) and *Straw Dogs* (1971).
peck·ish (pĕk′ĭsh) *adj. Informal.* **1.** Somewhat hungry. **2.** Peevish; irritable.
Peck·sniff·i·an (pĕk-snĭf′ē-ən) *adj.* Addicted to fatuous and hypocritical talk of benevolence and other virtues. [After Seth *Pecksniff,* a character in Dickens' novel *Martin Chuzzlewit* (1844).]
pec·o·ri·no (pĕk′ə-rē′nō) *n.* A hard, pale yellow Italian cheese made from ewe's milk. [Italian (adjective), of ewes, from *pecora,* sheep, from Latin, cattle, plural of *pecu* (stem *pecor-*), herd, cattle.]
Pe·cos (pā′kəs). River of the southern United States. It flows 1,180 kilometers (735 miles) across New Mexico and Texas to join the Rio Grande.
pec·tase (pĕk′tās′, -tāz′) *n.* An enzyme found in certain fruits that catalyzes the conversion of pectins to pectic acids. [PECT(IN) + -ASE.]
pec·tate (pĕk′tāt′) *n.* A salt or ester of pectic acid. [PECT(IC ACID) + -ATE.]
pec·ten (pĕk′tən) *n., pl.* **-tens** or **-tines** (-tə-nēz′). *Zoology.* **1.** Any body structure or organ resembling a comb, such as the ridged part of the eye of reptiles and birds. **2.** A scallop of the genus *Pecten.* [New Latin, from Latin, comb.]
pec·tic acid (pĕk′tĭk) *n. Chemistry.* Any of several colloidal substances, essentially complex organic acids, derived from the sugar galactose. [French *pectique,* related to pectin. See **pectin.**]
pec·tin (pĕk′tĭn) *n.* Any of a group of complex colloidal substances of high molecular weight found in ripe fruits, such as apples, and used to form a gel when heated with sugar, as in making jam. [French *pectine,* from *pectique,* from Greek *pēktikos,* coagulating, from *pēktos,* coagulated, from *pēgnunai,* to coagulate.] —**pec·tic** (pĕk′tĭk), **pec·tin·ous** (-tĭ-nəs) *adj.*
pec·tin·ase (pĕk′tə-nās′, -nāz′) *n.* A plant enzyme that catalyzes the hydrolysis of pectin.
pec·ti·nate (pĕk′tə-nāt′) *adj.* Also **pec·ti·nat·ed** (-nā′tĭd). Shaped like a comb; comblike. [Latin *pecten* (stem *pectin-*), comb, PECTEN + -ATE.] —**pec·ti·na·tion** *n.*
pec·to·ral (pĕk′tər-əl) *adj.* **1.** *Anatomy.* Pertaining to the breast or chest: *a pectoral muscle.* **2.** *Medicine.* Useful in diseases of the chest. **3.** Worn on the chest or breast: *a pectoral cross.*
∼*n.* **1.** A chest muscle or organ. **2.** A pectoral fin. **3.** A medicine for chest diseases. **4.** An ornament or decoration worn on the chest. [Middle English, from Old French, of or worn on the chest, from Latin *pectorālis,* from *pectus* (stem *pector-*), breast.]
pectoral arch *n.* The **pectoral girdle** *(see).*
pectoral fin *n.* Either of the anterior pair of fins attached to the pectoral girdle of fishes. Also called "pectoral."
pectoral girdle *n. Zoology.* A skeletal structure in vertebrates, attached to and supporting the forelimbs or fins. Also called "pectoral arch," and, chiefly in humans, "shoulder girdle."
pec·u·late (pĕk′yə-lāt′) *v.* **-lated, -lating, -lates.** —*tr.* To embezzle or take for one's own use. —*intr.* To steal money or goods entrusted to one. [Latin *pecūlārī,* to embezzle, from *pecūlium,* "wealth in cattle," private property, from *pecu,* cattle.] —**pec·u·la·tion** *n.* —**pec·u·la·tor** *n.*
pe·cu·liar (pĭ-kyōōl′yər) *adj.* **1.** Unusual or eccentric; strange; queer. **2.** Calling for special consideration or attention; distinct and particular. **3. a.** Exclusive; unique: *the peculiar attributes of beauty.* **b.** Belonging distinctively or especially to one person, group, or kind: *He spoke with an accent peculiar to his native county.* —See Synonyms at **characteristic, strange.**
∼*n.* **1.** Some privilege or property that belongs exclusively to one. **2.** *British.* A church or parish under the jurisdiction of a diocese different from that in which it lies. **3.** *Printing.* A **special sort** *(see).* [Middle English *peculier,* from Latin *pecūliāris,* individual, peculiar, of private property, from *pecūlium,* "wealth in cattle," private property, from *pecu,* cattle, wealth.] —**pe·cu·liar·ly** *adv.*
pe·cu·li·ar·i·ty (pĭ-kyōō′lē-ăr′ə-tē, pĭ-kyōōl-yăr′-) *n., pl.* **-ties. 1.** The quality or state of being peculiar. **2. a.** A notable or distinctive feature or characteristic. **b.** An eccentricity; an idiosyncrasy; a quirk.
pe·cu·ni·ar·y (pĭ-kyōō′nē-ĕr′ē) *adj.* **1.** Consisting of or pertaining to money: *a pecuniary loss; pecuniary motives.* **2.** Requiring the payment of money: *a pecuniary offense.* —See Synonyms at **financial.** [Latin *pecūniārius,* from *pecūnia,* "wealth in cattle," property, money, from *pecu,* cattle.]
ped–. 1. Variant of **pedo-** (soil). **2.** Variant of **pedo-** (child).
–ped, –pede *suffix.* Indicates foot or feet; for example, **biped, centipede.** [Latin *pēs* (stem *ped-*), foot.]
ped·a·gog·ic (pĕd′ə-gŏj′ĭk, -gō′jĭk) *adj.* Also **ped·a·gog·i·cal** (-gŏj′ĭ-kəl, -gō′jĭ-kəl) *adj.* **1.** Of, pertaining to, or characteristic of teaching or teachers. **2.** Characterized by pedantic formality. —**ped·a·gog·i·cal·ly** *adv.*
ped·a·gog·ics (pĕd′ə-gŏj′ĭks, -gō′jĭks) *n. Used with a singular verb.* The art of teaching; education; pedagogy.
ped·a·gogue (pĕd′ə-gŏg′, -gôg′) *n.* **1.** A schoolteacher; an educator. **2.** One who instructs in a pedantic or dogmatic manner. [Middle English *pedagoge,* from Old French *pedagogue,* from Latin *paedagōgus,* from Greek *paidagōgos,* teacher, trainer (of boys) : *paid-,* PEDO- + *agōgos,* leader, from *agein,* to lead.] —**ped·a·gogu·ish** *adj.*
ped·a·go·gy (pĕd′ə-gō′jē, -gŏj′ē) *n.* **1.** The art or profession of teaching. **2.** Preparatory training or instruction.
ped·al (pĕd′l) *n.* **1. a.** A lever operated by the foot on various musical instruments, such as the piano, organ, or harp. **b.** Any of various electronic devices used to modify the signal from an electronic instrument, especially a guitar. **2.** A pedal point. **3.** A lever worked by the foot in a machine, such as a motor vehicle, bicycle, or sewing machine.
∼*adj.* **1.** Pertaining to a foot or footlike part: *the pedal extremities.* **2.** *Music.* Pertaining to a pedal.
∼*v.* **pedaled, -aling, -als.** Also *chiefly British* **-alled, -alling.** —*intr.* **1.** To use or operate a pedal or pedals. **2.** To ride a bicycle. —*tr.* To operate the pedals of. [French *pédale,* from Italian *pedale,* (organ) pedal, from Latin *pedālis,* of the foot, from *pēs,* foot.]
ped·al·board (pĕd′l-bôrd′, -bōrd′) *n.* A bank of foot-operated keys, as on an organ.
pe·dal·fer (pĭ-dăl′fər) *n. Geology.* Soil rich in aluminum and iron and deficient in carbonates, characteristic of humid, high-temperature regions with forest cover. Compare **pedocal.** [PED(O)- (soil) + AL(UM) + Latin *ferrum,* iron.]
ped·a·lo (pĕd′l-ō′) *n., pl.* **-los** or **-loes.** *Chiefly British.* A small pleasure boat propelled by paddle wheels operated by pedals. [From PEDAL.]
pedal point *n. Music.* A note, usually in the bass and on the tonic or the dominant, sustained through harmonic changes in the other parts. Also called "pedal."
pedal pushers *pl.n.* Calf-length women's and girls' slacks, originally worn for cycling.
ped·ant (pĕd′ənt) *n.* **1.** One who pays undue attention to book learning and formal rules or details without having true insight or understanding. **2.** One who exhibits his learning or scholarship ostentatiously. **3.** *Archaic.* A schoolmaster; a pedagogue. [Old French, from Old Italian *pedante,* probably from Latin *paedagōgāns,* present participle of *paedagōgāre,* to instruct, from *paedagōgus,* PEDAGOGUE.] —**pe·dan·tic** (pə-dăn′tĭk), **pe·dan·ti·cal** *adj.* —**pe·dan·ti·cal·ly** *adv.*
ped·ant·ry (pĕd′n-trē) *n., pl.* **-ries. 1.** Excessive attention to detail or rules in learning or teaching. **2. a.** The habit of mind or manner characteristic of a pedant. **b.** An instance of pedantic behavior.
ped·ate (pĕd′āt′) *adj.* **1.** *Zoology.* Having feet. **2.** Resembling or functioning as a foot or feet: *pedate appendages.* **3.** *Botany.* Having radiating lobes or divisions, with the lateral lobes cleft or divided: *a pedate leaf.* [Latin *pedātus,* from *pēs* (stem *ped-*), foot.]
ped·dle (pĕd′l) *v.* **-dled, -dling, -dles.** —*tr.* **1.** To travel about selling (wares): *peddling goods from door to door.* **2.** To sell (narcotic drugs, for example), especially in small quantities. **3.** To try to spread or circulate (ideas or opinions). —*intr.* To travel about selling wares. [Back-formation from PEDDLER.]
ped·dler, ped·lar, ped·ler (pĕd′lər) *n.* One who peddles for a liv-

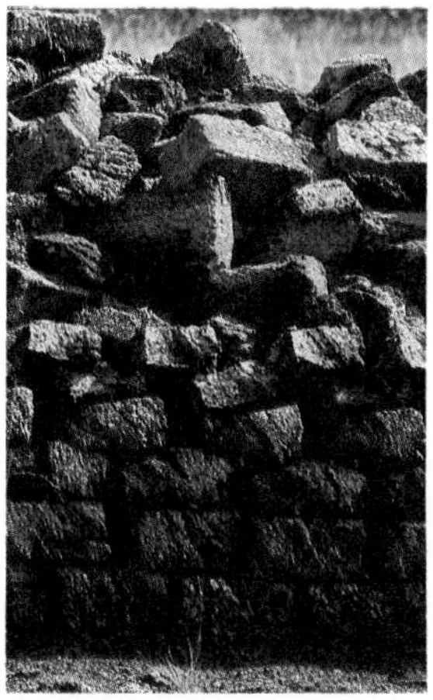

peat *The remains of decomposing vegetable matter, peat is found in boggy regions with temperate climates. It is the first stage in nature's production of coal and is cut from the ground in blocks, dried, and used as a fuel.*

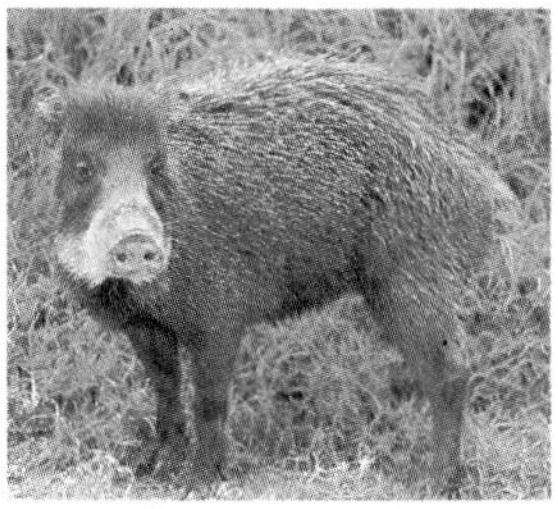

peccary *Peccaries live in packs of about a dozen animals in southern North America, Central and South America. A full-grown peccary can weigh about 30 kilograms (65 pounds).*

ing; a hawker. Also called "packman." [Middle English *pedlere*, probably altered from *peddere*, from *peddet*, covered basket.] —**ped·dler·y** *n.*

ped·er·ast (pĕd′ə-răst′) *n.* One who practices pederasty. [Back-formation from PEDERASTY.]

ped·er·as·ty (pĕd′ə-răs′tē) *n.* Homosexual relations, especially between a male adult and a boy or young man. [New Latin *paederastia*, from Greek *paiderastia* : *pais* (stem *paid*-), boy + *erastēs*, lover (from *eros*, sexual love, EROS).]

ped·es. Plural of **pes.**

ped·es·tal (pĕd′ə-stəl) *n.* **1.** An architectural support or base, as for a column or statue. **2.** Either of the supports for a kneehole desk, usually consisting of a set of drawers. **3.** Any support or foundation. —**put on a pedestal.** To treat with exaggerated regard, ignoring imperfections.
~*tr.v.* **pedestaled, -taling, -tals.** Also chiefly British **-talled, -talling.** To place on or provide with a pedestal. [Old French *piedestal*, from Old Italian *piedestallo*, from *pie di stallo*, "foot of a stall" : *pie*, foot, from Latin *pēs* + *di*, of + *stallo*, stall.]

pe·des·tri·an (pə-dĕs′trē-ən) *n.* A person traveling on foot; a walker, especially in a town or city.
~*adj.* **1.** Of, suitable for, pertaining to, or designed for pedestrians: *pedestrian traffic.* **2.** Going or performed on foot: *a pedestrian journey.* **3.** Commonplace; undistinguished; ordinary. [Latin *pedester*, going on foot, hence prosaic, from *pedes*, one who goes on foot, from *pēs* (stem *ped*-), a foot.] —**pe·des·tri·an·ism** *n.*

pedestrian crossing *n.* A crosswalk.

pedi- *prefix.* Indicates foot; for example, **pediform.** [Latin, from *pēs* (stem *ped*-), foot.]

pe·di·a·tri·cian (pē′dē-ə-trĭsh′ən) *n.* Also **pe·di·at·rist** (pē′dē-ăt′rĭst). A physician who specializes in pediatrics.

pe·di·at·rics (pē′dē-ăt′rĭks) *n. Used with a singular verb.* The branch of medicine that deals with the care of babies and children and the treatment of their diseases. [PED(O)- + -IATRICS.] —**pe·di·at·ric** *adj.* —**pe·di·at·ri·cal·ly** *adv.*

ped·i·cel (pĕd′ə-səl, -sĕl′) *n.* Also **ped·i·cle** (pĕd′ĭ-kəl). **1.** *Biology.* A small stalk, part, or organ, especially one serving as a support. **2.** *Botany.* **a.** Any of several small stalks bearing a single flower in an inflorescence. **b.** A support for a fern sporangium or moss capsule. **3.** The second segment of an insect's antenna. [New Latin *pedicellus*, diminutive of Latin *pedīculus*, little foot, pedicel, from *pēs*, a foot.]

ped·i·cel·late (pĕd′ə-sĕl′ĭt, -āt′) *adj.* Also **ped·i·cel·lar** (-ər). Having or supported by a pedicel.

pedicle *n.* Variant of **pedicel.**

pe·dic·u·lar (pə-dĭk′yə-lər) *adj.* Of or caused by lice. [Latin *pedīculāris*, from *pedīculus*, louse, diminutive of *pedis*, louse.]

pe·dic·u·late (pə-dĭk′yə-lĭt, -lāt′) *adj.* Of or pertaining to marine fishes of the order Pediculati (or Lophiiformes), which includes the anglerfish.
~*n.* A fish of this order. [New Latin *Pediculati*, "little-footed ones" (from the shape of their pectoral fins), from Latin *pedīculus*, little foot. See **pedicel.**]

pe·dic·u·lo·sis (pə-dĭk′yə-lō′sĭs) *n.* Infestation with lice. [New Latin : Latin *pēdīculus*, louse (see **pedicular**) + -OSIS.] —**pe·dic·u·lous** (pə-dĭk′yə-ləs) *adj.*

ped·i·cure (pĕd′ĭ-kyŏŏr′) *n.* **1. a.** Cosmetic care of the feet and toenails. **b.** A single cosmetic treatment of the feet and toenails. **2.** A chiropodist.
~*tr.v.* **pedicured, -curing, -cures.** To give a pedicure to. [French *pédicure* : PEDI- + Latin *cūrāre*, to take care of, from *cūra*, care.] —**ped·i·cur·ist** *n.*

ped·i·form (pĕd′ə-fôrm′) *adj.* Shaped like a foot. [French *pédiforme* : PEDI- + -FORM.]

ped·i·gree (pĕd′ə-grē′) *n.* **1.** Recorded ancestry; lineage: *"Every form in literature has a pedigree"* (Northrop Frye). **2.** A list of ancestors; a family tree. **3.** The recorded descent of a purebred animal. Also used adjectivally: *a pedigree horse.* **4.** A source or derivation. [Middle English *pedegru*, from Old French *pie de grue*, "crane's foot," from the three-line, claw-shaped mark formerly used to show the succession in a pedigree : *pie*, foot, from Latin *pēs* + *de*, of + *grue*, crane, from Latin *grūs*.] —**ped·i·greed** *adj.*

ped·i·ment (pĕd′ə-mənt) *n.* **1.** A wide, low-pitched gable surmounting the façade of a building in the Grecian style. **2.** A similar or derivative element used widely in architecture and decoration. **3.** A sloping rock surface, usually covered with alluvium, found in desert areas at the base of mountains. [Variant of earlier *perement*, probably variant (influenced by PEDI-) of PYRAMID.] —**ped·i·men·tal** (pĕd′ə-mĕnt′l) *adj.* —**ped·i·ment·ed** *adj.*

ped·i·palp (pĕd′ə-pălp′) *n.* Either of the second pair of appendages in arachnids that are attached to the head and may be adapted as sensory organs, as in spiders, or as claws, as in scorpions. Also called "palp." [New Latin *pedipalpus.* See **pedi-, palp.**]

pedlar, pedler *n.* Variants of **peddler.**

pedo-¹, ped- *prefix.* Indicates soil; for example, **pedalfer, pedocal.** [Greek *pedon*, earth, soil.]

pedo-², ped- Also chiefly British **paedo-, paed-.** *prefix.* Indicates child; for example, **pediatrics, pedodontia.** [Greek *paido-*, from *pais*, child.]

ped·o·cal (pĕd′ə-kăl′) *n. Geology.* A lime-rich soil of cool, semiarid, and arid regions. Compare **pedalfer.** [PEDO- (soil) + Latin *calx*, lime, limestone, from Greek *khalix*, pebble, small stone.] —**ped·o·cal·ic** (pĕd′ə-kăl′ĭk) *adj.*

pe·do·don·tia (pē′də-dŏn′shə, -shē-ə) *n.* The dentistry of children's teeth. [PED(O)- (child) + -ODONT + -IA.] —**pe·do·don·tist** *n.*

pe·dol·o·gy¹ (pē-dŏl′ə-jē) *n.* The study of the behavior and development of children. [PEDO- (child) + -LOGY.] —**pe·do·log·ic** (pē′də-lŏj′ĭk), **pe·do·log·i·cal** *adj.* —**pe·do·log·i·cal·ly** *adv.* —**pe·dol·o·gist** *n.*

ped·o·log·y² (pĭ-dŏl′ə-jē, pĕ-dŏl′-) *n.* The scientific study of soils, their origins, characteristics, and uses. Compare **agrology.** [PEDO- (soil) + -LOGY.] —**ped·o·log·ic** (pĕd′ə-lŏj′ĭk), **ped·o·log·i·cal** *adj.* —**ped·o·log·i·cal·ly** *adv.* —**pe·dol·o·gist** *n.*

pe·dom·e·ter (pĭ-dŏm′ə-tər) *n.* An instrument that gauges the approximate distance traveled on foot by registering the number of steps taken. [French *pédomètre* : *pedo-*, variant of PEDI- + -METER.]

pe·dun·cle (pĭ-dŭng′kəl, pē′dŭng′kəl) *n.* **1.** *Botany.* The main stalk of an inflorescence, or a stalk or stem bearing a solitary flower. **2.** *Zoology.* A stalklike structure in various invertebrate animals. **3.** *Anatomy.* A stalklike bundle of fibers, especially of nerve fibers, connecting different parts of the central nervous system. [New Latin *pedunculus*, diminutive of Latin *pēs* (stem *ped*-), a foot.] —**pe·dun·cu·lar** (pĭ-dŭng′kyə-lər) *adj.*

pe·dun·cu·late (pĭ-dŭng′kyə-lĭt, -lāt′) *adj.* Also **pe·dun·cu·lat·ed** (-lā′tĭd). Having or supported on a peduncle.

pedunculate oak *n.* The common or English oak, *Quercus robur*, having acorns borne on long peduncles. See **oak.**

Pee·bles·shire (pē′bəl-shĭr′, -shər). Former county of southeastern Scotland, now part of the Borders Region. Peebles was its county town.

peek (pēk) *intr.v.* **peeked, peeking, peeks. 1.** To glance quickly. **2.** To look or peer furtively, as from a place of concealment.
~*n.* A furtive or brief look. [Middle English *piken*†.]

peek·a·boo (pē′kə-bōō′) *n.* A child's game in which one repeatedly covers and exposes one's face, exclaiming "peekaboo!"
~*adj.* Having a pattern of small holes. Said of a garment or fabric. [PEEK + BOO; akin to Dutch *kiekeboe*.]

peel¹ (pēl) *n.* The skin or rind of certain fruits, such as the orange or apple.
~*v.* **peeled, peeling, peels.** —*tr.* **1.** To strip or cut away the skin, rind, or bark from; pare. **2.** To strip away; pull off (an outer covering). **3.** To put (another player's ball) through a hoop in croquet. —*intr.* **1.** To lose or shed skin, bark, or other covering. **2.** To come off in thin strips or pieces, as bark, skin, or paint may. **3.** *Slang.* To remove one's clothes; undress. —**peel off.** To leave flight formation in order to land or make a dive. Used of an aircraft. [Middle English *pelen*, from Old French *peler*, to peel, remove hair from, from Latin *pilāre*, to plunder, "pile up (booty)," from *pīa*, "pile," PILLAR.]

peel² *n.* **1.** A long-handled, shovellike tool used by bakers to move bread or pastries into and out of an oven. **2.** Formerly, a T-shaped pole used by printers for hanging freshly printed sheets of paper to dry. [Middle English *pele*, from Old French, shovel, from Latin *pāla*, spade.]

peel³ *n.* Any of several fortified houses or towers constructed in the border area between Scotland and England in the 16th century. [Middle English *pel(e)*, castle, small tower, (originally) palisade, from Norman French, from Latin *pālus*, stake.]

Peel (pēl), **Sir Robert** (1788-1850). British Conservative prime minister (1834-35 and 1841-46). Entering Parliament as a Tory (1809), he served as secretary for Ireland (1812-18) and was home secretary (1821-27, 1828-30), during which time he reorganized and consolidated the London police as the Metropolitan Police (1829) and helped pass the Catholic Emancipation Act (1829). After the passing of the parliamentary Reform Bill (1832), he outlined the reform program of the emergent Conservative Party with the Tamworth Manifesto (1834). Following the split between the traditional protectionist Tories and the new Conservatives over free trade and the repeal of the Corn Laws (1846), his government fell, after which he gave his support to the Whigs.

peel·er¹ (pē′lər) *n.* **1.** A person or device that peels; especially, a kitchen implement for peeling the rind or skin from a fruit or vegetable. **2.** *Slang.* A stripteaser.

peeler² *n. British Slang.* A policeman. Not in current usage. [After Sir Robert PEEL.]

peel·ing (pē′lĭng) *n.* A piece or strip that has been peeled off, as of skin, bark, or rind.

peen (pēn) *n.* The end of a hammerhead opposite the flat striking surface, often wedge-shaped or ball-shaped and used for chipping, indenting, and metalworking.
~*tr.v.* **peened, peening, peens.** To hammer, bend, or shape with a peen. [*Peen, pane*, perhaps from French *panne*, from Dutch *pen*, from Latin *pinna*, point.]

Pee·ne·mün·de (pā′nə-mōōn′də). Fishing village in East Germany. Situated on the Isle of Usedom on the Baltic coast, it was a center for the development of guided missiles prior to and during World War II (1937-45), producing the V-1 robot bomb and the V-2 rocket.

peep¹ (pēp) *n.* **1.** A weak, shrill sound or utterance, like that of a young bird. **2.** Any slight sound or utterance: *I don't want to hear a peep out of you.* **3.** Any of various North American sandpipers.
~*intr.v.* **peeped, peeping, peeps. 1.** To utter short, soft, high-pitched sounds, like those of a baby bird. **2.** To speak in a thin, high-pitched voice. [Middle English *pepen* (imitative).]

peep² *v.* **peeped, peeping, peeps.** —*intr.* **1.** To look furtively; steal a quick glance. **2.** To peer through a small opening or from behind

something: *"She stretched herself up on tiptoe, and peeped over the edge of the mushroom"* (Lewis Carroll). **3.** To become visible gradually, as though emerging from a hiding place: *At dawn the sun peeped over the horizon.* —*tr.* To cause to emerge or become partly visible.
∼*n.* **1.** A quick or furtive look; a glance. **2.** A first glimpse or first appearance: *the peep of dawn.* [Middle English *pepen,* alteration of *pken,* to PEEK.]

peep-bo (pēp′bō′) *n. British.* The game of peekaboo.

peep·er[1] (pē′pər) *n.* A creature that peeps.

peeper[2] *n.* **1.** Someone who looks furtively. **2.** *Slang.* An eye.

peep·hole (pēp′hōl′) *n.* A small hole or crevice through which one may peep.

peeping Tom *n.* A man who derives sexual gratification from pruriently and secretly spying on the intimate behavior of others; a voyeur. [From the story of *Peeping Tom* of Coventry, a tailor who was the sole person to peep at the naked Lady Godiva (and was struck blind).]

peep·show (pēp′shō′) *n.* **1.** An exhibition of pictures or objects, especially of an erotic nature, viewed through a small hole or magnifying glass. Also called "raree show." **2.** A short, sexually explicit film seen usually in a small, coin-operated projection booth.

peep sight *n.* A rear sight of a firearm consisting of an adjustable eyepiece with a small opening through which the front sight and the target are aligned.

pee·pul, pi·pal (pē′pəl) *n.* A fig tree, *Ficus religiosa,* of India, regarded as sacred by Buddhists. According to Buddhist tradition, this is the tree under which the Buddha attained enlightenment. Also called "bo tree." [Hindi *pīpal,* from Sanskrit *pippala.*]

peer[1] (pîr) *intr.v.* **peered, peering, peers. 1.** To look intently, searchingly, or with difficulty: *We peered through the mist.* **2.** To be partially visible; show: *The moon peered from behind a cloud.* —See Synonyms at **gaze.** [Perhaps alteration of APPEAR.]

peer[2] *n.* **1. a.** A nobleman. **b.** A member of the British peerage; a duke, marquis, earl, viscount, or baron. **2.** A person who has equal standing with another, as in rank, class, or age. Also used adjectivally: *a peer group.* **3.** *Archaic.* A companion; a fellow. [Middle English *peer(e),* from Old French *per,* equal, one's equal, (hence) nobleman, from Latin *pār,* equal.]

peer·age (pîr′ĭj) *n.* **1.** The rank or title of a peer. **2.** The body of peers. **3.** A book listing peers and their families.

peer·ess (pîr′ĭs) *n.* **1.** A woman who holds a life peerage. **2.** The wife or widow of a peer.

peer·less (pîr′lĭs) *adj.* Without peer; unmatched; unequaled. **—peer·less·ly** *adv.* **—peer·less·ness** *n.*

peer of the realm *n., pl.* **peers of the realm.** *British.* A hereditary peer who has the right to sit in the House of Lords on his majority.

peeve (pēv) *tr.v.* **peeved, peeving, peeves.** *Informal.* To annoy or make resentful; vex.
∼*n. Informal.* **1.** A vexation; a grievance: *a pet peeve.* **2.** A resentful mood: *be in a peeve.* [Back-formation from PEEVISH.]

pee·vish (pē′vĭsh) *adj.* **1.** Querulous; discontented; fretful. **2.** Ill-tempered. **3.** Contrary; fractious. [Middle English *pevish*†.] **—pee·vish·ly** *adv.* **—pee·vish·ness** *n.*

pee·wee (pē′wē) *n.* **1.** *Informal.* Any relatively or unusually small person or thing. **2.** Variant of **pewee.** [Whimsical formation based on WEE.] **—pee·wee** *adj.*

pee·wit, pe·wit (pē′wĭt′) *n.* A bird, the **lapwing** *(see).* [Imitative of its call.]

peg (pĕg) *n.* **1.** A small cylindrical or tapered pin, as of wood, used to fasten things, such as floorboards, to mark a point, such as a boundary, or to plug a hole, such as the vent of a barrel. **2.** A similar pin forming a projection that may be used as a support, as for hanging clothes on. **3.** Any of the pins of a stringed musical instrument that are turned to tighten or slacken the strings so as to regulate their pitch. **4.** An implement fitted with a pointed prong or claw for tearing or catching. **5.** A degree or notch, especially in estimation. **6.** *Chiefly British.* A small alcoholic drink, especially brandy or whiskey and soda. **7.** A pretext or occasion: *a peg to hang one's grievances upon.* **8.** *Baseball.* A low and fast throw of the ball to a baseman to retire a runner. **9.** A **clothespin** *(see).* **10.** *Informal.* A wooden leg. **—a square peg in a round hole.** A misfit. **—take someone down a peg.** To reduce the pride of; humble.
∼*v.* **pegged, pegging, pegs.** —*tr.* **1. a.** To put or insert a peg into. **b.** To provide (a barrel) with a vent and peg. **c.** To pierce or strike with or as if with a peg. **2.** To designate or mark by means of pegs: *pegging the score in a cribbage game.* **3.** *Finance.* **a.** To stabilize or fix the prices of (securities, stocks, or the like) so as to minimize fluctuation. **b.** To fix levels of (prices, wages, or the like), as by government legislation. **4.** To aim and throw (a missile, such as a stone or a ball) at or to a person or target. **5.** *Baseball.* **a.** To throw (the ball) fast and low to a baseman to retire a runner. **b.** To retire (a runner) in this manner. **6.** *Informal.* To classify; categorize. —*intr.* To proceed doggedly and steadily; hammer away; persist. Often followed by *away: pegging steadily away until the work's done.* [Middle English *pegge,* probably from Middle Dutch.]

Peg·a·sus[1] (pĕg′ə-səs). *Greek Mythology.* The winged steed that caused Hippocrene, the fountain of the Muses on Helicon, to well forth with a stroke of his hoof; the mount of Bellerophon. [Latin, from Greek *Pegasos,* from *pēgē,* spring.]

Pegasus[2] *n.* A constellation in the Northern Hemisphere near Aquarius and Andromeda. [After PEGASUS.]

peg·board (pĕg′bôrd′, -bōrd′) *n.* **1.** A board for playing games such as cribbage, having holes into which pegs are inserted. **2.** A board with rows of small perforations into which hooks or pegs may be inserted for displaying or storing articles such as pots.

peg leg *n. Informal.* An artificial leg, especially one made of wood.

peg·ma·tite (pĕg′mə-tīt′) *n. Geology.* A very coarse-grained igneous rock, sometimes rich in rare elements such as uranium, tungsten, and tantalum. Most pegmatites are granite. [French : Greek *pēgma* (stem *pēgmat-*), framework, from *pēgnunai,* to fasten + -ITE.] **—peg·ma·tit·ic** (pĕg′mə-tĭt′ĭk) *adj.*

peg top *n.* A wooden spinning top, tapering to a usually metal point on which it rotates.

Pé·guy (pā-gē′), **Charles Pierre** (1873–1914). French poet and publisher. He founded the journal *Cahiers de la Quinzaine* (1900–14), in which he published his own work and that of other writers.

Pehlevi. Variant of **Pahlavi.**

Pei (pā), **Ieoh Ming,** known as "I.M. Pei" (1917–). U.S. architect, born in China. He came to the United States in 1935 and later taught at Harvard University. Pei has designed numerous projects in the United States and Canada, including Government Center in Boston, Kips Bay Plaza in New York City, and Place Ville Marie in Montreal.

P.E.I. Prince Edward Island.

pei·gnoir (pān-wär′, pĕn-) *n.* A woman's loose-fitting dressing gown; a negligee. [French, "garment worn while combing the hair," from Old French *peigner,* to comb the hair, from Latin *pectināre,* from *pecten* (stem *pectin-*), comb.]

Peiping. See **Beijing.**

Peirce (pîrs), **Charles Sanders** (1839–1914). U.S. philosopher and logician. He founded pragmatism as a reaction against metaphysical speculation and theorizing. He was also a pioneer in the development of modern formal logic.

pej·o·rate (pĕj′ə-rāt′) *tr.v.* **-rated, -rating, -rates.** To diminish in quality, status, or worth. [Back-formation from PEJORATIVE.]

pej·o·ra·tion (pĕj′ə-rā′shən, pē′jə-) *n.* **1.** The process or condition of worsening or degenerating. **2.** *Linguistics.* The process by which the semantic status of a word changes for the worse over a period of time. For example, *egregious,* which formerly meant "distinguished," has come to mean "conspicuously bad." Compare **amelioration.** [Medieval Latin *pējōrātiō* (stem *pējōrātiōn-*), from Late Latin *pējōrāre,* to become or make worse, from Latin *pējor,* worse.]

pe·jor·a·tive (pĭ-jôr′ə-tĭv, -jŏr′ə-tĭv, pĕj′ə-rā′tĭv, pē′jə-) *adj.* **1.** Tending to make or become worse. **2.** Expressing disapproval.
∼*n.* A pejorative word. **—pe·jor·a·tive·ly** *adv.*

pek·an (pĕk′ən) *n.* A mammal, the **fisher** *(see).* [Canadian French *pékan,* of Algonquian origin, akin to Abnaki *pékané.*]

peke (pēk) *n. Informal.* A Pekingese dog.

Pe·kin (pĭ-kĭn′, pē′kĭn′) *n.* A large white duck of an Oriental breed, widely reared in the United States for food. [French *pékin,* from *Pékin,* Peking (Beijing).]

Peking. See **Beijing.**

Pe·king·ese (pē′kĭng-ēz′, -ēs′ *for senses 1, 2;* pē′kə-nēz′, -nēs′ *for sense 3*) *n., pl.* **Pekingese.** Also **Pe·kin·ese** (pē′kə-nēz′, -nēs′) *pl.* **Pekinese. 1.** A resident or native of Peking (Beijing), China. **2.** The Chinese dialect of Peking (Beijing). **3.** A toy dog of a breed developed in China, having a flat nose, long hair, and short, bowed forelegs. **—Pe·king·ese** *adj.*

Pe·king man (pē′kĭng′) *n.* An extinct hominid primate of the genus *Sinanthropus,* known from fossil remains of the Pleistocene epoch. [After *Peking* (Beijing), China, near which the remains were found.]

pe·koe (pē′kō, pĕk′ō) *n.* A high-quality variety of black tea made from the leaves around the buds. [Chinese (Amoy) *peh ho* : *peh,* white + *ho,* down (referring to the downy appearance of the young leaves).]

pel·age (pĕl′ĭj) *n.* The coat of a mammal, consisting of hair, fur, wool, or other soft covering, as distinct from bare skin. [French, from Old French *pel, poil,* hair, from Latin *pilus.*]

Pe·la·gi·an·ism (pə-lā′jē-ə-nĭz′əm) *n.* The theological doctrine propounded by Pelagius and condemned as heresy by the Roman Catholic Church in A.D. 417. Among its tenets were denial of original sin and affirmation of man's ability to be righteous by the exercise of free will. **—Pe·la·gi·an** *adj.* & *n.*

pe·lag·ic (pə-lăj′ĭk) *adj.* Of, pertaining to, or living in open oceans or seas rather than waters adjacent to land or inland waters. See **plankton, nekton.** [Latin *pelagicus,* from Greek *pelagikos,* from *pelagos,* sea.]

Pe·lag·i·us (pə-lā′jē-əs) (*c.* A.D. 360–420). British heretical theologian. Settling in Rome (*c.* 380), he rejected St. Augustine's teachings on predestination and original sin and in the heretical doctrine of Pelagianism proclaimed the free will of man to do good or evil. He was condemned by Pope Innocent I (417) and by the Council of Ephesus (431).

pel·ar·gon·ic acid (pĕl′är-gŏn′ĭk, -gō′nĭk) *n.* A colorless or yellow oil, $CH_3(CH_2)_7COOH$, used as a gasoline additive and in the manufacture of lacquers, plastics, and pharmaceuticals. Also called "nonanoic acid." [PELARGON(IUM) + -IC.]

pel·ar·go·ni·um (pĕl′är-gō′nē-əm) *n.* Any of various plants and shrubs of the genus *Pelargonium,* which includes the geraniums. [New Latin, from Greek *pelargos,* a stork (from the long, beak-shaped capsules of the plants).]

Pe·las·gi·an (pə-lăz′jē-ən) *n.* A member of a people living in the region of the Aegean Sea before the coming of the Greeks. [Greek

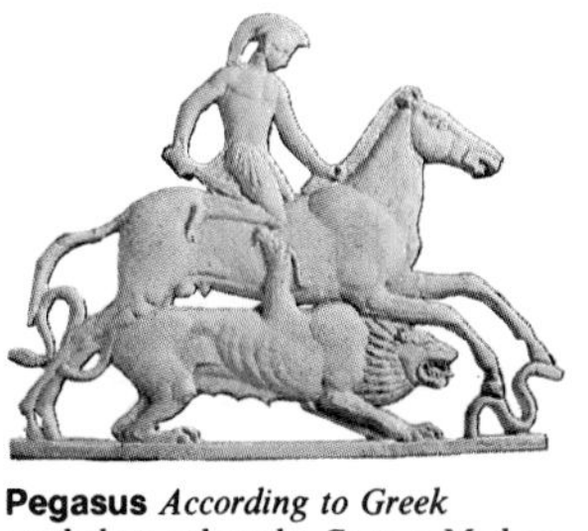

Pegasus *According to Greek mythology, when the Gorgon Medusa was slain by the hero Perseus, the flying horse Pegasus rose from her blood. Later Bellerophon rode the horse in his fight with the Chimera (above). Pegasus became a constellation in the sky when Bellerophon fell off while attempting to ride him to heaven.*

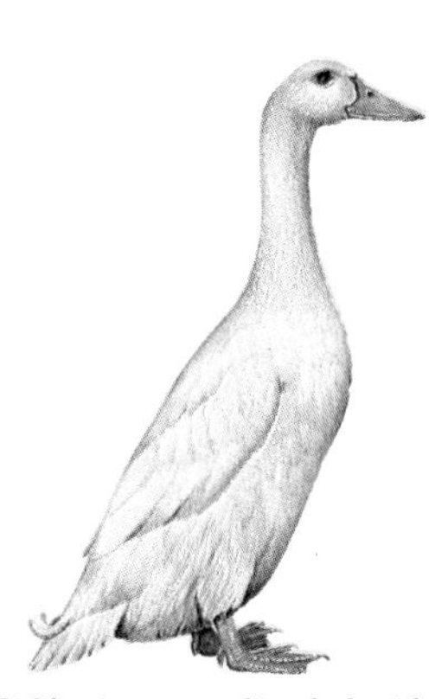

Pekin *A creamy white duck with a bright yellow bill. It is found in farmyards throughout the world.*

Pelasgoi, native name of unknown origin, probably altered by folk etymology as if to mean "sea people," from *pelagos,* sea.] **—Pe·las·gi·an, Pe·las·gic** (pə-lăz′jĭk) *adj.*

Pe·lé (pā′lā, pā-lā′), born Edson Arantes do Nascimento (1940–). Brazilian soccer player. One of the world's greatest inside forwards, he helped win the World Cup for Brazil in 1958, 1962, and 1970. Playing for Santos (1955–74) and the New York Cosmos (1975–77), he scored more than 1,200 goals.

Pe·lée, Mount (pə-lā′). Volcano on the West Indian island of Martinique. Its eruption (1902), with clouds of incandescent gas, destroyed the town of St. Pierre.

pel·er·ine (pĕl′ə-rēn′, pĕl′ər-ĭn) *n.* A woman's cape, usually short, with points hanging in front. [French *pèlerine,* from the feminine of *pèlerin,* a pilgrim, from Late Latin *pelegrīnus,* PILGRIM.]

Pe·le·us (pē′lē-əs, pēl′yo͞os′) *n. Greek Mythology.* A son of Aeacus and father of Achilles. [Latin, from Greek *Pēleus.*]

pelf (pĕlf) *n.* Wealth or riches, especially when dishonestly acquired. [Middle English, booty, from Old French *pelfre.* See **pilfer.**]

pel·ham (pĕl′əm) *n.* A horse's bit combining a curb and a snaffle. [Probably from the surname *Pelham.*]

pel·i·can (pĕl′ĭ-kən) *n.* Any of various large, web-footed birds of the genus *Pelecanus,* of tropical and warm regions, having under the lower bill a large pouch used for catching and holding fish. [Middle English *pelican,* Old English *pellican,* from Late Latin *pelicānus,* from Greek *pelekan, pelekinos,* from *pelekus,* an ax (probably from the shape of its bill), akin to Sanskrit *parasu,* an ax, probably of Mesopotamian origin.]

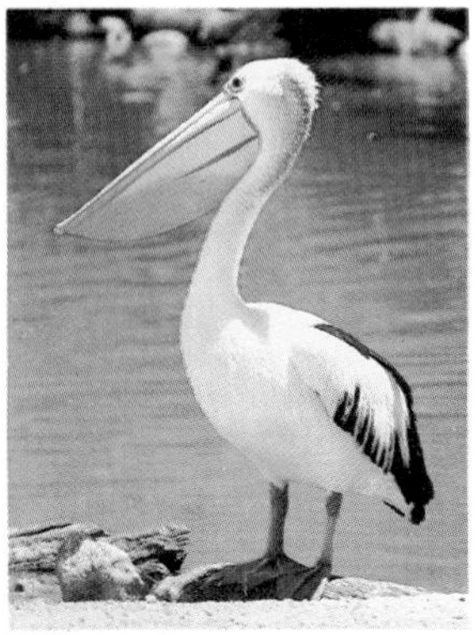

pelican *The pelican's huge beak pouch is used as a fishing net. Clumsy on land, pelicans are impressive fliers. This is the Australian pelican,* Pelecanus conspicillatus.

pe·lisse (pə-lēs′) *n.* **1.** A long cloak or outer robe, usually of fur or with a fur lining. **2.** A woman's loose, light cloak, often with openings for the arms. [French, from Medieval Latin *pellicia,* leather garment, cloak, from Latin *pellicius,* made of skin, from *pellis,* skin.]

pe·lite (pē′līt′) *n.* Rock composed of fine fragments, as of clay, quartz particles, or rock flour. [Greek *pēlos*†, clay + -ITE.] **—pe·lit·ic** (pə-lĭt′ĭk) *adj.*

Pel·la (pĕl′ə). Ancient city of Greece. Capital of Macedonia under Philip II (382–336 B.C.), it was the birthplace of his son Alexander the Great (356 B.C.).

pel·lag·ra (pə-lăg′rə, -lā′grə, -lă′grə) *n.* A chronic disease caused by niacin deficiency, and characterized by skin eruptions, digestive and nervous disturbances, and eventual mental deterioration. [Italian : *pelle,* skin, from Latin *pellis* + Greek *agra,* seizure.] **—pel·lag·rous** *adj.*

pel·lag·rin (pə-lăg′rĭn, -lā′grĭn, -lă′grĭn) *n.* A person afflicted with pellagra. [From PELLAGRA.]

pel·let (pĕl′ĭt) *n.* **1.** A small, solid or densely packed ball or mass, as of bread, wax, or medicine. **2.** A bullet or piece of small shot. **3.** A stone ball used as a catapult missile or as a primitive cannonball. **4.** A hard mass of indigestible food that is regurgitated by certain birds, especially birds of prey.

~tr.v. **pelleted, -leting, -lets. 1.** To make or form into pellets. **2.** To strike with pellets. [Middle English *pelet,* from Old French *pelote,* from Vulgar Latin *pilotta* (unattested), diminutive of Latin *pila,* ball, PILL.]

pel·li·cle (pĕl′ĭ-kəl) *n.* **1.** A thin skin or film, such as an organic membrane or a liquid film. **2.** A rigid outer layer of cytoplasm in certain single-celled organisms such as the euglenas. **3.** The thin outer covering of a mushroom cap. [Old French *pellicule,* from Medieval Latin *pellicula,* from Latin, diminutive of *pellis,* skin.] **—pel·lic·u·lar** (pə-lĭk′yə-lər) *adj.*

pel·li·to·ry (pĕl′ə-tôr′ē, -tōr′ē) *n., pl.* **-ries. 1.** Any of various plants of the genus *Parietaria,* growing on walls, rocks, and the like and having clusters of small flowers arising at the leaf bases. **2.** A small plant, *Anacyclus pyrethrum,* of the Mediterranean region, containing a volatile oil once used for the relief of toothache and facial neuralgia. [Sense 1, altered from Middle English *peritorie, paritorie,* from Old French *paritaire,* from Late Latin *parietāria (herba),* "herb of the wall," from *parietārius,* belonging to walls, from Latin *pariēs* (stem *pariet-*), wall. See **paries.** Sense 2, altered from earlier *peletyr,* Middle English *peletre, peretre,* from Latin *pyrethrum,* PYRETHRUM.]

pell-mell (pĕl′mĕl′) *adv.* **1.** In a jumbled, confused manner; helter-skelter. **2.** In frantic, disorderly haste; headlong. [French *pêle-mêle,* Old French *pesle mesle, mesle mesle,* reduplications of *mesle,* imperative of *mesler,* to mix, from Vulgar Latin *misculāre* (unattested), from Latin *miscēre.*] **—pell-mell** *adj. & n.*

pel·lu·cid (pə-lo͞o′sĭd) *adj.* **1.** Admitting the passage of light; transparent; translucent. **2.** Transparently clear in style or meaning: *pellucid prose.* [Latin *pellūcidus,* from *pellūcēre, perlūcēre,* to shine through : *per,* through + *lūcēre,* to shine.] **—pel·lu·cid·i·ty** (pĕl′yo͞o-sĭd′ə-tē), **pel·lu·cid·ness** *n.* **—pel·lu·cid·ly** *adv.*

pel·met (pĕl′mət) *n.* A piece of board or draped material fixed above a window or door to hide a curtain rod. [Probably from French *palmette,* PALMETTE.]

Pel·o·pon·nese (pĕl′ə-pə-nēz′, -nēs′). Also **Pel·o·pon·ne·sus** (-nē′səs). *Medieval name* **Mo·re·a** (mô-rē′ə, mō-). Peninsula of southern Greece. Joined to the mainland by the Isthmus of Corinth, it is largely mountainous, with fertile coastal lowlands in the west and north. Ruled by Sparta until the 4th century B.C., it has many ruins and produces currants, wine, and olives. **—Pel·o·pon·ne·sian** (pĕl′ə-pə-nē′zhən, -shən) *adj. & n.*

Peloponnesian War. A war between Athens and Sparta with their allies (431–404 B.C.) that was won by Sparta.

Pe·lops (pē′lŏps′). *Greek Mythology.* The son of Tantalus and father of Atreus. [Latin, from Greek : *pelios,* dark + *ops,* face.]

pe·lo·ri·a (pə-lôr′ē-ə, -lōr′ē-ə) *n. Botany.* Unusual regularity in the form of a flower or other structure that is normally irregular. [New Latin, from Greek *pelōros,* monstrous, from *pelōr,* monster, prodigy.] **—pe·lo·ric** (pə-lôr′ĭk, -lōr′ĭk) *adj.*

pe·lo·rus (pə-lôr′əs, -lōr′əs) *n., pl.* **-ruses.** A fixed compass card on which bearings relative to a ship's heading are taken. [Perhaps after *Pelorus,* pilot of Hannibal.]

pe·lo·ta (pə-lō′tə) *n.* **1.** The game of **jai alai** *(see).* **2.** The ball used in jai alai. [Spanish, ball, augmentative of *pella,* from Latin *pila,* ball.]

pelt[1] (pĕlt) *n.* **1. a.** The skin of an animal with the fur or hair still on it. **b.** A stripped animal skin ready for tanning. **2.** An animal hide, especially one used as a garment. [Middle English, perhaps back-formation from PELTRY.]

pelt[2] *v.* **pelted, pelting, pelts.** *—tr.* **1.** To strike or assail repeatedly with or as if with blows or missiles; bombard. **2.** To cast, hurl, or throw (missiles). *—intr.* **1.** To beat or strike heavily and repeatedly. **2.** To move at a fast speed. **3.** To pour with rain. Often used with *down.*

~n. **1.** A sharp blow; a whack. **2.** A rapid pace; speed. Used chiefly in the phrase *at full pelt.* [Middle English *pelten,* perhaps from Latin *pultāre.*] **—pelt·er** *n.*

pel·tast (pĕl′tăst′) *n.* In ancient Greece, a foot soldier who carried a spear and small leather shield. [Latin *peltasta,* from Greek *peltastēs,* from *peltē,* small shield.]

pel·tate (pĕl′tāt′) *adj. Botany.* Having the leaf stalk attached near the center of the surface, rather than at or near the margin. [New Latin *peltatus,* "having a shield," from Latin *pelta,* small light shield, from Greek *peltē.*] **—pel·tate·ly** *adv.*

Pel·ti·er effect (pĕl′tē-ā′) *n.* The generation of heat at either of the two junctions of a thermocouple when it is passing current. Compare **Seebeck effect.** [After Jean *Peltier* (1785–1845), French physicist.]

Peltier element *n.* An electronic device consisting of metal strips that alternate with strips of n-type and p-type semiconductor so that when a current is passed heat is absorbed from one set of metallic strips and emitted from the other set as a result of the Peltier effect. [After Jean *Peltier.*]

pelt·ing (pĕl′tĭng) *adj. Archaic.* Paltry; petty; contemptible. [Origin unknown.]

pelt·ry (pĕl′trē) *n.* Undressed pelts collectively. [Middle English, from Old French *peleterie,* from *peletier,* furrier, from *pel,* skin, from Latin *pellis.*]

pel·vic (pĕl′vĭk) *adj.* Of, in, near, or pertaining to the pelvis.

pelvic fin *n.* Either of a pair of lateral hind fins of fishes, attached to the pelvic girdle. Also called "ventral fin."

pelvic girdle *n.* The skeletal structure of bone or cartilage by which the hind limbs or analogous parts are supported and joined to the vertebral column. Also called "pelvic arch," and in humans "hip girdle."

pel·vis (pĕl′vĭs) *n., pl.* **-vises** or **-ves** (-vēz′). *Anatomy.* **1.** A basin-shaped skeletal structure, composed of the innominate bones on the sides, the pubis in front, and the sacrum and coccyx behind. **2.** The **renal pelvis** *(see).* [New Latin, from Latin *pēlvis,* basin.]

pem·broke (pĕm′brŏk′, -bro͝ok′) *n.* A Welsh corgi of a breed characterized by a short tail and pointed ears. [After *Pembroke,* England.]

Pem·broke·shire (pĕm′bro͝ok-shîr′, -shər). Former county of southwestern Wales, now part of Dyfed. Its coast is a national park, and tourism and dairy farming are important sources of revenue. Its county town was Haverfordwest.

pem·mi·can, pem·i·can (pĕm′ĭ-kən) *n.* **1.** A food originally prepared by North American Indians from lean, dried strips of meat pounded into paste, mixed with fat and berries, and pressed into small cakes. **2.** A similar food made chiefly from beef, dried fruit, and suet, used as emergency rations. [Cree *pimikân,* from *pimii,* grease, fat.]

pem·phi·gus (pĕm′fĭ-gəs, pĕm-fī′gəs) *n.* Any of several acute or chronic skin diseases characterized by itching blisters. The variety *Pemphigus vulgaris* is a serious disease that spreads from the mucous membranes to large areas of skin. [New Latin, from Greek *pemphix* (stem *pemphig-*), drop, pustule, of imitative origin.]

pen[1] (pĕn) *n.* **1.** An instrument for writing or drawing with ink, especially: **a.** One made from a large quill with the nib split and sharpened. **b.** A tapering metal device with a split point fitted to a metal, plastic, or wooden holder. It may be dipped in ink or supplied by a reservoir within the holder. **c.** A penholder and its pen together. See **ball-point pen, fountain pen. 2.** A writing instrument viewed as the writer's weapon or means of expression of ideas or opinions. **3.** A writer or author: *a hired pen.* **4.** A style of writing: *a witty pen.* **5.** The chitinous internal shell of a squid.

~tr.v. **penned, penning, pens.** To write or compose with a pen. [Middle English *penne,* from Old French, feather, pen, from Latin *penna,* feather (in Late Latin, also "pen").] **—pen·ner** *n.*

pen[2] *n.* **1.** A fenced enclosure for animals. **2.** The animals kept in such an enclosure. **3.** Any of various other enclosures, such as a bullpen or a playpen. **4.** A repair dock for submarines. **5.** In Jamaica: **a.** A farm where livestock is bred. **b.** A country estate.

~tr.v. **penned, penning, pens.** To confine in or as if in a pen. [Middle English *pen,* Old English *penn.*]

pen[3] *n.* A female swan. Compare **cob.** [Origin unknown.]

pen[4] *n. Slang.* A penitentiary (sense 2). [Short for PENITENTIARY.]

pen., Pen. peninsula.

P.E.N. (pĕn) *n.* International Association of Poets, Playwrights, Editors, Essayists, and Novelists.

pe·nal (pē'nəl) *adj.* **1.** Of or pertaining to punishment, especially for breaking the law. **2.** Subject to punishment; legally punishable: *a penal offense.* **3.** Prescribing or enumerating punishments or penalties for offenses: *penal laws.* **4.** Serving as or constituting a means or place of punishment: *penal servitude.* [Middle English, from Old French, from Latin *poenālis,* from *poena,* penalty.] —**pe·nal·ly** *adv.*

penal code *n.* The body of laws relating to crimes and offenses and the penalties for their commission.

pe·nal·ize (pē'nə-līz', pĕn'ə-) *tr.v.* **-ized, -izing, -izes. 1.** To subject to a penalty, especially for infringement of a law or official regulation. **2.** To impose a handicap on; place at a disadvantage. **3.** To make punishable by a penalty. —See Synonyms at **punish.** —**pe·nal·i·za·tion** *n.*

pen·al·ty (pĕn'əl-tē) *n., pl.* **-ties. 1.** A punishment established by law or authority for a crime or offense. **2.** Something, especially a sum of money, required as a forfeit for an offense or a failure to fulfill a contract or obligation. **3.** The disadvantage or painful consequences resulting from an action or condition. **4.** *Sports.* A handicap or loss of advantage imposed on a team or competitor for infraction of a rule. **5.** *Often* **penalties.** In contract bridge, points scored by the opponents when the declarer fails to make his bid. [Norman French *penalte* (unattested), from Medieval Latin *poenālitās* (stem *poenālitāt-*), from Latin *poenālis,* PENAL.]

penalty area *n.* In soccer, the area in front of the goal where the goalkeeper may handle the ball and where a penalty kick may be awarded. Also called "penalty box."

penalty box *n.* **1.** In soccer, the penalty area. **2.** In ice hockey, the enclosure where penalized players sit.

penalty kick *n.* **1.** In soccer, a direct free kick at the goal awarded following a foul committed in the penalty area of the defending team and taken from the penalty spot, with only the goalkeeper in defense. **2.** In Rugby football, a kick awarded against a team for an infringement, such as a player's being offside.

pen·ance (pĕn'əns) *n.* **1.** An act of self-mortification or devotion performed by way of demonstrating contrition for sin. **2.** *Ecclesiastical.* **a.** A sacrament that includes contrition, confession to a priest, acceptance of punishment, and absolution. **b.** A punishment imposed as a condition of absolution. **3.** A feeling of sorrow for one's wrongdoing or sin. —**do penance.** To show repentance by undergoing imposed or voluntary punishment. [Middle English *penaunce,* from Old French *penance,* from Latin *paenitentia,* penitence, from *paenitēns,* PENITENT.]

Pe·nang[1] (pē-năng', pə-). Also **Pi·nang.** State of Peninsular Malaysia. It is made up of Penang Island at the north end of the Strait of Malacca and Wellesley province on the mainland, and produces coconuts, rice, and rubber. George Town is the capital.

Penang[2], **Pinang.** See **George Town.**

pe·na·tes (pə-nā'tēz, -nä'tēz) *pl.n.* The Roman gods of the household, tutelary deities of the home and of the state, whose cult was closely connected and often identified with that of the **lares** *(see).* [Latin *Penātēs,* household gods, akin to *penus*†, the interior of a house (compare **penetrate**).]

pence (pĕns). *British.* Alternate plural of **penny.** Often used in combination: *twopence.*

pen·cel, pen·sil (pĕn'səl) *n.* A narrow flag, streamer, or pennon, especially one carried at the top of a lance or spear. [Middle English, from Norman French, contracted from Old French *penoncel,* diminutive of *penon,* PENNON.]

pen·chant (pĕn'chənt) *n.* A strong inclination; a definite and continued liking. [French, from the present participle of *pencher,* to incline, from Vulgar Latin *pendicāre* (unattested), from Latin *pendēre,* to hang.]

pen·cil (pĕn'səl) *n.* **1.** A narrow, generally cylindrical implement for writing, drawing, or marking, consisting of a thin rod of graphite, crayon, or similar substance encased in wood or held in a plastic or metal mechanical device. **2.** Something shaped or used like a pencil; especially, a narrow medicated or cosmetic stick: *a styptic pencil; an eyebrow pencil.* **3. a.** *Archaic.* An artist's brush, especially a fine one. **b.** An artist's style or technique in drawing or delineating. **c.** Descriptive skill. **4.** A narrow cone or cylinder of rays, especially light rays, forming a beam of small diameter. **5.** *Mathematics.* A family of geometric figures that share a common property, such as all straight lines in a plane that pass through a fixed point.
~*tr.v.* **penciled, -ciling, -cils.** Also *chiefly British* **-cilled, -cilling. 1.** To write or produce by using a pencil: *pencil a note.* **2.** To mark, shade, or color with or as if with a pencil. —**pencil in.** To enter or note down provisionally in a diary, timetable, or the like. [Middle English *pensel, pencel,* from Old French *pincel,* from Vulgar Latin *pēnicellus* (unattested), from Latin *pēnicillus,* a brush, pencil, "small tail," diminutive of *pēnis,* tail.] —**pen·cil·er** *n.*

pencil pusher *n. Informal.* One whose job involves writing. Also called "pen pusher."

pencil sharpener *n.* A device consisting of a blade for giving a sharp point to a lead pencil.

pend (pĕnd) *intr.v.* **pended, pending, pends. 1.** To wait for a decision or judgment. **2.** *Regional.* To hang; depend. [Latin *pendere,* to suspend, hang.]

pen·dant, pen·dent (pĕn'dənt) *n.* **1.** Something suspended from something else; especially, an ornament or piece of jewelry attached to a necklace or bracelet. **2.** A hanging lamp or chandelier. **3.** A sculptured ornament suspended from a vaulted Gothic roof or ceiling. **4. a.** Either of a matched pair; a parallel or companion piece. **b.** An additional thing or part that supplements or complements another; complement. **5.** A short rope hanging from a mast or spar with an eye at its lower end to which fittings may be attached. **6.** *Nautical.* See **pennant** (sense 1).
~*adj.* Variant of **pendent.** [Middle English *pendaunt,* from Old French *pendant,* from the present participle of *pendre,* to hang, from Vulgar Latin *pendere* (unattested), to hang, variant of Latin *pendēre,* to hang.]

pen·dent, pen·dant (pĕn'dənt) *adj.* **1.** Hanging down; dangling; suspended. **2.** Projecting; jutting; overhanging. **3.** Awaiting settlement; undecided; pending.
~*n.* Variant of **pendant.** [Middle English *penda(u)nt,* from Old French *pendant,* hanging. See **pendant.**] —**pen·dent·ly** *adv.*

pen·den·te li·te (pĕn-dĕn'tē lī'tē) *adv. Law.* While a lawsuit is pending; during litigation. [Latin, "with litigation pending."]

pen·den·tive (pĕn-dĕn'tĭv) *n. Architecture.* An overhanging, triangular section of vaulting between the rim of a dome and each adjacent pair of the arches that support it. [French *pendentif,* "overhanging feature," from Latin *pendēns* (stem *pendent-*), present participle of *pendēre,* to hang.]

pend·ing (pĕn'dĭng) *adj.* **1.** Not yet dealt with, decided, or settled; awaiting conclusion or confirmation. **2.** Impending; imminent.
~*prep.* **1.** While in process of; during. **2.** While awaiting; until. [Anglicized form of French *pendant,* from Old French, "hanging" (after Latin *pendēns* (stem *pendent-*), hanging, pending).]

pen·drag·on (pĕn-drăg'ən) *n.* The supreme war leader of the post-Roman Celts of England and Wales. [Middle English, from Welsh : *pen,* chief, head, from Common Celtic *gwenno-* (unattested) + *dragon,* standard, from Latin *dracō,* cohort's standard, DRAGON.] —**pen·drag·on·ship** *n.*

pen·du·lar (pĕn'jo͝o-lər, pĕn'dyə-) *adj.* Of or resembling the motion of a pendulum; swinging back and forth.

pen·du·lous (pĕn'jo͝o-ləs, pĕn'dyə-) *adj.* **1.** Hanging loosely. **2.** Wavering; undecided. [Latin *pendulus,* from *pendēre,* to hang.] —**pen·du·lous·ly** *adv.* —**pen·du·lous·ness** *n.*

pen·du·lum (pĕn'jo͝o-ləm, pĕn'dyə-, pĕn'də-) *n.* **1. a.** A mass suspended from a fixed low-friction support at the end of a relatively light thread so that it is free to swing in a vertical plane under the influence of gravitational force only. Also called "simple pendulum." **b.** Any of several related, freely swinging configurations differing in mass distribution, suspension, and possible modes of motion. Also called "compound pendulum." **2.** Any such object used to regulate the movement of various devices, especially clocks. **3.** Something that swings back and forth from one course, opinion, or condition to another: *the pendulum of public opinion.* [New Latin, from Latin, neuter of *pendulus,* PENDULOUS.]

Pe·nel·o·pe (pə-nĕl'ə-pē). In the *Odyssey,* the wife of Odysseus and mother of Telemachus, celebrated for her constancy.

pe·ne·plain, pe·ne·plane (pē'nə-plān') *n. Geology.* A nearly flat land surface representing an advanced stage of erosion. [Latin *paene, pēne,* almost + PLAIN.] —**pe·ne·pla·na·tion** (pē'nə-plə-nā'shən) *n.*

pe·nes. Alternate plural of **penis.**

pen·e·tra·li·a (pĕn'ə-trā'lē-ə) *pl.n.* **1.** The innermost parts of a building; especially, the sanctuary of a temple. **2.** Innermost or hidden parts; recesses: *the penetralia of the soul.* [Latin *penetrālia,* plural of *penetrāle,* innermost part, from *penetrālis,* inner, interior, from *penetrāre,* to PENETRATE.]

pen·e·trance (pĕn'ə-trəns) *n. Genetics.* The degree of frequency with which a gene manifests its effect. Also called "expression." [From PENETRANT.]

pen·e·trant (pĕn'ə-trənt) *adj.* Penetrating; piercing.
~*n.* Something that penetrates or is capable of penetrating. [Latin *penetrāns* (stem *penetrant-*), present participle of *penetrāre,* to PENETRATE.]

pen·e·trate (pĕn'ə-trāt') *v.* **-trated, -trating, -trates.** —*tr.* **1.** To enter or force a way into; pierce: *penetrated the enemy's territory.* **2. a.** To enter into and permeate: *The smell penetrated the entire building.* **b.** To cause to be permeated or diffused; steep. **3.** To grasp the inner significance of; understand: *penetrate a mystery.* **4.** To see through. **5.** To affect deeply, as by piercing the consciousness or emotions. **6.** To infiltrate: *The spy penetrated the enemy's intelligence service.* —*intr.* **1.** To pierce or enter into something; make a way in or through something. **2.** To gain admittance or access. **3.** To gain insight into something. [Latin *penetrāre,* from *penitus,* deeply, from *penus*†, the interior of a house.] —**pen·e·tra·bil·i·ty** *n.* —**pen·e·tra·ble** (pĕn'ə-trə-bəl) *adj.* —**pen·e·tra·bly** *adv.* —**pen·e·tra·tor** *n.* —**pen·e·tra·tive** (pĕn'ə-trā'tĭv) *adj.*

pen·e·trat·ing (pĕn'ə-trā'tĭng) *adj.* **1.** Able or seeming to penetrate: *a penetrating wind.* **2.** Keenly perceptive or understanding: *penetrating insight.* —**pen·e·trat·ing·ly** *adv.*

pen·e·tra·tion (pĕn'ə-trā'shən) *n.* **1.** The act or process of piercing or penetrating something. **2.** The power or ability to penetrate. **3.** The extent to which a person or thing penetrates, especially: **a.** The extent to which an incursion or infiltration by a hostile force is successful. **b.** The depth reached by a projectile after hitting its target. **c.** In ball games, the depth to which the ball is sent into an opponent's playing area. **4.** Understanding; insight.

pen·e·trom·e·ter (pĕn'ə-trŏm'ə-tər) *n.* **1.** A device for measuring the penetrating power of x-rays. **2.** A device for measuring the penetrability of semisolids. [PENETR(ATION) + -METER.]

pen·guin (pĕn'gwĭn, pĕng'gwĭn) *n.* **1.** Any of various flightless marine birds of the family Spheniscidae, of cool regions of the Southern Hemisphere. They have scalelike, barbless feathers, flipperlike

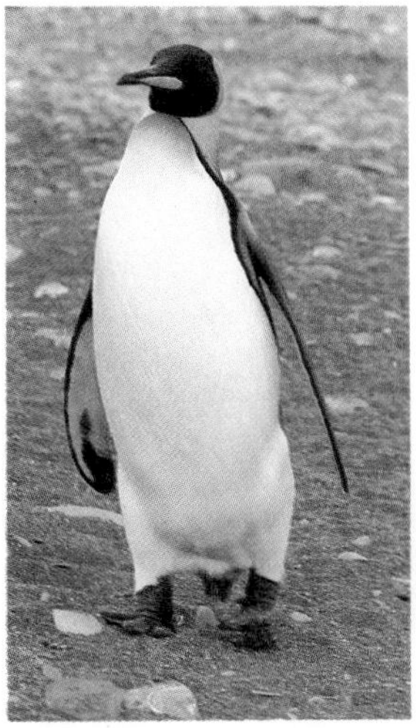

penguin *Flightless, but good swimmers, all 18 species of penguin live in the Southern Hemisphere, feeding on fish, squid, and crustaceans. This is the king penguin,* Aptenodytes patagonicus.

PRONUNCIATION KEY

ă, pat; ā, pay; âr, care;
ä, father, are; b, bib;
ch, church; d, deed; ĕ, pet;
ē, be; f, fife; g, gag; h, hat;
hw, which; ĭ, pit; ī, pie;
îr, pier; j, judge; k, kick;
l, lid, needle; m, mum;
n, no, sudden; ng, thing;
ŏ, pot; ō, toe; ô, paw, for;
oi, noise; ou, out; o͝o, book;
o͞o, boot; p, pop; r, roar;
s, sauce; sh, ship, dish;
t, tight; th, thin, path;
th, this, bathe; ŭ, cut; ûr, fur;
v, valve; w, with; y, yes;
z, zebra, size; zh, vision;
ə, about, item, edible,
gallop, circus, peaceful

IN FOREIGN WORDS:

à, *Fr.* ami; œ, *Fr.* feu, *Ger.* schön; ü, *Fr.* tu, *Ger.* über; KH, *Ger.* ich, *Scot.* loch; N, *Fr.* bon; y', *Fr.* Compiègne

STRESS MARKS:

Primary stress: '
in·cite' (ĭn-sīt')
Secondary stress: '
in'sight' (ĭn'sīt')

wings, and webbed feet. See **Adélie penguin, emperor penguin.** **2.** *Obsolete.* The great auk. [16th century : origin obscure.]

–penia *suffix.* Indicates lack or deficiency; for example, **leukopenia.** [New Latin, from Greek *penia,* poverty, lack.]

pen·i·cil·la·mine (pĕn′ĭ-sĭl′ə-mēn′) *n.* A drug that is a chelating agent and is used to treat severe rheumatoid arthritis and poisoning by various metals. [PENICILL(IN) + AMINE.]

pen·i·cil·late (pĕn′ə-sĭl′ĭt, -āt′) *adj.* Having or resembling a tuft or brush of fine hairs, such as those on caterpillars and certain grasses. [Latin *pēnicillus,* brush, PENCIL + -ATE.] —**pen·i·cil·late·ly** *adv.* —**pen·i·cil·la·tion** (pĕn′ə-sĭ-lā′shən) *n.*

pen·i·cil·lin (pĕn′ə-sĭl′ĭn) *n.* Any of several isomeric antibiotic compounds obtained from penicillium molds, especially *Penicillium notatum* and *P. chrysogenum,* or produced biosynthetically, and used to treat a wide variety of bacterial infections. [New Latin *penicillium,* PENICILLIUM.]

pen·i·cil·lin·ase (pĕn′ĭ-sĭl′ĭ-nās′, -nāz′) *n.* A bacterial enzyme that inactivates penicillin by hydrolysis.

pen·i·cil·li·um (pĕn′ə-sĭl′ē-əm) *n., pl.* **-cilliums** or **-cillia** (-sĭl′ē-ə). Any of various molds of the genus *Penicillium,* having a characteristic blue-green color and producing tufts of fine filaments. They grow on decaying fruits and ripening cheese and are used in the production of penicillin and in making cheese. [New Latin, from Latin *pēnicillus,* brush, PENCIL.]

pe·nile (pē′nīl′) *adj.* Of or relating to the penis. [New Latin *penilis.*]

pen·in·su·la (pə-nĭn′syə-lə, -sə-lə) *n. Abbr.* **pen., Pen.** A long projection of land into water. Compare **cape.** [Latin *pēninsula* : *paene,* almost + *īnsula,* an island.]

pen·in·su·lar (pə-nĭn′syə-lər, -sə-lər) *adj.* Of, pertaining to, or resembling a peninsula.
~*n.* An inhabitant of a peninsula.

Peninsular Malaysia. See **Malaya.**

Peninsular War *n.* The part of the Napoleonic Wars fought against France in the Iberian Peninsula from 1808 to 1814 by Britain, Portugal, and Spain.

pe·nis (pē′nĭs) *n., pl.* **-nises** or **-nes** (-nēz′). **1.** *Anatomy.* The male organ of copulation in higher vertebrates, and of urinary excretion in mammals. **2.** Any of various copulatory organs in males of lower animals. [Latin *pēnis,* tail, penis.]

penis envy *n.* In Freudian psychoanalytic theory, an emotional and sexual drive in women supposed to originate when a girl perceives her genitalia as a lack or castration.

pen·i·tent (pĕn′ə-tənt) *adj.* Feeling or expressing remorse for one's misdeeds or sins.
~*n.* **1.** One who is penitent. **2.** A person performing penance under the direction of a confessor. [Middle English, from Old French, from Latin *paenitēns* (stem *paenitent-*), present participle of *paenitēre,* to repent.] —**pen·i·tence** *n.* —**pen·i·tent·ly** *adv.*

pen·i·ten·tial (pĕn′ə-tĕn′shəl) *adj.* **1.** Of, pertaining to, or expressing penitence. **2.** Pertaining to or of the nature of penance.
~*n.* **1.** A book or set of church rules concerning the sacrament of penance. **2.** A penitent. —**pen·i·ten·tial·ly** *adv.*

pen·i·ten·tia·ry (pĕn′ə-tĕn′shə-rē) *n., pl.* **-ries. 1.** *Roman Catholic Church.* A tribunal of the Roman Curia, presided over by a cardinal designated in this office as the Grand Penitentiary, having jurisdiction in matters relating to penance, dispensations, and papal absolutions. **2.** A prison, especially one for those convicted of serious crimes.
~*adj.* **1.** Of or for the purpose of penance; penitential. **2.** Pertaining to or used for punishment or reform of wrongdoers. **3.** Resulting in or punishable by imprisonment in a penitentiary: *a penitentiary offense.* [Middle English *penitenciary,* penance officer, from Medieval Latin *penitentiārius,* from Latin *paenitentia,* repentance, from *paenitēns* (stem *paenitent-*), PENITENT.]

pen·knife (pĕn′nīf′) *n., pl.* **-knives** (-nīvz′). A small pocketknife, usually with one or more blades that fold into the handle, originally used to make or sharpen quill pens.

pen·light (pĕn′līt′) *n.* A small flashlight having the size and shape of a fountain pen.

pen·man (pĕn′mən) *n., pl.* **-men** (-mĭn). **1.** An author; writer. **2.** An expert in penmanship. **3.** A copyist; scribe.

pen·man·ship (pĕn′mən-shĭp′) *n.* The art, skill, style, or manner of handwriting; calligraphy.

Penn (pĕn), **William** (1644–1718). English Quaker. Converted to Quakerism (1667), he was imprisoned in the Tower of London for his views (1668). In 1681 he was given a charter in Pennsylvania by the Crown in lieu of a debt to his late father and proceeded to establish a colony practicing religious toleration (1682).

pen·na (pĕn′ə) *n., pl.* **pennae** (pĕn′ē). Any of the larger feathers forming the visible plumage of a bird, as distinguished from the down feathers. [Latin, feather.] —**pen·na·ceous** (pə-nā′shəs) *adj.*

pen name *n.* A literary pseudonym.

pen·nant (pĕn′ənt) *n.* **1.** *Nautical.* A long, narrow, relatively small flag, often triangular, used for signaling or for identification. Also called "pendant." **2.** Any similar flag; a pennon. **3. a.** A flag used as an emblem or one awarded to the winner of a contest. **b.** A flag that serves as the emblem of the championship in a professional baseball league. **c.** The yearly championship in such a league. [Blend of PENDANT and PENNON.]

pen·nate (pĕn′āt′) *adj.* Also **pen·nat·ed** (pĕn′ā′tĭd). Feathered or winged. [Latin *pennātus,* winged, from *penna,* feather, wing.]

pen·ni (pĕn′ē) *n., pl.* **-nis** or **penniä** (pĕn′ē-ə). A coin equal to ¹/₁₀₀ of the markka of Finland. See feature at **currency.** [Finnish, perhaps

from Middle Low German *pennige,* from West Germanic *panninga* (unattested).]

pen·ni·less (pĕn′ē-lĭs, pĕn′ə-lĭs) *adj.* Entirely without money; very poor. —**pen·ni·less·ly** *adv.* —**pen·ni·less·ness** *n.*

Pen·nines (pĕn′īnz′). Also **Pen·nine Chain** (pĕn′īn′). Range of hills in northern England. It extends from the Cheviot Hills in the north to the Vale of Trent in the south; its maximum height, 893 meters (2,930 feet), is at Cross Fell.

pen·ni·nite (pĕn′ə-nīt′) *n.* A bluish-green form of **chlorite** (see). [German *Pennin,* Pennine Alps along the Swiss-Italian border (where it was discovered) + -ITE.]

pen·non (pĕn′ən) *n.* **1.** A long, narrow banner or streamer, often forked or triangular in shape, borne upon a lance. **2.** A pointed or tapering banner or flag flown by a boat. **3.** Any banner, flag, or pennant. **4.** A pinion; wing. [Middle English, from Old French *penon,* augmentative of *penne,* feather, wing, from Latin *penna.*] —**pen·noned** *adj.*

pen·non·cel, pen·on·cel, pen·non·celle (pĕn′ən-sĕl′) *n.* A small pennon, flag, or streamer borne upon a lance. [Middle English *penoncelle,* from Old French *penoncel,* diminutive of *penon,* PENNON.]

Penn·syl·va·nia (pĕn′səl-vān′yə, -vā′nē-ə). *Abbr.* **Pa.** State of the northeastern United States. It was established as a colony (1681) by William Penn, who aimed to promote religious tolerance. Its many industrial towns include Pittsburgh, Philadelphia, and the capital, Harrisburg; and agriculture and dairy farming are important.

Pennsylvania Dutch *n.* **1.** *Used with a plural verb.* The descendants of German and Swiss immigrants who settled in Pennsylvania in the 17th and 18th centuries. **2.** The dialects of German spoken by this group. Also called "Pennsylvania German."

Penn·syl·va·nian (pĕn′səl-vān′yən, -vā′nē-ən) *adj.* **1.** Of or pertaining to the state of Pennsylvania. **2.** *Geology.* Of, belonging to, or designating the geologic time, system of rocks, and sedimentary deposits of the sixth period of the Paleozoic era, characterized by the development of coal-bearing rock formations. In Europe, called "Upper Carboniferous."
~*n.* **1.** A native or inhabitant of Pennsylvania. **2.** *Geology.* The Pennsylvanian period. Preceded by *the.*

pen·ny (pĕn′ē) *n., pl.* **-nies** or **pence** (pĕns) (for senses 2, 3). **1.** *Abbr.* **p.** A coin of the United States and Canada, the **cent** (see). **2. a.** *Abbr.* **p.** A coin of the United Kingdom equal to ¹/₁₀₀ of a pound. **b.** *Abbr.* **d.** Formerly, a coin of the United Kingdom equal to ¹/₂₄₀ of a pound, or ¹/₁₂ of a shilling. **c.** A coin of the Republic of Ireland and of various dependent territories of the United Kingdom. See feature at **currency. 3.** Any of various coins of small denomination. —**pretty penny.** A relatively large sum of money: *That car must have cost a pretty penny.* [Middle English *penny,* Old English *penig, penning,* from West Germanic *panninga* (unattested); probably akin to PAWN (security).]

penny ante *n.* **1.** A poker game in which the highest bet is limited to a penny or some other small sum. **2.** *Informal.* A business transaction on a small scale. —**pen·ny-an·te** (pĕn′ē-ăn′tē) *adj.*

penny arcade *n.* A hall or building, especially in an amusement park, where various coin-operated devices are played for entertainment.

pen·ny·cress (pĕn′ē-krĕs′) *n.* Any of several plants of the genus *Thlaspi,* native to Europe, and characteristically having small, winged seed pods; especially, *T. arvense,* which grows as a weed throughout North America. [Perhaps variant of *penny grass,* from its round, flat pods.]

penny dreadful *n. Informal.* A piece of cheap, sensational popular fiction, such as a book or magazine.

penny pincher *n. Informal.* A frugal or stingy person.

pen·ny-pinch·ing (pĕn′ē-pĭn′chĭng) *adj. Informal.* Very stingy with money. —**pen·ny-pinch·ing** *n.*

pen·ny·roy·al (pĕn′ē-roi′əl, pĕn′ē-roi′əl) *n.* **1.** A Eurasian plant, *Mentha pulegium,* having hairy leaves and small lilac-blue flowers. It yields a useful aromatic oil. **2.** An aromatic plant, *Hedeoma pulegioides,* of eastern North America, having a similar appearance and uses. [Variant of Middle English *puliol real,* from Norman French : Old French *poliol,* pennyroyal, from Latin *pūlegium†,* fleabane + *real, roial,* ROYAL.]

pen·ny·weight (pĕn′ē-wāt′) *n. Abbr.* **dwt., pwt.** A unit of troy weight equal to 24 grains, ¹/₂₀ of a troy ounce or approximately 1.555 grams.

penny whistle *n.* A type of metal flageolet with six finger holes. Also called "tin whistle."

pen·ny-wise (pĕn′ē-wīz′) *adj.* Careful only in dealing with small sums of money or small matters. —**penny-wise, pound-foolish.** Careful with small sums but wasteful with large sums of money.

pen·ny·wort (pĕn′ē-wûrt′, -wôrt′) *n.* Any of several plants having rounded leaves suggestive of pennies, such as: **1.** A Eurasian plant, *Umbilicus rupestris* (or *Cotyledon umbilicus*), having thick, rounded leaves and yellowish-green, bell-shaped flowers. This species is also called "navelwort." **2.** A North American plant, *Obolaria virginica,* having fleshy leaves and small white or purplish flowers. **3.** A small, prostrate plant, *Hydrocotyle vulgaris,* having tiny pink flowers.

pen·ny·worth (pĕn′ē-wûrth′) *n.* **1.** As much as a penny will buy. **2.** A small amount; a modicum. **3.** A bargain.

Pe·nob·scot[1] (pə-nŏb′skət, -skŏt′) *n., pl.* **-scots** or collectively **Penobscot. 1. a.** A tribe of North American Indians who were part of

the Algonquin federation and formerly inhabited central Maine.
b. A member of this Indian tribe. **2.** The Algonquian language of
the Penobscot. —**Pe·nob·scot** *adj.*

Penobscot². River rising in numerous lakes in central Maine and
flowing generally east, then south to Penobscot Bay, an inlet of the
Atlantic Ocean. The river is an important source of power for pulp-
wood and paper mills.

pe·nol·o·gy, poe·nol·o·gy (pē-nŏl′ə-jē) *n.* The theory and practice
of prison management and criminal treatment and rehabilitation.
Compare **criminology.** [Latin *poena,* penalty, from Greek *poinē* +
-LOGY.] —**pe·no·log·i·cal** (pē′nə-lŏj′ĭ-kəl) *adj.* —**pe·no·log·i·cal·ly**
adv. —**pe·nol·o·gist** *n.*

penoncel. Variant of **pennoncel.**

pen pal *n.* A person with whom one corresponds regularly and
forms a friendship, usually without meeting.

pen pusher *n. Informal.* A **pencil pusher** (see).

Pen·sa·co·la (pĕn′sə-kō′lə). City of extreme northwestern Florida,
on Pensacola Bay, an inlet of the Gulf of Mexico. It is a port of
entry with a good natural harbor and shipping and fishing industries. A U.S. naval station was established here in 1914. There are
several historical ruins here.

pensil. Variant of **pencel.**

pen·sile (pĕn′sīl) *adj.* **1.** Hanging down loosely; suspended: *a pen-
sile nest.* **2.** Building a hanging nest. Said of birds. [Latin *pēnsilis,*
from *pendēre* (past participle *pēnsus*), to hang.] —**pen·sile·ness,**
pen·sil·i·ty (pĕn-sĭl′ə-tē) *n.*

pen·sion¹ (pĕn′shən) *n.* **1.** A fixed sum of money paid regularly to an
individual, as by a government or a former employer, as a retirement or injury benefit, in return for a service, or by way of patronage.
~*tr.v.* **pensioned, -sioning, -sions. 1.** To grant a pension to. **2.** To
retire or dismiss with a pension. Usually used with *off.* [Middle
English *pensioun,* from Old French *pension,* from Medieval Latin
pēnsiō (stem *pēnsiōn-*), from Latin, payment, from *pendere* (past
participle *pēnsus*), to weigh, pay.]

pen·sion² (päN-syôN′) *n.* A boarding house or small hotel in continental Europe, especially France. [French, boarding house, boarding school, originally "payment for the board and education of a
child," extended use of Old French *pension,* payment, PENSION
(grant).]

pen·sion·a·ble (pĕn′shə-nə-bəl) *adj.* **1.** Entitling one to receive a
pension: *reached a pensionable age.* **2.** Conferring the right to a
pension: *a pensionable job.*

pen·sion·ar·y (pĕn′shə-nĕr′ē) *adj.* **1.** Constituting a pension. **2.** Receiving a pension. **3.** Mercenary; venal.
~*n., pl.* **pensionaries. 1.** A pensioner. **2.** A hireling.

pen·sion·er (pĕn′shə-nər) *n.* **1.** One who receives a pension; especially, one who receives a government retirement pension. **2.** One
who is dependent on the bounty of another.

pension fund *n.* A fund contributed to by employers and usually
also employees to provide retirement and widows' pensions for employees.

pen·sive (pĕn′sĭv) *adj.* **1.** Deeply or seriously thoughtful. **2.** Suggesting or expressing deep, often melancholy thoughtfulness. [Mid-
dle English *pensif,* from Old French, from *penser,* to think, from
Latin *pēnsāre,* frequentative of *pendere* (past participle *pēnsus*), to
weigh.] —**pen·sive·ly** *adv.* —**pen·sive·ness** *n.*

   Synonyms: pensive, contemplative, reflective, meditative. These
describe the quality or nature of being mentally or spiritually preoccupied, usually in a quiet way but one that is or would be apparent
to other people. One is *pensive* when one is silently thinking in a
serious way about some matter or problem, frequently despite oneself. It can be in a rational (if troubled) way, but it more often has
a wistful, dreamy, or sad sense. *Contemplative* implies a slow, directed consideration of a lofty object of thought, or physical object,
with conscious intent of better understanding of or spiritual or aesthetic enrichment: *a contemplative attitude toward nature. Reflective*
expresses a more analytical deliberation about past experience or
about something that has just happened, often as a process of second thought or reappraisal of a particular occurrence. *Meditative*
means to be consciously intent or reflective in a spiritual sense. It
differs from *contemplative* in that the object of one's thought is
usually inward, as in self-examination, rather than outward.

pen·ste·mon, pent·ste·mon (pĕn-stē′mən, pĕnt-, pĕn′stə-mən,
pĕnt′stə-) *n.* Any of numerous plants of the North American genus
Penstemon, having four fertile stamens and one bearded sterile stamen. [New Latin, irregularly from PENT(A)- + Greek *stēmōn,* warp
(here representing "stamen").]

pen·stock (pĕn′stŏk′) *n.* **1.** A sluice or gate used to control a flow of
water. **2.** A pipe or conduit used to carry water to a water wheel or
turbine. [PEN (enclosure) + STOCK.]

pent (pĕnt). Alternate past tense and past participle of **pen** (to confine).

penta-, pent- *prefix.* Indicates five; for example, **pentameter, pen-
tangular.** [Greek, from *pente,* five.]

pen·ta·chlo·ro·phe·nol (pĕn′tə-klôr′ə-fē′nôl′, -nôl′, pĕn′tə-klōr′-) *n.*
A compound, C₆Cl₅OH, used in solution as a fungicide and wood
preservative.

pen·ta·chord (pĕn′tə-kôrd′, -kōrd′) *n. Music.* **1.** An ancient instrument with five strings. **2.** A series of five tones in a diatonic scale.

pen·ta·cle (pĕn′tə-kəl) *n.* A five-pointed star, often thought to have
magical or mystical significance, formed by five straight lines connecting the vertices of a pentagon and enclosing another pentagon

in the completed figure. [Medieval Latin *pentaculum* (unattested) :
Greek *penta-,* PENTA- + *-culum,* diminutive suffix.]

pen·tad (pĕn′tăd′) *n.* **1.** A group or series of five members. **2.** A
five-year period. [Greek *pentas* (stem *pentad-*), from *pente,* five.]

pen·ta·dac·tyl (pĕn′tə-dăk′təl) *adj.* Also **pen·ta·dac·ty·late** (-tə-lĭt,
-lāt′). Having five fingers or toes on each hand or foot. [Latin
pentadactylus, from Greek *pentadaktulos* : PENTA- + *daktulos,* finger, DACTYL.]

pen·ta·gon (pĕn′tə-gŏn′) *n.* **1.** A polygon having five sides and five
angles. **2. Pentagon.** The U.S. Department of Defense; the U.S.
military command. [Latin *pentagōnum,* from Greek *pentagōnon* :
PENTA- + -GON.]

pen·tag·o·nal (pĕn-tăg′ə-nəl) *adj.* **1.** Having five sides and five angles. **2.** Of or formed in pentagons. —**pen·tag·o·nal·ly** *adv.*

pen·ta·he·dron (pĕn′tə-hē′drən) *n., pl.* **-drons** or **-dra** (-drə). A
polyhedron having five plane surfaces. [New Latin : PENTA- +
-HEDRON.] —**pen·ta·he·dral** *adj.*

pen·tam·er·ous (pĕn-tăm′ər-əs) *adj.* **1.** Having or divided into five
similar parts. **2.** *Botany.* Having flower parts, such as petals, sepals,
and stamens, in sets of five. [New Latin *pentamerus* : PENTA- +
-MEROUS.] —**pen·tam·er·ism** *n.*

pen·tam·e·ter (pĕn-tăm′ə-tər) *n.* **1.** A line of verse composed of five
metrical feet; especially, a line of classical verse having a set metrical pattern consisting of four dactyls and two stressed feet. **2.** English verse composed in iambic pentameter. [Latin, from Greek
pentametros : PENTA- + -METER.] —**pen·tam·e·ter** *adj.*

pen·tane (pĕn′tān′) *n.* Any of three isomeric alkanes, C₅H₁₂:
1. *Normal pentane.* A colorless flammable liquid used as an anesthetic, solvent, and in the manufacture of artificial ice. **2.** *Isopen-
tane.* A colorless flammable liquid used as a solvent and in the
manufacture of polystyrene foam. **3.** *Neopentane.* A colorless gas
used in the manufacture of synthetic rubber. [PENT(A)- + -ANE.]

pen·tan·gu·lar (pĕn-tăng′gyə-lər) *adj.* Having five angles.

pen·ta·no·ic acid (pĕn′tə-nō′ĭk). A colorless liquid,
CH₃(CH₂)₃COOH, used in making perfumes, flavorings, and pharmaceuticals. Also called "valeric acid." [PENTAN(E) + -OIC.]

pen·ta·prism (pĕn′tə-prĭz′əm) *n.* A prism with a pentagonal cross
section, used especially in single-lens reflex cameras to deflect an
image through the lens to the view finder.

pen·ta·quine (pĕn′tə-kwēn′, -kwĭn) *n.* A drug used in the treatment
of malaria. [PENTA- + QUIN(OLINE).]

pen·tar·chy (pĕn′tär′kē) *n., pl.* **-chies. 1.** Government by five rulers.
2. A body of five rulers governing jointly. **3.** A country governed by
five joint rulers. **4.** An association or federation of five governments, each ruled by a different leader. [Greek *pentarkhia* : PENTA-
+ -ARCHY.] —**pen·tar·chi·cal** (pĕn-tär′kĭ-kəl) *adj.*

pen·ta·stich (pĕn′tə-stĭk′) *n.* A poem, strophe, or stanza containing
five lines. [Late Greek *pentastikhos,* of five verses : PENTA- + *stikhos,* -STICH.]

Pen·ta·teuch (pĕn′tə-tōōk′, -tyōōk′) *n.* The first five books of the
Old Testament: Genesis, Exodus, Leviticus, Numbers, and Deuteronomy. [Late Latin *Pentateuchus,* from ecclesiastical Greek *Penta-
teukhos* : PENTA- + *teukhos,* a tool, case for papyrus rolls, scroll.]
—**Pen·ta·teuch·al** *adj.*

pen·tath·lon (pĕn-tăth′lən, -lŏn′) *n.* An athletic contest consisting of
five events for each participant. Originating in the ancient Olympics, it was revived in the modern Olympics as the *modern pentathlon,* and consists of running, riding, swimming, fencing, and pistol
shooting. [Greek : PENT(A)- + *athlon,* contest (see **athlete**).] —**pen·
tath·lete** (pĕn-tăth′lēt′) *n.*

pen·ta·tom·ic (pĕn′tə-tŏm′ĭk) *adj. Chemistry.* Designating a molecule that contains five atoms.

pen·ta·ton·ic scale (pĕn′tə-tŏn′ĭk) *n.* Any of various five-tone musical scales, especially one composed of the first, second, third, fifth,
and sixth tones of a diatonic scale.

pen·ta·va·lent (pĕn′tə-vā′lənt) *adj. Chemistry.* Having a valence of
5; quinquevalent.

Pen·te·cost (pĕn′tĭ-kôst′, -kŏst′) *n.* **1.** A festival of the Christian
Church occurring on the seventh Sunday after Easter, to celebrate
the descent of the Holy Ghost upon the disciples. Also called
"Whitsunday." **2.** A Jewish festival, **Shavuot** (see). [Middle English
Pentecost, Old English *Pentecosten,* from Late Latin *Pentēcostē,*
from Greek *pentēkostē (hēmera),* the fiftieth day (after the Resurrection), Pentecost, from *pentēkostos,* fiftieth, from *pentēkonta,* fifty :
pente, five + *-konta,* "ten times."]

Pen·te·cos·tal (pĕn′tĭ-kŏ′stəl, -kô′stəl) *adj.* **1.** Of, pertaining to, or
occurring at Pentecost. **2.** Of, pertaining to, or designating any of
various Christian religious congregations that seek to be filled with
the Holy Ghost, in emulation of the disciples at Pentecost. —**Pen·
te·cos·tal** *n.* —**Pen·te·cos·tal·ism** *n.*

pen·tene (pĕn′tēn′) *n.* A colorless flammable alkene, C₅H₁₀, occurring in several isomeric forms. Formerly called "amylene."
[PENT(A)- + -ENE.]

pent·house (pĕnt′hous′) *n.* **1. a.** An apartment or dwelling situated
on the roof of a building. **b.** A residence, often with a terrace,
comprising the top floor of an apartment house. **c.** A structure
housing machinery on the roof of a building. **2.** A shed or sloping
roof attached to the side of a building or wall. [Alteration (assimilated to HOUSE) of Middle English *pentis,* from Old French *appentis,*
from Medieval Latin *appenticium,* appendage, from Latin *appendix,*
from *appendēre,* to append : *ad,* on + *pendēre,* to suspend, hang.]

pen·ti·men·to (pĕn′tĭ-mĕn′tō) *n., pl.* **-ti** (-tē). The emergence in a
painting of an underlying image, as an earlier painting, part of a

painting, or original draft, that shows through, usually when the top layer of paint has become transparent with age. [Italian, "repentance," correction.]

Pent·land Firth (pĕnt′lənd). Strait, 32 kilometers (20 miles) long, separating northern Scotland from the Orkney Islands. Despite its strong currents, it is a major shipping route.

pent·land·ite (pĕnt′lən-dīt′) n. The principal ore of nickel, a light-brown nickel iron sulfide. [French, after Joseph B. *Pentland* (died 1873), Irish scientist.]

pen·to·bar·bi·tal sodium (pĕn′tə-bär′bə-tôl′, -tōl′) n. A white crystalline or powdery barbiturate, C₁₁H₁₇N₂NaO₃, used as a sedative. Also called "sodium pentobarbital."

pen·tode (pĕn′tōd′) n. An electronic valve with five electrodes. In addition to a cathode and an anode it has a control grid, a screen grid, and a suppressor grid situated between the screen and the anode. [PENTA- + Greek *hodos*, way.]

pen·to·san (pĕn′tə-săn′) n. Any of a group of complex carbohydrates found with cellulose in many woody plants and yielding pentoses on hydrolysis. [PENTOS(E) + -AN.]

pen·tose (pĕn′tōs′, -tōz′) n. A sugar having five carbon atoms per molecule. [PENT(A)- + -OSE.]

pent·ox·ide (pĕnt-ŏk′sīd′) n. An oxide having five atoms of oxygen in the molecule. [PENT(A)- + OXIDE.]

pentstemon. Variant of **penstemon.**

pent-up (pĕnt′ŭp′) adj. Not given expression; repressed: *pent-up anger.*

pen·tyl (pĕn′təl) n. Chemistry. The univalent organic radical C₅H₁₁, occurring in several isomeric forms in many organic compounds. Formerly called "amyl." [PENT(A)- + -YL.]

pentyl acetate n. A colorless combustible liquid, CH₃COOC₅H₁₁, used as a paint solvent and in flavorings, photographic films, and the extraction of penicillin.

pen·tyl·ene·tet·ra·zol (pĕn′tə-lēn′tĕt′rə-zôl′, -zŏl′) n. A drug, C₆H₁₀N₄, used as a stimulant of the central nervous system. [PENT(A)- + (METH)YLENE + TETR(A)- + AZ(O)- + -OL.]

penuchle. Variant of **pinochle.**

pe·nult (pē′nŭlt′, pĭ-nŭlt′) n. Also **pe·nul·ti·ma** (pə-nŭl′tə-mə). **1.** The next to last syllable in a word. **2.** The next to last item in a series. [Latin *paenultimus*, last but one : *paene*, *pēne*†, almost + *ultimus*, farthest away, last, from *uls*, beyond.]

pe·nul·ti·mate (pə-nŭl′tə-mĭt) adj. **1.** Next to last. **2.** Of or pertaining to the penult of a word: *penultimate stress.*
~n. The next to the last. [Latin *paenultimus*, PENULT.]

pe·num·bra (pĭ-nŭm′brə) n., pl. **-brae** (-brē) or **-bras. 1.** A partial shadow between regions of complete shadow and complete illumination, as during an eclipse. **2.** Astronomy. The partly darkened fringe around a sunspot. **3.** An outlying surrounding region; periphery. [New Latin : Latin *paene*, *pēne*†, almost + UMBRA.] —**pe·num·bral, pe·num·brous** adj.

pe·nu·ri·ous (pə-nŏŏr′ē-əs, -nyŏŏr′ē-əs) adj. **1.** Miserly; stingy. **2.** Poverty-stricken; needy. **3.** Yielding little; barren: *a penurious land.* [Medieval Latin *pēnūriōsus*, from *pēnūria*, PENURY.] —**pe·nu·ri·ous·ly** adv. —**pe·nu·ri·ous·ness** n.

pen·u·ry (pĕn′yə-rē) n. **1.** Extreme want or poverty; destitution. **2.** Extreme dearth; barrenness; insufficiency. [Middle English, from Latin *paenūria*, *pēnūria*†, want, scarcity.]

Pe·nu·ti·an (pə-nŏŏ′tē-ən, -shən) n. A family or phylum of North American Indian languages of Pacific coastal areas from California to British Columbia.

Pen·zance (pĕn-zăns′, pən-). Seaside resort in Cornwall, southwestern England. It serves as a port for early crops from the Scilly Isles; its other industries include tourism and fishing.

pe·on (pē′ŏn′, pē′ən) n. **1. a.** An unskilled laborer or farm worker of Latin America or the southwestern United States. **b.** Such a worker bound in servitude to a creditor. **2.** A native Indian or Ceylonese messenger, servant, or foot soldier. **3.** Any menial worker; drudge. [Spanish *peon*, Portuguese *peão*, and French *pion*, all from Medieval Latin *pedo* (stem *pedōn-*), a foot soldier, from Latin *pēs* (stem *ped-*), a foot.]

pe·on·age (pē′ə-nĭj) n. Also **pe·on·ism** (-nĭz′əm). **1.** The condition of being a peon. **2.** A system by which debtors are bound in servitude to their creditors until the debts are paid.

pe·o·ny (pē′ə-nē) n., pl. **-nies.** Any of various garden plants of the genus *Paeonia*, having large pink, red, white, or creamy globular flowers. [Middle English *pione*, Old English *peonie*, from Latin *peōnia*, from Greek *paiōniā*, supposedly discovered by *Paiōn*, physician (of the gods). See **paean.**]

peo·ple (pē′pəl) n., pl. **people** or **peoples** (for senses 1, 2). **1.** A body of persons living in the same country under one national government; nationality. **2.** A body of persons sharing a common religion, culture, language, or inherited condition of life. **3.** Persons in general; men, women, and children; human individuals collectively. **4.** The mass of ordinary persons; the populace. Usually preceded by *the.* **5. a.** The citizens of a nation, state, or other political unit. **b.** In certain forms of Marxist ideology, the proletariat: *a people's court.* **6.** Persons subordinate to or loyal to a ruler, superior, or employer. **7. a.** Family, relatives, or ancestors. **b.** Visitors; guests: *We're having people over for the weekend.* **8.** Persons with regard to some characteristic, or considered as a group: *working people; young people.* **9.** Human beings considered as distinct from lower animals or inanimate things. **10.** A race or kind of beings distinct from human beings: *the little people.* —See Usage note at **nation.**
~tr.v. **peopled, -pling, -ples.** To furnish with a population; populate. [Middle English *peple*, *poeple*, from Old French *pueple*, *pople*, from Latin *populus*.] —**peo·pler** (pē′plər) n.

Usage: **People** is the usual word for a group of human beings considered collectively and without differentiation: *Several people were in the room.* **Persons** is more restricted in use; it tends to be found in more formal and impersonal contexts and is therefore typical of written rather than spoken English, particularly administrative and official English. In its singular form *person* takes a singular pronoun (*If a person has an interest in politics, he will . . .*), though a plural form *(they)* is sometimes used in informal speech.

people's front n. A political coalition, a **popular front** *(see).*

People's Republic of China. See **China.**

Pe·o·ri·a (pē-ôr′ē-ə, -ōr′ē-ə). City in north-central Illinois. Located where the Illinois River becomes Lake Peoria, it is a port and agricultural center for the Corn Belt and manufactures machinery.

pep (pĕp) n. Informal. Energy; high spirits; vim.
~tr.v. **pepped, pepping, peps.** Informal. To bring energy or liveliness to; invigorate. Usually followed by *up.* [Short for PEPPER.] —**pep·pi·ness** n. —**pep·py** adj.

Pep·in the Short (pĕp′ĭn), also known as Pepin III (c. 715–68). King of the Franks (751–68). The father of Charlemagne, he came to the defense of Pope Stephen II against the king of the Lombards, Aistulf (754), and established the core territory of the Papal States.

pep·los (pĕp′ləs, -lŏs′) n., pl. **-loses.** Also **pep·lus** (pĕp′ləs), pl. **-luses.** A loose outer robe worn by women in ancient Greece. Also called "peplum." [Greek *peplos†.*]

pep·lum (pĕp′ləm) n., pl. **-lums. 1.** A short overskirt or ruffle attached at the waistline of a jacket, blouse, or dress. **2.** A peplos. [Latin, from *peplus*, PEPLOS.]

pe·po (pē′pō) n., pl. **-pos.** The fruit of any of various related plants, such as the cucumber and melon, having a hard rind, fleshy pulp, and numerous seeds. [Latin, melon, from Greek *pepōn.*]

pep·per (pĕp′ər) n. **1.** A woody vine, *Piper nigrum*, of the East Indies, having small, berrylike fruit. **2.** The dried, blackish fruit of this plant, used as a pungent condiment. When ground whole, it is called *black pepper*, and with the shell removed, *white pepper.* **3.** Any of several other plants of the genus *Piper*, such as cubeb, betel, and kava. **4.** Any of several varieties of a tropical plant, *Capsicum annuum* (or *C. frutescens*). **5.** The podlike fruit of any of these plants, varying in size, shape, color, and degree of pungency. The milder types include the **sweet pepper** and **pimiento** *(both of which see),* and the more pungent types include the **chili** *(see).* **6.** Any of various condiments made from the more pungent varieties of *C. annuum* (or *C. frutescens*), such as **cayenne pepper, chili pepper,** and **paprika** *(all of which see).* In this sense, also called "hot pepper."
~tr.v. **peppered, -pering, pers. 1.** To season or sprinkle with pepper. **2.** To sprinkle liberally; dot. **3.** To pelt or shower with small missiles. **4.** To make (a speech or article, for example) lively and vivid, as with wit or invective. [Middle English *peper*, Old English *pipor*, from Latin *piper*, from Greek *peperi*, from Sanskrit *pippalī*, berry.]

pep·per-and-salt (pĕp′ər-ən-sôlt′) adj. Having a close mixture of black and white or brown and white. Said of hair or fabrics.

pep·per·box (pĕp′ər-bŏks′) n. A container with small holes in the top for sprinkling pepper.

pep·per·corn (pĕp′ər-kôrn′) n. **1.** A dried berry of the pepper vine *Piper nigrum.* **2.** Any small or insignificant thing.

peppered moth n. A European moth, *Biston betularia*, that exists in two distinct forms, a black and white speckled form predominating in rural regions and a black or melanic form that flourishes in industrial areas. See **pigmentation.**

pep·per·grass (pĕp′ər-grăs′, -gräs′) n. Any of several plants of the genus *Lepidium*; especially, *L. virginicum*, having small white flowers and pungent seeds. Also called "pepperwort."

pepper mill n. A utensil for grinding peppercorns.

pep·per·mint (pĕp′ər-mĭnt′) n. **1.** A plant, *Mentha piperita*, having small purple or white flowers and downy leaves that yield a pungent oil. **2.** The oil from this plant, or a preparation made from it, used as flavoring. **3.** A candy with this flavoring.

pep·per·o·ni (pĕp′ə-rō′nē) n. A highly spiced pork and beef sausage. [Italian *peperone*, chili, from *pepere*, pepper.]

pepper pot n. **1.** A thick soup that is made with tripe and other meat, vegetables, and often dumplings and that is highly seasoned with pepper. Also called "Philadelphia pepper pot." **2.** A thick West Indian stew of meat or fish, vegetables, and regional condiments. **3.** A pepperbox.

pepper tree n. Any of several trees of the genus *Schinus*; especially, *S. molle*, native to South America, having yellowish-white flowers and red ornamental fruits with seeds that are used as a condiment.

pep·per·wort (pĕp′ər-wûrt′, -wôrt′) n. A plant, **peppergrass** *(see).*

pep·per·y (pĕp′ə-rē) adj. **1.** Of, like, or containing pepper; sharp or pungent in flavor. **2.** Vigorously sharp-tempered in disposition and manner: *a peppery general.* **3.** Sharp and stinging in style or content: *a peppery speech.* —**pep·per·i·ness** n.

pep pill n. Slang. Any tablet or capsule containing an ingredient that stimulates the central nervous system; especially, any of the amphetamines.

pep·sin, pep·sine (pĕp′sĭn) n. **1.** A digestive enzyme found in gastric juice that catalyzes the breakdown of protein to peptides. **2.** A substance containing this enzyme, obtained from the stomachs of pigs and used as a digestive aid. [German *Pepsin*, from Greek *pepsis*, digestion, from *peptein*, to digest, cook.]

pep·sin·o·gen (pĕp-sĭn′ə-jən) *n.* An inert substance found in the cells of the gastric mucosa that is converted to pepsin during digestion by the action of hydrochloric acid. [PEPSIN + -GEN.]

pep talk *n.* A speech of exhortation delivered by a leader, as to team members or staff.

pep·tic (pĕp′tĭk) *adj.* **1. a.** Of or assisting digestion: *peptic secretion.* **b.** Induced by or associated with the action of digestive secretions. **2.** Of or involving pepsin. **3.** Capable of digesting.
∼*n.* A digestive agent. [Latin *pepticus,* from Greek *peptikos,* from *peptein,* to digest.]

peptic ulcer *n.* An ulcer of the mucous membrane, especially of the stomach or esophagus, caused by the action of digestive secretions.

pep·ti·dase (pĕp′tĭ-dās′, -dāz′) *n.* An enzyme that hydrolyzes peptides, releasing amino acids. [PEPTID(E) + -ASE.]

pep·tide (pĕp′tīd′) *n.* Also **pep·tid** (pĕp′tĭd). Any of various natural or synthetic compounds containing two or more amino acids linked by the carboxyl group of one amino acid and the amino group of another. [PEPT(ONE) + -IDE.]

peptide bond *n.* The chemical bond between the organic acid groups and amine groups of neighboring amino acids, constituting the primary linkage of all protein structures.

pep·tize (pĕp′tīz′) *tr.v.* **-tized, -tizing, -tizes. 1.** To increase the dispersion of (a colloidal solution) by the addition of an electrolyte. **2.** To liquefy (a colloidal gel) by the addition of an electrolyte to form a sol. [Greek *peptein,* to digest + -IZE.] **—pep·ti·za·tion** *n.*

pep·tone (pĕp′tōn′) *n.* Any of various protein compounds obtained by acid or enzyme hydrolysis of natural protein and used as nutrients and culture media. [German *Pepton,* from Greek *pepton,* from *peptein,* to digest, cook.] **—pep·ton·ic** (pĕp-tŏn′ĭk) *adj.*

pep·to·nize (pĕp′tə-nīz′) *tr.v.* **-nized, -nizing, -nizes. 1.** To convert (protein) into a peptone. **2.** To dissolve (food) by means of a proteolytic enzyme. **3.** To combine with peptone. **—pep·to·ni·za·tion** *n.* **—pep·to·niz·er** *n.*

Pepys (pēps), **Samuel** (1633–1703). English diarist. His diary, a detailed account of everyday life, includes descriptions of the Great Fire of London and the Great Plague.

Pe·quot (pē′kwŏt′) *n., pl.* **-quots** or collectively **Pequot. 1.** A member of an Algonquian-speaking North American Indian people formerly living in southern New England. **2.** The language of this tribe. **—Pe·quot** *adj.*

per (pûr) *prep. Abbr.* **p. 1.** Through; by means of: *per bearer.* Used in business. **2.** To, for, or by each; for every: *40 miles per gallon.* **3.** According to; by the. Often used with *as*: *as per instructions.* [Latin.]

per– *prefix. Chemistry.* Indicates: **1.** A compound that includes an element in its highest oxidation state; for example, **perchloric acid. 2.** A compound that includes the peroxy group in its structure; for example, **hydrogen peroxide. 3.** A complete substitution or addition in an organic compound; for example, **perchloroethylene.** [Latin, from preposition *per,* through, by, away. In borrowed Latin compounds, *per-* indicates: 1. Through, as in **percolate.** 2. Throughout, to the end, as in **perennial, perorate.** 3. Thoroughly, completely, as in **perfect, perceive.** 4. Away, as in **perdition, peregrine.** 5. Destruction, as in **perfidy, perjure.** 6. Intensified action, as in **perfervid, perform.**]

per. 1. period. **2.** person.

per·ac·id (pûr′ăs′ĭd) *n.* **1.** Any acid containing the peroxy group. **2.** An inorganic acid, such as perchloric acid, containing the largest proportion of oxygen in a series of related acids.

per·ad·ven·ture (pûr′əd-vĕn′chər, pĕr′-) *adv. Archaic.* Perhaps; perchance; it may be.
∼*n. Archaic.* Uncertainty; doubt: *beyond peradventure.* [Middle English *per aventure* : Old French *per,* by + *aventure,* ADVENTURE.]

Pe·rak (pā′răk′, -räk′). State in the west of Peninsular Malaysia. It has rich tin deposits and produces sugar, rubber, rice, and coconuts. Ipoh is the capital.

per·am·bu·late (pə-răm′byə-lāt′) *v.* **-lated, -lating, -lates.** —*tr.* To traverse, especially in order to inspect. —*intr.* To walk about; roam; stroll. [Latin *perambulāre* : *per-,* through + *ambulāre,* to walk, AMBULATE.] **—per·am·bu·la·tion** *n.* **—per·am·bu·la·to·ry** (pə-răm′byə-lə-tôr′ē, -tōr′ē) *adj.*

per·am·bu·la·tor (pə-răm′byə-lā′tər) *n. Chiefly British.* A baby carriage. Also called "pram."

per an·num (ăn′əm) *adv. Abbr.* **p.a., per an., per ann.** By the year; annually. [Latin.]

per·bo·rate (pər-bôr′āt′, -bōr′āt′) *n.* A salt containing the radical BO_3, formed from a borate and hydrogen peroxide.

per·cale (pər-kāl′) *n.* An opaque cotton fabric used to make sheets and clothing. [French, from Persian *pargālah*†.]

per·ca·line (pûr′kə-lēn′) *n.* A glazed fine cotton fabric used for linings. [French, from PERCALE.]

per cap·i·ta (kăp′ə-tə) *adv.* **1.** Per person: *income per capita.* **2.** Equally to each heir. [Latin, "by heads."]

per·ceive (pər-sēv′) *tr.v.* **-ceived, -ceiving, -ceives. 1.** To become aware of directly through any of the senses; especially, to see or hear. **2.** To take notice of; observe; detect. **3.** To become aware of in one's mind; achieve understanding of; apprehend. —See Synonyms at **see.** [Middle English *perceiven,* from Old French *perceivre,* from Latin *percipere,* "to seize wholly," "see all the way through" : *per-,* thoroughly + *capere,* to seize.] **—per·ceiv·a·ble** *adj.* **—per·ceiv·a·bly** *adv.*

perceived noise decibel *n. Abbr.* **PNdB.** A unit used to measure perceived noise levels by comparing them with the level of sound pressure of a reference sound that is judged to be of equal level by a normal listener.

per·cent, per cent (pər-sĕnt′) *adv. Abbr.* **p.c., pct.** *Symbol* **%** Per hundred; for or out of each hundred. Used to indicate that the preceding number is a percentage: *A quarter of ten is 25 percent.*
∼*n.* **1.** One part in a hundred. **2.** A percentage: *paid a large percent of her salary for rent.* [Short for Latin *per centum,* by the hundred : *per,* by + *centum,* hundred.]

Usage: *Percent* and *percentage* are both used to express quantity with relation to a whole. *Percent* is always used in a specific sense with a number: *60 percent of the population agreed. Percentage* is never preceded by a number and is generally qualified by a term indicating size: *A large percentage agreed.* It is also often used loosely in the sense of "a certain proportion" *(A percentage of the population objected),* but this has attracted criticism. The construction of the verb following is governed by the number of the noun used with *percent/percentage*: *A large percentage of the patients are . . . .; A large percentage of the population is . . .*

per·cent·age (pər-sĕn′tĭj) *n.* **1.** A fraction or ratio with 100 fixed and understood as the denominator. It is formed by multiplying a decimal equivalent of a fraction by 100. For example, 0.98 equals a percentage of 98. **2. a.** A specified proportion or share in relation to the whole: *in a high percentage of cases.* **b.** *Informal.* A certain proportion: *A percentage of the electorate never votes.* **3.** An allowance, commission, or the like that varies in proportion to a larger sum, such as total sales: *work for a percentage.* **4.** *Informal.* Advantage; gain. —See Usage note at **percent.**

per·cen·tile (pər-sĕn′tīl′) *n. Statistics.* A number scale of 100 equal divisions of a range of a set of statistical data that indicates the value below which that percentage of the data lies. For example, a score higher than 97 percent in an examination is in the 97th percentile. [From PERCENT.]

per·cept (pûr′sĕpt′) *n.* **1.** The object of perception. **2.** An impression in the mind of something perceived by the senses, viewed as the basic component in the formation of concepts. [Back-formation from PERCEPTION.]

per·cep·ti·ble (pər-sĕp′tə-bəl) *adj.* Capable of being perceived; discernible by the senses or mind. **—per·cep·ti·bil·i·ty** *n.* **—per·cep·ti·bly** *adv.*

Synonyms: *appreciable, discernible, noticeable, palpable.*

per·cep·tion (pər-sĕp′shən) *n.* **1.** The process, act, or faculty of perceiving. **2.** The effect or product of perceiving. **3.** The awareness of the external world, or some aspect of it, through physical sensations and the interpretation of these by the mind. **4.** Any insight, intuition, or knowledge gained by perceiving. **5.** The ability or capacity to gain insight by perceiving. [Latin *perceptiō* (stem *perceptiōn-*), from *percipere* (past participle *perceptus*), to PERCEIVE.] **—per·cep·tion·al** *adj.*

per·cep·tive (pər-sĕp′tĭv) *adj.* **1.** Of or pertaining to perception. **2. a.** Having the ability to perceive; keen in discernment. **b.** Marked by discernment and understanding; sensitive. **—per·cep·tive·ly** *adv.* **—per·cep·tiv·i·ty** (pûr′sĕp-tĭv′ə-tē) *n.*

per·cep·tu·al (pər-sĕp′cho͞o-əl) *adj.* Of, based on, or involving perception. **—per·cep·tu·al·ly** *adv.*

Perceval. Variant of **Percival.**

perch[1] (pûrch) *n.* **1.** A rod or branch serving as a roost for a bird. **2. a.** A place for resting or sitting, especially one that is high. **b.** A secure position. **3.** A pole used in acrobatics. **4.** *British.* **a.** A unit of length, the **rod** (sense 12a) *(see).* **b.** One square rod of land. **5.** A unit of cubic measure used in stonework, usually 16.5 feet by 1 foot by 1.5 feet, or 24.75 cubic feet. **6.** A frame on which cloth is laid for examination of quality. **7.** A pole connecting the front and back axles in a wagon, carriage, or the like.
∼*v.* **perched, perching, perches.** —*intr.* **1.** To alight or rest on a perch; roost. **2.** To stand, sit, rest, or be situated on some elevated place or position: *The child perched on the windowsill.* —*tr.* **1.** To place on or as if on a perch. **2.** To lay (cloth) on a perch in order to examine it. [Middle English *perche,* from Old French, from Latin *pertica,* stick, from Italic root *pert-* (unattested), pole.]

perch[2] *n., pl.* **perches** or collectively **perch. 1.** Any of various freshwater fishes of the genus *Perca*; especially, either of two edible species, *P. fluviatilis,* of Europe, and *P. flavescens,* of North America. **2.** Any of various related or similar fishes, such as the **pike-perch** *(see).* [Middle English *perche,* from Old French, from Latin *perca,* from Greek *perkē.*]

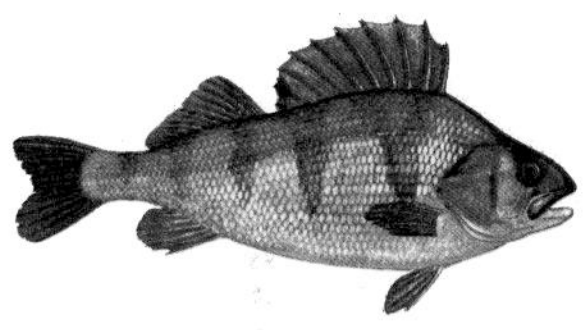

perch *The European perch,* Perca fluviatilis *(above), can live for ten years, growing to more than 3 kilograms (6 1/2 pounds). Adult perch feed on smaller fish.*

per·chance (pər-chăns′, -chäns′) *adv.* Perhaps; possibly. [Middle English *perchaunce,* from Old French *per chance, par chance* : *per, par,* by + CHANCE.]

Per·che·ron (pûr′chə-rŏn′, pûr′shə-) *n.* A large draft horse of a breed developed in France. [French, a native of *le Perche,* district south of Normandy.]

perch·ing (pûr′chĭng) *adj.* Having feet especially adapted for grasping a perch. Said of certain birds.

per·chlo·rate (pər-klôr′āt′, -klōr′āt′) *n.* An ester or a salt of perchloric acid.

per·chlo·ric acid (pər-klôr′ĭk, -klōr′ĭk) *n.* A clear, colorless, hygroscopic liquid, $HClO_4$, explosively unstable under some conditions. It is a powerful oxidant and is used as a catalyst and in explosives.

per·chlor·o·eth·yl·ene (pər-klôr′ō-ĕth′ə-lēn′, pər-klōr′-) *n.* A clear, colorless, nonflammable organic solvent, $Cl_2C{:}CCl_2$, used in dry-cleaning solutions and to dissolve a variety of waxes, tars, rubbers, and gums.

percussion instruments

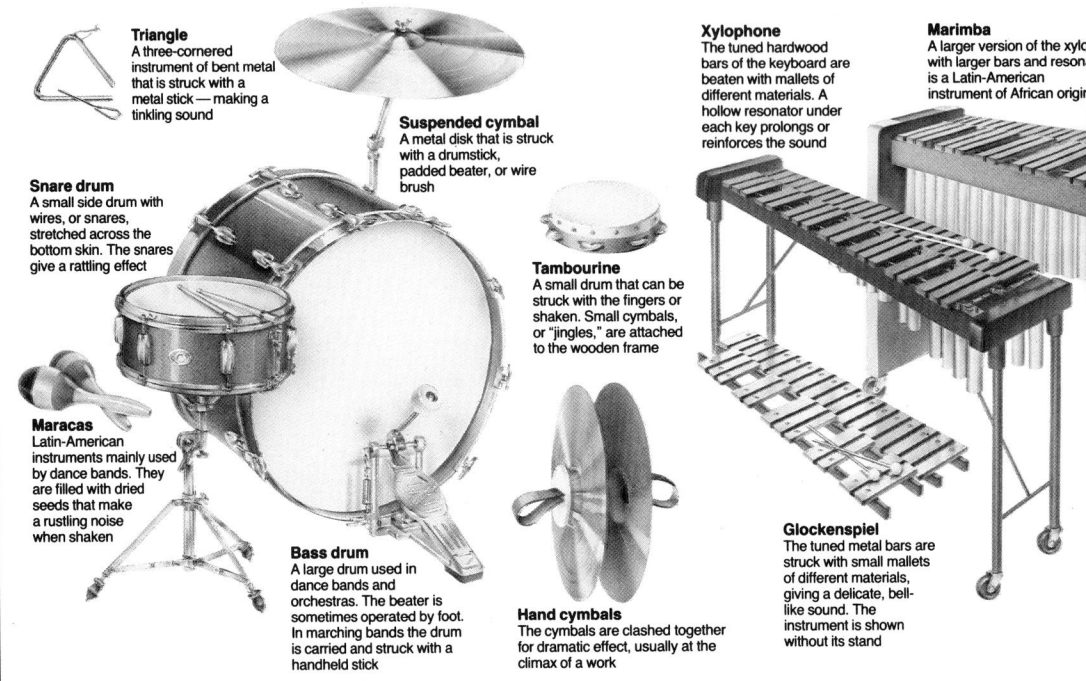

THE BEAT BEHIND AN ORCHESTRA
Musical instruments that are struck with a stick, beater, or hand

Music for a symphony orchestra, a band, or a pop group underlines its rhythms with percussion instruments—the instruments that are played by being struck. In most cases they are struck directly by hand or with a stick or padded beater; but sometimes a pedal-operated beater is used, as with the bass drum.

The ancient Greeks used a small drum called a *tympanum*—a forerunner of the kettledrum—and large kettledrums appeared in European orchestras in the 17th century. Today's kettledrums, or timpani, are tuned to a definite pitch that can be altered mechanically by means of a pedal or by screws around the drumhead.

Other tuned percussion instruments include the glockenspiel, chimes, xylophone, and marimba. Those not tuned, which always produce the same note when struck, include the bass drum, snare drum, tambourine, triangle, maracas, and cymbals.

Triangle
A three-cornered instrument of bent metal that is struck with a metal stick — making a tinkling sound

Suspended cymbal
A metal disk that is struck with a drumstick, padded beater, or wire brush

Snare drum
A small side drum with wires, or snares, stretched across the bottom skin. The snares give a rattling effect

Tambourine
A small drum that can be struck with the fingers or shaken. Small cymbals, or "jingles," are attached to the wooden frame

Maracas
Latin-American instruments mainly used by dance bands. They are filled with dried seeds that make a rustling noise when shaken

Bass drum
A large drum used in dance bands and orchestras. The beater is sometimes operated by foot. In marching bands the drum is carried and struck with a handheld stick

Hand cymbals
The cymbals are clashed together for dramatic effect, usually at the climax of a work

Xylophone
The tuned hardwood bars of the keyboard are beaten with mallets of different materials. A hollow resonator under each key prolongs or reinforces the sound

Marimba
A larger version of the xylo with larger bars and reson is a Latin-American instrument of African origin

Glockenspiel
The tuned metal bars are struck with small mallets of different materials, giving a delicate, bell-like sound. The instrument is shown without its stand

per·cip·i·ent (pər-sĭp′ē-ənt) *adj.* Having the power of perceiving; especially, perceiving keenly and readily.
—*n.* One that perceives. [Latin *percipiēns* (stem *percipient-*), present participle of *percipere,* to PERCEIVE.] —**per·cip·i·ence** *n.*

Per·ci·val, Per·ce·val (pûr′sə-vəl). Also **Par·si·fal** (pär′sə-fəl), **Par·si·val** (-vəl). *Arthurian Legend.* A naive and virtuous young knight who is eventually granted a sight of the Holy Grail.

per·coid (pûr′koid′) *n.* Also **per·coi·de·an** (pər-koi′dē-ən). Any member of the Percoidea, a large suborder of fishes that includes the perches, sunfishes, and groupers. [New Latin *Percoidea* : Latin *perca,* PERCH (fish) + -OID.] —**per·coid, per·coi·de·an** *adj.*

per·co·late (pûr′kə-lāt′) *v.* **-lated, -lating, -lates.** —*tr.* **1.** To cause (liquid, powder, or small particles) to pass through a porous substance or small holes; filter; sift. **2.** To pass or ooze through: *Water percolated the sand.* **3.** To make (coffee, for example) in a percolator. —*intr.* **1.** To drain or seep through a porous substance or filter. **2.** *Informal.* To become lively or active. **3.** *Informal.* To pass along gradually: *The news percolated down to me.*
—*n.* (pûr′kə-lĭt, -lāt′). A liquid that has been percolated. [Latin *percōlāre* : *per-,* through + *cōlāre,* to filter, strain, from *cōlum,* sieve.] —**per·co·la·tion** *n.*

per·co·la·tor (pûr′kə-lā′tər) *n.* A type of coffeepot in which boiling water is forced repeatedly up through a center tube to filter back down through a perforated container of ground coffee.

per con·tra (pər kŏn′trə) *adv.* **1. a.** On the contrary. **b.** By way of contrast. **2.** As an offset. [Latin.]

per·cuss (pər-kŭs′) *tr.v.* **-cussed, -cussing, -cusses.** To strike or tap firmly, as in medical percussion: *percuss a patient's chest.* [Latin *percutere* (past participle *percussus*), to strike hard : *per-* (intensive) + *quatere,* to strike.]

per·cus·sion (pər-kŭsh′ən) *n.* **1.** The striking together of two bodies, especially when noise is produced. **2.** The sound, vibration, or shock caused by such a striking together. **3.** The act of detonating a percussion cap in a firearm. **4.** A method of medical diagnosis in which various areas of the body, especially the chest, back, and abdomen, are tapped to determine by resonance the condition of internal organs. **5. a.** Musical percussion instruments collectively. **b.** The section of an orchestra consisting of these instruments. [Latin *percussiō* (stem *percussiōn-*), from *percutere,* to PERCUSS.]

percussion cap *n.* A thin metal cap containing gunpowder or some other detonator that explodes on being struck.

percussion instrument *n.* A musical instrument in which sound is produced by striking, such as a drum, xylophone, or cymbal.

per·cus·sion·ist (pər-kŭsh′ə-nĭst) *n.* One who plays percussion instruments.

per·cus·sive (pər-kŭs′ĭv) *adj.* Of, pertaining to, or characterized by percussion. —**per·cus·sive·ly** *adv.* —**per·cus·sive·ness** *n.*

per·cu·ta·ne·ous (pûr′kyōō-tā′nē-əs) *adj.* Passed, done, or effected through or by means of the skin. —**per·cu·ta·ne·ous·ly** *adv.*

Per·cy (pûr′sē), **Sir Henry,** known as "Hotspur" (1364–1403). English soldier. He plotted with his father, the Earl of Northumberland, to overthrow Henry IV. He was killed in battle at Shrewsbury.

Percy, Thomas (1729–1811). English antiquary and poet and the bishop of Dromore from 1782. His chief work is *The Reliques of Ancient English Poetry* (1765), a selection of medieval ballads and songs that stimulated the romantic revival.

per di·em (dē′əm, dī′əm) *adv. Abbr.* **p.d., P.D.** Per day.
—*n. Abbr.* **p.d., P.D.** An allowance for daily expenses.
—*adj. Abbr.* **p.d., P.D.** Reckoned on a daily basis: *per diem costs.* [Latin, "by the day."]

per·di·tion (pər-dĭsh′ən) *n.* **1. a.** The loss of the soul; eternal damnation. **b.** Hell. **2.** *Archaic.* Utter loss or ruin. [Middle English *perdicioun,* from Late Latin *perditiō* (stem *perditiōn-*), from Latin *perdere* (past participle *perditus*), to throw away, destroy, lose : *per-,* away + *dare,* to give.]

per·du, per·due (pər-dōō′, -dyōō′, -dū′) *adj.* Being out of sight; concealed. Used chiefly in the phrase *lie perdu.*
—*n. Obsolete.* A soldier sent on a dangerous mission. [French, "lost," from the past participle of *perdre,* to lose, from Latin *perdere.* See **perdition.**]

per·du·ra·ble (pər-dŏor′ə-bəl, -dyŏor′ə-bəl) *adj.* Extremely durable; permanent. [Middle English, from Old French, from Late Latin *perdūrābilis,* from Latin *perdūrāre,* "to last throughout," endure : *per-,* throughout + *dūrāre,* to last.] —**per·du·ra·bil·i·ty** *n.* —**per·du·ra·bly** *adv.*

père (pâr) *n. French.* Father. Used after a proper name to distinguish a father from a son who has the same name: *Dumas père.* Compare **fils.**

Père Da·vid's deer (pâr′ dä-vēdz′, pâr-dä′vĭdz) *n.* A large reddish-gray Chinese deer, *Elaphurus davidianus,* that survives only in domesticated herds. [After Père Armand *David* (1826–1900), French missionary and naturalist.]

per·e·gri·nate (pĕr′ə-grə-nāt′) *v.* **-nated, -nating, -nates.** —*intr.* To journey or travel from place to place usually for a long time and

Chimes
The free-hanging tubular
bells are struck by hand
with a small hammer

Gong
The bronze disk,
suspended from a stand,
is struck with hard,
medium, or soft hammers

Kettledrum
The drumhead is attached
to a deep metal bowl. The
tone quality varies according
to the kind of drumstick used
and the point of impact

over great distances. —*tr.* To travel through or over. [Latin *peregrīnārī,* to travel in foreign lands, from *peregrīnus,* foreigner. See **peregrine.**] —**per·e·gri·na·tion** *n.* —**per·e·gri·na·tor** *n.*

per·e·grine (pĕr′ə-grĭn, -grēn′) *adj.* **1.** Foreign; alien. **2.** Roving or wandering; migratory.
~*n.* The peregrine falcon. [Medieval Latin *peregrīnus,* from Latin, a foreigner, stranger, from *pereger,* being abroad : *per-,* away + *ager,* land, field.]

peregrine falcon *n.* A widely distributed bird of prey, *Falco peregrinus,* having gray and white plumage, formerly much used in falconry. Also called "peregrine." [Middle English, translation of Medieval Latin *falco peregrinus,* "pilgrim falcon"; so named because young peregrines were caught in passage ("pilgrimage") from their breeding place, rather than taken from the nest.]

Per·el·man (pĕr′əl-mən), **S(idney) J(oseph)** (1904–79). U.S. humorist. Beginning as a cartoonist, he became a scriptwriter on the Marx Brothers' films.

per·emp·to·ry (pə-rĕmp′tə-rē) *adj.* **1.** Overbearing; imperious: *a peremptory manner.* **2.** Having the nature of or expressing command; urgent: *"a bell began to toll with a peremptory clang."* (Thomas Hardy). **3.** Not admitting denial or refusal; imperative: *a peremptory command.* **4.** *Law.* Precluding further debate or action: *a peremptory decree.* [Late Latin *peremptōrius,* "precluding debate," decisive, from *perimere* (past participle *peremptus*), to take away completely : *per-,* completely + *emere,* to obtain.] —**per·emp·to·ri·ly** *adv.* —**per·emp·to·ri·ness** *n.*

peremptory challenge *n. Law.* A challenge of a juror that is issued as a right and requires no explanation or justification.

per·en·nate (pĕr′ə-nāt′, pə-rĕn′āt′) *intr.v.* **-nated, -nating, -nates.** To survive from one growing season to the next, often with a period of reduced or arrested growth between seasons. Used of plants. [Latin *perennātus,* past participle of *perennāre,* to survive, continue : PER- (through) + *-ennāre,* from *annus,* year.]

per·en·ni·al (pə-rĕn′ē-əl) *adj.* **1.** Lasting or active through the year or through many years: *the perennial snowcaps of the Alps.* **2. a.** Lasting an indefinitely long time; everlasting; perpetual: *perennial happiness.* **b.** Appearing again and again; continually recurring. **3.** *Botany.* Having a life span of more than two years. Compare **annual, biennial.** —See Synonyms at **continual.**
~*n. Botany.* A perennial plant. [Latin *perennis : per-,* throughout + *annus,* year.] —**per·en·ni·al·ly** *adv.*

Per·es (pĕr′ĕz′), **Shimon** (1923–). Israeli politician, prime minister

(1984–). He served as minister of defense (1974–77) and was acting prime minister in 1977. In 1984 he won a general election without an overall majority and formed a government of national unity with the outgoing prime minister, Yitzhak Shamir.

perf. 1. perfect. **2.** perforated.

per·fect (pûr′fĭkt) *adj. Abbr.* **perf. 1.** Lacking nothing essential to the whole; complete of its nature or kind. **2.** In a state of undiminished or highest excellence; without defect; flawless. **3.** Highly skilled or talented in a certain field or area. **4. a.** Faithfully reproducing an original; accurate; exact: *a perfect reproduction of a painting.* **b.** Corresponding in every respect to an ideal or conventionally recognized standard: *the perfect host.* **c.** Precise; correct: *perfect pitch; perfect timing.* **5.** Complete; thorough; utter: *a perfect fool.* **6.** Pure; undiluted; unmixed: *perfect red.* **7.** Excellent and delightful in all respects: *a perfect day.* **8.** *Botany.* Having both stamens and pistils in the same flower; monoclinous. **9.** *Grammar.* Of, pertaining to, or designating a verb form expressing action completed prior to a fixed point of reference in time. English verbs have three perfect tenses: the present (or simple) perfect, the pluperfect (or past perfect), and the future perfect. **10.** Of, pertaining to, or designating a number or quantity equal to an integral power of another number or quantity: *4, 9, and 16 are perfect squares.* **11.** *Music.* **a.** Designating the three basic intervals of the octave, fourth, and fifth. **b.** Designating a cadence in which the final chord has its root in both bass and soprano. **12.** Designating a gas that obeys the ideal gas laws.
~*n. Abbr.* **perf.** *Grammar.* **1.** The perfect tense. **2.** A verb or verb form in this tense.
~*tr.v.* (pər-fĕkt′) **perfected, -fecting, -fects. 1.** To bring to perfection or completion. **2.** To improve. **3.** To complete the printing of (a sheet) by printing the reverse side. [Middle English *perfit, parfit,* from Old French *parfit,* from Latin *perfectus,* finished, complete, excellent, from the past participle of *perficere,* to complete : *per-,* completely + *facere,* to do.] —**per·fect·er** *n.* —**per·fect·ness** *n.*
Usage: In its absolute senses, it is not possible to use comparative and superlative forms with *perfect* in standard English. However, in the more general sense of "excellent," these forms are often used loosely: *That's one of the most perfect specimens I've ever seen.*

perfect binding *n.* A common method of binding books in which each cut sheet is glued by one edge onto a stiff backing. —**per·fect-bound** (pûr′fĭkt-bound′) *adj.*

per·fect·i·ble (pər-fĕk′tə-bəl) *adj.* Capable of becoming or being made perfect. —**per·fect·i·bil·i·ty** *n.*

per·fec·tion (pər-fĕk′shən) *n.* **1.** The state or quality of being perfect. **2.** The process or act of perfecting: *Perfection of the plan took years.* **3.** A person or thing that perfectly embodies something: *Her pastry is culinary perfection.* **4.** An instance or quality of excellence. —**to perfection.** Perfectly: *cooked to perfection.*

per·fec·tion·ism (pər-fĕk′shə-nĭz′əm) *n.* **1.** A belief that moral or spiritual perfection can be achieved by man in this life. **2.** A propensity for setting extremely high standards and being displeased with anything less. —**per·fec·tion·ist** *n. & adj.* —**per·fec·tion·is·tic** (pər-fĕk′shə-nĭs′tĭk) *adj.*

per·fec·tive (pər-fĕk′tĭv) *adj.* **1.** Tending toward perfection. **2.** *Grammar.* Of or designating a verb in the perfective aspect.
~*n. Grammar.* **1.** The perfective aspect. **2.** A verb in the perfective aspect. —**per·fec·tive·ly** *adv.* —**per·fec·tive·ness, per·fec·tiv·i·ty** (pûr′fĕk-tĭv′ə-tē) *n.*

perfective aspect *n.* An aspect of verbs that expresses a completed action as distinct from a continuing or not necessarily completed action. Compare **imperfective aspect.** See **aspect.**

per·fect·ly (pûr′fĭkt-lē) *adv.* **1.** In a perfect manner or to a perfect degree. **2.** Completely; fully; wholly: *perfectly ridiculous.*

perfect number *n.* A number that is equal to the sum of its integral factors, as 28, whose divisors are 1, 2, 4, 7, and 14. The first four perfect numbers are 6, 28, 496, and 8,128.

per·fec·to (pər-fĕk′tō) *n., pl.* **-tos.** A cigar of standard length, thick in the center and tapering at each end. [Spanish, perfect, from Latin *perfectus,* PERFECT.]

perfect participle *n.* The **past participle** (see).

perfect pitch *n.* **Absolute pitch** (see).

perfect rhyme *n.* The commonest English rhyme, having identity in sound for the last accented vowel and any final consonants or syllables but with variation in the preceding consonant, as *great, late; rider, spider; dutiful, unbeautiful.* Also called "full rhyme," "true rhyme."

perfect square *n.* An integer that is the square of an integer.

perfect year *n.* In the Hebrew calendar, a year having 355 days or a leap year having 385 days. See feature at **calendar.**

per·fer·vid (pər-fûr′vĭd) *adj.* Impassioned; zealous; extravagantly eager. [New Latin *perfervidus : per-* (intensifier) + Latin *fervidus,* FERVID.] —**per·fer·vid·ly** *adv.* —**per·fer·vid·ness** *n.*

per·fid·i·ous (pər-fĭd′ē-əs) *adj.* Of, pertaining to, or marked by perfidy. —See Synonyms at **faithless.** —**per·fid·i·ous·ly** *adv.*

per·fi·dy (pûr′fə-dē) *n., pl.* **-dies.** Deliberate breach of faith; calculated violation of trust; treachery. [Latin *perfidia,* from *perfidus,* treacherous : *per-* (destruction) + *fidēs,* faith.]

per·fo·li·ate (pər-fō′lē-ĭt) *adj.* Designating a leaf that completely clasps the stem and is apparently pierced by it. [New Latin *perfoliatus,* "pierced through the leaf" : Latin *per-,* through + *foliātus,* "leaved," FOLIATE.] —**per·fo·li·a·tion** *n.*

per·fo·rate (pûr′fə-rāt′) *tr.v.* **-rated, -rating, -rates. 1.** To pierce, punch, or bore a hole or holes in. **2.** To pierce or stamp (a sheet of

peregrine *This falcon can dive on its prey—often a grouse or pigeon—at speeds of up to 130 kilometers (80 miles) per hour. It kills the victim in midair with a single blow of its talons, then circles back to retrieve the body from the ground. Peregrines mate for life, often returning to the same aerie year after year; they are found on all of the world's continents except Antarctica.*

Pericles *A Greek bust of the Athenian orator and statesman who was responsible for the building of the Parthenon in Athens. The bust, now in the British Museum in London, bears Pericles' name in Greek characters across its base.*

PRONUNCIATION KEY

ă, pat; ā, pay; âr, care;
ä, father, are; b, **bib**;
ch, **church**; d, **deed**; ĕ, pet;
ē, be; f, **fife**; g, **gag**; h, **hat**;
hw, **which**; ĭ, pit; ī, pie;
îr, **pier**; j, **judge**; k, **kick**;
l, lid, needle; m, **mum**;
n, no, sudden; ng, **thing**;
ŏ, pot; ō, **toe**; ô, **paw**, **for**;
oi, noise; ou, **out**; o͝o, **book**;
o͞o, **boot**; p, **pop**; r, **roar**;
s, **sauce**; sh, **ship**, **dish**;
t, **tight**; th, **thin**, **path**;
th, this, bathe; ŭ, cut; ûr, **fur**;
v, valve; w, **with**; y, **yes**;
z, zebra, **size**; zh, **vision**;
ə, about, item, edible, gallop, circus, peaceful

IN FOREIGN WORDS:

à, *Fr.* ami; œ, *Fr.* **feu**, *Ger.* **schön**; ü, *Fr.* **tu**, *Ger.* **über**; KH, *Ger.* **ich**, *Scot.* **loch**; N, *Fr.* bon; y', *Fr.* Compiègne

STRESS MARKS:

Primary stress: ′
in·cite′ (ĭn-sīt′)
Secondary stress: ′
in′sight′ (ĭn′sīt′)

paper, for example) with rows of holes, such as those between postage stamps, to allow easy separation.
~*adj.* (pûr′fər-ĭt, -fə-rāt′). Perforated. [Latin *perforāre* : *per-*, through + *forāre*, to bore.] —**per·fo·ra·ble** (pûr′fər-ə-bəl) *adj.* —**per·fo·ra·tive** (pûr′fə-rā′tĭv), **per·fo·ra·to·ry** (pûr′fər-ə-tôr′ē, -tōr′ē) *adj.* —**per·fo·ra·tor** (-fə-rā′tər) *n.*

per·fo·rat·ed (pûr′fə-rā′tĭd) *adj. Abbr.* **perf.** Having a perforation or perforations.

per·fo·ra·tion (pûr′fə-rā′shən) *n.* **1.** The act of perforating or state of being perforated. **2.** A hole or series or set of holes punched or bored through something. **3.** In stamp collecting: **a.** Any of the small holes, or the set of such holes, punched between or around individual stamps on a sheet or roll for the purpose of easy separation. **b.** The method of dividing sheets or rolls of stamps in this way. Compare **roulette**. **4.** The series of ridges and indentations along the edge of an object, especially a postage stamp, that has been detached by tearing along a perforated line.

per·force (pər-fôrs′, -fōrs′) *adv.* By necessity; willy-nilly. [Middle English *par force*, from Old French : *par*, by + FORCE.]

per·form (pər-fôrm′) *v.* **-formed, -forming, -forms.** —*tr.* **1.** To begin and carry through to completion; do: *perform an operation.* **2.** To take action in accordance with the requirements of; fulfill (a promise or duty, for example). **3. a.** To enact (a feat or role) before an audience. **b.** To give a public presentation of (a piece of music, for example). —*intr.* **1.** To carry out a particular activity; function, especially in a specified way: *My car performs badly on wet roads.* **2.** To fulfill an obligation or requirement; accomplish something as promised or expected. **3.** To portray a role or demonstrate some skill before an audience. **4.** To present a dramatic or musical work or other entertainment before an audience. [Middle English *performen*, from Norman French *parformer*, variant of Old French *parfornir* (assimilated to *forme*, FORM) : *par-* (intensifier), from Latin *per-* + *fornir*, to FURNISH.] —**per·form·a·ble** *adj.* —**per·form·er** *n.*
Synonyms: *accomplish, achieve, discharge, effect, execute, fulfill.*

per·form·ance (pər-fôr′məns) *n.* **1.** The act of performing, or the state of being performed. **2.** The act or style of performing a work or role before an audience. **3. a.** The way in which someone or something functions. **b.** Excellence in functioning. Also used adjectivally: *a high-performance car.* **4.** A presentation, especially a theatrical one, before an audience. **5.** Something performed; an accomplishment; a deed. **6.** *Informal.* An instance of bad behavior, such as a display of temper, usually in public. **7.** *Informal.* Something involving effort or difficulty: *Moving from the city was quite a performance.* **8.** *Linguistics.* The collective spoken utterances of a user of language as opposed to his linguistic **competence** *(see).*

performance test *n.* A psychological test that requires only nonverbal responses, as one used to test the intellectual ability of children with speech problems.

per·form·a·tive (pər-fôr′mə-tĭv) *adj. Philosophy.* **1.** Designating an utterance that is itself an instance of the action it describes; for example, utterances such as *I promise that* . . . or *I command that* . . . are instances of promising or commanding. **2.** Designating a verb used in such an utterance.
~*n. Philosophy.* A performative verb or utterance.

performing arts *pl.n.* Arts, such as drama and music, that are realized in public performance.

per·fume (pûr′fyo͞om′, pər-fyo͞om′) *n.* **1.** A volatile liquid, distilled from flowers or prepared synthetically, that emits and diffuses a fragrant odor. **2.** Any agreeable scent or odor. —See Synonyms at **smell.**
~*tr.v.* (pər-fyo͞om′) **perfumed, -fuming, -fumes.** To impregnate with fragrance; impart a pleasant odor to. [French *parfum*, probably from obsolete Italian *parfumare*, to smoke through : *par-*, through, from Latin *per-* + *fumare*, to smoke, from Latin *fūmāre*, from *fūmus*, smoke.]

per·fum·er (pər-fyo͞o′mər) *n.* A maker or seller of perfumes.

per·fum·er·y (pər-fyo͞o′mə-rē) *n., pl.* **-ies.** **1.** Perfumes in general. **2.** An establishment that specializes in making or selling perfume. **3.** The art of making perfume.

per·func·to·ry (pər-fŭngk′tə-rē) *adj.* Done or acting routinely and with little interest or care. —See Synonyms at **superficial.** [Late Latin *perfunctōrius*, from Latin *perfungī* (past participle *perfunctus*), "to get through with" : *per-*, completely + *fungī*, to perform.] —**per·func·to·ri·ly** *adv.* —**per·func·to·ri·ness** *n.*

per·fuse (pər-fyo͞oz′) *tr.v.* **-fused, -fusing, -fuses.** **1.** To coat, suffuse, or permeate with liquid, color, or light. **2.** To pour or diffuse (a liquid) over or through something. [Latin *perfundere* (past participle *perfusus*), to pour over or through : *per-*, through + *fundere*, to pour.] —**per·fu·sive** (pər-fyo͞o′sĭv, -zĭv) *adj.*

Per·ga·mum (pûr′gə-məm). Ancient Greek city of northwestern Asia Minor. It became important (*c.* 300 B.C.) after the breakup of the Macedonian Empire. Known chiefly for its sculpture, it also had a library second in size only to the one at Alexandria.

per·go·la (pûr′gə-lə) *n.* An arbor or passageway with a roof of trelliswork on which climbing plants grow. [Italian, from Latin *pergula*, projecting roof, from *pergere*, to proceed.]

Per·go·le·si (pĕr′gō-lā′zē), **Giovanni Battista** (1710–36). Italian composer. Although he also composed sacred music, he is best known for his comic opera *La Serva Padrona* ("The Maid as Mistress"), written in 1733.

per·haps (pər-hăps′) *adv.* Possibly; maybe; it may be that. [PER (by) + plural of HAP (chance).]

pe·ri (pîr′ē) *n.* **1.** In Persian mythology, a beautiful fairy. **2.** A fairylike being, especially a beautiful young girl. [Persian *pāri*; akin to Avestan *pairika*, witch.]

peri– *prefix.* Indicates: **1.** About, around, encircling, or enclosing; for example, **periotic, periscope. 2.** Close at hand, adjacent, or near; for example, **perihelion.** [Latin, from Greek, from *peri*, about, near, around.]

per·i·anth (pĕr′ē-ănth′) *n. Botany.* The outer organs of a flower, consisting of the calyx and corolla (the sepals and petals), or of either of these if the other is absent. [French *périanthe*, from New Latin *perianthium* : PERI- + ANTH(O)- + -IUM.]

per·i·apt (pĕr′ē-ăpt′) *n.* An amulet or charm worn as protection against harm and disease. [Old French *periapte*, from Greek *periapton*, from *periaptos*, appended, from *periaptein*, to hang or fasten around : *peri-*, PERI- + *haptein*, to fasten (see **synapse**).]

per·i·blem (pĕr′ə-blĕm′) *n. Botany.* A zone of tissue in the apical meristem of a root that develops into the cortex. [German, from Greek *periblēma*, protection, from *periballein*, to throw around : *peri-*, PERI- + *ballein*, to throw.]

per·i·car·di·tis (pĕr′ĭ-kär-dī′tĭs) *n.* Inflammation of the pericardium. [New Latin : PERICARD(IUM) + -ITIS.]

per·i·car·di·um (pĕr′ĭ-kär′dē-əm) *n., pl.* **-dia** (-dē-ə). The membranous sac enclosing the heart. [New Latin, from Greek *perikardion*, from *perikardios*, around the heart : PERI- + *kardia*, heart.] —**per·i·car·di·ac** (pĕr′ĭ-kär′dē-ăk′), **per·i·car·di·al** *adj.*

per·i·carp (pĕr′ĭ-kärp′) *n. Botany.* The casing of the seed or seeds within a fruit, developed from the ovary wall. [New Latin *pericarpium*, from Greek *perikarpion*, pod, shell : *peri-*, PERI- + -CARP.] —**per·i·car·pi·al** (pĕr′ĭ-kär′pē-əl) *adj.*

per·i·chon·dri·um (pĕr′ĭ-kŏn′drē-əm) *n., pl.* **-dria** (-drē-ə). *Anatomy.* The fibrous membrane covering the surface of cartilage except at joint endings. [New Latin : PERI- + CHONDR(O)- + -IUM.] —**per·i·chon·dri·al** *adj.*

per·i·clase (pĕr′ĭ-klās′, -klāz′) *n.* A mineral form of magnesium oxide, MgO, usually occurring in isomeric crystals or grains. [German *Periklas*, from New Latin *periclasia*, "perfect cleavage (of the crystals)" : PERI- (around, hence above others, exceedingly) + -CLASE.]

Per·i·cles (pĕr′ĭ-klēz′) (*c.* 495–429 B.C.). Athenian statesman and general. A great democrat and skilled orator, he controlled Athenian affairs during the city's most glorious era. He fostered cultural life, encouraging Sophocles and Phidias among others, and ordered the building of the Parthenon. —**Per·i·cle·an** (pĕr′ĭ-klē′ən) *adj.*

per·i·cli·nal (pĕr′ĭ-klī′nəl) *adj.* **1.** Of or pertaining to a pericline. **2.** *Botany.* **a.** Designating a line of cell division parallel to the surface of the organ, as found in a meristem. **b.** Having tissue of one origin completely enclosed by tissue of a different origin. Said of certain chimeras.

per·i·cline (pĕr′ĭ-klīn′) *n.* **1.** A variety of albite occurring as elongated white crystals. **2.** A formation of stratified rock shaped like a dome or basin in which the slopes follow the direction of folding. Also called "dome." [Greek *periklinēs*, sloping on all sides : *peri-*, PERI- + *klinein*, to slope, lean.]

per·i·cra·ni·um (pĕr′ĭ-krā′nē-əm) *n., pl.* **-nia** (-nē-ə). *Anatomy.* The external **periosteum** *(see)* that covers the outer surface of the skull. [New Latin, from Greek *perikranion*, from *perikranios*, around the skull : PERI- + *kranion*, CRANIUM.] —**per·i·cra·ni·al** *adj.*

per·i·cy·cle (pĕr′ĭ-sī′kəl) *n. Botany.* The outermost layer of the stele of a plant, usually though not always consisting of a layer of cells. [French *péricycle*, from Greek *perikuklos*, spherical : *peri-*, PERI- + *kuklos*, CYCLE.] —**per·i·cy·clic** (pĕr′ĭ-sī′klĭk) *adj.*

per·i·cyn·thi·on (pĕr′ə-sĭn′thē-ən) *n.* The point at which a spacecraft launched from the earth into orbit around the moon is nearest to the moon. Compare **apocynthion, perilune.** [PERI- + *-cynthion*, from CYNTHIA (the moon).]

per·i·derm (pĕr′ə-dûrm′) *n. Botany.* An outer layer of tissue of plant roots and stems, consisting of the bark and the layer of growing tissue beneath the bark. [New Latin *peridermis* : PERI- + -DERM.] —**per·i·der·mal** (pĕr′ə-dûr′məl), **per·i·der·mic** *adj.*

pe·rid·i·um (pə-rĭd′ē-əm) *n., pl.* **-ridia** (-rĭd′-ē-ə). The covering of the spore-bearing organ in many fungi. [New Latin, from Greek *pēridion*, diminutive of *pēra*†, leather bag.] —**pe·rid·i·al** *adj.*

per·i·dot (pĕr′ə-dŏt′, -dō′) *n.* A transparent, pale-green variety of **olivine** *(see).* [French *péridot*, from Old French *peritot*†.] —**per·i·dot·ic** (pĕr′ə-dŏt′ĭk, -dō′tĭk) *adj.*

per·i·do·tite (pĕr′ə-dō-tīt′, pə-rĭd′ə-tīt′) *n.* Any of a group of igneous rocks composed mainly of olivine and various pyroxenes and amphiboles. [French *péridotite*, from *péridot*, PERIDOT.]

per·i·gee (pĕr′ə-jē) *n.* The point nearest the earth in the orbit of the moon or a satellite. Compare **apogee.** [French *périgée*, from New Latin *perigeum*, from Greek *perigeion*, from *perigeios*, near the earth : *peri-*, PERI- + *gē*, the earth.] —**per·i·ge·an** (pĕr′ə-jē′ən) *adj.*

per·i·gla·cial (pĕr′ĭ-glā′shəl) *adj.* Designating a region around a glacier.

per·i·gon (pĕr′ĭ-gŏn′, -gən) *n.* An angle of 360°; a round angle. [PERI- + -GON.]

Pér·i·gueux (pĕr′ə-gō′). Town in southwestern France. Situated on the Isle River, it is the capital of the Dordogne department.

pe·rig·y·nous (pə-rĭj′ə-nəs) *adj. Botany.* **1.** Having sepals, petals, and stamens around the edge of a flat or cuplike receptacle containing the ovary. **2.** Designating flower parts arranged in this way: *perigynous stamens.* [New Latin *perigynus* : PERI- + -GYNOUS.] —**pe·rig·y·ny** (pə-rĭj′ə-nē) *n.*

per·i·he·li·on (pĕr′ə-hē′lē-ən, -hēl′yən) *n., pl.* **-helia** (-hē′lē-ə, -hēl′yə). The point nearest the sun in the orbit of a planet or other body. Compare **aphelion.** [New Latin : PERI- + Greek *hēlios,* sun.] —**per·i·he·li·al** *adj.*

per·il (pĕr′əl) *n.* **1.** A condition of imminent danger; exposure to the risk of harm or loss. **2.** Something that endangers; a serious risk. —**at one's peril.** At the risk of danger or punishment. —See Synonyms at **danger.** ~*tr.v.* **periled, -il·ing, -ils.** Also chiefly British **-illed, -illing.** To expose to danger or the chance of injury; imperil. [Middle English, from Old French, from Latin *perīculum,* trial, danger.] —**per·il·ous** *adj.* —**per·il·ous·ly** *adv.*

per·i·lune (pĕr′ə-loōn′) *n.* The point at which a spacecraft launched from the moon into lunar orbit is nearest to the moon. Compare **apolune, pericynthion.** [PERI- + Latin *lūna,* moon, by analogy with *perigee.*]

per·i·lymph (pĕr′ə-lĭmf′) *n.* The fluid surrounding the structures of the internal ear in vertebrates.

pe·rim·e·ter (pə-rĭm′ə-tər) *n.* **1.** *Mathematics.* **a.** A closed curve bounding a plane area. **b.** The length of such a boundary. **2.** Any outer boundary, such as the edge of a playing field or a fortified strip protecting a military position. **3.** A diagnostic instrument used to measure the extent of a person's field of vision. [French *périmètre,* from Latin *perimetros,* from Greek : *peri-,* PERI- + -METER.] —**per·i·met·ric** (pĕr′ə-mĕt′rĭk), **per·i·met·ri·cal** *adj.* —**per·i·met·ri·cal·ly** *adv.*

per·i·morph (pĕr′ə-môrf′) *n.* A mineral that encloses a different mineral. Compare **endomorph.** [PERI- + -MORPH.] —**per·i·mor·phic** (pĕr′ə-môr′fĭk), **per·i·mor·phous** *adj.* —**per·i·mor·phism** (pĕr′ə-môr′fĭz′əm) *n.*

per·i·my·si·um (pĕr′ə-mĭzh′ē-əm, -mĭz′ē-əm) *n., pl.* **-mysia** (-mĭzh′ē-ə, -mĭz′ē-ə). A sheath of connective tissue enveloping bundles of muscle fibers. [New Latin : PERI- + Greek *mus,* muscle.]

per·i·na·tal (pĕr′ə-nāt′l) *adj.* Of, pertaining to, or occurring in the period from approximately three months before to one month after birth: *perinatal mortality.*

per·i·neph·ri·um (pĕr′ə-nĕf′rē-əm) *n., pl.* **-ria** (-rē-ə). The connective and fatty tissue surrounding the kidney. [New Latin, from Greek *perinephros,* fat around the kidney : *peri-,* PERI- + *nephros,* kidney.] —**per·i·neph·ral, per·i·neph·ric** *adj.*

per·i·ne·um (pĕr′ə-nē′əm) *n., pl.* **-nea** (-nē′ə). **1.** The portion of the body in the pelvis occupied by the urogenital passages and the rectum. **2.** The region between the scrotum and the anus in males, and between the posterior vulva junction and the anus in females. [New Latin, from Late Latin *perinaion,* from Greek : *peri-,* PERI- + *inan*†, to excrete.] —**per·i·ne·al** *adj.*

per·i·neu·ri·um (pĕr′ə-noōr′ē-əm, -nyoōr′ē-əm) *n., pl.* **-neuria** (-noōr′ē-ə, -nyoōr′ē-ə). A sheath of connective tissue enclosing a bundle of nerve fibers. [New Latin : PERI- + NEUR(O)- + -IUM.] —**per·i·neu·ri·al** *adj.*

pe·ri·od (pîr′ē-əd) *n.* *Abbr.* **per. 1.** An interval of time characterized by the occurrence of certain conditions or events: *slack periods.* **2.** An interval of time characterized by the prevalence of a specified culture, ideology, or technology: *artifacts of the pre-Columbian period.* **3.** A unit of geologic time longer than an epoch and shorter than an era. **4.** An interval regarded as a distinct evolutionary or developmental phase; a stage: *Picasso's blue period.* **5.** Any of various arbitrary temporal units, especially: **a.** A division of time allotted for teaching a class. **b.** A division of the playing time of a game. **6.** *Physics.* The time interval between two successive occurrences of any recurrent event or cycle; the reciprocal of frequency. **7.** An instance or occurrence of menstruation. **8.** A point or portion of time at which something is ended; a completion; a conclusion. **9.** The full pause at the end of a spoken sentence. **10.** A punctuation mark (.) indicating a full stop, placed at the end of declarative sentences and other statements thought to be complete, and after many abbreviations. **11.** In formal literary composition, a sentence of several carefully balanced clauses. **12.** A metrical unit of Greek verse consisting of two or more cola. **13.** *Music.* A group of two or more phrases within a composition, made up of eight or sixteen measures and terminating with a cadence. **14.** *Mathematics.* **a.** The smallest interval in the range of the independent variable required for a periodic function to begin another cycle. **b.** A group of digits separated by commas in a written number. **c.** The number of digits that repeat in a repeating decimal. For example, $\frac{1}{7}$ = 0.142857142857 . . . has a six-digit period. **15.** *Astronomy.* **a.** The time taken for a heavenly body to complete one orbit or one rotation on its axis. **b.** The interval between two maximum emissions from a variable star. **16.** *Chemistry.* Any of the horizontal rows of elements in the periodic table. Compare **group.** ~*adv.* Used to add finality and emphasis to a preceding statement: *I'm going, period!* ~*adj.* Of, belonging to, or representing a particular historical age or time: *a period piece; period furniture.* [Middle English *paryode,* from Old French *periode,* from Late Latin *periodus,* period of time, from Latin, sentence, from Greek *periodos,* circuit : *peri-,* PERI- + *hodos,* way.]

per·i·o·date (pĕr′ē-ə-dāt′) *n.* A salt or ester of a periodic acid. [PE-RIOD(IC ACID) + -ATE.]

pe·ri·od·ic (pîr′ē-ŏd′ĭk) *adj.* **1.** Having periods or repeated cycles. **2.** Happening or appearing at regular intervals. **3.** Taking place now and then; intermittent. [French *périodique,* from Late Latin *periodicus,* from Greek *periodikos,* from *periodos,* PERIOD.] —**pe·ri·od·i·cal·ly** *adv.*

Synonyms: *fitful, intermittent, occasional, sporadic.*

per·i·od·ic acid (pûr′ī-ŏd′ĭk) *n.* Any of several acids that contain more oxygen than iodic acid, especially HIO_4 and H_5IO_6. [From PER- + IODIC.]

pe·ri·od·i·cal (pîr′ē-ŏd′ĭ-kəl) *adj.* **1.** Periodic. **2. a.** Published at regular intervals of more than one day. **b.** Of or pertaining to a publication issued at such intervals. ~*n.* A periodical publication.

periodic function *n.* A mathematical function, such as sin *x* or cos *x,* whose value is repeated at regular invervals.

pe·ri·o·dic·i·ty (pîr′ē-ə-dĭs′ə-tē) *n.* The quality of being periodic; recurrence at regular intervals.

periodic law *n. Chemistry.* The principle that the properties of the elements recur periodically with increasing atomic number.

periodic system *n.* The classification of the chemical elements on the basis of the periodic law.

periodic table *n. Chemistry.* A tabular arrangement of the elements according to their atomic number. See feature, next page.

per·i·o·don·tal (pĕr′ē-ō-dŏnt′l) *adj.* Of or designating tissue and structures surrounding and supporting the teeth. [PERI- + ODONT(O)- + -AL.]

per·i·o·don·tics (pĕr′ē-ō-dŏn′tĭks) *n.* *Used with a singular verb.* Also **per·i·o·don·tia** (-shə). The branch of dentistry dealing with periodontal disease. [New Latin *periodontium,* periodontal tissue : PERI- + ODONT(O)- + -IUM.] —**per·i·o·don·tic** *adj.* —**per·i·o·don·tist** *n.*

per·i·os·te·um (pĕr′ē-ŏs′tē-əm) *n., pl.* **-tea** (-tē-ə). A fibrous membrane covering all bones, except at points of articulation. [New Latin, from Late Latin *periosteon,* from Greek, from *periosteos,* around the bones : *peri-,* PERI- + *osteon,* bone.] —**per·i·os·te·al, per·i·os·te·ous** *adj.*

per·i·os·ti·tis (pĕr′ē-ŏ-stī′tĭs) *n.* Inflammation of the periosteum. —**per·i·os·tit·ic** (pĕr′ē-ŏ-stĭt′ĭk) *adj.*

per·i·ot·ic (pĕr′ē-ō′tĭk) *adj.* **1.** Situated around the ear. **2.** Of or designating the bones immediately around the inner ear. [PERI- + OTIC.]

per·i·pa·tet·ic (pĕr′ə-pə-tĕt′ĭk) *adj.* **1.** Walking about from place to place in the pursuit of one's business; itinerant. **2.** Carried on while walking or moving from place to place: *a peripatetic conversation.* ~*n.* One who walks from place to place; an itinerant. [From PERI-PATETIC.]

Per·i·pa·tet·ic (pĕr′ə-pə-tĕt′ĭk) *adj.* Of or pertaining to the philosophy or methods of teaching of Aristotle, who conducted discussions while walking about in the Lyceum of ancient Athens. ~*n.* A follower of the philosophy of Aristotle; an Aristotelian. [Middle English, from Old French *peripatetique,* from Latin *peripatēticus,* from Greek *peripatētikos,* from *peripatein,* to walk about while teaching : *peri-,* PERI- + *patein,* to tread, walk.]

per·i·pe·te·ia (pĕr′ə-pə-tē′ə, -tī′ə) *n.* Also **pe·rip·e·ty** (pə-rĭp′ə-tē). An abrupt or unexpected change in a course of events or situation, especially in a drama or literary work. [Greek, from *peripiptein,* to change suddenly, "fall around" : *peri-,* PERI- + *piptein,* to fall.]

pe·riph·er·al (pə-rĭf′ər-əl) *adj.* Also **per·i·pher·ic** (pĕr′ə-fĕr′ĭk). **1.** Pertaining to, located on, or constituting the periphery. **2.** Not of central importance; minor or incidental. ~*n. Computer Science.* A peripheral device. —**pe·riph·er·al·ly** *adv.*

peripheral device *n.* A device used to feed information into or extract information from a computer, such as a keyboard, printer, or magnetic tape unit, or a device outside the main store in which information is stored. Also called "peripheral," "peripheral unit."

peripheral nervous system *n.* The part of the nervous system comprising the cranial nerves, the spinal nerves, and the autonomic nervous system.

peripheral vision *n. Antomaty.* Vision in which images fall upon parts of the retina outside the macula lutea.

pe·riph·er·y (pə-rĭf′ə-rē) *n., pl.* **-ies. 1. a.** The outermost part or region within a precise boundary. **b.** The region or area immediately beyond a precise boundary. **c.** Broadly, an area forming an imprecise boundary; the fringe or edge of something, especially of a social group. **2.** *Mathematics.* **a.** A perimeter *(see).* **b.** The surface of a solid. **3.** *Anatomy.* A region in which nerves end. [Middle English *peripherie,* from Late Latin *peripherīa,* from Greek *periphereia,* from *peripherēs,* carrying around, from *peripherein,* to carry around : *peri-,* PERI- + *pherein,* to carry.]

pe·riph·ra·sis (pə-rĭf′rə-sĭs) *n., pl.* **-ses** (-sēz′). **1.** The use of indirect or roundabout methods of expression. **2.** An indirect expression; a circumlocution. [Latin, from Greek, from *periphrazein,* to express in a roundabout way : *peri-,* PERI- + *phrazein,* to say.]

per·i·phras·tic (pĕr′ə-frăs′tĭk) *adj.* **1.** Of or characterized by periphrasis. **2.** *Grammar.* Constructed by using an auxiliary word rather than an inflected form; for example, the phrases *the word of his father* and *his father did say* are periphrastic, while *his father's word* and *his father said* are inflected. —**per·i·phras·ti·cal·ly** *adv.*

pe·riph·y·ton (pə-rĭf′ĭ-tŏn′) *n.* Sessile organisms that live attached to surfaces projecting from the bottom in a freshwater aquatic environment. [New Latin, from Greek *periphutos,* planted all over : *peri,* around + *phuein,* to grow.]

pe·rip·ter·al (pə-rĭp′tər-əl) *adj. Architecture.* Built with a row of columns on all sides. [Latin *peripteros,* from Greek, "flying around" : *peri-,* PERI- + *pteron,* wing.]

pe·rique (pə-rēk′) *n.* A strongly flavored, black tobacco grown in Louisiana and used in various blends. [Louisiana French, said to be after *Périque,* nickname of *Pierre* Chenet, planter who introduced tobacco growing in Louisiana.]

per·i·sarc (pĕr'ə-särk') n. Zoology. A horny external covering that encloses the polyp colonies of certain hydrozoans. [PERI- + Greek sarx (stem sark-), flesh.] —**per·i·sar·cal** (pĕr'ə-sär'kəl), **per·i·sar·cous** adj.

per·i·scope (pĕr'ə-skōp') n. Any of various optical instruments that contain reflecting elements, such as mirrors and prisms, to permit observation from a position displaced from a direct line of sight, as from a submerged submarine or a trench below ground level. [PERI- + -SCOPE.] —**per·i·scop·ic** (pĕr'ə-skŏp'ĭk) adj.

per·ish (pĕr'ĭsh) v. -ished, -ishing, -ishes. —intr. 1. To die, especially in a violent or untimely manner. 2. To pass from existence; die out or away. 3. To decay; rot away. —tr. British. To cause to perish; destroy. [Middle English perisshen, from Old French perir

(present stem periss-), from Latin perīre, to pass away : per-, away + īre, to go.]

per·ish·a·ble (pĕr'ĭ-shə-bəl) adj. Liable to perish, decay, or spoil. ~n. **perishables.** Perishable foodstuffs. —**per·ish·a·bil·i·ty, per·ish·a·ble·ness** n. —**per·ish·a·bly** adv.

per·ished (pĕr'ĭsht) adj. British Informal. 1. Debilitated or distressed by cold. 2. Feeling extremely cold; frozen.

per·i·sperm (pĕr'ə-spûrm') n. Botany. The nutritive tissue in the seeds of many plants that is derived from the nucellus and deposited outside the embryo sac.

pe·ris·so·dac·tyl (pə-rĭs'ō-dăk'təl) adj. Zoology. 1. Having an odd number of toes. 2. Of or designating certain hoofed mammals, such

---

periodic table

HOW NATURE'S ELEMENTS ARE RELATED
Discovering the pattern that puts atoms into families

Ninety-two chemical elements are found in nature. Each has a different number of protons in the nucleus of its atoms. Hydrogen has one proton, helium two, lithium three, and so on to uranium with 92. This number is known as the atomic number.

If the elements are set out in horizontal rows in order of their atomic number, they can be arranged in a pattern, or table, that brings out the similarities in their chemical properties. The pattern is known as the periodic table because elements with similar properties appear at regular, predictable intervals in the numerical order and fall into columns in the table. In this way

elements can be grouped into "families."

The periodic relationship between the elements was discovered by a Russian-born physicist, Dmitri Mendeleyev (1834–1907). He did not know of the existence of protons, but he did know that the atom of each element—and not all 92 were known at that time—had a different weight and that the weights increased at a regular, progressive rate.

In 1869 Mendeleyev wrote the names of the known elements on cards and placed the cards in rows and columns as in some fantastic game of solitaire. He shuffled his cards about for two years—and the results

were astonishing. When placed in a certain pattern in order of their atomic weight, with blank cards for obvious gaps in the progression, the elements in the vertical columns all had similarities in their chemical properties.

Using his table of elements, Mendeleyev was able to predict the existence, weight, and chemical properties of elements then unknown to man. Only in the 1930's, with the discovery of the internal structure of the atom, was the accuracy of Mendeleyev's table finally proved. By then the elements he had predicted had been identified.

Group Elements in the same column are alike in the number of electrons in the outer "shell" of their atom. All those in column 2A, for example, have two

Period Elements in the same row, or period, show a progressive increase in the number of electrons in outer "shell" of the atom — Lithium (3) has 1 electron, Neon (10) has 8 electrons

1A	2A	3B	4B	5B	6B	7B	8B			1B	2B	3A	4A	5A	6A	7A	0
H (1) 1.008																	He (2) 4.003
Li (3) 6.939	Be (4) 9.012											B (5) 10.811	C (6) 12.011	N (7) 14.007	O (8) 15.999	F (9) 18.998	Ne (10) 20.183
Na (11) 22.990	Mg (12) 24.312											Al (13) 26.982	Si (14) 28.086	P (15) 30.974	S (16) 32.064	Cl (17) 35.453	Ar (18) 39.948
K (19) 39.102	Ca (20) 40.08	Sc (21) 44.956	Ti (22) 47.90	V (23) 50.942	Cr (24) 51.996	Mn (25) 54.938	Fe (26) 55.847	Co (27) 58.933	Ni (28) 58.71	Cu (29) 63.54	Zn (30) 65.37	Ga (31) 69.72	Ge (32) 72.59	As (33) 74.922	Se (34) 78.96	Br (35) 79.909	Kr (36) 83.80
Rb (37) 85.47	Sr (38) 87.62	Y (39) 88.905	Zr (40) 91.22	Nb (41) 92.906	Mo (42) 95.94	Tc (43) 99	Ru (44) 101.07	Rh (45) 102.905	Pd (46) 106.4	Ag (47) 107.870	Cd (48) 112.40	In (49) 114.82	Sn (50) 118.69	Sb (51) 121.75	Te (52) 127.60	I (53) 126.904	Xe (54) 131.30
Cs (55) 132.905	Ba (56) 137.34	La (57) 138.91	Hf (72) 178.49	Ta (73) 180.948	W (74) 183.85	Re (75) 186.2	Os (76) 190.2	Ir (77) 192.2	Pt (78) 195.09	Au (79) 196.967	Hg (80) 200.59	Tl (81) 204.37	Pb (82) 207.19	Bi (83) 208.980	Po (84) 210	At (85) 210	Rn (86) 222
Fr (87) 223	Ra (88) 226	Ac (89) 227	Rf (104) 259	Ha (105) 260	Unnamed (106) 263												

Ce (58) 140.12	Pr (59) 140.907	Nd (60) 144.24	Pm (61) 145	Sm (62) 150.35	Eu (63) 151.96	Gd (64) 157.25	Tb (65) 158.924	Dy (66) 162.50	Ho (67) 164.930	Er (68) 167.26	Tm (69) 168.934	Yb (70) 173.04	Lu (71) 174.97
Th (90) 232.038	Pa (91) 231	U (92) 238.03	Np (93) 237	Pu (94) 244	Am (95) 243	Cm (96) 247	Bk (97) 247	Cf (98) 251	Es (99) 254	Fm (100) 257	Md (101) 256	No (102) 254	Lr (103) 257

MODERN PERIODIC TABLE *Each square of the table represents a different element, identified by its chemical symbol, atomic number (in brackets), and atomic weight. The elements are ranged in seven horizontal rows, or periods, and 18 vertical groups. The blue squares represent metallic elements and the yellow squares nonmetallic elements. The two rows shown separately at the foot of the table represent elements 58–71 and 90–103, which interrupt the sequence and fit in by a different analysis of their atomic structure.*

Since 1934 scientists have created elements beyond uranium—transuranium elements—by bombarding an element with neutrons. This transforms part of it into the element with the next highest atomic number. The method had been used to create 14 transuranium elements by 1982, giving a table of 106 elements.

Ac	Actinium (89)	Co	Cobalt (27)	I	Iodine (53)	O	Oxygen (8)	Se	Selenium (34)
Ag	Silver (47)	Cr	Chromium (24)	In	Indium (49)	Os	Osmium (76)	Si	Silicon (14)
Al	Aluminum (13)	Cs	Cesium (55)	Ir	Iridium (77)	P	Phosphorus (15)	Sm	Samarium (62)
Am	Americium (95)	Cu	Copper (29)	K	Potassium (19)	Pa	Proctactinium (91)	Sn	Tin (50)
Ar	Argon (18)	Dy	Dysprosium (66)	Kr	Krypton (36)	Pb	Lead (82)	Sr	Strontium (38)
As	Arsenic (33)	Er	Erbium (68)	La	Lanthanum (57)	Pd	Palladium (46)	Ta	Tantalum (73)
At	Astatine (85)	Es	Einsteinium (99)	Li	Lithium (3)	Pm	Promethium (61)	Tb	Terbium (65)
Au	Gold (79)	Eu	Europium (63)	Lr	Lawrencium (103)	Po	Polonium (84)	Tc	Technetium (43)
B	Boron (5)	F	Fluorine (9)	Lu	Lutetium (71)	Pr	Praseodymium (59)	Te	Tellurium (52)
Ba	Barium (56)	Fe	Iron (26)	Md	Mendelevium (101)	Pt	Platinum (78)	Th	Thorium (90)
Be	Beryllium (4)	Fm	Fermium (100)	Mg	Magnesium (12)	Pu	Plutonium (94)	Ti	Titanium (22)
Bi	Bismuth (83)	Fr	Francium (87)	Mn	Manganese (25)	Ra	Radium (88)	Tl	Thallium (81)
Bk	Berkelium (97)	Ga	Gallium (31)	Mo	Molybdenum (42)	Rb	Rubidium (37)	Tm	Thulium (69)
Br	Bromine (35)	Gd	Gadolinium (64)	N	Nitrogen (7)	Re	Rhenium (75)	U	Uranium (92)
C	Carbon (6)	Ge	Germanium (32)	Na	Sodium (11)	Rf	Rutherfordium (104)	V	Vanadium (23)
Ca	Calcium (20)	H	Hydrogen (1)	Nb	Niobium (41)	Rh	Rhodium (45)	W	Tungsten (74)
Cd	Cadmium (48)	Ha	Hahnium (105)	Nd	Neodymium (60)	Rn	Radon (86)	Xe	Xenon (54)
Ce	Cerium (58)	He	Helium (2)	Ne	Neon (10)	Ru	Ruthenium (44)	Y	Yttrium (39)
Cf	Californium (98)	Hf	Hafnium (72)	Ni	Nickel (28)	S	Sulfur (16)	Yb	Ytterbium (70)
Cl	Chlorine (17)	Hg	Mercury (80)	No	Nobelium (102)	Sb	Antimony (51)	Zn	Zinc (30)
Cm	Curium (96)	Ho	Holmium (67)	Np	Neptunium (93)	Sc	Scandium (21)	Zr	Zirconium (40)

as horses and rhinoceroses, of the order Perissodactyla, that have an odd number of toes. ~n. *Zoology.* A hoofed mammal of this order. [Greek *perissodaktulos* : *perissos,* excessive, uneven, from *peri-,* PERI- (around, hence beyond) + *daktulos,* DACTYL.] —**per·is·so·dac·ty·lous** *adj.*

per·i·stal·sis (pĕr′ə-stôl′sĭs, -stăl′sĭs) *n., pl.* -**ses** (-sēz′). Involuntary wavelike muscular contractions that propel contained matter along tubular organs, as in the alimentary canal. [New Latin, from *peristalticus,* of peristalsis, from Greek *peristaltikos,* compressing around, from *peristellein,* to wrap around : *peri-,* PERI- + *stellein,* to place, set.] —**per·i·stal·tic** *adj.*

per·i·stome (pĕr′ə-stōm′) *n.* **1.** *Botany.* A circular row of toothlike appendages surrounding the mouth of a moss capsule. **2.** *Zoology.* The area around the mouth in certain invertebrates. [New Latin *peristoma* : PERI- + -STOME.] —**per·i·sto·mal, per·i·sto·mi·al** *adj.*

per·i·style (pĕr′ə-stīl′) *n. Architecture.* **1.** A series of columns surrounding a temple or other structure, or enclosing a court. **2.** A court enclosed by such columns. [French *péristyle,* from Latin *peristylum,* from Greek *peristulon,* from *peristulos,* surrounded by columns : *peri-,* PERI- + *stulos,* pillar.] —**per·i·sty·lar** (pĕr′ə-stī′lər) *adj.*

per·i·the·ci·um (pĕr′ə-thē′shē-əm, -sē-əm) *n., pl.* -**cia** (-shē-ə, -sē-ə). A flask-shaped fruiting body in certain fungi, containing ascospores. [New Latin : PERI- + Greek *thēkion,* diminutive of *thēkē,* a case, chest.]

per·i·to·ne·um (pĕr′ə-tə-nē′əm) *n., pl.* -**nea** (-nē′ə). The membrane lining the walls of the abdominal cavity and covering the viscera. [Late Latin *peritonēum,* from Greek *peritonaion,* neuter of *peritonaios,* stretched across, from *peritonos,* stretched around or over : *peri-,* PERI- + *tenein,* to stretch.] —**per·i·to·ne·al** *adj.*

per·i·to·ni·tis (pĕr′ə-tə-nī′tĭs) *n.* Inflammation of the peritoneum. [New Latin : PERITON(EUM) + -ITIS.]

pe·rit·ri·cha (pə-rĭt′rĭ-kə) *pl.n.* Singular **per·i·trich** (pĕr′ə-trĭk′). **1.** Bell-shaped or tubular microorganisms of the order Peritrichida, characterized by a wide oral opening surrounded by cilia. **2.** Bacteria entirely covered with cilia. [New Latin : PERI- + Greek *thrix* (stem *trikh-*), hair.] —**pe·rit·ri·chous** (pə-rĭt′rĭ-kəs) *adj.*

per·i·wig (pĕr′ĭ-wĭg′) *n.* A wig or peruke. [Earlier *perwyke,* from Old French *perruque,* PERUKE.]

per·i·win·kle¹ (pĕr′ĭ-wĭng′kəl) *n.* **1.** Any of several small, edible marine snails, especially of the genus *Littorina,* having thick, cone-shaped, whorled shells. **2.** The shell of any of these snails. Also called "winkle." [16th century : origin obscure.]

periwinkle² *n.* **1.** Any of several trailing, evergreen plants of the genus *Vinca;* especially, *V. minor,* having glossy, dark-green leaves and blue flowers. Also called "myrtle." **2.** Light purplish-blue. Also called "periwinkle blue." [Variant (influenced by PERIWINKLE, snail) of Middle English *pervenke,* from Old French *pervenche,* from Latin *pervinca,* shortening of *vincapervinca†.*] —**per·i·win·kle** *adj.*

per·jure (pûr′jər) *tr.v.* -**jured,** -**juring,** -**jures.** To render (oneself) guilty of perjury by deliberately giving false evidence or testifying falsely under oath. [Middle English *perjuren,* from Old French *perjurer,* from Latin *perjūrāre* : *per-* (destruction) + *jūrāre,* to swear.] —**per·jur·er** *n.*

per·ju·ry (pûr′jə-rē) *n., pl.* -**ries. 1.** *Law.* The deliberate, willful giving of false, misleading, or incomplete evidence or testimony by a witness under oath in a judicial proceeding, whether given in a court or by affidavit. **2.** Any violation of an oath or promise. [Middle English *perjurie,* from Norman French *parjurie,* from Latin *perjūrium,* from *perjūrus,* perjured, from *perjūrāre,* to PERJURE.] —**per·ju·ri·ous** (pər-jŏŏr′ē-əs) *adj.* —**per·ju·ri·ous·ly** *adv.*

perk¹ (pûrk) *v.* **perked, perking, perks.** —*intr.* **1.** To stick up or jut out jauntily, as a dog's ears might. Often used with *up.* **2.** To regain one's animation or good spirits. Used with *up.* —*tr.* **1.** To raise smartly and quickly. Often used with *up.* **2.** To make vigorous and lively again; cheer. Often used with *up.* **3.** To make more attractive, trim, or smart in appearance. Often used with *up.* [Middle English *perken,* perhaps from Norman French *perquer,* to perch, from *perque,* rod, from Latin *pertica.* See **perch** (roost).]

perk² *n.* Often **perks.** A perquisite. —See Synonyms at **right.** [Shortened from PERQUISITE.]

perk³ *v.* **perked, perking, perks.** —*intr.* To percolate. Used of coffee. —*tr.* To cause (coffee) to percolate. [Shortened from PERCOLATE.]

Per·kins (pûr′kĭnz), **Frances** (1882-1965). U.S. social worker. She worked at Hull House in Chicago and as a labor commissioner for New York State. Appointed U.S. secretary of labor in 1933, she was the first woman to serve in the Cabinet.

Per·kin's mauve (pûr′kĭnz) *n.* A dye, **mauveine** *(see).* [After Sir William *Perkin* (1838-1907), British chemist who developed it.]

perk·y (pûr′kē) *adj.* -**ier,** -**iest. 1.** Cheerful and brisk; jaunty. **2.** Assertive and confident. —**perk·i·ly** *adv.* —**perk·i·ness** *n.*

per·lite, pearl·ite (pûr′līt′) *n.* A natural volcanic glass similar to obsidian but having distinctive concentric cracks and a relatively high water content. In a fluffy heat-expanded form it is used as a lightweight aggregate in plaster and concrete and in thermal and acoustic insulation. [French. See **pearl, -ite.**] —**per·lit·ic** (pər-lĭt′ĭk) *adj.*

Perl·man (pûrl′mən), **Itzhak** (1945-). U.S. violinist, born in Israel. He first performed in public in Tel Aviv at the age of nine and came to the United States in 1958 to study at the Juilliard School in New York City. Perlman is known for his brilliant virtuoso technique.

perm (pûrm) *n.* A **permanent wave** *(see).* ~*tr.v.* **permed, perming, perms.** To wave (hair) by applying

---

periscope

BENDING THE LINE OF SIGHT

How prisms and mirrors can move an image

The simplest form of periscope consists of two mirrors angled at 45° and placed with one higher than the other so that an image is reflected from the top of the instrument down to the observer at its base. This simple device was much used for observation in the trenches during World War I, when sniper fire made it dangerous for a man to poke his head out. It is often used by people in crowds to see a procession, for example, over the heads of those in front.

More sophisticated periscopes, such as those used in submarines, work on the same basic principle but use prisms instead of mirrors. When set at a certain angle, a right-angled prism reflects a beam of light through 90° and allows only about 4 percent of the light to be lost, so the intensity of the image is retained even when the periscope is very long. Submarine periscopes incorporate several lenses to increase magnification and alter the field of view.

Not all periscopes are designed to give a simple vertical shift to the image. For example, those used in armored cars may also shift the image horizontally. Different prisms can be used to move the image through any angle.

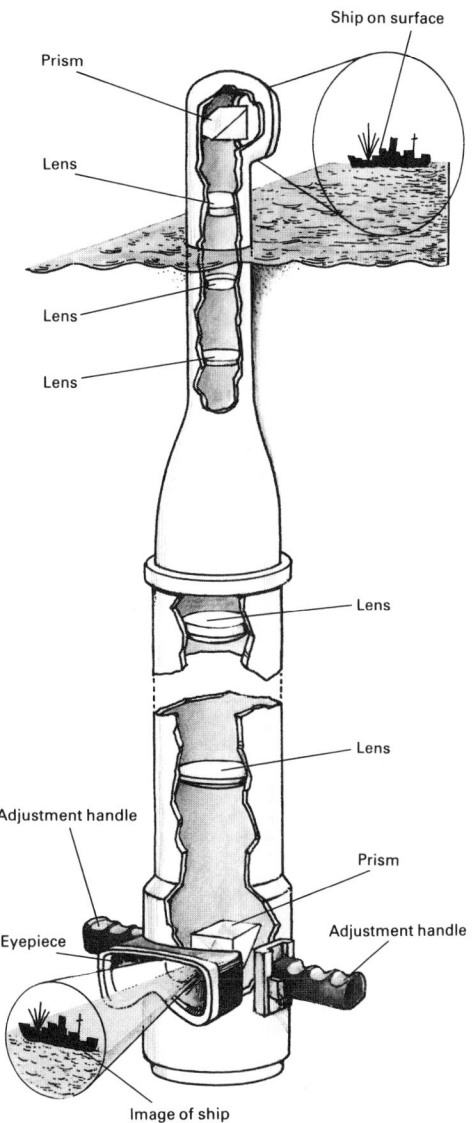

ADJUSTABLE LENSES *Handles at the base of a submarine periscope enable the observer to adjust the lenses in order to obtain a magnified image and a wider field of vision.*

chemicals, winding it on curlers, and drying it with heat. [Shortened from PERMANENT WAVE.]

Perm (pûrm, pârm). City and region of the R.S.F.S.R., U.S.S.R., on the Kama River.

perm. permanent.

per·ma·frost (pûr′mə-frôst′, -frŏst′) *n.* Permanently frozen rock, soil, and subsoil continuous in polar regions and occurring locally in perennially frigid areas. [PERMA(NENT) + FROST.]

perm·al·loy (pûr′mə-loi′, pûrm-ăl′oi′) *n.* Any of several alloys of nickel and iron, often with small amounts of other elements, having exceptionally high magnetic permeability. [PERM(EABLE) + ALLOY.]

per·ma·nence (pûr′mə-nəns) *n.* The condition or quality of being permanent.

per·ma·nen·cy (pûr′mə-nən-sē) *n.,* *pl.* **-cies.** **1.** Permanence. **2.** Someone or something permanent.

per·ma·nent (pûr′mə-nənt) *adj.* *Abbr.* **perm. 1.** Fixed and changeless; lasting or meant to last indefinitely. **2. a.** Not expected to change for a long or indefinite period: *my permanent address.* **b.** *Often* **Permanent.** *Chiefly British.* Designating a high-ranking member of a governmental department whose position is not affected by changes in the government: *Permanent Secretary to the Treasury.* ~*n.* A **permanent wave** *(see).* [Middle English, from Old French, from Latin *permanēns* (stem *permanent-*), present participle of *permanēre,* to remain throughout : *per-,* throughout + *manēre,* to remain.] —**per·ma·nent·ly** *adv.*

permanent magnet *n.* A material that retains induced magnetic properties after it is removed from a magnetic field; a ferromagnet.

permanent press *n.* **1.** A chemical process in which fabrics are permanently shaped and treated for wrinkle resistance. **2.** A fabric treated by permanent press. **3.** The condition of fabric treated by permanent press.

permanent wave *n.* **1.** Artificial waves or curls in the hair produced by applying chemicals to it while wet, winding it on curlers, and drying it with heat. **2.** The process used in making these waves or curls. **3.** A preparation used in this process. Compare **cold wave** (sense 2). Also called "perm," "permanent."

per·man·ga·nate (pər-măn′gə-nāt′) *n.* Any of the salts of permanganic acid, all of which are strong oxidizing agents. [PERMANGAN(IC ACID) + -ATE.]

permanganate of potash *n.* Potassium permanganate *(see).*

per·man·gan·ic acid (pûr′măn-găn′ĭk, -măng-găn′ĭk) *n.* An unstable inorganic acid, $HMnO_4$, existing as a strongly oxidizing, aqueous solution.

per·me·a·bil·i·ty (pûr′mē-ə-bĭl′ə-tē) *n.* **1.** The property or condition of being permeable. **2.** *Physics.* **Magnetic permeability** *(see).* **3.** The rate of diffusion of a pressurized gas through a porous material.

per·me·a·ble (pûr′mē-ə-bəl) *adj.* Capable of being permeated. [Late Latin *permeābilis,* from Latin *permeāre,* to PERMEATE.] —**per·me·a·bly** *adv.*

per·me·ance (pûr′mē-əns) *n.* **1.** The act of permeating. **2.** A measure of the ability of a magnetic circuit to conduct magnetic flux; the reciprocal of **reluctance** *(see).* [Latin *permeāns,* present participle of *permeāre,* to PERMEATE.]

per·me·ate (pûr′mē-āt′) *v.* **-ated, -ating, -ates.** —*tr.* **1.** To spread or flow throughout; pervade. **2.** To pass through the openings or interstices of: *liquid permeating a membrane.* —*intr.* To spread; penetrate; diffuse. [Latin *permeāre : per-,* through + *meāre,* to go, pass.] —**per·me·ant** (pûr′mē-ənt), **per·me·a·tive** (pûr′mē-ā′tĭv) *adj.* —**per·me·a·tion** (pûr′mē-ā′shən) *n.*

per men·sem (pûr mĕn′səm) *adv.* By the month or for each month. [Latin.]

Per·mi·an (pûr′mē-ən, pĕr′-) *adj.* Of, belonging to, or designating the geologic time, system of rocks, and sedimentary deposits of the last period of the Paleozoic era. ~*n.* *Geology.* The Permian period. Preceded by *the.* [After *Perm,* former Russian province (see PERM) where the rock strata were first identified.]

per mil, per mil (pûr mĭl′) *adv.* By the thousand; per thousand. [*mill, mil,* from Latin *mille,* a thousand.]

per·mis·si·ble (pər-mĭs′ə-bəl) *adj.* That can be permitted, tolerated, or accepted; allowable: *maximum permissible dosage.* —**per·mis·si·bil·i·ty, per·mis·si·ble·ness** *n.* —**per·mis·si·bly** *adv.*

per·mis·sion (pər-mĭsh′ən) *n.* **1.** The act of permitting. **2.** Consent, especially formal consent; leave; authorization. [Middle English, from Old French, from Latin *permissiō* (stem *permissiōn-*), from *permittere* (past participle *permissus*), to PERMIT.]

per·mis·sive (pər-mĭs′ĭv) *adj.* **1.** Granting permission; allowing. **2.** Permitting discretion, as distinct from prescriptive. **3.** Lenient, tolerant, or liberal, especially when based on or reflecting a belief that there should be as few restraints as possible in matters of sexual morality. **4.** Not forbidden; permitted. —**per·mis·sive·ly** *adv.* —**per·mis·sive·ness** *n.*

per·mit (pər-mĭt′) *v.* **-mitted, -mitting, -mits.** —*tr.* **1.** To allow (something); consent to; tolerate. **2.** To give permission to; authorize. **3. a.** To afford opportunity for; make possible. **b.** To allow as possible; admit of. —*intr.* To afford opportunity; allow. —**permit of.** To allow as a possibility; permit. ~*n.* (pûr′mĭt, pər-mĭt′). **1.** Permission; leave. **2.** A document or certificate giving permission to do something; license; warrant. [Latin *permittere : per-,* through + *mittere,* to let go, send.] —**per·mit·ter** *n.*

Usage: **Permit of** is sometimes used for the transitive verb *per-*

mit (to allow, to admit), as in *The wording permits of two interpretations.*

per·mit·tiv·i·ty (pûr′mĭ-tĭv′ə-tē) *n., pl.* **-ties.** *Physics.* **1.** A measure of the ability of a medium to transmit an electric field, expressed as the ratio of its electric displacement to the intensity of the field at some point. Also called "absolute permittivity." See **electric constant. 2.** The ratio of electric flux density produced by an electric field in a medium to that produced in a vacuum by the same field. Also called "relative permittivity," "dielectric constant." [From PERMIT.]

per·mu·ta·tion (pûr′myŏŏ-tā′shən) *n.* **1.** A complete change; a transformation. **2.** The act of changing the arrangement or order of a given set of objects in a group. **3.** *Mathematics.* An ordered arrangement of all or some of the elements of a set. **4.** Broadly, any of the variations possible in a given situation: *permutations of our original plan.* —**per·mu·ta·tion·al** *adj.*

per·mute (pər-myŏŏt′) *tr.v.* **-muted, -muting, -mutes. 1.** To change the order of. **2.** *Mathematics.* To subject to permutation. [Middle English *permuten,* from Old French *permuter,* from Latin *permūtāre : per-,* completely + *mūtāre,* to change.] —**per·mut·a·ble** *adj.*

per·ni·cious (pər-nĭsh′əs) *adj.* **1. a.** Tending to cause death or serious injury; deadly. **b.** Causing great harm; destructive; ruinous. **2.** Causing moral injury; evil: *a pernicious philosophy.* [Latin *perniciōsus,* from *perniciēs,* destruction : *per-,* completely + *nex* (stem *nec-*), death.] —**per·ni·cious·ly** *adv.* —**per·ni·cious·ness** *n.*

pernicious anemia *n.* A severe anemia associated with failure to absorb vitamin B_{12}, and characterized by the presence of abnormally large red blood cells, gastrointestinal disturbances, and lesions of the spinal cord.

pernickety. Variant of **persnickety.**

Pe·rón (pā-rōn′), **Juan Domingo** (1895–1974). Argentinian soldier and politician, president (1946–55 and 1973–74). As vice president (1944) in a right-wing military government he developed a personal following among urban workers. Imprisoned by democrats in 1945, he was released following street demonstrations in his favor and was elected president in 1946. While restricting civil liberties he carried out social reforms. His second wife, **(María) Eva Duarte de Perón** (1919–52), known as "Evita," won popularity for her charitable works. Perón was overthrown by the army in 1955 but returned from exile to become president again in 1973. He was succeeded in office by his third wife, **María Estela Martínez de Perón** (1931–), known as "Isabelita," who was ousted by the army in 1976.

per·o·ne·al (pĕr′ə-nē′əl) *adj.* *Anatomy.* Of or pertaining to the fibula or to the outer portion of the leg. [New Latin *peroneus,* of the fibula, from *perone,* fibula, from Greek *peronē,* "pin," "buckle."]

per·o·ral (pər-ôr′əl, -ōr′əl, -ōr′əl) *adj.* Administered by way of the mouth. [Latin *per,* through + Latin *ōs, ōr-,* mouth.] —**per·o·ral·ly** *adv.*

per·o·rate (pĕr′ə-rāt′) *intr.v.* **-rated, -rating, -rates. 1.** To make a peroration. **2.** To speak at great length, often in an inflated, pompous manner; declaim. [Latin *perōrāre,* to harangue at length : *per-,* thoroughly, to the end + *ōrāre,* to speak.]

per·o·ra·tion (pĕr′ə-rā′shən) *n.* The concluding part of a speech or written discourse, usually consisting of a formal recapitulation.

per·ox·i·dase (pə-rŏk′sə-dās′, -dāz′) *n.* An enzyme found in most plant cells and some animal cells that catalyzes peroxide oxidation reactions. [PEROXID(E) + -ASE.]

per·ox·ide (pə-rŏk′sīd′) *n.* *Chemistry.* **1.** Hydrogen peroxide *(see).* **2.** Any compound containing oxygen that yields hydrogen peroxide with an acid, such as sodium peroxide, Na_2O_2. ~*tr.v.* **peroxided, -iding, -ides. 1.** To treat with peroxide. **2.** To bleach (hair) with hydrogen peroxide.

per·ox·i·some (pə-rŏk′sĭ-sōm′) *n.* A cell organelle containing enzymes that catalyze the production and breakdown of hydrogen peroxide. [PEROXI(DE) + -SOME (body).] —**per·ox·i·som·al** *adj.*

per·ox·y (pə-rŏk′sē) *adj.* Containing the bivalent group O_2. [PER- + OXY-.]

per·ox·y·sul·fu·ric acid (pə-rŏk′sē-sŭl-fyŏŏr′ĭk) *n.* A white unstable crystalline acid, H_2SO_5, used as an oxidizing agent. Also called "Caro's acid," "persulfuric acid."

per·pend (pər-pĕnd′) *v.* **-pended, -pending, -pends.** *Archaic.* —*tr.* To wonder about; ponder. —*intr.* To wonder; reflect. [Latin *perpendere,* to consider carefully : *per-,* thoroughly + *pendere,* to consider, weigh.]

per·pen·dic·u·lar (pûr′pən-dĭk′yə-lər) *adj.* **1.** *Mathematics.* Intersecting at or forming right angles. **2.** At right angles to the horizontal; vertical. **3.** Vertical or very steep; precipitous, as a cliff face or mountainside might be. **4. Perpendicular.** Designating a style of English Gothic architecture of the 14th–16th centuries, characterized by emphasis of the vertical element and especially by vertical lines in window tracery. —See Synonyms at **vertical.** ~*n.* **1.** A line or plane perpendicular to a given line or plane. **2.** A perpendicular position. **3.** A device, such as a plumb line, used in marking the vertical from a given point. **4.** A vertical or nearly vertical line or plane. [Middle English *perpendiculer,* from Old French, from Latin *perpendiculāris,* from *perpendiculum,* plumb line : *per-,* thoroughly + *pendēre,* to hang + *-culum,* instrumental suffix.] —**per·pen·dic·u·lar·i·ty** (pûr′pən-dĭk′yə-lār′ə-tē) *n.* —**per·pen·dic·u·lar·ly** *adv.*

per·pe·trate (pûr′pə-trāt′) *tr.v.* **-trated, -trating, -trates. 1.** To be guilty of; commit: *perpetrate a crime.* **2.** To carry out; perform (an act, especially one considered outrageous or bad): *perpetrate a practical joke.* [Latin *perpetrāre,* to accomplish : *per-,* completely +

patrāre, to do, "perform in the capacity of a father," from *pater,* father.] **—per·pe·tra·tion** *n.* **—per·pe·tra·tor** *n.*

per·pet·u·al (pər-pĕch′ōō-əl) *adj.* **1.** Lasting for eternity. **2.** Lasting for an indefinitely long time. **3.** Having effect or having tenure for an unlimited duration or for a complete lifetime: *a treaty of perpetual friendship.* **4.** Ceaselessly repeated or continuing without interruption: *perpetual nagging.* **5.** Flowering throughout the growing season. —See Synonyms at **continual.**

~*n.* A plant that flowers throughout the growing season. [Middle English *perpetuel,* from Old French, from Latin *perpetuālis,* from *perpetuus,* continuous, permanent, from *perpes* (stem *perpet-*), throughout, uninterrupted : *per-,* thoroughly + *petere,* to go toward.] **—per·pet·u·al·ly** *adv.* **—per·pet·u·al·ness** *n.*

perpetual calendar *n.* A chart or mechanical device that indicates the day of the week corresponding to any given date over a period of many years.

perpetual motion *n.* The hypothetical continuous and perpetual operation of an isolated mechanical device or other closed system without loss of energy and without an external energy source.

per·pet·u·ate (pər-pĕch′ōō-āt′) *tr.v.* **-ated, -ating, -ates. 1.** To make perpetual. **2.** To prolong the existence or memory of: *a myth perpetuated by repetition.* [Latin *perpetuāre,* from *perpetuus,* PERPETUAL.] **—per·pet·u·a·tion,** per·pet·u·ance *n.* **—per·pet·u·a·tor** *n.*

per·pe·tu·i·ty (pûr′pə-tōō′ə-tē, -tyōō′ə-tē) *n., pl.* **-ties. 1.** The quality, state, or condition of being perpetual: *"The perpetuity of the Church was an article of faith"* (Morris West). **2.** Time without end; eternity. **3.** *Law.* **a.** The condition of an estate that is limited so as to be inalienable either perpetually or longer than the period determined by law. **b.** An estate so limited. **4.** *Finance.* An annuity payable indefinitely. Forever. **—in perpetuity.** Forever.

Per·pi·gnan (pĕr′pēn-yän′). Town in southern France, capital of Pyrénées-Orientales department. Located on the Têt River, it is a tourist and agricultural center.

per·plex (pər-plĕks′) *tr.v.* **-plexed, -plexing, -plexes. 1.** To fill with uncertainty or bewilderment; confuse or puzzle. **2.** To make confusedly intricate; complicate: *Her explanation only perplexed the matter even more.* —See Synonyms at **puzzle.** [From obsolete adjective *perplex,* involved, perplexed, from Latin *perplexus,* intricate : *per-,* thoroughly + *plectere* (past participle *plexus*), to weave, entwine.] **—per·plex·ed·ly** (pər-plĕk′sĭd-lē) *adv.*

per·plex·i·ty (pər-plĕk′sə-tē) *n., pl.* **-ties. 1.** The state or condition of being perplexed or puzzled; bewilderment. **2.** The state or condition of being intricate or complicated: *the perplexity of life in the 20th century.* **3.** Something that perplexes.

per·qui·site (pûr′kwə-zĭt) *n.* **1.** A payment or profit received in addition to a regular wage or salary, especially a benefit expected as one's due. **2.** A tip; a gratuity. **3.** Something claimed as an exclusive right: *"Politics was the perquisite of the upper class"* (Richard B. Sewall). —See Synonyms at **right.** [Middle English, from Medieval Latin *perquīsītum,* acquisition, perquisite, from the past participle of Latin *perquīrere,* to search for : *per-,* thoroughly + *quaerere,* to seek.]

Per·rault (pə-rō′, pĕ-), **Charles** (1628–1703). French writer. His *Tales of Mother Goose* (*c.* 1697) includes "Tom Thumb," "Puss in Boots," and "Sleeping Beauty."

Per·rin (pĕ-răn′), **Jean Baptiste** (1870–1942). French physicist and chemist. He was a professor at the University of Paris (1910–40) and came to the United States in 1941. For his work on the discontinuous structure of matter and his discovery of the equilibrium of sedimentation he received the Nobel Prize for physics (1926).

per·ron (pĕr′ən, pĕ-rôn′) *n.* **1.** A platform at the entrance of a large building or a church. **2.** A flight of steps leading to a perron. [Middle English, from Old French, from Vulgar Latin *petro* (stem *petron-*) (unattested), augmentative of *petra,* stone.]

per·ry (pĕr′ē) *n., pl.* **-ries.** A fermented alcoholic beverage made from pears. [Middle English *pereye,* from Old French *pere,* from Vulgar Latin *pirātum* (unattested), from Latin *pirum,* PEAR.]

Per·ry (pĕr′ē), **Matthew Calbraith** (1794–1858). U.S. naval officer. He commanded the first steam vessel in the U.S. Navy and encouraged the broadening of naval education. In 1853 to 1854 he sailed to Japan, concluding a treaty that opened the country to American trade.

Perry, Oliver Hazard (1785–1819). U.S. naval officer, brother of Matthew C. Perry. In the War of 1812 he won the Battle of Lake Erie (1813). His victory and his report of the battle—"We have met the enemy, and they are ours"—made him a national hero.

Pers. Persia; Persian.

per·salt (pĕr′sôlt′) *n.* A salt of a peracid.

per se (pər sā′, sĕ′) *adv.* In or by itself; as such; intrinsically. [Latin *per sē* : *per,* by, PER + *sē* (accusative), self.]

Perse (pĕrs, pûrs), **Saint John,** real name Alexis Saint-Léger Léger (1887–1975). French poet and diplomat. Known for his opposition to appeasement of the Nazis, he was one of Europe's foremost diplomats. After his self-imposed exile to the United States (1940), his reputation as a lyric poet grew, earning him a Nobel Prize in literature (1960).

per·se·cute (pûr′sə-kyōōt′) *tr.v.* **-cuted, -cuting, -cutes. 1.** To oppress or harass with ill-treatment; especially, to subject to severe penalties because of political or religious dissent. **2.** To annoy persistently; bother. [Middle English, from Old French *persecuter,* back-formation from *persecuteur,* pursuer, from Late Latin *persecutor,* from Latin *persequī* (past participle *persecūtus*), to pursue : *per-,* throughout, to the end + *sequī,* to follow.] **—per·se·cu·tive, per·se·**

Perpendicular

SOARING TO THE HEAVENS

Tall towers that marked the climax of English Gothic architecture

Most medieval churches in Britain—those built between the late 12th century and early 16th—were designed in one of three distinct styles known collectively as Gothic. Perpendicular, the last of these styles to be developed, began in about 1380 and dominated English architecture for more than 200 years.

During this period, builders turned away from the narrow arches of earlier Gothic designs. With the broader arches were larger windows with rectilinear tracery, slender columns, and tall, majestic towers. The effect was to make churches seem to be reaching toward heaven, and it is this vertical emphasis that gives the Perpendicular style its name. Several outstanding examples of the style, also noted for its fan vaulting, still survive. Among them are King's College Chapel in Cambridge (1446–1515) and the Henry VII Chapel in Westminster Abbey (1503–12).

POINTING THE WAY *Strong vertical lines in the stonework and a huge stained-glass window—both typical of Perpendicular architecture—dominate the 14th-century east front of York Minster.*

WHEELS WITHIN WHEELS *Decorative ribs radiate from supporting columns to form a complex cluster of fan vaults with pendants in the Henry VII Chapel in Westminster Abbey.*

persimmon *The edible fruit of some trees of the genus* Diospyros. *Approximately the size of an orange, the fruit is grown extensively in China and Japan and remains on the trees in autumn long after the leaves have fallen. It is extremely bitter until ripe.*

cu•to•ry (pûr′sə-kyo͞o-tôr′ē, -tōr′ē, pûr′sə-kyo͞o′tə-rē) *adj.* **—per•se•cu•tor** *n.*

per•se•cu•tion (pûr′sə-kyo͞o′shən) *n.* **1.** The act or practice of persecuting. **2.** The state or condition of being persecuted. **3.** A period during which people are persecuted. **—per•se•cu•tion•al** *adj.*

persecution complex *n.* A psychological delusion that one is being persecuted or victimized.

Per•se•id (pûr′sē-ĭd) *n., pl.* **-ids** or **Perseides** (pər-sē′ə-dēz′). *Astronomy.* Any of a shower of meteors that appears to originate in the vicinity of the constellation Perseus during August. [New Latin *Perseïdes,* plural of *Perseïs,* daughter of PERSEUS.]

Per•seph•o•ne (pər-sĕf′ə-nē). *Greek Mythology.* The wife of Hades and queen of the underworld; identified with Proserpina.

Per•sep•o•lis (pər-sĕp′ə-lĭs). Ruined city of ancient Persia, northeast of modern Shiraz, Iran. It was the capital of the Achaemenid empire under Darius I and his successors.

Per•se•us[1] (pûr′sē-əs, -so͞os′). *Greek Mythology.* The son of Zeus and Danae who slew Medusa and rescued Andromeda.

Perseus[2] *n.* A constellation in the Northern Hemisphere near Andromeda and Auriga. [After PERSEUS.]

per•se•ver•ance (pûr′sə-vîr′əns) *n.* **1.** The holding to a course of action, belief, or purpose without giving way; steadfastness. **2.** The Calvinistic doctrine that those who have been chosen by God will continue in a state of grace to the end and will finally be saved.

Synonyms: *persistence, steadfastness, tenacity.*

per•sev•er•a•tion (pər-sĕv′ə-rā′shən) *n. Psychology.* **1.** Continued or repetitive activity or actions, specifically: **a.** The uncontrollable repetition of a word, phrase, or gesture. **b.** The spontaneous recurrence of a thought, image, phrase, or tune in the mind. **2.** The retention in new and inappropriate circumstances of a form of behavior or a working pattern from other circumstances. **—per•sev•er•ate** (pər-sĕv′ə-rāt′) *v.*

per•se•vere (pûr′sə-vîr′) *intr.v.* **-vered, -vering, -veres.** To persist in or remain constant to a purpose, idea, or task in the face of obstacles or discouragement. [Middle English *perseveren,* from Old French *perseverer,* from Latin *persevērāre,* from *persevērus,* very serious : *per-* (intensifier) + *sevērus,* serious, severe.] **—per•se•ver•ing•ly** *adv.*

Per•shing (pûr′shĭng), **John Joseph,** known as "Black Jack" (1860–1948). U.S. general. He commanded the U.S. Expeditionary Force sent to Europe in 1917 and later became U.S. chief of staff (1921–24).

Persia. *Abbr.* **Pers.** See **Iran.** See also feature, next page.

Per•sian (pûr′zhən) *adj. Abbr.* **Pers.** Of or pertaining to Persia or Iran or their people, languages, or culture.

~n. Abbr. **Pers. 1.** A native or inhabitant of ancient Persia or modern Iran. **2.** The Iranian language of the Persians, of the West Iranian group of Indo-European languages, in any of its several historical forms, Old Persian, Avestan, Pahlavi, Middle Persian, and modern Iranian.

Persian cat *n.* A domestic cat of a breed having long, silky fur.

Persian Gulf, also known as "the Gulf." Arm of the Indian Ocean, between Iran and the Arabian Peninsula. Bounded in the south by the Strait of Hormuz, it is 816 kilometers (507 miles) long and is strategically important because of the access it gives to large offshore oil reserves.

Persian lamb *n.* **1.** The lamb of the karakul sheep of Asia. **2.** The glossy, tightly curled fur obtained from such a lamb, usually when it is three or four days old.

Persian melon *n.* A melon, *Cucumis melo inodorus,* with light-colored unridged rind and orange-colored flesh.

per•si•car•i•a (pûr′sə-kâr′ē-ə) *n.* Any of various plants of the genus *Polygonum,* having spikes of pink or white flowers. Common persicaria, *P. persicaria,* is also called "redshank." [New Latin, from Latin *persicum,* peach.]

per•si•flage (pûr′sə-fläzh′) *n.* **1.** A light, bantering style in writing or speaking. **2.** Idle, good-natured banter. [French, from *persifler,* to banter : *per-* (intensive), from Latin + *siffler,* to whistle, hiss, boo, from Vulgar Latin *sīfilāre* (unattested), from Latin *sībilāre.*]

per•sim•mon (pər-sĭm′ən) *n.* **1.** Any of various chiefly tropical trees of the genus *Diospyros,* such as the Chinese persimmon *D. Kaki,* having orange-red fruit that is edible only when completely ripe. **2.** The fruit of any of these trees. [Of Algonquian origin; akin to Cree *pasiminan* and Delaware *pasĭmĕnan,* dried fruit.]

per•sist (pər-sĭst′, -zĭst′) *intr.v.* **-sisted, -sisting, -sists. 1.** To hold firmly and steadfastly to some purpose, state, belief, or course of action despite obstacles, warnings, or setbacks. **2.** To continue in existence; last: *The pain persisted for several months.* [Latin *persistere : per-* (intensive) + *sistere,* to stand firm.]

per•sist•ence (pər-sĭs′təns, -zĭs′təns) *n.* Also **per•sis•ten•cy** (-tən-sē). **1.** The act of persisting. **2.** The quality of being persistent; perseverance; tenacity. **3.** The continuance of an effect after the cause is removed: *persistence of vision.* —See Synonyms at **perseverance.**

per•sist•ent (pər-sĭs′tənt, -zĭs′tənt) *adj.* **1.** Refusing to give up or let go; persevering obstinately. **2.** Insistently repetitive or continuous. **3.** Continuing to exist, often in spite of action designed to prevent this; enduring: *a persistent rumor; a persistent superconducting current.* **4.** *Botany.* Lasting past maturity without falling off. Said of certain leaves or flowers. **5.** *Zoology.* **a.** Retained permanently, rather than disappearing in an early stage of development: *the persistent gills of axolotls.* **b.** Continuing to grow after the normal period of growth. **—per•sist•ent•ly** *adv.*

per•snick•e•ty (pər-snĭk′ə-tē) *adj.* Also **per•nick•e•ty** (pər-nĭk′ə-tē). *Informal.* **1.** Fastidious; exacting. **2.** Requiring strict attention to detail. [Origin unknown.] **—per•snick•e•ti•ness** *n.*

per•son (pûr′sən) *n. Abbr.* **per. 1.** A living human being, especially as distinguished from an animal or thing. **2.** A human being considered without reference to his or her sex. See **-person. 3.** The composite of characteristics that make up an individual personality. **4. a.** The living body of a human being. **b.** The body together with its clothing: *a pistol concealed about his person.* **5.** Guise; character. **6.** Physique and general appearance. **7.** *Law.* A human being or organization with legal rights and duties. **8.** *Theology.* The separate individualities of the Father, Son, and Holy Spirit as distinguished from the essence of the Godhead that unites them. **9.** *Grammar.* **a.** Any of three groups of pronoun forms with corresponding verb inflections that distinguish between the speaker (first person), the individual addressed (second person), and the individual or thing spoken of (third person). **b.** Any of the different forms or inflections expressing these distinctions. —See Usage notes at **individual** and **people. —in person.** Physically present. [Middle English *persone, person,* from Old French *persone,* from Latin *persōna,* mask (especially one worn by an actor), hence the character played by an actor, probably from Etruscan *phersu,* mask.]

-person *suffix.* Indicates one holding a specified position or doing a specified job; for example, **salesperson, chairperson.**

Usage: In recent years titles or job descriptions in which a person's sex is explicitly represented (such as *chairman, barman*) have attracted the criticism of those concerned with the status of women's rights in society. It is argued that such suffixes as *-man* symbolize the biases of a male-dominated society and should be avoided where possible. Consequently the neutral *-person* form has come to be increasingly used. See also Usage note at **-ess.**

per•so•na (pər-sō′nə, -nä′) *n., pl.* **-nae** (-nē) (for sense 1) or **-nas** (for senses 2, 3). **1.** A character in a dramatic or literary work. **2.** *Psychology.* The role that a person assumes in order to display his conscious intentions to himself and to others. Compare **anima. 3.** A person's public image. [Latin *persōna,* mask, PERSON.]

per•son•a•ble (pûr′sə-nə-bəl) *adj.* Pleasing in appearance or personality; attractive. **—per•son•a•ble•ness** *n.*

per•son•age (pûr′sə-nĭj) *n.* **1. a.** A person. **b.** A person of distinction. **2.** A historical or fictional character. [Middle English, from Old French, from *persone,* PERSON.]

per•so•na gra•ta (pər-sō′nə grä′tə, grăt′ə) *n., pl.* **personae gratae** (pər-sō′nē grä′tē, grăt′ē). A person who is acceptable; especially, a diplomat who is fully acceptable to a foreign government. [Latin, "an acceptable person."]

per•son•al (pûr′sə-nəl) *adj.* **1.** Of or pertaining to a particular person; private; one's own: *personal affairs.* **2.** Characterized by or involving action on the part of a particular person rather than of a representative: *a personal appearance; took a personal interest in the case.* **3.** Done to or for or directed toward a particular person: *a personal favor.* **4. a.** Concerning or referring to a person's individual character and his intimate affairs or interests, especially in a critical or hostile manner: *an uncalled-for, highly personal remark.* **b.** Making or tending to make personal remarks: *He always becomes personal in an argument.* **5.** Of or pertaining to the body or physical being: *personal cleanliness.* **6.** Pertaining to or having the nature of a person or self-conscious being: *a personal God.* **7.** *Law.* Pertaining to a person's movable property: *personal possessions.* Compare **real. 8.** *Grammar.* Of or pertaining to grammatical person.

~n. A personal notice or item in a newspaper.

personal column *n.* The section of a newspaper or magazine containing brief classified advertisements, announcements, and especially private messages.

personal effects *pl.n.* Privately owned items, as keys, a wallet, or a watch, that are regularly worn or carried on one's person.

personal equation *n.* **1.** The tendency of a person, based on his individual characteristics, to subjectivity or error. **2.** The resulting variation in observation, judgment, and reasoning. **3.** The allowance or correction made for such variation.

per•son•al•ism (pûr′sə-nə-lĭz′əm) *n.* **1.** The quality of being characterized by purely personal modes of expression or behavior; idiosyncrasy. **2.** *Philosophy.* Any of various trends of subjective idealism emphasizing the importance of individuals and regarding personality as the key to the interpretation of reality. **—per•son•al•ist** *n.* **—per•son•al•is•tic** (pûr′sə-nə-lĭs′tĭk) *adj.*

per•son•al•i•ty (pûr′sə-năl′ə-tē) *n., pl.* **-ties. 1.** The state or quality of being a person. **2. a.** The dynamic character, self, or psyche that constitutes and animates the individual person and makes his experience of life unique. **b.** A person as the embodiment of distinctive traits of mind and behavior. **3.** The pattern of collective behavioral, temperamental, emotional, and mental traits of an individual. **4.** The distinctive qualities of an individual; especially, those distinguishing personal characteristics that make one socially appealing. **5. a.** A person of prominence or notoriety; a celebrity: *personalities in the news.* **b.** A person with an amusing or striking turn of mind; a character. **6.** *Often* **personalities.** A remark of a personal nature, especially when offensive. **7.** The characteristics of a place or situation that give it a distinctive quality. —See Synonyms at **disposition.** [Middle English *personalite,* from Old French, from Late Latin *persōnālitās* (stem *persōnālitāt-*), from Latin *persōnālis,* personal, from *persōna,* PERSON.]

per•son•al•ize (pûr′sə-nə-līz′) *tr.v.* **-ized, -izing, -izes. 1.** To endow with personal or human qualities; personify. **2.** To have printed or marked with one's initials or name: *personalized stationery.* **3.** To

Persia

THE FIRST OF THE FABULOUS EMPIRES
Cyrus II founded Persia's lasting civilization

Almost 3,000 years ago, Aryan tribes settled at the cross-roads of Europe and Asia and formed one of the world's most durable civilizations. They called it Iran, land of the Aryans, but it is better known as Persia after the Parsua, the warrior tribe that turned it into the first of the great empires.

About 546 B.C. Cyrus II, King of Persia, overthrew the other dominant tribe of Iran, the Medes, and conquered all the neighboring lands from Assyria in the west to India in the east. He named this the Achaeminid empire after an ancestor, Achaemenes. The empire reached its peak under Darius I (521–486 B.C.) and his son, Xerxes (486–465 B.C.); during this time the Persians administered 20 provinces and narrowly failed to conquer Greece, when Xerxes was defeated at the sea battle of Salamis (480).

Since then, waves of invaders have poured across Persia's temperate plateau, only to have their culture absorbed into the Persian way of life. Alexander the Great conquered the empire (334 B.C.) and stayed there, seduced by its attractions. For 500 years (223 B.C. to A.D. 226) Parthians, fearsome horsemen from central Asia, ruled Persia, keeping the Romans at bay and preserving the country's personality.

The Sassanids (A.D. 246–642) restored Persian sovereignty and built a network of roads and a capital at Ctesiphon. This brilliant dynasty fell to the most cataclysmic of all Persia's invaders, Bedouin Arabs, who swarmed into the country, lured by its wealth. Although poorly armed, they were inspired by a new faith, Islam. They swept aside the Sassanids and grafted their religion, Shi'ism, onto the Persian culture. Under their dynamism, mathematics and science flowered and the Persian language, enriched by Arabic, became the literary idiom of Islam.

Alongside this renaissance, Persia retained its old customs and crafts. Goldsmiths and brass beaters worked in the open bazaars; architecture and the decorative art of tile glazing reached new heights; carpet weaving flourished. There were later invasions: the Seljuks, a Turkish tribe (1037–1220); the Mongols (1220–1380); Tamerlane's Timurids (1380–1500); the Qajars, another Turkish tribe (1787–1925). None had the impact of the Islamic incursion. Modern Persia became known as Iran in 1935.

EMPIRE BUILDER *This ancient marble head of an Achaeminid king is most likely a bust of the Persian empire's first great ruler, Cyrus II. In 546 B.C. this warlord molded the lands of Media and Parsa into a single kingdom, then swept out to bring most of Middle Eastern Asia under his heel.*

take (remarks, for example) as applying to oneself, and usually as an insult.

per·son·al·ly (pûr′sə-nə-lē) *adv.* **1.** In person; without the intervention of another. **2.** As far as oneself is concerned: *Personally, I don't care how much it costs.* **3.** As a person: *I admire his skill but dislike him personally.* **4.** As applying to oneself, and usually as a criticism: *Don't take his remarks personally.*

personal pronoun *n.* A pronoun indicating speaker, person spoken to, or person or thing spoken about. The personal pronouns in the subject form in current English are *I, we, you, he, she, it, they.*

personal property *n. Law.* Temporary or movable property as distinguished from real property.

per·son·al·ty (pûr′sə-nəl-tē) *n., pl.* **-ties.** *Law.* Personal property. [Norman French *personalté,* from Late Latin *personālitās,* PERSONALITY.]

per·so·na non gra·ta (pər-sō′nə nŏn grä′tə, grăt′ə) *n., pl.* **personae non gratae** (pər-sō′nē nŏn grä′tē, grăt′ē) or **persona non grata.** *Abbr.* **p.n.g.** A person who is not acceptable or welcome; especially, a diplomat not acceptable to a foreign government. [Latin, "unacceptable person."]

per·son·ate¹ (pûr′sə-nāt′) *tr.v.* **-ated, -ating, -ates. 1.** To impersonate (a character); play the role or portray the part of. **2.** To endow with personal qualities; personify. **3.** *Law.* To assume the identity of (a person) with intent to deceive. [From PERSON.] **—per·son·a·tion** *n.* **—per·son·a·tive** *adj.* **—per·son·a·tor** *n.*

per·son·ate² (pûr′sə-nĭt) *adj. Botany.* Designating a corolla having the upper lip arched and the lower lip protruding so that the throat is nearly closed. [Latin *persōnātus,* masked, from *persōna,* mask, PERSON.]

per·son·i·fi·ca·tion (pər-sŏn′ə-fĭ-kā′shən) *n.* **1.** The personifying of something abstract or inanimate, as: **a.** A rhetorical figure of speech in which objects or abstractions are endowed with human qualities or are represented as possessing human form, as in *Hunger sat shivering on the road* or *Flowers danced about the lawn.* **b.** The artistic representation of an abstract quality or idea as a person. **2.** A person or thing exemplifying to a remarkable degree a specified quality or idea; an embodiment: *a personification of bigotry.*

per·son·i·fy (pər-sŏn′ə-fī′) *tr.v.* **-fied, -fying, -fies. 1.** To think of or represent (an object or abstraction) as having personality or the qualities, thoughts, or movements of a living human being. **2.** To represent (an object or abstraction) by a human figure. **3.** To represent (an abstract quality or idea): *He personifies evil.* **4.** To be the embodiment or perfect example of: *She personified liberalism.* [French *personnifier,* from *personne,* person, from Old French *persone,* PERSON.] **—per·son·i·fi·er** *n.*

per·son·nel (pûr′sə-nĕl′) *n.* **1.** The body of persons employed by or active in an organization, business, or service: *military personnel.* **2.** The administrative division of an organization concerned with the recruitment and well-being of its personnel. [French, from Old French *personal,* personal, from Late Latin *persōnālis,* from Latin *persōna,* mask, PERSON.]

per·spec·tive (pər-spĕk′tĭv) *n.* **1.** Any of various techniques for representing three-dimensional objects and depth relationships on a two-dimensional surface. *Linear perspective* renders depth by using actual or suggested lines that intersect in the background to delimit relative size from background to foreground. *Aerial* or *atmospheric perspective* renders depth by changes of form, size, tone, and color with recession of objects from the picture plane. **2.** Any picture representing objects in this way. **3.** A view or vista. **4.** The appearance of objects in depth as perceived by normal binocular vision. **5. a.** The relationship of aspects of a subject to one another and to a whole: *a perspective of history.* **b.** Any of such aspects. **6.** Subjective evaluation of the relative significance of facts or things; one's personal point of view. **7.** An objective and well-balanced evaluation or point of view: *get things in perspective.* [Middle English, from Medieval Latin *perspectīva (ars),* optics, from Late Latin *perspectīvus,* of a view, from Latin *perspicere* (past participle *perspectus*), to see through or into, inspect : *per-* (intensive) + *specere,* to look.] **—per·spec·tive** *adj.* **—per·spec·tive·ly** *adv.* See feature, next page.

per·spec·tiv·ism (pər-spĕk′tĭ-vĭz′əm) *n. Sometimes* **Perspectivism.** *Philosophy.* The doctrine that reality can be accurately understood only from several different points of view.

per·spi·ca·cious (pûr′spĭ-kā′shəs) *adj.* Acutely discerning, perceptive, or understanding. [Latin *perspicāx,* clear-sighted, from *perspicere,* to see through. See **perspective.**] **—per·spi·ca·cious·ly** *adv.* **—per·spi·cac·i·ty** (pûr′spĭ-kăs′ə-tē), **per·spi·ca·cious·ness** *n.*

per·spi·cu·i·ty (pûr′spĭ-kyōō′ə-tē) *n.* **1.** The quality of being perspicuous; clarity of expression or exposition. **2.** Perspicacity.

per·spic·u·ous (pər-spĭk′yōō-əs) *adj.* Clearly expressed or presented; easy to understand; lucid. [Latin *perspicuus,* from *perspicere,* to see through. See **perspective.**] **—per·spic·u·ous·ly** *adv.* **—per·spic·u·ous·ness** *n.*

per·spi·ra·tion (pûr′spə-rā′shən) *n.* **1.** The salty moisture excreted through the pores of the skin by the sweat glands; sweat. **2.** The act or process of perspiring. **—per·spir·a·to·ry** (pər-spīr′ə-tôr′ē, -tōr′ē, pûr′spə-rə-) *adj.*

per·spire (pər-spīr′) *v.* **-spired, -spiring, -spires.** *—intr.* To excrete perspiration through the pores of the skin. *—tr.* To expel through external pores; exude. [French *perspirer,* from Old French, from Latin *perspīrāre,* to breathe through : *per-,* through + *spīrāre,* to blow, breathe.]

per·suade (pûr-swād′) *tr.v.* **-suaded, -suading, -suades. 1. a.** To

PRONUNCIATION KEY

ă, pat; ā, pay; âr, care;
ä, father, are; b, bib;
ch, church; d, deed; ĕ, pet;
ē, be; f, fife; g, gag; h, hat;
hw, which; ĭ, pit; ī, pie;
îr, pier; j, judge; k, kick;
l, lid, needle; m, mum;
n, no, sudden; ng, thing;
ŏ, pot; ō, toe; ô, paw, for;
oi, noise; ou, out; ŏŏ, book;
ōō, boot; p, pop; r, roar;
s, sauce; sh, ship, dish;
t, tight; th, thin, path;
th, this, bathe; ŭ, cut; ûr, fur;
v, valve; w, with; y, yes;
z, zebra, size; zh, vision;
ə, about, item, edible,
gallop, circus, peaceful

IN FOREIGN WORDS:

à, *Fr.* ami; œ, *Fr.* feu, *Ger.*
schön; ü, *Fr.* tu, *Ger.* über;
KH, *Ger.* ich, *Scot.* loch;
N, *Fr.* bon; y′, *Fr.* Compiègne

STRESS MARKS:

Primary stress: ′
in·cite′ (ĭn-sīt′)
Secondary stress: ′
in′sight′ (ĭn′sīt′)

induce to do something by means of argument, reasoning, or entreaty: *persuaded him to part with his money.* **b.** To win over to a course of action by reasoning or inducement. **2.** To make (someone or oneself) believe something; convince: *persuaded me that she was right.* [Latin *persuādēre* : *per-* (intensive) + *suādēre*, to persuade, urge.] —**per·suad·a·ble** *adj.* —**per·suad·er** *n.*
    Synonyms: *convince, induce, prevail on.*
per·sua·si·ble (pər-swā′zə-bəl, -sə-bəl) *adj.* That can be persuaded; persuadable. —**per·sua·si·bil·i·ty** *n.*
per·sua·sion (pər-swā′zhən) *n.* **1. a.** The act of persuading or attempting to persuade. **b.** The state of being persuaded. **2.** The ability or power to persuade. **3.** A strong conviction or belief. **4. a.** A body of religious beliefs; a religion: *worshipers of various persuasions.* **b.** Those who adhere to such beliefs; a sect. **5.** Any grouping or faction. —See Synonyms at **opinion.** [Latin *persuāsiō* (stem *persuāsiōn-*), from *persuādēre*, to PERSUADE.]
per·sua·sive (pər-swā′sĭv, -zĭv) *adj.* Tending or having the power to persuade: *a persuasive argument.* —**per·sua·sive·ly** *adv.* —**per·sua·sive·ness** *n.*
per·sul·fu·ric acid (pûr′sŭl-fyŏŏr′ĭk) *n.* **Peroxysulfuric acid** *(see).*
pert (pûrt) *adj.* **perter, pertest. 1.** Impudently bold; saucy: *a pert little girl.* **2.** High-spirited; vivacious: *a pert old lady.* **3.** Jaunty: *a pert little hat.* [Middle English, short for Old French *apert*, straightforward, open, from Latin *aperīre* (past participle *apertus*), to open, and from Old French *aspert*, from Latin *expertus*, EXPERT.] —**pert·ly** *adv.* —**pert·ness** *n.*
pert. pertaining.
per·tain (pər-tān′) *intr.v.* **-tained, -taining, -tains. 1.** To have reference; relate: *evidence pertaining to the accident.* **2.** To belong as an adjunct or accessory: *the farm and all the lands that pertain to it.* **3.** To be fitting or suitable. [Middle English *partenen*, from Old French *partenir*, from Latin *pertinēre*, to relate to, reach to : *per-*, to, thoroughly + *tenēre*, to hold.]
Perth[1] (pûrth). City in Tayside Region, eastern Scotland, on the Tay River. A former capital of Scotland, it is where James I was murdered (1437) and where John Knox preached against idolatry (1559).
Perth[2]. Capital of Western Australia, on the Swan River. It was founded in 1829 and expanded with the discovery of gold at Coolgardie in the 1890's. It is now a commercial and cultural center and a market center for agricultural products.
Perth·shire (pûrth′shĭr′, -shər). Former county of Scotland, now in the Central and Tayside regions. It is largely mountainous.
per·ti·na·cious (pûr′tə-nā′shəs) *adj.* **1.** Holding firmly or tenaciously to some purpose, belief, or opinion. **2.** Stubbornly or perversely persistent. —See Synonyms at **obstinate.** [Latin *pertināx* : *per-*, thoroughly, completely + *tenāx*, tenacious, from *tenēre*, to hold.] —**per·ti·na·cious·ly** *adv.* —**per·ti·na·cious·ness** *n.*
per·ti·nac·i·ty (pûr′tə-năs′ə-tē) *n.* The quality or state of being pertinacious.
per·ti·nent (pûr′tə-nənt) *adj.* Having a clear connection with a specific matter; apposite. —See Synonyms at **relevant.** [Middle English, from Old French, from Latin *pertinēns* (stem *pertinent-*), present participle of *pertinēre*, to reach, concern, PERTAIN.] —**per·**

ti·**nence, per·ti·nen·cy** *n.* —**per·ti·nent·ly** *adv.*
per·turb (pər-tûrb′) *tr.v.* **-turbed, -turbing, -turbs. 1.** To disturb greatly; make uneasy or anxious. **2.** To throw into great disorder. **3.** *Physics.* To cause perturbation to (an electron or celestial body). [Middle English *perturben*, from Old French *perturber*, from Latin *perturbāre* : *per-*, thoroughly + *turbāre*, to throw into disorder, from *turba*, confusion, probably from Greek *turbē*, disorder.]
per·tur·ba·tion (pûr′tər-bā′shən) *n.* **1. a.** The act of perturbing. **b.** The state or condition of being perturbed; agitation. **2.** Something that perturbs. **3.** *Physics.* Variation in a designated orbit, as of an electron or planet, resulting from the influence of one or more external bodies.
per·tus·sis (pər-tŭs′ĭs) *n.* A disease, **whooping cough** *(see).* [New Latin : Latin *per-* (intensive) + *tussis*, a cough, TUSSIS.] —**per·tus·sal** *adj.*
Pe·ru (pə-rōō′). Republic of western South America. It rises from the Pacific Ocean to the Andes, 6,768 meters (22,205 feet) at Mt. Huascaran, descending again to the forested Amazon Basin. Conquered by the Spanish (1533), who destroyed its Inca civilization, it regained its independence in 1824 and lost its southern territories to Chile in the War of the Pacific (1879–83). It has considerable mineral resources, including copper, iron, silver, zinc, and oil, while its agricultural products include corn, cotton, sugar, and coffee. Fishing and livestock breeding are also important, and industrial production is expanding rapidly. Area, 1,285,216 square kilometers (496,225 square miles). Population, 17,100,000. Capital, Lima.
Peru Current. Also **Hum·boldt Current** (hŭm′bōlt′). A cold ocean current of the South Pacific, flowing northward along the northern coast of Chile and Peru to southern Ecuador.
Pe·ru·gia (pə-rōō′jə). Capital of mountainous Perugia province, Umbria, central Italy. It is an agricultural trade center, and its products include furniture, glassware, and chocolates.
Pe·ru·gi·no (pĕr′ə-jē′nō), **Il,** born Pietro di Cristoforo Vannucci (c. 1445–1523). Italian painter, born near Perugia (from which his name derives). His outstanding works include a fresco in the Sistine Chapel, *Christ Giving the Keys to St. Peter.*
pe·ruke (pə-rōōk′) *n.* A wig, especially one of a type worn by men in the 17th and 18th centuries; a periwig. [French *perruque*, from Italian *parrucca, perrucca†*, head of hair, wig.]
pe·rus·al (pə-rōō′zəl) *n.* The act or an instance of perusing.
pe·ruse (pə-rōōz′) *tr.v.* **-rused, -rusing, -ruses. 1.** To read, especially with great care. **2.** To read, especially in a casual or leisurely fashion. [Middle English *perusen*, to use up, perhaps from Medieval Latin *perusāre* (unattested) : *per-* (intensive) + Vulgar Latin *usāre* (unattested), to USE.] —**pe·rus·er** *n.*
Pe·ru·vi·an (pə-rōō′vē-ən) *adj.* Of or pertaining to Peru, its inhabitants, or their culture.
    ~*n.* A native or inhabitant of Peru. [New Latin *Peruvia*, Peru + -AN.]
Peruvian bark *n.* A medicinal bark, **cinchona** *(see).*
Pe·ruz·zi (pə-rōōt′sē, pä-), **Baldassare** (1481–1536). Italian architect and painter. As architect for St. Peter's in Rome (after 1520) and in his paintings, he reflected the High Renaissance and mannerist periods, adapting forms derived from ancient art to his singu-

---

perspective

SPACE AND MOVEMENT IN PAINTING
Perspective creates the illusion of a three-dimensional space on a flat surface

It was not until the 15th century that artists learned how to introduce the effect of space and movement into their work. The ancient Egyptians, for example, were more interested in telling a story or showing objects separately than in giving an appearance of depth and solidity. The study of perspective by Renaissance artists and mathematicians resulted in the discovery of a means of projecting the illusion of a three-dimensional space onto a two-dimensional surface.

Pioneered by the Florentine architect Filippo Brunelleschi (1377–1446), the new discovery was quickly taken up by Italian painters like Masaccio (1401–28), Paolo Uccello (1397–1475), and Piero della Francesca (c. 1410–92), and by the German Albrecht Dürer (1471–1528). For 400 years linear perspective dominated European painting, and it was only in the late 19th century that artists turned to color and shading to give the impression of depth.

Linear perspective makes use of the observation that objects appear to get smaller and parallel lines to converge, the closer they are to the horizon. The architect Leone Battista Alberti (1404–72) formulated mathematical rules to show how this effect could be created in art. On a flat surface like a painting, roofs, pavements, and other horizontal lines converge. If continued, they would meet at a vanishing point on the horizon. Vertical shapes like trees and pillars diminish in size as they recede.

PERSPECTIVE IN ART *In this picture,* The Tribute Money, *painted by the Italian artist Masaccio about 1427, perspective is used to indicate relative distances between objects. The horizontal lines of the building on the right are drawn so that they would converge at a vanishing point on the horizon roughly at the center of the picture. The figures and trees in the painting get gradually smaller in size the nearer they are to the horizon, giving the effect of distance.*

larly elegant and sophisticated style.

per·vade (pər-vād′) tr.v. **-vaded, -vading, -vades.** To spread right through; be present throughout; permeate: *"A marvellous stillness pervaded the world"* (Joseph Conrad). [Latin *pervādere* : *per-,* through + *vādere,* to go.] **—per·va·sion** (pər-vā′zhən) n.

per·va·sive (pər-vā′sĭv, -zĭv) adj. Having the quality of pervading or tendency to pervade. [Latin *pervāsus,* past participle of *pervādere,* to PERVADE.] **—per·va·sive·ly** adv. **—per·va·sive·ness** n.

per·verse (pər-vûrs′) adj. **1. a.** Having a disposition to oppose and contradict. **b.** Characterized by or arising from such a disposition. **2.** Directed away from what is right or good; perverted. **3.** Obstinately persisting in an error or fault; wrongly self-willed or stubborn. **4.** Irritable; peevish. **—See Synonyms at contrary.** [Middle English *pervers,* from Old French, from Latin *pervertere* (past participle *perversus*), to PERVERT.] **—per·verse·ly** adv. **—per·verse·ness** n.

per·ver·sion (pər-vûr′zhən, -shən) n. **1.** The act of perverting or the state of being perverted. **2.** A sexual practice or act considered abnormal. **3.** An incorrect interpretation or perverted form. **—per·ver·sive** (pər-vûr′sĭv, -zĭv) adj.

per·ver·si·ty (pər-vûr′sə-tē) n., pl. **-ties. 1.** The quality or state of being perverse. **2.** An instance of being perverse.

per·vert (pər-vûrt′) tr.v. **-verted, -verting, -verts. 1. a.** To cause to turn from what is considered morally right; corrupt. **b.** To cause to deviate from what is natural or normal. **2.** To employ for a wrong or improper purpose; misuse. **3.** To interpret incorrectly; distort; misconstrue. **4.** To bring to a worse condition; debase. ~n. (pûr′vûrt). One who practices sexual perversion. [Middle English *perverten,* from Old French *pervertir,* from Latin *pervertere,* to turn the wrong way, turn around : *per-,* completely + *vertere,* to turn.] **—per·vert·er** n. **—per·vert·i·ble** adj.

per·vert·ed (pər-vûr′tĭd) adj. **1.** Deviating greatly from what is considered proper and correct: *a perverted idea of justice.* **2.** Of, pertaining to, or practicing sexual perversion. **—per·vert·ed·ly** adv.

per·vi·ous (pûr′vē-əs) adj. **1.** Allowing passage or entrance; permeable: *material pervious to water.* **2.** Open to arguments, ideas, or change. [Latin *pervius* : *per-,* through + *via,* way, road.] **—per·vi·ous·ly** adv. **—per·vi·ous·ness** n.

pes (pās) n., pl. **pedes** (pěd′ās′). *Biology.* A foot or footlike part, especially: **1.** The human foot. **2.** The corresponding part in other higher vertebrates. [New Latin, from Latin *pēs,* foot.]

Pe·sach, Pe·sah (pä′säKH′) n. Passover (see). [Hebrew *pesaḥ,* a passing over, from *pāsaḥ,* to pass over.]

pe·sade (pə-säd′, -zäd′) n. The act or position of a horse when rearing on its hind legs with its forelegs in the air. [French, variant of obsolete *posade,* from Old French, from Old Italian *posata,* "a pause," from *posare,* to pause, from Late Latin *pausāre,* from Latin *pausa,* PAUSE.]

pe·se·ta (pə-sā′tə) n. Abbr. **p., pta. 1.** The basic monetary unit of Spain, equal to 100 céntimos. **2.** A coin worth one peseta. See feature at **currency.** [Spanish, diminutive of PESO.]

pe·se·wa (pā-sā′wä) n., pl. **pesewa** or **pesewas.** A monetary unit equal to ¹/₁₀₀ of the cedi of Ghana. See feature at **currency.** [Native word in Ghana.]

Pe·sha·war (pə-shä′wər). Strategic city in northern Pakistan. Situated 18 kilometers (11 miles) from the eastern end of the Khyber Pass, it has for centuries been a major trading center for central Asia.

pes·ky (pěs′kē) adj. **-kier, -kiest.** *Informal.* Troublesome; annoying: *a pesky mosquito.* [Probably alteration of PEST.] **—pes·ki·ly** adv. **—pes·ki·ness** n.

pe·so (pā′sō, pěs′ō) n., pl. **-sos.** Abbr. **p. 1.** The basic monetary unit of Argentina, Bolivia, Chile, Colombia, Cuba, the Dominican Republic, Guinea-Bissau, Mexico, and the Philippines, equal to 100 centavos. See feature at **currency.** **2.** A coin or note worth one peso. [Spanish, "weight," from Latin *pēnsum,* from *pendere* (past participle *pēnsus*), to weigh.]

pes·sa·ry (pěs′ə-rē) n., pl. **-ries.** *Medicine.* **1.** Any of various contraceptive or supportive devices placed and worn in the vagina. **2.** A medicated vaginal suppository. [Middle English *pessarie,* from Medieval Latin *pessārium,* from Late Latin *pessum, pessus,* from Greek *pessos,* pessary, oval stone for games.]

pes·si·mism (pěs′ə-mĭz′əm) n. **1.** A tendency to take the gloomiest and least hopeful possible view of a situation. **2.** The doctrine or belief that this is the worst of all possible worlds and that all things ultimately tend toward evil. **3.** The doctrine or belief that the evil in the world outweighs the good. [French *pessimisme,* from Latin *pessimus,* worst.] **—pes·si·mist** n. **—pes·si·mis·tic** (pěs′ə-mĭs′tĭk) adj. **—pes·si·mis·ti·cal·ly** adv.

pest (pěst) n. **1.** An annoying person or thing; a nuisance. **2.** An injurious plant or animal, especially one that is harmful to man, crops, or livestock. **3.** A pestilence. [French *peste,* from Latin *pestis*†, plague.]

Pes·ta·loz·zi (pěs′tə-lŏt′sē), **Johann Heinrich** (1746–1827). Swiss educator. He opened homes and schools for poor children and in works such as *How Gertrude Teaches Her Children* (1801) described his theory that a child should be taught to think rather than learn by rote.

pes·ter (pěs′tər) tr.v. **-tered, -tering, -ters.** To harass with petty annoyances or repeated demands; bother. **—See Synonyms at harass.** [Probably from Old French *empestrer,* to tie up (an animal), impede, from Vulgar Latin *impastōriāre* (unattested) : *in,* on, in + *pastōria* (unattested), the tying up of an animal, from Late Latin *pāstūra,* PASTURE; influenced by PEST.] **—pes·ter·er** n.

pest·house (pěst′hous′) n. Formerly, a hospital for patients suffering from plague or some other infectious disease; a lazaretto.

pes·ti·cide (pěs′tə-sīd′) n. Any chemical that is used to kill pests, especially insects and rodents. [PEST + -CIDE.] **—pes·ti·cid·al** (pěs′tə-sīd′l) adj.

pes·tif·er·ous (pě-stĭf′ər-əs) adj. **1.** Producing or breeding infectious disease. **2.** Infected with or contaminated by an epidemic disease. **3.** Morally evil or corrupting; pernicious. **4.** *Informal.* Irritating; annoying. [Middle English, from Latin *pestiferus* : *pestis,* PEST + -FEROUS.] **—pes·tif·er·ous·ly** adv.

pes·ti·lence (pěs′tə-ləns) n. **1.** Any usually fatal epidemic disease, especially bubonic plague. **2.** An epidemic of such a disease. **3.** A pernicious, evil influence or agent.

pes·ti·lent (pěs′tə-lənt) adj. **1.** Tending to cause death; deadly; fatal. **2.** Infected or contaminated with a contagious disease. **3.** Morally, socially, or politically harmful; pernicious. **4.** Extremely irritating or annoying. [Middle English, from Latin *pestilēns* (stem *pestilent-*), from *pestis,* plague, PEST.]

pes·ti·len·tial (pěs′tə-lěn′shəl) adj. **1.** Of or pertaining to pestilence. **2.** Tending to cause epidemic disease; pestiferous. **3.** Pernicious or troublesome; pestilent.

pes·tle (pěs′əl, pěs′təl) n. **1.** A club-shaped hand tool for grinding or mashing substances in a mortar. **2.** A large bar moved vertically to stamp or pound, as in a press or mill. ~v. **pestled, -tling, -tles.** —tr. To pound, grind, or mash with a pestle. —intr. To use a pestle. [Middle English *pestel,* from Old French, from Latin *pistillum.*]

pet¹ (pět) n. **1.** A tame animal kept for amusement or companionship. **2.** Any object of the affections. **3.** A person especially loved or indulged; a favorite: *teacher's pet.* ~adj. **1.** Kept as a pet: *a pet cat.* **2.** Of or pertaining to pets: *pet food.* **3.** Especially cherished or indulged; favorite: *a pet daughter.* ~v. **petted, petting, pets.** —tr. **1.** To treat or regard as a pet; indulge or pamper. **2.** To stroke or caress gently. **3.** To fondle or caress in an erotic way. —intr. To fondle and caress in an erotic way. [16th century (Scottish and northern English dialect) : origin obscure.] **—pet·ter** n.

pet² n. A fit of bad temper or pique. ~intr.v. **petted, petting, pets.** To be sulky and peevish. [16th century : origin obscure.]

Pé·tain (pā-tăn′), **Henri Philippe** (1856–1951). French military leader. As a general in World War I he became a national hero for successfully defending Verdun (1916). Appointed head of state in 1940, he accepted the terms of surrender to Germany and headed the pro-German government of unoccupied Vichy France until 1942. After the end of World War II he was condemned to death, a sentence later commuted to life imprisonment.

pet·al (pět′l) n. *Botany.* A separate, often brightly colored segment

of a corolla. Compare **sepal**. [New Latin *petalum*, from Greek *petalon*, leaf.] —**pet·aled, pet·alled** *adj.*

-petal *suffix*. Indicates a moving toward or seeking; for example, **centripetal**. [New Latin *-petus*, from Latin *petere*, to seek.]

pet·al·if·er·ous (pĕt'l-ĭf'ər-əs) *adj.* Bearing petals. [From PETAL + -FEROUS.]

pet·al·ine (pĕt'l-ĭn, -īn') *adj.* Of or resembling a petal.

pet·al·o·dy (pĕt'l-ō'dē) *n.* A condition in some plants where the stamens or other floral parts take on the appearance and function of petals. [Greek *petalōdēs*, leaflike, from *petalon*, leaf, PETAL.] —**pet·al·od·ic** (pĕt'l-ŏd'ĭk) *adj.*

pet·al·oid (pĕt'l-oid') *adj.* Resembling a petal; petallike.

pet·al·ous (pĕt'l-əs) *adj.* Having petals; petaled.

pe·tard (pĭ-tärd') *n.* **1.** Formerly, a small bell-shaped bomb used to breach a gate or wall. **2.** A firecracker that explodes with a loud noise. —**hoist with one's own petard**. Suffering harm as a result of one's own cleverness or scheming. [French *pétard*, from *péter*, to break wind, from *pet*, a fart, from Latin *pēditum*, from *pēdere*, to break wind.]

pet·cock (pĕt'kŏk') *n.* A small valve or faucet used to drain or reduce pressure from pipes, radiators, and boilers. [Perhaps PET(TY) + COCK.]

pe·te·chi·a (pə-tē'kē-ə, -tĕk'ē-ə) *n., pl.* **-techiae** (-tē'kē-ē', -tĕk'ē-ē'). A small spot on a body surface, such as the skin or mucous membrane, caused by a minute hemorrhage. [New Latin, from Italian *petecchia†*, skin spot.] —**pe·te·chi·al** *adj.* —**pe·te·chi·ate** (pə-tē'kē-īt, -āt', pə-tĕk'ē-īt, -āt') *adj.*

pe·ter[1] (pē'tər) *intr.v.* **-tered, -tering, -ters**. **1.** To diminish gradually. Usually used with *out*. **2.** To become exhausted. Used with *out*: *all petered out*. [Origin unknown.]

peter[2] *n.* In bridge and other card games, a conventional sequence of play designed to indicate to one's partner the strength of one's hand in a particular suit. It usually involves playing a high card and then a low card in that suit.
~*intr.v.* **petered, -tering, -ters**. To play a peter. [From PETER (verb), to give out, diminish gradually.]

Pe·ter (pē'tər) *n.* Either of the two books of the New Testament attributed to St. Peter.

Peter I, known as "Peter the Great" (1672–1725). Czar of Russia (1682–1725), who turned his country into a major European power. From 1682 he ruled jointly with his half-brother Ivan V, under the regency of Ivan's elder sister, Sophia. Effectively sole ruler from 1689, Peter campaigned against the Turks and Persians and led Russia, Poland, and Denmark to victory over Sweden in the Battle of Poltava (1709). Extending Russian territory around the Baltic and Caspian shores, he also founded the Russian navy and reformed the administration of the state.

Peter, Saint, called "Simon Peter" (died *c.* A.D. 67). The chief of the Apostles; traditionally regarded as the first bishop of Rome. [Greek *petros*, stone, rock, translation of Aramaic *Kēphā*, surname conferred upon the Apostle by Jesus: *"thou art Peter, and upon this rock I will build my church"* (Matthew 16:1).]

Pe·ter·bor·ough (pē'tər-bûr'ō, -bər-ə). City in Cambridgeshire, eastern England, on the Nene River. Catherine of Aragon is buried in its 12th-century cathedral. It is an agricultural center and produces bricks and diesel engines.

Pe·ter·loo massacre (pē'tər-lōō'). The violent dispersion by cavalry of a meeting of English radicals in Manchester on August 16, 1819. The incident became a symbol of repression. [After St. Peter's Fields (in Manchester) + (WATER)LOO.]

Peter Pan *n.* **1.** A man who clings to his childhood and remains emotionally or psychologically a boy; a chronically immature man. **2.** A man who looks much younger than he is. [After the central character in J.M. Barrie's play *Peter Pan* (1904).]

Peter principle *n.* The principle that in a hierarchy a person competent for certain tasks will be promoted to others he is less able to fulfill and will thus find his own level of incompetence. [From *The Peter Principle* (1969), book by L. Peter and R. Hull.]

Pe·ters·burg (pē'tərz-bûrg'). City in southeastern Virginia, on the Appomattox River south of Richmond. It was the site of a prolonged siege in the Civil War (June 15, 1864–April 3, 1865). The Petersburg National Battlefield preserves many of the old earthworks and tunnels.

pe·ter·sham (pē'tər-shəm) *n.* **1.** A thick woolen fabric. **2.** An overcoat made of such a fabric. **3.** A stiff, ribbed silk braid. [After Viscount *Petersham* (died 1851), British army officer.]

Pe·ter·son (pē'tər-sən), **Oscar Emmanuel** (1925–). Canadian jazz pianist. His style is noted for its technical accomplishment.

Peter's pence *n.* Also **Peter pence**. **1.** A tax, originally of one penny per household, paid in medieval England to the Papal See. **2.** An annual voluntary contribution made by Roman Catholics toward the expenses of the Holy See. [From St. PETER, as symbolizing the papacy.]

Peter the Hermit, known as "Peter of Amiens" (*c.* 1050–1115). French monk. In 1095 he began successfully preaching the First Crusade, and he led one of its bands to Constantinople in 1096. After the conquest of Jerusalem he returned to France (late 1099).

pet·i·o·lar (pĕt'ē-ō'lər) *adj. Biology.* Of, pertaining to, or growing on a petiole.

pet·i·o·late (pĕt'ē-ə-lāt', pĕt'ē-ō'lĭt) *adj.* Also **pet·i·o·lat·ed** (pĕt'ē-ə-lā'tĭd). *Biology.* Having a petiole.

pet·i·ole (pĕt'ē-ōl') *n.* **1.** *Botany.* The stalk by which a leaf is attached to a stem; a leafstalk. **2.** *Zoology.* The slender, stalklike connection between the thorax and abdomen in certain insects. [New Latin *petiolus*, from Late Latin *petiolus, peciolus*, small foot, fruit stalk, irregularly from Latin *pediculus*, diminutive of *pēs* (stem *ped-*), foot.]

pet·i·o·lule (pĕt'ē-ō-lōōl', pĕt'ē-ōl'yōōl) *n. Botany.* The stalk of a leaflet in a compound leaf. [New Latin *petiolulus*, diminutive of *petiolus*, PETIOLE.]

pet·it, pet·ty (pĕt'ē) *adj. Law.* Lesser; minor. [Middle English, from Old French *petit*, "small," perhaps from Gallo-Roman (unattested) *pittitto-* (perhaps imitative of children's speech).]

Pe·tit (pə-tē'), **Roland** (1924–). French dancer and choreographer. An innovator in contemporary ballet, he has introduced both realism and fantasy in works that include *The Strolling Players* (1945) and *Carmen* (1949).

pe·tit bour·geois (pĕt'ē bŏŏr-zhwä', pə-tē') *n., pl.* **petits bourgeois** (*pronounced as singular*). Also **petty bourgeois**. A member of the petite bourgeoisie, often considered as narrow-minded, conservative, and self-righteous. —**pe·tit-bour·geois** (pĕt'ē-bŏŏr-zhwä', pə-tē'-) *adj.*

pe·tite (pə-tēt') *adj.* Small, slender, and trim. Said of a girl or woman.
~*n.* A clothing size for short women. [French, feminine of PETIT.]

petite bour·geoi·sie (bŏŏr'zhwä-zē') *n.* Also **petty bourgeoisie**. The class that includes small businessmen, skilled manual workers, and low-ranking white-collar staff.

petite mar·mite (mär-mēt') *n.* A broth made of brown stock and served in a small, covered earthenware casserole. [French : *petite*, little + *marmite*, kettle.]

pet·it four (pĕt'ē fôr', fôr') *n., pl.* **petits fours** or **petit fours** (pĕt'ē fôrz', fôrz'). A small, rich tea cake, often frosted and decorated. [French, small cake, from *four*, oven.]

pe·ti·tion (pə-tĭsh'ən) *n.* **1.** A written document bearing many signatures, requesting action on a particular issue from those in authority. **2.** A solemn supplication or request to a superior authority; an entreaty. **3.** *Law.* **a.** A formal written application asking a court for a specific judicial action: *a petition for appeal*. **b.** The act of making such a request. **c.** That which is asked for in any such request.
~*v.* **petitioned, -tioning, -tions.** —*tr.* **1.** To address a petition to. **2.** To ask for by petition; request formally. —*intr.* To make a request or entreaty. Often followed by *for: The defendant petitioned for retrial*. [Middle English *peticioun*, from Old French *petition*, from Latin *petītiō* (stem *petītiōn-*), attack, solicitation, from *petere* (past participle *petītus*), to seek; demand.] —**pe·ti·tion·ar·y** (pə-tĭsh'ə-nĕr'ē) *adj.* —**pe·ti·tion·er** *n.*

pe·ti·ti·o prin·ci·pi·i (pə-tĭsh'ē-ō' prĭn-sĭp'ē-ē') *n. Logic.* The fallacy of assuming in the premise of an argument that which one wishes to prove in the conclusion; begging the question. [Medieval Latin, "postulation of the beginning."]

pet·it juror (pĕt'ē) *n.* A member of a petit jury.

pet·it jury (pĕt'ē) *n.* A jury of 12 persons that sits at civil and criminal trials. Also called "trial jury." Compare **grand jury**.

pet·it larceny (pĕt'ē) *n.* The theft of objects whose value is below a certain designated figure. Compare **grand larceny**.

pe·tit maî·tre (pə-tē' mā'trə) *n., pl.* **petits maîtres** or **petit maîtres** (*pronounced as singular*). A dandy. [French, "small master."]

pet·it mal (pĕt'ē mäl', mäl') *n. Pathology.* A mild form of epilepsy characterized by frequent but transient lapses of consciousness and only rare spasms or falling. Compare **grand mal**. [French, "small illness."]

pet·it point (pĕt'ē point') *n.* **1.** A small stitch used in needlepoint. **2.** Needlepoint done with such a stitch. Compare **gros point**. [French, "small point."]

pet·nap (pĕt'năp') *tr.v.* **-napped, -napping, -naps**. To steal (a pet), usually for profit. [PET + (KID)NAP.] —**pet·nap·per** *n.* —**pet·nap·ping** *n.*

Pe·tra (pē'trə, pĕt'rə). Ancient ruined city of southwestern Jordan. It was the capital of the Nabataeans, prospering as an important trading post from the 4th century B.C. until its capture by the Romans (A.D. 106). It was rediscovered in 1812.

Pe·trarch (pē'trärk', pĕt'rärk'), born Francesco Petrarca (1304–74). Italian poet and scholar who, with Dante and Boccaccio, instituted the literary Renaissance in Italy. A Florentine by birth, his works unite classical scholarship with Christian belief in the spirit of humanism. He is especially remembered for his love sonnets dedicated to Laura. —**Pe·trarch·an** (pĭ-trär'kən) *adj.*

Petrarchan sonnet *n.* A sonnet in a form of Italian origin comprising an octave with the rhyme pattern *abbaabba* and a sestet of various rhyme patterns such as *cdccdc* or *cdecde*. Also called "Italian sonnet." [After PETRARCH.]

pet·rel (pĕt'rəl) *n.* Any of various sea birds of the order Procellariiformes, especially the **storm petrel** (see). [Variant of earlier *pitteral†*.]

Pe·tri dish (pē'trē) *n.* A shallow dish with a loose-fitting cover, used especially to culture microorganisms for research. [After Julius R. *Petri* (1852–1921), German bacteriologist.]

Pe·trie (pē'trē), **Sir (William Matthew) Flinders** (1853–1942). British archaeologist, especially known for his excavations in Egypt, which began (1880) with work on the pyramids at Giza. His published works include *Methods and Aims of Archaeology* (1904).

pet·ri·fac·tion (pĕt'rə-făk'shən) *n.* Also **pet·ri·fi·ca·tion** (-fĭ-kā'shən). **1. a.** The process of petrifying; the conversion of organic matter into stone or a stony substance. **b.** Something resulting from this process. **2.** The state of being petrified, as by fear.

Petrified Forest National Park. Area of 38,147 hectares (94,189 acres) in eastern Arizona. Part of the Painted Desert, it contains the largest known display of petrified wood in the world. The "stone trees" date from the Triassic period, more than two million years ago.

pet·ri·fy (pĕt′rə-fī′) *v.* **-fied, -fying, -fies.** —*tr.* **1.** To convert (wood or other organic matter) into stone or a stony substance by structural impregnation with dissolved minerals. **2.** To cause to become stiff or stonelike; deaden. **3.** To stun or paralyze with terror. —*intr.* To become stony, especially by mineral replacement of organic matter. [French *petrifier* : Latin *petra,* stone, from Greek + *facere,* to make.]

Pe·trine (pē′trīn′) *adj.* **1.** Of or pertaining to St. Peter. **2.** Of or pertaining to the pope considered as a successor of St. Peter.

petro– *prefix.* Indicates: **1.** Rock or stone; for example, **petrology. 2.** Petroleum; for example, **petrochemistry.** [Greek *petros,* stone, and *petra,* rock.]

pet·ro·chem·i·cal (pĕt′rō-kĕm′ĭ-kəl) *n.* Any chemical derived from petroleum or natural gas. **—pet·ro·chem·i·cal** *adj.*

pet·ro·chem·is·try (pĕt′rō-kĕm′ĭ-strē) *n.* The chemistry of petroleum and its derivatives.

pet·ro·dol·lar (pĕt′rō-dŏl′ər) *n.* A dollar earned by an oil-producing country from its exports, especially as part of a reserve to be invested abroad.

pet·ro·gen·e·sis (pĕt′rō-jĕn′ə-sĭs) *n.* A branch of petrology that deals with the origin of rocks. **—pet·ro·ge·net·ic** (pĕt′rō-jə-nĕt′ĭk) *adj.*

pet·ro·glyph (pĕt′rə-glĭf′) *n.* A usually prehistoric carving or line drawing on rock. **—pet·ro·glyph·ic** (pĕt′rə-glĭf′ĭk) *adj.*

Petrograd. See **Leningrad.**

pe·trog·ra·phy (pə-trŏg′rə-fē) *n.* The description and classification of rocks. [PETRO- + -GRAPHY.] **—pe·trog·ra·pher** *n.* **—pet·ro·graph·ic** (pĕt′rə-grăf′ĭk), **pet·ro·graph·i·cal** *adj.* **—pet·ro·graph·i·cal·ly** *adv.*

pet·rol (pĕt′rəl) *n. Chiefly British.* Gasoline. [French *pétrole* (in the phrase *essence de pétrole*), from Old French *petrole,* from Medieval Latin *petroleum,* PETROLEUM.]

pet·ro·la·tum (pĕt′rə-lā′təm, -lä′təm) *n.* A colorless to amber gelatinous semisolid obtained from petroleum, consisting of various alkanes and alkenes, and used in lubricants and medicinal ointments. Also called "petroleum jelly." [New Latin, from Medieval Latin *petroleum,* PETROLEUM.]

pe·tro·le·um (pə-trō′lē-əm) *n. Abbr.* **pet.** A natural, yellow-to-black, thick, flammable liquid hydrocarbon mixture found principally beneath the earth's surface and processed for fractions including natural gas, gasoline, naphtha, kerosene, fuel and lubricating oils, paraffin wax, asphalt, and a wide variety of derivative products. Also called "crude oil," *chiefly British* "rock oil." [Medieval Latin : PETRO- + *oleum,* oil.]

petroleum ether *n.* A volatile mixture of the higher alkane liquids obtained as a fraction of petroleum distillation and used as a solvent.

petroleum jelly *n.* Petrolatum.

pe·trol·ic (pə-trŏl′ĭk) *adj.* Derived from petroleum.

pe·trol·o·gy (pə-trŏl′ə-jē) *n.* The study of the origin, composition, structure, and alteration of rocks. [PETRO- + -LOGY.] **—pet·ro·log·ic** (pĕt′rə-lŏj′ĭk), **pet·ro·log·i·cal** *adj.* **—pet·ro·log·i·cal·ly** *adv.* **—pe·trol·o·gist** *n.*

pet·ro·nel (pĕt′rə-nĕl′) *n.* A firearm or large pistol used by cavalry soldiers in the 16th and 17th centuries. [French *petrinal,* variant of *poitrinal* (noun), from adjective, "of the chest" (the butt end was designed to rest on the chest while the weapon was being fired), from *poitrine,* chest, from Vulgar Latin *pectorina* (unattested), from Latin *pectus* (stem *pectŏr-*), chest.]

Pe·tro·ni·us (pə-trō′nē-əs), **Gaius,** known as "Petronius Arbiter" (*fl.* 1st century A.D.). Roman courtier and wit and the supposed author of the *Satyricon,* a bitingly satirical character study written in both prose and verse that survives only in fragments.

pet·ro·pol·i·tics (pĕt′rō-pŏl′ĭ-tĭks) *n. Used with a singular or plural verb.* The strategic practice of controlling petroleum sales so as to achieve international political and economic ends and goals.

pe·tro·sal (pə-trō′səl) *adj.* Also **pet·rous** (pĕt′rəs). *Anatomy.* Pertaining to or located near the portion of the temporal bone that surrounds the inner ear. [Latin *petrōsus,* PETROUS.]

pet·rous (pĕt′rəs) *adj.* **1.** Of, pertaining to, or resembling rock; stony; hard. **2.** *Anatomy.* Variant of **petrosal.** [Latin *petrōsus,* rocky, from *petra,* rock, from Greek.]

pet·ti·coat (pĕt′ē-kōt′) *n.* **1.** A skirt, especially a woman's slip or underskirt. **2.** *Slang.* A woman or girl.
~*adj.* **1.** Female; feminine. **2.** Of or by women: *petticoat government.* [Middle English *petycote* : PETTY + COAT.]

petticoat narcissus *n.* A small daffodil, *Narcissus bulbocodium,* native to the Mediterranean region, having yellow or white flowers. Also called "hoop-petticoat narcissus."

pet·ti·fog (pĕt′ē-fŏg′, -fôg′) *intr.v.* **-fogged, -fogging, -fogs.** To act like a pettifogger. [Back-formation from PETTIFOGGER.]

pet·ti·fog·ger (pĕt′ē-fŏg′ər, -fô′gər) *n.* **1.** An unscrupulous lawyer. **2.** A person who pays excessive attention to small details; an extremely fussy person; a quibbler. [Origin unknown.]

pet·tish (pĕt′ĭsh) *adj.* Ill-tempered; peevish; petulant. [Probably from PET (ill temper).] **—pet·tish·ly** *adv.* **—pet·tish·ness** *n.*

pet·ti·toes (pĕt′ē-tōz′) *pl.n.* Pig's trotters considered as food. [16th century (originally, offal), from Old French *petite oie,* "little goose," giblets of a goose; assimilated to *petty toes.*]

pet·ty (pĕt′ē) *adj.* **-tier, -tiest. 1.** Small, trivial, or insignificant in quantity or quality: *petty grievances.* **2.** Having or showing a contemptibly narrow-minded and ungenerous nature: *a petty outlook.* **3.** Of subordinate or inferior rank. **4.** *Law.* Variant of **petit.** —See Synonyms at **trivial.** [Middle English *pety,* small, variant of *petit,* PETIT.] **—pet·ti·ly** *adv.* **—pet·ti·ness** *n.*

petty bourgeois. Variant of **petit bourgeois.**

petty bourgeoisie. Variant of **petite bourgeoisie.**

petty cash *n. Abbr.* **p.c., p/c, P/C** A small fund of money for incidental expenses, as in an office.

petty officer *n. Abbr.* **P.O., p.o.** A naval noncommissioned officer.

pet·u·lant (pĕch′o͞o-lənt) *adj.* Unreasonably irritable or ill-tempered; peevish. [French *pétulant,* saucy, from Latin *petulāns* (stem *petulant-*), present participle of *petulāre* (unattested), to jab at, frequentative of *petere,* to attack.] **—pet·u·lance, pet·u·lan·cy** *n.* **—pet·u·lant·ly** *adv.*

pe·tu·ni·a (pə-to͞on′yə, -tyo͞on′yə) *n.* Any of various widely cultivated plants of the genus *Petunia,* native to tropical America, having funnel-shaped flowers in various shades. [New Latin, from obsolete French *petun,* tobacco, from Tupi *petyn, petyma.*]

pe·tun·tse, pe·tun·tze (pə-to͞on′tsē) *n.* A variety of feldspar sometimes mixed with kaolin in Chinese porcelain. [Chinese *bái dùn zi,* "white heap."]

Pev·en·sey (pĕv′ən-zē). Village in East Sussex, southeastern England. Now located inland as a result of the retreating sea, it is where William the Conqueror landed in 1066. It is one of the Cinque Ports and has the remains of a Norman castle and Roman fort.

pew (pyo͞o) *n.* **1.** A bench for the congregation in a church. **2.** A small enclosure or box of seats in a church, especially one formerly reserved for a particular family or group of regular churchgoers. [Middle English *pewe, puwe,* from Old French *puie,* raised seat, balcony, from Latin *podia,* plural of *podium,* podium, balcony, from Greek *podion,* small foot, base, diminutive of *pous* (stem *pod-*), foot.]

pe·wee, pee·wee (pē′wē) *n.* Any of various small, olive-brown North American woodland birds of the genus *Contopus.* [Imitative of its cry.]

pewit. Variant of **peewit.**

pew·ter (pyo͞o′tər) *n.* **1.** Any of numerous silver-gray alloys of tin with various amounts of antimony, copper, and lead, formerly used widely for fine kitchen utensils and tableware. **2.** Pewter articles collectively. [Middle English *pewtre,* from Old French *peutre, peautre,* variant of *peltre,* tin, from (unattested) Vulgar Latin *peltrum*†.] **—pew·ter** *adj.*

pe·yo·te (pā-ō′tē) *n.* Also **pe·yo·tl** (pā-ōt′l). **1.** A cactus, **mescal** *(see).* **2.** A hallucinatory drug derived from the tubercles of this cactus. [Mexican Spanish, from Nahuatl.]

pf. **1.** pfennig. **2.** preferred.

pfen·nig (fĕn′ĭg) *n., pl.* **-nigs** or **pfennige** (fĕn′ĭ-gə). *Abbr.* **pf., pfg.** A coin equal to $^{1}/_{100}$ of the Deutsche Mark of West Germany and the Mark of East Germany. See feature at **currency.** [German *Pfennig,* from Old High German *pfenning,* from West Germanic *panninga* (unattested). See also **penny, penni.**]

pfg. pfennig.

PG (pē′jē′) *adj.* Indicating a motion-picture rating that allows admission of persons of all ages but suggests parental guidance in the case of children. [*p*arental *g*uidance.]

Pg. Portuguese.

P.G. **1.** paying guest. **2.** postgraduate.

PGA Professional Golfers' Association.

pH (pē′āch′) *n. Chemistry.* A measure of the acidity or alkalinity of a solution calculated as the common logarithm of the reciprocal of the hydrogen ion concentration in moles per cubic decimeter of solution and numerically equal to 7 for neutral solutions. pH increases with increasing alkalinity and decreases with increasing acidity. [*p*otential of *h*ydrogen.]

ph. phase.

Phae·drus (fē′drəs) (1st century A.D.). A Thracian-born freedman, he was the author of a collection of fables based on those attributed to Aesop.

phae·ton (fā′ə-tən) *n.* A light, open, four-wheeled carriage, usually drawn by a pair of horses. [French *phaéton,* after *Phaéton,* French form of *Phaethon,* son of Helios who attempted to drive the chariot of the sun.]

phage (fāj) *n.* A **bacteriophage** *(see).*

-phage *suffix.* Indicates something that eats or destroys; for example, **bacteriophage.** [Greek *-phagos,* from *phagein,* to eat.]

phag·e·de·na, phag·e·dae·na (făj′ə-dē′nə) *n.* An ulcer of the skin and subcutaneous tissues that spreads rapidly and causes sloughing off of the skin. [Latin, from Greek *phagedaina,* from *phagein,* to consume, eat.]

phago– *suffix.* Indicates eating or destroying; for example, **phagocyte.** [Greek, from *phagein,* to eat.]

phag·o·cyte (făg′ə-sīt′) *n. Physiology.* A cell such as a leukocyte that engulfs and digests cells, microorganisms, or other foreign bodies in the bloodstream and tissues. [PHAGO- + -CYTE.] **—phag·o·cyt·ic** (făg′ə-sĭt′ĭk) *adj.*

phag·o·cy·to·sis (făg′ə-sī-tō′sĭs) *n. Physiology.* The envelopment and digestion of bacteria or other foreign bodies by phagocytes. [New Latin : PHAGOCYT(E) + -OSIS.]

-phagous *suffix.* Indicates eating or tending to eat; for example, **phyllophagous.** [Latin *-phagus,* from Greek *-phagos,* eating, from *phagein,* to eat.]

petrifaction *These jumbled rocks were trees about 170 million years ago. Long after the trees fell and were buried by layers of mud, sand, and volcanic ash, they became petrified—turned into stone—as mineral-rich water seeped into the trunks, eventually replacing each cell in the wood with a matching crystal of quartz. Later, erosion brought the stone trees back to the surface, where they now form part of the Petrified Forest National Park in Arizona.*

pewter *In the Middle Ages this tin-based alloy replaced wood as a material for tableware. It remained unrivaled until the end of the 18th century, when manufacturers first produced relatively cheap porcelain and earthenware in large quantities. This pewter tableware was made in the United States in the mid-19th century.*

pharaoh *This solid gold funeral mask of the Egyptian pharaoh Tutankhamen was placed over the head and shoulders of his linen-wrapped mummy more than 3,000 years ago. It was found when his tomb was rediscovered in 1922 by the British archaeologist Howard Carter.*

–phagy, –phagia *suffix.* Indicates an eating or consumption; for example, **cytophagy, dysphagia.** [Greek *-phagia,* from *phagein,* to eat.]

pha·lan·ge·al (fə-lăn′jē-əl, fā-) *adj. Anatomy.* Of or pertaining to a phalanx or phalanges.

pha·lan·ger (fə-lăn′jər) *n.* Any of various small, arboreal marsupials of the family Phalangeridae, of Australia and adjacent islands, having a long tail and dense, woolly fur. [New Latin, from PHALANX, "toe bone" (with reference to the peculiar structure of the second and third toes of its hind feet).]

pha·lange (fă′lănj′, fə-lănj′) *n. Anatomy.* See **phalanx** (sense 4). [French, from New Latin *phalanx* (stem *phalang-*), PHALANX.]

phal·an·ster·y (făl′ən-stĕr′ē, fə-lăn′stə-rē) *n., pl.* **-ies. 1.** A community of the followers of Charles **Fourier** *(see).* Also called "phalanx." **2.** The buildings of such a community. [French *Phalanstère* : *phalange,* phalanx, from New Latin *phalanx,* PHALANX + *monastère,* monastery, from Late Latin *monastērium,* MONASTERY.] **—phal·an·ste·ri·an** (făl′ən-stîr′ē-ən) *n.* & *adj.* **—phal·an·ste·ri·an·ism** *n.*

pha·lanx (fā′lăngks′; *British* făl′ăngks′) *n., pl.* **-lanxes** or **phalanges** (fə-lăn′jēz, fā-) (only form for sense 4). **1.** An ancient Greek formation of infantry carrying overlapping shields and long spears, perfected by Philip II of Macedon and used by Alexander the Great. **2.** A close-knit or compact body of people: *"formed a solid phalanx in defence of the Constitution and Protestant religion"* (G.M. Trevelyan). **3.** A **phalanstery** *(see).* **4.** *Anatomy.* A bone of a finger or toe. Also called "phalange." [Latin, from Greek, wooden beam, finger bone, line of battle.]

phal·a·rope (făl′ə-rōp′) *n.* Any of several wading birds of the family Phalaropodidae, having lobed toes that enable them to swim. [French, from New Latin *phalaropus* : Greek *phalaris,* coot (which has a white patch on the head), from *phalaros,* having a white spot + *-pus,* from Greek *pous,* foot.]

phal·lic (făl′ĭk) *adj.* **1.** Of, pertaining to, or resembling a phallus. **2.** Of or pertaining to the cult of the phallus as an embodiment of generative power. [Greek *phallikos,* from *phallos,* PHALLUS.]

phal·lus (făl′əs) *n., pl.* **phalli** (făl′ī′) or **-luses. 1.** A representation of the penis and testes as an embodiment of generative power. **2. a.** The penis. **b.** The sexually undifferentiated tissue in the embryo that becomes the penis or clitoris. [Late Latin *phallus,* penis, from Greek *phallos.*]

–phane *suffix.* Indicates resemblance or similarity to a specified material; for example, **cellophane.** [Greek *-phanēs,* appearing, shining, from *phainesthai,* to appear.]

phan·er·o·crys·tal·line (făn′ə-rō-krĭs′tə-lĭn, -līn′) *adj.* Designating igneous or metamorphic rocks having a crystalline structure in which the crystals are visible to the naked eye. [Greek *phaneros,* visible + CRYSTALLINE.]

phan·er·o·gam (făn′ər-ə-găm′) *n. Botany.* A plant that produces flowers and true seeds; a spermatophyte. No longer in technical usage. Compare **cryptogam.** [New Latin *phanerogamus,* "one having visible reproductive parts" : Greek *phaneros,* visible, from *phainein,* to show + -GAMOUS.] **—phan·er·o·gam·ic** (făn′ər-ə-găm′ĭk), **phan·er·og·a·mous** (făn′ə-rŏg′ə-məs) *adj.*

phan·er·o·phyte (făn′ər-ə-fīt′) *n.* A perennial plant that bears its dormant buds well above soil level. [Greek *phaneros,* visible + -PHYTE.]

phan·tasm (făn′tăz′əm) *n.* **1.** Something apparently seen but having no physical reality; a phantom. **2.** An illusory mental image. **3.** In Platonic philosophy, objective reality as perceived and distorted by the five senses. [Middle English *fantasme,* from Old French, from Latin *phantasma,* apparition, specter, from Greek, from *phantazein,* to make visible, from *phainein,* to show.] **—phan·tas·mal** (făn-tăz′məl), **phan·tas·mic** (făn-tăz′mĭk) *adj.*

phan·tas·ma·go·ri·a (făn-tăz′mə-gôr′ē-ə, -gōr′ē-ə) *n.* **1.** A fantastic sequence of haphazardly associative imagery, as seen in dreams or fever. **2.** Fantastic imagery as represented in art. **3.** A scene of constant and bewildering change. [Possibly from Greek *phantasma,* PHANTASM + *agora,* assembly.] **—phan·tas·ma·gor·ic** (făn-tăz′mə-gôr′ĭk, -gŏr′ĭk), **phan·tas·ma·gor·i·cal** *adj.*

phantasy. Variant of **fantasy.**

phan·tom (făn′təm) *n.* **1.** Something apparently seen, heard, or sensed, but having no physical reality; ghost; specter. **2.** An image that appears only in the mind.
~*adj.* **1.** Unreal; ghostlike. **2.** *Pathology.* Designating an organ, structure, or condition that does not exist but appears to from various signs and symptoms. [Middle English *fantosme, fantome,* from Old French, from Latin *phantasma,* PHANTASM.]

phantom limb *n.* The sensation that a limb or part of a limb still exists after it has been amputated, usually because pain appears to come from the amputated part.

phantom pregnancy *n.* A condition in which symptoms of pregnancy, such as an enlarged abdomen, occur in a nonpregnant woman. Caused by the secretion of pituitary hormones, it is usually the result of an emotional disorder. Also called "pseudocyesis."

–phany *suffix.* Indicates a manifestation or sudden appearance; for example, **epiphany.** [Greek *-phania,* from *phainein,* to show.]

phar·aoh (fâr′ō, fā′rō) *n. Often* **Pharaoh. 1.** A king of ancient Egypt. **2.** A tyrant. [Late Latin *Pharaō,* from Greek *Pharaō,* transcription of Hebrew *Par'ōh,* from an Egyptian word meaning "great house."] **—Phar·a·on·ic** (fâr′ā-ŏn′ĭk) *adj.*

pharaoh ant *n.* A small reddish ant, *Monomorium pharaonis,* originally of tropical countries but now a pest of heated buildings in temperate regions.

Phar·i·sa·ic (făr′ə-sā′ĭk) *adj.* **1.** Of or pertaining to the Pharisees. **2. pharisaic.** Variant of **pharisaical.**

phar·i·sa·i·cal (făr′ə-sā′ĭ-kəl) *adj.* Also **phar·i·sa·ic** (-sā′ĭk). Hypocritically self-righteous and censorious. **—phar·i·sa·i·cal·ly** *adv.* **—phar·i·sa·i·cal·ness** *n.*

phar·i·sa·ism (făr′ə-sā-ĭz′əm) *n.* Also **phar·i·see·ism** (-sē-ĭz′əm). **1.** Hypocritical observance of the letter of religious or moral law without regard for the spirit; sanctimoniousness. **2. Pharisaism.** The doctrines and practices of the Pharisees.

phar·i·see (făr′ə-sē) *n.* **1. Pharisee.** A member of an ancient Jewish sect that emphasized strict interpretation and observance of the Mosaic law in both its oral and written form. Compare **Sadducee. 2.** A hypocritically self-righteous person. [Middle English *pharise,* Old English *farise,* from Late Latin *pharisaeus,* from Greek *pharisaios,* from Aramaic *perīshayyā,* plural of *perīsh,* "separated."]

phar·ma·ceu·ti·cal (fär′mə-so͞o′tĭ-kəl) *adj.* Also **phar·ma·ceu·tic** (-tĭk). Of or pertaining to pharmacy or pharmacists.
~*n.* A pharmaceutical product or preparation. [Late Latin *pharmaceuticus,* from Greek *pharmakeutikos,* from *pharmakeutēs,* pharmacist, from *pharmakeuein,* to give drugs, from *pharmakon,* drug. See **pharmaco-.**] **—phar·ma·ceu·ti·cal·ly** *adv.*

phar·ma·ceu·tics (fär′mə-so͞o′tĭks) *n. Used with a singular verb.* See **pharmacy** (sense 1).

phar·ma·cist (fär′mə-sĭst) *n.* A person trained in pharmacy.

pharmaco– *prefix.* Indicates drugs; for example, **pharmacology.** [Greek *pharmakon*†, drug, poison, potion.]

phar·ma·cog·no·sy (fär′mə-kŏg′nə-sē) *n.* The branch of pharmacology dealing with crude natural drugs. [PHARMACO- + Greek *-gnōsia,* knowledge, from -GNOSIS.] **—phar·ma·cog·no·sist** *n.* **—phar·ma·cog·nos·tic** (fär′mə-kŏg-nŏs′tĭk) *adj.*

phar·ma·col·o·gy (fär′mə-kŏl′ə-jē) *n.* The science of drugs, including their composition, uses, and effects. [PHARMACO- + -LOGY.] **—phar·ma·co·log·ic** (fär′mə-kə-lŏj′ĭk), **phar·ma·co·log·i·cal** *adj.* **—phar·ma·co·log·i·cal·ly** *adv.* **—phar·ma·col·o·gist** *n.*

phar·ma·co·poe·ia, phar·ma·co·pe·ia (fär′mə-kə-pē′ə) *n.* **1.** A book containing an official list of medicinal drugs together with articles on their preparation and use. **2.** The range of drugs used in medicine. [New Latin, from Greek *pharmakopoiia,* preparation of drugs, from *pharmakopoios,* preparing drugs : PHARMACO- + *-poios,* "making," from *poiein,* to make.] **—phar·ma·co·poe·ial** *adj.* **—phar·ma·co·poe·ist** *n.*

phar·ma·cy (fär′mə-sē) *n., pl.* **-cies. 1.** The science of preparing and dispensing drugs. Also called "pharmaceutics." **2.** A place where drugs are prepared or dispensed. **3.** A **drugstore** *(see).* [Middle English *farmacie,* from Old French, from Late Latin *pharmacia,* from Greek *pharmakeia,* from *pharmakon,* drug.]

pha·ros (fâr′ŏs′) *n.* A lighthouse. [Latin, from Greek, after *Pharos,* an island in the bay of Alexandria, Egypt, celebrated in antiquity for its lighthouse.]

pha·ryn·ge·al (fə-rĭn′jē-əl, -jəl, făr′ĭn-jē′əl) *adj.* Also **pha·ryn·gal** (fə-rĭng′gəl). Of, pertaining to, located in, going to, or coming from the pharynx: *pharyngeal air-stream mechanism.*
~*n.* Also **pha·ryn·gal.** A speech sound produced in the pharynx. [New Latin *pharyngeus,* from *pharynx,* PHARYNX.]

phar·yn·gi·tis (făr′ĭn-jī′tĭs) *n.* Inflammation of the pharynx. [New Latin : PHARYNG(O)- + -ITIS.]

pharyngo–, pharyng– *prefix.* Indicates pharynx; for example, **pharyngoscope, pharyngitis.** [New Latin, from Greek *pharungo-,* from *pharunx,* PHARYNX.]

phar·yn·gol·o·gy (făr′ĭng-gŏl′ə-jē) *n.* The medical study of the pharynx and its diseases. [PHARYNGO- + -LOGY.] **—phar·yn·go·log·i·cal** (fə-rĭng′gə-lŏj′ĭ-kəl) *adj.* **—phar·yn·gol·o·gist** *n.*

pha·ryn·go·scope (fə-rĭng′gə-skōp′) *n.* An instrument used in examining the pharynx. [PHARYNGO- + -SCOPE.] **—phar·yn·gos·co·py** (făr′ĭng-gŏs′kə-pē) *n.*

phar·yn·got·o·my (făr′ĭng-gŏt′ə-mē) *n., pl.* **-mies.** A surgical incision of the pharynx. [PHARYNGO- + -TOMY.]

phar·ynx (făr′ĭngks) *n., pl.* **pharynges** (fə-rĭn′jēz) or **pharynxes.** The section of the digestive tract that extends from the nasal cavities and mouth to the esophagus. [New Latin, from Greek *pharunx,* throat, pharynx.]

phase (fāz) *n. Abbr.* **ph. 1.** Any one of a sequence of distinct apparent forms. **2.** A distinct stage of development: *The war fell into three clear phases.* **3.** A temporary manner, attitude, or pattern of behavior: *a passing phase.* **4.** *Astronomy.* Any of the cyclically recurring apparent forms of the moon or a planet. **5.** *Physics.* **a.** A particular stage in a periodic process or phenomenon. **b.** The fraction of a complete cycle elapsed as measured from a given reference point and often expressed as an angle. **6.** *Chemistry.* A discrete homogeneous part of a material system that is mechanically separable from the rest, as is ice from water. **7.** *Biology.* A characteristic form or appearance that occurs in a cycle or that distinguishes some individuals of a group. **8.** *Biology.* A stage in cell division. **—in** (or **out of**) **phase.** *Physics.* Reaching (or not reaching) corresponding phases at the same time, as two waves might.
~*tr.v.* **phased, phasing, phases. 1.** To plan or carry out systematically by phases: *a phased withdrawal of troops.* **2.** To bring into harmony or efficient joint functioning. Often used with *with*: *phase one process with another.* **—phase in.** To introduce slowly one stage at a time. **—phase out.** To eliminate or withdraw slowly one stage at a time. [Back-formation from *phases* (plural), from New Latin *phasis,* from Greek, appearance, phase of the moon, from *phainein,* to show.] **—pha·sic** (fā′zĭk) *adj.*

phase-con·trast microscope (fāz′kŏn′trăst′) *n.* A microscope that renders differences in the phase of light transmitted or reflected by a specimen as variations in contrast. Also called "phase microscope."

phase modulation *n.* In telecommunications, the variation of the phase of a carrier wave by an amount proportional to the amplitude of a modulating signal.

phase rule *n.* A rule stating that the number of degrees of freedom in a material system at equilibrium is equal to the number of components minus the number of phases plus the constant 2. For example, the system of water vapor, water, and ice has zero degrees of freedom, since three phases of one component coexist.

-phasia *suffix.* Indicates a specified type of speech disorder; for example, **dysphasia.** [New Latin, from Greek, speech, from *phasis,* utterance, from *phanai,* to say, speak.]

phat·ic (făt′ĭk) *adj.* Designating utterances that assert a friendly social relationship rather than conveying specific thoughts or ideas. Much conversation about the weather, for example, is merely phatic. [From the term *phatic communion,* coined by Bronislaw MALINOWSKI : Greek *phatos,* spoken, from *phanai,* to speak.]

Ph.D. Doctor of Philosophy. [Latin *Philosophiae Doctor.*]

pheas·ant (fĕz′ənt) *n.,* pl. **-ants** or collectively **pheasant.** **1.** Any of various game birds of the family Phasianidae, native to the Old World, characteristically having long tails and, in the males of many species, brilliantly colored plumage. **2.** Any of various similar birds, such as the **ruffed grouse** (see). [Middle English *fesaunt, fesant,* from Old French *fesan, faisan,* from Latin *phasiānus,* from Greek *phasianos,* "the Phasian (bird)," of the river Phasis in the Caucasus, from *Phāsis,* the river Phasis.]

pheasant's eye *n.* **1.** Any of various plants of the genus *Adonis;* especially, *A. annua,* which has small scarlet flowers and finely divided leaves. **2.** A narcissus, *Narcissus poeticus,* having white petals and a shallow, red-rimmed, yellow corona. In this sense, also called "narcissus."

phel·lem (fĕl′əm) *n. Botany.* **Cork cambium** (see). [Greek *phellos,* cork + *-em,* as in PHLOEM.]

phel·lo·derm (fĕl′ə-dûrm′) *n.* The soft cortex tissue that forms on the inner side of the phellogen of some trees. [Greek *phellos,* cork + -DERM.] —**phel·lo·der·mal** (fĕl′ə-dûr′məl) *adj.*

phel·lo·gen (fĕl′ə-jən) *n.* A tissue in woody plants from which cork and phelloderm develop. [Greek *phellos,* cork + -GEN.] —**phel·lo·ge·net·ic** (fĕl′ə-jə-nĕt′ĭk), **phel·lo·gen·ic** (fĕl′ə-jĕn′ĭk) *adj.*

phe·nac·e·tin (fə-năs′ə-tĭn) *n.* An analgesic drug, **acetophenetidin** (see). [PHEN(O)- + ACET(O)- + -IN.]

phen·a·cite (fĕn′ə-sīt′) *n.* A rare natural beryllium silicate, yellow, brown, or pale rose in color, occurring as vitreous crystals sometimes used as gems. [Greek *phenax†* (stem *phenak-*), an impostor (from its resemblance to quartz).]

phe·nan·threne (fə-năn′thrēn′) *n.* A colorless crystalline compound, $C_{14}H_{10}$, obtained by fractional distillation of coal-tar oils and used in dyes, drugs, and explosives. [PHEN(O)- + ANTHR(A-C)ENE.]

phen·ar·sa·zine chloride (fĭ-när′sə-zēn′) *n.* A highly poisonous yellow crystalline compound, $C_{12}H_9AsClN$, used as a poison gas. [PHEN(O)- + ARS(ENIC) + AZINE.]

phen·a·zine (fĕn′ə-zēn′) *n.* A yellow crystalline compound, $C_6H_4N_2C_6H_4$, used in the manufacture of dyes.

phe·net·ic (fə-nĕt′ĭk) *adj. Biology.* Of, pertaining to, or designating a system of classification based on observed similarities and differences between organisms rather than on their supposed evolutionary relationships. [*Phenotype* + *genetic.*]

phen·e·tole (fĕn′ə-tōl′, -tŏl′) *n.* A colorless, oily phenyl ether, $C_6H_5OC_2H_5$.

phenix. Variant of **phoenix.**

pheno-, phen- *prefix. Chemistry.* Indicates: **1.** Showing or displaying; for example, **phenocryst. 2.** A compound derived from, containing, or related to benzene; for example, **phenol, phenothiazine.** [Greek *phainein,* to show. Sense 2 is from French *(acide) phénique,* an early name for phenol, from Greek *phainein* (so named because it was originally extracted from illuminating gas).]

Phe·no·bar·bi·tal (fē′nō-bär′bə-tôl′, -tŏl′) *n.* A trademark for a white, shiny crystalline compound, $C_{12}H_{12}N_2O_3$, used in medicine as a sedative, for treating insomnia, and as a hypnotic.

phe·no·cop·y (fē′nə-kŏp′ē) *n.,* pl. **-ies.** *Genetics.* **1.** An environmentally induced phenotypic variation that closely resembles a genetically determined character. **2.** A characteristic or organism existing as such a variation. [PHENO(TYPE) + COPY.]

phe·no·cryst (fē′nə-krĭst′) *n.* A conspicuous crystal embedded in a finer-grained groundmass giving a porphyritic texture. [PHENO- + CRYST(AL).] —**phe·no·crys·tic** (fē′nə-krĭs′tĭk) *adj.*

phe·nol (fē′nōl′, -nŏl′) *n. Chemistry.* **1.** A caustic, poisonous, white, crystalline compound, C_6H_5OH, derived from benzene and used in various resins, plastics, disinfectants, and pharmaceuticals. Also called "carbolic acid." **2.** A class of aromatic organic compounds having at least one hydroxyl group attached directly to the benzene ring. [PHEN(O)- + -OL.] —**phe·no·lic** (fĭ-nō′lĭk, -nŏl′ĭk) *adj.*

phenolic resin *n.* Any of various synthetic thermosetting resin, obtained by the reaction of phenols with simple aldehydes and used to make molded products and as coatings and adhesives.

phe·nol·o·gy (fĭ-nŏl′ə-jē) *n.* The study of periodic biological phenomena, such as flowering, breeding, and migration, especially as related to climate. [PHENO(MENON) + -LOGY.] —**phe·no·log·i·cal** (fē′nə-lŏj′ĭ-kəl) *adj.* —**phe·nol·o·gist** *n.*

phe·nol·phthal·ein (fē′nōl-thăl′ēn, -thăl′ē-ĭn, -thā′lēn′, -thā′lē-ĭn) *n.* A pale yellow crystalline powder, $(C_6H_4OH)_2C_2O_2C_6H_4$, used as an acid-base indicator, in making dyes, and as a cathartic.

phe·nom·e·nal (fĭ-nŏm′ə-nəl) *adj.* **1.** Of or pertaining to a phenomenon or phenomena. **2.** Extraordinary; outstanding; remarkable. **3.** *Philosophy.* Known or derived through the senses rather than through the mind. —**phe·nom·e·nal·ly** *adv.*

phe·nom·e·nal·ism (fĭ-nŏm′ə-nə-lĭz′əm) *n. Philosophy.* The doctrine that the sole objects of knowledge are perceptual experiences. —**phe·nom·e·nal·ist** *n.* —**phe·nom·e·nal·is·tic** (fĭ-nŏm′ə-nə-lĭs′tĭk) *adj.* —**phe·nom·e·nal·is·ti·cal·ly** *adv.*

phe·nom·e·nol·o·gy (fĭ-nŏm′ə-nŏl′ə-jē) *n.* **1.** The study of all possible appearances in human experience, during which considerations of objective reality and of purely subjective response are temporarily left out of account. **2.** A philosophical movement based on such study, originated by Edmund Husserl about 1905. [German *Phänomenologie* : PHENOMENO(N) + -LOGY.] —**phe·nom·e·no·log·i·cal** (fĭ-nŏm′ə-nə-lŏj′ĭ-kəl) *adj.* —**phe·nom·e·no·log·i·cal·ly** *adv.* —**phe·nom·e·nol·o·gist** *n.*

phe·nom·e·non (fĭ-nŏm′ə-nŏn′, -nən) *n.,* pl. **-na** (-nə) or **-nons** (for sense 2). **1.** Any occurrence or fact that is directly perceptible by the senses. **2. a.** An unusual, significant, or unaccountable fact or occurrence; a marvel. **b.** A person outstanding for some extreme quality or achievement: *"I thought Mr. Barkis a phenomenon of respectability."* (Charles Dickens). **3.** *Philosophy.* That which appears real to the senses, regardless of whether its underlying existence is proved or its nature understood. Compare **noumenon.** **4.** *Physics.* An observable event. [Late Latin *phaenomenon,* from Greek *phainomenon,* from *phainomenos,* present participle of *phainesthai,* to appear, from *phainein,* to show.]

phe·no·thi·a·zine (fē′nō-thī′ə-zēn′) *n.* A greenish organic compound, $C_{12}H_9NS$, used in insecticides, anthelmintics, and dyes.

phe·no·type (fē′nə-tīp′) *n. Genetics.* **1.** The environmentally and genetically determined observable appearance of an organism. Compare **genotype. 2.** An individual or group of organisms exhibiting a particular phenotype. [German *Phänotypus* : PHENO- + TYPE.] —**phe·no·typ·ic** (fē′nə-tīp′ĭk), **phe·no·typ·i·cal** *adj.* —**phe·no·typ·i·cal·ly** *adv.*

phen·ox·ide (fĭ-nŏk′sīd′) *n.* Any of various salts of phenol containing the ion $C_6H_5O^-$.

phen·yl (fĕn′əl, fē′nəl) *adj. Chemistry.* Designating, containing, or combined with the group C_6H_5, derived from benzene. Usually used in combination: *phenylalanine.* [PHEN(O)- + -YL.] —**phe·nyl·ic** (fĭ-nĭl′ĭk) *adj.*

phen·yl·al·a·nine (fĕn′əl-ăl′ə-nēn′, fē′nəl-) *n.* A natural amino acid, $C_6H_5CH_2CH(NH_2)COOH$, that occurs as a constituent of many proteins and is extracted for use as a dietary supplement. It is normally converted to tyrosine in the body; a failure in this reaction causes phenylketonuria.

phen·yl·ene (fĕn′ə-lēn′, fē′nə-) *n.* An organic radical, C_6H_4, derived from benzene by removal of two hydrogen atoms.

phenylene blue *n.* An organic base, **indamine** (see).

phen·yl·ke·to·nu·ri·a (fĕn′əl-kēt′n-ŏŏr′ē-ə, -kēt′n-yŏŏr′ē-ə, fē′nəl-) *n.* A congenital defect of protein metabolism that causes excessive accumulation of phenylalanine in the blood and leads to mental retardation unless detected and remedied. [New Latin : PHENYL + KETON(E) + -URIA.] —**phen·yl·ke·to·nu·ric** *adj. & n.*

phen·yl·thi·o·car·ba·mide (fĕn′əl-thī′ō-kär′bə-mīd′, fē′nəl-) *n. Abbr.* **PTC** A crystalline compound, $C_7H_8N_2S$, the taste of which is determined by a pair of genes. If one or both genes are dominant the compound is bitter to the taster; if neither is dominant it is tasteless. Also called "phenylthiourea."

pher·o·mone (fĕr′ə-mōn′) *n.* A substance that is externally secreted by certain animals and induces a behavioral or physiological response in other animals of the same species. [Greek *pherein,* to bear + *hormone.*] —**pher·o·mo·nal** (fĕr′ə-mō′nəl) *adj.*

phew (fyŏŏ) *interj.* Used to express relief, fatigue, surprise, or disgust.

phi (fī) *n.* The 21st letter in the Greek alphabet, written Φ, φ. Transliterated in English as *ph,* or *f* in modern Greek words. See feature at **alphabet.** [Greek.]

phi·al (fī′əl) *n.* A small bottle, a **vial** (see). [Middle English *fiole,* from Old French, from Old Provençal *fiola,* from Latin *phiala,* vessel, saucer, from Greek *phialē,* broad vessel.]

Phi Be·ta Kap·pa (fī′bā′tə kăp′ə) *n.* **1.** A fraternity of American university students and graduates whose members are chosen on the basis of high academic standing. It is the oldest fraternity in the United States (founded 1776). **2.** A member of this fraternity. [From the initials of the Greek phrase *philosophia biou kubernētēs,* "philosophy the guide of life" (motto of the society).]

Phid·i·as (fĭd′ē-əs) (c. 500–430 B.C.). Athenian sculptor, considered by his contemporaries the greatest in Greece. He supervised work on the Parthenon, and his statue of Zeus at Olympia was listed as one of the Seven Wonders of the World.

phil. philosopher; philosophical; philosophy.

Phil. 1. Philippians (New Testament). **2.** Philippines.

phil-. Variant of **philo-.**

Phil·a·del·phi·a (fĭl′ə-dĕl′fē-ə). City in southeastern Pennsylvania, on the Delaware River. It was founded in 1681 by William Penn. Its industries include textiles and oil refining, and its port exports grain and timber. The signing of the Declaration of Independence (1776) and the drafting of the U.S. Constitution (1787) both took place here.

Philadelphia lawyer *n.* A lawyer of great ingenuity in the discovery and manipulation of subtle legalisms. [After PHILADELPHIA.]

Philadelphia pepper pot *n.* A soup, **pepper pot** *(see)*.

phil·a·del·phus (fĭl′ə-dĕl′fəs) *n. Botany.* The **mock orange** *(see)*.

Phi·lae (fī′lē). Submerged island in the Nile River, southeastern Egypt. It is the former site of ancient ruins, most of which were removed before the completion of the Aswan High Dam.

phi·lan·der (fĭ-lăn′dər) *intr.v.* **-dered, -dering, -ders.** To engage in love affairs frivolously or casually; flirt. Used of a man. [From *Philander,* a traditional literary name for a lover, mistakenly adopted from Greek *philandros,* "loving men," "loving one's husband" : PHIL(O)- + *anēr* (stem *andr-*), man.] **—phi·lan·der·er** *n.*

phil·an·throp·ic (fĭl′ən-thrŏp′ĭk) *adj.* Also **phil·an·throp·i·cal** (-ĭ-kəl). Of, pertaining to, marked by, engaged in, or practicing philanthropy: *a philanthropic gesture; a philanthropic institution.* **—phil·an·throp·i·cal·ly** *adv.*

phi·lan·thro·py (fĭ-lăn′thrə-pē) *n., pl.* **-pies. 1.** The effort or wish to increase the well-being of humanity, as by charitable works. **2.** Love of humanity in general. **3.** An action or institution designed to promote human welfare. [Late Latin *philanthrōpia,* from Greek *philanthrōpia,* benevolence, from *philanthrōpos,* "lover of mankind" : PHIL(O)- + *anthrōpos,* man.] **—phi·lan·thro·pist** *n.*

phil·at·e·ly (fĭ-lăt′l-ē) *n.* The collection and study of postage stamps, postmarks, and related materials; stamp collecting. [French *philatélie* : PHIL(O)- + Greek *atelēs,* tax-free (here used as a rendering of the old postmark *franc de port,* "carriage-free"; see **frank**) : A- (without) + *telos,* charge.] **—phil·a·tel·ic** (fĭl′ə-tĕl′ĭk) *adj.* **—phil·a·tel·i·cal·ly** *adv.* **—phil·at·e·list** *n.*

–phile, –phil *suffix.* Indicates one having a strong affinity or fondness for; for example, **Anglophile.** [French *-phile* or New Latin *-philus,* from Greek *-philos,* beloved, dear, loving.]

Phi·le·mon[1] (fĭ-lē′mən, fī-). A friend and convert of Saint Paul.

Philemon[2] *n. Abbr.* **Philem.** A book of the New Testament, a short epistle to Philemon by Saint Paul.

phil·har·mon·ic (fĭl′här-mŏn′ĭk, fĭl′ər-) *adj. Often* **Philharmonic.** Devoted to or appreciative of music. Used chiefly in the names of symphony orchestras, choirs, or musical societies.

~*n. Often* **Philharmonic.** A symphony orchestra or the group that supports it. [French *philharmonique,* from Italian *filarmonico* : *fil-,* PHILO- + *armonico,* harmonic.]

phil·hel·lene (fĭl-hĕl′ēn′) *n.* Also **phil·hel·len·ist** (fĭl-hĕl′ə-nĭst). **1.** One who admires Greece or the Greeks. **2.** Formerly, one who advocated the national independence of Greece. [Greek *philellēn* : PHIL(O)- + HELLENE.] **—phil·hel·len·ic** (fĭl′hĕ-lĕn′ĭk) *adj.* **—phil·hel·len·ism** (fĭl′hĕl′ə-nĭz′əm) *n.*

–philia *suffix.* Indicates: **1.** Tendency toward; for example, **hemophilia. 2.** Abnormal attraction to; for example, **necrophilia.** [New Latin, from Greek *philia,* friendship, from *philos,* loving.]

–philiac *suffix.* Indicates: **1.** One that has a tendency toward: **hemophiliac. 2.** One that has an abnormal attraction to: **coprophiliac.** [New Latin *-philia,* -PHILIA + Greek *-akos,* adjective suffix.]

–philic. Variant of **-philous.**

Phil·ip II[1] (fĭl′ĭp) (*c.* 382–336 B.C.). King of Macedon (359–336) and father of Alexander the Great. He created a powerful army that finally defeated a Greek coalition at Chaeronea (338) and achieved a peace settlement in which all the states except Sparta took part.

Philip II[2], known as "Philip Augustus" (1165–1223). King of France. During his reign (1180–1223), he more than doubled the territory of the royal domains and strengthened the power of the monarchy over the feudal lords.

Philip II[3] (1527–98). King of Spain (1556–98). A devout Catholic, he married Mary I of England (1554) to seal an alliance in defense of the Netherlands. From his father, Charles V, he acquired the kingdom of Naples and Sicily (1554) and the duchy of Milan (1540), the Low Countries (1555), and territories in the Americas (1556). When Charles abdicated in 1556, Philip was left a huge empire that he tried to maintain through a series of costly wars. In 1588 he launched the ill-fated Armada against England.

Philip IV, known as "Philip the Fair" (1268–1314). King of France (1285–1314). His policies greatly strengthened the French monarchy and expanded the royal revenues. His support of Clement V as pope led to the transfer of the papal residence to Avignon and the beginning of the Babylonian captivity.

Philip, Prince, Duke of Edinburgh (1921–). Husband of Queen Elizabeth II. He was born in Corfu but educated mainly in Britain. He served in the Royal Navy in World War II and took up British citizenship in 1947. He was created Duke of Edinburgh on the eve of his wedding to Elizabeth later that year.

Philip, Saint[1]. One of the Apostles; said to have spread the Gospel in Asia Minor. Matthew 10:3; Acts 1:13.

Philip, Saint[2]. Called "the Evangelist." Christian leader of the 1st century A.D.

Phi·lip·pi (fĭl′ə-pī′, fĭ-lĭp′ī′). Ancient town in Macedonia, Greece; the scene of the defeat of Brutus and Cassius by Mark Antony and Octavian (42 B.C.). **—Phi·lip·pi·an** (fĭ-lĭp′ē-ən) *n. & adj.*

Phi·lip·pi·ans (fĭ-lĭp′ē-ənz) *n. Used with a singular verb. Abbr.* **Phil.** A book of the New Testament, the epistle of Saint Paul to the Christians of Philippi.

Phi·lip·pic (fĭ-lĭp′ĭk) *n.* **1.** Any of the orations of Demosthenes against Philip of Macedon in the 4th century B.C. **2.** Any of the

orations of Cicero against Mark Antony in 44 B.C. **3. philippic.** A verbal denunciation characterized by invective.

Phil·ip·pine mahogany (fĭl′ə-pēn′) *n.* Any of various Philippine hardwood trees of the genus *Shorea* and related genera.

Phil·ip·pines (fĭl′ə-pēnz′). Republic of Southeast Asia. It consists of more than 7,000 islands, most of which are uninhabited. The largest islands are Luzon and Mindanao. The country is mountainous and heavily forested and relies on agriculture, but manufacturing is expanding. Coconut products, copper, sugar, and forest products are the chief exports. The islands were colonized by the Spaniards, transferred to the United States (1898) following the Spanish-American War, and, after Japanese occupation in World War II, granted independence (1946). Ferdinand Marcos, elected president in 1965, became virtually president for life with dictatorial powers in 1976; he went into exile in 1986 after the election of Corazon Aquino. Area, 300,000 square kilometers (115,831 square miles). Population, 48,000,000. Capital, Manila. **—Phil·ip·pine** *adj.*

Philippine Sea. Region of the western Pacific Ocean, immediately to the east of the Philippines. It reaches its maximum depth in the Philippines Trench (10,540 meters; 34,578 feet).

Phil·is·tine (fĭl′ĭ-stēn′, fĭ-lĭs′tĭn, -tēn′) *n.* **1.** A member of the warlike people of ancient Philistia in southwestern Palestine. **2.** *Usually* **philistine.** A boorish and uncultured person, especially one who is proud of his ignorance and actively antagonistic to intellectual or artistic matters.

~*adj.* **1.** Of or pertaining to the ancient Philistines. **2.** *Sometimes* **philistine.** Lacking in or hostile to culture: *philistine cuts in arts spending.* [Middle English, from Late Latin *Philistīnus,* from Late Greek *Philistinos,* from Hebrew *Pelishtī,* Philistia, from *pelesheth,* "land of the Philistines."] **—Phil·is·tin·ism** (fĭl′ĭ-stē-nĭz′əm, fĭ-lĭs′tə-nĭz′əm, -tē-nĭz′əm) *n.*

Phil·lips (fĭl′ĭps), **Wendell** (1811–84). U.S. lawyer, orator, and reformer. A rabid abolitionist, he traveled widely on the lyceum circuit, passionately speaking against slavery and ultimately calling for the secession of the North in the 1850's. After the Civil War he campaigned for prohibition and fair treatment of the Indians.

Phillips Screw *n.* A trademark for a screw with a cross-shaped groove in its head, used with a matching screwdriver.

phil·lu·me·ny (fə-lōō′mə-nē) *n.* The collection and study of matchbooks or of matchboxes and matchbox labels. [PHIL(O)- + Latin *lumen,* light + -Y.] **—phil·lu·me·nist** *n.*

Phi·lo Ju·dae·us (fī′lō jōō-dē′əs, -dā′əs) (died *c.* A.D. 50). Jewish philosopher and historian. The author of many treatises, he is especially known for trying to interpret the Scriptures in terms of Greek philosophy.

philo–, phil– *prefix.* Indicates love; for example, **philology, philanthropy.** [New Latin, from Greek, from *philos,* loving.]

phil·o·den·dron (fĭl′ə-dĕn′drən) *n., pl.* **-drons** or **-dra** (-drə). Any of various climbing tropical American plants of the genus *Philodendron,* many of which are cultivated as house plants for their heartshaped, glossy green leaves. [New Latin, from Greek, from *philodendros,* "tree-loving" : PHILO- + *dendron,* tree.]

phi·lol·o·gy (fĭ-lŏl′ə-jē) *n. Abbr.* **philol. 1.** The study of language; especially, **historical linguistics** *(see)*. **2.** Literary study or classical scholarship. [French *philologie,* from Old French, from Latin *philologia,* love of learning, from Greek : PHILO- + -LOGY.] **—phil·o·log·ic** (fĭl′ə-lŏj′ĭk), **phil·o·log·i·cal** *adj.* **—phil·o·log·i·cal·ly** *adv.* **—phi·lol·o·gist** (fĭ-lŏl′ə-jĭst), **phi·lol·o·ger** *n.*

phil·o·mel (fĭl′ə-mĕl′) *n.* Also **phil·o·me·la** (fĭl′ə-mā′lə, -mē′lə). Poetic. A nightingale. [From PHILOMELA.]

Phil·o·me·la (fĭl′ə-mā′lə, -mē′lə). Greek Mythology. A princess of Athens who, after being raped and having her tongue cut out by Tereus, king of Thrace, was turned into either a swallow or a nightingale.

phil·o·pro·gen·i·tive (fĭl′ō-prō-jĕn′ə-tĭv) *adj.* **1.** Producing many offspring; prolific. **2.** Loving one's own offspring or children in general. **3.** Of or pertaining to love of children. **—phil·o·pro·gen·i·tive·ly** *adv.* **—phil·o·pro·gen·i·tive·ness** *n.*

philos. philosopher; philosophical; philosophy.

phi·lo·sophe (fē′lə-zôf′) *n.* Any of the leading philosophical, political, and social writers of the French Enlightenment. [French, "philosopher", from Old French, PHILOSOPHER.]

phi·los·o·pher (fĭ-lŏs′ə-fər) *n.* **1.** *Abbr.* **phil., philos.** A student of or specialist in philosophy. **2.** A person who lives and thinks according to a particular philosophy. **3.** A writer or thinker whose intellectual or ideological theories are used as the basis of a policy, cult, or school of thought: *the philosopher of monetarism.* **4.** A person who remains calm and rational even under the most trying of circumstances. **5.** *Archaic.* An alchemist. [Middle English *philosophre,* from Old French *philosophe,* from Latin *philosophus,* from Greek *philosophos,* "loving wisdom" : PHILO- + *sophos,* wise.]

philosophers' stone, philosopher's stone *n.* **1.** *Alchemy.* **a.** The substance held to have the power of transmuting baser metals into gold. **b.** See **elixir** (sense 3a). **2.** Anything, such as a principle or idea, thought capable of effecting spiritual or other regeneration.

phil·o·soph·i·cal (fĭl′ə-sŏf′ĭ-kəl) *adj.* Also **phil·o·soph·ic** (-ĭk). *Abbr.* **phil., philos. 1.** Of, pertaining to, or based on a system of philosophy. **2.** Characteristic of or befitting a philosopher; enlightened; wise. **3.** Serene and stoical in the face of difficulties. **—phil·o·soph·i·cal·ly** *adv.*

phi·los·o·phize (fĭ-lŏs′ə-fīz′) *v.* **-phized, -phizing, -phizes.** *—intr.* **1.** To talk or speculate in a philosophical manner. **2.** To indulge in

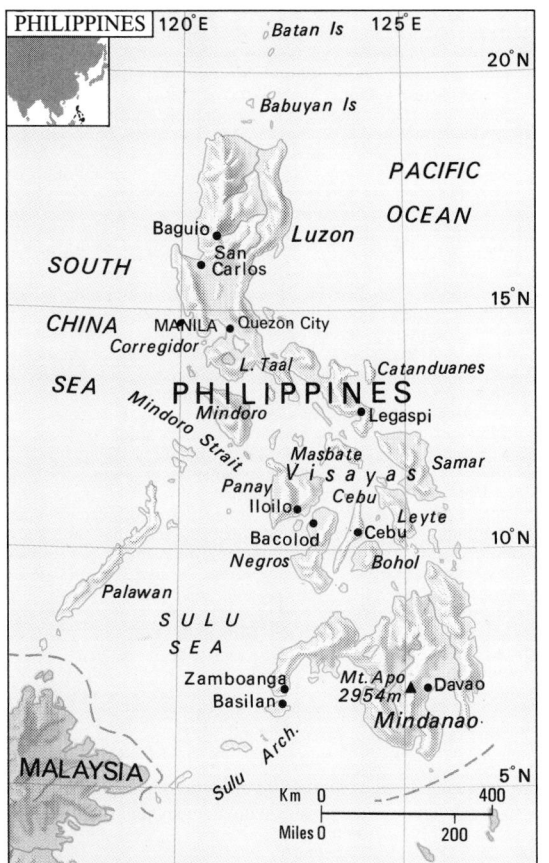

PHILIPPINES

moralistic and often superficial reasoning. —*tr.* **1.** To make (a theory or view) philosophical. **2.** To explain (an event, decision, or the like) in a philosophical way. —**phi·los·o·phiz·er** *n.*

phi·los·o·phy (fĭ-lŏs′ə-fē) *n., pl.* **-phies.** *Abbr.* **phil., philos.** **1. a.** Love and pursuit of wisdom by intellectual means. **b.** The investigation of causes and laws underlying reality. **c.** A particular system of philosophical inquiry or demonstration. **2.** Inquiry into the nature of things based on logical reasoning rather than empirical methods. **3.** The critique and analysis of fundamental beliefs as they come to be conceptualized and formulated. **4.** The investigation of natural phenomena and its systematization in theory and experiment, as in alchemy, astrology, or astronomy: *natural philosophy.* **5.** All the disciplines presented in university curricula of science and the liberal arts except medicine, law, and theology: *Doctor of Philosophy.* **6.** The science comprising logic, ethics, aesthetics, metaphysics, and epistemology. **7.** The general principles underlying a particular branch of study, field of activity, or approach to practical problems: *the philosophy of history; monetarist philosophy.* **8.** The system of values by which one lives. **9.** The calmness and detachment thought to befit a philosopher. [Middle English *philosophie,* from Old French, from Latin *philosophia,* from Greek, from *philosophos,* "loving wisdom." See **philosopher.**]

–philous, –philic *suffix.* Indicates a love of or attraction to something; for example, **photophilous, lyophilic.** [Greek *philos,* beloved, dear, loving.]

phil·ter, phil·tre (fĭl′tər) *n.* **1.** A love potion. **2.** Any magic potion or charm. [French *philtre,* from Latin *philtrum,* from Greek *philtron,* "love charm," from *philein,* to love, from *philos,* beloved.]

phi·mo·sis (fī-mō′sĭs) *n.* Abnormal narrowing of the opening of the foreskin, which prevents its being drawn back over the tip of the penis. [New Latin, from Greek, a muzzling, from *phimos,* muzzle.]

phiz (fĭz) *n.* Also **phi·zog** (fĭ-zŏg′). *Slang.* A face or facial expression. [Alteration and shortening of PHYSIOGNOMY.]

Phiz (fĭz). Pseudonym of Hablot Knight **Browne** (*see*).

phle·bi·tis (flĭ-bī′tĭs) *n. Pathology.* Inflammation of a vein. [PHLEB(O)- + -ITIS.] —**phle·bit·ic** (flĭ-bĭt′ĭk) *adj.*

phlebo–, phleb– *prefix.* Indicates a vein; for example, **phlebotomy, phlebitis.** [Greek, from *phleps†* (stem *phleb-*), vein.]

phle·bot·o·mize (flĭ-bŏt′ə-mīz′) *tr.v.* **-mized, -mizing, -mizes.** *Medicine.* To perform a phlebotomy.

phle·bot·o·my (flĭ-bŏt′ə-mē) *n., pl.* **-mies.** *Medicine.* The therapeutic practice of opening a vein to draw blood. Also called "venesection." [Middle English *flebotomye,* from Old French *flebotomie,* from Late Latin *phlebotomia,* from Greek, "blood-letting" : PHLEBO- + -TOMY.] —**phleb·o·tom·ic** (flĕb′ə-tŏm′ĭk), **phleb·o·tom·i·cal** *adj.* —**phle·bot·o·mist** *n.*

Phleg·e·thon (flĕg′ə-thŏn′) *n. Greek Mythology.* A river of fire, one of the six rivers of Hades. [Greek, from *phlegethein,* to blaze, from *phlegein,* to burn.]

phlegm (flĕm) *n.* **1.** *Physiology.* Thick mucus secreted by the respiratory mucosa. **2.** One of the four humors of ancient physiology. **3.** Sluggishness of temperament. **4.** Calm self-possession; equanimity. [Middle English *fleume,* from Old French, from Late Latin *phlegma,* body moisture, from Greek, flame, inflammation, phlegm, from *phlegein,* to burn.] —**phlegm·y** (flĕm′ē) *adj.*

phleg·mat·ic (flĕg-măt′ĭk) *adj.* Having or suggesting a calm, unexcitable temperament; unemotional. [Middle English from Old French, from Late Latin *phlegmaticus,* from Greek *phlegmatikos,* having phlegm, from *phlegma* (stem *phlegmat-*), PHLEGM.]

phlo·em (flō′ĕm) *n. Botany.* The nutrient-conducting tissue of vascular plants, consisting of sieve tubes and other cellular material. Also called "bast." Compare **xylem.** [German *Phloem,* from Greek *phloios, phloos,* bark.]

phlo·gis·tic (flō-jĭs′tĭk) *adj.* **1.** Of or pertaining to phlogiston. **2.** *Medicine.* Of or pertaining to inflammation or fever.

phlo·gis·ton (flō-jĭs′tŏn′, -tən) *n.* A hypothetical substance formerly thought to be a volatile constituent of all combustible substances released as flame in combustion. [New Latin, from Greek, from *phlogistos,* "inflammable," from *phlogizein,* to set on fire, from *phlox* (stem *phlog-*), flame, from *phlegein,* to burn.]

phlog·o·pite (flŏg′ə-pīt′) *n.* A yellow to dark-brown mica, $KMg_3AlSi_3O_{10}(OH)_2$, used in insulation. [German *Phlogopit,* from Greek *phlogōpos,* "fiery-looking" : *phlox* (stem *phlog-*), flame (see **phlogiston**) + *ōps,* eye.]

phlox (flŏks) *n., pl.* **phlox** or **phloxes.** Any plant of the genus *Phlox,* chiefly native to North America but widely cultivated, having lance-shaped leaves and clusters of white, red, or purple flowers. [New Latin, from Latin, a flower, from Greek, wallflower, flame, from *phlegein,* to burn.]

phlyc·te·na, phlyc·tae·na (flĭk-tē′nə) *n., pl.* **-nae** (-nē). *Medicine.* A small blister; a vesicle. [New Latin, from Greek *phluktaina,* blister, from *phluein, phluzein,* to boil over.]

Phnom Penh (pə-nôm′ pĕn′). Capital of Kampuchea (Cambodia), at the head of the Mekong delta. It was a loyalist stronghold during the civil war (1970–75) but suffered greatly, with most of its population being dispersed after its fall to the Khmer Rouge (1976). The city was a thriving port and a cultural and commercial center, producing textiles, shipping, and dried fish.

–phobe *suffix.* Indicates one that fears, often irrationally, is averse to, or lacks an affinity for something specified; for example, **xenophobe.** [Greek *-phobos,* fearing, from *phobos,* fear, flight.]

pho·bi·a (fō′bē-ə) *n.* **1.** A persistent, abnormal, or irrational fear of something specified. **2.** A strong fear, dislike, or aversion. [New Latin, independent use of *-phobia,* -PHOBIA.] —**pho·bic** (fō′bĭk) *adj.*

–phobia *suffix.* Indicates persistent, irrational, abnormal, or intense fear; for example, **agoraphobia.** [New Latin, from Late Latin, from Greek, from *phobos,* fear, flight.]

–phobic *suffix.* **1.** Having an abnormal fear or dread of; for example, **arachnophobic.** **2.** Lacking an affinity for; for example, **lyophobic.** [-PHOBIA + -IC.]

Pho·bos (fō′bŏs′, fōb′ŏs′) *n. Astronomy.* The larger and inner of the two satellites of the planet Mars. [Greek *phobos,* fear.]

phoe·be (fē′bē) *n.* Any of several small dull-colored North American birds of the genus *Sayornis.* [Imitative of its call.]

Phoe·be¹ (fē′bē). *Greek Mythology.* The goddess Artemis. [Greek *Phoibē,* from *phoibos,* shining.]

Phoebe² *n.* **1.** *Poetic.* The moon. **2.** *Astronomy.* The ninth, smallest, and outermost of the major satellites of Saturn. [From PHOEBE.]

Phoe·bus (fē′bəs). *Greek Mythology.* Apollo, the god of the sun. [Greek *phoibos,* radiant.]

Phoe·ni·cia (fī-nĭsh′ə, -nē′shə). Ancient name for the coastal areas of modern Syria and Lebanon. It was settled by a Semitic people descended from the Canaanites, who established a trading empire (*c.* 1200 B.C.) along the Mediterranean. Its chief colony was at Carthage, with others in Spain, Cyprus, and Sicily, and its chief towns were Sidon and Tyre.

Phoe·ni·cian (fī-nĭsh′ən, -nē′shən) *n.* **1.** A native, inhabitant, or subject of ancient Phoenicia. **2.** The Northwest Semitic language of ancient Phoenicia. [Middle English *Phenicien,* from Old French, from Latin *Phoenīcius,* from Greek *phoinix,* PHOENIX, also a Phoenician (the association is unexplained).] —**Phoe·ni·cian** *adj.*

phoe·nix, phe·nix (fē′nĭks) *n.* **1.** A bird in Egyptian mythology that consumed itself by fire after 500 years, and rose renewed from its ashes. **2.** A person or thing that has been restored to a new existence from destruction, downfall, or ruin. **3.** A person or thing of unsurpassed excellence or beauty; a paragon. [Middle English *fenix,* from Old French, from Latin *phoenix,* from Greek *phoinix,* phoenix, purple, Phoenician.]

Phoe·nix¹ (fē′nĭks). Capital of Arizona, in the south-central part of the state, on the Salt River. It is in a dairy and citrus fruit region, is a health resort, and produces textiles, aircraft, steel, and aluminum.

Phoenix² *n. Astronomy.* A constellation in the Southern Hemisphere near Tucana and Sculptor.

Phoenix Islands. Group of eight islands in the central Pacific, part of Kiribati. The islands were discovered between 1823 and 1840 and were annexed by Great Britain in the late 19th century.

phon (fŏn) *n.* A unit of loudness equal to the number of decibels a sound is above a reference tone having a frequency of 1,000 hertz and a given root-mean-square sound pressure. [Greek *phōnē,* sound.]

phon. phonetic; phonetics; phonology.

pho·nate (fō'nāt') v. -nated, -nating, -nates. —*intr.* To utter vocal sounds; vocalize. —*tr.* To utter (a sound). [PHON(O)- + -ATE.] —**pho·na·tion** (fō-nā'shən) n. —**pho·na·to·ry** (fō'nə-tôr'ē, -tōr'ē) adj.

phone¹ (fōn) n. Linguistics. Any individual sound as realized in speech. [Greek *phōnē*, sound, voice.]

phone² n. Informal. A telephone. ~v. **phoned, phoning, phones.** Informal. —*intr.* To telephone. —*tr.* **1.** To telephone (someone). **2.** To impart (information or news, for example) by telephone. [Short for TELEPHONE.]

-phone suffix. Indicates: **1.** A sound or sound-emitting device; for example, **radiophone. 2.** A speaker of a specified language; for example, **Anglophone.** [Greek *phōnē*, sound, voice.]

pho·neme (fō'nēm) n. Linguistics. One of the set of the smallest units of speech, as the *m* of *mat* and the *b* of *bat* in English, that distinguish one utterance or word from another in a given language. [French *phonème*, from Greek *phōnēma*, an utterance, from *phōnein*; see **phonetic.**]

pho·ne·mic (fə-nē'mĭk, fō-) adj. Also **pho·ne·mat·ic** (fō'nə-măt'ĭk). **1.** Of, pertaining to, or having the characteristics of a phoneme. **2.** Of or pertaining to phonemics. **3.** Serving to differentiate the meaning of otherwise identical utterances. **4.** Of, pertaining to, or being members of different phonemes. —**pho·ne·mi·cal·ly** adv.

pho·ne·mi·cize (fə-nē'mĭ-sīz', fō-) tr.v. -cized, -cizing, -cizes. To analyze (speech sounds) into phonemes. —**pho·ne·mi·ci·za·tion** n.

pho·ne·mics (fə-nē'mĭks, fō-) n. Used with a singular verb. Linguistics. The study and establishment of the phonemes of a language. —**pho·ne·mi·cist** (fō-nē'mĭ-sĭst) n.

phonet. phonetic; phonetics.

pho·net·ic (fə-nĕt'ĭk) adj. Abbr. **phon., phonet. 1.** Of or pertaining to phonetics. **2.** Representing the sounds of speech with a set of distinct symbols, each denoting a single sound: *phonetic spelling.* **3.** Being an alteration of the conventional spelling of a word that better represents its actual pronunciation, as the spelling *kwik* for *quick.* **4.** Employing more than the minimum number of symbols necessary to differentiate the meaning of utterances. [New Latin *phoneticus,* from Greek *phōnētikos,* from *phōnein,* to sound, from *phōnē,* sound, voice.] —**pho·net·i·cal·ly** adv.

phonetic alphabet n. **1.** A standardized set of symbols used in phonetic transcription. See **International Phonetic Alphabet. 2.** In telecommunications, any of various systems of code words for identifying letters in voice communication, such as *Charlie* standing for *C, Foxtrot* for *F,* and the like.

pho·ne·ti·cian (fō'nə-tĭsh'ən) n. Also **pho·net·i·cist** (fə-nĕt'ə-sĭst), **pho·ne·tist** (fō'nə-tĭst). An expert in phonetics.

pho·net·ics (fə-nĕt'ĭks) n. Used with a singular verb. Abbr. **phon., phonet. 1.** The science or study of the sounds of speech and their production, reception, combination, description, classification, and representation by written symbols. **2.** The system of sounds of a particular language.

phoney. Variant of **phony.**

-phonia suffix. Indicates a speech disorder of a specified kind; for example, **dysphonia.** [Greek *-phōnia,* from *phōnē,* sound.]

phon·ic (fōn'ĭk) adj. **1.** Of, pertaining to, or having the nature of sound, especially speech sound. **2.** Of or pertaining to phonics. [PHON(O)- + -IC.] —**phon·i·cal·ly** adv.

phon·ics (fōn'ĭks) n. Used with a singular verb. **1.** The study or science of sound; acoustics. Not in current technical usage. **2.** A method of teaching reading and pronunciation by training learners to recognize the phonetic value of letters and syllables.

phono-, phon- prefix. Indicates sound or a voice; for example, **phonology.** [Greek *phōnē,* sound, voice.]

pho·no·car·di·o·gram (fō'nə-kär'dē-ə-grăm') n. A graphic record of heart sounds.

pho·no·car·di·o·graph (fō'nə-kär'dē-ə-grăf', -gräf') n. An instrument used in making phonocardiograms. —**pho·no·car·di·o·graph·ic** (fō'nə-kär'dē-ə-grăf'ĭk) adj. —**pho·no·car·di·o·graph·i·cal·ly** adv. —**pho·no·car·di·og·ra·phy** (fō'nə-kär'dē-ŏg'rə-fē) n.

pho·no·gram (fō'nə-grăm') n. A character, symbol, or sequence of symbols, as in a phonetic alphabet, representing a word or phoneme in speech. [PHONO- + -GRAM.] —**pho·no·gram·ic, pho·no·gram·mic** (fō'nə-grăm'ĭk) adj.

pho·no·graph (fō'nə-grăf', -gräf') n. A machine that reproduces sound from a disc. [PHONO- + -GRAPH.] —**pho·no·graph·ic** (fō'-nə-grăf'ĭk) adj. —**pho·no·graph·i·cal·ly** adv.

pho·nog·ra·phy (fə-nŏg'rə-fē, fō-) n. **1.** The science or practice of transcribing speech by means of symbols representing elements of sound; phonetic transcription. **2.** Any system of writing or shorthand based on phonetic transcription. [PHONO- + -GRAPHY.] —**pho·nog·ra·pher, pho·nog·ra·phist** n.

pho·no·lite (fō'nə-līt') n. A volcanic rock composed principally of orthoclase and nepheline. Also called "clinkstone." [French, from German *Phonolith* : Greek *phōnē,* sound + Greek *lithos,* stone.] —**pho·no·lit·ic** (fō'nə-lĭt'ĭk) adj.

pho·nol·o·gy (fə-nŏl'ə-jē, fō-) n. Abbr. **phon., phonol. 1.** The science of speech sounds, including phonetics and phonemics. **2.** The study of the sound system of a language or of two or more related languages. **3.** The sound system of a given language. [PHONO- + -LOGY.] —**pho·no·log·ic** (fō'nə-lŏj'ĭk), **pho·no·log·i·cal** adj. —**pho·no·log·i·cal·ly** adv. —**pho·nol·o·gist** n.

pho·nom·e·ter (fə-nŏm'ə-tər, fō-) n. A device that measures the intensity of sound, usually calibrated in phons. [PHONO- + -ME-

phonograph *Thomas Edison's standard phonograph in the Science Museum, London. These early clockwork phonographs, which used a needle running in the grooves of a cylinder, were the forerunners of modern record players.*

TER.] —**pho·no·met·ric** (fō'nə-mĕt'rĭk), **pho·no·met·ri·cal** adj.

pho·non (fō'nŏn') n. Physics. The quantum of thermal energy in a crystal lattice, used especially in mathematical models to calculate vibrational properties of solids. There are two types of phonon: *acoustic,* corresponding to longitudinal motion of the lattice points, and *optic,* corresponding to transverse motion. [PHON(O)- + -ON.]

pho·no·re·cep·tion (fō'nō-rĭ-sĕp'shən) n. Perception of or response to sound waves. —**pho·no·re·cep·tor** n.

pho·no·scope (fō'nə-skōp') n. A device that produces a visible display of the mechanical properties of a sounding body, especially of musical instruments. [PHONO- + -SCOPE.]

pho·no·type (fō'nə-tīp') n. **1.** A phonetic symbol used in printing. **2.** Text printed in phonetic symbols. —**pho·no·typ·ic** (fō'nə-tĭp'ĭk), **pho·no·typ·i·cal** adj. —**pho·no·typ·i·cal·ly** adv.

pho·no·typ·y (fō'nə-tī'pē) n. The practice of transcribing speech sounds by means of phonetic symbols. —**pho·no·typ·ist** n.

pho·ny, pho·ney (fō'nē) adj. -nier, -niest. Informal. **1.** Not genuine or real; spurious: *a phony painting.* **2.** False in manner; insincere. ~n., pl. **phonies** or **-neys.** Informal. **1.** Something not genuine; a fake. **2.** An insincere or hypocritical person. [Origin unknown.] —**pho·ni·ly** adv. —**pho·ni·ness** n.

-phony suffix. Indicates sound of a specified kind; for example, **telephony.** [Greek *-phōnia,* from *phōnē,* sound.]

phoo·ey (fōo'ē) interj. Used as an exclamation of disgust, disbelief, disappointment, or contempt. [Imitative.]

-phore suffix. Indicates a bearer or producer of; for example, **semaphore.** [Greek *-phoros,* bearing, from *pherein,* to bear.]

-phoresis suffix. Indicates transmission; for example, **electrophoresis.** [Greek *phorēsis,* a bearing, from *phorein,* frequentative of *pherein,* to bear.]

-phorous suffix. Indicates bearing or producing; for example, **gonophorous.** [Greek *-phoros,* from *pherein,* to bear.]

phos- prefix. Indicates the presence of light; for example, **phosgene.** [Greek *phōs,* light.]

phos·gene (fŏs'jēn', fŏz'-) n. A colorless volatile liquid or gas, $COCl_2$, used as a poison gas and in making glass, dyes, resins, and plastics. Also called "carbonyl chloride." [PHOS- (from the former method of obtaining the compound by exposure to sunlight) + -gene, variant of -GEN.]

phos·gen·ite (fŏz'jə-nīt') n. A rare fluorescent secondary mineral, $Pb_2(Cl_2CO_3)$, occurring as white, yellow, or gray tetragonal crystals. [German *Phosgenit* : PHOSGENE + -ITE.]

phosph-. Variant of **phospho-.**

phos·pha·gen (fŏs'fə-jən, -jĕn') n. Phosphocreatine (see). [PHOS-PHA(TE) + -GEN.]

phos·pha·tase (fŏs'fə-tās', -tāz') n. Any of numerous enzymes that catalyze the hydrolysis of phosphoric acid esters to phosphate ions. [PHOSPHAT(E) + -ASE.]

phos·phate (fŏs'fāt') n. **1.** Chemistry. Any salt or ester of phosphoric acid containing mainly pentavalent phosphorus and oxygen. **2.** A fertilizer containing phosphorus compounds. [French *phosphat,* from *phosphore,* phosphorous, from New Latin *phosphorus,* PHOSPHORUS.] —**phos·phat·ic** (fŏs-făt'ĭk) adj.

phosphate rock n. Any of various sedimentary rocks composed largely of apatite or guano deposits, both of which are used as fertilizer and as a source of phosphorous compounds.

phos·pha·tide (fŏs'fə-tīd') n. A phospholipid.

phos·pha·tize (fŏs'fə-tīz') v. -tized, -tizing, -tizes. —*tr.* **1.** To change into a phosphate or phosphates. **2.** To treat with phosphate or phosphoric acid. —*intr.* To change into or become a phosphate. —**phos·pha·ti·za·tion** n.

phos·pha·tu·ri·a (fŏs'fə-tŏor'ē-ə, -tyŏor'ē-ə) n. A condition in which excessive phosphates are discharged in the urine. [New Latin : PHOSPHAT(E) + -URIA.] —**phos·pha·tu·ric** adj.

phos·phene (fŏs'fēn') n. A luminous visual sensation experienced when the eyeball is pressed. [PHOS- + Greek *phainein,* to show.]

phos·phide (fŏs'fīd') n. A compound of phosphorus and a more electropositive element. [PHOSPH(O)- + -IDE.]

phos·phine (fŏs'fēn') n. **1.** A colorless, spontaneously flammable poisonous gas, PH_3, having a garliclike smell and used as a doping agent for solid-state components. **2.** A synthetic yellow dye. [PHOSPH(O)- + -INE.]

phos·phite (fŏs'fīt') n. Any salt of phosphorous acid.

phospho-, phosph- prefix. Indicates the presence of phosphorus; for example, **phosphocreatine.** [French, from *phosphore,* phosphorus, from New Latin *phosphorus,* PHOSPHORUS.]

phos·pho·cre·a·tine (fŏs'fō-krē'ə-tēn') n. Also **phos·pho·cre·a·tin** (-tĭn). An organic compound, $C_4H_{10}N_3O_5P$, found in vertebrate tissues, capable of providing physiological energy, as in muscular contraction. Also called "creatine phosphate," "phosphagen."

phos·pho·lip·id (fŏs'fō-lĭp'ĭd) n. Any of a group of compound lipids consisting of phosphoric acid, fatty acids, and a nitrogenous base, forming an important part of cell membranes. Also called "phosphatide."

phos·pho·ni·um (fŏs-fō'nē-əm) n. A univalent radical, PH_4, derived from phosphine. [PHOSPH(O)- + (AMM)ONIUM.]

phos·pho·pro·tein (fŏs'fō-prō'tēn', -prō'tē-ĭn) n. Any of a group of proteins containing chemically bound phosphoric acid.

phos·phor (fŏs'fər, -fôr) n. **1.** Any substance that can be stimulated to emit light by incident radiation. **2.** Something exhibiting phosphorescence. [French *phosphore,* from New Latin *phosphorus,* PHOSPHORUS.]

phosphor bronze n. A hard, strong, corrosion-resistant bronze containing up to 0.5 percent phosphorus and used in electric switches, springs, and chains.

phos·pho·resce (fŏs'fə-rĕs') *intr.v.* **-resced, -rescing, -resces.** To exhibit phosphorescence. [Back-formation from *phosphorescent* : PHOSPHOR + -ESCENT.]

phos·pho·res·cence (fŏs'fə-rĕs'əns) *n.* Persistent emission of light following exposure to and removal of incident radiation. Compare **fluorescence, bioluminescence.** [From PHOSPHOR.] **—phos·pho·res·cent** *adj.* **—phos·pho·res·cent·ly** *adv.*

phos·phor·ic (fŏs-fôr'ĭk, -fŏr'ĭk) *adj.* Of, pertaining to, or containing phosphorus, especially in a valence state higher than that of a comparable phosphorous compound.

phosphoric acid *n.* A clear colorless liquid, H_3PO_4, used in fertilizers, soaps and detergents, food flavoring, and pharmaceuticals.

phos·pho·rism (fŏs'fə-rĭz'əm) *n.* Chronic phosphorus poisoning from ingestion or inhalation. [PHOSPHOR(US) + -ISM.]

phos·pho·rite (fŏs'fə-rīt') *n.* **1.** A fibrous variety of **apatite** (*see*). **2.** A concretionary mass of rock consisting predominantly of calcium phosphate. [PHOSPHOR(US) + -ITE.]

phos·phor·o·scope (fŏs-fôr'ə-skōp') *n.* A device for studying phosphorescence, especially its rate of decay.

phos·pho·rous (fŏs'fər-əs, fŏs-fôr'əs, fŏs-fōr'əs) *adj.* Of, pertaining to, or containing phosphorus, especially in the trivalent state.

phosphorous acid *n. Chemistry.* A white or yellowish hygroscopic crystalline solid, H_3PO_3, used as a reducing agent and to produce phosphite salts.

phos·pho·rus (fŏs'fər-əs) *n.* **1.** *Symbol* **P** A highly reactive, poisonous, nonmetallic element occurring naturally in phosphates, especially apatite, and existing in three allotropic forms, white (sometimes yellow), red, and black. It is an essential constituent of living cells and, depending on the allotropic form, is used in safety matches, pyrotechnics, incendiary shells, fertilizers, glass, and steel. Atomic number 15, atomic weight 30.9738, melting point (white) 44.1°C, boiling point 280°C, specific gravity (white) 1.83, valences 3, 5. **2.** Any phosphorescent substance. [New Latin, from Greek *phōsphoros,* "light-bearing" (so named from the fact that white phosphorus is phosphorescent in air) : PHOS- + -PHOROUS.]

phosphorus pentoxide *n.* A white solid, P_2O_5, produced by burning phosphorus. It has an affinity for water, with which it forms phosphoric acid.

phos·pho·ryl·ase (fŏs'fər-ə-lās', -lāz') *n. Biochemistry.* Any of a group of enzymes that catalyze the production of glucose-1-phosphate from glycogen. [PHOSPHOR(US) + -YL + -ASE.]

phos·pho·ryl·ate (fŏs'fər-ə-lāt') *tr.v.* **-ated, -ating, -ates.** To change (an organic substance) into an organic phosphate. [PHOSPHOR(US) + -YL + -ATE.] **—phos·pho·ryl·a·tion** *n.*

phot (fōt, fŏt) *n. Physics.* A unit of illumination equal to one **lumen** (*see*) per square centimeter. [Greek *phōs* (stem *phōt*-), light.]

pho·tic (fō'tĭk) *adj.* **1.** Of or pertaining to light. **2.** *Biology.* Pertaining to the production of light by organisms. **3.** Pertaining to or designating the upper zone or region of a body of water, into which sunlight penetrates. [PHOT(O)- + -IC.]

pho·to (fō'tō) *n., pl.* **-tos.** *Informal.* A photograph.

photo-, phot- *prefix.* Indicates: **1.** Light; for example, **photosynthesis, photic. 2.** Photographic; for example, **photomontage.** [Greek *phōs* (stem *phōt*-), light.]

pho·to·ac·tin·ic (fō'tō-ăk-tĭn'ĭk) *adj.* Able to emit actinic radiation.

pho·to·ac·tive (fō'tō-ăk'tĭv) *adj.* **1.** Capable of responding to photoelectric stimulation. **2.** Capable of responding to light by chemical reaction. **—pho·to·ac·tiv·i·ty** (fō'tō-ăk-tĭv'ə-tē) *n.*

pho·to·au·to·troph·ic (fō'tō-ô'tə-trŏf'ĭk, -trō'fĭk) *adj. Biology.* Capable of using light as a source of energy in the synthesis of food from inorganic materials.

pho·to·bi·ot·ic (fō'tō-bī-ŏt'ĭk) *adj. Biology.* Depending on light for the continuance of life and growth.

pho·to·cath·ode (fō'tō-kăth'ōd') *n.* A cathode that emits electrons when it is illuminated.

pho·to·cell (fō'tō-sĕl') *n. Electronics.* A **photoelectric cell** (*see*).

pho·to·chem·is·try (fō'tō-kĕm'ĭ-strē) *n.* The chemistry of the interactions of radiant energy and chemical systems. **—pho·to·chem·i·cal** (fō'tō-kĕm'ĭ-kəl) *adj.*

pho·to·chro·mic (fō'tō-krō'mĭk) *adj.* **1.** Of or designating a substance exhibiting photochromism. **2.** Of or pertaining to transparent materials containing compounds exhibiting photochromism.

pho·to·chro·mism (fō'tō-krō'mĭz'əm) *n.* The ability of certain compound materials, especially treated plastics, to darken or change color when exposed to visible or near ultraviolet light and to revert to their original transparency or color when the light source is removed.

pho·to·chron·o·graph (fō'tō-krŏn'ə-grăf', -grăf') *n.* A device for measuring small intervals of time by the length of a trace made by a light beam on a moving photographic film. **—pho·to·chro·nog·ra·phy** (fō'tō-krə-nŏg'rə-fē) *n.*

pho·to·co·ag·u·la·tion (fō'tō-kō-ăg'yə-lā'shən) *n.* The surgical coagulation of tissue by means of intense light energy, as a laser beam.

pho·to·com·pose (fō'tō-kəm-pōz') *tr.v.* **-posed, -posing, -poses.** To prepare (written or graphic matter) for printing by photocomposition; photoset. **—pho·to·com·pos·er** *n.*

pho·to·com·po·si·tion (fō'tō-kŏm'pə-zĭsh'ən) *n.* The projection of the image of type characters, by photomechanical or electronic means, onto photographic film, which is used to prepare printing plates. Also called "filmsetting," "phototypesetting."

pho·to·con·duc·tiv·i·ty (fō'tō-kŏn'dŭk-tĭv'ə-tē) *n. Physics.* The increase in electrical conductivity of certain semiconductors when exposed to light. **—pho·to·con·duc·tion** (fō'tō-kən-dŭk'shən) *n.* **—pho·to·con·duc·tive** (fō'tō-kən-dŭk'tĭv) *adj.*

pho·to·cop·i·er (fō'tō-kŏp'ē-ər) *n.* A device for photographically reproducing written, printed, or graphic material.

pho·to·cop·y (fō'tō-kŏp'ē) *tr.v.* **-copied, -copying, -copies.** To make a photographic reproduction of (printed, written, or graphic material).
~*n., pl.* **photocopies.** A photographic reproduction.

pho·to·cur·rent (fō'tō-kûr'ənt) *n. Physics.* An electric current produced by illumination of a photoelectric material.

pho·to·de·com·po·si·tion (fō'tō-dē-kŏm'pə-zĭsh'ən) *n.* Chemical breakdown caused by radiant energy.

pho·to·dis·in·te·gra·tion (fō'tō-dĭs-ĭn'tə-grā'shən) *n. Physics.* Nuclear disintegration or transformation caused by absorption of gamma rays or other high-energy radiation.

pho·to·dy·nam·ic (fō'tō-dī-năm'ĭk) *adj. Biology.* Of or pertaining to the effect of light on organisms. **—pho·to·dy·nam·ics** *n.*

pho·to·e·las·tic·i·ty (fō'tō-ĭ-lă-stĭs'ə-tē, fō'tō-ē'lă-) *n. Physics.* The effect of distortion of a solid on its optical properties; especially, the production of double refraction in crystals by applied stress. **—pho·to·e·las·tic** (fō'tō-ĭ-lăs'tĭk) *adj.*

pho·to·e·lec·tric (fō'tō-ĭ-lĕk'trĭk) *adj.* Also **pho·to·e·lec·tri·cal** (-trĭ-kəl). Of or pertaining to electric effects, such as increased electrical conduction, caused by illumination. **—pho·to·e·lec·tri·cal·ly** *adv.* **—pho·to·e·lec·tric·i·ty** (fō'tō-ĭ-lĕk-trĭs'ə-tē) *n.*

photoelectric cell *n.* An electronic device having an electrical output that varies in response to incident radiation, especially to visible light. Also called "electric eye," "magic eye," "photocell."

photoelectric effect *n. Physics.* The ejection of electrons from a substance by incident electromagnetic radiation, especially by visible and ultraviolet light.

pho·to·e·lec·tron (fō'tō-ĭ-lĕk'trŏn') *n. Physics.* An electron released or ejected from a substance by the photoelectric effect.

pho·to·e·mis·sion (fō'tō-ĭ-mĭsh'ən) *n. Physics.* The emission of photoelectrons, especially from metallic surfaces.

pho·to·en·grave (fō'tō-ĕn-grāv') *tr.v.* **-graved, -graving, -graves.** To reproduce by photoengraving. **—pho·to·en·grav·er** *n.*

pho·to·en·grav·ing (fō'tō-ĕn-grā'vĭng) *n.* **1.** The process of reproducing graphic or printed material by transferring the image photomechanically to a plate or other surface in etched relief for printing. **2.** A plate prepared by this method. **3.** A reproduction made by this method.

photo finish *n.* **1.** The end of a race in which the leading contestants cross the finishing line so close together that the winner must be determined by a photograph taken at the moment of crossing. **2.** *Informal.* Any extremely close finish or result.

pho·to·flash (fō'tō-flăsh') *n.* In photography, a **flash bulb** (*see*).

pho·to·flood (fō'tō-flŭd') *n.* A reusable electric lamp that produces a bright continuous light for photographic illumination.

pho·to·fluor·og·ra·phy (fō'tō-floo-rŏg'rə-fē) *n. Medicine.* The process of taking photographs (*photofluorograms*) of fluoroscopic images. [PHOTO- + FLUORO- + -GRAPHY.] **—pho·to·fluor·o·graph·ic** (fō'tō-floor'ə-grăf'ĭk) *adj.*

photog. photograph; photographer; photography.

pho·to·gel·a·tin process (fō'tō-jĕl'ə-tĭn) *n.* In photography, **collotype** (*see*).

pho·to·gene (fō'tə-jēn') *n. Physiology.* A retinal **afterimage** (*see*). [PHOTO- + *-gene,* variant of -GEN.]

pho·to·gen·ic (fō'tə-jĕn'ĭk) *adj.* **1.** Attractive as a subject for photography. **2.** *Biology.* Producing or emitting light; phosphorescent. **3.** Caused or produced by light. [PHOTO- + -GENIC.] **—pho·to·gen·i·cal·ly** *adv.*

pho·to·ge·ol·o·gy (fō'tō-jē-ŏl'ə-jē) *n.* The study of geology and geological phenomena by means of aerial and satellite photography.

pho·to·gram (fō'tə-grăm') *n.* **1.** A shadowy image produced without a camera by placing an object in contact with film or photosensitive paper and exposing it to light. **2.** A photograph. [PHOTO- + -GRAM.]

pho·to·gram·me·try (fō'tə-grăm'ə-trē) *n.* **1.** The process of making maps or scale drawings by aerial or other photography. **2.** The process of making precise measurements by the use of photography. [PHOTOGRAM + -METRY.] **—pho·to·gram·met·ric** (fō'tə-grə-mĕt'rĭk) *adj.* **—pho·to·gram·me·trist** *n.*

pho·to·graph (fō'tə-grăf', -grăf') *n. Abbr.* **photog.** An image, especially a positive print, recorded by a camera and reproduced on a photosensitive surface.
~*v.* **photographed, -graphing, -graphs.** *—tr.* To take a photograph of. *—intr.* **1.** To practice photography. **2.** To appear in photographs in a specified way: *She photographs well.* [PHOTO- + -GRAPH.]

pho·tog·ra·pher (fə-tŏg'rə-fər) *n. Abbr.* **photog.** A person who takes photographs, especially as a profession.

pho·to·graph·ic (fō'tə-grăf'ĭk) *adj.* Also **pho·to·graph·i·cal** (-ĭ-kəl). **1.** Of, pertaining to, or produced by photography. **2.** Used in photography: *a photographic lens.* **3.** Resembling a photograph; especially, representing or simulating something with great accuracy and fidelity of detail. **4.** Capable of retaining facts or forming accurate and lasting impressions, often after reading or seeing something for only a short time: *had a photographic memory.* **—pho·to·graph·i·cal·ly** *adv.*

photographic magnitude *n.* The magnitude of a star as measured from a photographic plate, taking into account the difference in color sensitivity between the emulsion and the eye.

pho·tog·ra·phy (fə-tŏg′rə-fē) n. Abbr. **photog.** 1. The process of creating optical images on photosensitive surfaces. 2. The art, practice, or occupation of taking and printing photographs, slides, or films. [PHOTO- + -GRAPHY.]

pho·to·gra·vure (fō′tə-grə-vyŏŏr′) n. 1. The process of printing from an intaglio plate on which an image has been engraved by means of photography. 2. A picture or reproduction, or graphic material generally, produced by this process.

pho·to·he·li·o·graph (fō′tō-hē′lē-ə-grăf′, -gräf′) n. A refracting telescope equipped to photograph the sun.

pho·to·i·on·i·za·tion (fō′tō-ī′ə-nə-zā′shən) n. The ionization of an atom or molecule as a result of exposure to radiation. See **ionizing radiation**.

pho·to·jour·nal·ism (fō′tō-jûr′nə-lĭz′əm) n. Journalism making extensive use of photographs rather than written material as a means of reporting news. —**pho·to·jour·nal·ist** n.

pho·to·ki·ne·sis (fō′tō-kĭ-nē′sĭs, -kī-nē′sĭs) n. Biology. Movement as a response to light. —**pho·to·ki·net·ic** (fō′tō-kĭ-nĕt′ĭk) adj.

pho·to·lith·o·graph (fō′tō-lĭth′ə-grăf′, -gräf′) tr.v. -**graphed**, -**graphing**, -**graphs**. To reproduce by means of photolithography.
~n. A picture made by photolithography.

pho·to·li·thog·ra·phy (fō′tō-lĭ-thŏg′rə-fē) n. 1. A planographic printing process using plates prepared by photographic means. Also called "photolith." 2. Electronics. A technique for making printed circuits, integrated circuits, and the like by photographically reproducing a pattern for electroplating, etching, or diffusion. —**pho·to·li·thog·ra·pher** (fō′tō-lĭ-thŏg′rə-fər) n. —**pho·to·lith·o·graph·ic** (fō′tō-lĭth′ə-grăf′ĭk) adj.

pho·to·lu·mi·nes·cence (fō′tō-lŏŏ′mə-nĕs′əns) n. **Luminescence** (see) produced by infrared radiation, visible light, or ultraviolet radiation. —**pho·to·lu·mi·nes·cent** adj.

pho·tol·y·sis (fō-tŏl′ə-sĭs) n. Chemical decomposition induced by light or other radiant energy. [New Latin : PHOTO- + -LYSIS.] —**pho·to·lyt·ic** (fō′tə-lĭt′ĭk) adj.

photom. photometry.

pho·to·map (fō′tə-măp′) n. A map made by superimposing orienting data on an aerial photograph.

pho·to·me·chan·i·cal (fō′tō-mĭ-kăn′ĭ-kəl) adj. Of, pertaining to, or designating any of various methods by which plates are prepared for printing by means of photography.
~n. A piece of artwork or paste-up of typeset material that is ready to be processed into a printing plate by photographic means. —**pho·to·me·chan·i·cal·ly** adv.

pho·tom·e·ter (fō-tŏm′ə-tər) n. An instrument for measuring a property of light, especially luminous intensity or flux. [PHOTO- + -METER.]

pho·tom·e·try (fō-tŏm′ə-trē) n. Abbr. **photom.** Physics. The measurement of the properties of light, especially of luminous intensity. [PHOTO- + -METRY.] —**pho·to·met·ric** (fō′tə-mĕt′rĭk), **pho·to·met·ri·cal** adj. —**pho·tom·e·trist** n.

pho·to·mi·cro·graph (fō′tō-mī′krə-grăf′, -gräf′) n. A photograph made through a microscope. Compare **microphotograph**.
~tr.v. **photomicrographed**, -**graphing**, -**graphs**. To photograph through a microscope. —**pho·to·mi·crog·ra·pher** (fō′tō-mī-krŏg′rə-fər) n. —**pho·to·mi·cro·graph·ic** (fō′tō-mī′krə-grăf′ĭk) adj. —**pho·to·mi·crog·ra·phy** (fō′tō-mī-krŏg′rə-fē) n.

pho·to·mon·tage (fō′tō-mŏn-täzh′, -môn-täzh′) n. 1. A technique of making a composite picture by assembling several photographs or pieces of photographs, often in combination with other types of graphic material. 2. A composite picture produced by this technique.

pho·to·mul·ti·pli·er (fō′tō-mŭl′tə-plī′ər) n. A device for detecting and measuring electromagnetic radiation, consisting of a photocathode to detect the radiation and an electron multiplier to amplify it and produce a detectable electric signal.

pho·to·mu·ral (fō′tō-myŏŏr′əl) n. A mural made from a very much enlarged photograph or a montage of photographs.

pho·ton (fō′tŏn′) n. Physics. The quantum of electromagnetic energy, generally regarded as a discrete, stable particle having zero mass and no electric charge and carrying angular and linear momentum. [PHOT(O)- + -ON.] —**pho·ton·ic** (fō-tŏn′ĭk) adj.

pho·to·nas·ty (fō′tō-năs′tē) n. Botany. A nastic movement in which the stimulus is light. [PHOTO- + -NASTY.] —**pho·to·nas·tic** (fō′tō-năs′tĭk) adj.

pho·to·neu·tron (fō′tō-nŏŏ′trŏn′, -nyŏŏ′trŏn′) n. A neutron produced by an atomic nucleus as a result of a photodisintegration.

pho·to·nu·cle·ar (fō′tō-nŏŏ′klē-ər, -nyŏŏ′klē-ər) adj. Physics. Of, pertaining to, or being a nuclear reaction induced by photons.

pho·to·off·set (fō′tō-ôf′sĕt′, -ŏf′sĕt′) n. A method of printing, **offset** (see).

pho·to·pe·ri·od (fō′tō-pîr′ē-əd) n. Biology. The relative exposure of an organism to daylight as a proportion of the total day, considered especially with regard to the effect on growth and functioning. —**pho·to·pe·ri·od·ic** (fō′tō-pîr′ē-ŏd′ĭk), **pho·to·pe·ri·od·i·cal** adj. —**pho·to·pe·ri·od·ism** n.

pho·toph·i·lous (fō-tŏf′ə-ləs) adj. Also **pho·to·phil·ic** (fō′tə-fĭl′ĭk). Biology. Growing or functioning best in strong light. [PHOTO- + -PHILOUS.] —**pho·toph·i·ly** (fō-tŏf′ə-lē) n.

pho·to·pho·bi·a (fō′tə-fō′bē-ə) n. 1. Abnormal sensitivity, especially of the eyes, to light. 2. Psychology. An abnormal dread of or aversion to sunlight or well-lit places. [PHOTO- + -PHOBIA.] —**pho·to·pho·bic** (fō′tə-fō′bĭk) adj.

pho·to·pi·a (fō-tō′pē-ə) n. Daylight vision with eyes adapted to nor-

mal bright light. [New Latin : PHOT(O)- + -OPIA.] —**pho·to·pic** (fō-tō′pĭk, -tŏp′ĭk) adj.

pho·to·pol·y·mer (fō′tō-pŏl′ə-mər) n. Any polymeric material that is sensitive to light.

pho·to·re·al·ism (fō′tō-rē′ə-lĭz′əm) n. A style of painting that attempts to imitate the effects of still photography, especially by painting in very fine detail and using commonplace subject matter. —**pho·to·re·al·ist** n.

pho·to·re·cep·tion (fō′tō-rĭ-sĕp′shən) n. Biology. The detection or perception of visible light; vision; sight. —**pho·to·re·cep·tive** adj.

pho·to·re·cep·tor (fō′tō-rĭ-sĕp′tər) n. A photoreceptive nerve and the cell or organ that it serves.

pho·to·re·con·nais·sance (fō′tō-rĭ-kŏn′ə-səns, -zəns) n. Military. Photographic aerial reconnaissance.

pho·to·sen·si·tive (fō′tō-sĕn′sə-tĭv) adj. Sensitive to light. —**pho·to·sen·si·tiv·i·ty** (fō′tō-sĕn′sə-tĭv′ə-tē) n.

pho·to·sen·si·tize (fō′tō-sĕn′sə-tīz′) tr.v. -**tized**, -**tizing**, -**tizes**. To make (an organism or substance) sensitive to light. —**pho·to·sen·si·ti·za·tion** n.

pho·to·set (fō′tō-sĕt′) tr.v. -**set**, -**setting**, -**sets**. Printing. To photocompose. —**pho·to·set·ter** n.

pho·to·sphere (fō′tə-sfîr′) n. The surface of a star, especially of the sun. —**pho·to·spher·ic** (fō′tə-sfîr′ĭk, -sfĕr′ĭk) adj.

Pho·to·stat (fō′tə-stăt′) n. 1. A trademark for a device used to make quick, direct-reading negative or positive photographic copies, as of printed material. 2. A copy made by Photostat.
~tr.v. **Photostated**, -**stating**, -**stats**. Also -**statted**, -**statting**. To make a copy of by Photostat. [PHOTO- + -STAT.] —**Pho·to·stat·er** n. —**Pho·to·stat·ic** (fō′tə-stăt′ĭk) adj.

pho·to·syn·the·sis (fō′tō-sĭn′thə-sĭs) n. 1. The process by which chlorophyll-containing cells in green plants convert incident light to chemical energy and synthesize organic compounds from inorganic compounds, especially carbohydrates from carbon dioxide and water, with the simultaneous release of oxygen. 2. A similar process occurring in certain bacteria. —**pho·to·syn·thet·ic** (fō′tō-sĭn-thĕt′ĭk) adj. —**pho·to·syn·thet·i·cal·ly** adv.

pho·to·syn·the·size (fō′tō-sĭn′thə-sīz′) v. -**sized**, -**sizing**, -**sizes**. —tr. To synthesize by the process of photosynthesis. —intr. To perform the process of photosynthesis.

pho·to·tax·is (fō′tō-tăk′sĭs) n. Also **pho·to·tax·y** (fō′tō-tăk′sē). Biology. The movement of an organism in response to a source of light. [PHOTO- + -TAXIS.] —**pho·to·tac·tic** (fō′tō-tăk′tĭk) adj.

pho·to·tel·e·graph (fō′tō-tĕl′ə-grăf′, -gräf′) tr.v. -**graphed**, -**graphing**, -**graphs**. To transmit (printed or other graphic material) by **facsimile** (see). —**pho·to·tel·e·graph·ic** (fō′tō-tĕl′ə-grăf′ĭk), **pho·to·tel·e·graph·i·cal** adj. —**pho·to·tel·e·graph·i·cal·ly** adv. —**pho·to·te·leg·ra·phy** (fō′tō-tə-lĕg′rə-fē) n.

pho·to·ther·a·py (fō′tō-thĕr′ə-pē) n. The treatment of disease, especially certain skin conditions, with light, including infrared and ultraviolet radiation. Also called "phototherapeutics."

pho·tot·o·nus (fō-tŏt′n-əs) n. Biology. Sensitivity of an organism caused by exposure to light. [PHOTO- + TONUS.] —**pho·to·ton·ic** (fō′tə-tŏn′ĭk) adj.

pho·to·tran·sis·tor (fō′tō-trăn-zĭs′tər, -sĭs′tər) n. Electronics. A transistor having highly photosensitive electrical characteristics.

pho·tot·ro·pism (fō-tŏt′rə-pĭz′əm) n. Also **pho·tot·ro·py** (-pē). Botany. Growth or movement of a plant part in response to a source of light. [PHOTO- + -TROPISM.] —**pho·to·trop·ic** (fō′tə-trŏp′ĭk) adj. —**pho·to·trop·i·cal·ly** adv.

pho·to·tube (fō′tə-tŏŏb′, -tyŏŏb′) n. Electronics. An electron tube with a photocathode.

pho·to·type·set·ter (fō′tō-tīp′sĕt′ər) n. Any of various machines used in photocomposition.

pho·to·type·set·ting (fō′tō-tīp′sĕt′ĭng) n. Printing. **Photocomposition** (see).

pho·to·ty·pog·ra·phy (fō′tō-tī-pŏg′rə-fē) n. Photomechanical printing that resembles the work produced by metal typography. —**pho·to·ty·po·graph·ic** (fō′tō-tī′pə-grăf′ĭk), **pho·to·ty·po·graph·i·cal** adj. —**pho·to·ty·po·graph·i·cal·ly** adv.

pho·to·vol·ta·ic (fō′tō-vŏl-tā′ĭk, -vōl-tā′ĭk) adj. Electronics. Capable of producing a voltage when exposed to radiant energy, especially visible light.

photovoltaic effect n. The difference in potential produced when electromagnetic radiation falls on a thin film of one solid deposited on the surface of another solid, especially when those solids are semiconductors.

pho·to·zin·co·graph (fō′tō-zĭng′kə-grăf′, -gräf′) tr.v. -**graphed**, -**graphing**, -**graphs**. To make (a print) by photozincography.
~n. A print produced by photozincography.

pho·to·zin·cog·ra·phy (fō′tō-zĭng-kŏg′rə-fē) n. A photoengraving process in which sensitized zinc plates are used.

phr. phrase.

phras·al (frāz′əl) adj. Of, pertaining to, or consisting of a phrase or phrases. —**phras·al·ly** adv.

phrasal verb n. Grammar. A verb combined with an adverb or preposition or both that functions as a unit and usually means more than the sum of its parts; for example, give in, meaning to yield, or hang back, meaning to hesitate, are phrasal verbs.

phrase (frāz) n. Abbr. **phr.** 1. Any sequence of words intended to have meaning. 2. A brief, apt, and cogent expression, such as at a stroke. 3. A particular or characteristic style of verbal expression. 4. Grammar. A group of two or more words in sequence that form a syntactic unit or group of syntactic units but, especially in English,

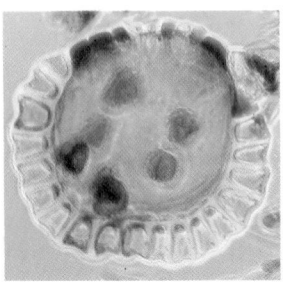

photomicrograph A photograph taken through a microscope. This example is of the spore-bearing structure in a fern.

do not contain a finite verb. **5.** A series of dance movements forming a unit in a choreographic pattern. **6.** *Music.* A segment of a composition usually consisting of four or eight bars and ending in a cadence.
~*tr.v.* **phrased, phrasing, phrases. 1.** To express in words: *a tactfully phrased reply.* **2.** To pace or mark off (something read aloud or spoken) by pauses. **3.** *Music.* To divide (a passage) into phrases. [Latin *phrasis,* from Greek, speech, style of speech, from *phrazein,* to show, explain.]

phrase book *n.* A book, often pocket-sized, that gives common and useful expressions in a foreign language with their translations.

phrase marker *n. Linguistics.* The representation of a sentence's grammatical structure, usually by a tree diagram.

phra·se·o·gram (frā′zē-ə-grăm′) *n.* A symbol, such as one used in shorthand, that denotes a particular phrase.

phra·se·o·graph (frā′zē-ə-grăf′, -gräf′) *n.* A phrase having a phraseogram. **—phra·se·o·graph·ic** (frā′zē-ə-grăf′ĭk) *adj.*

phra·se·ol·o·gist (frā′zē-ŏl′ə-jĭst) *n.* A person who uses epigrammatic phrases or a particular phraseology.

phra·se·ol·o·gy (frā′zē-ŏl′ə-jē) *n., pl.* **-gies. 1.** The way in which words and phrases are used in speech or writing; style. **2.** The characteristic mode of expression used by a particular person or group; parlance: *nautical phraseology.* [New Latin *phraseologia* : PHRASE + -LOGY.] **—phra·se·o·log·i·cal** (frā′zē-ə-lŏj′ĭ-kəl) *adj.*

phras·ing (frā′zĭng) *n.* **1.** The manner in which an expression is phrased; wording. **2.** *Music.* **a.** The division of a passage into phrases. **b.** The manner in which a phrase is rendered or interpreted.

phra·try (frā′trē) *n., pl.* **-tries. 1.** In ancient Greece, a subdivision of a tribe or phyle, being originally a kinship group and surviving in classical Athens as a division in the political and military organization of the state. **2.** *Anthropology.* An exogamous subdivision of the tribe, comprising two or more related clans. [Greek *phratria,* from *phratēr,* fellow clan member.] **—phra·tric** *adj.*

phre·at·ic (frē-ăt′ĭk) *adj. Geology.* Of, pertaining to, or designating **ground water** (see). [Greek *phrear* (stem *phreat-*), a well.]

-phrenia *suffix.* Indicates mental disorder; for example, **schizophrenia.** [Greek *phrēn,* mind.]

phren·ic (frĕn′ĭk, frē′nĭk) *adj.* **1.** Of or pertaining to the mind. **2.** *Anatomy.* Of or pertaining to the diaphragm: *the phrenic nerve.* [New Latin *phrenicus* : PHREN(O)- + -IC.]

phre·ni·tis (frĭ-nī′tĭs) *n. Pathology.* **1.** Encephalitis (see). **2.** Inflammation of the diaphragm. **3.** Frenzy; delirium. [Late Latin *phrenītis,* from Greek *phrenitis* : *phrēn,* diaphragm, mind + -ITIS.] **—phre·nit·ic** (frĭ-nĭt′ĭk) *adj.*

phreno-, phren- *prefix.* Indicates: **1.** The mind; for example, **phrenology. 2.** The diaphragm; for example, **phrenic.** [Greek *phrēn,* diaphragm, mind.]

phre·nol·o·gy (frĭ-nŏl′ə-jē) *n. Abbr.* **phrenol.** The now discredited practice of studying character and mental capacity from the shape and irregularities of the skull. [PHRENO- + -LOGY.] **—phren·o·log·ic** (frĕn′ə-lŏj′ĭk, frē′nə-), **phren·o·log·i·cal** *adj.* **—phre·nol·o·gist** *n.*

Phryg·i·a (frĭj′ē-ə). Former kingdom of western and central Asia Minor. It reached the peak of its prosperity in the 8th century B.C.

Phryg·i·an (frĭj′ē-ən) *adj.* **1.** Of or pertaining to Phrygia or its people, language, and culture. **2.** *Music.* **a.** Of or designating a mode of the ancient Greeks. **b.** Of or designating an authentic church mode with tonic E and dominant C.
~*n.* **1.** A native or inhabitant of Phrygia. **2.** The Indo-European language of the Phrygians.

Phrygian cap *n.* A soft cap with a forward-curving peak, represented in ancient Greek art as part of the attire worn by Phrygians. Compare **liberty cap.**

PHS Public Health Service.

phthal·ein (thăl′ēn′, thăl′ē-ĭn, thă′lēn′, thă′lē-ĭn) *n.* Any of a group of chemical compounds formed by a combination of phthalic anhydride with a phenol, from which certain synthetic dyes are derived. [PHTHAL(IC) + -EIN.]

phthal·ic (thăl′ĭk, thă′lĭk) *adj. Chemistry.* **1.** Of, pertaining to, or derived from naphthalene. **2.** Pertaining to phthalic acid. [Short for *naphthalic* : (NA)PHTH(A) + AL(COHOL) + -IC.]

phthalic acid *n.* A colorless, crystalline organic acid, $C_6H_4(COOH)_2$, prepared from naphthalene and used in the synthesis of dyes, perfumes, and other organic compounds.

phthalic anhydride *n.* A white, crystalline compound, $C_6H_4(CO)_2O$, used in the manufacture of phthaleins and other dyes, resins, plasticizers, and insecticides.

phthal·in (thăl′ĭn, thă′lĭn) *n.* Any of various colorless compounds derived from the reduction of phthaleins.

phthal·o·cy·a·nine (thăl′ō-sī′ə-nēn′, thă′lō-) *n.* Any of several stable, light-fast, blue or green organic pigments derived from the basic compound $(C_6H_4C_2N)_4N_4$ and used in enamels, printing inks, linoleum, and plastics. [PHTHAL(IC) + CYANINE.]

phthi·ri·a·sis (thĭ-rī′ə-sĭs, thī-) *n. Pathology.* Infestation with lice; pediculosis. [Latin *phthiriasis,* from Greek *phtheiriasis* : *phtheir,* louse + -IASIS.]

phthis·ic (tĭz′ĭk) *n.* **1.** Variant of **phthisis. 2.** *Archaic.* **Asthma** (see). [Sense 2, from Middle English *ptisike,* from Old French *tisique,* from Latin *phthisicus,* from Greek *phthisikos,* consumptive, from *phthisis,* PHTHISIS.] **—phthis·ic, phthis·i·cal** *adj.*

phthi·sis (thī′sĭs) *n.* Also **phthis·ic** (tĭz′ĭk). *Pathology.* **1.** Tuberculosis (see) of the lungs. **2.** A wasting away or emaciation and atrophy

---

HOW PLANTS USE THE SUN'S ENERGY
Green cells trigger all the world's food chains

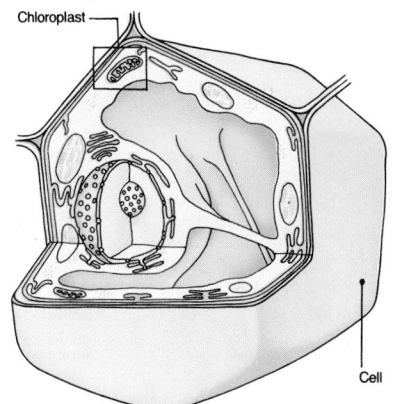

Chloroplast

Cell

The power of the sun is trapped by the leaves of plants on earth and used to produce food by a process called photosynthesis. When sunlight strikes the plant leaves, chlorophyll molecules—which give the leaves their green color—are agitated into generating tiny electric currents. These electric currents split the water that has been sucked into the plant by its roots into separate particles involving oxygen gas and hydrogen atoms.

The oxygen is given off into the atmosphere to form a vital part of the air we breathe. The hydrogen is combined with carbon dioxide absorbed from the surrounding air by pores in the leaves to form a sugar. Such sugars are the basic building blocks of plants. Photosynthesis not only provides the oxygen that keeps most animals alive, but it is the basis of all the world's food chains. Animals such as sheep and cattle eat plants and convert them into protein, which is consumed by meat eaters such as man. In water, bacteria and blue-green and other algae carry out a similar photosynthesis, creating a waterborne food chain similar to that on land.

KEY TO LIFE *Inside the plant cell, chloroplasts trigger the photosynthesis by converting sunlight to electricity. This creates the food for plant growth that is the starting point for all the food chains of the living world.*

HOW SUNLIGHT, WATER, AND CARBON DIOXIDE CREATE SUGARS IN A CHLOROPLAST

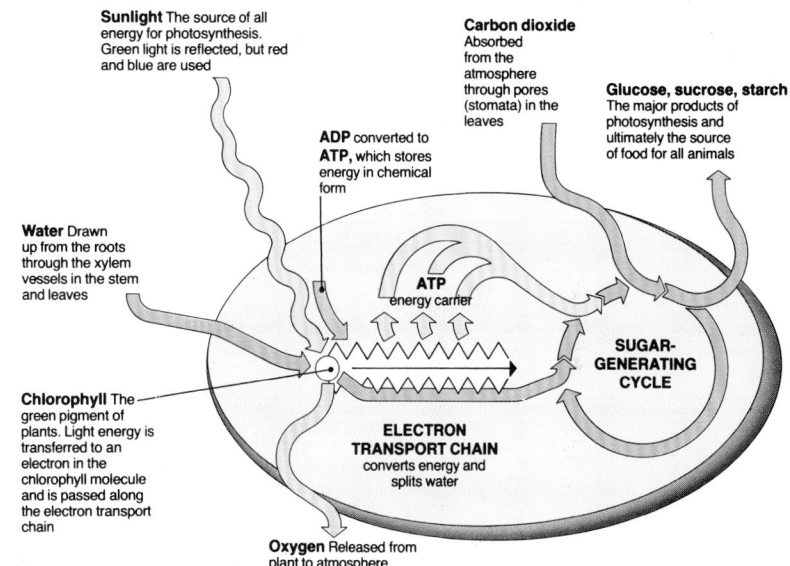

Sunlight The source of all energy for photosynthesis. Green light is reflected, but red and blue are used

Carbon dioxide Absorbed from the atmosphere through pores (stomata) in the leaves

Glucose, sucrose, starch The major products of photosynthesis and ultimately the source of food for all animals

ADP converted to **ATP,** which stores energy in chemical form

Water Drawn up from the roots through the xylem vessels in the stem and leaves

ATP energy carrier

SUGAR-GENERATING CYCLE

Chlorophyll The green pigment of plants. Light energy is transferred to an electron in the chlorophyll molecule and is passed along the electron transport chain

ELECTRON TRANSPORT CHAIN converts energy and splits water

Oxygen Released from plant to atmosphere

The electric charge that is created in photosynthesis is used to form adenosine triphosphate (ATP) from adenosine diphosphate (ADP) by the addition of a phosphate molecule. ATP holds in chemical form energy that is later needed to convert carbon dioxide to sugar.

---

of the body or part of the body. [Latin, from Greek, from Greek *phthinein, phthien,* to decay, waste away.]

phut (fŭt) *n.* A heavy, dull sound, as of impact with an inflatable object. **—go phut.** *Informal.* To collapse or fail. [Hindi *phatnā,* to burst, collapse (imitative).]

phyco- *prefix.* Indicates algae; for example, **phycology.** [Greek *phukos†,* seaweed.]

phy·col·o·gy (fī-kŏl′ə-jē) *n.* The branch of botany concerned with the study of algae. [PHYCO- + -LOGY.] **—phy·co·log·i·cal** (fī′kə-lŏj′ĭ-kəl) *adj.* **—phy·col·o·gist** *n.*

phy·co·my·cete (fī′kō-mī′sēt′, -mī-sēt′) *n. Botany.* Any of various filamentous aquatic fungi, including certain molds and mildews. [New Latin *phycomycetes* : PHYCO- + -MYCETE.] **—phy·co·my·ce·tous** *adj.*

Phyfe (fīf), **Duncan** (c. 1768–1854). U.S. cabinetmaker, born in Scotland. An elegant interpreter of classic European furniture design, he is considered among America's foremost cabinetmakers. In the 1830's his New York City shop became one of the first to use factory methods of furniture construction.

phy·la. Plural of **phylum.**

phy·lac·ter·y (fĭ-lăk′tə-rē) *n., pl.* **-ies. 1.** *Judaism.* Either of two small leather boxes, each containing strips of parchment inscribed

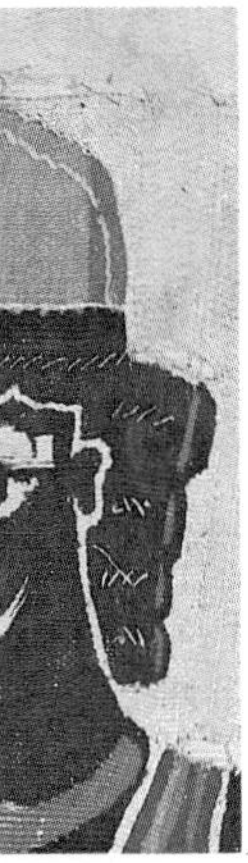

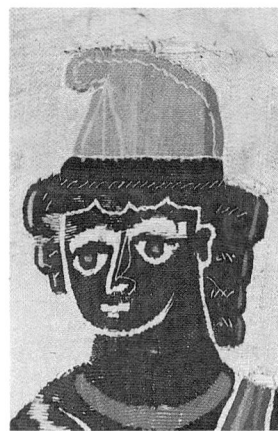

Phrygian cap *A detail from a Coptic textile of the fourth or fifth century* A.D. *The cap was the typical headgear of the Phrygians, a people who settled in central Turkey in the eighth century* B.C. *Caps of the same shape, called liberty caps, were popular in France and the United States during the decade before 1800.*

with quotations from the Hebrew Scriptures. One is strapped to the forehead and the other to the left arm by religiously observant Jewish men during morning worship, except on Sabbath and holidays. **2.** *Archaic.* **a.** An amulet **b.** A reminder. [Middle English *filakterie,* from Late Latin *phylactērium,* from Greek *phulaktērion,* safeguard, from *phulaktēr,* guard, from *phulax* (stem *phulak-*), guard.]

phy·lax·is (fī-lăk′sĭs) *n.* Inhibiting of infection by the body. [Greek *phulaxis,* "a guarding," from *phulassein,* to guard.] **—phy·lac·tic** (fī-lăk′tĭk) *adj.*

phy·le (fī′lē) *n., pl.* **-lae** (-lē). A large grouping of citizens, based on kinship, constituting the largest political subdivision of an ancient Greek city-state. [Greek *phulē,* tribe.] **—phy·lic** *adj.*

phy·let·ic (fī-lĕt′ĭk) *adj. Biology.* Of, pertaining to, or reflecting the phylogeny or evolutionary development of an organism. [New Latin *phylesis,* a genus development, from Greek *phulon,* tribe, class, race.] **—phy·let·i·cal·ly** *adv.*

-phyll *suffix.* Indicates leaf; for example, **chlorophyll.** [Greek *phullon,* leaf.]

phyl·lite (fĭl′īt′) *n.* A metamorphic rock similar to slate but often having a wavy, silky luster and a distinctive cleavage. [PHYLL(O)- + -ITE.]

phyllo-, phyll- *prefix.* Indicates leaf; for example, **phylloclade.** [New Latin, from Greek *phullon,* leaf.]

phyl·lo·clade (fĭl′ə-klād′) *n.* Also **phyl·lo·clad** (-klăd′). *Botany.* A **cladophyll** *(see).* [New Latin *phyllocladium* : PHYLLO- + Greek *klados,* a branch.]

phyl·lode (fĭl′ōd′) *n.* Also **phyl·lo·di·um** (fĭ-lō′dē-əm) *pl.* **-dia** (-dē-ə). *Botany.* A flattened leafstalk that performs the functions of a leaf. [New Latin *phyllodium,* from Greek *phullōdēs,* like a leaf : PHYLL(O)- + -ODE (like).] **—phyl·lo·di·al** *adj.*

phyl·loid (fĭl′oid′) *adj. Botany.* Resembling a leaf; leaflike. [New Latin *phylloides* : PHYLL(O)- + -OID.]

phyl·lome (fĭl′ōm′) *n. Botany.* A leaf, or a plant structure that functions as a leaf. [PHYLL(O)- + -OME.] **—phyl·lom·ic** (fĭ-lŏm′ĭk, -lō′mĭk) *adj.*

phyl·loph·a·gous (fĭ-lŏf′ə-gəs) *adj. Zoology.* Feeding on leaves. [PHYLLO- + -PHAGOUS.]

phyl·lo·pod (fĭl′ə-pŏd′) *n.* Any of various crustaceans of the order Phyllopoda, having swimming and respiratory appendages that resemble leaves.
~adj. Also **phyl·lop·o·dous** (fĭ-lŏp′ə-dəs). **1.** Possessing leaflike feet. **2.** Of or pertaining to the phyllopods. [New Latin *phyllopoda,* "leaf-footed" : PHYLLO- + -POD.] **—phyl·lop·o·dan** (fĭ-lŏp′ə-dən) *adj.* & *n.*

phyl·lo·qui·none (fĭl′ō-kwĭ-nōn′, -kwĭn′ōn′) *n.* A form of **vitamin K** *(see),* occurring in plants.

phyl·lo·tax·y (fĭl′ə-tăk′sē) *n.* Also **phyl·lo·tax·is** (fĭl′ə-tăk′sĭs). *Botany.* **1.** The arrangement of leaves on a stem. **2.** The principles governing leaf arrangement. [New Latin : PHYLLO- + -TAXIS.] **—phyl·lo·tac·tic** (fĭl′ə-tăk′tĭk), **phyl·lo·tac·ti·cal** *adj.*

-phyllous *suffix.* Indicates a specified kind or number of leaves; for example, **heterophyllous.** [New Latin *-phyllus,* from Greek *phullon,* leaf.]

phyl·lox·e·ra (fĭl′ŏk-sîr′ə, fĭ-lŏk′sər-ə) *n., pl.* **-rae** (-rē′) or **-ras.** Any of several small insects of the genus *Phylloxera*; especially, *P. vitifoliae,* a species very destructive to grape crops. [New Latin : PHYLLO- + Greek *xēros,* dry.] **—phyl·lox·e·ran** *adj.* & *n.*

phy·log·e·ny (fī-lŏj′ə-nē) *n., pl.* **-nies.** Also **phy·lo·gen·e·sis** (fī′lō-jĕn′ə-sĭs) *pl.* **-ses** (-sēz′). *Biology.* The evolutionary development of a species, genus, or other taxonomic rank. Compare **ontogeny.** [Greek *phulē,* tribe, clan, and *phulon,* tribe, race + -GENY.] **—phy·lo·ge·net·ic** (fī′lō-jə-nĕt′ĭk), **phy·lo·gen·ic** (-jĕn′ĭk) *adj.* **—phy·lo·ge·net·i·cal·ly** *adv.*

phy·lum (fī′ləm) *n., pl.* **-la** (-lə). **1.** *Biology.* A taxonomic division of the animal kingdom or, less commonly, the plant kingdom, directly above a class in size. **2.** *Linguistics.* A large division of related families of languages or linguistic stocks, especially of the New World. [New Latin, from Greek *phulon,* tribe, class, race.]

phys. 1. physical. **2.** physician. **3.** physicist; physics. **4.** physiological; physiology.

phys·i·at·rics (fĭz′ē-ăt′rĭks) *n. Used with a singular verb.* **Physical therapy** *(see).* [PHYS(IO)- + -IATRICS.] **—phys·i·at·ric, phys·i·at·ri·cal** *adj.*

phys·i·at·rist (fĭz′ē-ăt′rĭst) *n.* A physician who specializes in physical medicine or physical therapy.

phys·ic (fĭz′ĭk) *n.* **1.** A medicine or drug. **2.** A cathartic. **3.** *Archaic.* The profession of medicine. **4.** *Obsolete.* Physics.
~tr.v. **physicked, -icking, -ics. 1.** *Archaic.* To treat with or as if with medicine. **2.** To act upon as a cathartic. [Middle English *fisike,* from Old French *fisique,* from Latin *physica,* natural medicine or science, physics, from Greek *phusikē,* from *phusikos,* natural, from *phusis,* nature, from *phuein,* to bring forth, make grow.]

phys·i·cal (fĭz′ĭ-kəl) *adj. Abbr.* **phys. 1.** Of or pertaining to the body, as distinguished from the mind or spirit; bodily; corporeal: *physical strength.* **2.** Of or pertaining to material things: *physical environment.* **3.** Of or pertaining to matter and energy or the sciences dealing with them, especially physics. **4. a.** Highly conscious of or communicating through one's body. **b.** Involving a great deal of physical contact: *a physical game, with a lot of hard tackles.*
~n. A physical examination. [Middle English *phisycal,* from Medieval Latin *physicālis,* medicinal, from Latin *physica,* natural medicine. See **physic.**] **—phys·i·cal·ly** *adv.*

physical anthropology *n.* The science of human evolutionary biology, genetic development, racial variation, and classification. Also called "somatology." Compare **cultural anthropology.**

physical chemistry *n.* The scientific analysis of the properties and behavior of chemical systems primarily by physical theory and technique as, for example, the thermodynamic analysis of macroscopic chemical phenomena.

physical education *n. Abbr.* **PE** Education, training, and practice in physical exercise, team games, gymnastics, and the like, especially as part of a school curriculum.

physical examination *n.* A medical examination to detect illness or dysfunction and, especially, to determine physical fitness for a particular activity or service. Also called "physical."

physical geography *n.* The study of the natural features of the earth's surface, including land forms, oceans, seas, soils, the atmosphere, and the distribution of fauna and flora. Also called "physiography."

phys·i·cal·ism (fĭz′ĭ-kə-lĭz′əm) *n. Philosophy.* The doctrine that all phenomena can be described in terms of time and space and consequently that any meaningful statement other than an analytic and tautologous one can in principle be reduced to an empirically verifiable physical statement. **—phys·i·cal·ist** *n.* **—phys·i·cal·is·tic** (fĭz′ĭ-kə-lĭs′tĭk) *adj.*

physical medicine *n.* The branch of medicine that diagnoses and treats disease by essentially physical means, including manipulation, massage, and exercise, often with mechanical devices, and the application of heat, cold, electricity, radiation, and water.

physical quantity *n. Physics.* A **quantity** *(see).*

physical science *n.* Any of the sciences, such as physics, chemistry, astronomy, and geology, that analyze the nature and properties of energy and nonliving matter. Compare **life science.**

physical therapy *n.* The treatment of disease and injury by mechanical means such as exercise, light, heat, and massage. Also called "physiatrics," "physiotherapy."

phy·si·cian (fĭ-zĭsh′ən) *n. Abbr.* **phys. 1.** A person qualified to practice medicine, especially in areas other than surgery; a medical doctor. **2.** *Archaic.* Any person who heals or exerts a healing influence. [Middle English *fisicien,* from Old French, from *fisique,* PHYSIC.]

phys·i·cist (fĭz′ə-sĭst) *n. Abbr.* **phys.** A scientist who specializes in physics.

phys·i·co·chem·i·cal (fĭz′ĭ-kō-kĕm′ĭ-kəl) *adj.* Of or pertaining to physical chemistry or the physical and chemical aspects of a phenomenon. [*Physico-,* "physics and" + CHEMICAL.]

phys·ics (fĭz′ĭks) *n. Used with a singular verb. Abbr.* **phys. 1.** The science of matter and energy and of interactions between the two. It is based on mathematics and grouped in traditional fields such as acoustics, optics, mechanics, thermodynamics, and electromagnetism. In modern physics, relativity and quantum theory are used and other areas of study include atomic and nuclear physics, cryogenics, solid-state physics, particle physics, and astrophysics. **2.** Physical properties, interactions, processes, or laws: *the physics of supersonic flight.* **3.** *Archaic.* The study of the natural or material world and phenomena; natural science or natural philosophy. [Plural of PHYSIC (translation of Latin plural *physica,* natural science).]

physio-, phys- *prefix.* Indicates: **1.** Natural or nature; for example, **physiography. 2.** Physical; for example, **physiotherapy.** [Greek *phusio-,* from *phusis,* nature, from *phuein,* to make grow.]

phys·i·og·no·my (fĭz′ē-ŏg′nə-mē, -ŏn′ə-mē) *n., pl.* **-mies. 1.** The art or practice of judging human character from facial features. **2.** Facial features, especially when regarded as revealing character. **3.** The aspect and character of an inanimate or abstract entity: *the physiognomy of New England.* [Learned respelling of Middle English *fysnamye, phisnomye,* from Old French *phizonomie,* from Medieval Latin *physionomia,* from Late Greek *phusiognōmia,* short for Greek *phusiognōmonia* : PHYSIO- + *gnōmōn,* "judge," "interpreter."] **—phys·i·og·nom·ic** (fĭz′ē-ŏg-nŏm′ĭk, fĭz′ē-ə-nŏm′ĭk), **phys·i·og·nom·i·cal** *adj.* **—phys·i·og·nom·i·cal·ly** *adv.* **—phys·i·og·no·mist** *n.*

phys·i·og·ra·phy (fĭz′ē-ŏg′rə-fē) *n.* **Physical geography** *(see).* [PHYSIO- + -GRAPHY.] **—phys·i·og·ra·pher** *n.* **—phys·i·o·graph·ic** (fĭz′ē-ə-grăf′ĭk), **phys·i·o·graph·i·cal** *adj.* **—phys·i·o·graph·i·cal·ly** *adv.*

physiol. physiological; physiology.

phys·i·o·log·i·cal (fĭz′ē-ə-lŏj′ĭ-kəl) *adj.* Also **phys·i·o·log·ic** (-ĭk). *Abbr.* **phys., physiol. 1.** Of or pertaining to physiology. **2.** In accordance with or characteristic of the normal functioning of a living organism. **—phys·i·o·log·i·cal·ly** *adv.*

physiological saline *n.* A salt solution, **saline** *(see).*

phys·i·ol·o·gy (fĭz′ē-ŏl′ə-jē) *n. Abbr.* **phys., physiol. 1.** The biological science of essential and characteristic life processes, activities, and functions. **2.** All the vital processes of an organism, organ, or tissue. [Latin *physiologia,* from Greek *phusiologia,* study of nature : PHYSIO- + -LOGY.] **—phys·i·ol·o·gist** *n.*

phys·i·o·ther·a·py (fĭz′ē-ō-thĕr′ə-pē) *n. Medicine.* **Physical therapy** *(see).* **—phys·i·o·ther·a·peu·tic** (fĭz′ē-ō-thĕr′ə-pyōō′tĭk) *adj.* **—phys·i·o·ther·a·pist** *n.*

phy·sique (fĭ-zēk′) *n.* The body considered with reference to its proportions, muscular development, and appearance: *the physique of an athlete.* [French, from adjective, "physical," from Latin *physicus,* natural, from Greek *phusikos*; see **physic.**]

phy·so·clis·tous (fī′sə-klĭs′təs) *adj.* Having an air bladder that is not joined to the alimentary canal, as in certain fishes. [Greek *phusa,* bladder + *-clistous,* from Greek *kleistos,* closed.]

phy·so·stig·mine (fī′sō-stĭg′mēn′) *n.* A colorless or pink alkaloid, $C_{15}H_{21}N_3O_2$, extracted from the Calabar bean and used especially in eyedrops to restrict the size of the pupil and to relieve pressure in

the eyeball. Also called "eserine." [New Latin *Physostigma* (genus of the Calabar bean) : Greek *phusa*, bellows, bladder + STIGMA.]

phy·sos·to·mous (fĭ-sŏs'tə-məs) *adj.* Having a connecting tube between the air bladder and a part of the alimentary canal, as in certain fishes. [Greek *phusa*, bellows, bladder + -STOME + -OUS.]

-phyte *suffix. Botany.* Indicates a plant with a specified character or habitat; for example, **xerophyte**. [Greek *phuton*, plant, from *phuein*, to make grow.]

phyto-, phyt- *prefix.* Indicates plant or plant life; for example, **phytogenesis**. [New Latin, from Greek *phuto-*, from *phuton*, plant, from *phuein*, to make grow.]

phy·to·gen·e·sis (fī'tō-jĕn'ə-sĭs) *n.* Also **phy·tog·e·ny** (fī-tŏj'ə-nē). The origin and evolutionary development of plants. [PHYTO- + -GENESIS.] —**phy·to·ge·net·ic** (fī'tō-jə-nĕt'ĭk) *adj.* —**phy·to·ge·net·i·cal·ly** *adv.*

phy·to·gen·ic (fī'tō-jĕn'ĭk) *adj.* Also **phy·tog·e·nous** (fī-tŏj'ə-nəs). Having a plant origin, as coal has. [PHYTO- + -GENIC.]

phy·to·ge·og·ra·phy (fī'tō-jē-ŏg'rə-fē) *n.* The study of the distribution of plants. —**phy·to·ge·og·ra·pher** *n.* —**phy·to·ge·o·graph·ic** (fī'tō-jē'ə-grăf'ĭk), **phy·to·ge·o·graph·i·cal** *adj.*

phy·tog·ra·phy (fī-tŏg'rə-fē) *n.* The science of plant description; descriptive botany. [PHYTO- + -GRAPHY.]

phy·to·hor·mone (fī'tō-hôr'mōn) *n.* A growth substance (see).

phy·tol (fī'tŏl', -tōl') *n.* A liquid alcohol, $C_{20}H_{40}O$, used in the synthesis of vitamins E and K.

phy·to·lite (fī'tə-līt') *n.* Also **phy·to·lith** (fī'tə-lĭth'). A fossil plant. [PHYTO- + -LITE.]

phy·tol·o·gy (fī-tŏl'ə-jē) *n.* The study of plants; botany. [New Latin *phytologia* : PHYTO- + -LOGY.] —**phy·to·log·ic** (fī'tə-lŏj'ĭk), **phy·to·log·i·cal** *adj.*

phy·ton (fī'tŏn') *n.* A segment of a plant sufficiently large to be able to grow independently if given appropriate conditions. [New Latin, from Greek *phuton*, plant, from *phuein*, to make grow.] —**phy·ton·ic** (fī-tŏn'ĭk) *adj.*

phy·to·pa·thol·o·gy (fī'tō-pə-thŏl'ə-jē) *n.* The study of the origin, nature, and prevention of plant diseases. —**phy·to·path·o·log·ic** (fī'tō-păth'ə-lŏj'ĭk), **phy·to·path·o·log·i·cal** *adj.* —**phy·to·pa·thol·o·gist** *n.*

phy·toph·a·gous (fī-tŏf'ə-gəs) *adj.* Feeding on plants, including shrubs and trees. Said especially of certain insects. [PHYTO- + -PHAGOUS.] —**phy·toph·a·gy** (fī-tŏf'ə-jē) *n.*

phy·to·plank·ton (fī'tō-plăngk'tən) *n.* Minute, floating aquatic plants. —**phy·to·plank·ton·ic** (fī'tō-plăngk-tŏn'ĭk) *adj.*

phy·to·so·ci·ol·o·gy (fī'tō-sō'sē-ŏl'ə-jē, -sō'shē-ŏl'ə-jē) *n.* The branch of ecology that deals with the characteristics, relationships, and distribution of associated plants. —**phy·to·so·ci·o·log·i·cal** (fī'tō-sō'sē-ə-lŏj'ĭ-kəl, -sō'shē-ə-lŏj'ĭ-kəl) *adj.* —**phy·to·so·ci·o·log·i·cal·ly** *adv.* —**phy·to·so·ci·ol·o·gist** *n.*

phy·to·tox·ic (fī'tō-tŏk'sĭk) *adj.* Poisonous to plants. —**phy·to·tox·ic·i·ty** (fī'tō-tŏk-sĭs'ə-tē) *n.*

phy·to·tox·in (fī'tō-tŏk'sĭn) *n.* Any poison, such as curare or strychnine, that is derived from a plant.

phy·to·tron (fī'tō-trŏn') *n.* A building, often divided into many compartments, in which plants can be grown under controlled conditions. [PHYTO- + -TRON.]

pi¹ (pī) *n., pl.* **pis.** **1.** The 16th letter in the Greek alphabet, written Π, π. Transliterated in English as *P, p.* See feature at **alphabet.** **2.** *Symbol* π *Mathematics.* A transcendental number, approximately 3.14159, representing the ratio of the circumference to the diameter of a circle and appearing as a constant in a wide range of mathematical problems. [Greek. The mathematical sense is from the first letter of Greek *periphireia*, PERIPHERY, and *perimetros*, PERIMETER.]

pi², **pie** (pī) *n., pl.* **pies.** *Printing.* An amount of type that has been jumbled or thrown together at random.

~*v.* **pied**, **piing**, **pies.** Also **pie, pied, pieing, pies.** —*tr.* To jumble or mix up (type). —*intr.* To become jumbled. [Origin unknown.]

pi·a (pī'ə, pē'ə) *n. Anatomy.* The pia mater (see). —**pi·al** *adj.*

pi·ac·u·lar (pī-ăk'yə-lər) *adj. Ecclesiastical.* **1.** Making expiation or atonement for a sacrilege: *piacular sacrifice.* **2.** Requiring expiation; wicked; blameworthy. [Latin *piāculāris*, from *piāculum*, sin offering, propitiatory sacrifice, from *piāre*, to appease, atone for, from *pius*, pious.]

Pi·af (pē-äf', pē'äf'), **Edith**, born Edith Giovanna Gassion (1915-63). French cabaret singer. Her songs include *La Vie en Rose* and *Non, Je ne Regrette Rien*, which became a signature tune.

piaffe (pyäf) *intr.v.* **piaffed, piaffing, piaffes.** *Dressage.* To perform the piaffer. [French *piaffer*, to strut.]

piaff·er (pyäf'ər) *n. Dressage.* A movement in which a horse trots very slowly or on the spot with high action of the legs. [French, from *piaffer*, to strut.]

Pia·get (pyä-zhā'), **Jean** (1896-1980). Swiss child psychologist. He studied the development of intellectual awareness through the successive stages of childhood, systematically observing changes in such conceptions as justice and guilt.

pi·a ma·ter (pī'ə mā'tər, pē'ə mä'tər) *n. Anatomy.* The fine vascular membrane that envelops the brain and spinal cord under the arachnoid membrane and the dura mater. Also called "pia." [Medieval Latin (translation of Arabic *al'umm raqīgah*, "tender mother").]

pi·an·ism (pē-ăn'ĭz'əm, pē'ə-nĭz'əm) *n.* Technique, artistry, or execution in piano playing.

pi·a·nis·si·mo (pē'ə-nĭs'ə-mō') *adv. Abbr.* **pp, pp.** *Music.* Very softly or quietly. Used as a direction.

~*n., pl.* **pianissimos.** *Music.* A part of a composition that is to be played pianissimo. [Italian, superlative of PIANO (softly).] —**pi·a·nis·si·mo** *adj.*

pi·an·ist (pē-ăn'ĭst, pē'ə-nĭst) *n.* One who plays the piano.

pi·a·nis·tic (pē'ə-nĭs'tĭk) *adj.* **1.** Of or pertaining to the piano. **2.** Well-adapted to the piano. —**pi·a·nis·ti·cal·ly** *adv.*

pi·an·o¹ (pē-ăn'ō, -ä'nō) *n., pl.* **-os.** A musical instrument with a manual keyboard actuating hammers that strike wire strings set vertically in an upright frame or horizontally in a roughly triangular frame, producing sounds that may be softened or sustained by means of pedals. [Italian, short for PIANOFORTE.]

pi·a·no² (pē-ä'nō) *adv. Abbr.* **p, p.** *Music.* Softly; quietly. Used as a direction.

~*n., pl.* **pianos.** *Music.* A passage to be played softly. [Italian, from Late Latin *plānus*, smooth, from Latin, even.] —**pi·a·no** *adj.*

piano accordion *n.* An accordion that has a pianolike keyboard played by the right hand.

pi·an·o·for·te (pē-ăn'ō-fôr'tā, -fôr'tē, -fôrt', pē-ä'nō-) *n.* A piano. [Italian, from *piano e forte*, soft and loud.]

piano hinge *n.* A long narrow hinge with a pin running the entire length of its joint.

piano trio *n.* **1.** An instrumental ensemble for playing chamber music that consists of a piano and two other instruments, often a violin and a cello. **2.** A piece of music written for a piano trio.

pi·as·sa·va (pē'ə-sä'və) *n.* Also **pi·as·sa·ba** (pē'ə-sä'bə). **1.** Either of two Brazilian palm trees, *Attalea funifera* or *Leopoldinia piassaba*, from which a strong, coarse fiber is obtained. **2.** The fiber of either of these trees, used for making ropes, brushes, and brooms. [Portuguese *piassaba*, from Tupi *piaçába*.]

pi·as·ter, pi·as·tre (pē-ăs'tər, -ä'stər) *n.* **1.** A coin equal to ¹⁄₁₀₀ of the pound of Egypt, Lebanon, Sudan, and Syria. **2.** A monetary unit equal to ¹⁄₁₀₀ of the lira (or pound) of Turkey. **3.** The basic monetary unit of what was formerly South Vietnam, equal to 100 cents. See feature at **currency.** **4.** A Spanish piece of eight. [French *piastre*, from Italian *piastra (d'argento)*, plate (of silver), from Latin *emplastra, emplastrum*, PLASTER.]

pi·az·za (pē-ăz'ə, -ä'zə, -ät'sə, -ät'sə) *n., pl.* **-zas** (for all senses) or **piazze** (pē-ät'sā) (for sense 1). **1.** A public square in an Italian town. **2.** A roofed and arcaded passageway; colonnade. **3.** A verandah; porch. [Italian, from Latin *platea*, broad street, courtyard, from Greek *plateia*, from *platus*, broad, flat.]

pi·broch (pē'brŏкн) *n.* A series of variations on a traditional dirge or martial theme for the highland bagpipes. [Scottish Gaelic *piobaireachd*, pipe music, from *piobair*, piper, from *píob*, pipe.]

pi·ca¹ (pī'kə) *n.* **1.** A printer's unit of type size equal to 12 points or about 0.42 centimeters (⅙ inch). **2.** An equivalent unit of composition measurement used in determining the dimensions of lines, illustrations, or printed pages. **3.** A size of letters in typewriting having 10 characters to the inch, the equivalent of 12-point printing type. [Probably from Medieval Latin *pīca*, PIE (church almanac).]

pica² *n.* A craving for unnatural food such as mud or cloth, as occurs occasionally in hysteria and pregnancy. [New Latin, from Latin *pīca*, magpie (from its omnivorous nature).]

pic·a·dor (pĭk'ə-dôr') *n., pl.* **-dors** or **picadores** (pĭk'ə-dôr'ās'). A horseman in a bullfight who lances the bull's neck muscles so that it will tend to keep its head low for the subsequent stages. [Spanish, from *picar*, to prick, pierce. See **picaro**.]

Pic·ar·dy (pĭk'ər-dē). Region and former province of northern France, now mainly in the Somme department. It stretches from the English Channel along the Somme and Oise rivers and was the scene of heavy fighting during both world wars. Its main industries are agriculture and the production of textiles.

pic·a·resque (pĭk'ə-rĕsk', pē'kə-) *adj.* **1.** Of or involving clever rogues or adventurers. **2.** Of, pertaining to, or characteristic of the *picaresque novel*, in which the rogue-hero and his escapades are depicted episodically with broad realism and satire. [French, from Spanish *picaresco*, from *picaro*, rogue, PICARO.]

pi·ca·ro (pē'kä-rō') *n., pl.* **-ros** (-rōz', -rōs'). An adventurer; a rogue. [Spanish, "rogue," from *picar*, to wound lightly, "to prick," from Vulgar Latin *piccāre* (unattested), to pick, from *piccus* (unattested), woodpecker, from Latin *pīcus*.]

pic·a·roon (pĭk'ə-rōōn') *n.* **1. a.** A pirate. **b.** A rogue or thief. **2.** A pirate ship.

~*intr.v.* **picarooned, -rooning, -roons.** To act as a pirate. [Spanish *picarón*, augmentative of *picaro*, PICARO.]

Pi·cas·so (pĭ-kä'sō, pē-), **Pablo Ruiz y** (1881-1973). Spanish painter, perhaps the most prolific and versatile artist of this century. Among his many works are *Les Demoiselles d'Avignon* (1907) and *Guernica* (1937). See feature, next page.

pic·a·yune (pĭk'ē-yōōn') *adj.* **1.** Of little value or importance; paltry. **2.** Petty; mean.

~*n.* **1.** A Spanish-American half-real piece, formerly used in parts of the southern United States. **2.** A five-cent piece. **3.** Something of very small value; a trifle: *not worth a picayune.* [French *picaillon*, small copper coin, from Provençal *picaioun†*.]

Pic·ca·dil·ly (pĭk'ə-dĭl'ē). Famous thoroughfare in western London, England, running west from Piccadilly Circus to Hyde Park Corner. It forms the boundary of the Mayfair district.

pic·ca·lil·li (pĭk'ə-lĭl'ē) *n., pl.* **-lis.** A pickled relish made of various chopped vegetables, mustard, and hot spices. [Perhaps blend of PICKLE and CHILI.]

Pic·card (pē-kär', -kärd'), **Auguste** (1884-1962). Swiss physicist and inventor. Known for his innovative experiments at extreme altitudes and depths, he designed a balloon that carried him to

Picasso

THE PRODIGIOUS MASTER OF 20TH-CENTURY ART
Picasso's restless mind sought the shapes behind the shapes

Pablo Picasso (1881-1973) is the dominant figure of 20th-century art. He was born in Málaga, Spain, the son of an art teacher. He showed precocious talent while a pupil at Barcelona (1895-1903), and from 1900 spent much of his time in Paris, settling there in 1904. Paris was the inspiration of his blue period, during which he painted—with blue predominant—the city's prostitutes and destitutes.

His rose period (1905-7), all circuses and harlequins, was more cheerful. Picasso became influenced by Gauguin's primitive art and Cézanne's search for color and form. Cézanne told him: "Look for the spheres, cones, and cylinders in life." Picasso took him at his word. With Georges Braque, he launched cubism (1908-14), looking in analytical ways at the outlines of familiar subjects, as in *Portrait of Clovis Sagot* (1909), *Violin and Grapes* (1912), and *Girl and Mandolin* (1910). Picasso broke up his pictures into solid fragments, looking for shapes and the space behind.

In the 1920's and 1930's, Picasso's restless imagination switched to etching, sculpture, surrealism, and stage designing. *Guernica* (1937), his most famous painting, was inspired by the bombing of the Basque town of Guernica by German airplanes. Picasso became a Communist. He twice accepted the Lenin Peace Prize, but angered the French by rejecting their Legion of Honor (1967). He died leaving a hoard of his work. Much of it was given to the French government in lieu of death duties and is to be permanently housed in the Musée Picasso in Paris.

A MASTER'S MASTERPIECE *Picasso's huge protest of war and fascism was finished within a few weeks of Guernica's destruction by German bombs. A tangle of people and horses shriek in protest at the carnage, apparently overseen by a rampant bull. A naked electric light bulb offers the bare promise of hope. The work was given to the Spanish Republican government and kept in New York at Picasso's request "Until democracy returned to Spain." It was taken to a permanent place at the Prado, Madrid, in 1981.*

16,940 meters (55,567 feet) in 1932 and invented the bathyscaphe, named *Trieste,* that descended 3,150 meters (10,330 feet) in 1953.

pic·co·lo¹ (pĭk′ə-lō′) *n., pl.* **-los.** A small flute pitched an octave above a regular flute. [Shortened from *piccolo flute,* from PICCOLO (adjective).]

piccolo² *adj.* Designating a musical instrument considerably smaller than the usual size: *a piccolo trumpet; a piccolo concertina.* [Italian *piccolo†,* small.]

pice (pīs) *n., pl.* **pice.** An Indian coin of low value, a **paisa** *(see).* See feature at **currency.** [Hindi *paisā.*]

pi·ce·ous (pī′sē-əs) *adj.* **1.** Of, pertaining to, or resembling pitch. **2.** Glossy black in color. [Latin *piceus,* from *pix* (stem *pic-*), pitch.]

pich·i·ci·e·go (pĭch′ə-sē-ā′gō) *n., pl.* **-gos.** Also **pich·i·ci·a·go** (-ä′gō, -ä′gō), *pl.* **-gos. 1.** A small armadillo, *Chlamyphorus truncatus,* of Argentina, having pale-pink armor and white hair. **2.** A similar South American armadillo, *Burmeisteria retusa,* having yellow-brown armor and whitish hair. [Spanish, perhaps from Guarani *pichey,* armadillo + Spanish *ciego,* blind, from Latin *caecus.*]

pick¹ (pĭk) *v.* **picked, picking, picks.** —*tr.* **1.** To select from or as if from a group: *picked the best.* **2. a.** To pull or pluck off: *pick an apple.* **b.** To gather in by picking: *pick cotton.* **c.** To gather the harvest from: *picked a field.* **3. a.** To remove the outer covering of; pluck: *pick a chicken clean of feathers.* **b.** To tear off bit by bit: *pick meat from the bones.* **4. a.** To probe (the teeth, for example) to remove extraneous matter. **b.** To scratch or try to remove (a spot, for example) with the fingernails. **5.** To untangle and isolate (threads), as in weaving. **6.** To break up, pierce, or dig by means of a sharp, pointed instrument, such as a pick. **7.** To make (a hole) with a sharp instrument. **8.** To seek and discover (a flaw): *He picked holes in their argument.* **9.** To take up (food) with the beak; peck: *The parrot picked its seed.* **10. a.** To steal the contents of (a person's pocket). **b.** To steal (money, for example) from a person's pocket. **11.** To open (a lock) without the use of a key. **12.** To make (one's way) carefully: *picked her way through the mud.* **13.** To provoke: *pick a fight.* **14.** To pluck the strings of (a musical instrument). —*intr.* **1.** To decide with care or forethought: *pick and choose.* **2.** To work with a pick. **3.** To harvest or gather fruit, crops, or the like. **4.** To eat food sparingly and without apparent appetite: *just picked at his meal.* —See Synonyms at **choose.** —**pick apart. 1.** To separate into pieces by picking. **2.** To refute or find flaws in by close examination: *The lawyer picked apart the defendant's testimony.* —**pick at.** *Informal.* To find fault with or make petty criticisms about; nag: *She picks at him day and night.* —**pick off. 1.** To shoot after singling out: *I picked the ducks off one by one.* **2.** *Baseball.* To put (a base runner) out with a quick throw, as from the pitcher or catcher. **3.** *Sports.* To intercept, as in a football pass. —**pick on. 1.** To tease or bully. **2.** To select, especially for something unpleasant. —**pick out. 1.** To choose or select. **2.** To discern from the surroundings; distinguish: *At last we managed to pick out his face in the crowd.* **3.** To play (music) slowly by or as if by ear: *He managed to pick out the tune.* —**pick over.** To sort out or examine item by item, especially in order to select the best.

~*n.* **1. a.** The act of picking, especially with a pointed instrument. **b.** A long-toothed comb used in grooming the hair. **2.** The act of selecting or choosing; choice: *Take your pick.* **3.** That which is selected or regarded as the most desirable; the best or choicest one: *the pick of the crop.* **4.** The amount or quantity of a crop that is picked by hand. [Middle English *piken,* to pierce, probably from Old French *piquer,* to prick, pick, from Vulgar Latin *piccāre* (unattested), to prick, pierce.]

pick² *n.* **1.** A tool for breaking hard surfaces, consisting of a curved bar sharpened at one or both ends and fitted to a long handle. **2.** Anything used for picking, such as an ice pick or a toothpick. **3.** *Music.* A plectrum *(see).* [Middle English *pik,* probably a variant of PIKE (pole).]

pick³ *n.* **1.** A weft thread in weaving. **2.** A passage or throw of the shuttle in a loom. ~*tr.v.* **picked, picking, picks. 1.** To throw (a shuttle) across the loom. **2.** *Archaic.* To cast; pitch: *"as high as I could pick my lance"* (Shakespeare). [Middle English *pykken,* to throw (a shuttle), to cast, variant of *picchen,* to PITCH.]

pickaback. Variant of **piggyback.**

pick·ax, pick·axe (pĭk′ăks′) *n.* A pick, usually with a point at one end of the head and a chisel edge at the other.

~*v.* **pickaxed, -axing, -axes.** —*intr.* To use a pickax. —*tr.* To use a pickax on. [Alteration (influenced by AX) of Middle English *pikois, pikeis,* pickax, from Old French *picois,* from *pic,* pickax, perhaps from *piquer,* to prick. See **picket.**]

picked (pĭkt) *adj.* Chosen by careful selection.

pick·er[1] (pĭk′ər) *n.* **1.** One that picks; especially, a machine or person that harvests crops or gathers fruit. **2.** A machine that separates and cleans the fibers of wool, cotton, or the like.

picker[2] *n.* In weaving, the part of a loom that throws the shuttle across it.

pick·er·el (pĭk′ər-əl, pĭk′rəl) *n., pl.* **-els** or collectively **pickerel. 1.** Any of several North American freshwater game and food fishes of the genus *Esox,* especially *E. niger* and *E. vermiculatus.* **2.** Any of various similar or related fishes, such as the walleye. **3.** *British.* A young pike. [Middle English *pikerel,* diminutive of *pik, pike,* PIKE (fish).]

Pick·er·ing (pĭk′ər-ĭng). Prominent U.S. family, including **Timothy** (1745–1829), a Revolutionary War soldier, statesman, and legislator. His son **John** (1777–1846), a philologist, compiled a Greek lexicon and the first dictionary of Americanisms. John's nephew **Charles** (1805–78), a naturalist, wrote several books, including *Races of Men and Their Geographical Distribution* (1848). John's nephews **Edward Charles** (1846–1919) and **William Henry** (1858–1938), both astronomers, made notable contributions to their field, Edward's in the area of stellar observation and photography, and John's being the discovery of Phoebe, a satellite of Saturn (1899), and the planet Pluto (1919).

pick·et (pĭk′ĭt) *n.* **1. a.** A person or persons stationed outside a place of employment, usually during a strike, to express grievance or protest and discourage entry by nonstriking employees or customers. **b.** A person or persons present outside any building to protest. **2.** A pointed stake driven into the ground to support a fence, secure a tent, tether animals, mark points in surveying, or, when pointed at the top, serve as part of a defensive barrier. **3.** *Military.* A detachment of one or more soldiers positioned in front of their lines to give advance warning of enemy approach.
~*v.* **picketed, -eting, -ets.** —*tr.* **1.** To enclose, secure, tether, mark out, or fortify with pickets. **2.** *Military.* **a.** To post as a picket. **b.** To guard with a picket. **3.** To post a picket or act as a picket at (a place of work, for example) during a strike or demonstration. —*intr.* To act or serve as a picket. [French *piquet,* from *piquer,* to prick, from *pic,* PICK (tool).] —**pick·et·er** *n.*

picket fence *n.* A fence of pointed, upright pickets.

picket line *n.* A line or procession of people picketing a place of business or otherwise staging a public protest.

Pick·ett (pĭk′ĭt), **George Edward** (1825–75). U.S. Confederate general. A West Point graduate and distinguished veteran of the Mexican War, he joined the Confederate Army in 1861. He is primarily remembered for the disastrous Pickett's Charge at Gettysburg (1863), a pivotal point of that battle and the Civil War.

Pick·ford (pĭk′fərd), **Mary,** born Gladys Mary Smith (1893–1979). U.S. star of the silent screen, born in Canada. She was known as "America's Sweetheart"; her films included *Pollyanna* (1919).

pick·ings (pĭk′ĭngz′) *pl.n.* Something that is or may be picked, as: **a.** Leftovers. **b.** Profits, spoils, or a share of spoils.

pick·le (pĭk′əl) *n.* **1. a.** An edible product, especially vegetables or fruit, that has been preserved and flavored in a solution of brine or vinegar. **b.** A relish containing such vegetables or fruit. **c.** A cucumber thus preserved and flavored. **2.** A solution of brine or vinegar, often spiced, for preserving and flavoring food. **3.** An acid or other chemical solution used as a bath to remove scale and oxides from the surface of metals before plating or finishing. **4.** *Informal.* A troublesome, embarrassing, or difficult situation.
~*tr.v.* **pickled, -ling, -les. 1.** To preserve or flavor in a solution of brine or vinegar. **2.** To treat (metal) in a chemical bath. [Middle English *pekille,* from Middle Dutch and Middle Low German *pekel*†.]

pick·led (pĭk′əld) *adj.* **1.** Preserved in or treated with pickle. **2.** *Informal.* Drunk.

pick·lock (pĭk′lŏk′) *n.* **1.** A person who picks locks; especially, a thief. **2.** An instrument for picking a lock.

pick-me-up (pĭk′mē-ŭp′) *n. Informal.* A drink, often alcoholic, taken as a stimulant or restorative.

pick·pock·et (pĭk′pŏk′ĭt) *n.* One who steals from pockets or handbags.

pick·proof (pĭk′pro͞of′) *adj.* Designed to prevent picking: *a pickproof lock.*

pick up *tr.v.* **1.** To take up or gather up by hand: *pick up your toys.* **2.** To take on (passengers, freight, survivors, hitchhikers, or the like). **3.** *Informal.* **a.** To go and fetch; collect: *pick the kids up from school.* **b.** To get or acquire without deliberate planning: *pick up a bargain.* **c.** To acquire (skill, knowledge, or understanding) over a period of time. **4.** To bring by chance or intent within sight or hearing: *picked up a foreign station.* **5.** To gain or recover (speed). **6.** *Informal.* To take into custody; arrest: *The coast guard picked up five smugglers.* **7.** To accept the responsibility of paying: *pick up the bill.* **8.** *Slang.* To make casual acquaintance with, usually in anticipation of sexual relations. —*intr.v. Informal.* To improve in condition or activity: *Sales will pick up next autumn.*

pick·up, pick-up (pĭk′ŭp′) *n.* **1. a.** The action or process of picking up: *the pickup and delivery of farm produce.* **b.** Capacity for acceleration: *a sports car with good pickup.* **c.** *Informal.* An improvement in condition or activity: *a pickup in sales.* **2.** *Informal.* **a.** A place where passengers, freight, or the like are picked up. Also used adjectivally: *a pickup point.* **b.** Passengers, freight, or the like to be picked up. **3.** *Slang.* A stranger with whom casual acquaintance is made, usually in anticipation of sexual relations. Often used derogatorily. **4.** A light truck with an open body and low sides used for making light deliveries. Also called "pickup truck." **5. a.** *Electronics.* A device that converts the oscillations of a phonograph needle into electrical impulses for subsequent conversion into sound. **b.** A device on an electric guitar that converts the vibrations of the strings into electric signals for subsequent amplification and conversion into sound. See **crystal pickup, magnetic pickup. 6.** In radio and television: **a.** The reception of waves for conversion to electrical impulses. **b.** The apparatus used for such reception.

Pick·wick·i·an (pĭk-wĭk′ē-ən) *adj.* **1.** Characterized by simplicity and benevolence. **2.** Understood or meant in a sense other than the obvious or literal one. Said of words. [After Mr. *Pickwick* in Dickens' *The Pickwick Papers* (1837).]

pick·y (pĭk′ē) *adj.* **-ier, -iest.** *Informal.* Excessively meticulous; fussy.

pic·nic (pĭk′nĭk′) *n.* **1. a.** A meal taken to be eaten in the open air on an excursion, as to the seaside or the country. **b.** An excursion or outing in which food is taken to be eaten in the open air. **2.** *Slang.* An easy task or pleasant experience: *Teaching's no picnic.*
~*intr.v.* **picnicked, -nicking, -nics.** To go on or participate in a picnic. [French *piquenique,* perhaps a reduplication (influenced by obsolete French *nique,* a trifle) of *piquer,* to pick, peck, from Old French. See **picket.**] —**pic·nick·er** *n.*

pico– *prefix. Symbol* **p** Indicates one trillionth; for example, **picosecond.** [Spanish *pico,* small quantity, peak, from *picar,* to prick. See **picaro.**]

Pi·co Bo·lí·var (pē′kō bō-lē′vär′). Highest mountain in Venezuela, rising to 5,003 meters (16,411 feet). It is in the western part of the country, south of Lake Maracaibo.

Pico de A·ne·to (dā ə-nä′tō). Mountain in northeastern Spain near the border with France. Rising to 3,406 meters (11,168 feet), it is the highest mountain in the Pyrenees.

Pico del·la Mi·ran·do·la (dĕl′ə mə-răn′də-lə), **Giovanni, Count** (1463–94). Italian humanist and philosopher. He tried to reconcile Christianity, Platonism, and Hebrew philosophy.

pic·o·line (pĭk′ə-lēn′, pī′kə-) *n.* Any of three isomeric liquid methylpyridine bases, C_6H_7N, derived from coal tar, horse urine, and bone oil and used as an industrial solvent. [Latin *pix* (stem *pic-*), pitch + -OL + -INE.]

pi·co·sec·ond (pē′kə-sĕk′ənd, pī′kə-) *n.* One trillionth (10^{-12}) of a second.

pi·cot (pē′kō, pē-kō′) *n.* A small embroidered loop forming an ornamental edging, as on ribbons, handkerchiefs, or hems.
~*tr.v.* **picoted** (pē′kōd, pē-kōd′), **picoting** (pē′kō-ĭng, pē-kō′ĭng), **picots** (pē′kōz, pē-kōz′). To trim with edging. [French, "small point," diminutive of *pic,* peak, point, prick, from *piquer,* to prick. See **picket.**]

pic·o·tee (pĭk′ə-tē′) *n.* A carnation of a type having pale petals bordered by a darker color. [French *picoté,* furnished with points, from *picoter,* to mark with points or pricks, from PICOT.]

pic·rate (pĭk′rāt′) *n.* A salt or ester of picric acid. [PICR(O)- + -ATE.]

pic·ric acid (pĭk′rĭk) *n.* A poisonous, explosive yellow crystalline solid, $C_6H_2(NO_2)_3OH$, used in explosives, dyes, and antiseptics. Also called "trinitrophenol." [PICR(O)- + -IC.]

pic·rite (pĭk′rīt′) *n.* A coarse-grained igneous rock consisting of olivine and augite with small quantities of plagioclase feldspar. [PICRO- (containing magnesium) + -ITE.]

picro– *prefix.* Indicates something bitter; for example, **picrotoxin.** [Greek *pikro-,* from *pikros,* bitter.]

pic·ro·tox·in (pĭk′rə-tŏk′sĭn) *n.* A bitter powder, $C_{30}H_{34}O_{13}$, used as a stimulant and antidote for barbiturate poisoning.

Pict (pĭkt) *n.* A member of an ancient northern British people. They came into conflict with the Britons, and later made raids on Roman garrisons. By about A.D. 900, they had effectively disappeared, having been assimilated with the Scots. [Middle English, from Late Latin *Pictī,* Picts.]

Pict·ish (pĭk′tĭsh) *adj.* Of or pertaining to the Picts or their language.
~*n.* The language of the Picts, extinct by the 10th century and known chiefly from place names.

pic·to·graph (pĭk′tə-grăf′, -gräf′) *n.* Also **pic·to·gram** (-grăm′). **1.** A picture representing a word or idea; a hieroglyph. **2.** A record in hieroglyphic symbols. **3.** A pictorial representation of numerical data or relationships, as by charts or symbols. [Latin *pictus,* past participle of *pingere,* to paint + -GRAPH.] —**pic·to·graph·ic** (pĭk′tə-grăf′ĭk) *adj.* —**pic·to·graph·i·cal·ly** *adv.* —**pic·tog·ra·phy** (pĭk-tŏg′rə-fē) *n.*

Pic·tor (pĭk′tər) *n.* A constellation in the Southern Hemisphere near Columba and Dorado. [Latin, painter, from *pingere* (past participle *pictus*), to paint.]

pic·to·ri·al (pĭk-tôr′ē-əl, -tōr′ē-əl) *adj.* **1.** Pertaining to, characterized by, or composed of pictures. **2.** Of or pertaining to painting, drawing, or etching. **3.** Represented in a picture. **4.** Having vivid imagery; graphic: *pictorial prose.* **5.** Illustrated by pictures.
~*n.* An illustrated periodical. [Late Latin *pictōrius,* from Latin *pictor,* painter. See **Pictor.**] —**pic·to·ri·al·ly** *adv.*

pic·ture (pĭk′chər) *n.* **1. a.** A visual representation or image painted, drawn, photographed, or otherwise rendered on a surface. Also used adjectivally: *a picture postcard.* **b.** An image in the mind: *a vivid picture of the attack.* **2.** Any visible image, especially one on a

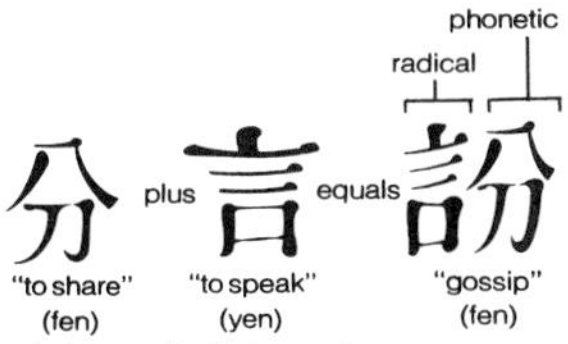

pictograph *Chinese characters are pictographic in origin, but the relationship between image and meaning is no longer immediately apparent because the original pictures used have been reduced to symbols. Modern Chinese characters—as in the word for "gossip" (above)—are made up of two pictographic elements: a radical, which indicates the general meaning, and a phonetic component, which indicates the pronunciation.*

PRONUNCIATION KEY

ă, pat; ā, pay; âr, care;
ä, father, are; b, bib;
ch, church; d, deed; ĕ, pet;
ē, be; f, fife; g, gag; h, hat;
hw, which; ĭ, pit; ī, pie;
îr, pier; j, judge; k, kick;
l, lid, needle; m, mum;
n, no, sudden; ng, thing;
ŏ, pot; ō, toe; ô, paw, for;
oi, noise; ou, out; o͝o, book;
o͞o, boot; p, pop; r, roar;
s, sauce; sh, ship, dish;
t, tight; th, thin, path;
th, this, bathe; ŭ, cut; ûr, fur;
v, valve; w, with; y, yes;
z, zebra, size; zh, vision;
ə, about, item, edible, gallop, circus, peaceful

IN FOREIGN WORDS:

à, *Fr.* ami; œ, *Fr.* feu, *Ger.* schön; ü, *Fr.* tu, *Ger.* über; KH, *Ger.* ich, *Scot.* loch; N, *Fr.* bon; y′, *Fr.* Compiègne

STRESS MARKS:

Primary stress: ′
in·cite′ (ĭn-sīt′)
Secondary stress: ′
in′sight′ (ĭn′sīt′)

flat surface: *the picture reflected in the lake.* **3.** A vivid or realistic verbal description: *a Shakespearean picture of guilt.* **4.** A person or object that bears a striking resemblance to another: *the picture of her mother.* **5.** A person, object, or scene that typifies or embodies an emotion, state of mind, or mood: *a picture of embarrassment.* **6.** The circumstances of an event or time considered as a scene; a situation: *Their defeat changed the picture.* **7. a.** A motion picture. **b.** *British.* **pictures.** Movies. **8.** A **tableau vivant** *(see).* ~*tr.v.* **pictured, -turing, -tures. 1.** To make a visible representation or picture of. **2.** To form a mental image of; visualize: *I can't picture him as a nurse.* **3.** To describe vividly in words; make a verbal picture of: *pictured her heroism glowingly.* [Middle English, from Latin *pictūra,* from *pingere* (past participle *pictus*), to paint.]

picture book *n.* A book composed chiefly of pictures.

picture hat *n.* A wide-brimmed hat, often highly decorated, originally worn by women in the 18th century.

Pic·ture·phone (pĭk′chər-fōn′) *n.* A trademark for a device that combines telephone and television communications.

picture puzzle *n.* A **jigsaw puzzle** *(see).*

pic·tur·esque (pĭk′chə-rĕsk′) *adj.* **1.** Constituting or suggesting a striking or attractive picture; suitable for a picture: *the picturesque emerald hills of Ireland.* **2.** Striking or interesting in an unusual way; irregularly or quaintly attractive. **3.** Strikingly expressive or vivid: *picturesque language.* [Alteration (influenced by PICTURE) of French *pittoresque,* from Italian *pittoresco,* from *pittore,* painter, from Latin *pictor,* from *pingere* (past participle *pictus*), to paint.] —**pic·tur·esque·ly** *adv.* —**pic·tur·esque·ness** *n.*

picture tube *n.* A **television tube** *(see).*

picture window *n.* A large window, usually of a single sheet of glass, that provides a broad, attractive outside view.

picture writing *n.* **1.** The recording of events using pictures or symbols, such as in early hieroglyphs. **2.** A writing system that uses pictographs.

pic·ul (pĭk′əl) *n.* Any of various units of weight used in the Far East; especially, a Chinese unit equal to about 60 kilograms (133 pounds). [Malay *pīkul,* a man's load.]

pid·dle (pĭd′l) *intr.v.* **-dled, -dling, -dles. 1.** To spend time aimlessly; diddle. **2.** *Informal.* To urinate. [Origin unknown.]

pid·dling (pĭd′lĭng) *adj. Informal.* Beneath consideration; trifling; trivial.

pid·dock (pĭd′ək) *n.* Any of various marine bivalve mollusks of the family Pholadidae, capable of boring into wood, rock, and other materials. [18th century : origin obscure.]

pidg·in (pĭj′ən) *n.* A simplified form of speech, usually a mixture of two or more languages, that has a rudimentary grammar and vocabulary and is used for communication between groups speaking different languages. Compare **creolized language.** [From PIDGIN ENGLISH.] —**pidg·in** *adj.*

pidgin English *n. Sometimes* **Pidgin.** A pidgin based on English and used originally as a trade language in Far Eastern ports. [Alteration of *business English.*]

pie¹ (pī) *n.* A baked food consisting of a shell of pastry and a filling of fruit, meat, cheese, or other ingredients, usually covered with a pastry crust. —**pie in the sky.** A promise or prospect of future happiness or wealth. [Middle English *pie,* perhaps "magpie" (comparing the mixture in a pie to the various items a magpie might collect).]

pie² *n.* A bird, the **magpie** *(see).* [Middle English, from Old French, from Latin *pīca.*]

pie³ *n.* A former monetary unit of India and Pakistan. [Hindi *pā′ī,* from Sanskrit *pādikā,* quarter, from *pāda,* foot, leg, quarter.]

pie⁴ *n.* An almanac of services used in the English church before the Reformation. [Medieval Latin *pīca,* almanac, PICA.]

pie⁵. *Printing.* Variant of **pi** (type).

pie·bald (pī′bôld′) *adj.* Spotted or patched, especially in black and white: *a piebald horse.* ~*n.* A piebald animal, especially a horse. Compare **skewbald.** [PIE (magpie) + BALD.]

piece (pēs) *n.* **1.** A thing considered as a unit or element of a larger quantity or class; a portion: *a piece of string.* **2.** A portion or part that has been separated from a whole: *a piece of cake.* **3. a.** An object that is one member of a group or class: *a piece of furniture.* **b.** Such an object considered as particularly fine, valuable, or rare: *a collector's piece.* **4.** An artistic, musical, or literary work or composition. **5.** An instance; a specimen: *a piece of folly.* **6.** *Informal.* One's fully expressed opinion; one's mind: *speak one's piece.* **7.** A coin or counter: *a ten-cent piece.* **8.** In various board games, any of the counters or men used in playing. **9.** In chess, any of the figures other than a pawn. **10.** A firearm, especially a rifle. **11.** *Chiefly Regional.* A short or manageable distance. —**a piece of one's mind.** *Informal.* Frank or aggressive criticism or censure. —**go to pieces. 1.** To break into small pieces; fall apart. **2.** *Informal.* To lose mental and emotional self-control; break down. —**of a piece. 1.** Belonging to the same kind or class. **2.** Internally consistent and predictable; forming a coherent whole. —**piece of the action.** *Informal.* A share of an activity or of profits. ~*tr.v.* **pieced, piecing, pieces. 1. a.** To mend or put together by joining or uniting the pieces of: *He pieced together the vase.* **b.** To combine the parts or pieces of in such a way as to be able to understand or draw conclusions: *tried to piece the story together.* **2.** To join (broken threads) when spinning. [Middle English, from Norman French, from Old French *pece,* from Medieval Latin *pecia, petia,* from Gaulish *pettia†* (unattested).]

pièce de ré·sis·tance (pyĕs′ də rā′zē-stäNs′) *n.* **1.** The principal dish of a meal. **2.** The most outstanding item or event in a group or series, especially in a series of artistic works. [French.]

piece goods *pl.n.* Fabrics made and sold in standard lengths. Also called "yard goods."

piece·meal (pēs′mēl′) *adv.* **1.** Piece by piece; gradually: *articles acquired piecemeal.* **2.** In pieces; apart. ~*adj.* Accomplished or made piece by piece or in separate stages; fragmentary. [Middle English *pecemele : pece,* PIECE + *-mele,* by a certain measure, Old English *mǣlum,* dative plural of *mǣl,* a point of time. See **meal.**]

piece of cake *n. Informal.* Something that is very easy to perform, obtain, operate, or the like.

piece of eight *n., pl.* **pieces of eight.** An obsolete Spanish silver coin.

piece rate *n.* A fixed rate of payment per number of items turned out.

piece·work (pēs′wûrk′) *n.* Work paid for according to the number of items produced. —**piece·work·er** *n.*

pie chart *n.* A circular chart having radii dividing the circle into sectors proportional to the relative size of the quantities represented. Also called "pie graph." [From PIE (pastry).]

pie·crust (pī′krŭst′) *n.* The pastry shell of a pie. ~*adj.* Designating a piece of furniture with an ornamental molding like the edge of a piecrust.

pied¹ (pīd) *adj.* Patchy in color; splotched; piebald. [Middle English, from PIE (magpie), from its piebald coloring.]

pied². *Printing.* A past tense and a past participle of **pi** (type).

pied-à-terre (pyä′dä-târ′) *n., pl.* **pieds-à-terre** (*pronounced as singular*). A secondary or temporary lodging: *a small pied-à-terre in the city.* [French, "foot to the ground."]

pied·mont (pēd′mŏnt′) *adj. Geology.* Formed or lying at the foot of a mountain or mountain range: *a piedmont plain.* ~*n. Geology.* A piedmont area or region. [French, from Italian *piémonte,* PIEDMONT.]

Pied·mont (pēd′mŏnt′). Autonomous region of northwestern Italy. It includes part of the Alps and the Po valley. Asti, Novara, and Turin are among its provinces. It was the heartland of modern Italy in the Risorgimento (from 1814), and its capital, Turin, was Italy's first capital. —**Pied·mon·tese** (pēd′mŏn-tēz′, -tēs′) *n. & adj.*

Pied Piper *n.* **1.** In German legend, a piper who rid the town of Hamelin of its rats by leading them away with his music. When he was refused due payment he led away the children of the town as well. Also called "Pied Piper of Hamelin." **2. pied piper. a.** A person who lures away others to follow him. **b.** A leader who makes promises irresponsibly.

pied wagtail *n.* A British subspecies of the white wagtail (*Motacilla alba*), *Motacilla alba yarrellii,* having black and white plumage and a long black tail. Also called "water wagtail."

pie-eyed (pī′īd′) *adj. Slang.* Drunk.

pie graph *n.* A **pie chart** *(see).*

pie·man (pī′mən) *n., pl.* **-men** (-mĭn). *Archaic.* A person who sells pies.

pie·plant (pī′plănt′, -plänt′) *n.* A plant, **rhubarb** *(see).*

pier (pîr) *n.* **1. a.** A platform extending from a shore over water and supported by piles or pillars, used to secure, protect, and provide access to ships or boats. **b.** Such a structure supporting various buildings used predominantly for entertainment. **2.** A supporting structure at the junction of connecting spans of a bridge. **3.** *Architecture.* Any of various vertical supporting structures, especially: **a.** A pillar, rectangular in cross section, supporting an arch or roof. **b.** The portion of a wall between windows or openings. **c.** A reinforcing structure that projects from a wall; buttress. [Middle English *per,* from Old English, from Medieval Latin *perat†.*]

pierce (pîrs) *tr.v.* **pierced, piercing, pierces. 1.** To cut or pass through or into with or as if with a sharp instrument; stab; penetrate. **2.** To make a hole or opening in; perforate. **3.** To make a way through: *The path pierced the wilderness.* **4. a.** To sound sharply through: *His shout pierced the din.* **b.** To shine through: *His torch pierced the darkness.* **5.** To succeed in discerning or understanding: *She pierced the heart of the mystery.* **6.** To affect penetratingly; move deeply; transfix: *pierced by anguish.* —*intr.* To penetrate into or through something: *The rocket pierced through space.* [Middle English *percen,* from Old French *percer, percier,* from Vulgar Latin *pertūsiāre* (unattested), from Latin *pertundere* (past participle *pertūsus*), to pierce through : *per,* through + *tundere,* to thrust.] —**pierc·er** *n.* —**pierc·ing·ly** *adv.*

Pierce (pîrs), **Franklin** (1804–69). 14th U.S. president (1853–57). A New Hampshire lawyer and politician, he was elected president in 1852. He supported the expansion of American territory and encouraged settlement of the Northwest. He was criticized for his inability to treat the continuing slavery controversy that was further fueled by the Kansas-Nebraska Act of 1854.

pierced (pîrst) *adj.* **1.** Designating an ear having a tiny hole made in the lobe to hold an earring. **2.** Designed for pierced ears: *pierced earrings.*

pier glass *n.* A long mirror to be hung on a portion of a wall between windows.

Pi·e·ri·an (pī-îr′ē-ən) *adj.* Of or pertaining to the Muses or to artistic inspiration. [After the PIERIAN SPRING.]

Pierian Spring *n.* **1.** *Greek Mythology.* A fountain in Pieria in ancient Macedonia, sacred to the Muses. **2.** A source of inspiration, especially to artists and poets.

Pie·ro del·la Fran·ces·ca (pyâr′ō dĕl′ə frän-chĕs′kə) (*c.* 1420–92). Italian painter of the Renaissance. His mature works include a fresco cycle, *The Story of the True Cross* (1452–66).

Pierre (pîr). Capital of South Dakota, in the central part of the state, on the east bank of the Missouri River. Its economy is centered on agriculture and the state government. Originally a small trading center, the city boomed with the coming of the railroad (1880).

Pier·rot (pē′ə-rō′, pyĕ-rō′) *n.* **1.** A stock male character in traditional French pantomime having a whitened face and floppy white clothing. **2. pierrot.** A clown, doll, or the like similarly dressed and made up. [French, diminutive of *Pierre,* from Latin *Petrūs,* the name Peter.]

pier table *n.* A table designed to stand under a pier glass.

pie·tà (pyā-tä′) *n.* *Often* **Pietà.** A painting, drawing, or sculpture of the Virgin Mary holding and mourning over the dead body of Jesus. [Italian, "pity," from Latin *pietās,* PIETY.]

Pie·ter·mar·itz·burg (pē′tər-măr′ĭts-bûrg′). Capital of Natal province, Republic of South Africa. Founded (1838) by the Boers, it is in an agricultural region.

pi·e·tism (pī′ə-tĭz′əm) *n.* **1.** Piety. **2.** Affected or exaggerated piety. **3. Pietism.** A reform movement in the German Lutheran Church during the 17th and 18th centuries that strove to renew the devotional ideal in the Protestant religion. [German *Pietismus,* from Latin *pietās,* PIETY.] **—pi·e·tist** *n.* **—pi·e·tis·tic** (pī′ə-tĭs′tĭk), **pi·e·tis·ti·cal** *adj.* **—pi·e·tis·ti·cal·ly** *adv.*

pi·e·ty (pī′ə-tē) *n., pl.* **-ties.** **1.** Religious devotion and reverence to God. **2.** Devotion and reverence to parents and family. **3.** A pious act or thought. **4.** The state or quality of being pious. [French *piété,* from Latin *pietās* (stem *pietāt-*), from *pius,* PIOUS.]

piezo- *prefix.* Indicates pressure; for example, **piezometer.** [Greek *piezein,* to squeeze, press.]

pi·e·zo·e·lec·tric crystal (pī-ē′zō-ĭ-lĕk′trĭk, pē-ā′zo-) *n.* Any of certain crystals lacking a center of symmetry, such as quartz, that when subjected to stress produce a **potential difference** *(see)* between their two stressed surfaces.

pi·e·zo·e·lec·tric·i·ty (pī-ē′zō-ə-lĕk′trĭs′ə-tē, pē-ā′zō-) *n.* The generation of electricity or of electric polarity in dielectric crystals subjected to mechanical stress, and, conversely, the generation of stress in such crystals subjected to an applied voltage. Also called "piezoelectric effect." **—pi·e·zo·e·lec·tric, pi·e·zo·e·lec·tri·cal** *adj.* **—pi·e·zo·e·lec·tri·cal·ly** *adv.*

pi·e·zom·e·ter (pī′ə-zŏm′ə-tər, pē′ə-) *n.* Any instrument for measuring pressure, especially high pressure. [PIEZO- + -METER.] **—pi·e·zo·met·ric** (pī-ē′zə-mĕt′rĭk, pē-ā′zə-), **pi·e·zo·met·ri·cal** *adj.* **—pi·e·zom·e·try** (pī′ə-zŏm′ə-trē, pē′ə-) *n.*

pif·fle (pĭf′əl) *intr.v.* **-fled, -fling, -fles.** *Informal.* To talk or act in a feeble or futile way.
~n. Informal. Foolish or futile talk or ideas; nonsense. [Imitative.]

pif·fling (pĭf′lĭng) *adj.* Futile and trivial; silly.

pig (pĭg) *n.* **1.** Any of several mammals of the family Suidae, having short legs, cloven hoofs, bristly hair, and a cartilaginous snout used for digging; especially, the domesticated pig, *Sus scrofa.* **2.** The edible parts of a pig; pork. **3.** *Informal.* A person regarded as being unpleasantly dirty, piglike, greedy, or gross. **4.** See **guinea pig** (sense 1). **5. a.** An oblong block of metal, chiefly iron or lead, poured from a smelting furnace. **b.** A mold in which such metal is cast. **c. Pig iron** *(see).* **—a pig in a poke.** Something that is obtained without first being inspected or whose value is unknown. **—make a pig of oneself.** To be greedy or self-indulgent.
~v. **pigged, pigging, pigs.** *—intr.* **1.** To give birth to pigs; farrow. **2.** To act in a greedy, dirty, or piggish way. *—tr. Informal.* To eat (food) greedily; gobble. **—pig it.** To live in a piglike way. **—pig out.** *Slang.* To eat greedily and especially in large amounts. [Middle English *pigge,* probably from Old English *picgat†* (unattested).]

pig bed *n.* A bed of sand in which pigs of iron are cast.

pi·geon (pĭj′ən) *n.* **1.** Any of various birds of the widely distributed family Columbidae, characteristically having deep-chested bodies, small heads, and short legs; especially, *Columba livia* or any of its domesticated varieties. This species is also called "rock dove." **2.** *Slang.* One who is easily swindled; a dupe. **3.** *British Informal.* Responsibility; business: *It's not my pigeon.* [Middle English *pijon,* from Old French, young bird, pigeon, from Late Latin *pīpiō* (stem *pīpiōn-*), squab, young chirping bird, from *pīpīre,* to chirp.]

pigeon chest *n.* A chest deformity marked by a projecting sternum, often the result of rickets.

pigeon hawk *n.* A small falcon, *Falco columbarius.* Also called "merlin."

pi·geon·hole (pĭj′ən-hōl′) *n.* **1.** The small hole or holes for nesting in a pigeon loft. **2.** A small compartment or recess for holding papers; cubbyhole. **3.** *Informal.* A category or classification.
~tr.v. **pigeonholed, -holing, -holes.** **1.** To place or file in a pigeonhole. **2.** To classify mentally; categorize. **3.** To put aside and ignore; shelve.

pigeon pea *n.* **Dhal** *(see).*

pi·geon-toed (pĭj′ən-tōd′) *adj.* Having the toes turned inward.

pi·geon·wing (pĭj′ən-wĭng′) *n.* A dance step performed by jumping and clapping the feet together. [Probably a translation of French *ailes de pigeon,* a ballet term for a leap in which the dancer's legs imitate the motion of a bird's wings.]

pig·fish (pĭg′fĭsh′) *n., pl.* **-fishes** or collectively **pigfish.** A marine fish, *Orthopristis chrysopterus,* of Atlantic waters along the U.S. coast. Also called "hogfish." [It grunts like a pig.]

pig·ger·y (pĭg′ə-rē) *n., pl.* **-ies.** **1.** A place where pigs are kept. **2.** Greediness or slovenliness; piggishness. [PIG + -ERY.]

pig·gin (pĭg′ĭn) *n.* A small wooden bucket with one stave projecting above the rim for use as a handle. Also called "pipkin." [16th century : origin obscure.]

pig·gish (pĭg′ĭsh) *adj.* **1.** Like a pig; greedy; dirty. **2.** *British Informal.* Stubborn; pig-headed. **—pig·gish·ly** *adv.* **—pig·gish·ness** *n.*

pig·gy (pĭg′ē) *n., pl.* **-gies.** A little pig. Used especially by children.
~adj. **piggier, -giest.** Piggish.

pig·gy·back (pĭg′ē-băk′) *n.* Also **pick·a·back** (pĭk′ə-băk′). **1.** A ride on the shoulders or back of another person. **2.** A method of transporting vehicles by loading them onto another vehicle such as a train or a specially designed truck.
~v. **piggybacked, -backing, -backs.** Also **pick·a·back.** *—tr.* **1.** To carry or transport by piggyback. **2.** To cause to be aligned with something, such as an issue, that is larger or more important. *—intr.* To function as if carried on the back of another.
~adj. **1.** Of, pertaining to, or designating a piggyback. **2.** *Informal.* Of or pertaining to a method of transplant surgery in which the new organ is initially supported by the existing organ, which is left in the body until the transplant has established itself: *a piggyback heart.* **—pig·gy·back** *adv.*

piggy bank *n.* A child's receptacle for holding money that is shaped like a pig and has a slot into which coins are inserted.

pig-head·ed (pĭg′hĕd′ĭd) *adj.* Stubborn, especially in a stupid or belligerent way. —See Synonyms at **obstinate.** **—pig-head·ed·ly** *adv.* **—pig-head·ed·ness** *n.*

pig iron *n.* Crude iron cast in blocks or pigs. Also called "pig."

pig Latin *n.* A coded jargon in which the initial consonant of each word is transposed to the end of that word with *-ay* (ay) added to form a new syllable, as *igpay atinlay* for *pig Latin.*

pig lead *n.* Crude lead cast in blocks.

pig·let (pĭg′lĭt) *n.* A young pig.

pig·ment (pĭg′mənt) *n.* **1.** Any substance or matter used as coloring. **2.** Dry coloring matter, usually an insoluble powder to be mixed with a liquid base to produce paint and similar products. **3.** *Biology.* A substance, such as chlorophyll or hemoglobin, that produces a characteristic color in plant or animal tissue.
~tr.v. (pĭg′mənt, -mĕnt′) **pigmented, -menting, -ments.** To color with pigment. [Latin *pigmentum,* from *pingere,* to paint.] **—pig·men·tar·y** (pĭg′mən-tĕr′ē) *adj.*

pig·men·ta·tion (pĭg′mən-tā′shən) *n. Biology.* **1.** Coloration of tissues by pigment. **2.** Deposition of pigment by cells.

pigment cell *n.* A **chromatophore** *(see).*

pigmy. Variant of **pygmy.**

Pigmy. Variant of **Pygmy.**

pig·nut (pĭg′nŭt′) *n.* **1.** Either of two trees, *Carya glabra* or *C. ovalis,* of the eastern United States, bearing nuts with slightly bitter kernels. **2.** The nut of either of these trees. **3.** A plant, the **earthnut** *(see),* or its tuberous root.

pig·pen (pĭg′pĕn′) *n.* **1.** A pen for pigs. **2.** A dirty or messy place.

pig·skin (pĭg′skĭn′) *n.* **1.** The skin of a pig. **2.** Leather made from this. **3.** *Informal.* **a.** A football. **b.** A saddle. **—pig·skin** *adj.*

pig·stick (pĭg′stĭk′) *intr.v.* **-sticked, -sticking, -sticks.** To hunt wild boar on horseback with a spear. **—pig·stick·er** *n.* **—pig·stick·ing** *n.*

pig·sty (pĭg′stī′) *n., pl.* **-sties.** **1.** A shelter or pen where pigs are kept. **2.** A filthy or very untidy place.

pig·tail (pĭg′tāl′) *n.* **1. a.** A plait of braided hair that hangs down behind the head. **b.** Either of a pair of similar plaits at the sides of the head. **2.** A twisted roll of tobacco. **—pig·tailed** *adj.*

pig·weed (pĭg′wēd′) *n.* **1.** A coarse weed, *Amaranthus retroflexus,* having hairy leaves and spikes of green flowers. **2.** A common wild plant, *Chenopodium album,* having leaves with a mealy surface and small green flowers. Also *chiefly British* "fat hen."

pi·ing. *Printing.* Present participle of **pi** (to jumble type).

pi·ka (pē′kə) *n.* Any of several small, tailless, harelike mammals of the genus *Ochotona,* of the mountains of North America and Eurasia. Also called "cony." [Tungus *piika.*]

pike[1] (pīk) *n.* **1.** A weapon consisting of a long wooden shaft with a pointed steel or iron head, formerly used by infantry. **2.** Any spike or sharp point, such as the tip of a spear.
~tr.v. **piked, piking, pikes.** To pierce or kill with a pike. [Middle English, Old English *pīc†,* prick, point.]

pike[2] *n., pl.* **pikes** or collectively **pike.** **1.** A freshwater game and food fish, *Esox lucius,* of the Northern Hemisphere, having a long snout and sometimes attaining a length of over 1½ meters (four feet). **2.** Any of various similar or related fishes. [Middle English, perhaps from PIKE (spike), referring to the shape of its jaw.]

pike[3] *n.* **1.** A turnpike. **2. a.** A tollgate on a turnpike. **b.** The toll paid.
~intr.v. **piked, piking, pikes.** To move quickly. Often used with *along.* [Short for TURNPIKE.]

pike[4] *n. Chiefly British Regional.* A mountain or hill peak. [Middle English, akin to Norwegian dialectal *pīk†.*]

pike·man (pīk′mən) *n., pl.* **-men** (-mĭn). **1.** The keeper of a turnpike. **2.** Formerly, a soldier armed with a pike.

pike perch *n.* Any of various fishes related to the perches and resembling the pike, such as the **walleye** *(see).*

pik·er (pī′kər) *n. Slang.* A stingy, petty person, especially one who gambles with small amounts of money. [Origin unknown.]

Pikes Peak (pīks). Mountain, 4,304 meters (14,110 feet) high, in the Front Range of the Rocky Mts. in central Colorado. Though not the highest of the Rockies, it is the best known and most conspicu-

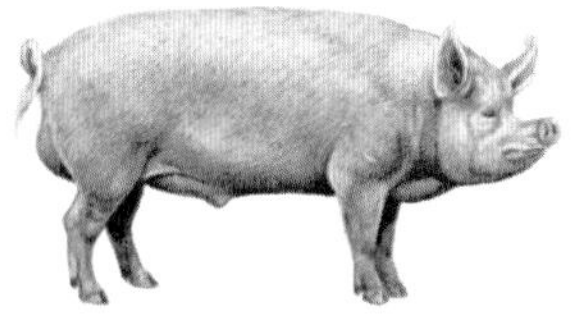

pig *One of the most useful farm animals, its flesh is used for food, its bristles for brushes, and its skin for hides; the Large White pig (above) is primarily reared for bacon.*

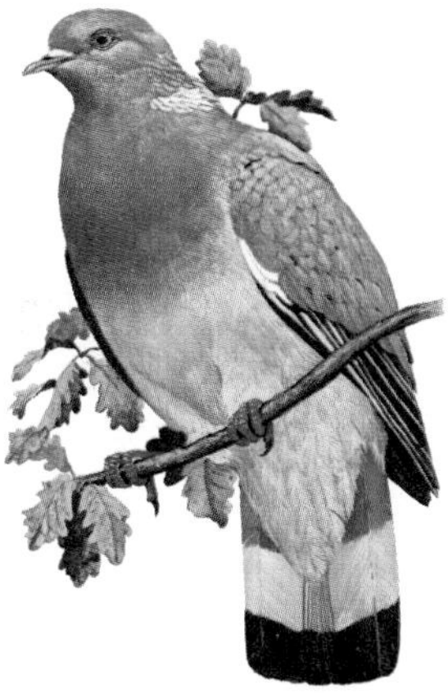

pigeon *Grain and plants are the pigeon's chief diet. The young are fed on a milky substance secreted in the adults' crop that provides them with protein. Pigeons are the only birds to produce a milk similar to that of mammals.*

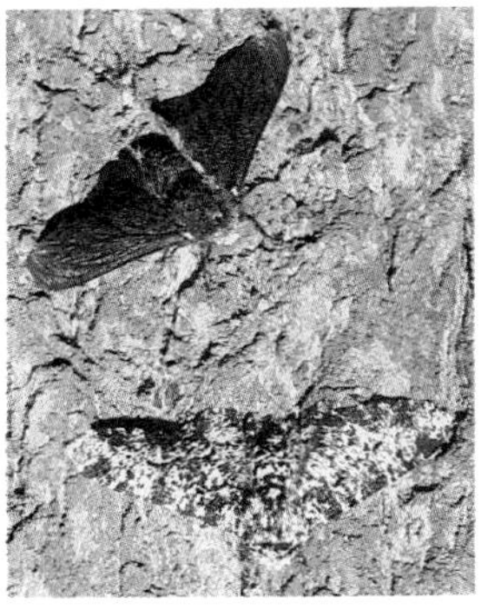

pigmentation *Many animals, such as chameleons and some fish, can change their coloring, or pigmentation, to match their surroundings. These two peppered moths are both of the same species, but have adapted to different environments. The original type (bottom) is speckled and is therefore unobtrusive on lichen-covered trees. The upper one is more common near sooty, polluted cities.*

ous because of its location at the edge of the Great Plains. It was discovered by the explorer Zebulon Pike (1779–1813) in 1806.

pike·staff (pīk′stăf′, -stäf′) *n., pl.* **-staffs** or **-staves** (-stāvz′). **1.** The shaft of a pike. **2.** A walking stick tipped with a metal spike. [PIKE (point) + STAFF.]

pi·laf, pi·laff (pĭ-läf′, pē-) *n.* Also **pi·lau** (pĭ-lô′, pē-). A dish made of seasoned rice and often meat and vegetables. [Turkish *pilāw,* from Persian *pilāw,* from Osmanli *pilau*†, "rice porridge."]

pi·lar (pī′lər) *adj.* Of or covered with hair. [New Latin *pilaris,* from Latin *pilus,* a hair.]

pi·las·ter (pĭ-lăs′tər) *n. Architecture.* A rectangular column with a capital and base, set into a wall to ornament it. [Old French *pilastre,* from Italian *pilastro,* from Medieval Latin *pilastrum,* from Latin *pīla,* PILLAR.]

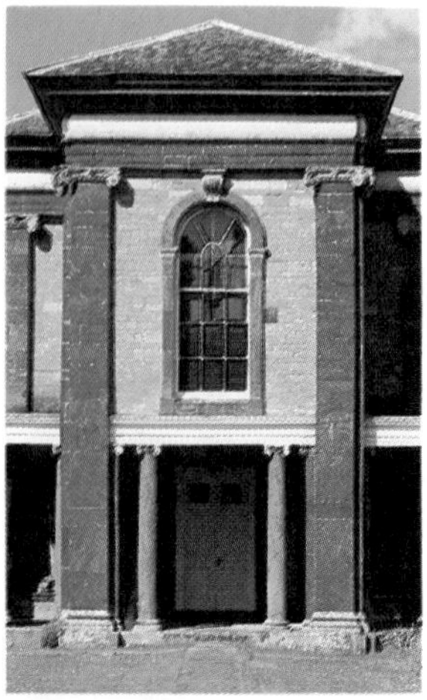

pilaster *A pavilion framed by the rectangular columns known as pilasters at Stoke Bruerne, Northamptonshire, England. It was designed by the architect Inigo Jones (1573–1652).*

Pi·late (pī′lət), **Pontius** (1st century A.D.). Roman governor of Judea (*c.* A.D. 26–36). He ordered Christ's crucifixion (allegedly with some reluctance). He is referred to by the Jewish authors Josephus and Philo, who both allude to his political insensitivity.

pil·chard (pĭl′chərd) *n.* Any of various small marine fishes related to the herrings; especially, a commercially important edible species, *Sardina pilchardus,* of European waters. [16th century : *pilchert*†.]

pile¹ (pīl) *n.* **1.** A quantity of objects stacked, thrown, or having fallen together in a heap; a mound. **2.** *Often* **piles.** *Informal.* A large accumulation or quantity: *a pile of trouble.* **3.** *Slang.* A large sum of money; a fortune. **4.** A funeral pyre. **5.** A very large building or complex of buildings. **6.** *Physics.* A **nuclear reactor** *(see).* **7.** *Electricity.* A **voltaic pile** *(see).*
~*v.* **piled, piling, piles.** —*tr.* **1.** To set or stack in a pile or heap. Sometimes used with *up.* **2.** To load with a pile: *He piled the table with books.* —*intr.* **1.** To become or form a heap or pile. Often used with *up.* **2.** *Informal.* To move in a disorderly mass or group. Used with *in, on, off,* or *out: pile out of a car.* —**pile it on.** *Informal.* To exaggerate. [Middle English, from Old French, heap, heap of stone, from Latin *pīla,* PILLAR.]

pile² *n.* **1.** A heavy beam of timber, concrete, or steel, driven into the earth as a foundation or support for a structure. **2.** *Heraldry.* A wedge-shaped charge, usually pointing downward.
~*tr.v.* **piled, piling, piles.** **1.** To drive piles into. **2.** To support or provide with piles. [Middle English *pile,* pointed shaft, stake, Old English *pīl,* from West Germanic *pīla* (unattested), from Latin *pīlum,* heavy javelin, pestle.]

pile³ *n.* **1. a.** Cut or uncut loops of yarn forming the surface of certain fabrics, such as velvet, plush, and carpeting. Compare **nap. b.** Any such filament or loop of yarn. **2.** The surface so formed. **3.** Soft, fine hair, fur, or wool. [Middle English, probably from Norman French *pyle,* from Latin *pilus,* hair.] —**piled** *adj.*

pi·le·at·ed (pī′lē-ā′tĭd, pĭl′ē-) *adj.* Also **pi·le·ate** (pī′lē-ĭt, -āt′, pĭl′ē-). **1.** *Botany.* Having a pileus. **2.** *Zoology.* Having a crest, as certain birds do. [Latin *pīleātus,* from PILEUS.]

pileated woodpecker *n.* A large North American woodpecker, *Dryocopus pileatus,* having black and white plumage and a bright red crest.

pile driver *n.* **1.** A machine that drives piles into the earth by means of a steam hammer or by raising a weight between guideposts and dropping it on the head of the pile. **2.** One who operates a pile driver.

pi·le·ous (pī′lē-əs, pĭl′ē-) *adj. Biology.* Hairy. [Latin *pilus,* hair.]

piles (pīlz) *pl.n.* **Hemorrhoids** *(see).* Not in technical usage. [Plural of *pile,* from Latin *pila,* ball. See **pill.**]

pi·le·um (pī′lē-əm, pĭl′ē-) *n., pl.* **pilea** (pī′lē-ə, pĭl′ē-ə). *Zoology.* The top of a bird's head, extending from the base of the bill to the nape. [New Latin, from Latin *pīleus,* felt cap, PILEUS.]

pile up *intr.v. Informal.* To crash; collide. Used especially of motor vehicles. —*tr. Informal.* To cause to crash or collide.

pile-up (pīl′ŭp′) *n. Informal.* A collision involving several motor vehicles.

pi·le·us (pī′lē-əs, pĭl′ē-) *n., pl.* **pilei** (pī′lē-ī′, pĭl′ē-ī′). **1.** *Botany.* The umbrellalike cap of the reproductive body of certain fungi, such as mushrooms. **2.** A round, brimless skullcap worn in ancient Rome. [New Latin, from Latin *pīleus, pilleus,* felt cap.]

pile·wort (pīl′wûrt′, -wôrt′) *n.* The **lesser celandine** *(see).*

pil·fer (pĭl′fər) *v.* **-fered, -fering, -fers.** —*tr.* To steal (a small amount or inexpensive item); filch. —*intr.* To steal or filch. —See Synonyms at **rob.** [Middle English, from Norman French, from Old French *pelfrer,* to rob, despoil, from *pelfre*†, booty.] —**pil·fer·age** (pĭl′fər-ĭj) *n.* —**pil·fer·er** *n.*

pil·grim (pĭl′grĭm, -grəm) *n.* **1.** A religious devotee who journeys to a shrine or sacred place. **2.** One who embarks on a quest for some end conceived as sacred. **3.** Any traveler. **4. Pilgrim.** One of the English Puritans who founded the colony of Plymouth in New England (1620). [Middle English *pelegrim,* from Old French *peligrin,* from Late Latin *pelegrīnus,* alteration of Latin *peregrīnus,* PEREGRINE.]

pil·grim·age (pĭl′grə-mĭj) *n.* **1.** A journey to a sacred place or shrine. **2.** Any long journey or search, especially one of exalted purpose or moral significance.
~*intr.v.* **pilgrimaged, -aging, -ages.** To go on a pilgrimage.

pi·lif·er·ous (pī-lĭf′ər-əs, pĭ-) *adj.* **1.** *Botany.* Designating the outermost layer of cells in the region behind a root apex that are elongated to form root hairs. **2.** Bearing or terminating in a hair or hairs. [Latin *pilus,* hair + -FEROUS.]

pi·li·form (pī′lĭ-fôrm′, pĭl′ĭ-) *adj. Botany.* Resembling a hair. [Latin *pilus,* hair + -FORM.]

pil·ing (pī′lĭng) *n.* **1.** The act of driving building piles into the earth. **2.** Building piles collectively. **3.** A structure composed of piles.

Pil·i·pi·no (pĭl′ə-pē′nō) *n.* The national language of the Philippines, based primarily on Tagalog and having many Spanish and local dialectal elements. [Tagalog, from *pilipino,* Filipino, from Philippine Spanish, FILIPINO.]

pill¹ (pĭl) *n.* **1.** A small pellet or tablet of medicine, sometimes coated, taken by swallowing whole or chewing. **2.** *Informal.* An oral contraceptive. Usually preceded by *the.* **3.** *Slang.* Something considered to resemble a pill, as a baseball. **4.** Something distasteful or unpleasant, but necessary: *a bitter pill to swallow.* **5.** *Slang.* An insipid or ill-natured person.
~*v.* **pilled, pilling, pills.** —*tr.* **1.** To dose with pills. **2.** To make into pills. —*intr.* To form small balls resembling pills: *a sweater that pills.* [Middle Dutch *pile,* probably, from Latin *pilula,* diminutive of *pila*†, ball.]

pill² *v.* **pilled, pilling, pills.** —*tr.* **1.** *Archaic.* To pillage (people or a place). **2.** *Regional.* To strip away; peel. —*intr. Archaic.* To pillage. [Middle English *pillen,* from Old French *piller,* to plunder.]

pil·lage (pĭl′ĭj) *v.* **-laged, -laging, -lages.** —*tr.* **1.** To rob (people or a place) of goods by violent seizure; plunder. **2.** To take as spoils. —*intr.* To take spoils by robbery and violence.
~*n.* **1.** The act of pillaging. **2.** Something pillaged; spoils. [Middle English, from Old French, from *piller,* to tear up, maltreat, plunder, from *pille,* dialectal variant of *peille,* rag, cloth, probably from Latin *pilleus,* felt cap.] —**pil·lag·er** *n.*

pil·lar (pĭl′ər) *n.* **1.** *Architecture.* A slender, freestanding, vertical support; column. **2.** Any similar structure used for decoration. **3.** One similar in function or shape to a pillar: *a pillar of strength; a pillar of flame.* **4.** One who occupies a central or responsible position: *a pillar of the state.* —**from pillar to post.** From one place or situation to another; hither and thither.
~*tr.v.* **pillared, -laring, -lars.** To support or decorate with a pillar or pillars. [Middle English *piler, piller,* from Old French *pilier,* from Vulgar Latin *pīlāre* (unattested), extension of Latin *pīla*†, pillar.]

pillar box *n. British.* A bright-red pillar-shaped public mailbox.

Pillars of Her·cu·les (hûr′kyə-lēz′). Two peaks, Gibraltar and Jebel Musa, one on each side of the Strait of Gibraltar, at the entrance to the Mediterranean Sea.

pill·box (pĭl′bŏks′) *n.* **1.** A small box for pills, usually having a shallow, cylindrical shape. **2.** A woman's small, round hat. **3.** A roofed concrete emplacement for a machine gun or other weapon.

pill bug *n.* A **woodlouse** *(see).*

pil·lion (pĭl′yən) *n.* A pad or cushion for a passenger behind the saddle on a motorcycle, scooter, or horse. Also used adjectivally: *a pillion passenger.*
~*adv.* On a pillion: *ride pillion.* [Scottish Gaelic *pillean,* diminutive of *peall,* covering, cushion, from Latin *pellis,* skin, hide.]

pil·lo·ry (pĭl′ə-rē) *n., pl.* **-ries.** **1.** A wooden framework with holes for the head and hands in which offenders were formerly locked to be exposed to public scorn as punishment. **2.** Public humiliation or exposure to scorn.
~*tr.v.* **pilloried, -rying, -ries.** **1.** To put in a pillory as punishment. **2.** To expose to public ridicule and abuse. [Middle English, from Old French *pilori,* from Medieval Latin *pīlōrium,* probably from Latin *pīla,* PILLAR.]

pil·low (pĭl′ō) *n.* **1.** A cushion for the head, used especially during sleep, consisting of a cloth case stuffed with something soft, such as down, feathers, or foam rubber. **2.** Something similar in function or shape: *a pillow of moss.* **3.** The pad on which bobbin lace is made.
~*tr.v.* **pillowed, -lowing, -lows.** **1.** To rest (one's head) on or as if on a pillow. **2.** To act as a pillow for. [Middle English *pilwe,* Old English *pyle, pylu,* from Latin *pulvīnus*†, pillow.] —**pil·low·y** *adj.*

pillow block *n. Engineering.* A block that encloses and supports a journal or shaft; a bearing.

pil·low·case (pĭl′ō-kās′) *n.* A removable covering for a pillow, usually of cotton or linen. Also called "pillowslip."

pill·wort (pĭl′wûrt′, -wôrt′) *n.* An aquatic Eurasian fern, *Pilularia globulifera,* with pill-like spore-producing bodies.

pillow lace *n.* **Bobbin lace** *(see).*

pi·lo·car·pine (pī′lō-kär′pēn′) *n.* Also **pi·lo·car·pin** (-pĭn). A poisonous alkaloid, $C_{11}H_{16}N_2O_2$, obtained from the leaves of the **jaborandi tree** *(see)* and used to increase the secretion of various glands, and, as eye drops, to constrict the pupil. [From New Latin *Pilocarpus,* genus of the jaborandi : Greek *pilos,* felt + -CARPOUS.]

pi·lose (pī′lōs′) *adj.* Covered with fine, soft hair. [Latin *pilōsus,* from *pilus,* a hair.]

pi·lot (pī′lət) *n.* **1.** One who operates or is licensed to operate an aircraft or spacecraft in flight. **2. a.** One who is licensed to take charge of and steer a ship into and out of port or through dangerous waters, though not himself belonging to the ship's crew. **b.** The helmsman of a ship. **3.** One who guides or directs a course of action for others. **4.** The part of a tool, device, or machine that leads or guides the whole. **5.** A **pilot light** *(see).* **6.** Something that serves as a test, trial, or model, such as a television program produced as a prototype of a series being considered for adoption by a network.
~*tr.v.* **piloted, -loting, -lots.** **1.** To serve as the pilot of. **2.** To steer or control the course of.
~*adj.* **1.** Serving as a tentative model for future experiment or development: *a pilot film; a pilot study.* **2.** Serving or leading as a guide: *a pilot beacon.* [French *pilote,* from Italian *pilota,* alteration of obsolete *pedota,* from Medieval Greek *pēdōtēs* (unattested), from Greek *pēda,* plural of *pēdon,* rudder, steering oar.]

pi·lot·age (pī'lə-tĭj) *n.* **1.** *Nautical.* **a.** The technique or act of piloting. **b.** The fee paid to a pilot. **2.** Navigation of an aircraft by visual identification of landmarks.

pilot balloon *n.* A small balloon used to determine wind velocity.

pilot bread *n.* Hardtack *(see).*

pilot cell *n.* A storage battery cell tested to determine the condition of the entire battery.

pilot cloth *n.* A thick, dark-blue cloth used for seamen's coats and similar garments.

pilot engine *n.* A locomotive engine sent ahead of a train to check the track for safety.

pilot fish *n.* A marine fish, *Naucrates ductor,* that often swims in company with larger fishes, especially sharks.

pi·lot·house (pī'lət-hous') *n.* An enclosed area on the deck or bridge of a vessel from which the vessel is controlled when under way. Also called "wheelhouse."

pi·lot·ing (pī'lə-tĭng) *n.* **1.** The occupation or service of a pilot. **2.** *Nautical.* Coastal navigation by reference to landmarks, buoys, soundings, and the like. See **celestial navigation.**

pilot lamp *n.* A small electric lamp wired to light in response to specified conditions in an electric circuit. Also called "pilot light."

pilot light *n.* **1.** A small gas flame that is kept burning constantly in order to ignite a gas burner, as in a stove, or the main burner, as in a boiler. Also called "pilot." **2.** A pilot lamp.

pilot officer *n.* The lowest-ranking commissioned officer in the Royal Air Force and various other air forces, ranking below a flying officer and equivalent in rank to a second lieutenant in the Army or a midshipman in the Navy.

pilot whale *n.* Any of several small, dark-colored whales of the genus *Globicephala.* Also called "blackfish."

Pilsen. See **Plzeň.**

pils·ner, pil·sen·er (pĭlz'nər, pĭl'snər) *n.* **1.** A strong-flavored light beer. **2.** A tall, footed glass for beer. [After *Pilsen* (PLZEŇ), Czechoslovakia, where it was originally brewed.]

Pil·sud·ski (pĭl-sōōt'skē, -zōōt'skē), **Józef** (1867–1935). Polish statesman. A Polish Socialist Party member and publisher of an underground newspaper after 1892, he secretly organized a Polish army (1908–10) and commanded it during World War I. In 1918 he became president of the newly independent Poland. He stepped down from power in 1922, but in 1926, displeased with the current government, he marched on Warsaw, where he established another government in which he served as minister of defense.

Pilt·down man (pĭlt'doun') *n.* A species of early man, *Eoanthropus dawsoni,* postulated from bones found in an early Pleistocene gravel bed in 1912, and proved in 1953 to be a forgery based on the artificial modification and juxtaposition of the cranium of a modern man and the mandible of an orangutan. [After the site near *Piltdown* Common, Sussex, England, identified by Charles Dawson (died 1916), English lawyer and amateur paleontologist.]

pil·ule (pĭl'yōol) *n.* A small pill. [French, from Latin *pilula,* diminutive of *pila,* ball. See **pill.**] —**pil·u·lar** (pĭl'yə-lər) *adj.*

Pi·ma (pē'mə) *n., pl.* **-mas** or collectively **Pima. 1.** A member of a North American Indian people living in southern Arizona and northern Mexico. **2.** The Uto-Aztecan language of this people. —**Pi·man** *adj.*

pi·men·to (pĭ-mĕn'tō) *n., pl.* **-tos. 1.** A tree, the **allspice** *(see),* or its berries. **2.** The pimiento. [Spanish *pimiento,* pepper, from Late Latin *pigmenta,* plural of *pigmentum,* plant juice, PIGMENT.]

pi meson (pī' mĕz'ŏn', mē'zŏn', mĕs'ŏn', mē'sŏn') *n.* *Physics.* A subatomic particle, the **pion** *(see).*

pi·mien·to (pĭ-mĕn'tō, -myĕn'tō) *n., pl.* **-tos.** A garden pepper, *Capsicum anuum,* or its mild, ripe, red fruit used in salads, cookery, and as stuffing for green olives. Also called "red pepper." [Spanish, pepper, allspice, PIMENTO.]

pimp (pĭmp) *n.* **1.** A man who solicits clients for a prostitute or brothel. **2.** A man who procures prostitutes for a client or patron; pander. ~*intr.v.* **pimped, pimping, pimps.** To serve as a pimp. [19th century : origin obscure.]

pim·per·nel (pĭm'pər-nĕl', -nəl) *n.* **1.** Any plant of the genus *Anagallis,* especially the scarlet pimpernel, *A. arvensis,* whose small, red, starlike flowers close in bad weather. Also called "poor man's weatherglass," "shepherd's weatherglass." **2.** Any of various similar or related plants, such as the yellow pimpernel, *Lysimachia nemorum.* [Middle English *pympernele,* from Old French *pimpernelle,* from Vulgar Latin *piperīnella* (unattested), from Latin *piper,* PEPPER.]

pim·ple (pĭm'pəl) *n.* A small swelling of the skin, sometimes containing pus; a papule or pustule. [Middle English *pinple,* nasalized form from Old English *piplian†,* to break out in pimples.] —**pim·pled, pim·ply** *adj.*

pin (pĭn) *n.* **1.** A short, straight, stiff piece of wire with a blunt head and a sharp point, used especially for fastening. **2.** Anything resembling a pin in shape or use, such as a hairpin or safety pin. **3.** An ornament, brooch, or badge, especially a thin one, fastened to the clothing by means of a pin. **4.** Something of little or no value: *"I would not care a pin"* (Shakespeare). **5.** A slender, cylindrical piece of wood or metal for holding or fastening parts together or serving as a support for suspending one thing from another, as: **a.** A thin rod for securing the ends of fractured bones. **b.** A peg for fixing a crown to the root of a tooth. **c.** A **cotter pin** *(see).* **6.** *Nautical.* **a.** A **belaying pin** *(see).* **b.** A wooden peg, a **thole** *(see).* **7.** *Music.* Any of the pegs securing the strings and regulating their tension on a

stringed instrument. **8.** The part of a key stem entering a lock. **9.** The safety clasp on a hand grenade, whose removal releases the spring that activates the detonation process. **10.** A **rolling pin** *(see).* **11.** Any of the wooden clubs at which the ball is aimed in various bowling games. **12.** In golf, the pole bearing a pennant to mark a hole. **13.** In wrestling, a hold that prevents one's opponent from moving, especially one pressing both his shoulders to the ground. **14. pins.** *Informal.* The legs: *steady on his pins.* ~*tr.v.* **pinned, pinning, pins. 1.** To fasten or secure with or as if with a pin or pins. **2. a.** To transfix. **b.** To place in a position of trusting dependence. Used with *on* or *to: pinned his faith on an absurdity.* **3. a.** In wrestling, to secure (one's opponent) in an immobilizing hold, especially when pressing both his shoulders to the ground. **b.** To hold fast; immobilize: *He was pinned under the wreckage.* **4.** *Informal.* To attribute (a wrongdoing or crime). Used with *on: The murder was pinned on the wrong man.* **5.** In chess, to prevent the moving of (a piece) without exposing a more valuable piece to capture. —**pin down. 1.** To oblige (someone) to make a definite response or commitment. **2.** To specify clearly or locate precisely: *had a feeling of sadness but couldn't pin down its cause.* ~*adj.* Having a grain suggestive of the heads of pins: *pin leather.* [Middle English *pin,* peg, Old English *pinn,* probably from Latin *pinna,* quill.]

pi·ña cloth (pēn'yə) *n.* A soft, sheer fabric made from the fibers of pineapple leaves. [Spanish *piña,* pineapple, pine cone, from Latin *pīnea,* from *pīnus,* PINE.]

pi·ña co·la·da (pēn'yə kō-lä'də, kə-lä'də, pĭn'yə) *n.* A cocktail consisting of dark rum, pineapple juice, and coconut milk or syrup. [Spanish, "strained pineapple."]

pin·a·fore (pĭn'ə-fôr', -fōr') *n.* A sleeveless garment like an apron, usually with a bib, worn especially by small girls as a dress or an overdress. [PIN (verb) + AFORE (originally pinned on dress).]

Pinang. See **Penang.**

pi·nas·ter (pī-năs'tər) *n.* A pine tree, *Pinus pinaster,* native to the Mediterranean region, having large cones and a characteristic pyramidal form. Also called "maritime pine," "cluster pine." [Latin *pīnaster,* a wild pine : *pīnus,* PIN(E) + -ASTER.]

pi·ña·ta (pēn-yä'tə) *n.* A decorated container filled with candy and toys and suspended from the ceiling to be broken by a blindfolded child with a stick as part of the Christmas celebration in some Latin-American countries.

pin·ball (pĭn'bôl') *n.* A game played on a board or machine in which the player operates a plunger to shoot a ball down a slanted surface having obstacles and targets; especially, a slot-machine game in which a player propels a number of small steel balls, one at a time, into a slanted area containing electronic devices that when touched by the ball register points for the contestant. Also used adjectively: *a pinball machine.*

pince-nez (păns'nā', pĭns'-) *n., pl.* **pince-nez** (-nāz', -nā'). Glasses that are held in position by being clipped to the bridge of the nose. [French, "pinch-nose" : *pincer,* to PINCH + *nez,* nose, from Latin *nāsus.*]

pin·cer (pĭn'sər) *n.* Anything resembling either of the grasping parts of pincers.

pincer movement *n.* Also **pincers movement.** A military maneuver in which the enemy is attacked from two flanks with the aim of encirclement.

pin·cers (pĭn'sərz) *pl.n.* **1.** A grasping tool having a pair of jaws and handles pivoted together to work in opposition. **2.** The articulated, prehensile claws of certain arthropods, such as the lobster. [Middle English *pynsour,* a pincer, from Old French *pinceour* (unattested), from *pincier,* to PINCH.]

pinch (pĭnch) *v.* **pinched, pinching, pinches.** —*tr.* **1.** To squeeze between the thumb and a finger, the jaws of a tool, or other edges. **2.** To squeeze or bind (a part of the body) in such a way as to cause discomfort or pain: *The shoes pinch my toes.* **3.** To nip, wither, or shrivel: *buds pinched by the frost.* **4.** To cause to become thin or tired-looking, as from lack of food, emotional stress, or the like: *Her face was pinched with grief.* **5.** To cause extreme hardship to; straiten: *Many families were pinched by the recession.* **6.** *Informal.* To steal. **7.** *Slang.* To arrest. **8.** To move by means of a pinch bar. **9.** *Nautical.* To head (a boat) too close into the wind. **10.** To cause to have very little money. Usually used in the passive: *very pinched for cash at the moment.* **11.** To cut off the tips of (buds or shoots). Usually used with *back* or *down.* —*intr.* **1.** To press, squeeze, or bind painfully: *This collar pinches.* **2.** To be miserly or excessively frugal. **3.** *Nautical.* To sail too close to the wind. **4.** To become narrow and then give out altogether. Used of a vein of ore. ~*n.* **1.** The act or an instance of pinching. **2. a.** An amount of something that can be held between thumb and forefinger: *a pinch of rosemary.* **b.** A very small amount. **3.** A painful, difficult, or straitened circumstance: *to feel the pinch.* **4.** *Slang.* A theft or robbery. **5.** *Slang.* An arrest or police raid. —**in** (or **at**) **a pinch.** In extreme circumstances; if unavoidable. —**pinch pennies.** To be very thrifty or miserly. [Middle English *pinchen,* to pinch, prick, from Old North French *pinchier* (unattested), variant of Old French *pincier,* from Gallo-Roman *pinctiare, punctiare* (unattested), from Latin *pungere* (past participle *punctus*), to prick.]

pinch bar *n.* A crowbar with a pointed projection at one end.

pinch·beck (pĭnch'bĕk') *n.* **1.** An alloy of zinc and copper used as imitation gold. **2.** A cheap imitation. ~*adj.* **1.** Made of pinchbeck. **2.** Imitation; spurious. [Invented by Christopher *Pinchbeck* (c. 1670–1732), English watchmaker.]

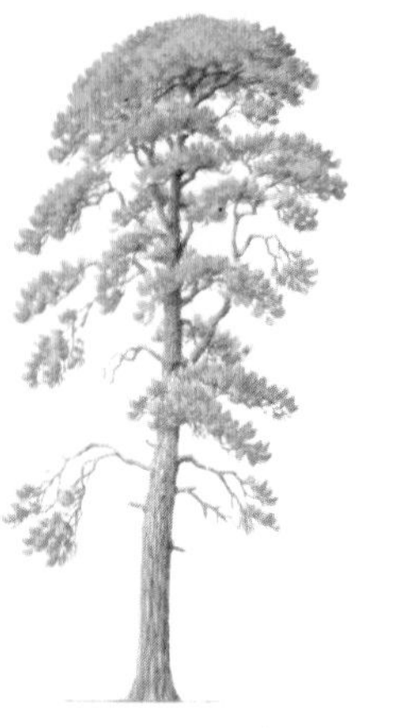

pine *Any evergreen conifer with needles arranged in groups of two, three, or five qualifies as a pine. This is a Scots pine, which survives in a few natural forests in the Scottish Highlands, but is usually grown as a timber tree in commercial plantations.*

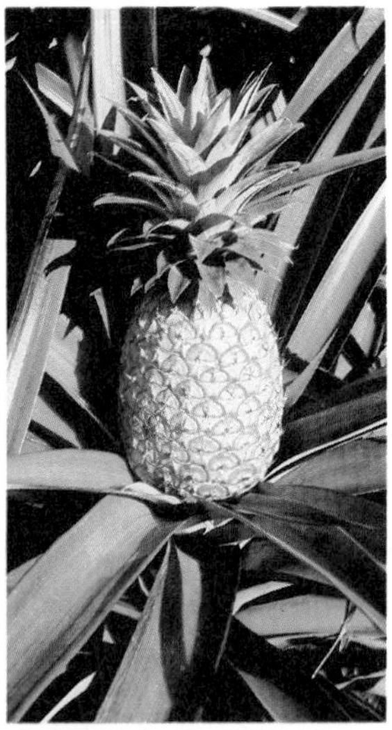

pineapple *The pineapple plant is a native of South and Central America and resembles a small yucca tree. The edible aromatic fruit weighs up to 2 kilograms (4½ pounds).*

pinch·cock (pĭnch′kŏk′) *n.* A clamp used to regulate or close a flexible tube, especially in laboratory apparatus.

pinch effect *n. Physics.* The radial constriction of a **plasma** *(see),* caused by the interaction of its internal electric currents and its self-generated magnetic field.

pinch-hit (pĭnch′hĭt′) *intr.v.* **-hit, -hitting, -hits. 1.** *Baseball.* To bat in place of a player scheduled to bat, especially when a hit is badly needed. **2.** *Informal.* To substitute for another in an emergency. **—pinch hitter** *n.*

Pinck·ney (pĭngk′nē). Family of U.S. Revolutionary War soldiers, politicians and diplomats, including **Charles Cotesworth** (1746–1825), a South Carolina legislator, member of the Constitutional Convention (1787), and a diplomat in France during the XYZ Affair (1798). His brother **Thomas** (1750–1828), governor of South Carolina (1787–89) and minister to Great Britain (1792–96), negotiated the Treaty of San Lorenzo with Spain in 1795. Their cousin **Charles** (1757–1824), also a member of the Constitutional Convention, profoundly influenced the form and content of the U.S. Constitution and served as South Carolina governor (1796–98 and 1806–08), U.S. senator (1798–1801), U.S. representative (1819–21), and minister to Spain (1801–05).

pin clover *n.* A plant, the **alfilaria** *(see).*

pin curl *n.* A coiled strand of hair, usually damp, secured with a bobby pin or clip and combed into a wave or curl when dry.

pin·cush·ion (pĭn′kŏŏsh′ən) *n.* A small, firm cushion in which pins are stuck when not in use.

Pin·dar (pĭn′dər, -där′) (*c.* 522–443 B.C.). Greek poet. He is remembered especially for his *Odes.*

Pin·dar·ic (pĭn-dăr′ĭk) *adj.* **1.** Pertaining to or characteristic of the poetic style of Pindar. **2.** Of or characteristic of a Pindaric ode. *~n.* A Pindaric ode.

Pindaric ode *n.* **1.** An ode in the form developed by Pindar, consisting of a series of triads formed by the strophe, antistrophe, and epode. **2.** An ode based on an adaptation of this form, with irregular stanzas and rhyme schemes, especially as practiced by English poets of the 17th and 18th centuries.

pine¹ (pīn) *n.* **1.** Any of various evergreen trees of the genus *Pinus,* having needle-shaped leaves in clusters and bearing cones. Many are valued for shade and ornament and for their wood and resinous sap, which yields turpentine and pine tar. **2.** Loosely, any coniferous tree, especially of the family Pinaceae, such as the cedar, spruce, or fir. **3.** The wood of any of these trees. **4.** Any of various similar but unrelated plants, such as the screw pine or ground pine. [Middle English *pine,* from Old English *pīn* and Old French *pin,* from Latin *pīnus.*]

pine² *v.* **pined, pining, pines.** *—intr.* **1.** To suffer intense longing or yearning. Usually used with *for*: *pining for home.* **2.** To wither or waste away from longing or grief. Usually used with *away.* *—tr. Archaic.* To grieve or mourn for. —See Synonyms at **yearn.**
~n. Archaic. Intense longing or grief. [Middle English *pinen,* Old English *pīnian,* from *pīne* (unattested), torture, from Latin *poena,* penalty, from Greek *poinē,* punishment.]

pin·e·al (pĭn′ē-əl, pī′nē-) *adj.* Of or pertaining to the pineal body. [French *pinéal,* from Latin *pīnea,* pine cone, from *pīneus,* of the pine, from *pīnus,* PINE.]

pineal body *n.* A small glandlike structure in the brain of vertebrates. In animals it secretes melatonin, but its functions in humans are uncertain. Also called "pineal gland," "epiphysis."

pineal eye *n.* An extension of the pineal body that forms an eyelike protuberance on the head in certain reptiles and primitive cartilaginous fish.

pine·ap·ple (pīn′ăp′əl) *n.* **1.** A tropical American plant, *Ananas comosus,* having large, swordlike leaves and a large, fleshy, edible fruit consisting of the flowers fused into a compound whole with a terminal tuft of leaves. **2.** The fruit of this plant. **3.** *Slang.* A small hand grenade. [Originally "pine cone" (from the resemblance of the fruit to a pine cone), Middle English *pinappel* : PINE + APPLE.]

pineapple weed *n.* A low-growing annual plant, *Matricaria matricarioides,* having greenish-yellow, rayless flower heads and a smell of pineapple when crushed.

pine cone *n.* The woody conical reproductive structure of a pine tree.

pine marten *n.* An arboreal musteline mammal, *Martes martes,* found in woods, especially pine woods, of northern Europe.

pi·nene (pī′nēn′) *n.* Either of two isomeric terpene liquids, $C_{10}H_{16}$, that are the main constituents of oil or spirits of turpentine. [PIN(E) + -ENE.]

pine needle *n.* The needle-shaped leaf of a pine tree.

pine nut *n.* The edible seed of certain pines, such as the piñon.

Pi·ne·ro (pĭ-nîr′ō), **Sir Arthur Wing** (1855–1934). British playwright. Abandoning a career in law, he won fame as a writer of immensely popular farces, such as *Dandy Dick* (1887). His later plays include *The Second Mrs. Tanqueray* (1893).

pin·er·y (pī′nə-rē) *n., pl.* **-ies. 1.** A hothouse or plantation for the cultivation of pineapples. **2.** A forest of pine trees.

pine siskin *n.* A North American finch, *Spinus pinus,* having streaked, brownish plumage.

pine tar *n.* A viscous or semisolid brown to black substance produced by the destructive distillation of pine wood and used in roofing preparations, paints and varnishes, and as an antiseptic.

pi·ne·tum (pī-nē′təm) *n., pl.* **-ta** (-tə). An area planted with pine trees or related conifers, especially for botanical study. [Latin *pīnētum,* pine grove, from *pīnus,* PINE.]

piney. Variant of **piny.**

pin·feath·er (pĭn′fĕth′ər) *n.* In birds, a growing feather still enclosed in its horny sheath; especially, one just emerging through the skin.

pin·fold (pĭn′fōld′) *n.* A pound for stray animals, such as sheep. *~tr.v.* **pinfolded, -folding, -folds.** To confine in or as if in a pinfold. [Middle English *pyn(de)fold,* Old English *pundfald* : *pund-,* POUND (enclosure) + *fald,* FOLD.]

ping (pĭng) *n.* A brief, high-pitched sound, such as that made by a bullet striking metal.
~intr.v. **pinged, pinging, pings.** To produce a ping. [Imitative.]

pin·go (pĭng′gō′) *n.* A mound of gravel or earth occurring in Arctic regions as a result of pressure from water trapped between newly frozen ice and the permafrost beneath it. [Eskimo.]

Ping-Pong (pĭng′pông′, -pŏng′) *n.* **1.** A trademark for table-tennis equipment. **2. ping-pong.** The game of table tennis.

pin·guid (pĭng′gwĭd) *adj.* **1.** Oily, greasy, or fatty. **2.** Designating soil that is rich and fertile. [Latin *pinguis,* fat + -ID.] **—pin·guid·i·ty** (pĭng-gwĭd′ə-tē) *n.*

pin·head (pĭn′hĕd′) *n.* **1.** The head of a pin. **2.** Anything small, trifling, or insignificant. **3.** *Slang.* A stupid person. **—pin·head·ed** *adj.* **—pin·head·ed·ness** *n.*

pin·hole (pĭn′hōl′) *n.* A tiny puncture made by or as if by a pin.

pin·ion¹ (pĭn′yən) *n.* **1.** A bird's wing. **2.** The outer rear edge of a bird's wing, containing the primary feathers. **3.** A primary feather of a bird.
~tr.v. **pinioned, -ioning, -ions. 1. a.** To remove or bind the wing feathers of (a bird) to prevent flight. **b.** To cut or bind (the wings of a bird). **2.** To restrain or immobilize (a person) by binding the arms. **3.** To fix in one place; make fast: *He jabbed with his fork and pinioned a piece of meat.* [Middle English *pynyon,* from Old French *pignon,* from Vulgar Latin *pinniō,* stem *pinniōn-* (unattested), augmentative of Latin *pinna, penna,* a feather, wing.]

pinion² *n.* A small cogwheel that engages or is engaged by a larger cogwheel or a rack. [French *pignon,* alteration of obsolete *pignol,* from Vulgar Latin *pīneolus,* from Latin *pīnea,* pine cone, from *pīnus,* PINE.]

pin·ite (pĭn′īt′, pē′nīt′) *n.* A hydrous, usually amorphous mineral silicate of aluminum and potassium. [German *Pinit* after *Pini,* a mine in Saxony where it was found.]

pink¹ (pĭngk) *n.* **1.** Any of various plants of the genus *Dianthus,* often cultivated for their fragrant flowers. **2.** Any of various similar plants of other genera. **3.** A flower of any of these plants. **4.** The highest degree of excellence or perfection: *He is in the pink of condition.* **5.** Any of a group of colors pale reddish in hue, of medium to high lightness, and low to moderate saturation. **6. a.** Pink clothing. **b. pinks.** Light-brown trousers formerly worn as part of the winter semidress uniform by U.S. Army officers. **7.** *British.* **a.** The scarlet coat of a fox hunter. **b.** A fox hunter wearing a scarlet coat. **8.** *Slang.* A person regarded as sympathetic with or influenced by Communist doctrine. **—in the pink.** In excellent health.
~adj. **pinker, pinkest. 1.** Of the color pink. **2.** Designating the scarlet coat worn by a fox hunter. **3.** *Slang.* Sympathetic with or influenced by Communist doctrine. [Perhaps short for obsolete *pink eye,* "small eye" (from the shape of the flower), from obsolete Dutch *pinck oog(en),* "small eye(s)," also "conjunctivitis" : *pin(c)k*†, small, the little finger + *oog,* eye.] **—pink·ish** *adj.* **—pink·ness** *n.*

pink² *tr.v.* **pinked, pinking, pinks. 1.** To stab lightly with a pointed weapon; prick. **2.** To decorate with a perforated pattern. **3.** To cut with pinking shears. [Middle English *pynken,* probably of Low German origin; akin to Low German *pinken*†, to peck.]

pink³ *n.* Also **pink·ie, pink·y** (pĭng′kē), *pl.* **-ies.** *Nautical.* A sailing vessel with a narrow stern. [Middle English *pynk,* from Middle Dutch *pin(c)ke*†.]

pink elephants *pl.n.* Hallucinations resulting from excessive consumption of alcohol. Used humorously.

Pink·er·ton (pĭng′kər-tən), **Allan** (1819–84). U.S. detective, born in Scotland. In 1850 he founded Pinkerton's National Detective Agency, later the most famous in the United States.

pink·eye (pĭngk′ī′) *n.* Acute contagious conjunctivitis, characterized by inflamed eyelids and eyeballs. Not in technical usage. [See **pink** (color).]

Pink·ham (pĭng′kəm), **Lydia Estes** (1819–83). U.S. patent-medicine manufacturer. After concocting "Vegetable Compound" for her family and neighbors, she began marketing the potion for the general public (1875). Her likeness was used in numerous advertisements for the product, which supposedly relieved all feminine ills and had an alcohol content of 18 percent.

pink·ie, pink·y (pĭng′kē) *n., pl.* **-ies.** *Informal.* **1.** The little finger. **2.** Variant of **pink** (sailing vessel). [Dutch *pinkje,* diminutive of *pink,* little finger, from obsolete *pin(c)k*†.]

pinking shears *pl.n.* Sewing scissors with notched or serrated blades. They are used to finish edges of cloth with a scalloped or zigzag pattern, for decoration or to prevent fraying.

pink lady *n.* A cocktail of gin, brandy, lemon or lime juice, egg white, and grenadine, shaken with ice and strained.

pink·root (pĭngk′rōōt′, -rŏŏt′) *n.* A plant, *Spigelia marilandica,* of eastern North America, having red and yellow flowers. Its root was once used as a vermifuge.

Pink·ster, Pinx·ster (pĭngk′stər) *n. Regional.* Whitsunday or Whitsuntide. [Dutch, PENTECOST.]

pin money *n.* Money for incidental expenses. [Originally, a small sum for buying hat pins or hairpins.]

pin·na (pĭn′ə) *n., pl.* **pinnae** (pĭn′ē) or **-nas. 1.** *Botany.* Any of the leaflets of a pinnate leaf. **2.** *Zoology.* A feather, wing, fin, or similar appendage. **3.** *Anatomy.* The external part of the ear; the auricle. [Latin *pinna, penna,* wing, feather.] **—pin·nal** *adj.*

pin·nace (pĭn′ĭs) *n.* *Nautical.* **1.** A small sailing boat formerly used as a tender for merchant and war vessels. **2.** Any small ship or ship's boat. [French *pinace,* from Old Spanish *pinaza* or Italian *pinaccia,* from (unattested) Vulgar Latin *pīnācea (nāvis),* "(ship) of pine wood," from Latin *pīnus,* pine tree.]

pin·na·cle (pĭn′ə-kəl) *n.* **1.** *Architecture.* A small turret or spire on a roof or buttress. **2.** Any tall, pointed formation, such as a mountain peak. **3.** The highest point; summit; acme: *the pinnacle of achievement.* —See Synonyms at **summit.**
~*tr.v.* **pinnacled, -cling, -cles. 1.** To furnish with a pinnacle. **2.** To place on or as if on a pinnacle. [Middle English *pin(n)acle,* from Old French, from Late Latin *pinnāculum,* "little wing," from Latin *pinna,* feather, wing.]

pin·nate (pĭn′āt′) *adj.* Also **pin·nat·ed** (pĭn′ā′tĭd). **1.** Resembling a feather; pennate. **2.** *Botany.* Having leaflets, lobes, or divisions in a featherlike arrangement on each side of a common axis, as many compound leaves do. [Latin *pinnātus,* feathered, from *pinna,* feather.] **—pin·nate·ly** *adv.*

pin·nat·i·fid (pĭ-năt′ə-fĭd) *adj.* *Botany.* Having pinnately cleft lobes or divisions reaching over halfway to the midrib. Said of certain leaves. [Latin *pinnātus,* PINNATE + -FID.] **—pin·nat·i·fid·ly** *adv.*

pin·nat·i·sect (pĭ-năt′ə-sĕkt′) *adj.* *Botany.* Divided nearly to the midrib. Said of certain leaves. [PINNATI- + -SECT.]

pin·ni·ped (pĭn′ə-pĕd′) *adj.* Also **pin·ni·pe·di·an** (-pē′dē-ən). *Zoology.* Of or belonging to the Pinnipedia, an order of aquatic mammals that includes the seals, walruses, and similar animals having finlike flippers for locomotion.
~*n.* A mammal belonging to this order. [Latin *pinna,* feather, wing, PINNA + -PED.]

pin·nule (pĭn′yo͞ol) *n.* Also **pin·nu·la** (pĭn′yə-lə) *pl.* **-lae** (-lē′). **1.** *Botany.* Any of the lobes of a leaflet of a pinnately compound leaf. **2.** *Zoology.* A featherlike or plumelike organ or part, such as a small fin, or any of the appendages of a crinoid. [New Latin *pinnula,* from Latin, diminutive of *pinna, penna,* feather, wing, fin.] **—pin·nu·lar** (pĭn′yə-lər) *adj.*

Pi·no·chet U·gar·te (pē′nō-shā o͞o-gär′tā; *Spanish* pē′nō-chĕt o͞o-gär′tä), **Augusto** (1915–). Chilean general. He led the group of officers who, in 1973, overthrew the elected government of Salvador Allende. Appointed president in 1974, he directed a notoriously brutal junta.

pi·noch·le, pi·noc·le, pe·nuch·le (pē′nŭk′əl, -nŏk′əl) *n.* **1.** A game of cards for two to four persons, played with a special pack of 48 cards, with points being scored by taking tricks and forming certain combinations. **2.** The combination of the queen of spades and jack of diamonds in this game. [19th century : origin obscure.]

pi·ñon (pĭn′yŏn′, -yən) *n., pl.* **piñons** or **piñones** (pĭn-yō′nēz). Also **pin·yon.** Any of several pine trees bearing edible, nutlike seeds, especially *Pinus cembroides edulis,* of the western United States and Mexico. [Spanish, pine cone, from *piña,* from Latin *pinea,* feminine of *pineus,* of pine, from *pīnus,* pine.]

pi·not noir (pē′nō nwär′) *n.* A variety of black grape used in winemaking. [French, "black pinot" : *pinot,* variant of *pineau,* diminutive of *pin,* pine (tree); comparing the shape of its grape clusters to pine cones.]

pin·point (pĭn′point′) *n.* **1.** An extremely small thing; particle; bit: *a pinpoint of light.* **2.** A tiny or insignificant spot: *the pinpoint of ground upon which we stand.* **3.** *Military.* **a.** A point on a map indicating a strictly defined target. **b.** A precisely identified and limited target. **4.** The sharp tip of a pin.
~*tr.v.* **pinpointed, -pointing, -points. 1. a.** To locate and identify precisely: *Our radar pinpointed the planes.* **b.** To define or delimit precisely. **2.** *Military.* To take precise aim at: *pinpoint a target.*
~*adj.* **1.** Characterized by meticulous precision: *He spots flaws with pinpoint accuracy.* **2.** Minuscule; tiny: *pinpoint creatures.*

pin·prick (pĭn′prĭk′) *n.* **1.** A slight puncture made by or as if by a pin. **2.** An insignificant wound. **3.** A minor annoyance.
~*v.* **pinpricked, -pricking, -pricks.** —*tr.* To puncture with or as if with a pin. —*intr.* To make a slight puncture with a pin.

pins and needles *pl.n.* A tingling felt in a part of the body numbed from lack of circulation. **—on pins and needles.** In a state of anxiety or tense anticipation.

pin·scher (pĭn′shər) *n.* A **Doberman pinscher** *(see).*

pin·stripe (pĭn′strīp′) *n.* **1.** A thin stripe on a fabric. **2.** A kind of fabric with thin stripes, often used for men's suits. Also used adjectivally: *a pinstripe suit.*

pint (pīnt) *n.* *Abbr.* **p., pt., o. 1. a.** A unit of volume or capacity in the U.S. Customary System, used in liquid measure, equal to 16 fluid ounces (.473 liter). **b.** A unit of volume or capacity in the U.S. Customary System, used in dry measure, equal to 1/2 quart (.551 liter). **c.** A unit of volume or capacity in the British Imperial System, used in dry and liquid measure, equal to .568 liter. **2. a.** A container with a pint capacity. **b.** The amount of a substance that can be held in such a container. [Middle English *pinte,* from Old French, probably from Medieval Latin *pincta,* "painted mark (on a measuring container)," from Vulgar Latin *pinctus* (unattested), painted. See **pinto.**]

pin·ta (pĭn′tə, pĕn′tä) *n.* A contagious skin disease, prevalent in tropical America, caused by spirochete microorganisms and characterized by extreme thickening and localized discoloration of the skin. [American Spanish, from Spanish, painted mark, from the feminine of Vulgar Latin *pinctus* (unattested), painted. See **pinto.**]

pin·tail (pĭn′tāl′) *n., pl.* **-tails** or collectively **pintail.** A duck, *Anas acuta,* of the Northern Hemisphere, having gray, brown, and white plumage and a sharply pointed tail in the male.

Pin·ter (pĭn′tər), **Harold** (1930–). British playwright, actor, and director. His plays, which include *The Caretaker* (1959) and *The Homecoming* (1965), are known for their elusive dialogue and atmosphere of menace. **—Pin·ter·esque** (pĭn′tə-rĕsk′) *adj.*

pin·tle (pĭnt′l) *n.* An upright pin or bolt used as a pivot; specifically: **1.** *Nautical.* The pin on which a rudder turns. **2.** The pin on a gun carriage. **3.** A pin or bolt on the back of a towing vehicle to which a towed vehicle is attached. [Middle English *pintel,* "penis," Old English *pintel*†.]

pin·to (pĭn′tō) *n., pl.* **-tos** or **-toes.** Any horse with irregular spots or markings.
~*adj.* Irregularly marked; piebald. [American Spanish, from obsolete Spanish, "painted," "spotted," from Vulgar Latin *pinctus* (unattested), variant of Latin *pictus,* past participle of Latin *pingere,* to paint.]

pinto bean *n.* A form of the common string bean that has mottled seeds and is grown chiefly in the southwestern United States.

pint-size (pīnt′sīz′) *adj.* Also **pint-sized** (-sīzd′). *Informal.* Of small dimensions; diminutive.

pin-up (pĭn′ŭp′) *n.* **1.** A picture to be pinned up on a wall; especially, a photograph of a sexually attractive person or a nude or partially dressed person, especially a woman. **2.** A person considered as a suitable model for such a picture. **3.** A photograph of a celebrity.
~*adj.* Designed to be attached to a wall: *a pin-up lamp.*

Pin·tu·ric·chi·o (pēn′to͞o-rē′kē-ō′) (1454–1513). Italian painter. Noted for his brilliantly colored frescoes, he assisted Perugino on works in the Sistine Chapel (1481–82), completed six frescoes in the Vatican for Pope Alexander VI (1492–94), and painted 10 scenes from the life of Pius II in the Siena cathedral (1503–08).

pin·wale (pĭn′wāl′) *n.* A corduroy made with narrow ribs or wales. **—pin·wale** *adj.*

pin·wheel (pĭn′hwēl′) *n.* **1.** A toy consisting of vanes of colored paper or plastic pinned to the end of a stick in such a way that they turn when blown upon. **2.** A cogwheel with a circle of pins at right angles to its face, used as a tripping device. **3.** A firework that forms a rotating wheel of colored flames.

pin·work (pĭn′wûrk′) *n.* The fine stitches raised in needlepoint lace from the surface of a motif.

pin·worm (pĭn′wûrm′) *n.* A small nematode worm, *Enterobius vermicularis,* that infects the human intestines and rectum, especially in children. Also called "threadworm."

pin·wrench, pin wrench (pĭn′rĕnch′) *n.* A wrench having a projection designed to fit a hole in the object to be turned.

pinx·it (pĭngk′sĭt) *n.* *Abbr.* **pinx.** *Latin.* He or she painted (this). Formerly used as part of the painter's signature on a painting.

Pinxter. Variant of **Pinkster.**

pin·y, pine·y (pī′nē) *adj.* **-ier, -iest.** Resembling, characteristic of, consisting of, or covered with pines.

pin·yin, Pin·yin (pĭn′yĭn′, -yĭn) *n.* A system of transliteration of Chinese characters into Roman characters, introduced in China in 1957. [Chinese, "spell sound."]

Pin·za (pĭn′zə, pĕn′tsä), **Ezio** (1895–1957). U.S. basso; born in Italy. After his Rome debut in Wagner's *Tristan und Isolde* (1920), he performed in Europe until 1926, when he appeared in Gasparo Spontini's *La Vestale* at the Metropolitan Opera House in New York City, beginning his 22 years as the Metropolitan's leading basso.

pi·o·let (pē′ə-lā′) *n.* A kind of ice ax. [French, diminutive of French dialectal *piola,* small ax, ultimately from Old Provençal *apcha, apia,* ax, from Germanic; akin to Old High German *hāppa,* sickle.]

pi·on (pī′ŏn′) *n.* *Symbol* π *Physics.* Any of three elementary particles in the meson family, *pi zero, pi minus,* and *pi plus,* having zero spin, negative parity, and 0, +1, and −1 times the charge of the electron respectively. The pi zero has a lifetime of 9×10^{-16} second and decays into photons, while the two pions have lifetimes of about 2.5×10^{-8} and decay into leptons. They are exchanged between particles in the strong remaining interaction. Also called "pi meson." [Shortened from PI MESON.]

pi·o·neer (pī′ə-nîr′) *n.* **1.** One who ventures into unknown or unclaimed territory to settle. Also used adjectivally: *a pioneer spirit.* **2.** An innovator in a particular field: *a pioneer in aviation.* Also used adjectivally: *pioneer research.* **3.** A military engineer employed in the construction and fortification of roads, bridges, or the like, and the maintenance of communication lines. **4.** *Ecology.* A plant species that is one of the first to establish itself in a previously barren environment.
~*v.* **pioneered, -neering, -neers.** —*tr.* **1.** To initiate or participate in the development of: *men who pioneered the submarine.* **2. a.** To explore or open up (a region). **b.** To be a pioneer to (travelers, for example); conduct. —*intr.* To act as a pioneer. [French *pionnier,* from Old French *peon(n)ier,* originally "a foot soldier sent out to clear the way," from *pion, peon,* foot soldier. See **peon.**]

pi·ous (pī′əs) *adj.* **1.** Having or showing reverence and earnest compliance in the observance of religion; devout. **2. a.** Marked by conspicuous devoutness. **b.** Marked by false devoutness; solemnly hypocritical. **3.** Not secular; devotional: *pious readings.* **4.** Professing or exhibiting a strict, traditional sense of virtue and morality;

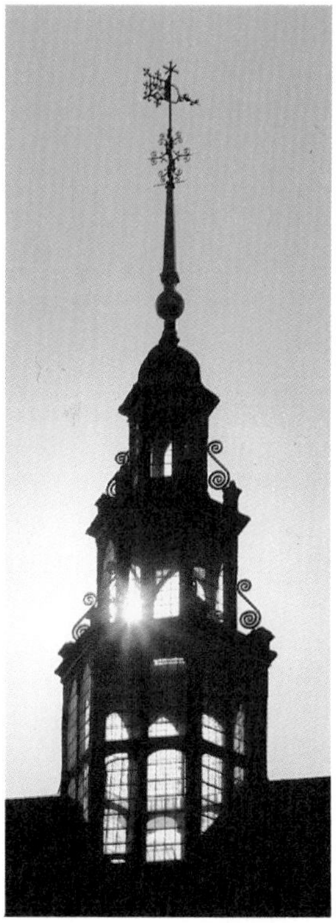

pinnacle *The slender outlines of the pinnacled clock tower at Trinity College in Cambridge, England.*

PRONUNCIATION KEY

ă, pat; ā, pay; âr, care;
ä, father, are; b, bib;
ch, church; d, deed; ĕ, pet;
ē, be; f, fife; g, gag; h, hat;
hw, which; ĭ, pit; ī, pie;
îr, pier; j, judge; k, kick;
l, lid, needle; m, mum;
n, no, sudden; ng, thing;
ŏ, pot; ō, toe; ô, paw, for;
oi, noise; ou, out; o͝o, book;
o͞o, boot; p, pop; r, roar;
s, sauce; sh, ship, dish;
t, tight; th, thin, path;
th, this, bathe; ŭ, cut; ûr, fur;
v, valve; w, with; y, yes;
z, zebra, size; zh, vision;
ə, about, item, edible,
gallop, circus, peaceful

IN FOREIGN WORDS:

à, *Fr.* ami; œ, *Fr.* feu, *Ger.* schön; ü, *Fr.* tu, *Ger.* über;
KH, *Ger.* ich, *Scot.* loch;
N, *Fr.* bon; y′, *Fr.* Compiègne

STRESS MARKS:

Primary stress: ′
in·cite′ (ĭn-sīt′)
Secondary stress: ′
in′sight′ (ĭn′sīt′)

high-minded: *the pious instructions of his parents.* **5.** Commendable; worthy: *a pious attempt.* **6.** *Archaic.* Having filial reverence; dutiful. [Latin *pius.*] **—pi·ous·ly** *adv.* **—pi·ous·ness** *n.*

Pioz·zi (pyôt′sē), **Hester Lynch,** also called "Mrs. Thrale" (1741–1821). English writer and socialite. Her books *Anecdotes of the Late Samuel Johnson* (1796) and *Letters to and from the Late Samuel Johnson* (1788) recount her 20-year friendship with the famed lexicographer, whom she met in 1765.

pip¹ (pĭp) *n.* **1.** The seed of a fleshy fruit, such as an apple or orange. **2.** A rootstock of certain flowering plants, especially lily of the valley. **3.** *Informal.* Something remarkable of its kind: *a pip of a plan.* [Shortened from PIPPIN.]

pip² *tr.v.* **pipped, pipping, pips.** *British Slang.* **1.** To strike with a gunshot; hit. **2.** To defeat, especially at the last moment: *He was pipped at the post.* **3.** To blackball. [Perhaps from PIP (dot on dice, hence, "small ball").]

pip³ *n.* **1.** A dot indicating a unit of numerical value on playing cards, dice, or dominoes. **2.** *British Informal.* A shoulder insignia indicating the rank of certain officers in the British Army. **3.** A radar signal. **4.** Any of the segments found on the surface of a pineapple. [16th century : *peepe*†.]

pip⁴ *v.* **pipped, pipping, pips.** *—tr.* To break through (an eggshell) in hatching. *—intr.* To peep or chirp, as a young bird does.
~n. A short, high-pitched signal, especially one of a series constituting a time signal in a radio transmission. [Variant of PEEP (to peek) and PEEP (to cheep).]

pip⁵ *n.* **1. a.** A disease of birds, characterized by a thick mucous discharge that forms a crust in the mouth and throat. **b.** The crust symptomatic of this disease. **2.** *Slang.* Any minor or imaginary ailment, or a feeling of depression. Preceded by *the*: *She gives me the pip.* [Middle English *pippe,* from Middle Dutch, phlegm, mucus, from West Germanic *pipit* (unattested), probably from Vulgar Latin *pīppīta,* (earlier) *pītīta* (both unattested), alterations of Latin *pītuīta,* phlegm.]

pi·pa (pē′pə) *n.* A South American toad, *Pipa pipa,* the female of which carries her fertilized eggs on her back, where they develop in pits in the skin. Also called "Surinam toad." [Surinam dialectal *pipá* (feminine), *pipál* (masculine), of African origin.]

pip·age (pī′pĭj) *n.* **1.** The transmission of liquids through pipes. **2.** The charge for such transmission. **3.** Pipes; piping.

pipal. Variant of **peepul.**

pipe (pīp) *n.* **1. a.** Any hollow cylinder or tubular conveyance for a fluid or gas. **b.** A section or piece of such a tube. **2. a.** An instrument for smoking, consisting of a tube of wood or clay with a mouthpiece at one end and a small bowl at the other. **b.** The amount of tobacco or other substance to fill the bowl of a smoking pipe; a pipeful. **3. a.** *Biology.* A tubular part or organ. **b. pipes.** *Informal.* The human respiratory system or vocal cords. **4.** *Abbr.* **p. a.** A wine cask having a capacity of 105 gallons (457 liters). **b.** This volume as a unit of liquid measure. **5.** *Abbr.* **p.** *Music.* **a.** A tubular wind instrument, such as a flute. **b.** Any of the tubes in an organ. **c. pipes.** A small wind instrument consisting of tubes of different lengths bound together: *pipes of Pan.* **d. pipes.** A set of bagpipes. **e.** A primitive type of flute that was played with one hand while the other beat a drum or tabor. **6.** The sound of the voice, especially as used in singing or acting. **7.** A birdcall. **8. a.** *Nautical.* A kind of whistle used for signaling crew members: *a boatswain's pipe.* **b.** The sound this pipe makes. **9.** *Mining.* **a.** A vertical, cylindrical vein of ore. **b.** Any of the vertical veins of eruptive origin in which diamonds are found in South Africa. **10.** *Geology.* An eruptive passageway opening into the crater of a volcano. **11.** A cone-shaped cavity in a steel ingot, formed during cooling by unequal contraction. **—put that in your pipe and smoke it.** That is the situation whether you like it or not.
~v. **piped, piping, pipes.** *—tr.* **1. a.** To convey (liquid or gas) by means of pipes. **b.** To supply or convey as if by means of a pipe. **2.** To provide or connect with pipes. **3. a.** To play (a tune) on a pipe or pipes: *"Piper, pipe that song again"* (William Blake). **b.** To lead by playing on pipes. **4.** *Nautical.* To call (crew members, for example) by sounding the boatswain's pipe. **5.** To utter in a shrill, reedy tone. **6.** To furnish (a garment or fabric) with piping. *—intr.* **1.** To play on a pipe. **2.** To speak shrilly; make a shrill sound. **3.** To chirp or whistle, as a bird does. **4.** *Nautical.* To call on a boatswain's pipe. **5.** In metallurgy, to develop conical cavities. **—pipe down.** *Informal.* To stop talking; be quiet. **—pipe up.** To speak up, especially in a small, shrill voice. [Middle English *pipe,* Old English *pīpe,* from Common Germanic *pīpa* (unattested), from Common Romance *pīpa* (unattested), from Latin *pīpāre,* to chirp.] **—pip·y** *adj.*

pipe clay *n.* A fine white clay used in making tobacco pipes and pottery, in calico printing, and in whitening leather.

pipe cleaner *n.* A pliant, tufted piece of wire used for cleaning the stem of a tobacco pipe.

pipe dream *n.* A wishful, fantastic notion or hope. [From the fantasies induced by opium.]

pipe·fish (pīp′fĭsh′) *n., pl.* **-fishes** or collectively **pipefish.** Any of various slim, elongated marine or freshwater fishes of the family Syngnathidae, characterized by a tubelike snout and an external covering of bony plates. Also called "needlefish."

pipe fitter *n.* One who installs and repairs piping systems.

pipe·fit·ting (pīp′fĭt′ĭng) *n.* **1. a.** The act or work of joining pipes together. **b.** A branch of the plumbing trade that deals specifically with the installation and repair of piping systems. **2.** A section of pipe used to join two or more pipes together.

pipe·ful (pīp′fo͝ol′) *n., pl.* **-fuls.** The amount required to fill a pipe.

pipe·line (pīp′līn′) *n.* **1.** A long pipe, often buried underground, for the conveyance of water, gas, or petroleum products. **2.** A channel by which information of a generally secret or confidential nature is transmitted. **3.** A line of communication or route of supply: *a new pipeline for medical supplies.*
~tr.v. **pipelined, -lining, -lines. 1.** To convey by means of a pipeline. **2.** To lay a pipeline through.

pipe organ *n.* A musical instrument, an **organ** (sense 1) *(see).*

pip·er (pī′pər) *n.* One who plays a pipe or the bagpipes.

pi·per·a·zine (pī-pĕr′ə-zēn′, pĭ-) *n.* A colorless crystalline compound, $C_4H_{10}N_2$, used to inhibit corrosion, in insecticides, and as an anthelmintic. [PIPER(INE) + AZ(O)- + -INE.]

pi·per·i·dine (pī-pĕr′ə-dēn′, pĭ-) *n.* A colorless liquid, $C_5H_{10}NH$, a strong base used in the manufacture of rubber and as a curing agent in epoxy resins. [PIPER(INE) + -ID(E) + -INE.]

pip·er·ine (pĭp′ə-rēn′) *n.* A crystalline alkaloid, $C_{17}H_{19}NO_3$, extracted from black pepper and used as flavoring and as an insecticide. [Latin *piper,* PEPPER + -INE.]

pi·per·o·nal (pī-pĕr′ə-năl′, pĭ-) *n.* A white powder, $C_8H_6O_3$, having a floral odor, used as flavoring and in perfume. Also called "heliotropin." [PIPER(INE) + -ON(E) + -AL.]

pipe·stone (pīp′stōn′) *n.* A heat-hardened compacted red clay used by American Indians for making tobacco pipes.

pi·pette, pi·pet (pī-pĕt′) *n. Chemistry.* Any of variously shaped glass tubes, open at both ends, usually calibrated, and used especially to transfer small volumes of liquid from one container to another. [French, diminutive of *pipe,* PIPE.]

pipe vine *n.* A woody vine, *Aristolochia durior,* of the eastern United States, having greenish, brown-mottled flowers shaped like a curved pipe.

pipe wrench *n.* A wrench with two serrated jaws, one adjustable, used for gripping and turning pipes. Compare **Stillson wrench.**

pip·ing (pī′pĭng) *n.* **1.** A system of pipes, such as one used in plumbing. **2.** *Music.* **a.** The act of playing on a pipe. **b.** The music produced by a pipe. **3.** A shrill, high-pitched sound. **4.** A rounded strip of cloth, sometimes covering a cord, used for trimming the seams and edges of garments or furniture covers. **5.** Rounded strands produced by forcing a substance such as icing through a pastry tube.
~adj. **1.** Playing on a pipe. **2.** Making a high-pitched sound with little resonance, as does a pipe.
~adv. Used as an intensive: *piping hot.*

pip·i·strelle (pĭp′ĭ-strĕl′) *n.* Any small bat of the genus *Pipistrellus,* especially *P. pipistrellus.* [French, from Italian *pipistrello, vipistrello,* ultimately from Latin *vespertilio,* bat, from *vesper,* evening.]

pip·it (pĭp′ĭt) *n.* Any of various widely distributed songbirds of the genus *Anthus,* characteristically having brownish upper plumage and a light, streaked breast. The meadow pipit, *A. pratensis,* was formerly also called "titlark." [Imitative of its song.]

pip·kin (pĭp′kĭn) *n.* **1.** A small earthenware or metal cooking pot. **2.** A piggin *(see).* [16th century : origin obscure.]

pip·pin (pĭp′ĭn) *n.* **1.** Any of several varieties of eating apple. **2.** *Informal.* An admired person or thing. [Middle English *pepin, pipin,* seed, seedling apple, from Old French *pepin,* from Common Romance stem *pipp-* (suggestive of the small size of the seed).]

pip·sis·se·wa (pĭp-sĭs′ə-wô′) *n.* Any of several North American evergreen plants of the genus *Chimaphila*; especially, *C. umbellata,* having white or pinkish flowers. [Cree *pipisisikweu,* "it breaks it (i.e., a gallstone) into small pieces," from its use as a diuretic.]

pip·squeak (pĭp′skwēk′) *n.* A contemptibly small or insignificant person. [Originally a name given to a small artillery shell used by the Germans in World War I : PIP (dot) + SQUEAK.]

pi·quant (pē′kənt, -känt′, pē-känt′) *adj.* **1.** Pleasantly pungent in taste or odor; spicy. **2. a.** Appealing; engaging: *the piquant faces of children.* **b.** Interesting yet having a disconcerting or troubling effect: *a piquant reversal of roles.* **3.** *Archaic.* Causing hurt pride or feelings; stinging: *a piquant answer.* [Old French, present participle of *piquer,* to pierce, prick, PIQUE.] **—pi·quan·cy** *n.* **—pi·quant·ly** *adv.*

pique (pēk) *n.* A feeling of resentment or vexation arising from wounded pride or vanity: *a fit of pique.*
~tr.v. **piqued, piquing, piques. 1.** To cause to feel resentment or vexation; injure the pride of: *piqued by her snub.* **2.** To provoke; arouse: *The portrait piqued my curiosity.* **3.** To pride (oneself). Used with *on* or *upon*: *piqued themselves on their style.* [Old French, "a pricking," from *piquer,* to prick, from Vulgar Latin *piccāre* (unattested), perhaps from Latin *pīcus,* magpie, woodpecker.]

pi·qué (pĭ-kā′, pē-) *n.* A tightly woven fabric with various raised patterns, produced especially by a double warp. [French, "quilting," from *piquer,* to backstitch (as in quilting), to prick, PIQUE.]

pi·quet (pĭ-kā′) *n.* A card game for two people, played with a pack from which all cards below the seven (aces being high) are removed. [French, of obscure origin.]

pi·ra·cy (pī′rə-sē) *n., pl.* **-cies. 1.** Robbery committed at sea. **2.** Any illegal act, such as kidnapping, committed at sea or in the air. **3.** The unauthorized use or reproduction of copyright material.

Pi·rae·us (pī-rē′əs). Port of Athens, Greece, situated on the Saronic Gulf. It is the main industrial part of the city.

pi·ra·gua (pĭ-rä′gwə) *n.* **1.** A canoe made by hollowing out a tree

PRONUNCIATION KEY

ă, pat; ā, pay; âr, care;
ä, father, are; b, bib;
ch, church; d, deed; ĕ, pet;
ē, be; f, fife; g, gag; h, hat;
hw, which; ĭ, pit; ī, pie;
îr, pier; j, judge; k, kick;
l, lid, needle; m, mum;
n, no, sudden; ng, thing;
ŏ, pot; ō, toe; ô, paw, for;
oi, noise; ou, out; o͝o, book;
o͞o, boot; p, pop; r, roar;
s, sauce; sh, ship, dish;
t, tight; th, thin, path;
th, this, bathe; ŭ, cut; ûr, fur;
v, valve; w, with; y, yes;
z, zebra, size; zh, vision;
ə, about, item, edible,
gallop, circus, peaceful

IN FOREIGN WORDS:

à, *Fr.* ami; œ, *Fr.* feu, *Ger.* schön; ü, *Fr.* tu, *Ger.* über; KH, *Ger.* ich, *Scot.* loch; N, *Fr.* bon; y′, *Fr.* Compiègne

STRESS MARKS:

Primary stress: ′
in·cite′ (ĭn-sīt′)
Secondary stress: ′
in′sight′ (ĭn′sīt′)

trunk; a dugout. **2.** A flat-bottomed sailing boat with two masts. [Spanish, from Carib *piraguas.*]

Pi·ran·del·lo (pîr′ən-dĕl′ō), **Luigi** (1867–1936). Italian playwright, novelist, and short-story writer. His work examines the relativity of truth and the elusiveness of identity, as in *Six Characters in Search of an Author* (1922) and *Henry IV* (1922). Pirandello won the Nobel Prize for literature in 1934.

Pi·ra·ne·si (pîr′ə-nā′zē), **Giovanni Battista** (1720–78). Italian artist, known for his architectural etchings. His studies of Rome and its ruins contributed to the emergence of neoclassicism.

pi·ra·nha (pĭ-rän′yə, -răn′yə) *n.* Any of several tropical American freshwater fishes of the genus *Serrasalmus.* They are voraciously carnivorous and often attack and destroy living animals. [Portuguese, from Tupi, variant of *piraya,* scissors.]

pi·ra·ru·cu (pĭ-rär′ə-ko͞o′) *n.* A fish, the **arapaima** *(see).* [Portuguese *pirarucú,* from Tupi *pirá-rucú,* "red fish" : *pirá,* fish + *(u)rucú,* red.]

pi·rate (pī′rĭt) *n.* **1.** One who robs at sea or plunders the land near the sea without commission from a sovereign nation. **2.** A ship used for this purpose. **3.** One who operates without proper authorization, especially: **a.** One who makes use of or reproduces the work, especially the copyrighted material, of another, illicitly or without permission: *a video pirate.* **b.** One who broadcasts on an unauthorized radio wavelength.
~*v.* **pirated, -rating, -rates.** —*tr.* **1.** To attack and rob (a ship at sea). **2.** To seize (goods) by piracy. **3.** To make use of or reproduce (another's work) illicitly. —*intr.* To act as a pirate. [Middle English, from Latin *pīrāta,* from Greek *peiratēs,* "attacker," from *peiran,* to attempt, attack, from *peira,* an attempt.] —**pi·rat·ic** (pī-răt′ĭk), **pi·rat·i·cal** *adj.* —**pi·rat·i·cal·ly** *adv.*

pi·rog (pĭ-rōg′) *n., pl.* **-rogen** (-rō′gən) or **-roghi** (-rō′gē) or **-rogi.** A large pastry made of dough with various stuffings of meat, fish, rice, eggs, and vegetables. [Russian, probably from *pir,* feast.]

pi·rogue (pĭ-rōg′) *n.* A canoe made from a hollowed tree trunk; a piragua. [French, from Spanish *piragua,* PIRAGUA.]

pir·ou·ette (pîr′o͞o-ĕt′) *n.* In ballet, a full turn of the body on the tip of the toe or on the ball of the foot.
~*intr.v.* **pirouetted, -etting, -ettes.** To execute a pirouette. [French, from Old French *pirouet*†, a spinning top.]

pi·rozh·ki, pi·rosh·ki (pĭ-rôzh′kē) *pl.n.* Small pastries made especially with meat or cabbage fillings. [Russian, small pocket of pastry, diminutive of PIROG.]

Pi·sa (pē′zə). Capital of Pisa province, Tuscany, Italy, on the Arno River near the Ligurian Sea. It was a commercial and artistic center (12th and 13th centuries); its many historical monuments include its leaning Romanesque bell tower.

pis al·ler (pē′ ză-lā′) *n.* A course of action adopted for want of a better alternative. [French, "to go worse."]

Pi·sa·nel·lo (pē′zä-nĕl′lō), born Antonio Pisano, also called Vittore Pisano (*c.* 1395–*c.* 1455). Italian artist and medalist. In his own day he was celebrated for his medallions; he is especially admired today for his sketches of the natural world.

Pi·sa·no (pē-zä′nō), **Andrea,** born Andrea da Pontedera (*c.* 1290–*c.*1348). Italian sculptor and architect. He worked mainly in Florence, where he executed the bronze door of the Baptistery.

pis·ca·ry (pĭs′kə-rē) *n., pl.* **-ries. 1.** *Law.* The right to fish. Used chiefly in the phrase *common of piscary,* meaning the right to fish in waters belonging to another. **2.** A place in which to fish. [Middle English *piscairie,* from Medieval Latin *piscāria,* right to fish, from Latin, neuter plural of *piscārius,* of fish or fishing, from *piscis,* fish.]

pis·ca·to·ri·al (pĭs′kə-tôr′ē-əl, -tōr′ē-əl) *adj.* Also **pis·ca·to·ry** (pĭs′kə-tôr′ē, -tōr′ē). **1.** Of or pertaining to fish, fishermen, or fishing. **2.** Involved in or devoted to fishing. [Latin *piscātōrius,* of fish or fishing, from *piscātor,* fisherman, from *piscārī,* to fish, from *piscis,* fish.] —**pis·ca·to·ri·al·ly** *adv.*

Pi·sces (pī′sēz) *n.* **1.** A constellation in the equatorial region of the Northern Hemisphere near Aries and Pegasus. **2. a.** The 12th sign of the **zodiac** *(see).* Also called "Fish," "Fishes." **b.** One born under this sign. **3.** A taxonomic group that includes the cartilaginous and bony fishes. [Middle English, from Latin, from the plural of *piscis,* fish.] —**Pi·sce·an** (pī′sē-ən) *n. & adj.*

pisci- *prefix.* Indicates fish; for example, **pisciform.** [From Latin *piscis,* fish.]

pi·sci·cul·ture (pī′sĭ-kŭl′chər, pĭs′ĭ-) *n.* The breeding, hatching, and rearing of fish under controlled conditions. —**pi·sci·cul·tur·al** (pī′sĭ-kŭl′chər-əl, pĭs′ĭ-) *adj.* —**pi·sci·cul·tur·ist** *n.*

pi·sci·form (pī′sĭ-fôrm′, pĭs′ĭ-) *adj.* Having the shape of a fish. [PISCI- + -FORM.]

pi·sci·na (pĭ-sī′nə, -sē′nə, -shē′nə) *n., pl.* **-nae** (-nē′) or **-nas.** *Ecclesiastical.* A stone basin with a drain for carrying away the water used in ceremonial ablutions. Also called "sacrarium." [Medieval Latin, from Latin, fish tank, from *piscis,* fish.] —**pis·ci·nal** *adj.*

pi·scine (pī′sēn′, pĭs′īn′) *adj.* Of, pertaining to, or typical of a fish or fishes. [Medieval Latin *piscīnus,* from *piscis,* fish.]

Pi·scis Aus·tri·nus (pī′sĭs ô-strī′nəs) *n.* A constellation in the Southern Hemisphere near Aquarius and Grus. [New Latin, "(the) Southern Fish."]

pi·sciv·o·rous (pĭ-sĭv′ər-əs, pī-) *adj.* Feeding on fish; fish-eating. [PISCI- + -VOROUS.]

pish (pĭsh) *interj.* Used to express disdain.

pi·shogue (pĭ-shōg′) *n. Irish.* **1.** Black magic; sorcery; witchcraft. **2.** An evil spell; incantation. [Irish *piseog,* witchcraft.]

pi·si·form (pī′sə-fôrm′) *adj.* Suggestive of a pea in size or shape; pealike.
~*n. Anatomy.* A small bone at the junction of the ulna and the wrist. [Latin *pīsum,* PEA + -FORM.]

Pi·sis·tra·tus (pī-sĭs′trə-təs, pĭ-) (died 527 B.C.). Athenian tyrant (560–27). Although he attained and maintained his power by force, he was a popular leader who improved the water supply and judicial system and encouraged athletic contests and literary efforts, helping Athens develop into the pre-eminent ancient Greek city.

pis·mire (pĭs′mîr′, pĭz′-) *n.* An ant. [Middle English *pissemyre,* from *pisse,* PISS (from the urinous smell of an anthill) + obsolete *mire,* ant, probably from Scandinavian; akin to Danish *myre,* ant.]

pis·mo clam (pĭz′mō) *n.* An edible marine clam, *Tivela stultorum,* of the southern Pacific coast of North America. [After *Pismo* Beach, California.]

pi·so·lite (pī′sə-līt′) *n. Geology.* A concretionary limestone composed of globules more than 2 millimeters in diameter. [New Latin *pisolithus,* "pea stone" : Greek *pisos, pison,* PEA + -LITE.] —**pi·so·lit·ic** (pī′sə-lĭt′ĭk) *adj.*

Pis·sar·ro (pĭ-sär′ō), **Camille** (1830–1903). French impressionist painter. He took part in all eight impressionist exhibitions (1874–86), chiefly producing rural scenes.

pis·ta·chi·o (pĭ-stăsh′ē-ō′, -stä′shē-ō′) *n., pl.* **-os.** Also **pis·tache** (pĭ-stăsh′, -stäsh′). **1.** A tree, *Pistacia vera,* of the Mediterranean region and western Asia, bearing small hard-shelled nuts. **2.** The nut of this tree, having an edible, oily, green kernel. Also called "pistachio nut." **3.** A moderate to light yellowish green. [Italian *pistaccio,* from Latin *pistācium,* from Greek *pistakion,* pistachio nut, from *pistakē,* pistachio tree, from Persian *pistah*†.]

pis·ta·reen (pĭs′tə-rēn′) *n.* A small silver coin used in America and the West Indies during the 18th century. [Probably altered from Spanish *peseta,* PESETA.]

piste (pēst) *n.* **1.** A ski slope or run of densely packed snow. **2.** The area in which a fencing bout takes place. [French, racetrack.]

pis·til (pĭs′təl) *n. Botany.* The female reproductive organ of a flower, including the stigma, style, and ovary. [French *pistil,* from Latin *pistillum,* PESTLE.]

pis·til·late (pĭs′tə-lāt′, -lĭt) *adj. Botany.* **1.** Having a pistil or pistils. **2.** Bearing pistils but no stamens: *pistillate flowers.*

pis·tol (pĭs′təl) *n.* A firearm designed to be held and fired with one hand.
~*tr.v.* **pistoled, -toling, -tols.** Also *chiefly British* **-tolled, -tolling.** To shoot with a pistol. [French *pistole,* from German *Pistole,* from Czech *pištala,* "pipe," akin to Russian *pischal,* shepherd's pipe.]

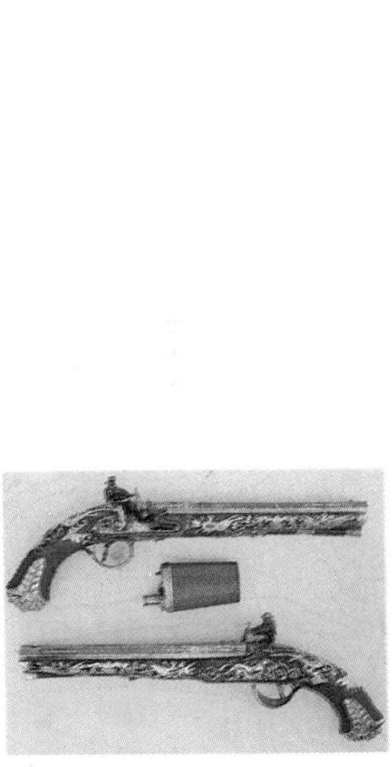

pistol *The handgun appeared in the first half of the 16th century. This pair of flintlock pistols was made in London in 1815 for the Prince Regent.*

pis·tole (pĭ-stōl′) *n.* An obsolete gold coin used in various European countries until the late 19th century. [French, variant of *pistolet,* perhaps "small pistol" (originally a name given in jest to Spanish coins, which were smaller than French coins, as a pistol is smaller than a harquebus), from *pistole,* PISTOL.]

pis·to·leer (pĭs′tə-lîr′) *n.* One armed with a pistol.

pistol grip *n.* **1.** The grip of a pistol, shaped to fit the hand. **2.** A similar grip sometimes used on a rifle or other firearm. **3.** A grip used on certain tools, such as a saw, shaped to fit the hand.

pis·tol-whip (pĭs′təl-hwĭp′) *tr.v.* **-whipped, -whipping, -whips.** To beat with a pistol barrel.

pis·ton (pĭs′tən) *n.* **1.** A solid cylinder or disk that fits into a larger cylinder and moves back and forth under fluid pressure, as in a reciprocating engine, or displaces or compresses fluids, as in pumps and compressors. **2.** *Music.* A valve mechanism in brass instruments for altering pitch. [French, from Old French, from Old Italian *pistone, pestone,* augmentative of *pestello,* PESTLE.]

piston ring *n.* An adjustable split metal ring that fits around a piston and closes the gap between the piston and cylinder wall.

piston rod *n.* A **connecting rod** *(see)* that is attached to a piston.

pit[1] (pĭt) *n.* **1.** A relatively deep hole in the ground. **2. a.** An area excavated for minerals. Often used in combination: *a chalkpit.* **b.** A coal mine. **c.** The shaft of a coal mine. **3.** A trap consisting of a concealed hole in the ground; a pitfall. **4.** Hell. Preceded by *the.* **5.** An enclosed space, often one dug in the ground, in which animals, such as dogs or gamecocks, are placed for fighting. Often used in combination: *a cockpit.* **6. a.** The lowest surface of a body, organ, or part: *the pit of the stomach.* **b.** A small indentation in the skin left by disease or injury; a pockmark. **7. a.** An **orchestra pit** *(see).* **b.** *Chiefly British.* The ground floor of a theater. **c.** Those who sit in this area. **8.** The section of an exchange where trading in a specific commodity is carried on. **9.** *Botany.* A thin-walled area in the wall of lignified plant cells. **10.** An area filled with material such as sand or sawdust to cushion the fall of athletes, as those taking part in the long jump or the pole vault. **11. a.** A sunken area in a garage floor from which mechanics may inspect or work on the underside of vehicles. **b.** *Often* **pits.** A place beside an auto racecourse where cars or motorcycles may be serviced during a race. **12.** *Football.* The middle areas of the defensive and offensive lines. **13. pits.** *Slang.* The worst imaginable: *That dinner was the pits.* —See Synonyms at **hole.**
~*v.* **pitted, pitting, pits.** —*tr.* **1.** To make cavities, depressions, or scars in: *"the mountain was pitted with deep craters"* (Muriel Spark). **2.** To place in contest against another; set in direct opposition: *"a man pitted in conflict against the sea"* (D.H. Lawrence). **3.** To put, bury, or store in a pit. —*intr.* **1.** To become marked with small pits. **2.** To retain an impression after being indented, as by a fingernail. Used of skin. [Middle English *pitt,* Old English *pytt,* from West Germanic *putti* (unattested), from Latin *puteus,* a pit, well.]

pit[2] *n.* The single, central kernel of certain fruits, such as a peach or cherry; a stone.

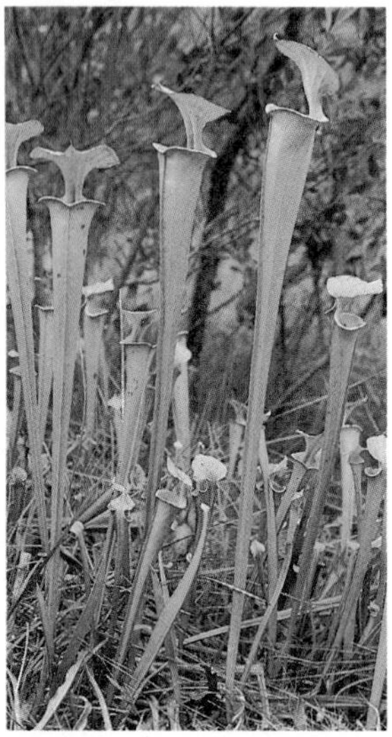

pitcher plant *A type of carnivorous plant that attracts insects by means of nectar secreted inside its lip. Once inside the vaselike pitcher, the insects slide down into a pool of enzymes, where they drown and are digested. This is a North American species,* Sarracenia flava.

~*tr.v.* **pitted, pitting, pits.** To extract pits from (fruit). [Perhaps from Dutch, from Middle Dutch *pit(te),* from West Germanic *pithan* (unattested), PITH.]

pi·ta[1] (pē′tə) *n.* Any of several plants of the genus *Agave* that yield a strong fiber. Also called "istle," "ixtle." [Spanish, from Quechua.]

pita[2] *n.* Round, flat bread that can be slit open to form a pocket. [Modern Greek, "pie, cake."]

pit·a·pat (pĭt′ə-păt′) *intr.v.* **-patted, -patting, -pats. 1.** To move with a series of quick, tapping steps. **2.** To make a repeated tapping sound.
~*n.* A series of quick steps, taps, or beats.
~*adv.* With a rapid tapping sound. [Imitative.]

Pit·cairn Islands (pĭt′kârn′). Small group of volcanic islands in the South Pacific. The largest, Pitcairn Island, was settled by nine fleeing mutineers of the *Bounty* (1790) together with some Tahitians. It is a British dependency. See map at **Pacific Ocean.**

pitch[1] (pĭch) *n.* **1.** Any of various thick, dark, sticky substances obtained from the distillation residue of coal tar, wood tar, or petroleum, and used for waterproofing, roofing, caulking, and paving. **2.** Any of various natural bitumens, such as mineral pitch or asphalt, having similar uses. **3.** A resin derived from the sap of various coniferous trees, such as the pines.
~*tr.v.* **pitched, pitching, pitches.** To smear or cover with or as if with pitch. [Middle English *pich,* Old English *pic,* from Latin *pix* (stem *pic-*).] **—pitch·i·ness** *n.* **—pitch·y** *adj.*

pitch[2] *v.* **pitched, pitching, pitches.** —*tr.* **1.** To throw, usually forcefully, in a specified direction. **2.** *Baseball.* **a.** To throw (the ball) from the mound to the batter. **b.** To play (a game, or part of one) in the position of pitcher. **3.** To put up or in position; establish: *pitch a tent.* **4.** To set firmly; implant; embed: *pitched the stakes in the ground.* **5. a.** To fix the level of: *pitch one's expectations high.* **b.** To set the character and course of: *He pitched his speech to the party line.* **6.** To set in a particular musical key. **7.** In card games, to lead (a card), thus establishing the trump suit. **8.** In golf, to strike (a ball) with great elevation and backspin so as to minimize movement on landing. —*intr.* **1.** To throw or toss something, such as a ball, horseshoe, or bale. **2.** In baseball, to play in the position of pitcher. **3.** To plunge; fall, especially forward: *He pitched over the railing.* **4.** To stumble around; lurch. **5.** To dip bow and stern alternately. Used of a ship or an aircraft. Compare **roll. 6.** To slope downward: *The hill pitched steeply.* **7.** To set up living quarters; encamp; settle. **—pitch in.** *Informal.* **1.** To set to work vigorously. **2.** To join forces with others; help; cooperate. **—pitch into.** *Informal.* To attack verbally or physically; assault. **—pitch on.** *Informal.* To choose: *They pitched on her solution as the best.*
~*n.* **1.** An act or instance of pitching. **2. a.** In baseball, a throw of the ball by the pitcher for action by the batter. **b.** The ball so thrown. **3.** *British.* **a.** The playing area in certain ball games, as football or hockey. **b.** In cricket, the rectangular area between the wickets, 22 yards by 10 feet. In this sense, also called "wicket." **4.** *Nautical.* The alternate dip and rise of a craft's bow and stern. **5. a.** Any steep downward slant. **b.** The degree of such a slant. **6.** *Architecture.* **a.** The angle of a roof. **b.** The highest point of a structure: *the pitch of an arch.* **7.** A point or stage of development or intensity, especially an extreme point: *reached a pitch of excitement; worked at a feverish pitch.* **8.** The subjective quality of a complex sound, dependent on frequency, loudness, and intensity and often measured as the frequency of a pure note of a given intensity judged equivalent to the complex sound by a normal ear. **9.** *Music.* **a.** The relative position of a tone in a scale as determined by its frequency. **b.** Any of various standards that establish a frequency for each musical tone, used in the tuning of instruments. See **concert pitch. 10. a.** The distance traveled by a screw in a single revolution. **b.** The distance between two corresponding points on adjacent screw threads or gear teeth. **c.** The distance between two corresponding points on a helix. **11.** The distance a propeller would travel in an ideal medium during one complete revolution, measured parallel to the shaft of the propeller. **12. a.** *Slang.* A set talk designed to persuade: *a slick sales pitch.* **b.** The place or stand of a vender, hawker, or the like. **13.** A card game, **seven-up** *(see).* **14.** In golf, a shot that is pitched. In this sense, also called "pitch shot." [Middle English *picchen,* to pierce, fix, set, throw, Old English *picc(e)an* (unattested), to prick, thrust, peculiar causative of *pician* (unattested), to PICK (prick).]

pitch accent *n. Linguistics.* **Tonic accent** *(see).*

pitch-black (pĭch′blăk′) *adj.* Extremely dark or black.

pitch·blende (pĭch′blĕnd′) *n.* The principal ore of uranium, a brownish-black mineral of uranium dioxide with small amounts of uranium decay products. It is the chief source of radium. [German *Pechblende* : *Pech,* pitch (from its black color), from Latin *pix* + BLENDE.]

pitch circle *n.* An imaginary circle passing through the teeth of a gearwheel, having a radius that would enable it to touch but not overlap a similar circle on a mating gear.

pitch-dark (pĭch′därk′) *adj.* Extremely dark.

pitched battle *n.* **1.** A fierce, intense battle fought in close contact, as by troops whose formation and tactics have been carefully planned. **2.** A fierce combat or dispute. [From the past participle of PITCH (to put in position, array for battle).]

pitched roof *n.* A roof with a downward slant.

pitch·er[1] (pĭch′ər) *n.* **1.** One that pitches. **2.** In baseball, the player who throws the ball from the mound to the batter. **3.** In golf, an iron club with a sharply inclined head.

pitcher[2] *n.* **1. a.** A large vessel for liquids made of clay, earthenware, or the like, and usually having two handles and a spout for pouring. **b.** Any large jug. **2.** *Botany.* A juglike part, such as the leaf of a pitcher plant. [Middle English *picher,* from Old French *pichier, bichier,* from Frankish *bikari* (unattested), BEAKER.]

Pitcher, Molly. See Mary **McCauley.**

pitcher plant *n.* Any of various insectivorous plants of the genera *Sarracenia, Heliamphora, Darlingtonia, Nepenthes,* and *Cephalotus,* having leaves modified to form juglike organs that trap insects.

pitch·fork (pĭch′fôrk′) *n.* A large fork with sharp, widely spaced prongs for lifting and pitching hay.
~*tr.v.* **pitchforked, -forking, -forks. 1.** To lift or toss with a pitchfork. **2.** To force or thrust into a place or position very suddenly. [Middle English *pychforke,* alteration of *pikforke* (through wrong association with *picchen,* to toss, PITCH) : probably PICK + FORK.]

pitch·man (pĭch′mən) *n., pl.* **-men** (-mĭn). *Informal.* A pedler or vender of small wares, especially one with a colorful sales talk.

pitch·out (pĭch′out′) *n.* **1.** *Baseball.* A pitch deliberately thrown high and away from the batter to make it easier for the catcher to throw out a base runner attempting to steal. **2.** *Football.* A lateral pass from the back receiving the snap from the center to another back behind the line of scrimmage.

pitch pine *n.* **1.** Any of various American pine trees yielding pitch or turpentine, such as *Pinus rigida* of eastern North America. **2.** The wood of any of these trees.

pitch pipe *n. Music.* A small pipe that when sounded gives the standard pitch for a piece of music or for tuning an instrument.

pitch·stone (pĭch′stōn′) *n.* Any of various glassy volcanic rocks distinguished by their dark luster and relatively high water content. [Translation of German *Pechstein.*]

pit·e·ous (pĭt′ē-əs) *adj.* **1.** Arousing pity; pathetic. **2.** *Archaic.* Pitying; compassionate. [Middle English *piteus, pitous,* from Old French *piteus,* from *pite,* PITY.] **—pit·e·ous·ly** *adv.* **—pit·e·ous·ness** *n.*

pit·fall (pĭt′fôl′) *n.* **1.** A trap made by digging a hole in the ground and concealing its opening. **2.** Any danger or difficulty that is not easily anticipated or avoided.

pith (pĭth) *n.* **1.** *Botany.* The soft, spongelike substance in the center of stems and branches of most vascular plants. Also called "medulla." **2.** The white fibrous tissue between the rind and the pulp in such fruits as oranges and grapefruits. **3.** The essential or central part of anything; the essence; the gist. **4.** Force; strength; vigor.
~*tr.v.* **pithed, pithing, piths. 1.** To remove the pith from (a plant stem). **2.** To sever or destroy the spinal cord of (a laboratory animal), usually by means of a needle inserted into the vertebral canal. **3.** To kill (animals) by cutting the spinal cord. [Middle English *pithe,* Old English *pitha,* from West Germanic *pithon*† (unattested). See also **pit** (stone of fruit).]

pith·e·can·thro·pus (pĭth′ĭ-kăn′thrə-pəs, -kăn-thrō′pəs) *n., pl.* **-pi** (-pī′). A member of the former genus *Pithecanthropus,* thought to indicate the existence of a primate between man and ape. It is now reclassified as *Homo erectus.* Also called "Java man." See **Peking man.** [New Latin : Greek *pithēkos*†, ape + -ANTHROPUS.] **—pith·e·can·thro·poid** (pĭth′ĭ-kăn′thrə-poid′) *adj.*

pith helmet *n.* A light sun hat made from dried pith; a topi.

pith·os (pĭth′ŏs′) *n., pl.* **piththoi** (pĭth′oi′). *Archaeology.* A large jar used for storing goods such as oil or grain. [Greek.]

pith·y (pĭth′ē) *adj.* **-ier, -iest. 1.** Consisting of or resembling pith. **2.** Precisely meaningful; cogent and terse. —See Synonyms at **concise. —pith·i·ly** *adv.* **—pith·i·ness** *n.*

pit·i·a·ble (pĭt′ē-ə-bəl) *adj.* **1.** Arousing or deserving of pity or compassion. **2.** Arousing disdainful pity; paltry; despicable. **—pit·i·a·ble·ness** *n.* **—pit·i·a·bly** *adv.*

pit·i·ful (pĭt′ĭ-fəl) *adj.* **1.** Arousing pity; pathetic. **2.** So inferior or insignificant as to be contemptible; mean; paltry. **3.** *Archaic.* Filled with pity or compassion. —See Synonyms at **pathetic. —pit·i·ful·ly** *adv.* **—pit·i·ful·ness** *n.*

pit·i·less (pĭt′ĭ-lĭs) *adj.* Having no pity; without mercy. —See Synonyms at **cruel. —pit·i·less·ly** *adv.* **—pit·i·less·ness** *n.*

pit·man (pĭt′mən) *n., pl.* **-men** (-mĭn) (for sense 1), **-mans** (-mənz) (for sense 2). **1.** A worker employed inside a pit in various industrial operations, as in a coal mine. **2.** A **connecting rod** *(see).*

Pit·man (pĭt′mən), **Sir Isaac** (1813–97). British inventor of the Pitman shorthand system (1837). It was based on the sound rather than the written appearance of words.

pi·ton (pē′tŏn′) *n.* A metal spike fitted at one end with an eye or ring through which to pass a rope, used in mountain climbing. [French, from Old French, "nail."]

Pi·tot-stat·ic tube (pē′tō-stăt′ĭk, pē-tō′-) *n.* A device consisting of a Pitot tube and a static tube combined to measure simultaneously total and static pressure in a fluid stream. It can be used in aircraft to determine relative wind speed.

Pi·tot tube (pē′tō, pē-tō′) *n.* A device used to measure the total pressure of a fluid stream. It is essentially a tube attached to a manometer at one end with its other end pointing upstream. [After Henri *Pitot* (1695–1771), French physicist.]

pit·saw (pĭt′sô′) *n.* A large saw for cutting logs, hand-operated by two men, one of whom stands on the log and the other in a pit underneath.

pit stop *n.* **1.** A stop at a pit for refueling or service during an auto race. **2.** *Informal.* **a.** A stop during a trip for rest, food, or fuel. **b.** A place where such a stop is made.

Pitt (pĭt), **William, 1st Earl of Chatham,** known as "Pitt the Elder"

(1708–78). British statesman and orator. He became an M.P. in 1735 and was associated with the Whig faction, opposing Robert Walpole. He was paymaster general (1746–55) and secretary of state (1756–57, 1757–61) for much of the Seven Years' War. In 1766–68 he formed an all-party ministry that failed to cope with the crisis in the American colonies, and he resigned through ill health.

Pitt, William, known as "Pitt the Younger" (1759–1806). British statesman and prime minister (1783–1801 and 1804–06). The son of William Pitt the Elder, he became an M.P. in 1781 and as Chancellor of the Exchequer (1782–83) began a lifelong rivalry with Charles James Fox. He became at 24 the youngest prime minister in British history. His India Act (1784) and Canada Act (1791) laid the basis of future colonial administration. In response to Irish unrest, he accomplished the Act of Union between Ireland and Britain (1800). The Napoleonic Wars dominated Pitt's second ministry. He negotiated an alliance with Russia and Austria that collapsed after Napoleon's victory at Austerlitz (1805).

pit·tance (pĭt′ns) *n.* **1.** A meager allowance of money: *She lives on a pittance.* **2.** A very small salary or remuneration. **3.** A small amount or portion of anything. [Middle English *pitaunce,* from Old French *pitance,* from Medieval Latin *pittantia,* from Vulgar Latin *pietantia* (unattested), pious donation, portion (of food) given to monastics, from *pietārī,* to be charitable, from Latin *pietās,* piety, from *pius,* pious.]

pit·ter-pat·ter (pĭt′ər-păt′ər) *n.* A rapid series of light, tapping sounds.
~*intr.v.* **-tered, -tering, -ters.** To move with or make a pitter-patter: *Rain pitter-pattered on the roof.*
~*adv.* With a series of light, tapping sounds. [Imitative.]

Pitts·burgh (pĭts′bûrg′). City in southwestern Pennsylvania. At the confluence of the Allegheny, Monongahela, and Ohio rivers, it is the country's largest inland river port. It produces coal and steel.

pi·tu·i·tar·y (pĭ-tōō′ĭ-tĕr′ē, pĭ-tyōō′-) *n., pl.* **-ies. 1.** *Anatomy.* The pituitary gland. **2.** *Medicine.* An extract from the anterior or posterior lobes of the pituitary gland, prepared for therapeutic use.
~*adj.* **1.** Of or pertaining to the pituitary gland. **2.** Of or secreting phlegm or mucus; mucous. [Latin *pītuītārius,* from *pītuīta,* phlegm.]

pituitary gland *n. Anatomy.* A small, oval endocrine gland attached to the base of the vertebrate brain, the secretions of which control the other endocrine glands and influence growth, metabolism, and maturation. Also called "hypophysis," "pituitary body."

pit·u·ri (pĭch′ə-rē) *n.* An Australian shrub, *Duboisia hopwoodii,* the leaves of which yield a narcotic. [From a native Australian name.]

pit viper *n.* Any of various venomous snakes of the family Crotalidae, such as the copperhead or rattlesnake, characterized by a small pit on each side of the head.

pit·y (pĭt′ē) *n., pl.* **-ies. 1. a.** Sorrow or grief aroused by the misfortune of another; compassion for another's suffering. **b.** Concern or regret for one considered inferior or less favored; condescending sympathy. **2.** A regrettable or disagreeable fact or necessity. —**for pity's sake.** Used to express angry frustration or an embittered plea: *Go away, for pity's sake!* —**more's the pity.** Regrettably; so much the worse: *I didn't see it, more's the pity.* —**take pity on.** To attempt to alleviate the misfortune of.
~*v.* **pitied, pitying, pities.** —*tr.* To feel pity for. —*intr.* To feel pity. [Middle English *pite,* from Old French *pit(i)e,* from Late Latin *pietās* (stem *pietāt-*), compassion, extended sense of Latin *pietās,* piety, from *pius,* pious.] —**pit·y·ing·ly** *adv.*

Synonyms: commiseration, compassion, condolence, sympathy.

pit·y·ri·a·sis (pĭt′ĭ-rī′ə-sĭs) *n.* Any of various skin diseases of humans and animals, characterized by epidermal shedding of flaky scales. [Greek *pituriasis,* from *pituron*†, grain husk, dandruff.]

più (pyōō) *adv. Music.* More. Used in directions to performers, as in *più forte,* more loudly. [Italian, from Latin *plūs,* more.]

Pi·us V (pī′əs), **Saint,** born Michele Ghislieri (1504–72). Pope (1566–72). He supported the Inquisition and encouraged the suppression of Protestantism in France and the Netherlands. In 1570 he excommunicated Elizabeth I of England.

Pius IX, born Giovanni Mastai-Ferretti (1792–1878). Italian pope (1846–78). In the longest papacy in Roman Catholic Church history, he led a shift from liberal to conservative theology, including the declaration of the Immaculate Conception (1854). During the First Vatican Council (1869–70) the doctrine of papal infallibility was defined.

Pius X, Saint, born Giuseppe Melchiorre Sarto (1835–1914). Italian pope (1903–14). Both politically and religiously conservative, he opposed Christian Democrats and the separation of church and state in France (1905) and repressed Modernism throughout his papacy.

Pius XI, born Ambrogio Ratti (1857–1939). Italian pope (1922–39). Dedicated to establishing world peace as the goal of Christianity, he directed the Church's attention toward contemporary issues. He and Mussolini signed the Lateran Treaty (1929) that established Vatican City as an independent state.

Pius XII, born Eugenio Pacelli (1876–1958). Italian pope (1939–58). As papal secretary of state he negotiated the concordat with Nazi Germany (1933). During World War II he believed the best way to achieve peace was to maintain formal relations with all the belligerents, but he was much criticized for not speaking out against the persecution of the Jews.

Piute. Variant of **Paiute.**

piv·ot (pĭv′ət) *n.* **1.** A short rod or pointed shaft on which a related part rotates or swings; a fulcrum. **2.** A person or thing that chiefly determines the course or effect of something; the essential component. **3.** A person who helps to keep the order and direction of wheeling troops.
~*v.* **pivoted, -oting, -ots.** —*tr.* To mount on, attach by, or furnish with a pivot or pivots. —*intr.* To turn on or as if on a pivot: *It all pivots on her decision.* [French, of obscure origin.]

piv·ot·al (pĭv′ə-təl) *adj.* **1.** Of, pertaining to, or being a pivot. **2.** Of vital importance; crucial. —**piv·ot·al·ly** *adv.*

pix¹ (pĭks) *pl.n. Informal.* Photographs or motion pictures. [Abbreviation of *pictures.*]

pix². Variant of **pyx.**

pix·el (pĭk′səl) *n.* An element of a computer graphics display on a video terminal. [PIX (photographs) + EL(EMENT).]

pix·ie, pix·y (pĭk′sē) *n., pl.* **-ies.** A fairylike or elfin creature. [17th century : origin obscure.]

pix·i·lat·ed (pĭk′sə-lā′tĭd) *adj.* **1.** Behaving as if led by pixies; bemused; whimsical; eccentric. **2.** *Slang.* Drunk. [From PIXIE.] —**pix·i·la·tion** *n.*

Pi·zar·ro (pĭ-zär′ō), **Francisco** (1475–1541). Spanish conquistador. In 1530 with some 180 men he crossed the Andes and in 1532 reached the heart of the Incan empire. He captured and killed its emperor, Atahualpa, at Cajamarca and entered Cuzco in 1533. Within two years he subdued the whole empire and founded Lima as his capital (1535).

pizz. *Music.* pizzicato.

piz·za (pēt′sə) *n.* A baked dish of Italian origin consisting of a shallow breadlike crust typically covered with a spiced mixture of tomatoes and cheese, and sometimes other ingredients, such as anchovies, meat, or olives. [Italian.]

piz·zazz, pe·zazz (pĭ-zăz′) *n. Slang.* Flamboyance; zest or flair. [Origin unknown.]

piz·ze·ri·a (pēt′sə-rē′ə) *n.* A place where pizzas are made, sold, and eaten. [Italian, from PIZZA.]

piz·zi·ca·to (pĭt′sĭ-kä′tō) *adj. Abbr.* **pizz.** *Music.* Played by plucking rather than bowing the strings of an instrument such as a violin.
~*n., pl.* **-tos** or **-ti** (-tē). *Abbr.* **pizz.** A pizzicato passage or note. [Italian, past participle of *pizzicare,* to pluck, from *pizzare,* to prick, from Old Italian *pizza,* a point, edge, from Gallo-Roman *pīnts-, pīts-* (unattested). See also **pinch.**] —**piz·zi·ca·to** *adv.*

piz·zle (pĭz′əl) *n.* The penis of an animal, especially that of a bull. [Earlier *peezel,* from Low German *pēsel,* diminutive of Middle Low German *pēse,* sinew, penis, perhaps an early borrowing of Latin *pēniculus,* diminutive of *pēnis,* PENIS.]

PK psychokinesis.

pk. 1. pack. **2.** park. **3.** peak. **4.** peck.

pkg. package.

pkt. packet.

pl. 1. place. **2.** plate. **3.** plural.

Pl. Place (used in street names).

PL/1 (pē′ĕl-wŭn′) *n.* A high-level symbolic language designed for programming computers. [Program Language Number *1.*]

plac·a·ble (plăk′ə-bəl, plā′kə-) *adj.* Easily calmed or pacified; tolerant. [Middle English, agreeable, from Old French, placable, from Latin *plācābilis,* from *plācāre,* to calm, appease.] —**plac·a·bil·i·ty** *n.* —**plac·a·bly** *adv.*

plac·ard (plăk′ärd′, -ərd) *n.* **1.** A printed or written announcement for display in a public place; poster: *demonstrators carrying placards with slogans.* **2.** A nameplate, as on the door of a house.
~*tr.v.* **placarded, -arding, -ards. 1.** To announce or advertise (a message or product) on a placard. **2.** To post placards on or in. **3.** To display as a placard. [Middle English *placquart,* plate, breastplate, from Old French *plaquart,* from *plaquier,* to plaster, from Middle Dutch *placken*†, to patch, paste. See also **plaque.**] —**plac·ard·er** *n.*

pla·cate (plā′kāt′, plăk′āt′) *tr.v.* **-cated, -cating, -cates.** To allay the anger of, especially by making concessions; appease. —See Synonyms at **pacify.** [Latin *plācāre,* to calm, appease.] —**pla·cat·er** *n.* —**pla·ca·tion** (plā-kā′shən) *n.* —**pla·ca·to·ry** (plā′kə-tôr′ē, -tōr′ē, plăk′ə-), **pla·ca·tive** (plā′kā′tĭv) *adj.*

place (plās) *n.* **1.** A portion of space; an area with definite or indefinite boundaries. **2.** Such an area, as a building, set aside for a specified activity: *a place of worship.* **3.** A definite location, especially: **a.** A house, apartment, or other residence: *My place or yours?* **b.** A business establishment or office. **c.** A particular town or city. **4.** *Usually* **Place.** *Abbr.* **Pl.** A public square or street with houses in a town. **5. a.** A space in which one person, as a passenger or spectator, can sit or stand. **b.** A setting for one person at a table. **6.** A position regarded as belonging to someone or something else; stead: *I was chosen in his place.* **7.** A particular point that one has reached; especially, a point up to which one has read in a book: *I lost my place.* **8.** A position figuratively occupied by a thing, group, or activity in a larger complex; an existing function; a role: *the place of labor unions in society.* **9.** Proper or customary location or order: *Everything is in place.* **10. a.** A social status entailing a certain mode of behavior: *He overstepped his place.* **b.** An appropriate right or duty: *It's not my place to criticize.* **c.** A location or situation requiring a particular mode of behavior: *This is not the place for flippancy.* **11. a.** A position of eminence: *a place in history.* **b.** A position as a member of a selective body, as a post in a business firm or membership in a team. **12. a.** A relative position in a series, especially in a series classified according to achievement: *was in third place.* **b.** *British.* A position as one of the first three (or, sometimes, four) horses to finish a race, and especially as either the

second or third horse. **c.** A specified stage in a list of points to be made, as in an argument: *In the first place, they have no right to protest.* **13.** *Abbr.* **pl.** The position of a number in relation to other numbers in a series. See **decimal place.** **—go places.** *Informal.* To enjoy increasing success. **—in place of.** Instead of. **—out of place. 1.** Inappropriate. **2.** In the wrong place. **—put someone in his place.** To cause (someone who is arrogant or conceited) to be humbled. **—take one's place.** To take up a usual or specified position: *took his place at the front.* **—take place.** To occur; happen.
~*v.* **placed, placing, places.** *—tr.* **1.** To put in a specified position; set. **2.** To put in a specified relation or order: *Place the words in alphabetical order.* **3.** To arrange for (a person or thing) to receive appropriate treatment, especially: **a.** To find accommodation or employment for. **b.** To invest (money). **c.** To lay (an order or bet, for example). **d.** To find a publisher for (a book). **e.** To have (an advertisement, for example) displayed or published. **4.** To appoint to a post: *placed in a key position.* **5.** To rank in an order or sequence: *I'd place him second best.* **6.** To put, lay, or fix: *placed emphasis on her appearance.* **7.** To recollect clearly the circumstances or context of: *I can't place him now.* **8.** To adjust (one's speaking or singing voice) for the best possible effects. **9.** To declare the position of (a horse, runner, or other contestant), especially among the first three finishers in a race. *—intr.* To arrive among the first three finishers in a race; especially, to finish in second place. [Middle English, space, locality, from Old French, from Latin *platea,* "broad street," space, from Greek *plateia (hodos),* "broad (way)," from feminine of *platus,* broad.]

pla·ce·bo (plä-chā'bō *for sense 1;* plə-sē'bō *for senses 2 and 3*) *n., pl.* **-bos** or **-boes. 1.** *Roman Catholic Church.* The service or office of vespers for the dead. **2. a.** *Medicine.* A substance containing no active drug given to a patient who believes it to be an active drug in order to humor him or to effect a cure *(the placebo effect)* by changing his psychological attitude. **b.** An inactive substance used as a control in an experiment. **3.** Anything lacking intrinsic remedial value, done or given to humor another. [Medieval Latin, from the first word of the first antiphon of the service, *Placēbo (Dominō in rēgiōne vivōrum),* "I shall please (the Lord in the land of the living)," from *placēre,* to please.]

place card *n.* A card that bears a name indicating where a person must sit at a dinner table.

place kick *n. Football.* A kick, as for a field goal, for which the ball is propped up in a fixed position on the ground. **—place-kick** (plās'kĭk') *v.* **—place-kick·er** *n.*

place mat *n.* A protective table mat, often decorative, on which dishes and plates are placed at mealtimes.

place·ment (plās'mənt) *n.* **1. a.** The act of placing or arranging. **b.** The state of being placed or arranged. **2.** The act or business of finding jobs, lodgings, or other positions for applicants. **3.** In racket games such as tennis or squash, the act or practice of accurately placing the ball in parts of the court. **4.** *Football.* **a.** The setting of the ball in position for a place kick. **b.** A place kick.

pla·cen·ta (plə-sĕn'tə) *n., pl.* **-tas** or **-tae** (-tē). **1.** *Anatomy.* A vascular, membranous organ that develops in female mammals during pregnancy and provides the fetus with nutrients and removes waste products via the umbilical cord. Following birth, the placenta is expelled as part of the afterbirth. **2.** *Botany.* **a.** The part of the ovary to which the ovules are attached. **b.** In nonflowering plants, the tissue that bears the spore cases. [Latin, flat cake, from Greek *plakoenta,* accusative of *plakoeis, plakous,* flat, flat cake, from *plax* (stem *plak-*), flat surface.]

pla·cen·tal (plə-sĕn'təl) *adj.* Also **pla·cen·tate** (-sĕn'tāt'). Having a placenta. Said especially of animals.

plac·en·ta·tion (plăs'ən-tā'shən) *n.* **1.** *Zoology.* **a.** The formation of a placenta. **b.** The type or structure of a placenta. **2.** *Botany.* The way in which the placenta is arranged in or attached to the ovary.

plac·er (plăs'ər) *n.* **1.** A glacial or alluvial deposit of sand or gravel containing deposits of heavy minerals such as gold, platinum, and diamonds. **2.** A place where such a deposit is washed to extract its mineral content. [American Spanish, "shoal," from *plaza,* place, from Latin *platea,* "broad road," PLACE.]

placer mining *n.* The obtaining of minerals from placers by washing or dredging. **—placer miner** *n.*

place setting *n.* A table service for one person.

plac·id (plăs'ĭd) *adj.* Having a calm appearance or temperament; not easily excited or upset. —See Synonyms at **calm.** [French, from Latin *placidus,* pleasing, gentle, from *placēre,* to please.] **—pla·cid·i·ty** (plə-sĭd'ĭ-tē), **plac·id·ness** *n.* **—plac·id·ly** *adv.*

plack·et (plăk'ĭt) *n.* A slit in a dress, blouse, or skirt to make the garment easy to put on or take off or to give access to a pocket. [Earlier *plackerd,* dress, petticoat, originally, "breastplate," variant of PLACARD.]

plac·oid (plăk'oid') *adj. Zoology.* Platelike, as the hard, toothlike scales of sharks, skates, and rays are. [Greek *plax* (stem *plak-*), flat surface, plate + -OID.]

pla·fond (plä-fōɴ') *n.* A ceiling, especially one that is decorated, as with paintings. [French, from *plat,* flat + *fond,* bottom.]

pla·gal (plā'gəl) *adj. Music.* **1.** Designating a medieval mode having a range from the fourth below to the fifth above its final tone. **2.** Designating a cadence with the subdominant chord immediately preceding the tonic chord. Compare **authentic.** [Medieval Latin *plagālis,* from *plaga,* plagal mode, from *plagius,* plagal, from Medieval Greek *plagios (ēkhos),* plagal (mode), from Greek *plagios,* placed sideways, oblique, from *plagos,* side.]

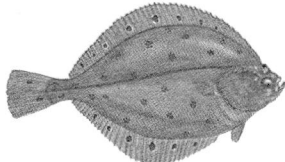

plaice *An edible flatfish that feeds on flat-bottomed, sandy seabeds in the North Atlantic. Newly hatched fish have an eye on each side of the head. As they grow, the left eye moves up and over the head, and the fish's right side becomes its back. This is the European species,* Pleuronectes platessa.

plage (pläzh) *n. Astronomy.* See **flocculus** (sense 3). [French, from Italian *piaggia,* beach, slope, from Greek *plagios,* oblique, from *plagos,* side.]

pla·gia·rism (plā'jə-rĭz'əm) *n.* **1.** The act of plagiarizing. **2.** That which is plagiarized. [From PLAGIARY.] **—pla·gia·rist** *n.* **—pla·gia·ris·tic** (plā'jə-rĭs'tĭk) *adj.*

pla·gia·rize (plā'jə-rīz') *v.* **-rized, -rizing, -rizes.** *—tr.* **1.** To steal and use (the ideas or writings of another) as one's own. **2.** To appropriate passages or ideas from (another) to use as one's own. *—intr.* To take and use as one's own the writings or ideas of another. [From PLAGIARY.] **—pla·gia·riz·er** *n.*

pla·gia·ry (plā'jə-rē) *n., pl.* **-ries. 1.** Plagiarism. **2.** *Archaic.* A plagiarist. [Originally "kidnapper," from Latin *plagiārius,* from *plagium,* kidnapping, from *plaga,* net.]

plagio– *prefix.* Indicates a slanting or inclining; for example, **plagiotropism.** [Greek *plagios,* placed sideways, oblique, from *plagos,* side.]

pla·gi·o·clase (plā'jē-ə-klās', -klāz', plăj'ē-) *n.* Any of a common rock-forming series of triclinic feldspars consisting of mixtures of sodium and calcium aluminum silicates. Also called "plagioclase feldspar." [German *Plagioklas* : PLAGIO- + -CLASE.] **—pla·gi·o·clas·tic** (plā'jē-ə-klăs'tĭk, plăj'ē-) *adj.*

pla·gi·o·cli·max (plā'jē-ō-klī'măks', plăj'ē-) *n. Ecology.* A stable plant community that because of environmental factors such as grazing pressure cannot develop into a natural climax.

pla·gi·ot·ro·pism (plā'jē-ŏt'rə-pĭz'əm, plăj'ē-) *n. Biology.* A tendency, especially in lateral roots, to grow at an oblique angle to the direction of the stimulus. [PLAGIO- + -TROPISM.] **—pla·gi·o·trop·ic** (plā'jē-ə-trŏp'ĭk, plăj'ē-) *adj.* **—pla·gi·o·trop·i·cal·ly** *adv.*

plague (plāg) *n.* **1.** A highly infectious, usually fatal epidemic disease, especially bubonic plague. **2.** A sudden influx, as of destructive or harmful insects: *a plague of locusts.* **3.** *Informal.* Any cause for annoyance; a nuisance: *the plague of their chatter.* **4.** A disaster, affliction, or calamity, especially one seen as a punishment. **—a plague on.** *Archaic.* Used as a curse: *A plague on your good deeds!*
~*tr.v.* **plagued, plaguing, plagues. 1.** To harass, pester, or annoy: *plagued their parents with silly questions.* **2.** To afflict with or as if with plague or any other evil. —See Synonyms at **harass.** [Middle English, a blow, calamity, malignant disease, from Old French, from Late Latin *plāga,* from Latin, a stroke, wound, probably from Greek *plaga, plēgē,* stroke.] **—plagu·er** *n.*

pla·guy, pla·guey (plā'gē) *adj.* Irritating; bothersome. **—pla·gui·ly** (plā'gə-lē) *adv.*

plaice (plās) *n., pl.* **plaices** or collectively **plaice. 1.** An edible marine flatfish, *Pleuronectes platessa,* of western European waters. **2.** Any related flatfish, such as *Hippoglossoides platessoides* of North American Atlantic waters. [Middle English, from Old French *plaïs, plaïz,* from Late Latin *platessa,* "flatfish."]

plaid (plăd) *n.* **1.** A long, rectangular piece of woolen cloth of a tartan or checked pattern worn over one shoulder as part of Scottish Highland costume. **2.** Cloth with a tartan or checked pattern.
~*adj.* **1.** Made of plaid. **2.** Having a tartan or checked pattern. [Scottish Gaelic *plaide*†.]

plain (plān) *adj.* **plainer, plainest. 1.** Free from obstructions; open to view; clear: *plain sight.* **2.** *Archaic.* Having no visible elevation or depression; flat; level. **3.** Easily understood; clearly evident; obvious to the mind: *make one's intention plain.* **4.** Uncomplicated; easily done; simple: *plain needlework.* **5.** Straightforward; frank; candid: *plain speaking.* **6. a.** Not mixed with other substances; pure: *plain water.* **b.** Containing no raising agents: *plain flour.* **7. a.** Common in rank or station; ordinary: *a plain man.* **b.** Without affectation or pretension. **8.** Not ruled; without lines. Said of paper. **9.** Not rich or elaborate: *plain food.* **10.** With little ornamentation or decoration: *a plain dress.* **11.** Not dyed, twilled, or patterned: *a plain fabric.* **12.** Not beautiful or handsome: *a plain face.* **13.** Sheer; utter; unqualified: *plain stupidity.* **14.** Not in code: *a plain message.* **15.** Designating the basic, simple knitting stitch. —See Synonyms at **evident.**
~*n.* **1.** An extensive, level, treeless land region, such as a valley floor or a plateau summit. **2.** In knitting, plain stitch.
~*adv.* In a clear or obvious manner: *plain stubborn.* [Middle English, from Old French, from Latin *plānus,* flat, clear.] **—plain·ly** *adv.* **—plain·ness** *n.*

plain·chant (plān'chănt', -chänt') *n.* See **plainsong** (sense 2). [French, from Medieval Latin *cantus plānus,* PLAINSONG.]

plain·clothes (plān'klōz') *adj.* Not wearing a uniform, especially a police uniform, while on duty.

plain·clothes·man (plān'klōz'mən) *n., pl.* **-men** (-mĭn). Also **plain·clothes man.** A plainclothes member of a police force, especially a detective.

plain-laid (plān'lād') *adj.* Designating a rope made of three strands laid together with a right-hand twist.

plain sailing *n.* **1.** Easy sailing over a direct course. **2.** Easy, unimpeded progress. [Alteration of *plane sailing* (navigation using PLANE angles).]

Plains Indian *n.* A member of any of the North American Indian peoples that once inhabited the Great Plains of North America.

plains·man (plānz'mən) *n., pl.* **-men** (-mĭn). An inhabitant or settler of a plains region, especially the prairie regions of the United States.

Plains of Abraham. See **Abraham, Plains of.**

plain·song (plān'sông', -sŏng') *n. Music.* **1. Gregorian chant** *(see).* **2.** Any medieval liturgical music without strict meter and traditionally sung without accompaniment. Also called "plainchant." [Translation of Medieval Latin *cantus plānus.*]

plain·spo·ken (plān'spō'kən) *adj.* Blunt; frank.

plain stitch *n.* In knitting, the basic, simple stitch, producing either a flat surface, as in stocking stitch, or a ribbed surface, as in garter stitch. Compare **purl stitch.**

plaint (plānt) *n.* **1. a.** A complaint. **b.** An utterance of grief or sorrow; lamentation. **2.** *Law.* A statement of grievance submitted to a court as a request for redress. [Middle English *pleinte, plaint,* from Old French *plainte,* from Latin *planctus,* past participle of *plangere,* to strike (one's breast), lament.]

plain·tiff (plān'tĭf) *n. Law.* The party that institutes a suit in a court. Compare **defendant.** [Middle English *plaintif,* from Old French, from adjective *plaintif,* PLAINTIVE.]

plain·tive (plān'tĭv) *adj.* Expressing restrained sorrow; mournful; melancholy: *the plaintive sound of wind in the trees.* [Middle English *pleintif,* from Old French *plaintif,* from *plainte,* lamentation, PLAINT.] —**plain·tive·ly** *adv.* —**plain·tive·ness** *n.*

plain weave *n.* A weave in which the filling threads and the warp threads interlace alternately, forming a checked pattern. Also called "taffeta weave."

plait (plāt, plăt) *n.* **1.** A length of interwoven strands, especially of hair. **2.** A pleat.

~*tr.v.* **plaited, plaiting, plaits. 1.** To interweave (hair, grass, thread, or the like) into a plait. **2.** To make by plaiting. [Middle English, fold, crease, from Old French *pleit,* from Vulgar Latin *plic(i)tus* (unattested), from Latin *plicitus,* variant past participle of *plicāre,* to fold.] —**plait·er** *n.*

plan (plăn) *n.* **1.** Any detailed scheme, program, or method worked out beforehand for the accomplishment of an object: *a plan of attack.* **2.** A proposed or tentative project or course of action: *Do you have any plans for the evening?* **3.** A systematic arrangement of details; an outline or sketch: *the plan of a story.* **4.** A drawing or diagram made to scale showing the structure or arrangement of something: *a town plan; the plan of a building.* **5.** In rendering perspective, one of several imaginary planes perpendicular to the line of vision between the viewer and the object being depicted.

~*v.* **planned, planning, plans.** —*tr.* **1.** To formulate a scheme or program for the accomplishment or attainment of: *plan a campaign.* **2.** To have as a specified aim or purpose; intend: *They plan to go to the beach.* **3.** To draw or make a graphic representation of. —*intr.* To make a plan. Often used with *on* or *for.* [French, as "level ground," "plane," from Latin *plānum,* from *plānus,* flat; as "ground plan," "map," altered from *plant* (in sense influenced by Italian *pianta,* ground plan or design), from *planter,* to plant, from Latin *plantāre.* See **plant.**]

pla·nar (plā'nər) *adj.* **1.** Of, pertaining to, or situated in a plane. **2.** Flat: *a planar surface.* **3.** Having a two-dimensional characteristic. [Late Latin *plānāris,* from Latin *plānum,* level surface, from *plānus,* flat, PLAIN.] —**pla·nar·i·ty** (plə-năr'ə-tē) *n.*

pla·nar·i·an (plə-nâr'ē-ən) *n.* Any of various flatworms of the order Tricladida, having broad, ciliated bodies and a three-branched digestive cavity. [New Latin *Planaria* (genus), from Latin *plānus,* flat.]

planar process *n.* A method of manufacturing semiconductor devices in which impurities are diffused through holes etched into an oxide layer formed on a silicon substrate, producing a diffused junction.

pla·na·tion (plā-nā'shən) *n.* Lateral erosion, as of a valley, by a running stream. [From PLANE (level surface).]

planch·et (plăn'chĭt) *n.* **1.** A flat disk of metal ready for stamping as a coin; a coin blank. **2.** A small disk of metal on which a radioactive substance is deposited for measurement of its activity. [Diminutive of *planch,* board, Middle English *plaunche,* from Old French *planche,* from Latin *planca.* See **plank.**]

plan·chette (plăn-shĕt') *n.* A small triangular board with a pointer supported by two casters and a vertical pencil that is said to spell out messages from the spirit world when the operator's fingers are placed lightly upon it. [French, diminutive of Old French *planche,* board. See **planchet.**]

Planck (plăngk), **Max Karl Ernst Ludwig** (1858–1947). German physicist. While a professor at the University of Berlin (1889–1928) he originated the quantum theory (1900); he was awarded the Nobel Prize (1918), and his theory was applied by Einstein, Bohr, and others to transform 20th-century physics.

Planck's constant *n.* Symbol **h** *Physics.* The constant of proportionality relating the quantum of energy that can be possessed by radiation to the frequency of that radiation. Its value is approximately 6.6262×10^{-34} joule seconds. [After Max PLANCK.]

Planck's formula *n.* The formula by which the distribution of energy in **blackbody radiation** *(see)* over a narrow frequency range is expressed as a function of frequency and temperature. [After Max PLANCK.]

plane¹ (plān) *n.* **1.** *Geometry.* A surface containing all the straight lines connecting any two points on it. **2.** Any flat or level surface. **3.** A level of development, existence, or achievement. **4.** An airplane or hydroplane. **5.** *Aeronautics.* A supporting surface of an aircraft; an airfoil or wing.

~*adj.* **1.** *Geometry.* Designating a figure lying in a plane: *a plane curve.* **2.** Flat. —See Synonyms at **level.** [Latin *plānum,* a flat surface, from *plānus,* flat.] —**plane·ness** *n.*

plane² *n.* **1.** A carpenter's tool with an adjustable blade for smooth-

ing and leveling wood. **2.** A flat, trowel-shaped tool for smoothing the surface of clay, sand, or plaster in a mold.

~*v.* **planed, planing, planes.** —*tr.* **1.** To smooth or finish with or as if with a plane. **2.** To remove with a plane. Used with *off* or *away.* —*intr.* **1.** To work with a plane. **2.** To act as a plane. [Middle English, from French *plane, plaine,* from Late Latin *plāna,* from *plānāre,* to plane, from *plānus,* level.]

plane³ *intr.v.* **planed, planing, planes. 1.** To rise partly out of the water, as a hydroplane does at high speeds. **2.** To soar or glide. **3.** To travel by airplane. [French *planer,* to glide, from *plan,* a level surface, from Latin *plānum,* from *plānus,* flat.]

plane⁴ *n.* The **plane tree** *(see).*

plane angle *n.* An angle formed by two straight lines in a plane.

plane geometry *n.* The geometry of planar figures.

plane polarization *n.* A form of polarization of electromagnetic radiation in which the waves are restricted to vibration in one plane.

plan·er (plā'nər) *n.* **1.** One that planes. **2.** A machine tool for smoothing and planing the surfaces of wood or metal. **3.** *Printing.* A smooth block of wood used to level a form of type.

plane sailing *n.* **1.** The calculation of the position of a ship on the basis that it is sailing on a plane and not the curved surface of the earth. **2.** See **plain sailing.**

plan·et (plăn'ĭt) *n.* **1.** A nonluminous celestial body illuminated by light from a star, such as the sun, around which it revolves. In the **solar system** *(see)* there are nine known major planets: Mercury, Venus, Earth, Mars, Jupiter, Saturn, Uranus, Neptune, and Pluto. **2.** In ancient astronomy, any of the seven celestial bodies (Mercury, Venus, the moon, the sun, Mars, Jupiter, and Saturn) visible to the naked eye and thought to revolve about a fixed Earth. **3.** *Astrology.* Any of the seven revolving celestial bodies that in conjunction with the stars are supposed to influence human affairs and personalities. [Middle English *planete,* from Old French, from Late Latin *planēta,* from Greek *planēs, planētēs,* plural of *planētos,* wandering planet, from *planasthai,* to wander.] See feature, next page.

plane table *n.* A portable surveying instrument consisting essentially of a drawing board and a ruler mounted on a tripod and used to sight and map topographical details.

plan·e·tar·i·um (plăn'ə-târ'ē-əm) *n., pl.* **-iums** or **-ia** (-ē-ə). **1.** An apparatus or model representing the solar system. **2.** A device for projecting images of celestial bodies in their courses on the inner surface of a hemispherical dome. **3.** A building or room containing such a device, with seats for an audience. [PLANET + -ARIUM.]

plan·e·tar·y (plăn'ə-tĕr'ē) *adj.* **1.** Of, pertaining to, or resembling the physical or orbital characteristics of a planet or the planets. **2.** Terrestrial; mundane; earthly. **3.** Wandering; erratic: *planetary life.* **4.** Designating or pertaining to a **gear train** *(see)* consisting of a central gear with an internal ring gear and one or more pinions.

planetary nebula *n.* Any of several objects in the Galaxy consisting of a hot, blue-white central star surrounded by an envelope of expanding gas. See **Ring Nebula.**

plan·e·tes·i·mal (plăn'ə-tĕs'ə-məl, -tĕz'ə-məl) *n. Astronomy.* **1.** Any of the innumerable small bodies consisting of interstellar dust thought to have been present in the presolar medium. **2.** In the planetesimal hypothesis, any of the innumerable small bodies thought to have been formed from gaseous solar material. [PLANET + (INFINIT)ESIMAL.] —**plan·e·tes·i·mal** *adj.*

planetesimal hypothesis *n.* The hypothesis put forward by T.C. Chamberlain and F.R. Moulton in 1906 to account for the formation of the planets in the solar system. It states that gas drawn off from the young sun and another star as they passed close to each other condensed into planetesimals, which then by gravitational aggregation and accretion formed the planets. Compare **nebular hypothesis, presolar nebular hypothesis.**

plan·e·toid (plăn'ə-toid') *n. Astronomy.* An **asteroid** *(see).* —**plan·e·toid·al** (plăn'ə-toid'l) *adj.*

plane tree *n.* Any of several trees of the genus *Platanus,* having ball-shaped fruit clusters, large leaves with pointed lobes, and, usually, outer bark that flakes off in patches. Also called "plane," "platan." See **London plane.** [*Plane,* from Middle English, from Old French, from Latin *platanus,* from Greek *platanos,* from *platus,* broad (from its broad leaves).]

planet wheel *n.* Any of the small gear wheels in an **epicyclic train** *(see).*

plan·gent (plăn'jənt) *adj.* **1.** Striking with a reverberating sound, as waves do against the shore. **2. a.** Loud and resounding, as is the sound of bells. **b.** Expressing sadness; plaintive: *plangent strains.* [Latin *plangens* (stem *plangent-*), present participle of *plangere,* to strike (one's breast).] —**plan·gen·cy** *n.* —**plan·gent·ly** *adv.*

plani-. Variant of **plano-.**

pla·nim·e·ter (plə-nĭm'ə-tər, plā-) *n.* An instrument that measures the area of a plane figure as a mechanically coupled pointer traverses the figure's perimeter. [French *planimètre* : PLANI- + -METER.] —**pla·ni·met·ric** (plā'nə-mĕt'rĭk), **pla·ni·met·ri·cal** *adj.* —**pla·ni·met·ri·cal·ly** *adv.* —**pla·nim·e·try** *n.*

plan·ish (plăn'ĭsh) *tr.v.* **-ished, -ishing, -ishes.** To flatten, smooth, toughen, or polish (metal) by rolling or hammering. [French *planir* (present stem *planiss-*), to make level, from *plan,* level, from Latin *plānus.*] —**plan·ish·er** *n.*

pla·ni·sphere (plā'nə-sfîr') *n.* **1.** A representation of a sphere or part of a sphere on a plane surface. **2.** *Astronomy.* A polar projection of the celestial sphere on a chart equipped with an adjustable overlay to show the stars visible at a particular time and place.

THE ROTATING SATELLITES OF OUR OWN SOLAR SYSTEM
Nine major bodies constantly circle the sun

A planet is a nonluminous body of matter in space, revolving around a luminous star from which it gets its light. There are nine known major planets circling the sun in our Solar System and they are listed below. It is not known precisely how the planets were created, but one widely accepted theory is that they were formed about 4.6 billion years ago from a cloud of swirling gas and dust. Matter collided and contracted under its own gravitational force and coalesced into the planets with, at their center, the largest body of all, the sun, which contains 99.9 percent of all the matter in the Solar System.

PLANET	Distance from Sun Kilometers (miles)	Diameter Kilometers (miles)	Length of day	Length of year	Mass relative to Earth	Escape velocity Kilometers/sec (miles/sec)	Mean surface temperature	Number of known satellites (moons)
MERCURY	57,900,000 (36,000,000)	4,880 (3,032)	58 days 15 hr 36 min	87.97 days	0.055	4.25 (2.64)	+350°C	0
VENUS	108,200,000 (67,200,000)	12,104 (7,521)	243 days	224.7 days	0.815	10.36 (6.43)	+475°C	0
EARTH	149,600,000 (92,960,000)	12,756 (7,926)	23 hr 56 min 4 sec	365.26 days	1.0	11.18 (6.95)	+22°C	1
MARS	227,900,000 (141,600,000)	6,787 (4,217)	24 hr 37 min 23 sec	686.98 days	0.108	5.02 (3.12)	-23°C	2
JUPITER	778,300,000 (483,600,000)	142,800 (88,700)	9 hr 50 min 30 sec	4,332.59 days	317.943	59.64 (37.06)	-123°C	16
SATURN	1,427,000,000 (886,700,000)	120,000 (74,500)	10 hr 14 mins	10,759.22 days	95.195	35.41 (22.0)	-180°C	21+
URANUS	2,869,600,000 (1,783,100,000)	51,800 (32,200)	16 hr (?)	30,685.4 days	14.605	21.41 (13.3)	-218°C	5
NEPTUNE	4,496,600,000 (2,794,100,000)	49,500 (30,800)	18 hr (?)	60,195 days	17.232	23.52 (14.61)	-228°C	2
PLUTO	5,900,000,000 (3,666,000,000)	2,320 (1,440)	6 days 9 hr 18 min	90,475 days	0.002	1.0 (0.6)	-230°C (?)	1

DETAILS OF THE PLANETS *The distance from the sun is an average, as the planets' orbits are elliptical. The day is the length of axial rotation, and the year is the time each planet takes to complete a revolution around the sun. Both are measured in units of earth time. The mass, or the amount of matter that each planet consists of, is given as a multiple of earth's mass. Escape velocity is the minimum speed a body must reach in order to escape the planet's gravity.*

[Middle English *planispherie,* from Medieval Latin *plānisphaerium* : PLANI- + -SPHERE.] —**pla·ni·spher·ic** (plă′nə-sfĭr′ĭk, -sfĕr′ĭk), **pla·ni·spher·i·cal** *adj.*

plank (plăngk) *n.* **1.** A long piece of timber cut thicker than a board. **2. a.** Any of the policies of a political platform. **b.** Loosely, anything that supports a position: *the chief plank in their argument.* —**walk the plank.** To be forced, as by pirates, to walk down a plank extended over the side of a ship so as to drown. ~*tr.v.* **planked, planking, planks. 1.** To furnish, lay, or cover with planks. **2.** To put or set down emphatically or with force. **3.** To bake or grill and serve (fish or meat) on a plank. **4.** *Informal.* To pay at once. Usually used with *down* or *out.* [Middle English *plank(e),* from Old North French *planke,* from Latin *planca.*]

plank-sheer (plăngk′shĭr′) *n.* A horizontal timber forming the outer edge of the upper deck of a wooden ship. Also called "covering board." [Altered (by association with PLANK and SHEER) from earlier *planshire,* Middle English *plancher,* from Old French *planchier,* from *planche,* plank, from Latin *planca.*]

plank-ton (plăngk′tən) *n. Biology.* Plant and animal organisms, generally microscopic, that float or drift in great numbers in fresh or salt water. Compare NEKTON. [German, from Greek, "wanderer," neuter of *planktos,* wandering, from *plazesthai,* to wander, drift.] —**plank-ton-ic** (plăngk-tŏn′ĭk) *adj.*

Planned Parenthood. An organization that provides family planning services.

plan·ner (plăn′ər) *n.* One who plans; especially, an official responsible for planning architectural development and the use of land.

plano-, plani- *prefix.* Indicates flatness; for example, **planometer, planimeter.** [Latin *plānus,* flat.]

pla·no·con·cave (plă′nō-kŏn-kāv′, -kŏn′kāv′) *adj.* Flat or plane on one side and concave on the other. Said of a lens.

pla·no·con·vex (plă′nō-kŏn-vĕks′, -kŏn′vĕks′) *adj.* Flat or plane on one side and convex on the other. Said of a lens.

pla·nog·ra·phy (plə-nŏg′rə-fē, plā-) *n.* A process for printing from a smooth surface, such as lithography or offset. [PLANO- + -GRAPHY.] —**pla·no·graph** (plă′nə-grăf′, -gräf′) *tr.v.* —**pla·no·graph·ic** (plă′nə-grăf′ĭk) *adj.* —**pla·no·graph·i·cal·ly** *adv.*

pla·nom·e·ter (plə-nŏm′ə-tər, plā-) *n.* A flat metal plate for gauging the accuracy of a plane surface in precision metalworking. Also called "faceplate," "surface plate." [PLANO- + -METER.] —**pla·no·met·ric** (plă′nə-mĕt′rĭk) *adj.* —**pla·nom·e·try** *n.*

plant (plănt, plänt) *n.* **1.** Any organism that characteristically has cellulose cell walls, grows by synthesizing inorganic substances, lacks the power of locomotion, and lacks specialized sensory organs and nervous tissue. **2.** A plant having no permanent woody stem; an herb as distinguished from a tree or shrub. *Note:* In this dictionary *plant* is used in this sense rather than the word *herb,* to prevent confusion with the medicinal and cookery senses of the latter term. **3. a.** Equipment, including machinery, tools, instruments, and fixtures, and the buildings containing them, necessary for any industrial or manufacturing operation. **b.** A factory or other place where industrial processes are carried out. **4.** The buildings, equipment, and fixtures of any institution. **5.** *Informal.* A person secretly placed among others in order to observe, spy on, or mislead them. **6.** *Informal.* **a.** A misleading piece of evidence placed so as to be discovered. **b.** Something, especially stolen goods, fraudulently placed so as to incriminate a person. **7.** *Slang.* A scheming trick; a swindle. ~*tr.v.* **planted, planting, plants. 1.** To place or set (seeds, roots, cuttings, or young plants) in the ground to grow. **2. a.** To furnish or supply (a plot of land) with plants or seeds. **b.** To stock (water) with fish or spawn. **c.** To introduce (an animal) into an area. **3.** To fix or set firmly in position: *He planted both feet on the ground.* **4.** To establish or set up; found: *plant a colony.* **5.** To implant (an idea, sentiment, or the like) in the mind; introduce and establish firmly. **6.** *Informal.* **a.** To place or station (a person) for the purposes of observation, spying, misleading, or the like: *Detectives were planted all over the store.* **b.** To place (something) for the purpose of deception: *plant false evidence.* **7.** *Informal.* To hide by burying. **8.** *Slang.* To deliver (a blow or punch). [Middle English *plante,* from Old French and Old English, from Latin *planta,* shoot, from *plantāre,* to plant, "drive in with the sole of the foot," from *planta,* sole of the foot.] —**plant·a·ble** *adj.*

Plan·tag·e·net (plăn-tăj′ə-nĭt). Family name of a line of English kings from Henry II to Richard III (1154–1485) who succeeded the Norman monarchs and descended from Queen Matilda's marriage to Geoffrey, Count of Anjou. The line includes the Angevin, Lancastrian, and Yorkist kings and ended with the accession of the

Tudors. [Middle English, from Old French, sprig of broom (an insignia in the crest of the counts of Anjou) : Latin *planta,* sprig + *genista,* broom.] **—Plan·tag·e·net** *adj.*

plan·tain¹ (plăn′tən) *n.* Any of various plants of the genus *Plantago;* especially, *P. major,* a weed with a rosette of broad leaves and a spike of small, greenish flowers. [Middle English, from Old French, from Latin *plantāgō* (stem *plantagin-*), from *planta,* sole of the foot (from its broad leaves).]

plantain² *n.* **1.** A large tropical plant, *Musa paradisiaca,* resembling the banana and bearing similar fruit. **2.** The green-skinned, starchy fruit of this plant, used as a staple food in tropical regions. [Spanish *plántano,* plane tree, from Medieval Latin *plantanus,* variant of Latin *platanus,* PLANE TREE.]

plantain lily *n.* Any of several plants of the genus *Hosta,* native to Asia, widely cultivated for their broad leaves and white, blue, or lilac flowers. Also called "hosta," "day lily."

plan·tar (plăn′tər, -tär′, plän′-) *adj.* Of, pertaining to, or located on the sole of the foot. [Latin *plantāris,* from *planta,* sole of the foot.]

plan·ta·tion (plăn-tā′shən) *n.* **1.** An area under cultivation. **2.** A group of cultivated trees or plants. **3.** A large estate or farm on which crops such as cotton, tobacco, or sugar are grown and harvested, often by resident workers. **4.** Formerly, a newly established colony or settlement.

plant·er (plăn′tər, plän′-) *n.* **1. a.** One who plants. **b.** A machine or tool for planting or sowing seeds. **2.** The owner or manager of a plantation. **3.** An early settler or colonist. **4.** A decorative container for house plants.

planter's punch *n.* A drink of rum with lemon or lime juice, sugar syrup, water or soda, bitters, and grenadine.

plant hormone *n.* **Growth substance** *(see).*

plan·ti·grade (plăn′tə-grăd′, plän′-) *adj. Zoology.* Walking with the entire lower surface of the foot on the ground, as humans do. ~*n.* A plantigrade animal. Compare **digitigrade.** [French, from New Latin *plantigradus* : Latin *planta,* sole of the foot + -GRADE.]

plant kingdom *n.* One of the main divisions of the living world, comprising the algae, bryophytes, pteridophytes, and seed plants, and usually the fungi. Compare **animal kingdom, mineral kingdom.**

plant louse *n.* An **aphid** *(see).*

plan·u·la (plăn′yə-lə) *n., pl.* **-lae** (-lē′). The free-swimming, ciliated larva of a coelenterate. [New Latin, from Latin, little plane (from the flatness of the larva), from *plānus,* flat, level.] **—plan·u·lar** *adj.*

plaque (plăk) *n.* **1.** A flat plate, slab, or disk that is ornamented or engraved for mounting, as on a wall for decoration or on a monument for information. **2.** A small pin or brooch worn as an ornament or a badge of membership. **3.** *Pathology.* A small, disk-shaped formation or growth; patch. **4. Dental plaque** *(see).* **5.** In bacteriology, a clear area in a colony of bacterial cells caused by the localized destruction of bacteria by a bacteriophage. [French, from Old French, metal plate, coin, from Middle Dutch *placke,* from *placken†,* to patch, paste. See also **placard.**]

plash¹ (plăsh) *n.* **1.** A light splash. **2.** The sound of such a splash. ~*v.* **plashed, plashing, plashes.** —*tr.* To spatter (liquid) about; splash. —*intr.* To splash lightly. [Perhaps from Dutch *plassen,* from Middle Dutch *plasschen* (imitative).]

plash² *tr.v.* **plashed, plashing, plashes.** To interweave (branches, for example); pleach. [Middle English, from Old French *plassier,* from Vulgar Latin *plectiare* (unattested), from Latin *plectere,* to plait.]

plash·y (plăsh′ē) *adj.* **-ier, -iest. 1.** Marshy; wet. **2.** Plashing or splashing.

-plasia, -plasy *suffix.* Indicates growth or change; for example, *hypoplasia, heteroplasy.* [New Latin, from Greek *plasis,* molding, from *plassein,* to mold.]

plasm (plăz′əm) *n.* **1. Germ plasm** *(see).* **2.** Variant of **plasma.**

plasm-. Variant of **plasmo-.**

-plasm *suffix. Biology.* Indicates the material characteristically forming cells; for example, **protoplasm.** [From PLASMA.]

plas·ma (plăz′mə) *n.* Also **plasm** (plăz′əm). **1. a.** *Physiology.* The clear, yellowish fluid portion of blood, lymph, or intramuscular fluid in which cells are suspended. **b.** *Medicine.* Cell-free, sterilized **blood plasma** *(see),* used in transfusions. **2.** Protoplasm or cytoplasm. **3.** The fluid portion of milk from which the curd has been separated by coagulation; whey. **4.** *Physics.* An electrically neutral, highly ionized gas composed of ions, electrons, and neutral particles. [New Latin, extended use of Late Latin *plasma,* a form, mold, from Greek, from *plassein,* to mold.] **—plas·mat·ic** (plăz-măt′ĭk), **plas·mic** (plăz′mĭk) *adj.*

plasma engine *n.* A hypothetical engine for use in space that generates thrust by emitting a jet of plasma.

plas·ma·gel (plăz′mə-jĕl′) *n. Biology.* A jellylike state of cytoplasm, characteristically occurring in the periphery of the cell.

plas·ma·gene (plăz′mə-jēn′) *n. Genetics.* A self-reproducing hereditary structure in cell cytoplasm that functions in a manner analogous to but independent of chromosomal genes. **—plas·ma·gen·ic** (plăz′mə-jĕ′nĭk, -jĕn′ĭk) *adj.*

plasma membrane *n. Biology.* The semipermeable membrane that encloses the cytoplasm of a cell.

plas·ma·pher·e·sis (plăz′mə-fĕr′ə-sĭs) *n.* A method of obtaining quantities of plasma rather than whole blood from donors for the purpose of transfusion. [New Latin, from PLASMA + Greek *aphesis,* a removal, from *aphairein,* to take away: *apo,* off, away + *hairein,* to take.]

plas·ma·sol (plăz′mə-sôl′, -sōl′, -sŏl′) *n. Biology.* A state of cyto-

plasm that is more liquid than plasmagel and is found in the interior of the cell. [PLASMA + SOL (colloid).]

plas·min (plăz′mĭn) *n. Biochemistry.* A proteolytic enzyme in plasma that dissolves fibrin in blood clots. Also called "fibrinolysin." [PLASM(O)- + -IN.]

plas·min·o·gen (plăz-mĭn′ə-jən) *n.* The precursor to plasmin that is found in body fluids and in blood plasma.

plasmo-, plasm- *prefix.* Indicates plasma or resemblance to plasma; for example, **plasmolysis, plasmin.** [New Latin PLASMA.]

plas·mo·des·ma (plăz′mə-dĕz′mə) *n., pl.* **-mata** (-mə-tə). Also **plas·mo·desm** (plăz′mə-dĕz′əm). *Biology.* A strand of living cytoplasm connecting two plant cells that are otherwise functionally separate. [New Latin : PLASMO- + Greek *desma,* a bond, from *dein,* to bind.]

plas·mo·di·um (plăz-mō′dē-əm) *n., pl.* **-dia** (-dē-ə). **1.** Any protozoan of the genus *Plasmodium,* which includes the parasites that cause malaria. **2.** A naked, multinucleate mass of protoplasm such as that characteristic of the vegetative phase of the slime molds. [New Latin : PLASM(O)- + -OD(E) + -IUM.]

plas·mol·y·sis (plăz-mŏl′ə-sĭs) *n. Biology.* Shrinkage or contraction of the protoplasm in a plant or bacterial cell, caused by loss of water through osmosis. [PLASMO- + -LYSIS.] **—plas·mo·lyt·ic** (plăz′mə-lĭt′ĭk) *adj.* **—plas·mo·lyt·i·cal·ly** *adv.*

plas·mo·lyze (plăz′mə-līz′) *v.* **-lyzed, -lyzing, -lyzes.** —*tr.* To subject to plasmolysis. —*intr.* To undergo plasmolysis. [Back-formation from PLASMOLYSIS.]

plas·mo·some (plăz′mə-sōm′) *n. Biology.* A **nucleolus** *(see).*

-plast *suffix.* Indicates an organized unit of living matter; for example, **protoplast.** [Greek *plastos,* molded. See **plastic.**]

plas·ter (plăs′tər, plä′stər) *n.* **1.** A mixture of lime, sand, and water, sometimes with hair or other fiber added, that hardens to a smooth solid and is used for coating walls and ceilings. **2.** A piece of adhesive material used to protect a wound or hold a dressing in place. Also called "sticking plaster." **3. Plaster of Paris** *(see).* **4.** A paste-like mixture applied to a part of the body for healing or cosmetic purposes. **5.** A **mustard plaster** *(see).* ~*tr.v.* **plastered, -tering, -ters. 1.** To cover, coat, or repair with plaster or similar material. **2.** To cover by or as if by pasting; especially, to cover conspicuously or to excess. **3.** To apply a plaster to. **4.** To cause to adhere to another surface: *"His hair was plastered to his forehead"* (William Golding). **5.** To make smooth by applying a sticky substance: *plastered his hair with pomade.* **6.** *Slang.* To inflict injury, damage, or defeat on. [Middle English *plaster,* Old English *plaster,* from Medieval Latin *plastrum,* short for Latin *emplastrum,* from Greek *emplastron, emplaston,* salve, from *emplastos,* past participle of *emplassein,* to daub on, plaster : *em-, en,* in + *plassein,* to mold, plaster.] **—plas·ter·er** *n.*

plas·ter·board (plăs′tər-bôrd′, -bōrd′, plä′stər-) *n.* A thin, rigid board or sheet of layers of fiberboard or paper, with a plaster core, used to cover walls and ceilings.

plaster cast *n.* **1.** A mold or cast of a piece of sculpture or other object made with plaster of Paris. **2.** *Medicine.* See **cast** (sense 1).

plas·tered (plăs′tərd, plä′stərd) *adj. Slang.* Drunk.

plas·ter·ing (plăs′tər-ĭng, plä′stər-) *n.* **1.** A layer or coating of plaster. **2.** *Informal.* A heavy defeat.

plaster of Paris *n.* Any of a group of gypsum cements, essentially hemihydrated calcium sulfate, $2CaSO_4 \cdot H_2O$, a white powder that forms a paste when mixed with water and hardens into a solid, used in making small molded articles and in surgical casts. Also called "plaster." [After Paris, France, where it was originally made.]

plas·tic (plăs′tĭk) *adj.* **1.** Capable of being shaped or formed; pliable: *Clay is a plastic substance.* **2.** Pertaining to or dealing with shaping or modeling: *the plastic arts.* **3.** Giving form or shape to a substance. **4.** Easily influenced; impressionable. **5.** Made of a plastic or plastics: *a plastic garden hose.* **6.** *Informal.* Synthetic or artificial in taste or appearance: *plastic food.* **7.** *Physics.* Capable of undergoing continuous deformation without breaking or returning to the original size. Said of solids. **8.** *Biology.* Capable of changing or developing tissue; formative. Said of cells and tissues. —See Synonyms at **flexible.**
~*n.* Any of various materials based on polymerized organic compounds, often with additives such as pigments, fillers, or plasticizers. They can be molded, extruded, or cast into various shapes and coatings, or drawn into filaments used as textile fibers. [French *plastique,* from Latin *plasticus,* from Greek *plastikos,* fit for molding, from *plastos,* molded, from *plassein,* to mold.] **—plas·ti·cal·ly** *adv.* **—plas·tic·i·ty** (plă-stĭs′ə-tē) *n.*

-plastic *suffix.* Indicates a forming or growing; for example, **cytoplastic.** [Greek *plastikos,* fit for molding, PLASTIC.]

plastic explosive *n.* A type of high explosive in the form of a moldable jelly, used with a detonator.

Plas·ti·cine (plăs′tə-sēn′) *n.* A trademark for a puttylike modeling material used especially by children.

plas·ti·cize (plăs′tə-sīz′) *v.* **-cized, -cizing, -cizes.** —*tr.* To make plastic. —*intr.* To become plastic.

plas·ti·ciz·er (plăs′tə-sī′zər) *n.* Any of various substances added to plastics or other materials to keep them soft or pliable.

plastic surgery *n.* Cosmetic or remedial surgery to remodel, repair, or restore injured or defective tissue or body parts. **—plastic surgeon** *n.*

plas·tid (plăs′tĭd) *n. Biology.* Any of several specialized cytoplasmic structures occurring in plant cells and in some plantlike organisms, and having various physiological functions. [German *Plastid, Plas-*

tiden (plural), from Greek *plastides,* feminine plural of *plastēs,* molder, sculptor, from *plastos,* molded, from *plassein,* to mold.] **—plas·tid·i·al** (plă-stĭd'ē-əl) *adj.*

plas·to·mer (plăs'tə-mər) *n.* Any of various tough, hard polymers, such as acrylate resin. [Greek *plastos,* molded + (POLY)MER.]

plas·tron (plăs'trən) *n.* **1.** A breastplate worn under a coat of mail. **2.** A protective breastplate worn by fencers. **3.** A trimming on the front of a bodice. **4.** The front of a man's dress shirt. **5.** *Zoology.* The ventral surface of the shell of a turtle or tortoise. **6.** *Anatomy.* The breastbone together with the cartilages associated with it. [Old French, from Old Italian *piastrone,* augmentative of *piastra,* "metal plate," from Latin *emplastra, emplastrum,* PLASTER.] **—plas·tral** (plăs'trəl) *adj.*

-plasty *suffix.* Indicates plastic surgery; for example, **dermatoplasty.** [Greek *-plastia,* from *plastos,* molded. See **plastic.**]

-plasy. Variant of **-plasia.**

plat¹ (plăt) *tr.v.* **platted, platting, plats.** To plait or braid.
~n. A plait. [Middle English *platen,* variant of *plaiten,* to PLAIT.]

plat² *n.* **1.** *Archaic.* A small area of ground; a plot. **2.** A chart, plan, or the like, especially one showing the proposed design of a town or group of buildings. [Variant of PLOT.]

plat. **1.** platform. **2.** platoon.

Pla·ta, Rí·o de la (rē'ō dā lä plä'tä). Estuary in South America formed by the confluence of the Paraná and Uruguay rivers and flowing to the Atlantic Ocean.

plat·an (plăt'n) *n.* A **plane tree** *(see).* [Middle English, from Latin *platanus,* PLANE TREE.]

plat·an·na (plăt'ăn'ə) *n. South African.* A **xenopus** *(see).* [Afrikaans.]

plate (plāt) *n.* **1. a.** A shallow dish in which food is served or from which it is eaten. **b.** The contents of such a dish. **c.** The amount a plate will hold; a plateful. **d.** A whole course served on such a dish. **2.** Food and service for one person at a meal: *dinner at a set price per plate.* **3. a.** Household utensils covered with a thin layer of precious metal, such as gold or silver. **b.** Articles, as in a church, made of gold or silver. **4.** A dish passed among a congregation for the collection of offerings. **5.** A smooth, flat, relatively thin, rigid body of uniform thickness. **6. a.** A sheet of hammered, rolled, or cast metal. **b.** A very thin plated coat or layer of metal. **c.** Metal or metal objects coated with such a layer. **7. a.** A flat piece of metal forming part of a machine: *a boiler plate.* **b.** A flat piece of metal on which something is engraved. **c.** A number plate on a motor vehicle. **8. a.** A thin piece of metal used for armor. **b.** Armor made of this. **9.** *Abbr.* **pl.** *Printing.* **a.** A sheet of metal, plastic, rubber, paperboard, or other material converted into a printing surface, such as an electrotype or stereotype. **b.** A print of a woodcut, lithograph, or other engraved material, especially when reproduced in a book. **c.** A full-page book illustration, often in color and printed on paper different from that used on the text pages. **10.** *Abbr.* **pl.** *Photography.* A light-sensitive sheet of glass or metal upon which an image can be recorded. **11.** A thin metallic or plastic support fitted to the gums to anchor artificial teeth; a dental plate. **12.** *Architecture.* In wood-frame construction, a horizontal member, capping the exterior wall studs, upon which the roof rafters rest. **13.** In baseball, a flat piece of heavy rubber set in the ground that is used to define the place over which the ball must be thrown by a pitcher for a strike. Also called "home base." **14.** *Sports.* **a.** A dish, cup, or other trophy offered as a prize. **b.** A contest, especially a horse race, offering such a prize. **15.** *Anatomy & Zoology.* **a.** A thin, flat layer or scale. **b.** A platelike part or organ. **16.** *Electronics.* **a.** An electrode, as in a storage battery or capacitor. **b.** The anode in a thermionic valve. **17.** Any of the regions of the earth's crust. See **plate tectonics.**
~tr.v. **plated, plating, plates.** **1.** To coat or cover with a thin layer of metal. **2.** To armor. **3.** *Printing.* To make a stereotype or electrotype from. **4.** To give a glossy finish to (paper) by pressing between metal sheets or rollers. [Middle English, from Old French, from feminine of *plat,* flat, from Vulgar Latin *plattus* (unattested), from Greek *platus,* broad, flat.]

pla·teau (plă-tō') *n., pl.* **-teaus** or **-teaux** (-tōz'). **1.** An elevated and comparatively level expanse of land; tableland. **2.** A relatively stable or quiescent period or state; a leveling off: *a plateau of business activity.* **3.** A flat region on a graph. [French, from Old French *platel,* a flat piece, from *plat,* flat, from Vulgar Latin *plattus* (unattested), from Greek *platus,* broad, flat.]

plat·ed (plā'tĭd) *adj.* **1.** Coated with a thin layer of metal. Often used in combination: *gold-plated.* **2.** Covered or furnished with plates or sheets of metal. Often used in combination: *armor-plated.* **3.** Knitted with two kinds of wool, one on the face and one on the back.

plate·ful (plāt'fo͝ol') *n., pl.* **-fuls.** **1.** The amount of food or other substance that a plate will hold. **2.** A generous portion of food.

plate glass *n.* Rolled and polished flat glass containing few impurities, used for mirrors and windows.

plate·let (plāt'lĭt) *n.* A protoplasmic disk smaller than a red blood cell that is found in the blood of vertebrates and promotes coagulation. Also called "blood platelet," "thrombocyte." [Diminutive of PLATE.]

plate·mark (plāt'märk') *n. British.* A mark on metal, a **hallmark** (sense 1) *(see).*

plat·en (plăt'n) *n.* **1.** A flat plate in a printing press that serves to position the paper and hold it against the inked type. **2.** The roller on a typewriter against which the keys strike. [Earlier *plattin,* from Old French *platine,* from *plate,* PLATE.]

plate proof *n.* A proof taken from a master printing plate.

plat·er (plā'tər) *n.* **1.** One that plates. **2.** *Slang.* An inferior racehorse.

plate tectonics *n.* **1.** The theory that the earth's crust is composed of a series of rigid plates and that movement of these plates in relation to each other is responsible for all the features of the earth's surface. **2.** The study of the earth's crust based on this theory.

plat·form (plăt'fôrm') *n. Abbr.* **plat.** **1.** A floor or horizontal surface raised above the level of the adjacent area, especially: **a.** A stage for public speaking. **b.** A raised area alongside the tracks in a railway station where passengers may alight from or board trains. **2.** A vestibule and the end of a railway car. **3.** A thick raised sole or heel on certain types of shoes and boots. Also used adjectivally: *platform soles.* **4.** The declared policies with which a political figure or group makes an appeal to an electorate. [French, "ground plan," from Old French, "flat form" : feminine of *plat,* flat (see **plateau**) + *forme,* FORM.]

platform balance *n.* An equal-arm balance having two flat platforms above the beam and frequently using a sliding rider instead of weights.

platform scale *n.* A weighing instrument consisting of a platform coupled to an automatic system of levers and adjustable weights, designed to move a pointer over a scale.

Plath (plăth), **Sylvia** (1932–63). U.S. poet. She established her reputation with her collection *The Colossus* (1960). In 1963 she committed suicide, and her collection *Ariel,* published posthumously (1968), contains poems of intense anguish.

pla·ti·na (plə-tē'nə) *n.* Platinum, especially as found naturally. [Spanish, diminutive of *plata,* silver, flat, from Vulgar Latin *platus*†, from Greek *platus,* flat.]

plat·ing (plā'tĭng) *n.* **1.** A thin layer or coating of metal, such as gold or silver. **2.** A covering or layer of metal sheets or plates.

pla·tin·ic (plə-tĭn'ĭk) *adj. Chemistry.* Of, pertaining to, or containing platinum. Said especially of compounds containing platinum with a valence of 4. [PLATIN- + -IC.]

plat·i·nize (plăt'n-īz') *tr.v.* **-nized, -nizing, -nizes.** To coat with platinum, as by electroplating or vacuum evaporation. [PLATIN(I)- + -IZE.]

plat·i·nized (plăt'n-īzd') *adj.* Coated or treated with platinum; especially, coated with finely divided platinum: *platinized asbestos.*

platino-, platin-, platini- *prefix.* Indicates the presence or characteristics of platinum; for example, **platinotype, platinoid.** [From PLATINUM.]

plat·i·noid (plăt'n-oid') *adj.* Like platinum.
~n. **1.** An alloy of copper, nickel, tungsten, and zinc, formerly used in electric coils. **2.** Any metal resembling platinum chemically, especially osmium, iridium, or palladium. [PLATIN(O)- + -OID.]

plat·i·no·type (plăt'n-ō-tīp') *n.* **1.** A process formerly used for making photographic prints, using a finely precipitated platinum salt and an iron salt in the sensitizing solution to produce photographic prints in platinum black. **2.** A photographic print produced by this process. [PLATINO- + -TYPE.]

plat·i·nous (plăt'n-əs) *adj. Chemistry.* Of, pertaining to, or containing platinum. Said especially of compounds containing platinum with a valence of 2.

plat·i·num (plăt'n-əm) *n.* **1.** *Symbol* **Pt** A silver-white metallic element occurring worldwide, usually mixed with other metals such as iridium, osmium, or gold. It is ductile and malleable, does not oxidize in air, and is used in electrical components, jewelery, dentistry, electroplating, and as a catalyst. Atomic number 78, atomic weight 195.09, melting point 1773.5°C, boiling point 3827°C, specific gravity 21.45, valences 2, 4. **2.** Medium to light bluish gray. [New Latin, from Spanish *platina,* PLATINA.]

platinum black *n.* A fine black powder of metallic platinum, used as a catalyst and as a gas absorbent.

platinum blond *n.* **1.** A very light silver-blond hair color, especially when artificially produced. **2.** A person having hair of this color. —See Usage note at **blond.**

platinum metals *pl.n.* The group of chemically related elements ruthenium, osmium, rhodium, iridium, palladium, and platinum.

plat·i·tude (plăt'ə-to͞od', -tyo͞od') *n.* **1.** A trite, unoriginal, sententious remark or statement. **2.** Lack of originality; triteness. [French, "flatness," from *plat,* flat, from Old French, from Vulgar Latin *plattus* (unattested), from Greek *platus,* broad, flat.] **—plat·i·tu·di·nize** (plăt'ə-to͞od'n-īz', plăt'ə-tyo͞od'-) *v.* **—plat·i·tu·di·nous** *adj.*

Pla·to (plā'tō) (*c.* 428–347 B.C.). Greek philosopher, a major influence on Western thought. An Athenian aristocrat, he became a devoted admirer of Socrates. In about 386 he founded the Academy, where he taught and wrote for much of the rest of his life. Plato presented his philosophy in the form of dramatic *Dialogues* in which Socrates conducts the discussions, as in *The Republic.*

Pla·ton·ic (plə-tŏn'ĭk, plā-) *adj.* Also **Pla·ton·i·cal** (plə-tŏn'ĭ-kəl, plā-). **1.** Of, pertaining to, or characteristic of Plato or his philosophy. **2. a.** *Often* **platonic.** Transcending physical desire and tending toward the purely spiritual or ideal: *platonic love.* **b. platonic.** Intimate but not indulging in sexual intimacy: *a platonic relationship.* [Latin *Platonicus,* from Greek *Platōn,* Plato.] **—Pla·ton·i·cal·ly** *adv.*

Pla·to·nism (plāt'n-ĭz'əm) *n.* The philosophy of Plato, especially the view that asserts that the phenomena of the world are an imperfect and transitory copy of a transcendent world of archetypal forms. **—Pla·to·nist** *n.*

pla·toon (plə-to͞on') *n. Abbr.* **plat.** **1.** A subdivision of a military

PRONUNCIATION KEY

ă, pat; ā, pay; âr, care; ä, father, are; b, bib; ch, church; d, deed; ĕ, pet; ē, be; f, fife; g, gag; h, hat; hw, which; ĭ, pit; ī, pie; îr, pier; j, judge; k, kick; l, lid, needle; m, mum; n, no, sudden; ng, thing; ŏ, pot; ō, toe; ô, paw, for; oi, noise; ou, out; o͝o, book; o͞o, boot; p, pop; r, roar; s, sauce; sh, ship, dish; t, tight; th, thin, path; *th*, this, bathe; ŭ, cut; ûr, fur; v, valve; w, with; y, yes; z, zebra, size; zh, vision; ə, about, item, edible, gallop, circus, peaceful

IN FOREIGN WORDS:

à, *Fr.* ami; œ, *Fr.* feu, *Ger.* schön; ü, *Fr.* tu, *Ger.* über; KH, *Ger.* ich, *Scot.* loch; N, *Fr.* bon; y', *Fr.* Compiègne

STRESS MARKS:

Primary stress: '
in·cite' (ĭn-sīt')
Secondary stress: '
in'sight' (ĭn'sīt')

plate tectonics

THE WORLD'S CONTINENTS ARE ON THE MOVE
Mountains rise up and earthquakes shake the earth

Some 200 million years ago, all the continents of the world were grouped together in a single supercontinent that geologists call Pangaea (from the Greek word that means "all earth"). Beneath the earth's outer shell, or lithosphere, there is a molten layer, called the asthenosphere, through which slow convection currents exercised their force on Pangaea. Gradually the single landmass broke up and separate pieces of it began moving to their present positions.

The lithosphere is composed of a number of rigid plates colliding or growing apart or sliding past each other. This movement is continuous and measurable—the Atlantic Ocean expands by a few inches a year as Europe and North America draw apart. The Indian Ocean is also expanding but the Pacific and the Mediterranean are becoming smaller.

Where continental plates collide they cause the earth's crust to buckle and throw up mountains—the

Himalayas have been pushed up by the constant pressure of the Indian plate on the Asian plate.

Ocean ridges occur where molten rock rises through a rift fault in the ocean floor to form new lithosphere. The oceanic plate becomes larger and is forced against a continental plate, forming a subduction zone. Here the less dense ocean floor sinks back into the earth's molten interior, perhaps under the pressure of gravity or convection currents.

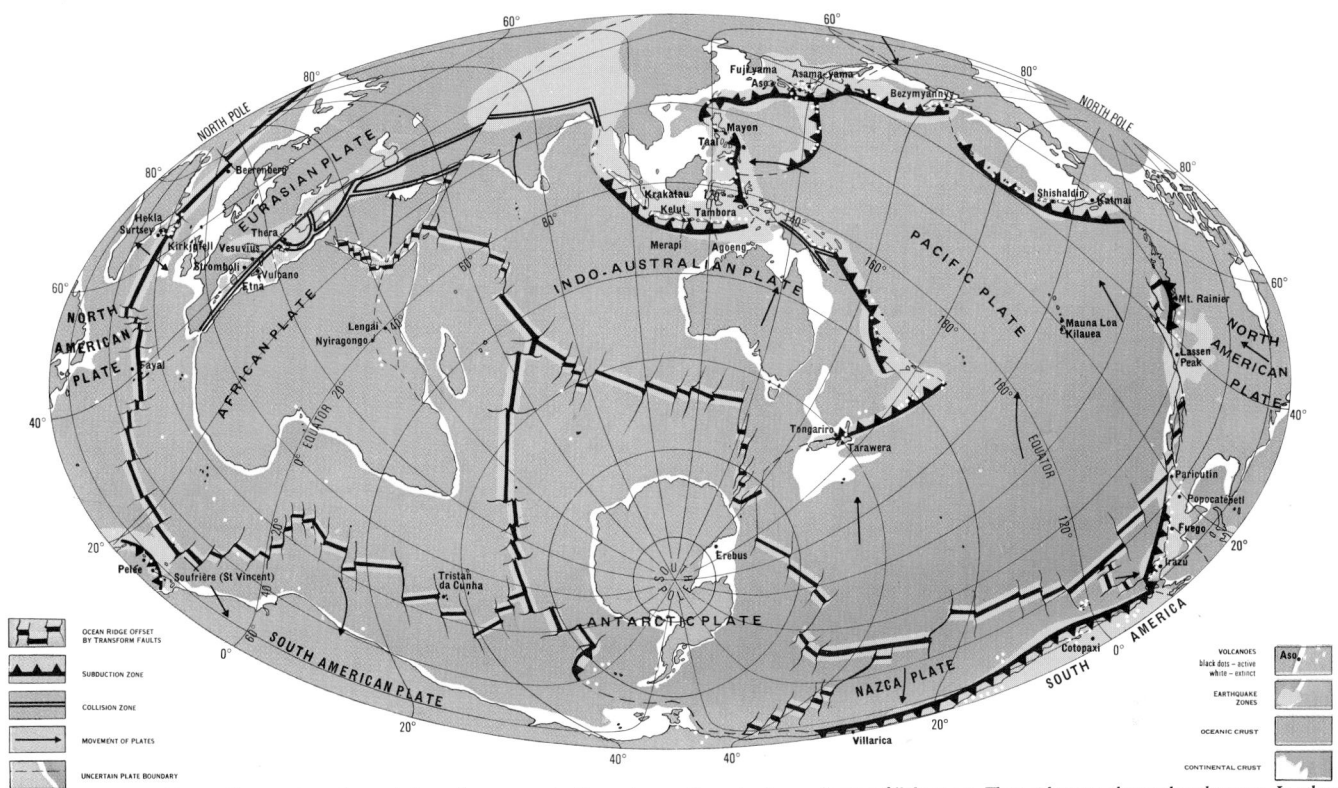

ZONES OF UPHEAVAL The earth's crust is made up of plates that are constantly moving. The areas where two plates push together—subduction or collision zones—make up the world's volcano and earthquake belts. Where plates move apart, midocean ridges are *formed as lava wells up to fill the space. These ridges are also earthquake areas. In other parts of the world, including California, two plates traveling in the same direction at slightly different speeds grind jerkily past each other.*

---

company divided into squads or sections. **2.** A body of persons working together. [French *peloton,* "little ball," group of soldiers, from Old French *pelote,* from Vulgar Latin *pilotta* (unattested), diminutive of Latin *pila,* ball. See **pill.**]

Platt·deutsch (plăt′doich′) *n.* The Low German vernacular of northern Germany. [German, from Dutch *platduits : plat,* flat, low, clear, from Middle Dutch, from Old French, flat (see **platitude**) + *Duitsch,* German, from Middle Dutch *duutsch.*]

Platte (plăt). River, c. 500 kilometers (310 miles) long, formed by the confluence of the North Platte (1,095 kilometers; 680 miles) and the South Platte (690 kilometers; 430 miles) in west-central Nebraska. It flows generally east to join the Missouri River south of Omaha.

plat·ter (plăt′ər) *n.* **1. a.** A large, shallow, often wooden dish or plate used especially for serving food. **b.** A meal served on such a dish. **2.** *Slang.* A phonograph record. —**on a platter.** With great ease; effortlessly. [Middle English *plater,* from Norman French, from Old French *plate,* PLATE.]

Platts·burgh (plăts′bûrg′). City of northeastern New York State, on Lake Champlain. It is a resort center, with a U.S. Air Force strategic command base nearby. In the War of 1812 it was the site of a U.S. naval victory over the British.

plat·y¹ (plā′tē) *adj.* **-i·er, -i·est.** Designating soil or minerals occurring in flaky layers.

plat·y² (plăt′ē) *n., pl.* **platys** or **platies** or collectively **platy.** Any of several small freshwater fishes of the genus *Xiphophorus,* of southern North America; especially, *X. maculatus,* a colorful aquarium fish. [New Latin *Platypoecilus,* "flat and colorful" (Greek *poikilos,* variegated), from Greek *platus,* broad, flat.]

platy- *prefix.* Indicates flatness; for example, **platyhelminth.** [Greek *platus,* broad, flat.]

plat·y·hel·minth (plăt′ĭ-hĕl′mĭnth′) *n. Zoology.* Any of various parasitic and nonparasitic worms of the phylum Platyhelminthes, such as a tapeworm, characteristically having a flattened body. Also called "flatworm." [PLATY- + Greek *helmis* (stem *helminth-*), parasitic worm.] —**plat·y·hel·min·thic** (plăt′ĭ-hĕl-mĭn′thĭk) *adj.*

plat·y·pus (plăt′ĭ-pəs) *n., pl.* **-puses.** The **duck-billed platypus** (*see*). [New Latin, from Greek *platupous,* "flat-footed" : PLATY- + *pous,* foot.]

plat·yr·rhine (plăt′ĭ-rīn′) *adj.* Also **plat·yr·rhin·i·an** (plăt′ĭ-rīn′ē-ən). **1.** *Anthropology.* Having a broad, flat nose. **2.** *Zoology.* Of or designating the New World monkeys, many of which are characterized by widely separated nostrils.
~*n.* Also **plat·yr·rhin·i·an.** A platyrrhine person or monkey. [New Latin *Platyrrhina,* "flat-nosed ones," from *platyrrhinus,* flat-nosed, from Greek *platurrhis, platurrhinos* : PLATY- + Greek *rhis* (stem *rhin-*), nose (see **rhino-**).]

plau·dit (plô′dĭt) *n. Usually* **plaudits.** Enthusiastic approbation or praise; especially, critical approval. [Originally "an appeal for applause," from Latin *plaudite,* imperative of *plaudere,* to applaud.]

plau·si·ble (plô′zə-bəl) *adj.* **1.** Seemingly or apparently valid, likely, or acceptable: *a plausible excuse.* **2.** Giving a deceptive impression of truth, acceptability, or reliability; specious. [Originally "deserving applause," acceptable, from Latin *plausibilis,* from *plaudere* (past participle *plausus*), to applaud, acclaim.] —**plau·si·bil·i·ty, plau·si·ble·ness** *n.* —**plau·si·bly** *adv.*

plau·sive (plô′zĭv, -sĭv) *adj.* **1.** Showing or expressing praise or approbation; applauding. **2.** *Obsolete.* Plausible. [From Latin *plaudere,* to applaud.]

Plau·tus (plô′təs), **Titus Maccius** (c. 254–184 B.C.). Roman comic dramatist. Twenty-one of his comedies survive, all adapted from Greek sources, to which he added his own earthy Roman humor.

His imitators included Shakespeare and Molière.

play (plā) *v.* **played, playing, plays.** *—intr.* **1.** To occupy oneself in amusing or diverting activities. **2. a.** To take part in a game. **b.** To participate in a betting game; gamble. **3.** To act in jest or sport. **4.** To deal or behave carelessly or indifferently; toy; trifle. Usually used with *with.* **5.** To act or behave in a specified way: *play fair.* **6.** To act or perform, especially in a dramatic production. **7.** To perform on a musical instrument. **8.** To emit sound or be sounded in performance: *The band is playing.* **9.** To be performed or shown, as in a theater: *Othello is playing next week.* **10.** To move or seem to move quickly, lightly, or irregularly: *The breeze played on the water.* **11.** To function or operate uninterruptedly; especially, to discharge a steady stream: *The fountains played in the courtyard.* **12.** To move or operate freely within a bounded space, as machine parts do. *—tr.* **1. a.** To perform or act (a role or part) in a dramatic performance. **b.** To assume the role of; act as: *play the villain.* **2.** To put on or perform (a drama or other theatrical work) on or as if on the stage. **3.** To put on or produce a theatrical, musical, or other performance in (a specified place): *played Boston last week.* **4.** To pretend to be; mimic the activities of: *The boys played cowboys and Indians.* **5.** To participate in (a game or sport). **6.** To compete against in a game or sport. **7. a.** To occupy or work at (a position) in a game: *She plays first base.* **b.** To employ the position of in a game: *play her at first base.* **c.** To use or move (a card, piece, or the like) in a game: *play the ace.* **d.** To make (a shot or stroke), as in tennis: *played a forehand.* **8.** To perform or put into effect, especially as a trick or deception: *play a joke on someone.* **9.** To use or manipulate (two or more competitors, for example) for one's own interests: *play them against each other.* **10. a.** To bet or wager. **b.** To make a wager on. **11. a.** To perform on (a musical instrument): *play the guitar.* **b.** To perform (music) on an instrument or instruments. **12.** To cause (a record or record player, for example) to emit recorded sounds. **13.** To discharge, set off, or cause to operate in or as if in a continuous stream: *play a hose on a fire.* **14.** To cause to move rapidly, lightly, or irregularly: *play lights over the dance floor.* **15.** In angling, to exhaust (a hooked fish) by allowing it to pull on the line. **—play along.** *Informal.* To cooperate, as with a plan or person, especially out of self-interest. **—play at.** To participate in or engage in half-heartedly or frivolously. **—play down.** To minimize the importance of; make little of: *play down one's successes.* **—play on** (or **upon**). To take advantage of (another's attitudes or feelings) for one's own interests. **—play out. 1.** To do or play until completed; finish. **2.** To use up; exhaust. **—play up.** *Informal.* To emphasize or publicize: *play up one's conquests.* **—play up to.** *Informal.* To try to ingratiate oneself with.
~n. **1. a.** A dramatic work written for performance on the stage; a drama. **b.** The performance of such a work. **2.** Activity engaged in for enjoyment or recreation. **3.** Fun or jesting: *done in play.* **4. a.** The act of carrying on or engaging in a game or sport. **b.** The manner or way of playing a game or sport. **5.** A manner or method of dealing with people generally. Used especially in the phrases *foul play* and *fair play.* **6.** A turn, move, or action in a game: *It's your play.* **7.** Participation in betting; gambling. **8.** *Sports.* The condition of a ball, puck, or similar object in active or legitimate use or motion during a game. Used in the phrases *in play* and *out of play.* **9.** Action, motion, or use: *the play of the imagination.* **10.** Quick, often irregular movement or action, especially of light or color: *the play of the light.* **11.** Movement or space or scope for movement: *give the rope more play.* **—bring** (or **call**) **into play.** To cause to operate; activate. **—make a play for.** *Informal.* To attempt to attract or obtain by using art, wiles, or skill. **—play both ends against the middle.** To set opposing parties or interests against each other so as to advance one's own goals. **—play possum.** To pretend to be sleeping or dead. **—play the field.** To date more than one person. [As verb, Middle English *playen,* from Old English *plegan*; as noun, Middle English *pley, play,* Old English *plega.*] **—play·a·ble** *adj.*

pla·ya (plī'ə) *n.* **1.** The beach or bank of a river. **2. a.** An inland drainage basin, surrounded by sheets of saline or alkaline crust and containing a shallow lake. **b.** The lake in such a basin. [Spanish, "shore," from Medieval Latin *plagia,* from Greek, sides, neuter plural of *plagios.* See **plagio-.**]

play-act (plā'ăkt') *intr.v.* **-acted, -acting, -acts. 1.** To play a pretended role; make believe. **2.** To behave in an overdramatic or artificial manner. **—play-act·ing** *n.* **—play-ac·tor** *n.*

play back *tr.v.* To perform a playback of (a recently recorded tape or disc).

play·back (plā'băk') *n.* **1.** The act or process of replaying a newly made record or tape. **2.** A method of or apparatus for reproducing sound recordings.

play·bill (plā'bĭl') *n.* **1.** A poster announcing a theatrical performance. **2.** A program for a theatrical performance.

play·boy (plā'boi') *n.* A man who is devoted to the pursuit of pleasurable activities.

play-by-play (plā'bī-plā') *adj.* Consisting of a detailed running commentary or account, as of the action of a sports event.

play·er (plā'ər) *n.* **1.** One who participates in a game or sport, especially professionally. **2.** One who performs in theatrical roles. **3.** One who plays a musical instrument. **4.** The mechanism actuating a player piano. **5.** An apparatus for reproducing recorded sound: *a cassette player.* **6.** A gambler. **7.** A trifler.

player piano *n.* A mechanically operated piano that uses a perforated paper roll to actuate the keys.

play·ful (plā'fəl) *adj.* **1.** Full of fun and good spirits; frolicsome; sportive: *a playful kitten.* **2.** Humorous; jesting: *a playful comment.* **—play·ful·ly** *adv.* **—play·ful·ness** *n.*
Synonyms: *frivolous, impish, mischievous, waggish.*

play·girl (plā'gûrl') *n.* A woman who is devoted to the pursuit of pleasurable activities.

play·go·er (plā'gō'ər) *n.* One who regularly attends the theater.

play·ground (plā'ground') *n.* **1.** An outdoor area set aside for recreation and play, as in a school; especially, one containing seesaws, swings, and the like. **2.** Broadly, any area in which one may enjoy oneself: *The Riviera is a millionaires' playground.*

play·group (plā'gro͞op') *n.* A supervised gathering of children of preschool age where they can engage in games and other activities.

play·house (plā'hous') *n.* **1.** A theater. **2.** A small house for children to play in. **3.** A child's toy house; a dollhouse.

playing card *n.* Any of a pack of cards with a design designating its value in the color of one of the four **suits** *(see)* that is used in various card games.

playing field *n.* A field for games such as cricket and soccer.

play·mate (plā'māt') *n.* A companion in play or recreation.

play off *tr.v.* **1.** *Sports.* **a.** To establish the winner of (a tie) by playing in an additional game or series of games. **b.** To participate in a playoff. **2.** To set (one individual or party) in opposition to another so as to advance one's own interests.

play-off (plā'ôf', -ŏf') *n. Sports.* **1.** A final game or series of games played to break a tie. **2.** A series of games played to determine a championship.

play·pen (plā'pĕn') *n.* A portable enclosure in which a baby or young child can be left to play.

play·room (plā'ro͞om', -ro͝om') *n.* A room designed or set aside for recreation or playing.

play·school (plā'sko͞ol') *n.* A program of educational activities based on play for preschool children.

play·thing (plā'thĭng') *n.* **1.** Something to play with; a toy. **2.** One treated as a toy: *a plaything of fate.*

play·time (plā'tīm') *n.* Time devoted to recreation, especially as a break from school lessons.

play·wright (plā'rīt') *n.* One who writes plays; a dramatist.

pla·za (plä'zə, plăz'ə) *n.* **1.** A public square or similar open area, especially in towns or cities of Spanish-speaking countries. **2.** A broad paved area for automobiles, especially: **a.** The widened roadway forming the approach to tollbooths on a highway. **b.** A parking or servicing area next to a highway. **3.** A **shopping center** *(see).* [Spanish, from Vulgar Latin *plattea* (unattested), variant of Latin *platea,* broad street. See **place.**]

plea (plē) *n.* **1.** An appeal or entreaty: *a plea for leniency.* **2.** An excuse; a pretext: *"Necessity, the tyrant's plea"* (Milton). **3.** *Law.* **a.** An allegation offered in pleading a case. **b.** In common law, a defendant's establishment of an allegation of fact in answer to the declaration made by the plaintiff. Compare **demurrer. c.** In criminal law, the answer of the accused to a charge or indictment. **d.** In equity law, a special answer depending upon or demonstrating one or more reasons why a suit should be delayed, dismissed, or barred. **e.** Formerly, an action or suit. [Middle English *plai(d), plee,* a lawsuit, pleading, from Norman French *plai, ple,* Old French *plaid,* legal action, agreement, decree, from Medieval Latin *placitum,* from Latin, "something agreeable," opinion, decision, from the neuter of *placitus,* pleasing, agreeable, from the past participle of *placēre,* to please.]

plea bargaining *n.* The practice, especially between defending and prosecuting counsel, of reaching agreement over the charge on which the defendant should stand trial, normally resulting in the defendant pleading guilty to a less serious offense than that with which he could otherwise be charged (and would be so charged, were he to plead not guilty).

pleach (plēch, plāch) *tr.v.* **pleached, pleaching, pleaches.** To plait or interlace (branches or twigs, for example), especially in making a hedge or an arbor. [Middle English *plechen,* from Old North French *plechier,* from Latin *plectere* (past participle *plexus*), to weave, plait.]

plead (plēd) *v.* **pleaded** or **pled** (plĕd), **pleading, pleads.** *—intr.* **1.** To appeal earnestly; implore; beg: *pleaded with her to stay.* **2.** To argue or offer persuasive reasons for or against something. **3.** To furnish or provide an argument or appeal: *His misfortunes plead for him.* **4.** *Law.* **a.** To put forward a plea of a specified nature in a court of law: *plead guilty.* **b.** To enter an answer or pleading on behalf of a defendant or as part of the prosecution in a law action. **c.** To address a court as a lawyer or advocate. *—tr.* **1.** To assert or put forward as defense, vindication, or excuse; submit as a plea: *plead illness.* **2.** To present as an answer to a charge, indictment, or declaration made against one. **3. a.** *Law.* To argue or present (a case) in a court of law. **b.** To present the arguments for (a cause). [Middle English *pleden,* from Norman French, from Old French *plaidier.* See **plea.**] **—plead·a·ble** *adj.* **—plead·er** *n.*

plead·ing (plē'dĭng) *n.* **1. a.** The act of entreating or making a plea. **b.** A plea or entreaty thus made. **2.** *Law.* **a.** The art or procedure of one who acts as an advocate in a law court. **b.** The act or technique of drawing up or presenting pleas in legal cases. **c.** A formal statement, generally written, propounding the cause of action or the defense of a legal case. **d. pleadings.** The consecutive statements, allegations, and counterallegations made in turn by plaintiff and defendant, or prosecutor and accused, until a single issue is reached upon which the trial may be held. **—plead·ing·ly** *adv.*

PRONUNCIATION KEY

ă, pat; ā, pay; âr, care;
ä, father, are; b, bib;
ch, church; d, deed; ĕ, pet;
ē, be; f, fife; g, gag; h, hat;
hw, which; ĭ, pit; ī, pie;
îr, pier; j, judge; k, kick;
l, lid, needle; m, mum;
n, no, sudden; ng, thing;
ŏ, pot; ō, toe; ô, paw, for;
oi, noise; ou, out; o͝o, book;
o͞o, boot; p, pop; r, roar;
s, sauce; sh, ship, dish;
t, tight; th, thin, path;
th, this, bathe; ŭ, cut; ûr, fur;
v, valve; w, with; y, yes;
z, zebra, size; zh, vision;
ə, about, item, edible,
gallop, circus, peaceful

IN FOREIGN WORDS:

à, *Fr.* ami; œ, *Fr.* feu, *Ger.* schön; ü, *Fr.* tu, *Ger.* über; KH, *Ger.* ich, *Scot.* loch; N, *Fr.* bon; y', *Fr.* Compiègne

STRESS MARKS:

Primary stress: '
in·cite' (ĭn-sīt')
Secondary stress: '
in'sight' (ĭn'sīt')

pleas·ance (plĕz′əns) *n. Archaic.* **1.** A secluded, landscaped area, such as the garden of a mansion. **2.** Pleasure or a source of pleasure. [Old French (*maison de*) *plaisance*, "(house of) pleasure," from *plaisant*, PLEASANT.]

pleas·ant (plĕz′ənt) *adj.* **1.** Giving or affording pleasure or enjoyment; agreeable. **2.** Pleasing in manner, appearance, or other personal qualities. **3.** Fair and comfortable. **4.** *Obsolete.* Merry; lively. [Middle English *plesaunt*, from Old French *plaisant*, from the present participle of *plaisir*, to PLEASE.] —**pleas·ant·ly** *adv.* —**pleas·ant·ness** *n.*

Pleasant Island. See Nauru.

pleas·ant·ry (plĕz′ən-trē) *n., pl.* **-ries. 1.** A jesting, entertaining, or humorous remark or action: *exchanged pleasantries.* **2.** Pleasingly humorous style or manner in conversation or at social occasions. [French *plaisanterie*, from *plaisant*, PLEASANT.]

Pleas·ant·ville (plĕz′ənt-vĭl′). Residential community of south-eastern New York State, north-northeast of New York City. It has a publishing industry and is the headquarters for the Reader's Digest Association, Inc.

please (plēz) *v.* **pleased, pleasing, pleases.** —*tr.* **1.** To give enjoyment, pleasure, or satisfaction to; make glad or contented. **2.** To be the will or desire of. Used impersonally with *it: May it please you to accept our gifts.* —*intr.* **1.** To give satisfaction or pleasure; be agreeable. **2.** To have the will or desire; wish: *Do whatever you please.* —**be pleased to.** *Formal.* To be willing to; agree to: *He was pleased to grant me an audience.* —**if you please. 1.** If it is your will, desire, or pleasure. **2.** If you can believe or imagine it. Used as an ironical expression of indignation or surprise. —**please oneself.** To do or act as one likes.
~*interj.* Used: **1.** To indicate a polite request. **2.** To express an earnest wish or protest. [Middle English *plaisen, plesen,* from Old French *plaisir,* from Latin *placēre.*]

---

playing cards

THE MYSTERIOUS ORIGINS OF PLAYING CARDS

Were they first known in China, Arabia, or Europe?

Playing cards may have originated in China, where they were developed from paper money, or they may have been invented independently in Europe, where they were first heard of in Italy in 1300. Or they may have been introduced to Europe by the Arabs, after they conquered Sicily and Spain.

The modern deck was developed from the 78-card Tarot deck, used for both fortunetelling and games, which has four suits— swords, cups, coins, and batons. Today's familiar 52-card deck emerged in France in the early 15th century. Italian and Spanish cards still have the Tarot suits. The German suits are hearts, bells, acorns, and leaves. The French and English suits are spades, hearts, diamonds, and clubs, although the club of English-speaking countries is really a trefoil, and the spade is the head of a pike.

1500 *German card suits are bells, leaves, hearts, and acorns. This bell of 1500 is probably a knave.*

1678 *An English card illustrating the Popish Plot of 1678, a supposed plan to murder Charles II.*

ORIENTAL CARDS

In India and Iran cards are all handmade on slivers of wood, cardboard, fabric, or leather. The cards are hand-painted and coated with lacquer, making them much thicker than factory-produced European cards.

IRAN *This Shah (or King) is one of 25 cards in the Iranian pack of five suits.*

1840 *Some English cards of the 19th century made the suit signs into scenes—in this case a sword fight.*

MODERN *Double-headed cards were introduced in the 18th century, but did not become standard until after 1870.*

INDIA *A Mir (or King) of the Moon suit in one type of pack. Most Indian cards are circular.*

pleas·ing (plē'zĭng) *adj.* Giving pleasure or enjoyment; agreeable; gratifying. **—pleas·ing·ly** *adv.* **—pleas·ing·ness** *n.*

pleas·ur·a·ble (plĕzh'ər-ə-bəl) *adj.* Agreeable; gratifying. **—pleas·ur·a·ble·ness** *n.* **—pleas·ur·a·bly** *adv.*

pleas·ure (plĕzh'ər) *n.* **1. a.** An enjoyable sensation or emotion: *got pleasure from swimming.* **b.** Satisfaction; delight: *I'll do it with pleasure.* **2.** A source of enjoyment, gratification, or delight. **3.** Amusement, diversion, or worldly enjoyment. Also used adjectivally: *a pleasure cruise.* **4.** Sensual gratification or indulgence. **5.** One's preference, wish, or choice: *What is your pleasure?*
~*v.* **pleasured, -uring, -ures.** —*tr.* **1.** To give pleasure or enjoyment to; please; gratify. **2.** To gratify sexually. —*intr.* **1.** To take pleasure; delight. Often used with *in.* **2.** To search for pleasure or enjoyment. [Middle English *plesure,* (earlier) *plesir,* from Old French *plaisir,* noun use of *plaisir,* to PLEASE.]
***Synonyms:** delight, enjoyment, joy.*

pleasure principle *n.* The tendency for individuals to seek immediate gratification of instinctual needs and to reduce pain. [Translation of German *Lustprinzip.*]

pleat (plēt) *n.* A fold in cloth or other material made by doubling the material upon itself and then pressing or stitching into place.
~*tr.v.* **pleated, pleating, pleats.** To press or arrange in pleats. [Middle English, variant of PLAIT.]

pleb (plĕb) *n.* **1.** A person of the lower classes; a plebeian. **2.** A plebe. [Short for PLEBEIAN.]

plebe (plēb) *n.* A freshman at the U.S. Military or Naval Academy. [Short for PLEBEIAN.]

ple·be·ian (plĭ-bē'ən) *adj.* **1.** Of or pertaining to the Roman plebs. In this sense, compare **patrician. 2.** Of, belonging to, or characteristic of common people. **3.** Crude; vulgar; low: *plebeian tastes.*
~*n.* **1.** A member of the Roman plebs. **2.** A member of the lower classes. **3.** Someone who is vulgar or coarse. [Latin *plēbēius,* from *plēbs,* common people.] **—ple·be·ian·ism** *n.*

pleb·i·scite (plĕb'ə-sīt', -sĭt) *n.* **1.** A direct vote in which the entire electorate of a country, region, or other political unit is invited to accept or refuse the measure, program, or government of the person or party initiating the consultation. **2.** Such a vote whereby a population exercises the right of national self-determination. Compare **referendum.** [French *plébiscite,* from Latin *plēbiscītum,* people's decree : *plēbi,* genitive of *plēbs,* common people + *scītum,* decree, from *sciscere* (past participle *scītus*), to approve, decree, "to seek to know," from *scīre,* to know.]

plebs (plĕbz) *n., pl.* **plebes** (plē'bēz). **1.** The common people of ancient Rome. **2.** The common people; the populace. [Latin *plēbs.*]

plec·tog·nath (plĕk'tŏg-năth') *n.* Any of various tropical marine fishes of the order Tetraodontiformes (or Plectognathi), which includes the triggerfishes, puffers, trunkfishes, and others. [New Latin *Plectognathi,* "ones having twisted jaws" (from their ankylosed jaws) : Greek *plektos,* past participle of *plekein,* to weave, twist + *-gnathi,* plural of *-gnathus,* -GNATHOUS.] **—plec·tog·nath** *adj.*

plec·trum (plĕk'trəm) *n., pl.* **-trums** or **-tra** (-trə). Also **plec·tron** (plĕk'trŏn'). A small, thin, flexible piece of metal, plastic, bone, or other material, used to pluck the strings of certain musical instruments, such as the guitar or lute. Also called "pick." [Latin, from Greek *plēktron,* from *plēssein* (stem *plek-*), to strike + *-tron,* instrumental suffix.]

pled. Alternate past tense and past participle of **plead.**

pledge (plĕj) *n.* **1.** A formal promise to do something, such as the performance of an obligation or duty, or to refrain from doing something. **2. a.** Something given or held as security to guarantee payment of a debt or fulfillment of an obligation. **b.** The condition of something thus given or held: *put an article in pledge.* **3.** Something, such as an item of personal property, put in pawn. **4.** Something given as a token or sign. **5.** The act of drinking to someone; a toast. **—take the pledge.** To make a solemn vow to abstain from drinking alcoholic liquor.
~*tr.v.* **pledged, pledging, pledges. 1.** To offer or guarantee by a solemn promise. **2.** To bind or secure by or as if by a pledge. **3.** To deposit as security; pawn. **4.** To drink a toast to. —See Synonyms at **devote.** [Middle English *pleg(g)e,* from Old French *plege,* from Late Latin *plebium,* from *plebire,* to pledge, probably from Frankish *plegan* (unattested), to guarantee (influenced by Latin *praebēre,* to offer).]

pledg·ee (plĕ-jē') *n.* **1.** A person to whom something is pledged. **2.** A person with whom something is deposited as a pledge.

pledg·er (plĕj'ər) *n.* One who makes or gives a pledge.

pledg·or, pledge·or (plĕj'ər, plĕ-jôr') *n. Law.* A person who deposits its property as a pledge.

-plegia *suffix. Medicine.* Indicates a form of paralysis; for example, **paraplegia.** [New Latin, from Greek *plēgē,* a stroke, blow, from *plēssein* (stem *plēg-*), to strike.]

Plei·ad[1] (plē'əd) *n., pl.* **Pleiades** (plē'ə-dēz'). *Sometimes* **pleiad.** A group of seven illustrious persons. [French *Pléiade,* the name adopted by Ronsard (*c.* 1553) to designate himself and his six most eminent companions among the poets of the "brigade," in allusion to a group of Alexandrian poets named after the PLEIADES.]

Pleiad[2], **Pleiade.** *Greek Mythology.* Any of the Pleiades.

Pleiad[3], **Pleiade** *n. Astronomy.* Any of the stars in the Pleiades.

Plei·a·des[1] (plē'ə-dēz'). *Greek Mythology.* The seven daughters of Atlas (Maia, Electra, Celaeno, Taygeta, Merope, Alcyone, and Sterope), who were changed into stars.

Pleiades[2] *pl.n. Astronomy.* An open star cluster in the constellation Taurus, consisting of several hundred stars, of which six or seven are visible to the naked eye. Also called "Seven Sisters."

pleio-. Variant of **pleo-.**

Pleiocene. Variant of **Pliocene.**

plei·ot·ro·pism (plī-ŏt'rə-pĭz'əm) *n.* Also **plei·ot·ro·py** (plī-ŏt'rə-pē). *Genetics.* The control or determination of more than one characteristic or function by a single gene. [Greek *ple(i)ōn,* more + -TROPISM.] **—plei·o·trop·ic** (plī'ə-trŏp'ĭk) *adj.* **—plei·o·trop·i·cal·ly** *adv.*

Pleis·to·cene (plī'stə-sēn') *adj. Geology.* Of, belonging to, or designating the geologic time, rock series, and sedimentary deposits of the earlier of the two epochs of the Quaternary period, characterized by the alternate appearance and recession of northern glaciation and the appearance of the progenitors of man.
~*n. Geology.* The Pleistocene epoch or system of deposits. Preceded by *the.* [Greek *pleistos,* most + -CENE.]

Ple·kha·nov (plĭ-kä'nôf', -KHä'nəf), **Georgi Valentinovich** (1857–1918). Russian revolutionary and political philosopher. Fleeing Russia in 1880 to avoid political persecution, he developed his influential Marxist theories in exile and published them in *Socialism and Political Struggle* (1883) and other works. He helped organize the first Russian Marxist revolutionary group (1883). A Menshevik, he returned to Russia in 1917, but was harassed by the newly formed Bolshevik government. He died in exile.

ple·na·ry (plē'nə-rē, plĕn'ə-) *adj.* **1.** Complete in all aspects or essentials; full; absolute: *plenary powers.* **2.** Fully attended by all qualified members: *a plenary session.*
~*n., pl.* **-ries.** A plenary session or meeting of an organization; a plenum. [Late Latin *plēnārius,* from Latin *plēnus,* full.] **—ple·na·ri·ly** (plē'nər-ə-lē, plĭ-nâr'ə-) *adv.* **—ple·na·ri·ness** *n.*

plenary indulgence *n. Roman Catholic Church.* An indulgence that remits the full temporal punishment incurred by a sinner.

plen·i·po·ten·ti·ar·y (plĕn'ē-pə-tĕn'shē-ĕr'ē, -shə-rē) *adj.* **1.** Invested with or conferring full powers. **2.** Absolute; full: *plenipotentiary power.*
~*n., pl.* **plenipotentiaries.** A person, especially an ambassador or diplomat, fully authorized to represent a government. [Medieval Latin *plēnipotentiārius,* from Late Latin *plēnipotens* : Latin *plēnus,* full + *potens,* POTENT.]

plen·i·tude (plĕn'ə-to͞od', -tyo͞od') *n.* **1.** Abundance; copiousness. **2.** The condition of being full, ample, or complete. [Middle English, fullness, from Old French, from Latin *plēnitūdō,* from *plēnus,* full.]

plen·te·ous (plĕn'tē-əs) *adj.* **1.** Abundant; copious. **2.** Producing or yielding in abundance. [Middle English *plenti(v)ous,* from Old French *plentiveus,* from *plentif,* abundant, from *plente(t),* PLENTY.] **—plen·te·ous·ly** *adv.* **—plen·te·ous·ness** *n.*

plen·ti·ful (plĕn'tĭ-fəl) *adj.* **1.** Existing in great quantity or ample supply. **2.** Providing or producing an abundance: *a plentiful harvest.* **—plen·ti·ful·ly** *adv.* **—plen·ti·ful·ness** *n.*

plen·ty (plĕn'tē) *n.* **1.** A full or wholly adequate amount or supply; as much as one could want: *plenty of time.* **2.** A large quantity or amount; abundance: *goods in plenty.* **3.** A condition of general abundance or prosperity: *peace and plenty.*
~*adj.* Plentiful; abundant. Always used after the noun or pronoun: *That's plenty.*
~*adv. Informal.* Sufficiently; quite: *It's plenty hot.* [Middle English *plent(i)e, plentet,* from Old French *plente(t),* from Latin *plēnitās* (stem *plēnitat*), from *plēnus,* full.]

ple·num (plē'nəm, plĕn'əm) *n., pl.* **-nums** or **plena** (plē'nə, plĕn'ə). **1. a.** A condition in which air or other gas in an enclosure is at a pressure greater than that outside the enclosure. **b.** An enclosure in which such a condition exists. **2.** In the philosophy of the Stoics, the whole of space regarded as being filled with matter. **3.** An assembly or meeting with all members present. **4.** Fullness. [Latin, neuter of *plēnus,* full.] **—ple·num** *adj.*

pleo-, pleio-, plio- *prefix.* Indicates more; for example, **pleomorphism, pleiotropism, Pliocene.** [Greek *pleiōn, pleōn,* more.]

ple·och·ro·ism (plē-ŏk'rō-ĭz'əm) *n.* The property possessed by some crystals of exhibiting different colors when viewed along different axes. Compare **dichroism.** [PLEO- + -CHRO(OUS) + -ISM.] **—ple·o·chro·ic** (plē'ə-krō'ĭk) *adj.*

ple·o·mor·phism, plei·o·mor·phism (plē'ə-môr'fĭz'əm) *n.* **1.** *Chemistry.* **Polymorphism** *(see).* **2.** *Biology.* The occurrence of two or more structural forms during a life cycle, especially of certain plants. [PLEO- + -MORPH + -ISM.] **—ple·o·mor·phic** *adj.*

ple·o·nasm (plē'ə-năz'əm) *n.* **1.** The use of more words than are required to express an idea; redundancy. **2.** An instance of this. **3.** A superfluous word or phrase. [Late Latin *pleonasmus,* from Greek *pleonasmos,* "superabundance," from *pleonazein,* to be more than enough, from *ple(i)ōn,* more.] **—ple·o·nas·tic** (plē'ə-năs'tĭk) *adj.* **—ple·o·nas·ti·cal·ly** *adv.*

ple·o·pod (plē'ə-pŏd') *n. Zoology.* An appendage of crustaceans, a **swimmeret** *(see).* [PLEO- + -POD.]

ple·si·o·sau·rus (plē'sē-ə-sôr'əs, plē'zē-) *n., pl.* **-sauri** (-sôr'ī'). Also **ple·si·o·saur** (plē'sē-ə-sôr', plē'zē-). A large, long-necked marine reptile of the extinct suborder Plesiosauria, common in Europe and North America during the Mesozoic era. [New Latin, from Greek *plēsios,* near + -SAURUS.]

plessor. *Medicine.* Variant of **plexor.**

pleth·o·ra (plĕth'ər-ə) *n.* **1.** A superabundance; an excess. **2.** An excess of blood in the circulatory system or in one organ or area. [Late Latin *plēthōra,* from Greek *plēthōra, plēthōrē,* fullness, from *plēthein,* to be full.]

ple·thor·ic (plĕ-thôr'ĭk, -thŏr'ĭk, plĕth'ər-ĭk) *adj.* **1. a.** Excessive in quantity; superabundant: *plethoric wealth.* **b.** Inflated in style; tur-

PRONUNCIATION KEY
ă, pat; ā, pay; âr, care;
ä, father, are; b, bib;
ch, church; d, deed; ĕ, pet;
ē, be; f, fife; g, gag; h, hat;
hw, which; ĭ, pit; ī, pie;
îr, pier; j, judge; k, kick;
l, lid, needle; m, mum;
n, no, sudden; ng, thing;
ŏ, pot; ō, toe; ô, paw, for;
oi, noise; ou, out; o͝o, book;
o͞o, boot; p, pop; r, roar;
s, sauce; sh, ship, dish;
t, tight; th, thin, path;
th, this, bathe; ŭ, cut; ûr, fur;
v, valve; w, with; y, yes;
z, zebra, size; zh, vision;
ə, about, item, edible,
gallop, circus, peaceful

IN FOREIGN WORDS:
à, *Fr.* ami; œ, *Fr.* feu, *Ger.* schön; ü, *Fr.* tu, *Ger.* über; KH, *Ger.* ich, *Scot.* loch; N, *Fr.* bon; y', *Fr.* Compiègne

STRESS MARKS:
Primary stress: '
in·cite' (ĭn-sīt')
Secondary stress: '
in'sight' (ĭn'sīt')

gid: *plethoric prose.* **2.** Characterized by an overabundance of blood. —**ple·thor·i·cal·ly** *adv.*

ple·thys·mo·graph (plĕ-thĭz′mə-grăf′, -grăf′, plə-) *n.* An instrument used to measure changes in the volume of fluid in a part of the body, such as a limb, caused by fluctuations in blood pressure. [Greek *plēthusmos,* enlargement + -GRAPH.] —**ple·thys·mo·graph·ic** (plĕ-thĭz′mə-grăf′ĭk, plə-) *adj.* —**pleth·ys·mo·graph·i·cal·ly** *adv.* —**pleth·ys·mog·ra·phy** (plĕth′ĭz-mŏg′rə-fē) *n.*

pleu·ra¹ (plŏor′ə) *n., pl.* **pleurae** (plŏor′ē′). *Anatomy.* Either of two membranous sacs, each of which lines one side of the thoracic cavity and envelops the contiguous lung, reducing the friction of respiratory movements to a minimum. [Medieval Latin, from Greek *pleura†,* side, rib.] —**pleu·ral** *adj.*

pleu·ra². Plural of **pleuron.**

pleu·ri·sy (plŏor′ə-sē) *n. Pathology.* Inflammation of the pleura, characterized by pain in the chest or side that becomes worse on deep breathing or coughing. [Middle English *pleresye, pluresy,* from Old French *pleurisie,* from Medieval Latin *pleurisis,* from Late Latin *pleurītis,* from Greek *pleuritis,* from *pleura†,* side, rib.] —**pleu·rit·ic** (plŏo-rĭt′ĭk) *adj.*

pleurisy root *n.* A plant, **butterfly weed** (*see*).

pleuro-, pleur– *prefix.* Indicates: **1.** The side; for example, **pleurodont. 2.** The pleura; for example, **pleuropneumonia.** [New Latin, from Greek *pleura†,* side, rib.]

pleu·ro·dont (plŏor′ə-dŏnt′) *adj. Zoology.* **1.** Having the teeth attached by their sides to the inner side of the jaw, as in some lizards. **2.** Attached in this way: *pleurodont teeth.*
~*n.* An animal with pleurodont teeth. [PLEUR(O)- + -ODONT.]

pleu·ron (plŏor′ŏn) *n., pl.* **pleura** (plŏor′ə). *Zoology.* Either of the two lateral parts of the cuticle covering each of the body segments of arthropods. [New Latin, from Greek *pleuron, pleura†,* rib, side.]

pleu·ro·pneu·mo·nia (plŏor′ō-nŏo-mōn′yə, -nyŏo-mōn′yə) *n. Pathology.* Pneumonia aggravated by pleurisy.

pleu·ro·pneu·mo·nia-like organism (plŏor′ō-nŏo-mōn′yə-līk′, -nyŏo-mōn′yə-līk′) *n. Abbr.* **PPLO** Any of a group of tiny, nonmotile, bacterialike organisms formerly thought to cause a disease resembling pneumonia but now known to be harmless.

pleu·rot·o·my (plŏo-rŏt′ə-mē) *n., pl.* **-mies.** Surgical incision into the pleura. [PLEURO- + -TOMY.]

pleus·ton (plŏo′stən, -stŏn′) *n.* Vegetation, as algae, that floats upon the surface of bodies of fresh water. [Greek *pleusis,* sailing, from *plein,* to sail + (PLANK)TON.] —**pleus·ton·ic** (plŏo-stŏn′ĭk) *adj.*

plex·i·form (plĕk′sə-fôrm′) *adj.* Similar to or having the form of a plexus; complicated in structure. [PLEX(US) + -FORM.]

Plex·i·glas (plĕk′sĭ-glăs′, -gläs′) *n.* A trademark for a light, permanently transparent, weather-resistant thermoplastic form of polymethyl methacrylate.

plex·im·e·ter (plĕk-sĭm′ə-tər) *n. Medicine.* A small, thin plate held against the body and struck with a plexor in the technique of **percussion** (*see*). [PLEX(OR) + -METER.] —**plex·i·met·ric** (plĕk′sĭ-mĕt′rĭk) *adj.* —**plex·im·e·try** *n.*

plex·or (plĕk′sər) *n.* Also **ples·sor** (plĕs′ər). *Medicine.* A small rubber-headed hammer used with a pleximeter in diagnosis by **percussion** (*see*) and also in testing nervous reflexes. [Greek *plēxis,* stroke, from *plēssein,* to strike.]

plex·us (plĕk′səs) *n., pl.* **plexus** or **-uses. 1.** *Anatomy.* A structure in the form of a network, especially of nerves, blood vessels, or lymphatics: *the solar plexus.* **2.** Any interlacing of parts; network. [New Latin, from Latin, network, from *plexus,* past participle of *plectere,* to plait.]

pli·a·ble (plī′ə-bəl) *adj.* **1.** Easily bent or shaped; flexible. **2. a.** Receptive to change; adaptable. **b.** Easily influenced, persuaded, or swayed; tractable. —See Synonyms at **flexible.** —**pli·a·bil·i·ty, pli·a·ble·ness** *n.* —**pli·a·bly** *adv.*

pli·an·cy (plī′ən-sē) *n.* The quality or condition of being pliant.

pli·ant (plī′ənt) *adj.* **1.** Easily bent or flexed; supple; limber. **2.** Easily altered or modified to fit conditions; adaptable. **3.** Yielding readily to influence or domination; docile; compliant. —See Synonyms at **flexible.** [Middle English, from Old French, present participle of *plier,* to bend, fold, from Latin *plicāre,* to fold.] —**pli·ant·ly** *adv.* —**pli·ant·ness** *n.*

pli·ca (plī′kə) *n., pl.* **plicae** (plī′sē′). **1.** *Zoology & Anatomy.* A fold or ridge, as of skin, membrane, or shell. **2.** A matted and encrusted state of the hair, resulting from dirt and vermin. [Medieval Latin, a fold, plait, from Latin *plicāre,* to fold.] —**pli·cal** (plī′kəl) *adj.*

pli·cate (plī′kāt′) *adj.* Also **pli·cat·ed** (plī′kā′tĭd). Arranged in folds like those of a fan; pleated: *plicate leaves.* [Latin *plicātus,* past participle of *plicāre,* to fold.] —**pli·cate·ly** *adv.* —**pli·cate·ness** *n.*

pli·ca·tion (plī-kā′shən) *n.* Also **plic·a·ture** (plĭk′ə-chŏor′). **1. a.** The act or process of folding. **b.** The state of being folded. **2.** A fold. **3.** A surgical technique in which folds are sutured in the walls of a hollow organ to reduce its size.

pli·é (plē-ā′) *n.* A movement in ballet in which the knees are bent while the back remains straight and the feet remain flat on the floor. [French, from the past participle of *plier,* to bend.]

plied. **1.** Past tense and past participle of **ply** (to join). **2.** Past tense and past participle of **ply** (to use or traverse).

pli·er (plī′ər) *n.* One who plies a trade.

pli·ers (plī′ərz) *pl.n.* Any of variously shaped tools having a pair of pivoted jaws, used for holding, bending, or cutting.

plies. 1. Third person singular present tense of **ply** (to join). **2.** Third person singular present tense of **ply** (to use or traverse).

plight¹ (plīt) *n.* A condition or situation of difficulty or adversity. —See Synonyms at **predicament.** [Middle English *plit,* from Norman French, from Old French *pleit, ploit,* "a fold," from Vulgar Latin *plicitum* (unattested), from Latin *plicitus,* past participle of *plicāre,* to fold.]

plight² *tr.v.* **plighted, plighting, plights. 1.** To promise or bind by a solemn pledge; especially, to betroth. **2.** To give or pledge (one's word or oath, for example): *plight one's troth.*
~*n.* **1.** A solemn pledge, as of faith. **2.** An engagement. [Middle English, Old English *pliht* (noun), peril.] —**plight·er** *n.*

plim·soll (plĭm′səl, -sôl′) *n.* Also **plim·sole** (-sōl′). *British.* A light rubber-soled cloth shoe; sneaker. [Probably because the rubber rim resembles a PLIMSOLL LINE.]

Plimsoll line *n.* Any of a set of lines on the hull of a merchant ship to indicate the depth to which it may be legally loaded under specific conditions. Also called "load line," "Plimsoll mark." [After Samuel *Plimsoll* (1824–98), Member of Parliament who supported the British Merchant Shipping Act (1876).]

plink (plĭngk) *n.* A light tinkling sound.
~*v.* **plinked, plinking, plinks.** —*intr.* To produce a plink. —*tr.* To cause to plink. [Imitative.]

plinth (plĭnth) *n.* **1.** A block or slab upon which a pedestal, column, or statue is placed. **2.** The base block at the intersection of the horizontal baseboard and the vertical frame around a doorway. **3.** A continuous course of stones supporting a wall. Also called "plinth course." **4.** A square base, as on a vase. [French *plinthe,* from Latin *plinthus,* from Greek *plinthos†,* brick, square stone block.]

Plin·y¹ (plĭn′ē), Latin name Gaius Plinius Secundus, known as "the Elder" (A.D. 23–79). Roman writer and administrator. He is remembered chiefly for his encyclopedic *Natural History.*

Pliny². Latin name Gaius Plinius Caecilius Secundus, known as "the Younger" (*c.* A.D. 61–113). Roman politician and writer, the nephew of Pliny the Elder. His correspondence provides much valuable information about Roman life and includes a letter from Bithynia that gives one of the first accounts of the early Christians.

plio-. Variant of **pleo-.**

Pli·o·cene (plī′ə-sēn′) *adj. Geology.* Of, belonging to, or designating the geologic time, rock series, and sedimentary deposits of the last of the five epochs of the Tertiary period, characterized by the appearance of distinctly modern plants and animals.
~*n. Geology.* The Pliocene epoch or system of deposits. Preceded by *the.* [Greek *pleiōn,* more + -CENE.] —**Pli·o·cen·ic** (plī′ə-sēn′ĭk, -sē′nĭk) *adj.*

Pli·o·film (plī′ə-fĭlm′) *n.* A trademark for a pliant, transparent rubber compound used for waterproof items.

pli·o·tron (plī′ə-trŏn′) *n.* A vacuum tube run with a high-temperature cathode that has one or more grids. [Originally a trademark.]

plis·sé (plĭ-sā′) *n.* **1.** A puckered texture of cloth created by treating fabric with a caustic soda. **2.** Fabric having such a texture. [French, past participle of *plisser,* to fold, pleat.]

PLO Palestine Liberation Organization.

plod (plŏd) *v.* **plodded, plodding, plods.** —*intr.* **1.** To move or walk heavily or laboriously; trudge. **2.** To work or act perseveringly or monotonously; drudge. Used with *at, on,* or *upon.* —*tr.* To make (one's way) or trudge heavily and slowly along or over.
~*n.* **1.** The act of moving or walking heavily and slowly. **2. a.** A laborious journey. **b.** A laborious piece of work. **3.** The sound made by a heavy step. [16th century : imitative] —**plod·ding·ly** *adv.*

plod·der (plŏd′ər) *n.* One who moves or, especially, works steadily but laboriously and unimaginatively.

–ploid *suffix. Biology.* Indicates a specified multiple of a set of chromosomes; for example, **polyploid.** [Greek *-ploos,* -fold + -OID.]

ploi·dy (ploi′dē) *n.* A multiple of a set of chromosomes. [Back-formation from DIPLOIDY and HAPLOIDY.]

plonk¹. Variant of **plunk.**

plonk² *n. Chiefly British Informal.* Wine of indifferent quality. [Originally Australian slang, probably from French *(vin) blanc,* white (wine).]

plop (plŏp) *v.* **plopped, plopping, plops.** —*intr.* To fall or move with a sound like that of an object falling into water without splashing. —*tr.* To drop or move so as to make such a sound.
~*n.* A plopping sound or movement. [19th century : imitative.] —**plop** *adv.*

plo·sion (plō′zhən) *n. Phonetics.* The sudden release of breath in the articulation of a plosive. Also called "explosion." Compare **implosion.** [From EXPLOSION.]

plo·sive (plō′sĭv, -zĭv) *adj. Phonetics.* Designating a speech sound whose articulation requires, at some stage, the complete closure of both the nasal and the oral passage, as in the sound of (p) in *top.*
~*n. Phonetics.* A plosive speech sound. Also called "explosive." [French, from *explosif,* EXPLOSIVE.]

plot (plŏt) *n.* **1.** A small piece of ground, generally used for a specific purpose. **2. a.** A graphic representation, as on a chart. **b.** Something located on a graph. **c.** A ground plan, as for a building; chart; diagram. **3.** A plan of the main series of events or an outline of the action of a story, drama, or the like. **4.** A secret plan, usually to accomplish a hostile or illegal purpose; scheme. —See Synonyms at **conspiracy.** —**the plot thickens.** Matters are becoming more complex, often with intriguing or sinister overtones.
~*v.* **plotted, plotting, plots.** —*tr.* **1.** To represent graphically, as on a chart: *plot a ship's course.* **b.** To make a plan or map of. **2.** To prearrange secretly or deviously: *plot an assassination.* **3.** To con-

plover Pluvialis squatarola, *the gray plover (above), is a shore bird, foraging for small shellfish, worms, and insects along beaches and mudflats. It breeds only in the high arctic tundras of Canada and Russia; but after the northern summer, some birds migrate as far south as the coasts of South America and Australia.*

plum *Some species of this Northern Hemisphere fruit tree grow up to 10 meters (33 feet) high, others are merely shrubs. The fruit become prunes when dried.*

ceive and arrange the action and incidents of: *plot a novel.* **4. a.** To locate (points or other figures) on a graph mathematically by means of coordinates. **b.** To draw (a curve) connecting points on a graph. *—intr.* To devise secretly; conspire. [In the sense "a piece of ground" (and hence the extended senses "plan," "diagram"), Middle English *plot(te),* Old English *plot*†. In the sense "secret plan," from *complot,* from Old French *complote*†.] **—plot·ter** *n.*

Plo·ti·nus (plō-tī'nəs) (*c.* A.D. 205–70). Greek philosopher. He initiated Neo-Platonism, developing Plato's teaching along mystic lines that suggest some knowledge of Oriental philosophy.

plotting board *n.* A computer output device that plots the curves of functions of variables.

plough. *Chiefly British.* Variant of **plow.**

plov·er (plŭv'ər, plō'vər) *n., pl.* **-ers** or collectively **plover. 1.** Any of various widely distributed wading birds of the family Charadriidae, including the lapwing, having rounded bodies, short tails, and short bills. **2.** Any of various similar or related birds. [Middle English, from Old French *plovier,* from Vulgar Latin *pluviārius, ploviārius* (unattested), "rain-bird" (reason for naming obscure), from Latin *pluvia,* rain, from *pluere,* to rain.]

plow (plou) *n.* Also *chiefly British* **plough. 1.** A farm implement consisting of a heavy blade or blades at the end of a beam, usually pulled by a draft animal or tractor and used for breaking up and turning over soil in preparation for sowing. **2.** Any implement with a similar function, such as a snowplow. **3.** Plowed land. **4. Plow.** *Astronomy.* The **Big Dipper** *(see).*
~v. **plowed, plowing, plows.** Also *chiefly British* **ploughed, ploughing, ploughs.** *—tr.* **1.** To break and turn over (earth) with a plow. **2. a.** To form (a furrow, for example) with a plow. **b.** To make or form with driving force: *plowed his way through the crowd.* **3.** To make furrows or indentations in. **4.** To cut through (water): *plow the high seas.* *—intr.* **1.** To break and turn up earth with a plow. **2.** To admit of being plowed: *Rocky earth plows poorly.* **3.** To move or progress in the manner of a plow. Usually used with *through.* **4.** To proceed laboriously; plod. **—plow back.** To reinvest (earnings or profits) in one's business. **—plow into.** *Informal.* **1.** To strike with force. **2.** To undertake (a task, for example) with eagerness and vigor. **—plow under. 1.** To overwhelm. **2.** To cause to vanish. [Middle English *plou, plogh,* Old English *plōg, plōh,* from late Germanic *plōgaz* (unattested), of Italic origin.] **—plow·a·ble** *adj.* **—plow·er** *n.*

plow·boy (plou'boi') *n.* **1.** A boy who leads or guides a team of animals in plowing. **2.** A country boy.

plow·head (plou'hĕd') *n.* The metal shackle at the leading end of the beam of a plow, used to attach the plow to a tractor or draft animal.

plow·land (plou'lănd') *n.* **1.** In medieval England, a unit of land area roughly equivalent to the area capable of being plowed by a team of eight oxen in a single year. **2.** Land under cultivation or suitable for cultivation.

plow·man (plou'mən) *n., pl.* **-men** (-mĭn). **1.** A person who plows. **2.** A farmer or rustic.

Plow·right (plou'rīt'), **Joan (Anne),** The Lady Olivier (1929–). British actress. She is admired for her work in the modern theater, especially in the socially aware plays of the 1950's, including Osborne's *The Entertainer* (1958, filmed 1960).

plow·share (plou'shâr') *n.* The cutting blade of a plow; a share.

plow steel *n.* A high-strength steel having a carbon content of 0.5 to 0.95 percent and used primarily to make wire rope.

ploy (ploi) *n.* **1.** A tactic or stratagem, as in a conversation or game, to obtain an advantage. **2.** An escapade or amusement. [18th century (Scottish) : origin obscure.]

plu. plural.

pluck (plŭk) *v.* **plucked, plucking, plucks.** *—tr.* **1.** To detach by grasping and pulling abruptly with the fingers; pick: *pluck a flower.* **2.** To pull out the hair or feathers of: *pluck a chicken.* **3.** To give an abrupt pull to; tug at: *pluck a sleeve.* **4.** *Music.* To sound (the strings of an instrument) by pulling and releasing them with the fingers or a plectrum. **5.** *Slang.* To rob or swindle. *—intr.* To give an abrupt pull; tug. Used with *at.*
~n. **1.** The act of plucking; tug; snatch. **2.** Resourceful courage and daring in the face of difficulties; spirit. **3.** The heart, liver, windpipe, and lungs of a slaughtered animal. [Middle English *plukken,* Old English *pluccian,* from West Germanic *plukkōn* (unattested), from Vulgar Latin *piluccāre* (unattested), to remove the hair, pluck, irregularly from *pilus,* hair.] **—pluck·er** *n.*

pluck·y (plŭk'ē) *adj.* **-ier, -iest.** Having or showing courage or spirited resourcefulness in trying circumstances. —See Synonyms at **brave. —pluck·i·ly** *adv.* **—pluck·i·ness** *n.*

plug (plŭg) *n.* **1.** An object, such as a cork, rubber disk, or wad of cloth, used to stop a hole or gap. **2.** A fitting, with metal prongs for insertion in a fixed socket, used to connect an appliance to a power supply. **3.** A **spark plug** *(see).* **4. a.** A flat cake of pressed or twisted tobacco. **b.** A portion of chewing tobacco. **5.** *Geology.* A mass of igneous rock filling the opening, or vent, of a volcano. **6.** *Informal.* A favorable public mention, as of a commercial product, especially on television or radio. **7.** *Slang.* Something inferior, useless, or defective; especially, an old, worn-out horse.
~v. **plugged, plugging, plugs.** *—tr.* **1.** To fill (a hole) tightly with or as if with a plug or stopper; stop up. **2.** To use as a plug: *plugged a cork in a bottle.* **3.** To connect (an electrical appliance) to a socket. Used with *in.* **4.** *Slang.* **a.** To hit with a bullet; shoot. **b.** To hit with the fist; punch. **5.** *Informal.* **a.** To make favorable public mention of (a product, for example). **b.** To advertise or publicize (a song, for example) by constant repetition. *—intr.* **1.** To function by being connected to an electrical outlet. Used with *in.* **2.** *Informal.* To work doggedly and persistently at some activity. Often used with *away* or *along: plug away at homework.* **3.** *Slang.* To fire bullets. [Middle Dutch *plugge*†.] **—plug·ger** *n.*

plug·board, plug board (plŭg'bôrd', -bōrd') *n.* **1.** *Electronics.* A board containing a number of sockets used for patching circuits. Also called "patch board." **2.** A removable panel in a computing device that may be rewired at will to sort data by a prescribed pattern.

plug-com·pat·i·ble (plŭg'kəm-păt'ə-bəl) *adj.* Capable of being connected peripherally to a computer without modification.

plug hat *n. Slang.* A man's high silk hat. [Probably because the head fits into it like a plug.]

plug·hole (plŭg'hōl') *n.* The main drainage hole in a bathtub, basin, or other fixture into which a plug fits.

plug in *intr.v.* **1.** To connect an appliance to an electrical power source by inserting its plug into a socket. **2.** *Slang.* To become aware of or in touch with something: *It's time to face facts and plug in to the real world.* *—tr.v.* To cause to be plugged in.

plug-in (plŭg'ĭn') *adj.* Designating an appliance that works by being plugged in to an electrical power source.
~n. A plug-in appliance or piece of equipment.

plug-ug·ly (plŭg'ŭg'lē) *n., pl.* **-lies.** *Slang.* A gangster or ruffian.
~adj. Very ugly. [After the *plug-ugly* gangs in 19th-century New York, whose members wore PLUG HAT(S).]

plum¹ (plŭm) *n.* **1.** Any of several shrubs or small trees of the genus *Prunus*; especially, *P. domestica,* bearing smooth-skinned, fleshy, edible fruit with a single hard-shelled seed. **2.** The fruit of any of these trees. **3. a.** Any of several trees bearing plumlike fruit. **b.** The fruit of such a tree. **4.** A raisin, when added to a pudding or cake. **5.** Dark purple to deep reddish purple. **6.** *Informal.* Something that is the best of its kind or that is especially desirable, such as a good position. [Middle English *plum(me), plowme,* Old English *plūme,* from West Germanic, from Latin *prūnum.* See **prune.**]

plum². *Informal.* Variant of **plumb.**

plum·age (plo͞o'mĭj) *n.* **1.** The feathers of a bird. **2.** Feathers used ornamentally. **3.** Elaborate dress; finery. [Middle English, from Old French, from *plume,* PLUME.]

plu·mate (plo͞o'māt') *adj.* *Biology.* Resembling or possessing a plume or feather. [Latin *plūmātus,* feathered, from *plūma,* a feather.]

plumb (plŭm) *n.* **1.** A weight suspended from the end of a line, used to determine water depth or to establish a true vertical. **2.** The truly vertical position of a freely suspended plumb line. **—out of** (or **off**) **plumb.** Not vertical.
~adj. Also **plum** (for sense 2). **1.** Exactly vertical. **2.** *Informal.* Utter; sheer: *a plumb fool.* —See Synonyms at **vertical.**
~adv. Also **plum** (for sense 2). **1.** In a vertical or perpendicular line. **2.** *Informal.* Utterly; completely: *plumb tired.*
~v. **plumbed, plumbing, plumbs.** *—tr.* **1.** To test the alignment or angle of with a plumb line. **2.** To straighten or make perpendicular. Usually used with *up.* **3.** To determine the depth of; sound. **4.** To reach or experience (the lowest point or worst extreme of something). **5.** To examine closely; probe into. **6.** To seal with lead. *—intr.* To work as a plumber. [Middle English *plumbe, plombe,* from Old French *plombe,* from Latin *plumbum,* lead.] **—plumb·a·ble** *adj.*

plum·ba·go (plŭm-bā'gō) *n., pl.* **-gos. 1.** Graphite. **2.** Any plant of the genus *Plumbago,* the **leadwort** *(see).* [Latin *plumbāgō,* lead ore, leadwort, from *plumbum,* lead.]

plumb bob *n.* A usually conical piece of metal attached to the end of a plumb line. Also called "plummet."

plumb·er (plŭm'ər) *n.* A workman who installs and repairs pipes and plumbing fixtures for water and drainage. [Middle English *plummer,* from Old French *plommier,* from Late Latin *plumbārius,* lead worker, from Latin *plumbum,* lead.]

plumber's helper *n.* A device having a large suction cup at the end of a handle, used to clear drains; a plunger.

plumber's snake *n.* A plumber's tool, a **snake** *(see).*

plumb·er·y (plŭm'ə-rē) *n., pl.* **-ies. 1.** A plumber's workshop or place of business. **2.** A plumber's work; plumbing.

plum·bic (plŭm'bĭk) *adj. Chemistry.* Of, pertaining to, or containing lead. Said especially of compounds that contain lead with a valence of 4. [From Latin *plumbum,* lead.]

plum·bi·con (plŭm'bĭ-kŏn') *n. Electronics.* A type of television camera tube in which the optical image is detected by a semiconducting lead oxide layer. [From Latin *plumbum,* lead + ICON.]

plum·bif·er·ous (plŭm-bĭf'ər-əs) *adj.* Containing lead. [Latin *plumbum,* lead + -FEROUS.]

plumb·ing (plŭm'ĭng) *n.* **1.** The pipes, fixtures, and other apparatus of a water or sewage system. **2.** The work or trade of a plumber. **3.** The act of using a plumb line.

plum·bism (plŭm'bĭz'əm) *n.* **Lead poisoning** *(see).*

plumb line *n.* **1.** A line from which a weight is suspended to determine verticality or depth. **2.** A line regarded as directed exactly toward the earth's center of gravity.

plum·bous (plŭm'bəs) *adj.* Of, pertaining to, or containing lead. Said especially of compounds that contain lead with a valence of 2. [Late Latin *plumbōsus,* full of lead, from *plumbum,* lead.]

plumb rule *n.* A narrow strip of wood with a plumb line and bob attached, used to test for a true vertical.

plum cake *n.* A kind of rich cake containing raisins, currants, and often other dried fruit.

plum duff *n.* A flour pudding made with raisins or currants, boiled in a cloth bag.

plume (plōm) *n.* 1. A feather, especially one that is large and ornamental. 2. A large feather or cluster of feathers worn as an ornament or symbol of rank, as on a helmet. 3. A token of honor or achievement. 4. A featherlike structure, form, or object: *a plume of smoke.* 5. *Biology.* A feathery structure, such as the cluster of fine hairs on certain fruits and seeds. *—tr.v.* **plumed, pluming, plumes.** 1. To decorate, cover, or supply with or as if with plumes. 2. To smooth (feathers); preen. Used of a bird. 3. To pride or congratulate (oneself). Used with *on* or *upon.* [Middle English, from Old French, from Latin *plūma.*] **—plum·y** *adj.*

plume·let (plōm′lĭt) *n.* A small plume.

plum·met (plŭm′ĭt) *n.* 1. A **plumb bob** (see). 2. Anything that weighs down or oppresses. *—intr.v.* **plummeted, -meting, -mets.** To drop straight down; plunge. [Middle English *plomet,* from Old French *plombet,* ball of lead, diminutive of *plomb,* lead, from Latin *plumbum.*]

plum·my (plŭm′ē) *adj.* **-mier, -miest.** 1. Made of, resembling, or full of plums. 2. Mellow and rich, often to the point of sounding affected: *a plummy voice.* 3. *Informal.* Desirable; good: *a plummy job.*

plu·mose (plōo′mōs′) *adj.* 1. Having plumes or feathers; feathered. 2. Resembling a feather or plume; feathery. [Latin *plūmōsus,* from *plūma,* a feather.] **—plu·mose·ly** *adv.* **—plu·mos·i·ty** (plōo-mŏs′ə-tē) *n.*

plump¹ (plŭmp) *adj.* **plumper, plumpest.** 1. a. Overweight in an attractive way. b. Well-rounded and full in form: *plump cheeks.* 2. Abundant; ample: *a plump reward.* —See Synonyms at **fat.** *—v.* **plumped, plumping, plumps.** *—tr.* To make full or well-rounded. Often used with *up: plump up a pillow.* *—intr.* To become rounded or full. Often used with *up.* [Middle English, from Middle Dutch, from Middle Low German *plomp, plump,* thick, blunt, dull, probably akin to *plumpen,* to PLUMP.] **—plump·ish** *adj.* **—plump·ly** *adv.* **—plump·ness** *n.*

plump² *v.* **plumped, plumping, plumps.** *—intr.* 1. To drop abruptly or heavily: *plump into a chair.* 2. To give all one's support or praise. Used with *for: plumped for her appointment as department head.* *—tr.* To drop or throw down heavily or abruptly: *plump an ice cube into a glass.* *—n.* 1. A heavy or abrupt fall or collision. 2. The sound of this. *—adj.* Blunt; direct. *—adv.* 1. With a heavy or abrupt impact. 2. Straight down. 3. Without qualification; bluntly. [Middle English, from Middle Low German *plumpen,* to plunge into water (probably imitative).]

plum pudding *n.* A rich boiled or steamed pudding containing raisins, currants, citron, and spices. Also called "Christmas pudding."

plum tomato *n.* A variety of cherry tomato that produces long, oval fruits, which are often canned.

plu·mule (plōom′yōol) *n.* 1. A down feather. 2. *Botany.* The rudimentary bud of a plant embryo, which becomes the shoot of the seedling. [Latin *plūmula,* diminutive of *plūma,* feather.] **—plu·mu·lose** (plōom′yə-lōs′) *adj.*

plun·der (plŭn′dər) *v.* **-dered, -dering, -ders.** *—tr.* 1. To rob (a person or place) of goods by force, especially in time of war; pillage; loot. 2. To seize wrongfully or by force; steal. *—intr.* To take booty; rob; pillage. —See Synonyms at **rob.** *—n.* 1. Property stolen by fraud or force; booty. 2. The act or practice of plundering. [Middle Dutch *plunderen* or Frisian *plunderje,* "to rob (of household goods)," akin to Middle Dutch *plunde, plunnet†,* household goods, clothes.] **—plun·der·a·ble** *adj.* **—plun·der·er** *n.* **—plun·der·ous** *adj.*

plun·der·age (plŭn′dər-ĭj) *n.* 1. The act of plundering; pillage. 2. *Maritime Law.* a. The embezzling of goods on board a ship. b. The goods so acquired.

plunge (plŭnj) *v.* **plunged, plunging, plunges.** *—tr.* 1. To thrust or throw forcefully into a substance or place: *Plunge the lobsters into boiling salted water.* 2. To cast suddenly or violently into a specified state or situation: *The room was plunged into darkness.* *—intr.* 1. To throw oneself into a substance or place. 2. To throw oneself earnestly or wholeheartedly into a specified state or activity. 3. To enter violently or speedily. 4. To descend steeply; fall precipitously, as a road or cliff might. 5. To move forward and downward violently. 6. *Informal.* To speculate or gamble extravagantly. *—n.* 1. An act or instance of plunging. 2. a. A place or area for diving or plunging, as a swimming pool. b. A swim; a dip. **—take the plunge.** 1. To take a decisive, difficult step. 2. *Informal.* To get married. [Middle English *plungen, plongen,* from Old French *plonger, plungier,* from Vulgar Latin *plumbicāre* (unattested), to sound with a plumb, from Latin *plumbum,* lead.]

plung·er (plŭn′jər) *n.* 1. One that plunges. 2. A part that operates with a repeated thrusting or plunging movement, such as a piston. 3. A device consisting of a rubber suction cup attached to the end of a stick, used to clean out clogged drains and pipes.

plunk (plŭngk) *v.* **plunked, plunking, plunks.** *Informal.* *—tr.* 1. To strum or pluck (the strings of a musical instrument). 2. To throw or place heavily or abruptly. Used with *down: plunk one's money down.* *—intr.* 1. To emit a hollow, twanging sound. 2. To drop or fall abruptly or heavily; plump.

—n. *Informal.* 1. A short, hollow, twanging sound. 2. A heavy blow or stroke. *—adv.* *Informal.* 1. With a short, hollow thud. 2. Exactly; precisely: *plunk in the center.* [Imitative.] **—plunk·er** *n.*

plu·per·fect (plōo-pûr′fĭkt) *adj.* *Abbr.* **plup., plupf.** *Grammar.* Of or designating a verb tense used to express action completed prior to a stated or implied past time. *—n.* *Abbr.* **plup., plupf.** 1. The pluperfect tense, formed in English with the past participle of a verb and one or more auxiliaries; for example, in the sentence *He had gone by the time we arrived, had gone* is in the pluperfect. 2. A verb or form in this tense. Also called "past perfect." [New Latin *plūsperfectum,* contracted from Latin *(tempus praeteritum) plūs quam perfectum,* "(past tense) more than perfect" (translation of Greek *khronos hupersuntelikos*) : Latin *plūs,* more + *quam,* than + *perfectus,* PERFECT (tense).]

plu·ral (plōor′əl) *adj.* *Abbr.* **pl., plu., plur.** 1. Of or composed of more than one member, set, or kind. 2. Of or relating to a grammatical form that designates more than one of the things or persons stated. Compare **dual, singular.** *—n.* *Abbr.* **pl., plu., plur.** *Grammar.* 1. The plural number or form. 2. A word or word element in this form. [Middle English *plurel, plural,* from Old French *plurel,* from Latin *plūrālis,* from *plūs* (stem *plūr-*), more.] **—plu·ral·ly** *adv.*

plu·ral·ism (plōor′ə-lĭz′əm) *n.* 1. The condition of being plural. 2. A condition of society in which numerous ethnic, religious, or cultural groups remain distinct but coexist within one nation. 3. The belief that political power should not be wielded by central government alone, but shared by regional councils and organizations. 4. The holding by one person of more than one position or office, especially two or more ecclesiastical benefices, at one time. 5. *Philosophy.* a. The doctrine that reality is composed of many ultimate substances. b. The belief that no single explanatory system or view of reality can account for all the phenomena of life. Compare **monism, dualism.**

plu·ral·ist (plōor′ə-lĭst) *n.* 1. A person who holds more than one office, especially two or more ecclesiastical benefices, at one time. 2. One who adheres to philosophical pluralism. 3. One who advocates cultural pluralism. **—plu·ral·is·tic** (plōor′ə-lĭs′tĭk) *adj.*

plu·ral·i·ty (plōo-răl′ə-tē) *n., pl.* **-ties.** *Abbr.* **plur.** 1. The state or fact of being plural. 2. A large number or amount; multitude. 3. *Ecclesiastical.* a. Pluralism. b. The offices or benefices held by a pluralist. 4. a. In a contest of more than two selections, the number of votes cast for the winning selection if this number is not more than one half of the total votes cast. b. The number by which the vote of a winning candidate exceeds that of the closest opponent. Compare **majority.** 5. The larger or greater part of anything.

plu·ral·ize (plōor′ə-līz′) *v.* **-ized, -izing, -izes.** *—tr.* 1. To make plural. 2. To express in the plural. *—intr.* 1. To become plural. 2. To hold more than one position or ecclesiastical benefice at one time. **—plu·ral·i·za·tion** *n.*

plural marriage *n.* Marriage to more than one partner at the same time or during one period; polygamy.

pluri- *prefix.* Indicates more than one or many; for example, **pluricellular.** [Latin *plūs* (stem *plūr-*), more, *plures* (plural); several.]

plus (plŭs) *prep.* 1. Added to. 2. Increased by; along with: *earnings plus dividends.* *—adj.* 1. a. Involving or pertaining to addition. b. Positive, as on a scale; more than zero. 2. Added or extra: *a plus benefit.* 3. *Informal.* Increased to a further degree: *personality plus.* 4. Slightly more than: *a mark of C plus.* 5. *Electricity.* Positive. *—conj.* *Informal.* In addition; and. *—n., pl.* **pluses** or **plusses.** 1. The plus sign (+). 2. A positive quantity. 3. A favorable factor: *Clear weather was a plus for the trip.* [Latin *plūs,* more.]

plus fours *pl.n.* Loose knickerbockers bagging below the knees, traditionally worn by men for golf. [From the fact that they are four inches longer than ordinary knickerbockers.]

plush (plŭsh) *n.* A fabric of silk, rayon, cotton, or other material, having a thick, deep pile. *—adj.* 1. Made of or covered with plush. 2. *Informal.* Ostentatiously luxurious, as in furnishings. [From obsolete French *pluche,* from Old French *p(e)luche,* from *peluch(i)er,* to pluck, from Vulgar Latin *pilūccāre,* "to remove the hair," irregularly from *pilus,* hair.] **—plush·ly** *adv.* **—plush·ness** *n.*

plush·y (plŭsh′ē) *adj.* **-ier, -iest.** 1. Resembling plush in texture. 2. *Informal.* Plush; luxurious: *a plushy office.* **—plush·i·ly** *adv.* **—plush·i·ness** *n.*

plus sign *n.* The symbol (+), as in 2 + 2 = 4, used to indicate addition or a positive quantity. Also called "plus." Compare **minus sign.**

Plu·tarch (plōo′tärk′) (c. A.D. 46–120). Greek academic. He wrote *Parallel Lives,* a collection of biographies that Shakespeare used in his Roman plays.

Plu·to¹ (plōo′tō). *Roman Mythology.* The god of the dead and ruler of the underworld, identified with the Greek Hades. [Latin, from Greek *Ploutōn,* "rich one," from *ploutos,* wealth.]

Pluto² *n.* The ninth and farthest planet from the sun, having a sidereal period of revolution about the sun of 248.4 years, 4.5 billion kilometers (2.8 billion miles) distant from the earth at perihelion and 7.4 billion kilometers (4.6 billion miles) at aphelion, and a diameter approximately half that of the earth. [After PLUTO (god).] See feature, next page.

plu·toc·ra·cy (plōo-tŏk′rə-sē) *n., pl.* **-cies.** 1. Government by the wealthy. **2.** A wealthy class that controls a government. **3.** A government or state in which the wealthy rule. [Greek *ploutokratia* : *ploutos*, wealth + -CRACY.] **—plu·to·crat** (plōō'tə-krăt') *n.* **—plu·to·crat·ic** (plōō'tə-krăt'ĭk) *adj.* **—plu·to·crat·i·cal·ly** *adv.*

plu·ton (plōō'tŏn') *n.* Igneous rock formed beneath the surface of the earth by consolidation of magma. [Probably back-formation from PLUTONIC.]

Plu·to·ni·an (plōō-tō'nē-ən) *adj.* Also **Plu·ton·ic** (-tŏn'ĭk). **1.** Of or pertaining to Pluto or the underworld. **2.** Of or pertaining to the planet Pluto.

plu·ton·ic (plōō-tŏn'ĭk) *adj.* *Geology.* **1.** Of deep igneous or magmatic origin: *plutonic water.* **2.** Plutonic. Variant of **Plutonian.** [From PLUTO (referring to the infernal regions).]

plu·to·ni·um (plōō-tō'nē-əm) *n.* *Symbol* **Pu** A naturally radioactive, silvery, metallic transuranic element, occurring in uranium ores and produced artificially by neutron bombardment of uranium, having fifteen isotopes with masses ranging from 232 to 246 and half-lives from 20 minutes to 76 million years. It is a radiological poison, specifically absorbed by bone marrow, and is used, especially in the highly fissionable isotope Plutonium-239, as a reactor fuel and in nuclear weapons. Atomic number 94, melting point 639.5°C, boiling point 3,226.8°C, specific gravity 19.8, valences 3, 4, 5, 6. [Latin *Pluto, Pluton-,* PLUTO + -IUM.]

plu·vi·al (plōō'vē-əl) *adj.* **1.** Of or pertaining to rain; rainy. **2.** *Geology.* Caused by rain.
~n. A period of prolonged rain causing geologic change. [Latin *pluviālis,* from *pluvia,* rain. See **pluvious.**]

pluvio– *prefix.* Indicates rain; for example, **pluviometer.** [Latin *pluvia,* rain. See **pluvious.**]

plu·vi·om·e·ter (plōō'vē-ŏm'ə-tər) *n.* A device for measuring rainfall, a **rain gauge** (see). [French *pluviomètre* : PLUVIO- + -METER.] **—plu·vi·o·met·ric** (plōō'vē-ə-mĕt'rĭk), **plu·vi·o·met·ri·cal** *adj.* **—plu·vi·o·met·ri·cal·ly** *adv.* **—plu·vi·om·e·try** *n.*

plu·vi·ous (plōō'vē-əs) *adj.* Also **plu·vi·ose** (plōō'vē-ōs'). Characterized by heavy rainfall; rainy. [Middle English *pluvyous,* from Latin *pluviōsus,* from *pluvia,* rain, from *pluvius,* rainy, from *pluvere,* to rain.] **—plu·vi·os·i·ty** (plōō'vē-ŏs'ə-tē) *n.*

ply¹ (plī) *tr.v.* **plied, plying, plies. 1.** To join together, as by molding or twisting. **2.** To double over (cloth, for example).
~n., *pl.* **plies. 1.** A layer, as of doubled-over cloth or of paper. **2.** Any of the sheets of wood glued together to form plywood. **3.** Any of the strands twisted together to make yarn, rope, or thread. Used in combination to indicate a specified number of strands, twists, or folds: *three-ply.* **4.** A bias; inclination. [Middle English *plien,* from Old French *plier,* from Latin *plicāre,* to fold.]

ply² *v.* **plied, plying, plies. —tr. 1.** To use diligently as a tool or weapon; wield: *plies an ax.* **2.** To engage in (a trade, for example); practice diligently. **3.** To traverse or sail over regularly: *plied the coastal routes.* **4.** To continue supplying or offering to: *plying her guests with food.* **5.** To assail vigorously. **—intr. 1.** To traverse a route or course regularly: *A boat plies between the islands.* **2.** To perform or work diligently or regularly: *plied at the weaver's trade.* **3.** *Nautical.* To work against the wind by a zigzag course; tack. —See Usage note at **handle.** [Middle English *(ap)plien,* to employ, APPLY.]

Plym·outh¹ (plĭm'əth). Port of Devonshire, southwestern England. On Plymouth Sound between the Plym and Tamar estuaries, it has long been important as a naval station. Sir Francis Drake sailed from here to fight the Spanish Armada, and it was the last port of call for the *Mayflower* before it sailed to America (1620).

Plymouth². Town in Massachusetts, southeast of Boston on Plymouth Bay. It was the landing point for the Pilgrim Fathers and the *Mayflower* (1620). Tourism, fishing, and electronics are important.

Plymouth Brethren *n.* A strict puritanical Protestant sect founded in 1830 in Plymouth, England.

Plymouth Rock *n.* **1.** A boulder on the coast of Massachusetts,

---

Pluto

A REMOTE AND FRIGID WORLD

The planet that proved to be much smaller than predicted

Pluto, the ninth planet, was discovered in 1930 by the American astronomer Clyde Tombaugh. Its position had been predicted by another American, Percival Lowell, who died in 1916. The prediction had been made on the basis of irregularities in the movements of the giant planets Uranus and Neptune, which indicated that they were being influenced by an invisible body. When Pluto's size was measured, however, it was surprisingly small—no more than 2,320 kilometers (1,440 miles) in diameter, or one-fifth of the diameter of the earth. It is probably made up of a mixture of ice and rock, with a surface temperature of –230°C (–382°F). It is not massive enough to cause any measurable effects upon other planets, and so the planet Lowell sought may remain to be discovered.

Pluto has a much more eccentric orbit than those of the other planets. It takes 248 years to go once around the Sun, and at its closest it moves farther in toward the Sun than the orbit of Neptune, so between 1979 and 1999 Neptune, not Pluto, is "the outermost planet." In 1977 it was found that Pluto has a moon, which is one-third the diameter of Pluto, and moves around it every 6.3 days. Both Pluto and its moon, Charon, may have layers of frozen methane on their surfaces.

Even in the world's largest telescopes Pluto looks like nothing more than a dim star, and very sensitive techniques are needed to show Pluto and Charon separately.

HOW A PLANET WAS FOUND *Clyde Tombaugh found Pluto when checking two photographs of the same area of sky taken on January 23 and 29, 1930, at the Lowell Observatory in Arizona, as part of an intensive search for the planet. He noticed that one point had* *moved position. It was indeed a planet, but it was not exactly what he was looking for. Scientists had predicted a gaseous giant, not a tiny lump of ice and rock. But Pluto's discovery was a triumph: it was the first planet to be discovered with photography.*

Planet location guide

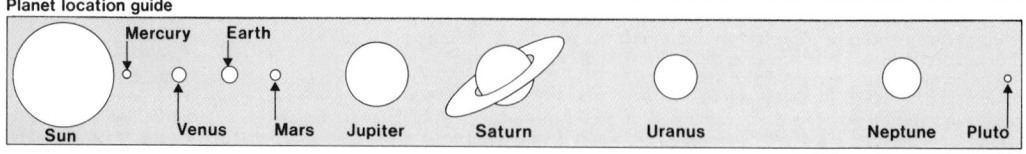

traditionally regarded as the landing place of the Pilgrims. **2.** An American breed of fowl raised for both meat and eggs.

ply·wood (plī′wŏŏd′) *n.* A structural material made of thin layers of wood glued tightly together, usually with the grains of adjoining layers at right angles to each other. [PLY (layer) + WOOD.]

Pl·zeň (pŭl′zĕn′, -zĕn′yə). German **Pil·sen** (pĭl′zən). Capital of West Bohemia, Czechoslovakia. On the Berounka River, it is famous for its pilsner beer, brewed since the Middle Ages.

Pm The symbol for the element promethium.

PM postmaster; postmistress.

pm. **1.** paymaster. **2.** premium.

p.m. **1.** post meridiem. **2.** post-mortem. **3.** post-mortem examination.

P.M. **1.** past master. **2.** postmaster; postmistress. **3.** post meridiem. **4.** post-mortem examination. **5.** prime minister. **6.** provost marshal.

PMBX private manual branch (telephone) exchange.

P.M.G. **1.** paymaster general. **2.** postmaster general.

PMS premenstrual syndrome.

PMT (pē′ĕm-tē′) *n.* A photomechanical transfer.

p.n., P/N promissory note.

PNdB. perceived noise decibel.

pneum. pneumatic.

pneu·ma (nŏŏ′mə, nyŏŏ′-) *n.* The soul or vital spirit. [Greek *pneuma,* blast of wind, breath, divine inspiration, spirit.]

pneu·mat·ic (nŏŏ-măt′ĭk, nyŏŏ′-) *adj. Abbr.* **pneum. 1.** Of or pertaining to air or other gases. **2.** Of or pertaining to pneumatics. **3.** Run by or using compressed air. **4.** Filled with air, especially compressed air: *a pneumatic tire.* **5.** Having air cavities, as do the bones of many birds. **6.** Having or pertaining to shapely, full breasts. **7.** Of or pertaining to the pneuma; spiritual. [French *pneumatique,* from Latin *pneumaticus,* from Greek *pneumatikos,* from *pneuma* (stem *pneumat-*), wind, spirit.] —**pneu·mat·i·cal·ly** *adv.* —**pneu·ma·tic·i·ty** (nŏŏ′mə-tĭs′ə-tē, nyŏŏ′-) *n.*

pneu·mat·ics (nŏŏ-măt′ĭks, nyŏŏ′-) *n. Used with a singular verb.* The study of the mechanical properties of air and other gases.

pneumatic trough *n. Chemistry.* A flat dish filled with water or other liquid, used in laboratory experiments for collecting gases by displacement of liquid from an inverted container.

pneumato– *prefix.* Indicates: **1.** Air; for example, **pneumatophore. 2.** Breath or breathing; for example, **pneumatometer. 3.** Spirit or spirits; for example, **pneumatology.** [Greek *pneuma* (stem *pneumat-*), blast of wind, breath, spirit.]

pneu·ma·tol·o·gy (nŏŏ′mə-tŏl′ə-jē, nyŏŏ′-) *n.* **1.** The doctrine or study of spiritual beings and phenomena; especially, the belief in spirits intervening between man and God. **2.** The Christian doctrine of the Holy Ghost. **3.** *Archaic. Psychology.* [New Latin *pneumatologia* : PNEUMATO- + -LOGY.] —**pneu·ma·to·log·ic** (nŏŏ′mə-tə-lŏj′ĭk, nyŏŏ′-), **pneu·ma·to·log·i·cal** *adj.* —**pneu·ma·tol·o·gist** *n.*

pneu·ma·tom·e·ter (nŏŏ′mə-tŏm′ə-tər, nyŏŏ′-) *n.* A device for measuring the pressure of inspiration or expiration in the lungs. [PNEUMATO- + -METER.] —**pneu·ma·tom·e·try** *n.*

pneu·mat·o·phore (nŏŏ-măt′ə-fôr′, -fōr′, nyŏŏ-) *n.* **1.** *Zoology.* A gas-filled sac serving as a float in certain colonial organisms, such as the Portuguese man-of-war. **2.** *Botany.* A specialized root in certain aquatic plants, such as the mangrove, that grows upward and through which exchange of respiratory gases occurs.

pneumo–, pneum– *prefix.* **1.** The lung or respiratory organs; for example, **pneumograph. 2.** Air or gas; for example, **pneumothorax.** [Greek *pneuma,* wind, breath, spirit.]

pneu·mo·ba·cil·lus (nŏŏ′mō-bə-sĭl′əs, nyŏŏ′-) *n., pl.* **-cilli** (-sĭl′ī). A rod-shaped bacterium, *Klebsiella pneumoniae,* associated with respiratory infections, especially pneumonia.

pneu·mo·coc·cus (nŏŏ′mə-kŏk′əs, nyŏŏ′-) *n., pl.* **-cocci** (-kŏk′sī, -kŏk′ī). A spherical bacterium, *Streptococcus pneumoniae,* that causes pneumonia. —**pneu·mo·coc·cal** *adj.*

pneu·mo·co·ni·o·sis (nŏŏ′mō-kō′nē-ō′sĭs, nyŏŏ′-) *n.* A lung disease caused by prolonged inhalation of mineral or metallic dusts and characterized by breathlessness and coughing. [New Latin : PNEUMO- + Greek *konia, konis,* dust + -OSIS.]

pneu·mo·gas·tric (nŏŏ′mō-găs′trĭk, nyŏŏ′-) *adj.* **1.** Of or involving the lungs and the stomach. **2.** Relating to the vagus nerve. In this sense, not in current technical usage.

pneumogastric nerve *n. Anatomy.* The **vagus** *(see).* Not in current technical usage.

pneu·mo·graph (nŏŏ′mə-grăf′, -gräf′, nyŏŏ′-) *n.* A device for recording chest movements during respiration. [PNEUMO- + -GRAPH.] —**pneu·mo·graph·ic** (nŏŏ′mə-grăf′ĭk, nyŏŏ′-) *adj.*

pneu·mo·nec·to·my (nŏŏ′mə-nĕk′tə-mē, nyŏŏ′-) *n., pl.* **-mies.** Also **pneu·mec·to·my** (nŏŏ-mĕk′tə-mē, nyŏŏ′-). Surgical removal of a lung or of lung tissue. [Greek *pneumōn,* lung (see **pneumonic**) + -ECTOMY.]

pneu·mo·nia (nŏŏ-mōn′yə, nyŏŏ′-) *n.* A disease marked by inflammation of one lung *(single pneumonia)* or both lungs *(double pneumonia)* and caused by viruses, bacteria, and physical and chemical agents. [New Latin, from Greek, from *pneumōn,* lung, from *pneuma,* breath.]

pneu·mon·ic (nŏŏ-mŏn′ĭk, nyŏŏ′-) *adj.* **1.** Pertaining to, affected by, or similar to pneumonia. **2.** Of, affecting, or pertaining to the lungs; pulmonary. [New Latin *pneumonicus,* from Greek *pneumonikos,* of the lungs, from *pneumōn,* lung.]

pneu·mo·ni·tis (nŏŏ′mə-nī′tĭs, nyŏŏ′-) *n.* Inflammation of the lungs

that is restricted to the walls of the air sacs. [PNEUMON- + -ITIS.]

pneu·mo·tho·rax (nŏŏ′mō-thôr′ăks, -thōr′ăks, nyŏŏ′-) *n.* Accumulation of air or gas in the pleural cavity, occurring as a result of disease or injury or sometimes induced to collapse the lung in the treatment of tuberculosis and other lung diseases.

p.n.g. persona non grata.

p-n junction (pē′ĕn′) *n. Electronics.* A junction between a p-type and an n-type semiconducting region, used in rectifiers and in transistors. [*P-n,* abbreviation of *Positive-negative.*]

Po¹ The symbol for the element polonium.

Po² (pō). Italy's longest river, 652 kilometers (405 miles). Rising in the western Alps, it flows eastward to a delta on the Adriatic Sea.

p.o. **1.** petty officer. **2.** post office.

P.O. **1.** Personnel Officer. **2.** petty officer. **3.** postal order. **4.** post office.

poach¹ (pōch) *tr.v.* **poached, poaching, poaches.** To cook gently in a boiling or simmering liquid: *fish poached in wine.* [Middle English *pochen,* from Old French *poch(i)er* (originally of shelled eggs, to cook so that the whites form pockets), from *poche,* pocket, from Frankish *pokka* (unattested).]

poach² (pōch) *v.* **poached, poaching, poaches.** —*intr.* **1.** To trespass on another's property in order to take fish or game. **2.** To take fish or game in a forbidden area. **3.** To take, acquire, or appropriate something or someone by devious or unfair means. **4.** To become muddy or broken up from being trampled. Used of land. —*tr.* **1.** To trespass on (another's property) for fishing or hunting. **2.** To take (fish or game) illegally. **3.** To take, acquire, or appropriate (something or someone) by devious or unfair means: *was accused of poaching staff from a rival company.* **4.** In tennis and similar games, to play (a shot that should have been taken by one's partner). **5.** To make (land) muddy or broken up by trampling. [Earlier *poche,* perhaps from French *pocher,* to pocket. See **poach** (cookery).]

poach·er¹ (pō′chər) *n.* A vessel or dish designed for the poaching of food, such as eggs or fish.

poacher² *n.* A person who poaches on the property of another.

Po·ca·hon·tas (pō′kə-hŏn′təs) (c. 1595-1617). An American Indian, she befriended the colonists who settled near Chesapeake Bay in 1607. Her appeals to her powerful father saved the life of the captured Capt. John Smith. She married another colonist, John Rolfe, in 1614 and accompanied him to England, where she contracted a fatal case of smallpox.

po·chard (pō′chərd) *n.* Any of various diving ducks of the genera *Aythya* and *Netta;* especially, *A. ferina,* of Europe, having gray and black plumage and a reddish head. [Origin unknown.]

pock (pŏk) *n.* **1.** A pustule caused by smallpox or a similar eruptive disease. **2.** A mark or scar left in the skin by such a pustule; pockmark.
~*tr.v.* **pocked, pocking, pocks.** To mark with pocks; pit. [Middle English *pokke,* Old English *pocc,* from Germanic.]

pock·et (pŏk′ĭt) *n.* **1. a.** A small, flat pouch or pouchlike piece of material sewn into a garment and used to carry small articles. **b.** A piece of material sewn onto the outside of a garment with the top edge open. **2.** A small sack or bag. **3.** Any receptacle, cavity, or opening similar in shape or purpose to a garment pocket, such as a compartment on the inside of a car door, or a receptacle on the back of an airplane seat or inside a suitcase. **4.** Supply of money; financial means. **5.** *Mining.* **a.** A small cavity in the earth containing ore. **b.** A small body or accumulation of ore. **6.** Any of the pouchlike receptacles at the corners and sides of a billiard table. **7.** A small, isolated or protected area or group. **8.** An **air pocket** *(see).* —See Synonyms at **hole.** —**in** (or **out of) pocket.** Having gained (or lost) money. —**line one's pockets.** To profit dishonestly by one's position.
~*adj.* **1.** Suitable for or capable of being carried in one's pocket: *a pocket edition.* **2.** Small; miniature.
~*tr.v.* **pocketed, -eting, -ets. 1.** To place in or as if in one's pocket. **2.** To take possession of for oneself, especially dishonestly. **3.** To accept or tolerate (an insult, for example). **4.** To suppress or conceal: *He pocketed his pride.* **5.** To prevent (a bill) from becoming law by delaying its signing until the adjournment of the legislative body. See **pocket veto. 6.** In billiards, snooker, and similar games, to hit (a ball) directly or indirectly into a pocket. [Middle English *poket,* from Norman French *poket(e),* diminutive of *poke, poque,* bag, POKE.] —**pock·et·a·ble** *adj.* —**pock·et·er** *n.*

pocket billiards *n.* The game of **pool** (sense 6) *(see).*

pock·et·book (pŏk′ĭt-bŏŏk′) *n.* **1.** A pocket-sized folder or case used to hold money and papers. **2.** A bag used to carry money, papers, and other small articles; purse. **3.** Also **pocket book.** A pocket-sized, usually paperbound book. **4.** Supply of money; financial resources.

pocket borough *n.* A borough in England, prior to the Reform Act of 1832, whose representation was controlled by a single person or family. Compare **rotten borough.**

pocket bread *n.* Pita bread.

pocket calculator *n.* A small calculator designed to be carried in a pocket.

pock·et·ful (pŏk′ĭt-fŏŏl′) *n., pl.* **-fuls** or **pocketsful.** As much as a pocket will hold.

pocket gopher *n.* A gopher (sense 1) *(see).*

pocket handkerchief *n.* A small handkerchief kept in a garment pocket.

pock·et·knife (pŏk′ĭt-nīf′) *n., pl.* **-knives** (-nīvz′). A small knife with a blade or blades folding into the handle.

pochard *A freshwater duck of European lakes and rivers that can dive to 3 meters (about 10 feet) to feed on roots, buds, and seeds. The adult female (above, foreground) has brown plumage; the male has a red head, a black breast, and a pale gray body. The pochard closely resembles the North American duck known as "redhead."*

pocket money *n.* Money for incidental or minor expenses.

pocket mouse *n.* Any of various small, North American burrowing rodents of the genus *Perognathus*, having external cheek pouches.

pocket veto *n.* **1.** The President's indirect veto of a bill presented to him within ten days of Congressional adjournment, by his retaining the bill unsigned until Congress adjourns. **2.** A similar action exercised by a state governor or other chief executive.

pock·mark (pŏk'märk') *n.* **1.** A pitlike scar left on the skin by smallpox or another eruptive disease. **2.** A pit or scar on a surface. —*tr.v.* **pockmarked, -marking, -marks.** To disfigure with pockmarks. —**pock·marked** *adj.*

po·co (pō'kō) *adv. Music.* Somewhat; a little. Used as a direction: *poco adagio.* [Italian, little, from Latin *paucus,* little, few.]

po·co a po·co (pō'kō ä pō'kō) *adv. Music.* Gradually; little by little. Used as a direction: *poco a poco diminuendo.* [Italian.]

po·co·cu·ran·te (pō'kō-kŏŏ-rän'tē, -rän'tē) *adj.* Indifferent; unconcerned; apathetic.
~*n.* One who does not care; an unconcerned person. [Italian, "little caring."] —**po·co·cu·ran·tism** *n.*

Po·co·no Mountains (pō'kə-nō'). Also **Po·co·nos** (-nōz'). Range of the Appalachian Mts. in northeastern Pennsylvania. Forested and having many lakes and streams, the Poconos are a major resort area.

po·co·sin (pə-kō'sĭn) *n. Chiefly Southeastern U.S.* A swamp in an upland coastal region. [Delaware *pâkwesen.*]

pod¹ (pŏd) *n.* **1.** *Botany.* **a.** The long, two-valved fruit of a leguminous plant, such as the pea, which contains several seeds and usually dries and splits open when ripe. **b.** The seed case of such a fruit. **c.** Any of several similar fruits. **2.** A podlike protective covering. **3.** A compartment for personnel or instrumentation that may be detached from the spacecraft carrying it.
~*v.* **podded, podding, pods.** —*intr.* **1.** To bear or produce pods. **2.** To expand or swell like a pod. —*tr.* To remove (seeds, peas, beans, or the like) from a pod. [17th century : back-formation from dialectal *podware†,* crops, bagged vegetables.]

pod² *n.* **1.** A school of seals or whales. **2.** A small flock of birds. [Origin unknown.]

pod³ *n.* **1.** The lengthwise groove in certain boring tools, such as augers. **2.** The socket for holding the bit in a boring tool. [16th century : perhaps variant of PAD (cushion).]

–pod, –pode *suffix.* Indicates a specified kind or number of feet; for example, **cephalopod, tripod.** [New Latin *-podius, -poda,* from Greek *pous* (stem *pod-*), foot.]

po·dag·ra (pə-dăg'rə) *n. Pathology.* Gout, especially of the big toe. [Middle English, from Latin, from Greek, "trap for the feet," foot disease, gout : *pous* (stem *pod-*), foot + *agra, agrē,* seizure.] —**po·dag·ral, po·dag·ric** *adj.*

po·des·ta (pō-děs'tə, pō'dě-stä') *n.* **1.** A governor appointed by Frederick Barbarossa to rule over one or more of the Lombard cities. **2.** The chief magistrate or officer in any of the republics of medieval Italy. **3.** Under the Fascist regime in Italy, the chief magistrate or mayor in any of the Italian communes except Rome and Naples. **4.** A subordinate magistrate or judge in some modern Italian towns. [Italian *podestà, potestà,* from Latin *potestās* (stem *potestāt-*), power, magistrate, from *potis,* able.]

Pod·gor·ny (pŏd-gôr'nē), **Nikolai Viktorovich** (1903–83). Soviet politician. He became president of the U.S.S.R. (1965), but resigned (1977) when displaced by Brezhnev.

podgy *Chiefly British.* Variant of **pudgy.**

po·di·a·try (pə-dī'ə-trē) *n.* The study, care, and treatment of the human foot. Also called "chiropody." [Greek *pous* (stem *pod-*), foot + -IATRY.] —**po·di·a·trist** *n.*

po·di·um (pō'dē-əm) *n., pl.* **-dia** (-dē-ə) or **-ums. 1.** An elevated platform, as for an orchestra conductor or lecturer; dais. **2.** *Architecture.* A low wall serving as foundation. **3.** A wall circling the arena of an ancient amphitheater. **4.** *Zoology.* A structure resembling or functioning as a foot. [Latin, raised platform, balcony, from Greek *podion,* "small foot," base, from *pous* (stem *pod-*), foot.]

–podium *suffix.* Indicates a part that resembles a foot; for example, **monopodium.** [New Latin, from Greek *podion,* "small foot," from *pous* (stem *pod-*), foot.]

pod·o·phyl·lin (pŏd'ə-fĭl'ĭn) *n.* A bitter-tasting resin obtained from the dried root of the May apple *(see)* and used as a laxative. [New Latin *podophyllum,* "(plant with) footlike leaves" : Greek *pous* (stem *pod-*), foot + *phullon,* a leaf + -IN.]

–podous *suffix.* Having a specified kind or number of feet or footlike parts: *gastropodous.* [-POD + -OUS.]

Po·dunk (pō'dŭngk') *n. Slang.* Any small, isolated, and unimportant town. [After *Podunk,* locality in Connecticut or town in Massachusetts.]

pod·zol (pŏd'zôl') *n.* A leached soil formed mainly in cool, humid climates. [Russian, "ash ground" : *pod,* bottom, ground + *zola,* ashes.] —**pod·zol·ic** (pŏd-zŏl'ĭk, -zō'lĭk) *adj.*

pod·zol·ize (pŏd'zō-līz') *v.* **-ized, -izing, -izes.** —*tr.* To make (soil) acidic by leaching out bases; form into a podzol. —*intr.* To become acidic by leaching; become a podzol. Used of soil. —**pod·zol·i·za·tion** *n.*

Poe (pō), **Edgar Allan** (1809–49). U.S. author. His macabre stories and poems, such as *The Fall of the House of Usher* (1839) and *Ligeia* (1840), had widespread influence, especially on Baudelaire and Mallarmé in France.

P.O.E. 1. port of embarkation. **2.** port of entry.

po·em (pō'əm, -ĭm) *n.* **1.** A composition designed to convey a vivid

and imaginative sense of experience, characterized by the use of condensed language chosen for its sound and suggestive power as well as its meaning, and by the use of such literary techniques as structured meter, natural cadences, rhyme, and imagery. **2.** Any composition in verse rather than in prose. **3.** Any literary composition written with an intensity of language or conscious use of stylistic devices more characteristic of poetry than of prose: *a prose poem.* **4.** Any creation, object, or experience thought to embody the lyrical beauty or structural perfection characteristic of poetry. [Old French *poeme,* from Latin *poēma,* from Greek *poiēma, poēma,* "created thing," work, poem, from *poiein,* to make, create.]

poenology. Variant of **penology.**

po·e·sy (pō'ə-zē, -sē) *n., pl.* **-sies. 1.** Poetry. **2. a.** The art or practice of composing poems. **b.** The inspiration involved in composing poetry. **3.** Poems collectively. [Middle English *poesie,* from Old French, from Common Romance *poēsia* (unattested), variant of Latin *poēsis,* from Greek *po(i)ēsis,* "a making," "creation," poetry, from *poiein,* to make, create.]

po·et (pō'ĭt) *n.* **1.** A writer of poems. **2.** One who is especially gifted in the perception and expression of the beautiful or lyrical. [Middle English *poete,* from Old French, from Latin *poēta,* from Greek *poiētēs,* "maker," poet, from *poiein,* to make, create.]
Synonyms: bard, poetaster, rhymer, rhymester, versifier.

po·et·as·ter (pō'ĭt-ăs'tər) *n.* An inferior poet. —See Synonyms at **poet.** [New Latin : Latin *poēt(a),* POET + -ASTER.]

po·et·ess (pō'ĭ-tĭs) *n.* A woman who writes poems. —See Usage note at **-ess.**

po·et·ic (pō-ĕt'ĭk) *adj.* Also **po·et·i·cal** (-ĭ-kəl). **1.** Of or pertaining to poetry. **2.** Having a quality or style characteristic of poetry: *poetic diction.* **3.** Suitable as a subject for poetry: *a poetic love affair.* **4.** Of, pertaining to, or befitting a poet: *poetic insight.* **5.** Having or showing the sensitivity or insight of a poet. **6.** Characterized by romantic imagery: *a poetic account.* [From French *poétique,* from Latin *poēticus,* from Greek *poiētikos,* inventive, ingenious, from *poiētēs,* "maker," POET.]

po·et·i·cal (pō-ĕt'ĭ-kəl) *adj.* **1.** Variant of **poetic. 2.** Fancifully depicted or embellished; idealized. —**po·et·i·cal·ly** *adv.*

po·et·i·cism (pō-ĕt'ĭ-sĭz'əm) *n.* A poetic term or expression that has become no longer vivid or evocative.

po·et·i·cize (pō-ĕt'ĭ-sīz') *tr.v.* **-cized, -cizing, -cizes.** To give a poetic quality to.

poetic justice *n.* An outcome whereby a person receives his just deserts in a manner peculiarly or ironically appropriate.

poetic license *n.* The liberty taken, especially by an artist or writer, in deviating from conventional form or fact to achieve a desired effect.

po·et·ics (pō-ĕt'ĭks) *n. Used with a singular verb.* **1.** Literary criticism that deals with the nature, forms, and laws of poetry. **2.** A treatise on or study of poetry or aesthetics. **3.** Poetic utterances or feelings.

po·et·ize (pō'ĭ-tīz') *v.* **-ized, -izing, -izes.** —*intr.* To write or express oneself in poetry. —*tr.* To give poetic expression to. —**po·et·iz·er** *n.*

poet laureate *n., pl.* **poets laureate** or **poet laureates. 1.** A poet who is appointed by the British sovereign to compose poems for state occasions and who is a member of the royal household. **2.** A poet acclaimed as the most excellent or most representative of a locality or group. **3.** A poet honored for excellence.

po·et·ry (pō'ĭ-trē) *n.* **1.** The art or work of a poet. **2. a.** Poems regarded as forming a division of literature. **b.** The poetic works of a given author, group, nation, or genre. **3.** Any piece of literature written in meter; verse. **4.** Prose that resembles a poem, as in form, sound, or other qualities. **5.** The essence of or characteristic quality possessed by a poem or poems. **6.** A quality that suggests poetry, as in grace, beauty, or harmony: *the poetry of dance movements.* [Middle English, from Medieval Latin *poētria,* from Latin *poēta,* POET.]

pogge (pŏg) *n.* A European marine fish, *Agonus cataphractus,* with a body covering of bony plates, a large broad head, and a long tapering tail. [17th century : origin obscure.]

po·go·ni·a (pə-gō'nē-ə, -gōn'yə) *n.* Any of various small terrestrial orchids of the genus *Pogonia,* of the North Temperate Zone, having pink or whitish flowers. [New Latin, "bearded plant" (from the yellow hair covering the lip of its flower), from Greek *pōgōn†,* beard.]

po·go stick (pō'gō) *n.* A strong stick with footrests and a heavy spring set into the bottom end, propelled along the ground by hopping. [From *Pogo,* a former trademark.]

po·grom (pō'grəm, pō-grŏm') *n.* An organized and often officially encouraged massacre or persecution of a minority group, especially a Jewish community.
~*tr.v.* **pogromed, -groming, -groms.** To massacre in a pogrom. [Russian, "like thunder," devastation : *po-,* like, from *po,* at, by, next to + *grom,* thunder.]

Po Hai. See **Bo Hai.**

poi (poi) *n.* A Hawaiian food made from taro root cooked, pounded to a paste, and fermented. [Hawaiian.]

–poiesis *suffix.* Indicates making, creating, or producing; for example, **hematopoiesis.** [From Greek *poiēsis,* a making, creation, from *poiein,* to make.]

–poietic *suffix.* Indicates productive or formative; for example, **hematopoietic.** [From Greek *poiētikos,* creative, productive, from *poiētēs,* maker, creator, from *poiein,* to make.]

poign·ant (poin'yənt) *adj.* **1.** Appealing to the emotions; affecting;

touching: *poignant sentiment.* **2.** Piercing; incisive: *poignant criticism.* **3.** Keenly distressing to the mind: *poignant anxiety.* **4.** Relevant; to the point: *"Her illustrations were apposite and poignant."* (Charles Lamb). **5.** Agreeably intense or stimulating: *poignant delight.* **6. a.** *Archaic.* Sharp or sour to the taste. **b.** Sharp or pungent to the smell: *a poignant perfume.* —See Synonyms at **moving.** [Middle English *poynaunt, pugnaunt,* pointed, sharp, from Old French *puignant,* present participle of *poindre,* from Latin *pungere,* to prick, pierce.] **—poign·an·cy, poign·ance** *n.* **—poign·ant·ly** *adv.*

poi·kil·o·therm (poi-kĭl'ə-thûrm') *n. Zoology.* A poikilothermic organism, such as a fish or reptile. [Greek *poikilos,* various, variant + -THERM.]

poi·kil·o·ther·mic (poi-kĭl'-ə-thûr'mĭk) *adj.* Also **poi·kil·o·ther·mal** (-məl). *Zoology.* Having a body temperature that varies with the external environment; cold-blooded. Compare **homoiothermic.** **—poi·kil·o·ther·mism** *n.*

poi·lu (pwä-lo͞o') *n. Slang.* A French front-line soldier in World War I. [French, "hirsute," hence (slang) pugnacious, from *poil,* hair, from Latin *pilus.*]

Poin·ca·ré (pwăɴ'kä-rā'), **Jules Henri** (1854–1912). French mathematician. He made a distinguished contribution to experimental physics and theoretical astronomy, as well as pure and applied mathematics, anticipating Einstein's work on relativity.

Poincaré, Raymond (1860–1934). French politician. A cousin of Jules Henri Poincaré, he held office as ninth president of the Republic (1913–20) and served for three terms as prime minister (1912–13, 1922–24, and 1926–29).

poin·ci·an·a (poin'sē-ăn'ə, -ä'nə) *n.* **1.** Any of various tropical trees of the genus *Poinciana,* having large orange or red flowers. **2.** A related tree, the **royal poinciana** *(see).* [New Latin, after M. de *Poinci,* 17th-century governor of French Antilles.]

poin·set·ti·a (poin-sĕt'ē-ə, -sĕt'ə) *n.* A tropical American shrub, *Euphorbia pulcherrima,* having petallike, usually scarlet bracts beneath small yellow flowers, widely grown as a house plant. [New Latin; discovered by J.R. *Poinsett* (1799–1851), U.S. minister to Mexico.]

point (point) *n. Abbr.* **pt. 1.** The sharp or tapered end of something: *the point of a knife.* **2.** Something that has a sharp or tapered end, such as a knife or needle. **3.** A tapering extension of land projecting into water; promontory; cape. **4.** A mark formed by or as if by the sharp end of something. **5.** A mark or dot used in printing or writing. **6.** A mark used in punctuation; especially, a period. **7.** See **decimal point. 8.** *Phonetics.* A diacritical mark used to differentiate or modify vowels and consonants, such as a **vowel point** *(see).* **9.** Any of the protruding marks used in certain methods, such as Braille, of writing and printing for the blind. **10.** *Geometry.* A dimensionless geometric object having no property but position. **11.** A position, place, or situation; spot: *a good point to begin.* **12.** A specified degree, condition, or limit in a scale, course, or the like: *a melting point.* **13. a.** One of the 32 equal divisions marked at the circumference of a mariner's compass card that indicate direction. **b.** The distance or interval of 11 degrees, 15 minutes between any two adjacent markings. **14.** Any distinct condition or degree: *the point of no return.* **15.** A specific moment in time: *At this point she left.* **16.** A crucial situation in a course of events. **17.** An important, essential, or primary factor: *missed the whole point.* **18.** A purpose, goal, advantage, or reason: *can't see any point in continuing.* **19.** The major idea or essential part of a concept or narrative: *get to the point of the story.* **20.** A significant, outstanding, or effective idea, argument, or suggestion: *made some excellent points.* **21.** A separate or individual item or element; detail: *several points worth noting.* **22. a.** A striking or distinctive characteristic or quality: *his good points.* **b.** A quality or characteristic that is important or distinctive; especially, a standard characteristic used to judge an animal. **c. points.** The extremities of a horse, dog, or the like: *a bay pony with white points.* **23.** A single unit, as in counting, rating, or measuring. **24. a.** A unit of academic credit usually equal to one hour of class work per week during one semester. **b.** A numerical unit equal to a letter grade in grading academic achievement. **25.** A unit of scoring or counting in a game or sport: *won the match on points.* **26.** The stiff and attentive stance taken by a hunting dog. **27.** *Electricity.* **a.** An electrical contact, especially one in the distributor of a car engine or crystal set. **b.** *Chiefly British.* A socket or outlet. **28.** *Finance.* A unit of value used to quote or state the current prices of stocks, commodities, or the like. **29.** A unit equal to .0001 used in calculating a rate of exchange in U.S. dollars: *The pound gained three points against the dollar.* **30.** *Printing.* A unit of type size equal to 0.01384 inch, or approximately $^1/_{72}$ of an inch. **31.** A jeweler's unit of mass equal to 2 milligrams or 0.01 carat. **32. a.** Needlepoint. **b.** Bobbin lace. **33.** *British.* **a.** A railway **switch** *(see).* **b.** The junction of railroad tracks at such a device. **34.** A ribbon or cord with a metal tag at the end, used to fasten clothing in the 16th and 17th centuries. **35.** In boxing, the top of the chin as a spot for delivering a blow. **36.** In backgammon, any of the tapered divisions of the board. **37.** A small body of troops that goes ahead of or behind the main force to reconnoiter. **38.** An aggressive stance or stroke made while holding a bayonet. **—beside the point.** Having nothing to do with the subject; irrelevant. **—in point.** By way of example. Used chiefly in the phrase *a case in point.* **—in point of fact.** As a matter of fact. **—make a point of.** To take special care or pains to. **—make one's point.** To prove oneself successfully to be right. **—stretch a point. 1.** To make an exception. **2.** To exaggerate. **—to the point.** Relevant; apposite.
~*v.* **pointed, pointing, points.** —*tr.* **1.** To direct or aim: *point a weapon.* **2.** To cause to head: *pointed us in the right direction.* **3.** To indicate the position or direction of: *point the way.* **4.** To sharpen (a pencil, for example); provide with a point. **5.** To separate with a decimal point. Used with *off.* **6.** To mark with a point or period; punctuate. **7.** To mark (a consonant) with a vowel point. **8.** To give emphasis to (a remark, for example); stress. **9.** To indicate the presence and position of (game) by standing immobile and directing the muzzle toward it. Said of a hunting dog. **10.** To fill and finish the joints of (brickwork, for example) with cement or mortar. —*intr.* **1.** To direct attention or indicate position with or as if with the finger. Usually used with *at* or *to.* **2.** To turn the mind or thought in a particular direction: *The facts all point to one conclusion.* **3.** To be turned or faced in a given direction; aim. **4.** To perform the action of a hunting dog scenting game and gazing toward it fixedly. **5.** *Nautical.* To sail close to the wind. **—point out.** To call attention to; indicate. [Middle English *poynt,* from Old French *point,* a prick, dot, small particle, and *pointe,* pointed end or tip, respectively from Latin *punctum* and *puncta,* from the neuter and feminine of *punctus,* past participle of *pungere,* to pierce, prick.]

Point Bar·row (băr'o). Northernmost point of Alaska, on the Arctic Ocean. It was discovered in 1826 and named for the British geographer Sir John Barrow (1764–1848).

point-blank (point'blăngk') *adj.* **1.** Aimed straight at the mark or target; especially, aimed straight without allowing for the drop in a projectile's course: *a point-blank shot.* **2. a.** So close to a target that a weapon may be aimed directly at it. **b.** Close enough so that missing the target is unlikely or impossible: *point-blank range.* **3.** Straightforward; blunt: *a point-blank accusation.*
~*adv.* **1.** With a straight aim; directly; straight: *The policeman fired point-blank.* **2.** Without hesitation, deliberation, or equivocation: *answer point-blank.* [Probably POINT (verb) + BLANK (white center spot of a target).]

point d'ap·pui (pwăɴ' dä-pwē') *n., pl.* **points d'appui** *(pronounced as singular).* **1.** *Military.* A secure position or base serving as a support for operations in the field. **2.** A base or support. [French, point of support.]

point defect *n. Crystallography.* A defect in a crystal lattice occurring at a single lattice point; a vacancy or an interstitial.

Point de Galle. See **Galle.**

point-de·vice (point'dĭ-vīs') *adj. Archaic.* Scrupulously correct or neat; precise. [Middle English *at point devis,* probably from Norman French *à point devis* (unattested), "arranged to (the) point" : *à point,* to perfection + *devis,* "divided," arranged, from Latin *divisus,* past participle of *dīvidere,* to divide.] **—point-de·vice** *adv.*

pointe (pwăɴt, point) *n.* In ballet, the position of being balanced on the tip of the toes. [French.]

point·ed (poin'tĭd) *adj.* **1.** Having an end coming to a point. **2.** Sharp; cutting: *a pointed question.* **3.** Obviously directed at or making reference to a particular target: *pointed wit.* **4.** Clearly evident or conspicuous; emphasized; marked: *a pointed lack of interest.* **5.** Characterized by the use of a pointed crown, as in Gothic architecture: *a pointed arch.* **—point·ed·ly** *adv.* **—point·ed·ness** *n.*

point·er (poin'tər) *n.* **1.** One that sharpens, directs, indicates, or points. **2.** A scale indicator on a watch, balance, or other measuring instrument. **3.** A long, tapered stick for indicating objects on a chart, blackboard, or the like. **4.** A hunting dog of a breed having a short-haired coat that is usually white with black or brownish spots. **5.** *Informal.* A suggestion; hint; piece of advice. **6.** *Computer Science.* A computer word that directs the user to the address of a core storage location. **6. Pointers.** In the constellation of the Big Dipper, the two stars that align with the Pole Star and can be used to indicate north.

poin·til·lism (pwăɴ'tē-ĭz'əm, poin'tə-lĭz'-) *n.* A method of painting exemplified by Seurat and his followers in late 19th-century France consisting of the juxtaposition of dots of primary colors that blend in the viewer's eye from a distance, giving brighter secondary colors. Compare **divisionism.** [French *pointillisme,* from *pointiller,* to paint small dots, from *pointille,* small dot, from Italian *puntiglio,* diminutive of *punto,* point, from Latin *punctum,* from the neuter past participle of *pungere,* to pierce, prick.] **—poin·til·list** *n. & adj.* **—poin·til·lis·tic** (pwăɴ'tē-ĭs'tĭk, poin'tə-lĭs'-) *adj.*

Point Ju·dith (jo͞o'dĭth). A cape in south-central Rhode Island on the western side of the entrance to Narragansett Bay.

point lace *n.* A type of handmade lace, **needlepoint** *(see).*

point·less (point'lĭs) *adj.* **1.** Meaningless; irrelevant: *a pointless remark.* **2.** Ineffectual; futile: *It would be pointless to complain.* **—point·less·ly** *adv.* **—point·less·ness** *n.*

point of honor *n., pl.* **points of honor.** A matter that affects one's honor or reputation.

point of inflection *n. Mathematics.* A stationary point on a curve at which the tangent to the curve changes from rotating in one direction to rotating in the other as the curve passes through the point.

point of no return *n.* A stage or point reached in a course of action after which turning back or stopping is no longer possible.

point of order *n.* A question as to whether that which is being discussed is in order or allowed by the rules.

point of reference *n.* A **reference** (sense 9) *(see).*

point-of-sale (point'əv-sāl') *adj.* Of, provided for, or situated at the place where purchases are made: *point-of-sale advertising.*

point of view *n.* **1.** The position from which something is observed or considered; a standpoint. **2.** A manner of viewing things; an attitude.

point source *n. Optics.* A source of light or other radiation that can be regarded as having negligible size.

point system *n.* **1.** *Printing.* A system of measurement by the **point** *(see).* **2.** Any system of printing or writing for the blind that uses an alphabet of raised symbols or dots that correspond to letters, such as Braille. **3.** A system of evaluating and averaging achievement, as in education, by awarding numerical units or points.

poise¹ (poiz) *v.* **poised, pois·ing, pois·es.** —*tr.* **1.** To carry or hold in equilibrium; balance. **2.** To hold steady or raised, as in readiness: *with hands poised.* —*intr.* To be balanced or held in suspension; hover: *poise on the brink.*
~*n.* **1.** The state or condition of being balanced or held in equilibrium; stability; balance. **2.** Freedom from awkwardness or embarrassment; assurance; composure. **3.** The bearing or deportment of the head or body; mien. **4.** A state or condition of hovering or being suspended. [Middle English *poisen, peisen,* to weigh, from Old French *poiser, peser,* from Vulgar Latin *pēsāre* (unattested), variant of Latin *pensāre,* frequentative of *pendere,* to weigh.]

poise² (pwäz, poiz) *n.* A centimeter-gram-second unit of dynamic viscosity equal to one dyne-second per square centimeter. [French, after Jean Louis Marie *Poiseuille* (1799–1869), French physician.]

poised (poizd) *adj.* **1.** Assured; composed. **2.** Held balanced or steady in readiness: *stood poised for the jump.*

poi·son (poi′zən) *n.* **1.** Any substance that causes injury, illness, or death, especially by chemical means. **2.** Anything that is destructive, corruptive, or fatal: *the poison of her criticism.* **3.** A substance that inhibits or retards a chemical reaction or deactivates a catalyst. **4.** A substance in a nuclear reactor that absorbs neutrons without undergoing fission, thereby slowing down the chain reaction.
~*tr.v.* **poisoned, -son·ing, -sons.** **1.** To give poison to; kill or harm with poison. **2.** To put poison on or into: *poison a cup.* **3. a.** To pollute: *Fumes poisoned the air.* **b.** To have a harmful influence on; corrupt, ruin, taint, or embitter: *Jealousy poisoned their friendship.* **4.** To inhibit or retard (a chemical or nuclear reaction).
~*adj.* Poisonous. [Middle English *poysoun,* potion, poisonous drink, from Old French *poison,* from Latin *pōtiō* (stem *pōtiōn-*), from *pōtāre,* to drink.] —**poi·son·er** *n.*

poison gas *n.* A lethal or crippling vapor, such as phosgene or chlorine, used in warfare.

poison hemlock *n.* A poisonous plant, *Conium maculatum,* native to Eurasia but naturalized in North America, having compound leaves and umbels of small, white flowers.

poison ivy *n.* A North American shrub or vine, *Rhus radicans,* having leaflets in groups of three, small green flowers, and whitish berries and causing a rash on contact.

poison oak *n.* **1.** Either of two shrubs, *Rhus toxicodendron* of the southeastern United States or *R. diversiloba* of western North America, related to poison ivy and causing a similar rash. **2.** Loosely, poison ivy.

poi·son·ous (poi′zə-nəs) *adj.* **1. a.** Capable of harming or killing by or as if by poison. **b.** Broadly, toxic or venomous. **2.** Containing a poison. **3.** Marked by apparent ill will; malicious: *a poisonous glance.* **4.** *Informal.* Objectionable; unpleasant. —**poi·son·ous·ly** *adv.* —**poi·son·ous·ness** *n.*

poi·son-pen letter (poi′zən-pĕn′) *n.* A letter or note, usually anonymous, containing abusive or malicious information about the recipient or a third party.

poison sumac *n.* A swamp shrub, *Rhus vernix,* of the southeastern United States, having compound leaves and greenish-white berries, and causing an itching rash on contact with the skin.

Pois·son distribution (pwä-sôn′) *n. Statistics.* A probability distribution used to describe the occurrence of events in a large number of independent repeated trials. [After S.D. *Poisson* (1781–1840), French mathematician.]

Poi·tier (pwä′tyā′, pwä′tē-ā′), **Sidney** (1924-). U.S. actor and director. With his acclaimed performances in motion pictures such as *The Defiant Ones* (1958) and *Lilies of the Field* (1963), for which he won an Academy Award, he helped break through the color barrier of the movie industry. He has also directed several films.

Poi·tiers (pwä-tyā′). Capital of Vienne department, western France. It was the capital of the former province of Poitou and the site of many battles, including the defeat of the French (under John II) by the English (under Edward the Black Prince) in 1356. An agricultural center, it also produces chemicals and electrical equipment.

Poi·tou (pwä-tōō′). Region and former province of western France, stretching from the Atlantic coast east beyond the Vienne River. Part of the Roman province of Aquitaine, Poitou fell to the Visigoths (5th century) and the Franks (507). The area was frequently contested by England and France during the Hundred Years' War.

poke¹ (pōk) *v.* **poked, pok·ing, pokes.** —*tr.* **1.** To push or jab at, as with a finger or arm; prod. **2.** To make (a hole or pathway, for example) by or as if by prodding, thrusting, or poking. **3.** To cause to project; stick: *A seal poked its head out of the water.* **4.** To stir (a fire) by prodding the wood or coal with a poker or stick. **5.** To strike; punch. —*intr.* **1.** To make thrusts or jabs with a stick, poker, or the like. Used with *at.* **2.** To pry or meddle; intrude: *poking into another's business.* **3.** To search or look in a curious manner: *poking around in the drawer.* **4.** To thrust forward; appear; protrude: *His head poked from under the blankets.* **5.** To live or proceed in a slow or lazy manner; dawdle; putter. Often used with *along.*
~*n.* **1.** A push, thrust, or jab. **2.** A punch or blow with the fist. **3.** A person who moves slowly or aimlessly; dawdler. —**poke fun**

at. To ridicule in a mischievous way; tease. [Middle English *poken,* from Middle Dutch and Middle Low German *poken,* to strike, thrust (probably imitative).]

poke² *n.* **1.** A large bonnet having a projecting brim at the front, worn especially in the 18th and 19th centuries. Also called "poke bonnet." **2.** The brim of such a bonnet. [From POKE (to thrust).]

poke³ *n. Chiefly Regional.* A sack or bag. [Middle English, from Old North French *poque,* variant of Old French *poche,* pocket, from Frankish *pokka* (unattested), bag.]

poke⁴ *n.* A plant, **pokeweed** *(see).* [Algonquian (Virginia) *pakon,* any plant used for dyeing, from *pak,* blood.]

pok·er¹ (pō′kər) *n.* One that pokes; specifically, a metal rod used to stir a fire.

poker² *n.* Any of various card games played by two or more players who bet on the value of their hands. [19th century : origin obscure.]

poker face *n.* A face lacking any interpretable expression. [From the impassive face of an expert poker player.] —**pok·er-faced** (pō′kər-fāst′) *adj.*

poke·weed (pōk′wēd′) *n.* A tall North American plant, *Phytolacca americana,* having small white flowers, blackish red berries, and a poisonous root. Also called "poke," "pokeberry," "pokeroot," "inkberry." [POKE⁴ + WEED.]

po·key (pō′kē) *n., pl.* **-keys.** Also **po·ky** *pl.* **-kies.** *Slang.* Jail; prison. [Origin unknown.]

pok·y, poke·y (pō′kē) *adj.* **-ier, -iest.** *Informal.* **1.** Small and cramped: *a poky apartment.* **2.** Frumpish; shabby: *poky old clothes.* **3.** Dawdling; slow. [From POKE (to thrust).]

Pol. Poland; Polish.

Po·land (pō′lənd). *Polish* **Pol·ska** (pôl′skä). *Abbr.* **Pol.** Country in eastern Europe. It is largely an undulating plain rising to the Carpathian Mts. in the south and is crossed by the Vistula and Warta rivers. Becoming a united state in the 10th century, it was a great power during the 15th and 16th centuries but was partitioned in 1772, 1793, and 1795, after which it disappeared until re-formed in 1918. Occupied by the Germans from 1939 to 1945, it has been under Communist rule since 1948. Poland is largely an agricultural country, although industry has grown considerably since World War II. Economic troubles led to riots over the price of food in 1970, 1976, and 1980–81, culminating in strikes, the declaration of martial law, and the suppression of the free trade union, Solidarity, coupled with the threat of Soviet invasion (1981–82). Area, 312,677 square kilometers (120,725 square miles). Population, 35,800,000. Capital, Warsaw.

Po·lan·ski (pə-lăn′skē), **Roman** (1933–). Polish film director. His films, such as *Rosemary's Baby* (1968), *Chinatown* (1974), and *Tess* (1980), are notable for their brooding menace and black humor.

po·lar (pō′lər) *adj.* **1. a.** Of, pertaining to, or designating a pole. **b.** Measured from or referred to a pole or poles: *polar diameter.* **2.** Pertaining to, connected with, or located near the North Pole or South Pole. **3.** Occupying or characterized by opposite extremes. **4.** Serving as a guide, as a polestar or a pole of the earth might. **5.** Central or pivotal. [New Latin *polāris,* from Latin *polus,* POLE.]

polar angle *n.* The angle formed by the polar axis and the radius vector in a polar coordinate system.

polar axis *n.* The fixed reference axis from which the polar angle is measured in a polar coordinate system.

polar bear *n.* A large, white-furred bear, *Thalarctos maritimus,* of Arctic regions.

polar body *n. Genetics.* A minute cell produced and ultimately discarded in the development of an ovum, containing little or no cytoplasm but having one of the nuclei derived from the first or second meiotic division of the oocyte.

polar cap *n.* **1. a.** A high-altitude icecap. **b.** The polar regions of ice. **2.** *Astronomy.* Any differentiated polar region of a planet.

polar bear *These wandering arctic hunters feed mainly on seals. When fully grown, they can be 2.5 meters (more than 8 feet) long and can weigh up to 720 kilograms (nearly 1,600 pounds).*

polar circle *n.* The **Arctic Circle** or **Antarctic Circle** *(both of which see).*
polar coordinate *n.* Either of two coordinates, the radius vector or the polar angle, that together can be used to specify the position of any point in a plane.
polar distance *n. Astronomy.* The angular distance between the celestial pole and a point to be measured on the celestial sphere.
po·lar·im·e·ter (pō′lə-rĭm′ə-tər) *n.* An instrument used to measure the rotation of the plane of polarization of polarized light, or the degree of polarization of light passing through an optically active compound or sample. **—po·lar·i·met·ric** (pō-lăr′ə-mĕt′rĭk) *adj.* **—po·lar·im·e·try** *n.*
Po·lar·is (pō-lăr′ĭs, -lâr′ĭs) *n.* **1.** A star of the second magnitude at the end of the handle of the Little Dipper and almost at the north celestial pole. Also called "North Star," "polar star," "polestar." **2.** A U.S. Navy intermediate range surface-to-surface ballistic missile. [New Latin *(Stella) Polāris,* polar (star).]
po·lar·i·scope (pō-lăr′ə-skōp′, pō-lâr′-) *n.* An instrument for ascertaining, measuring, or exhibiting the properties of polarized light, or for studying the interactions of polarized light with optically transparent media.
po·lar·i·ty (pō-lăr′ə-tē, pō-lâr′-) *n., pl.* **-ties. 1.** Intrinsic separation into contrasting or opposite poles; intrinsic polar alignment or orientation, especially with respect to a physical property: *magnetic polarity.* **2.** The possession or manifestation of two opposing attributes, tendencies, or principles: *political polarity.* **3.** A specified polar extreme: *an electric terminal with positive polarity.*
po·lar·i·za·tion (pō′lər-ə-zā′shən, -ī-zā′shən) *n.* **1.** The uniform and nonrandom elliptical, circular, or linear variation of a wave characteristic, especially of vibrational orientation, in light or other radiation. **2.** The partial or complete polar separation of positive and negative electric charge in a nuclear, atomic, molecular, or chemical system. **3.** A concentration, as of groups, forces, or interests, about two conflicting or contrasting positions.
po·lar·ize (pō′lə-rīz′) *v.* **-ized, -izing, -izes.** *—tr.* **1.** To induce polarization in or impart polarity to. **2.** To cause to concentrate about two conflicting or contrasting positions. *—intr.* To become polarized. **—po·lar·iz·a·ble** *adj.* **—po·lar·iz·er** *n.*
po·lar·og·ra·phy (pō′lə-rŏg′rə-fē) *n.* An electrochemical method of quantitative or qualitative analysis based on the relationship between an increasing current passing through the solution being analyzed and the increasing voltage used to produce the current. [POLAR(IZATION) + -GRAPHY.] **—po·lar·o·graph·ic** (pō-lăr′ə-grăf′ĭk) *adj.* **—po·lar·o·graph·i·cal·ly** *adv.*
Po·lar·oid (pō′lə-roid′) *n.* **1.** A trademark for a specially treated transparent plastic capable of polarizing light passing through it, used in sunglasses and other glare-reducing optical devices. **2. a.** A trademark for a type of camera that develops the film and produces prints within a few seconds of taking the photograph. **b.** A photograph taken with such a camera.
Polar Regions. The land and water areas surrounding the North and South poles.
polar star *n.* A star, **Polaris** *(see).*
pol·der (pōl′dər) *n.* An area of low-lying land, especially in the Netherlands, that has been reclaimed from a body of water and is protected by dikes. [Middle Dutch *polre, polder*†.]
pole[1] (pōl) *n. Abbr.* **p. 1.** Either axial extremity of any axis through a sphere. **2.** Either of the regions contiguous to the extremities of the earth's rotational axis, the **North Pole** or the **South Pole** *(both of which see).* **3.** *Physics.* A **magnetic pole** *(see).* **4.** *Electricity.* Either of two oppositely charged terminals, as in an electric cell or battery. **5.** *Astronomy.* A **celestial pole** *(see).* **6.** *Biology.* **a.** A structurally or physiologically distinct region at either axial extremity of a nucleus, cell, or organism. **b.** Either end of the spindle formed in a cell during mitosis or meiosis. **7.** Either of two antithetical ideas, propensities, forces, or positions. **8.** Any fixed point of reference. **9.** *Geometry.* The origin in a polar coordinate system; the polar angle vertex. **—poles apart.** Having very different opinions, views, tastes, or the like. [Middle English, from Latin *polus,* from Greek *polos,* axis of the sphere, firmament.]
pole[2] *n.* **1.** A long, relatively slender and generally rounded piece of wood or other material. **2.** The long, tapering wooden shaft extending up from the front axle of a vehicle to the collars of the animals drawing it; a tongue. **3. a.** A unit of length, a **rod** *(see).* **b.** A unit of area equal to a square rod (30 1/4 square yards). **4.** *Nautical.* A small or light spar. **5.** In horseracing, the starting position nearest the inner rail on the inside lane. **—under bare poles.** *Nautical.* Having no sails up. Said of a sailing vessel.
~v. **poled, poling, poles.** *—tr.* **1.** To propel with a pole. **2.** To support (plants) with a pole. **3.** To strike, poke, or stir with a pole. **4.** To stir (molten metal) with a green pole that introduces carbon and deoxidizes the substance by reacting with the oxygen. *—intr.* **1.** To propel a boat, raft, or the like with a pole. **2.** To use ski poles to gain speed or to turn. [Middle English *po(o)le,* Old English *pāl,* from Common Germanic, from Latin *pālus,* stake.]
Pole (pōl) *n.* A native or inhabitant of Poland.
pole·ax, pole·axe (pōl′ăks′) *n.* **1.** A battle-ax used in the Middle Ages, consisting of an ax, or an ax, hammer, and pick combination, with a long shaft. **2.** An ax having a hammer face opposite the blade, used to slaughter cattle.
~tr.v. **poleaxed, -axing, -axes.** To strike or fell with or as if with a poleax. [Middle English *pollax* : POLL (head) + AX.]
pole bean *n.* Any of various cultivated climbing beans trained to grow on poles or supports.
pole·cat (pōl′kăt′) *n.* **1.** A carnivorous mammal, *Mustela putorius,* of Europe, Asia, and northern Africa, having dark brown or black fur. It emits a foul-smelling fluid when alarmed. **2.** Any of several similar or related animals, especially the skunk. [Middle English *polcat* : *pol-*† (meaning unknown) + CAT.]
pole horse *n.* A horse harnessed to the pole, or tongue, of a vehicle. Also called "poler."
po·lem·ic (pə-lĕm′ĭk) *n.* **1. a.** A controversy or argument, especially one that is a refutation of or an attack upon a particular opinion, doctrine, or the like. **b.** Loosely, any virulent criticism. **2.** A person engaged in or inclined to controversy, argument, or refutation.
~adj. Also **po·lem·i·cal** (pə-lĕm′ĭ-kəl). Of, pertaining to, or given to controversy, argument, or refutation. [Medieval Latin *polemicus,* controversialist, from Greek *polemikos,* of war, hostile, opposed, from *polemos*†, war.] **—po·lem·i·cal·ly** *adv.*
po·lem·i·cist (pə-lĕm′ə-sĭst) *n.* Also **pol·e·mist** (pŏl′ə-mĭst, pə-lĕm′ĭst). A person who writes or is skilled in polemics.
po·lem·ics (pə-lĕm′ĭks) *n. Used with a singular verb.* The art or practice of argument or controversy, especially in support of or against a doctrine or belief.
po·len·ta (pō-lĕn′tə) *n.* A thick mush made of farina or cornmeal. [Italian, from Latin, pearl barley.]
pol·er (pō′lər) *n.* **1.** One that propels, supports, conveys, or strikes with a pole. **2.** A **pole horse** *(see).*
pole·star (pōl′stär′) *n.* **1.** The star, **Polaris** *(see).* **2.** A guiding principle.
pole vault *n. Sports.* A field event in which the contestant jumps or vaults over a high crossbar with the aid of a long flexible pole.
pole-vault (pōl′vôlt′) *intr.v.* **-vaulted, -vaulting, -vaults.** *Sports.* To perform or compete in the pole vault. **—pole-vault·er** *n.*
po·leyn (pō′lān′) *n.* A piece of armor protecting the knee. [Middle English, from Old French *polain.*]
po·lice (pə-lēs′) *n., pl.* **police. 1. a.** The government department established to maintain order, enforce the law, and prevent and detect crime. **b.** A police force. **c.** *Used with a plural verb.* The members of such a force. **2. a.** A group of persons resembling the police force of a community in organization or function: *campus police.* **b.** *Used with a plural verb.* The members of such a group. **3.** The regulation and control of the affairs of a community, especially with respect to the maintenance of order, law, health, morals, safety, and other matters affecting general welfare. **4.** The cleaning of a military base or other military area. **5.** Soldiers who are assigned to a particular maintenance duty: *kitchen police.*
~tr.v. **policed, -licing, -lices. 1.** To regulate, control, or keep in order with or as if with police. **2.** To make (a military area) neat in appearance. [Originally "policy," "government organization," from French, from Late Latin *polītia,* administration of the commonwealth, from Latin *polītīa,* the state, from Greek *politeia,* polity, citizenship, from *politēs,* citizen, from *polis,* city.]
police action *n.* A localized military action undertaken without a formal declaration of war.
police court An inferior court having the power to prosecute minor criminal offenses and to hold for trial persons charged with more serious offenses.
police dog *n.* A dog, especially a German shepherd, trained to aid the police.
police force *n.* A body of persons trained in methods of law enforcement and crime prevention and detection, and given authority to maintain the peace, safety, and order of the community.
po·lice·man (pə-lēs′mən) *n., pl.* **-men** (-mĭn). A male member of a police force.
police officer *n.* A policeman or policewoman.
police state *n.* A country or other political unit in which the government exercises rigid and repressive controls over social, economic, and political life, especially by means of a secret police force.
police station *n.* The headquarters of a unit of a police force where those under arrest are first charged.
po·lice·wom·an (pə-lēs′wo͝om′ən) *n., pl.* **-women** (-wĭm′ĭn). A female member of a police force.
pol·i·cy[1] (pŏl′ə-sē) *n., pl.* **-cies. 1.** An overall plan or course of action, as of a government, political party, or business organization, designed to influence and determine immediate and long-term decisions or actions: *foreign policy; company personnel policy.* **2. a.** A course of action, guiding principle, or procedure considered to be expedient, prudent, or advantageous: *Honesty is the best policy.* **b.** Prudence, shrewdness, or sagacity in practical matters. [Middle English *policye,* polity, commonwealth, policy, from Old French *policie,* from Latin *polītīa,* state, from Greek *politeia,* citizenship, from *politēs,* citizen, from *polis,* city.]
policy[2] *n., pl.* **-cies.** A written contract or certificate of insurance. [French *police,* from Provençal *poliss(i)a* or Italian *polizza,* probably from Medieval Latin *apodixa,* from Latin *apodīxis,* from Greek *apodeixis,* "a showing or making known," proof, from *apodeiknunai,* to show off, make known : *apo,* off, from + *deiknunai,* to show.]
pol·i·cy·hold·er (pŏl′ə-sē-hōl′dər) *n.* A person or organization that holds an insurance policy.
pol·i·cy·mak·ing, pol·i·cy-mak·ing (pŏl′ə-sē-mā′kĭng) *n.* The top-level development of policy, especially official government policy. **—pol·i·cy·mak·er** *n.*
po·li·o (pō′lē-ō′) *n.* Poliomyelitis.

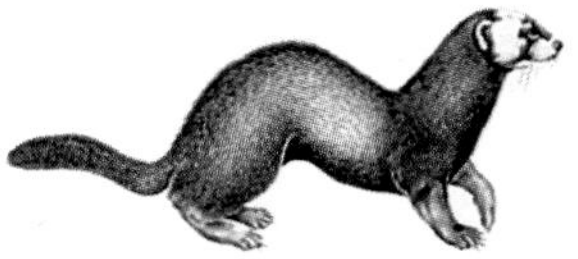

polecat *A relative of the weasel, the common Eurasian polecat usually lives in a woodland burrow. It is a good swimmer, but a poor climber. Polecats are meat eaters, hunting small animals such as rabbits, birds, and snakes. They are also known to have made stores of frogs for winter food—sometimes hoarding as many as 120 in larders in their burrows. The polecat bites the frogs at the base of their skulls, paralyzing but not killing them, so that they stay fresh for long periods.*

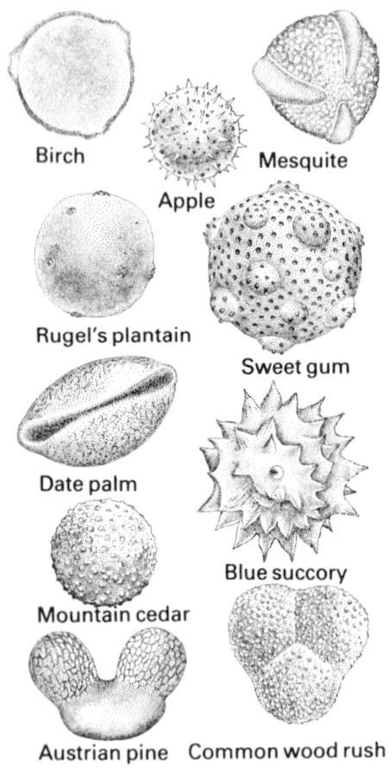
Birch
Apple
Mesquite
Rugel's plantain
Sweet gum
Date palm
Blue succory
Mountain cedar
Austrian pine
Common wood rush

pollen *Each type of pollen has a distinctive shape. The material of the protective spore coat is so durable that botanists have been able to use pollen grains found in ancient rocks to identify plant species that grew millions of years ago.*

po·li·o·my·e·li·tis (pō'lē-ō-mī'ə-lī'tĭs) *n.* An infectious viral disease occurring mainly in children and in its severest form attacking the central nervous system and producing paralysis, muscular atrophy, and often deformity. Also called "infantile paralysis," "polio." [Greek *polios,* gray + MYELITIS.]

po·lis (pō'lĭs) *n., pl.* **-leis** (-lās'). A city-state of ancient Greece. [Greek *polis,* city.]

pol·ish (pŏl'ĭsh) *v.* **-ished, -ishing, -ishes.** —*tr.* **1.** To make smooth and shiny by abrasion or chemical action. **2.** To free from coarseness; make elegant; refine: *polish one's manners.* **3.** To remove flaws from; perfect or complete: *polish one's piano technique.* —*intr.* **1.** To become smooth or shiny by or as if by rubbing. **2.** To become perfect or refined. **—polish off.** *Informal.* To finish or dispose of quickly and easily.

~*n.* **1.** Smoothness or shininess of surface or finish. **2.** A substance applied to smooth, color, or shine a surface: *shoe polish.* **3.** The act or process of polishing. **4.** Elegance of style or manners; refinement. [Middle English *polisshen,* from Old French *polir* (present stem *poliss-*), from Latin *polīre.*] **—pol·ish·er** *n.*

Po·lish (pō'lĭsh) *adj. Abbr.* **Pol.** Of or pertaining to Poland, its inhabitants, or their language or culture.

~*n. Abbr.* **Pol. 1.** The West Slavic language that is the major language of Poland. **2.** *Used with a plural verb.* The people of Poland.

Polish Corridor. Strip of German territory, 32 to 113 kilometers (20 to 70 miles) wide, awarded to newly independent Poland by the Treaty of Versailles (1919). It separated East Prussia from the rest of Germany and afforded Poland access to the Baltic Sea. Friction between Poland and Germany over the corridor was a major cause of the outbreak of World War II.

pol·ished (pŏl'ĭsht) *adj.* **1. a.** Made shiny and smooth. **b.** Refined; elegant; cultured. **2.** Naturally shiny and smooth. **3.** Having the husk removed. Said of grains of rice. **4.** Having no imperfections or errors; flawless.

pol·it·bu·ro (pŏl'ĭt-byŏŏr'ō, pə-lĭt'-) *n., pl.* **-ros.** The chief political and executive committee of a Communist party, as in the U.S.S.R. [Russian *Polit(icheskoe) Buro,* political bureau.]

po·lite (pə-līt') *adj.* **-liter, -litest. 1.** Marked by consideration for others, correct manners, or tact; courteous. **2.** Refined; elegant; cultivated: *polite society.* [Middle English *polyt,* polished, smoothed, from Latin *polītus,* past participle of Latin *polīre,* to POLISH.] **—po·lite·ly** *adv.* **—po·lite·ness** *n.*

Synonyms: *civil, courteous, genteel.*

pol·i·tesse (pŏl'ĭ-tĕs', pô'lĭ-) *n.* Courteous formality; politeness. [French, from Italian *politezza, pulitezza,* cleanliness, from *pulīto,* "polished," clean, from Latin *polītus,* past participle of *polīre,* to POLISH.]

pol·i·tic (pŏl'ə-tĭk) *adj.* **1.** Artful; ingenious; shrewd: *a politic diplomat.* **2.** Using, displaying, or proceeding from policy; prudent; judicious: *a politic decision.* **3.** Crafty; unscrupulous; cunning. **4.** Political. Now archaic except in the phrase *the body politic.* [Middle English *polytyk,* "political," pursuing a policy, prudent, from Old French *politique,* from Latin *polīticus,* from Greek *politikos,* of a citizen, from *politēs,* citizen, from *polis,* city.] **—pol·i·tic·ly** *adv.*

po·lit·i·cal (pə-lĭt'ĭ-kəl) *adj.* **1.** Of or pertaining to the study, structure, or affairs of government or the state, especially in regard to civil policymaking rather than military, legal, or administrative matters. **2.** Having a definite or organized policy or structure of government. **3.** Of or pertaining to policies or parties within a state: *strong political views.* **4.** Of or pertaining to the citizens of a state: *political rights.* **5.** Of or pertaining to the security of a government or state: *a political offense.* **6.** Active in politics: *political college students.* **7.** Arising from or influenced by partisan factors rather than merit: *a purely political promotion.* **—po·lit·i·cal·ly** *adv.*

political asylum *n.* The protection offered by a state to a foreigner who has left or wishes to leave his own country for political reasons.

political economy *n.* The science of economics. Not in current usage.

political prisoner *n.* A person imprisoned for any act a state considers hostile, especially the expression of views in conflict with its ideology, or for any offense it may consider dangerous to its security. Compare **prisoner of conscience.**

political science *n.* The study of the history, processes, principles, and structure of government and of political institutions. **—political scientist** *n.*

pol·i·ti·cian (pŏl'ə-tĭsh'ən) *n.* **1. a.** One who is actively involved in politics, especially party politics. **b.** One who holds or seeks a political office. **2.** One skilled or experienced in the science or administration of government. **3.** One skilled at or given to scheming and maneuvering. —Compare **statesman.**

po·lit·i·cize (pə-lĭt'ə-sīz') *v.* **-cized, -cizing, -cizes.** —*intr.* To engage in or discuss politics. —*tr.* To make political in character or awareness. **—po·lit·i·ci·za·tion** *n.*

pol·i·tick (pŏl'ə-tĭk') *intr.v.* **-ticked, -ticking, -ticks.** To engage in or talk politics. **—pol·i·tick·ing** *n.*

po·lit·i·co (pə-lĭt'ĭ-kō') *n., pl.* **-cos.** *Informal.* A politician or political agitator. Often used derogatorily. [Italian and Spanish, "political," from Latin *polīticus,* POLITIC.]

pol·i·tics (pŏl'ə-tĭks) *n. Usually used with a singular verb.* **1.** The art or science of power and government. **2.** The policies, goals, or affairs of a government or state or of the groups or parties within it. **3. a.** The conducting of or engaging in political affairs, often professionally. **b.** The business, activities, or profession of a person so involved. **4.** The methods or tactics involved in managing a state or government. **5. a.** The scheming and maneuvering for power and personal advantage that occurs within a given group: *office politics.* **b.** A political aspect inherent in a given situation or sphere: *sexual politics.* **6.** *Used with a plural verb.* Opinions or principles dealing with political subjects: *Her politics are conservative.*

pol·i·ty (pŏl'ə-tē) *n., pl.* **-ties. 1.** The form of government of a nation, state, church, or organization. **2.** Any organized society, such as a nation, having one specific form of government. **3.** The supervision of public affairs; political administration. **4.** The condition of having a government or being politically organized. [From Latin *polītīa,* POLICY.]

Polk (pōk), **James Knox** (1795–1849). 11th U.S. president (1845–49). Experienced as a U.S. representative from Tennessee (1825–39), he brought his intense party loyalty and urgent sense of duty to his presidency, which was marked by the annexation of Texas (1843), the establishment of the 49th parallel as America's northern border (1849), and the formation of the Department of the Interior, the U.S. Naval Academy of Annapolis, and the Smithsonian Institution.

pol·ka (pōl'kə, pō'kə) *n.* **1.** A lively dance consisting of three steps and a skip, originating in Bohemia, performed by couples in duple time. **2.** A piece of music for this dance. [French and German, from Czech *pulka,* half-step, from *pul,* half.] **—pol·ka** *v.*

pol·ka dot (pō'kə) *n.* **1.** Any of a number of dots or round spots forming a pattern on cloth. **2.** A pattern or fabric marked with such dots. [Perhaps a respelling of *poke a dot.*]

poll (pōl) *n.* **1.** The casting and registering of votes in an election. **2.** The number of votes cast or recorded. **3.** A tax required for voting, a **poll tax** *(see).* **4.** A list or record of persons, especially for taxing or voting purposes. **5. a.** Any sampling of opinion on an issue in a given group: *took a poll of the class.* **b.** An **opinion poll** *(see).* **6.** The head, especially the top of the head where hair grows. **7.** The blunt or broad end of a hammer, ax, or other similar tool. **—go to the polls.** To vote. Used of a country or electorate.

~*v.* **polled, polling, polls.** —*tr.* **1.** To receive (a specified number of votes). **2.** To register (a person), especially for voting purposes. **3.** To receive or record the votes of. **4.** To cast (a vote or ballot). **5.** To canvass (a person, area, or sample group of persons) to survey general opinion. **6.** To cut off or trim (hair, horns, or wool, for example). **7.** To trim or cut off the hair, wool, branches, or horns of: *poll sheep.* —*intr.* To vote in an election. [Middle English *pol, polle,* head (whence the Modern English senses of counting by heads and registering of votes), of Low German origin; perhaps akin to Middle Low German *polle*†.] **—poll·er** *n.*

pol·lack, pol·lock (pŏl'ək) *n., pl.* **-lacks** or collectively **pollack,** also **-locks** or collectively **pollock.** A marine food and game fish, *Pollachius virens,* related to the cod, occurring chiefly in northern Atlantic waters. [17th century : from Scottish *podlock*†.]

pol·lard (pŏl'ərd) *n.* **1.** A tree whose top branches have been cut back to the trunk so that it may produce a dense growth of new shoots. **2.** An animal, such as an ox, goat, or sheep, that no longer has its horns.

~*tr.v.* **pollarded, -larding, -lards.** To change into a pollard. [From POLL.]

polled (pōld) *adj.* Having no horns; hornless.

pol·len (pŏl'ən) *n. Botany.* The fine, powderlike material produced by the anthers of flowering plants and by the male cones of conifers, which contains the male gametes and functions as the male element in fertilization. [New Latin, from Latin, flour, dust.]

pollen analysis *n.* **Palynology** *(see).*

pollen count *n.* The average number of pollen grains in a cubic yard or other standard volume of air over a 24-hour period at a particular time and place, used to estimate the possible severity of hay-fever attacks.

pollen tube *n. Botany.* The slender tube that grows from a grain of pollen down the style of a pollinated plant to the ovule and conveys male gametes that fertilize the egg cell.

pol·lex (pŏl'ĕks') *n., pl.* **pollices** (pŏl'ə-sēz'). The innermost forelimb digit; the thumb. [Latin, thumb.] **—pol·li·cal** (pŏl'ĭ-kəl) *adj.*

pollin-, pollini- *prefix.* Indicates pollen; for example, **pollinosis, polliniferous.** [New Latin *pollen* (stem *pollin-*), POLLEN.]

pol·li·nate, pol·le·nate (pŏl'ə-nāt') *tr.v.* **-nated, -nating, -nates.** *Botany.* To convey or transfer pollen from an anther or male cone to a stigma or female cone of (a plant or flower) in the process of fertilization. [New Latin *pollen* (stem *pollin-*), POLLEN.] **—pol·li·na·tion** *n.* **—pol·li·na·tor** *n.*

pol·lin·ic (pō-lĭn'ĭk) *adj. Botany.* Of or pertaining to pollen.

pol·li·nif·er·ous, pol·len·if·er·ous (pŏl'ə-nĭf'ər-əs) *adj.* **1.** Producing or yielding pollen. **2.** Adapted for carrying pollen, as a bee's legs are. [POLLINI- + -FEROUS.]

pol·lin·i·um (pŏ-lĭn'ē-əm) *n., pl.* **-ia** (-ē-ə). *Botany.* A mass of agglutinated pollen grains, found in the flowers of most orchids and milkweeds. [New Latin : POLLIN- + -IUM.]

pol·li·nize (pŏl'ə-nīz') *tr.v.* **-nized, -nizing, -nizes.** To pollinate. **—pol·li·ni·za·tion** *n.* **—pol·li·niz·er** *n.*

pol·li·no·sis, pol·len·o·sis (pŏl'ə-nō'sĭs) *n. Pathology.* Allergic reaction to pollen, as in disorders such as hay fever or asthma. [New Latin : POLLIN- + -OSIS.]

pol·li·wog, pol·ly·wog (pŏl'ē-wŏg', -wôg') *n.* An immature frog or toad; a tadpole. [Middle English *polwygle* : *pol, polle,* POLL (head) + *wiglen, wigelen,* to WIGGLE.]

pollock. Variant of **pollack.**

Pol·lock (pŏl'ək), **Jackson** (1912–56). U.S. artist. After early surrealistic work, he turned to the technique of action painting, throwing or dripping paint onto a very large canvas.

poll·ster (pōl′stər) *n.* A person who conducts opinion polls.

poll tax *n.* A tax levied on persons rather than on property, often as a requirement for voting. Also called "poll."

pol·lut·ant (pə-lōōt′nt) *n.* Anything that pollutes; especially, any gaseous, chemical, or organic waste that contaminates air, soil, or water.

pol·lute (pə-lōōt′) *tr.v.* **-luted, -luting, -lutes.** **1.** To contaminate (the environment) with harmful or poisonous substances. **2.** To render morally impure; corrupt. **3.** To make ceremonially impure; profane; desecrate. [Middle English *polluten,* from Latin *polluere* (past participial stem *pollut-*).] **—pol·lut·er** *n.* **—pol·lu·tive** *adj.*

pol·lu·tion (pə-lōō′shən) *n.* **1.** The act or process of polluting or the state of being polluted. **2.** The contamination of soil, water, or the atmosphere by the discharge of noxious substances. **3.** Broadly, any public nuisance attributable to a particular cause: *noise pollution.*

Pol·lux[1] (pŏl′əks). *Greek Mythology.* One of the twin sons of Zeus and Leda. See **Castor and Pollux.**

Pollux[2] *n. Astronomy.* A first-magnitude star in the constellation Gemini. [After the mythical twin POLLUX.]

Pol·ly (pŏl′ē) *n.* A name for a parrot.

Pol·ly·an·na (pŏl′ē-ăn′ə) *n.* A foolishly or blindly optimistic person. [After the title character in *Pollyanna* (1913), novel by Eleanor Porter (1868–1920).]

po·lo (pō′lō) *n.* **1.** A game of Oriental origin played by two teams of three or four players on horseback, equipped with long-handled mallets for driving a small wooden ball through the opponents' goal. **2.** Any similar game, such as water polo. [Balti *polo,* "ball," akin to Tibetan *bo·lo.*] **—po·lo·ist** *n.*

Po·lo (pō′lō), **Marco** (c. 1254–1324). Venetian traveler. His father and uncle had already made one successful trading expedition to the court of the Mongol emperor Kublai Khan in China before they took Marco with them in 1271. He entered Kublai's diplomatic service and undertook missions to all parts of the Mongol Empire before returning to Venice in 1295. His memoirs were for hundreds of years the West's chief source of knowledge of the Orient.

polo coat *n.* A kind of loose-fitting, tailored overcoat made from camel's hair or a similar material.

pol·o·naise (pŏl′ə-nāz′, pō′lə-) *n.* **1.** A stately, marchlike dance in triple time, consisting mainly of a promenade of couples. **2.** A piece of music for this dance. **3.** A woman's dress of the 18th century, having a fitted bodice and draped cutaway skirt, worn over an elaborate underskirt. [French, from the feminine of *polonais,* Polish, from Medieval Latin *Polōnia,* Poland.]

po·lo·ni·um (pə-lō′nē-əm) *n. Symbol* **Po** A naturally radioactive metallic element, occurring in minute quantities as a product of radium disintegration and produced by bombarding bismuth with neutrons. It has many isotopes ranging in mass number from 193 to 218, of which polonium-210, with a half-life of 134.8 days, is the most readily available. Atomic number 84, melting point 254°C, boiling point 962°C, specific gravity 9.32, valences 2, 4, 6. [Latin *Polōnia,* Poland, native country of its discoverers, the Curies.]

polo shirt *n.* A pullover sport shirt of knitted cotton.

Pol Pot (pŏl pŏt′) (1928–). Cambodian political leader. A Communist Party member since the 1940's, he led the Khmer Rouge movement that overthrew the Cambodian government in 1975. He established a regime that allegedly caused the deaths of millions of citizens. He fled the country in 1979 when Vietnamese forces overthrew his government.

Polska. See **Poland.**

pol·ter·geist (pōl′tər-gīst′) *n.* A noisy, mischievous spirit that manifests itself by slamming doors, moving objects, and the like. [German *Poltergeist : poltern,* to make noises, rattle, knock, from Middle High German *boldern, buldern* + German *Geist,* ghost, from Old High German *geist.*]

pol·troon (pŏl-trōōn′) *n. Archaic.* A base coward. [French *poltron,* from Italian *poltrone,* perhaps augmentative of *poltro,* lazy person.] **—pol·troon·er·y** *n.*

poly– *prefix.* Indicates: **1.** More than one, many, or much; for example, **polygamy. 2.** More than usual; abnormal or excessive; for example, **polydipsia. 3.** A polymer; for example, **polythene, polyester.** [Greek *polus,* much, many.]

pol·y·a·cryl·a·mide (pŏl′ē-ə-krĭl′ə-mīd′) *n.* A white polyamide (-CH₂CHCONH₂) of acrylic acid. [POLY- + ACRYL(IC ACID) + AMIDE.]

pol·y·a·del·phous (pŏl′ē-ə-dĕl′fəs) *adj. Botany.* Having or designating stamens arranged in three or more groups by means of their united stalks or filaments. Said of flowers. [POLY- + Greek *adelphos,* brother + -OUS.]

pol·y·am·ide (pŏl′ē-ăm′īd′) *n. Chemistry.* A polymer containing repeated amide linkages, as in various kinds of nylon.

pol·y·a·mine (pŏl′ē-ə-mēn′, pŏl′ē-ăm′ēn′) *n.* Any of a group of organic compounds that contain two or more amino groups.

pol·y·an·dry (pŏl′ē-ăn′drē) *n.* **1.** The state or practice of having more than one husband at a single time. **2.** *Botany.* The condition in flowers of having an indefinite number of stamens. **3.** The practice of a female animal's mating with more than one male during a single breeding season. [Greek *poluandria,* from *poluandros :* POLY- + -ANDROUS.] **—pol·y·an·drous** *adj.*

pol·y·an·thus (pŏl′ē-ăn′thəs) *n., pl.* **-thuses.** Any of a group of hybrid garden primroses, especially *Primula polyantha,* having clusters of variously colored flowers. [New Latin, from Greek *poluanthos,*

"having many flowers" : POLY- + -ANTHOUS.]

polyanthus narcissus *n.* A bulbous plant, *Narcissus tazetta,* native to Eurasia, having clusters of fragrant white or yellow flowers.

pol·y·a·tom·ic (pŏl′ē-ə-tŏm′ĭk) *adj. Chemistry.* Having three or more atoms as constituents. Said especially of molecules.

pol·y·ba·sic (pŏl′ē-bā′sĭk) *adj. Chemistry.* Polyprotic.

pol·y·ba·site (pŏl′ē-bā′sīt′) *n.* A black mineral with a metallic luster, containing silver, copper, antimony, arsenic, and sulfur, essentially (Ag,Cu)₁₆(Sb,As)₂S₁₁, often found in veins of silver. [German *Polybasit :* POLY- + BAS(IS) + -ITE.]

Po·lyb·i·us (pə-lĭb′ē-əs) (c. 201–120 B.C.). Greek historian. His 40-volume history of Rome in the 2nd and 3rd centuries B.C. has mostly been lost.

pol·y·car·bon·ate (pŏl′ē-kär′bə-nāt′, -nĭt) *n.* Any of a class of clear, strong polyester resins made from phosgene and dihydric phenols and used in molded articles.

pol·y·car·pel·lar·y (pŏl′ē-kär′pə-lĕr′ē) *adj.* Having or consisting of many carpels. [POLY- + CARPEL + -ARY.]

pol·y·car·pic (pŏl′ē-kär′pĭk) *adj.* Also **pol·y·car·pous** (-pəs) (for sense 1). *Botany.* **1.** Having fruit with two or more carpels. **2.** Producing flowers and fruit several times in one season. [POLY- + -CARPOUS.] **—pol·y·car·py** (pŏl′ē-kär′pē) *n.*

pol·y·cen·trism (pŏl′ē-sĕn′trĭz′əm) *n.* The principle or advocacy, especially in Communism, of more than one possible dogma or political center. **—pol·y·cen·trist** *n. & adj.*

pol·y·chaete (pŏl′ī-kēt′) *n.* Any of various marine worms of the class Polychaeta, including the lugworms, bristleworms, and ragworms, having paired, flattened, bristle-tipped organs of locomotion. [New Latin *Polychaeta,* from Greek *polukhaitēs,* with much hair : POLY + *khaitē,* long hair, CHAETA.] **—pol·y·chaete, pol·y·chae·tous** (pŏl′ī-kē′təs) *adj.*

pol·y·chro·mat·ic (pŏl′ē-krō-măt′ĭk) *adj.* Also **pol·y·chro·mic** (-krō′mĭk), **pol·y·chro·mous** (-krō′məs). **1.** Having many colors or manifesting changes of color. **2.** *Physics.* Having a mixture of wavelengths. Said of light and other electromagnetic radiation. **3.** *Physics.* Having a mixture of energies. Said of streams of particles. **—pol·y·chro·ma·tism** (pŏl′ē-krō′mə-tĭz′əm) *n.*

pol·y·chro·mato·phil·i·a (pŏl′ē-krō-măt′ə-fĭl′ē-ə) *n.* Also **pol·y·chro·mo·phil·i·a** (-krō′mə-fĭl′ē-ə). Susceptibility to staining with more than one type of dye, as seen in diseased red blood cells. [POLY- + CHROMATO- + -PHILIA.] **—pol·y·chro·mato·phil·ic** *adj.*

pol·y·chrome (pŏl′ē-krōm′) *adj.* **1.** Having many or various changing colors; polychromatic. **2.** Made or decorated in many or various colors.

~n. An object having or decorated in many colors. [Greek *polukhrōmos :* POLY- + -CHROME.]

pol·y·chro·my (pŏl′ē-krō′mē) *n.* The art of employing many colors in decoration, especially as used in ancient architecture or pottery.

pol·y·con·ic projection (pŏl′ē-kŏn′ĭk) *n. Geography.* A conic map projection having distances between meridians along every parallel of latitude equal to those distances on a globe. The central geographic meridian is a straight line and the others are curved, while the parallels are arcs of circles.

pol·y·cot·ton (pŏl′ē-kŏt′n) *n.* A textile composed of a mixture of cotton and polyester fibers.

pol·y·cot·y·le·don (pŏl′ē-kŏt′l-ēd′n) *n. Botany.* A plant having several cotyledons. **—pol·y·cot·y·le·don·ous** *adj.*

pol·y·cy·clic (pŏl′ē-sī′klĭk, -sĭk′lĭk) *adj. Chemistry.* Of or designating a compound with molecules that contain three or more rings of atoms.

pol·y·cy·the·mi·a (pŏl′ē-sī-thē′mē-ə) *n. Pathology.* A condition marked by an abnormally large number of red cells in the blood. [POLY- + CYT(O)- + -HEMIA.]

pol·y·dac·tyl (pŏl′ē-dăk′təl) *adj.* Also **pol·y·dac·ty·lous** (-tə-ləs). Having more than the normal number of fingers or toes.

~n. polydactyl. A polydactyl person or animal. [Greek *poludaktulos :* POLY- + DACTYL.] **—pol·y·dac·tyl·ism, pol·y·dac·ty·ly** *n.*

pol·y·dem·ic (pŏl′ē-dĕm′ĭk) *adj. Ecology.* Occurring in or inhabiting two or more regions. [POLY- + (EN)DEMIC.]

pol·y·dip·si·a (pŏl′ē-dĭp′sē-ə) *n.* Excessive or abnormal thirst. [New Latin : POLY- + Greek *dipsa,* thirst.] **—pol·y·dip·sic** *adj.*

pol·y·em·bry·o·ny (pŏl′ē-ĕm′brē-ə-nē, -ĕm-brī′ə-nē) *n. Biology.* The development of more than one embryo from a single egg or ovule, as occurs in the development of identical twins. [POLY- + Late Latin *embryō* (stem *embryōn-*) + -Y.] **—pol·y·em·bry·on·ic** (pŏl′-ē-ĕm′brē-ŏn′ĭk) *adj.*

pol·y·es·ter (pŏl′ē-ĕs′tər) *n. Chemistry.* Any of numerous synthetic resins produced chiefly by reaction of dibasic acids with dihydric alcohols. Reinforced polyester resins are light, strong, and weather-resistant, and are used in boat hulls, swimming pools, waterproof fibers, adhesives, and molded parts. [POLY(MER) + ESTER.] **—pol·y·es·ter·i·fi·ca·tion** (pŏl′ē-ĕs-stĕr′ə-fĭ-kā′shən) *n.*

pol·y·e·ther (pŏl′ē-ē′thər) *n.* Any of a large number of synthetic polymeric materials containing C-O-C linkages, as in the epoxy resins.

pol·y·eth·yl·ene (pŏl′ē-ĕth′ə-lēn′) *n.* Also *chiefly British* **pol·y·thene** (pŏl′ə-thēn′). *Chemistry.* A polymerized ethylene resin used especially in the form of films and sheets for packaging or molded for a wide variety of containers, kitchenware, and tubing. [POLY(MER) + ETHYLENE.]

po·lyg·a·la (pə-lĭg′ə-lə) *n.* A plant, the **milkwort** (see). [New Latin *Polygala,* from Latin, from Greek *polugalon :* POLY- + *gala,* milk.]

po·lyg·a·mist (pə-lĭg′ə-mĭst) *n.* One who practices polygamy.

polo *Polo is thought to have been first played by the Persians, possibly as long ago as 500 B.C. It spread, in the 19th century, to Europe and the United States from India, where it had become popular with the British stationed there.*

po·lyg·a·my (pə-lĭg′ə-mē) *n.* **1. a.** The state or practice of having more than one spouse at one time. **b.** *Zoology.* The state of having more than one mate at one time. **2. a.** The condition of having both hermaphroditic and unisexual flowers on the same plant. **b.** The condition of having hermaphroditic and unisexual flowers on different plants of the same species. [Old French *polygamie,* from Late Latin *polygamia,* from Greek *polugamia* : POLY- + -GAMY.] **—po·lyg·a·mous** *adj.* **—po·lyg·a·mous·ly** *adv.*

pol·y·gene (pŏl′ē-jēn′) *n.* Any of a set of cooperating genes, each producing a small quantitative effect on a single characteristic.

pol·y·gen·e·sis (pŏl′ē-jĕn′ə-sĭs) *n.* The derivation of a species or type from more than one ancestor. Compare **monogenesis. —pol·y·ge·net·ic** (pŏl′ē-jə-nĕt′ĭk), **pol·y·gen·ic** (pŏl′ē-jĕn′ĭk) *adj.*

pol·y·glot (pŏl′ē-glŏt′) *adj.* Speaking, writing, written in, or composed of several languages.
∼*n.* **1.** A person with a reading, writing, or speaking knowledge of several languages. **2.** A book, especially the Bible, containing versions of the same text in different languages. **3.** A mixture or confusion of languages. [French *polyglotte,* from Greek *poluglōttos* : POLY- + *glōtta, glōssa,* tongue.] **—pol·y·glot·ism, pol·y·glot·tism** *n.*

pol·y·gon (pŏl′ē-gŏn′) *n.* A closed plane figure bounded by three or more line segments. [Late Latin *polygōnum,* from Greek *polugōnon,* from *polugōnos,* "having many angles" : POLY- + -GON.] **—po·lyg·o·nal** (pə-lĭg′ə-nəl) *adj.* **—po·lyg·o·nal·ly** *adv.*

po·lyg·o·num (pə-lĭg′ə-nəm) *n.* Any of numerous plants of the widely distributed genus *Polygonum,* including knotgrass and bistort, characterized by stems with knotlike joints and heads of small pink or white flowers. [New Latin, from Greek *polugonon,* knotgrass : POLY- + *gonu,* knee.]

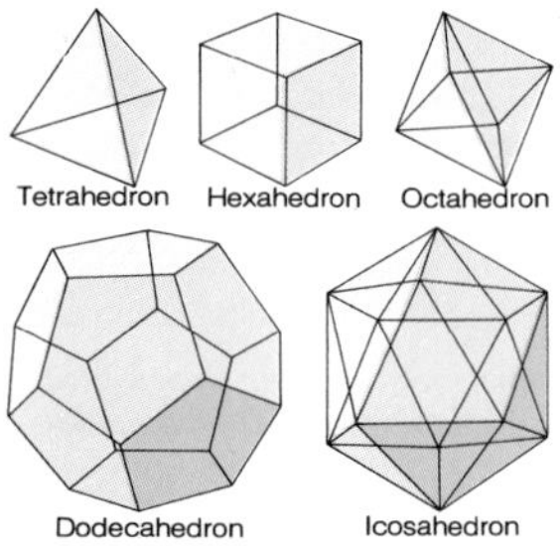
Tetrahedron
Hexahedron
Octahedron
Dodecahedron
Icosahedron

polyhedron *Each of these five regular polyhedrons has identical regular faces and identical angles. There are no other shapes with these properties.*

pol·y·graph (pŏl′ē-grăf′, -gräf′) *n.* **1.** An instrument that simultaneously records changes in such physiological processes as heartbeat, blood pressure, and respiration, and is sometimes used in lie detection. **2.** A device that produces simultaneous copies of matter written, printed, or drawn. **3.** An author who is prolific or who writes many varying works. [Greek *polugraphos,* "writing a lot" : POLY- + -GRAPH.] **—po·lyg·ra·pher** (pə-lĭg′rə-fər) *n.* **—pol·y·graph·ic** (pŏl′ē-grăf′ĭk) *adj.*

po·lyg·y·ny (pə-lĭj′ə-nē) *n.* **1.** The condition or practice of having more than one wife or female mate at a single time. **2.** The condition in flowers of having many styles. [POLY- + Greek *gunē,* woman.] **—po·lyg·y·nous** *adj.*

pol·y·he·dral angle (pŏl′ē-hē′drəl) *n. Geometry.* A configuration formed by three or more planes having intersections that form a common vertex. Compare **solid angle.**

pol·y·he·dron (pŏl′ē-hē′drən) *n., pl.* **-drons** or **-dra** (-drə). *Geometry.* A solid bounded by polygons. [New Latin, from Greek *poluedron,* neuter of *poluedros,* having many sides or seats : POLY- + -HEDRON.] **—pol·y·he·dral** *adj.*

pol·y·his·tor (pŏl′ē-hĭs′tər) *n.* A polymath. [Greek *poluistōr* : POLY- + *histōr,* learned.] **—pol·y·his·tor·ic** (pŏl′ē-hĭ-stôr′ĭk, -stŏr′ĭk) *adj.*

pol·y·hy·dric (pŏl′ē-hī′drĭk) *adj. Chemistry.* Containing at least two hydroxyl groups.

Pol·y·hym·ni·a (pŏl′ē-hĭm′nē-ə). *Greek Mythology.* The Muse of sacred song, poetry, and mime. [Latin, from Greek *Polumnia,* from *polumnos,* abounding in songs : POLY- + *humnos,* HYMN.]

pol·y·mas·ti·gote (pŏl′ē-măs′tĭ-gōt′) *adj. Zoology.* Having a tuftlike arrangement of flagella. [POLY- + Greek *mastix*† (stem *mastig-*), whip + -ATE.]

pol·y·math (pŏl′ē-măth′) *n.* A person of great or varied learning. [Greek *polumathēs* : POLY- + *math-,* stem of *manthanein,* to learn.] **—pol·y·math, pol·y·math·ic** (pŏl′ē-măth′ĭk) *adj.*

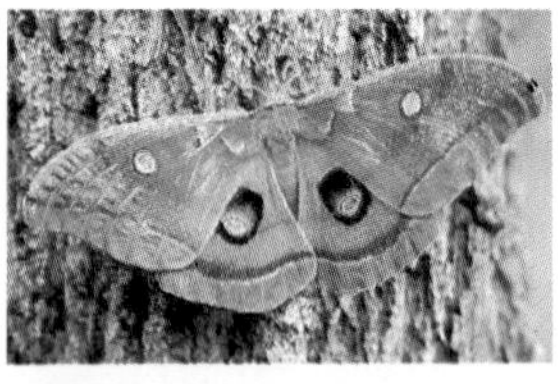

polyphemus moth *In Greek mythology, Polyphemus was a one-eyed giant, and this silkworm moth is so named because of the single eyelike marking on each of its hind wings.*

pol·y·mer (pŏl′ə-mər) *n. Chemistry.* A substance formed by linkage of numerous natural and synthetic compounds of usually high molecular weight of two or more repeated units. [Back-formation from POLYMERIC.]

pol·y·mer·ic (pŏl′ə-mĕr′ĭk) *adj. Chemistry.* Of, pertaining to, or consisting of a polymer. [Greek *polumerēs,* having many parts : POLY- + -MEROUS.] **—pol·y·mer·i·cal·ly** *adv.* **—po·lym·er·ism** (pə-lĭm′ə-rĭz′əm, pŏl′ə-mə-) *n.*

pol·y·mer·ize (pŏl′ə-mə-rīz′, pə-lĭm′ə-) *v.* **-ized, -izing, -izes.** *Chemistry.* —*tr.* To cause (a chemical compound) to form a polymer. —*intr.* To react to form a polymer. Used of compounds. **—pol·y·mer·i·za·tion** *n.*

po·lym·er·ous (pə-lĭm′ər-əs) *adj. Biology.* Consisting of numerous parts. [POLY- + -MEROUS.]

pol·y·meth·yl methacrylate (pŏl′ē-mĕth′əl) *n.* A clear synthetic material used extensively as a substitute for plate glass.

pol·y·morph (pŏl′ē-môrf′) *n.* **1.** *Biology.* An organism characterized by polymorphism. **2.** *Chemistry.* A specific crystalline form of a compound or mineral that can crystallize in different forms. **3.** Any of a group of white blood cells that have a lobed nucleus and granular cytoplasm. Also called "polymorphonuclear leukocyte." [From *polymorphous,* having many forms, from Greek *polumorphos* : POLY- + -MORPHOUS.]

pol·y·mor·phism (pŏl′ē-môr′fĭz′əm) *n.* **1.** *Biology.* The occurrence of different forms, stages, or color types in organisms of the same species. **2.** *Chemistry.* Crystallization of a compound or mineral in at least two distinct forms. **—pol·y·mor·phic, pol·y·mor·phous** *adj.*

pol·y·myx·in (pŏl′ē-mĭk′sĭn) *n. Medicine.* Any of various mainly toxic antibiotics derived from strains of the soil bacterium *Bacillus polymixa* and used to treat a variety of infections. [New Latin *(Bacillus) polymixa* : POLY- + MYX(O)- + -IN.]

Pol·y·ne·sia (pŏl′ə-nē′zhə, -shə). A division of the Pacific islands, including New Zealand and the many smaller islands in the southern and central Pacific. The smaller islands are mostly coral islands, and the larger ones volcanic. See also **Melanesia, Micronesia.** See map at **Pacific Ocean.**

Pol·y·ne·sian (pŏl′ə-nē′zhən, -shən) *adj.* Of or pertaining to Polynesia, its inhabitants, culture, or languages.
∼*n.* **1.** A member of one of the native peoples of Polynesia, including the Hawaiians, Maoris, Samoans, and Tahitians. **2.** A subfamily of the Austronesian language family spoken in Polynesia.

pol·y·neu·ri·tis (pŏl′ē-no͝o-rī′tĭs, -nyo͝o-rī′tĭs) *n.* Any disorder involving inflammation of all the peripheral nerves.

pol·y·no·mi·al (pŏl′ē-nō′mē-əl) *adj.* Of, pertaining to, or consisting of more than two names or terms.
∼*n.* **1.** *Biology.* A taxonomic name consisting of more than two terms. **2.** *Mathematics.* **a.** An algebraic function of two or more summed terms, each term consisting of a constant multiplier and one or more variables raised, in general, to integral powers. For example, the general form of a polynomial of degree *n* in a single real variable *x* is $a_0x^n + a_1x^{n-1} + \ldots + a_{n-1}x + a_n$ where $a_0, a_1, \ldots, a_n$ are real numbers with $a_0 \neq 0$ and *n* is a positive integer. **b.** Any mathematical expression of two or more terms. Also called "multinomial." [POLY- + (BI)NOMIAL.]

pol·y·nu·cle·o·tide (pŏl′ē-no͞o′klē-ə-tīd′, -nyo͞o′klē-ə-tīd′) *n.* A compound consisting of a chain of linked nucleotides, such as the nucleic acids DNA and RNA.

po·lyn·ya (pŏl′ən-yä′) *n.* A large area of open water surrounded by sea ice. [Russian *polyn′ya,* from *polyĭ,* open.]

pol·y·on·y·mous (pŏl′ē-ŏn′ə-məs) *adj.* Having or called by several different names. [POLY- + -ONYM + -OUS.]

pol·yp (pŏl′ĭp) *n.* **1.** *Zoology.* A coelenterate having a cylindrical body and an oral opening usually surrounded by tentacles, such as a hydra or coral. Compare **medusa. 2.** *Pathology.* A growth protruding from the mucous lining of an organ, such as the nose. In this sense, also called "polypus." [French *polype,* octopus, from Latin *polypus,* from Greek *polupous,* "many-footed" : POLY- + *pous,* foot.] **—pol·yp·oid** (pŏl′ə-poid′) *adj.*

pol·y·par·y (pŏl′ə-pĕr′ē) *n., pl.* **-ies.** Also **pol·y·par·i·um** (pŏl′ə-pâr′ē-əm) *pl.* **-ia** (-ē-ə). *Zoology.* The common framework and base of a polyp colony, especially of coral. [From POLYP.]

pol·y·pep·tide (pŏl′ē-pĕp′tīd′) *n. Biochemistry.* A **peptide** *(see)* containing between 10 and 100 amino acids.

pol·y·pet·al·ous (pŏl′ē-pĕt′l-əs) *adj. Botany.* Having distinctly separate petals: *a polypetalous corolla.*

pol·y·pha·gi·a (pŏl′ē-fā′jē-ə, -jə) *n.* An excessive or pathological desire to eat. [New Latin, from Greek *poluphagia,* from *poluphagos,* eating much, POLYPHAGOUS.] **—pol·y·pha·gi·an** *adj.*

po·lyph·a·gous (pə-lĭf′ə-gəs) *adj. Zoology.* Feeding on or utilizing a variety of foods. [Greek *poluphagos,* eating much : POLY- + -PHAGOUS.]

Pol·y·phe·mus (pŏl′ə-fē′məs). *Greek Mythology.* The Cyclops who confined Odysseus and his companions in a cave until Odysseus blinded him and escaped.

polyphemus moth *n.* A large North American moth, *Anteraea polyphemus,* having an eyelike spot on each hind wing. [New Latin, after POLYPHEMUS.]

pol·y·phone (pŏl′ē-fōn′) *n. Phonetics.* A written character or combination of characters having two or more phonetic values, such as the letter *c* in *cake* and *certain.* [POLY- + -PHONE.]

pol·y·phon·ic (pŏl′ē-fŏn′ĭk) *adj.* **1.** *Music.* **a.** Of or pertaining to polyphony. **b.** Of or designating an instrument that can sound more than one note at a time. **2.** Having many voices. **3.** *Phonetics.* Of, pertaining to, or being a polyphone. **—pol·y·phon·i·cal·ly** *adv.*

polyphonic prose *n.* Prose that has a distinct rhythmic pattern and uses poetic devices so as to give the effect of verse, especially when read aloud.

po·lyph·o·ny (pə-lĭf′ə-nē) *n., pl.* **-nies. 1.** *Music.* **a.** The simultaneous combination of two or more independent melodic parts, especially when in close harmonic relationship; counterpoint. Compare **homophony, monophony. b.** Musical composition marked by polyphony. **2.** The representation of two or more sounds by one written character, such as the *c* in *cake* and *certain.* [Greek *poluphōnia,* variety of tones, from *poluphōnos,* having many tones : POLY- + *phōnē,* sound, PHONE.] **—po·lyph·o·nous** *adj.* **—po·lyph·o·nous·ly** *adv.*

pol·y·phy·let·ic (pŏl′ē-fī-lĕt′ĭk) *adj. Biology.* Pertaining to or characterized by development from more than one ancestral type. **—pol·y·phy·let·i·cal·ly** *adv.*

pol·y·phy·o·dont (pŏl′ē-fī′ə-dŏnt′) *adj.* Having many sets of teeth that develop and are shed in succession. [New Latin, "producing many teeth," from Greek *poluphuēs* (POLY- + *-phuēs,* from *phuein,* to bring forth) + -ODONT.]

pol·y·ploid (pŏl′ē-ploid′) *adj. Genetics.* Having more than twice the normal haploid chromosome number.
∼*n. Genetics.* An organism with more than two sets of chromosomes. [POLY- + -PLOID.] **—pol·y·ploi·dic** (pŏl′ē-ploi′dĭk) *adj.* **—pol·y·ploi·dy** (pŏl′ē-ploi′dē) *n.*

pol·yp·ne·a (pŏl′ĭp-nē′ə) *n.* Very rapid breathing; panting. [New Latin : POLY- + Greek *pnoia,* breathing, from *pnein,* to breathe.] **—pol·yp·ne·ic** *adj.*

pol·y·pod (pŏl′ē-pŏd′) *adj.* Also **po·lyp·o·dous** (pə-lĭp′ə-dəs). Having numerous legs. Said of insect larvae and similar organisms.
∼*n.* A polypod animal or organism. [Greek *polypous* (stem *polypod-*), "many-footed" : POLY- + *pous,* foot.]

pol·y·po·dy (pŏl′ē-pō′dē) *n., pl.* **-dies.** Any of various ferns of the widely distributed genus *Polypodium,* having simple or compound fronds and creeping rootstocks. Also called "wall fern." [Middle English *polypodie,* from Latin *polypodium,* from Greek *polupodion,* diminutive of *polupous,* POLYPOD.]

pol·y·pore (pŏl′ē-pôr′, -pōr′) *n.* A pore fungus *(see).*

pol·y·pro·pyl·ene (pŏl′ī-prō′pə-lēn′) *n.* A strong synthetic polymeric material made from propene and used extensively in molded articles, such as kitchenware, toys, and chairs.

pol·y·pro·tic (pŏl′ē-prō′tĭk) *adj. Chemistry.* Designating an acid with two or more replaceable hydrogen atoms in each molecule; polybasic. [POLY- + PROT(ON) + -IC.]

pol·yp·tych (pŏl′ĭp-tĭk′) *n.* A decorated altarpiece or panel having four or more hinged sections that can be folded together. [Greek *poluptukhos,* having many folds : POLY- + *ptukhē,* a fold, from *ptussein†,* to fold.]

pol·y·pus (pŏl′ə-pəs) *n., pl.* **-pi** (-pī′) or **-puses.** *Pathology.* A polyp *(see).* [Latin, POLYP.]

pol·y·rhyth·mic (pŏl′ē-rĭth′mĭk) *adj. Music.* Of, pertaining to, having, or using several different rhythms, as for different parts, simultaneously. —**pol·y·rhythm** (pŏl′ē-rĭth′əm) *n.*

pol·y·sac·cha·ride (pŏl′ē-săk′ə-rīd′) *n.* Also **pol·y·sac·cha·rose** (pŏl′ē-săk′ə-rōs′, -rōz′). A carbohydrate consisting of a group of nine or more monosaccharides joined by glycosidic bonds, such as starch and cellulose.

pol·y·se·my (pŏl′ĭ-sē′mē, pə-lĭs′ə-mē) *n.* The fact of having two or more different meanings. Used of a word or phrase. —**pol·y·se·mous** (pŏl′ĭ-sē′məs, pə-lĭs′ə-məs) *adj.*

pol·y·sep·al·ous (pŏl′ē-sĕp′ə-ləs) *adj. Botany.* Having distinctly separated sepals.

pol·y·some (pŏl′ē-sōm′) *n.* A structure in the cytoplasm of cells that consists of a group of ribosomes associated with messenger RNA. Also called "polyribosome." [POLY- + -SOME.]

pol·y·so·mic (pŏl′ē-sō′mĭk) *adj. Genetics.* Having an excess number of one or more chromosomes, but not all. [POLY- + (CHROMO)-SOM(E) + -IC.] —**pol·y·so·my** (pŏl′ē-sō′mē) *n.*

pol·y·sper·my (pŏl′ē-spûr′mē) *n.* The entry of several sperms into an ovum during fertilization. —**pol·y·sper·mic** (pŏl′ē-spûr′mĭk) *adj.*

po·lys·ti·chous (pə-lĭs′tĭ-kəs) *adj.* Arranged in two or more series or rows. Said especially of leaves on a stem.

pol·y·sty·rene (pŏl′ē-stī′rēn′) *n.* A polymeric form of styrene used either as a hard, rigid plastic for molded articles, or as a white, light, expanded foam for packing and thermal insulation.

pol·y·sul·fide (pŏl′ē-sŭl′fīd′) *n. Chemistry.* A sulfur compound containing at least two sulfur atoms linked together per molecule.

pol·y·syl·lab·ic (pŏl′ē-sĭ-lăb′ĭk) *adj.* 1. Having more than three syllables. 2. Characterized by words having more than three syllables. —**pol·y·syl·lab·i·cal·ly** *adv.*

pol·y·syl·la·ble (pŏl′ē-sĭl′ə-bəl) *n.* A polysyllabic word. [Medieval Latin *polysyllaba,* feminine of *polysyllabus,* polysyllabic, from Greek *polusullabos* : POLY- + *sullabē,* SYLLABLE.] —**pol·y·syl·lab·i·cism** (pŏl′ē-sĭ-lăb′ə-sĭz′əm), **pol·y·syl·la·bism** (-sĭl′ə-bĭz′əm) *n.*

pol·y·syn·de·ton (pŏl′ē-sĭn′də-tŏn′) *n.* The repetition of connectives or conjunctions in close succession for rhetorical effect, as in the phrase *here and there and everywhere.* [Late Greek *polusundeton,* from *polusundetos,* using many connectives : Greek, POLY- + *sundetos,* bound together (see **syndetic**).]

pol·y·syn·thet·ic (pŏl′ē-sĭn-thĕt′ĭk) *adj. Linguistics.* Designating a language, such as Eskimo, in which many of the element·s of a sentence or phrase are combined into one word and do not exist separately; holophrastic. Compare **synthetic.**

pol·y·tech·nic (pŏl′ē-tĕk′nĭk) *adj.* 1. Pertaining to technical training. 2. Pertaining to or dealing with many arts or sciences.
~*n.* A school specializing in the teaching of technical and vocational subjects and applied sciences. [French *polytechnique,* from Greek *polutekhnos,* skilled in many arts : POLY- + *tekhnē,* art.]

pol·y·tene (pŏl′ĭ-tēn′) *adj. Genetics.* Designating a chromosome in which the chromatids have remained unseparated after duplicating, resulting in a very large chromosome with conspicuous transverse bands. [POLY- + Latin *taenia,* band, from Greek *tainia,* ribbon.]

pol·y·tet·ra·fluor·o·eth·y·lene (pŏl′ē-tĕt′rə-floŏr′ō-ĕth′ə-lēn′) *n. Abbr.* **PTFE** A waxy, opaque-white thermoplastic resin, (C₂F₄)*n,* thermally stable, resistant to acids, alkalis, and oxidizing agents, and having an extremely low coefficient of friction. It is used as a low-friction coating, especially for nonstick pans, and for chemical-resistant gaskets, seals, and hoses. A trademark is Teflon.

pol·y·the·ism (pŏl′ē-thē-ĭz′əm) *n.* The worship of or belief in more than one god. [French *polythéisme,* from Greek *polutheos,* believing in many gods : POLY- + *theos,* god.] —**pol·y·the·ist** *n.* —**pol·y·the·is·tic** (pŏl′ē-thē-ĭs′tĭk) *adj.*

pol·y·thene. *Chiefly British.* Variant of **polyethylene.**

po·lyt·o·cous (pə-lĭt′ə-kəs) *adj. Biology.* Producing many offspring or ova at a single time. [Greek *polutokos,* bearing numerous offspring : POLY- + *tokos,* offspring, from *tiktein,* to beget.]

pol·y·to·nal·i·ty (pŏl′ē-tō-năl′ə-tē) *n. Music.* The use or occurrence of two or more keys simultaneously in a composition. —**pol·y·ton·al** (pŏl′ē-tō′nəl) *adj.* —**pol·y·ton·al·ly** *adv.*

pol·y·troph·ic (pŏl′ē-trŏf′ĭk, -trō′fĭk) *adj.* 1. *Biology.* Obtaining nourishment from various types of organic material. 2. *Pathology.* Characterized by or pertaining to excessive nutrition. [Greek *polytrophos,* well-fed : POLY- + *trephein,* to feed.]

pol·y·typ·ic (pŏl′ē-tĭp′ĭk) *adj.* Also **pol·y·typ·i·cal** (-ĭ-kəl). Existing in, having, or involving many different forms or types.

pol·y·un·sat·u·rat·ed (pŏl′ē-ŭn-săch′ə-rā′tĭd) *adj.* Of, pertaining to, or containing long chains of carbon atoms with numbers of double carbon-carbon linkages. Said especially of natural fats and oils used in margarines and cooking oils.

pol·y·u·re·thane (pŏl′ē-yoŏr′ə-thān′) *n.* Any of various thermoplastic or thermosetting resins, of varying flexibility, used in paints, varnishes, adhesives, foams, and electrical insulation. Also called "urethane."

pol·y·u·ri·a (pŏl′ē-yoŏr′ē-ə) *n. Pathology.* Excessive passage of urine, as in diabetes. [POLY- + -URIA.] —**pol·y·u·ric** *adj.*

pol·y·va·lent (pŏl′ē-vā′lənt) *adj.* 1. *Microbiology.* Containing, sensitive to, or interacting with more than one kind of antigen, antibody, toxin, or microorganism. 2. *Chemistry.* **a.** Having more than one valence. **b.** Having a valence of 3 or higher; multivalent. [POLY- + *valent,* from VALENCE.] —**pol·y·va·lence, pol·y·va·len·cy** *n.*

pol·y·vi·nyl (pŏl′ē-vī′nəl) *adj.* Designating any of a group of polymerized thermoplastic vinyl compounds, such as PVC.

polyvinyl acetate *n.* A common clear thermoplastic resin used in paints and adhesives.

polyvinyl chloride *n.* See **PVC.**

pol·y·zo·an (pŏl′ē-zō′ən) *n. Zoology.* A bryozoan *(see).* [New Latin *Polyzoa* : POLY- + -ZOA.] —**pol·y·zo·an** *adj.*

pol·y·zo·ar·i·um (pŏl′ē-zō-âr′ē-əm) *n., pl.* **-aria** (-âr′ē-ə). Also **pol·y·zo·a·ry** (-zō′ə-rē) *pl.* **-ries.** *Zoology.* A polyzoan colony or its supporting skeletal structure. [POLY- + -ZO(A) + -ARIUM.] —**pol·y·zo·ar·i·al** *adj.*

pol·y·zo·ic (pŏl′ē-zō′ĭk) *adj. Biology.* 1. Forming or consisting of a colony of zooids. 2. Having many sporozoites. [POLY- + -ZOIC.]

pom·ace (pŭm′ĭs, pŏm′-) *n.* 1. The pulpy refuse remaining after the juice has been pressed from apples or other fruit. 2. Any similar pulpy material, such as that remaining after the extraction of oil from nuts, seeds, or fish. [Middle English, from Medieval Latin *pōmācium,* cider, from Latin *pōmum,* apple.]

po·ma·ceous (pō-mā′shəs) *adj.* 1. Of, pertaining to, or characteristic of apples. 2. Of, pertaining to, or bearing pomes. [New Latin *pomaceus* : Latin *pōmum,* apple (see **pomace**) + -ACEOUS.]

po·made (pə-mād′, -mäd′, pō-) *n.* A perfumed ointment applied to the hair.
~*tr.v.* **pomaded, -mading, -mades.** To apply pomade to. [French *pommade,* from Italian *pomata,* hair ointment (originally apple-scented), from *pomo,* apple, from Latin *pōmum.*]

po·man·der (pō′măn′dər, pō-măn′-) *n.* 1. A mixture of aromatic substances formerly worn in a bag as a protection against odor and infection and now used to perfume rooms, closets, or the like. 2. A case or box for holding this mixture. [Middle English, variant of Old French *pome d'embre,* from Medieval Latin *pōmum de ambra,* "apple" or "ball of amber" : *pōmum,* apple, POME + *de,* of + *ambra,* AMBER.]

pom·be (pŏm′bā′) *n. East African.* An alcoholic drink made from grain, especially from millet. [Swahili.]

pome (pōm) *n. Botany.* A fleshy fruit in which the ovary and seeds are enclosed in an enlarged receptacle, such as the apple, pear, or quince. [Middle English, from Old French *pomme, pome,* apple, from Vulgar Latin *pōma* (unattested), from Latin *pōmum.*]

pome·gran·ate (pŏm′grăn′ĭt, pŭm′-) *n.* 1. A semitropical shrub or small tree, *Punica granatum,* native to Asia and widely cultivated for its edible fruit. 2. The fruit of this tree, having a tough, reddish rind and containing many seeds enclosed in a juicy red pulp with a mildly acid flavor. [Middle English *poumgarnei, pomegranard,* from Old French *pome grenate* : *pome,* apple, POME + *grenate,* having many seeds, from Latin *grānātus,* from *grānum,* grain.]

pom·e·lo (pŏm′ə-lō′) *n.* The **grapefruit** or **shaddock** *(both of which see).* [Alteration of POMPELMOUS.]

Pom·er·a·ni·a (pŏm′ə-rā′nē-ə, -rān′yə). Former region of central Europe, now absorbed into East Germany and Poland (1945). It extends from the Baltic Sea to the Vistula River in a low-lying plain.

Pom·er·a·ni·an (pŏm′ə-rā′nē-ən, -rān′yən) *adj.* Of or relating to Pomerania or its people.
~*n.* 1. A native or inhabitant of Pomerania. 2. A toy dog of a breed having long, silky hair and a small body.

po·mi·cul·ture (pō′mĭ-kŭl′chər) *n.* The cultivation of fruit. [Latin *pōmum,* fruit, POME + CULTURE.]

po·mif·er·ous (pō-mĭf′ər-əs) *adj. Botany.* Bearing pomes. [Latin *pōmifer,* fruit-bearing : *pōmum,* fruit, POME + -FER.]

pom·mel (pŭm′əl, pŏm′-) *n.* 1. A knob on the hilt of a sword or other weapon. 2. The raised front part of a saddle; saddlebow.
~*tr.v.* **pommeled, -meling, -mels.** Also *chiefly British* **-melled, -melling.** To beat; pummel. [Middle English *pomel,* from Old French, from Vulgar Latin *pōmellum* (unattested), rounded knob, diminutive of Latin *pōmum,* fruit, apple, POME.]

po·mol·o·gy (pō-mŏl′ə-jē) *n.* The scientific study and cultivation of fruit. [New Latin *pomologia* : Latin *pōmum,* fruit, POME + -LOGY.] —**po·mo·log·i·cal** (pō′mə-lŏj′ĭ-kəl) *adj.* —**po·mo·log·i·cal·ly** *adv.* —**po·mol·o·gist** *n.*

Pomona. See **Mainland** (Orkney Islands).

pomp (pŏmp) *n.* 1. Dignified or magnificent display; splendor. 2. Vain or ostentatious display. [Middle English, from Old French *pompe,* from Latin *pompa,* from Greek *pompē,* "a sending," solemn procession, from *pempein,* to send.]

pom·pa·dour (pŏm′pə-dôr′, -dōr′) *n.* 1. A woman's hairstyle formed by sweeping the hair straight up from the forehead into a high, turned-back roll. 2. A man's hairstyle with the hair brushed up

pomegranate *Originally the pomegranate grew only in Asia. But it is now grown in most parts of the world for its edible fruit (above) and as an ornamental tree for its scarlet flowers.*

from the forehead. [Invented by the Marquise de POMPADOUR.]

Pom·pa·dour (pŏm′pə-dôr′, -dōr′, -dŏŏr′, pôn′pä-dōōr′), **Marquise de,** born Jeanne Antoinette Poisson, known as "Madame de Pompadour" (1721–64). Mistress of King Louis XV of France. She was popularly blamed for engineering France's alliance with Austria, which led to the Seven Years' War (1756–63).

pom·pa·no (pŏm′pə-nō′, pŭm′-) *n.*, *pl.* **-nos** or collectively **pompano. 1.** Any of several marine food fishes of the genus *Trachinotus*; especially, *T. glancus*, of tropical and temperate Atlantic waters. **2.** Any of several fishes, such as *Palometa simillima*, a butterfish of American Pacific coastal waters. [Spanish *pámpano†*.]

Pom·pe·ian red (pŏm-pā′ən) *n.* A grayish to moderate red.

Pom·pe·ii (pŏm-pā′, -pā′ē′). Ancient city of Campania, southern Italy, on the Gulf of Naples. It was buried by the eruption of Mt. Vesuvius (A.D. 79). Since its rediscovery (1748), excavations have provided an invaluable insight into ancient Roman life.

pom·pel·mous (pŏm′pəl-mōōs′) *n.* A tree, the **shaddock** (*see*), or its fruit. [Dutch *pompelmoes*].

Pom·pey (pŏm′pē), Latin name Gnaeus Pompeius Magnus, known as "the Great" (106–48 B.C.). Roman general and statesman. He suppressed the slave revolt led by Spartacus and campaigned on the empire's eastern frontiers. Pompey joined Julius Caesar and Crassus to form a ruling triumvirate in 60 B.C. He broke with Caesar in 50 B.C., but was defeated by him at Pharsala in 48 B.C. and fled to Egypt, where he was murdered.

Pom·pi·dou (pŏm′pĭ-dōō′, pôn′pē-dōō′), **Georges Jean Raymond** (1911–74). French statesman and president. He served as adviser (1944–46) and personal assistant (1958–59) to De Gaulle, helping draft the constitution of the Fifth Republic. He was prime minister four times and helped negotiate a settlement between France and the Algerians (1961) and defuse the student revolt (1968). He succeeded De Gaulle as president (1969–74).

pom·pom¹ (pŏm′pŏm′) *n.* **1.** In World War I, a variety of large machine gun using one-pound shells. **2.** In World War II, an automatic, rapid-fire, antiaircraft cannon. [Imitative.]

pom·pom² (pŏm′pŏm′) *n.* Also **pom·pon** (pŏm′pŏn′). **1.** A tuft or ball of wool, feathers, or other material worn as a decoration, especially on a hat. **2.** A small, buttonlike flower of certain chrysanthemums and dahlias. [French *pompon†*.]

pom·pous (pŏm′pəs) *adj.* **1.** Characterized by an exaggerated show of dignity or self-importance; pretentious. **2.** Self-important in speech or manner. **3.** Characterized by pomp or stately display; ceremonious. [Middle English, from Old French *pompeux*, from Late Latin *pompōsus*, from Latin *pompa*, POMP.] —**pom·pos·i·ty** (pŏm-pŏs′ə-tē), **pom·pous·ness** *n.* —**pom·pous·ly** *adv.*

ponce (pŏns) *n. Chiefly British.* A man who lives off the earnings of a prostitute; a pimp. [Perhaps from POUNCE.]

Ponce de Le·ón (pŏns′ də lē′ən, lē-ōn′), **Juan** (1460–1521). Spanish explorer. He sailed with Columbus on his second voyage (1493–94) and started the settlement of Puerto Rico in 1508, becoming its governor (1509–12). He discovered Florida in 1513, but while starting a settlement there in 1521 he was killed in a skirmish with the local Indians.

pon·cho (pŏn′chō) *n., pl.* **-chos. 1.** A blanketlike cloak having a hole in the center for the head, worn originally in South America. **2.** A similar garment worn instead of a jacket or coat, or as a shawl. [American Spanish, from Araucanian *pontho*, woolen fabric.]

pond (pŏnd) *n.* A still body of water, smaller than a lake, often of artificial construction.
~*v.* **ponded, ponding, ponds.** —*intr.* To form a pond. —*tr.* To confine in or as if in a pond; dam up. [Middle English *ponde, pounde,* enclosure, Old English *pund-.*]

pon·der (pŏn′dər) *v.* **-dered, -dering, -ders.** —*tr.* To weigh mentally; consider carefully. —*intr.* To meditate; deliberate; reflect. Often used with *on* or *upon.* [Middle English *ponderen,* from Old French *ponderer,* from Latin *ponderāre,* to weigh, ponder, from *pondus* (stem *ponder-*), weight.] —**pon·der·er** *n.*

pon·der·a·ble (pŏn′dər-ə-bəl) *adj.* Capable of being weighed or assessed; appreciable. —**pon·der·a·bil·i·ty** *n.*

pon·der·o·sa pine (pŏn′də-rō′sə) *n.* A tall timber tree, *Pinus ponderosa,* of western North America, having long, dark-green needles. [New Latin *Pinus ponderosa,* ponderous pine.]

pon·der·ous (pŏn′dər-əs) *adj.* **1.** Having great weight; massive; huge. **2.** Graceless or unwieldy from weight. **3.** Lacking fluency; labored; dull: *a ponderous speech.* —See Synonyms at **heavy.** [Middle English, from Old French *pondereux,* from Latin *ponderōsus,* from *pondus* (stem *ponder-*), weight.] —**pon·der·os·i·ty** (pŏn′də-rŏs′ə-tē), **pon·der·ous·ness** *n.* —**pon·der·ous·ly** *adv.*

Pon·di·cher·ry (pŏn′dĭ-chěr′ē, -shěr′ē). Union territory of southeastern India. On the Coromandel Coast, it was a former French territory (founded 1674), reverting to Indian control in 1954.

pond lily *n.* The **water lily** (*see*).

pond scum *n.* Any of various freshwater algae that form a usually greenish scum on the surface of stagnant water.

pond skater *n.* An insect, the **water strider** (*see*).

pond·weed (pŏnd′wēd′) *n.* Any of various submerged or floating aquatic plants of the genus *Potamogeton.*

pone (pōn) *n.* **Corn pone** (*see*). [Of Algonquian origin, akın to Delaware *ăpân,* baked, Passamaquoddy *ābân.*]

pon·gee (pŏn-jē′, pŏn′jē) *n.* **1.** A soft, thin undyed cloth of Chinese or Indian silk with a knotty weave. **2.** A synthetic fabric resembling this. [Mandarin Chinese *běn zhī,* "homemade" : *běn,* own, self + *zhī,* weave.]

Pompeii *The temple of Apollo at Pompeii, with Vesuvius in the background. The building was preserved, like others in the town, by the ash that buried it when Vesuvius erupted in A.D. 79.*

pon·gid (pŏn′jĭd, pŏng′gĭd) *n.* Any primate of the family Pongidae; an **anthropoid** (*see*).
~*adj.* Of or pertaining to the family Pongidae. [New Latin *Pongidae,* from *Pongo* (genus), from Congolese *mpongo,* ape.]

pon·iard (pŏn′yərd) *n.* A dagger.
~*tr.v.* **poniarded, -iarding, -iards.** To stab with a poniard. [French *poignard,* from *poing,* fist, from Old French, from Latin *pugnus.*]

pons (pŏnz) *n., pl.* **pontes** (pŏn′tēz′). *Anatomy.* **1.** Any slender tissue joining two parts of an organ. **2.** The **pons varolii.** [Latin *pōns,* bridge.]

Pons (pôns, pŏnz), **Lily** (1904–76). U.S. operatic soprano, born in France. A principal soprano with the Metropolitan Opera for 30 years (1931–61), she was noted for her vocal range and her expressive performance.

pons as·i·no·rum (pŏnz′ ăs′ə-nôr′əm, -nōr′əm) *n.* **1.** A proposition in the first book of Euclid stating that the angles opposite the equal sides of an isosceles triangle are equal. **2.** A problem difficult for beginners. [Latin, "asses' bridge" : *pōns,* PONS + *asinōrum,* genitive plural of *asinus,* ASS.]

Pon·selle (pŏn-sĕl′), **Rosa Melba** (1897–1981). U.S. operatic soprano. Discovered at the age of 21 by Enrico Caruso, she made her debut in Verdi's *La Forza del Destino* (1918). She spent all but two years of her career with the Metropolitan Opera Company and is considered one of America's greatest native opera singers.

pons va·ro·li·i (pŏnz′ və-rō′lē-ī′) *n.* A band of nerve fibers in the brain connecting the medulla oblongata and the mesencephalon below the cerebellum. Also called "pons." [New Latin, "bridge of Varoli," after Constanzo *Varoli* (1542–75), Italian surgeon and anatomist.]

Pon·ta Del·ga·da (pŏn′tə dĕl-gä′də). Capital and largest city of the Azores, on São Miguel Island. It is a tourist center and fueling point for shipping.

Pont·char·train (pŏn′chər-trān′). Shallow lake, *c.* 1,630 square kilometers (630 square miles), in southern Louisiana north of New Orleans. It is linked with the Mississippi River by canal and with the Gulf of Mexico through Lake Borgne.

Pon·te·fract (pŏn′tə-frăkt; *British* pŭm′frĭt). Town in West Yorkshire, northern England. Britain's first parliamentary election by secret ballot was held here in 1872. Coal mining and the production of licorice confections, called pomfret cakes, are important.

Pon·ti·ac (pŏn′tē-ăk′) (*c.* 1720–69). U.S. Indian leader. He organized his people, the Ottawas, and virtually every Native American tribe from Lake Superior to the lower Mississippi River in a highly successful effort to expel the British military and settlers in the region. He negotiated a peace treaty with the British in 1766.

Pon·tic (pŏn′tĭk) *adj.* Of or pertaining to the Black Sea region. [Latin *Ponticus,* from Greek *Pontikos,* from *Pontos,* PONTUS.]

pon·ti·fex (pŏn′tə-fĕks′) *n., pl.* **pontifices** (pŏn-tĭf′ə-sēz′). **1.** In ancient Rome, a member of the Pontifical College, the highest college of priests, headed by the *Pontifex Maximus.* **2.** A pontiff. [Latin, probably from Etruscan, reshaped by folk etymology as if to mean "bridge-maker."]

pon·tiff (pŏn′tĭf) *n.* **1. a.** The pope. **b.** A bishop. **2.** A pontifex. [French *pontif,* from Latin *pontifex,* PONTIFEX.]

pon·tif·i·cal (pŏn-tĭf′ĭ-kəl) *adj.* **1.** Pertaining to, characteristic of, or suitable for a pope or bishop. **2.** Having the dignity, pomp, or authority of a pontiff. **3.** Pompously authoritative.
~*n.* **1. pontificals.** The vestments and insignia of a pontiff. **2.** A book of ceremonies and rites for a bishop. [Latin *pontificālis,* from *pontifex,* PONTIFEX.] —**pon·tif·i·cal·ly** *adv.*

pon·tif·i·cate (pŏn-tĭf′ĭ-kĭt, -kāt′) *n.* The office or term of office of a pontiff.
~*intr.v.* (pŏn-tĭf′ĭ-kāt′) **pontificated, -cating, -cates. 1.** To serve as a pontiff. **2.** To speak or behave with pompous authority. [Latin *pontificātus,* from *pontifex,* PONTIFEX.]

pon·ti·fy (pŏn′tĭ-fī′) *intr.v.* **-fied, -fying, -fies.** To speak or behave with pompous authority; pontificate.

pon·til (pŏn′tĭl) *n.* A glassmaker's tool, a **punty** (*see*). [French, perhaps from Italian *puntello,* diminutive of *punto,* point, from Latin *punctum,* from the neuter past participle of *pungere,* to prick.]

pon·tine (pŏn′tīn′) *adj.* **1.** Of or pertaining to bridges. **2.** Pertaining to the **pons varolii** (*see*). [Latin *pōns* (stem *pont-*), bridge.]

Pon·tine Marshes (pŏn′tīn′). Reclaimed area in south Latium, central Italy. Drainage was completed in the 1930's, destroying malarial breeding grounds and providing rich agricultural land.

Pon·tius Pilate (pŏn′chəs). See **Pilate.**

Pont l'É·vêque (pôn′ lā-věk′) *n.* A soft-centered French cheese made of whole cows' milk. [After *Pont l'Évêque,* town in northern France.]

pon·to·nier (pŏn′tə-nîr′) *n. Military.* A person in charge of pontoons or engaged in the construction of pontoon bridges. [French *pontonnier,* from *ponton,* PONTOON.]

pon·toon¹ (pŏn-tōōn′) *n.* **1. a.** A flat-bottomed boat or other structure used to support a floating bridge. **b.** A floating structure serving as a dock. **2.** A float on a seaplane. [French *ponton,* floating bridge, from Old French, from Latin *pontō* (stem *pontōn-*), boat bridge, from *pōns,* bridge.]

pontoon² *n.* **1.** A card game in which the aim is to hold cards that have a score higher than those of the banker, but no higher than 21. **2.** A winning hand in this game, consisting of an ace and a court card or ten, that adds up to exactly 21. Also called "vingt-et-un," "twenty-one." [Probably from French *vingt-et-un,* twenty-one.]

pontoon bridge *n.* A temporary floating bridge using pontoons for support.

Pon·tus (pŏn′təs). Ancient kingdom in northeastern Asia Minor, on the south shore of the Black Sea. It reached its peak under Mithridates VI but declined after his defeat by Pompey (*c.* 65 B.C.).

po·ny (pō′nē) *n., pl.* **-nies. 1.** A horse of any of several small breeds, not over 14.2 hands high. **2.** *Informal.* A racehorse. **3.** A translation or summary used as an aid in studying or examinations. Also called "trot," *chiefly British* "crib." **4.** Something small for its kind, as a liqueur glass. **5.** *British Slang.* The sum of 25 pounds. —*intr.v.* **ponied, -nying, -nies.** *Slang.* To pay money owed or due. Used with *up.* [Earlier *powny*, probably from obsolete French *poulenet*, diminutive of *poulain*, from Late Latin *pullāmen*, from Latin *pullus*, foal.]

pony express *n.* A postal system using relays of ponies; specifically, the system in operation from St. Joseph, Missouri, to Sacramento, California (1860–61).

po·ny·tail (pō′nē-tāl′) *n.* A hairstyle, as for girls or women, in which the hair is clasped at the back so as to hang down like a tail.

pooch (pōōch) *n. Informal.* A dog. [20th century : origin obscure.]

pood (pōōd) *n.* A former Russian weight equivalent to about 16.4 kilograms (36 pounds). [Russian *pud*, from Old Norse *pund*, POUND.]

poo·dle (pōōd′l) *n.* A dog of any of various breeds originally developed in Europe as hunting dogs, having thick, curly hair, and ranging in size from the fairly large standard poodle to the very small toy poodle. [German *Pudel(hund)*, "poodle (dog)," probably from Low German (*pudeln*, to splash), "splashing dog" (because the poodle was originally trained as a water dog); akin to Old English *pudd*, ditch. See **puddle.**]

pooh (pōō) *interj.* Used to express disdain or disgust. [Imitative.]

Pooh-Bah (pōō′bä′) *n.* **1.** A pompous, ostentatious official; especially, one who, holding many offices, fulfills none of them. **2.** A person who holds high office. [After *Pooh-Bah*, Lord-High-Everything-Else in W.S. Gilbert's *Mikado* (1885).]

pooh-pooh (pōō′pōō′) *tr.v.* **-poohed, -poohing, -poohs.** *Informal.* To express contempt or disdain for; dismiss or make light of. [Reduplication of POOH.]

pool¹ (pōōl) *n.* **1.** A small body of still water; a small pond. **2.** A puddle of any liquid. **3.** A deep place in a river or stream. **4.** A **swimming pool** (*see*). **5.** An underground reservoir, as of oil or gas. [Middle English, Old English *pōl*, from West Germanic *pōla-, pōl-* (unattested).]

pool² *n.* **1.** In certain gambling games, the total amount staked by all players. **2. a.** A supply of people with certain skills, material resources, or the like that can be drawn on: *a typing pool.* **b.** Any grouping of resources for the common advantage of the participants: *a car pool.* **3.** *Finance.* **a.** A mutual fund established by a group of shareholders for speculating in or manipulating prices of securities. **b.** The persons or parties participating in such a combination. **4. a.** An agreement between competing business concerns to establish controls over production, market, and prices for common profit. **b.** The group of concerns participating in such an agreement. **5.** In fencing, a match in which each member of a team fences successively with each member of an opposing team. **6.** Any of several games played on a 6-pocket billiard table, usually with 15 object balls and a cue ball. Also called "pocket billiards." Compare **billiards.** —*v.* **pooled, pooling, pools.** —*tr.* To combine (money, funds, or interests) into a common stock for mutual benefit. —*intr.* To join in or form a pool. [French *poule*, stakes, target (as in *jeu de la poule*, "game of the hen"), hen, from Late Latin *pullus*, hen, from Latin, young of an animal.]

pool·room (pōōl′rōōm′, -rōōm′) *n.* A commercial establishment or room for the playing of pool or billiards.

pool table *n.* A six-pocket billiard table on which pool is played.

poon (pōōn) *n.* **1.** Any of several trees of the genus *Calophyllum,* of southern and eastern Asia, having light, hard wood used for masts and spars. **2.** The wood or medicinal oil obtained from any of these trees. [Singhalese *pūna,* probably from Tamil *punnai.*]

Poo·na (pōō′nə). City of west-central India, in the Western Ghats, Maharashtra state. It was captured by the British in 1817. Mild in climate, it is a resort town and military center. It also has cotton and paper mills.

poop¹ (pōōp) *n. Nautical.* **1.** The superstructure at the stern of a ship. **2.** The **poop deck** (*see*). —*tr.v.* **pooped, pooping, poops.** *Nautical.* **1.** To break over the stern of (a ship). Used of waves. **2.** To be subjected to the breaking of (waves). Used of a ship or ship's stern. [Middle English, from Old French *poupe,* from Latin *puppis†.*]

poop² *tr.v.* **pooped, pooping, poops.** *Slang.* To cause to become fatigued or exhausted; tire. —**poop out. 1.** To give up because of exhaustion: *poop out of the race.* **2.** To decide not to participate, especially at the last minute. [Origin unknown.]

poop³ *n. Slang.* Inside information. [20th century : origin obscure.]

poop deck *n. Nautical.* The deck at the stern of a ship built above the main deck. Also called "poop."

poor (pōōr) *adj.* **poorer, poorest. 1. a.** Having little or no wealth and few or no possessions; poverty-stricken. **b.** *Law.* Dependent on charity or public funds; destitute. **c.** Wanting or lacking in financial or other resources: *an area poor in timber and coal.* **2. a.** Lacking in mental or moral quality; ignoble: *a poor loser; a poor spirit.* **b.** Inferior; inadequate; inefficient: *a poor memory.* **3. a.** Lacking

desirable elements or constituents: *Poor soil leads to poor milk.* **b.** Bad or ill; weak: *poor health.* **4. a.** Lacking in value or quality; trivial: *a poor exchange.* **b.** Lacking in quantity: *poor attendance.* **5. a.** Humble: *in my poor opinion.* **b.** Needing or deserving pity; pitiable: *the poor fellow.* [Middle English *povere, poure,* from Old French *povre,* from Latin *pauper.*] —**poor·ness** *n.*

poor box *n.* A box, especially in a church, for collecting charitable donations.

poor boy *n.* A **hero** (sense 5) (*see*).

poor farm *n.* A farm that houses, supports, and employs paupers at public expense.

poor·house (pōōr′hous′) *n.* An establishment maintained at public expense as a place for the accommodation and sometimes employment of paupers; a workhouse.

poo·ri, pu·ri (pōōr′ē) *n.* A light, flat wheat cake of Pakistan and northern India, usually fried in deep fat. [Hindi *puri,* from Sanskrit *puraḥ,* cake.]

poor law *n.* A law or system of laws providing for public relief and support of the poor.

poor·ly (pōōr′lē) *adv.* In a poor manner. —*adj.* In poor health; ailing; ill: *feeling poorly.* —See Synonyms at **sick.**

poor man's weatherglass *n.* A plant, the scarlet pimpernel. See **pimpernel.** [So called because its blossoms open only in fair weather.]

pop¹ (pŏp) *v.* **popped, popping, pops.** —*intr.* **1.** To make a short, light, explosive sound. **2.** To burst open with such a sound. **3.** To move quickly or unexpectedly; appear abruptly: *She popped up from nowhere.* **4.** To open wide suddenly so as to protrude: *His eyes popped with interest.* **5.** In baseball, to hit a short high fly ball that can be caught by an infielder. **6.** To shoot a pistol or other firearm. —*tr.* **1.** To cause to make a sharp bursting sound: *beer bottles being popped open.* **2.** To cause to burst open or explode with such a sound. **3.** To put or thrust quickly or suddenly: *She popped the shrimp into her mouth.* **4.** To fire (a pistol or other firearm). **5.** To fire at; shoot. **6.** *Slang.* To take or swallow (drugs in pill form), usually habitually. —**pop off.** *Informal.* **1.** To leave abruptly or hurriedly. **2.** To die. **3.** To speak in a burst of vehement anger. —**pop the question.** *Informal.* To propose marriage. —*n.* **1.** A sudden, light, explosive sound. **2.** A shot with a firearm. **3.** *Informal.* A nonalcoholic, flavored, carbonated drink. **4.** *Baseball.* A pop fly. —*adv.* **1.** With a popping sound. **2.** Abruptly or unexpectedly. [Middle English *poppen* (imitative).]

pop² *n.* Father. Used as a familiar term of address. [Short for *poppa,* variant of PAPA.]

pop³ *n.* Pop music (*see*). —*adj.* **1.** Of, pertaining to, or specializing in pop. **2.** Of, pertaining to, or suggestive of pop art. [Short for POPULAR.]

pop. 1. popular. **2.** population.

pop art *n.* A form of art that depicts objects of everyday life and adapts techniques of commercial art, such as comic strips. See feature, next page.

pop·corn (pŏp′kôrn′) *n.* **1.** A variety of corn, *Zea mays everta,* having hard kernels that burst when heated to form white, irregularly shaped puffs. **2.** The edible, popped kernels of popcorn. [Contraction of *popped corn.*]

pope¹ (pōp) *n.* **1.** *Often* **Pope.** The bishop of Rome and head of the Roman Catholic Church on earth, considered by Catholics to be, by apostolic succession from St. Peter, the vicar of Christ on earth. **2.** *Eastern Orthodox Church.* **a.** A priest. **b.** The patriarch of Alexandria. **3.** The head of the Coptic Church in Egypt. **4.** A figure considered to have unquestioned authority: *the pope of surrealism.* [Middle English, Old English *pāpa,* from Late Latin, from Greek *pappas,* title of bishops, PAPA.]

pope² *n.* A fish, the **ruffe** (*see*). [From POPE (prelate).]

Pope, Alexander (1688–1744). English poet. He is best known for the famous satirical, mock-epic poems *The Rape of the Lock* (1712; 1714) and *The Dunciad* (1728; 1743). He also wrote philosophical poems such as *An Essay on Man* (1733–34) and edited Shakespeare and translated Homer.

pope·dom (pōp′dəm) *n.* The office, jurisdiction, or tenure of a pope; the papacy.

pop·er·y (pōp′ə-rē) *n.* The doctrines, practices, and rituals of the Roman Catholic Church. Used derogatorily.

pope's nose *n.* The fatty end part of the rump of a cooked fowl. Also called "parson's nose."

pop·eyed (pŏp′īd′) *adj.* **1.** Having bulging eyes. **2.** Amazed; astonished: *popeyed at the spectacle.*

pop fly *n. Baseball.* A short high fly ball. Also called "pop," "pop-up."

pop·gun (pŏp′gŭn′) *n.* A toy gun that operates by compressed air, firing corks or pellets with a popping noise.

pop·in·jay (pŏp′ĭn-jā′) *n.* **1.** A vain, supercilious person; fop. **2.** *Obsolete.* A parrot. [Middle English *papejay, papengay,* parrot, from Old French *papegai,* from Spanish *papagayo,* from Arabic *babaghā.*]

pop·ish (pō′pĭsh) *adj.* Of or pertaining to the popes or the Roman Catholic Church. Used derogatorily. —**pop·ish·ly** *adv.* —**pop·ish·ness** *n.*

pop·lar (pŏp′lər) *n.* **1.** Any of several fast-growing deciduous trees of the genus *Populus,* having triangular leaves and soft, light wood. See **aspen, cottonwood, Lombardy poplar. 2.** The wood of any of these trees. **3.** Loosely, the **tulip tree** (*see*). [Middle English *poplere,*

THE COMIC-STRIP WORLD OF POP ART

A dynamic glorification of 20th-century mass-produced objects and images

Pop art originated in England and the United States in the late 1950's and early 1960's. It aimed to portray all aspects of popular culture, and in order to do this the movement focused on contemporary personalities and celebrities as well as on commercial and mundane objects that were in daily use; for the first time products such as soup cans, Coca-Cola bottles, advertisements, and comic strips were invested with aesthetic interest. Roy Lichtenstein, Andy Warhol, and Robert Raushenberg were among the foremost American pop artists. In England the leading artists were Richard Hamilton, Peter Blake, and David Hockney.

WHAAM *Oil on two canvas panels by Roy Lichtenstein (1963). Born in 1923, Lichtenstein pioneered the pop art movement in the United States. He concentrated on comic-strip cartoons, reproducing them so exactly that he even incorporated the color dots used in commercial printing. Later he made use of the comic strip to portray subjects other than cartoons.*

CAMPBELL SOUP CAN *This painting by Andy Warhol (1965) is in the Museum of Modern Art in New York City.*

from Norman French, Old French *poplier,* earlier *pople,* from Latin *pōpulus.*]

pop·lin (pŏp'lĭn) *n.* A light, ribbed fabric of silk, rayon, wool, or cotton, used in making clothing and upholstery. [Obsolete French *papeline,* from Italian *papalina,* feminine of *papalino,* papal, from Medieval Latin *papalis,* from Late Latin *papa,* POPE (the fabric was first made at the papal town of Avignon).]

pop·lit·e·al (pŏp-lĭt'ē-əl, pŏp'lĭ-tē'əl) *adj.* Of or pertaining to the part of the leg behind the knee joint. [New Latin *popliteus,* from Latin *poples*† (stem *poplit-*), the hollow of the knee.]

pop music *n.* Modern music, often electrically amplified, typically using simple melodies and strong rhythms and having a broad, popular appeal, especially to young people. Also called "pop."

Po·po·ca·té·petl, Mount (pŏp'pō-kăt'ə-pĕt'l). Dormant volcano in central Mexico. It is 5,452 meters (17,887 feet) high.

pop·o·ver (pŏp'ō'vər) *n.* A very light, puffy, hollow muffin made with eggs, milk, and flour. [So called because it pops up over the rim of the baking tin.]

poppa. Variant of *papa.*

pop·per (pŏp'ər) *n.* **1.** One that pops. **2.** A container or pan in which popcorn is popped. **3.** *Slang.* A drug, **amyl nitrite** *(see),* inhaled for sensual gratification.

Pop·per (pŏp'ər), **Sir Karl Raimund** (1902–). British philosopher, born in Austria. His best-known works are *The Open Society and Its Enemies* (1945) and *The Poverty of Historicism* (1957).

pop·pet (pŏp'ĭt) *n.* **1.** A **poppet valve** *(see).* **2.** *Nautical.* **a.** A small wooden strip on the gunwale of a boat that forms or supports the oarlocks. **b.** Any of the beams of a launching cradle supporting a ship's hull. **3.** *Chiefly British.* A sweet, endearing person, animal, or child; darling. [Middle English *popet,* child, doll, PUPPET.]

poppet valve *n.* An intake or exhaust valve, operated by springs and cams, that opens by axial motion. Also called "poppet."

pop·ple[1] (pŏp'əl) *intr.v.* **-pled, -pling, -ples.** To move in a tossing, bubbling, or rippling manner, as choppy water does.
~*n.* **1.** Choppy or bubbling water. **2.** The sound made by boiling liquid. [Middle English *poplen,* from Middle Dutch *popelen*†, to quiver (imitative).]

popple[2] *n. Informal.* A poplar. [Middle English *popul,* Old English *popul,* from Latin *pōpulus,* POPLAR.]

pop·py (pŏp'ē) *n., pl.* **-pies. 1.** Any of numerous plants of the genus *Papaver,* of temperate regions, having conspicuous red, orange, or white flowers and milky white juice. See **opium poppy. 2.** Any of several similar or related plants, such as the **California poppy** and the **horned poppy** *(both of which see).* **3.** The narcotic extracted from the opium poppy. **4.** A vivid red to reddish orange. [Middle English *popi,* Old English *popig, popaeg,* altered from Vulgar Latin *papāvum* (unattested), variant of Latin *papāver*†.]

pop·py·cock (pŏp'ē-kŏk') *n.* Senseless talk; nonsense. [Dutch dialectal *pappekak,* "soft dung" : *pap,* soft food, pap, from Middle Dutch *pappe,* probably from Latin *pappa,* father, food + *kak,* dung, from *kakken,* to defecate, from Latin *cacāre.*]

pop·py·head (pŏp'ē-hĕd') *n.* **1.** The seed capsule of a poppy. **2.** An ornamental carving on the top end of a church bench or pew.

Pop·si·cle (pŏp'sĭ-kəl, -sĭk'əl) *n.* A trademark for colored, flavored ice molded into a rectangle with two flat sticks for handles.

pop·u·lace (pŏp'yə-lĭs) *n.* **1.** The common people; the masses. **2.** A population. [French, from Italian *popolaccio,* rabble, from *popolo,* the people, from Latin *populus.*]

pop·u·lar (pŏp'yə-lər) *adj. Abbr.* **pop. 1.** Widely liked or appreciated by the public. **2. a.** Liked by friends, associates, or acquaintances; sought after for company. **b.** Liked or appreciated by an individual or group: *Cats are not popular with me.* **3.** Of, representing, or carried on by the common people or the people at large: *a popular uprising.* **4.** Fit for or reflecting the taste and intelligence of the broad mass of people: *a popular newspaper.* **5.** Accepted by, originating with, or prevalent among the people in general: *a popular misunderstanding.* **6.** Suited or appealing to ordinary people, as by being within their financial means: *popular prices.* [Latin *populāris,* of the people, from *populus,* people.] —**pop·u·lar·ly** *adv.*

popular front *n.* Any of various political coalitions formed in European countries during the 1930's, as an alliance of democratic, left-wing, and revolutionary parties having common interests in the struggle against reaction and fascism.

pop·u·lar·i·ty (pŏp'yə-lăr'ə-tē) *n.* The quality or state of being popular, especially of being widely admired or sought after.

pop·u·lar·ize (pŏp'yə-lə-rīz') *tr.v.* **-ized, -izing, -izes.** To make popular; especially, to cause to become readily intelligible to the layman: *a program popularizing science.* —**pop·u·lar·i·za·tion** *n.* —**pop·u·lar·iz·er** *n.*

popular music *n.* Light music, typically being melodic and emotionally evocative, and having a broad, popular appeal.

pop·u·late (pŏp'yə-lāt') *tr.v.* **-lated, -lating, -lates. 1.** To supply with inhabitants, as by colonization; fill with people. **2.** To inhabit or become inhabitants of. **3.** *Physics & Chemistry.* To cause (quantum states or energy levels) to be occupied. [Medieval Latin *populāre,* to people, from Latin *populus,* people.]

pop·u·la·tion (pŏp'yə-lā'shən) *n. Abbr.* **p., pop. 1. a.** All the people inhabiting a specified area. **b.** The total number of such people. **2.** The total number of inhabitants of a particular race, class, or group in a specified area. **3.** The act or process of furnishing with inhabitants. **4.** *Ecology.* All the organisms that constitute a specific interbreeding group, especially a species, inhabiting a specified habitat. **5.** *Statistics.* The entire set of individuals, items, or scores from which a sample is drawn. Also called "universe." **6.** *Astronomy.* Either of two classes to which stars can be assigned according to their age, distribution, and content of metal: *population I,* which contains young, luminous, metal-rich stars found in the spiral arms of galaxies; and *population II,* which contains older, metal-deficient stars found in the Galactic halo. [Late Latin *populātiō,* from Latin *populus,* people.]

population density *n.* See **density** (sense 3).

population explosion *n.* A sudden sharp increase in population caused by a rise in the birth rate or a decline in the death rate or both.

poppy *The field poppy,* Papaver rhoeas, *sheds its petals after only one day, but a vigorous plant may produce up to 400 flowers in succession during the summer. Often the first wildflower to colonize wasteland, the poppy became a symbol of remembrance for the war dead because it thrived on the battlefields of Flanders after World War I.*

population inversion *n. Physics.* A condition in which the usual or unexcited energy level of atoms in laser material is less heavily populated than a higher level, making stimulated emission and laser action possible.
Pop·u·lism (pŏp′yə-lĭz′əm) *n.* **1.** The philosophy of the Populist Party. **2. populism.** A political philosophy directed to the needs of the common people and advocating a more equitable distribution of wealth and power. **3. populism.** A style of political or personal conduct displaying identification with the interests, attitudes, or activities of the common people.
Pop·u·list (pŏp′yə-lĭst) *n.* **1.** A member or supporter of the Populist Party. **2. populist.** An advocate of populism.
∼*adj.* **1.** Of or pertaining to the Populist Party. **2. populist.** Pertaining to or characteristic of populism or its advocates.
Populist Party *n.* An American political party formed to represent agrarian interests in the Presidential election of 1892. It advocated increased currency issue, free coinage of gold and silver, public ownership of railroads, and a graduated federal income tax. Also called "People's Party."
pop·u·lous (pŏp′yə-ləs) *adj.* Containing many people or inhabitants; thickly settled or populated. [Middle English *populus,* from Latin *populōsus,* from *populus,* people.] **—pop·u·lous·ly** *adv.* **—pop·u·lous·ness** *n.*
pop-up (pŏp′ŭp′) *adj.* **1.** Having a mechanism that springs upward or makes an object spring upward: *a pop-up toaster.* **2.** Designating a book having paper or pages cut and folded in such a way that when it is opened pictures of figures and objects spring up.
∼*n.* **1.** A pop-up book. **2.** *Baseball.* A **pop fly** *(see).*
por·bea·gle (pôr′bē′gəl) *n.* A shark, *Lamna nasus,* of temperate Atlantic waters. Also called "mackerel shark." [Cornish *porghbugel*†.]
por·ce·lain (pôrs′lĭn, pōrs′-, pôr′sə-lĭn, pōr′sə-) *n.* **1.** A hard, white, translucent ceramic made by firing a pure clay and glazing with variously colored fusible materials; china. Also used adjectivally: *a porcelain vase.* **2.** An object or objects collectively made of this material. [French *porcelaine,* from Old French *pourcelaine,* from Italian *porcellana,* "of a sow," hence cowry shell, hence porcelain (from the resemblance of the shell to a sow's vulva), from *porcella,* diminutive of *porca,* sow, from Latin, feminine of *porcus,* swine.] **—por·ce·la·ne·ous** (pôr′sə-lā′nē-əs, pōr′-) *adj.* See feature, next page.
porcelain clay *n.* **Kaolin** *(see).*
porcelain enamel *n.* A silicate glass fired on metal. Also called "vitreous enamel."
porch (pôrch, pōrch) *n.* **1.** A covered platform, usually having a separate roof, at an entrance to a house. **2.** An open or enclosed gallery or room attached to the outside of a building; a verandah. **3.** *Obsolete.* A portico or covered walk. [Middle English *porche,* from Old French, from Latin *porticus,* PORTICO.]
por·cine (pôr′sīn′) *adj.* Of, pertaining to, or resembling a pig. [Latin *porcīnus,* from *porcus,* pig.]
por·cu·pine (pôr′kyə-pīn′) *n.* Any of various rodents, especially of the genera *Hystrix* and *Erethizon,* characteristically covered with long, sharp quills or spines. [Middle English *porkepin,* from Old French *porc espin,* "spiny pig," from Vulgar Latin *porcospīnus* (unattested) : Latin *porcus,* pig + *spīna,* thorn.]
porcupine fish *n.* Any of various spiny tropical marine fishes of the family Diodontidae; especially, *Diodon holocanthus,* capable of inflating itself when attacked.
porcupine grass *n.* Any of various Australian grasses of the genus *Triodia.* See **spinifex.**
pore¹ (pôr, pōr) *intr.v.* **pored, poring, pores. 1.** To read or study carefully and attentively. Usually used with *over*: *pore over a book.* **2.** To meditate deeply; ponder. Usually used with *over.* **3.** To gaze steadily or earnestly. [Middle English *pouren*†.]
pore² *n.* **1.** A minute orifice, such as one in the skin of an animal, serving as an outlet for perspiration, or in a plant leaf or stem, serving as a means of absorption and transpiration. **2.** Any minute surface opening or passageway, as in a rock. [Middle English, from Old French, from Latin *porus,* from Greek *poros,* passage.]
pore fungus *n.* Any fungus having a crustlike fruiting body with a pitted or porous surface. Also called "polypore."
por·gy (pôr′gē) *n., pl.* **-gies** or collectively **porgy. 1.** Any of various North American marine fishes of the family Sparidae. **2.** Any of several similar or related fishes. [18th century : origin obscure.]
po·rif·er·an (pə-rĭf′ər-ən) *n.* Any animal of the phylum Porifera, which includes the sponges. [New Latin *Porifera,* neuter plural of *porifer,* bearing pores : Latin *porus,* PORE + -FER.] **—po·rif·er·al, po·rif·er·an** *adj.*
po·rif·er·ous (pə-rĭf′ər-əs) *adj.* **1.** Having pores. **2.** *Zoology.* Of or pertaining to the phylum Porifera, which includes the sponges. [PORE + -FEROUS.]
pork (pôrk, pōrk) *n.* **1.** The flesh of a pig used as food. **2.** *Slang.* Government funds, appointments, or other favors acquired by a representative for his constituency as political patronage. [Middle English, from Old French *porc,* pig, from Latin *porcus.*]
pork barrel *n. Slang.* A government project or appropriation benefiting a specific area and a legislator's constituents.
pork·er (pôr′kər, pōr′-) *n.* **1.** A fattened young pig. **2.** *Informal.* One who resembles a pig, as in being fat and greedy.
pork·pie, pork pie (pôrk′pī′, pōrk′-) *n.* **1.** A thick-crusted pie filled with chopped pork. **2.** A man's hat having a low, flat crown and a brim that can be turned up or down.
pork·y (pôr′kē, pōr′-) *adj.* **-ier, -iest. 1.** Pertaining to or resembling pork. **2.** *Informal.* Fat or fleshy. **—pork·i·ness** *n.*
porn (pôrn) *n.* Also **por·no** (pôr′nō). *Slang.* Pornography.
∼*adj.* Also **por·no.** *Slang.* Pornographic.
por·nog·ra·phy (pôr-nŏg′rə-fē) *n.* **1.** Written, graphic, or other material intended solely to excite feelings of sexual lust, and usually considered obscene. **2.** The trade in or production of such material. **3.** Any activity, or representations of it, considered obscene or offensive: *the pornography of violence.* [Greek *pornographos,* writing about prostitutes : *pornē,* harlot, prostitute + -GRAPH.] **—por·nog·ra·pher** *n.* **—por·no·graph·ic** (pôr′nə-grăf′ĭk) *adj.*
po·ro·mer·ic (pôr′ə-mĕr′ĭk, pōr′-) *adj.* Permeable to water vapor. Said of synthetic materials, as those used in making shoes.
∼*n.* A poromeric material. [Greek *poros,* PORE + (POLY)MERIC.]
po·ros·i·ty (pə-rŏs′ə-tē, pô-) *n., pl.* **-ties. 1.** The state or property of being porous. **2.** *Geology.* A measure of this property, equal to the volume of air in a rock divided by the total volume. **3.** A structure or part that is porous. [Middle English, from Medieval Latin *porōsitās* (stem *porōsitāt-*), from *porōsus,* POROUS.]
po·rous (pôr′əs, pōr′-) *adj.* **1.** Having or full of pores. **2.** Admitting the passage of gas or liquid through pores or interstices. [Middle English, from Medieval Latin *porōsus,* from Latin *porus,* PORE.] **—po·rous·ly** *adv.* **—po·rous·ness** *n.*
porous pot *n. Chemistry.* A plate or container of porous fire clay used to separate electrolytes in a cell or to support a semipermeable membrane.
por·phyr·i·a (pôr-fîr′ē-ə) *n.* A hereditary disease involving disturbance in the metabolism of porphyrins and producing symptoms of mental confusion, neuritis, and abdominal pain. [New Latin, from PORPHYRIN, which colors the feces of porphyria patients.]
por·phy·rin (pôr′fər-ĭn) *n. Biochemistry.* Any of various nitrogen-containing, heterocyclic organic compounds occurring widely in plant and animal tissues and providing the foundation structure for hemoglobin, chlorophyll, and certain enzymes. [Greek *porphura,* PURPLE (from its color).]
por·phy·rit·ic (pôr′fə-rĭt′ĭk) *adj. Geology.* Of or pertaining to porphyry.
por·phy·roid (pôr′fə-roid′) *n.* Metamorphic rock having porphyritic texture.
por·phy·ry (pôr′fə-rē) *n., pl.* **-ries.** *Geology.* Igneous rock containing relatively large conspicuous crystals, especially feldspar, in a fine-grained matrix. [Middle English *porfurie,* red or purple stone, from Medieval Latin *porphyrium,* from Latin *porphyrītēs,* purple-colored stone, from Greek *porphuritēs,* from *porphura,* PURPLE.]
por·poise (pôr′pəs) *n., pl.* **-poises** or collectively **porpoise. 1.** Any of several gregarious aquatic mammals of the genus *Phocaena* and related genera, of oceanic waters, characteristically having a blunt snout and a triangular dorsal fin. **2.** Broadly, any of several related mammals, such as the **dolphin** *(see).* [Middle English *porpoys,* from Old French *porpois,* from Vulgar Latin *porcopiscis* (unattested) : Latin *porcus,* a pig + *piscis,* fish.]
por·ridge (pôr′ĭj, pōr′-) *n.* Cereal, as oatmeal, boiled in milk or water. [Alteration of POTTAGE.]
por·rin·ger (pôr′ĭn-jər, pŏr′-) *n.* A shallow cup or bowl with a handle. [Alteration of *pottinger,* Middle English *potinger, poteger,* from Old French *potager,* from *potage,* POTTAGE.]
Por·son (pôr′sən), **Richard** (1759–1808). English classical scholar. Particularly attentive to Greek meter and diction, he was the pre-eminent member of a group of scholars dedicated to restoring Greek texts spoiled by centuries of academic tinkering. His editions of four Euripides plays were published between 1797 and 1802.
port¹ (pôrt, pōrt) *n. Abbr.* **pt. 1. a.** A town having a harbor for ships taking on or discharging cargoes. **b.** A place on a waterway that provides a harbor for a nearby town. **2.** A place of shelter; a haven. **3.** A **port of entry** *(see).* [Middle English, from Old English and Old French, both from Latin *portus,* house door, port.]
port² *n.* The left-hand side of a ship or aircraft when facing forward. Compare **starboard.**
∼*adj.* On the left-hand side.
∼*tr.v.* **ported, porting, ports.** To turn or shift (the helm of a vessel) to the left. [17th century : probably referring to the side of a ship usually facing the port.]
port³ *n.* **1.** *Nautical.* **a.** An opening in the side of a ship used for access. **b.** A porthole. **2.** An opening for a gun to be fired through, as in a tank or wall. **3.** An opening, as in a cylinder or valve face, for the passage of steam or fluid. **4.** *Scottish.* A gateway or portal, as to a town. **5.** A point at which data can be input or output for a computer. [Middle English, opening, from Old French *porte,* gate, door, from Latin *porta.*]
port⁴ *n.* **1.** A rich, sweet fortified wine of Portugal. **2.** Any of various similar wines produced in other countries. [Short for *Oporto,* port in northwestern Portugal from which it was shipped.]
port⁵ *tr.v.* **ported, porting, ports.** *Military.* To carry (a rifle, sword, or other weapon) diagonally across the body, with the muzzle or blade near the left shoulder.
∼*n.* **1.** *Military.* The position of a rifle or other weapon when ported. **2.** The manner in which a person carries himself; bearing. [Middle English, "a bearing," from Old French, from *porter,* to bear, from Latin *portāre.*]
Port. Portugal; Portuguese.
port·a·ble (pôr′tə-bəl, pōr′-) *adj.* **1.** Capable of being carried. **2.** Easily carried or moved. **3.** *Archaic.* Endurable; bearable.
∼*n.* Something that is portable, such as a light typewriter. [Middle English, from Old French, from Late Latin *portābilis,* from Latin

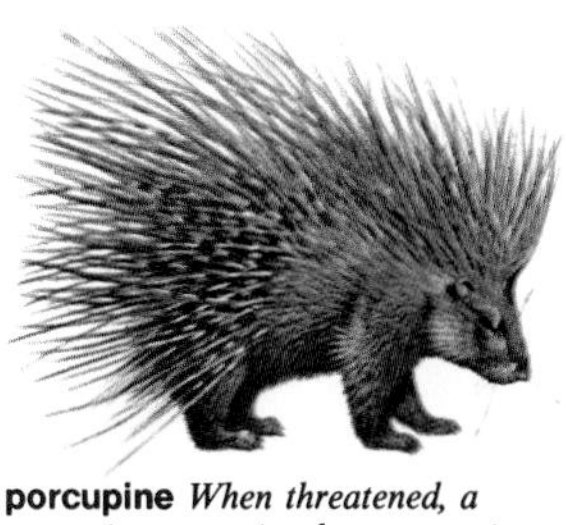

porcupine *When threatened, a porcupine erects its sharp, sometimes barbed, quills and shakes them in warning. If actually attacked, it turns its back to drive the quills into the attacker's face. The quills are easily detached and may remain embedded in the attacker, but the porcupine cannot shoot its quills. Porcupines are found in the Americas, Europe, Asia, and Africa.*

PRONUNCIATION KEY

ă, pat; ā, pay; âr, care;
ä, father, are; b, bib;
ch, church; d, deed; ĕ, pet;
ē, be; f, fife; g, gag; h, hat;
hw, which; ĭ, pit; ī, pie;
îr, pier; j, judge; k, kick;
l, lid, needle; m, mum;
n, no, sudden; ng, thing;
ŏ, pot; ō, toe; ô, paw, for;
oi, noise; ou, out; ŏŏ, book;
ōō, boot; p, pop; r, roar;
s, sauce; sh, ship, dish;
t, tight; th, thin, path;
th, this, bathe; ŭ, cut; ûr, fur;
v, valve; w, with; y, yes;
z, zebra, size; zh, vision;
ə, about, item, edible,
gallop, circus, peaceful

IN FOREIGN WORDS:

à, *Fr.* ami; œ, *Fr.* feu, *Ger.* schön; ü, *Fr.* tu, *Ger.* über; KH, *Ger.* ich, *Scot.* loch; N, *Fr.* bon; y′, *Fr.* Compiègne

STRESS MARKS:

Primary stress: ′
in·cite′ (ĭn-sīt′)
Secondary stress: ′
in′sight′ (ĭn′sīt′)

porcelain

THE SEARCH TO MAKE TRUE PORCELAIN
Chinese porcelain exported to Europe starts a craze for "Chinaware"

CHINESE PORCELAIN *The owner of this vase, which was made during the Yuan dynasty in the 14th century, buried it for safety. It was excavated in China in 1964.*

ITALIAN PORCELAIN *This soft-paste vase, with its enameled Chinese figures, was made in the Capodimonte factory in Italy in the 1740's.*

The type of ceramic called porcelain was being produced in China in the 8th century. It was composed of kaolin (china clay) and petuntze (a mineral similar to English Cornish stone). When fired to about 1300°C (2372°F) it becomes a tough, vitreous material, cool white in color and translucent when thin.

Ming porcelain exported to Europe in the 15th century started a craze for blue-and-white chinaware, and European potters began to imitate it. About 1580, potters in Italy created a glassy material, called Medici porcelain, that looked something like porcelain. It was a mixture of white clay and powdered glass, fired to less than 1050°C (1922°F). French potters of the 17th century made "soft-paste" porcelain in a similar way. Because this glassy material was more fragile than true "hard-paste" porcelain, the search for true porcelain continued.

Johann Böttger, a ceramist in Saxony, discovered how to make porcelain early in the 18th century and the Royal Saxon Porcelain factory at Meissen had a virtual monopoly for 40 years. But by 1750 there were hard-paste porcelain factories all over Europe. Soft-paste porcelain was made until about 1800 at many centers, including Sèvres in France and Chelsea, Bow, and Derby in England.

By 1800 a hybrid porcelain paste that included bone ash had been developed in England. Called bone china, it is tough, white, translucent when thin, and cheaper to make than hard-paste porcelain.

GERMAN PORCELAIN *Johann Böttger, the first European to make hard-paste porcelain, produced this coffeepot in Meissen, about 1719.*

ENGLISH BONE CHINA *This modern cup and saucer is made from a hybrid paste containing bone ash, probably first used about 1750.*

portāre, to carry.] **—port·a·bil·i·ty, port·a·ble·ness** *n.* **—port·a·bly** *adv.*

port·age (pôr′tĭj, pōr′-, pôr-täzh′) *n.* **1. a.** The act or process of carrying; transport. **b.** The cost of such transporting. **2. a.** The carrying of boats and supplies overland between two waterways. **b.** A place, track, or route used in such transporting. ~*v.* **portaged, -aging, -ages.** —*tr.* To transport by portage. —*intr.* To carry boats and supplies overland. [Middle English, from Old French, from Medieval Latin *portāgium,* from Latin *portāre,* to carry.]

por·tal (pôr′tl, pōr′tl) *n.* **1.** A doorway, entrance, or gate, especially one that is large and imposing. **2.** *Often* **portals.** Any entrance or means of entrance: *portals of knowledge.* ~*adj.* Of or pertaining to the portal vein. [Middle English, from Old French, from Medieval Latin *portāle,* a city gate, porch, from *portālis,* of a gate, from Latin *porta,* a gate.]

portal system *n.* A vein or group of veins that terminates at both ends in a capillary bed, such as the *hepatic portal system.*

por·tal-to-por·tal (pôr′tl-tə-pôr′tl, pōrt′l-tə-pōrt′l) *adj.* Of or based on the time spent on an employer's property, from the moment of arrival to that of departure: *portal-to-portal pay.*

portal vein *n. Anatomy.* A vein that conducts blood from one organ to another organ other than the heart.

por·ta·men·to (pôr′tə-mĕn′tō, pōr′-) *n., pl.* **-ti** (-tē). *Music.* A smooth, uninterrupted glide in passing from one tone to another, especially with the voice or a bowed string instrument. Also called "slide." [Italian, "a carrying," from *portare,* to carry, from Latin *portāre.*]

Port Arthur. See **Lü-da.**

por·ta·tive (pôr′tə-tĭv, pōr′-) *adj.* **1.** Portable. **2.** Of or pertaining to carrying. [Middle English *portatif,* from Old French, from Latin *portāre,* to carry.]

Port-au-Prince (pôrt′ō-prĭns′, pōrt′-, pôr′tō-prăns′). Capital of Haiti. It is the country's chief port and commercial center.

Port Blair (blâr). Administrative center and main port of the Andaman and Nicobar Islands, on South Andaman Island.

port·cul·lis (pôrt-kŭl′ĭs, pōrt-) *n.* A sliding grille of iron or wood suspended in the gateway of a fortified place in such a way that it can be quickly lowered in case of attack. [Middle English *porculis, port colice,* from Old French *porte coleïce : porte,* gate, from Latin *porta* + *coleïce,* feminine of *couleïs,* sliding, from *couler,* to slide, from Latin *colāre,* to strain, from *cōlum,* sieve.]

Porte (pôrt, pōrt) *n.* The government or court of the Ottoman Empire. [French *(la Sublime) Porte,* "(the High) Gate" (translation of Turkish *Bab-i Ali),* from Old French *porte,* gate, PORT.]

porte-co·chère, porte-co·chere (pôrt′kō-shâr′, pōrt′-) *n.* **1.** A supported roof projecting from an entrance to a building, such as a hotel, providing shelter for those getting in and out of vehicles. **2.** Formerly, a carriage entrance leading into a courtyard. [French *porte cochère,* "coach-door" : Old French *porte,* gate, PORT + *co-chère,* for coaches, from *coche,* COACH.]

Port E·liz·a·beth (ĭ-lĭz′ə-bəth). Seaport and city of southeastern Cape Province, South Africa. It was settled by the British in 1799. Its industries include vehicle assembly and fruit canning.

por·tend (pôr-tĕnd′, pōr-) *tr.v.* **-tended, -tending, -tends.** To serve as an omen or warning of; presage. —See Synonyms at **foretell.** [Middle English *portenden,* from Latin *portendere : por-,* variant of PRO- + *tendere,* to stretch.]

por·tent (pôr′tĕnt, pōr′-) *n.* **1.** An indication of something momentous or calamitous to occur; an omen. **2.** Prophetic or threatening significance: *a vision of dire portent.* **3.** Something amazing or miraculous; a marvel. [Latin *portentum,* from *portendere* (past participle *portentus*), to PORTEND.]

por·ten·tous (pôr-tĕn′təs, pōr-) *adj.* **1.** Marked by pompousness; pretentiously weighty. **2.** Full of unspecifiable significance; exciting wonder and awe; prodigious: *a portentous monster.* **3.** Of the nature of or constituting a portent; foreboding; ominous. **—por·ten·tous·ly** *adv.* **—por·ten·tous·ness** *n.*

por·ter[1] (pôr′tər, pōr′-) *n.* **1. a.** A person employed to carry luggage, as at a hotel or railroad station. **b.** A person who accompanies an expedition of explorers or mountaineers and carries equipment and supplies; a bearer. **2.** A railroad employee who waits on passengers. [Middle English *portour,* from Old French *porteur,* from Late Latin *portātor,* from Latin *portāre,* to carry.]

porter[2] *n. Chiefly British.* **1.** A gatekeeper; a doorman, especially in a large building. **2.** A person in charge of the entrance and entrance hall of a building, such as a college, who deals with inquiries and often has caretaking responsibilities. **3.** *Roman Catholic Church.* Formerly, an ordinand in the lowest of the minor orders. [Middle English, from Old French *portier,* from Late Latin *portārius,* from Latin *porta,* a gate.]

porter[3] *n.* A dark beer resembling light stout, made from malt browned by drying at a high temperature. [Shortened from *porter's beer* or *ale* (originally brewed especially for porters).]

Por·ter (pôr′tər, pōr′-), **Cole** (1893-1964). U.S. composer. He wrote the music and lyrics for musical comedies such as *High Society* and *Kiss Me Kate.* Among his popular songs is *Night and Day.*

Porter, Katherine Anne (1890-1980). U.S. writer. Her volumes of short stories include *Flowering Judas* (1930) and *Pale Horse, Pale Rider* (1939). Her only novel is *Ship of Fools* (1962).

Porter, William Sidney, known as "O. Henry" (1862-1910). U.S. author. A prolific short-story writer between 1903 and 1906, he often depicted commonplace characters and events in romantic, humorous fashion. Originally published in magazines, his many works were later collected in books such as *Whirligigs* (1910).

por·ter·age (pôr′tər-ĭj, pōr′-) *n.* **1.** The carrying of parcels or goods as done by porters. **2.** The charge for this.

por·ter·house (pôr′tər-hous′, pōr′-) *n.* **1.** In 19th-century America, an alehouse or chophouse. **2.** A cut of beef taken from the thick end of the sirloin, having a T-bone and a sizable piece of tenderloin. In this sense also called "porterhouse steak." [PORTER (beer) + HOUSE.]

port·fo·li·o (pôrt-fō′lē-ō′, pōrt-) *n., pl.* **-os. 1. a.** A portable case used for holding loose sheets of paper, drawings, maps, and the like. **b.** Such a case used for holding official documents such as those of a government ministry. **2.** The office, post, or responsibility of a cabinet member or minister of state. **3. a.** An itemized list of the investments, securities, and other financial assets owned by a bank, investment organization, or other investor. **b.** The investments and assets so listed. [Italian *portafoglio* : *portare,* to carry, from Latin *portāre* + *foglio,* leaf, sheet, from Latin *folium.*]

port·hole (pôrt′hōl′, pōrt′-) *n.* **1.** A small, usually circular window in a ship's side. **2.** An opening in a fortified wall; an embrasure.

por·ti·co (pôr′tĭ-kō′, pōr′-) *n., pl.* **-coes** or **-cos.** A porch or walkway with a roof supported by columns, often leading to the entrance of a building. [Italian, from Latin *porticus,* porch, from *porta,* a gate.] **—por·ti·coed** *adj.*

por·tière, por·tiere (pôr-tyâr′, pōr-) *n.* A heavy curtain hung across a doorway. [French *portière,* from *porte,* door, from Old French, gate, PORT.]

por·tion (pôr′shən, pōr′-) *n.* **1.** A section or quantity within a larger thing; a part of a whole. **2.** A part separated from a whole. **3.** A part that is allotted to a person or group, as: **a.** The amount of food or of a specific dish served to one person at a meal; a helping. **b.** The part of an estate received by an heir. **4.** A woman's dowry. **5.** One's allotment of human destiny; one's lot or fate.
~tr.v. **portioned, -tioning, -tions. 1.** To divide into parts or shares for distribution; parcel out. Usually used with *out.* **2.** To provide with a share, inheritance, or dowry. [Middle English, from Old French, from Latin *portiō* (stem *portiōn-*).] **—por·tion·a·ble** *adj.* **—por·tion·er** *n.* **—por·tion·less** *adj.*

Port·land[1] (pôrt′lənd). City of southwestern Maine, with a large, deep-water harbor on Casco Bay. It is a rail, shipping, and processing center for a farming, lumbering, and resort area. Founded *c.* 1632, Portland is today the commercial hub of the state.

Portland[2]. Deep-water port and largest city in Oregon. It is a major exporter of wood, grain, and fruit.

Portland[3], Isle of. Peninsula in Dorset, southern England, connected to the mainland by Chesil Bank. Its limestone quarries have provided the stone for such buildings as St. Paul's Cathedral, London.

Portland cement *n.* A hydraulic cement made by heating a mixture of limestone and clay in a kiln and pulverizing the resultant clinker. [After the Isle of PORTLAND.]

Port Laoi·se or **Port Laoighi·se** (lē′shə). County town of Leix, Leinster province, Republic of Ireland. It is a market town, and its industries include malting and flour milling.

Port Lou·is (lo͞o′ĭs, lo͞o′ē). Capital and seaport of Mauritius. Founded in 1735 by the French, it exports sugar and rum.

port·ly (pôrt′lē, pōrt′-) *adj.* **-lier, -liest. 1.** Being stout and corpulent and having a dignified bearing. Said especially of an adult man. **2.** *Archaic.* Stately; majestic; imposing. —See Synonyms at **fat.** [From PORT (bearing).] **—port·li·ness** *n.*

port·man·teau (pôrt-măn′tō, pōrt-, pôrt′măn-tō′, pōrt′-) *n., pl.* **-teaus** or **-teaux** (-tōz). *Chiefly British.* A large suitcase that opens into two hinged compartments. [French *portemanteau,* from Old French, "coat-carrier" : *porter,* to carry, from Latin *portāre* + MANTEAU.]

portmanteau word *n.* A word formed by merging the sounds and meanings of two different words; a blend as *chortle* from *chuckle* and *snort.* ["You see, it's like a *portmanteau* . . . there are two meanings packed up in one word" (Lewis Carroll).]

Port Mores·by (môrz′bē, mōrz′-). Capital of Papua New Guinea. It is a major commercial center and port.

port of call *n.* **1.** A port where ships dock in the course of voyages to load or unload cargo, obtain supplies, or undergo repairs. **2.** A stopping place on a journey; a place visited.

port of entry *n. Abbr.* **P.O.E.** A place where travelers or goods may officially enter or leave a country. Also called "port."

Port of Spain (spān). Capital and chief port of Trinidad and Tobago, West Indies. It is on the island of Trinidad, on the Gulf of Paria.

Por·to No·vo (pôr′tō nō′vō, pōr′-). Capital and chief port of Benin, West Africa. It was an important center of the slave trade and the capital of a native kingdom during the 19th century.

por·trait (pôr′trĭt, -trāt′, pōr′-) *n.* **1.** A painting, photograph, or other visual likeness, usually of a person; especially, one showing the face. **2.** A verbal picture or description, especially of a person. **3.** Any close likeness of one thing to another. [French, from Old French, from the past participle of *portraire,* to PORTRAY.]

por·trait·ist (pôr′trə-tĭst, pōr′-) *n.* A person who makes portraits, especially a painter or photographer.

por·trai·ture (pôr′trĭ-cho͝or′, -chər, pōr′-) *n.* **1.** The practice or art of making portraits. **2.** A portrait. **3.** Portraits collectively.

por·tray (pôr-trā′, pōr-) *tr.v.* **-trayed, -traying, -trays. 1.** To depict or represent pictorially; make a picture of. **2.** To depict or describe in words. **3.** To represent dramatically, as on the stage. [Middle English *portraien,* from Old French *portraire,* from Latin *prōtrahere,* to draw forth, reveal (in Medieval Latin, also "to portray") : *prō,* forth + *trahere,* to draw.] **—por·tray·a·ble** *adj.* **—por·tray·er** *n.*

por·tray·al (pôr-trā′əl, pōr-) *n.* **1.** The act or process of depicting or portraying. **2.** A representation or description.

por·tress (pôr′trĭs, pōr′-) *n.* A female doorkeeper or porter, especially in a convent.

Port Sa·id (sä-ēd′). City in northeastern Egypt, on the Mediterranean coast. It was founded in 1859 at the entrance to the new Suez Canal. Its main industry is the fueling and servicing of ships.

Port Sa·lut (pôr′ să-lo͞o′) *n.* Also **Port du Sa·lut** (pôr′ dü să-lo͞o′). A mild, semihard fermented cheese, made originally by Trappist monks in France. [After *Port de Salut,* Trappist abbey in northwestern France.]

Ports·mouth[1] (pôrts′məth, pōrts′-). City in Hampshire, southern England. It is situated on Portsea Island at the entrance to Portsmouth Harbor and is Britain's main naval base.

Portsmouth[2]. City of southeastern New Hampshire, at the mouth of the Piscataque River opposite Kittery, Maine. Tourism and fishing are important to its economy. There are many fine old houses at Strawberry Banke, a restored colonial community.

Port Stan·ley (stăn′lē). Also **Stanley.** Capital of the Falkland Islands, lying on East Falkland Island. It is the islands' only town and chief port.

Por·tu·gal (pôr′chə-gəl, pōr′-). Ancient name **Lu·si·ta·ni·a** (lo͞o′sə-tā′nē-ə). *Abbr.* **Port.** Republic of southwestern Europe, on the Iberian Peninsula. Its coastal plain rises to mountains in the north and east. It is one of western Europe's poorer countries, but manufacturing is expanding and in 1979 provided nearly as many jobs as farming. Textiles and clothing, chemicals, cork, wine, wood, fish, and fruit are the main exports. There are rich mineral resources, including tungsten, copper, and uranium. Tourism is important to its economy. Portugal became a kingdom in the 12th century and during the 15th century established an empire as a result of exploring Africa, discovering Brazil, and finding the sea route to India. It was ruled by Spain (1580–1640), invaded by France (1807), and in 1910 became a republic, later ruled by the fascist dictator Antonio de Oliveira Salazar. A peaceful military coup (1974) overthrew Salazar's successor, Marcello Caetano, and 1975 saw the return to democratic civilian rule. Madeira and the Azores are integral parts of Portugal, but its African territories achieved independence in the 1970's. Area, 92,082 square kilometers (35,553 square miles). Population, 9,900,000. Capital, Lisbon. See map, next page.

Por·tu·guese (pôr′chə-gēz′, -gēs′, pōr′-) *adj. Abbr.* **Pg., Port.** Of or pertaining to Portugal, its people, culture, or language.
~n., pl. **Portuguese.** *Abbr.* **Pg., Port. 1.** A native or inhabitant of Portugal. **2.** The Romance language of Portugal, Brazil, and various former Portuguese territories.

Portuguese East Africa. See **Mozambique.**

Portuguese Guinea. See **Guinea-Bissau.**

Portuguese man-of-war *n.* A complex colonial hydrozoan organism of the genus *Physalia,* of warm seas, having a bluish, bladderlike float from which are suspended numerous long, stinging tentacles capable of inflicting severe injury.

Portuguese Ti·mor (tē′môr′, tē-môr′). An overseas territory of Portugal, comprising the eastern part of the island of Timor, Oe-Cusse, in the northwest, and several offshore islands. It occupies approximately 19,130 square kilometers (7,286 square miles) and its capital is Dili.

Portuguese West Africa. See **Angola.**

por·tu·lac·a (pôr′chə-lăk′ə, pōr′-) *n.* Any plant of the genus *Portulaca,* having fleshy stems and leaves; especially, *P. grandiflora,* cultivated for its showy flowers that open only in sunlight. This species is also called "rose moss." See **purslane.** [New Latin, from Latin *portulāca,* purslane, from *portula,* diminutive of *porta,* gate, from the gatelike covering on its capsule.]

pos. 1. position. **2.** positive.

pose[1] (pōz) *v.* **posed, posing, poses.** *—intr.* **1.** To assume or hold a particular position or posture, as in sitting for a portrait. **2.** To affect a particular mental attitude or play a part, usually in order to impress. **3.** To represent oneself in a given character or as other than what one is: *He posed as a minister in order to enter people's houses.* *—tr.* **1.** To place (a model, for example) in a specific position. **2.** To propound or assert; put forward: *pose a threat.*
~n. **1.** A bodily attitude or position, especially one assumed for an artist or photographer. **2.** An affected attitude of mind or body. [Middle English *posen,* from Old French *poser,* from Late Latin *pausāre,* to cease, from Latin *pausa,* a pause, from Greek *pausis,* from *pauein,* to pause; confused in some senses with Latin *pōnere* (past participle *positus*), to place.]

pose[2] *tr.v.* **posed, posing, poses.** To puzzle or confuse with a difficult question or problem. [Short for *appose,* Middle English *apposen, opposen,* to confront with objections, from Old French *opposer,* to OPPOSE.]

Po·sei·don (pō-sīd′n). *Greek Mythology.* The god of the sea, earthquakes, and horses; brother of Zeus; identified with the Roman god Neptune. [Latin, from Greek *Poseidōn*†.]

Posen. See **Poznán.**

pos·er[1] (pō′zər) *n.* A person who poses.

poser[2] *n.* A baffling question or problem.

po·seur (pō-zœr′) *n.* A person who affects a particular attitude,

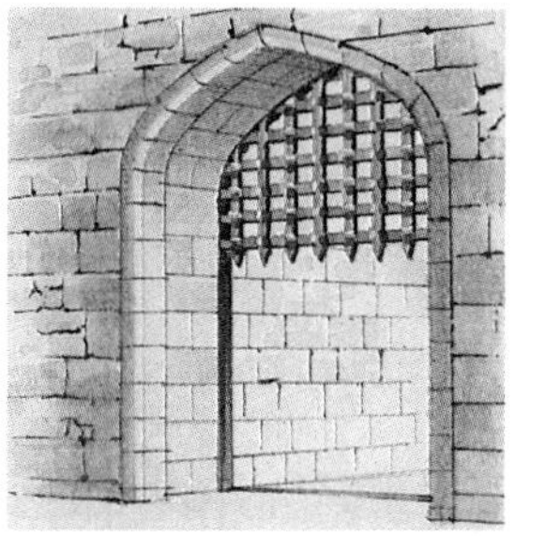

portcullis *A grating—usually made of metal or iron-plated oak—used to block the entrances to medieval castles. It was raised and lowered by rope and pulley.*

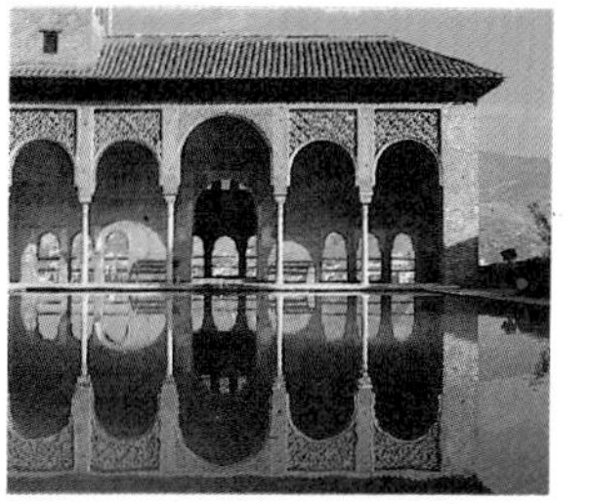

portico *A portico, or colonnaded porch, at the Alhambra, seat of the Moorish kings of Spain at Granada.*

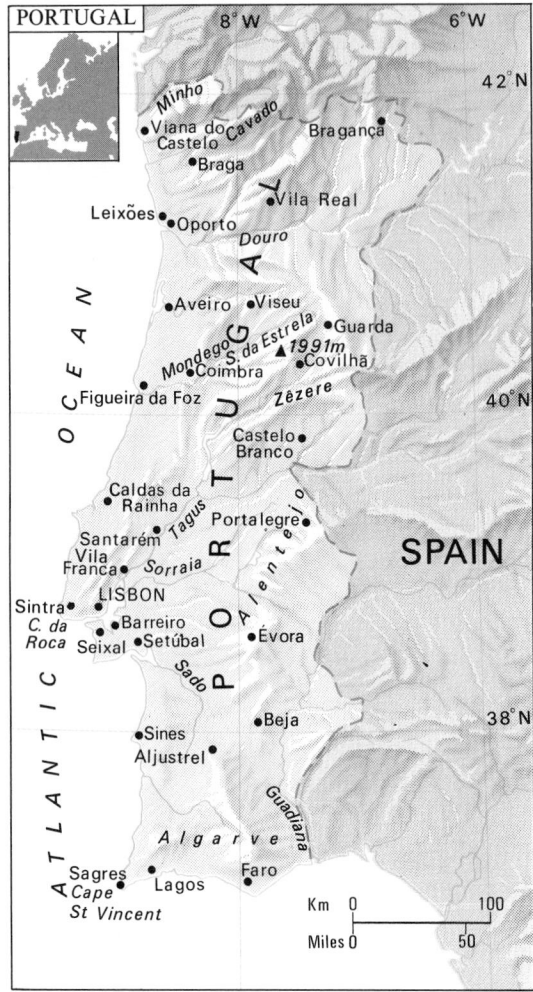

PORTUGAL

so the decimal 12 is indicated by 1100; that is, $(1 \times 2^3) + (1 \times 2^2) + (0 \times 2) + 0$. The same number in octal notation would be 14; that is, $(1 \times 8) + 4$.

position paper *n.* A detailed policy report that explains, justifies, or recommends a particular course of action.

pos·i·tive (pŏz′ə-tĭv) *adj. Abbr.* **pos.** **1.** Characterized by or displaying certainty, acceptance, or affirmation: *a positive answer.* **2.** Measured or moving in a direction of increase, progress, improvement, or forward motion. **3.** Explicitly or openly expressed or laid down: *a positive demand.* **4.** Admitting of no doubt; irrefutable. **5.** Determined or settled in opinion or assertion; confident; sure: *a positive manner.* **6.** Overconfident; dogmatic. **7.** Constructive rather than censorious or destructive; helpful or beneficial: *positive criticism.* **8.** Concerned with matters of fact rather than value; descriptive and empirical: *positive economics.* **9.** Composed of or characterized by the presence, rather than the absence, of particular qualities or attributes; real: *a positive benefit.* **10.** Without relation to or comparison with anything else; absolute. **11.** *Informal.* Used as an intensive: *She is a positive angel.* **12.** *Mathematics.* Pertaining to or designating: **a.** A quantity greater than zero. **b.** The sign (+). **c.** A quantity, number, angle, or direction opposite to another designated as negative. **13.** *Physics.* Pertaining to or designating electric charge of a sign opposite to that of an electron. **14.** *Medicine.* **a.** Indicating the presence of a particular disease, condition, or organism: *a positive Wassermann test.* **b.** Indicating the presence of the **Rh factor** *(see).* **15.** *Biology.* Indicating or characterized by response or motion toward the source of a stimulus: *positive tropism.* Compare **negative.** **16.** In photography, having the areas of light and dark in their original and normal relationship, or having natural colors, as in a print made from a negative. **17.** *Grammar.* Expressing or involving the simple, uncompared degree of comparison of adjectives or adverbs. Compare **comparative, superlative.** **18.** Driven by or generating power directly through intermediate parts having little or no play: *positive drive.* **19.** Designating a lens or mirror capable of converging a beam of radiation.
—*n. Abbr.* **pos.** **1.** Something that is positive. **2.** *Philosophy.* Something that is given or perceptible to the senses. **3.** *Mathematics.* A quantity greater than zero. **4.** *Physics.* A positive electric charge. **5.** In photography, an image in which the lights and darks or colors appear as they do in nature. **6.** *Grammar.* **a.** The positive degree of an adjective or adverb. **b.** An adjective or adverb expressing the positive degree; for example, the simple form *bright* as opposed to the forms *brighter* or *brightest.* [Middle English, from Old French *positif,* from Latin *positīvus,* arbitrarily laid down, dogmatic, from *pōnere* (past participle *positus*), to place.] —**pos·i·tive·ness** *n.*

positive discrimination *n.* Discrimination designed to remedy previous injustices or to make up for an existing discriminatory state of affairs; especially, the treating of a person or social group more favorably because of some disadvantage possessed, such as being physically handicapped or being a member of a racial minority.

positive feedback *n.* A type of **feedback** *(see)* in which an increase in output causes an increase in input.

pos·i·tive·ly (pŏz′ə-tĭv-lē, pŏz′ə-tĭv′lē) *adv.* **1.** In a positive manner. **2.** *Informal.* Used as an intensive: *Smart?—She's positively brilliant.*

positive prescription *n. Law.* Prescription (sense 4.a.) *(see).*

pos·i·tiv·ism (pŏz′ə-tĭ-vĭz′əm) *n.* **1. a.** A philosophical doctrine contending that sense perceptions are the only admissible basis of human knowledge and precise thought. **b.** A philosophical system based upon this doctrine; especially, the system of Auguste **Comte** *(see),* designed to supersede theology and metaphysics, and depending on a hierarchy of the sciences, beginning with mathematics and culminating in sociology. **2.** The application of positivism in logic, epistemology, and ethics. See **logical positivism.** **3.** Dogmatic certainty, as in speculation and argument. —**pos·i·tiv·ist** *n.* —**pos·i·tiv·is·tic** (pŏz′ə-tĭ-vĭs′tĭk) *adj.*

pos·i·tron (pŏz′ə-trŏn′) *n. Symbol* e+ The **antiparticle** *(see)* of the electron. Also called "antielectron." [POSI(TIVE) + (ELEC)TRON.]

pos·i·tro·ni·um (pŏz′ə-trō′nē-əm) *n. Physics.* A short-lived entity formed when an electron and a positron are bound together in a configuration resembling the hydrogen atom. [From POSITRON.]

po·sol·o·gy (pə-sŏl′ə-jē, pō-) *n.* The branch of medicine concerned with the science of the dosage of drugs and other agents. [French *posologie,* from Greek *posos,* how much.]

poss. **1.** possession. **2.** possessive. **3.** possible; possibly.

pos·se (pŏs′ē) *n.* **1.** A **posse comitatus** *(see).* **2.** A body of armed men with legal authority. **3.** *Informal.* A large body of people, usually with a shared purpose. —**in posse.** *Law.* Possible; potential. [Short for POSSE COMITATUS.]

posse com·i·ta·tus (kŏm′ə-tā′təs) *n.* A body of men that a sheriff or other peace officer is empowered to summon, as to aid in maintaining the peace or capturing a criminal. Also called "posse." [Medieval Latin *posse comitātūs,* "force of the county" : *posse,* power, from Latin, to be able, have power (see **potent**) + *comitātūs,* genitive of *comitātūs,* COUNTY.]

pos·sess (pə-zĕs′) *tr.v.* **-sessed, -sessing, -sesses. 1.** To have as property; own. **2.** To have as a quality, characteristic, or other attribute. **3.** To acquire mastery of or have knowledge of: *possess valuable data.* **4.** To gain or exert influence or control over; dominate: *Fury possessed him.* **5.** To control or maintain (one's nature) in a particular state or condition: *possessed his temper despite the insult.* **6.** To have sexual intercourse with. Used of a man. **7.** *Obsolete.* To gain or seize. [Middle English *possessen,* from Old French *possesser,* from Latin *possīdēre* (past participle *possessus*), "to sit as master,"

---

character, or manner to impress others. [French, from Old French *poser,* to POSE.]

posh (pŏsh) *adj. Informal.* **1.** Smart, rich, or fashionable; exclusive: *a posh car.* **2.** Refined; upper-class: *a posh accent.* [19th century : origin obscure. One unsubstantiated explanation cites the acronym for "port (side) out, starboard home," referring to accommodation on the shady and hence expensive side of ships sailing between England and India.]

pos·it (pŏz′ĭt) *tr.v.* **-ited, -iting, -its. 1.** To place in position. **2.** To put forward as a fact or truth or for the sake of argument; postulate. —See Synonyms at **presume.** [Latin *pōnere* (past participle *positus*), to place. See **position.**]

po·si·tion (pə-zĭsh′ən) *n. Abbr.* **pos. 1.** A place or location. **2. a.** The right or appropriate place: *The guns were in position.* **b.** An advantageous place: *maneuver for position.* **c.** *Military.* An area occupied by troops for a strategic purpose. **3. a.** The way in which something is placed. **b.** The arrangement of bodily parts; posture: *a standing position.* **c.** The arrangement of the pieces at any one time in a game of chess, checkers, or the like. **4.** A mental posture; a point of view: *the senator's position on foreign aid.* **5.** A situation or state relative to certain circumstances: *in a difficult position.* **6.** Social standing or status; rank. **7.** A post of employment; job. **8.** *Sports.* In team games, the part of the playing area for which a particular player is responsible. **9. a.** The act or process of positing. **b.** The principle or proposition posited. **10.** *Music.* **a.** One of the points on the fingerboard of a stringed instrument, as a violin, viola, or cello, at which the string may be stopped by the finger to produce a particular pitch. **b.** Any of seven lengths to which a trombone slide is extended to alter the pitch. **11.** In Greek and Latin verse, the condition in which a syllable is metrically long as a result of the placing of a short vowel before at least two successive consonants. **12.** *Finance.* The holding of securities or commodities by a dealer, either above *(long position)* or below *(short position)* the quantity he has undertaken to deliver.
—*tr.v.* **positioned, -tioning, -tions.** To place in position. [Old French, from Latin *positiō* (stem *positiōn-*), from *pōnere* (past participle *positus*), to place.] —**po·si·tion·al** *adj.* —**po·si·tion·er** *n.*

positional notation *n.* The common method of representing numbers by a set of digits, with the position of a digit in a string giving the power of the base of the system. For example, in decimal notation the number 12 indicates $(1 \times 10) + 2$; the number 212 indicates $(2 \times 10^2) + (1 \times 10) + 2$. In binary notation the base is 2,

take possession of : *posse,* to be able + *sīdere,* to sit down, and from Latin *possidēre* (past participle *possessus*), to own, possess : *posse,* to be able + *sedēre,* to sit.] **—pos·ses·sor** *n.*

pos·sessed (pə-zĕst′) *adj.* **1.** Owning, having, or mastering something such as property or knowledge. Used with *of*: *possessed of vital secrets; possessed of a sharp tongue.* **2.** Influenced or controlled by a strong emotion or idea or by or as if by an evil spirit or other force. Often used with *by* or *with*: *possessed with an urge to kill; a man possessed.* **3.** Self-possessed; calm or collected.

pos·ses·sion (pə-zĕsh′ən) *n.* **1.** The act or fact of possessing. **2.** The state of being possessed. **3.** *Abbr.* **poss.** That which is owned or possessed. **4. possessions.** Wealth or property. **5.** *Abbr.* **poss.** *Law.* Actual control, holding, or occupancy with or without rightful ownership. **6.** Any territory subject to foreign control. **7.** Self-control. **8.** The state of being dominated by or as if by evil spirits or by a strong emotion or idea. **9.** *Sports.* Control of the ball, puck, or the like. **—**See Synonyms at **assets.**

pos·ses·sive (pə-zĕs′ĭv) *adj. Abbr.* **poss. 1.** Of or pertaining to ownership or possession. **2.** Having or manifesting a desire to control or dominate: *a possessive husband.* **3.** *Grammar.* Of, pertaining to, or designating a noun or pronoun case that expresses belonging or a similar relation.
~*n. Grammar.* **1.** The possessive case. **2.** A possessive form or construction. **—pos·ses·sive·ly** *adv.* **—pos·ses·sive·ness** *n.*

possessive adjective *n. Grammar.* A pronominal adjective expressing possession. In the sentences *This is my duty* and *It is their fate,* the possessive adjectives are *my* and *their.*

possessive pronoun *n. Grammar.* Any of several pronouns expressing possession and capable of replacing noun phrases. In current English, they are *mine, his, hers, its, ours, yours, theirs, whose.*

pos·ses·so·ry (pə-zĕs′ə-rē) *adj.* **1.** Of, pertaining to, or having possession. **2.** *Law.* Depending on or arising from possession.

pos·set (pŏs′ĭt) *n.* A spiced drink of hot sweetened milk curdled with wine or ale. [Middle English *poshet, poshot*†.]

pos·si·bil·i·ty (pŏs′ə-bĭl′ə-tē) *n., pl.* **-ties. 1.** The fact or state of being possible. **2.** Something possible. **3.** A contestant or candidate capable of winning or being chosen. **4. possibilities.** Capacity for favorable development; potential: *The possibilities of microtechnology are unlimited.*

pos·si·ble (pŏs′ə-bəl) *adj. Abbr.* **poss. 1.** Capable of happening, existing, or being true without contradicting proven facts, laws, or circumstances. **2.** Capable of occurring or being done without offense to character, nature, or custom; suitable or acceptable: *the only possible answer.* **3.** Capable of favorable development; potential. **4.** Of uncertain likelihood.
~*n.* A possibility; especially, a candidate or contestant who has a strong chance of being selected or achieving success. [Middle English, from Old French, from Latin *possibilis,* from *posse,* to be able.]
Synonyms: *feasible, practicable, practical, viable, workable.*

pos·si·bly (pŏs′ə-blē) *adv.* **1.** Perhaps; maybe. **2.** In any way at all; under any circumstances: *She can't possibly have said that.*

pos·sum (pŏs′əm) *n.* **1.** An opossum. **2.** *Australian & New Zealand.* A **phalanger** *(see).* **—play possum.** To pretend to be dead, asleep, or unaware in order to deceive an opponent.

Pos·sum (pŏs′əm) *n.* A trademark for a device that enables paralyzed patients to operate such instruments as typewriters by means of blowing or extremely light touch.

possum haw *n.* **1.** A holly, *Ilex decidua,* of the southeastern United States, having bright-red fruit. **2.** A shrub, *Viburnum nudum,* of the eastern United States, having white flowers and bluish-black fruit.

post¹ (pōst) *n.* **1.** A long piece of wood, metal, or other material set upright in the ground to serve as a marker or support. **2.** Anything resembling this. **3.** The starting or finishing point at a racetrack, usually marked by a pole. **4.** A goal post.
~*tr.v.* **posted, posting, posts. 1. a.** To fasten up (an announcement) in a place of public view. **b.** To cover (a wall, for example) with posters; placard. Often used with *over.* **2.** To announce by or as if by posters: *post banns.* **3.** To put up signs on (property) warning against trespassing. **4.** To denounce publicly. **5.** To publish (a name) on a list. [Middle English *post,* Old English *post,* from West Germanic *posta* (unattested), from Latin *postis.*]

post² *n.* **1.** A military base where troops are stationed. **2.** The grounds and buildings of a military base. **3.** *British Military.* Either of two bugle calls, *first post* or *last post,* sounded in the evening as a signal to retire to quarters. **4.** An assigned position or station, as of a guard or sentry. **5.** A position of employment; especially, an appointed public office. **6.** A place to which anyone is assigned for duty or work. **7.** A **trading post** *(see).*
~*tr.v.* **posted, posting, posts. 1.** To assign to a position or station: *post a sentry.* **2.** To appoint to a naval or military command. **3.** To appoint or assign (someone) to a position or job in a distant location: *was posted to Libya as consul.* [French *poste,* from Old Italian *posto,* from Vulgar Latin *postum* (unattested), contraction of Latin *positum,* neuter past participle of *pōnere,* to place.]

post³ *n.* **1. a.** Formerly, any of a series of relay stations along a fixed route, furnishing fresh riders and horses for the delivery of mail on horseback. **b.** A rider on such a mail route; a courier. **2.** *British.* **a.** A governmental system for transporting and delivering the mail. **b.** A post office. **3. a.** A delivery of mail. **b.** The mail delivered. **4. Post.** Used as part of the title of certain newspapers: *The Sunday Post.*
~*v.* **posted, posting, posts.** *—intr.* **1.** To travel in stages or relays. **2.** *Archaic.* To travel quickly; speed or hasten. **3.** To bob up and down in the saddle in rhythm with a horse's trotting gait. *—tr.* **1.** To send (a letter, package, or the like) by post. **2.** To inform of the latest news. Usually used in the passive: *keep me posted.* **3.** To send by mail in a system of relays on horseback. **4.** In bookkeeping: **a.** To transfer (an item or items) to a ledger. **b.** To make the necessary entries in (a ledger). **5.** *Computer Science.* To enter a unit of information on a record or into a section of computer storage.
~*adv.* **1.** By post. **2.** By post horse. **3.** With great speed; rapidly. [French *poste,* from Italian *posta,* from Vulgar Latin *posta* (unattested), contraction of Latin *posita,* feminine past participle of *pōnere,* to place.]

Post (pōst), **Emily Price** (1872–1960). U.S. etiquette authority. In her highly popular book *Etiquette: The Blue Book of Social Usage,* first published in 1922 under another title, she advised millions of people on matters of manners. The tremendous response to the book prompted her to write a popular syndicated newspaper column.

Post, Wiley (1899–1935). U.S. aviator. A colorful character in the fledgling years of American aviation, he set many records, including the first solo around-the-world flight (1933). He was killed along with Will Rogers when his plane crashed in Alaska.

post– *prefix.* Indicates: **1.** After in time; later; subsequent to; for example, **postdate, postgraduate. 2.** After in position; behind; posterior to; for example, **postfix, postaxial.** ***Note:*** Many compounds other than those entered here may be formed with *post-.* In forming compounds, *post-* is now usually joined with the following element without space or hyphen: *postwar.* However, if the second element begins with a *t* or a capital letter, it is separated with a hyphen: *post-traumatic; post-Victorian.* Compounds made up of the Latin word *post* and another Latin form are hyphenated. Those entered here are **post-bellum, post-mortem,** and **post-obit.** [Latin, from *post,* behind, after.]

post·age (pō′stĭj) *n.* The charge for mailing an item.

postage meter *n.* A machine used in bulk mailing to print the correct amount of postage on each piece of mail.

postage stamp *n.* A small printed, usually adhesive label issued by a government and sold in various denominations to be affixed to items of mail as evidence of the payment of postage.

post·al (pō′stəl) *adj.* Of or pertaining to the post office or mail service.
~*n.* A **postal card** *(see).* **—post·al·ly** *adv.*

postal card *n.* A card printed with a postage stamp, issued by a government and sold by a governmental agency, for sending messages at low rates. Also called "postal," "postcard."

postal order *n. Chiefly British.* A **money order** *(see).*

postal service *n.* The **post office** (sense 1) *(see).*

post·ax·i·al (pōst-ăk′sē-əl) *adj. Anatomy.* Located behind an axis of the body, especially behind the fibula or the ulna.

post·bag (pōst′băg′) *n. British.* A **mailbag** *(see).*

post-bel·lum (pōst′bĕl′əm) *adj.* Of, during, or designating the period after a war, especially the American Civil War. [Latin *post,* after + *bellum,* war.]

post·box (pōst′bŏks′) *n.* A **mailbox** *(see).*

post·boy (pōst′boi′) *n.* A **postilion** *(see).*

post·card, post card (pōst′kärd′) *n. Abbr.* **p.c. 1.** A card, usually bearing a picture on one side, with space for an address, postage stamp, and short message. **2.** A **postal card** *(see).*

post·ca·va (pōst-kä′və, -kā′və) *n. Anatomy.* The inferior **vena cava** *(see).* **—post·ca·val** *adj.*

post chaise *n.* A closed, four-wheeled, horse-drawn carriage, formerly used to transport mail and passengers. Also called "chaise." [POST (mail) + CHAISE.]

post·clas·si·cal (pōst-klăs′ĭ-kəl) *adj.* Of, relating to, or being a time following a classical period, as in art or literature.

post·co·lo·ni·al (pōst′kə-lō′nē-əl) *adj.* Of, relating to, or being the time following the establishment of independence in a colony: *postcolonial economics.*

post·con·cil·i·ar (pōst′kən-sĭl′ē-ər) *adj.* Designating, pertaining to, or characteristic of the Roman Catholic Church since the Second Vatican Council (1962–65).

post·date (pōst-dāt′) *tr.v.* **-dated, -dating, -dates. 1.** To put a date on (a check, letter, or document) that is later than the actual date. **2.** To occur later than; follow in time.

post·di·lu·vi·an (pōst′dĭ-lo͞o′vē-ən) *adj.* Also **post·di·lu·vi·al** (-əl). Existing or occurring after the biblical Flood.
~*n.* A person or thing living after the biblical Flood.

post·doc·tor·al (pōst-dŏk′tər-əl) *adj.* Of, pertaining to, designating, or engaged in academic study beyond a doctoral degree.

post·er (pō′stər) *n.* **1. a.** A large printed placard, bill, or announcement, often illustrated, posted to advertise or publicize something. **b.** An illustration, picture, reproduction of a painting, or the like on a large sheet of paper, often used to decorate the wall of a room. **2.** One who posts bills or notices.

poster art *n.* An art form characteristically used in advertising or decorative posters.

poste res·tante (pōst′ rĕ-stänt′) *n. Chiefly British.* **1.** A notation written on an item such as a letter to indicate that it should be held at a particular post office until claimed by the addressee. **2.** See **general delivery** (sense 1). [French, "remaining mail" : *poste,* POST (mail) + *restante,* present participle of *rester,* to REST.]

pos·te·ri·or (pŏ-stîr′ē-ər, pō-) *adj.* **1.** Located behind a part or toward the rear of a structure. **2.** *Zoology & Anatomy.* Pertaining to the caudal (hind) end of the body in an animal or the dorsal (back)

PRONUNCIATION KEY

ă, pat; ā, pay; âr, care; ä, father, are; b, bib; ch, church; d, deed; ĕ, pet; ē, be; f, fife; g, gag; h, hat; hw, which; ĭ, pit; ī, pie; îr, pier; j, judge; k, kick; l, lid, needle; m, mum; n, no, sudden; ng, thing; ŏ, pot; ō, toe; ô, paw, for; oi, noise; ou, out; o͝o, book; o͞o, boot; p, pop; r, roar; s, sauce; sh, ship, dish; t, tight; th, thin, path; *th*, this, bathe; ŭ, cut; ûr, fur; v, valve; w, with; y, yes; z, zebra, size; zh, vision; ə, about, item, edible, gallop, circus, peaceful

IN FOREIGN WORDS:

à, *Fr.* ami; œ, *Fr.* feu, *Ger.* schön; ü, *Fr.* tu, *Ger.* über; KH, *Ger.* ich, *Scot.* loch; N, *Fr.* bon; y′, *Fr.* Compiègne

STRESS MARKS:

Primary stress: ′ in·cite′ (ĭn-sīt′)
Secondary stress: ′ in′sight′ (ĭn′sīt′)

side in man. **3.** *Botany.* Next to or nearest the main stem or axis. Said of flowers and buds. **4.** Coming after in order; following. **5.** Following in time; later; subsequent. Compare **anterior.** ~*n.* The buttocks. [Latin, comparative of *posterus,* coming after, next, from *post,* after.] —**pos·te·ri·or·ly** *adv.*

pos·te·ri·or·i·ty (pŏ-stîr′ē-ôr′ə-tē, -ŏr′ə-tē, pō-) *n.* The condition of being posterior in location or time.

pos·ter·i·ty (pŏ-stĕr′ə-tē) *n.* **1.** Future generations. **2.** All of a person's descendants. [Middle English *posterite,* from Old French *posterite,* from Latin *posteritās* (stem *posteritāt-*), from *posterus,* next. See **posterior.**]

pos·tern (pō′stərn, pŏs′tərn) *n.* A small, usually private rear gate, especially one in a fort or castle. ~*adj.* Situated at the back or side. [Middle English *posterne,* from Old French, variant of *posterle,* from Late Latin *posterula,* diminutive of *postera,* back door, from the feminine of *posterus,* coming after. See **posterior.**]

poster paint *n.* Opaque watercolor paint in bright colors. Also called "poster color."

Post Exchange *n. Abbr.* **PX** A trademark for a store on a military base for the sale of tax-free merchandise and services to military personnel and their families, or to authorized civilians.

post·ex·il·i·an (pōst′ĕg-zĭl′ē-ən, -zĭl′yən, -ĕk-sĭl′ē-ən, -sĭl′yən) *adj.* Also **post·ex·il·ic** (-ĕg-zĭl′ĭk, -ĕk-sĭl′ĭk). Of, pertaining to, or designating the period of Jewish history following the Babylonian captivity (after 586 B.C.).

post·fix (pōst-fĭks′) *tr.v.* **-fixed, -fixing, -fixes.** To add at the end; especially, to suffix. ~*n.* (pōst′fĭks′). A suffix. —**post·fix·al** (pōst-fĭk′səl) *adj.*

post-free (pōst′frē′) *adj. Chiefly British.* Postpaid. —**post-free** *adv.*

post·gan·gli·on·ic (pōst′găng′glē-ŏn′ĭk) *adj.* Located posterior or distal to a ganglion.

post·gla·cial (pōst-glā′shəl) *adj. Geology.* Pertaining to or occurring during the time following a glacial period.

post·grad·u·ate (pōst-grăj′ōō-ĭt, -āt′) *adj. Abbr.* **P.G.** Of, pertaining to, designating, or pursuing advanced study beyond the level of a bachelor's or equivalent degree. ~*n.* A person engaged in such study.

post·haste (pōst′hāst′) *adv.* With great speed; hastily; rapidly. ~*n. Archaic.* Great speed; rapidity. [Originally *post, haste,* a direction on letters : POST (courier) + HASTE (imperative).]

post hoc (pōst′hŏk′) *n.* The fallacy of assuming or arguing that because one event or situation comes after another, it must in some way be the result of it. [Shortened from Latin *post hoc ergo propter hoc,* "after this, therefore on account of this."]

post horn *n.* A small copper or brass wind instrument originally blown to announce the arrival of a coach, especially a mail coach.

post horse *n.* Formerly, a horse kept especially for use by couriers or mail carriers.

post·hu·mous (pŏs′chōō-məs) *adj.* **1.** Occurring or continuing after one's death: *a posthumous award; posthumous fame.* **2.** Published after the author's death: *a posthumous book.* **3.** Born after the death of the father: *a posthumous child.* [Latin *posthumus,* "last," alteration (influenced by *humus,* earth, and taken as "after burial") of *postumus,* superlative of *posterus,* coming after, next. See **posterior.**] —**post·hu·mous·ly** *adv.* —**post·hu·mous·ness** *n.*

post·hyp·not·ic suggestion (pōst′hĭp-nŏt′ĭk) *n.* A suggestion made to a hypnotized person specifying an action to be performed in a subsequent waking state.

pos·tiche (pŏ-stēsh′, pō-) *adj.* **1.** Added superfluously or inappropriately. Said especially of architectural ornamentation. **2.** Artificial; false. ~*n.* **1.** Something false; a sham. **2.** A small hairpiece; toupee. [French, from Italian *posticcio,* fake, counterfeit, from *posto,* added, placed, from Latin *positus,* past participle of *pōnere,* to place.]

pos·til·ion, pos·til·lion (pō-stĭl′yən, pŏ-) *n.* A person who rides the near (left-hand) horse of the leading pair to guide a team of horses drawing a coach. [French *postillon,* from Italian *postiglione,* from *posta,* POST (mail).]

post·im·pres·sion·ism, post-im·pres·sion·ism (pōst′ĭm-prĕsh′ə-nĭz′əm) *n.* A school of painting in France in the late 19th century, exemplified by artists such as Cézanne, Gauguin, and van Gogh, who rejected the objective naturalism of impressionism and used form and color in freer and more individually subjective ways. —**post·im·pres·sion·ist** *n. & adj.* —**post·im·pres·sion·is·tic** (pōst′ĭm-prĕsh′ə-nĭs′tĭk) *adj.*

post·ing (pō′stĭng) *n.* An appointment to a job or post, especially to a military position or to one overseas.

post·lude (pōst′lōōd′) *n.* **1. a.** An organ voluntary played at the end of a church service. **b.** A concluding piece of music. **2.** A final chapter or phase. [POST- + (PRE)LUDE.]

post·man (pōst′mən) *n., pl.* **-men** (-mĭn). A mailman *(see).*

post·mark (pōst′märk′) *n.* An official mark printed over the stamp on a piece of mail; especially, one that cancels the stamp and records the date and place of mailing. ~*tr.v.* **postmarked, -marking, -marks.** To stamp with a postmark.

post·mas·ter (pōst′măs′tər, -mä′stər) *n. Abbr.* **PM, P.M.** An official in charge of a local post office. —**post·mas·ter·ship** *n.*

postmaster general *n., pl.* **postmasters general.** *Abbr.* **P.M.G.** The executive head of certain national postal services.

post·me·rid·i·an (pōst′mə-rĭd′ē-ən) *adj.* Of, pertaining to, or taking place in the afternoon. [Latin *postmerīdiānus* : *post,* after + *merīdiānus,* MERIDIAN.]

post me·rid·i·em (pōst′ mə-rĭd′ē-əm) *adv. Abbr.* **p.m., P.M.** After noon. Used chiefly in the abbreviated form to specify the hour: *10:30 p.m.* [Latin *post merīdiem,* after midday : *post,* after + *merīdiem,* accusative of *merīdiēs,* midday, noon (see **meridian**).]

post·mil·le·nar·i·an (pōst′mĭl-ə-nâr′ē-ən) *adj.* Of or pertaining to postmillennialism. ~*n.* A person who believes in postmillennialism. Compare **premillenarian.** —**post·mil·le·nar·i·an·ism** *n.*

post·mil·len·ni·al·ism (pōst′mə-lĕn′ē-ə-lĭz′əm) *n.* The doctrine that Christ's second coming will follow the millennium. Also called "postmillenarianism." Compare **premillennialism.** —**post·mil·len·ni·al** *adj.* —**post·mil·len·ni·al·ist** *n.*

post·mis·tress (pōst′mĭs′trĭs) *n. Abbr.* **PM, P.M.** A woman official in charge of a local post office.

post·mod·ern·ism, post-mod·ern·ism (pōst-mŏd′ər-nĭz′əm) *n.* Either of two trends in art, literature, and architecture that largely reject the theories and practices of modernism. One of the trends reverts to more traditional, formal, even classical approaches; the other seeks to go beyond art, form, and meaning altogether and favors works that are anarchic, outrageous, or transitory.

post·mor·tem (pōst-môr′təm) *adj. Abbr.* **p.m. 1.** Occurring or done after death. **2.** Of or pertaining to a post-mortem examination. ~*n.* **1.** A post-mortem examination, especially an **autopsy** *(see).* **2.** *Informal.* An analysis or review of some completed event, especially of a failure or defeat. [Latin, after death.]

post·na·sal (pōst-nā′zəl) *adj.* At the rear part of the nasal cavity.

postnasal drip *n.* The chronic secretion of mucus from the posterior nasal cavities, resulting in congestion and coughing.

post·na·tal (pōst-nāt′l) *adj.* Of or occurring during the period immediately after birth. —**post·na·tal·ly** *adv.*

postnatal depression *n.* A period of depression and anxiety experienced by a mother after having given birth, sometimes manifested by aggression toward the baby.

post·nup·tial (pōst-nŭp′shəl, -chəl) *adj.* Happening after marriage. —**post·nup·tial·ly** *adv.*

post·o·bit (pōst-ō′bĭt, -ŏb′ĭt) *adj.* Also **post·o·bit·u·ar·y** (pōst′ō-bĭch′ōō-ĕr′ē). Coming into effect after a person's death. ~*n.* A bond given by a borrower promising to repay a debt after the death of a person from whose estate he expects to inherit. Also called "post-obit bond." [Latin *post obitum,* after death : *post,* after + *obitum,* accusative of *obitus,* death (see **obituary**).]

post office *n. Abbr.* **p.o., P.O. 1.** The public department responsible for all postal services, and, in many countries, for telecommunications as well. **2.** Any local office where mail is received, sorted, and delivered, and stamps and other postal matter are sold.

post office box *n. Abbr.* **P.O.B.** A private rented box, pigeonhole, or the like in a post office to which mail can be addressed and delivered and where it is kept until collected.

post·op·er·a·tive (pōst-ŏp′ər-ə-tĭv, -ŏp′rə-tĭv, -ŏp′ə-rā′tĭv) *adj.* Of, administered, or occurring in the period shortly after surgery. —**post·op·er·a·tive·ly** *adv.*

post·or·bi·tal (pōst-ôr′bĭ-təl) *adj. Anatomy.* Located behind the eye or eye socket: *a postorbital bone.*

post·paid (pōst′pād′) *adj. Abbr.* **p.p., ppd.** With the postage paid in advance.

post·par·tum (pōst-pär′təm) *adj.* Of or occurring in the period shortly after childbirth. [Latin *post partum,* after birth : *post,* after + *partum,* accusative of *partus,* a bringing forth, from the past participle of *parere,* to bear.]

post·pone (pōst-pōn′, pōs-pōn′) *tr.v.* **-poned, -poning, -pones. 1.** To delay until a future time; put off. **2.** To place after in importance; subordinate. [Latin *postpōnere,* to place after : *post,* after + *pōnere,* to put, place.] —**post·pon·a·ble** *adj.* —**post·pone·ment** *n.* —**post·pon·er** *n.*

post·po·si·tion (pōst′pə-zĭsh′ən, pōst′pə-zĭsh′ən) *n. Grammar.* **1.** The placing of a word or particle after the word to which it is grammatically related. **2.** A word or particle so placed, as *-ward* in *homeward.* [French, from Old French *postposer,* to place after, from Latin *postpōnere,* to POSTPONE.] —**post·po·si·tion·al** *adj.* —**post·po·si·tion·al·ly** *adv.*

post·pos·i·tive (pōst-pŏz′ə-tĭv) *adj. Grammar.* Of, pertaining to, or designating a word or particle characterized by postposition: *a postpositive adjective.* Compare **prepositive.** ~*n.* A postpositive word or particle. [Late Latin *postpositīvus,* from Latin *postpōnere* (past participle *postpositus*), to place after, POSTPONE.] —**post·pos·i·tive·ly** *adv.*

post·pran·di·al, post-pran·di·al (pōst-prăn′dē-əl) *adj.* Following or after any meal, especially dinner.

post·script (pōst′skrĭpt′, pōs′skrĭpt′) *n. Abbr.* **p.s., P.S. 1.** A message appended at the end of a letter after the writer's signature. **2.** Additional information appended to a book, article, or the like. [Latin *postscriptum,* from *postscrībere* (past participle *postscriptus*), to write after : *post,* after + *scrībere,* to write.]

post time *n.* The time set immediately before the official start of a race after which point no further betting is allowed.

post·trau·mat·ic (pōst′trou-măt′ĭk, -trō-măt′ĭk) *adj.* Following injury or resulting from it: *post-traumatic amnesia.*

pos·tu·lant (pŏs′chōō-lənt) *n.* **1.** A person submitting a request or application; petitioner. **2.** A candidate for admission into a religious order. Compare **novice.** [French, from Latin *postulāns* (stem *postulānt-*), present participle of *postulāre,* to demand, POSTULATE.] —**pos·tu·lan·cy, pos·tu·lant·ship** *n.*

pos·tu·late (pŏs′chōō-lāt′) *tr.v.* **-lated, -lating, -lates. 1.** To make

claim for; demand. **2.** To put forward for consideration as true or real with no proof: *He postulated the presence of ghosts to explain the strange noises.* **3.** To assume as a premise or axiom; take for granted, especially in a mathematical or logical proof or theorem. **4.** To appoint or promote (a person) provisionally, subject to higher authorization. —See Synonyms at **presume.**
~*n.* (pŏs′chŏŏ-lĭt, -lāt′). **1.** Something assumed as being self-evident or generally accepted, as used as a basis for an argument. **2.** A fundamental element; a basic principle. **3.** *Logic & Mathematics.* An axiom. **4.** A requirement; prerequisite. [Latin *postulāre*, to request, demand.] —**pos·tu·la·tion** *n.*
pos·tu·la·tor (pŏs′chŏŏ-lā′tər) *n.* **1.** One who postulates. **2.** *Roman*

Catholic Church. A church official who presents a plea for canonization or beatification. [Medieval Latin. See **postulate.**]
pos·ture (pŏs′chər) *n.* **1.** A position or attitude of the body or of bodily parts: *a sitting posture.* **2.** A characteristic way of bearing one's body, especially the trunk and head; carriage: *learning good posture.* **3.** A particular bodily position, such as one assumed by an artist's model. **4.** The arrangement of the parts of any object. **5.** The present condition or tendency of something: *the military posture of a nation.* **6.** A frame of mind affecting one's behavior; an overall attitude: *a posture of tolerance.* **7.** An exaggerated or unnatural attitude or mode of behavior.
~*v.* **postured, -turing, -tures.** —*intr.* To assume an exaggerated or unnatural pose or mental attitude; pose for effect. —*tr.* To put in

---

postimpressionism

THE POSTIMPRESSIONIST SCHOOL

A group of 19th-century painters who influenced 20th-century art

The term postimpressionism was never used by the postimpressionist painters; it was coined retrospectively in 1910 by the English art critic Roger Fry when he mounted an exhibition in London of the work of the French painters Paul Cézanne (1839–1906) and Paul Gauguin (1848–1903) and the Dutch painter Vincent van Gogh (1853–90).

Postimpressionism describes a school of painting

that flourished in France in the last two decades of the 19th century. Most postimpressionist artists began as impressionists and continued to base their style on the color innovations of the impressionist movement. However, they moved away from the objectivity of the impressionists, who tried to represent what the eye actually sees. The postimpressionists painted pictures that were entirely subjective and that captured the art-

ist's own highly personalized ideas, emotions, and imagination.

This individualistic and intellectual approach to art led to an increased interest in ways of showing emotion in its most dramatic and compelling form and in the structural qualities of a subject. And it heralded the surrealist, futurist, cubist, expressionist, and fauvist movements of 20th-century art.

VAN GOGH Poppy Field *was painted in 1890 by van Gogh at Saint-Rémy, near Arles in France. The artist moved to France in 1886, and there, inspired by the landscape, created his most outstanding work. His rich, energetic brushstrokes and dynamic use of brilliant color portray his innermost perceptions.*

GAUGUIN *Paul Gauguin painted* Contes Barbares *(above) in 1902 in the Marquesas Islands. He died there a year later. His style, one of the most distinctive, uses large areas of strong unbroken color to create a direct emotional effect. His paintings are full of symbolic and psychological depth; one of his main themes is the contrast between the primitive and civilized world.*

CÉZANNE Mont Sainte-Victoire *(left) typifies Cézanne's striving to give a feeling of monumental permanence to his subject matter instead of portraying a fleeting moment, as impressionist art did. He juxtaposed subtle colors to create the illusion of depth and volume in his work. He painted many landscapes and still lifes, but also figure groups and some portraits.*

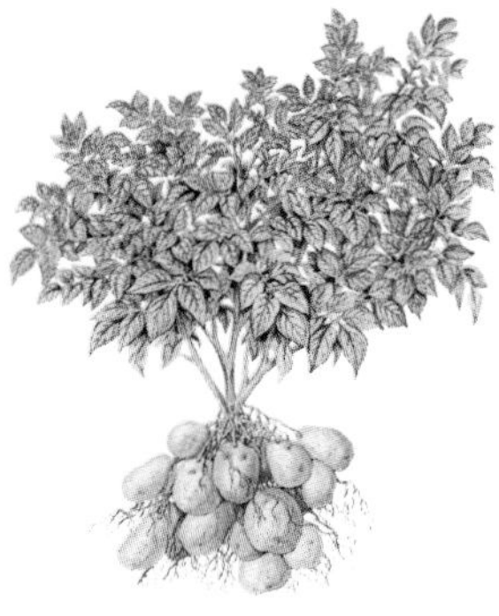

potato *This native South American plant, which is related to the tomato, has also flourished in Europe since the 16th century. The flower is inconspicuous, but the underground tubers from which the plant is propagated are a staple food in many countries.*

PRONUNCIATION KEY

ă, pat; ā, pay; âr, care;
ä, father, are; b, **bib**;
ch, **church**; d, **deed**; ĕ, pet;
ē, be; f, **fife**; g, **gag**; h, **hat**;
hw, **which**; ĭ, pit; ī, pie;
îr, **pier**; j, **judge**; k, **kick**;
l, lid, needle; m, **mum**;
n, no, sudden; ng, **thing**;
ŏ, pot; ō, **toe**; ô, **paw**, **for**;
oi, **noise**; ou, **out**; o͝o, **book**;
o͞o, **boot**; p, **pop**; r, **roar**;
s, sauce; sh, **ship**, **dish**;
t, **tight**; th, **thin**, **path**;
th, **this**, **bathe**; ŭ, **cut**; ûr, **fur**;
v, **valve**; w, **with**; y, **yes**;
z, zebra, size; zh, vision;
ə, about, item, edible,
gallop, circus, peaceful

IN FOREIGN WORDS:

à, *Fr.* ami; œ, *Fr.* **feu**, *Ger.* **schön**; ü, *Fr.* **tu**, *Ger.* **über**;
KH, *Ger.* **ich**, *Scot.* **loch**;
N, *Fr.* bon; y', *Fr.* **Compiègne**

STRESS MARKS:

Primary stress: ′
in·cite′ (ĭn-sīt′)
Secondary stress: ′
in′sight′ (ĭn′sīt′)

a posture; position. [French, from Italian *postura,* from Latin *positūra,* position, from *pōnere* (past participle *positus*), to place.] **—pos·tur·al** *adj.* **—pos·tur·er, pos·tur·ist** *n.*

post·vo·cal·ic (pōst′vō-kăl′ĭk) *adj.* Designating a consonant or consonantal sound directly following a vowel.

post·war (pōst′wôr′) *adj.* Occurring after a particular war.

po·sy (pō′zē) *n., pl.* **-sies.** **1.** A flower or small bunch of flowers. **2.** *Archaic.* A brief verse or sentimental phrase, especially when inscribed on a trinket. [Variant of POESY.]

pot[1] (pŏt) *n.* **1. a.** Any of various usually domestic containers made of metal, glass, or pottery, such as a short, cylindrical vessel for holding jam, a rounded juglike vessel for liquid tea or coffee, or a round, fairly deep cooking vessel with a handle. **b.** Such a vessel and its contents: *a pot of soup; a pot of tea.* **c.** The amount that such a vessel will hold. **2. a.** A large drinking cup; tankard. **b.** A drink, usually of beer, contained in such a cup. **3.** An artistic or decorative ceramic vessel of any size or shape. **4. a.** A flowerpot. **b.** Something resembling a domestic pot in appearance or function, such as a chimney pot or chamber pot. **5.** A trap for fish, crustaceans, or eels, consisting of a wicker, wood, or wire basket: *a lobster pot.* **6.** In gambling card games, the total amount staked by all the players in one hand. **7.** *Informal.* A common fund to which the members of a group contribute and upon which they draw for certain stated purposes. **8.** *Informal.* **a. pots.** A great deal; a large amount: *pots of money.* **b.** A large amount of money: *made a pot.* **9.** *Informal.* A **potbelly** *(see).* **10.** In billiards, snooker, and similar games, a shot intended to send a ball into a pocket. **11.** *Informal.* A **pot shot** *(see).* **12.** *Computer Science.* A section of computer storage reserved for storing accumulated data. **—go to pot.** *Informal.* To deteriorate.
~*v.* **potted, potting, pots.** *—tr.* **1.** To place or plant in a pot: *pot a plant.* **2.** To preserve (food) in a pot. **3.** To cook in a pot. **4.** To shoot (game) for food rather than for sport. **5.** *Informal.* To shoot with a pot shot. **6.** *Informal.* To win or capture; bag. **7.** In billiards, snooker, and similar games, to hit (a ball) directly or indirectly into a pocket. *—intr. Informal.* To take a pot shot. [Middle English, Old English *pott,* from Vulgar Latin *pottus* (attested only in Late Latin).]

pot[2] *n. Slang.* **Marijuana** *(see).* [Perhaps shortened from Mexican Spanish *potiguaya*†.]

pot. potential.

po·ta·ble (pō′tə-bəl) *n. Often* **potables.** Drinkable liquid.
~*adj.* Fit to drink. [French, from Late Latin *pōtābilis,* from Latin *pōtāre,* to drink.] **—po·ta·bil·i·ty, po·ta·ble·ness** *n.*

po·tage (pō-täzh′) *n.* A thick soup. [French, from Old French, contents of a pot, from *pot,* POT.]

po·tam·ic (pə-tăm′ĭk, pō-) *adj.* Of or pertaining to rivers. [Greek *potamos,* river.]

pot·a·mol·o·gy (pŏt′ə-mŏl′ə-jē) *n.* The scientific study of rivers. [Greek *potamos,* river + -LOGY.]

pot·ash (pŏt′ăsh′) *n.* **1.** Potassium carbonate. **2.** Potassium hydroxide. **3.** Any of several compounds containing potassium, especially soluble compounds, such as potassium oxide, potassium chloride, and various potassium sulfates, used chiefly in fertilizers. [Singular of earlier *pot ashes* (translation of obsolete Dutch *potasschen*) : POT + plural of ASH (so called because first obtained by evaporating the lye of wood ashes in iron pots).]

potash feldspar *n.* **Potassium feldspar** *(see).*

potash muriate *n. Chemistry.* **Potassium chloride** *(see).*

po·tas·si·um (pə-tăs′ē-əm) *n. Symbol* **K** A soft, silver-white, light, highly or explosively reactive metallic element obtained by electrolysis of its common hydroxide and found in, or converted to, a wide variety of salts used in fertilizers and soaps. Atomic number 19, atomic weight 39.102, melting point 63.2°C, boiling point 765.5°C, specific gravity 0.856, valence 1. [New Latin, from *potassa,* potassium monoxide, from English POTASH.] **—po·tas·sic** *adj.*

po·tas·si·um-ar·gon dating (pə-tăs′ē-əm-är′gŏn′) *n.* A method of dating rocks and minerals by measuring the isotope argon-40 in the sample, present as a result of the radioactive decay of the naturally occurring isotope potassium-40. The technique can be used for ages up to 10^{10} years.

potassium bitartrate *n.* A white crystalline solid or powder, $KHC_4H_4O_6$, used in baking powder, in the tinning of metals, and as a component of laxatives. Also called "cream of tartar."

potassium bromide *n.* A white crystalline solid or powder, KBr, used as a sedative, in photographic emulsion, and in spectroscopy. Also called "bromide."

potassium carbonate *n.* A transparent, white, deliquescent, granular powder, K_2CO_3, used in making glass, pigments, ceramics, and soaps. Also called "pearl ash," "potash."

potassium chlorate *n.* A moderately poisonous crystalline compound, $KClO_3$, used as an oxidizing agent, bleach, and disinfectant, and in making explosives, matches, and fireworks.

potassium chloride *n.* A colorless crystalline solid or powder, KCl, used in fertilizers and in the preparation of potassium compounds. Also called "potassium muriate," "potash muriate."

potassium cyanide *n.* A poisonous white compound, KCN, used in extracting gold and silver from ores, electroplating, photography, and as a fumigant and insecticide. Also called "cyanide."

potassium dichromate *n.* A bright yellowish-red crystalline compound, $K_2Cr_2O_7$, used as an oxidizing agent, and in pyrotechnics, explosives, and safety matches.

potassium feldspar *n.* Any member of the feldspar group of minerals that comprises silicates of aluminum and potassium. Orthoclase and microcline are the most common members of the group. Also called "potash feldspar."

potassium hydroxide *n.* A caustic deliquescent solid, KOH, used as a bleach and in detergents and soaps, matches, and many potassium compounds. Also called "caustic potash," "lye," "potash."

potassium nitrate *n.* A transparent or white crystalline compound, KNO_3, used to pickle meat and in explosives, matches, rocket propellants, and fertilizers. Also called "niter," "saltpeter."

potassium permanganate *n.* A dark purple crystalline compound, $KMnO_4$, used as an oxidizing agent, disinfectant, and in deodorizers and dyes. Also called "permanganate of potash," "purple salt."

potassium sulfate *n.* A colorless or white crystalline compound, K_2SO_4, used in medicine, glassmaking, fertilizers, and as a reagent in analytical chemistry.

po·ta·tion (pō-tā′shən) *n.* **1.** The act of drinking. **2.** A drink, especially an alcoholic drink. [Middle English *potacioun,* from Old French *potation,* from Latin *pōtātiō* (stem *pōtātiōn-*), from *pōtāre,* to drink.]

po·ta·to (pə-tā′tō) *n., pl.* **-toes.** **1.** A plant, *Solanum tuberosum,* native to South America and widely cultivated for its starchy, edible tubers. **2.** A tuber of the potato plant cooked and eaten as a vegetable. **3.** Any of several similar plants; especially, the **sweet potato** *(see).* [Spanish *patata,* from Taino *batata.*]

potato beetle *n.* The **Colorado beetle** *(see).*

potato blight *n.* Any of various highly destructive fungus diseases of the potato.

potato chip *n.* A thin slice of potato fried in deep fat until crisp and then usually salted.

po·ta·to·ry (pō′tə-tôr′ē, -tōr′ē) *adj.* Of, pertaining to, or given to drinking. [Latin *pōtātōrius,* from *pōtāre,* to drink.]

pot-au-feu (pô′tō-fœ′) *n.* A French dish in which meat and vegetables are simmered together. [French, "pot on the fire."]

pot·bel·ly (pŏt′bĕl′ē) *n., pl.* **-lies.** **1.** A protruding abdominal region; a fat, rounded stomach. Also informally called "pot." **2.** A **potbelly stove** *(see).* **—pot·bel·lied** *adj.*

potbelly stove *n.* A short rounded stove in which wood or coal is burned. Also called "potbellied stove," "potbelly."

pot·boil·er (pŏt′boi′lər) *n.* A literary or artistic work of poor quality, produced as quickly as possible for profit. [So called because the income enables one to keep a cooking pot on the boil, that is, to sustain the necessities of life.]

pot-bound (pŏt′bound′) *adj.* Designating a pot plant whose roots no longer have enough space in the flowerpot to grow, and whose growth above the surface is consequently poor or retarded.

po·teen (pō-tēn′) *n.* Irish whiskey that is distilled unlawfully. [Irish Gaelic *poitīn,* small pot, whiskey made in a private still, diminutive of *pota,* POT.]

Po·tem·kin (pō-tĕm′kĭn, pə-), **Grigory Alexandrovich, Prince** (1739–91). Russian soldier and statesman. He became Catherine II's lover and lifelong favorite. He built up the Black Sea fleet, annexed the Crimea, and campaigned against the Turks (1787–91).

po·tence (pōt′ns) *n.* Potency.

po·ten·cy (pōt′n-sē) *n., pl.* **-cies.** **1.** The quality or state of being potent. **2.** Inherent capacity for growth and development; potentiality. —See Synonyms at **strength.**

po·tent (pōt′nt) *adj.* **1.** Possessing inner or physical strength; powerful. **2.** Capable of commanding attention; able to convince: *potent arguments.* **3.** Having great control or authority. **4.** Capable of causing strong physiological or chemical effects, as medicines or alcoholic drinks might. **5.** Able to achieve sexual penetration of the female. Said of a male. [Middle English (Scottish), from Latin *potēns* (stem *potent-*), present participle of Old Latin *potēre* (unattested) (superseded by *posse*), to be able, have power.] **—po·tent·ly** *adv.* **—po·tent·ness** *n.*

po·ten·tate (pōt′n-tāt′) *n.* **1.** One who has the power and position to rule over others; a monarch. **2.** One who dominates or leads any group or endeavor: *an industrial potentate.* [Middle English *potentat,* from Old French, from Late Latin *potentātus,* from Latin, power, rule, from *potēns,* POTENT.]

po·ten·tial (pə-tĕn′shəl) *adj. Abbr.* **pot.** **1.** Possible but not yet realized; capable of being but not yet in existence; latent: *"Every admirer is a potential enemy"* (Cyril Connolly). **2.** *Grammar.* Expressing possibility, capability, or power. Said of a verb or verb form: *the potential subjunctive.* —See Synonyms at **latent.**
~*n. Abbr.* **pot.** **1.** The inherent ability or capacity for growth, development, or coming into being: *Women have a potential for political influence that has never been realized.* **2.** The ability to succeed; unrealized talent: *She has great potential.* **3.** *Grammar.* A potential verb form. **4.** *Physics.* The work required to bring a unit electric charge, magnetic pole, or mass from an infinitely distant position to a designated point in a static electric, magnetic, or gravitational field, respectively. **5.** *Electricity.* The potential energy of a unit charge at any point in an electric circuit measured with respect to a specified reference point in the circuit or to earth; voltage. [Middle English *potencial,* from Old French, from Late Latin *potentiālis,* powerful, from *potentia,* latent power, from Latin, potency, from *potēns,* POTENT.] **—po·ten·tial·ly** *adv.*

potential difference *n. Symbol* **V** The difference in electrical potential between two points in a circuit or other system; the work done in moving unit electric charge from one point to the other.

potential energy *n.* The energy of a particle or system of particles derived from position, rather than motion, with respect to a specified reference state taken as zero energy. Compare **kinetic energy**.

po·ten·ti·al·i·ty (pə-tĕn′shē-ăl′ə-tē) *n., pl.* **-ties. 1.** Inherent capacity for growth, development, or coming into existence. **2.** Something possessing this capacity.

po·ten·ti·ate (pə-tĕn′shē-āt′) *tr.v.* **-ated, -ating, -ates. 1.** To make possible or effective. **2.** To increase the effectiveness of (two drugs, hormones, or the like) by administering them in combination. [POTENCY + -ATE, by analogy with *substantiate.*] **—po·ten·ti·a·tion** *n.*

po·ten·til·la (pŏt′n-tĭl′ə) *n.* Any of numerous plants or shrubs of the genus *Potentilla,* of the North Temperate Zone. See **cinquefoil.** [New Latin, from Medieval Latin, garden valerian, from Latin *potēns,* POTENT.]

po·ten·ti·om·e·ter (pə-tĕn′shē-ŏm′ə-tər) *n. Electricity.* **1.** An instrument for measuring an unknown voltage or potential difference by comparison with a standard voltage. **2.** Any three-terminal resistor with an adjustable center connection, widely used for volume control in radio and television receivers.

pot·head (pŏt′hĕd′) *n. Slang.* A person who habitually smokes marijuana.

poth·er (pŏ*th*′ər) *n.* **1.** A commotion; disturbance. **2.** A state of nervous activity; fuss. **3.** A choking cloud of smoke or dust.
∼*v.* **pothered, -ering, -ers.** *—tr.* To make confused; trouble; worry. *—intr.* To be excessively concerned with trifles; fuss. [16th century : origin obscure.]

pot·herb (pŏt′ûrb′, -hûrb′) *n.* Any plant whose leaves, stems, or flowers are cooked and eaten or used as seasoning.

pot·hold·er (pŏt′hōl′dər) *n.* A small fabric pad used to hold hot cooking utensils.

pot·hole (pŏt′hōl′) *n.* **1.** A hole in the rocky bed of a stream, formed by the grinding effect of pebbles whirled around by eddies. **2.** A deep hole or pit, especially in a road surface. **3.** *Western U.S.* A place filled with mud or quicksand that is a hazard to cattle. **4.** Loosely, a vertical cave system, especially in the Pennines of northern England.
∼*intr.v.* **potholed, -holing, -holes.** To explore underground caves, especially vertical cave systems, as a hobby or sport. **—pot·hol·er** *n.* **—pot·hol·ing** *n.*

pot·hook (pŏt′ho͝ok′) *n.* **1.** A bent or hooked piece of iron for hanging a pot or kettle over an open fire. **2.** A curved iron rod with a hooked end used for lifting hot pots, irons, or stove lids. **3.** A curved, S-shaped mark made in writing. **4.** *Often* **pothooks.** Illegible handwriting or aimless scribbling.

pot·hunt·er (pŏt′hŭn′tər) *n.* **1.** One who hunts game for food, ignoring the rules of sport. **2.** One who participates in contests simply to win prizes. **—pot·hunt·ing** *adj.* & *n.*

po·tiche (pô-tēsh′) *n.* A vase or jar with a round or polygonal body tapering at the neck and having a removable cover. [French, from *pot,* POT.]

po·tion (pō′shən) *n.* A liquid drink or dose, especially of medicinal, magic, or poisonous content. [Middle English *pocioun,* from Old French *potion,* from Latin *pōtiō* (stem *pōtiōn-*), from *pōtāre* (alternative past participle *pōtus*), to drink.]

Pot·i·phar (pŏt′ə-fər). Pharaoh's chief officer, who purchased Joseph as a slave. Genesis 39:1–20.

pot·latch (pŏt′lăch′) *n.* A ceremonial feast among North American Indians living on the Pacific coast of Washington, British Columbia, and Alaska, at the end of which the host distributes valuable gifts or destroys property to show that he can afford to do so. [Chinook, from Nootka *patlatsh,* giving, gift.]

pot luck *n.* Whatever food happens to be available for a meal, especially when offered to a guest. **—take pot luck. 1.** To take whatever food is offered. **2.** To choose at random.

pot marigold *n.* A plant, *Calendula officinalis,* native to southern Europe, often grown for its showy yellow or orange flowers, the dried florets of which were formerly used for seasoning.

pot marjoram *n.* **Marjoram** (sense 3) *(see).*

Po·to·mac (pə-tō′mək). River in the eastern United States. Rising in the Allegheny Mts. of West Virginia, it flows 462 kilometers (287 miles) to the Atlantic Ocean at Chesapeake Bay. Washington, D.C., is at its highest navigable point.

po·to·roo (pō′tə-ro͞o′) *n., pl.* **-roos.** *Australian.* A **kangaroo rat** *(see).* [From a native Australian name.]

pot·pie (pŏt′pī′) *n.* A mixture of meat or poultry and vegetables covered with a pastry crust and baked in a deep dish.

pot plant *n.* **1.** A cultivated plant grown in a flowerpot; especially, one used as a house plant. **2.** *Informal.* A marijuana plant.

pot·pour·ri (pō′po͞o-rē′) *n., pl.* **-ris. 1.** A combination of various incongruous elements. **2.** A miscellaneous anthology or collection. **3.** A mixture of dried flower petals and spices, kept in a jar and used to scent the air. [French *pot pourri* (translation of Spanish OLLA PODRIDA) : POT + *pourri,* rotten, from the past participle of *pourrir,* to rot, from Vulgar Latin *putrīre* (unattested), variant of Latin *putrēre, putrēscere,* from *puter,* rotten.]

pot roast *n.* A piece of meat, usually beef, that is browned and then cooked until tender, often with vegetables, in a covered pot.

Pots·dam (pŏts′dăm′). City in East Germany, on the Havel River. It was the administrative capital of the Prussian province of Brandenburg and the site of the Potsdam Conference (1945).

pot·sherd (pŏt′shûrd′) *n.* Also **pot·shard** (-shärd′). A fragment of broken pottery, as found in an archaeological excavation. Also called "shard," "sherd." [Middle English : POT + SHARD.]

pot·shot (pŏt′shŏt′) *n.* **1.** A shot aimed to kill, without regard for sporting rules. **2. a.** A random shot. **b.** A shot fired at an animal or person within easy range. **3.** A criticism made thoughtlessly and aimed at a handy target for attack: *reporters taking potshots at the mayor.* [Referring to shots fired by a hunter who kills game only for his pot.] **—pot·shot** *v.*

pot still *n.* A still used in whiskey making in which the mash is heated directly.

pot·stone (pŏt′stōn′) *n.* An impure variety of soapstone once used to make cooking vessels.

pot·ta·ble (pŏt′ə-bəl) *adj.* Designating a ball in billiards, snooker, or similar games that can be potted relatively easily.

pot·tage (pŏt′ĭj) *n.* **1.** A thick soup or stew of vegetables and sometimes meat. **2.** *Archaic.* Porridge. [Middle English *potage,* from Old French, *potage,* POTAGE.]

pot·ted (pŏt′ĭd) *adj.* **1. a.** Placed in a pot. **b.** Grown in a pot, as a plant. **2.** Preserved in a pot or jar. **3.** *Chiefly British Informal.* Shortened or summarized, often in a crude or superficial way: *a potted history of the Church.* **4.** *Slang.* Intoxicated.

pot·ter¹ (pŏt′ər) *n.* A person who makes earthenware pots, dishes, or other vessels. [Middle English, Old English *pottere,* from POT.]

potter². *Chiefly British.* Variant of **putter** (to idle).

Pot·ter (pŏt′ər), **Beatrix** (1866–1943). British writer and illustrator of children's books. *The Tale of Peter Rabbit* (1902) was the first in a series of perennially popular works.

potter's clay *n.* A clay suitable for making pottery or for modeling, low in iron content. Also called "potter's earth."

potter's field *n.* A place for the burial of indigent or unknown persons. [From the potter's field mentioned in the Gospel according to Saint Matthew.]

potter's wheel *n.* A revolving, horizontal disk, operated electrically or by treadle, upon which clay is shaped manually.

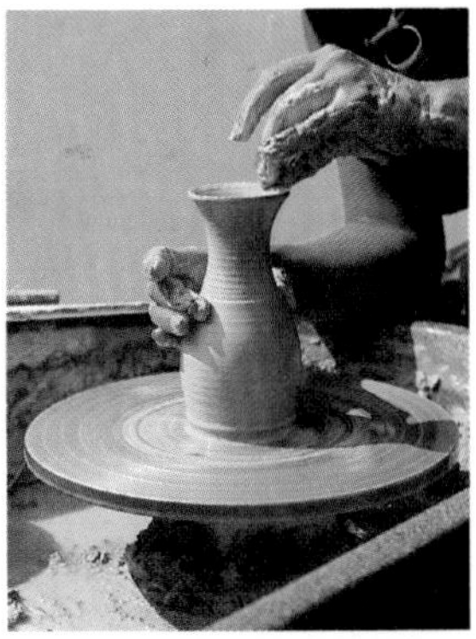

potter's wheel *The invention of the potter's wheel in Mesopotamia in about 3500 B.C. revolutionized the making of ceramics shortly before the invention of the wheel itself revolutionized transportation.*

potter wasp *n.* Any of various wasps of the genus *Eumenes,* characteristically building pot-shaped nests of clay.

pot·ter·y (pŏt′ə-rē) *n., pl.* **-ies. 1.** Ware, such as vases, pots, bowls, or plates, made of stoneware, earthenware, or porcelain. **2.** The craft or occupation of a potter. **3.** The establishment in which this craft is pursued. [Middle English, from Old French *poterie,* from *potier,* POTTER.] See feature, next page.

potting shed *n.* A garden shed in which plants can be grown and protected from harsh weather before being planted outside.

pot·tle (pŏt′l) *n.* **1.** A pot or drinking vessel with a two-quart capacity. **2.** The liquid contained in such a vessel. **3.** An old liquid measure equal to about two quarts. [Middle English *potel,* from Old French, diminutive of POT.]

pot·to (pŏt′ō) *n., pl.* **-tos. 1.** Any of several small African primates of the genera *Perodicticus* and *Arctocebus*; especially *P. potto,* having woolly fur. **2.** The **kinkajou** *(see).* [Probably from Guinea dialect; akin to Wolof *pata,* a tailless monkey.]

Pott's disease (pŏts) *n.* Tuberculosis of the spine, often resulting in deformity. [After Percivall *Pott* (1714–88), British surgeon.]

pot·ty¹ (pŏt′ē) *adj.* **-tier, -tiest.** *Chiefly British Informal.* **1.** Somewhat silly or crazy; foolish. **2.** Of little importance; trivial. [Perhaps from the phrase *go to pot,* to deteriorate, and from POT (liquor).]

potty² *n., pl.* **-ties.** A young child's pot for use as a toilet.

pot·ty-chair (pŏt′ē-châr′) *n.* A small chair with an opening in the seat and a receptacle beneath, used for toilet-training young children.

pot·ty-trained (pŏt′ē-trānd′) *adj. Informal.* Designating a child who has learned to use a potty or toilet; toilet-trained.

pouch (pouch) *n.* **1.** A small flexible receptacle; bag. **2.** A small bag of leather or other relatively nonporous material for carrying loose pipe tobacco. **3.** *Archaic.* A purse for small coins. **4.** A leather bag for carrying powder or small-arms ammunition. **5.** A bag for mail, especially one for diplomatic dispatches. **6.** Anything resembling a bag in shape: *He had pouches under his eyes.* **7.** *Zoology.* A saclike structure, such as the cheek pockets of the hamster, or the external abdominal pocket in which marsupials carry their young. **8.** *Anatomy.* A small saclike structure occurring as an outgrowth of a larger structure. **9.** *Scottish.* A pocket.
∼*v.* **pouched, pouching, pouches.** *—tr.* **1.** To place in or as if in a pouch; pocket: *He pouched all the money.* **2.** To cause to resemble a pouch in shape. **3.** To swallow. Used of certain birds and fishes. *—intr.* To assume the form of a pouch or pouchlike cavity. [Middle English *pouche,* from Old French *po(u)che,* from Frankish *pokka* (unattested).] **—pouch·y** *adj.*

pouf, pouffe (po͞of) *n.* **1. a.** A large, firm cushion used as a seat. **b.** A small, soft, backless couch. **2.** A woman's hairstyle popular in the 18th century, characterized by high rolled puffs. **3.** Any part of a dress or other garment gathered into a puff. **4.** A rounded soft pad used to stiffen or give body to puffs in the hair or to puffs in a garment. [French (imitative).]

Pough·keep·sie (pə-kĭp′sē). City of southeastern New York State, on the Hudson River. A trade center with a great variety of industries, it is the site of Vassar College. From 1777 to 1797 it was the state capital.

pouil·ly-fuis·sé (po͞o-yē′fwē-sā′) *n.* A dry white Burgundy. [After Solutré-*Pouilly* and *Fuissé,* villages in France.]

pou·lard, pou·larde (po͞o-lärd′) *n.* A young hen that has been spayed for fattening. Compare **capon.** [French *poularde,* from Old French *pollarde,* from *polle, poule,* hen, from Vulgar Latin *pulla* (unattested), from Latin *pullus,* young of an animal.]

Pou·lenc (po͞o-lănk′), **Francis** (1899–1963). French composer, member of Les Six. His works range from song cycles like *Le Bes-*

tiaire (1919) to the operas *Les Mamelles de Tirésias* (1947) and *Dialogue des Carmélites* (1957).

poult (pōlt) *n.* A young domestic fowl or related bird. [Middle English *pult,* short for *polet, poulet,* pullet, from Old French *poulet,* diminutive of *poule,* hen, chicken. See **poulard.**]

poul·ter·er (pōl′tər-ər) *n. British.* A poultry dealer. [Middle English *poulter,* from Old French *pouletier,* from *poulet,* POULT.]

poul·tice (pōl′tĭs) *n.* A moist, soft mass of bread, meal, kaolin, or other adhesive substance, usually heated, spread on cloth, and applied to warm, moisten, or stimulate an aching or inflamed part of the body. Also called "cataplasm." [Earlier *pultes* (taken as singular), from Medieval Latin *pultēs,* pulp, thick paste, from Latin, plural of *puls* (stem *pult-*), pap, possibly from Greek *poltos,* porridge.] —**poul·tice** *v.*

poul·try (pōl′trē) *n.* Domestic fowls, such as chickens, turkeys, ducks, or geese. [Middle English *pultrie,* from Old French *pouleterie,* from *pouletier,* POULTERER.]

pounce¹ (pouns) *v.* **pounced, pouncing, pounces.** —*intr.* **1.** To spring or swoop with intent to seize someone or something. Used

THE FINE ART OF BAKING AND GLAZING CLAY

Ancient techniques adapted for by artists through the ages

The main types of pottery—earthenware, stoneware, and porcelain—differ in their clays and in the degree of heat that is needed to harden them. Throughout history, clay has been used to make vessels—simply pressed into shape, built up in rolls, or formed on a wheel. About 25,000 years ago man found that clay models hardened when they were baked in a fire, but pottery was first made about 7000 B.C. in western Asia. And by about 3500 B.C. the potter's wheel was in use in Mesopotamia.

Early earthenware pots were fired at a relatively low temperature, about 500°C (932°F), and were porous. By 1500 B.C. potters were using a glassy paste to decorate pots, but it was 300 B.C. before a waterproof glaze for earthenware was developed. Stoneware was first made by the Chinese about 1400 B.C. They discovered a clay that would become nonporous if it was fired at about 1150°C (2102°F), and therefore needed no glaze. The Chinese were also the first to make porcelain, during the T'ang dynasty (A.D. 618–907). It was made from kaolin and petuntze and it needed firing at about 1300°C (2372°F). It is the hardest type of pottery and can be made very thin.

Fine pottery was made in ancient Greece, 7th–17th century China, America before Columbus, and Islamic Persia, Turkey, and Spain. Meissen in Germany, Sèvres in France, and Chelsea and Worcester in England were famed for porcelain in the 18th and 19th centuries.

PERSIAN POTTERY *This earthenware ewer was made in the 12th century in Kashan, a province of Persia noted for its lusterware. The ewer was press-molded and decorated with metallic luster, a carved pattern, and blue and turquoise glaze.*

CHELSEA PORCELAIN *This figure group, made about 1750, shows how fine, hard clay will hold minute detail with great sharpness.*

MODERN VASE *The ancient techniques were used to produce this simply shaped stoneware vase made by the British artist Hans Coper in 1968.*

with *on, upon,* or *at.* **2.** To attack suddenly and unexpectedly. —*tr. Rare.* To seize with or as if with talons. ~*n.* **1.** The act of pouncing. **2.** The talon or claw of a bird of prey. [Middle English, talon, claw (hence verb, to seize), probably variant of *punson,* PUNCHEON.] —**pounc·er** *n.*

pounce² *n.* **1.** A fine powder formerly used to seal the porous surfaces of paper and parchment and prepare them for writing on. **2.** A fine powder, such as pulverized charcoal, dusted over a stencil to transfer a design to an underlying surface. ~*tr.v.* **pounced, pouncing, pounces.** **1.** To sprinkle, smooth, or treat with pounce. **2.** To transfer (a stenciled design) with pounce. [French *ponce,* from Vulgar Latin *pōmex* (unattested), variant of Latin *pūmex,* PUMICE.] —**pounc·er** *n.*

pounce³ *tr.v.* **pounced, pouncing, pounces.** To ornament (metal, for example) by perforating from the back with a pointed implement. [Middle English *pounsen,* variant of *pounsonen,* from Old French *poinçonner,* to prick, stamp, from *poinçon,* pointed tool. See **punch, puncheon.**]

pounce box *n.* A small box with a perforated top, formerly used to sprinkle sand or pounce on writing paper to dry the ink.

poun·cet box (poun′sĭt) *n.* A small perfume box with a perforated top. [Probably alteration of POUNCE BOX.]

pound¹ (pound) *n., pl.* **pound** or **pounds.** **1.** *Abbr.* **lb.** **a.** A unit of mass in the avoirdupois system equal to 7,600 grains and divided into 16 ounces. It is equivalent to 0.453592 kilogram. Also called "pound avoirdupois." **b.** A unit of weight in the troy system equal to 5,760 grains and divided into 12 ounces. It is equal to 0.373242 kilogram. Also called "pound troy." **c.** A unit of weight in the apothecaries' system equal to 5,760 grains or one pound troy. **2.** A unit of weight differing in various countries and times, especially one equal to half a kilogram. **3.** A British unit of force equal to the weight of a standard one-pound mass where the local acceleration of gravity is 32.174 feet per second per second. Also called "pound force." **4.** *Symbol* **£** **a.** The basic monetary unit of the United Kingdom, equal to 100 new pence; before 1971 it was equal to 20 shillings or 240 old pence. Also called "pound sterling." **b.** The basic monetary unit of various dependent territories of the United Kingdom, equal to 100 pence. **c.** The Irish **punt** (see). See feature at **currency.** **5. a.** The basic monetary unit of Lebanon and Syria, equal to 100 piastres. **b.** The basic monetary unit of Egypt and Sudan, equal to 100 piastres or 1,000 millièmes. **c.** The basic monetary unit of Cyprus and Malta, equal to 100 cents or 1,000 mils. **d.** Formerly, the basic monetary unit of Israel, equal to 100 agorot. It is now worth ¹/₁₀ of the shekel. See feature at **currency.** **6.** A former monetary unit of Scotland before the Union, usually worth a small fraction of the pound sterling. Also called "pound Scots." **7.** A coin or note worth one pound. [Middle English *po(u)nd,* Old English *pund,* from Latin *pondō* (a weight of 12 ounces).]

pound² *v.* **pounded, pounding, pounds.** —*tr.* **1.** To strike or hammer with a heavy blow or blows. **2.** To drive (something) in or out with repeated blows; hammer. **3.** To beat to a powder or pulp; pulverize or crush. **4.** To instill by persistent and emphatic repetition: *pound knowledge into their heads.* **5.** To assault with heavy gunfire. —*intr.* **1.** To strike vigorous, repeated blows. Often used with *on* or *at: He pounded on the table.* **2.** To move along heavily and noisily. **3.** To pulsate rapidly and heavily: *Her heart pounded.* **4.** To work or move laboriously: *a ship pounding through heavy seas.* **5.** To do something in a vigorous attacking way: *pounded away at the typewriters.* —**pound out.** To produce (something) by or as if by pounding: *pounding out his new novel.* ~*n.* **1.** A heavy blow. **2.** The sound of a heavy blow; a thump. **3.** The act of pounding. [Middle English *pounen,* from Old English *pūnian†,* probably from Germanic.]

pound³ *n.* **1.** A public enclosure for the confinement of stray dogs or livestock. **2.** A place in which impounded property is held until redeemed. **3.** An enclosure in which animals or fish are trapped or kept. **4.** A place of confinement for lawbreakers. ~*tr.v.* **pounded, pounding, pounds.** To impound. [Middle English *pound,* from Old English *pund-.* Compare PINFOLD.]

Pound (pound), **Ezra Loomis** (1885–1972). U.S. poet. He was instrumental in establishing the modernist movement in poetry. As a result of his profascist stance during World War II, he was confined to a mental hospital in the United States until 1958, when he returned to Italy. His best-known work is an unfinished sequence of poems, the *Cantos* (1925–60).

pound·age¹ (poun′dĭj) *n.* **1.** A tax or commission based on value per pound (sterling). **2.** A rate or charge based on weight in pounds. **3.** Weight measured in pounds.

poundage² *n.* **1.** The act of impounding or the state of being impounded. **2.** A fee charged for the redemption of impounded animals or other property.

pound·al (poun′dl) *n. Abbr.* **pdl.** A unit of force in the foot-pound-second system of measurement equal to the force required to accelerate a standard one-pound mass one foot per second per second. [*pound* quint*al.*]

pound cake *n.* A rich cake containing eggs and originally made with a pound each of flour, butter, and sugar.

pound·er (poun′dər) *n.* **1. a.** Something weighing a pound. **b.** Something weighing a specified number of pounds. Used in combination: *a quarter-pounder.* **2.** A gun firing shells that weigh a specified number of pounds. Used in combination: *an eighteen-pounder.*

pound-fool·ish (pound′fo͞o′lĭsh) *adj.* Unwise in dealing with large sums of money or important matters. See **penny-wise.**

pour (pôr, pōr) *v.* **poured, pouring, pours.** —*tr.* **1.** To make (a fluid or granular solid) stream or flow. **2.** To send forth, produce, express, or utter copiously as if in a stream or flood: *poured money into the project; poured out his tale of woe.* —*intr.* **1.** To stream or flow continuously or profusely. **2.** To rain hard or heavily. **3.** To go forth or stream in large numbers or quantities. **4.** To fill cups with tea, coffee, or the like: *Will you pour?*
~*n.* A pouring or flowing forth; especially, a downpour of rain. [Middle English *pourent*.] —**pour·er** *n.*

pour·boire (po͝or-bwär′) *n.* Money given as a gratuity; a tip. [French, "for drinking."]

pour·par·ler (po͝or′pär-lā′) *n.* Conversation or discussion preliminary to negotiation. [French, "for speaking."]

pour point *n.* The lowest temperature at which an oil or other liquid will pour when cooled under given conditions.

pousse-ca·fé (po͞os′kă-fā′) *n.* **1.** A brandy or liqueur served after dinner with coffee. **2.** A drink consisting of several liqueurs of different densities poured to form layers of different colors. [French : *pousse,* a push + *café,* coffee.]

pous·sette (po͞o-sĕt′) *n.* A country-dance figure in which a couple or couples join hands and swing around the floor. [French, from *pousse,* a push, from *pousser,* to push, from Old French, from Latin *pulsāre,* frequentative of *pellere,* to push, beat.] —**pous·sette** *intr.v.*

pous·sin (po͞o-săɴ′) *n.* A young chicken weighing about one and a half pounds and raised for eating. [French.]

Pous·sin (po͞o-săɴ′), **Nicolas** (1594–1665). French painter. His landscapes and historical and religious subjects are considered some of the finest examples of the classical style.

pout¹ (pout) *v.* **pouted, pouting, pouts.** —*intr.* **1.** To protrude the lips in an expression of displeasure or sulkiness. **2.** To show displeasure or disappointment; sulk. **3.** To project or protrude: *His lips pouted in expectation of a kiss.* —*tr.* **1.** To push out or protrude (the lips). **2.** To utter or express with a pout.
~*n.* **1.** A protrusion of the lips, especially as an expression of sullen or childish discontent. **2.** *Sometimes* **pouts.** A fit of petulant sulkiness. [Middle English *pouten,* perhaps from Old English *pūtian* (unattested), to swell, be inflated, from Germanic.]

pout² *n., pl.* **pouts** or collectively **pout. 1.** Any of various European food fishes related to the cod; especially, the **bib** or the **Norway pout** *(both of which see).* **2.** Any of various freshwater or marine fishes such as the **eelpout** *(see).* [Middle English *poute* (unattested), Old English *-pūte* (as in *aele-pūte,* eelpout), from Germanic.]

pout·er (pou′tər) *n.* **1.** Any of a breed of pigeons capable of distending the crop until the breast becomes puffed out. **2.** One who pouts.

pov·er·ty (pŏv′ər-tē) *n.* **1. a.** The state or condition of being poor; lack of the means of providing material needs or comforts. **b.** The renunciation by a member of a religious order of the right to personal property. **2.** Lack of something necessary or desirable; insufficiency; paucity: *a poverty of talent.* **3.** Deficiency in amount; scantiness: *the poverty of his vocabulary.* **4.** Unproductiveness; infertility: *the poverty of the soil.* [Middle English *poverte,* from Old French, from Latin *paupertās* (stem *paupertāt-*), from *pauper,* poor.]

poverty grass *n.* Any of several North American grasses that grow in poor or sandy soil.

poverty level *n.* A minimum income level below which a person is considered to lack adequate subsistence and to be living in poverty.

pow (pou) *n.* The sound of a blow, collision, or explosion.
~*interj.* Used to imitate the sound of a blow, collision, or explosion. [Imitative.]

POW, P.O.W. prisoner of war.

pow·an (pō′ən) *n.* Any of various related freshwater fishes; especially, a whitefish, *Coregonus clupeoides,* found in Scottish lakes. Also called "lake herring." [Scottish variant of POLLAN.]

pow·der (pou′dər) *n.* **1. a.** A substance consisting of ground, pulverized, or otherwise finely dispersed solid particles. **b.** Any of various preparations in this form, as certain medicines; especially, a flesh-colored cosmetic used on the face. **2. a.** An explosive mixture, **gunpowder** *(see).* **b.** Any of various similar explosive substances. **3. Powder snow** *(see).* —**take a powder.** *Slang.* To make a quick departure; leave in a hurry.
~*v.* **powdered, -dering, -ders.** —*tr.* **1.** To reduce to powder; pulverize. **2. a.** To dust or cover with or as if with powder. **b.** To apply powder to. —*intr.* **1.** To become pulverized; turn to powder. **2.** To use powder as a cosmetic. [Middle English *poudre,* from Old French, from Latin *pulvis* (stem *pulver-*).] —**pow·der·er** *n.*

powder blue *n.* A moderate to pale blue. [From the color of powdered smalt.] —**pow·der-blue** (pou′dər-blo͞o′) *adj.*

pow·dered (pou′dərd) *adj.* Covered or dotted with small objects: *The meadow was powdered with daisies.*

powder flask *n.* A small flask or similar receptacle used for carrying gunpowder.

powder horn *n.* A container consisting of an animal's horn capped at the open end used to carry gunpowder.

powder keg *n.* **1.** A small barrel for holding gunpowder or other explosives. **2.** A potentially explosive thing or situation.

powder magazine *n.* A storage place for gunpowder.

powder metallurgy *n.* The technology of powdered metals, especially the production and use of metallic powders for making objects by pressure and heating.

powder puff *n.* A soft pad for applying cosmetic or talcum powder to the skin.

powder room *n.* A lavatory for women.

powder snow *n.* Loose, dry snow on the ground, making an ideal skiing surface. Also called "powder."

pow·der·y (pou′də-rē) *adj.* **1.** Composed of or similar to powder. **2.** Dusted or covered with or as if with powder. **3.** Easily made into powder; friable.

powdery mildew *n.* **1.** Any of various plant diseases caused by fungi of the family Erysiphaceae and resulting in a white, powdery growth appearing mostly on the upper surface of leaves. **2.** Any of the fungi causing such a disease.

Pow·ell (pou′əl), **Anthony** (1905–). British novelist. His 12-volume novel cycle, *A Dance to the Music of Time,* is a social satire portraying Nicholas Jenkins and his upper-class friends.

pow·er (pou′ər) *n.* **1.** The ability or capacity to act or perform effectively. **2.** *Often* **powers. a.** A specific capacity, faculty, or aptitude: *his powers of concentration.* **b.** Natural abilities or capacities: *at the height of her powers.* **3.** Strength or force exerted or capable of being exerted; might. **4. a.** The ability or official capacity to exercise control; authority. **b.** A privilege or right; prerogative. **5.** A person, group, or nation having great influence or control over others. **6.** The might of a nation, political organization, or similar group. **7.** Forcefulness; effectiveness: *a novel of great power.* **8.** *Regional.* A large number or amount: *a power of good.* **9.** *Physics.* The rate at which work is done, mathematically expressed as the first derivative of work with respect to time and commonly measured in units such as the watt and horsepower. **10. a.** The capacity to supply physical systems, as machines, with the energy to operate or to generate light and heat: *wave power.* **b.** Electrical or mechanical energy as opposed to unaided human energy. **11.** *Mathematics.* **a.** An **exponent** *(see).* **b.** The number of elements in a finite set. **12.** *Optics.* A measure of the **magnification** *(see)* of an optical instrument, such as a microscope or telescope. **13. powers. a.** Supernatural spirits. **b.** *Theology.* The sixth group of angels in the hierarchical order of nine. See **angel. 14.** *Archaic.* An armed force. —See Synonyms at **strength.**
~*tr.v.* **powered, -ering, -ers.** To supply with power, especially mechanical power.
~*adj.* Of, pertaining to, or being a mechanical device in which the force or torque applied by an operator is amplified by an engine: *power brakes; power steering.* [Middle English *pouer,* from Old French *poeir, povoir,* from *poeir,* to be able, from Old Latin *potēre* (unattested) (superseded by *posse*).]

Pow·er (pou′ər), **Tyrone** (1914–58). U.S. actor. A versatile performer, he toured with the Shakespeare Repertoire Company before becoming a popular motion-picture leading man. Among his many film credits are *Café Metropole* (1937), *The Razor's Edge* (1946), and *Witness for the Prosecution* (1957).

power base *n.* A position that allows a person or group to build up and consolidate power, usually through the support of a committed following: *The young conservatives of the party were his power base.*

pow·er·boat (pou′ər-bōt′) *n.* A **motorboat** *(see).*

power broker *n.* One who exerts influence over those in power, especially by promising or withdrawing the support of his followers.

power dive *n.* A downward plunge of an aircraft accelerated by both gravity and engine power. —**pow·er-dive** (pou′ər-dīv′) *v.*

power drill *n.* **1.** A portable electric drill. **2.** A large drilling machine having a vertical motorized drill set in a table stand.

pow·er·ful (pou′ər-fəl) *adj.* **1.** Having or capable of exerting power. **2.** Strong in effect; potent: *a powerful drug.* **3.** *Regional.* Great: *It did a powerful lot of good.*
~*adv. Regional.* Very: *It was powerful hot.* —**pow·er·ful·ly** *adv.*

pow·er·house (pou′ər-hous′) *n.* **1.** A power plant. **2.** A person or group having great strength or contributing greatly to the activity of a body: *the nation's intellectual powerhouse.*

pow·er·less (pou′ər-lĭs) *adj.* **1.** Lacking strength or power; helpless; ineffectual. **2.** Lacking legal or other authority. —**pow·er·less·ly** *adv.* —**pow·er·less·ness** *n.*

power mower *n.* A lawn mower that is powered by a gasoline or electric motor.

power of appointment *n. Law.* A power, granted by deed or will, giving a person the authority to assign an estate or an interest in it.

power of attorney *n. Abbr.* **P/A, P.A.** *Law.* A legal instrument authorizing a person to act as another's attorney, legal representative, or agent; legal authority to act on behalf of another. Also called "procuration."

power pack *n. Electronics.* A compact, often portable device that converts supply current to direct or alternating current as required by specific equipment.

power plant *n.* **1.** All the equipment, including structural members, that constitutes a unit power source: *the power plant of a truck.* **2.** A complex of structures, machinery, and associated equipment for generating power, especially electric power.

power play *n.* **1.** *Sports.* **a.** An offensive maneuver in football in which a massive concentration of players is used to block in a particular area. **b.** A situation in ice hockey in which one team has an advantage because the other team has a player or players in the penalty box. **2.** A strategic action or maneuver, as in politics, diplomacy, business, or warfare, based on the use or threatened use of power.

power point *n.* A device into which an electric plug can be inserted in order to connect it with a circuit. Also called "point."

power politics *n. Used with a singular or plural verb.* International diplomacy in which each nation uses or threatens to use military or

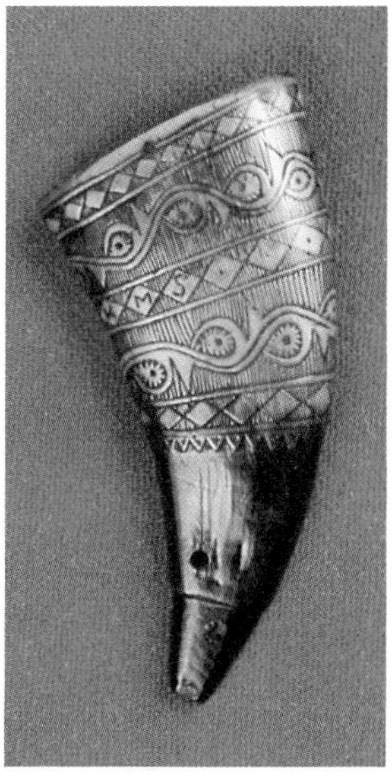

powder horn *Gunpowder for flintlock firearms was kept in an animal's horn. A hole in the base of the horn acted as a funnel for loading the powder into the weapon.*

economic power to further its own interests. [Translation of German *Machtpolitik*.]

power series *n.* *Mathematics.* A sum of successively higher integral powers of a variable or combination of variables, each multiplied by a constant coefficient.

power sharing *n.* A system whereby minority parties or interests exercise some measure of political power in cooperation with the majority. —**pow·er-shar·ing** (pou′ər-shâr′ĭng) *adj.*

power shovel *n.* A large, usually mobile machine having a boom, a dipper stick, and a bucket for excavating.

power station *n.* A power plant for generating electricity.

Pow·ha·tan (pou′ə-tăn′, pou-hăt′n) (c. 1550-1618). American Indian chief. When the English settlers established Jamestown in 1607, he was the powerful leader of 30 unified tribes in the area. At first opposed to the newcomers, he maintained peace with them after the marriage of his daughter Pocahontas to a colonist (1614).

pow·wow (pou′wou′) *n.* **1. a.** A conference or meeting with or of North American Indians. **b.** *Informal.* A conference or gathering for discussion. **2.** A North American Indian medicine man. **3.** A North American Indian ceremony in which incantations and dancing are used to invoke divine aid in hunting, in battle, or against disease.

~*intr.v.* **powwowed, -wowing, -wows.** To hold a powwow. [Algonquian; akin to Narraganset *powwaw*, magician.]

pox (pŏks) *n.* **1.** A disease characterized by purulent skin eruptions, as chicken pox or smallpox. **2.** Syphilis. —**a pox on someone** or **something.** *Archaic.* Used to wish misfortune and calamity on someone or something. [Alteration of *pocks*, plural of POCK (mark).]

Poz·nań (pôz′nän′, -nän′yə). *German* **Pos·en** (pō′zən). Capital of Poznań province in western Poland, on the Warta River. It was the residence of the Polish kings until 1296. During World War II it was occupied by Germany and badly damaged. In 1956 it was the scene of severe rioting over economic and political problems.

poz·zuo·la·na (pŏt′swə-lä′nə) *n.* Also **poz·zo·la·na** (pŏt′sə-). **1.** A siliceous volcanic ash used to produce hydraulic cement. **2.** Any of various artificially produced substances resembling this ash. [Italian *pozzolana*, "of Pozzuoli," town near Vesuvius.] —**poz·zuo·la·nic** *adj.*

pp *Music.* pianissimo.

pp. **1.** pages. **2.** past participle. **3.** *Music.* pianissimo.

p.p. **1.** parcel post. **2.** parish priest. **3.** past participle. **4.** per procurationem. **5.** postpaid.

P.P. parish priest.

ppd. **1.** postpaid. **2.** prepaid.

pph. pamphlet.

P.P.S. additional postscript [Latin *post postscriptum*].

p.q. previous question.

P.Q. Province of Quebec.

Pr The symbol for the element praseodymium.

PR public relations.

pr. **1.** pair. **2.** *Grammar.* present. **3.** price. **4.** printing. **5.** pronoun.

Pr. **1.** priest. **2.** prince. **3.** Provençal.

P.R. **1.** proportional representation. **2.** public relations. **3.** Puerto Rico.

praam, pram (präm) *n.* **1.** A flat-bottomed boat used especially in the Baltic as a barge. **2.** *Chiefly British.* A small dinghy having a flat, snub-nosed bow. [Dutch, from Middle Dutch *praem*, from Czech *prám*.]

prac·ti·ca·ble (prăk′tĭ-kə-bəl) *adj.* **1.** Capable of being effected, done, or executed; feasible. **2.** Capable of being used for a specified purpose: *a practicable way of entry.* —See Synonyms at **possible.** —See Usage note at **practical.** [French *practicable*, from *pratiquer*, to PRACTICE.] —**prac·ti·ca·bil·i·ty** *n.* —**prac·ti·ca·bly** *adv.*

prac·ti·cal (prăk′tĭ-kəl) *adj.* **1.** Of, pertaining to, governed by, or acquired through practice or action rather than theory, speculation, or ideals. **2.** Manifested in or involving practice. **3.** Actually engaged in some work or occupation. **4.** Capable of being used or put into effect; useful: *a practical knowledge of German.* **5.** Designed to serve a purpose without elaboration: *practical low-heeled shoes.* **6.** Concerned with the production or operation of something useful: *Woodworking is a practical art.* **7.** Level-headed, efficient, and down-to-earth. **8.** Being actually so in almost every respect; virtual: *a practical disaster.* —See Synonyms at **possible.** ~*n.* An examination testing a student's practical ability in a subject: *a chemistry practical.* [Late Latin *practicus*, practical, from Greek *praktikos*, from *praktos*, to be done, from *prattein, prassein,* to practice.] —**prac·ti·cal·i·ty** (prăk′tĭ-kăl′ə-tē), **prac·ti·cal·ness** *n.*

   Usage: *Practical* and *practicable* are sometimes confused. A *practical* solution to a problem is one of proven effectiveness; a *practicable* solution is one that is capable of being put into effect, though it may not necessarily solve the problem. There may be several *practicable* suggestions for dealing with a situation, but not all of these may be *practical* ones. *Practicable* is not used of people and thus lacks the sense of down-to-earth efficiency that is apparent in such contexts as *John is a very practical person.* In contemporary usage, *practical* seems to be taking over some of the senses of *practicable*, but the trend is open to criticism.

practical joke *n.* A mischievous trick played on a person especially to cause him or her to feel embarrassment or indignity.

prac·ti·cal·ly (prăk′tĭk-lē) *adv.* **1.** In a way that is practical. **2.** In every important respect; virtually. **3.** Almost.

   Usage: *Practically* is used unexceptionally in its primary sense of "in a way that is practical." In other senses it has become almost interchangeable with *virtually.* Such use is acceptable when the meaning is "for all practical purposes." Thus, a man whose liabilities exceed his assets may be said to be *practically bankrupt,* even though he has not been legally declared insolvent. By a slight extension of this meaning, however, *practically* is often used to mean "nearly" or "all but": *He had practically finished his meal when I arrived.* In this sense it should be avoided in writing.

practical nurse *n.* A licensed practical nurse (see).

prac·tice (prăk′tĭs) *n.* **1.** A habitual or customary action or way of doing something: *make a practice of being punctual.* **2. a.** Repeated performance of an activity in order to learn or perfect a skill. **b.** *Archaic.* The skill so learned or perfected. **c.** The condition of being skilled through repeated performance: *He is out of practice at golf.* **3.** The act or process of doing something; performance. **4.** The exercise of an occupation or profession, such as medicine or law. **5.** The business of a professional person, such as a lawyer or doctor: *How large is the practice?* **6.** Often **practices.** A habitual action or act: *questionable business practices; a standard accounting practice.* **7.** The methods of procedure used in a court of law. **8.** *Archaic.* **a.** The act of tricking. **b.** A stratagem; a trick. —See Synonyms at **habit.**

~*v.* **practiced, -ticing, -tices.** Also *chiefly British* **prac·tise, -tised, -tising, -tises.** —*tr.* **1.** To do or perform habitually or customarily; make a habit of. **2.** To exercise or perform repeatedly in order to acquire or polish a skill: *practice a dance step.* **3.** To give lessons or repeated instructions to; drill. **4.** To work at, especially as a profession: *practice law.* **5.** To carry out in action; act in accordance with: *practice one's religion.* **6.** *Obsolete.* To prearrange secretly or deviously; plot. —*intr.* **1.** To do or perform something habitually or repeatedly. **2.** To do something repeatedly in order to acquire or polish a skill. **3.** To work at a profession. **4.** *Obsolete.* To intrigue or plot. [Middle English *practisen,* from Old French *practiser, pratiquer,* from Medieval Latin *practicāre,* from Late Latin *practicus,* PRACTICAL.]

prac·ticed (prăk′tĭst) *adj.* **1.** Proficient; skilled; expert. **2.** Acquired or brought to perfection by practice.

practice teaching *n.* Classroom teaching by a college student under the supervision of an experienced teacher that is done as an internship in teaching methodology prior to certification as a professional teacher.

prac·tic·ing (prăk′tĭ-sĭng) *adj.* **1.** Actively professing and adhering to a particular set of beliefs or way of life: *a practicing Christian.* **2.** Actively engaged in a particular profession or occupation: *She is both a novelist and a practicing physician.*

prac·ti·cum (prăk′tĭ-kəm) *n.* Supervised practical application of a previously studied theory: *an advanced practicum for teaching reading to visually impaired pupils.* [German *Praktikum,* from Late Latin *practicum,* neuter of *practicus,* PRACTICAL.]

prac·ti·tion·er (prăk-tĭsh′ə-nər) *n.* **1.** One who practices an occupation, profession, or technique: *a medical practitioner.* **2.** *Christian Science.* A person engaged in the public ministry of spiritual healing. [From earlier *practician,* from obsolete French *practicien,* from *pra(c)tique,* practice, from Late Latin *practicus,* PRACTICAL.]

prae-. Variant of **pre-.**

prae·di·al, pre·di·al (prē′dē-əl) *adj.* **1.** Pertaining to land or its products. **2.** Attached to or arising from land or landed property: *praedial serfs.* [Medieval Latin *praediālis,* of an estate, from Latin *praedium,* estate, from *praes,* surety.]

praefect. Variant of **prefect.**

prae·mu·ni·re (prē′myōō-nī′rē) *n.* *Law.* **1.** Formerly in Britain, the offense of appealing to or obeying a foreign court or authority, such as that of the pope, thus challenging the supremacy of the Crown. **2.** The writ charging this offense. **3.** The penalty for this offense. [Middle English, from Medieval Latin *praemūnīre (facias),* "that you warn (someone to appear)" (words in the writ), from Latin *praemūnīre,* to fortify (meaning influenced by *praemonēre,* to forewarn) : *prae,* before + *mūnīre,* to fortify.]

prae·no·men (prē-nō′mən) *n., pl.* **-nomina** (-nŏm′ə-nə, -nō′mə-nə) or **-nomens.** The first or given name of an ancient Roman. Compare **cognomen, nomen.** [Latin *praenōmen* : *prae,* before + *nōmen,* name.] —**prae·nom·i·nal** (prē-nŏm′ə-nəl) *adj.*

prae·tor (prē′tər) *n.* A high elected magistrate of the ancient Roman Republic, ranking below the consuls and serving as a judge. [Latin *praetor,* "leader," "chief," from *praeīre,* to go before : *prae-,* in front of + *īre,* to go.] —**prae·tor·ship** *n.*

prae·to·ri·an (prē-tôr′ē-ən, -tōr′ē-ən) *adj.* **1.** Of or pertaining to a praetor. **2. Praetorian.** Of, pertaining to, comprising, or belonging to the bodyguard of the Roman emperors. ~*n.* **1.** A praetor. **2. Praetorian.** A member of the bodyguard of the Roman emperors.

Prae·to·ri·us (prī-tôr′ē-əs, -tōr′ē-əs), **Michael,** born Michael Schultheiss; also known as Michael Schulz (1571-1621). German composer. He wrote a number of hymns, dances, and madrigals. His *Syntagma Musicum* (1615-19) is an account of the musical theory and instruments employed in his time.

prag·mat·ic (prăg-măt′ĭk) *adj.* **1. a.** Dealing with facts or actual occurrences; based on or dealing with immediate circumstances rather than theoretical considerations; practical. **b.** Active rather than contemplative. **2.** Pertaining to the study of events and historical phenomena with emphasis on their practical outcome. **3.** Of or pertaining to pragmatism. **4.** Of or pertaining to the affairs of a state. **5.** Interfering; meddling.

~n. **1.** A pragmatic sanction *(see).* **2.** A meddler; busybody. [Latin *pragmaticus,* skilled in affairs, from Greek *pragmatikos,* from *pragma* (stem *pragmat-*), deed, affair, from *prattein,* to do.] **—prag·mat·i·cal** *adj.* **—prag·mat·i·cal·ly** *adv.*

prag·mat·ics (prăg-măt′ĭks) *n. Used with a singular or plural verb.* The branch of semiotics concerned with the relations between signs or expressions and their users.

pragmatic sanction *n.* An edict issued by a sovereign that becomes part of the fundamental law of the land. Also called "pragmatic."

prag·ma·tism (prăg′mə-tĭz′əm) *n.* **1.** *Philosophy.* The theory, developed by Charles S. Peirce and William James, that the meaning of a proposition or course of action lies in its observable consequences and that the sum of these consequences constitutes its meaning. **2.** A method or tendency in the conduct of political affairs that is characterized by the rejection of theory and precedent and by the use of practical means and expedients. **3.** A pragmatic outlook or way of solving problems. **—prag·ma·tist** (prăg′mə-tĭst) *n.* **—prag·ma·tis·tic** (prăg′mə-tĭs′tĭk) *adj.*

prag·ma·tize (prăg′mə-tīz′) *tr.v.* **-tized, -tizing, -tizes.** To consider or represent as real or actual.

Prague (prāg). *Czech* **Pra·ha** (prä′hä). Capital of Czechoslovakia, on the Vltava River in central Bohemia. It became the capital of newly independent Czechoslovakia in 1918. In 1968 Soviet forces entered the city following the "Prague Spring," a period in which the city had become the focus of the movement for greater economic and political freedom led by Alexander Dubček. Prague is the leading Czech industrial center.

prai·rie (prâr′ē) *n.* An extensive area of flat or rolling grassland, especially in central North America. [French, from Old French *praerie,* from Vulgar Latin *prātāria* (unattested), from Latin *prā-tum†,* meadow.]

prairie breaker *n.* A plow that cuts a wide furrow and turns the earth completely over.

prairie chicken *n.* Either of two birds, *Tympanuchus cupido* or *T. pallidicinctus,* of western North America, having deep-chested bodies and mottled brownish plumage. Also called "prairie hen."

prairie dog *n.* Any of several burrowing rodents of the genus *Cynomys,* of west-central North America. They have yellowish fur and a barklike call and live in large communities.

prairie hen *n.* A prairie chicken.

prairie oyster *n.* **1.** *Slang.* A raw egg immersed in a liquid, as Worcestershire sauce or vinegar, and swallowed whole, especially as a remedy for a hangover. **2.** *Chiefly Regional.* A testicle of a calf cooked and served as food.

Prairie Provinces. Region of west-central Canada: the provinces of Manitoba, Alberta, and Saskatchewan.

prairie schooner *n.* A canvas-covered wagon, similar to but lighter than the Conestoga wagon, used by pioneers crossing the North American prairies. Also called "schooner."

prairie wolf *n.* The **coyote** *(see).*

praise (prāz) *n.* **1.** An expression of warm approval or admiration; strong commendation. **2.** The glorification and extolling of a deity, ruler, or hero. **3.** *Archaic.* A reason for praise; merit. **—praise be.** Used to express gratitude or relief. **—sing the praises of.** To praise highly and publicly.
~tr.v. **praised, praising, praises.** **1.** To express warm approval of or admiration for; commend; applaud. **2.** To extol or exalt; worship. [Middle English *preisen,* from Old French *preisier,* to prize, praise, from Late Latin *pretiāre,* from Latin *pretium,* price.] **—prais·er** *n.*
Synonyms: acclaim, commend, extol, laud.

praise·wor·thy (prāz′wûr′thē) *adj.* Meriting praise; highly commendable. **—praise·wor·thi·ly** *adv.* **—praise·wor·thi·ness** *n.*

Pra·krit (prä′krĭt) *n.* **1.** Any of the vernacular languages of India, as opposed to the literary language, **Sanskrit** *(see).* **2.** Any of the various ancient Indic languages on which the modern vernaculars are based. [Sanskrit *prākṛta,* vulgar, vernacular : *pra-,* before + *kṛta,* made, from *kṛ,* to make.] **—Pra·krit·ic** (pră-krĭt′ĭk) *adj.*

pra·line (prä′lēn′, prā′-, prô′-) *n.* A crisp confection made of nut kernels stirred in boiling sugar syrup until brown. It is often crushed and used as a flavoring. [French, invented by the cook of César de Choiseul, Count du Plessis-*Praslin,* French field marshal (1598–1675).]

prall·tril·ler (präl′trĭl′ər) *n. Music.* A melodic detail or embellishment consisting of a mordent with the auxiliary note above the principal note. Also called "inverted mordent." [German *Pralltriller,* "elastic trill" : *prallen,* to rebound (akin to Middle High German *prellen†*) + *triller,* trill, from Italian *trillo,* TRILL.]

pram¹ (prăm) *n. Chiefly British.* A baby carriage; perambulator. [Shortened from PERAMBULATOR.]

pram². Variant of **praam.**

prance (prăns, präns) *intr.v.* **pranced, prancing, prances.** **1. a.** To spring forward on the hind legs. Used of a horse. **b.** To move with a succession of such springs or bounds. **2.** To ride a horse that moves in this way. **3.** To walk or move about in a lively manner; spring; strut.
~n. An act of prancing. [Middle English *prauncen†.*] **—pranc·er** *n.* **—pranc·ing·ly** *adv.*

pran·di·al (prăn′dē-əl) *adj.* Of or relating to a meal, especially dinner. [Latin *prandium,* late breakfast.] **—pran·di·al·ly** *adv.*

prang (prăng) *n. Informal.* **1.** A crash, accident, or collision, especially in an aircraft or car. **2.** The destruction of a target by bombing.

~v. **pranged, pranging, prangs.** *Informal.* **—tr. 1.** To crash or damage in a collision. **2.** To bomb. **—intr.** To crash an aircraft or other vehicle. [Imitative.]

prank¹ (prăngk) *n.* A mischievous trick; a practical joke. [16th century : origin obscure.]

prank² *v.* **pranked, pranking, pranks.** **—tr.** To decorate or dress ostentatiously or gaudily. **—intr.** To make an ostentatious display. [Akin to Dutch *pronk†,* finery, and *pronken†,* to strut.]

prank·ish (prăng′kĭsh) *adj.* Characterized by impish, mischievous behavior. **—prank·ish·ly** *adv.* **—prank·ish·ness** *n.*

prank·ster (prăngk′stər) *n.* One who plays tricks or pranks.

pra·se·o·dym·i·um (prā′zē-ō-dĭm′ē-əm, prā′sē-) *n. Symbol* **Pr** A soft, yellow, malleable, ductile rare-earth element that develops a characteristic green tarnish in air. It occurs naturally with other rare earths in monazite and is used to color glass yellow, as a core material for carbon arcs, and in metallic alloys. Atomic number 59, atomic weight 140.907, melting point 935°C, boiling point 3,127°C, specific gravity 6.64, valences 3, 4. [New Latin, contraction of *praseodidymium* : Greek *prasios,* leek-green, from *prason,* leek + DIDYMIUM.]

prat (prăt) *n.* **1.** *Slang.* The buttocks. **2.** *British Informal.* A stupidly pretentious or incompetent person. [Perhaps imitative of the sound of spanking.]

prate (prāt) *v.* **prated, prating, prates.** **—intr.** To talk idly and at great length; chatter. **—tr.** To utter idly or to little purpose.
~n. Empty, foolish, or trivial talk. [Middle English *praten,* akin to Middle Dutch and Middle Low German *prāten* (perhaps imitative).] **—prat·er** *n.* **—prat·ing·ly** *adv.*

prat·fall (prăt′fôl′) *n.* **1.** An embarrassing mistake or failure. **2.** A fall on the buttocks. [PRAT + FALL.]

prat·in·cole (prăt′ĭng-kōl′, prā′tĭng-) *n.* Any of several swallowlike Old World birds of the genus *Glareola* and related genera, having brown and black plumage, long, pointed wings, and a forked tail. [New Latin *pratincola,* "meadow-dweller" : Latin *prātum,* meadow (see prairie) + *incola,* inhabitant.]

pra·tique (pră-tēk′) *n. Nautical.* Clearance granted to a ship to proceed into port after compliance with quarantine or health regulations. [French, from PRACTICE.]

prat·tle (prăt′l) *v.* **-tled, -tling, -tles.** **—intr.** To talk idly or meaninglessly; babble. **—tr.** To utter in a childish or silly way.
~n. Childish or meaningless sounds; babble. [Frequentative of PRATE (akin to Low German *prateln*).] **—prat·tler** *n.*

prawn (prôn) *n.* Any of various edible marine crustaceans of the genus *Palaemonetes* and related genera, closely related to and resembling the shrimps.
~intr.v. **prawned, prawning, prawns.** To fish for prawns. [Middle English *prayne†.*] **—prawn·er** *n.*

prax·i·ol·o·gy, prax·e·ol·o·gy (prăk′sē-ŏl′ə-jē) *n.* The study of human conduct. [PRAXI(S) + -LOGY.] **—prax·i·o·log·i·cal** (prăk′sē-ə-lŏj′ĭ-kəl) *adj.*

prax·is (prăk′sĭs) *n., pl.* **-es** (-sēz′). **1.** Practical application or exercise of a branch of learning. **2.** Habitual or established practice; custom. [Medieval Latin, from Greek, doing, action, from *prattein,* to do.]

Prax·it·e·les (prăk-sĭt′l-ēz′) (mid-4th century B.C.). Athenian sculptor. His few surviving works include *Hermes Carrying Dionysus,* discovered at Olympia (1877).

pray (prā) *v.* **prayed, praying, prays.** **—intr. 1.** To utter or address a petition to God, a god, or an object of worship. **2.** To make a fervent request; beg. **—tr. 1.** To say a prayer or prayers to. **2.** To ask (someone) imploringly; beseech. Often used to introduce an entreaty or question: *Pray, be careful.* **3.** To make a devout or earnest request for: *I pray your indulgence.* **4.** To move or bring by prayer or entreaty. [Middle English *preyen,* from Old French *preier,* from Latin *precārī,* to entreat, from *prex* (stem *prec-*), prayer.]

pray·er¹ (prā′ər) *n.* One who prays.

prayer² (prâr) *n.* **1. a.** The act or practice of addressing God or a god in words or through meditation, as in praise, gratitude, sorrow, or intercession. **b.** An instance of this. **c.** A specially worded form used in addressing God. **d.** A petition or act of devotion to an object of worship. **2.** *Sometimes* **Prayer.** A religious service in which praying predominates: *morning prayer.* **3. a.** A fervent request. **b.** The thing requested: *His safe arrival was their prayer.* **4.** The slightest chance or hope: *You haven't a prayer of winning.* [Middle English *preyere,* from Old French *preiere,* from Medieval Latin *precāria,* written petition, prayer, from Latin, feminine of *precārius,* obtained by entreaty, from *precārī,* to entreat, from PRAY.]

prayer beads *pl.n.* A string of beads for keeping count of the prayers one is saying; a rosary.

prayer book *n.* **1.** A book containing prayers and other forms of worship. **2.** *Usually* **Prayer Book.** *Abbr.* **P.B.** The Book of Common Prayer.

prayer·ful (prâr′fəl) *adj.* **1.** Inclined to pray frequently; devout. **2.** Characterized by or conducive to prayer. **—prayer·ful·ly** *adv.* **—prayer·ful·ness** *n.*

prayer mat *n.* A small mat or carpet knelt on by Muslims when praying. Also called "prayer rug."

prayer meeting *n.* An evangelical service, especially one held on a weekday evening, in which the laity participate by singing, praying, or testifying.

prayer rug *n.* A prayer mat *(see).*

prayer shawl *n.* A large shawl worn, especially by Jewish men, during prayer. See **tallith.**

prairie dog *This rodent of the North American plains lives underground in communal burrows containing up to 1,000 animals. It gets its name from its doglike warning bark.*

prayer wheel n. A cylinder inscribed with or containing written prayers and revolved on an axis, used especially by the Buddhists of Tibet.

praying mantis n. A green or brownish predatory insect, *Mantis religiosa*, that while at rest folds its front legs as if in prayer.

P.R.B. Pre-Raphaelite Brotherhood.

pre-, prae– *prefix.* Indicates: **1.** An earlier or prior time; for example, **prearrange**, **pre-Columbian**. **2.** Preliminary or preparatory work or activity; for example, **preschool**. **3.** A location in front or anterior; for example, **preaxial**. *Note:* Many compounds other than those entered here may be formed with *pre-*. In this dictionary, *pre-* is normally joined with the following element without space or hyphen: *prearrange*. However, many users prefer the hyphenated form, especially if the second element begins with a capital letter *(pre-Christian)* or the letter *e (pre-eminent)*. [Middle English, from Old French, from Latin *prae-*, from *prae*, before, in front. In Latin compounds, *prae-* indicates: 1. Before in time, as in **prescience**. 2. Before in position, in front, as in **premorse**. 3. Before in degree or importance, superior, exceeding, as in **preponderate**. 4. Intensifying action, as in **prepotent**.]

preach (prēch) v. **preached, preaching, preaches.** —*tr.* **1.** To expound upon in writing or speech; especially, to urge acceptance of or compliance with (specified religious or moral principles). **2.** To deliver (a sermon or advice, for example). —*intr.* **1.** To deliver a sermon. **2.** To give religious or moral instruction, especially in a drawn-out, tiresome manner. [Middle English *prechen*, from Old French *prechier*, from Late Latin *praedĭcāre*, from Latin, to proclaim : *prae*, before + *dĭcāre*, to say.]

preach·er (prē′chər) n. **1.** A Protestant clergyman; a minister. **2.** One who preaches.

preach·i·fy (prē′chə-fī′) *intr.v.* **-fied, -fying, -fies.** *Informal.* To preach tediously and didactically. —**preach·i·fi·ca·tion** n.

preach·ment (prēch′mənt) n. **1.** The act of preaching. **2.** A tiresome or unwelcome moral lecture; tedious sermonizing.

preach·y (prē′chē) *adj.* **-ier, -iest.** Inclined to preach. —**preach·i·ly** *adv.* —**preach·i·ness** n.

pre·ad·am·ite (prē-ăd′ə-mīt′) n. **1.** One supposed to have been in existence before Adam, traditionally thought to have been the first man, created by God. **2.** One who holds that there were people in existence before Adam. [PRE- + ADAM + -ITE.] —**pre·ad·am·ite** *adj.*

pre·ad·ap·ta·tion (prē-ăd′ăp-tā′shən) n. The possession by an organism or group of organisms of one or more characteristics that would be advantageous and therefore enhance its chances of survival in a changed environment.

pre·ad·o·les·cence (prē-ăd′l-ĕs′əns) n. The period between childhood and adolescence, often designated as between the ages of ten and twelve. —**pre·ad·o·les·cent** n. & *adj.*

pre·ag·ri·cul·tur·al (prē-ăg′rĭ-kŭl′chər-əl) *adj.* Occurring or existing before the advent of agriculture.

pre·am·ble (prē′ăm′bəl, prē-ăm′-) n. **1.** A preliminary statement; especially, the introduction to a formal document that explains its purpose. **2.** An introductory occurrence or fact; a preliminary. [Middle English, from Old French *preambule*, from Medieval Latin *praeambulum*, from Late Latin *praeambulus*, walking in front : *prae*, in front + *ambulāre*, to walk.] —**pre·am·bu·lar** (prē-ăm′byə-lər), **pre·am·bu·lar·y** (-lĕr′ē) *adj.*

pre·am·pli·fi·er (prē-ăm′plə-fī′ər) n. An electronic circuit or device that detects and sufficiently amplifies weak signals, especially from a radio receiver, for subsequent amplification stages.

pre·ar·range (prē′ə-rānj′) *tr.v.* **-ranged, -ranging, -ranges.** To arrange in advance. —**pre·ar·range·ment** n.

pre·as·signed (prē′ə-sīnd′) *adj.* Assigned beforehand.

pre·a·tom·ic (prē′ə-tŏm′ĭk) *adj.* Of or pertaining to the period preceding the use of atomic energy.

pre·au·di·ence (prē-ô′dē-əns) n. In Britain, the right of certain lawyers to be heard before others when there is no particular order in which business is to be heard in court.

pre·ax·i·al (prē-ăk′sē-əl) *adj.* Anatomically positioned in front of a body axis. —**pre·ax·i·al·ly** *adv.*

preb·end (prĕb′ənd) n. **1.** A clergyman's stipend, drawn from a special endowment belonging to his cathedral or church. **2.** The property or tithe providing the endowment for such a stipend. **3.** The clergyman who receives such a stipend; a prebendary. [Middle English *prebende*, from Old French, from Medieval Latin *praebenda*, from Late Latin, "things to be given," from *praebēre*, to grant : *prae*, forth + *habēre*, to hold, offer.] —**pre·ben·dal** (prĭ-bĕn′dəl, prĕb′ən-dəl) *adj.*

preb·en·dar·y (prĕb′ən-dĕr′ē) n., pl. **-ies. 1.** A clergyman who receives a prebend. **2.** In the Anglican Church, a clergyman holding the honorary title of prebend without a stipend.

prec. preceding.

Pre·cam·bri·an (prē-kăm′brē-ən) *adj.* Of, belonging to, or designating the oldest and largest division of geologic time, preceding the Cambrian, often subdivided into the Archeozoic and Proterozoic eras, and characterized by the appearance of primitive forms of life. —n. The Precambrian era. Preceded by *the*.

pre·can·cel (prē-kăn′səl) *tr.v.* **-celed** or **-celled, -celing** or **-celling, -cels.** To cancel (a postage stamp) before mailing. —n. A precanceled stamp or envelope.

pre·can·cer·ous (prē-kăn′sər-əs) *adj.* Exhibiting a likelihood of becoming cancerous: *precancerous cells*.

pre·car·i·ous (prĭ-kâr′ē-əs) *adj.* **1.** Dangerously lacking in security or stability. **2.** Subject to chance or unknown conditions. **3.** Based upon uncertain or unproved premises: *a precarious argument*. **4.** *Archaic.* Dependent on the will or favor of another. [Latin *precārius*, dependent on prayer, from *precārī*, to entreat, from *prex* (stem *prec-*), entreaty, prayer.] —**pre·car·i·ous·ly** *adv.* —**pre·car·i·ous·ness** n.

pre·cast (prē-kăst′, -käst′) *tr.v.* **-cast, -casting, -casts.** To form (concrete or other building materials) into structurally useful shapes, typically blocks, before use.

prec·a·to·ry (prĕk′ə-tôr′ē, -tōr′ē) *adj.* Also **prec·a·tive** (-tĭv). Relating to or expressing entreaty or supplication. [Late Latin *precātōrius*, from *precārī*, to entreat. See **precarious**.]

pre·cau·tion (prĭ-kô′shən) n. **1.** An action taken in advance to protect against possible failure or danger; a safeguard. **2.** Caution practiced in advance; circumspection. [French *précaution*, from Late Latin *praecautiō*, from Latin *praecavēre*, to guard against before : *prae*, before + *cavēre*, to guard against.]

pre·cau·tion·ar·y (prĭ-kô′shə-nĕr′ē) *adj.* Also **pre·cau·tion·al** (-nəl). **1.** Of or constituting a precaution. **2.** Advising or exercising precaution.

pre·cau·tious (prĭ-kô′shəs) *adj.* Exercising precaution. —**pre·cau·tious·ly** *adv.* —**pre·cau·tious·ness** n.

pre·cede (prĭ-sēd′) v. **-ceded, -ceding, -cedes.** —*tr.* **1.** To come before in time; exist or occur prior to. **2.** To come before in order or rank; surpass; outrank. **3.** To be or go in a position in front of or in advance of. **4.** To preface; introduce: *precede a speech with an anecdote.* —*intr.* To exist or go before. [Middle English *preceden*, from Old French *preceder*, from Latin *praecēdere* : *prae*, before + *cēdere*, to go.]

pre·ced·ence (prĭ-sēd′ns, prĕs′ə-dəns) n. Also **pre·ced·en·cy** (prĭ-sēd′n-sē, prĕs′ə-dən-). **1.** The act, state, or right of preceding. **2.** Priority in importance, position, or rank. **3.** A ceremonial order of rank, observed especially on formal occasions.
    Usage: The preposition that follows the phrase *take* or *have precedence* is *over* (less often *of*, which tends to be more formal). One also gives precedence *to*. The noun *precedent* may be followed by *of* (the precedent of staying for a year) or for (there is no precedent for doing that). The adjective is followed by *to* when it is used after a verb *(His statement was precedent to mine).*

prec·e·dent (prĕs′ə-dənt) n. **1.** An act or instance that may be used as an example in dealing with or justifying subsequent similar cases. **2.** *Law.* A judicial decision that may be used as a standard in subsequent similar cases. —*adj.* (prĭ-sēd′ənt). Preceding; prior. [Middle English, from Old French, from Latin *praecēdēns*, present participle of *praecēdere*, to PRECEDE.] —See Usage note at **precedence**.

prec·e·den·tial (prĕs′ə-dĕn′shəl) *adj.* **1.** Of, pertaining to, or serving as a precedent. **2.** Having precedence.

pre·ced·ing (prĭ-sē′dĭng) *adj.* Abbr. **prec.** Existing or coming before in time, place, rank, or sequence; previous.

pre·cen·tor (prĭ-sĕn′tər) n. **1.** One who directs the singing of the congregation or choir in a church. **2.** In some cathedrals, a member of the clergy who is in charge of music. [Late Latin, from Latin *praecinere*, to sing before : *prae*, before + *canere*, to sing.] —**pre·cen·to·ri·al** (prē′sĕn-tôr′ē-əl, -tōr′ē-əl) *adj.* —**pre·cen·tor·ship** (prĭ-sĕn′tər-shĭp′) n.

pre·cept (prē′sĕpt′) n. **1.** A rule or principle imposing a particular standard of action or conduct. **2.** *Law.* An order or direction from one official to another, as: **a.** A writ or warrant. **b.** *British.* A written order from a sheriff with instructions for holding an election. **3.** *British.* An order from a county council to a rating authority for the levying of rates. [Middle English, from Latin *praeceptum*, from *praecipere* (past participle *praeceptus*), to take beforehand, warn, teach : *prae*, before + *capere*, to take.]

pre·cep·tive (prĭ-sĕp′tĭv) *adj.* **1.** Of or expressing a precept. **2.** Giving precepts; didactic. —**pre·cep·tive·ly** *adv.*

pre·cep·tor (prĭ-sĕp′tər, prē′sĕp′-) n. A teacher; an instructor. [Middle English *preceptur*, from Latin *praeceptor*, teacher, from *praecipere*, to teach. See **precept**.] —**pre·cep·to·ri·al** (prē′sĕp-tôr′ē-əl, -tōr′ē-əl) *adj.* —**pre·cep·to·ri·al·ly** *adv.* —**pre·cep·tor·ship** (prĭ-sĕp′tər-shĭp′, prē′sĕp′-) n.

pre·cep·to·ry (prĭ-sĕp′tə-rē, prē′sĕp′-) n., pl. **-ries.** In the Order of the Knights Templars: **1.** A subordinate community. **2.** The buildings of such a community.

pre·cep·tress (prĭ-sĕp′trĭs, prē′sĕp′-) n. A female preceptor.

pre·cess (prĭ-sĕs′, prē′sĕs′) *intr.v.* **-cessed, -cessing, -cesses.** *Physics & Astronomy.* To move in or be subjected to precession. [Back-formation from PRECESSION.]

pre·ces·sion (prĭ-sĕsh′ən) n. **1.** The act or state of preceding; precedence. **2.** *Physics.* A complex motion executed by a rotating body in which the axis of rotation changes orientation when the body is subject to an applied torque. A torque of constant magnitude will cause the axis to describe a conical locus at a constant angular velocity. **3.** *Astronomy.* Precession of the equinoxes. [New Latin *praecessio*, from Medieval Latin *praecessiō* (stem *praecessiōn-*), a going forward, from Latin *praecēdere* (past participle *praecessus*), to PRECEDE.] —**pre·ces·sion·al** *adj.*

precession of the equinoxes n. *Astronomy.* A slow westward shift of the equinoctial points along the plane of the ecliptic at a rate of 50.27 seconds of arc per year, resulting from precession of the earth's axis of rotation.

pre·cinct (prē′sĭngkt′) n. **1.** *Often* **precincts. a.** A place or enclosure marked off by definite limits, as one that surrounds a church or cathedral. **b.** A boundary. **2. precincts.** Neighborhood; environs. **3.** *Often* **precincts.** An area of thought or action; province. **4. a.** A subdivision or district of a city patrolled by a unit of its police force. **b.** The police station in such a district. **5.** An election district of a city or town. [Middle English *precincte,* from Medieval Latin *praecinctum,* "enclosure," from Latin *praecingere* (past participle *praecinctus*), to gird about : *prae,* before, around + *cingere,* to gird.]

pre·ci·os·i·ty (prĕsh'ē-ŏs'ə-tē, prĕs'ē-) *n., pl.* **-ties.** Extreme meticulousness or overrefinement, as in language. [Middle English *preciousite,* from Old French *precieusite,* from Latin *pretiōsitās,* from *pretiōsus,* PRECIOUS.]

pre·cious (prĕsh'əs) *adj.* **1.** Of high cost or worth; valuable: *precious metal.* **2.** Highly esteemed; cherished. **3.** Dear; beloved. **4.** Affectedly dainty or overrefined. **5.** *Informal.* **a.** Arrant; thoroughgoing. **b.** Used as an intensive: *Take your precious books, for all I care!* —See Synonyms at **costly.**
∼*n.* One who is precious; a darling.
∼*adv.* Used as an intensive: *precious little to eat.* [Middle English, from Old French *precieus, precios,* from Latin *pretiōsus,* from *pretium,* price.] —**pre·cious·ly** *adv.* —**pre·cious·ness** *n.*

precious stone *n.* Any of various minerals, such as diamond, ruby, or sapphire, valued for their rarity or appearance.

prec·i·pice (prĕs'ə-pĭs) *n.* **1.** An extremely steep, high face of a cliff or mass of rock. **2.** The brink of a dangerous situation. [Old French, from Latin *praecipitium,* from *praecipitāre,* to throw headlong. See **precipitate.**]

pre·cip·i·ta·ble (prĭ-sĭp'ə-tə-bəl) *adj.* Capable of being precipitated. [From PRECIPITATE.]

pre·cip·i·tant (prĭ-sĭp'ə-tənt) *adj.* **1.** Rushing or falling headlong. **2.** Impulsive in thought or action; rash. **3.** Abrupt or unexpected; sudden. —See Usage note at **precipitate.**
∼*n.* Any substance that causes precipitation. [French *précipitant,* from Latin *praecipitāns,* present participle of *praecipitāre,* to throw headlong, PRECIPITATE.] —**pre·cip·i·tance, pre·cip·i·tan·cy** *n.* —**pre·cip·i·tant·ly** *adv.*

pre·cip·i·tate (prĭ-sĭp'ə-tāt') *v.* **-tated, -tating, -tates.** —*tr.* **1.** To throw from or as if from a great height; hurl downward. **2.** To cause to happen before anticipated or required. **3.** *Meteorology.* To cause (water vapor) to condense as rain, snow, dew, frost, sleet, or hail. **4.** *Chemistry.* To cause (a solid substance) to be separated from a solution. —*intr.* **1.** *Meteorology.* To condense and fall. **2.** *Chemistry.* To be separated from a solution as a precipitate. **3.** To fall headlong. —See Synonyms at **speed.**
∼*adj.* (-tĭt). **1.** Speeding headlong; moving rapidly and heedlessly. **2.** Acting with excessive haste or impulse; lacking due deliberation. **3.** Occurring suddenly or unexpectedly. —See Synonyms at **reckless.**
∼*n.* (-tāt', -tĭt). *Chemistry.* A solid or solid phase separated from a solution, usually as a suspension of particles that may subsequently settle. [Latin *praecipitāre,* to throw headlong, from *praeceps,* headlong : *prae,* in front + *caput,* head.] —**pre·cip·i·tate·ly** *adv.* —**pre·cip·i·tate·ness** *n.* —**pre·cip·i·ta·tive** (prĭ-sĭp'ə-tā'tĭv, -tə-tĭv) *adj.* —**pre·cip·i·ta·tor** *n.*

Usage: The adjectives *precipitate, precipitant,* and *precipitous* and their corresponding adverbs are sometimes confused. *Precipitate* and *precipitant* apply primarily to rash, overhasty human actions: *That was a very precipitate remark. He acted precipitantly when he resigned. Precipitous* is used primarily of physical steepness: *the precipitous west face of the mountain.*

pre·cip·i·ta·tion (prĭ-sĭp'ə-tā'shən) *n.* **1. a.** The act of precipitating. **b.** The state of being precipitated. **2.** Abrupt or impulsive haste. **3.** *Meteorology.* **a.** Deposition of water droplets or ice particles condensed from atmospheric water vapor as rain, snow, dew, frost, sleet, or hail. **b.** The quantity of such substances falling in a specific area within a specific period. **4.** *Chemistry.* The production of a precipitate.

pre·cip·i·tin (prĭ-sĭp'ə-tĭn) *n. Biochemistry.* An antibody that reacts with an antigen to form a precipitate. [PRECIPIT(ATE) + -IN.]

pre·cip·i·tous (prĭ-sĭp'ə-təs) *adj.* **1.** Like a precipice; extremely steep. **2.** Having several precipices. **3.** Abrupt and ill considered; precipitate. —See Usage note at **precipitate.** [French *précipiteux,* from Old French, from Latin *praecipitium,* PRECIPICE.] —**pre·cip·i·tous·ly** *adv.* —**pre·cip·i·tous·ness** *n.*

pré·cis (prā'sē, prā-sē') *n., pl.* **pré·cis** (prā'sēz, prā-sēz'). A concise summary of the essential facts or statements of a book, article, or other text; an abstract.
∼*tr.v.* **précised, -cising, -cises.** To make a précis of. [French *précis,* "precise," from Old French *precis,* PRECISE.]

pre·cise (prĭ-sīs') *adj.* **1.** Clearly expressed or delineated; distinct; definite: *precise ideas.* **2.** Of or producing great exactness or accuracy: *a precise measurement; precise instruments.* **3.** Exactly corresponding to what is indicated; correct: *the precise amount of seasoning.* **4.** Strictly distinguished from others; very: *at that precise moment.* **5.** Strictly correct in manners, behavior, or the like: *precise in his dress.* [Old French *precis,* from Latin *praecīsus,* shortened, from *praecīdere,* to cut off in front, shorten : *prae,* in front + *caedere,* to cut.] —**pre·cise·ly** *adv.* —**pre·cise·ness** *n.*

pre·ci·sian (prĭ-sĭzh'ən) *n.* A person who is strict and precise in adherence to established rules, forms, or standards; especially, one who is strict in matters of religion or morality. [From PRECISE.] —**pre·ci·sian·ism** *n.*

pre·ci·sion (prĭ-sĭzh'ən) *n.* The state or quality of being precise.
∼*adj.* Precise in nature, action, or performance: *a precision tool; precision handling.* [French *précision,* from Latin *praecīsiō* (stem *praecīsiōn-*), act of cutting, from *praecīdere,* to cut off in front, abridge. See **precise.**] —**pre·ci·sion·ism** *n.* —**pre·ci·sion·ist** *n.*

pre·clin·i·cal (prē-klĭn'ĭ-kəl) *adj.* **1.** Occurring in the early stages of a disease, before diagnosis is possible. **2.** Preparing for or pertaining to the studies that prepare for the study of medicine.

pre·clude (prĭ-klo͞od') *tr.v.* **-cluded, -cluding, -cludes.** **1.** To make impossible or impracticable by previous action; prevent. **2.** To bar or prevent (a person) from something; debar. —See Synonyms at **prevent.** [Latin *praeclūdere* : *prae,* in front + *claudere,* to close.] —**pre·clu·sion** (prĭ-klo͞o'zhən) *n.* —**pre·clu·sive** (-klo͞o'sĭv, -zĭv) *adj.* —**pre·clu·sive·ly** *adv.*

pre·co·cial (prĭ-kō'shəl) *adj.* Covered with down and capable of moving around when first hatched. Said of birds. Compare **altricial.** [New Latin *praecoces,* precocial birds, from Latin *praecox,* PRECOCIOUS.]

pre·co·cious (prĭ-kō'shəs) *adj.* **1.** Characterized by unusually early development or maturity, especially in mental aptitude: *A precocious child, he could read fluently by the age of three.* **2.** Manifesting or characterized by premature or unusually early development. **3.** *Botany.* Blossoming before the leaves sprout. [Latin *praecox,* "ripening before its time," from *praecoquere,* to cook or ripen before : *prae,* before + *coquere,* to cook, ripen.] —**pre·co·cious·ly** *adv.* —**pre·co·cious·ness, pre·coc·i·ty** (prĭ-kŏs'ə-tē) *n.*

pre·cog·ni·tion (prē'kŏg-nĭsh'ən) *n.* **1.** Knowledge of something in advance of its occurrence. **2.** In Scots law, an unsworn statement given by a witness in advance of a trial. [Late Latin *praecognitiō,* from Latin *praecognōscere* (past participle *praecognitus*), to know before : *prae,* before + *cognōscere,* to know (see **cognition**).] —**pre·cog·ni·tive** (prē-kŏg'nə-tĭv) *adj.*

pre-Co·lum·bi·an (prē'kə-lŭm'bē-ən) *adj.* Of, relating to, or originating in the Americas before the voyages of Columbus.

pre·con·ceive (prē'kən-sēv') *tr.v.* **-ceived, -ceiving, -ceives.** To form an opinion or conception of (a matter) beforehand, without knowledge or experience: *preconceived ideas.*

pre·con·cep·tion (prē'kən-sĕp'shən) *n.* **1.** An opinion or conception formed in advance of actual knowledge. **2.** A prejudice.

pre·con·di·tion (prē'kən-dĭsh'ən) *n.* A condition that must exist or be established before something can occur or be considered; a prerequisite.
∼*tr.v.* **preconditioned, -tioning, -tions.** To condition, train, or accustom in advance.

pre·co·nize (prē'kə-nīz') *tr.v.* **-nized, -nizing, -nizes.** **1.** To command or announce in public. **2.** To call or summon in public. **3.** *Roman Catholic Church.* To approve the nomination of (a new bishop) publicly. Used of the pope. [Middle English, from Medieval Latin *praeconizare,* from *praeco* (stem *praecon-*), herald.]

pre·con·scious (prē-kŏn'shəs) *adj.* **1.** *Psychoanalysis.* **a.** Capable of being recalled although not present in the conscious mind. **b.** Of, pertaining to, or being the part of the mind held to be the origin or repository of preconscious processes. **2.** Before the development of consciousness. —See Usage note at **conscious.** —**pre·con·scious·ly** *adv.* —**pre·con·scious·ness** *n.*

pre·con·tract (prē-kŏn'trăkt') *n.* An agreement or contract, as of marriage, entered into beforehand.
∼*v.* (prē'kən-trăkt') **precontracted, -tracting, -tracts.** —*tr.* **1.** To engage (a person) in a contract of marriage by previous agreement. **2.** To establish previously by contract. —*intr.* To enter into a precontract.

pre·cook (prē-ko͝ok') *tr.v.* **-cooked, -cooking, -cooks.** **1.** To cook in advance. **2.** To cook partially before final cooking.

pre·crit·i·cal (prē-krĭt'ĭ-kəl) *adj.* Prior to the occurrence of a critical condition.

pre·cur·sor (prĭ-kûr'sər, prē'kûr'-) *n.* **1.** One that precedes and indicates or announces someone or something to come; a forerunner; a harbinger. **2.** One that precedes another; a predecessor. **3.** A substance that is converted into another substance during a chemical or biochemical reaction. [Latin *praecursor,* from *praecurrere,* to run before : *prae,* before + *currere,* to run.]

pre·cur·so·ry (prĭ-kûr'sə-rē) *adj.* Also **pre·cur·sive** (-sĭv). **1.** Preceding in the manner of a precursor; preliminary; introductory. **2.** Suggesting or indicating something to follow; premonitory.

pred. predicate.

pre·da·cious, pre·da·ceous (prĭ-dā'shəs) *adj.* Living by seizing or taking prey; predatory. Said of such animals as lions and hawks. [Latin *praedārī,* to plunder. See **predatory.**] —**pre·da·cious·ness, pre·dac·i·ty** (prĭ-dăs'ə-tē) *n.*

pre·date (prē-dāt') *tr.v.* **-dated, -dating, -dates.** **1.** To mark or designate with an earlier date than the actual one. **2.** To precede in time; antedate.

pre·da·tion (prĭ-dā'shən) *n.* **1.** The act or practice of plundering or marauding. **2.** A feeding relationship in an ecological community in which one species of animal (the predator) captures, kills, and eats another (the prey). [Latin *praedātiō* (stem *praedātiōn-*), from *praedārī,* to plunder. See **predatory.**]

pred·a·tor (prĕd'ə-tər, -tôr') *n.* One that is predatory; especially, an animal that lives by preying upon others. [Latin *praedātor,* from *praedārī,* to plunder. See **predatory.**]

pred·a·to·ry (prĕd'ə-tôr'ē, -tōr'ē) *adj.* **1.** Of, pertaining to, or characterized by plundering, pillaging, or marauding. **2.** Preying on other animals; predacious. **3.** Characterized by a tendency to exploit or destroy others for one's own gain. [Latin *praedātōrius,* from *prae-*

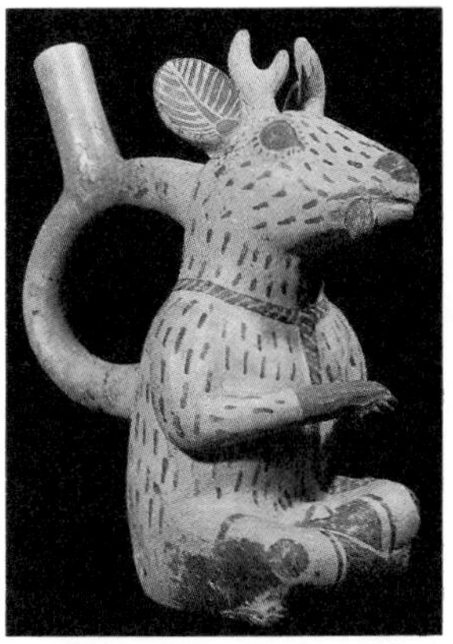

pre-Columbian pottery *A Mochica pot in the form of a man in a deerskin with a rope around his neck, possibly indicating a sacrificial role. The Mochica civilization—in the Moche Valley, on the north coast of Peru—flourished from about 100 B.C. It ended in about A.D. 750, more than 700 years before the arrival of Columbus.*

PRONUNCIATION KEY

ă, pat; ā, pay; âr, care; ä, father, are; b, bib; ch, church; d, deed; ĕ, pet; ē, be; f, fife; g, gag; h, hat; hw, which; ĭ, pit; ī, pie; îr, pier; j, judge; k, kick; l, lid, needle; m, mum; n, no, sudden; ng, thing; ŏ, pot; ō, toe; ô, paw, for; oi, noise; ou, out; o͝o, book; o͞o, boot; p, pop; r, roar; s, sauce; sh, ship, dish; t, tight; th, thin, path; *th,* this, bathe; ŭ, cut; ûr, fur; v, valve; w, with; y, yes; z, zebra, size; zh, vision; ə, about, item, edible, gallop, circus, peaceful

IN FOREIGN WORDS:

à, *Fr.* ami; œ, *Fr.* feu, *Ger.* schön; ü, *Fr.* tu, *Ger.* über; KH, *Ger.* ich, *Scot.* loch; N, *Fr.* bon; y', *Fr.* Compiègne

STRESS MARKS:

Primary stress: ′
in·cite′ (ĭn-sīt′)
Secondary stress: ′
in′sight′ (ĭn′sīt′)

dārī, to plunder, from *praeda,* booty.] —**pred·a·to·ri·ly** (prĕd'ə-tôr'ə-lē, -tōr'ə-lē) *adv.* —**pred·a·to·ri·ness** *n.*

pre·de·cease (prē'dĭ-sēs') *tr.v.* **-ceased, -ceasing, -ceases.** To die before (some other person). —**pre·de·cease** *n.*

pred·e·ces·sor (prĕd'ə-sĕs'ər, prē'də-) *n.* **1.** One who precedes another in time, especially in an office or position. **2.** Something that has been succeeded by another. **3.** An ancestor or forefather. [Middle English *predecessour,* from Old French *predecesseur,* from Late Latin *praedecessor* : Latin *prae,* before + *dēcessor,* one who leaves, from *dēcessus,* past participle of *dēcēdere,* to die, go away : *dē,* away + *cēdere,* to go.]

pre·del·la (prĭ-dĕl'ə) *n., pl.* **-delle** (-dĕl'ē, -dĕl'ā). **1. a.** An altar platform. **b.** Ornamentation on the front side of this platform. **2. a.** A raised shelf at the back of an altar. **b.** Ornamentation on the front side of this shelf. [Italian, stool, step, perhaps from Old High German *bret,* board.]

pre·des·ti·nar·i·an (prē-dĕs'tə-nâr'ē-ən) *adj.* **1.** Of or pertaining to predestination. **2.** Believing in or based on the doctrine of predestination.
~*n.* One who believes in the doctrine of predestination. —**pre·des·ti·nar·i·an·ism** *n.*

pre·des·ti·nate (prē-dĕs'tə-nāt') *tr.v.* **-nated, -nating, -nates. 1.** To destine or determine in advance; foreordain. **2.** *Theology.* To predestine.
~*adj.* (-nĭt, -nāt'). Foreordained; predestined. [Middle English *predestinaten,* from Latin *praedestināre,* to PREDESTINE.]

pre·des·ti·na·tion (prē-dĕs'tə-nā'shən) *n.* **1.** The act of predestining or the condition of being predestined. **2.** *Theology.* **a.** The act whereby God is believed to have foreordained all things. **b.** The doctrine that God has foreordained all things, especially the salvation or damnation of individual souls. **3.** Destiny.

pre·des·tine (prē-dĕs'tĭn) *tr.v.* **-tined, -tining, -tines. 1.** To fix upon, decide, or decree in advance; foreordain. **2.** *Theology.* To foreordain by divine will or decree; predestinate. [Middle English *predestinen,* from Old French *predestiner,* from Latin *praedestināre* : *prae,* before + *dēstināre,* to determine, DESTINE.]

pre·de·ter·mi·nate (prē'dĭ-tûr'mə-nĭt) *adj.* Determined or established beforehand.

pre·de·ter·mine (prē'dĭ-tûr'mĭn) *tr.v.* **-mined, -mining, -mines. 1.** To determine, decide, or establish in advance. **2.** To influence or sway toward an action or opinion; give a tendency to beforehand; predispose. [Late Latin *praedētermināre* : *prae,* before + *dētermināre,* to DETERMINE.] —**pre·de·ter·mi·na·tion** *n.* —**pre·de·ter·mi·na·tive** (prē'dĭ-tûr'mə-nā'tĭv, -nə-tĭv) *adj.* —**pre·de·ter·min·er** *n.*

predial. Variant of **praedial.**

pred·i·ca·ble (prĕd'ĭ-kə-bəl) *adj.* Capable of being stated or predicated.
~*n.* **1.** Something that can be predicated; a quality or attribute. **2.** *Logic.* Any of five general attributes of the Aristotelian class, *genus, species, property, difference,* and *accident,* designating the peculiar relation that a predicate bears to its subject regardless of the quantity or quality of a proposition. [Medieval Latin *praedicābilis,* from Late Latin *praedicāre,* to proclaim, PREDICATE.] —**pred·i·ca·bil·i·ty, pred·i·ca·ble·ness** *n.*

pre·dic·a·ment (prĭ-dĭk'ə-mənt *for senses 1, 2;* prĕd'ĭ-kə- *for sense 3*) *n.* **1.** A troublesome, embarrassing, or ludicrous situation. **2.** *Archaic.* A specific state or condition. **3.** *Logic.* A state or classification of existence. [Middle English, from Late Latin *praedicāmentum* (translation of Greek *katēgoria,* category), something predicated, condition (especially an unpleasant one), from *praedicāre,* to proclaim, PREDICATE.] —**pre·dic·a·men·tal** (prĭ-dĭk'ə-mĕn'təl) *adj.* —**pre·dic·a·men·tal·ly** *adv.*
Synonyms: *dilemma, plight, quandary.*

pred·i·cant (prĕd'ĭ-kənt) *adj.* Concerned with or dedicated to preaching: *a predicant order of priests.*
~*n.* A member of a religious order dedicated to preaching. [Latin *praedicāns* (stem *praedicānt-*), present participle of *praedicāre,* to speak in public. See **predicate.**]

pred·i·cate (prĕd'ĭ-kāt') *v.* **-cated, -cating, -cates.** —*tr.* **1.** To base or establish (a concept, statement, or action). Used with *on* or *upon*: *He predicates his argument on these facts.* **2.** *Logic.* **a.** To state or affirm as an attribute or quality of something: *predicate the perfectibility of mankind.* **b.** To make (a term or expression) the predicate of a proposition. **3.** To carry the connotation of; imply. **4.** To proclaim; assert; declare. —*intr.* To make a statement or assertion.
~*n.* (-kĭt). *Abbr.* **pred. 1.** *Grammar.* The part of a sentence or clause that expresses something about the subject. It regularly consists of a verb and may include objects, modifiers, or complements of the verb. In the simple sentences *The house is white* and *The man hit the dog,* the words *is white* and *hit the dog* are predicates. **2.** *Logic.* Whatever is stated about the subject of a proposition.
~*adj.* (-kĭt). **1.** *Grammar.* Of or belonging to the predicate of a sentence or clause. **2.** Predicated; stated. [Late Latin *praedicāre,* to proclaim, from Latin : *prae,* in front of, in public + *dicāre,* to say.] —**pred·i·ca·tion** *n.*

predicate adjective *n. Grammar.* An adjective that follows certain verbs and describes the subject of the verb. In the sentence *The man is good,* the predicate adjective is *good.*

predicate calculus *n.* The branch of symbolic logic dealing not only with relations between propositions as a whole but also with their internal structure, especially the relation between subject and predicate. Symbols are used to represent the subject and predicate of the proposition, and the existential or universal quantifier is used to denote whether the proposition is universal or particular in its application. Compare **propositional calculus.**

predicate nominative *n. Grammar.* A noun or a pronoun in the subject form that follows certain verbs and is identified with the subject of the verb. In the sentences *It is I* and *He became president,* the predicate nominatives are *I* and *president.*

pred·i·ca·tive (prĕd'ĭ-kā'tĭv, -kə-tĭv) *adj. Grammar.* Pertaining to or designating an adjective, noun, or construction that follows certain verbs, typically copulative verbs, and applies directly to the subject of the verb. For example, in the sentence *The young girl is ill, ill* is predicative. Compare **attributive.**
~*n. Grammar.* A predicative word or construction, especially an adjective. See **predicate adjective, predicate nominative.** —**pred·i·ca·tive·ly** *adv.* —**pred·i·ca·tive·ness** *n.*

pred·i·ca·to·ry (prĕd'ĭ-kə-tôr'ē, -tōr'ē) *adj.* Of, pertaining to, or characteristic of preaching or a preacher. [Late Latin *praedicātōrius,* from *praedicāre,* to proclaim, PREDICATE.]

pre·dict (prĭ-dĭkt') *v.* **-dicted, -dicting, -dicts.** —*tr.* To state, tell about, or make known in advance, especially on the basis of special knowledge; foretell: *predict the weather.* —*intr.* To foretell what will happen; prophesy. —See Synonyms at **foretell.** [Latin *praedīcere* (past participle *praedictus*), to foretell : *prae,* before + *dīcere,* to tell, say.]

pre·dict·a·ble (prĭ-dĭk'tə-bəl) *adj.* **1.** Capable of being predicted or anticipated. **2.** Having no element of originality: *predictable opinions.* —**pre·dict·a·bil·i·ty** *n.* —**pre·dict·a·bly** *adv.*

pre·dic·tion (prĭ-dĭk'shən) *n.* **1.** The act of foretelling or predicting. **2.** Something foretold or predicted; a prophecy. —**pre·dic·tive** *adj.* —**pre·dic·tive·ly** *adv.* —**pre·dic·tive·ness** *n.*

pre·dic·tor (prĭ-dĭk'tər) *n.* **1.** One that predicts. **2.** An instrument that enables an antiaircraft gun to track enemy aircraft.

pre·di·gest (prē'dĭ-jĕst', -dī-jĕst') *tr.v.* **-gested, -gesting, -gests.** To subject (food) to partial digestion. —**pre·di·ges·tion** (prē'dĭ-jĕs'chən, -dī-jĕs'chən) *n.*

pred·i·kant (prĕd'ĭ-känt', prā'dĭ-) *n.* A minister of the Dutch Reformed Church, especially in South Africa. [Dutch, from Latin *praedicāns* (stem *praedicant-*). See **predicant.**]

pred·i·lec·tion (prĕd'l-ĕk'shən, prēd'l-) *n.* A preference or partiality in favor of something; predisposition. [French *prédilection,* from Medieval Latin *praedīligere,* to prefer : Latin *prae,* before + *dīligere,* to love, choose (see **diligent**).]

pre·dis·pose (prē'dĭ-spōz') *tr.v.* **-posed, -posing, -poses. 1.** To make (someone) inclined to something in advance; put into a certain frame of mind for something: *His good manners predispose people to like him.* **2.** To make susceptible or liable. **3.** *Archaic.* To settle or dispose of in advance. —**pre·dis·pos·al** *n.*

pre·dis·po·si·tion (prē-dĭs'pə-zĭsh'ən) *n.* **1.** The state of being predisposed; a tendency or inclination. **2.** Susceptibility to a particular type of disease.

pred·ni·sone (prĕd'nĭ-sōn', -zōn') *n.* A synthetic corticosteroid drug, similar to cortisone, used to treat rheumatic, inflammatory, and allergic conditions. [English *pregnane* (a hydrocarbon) + D(I)- + -(E)N(E) + (CORT)ISONE.]

pre·dom·i·nant (prĭ-dŏm'ə-nənt) *adj.* **1.** Having greatest ascendancy, importance, influence, authority, or force. **2.** Most common or conspicuous; prevailing: *The predominant color was red.* —See Synonyms at **dominant.** [Old French, from Medieval Latin *praedomināns* (stem *praedominant-*), present participle of *praedominārī,* to PREDOMINATE.] —**pre·dom·i·nance, pre·dom·i·nan·cy** *n.* —**pre·dom·i·nant·ly** *adv.*

pre·dom·i·nate (prĭ-dŏm'ə-nāt') *v.* **-nated, -nating, -nates.** —*intr.* **1.** To be of greater power, importance, or quantity; be most important or outstanding. **2.** To have authority, power, or controlling influence; prevail. Often used with *over.* —*tr.* To dominate or prevail over. [Latin *praedominārī,* to subdue beforehand : *prae,* before + *dominārī,* to DOMINATE.] —**pre·dom·i·nate·ly** (prĭ-dŏm'ə-nĭt-lē) *adv.* —**pre·dom·i·nat·ing·ly** *adv.* —**pre·dom·i·na·tion** *n.* —**pre·dom·i·na·tor** *n.*

pre-e·clamp·si·a (prē'ĭ-klămp'sē-ə) *n.* A condition affecting pregnant women that is marked by high blood pressure, swelling of the ankles, and the presence of protein in the urine.

pre-em·i·nent (prē-ĕm'ə-nənt) *adj.* Superior to or notable above all others; outstanding. —See Synonyms at **dominant.** [Late Latin *praeēminēns* (stem *praeēminent-*), from Latin, present participle of *praeēminēre,* to excel : *prae,* in front of + *ēminēre,* to stand out (see **eminent**).] —**pre-em·i·nence** *n.* —**pre-em·i·nent·ly** *adv.*

pre-empt (prē-ĕmpt') *v.* **-empted, -empting, -empts.** —*tr.* **1.** To gain possession of (land, for example) by pre-emption. **2.** To appropriate, seize, or act for oneself before others. **3.** To be presented in place of: *A special news program pre-empted the scheduled show.* **4.** To gain a pre-eminent position in. —*intr.* In bridge, to make a pre-emptive bid. [Back-formation from PRE-EMPTION.] —**pre-emp·tor** (prē-ĕmp'tôr') *n.* —**pre-emp·to·ry** (-tə-rē) *adj.*

pre-emp·tion (prē-ĕmp'shən) *n.* **1. a.** The right to purchase something, especially government-owned land, before others. **b.** A purchase made using such a right. **2.** Acquisition or appropriation of something in advance of others. [Medieval Latin *praeemptiō* (stem *praeemptiōn-*), from *praeemere,* to buy beforehand : *prae,* before + *emere,* to buy.]

pre-emp·tive (prē-ĕmp'tĭv) *adj.* **1.** Of, pertaining to, or characteristic of pre-emption. **2.** Designed to anticipate and frustrate opposition: *a pre-emptive strike against the enemy.* **3.** Designating or characteristic of a high bid in bridge that is intended to prevent the opposing players from bidding. **—pre·emp·tive·ly** *adv.*

preen (prēn) *v.* **preened, preening, preens.** *—tr.* **1.** To smooth or clean (feathers) with the bill. Used of a bird. **2.** To dress or groom (oneself) carefully; primp. **3.** To take pride or satisfaction in (oneself); gloat: *preening themselves on having won another victory.* *—intr.* **1.** To dress up; primp. **2.** To smooth or clean feathers with the bill. Used of a bird. [Middle English *preinen, proinen, prunen,* perhaps a variant of PRUNE, influenced by dialectal *preen*†, to pierce.] **—preen·er** *n.*

pre·ex·il·i·an (prē'ĕg-zĭl'ē-ən, -zĭl'yən, -ĕk-sĭl'ē-ən, -sĭl'yən) *adj.* Also **pre·ex·il·ic** (-ĕg-zĭl'ĭk, -ĕk-sĭl'ĭk). Of or pertaining to the history of the Jewish people prior to their exile in Babylonia at the end of the 6th century B.C.

pre·ex·ist (prē'ĭg-zĭst') *v.* **-isted, -isting, -ists.** *—intr.* To exist before. *—tr.* To exist before (something): *dinosaurs that pre-existed mammals.* **—pre·ex·ist·ence** *n.* **—pre·ex·ist·ent** *adj.*

pref. **1.** preface; prefatory. **2.** preference; preferred. **3.** prefix.

pre·fab (prē'făb') *n.* A prefabricated part or building.

pre·fab·ri·cate (prē-făb'rĭ-kāt') *tr.v.* **-cated, -cating, -cates. 1.** To construct or manufacture in advance. **2.** To produce standard sections of (a house, for example) that can be easily assembled. **—pre·fab·ri·ca·tion** *n.* **—pre·fab·ri·ca·tor** *n.*

pref·ace (prĕf'ĭs) *n. Abbr.* **pref. 1. a.** A statement or essay, usually by the author, introducing a book and explaining its scope, intention, or background. **b.** The introductory section of a speech. **2.** Something introductory or preliminary. **3.** *Usually* **Preface.** A thanksgiving prayer ending with the Sanctus and introducing the Eucharistic prayer of the Roman Catholic Mass.

~tr.v. **prefaced, -acing, -aces. 1.** To introduce by or provide with a preliminary statement or essay. **2.** To serve as an introduction to. [Middle English, from Old French, from Medieval Latin *prefātia,* alteration of Latin *praefātiō,* a saying beforehand, from *praefārī,* to say beforehand : *prae,* before + *fārī,* to speak.] **—pref·ac·er** *n.*

pref·a·to·ry (prĕf'ə-tôr'ē, -tōr'ē) *adj.* Also **pref·a·to·ri·al** (prĕf'ə-tôr'ē-əl, -tōr'ē-əl). *Abbr.* **pref.** Of the nature of or serving as an introductory statement or essay; preliminary. [Latin *prefātiō,* PREFACE.]

pre·fect (prē'fĕkt') *n.* Also **prae·fect** (for senses 1, 3). **1.** Any of several high military or civil officials, such as magistrates or administrators, of ancient Rome. **2. a.** In some countries, such as France or Italy, a high-ranking administrative official in the provinces. **b.** The chief of police in Paris, France. **3.** *Roman Catholic Church.* A cardinal presiding over a congregation of the Curia. **4.** A senior pupil with limited disciplinary power over other pupils, especially in a private school. [Middle English, from Old French, from Latin *praefectus,* overseer, chief, from the past participle of *praeficere,* to place at the head of : *prae,* before + *facere,* to do.]

prefect apostolic *n., pl.* **prefects apostolic.** A Roman Catholic priest with broad jurisdiction in an area where no bishop has been appointed.

pre·fec·ture (prē'fĕk'chər) *n.* **1. a.** The office or authority of a prefect. **b.** The district of a prefect. **2.** The residence or offices of a prefect. **—pre·fec·tur·al** (prĭ-fĕk'chər-əl) *adj.*

pre·fer (prĭ-fûr') *tr.v.* **-ferred, -ferring, -fers. 1.** To choose rather than another or others as better or more to one's taste; value more highly; like better: *prefer to walk; prefers cider to beer.* **2.** *Law.* To give priority or precedence to (a creditor). **3.** *Law.* To enter, prosecute, or offer for consideration or resolution before a legal body: *He preferred charges against her for theft.* **4.** *Archaic.* To recommend for advancement or appointment. [Middle English *preferren,* from Old French *preferer,* from Latin *praeferre,* to hold or set before : *prae,* before + *ferre,* to bear.] **—pre·fer·rer** *n.*

Usage: When the object of *prefer* is an infinitive, the construction following is introduced by *rather than*: *I prefer to ride rather than to walk.* It is possible to omit the second *to* (*. . . to ride rather than walk*), but it is not acceptable in standard English to omit *rather.* In all other constructions *prefer* is followed by *to*: *I prefer riding to walking. I prefer coffee to tea. Than* can never be used in such constructions, though *rather than* is sometimes heard in informal speech (*I prefer coffee rather than tea*). In such cases stricter usage prefers the *to* construction or an alternative containing *have* (*I would rather have coffee than tea*) or *instead of* (*I would rather have coffee instead of tea*).

pref·er·a·ble (prĕf'ər-ə-bəl, prĕf'rə-) *adj.* More desirable or worthy; preferred. **—pref·er·a·bil·i·ty, pref·er·a·ble·ness** *n.* **—pref·er·a·bly** *adv.*

pref·er·ence (prĕf'ər-əns, prĕf'rəns) *n. Abbr.* **pref. 1. a.** The selecting of someone or something over another or others. **b.** Someone or something so chosen. **2.** The state of being better liked or more highly valued. **3.** *Law.* **a.** The paying of one or more creditors by an insolvent debtor before or to the exclusion of other creditors. **b.** The right to be so paid. **4.** The granting of precedence or advantage to one over all others, as to one country or group of countries in levying duties. —See Synonyms at **choice.** [French *préférence,* from Medieval Latin *praeferentia,* from Latin *praeferēns,* present participle of *praeferre,* to PREFER.]

preference shares *pl.n. British.* Preferred stock.

pref·er·en·tial (prĕf'ə-rĕn'shəl) *adj.* **1.** Of, having, providing, or obtaining advantage or preference: *The old patients receive preferential treatment.* **2.** Manifesting or originating from partiality or preference, as in international trade: *preferential tariff rates.* **—pref·er·en·tial·ism** *n.* **—pref·er·en·tial·ist** *n.* **—pref·er·en·tial·ly** *adv.*

preferential voting *n.* A system of voting in which the voter indicates his choices in order of preference.

pre·fer·ment (prĭ-fûr'mənt) *n.* **1.** The act of advancing to a higher position or office; promotion. **2.** A position, appointment, or rank giving advancement. [Middle English *preferrement,* from *preferren,* to PREFER.]

preferred stock *n.* The portion of a corporation's stock having a priority or preference over the common stock in the distribution of dividends and assets.

pre·fig·u·ra·tion (prē-fĭg'yə-rā'shən) *n.* **1.** The act of representing, suggesting, or imagining in advance. **2.** Something that prefigures. **—pre·fig·ur·a·tive** (prē-fĭg'yər-ə-tĭv) *adj.* **—pre·fig·ur·a·tive·ly** *adv.* **—pre·fig·ur·a·tive·ness** *n.*

pre·fig·ure (prē-fĭg'yər) *tr.v.* **-ured, -uring, -ures. 1.** To suggest, indicate, or represent by an antecedent form or model; presage; foreshadow: *The art and theories of Cézanne prefigured the cubist school of art.* **2.** To imagine or picture to oneself in advance. [Middle English *prefiguren,* from Late Latin *praefigūrāre,* to shape beforehand : *prae,* before + *figūrāre,* to shape, from *figūra,* FIGURE.] **—pre·fig·ure·ment** *n.*

pre·fix (prē-fĭks', prē'fĭks') *tr.v.* **-fixed, -fixing, -fixes. 1.** To put or fix in advance. **2.** To add as a prefix.

~n. (prē'fĭks'). **1.** *Abbr.* **pref.** *Grammar.* An affix, such as *dis-* in *disbelieve,* put before a word to produce a derivative word or an inflected form. **2.** A title placed before a person's name. [New Latin *praefixum,* a prefix, from Latin *praefīgere* (past participle *praefīxus*), to fix before : *prae,* before + *fīgere,* to fix.] **—pre·fix·al** (prē'fĭk'səl, prē-fĭk'səl) *adj.* **—pre·fix·al·ly** *adv.*

pre·for·ma·tion (prē'fôr-mā'shən) *n.* **1.** The act of shaping or forming in advance; prior formation. **2.** *Biology.* A now invalidated biological theory that all parts of a future organism exist completely formed in the germ cell and develop only by increasing in size. **—pre·for·ma·tion·ism** *n.*

pre·fron·tal lobe (prē-frŭnt'l) *n.* The part of each cerebral hemisphere of the brain situated in front of the frontal lobe.

prefrontal lobotomy *n.* An operation in which the white fibers connecting the prefrontal and frontal lobes of the brain to the thalamus are severed.

preg·na·ble (prĕg'nə-bəl) *adj.* Vulnerable to seizure or capture, as a fort. [Earlier *preignable,* Middle English *prenable,* from Old French, from *prendre,* to take, capture, from Latin *prehendere.*] **—preg·na·bil·i·ty** *n.*

preg·nan·cy (prĕg'nən-sē) *n., pl.* **-cies. 1.** The condition of being pregnant. **2.** An instance of being pregnant. **3.** The period during which a developing fetus is carried within the uterus.

preg·nant (prĕg'nənt) *adj.* **1.** Carrying a developing fetus within the uterus. **2.** Creative; inventive. **3.** Fraught with significance or implication: *a pregnant silence.* **4. a.** Abounding; profuse. **b.** Filled; fraught: *pregnant with fate.* **5.** Producing results; fruitful: *a pregnant decision.* [Middle English, from Latin *praegnāns* (stem *praegnānt-*), variant of *praegnās,* probably *prae,* before + *gnascī,* to be born.] **—preg·nant·ly** *adv.*

pre·heat (prē-hēt') *tr.v.* **-heated, -heating, -heats.** To heat beforehand: *preheat the oven for 30 minutes.*

pre·hen·sile (prē-hĕn'səl, -sīl') *adj.* Adapted for seizing or holding, especially by wrapping around an object: *a prehensile tail.* [French *préhensile,* from Latin *prehendere* (past participle *prehensus*), to seize.] **—pre·hen·sil·i·ty** (prē'hĕn-sĭl'ə-tē) *n.*

pre·hen·sion (prĭ-hĕn'shən) *n.* **1.** The act of grasping or seizing. **2. a.** Apprehension by the senses. **b.** Understanding. [Latin *prehensiō* (stem *prehensiōn-*), from *prehendere* (past participle *prehensus*), to seize.]

pre·his·tor·ic (prē'hĭ-stôr'ĭk, -stŏr'ĭk) *adj.* Also **pre·his·tor·i·cal** (-ĭ-kəl). **1.** Of, pertaining to, or belonging to the era before recorded history. **2.** Very old-fashioned or out-of-date. Used humorously. **—pre·his·tor·i·cal·ly** *adv.*

pre·his·to·ry (prē-hĭs'tə-rē) *n.* **1. a.** The history of mankind in the period before written or recorded history, investigated by archaeology. **b.** The study of prehistory. **2.** The history of the earlier stages of an event or incident. **—pre·his·to·ri·an** (prē'hĭ-stôr'ē-ən, -stŏr'ē-ən) *n.*

pre·ig·ni·tion (prē'ĭg-nĭsh'ən) *n.* The ignition of fuel in an internal-combustion engine before the spark passes through the fuel.

pre·judge (prē-jŭj') *tr.v.* **-judged, -judging, -judges.** To judge beforehand without adequate evidence. [French *préjuger,* from Latin *praejūdicāre* : *prae,* before + *jūdicāre,* to judge, from *jūdex,* JUDGE.] **—pre·judg·er** *n.* **—pre·judg·ment, pre·judge·ment** *n.*

prej·u·dice (prĕj'ə-dĭs) *n.* **1. a.** An adverse judgment or opinion formed beforehand or without knowledge or examination of the facts. **b.** A preconceived preference or idea; a bias. **2.** The act or state of holding unreasonable preconceived judgments or convictions. **3.** Irrational suspicion or hatred of a particular group, race, or religion. **4.** Detriment or injury caused to a person by the preconceived and unfavorable conviction of another or others. Now rare except in the phrase *in* or *to the prejudice of.* **—without prejudice.** *Law.* Without affecting any right or claim.

~tr.v. **prejudiced, -dicing, -dices. 1.** To cause (a person) to judge prematurely and irrationally; bias. **2.** To affect injuriously or detrimentally by some judgment or act. [Middle English, from Old French, from Latin *praejūdicium* : *prae,* before + *jūdicium,* judgment, from *jūdex,* JUDGE.]

prej·u·di·cial (prĕj'ə-dĭsh'əl) *adj.* Causing or of the nature of prejudice; detrimental. **—prej·u·di·cial·ly** *adv.*

prel·a·cy (prĕl'ə-sē) *n., pl.* **-cies. 1. a.** The office or station of a

PRONUNCIATION KEY

ă, pat; ā, pay; âr, care;
ä, father, are; b, bib;
ch, church; d, deed; ĕ, pet;
ē, be; f, fife; g, gag; h, hat;
hw, which; ĭ, pit; ī, pie;
îr, pier; j, judge; k, kick;
l, lid, needle; m, mum;
n, no, sudden; ng, thing;
ŏ, pot; ō, toe; ô, paw, for;
oi, noise; ou, out; ŏŏ, book;
ōō, boot; p, pop; r, roar;
s, sauce; sh, ship, dish;
t, tight; th, thin, path;
th, this, bathe; ŭ, cut; ûr, fur;
v, valve; w, with; y, yes;
z, zebra, size; zh, vision;
ə, about, item, edible, gallop, circus, peaceful

IN FOREIGN WORDS:

à, *Fr.* ami; œ, *Fr.* feu, *Ger.* schön; ü, *Fr.* tu, *Ger.* über; KH, *Ger.* ich, *Scot.* loch; N, *Fr.* bon; y', *Fr.* Compiègne

STRESS MARKS:

Primary stress: '
in·cite' (ĭn-sīt')
Secondary stress: '
in'sight' (ĭn'sīt')

prelate. **b.** Prelates collectively. **2.** Church government administrated by prelates.

prel·ate (prĕl′ĭt) *n.* A high-ranking clergyman such as a bishop or an abbot. [Middle English *prelat,* from Old French, from Medieval Latin *praelātus,* from Latin (past participle of *praeferre,* to bear before, prefer) : *prae,* before + *-lātus,* "carried."] **—pre·lat·ic** (prī-lăt′ĭk) *adj.*

prelate nul·li·us (nŏŏ-lē′əs) *n.* A Roman Catholic prelate, usually a titular bishop, who has jurisdiction over a territory not in a diocese but subject directly to the Holy See. [PRELATE + Latin *nūllius,* of nobody, from *nūllus,* NULL.]

pre·lect (prī-lĕkt′) *intr.v.* **-lected, -lecting, -lects.** To lecture or discourse in public. [Latin *praelegere* (past participle *praelectus*) : *prae,* in front of, in public + *legere,* to read.] **—pre·lec·tion** *n.* **—pre·lec·tor** *n.*

pre·li·ba·tion (prē′lī-bā′shən) *n.* A foretaste. [Latin *praelībātiō* (stem *praelībātiōn-*), from *praelībāre,* to taste beforehand : *prae,* before + *lībāre,* to taste.]

pre·lim (prē′lĭm, prī-lĭm′) *n. Informal.* A preliminary.
~*adj. Informal.* Preliminary.

pre·lim·i·nar·y (prī-lĭm′ə-nĕr′ē) *adj.* Prior to or preparing for the main matter, action, or business; introductory; prefatory.
~*n., pl.* **preliminaries. 1.** Something, such as a statement or action, that is antecedent or preparatory. **2. a.** An academic test or examination that is preparatory to one that is longer, more complex, or more important. **b.** *Sports.* An event that precedes the main event of a program, especially in boxing or wrestling. **3. preliminaries.** *Printing.* Material that precedes the actual text of a book, as the title pages, preface, or dedication. [French *préliminaire,* from Medieval Latin *praelīmināris* : *prae,* before + *līmināris,* of a threshold, from *līmen,* threshold, lintel (see **limen**).] **—pre·lim·i·nar·i·ly** (prī-lĭm′ə-nâr′ə-lē) *adv.*

pre·lit·er·ate (prē-lĭt′ər-ĭt) *adj.* Of or pertaining to any culture not having a written language.

prel·ude (prĕl′yŏŏd, prā′lŏŏd, prē′-) *n.* **1.** Something that precedes or introduces a performance, event, or action. **2.** *Music.* A piece or movement serving as an introduction to a musical composition, as: **a.** An independent piece of moderate length that precedes a fugue. **b.** The opening section of a suite. **c.** The overture to an opera or oratorio or a similar piece played before one of the acts of an opera. **d.** A piece played before a church service; an introductory voluntary. **e.** A relatively short composition in a free style, usually for piano or orchestra.
~*v.* **preluded, -uding, -udes.** —*tr.* **1.** To serve as a prelude to. **2.** To introduce with or as if with a prelude. —*intr.* To serve as a prelude or introduction. [Old French, from Medieval Latin *praelūdium,* from Latin *praelūdere,* to play beforehand : *prae,* before + *lūdere,* to play, from *lūdus,* game.] **—prel·ud·er** *n.* **—pre·lu·di·al** (prī-lŏŏ′dē-əl) *adj.*

prem. premium.

pre·mar·i·tal (prē-măr′ə-təl) *adj.* Occurring before marriage: *premarital sex.*

pre·ma·ture (prē′mə-chŏŏr′, -tŏŏr′, -tyŏŏr′) *adj.* **1.** Occurring, growing, or existing prior to the customary, correct, or assigned time; uncommonly or unexpectedly early: *a premature end.* **2.** Too hurried or impulsive. **3.** Born or occurring after a gestation period of less than the normal time: *a premature baby.* [Latin *praemātūrus* : *prae,* before + *mātūrus,* ripe, MATURE.] **—pre·ma·ture·ly** *adv.* **—pre·ma·ture·ness, pre·ma·tu·ri·ty** (prē′mə-chŏŏr′ə-tē, -tŏŏr′ə-tē, -tyŏŏr′ə-tē) *n.*

pre·max·il·la (prē′măk-sĭl′ə) *n., pl.* **-maxillae** (-măk-sĭl′ē). Either of two bones located in front of and between the maxillary bones in the upper jaw of vertebrates. **—pre·max·il·lar·y** (prē-măk′sə-lĕr′ē) *adj.*

pre·med (prē′mĕd′) *n. Informal.* **1.** A premedical student. **2.** Premedication.
~*adj. Informal.* Premedical.

pre·med·i·cal (prē-mĕd′ĭ-kəl) *adj.* Preparing for or preparatory to the study of medicine.

pre·med·i·ca·tion (prē-mĕd′ĭ-kā′shən) *n.* Drugs, including a sedative, administered before a general anesthetic to prepare a patient for surgery.

pre·med·i·tate (prē-mĕd′ə-tāt′) *v.* **-tated, -tating, -tates.** —*tr.* To plan, arrange, or plot (a deed or events) in advance. —*intr.* To meditate or deliberate beforehand. [Latin *praemeditārī* : *prae,* before + *meditārī,* to MEDITATE.] **—pre·med·i·ta·tive** (prē-mĕd′ə-tā′tĭv) *adj.* **—pre·med·i·ta·tor** *n.*

pre·med·i·tat·ed (prē-mĕd′ə-tā′tĭd) *adj.* Characterized by deliberate purpose, previous consideration, and some degree of planning. **—pre·med·i·tat·ed·ly** *adv.*

pre·med·i·ta·tion (prē-mĕd′ə-tā′shən) *n.* **1.** The act of speculating, arranging, or plotting in advance. **2.** *Law.* The contemplation and plotting of a crime in advance, showing intent to commit the crime.

pre·men·stru·al syndrome (prē-mĕn′strŏŏ-əl) *n. Abbr.* **PMS** A group of symptoms including emotional disturbance, fatigue, irritability, and sometimes depression that affects some women for up to about a week before menstruation. It is associated with retention of water and salts in the tissues. Also called "premenstrual stress."

pre·mi·er (prē-mēr′, prĕm′ē-ər, prĕm′ē-, prī-mîr′) *adj.* **1.** First in status or importance; chief. **2.** First to occur or exist; earliest.
~*n.* **1.** The head of government in some countries; especially, a prime minister. **2.** The chief executive of a Canadian province or an Australian state. [Middle English *primier,* from Old French *pre-*

mier, first, chief, from Latin *prīmārius,* of the first rank, from *prīmus,* first.] **—pre·mier·ship** (prī-mîr′shĭp′) *n.*

pre·mière (prī-mîr′, prĭm-yâr′) *n.* **1.** The first public presentation of a performance, as a film or play. **2.** The leading lady of a theatrical company.
~*v.* **premièred, -mièring, -mières.** —*tr.* To present the first public performance of. —*intr.* To have the first public presentation.
~*adj.* Outstanding; premier. [French, feminine of *premier,* first, chief, PREMIER.]

pre·mil·le·nar·i·an (prē-mĭl′ə-nâr′ē-ən) *adj.* Of or pertaining to premillennialism.
~*n.* A person who believes in premillennialism. Compare **postmillenarian.**

pre·mil·len·ni·al (prē′mĭ-lĕn′ē-əl) *adj.* Of or happening before the millennium.

pre·mil·len·ni·al·ism (prē′mĭ-lĕn′ē-ə-lĭz′əm) *n.* The belief that Christ's second coming will immediately precede the millennium. Compare **postmillennialism. —pre·mil·len·ni·al·ist** *n.*

Prem·in·ger (prĕm′ĭn-jər), **Otto Ludwig** (1906–86). Austrian-born U.S. film director. Among his most successful films are *Laura* (1944) and *Anatomy of a Murder* (1959).

prem·ise (prĕm′ĭs) *n.* **1. a.** A proposition upon which an argument is based or from which a conclusion is drawn. **b.** *Logic.* One of the first two propositions (major or minor) of a syllogism, from which the conclusion is drawn. **2. premises.** *Law.* **a.** Matter previously referred to in a document; the aforesaid. **b.** The preliminary or explanatory statements or facts of a document, as in a conveyance or deed. **3. premises. a.** Land and the buildings upon it. **b.** A building or part of a building.
~*v.* **premised, -ising, -ises.** —*tr.* **1.** To state in advance as an introduction or explanation. **2.** To state or assume as a proposition in an argument. —*intr.* To make a premise. [Middle English *premisse,* from Old French, from Medieval Latin *praemissa (prōpositiō),* "(proposition) put before," from *praemissus,* past participle of *praemittere,* to send ahead : *prae,* before + *mittere,* to send.]

pre·mi·um (prē′mē-əm) *n., pl.* **-ums.** *Abbr.* **pm., prem. 1.** A prize awarded for a particular act. **2.** Something offered free or at a reduced price as an inducement to buy. **3.** A sum of money or bonus paid in addition to a regular price, salary, or other amount. **4.** The amount paid, often in addition to the interest, to obtain a loan. **5.** The amount paid or payable, often in installments, for an insurance policy. **6.** The amount at which something is valued above its par or nominal value, as money or securities. **7.** Payment for training in a trade or profession. **8.** An unusual or high value: *put a premium on honesty and hard work.* —See Synonyms at **bonus.** **—at a premium. 1.** Above par or an average. **2.** In great demand; more valuable than usual.
~*adj.* Of high quality. [Latin *praemium,* profit derived from booty, "that which is obtained before others" : *prae,* before + *emere,* to take.]

pre·mo·lar (prē-mō′lər) *n.* Any of eight bicuspid teeth located in pairs on each side of the upper and lower jaws behind the canines and in front of the molars. **—pre·mo·lar** *adj.*

pre·mo·ni·tion (prē′mə-nĭsh′ən, prĕm′ə-) *n.* **1.** A warning in advance; a forewarning. **2.** A presentiment of the future; a foreboding. [Old French, from Late Latin *praemonitiō* (stem *praemonitiōn-*), from Latin *praemonēre,* to warn beforehand : *prae,* before + *monēre,* to warn.] **—pre·mon·i·to·ri·ly** (prē-mŏn′ə-tôr′ə-lē, -tôr′ə-lē) *adv.* **—pre·mon·i·to·ry** (prē-mŏn′ə-tôr′ē, -tôr′ē) *adj.*

pre·morse (prī-môrs′) *adj. Biology.* Abruptly truncated, as though bitten or broken off: *premorse leaves.* [Latin *praemorsus,* past participle of *praemordēre,* to bite off in front : *prae,* in front + *mordēre,* to bite.]

pre·mu·ni·tion (prē′myŏŏ-nĭsh′ən) *n.* Relative immunity to severe infection as a result of inducing an active low-grade infection. [Latin *praemūnitiō* (stem *praemūnitiōn-*), fortification beforehand, from *praemūnīre,* to fortify beforehand : *prae,* before + *mūnīre,* to fortify.] **—pre·mune** (prē-myŏŏn′) *adj.*

pre·name (prē′nām′) *n.* A first name.

pre·na·tal (prē-nāt′l) *adj.* Existing or taking place prior to birth; preceding birth. **—pre·na·tal·ly** *adv.*

prenatal diagnosis *n.* Examination of a pregnant woman in order to discover genetic, developmental, or other abnormalities in the fetus. Techniques used include amniocentesis.

pren·tice (prĕn′tĭs) *n. Archaic.* An apprentice.
~*adj. Archaic.* **1.** Of or pertaining to an apprentice. **2.** Inexperienced; unskilled.
~*tr.v.* **-ticed, -ticing, -tices.** *Archaic.* To take on or place as an apprentice.

pre·oc·cu·pan·cy (prē-ŏk′yə-pən-sē) *n.* **1.** The act or right of taking possession before others; preoccupation. **2.** The state of being preoccupied or engrossed.

pre·oc·cu·pa·tion (prē-ŏk′yə-pā′shən) *n.* **1.** The state of being preoccupied; absorption of the attention or intellect. **2.** Something that preoccupies or engrosses the mind: *Increasing the profits of his factory was his sole preoccupation.* **3.** Possession or occupation in advance; preoccupancy.

pre·oc·cu·pied (prē-ŏk′yə-pīd′) *adj.* **1. a.** Absorbed in thought; engrossed. **b.** Excessively concerned with something; distracted. **2.** Formerly or already occupied. **3.** Already used and therefore unavailable for further use. Said of taxonomic names.

pre·oc·cu·py (prē-ŏk′yə-pī′) *tr.v.* **-pied, -pying, -pies. 1.** To occupy completely the mind or attention of; engross. **2.** To occupy or take possession of in advance or before another. [Latin *praeoccupāre* : *prae,* before + *occupāre,* to OCCUPY.]

pre·or·dain (prē′ôr-dān′) *tr.v.* **-dained, -daining, -dains.** To appoint, decree, or ordain in advance; foreordain. **—pre·or·dain·ment, pre·or·di·na·tion** (prē-ôr′də-nā′shən) *n.*

prep (prĕp) *adj. Informal.* Preparatory: *a prep course.*
—n. Informal. **1.** A preparatory school. **2.** *British.* **a.** The preparing of lessons; homework. **b.** Time set aside for this.
—v. **prepped, prepping, preps.** *Informal. —intr.* **1.** To attend a preparatory school. **2.** To study or train in preparation for something. *—tr.* To prepare (a person) for medical examination or surgery.

prep. 1. preparation; preparatory. **2.** preposition.

pre·pack·age (prē-păk′ĭj) *tr.v.* **-aged, -aging, -ages.** To wrap or pack (products) before marketing to consumers.

prep·a·ra·tion (prĕp′ə-rā′shən) *n. Abbr.* **prep. 1.** The act or process of preparing. **2.** The state of being made ready beforehand; readiness. **3.** *Often* **preparations.** A preliminary measure that serves to make ready for something: *preparations for the wedding reception.* **4.** A substance, such as a medicine, prepared for a particular purpose. **5.** *Music.* **a.** The anticipation of a dissonant note by means of its introduction as a consonant note in the preceding chord. **b.** The note so used.

pre·par·a·tive (prĭ-păr′ə-tĭv, prĭ-pâr′-) *adj.* Serving or tending to prepare or make ready; preparatory.
—n. Something that prepares for something following. **—pre·par·a·tive·ly** *adv.*

pre·par·a·to·ry (prĭ-păr′ə-tôr′ē, -tōr′ē, prĭ-pâr′-) *adj. Abbr.* **prep. 1.** Serving to make ready or prepare. **2.** Preliminary; introductory. **3.** Occupied in or pertaining to preparation, especially for admission to college. **—preparatory to.** In preparation for. **—pre·par·a·to·ri·ly** (prĭ-păr′ə-tôr′ə-lē, -tōr′ə-lē, prĭ-pâr′-) *adv.*

preparatory school *n.* **1.** A secondary school, usually private, preparing students for college. **2.** In Britain, a school, usually private, for pupils up to the age of 13, attended in preparation for public schools.

pre·pare (prĭ-pâr′) *v.* **-pared, -paring, -pares.** *—tr.* **1.** To make ready beforehand for a specific purpose, event, occasion, or experience: *prepared the fish for cooking; wasn't prepared for the shock.* **2. a.** To put together or make by combining various elements or ingredients; manufacture or compound: *The druggist prepared the prescription while I waited.* **b.** To compose (a speech, for example) in writing for subsequent use. **3.** To fit out; equip: *The troops were prepared for service in the Arctic.* **4.** *Music.* To lead up to and soften (a dissonance or its impact) by means of preparation. *—intr.* To put things or oneself in readiness; get ready: *We prepared for our trip.* [Middle English *preparen,* from Old French *preparer,* from Latin *praeparāre,* to prepare in advance : *prae,* before + *parāre,* to make ready.] **—pre·par·er** *n.*

pre·pared (prĭ-pârd′) *adj.* **1.** Subjected to preparation. **2.** Being in an appropriate frame of mind: *Both sides were prepared to meet.* **—pre·par·ed·ly** (prĭ-pâr′ĭd-lē) *adv.*

pre·par·ed·ness (prĭ-pâr′ĭd-nĭs) *n.* The state of being prepared; especially, military readiness for war.

pre·pay (prē-pā′) *tr.v.* **-paid** (-pād′), **-paying, -pays.** To pay or pay for beforehand. **—pre·pay·ment** *n.*

pre·pense (prĭ-pĕns′) *adj. Law.* Contemplated in advance; premeditated. Used chiefly in the phrase *malice prepense.* [Variant of obsolete *prepensed, purpensed,* from Middle English *purpensen,* to think of in advance, from Old French *pourpenser,* to premeditate : *pour,* forth, before, from Latin *prō-* + *penser,* to think, from Latin *pensāre,* frequentative of *pendere,* to weigh.] **—pre·pense·ly** *adv.*

pre·pon·der·ance (prĭ-pŏn′dər-əns) *n.* Also **pre·pon·der·an·cy** (-ən-sē). Superiority, as in weight, quantity, power, or importance.

pre·pon·der·ant (prĭ-pŏn′dər-ənt) *adj.* Being superior, as in power, force, or importance; predominant. —See Synonyms at **dominant.** **—pre·pon·der·ant·ly** *adv.*

pre·pon·der·ate (prĭ-pŏn′də-rāt′) *intr.v.* **-ated, -ating, -ates. 1.** To exceed something else in weight. **2.** To be greater, as in power, force, quantity, or importance; predominate. **3.** *Archaic.* To be weighed down, as one end of a balance.
—adj. (-dər-ĭt). Preponderant. [Latin *praeponderāre* : *prae,* in front of, exceeding + *ponderāre,* to weigh, from *pondus* (stem *ponder-*), weight.] **—pre·pon·der·ate·ly, pre·pon·der·at·ing·ly** *adv.* **—pre·pon·der·a·tion** *n.*

prep·o·si·tion (prĕp′ə-zĭsh′ən) *n. Abbr.* **prep.** *Grammar.* **1.** In some languages, a word that indicates the relation of a substantive to a verb, an adjective, or another substantive. Some English prepositions are *at, by, in, to, from,* and *with.* **2.** A word or construction similar in function to a preposition, as *with regard to* or *concerning.* [Middle English *preposicioun,* from Latin *praepositiō* (translation of Greek *prothesis*), from *praepōnere* (past participle *praepositus*), to place in front : *prae,* in front + *pōnere,* to place.]

prep·o·si·tion·al (prĕp′ə-zĭsh′ə-nəl) *adj.* **1.** Pertaining to, composed of, or used as a preposition. **2.** Designating, pertaining to, or inflected in the prepositional.
—n. **1.** The grammatical case in certain Indo-European languages, such as Russian, that is used only as the object of prepositions. **2.** A form or construction in this case. **—prep·o·si·tion·al·ly** *adv.*

prepositional phrase *n. Grammar.* A phrase consisting of a preposition and the noun it governs and having adjectival or adverbial value; for example, in the phrases *a dress of wool* and *written in haste,* the prepositional phrases are *of wool* (adjectival value) and *in haste* (adverbial value).

pre·pos·i·tive (prē-pŏz′ə-tĭv) *adj. Grammar.* Put before; prefixed: *a prepositive adjective.* Compare **postpositive.**
—n. Grammar. A word or particle put before another word. [Late Latin *praepositīvus,* from *praepōnere* (past participle *praepositus*), to place in front. See **preposition.**] **—pre·pos·i·tive·ly** *adv.*

pre·pos·sess (prē′pə-zĕs′) *tr.v.* **-sessed, -sessing, -sesses. 1.** To preoccupy the mind of to the exclusion of other thoughts or feelings. **2.** To influence beforehand for or against someone or something; prejudice; bias. **3.** To impress favorably in advance.

pre·pos·sess·ing (prē′pə-zĕs′ĭng) *adj.* Impressing favorably; pleasing. **—pre·pos·sess·ing·ly** *adv.* **—pre·pos·sess·ing·ness** *n.*

pre·pos·ses·sion (prē′pə-zĕsh′ən) *n.* **1.** A preconception or prejudice. **2.** The state of being preoccupied with thoughts, opinions, or feelings, especially favorable ones.

pre·pos·ter·ous (prĭ-pŏs′tər-əs) *adj.* Contrary to nature, reason, or common sense; absurd. —See Synonyms at **foolish.** [Latin *praeposterus,* "inverted," perverted, absurd : *prae-,* before + *posterus,* coming after, following, next, from *post,* after.] **—pre·pos·ter·ous·ly** *adv.* **—pre·pos·ter·ous·ness** *n.*

pre·po·ten·cy (prē-pŏt′n-sē) *n.* **1.** The state or condition of being prepotent; predominance. **2.** *Genetics.* The capacity of one parent to transmit more characteristics to the offspring than the other parent. **3.** *Botany.* The capacity of some pollen to cause fertilization more readily than pollen from another source.

pre·po·tent (prē-pōt′ənt) *adj.* Also **pre·po·ten·tial** (prē′pə-tĕn′shəl). **1.** Greater in power, influence, or force; predominant. **2.** *Genetics.* Showing prepotency. [Middle English, from Latin *praepotēns* (stem *praepotent-*), present participle of *praeposse,* to be very powerful : *prae-* (intensifier) + *posse,* to be able or powerful.] **—pre·po·tent·ly** *adv.*

prep·pie, prep·py (prĕp′ē) *n., pl.* **-pies.** *Informal.* **1.** A student in or graduate of a preparatory school. **2.** A student or young adult whose manner and dress are traditional and conservative.
—adj. Informal. Of, pertaining to, or being a preppie; especially, having the conservative tastes and values or way of dressing characteristic of a preppie. [Shortening and alteration of PREPARATORY SCHOOL.]

prep school *n. Informal.* A **preparatory school** *(see).*

pre·puce (prē′pyo͞os′) *n.* **1.** The **foreskin** *(see).* **2.** A structure corresponding to the foreskin that covers the glans of the clitoris. [Middle English, from Old French, from Latin *praepūtium.*] **—pre·pu·tial** (prĭ-pyo͞o′shəl) *adj.*

pre·quel (prē′kwəl) *n.* A work such as a film or book that is based on an earlier work about the same subject but that relates events that occurred prior to those related in the earlier work. [PRE- or PRE(VIOUS) + (SE)QUEL.]

pre-Raph·a·el·ite (prē-răf′ē-ə-līt′, prē-rā′fē-) *n.* A painter or writer belonging to or influenced by the pre-Raphaelite Brotherhood, a society founded in 1848 to advance the style and spirit of Italian painting before Raphael. **—pre-Raph·a·el·ite** *adj.*

pre·re·cord (prē′rĭ-kôrd′) *tr.v.* **-corded, -cording, -cords.** To record beforehand; especially, to record (a radio or television broadcast) in advance of transmission.

pre·req·ui·site (prē-rĕk′wə-zĭt) *adj.* Required as a prior condition to something. —See Synonyms at **necessary.**
—n. Something that is prerequisite.
Usage: As a noun, *prerequisite* is followed by *of* or *for* and occasionally by *to*: *Hard work is a prerequisite for success.* As an adjective, it is followed by *to*: *Hard work is prerequisite to success.*

pre·rog·a·tive (prĭ-rŏg′ə-tĭv) *n.* **1.** An exclusive right or privilege held by a person or group, especially a hereditary or official right. **2.** A characteristically exclusive right or privilege: *It's my prerogative to change my mind.* **3.** A natural advantage making one superior: *Thinking is one of man's prerogatives.* —See Synonyms at **right.**
—adj. Of, arising from, or exercising a prerogative. [Middle English, from Old French, from Latin *praerogātīva (centuria),* "(century) chosen to vote first," from *praerogātīvus,* asked to vote first, from *praerogāre,* to ask before others : *prae-,* before + *rogāre,* to ask.]

pres. 1. present (time). **2.** president.

Pres. President.

pres·age (prĕs′ĭj) *n.* **1.** An indication or warning of a future occurrence; an omen. **2.** A feeling or intuition of what is going to occur; a presentiment. **3.** *Archaic.* A prediction.
—v. **pre·sage** (prĭ-sāj′, prĕs′ĭj) **presaged, -saging, -sages.** *—tr.* **1.** To indicate or warn of in advance; portend. **2.** To have a presentiment of. **3.** To foretell or predict. *—intr.* To make or utter a prediction. —See Synonyms at **foretell.** [Middle English, from Latin *praesāgium,* foreboding, from *praesāgīre,* to perceive beforehand : *prae-,* before + *sāgīre,* to perceive.] **—pre·sage·ful** (prĭ-sāj′fəl) *adj.*

pres·by·o·pi·a (prĕz′bē-ō′pē-ə, prĕs′-) *n.* The inability of the eye to focus sharply on nearby objects, resulting from hardening of the lens with advancing age. [New Latin : Greek *presbus,* old man + ′-OPIA.] **—pres·by·op·ic** (prĕz′bē-ŏp′ĭk, -ō′pĭk, prĕs′-) *adj.*

pres·by·ter (prĕz′bə-tər, prĕs′-) *n.* **1.** In the early Christian church, an elder of the congregation. **2.** In various hierarchical churches, a priest. **3.** In the Presbyterian Church: **a.** A teaching elder. **b.** A

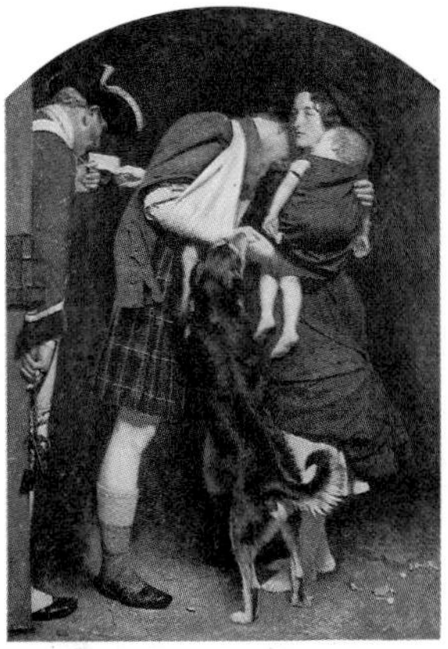

pre-Raphaelite painting The Order of Release *by John Everett Millais (1829–96), one of the founders of the pre-Raphaelite movement. The pre-Raphaelites reacted to the thrusting materialism of the 19th century by seeking a return to what they saw as the innocence and sincerity of early Renaissance painting.*

ruling elder. [Late Latin, an elder, from Greek *presbuteros,* a priest, "older," comparative of *presbus,* old man.]

pres·byt·er·ate (prĕz-bĭt′ər-ĭt, -ə-rāt′, prĕs-) *n.* **1.** The office of a presbyter. **2.** The body or order of presbyters.

pres·by·te·ri·al (prĕz′bə-tîr′ē-əl, prĕs′-) *adj.* Of or pertaining to a presbyter or the presbytery. **—pres·by·te·ri·al·ly** *adv.*

pres·by·te·ri·an (prĕz′bə-tîr′ē-ən, prĕs′-) *adj.* **1.** Of or pertaining to ecclesiastical government by presbyters. **2. Presbyterian.** Of or pertaining to a Presbyterian Church.

~n. **Presbyterian.** A member or adherent of a Presbyterian Church. **—Pres·by·te·ri·an·ism** *n.*

Presbyterian Church *n.* Any of various Protestant churches governed by presbyters and traditionally Calvinist in doctrine.

pres·by·ter·y (prĕz′bə-tĕr′ē, prĕs′-) *n., pl.* **-ies. 1.** In the Presbyterian Church: **a.** A court composed of the ministers and representative elders of a particular locality. **b.** The district represented by this court. **2.** Presbyters collectively. **3.** Government of a church by presbyters. **4.** The section of a church east of the choir where the main altar is situated; sanctuary. **5.** *Roman Catholic Church.* The residence of a priest. [Middle English *presbytory,* from Late Latin *presbyterium,* a council of presbyters, from Greek *presbuterion,* from *presbuteros,* priest, PRESBYTER.]

pre·school (prē′sko͞ol′) *adj.* Of, pertaining to, or designed for a child of nursery-school age.

~n. A nursery school. **—pre·school·er** *n.*

pre·sci·ence (prē′shē-əns, prĕsh′ē-) *n.* Knowledge of actions or events before they occur; foreknowledge; foresight. **—pre·sci·ent** (prē′shē-ənt, prĕsh′ē-) *adj.* **—pre·sci·ent·ly** *adv.*

pre·scind (prĭ-sĭnd′) *v.* **-scinded, -scinding, -scinds.** *—tr.* To separate or divide, especially so as to consider individually. Used with *from.* *—intr.* To withdraw one's attention. Used with *from.* [Latin *praescindere,* to cut off in front : *prae-,* in front + *scindere,* to cut off.]

Pres·cott (prĕs′kət, -kŏt′), **Samuel** (1751–*c.* 1777). U.S. Revolutionary patriot. On April 18, 1775, he joined Paul Revere and William Dawes on their famous ride to spread the news of the British advance. Because Revere was captured and Dawes was forced to retreat, it was Prescott who completed the ride, first alerting the Lincoln minutemen and then warning the Concord militia.

Prescott, William (1726–95). U.S. Revolutionary officer. While commanding the defense of Breed's Hill during the Battle of Bunker Hill (1775), he inspired his men and displayed remarkable coolness by donning a light jacket and wide-brimmed hat and pacing the battlements amid a hail of British bullets.

Prescott, William Hickling (1796–1859). U.S. historian. Fascinated by Spanish history, he concentrated on that subject in his voluminous endeavors. His dramatic writing style contributed to the success of his books, including *History of the Conquest of Mexico* (1843).

pre·scribe (prĭ-skrīb′) *v.* **-scribed, -scribing, -scribes.** *—tr.* **1.** To set down as a rule or guide; ordain; enjoin. **2.** *Medicine.* To order or recommend the use of (a drug, treatment, or the like). *—intr.* **1.** To establish rules, laws, or directions. **2.** *Medicine.* To order or recommend a remedy or treatment. **3.** *Law.* To assert a right or title to something on the grounds of prescription. [Middle English *prescriben,* to hold by right of prescription, from Medieval Latin *prescrībere,* to claim by such right, from Latin *praescrībere,* to write at the beginning, prescribe : *prae-,* before, in front + *scrībere,* to write.] **—pre·scrib·er** *n.*

pre·script (prē′skrĭpt′) *n.* Something prescribed, especially a rule or regulation of conduct.

~adj. (prē′skrĭpt′, prĭ-skrĭpt′). Established as a rule; set down; prescribed. [Latin *praescriptum,* from *praescrībere* (past participle *praescriptus*), to PRESCRIBE.]

pre·scrip·ti·ble (prĭ-skrĭp′tə-bəl) *adj.* Capable of, subject to, or derived from prescription. **—pre·scrip·ti·bil·i·ty** *n.*

pre·scrip·tion (prĭ-skrĭp′shən) *n.* **1. a.** The act of prescribing. **b.** That which is prescribed. **2.** *Medicine.* **a.** A written instruction by a doctor for the preparation and administration of a medicine. **b.** A prescribed medicine. **c.** An ophthalmologist's or optometrist's written instruction for the grinding of corrective lenses. **3.** A formula directing the preparation or correction of something. **4.** *Law.* **a.** The process of acquiring title to property by reason of uninterrupted possession of specified duration. Also called "positive prescription." **b.** The limitation of time beyond which an action, debt, or crime is no longer valid or enforceable. Also called "negative prescription." [Middle English *prescripcion,* from Old French *prescription,* from Latin *praescriptiō* (stem *praescriptiōn-*), a writing in front, from *praescrībere,* to PRESCRIBE.]

prescription drug *n.* A controlled drug that is available only by the order of a physician's prescription.

pre·scrip·tive (prĭ-skrĭp′tĭv) *adj.* **1.** Sanctioned or authorized by long-standing custom or usage. **2.** Making or giving injunctions, directions, laws, or rules. **3.** *Law.* Acquired by or based upon uninterrupted possession. **4.** *Linguistics.* Of, pertaining to, or being a study that seeks to lay down rules for the usage of language, as opposed to just describing it. **—pre·scrip·tive·ly** *adv.*

pre·scrip·tiv·ism (prĭ-skrĭp′tə-vĭz′əm) *n.* **1.** *Philosophy.* The doctrine that ethical propositions prescribe a course of action or a code of morality and are not true or false. Compare **emotivism, descriptivism. 2.** *Linguistics.* The doctrine that a grammar should be prescriptive. Compare **descriptivism.**

pres·ence (prĕz′əns) *n.* **1.** The state or fact of being present. **2.** Immediate proximity in time or space. **3.** The area immediately surrounding a great personage, especially a sovereign. **4.** A person's manner of carrying himself; bearing. **5.** A supernatural influence or being that is felt to be nearby. **6.** A person or body of persons present in a given place. **7.** Charismatic bearing or authority, as in an actor. —See Synonyms at **bearing.**

presence of mind *n.* Ability to think and act efficiently, especially when under pressure.

pre·se·nile dementia (prē-sē′nīl′, -sĕn′īl) *n.* Any of several conditions, especially **Alzheimer's disease** *(see),* characterized by the deterioration of mental faculties in young or middle-aged people.

pres·ent[1] (prĕz′ənt) *n.* **1.** A moment or period in time designated as being intermediate between past and future; now. **2.** *Abbr.* **pr., pres.** *Grammar.* **a.** The present tense. **b.** A verb form in the present tense. **3. presents.** *Law.* The document or instrument in question: *be it known by these presents.*

~adj. **1.** Being, pertaining to, existing, or occurring at a moment or period in time considered as the present: *present events.* **2.** Being at hand; nearby. **3.** *Abbr.* **pr., pres.** *Grammar.* Designating a verb tense or form that expresses current time. **4.** *Archaic.* Readily available; immediate. [Middle English, from Old French, from Latin *praesēns* (stem *praesent-*), present participle of *praeesse,* to be before one, be present : *prae-,* in front of + *esse,* to be.]

pre·sent[2] (prĭ-zĕnt′) *v.* **-sented, -senting, -sents.** *—tr.* **1. a.** To introduce, especially with formal ceremony: *She was presented to the king.* **b.** To introduce (a young woman) to society with conventional ceremony. **2.** To bring before the public: *present a play.* **3. a.** To hand over or give, especially as a gift or award: *presented a huge bill; presented the check to the winner.* **b.** To hand over or give to, especially formally: *presented him with a gold watch.* **4.** To offer to view; show: *presented a sharp contrast.* **5. a.** To constitute or entail: *This presents a challenge to us all.* **b.** To face; confront: *presented me with a dilemma.* **6.** To offer for consideration: *An idea presented itself.* **7. a.** To point or aim (a weapon). **b.** To salute with (a weapon). **8.** To recommend (a clergyman) for a benefice. **9.** *Law.* **a.** To offer to a legislature or court for consideration. **b.** To bring a charge or indictment against. **10.** To represent or depict in a particular manner: *He presented himself to us as a benefactor.* *—intr.* To be directed toward the neck of the uterus and vagina during labor. Used of part of an unborn child. —See Synonyms at **offer.**

~n. **pres·ent** (prĕz′ənt). Something presented; a gift. [Middle English *presenten,* from Old French *presenter,* from Latin *praesentāre,* from *praesēns,* PRESENT (adjective).] **—pre·sent·er** (prĭ-zĕn′tər) *n.*

pre·sent·a·ble (prĭ-zĕn′tə-bəl) *adj.* **1.** Capable of being given, displayed, or offered. **2.** Of decent enough appearance or manner to be fit for introduction to others. **—pre·sent·a·bil·i·ty, pre·sent·a·ble·ness** *n.* **—pre·sent·a·bly** *adv.*

pres·en·ta·tion (prĕz′ən-tā′shən, prē′zən-) *n.* **1. a.** The act of presenting or offering, as for acceptance or approval. **b.** The state of being presented. **c.** The manner or style in which someone or something is presented; especially, the way in which a commercial product is promoted through design, packaging, and advertising. **2.** A performance, as of a play. **3. a.** A formal ceremony at which something, such as an award or prize, is presented. **b.** Something that is presented. Also used adjectivally: *a presentation copy of a book.* **4.** A formal introduction, as at court. **5.** The act or right of nominating a clergyman to a benefice. **6.** The process of offering for consideration. **7.** *Medicine.* The position of a fetus in the uterus at birth with respect to the neck of the uterus. **—pres·en·ta·tion·al** *adj.*

pre·sent·a·tive (prĭ-zĕn′tə-tĭv) *adj.* **1.** Having the capacity or function of bringing an idea or image to mind. **2.** *Philosophy.* **a.** Perceived or capable of being perceived directly rather than through association. **b.** Having the ability to so perceive. **3.** Capable of nominating or of being nominated to an ecclesiastical benefice. **—pre·sent·a·tive·ness** *n.*

pres·ent-day (prĕz′ənt-dā′) *adj.* Current.

pres·ent·ee (prĕz′ən-tē′, prĭ-zĕn′-) *n.* **1.** A person who is presented. **2.** A person to whom something is given.

pre·sen·tient (prē-sĕn′shənt, -shē-ənt) *adj.* Having a presentiment. [Latin *praesentiēns* (stem *praesentient-*), present participle of *praesentīre,* to have a presentiment. See **presentiment.**]

pre·sen·ti·ment (prĭ-zĕn′tə-mənt) *n.* A sense of something about to occur; a premonition. —See Synonyms at **apprehension.** [Obsolete French, from Old French *presentir,* to have a presentiment, from Latin *praesentīre,* to perceive beforehand : *prae-,* before + *sentīre,* to perceive.]

pres·ent·ly (prĕz′ənt-lē) *adv.* **1.** In a short time; soon: *She will arrive presently.* **2.** At this time or period; now: *He is presently staying with us.* **3.** *Obsolete.* At once; immediately. —See Usage note at **immediately.**

pre·sent·ment (prĭ-zĕnt′mənt) *n.* **1.** The act of presenting; presentation. **2.** Something presented, as a picture or exhibition. **3.** *Law.* **a.** The act of submitting or presenting a formal statement of a legal matter to a court or authorized person. **b.** The report concerning an offense written by a grand jury and based on the jury's own knowledge and observation. **4.** *Finance.* The presenting of a bill or note for payment.

present participle *n. Grammar.* A participle expressing present action, in English formed by the infinitive plus *-ing* and used: **1.** To express present action in relation to the time indicated by the finite verb in its clause. **2.** To form certain compound tenses of the verb. **3.** To function as a verbal adjective.

present perfect *n. Grammar.* **1.** The verb tense expressing action completed at the present time. This tense is formed in English by combining the present tense of *have* with a past participle; for example, in the sentence *He has spoken,* the words *has spoken* constitute the present perfect. **2.** A verb in the present perfect tense.

present tense *n. Grammar.* The verb tense expressing action in the present time or habitual action in the past and future; for example, in the sentence *She drinks her coffee quickly,* the verb *drinks* is in the present tense.

pres·er·va·tion·ist (prĕz′ər-vā′shə-nĭst) *n.* One who advocates preservation, as of a building having historical value.

pre·serv·a·tive (prĭ-zûr′və-tĭv) *n.* Something used to preserve; especially, a chemical used in foods to inhibit decay. —**pre·serv·a·tive** *adj.*

pre·serve (prĭ-zûrv′) *v.* **-served, -serving, -serves.** —*tr.* **1.** To protect from injury, peril, or other adversity; maintain in safety. **2. a.** To keep in a good, healthy condition: *Moisturizing cream is said to preserve the skin.* **b.** To keep or maintain in an unchanged form: *a project to preserve the old state house.* **3.** To keep or maintain intact: *tried to preserve family harmony.* **4. a.** To prepare so as to prevent decomposition, as by salting or refrigerating. **b.** To prepare (fruits or vegetables, for example) for future use, as by canning or bottling. **5.** To prevent (organic bodies) from decaying or spoiling. **6.** To keep or protect (game or fish) for one's private hunting or fishing. —*intr.* **1.** To treat foods, as fruit, so as to prevent decay. **2.** To maintain a private area stocked with game or fish. —See Synonyms at **defend.** ~*n.* **1.** Something that acts to preserve; a preservative. **2.** *Often* **preserves.** Fruit that has been preserved by boiling with sugar, especially for use as jam. **3.** An area maintained for the protection of wildlife or of natural resources. **4.** Something considered to be the special domain or sphere of certain persons: *Ancient Greek is the preserve of scholars.* [Middle English *preserven,* from Old French *preserver,* from Medieval Latin *praeservāre,* "to guard beforehand": Latin *prae-,* before + *servāre,* to keep, guard.] —**pre·serv·a·bil·i·ty** *n.* —**pre·serv·a·ble** *adj.* —**pres·er·va·tion** (prĕz′ər-vā′shən) *n.* —**pre·serv·er** *n.*

pre·set (prē-sĕt′) *tr.v.* **-set, -setting, -sets.** To set (controls, for example) in advance.

pre·shrunk (prē′shrŭngk′) *adj.* Shrunk during manufacture to minimize subsequent shrinkage.

pre·side (prĭ-zīd′) *intr.v.* **-sided, -siding, -sides.** **1.** To occupy the position of authority; act as chairperson or president. **2.** To possess or exercise authority or control. **3.** *Music.* To be the featured instrumental performer: *presided at the piano.* [French *presider,* from Latin *praesidēre,* "to sit in front of," superintend : *prae-,* before + *sedēre,* to sit.] —**pre·sid·er** *n.*

pres·i·den·cy (prĕz′ə-dən-sē, -dĕn′sē) *n., pl.* **-cies.** **1.** The office, function, or term of a president. **2.** *Often* **Presidency.** The office of the president of a republic, especially of the United States. **3.** *Mormon Church.* **a.** A local governing body consisting of three men. **b.** *Often* **Presidency.** The chief administrative body of the church.

pres·i·dent (prĕz′ə-dənt, -dĕnt′) *n. Abbr.* **p., P., pres., Pres. 1.** One appointed or elected to preside over an organized body of people, such as an assembly or meeting. **2.** *Often* **President.** The chief executive of a republic, especially of the United States. **3.** The chief officer of a body such as a branch of government, a corporation, a board of trustees, a university, a college, or a club. [Middle English, from Old French, from Latin *praesidēns* (stem *praesident-*), present participle of *praesidēre,* to PRESIDE.] —**pres·i·den·tial** (prĕz′ə-dĕn′shəl) *adj.* —**pres·i·den·tial·ly** *adv.* —**pres·i·dent·ship** *n.*

pres·i·dent-e·lect (prĕz′ə-dənt-ĭ-lĕkt′) *n.* A person who has been elected president but has not yet begun his term of office.

pre·si·di·o (prĭ-sē′dē-ō′, -sĭd′ē-ō′) *n., pl.* **-os.** A military post, especially a garrison in a country under Spanish control. [Spanish, from Latin *praesidium,* garrison, fortification, from *praesidēre,* "to sit in front of," guard, PRESIDE.]

pre·sid·i·um (prĭ-sĭd′ē-əm) *n., pl.* **-ia** (-ē-ə) or **-iums.** **1.** Any of various permanent executive committees in Communist countries having power to act for a larger governing body. **2. Presidium.** A committee of the Supreme Soviet headed by the premier and constituting the highest policy-making body of the Soviet Union. [Russian *prezidium,* from Latin *praesidium.* See presidio.]

pre·sig·ni·fy (prē-sĭg′nə-fī′) *tr.v.* **-fied, -fying, -fies.** To betoken or signify beforehand; prefigure; foreshadow.

Pres·ley (prĕs′lē, prĕz′-), **Elvis Aaron** (1935-77). U.S. rock 'n' roll singer. Following his first popular record success, *Heartbreak Hotel* (1956), he embarked on a career that was to encompass more than 30 films and the sale of over 150 million copies of his records.

pre·so·lar nebular hypothesis (prē-sō′lər) *n.* A theory put forward to account for the origin of the sun and the solar system in which gas and dust from the interstellar medium contracted under the influence of gravity to form a nebula. The dust particles in the nebula became centers of accretion for matter, forming planetismals that in turn coalesced and accreted matter to form the bodies in the solar system. Compare **planetismal hypothesis, primitive solar-nebula hypothesis.**

press¹ (prĕs) *v.* **pressed, pressing, presses.** —*tr.* **1.** To exert steady weight or force against; bear down on: *The mailman pressed the doorbell.* **2. a.** To squeeze the juice or other contents from. **b.** To extract (juice, for example) by squeezing or compressing. **3. a.** To apply steady force to so as to make compact, reshape, or flatten: *pressed flowers.* **b.** To smooth, flatten, or shape (clothing) using steam or steady pressure from an iron. **4.** To clasp or embrace closely. **5.** To seek to influence, as by insistent arguments; entreat persistently. **6.** To attempt to force to action; urge on; spur. **7.** To place in trying or constraining circumstances; harass: *pressed by lack of money; pressed for time.* **8.** To lay stress upon; emphasize: *pressed her point.* **9.** To advance or carry on vigorously: *pressed his attack.* **10.** To put forward importunately or insistently: *They pressed their claim.* **11.** To manufacture (a record) from a mold or matrix. **12.** To lift (a weight) first to the shoulders and then above the head. Used of a weight lifter. —*intr.* **1.** To exert force or pressure. **2.** To weigh heavily, as on the mind. **3.** To advance eagerly; push forward: *Let's press on with our business.* **4.** To require haste; be urgent. **5.** To press clothes or other material. **6.** To assemble closely and in large numbers; crowd. **7.** To employ urgent persuasion or entreaty; ask earnestly or persistently. —See Synonyms at **urge.** ~*n.* **1.** Any of various machines or devices that apply pressure. Often used in combination: *a winepress.* **2.** Any of various machines used for printing; a printing press. **3.** A place or establishment where matter is printed. **4.** The method, art, or business of printing. **5. a.** The news media as a whole; especially, newspapers and magazines. **b.** The people involved in the news media; especially, editors, reporters, and photographers. **c.** The material dealt with in the news media; especially, reviews or editorial comment: *The new play received a bad press.* **6.** The act of gathering in large numbers or of pushing forward. **7.** A large gathering; a throng. **8. a.** The act of applying pressure. **b.** The state of being pressed. **9.** The haste or urgency of business or affairs. **10.** The set of proper creases in a garment or fabric, formed by ironing. **11.** An upright closet or case used for storing articles such as clothing or books. **12.** In weightlifting, the act of pressing a weight. [Middle English *pressen,* from Old French *presser,* from Latin *pressāre,* frequentative of *premere* (past participle *pressus*), to press.]

press² *tr.v.* **pressed, pressing, presses. 1.** To force into service in the army or navy; impress. **2.** To use in a manner different from the usual or intended. ~*n.* **1.** Conscription or impressment into service, especially into the navy. **2.** An official warrant for impressing men. [Alteration (by association with PRESS, to apply pressure, compel) of earlier *prest,* to give money to (recruits), from Middle English *prest,* money given to recruits, from Old French, "loan," from *prester,* to lend, from Latin *praestāre,* to place something at someone's disposal, furnish : *prae-,* PRE- + *stāre,* to stand.]

press agency *n.* A news agency (see).

press agent *n. Abbr.* **P.A.** A person employed to arrange advertising and publicity, as for an actor or theater.

press·a·gent·ry (prĕs′ā′jən-trē) *n.* **1.** The work of a press agent. **2.** The techniques and methods used by a press agent.

press association *n.* A news agency (see).

press·board (prĕs′bôrd′, -bōrd′) *n.* **1.** A heavy glazed paper or pasteboard used especially to cover the platen or cylinder of a printing press. **2.** A small ironing board.

press box *n.* A section reserved for reporters, as in a sports stadium.

press conference *n.* An interview held for news reporters and photographers by a politician or other public figure.

press·er (prĕs′ər) *n.* **1.** A person who presses clothes. **2.** Any of various devices that apply pressure to a product in manufacturing or canning.

press gallery *n.* An area above the ground floor reserved for the press, especially in a legislative chamber.

press gang, press·gang (prĕs′găng′) *n.* A company under an officer with the task of pressing men into military or naval service.

press-gang (prĕs′găng′) *tr.v.* **-ganged, -ganging, -gangs. 1.** To press into military or naval service. **2.** To force a person to do something unwillingly.

press·ing (prĕs′ĭng) *adj.* **1.** Demanding immediate attention; urgent: *a pressing need.* **2.** Importunate; insistent: *a pressing invitation.* —See Synonyms at **urgent.** ~*n.* A series of phonograph records produced at one time. —**press·ing·ly** *adv.*

press·man (prĕs′mən, -măn′) *n., pl.* **-men** (-mĭn, -mĕn′). **1.** A printing press operator. **2.** *British.* A journalist.

press·mark (prĕs′märk′) *n.* **1.** A mark in or on a book indicating where it should be placed in a library. **2.** A notation or figure in the margin of a printed sheet indicating the press upon which it was printed.

press officer *n.* A person employed by an organization to communicate with and answer inquiries from the press.

press of sail *n. Nautical.* The greatest amount of sail that a ship can carry safely.

pres·sor (prĕs′ôr, -ər) *adj.* Causing an increase in blood pressure. [From Latin *premere* (stem *press-*), to PRESS.] —**pres·sor** *n.*

press release *n.* An announcement or official account of an event, performance, or other news or publicity item issued to the press.

press·room (prĕs′rōom′, -rŏom′) *n.* The room in a printing or newspaper publishing establishment that contains the presses.

press·run (prĕs′rŭn′) *n.* **1.** A single uninterrupted operation of a printing press producing a specific number of copies. **2.** The number of copies produced in a pressrun.

press secretary *n.* A person who manages the public affairs and press conferences of a public figure.

press-stud (prĕs'stŭd') *n. Chiefly British.* A **snap fastener** *(see).*

press-up (prĕs'ŭp') *n. British.* See **pushup** (sense 1).

pres-sure (prĕsh'ər) *n.* **1. a.** The act of pressing. **b.** The condition of being pressed. **2.** The application of continuous force by one body upon another that it is touching; compression. **3. a.** *Abbr.* **P** *Physics.* Force applied over a surface, measured as force per unit of area. It is measured in pascals, pounds per square inch, or the like. **b.** *Meteorology.* **Atmospheric pressure** *(see).* **4.** A constraining influence, as a moral force, upon the mind or will: *brought pressure to bear upon the government to make peace with the enemy.* **5.** Urgent claim or demand: *seems to enjoy working under pressure.* **6.** A burdensome, distressing, oppressive, or weighty condition: *couldn't cope with the pressure of illness.* **7.** *Archaic.* A mark made by the application of force or weight; impression. ~*tr.v.* **pressured, -suring, -sures.** To bring pressure upon (a person), as by influence or persuasion. [Middle English, from Latin *pressūra,* from *premere,* to PRESS.]

pressure cabin *n.* A pressurized section of an aircraft.

pressure cooker *n.* **1.** An airtight metal pot that uses steam under pressure at high temperature to cook food quickly. **2.** A position of difficulty, stress, or anxiety.

pressure gauge *n.* **1.** A device for measuring fluid pressure. **2.** A device for measuring the pressure of explosions.

pressure group *n.* Any group that exerts pressure on legislators and public opinion to advance or protect its interests.

pressure point *n.* Any of several places on the skin where an artery lies over a bone and where pressure may be applied to stop or control bleeding from a wound.

pressure ridge *n.* A ridge of floating ice formed as two ice floes push against each other.

pressure sore *n.* A **bedsore** *(see).*

pressure suit *n.* A garment that is worn in high-altitude aircraft or in spacecraft to compensate for low-pressure conditions. Compare **G-suit.**

pressure system *n.* A system of high or low atmospheric pressure, as a depression or an anticyclone.

pres-sur-ize (prĕsh'ə-rīz') *tr.v.* **-ized, -izing, -izes.** **1.** To maintain normal air pressure in (an enclosure, such as an aircraft or submarine). **2.** To put (gas or liquid) under a greater than normal pressure. **3.** To design to resist pressure. **4.** To bring pressure to bear on. —**pres·sur·i·za·tion** *n.* —**pres·sur·iz·er** *n.*

press-work (prĕs'wûrk') *n.* **1.** The direction or operation of a printing press. **2.** The matter printed by a printing press.

pres-ti-dig-i-ta-tion (prĕs'tə-dĭj'ə-tā'shən) *n.* Manual skill and dexterity in the execution of tricks; sleight of hand. [French, from *prestidigitateur,* juggler, from *preste,* nimble, from Latin *praestus* (see **presto**) + Latin *digitus,* finger.] —**pres·ti·dig·i·ta·tor** *n.*

pres-tige (prĕ-stēzh', -stēj') *n.* **1.** Prominence or influential status achieved through success, renown, or wealth. **2.** The power to command admiration in a group. ~*adj.* Possessing or conferring prestige. [French, originally "illusion brought on by magic," phantasmagoria, from Latin *praestigiae,* "juggler's tricks," illusions, alteration of *praestrigiae* (unattested), from *praestringere,* to bind up, dazzle, blind : *prae-,* before + *stringere,* to bind, tighten.] —**pres·tig·ious** (prĕ-stē'jəs, -stĭj'əs) *adj.* —**pres·tig·ious·ly** *adv.* —**pres·tig·ious·ness** *n.*

pres-tis-si-mo (prĕs-tĭs'ə-mō') *adv. Music.* At as fast a tempo as possible. Used as a direction. ~*n., pl.* **prestissimos.** *Music.* A section or passage to be played prestissimo. [Italian, superlative of PRESTO.] —**pres·tis·si·mo** *adj.*

pres-to (prĕs'tō) *adv.* **1.** *Music.* In rapid tempo. Used as a direction. **2.** Suddenly and speedily: *I turned around, and presto! There they were.* ~*n., pl.* **prestos.** *Music.* A section or passage to be played presto. [Italian, from Latin *praestus,* ready, from *praestō†,* at hand.] —**pres·to** *adj.*

pre-stress (prē-strĕs') *tr.v.* **-stressed, -stressing, -stresses.** To subject (material) to stress before applying a load so as to counterbalance applied stresses under loaded conditions.

prestressed concrete *n.* Reinforced concrete in which the reinforcing wires or bars have been prestressed.

Prest-wick (prĕst'wĭk'). Town in Strathclyde Region, Scotland, on the Firth of Clyde. It is famous for its golf course. Scotland's international airport is located here.

pre-sum-a-ble (prĭ-zōō'mə-bəl) *adj.* Capable of being presumed or taken for granted; reasonable as a supposition; probable. —**pre·sum·a·bly** *adv.*

pre-sume (prĭ-zōōm') *v.* **-sumed, -suming, -sumes.** —*tr.* **1.** To take for granted; assume: *I presume you're joining us.* **2.** *Law.* To take as being proved in the absence of contrary evidence. **3.** To engage oneself in without authority or permission; dare: *He presumed to invite himself to dinner.* —*intr.* **1.** To act overconfidently; take liberties. **2.** To take unwarranted advantage of something: *Don't presume on her kindness.* —See Synonyms at **conjecture.** [Middle English *presumen,* from Old French *presumer,* from Late Latin *praesūmere,* to venture, from Latin, "to take in advance," presuppose, foresee, assume : *prae-,* before + *sūmere,* to take.] —**pre·sum·ed·ly** (prĭ-zōō'mĭd-lē) *adv.* —**pre·sum·er** *n.*

Synonyms: assume, posit, postulate, suppose.

pre-sump-tion (prĭ-zŭmp'shən) *n.* **1.** Behavior or language that is boldly arrogant or offensive; effrontery. **2.** The act of presuming or

accepting as true. **3.** Acceptance or belief based on reasonable evidence; an assumption or supposition. **4.** A condition or basis for accepting or presuming. **5.** *Law.* An inference as to the truth of an allegation or proposition, based on probable reasoning in the absence of or prior to actual proof or disproof. [Middle English *presumpcion,* from Old French, from Latin *praesumptiō* (stem *praesumptiōn-*), from *praesūmere,* to PRESUME.]

pre-sump-tive (prĭ-zŭmp'tĭv) *adj.* **1.** Providing a reasonable basis for belief or acceptance. **2.** Founded on probability or presumption: *an heir presumptive.* **3.** *Zoology.* Designating a cell or cells of an embryo that differentiate into a particular structure or organ. —**pre·sump·tive·ly** *adv.*

pre-sump-tu-ous (prĭ-zŭmp'chōō-əs) *adj.* **1.** Excessively forward or bold, especially because of undue self-confidence; arrogant. **2.** *Obsolete.* Presumptive. [Middle English, from Old French *presumptueux,* from Late Latin *praesumptuōsus,* audacious, from *praesumptiō,* audacity, PRESUMPTION.] —**pre·sump·tu·ous·ly** *adv.* —**pre·sump·tu·ous·ness** *n.*

pre-sup-pose (prē'sə-pōz') *tr.v.* **-posed, -posing, -poses.** **1.** To assume or suppose in advance; take for granted. **2.** To require or involve necessarily as an antecedent condition: *Intelligent speaking presupposes intelligent thinking.* [Middle English *presupposen,* from Old French *presupposer,* from Medieval Latin *praesuppōnere* : *prae-,* before + *suppōnere,* to SUPPOSE.] —**pre·sup·po·si·tion** (prē-sŭp'ə-zĭsh'ən) *n.*

pret. preterit.

pre-tax (prē'tăks') *adj.* Before taxation.

pre-teen (prē'tēn') *adj.* **1.** Of, pertaining to, or for preadolescent children: *preteen clothing.* **2.** Being a preadolescent child. ~*n.* A preadolescent child.

pre-tend (prĭ-tĕnd') *v.* **-tended, -tending, -tends.** —*tr.* **1.** To affect; feign. **2.** To claim or allege insincerely or falsely; profess: *She pretended to be stupid.* **3.** To represent fictitiously in play; make believe: *You pretend to be an astronaut.* **4.** To take upon oneself; venture: *I won't pretend to tell you, a novelist, how to write.* —*intr.* **1.** To feign an action, role, or character, as in play. **2.** To put forward a claim: *I don't pretend to any expertise.* ~*adj. Informal.* Imaginary; taken as such, especially for the purposes of a game: *pretend money.* [Middle English *pretenden,* from Latin *praetendere,* "to stretch forth," hold out as a pretext, assert : *prae-,* before + *tendere,* to stretch.]

Synonyms: dissemble, fake, feign, simulate.

pre-tend-ed (prĭ-tĕn'dĭd) *adj.* **1.** Falsely asserted or alleged: *pretended loyalty.* **2.** False; untrue; feigned. —**pre·tend·ed·ly** *adv.*

pre-tend-er (prĭ-tĕn'dər) *n.* **1.** One who simulates, pretends, or alleges falsely; a hypocrite or dissembler. **2. a.** One who sets forth a claim. **b.** A claimant to a throne. **3. Pretender.** In British history: **a.** James Edward **Stuart** *(see),* the Old Pretender. **b.** Charles Edward **Stuart** *(see),* the Young Pretender.

pre-tense (prē'tĕns', prĭ-tĕns') *n.* Also *chiefly British* **pre-tence.** **1.** The act of pretending; a false appearance or action intended to deceive. **2.** A false or studied show of something; an affectation. **3.** A false reason or excuse; a pretext. **4.** Something imagined or pretended; a piece of make-believe. **5.** A mere show without reality; an outward appearance. Used with *at: There was some pretense at negotiating.* **6.** A right asserted with or without foundation; a claim. **7.** Ostentation; pretentiousness. [Middle English, from Norman French *pretense,* from Medieval Latin *praetensa* (unattested), from Latin *praetendere,* to PRETEND.]

pre-ten-sion (prĭ-tĕn'shən) *n.* **1.** A specious allegation; a pretext. **2.** An asserted but usually unproved claim to something, such as a privilege, right, or position of distinction or importance. **3.** An asserted but unsupported claim, as to some merit or skill: *no pretensions to being a chess player.* **4.** Pretentiousness; ostentation; display.

pre-ten-tious (prĭ-tĕn'shəs) *adj.* **1. a.** Claiming or demanding a position of distinction or merit, especially when unjustified: *a pretentious play.* **b.** Affecting or adopting a mannerism, habit, style of dress, or the like, simply for the sake of appearance. **2.** Making an extravagant outward show; ostentatious. —**pre·ten·tious·ly** *adv.* —**pre·ten·tious·ness** *n.*

pret-er-it, pret-er-ite (prĕt'ər-ĭt) *adj. Abbr.* **pret., pt.** *Grammar.* Designating the verb tense that expresses or describes a past or completed action or condition; for example, in the sentence *Mary bought cakes, bought* is in the preterit tense. ~*n. Abbr.* **pret., pt.** *Grammar.* **1.** The verb form expressing or describing a past or completed action or condition; the past tense. **2.** A verb in this form. [Middle English, past, past tense, from Old French, from Latin *praeteritus,* gone by, past, past participle of *praeterīre,* to go by, pass : *praeter,* beyond, comparative of *prae-,* before + *īre,* to go.]

pret-er-i-tion (prĕt'ə-rĭsh'ən) *n.* **1.** The act of passing by, disregarding, or omitting. **2.** In Roman law, the neglect of a testator to mention a legal heir or heirs in his will. **3.** *Theology.* The passing over of the nonelect by God. [Late Latin *praeteritiō* (stem *praeteritiōn-*), from *praeterīre,* to go by, pass over. See **preterit.**]

pret-er-i-tive (prĭ-tĕr'ə-tĭv) *adj. Grammar.* Designating a verb limited to a past tense or past tenses.

pre-ter-mit (prē'tər-mĭt') *tr.v.* **-mitted, -mitting, -mits.** **1.** To disregard intentionally or allow to pass unnoticed or unmentioned. **2.** To fail to do or include; omit; neglect. **3.** To desist from temporarily. [Latin *praetermittere,* to let go by : *praeter,* beyond (see **pret-**

erit) + *mittere*, to let go.] —**pre·ter·mis·sion** (prē'tər-mĭsh'ən) *n.* —**pre·ter·mit·ter** *n.*

pre·ter·nat·u·ral (prē'tər-năch'ər-əl) *adj.* **1.** Out of or beyond the normal course of nature; differing from the natural. **2.** Transcending the natural or material order, often connoting divinity; supernatural. [Medieval Latin *praeternātūrālis*, from Latin *praeter nātūram*, beyond nature : *praeter*, beyond + accusative of *nātūra*, NATURE.] —**pre·ter·nat·u·ral·ism** *n.* —**pre·ter·nat·u·ral·ly** *adv.* —**pre·ter·nat·u·ral·ness** *n.*

pre·text (prē'tĕkst') *n.* An ostensible or professed purpose. ~*tr.v.* **pretexted, -texting, -texts.** To allege as an excuse: *"I shall pretext a catastrophe"* (Aldous Huxley). [Latin *praetextus*, outward show, pretense, from the past participle of *praetexere*, to weave in front, cloak, disguise, pretend : *prae-*, before + *texere*, to weave.]

Pre·to·ri·a (prĭ-tôr'ē-ə, -tōr'ē-ə). Administrative capital of Transvaal province and the Republic of South Africa, founded in 1855. Its industries include steel making and food processing.

Pre·to·ri·us (prĭ-tôr'ē-əs, -tōr'ē-əs), **Andries Wilhelmus Jacobus** (1799–1853). Afrikaner politician and soldier. Leading the trek to the Natal, he defeated the Zulus (1838), then, seeking independence from the British, trekked on to the Transvaal. Following the Boer victory (1848), he secured independence for the area as a republic, and for the Orange Free State. His son, **Marthinus Wessel Pretorius** (1819–1901), was president of both states and leader of the Boers in the first Boer War (1880–81).

pret·ti·fy (prĭt'ə-fī') *tr.v.* **-fied, -fying, -fies.** To make pretty, especially in a superficial or insubstantial way. —**pret·ti·fi·ca·tion** *n.* —**pret·ti·fi·er** *n.*

pret·ty (prĭt'ē) *adj.* **-tier, -tiest. 1.** Pleasing or attractive to the eye or ear, especially in a graceful or delicate way: *a pretty girl; a pretty tune.* **2.** Excellent; fine; good. Often used ironically: *That's a pretty mess you've gotten us into!* **3.** *Archaic.* Elegant; fine. **4.** Effeminate; foppish: *a pretty boy.* **5.** *Informal.* Considerable in size or extent: *a pretty fortune.* —See Synonyms at **beautiful.** ~*adv.* **1.** To a fair degree; somewhat; moderately: *He is a pretty good student.* **2.** Very; extremely: *a pretty good judge of character.* —**sitting pretty.** *Informal.* In favorable circumstances; in a good position. ~*n., pl.* **pretties.** *Informal.* One that is pleasing or pretty. ~*tr.v.* **prettied, -tying, -ties.** *Informal.* To make pretty: *tried to pretty up the house before the guests arrived.* [Middle English *prety, praty*, clever, skillfully made, fine, Old English *prættig*, cunning, tricky, from *prætt*, trick, wile, craft, from West Germanic *pratt-*† (unattested).] —**pret·ti·ly** *adv.* —**pret·ti·ness** *n.*

pre·tu·ber·cu·lous (prē'tōō-bûr'kyə-ləs, prē'tyōō-) *adj.* Of, pertaining to, or being at the stage at which tuberculosis is established but before the actual development of symptoms.

pret·zel (prĕt'səl) *n.* A glazed, salted biscuit that is usually baked in the form of a loose knot or stick. [German *Pretzel, Brezel*, from Old High German *brezitella*, from Medieval Latin *brachiatellum* (unattested), diminutive of *brachītum* (unattested), "armlet," hence a ring-shaped cake, from Latin *bracchium*, arm, from Greek *brakhiōn*.]

pre·vail (prĭ-vāl') *intr.v.* **-vailed, -vailing, -vails. 1.** To be greater in strength or influence; triumph or win a victory: *prevailed against great odds; will prevail over the enemy; hoping that common sense would prevail.* **2.** To be most common or frequent; be predominant. **3.** To be in force, use, or effect; be current. —**prevail on** (or **upon**). To use persuasion or inducement successfully. —See Synonyms at **persuade.** [Middle English *prevayllen*, from Latin *praevalēre*, to be more powerful : *prae-*, before, beyond + *valēre*, to be strong.] —**pre·vail·er** *n.*

pre·vail·ing (prĭ-vā'lĭng) *adj.* **1.** Most frequent or common; predominant. **2.** Generally current; widespread. **3.** Being more influential or forceful: *the prevailing scientific theory.* —**pre·vail·ing·ly** *adv.* —**pre·vail·ing·ness** *n.*

Synonyms: *current, prevalent, rife.*

prev·a·lent (prĕv'ə-lənt) *adj.* **1.** Widely or commonly occurring. **2.** Generally accepted or practiced. —See Synonyms at **common, prevailing.** [Latin *praevalēns* (stem *praevalent-*), present participle of *praevalēre*, to PREVAIL.] —**prev·a·lence** *n.* —**prev·a·lent·ly** *adv.*

pre·var·i·cate (prĭ-văr'ĭ-kāt') *intr.v.* **-cated, -cating, -cates. 1.** To stray from or evade the truth; equivocate. **2.** To speak or act evasively; quibble. [Latin *praevāricārī*, to walk crookedly, deviate from one's course, collude : *prae-*, before, beyond + *vāricāre*, to straddle, from *vāricus*, straddling, from *vārus*, stretched, bent, knock-kneed (see **varus**).] —**pre·var·i·ca·tion** *n.* —**pre·var·i·ca·tive** (prĭ-văr'ĭ-kā'tĭv) *adj.* —**pre·var·i·ca·tor** *n.*

pre·ven·ient (prĭ-vēn'yənt) *adj.* **1.** Antecedent; previous. **2.** Expectant; anticipatory. [Latin *praeveniēns* (stem *praevenient-*), present participle of *praevenīre*, to come before, precede, anticipate : *prae-*, before + *venīre*, to come.] —**pre·ven·ience** *n.* —**pre·ven·ient·ly** *adv.*

pre·vent (prĭ-vĕnt') *v.* **-vented, -venting, -vents.** —*tr.* **1.** To keep from happening, as by some prior action; avert: *tried to prevent a strike.* **2.** To keep (someone) from doing something; impede: *Serious illness prevented him from competing in the marathon.* **3.** To anticipate or counter in advance. **4.** *Archaic.* To come before; precede. —*intr.* To be an obstacle: *There will be a picnic if nothing prevents.* [Middle English *preventen*, to anticipate, from Latin *praevenīre*, to come before, anticipate : *prae-*, before + *venīre*, to come.] —**pre·vent·a·bil·i·ty, pre·vent·i·bil·i·ty** *n.* —**pre·vent·a·ble, pre·vent·i·ble** *adj.* —**pre·vent·er** *n.*

Synonyms: *forestall, obviate, preclude.*

Usage: When *prevent* is followed by the *-ing* form of a verb, formal English requires that any preceding noun be in the possessive case: *He prevented Jean's leaving.* The noun may also be used without any possessive marker and followed by *from*: *He prevented Jean from leaving.* A construction lacking both *from* and the possessive ending is sometimes used, but attracts criticism: *He prevented Jean leaving.*

pre·ven·tion (prĭ-vĕn'shən) *n.* **1.** The act of preventing. **2.** A hindrance; an obstacle.

pre·ven·tive (prĭ-vĕn'tĭv) *adj.* Also **pre·ven·ta·tive** (-tə-tĭv). **1.** Designed or used to prevent or hinder; acting as an obstacle. **2.** *Medicine.* Thwarting or warding off illness or disease; prophylactic. **3.** In Britain, designating the branch of customs that is concerned with intercepting smuggling. ~*n.* Also **preventative. 1.** Something that prevents; an obstacle. **2.** *Medicine.* Something used to ward off illness. —**pre·ven·tive·ly** *adv.* —**pre·ven·tive·ness** *n.*

pre·view, pre·vue (prē'vyōō') *n.* **1.** An advance showing of an event such as a motion picture or an art exhibition to an invited audience prior to public presentation. **2.** An advance viewing or exhibition. **3.** An introductory or limited experience. ~*v.* **previewed, -viewing, -views.** Also **prevued, -vuing, -vues.** —*tr.* To view or exhibit in advance. —*intr.* To be shown or exhibited in advance.

Prev·in (prĕv'ĭn), **André George**, born Andreas Ludwig Priwin (1929–). German-born U.S. conductor, arranger, and composer. Winner of four Academy Awards for his film scores, he later gained recognition in the world of classical music.

pre·vi·ous (prē'vē-əs) *adj.* **1.** Existing or occurring prior to something else in time or order; antecedent. **2.** *Informal.* Premature; hasty. —**previous to.** Prior to; before. [Latin *praevius*, going before, leading the way : *prae-*, before + *via*, way.] —**pre·vi·ous·ly** *adv.* —**pre·vi·ous·ness** *n.*

previous question *n. Abbr.* **p.q.** In parliamentary procedure, a motion to take an immediate vote on the issue being debated, which if carried ends the debate but if defeated means that debate can be resumed. Compare **cloture.**

pre·vise (prĭ-vīz') *tr.v.* **-vised, -vising, -vises. 1.** To foresee. **2.** To notify in advance. [Latin *praevidēre* (stem *praevīs-*) : *prae-*, before + *vidēre*, to see.] —**pre·vi·sion** (prĭ-vĭzh'ən) *n.* —**pre·vi·sion·al, pre·vi·sion·ar·y** (-ə-nĕr'ē) *adj.*

pre·vo·cal·ic (prē'vō-kăl'ĭk) *adj. Phonetics.* Preceding a vowel.

Pré·vost d'Ex·iles (prā-vō' dĕg-zēl'), **Antoine François**, known as "Abbé Prévost" (1697–1763). French novelist. Though he was ordained a priest in 1728, he was often involved in love affairs and was regularly in financial straits. He is primarily remembered for *Manon Lescaut* (1731), the story of a well-bred young man who falls in love with a harlot.

prevue. Variant of **preview.**

pre·war (prē'wôr') *adj.* Existing or occurring before a war: *Prewar housing was better constructed and less expensive.*

prex·y (prĕk'sē) *n., pl.* **-ies.** *Slang.* A president, especially of a college or university. [Shortened variant of PRESIDENT.]

prey (prā) *n.* **1.** A creature hunted or caught for food; a quarry. **2.** One that can be damaged or hurt; a victim: *The district fell prey to the developers.* **3.** The act of preying. ~*intr.v.* **preyed, preying, preys. 1.** To hunt, catch, or eat as prey. **2.** To victimize someone or make a profit at someone's expense. **3.** To plunder or pillage. **4.** To exert a grave or harmful effect: *Remorse preyed upon his mind.* [Middle English *preye*, from Old French *preie*, from Latin *praeda*, booty, prey.] —**prey·er** *n.*

Pri·am (prī'əm). *Greek Mythology.* King of Troy, the father of Paris and Hector, killed when his city fell to the Greeks.

pri·ap·ic (prī-ăp'ĭk, -ā'pĭk) *adj.* Also **pri·a·pe·an** (prī'ə-pē'ən). Phallic. [From PRIAPUS.]

pri·a·pism (prī'ə-pĭz'əm) *n.* Persistent, usually painful erection of the penis, especially as a consequence of disease. [French *priapisme*, from Late Latin *priāpismus*, from Greek *priapismos*, from *priapizein*, "to act like Priapus," be lewd, from *Priapos*, PRIAPUS.]

pri·a·pus (prī-ā'pəs) *n.* **1. Priapus.** The Greco-Roman god of procreation, guardian of gardens and vineyards, and personification of the erect phallus. **2.** An image of the god Priapus, such as a statuette with a large, erect penis. [Latin, from Greek *Priapos*†.]

Prib·i·lof Islands (prĭb'ə-lôf'). Group of volcanic islands in the central Bering Sea, the breeding ground of the Alaska fur seal and an internationally recognized seal preserve.

price (prīs) *n. Abbr.* **pr. 1.** The sum of money or quantity of goods asked or given for something. **2.** The cost at which something is obtained: *Victory must be achieved at any price.* **3.** The cost of bribing someone: *Cynics think that every man has his price.* **4.** A reward offered for the capture or killing of a person: *There was a price on his head.* **5.** *Archaic.* Value or worth. **6.** Betting odds. —**at a price.** At considerable cost: *We finally bought the house—but at a price.* ~*tr.v.* **priced, pricing, prices. 1.** To fix or establish a price for: *shoes priced at nineteen dollars.* **2.** To find out the price of: *spent the day pricing dresses.* —**price out of the market.** To charge so much for goods or services that people no longer buy or use them. [Middle English *pris*, price, value, praise, from Old French, from Latin *pretium*, price, value, reward.]

Synonyms: *charge, cost, expenditure, expense, fee, outlay.*

Price (prīs), **(Mary) Leontyne** (1927–). U.S. operatic soprano. After her debut in *Four Saints in Three Acts* (1952), she appeared as

Bess in *Porgy and Bess* (1952–54) and attracted national attention in a television production of *Tosca* (1955). She spent three seasons with the San Francisco Opera (1957–60) and has appeared in several Metropolitan Opera Company productions.

Price, Vincent (1911–). U.S. actor. An accomplished stage, screen, and television actor, he has appeared in numerous horror films and thrillers as a menacingly intelligent villain.

price control *n.* The imposition of a maximum level upon the prices of certain goods by a government, especially in a time of economic crisis.

price index *n.* A number relating prices of a group of commodities to their prices during a particular base period.

price·less (prīs′lĭs) *adj.* **1.** Of inestimable worth; invaluable. **2.** Highly amusing, absurd, or odd. —See Synonyms at **costly.**

price support *n. Economics.* A system of maintaining a minimum price for certain goods in which a government undertakes to buy them if the market price falls below an agreed level.

price tag *n.* **1.** A label attached to a piece of merchandise indicating its price. **2.** The cost of something: *Success carried a high price tag.*

price war *n.* A situation in which suppliers in the same market cut their prices in a competitive battle to increase their sales.

pric·ey (prī′sē) *adj.* **-ier, -iest.** *Informal.* Expensive.

prick (prĭk) *n.* **1. a.** The act of puncturing lightly. **b.** The sensation of being punctured lightly: *I felt a slight prick when the thorn pierced my finger.* **2.** A painful or stinging feeling, as of sorrow: *the pricks of remorse.* **3.** A small mark or puncture made by a pointed object. **4.** A pointed object, such as an ice pick, goad, thorn, or bee stinger. ∼*v.* **pricked, pricking, pricks.** —*tr.* **1. a.** To puncture lightly. **b.** To puncture so as to cause injury. **2.** To sting with a mental or emotional pang. **3.** To urge forward or onward; impel: *"My duty pricks me on"* (Shakespeare). **4.** To mark or delineate on a surface by means of small punctures: *prick a pattern on a board.* **5.** *Nautical.* To measure with dividers on a chart. **6.** To cause to rise sharply or stiffly: *The dog pricked his ears.* **7.** To transplant (seedlings) prior to a final planting. **8.** To pierce the quick of (a horse's hoof) while shoeing. —*intr.* **1.** To pierce or puncture something. **2.** To feel a stinging or pricking sensation. **3.** To ride at a gallop. —**prick up one's ears.** To listen with attentive interest. [Middle English *prik(ke),* Old English *prica,* pricked mark, puncture, from West Germanic *prikk-* (unattested).]

prick·er (prĭk′ər) *n.* **1.** Something, such as a tool, that pricks. **2.** A prickle or thorn.

prick·et (prĭk′ĭt) *n.* **1. a.** A small spike for holding a candle upright. **b.** A candlestick having such a spike. **2.** A male deer before his antlers branch. [Middle English *priket,* from *prik,* PRICK.]

prick·le (prĭk′əl) *n.* **1.** A small, sharp point arising from the epidermis of a branch, leaf, or other plant structure and containing no woody or vascular tissue. **2.** A spine, as on a hedgehog. **3.** A pricking or tingling sensation.
∼*v.* **prickled, -ling, -les.** —*tr.* **1.** To prick, as with a thorn. **2.** To cause a tingling sensation in. —*intr.* **1.** To feel a tingling sensation. **2.** To rise or stand up like prickles. [Middle English *prikle, prikel,* from Old English *pricel(s),* from West Germanic *prikkil-* (unattested), diminutive of *prikk-,* PRICK.]

prick·ly (prĭk′lē) *adj.* **-lier, -liest. 1.** Having prickles or sharp spines. **2.** Tingling; smarting; stinging. **3. a.** Touchy; irritable. **b.** Causing irritation: *a prickly problem.* —**prick·li·ness** *n.*

prickly heat *n.* A noncontagious skin disease, **miliaria** *(see).*

prickly pear *n.* **1.** Any of various cacti of the genus *Opuntia,* having bristly flattened or cylindrical joints, showy, usually yellow flowers, and ovoid, sometimes edible fruit. See **cholla, nopal. 2.** The fruit of any of these plants.

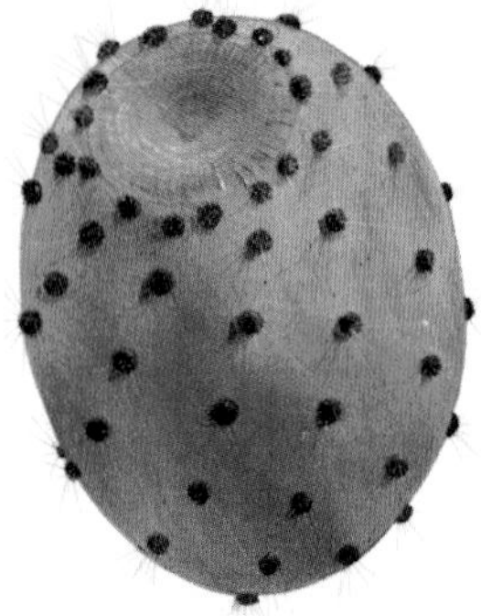

prickly pear *The edible fruit of some species of* Opuntia *cacti.* Opuntia ficus-indica, *shown here, is a native of Mexico.*

prickly poppy *n.* Any of various plants of the genus *Argemone,* chiefly of tropical America, having large yellow or white flowers and prickly leaves, stems, and pods.

pride (prīd) *n.* **1.** A sense of one's own proper dignity or value; self-respect: *Failure robbed them of their pride.* **2.** Pleasure or satisfaction taken in one's work, achievements, or possessions: *took pride in her garden.* **3. a.** A cause or source of pride: *These men were their country's pride.* **b.** The best representative or member, as of a group or class. **c.** The most successful or thriving condition; prime: *was in the flush and pride of her youth.* **4. a.** An excessively high opinion of oneself; conceit. **b.** *Theology.* The consideration or personification of this condition as the first of the seven deadly sins. **5. a.** Mettle or spirit in horses. **b.** *Archaic.* The state of sexual desire or heat, especially in female animals; rut. **6.** A company of lions. —**pride of place.** The best or most important position: *Her porcelain collection took pride of place in the dining room.*
∼*v.* **prided, priding, prides.** —*tr.* To esteem (oneself) for: *The musician prided himself on his great virtuosity.* —*intr.* To indulge in self-esteem; glory. [Middle English *pride, prude, prute,* Old English *prȳte, prȳde,* from *prūt, prūd,* PROUD.] —**pride·ful** *adj.* —**pride·ful·ly** *adv.* —**pride·ful·ness** *n.*

Pride (prīd), **Thomas** (died 1658). English colonel in the Parliamentary army. In 1648 he led his regiment to Parliament and expelled some 150 Presbyterian and Royalist members who were opposed to the condemnation of Charles I ("Pride's Purge"); he was one of the signatories of Charles's death warrant.

prie-dieu (prē-dyœ′) *n., pl.* **-dieus** or **-dieux** (-dyœz′). A low desk with space for a book above and with a foot piece below for kneeling in prayer. [French *prie Dieu,* "pray God."]

pri·er, pry·er (prī′ər) *n.* One who pries.

priest (prēst) *n.* **1.** *Abbr.* **P., Pr.** In the Roman Catholic, Eastern Orthodox, Anglican, Armenian, and separated Catholic hierarchies, an ordained clergyman ranking below a bishop but above a deacon and having authority to pronounce absolution and administer sacraments. **2.** A minister in a non-Christian religion.
∼*tr.v.* **priested, priesting, priests.** To ordain or admit to the priesthood. [Middle English *pre(e)st, preost,* from Old English *prēost,* from Vulgar Latin *prester* (unattested), contracted from Late Latin *presbyter,* from Greek *presbuteros,* "elder," comparative of *presbus,* old man.]

priest·ess (prē′stĭs) *n.* A female priest, especially in a non-Christian religion.

priest·hood (prēst′ho͝od′) *n.* **1.** The character, office, or vocation of a priest. **2.** The clergy.

Priest·ley (prēst′lē), **J(ohn) B(oynton)** (1894–1984). British author. His robust and perceptive novels, including *The Good Companions* (1929), have enjoyed great popularity, as have his plays. These include *Laburnum Grove* (1933), a social comedy, and *Dangerous Corner* (1932), an examination of the nature of time and perception.

Priestley, Joseph (1733–1804). English scientist. He is best known for his work on the isolation of gases and for the discovery of oxygen (1774).

priest·ly (prēst′lē) *adj.* **-lier, -liest.** Of, pertaining to, or befitting a priest or priests. —**priest·li·ness** *n.*

prig (prĭg) *n.* **1.** A person regarded as overprecise, affectedly arrogant, smug, or narrow-minded. **2.** *Archaic.* A coxcomb: *"A cane is part of the dress of a prig"* (Steele). [16th century (cant, "tinker") : origin obscure.] —**prig·ger·y** (prĭg′ə-rē) *n.* —**prig·gish** *adj.* —**prig·gish·ly** *adv.* —**prig·gish·ness** *n.*

prim (prĭm) *adj.* **primmer, primmest. 1.** Precise, neat, or trim. **2.** Excessively formal or strict in matters of convention or morality.
∼*v.* **primmed, primming, prims.** —*tr.* To fix (the face or mouth) in a prim expression. —*intr.* To assume a prim expression. [Old French *prin, prime,* very fine, excellent, from Latin *prīmus,* first, PRIME.] —**prim·ly** *adv.* —**prim·ness** *n.*

prim. **1.** primary. **2.** primitive.

pri·ma ballerina (prē′mə) *n., pl.* **prima ballerinas.** The leading female dancer in a ballet company. Compare **ballerina.** [Italian, "first ballerina."]

pri·ma·cy (prī′mə-sē) *n., pl.* **-cies. 1.** The state or condition of being first or foremost. **2.** The office or province of an ecclesiastical primate. [Middle English, from Medieval Latin *prīmātia,* from *prīmās,* PRIMATE.]

pri·ma donna (prē′mə, prĭm′ə) *n., pl.* **prima donnas. 1.** The leading female soloist in an opera company. **2.** A temperamental and conceited person. [Italian, "first lady."]

pri·ma fa·cie (prī′mə fā′shē, fā′shə) *adv.* At first sight; before closer inspection. [Latin.] —**pri·ma-fa·cie** *adj.*

prima-facie evidence *n. Law.* Evidence that would if uncontested establish a fact or raise a presumption of a fact.

pri·mal (prī′məl) *adj.* **1.** Being first in time; original or primitive. **2.** Of first importance; primary. [Medieval Latin *prīmālis,* from Latin *prīmus,* first.]

primal scream therapy *n.* Primal therapy.

primal therapy *n.* A form of psychotherapy in which attempts are made to make patients relive painful earlier experiences, as of infancy and sometimes birth, the reliving of which with full intensity is held to produce permanent positive physical and psychological changes. —**primal therapist** *n.*

pri·mar·i·ly (prī-mâr′ə-lē, -mĕr′ə-lē) *adv.* **1.** At first; originally. **2.** Chiefly; principally.

pri·mar·y (prī′mĕr′ē, -mə-rē) *adj. Abbr.* **prim. 1.** Occurring first in time, development, or sequence; earliest and original: *The author's personal correspondence constitutes a primary source.* **2.** Of or pertaining to a primary school. **3.** Of, being, or standing first in a list, series, or sequence: *The chairman of the board is our primary negotiator.* **4.** First or best in degree, quality, or importance: *Safety must be the primary consideration.* **5.** *Geology.* **a.** Of, pertaining to, or designating the earliest periods of geological development up to and including the Paleozoic era; Precambrian. **b.** Designating features of a rock that developed at the time of formation. **6. a.** Of, pertaining to, or being a fundamental or basic part of an organized whole: *Play on words is a primary element in Shakespeare's language.* **b.** Of or designating certain basic natural industries, such as agriculture, fishing, or forestry, or their products. **7.** Immediate; direct: *A primary effect of eating is a feeling of satiety.* **8.** Of or pertaining to the basic colors from which all other colors may be derived. See **primary color. 9.** *Linguistics.* **a.** Having a word root or other linguistic element as a basis that cannot be further analyzed or broken down. Said of the derivation of a word or word element. **b.** Referring to present or future time. Said of the various present and future tenses in Latin, Greek, and Sanskrit. **10.** *Electricity.* Of, pertaining to, or designating an inducting current, circuit, or coil. **11.** Of, pertaining to, or designating the main flight feathers projecting along the outer edge of a bird's wing. **12.** *Chemistry.* **a.** Pertaining to the replacement of one of several atoms or radicals in a compound by another atom or radical. **b.** Having a carbon atom attached solely to one other carbon atom in a molecule. **13.** Of, pertaining to, or designating plant growth derived solely from apical meristems present in the embryo. **14.** *Biochemistry.* Of, pertaining to, or being the sequence of amino acids in a protein. —See Synonyms at **chief.**
∼*n., pl.* **primaries.** *Abbr.* **prim. 1. a.** One that is first in time, order, or sequence. **b.** One that is first or best in degree, quality, or impor-

tance. **c.** One that is fundamental or basic. **2.** A primary color. **3.** Any of the main flight feathers projecting along the outer edge of a bird's wing. **4.** An inducting electric current, circuit, or coil. **5.** *Astronomy.* A celestial body, especially a star, to which the orbit of a satellite, or secondary, is referred. **6.** A cosmic ray. **7. a.** A meeting of the registered voters of a political party for the purpose of nominating candidates and for choosing delegates to their party convention. **b.** A preliminary election in which the registered voters of a political party nominate candidates for office. [Middle English, from Latin *prīmārius,* of the first rank, chief, basic, from *prīmus,* first.]

primary accent *n.* **Primary stress** *(see).*

primary atypical pneumonia *n.* A mild pneumonia that is probably caused by a virus.

primary cell *n.* A cell in which an irreversible chemical reaction generates electricity. Also called "galvanic cell," "voltaic cell." Compare **secondary cell.**

primary coil *n.* An electrically conducting coil, as in a transformer, that carries an inducting current.

primary color *n.* A color belonging to any of three groups, each of which is regarded as generating all colors. These groups are: **1.** *Additive, physiological,* or *light* primaries—red, green, and blue. Lights of red, green, and blue wavelengths may be mixed to produce all colors. **2.** *Subtractive* or *colorant* primaries—magenta, yellow, and cyan. Substances that reflect light of one of these wavelengths and absorb (subtract) other wavelengths may be mixed to produce all colors. **3.** *Psychological* primaries—red, yellow, green, and blue, plus the achromatic pair black and white. All colors may be subjectively conceived as mixtures of these.

primary group *n. Sociology.* A group of people in regular personal and social contact, as a family or a team of workers. Compare **secondary group.**

primary radiation *n.* Cosmic radiation as it enters the earth's atmosphere.

primary school *n.* A school that usually comprises the first three or four grades of elementary school and sometimes kindergarten.

primary stress *n.* **1.** The strongest stress or accent in a word; for example, in the word *typical,* the first syllable carries the primary stress. **2.** The mark (′) used to indicate the primary stress in the pronunciation of a word. In both senses, also called "primary accent." Compare **secondary stress, tertiary stress.**

pri·mate (prī′mĭt, -māt′ *for sense 1;* prī′māt′ *for sense 2*) *n.* **1.** *Often* **Primate.** A bishop of the highest rank in a province or country. **2.** A member of the order Primates, which includes the monkeys, apes, and humans, typically having dexterous hands and feet, binocular vision, and a well-developed brain.
~*adj.* Of, pertaining to, or belonging to the order Primates. [Middle English *primat,* from Old French, from Medieval Latin *prīmās* (stem *prīmāt-*), archbishop, from Latin, "of the first rank," chief, leader, from *prīmus,* first.] —**pri·mate·ship** *n.* —**pri·ma·tial** (prī-mā′shəl) *adj.*

pri·ma·ve·ra (prē′mə-vĕr′ə) *n.* **1.** A tree, *Cybistax donnellsmithii,* of Central America, having yellow flowers and close-grained light-colored wood. **2.** The wood of the primavera, used in cabinetwork. [American Spanish, from Spanish, "spring," from Late Latin *prīma vēra,* early spring, feminine of Latin *prīmum vēr* : *prīmum,* first part, from neuter of *prīmus,* first + *vēr,* spring.]

prime (prīm) *adj.* **1.** First in excellence, quality, or value: *prime beef.* **2.** First in degree or rank; chief: *Money was his prime motive.* **3.** First or early in time, order, or sequence. **4.** *Mathematics.* Designating a prime number.
~*n.* **1. a.** The earliest hours of the day. **b.** The season of spring. **2.** *Mathematics.* A prime number. **3.** The age of maximum physical health and intellectual vigor: *the prime of life.* **4.** The period or phase of ideal or peak condition. **5.** In fencing, the first of eight positions of thrust and parry. **6.** A mark (′) written above and to the right of a letter in order to distinguish it from the same letter already in use or to designate a related quantity or thing, such as feet, minutes of angle, or minutes of time. **7.** *Theology.* **a.** The second of the seven **canonical hours** *(see).* **b.** The time of day set aside for this prayer, usually about 6:00 A.M. **8.** *Music.* **a.** The tonic of a scale. **b.** A zero interval between notes.
~*v.* **primed, priming, primes.** —*tr.* **1.** To make ready; prepare. **2.** To prepare (a gun or mine) for firing by inserting a charge of gunpowder or a primer. **3.** To prepare for operation, as by pouring water into a pump or gasoline into a carburetor. **4.** To prepare (a surface) for painting by covering with size, primer, or an undercoat. **5.** To prepare with information; coach. —*intr.* To prepare someone or something for future action or operation. [Middle English, from Old French, feminine of *prin,* from Latin *prīmus,* first; the canonical hour derives from Old English *prīm,* from Latin *prīma (hōra),* first (hour), from the feminine of *prīmus.*] —**prime·ly** *adv.* —**prime·ness** *n.*

prime meridian *n.* The zero meridian (0°), used as a reference line from which longitude east and west is measured and which passes through Greenwich, England.

prime minister *n. Abbr.* **P.M. 1.** A chief minister appointed by a ruler. **2.** *Often* **Prime Minister.** In a parliamentary democracy, such as Britain, the chief minister who leads the government. —**prime ministership, prime ministry** *n.*

prime mover *n.* **1.** The initial force, such as electricity, wind, or gravity, that engages or moves a machine. **2.** Something regarded as the initial source of energy directed toward a goal. **3.** A machine or mechanism that converts natural energy into work. **4.** In Aristotelian philosophy, the self-moved being that causes all motion.

prime number *n.* A number that has itself and one as its only factors.

prim·er[1] (prĭm′ər) *n.* **1.** A school textbook. **2.** A book that covers the basic elements of any subject: *a primer of Freudian psychology.* [Middle English, from Norman French, from Medieval Latin *prīmārium (manuāle),* "basic (handbook)," from Latin *prīmārius,* basic, PRIMARY.]

prim·er[2] (prī′mər) *n.* **1.** A cap or tube containing a small amount of explosive used to detonate the main explosive charge of a firearm or mine. **2.** Someone or something that primes or causes to be primed. **3.** An undercoat of paint or size applied to prepare a surface, as for painting. [From PRIME (verb).]

prime rate *n.* The lowest rate of interest on bank loans at any given time and place, offered to preferred borrowers.

pri·me·ro (prĭ-mâr′ō) *n.* A gambling card game popular in Elizabethan England. [Alteration of Spanish *primera,* feminine of *primero,* "first," from Latin *prīmārius,* principal, from *prīmus,* first.]

prime time *n.* The hours, usually during the evening, when television attracts its largest audience.

pri·me·val (prī-mē′vəl) *adj.* Belonging to the first or earliest age; original: *the primeval swamp.* [Latin *prīmaevus,* in the first period of life : *prīmus,* first + *aevum,* age.] —**pri·me·val·ly** *adv.*

prime vertical *n. Astronomy.* The great circle that passes through an observer's zenith at right angles to the celestial meridian and intersects the horizon at the east and west points.

pri·mi·grav·i·da (prī′mə-grăv′ĭ-də) *n., pl.* **-das** or **-dae** (-dē). *Medicine.* A woman who is pregnant for the first time. [New Latin, from Latin (feminine) *prima,* first + *gravida,* GRAVID.]

prim·ing (prī′mĭng) *n.* **1.** The explosive used to ignite a charge. **2.** A preliminary coat of paint or size applied to a surface.

pri·mip·a·ra (prī-mĭp′ər-ə) *n., pl.* **-aras** or **-arae** (-ə-rē′). *Medicine.* A woman who has borne only one child. [Latin : *prīmus,* first + *-para,* feminine of *-parus,* -PAROUS.] —**pri·mi·par·i·ty** (prī′mə-păr′ə-tē) *n.* —**pri·mip·a·rous** (prī-mĭp′ər-əs) *adj.*

prim·i·tive (prĭm′ə-tĭv) *adj. Abbr.* **prim. 1.** Of or pertaining to an earliest or original stage or state: *the primitive church.* **2.** Characterized by simplicity or crudity; unsophisticated: *primitive weapons.* **3.** Of or pertaining to early stages in the evolution of human culture: *primitive societies.* **4.** *Linguistics.* **a.** Serving as the basis for derived or inflected forms. **b.** Being a protolanguage: *primitive Germanic.* **5.** *Mathematics.* Being a form in geometry or algebra from which another form is derived. **6. a.** Of or pertaining to late medieval or pre-Renaissance European painters. **b.** Of, pertaining to, or having an unsophisticated style of painting. **c.** Of, pertaining to, or being one who paints in a primitive style. **d.** Self-taught: *a primitive cabinetmaker.* **7.** *Geology.* Of or pertaining to rocks formed by the first solidification of the earth's crust. **8.** *Biology.* Occurring in or characteristic of an early stage of development or evolution.
~*n.* **1.** A person belonging to a primitive society. **2.** One that is at a low or early stage of development. **3. a.** One belonging to an early stage in the development of a culture or artistic trend; especially, a painter of the pre-Renaissance period. **b.** An artist having or affecting a primitive style. **c.** A self-taught artist. **d.** A work by a primitive painter. **4.** *Linguistics.* A word or word element from which another word or inflected form of the word is derived. Compare **derivative. 5.** *Computer Science.* A basic or fundamental unit of machine instruction or translation. [Middle English *primitif,* from Old French, from Latin *prīmitīvus,* first of its kind, from *prīmitus,* at first, in the first place, from *prīmus,* first.] —**prim·i·tive·ly** *adv.* —**prim·i·tive·ness, prim·i·tiv·i·ty** (prĭm′ə-tĭv′ə-tē) *n.*

primitive so·lar-neb·u·la hypothesis (sō′lər-nĕb′yə-lə) *n.* A theory of the origin of the solar system that combines elements of the **nebular hypothesis** and the **planetismal hypothesis** (*both of which see*). It states that dust and gas condensed from galactic matter, forming a *presolar medium* that contracted under its own gravity and eventually led to the formation of the sun and planetismals, which in turn accreted further matter to form the planets, their satellites, and the rest of the bodies in the solar system.

prim·i·tiv·ism (prĭm′ə-tĭ-vĭz′əm) *n.* **1.** The state or quality of being primitive. **2.** A belief that modern civilization would benefit by a return to or consideration of primitive culture, customs, or ideas. **3.** The style of primitive painters. —**prim·i·tiv·ist** *adj.* & *n.* —**prim·i·tiv·is·tic** (prĭm′ə-tĭ-vĭs′tĭk) *adj.*

pri·mo (prē′mō) *n., pl.* **-mos** or **-mi** (-mē). *Music.* The principal part in a duet or ensemble composition. [Italian, "first," from Latin *prīmus.*] —**pri·mo** *adj.*

Pri·mo de Ri·ve·ra (prē′mo də rĭ-vĕr′ə), **Miguel** (1870–1930). Spanish general and politician. He seized power (1923) and established a military directorate to run the country. Political dissent and ill health forced his resignation (1930). His son **José Antonio** (1903–36) founded the Falangist movement and was executed by the Loyalists in the Civil War.

pri·mo·gen·i·tor (prī′mō-jĕn′ə-tər) *n.* The earliest ancestor or forefather. [Medieval Latin : Latin *prīmus,* first + GENITOR.]

pri·mo·gen·i·ture (prī′mō-jĕn′ə-chŏŏr′, -chər) *n.* **1.** The state of being the first-born or eldest child of the same parents. **2.** *Law.* The right of the eldest child, especially the eldest son, to inherit the entire estate of one or both parents. Compare **ultimogeniture.** [Medieval Latin *prīmōgenitūra* : Latin *prīmus,* first + *genitūra,* birth, from *gignere* (stem *genit-*), to beget.] —**pri·mo·gen·i·tar·y** (prī′mō-jĕn′ə-tĕr′ē), **pri·mo·gen·i·tal** (-ə-təl) *adj.*

PRONUNCIATION KEY

ă, **pat**; ā, **pay**; âr, **care**; ä, **father**, **are**; b, **bib**; ch, **church**; d, **deed**; ĕ, **pet**; ē, **be**; f, **fife**; g, **gag**; h, **hat**; hw, **which**; ĭ, **pit**; ī, **pie**; îr, **pier**; j, **judge**; k, **kick**; l, **lid**, **needle**; m, **mum**; n, **no**, **sudden**; ng, **thing**; ŏ, **pot**; ō, **toe**; ô, **paw**, **for**; oi, **noise**; ou, **out**; ŏŏ, **book**; ōō, **boot**; p, **pop**; r, **roar**; s, **sauce**; sh, **ship**, **dish**; t, **tight**; th, **thin**, **path**; *th*, **this**, **bathe**; ŭ, **cut**; ûr, **fur**; v, **valve**; w, **with**; y, **yes**; z, **zebra**, **size**; zh, **vision**; ə, **about**, **item**, **edible**, **gallop**, **circus**, **peaceful**

IN FOREIGN WORDS:

à, *Fr.* **ami**; œ, *Fr.* **feu**, *Ger.* **schön**; ü, *Fr.* **tu**, *Ger.* **über**; KH, *Ger.* **ich**, *Scot.* **loch**; N, *Fr.* **bon**; y′, *Fr.* **Compiègne**

STRESS MARKS:

Primary stress: ′
in·cite′ (ĭn-sīt′)
Secondary stress: ′
in′sight′ (ĭn′sīt′)

pri·mor·di·al (prī-môr′dē-əl) *adj.* **1.** Happening at, belonging to, or characteristic of the beginning of time or history. **2.** Fundamental; seeming to have always existed: *primordial images in myths.* **3.** *Biology.* Belonging to or characteristic of the earliest stage of development of an organism or part.
~*n.* A basic principle. [Middle English, from Late Latin *prīmōrdiālis,* from Latin *prīmōrdium,* origin, from *prīmōrdius,* original : *prīmus,* first + *ordīrī,* to begin.] **—pri·mor·di·al·ly** *adv.*

primordial soup *n.* The suspension of organic molecules thought to have been the origin of life. Compare **spontaneous generation, abiogenesis.**

pri·mor·di·um (prī-môr′dē-əm) *n., pl.* **-dia** (-dē-ə). An organ or part in its earliest stage of development. [Latin, "origin." See **primordial.**]

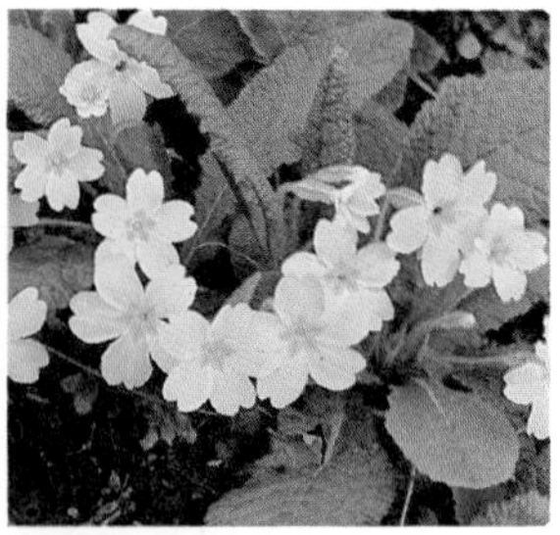
primrose *There are over 500 species in the primrose genus; this is* Primula vulgaris. *They grow wild throughout the Northern Hemisphere in cool or mountainous areas and are common garden plants.*

primp (prĭmp) *v.* **primped, primping, primps.** *—tr.* To neaten (one's hair, for example) with considerable attention to detail. *—intr.* To groom oneself with great care. [Dialectal variant of PRIM.]

prim·rose (prĭm′rōz′) *n.* **1.** Any of various plants of the genus *Primula;* especially, *P. vulgaris,* which has single pale-yellow flowers on long hairy stalks. **2.** The **evening primrose** *(see).* **3.** A pale yellow. [Middle English *primerose,* from Old French, from Medieval Latin *prīma rosa,* "first (or earliest) rose" : Latin *prīma,* feminine of *prīmus,* first + *rosa,* ROSE.]

primrose path *n.* A life of ease or pleasure, especially at the risk of eventual ruin.

prim·u·la (prĭm′yə-lə) *n.* A plant of the genus *Primula,* which includes the primrose, cowslip, oxlip, and polyanthus. [Medieval Latin, feminine noun from *primulus,* diminutive of *prīmus,* first.]

pri·mum mo·bi·le (prī′məm mō′bə-lē′, prē′məm mō′bə-lā′) *n.* **1.** In medieval astronomy, the tenth and outermost concentric sphere of the universe, thought to revolve around the earth from east to west in 24 hours and believed to cause the other nine spheres to revolve with it. **2.** A prime mover. [Medieval Latin, "first moving (thing)," a translation of Arabic *al-muḥarrik al-awwal.*]

pri·mus (prī′məs) *n., pl.* **-muses.** The first in rank of the bishops of the Scottish Episcopal Church. [Medieval Latin *prīmus,* from Latin, first.]

Pri·mus (prī′məs) *n.* A trademark for a small, portable oil-burning stove.

pri·mus in·ter pa·res (prī′məs ĭn′tər pâr′ēz′, prē′məs) *n.* The first among equals. [Latin.]

prin. **1.** principal. **2.** principle.

prince (prĭns) *n.* **1.** A hereditary ruler; a king. **2.** *Abbr.* **p., P., Pr.** The ruler of a principality or a small state. **3.** *Abbr.* **p., P., Pr.** A male member of a royal family other than the monarch; especially, in Britain, the son or grandson of a monarch. **4.** *Abbr.* **p., P., Pr.** A nobleman of varying status or rank. **5.** An outstanding man in a group or class: *a merchant prince.* [Middle English, from Old French, from Latin *princeps* (stem *princip-*), first in rank, sovereign, ruler : *prīmus,* first + *cipere,* variant of *capere,* to take.]

Prince Al·bert (ăl′bərt) *n.* A man's long, double-breasted frock coat. [Popularized by Prince *Albert* Edward, later Edward VII.]

prince consort *n.* The husband of a sovereign queen.

prince·dom (prĭns′dəm) *n.* **1.** The territory ruled by a prince; a principality. **2.** The rank or status of a prince.

Prince Ed·ward Island (ĕd′wərd). *Abbr.* **P.E.I.** Island province of southeastern Canada, in the Gulf of St. Lawrence and separated from the mainland by Northumberland Strait. Its capital is Charlottetown.

prince·ling (prĭns′lĭng) *n.* Also **prince·let** (-lĭt). A prince of minor status or importance.

prince·ly (prĭns′lē) *adj.* **-lier, -liest. 1.** Of or befitting a prince. **2.** Sumptuous; lavish. **—prince·li·ness** *n.* **—prince·ly** *adv.*

Prince of Darkness *n.* Satan.

Prince of Peace *n.* Christ.

Prince of the Church *n.* A cardinal in the Roman Catholic Church.

Prince of Wales *n.* **1.** A title given to the eldest son of a British sovereign. **2.** A male holding the title Prince of Wales.

prince regent *n.* A prince who rules a country during the minority, absence, or incapacity of a sovereign.

prince royal *n.* The eldest son of a sovereign.

prince's-feath·er (prĭn′sĭz-fĕth′ər) *n.* **1.** An annual plant, *Amaranthus hybridus hypochondriacus,* having dense, feathery red flower clusters. **2.** A tall plant, *Polygonum orientale,* having hairy stems and long spikes of pink or rose flowers.

prin·cess (prĭn′sĭs, -sĕs′, prĭn-sĕs′) *n.* **1.** *Archaic.* A hereditary female ruler; a queen. **2.** The female ruler of a principality. **3.** A female member of a royal family other than the monarch; especially, in Britain, the daughter or granddaughter of a monarch. **4.** A noblewoman of varying status or rank. **5.** The wife of a prince. **6.** A woman thought of as having the status or qualities of a princess.
~*adj.* Also **prin·cesse** (prĭn-sĕs′). Designed to hang in smooth, close-fitting, unbroken lines from shoulder to flared hem: *a princess dress; a princess coat.* [Middle English *princesse,* from Old French, feminine of PRINCE.]

princess royal *n.* The eldest daughter of a sovereign.

Prince·ton (prĭn′stən). Town in west-central New Jersey. It is the site of the defeat of the British under James Grant and Lord Cornwallis by George Washington's forces (1777). Today it is noted chiefly for its university.

prin·ci·pal (prĭn′sə-pəl) *adj. Abbr.* **prin.** First, highest, or foremost in importance, rank, worth, or degree; chief: *My principal reason for asking is that I'm concerned.* —See Synonyms at **chief.**
~*n. Abbr.* **prin. 1.** One who holds a position of presiding rank; especially, the head of an elementary school or a high school. **2.** A main participant in a given situation. **3.** A person having a leading or starring role, as in a dramatic work. **4.** *Finance.* **a.** The capital or main body of an estate or financial holding as distinguished from the interest or revenue from it. **b.** A sum of money owed as a debt, upon which interest is calculated. **5.** *Law.* **a.** A person who empowers another to act as his representative. **b.** The person having prime responsibility for an obligation as distinguished from one who acts as surety or as an endorser. **c.** One who commits or is an accomplice to a crime. **6.** The main truss or rafter that supports and gives form to a roof. **7.** Either of the participants in a duel. **8. Principal.** *British.* An administrative officer of the government service in the grade between Assistant Secretary and Senior Executive Officer. **9.** *Music.* **a.** A player leading any of the instrumental groups in an orchestra. **b.** A four-foot diapason stop on an organ. [Middle English, from Old French, from Latin *principālis,* first, original, hence overseer, ruler, from *princeps,* first one in rank, chief, PRINCE.] **—prin·ci·pal·ly** *adv.*
Usage: *Principal* and *principle* are often confused in spelling, but they have no senses in common. *Principal* is both an adjective and a noun, with senses to do with "leading, chief": *the principal violinist; the principal of the college. Principle* is only a noun, pertaining to basic truths, laws, or rules: *the principle of self-government.*

principal axis *n.* **1.** An imaginary line that passes through the centers of curvature of a system of lenses or mirrors. **2.** Any of the three mutually perpendicular axes about which the moment of inertia of a body is a maximum.

principal diagonal *n.* The diagonal in a square matrix that goes from the upper left corner to the lower right corner.

principal focus *n.* A **focal point** *(see).*

prin·ci·pal·i·ty (prĭn′sə-păl′ə-tē) *n., pl.* **-ties. 1.** A territory ruled by a prince or from which a prince derives his title. **2.** The position, authority, or jurisdiction of a prince; sovereignty. **3. principalities.** In medieval angelology, one of the nine orders of angels. See **angel.**

principal parts *pl.n.* In traditional grammars of inflected languages, the primary forms of a verb from which all other forms may be derived. In English, the principal parts are generally considered to be the present infinitive *(play, eat),* the past tense *(played, ate),* the past participle *(played, eaten),* and the present participle *(playing, eating).* ***Note:*** In this dictionary, all inflected forms of verbs are given. For regular verbs, this includes, in addition to the principal parts, the third-person singular form *(plays, eats),* which is listed following the present participle.

prin·cip·i·um (prĭn-sĭp′ē-əm) *n., pl.* **-ia** (-ē-ə). A principle, especially one that is basic. [Latin, basis, origin, PRINCIPLE.]

prin·ci·ple (prĭn′sə-pəl) *n. Abbr.* **prin. 1.** A basic truth, law, or assumption: *the principles of democracy.* **2. a.** A rule or standard, especially of good behavior. **b.** Moral or ethical standards or judgments collectively. **3.** A fixed or predetermined policy or mode of action: *acting on the principle of every man for himself.* **4.** A basic or essential quality or element determining intrinsic nature or characteristic behavior. **5.** A scientific rule or law, as one concerning: **a.** Natural phenomena: *the principle of relativity.* **b.** Mechanical processes: *the principle of jet propulsion.* **6.** A basic source; an origin. **7.** A constituent imparting a distinctive character. **8. Principle.** *Christian Science.* God. —See Usage note at **principal. —in principle.** With regard to basic elements: *We accept your proposal in principle, but the details will have to be discussed.* [Middle English, origin, commencement, hence fundamental quality or truth, modification of Old French *principe,* from Latin *principium,* from *princeps,* first. See **prince.**]

prin·ci·pled (prĭn′sə-pəld) *adj.* Motivated by or based on moral or ethical principles.

prink (prĭngk) *v.* **prinked, prinking, prinks.** *—tr.* To adorn (oneself) in a showy manner. *—intr.* To primp. [Probably alteration of PRANK (to adorn).] **—prink·er** *n.*

print (prĭnt) *n.* **1.** A mark or impression made in or upon a surface by pressure: *the print of footsteps in the sand.* **2. a.** A device or implement, such as a stamp, die, or seal, used to press markings on or into a surface. **b.** Something formed or marked by such a device: *a print of butter.* **3. a.** Lettering or other impressions produced in ink from type by a printing press or other means. **b.** Matter, such as newspaper publications, produced by such a process. **c.** The state or form of matter so produced. **d.** A newspaper or periodical. **4.** A design or picture transferred from an engraved plate, wood block, lithographic stone, or other medium. **5.** A photographic image transferred to paper or a similar surface, usually from a negative. **6. a.** A fabric or garment with a dyed pattern that has been pressed onto it, usually by engraved rollers. **b.** The pattern itself. **7.** A fingerprint. **—in print. 1.** In printed or published form. **2.** Still offered for sale by the publisher: *books in print.* **—out of print.** No longer offered for sale by the publisher.
~*v.* **printed, printing, prints.** *—tr.* **1.** To press (a mark or design, for example) onto or into a surface. **2.** To make an impression on or in (a surface) with a stamp, seal, die, or similar device. **3.** To press (a stamp or similar device) onto or into a surface to leave a marking. **4.** To produce by means of pressed type on a paper surface with or as if with a printing press. **5.** To offer in printed form; publish. **6.** To write in unjoined characters similar to those commonly used in print. **7.** To impress firmly in the mind or memory. **8.** To produce (a positive photograph) by passing light through a

PRONUNCIATION KEY

ă, pat; ā, pay; âr, care;
ä, father, are; b, bib;
ch, church; d, deed; ĕ, pet;
ē, be; f, fife; g, gag; h, hat;
hw, which; ĭ, pit; ī, pie;
îr, pier; j, judge; k, kick;
l, lid, needle; m, mum;
n, no, sudden; ng, thing;
ŏ, pot; ō, toe; ô, paw, for;
oi, noise; ou, out; o͝o, book;
o͞o, boot; p, pop; r, roar;
s, sauce; sh, ship, dish;
t, tight; th, thin, path;
th, this, bathe; ŭ, cut; ûr, fur;
v, valve; w, with; y, yes;
z, zebra, size; zh, vision;
ə, about, item, edible,
gallop, circus, peaceful

IN FOREIGN WORDS:

à, *Fr.* ami; œ, *Fr.* feu, *Ger.* schön; ü, *Fr.* tu, *Ger.* über;
KH, *Ger.* ich, *Scot.* loch;
N, *Fr.* bon; y′, *Fr.* Compiègne

STRESS MARKS:

Primary stress: ′
in·cite′ (ĭn-sīt′)
Secondary stress: ′
in′sight′ (ĭn′sīt′)

negative onto sensitized paper. —*intr.* **1.** To work as a printer. **2.** To write in unjoined characters similar to those commonly used in print. **3.** To produce or receive an impression, marking, or image. **4.** To produce a book, newspaper, or the like by printing. [Middle English *pri(e)nte, pre(i)nte,* from Old French *preinte,* from the past participle of *preindre,* to press, from Latin *premere.*]

print. printing.

print·a·ble (prĭn′tə-bəl) *adj.* **1.** Capable of being printed or of producing a print. **2.** Regarded as fit for publication.

printed circuit *n.* An electronic circuit in which the conducting connections are formed by depositing a metal, such as copper, in predetermined patterns on an insulating substrate. Other materials, especially semiconductors, may also be deposited to form various electronic components.

printed matter *n.* Printed material, as a book or magazine, that is not considered first-class mail and qualifies for a special postal rate.

print·er (prĭn′tər) *n.* **1.** A person who operates a printing press. **2.** A typesetter. **3.** Loosely, a person involved in the business of printing. **4.** One that prints. **5.** The part of a word processor or computer that produces printed matter.

printer's devil *n.* An apprentice in a printing establishment.

print·er·y (prĭn′tə-rē) *n., pl.* **-ies. 1.** A place where typographic printing is done. **2.** A factory where fabrics are printed.

print·ing (prĭn′tĭng) *n. Abbr.* **pr., print., ptg. 1.** The process, art, or business of producing printed material by means of inked type and a printing press or by similar means. **2. a.** The act of one that prints. **b.** Matter that is printed. **3.** All the copies of a book or other publication that are printed at one time. Compare **edition. 4.** Written unjoined characters resembling those appearing in print.

printing office *n.* An establishment where printed material is produced, especially one that is officially authorized.

printing press *n.* A machine that transfers lettering or images by the contact of various forms of inked surface with paper or similar material fed into it. Also called "press." See **flat-bed press, rotary press, web press.**

print·mak·ing (prĭnt′mā′kĭng) *n.* The artistic design and manufacture of prints, as woodcuts or silkscreens. **—print·mak·er** *n.*

print out *intr.v.* To print as a computer function; produce print-out. *—tr.v.* To produce (information) as print-out.

print-out (prĭnt′out′) *n.* The printed output of a computer.

print run *n.* The number of copies printed during a continuous operation of a printing press.

print shop *n.* A printers' workplace.

print wheel *n.* A disk-shaped mechanism in a printing device that carries the template of the characters to be printed around its rim and prints one character at a time, revolving after each character to the proper position for the next.

pri·or¹ (prī′ər) *adj.* **1.** Preceding in time or order: *a prior commitment.* **2.** Preceding in importance or value: *a prior consideration.* **—prior to.** Before; earlier than. [Latin. See **prior** (cleric).]

prior² *n.* **1.** A monk in charge of a priory, or ranking next under the abbot of an abbey. **2.** One of the ruling magistrates of the medieval Italian republic of Florence. [Middle English *pri(o)ur,* from Old English and Old French *prior,* both from Medieval Latin *prior,* from Late Latin, superior officer, administrator, from Latin, former, superior.] **—pri·or·ate** *n.* **—pri·or·ship** *n.*

pri·or·ess (prī′ər-ĭs) *n.* A nun at the head of a priory or ranking next below an abbess in an abbey. [Middle English *prioresse,* from Old French, feminine of PRIOR.]

pri·or·i·ty (prī-ôr′ə-tē, -ŏr′ə-tē) *n., pl.* **-ties. 1.** Precedence, especially as established by order of importance or urgency. Also used adjectivally: *priority booking.* **2. a.** An established right to precedence. **b.** Something that has or claims precedence: *Accuracy was not one of her priorities.* **3.** A preceding or coming earlier in time. [Middle English *priorite,* from Old French, from Medieval Latin *priōritās* (stem *priōritāt-*), from Latin *prior,* PRIOR.]

pri·or·y (prī′ə-rē) *n., pl.* **-ies.** A monastery or convent governed by a prior or prioress. [Middle English *priorie,* from Norman French, from Medieval Latin *priōria,* from PRIOR.]

Prip·et (prĭp′ĕt′, prē′pĕt′). *Russian* **Pri·pyat** (prē′pyət). River in western U.S.S.R. Rising near the Polish border in northwestern Ukraine, it flows 800 kilometers (500 miles) generally eastward through the Pripet Marshes to join the Dnieper River near Kiev.

prise. Variant of **prize** (to move with a lever).

pri·sere (prī′sîr′) *n.* The succession of vegetation that occurs in an area not previously occupied by a community as it passes from barren earth or water to a climax community. [PRI(MARY) + SERE (sequence).]

prism (prĭz′əm) *n.* **1.** *Mathematics.* A polyhedron having parallel, congruent polygons as bases and parallelograms as sides. **2.** A homogeneous transparent solid, usually with triangular bases and rectangular sides, used to produce or analyze a continuous spectrum. **3.** A crystalline solid having three or more similar faces parallel to a single axis. [Late Latin *prisma,* from Greek, "a thing sawed," prism, from *priein†,* to saw.]

pris·mat·ic (prĭz-măt′ĭk) *adj.* Also **pris·mat·i·cal** (-ĭ-kəl). **1.** Of, pertaining to, or resembling a prism. **2.** Refracting light as a prism does. **3.** Multicolored; iridescent. **—pris·mat·i·cal·ly** *adv.*

pris·ma·toid (prĭz′mə-toid′) *n. Mathematics.* A polyhedron having all vertices lying in one of two parallel planes. [New Latin *prismatoides* : Greek *prisma* (stem *prismat-*), PRISM + -OID.] **—pris·ma·toi·dal** (prĭz′mə-toid′l) *adj.*

SPREADING THE WORD QUICKLY AND ACCURATELY
How letterpress printing opened up mass communication

Printing, the repeated reproduction on paper of words in ink, gave man the means of mass communication. Suddenly, thousands of leaflets, pamphlets, or books could be reproduced in a fraction of the time it took a whole team of men to copy by hand a single publication.

Ancient Babylonians had put their information in seals of baked clay. The Egyptians wrote on papyrus; the Romans on parchment, an untanned leather. Medieval monks copied prayers and bibles on paper, once the secret of papermaking had been learned from the Chinese. But, until printing was invented, the main forms of communication were speech and drama.

In the 1040's in China, books were first printed from individual clay characters held in an iron frame. Metal type was used in Korea around 1400. The process—letterpress printing—was invented independently in Europe about 1440 by Johann Gutenberg of Mainz, West Germany. Using single molds, he was able to cast, in a mixture of tin and lead, all the letters he wanted. Composed together into words and sentences and locked into frames and inked, they could be printed over and over again. Gutenberg's technique, printing from a raised surface, has scarcely changed and has been used to produce most of the millions upon millions of books and newspapers printed since. The development of lithography in Germany (1798) made it simpler to reproduce color pictures, and in 1895, the engraving of copper plates was adapted to reproduce photographs, by etching light and shade onto the plate in a series of dots.

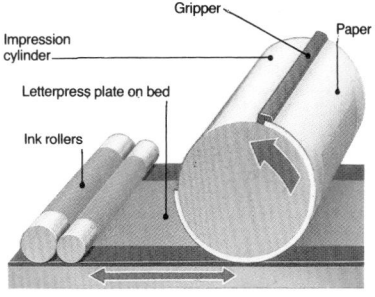

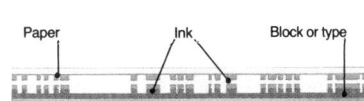

LETTERPRESS *In the oldest form of printing, letterpress, the letters and images to be reproduced are raised above the areas to be left blank. The type and plates are locked into a frame, placed on a flat bed, inked by rollers, and the paper to be printed is gently rolled across it. For high-speed printing of newspapers and magazines, the raised images are impressed on a curved metal stereotype cast from a papier-mâché mold, then fixed to a cylinder on a rotary press.*

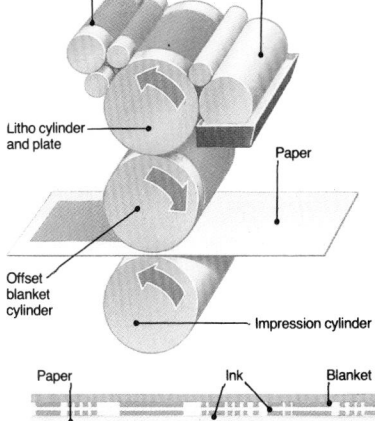

LITHOGRAPHY *Images are photographically exposed onto a flexible metal plate that is developed chemically so that image areas accept greasy ink and nonimage areas only water (grease and water repel each other). The plate is wetted and inked and the image printed onto paper. In offset lithography the image is transferred to a rubber blanket and then onto the paper.*

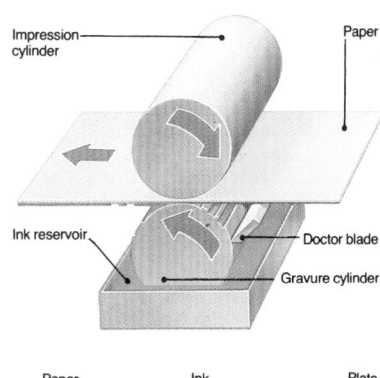

PHOTOGRAVURE *Printing images are exposed photographically onto a plate or copper cylinder that is then etched into cells or recesses. The cylinder runs in an ink reservoir that fills the recesses with ink. A "doctor" blade wipes off surface ink, then the image is printed on paper carried by an impression cylinder. The deeper ink-filled cells create the darker areas.*

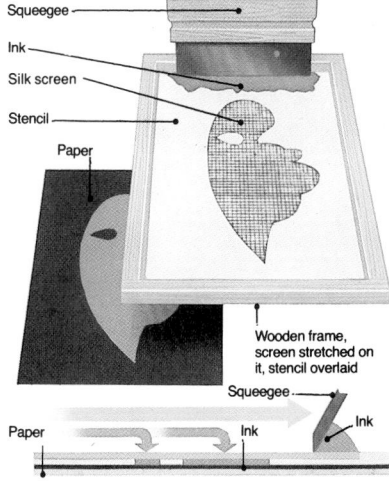

SILK SCREEN *A process used for advertising and display work. A stencil to blank out the nonimage areas is hand-cut or photographically reproduced. A screen of silk, nylon, or metal mesh is stretched over a frame, and the stencil is laid on it. Ink is forced with a rubber squeegee through the screen and onto the paper. The process is repeated for each different color used.*

pris·moid (prĭz′moid′) *n.* A prismatoid whose bases and sides are equal in number and whose faces are parallelograms or trapezoids. [French *prismoïde* : *prisme,* prism, from Late Latin *prisma,* PRISM + -OID.] —**pris·moi·dal** (prĭz-moid′l) *adj.*

pris·on (prĭz′ən) *n.* **1.** A place where persons convicted or accused of crimes are confined; a jail. **2.** Any place or condition of forced confinement or constraint. **3.** Imprisonment.
~*tr.v.* **prisoned, -oning, -ons.** To imprison. [Middle English *priso(u)n, prisun,* from Old French *prison,* "seizure, imprisonment," from Latin *pre(n)siō,* contraction from *prehensiō* (stem *prehensiōn*-), from *prehendere,* to seize.]

pris·on·er (prĭz′ə-nər, prĭz′nər) *n.* **1.** A person held in custody, captivity, or a condition of forcible restraint, especially while awaiting trial or serving a prison sentence. **2.** One deprived of freedom of action or expression: *a prisoner of fate.*

prisoner of conscience *n.* A person imprisoned for political or religious views. Compare **political prisoner.**

prisoner of war *n. Abbr.* **POW, P.O.W.** A person, especially a member of the armed services, taken captive by or surrendering to enemy forces during wartime.

pris·sy (prĭs′ē) *adj.* **-sier, -siest.** Finicky, fussy, and prudish. [Blend of PRIM and SISSY.] —**pris·si·ly** *adv.* —**pris·si·ness** *n.*

pris·tine (prĭs′tēn′, prĭ-stēn′) *adj.* **1.** Of, pertaining to, or typical of the earliest time or condition; primitive or original. **2. a.** Remaining in a pure state; uncorrupted. **b.** Loosely, not soiled; fresh; clean. [Latin *prīstīnus,* original.]

prith·ee (prĭth′ē, prĭth′ē) *interj. Archaic.* Please; I pray thee. [Earlier *preythe,* from (I) *pray thee.*]

priv. private.

pri·va·cy (prī′və-sē) *n., pl.* **-cies. 1.** The condition of being secluded or isolated from the view of, or from contact with, others. **2.** Concealment; secrecy.

pri·vate (prī′vĭt) *adj. Abbr.* **priv., pvt. 1.** Secluded from the sight, presence, or intrusion of others: *a private bathroom.* **2. a.** Of or confined to one person; personal: *private opinions.* **b.** Exclusive to a small group, usually a pair: *a private joke.* **3.** Not available for public use, control, or participation: *a private club.* **4.** Belonging to a particular person or persons, as opposed to the public or the government: *private property.* **5.** Not holding an official or public position: *"Othello himself is no mere private person; he is the general of the Republic"* (A.C. Bradley). **6.** Not public; intimate; secret: *private tragedy.*
~*n.* **1.** *Abbr.* **Pvt.** An enlisted person ranking below private first class in the Army or Marine Corps. **2. privates.** The genitals. —**in private.** Secretly; confidentially. [Middle English *privat,* from Latin *prīvātus,* not belonging to the state, not in public life, deprived of office, from the past participle of *prīvāre,* to deprive, release, from *prīvus,* single, individual, deprived of.] —**pri·vate·ly** *adv.* —**pri·vate·ness** *n.*

private bill *n.* A bill put before a legislative body that deals with the affairs of an individual or organization, such as a local authority, rather than with national matters.

private carrier *n.* A carrier by land, water, or air, as an airline company, that reserves the right to decide whether it will carry particular passengers or goods. Compare **common carrier.**

private detective *n.* A privately employed detective as distinguished from one belonging to a public police force. Also informally called "private eye."

private enterprise *n.* **1.** Business activities unregulated by state ownership or control; privately owned business in general. **2.** A privately owned business enterprise, especially one in a system of free enterprise or laissez-faire capitalism.

pri·va·teer (prī′və-tîr′) *n.* **1.** A ship privately owned and manned but authorized by a government during wartime to attack enemy vessels. **2.** The commander or any crew member of such a ship.
~*intr.v.* **privateered, -teering, -teers.** To sail or serve as a privateer. [From PRIVATE (adjective) by analogy with *volunteer.*]

private first class *n. Abbr.* **Pfc, Pfc.** An enlisted person ranking below corporal and above private in the Army or Marine Corps.

private income *n.* An income derived from trusts, investments, or the like, rather than from employment.

private law *n.* The branch of law that deals with or affects the rights of, and the relations between, private individuals. Compare **public law.**

private member *n.* A member of the British Parliament who does not hold office in the government or in his party.

private parts *pl.n.* The genitals. Used euphemistically.

private school *n.* A school run and supported by private individuals or by a charity or other body rather than by a government or public agency, and usually charging fees. See **public school.**

private sector *n.* The section of a state's economy that is under the control of privately owned enterprises, rather than of government departments or public corporations. Compare **public sector.**

pri·va·tion (prī-vā′shən) *n.* **1. a.** Lack of the basic necessities or comforts of life. **b.** The condition resulting from such lack. **2.** An act, condition, or result of deprivation or loss. [Middle English *privacion,* from Old French *privation,* from Latin *prīvātiō* (stem *prīvātiōn*-), from *prīvāre,* to deprive. See **private.**]

pri·vat·ism (prī′və-tĭz′əm) *n.* The social position of being noncommittal to or uninvolved with anything other than one's own immediate interests and lifestyle. —**pri·va·tis·tic** (prī′və-tĭs′tĭk) *adj.*

priv·a·tive (prĭv′ə-tĭv) *adj.* **1.** Causing deprivation, lack, or loss. **2.** *Grammar.* Altering the meaning of a term from positive to negative.
~*n. Grammar.* A privative prefix or suffix, such as *a-, non-, un-,* or *-less.* [Latin *prīvātīvus,* from *prīvāre,* to deprive. See **private.**] —**priv·a·tive·ly** *adv.*

priv·et (prĭv′ĭt) *n.* Any of several trees or shrubs of the genus *Ligustrum,* having pointed leaves, clusters of white tubular flowers, and black to purple berries; especially, *L. ovalifolium,* which is widely planted as hedging. [16th century : origin obscure.]

privet hawk *n.* A large hawk moth, *Sphinx ligustri,* the larvae of which feed mostly on privet and lilac.

priv·i·lege (prĭv′ə-lĭj) *n.* **1. a.** A special advantage, immunity, permission, right, or benefit granted to or enjoyed by an individual, race, sex, class, or caste. **b.** Such a right or advantage held as a result of status or rank, and exercised to the exclusion or detriment of others. **2.** The principle of granting and maintaining privileges: *a society based on privilege.* **3.** Any of the basic rights to which a nation's citizen is entitled by the constitution. **4.** The rights and immunities of members of legislative bodies enjoyed by virtue of their position. **5.** The right extended to or claimed by priests, lawyers, and certain public officials to withhold confidential information. **6.** *Finance.* Any option to buy or sell a stock, including **put, call, spread,** and **straddle** *(all of which see).* —See Synonyms at **right.**
~*tr.v.* **privileged, -leging, -leges. 1.** To grant a privilege to. **2.** To free or exempt. Used with *from.* [Middle English, from Old French, from Latin *prīvilēgium,* law affecting an individual, prerogative : *prīvus,* single, individual + *lēx* (stem *lēg*-), law.]

priv·i·leged (prĭv′ə-lĭjd) *adj.* **1.** Enjoying a privilege or having privileges: *a privileged childhood.* **2.** Protected against any action for defamation: *a privileged remark.* **3.** Protected against demands for publication or access: *privileged information.*

priv·i·ty (prĭv′ə-tē) *n., pl.* **-ties. 1.** Knowledge of something private or secret shared between individuals, especially with the implication of approval or consent. **2.** *Law.* **a.** A relationship between parties that is held to be sufficiently close and direct to support a legal claim on behalf of or against another person with whom this relationship exists. **b.** A successive or mutual interest in or relationship to the same property. [Middle English *privete, privite,* a secret, privacy, from Old French, from Medieval Latin *prīvitās* (stem *prīvitāt*-), from Latin *prīvus,* single, private.]

priv·y (prĭv′ē) *adj.* **-ier, -iest. 1.** Sharing in or having knowledge of something private or secret. Used with *to*: *privy to another's thoughts and desires.* **2.** Belonging or proper to a person, such as the British sovereign, in his private rather than his official capacity: *Privy Council.* **3.** *Archaic.* Concealed; secret.
~*n., pl.* **privies. 1. a.** A latrine. **b.** An outhouse. **2.** *Law.* Any of the parties having an interest in the same matter. [Middle English *prive,* secret, private, acquainted with, from Old French *prive,* from Latin *prīvātus,* PRIVATE.] —**priv·i·ly** *adv.*

Privy Council *n. Abbr.* **P.C. 1.** A council of the British sovereign that now consists of all current and former cabinet ministers and certain senior legal and ecclesiastical officials in private capacity and others appointed as a high honor, membership being for life. In certain cases its Judicial Committee acts as a supreme appellate court in the Commonwealth. **2.** A similar council in various other countries that serves as an advisory body to the head of state. —**Privy Councillor** *n.*

Privy Purse, privy purse *n.* **1.** The sum of money assigned to the British sovereign, or any of various other sovereigns, for the private expenses of the royal household. **2.** The official in charge of the private expenses of the British royal household.

Privy Seal *n.* In Britain, a royal seal attached to certain documents as proof that they are issued by royal authority.

prix fixe (prē′ fēks′) *n., pl.* **prix fixes** *(pronounced as singular).* **1.** A **table d'hôte** *(see).* **2.** The price at which a table d'hôte meal is offered. Compare **à la carte.** [French, "fixed price."]

prize[1] (prīz) *n.* **1.** Something offered or won as an award for achieving superiority or excellence in competition with others. **2.** Something offered for winning in a raffle, lottery, or other game of chance. **3.** Anything worth striving for or aspiring to.
~*adj.* **1.** Offered or given as a prize: *a prize cup.* **2.** Given a prize, or likely to win a prize: *a prize cow.* **3.** Worthy of a prize; first-class. Often used ironically: *a prize idiot.*
~*tr.v.* **prized, prizing, prizes. 1.** To value highly; esteem, cherish, or treasure. **2.** To estimate the worth of; appraise; evaluate. —See Synonyms at **appreciate.** [Middle English *pris,* value, PRICE.]

prize[2] *n.* **1.** Something seized by force or taken as booty; especially, an enemy ship and cargo captured at sea during wartime. **2.** Something valuable taken from another. **3.** The act of seizing; capture. [Middle English *pris(e),* from Old French *prise,* from Vulgar Latin *pre(n)sa* (unattested), "something seized," from the past participle of Latin *pre(he)ndere,* to seize.]

prize[3], **prise** *tr.v.* **prized, prizing, prizes** or **prised, prising, prises.** To move, open, or force with or as if with a lever.
~*n.* Also **prise** (prīz). **1.** Leverage. **2.** *Regional.* Something used as a lever. [Middle English *prisen* (verb, from noun), from Old French *prise,* lever, instrument for forcing, from the past participle of *prendre,* from Latin *prehendere,* to seize.]

prize court *n. Law.* A court authorized to determine and allocate claimants' shares to goods seized at sea during wartime.

prize·fight (prīz′fīt′) *n.* A match fought between professional boxers for money. —**prize·fight·er** *n.* —**prize·fight·ing** *n.*

PRONUNCIATION KEY

ă, pat; ā, pay; âr, care;
ä, father, are; b, bib;
ch, church; d, deed; ĕ, pet;
ē, be; f, fife; g, gag; h, hat;
hw, which; ĭ, pit; ī, pie;
îr, pier; j, judge; k, kick;
l, lid, needle; m, mum;
n, no, sudden; ng, thing;
ŏ, pot; ō, toe; ô, paw, for;
oi, noise; ou, out; ŏŏ, book;
ōō, boot; p, pop; r, roar;
s, sauce; sh, ship, dish;
t, tight; th, thin, path;
th, this, bathe; ŭ, cut; ûr, fur;
v, valve; w, with; y, yes;
z, zebra, size; zh, vision;
ə, about, item, edible,
gallop, circus, peaceful

IN FOREIGN WORDS:

à, *Fr.* ami; œ, *Fr.* feu, *Ger.* schön; ü, *Fr.* tu, *Ger.* über; KH, *Ger.* ich, *Scot.* loch; N, *Fr.* bon; y′, *Fr.* Compiègne

STRESS MARKS:

Primary stress: ′
in·cite′ (ĭn-sīt′)
Secondary stress: ′
in′sight′ (ĭn′sīt′)

prize money *n.* **1.** Money constituting a prize or prizes. **2.** Money representing a part of the value of ships or property captured at sea, formerly allocated for division between those taking part in the capture. In this sense, also called "prize bounty."

prize ring *n.* **1.** The platform enclosed by ropes in which contending boxers meet. **2.** Professional boxing.

p.r.n. *Medicine.* as the situation demands. [Latin *pro re nata.*]

pro¹ (prō) *n., pl.* **pros.** *Abbr.* **p. 1.** An argument in favor of something; an affirmative consideration. Used chiefly in the phrase *pros and cons.* **2.** One who supports a proposal or takes the affirmative side in debate.
~*prep.* In favor of.
~*adv.* In favor of something; affirmatively.
~*adj.* Favoring; supporting. [Middle English, from Latin *prō,* for.]

pro² *n., pl.* **pros.** *Informal.* **1.** A professional, especially in sports. **2.** An expert in any field of endeavor.
~*adj. Informal.* Professional: *pro football.* [Short for PROFESSIONAL.]

pro–¹ *prefix.* Indicates: **1.** Favor or support; for example, **prorevolutionary. 2.** Acting as; for example, **proconsul, properdin.** *Note:* Many compounds other than those entered here may be formed with *pro-.* In this dictionary, when forming compounds, *pro-* is normally joined with the following element without space or hyphen: *profascist.* However, many users prefer the hyphenated form, especially when the second element begins with a capital letter: *pro-American.* It is also preferable to use the hyphen when the second element begins with *o* or when forming the compound brings together three or more vowels that would be confusing to read: *proaesthetic.* [In borrowed Latin compounds, *pro-* indicates: **1.** Forward, forth, in public, as in **project, proclaim. 2.** Forward and downward, as in **profligate. 3.** Away, as in **prodigal. 4.** In front of, before, as in **prohibit. 5.** Anterior, before, in anticipation of, as in **provide. 6.** Onward, forward, as in **progress. 7.** Extending out, as in **prolong. 8.** Substituting for, acting as, as in **pronominal. 9.** On behalf of, for, as in **prosit. 10.** Intensified action, as in **promiscuous.** Latin *prō-,* from *prō,* before, in front of, according to, for.]

pro–² *prefix.* Indicates before in time or position, or forward; for example, **prophage, procarp, procephalic.** [Greek *pro,* before, in front of, forward.]

pro., Pro. professional.

P.R.O. public relations officer.

pro·a (prō'ə) *n.* A swift Malayan sailing boat with a triangular sail and a single outrigger. [Earlier *parao, prau,* from Malay *pĕrāhū,* probably from Marathi *pạḍāv.*]

pro·am (prō'ăm') *adj.* Of, pertaining to, or designating a sports competition in which both professional and amateur players take part. [PRO(FESSIONAL) + AM(ATEUR)]

pro and con *adj.* Also **pro and contra.** For and against.
~*prep.* For and against. See **pro.** [Latin *pro,* for + *contra,* against.]

prob. 1. probable; probably. **2.** problem.

prob·a·bi·lism (prŏb'ə-bə-lĭz'əm) *n.* **1.** *Philosophy.* The doctrine that probability is a sufficient basis for belief and action, since certainty in knowledge is unattainable. **2.** *Roman Catholic Church.* A principle that when there is doubt as to the moral rectitude of an action, the opinion that favors liberty may be followed provided that it is theologically probable, even though the contrary may be equally or even more probable. —**prob·a·bi·list** *n.* —**prob·a·bi·lis·tic** (prŏb'ə-bə-lĭs'tĭk) *adj.*

prob·a·bil·i·ty (prŏb'ə-bĭl'ə-tē) *n., pl.* **-ties. 1.** The quality or condition of being probable; likelihood. **2.** A probable situation, condition, or event. **3.** *Statistics.* A number expressing the likelihood of occurrence of a specific event, such as the ratio of the number of experimental results that would produce the event to the total number of results considered possible. If the probability is 1 the event is certain to happen; if it is 0 it is certain not to happen. —**in all probability.** Most probably; very likely.

probability density function *n. Statistics.* A function that enables the probability for any value or interval within a range to be determined and formulas for parameters to be established. Also called "density," "density function."

probability theory *n.* A branch of mathematics dealing with the statistical evaluation of the probability of random occurrences.

prob·a·ble (prŏb'ə-bəl) *adj. Abbr.* **prob. 1.** Likely to happen or to be true. **2.** Relatively or most likely but not certain; plausible. **3.** *Theology.* Of or pertaining to moral opinions and actions for the lawfulness of which intrinsic reasons or extrinsic authority may be adduced; possible; provable.
~*n. Informal.* A candidate or competitor who is likely to be selected or successful. [Middle English, from Old French, from Latin *probābilis,* provable, laudable, from *probāre,* to approve, PROVE.]

probable cause *n. Law.* Reasonable grounds for belief that an accused person is guilty as charged and accordingly that further legal action is justified.

prob·a·bly (prŏb'ə-blē) *adv. Abbr.* **prob.** Most likely; in all probability; presumably.

pro·band (prō'bănd') *n.* In genealogical or medical surveys, the ancestor or member of a family who is used as the starting point for the purposes of a genetic study. [Latin *probandus,* gerundive of *probāre,* to test.]

pro·bang (prō'băng') *n.* A long, slender, flexible rod having a tuft or sponge at the end, used to displace foreign bodies from the larynx or esophagus. [Alteration (influenced by PROBE) of earlier *provang* (so named by the inventor).]

pro·bate (prō'bāt') *adj.* Of or pertaining to a probate court or its action.
~*n.* **1.** Legal establishment of the validity of a will. **2.** A document certifying such validity. **3.** The right to validate wills.
~*tr.v.* **probated, -bating, -bates.** To establish the validity of (a will). [Middle English *probat,* from Latin *probātum,* something proved, from *probāre,* to examine, demonstrate as good, PROVE.]

probate court *n.* A court limited to the jurisdiction of probating wills and administering estates.

pro·ba·tion (prō-bā'shən) *n.* **1.** A trial period in which a person's fitness for membership in a working or social group is tested. **2.** *Law.* The action of suspending the sentence of one convicted of a minor offense and granting provisional freedom on the promise of good behavior. **3.** A trial period in which a student is permitted to redeem failing grades or bad conduct. **4.** The status of a person on probation. **5.** The act or process of testing or being tested. [Middle English *probacioun,* from Old French *probation,* from Latin *probātiō* (stem *probātiōn-*), from *probāre,* to try, PROVE.] —**pro·ba·tion·al, pro·ba·tion·ar·y** (prō-bā'shə-něr'ē) *adj.* —**pro·ba·tion·al·ly** *adv.*

pro·ba·tion·er (prō-bā'shə-nər) *n.* A person on probation.

probation officer *n.* A social worker who under the direction of a court supervises and gives support to an offender on probation.

pro·ba·tive (prō'bə-tĭv) *adj.* Also **pro·ba·to·ry** (-tôr'ē, -tōr'ē). **1.** Serving to test, try, or prove. **2.** Furnishing evidence or proof. [Middle English *probatiffe,* from Latin *probātīvus,* of proof, from *probāre,* to try, PROVE.]

probe (prōb) *n.* **1.** Any object or device used to investigate an unknown configuration or condition. **2.** A slender, flexible instrument used to explore a wound or body cavity. **3.** The act of exploring or searching with the aid of such an instrument. **4.** An investigation into the nature of something; especially, an investigation conducted by a legislative committee into corrupt practices. **5.** *Electronics.* An electrical lead attached to a measuring or detecting instrument, used for testing circuits. **6.** Loosely, any act of examining or testing. **7.** A space probe (*see*).
~*v.* **probed, probing, probes.** —*tr.* **1.** To explore with a probe. **2.** To test or examine: *probed their defenses; probing her motives.* **3.** To investigate (a matter, especially a public scandal) thoroughly; delve into. —*intr.* To conduct an exploratory investigation; search. [Medieval Latin *proba,* examination, from Late Latin, proof, test, from Latin *probāre,* to test, PROVE.] —**prob·er** *n.*

pro·bi·ty (prō'bə-tē) *n.* Complete and confirmed integrity; uprightness. —See Synonyms at **honesty.** [Old French *probite,* from Latin *probitās* (stem *probitāt-*), goodness, honesty, from *probus,* good, honest, virtuous.]

prob·lem (prŏb'ləm) *n. Abbr.* **prob. 1.** A question or situation that presents uncertainty, perplexity, or difficulty. **2.** A person who is difficult to deal with. **3.** A question put forward for consideration, discussion, or solution.
~*adj.* **1.** Difficult to deal with or handle: *a problem child.* **2.** Dealing with a social or moral problem: *a problem play.* [Middle English

---

probability

HEADS OR TAILS?

The mathematics behind the toss of a coin

Blaise Pascal, a 17th-century French mathematician, was one of the first scholars to study the laws of chance and so open the way for the science of statistics. The number triangle below—which gives the chances of each outcome possible when one or more coins are tossed together—was devised by him and is known as Pascal's triangle. In each row each number is the sum of the two above. The "6 coins" row shows the probabilities if six coins are tossed. The sum of the numbers in the row, 64, is the total number of possible results. One possible result is six heads and no tails; the chance of this happening is 1 in 64. Another possible result is five heads and one tail; the Pascal triangle shows that its probability is 6 in 64.

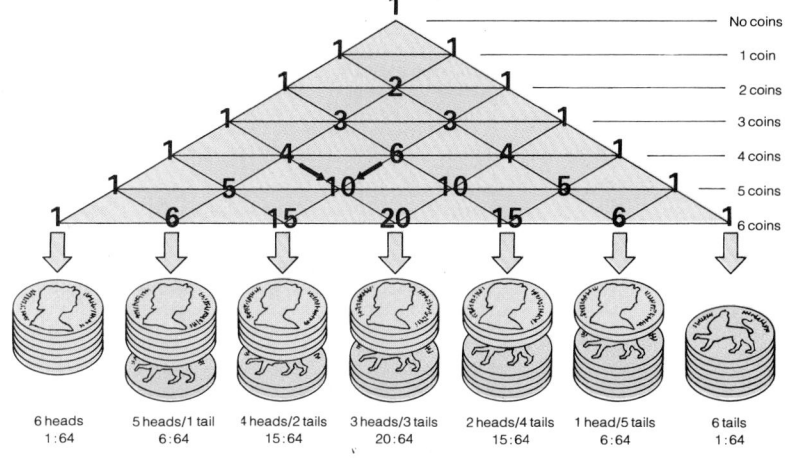

6 heads	5 heads/1 tail	4 heads/2 tails	3 heads/3 tails	2 heads/4 tails	1 head/5 tails	6 tails
1:64	6:64	15:64	20:64	15:64	6:64	1:64

proboscis *The only surviving member of the scientific order* Proboscidea—*the trunked animals—is the elephant. It uses its muscular proboscis to lift food and water to its mouth. The elephant is used in Asia both as a ceremonial means of transportation and as a draft animal.*

probleme, from Old French, from Latin *problēma,* from Greek *problēma,* "thing thrown forward," projection, obstacle, problem, from *proballein,* to throw forward : *pro-,* forward + *ballein,* to throw.]

prob·lem·at·i·cal (prŏb′lə-măt′ĭ-kəl) *adj.* Also **prob·lem·at·ic** (-măt′ĭk). **1.** Posing a problem; difficult to solve. **2.** Open to doubt; debatable. **—prob·lem·at·i·cal·ly** *adv.*

pro·bos·cid·i·an (prō′bŏ-sĭd′ē-ən) *n.* Also **pro·bos·ci·de·an** (prō-bŏs′ə-dē′ən, prō′bŏ-sĭd′ē-ən). An animal belonging to the Proboscidea, an order of mammals that is characterized by a trunk or proboscis and includes the elephant. **—pro·bos·cid·i·an** *adj.*

pro·bos·cis (prō-bŏs′ĭs) *n., pl.* **-cises** or **proboscides** (prō-bŏs′ə-dēz′). **1.** A long, flexible snout or trunk, such as that of an elephant. **2.** A slender, tubular feeding and sucking structure of some insects. **3.** A human nose, especially a prominent one. [Latin, from Greek *proboskis* : *pro-,* in front + *boskein,* to feed.]

proboscis monkey *n.* A monkey, *Nasalis larvatus,* native to the forests of Borneo, the male of which has a large, long nose.

proboscis worm *n.* A marine worm, the **nemertean** *(see).*

proc. **1.** proceedings. **2.** process.

pro·caine hydrochloride (prō′kān′) *n.* A white crystalline powder, $C_{13}H_{20}O_2N_2{\cdot}HCl$, used as a local anesthetic in medicine and dentistry. A trademark is "Novocain." [PRO- (in place of) + (CO)-CAINE.]

pro·cam·bi·um (prō-kăm′bē-əm) *n. Botany.* A layer of meristematic tissue from which the vascular tissue is formed. [PRO- (before) + CAMBIUM.] **—pro·cam·bi·al** *adj.*

pro·carp (prō′kärp′) *n. Botany.* A specialized female reproductive organ in certain algae. [New Latin *procarpium* : PRO- (before) + -CARP.]

procaryote. Variant of **prokaryote.**

pro·ca·the·dral (prō′kə-thē′drəl) *n.* A church functioning as the cathedral church of a diocese.

pro·ce·dur·al (prə-sē′jər-əl) *adj.* Of or concerning procedure, especially of a court of law or parliamentary body.

pro·ce·dure (prə-sē′jər) *n.* **1.** A manner of proceeding; a way of performing or effecting something. **2.** An act composed of steps; a course of action. **3.** A set of established forms or methods for conducting the affairs of a business, legislative body, or court of law. [French *procédure,* from Old French, from *proceder,* to PROCEED.]

pro·ceed (prō-sēd′, prə-) *intr.v.* **-ceeded, -ceeding, -ceeds. 1. a.** To go forward or onward, especially after an interruption; continue. **b.** To resume speaking. **2.** To undertake and carry on some action or process. **3.** To move on in an orderly manner. **4. a.** To come into being; arise. **b.** To issue forth; originate. Used of the Holy Spirit. **c.** To come out; emerge: *cries proceeding from next door.* **5.** To institute and conduct a legal action. Used with *against.* [Middle English *proceden,* from Old French *proceder,* from Latin *prōcēdere* : *prō-,* forward + *cēdere,* to go.] **—pro·ceed·er** *n.*

pro·ceed·ing (prō-sē′dĭng, prə-) *n.* **1.** A course of action; a procedure. **2.** A continuing of an action. **3. proceedings.** A sequence of events occurring at a particular place or time. **4. proceedings.** *Abbr.* **proc.** A record of business carried on by a society or other organization; minutes. **5.** *Law.* **a. proceedings.** Litigation. **b.** The instituting or conducting of litigation.

pro·ceeds (prō′sēdz′) *pl.n.* The amount of money derived from a commercial or fund-raising venture; profits; yield.

pro·ce·phal·ic (prō′sə-făl′ĭk) *adj. Anatomy.* Pertaining or belonging to the front of the head. [PRO- (in front) + -CEPHALIC.]

proc·ess[1] (prŏs′ĕs′, prō′sĕs′) *n. Abbr.* **proc. 1.** A system of operations in the production of something. **2.** A series of actions, changes, or functions that bring about an end or result: *the peacemaking process.* **3.** The course or passage of time. **4.** Ongoing movement; progression. **5.** *Law.* **a.** A summons or writ ordering a defendant to appear in court. **b.** The total set or number of summonses or writs issued in a particular proceeding. **c.** The entire course of a judicial proceeding. **6.** *Biology.* A part extending or projecting from an organ or organism; an appendage. **7.** Any of various photomechanical or photoengraving methods.

~*tr.v.* **processed, -essing, -esses. 1.** To put through the steps of a prescribed procedure. **2.** To prepare, treat, or convert by subjecting to some special process: *processed cheese; to process film.* **3.** *Law.* To serve with a summons or writ. **4.** To institute legal proceedings against; prosecute. **5.** *Computer Science.* To subject (numbers, text, or other data) to modification by program.

~*adj. Abbr.* **proc. 1.** Prepared or converted by a special treatment. **2.** Made by or used in photomechanical or photoengraving methods: *a process print.* [Middle English *proces(se),* from Old French *proces,* from Latin *prōcessus,* from the past participle of *prōcēdere,* to PROCEED.]

pro·cess[2] (prə-sĕs′) *intr.v.* **-cessed, -cessing, -cesses.** To move along or go in or as if in a procession. [Back-formation from PROCESSION.]

pro·ces·sion (prə-sĕsh′ən) *n.* **1.** The act of proceeding, moving along, or issuing forth. **2. a.** A group of persons, vehicles, or objects moving along in an orderly and formal manner, usually in a long line. **b.** The movement of such a group. **3.** Any continuous and orderly course: *the procession of the seasons.*

~*intr.v.* **processioned, -sioning, -sions.** To form or go in a procession. [Middle English, from Old French, from Late Latin *prōcessiō* (stem *prōcessiōn-*), religious procession, from Latin, a marching forward, from *prōcēdere,* to PROCEED.]

pro·ces·sion·al (prə-sĕsh′ə-nəl) *adj.* Of, pertaining to, or suitable for a procession.

~*n.* **1.** A book containing the ritual observed during a religious procession. **2.** A hymn sung when the clergy enter a church at the beginning of the service. **3.** Any music intended to be played or sung during a procession. **—pro·ces·sion·al·ly** *adv.*

proc·es·sor (prŏs′ĕs′ər, prō′sĕs′-) *n.* **1.** One who processes. **2.** The **central processing unit** *(see)* of a computer.

process printing *n.* Printing from multiple, usually four, halftone images, each inked with a different color such that the composite impression will reproduce the colors of the original.

process server *n.* A person who serves summonses or writs.

pro·cès-ver·bal (prō-sā′vĕr-bäl′) *n., pl.* **-baux** (-bō′). **1.** An official record of diplomatic negotiations. **2.** In France, a detailed official record of a legal charge or other proceeding. [French, "verbal proceedings," originally referring to evidence delivered orally by illiterate subaltern police officers.]

pro-choice (prō-chois′) *adj.* Supporting legalized abortion.

pro·chro·nism (prō′krə-nĭz′əm, prŏk′rə-) *n.* An anachronism consisting in assigning something too early a date. Compare **parachronism.** [PRO- + Greek *khronos,* time + -ISM.]

pro·claim (prō-klām′, prə-) *tr.v.* **-claimed, -claiming, -claims. 1.** To announce officially and publicly; declare. **2.** To indicate unmistakably; make plain. **3.** To praise; extol. [Middle English *procla(y)men,* from Old French *proclamer,* from Latin *prōclāmāre* : *prō-,* forward, forth + *clāmāre,* to cry out.] **—pro·claim·er** *n.*

proc·la·ma·tion (prŏk′lə-mā′shən) *n.* **1.** The act of proclaiming. **2.** Something proclaimed; especially, an official public announcement.

pro·clit·ic (prō-klĭt′ĭk) *adj. Linguistics.* Forming an accentual unit with the following word and thus having no independent accent. Compare **enclitic.**

~*n.* A proclitic word. [New Latin *procliticus,* formed by analogy with Late Latin *encliticus,* ENCLITIC : Greek *pro-,* forward + *klinein,* to lean.]

pro·cliv·i·ty (prō-klĭv′ĭ-tē) *n., pl.* **-ties.** A natural propensity or inclination; a predisposition. [Latin *prōclīvitās,* from *prōclīvus,* sloping forward : *prō-,* forward + *clīvus,* slope, hill.]

Pro·clus (prō′kləs, prŏk′ləs) (*c.* 410–85). Greek philosopher. The last major Greek philosopher, he was head of the academy originally established by Plato. He refined the views of previous Neo-Platonists and developed his own system of thought based on the belief that reality is fundamentally mental, not material.

pro·con·sul (prō-kŏn′səl) *n.* **1.** A provincial governor of consular rank in ancient Rome. **2.** A high administrator in any of various territories of the European colonial empires. [Middle English, from Latin, combined from *prō consule,* (one acting) for a consul : *prō-,* for + CONSUL.] **—pro·con·su·lar** *adj.* **—pro·con·su·late** *n.*

Pro·co·pi·us (prə-kō′pē-əs, prō-) (*fl.* 6th century A.D.). Byzantine historian. Active during the reign of Justinian I, he wrote histories of the Persian, Vandal, and Gothic wars and a secret work directed against Justinian, *Anecdota.*

pro·cras·ti·nate (prō-krăs′tə-nāt′, prə-) *v.* **-nated, -nating, -nates.** —*intr.* To put off doing something until a future time. —*tr.* To postpone or delay needlessly. [Latin *prōcrāstināre,* "to put forward to tomorrow" : *prō-,* forward + *crāstinus,* of tomorrow, from *crās†,* tomorrow.] **—pro·cras·ti·na·tion** *n.* **—pro·cras·ti·na·tor** *n.*

pro·cre·ate (prō′krē-āt′) *v.* **-ated, -ating, -ates.** —*tr.* **1.** To beget (offspring). **2.** To produce or create; originate. —*intr.* To beget offspring; reproduce. [Latin *prōcreāre* : *prō-,* forward, forth + *creāre,* to CREATE.] **—pro·cre·ant** *adj.* **—pro·cre·a·tion** *n.* **—pro·cre·a·tor** *n.*

pro·cre·a·tive (prō′krē-ā′tĭv) *adj.* **1.** Capable of reproducing; generative. **2.** Of or directed toward procreation: *procreative instinct.*

pro·crus·te·an (prō-krŭs′tē-ən) *adj.* Producing or designed to produce conformity by ruthless or arbitrary means. [After *Procrustes,* from Greek *Prokroustēs,* "stretcher," name of a legendary giant who stretched or shortened captives to fit an iron bed.]

procrustean bed *n. Often* **Procrustean bed.** An arbitrary standard to which exact conformity is forced.

pro·cryp·tic (prō-krĭp′tĭk) *adj. Zoology.* Having a pattern or coloration adapted for natural camouflage. [Probably PRO(TECT) + CRYPTIC.]

procto–, proct– *prefix.* Indicates rectum or anus; for example, **proctology.** [Greek *prōktos,* anus.]

proc·tol·o·gy (prŏk-tŏl′ə-jē) *n.* The physiology and pathology of the rectum and anus. [PROCTO- + -LOGY.] **—proc·to·log·ic** (prŏk′tə-lŏj′ĭk), **proc·to·log·i·cal** *adj.* **—proc·to·log·i·cal·ly** *adv.* **—proc·tol·o·gist** *n.*

proc·tor (prŏk′tər) *n.* **1.** In certain universities and schools, an official responsible for discipline and for supervising at examinations. **2.** An agent or representative, especially one hired to collect tithes or to conduct a court case on another's behalf. **3.** In the Church of England, an elected clerical member of a synod.

~*v.* **proctored, -toring, -tors.** —*tr.* To serve as proctor at (an examination). —*intr.* To serve as a proctor. [Middle English *proc(u)tour,* agent, deputy, contraction of *procuratour,* PROCURATOR.] **—proc·to·ri·al** (prŏk-tôr′ē-əl, -tōr′ē-əl) *adj.*

proc·to·scope (prŏk′tə-skōp′) *n.* An instrument for examining the rectum. [PROCTO- + -SCOPE.] **—proc·to·scop·ic** (prŏk′tə-skŏp′ĭk) *adj.* **—proc·tos·co·py** (prŏk-tŏs′kə-pē) *n.*

pro·cum·bent (prō-kŭm′bənt) *adj.* **1.** *Botany.* Trailing along the ground; prostrate: *a procumbent vine.* **2.** Lying face down; prone. [Latin *prōcumbens* (stem *prōcumbent-*), present participle of *prōcum-*

bere, to fall forward, bend down : *prō-,* forward, down + *cumbere,* to lie down.]
proc·u·ra·tion (prŏk′yə-rā′shən) *n.* **1. a.** The act or process of procuring. **b.** The state of being procured. **2.** *Law.* The criminal act of procuring women for purposes of prostitution. **3.** *Law.* **a.** The appointment or duties of an agent or legal representative. **b.** The document certifying such appointment or duties. **c. Power of attorney** *(see).*
proc·u·ra·tor (prŏk′yə-rā′tər) *n.* **1.** An agent having power of attorney. **2.** A Roman official acting as a financial agent of the emperor or as the administrator of a minor province. [Middle English *procuratour,* from Old French, from Latin *prōcūrātor,* from *prōcūrāre,* to take care of, PROCURE.] **—proc·u·ra·to·ri·al** (prŏk′yər-ə-tôr′ē-əl, -tōr′ē-əl), **proc·u·ra·to·ry** (prŏk′yər-ə-tôr′ē, -tōr′ē) *adj.*
procurator fiscal *n.* In Scotland, an official who serves as coroner and public prosecutor. Also called "fiscal."
pro·cure (prō-kyo͝or′, prə-) *v.* **-cured, -curing, -cures.** *—tr.* **1.** To obtain; acquire. **2.** To bring about; effect: *procure a solution.* **3.** To obtain (a child or woman) to serve as a prostitute. *—intr.* To obtain girls or women to serve as prostitutes. [Middle English *procuren,* to take care of, gain, obtain, from Old French *procurer,* from Late Latin *prōcūrāre,* to obtain, from Latin, to take care of, manage for someone else : *prō-,* for, on behalf of + *cūrāre,* to take care of.] **—pro·cure·ment** *n.*
pro·cur·er (prō-kyo͝or′ər, prə-) *n.* **1.** One who procures. **2.** A pander.
pro·cur·ess (prō-kyo͝or′ĭs, prə-) *n.* A female procurer.
Pro·cy·on (prō′sē-ŏn′) *n.* A double star in the constellation Canis Minor. Also called "Dog Star." [Latin, from Greek *Prokuōn,* "before the dog star" : *pro-,* before + *kuōn,* dog.]
prod (prŏd) *tr.v.* **prodded, prodding, prods. 1.** To jab or poke, as with a pointed instrument. **2.** To rouse to action; urge; goad.
∼*n.* **1.** The act or an instance of prodding. **2.** Anything pointed used to prod; a goad. **3.** An incitement or reminder; a stimulus. [16th century : perhaps imitative.] **—prod·der** *n.*
Prod (prŏd) *n.* In Ireland, a Protestant. Used derogatorily. **—Prod, Prod·dy** *adj.*
prod. **1.** produce; produced. **2.** product.
prod·i·gal (prŏd′ĭ-gəl) *adj.* **1.** Recklessly wasteful; extravagant. **2.** Extremely generous. **3.** Profuse; lavish: *prodigal praise.*
∼*n.* A person given to luxury or extravagance; a spendthrift or profligate. [Latin *prōdigus,* from *prōdigere,* to drive away, squander : *prōd-,* variant of *prō-,* forth, away + *agere,* to drive.] **—prod·i·gal·ly** *adv.*
prod·i·gal·i·ty (prŏd′ĭ-găl′ə-tē) *n., pl.* **-ties. 1.** Extravagant wastefulness. **2.** Profuse generosity. **3.** Extreme abundance; lavishness.
pro·di·gious (prə-dĭj′əs) *adj.* **1.** Impressively great in size, force, or extent; enormous. **2.** Extraordinary; marvelous. **3.** *Obsolete.* Portentous; ominous. [Latin *prōdigiōsus,* from *prōdigium,* omen, portent, PRODIGY.] **—pro·di·gious·ly** *adv.* **—pro·di·gious·ness** *n.*
prod·i·gy (prŏd′ə-jē) *n., pl.* **-gies. 1.** A person with exceptional talents or powers: *a child prodigy.* **2.** An act, object, or event so extraordinary or rare as to inspire wonder; a marvel. **3.** *Archaic.* An omen or portent. [Latin *prōdigium,* prophetic sign, marvel.]
pro·drome (prō′drōm′) *n.* An early symptom of a disease, often different in nature from the later symptoms. [French, from Greek *prodromos,* precursor : *pro-,* forward + *dromos,* running.] **—pro·dro·mal** (prō-drō′məl), **pro·drom·ic** (-drŏm′ĭk) *adj.*
pro·duce (prə-do͞os′, -dyo͞os′, prō-) *v.* **-duced, -ducing, -duces.** *—tr.* **1.** To bring forth; yield. **2.** To create by mental or physical effort. **3.** To manufacture. **4. a.** To cause to occur or exist; give rise to. **b.** To give birth to. **5.** To bring forward; exhibit. **6.** *British.* To interpret and supervise the acting and artistic design of (a play, for example). **7.** To sponsor and present to the public: *produce a film.* **8.** *Geometry.* To extend (an area or volume) or lengthen (a line). *—intr.* To make or yield the customary product or products.
∼*n.* (prŏd′o͞os, -yo͞os, prō′do͞os, -dyo͞os). *Abbr.* **prod.** Something produced; a product; especially, agricultural products collectively. [Latin *prōdūcere,* to lead or bring forth : *prō-,* forward + *dūcere,* to lead.] **—pro·duc·i·ble** *adj.*
pro·duc·er (prə-do͞o′sər, -dyo͞o′sər, prō-) *n.* **1.** One that produces. **2.** *Economics.* A person or organization that grows or manufactures goods or provides services for sale. **3. a.** A person who arranges the finance, hiring of actors, and other practical business in the making of a motion picture or the staging of a play. Compare **director. b.** *British.* The person who supervises and instructs the actors or participants in a radio or television production and is responsible for the overall artistic interpretation. **4.** A furnace that manufactures producer gas. **5.** *Ecology.* Any organism that is the first stage in a food chain, such as bacteria or green plants, building up foods from and feeding on inorganic matter. Compare **consumer.**
producer gas *n.* A gas used as fuel, generated by passing air with steam over burning coke or coal to yield a combustible mixture of nitrogen, carbon monoxide, and hydrogen. Also called "air gas."
producer goods *pl.n. Economics.* **Capital goods** *(see).*
prod·uct (prŏd′əkt) *n. Abbr.* **prod. 1. a.** Anything produced by human or mechanical effort or by a natural process. **b.** An article considered as merchandise: *redesign the product.* **c.** Marketable goods collectively: *What the company needs is product.* **d.** A person who has undergone a specified type of training or education: *a grammar school product.* **2.** A direct result; a consequence. **3.** *Chemistry.* A substance produced by a chemical change. **4.** *Mathematics.* **a.** The result obtained by performing multiplication. **b.** A **scalar product** *(see).* **c.** A **vector product** *(see).* [Latin *prōductum,* from the past participle of *prōdūcere,* to PRODUCE.]
pro·duc·tion (prə-dŭk′shən, prō-) *n.* **1.** The act or process of producing. **2.** *Economics.* The creation of value or wealth by producing goods and services. **3.** Something produced; a product. **4. a.** The total number of products; output. **b.** The rate at which products are produced. **5. a.** *British.* The artistic supervision and interpretation of a stage play or other live public entertainment. **b.** A public performance or showing of such an entertainment. **c.** A version of a play or similar work with a particular interpretation and staging: *a new production of Fidelio.* **6.** Mass production. Also used adjectivally: *a production model.* **7.** *Informal.* **a.** A great effort. **b.** An unnecessarily complicated procedure; a fuss. **—pro·duc·tion·al** *adj.*
production line *n.* **1.** An **assembly line** *(see).* **2.** A method of mass-producing goods using a continuous flow of components that are assembled on a moving conveyor. **3.** Any system or institution whose products or graduates emerge regularly and systematically and have standardized characteristics.
pro·duc·tive (prə-dŭk′tĭv, prō-) *adj.* **1.** Producing or capable of producing. **2.** Producing abundantly; fertile; prolific. **3.** Yielding favorable or useful results; constructive. **4.** *Economics.* Of or involved in the creation of goods and services to produce wealth or value. **5.** Resulting in. Used with *of: difficulties productive of dispute.* **—pro·duc·tive·ly** *adv.* **—pro·duc·tiv·i·ty, pro·duc·tive·ness** *n.*
product liability *n.* Legal responsibility on the part of a manufacturer, as opposed to a retailer, to ensure that a product is safe or of good quality and fit for its purpose.
pro·em (prō′ĕm′) *n.* A short introduction; a preface. [Middle English *proheme,* from Old French *pro(h)eme,* from Latin *prooemium,* from Greek *prooimion,* prelude : *pro-,* before + *oimē,* song, from *oimos,* way, path.] **—pro·e·mi·al** *adj.*
pro·es·trus (prō-ĕs′trəs) *n.* The period of preparation for pregnancy that immediately precedes estrus in most female mammals.
prof., Prof. professor.
prof·a·na·tion (prŏf′ə-nā′shən) *n.* The act or an instance of profaning; desecration.
pro·fane (prō-fān′, prə-) *adj.* **1.** Showing contempt or irreverence toward God or sacred things; blasphemous. **2.** Nonreligious in subject matter, form, or use; secular: *sacred and profane music.* **3.** Not initiated into the mysteries of ritual. **4.** Vulgar; coarse.
∼*tr.v.* **profaned, -faning, -fanes. 1.** To treat with irreverence. **2.** To put to an improper, unworthy, or degrading use; abuse. [Middle English *prophane,* from Old French, from Medieval Latin *prophānus,* variant of Latin *profānus,* "before (i.e., outside) the temple," hence not sacred, secular, impious : *prō-,* before + *fānum,* temple.] **—pro·fan·a·to·ry** *adj.* **—pro·fane·ly** *adv.* **—pro·fane·ness** *n.* **—pro·fan·er** *n.*
***Synonyms:** blasphemous, sacrilegious.*
pro·fan·i·ty (prō-făn′ə-tē, prə-) *n., pl.* **-ties. 1.** The condition or quality of being profane. **2. a.** Abusive, vulgar, or irreverent language. **b.** The use or an instance of such language.
pro·fess (prə-fĕs′, prō-) *v.* **-fessed, -fessing, -fesses.** *—tr.* **1.** To affirm openly; declare or claim. **2.** To make a pretense of. **3.** To claim skill in or knowledge of. **4.** To affirm belief in: *profess Catholicism.* **5.** To receive into a religious order. *—intr.* **1.** To make an open affirmation. **2.** To take the vows of a religious order. [Latin *prōfitērī* (past participle *prōfessus*), to declare publicly : *prō-,* forth, in public + *fatērī,* to acknowledge, confess.]
pro·fessed (prə-fĕst′, prō-) *adj.* **1.** According to one's own admission; self-confessed: *a professed hedonist.* **2.** Self-proclaimed but pretended. **3.** Belonging to a profession. **4.** Having taken the vows of a religious order. **—pro·fess·ed·ly** *adv.*
pro·fes·sion (prə-fĕsh′ən) *n.* **1.** An occupation or vocation requiring training, as in law, theology, or the sciences. **2.** The body of qualified persons of any specific occupation or field. **3.** The act or an instance of professing; a declaration; a claim. **4.** An avowal of faith in a religion, especially on first being accepted into it. **5.** The taking of vows by a person joining a religious order. [Middle English, vow made on entering a religious order, from Old French, from Latin *professiō* (stem *professiōn-*), declaration, confession, from *profitērī,* to PROFESS.]
pro·fes·sion·al (prə-fĕsh′ən-əl) *adj.* **1.** Of, pertaining to, engaged in, or suitable for a profession. **2.** Engaged in a specific activity as a source of livelihood. **3.** Performed by persons receiving pay. **4.** Having great skill or experience in a particular field or activity.
∼*n. Abbr.* **pro., Pro. 1.** A person following a profession. **2.** One who earns his or her livelihood as an athlete, either playing or coaching. **3.** One who has an assured competence in a particular field or occupation. **—pro·fes·sion·al·ly** *adv.*
professional foul *n. Sports.* In team games, a deliberate foul, usually committed when the opposing team seems certain of scoring.
pro·fes·sion·al·ism (prə-fĕsh′ən-ə-lĭz′əm) *n.* **1.** Professional status, methods, character, or standards. **2.** The use of professional players in organized sports.
pro·fes·sor (prə-fĕs′ər) *n.* **1.** *Abbr.* **prof., Prof. a.** A teacher of the highest rank in a university or comparable institution. **b.** A teacher or instructor. **2.** One who professes. [Middle English *professour,* from Latin *professor,* from *profitērī,* to PROFESS.] **—pro·fes·so·ri·al** *adj.* **—pro·fes·so·ri·al·ly** *adv.* **—pro·fes·sor·ship** *n.*
prof·fer (prŏf′ər) *tr.v.* **-fered, -fering, -fers.** To offer; tender. **—See Synonyms at offer.**
∼*n.* The act of proffering; an offer. [Middle English *profren,* from Old French *p(o)roffrir* : *por-,* from Latin *prō-,* forth + *offrir,* to

PRONUNCIATION KEY

ă, pat; ā, pay; âr, care;
ä, father, are; b, bib;
ch, church; d, deed; ĕ, pet;
ē, be; f, fife; g, gag; h, hat;
hw, which; ĭ, pit; ī, pie;
îr, pier; j, judge; k, kick;
l, lid, needle; m, mum;
n, no, sudden; ng, thing;
ŏ, pot; ō, toe; ô, paw, for;
oi, noise; ou, out; o͝o, book;
o͞o, boot; p, pop; r, roar;
s, sauce; sh, ship, dish;
t, tight; th, thin, path;
th, this, bathe; ŭ, cut; ûr, fur;
v, valve; w, with; y, yes;
z, zebra, size; zh, vision;
ə, about, item, edible, gallop, circus, peaceful

IN FOREIGN WORDS:

à, *Fr.* ami; œ, *Fr.* feu, *Ger.* schön; ü, *Fr.* tu, *Ger.* über;
KH, *Ger.* ich, *Scot.* loch;
N, *Fr.* bon; y′, *Fr.* Compiègne

STRESS MARKS:

Primary stress: ′
in·cite′ (ĭn-sīt′)
Secondary stress: ′
in′sight′ (ĭn′sīt′)

offer, from Latin *offerre,* "to carry toward" : *ob-,* to, toward + *ferre,* to carry.] **—prof·fer·er** *n.*

pro·fi·cien·cy (prə-fĭsh′ən-sē) *n., pl.* **-cies.** The state or quality of being proficient; skill; competence.

pro·fi·cient (prə-fĭsh′ənt) *adj.* Performing in a given art, skill, or branch of learning with expert correctness and facility; adept.
~n. An adept; expert. [Latin *prōficiens* (stem *prōficient-*), present participle of *prōficere,* to progress. See **profit.**] **—pro·fi·cient·ly** *adv.*
Synonyms: *adept, skilled, skillful.*

pro·file (prō′fīl′) *n.* **1. a.** A side view of an object or structure, especially of a human head. **b.** A representation of an object or structure seen from the side. **2.** An outline of any object. **3.** A biographical essay presenting the subject's most noteworthy characteristics and achievements. **4. a.** A graph or table representing numerically the extent to which a person or thing shows various tested characteristics: *an organizational profile.* **b.** The characteristics represented. **5. a.** A vertical section of the soil at any point of the earth's surface down to the parent rock, showing the different horizons. **b.** A graph representing this section. Also called "soil profile." **6. a.** A vertical section of the earth's crust at any point showing the different layers of rock. **b.** A graph representing this section. —See Synonyms at **form.**
~tr.v. **profiled, -filing, -files. 1.** To draw or shape a profile of. **2.** To write a profile of. [Italian *profilo,* from *profilare,* to draw in outline : *pro-,* forward + *filare,* to spin, draw a line, from Late Latin *fīlāre,* to spin, from Latin *fīlum,* thread, string.]

prof·it (prŏf′ĭt) *n.* **1.** An advantageous gain or return; a benefit. **2.** The return received on a business undertaking after all operating expenses have been met. **3.** *Economics.* The prospect of such return considered as the chief motivation in all activity in a capitalist economy. **4.** *Often* **profits. a.** The return received on an investment after all charges have been paid. **b.** The rate of increase in the net worth of a business enterprise in a given accounting period. **c.** Income received from investments or property. **d.** The amount received for a commodity or service in excess of the original cost.
~v. **profited, -iting, -its.** *—intr.* **1.** To make a gain or profit. **2.** To be advantageous; benefit. *—tr.* To be beneficial to. [Middle English, from Old French, from Latin *prōfectus,* advance, progress, success, profit, from the past participle of *prōficere,* to go forward, accomplish, be advantageous : *prō-,* for + *facere,* to do, make.] **—prof·it·a·bil·i·ty, prof·it·a·ble·ness** *n.* **—prof·it·a·ble** *adj.* **—prof·it·a·bly** *adv.*

profit and loss *n.* An account showing net and gross profit or loss over a given period. **—prof·it-and-loss** *adj.*

prof·i·teer (prŏf′ə-tîr′) *n.* One who makes excessive profits on commodities in short supply.
~intr.v. **profiteered, -teering, -teers.** To act as a profiteer.

profit sharing *n.* A system by which employees receive a share of the profits of a business enterprise. **—prof·it-shar·ing** *adj.*

prof·li·gate (prŏf′lĭ-gĭt, -gāt′) *adj.* **1.** Given over to dissipation; dissolute. **2.** Recklessly wasteful; wildly extravagant.
~n. A profligate person; a wastrel. [Latin *prōflīgātus,* from the past participle of *prōflīgāre,* to strike down, destroy, ruin : *prō-,* forward, down + *flīgere,* to strike.] **—prof·li·ga·cy** (prŏf′lĭ-gə-sē) *n.*

pro for·ma (prō fôr′mə) *adv.* As a matter of, or according to, form. [Latin, "for form."] **—pro for·ma** *adj.*

pro·found (prə-found′, prō-) *adj.* **-er, -est. 1.** Situated at, extending to, or coming from a great depth; deep. **2.** Coming as if from the depths of one's being: *profound contempt.* **3.** Thoroughgoing; far-reaching. **4.** Penetrating beyond what is superficial or obvious: *a profound thinker.* **5.** Unqualified; absolute; complete. [Middle English *profounde,* from Old French *profond, profund,* from Latin *profundus* : *prō-,* before + *fundus,* bottom.] **—pro·found·ly** *adv.* **—pro·found·ness** *n.*

pro·fun·di·ty (prə-fŭn′də-tē, prō-) *n., pl.* **-ties. 1.** Great depth. **2.** Depth of intellect, feeling, or meaning. **3.** Something profound or abstruse. [Middle English *profundite,* from Old French, from Late Latin *profunditās* (stem *profunditāt-*), from *profundus,* deep, PROFOUND.]

pro·fuse (prə-fyōōs′, prō-) *adj.* **1.** Plentiful; overflowing. **2.** Giving or given freely and abundantly; extravagant. Usually used with *in* or *with*: *profuse in his compliments.* [Middle English, from Latin *prōfūsus,* from the past participle of *prōfundere,* to pour forth : *prō-,* forth + *fundere,* to pour.] **—pro·fuse·ly** *adv.* **—pro·fuse·ness** *n.*

pro·fu·sion (prə-fyōō′zhən, prō-) *n.* **1.** The state of being profuse; abundance. **2.** Lavish or unrestrained expense; extravagance. **3.** A profuse outpouring or display.

prog. 1. program. **2.** progress; progressive.

pro·gen·i·tive (prō-jĕn′ə-tĭv) *adj.* Capable of producing offspring; fertile. [Middle English. See **progenitor.**]

pro·gen·i·tor (prō-jĕn′ə-tər) *n.* **1.** A direct ancestor. **2.** An originator of a line of descent. **3.** Any founder or precursor of a trend or tradition. [Middle English *progenitour,* from Old French *progeniteur,* from Latin *prōgenitor,* from *prōgenitus,* past participle of *prōgignere,* to beget : *prō-,* forth + *gignere,* to beget.]

prog·e·ny (prŏj′ə-nē) *n., pl.* **-nies. 1.** Children or descendants; offspring. **2.** A result of creative effort; a product. [Middle English *progenie,* from Old French, from Latin *prōgeniēs,* descent, descendants, from *prōgignere,* to beget. See **progenitor.**]

pro·ges·ta·tion·al (prō′jĕs-tā′shən-əl) *adj.* **1.** Preceding gestation. **2.** Preceding ovulation.

pro·ges·ter·one (prō-jĕs′tə-rōn′) *n.* A female hormone, $C_{21}H_{30}O_2$, secreted by the corpus luteum of the ovary prior to ovulation, which prepares the uterus for implantation of a fertilized ovum. [PRO- (acting for) + GES(TATION) + STER(OL) + -ONE.]

pro·ges·to·gen (prō-jĕs′tə-jən) *n.* Any substance having an action like progesterone. [PROGEST(ERONE) + -GEN.]

pro·glot·tid (prō-glŏt′ĭd) *n., pl.* **-tids.** Also **pro·glot·tis** (-ĭs), *pl.* **-tides** (-ə-dēz′). Any of the segments of a tapeworm. [New Latin *proglottis* (stem *proglottid-*), from Greek *proglōssis,* tip of the tongue (from its shape) : *pro-,* before + *glōssa, glōtta,* tongue.] **—pro·glot·tic, pro·glot·ti·de·an** *adj.*

prog·na·thous (prŏg′nə-thəs, prŏg-nā′-) *adj.* Also **prog·nath·ic** (prŏg-năth′ĭk). Having one or both jaws projecting forward to a considerable degree. [PRO- (in front, projecting) + -GNATHOUS.] **—prog·na·thism** *n.*

prog·no·sis (prŏg-nō′sĭs) *n., pl.* **-ses** (-sēz′). **1. a.** A prediction of the probable course and outcome of a disease. **b.** The likelihood of recovery from a disease. **2.** Any forecast or prediction. [Late Latin, from Greek *prognōsis,* from *progignōskein,* to foreknow, predict : *pro-,* before + *gignōskein,* to know.]

prog·nos·tic (prŏg-nŏs′tĭk) *adj.* **1.** Of, pertaining to, or acting as a prognosis. **2.** Predicting; foretelling.
~n. **1.** A sign or omen of some future happening. **2.** A symptom indicating the future course of a disease. [Medieval Latin *prognōsticus,* from Greek *prognōstikos,* from *progignōskein,* to predict. See **prognosis.**]

prog·nos·ti·cate (prŏg-nŏs′tĭ-kāt′) *tr.v.* **-cated, -cating, -cates. 1.** To predict, using present indications as a guide. **2.** To foreshadow; portend. [Medieval Latin *prognōsticāre,* from *prognōsticus,* PROGNOSTIC.] **—prog·nos·ti·ca·tor** *n.* **—prog·nos·ti·ca·tion** *n.*

pro·gram (prō′grăm′, -grəm) *n.* Also *chiefly British* **pro·gramme. 1. a.** A listing of the order of events and other pertinent information for some public presentation. **b.** A booklet containing such information sold at concerts, plays, and similar events. **2.** The presentation itself. **3.** A radio or television show. **4.** Any organized list or schedule of procedures or activities. **5.** A schedule of projects to be carried out: *a building program.* **6.** A set of instructions, written in a suitable programming language, that are fed into a computer to enable it to perform logical or arithmetical operations on data. **7.** A syllabus.
~tr.v. **programmed** or **programed, -gramming** or **-graming, -grams. 1.** To include or schedule in a program. **2.** To design (a plan, for example) as a definite program. **3.** To cause (a machine, animal, or person) to follow a set procedure; control or direct the behavior of. **4.** *Computer Science.* To provide (a computer) with a set of instructions for solving a problem. [French *programme,* from Late Latin *programma,* public notice, from Greek, from *prographein,* to set forth as a public notice : *pro-,* before + *graphein,* to write.] **—pro·gram·ma·bil·i·ty** *n.* **—pro·gram·ma·ble** *adj.* **—pro·gram·mat·ic** *adj.* **—pro·gram·mat·i·cal·ly** *adv.*

program director *n.* A radio or television director who is responsible for selecting, planning, and scheduling programs.

programme. *Chiefly British.* Variant of **program.**

pro·grammed, pro·gramed (prō′grămd′) *adj.* Of, pertaining to, or occurring by programmed instruction: *programmed learning.*

programmed instruction *n.* A method of teaching in which the information to be learned is presented in discrete units, with a correct response to each unit required from the learner before advancing to the next unit.

pro·gram·mer, pro·gram·er (prō′grăm′ər) *n.* **1.** One who prepares a computer program. **2.** A person who schedules radio or television programs.

pro·gram·ming, pro·gram·ing (prō′grăm′ĭng) *n.* The designating, scheduling, or planning of a program.

programming language *n.* Any of various coded systems of words and symbols used to write instructions to a computer in familiar notation rather than directly in a machine code. See **high-level language, low-level language.**

program music *n.* Music intended to convey ideas or suggest the episodes of a story. Compare **absolute music.**

prog·ress (prŏg′rĕs′, -rəs) *n.* **1.** Movement toward a goal. **2.** Development; unfolding. **3.** Steady improvement, as of a society or civilization: *a believer in progress.* **4.** *Chiefly British.* A state journey made by a sovereign through the realm. **—in progress.** Under way; currently being done or made.
~intr.v. **pro·gress** (prə-grĕs′), **-gressed, -gressing, -gresses. 1.** To advance; proceed. **2.** To advance toward a more desirable form or condition. [Middle English *progresse,* from Latin *prōgressus,* from past participle of *prōgredī,* to go forward : *prō-,* forward + *gradī,* to step, go.]

pro·gres·sion (prə-grĕsh′ən) *n.* **1.** The act of or an instance of progressing. **2. a.** A sequence, as of events. **b.** The movement from one item in such a sequence to the next. **3.** *Mathematics.* A series of numbers or quantities, each derived from the one preceding by some consistent operation. See **arithmetic progression, geometric progression. 4.** *Music.* A succession of notes or chords or the modulation from one to the next. —See Synonyms at **series. —pro·gres·sion·al** *adj.*

pro·gres·sive *adj.* **1.** Moving forward; ongoing; advancing. **2.** Proceeding in steps; continuing steadily by increments. **3. a.** Believing in or striving for constant improvement or new advances. **b.** Characterized by an advance over the established forms; very modern: *progressive rock music.* **c.** Promoting or favoring political and social reform. **4. Progressive.** Of or belonging to a Progressive Party. **5.** Of, designating, pertaining to, or influenced by a theory of educa-

PRONUNCIATION KEY

ă, pat; ā, pay; âr, care;
ä, father, are; b, bib;
ch, church; d, deed; ĕ, pet;
ē, be; f, fife; g, gag; h, hat;
hw, which; ĭ, pit; ī, pie;
îr, pier; j, judge; k, kick;
l, lid, needle; m, mum;
n, no, sudden; ng, thing;
ŏ, pot; ō, toe; ô, paw, for;
oi, noise; ou, out; ŏŏ, book;
ōō, boot; p, pop; r, roar;
s, sauce; sh, ship, dish;
t, tight; th, thin, path;
th, this, bathe; ŭ, cut; ûr, fur;
v, valve; w, with; y, yes;
z, zebra, size; zh, vision;
ə, about, item, edible,
gallop, circus, peaceful

IN FOREIGN WORDS:

à, *Fr.* ami; œ, *Fr.* feu, *Ger.* schön; ü, *Fr.* tu, *Ger.* über;
KH, *Ger.* ich, *Scot.* loch;
N, *Fr.* bon; y′, *Fr.* Compiègne

STRESS MARKS:

Primary stress: ′
in·cite′ (ĭn-sīt′)
Secondary stress: ′
in′sight′ (ĭn′sīt′)

tion characterized by emphasis on the individual needs and capacities of each child and informality of curriculum. **6.** Of or denoting a tax system in which the rate of taxation increases as the taxable amount increases. **7.** *Pathology.* Continuously spreading or increasing in severity. **8.** *Grammar.* Designating a verb form or aspect that expresses an action or condition in progress; continuous. In English, it is formed by adding the suffix *-ing* to the root verb form.
~*n.* **1.** A person who favors or strives for advances or reform in politics, education, or other fields. **2. Progressive.** One who belongs to a Progressive Party. **3. a.** The progressive form of a verb. **b.** A verb in this form. **—pro·gres·sive·ly** *adv.* **—pro·gres·sive·ness** *n.*

Progressive Party *n.* **1.** An American political party organized under the leadership of Theodore Roosevelt in 1912. **2.** A party with similar goals organized in 1924 and led by Robert M. La Follette. **3.** A party formed in 1948, originally led by Henry A. Wallace.

pro·gres·siv·ism (prə-grĕs'ĭ-vĭz'əm) *n.* The doctrines and practice of political or educational progressives.

pro·hib·it (prō-hĭb'ĭt) *tr.v.* **-ited, -iting, -its. 1.** To forbid by authority. **2.** To prevent or debar. [Middle English *prohibiten,* from Latin *prōhibēre,* to hold in front, hinder, hold back : *prō-,* in front + *habēre,* to hold.]
Usage: The usual preposition following this verb is *from (The law prohibits you from doing that),* but the following constructions are also used: *The law prohibits doing that; The law prohibits your doing that.* The construction *The law prohibits you doing that* is not acceptable. See also **forbid, prevent.**

pro·hi·bi·tion (prō'ə-bĭsh'ən) *n.* **1.** The act of prohibiting or state of being prohibited. **2.** A law, order, or decree that forbids something. **3.** *Law.* An order from the High Court forbidding a lower court or tribunal from deciding a particular case. **4. a.** The forbidding by law of the manufacture, transportation, sale, and possession of alcoholic drinks. **b. Prohibition.** The period (1920–33) during which such a law was in force in the United States.

pro·hi·bi·tion·ist (prō'ə-bĭsh'ən-ĭst) *n.* **1.** One in favor of banning the manufacture and sale of alcoholic drinks. **2.** *Often* **Prohibitionist.** A member of the Prohibition Party.

Prohibition Party. An American political party organized in 1869, advocating prohibition.

pro·hib·i·tive (prō-hĭb'ə-tĭv) *adj.* Also **pro·hib·i·to·ry** (-tôr'ē, -tōr'ē). **1.** Prohibiting or likely to prohibit. **2.** Preventing or discouraging something, such as purchase or use: *prohibitive costs.* **—pro·hib·i·tive·ly** *adv.*

proj·ect (prŏj'ĕkt', -ĭkt) *n.* **1.** A plan or proposal. **2.** An undertaking requiring concerted effort. **3.** A research undertaking.
~*v.* **pro·ject** (prə-jĕkt'), **-jected, -jecting, -jects.** *—tr.* **1.** To thrust outward or forward. Compare **retroject. 2.** To throw forward; hurl; impel. **3.** To transport in one's imagination. **4.** *Psychology.* To externalize and attribute (an emotion, for example) to someone or something else. **5.** To direct (one's voice) so as to be heard clearly at a distance. **6.** To form a plan or intention for; intend. Used especially in the past participle: *my projected tour of national parks.* **7. a.** To cause (an image) to appear on a surface. **b.** To cast (light or shadow). **8.** To produce a projection of. **9. a.** To use as a basis for estimates or predictions: *If you project these figures to next year, you will see that prices should rise.* **b.** To estimate; predict: *projected a ten percent rise.* **10.** To convey or represent vividly to an audience: *projects himself poorly.* *—intr.* **1.** To extend forward or out; protrude. **2.** To direct one's voice so as to be heard clearly at a distance. [Middle English *proiecte,* from Latin *prōjectum,* a projecting, projection, from the past participle of *prō(j)icere,* to throw forth : *prō-,* forth + *jacere,* to throw.]

pro·jec·tile (prə-jĕk'təl, -tīl') *n.* **1.** A fired, thrown, or otherwise projected object, such as a bullet, having no capacity for self-propulsion. **2.** A self-propelling missile, such as a rocket.
~*adj.* **1.** Capable of being impelled or hurled forward. **2.** Driving forward; impelling. **3.** *Zoology.* Capable of being thrust outward; protrusile. [New Latin *prōjectilis,* from Latin *prō(j)icere,* to throw forth, PROJECT.]

pro·jec·tion (prə-jĕk'shən) *n.* **1.** The act of projecting or state of being projected. **2.** Something that thrusts outward; a protuberance. **3.** A plan for an anticipated course of action. **4.** A prediction made after all available information has been examined. **5. a.** The process of projecting a filmed image onto a screen or other viewing surface. **b.** The image so projected. **6.** The image of a geometric figure produced by a coordinate mapping. **7.** A system of intersecting lines, such as the grid of a map, on which part or all of the globe or the celestial sphere may be represented as a plane surface. See **map projection. 8.** *Psychology.* The naive or unconscious attribution of one's own feelings, attitudes, or desires to others. **—pro·jec·tion·al** *adj.*

pro·jec·tion·ist (prə-jĕk'shən-ĭst) *n.* **1.** One who operates a motion-picture projector. **2.** A map-maker.

pro·jec·tive (prə-jĕk'tĭv) *adj.* *Mathematics.* **1.** Pertaining to or made by projection. **2.** Extending outward; projecting. **3.** Designating a property of a geometric figure that does not vary when the figure undergoes projection. **—pro·jec·tive·ly** *adv.*

projective geometry *n.* The study of geometric properties that are invariant under projection.

projective test *n.* A psychological test in which a subject's responses to relatively unstructured standard stimuli, such as a series of abstract patterns or incomplete sentences, are analyzed to obtain information about personality or sometimes cognition.

pro·jec·tor (prə-jĕk'tər) *n.* **1.** A machine for projecting an image onto a screen. **2.** A device for projecting a beam of light. **3.** One who devises plans or projects.

pro·kar·y·ote, pro·car·y·ote (prō-kăr'ē-ōt') *n.* Any organism in which the genetic material is not bounded by a nuclear membrane but exists free in the cytoplasm. Prokaryotes consist mainly of the bacteria and blue-green algae. Compare **eukaryote.** [PRO- + KARYO- + *-ote,* as in *zygote.*] **—pro·kar·y·ot·ic** (prō-kăr'ə-ŏt'ĭk) *adj.*

Pro·kof·iev (prō-kôf'yəf, -yĕf'), **Sergei Sergeyevich** (1891–1953). Russian composer. He wrote seven symphonies and several operas, ballets, and concertos. His glittering, inventive compositions include the opera *The Love for Three Oranges.*

pro·lac·tin (prō-lăk'tĭn) *n.* A pituitary hormone that, in mammals, stimulates and controls the secretion of milk and stimulates the production of progesterone by the corpus luteum in the ovary. Also called "luteotrophic hormone." [PRO- (forth) + LACT(O)- + -IN.]

pro·la·mine (prō'lə-mĭn, -mēn', prō-lăm'ĭn, -ēn') *n.* Also **pro·la·min** (prō'lə-mĭn, prō-lăm'ĭn). Any of a class of simple proteins found in wheat, rye, and other grains. [PROL(INE) + AM(MONIA) + -INE.]

pro·lan (prō'lăn') *n.* The gonadotropic hormone in pregnant women's urine, used to indicate pregnancy. [German *Prolan,* from Latin *prōlēs,* offspring.]

pro·lapse (prō-lăps') *intr.v.* **-lapsed, -lapsing, -lapses.** *Medicine.* To fall or slip out of place.
~*n.* Also **pro·lap·sus** (prō-lăp'səs). *Medicine.* The falling down or slipping out of place of an organ or part, such as the uterus. [Late Latin *prōlapsus,* a falling, from Latin, past participle of *prōlābī,* to fall or slip down : *prō-,* forward, down + *lābī,* to fall, slip.]

pro·late (prō'lāt') *adj.* Designating the shape of a solid, especially of a spheroid, having its polar axis longer than its equatorial diameter; cigar-shaped. Compare **oblate.** [Latin *prōlātus,* stretched out (used as past participle of *prōferre,* to bring forward, stretch out) : *prō-,* forth + *-lātus,* "carried."] **—pro·late·ly** *adv.* **—pro·late·ness** *n.*

pro·la·tive (prō-lā'tĭv) *adj.* *Grammar.* Serving to extend or complete predication, as an infinitive verb does when joined without *to* to an auxiliary verb. For example, the word *hope* in *we must hope* is a prolative verb or infinitive. [PROLAT(E) + -IVE.]

prole (prōl) *n.* *Informal.* A member of the working class; a proletarian. Used derogatorily. [Shortened from PROLETARIAN; popularized by George Orwell's novel *1984.*]

pro·leg (prō'lĕg') *n.* Any of the stubby limbs on the abdominal segments of insect larvae. [PRO- (for, serving as) + LEG.]

pro·le·gom·e·non (prō'lĭ-gŏm'ə-nŏn', -nən) *n., pl.* **-na** (-nə). A critical introduction, usually to a scholarly text. [Greek, from the present passive participle of *prolegein,* to say beforehand : *pro-,* before + *legein,* to say.] **—pro·le·gom·e·nous** *adj.*

pro·lep·sis (prō-lĕp'sĭs) *n., pl.* **-ses** (-sēz'). **1.** *Rhetoric.* The device of anticipating and answering an objection or argument before one's opponent has put it forward. **2.** The use of a descriptive word in anticipation of the act or circumstances that would make it applicable. In the sentence *That gambler is a dead man*: *Sam Sneak has sworn to get him,* the use of the adjective *dead* indicates a prolepsis. [Late Latin, rhetorical anticipation, from Greek *prolēpsis,* from *prolambanein,* to take beforehand, anticipate : *prō-,* before + *lambanein,* to take.] **—pro·lep·tic, pro·lep·ti·cal** *adj.*

pro·le·tar·i·an (prō'lə-târ'ē-ən) *adj.* Of, pertaining to, or characteristic of the proletariat.
~*n.* A member of the proletariat. [Latin *prōlētārius,* Roman citizen of the lowest class (who serves the state only by producing offspring), from *prōlēs,* offspring.] **—pro·le·tar·i·an·ism** *n.*

pro·le·tar·i·at (prō'lə-târ'ē-ĭt) *n.* **1. a.** The class of industrial wage earners who, possessing neither capital nor means of production, must earn their living from their labor power. **b.** The poorest class of working people. **2.** In ancient Rome, the people who possessed no property, constituting the lowest class of citizens. [French *prolétariat,* from Latin *prōlētārius,* PROLETARIAN.]

pro·lif·er·ate (prō-lĭf'ə-rāt') *v.* **-ated, -ating, -ates.** *—intr.* **1.** To reproduce or produce new growth or parts rapidly and repeatedly: *cells proliferating.* **2.** To increase or spread at a rapid rate. *—tr.* To cause to grow or increase rapidly. [French *prolifère,* from Medieval Latin *prōlifer,* producing offspring, PROLIFEROUS.] **—pro·lif·er·a·tion** *n.* **—pro·lif·er·a·tive** *adj.*

pro·lif·er·ous (prō-lĭf'ər-əs) *adj.* **1.** *Biology.* Reproducing freely by means of buds and side branches. **2.** *Botany.* Freely producing buds or offshoots, sometimes from abnormal places. [Medieval Latin *prōlifer,* producing offspring : Latin *prōlēs,* offspring + -FEROUS.]

pro·lif·ic (prō-lĭf'ĭk) *adj.* **1.** Producing offspring or fruit in great abundance; fertile. **2.** Producing abundant works or results. [Medieval Latin *prōlificus* : Latin *prōlēs,* offspring + *-ficus,* from *facere,* to make.] **—pro·lif·i·cal·ly** *adv.*

pro·line (prō'lēn') *n.* An amino acid, $C_5H_9O_2N$, found in proteins. [German *Prolin* : P(YR)ROL(E) + -INE.]

pro·lix (prō-lĭks', prō'lĭks) *adj.* **1.** Wordy and tedious. **2.** Tending to speak or write at great length; long-winded. [Middle English, from Old French *prolixe,* from Latin *prōlixus,* "poured forth," extended, abundant : *prō,* forth + *-lixus,* from *liquēre,* to be liquid.] **—pro·lix·i·ty** *n.* **—pro·lix·ly** *adv.*

pro·loc·u·tor (prō-lŏk'yə-tər) *n.* A presiding officer or chairman, especially of the lower house of a convocation in the Anglican Church. [Middle English, from Latin *prōlocūtor,* "one who speaks out," advocate, from *prōloquī,* to speak out, plead : *prō-,* forth + *loquī,* to speak.]

pro·logue (prō′lôg′, -lŏg′) *n.* **1.** The lines introducing a discourse or play. **2.** The character or actor who delivers these lines. **3.** An introductory act or event. [Middle English *prolog,* from Old French *prolog(u)e,* from Latin *prologus,* from Greek *prologos,* (speaker of) a prologue, : *pro-,* before + *legein,* to speak.]

pro·long (prə-lông′, -lŏng′) *tr.v.* **-longed, -longing, -longs.** Also **pro·lon·gate** (prə-lông′gāt′, -lŏng′-), **-gated, -gating, -gates. 1.** To lengthen in duration; protract. **2.** To lengthen in extent. [Middle English *prolongen,* from Old French *prolonguer,* from Late Latin *prōlongāre* : Latin *prō-,* out, extending + *longus,* LONG.] **—pro·lon·ga·tion** *n.*

> *Usage:* **prolong, protract, extend.** These verbs mean to lengthen in time or space. *Prolong* implies an increase in duration (time) beyond normal limits. *Protract* adds to *prolong* the idea of lengthening indefinitely or unnecessarily. *Extend* can refer to mere lengthening in time or space or to increase in range or scope of activities or influence.

pro·lu·sion (prō-lōō′zhən) *n.* **1.** A preliminary exercise in writing. **2.** An essay written as a preface to a more detailed work. [Latin *prōlūsiō* (stem *prōlūsiōn-*), from *prōlūdere* (past participle *prōlūsus*), to play or practice beforehand : *prō-,* before + *lūdere,* to play.] **—pro·lu·so·ry** *adj.*

prom (prŏm) *n.* **1.** A ball or formal dance held for a high school or college class. **2.** *British Informal.* **a.** A promenade. **b.** A promenade concert. [Short for PROMENADE.]

prom. promontory.

prom·e·nade (prŏm′ə-nād′, -näd′) *n.* **1.** A leisurely walk, especially one taken in a public place as a social activity. **2.** A public place for such walking. In this sense, also *British* "prom." **3. a.** A formal ball. **b.** A formal march by the guests at the opening of a ball. **4.** A march executed between the figures of a square dance or country dance. *~v.* **promenaded, -nading, -nades.** *—intr.* **1.** To go on a leisurely walk. **2.** To execute a promenade in square or country dancing. *—tr.* **1.** To take a promenade along or through. **2.** To take or display on or as if on a promenade. [French, from *se promener,* to take a walk, from Late Latin *prōmināre,* to drive forward : *prō-,* forward + *mināre,* to drive, from Latin *minārī,* to threaten, from *minae,* threats.] **—prom·e·nad·er** *n.*

promenade concert *n. Chiefly British.* A concert in which part of the audience stands rather than sits. Also informally called "prom."

promenade deck *n.* The upper deck or a section of the upper deck on a passenger ship where the passengers can promenade.

Pro·me·the·an (prə-mē′thē-ən) *adj.* **1.** Pertaining to or suggestive of Prometheus. **2.** Boldly creative; life-bringing. *~n.* One who is Promethean in manner or actions.

Pro·me·the·us (prə-mē′thē-əs, -thyōōs′). *Greek Mythology.* A Titan who stole fire from the gods to give to humankind and was punished by being chained to a rock where a vulture gnawed at his liver.

pro·me·thi·um (prə-mē′thē-əm) *n. Symbol* **Pm** A radioactive rare-earth element prepared by fission of uranium or by neutron bombardment of neodymium, having 14 isotopes with mass numbers ranging from 140 to 154, and used as a source of beta rays. Atomic number 61, melting point 1,080°C, boiling point 2,460°C, valence 3. [New Latin, after PROMETHEUS (referring to the fire of a nuclear furnace).]

prom·i·nence (prŏm′ə-nəns) *n.* Also **prom·i·nen·cy** (-nən-sē). **1.** The condition or quality of being prominent. **2.** Something that is prominent; a projection. **3.** Emphasis or importance. **4.** *Astronomy.* A tonguelike cloud of luminous gas rising from the sun's surface, visible as part of the corona during a total solar eclipse.

prom·i·nent (prŏm′ə-nənt) *adj.* **1.** Projecting outward; protuberant. **2.** Immediately noticeable; conspicuous. **3.** Widely known; eminent. [Latin *prōminēns* (stem *prōminent-*), present participle of *prōminēre,* to jut out, project : *prō-,* forth + *-minēre,* to jut.] **—prom·i·nent·ly** *adv.*

prom·is·cu·i·ty (prŏm′ĭ-skyōō′ə-tē, prō′mĭ-) *n., pl.* **-ties. 1.** The state or character of being promiscuous. **2.** Promiscuous sexual intercourse. **3.** An indiscriminate mixture; a hotchpotch.

pro·mis·cu·ous (prə-mĭs′kyōō-əs) *adj.* **1.** Characterized by casual association with many sexual partners. **2.** Consisting of diverse and unrelated parts or individuals; confused. **3.** Lacking standards of selection; indiscriminate. **4.** Casual; random. [Latin *prōmiscuus,* mixed : *prō-* (intensifier), thoroughly + *miscēre,* to mix.] **—pro·mis·cu·ous·ly** *adv.* **—pro·mis·cu·ous·ness** *n.*

prom·ise (prŏm′ĭs) *n.* **1.** A declaration giving assurance that one will or will not do something; a vow. **2.** Something that one has undertaken to give or perform. **3.** Indication of future excellence or success: *a child with great promise.* *~v.* **promised, -ising, -ises.** *—tr.* **1.** To pledge or offer assurance. Followed by an infinitive or clause. **2.** To make a promise of; pledge oneself to give. **3.** To afford a basis for expecting: *That clear sky promises a hot afternoon.* *—intr.* **1.** To make a promise. **2.** To afford a basis for expectation. Often used with *well* or *fair.* [Middle English *promys(se),* from Latin *prōmissum,* from the neuter past participle of *prōmittere,* "to send forth," promise : *prō-,* forth + *mittere,* to let go, send.] **—prom·is·er** *n.*

Promised Land *n.* **1.** The land of Canaan, promised to Abraham and his descendants. Genesis 12:7. **2. promised land.** Any place or time of anticipated happiness.

prom·is·ee (prŏm′ĭ-sē′) *n. Law.* An individual to whom a promise is made.

prom·is·ing (prŏm′ĭ-sĭng) *adj.* Likely to develop in a desirable or successful way. **—prom·is·ing·ly** *adv.*

prom·i·sor (prŏm′ĭ-sôr′) *n. Law.* An individual who makes a promise.

prom·is·so·ry (prŏm′ĭ-sôr′ē, -sōr′ē) *adj.* **1.** Containing, involving, or having the nature of a promise. **2.** *Insurance.* Of or designating the preliminary undertakings or guarantees indicating how the provisions of an insurance contract will be carried out after it is signed. [Medieval Latin *prōmissōrius,* from Latin *prōmissor,* one who promises, from *prōmittere,* to PROMISE.]

promissory note *n. Abbr.* **p.n., P/N** A written promise to pay or repay a specified sum of money at a stated time or on demand. Also called "note," "note of hand."

pro·mo (prō′mō) *n., pl.* **-mos.** *Informal.* An advertising or publicity campaign. Also used adjectively: *promo material.* [Shortened from PROMOTION or PROMOTIONAL.]

prom·on·to·ry (prŏm′ən-tôr′ē, -tōr′ē) *n., pl.* **-ries.** *Abbr.* **prom. 1.** A high ridge of land or rock jutting out into a sea or other expanse of water. **2.** *Anatomy.* A projecting bodily part. [Medieval Latin *prōmontōrium,* alteration of Latin *prōmunturium* : probably from *prō-,* forward + *mōns* (stem *mont-*), mountain.]

pro·mote (prə-mōt′) *tr.v.* **-moted, -moting, -motes. 1. a.** To raise to a more important or responsible job or rank. **b.** To advance (a student) to the next, higher course or class. **2.** To contribute to the progress or growth of; further. **3.** To urge the adoption of; advocate. **4.** To attempt to sell or popularize by advertising or by securing financial support. **—See Synonyms at advance.** [Middle English *promoten,* from Latin *prōmovēre* (past participle *prōmōtus*), to move forward, advance : *prō-,* forward, onward + *movēre,* to move.]

pro·mot·er (prə-mō′tər) *n.* **1.** An active supporter; an advocate. **2.** A finance and publicity organizer, as of a boxing match. **3.** *Chemistry.* A substance added to a catalyst in small amounts to increase its activity.

Promoter of the Faith *n. Roman Catholic Church.* The official name for a **devil's advocate** *(see).*

pro·mo·tion (prə-mō′shən) *n.* **1.** The act of promoting. **2.** An advancement in rank or responsibility. **3.** Encouragement; furtherance. **4. a.** Advertising or other publicity. **b.** An advertising or publicity campaign. **—pro·mo·tion·al** *adj.* **—pro·mo·tion·al·ly** *adv.*

pro·mo·tive (prə-mō′tĭv) *adj.* Tending to promote.

prompt (prŏmpt) *adj.* **1.** On time; punctual. **2.** Done without delay. **3.** Ready for action; quick to respond. *~tr.v.* **prompted, prompting, prompts. 1.** To press into action; incite. **2.** To give rise to; inspire. **3.** To assist with a reminder; remind. **4.** In theatrical productions, to give a cue to. *~n.* **1. a.** The act of prompting or giving a cue. **b.** The information suggested; a reminder or cue. **2.** A theatrical prompter. **3.** *Finance.* **a.** A prompt note. **b.** The time limit stipulated in a prompt note. [Middle English, from Old French, from Latin *promptus,* "brought to light," "visible," hence, at hand, ready, prompt, from the past participle of *prōmere,* to bring forth, make manifest : *prō-,* forth + *emere,* to take.] **—promp·ti·tude, prompt·ness** *n.*

prompt·book (prŏmpt′bŏok′) *n.* An annotated script used by a theater prompter.

prompt·er (prŏmp′tər) *n.* **1.** One who prompts. **2.** One who gives cues to actors.

prompt·ly (prŏmpt′lē) *adv.* In a prompt manner or way; on time. **—See Usage note at immediately.**

prompt neutron *n.* A neutron instantaneously emitted (within 10^{-8} second) in nuclear fission. Compare **delayed neutron.**

prompt note *n.* A notice sent to the purchaser of goods reminding him of the amount due to the seller and the date on which it is due. Also called "prompt."

prompt side *n. Abbr.* **P.S.** The side of the stage on which the prompter sits: in the United States, to the right of an actor facing the audience, in Britain, to the left.

prom·ul·gate (prŏm′əl-gāt′, prō-mŭl′gāt′) *tr.v.* **-gated, -gating, -gates. 1.** To make known (a decree, law, or doctrine) by public declaration; announce officially. **2.** To put (a law) into effect by formal public announcement. [Latin *prōmulgāre* : *prō-,* forth + *mulgēre,* to milk, cause to emerge.] **—prom·ul·ga·tion** *n.* **—prom·ul·ga·tor** *n.*

pro·my·ce·li·um (prō′mī-sē′lē-əm) *n., pl.* **-lia** (-lē-ə). *Botany.* A germ tube produced by certain fungal spores.

pron. 1. pronominal; pronoun. **2.** pronounced; pronunciation.

pro·nate (prō′nāt′) *tr.v.* **-nated, -nating, -nates.** To turn (the palm of the hand or inner surface of a forelimb) downward or backward. [Late Latin *prōnāre,* to bend forward, bow, from Latin *prōnus,* PRONE.] **—pro·na·tion** *n.*

pro·na·tor (prō′nā′tər) *n., pl.* **-tores** (-tôr′ēz′, -tōr′ēz′). A forearm or forelimb muscle that effects pronation.

prone (prōn) *adj.* **1.** Lying with the front or face downward; prostrate. **2.** Tending or liable: *prone to mischief.* Often used in combination: *accident-prone.* [Middle English, from Latin *prōnus,* "bending" or "leaning forward."] **—prone·ly** *adv.* **—prone·ness** *n.*

> *Usage:* **prone, supine, prostrate, recumbent.** *Prone* always means lying face downward. *Supine* also means lying down, but always on one's back. *Prostrate* can mean lying down in either position and suggests placing oneself, being thrown, or collapsing into this position. *Recumbent* means lying down but emphasizes a position of comfort or rest.

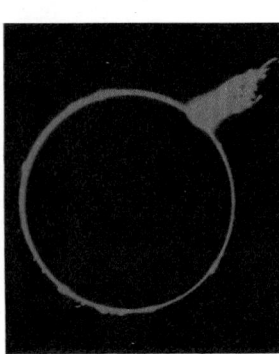

prominence *In a solar prominence, hot gases can lash out nearly 1,000,000 kilometers (600,000 miles) from the surface of the sun.*

pro·neph·ros (prō-něf′rəs, -rŏs′) *n., pl.* **-roi** (-roi′) or **-ra** (-rə). A primitive kidney that disappears early in the embryonic development of higher vertebrates. [New Latin : Greek *pro-*, before + *nephros,* kidney.] **—pro·neph·ric** *adj.*

prong (prŏng, prông) *n.* **1.** A sharply pointed part of a tool or instrument, such as a tine of a fork. **2.** Any sharply pointed projection. **3.** Something, as a unit of troops or a policy, that can be used in combination with something else to attack an enemy or tackle a problem: *the three prongs of our war on inflation.* ~*tr.v.* **pronged, pronging, prongs.** To pierce with a prong. [Middle English *pronge, prange,* forked instrument; perhaps akin to Middle Low German *prange,* pinching instrument, from Germanic *prang-* (unattested), pinch.]

pronged (prôngd, prŏngd) *adj.* **1.** Having a specified number of prongs. **2.** Coming from a specified number of directions at once.

prong·horn (prông′hôrn′, prŏng′-) *n., pl.* **-horns** or collectively **pronghorn.** A small deer, *Antilocapra americana,* resembling an antelope and having small forked horns, found on North American plains. Also called "pronghorn antelope."

pro·nom·i·nal (prō-nŏm′ə-nəl) *adj. Abbr.* **pron., pronom. 1.** Of, pertaining to, or functioning as a pronoun. **2.** Resembling a pronoun, as by specifying a person, place, or thing, while functioning primarily as another part of speech. *His* in *his choice* is a pronominal adjective. [Late Latin *prōnōminālis,* from Latin *prōnōmen,* PRO-NOUN.] **—pro·nom·i·nal·ly** *adv.*

pro·noun (prō′noun′) *n. Abbr.* **pron., pr.** Any of a class of words that function as substitutes for nouns or noun phrases and denote persons or things asked for, previously specified, or understood from the context. [Middle English *pronom,* from Latin *prōnōmen : prō-,* in place of + *nōmen,* name.]

pro·nounce (prə-nouns′) *v.* **-nounced, -nouncing, -nounces.** *—tr.* **1. a.** To articulate (a word or speech sound). **b.** To articulate in the approved manner. **2.** To transcribe (a word) in phonetic symbols. **3.** To state officially and formally; declare. **4.** To declare to be in a specified condition: *The doctor pronounced the victim dead.* **5.** To deliver (a verdict or opinion, for example). *—intr.* **1.** To declare one's opinion or make a pronouncement. Used with *on.* **2.** To articulate words. [Middle English *pronuncen, pronouncen,* from Old French *prononcier,* from Latin *prōnuntiāre,* to speak in public, declare : *prō-,* forth, in public + *nuntiāre,* to declare, from *nuntius,* message, messenger.] **—pro·nounce·a·ble** *adj.* **—pro·nounc·er** *n.*

pro·nounced (prə-nounst′) *adj. Abbr.* **pron. 1.** Spoken; voiced. **2.** Distinct; strongly marked. **—pro·nounc·ed·ly** (prə-noun′sĭd-lē) *adv.* **—pro·nounc·ed·ness** *n.*

pro·nounce·ment (prə-nouns′mənt) *n.* **1.** A formal declaration. **2.** An authoritative statement.

pron·to (prŏn′tō) *adv. Informal.* Without delay; quickly. [Spanish, from Latin *promptus,* PROMPT.]

pro·nu·cle·us (prō-nōō′klē-əs, -nyōō′klē-əs) *n., pl.* **-clei** (-klē-ī′). The haploid nucleus of a sperm or egg prior to fusion of the nuclei in fertilization. **—pro·nu·cle·ar** *adj.*

pro·nun·ci·a·mien·to (prō-nŭn′sē-ə-měn′tō) *n., pl.* **-tos** or **-toes. 1.** An edict or proclamation, especially when announcing a coup d'état. **2.** Any authoritarian pronouncement. [Spanish.]

pro·nun·ci·a·tion (prə-nŭn′sē-ā′shən) *n. Abbr.* **pron. 1.** The act or manner or an instance of articulating speech. **2.** A phonetic transcription of a word. **—pro·nun·ci·a·tion·al** *adj.*

proof (prōōf) *n.* **1.** The evidence establishing the validity of a given assertion. **2.** Conclusive demonstration of something. **3.** The proving or validation of something by experiment, test, or trial. **4.** *Archaic.* Proven impenetrability. **5.** *Law.* The evidence used to determine the verdict or judgment in a case. **6.** The validation of a proposition by application of specified rules, as of induction or deduction, to assumptions, axioms, and sequentially derived conclusions. **7.** The strength of a liquor with reference to **proof spirit** *(see).* **8.** *Printing.* A trial sheet of printed material that is checked against the original manuscript and on which corrections are made. Also called "proof sheet." **9.** *Engraving.* A trial impression of a plate, stone, or block taken at any of various stages of its execution. **10.** *Photography.* A trial print. ~*adj.* **1.** Fully or successfully resistant; impervious. Used with *against: proof against fire.* **2.** Of standard alcoholic strength. **3.** Used in proving or making corrections. ~*v.* **proofed, proofing, proofs.** *—tr.* **1.** To make or run off (a printed or engraved proof). **2.** To proofread (copy). **3.** To make resistant or impervious. **4.** To proofread. [Middle English *pre(o)ve, prof, prove,* from Old French *pre(o)ve,* from Late Latin *proba,* from Latin *probāre,* to test, PROVE.]

-proof *suffix.* Indicates impervious to or able to resist or withstand; for example, **shockproof, waterproof, rustproof.** [From PROOF (adjective).]

proof·read (prōōf′rēd′) *v.* **-read** (-rĕd′), **-reading, -reads.** *—tr.* To read (copy or a printer's proof) against the original typescript, printed version, or manuscript in order to check that they are correct. *—intr.* To correct a printer's proof while reading against the original version. **—proof·read·er** *n.*

proof spirit *n.* An alcohol-water mixture or an alcoholic drink containing a standard amount of alcohol, the U.S. standard being 100 proof, or 50 percent, or ethyl alcohol by volume at 60° F.

prop[1] (prŏp) *n.* **1.** Anything used to support or shore something up. **2.** A person or thing serving as a support or stay. ~*tr.v.* **propped, propping, props. 1.** To keep from falling; support, especially by means of a rigid object. Often used with *up.* **2.** To lean

or rest for support. Usually used with *against.* [Middle English *proppe,* probably from Middle Dutch *proppe†,* vine-prop, stopper.]

prop[2] *n.* A stage **property** *(see).*

prop[3] *n. Informal.* A propeller.

prop- *prefix. Chemistry.* Indicates derivation from propionic acid; for example, **propane.** [From PROPIONIC (ACID).]

prop. 1. proper; properly. **2.** property. **3.** proposition. **4.** proprietary; proprietor.

pro·pae·deu·tic (prō′pĭ-dōō′tĭk, -dyōō′tĭk) *adj.* Providing introductory instruction. ~*n. Often* **propaedeutics.** Preparatory instruction. [Greek *propaideuein,* to teach beforehand : *pro-,* before + *paideuein,* to rear or educate, from *pais* (stem *paid-*), child.]

prop·a·ga·ble (prŏp′ə-gə-bəl) *adj.* Capable of being propagated.

prop·a·gan·da (prŏp′ə-găn′də) *n.* **1.** The systematic propagation or discrediting of a given doctrine or cause by circulating polemical material, such as posters or leaflets. **2.** Material disseminated by the champions or opponents of a doctrine or cause. **3.** **Propaganda.** Propaganda Fide. [From PROPAGANDA FIDE.] **—prop·a·gan·dism** *n.* **—prop·a·gan·dist** *n.* **—prop·a·gan·dis·tic** *adj.* **—prop·a·gan·dis·ti·cal·ly** *adv.*

Propaganda Fi·de (fē′dā) *n. Roman Catholic Church.* The Congregation of the Roman Curia that has authority in the matters of preaching the gospel and of administering Church missions in territories where there is no properly organized hierarchy. Also called "Propaganda." [Italian, short for the New Latin title *Sacra Congregatio de Propaganda Fide,* Sacred Congregation for Propagating the Faith, from Latin *prōpāgandus,* gerundive of *prōpāgāre,* to PROPAGATE.]

prop·a·gan·dize (prŏp′ə-găn′dīz′) *v.* **-dized, -dizing, -dizes.** *—tr.* **1.** To spread (a doctrine or opinion) by means of propaganda. **2.** To subject (a person or group of persons) to propaganda. *—intr.* To spread propaganda.

prop·a·gate (prŏp′ə-gāt′) *v.* **-gated, -gating, -gates.** *—tr.* **1.** To cause (animals) to breed. **2.** To breed (offspring). **3.** To multiply (plants) by cuttings, graftings, or the like. **4.** To transmit (characteristics) from one generation to another. **5.** To make known; promote or spread; publicize. **6.** *Physics.* To cause (a wave, for example) to move through a medium; transmit. *—intr.* **1.** *Physics.* To move through a medium. **2.** To breed or multiply. [Latin *prōpāgāre,* to propagate (plants) by means of slips, from *prōpāgō, prōpāgēs,* slip, shoot, offspring : *prō,* forth + *pāgo,* from *pangere,* to layer.] **—prop·a·ga·tive** *adj.*

prop·a·ga·tion (prŏp′ə-gā′shən) *n.* **1.** Increase or spread, as by natural reproduction. **2.** Dissemination, as of a belief: *propagation of the Gospel.* **—prop·a·ga·tion·al** *adj.*

prop·a·ga·tor (prŏp′ə-gā′tər) *n.* One that propagates; especially, a tray with a clear glass or plastic cover containing soil in which seeds or cuttings are raised.

prop·a·gule (prŏp′ə-gyōōl′) *n.* A plant structure, such as a bud, bulb, or tuber, that becomes detached from the parent plant and develops into a new individual. [From PROPAGATE + -ULE.]

pro·pane (prō′pān′) *n.* A colorless alkane gas, C_3H_8, found in natural gas and petroleum, and used as fuel. [PROP- + -ANE.]

pro·pane-di·ol (prō′pān-dī′ôl) *n. Chemistry.* Propylene glycol *(see).*

pro·pa·no·ic ac·id (prō′pə-nō′ĭk) *n. Chemistry.* Propionic acid *(see).* [PROPANE + -IC.]

pro·pa·nol (prō′pə-nōl′, -nôl′) *n.* A colorless, liquid alcohol that occurs in two isomeric forms, 1-propanol, $CH_3CH_2CH_2OH$, and 2-propanol, $CH_3CHOHCH_3$. Both forms are used as solvents. Also called "propyl alcohol." [PROPAN(E) + -OL.]

pro·pa·none (prō′pə-nōn′) *n. Chemistry.* An organic ketone, **acetone** *(see).*

pro·par·ox·y·tone (prō′păr-ŏk′sĭ-tōn′) *adj.* Having an acute accent on the antepenult in Classical Greek. ~*n.* A proparoxytone word. [Greek *proparoxutonos : pro-,* before + PAROXYTONE.] **—pro·par·ox·y·ton·ic** (prō′păr-ŏk′sĭ-tŏn′ĭk) *adj.*

pro pa·tri·a (prō pä′trē-ə) *adv.* For one's country. [Latin.] **—pro pa·tri·a** *adj.*

pro·pel (prə-pĕl′) *tr.v.* **-pelled, -pelling, -pels.** To cause to move or sustain in motion. [Middle English *propellen,* from Latin *prōpellere : prō,* forward + *pellere,* to drive.]

pro·pel·lant, pro·pel·lent (prə-pĕl′ənt) *n.* **1.** Something that propels or provides thrust, such as an explosive charge or a rocket fuel. **2.** The gas used in a domestic aerosol spray. ~*adj.* Serving to propel; propelling.

pro·pel·ler (prə-pĕl′ər) *n.* Any of various related simple machines for propelling aircraft or boats, especially one having radiating blades mounted on a revolving power-driven shaft. Also called "prop," "screw," "screw propeller."

propeller shaft *n.* **1.** The shaft that drives a propeller. **2.** The shaft in a motor vehicle that transmits power from the gearbox to the differential. Also called "prop shaft."

pro·pe·nal (prō′pə-nāl′) *n. Chemistry.* An organic aldehyde, **acrolein** *(see).*

pro·pend (prō-pĕnd′) *intr.v.* **-pended, -pending, -pends.** To have a propensity toward. [Latin *prōpendēre,* to hang forward or downward, be inclined or favorable : *prō-,* forward, down + *pendēre,* to hang.]

pro·pene (prō′pēn′) *n.* A colorless, flammable alkene gas, C_3H_6, obtained by cracking petroleum and used in organic synthesis. Also called "propylene."

pronghorn *The only surviving member of the family* Antilocapridae, *the pronghorn resembles the antelope and was once found from Mexico to Canada. Now, however, it is confined to the plains of North America.*

pro·pe·no·ic acid (prō'pə-nō'ĭk) n. Chemistry. An organic acid, **acrylic acid** (see).

pro·pen·si·ty (prə-pĕn'sə-tē) n., pl. **-ties.** An innate inclination; a tendency; a bent. [From archaic propense, inclined, from Latin prōpensus, past participle of prōpendēre, to be inclined or favorable, PROPEND.]

prop·er (prŏp'ər) adj. **1.** Suitable; fitting; appropriate: the proper moment. **2.** Out-and-out; thorough: a proper rascal. **3.** Worthy of the name: take one's medicine like a proper man. **4.** Meeting a requisite standard of competence or validity. **5. a.** Within the strict limitation of the term. Used after the noun: France proper. **b.** Rigorously correct; exact. **6.** Characteristically belonging to the being or thing in question. Used after the noun and with to: an optical effect proper to fluids. **7. a.** Seemly; decorous in behavior. **b.** Displaying exaggerated propriety or gentility. **8.** Mathematics. Designating a subset of a given set when the latter has at least one element not in the subset. **9.** Ecclesiastical. Belonging to the proper of the day. —See Synonyms at **fit.**
~adv. Thoroughly: He got told off good and proper.
~n. Sometimes **Proper.** Ecclesiastical. **1.** The parts of the Mass or Divine Office that vary according to the particular day or feast. **2.** An office to be said on an appointed day or feast. Compare **ordinary.** [Middle English propre, one's own, distinctive, correct, proper, from Old French, from Latin proprius, one's own, personal, particular.] —**prop·er·ly** adv. —**prop·er·ness** n.

proper adjective n. An adjective formed from a proper noun.

pro·per·din (prō-pûr'dĭn) n. A natural protein in human blood serum that helps provide immunity to Gram-negative bacteria and viruses. Not in technical usage. [Perhaps PRO- (acting as) + Latin perdere, "to give away," squander, hence, to destroy : per-, away, to destruction + dare, to give + -IN.]

proper fraction n. **1.** A numerical fraction in which the numerator is less than the denominator; a common fraction that is less than one. **2.** A polynomial fraction in which the numerator is of lower degree than the denominator. Compare **improper fraction.**

proper motion n. Astronomy. The component of a star's motion in space, relative to the sun, that is perpendicular to the line of sight.

proper noun n. A noun designating by name a being or thing without a limiting modifier. Also called "proper name." Compare **common noun.**

prop·er·tied (prŏp'ər-tēd) adj. Owning land or securities as a principal source of revenue.

Pro·per·tius (prō-pûr'shəs, -shē-əs), **Sextus** (c. 50–15 B.C.). Roman elegiac poet. With his first book Cynthia, an elegy on his former lover, published in 29 B.C., he was recognized by the literary patron Maecenas and was introduced to a circle of important poets, including Virgil, Ovid, and Horace, who influenced his work.

prop·er·ty (prŏp'ər-tē) n., pl. **-ties.** Abbr. prop. **1.** The right of possession, use, and disposal of something; ownership. **2.** A possession, or possessions collectively. **3.** Something tangible or intangible to which its owner has legal title. **4.** A piece of land, such as that on which a house stands or that used for farming. **5.** Any article, except costumes and scenery, used on the set or stage of a film, play, or musical. Also called "prop." **6. a.** A characteristic trait or peculiarity. **b.** A special capability or power; a virtue. **c.** A quality serving to define or describe an object or substance. **d.** A characteristic attribute possessed by all members of a class. **e.** Logic. A predicable that is common and peculiar to the whole of a species and is necessarily predicated of its essence without being part of that essence. —See Synonyms at **assets, quality.** [Middle English proprete, from Old French propr(i)ete, from Latin proprietās (stem proprietāt-), ownership, peculiarity, from proprius, own, particular, PROPER.]

pro·phage (prō'fāj') n. A noninfectious association between a bacterial virus and a bacterium, in which the viral chromosomes link with the bacterial chromosomes but do not cause disruption of the bacterial cell or promote replication of the virus itself. [PRO- (before) + -PHAGE.]

pro·phase (prō'fāz') n. Biology. The first stage in cell division in meiosis and mitosis, during which chromosomes become visible and the nuclear membrane begins to disintegrate. See **diakinesis, diplotene, leptotene, pachytene, zygotene.**

proph·e·cy (prŏf'ə-sē) n., pl. **-cies. 1.** A prediction. **2. a.** The inspired utterance of a prophet, viewed as a declaration of divine will. **b.** Such a revelation transmitted orally or in writing. **c.** The quality or activity of receiving and transmitting such revelations. [Middle English prophecie, from Old French profecie, prophecie, from Latin prophētīa, from Greek prophēteia, from prophētēs, PROPHET.]

Usage: Prophecy and prophesy are sometimes confused in spelling. Prophecy is the noun; prophesy the verb. Their pronunciations are also different.

proph·e·sy (prŏf'ə-sī') v. **-sied, -sying, -sies.** —tr. **1.** To reveal by divine inspiration. **2.** To predict. **3.** To prefigure; foreshow. —intr. **1.** To reveal the will of God. **2.** To predict the future. **3.** To speak as a prophet. —See Synonyms at **foretell.** —See Usage note at **prophecy.** [Middle English prophecien, from Old French prophecier, from prophecie, PROPHECY.] —**proph·e·si·er** n.

proph·et (prŏf'ĭt) n. **1.** A person who speaks by divine inspiration or as the interpreter through whom divine will is expressed. **2.** One who predicts the future. **3.** The chief spokesman of some cause or movement. —**the Prophet. 1.** Islam. Muhammad. **2.** Mormon Church. Joseph Smith. —**the Prophets.** The prophetic writings of the Hebrew Scriptures; the second main division of the Old Testament. [Middle English prophet(e), profete, from Old French, from Latin prophēta, from Greek prophētēs, "one who speaks beforehand" : pro-, before + -phētēs, "speaker," from phanai, to say.]

proph·et·ess (prŏf'ĭ-tĭs) n. A female prophet.

pro·phet·ic (prə-fĕt'ĭk) adj. Also **pro·phet·i·cal** (-ĭ-kəl). **1.** Of or belonging to a prophet or prophecy. **2.** Of the nature of prophecy. —**pro·phet·i·cal·ly** adv. —**pro·phet·i·cal·ness** n.

pro·phy·lac·tic (prō'fə-lăk'tĭk, prŏf'ə-) adj. Acting to defend against or prevent something, especially disease; protective.
~n. **1.** A prophylactic medicine, device, or measure. **2.** Something intended as a precaution. **3.** Any contraceptive device, especially a condom. [Greek prophulaktikos, from prophulassein, to stand on guard before (a place), take precautions against : pro-, before + phulassein, to guard, protect, from phulax, a guard.] —**pro·phy·lac·ti·cal·ly** adv.

pro·phy·lax·is (prō'fə-lăk'sĭs, prŏf'ə-) n., pl. **-laxes** (-lăk'sēz'). The prevention of or protective treatment for disease. [New Latin, from Greek prophulaktikos, PROPHYLACTIC.]

pro·pin·qui·ty (prō-pĭng'kwə-tē) n. **1.** Nearness in place or time; proximity. **2.** Kinship. **3.** Similarity in nature. [Middle English propinquite, from Latin propinquitās (stem propinquitāt-), from propinquus, near.]

pro·pi·o·nate (prō'pē-ə-nāt') n. A salt or ester of propionic acid. [PROPION(IC ACID) + -ATE.]

pro·pi·on·ic acid (prō'pē-ŏn'ĭk) n. A fatty acid, $CH_3CH_2CO_2H$, prepared synthetically and used in a salt form as a mold inhibitor in bread. Also called "propanoic acid." [French propionique : Greek pro-, before, first (because this acid is first in order among the fatty acids) + piōn, fat + -IC.]

pro·pi·ti·ate (prō-pĭsh'ē-āt') tr.v. **-ated, -ating, -ates.** To conciliate (an offended power); appease. [Latin propitiāre, from propitius, PROPITIOUS.] —**pro·pi·ti·a·ble** adj. —**pro·pi·ti·at·ing·ly** adv. —**pro·pi·ti·a·tive** adj. —**pro·pi·ti·a·tor** n.

pro·pi·ti·a·tion (prō-pĭsh'ē-ā'shən) n. **1.** The act of propitiating. **2.** Something that propitiates; especially, an offering to a god.

pro·pi·ti·a·to·ry (prō-pĭsh'ē-ə-tôr'ē, -tōr'ē) adj. Of or offered in propitiation; conciliatory.
~n., pl. **propitiatories.** In ancient Jewish ceremony, the **mercy seat** (see). —**pro·pi·ti·a·to·ri·ly** adv.

pro·pi·tious (prə-pĭsh'əs) adj. **1.** Presenting favorable circumstances; auspicious. **2.** Kindly; gracious. —See Synonyms at **favorable.** [Middle English propycyous, from Old French propicius, from Latin propitius, favorable, kind.] —**pro·pi·tious·ly** adv. —**pro·pi·tious·ness** n.

prop·jet (prŏp'jĕt') n. A **turboprop** (see).

prop·o·lis (prŏp'ə-lĭs) n. A resinous substance used by bees in making their hives. [Latin, from Greek, "suburb," hence (unexplained sense development) "bee glue" : pro-, before, beyond + polis, city.]

pro·po·nent (prə-pō'nənt) n. **1.** One who argues in support of something; an advocate. **2.** Law. A person who applies for probate of a will. [Latin prōpōnēns (stem prōpōnent-), present participle of prōpōnere, to PROPOSE.]

Pro·pon·tis (prō-pŏn'tĭs). The ancient name for the Sea of Marmara.

pro·por·tion (prə-pôr'shən, -pōr'shən) n. **1.** A part considered in relation to the whole. **2.** A relationship between things or parts of things with respect to comparative magnitude, quantity, or degree. **3.** A relationship between quantities, such that if one varies, another varies in a manner dependent on the first; a ratio. **4.** Harmonious relationship; symmetry. **5.** Usually **proportions.** Dimensions; size: He has the proportions of a giant. **6.** Mathematics. A relationship of equality between two ratios. Four quantities, a, b, c, d, are said to be in proportion if $a/b = c/d$.
~tr.v. **proportioned, -tioning, -tions. 1.** To adjust so that proper relations between parts are attained. **2.** To adjust in degree, quantity, or other measure, in relation to something else. [Middle English proporcioun, from Old French proportion, from Latin prōportiō (stem prōportiōn-) (translation of Greek analogia, analogy), from the phrase prō portiōne, "for the share of," proportionally : prō, for + portiō, share, portion.] —**pro·por·tion·a·ble** adj. —**pro·por·tion·a·bly** adv. —**pro·por·tion·er** n. —**pro·por·tion·ment** n.

Synonyms: balance, harmony, symmetry.

pro·por·tion·al (prə-pôr'shən-əl, -pōr'shən-əl) adj. **1.** Forming a relationship with other parts or quantities; being in proportion. **2.** Properly related in size or other measurable characteristics. **3.** Mathematics. Having a constant ratio.
~n. Any of the quantities in a mathematical proportion. —**pro·por·tion·al·i·ty** n. —**pro·por·tion·al·ly** adv.

proportional representation n. Abbr. **P.R.** Representation of all parties in an elective body in proportion to their share of the total vote cast in an election.

pro·por·tion·ate (prə-pôr'shən-ĭt, prə-pōr'-) adj. Being in due proportion; proportional.
~tr.v. (prə-pôr'shə-nāt', prə-pōr'-) **proportionated, -ating, -ates.** To make proportionate. —**pro·por·tion·ate·ly** adv.

pro·pos·al (prə-pō'zəl) n. **1.** The act of proposing. **2.** A plan or scheme that is proposed; a suggestion. **3.** An offer of marriage.

pro·pose (prə-pōz') v. **-posed, -posing, -poses.** —tr. **1.** To put forward for consideration, discussion, or adoption: propose new methods. **2.** To present or nominate (a person) for a position, office, or membership. **3.** To offer (a toast). **4.** To purpose; intend. —intr. To form or make a proposal, especially of marriage. [Middle English *proposen,* from Old French *proposer,* from Latin *prōpōnere* (past participle *prōpositus*), to put or set forth, declare, propound : *prō,* forward + *pōnere,* to place.] **—pro·pos·er** *n.*

prop·o·si·tion (prŏp′ə-zĭsh′ən) *n. Abbr.* **prop. 1.** A plan or scheme suggested for consideration or acceptance. **2.** *Informal.* A matter or person requiring special handling. **3.** A suggested business offer, arrangement, or the like. **4.** A subject for discussion or analysis, as in a debate. **5.** *Logic.* **a.** A statement in which the subject is affirmed or denied by the predicate and can or is shown to be true or false. **b.** A statement containing only logical constants and having a fixed truth-value. **6.** *Informal.* A dubious or immoral proposal. ∼*tr.v.* **propositioned, -tioning, -tions.** *Informal.* To propose a private bargain to; especially, to make an offer of sexual intercourse to. [Middle English *proposicioun,* from Old French *proposition,* from Latin *prōpositiō* (stem *prōpositiōn-*), from *prōpōnere,* PROPOSE.] **—prop·o·si·tion·al** *adj.* **—prop·o·si·tion·al·ly** *adv.*

propositional calculus *n. Logic.* The branch of symbolic logic dealing with the relationships formed between propositions by such connectives as *and, or,* and *if* as opposed to their internal structure. Compare **predicate calculus.**

propositional function *n. Logic.* An expression having the form of a proposition, but containing undefined symbols for the substantive elements. It becomes a proposition when appropriate values are assigned to the symbols.

pro·pos·i·tus (prō-pŏz′ĭ-təs) *n., pl.* **-ti** (-tī′). *Law.* One from whom a line of descent is traced. [New Latin, specialized use of the past participle of Latin *prōpōnere,* to place before, PROPOSE.]

pro·pound (prə-pound′) *tr.v.* **-pounded, -pounding, -pounds. 1.** To put forward for consideration; set forth. **2.** *Law.* To present (a will) before the proper authority to obtain probate. [Alteration of earlier *propoune,* Middle English (Scottish) *proponen,* from Latin *prōpōnere,* to PROPOSE.] **—pro·pound·er** *n.*

propr. proprietor.

pro·prae·tor (prō-prē′tər) *n.* A Roman official appointed, usually immediately after holding the praetorship, to be the chief administrator of a province. [Latin, from *prō* *praetōre,* (one acting) for a praetor : *prō,* for + PRAETOR.] **—pro·prae·to·ri·al, pro·prae·to·ri·an** *adj.*

pro·pri·e·tar·y (prə-prī′ə-tĕr′ē) *adj. Abbr.* **prop., pty. 1.** Of or pertaining to a proprietor or to proprietors collectively. **2.** Exclusively owned; private. **3.** Befitting an owner: *a proprietary air.* **4.** Owned by a private individual or corporation under a trademark or patent. **5.** *Medicine.* Of or designating a medical preparation or agent made and distributed under a trade name. ∼*n., pl.* **proprietaries.** *Abbr.* **prop., pty. 1.** A proprietor. **2.** A group of proprietors. **3.** Ownership; proprietorship. **4.** The governor of a proprietary colony. **5.** A proprietary medicine or agent. [Late Latin *proprietārius,* from Latin *proprietās,* property, PROPRIETY.] **—pro·pri·e·tar·i·ly** *adv.*

proprietary colony *n.* Any of certain early North American colonies, such as Carolina and Pennsylvania, that were granted by the Crown in the 17th century to one or more lords proprietary, who had full governing rights.

pro·pri·e·tor (prə-prī′ə-tər) *n. Abbr.* **prop., propr. 1.** A person who has legal title to something; an owner. **2.** The owner or owner-manager of a business or other institution. [Alteration of PROPRI-ETARY (noun).] **—pro·pri·e·to·ri·al** *adj.* **—pro·pri·e·to·ri·al·ly** *adv.* **—pro·pri·e·tor·ship** *n.*

pro·pri·e·tress (prə-prī′ə-trĭs) *n.* A female proprietor.

pro·pri·e·ty (prə-prī′ĭ-tē) *n., pl.* **-ties. 1.** The quality of being fitting or proper; appropriateness. **2. a.** Conformity to prevailing customs and usages. **b. proprieties.** The usages and customs considered to be correct in polite society. Preceded by *the.* **—See Synonyms at etiquette.** [Middle English *propriete,* ownership, one's own nature, idiosyncrasy, from Old French, from Latin *proprietās* (stem *proprie-tāt-*), from *proprius,* PROPER.]

pro·pri·o·cep·tor (prō′prē-ə-sĕp′tər) *n.* A sensory receptor, chiefly in muscles, tendons, and joints, that responds to stimuli arising within the organism. [Latin *proprius,* one's own + (RE)CEPTOR.] **—pro·pri·o·cep·tive** *adj.*

prop root *n.* A root growing from above ground into the soil and helping to support the plant stem, as in maize.

prop shaft *n.* A propeller shaft (*see*).

prop·to·sis (prŏp-tō′sĭs) *n., pl.* **-ses** (-sēz′). Forward displacement of an organ, such as the eyeball. [Late Latin, from Greek *proptōsis,* a falling forward, from *propiptein,* to fall forward : *pro-,* forward + *piptein,* to fall.]

pro·pul·sion (prə-pŭl′shən) *n.* **1.** The process of driving or propelling. **2.** A driving or propelling force. [Medieval Latin *prōpulsiō* (stem *prōpulsiōn-*), from Latin *prōpellere* (past participle *prōpulsus*), to drive forward, PROPEL.] **—pro·pul·sive, pro·pul·so·ry** *adj.*

pro·pyl (prō′pŭl) *n. Chemistry.* A univalent organic radical with composition C_3H_7, derived from propane. [PROP- + -YL.]

prop·y·lae·um (prŏp′ə-lē′əm) *n., pl.* **-laea** (-lē′ə). *Architecture.* An entrance or vestibule to a temple or group of buildings. Also called "propylon." [Latin, from Greek *propulaion* : *pro-,* before + *pulē,* gate.]

propyl alcohol *n. Chemistry.* Propanol (*see*).

pro·pyl·ene (prō′pə-lēn′) *n. Chemistry.* Propene (*see*). [PROPYL + -ENE.]

propylene glycol *n.* A colorless viscous hygroscopic liquid, $CH_3CH(OH)CH_2OH$, used in antifreeze solutions, in hydraulic fluids, and as a solvent. Also called "propanediol."

pro ra·ta (prō rā′tə, răt′ə, rä′tə) *adj.* In proportion. [Latin *pro rata (parte),* according to the calculated (share).] **—pro ra·ta** *adv.*

pro·rate (prō-rāt′, prō′rāt′) *v.* **-rated, -rating, -rates.** *—tr.* To divide, distribute, or assess proportionately. *—intr.* To settle affairs on the basis of proportional distribution. [From PRO RATA.] **—pro·rat·a·ble** *adj.* **—pro·ra·tion** *n.*

pro·rogue (prō-rōg′) *v.* **-rogued, -roguing, -rogues.** To discontinue the sessions of (a parliament or similar body) for a period of time. [Middle English *prorogen,* from Old French *prorog(u)er,* from Latin *prōrogāre,* "to ask publicly (for an extension of one's term of office)," prolong, defer : *prō-,* forward, in public + *rogāre,* to ask.] **—pro·ro·ga·tion** *n.*

pros. prosody.

pros– *prefix.* Indicates: **1.** Near, to, or toward; for example, **pros-enchyma. 2.** In front; for example, **prosencephalon.** [Greek, from *pros,* near, at, toward, to.]

pro·sa·ic (prō-zā′ĭk) *adj.* **1.** Of or like prose; not poetic. **2. a.** Matter-of-fact; straightforward. **b.** Lacking in imagination and spirit; dull; ordinary. [Late Latin *prōsaicus,* from Latin *prōsa,* PROSE.] **—pro·sa·i·cal·ly** *adv.* **—pro·sa·ic·ness** *n.*

pro·sa·ism (prō′zā-ĭz′əm) *n.* **1.** A quality or style that is prosaic. **2.** A prosaic expression, phrase, or word.

pro·sce·ni·um (prō-sē′nē-əm) *n., pl.* **-nia** (-nē-ə). **1.** In a modern theater, the area located between the curtain and the orchestra. **2.** In an ancient theater, the stage, located between the background and the orchestra. [Latin, from Greek *proskēnion* : *pro-,* before + *skēnē,* "tent," stage-building used as background (see **scene**).]

proscenium arch *n.* In a traditional theater, the arch over the front of and framing the stage.

pro·sciut·to (prō-shōō′tō) *n., pl.* **-ti.** A type of spiced Italian ham. [Italian, from *pro-,* beforehand, PRE- + *asciutto,* dried.]

pro·scribe (prō-skrīb′) *tr.v.* **-scribed, -scribing, -scribes. 1.** To denounce or condemn; specifically, to outlaw or banish. **2.** To prohibit; forbid. **3.** In ancient Rome, to publish the name of (a person) as outlawed and confiscate his property. [Latin *prōscrībere,* to publish in writing, proscribe : *prō-,* in front, publicly + *scrībere,* to write.] **—pro·scrib·er** *n.*

pro·scrip·tion (prō-skrĭp′shən) *n.* **1.** The act of proscribing; prohibition. **2.** The condition of being proscribed. **—pro·scrip·tive** *adj.* **—pro·scrip·tive·ly** *adv.*

prose (prōz) *n.* **1.** Ordinary speech or writing, as distinguished from verse. **2.** Commonplace expression or quality. **3.** A piece of English prose to be translated into another language as an exercise. **4.** *Roman Catholic Church.* Formerly, a hymn of irregular meter sung after the gradual at Mass. ∼*adj.* Written in prose. ∼*v.* **prosed, prosing, proses.** *—tr.* To make into prose. *—intr.* **1.** To write prose. **2.** To speak or write in a dull, tiresome style. [Middle English, from Old French, from Latin *prōsa (ōrātiō),* "straightforward discourse," from *prōsus, prorsus,* straightforward, direct, from *prōversus,* past participle of *prōvertere,* to turn forward : *prō-,* forward + *vertere,* to turn.]

pros·e·cute (prŏs′ə-kyōōt′) *v.* **-cuted, -cuting, -cutes.** *—tr.* **1.** To pursue or persist in so as to complete. **2.** To carry on (a trade, for example); practice. **3. a.** To initiate legal or criminal court action against. **b.** To seek to obtain or enforce by legal action. *—intr.* **1.** To initiate and conduct legal proceedings. **2.** To act as prosecutor. [Middle English *prosecuten,* to follow, from Latin *prōsequī* (past participle *prōsecūtus*), to follow up or forward : *prō-,* forward + *sequī,* to follow.]

prosecuting attorney *n.* An attorney empowered to prosecute cases on behalf of a government and the people.

pros·e·cu·tion (prŏs′ə-kyōō′shən) *n.* **1. a.** The act of prosecuting. **b.** The state of being prosecuted. **2.** The institution and carrying out of a legal proceeding. **3.** A prosecuting attorney.

pros·e·cu·tor (prŏs′ə-kyōō′tər) *n.* **1.** One who prosecutes. **2.** One who initiates and carries out a legal action, especially criminal proceedings. **3.** A prosecuting attorney.

pros·e·lyte (prŏs′ə-līt′) *n.* A convert to a religion or doctrine, especially a recent convert. ∼*v.* Variant of **proselytize.** [Middle English *proselite,* from Late Latin *prosēlytus,* from Greek *prosēlutos,* "one who comes to a place," stranger, religious convert.] **—pros·e·lyt·er** *n.*

pros·e·lyt·ism (prŏs′ə-lə-tĭz′əm, -līt-ĭz′əm) *n.* **1.** The practice of proselytizing. **2.** The state of being a proselyte; conversion. **—pros·e·lyt·i·cal** (prŏs′ə-lĭt′ĭ-kəl) *adj.* **—pros·e·lyt·ist** *n.*

pros·e·lyt·ize (prŏs′ə-lə-tīz′) *v.* **-ized, -izing, -izes.** Also **proselyte, -lyted, -lyting, -lytes.** *—intr.* **1.** To make proselytes. **2.** Loosely, to promote or speak enthusiastically on behalf of a cause. **3.** *Archaic.* To become a proselyte; convert. *—tr.* **1.** To convert from one belief or faith to another. **2.** Loosely, to try to win (a person) to a cause one espouses. **—pros·e·lyt·i·za·tion** *n.* **—pros·e·lyt·iz·er** *n.*

pros·en·ceph·a·lon (prŏs′ĕn-sĕf′ə-lŏn′) *n. Anatomy.* The **forebrain** (*see*). [New Latin : PROS- (before, in front) + ENCEPHALON.] **—pros·en·ce·phal·ic** (prŏs′ĕn-sə-făl′ĭk) *adj.*

pros·en·chy·ma (prŏs-ĕng′kĭ-mə) *n. Botany.* Tissue consisting of elongated cells with tapering ends, occurring in supporting and conducting tissue. [New Latin : PROS- (near, toward) + (PAR)EN-CHYMA.] **—pros·en·chym·a·tous** (prŏs′ĕn-kĭm′ə-təs) *adj.*

prose poem *n.* A short work, often a single paragraph, written as prose but employing poetic techniques and imagery.

Pro·ser·pi·na (prō-sûr′pə-nə). Also **Pros·er·pi·ne** (prŏs′ər-pīn′, prō-sûr′pə-nē). *Roman Mythology.* The wife of Pluto and daughter of Jupiter and Ceres; the goddess of the underworld, corresponding to the Greek Persephone.

pro·sim·i·an (prō-sĭm′ē-ən) *adj.* Of or belonging to the Prosimii, a primitive suborder of primates that includes the lemurs, lorises, and tarsiers. [New Latin *Prosimii* : *pro-*, before + Latin *simia*, ape, from *simus*, snub-nosed, from Greek *simos* (see **simian**).] **—pro·sim·i·an** *n.*

pro·sit (prōst, prō′sĭt) *interj.* Your health! Used as a drinking toast. [German, from Latin, "may it be advantageous."]

pros·o·dist (prŏs′ə-dĭst) *n.* A specialist in prosody.

pros·o·dy (prŏs′ə-dē) *n. pl.* **-dies.** *Abbr.* **pros. 1.** The science of versification, covering such aspects as metrical, rhythmical, and stanzaic forms. **2.** A particular system of versification. [Middle English *prosodye*, from Latin *prosōdia*, tone or accent of a syllable, from Greek *prosōidia*, accompanied song, modulation of voice, pronunciation, diacritical mark : *pros-*, to, in addition to + *ōidē*, song, lay, ode.] **—pro·sod·ic** (prō-sŏd′ĭk) *adj.* **—pro·sod·i·cal·ly** *adv.*

pro·so·po·poe·ia, pro·so·po·pe·ia (prō-sō′pə-pē′ə) *n. Rhetoric.* **1.** The impersonation of an absent or imaginary speaker. **2.** Personification, as of abstractions or inanimate objects. [Latin *prosopopoiia*, from Greek *prosōpopoiia*, dramatization : *prosōpon*, face, mask, dramatic character : *pros*, toward + stem *op-*, to see + *poiein*, to make.] **—pro·so·po·poe·ial** *adj.*

pros·pect (prŏs′pĕkt′) *n.* **1. a.** Something expected; a possibility. **b.** Expectation: *no prospect of a job.* **2. prospects.** Chances for success, especially with regard to wealth or social position. **3. a.** A potential customer. **b.** A candidate deemed likely to succeed. **4.** The direction in which an object, such as a building, faces. **5.** An extensive or distant view or scene presented to the eye: *a pleasant prospect.* **6.** The act of surveying or examining. **7.** *Mining.* **a.** The location or probable location of a mineral deposit. **b.** An actual or probable deposit. **c.** The mineral yield obtained by working an ore.
~*v.* **prospected, -pecting, -pects.** *—tr.* To explore (a region) for gold or other mineral deposits. *—intr.* To explore for mineral deposits. Often used with *for.* [Middle English *prospecte*, from Latin *prōspectus*, distant view, vista, from the past participle of *prōspicere*, to look forward, foresee : *prō-*, forward + *specere*, to look.]

Usage: *prospect, outlook, expectation.* These nouns refer to envisioning or predicting future conditions or personal chances or hopes. *Prospect* and *outlook* are projections of what the future has in store, good or bad. *Expectation* more strongly suggests anticipation of success or fulfillment.

pro·spec·tive (prə-spĕk′tĭv) *adj.* **1.** Looking forward in time; characterized by foresight. **2.** Being in prospect; likely to become: *the prospective bridegroom.* **—pro·spec·tive·ly** *adv.*

pros·pec·tor (prŏs′pĕk′tər) *n.* One who explores an area for natural deposits, such as gold or oil.

pro·spec·tus (prə-spĕk′təs) *n.* **1.** A formal summary of a proposed commercial, literary, or other venture. **2.** A brochure published by an institution, such as a school or university, giving such details as facilities and charges. [Latin, PROSPECT.]

pros·per (prŏs′pər) *v.* **-pered, -pering, -pers.** *—intr.* To be fortunate or successful; thrive. *—tr. Archaic.* To cause to thrive. [Middle English *prosperen*, from Old French *prosperer*, from Latin *prosperāre*, to make fortunate, from *prosperus*, fortunate.]

pros·per·i·ty (prŏs-pĕr′ə-tē) *n., pl.* **-ties.** The condition of being prosperous and having good fortune or financial success.

pros·per·ous (prŏs′pər-əs) *adj.* **1.** Having success; flourishing. **2.** Affluent; well-to-do. **3.** Propitious; favorable. **—pros·per·ous·ly** *adv.* **—pros·per·ous·ness** *n.*

pros·ta·glan·din (prŏs′tə-glăn′dĭn) *n.* Any of various substances composed of fatty acids and having hormonelike activity, found especially in mammals. [From PROSTA(TE) + GLAND + -IN.]

pros·tate (prŏs′tāt′) *n.* A gland in male mammals that secretes a liquid that forms a part of the semen. Also called "prostate gland." [New Latin *prostata*, from Greek *prostatēs*, "stander before (the bladder)," from *proïstanai*, to cause to stand in front : *pro-*, in front + *histanai*, to cause to stand.] **—pros·tate, pros·tat·ic** (prō-stăt′ĭk) *adj.*

pros·ta·tec·to·my (prŏs′tə-tĕk′tə-mē) *n., pl.* **-mies.** The surgical removal of all or part of the prostate. [PROSTAT(E) + -ECTOMY.]

pros·ta·ti·tis (prŏs′tə-tī′tĭs) *n.* Inflammation of the prostate.

pros·the·sis (prŏs-thē′sĭs) *n., pl.* **-ses** (-sēz′). **1.** The artificial replacement of a limb, tooth, or other body part. **2.** An artificial device used in such replacement. **3.** *Linguistics.* Variant of **prothesis.** [Late Latin, addition of a letter or syllable, from Greek, attachment, addition, from *prostithenai*, to put to, add : *pros-*, in addition + *tithenai*, to place, put.] **—pros·thet·ic** (prŏs-thĕt′ĭk) *adj.* **—pros·thet·i·cal·ly** *adv.*

prosthetic group *n. Biochemistry.* The nonpeptide part of a conjugated protein, such as the heme group in hemoglobin.

pros·thet·ics (prŏs-thĕt′ĭks) *n. Used with a singular verb.* Prosthetic surgery. **—pros·the·tist** (prŏs′thə-tĭst) *n.*

pros·tho·don·tics (prŏs′thə-dŏn′tĭks) *n. Used with a singular verb.* Also **pros·tho·don·ti·a** (-shē-ə). Prosthetic dentistry. [From PROSTH(ESIS) + -ODONT + -ICS.] **—pros·tho·don·tist** *n.*

pros·ti·tute (prŏs′tə-to͞ot′, -tyo͞ot′) *n.* **1.** One who solicits and accepts payment for sexual services, especially a woman or girl who accepts payment from men, or a man or boy who engages in homosexual practices for payment. **2.** One who sells or degrades ability or name for money or an unworthy cause.
~*tr.v.* **prostituted, -tuting, -tutes. 1.** To offer (oneself or another) for sexual hire. **2.** To degrade (oneself or one's talents) for money or an unworthy cause. [Latin *prōstitūta*, from the past participle of *prōstituere*, to expose publicly, prostitute : *prō-*, forth, in public + *statuere*, to set, place, from *stare* (past participle *status*), to stand.] **—pros·ti·tu·tor** *n.*

pros·ti·tu·tion (prŏs′tə-to͞o′shən, -tyo͞o′shən) *n.* **1.** The act or practice of prostituting. **2.** The act of offering or devoting one's talents to an unworthy use or cause.

pro·sto·mi·um (prō-stō′mē-əm) *n.* The part of the head end of an earthworm or other annelid that bears tentacles, a sucker, or feeding appendages.

pros·trate (prŏs′trāt′) *tr.v.* **-trated, -trating, -trates. 1.** To make (oneself) bow or kneel down in humility or adoration. **2.** To throw down flat. **3. a.** To make very weak or exhausted; overcome. **b.** To cause to be submissive; overthrow.
~*adj.* **1.** Lying face down, as in submission. **2.** Lying down full-length. **3. a.** Physically or emotionally exhausted; incapacitated. **b.** Overthrown or defeated. **4.** *Botany.* Growing along the ground. —See Usage note at **prone.** [Middle English *prostrat* (adjective), from Latin *prōstrātus*, past participle of *prōsternere*, to throw down, prostrate : *prō-*, down before + *sternere*, to stretch out, cast down.] **—pros·tra·tor** *n.*

pros·tra·tion (prŏs-trā′shən) *n.* **1. a.** The act of prostrating oneself. **b.** The state of being prostrate. **2.** Total exhaustion.

pro·style (prō′stīl) *adj. Architecture.* Having a row of columns across the front only, as in some Greek temples.
~*n.* A prostyle building or portico. [Latin *prostylos*, from Greek *prostulos*, having pillars in front : *pro-*, in front + *stulos*, pillar.]

pros·y (prō′zē) *adj.* **-ier, -iest. 1.** Matter-of-fact; dry; prosaic. **2.** Dull; commonplace. **—pros·i·ly** *adv.* **—pros·i·ness** *n.*

prot-. Variant of **proto-.**

Prot. 1. Protectorate. **2.** Protestant.

pro·tac·tin·i·um (prō′tăk-tĭn′ē-əm) *n. Symbol* **Pa** A rare radioactive element chemically similar to uranium, having 12 known isotopes, the most common of which is protactinium 231 with a half-life of 32,480 years. Atomic number 91, melting point about 1,600°C, specific gravity 15.37, valence 4 or 5. [New Latin : PROT(O)- + ACTINIUM (because it disintegrates into actinium).]

pro·tag·o·nist (prō-tăg′ə-nĭst) *n.* **1. a.** The leading character in Greek drama. **b.** The leading character in any play, novel, or other literary work. **2.** Any leading or principal figure; especially, one who initiates a political policy. [Greek *prōtagōnistēs* : PROT(O)- + *agōnistēs*, actor, from *agōnizesthai*, to contend, from *agōnia*, a contest, from *agōn*, gathering, contest, from *agein*, to lead.]

Usage: Traditionally, *protagonist* has the sense of "leader" or (in literary works) "leading character." It is therefore considered improper to use a phrase such as *chief protagonist* (because it is redundant) or to use the word in the plural when only one literary work is being referred to. However, the word is extending its meaning and is now often used in the sense of "leader in a matter of importance," as well as in the sense of "partisan" or "champion": *She was a staunch protagonist of the liberation movement.*

Pro·tag·o·ras (prō-tăg′ər-əs) (*c.* 490–421 B.C.). Greek philosopher. He is said to have coined the maxim "Man is the measure of all things."

pro·ta·mine (prō′tə-mēn′, -mĭn) *n.* Also **pro·ta·min** (-mĭn). Any of the group of the simplest proteins that are highly basic, soluble in water, not coagulated by heat, and yield only amino acids, chiefly arginine, upon hydrolysis. [PROT(O)- + -AMINE.]

pro·tan·drous (prō-tăn′drəs) *adj.* Also **pro·tan·dric** (-tăn′drĭk). Having male gametes that mature before the female gametes. Said of certain plants and hermaphrodite animals. Compare **protogynous.** [PROTO- + -ANDROUS.] **—pro·tan·dry** *n.*

pro·ta·no·pi·a (prō′tə-nō′pē-ə) *n.* A form of partial colorblindness in which perception of red is defective, and reds, yellows, and greens are confused. [New Latin : PROT(O)- + AN- (without) + -OPIA.] **—pro·ta·nope** *n.* **—pro·ta·nop·ic** (prō′tə-nŏp′ĭk) *adj.*

prot·a·sis (prŏt′ə-sĭs) *n.* **1.** *Grammar.* A subordinate clause expressing the condition in a conditional sentence. Compare **apodosis. 2.** The introductory part of a classical drama. [Late Latin, proposition, from Greek, "a stretching forward," proposition, premise, from *proteinein*, to stretch forward, offer, propose : *prō-*, before + *teinein*, to stretch.]

pro·te·a (prō′tē-ə) *n.* Any shrub of the southern African genus *Protea*, having showy, conelike flower heads. [New Latin, from PROTEUS (referring to the many different forms of the shrub.]

pro·te·an (prō′tē-ən, prō-tē′-) *adj.* Readily taking on different characters or forms; changeable. [From PROTEUS.]

pro·te·ase (prō′tē-ās′) *n.* An enzyme that catalyzes the hydrolytic breakdown of proteins. Also called "proteolytic enzyme." [PROTE(IN) + -ASE.]

pro·tect (prə-tĕkt′) *tr.v.* **-tected, -tecting, -tects. 1.** To keep from harm, attack, or injury; guard. **2.** *Economics.* To help (domestic industry) by imposing tariffs on imported goods. **3.** *Commerce.* To assure payment of (drafts or notes, for example) by setting aside funds in advance. —See Synonyms at **defend.** [Latin *prōtegere* (past participle *prōtectus*), to cover in front, protect : *prō-*, in front + *tegere*, to cover.] **—pro·tect·ing·ly** *adv.*

pro·tec·tion (prə-tĕk′shən) *n.* **1.** The act of protecting. **2.** The condition of being protected. **3.** One that protects. **4.** A document, such as a passport, guaranteeing safe conduct to travelers. **5.** *Economics.* A tariff system protecting domestic industries from foreign competition. **6.** *Informal.* **a.** Money extorted by racketeers in exchange for a promise of freedom from molestation. Also called

PRONUNCIATION KEY

ă, pat; ā, pay; âr, care;
ä, father, are; b, **bib**;
ch, **church**; d, **deed**; ĕ, pet;
ē, be; f, **fife**; g, **gag**; h, **hat**;
hw, **which**; ĭ, pit; ī, pie;
îr, pier; j, **judge**; k, **kick**;
l, lid, needle; m, **mum**;
n, no, sudden; ng, thing;
ŏ, pot; ō, toe; ô, paw, for;
oi, noise; ou, **out**; o͝o, book;
o͞o, boot; p, **pop**; r, roar;
s, sauce; sh, **ship**, dish;
t, tight; th, **thin**, path;
th, **this**, bathe; ŭ, cut; ûr, **fur**;
v, valve; w, with; y, yes;
z, zebra, size; zh, vision;
ə, about, item, edible,
gallop, circus, peaceful

IN FOREIGN WORDS:

à, *Fr.* ami; œ, *Fr.* **feu**, *Ger.* schön; ü, *Fr.* **tu**, *Ger.* **über**;
KH, *Ger.* **ich**, *Scot.* **loch**;
N, *Fr.* bon; y′, *Fr.* Compiègne

STRESS MARKS:

Primary stress: ′
in·cite′ (ĭn-sīt′)
Secondary stress: ′
in′sight′ (ĭn′sīt′)

"protection money." **b.** Freedom from molestation obtained in this way. **—pro·tec·tion·al** *adj.*

pro·tec·tion·ism (prə-tĕk′shən-ĭz′əm) *n. Economics.* The theory, policy, or system of protecting domestic industries from foreign competition. **—pro·tec·tion·ist** *n. & adj.*

pro·tec·tive (prə-tĕk′tĭv) *adj.* **1.** Adapted or intended to afford protection. **2.** Of, pertaining to, or designed to protect domestic industries from foreign competition: *a protective tariff.* **3.** Showing or expressing often undue concern over the safety or welfare of others: *too protective toward him.* **—pro·tec·tive** *n.* **—pro·tec·tive·ly** *adv.* **—pro·tec·tive·ness** *n.*

protective coloring *n. Zoology.* **1.** Color and markings of an animal that help it to appear inconspicuous in its surroundings so that it is less likely to be seen by predators; camouflage. **2. Batesian mimicry** *(see).*

pro·tec·tor (prə-tĕk′tər) *n.* **1.** A person who protects; a guardian. **2.** *Usually* **Protector.** Formerly, a title given to one who ruled during the absence, minority, or illness of the monarch. **—pro·tec·tor·al** *adj.* **—pro·tec·tor·ship** *n.*

pro·tec·tor·ate (prə-tĕk′tər-ĭt) *n. Abbr.* **Prot 1.** A relationship of protection and partial control assumed by a superior power over a dependent country or region. **2.** The protected country or region. **3. Protectorate. a.** The government, office, or term of a protector. **b.** The government of England under Oliver Cromwell (1653–58) and his son Richard (1658–59).

pro·tec·to·ry (prə-tĕk′tə-rē) *n., pl.* **-ries.** Formerly, an institution run by the Roman Catholic Church providing for the welfare of destitute children.

pro·té·gé (prō′tə-zhā) *n. Feminine* **pro·té·gée** (prō′tə-zhā). One whose welfare, training, or career is promoted by an influential person. [French, from the past participle of *protéger,* to PROTECT.]

pro·te·id (prō′tē-ĭd) *n.* A protein. Not in technical usage.

pro·tein (prō′tēn, -tē-ĭn) *n.* **1.** Any of a group of complex nitrogenous organic compounds of high molecular weight that contain amino acids as their basic structural units and that occur in all living matter and are essential for the growth and repair of animal tissue. Foods containing a high proportion of protein include meat, eggs, and cheese. **2.** The nutritional value provided by food containing any or a combination of these compounds. [French *protéine,* "primary substance (to the body)," from Late Greek *proteios,* primary, from Greek *prōtos,* first.] **—pro·tein·a·ceous** (prō′tə-nā′shəs, prō′tē-nā′-), **pro·te·in·ic** (prō′tē-ĭn′ĭk), **pro·tei·nous** (prō-tē′nəs) *adj.*

pro·tein·ase (prō′tē-nās′, -tē-ĭ-nās′) *n.* A protease that hydrolyzes proteins into polypeptides.

pro·tein·ate (prō′tē-nāt′, -tē-ĭ-nāt′) *n.* A protein compound.

pro·tein·u·ri·a (prō′tē-nyŏŏr′ē-ə, prō′tē-ĭ-) *n. Pathology.* **Albuminuria** *(see).*

pro tem (prō tĕm′) *adv.* Pro tempore. **—pro tem** *adj.*

pro tem·po·re (prō tĕm′pə-rē) *adv. Abbr.* **p.t.** For the time being; temporarily. [Latin.] **—pro tem·po·re** *adj.*

proteo– *prefix.* Indicates protein; for example, **proteolysis.**

pro·te·o·clas·tic (prō′tē-ō-klăs′tĭk) *adj.* Of, pertaining to, or causing proteolysis; proteolytic. [PROTEO- + -CLASTIC.]

pro·te·ol·y·sis (prō′tē-ŏl′ə-sĭs) *n.* The breaking down of proteins into simpler, soluble substances, as in digestion. [PROTEO- + -LYSIS.] **—pro·te·o·lyt·ic** (prō′tē-ə-lĭt′ĭk) *adj.*

proteolytic enzyme *n.* **Protease** *(see).*

pro·te·ose (prō′tē-ōs′, -ōz′) *n.* Any of several water-soluble substances created as a product of partial digestion of protein. [PROTE(O)- + -OSE.]

Prot·er·o·zo·ic (prŏt′ər-ə-zō′ĭk, prō′tər-) *adj. Geology.* Of, belonging to, or designating the geological time and deposits of the Precambrian era between the Archeozoic era and the Cambrian period of the Paleozoic era.
~*n. Geology.* The Proterozoic era. Preceded by *the.* [Greek *proteros,* earlier, anterior + -ZOIC.]

pro·test (prə-tĕst′, prō-tĕst′, prō′tĕst′) *v.* **-tested, -testing, -tests.** *—tr.* **1.** To promise or affirm with earnest solemnity: *The accused protested innocence.* **2.** *Law.* To declare (a bill of exchange or promissory note) dishonored or refused. **3.** *Archaic.* To proclaim or make known. **4.** To object to, especially in a formal statement. *—intr.* **1. a.** To express strong objection, disagreement, or annoyance. Used with *about, against,* or *at.* **b.** To hold a rally or meeting to voice disapproval or objection. **2.** To make an earnest avowal or affirmation. —See Synonyms at **object.**
~*n.* (prō′tĕst′). **1.** A formal declaration of disapproval or objection issued by a concerned party. **2.** Any individual or collective gesture or display of objection or disapproval. Also used adjectivally: *a protest song.* **3.** *Law.* **a.** A formal statement drawn up by a notary for a creditor, declaring that the debtor has refused to accept or honor a bill of exchange or promissory note. **b.** A formal declaration made by a taxpayer, stating that the tax demanded is illegal or excessive and reserving the right to contest it. **4.** A formal written statement by the master of a ship giving the circumstances and details of a disaster, injury, or the like, that occurred at sea. **5.** *Sports.* A formal objection lodged against a player or other competitor. **—under protest.** Against one's will; expressing disagreement or objections. [Middle English *protesten,* from Old French *protester,* from Latin *prōtestārī,* to declare in public, testify, protest : *prō-,* forth, in public + *testārī,* to be a witness, make a will, from *testis,* a witness, will.] **—pro·test·er** *n.* **—pro·test·ing·ly** *adv.*

prot·es·tant (prŏt′ĭs-tənt, prə-tĕs′tənt) *n. Rare.* One who makes a declaration or protest. **—prot·es·tant** *adj.*

Prot·es·tant (prŏt′ĭs-tənt) *n. Abbr.* **Prot. 1.** A member of any of the Christian churches, such as the Baptist, Methodist, or Presbyterian, descending from those that seceded from the Church of Rome at the time of the Reformation, denying the universal authority of the Pope and emphasizing the principle of justification by faith. **2.** Any of those who adhered to the doctrine of Martin Luther and, in 1529, protested against the decree of the Diet of Spires commanding submission to the authority of Rome.
~*adj.* Of, concerning, or pertaining to Protestants or Protestantism. [Latin *prōtestāns* (stem *prōtestānt-*), present participle of *prōtestārī,* to PROTEST.]

Protestant Episcopal Church *n.* A church body in the United States originally associated with the Church of England, but since 1789 organized as a separate entity. Also called "Episcopal Church."

Prot·es·tant·ism (prŏt′ĭs-tənt-ĭz′əm) *n.* **1.** Adherence to a Protestant church. **2.** The religion fostered by the Protestant movement. **3.** Protestants or the Protestant churches collectively.

pro·tes·ta·tion (prŏt′ĭs-tā′shən, prō′tĭs-) *n.* **1.** An emphatic declaration. **2.** A strong or formal expression of dissent.

Pro·teus (prō′tē-əs, -tyōōs). *Greek Mythology.* A sea god who could change his shape at will.

pro·tha·la·mi·on (prō′thə-lā′mē-ən, -ŏn′) *n., pl.* **-mia** (-mē-ə). A song in celebration of a wedding; an epithalamium. [Coined by Edmund Spenser : PRO- (before) + Greek *epithalamion,* EPITHALAMIUM.]

pro·thal·lus (prō-thăl′əs) *n., pl.* **-thalli** (-thăl′ī′) Also **pro·thal·li·um** (prō-thăl′ē-əm), *pl.* **-thallia** (-thăl′ē-ə). *Botany.* A small, flat mass of tissue that is produced by a germinating spore of certain pteridophytes and gymnosperms and bears sexual organs. [New Latin : Greek *pro-,* in front of, before + *thallos,* a shoot.] **—pro·thal·li·al** *adj.*

proth·e·sis (prŏth′ə-sĭs) *n., pl.* **-ses** (-sēz′). Also **pros·the·sis** (for sense 1). **1.** *Linguistics.* The addition of a phoneme at the beginning of a word to ease pronunciation or to form a new word. **2.** *Eastern Orthodox Church.* The preparation of the Eucharistic elements for consecration. [Greek, from *protithenai,* to put before : *pro-,* before + *tithenai,* to put, place.] **—pro·thet·ic** (prō-thĕt′ĭk) *adj.* **—pro·thet·i·cal·ly** *adv.*

pro·thon·o·tar·y (prō-thŏn′ə-tĕr′ē, prō′thə-nō′tə-rē) *n., pl.* **-ies.** Also **pro·ton·o·tar·y** (-tŏn′ə-tĕr′ē, -tə-nō′tə-rē). **1.** Formerly, the principal clerk in certain courts of law. **2.** *Roman Catholic Church.* One of a college of twelve ecclesiastics charged with the registry of important pontifical proceedings. **3.** *Archaic.* A chief scribe. [Middle English *prothonotarie,* from Late Latin *prōtonotārius* : PROTO- + *notārius,* "of shorthand," secretary, from *nota,* mark, shorthand character.] **—pro·thon·o·tar·i·al** *adj.*

prothonotary warbler *n.* A small bird, *Protonotaria citrea,* of southeastern North America, having a deep-yellow head and breast and grayish wings. [Probably from the bright-yellow robes worn by ecclesiastics at important meetings.]

pro·tho·rax (prō-thôr′ăks′, -thōr′ăks′) *n., pl.* **-axes** or **-thoraces** (-thôr′ə-sēz′, -thōr′ə-sēz′). The anterior division of the thorax of an insect, bearing the first pair of legs. **—pro·tho·rac·ic** (prō′thô-răs′ĭk, -thō-răs′ĭk) *adj.*

pro·throm·bin (prō-thrŏm′bĭn) *n.* A plasma protein that is converted into thrombin during blood coagulation.

pro·tist (prō′tĭst) *n. Biology.* Any of the single-celled organisms of the kingdom Protista, which includes protozoans, bacteria, fungi, some algae, and other forms not readily classified as either plants or animals. [New Latin *Protista,* "simplest organisms," from Greek *prōtista,* neuter plural of *prōtistos,* the very first, primal, from *prōtos,* first.] **—pro·tis·tan** *adj. & n.* **—pro·tis·tol·o·gy** (prō′tĭs-tŏl′ə-jē) *n.*

pro·ti·um (prō′tē-əm, prō′shē-) *n.* The most abundant isotope of hydrogen, H^1, with atomic mass 1. [New Latin : PROT(O)- + -IUM.]

proto–, prot– *prefix.* Indicates: **1.** The earliest form or the first in rank or time; for example, **protium, protoplast, prototype. 2. Proto-.** The earliest form of a language as reconstructed by comparative linguistics; for example, **Proto-Germanic. 3.** *Chemistry.* The member of a series that has the least amount of a specified element or radical; for example, **protoporphyrin.** [Greek *prōtos,* first.]

Pro·to-Al·gon·qui·an (prō′tō-ăl-gŏng′kwē-ən, -kē-ən) *n.* The earliest reconstructed ancestor of the Algonquian languages.

pro·to·col (prō′tə-kôl′, -kōl′, -kŏl′) *n.* **1. a.** The forms of ceremony, precedence, and etiquette observed by diplomats and heads of state. **b.** Any rules or code of behavior or etiquette. **2.** The first copy of a treaty or other document prior to its ratification. **3.** Any official record of a transaction or negotiations, especially one that is used as a preliminary draft for a document, such as a treaty. —See Synonyms at **etiquette.**
~*v.* **protocoled** or **-colled, -coling** or **-colling, -cols.** *—intr.* To form or issue protocols. *—tr.* To record or embody in a protocol. [Earlier Scottish *prothocoll,* from Old French *prothocole,* from Medieval Latin *protocollum,* from Late Greek *prōtokollon,* first sheet glued to binding of a book, bearing a table of contents : PROTO- + *kolla,* glue.] **—pro·to·col·ar** (prō′tə-kŏl′ər), **pro·to·col·a·ry, pro·to·col·ic** *adj.*

Pro·to-East·ern-Al·gon·qui·an (prō′tō-ē′stərn-ăl-gŏng′kwē-ən) *n.* The earliest reconstructed ancestor of Eastern Algonquian.

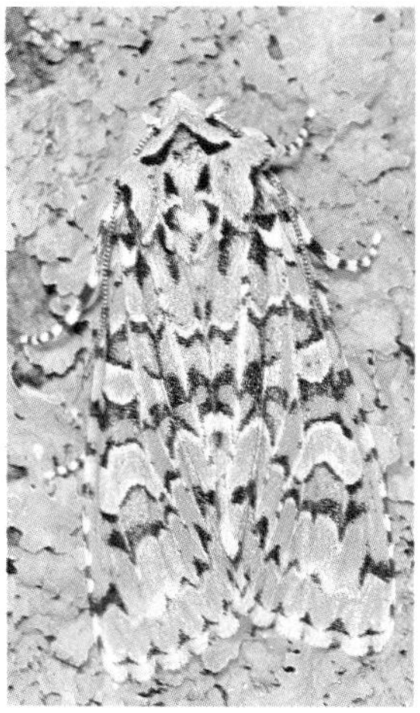

protective coloring *Many insect species have evolved elaborately patterned markings to enable them to hide from predators. This European moth,* Griposia aprilina, *has wings that match the lichen-covered trees on which it rests.*

Pro·to-Ger·man·ic (prō′tō-jûr-măn′ĭk) *n.* The hypothetical prehistoric language that was the ancestor of the Germanic languages.

Pro·to-Greek (prō′tō-grēk′) *n.* Prehistoric Greek after its separation from Indo-European and before its division into dialects.

pro·tog·y·nous (prō-tŏj′ə-nəs) *adj.* Having female gametes that mature before the male gametes. Said of certain plants and hermaphrodite animals. Compare **protandrous.** [PROTO- + -GYNOUS.] **—pro·tog·y·ny** *n.*

pro·to·his·to·ry (prō′tō-hĭs′tə-rē, -hĭs′trē) *n.* The study of human culture, or a particular instance of it, just prior to its earliest recorded history. **—pro·to·his·tor·ic** (prō′tō-hĭs-tôr′ĭk, -tŏr′ĭk) *adj.*

pro·to·hu·man (prō′tō-hyōō′mən) *n.* A member of any of several species of prehistoric primates resembling modern man but more primitive in development. **—pro·to·hu·man** *adj.*

Pro·to-In·do-Eur·o·pe·an (prō′tō-ĭn′dō-yŏŏr′ə-pē′ən) *n.* The hypothetical, reconstructed ancestor of the Indo-European languages.

pro·to·lan·guage (prō′tō-lăng′gwĭj) *n. Linguistics.* A language that is reconstructed by comparative linguistics as the hypothetical ancestor of another existing language or group of languages. Compare **Ursprache.**

pro·to·lith·ic (prō′tə-lĭth′ĭk) *adj.* Of, pertaining to, or characteristic of the very beginning of the Stone Age; eolithic. [PROTO- + -LITHIC.]

pro·to·mar·tyr (prō′tō-mär′tər) *n.* **1.** The first Christian martyr, Saint Stephen. **2.** The first martyr in a cause.

pro·to·mor·phic (prō′tə-môr′fĭk) *adj.* Primitive in structure or form. [PROTO- + -MORPHIC.]

pro·ton (prō′tŏn′) *n. Symbol* **p** *Physics.* A stable, positively charged elementary particle in the baryon family having a mass 1,836 times that of the electron. It is a constituent of all atomic nuclei. See **neutron, particle.** [Greek *prōton,* neuter of *prōtos,* first.] **—pro·ton·ic** *adj.*

pro·to·ne·ma (prō′tə-nē′mə) *n., pl.* **-nemata** (-nē′mə-tə, -nĕm′ə-tə). *Botany.* A green, threadlike structure that arises on germination of a moss spore and that eventually develops into a mature plant. [PROTO- + Greek *nēma,* thread.] **—pro·to·ne·mal** (prō′tə-nē′məl), **pro·to·ne·ma·tal** (prō′tə-nē′mə-təl, -nĕm′ə-təl) *adj.*

proton number *n.* **Atomic number** *(see).*

protonotary. Variant of **prothonotary.**

proton synchrotron *n. Physics.* A ring-shaped **synchrotron** *(see)* that uses a frequency modulated accelerating voltage to accelerate protons to energies of the order 10^9 electronvolts. Also called "proton accelerator."

pro·to·path·ic (prō′tə-păth′ĭk) *adj.* Of, pertaining to, or designating the cutaneous sensory reception of gross pressure, pain, heat, or cold. Compare **epicritic.** [Medieval Greek *prōtopathēs,* affected first, from Greek *prōtopathein,* to feel or be affected first : PROTO- + *paskhein,* to feel, experience.] **—pro·top·a·thy** (prō-tŏp′ə-thē) *n.*

pro·to·plasm (prō′tə-plăz′əm) *n.* A complex, jellylike colloidal substance constituting the living matter of plant and animal cells, and performing the basic life functions. See **cytoplasm, nucleoplasm.** [German *Protoplasma* : PROTO- + -PLASM.] **—pro·to·plas·mic, pro·to·plas·mal, pro·to·plas·mat·ic** *adj.*

pro·to·plast (prō′tə-plăst′) *n.* **1.** *Biology.* The protoplasm and plasma membrane of a plant or bacterial cell after the cell wall has been removed. **2.** *Rare.* A prototype. [Old French *protoplaste,* from Late Latin *prōtoplastus,* "first formed," from Greek *prōtoplastos* : PROTO- + -PLAST.] **—pro·to·plas·tic** *adj.*

pro·to·por·phy·rin (prō′tō-pôr′fə-rĭn) *n.* A metal-free porphyrin, $C_{34}H_{34}N_4O_4$, which, with iron, forms heme.

Pro·to-Sem·i·tic (prō′tō-sə-mĭt′ĭk) *n.* The hypothetical common ancestor of the Asiatic (Eastern) branch of Hamito-Semitic, from which Arabic, Canaanite, Aramaic, Ethiopic, and Ugaritic are descended.

pro·to·star (prō′tō-stär′) *n.* A mass of gas and dust in interstellar space that is thought to contract to form a star.

pro·to·stele (prō′tə-stēl′, prō′tə-stē′lē) *n. Botany.* A type of stele commonly found in roots that lacks pith and has a solid core of xylem. **—pro·to·ste·lic** (prō′tə-stē′lĭk) *adj.*

pro·to·troph·ic (prō′tə-trŏf′ĭk, -trō′fĭk) *adj.* Obtaining nourishment by the assimilation of inorganic materials. Said of plants and bacteria. [PROTO- + -TROPH(Y) + -IC.] **—pro·to·troph** *n.* **—pro·tot·roph·y** *n.*

pro·to·type (prō′tə-tīp′) *n.* **1.** An original type, form, or instance that serves as a model on which later stages are based or judged. **2.** An early and typical example. **3.** *Biology.* A primitive or ancestral form or species. [French, from Greek *prōtotupon,* original form, archetype, from neuter of *prōtotupos,* "in the first form," original : PROTO- + -TYPE.] **—pro·to·typ·al** (prō′tə-tī′pəl), **pro·to·typ·ic** (prō′tə-tĭp′ĭk), **pro·to·typ·i·cal** *adj.*

pro·to·xy·lem (prō′tō-zī′ləm) *n. Botany.* The first type of xylem that is formed from the procambium. Compare **metaxylem.**

pro·to·zo·an (prō′tə-zō′ən) *n., pl.* **-zoans** or **-zoa** (-zō′ə). Also **pro·to·zo·on** (-ŏn′), *pl.* **-zoons** or **-zoa.** Any of the single-celled, usually microscopic organisms of the phylum or subkingdom Protozoa, which includes the most primitive forms of animal life. [New Latin *Protozoa* : PROTO- + -ZOAN.] **—pro·to·zo·an, pro·to·zo·ic** (prō′tə-zō′ĭk) *adj.*

pro·to·zo·ol·o·gy (prō′tō-zō-ŏl′ə-jē) *n.* The biological study of protozoans. **—pro·to·zo·o·log·i·cal** (prō′tō-zō′ə-lŏj′ĭ-kəl) *adj.* **—pro·to·zo·ol·o·gist** *n.*

pro·tract (prō-trăkt′, prə-) *tr.v.* **-tracted, -tracting, -tracts. 1.** To draw out or lengthen in time; prolong, especially unnecessarily. **2.** *Surveying.* To draw to scale by means of a scale and protractor; plot. **3.** *Anatomy.* To extend or protrude. —See Usage note at **prolong.** [Latin *prōtrahere* (past participle *prōtractus*), to drag out, lengthen : *prō-,* out, extending + *trahere,* to drag, pull.] **—pro·tract·ed·ly** *adv.* **—pro·tract·ed·ness** *n.* **—pro·trac·tive** *adj.*

pro·trac·tile (prō-trăk′tĭl) *adj.* Also **pro·tract·i·ble** (-tə-bəl). *Zoology.* Capable of being protracted; extensible. **—pro·trac·til·i·ty** *n.*

pro·trac·tion (prō-trăk′shən) *n.* **1. a.** The act of protracting. **b.** The state of being protracted. **2.** A drawing made to scale. **3.** The irregular lengthening of a normally short syllable.

pro·trac·tor (prō-trăk′tər) *n.* **1.** A semicircular instrument for measuring and constructing angles. **2.** An adjustable pattern used by tailors. **3.** A surgical instrument for removing foreign objects, especially bullets, from the body.

pro·trude (prō-trōōd′) *v.* **-truded, -truding, -trudes.** *—tr.* To push or thrust outward. *—intr.* To jut out; project. [Latin *prōtrūdere* : *prō-,* forth + *trūdere,* to thrust.] **—pro·trud·ent** *adj.*

pro·tru·sile (prō-trōō′sĭl, -sīl′) *adj.* Also **pro·tru·si·ble** (prō-trōō′sə-bəl). Capable of being thrust outward, as the tongue is. [PROTRUS(ION) + -ILE.] **—pro·tru·sil·i·ty** (prō′trōō-sĭl′ə-tē) *n.*

pro·tru·sion (prō-trōō′zhən) *n.* **1. a.** The act of protruding. **b.** The state of being protruded. **2.** Something that protrudes.

pro·tru·sive (prō-trōō′sĭv, -zĭv) *adj.* **1.** Tending to protrude; protruding. **2.** Unduly or disagreeably conspicuous; obtrusive. **—pro·tru·sive·ly** *adv.* **—pro·tru·sive·ness** *n.*

pro·tu·ber·ance (prō-tōō′bər-əns, prō-tyōō′-) *n.* Also **pro·tu·ber·an·cy,** *pl.* **-cies. 1.** That which protrudes; a bulge or knob. **2.** The condition of being protuberant.

pro·tu·ber·ant (prō-tōō′bər-ənt, prō-tyōō′-) *adj.* Swelling outward; bulging. [Late Latin *prōtūberāns* (stem *prōtūberānt-*), present participle of *prōtūberāre,* to PROTUBERATE.] **—pro·tu·ber·ant·ly** *adv.*

pro·tu·ber·ate (prō-tōō′bə-rāt′, prō-tyōō′-) *intr.v.* **-ated, -ating, -ates.** To swell or bulge out. [Late Latin *prōtūberāre* : *prō-,* forth, outward + *tūber,* swelling, bump.] **—pro·tu·ber·a·tion** *n.*

proud (proud) *adj.* **prouder, proudest. 1.** Feeling pleasurable satisfaction over an attribute or act by which one's stature is measured. **2.** Occasioning pride; gratifying: *a proud moment.* **3.** Marked by exacting or constraining self-respect: *too proud to accept charity.* **4.** Having excessive self-esteem; haughty; arrogant. **5.** Of great dignity; honored: *a proud name.* **6.** Majestic; magnificent. **7.** Occasioned by pride, expressing pride: *a proud smile.* **8.** Spirited or excited. Said of animals: *a proud mare.* **9.** *British.* Projecting slightly from a surrounding surface; not flush: *The sockets are proud of the wall.* **—do someone proud.** To be very generous toward; especially, to entertain on a lavish scale. [Middle English *proud,* late Old English *prūt, prūd,* from Old French *prod, prud,* good, gallant, brave, from Late Latin *prōde,* advantageous, from Latin *prōdesse,* to be beneficial : *prōd-,* variant of *prō-,* for + *esse,* to be. **—proud·ly** *adv.* **—proud·ness** *n.*

Synonyms: *arrogant, disdainful, haughty, supercilious.*

proud flesh *n. Pathology.* The swollen flesh around a healing wound. [Middle English, *proud fleisch*; so called because of its swelling up.]

Prou·dhon (prōō-dôN′), **Pierre Joseph** (1809–65). French political theorist and economist, best known for his theory that "all property is theft" in his *Qu'est-ce que la Propriété* (1840).

Proust (prōōst), **Joseph Louis** (1754–1826). French chemist. He discovered that compounds contain fixed proportions of elements by weight and formulated the law of definite proportions.

Proust, Marcel (1871–1922). French novelist. His masterpiece was the 12-volume *A la Recherche du Temps Perdu* (published 1913–27), which is strongly autobiographical in theme and an exploration of memory and perception.

proust·ite (prōō′stīt′) *n.* A red silver ore, Ag_3AsS_3, occurring in hexagonal crystals often in association with other silver-bearing minerals. [After Joseph Louis PROUST.]

prov. 1. province; provincial. **2.** provisional.

Prov. 1. Provençal. **2.** Proverbs (Old Testament). **3.** Provost.

prove (prōōv) *v.* **proved, proved** or **proven** (prōō′vən), **proving, proves.** *—tr.* **1.** To establish the truth or validity of by presentation of argument or evidence. **2.** *Law.* To establish the authenticity of (a will). **3.** To determine the quality of by testing or scientific experiment. **4.** *Mathematics.* **a.** To validate (a hypothesis or proposition) by a proof. **b.** To verify (the result of a calculation). **5.** *Printing.* To make a sample impression of (type). **6.** *Archaic.* To experience: *"And we will all the pleasures prove"* (Christopher Marlowe). **7.** To raise (dough) to the desired degree before baking. *—intr.* To turn out: *"a very agreeable companion may . . . prove a very improper . . . friend"* (Lord Chesterfield). —See Synonyms at **confirm.** [Middle English *proven,* to put to test, prove, from Old French *prover,* from Latin *probāre,* to test, demonstrate as good, from *probus,* good, virtuous.] **—prov·a·bil·i·ty, prov·a·ble·ness** *n.* **—prov·a·ble** *adj.* **—prov·a·bly** *adv.* **—prov·er** *n.*

Usage: *Proved* is the preferred form of the past participle of the verb *prove*: *He has proved his point.* The form *proven* is a Scots variant made familiar through legal use: *The charges were not proven.* However, *proven* is more widely used as an adjective in the position immediately before the noun it modifies: *a proven actor.*

prov·en (prōō′vən) *adj.* Having been put to the test and shown to be valid: *proven ability.* —See Usage note at **prove.** **—prov·en·ly** *adv.*

prov·e·nance (prŏv′ə-nəns, -näns′) *n.* The place of origin; derivation. [French, from *provenant,* present participle of *provenir,* to

PRONUNCIATION KEY

ă, pat; ā, pay; âr, care; ä, father, are; b, bib; ch, church; d, deed; ĕ, pet; ē, be; f, fife; g, gag; h, hat; hw, which; ĭ, pit; ī, pie; îr, pier; j, judge; k, kick; l, lid, needle; m, mum; n, no, sudden; ng, thing; ŏ, pot; ō, toe; ô, paw, for; oi, noise; ou, out; ŏŏ, book; ōō, boot; p, pop; r, roar; s, sauce; sh, ship, dish; t, tight; th, thin, path; *th*, this, bathe; ŭ, cut; ûr, fur; v, valve; w, with; y, yes; z, zebra, size; zh, vision; ə, about, item, edible, gallop, circus, peaceful

IN FOREIGN WORDS:

à, *Fr.* ami; œ, *Fr.* feu, *Ger.* schön; ü, *Fr.* tu, *Ger.* über; KH, *Ger.* ich, *Scot.* loch; N, *Fr.* bon; y′, *Fr.* Compiègne

STRESS MARKS:

Primary stress: ′ in·cite′ (ĭn-sīt′)
Secondary stress: ′ in′sight′ (ĭn′sīt′)

come forth, originate, from Latin *prōvenīre* : *prō-*, forth + *venīre*, to come.]

Pro·ven·çal (prō′vən-säl′, prŏv′ən-; *French* prô-väN-sål′) *n. Abbr.* **Prov., Pr. 1.** A native or inhabitant of Provence, France. **2.** The Romance language of Provence, especially the literary language of the troubadours. —**Pro·ven·çal** *adj.*

Pro·vence (prō-väNs′). Region and former province of southeast France. It extends from the Alps westward to the Rhône valley and from the Mediterranean northward to the former province of Dauphiné and is a distinct cultural region with its own language, Provençal, in which the medieval troubadours composed their love lyrics. Tourism is important, especially along the Riviera, and wine and fruit are the chief products.

prov·en·der (prŏv′ən-dər) *n.* **1.** Dry food, such as hay, used as fodder for livestock. **2.** *Informal.* Food or provisions. [Middle English *provendre*, from Old French *provend(r)e*, from Medieval Latin *prōbenda*, fodder, alteration of Late Latin *praebenda*, support, subsistence, pension, "things to be supplied," from *praebendus*, gerundive of *prae(hi)bēre*, to hold forth, supply : *prae-*, before + *habēre*, to hold.]

pro·ve·ni·ence (prə-vēn′yəns, -vē′nē-əns) *n.* A source or origin of something. [Latin *prōveniēns* (stem *prōvenient-*), present participle of *prōvenīre*, to come forth. See **provenance**.]

pro·ven·tric·u·lus (prō′vĕn-trĭk′yə-ləs) *n., pl.* **-li** (-lī′). *Zoology.* **1.** The glandular part of the stomach anterior to the gizzard in birds. **2.** The thick-walled, muscular stomach of insects and crustaceans. Also called "gizzard." [New Latin : PRO- (in front of) + Latin *ventriculus*, stomach, gizzard, VENTRICLE.] —**pro·ven·tric·u·lar** *adj.*

prov·erb (prŏv′ûrb′) *n.* **1.** A short, pithy saying in frequent and widespread use, expressing a well-known truth or fact. **2.** A person or thing recognized as a typical example; one that is proverbial. —See Synonyms at **saying**.
~*tr.v.* **proverbed, -erbing, -erbs. 1.** To give the character of a proverb to. **2.** To make into a proverb. [Middle English *proverbe*, from Old French, from Latin *prōverbium*, "set of words put forth" : *prō-*, forth + *verbum*, word.]

pro·ver·bi·al (prə-vûr′bē-əl) *adj.* **1.** Of the nature of a proverb. **2.** Expressed in a proverb or proverbs. **3.** Widely referred to, as if the subject of a proverb; well known. —**pro·ver·bi·al·ly** *adv.*

Prov·erbs (prŏv′ûrbz′) *n. Used with a singular verb. Abbr.* **Prov.** A book of the Old Testament.

pro·vide (prə-vīd′) *v.* **-vided, -viding, -vides.** —*tr.* **1.** To furnish; supply: *You can provide the drinks.* **2.** To give; afford: *The delay provided an opportunity to reflect.* **3.** To set down as a stipulation: *The contract provides that in case of injury you will be excused.* **4.** *Ecclesiastical.* Formerly, to appoint to an ecclesiastical benefice, especially when the benefice has not yet become vacant. **5.** To make ready; prepare. —*intr.* **1.** To take measures in preparation. Used with *for* or *against.* **2.** To supply means of subsistence. Used with *for.* **3.** To make a stipulation or condition: *The will doesn't provide for such a contingency.* [Middle English *providen*, to foresee, make provision, from Latin *prōvidēre* : *prō-*, beforehand, in anticipation of + *vidēre*, to see.] —**pro·vid·er** *n.*

pro·vid·ed (prə-vī′dĭd) *conj.* On the condition; if and only if. Often followed by *that*: *She will go, provided that I stay behind.*
Usage: When a requirement is explicitly set forth, the standard construction is *provided that* (or simply *provided*): *You may leave, provided (that) you have finished the job.* The use of *providing* is common in informal speech, but attracts criticism in written English.

prov·i·dence (prŏv′ə-dəns, -dĕns′) *n.* **1.** Care or preparation in advance; foresight. **2.** Prudent management; economy. **3.** The care, guardianship, and control exercised by a deity. **4. Providence.** God, especially when viewed as a guardian and protector.

Prov·i·dence (prŏv′ə-dəns, -dĕns′). Seaport and capital of Rhode Island, in the northeastern part of the state where the Providence River joins Narragansett Bay. Its industries include jewelry making, printing, and textile manufacturing.

prov·i·dent (prŏv′ə-dənt, -dĕnt′) *adj.* **1.** Providing for future needs or events; showing foresight. **2.** Frugal; economical. [Middle English, from Latin *prōvidēns* (stem *prōvident-*), present participle of *prōvidēre*, to foresee, PROVIDE.] —**prov·i·dent·ly** *adv.*

prov·i·den·tial (prŏv′ə-dĕn′shəl) *adj.* **1.** Of or resulting from divine providence. **2.** Happening as if through divine intervention; fortunate; opportune. —**prov·i·den·tial·ly** *adv.*

pro·vid·ing (prə-vī′dĭng) *conj.* On the condition; provided. Sometimes followed by *that.* —See Usage note at **provided**.

prov·ince (prŏv′ĭns) *n. Abbr.* **prov. 1.** A territory governed as an administrative or political unit of a country or empire, such as Saskatchewan in Canada. **2.** Any of various lands outside Italy conquered by the Romans and administered by them as self-contained units. **3.** An ecclesiastical division of territory under the jurisdiction of an archbishop. **4. Provinces.** Areas of a country situated away from the capital or national cultural center. Preceded by *the.* **5.** A comprehensive area of knowledge, activity, or interest. **6.** The range of one's proper duties and functions; scope; jurisdiction. **7.** *Ecology.* A subdivision of a **region** *(see).* [Middle English *provynce*, from Old French *province*, from Latin *prōvincia*†.]

pro·vin·cial (prə-vĭn′shəl) *adj.* **1.** *Abbr.* **prov.** Of or pertaining to a province. **2.** Of or supposedly characteristic of people from the provinces; not fashionable or sophisticated. **3.** Limited in perspective; narrow and self-centered.
~*n.* **1.** A native or inhabitant of the provinces. **2.** A person who has supposedly provincial ideas or habits. —**pro·vin·cial·ism, pro·vin·ci·al·i·ty** *n.* —**pro·vin·cial·ly** *adv.*

proving ground *n.* A place for testing new devices or theories.

pro·vi·rus (prō-vī′rəs) *n.* A virus that does not cause lysis, has become part of the host cell, and is transmitted from one cell generation to the next in the chromosome.

pro·vi·sion (prə-vĭzh′ən) *n.* **1.** The act of supplying or fitting out. **2.** That which is provided. **3.** A preparatory measure: *make provision for our distinguished guest.* **4. provisions.** A stock of necessary supplies, especially food. **5.** A stipulation or qualification; especially, a clause in a document or agreement. **6.** The appointment of a clergyman to an ecclesiastical benefice before it is vacant.
~*tr.v.* **provisioned, -sioning, -sions.** To supply with provisions. [Middle English, foresight, precaution, from Old French, from Latin *prōvīsiō* (stem *prōvīsiōn-*), from *prōvīsus*, past participle of *prōvidēre*, to PROVIDE.] —**pro·vi·sion·er** *n.*

pro·vi·sion·al (prə-vĭzh′ən-əl) *adj.* Also **pro·vi·sion·ar·y** (-ə-nĕr′ē) (for sense 1). **1.** *Abbr.* **prov.** Provided for the time being, pending permanent arrangements: *a provisional plan.* —See Synonyms at **transient**. **2. Provisional.** Of, pertaining to, or designating the wing of both the Irish Republican Army and Sinn Fein formed by the split in those organizations, that emphasizes the use of terrorist methods to achieve the unification of Ireland.
~*n.* **1.** A stamp that is issued temporarily by a post office until the normal issue is available. **2. Provisional.** A member of the Provisional Irish Republican Army or Sinn Fein. —**pro·vi·sion·al·ly** *adv.*

pro·vi·so (prə-vī′zō) *n., pl.* **-sos** or **-soes. 1.** A clause in a document making a qualification, condition, or restriction. **2.** Any condition or stipulation. [Middle English, from Medieval Latin *prōvīsō (quod)*, provided (that), from *prōvīsus*, past participle of *prōvidēre*, to PROVIDE.]

pro·vi·so·ry (prə-vī′zə-rē) *adj.* Depending on a proviso; conditional. —**pro·vi·so·ri·ly** *adv.*

pro·vi·ta·min (prō-vī′tə-mĭn) *n.* A substance, such as carotene (provitamin A), that is converted into a vitamin in animal bodies.

Pro·vo (prō′vō) *n., pl.* **-vos.** A member of the Provisional IRA or Sinn Fein. —**Pro·vo** *adj.*

pro·vo·ca·teur (prō-vŏk′ə-tûr′) *n.* An **agent provocateur** *(see).*

prov·o·ca·tion (prŏv′ə-kā′shən) *n.* **1.** The act of provoking or inciting. **2.** Something that provokes; a cause of irritation. **3.** *Law.* Action by one person that causes another person to lose self-control and kill the doer, not amounting to a defense but reducing the gravity of the crime from murder to manslaughter.

pro·voc·a·tive (prə-vŏk′ə-tĭv) *adj.* Tending to arouse or excite a response, especially anger, curiosity, or sexual interest. —**pro·voc·a·tive·ly** *adv.* —**pro·voc·a·tive·ness** *n.*

pro·voke (prə-vōk′) *tr.v.* **-voked, -voking, -vokes. 1.** To incite to anger or resentment. **2.** To stir or incite to action; arouse. **3.** To bring on by inciting. —See Synonyms at **annoy**. [Middle English *provoken*, from Old French *provoquer*, from Latin *prōvocāre*, to call forth, challenge : *prō-*, forth + *vocāre*, to call.] —**pro·vok·ing·ly** *adv.*
Synonyms: *arouse, excite, incite, rouse, stimulate, stir.*

pro·vo·lo·ne (prō′və-lō′nē) *n.* A hard Italian curd cheese.

pro·vost (prō′vōst′, prŏv′əst, prō′vəst) *n. Abbr.* **Prov. 1.** The chief officer of a Scottish burgh. **2. a.** *Anglican Church.* The highest official in certain cathedrals, especially one of the modern foundation. **b.** *Roman Catholic Church.* The head of a cathedral chapter. **3.** The chief officer of some colleges. [Middle English *provost*, from Old English *profost* and Old French *provost*, both from Medieval Latin *prōpositus, praepositus*, from Latin *praepositus*, "(one) placed before (others)," president, superintendent, from the past participle of *praepōnere*, to place before or over : *prae-*, before + *pōnere*, to place.] —**pro·vost·ship** *n.*

pro·vost court (prō′vō) *n.* A military court for the trial of minor offenses committed in occupied hostile territories.

pro·vost guard (prō′vō) *n.* A detail of soldiers on police duty under a provost marshal.

pro·vost marshal (prō′vō) *n. Abbr.* **P.M. 1.** *U.S. Army.* The head of military police. **2.** *U.S. Navy.* An officer responsible for the disposition of prisoners facing court-martial.

prow (prou) *n.* **1.** The forward part of a ship's hull; the bow. **2.** A similar projecting part of anything, such as the forward end of a ski. [French *pro(u)e*, probably from Italian dialect *prua*, from Latin *prōra*, from Greek *prōira*.]

prow·ess (prou′ĭs) *n.* **1.** Outstanding skill or ability. **2.** Outstanding strength, courage, or daring, especially in battle. [Middle English *prowesse*, from Old French *proesse*, from *prou*, variant of *prod, prud*, gallant, brave, PROUD.]

prowl (proul) *v.* **prowled, prowling, prowls.** —*tr.* To roam through stealthily, as if in search of prey or plunder. —*intr.* To move around furtively or with predatory intent.
~*n.* An act of prowling: *on the prowl.* [Middle English *prollen*†.]

prowl car *n.* A **squad car** *(see).*

prowl·er (prou′lər) *n.* One who prowls; especially, a man who prowls at night, intent on theft, voyeurism, or sexual molestation.

prox. proximo.

prox·i·mal (prŏk′sə-məl) *adj.* **1.** Nearest; proximate. **2.** *Biology.* Near the central part of the body or a point of attachment or origin: *the proximal end of a bone.* Compare **distal**. [Latin *proximus*, nearest, next, PROXIMATE.] —**prox·i·mal·ly** *adv.*

prox·i·mate (prŏk′sə-mĭt) *adj.* **1.** Closely related in space, time, or order; nearest; next. **2.** Approximate. [Latin *proximātus*, past participle of *proximāre*, to come near, from *proximus*, nearest.] —**prox·i·mate·ly** *adv.*

prox·im·i·ty (prŏk-sĭm'ə-tē) *n.* The state, quality, or fact of being near or next in space or time; closeness. [Old French *proximite*, from Latin *proximitās*, from *proximus*, nearest. See **proximate**.]

proximity fuze *n.* An electronic device for detonating a projectile as it approaches a target, as in antiaircraft shells. Also "VT fuze."

prox·i·mo (prŏk'sə-mō') *adv. Abbr.* **prox.** *Archaic.* Of or in the following month: *on the 15th proximo.* Compare **ultimo, instant.** [Latin *proximō* (mense), in the next (month), ablative of *proximus*, nearest, next. See **proximate.**]

prox·y (prŏk'sē) *n., pl.* **-ies. 1.** A person authorized to act for another; an agent or substitute. **2.** The authority to act for another. **3.** The written authorization for such action. [Middle English *procusie, proxcy*, contractions of *procuracie*, from Norman French, from Medieval Latin *prōcūrātia*, from Latin *prōcūrātiō*, a caring for, from *prōcūrātus*, past participle of *prōcūrāre*, to take care of, PROCURE.]

prude (prōōd) *n.* A person who is overconcerned with being or seeming to be proper or modest, especially with regard to sex. [French, short for Old French *pr(e)udefemme*, virtuous woman, "fine thing of a woman" : *preu*, virtuous, variant of *prod, prud* (see **proud**) + *de*, of + *femme*, woman.] —**prud·er·y** *n.*

pru·dence (prōōd'əns) *n.* **1.** The state, quality, or fact of being prudent or sensible. **2.** Careful management; economy.

pru·dent (prōōd'ənt) *adj.* **1.** Wise in handling practical matters; exercising good judgment or common sense. **2.** Careful with regard to one's own interests; provident. **3.** Careful about one's conduct; circumspect; discreet. [Middle English, from Old French, from Latin *prūdēns* (stem *prūdent-*), foreseeing, wise, contraction of *prōvidēns*, PROVIDENT.] —**pru·dent·ly** *adv.*

pru·den·tial (prōō-dĕn'shəl) *adj.* **1.** Arising from or characterized by prudence. **2.** Exercising prudence, good judgment, or common sense. —**pru·den·tial·ly** *adv.*

Prud·hoe Bay (prōōd'hō, prŭd'-). Inlet of the Arctic Ocean, northern Alaska. Oil was discovered here (1968), and it is connected to Valdez on the south coast by the trans-Alaska pipeline.

prud·ish (prōō'dĭsh) *adj.* Having an excessive regard for propriety, modesty, or morality, especially that of others; prim. —**prud·ish·ly** *adv.* —**prud·ish·ness** *n.*

pru·i·nose (prōō'ə-nōs') *adj. Botany.* Having a white, powdery covering or bloom. [Latin *pruīnōsus*, covered with frost, from *pruīna*, hoarfrost.]

prune¹ (prōōn) *n.* **1.** The partially dried fruit of any of several varieties of the common plum, *Prunus domestica.* **2.** *Slang.* A crabbed or sour-natured person; spoilsport. **3.** *Chiefly British Informal.* A foolish or ineffectual person. [Middle English *prun(n)e*, from Old French *prune*, from Vulgar Latin *prūna* (unattested), from Latin, plural of *prūnum*, plum; akin to Greek *proumnon*, from an unknown source in Asia Minor.]

prune² *v.* **pruned, pruning, prunes.** —*tr.* **1.** To cut off or remove dead or living parts or branches of (a plant, shrub, or tree) to improve shape or growth. **2.** To remove or cut out as superfluous. **3.** To remove superfluous material from; cut down: *prune the budget.* —*intr.* To remove branches or parts from a plant. [Middle English *prouynen*, from Old French *pro(o)ignier*, from Vulgar Latin *prōrotundiāre* (unattested), to cut roundedly in front : Latin *prō-*, in front + *rotundus*, round, circular.] —**prun·er** *n.*

pru·nel·la (prōō-nĕl'ə) *n.* Also **pru·nel·lo** (-nĕl'ō). A strong, heavy fabric of worsted twill, used chiefly for shoe uppers, clerical robes, and academic gowns. [French *prunelle*, "sloe," here perhaps "sloe-colored stuff." See **prunelle.**]

pru·nelle (prōō-nĕl') *n.* A green, sloe-flavored French liqueur. [French, "sloe," diminutive of *prune*, plum.]

pruning hook *n.* A long pole with a curved saw blade and usually a clipping mechanism on one end, used especially for pruning small trees.

pru·ri·ent (prōōr'ē-ənt) *adj.* **1.** Obsessively interested in improper matters, especially those of a sexual nature. **2.** Characterized by or arousing such interest: *prurient thoughts.* [Latin *prūriēns* (stem *prūrient-*), present participle of *prūrīre*, to itch, be lascivious.] —**pru·ri·ence, pru·ri·en·cy** *n.* —**pru·ri·ent·ly** *adv.*

pru·ri·go (prōō-rī'gō) *n.* A chronic, inflammatory skin disease characterized by eruption and severe itching. [Latin, "an itching," from *prūrīre*, to itch.] —**pru·rig·i·nous** (prōō-rĭj'ə-nəs) *adj.*

pru·ri·tus (prōō-rī'təs) *n. Pathology.* **1.** Severe itching, usually of undamaged skin. **2.** Any condition characterized by this. [Latin, from *prūrīre*, to itch.] —**pru·rit·ic** (prōō-rĭt'ĭk) *adj.*

Prus·sia (prŭsh'ə). Former German state, now in West Germany, East Germany, the Soviet Union, and Poland. Bordering the Baltic Sea, it was established in the 13th century by the victory of the Teutonic Knights over the Prussians. It became a hereditary duchy in 1525 and united with the Mark of Brandenburg in 1618. It became the kingdom of Prussia in 1701 and under Frederick the Great took Silesia and parts of Poland. Prussia gained further territories at the Congress of Vienna (1815) and expanded under Bismarck to form the North German Confederation (1867) and the German Empire (1871). After World War I it became a republic much reduced in size (1918) and was dissolved completely after World War II (1946–47) by the Allies. Berlin was the capital.

Prus·sian (prŭsh'ən) *adj.* **1.** *Abbr.* **Prus., Pruss.** Of or pertaining to Prussia, its people, or their language and culture. **2.** Similar to or

suggestive of the Junkers and the military class of Prussia, especially in being sternly disciplined.
~*n.* **1.** Any of the western Balts inhabiting the region between the Vistula and the Neman in ancient times. **2.** A Baltic inhabitant of Prussia. **3.** A German inhabitant of Prussia. **4.** A language, **Old Prussian** (see).

Prussian blue *n.* **1.** An insoluble dark blue pigment and dye, ferric ferrocyanide or one of its modifications. **2. Iron blue** (see). **3.** Moderate to deep greenish blue. [Discovered in Berlin (1704) by H. de Diesbach, a maker of artist's colors.] —**Prus·sian-blue** *adj.*

Prus·sian·ize (prŭsh'ə-nīz') *tr.v.* **-ized, -izing, -izes.** To make Prussian in character or organization, as by imposing rigid discipline. —**Prus·sian·i·za·tion** *n.*

prus·si·ate (prŭs'ē-āt') *n. Chemistry.* **1.** A ferrocyanide or ferricyanide. **2.** A salt of hydrocyanic acid; a cyanide. [French : from *(acide) prussique*, PRUSSIC (ACID) + -ATE.]

prus·sic acid (prŭs'ĭk) *n. Chemistry.* **Hydrocyanic acid** (see). [French *acide prussique*, because obtained from PRUSSIAN BLUE.]

pry¹ (prī) *intr.v.* **pried, prying, pries.** To look or enquire closely, curiously, or inquisitively, especially in a furtive manner. Often used with *into.*
~*n., pl.* **pries. 1.** An act of prying. **2.** An excessively inquisitive person. [Middle English *prien*, perhaps related to PEER.] —**pry·ing·ly** *adv.*

pry² *tr.v.* **pried, prying, pries. 1.** To raise, move, or force open with a lever. **2.** To obtain with effort or difficulty: *pry a confession out of a suspect.*
~*n., pl.* **pries. 1.** Something used to apply leverage, such as a crowbar. **2.** Leverage. [From PRIZE, mistaken for third person singular, as if *pries.*]

pryer. Variant of **prier.**

Prynne (prĭn), **William** (1600–69). English political agitator. A Puritan, he was imprisoned (1633) and had his ears cut off for his pamphlet *Historiomastix*, an attack on the theater, which insulted the Queen. He was later branded on both cheeks for pamphleteering and again imprisoned (1650) for writings attacking the Commonwealth.

Prze·wal·ski's horse (prĕ'zhə-välz'kĕz) *n.* A Mongolian wild horse with an erect mane, *Equus przewalskii* (or *E. caballus przewalskii*), now an endangered species. [After N.M. *Przewalski* (1839–88), Russian explorer who discovered it.]

Ps. Psalm; Psalms (Old Testament).

p.s. 1. passenger steamer. **2.** postscript.

P.S. 1. permanent secretary. **2.** Police Sergeant. **3.** postscript. **4.** private secretary. **5.** prompt side. **6.** public school.

Psa. Psalm; Psalms (Old Testament).

psalm (säm) *n.* **1.** A sacred song; a hymn. **2.** *Usually* **Psalm.** *Abbr.* **Ps., Psa.** Any of the sacred songs or hymns collected in the Old Testament Book of Psalms.
~*tr.v.* **psalmed, psalming, psalms.** To sing of or celebrate in psalms. [Middle English *(p)salm*, Old English *(p)sealm*, from Late Latin *psalmus*, from Greek *psalmos*, song sung to the harp, psalm (translation of Hebrew *mizmōr*, song, psalm), from *psallein*, to pluck, play the harp.]

psalm·ist (sä'mĭst) *n.* A writer or composer of psalms. —**the Psalmist.** King David, to whom many of the scriptural psalms are traditionally attributed.

psalm·o·dy (sä'mə-dē, säl'mə-) *n., pl.* **-dies. 1.** The singing of psalms in divine worship. **2.** The composition or arranging of psalms for singing. **3.** A collection of psalms. [Middle English *psalmodie*, from Late Latin *psalmōdia*, from Late Greek, from Greek, "singing to the harp" : *psalmos*, PSALM + *ōidē*, song, ode.] —**psalm·o·dist** *n.*

Psalms (sämz). *Abbr.* **Ps., Psa.** A book of the Old Testament, the Book of Psalms, containing 150 songs.

Psal·ter (sôl'tər) *n. Often* **psalter. 1.** A book containing the Book of Psalms or a particular version of it in liturgical use. **2.** A musical setting for the Psalms. **3.** The Psalms. [Middle English *(p)salter, sauter*, from Old English *(p)saltere* and Old French *(p)sautier*, both from Late Latin *psaltērium*, early Christian transference of Greek *psaltērion*, psalm, song, PSALTERY.]

psal·te·ri·um (sôl-tûr'ē-əm) *n., pl.* **-teria** (-tîr'ē-ə). The third division of the stomach of ruminants, the **omasum** (see). [New Latin, from Late Latin, PSALTER (when slit open its folds fall apart like the leaves of a book).] —**psal·te·ri·al** *adj.*

psal·ter·y (sôl'tə-rē) *n., pl.* **-ies.** An ancient, stringed musical instrument played by plucking the strings with the fingers or a plectrum. [Middle English *(p)salterie, sautre*, from Old French *(p)salterie, sauter(i)e*, from Latin *psaltērium*, from Greek *psaltērion*, from *psallein*, to pluck, play on a stringed instrument.]

psam·mite (säm'īt') *n.* Metamorphosed arenaceous rock. [French : Greek *psammos*, sand + -ITE.] —**psam·mit·ic** (säm-ĭt'ĭk) *adj.*

p's and q's (pēz' ən kyōōz') *pl.n.* **1.** Socially correct behavior; manners. **2.** The way one acts; conduct: *was told to mind his p's and q's or he would be fired.*

pse·phite (sē'fīt') *n.* A rock consisting of relatively large fragments embedded in a finer matrix. [French, from Greek *psēphos*, pebble.] —**pse·phit·ic** (sē-fĭt'ĭk) *adj.*

pse·phol·o·gy (sē-fŏl'ə-jē) *n.* The study of electoral systems and voting trends and behavior. [Greek *psēphos*, pebble, vote (from the use of pebbles to cast votes in ancient Greece) + -LOGY.] —**pseph·o·log·i·cal** (sē'fə-lŏj'ĭ-kəl) *adj.* —**pse·phol·o·gist** *n.*

pseud (sōōd) *n. British Informal.* A pretentious, superficial, or affected person. [Shortened from PSEUDO.] —**pseud** *adj.*

pseud. pseudonym.

pseud–. Variant of **pseudo–.**

pseud·ax·is (sōō-dăk′sŭs) *n. Botany.* A **sympodium** *(see).* [PSEUD(O)- + AXIS.] —**pseud·ax·i·al** *adj.*

pseud·e·pig·ra·pha (sōō′dĭ-pĭg′rə-fə) *pl.n. Sometimes* **Pseud·epigrapha. 1.** Spurious writings; specifically, writings falsely attributed to Biblical characters or times. **2.** A body of Jewish religious texts written between 200 B.C. and A.D. 200 and spuriously ascribed to various prophets and kings of Hebrew Scriptures. [Greek, neuter plural of *pseudepigraphos*, falsely ascribed : PSEUDO- + *epigraphein*, to ascribe : *epi*, on, upon + *graphein*, to write.] —**pseud·e·pig·ra·phal, pseud·ep·i·graph·ic** (sōō′dĕp-ə-grăf′ĭk), **pseud·ep·i·graph·i·cal, pseud·e·pig·ra·phous** (sōō′dĭ-pĭg′rə-fəs) *adj.*

pseu·do (sōō′dō) *adj.* False or counterfeit; fake. [Middle English, from PSEUDO-.]

pseudo–, pseud– *prefix.* Indicates: **1.** Inauthenticity; sham; for example, **pseudoscience. 2.** Deceptive similarity; for example, **pseudopodium.** *Note:* Many compounds other than those entered here may be formed with *pseudo-.* In forming compounds, *pseudo-* is normally joined with the following element without a space or hyphen: *pseudoscience.* However, if the second element begins with a capital letter, it is separated with a hyphen: *pseudo-Americanism.* It is also preferable to use the hyphen if the second element begins with *o* or if forming the compound brings together three or more vowels that would be confusing to read. [Middle English, from Late Latin, from Greek *pseudēs*, false, from *pseudein†*, to lie.]

pseu·do·carp (sōō′də-kärp′) *n. Botany.* A fruit, such as the pear, apple, or strawberry, that contains fleshy tissue developed from floral parts as well as the ovary. Also called "accessory fruit," "false fruit." [PSEUDO- + -CARP.] —**pseu·do·car·pous** *adj.*

pseu·do·cy·e·sis (sōō′dō-sī-ē′sĭs) *n.* **Phantom pregnancy** *(see).*

pseu·do·her·maph·ro·dit·ism (sōō′dō-hər-măf′rə-dī′tĭz′əm) *n.* An abnormal condition, present at birth, in which the external genital organs resemble those of the opposite sex.

pseu·do·morph (sōō′də-môrf′) *n.* **1.** A false, deceptive, or irregular form. **2.** *Mineralogy.* A mineral having the crystalline form of another mineral rather than the form that is normally characteristic of its composition. [PSEUDO- + -MORPH.] —**pseu·do·mor·phic, pseu·do·mor·phous** *adj.* —**pseu·do·mor·phism** *n.*

pseu·do·nym (sōō′də-nĭm′) *n. Abbr.* **pseud.** A fictitious name, especially one assumed by an author. [French *pseudonyme*, from Greek *pseudōnumon*, neuter of *pseudōnumos* : PSEUD(O)- + -ONYM.] —**pseu·don·y·mous** (sōō-dŏn′ə-məs) *adj.*

pseu·do·po·di·um (sōō′də-pō′dē-əm) *n., pl.* **-dia** (-dē-ə). Also **pseu·do·pod** (sōō′də-pŏd′). A temporary protrusion of the cytoplasm of a cell, serving, in organisms such as the amoeba, as a means of locomotion and of surrounding and ingesting food. [PSEUDO- + -PODIUM.]

pseu·do·sci·ence (sōō′dō-sī′əns) *n.* An unscientific or trivially scientific theory, methodology, or activity that appears to be or is presented as scientific. —**pseu·do·sci·en·tif·ic** (sōō′dō-sī′ən-tĭf′ĭk) *adj.* —**pseu·do·sci·en·tist** *n.*

pseud·y (sōō′dē) *adj.* **-ier, -iest.** *British Informal.* Pretentious or insincere. [From PSEUD.] —**pseud·i·ly** *adv.* —**pseud·i·ness** *n.*

psf, p.s.f. pounds per square foot.

pshaw (shô) *interj.* Used to indicate impatience, irritation, disapproval, or disbelief.

psi (psī, sī) *n.* The 23rd letter in the Greek alphabet, written Ψ, ψ. Transliterated in English as *ps.* See feature at **alphabet.** [Late Greek, from Greek *psei*, originally (in the alphabet used at Athens) written ΦΣ.]

psi, p.s.i. pounds per square inch.

psi·lo·cy·bin (sī′lō-sī′bən) *n.* A phosphate, C₁₂H₁₇N₂O₄P, that is the hallucinogen in the fungus *Psilocybe mexicana.* [New Latin *Psilocybe*, from Greek *psīlos*, bald + *kubē*, head (referring to its appearance) + -IN.]

psi·lom·e·lane (sī-lŏm′ə-lān′) *n.* A black, hydrated oxide ore of manganese. [Greek *psilos*, mere, bare + *melas* (stem *melan-*), black.]

psi·lo·phyte (sī′lə-fīt′) *n.* Any of a group of simple vascular plants, the Psilophyta, that appeared early in the Paleozoic era and were the first of the land plants.

psi particle *n.* An elementary particle in the meson family, believed to consist of a charmed quark and the antiparticle of a quark, the discovery of which led to the concept of charm in physics. Also called "J particle," "J psi particle." [Greek *psi* (arbitrary designation).]

psit·ta·cine (sĭt′ə-sīn′) *adj.* Of, pertaining to, or characteristic of parrots. [Latin *psittacīnus*, from *psittacus*, parrot, from Greek *psittakos†*.]

psit·ta·co·sis (sĭt′ə-kō′sĭs) *n.* A virus disease of parrots and related birds, communicable to human beings, in whom it produces high fever, nosebleeds, and complications similar to pneumonia. Also called "parrot fever." [New Latin *psittacus*, parrot (see **psit·tacine**) + -OSIS.] —**psit·ta·cot·ic** (sĭt′ə-kŏt′ĭk, -kō′tĭk) *adj.*

pso·as (sō′əs) *n. Anatomy.* Either of two hip muscles, *psoas major* that flexes the hip joint, and *psoas minor*, a slender muscle that is often absent. [Greek, accusative plural of *psoa*, interpreted as singular.]

pso·ri·a·sis (sə-rī′ə-sĭs) *n.* A chronic, noncontagious skin disease characterized by inflammation and red, scaly patches. [New Latin, from Greek *psōriasis*, from *psōrian*, to have the itch, from *psōra*, itch, from *psēn*, to rub, scratch.] —**pso·ri·at·ic** (sôr′ē-ăt′ĭk, sōr′-) *adj.*

pst, psst *interj.* Used as a whisper to attract somebody's attention, especially without others noticing.

PST, P.S.T. Pacific Standard Time.

psych (sīk) *tr.v.* **psyched, psyching, psychs.** *Informal.* **1.** To put (a person, especially oneself) into the right psychological frame of mind, as for a performance or competition. Usually used with *up.* **2.** To undermine the confidence of by using psychological tactics. Often used with *out: She psyched out her opponent by insults.*

psych–. Variant of **psycho–.**

psych. psychological; psychologist; psychology.

psy·che (sī′kē) *n.* **1.** The soul or spirit, as distinguished from the body. **2.** *Psychiatry.* The mind functioning as the center of thought, feeling, and behavior, and consciously or unconsciously adjusting and relating the body to its social and physical environment. [Latin, from Greek *psukhē*, breath, life, soul.]

Psy·che (sī′kē). *Classical Mythology.* A maiden loved by Eros and united with him after Aphrodite's jealousy was overcome. She became the personification of the soul.

psy·che·del·i·a (sī′kĭ-dē′lē-ə, -dēl′yə) *pl.n.* **1.** The world of psychedelic drugs, those who take them, and the effects produced by them. **2.** The music, art, books, or other artifacts that deal with or are supposed to suggest or evoke psychedelic experiences. [PSYCHE-DELIC + -IA.]

psy·che·del·ic (sī′kə-dĕl′ĭk) *adj.* **1.** Of, pertaining to, or generating hallucinations, distortions of perception, and occasionally states resembling psychosis: *psychedelic drugs.* **2.** Producing an effect similar to the effects of psychedelic drugs: *psychedelic art.* ~*n.* A psychedelic drug. [From PSYCHE (mind) + Greek *dēlos*, clear, visible.]

psy·chi·a·trist (sĭ-kī′ə-trĭst, sī-) *n.* A doctor specially trained to practice psychiatry.

psy·chi·a·try (sĭ-kī′ə-trē, sī-) *n.* The medical study, diagnosis, treatment, and prevention of mental or emotional disorders. [PSYCH(O)- + -IATRY.] —**psy·chi·at·ric** (sī′kē-ăt′rĭk), **psy·chi·at·ri·cal** *adj.* —**psy·chi·at·ri·cal·ly** *adv.*

psy·chic (sī′kĭk) *adj.* Also **psy·chi·cal** (-kĭ-kəl). **1.** Of or pertaining to the human mind or psyche. **2. a.** Of or pertaining to extraordinary, especially extrasensory and nonphysical, mental processes or forces, such as extrasensory perception and telepathy. **b.** Proceeding from or produced by such processes or forces. **c.** Designating a person who is especially responsive to such processes or forces. ~*n.* **1.** A psychic person. **2.** A medium. [Greek *psukhikos*, from *psukhē*, soul, life, PSYCHE.] —**psy·chi·cal·ly** *adv.*

psy·chics (sī′kĭks) *n.* Used with a singular verb. The analysis, examination, and study of psychic phenomena.

psy·cho (sī′kō) *n., pl.* **-chos.** *Slang.* A psychopath. —**psy·cho** *adj.*

psycho–, psych– *prefix.* Indicates the mind or mental processes; as, **psychology.** [Greek *psukhē*, breath, life, PSYCHE.]

psy·cho·a·cous·tics (sī′kō-ə-kōō′stĭks) *n.* Used with a singular verb. The study of sound in relation to its reception, both physiological and psychological.

psy·cho·ac·tive (sī′kō-ăk′tĭv) *adj.* Having an effect on the mind.

psy·cho·a·nal·y·sis (sī′kō-ə-năl′ə-sĭs) *n.* **1.** A method of psychotherapy originated by Sigmund Freud, based on the exploration of unconscious mental processes as manifested in dreams and disturbed relationships with others. Its aim is to reveal repressed anxieties and overcome the effects of bad experiences in early childhood, typically using the technique of free association. **2.** A technique of research into human behavior and mental processes using the methods and theories of psychoanalysis. **3.** A theory of human psychology, based on the findings of psychoanalysis, concerning the structure of the mind and the effect of unconscious mental processes on behavior. —**psy·cho·an·a·lyst** (sī′kō-ăn′ə-lĭst) *n.* —**psy·cho·an·a·lyt·ic** (sī′kō-ăn′ə-lĭt′ĭk), **psy·cho·an·a·lyt·i·cal** *adj.* —**psy·cho·an·a·lyt·i·cal·ly** *adv.*

psy·cho·an·a·lyze (sī′kō-ăn′ə-līz′) *tr.v.* **-lyzed, -lyzing, -lyzes.** To analyze and treat by psychoanalysis. [Back-formation from PSYCHOANALYSIS.]

psy·cho·bab·ble (sī′kō-băb′əl) *n.* Psychoanalytic jargon. [Coined in 1975 by R.D. Rosen, author of *Psychobabble*.]

psy·cho·bi·ol·o·gy (sī′kō-bī-ŏl′ə-jē) *n.* The study of the interactions between mental and biological processes as they affect personality.

psy·cho·chem·i·cal (sī′kō-kĕm′ĭ-kəl) *adj.* Causing psychological changes or mental disorders. ~*n.* A psychochemical substance, such as a drug or gas.

psy·cho·dra·ma (sī′kō-drä′mə, -drăm′ə) *n.* **1.** A psychotherapeutic and analytic technique in which individuals spontaneously play out roles based on their personal histories. **2.** A psychological drama. —**psy·cho·dra·mat·ic** (sī′kō-drə-măt′ĭk) *adj.*

psy·cho·dy·nam·ics (sī′kō-dī-năm′ĭks) *n.* Used with a singular verb. **1.** The interaction of various mental or emotional processes, especially when they are considered as constituents of a system of interrelated forces. **2.** Behavioral analysis in terms of motives or drives. —**psy·cho·dy·nam·ic** *adj.*

psy·cho·gen·e·sis (sī′kō-jĕn′ə-sĭs) *n.* **1. a.** The origin and development of psychological processes, personality, or behavior. **b.** The origin of the soul. **2.** The psychological or mental, as opposed to the physiological or physical, origin of something. —**psy·cho·ge·net·ic** (sī′kō-jə-nĕt′ĭk) *adj.* —**psy·cho·ge·net·i·cal·ly** *adv.*

pseudomorph *A pseudomorph is a mineral appearing in the crystal form of another. This is pseudomorphous malachite found in the Ural Mountains of the U.S.S.R.*

psy·cho·gen·ic (sī′kō-jĕn′ĭk) *adj.* Having a psychological rather than physiological origin. Said of certain disorders. [PSYCHO- + -GENIC.] —**phy·cho·gen·ic·al·ly** *adv.*

psy·cho·ger·i·at·rics (sī′kō-jĕr′ē-ăt′rĭks) *n.* The psychiatry of the mental disorders of old people. —**psy·cho·ger·i·at·ric** *adj.*

psy·chog·no·sis (sī′kŏg-nō′sĭs) *n. Rare.* The study of the psyche. [PSYCHO- + -GNOSIS.] —**psy·chog·nos·tic** (sī′kŏg-nŏs′tĭk) *adj.*

psy·cho·his·to·ry (sī′kō-hĭs′tə-rē) *n.* The study of individual and collective psychology as it influences and is affected by the historical process: *the psychohistory of the Nazi holocaust.* —**psy·cho·his·tor·i·cal** *adj.* —**psy·cho·his·tor·i·cal·ly** *adv.*

psy·cho·ki·ne·sis (sī′kō-kĭ-nē′sĭs, -kī-nē′sĭs) *n.* **1.** *Abbr.* **PK** In parapsychology, the production of motion, especially in inanimate and remote objects, by the exercise of psychic powers. **2.** *Psychiatry.* Uninhibited, maniacal motor response. [PSYCHO- + -KINESIS.] —**psy·cho·ki·net·ic** *adj.*

psychol. psychological; psychologist; psychology.

psy·cho·lin·guis·tics (sī′kō-lĭng-gwĭs′tĭks) *n. Used with a singular verb.* A branch of linguistics concerned with the mental and psychological aspects of language and speech, such as the childhood acquisition of language. —**psy·cho·lin·guist** *n.* —**psy·cho·lin·guis·tic** *adj.*

psy·cho·log·i·cal (sī′kə-lŏj′ĭ-kəl) *adj.* Also **psy·cho·log·ic** (-lŏj′ĭk). *Abbr.* **psych., psychol. 1.** Of or pertaining to psychology. **2.** Of, pertaining to, or derived from the mind or emotions: *Your fear of water is purely psychological—you're a perfectly good swimmer.* **3.** Capable of influencing the mind or emotions. —**psy·cho·log·i·cal·ly** *adv.*

psychological moment *n.* The time when the mental state of a person is most likely to produce the desired response.

psychological warfare *n.* The use of tactics in warfare designed to undermine the courage, loyalty, or morale of the enemy.

psy·chol·o·gism (sī-kŏl′ə-jĭz′əm) *n.* The application or use, often spurious, of psychological theories to interpret or explain phenomena in other sciences or in the arts, as in history or literature.

psy·chol·o·gist (sī-kŏl′ə-jĭst) *n. Abbr.* **psych., psychol.** A person trained to perform psychological research or therapy.

psy·chol·o·gize (sī-kŏl′ə-jīz′) *v.* **-gized, -gizing, -gizes.** —*tr.* To explain (behavior) in terms of psychology. —*intr.* To investigate behavior using psychological concepts.

psy·chol·o·gy (sī-kŏl′ə-jē) *n., pl.* **-gies.** *Abbr.* **psych., psychol. 1.** The science concerned with understanding and explaining mental processes and behavior. **2.** The emotional and behavioral characteristics of an individual, group, or activity: *the psychology of war.* **3.** Subtle tactical action or argument: *She used poor psychology on her employer.* [New Latin *psychologia* : PSYCHO- + -LOGY.]

psy·cho·met·rics (sī′kō-mĕt′rĭks) *n. Used with a singular verb.* **1.** The measurement of psychological variables, such as intelligence, aptitude, or emotional disturbance. **2.** The mathematical, especially statistical, design of psychological tests and measures. —**psy·cho·met·ric, psy·cho·met·ri·cal** *adj.* —**psy·cho·met·ri·cal·ly** *adv.* —**psy·cho·me·tri·cian** (sī-kŏm′ə-trĭsh′ən) *n.*

psy·chom·e·try (sī-kŏm′ə-trē) *n.* **1.** Psychometrics. **2.** In parapsychology, the supposed ability to divine facts about events, objects, or people, through proximity to them or through touching them. [PSYCHO- + -METRY.] —**psy·chom·e·trist** *n.*

psy·cho·mo·tor (sī′kō-mō′tər) *adj.* Of or pertaining to muscular activity associated with mental processes.

psy·cho·neu·ro·sis (sī′kō-nŏŏ-rō′sĭs, -nyŏŏ-rō′sĭs) *n., pl.* **-ses** (-sēz). *Psychology.* Neurosis (see). —**psy·cho·neu·rot·ic** (sī′kō-nŏŏ-rŏt′ĭk, -nyŏŏ-rŏt′ĭk) *adj. & n.*

psy·cho·path (sī′kə-păth′) *n.* A person with a personality disorder, especially one manifested in aggressively antisocial behavior, amoral attitudes, and continually fluctuating moods. [From PSYCHOPATHY.] —**psy·cho·path·ic** *adj.*

psy·cho·pa·thol·o·gy (sī′kō-pə-thŏl′ə-jē) *n.* The study of pathological mental disorders. —**psy·cho·path·o·log·ic** (sī′kō-păth′ə-lŏj′ĭk), **psy·cho·path·o·log·i·cal** *adj.* —**psy·cho·pa·thol·o·gist** *n.*

psy·chop·a·thy (sī-kŏp′ə-thē) *n.* A mental disorder or disease. [PSYCHO- + -PATHY.]

psy·cho·phar·ma·col·o·gy (sī′kō-fär′mə-kŏl′ə-jē) *n.* A branch of pharmacology concerned with the study and use of drugs that affect the mind. —**psy·cho·phar·ma·co·log·i·cal** (sī′kō-fär′mə-kə-lŏj′ĭ-kəl) *adj.* —**psy·cho·phar·ma·col·o·gist** *n.*

psy·cho·phys·ics (sī′kō-fĭz′ĭks) *n. Used with a singular verb.* The psychological study of relationships between physical stimuli and sensory responses. —**psy·cho·phys·i·cal** *adj.* —**psy·cho·phys·i·cal·ly** *adv.* —**psy·cho·phys·i·cist** (sī′kō-fĭz′ə-sĭst) *n.*

psy·cho·phys·i·ol·o·gy (sī-kō-fĭz′ē-ŏl′ə-jē) *n.* The study of correlations between mental processes and physiology. —**psy·cho·phys·i·o·log·i·cal** (sī-kō-fĭz′ē-ə-lŏj′ĭ-kəl) *adj.* —**psy·cho·phys·i·o·log·i·cal·ly** *adv.*

psy·cho·pro·phy·lax·is (sī′kō-prō-fə-lăk′sĭs) *n.* The use of psychological conditioning to prepare a woman for natural childbirth. —**psy·cho·pro·phy·lac·tic** *adj.*

psy·cho·sex·u·al (sī′kō-sĕk′shŏŏ-əl) *adj.* Of or pertaining to the psychological aspects of sex or the mental processes relating to it. —**psy·cho·sex·u·al·i·ty** *n.*

psy·cho·sis (sī-kō′sĭs) *n., pl.* **-ses** (-sēz′). Any severe mental disorder, with or without organic damage, characterized by deterioration of normal intellectual and social functioning and by partial or complete withdrawal from reality. Compare **neurosis.** [New Latin : PSYCH(O)- + -OSIS.]

psy·cho·so·mat·ic (sī′kō-sō-măt′ĭk) *adj.* Of or pertaining to phenomena that exhibit an interaction of the physiological and the psychological, especially disorders, such as high blood pressure, that may be initiated or aggravated by mental stress.

psy·cho·sur·ger·y (sī′kō-sûr′jə-rē) *n.* Brain surgery when used to treat mental disorders. —**psy·cho·sur·gi·cal** *adj.*

psy·cho·tech·nics (sī′kō-tĕk′nĭks) *n. Used with a singular verb.* The practical or technological use of psychology, as in analysis of social or industrial problems. —**psy·cho·tech·ni·cal** *adj.* —**psy·cho·tech·ni·cian** (sī′kō-tĕk-nĭsh′ən) *n.*

psy·cho·ther·a·py (sī′kō-thĕr′ə-pē) *n.* **1.** Treatment of emotional and psychosomatic disorders based on the application of psychological knowledge, rather than exclusively on the use of drugs, surgery, or other physical treatment. **2.** Psychotherapy using depth psychology, by contrast with behavior therapy. —**psy·cho·ther·a·peu·tic** (sī′kō-thĕr′ə-pyŏŏ′tĭk) *adj.* —**psy·cho·ther·a·pist** *n.*

psy·chot·ic (sī-kŏt′ĭk) *n.* One suffering from a psychosis. [From PSYCHOSIS.] —**psy·chot·ic** *adj.* —**psy·chot·i·cal·ly** *adv.*

psy·chot·o·mi·met·ic (sī-kŏt′ō-mə-mĕt′ĭk, -mī-mĕt′ĭk) *adj.* Designating a drug, such as LSD, that is capable of causing psychosis or psychotic symptoms.
~*n.* A psychotomimetic drug. [PSYCHOT(IC) + MIMETIC.]

psy·cho·tro·pic (sī′kō-trō′pĭk, -trŏp′ĭk) *adj.* Affecting the moods or mental processes. Said of a drug. [PSYCHO- + -TROPIC.] —**psy·cho·tro·pic** *n.* —**psy·cho·trop·i·cal·ly** (sī′kə-trŏp′ĭk-lē, -trō′pĭk-) *adv.*

psychro– *prefix.* Indicates cold; for example, **psychrometer.** [Greek *psukhros†,* cold.]

psy·chrom·e·ter (sī-krŏm′ə-tər) *n.* A hygrometer that uses the difference in readings between two thermometers, one having a wet bulb that is ventilated to cause evaporation and the other having a dry bulb, as a measure of atmospheric moisture. Also called "wet-and-dry-bulb thermometer." [PSYCHRO- + -METER.]

psy·chro·phil·ic (sī′krō-fĭl′ĭk) *adj. Biology.* Thriving at relatively low temperatures, usually between 0 and 25°C. Said of certain bacteria. Compare **mesophilic, thermophilic.** [PSYCHRO- + -PHIL(E) + -IC.]

psyl·la (sĭl′ə) *n.* Also **psyl·lid** (-ĭd). Any of various plant lice of the family Chermidae (or Psyllidae), especially *Psylla mali,* a pest that infests apple trees. [Greek *psulla,* flea.]

Pt The symbol for the element platinum.

pt. 1. part. **2.** payment. **3.** pint. **4.** point. **5.** port. **6.** preterit.

p.t. 1. past tense. **2.** pro tempore.

P.T. 1. Pacific Time. **2.** physical therapy. **3.** physical training. **4.** postal telegraph.

pta. peseta.

P.T.A. Parent-Teacher Association.

Ptah (ptä, tä) *n.* In ancient Egypt, the creator god and the god of Memphis, represented in the form of a mummy.

ptar·mi·gan (tär′mĭ-gən) *n., pl.* **-gans** or collectively **ptarmigan.** A game bird, *Lagopus mutus,* of the grouse family, inhabiting arctic and subarctic regions of the Northern Hemisphere. It has feathered feet and plumage that is brownish-gray in summer, gray in autumn, and white in winter. [Alteration (by pseudolearned association with Greek *pteron,* wing) of Scottish Gaelic *tarmachan,* diminutive of *tarmach†.*]

PT boat (pē′tē′) *n.* A fast, maneuverable, lightly armed vessel used to torpedo enemy shipping. In full "patrol torpedo boat." Also *chiefly British* "mosquito boat."

–pter *suffix.* Indicates wings or winglike parts; for example, **ornithopter.** [New Latin *-ptera,* from Greek *-pteros,* -PTEROUS.]

pter·i·dol·o·gy (tĕr′ĭ-dŏl′ə-jē) *n.* The study of ferns. [Greek *pteris* (stem *pterid-*), fern, from *pteron,* feather + -LOGY.] —**pter·i·do·log·i·cal** (tĕr′ĭ-də-lŏj′ĭ-kəl) *adj.* —**pter·i·dol·o·gist** *n.*

pter·id·o·phyte (tə-rĭd′ə-fīt′, tĕr′ĭ-dō-) *n. Botany.* Any plant of the division Pteridophyta, including the ferns and horsetails, that reproduces by spores and that has vascular tissue. [New Latin *Pteridophyta* : Greek *pteris,* fern (see **pteridology**) + -PHYTE.] —**pter·id·o·phyt·ic** (tə-rĭd′ə-fĭt′ĭk), **pter·i·doph·y·tous** (tĕr′ĭ-dŏf′ə-təs) *adj.*

pter·id·o·sperm (tə-rĭd′ə-spûrm′, tĕr′ĭ-dō-) *n.* The **seed fern** (see).

ptero– *prefix.* Indicates feather, wing, or winglike part; for example, **pterodactyl.** [Greek *pteron,* feather, wing.]

pter·o·dac·tyl (tĕr′ə-dăk′tĭl) *n.* Any of various extinct flying reptiles of the family Pterodactylidae. See **pterosaur.** [New Latin *Pterodactylus,* "wing-finger" : PTERO- + DACTYL.]

pter·o·pod (tĕr′ə-pŏd′) *n.* Any of various small marine gastropod mollusks of the order Pteropoda, that swim with winglike expanded lobes of the foot. Also called "sea butterfly." [New Latin *Pteropoda,* "wing-footed ones," from Greek *pteropous,* wing-footed : PTERO- + *-pous,* -POD.] —**pter·o·pod** *adj.*

pter·o·saur (tĕr′ə-sôr′) *n.* Any of various extinct flying reptiles of the order Pterosauria, including the pterodactyls, of the Jurassic and Cretaceous periods, characterized by wings consisting of a flap of skin supported by the very long fourth digit on each front limb. [New Latin *Pterosauria,* "winged lizards" : PTERO- + *-sauria,* plural of -SAURUS.]

–pterous, –pteran *suffix.* Indicates a specified number or kind of wings; for example, **dipterous.** [Greek *-pteros,* -winged, from *pteron,* feather, wing.]

pter·y·goid (tĕr′ə-goid′) *adj. Anatomy.* Of or designating either of two processes in the skull attached to the body of the sphenoid bone.

~*n. Anatomy.* Either of these processes. Also called "pterygoid process." [Greek *pterugoeidēs : pterux,* wing, from *pteron,* feather, wing + -OID.]

PTFE polytetrafluoroethylene.

ptg. printing.

ptis·an (tĭz′ən, tī-zăn′) *n.* A **tisane** *(see).* [Middle English *tisan,* peeled barley, barley water, from Old French, from Medieval Latin *tisana,* variant of Latin *ptisana,* from Greek *ptisanē,* from *ptissein,* to peel, crush.]

Ptol·e·ma·ic (tŏl′ə-mā′ĭk) *adj.* **1.** Of or pertaining to the astronomer Ptolemy. **2.** Of or pertaining to the Ptolemies or to Egypt during their rule, 323 B.C. to 30 B.C.

Ptolemaic system *n.* The astronomical system of Ptolemy, having the earth at the center of the universe, with the moon, planets, and the stars revolving about it.

Ptol·e·ma·ist (tŏl′ə-mā′ĭst) *n.* An adherent of or believer in the astronomical system of Ptolemy.

Ptol·e·my (tŏl′ə-mē), born Claudius Ptolemaeus (*c.* A.D. 90-168). Greco-Egyptian mathematician and geographer. His work, preserved at the library in Alexandria, was translated into Arabic, spread across the Islamic world, and was reintroduced to Europe, where it had a great influence on medieval and Renaissance scholars. His *Geographike Hyphegesis* inspired Columbus.

Ptolemy I So·ter (sō′tər) *c.* 367-284 B.C.). Macedonian soldier, king, and historian. One of Alexander the Great's generals, he became governor of Egypt after his death and eventually (305) proclaimed himself king, founding the Ptolemaic dynasty. He founded the library at Alexandria and recorded Alexander's campaigns.

Ptolemy XIII (63-47 B.C.). King of Egypt. Following his succession to the throne (51 B.C.) with his sister and wife, Cleopatra, he exiled her (48 B.C.) to Syria. Julius Caesar, however, supported the reinstatement of Cleopatra, and Ptolemy was killed in the subsequent civil war.

pto·maine, pto·main (tō′mān′, tō-mān′) *n.* Any of various basic nitrogenous materials, some poisonous, produced by the putrefaction and decomposition of protein. [French *ptomaïne,* from Italian *ptomaina,* from Greek *ptōma,* "fall, fallen body," corpse, from *piptein,* to fall.]

ptomaine poisoning *n.* Food poisoning. Ptomaines were formerly erroneously considered a cause of all food poisoning.

pto·sis (tō′sĭs) *n.* Abnormal and permanent lowering of an organ; especially, drooping of the upper eyelid caused by muscle failure. [New Latin, from Greek *ptōsis,* fall, from *piptein,* to fall.] —**pto·tic** *adj.*

pts. **1.** parts. **2.** payments. **3.** pints. **4.** points. **5.** ports.

pty. proprietary.

pty·a·lin (tī′ə-lən) *n.* A salivary enzyme in humans and some other animals that hydrolyzes starch into dextrins and ultimately maltose. [Greek *ptualon,* saliva, from *ptuein,* to spit + -IN.]

pty·a·lism (tī′ə-lĭz′əm) *n.* Excessive flow of saliva. [Greek *ptualon,* saliva. See **ptyalin**.]

p-type (pē′tīp′) *adj. Electronics.* Of or designating a semiconductor or its type of conductivity, in which the majority of carriers are holes rather than electrons. Compare **n-type**. [*Positive type.*]

Pu The symbol for the element plutonium.

pub (pŭb) *n.* **1.** *Chiefly British.* A place where alcoholic drinks are sold under license to be consumed on or off the premises and that often also provides light meals. Also used adjectively: *a pub lunch.* **2.** A tavern; bar.

~*intr.v.* **pubbed, pubbing, pubs.** To have a drink in a pub. Used chiefly in the phrase *go pubbing.* [Short for PUBLIC HOUSE.]

pub. **1.** public. **2.** publication. **3.** published; publisher; publishing.

pub crawl *n. Slang.* A round of drinking in several pubs in succession. —**pub-crawl** (pŭb′krôl′) *v.* —**pub-crawl·er** *n.*

pu·ber·tal (pyōō′bər-təl) *adj.* Also **pu·ber·al** (-bər-əl). Of or pertaining to puberty.

pu·ber·ty (pyōō′bər-tē) *n.* The stage of maturation in early adolescence in which the individual becomes physiologically capable of sexual reproduction and the secondary sexual characteristics appear. [Middle English *puberte,* from Latin *pūbertās* (stem *pūbertāt-),* from *pūber,* adult.]

pu·ber·u·lent (pyōō-bĕr′yə-lənt, -bĕr′ə-lənt) *adj.* Also **pu·ber·u·lous** (-bĕr′yə-ləs, -bĕr′ə-ləs). *Biology.* Covered with minute hairs or very fine down; finely pubescent. [Latin *pūber,* grown up, adult, (of plants) downy.]

pu·bes (pyōō′bēz′) *n., pl.* **pubes. 1.** The pubic region. **2.** The pubic hair. **3.** Plural of **pubis**. [Latin *pūbēs.*]

pu·bes·cence (pyōō-bĕs′əns) *n.* **1.** The attainment or onset of puberty. **2. a.** A covering of soft down or short hairs, as on certain plants and insects. **b.** The state of being pubescent.

pu·bes·cent (pyōō-bĕs′ənt) *adj.* **1.** Reaching or having reached puberty. **2.** Covered with short hairs or soft down. [French, from Latin *pūbēscens* (stem *pūbēscent-),* present participle of *pūbēscere,* to reach puberty, from *pūber,* adult.]

pu·bic (pyōō′bĭk) *adj.* Of, pertaining to, or in the region of the lower part of the abdomen, the pubis, or the pubes. [From PUBES.]

pu·bis (pyōō′bĭs) *n., pl.* **-bes** (-bēz′). The forward portion of either of the hipbones, at the juncture forming the front arch of the pelvis. [New Latin *(os) pubis,* bone of the groin, from Latin *pūbis,* genitive of *pūbēs,* PUBES.]

publ. **1.** publication. **2.** published; publisher.

pub·lic (pŭb′lĭk) *adj. Abbr.* **pub. 1.** Of, concerning, or affecting the community or the people as a whole: *public affairs.* **2.** Maintained

for or open to be used by the whole community. **3.** Participated in or able to be attended by the whole community: *public worship.* **4.** Connected with or acting on behalf of the people, community, or government, rather than concerned with private matters or interests: *public office.* **5. a.** Open to the knowledge or judgment of all: *a public scandal.* **b.** Known or recognized by many people: *a public figure.* —**go public. 1.** To offer shares for sale to the public, especially for the first time. Used of a private company. **2.** To appeal directly to the public, as by means of the media, instead of going through the usual internal channels or complaints procedures. —**make public.** To cause to be known by several or many people or the people at large.

~*n. Abbr.* **pub. 1.** The community or the people as a whole. **2.** A group of people sharing a common specified interest: *the reading public.* **3.** Admirers or followers, especially of a famous person. [Middle English *publique, publyk,* from Old French *public, publique,* from Latin *pūblicus,* alteration of *poplicus,* from *populus,* people.] —**pub·lic·ness** *n.*

pub·lic-ad·dress system (pŭb′lĭk-ə-drĕs′) *n. Abbr.* **PA** An electronic amplification apparatus installed and used for broadcasting in public areas. Also called "PA system."

pub·li·can (pŭb′lĭ-kən) *n.* **1.** *Chiefly British.* The keeper of a pub; a tavernkeeper. **2.** A collector of public taxes or tolls in the ancient Roman Empire. [Middle English, from Old French *publicain,* from Latin *pūblicānus,* contractor for public revenues, from *pūblicum,* public revenue, from *pūblicus,* PUBLIC.]

pub·li·ca·tion (pŭb′lĭ-kā′shən) *n. Abbr.* **pub., publ. 1.** The act or process of publishing printed matter. **2.** Any printed material offered for sale or distribution, such as a book or periodical. **3.** The communication of information to the public. **4.** *Law.* The act of making defamatory information public. [Middle English *publicatioun,* from Old French, from Late Latin *pūblicātiō* (stem *pūblicā-tiōn-),* from *pūblicāre,* to make public, from Latin *pūblicus,* PUBLIC.]

public company *n.* A **public limited company** *(see).*

public corporation *n.* In Britain, a state-owned organization responsible for the management of a nationalized industry.

public defender *n.* A lawyer or staff of lawyers, usually publicly appointed, having responsibility for the legal defense of those unable to afford or obtain legal assistance.

public domain *n.* **1.** The status of publications, products, and processes that are not protected under patent or copyright. **2.** Land owned and controlled by the state or federal government.

public enemy *n.* A person, usually a criminal, who is considered to be especially dangerous to the community.

public health *n.* The art and science of protecting and improving community health by means of preventive medicine, health education, communicable disease control, and the application of the social and sanitary sciences.

public house *n. Chiefly British.* A pub.

pub·li·cist (pŭb′lə-sĭst) *n.* A person who publicizes something or someone; especially, a press or publicity agent.

pub·lic·i·ty (pŭ-blĭs′ə-tē) *n.* **1.** Information that concerns a person, group, event, or product and is disseminated through various forms of the media to attract public notice. **2.** Public interest, notice, or notoriety achieved by the spreading of such information. **3.** The act, process, or occupation of disseminating information to gain public interest. **4.** The condition of being public. [French *publicité,* from *public,* PUBLIC.]

pub·li·cize (pŭb′lə-sīz′) *tr.v.* **-cized, -cizing, -cizes.** To give publicity to; bring to public attention; advertise.

public law *n.* **1.** The branch of law dealing with the state or government and the way it relates to individuals or other governments. Compare **private law**. **2.** A law affecting the public.

public library *n.* A noncommercial library for the use of the general public, usually supported by public funds.

public limited company *n. Finance. Abbr.* **PLC, p.l.c., P.L.C.** A limited liability company whose shares are made available for subscription by the public rather than distributed privately, and can be transferred freely on the open market. Also called "public company."

pub·lic·ly (pŭb′lĭk-lē) *adv.* **1.** In a public manner; not privately; openly. **2.** By or with consent of the public.

public nuisance *n.* **1.** *Law.* An illegal act that causes harm to the community at large rather than to a particular individual. **2.** *Informal.* A person who is considered to be obnoxious by many people.

public opinion *n.* The views of the public, especially on a matter of public concern or interest.

public prosecutor *n.* **1.** A government official who prosecutes criminal actions on behalf of the state or community. **2.** A **prosecutor** *(see).*

public relations *n. Usually used with a singular verb. Abbr.* **PR, P.R. 1.** The methods and activities employed by an individual, organization, or government to promote a favorable relationship and good image with the public. **2.** The degree of success achieved in such a relationship. **3.** The staff employed to promote such a relationship. **4.** The art or science of establishing such a relationship.

public school *n.* **1.** *Abbr.* **P.S.** In the United States, an elementary or secondary school supported by public funds and providing free education for children of the community or district. **2.** In Britain, a private, independent, secondary, fee-paying school at which the pupils usually board.

public sector *n.* The section of the economy that is under the control of government departments or public corporations, including nationalized industries, national and local government, welfare, and education. Compare **private sector.** —**pub·lic·sec·tor** (pŭb′lĭk-sĕk′tər) *adj.*

public servant *n.* A person who holds a government position by election or by appointment.

public service *n.* **1.** Employment within a governmental system, especially within the civil services. **2.** A service performed for the benefit of the public.

pub·lic-serv·ice corporation (pŭb′lĭk-sûr′vĭs) *n.* A corporation providing utilities for the public.

public speaking *n.* The art or process of making speeches before an audience. —**public speaker** *n.*

pub·lic-spir·i·ted (pŭb′lĭk-spĭr′ĭ-tĭd) *adj.* Motivated by or showing active devotion to the good of the community; concerned for the public welfare. —**pub·lic-spir·it·ed·ness** *n.*

public television *n.* Noncommercial television that provides programs, especially of an educational nature, for the public.

public utility *n.* **1.** An industrial organization that provides an essential service or commodity, such as water, electricity, transportation, or communication, to the public. Also called "public utility company." **2.** *Usually* **public utilities.** *Finance.* Shares issued by such a company.

public works *pl.n.* Construction projects, such as highways or dams, financed by public funds and constructed by a government for the benefit or use of the general public.

pub·lish (pŭb′lĭsh) *v.* **-lished, -lishing, -lishes.** —*tr.* **1.** To prepare and issue (printed material) for public distribution or sale. **2.** To bring to the public attention; announce. —*intr.* **1.** To issue a publication. **2.** To be the author of a published work. [Middle English *publishen,* from Old French *publier* (stem *publiss-*), from Latin *pūblicāre,* to make public, from *pūblicus,* PUBLIC.] —**pub·lish·a·ble** *adj.*

pub·lish·er (pŭb′lĭsh-ər) *n. Abbr.* **pub., publ.** A person or company engaged in publishing printed material.

pub·lish·ing (pŭb′lĭsh-ĭng) *n.* The business, people, or work involved in the publication of books, periodicals, and the like.

Puc·ci·ni (pōō-chē′nē), **Giacomo** (1858-1924). Italian composer. He wrote in a style that is especially noted for its lyrical qualities. His works, which continue to enjoy enormous popularity, include *La Bohème* (1896), *Tosca* (1900), and *Madame Butterfly* (1904).

puc·coon (pə-kōōn′) *n.* **1.** Any of several North American plants of the genus *Lithospermum,* yielding a red or yellow dye; especially, *L. canescens,* having orange flowers. Sometimes called "alkanet." **2.** Any of several other plants yielding a reddish dye, as the bloodroot. **3.** The dye from any of these plants. [Earlier *pocoon,* from Algonquian (Virginia).]

puce (pyōōs) *n.* Deep red to dark grayish purple. [French *(couleur) puce,* "flea (color)," from Latin *pūlex,* flea.] —**puce** *adj.*

puck (pŭk) *n.* A hard rubber disk used in ice hockey as the playing and scoring medium. [19th century : origin obscure.]

Puck *n.* In English folklore, a mischievous sprite. Also called "Robin Goodfellow." [Middle English *p(o)uke,* Old English *pūca†.*]

pucka. Variant of **pukka.**

puck·er (pŭk′ər) *v.* **-ered, -ering, -ers.** —*tr.* To gather into small wrinkles or folds. —*intr.* To become contracted and wrinkled. ~*n.* A wrinkle or wrinkled part, as in tightly stitched cloth. [Originally "to form a pocket," perhaps from POCKET.]

puck·ish (pŭk′ĭsh) *adj.* Mischievous; impish: *a puckish grin.* [From PUCK.] —**puck·ish·ly** *adv.* —**puck·ish·ness** *n.*

pud·ding (pōōd′ĭng) *n.* **1. a.** A sweet dessert, usually containing flour or a cereal product, that has been boiled, steamed, or baked. **b.** A savory dish baked in suet pastry, with a puddinglike consistency. **2.** A sausagelike preparation made with minced meat or various other ingredients stuffed into a bag or skin and boiled. [Middle English, from Old French *boudin,* from Vulgar Latin *botellīnus* (unattested), diminutive of Latin *botellus,* sausage.]

pudding stone *n.* A rock, a **conglomerate** (see).

pud·dle (pŭd′l) *n.* **1.** A small pool of water, especially one formed by rain. **2.** A small pool of any liquid. **3.** A tempered paste of wet clay and sand used as waterproofing. ~*v.* **puddled, -dling, -dles.** —*tr.* **1.** To make muddy. **2.** To work (clay or sand) into a thick, watertight paste. **3.** *Metallurgy.* To process (impure metal) by puddling. —*intr.* To splash or dabble in or as if in a puddle. [Middle English *podel, pothel,* diminutive of Old English *pudd†,* ditch.] —**pud·dly** *adj.*

pud·dler (pŭd′lər) *n.* **1.** One who puddles iron or clay. **2.** One who puddles about.

pud·dling (pŭd′lĭng) *n.* **1.** *Metallurgy.* The purification of impure metal, especially pig iron, by agitation of a molten bath of the metal in an oxidizing atmosphere. **2.** Compaction of wet clay or a similar material to make a watertight paste.

pu·den·cy (pyōō′dən-sē) *n.* Modesty; shame; prudishness. [Late Latin *pudēntia,* shame, from Latin *pudēns* (stem *pudent-*), present participle of *pudēre,* to feel shame.]

pu·den·dum (pyōō-dĕn′dəm) *n., pl.* **-da** (-də). *Often* **pudenda.** The human external genital organs, especially a woman's. [New Latin, from Late Latin *pudenda,* from Latin *pudendus,* gerundive of *pudēre,* to be ashamed.] —**pu·den·dal** *adj.*

pudg·y (pŭj′ē) *adj.* **-i·er, -i·est.** Also *chiefly British* **podg·y.** Short and fat; chubby: *pudgy fingers.* —See Synonyms at **fat.** [Earlier *pudsy,* probably augmented from Scottish *pud,* belly, (hence) plump, healthy child, from Scottish Gaelic *poit,* ultimately from Vulgar Latin *pottus* (attested only in Late Latin).]

Pueb·la (pwĕb′lə). City and capital of Puebla state, east-central Mexico. It is an important agricultural, commercial, and manufacturing center and a popular tourist spot. The city is noted for the fine, colored tiles that decorate its buildings and churches.

pueb·lo (pwĕb′lō) *n., pl.* **-los. 1.** A community dwelling, up to five stories high, built of stone or adobe by Indian tribes of the southwestern United States. **2. Pueblo.** A member of a tribe, such as the Hopi or Zuñi, inhabiting such dwellings. **3.** An Indian village of the southwestern United States. [Spanish, "people," "population," from Latin *populus,* people.]

Pueb·lo (pwĕb′lō). City of south-central Colorado, on the Arkansas River in the foothills of the Rocky Mts. It is the center of shipping, trade, and industry for an extensive timber, coal, livestock, and farm area. A trading post was first established here in 1842.

puer·ile (pyōō′ər-ĭl, pyōōr′ĭl, pwĕr′ĭl, -īl′) *adj.* **1.** Immature; childish. **2.** Pertaining to childhood. [French *puéril,* from Latin *puerīlis,* from *puer,* child, boy.] —**puer·ile·ly** *adv.* —**puer·ile·ness** *n.*

puer·il·i·ty (pyōō′ə-rĭl′ə-tē, pyōō-rĭl′-, pwĕ-) *n., pl.* **-ties. 1.** The condition of being puerile. **2.** A childish action, idea, or utterance.

pu·er·per·al (pyōō-ûr′pər-əl) *adj. Medicine.* Connected with, resulting from, or following childbirth. [Latin *puerperus,* bearing young : *puer,* child + -PAROUS.]

puerperal fever *n.* Infection of the womb and of the bloodstream following childbirth. Also called "childbed fever."

pu·er·pe·ri·um (pyōō′ər-pûr′ē-əm) *n.* The approximate six-week period after childbirth to return of normal uterine size. [Latin, childbirth, from *puerperus,* PUERPERAL.]

Puer·to Ri·co (pwĕr′tō rē′kō, pôr′-). *Abbr.* **P.R.** Island in the West Indies. A self-governing commonwealth associated with the United States, it is largely mountainous and densely populated. Its chief industries include textiles, chemicals, cattle breeding, and sugar production. Large-scale emigration to the United States (1940's and 1950's) has declined, and there is a small independence movement. Area, 8,897 square kilometers (3,434 square miles). Population, 3,200,000. Capital, San Juan. —**Puer·to Ric·an** *adj. & n.*

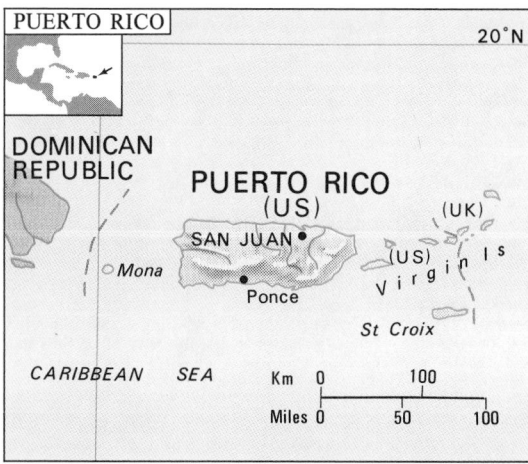

PUERTO RICO

puff (pŭf) *n.* **1. a.** A short, forceful exhalation of breath. **b.** A short, sudden gust of wind. **c.** A brief, sudden emission of air, vapor, or smoke. **d.** A short, sibilant sound produced by a puff. **2.** An amount of vapor, smoke, or similar material released in a puff. **3.** An act of drawing in and expelling the breath, as in smoking tobacco. **4.** A swelling or rounded protuberance. **5.** A light, flaky pastry. **6.** A powder puff. **7.** A soft roll of hair forming part of a hairstyle. **8.** A portion of fabric that is gathered at the edges and full in shape. **9.** An extravagantly flattering recommendation of a book, play, or the like, especially in a newspaper. **10.** An eiderdown. **11.** *Genetics.* A swelling seen in certain areas of giant chromosomes. ~*v.* **puffed, puffing, puffs.** —*intr.* **1.** To blow in puffs. **2.** To come forth in a puff or puffs. **3.** To breathe forcefully and rapidly; pant. **4.** To emit or move while emitting puffs of smoke, vapor, or the like: *The train puffed.* **5.** To take puffs on a cigarette, pipe, or cigar. **6.** To swell or seem to swell, as with air or pride. Often used with *up* or *out.* —*tr.* **1.** To emit or give forth in a puff or puffs. **2.** To impel with puffs. **3.** To smoke (a cigar, for example). **4.** To inflate or distend. **5.** To fill with pride or conceit. Used with *out* or *up: all puffed up by her recent success.* **6.** To publicize with exaggerated praise. **7.** To cause to be out of breath. Usually used in the passive with *out.* [Middle English *puffen,* Old English *puffan* (unattested), imitative.] —**puff·i·ly** *adv.* —**puff·i·ness** *n.*

puff adder *n.* **1.** A venomous African viper, *Bitis arietans,* having crescent-shaped yellowish markings. **2.** The **hognose snake** (see). [South African Dutch and Afrikaans *pofadder : pof,* puff + ADDER; so called because it inflates its body when aroused.]

puff·ball (pŭf′bôl′) *n.* Any of various fungi of the genus *Lycoperdon* and related genera, having a ball-shaped fruiting body that, when broken open, releases the enclosed spores in puffs of dust.

puffed sleeve *n.* A short sleeve, gathered at both ends so that it stands out from the shoulder. Also called "puff sleeve."

puff·er (pŭf′ər) *n.* **1.** One that puffs. **2.** Any of various marine fishes

pueblo *These multistoried buildings gave their Spanish name to the Native Americans whose traditional homes they are: the Pueblo peoples of the southwestern United States. Jutting beams support the roof of each house and take the weight of the rooms above.*

puffball *Many of these common fungi are edible until maturity. Then they become powdery inside and puff out spores if disturbed. Some species grow up to 120 centimeters (4 feet) across. The species shown above, Lycoperdon perlatum gemnatum, grows mostly in woodlands.*

puffer *A fish of Caribbean coral reefs, the puffer protects itself against predators by inflating its spiky body.*

of the family Tetraodontidae, that are capable of swelling up. In this sense, also called "blowfish," "swellfish."

puff·e·ry (pŭf′ə-rē) *n.* Exaggerated praise or recommendation.

puf·fin (pŭf′ĭn) *n.* Any of several sea birds of the genera *Fratercula* and *Lunda,* of northern regions, characteristically having black and white plumage and a vertically flattened, brightly colored bill. Also called "sea parrot." [Middle English *poffo(u)n, pophyn†.*]

puff pastry *n.* Dough that is rolled and folded in layers, and that expands in baking to form a rich, light, flaky pastry.

puff·y (pŭf′ē) *adj.* **-ier, -iest. 1.** Swollen or bloated: *puffy eyes after a night spent crying.* **2.** Breathless.

pug¹ (pŭg) *n.* A small dog of a breed originating in China, having a snub nose, wrinkled face, square body, short smooth hair, and a curled tail. [16th century : perhaps of Dutch origin.]

pug² *n.* **1.** Clay ground and kneaded with water into a plastic consistency for forming bricks or pottery. **2.** A machine for grinding and mixing clay. ~*tr.v.* **pugged, pugging, pugs. 1.** To knead (clay) with water. **2.** To fill in with clay or mortar. **3.** To cover or pack with clay, mortar, sawdust, or felt in order to soundproof. [16th century : origin obscure.]

pug³ *n.* A footprint, track, or trail, especially of an animal. [Hindi *pag,* probably from Sanskrit *padakah,* foot, from *pada.*]

pug⁴ *n. Slang.* A boxer. [Shortened from PUGILIST.]

Pu·get Sound (pyōō′jĭt) *n.* Arm of the Pacific Ocean, *c.* 160 kilometers (100 miles) long, in western Washington, extending from Admiralty Inlet to the city of Olympia. There are numerous scenic islands in the sound, which is navigable for large ships.

pug·gree, pug·ree (pŭg′rē) *n.* Also **pug·ga·ree, pug·a·ree** (pŭg′-ə-rē). A band or scarf wrapped around the crown of a hat. [Hindi *pagrī,* from Sanskrit *parikara;* akin to Arabic *pairikara,* turban.]

pu·gi·lism (pyōō′jə-lĭz′əm) *n.* The skill or practice of fighting with the fists; boxing. [Latin *pugil,* fighter, from *pugnus,* fist.]

pu·gi·list (pyōō′jə-lĭst) *n.* One who fights with the fists; especially, a professional boxer. —**pu·gi·lis·tic** *adj.*

Pu·gin (pōō′jĭn, pyōō′-), **Augustus Welby Northmore** (1812–52). British architect. A convert to Roman Catholicism and a leader of the neo-Gothic movement, which he advocated in his book *Contrasts* (1836), he designed many Catholic churches and cathedrals.

Puglia. See **Apulia.**

pug·na·cious (pŭg-nā′shəs) *adj.* Eager to fight; having a quarrelsome disposition. —See Synonyms at **belligerent.** [Latin *pugnāx* (stem *pugnāc-*), fond of fighting, from *pugnāre,* to fight, from *pugnus,* fist.] —**pug·na·cious·ly** *adv.* —**pug·na·cious·ness, pug·nac·i·ty** (pŭg-năs′ə-tē) *n.*

pug nose *n.* A short nose that is flattened and turned up at the end. [Probably from PUG (dog).] —**pug-nosed** (pŭg′nōsd′) *adj.*

puis·ne (pyōō′nē) *adj. Law.* Lower in rank; junior. ~*n. Law.* One of lesser rank; especially, an associate judge. [Old French, "born afterward." See **puny.**]

puis·sance (pwĭs′əns, pyōō′ə-səns, pyōō-ĭs′əns) *n.* **1.** An equestrian competition testing a horse's ability to jump heights. **2.** Power; potency; might.

puis·sant (pwĭs′ənt, pyōō′ə-sənt, pyōō-ĭs′ənt) *adj.* Mighty; powerful; potent. [Middle English *puissaunt,* from Old French, from Gallo-Roman *possiantem* (unattested), from Latin *posse,* to be powerful.] —**puis·sant·ly** *adv.*

puke (pyōōk) *v.* **puked, puking, pukes.** *Slang.* —*intr.* To vomit. Sometimes used with *up.* —*tr.* To vomit (something) up. ~*n. Slang.* **1.** Vomit. **2.** The act of vomiting. [16th century.]

puk·ka, puck·a (pŭk′ə) *adj. Anglo-Indian.* **1.** Genuine; authentic. **2.** Superior; first-class. **3.** Correct; right and proper. [Hindi *pakkā,* cooked, ripe, firm, from Sanskrit *pakva.*]

pul (pōōl) *n., pl.* **puls** or **puli** (pōō′lē). A monetary unit of Afghanistan, equal to ¹/₁₀₀ of the afghani. [Persian, from Turkish, possibly from Late Greek *phollis,* bellows, money bag, from Latin *follis.*]

pu·la (pōō′lä) *n., pl.* **-la** or **-las.** The basic monetary unit of Botswana, introduced in 1976 and equal to 100 thebe. [Tswana, "rain."]

Pu·las·ki (pōō-lăs′kē, pə-), **Casimir** or **Kazimierz** (*c.* 1748–79). Polish patriot and general in America. After earning military fame in the defenses of Berdichev (1768) and Częstochowa (1770–71) against the Russians, he joined American forces in the Revolutionary War at the request of Benjamin Franklin (1777). In his valiant charge on British troops in the siege of Savannah (1779), he was mortally wounded.

pul·chri·tude (pŭl′krĭ-tōōd′, -tyōōd′) *n.* Physical beauty. [Middle English *pulcritude,* from Latin *pulchritūdō,* from *pulcher†,* beautiful.] —**pul·chri·tu·di·nous** *adj.*

pule (pyōōl) *intr.v.* **puled, puling, pules.** To whine; fret. [Earlier *pewle, peule,* probably from French *piauler* (imitative).] —**pul·er** *n.*

pu·li¹ (pōō′lē, pyōō′lē) *n., pl.* **-lis** or **pulik** (pōō′lĕk, pyōō′lĕk). A long-haired sheepdog of a Hungarian breed. Also called "Hungarian puli." [Hungarian.]

pu·li². Alternate plural of **pul.**

Pu·lit·zer Prize (pōōl′ĭt-sər, pyōō′lĭt-) *n.* Any of several awards established by the U.S. publisher Joseph Pulitzer (1847–1911) and conferred annually for accomplishments in U.S. journalism, literature, and music.

pull (pōōl) *v.* **pulled, pulling, pulls.** —*tr.* **1.** To apply force to so as to cause or tend to cause motion toward the source of the force. **2.** To remove from a fixed position; extract: *pull teeth.* Usually used with *away, off,* or *out.* **3.** To tug at; jerk or tweak. **4.** To rip or tear;

rend. **5.** To stretch (taffy, for example) repeatedly. **6.** To strain (a muscle, for example) injuriously. **7.** *Informal.* To attract; draw. **8.** *Informal.* To perform or bring about successfully. Often used with *off: You'll never pull off a bank robbery.* **9.** *Slang.* To draw out (a knife or gun) in readiness for use. **10.** In golf or baseball, to hit (a ball) in the direction one is facing when the swing is carried through, as to the left of a right-handed player. **11. a.** To operate (an oar) in rowing. **b.** To transport or propel by rowing. **c.** To be rowed by: *That boat pulls six oars.* **12.** To rein in (a horse) to keep it from winning a race. **13.** *Printing.* To produce (a print or impression) from type. **14.** To remove the feathers from (a bird); pluck. —*intr.* **1. a.** To exert force in pulling something. **b.** To tug or jerk. Used with *at.* **2. a.** To move: *The bus pulled away from the curb.* **b.** To move in a vehicle: *She pulled away from the curb.* **3.** To drink or inhale deeply. Often used with *at* or *on.* **4.** To row a boat. **5.** To strain repeatedly at the bit. Used of a horse. —**pull a fast one.** *Informal.* To use a sly or underhand trick to gain advantage. —**pull ahead.** To move in front by going faster. —**pull down.** To dismantle or demolish (a building or structure). —**pull for.** To hope or cheer for the success of. —**pull in. 1.** To arrive at a destination: *We pulled in at midnight.* **2.** To rein in; restrain. **3.** *Informal.* To arrest: *The police pulled in three suspects for questioning.* —**pull oneself together.** To regain one's composure. —**pull together.** To make a joint effort; cooperate. ~*n.* **1.** The action or process of pulling or being pulled. **2.** Force exerted in pulling or required to overcome resistance in pulling. **3.** Any sustained effort: *a long pull across the mountains.* **4.** Something used for pulling, such as a knob on a drawer. **5.** A deep

puffin *The puffin's large brightly colored bill has given it the alternate name of sea parrot. The colors remain only during the breeding season; the outer layers of the bill are shed in the autumn.*

Pugin

ARCHITECT OF VICTORIAN ENGLAND'S GOTHIC REVIVAL
Pugin sought to express the spirit of Christianity

Augustus Welby Northmore Pugin was 21 years old when, in 1833, he was converted to the Roman Catholic faith, and resolved to build churches that would be "the perfect expression of all we should hold sacred."

Pugin hated what he called the "pagan" churches built in the classical style of the Renaissance. He felt that the architecture of a society reflected its moral quality, and that the Gothic architecture of the Middle Ages was a faithful expression of the Christian spirit. His book *True Principles of Pointed or Christian Architecture* appeared in 1841.

Born in London in 1812, Pugin was the son of an architectural draftsman and editor of books on Gothic details. In 1835—the year after the Houses of Parliament were burned down—it was Pugin who masterminded the detailed Gothic design and interior that won the architect Charles Barry the contract to rebuild them.

Four years later he began to design St. Chad's Cathedral in Birmingham, the first Gothic cathedral to be built in England for some 400 years. Among his other outstanding monuments are St. Giles's Church in Staffordshire (1841–46) and St. Augustine's Church in Kent (1846–51), where he lived.

For much of his life Pugin suffered from ill health and the effects of overwork. In 1851 he was committed to the London lunatic asylum known as Bedlam and died after his release the following year. "I have done the work of a hundred years in only forty," he declared shortly before the end. "It has worn me out."

FURNISHINGS OF THE HOUSE OF LORDS *During the last eight years of his life, Pugin made 2,000 designs for the interior of the House of Lords. Despite increasing ill health, he coped with orders for every kind of furnishing—from the royal throne down to fireguards, candlesticks, and inkstands.*

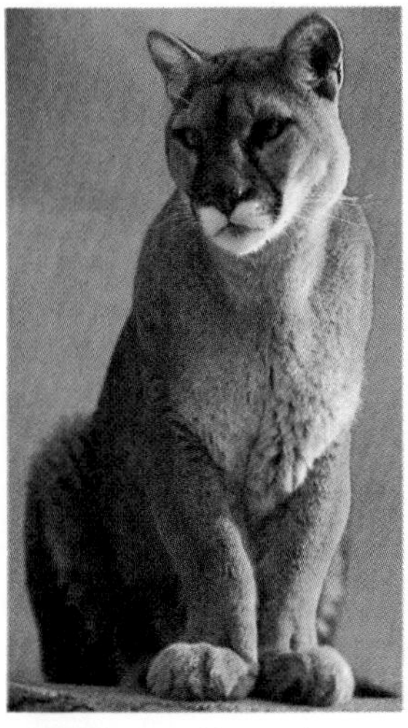

puma *The second-largest American wildcat after the jaguar, a full-grown puma can weigh more than 100 kilograms (220 pounds). Once ranging from British Columbia to Patagonia, it is now restricted to wilderness areas. It is also called mountain lion or cougar.*

inhalation or swallow, as on a cigar or of a drink. **6.** *Informal.* A means of gaining special advantage; influence: *He has pull with the boss.* **7.** *Informal.* Ability to draw or attract; popular appeal. **8.** A stroke or hit that pulls the ball in golf or baseball. **9.** A spell or period of rowing. **10.** The act of reining in a horse, especially when racing. **11.** *Printing.* A print or impression. **12.** The force required to draw back the trigger of a firearm or a bow. [Middle English *pullen,* to pull, pluck, Old English *pullian*†.] **—pull·er** *n.*

pull·back (pŏŏl′băk′) *n.* **1.** The act or process of pulling or moving something back; especially, an orderly withdrawal of troops. **2.** Any device for holding or drawing something back.

pul·let (pŏŏl′ĭt) *n.* A young hen, especially of the common domestic fowl, usually less than one year old. [Middle English *polet, pulet,* from Old French *poulet, pollet,* diminutive of *poul,* cock, *poule,* hen, from Latin *pullus,* young of an animal, chick.]

pul·ley (pŏŏl′ē) *n., pl.* **-leys. 1.** A simple machine used to change the direction and point of application of a pulling force, especially for lifting weights, consisting essentially of a wheel with a grooved rim in which a pulled rope or chain is run. **2.** A wheel turned by or driving a belt. [Middle English *po(u)ley,* from Old French *po(u)lie,* from Vulgar Latin *polidium* (unattested), probably from Late Greek *polidion* (unattested), diminutive of Greek *polos,* pole, pivot.]

Pull·man (pŏŏl′mən) *n.* A well-furnished railway carriage, usually with individual sleeping compartments. Also called "Pullman car." [After George M. *Pullman* (1831–97), U.S. industrialist.]

pul·lo·rum disease (pə-lôr′əm, -lōr′əm) *n.* A severe contagious diarrhea of young poultry, caused by the bacterium *Salmonella pullorum.* [Latin *pullorum,* genitive plural of *pullus,* young animal, PULLET.]

pull out *intr.v.* **1.** To depart from a station. Used of a train. **2. a.** To move from a stationary position at the side of a road. Used of a vehicle. **b.** To move out of a lane of traffic in order to pass another vehicle. **3.** To withdraw from a situation or commitment. **4.** *Military.* To withdraw from a site of battle. **5.** *Aeronautics.* To change from a dive into level flight. *—tr.v.* To withdraw (troops) from a battle.

pull·out (pŏŏl′out′) *n.* **1.** A withdrawal, especially of troops. **2.** *Aeronautics.* The change from a dive into level flight. **3.** Something designed to be pulled out, such as a leaflet in a book or magazine. **—pull·out** *adj.*

pull over *intr.v.* **1.** To bring a vehicle to a stop at the side of a road. **2.** To move to the side of the road in order to stop or to allow faster vehicles to pass.

pull·o·ver (pŏŏl′ō′vər) *n.* A garment, such as a sweater, that is put on by being drawn over the head. **—pull·o·ver** *adj.*

pull-tab (pŏŏl′tăb′) *n.* A **tab** (*see*) on a can.

pull through *intr.v.* To recover from an illness or setback. *—tr.v.* To cause to recover from an illness or setback.

pull·through (pŏŏl′thrōō′) *n.* Something designed to be pulled through; specifically, a long soft brush or piece of material for cleaning the inside of a wind instrument such as a saxophone.

pul·lu·late (pŭl′yə-lāt′) *intr.v.* **-lated, -lating, -lates. 1.** To put forth sprouts or buds; germinate. **2.** To breed rapidly or abundantly. **3.** To teem; swarm. [Latin *pullulāre,* to grow, sprout, from *pullulus,* diminutive of *pullus,* young animal, PULLET.] **—pul·lu·la·tion** *n.* **—pul·lu·la·tive** *adj.*

pull up *intr.v.* **1.** To come to a halt. Used of a vehicle. **2.** To move to a place or position that is level or ahead, as in a race. Used with *with.* *—tr.v.* **1.** To bring (a vehicle, horse, or the like) to a halt. **2.** To reprimand or scold. **3.** To stop (a person who is doing something wrong, making mistakes, or the like).

pull-up (pŏŏl′ŭp′) *n.* An exercise for strengthening the arms, performed by hanging by the hands from an overhead bar and pulling the body upward until the chin is even with or above the bar.

pul·mo·nar·y (pŏŏl′mə-nĕr′ē, pŭl′-) *adj.* **1.** Of or pertaining to the lungs. **2.** Having lungs or lunglike organs. [Latin *pulmōnārius,* from *pulmō,* (stem *pulmōn-*), lung.]

pulmonary artery *n.* An artery in which deoxygenated blood travels directly from the right ventricle of the heart to the lungs.

pulmonary vein *n.* A vein in which oxygenated blood travels directly from the lungs to the left atrium of the heart.

pul·mo·nate (pŏŏl′mə-nāt′, pŭl′-) *adj.* **1.** Having lungs or lunglike organs. **2.** Pertaining to the Pulmonata, an order of gastropods including snails and slugs, in which the mantle cavity is modified to function as a lung.
~n. A pulmonate mollusk. [Latin *pulmōnātus,* from *pulmō,* lung. See **pulmonary.**]

pul·mon·ic (pŏŏl-mŏn′ĭk, pŭl-) *adj.* Pulmonary.

pulp (pŭlp) *n.* **1.** A soft, moist, shapeless mass of matter. **2.** The soft, juicy part of fruit. **3.** A mass of pressed vegetable matter; *apple pulp.* **4.** A mixture of cellulose material, such as wood, paper, and rags, ground up and moistened to make paper. **5.** The soft inner structure of a tooth, consisting of nerve and blood vessels. **6.** *Mining.* A mixture of powdered ore and water. **7.** Magazines and books that contain sensational or pornographic subject matter and are characteristically printed on rough, unfinished paper. Also used adjectivally: *pulp fiction.* Compare **slick. —reduce someone to pulp.** To cause (someone) to be incapable of thought or action, as through fear, shock, or the like.
~v. **pulped, pulping, pulps.** *—tr.* **1.** To reduce to pulp. **2.** To remove the pulp from (fruit). *—intr.* To be reduced to a pulp. [Latin *pulpa*†, solid flesh, pulp.] **—pulp·ous, pulp·y** *adj.*

pul·pit (pŏŏl′pĭt, pŭl′-) *n.* **1.** An elevated platform, lectern, or stand used in preaching or conducting a religious service. **2.** Any similar raised platform, such as one used by harpooners in a fishing boat. **3. a.** Clergymen collectively. Preceded by *the.* **b.** The profession of preaching the Christian message. **4.** Any medium of communication through which a person expresses an opinion, especially regularly. [Middle English, from Latin *pulpitum*†, scaffold, platform.]

pulp·wood (pŭlp′wŏŏd′) *n.* Soft wood, such as spruce or pine, used in making paper.

pul·que (pŏŏl′kā′, -kē′, pŏŏl′-) *n.* An alcoholic milky drink made in Mexico from various species of agave. [Mexican Spanish; perhaps akin to Nahuatl *poliuhqui, puliuhqui,* decomposed, spoilt.]

pul·sar (pŭl′sär′) *n. Astronomy.* Any of numerous small, dense stars that emit regular pulses of radiation, usually radio waves, as a result of their rapid rotation. [From *puls*ating *star.*]

pul·sate (pŭl′sāt′) *intr.v.* **-sated, -sating, -sates. 1.** To expand and contract rhythmically; throb. **2.** To quiver. [Latin *pulsāre,* frequentative of *pellere* (past participle *pulsus*), to push, beat, strike.] **—pul·sa·tive** *adj.*
Synonyms: *beat, palpitate, throb.*

pul·sa·tile (pŭl′sə-tĭl) *adj.* Pulsating; vibrating. [Medieval Latin *pulsātilis,* from Latin *pulsāre,* to PULSATE.]

pulsating star *n.* A star that periodically becomes brighter as its outer layers expand and contract.

pul·sa·tion (pŭl-sā′shən) *n.* **1.** The act of pulsating. **2.** A single beat, throb, or vibration.

pul·sa·tor (pŭl-sā′tər) *n.* A pulsating device or machine, such as a pump.

pul·sa·to·ry (pŭl′sə-tôr′ē, -tōr′ē) *adj.* Having rhythmical vibration or movement; pulsating.

pulse¹ (pŭls) *n.* **1.** *Physiology.* The rhythmical throbbing of arteries produced by the regular contractions of the heart. **2.** Any regular beating rhythm. **3.** A single throb or beat. **4.** *Physics & Electronics.* A transient amplification or intensification of a characteristic of a system, especially of a wave characteristic, followed by return to equilibrium or steady state: *a signal pulse; a beam pulse.* **5.** The perceptible emotions or sentiments of a group: *the pulse of the electorate.* **6.** *Informal.* Energy; vitality: *the pulse of the party.*
~intr.v. **pulsed, pulsing, pulses.** To throb or vibrate; pulsate. [Middle English *pous, puls,* from Old French *pous, pols,* from Latin *pulsus,* beating, striking, from the past participle of *pellere,* to push, beat, strike.] **—pulse·less** *adj.*

pulse² *n.* **1.** The edible seeds of certain pod-bearing plants, such as lentils. **2.** A plant yielding such seeds. [Middle English *pols, puls,* from Old French *po(u)ls,* porridge, from Latin *puls,* pottage made of meal and pulse, possibly from Greek *poltos,* porridge.]

pulse-height analyzer (pŭls′hīt′) *n.* An electronic device that sorts signal pulses into predetermined ranges of amplitude.

pulse·jet (pŭls′jĕt′) *n.* A jet engine in which air intake and combustion occur intermittently, producing rapid periodic bursts of thrust.

pulse modulation *n. Electronics.* Modulation by coded variation of the amplitude or other characteristic of wave pulses.

pul·sim·e·ter (pŭl-sĭm′ə-tər) *n.* Also **pul·som·e·ter** (-sŏm′ə-tər). *Medicine.* An instrument that measures the frequency or strength of the pulse. [PULSE + -METER.]

pul·som·e·ter (pŭl-sŏm′ə-tər) *n.* **1.** A pump for raising water by the pulsed condensation of steam. Also called "vacuum pump." **2.** Variant of **pulsimeter.** [PULSE + -METER.]

pul·ver·a·ble (pŭl′vər-ə-bəl) *adj.* Capable of being pulverized.

pul·ver·ize (pŭl′və-rīz′) *v.* **-ized, -izing, -izes.** *—tr.* **1.** To pound, crush, or grind to a powder or dust. **2.** To demolish, defeat, or destroy. *—intr.* To be ground or reduced to powder or dust. [Old French *pulveriser,* from Late Latin *pulverizāre,* from Latin *pulvis* (stem *pulver-*), dust.] **—pul·ver·iz·a·ble** *adj.* **—pul·ver·i·za·tion** *n.* **—pul·ver·iz·er** *n.*

pul·ver·u·lent (pŭl-vĕr′yə-lənt) *adj.* **1.** Made of, covered with, or crumbling to fine powder or dust. **2.** Powdery; dusty; crumbly. [Latin *pulverulentus,* dusty, from *pulvis,* dust. See **pulverize.**]

pul·vil·lus (pŭl-vĭl′əs) *n., pl.* **-villi** (-vĭl′ī′). Any of the soft, cushionlike pads between the claws of an insect's foot. [Latin, diminutive of *pulvīnus*†, cushion.]

pul·vi·nate (pŭl′və-nāt′) *adj.* Also **pul·vi·nat·ed** (-nā′tĭd). **1.** Having a convex face. Said of a frieze. **2.** *Botany.* Having a swelling at the base. Said of a leafstalk. [Latin *pulvīnātus,* from PULVINUS.]

pul·vi·nus (pŭl-vī′nəs) *n., pl.* **-ni** (-nī′). *Botany.* A swelling of the stem at the base of a leafstalk. [Latin *pulvīnus*†, cushion.]

pu·ma (pyōō′mə) *n.* A large American wild cat, *Panthera concolor* (or *Felis concolor*), resembling a short-legged lioness; mountain lion. Also called "cougar." [Spanish, from Quechua.]

pum·ice (pŭm′ĭs) *n.* A porous, lightweight volcanic rock with the same composition as rhyolite, often used as an abrasive. Also called "pumice stone."
~tr.v. **pumiced, -icing, -ices.** To clean, polish, or smooth with pumice. [Middle English *pomys,* from Old French *pomis,* from Latin *pūmex.*] **—pu·mi·ceous** (pyōō-mĭsh′əs) *adj.* **—pum·ic·er** *n.*

pum·mel (pŭm′əl) *tr.v.* **-meled, -meling, -mels.** Also *chiefly British* **-melled, -melling.** To beat or hit with the fists; pommel.
~n. An act of pummeling. [From POMMEL (originally, to beat with the pommel of a sword).]

pump¹ (pŭmp) *n.* A machine or device for transferring a liquid or gas from a source or container through tubes or pipes to another container or receiver.
~v. **pumped, pumping, pumps.** *—tr.* **1.** To raise or cause to flow

by means of a pump. **2.** To inflate with gas by means of a pump. Often used with *up.* **3.** To remove the water from. Often used with *out.* **4.** To cause to operate with the up-and-down motion of a pump handle. **5.** To propel, eject, or insert with a pump. **6.** *Physics.* To supply (a laser) with sufficient energy to achieve population inversion. **7.** *Informal.* **a.** To question closely or persistently for information. **b.** To gain or force (information) from a person by persistent questioning: *They pumped the truth from him.* **8. a.** To fill with a steady stream of something, such as bullets or information. **b.** To supply or fill somebody or something with (a steady flow of something): *pumped money into the project.* —*intr.* **1.** To operate a pump. **2.** To raise or move gas or liquid with a pump. **3.** To gush or flow, especially in regular spurts. **4.** To move up and down in the manner of a pump handle. [Middle English *pumpe, pompe* (nautical use), from Middle Low German *pumpe* or Middle Dutch *pompe,* probably imitative.] —**pump·er** *n.*

pump² *n.* **1.** A low-heeled woman's shoe with no fastenings. **2.** A light shoe used for dancing and certain sports. [16th century.]

pum·per·nick·el (pŭm′pər-nĭk′əl) *n.* A dark, sourish bread made from whole, coarsely ground rye. [German *Pumpernickel* : early New High German *Pumpern,* a fart (imitative) + *Nickel,* "devil," general pejorative (see **nickel**); so named from being hard to digest.]

pump gun *n.* A gun or rifle that may be reloaded by means of a sliding magazine under the barrel.

pump·kin (pŭmp′kĭn, pŭm′-, pŭng′-) *n.* **1.** A coarse, trailing vine, *Cucurbita pepo,* cultivated for its fruit. **2.** The large, round fruit of this vine, with thick, orange-yellow rind, orange, pulpy flesh, and many seeds. **3.** Either of two similar vines, *C. maxima* or *C. moschata,* bearing large, pumpkinlike squashes. [Variant (influenced by -KIN) of earlier *pumpion, pompon,* from Old French *popon, pompon,* from Latin *pepō,* from Greek *pepōn,* a large melon (edible only when ripe), from *pepōn,* ripe, from *peptein,* to cook, ripen.]

pump·kin·seed (pŭmp′kĭn-sēd′, pŭm′-, pŭng′-) *n.* **1.** The seed of the pumpkin. **2.** A North American sunfish, *Lepomis gibbosus,* having brightly colored markings.

pun (pŭn) *n.* A play on words, sometimes on different senses of the same word and sometimes on the similar sense or sound of different words; for example, words of the dying Mercutio in *Romeo and Juliet: "Ask for me tomorrow, and you shall find me a grave man."* ~*intr.v.* **punned, punning, puns.** To make a pun or puns. [Probably short for obsolete *pundigrion,* perhaps a fanciful alteration of Italian *puntiglio,* "fine point," diminutive of *punto,* POINT.] —**pun·ning·ly** *adv.*

pu·na (po͞o′nə) *n.* **1.** A high, dry, bleak plateau within the Andes of Bolivia or Peru, sparsely covered with coarse grasses and stunted shrubs. **2.** The vegetation of a puna. [Quechua.]

punch¹ (pŭnch) *n.* **1.** A tool for making holes in a material: *a leather punch.* **2.** A tool for forcing a pin, bolt, or rivet in or out of a hole. **3.** A tool for stamping a design on a surface. **4.** A **countersink** *(see).* **5.** A device for punching cards *(card punch)* or paper tape *(tape punch)* for use in a computer.
~*v.* **punched, punching, punches.** —*tr.* To use a punch on. —*intr.* To use a punch. [Short for PUNCHEON (punching tool).]

punch² *tr.v.* **punched, punching, punches. 1.** To hit with a sharp blow of the fist. **2.** To poke or prod with a stick. **3.** *Western U.S.* To herd (cattle), especially as a profession.
~*n.* **1.** A blow with the fist. **2.** *Informal.* Vigor or forcefulness: *His writing lacks punch.* —**pull one's punches.** *Informal.* **1.** To hold back deliberately from giving full force to one's blows. **2.** To lessen deliberately the full impact of one's words; especially, to not be outspoken in one's criticism. [Middle English *punchen,* variant of *pounsen,* POUNCE (to perforate).] —**punch·er** *n.*

punch³ *n.* A mixed drink consisting of fruit juices, water, sugar, spices, or the like, usually with a wine or spirit base, and often hot. [Perhaps from Hindi *pānch,* from Sanskrit *pañca,* five (originally prepared with five ingredients).]

Punch *n.* The quarrelsome hook-nosed husband of **Judy** *(see)* in the comic puppet show, *Punch and Judy.* —**pleased as Punch.** Highly pleased; gratified. [Short for PUNCHINELLO.]

punch·ball (pŭnch′bôl′) *n.* **1.** A small inflated bag or ball, usually of leather, either suspended from above or supported on a springy pole and designed to be punched with the fists for exercise or boxing training. **2.** A punching bag.

punch bowl *n.* A large bowl from which punch or other drinks may be served by means of a ladle.

punch card *n.* Also **punched card.** A card punched with holes or notches to represent letters and numbers or with a pattern of holes to represent related data, for use in a computer.

punch-drunk (pŭnch′drŭngk′) *adj.* **1.** Suffering from the effects of repeated blows on the head. **2.** Acting in a dazed manner.

punched tape *n.* Also **punch tape.** Paper tape in which holes are punched to represent data to be processed by a computer.

pun·cheon¹ (pŭn′chən) *n.* **1.** A short, wooden upright used in structural framing. **2.** A piece of broad, heavy timber, roughly dressed, with one face finished flat. **3.** A punching, perforating, or stamping tool, especially one used by a goldsmith. [Middle English *ponchon, pons(y)on,* a sharp tool, from Old French *po(i)nchon, poinçon,* from Vulgar Latin *punctiō* (unattested), from *punctiāre* (unattested), to pierce, prick, from Latin *pungere* (past participle *punctus*), to prick.]

puncheon² *n.* **1.** A cask with a capacity of 84 U.S. gallons. **2.** This specific volume of liquid used as a measure. [Old French *po(i)nçon, po(i)nchon*†.]

Pun·chi·nel·lo (pŭn′chə-nĕl′ō) *n., pl.* **-los** or **-loes. 1.** The short, fat, comic-looking character in an Italian puppet show and probable prototype of the English Punch. **2.** A person thought to resemble this puppet. [Variant of earlier *policinello,* from Italian dialectal (Neapolitan) *polecenella,* perhaps diminutive of *polecena,* young turkey cock (from the puppet's beaklike nose), from *pulcino,* chicken, from Late Latin *pullicenus,* diminutive of Latin *pullus,* PULLET.]

punching bag *n.* A large, heavy, stuffed bag, usually of canvas, suspended from above and designed to be punched with the fists for exercise or boxing training.

punch line *n.* The line or part of a joke or humorous story that gives the point of the whole and causes amusement.

punch press *n.* A power press fitted with punches and dies for cutting, forming, or imprinting metal, plastic, or the like.

punch-up (pŭnch′ŭp′) *n. Chiefly British Slang.* A fistfight.

punch·y (pŭn′chē) *adj.* **-ier, -iest.** *Informal.* **1.** Having force, vigor, or zest: *a punchy ad.* **2.** Punch-drunk. —**punch·i·ly** *adv.*

punc·tate (pŭngk′tāt′) *adj.* Also **punc·tat·ed** (-tā′tĭd). Having tiny spots, points, or depressions. [New Latin *punctatus,* from Latin *punctum,* pricked mark, POINT.] —**punc·ta·tion** *n.*

punc·til·i·o (pŭngk-tĭl′ē-ō) *n., pl.* **-tilios. 1.** A fine or petty point of etiquette. **2.** Precise observance of formalities or etiquette. [Italian *puntiglio,* "fine point," diminutive of *punto,* POINT.]

punc·til·i·ous (pŭngk-tĭl′ē-əs) *adj.* **1.** Attentive to the finer points of etiquette and formal conduct. **2.** Showing attention to detail; precise; scrupulous. —See Synonyms at **meticulous.** [French *pointilleux,* from *pointille,* "fine point," from Italian. See **punctilio.**] —**punc·til·i·ous·ly** *adv.* —**punc·til·i·ous·ness** *n.*

punc·tu·al (pŭngk′cho͞o-əl) *adj.* **1. a.** Acting or arriving exactly at the time appointed; prompt. **b.** Always observant of or keeping to appointed times. **2.** Paid or accomplished at or by the appointed time. **3.** Precise; exact. **4.** Confined to or being a point in space. [Middle English, from Medieval Latin *punctuālis,* "to the point," from Latin *punctum,* pricked mark, POINT.] —**punc·tu·al·i·ty, punc·tu·al·ness** *n.* —**punc·tu·al·ly** *adv.*

punc·tu·ate (pŭngk′cho͞o-āt′) *v.* **-ated, -ating, -ates.** —*tr.* **1.** To provide (a text) with punctuation marks. **2.** To interrupt periodically. **3.** To stress; emphasize. —*intr.* To use punctuation. [Medieval Latin *punctuāre,* to mark with a point, punctuate, from Latin *punctum,* pricked mark, point, from the past participle of *pungere,* to prick, pierce.] —**punc·tu·a·tive** *adj.* —**punc·tu·a·tor** *n.*

punc·tu·a·tion (pŭngk′cho͞o-ā′shən) *n.* **1.** The use of standard marks and signs in writing and printing to separate words into sentences, clauses, and phrases in order to clarify meaning, give intonation, or provide emphasis. **2.** The marks so used. **3.** An act or instance of punctuating.

punctuation mark *n.* Any of a set of marks or signs used to punctuate texts; for example, the comma (,) or the period (.).

punc·ture (pŭngk′chər) *v.* **-tured, -turing, -tures.** —*tr.* **1.** To pierce with a pointed object. **2.** To make (a hole) by piercing. **3.** To cause to collapse by piercing. **4.** To depreciate; deflate: *She punctured his ego.* —*intr.* To be pierced or punctured.
~*n.* **1.** An act or instance of puncturing. **2.** A hole or depression made by a sharp object; especially, a hole in a pneumatic tire. [Middle English, from Latin *punctūra,* a pricking, puncture, from *pungere* (past participle *punctus*), to prick.] —**punc·tur·a·ble** *adj.*

pun·dit (pŭn′dĭt) *n.* Also **pan·dit** (păn′-) (for sense 1). **1.** A Brahmanic scholar, learned in Sanskrit and in Hindu philosophy, religion, and law. **2.** A learned person or a person who claims to be an expert. [Hindi *paṇḍit,* from Sanskrit *paṇḍita,* a learned man, from Dravidian (akin to Telegu *paṇḍa,* wisdom).] —**pun·dit·ry** *n.*

pung (pŭng) *n.* A low box sleigh drawn by one horse. [Shortened from *tom-pong, tow-pong,* of Algonquian origin, akin to TOBOGGAN.]

pun·gent (pŭn′jənt) *adj.* **1.** Having a sharp, acid taste or smell. **2.** Penetrating; biting; caustic: *pungent satire.* **3.** *Biology.* Pointed: *a pungent leaf.* [Latin *pungēns* (stem *pungent-*), present participle of *pungere,* to prick, sting.] —**pun·gen·cy** *n.* —**pun·gent·ly** *adv.*

Pu·nic (pyo͞o′nĭk) *adj.* **1.** Of or pertaining to ancient Carthage or its people. **2.** Having the characteristic of treachery attributed to the Carthaginians by the Romans.
~*n.* The West Semitic language of ancient Carthage, a dialect of Phoenician. [Latin *Pūnicus,* earlier *Poenicus,* from *Poenus,* a Carthaginian, from Greek *Phoinix,* Phoenician.]

Punic Wars *pl.n.* Three wars waged by Rome against Carthage (264–241, 218–201, and 149–146 B.C.) in which Rome finally defeated Carthage and annexed its territory.

pun·ish (pŭn′ĭsh) *v.* **-ished, -ishing, -ishes.** —*tr.* **1.** To subject (a person) to a penalty, such as imprisonment, a fine, or a beating, for a crime, fault, offense, or misbehavior. **2.** To inflict a penalty on a criminal or wrongdoer for (a crime or offense, for example). **3.** To handle roughly; injure; hurt. **4.** *Informal.* To deplete (a stock or supply) heavily. —*intr.* To give punishment. [Middle English *punissen, punyschen,* from Old French *punir* (stem *puniss-*), from Latin *pūnīre, poenīre,* from *poena,* penalty, punishment, from Greek *poinē.*] —**pun·ish·er** *n.* —**pun·ish·ing·ly** *adv.*
Synonyms: *castigate, chastise, discipline, penalize.*

pun·ish·a·ble (pŭn′ĭsh-ə-bəl) *adj.* Liable to punishment.

pun·ish·ment (pŭn′ĭsh-mənt) *n.* **1. a.** An act of punishing. **b.** The condition of being punished. **2.** A penalty imposed for wrongdoing, as for a crime or offense. **3.** *Informal.* Rough handling.

pu·ni·tive (pyo͞o′nə-tĭv) *adj.* Inflicting or aiming to inflict punishment; punishing. [French *punitif,* from Medieval Latin *pūnītīvus,*

PRONUNCIATION KEY

ă, pat; ā, pay; âr, care; ä, father, are; b, bib; ch, church; d, deed; ĕ, pet; ē, be; f, fife; g, gag; h, hat; hw, which; ĭ, pit; ī, pie; îr, pier; j, judge; k, kick; l, lid, needle; m, mum; n, no, sudden; ng, thing; ŏ, pot; ō, toe; ô, paw, for; oi, noise; ou, out; o͝o, book; o͞o, boot; p, pop; r, roar; s, sauce; sh, ship, dish; t, tight; th, thin, path; *th*, this, bathe; ŭ, cut; ûr, fur; v, valve; w, with; y, yes; z, zebra, size; zh, vision; ə, about, item, edible, gallop, circus, peaceful

IN FOREIGN WORDS:

à, *Fr.* ami; œ, *Fr.* feu, *Ger.* schön; ü, *Fr.* tu, *Ger.* über; KH, *Ger.* ich, *Scot.* loch; N, *Fr.* bon; y′, *Fr.* Compiègne

STRESS MARKS:

Primary stress: ′ **in·cite′** (ĭn-sīt′)
Secondary stress: ′ **in′sight′** (ĭn′sīt′)

from Latin *pūnīre* (past participle *pūnītus*), PUNISH.] **—pu·ni·tive·ly** *adv.* **—pu·ni·tive·ness** *n.*

punitive damages *pl.n.* Damages awarded by a court to a plaintiff as additional punishment to a defendant for a serious wrong.

Pun·jab (pŭn-jäb′, -jăb′). Region of the northwestern Indian subcontinent. It was ruled by the Sikhs until annexation by the British (1849) and was divided along religious lines in 1947. West Punjab passed to Pakistan and is now the province of Punjab. East Punjab remained Indian and was further divided (1966) into linguistic areas to form the present Indian states of Punjab and Haryana.

Pun·ja·bi (pŭn-jä′bē, -jăb′ē) *n.* Also **Pan·ja·bi** (for sense 2). **1.** A native or inhabitant of Punjab. **2.** The Indic language spoken in Punjab, belonging to the Indo-European family. **—Pun·ja·bi** *adj.*

punk¹ (pŭngk) *n.* **1.** A youth culture that developed in Britain in the late 1970's among fans of punk rock, characterized by a rejection of middle-class values and standard pop culture, and the adoption of a deliberately aggressive and outrageous personal appearance, often involving startling make-up and hairstyles, and leather clothing. **2.** A young person belonging to this culture. **3.** Punk rock. [Shortened from *punk rock(er).*]

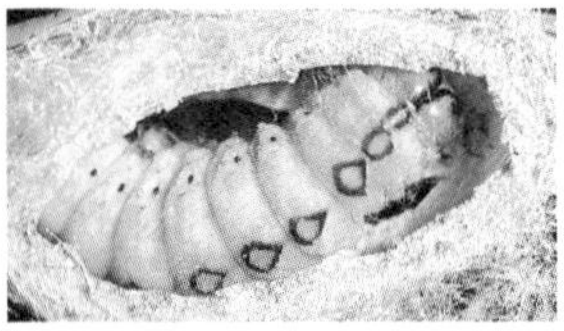

pupa *A caterpillar building the cocoon in which it will pupate, or undergo the transformation to adult. The pupa is the third stage—egg, larva, pupa, adult—in the metamorphic life cycle of insects such as bees, moths, and butterflies.*

punk² *n.* **1.** Dry, decayed wood, used as tinder. **2.** Any of various substances that smolder when ignited, used to light fireworks. **3. a.** An object of little value or poor quality. **b.** Such objects collectively; rubbish. **4.** *Slang.* Any disreputable or worthless person. **5.** *Slang.* **a.** A young ruffian or petty criminal. **b.** An inexperienced or callow youth.
~*adj. Slang.* Of poor quality; worthless. [18th century.]

pun·ka, pun·kah (pŭng′kə) *n.* A fan used especially in India, made of a palm frond or strip of cloth hung from the ceiling and moved manually or by machine. [Hindi *pankhā*, from Sanskrit *pakṣaka*, fan, from *pakṣa*, shoulder, wing.]

punk rock *n.* A type of rock music that developed in the late 1970's, characterized by a spirit of aggression and defiance embodied typically in loud, raucous singing, offensive lyrics, and driving rhythms. [PUNK (worthless, rotten) + ROCK (music).] **—punk rocker** *n.*

pun·net (pŭn′ĭt) *n. British.* A small, square basket used for holding soft fruit. [Perhaps diminutive of dialect *pun*, POUND (weight).]

pun·ster (pŭn′stər) *n.* A maker of puns.

punt¹ (pŭnt) *n.* An open, flat-bottomed boat with squared ends, propelled by a long pole and used in shallow waters.
~*v.* **punted, punting, punts.** *—tr.* **1.** To propel (a boat) with a pole. **2.** To carry in a punt. *—intr.* **1.** To propel a punt. **2.** To travel in a punt as a leisure activity. [Middle Low German *punte, punto*, ferryboat, from Latin *pontō*, a Gaulish vessel, apparently from *pōns* (stem *pont-*), bridge.] **—punt·er** *n.*

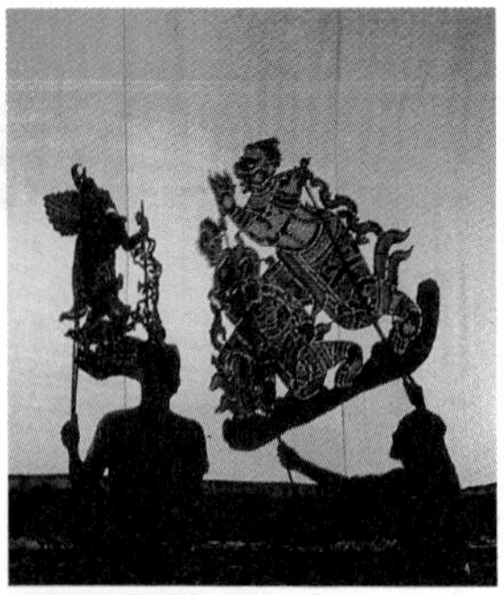

puppet *Richly painted two-dimensional puppets are operated by rods in a Javanese shadow play. This type of puppet theater was developed in Java about 1,000 years ago, and the puppets enact scenes from Indian and Javanese mythology.*

punt² *n. Football.* A kick in which the ball is dropped from the hands and kicked before it touches the ground.
~*v.* **punted, punting, punts.** *—tr.* To propel (a football) by means of a punt. *—intr.* To execute a punt. [Probably from dialectal *bunt, punt*†, to push, kick.]

punt³ *intr.v.* **punted, punting, punts.** **1.** In gambling games such as roulette or faro, to lay a bet against the bank. **2. a.** To gamble; bet. **b.** To bet on a horse race. [French *ponter*, from *ponte*, bet against the banker, from Spanish *punto*, "point," "ace," from Latin *punctum*, POINT.] **—punt·er** *n.*

punt⁴ *n.* **1.** The basic monetary unit of the Republic of Ireland, equal to 100 pence or pighne. See feature at **currency. 2.** A note worth one punt. Also called "pound."

Pun·ta A·re·nas (po͝on′tə ə-rā′nəs). The world's southernmost city, on the Strait of Magellan in Chile. It is an oil port, with military and naval installations, and a tourist center.

pun·ty (pŭn′tē) *n., pl.* **-ties.** In glassmaking, an iron rod on which molten glass is handled. Also called "pontil." [Variant of PONTIL.]

pu·ny (pyo͞o′nē) *adj.* **-nier, -niest. 1.** Of inferior size, strength, or significance; weak. **2.** Feeble; ineffectual: *a puny attempt.* [Phonetic spelling of PUISNE, from Old French "born afterward" : *puis*, afterward, from Vulgar Latin *postius* (unattested), comparative of Latin *post*, after + *ne*, born, from Latin *nātus*, past participle of *nāscī*, to be born.] **—pu·ni·ly** *adv.* **—pu·ni·ness** *n.*

pup (pŭp) *n.* **1.** A young dog; a puppy. **2.** The young of certain other animals, such as the seal. **3.** *British Informal.* An insolent person. **4.** *Informal.* An object or item that turns out to be worthless or inferior. Used chiefly in such phrases as *buy a pup* or *be sold a pup.* **—in pup.** Pregnant. Said of a bitch.
~*intr.v.* **pupped, pupping, pups.** To give birth to pups. [Backformation from PUPPY.]

pu·pa (pyo͞o′pə) *n., pl.* **-pae** (-pē′) or **-pas.** The nonmobile stage in the metamorphosis of many insects, following the larval stage and preceding the adult form, during which many internal changes occur. Compare **nymph.** [New Latin *pupa*, from Latin *pūpa*, girl, doll, feminine of *pūpus*, boy.] **—pu·pal** *adj.*

pu·pate (pyo͞o′pāt′) *intr.v.* **-pated, -pating, -pates.** To become a pupa. **—pu·pa·tion** (pyo͞o-pā′shən) *n.*

pu·pil¹ (pyo͞o′pəl) *n.* **1.** A student under the direct supervision of a teacher. **2.** *Law.* A minor under the supervision of a guardian. [Middle English *pupille*, orphan, ward, (hence) pupil, from Old French, from Latin *pūpillus*, diminutive of *pūpus*, boy.]

pupil² *n.* The apparently black circular aperture in the center of the iris of the eye through which light passes to the retina. [Middle English *pupilla* and Old French *pupille*, both from Latin *pūpilla*, "little orphan girl," pupil (by analogy with Greek *korē*, little girl, doll, pupil of the eye, originally referring to the miniature reflections that can be seen by looking closely at another's eye), feminine of *pūpillus*, PUPIL.]

pu·pil·age, pu·pil·lage (pyo͞o′pə-lĭj) *n.* **1.** The state or period of being a pupil. **2. a.** The practical training received by an inexperienced barrister in the chambers of an experienced barrister. **b.** The period of time spent in such training.

pu·pil·lar·y¹, pu·pi·lar·y (pyo͞o′pə-lĕr′ē) *adj.* Of or pertaining to a ward or a student.

pupillary², pupilary *adj.* Of or affecting the pupil of the eye.

pu·pip·a·rous (pyo͞o-pĭp′ər-əs) *adj.* Producing well-developed young that are ready to pupate. [PUPA + -PAROUS.]

pup·pet (pŭp′ĭt) *n.* **1.** A small figure of a person or animal, having jointed parts animated from above by strings or wires; a marionette. **2.** A similar figure having a cloth body and hollow head, designed to be fitted over and manipulated by the hand or finger. **3.** A toy representing a human figure; a doll. **4.** A person or group whose behavior is determined by the will of others.
~*adj.* **1.** Of or pertaining to puppets. **2.** Sponsored and controlled by another or others while professing autonomy: *a puppet state.* [Middle English *popet, popette*, small child, doll, from Old French *poupette*, diminutive of *poupe* (unattested), doll, from Vulgar Latin *puppa* (unattested), doll, from Latin *pūpa. See* **pupa.**]

pup·pet·eer (pŭp′ĭ-tîr′) *n.* A person who operates and entertains with puppets or marionettes.

pup·pet·ry (pŭp′ĭ-trē) *n., pl.* **-ries. 1.** The art of making puppets and presenting puppet shows. **2.** The actions of puppets. **3.** Stilted or artificial dramatic performance.

Pup·pis (pŭp′ĭs) *n.* A constellation in the Southern Hemisphere near Canis Major and Pyxis. [Latin, "the ship," from *puppis*, POOP (stern).]

pup·py (pŭp′ē) *n., pl.* **-pies. 1.** A young dog; a pup. **2.** A conceited or inexperienced youth. [Middle English *popi*, from Old French *po(u)pee*, doll, toy, plaything, from Vulgar Latin *puppa* (unattested). See **puppet.**] **—pup·py·ish** *adj.*

puppy fat *n.* The fatty tissue or fat appearance of a child or adolescent. It usually becomes less noticeable with age.

puppy love *n.* Adolescent love or infatuation.

pup tent *n.* A **shelter tent** *(see).*

Pur·beck marble (pûr′bĕk′) *n.* A nonmarine marble, used in architecture and sculpture on account of its high gloss. [After Isle of *Purbeck*, Dorset, England, the peninsula where it is quarried.]

pur·blind (pûr′blīnd′) *adj.* **1.** Having poor vision; nearly or partly blind. **2.** Slow in understanding or discernment; dull. [Middle English *pur(e)blind*, originally "totally blind" : PURE (completely) + BLIND.] **—pur·blind·ly** *adv.* **—pur·blind·ness** *n.*

Pur·cell (pûr′səl), **Henry** (1659–95). English composer. As organist at Westminster Abbey and composer to the Chapel Royal, he was the leading musical figure of Restoration England.

pur·chas·a·ble (pûr′chĭ-sə-bəl) *adj.* **1.** Capable of being bought. **2.** Capable of being bribed; venal. **—pur·chas·a·bil·i·ty** *n.*

pur·chase (pûr′chĭs) *tr.v.* **-chased, -chasing, -chases. 1.** To obtain in exchange for money or its equivalent; buy. **2.** To acquire by effort; earn. **3.** *Law.* To acquire (property) legally by means other than inheritance. **4.** To raise, haul, or hold with a mechanical device such as a lever or wrench.
~*n.* **1.** That which is bought. **2. a.** The act of buying. **b.** Acquisition through the payment of money or its equivalent. **3.** *Law.* **a.** The acquisition of property other than by inheritance. **b.** Annual rent or income, especially from land. **4.** A grip applied manually or mechanically to move something or prevent it from slipping. **5.** A tackle, lever, or other device used to obtain mechanical advantage. **6.** A position, as of a lever or one's feet, affording means to move or secure a weight. **7.** Any means of increasing power, influence, or advantage. [Middle English *po(u)rchasen*, from Old French *po(u)rchacier, purchacier*, to pursue, seek to obtain : *po(u)r-*, for, from Latin *prō* + *chacier*, to CHASE.] **—pur·chas·er** *n.*

purchasing agent *n. Abbr.* **P.A.** A person acting as another's agent in making purchases.

purchasing power *n.* **1.** The ability of a person or group to purchase, generally measured by income. **2.** The value of a particular monetary unit in terms of the goods or services it will buy.

pur·dah (pûr′də) *n.* **1.** A curtain used to screen Hindu or Muslim women from men or strangers, especially in India. **2.** In India, the system of secluding women, especially of high rank, from public view. **3.** Seclusion or ostracism resulting from embarrassment or disgrace. Used humorously: *After his blunder, he was in purdah for weeks.* [Hindi *pardā*, screen, veil, from Persian *pardah*†.]

pure (pyo͝or) *adj.* **purer, purest. 1.** Having a homogeneous or uniform composition; not mixed: *pure oxygen.* **2.** Free from adulterants or impurities; full-strength: *pure chocolate.* **3.** Free from dirt, defilement, or pollution; clean. **4.** Free from foreign elements: *keeping the language pure.* **5.** Containing nothing inappropriate or extraneous: *a pure production of Hamlet.* **6. a.** Complete: *by pure chance.* **b.** Thorough; utter: *pure folly.* **7.** Without faults; perfect; sinless. **8.** Chaste; virgin. **9.** Of unmixed blood or ancestry. **10.** *Genetics.* Breeding true to parental type; homozygous: *a pure line.* **11.** *Music.* Free from discordant qualities. **12.** *Phonetics.* Articulated with a single unchanging speech sound; monophthongal: *a pure vowel.* **13.** Theoretical rather than applied: *pure science.* **14.** *Philosophy.* Free from empirical elements: *pure reason.* [Middle English *pur, pure*, from Old French *pur* (feminine *pure*), from Latin *pūrus*, clean.] **—pure·ness** *n.*

pure·bred (pyo͝or′brĕd′) *adj.* Of a strain established through breeding many generations of unmixed stock. **—pure·bred** (pyo͝or′brĕd′) *n.*

pu·rée (pyo͝o-rā′, pyo͝or′ā) *tr.v.* **puréed, -réeing, -rées.** To convert (vegetables or fruit, for example) to a semisolid state, as by cooking and pressing through a strainer.
~n. Food so prepared. [French, from Old French *purer,* to purify, strain, from Latin *pūrāre,* to purify, from *pūrus,* PURE.]

Pure Land Buddhism *n.* A form of Buddhism widely followed in Japan, which teaches salvation through faith in and the calling on the name of the Buddha Amida. Also called "Jodo."

pure·ly (pyo͝or′lē) *adv.* **1.** In a pure manner. **2.** Innocently; chastely. **3.** Totally; entirely: *purely by chance.*

pur·fle (pûr′fəl) *tr.v.* **-fled, -fling, -fles.** To finish or decorate the border or edge of (a table or violin, for example).
~n. Also **pur·fling** (-flĭng). An ornamental border or edging. [Middle English *purfilen,* from Old French *porfiler,* to weave, from Vulgar Latin *prōfīlāre* (unattested), to draw in outline : Latin *prō,* forth, out + *fīlum,* thread.]

pur·ga·tion (pûr-gā′shən) *n.* The act of purging or purifying.

pur·ga·tive (pûr′gə-tĭv) *adj.* Tending to cleanse or purge.
~n. Medicine. A purgative agent, a **laxative** *(see).*

pur·ga·to·ri·al (pûr′gə-tôr′ē-əl, -tōr′ē-əl) *adj.* **1.** Serving to purify of sin; expiatory. **2.** Of, pertaining to, or resembling purgatory.

pur·ga·to·ry (pûr′gə-tôr′ē, -tōr′ē) *n., pl.* **-ries. 1.** *Roman Catholic Church.* A state in which the souls of those who have died in grace must expiate venial sins. **2.** Any place or condition of expiation, suffering, or remorse.
~adj. Tending to cleanse or purge. [Middle English *purgatorie,* from Medieval Latin *purgātōrium,* from Late Latin *purgātōrius,* from Latin *purgāre,* to PURGE.]

purge (pûrj) *v.* **purged, purging, purges.** *—tr.* **1. a.** To free from impurities; purify. **b.** To remove (impurities and other elements) by or as if by cleansing. **2.** To rid of sin, guilt, or defilement. **3.** *Law.* **a.** To clear (a person) of a charge or imputation. **b.** To atone for (an offense) by being punished. **4.** To rid (a nation, political party, or other group) of persons considered to be undesirable. **5.** *Medicine.* **a.** To cause evacuation of (the bowels). **b.** To induce evacuation of the bowels in (a patient). *—intr.* **1.** To become pure or clean. **2.** To undergo or cause an emptying of the bowels.
~n. **1.** The act or process of purging. **2.** Something that purges; especially, a medicinal purgative. **3.** The ridding of dissidents and others considered undesirable from a government, political party, or the like. [Middle English *purgen,* from Old French *purger,* from Latin *purgāre, pūrigāre* (unattested), to cleanse : *pūrus,* PURE + *agere,* to lead.] **—purg·er** *n.*

puri. Variant of **poori.**

Pu·ri (po͝or′ē). Seaport in Orissa, east-central India. It is a major center of pilgrimage for Hindus.

pu·ri·fi·ca·tor (pyo͝or′ə-fĭ-kā′tər) *n.* A cloth used to clean the chalice and paten and the lips and fingers of the celebrant at the Eucharist.

pu·ri·fy (pyo͝or′ə-fī′) *v.* **-fied, -fying, -fies.** *—tr.* **1.** To rid of impurities; cleanse. **2.** To rid of foreign or objectionable elements. **3.** To free from sin, guilt, or other defilement. *—intr.* To become clean or pure. [Middle English *purifien,* from Old French *purifier,* from Latin *pūrificāre,* to make pure : *pūrus,* PURE + *facere,* to make.] **—pu·ri·fi·ca·tion** (pyo͝or′ə-fĭ-kā′shən) *n.* **—pu·rif·i·ca·to·ry** (pyo͞o-rĭf′ĭ-kə-tôr′ē, -tōr′ē) *adj.* **—pu·ri·fi·er** *n.*

Pu·rim (po͝or′ĭm; *Hebrew* po͞o-rēm′) *n. Judaism.* A holiday in the month of Adar, celebrating the deliverance of the Jews from the threatened massacre by Haman. Esther 9:20–22. [Hebrew *pūrīm,* plural of *pūr,* lot (from the lots cast by Haman to determine the day of destruction of the Jews), from Akkadian *pūru,* stone.]

pu·rine (pyo͝or′ēn′) *n.* **1.** A colorless crystalline compound, $C_5H_4N_4$, used in organic synthesis and metabolism studies. **2.** Any of a group of naturally occurring organic compounds derived from or having molecular structures related to purine, including uric acid, adenine, guanine, and caffeine. [German *Purin* : blend of Latin *pūrus,* PURE + New Latin *uricus,* URIC (ACID) (in which it is found) + -INE.]

pur·ism (pyo͝or′ĭz′əm) *n.* Strict observance of or insistence upon traditional correctness, especially of language. [French *purisme,* from *pur,* PURE.]

pur·ist (pyo͝or′ĭst) *n.* One who practices or urges strict correctness, especially in the use of words.

pu·ris·tic (pyo͞o-rĭs′tĭk) *adj.* **1.** Characterized by purism. **2. Puristic.** Of or pertaining to Katharevousa. **—pu·ris·ti·cal·ly** *adv.*

Pu·ri·tan (pyo͝or′ə-tən) *n.* **1.** A member of a group of English Protestants who, in the 16th and 17th centuries, after the Reformation, sought further simplification of the ceremonies and creeds of the Church of England and strict religious discipline. **2. puritan.** One who lives in accordance with the precepts of the Puritans; especially, one who regards luxury or pleasure as sinful.
~adj. **1.** Of or pertaining to the Puritans or Puritanism. **2. puritan.** Characteristic of a puritan; puritanical. [Late Latin *pūritās,* purity, from *pūrus,* PURE, by analogy with *Catharan,* CATHAR.]

pu·ri·tan·i·cal (pyo͝or′ə-tăn′ĭ-kəl) *adj.* Also **pu·ri·tan·ic** (-tăn′ĭk). **1.** Rigorous in religious observance; marked by stern morality. **2. Puritanical.** Of, pertaining to, or characteristic of the Puritans. **—pu·ri·tan·i·cal·ly** *adv.* **—pu·ri·tan·i·cal·ness** *n.*

Pu·ri·tan·ism (pyo͝or′ə-tə-nĭz′əm) *n.* **1.** The practices and doctrines of the Puritans. **2. puritanism.** Scrupulous moral rigor; especially, hostility to social pleasures and indulgences.

pu·ri·ty (pyo͝or′ə-tē) *n.* **1.** The quality or condition of being pure. **2.** *Physics.* The proportion of a single-frequency spectral component in a mixture of achromatic and spectral colors.

purl[1] (pûrl) *intr.v.* **purled, purling, purls.** To flow or ripple with a murmuring sound. Used chiefly of water.
~n. The motion or sound made by rippling water. [16th century : probably imitative; akin to Norwegian *purla*†.]

purl[2] *v.* **purled, purling, purls.** Also **pearl** (for transitive sense 2 and intransitive sense 2). *—tr.* **1.** To knit with a purl stitch. **2.** To edge or finish with lace or embroidery. *—intr.* **1.** To do knitting with a purl stitch. **2.** To edge or finish with lace or embroidery.
~n. Also **pearl** (for senses 2 and 3). *Abbr.* **p. 1.** The inversion of a knit stitch; a purl stitch. **2.** A decorative edging of lace or embroidery. **3.** Gold or silver wire used in embroidery. [Earlier *pirl*†; perhaps akin to PURL (ripple).]

purl·er (pûr′lər) *n.* Also **pearl·er** (for sense 2). *Informal.* **1.** *British.* **a.** A blow throwing one forward. **b.** A headlong fall. Used chiefly in the phrases *come a purler* or *take a purler.* **2.** *Australian.* One that is outstanding or excellent.

pur·lieu (pûrl′yo͞o, pûr′lo͞o) *n.* **1.** Any outlying or neighboring area; specifically, in former times, land beyond the perimeter of a forest but still partly subject to hunting laws. **2. purlieus.** Outskirts; environs. **3.** A place that one frequents. [Middle English *purlewe,* perhaps alteration of Norman French *puralée,* perambulation, from the past participle of Old French *poraler, puraler,* to traverse : *por,* through, from Latin *prō,* forth + *aler,* to go, probably from Vulgar Latin *amlāre* (unattested), from Latin *ambulāre,* to walk.]

pur·lin, pur·line (pûr′lĭn) *n.* Any of several horizontal timbers supporting the rafters of a roof. [Middle English *purly(o)n*†.]

pur·loin (pər-loin′, pûr′loin′) *v.* **-loined, -loining, -loins.** *—tr.* To steal; filch. *—intr.* To commit theft. [Middle English *purloynen,* to remove, from Norman French *purloigner,* "to put far away" : Old French *pur-,* away, from Latin *prō-,* away + *loign,* far, from Latin *longē,* far, from *longus,* long.] **—pur·loin·er** *n.*

purl stitch *n.* An inverted knitting stitch. Also called "purl."

pur·ple (pûr′pəl) *n.* **1.** Any of a group of colors with a hue between that of violet and red. **2.** Cloth of this color, formerly worn as a symbol of royalty or high office. **3.** A pigment or dyeing agent used to produce such cloth. **4.** Imperial, royal, or other high rank. **5.** The cloth worn by or the rank or office of a cardinal or bishop.
~adj. **1.** Of the color purple. **2.** Royal or imperial; regal. **3.** Elaborate and ornate: *purple prose.*
~v. **purpled, -pling, -ples.** *—tr.* To make purple. *—intr.* To become purple. [Middle English *purpel, purpyl,* Old English *purple,* altered by dissimilation from *purpuran,* of purple, from *purpura,* purple cloth, from Latin, purple. See **purpura.**]

purple emperor *n.* A Eurasian butterfly, *Apatura iris,* having a purple sheen on the upper side of the wing in the male.

purple gallinule *n.* **1.** A dark, bluish-purple waterfowl, *Porphyrio porphyrio,* resembling a large moorhen. **2.** A similar American bird, *Porphyrula martinica,* with a blue-purple breast and green back.

purple heart *n.* Also **pur·ple·heart** (pûr′pəl-härt′) (for senses 1, 2). **1.** Any of several tropical American trees of the genus *Peltogyne,* valued for their decorative wood. **2.** The purplish heartwood of any of these trees. **3.** *Chiefly British Informal.* A purple, heart-shaped amphetamine tablet.

Purple Heart *n.* The U.S. Armed Forces medal of the Order of the Purple Heart, awarded to servicemen wounded in action.

purple loosestrife *n.* A marsh plant, *Lythrum salicaria,* having long spikes of purple flowers.

purple martin. A North American bird, *Progne subis,* related to the swallows, having a glossy, blue-black back, and, in the male, a dark breast.

purple patch *n.* **1.** An extravagant, florid, or ornate passage of literary writing. **2.** Broadly, any brief performance that is unusually stylish or effective. Also called "purple passage."

purple salt *n. Chemistry.* **Potassium permanganate** *(see).*

purple sprouting broccoli *n.* See **broccoli.**

pur·plish (pûr′plĭsh) *adj.* Having a somewhat purple tint.

pur·port (pər-pôrt′, -pōrt′, pûr′pôrt′, -pōrt′) *tr.v.* **-ported, -porting, -ports. 1.** To contain the claim or profession (to be or do something). **2.** To have or give the appearance, often falsely, of being, professing, or intending. —See Synonyms at **mean.**
~n. (pûr′pôrt′, -pōrt′). **1.** The apparent meaning; the import or significance. **2.** The purpose or intention. —See Synonyms at **meaning.** [Middle English *purporten,* to imply, from Old French *porporter,* to embody, contain, from Medieval Latin *prōportāre,* to carry forth : Latin *prō,* forth + *portāre,* to carry.] **—pur·port·ed·ly** (pər-pôr′tĭd-lē, pər-pōr′-) *adv.*

pur·pose (pûr′pəs) *n.* **1.** The object toward which one strives or for which something exists; a goal; an aim. **2.** A result or effect that is intended or desired. **3.** Determination; resolution. **4.** The matter at hand; the point at issue: *Let's return to the purpose.* —See Synonyms at **intention. —on purpose.** Deliberately.
~tr.v. **purposed, -posing, -poses.** To intend or resolve to perform or accomplish. [Middle English *porpos, purpos,* from Old French, from *porposer, purposer,* to design, intend, from Latin *prōpōnere* (past participle *prōpositus*), to put forward, PROPOSE.]

pur·pose-built (pûr′pəs-bĭlt′) *adj.* Built specifically for the purpose being served: *a purpose-built ski-resort.*

pur·pose·ful (pûr′pəs-fəl) *adj.* **1.** Having a purpose; intentional. **2.** Having or manifesting purpose; determined. —See Usage note at **purposely. —pur·pose·ful·ly** *adv.* **—pur·pose·ful·ness** *n.*

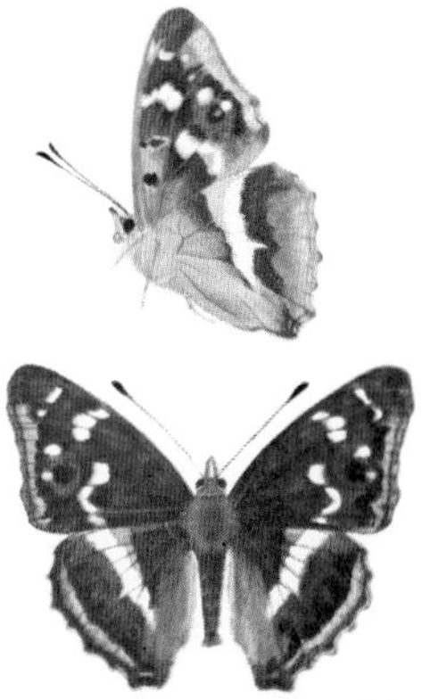

purple emperor *This beautiful woodland butterfly,* Apatura iris, *whose wings are differently colored on top (lower illustration) and underneath (upper illustration), is attracted to carrion, manure, and foul mud—possibly because of the presence of salts.*

PRONUNCIATION KEY

ă, pat; ā, pay; âr, care;
ä, father, are; b, bib;
ch, church; d, deed; ĕ, pet;
ē, be; f, fife; g, gag; h, hat;
hw, which; ĭ, pit; ī, pie;
îr, pier; j, judge; k, kick;
l, lid, needle; m, mum;
n, no, sudden; ng, thing;
ŏ, pot; ō, toe; ô, paw, for;
oi, noise; ou, out; o͝o, book;
o͞o, boot; p, pop; r, roar;
s, sauce; sh, ship, dish;
t, tight; th, thin, path;
th, this, bathe; ŭ, cut; ûr, fur;
v, valve; w, with; y, yes;
z, zebra, size; zh, vision;
ə, about, item, edible,
gallop, circus, peaceful

IN FOREIGN WORDS:

à, *Fr.* ami; œ, *Fr.* feu, *Ger.* schön; ü, *Fr.* tu, *Ger.* über;
KH, *Ger.* ich, *Scot.* loch;
N, *Fr.* bon; y′, *Fr.* Compiègne

STRESS MARKS:

Primary stress: ′
in·cite′ (ĭn-sīt′)
Secondary stress: ′
in′sight′ (ĭn′sīt′)

pur·pose·less (pûr'pəs-lĭs) *adj.* Without any purpose; aimless; pointless. —**pur·pose·less·ly** *adv.* —**pur·pose·less·ness** *n.*
pur·pose·ly (pûr'pəs-lē) *adv.* **1.** With a particular purpose in mind. **2.** On purpose; intentionally.
   Usage: Purposely, purposefully, and purposively are sometimes confused. Of the three, *purposely* is the most general term, meaning "deliberately, on purpose." *Purposefully* adds the nuance of "acting in a determined way," and *purposively* adds the nuance of "acting so as to achieve a particular end." Some contexts allow all three words, but usually a distinction is maintained: *He purposely left the room so I could sleep* and *He purposefully left the room to fetch the papers. Purposively* tends to be restricted to psychological or behavioral description: *This organism acts purposively.*
pur·pos·ive (pûr'pə-sĭv) *adj.* **1.** Having or serving a purpose. **2.** Purposeful as opposed to aimless or random. —See Usage note at **purposely.** —**pur·pos·ive·ly** *adv.* —**pur·pos·ive·ness** *n.*
pur·pu·ra (pûr'pə-rə, -pyə) *n.* A skin rash made up of small purple spots caused by subcutaneous bleeding. [Latin, from Greek *porphura,* purple (dye), shellfish from which it was obtained, from Semitic.]
pur·pure (pûr'pyər) *n. Heraldry.* The color purple. [Old English and Old French *purpre,* from Latin *purpura.* See **purpura.**] —**pur·pure** *adj.*
pur·pur·in (pûr'pyə-rĭn) *n.* A red crystalline derivative of anthraquinone, $C_{14}H_5O_2(OH)_3$, used as a stain in biology. [Latin *purpura,* purple (see **purpura**) + -IN.]
purr (pûr) *n.* **1.** The characteristic softly vibrant sound of a cat, understood to express pleasure or contentment. **2.** Any similar sound, such as the idling of a well-tuned motor car.
—*v.* **purred, purring, purrs.** —*intr.* To emit a purr. —*tr.* To utter or express by means of a purr: *purred their approval.* [Imitative.]
purse (pûrs) *n.* **1.** A small bag or pouch for carrying money, especially coins. **2.** A woman's handbag. **3.** Anything that resembles a bag or pouch. **4.** Available wealth or resources; money. **5.** A sum of money collected as a present or offered as a prize.
—*tr.v.* **pursed, pursing, purses.** To gather or contract (the lips or brow) into wrinkles or folds; pucker. [Middle English *purs,* Old English *purs,* from Late Latin *bursa,* bag, oxhide, from Greek *bursa,* leather, hide.]
purs·er (pûr'sər) *n.* The officer in charge of money matters and welfare of passengers on a ship. [Middle English, from *purs,* PURSE.]
purse seine (sān) *n.* A fishing seine that is pursed or drawn into the shape of a bag to enclose the catch.
purse strings *pl.n.* **1.** The strings that tighten and close the opening of an old-fashioned purse. **2.** Control of finance or money supply.
purs·lane (pûrs'lĭn, -lān') *n.* A trailing weed, *Portulaca oleracea,* having small yellow flowers, reddish stems, and fleshy leaves that are sometimes used in salads. Also called "pussley." [Middle English *purcelan, purslane,* from Old French *porcelaine,* cowrie shell, from Late Latin *porcillāgo,* from Latin *porcil(l)āca, portulāca.*]
pur·su·ance (pər-sōo'əns) *n.* The carrying out or putting into effect of a plan, idea, or the like.
pur·su·ant (pər-sōo'ənt) *adj.* Proceeding from and conformable to; in accordance with. Used with *to.*
—*adv.* Also **pur·su·ant·ly** (-lē). Accordingly; consequently. [Middle English *poursuiant,* from Old French, present participle of *poursuivre,* PURSUE.]
pur·sue (pər-sōo') *v.* **-sued, -suing, -sues.** —*tr.* **1.** To follow in an effort to overtake or capture; chase. **2.** To strive to gain or accomplish. **3.** To proceed along the course of; follow: *pursue the original plan.* **4.** To carry further; advance: *pursued the argument.* **5.** To be engaged in (a vocation or hobby, for example). **6.** To follow closely; harass. —*intr.* **1.** To chase; follow. **2.** To continue; carry on. [Middle English *pursuen,* from Norman French *pursuer,* from Old French *po(u)rsuivre, po(u)rsuir,* from Vulgar Latin *prōsequere* (unattested), from Latin *prōsequī : prō-,* forth, onward + *sequī,* to follow.] —**pur·su·a·ble** *adj.* —**pur·su·er** *n.*
pur·suit (pər-sōot') *n.* **1.** The act or an instance of chasing or pursuing. **2.** The act of striving: *pursuit of success.* **3.** An activity engaged in: *academic pursuits.* **4.** A cycling race, usually on a circular track, in which two riders or teams, beginning some distance apart, attempt to overtake each other. [Middle English *pursu(i)te,* from Old French *poursuite,* from *poursuivre,* PURSUE.]
pur·sui·vant (pûr'swĭ-vənt) *n.* **1.** In the British College of Heralds, an officer ranking below a herald. **2.** *Archaic.* A follower or attendant. [Middle English *pursevant,* from Old French *pours(u)ivant,* follower, from the present participle of *poursuivre,* PURSUE.]
pur·sy (pûr'sē) *adj.* **-sier, -siest.** **1.** Short-winded, especially because of being fat. **2.** Fat; corpulent. [Middle English *pursy, pursive,* from Norman French *porsif,* Old French *polsif,* from *polser,* to wheeze, be short of breath, from Latin *pulsāre,* to pulse. See **pulsate.**] —**purs·i·ness** *n.*
pur·te·nance (pûrt'n-əns) *n. Archaic.* An animal's viscera or inner organs, especially the heart, liver, and lungs. [Middle English *purtenaunce,* "appurtenance," "accessory," alteration of Old French *partenance,* pertinence, from PERTINENT.]
pu·ru·lence (pyōōr'ə-ləns, pyōōr'yə-) *n.* **1.** The condition of discharging or containing pus. **2.** Pus.
pu·ru·lent (pyōōr'ə-lənt, pyōōr'yə-) *adj.* Containing or discharging pus. [Latin *pūrulentus : pūs* (stem *pūr-*), pus + -ULENT.] —**pu·ru·lent·ly** *adv.*
pur·vey (pər-vā', pûr'vā') *tr.v.* **-veyed, -veying, -veys.** To supply (food or information, for example); furnish. [Middle English *pur-*

veien, porveien, from Old French *porveeir, porveioir,* from Latin *prōvidēre,* to foresee, PROVIDE.]
pur·vey·ance (pər-vā'əns) *n.* The act of procuring supplies.
pur·vey·or (pər-vā'ər) *n.* **1.** A person who furnishes provisions, especially food. **2.** A distributor; a dispenser.
pur·view (pûr'vyōō) *n.* **1.** The extent or range of function, power, or competence; scope. **2.** Range of vision, comprehension, or experience; outlook. **3.** *Law.* The body, scope, or limit of a statute. [Middle English *purveu, purvewe,* proviso, provisional clause, from Norman French *purveu,* "(it is) provided" (word used to introduce a proviso), from Old French *porveu,* past participle of *porveeir,* to provide, PURVEY.]
pus (pŭs) *n.* A viscous, yellowish-white fluid formed in infected tissue, consisting chiefly of leukocytes, cellular debris, and liquefied tissue elements. [Latin *pūs.*]
Pu·san (pōo'sän'). Seaport in southeastern Korea. Capital of South Kyongsang province, it is the nearest point on the Asiatic mainland to Japan and was a United Nations supply base during the Korean War. It is a commercial and industrial center.
push (pōosh) *v.* **pushed, pushing, pushes.** —*tr.* **1.** To exert force against (an object) to move it away. **2.** To move by exerting force in this manner; thrust; shove. **3.** To force (an enemy or opposing team) to move back or retreat: *pushed the tank battalion back.* **4.** To force (one's way): *He pushed his way through the crowd.* **5.** To urge on or encourage, especially in a forceful way: *They push us hard at school.* **6.** *Informal.* To bear hard upon; press: *pushed for time.* **7.** To extend or enlarge: *push civilization past the frontier.* **8.** *Informal.* **a.** To promote or market (a product). **b.** To sell (a narcotic) illegally. **c.** To advocate or seek support ·for: *push the idea.* **9.** *Sports.* To hit (a ball) with a slow, precise stroke, rather than with a sharp rap or swinging stroke. —*intr.* **1.** To exert outward force against something. **2.** To advance despite difficulty or opposition; press forward. **3.** To expend great or vigorous effort, especially to bring about or obtain something. Oten used with *for: pushing for an inquiry.* —**push along.** *Informal.* To depart; set out. —**push off. 1.** *Informal.* **a.** To depart; set out. **b.** To go away or withdraw hastily. Often used in the imperative. **2.** To cause (a boat, for example) to begin to move. —**push on.** To continue. —**push someone about** (or **around**). *Informal.* To bully someone or order someone about. —**push through.** To force the acceptance or adoption of (a bill or amendment, for example).
—*n.* **1.** The act of pushing; a thrust. **2.** A vigorous or insistent effort toward an end. **3.** A provocation to action; a stimulus. **4.** *Informal.* Persevering energy; enterprise. **5.** A struggle; a strain: *It'll be a push but we can do it.* **6.** *Australian Informal.* A group of people; a clique. —**at a push.** With some difficulty. —**give someone the push.** *Chiefly British Informal.* **1.** To dismiss (someone) from a job. **2.** To end an emotional relationship with (someone). [Middle English *posshen, pusshen,* from Old French *polser, poulser,* to push, beat, from Latin *pulsāre,* frequentative of *pellere* (past participle *pulsus*), to push, beat.]
push·ball (pōosh'bôl') *n.* **1.** A game in which two opposing teams attempt to push a heavy ball, six feet in diameter, across a goal. **2.** The ball so used.
push·bike (pōosh'bīk') *n. Chiefly British Informal.* A bicycle operated solely by pedaling, as distinct from a motorized bicycle.
push button *n.* A small button that activates an electric circuit.
push·but·ton (pōosh'bŭt'n) *adj.* Operated by or as if by push buttons: *push-button warfare.*
push·cart (pōosh'kärt') *n.* A light cart pushed by hand; a barrow.
push·chair (pōosh'châr') *n.* A light, folding, four-wheeled chair for wheeling small children about.
push·down (pōosh'doun') *n. Computer Science.* A section of stored data from which the most recently stored material must be the first to be utilized.
push·er (pōosh'ər) *n.* **1.** One that pushes. **2.** An energetically ambitious person. **3.** *Informal.* A person who sells drugs illegally. **4.** A utensil, used by a child, for pushing food onto a spoon or fork.
push·ing (pōosh'ĭng) *adj.* **1.** Energetic; enterprising. **2.** Aggressive; forward; presumptuous.
—*adv. Informal.* Almost; nearly: *pushing 40.* —**push·ing·ly** *adv.*
Push·kin (pōosh'kĭn), **Alexandr Sergeyevich** (1799-1837). Russian poet. He wrote the verse novel *Eugene Onegin* (1825-31), the play *Boris Godunov* (1831), and many narrative and lyrical poems and short stories, all considered classics of their genre. He is regarded as the founder of the Russian literary language.
push·o·ver (pōosh'ō'vər) *n. Informal.* **1.** Anything easily accomplished. **2.** A person or group easily defeated or taken advantage of.
push-pull (pōosh'pōol') *adj.* Designating an arrangement of two identical electronic devices that act 180° out of phase with each other in order to minimize distortion.
push-rod, push rod (pōosh'rŏd') *n.* A rod moved by a cam to operate the valves in an internal-combustion engine.
push-start (pōosh'stärt') *n.* A method of starting a motor vehicle by pushing it, then putting it into gear, so that the engine turns.
—*tr.v.* **push-started, -starting, -starts.** To start (a motor vehicle) in this way.
Push·tu (pŭsh'tōo) *n.* An Iranian language, **Pashto** (*see*).
push-up (pōosh'ŭp') *n.* **1.** An exercise for strengthening arm muscles, performed by lying with the face and palms to the floor and by pushing the body up and down with the arms. Also *British* "press-up." **2.** *Computer Science.* A section of stored data from which the earliest stored data must be the first to be utilized.

push·y (po͝osh′ē) *adj.* **-ier, -iest.** *Informal.* Disagreeably forward or aggressive. **—push·i·ly** *adv.* **—push·i·ness** *n.*

pu·sil·lan·i·mous (pyo͞o′sə-lăn′ə-məs) *adj.* Lacking courage; cowardly. [Late Latin *pūsillanimis* : Latin *pūsillus,* very small, weak, from *pūsus,* boy + *animus,* mind, soul.] **—pu·sil·la·nim·i·ty** (pyo͞o′sə-lə-nĭm′ə-tē) *n.* **—pu·sil·lan·i·mous·ly** *adv.*

puss[1] (po͝os) *n. Informal.* **1.** A cat. **2.** A girl or young woman. Used affectionately. **3.** *Archaic.* A hare. [Probably from Middle Low German *pūs*†.]

puss[2] *n. Slang.* **1.** The mouth. **2.** The face. [Irish *bus,* lip, mouth, from Old Irish, lip.]

puss moth *n.* A Eurasian moth, *Cerura vinula,* the caterpillar of which has a forked tail and prominent eyespots at the anterior end to alarm predators. [From PUSS (cat), referring to its furry body.]

puss·y[1] (po͝os′ē) *n., pl.* **-ies. 1.** *Informal.* A cat. **2.** A fuzzy catkin, especially of the pussy willow. [See **puss** (cat).]

pus·sy[2] (pŭs′ē) *adj.* **-sier, -siest.** Resembling or containing pus.

puss·y·foot (po͝os′ē-fo͝ot′) *intr.v.* **-footed, -footing, -foots. 1.** To move stealthily or cautiously. **2.** *Informal.* To act or proceed cautiously or timidly to avoid committing oneself.

pus·sy·toes (po͝os′ē-tōz′) *n. Used with a singular or plural verb.* Any of several low-growing plants of the genus *Antennaria,* having leaves with whitish down, and clusters of small white flowers. [The cluster resembles a cat's paw.]

pussy willow *n.* **1.** A North American shrub or small tree, *Salix discolor,* having silky, pale gray catkins. **2.** Any of several similar willows.

pus·tu·lant (pŭs′cho͞o-lənt, pŭs′tyə-) *adj.* Causing pustules to form. *~n.* An agent that produces pustules.

pus·tu·late (pŭs′cho͞o-lāt′, pŭs′tyə-) *v.* **-lated, -lating, -lates.** *—tr.* To cause (tissue) to form pustules. *—intr.* To form pustules. *~adj.* (-lĭt, -lāt′). Covered with pustules.

pus·tu·la·tion (pŭs′cho͞o-lā′shən, pŭs′tyə-) *n.* **1.** The formation or appearance of pustules. **2.** A pustule.

pus·tule (pŭs′cho͞ol, pŭs′tyo͞ol) *n.* **1.** A slight, inflamed raised area of the skin filled with pus. **2.** Any small swelling similar to a blister or pimple. [Middle English, from Old French, from Latin *pustula,* a blister.] **—pus·tu·lar** (pŭs′cho͞o-lər, pŭs′tyə-) *adj.*

pusz·ta (po͞osh′tə) *n.* Grassland on the plains of Hungary. [Hungarian, barren.]

put (po͝ot) *v.* **put, putting, puts.** *—tr.* **1.** To place in a specified location; set: *put the cat out; put words into her mouth.* **2.** To cause to be in a specified condition: *put one's room in order. She put his mind at rest.* **3.** To cause to undergo something; subject: *was put to death.* **4.** To assign; attribute: *put a false interpretation on events; put the blame on his wife.* **5.** To estimate. Used with *at*: *He put the time at five o'clock.* **6.** To impose or levy: *put a tax on cigarettes.* **7.** To bet; wager (a stake). **8.** To hurl with an overhand pushing motion: *put the shot.* **9.** To bring up for consideration or judgment: *The committee put the question.* **10.** To express; state: *putting it bluntly.* **11.** To render in a specified language or literary form: *put prose into verse.* **12.** To adapt: *lyrics put to music.* **13.** To urge or force to some action: *put an outlaw to flight.* **14.** To apply: *We must put our minds to it.* **15.** To impart; invest: *put some effort into it.* **16.** To cause to penetrate. Used with *through*: *put her hand through the window.* *—intr.* To proceed: *The ship put into the harbor.* **—put about. 1.** *Nautical.* **a.** To change direction; go from one tack to another. **b.** To cause (a ship) to put about. **2.** To spread (a rumor or news, for example). **—put across. 1.** To state so as to be understood or accepted. **2.** To convey (an impression): *She puts across an image of haughtiness.* **3.** To project or give a specified impression of (oneself): *He put himself across rather feebly at the interview.* **—put aside** (or **by**). **1.** To save for later use; reserve. **2.** To abandon; discard. **—put away. 1.** To save or keep in reserve. **2.** *Informal.* To confine in an institution, such as a mental hospital. **3.** To consume (food or drink), especially in large quantities. **—put back. 1.** To postpone for or until a specified time: *The meeting is being put back for 24 hours.* **2.** To cause delay or disruption to. **—put forth. 1.** To grow: *The plant put forth leaves.* **2.** To offer for consideration. **—put forward. 1.** To propose (an idea, for example). **2.** To nominate, as for a position of authority. **—put in. 1.** *Nautical.* To enter a port or harbor. **2.** To insert; interject. **3.** To submit (a form, for example). **4.** To apply or enter: *put in for the job.* **5.** To devote or contribute (work, time, or money, for example). **6.** To cause (a political party, for example) to be elected. **—put it about.** To spread information or rumor. **—put one across** (or **over on**). *Informal.* To trick or deceive (someone), especially into believing a claim or excuse. **—put out. 1.** To extinguish: *put out a fire.* **2.** *Nautical.* To leave, as from a port: *The ship put out to sea.* **3.** To blind (eyes), as by poking. **4.** To publish. **5.** To inconvenience: *I was put out by her late arrival.* **6.** To confuse; disconcert. **7.** To dislocate: *put his back out.* **—put over. 1.** To communicate or put across. **2.** *Informal.* To achieve (something). **—put through. 1. a.** To connect (a caller) by telephone. **b.** To make (a telephone call). **2.** To carry to a successful termination. **—put upon.** To impose on; take advantage of. Used in the passive: *He was put upon by his friends.* **—put up with.** To endure patiently.
~n. **1.** An act of putting the shot. **2.** *Finance.* An option to sell a stipulated amount of stock or securities within a stated time and at a fixed price. Compare **call, straddle.**
~adj. Informal. Fixed; stationary: *Stay put.* [Middle English *put(t)en* (unattested), Old English *pūtian*†, to push, thrust.]

pu·ta·men (pyo͞o-tā′mən) *n., pl.* **-tamina** (-tăm′ə-nə). *Botany.* A hard, shell-like covering, such as that enclosing the kernel of a peach. [New Latin, from Latin *putāmen,* clippings, prunings, shells, from *putāre,* to prune, cut.] **—pu·tam·i·nous** (pyo͞o-tăm′ə-nəs) *adj.*

pu·ta·tive (pyo͞o′tə-tĭv) *adj.* Generally regarded as such; supposed; reputed: *his putative mother.* [Middle English, from Old French *putatif,* from Late Latin *putātīvus,* from Latin *putāre,* to compute, consider.] **—pu·ta·tive·ly** *adv.*

put down *tr.v.* **1. a.** To write down; record. **b.** To record a promise or arrangement made by (someone): *Put her down for Tuesday.* **c.** To record or have recorded on a list. **d.** To list or table on an agenda: *put down a motion on overseas aid.* **2.** To repress; defeat. **3.** *Informal.* To express rejection or criticism of. **4.** To kill (an animal) mercifully. **5.** To attribute or ascribe: *Put it down to inexperience.* **6.** To regard or estimate: *I'd put her down for a liar.* **7.** To land (an aircraft). **8.** To stop reading (a book, for example). *—intr.v.* To land. Used of an aircraft.

put-down (po͝ot′doun′) *n. Slang.* A dismissal or rejection, especially in the form of a critical or slighting remark.

put·log (po͝ot′lôg′, -lŏg′, pŭt′-) *n.* Any of the short pieces of timber that support a scaffolding floor. [Earlier *putlock* : probably past participle of PUT + LOCK.]

Put·nam (pŭt′nəm), **Israel** (1718–90). U.S. soldier. The subject of numerous folk legends about his courage, he fought with Roger's Rangers in the French and Indian War and in the American Revolution was a hero in the Battle of Bunker Hill (1775). His promotion to general and subsequent military failures proved that his grit and tenacity served him better as a soldier than as an officer.

Putnam, Rufus (1738–1824). U.S. Revolutionary officer and pioneer. As a military engineer he organized the batteries on Dorchester Heights that forced the British to evacuate Boston (1776) and fortified West Point (1778). After the war he helped settle the Ohio Territory and served as surveyor general of the U.S. (1796–1803).

put off *tr.v.* **1.** To delay or postpone (a meeting, for example). **2.** To avoid meeting (a person) by giving an excuse. **3.** To annoy by distracting. **4.** To cause (someone) to feel dislike for (someone or something). **5.** To disconcert; make apprehensive.

put-off (po͝ot′ôf′, -ŏf′) *n.* A pretext for inaction.

put on *tr.v.* **1.** To clothe oneself with; don. **2.** To apply or activate: *put on the brake.* **3.** To present; perform: *put on a play.* **4.** To assume affectedly: *put on a funny accent.* **5.** To switch on (an electrical appliance). **6. a.** To increase in: *put on weight.* **b.** To add: *put on another layer of paint.* **7.** To cause to be connected, as on the telephone. **8.** To tease or mislead (someone).

put-on (po͝ot′ŏn′, -ôn′) *adj.* Pretended; feigned.
~n. Informal. **1.** The act of teasing or misleading someone, especially for amusement. **2.** Something intended as a hoax or joke.

put-put (pŭt′pŭt′) *n. Slang.* **1.** A small engine. **2.** The noise made by such an engine. **3.** A boat or vehicle operated by such an engine. Also used adjectivally: *a put-put engine.*
~intr.v. **put-putted, -putting, -puts. 1.** To make the sound of a put-put engine. **2.** To travel in or on or as if in or on a put-put boat or vehicle. [Imitative.]

pu·tre·fac·tion (pyo͞o′trə-făk′shən) *n.* **1.** The partial decomposition of organic matter by microorganisms, producing foul-smelling matter. **2.** Putrefied matter. **3.** The condition of being putrefied. [Middle English *putrefaccioun,* from Late Latin *putrefactiō* (stem *putrefactiōn-*), from Latin *putrefacere,* PUTREFY.] **—pu·tre·fac·tive, pu·tre·fa·cient** (pyo͞o′trə-fā′shənt) *adj.*

pu·tre·fy (pyo͞o′trə-fī′) *v.* **-fied, -fying, -fies.** *—tr.* **1.** To decompose (something); cause to decay. **2.** To make gangrenous. *—intr.* **1.** To decompose. **2.** To become gangrenous. —See Synonyms at **decay.** [Middle English *putrefien,* from Old French *putrefier,* from Latin *putrefacere* : *puter,* rotten + *facere,* to make.]

pu·tres·cence (pyo͞o-trĕs′əns) *n.* **1.** A putrescent character or condition. **2.** Putrid matter.

pu·tres·cent (pyo͞o-trĕs′ənt) *adj.* **1.** Becoming putrid; putrefying. **2.** Of or pertaining to putrefaction. [Latin *putrēscens,* present participle of *putrēscere* (stem *putrēscent-*), to grow rotten, inceptive of *putrēre,* to be rotten, from *puter,* rotten.]

pu·tres·ci·ble (pyo͞o-trĕs′ə-bəl) *adj.* Subject to putrefaction. [French, from Late Latin *putrēscibilis,* from Latin *putrēscere,* to grow rotten. See **putrescent.**] **—pu·tres·ci·bil·i·ty** *n.*

pu·tres·cine (pyo͞o-trĕs′ēn, -ĭn) *n.* A colorless amine, $NH_2(CH_2)_4NH_2$, occurring in putrefying animal substances; 1,4-diaminobutane. [Latin *putrēscere,* become rotten (see **putrescent**) + -INE.]

pu·trid (pyo͞o′trĭd) *adj.* **1.** In a decomposed, foul-smelling state; rotten. **2.** Proceeding from or displaying putrefaction. **3.** Corrupt; morally rotten. **4.** *Slang.* Extremely objectionable or worthless; vile. [Latin *putridus,* from *putrēre,* to be rotten. See **putrescent.**] **—pu·trid·i·ty, pu·trid·ness** *n.* **—pu·trid·ly** *adv.*

putsch (po͝och) *n. Sometimes* **Putsch.** A sudden attempt by a group to overthrow a government. [German, from Swiss German, a thrust (imitative).]

putt (pŭt) *n. Golf.* A light stroke made on the putting green in an effort to place the ball into the hole.
~v. **putted, putting, putts.** *—tr.* To hit (the ball) with such a stroke on the green. *—intr.* To putt the ball. [Variant of PUT.]

put·tee (pŭ-tē′, pŭt′ē) *n.* Also **put·ty,** *pl.* **-ties. 1.** A strip of cloth wound spirally around the leg from ankle to knee, for covering and protection. **2.** A rectangular canvas legging with small straps and

PRONUNCIATION KEY
ă, pat; ā, pay; âr, care;
ä, father, are; b, bib;
ch, church; d, deed; ĕ, pet;
ē, be; f, fife; g, gag; h, hat;
hw, which; ĭ, pit; ī, pie;
îr, pier; j, judge; k, kick;
l, lid, needle; m, mum;
n, no, sudden; ng, thing;
ŏ, pot; ō, toe; ô, paw, for;
oi, noise; ou, out; o͝o, book;
o͞o, boot; p, pop; r, roar;
s, sauce; sh, ship, dish;
t, tight; th, thin, path;
th, this, bathe; ŭ, cut; ûr, fur;
v, valve; w, with; y, yes;
z, zebra, size; zh, vision;
ə, about, item, edible, gallop, circus, peaceful

IN FOREIGN WORDS:
à, *Fr.* ami; œ, *Fr.* feu, *Ger.* schön; ü, *Fr.* tu, *Ger.* über;
KH, *Ger.* ich, *Scot.* loch;
N, *Fr.* bon; y′, *Fr.* Compiègne

STRESS MARKS:
Primary stress: ′
in·cite′ (ĭn-sīt′)
Secondary stress: ′
in′sight′ (ĭn′sīt′)

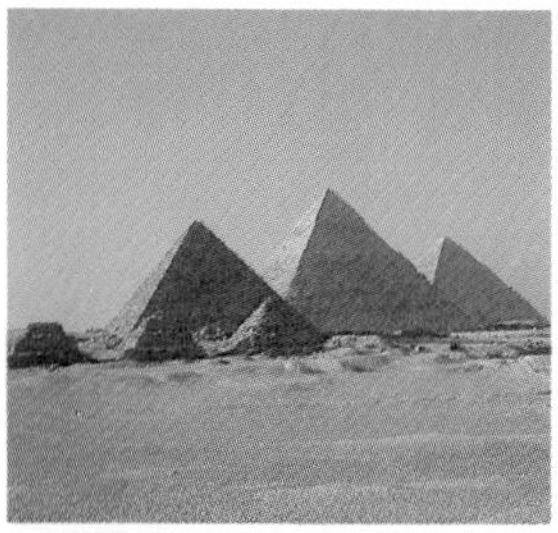

pyramid *Of the seven wonders of the ancient world, only the pyramids still stand. The pyramid on the left was built for the pharaoh Mycerinus and the one in the center for Chephren. But the oldest and largest of the three is the Great Pyramid of Khufu (Cheops), which was built about 2575* B.C. *and is 137 meters (450 feet) high.*

buckles, covering the lower leg between mid-calf and ankle. [Hindi *paṭṭī,* from Sanskrit *paṭṭikā,* from *paṭṭa†,* cloth band.]

put·ter¹ (pŭt′ər) *n. Golf.* **1.** A short, stiff-shafted club used for putting. **2.** A golfer who is putting.

put·ter² *n.* An athlete who puts the shot.

put·ter³ (pŭt′ər) *v.* **-tered, -tering, -ters.** Also *chiefly British* **pot·ter** (pŏt′ər). *—intr.* To occupy oneself in an aimless or desultory manner. *—tr.* To waste (especially time) in idling. Used with *away.* [Variant of dialectal *potter,* probably from *pote,* to punch, kick, Middle English *poten,* Old English *potian,* akin to Middle Dutch *pōten†,* to put in the ground.] **—put·ter·er** *n.*

putting green *n. Golf.* **1.** The area at the end of a fairway in which the hole is placed, having turf more closely mown than the rest of the course. **2.** An area for practicing putting.

put·to (po͞o′tō) *n., pl.* **-ti** (-tē). A figure of a small boy or cherub in painting, sculpture, and ornamentation.

put·ty (pŭt′ē) *n., pl.* **-ties. 1.** A doughlike cement made by mixing whiting and linseed oil, used to fill holes in woodwork and secure panes of glass. **2.** Any substance with a similar consistency or function. **3.** A fine lime cement used as a finishing coat on plaster. **4.** Yellowish or light grayish brown. **5.** A person or group that is very compliant, impressionable, or easily influenced: *His accomplices were putty in his hands.*
~*tr.v.* **puttied, -tying, -ties.** To fill, cover, or secure with putty. [French *potée,* from Old French, contents of a pot, a potful, from *pot,* a pot, from Middle Low German, from Vulgar Latin *pottus* (attested only in Late Latin).]

put·ty·root (pŭt′ē-ro͞ot′, -ro͝ot′) *n.* A North American orchid, *Aplectrum hyemale,* bearing a single leaf and yellowish-brown or purplish flowers. Also called "Adam-and-Eve." [From the use of the sticky substance in its corm as a cement.]

put up *tr.v.* **1.** To erect; build. **2.** To preserve, as in glass jars: *put up jam.* **3.** To nominate. **4.** To provide (funds) in advance. **5.** To provide lodgings for: *put someone up for the night.* **6.** To incite to some action: *put someone up to a prank.* **7.** To raise and arrange (long hair) in a style. **8.** To offer (property) for sale. **9.** To offer or show (resistance, for example), especially when hard-pressed: *put up a fight.* **10.** To raise or increase: *put up the price.* **11.** *Archaic.* To sheathe (a sword). *—intr.v.* **1.** To stay in lodgings. **2.** To nominate as a candidate. **—put up with.** To endure patiently; tolerate.

put-up (po͝ot′ŭp′) *adj. Informal.* Planned or prearranged secretly. Used chiefly in the phrase *a put-up job.*

Pu·vis de Cha·vannes (pü-vē də shä-vän′, -vēs′, pyo͞o-), **Pierre** (1824–98). French artist. Noted for his large works for the walls of public buildings, he remained independent from the prevalent art trends of the day and used pale colors and flowing lines in his uncomplicated and much admired works.

puy (pwē) *n.* A small extinct volcanic cone. [French.]

puz·zle (pŭz′əl) *v.* **-zled, -zling, -zles.** *—tr.* **1.** To cause uncertainty and indecision in; perplex. **2.** To clarify or solve (something confusing) by reasoning or study. Used with *out*: *He puzzled out the significance of her statement.* *—intr.* To ponder a problem in an effort to solve or understand it. Often used with *over* or *about.*
~*n.* **1.** One that puzzles. **2.** A game, toy, testing device, or the like, that tests ingenuity. See **jigsaw puzzle. 3.** The condition of being perplexed; bewilderment. [16th century : origin obscure.] **—puz·zle·ment** *n.* **—puz·zler** *n.*

Synonyms: *baffle, bewilder, confound, mystify, perplex.*

PVC *n.* A common thermoplastic resin used in a wide variety of manufactured products, including raincoats, garden hoses, phonograph records, and floor tiles. [*P*oly*v*inyl *c*hloride.]

pvt., Pvt. private.

pwt. pennyweight.

PX post exchange; Post Exchange.

py–. Variant of **pyo–.**

py·a (pē-ä′) *n., pl.* **-as.** A monetary unit equal to ¹⁄₁₀₀ of the kyat of Burma. See feature at **currency.** [Burmese.]

pyc·nid·i·um (pĭk-nĭd′ē-əm) *n., pl.* **-nidia** (-ē-ə). *Botany.* A rounded or flask-shaped asexual fruiting body containing spores. It occurs in certain fungi. [New Latin : Greek *puknos,* thick + *-idium,* Latin diminutive suffix, from Greek *-idion.*] **—pyc·nid·i·al** *adj.*

pyc·nom·e·ter (pĭk-nŏm′ə-tər) *n.* A standard vessel used in measuring the density or specific gravity of materials. [Greek *puknos,* thick, dense + METER.]

pye dog (pī) *n.* A stray, untamed domestic dog in Asia. Also called "pariah dog." [Hindi *pāhī,* pariah, outsider.]

py·e·li·tis (pī′ə-lī′tĭs) *n.* **Pyelonephritis** *(see).* [New Latin *pyelo-,* pelvis, from Greek *puelos,* basin + -ITIS.] **—py·e·lit·ic** *adj.*

py·e·log·ra·phy (pī′ə-lŏg′rə-fē) *n.* Examination of the kidneys by means of x-ray pictures *(pyelograms).* [New Latin *pyelo-,* pelvis (see **pyelitis**) + -GRAPHY.] **—py·e·lo·graph·ic** *adj.*

py·e·lo·ne·phri·tis (pī′ə-lō-nĭ-frī′tĭs) *n.* Inflammation of both the kidney and the pelvis of the ureter, usually caused by bacterial infection. Also called "pyelitis." [New Latin *pyelo-,* pelvis (see **pyelitis**) + NEPHRITIS.]

py·e·mi·a (pī-ē′mē-ə) *n.* Blood poisoning due to the presence of pus-forming bacteria. [New Latin : PY(O)- + -EMIA.] **—py·e·mic** *adj.*

py·gid·i·um (pī-jĭd′ē-əm) *n., pl.* **-ia** (-ē-ə). The posterior body region of certain invertebrates. [New Latin, from Greek *pugidion,* diminutive of *pugē†,* rump.] **—py·gid·i·al** *adj.*

Pyg·ma·li·on (pĭg-măl′yən, -mā′lē-ən). *Greek Mythology.* A king of Cyprus who carved and then fell in love with a statue of a woman that Aphrodite brought to life as Galatea.

pyg·moid (pĭg′moid′) *adj.* Resembling or characteristic of a Pygmy.

pyg·my, pig·my (pĭg′mē) *n., pl.* **-mies.** An individual of unusually small size or significance.
~*adj.* **1.** Unusually or atypically small. **2.** Of little importance or stature. [Middle English *pigmie,* from Latin *pygmaeus,* dwarfish, from Greek *pugmaios,* from *pugmē,* fist, the length from the elbow to the knuckles.] **—pyg·me·an** *adj.*

Pyg·my, Pig·my (pĭg′mē) *n., pl.* **-mies. 1.** A member of any of several African and Asian peoples with a hereditary stature of from four to five feet. **2.** *Greek Mythology.* A member of a race of dwarfs.
~*adj.* Of or pertaining to the Pygmies.

pyjamas. *Chiefly British.* Variant of **pajamas.**

pyk·nic (pĭk′nĭk) *adj. Anthropology.* Characterized by short, stocky, and powerful stature; endomorphic. [Greek *puknos,* thick, dense.] **—pyk·nic** *n.*

py·lon (pī′lŏn′) *n.* **1.** A steel tower supporting high-tension electric cables forming part of the grid system. **2.** *Aeronautics.* A tall tower used to guide pilots, especially as a marker for the turning point in a race. **3.** A large structure marking an entrance or approach; specifically, a monumental gateway in the form of a pair of truncated pyramids serving as the entrance to an ancient Egyptian temple. **4.** A streamlined casing for attaching an external engine pod or fuel tank to the body of an aircraft. **5.** A temporary artificial leg. [Greek *pulōn,* gateway, from *pulē,* a gate.]

py·lo·rus (pī-lôr′əs, -lōr′əs, pĭ-) *n., pl.* **-ri.** The passage connecting the stomach and the duodenum. [Late Latin *pylōrus,* from Greek *pulōros,* "a gatekeeper" : *pulē,* a gate + *ouros,* watcher, from *horan,* to see.] **—py·lor·ic** (pī′lôr′ĭk, -lŏr′ĭk, pĭ-) *adj.*

Py·los (pī′lŏs). Ancient harbor of southwestern Greece, on an arm of the Ionian Sea. Excavations have revealed a great Mycenaean palace of the 13th century B.C. and 600 clay tablets that were important in deciphering the late Minoan script.

Pym (pĭm), **John** (1584–1643). English politician. A Somerset squire, he became a leading Parliamentary opponent of Charles I, moving the bills of impeachment against his advisers. Charles's attempts to arrest him (1642) in the House of Commons precipitated the Civil War, in which his coordination of military activity earned him the title King Pym.

pyo–, py– *prefix.* Indicates pus; for example, **pyorrhea, pyemia.** [Greek *puon,* pus.]

py·o·der·ma (pī′ō-dûr′mə) *n.* Any skin disease in which pus is produced. [New Latin : PYO- + -DERMA.] **—py·o·der·mic** *adj.*

py·o·gen·e·sis (pī′ō-jĕn′ə-sĭs) *n. Pathology.* Pyosis. [PYO- + -GENESIS.] **—py·o·gen·ic** *adj.*

Pyong·yang (pyŭng′yăng′). Capital of North Korea. On the Taedong River, it was rebuilt after its destruction by U.S. bombing during the Korean War (1950–53). In a coal and iron region, its industries include heavy engineering and textiles.

py·or·rhe·a, py·or·rhoe·a (pī′ə-rē′ə) *n.* **1.** A discharge of pus. **2.** Inflammation of the gum and tooth sockets leading to loosening of the teeth. [New Latin : PYO- + -RRHEA.] **—py·or·rhe·al** *adj.*

py·o·sis (pī-ō′sĭs) *n.* The formation of pus. Also called "pyogenesis." [New Latin, from Greek *puōsis* : PY(O)- + -OSIS.]

pyr–. Variant of **pyro–.**

py·ra·can·tha (pī′rə-kăn′thə, pĭr′ə-) *n.* A shrub of the genus *Pyracantha,* the **firethorn** *(see).* [New Latin, from Greek *purakantha,* name of a shrub : PYR(O)- + Greek *akantha,* thorn.]

pyr·a·lid (pĭr′ə-lĭd) *n.* Also **py·ral·i·did** (pĭ-răl′ə-dĭd). Any of various small or medium-sized moths of the large, widely distributed family Pyralididae. [New Latin *pyralididae,* from *pyralis* (genus), from Greek *puralis,* fabulous insect supposed to live in fire, from *pur,* fire.] **—pyr·a·lid** *adj.*

pyr·a·mid (pĭr′ə-mĭd) *n.* **1.** *Geometry.* A polyhedron with a polygonal base and triangular faces meeting in a common vertex. **2.** Anything having such a shape or structure. **3.** A massive monument found especially in Egypt, having a rectangular base and four triangular faces culminating in a single apex and serving as a tomb or temple. **4. pyramids.** A game similar to billiards played with 15 colored balls and a cue ball. **5.** *Anatomy.* Any of various approximately pyramidal structures, as in the medulla of the kidney.
~*v.* **pyramided, -miding, -mids.** *—tr.* **1.** To place or build in the shape of a pyramid. **2.** To build (a thesis, for example) progressively from a basic general premise. **3.** *Finance.* To speculate in (securities or property) by making a series of buying and selling transactions in which paper profits are used as margin for making further purchases. *—intr.* **1.** To assume the shape of a pyramid. **2.** To increase rapidly and on a widening base. **3.** *Finance.* To pyramid securities or property. [Latin *pyramis* (stem *pyramid-*), from Greek *puramis†.*] **—py·ram·i·dal** (pĭ-răm′ə-dəl), **pyr·a·mid·ic** (pĭr′ə-mĭd′ĭk), **pyr·a·mid·i·cal** *adj.* **—py·ram·i·dal·ly** *adv.*

pyramiding *n. Finance.* A system of business organization in which a holding company controls subsidiary companies that are themselves holding companies, thereby achieving a concentration of power by means of limited capital ownership.

pyramid selling *n.* A system of selling in which one person with the right to sell certain goods sells part of this right or part of a consignment to others, who repeat this procedure, with only those at the bottom end of this pyramidal structure actually selling the goods.

py·ran (pī′răn′) *n.* An unsaturated ring compound, C_5H_5O, having two double bonds and, depending on the position of the bonds, two isomers. [PYR(O)- + -AN.]

PRONUNCIATION KEY

ă, pat; ā, pay; âr, care;
ä, father, are; b, **bib**;
ch, **church**; d, **deed**; ĕ, pet;
ē, be; f, **fife**; g, **gag**; h, **hat**;
hw, **which**; ĭ, pit; ī, pie;
îr, pier; j, **judge**; k, **kick**;
l, lid, needle; m, **mum**;
n, no, sudden; ng, thing;
ŏ, pot; ō, toe; ô, paw, for;
oi, noise; ou, **out**; o͝o, **book**;
o͞o, **boot**; p, **pop**; r, roar;
s, sauce; sh, **ship**, dish;
t, tight; th, **thin**, path;
th, **this**, bathe; ŭ, cut; ûr, **fur**;
v, valve; w, **with**; y, yes;
z, zebra, size; zh, vision;
ə, about, item, edible,
gallop, circus, peaceful

IN FOREIGN WORDS:

å, *Fr.* ami; œ, *Fr.* **feu**, *Ger.* schön; ü, *Fr.* tu, *Ger.* über;
KH, *Ger.* **ich**, *Scot.* **loch**;
N, *Fr.* bon; y′, *Fr.* Compiègne

STRESS MARKS:

Primary stress: ′
in·cite′ (ĭn-sīt′)
Secondary stress: ′
in′sight′ (ĭn′sīt′)

py·ra·nom·e·ter (pī′rə-nŏm′ə-tər) n. A **solarimeter** (see). [Greek *pur*, fire + *ano*, up + -METER.]

py·rar·gy·rite (pī-rär′jə-rīt′, pī-) n. A deep red to black silver ore with the composition Ag₃SbS₃. Also called "ruby silver." [German *Pyrargyrit* : PYR(O)- + Greek *arguros*, silver + -ITE.]

py·ra·zole (pī′rə-zōl′) n. A crystalline ring compound, C₃H₄N₂, consisting of a five-membered ring having two double bonds. [PYR(O)- + AZOLE.]

pyre (pīr) n. A heap of combustible material, especially one for burning a corpse as a funeral rite. [Latin *pyra*, from Greek *pura*, from *pur*, fire.]

py·rene¹ (pī′rēn, pī-rēn′) n. The one-seeded stone of certain single fruits. [New Latin *pyrena*, from Greek *purēn*.]

py·rene² (pī′rēn) n. A tetracyclic hydrocarbon, C₁₆H₁₀, obtained from coal tar. [PYR(O)- + -ENE.]

Pyrenean mountain dog n. A dog of an ancient breed originating in central Europe, typically having a large, powerful body with a coat of thick, fine, white hair.

Pyr·e·nees (pîr′ə-nēz′). Mountain range in southwestern Europe, separating France from the Iberian Peninsula. It rises to 3,404 meters (11,168 feet) at Pico de Aneto and includes Andorra. —**Pyr·e·ne·an** (pîr′ə-nē′ən) adj.

py·re·noid (pī-rē′noid′, pîr′ə-) n. Any of the protein granules of certain algae and some other lower plants in which starch is formed. [PYREN(E) (fruit stone; from the shape of its nucleus) + -OID.]

py·re·thrin (pī-rē′thrĭn, -rĕth′rĭn) n. Either of two viscous liquid esters, C₂₁H₂₈O₃ or C₂₂H₂₈O₅, extracted from pyrethrum flowers and used as insecticides. [French *pyréthrine* : PYRETHR(UM) + -IN.]

py·re·thrum (pī-rē′thrəm, -rĕth′rəm) n. 1. Any of various Old World plants of the genus *Chrysanthemum* (or *Tanacetum*) with showy, daisylike flowers; especially, *C. cinerariaefolium*, widely cultivated as a source of insecticide. 2. An insecticide made from the dried flowers of pyrethrum plants. 3. A medicinal preparation made from the root of a related plant, *Anacyclus pyrethrum*, used to stimulate saliva flow. In this sense, also called "pyrethrum root." [Latin, from Greek *purethron*, feverfew, from *puretos*, fever, from *pur*, fire.]

py·ret·ic (pī-rĕt′ĭk) adj. Characterized or affected by fever; feverish. [New Latin *pyreticus*, from Greek *puretikos*, from *puretos*, fever, from *pur*, fire.]

Py·rex (pī′rĕks′) n. A trademark for any of various types of heat- and chemical-resistant glass used for ovenware and tableware.

py·rex·i·a (pī-rĕk′sē-ə) n. Fever. [New Latin, from Greek *purexis*, from *puressein*, to have a fever, from *puretos*, fever. See **pyretic**.] —**py·rex·i·al**, **py·rex·ic** adj.

pyr·he·li·om·e·ter (pîr′hē-lē-ŏm′ə-tər) n. Any of various devices that measure all or restricted components of solar radiation. [PYR(O)- + HELIO- + -METER.]

pyr·i·dine (pĭr′ə-dēn′) n. A flammable, colorless or yellowish liquid base, C₅H₅N, used to synthesize vitamins and drugs and as a solvent and a denaturant for alcohol. [PYR(O)- + -ID + -INE.] —**py·rid·ic** (pī-rĭd′ĭk) adj.

pyr·i·dox·ine (pîr′ə-dŏk′sēn′, -sĭn) n. Also **pyr·i·dox·in** (-sĭn). A pyridine derivative, C₈H₁₁O₃N, occurring in plant and animal tissues and active in various metabolic processes. Also called "vitamin B₆." [PYRID(INE) + OX- + -INE.]

pyr·i·form (pîr′ə-fôrm′) adj. Pear-shaped: *a pyriform organ*. [New Latin *pyriformis* : Medieval Latin *pyrum*, variant of Latin *pirum*, PEAR + -FORM.]

py·rim·i·dine (pī-rĭm′ə-dēn′, pĭ-) n. 1. A liquid and crystalline organic base, C₄H₄N₂. 2. Any of several basic compounds, such as uracil, cytosine, or thymine, having a molecular structure similar to pyrimidine and found in living matter as a nucleotide component. [German *Pyrimidin*, variant of PYRIDINE.]

py·rite (pī′rīt′) n. A yellow to brown, widely occurring mineral sulfide, FeS₂, used as an iron ore and to produce sulfur dioxide for sulfuric acid. Also called "fool's gold," "iron pyrites." [Latin *pyrītēs*, PYRITES.] —**py·rit·ic** (pī-rĭt′ĭk), **py·rit·i·cal** adj.

py·ri·tes (pī-rī′tēz, pə-) n., pl. **pyrites**. Any of various natural metallic sulfides. [Latin *pyrītēs*, flint, pyrite, from Greek *purītēs* (*lithos*), "fire (stone)," from *purītēs*, of fire, from *pur*, fire.]

py·ro (pī′rō) adj. Chemistry. Of, pertaining to, or designating an acid derived from an anhydride and having a water content intermediate between those of the ortho and meta acids. Used in combination: *pyrosulfuric acid*. Compare **meta, ortho**.

pyro-, pyr– prefix. Indicates: 1. Fire or heat; for example, **pyrotechnic**. 2. Resulting from or by the action of fire or heat; for example, **pyrography**. 3. A mineral that changes its properties when heat is applied; for example **pyromorphite**. 4. Chemistry. A new substance obtained by heating another substance; for example **pyrophosphoric acid**. [From Greek *pur*, fire.]

py·ro·cat·e·chol (pī-rō-kăt′ə-chôl′, -chŏl′, -shôl′, -shŏl′) n. A colorless, crystalline organic compound, C₆H₄(OH)₂, used as an antiseptic and photographic developer. [PYRO- + CATECH(U) + -OL.]

py·ro·cel·lu·lose (pī-rō-sĕl′yə-lōs′, -lōz′) n. A cellulose nitrate used as a component of smokeless powder.

py·ro·chem·i·cal (pī′rō-kĕm′ə-kəl) adj. Of or designating high-temperature chemical activity. —**py·ro·chem·i·cal·ly** adv.

py·ro·clas·tic (pī′rō-klăs′tĭk) adj. Made up of fragments ejected from a volcano. Said of a rock. [PYRO- + -CLAST + -IC.]

py·ro·e·lec·tric (pī′rō-ə-lĕk′trĭk) adj. Exhibiting or pertaining to pyroelectricity.
~n. A pyroelectric material.

py·ro·e·lec·tric·i·ty (pī′rō-ə-lĕk-trĭs′ə-tē) n. The polarization of electric charge in a crystal by change of temperature.

py·ro·gal·lol (pī′rō-găl′ôl′, -ŏl′) n. A white lustrous crystalline compound, C₆H₃(OH)₃, used as a photographic developer and to treat skin diseases. Also called "pyrogallic acid." [PYRO- + GALL(IC) + -OL (hydroxyl group).] —**py·ro·gal·lic** adj.

py·ro·gen (pī′rə-jən) n. A substance that produces fever. [PYRO- + -GEN.]

py·ro·gen·ic (pī′rō-jĕn′ĭk) adj. Also **py·rog·e·nous** (pī-rŏj′ə-nəs). 1. Producing or produced by fever. 2. Caused by or generating heat. 3. Geology. Igneous.

py·rog·ra·phy (pī-rŏg′rə-fē) n. 1. The art or process of producing designs on wood, leather, or other material by using heated tools or a fine flame. 2. A design made by this process. [PYRO- + -GRAPHY.] —**py·ro·graph** (pī′rə-grăf′, -gräf′) n. —**py·rog·ra·pher** n. —**py·ro·graph·ic** adj.

py·ro·lig·ne·ous (pī′rō-lĭg′nē-əs) adj. Made by the destructive distillation of wood.

pyroligneous acid n. A mixture of methanol, acetic acid, acetone, various tars, and related products from wood distillation, used in meat smoking. Also called "wood vinegar."

py·ro·lu·site (pī′rō-lōō′sīt′) n. A soft, black to dark gray ore of manganese, consisting essentially of manganese dioxide. [German *Pyrolusit* : PYRO- + Greek *lousis*, a washing, from *louein*, to wash + -ITE (it is used in purifying glass).]

py·rol·y·sis (pī-rŏl′ə-sĭs) n. Chemical change caused by heat. [PYRO- + -LYSIS.] —**py·ro·lyt·ic** (pī′rə-lĭt′ĭk) adj.

py·ro·lyze (pī′rə-līz′) tr.v. **-lyzed, -lyzing, -lyzes**. To subject (something) to pyrolysis. [PYRO- + LYZE.]

py·ro·man·cy (pī′rə-măn′sē) n. Divination by fire or flames. [Middle English *piromance*, from Old French *pyromancie*, from Late Latin *pyromantīa*, from Greek *puromanteia* : PYRO- + -MANCY.] —**py·ro·man·tic** (pī′rə-măn′tĭk) adj.

py·ro·ma·ni·a (pī′rō-mā′nē-ə, -mān′yə) n. The uncontrollable impulse to start fires. [PYRO- + -MANIA.] —**py·ro·ma·ni·ac** (pī′-rō-mā′nē-ăk′) adj. & n. —**py·ro·ma·ni·a·cal** (pī′rō-mə-nī′ə-kəl) adj.

py·ro·met·al·lur·gy (pī′rō-mĕt′l-ûr′jē) n. Metallurgy that depends on the action of heat, involving such processes as smelting.

py·rom·e·ter (pī-rŏm′ə-tər) n. An electrical thermometer used for measuring high temperatures. [PYRO- + -METER.] —**py·ro·met·ric** (pī′rə-mĕt′rĭk), **py·ro·met·ri·cal** adj. —**py·rom·e·try** n.

py·ro·mor·phite (pī′rə-môr′fīt′) n. A lead ore (PbCl)Pb₄(PO₄)₃, occurring in green, brown, or yellow crystals. [German *Pyromorphit* : PYRO- + MORPH(O)- + -ITE.]

py·rone (pī′rōn′) n. Chemistry. A type of organic compound having a six-membered ring formed by five carbon atoms and one oxygen atom. [PYR(O)- + -ONE.]

py·rope (pī′rōp′) n. A deep-red garnet, Mg₃Al₂Si₃O₁₂, used as a gem. [Middle English *pirope*, from Old French, from Latin *pyrōpus*, gold bronze, fiery garnet, from Greek *purōpos*, "fiery-eyed" : PYR(O)- + Greek *ōps*, eye.]

py·ro·phor·ic (pī′rə-fôr′ĭk, -fōr′ĭk) adj. 1. Spontaneously igniting in air. 2. Producing sparks by friction. [Greek *purophoros*, "fire-bearing" : PYRO- + -PHOROUS.]

py·ro·phos·phate (pī′rō-fŏs′fāt′) n. A salt of pyrophosphoric acid.

py·ro·phos·phor·ic acid (pī′rō-fŏs-fôr′ĭk, -fōr′ĭk) n. A syrupy viscous liquid, H₄P₂O₇, used as a catalyst and in organic chemical manufacture. [PYRO- + PHOSPHORIC (it is made by heating a phosphoric acid).]

py·ro·phyl·lite (pī′rō-fĭl′īt′, pī-rŏf′ə-līt′) n. A silvery white or pale-green mineral, hydrous aluminium silicate, Al₂Si₄O₁₀(OH)₂, occurring naturally in soft, compact masses. [German *Pyrophyllit* : PYRO- + PHYLL(O)- + -ITE (its foliations spread when heated).]

py·ro·sis (pī-rō′sĭs) n. Heartburn. [Greek *purōsis*, a burning, from *pouroun*, to burn, from *pur*, fire.]

py·ro·stat (pī′rə-stăt′, pîr′-) n. 1. An automatic sensing device that activates an alarm or extinguisher in the event of fire. 2. A high-temperature thermostat. [PYRO- + -STAT.]

py·ro·sul·fate (pī′rə-sŭl′fāt′, pîr′-) n. A salt of pyrosulfuric acid. [PYROSULF(URIC ACID) + -ATE (salt).]

py·ro·sul·fu·ric acid (pī′rō-sŭl-fyŏŏr′ĭk, -pîr′ō-) n. A heavy, oily, colorless to dark-brown liquid, H₂S₂O₇, produced by adding sulfur trioxide to concentrated sulfuric acid and used in petroleum refining and explosives.

py·ro·tech·nic (pī′rō-tĕk′nĭk) adj. Also **py·ro·tech·ni·cal** (-nĭ-kəl). 1. Of or pertaining to fireworks. 2. Resembling fireworks; brilliant: *a pyrotechnic wit*. [PYRO- + Greek *tekhnikos*, of art or skill. See **technical**.] —**py·ro·tech·ni·cal·ly** adv.

py·ro·tech·nics (pī′rə-tĕk′nĭks, pîr′-) n. Also **py·ro·tech·ny** (-tĕk′nē) (for sense 1). 1. *Used with a singular verb*. The art of manufacturing or setting off fireworks. 2. *Used with a singular or plural verb*. A fireworks display. 3. *Used with a singular or plural verb*. A brilliant display, as of rhetoric or wit, or of virtuosity in the performing arts. —**py·ro·tech·nist** n.

py·rox·ene (pī-rŏk′sēn′) n. Any of a group of crystalline mineral silicates common in igneous and metamorphic rocks and containing two metallic oxides, usually magnesium, iron, calcium, or sodium. [French *pyroxène*, "stranger to fire" (i.e., foreign substance in igneous rocks) : PYRO- + Greek *xenos*, stranger.] —**py·rox·en·ic** (pī′-rŏk-sĕn′ĭk) adj.

py·rox·e·nite (pī-rŏk′sə-nīt′) n. An igneous rock consisting chiefly of pyroxenes.

pyrite *The name of this mineral comes from the Greek word for fire. Pyrite will make sparks if struck with a harder material. It is also known as fool's gold.*

pyrotechnics *Pyrotechnics in the form of a fireworks display. The term comes from Greek words meaning "skill with fire."*

py·rox·y·lin (pī-rŏk'sə-lĭn) *n.* Also **py·rox·y·line** (-lēn', -lĭn). A highly flammable nitrocellulose used in the manufacture of collodion, plastics, and lacquers. [PYRO- + XYL(O)- + -IN.]

pyr·rhic[1] (pĭr'ĭk) *n.* A Greek metrical foot composed of two short syllables. [Latin, from Greek *(pous) purrhikhios,* pyrrhic (foot), from *purrhikhē,* PYRRHIC (dance).] —**pyr·rhic** *adj.*

pyrrhic[2] *n.* An ancient Greek war dance imitative of actual fighting. [Latin, from Greek *purrhikhē,* traditionally supposed to be from *Purrhikhos,* the name of its creator.] —**pyr·rhic** *adj.*

Pyrrhic victory *n.* A victory involving great losses on the victor's part. [After *Pyrrhus,* (*c.* 318–272 B.C.), King of Epirus, whose tactical victories against the Romans failed to avert his defeat.]

Pyr·rhon·ism (pĭr'ə-nĭz'əm) *n.* **1.** The skeptical philosophy of Pyrrho of Elis (*c.* 360–270 B.C.); especially, the doctrine that nothing can be known as absolutely certain. **2.** Loosely, skepticism or philosophic doubt. —**Pyr·rhon·ist** *n.*

pyr·rho·tite (pĭr'ə-tīt') *n.* Also **pyr·rho·tine** (-tīn'). A brownish-bronze weakly magnetic mineral iron sulfide. When it contains nickel, it is a nickel ore, and is used for making sulfuric acid. Also called "magnetic pyrites." [German *Pyrrhotin,* from Greek *purrhotēs,* redness, from *purrhos,* fiery, red, from *pur,* fire.]

pyr·role (pĭ-rōl', pĭr'ōl') *n.* A yellowish or brown oil, C_4H_5N, with an odor similar to chloroform and used to manufacture a wide variety of drugs. Also called "azole." [Greek *purrhos,* red, tawny, from *pur,* fire + -OLE.] —**pyr·rol·ic** (pĭ-rōl'ĭk) *adj.*

pyr·rol·i·dine *n.* A colorless heterocyclic base, $C_4H_9N_1$, made synthetically by the hydrogenation of pyrrole and occurring in tobacco leaves. [PYRROLE + -IDE + -INE.]

py·ru·vic acid (pī-rōō'vĭk, pī-) *n.* A colorless liquid, $CH_3COCOOH$, formed as a fundamental intermediate in protein and carbohydrate metabolism. [PYR(O)- + Latin *ūva,* grape.]

Py·thag·o·ras (pĭ-thăg'ər-əs) (*c.* 580–500 B.C.). Greek philosopher, theologian, and mathematician. The school he founded in southern Italy taught spiritual growth through asceticism and the study of musical harmony and geometry. Though his famous theorem was known previously, he was the first to prove its universal validity. His insight into the relationship between numbers and the perceived universe gives him claim to be the first true mathematician.

Py·thag·o·re·an·ism (pĭ-thăg'ə-rē'ə-nĭz'əm) *n.* The philosophy of Pythagoras, chiefly distinguished by its description of reality in terms of arithmetical relationships and the doctrine of the transmigration of souls. —**Py·thag·o·re·an** (pĭ-thăg'ə-rē'ən) *n. & adj.*

Pythagorean theorem *n.* The theorem that in a right-angled triangle the square of the length of the hypotenuse is equal to the sum of the squares of the lengths of the other two sides.

Pyth·e·as (pĭth'ē-əs) (4th century B.C.). Greek navigator. Based in Marseilles, he passed through the Strait of Gibraltar and explored the Atlantic coasts of Europe, Britain, and possibly Iceland. His voyages are described by Strabo (*c.* 60 B.C.–A.D. 21).

Pyth·i·a (pĭth'ē-ə). The oracular priestess of Apollo at Delphi.

Pyth·i·an (pĭth'ē-ən) *adj.* **1.** Of or pertaining to Delphi, the temple of Apollo at Delphi, or its oracle. **2.** Of or pertaining to the Pythian games. [Latin *Pythius,* from Greek *Puthios,* from *Puthō, Puthōn,* ancient name of Delphi, after the serpent PYTHON.] —**Pyth·ic** *adj.*

Pythian games *pl.n.* In ancient Greece, a pan-Hellenic athletics festival held every four years at Delphi in honor of Apollo.

py·thon (pī'thŏn', -thən) *n.* Any of various large, nonvenomous Old World snakes of the family Pythonidae, that coil around and suffocate their prey. [After PYTHON.]

Py·thon (pī'thŏn', -thən). *Greek Mythology.* A dragon or serpent that was the tutelary demon of the oracular cult at Delphi until killed and expropriated by Apollo.

py·tho·ness (pī'thə-nĭs, pĭth'ə-) *n.* **1.** Pythia. **2.** A prophetess. [Middle English *phitonesse,* from Old French *phitonise, pithonise,* from Late Latin *pȳthōnissa,* from Greek *Puthōn,* PYTHON.]

py·thon·ic (pī-thŏn'ĭk) *adj.* **1.** Of, pertaining to, or resembling a python. **2.** Of or like an oracle; prophetic.

py·u·ri·a (pī-yōōr'ē-ə) *n.* The abnormal condition of pus in the urine. [New Latin : PY(O)- + -URIA.]

pyx, pix (pĭks) *n.* **1.** *Roman Catholic Church.* **a.** A container in which the Eucharist is carried. **b.** A container in which supplies of wafers for the Eucharist are kept. **2.** A chest in a mint in which specimen coins are placed to await assay. [Middle English *pyxe,* from Latin *pyxis,* box, from Greek *puxis,* box.]

pyx·id·i·um (pĭk-sĭd'ē-əm) *n., pl.* **-idia** (-ē-ə) *Botany.* A seed capsule having a circular lid that falls off to release the seeds. Also called "pyxis." [New Latin, from Greek *puxidion,* diminutive of *puxis,* PYXIS.]

pyx·ie (pĭk'sē) *n.* A creeping evergreen shrub, *Pyxidanthera barbulata,* native to pine barrens of the eastern United States, having small white or pinkish flowers. [Latin *Pyxidanthera:* PYXIS + ANTHER.]

pyx·is (pĭk'sĭs) *n., pl.* **pyxides** (pĭk'sə-dēz'). *Botany.* A pyxidium. [From Greek *puxis,* box.]

Pyxis *n.* A constellation in the Southern Hemisphere, near Antlia and Puppis. [New Latin *Pyxis (nautica),* "the Mariner's Compass," from Greek *puxis,* box, PYXIS.]

q, Q (kyōō) *n., pl.* **q's** or **Q's.** 1. The 17th letter of the modern English alphabet. See feature at **alphabet.** 2. Any of the speech sounds represented by this letter. 3. The 17th in a series; 16th when *J* is omitted.

q, Q, q., Q. *Note:* As an abbreviation or symbol, *q* may be a small or a capital letter, with or without a period. Established forms or those generally preferred precede the definition. When no form is given, all four forms are in general use in that sense. 1. **q.** quart. 2. **q.** quarter. 3. **q.** quarterly. 4. **q., Q.** quarto. 5. **Q** *Chess.* queen. 6. **q.** query. 7. **q.** question. 8. **Q** quetzal. 9. **q.** quintal. 10. **q.** quire.

Qad·da·fi or **Kad·da·fi** or **Kha·da·fy** (kə-dä'fē) or **Gad·da·fi** (gə-), **Muammar Muhammad el-** or **al-** (1942-). Libyan ruler. In 1969 he led an army coup that toppled the Libyan monarchy and imposed Islamic socialist policies on the country. He allegedly sponsors international terrorism to promote nationalistic and pro-Palestinian causes.

Qandahar. See **Kandahar.**

Qa·tar (kä'tär'). Independent country, bordering the Persian Gulf. It consists of the peninsula of Qatar, which is mainly desert. Its economy is primarily based on large resources of onshore and offshore oil and gas. Qatar was a British protectorate from 1916 until 1971. Area, 11,000 square kilometers (4,247 square miles). Population, 22,000. Capital, Doha. See map at **Gulf States.**

QB *Chess.* queen's bishop.

Q.B. Queen's Bench.

Q-boat (kyōō'bōt') *n.* A **Q-ship** *(see).*

QBP *Chess.* queen's bishop's pawn.

Q.C. Queen's Counsel.

Q.E.D. which was to be demonstrated or proved. Used to indicate that an incontrovertible conclusion has been reached. [Latin *quod erat demonstrandum.*]

Q.E.F. which was to be done. [Latin *quod erat faciendum.*]

Q factor *n.* 1. A measure of the efficiency of a resonant circuit given by (I/R) (L/C)^{1/2}, where R is the resistance, L the inductance, and C the capitance of the circuit. Also called "quality factor." 2. The heat released in a nuclear reaction, usually expressed in electron-volts. Also called "Q value." [Sense 2, *Q* (heat) + FACTOR.]

Q fever *n.* A disease of livestock caused by the rickettsia, *Coxiella burnettii,* that can be transmitted to humans and causes severe headaches and pneumonia. [From *Q*ueensland, Australia, where it was first identified.]

Qin or **Ch'in** (chĭn). A dynasty that ruled China from 221 to 206 B.C.

qindarka. Variant of **quintar.**

Qing or **Ch'ing** (chĭng). A Manchu dynasty that in 1644 took Beijing from the Ming and became the last ruling dynasty of China.

Qing·hai or **Ch'ing-hai** or **Tsing·hai** (chĭng'hī'). Province in northwestern China, named after one of the largest salt lakes in China, Qinghai Hu, which is also known by its Mongol name, Koko Nor, meaning "Blue Sea."

QKt *Chess.* queen's knight.

QKtP *Chess.* queen's knight's pawn.

ql. quintal.

Q.M. quartermaster.

Q.M.G. Quartermaster General.

qn. question.

Qom (kôm, kōm). Also **Qum** or **Kum** (kōōm). City in central Iran, on the main route connecting the capital Tehran with southern Iran. It is an important holy city for Shiite Muslims, and pilgrims flock to visit the tomb of Fatima, sister of Imam Riza.

qoph (kôf, kōf) *n.* The 19th letter of the Hebrew alphabet. See feature at **alphabet.** [Hebrew *qōph,* from a Northwest Semitic word meaning "eye of a needle."]

QP *Chess.* queen's pawn.

q. pl. as much as you please [Latin *quantum placet*].

qq. questions.

Qq. quartos.

qq.v. which (things) see [New Latin *quae vide*].

QR *Chess.* queen's rook.

qr. 1. quarter. 2. quarterly. 3. quire.

QRP *Chess.* queen's rook's pawn.

q.s. as much as suffices. [Latin *quantum sufficit.*]

Q-ship (kyōō'shĭp') *n.* A merchant ship carrying concealed guns as a trap for unsuspecting enemy submarines or ships. Also called "Q-boat." [From *Q,* perhaps representing *query.*]

QSO *Astronomy.* quasi-stellar object.

QSRS *Astronomy.* quasi-stellar radio source.

qt. 1. quantity. 2. quart.

q.t. *n. Slang.* Quiet: *The teenager sneaked out of the house on the q.t. and drove off in the family car.* [Short for QUIET.]

qto. quarto.

qty. quantity.

qu. 1. queen. 2. query. 3. question.

qua (kwā, kwä) *prep.* By virtue of being; in the capacity or character of: *The President, qua head of his party, mediated the dispute.* [Latin *quā,* ablative singular feminine of *quī,* who.]

Quaa·lude (kwā'lōōd') *n.* A trademark for **methaqualone** *(see).*

quack[1] (kwăk) *n.* The characteristic harsh, rasping call of a duck. ~*intr.v.* **quacked, quacking, quacks.** To emit a quack. [Imitative; compare Dutch *kwakken* and German *quacken.*]

quack[2] *n.* 1. An untrained person who pretends to have medical knowledge. 2. *Informal.* A person who pretends to possess knowledge or skill that he lacks; charlatan. ~*adj.* Of, pertaining to, or typical of a quack: *quack remedies.* ~*v.* **quacked, quacking, quacks.** ~*intr.* To act as a quack. ~*tr.* To offer (a remedy, for example) in fraudulent and extravagant terms. [Shortened from QUACKSALVER.] —**quack·er·y** *n.*

quack·sal·ver (kwăk'săl'vər) *n. Archaic.* A quack; a charlatan. [Dutch *quacksalver* : probably from obsolete *quacken,* to chatter + *salf,* SALVE.]

quad[1] (kwŏd) *n. Informal.* A quadrangle.

quad[2] *n. Printing.* A piece of type metal lower than the raised typeface that is used for filling spaces and blank lines. Also called "quadrat."

quad[3] *n. Informal.* A quadruplet.

quad. 1. quadrangle. 2. quadrant. 3. quadrilateral.

quadr–. Variant of **quadri–.**

quad·ran·gle (kwŏd'răng'gəl) *n. Abbr.* **quad.** 1. In geometry, a plane figure consisting of four points, no three of which are collinear, connected by straight lines. 2. **a.** A rectangular area surrounded on all four sides by buildings, as at some colleges and universities. **b.** The buildings bordering this area. 3. The area of land shown on one atlas sheet charted by the U.S. Geological Survey. [Middle English, from Old French, from Late Latin *quadr(i)angulum,* from Latin, neuter of *quadr(i)angulus,* having four angles : QUADR(I)- + *angulus,* ANGLE.] —**quad·ran·gu·lar** (kwŏ-drăng'gyə-lər) *adj.*

quad·rant (kwŏd'rənt) *n. Abbr.* **quad.** 1. In geometry: **a.** A circular arc subtending a central angle of 90°; a quarter of the circumference of a circle. **b.** The plane area bounded by two perpendicular radii and the arc they subtend. **c.** Any of the four areas into which a plane is divided by the reference axes in a coordinate system, designated *first, second, third,* and *fourth,* counting clockwise from the area in which both coordinates are positive. 2. Anything, such as a machine part, that is shaped like a quarter circle. 3. An early instrument for measuring altitudes, consisting of a graduated arc with a movable radius for measuring angles. [Middle English, quarter of a day, from Latin *quadrāns* (stem *quadrant-*), fourth part, quarter; akin to *quattuor,* four.]

quad·ra·phon·ic (kwŏd'rə-fŏn'ĭk) *adj.* Of, pertaining to, or reproduced by a high-fidelity sound system with equipment for the reproduction of sound from four separate channels. Compare **stereophonic.** [Irregularly from QUADR(I)- + PHONIC.] —**quad·ra·phon·ics, quad·raph·o·ny** (kwŏ-drăf'ə-nē) *n.*

quad·rat (kwŏd'rət, -răt') *n.* 1. *Printing.* A type metal, **quad** *(see).* 2. **a.** A square or rectangular area of vegetation, usually one square meter, selected at random for study of its plants, which are regarded as typical of the surrounding area. **b.** A rectangular frame used to mark out such an area. [Middle English, variant of QUADRATE.]

quad·rate (kwŏd′rāt′) *adj.* **1.** *Zoology.* Of, pertaining to, designating, or being a bone or cartilaginous structure of the skull that joins the upper and lower jaws in birds, fish, reptiles, and amphibians. **2.** Having four sides and four angles; square or rectangular. ~*n.* (-rāt′, -rĭt). **1.** A quadrate bone. **2.** An approximately square or cubic area, space, or object. ~*intr.v.* (-rāt′) **quadrated, -rating, -rates.** *Archaic.* To correspond; agree. [Middle English, square, from Latin *quadrātus,* past participle of *quadrāre,* to make square, from *quadrus,* a square.]

quad·rat·ic (kwŏ-drăt′ĭk) *adj.* Of, pertaining to, or containing mathematical equations whose terms are of the second degree or less. [From QUADRATE.] —**quad·rat·ic** *n.*

quadratic equation *n.* An equation of the second degree, having the general form $ax^2 + bx + c = 0$, where *a, b,* and *c* are constants.

quadratic formula *n.* The formula $x = [-b \pm \sqrt{(b^2 - 4ac)}]/2a$, used to calculate the roots of a quadratic equation.

quad·rat·ics (kwŏ-drăt′ĭks) *n. Used with a singular verb.* The algebra of quadratic equations.

quad·ra·ture (kwŏd′rə-chŏŏr′, -chər) *n.* **1.** The process of making something square. **2.** *Mathematics.* The process of constructing a square equal in area to a given surface. **3.** *Astronomy.* Any configuration in which the angular separation of two celestial bodies, as measured from a third, is 90°. **4.** *Electronics.* The state in which two alternating signals of the same frequency differ in phase by 90°.

quad·ren·ni·al (kwŏ-drĕn′ē-əl) *adj.* **1.** Happening once in four years. **2.** Lasting for four years. ~*n.* An event occurring every four years. —**quad·ren·ni·al·ly** *adv.*

quad·ren·ni·um (kwŏ-drĕn′ē-əm) *n., pl.* **-ums** or **-nia** (-ē-ə). A period of four years. [Latin *quadr(i)ennium* : QUADR(I)- + *annus,* year.]

quadri-, quadr- *prefix.* Indicates four; for example, **quadriceps, quadric.** [Latin; akin to *quattuor,* four.]

quad·ric (kwŏd′rĭk) *adj.* Of, pertaining to, or designating geometric surfaces that are defined by quadratic equations. [QUADR(I)- + -IC.]

quad·ri·cen·ten·ni·al (kwŏd′rĭ-sĕn-tĕn′ē-əl) *n.* A 400th anniversary. —**quad·ri·cen·ten·ni·al** *adj.*

quad·ri·ceps (kwŏd′rĭ-sĕps′) *n.* The large four-part extensor muscle at the front of the thigh. [New Latin : QUADRI- + (BI)CEPS.] —**quad·ri·cip·i·tal** (kwŏd′rĭ-sĭp′ə-təl) *adj.*

qua·dri·ga (kwŏ-drē′gə) *n.* In classical times, a chariot drawn by four horses.

quad·ri·lat·er·al (kwŏd′rə-lăt′ər-əl) *n. Abbr.* **quad.** In geometry, a four-sided polygon. ~*adj. Abbr.* **quad.** Having four sides.

qua·drille¹ (kwŏ-drĭl′, kwə-, kə-) *n.* **1.** A square dance of French origin composed of five figures and performed by four couples. **2.** A piece of music for the quadrille in 6/8 and 2/4 time. [French, originally "one of the four divisions of an army, group of knights at a tournament," from Spanish *cuadrilla,* diminutive of *cuadra,* "square," from Latin *quadra.*]

quadrille² *n.* A card game popular during the 18th century, played by four people with a pack of 40 cards. [French, perhaps from Spanish *cuartillo,* from *cuarto,* fourth, from Latin *quārtus;* assimilated to QUADRILLE (dance).]

quad·ril·lion (kwŏ-drĭl′yən) *n.* **1.** The cardinal number represented by 1 followed by 15 zeros, usually written 10¹⁵. **2.** *Chiefly British.* The cardinal number represented by 1 followed by 24 zeros, usually written 10²⁴. [French : QUADR(I)- + (M)ILLION.] —**quad·ril·lion** *adj.* —**quad·ril·lionth** *n., adj.,* & *adv.*

quad·ri·no·mi·al (kwŏd′rə-nō′mē-əl) *n.* A polynomial with four terms. [QUADRI- + -nomial (as in binomial).]

quad·ri·par·tite (kwŏd′rə-pär′tīt′) *adj.* **1.** Consisting of or divided into four parts. **2.** Involving four participants.

quad·ri·ple·gi·a (kwŏd′rə-plē′jē-ə, -jə) *n. Medicine.* Complete paralysis of the body from the neck down. [QUADRI- + -PLEGIA.] —**quad·ri·ple·gic** (kwŏd′rə-plē′jĭk) *adj. & n.*

quad·ri·va·lent (kwŏd′rə-vā′lənt) *adj. Chemistry.* **1.** Having four valences. **2.** Having a valence of four; tetravalent. —**quad·ri·va·lence, quad·ri·va·len·cy** *n.*

quad·riv·i·um (kwŏ-drĭv′ē-əm) *n., pl.* **-ia** (-ē-ə). The higher division of the seven liberal arts in the Middle Ages, composed of geometry, astronomy, arithmetic, and music. Compare **trivium.** [Late Latin, from Latin, "place where four ways meet" : QUADRI- + *via,* way.]

quad·roon (kwŏ-drōōn′) *n.* A person having one Negro grandparent. [Spanish *cuarterón,* from *cuarto,* quarter, from Latin *quārtus.*]

quad·ru·ma·nous (kwŏ-drōō′mə-nəs) *adj.* Also **quad·ru·ma·nal** (-nəl). Having four feet with opposable first digits, as primates other than humans do. [New Latin *quadrumana* (noun), neuter plural of *quadrumanus* : *quadru-,* variant of QUADRI- + *manus,* hand.]

quad·ru·ped (kwŏd′rə-pĕd′) *n.* A four-footed animal. ~*adj.* Four-footed. [Latin *quadrupēs* : *quadru-,* variant of QUADRI- + -PED.] —**quad·ru·pe·dal** (kwŏ-drōō′pə-dəl, kwŏd′rə-pĕd′l) *adj.*

quad·ru·ple (kwŏ-drōō′pəl, -drŭp′əl, kwŏd′rōō-pəl) *adj.* **1.** Consisting of or having four parts, members, or copies. **2.** Multiplied by four; four times as much, as many, or as large. **3.** *Music.* Having four beats to the measure: *quadruple time.* ~*n.* A fourfold amount. ~*v.* **quadrupled, -pling, -ples.** —*tr.* To multiply or increase by four; quadruplicate. —*intr.* To be multiplied fourfold. [French, from Latin *quadruplus* : *quadru-,* variant of QUADRI- + *-plus,* -fold.]

quad·ru·plet (kwŏ-drōō′plĭt, -drŭp′lĭt, kwŏd′rə-plĭt) *n.* **1.** A group

or combination of four associated by common properties or behavior. **2.** Any of four offspring born in a single birth.

quad·ru·pli·cate (kwŏ-drōō′plĭ-kĭt) *adj.* **1.** Multiplied by four; quadruple. **2.** Fourth in a group of four identical things. ~*n.* **1.** Any of a set of four. **2.** A set of four copies. ~*v.* (-kāt′) **quadruplicated, -cating, -cates.** —*tr.* To multiply by four. —*intr.* To become quadruplicated. [Latin *quadruplicātus,* past participle of *quadruplicāre,* to multiply by four, from *quadruplex,* fourfold : *quadru-,* variant of QUADRI- + *-plex,* -fold.] —**quad·ru·pli·cate·ly** *adv.* —**quad·ru·pli·ca·tion** *n.*

quad·ru·plic·i·ty (kwŏd′rə-plĭs′ə-tē) *n.* The state of being quadrupled. [Latin *quadruplex,* fourfold. See **quadruplicate.**]

quaes·tor (kwĕs′tər, kwē′stôr) *n.* Any of various public officials in ancient Rome responsible for finance or administration in various areas of government and the military. [Middle English *questor,* from Latin *quaestor,* from *quaerere* (past participial stem *quaesit-*), to seek, ask.] —**quaes·to·ri·al** (kwē-stôr′ē-əl, -stōr′ē-əl, kwĕ-) *adj.* —**quaes·tor·ship** *n.*

quaff (kwŏf, kwăf, kwôf) *v.* **quaffed, quaffing, quaffs.** —*tr.* To drink deeply. —*intr.* To take a long, deep drink. ~*n.* A long, deep drink. [Perhaps imitative.] —**quaff·er** *n.*

quag·ga (kwăg′ə, kwŏg′ə) *n.* A zebralike mammal, *Equus quagga,* of southern Africa, that has been extinct since the late 19th century. [Obsolete Afrikaans, from Xhosa *i-qwara,* perhaps from Hottentot *qûagga.*]

quag·gy (kwăg′ē, kwŏg′ē) *adj.* **-gier, -giest. 1.** Like a marsh; soggy. **2.** Soft; flabby. [From *quag,* marshy place; akin to dialect *quag,* to tremble, shake (imitative).]

quag·mire (kwăg′mīr′, kwŏg′-) *n.* **1.** A bog or swamp. **2.** A difficult or precarious situation from which extrication is almost impossible. [From *quag* (see QUAGGY) + MIRE.]

qua·hog (kwô′hôg′, -hŏg′, kwō′-, kwô′-, kō′-) *n.* An edible clam, *Venus mercenaria,* of the Atlantic coast of North America, having a hard, rounded shell. [Narraganset *poquaûhock.*]

quaich, quaigh (kwākʜ) *n.* A two-handled Scottish drinking cup of varying size. [Scottish Gaelic *cuach,* from Old Irish *cūach,* from Latin *caucus,* drinking cup, from Greek *kauka, kaukion.*]

Quai d'Or·say (kā dôr-sā′). Quay on the left bank of the Seine River in Paris, which has given its name to the French Ministry of Foreign Affairs located there.

quail¹ (kwāl) *n., pl.* **quails** or collectively **quail. 1.** Any of various small partridgelike Old World birds of the family Phasianidae; especially, *Coturnix coturnix,* having mottled brown plumage, a short tail, and a distinctive cry. **2.** Any of various New World birds that are similar or related to the quail, as the bobwhite. [Middle English *quaille,* from Old French, from Medieval Latin *coacula* (imitative of its cry).]

quail² *intr.v.* **quailed, quailing, quails. 1.** To lose courage; give way: *She quailed at the thought of giving testimony in a court of law.* **2.** To recoil in fear; cower. —See Synonyms at **recoil.** [Middle English *quailen†,* to decline, fail, give way.]

quaint (kwānt) *adj.* **quainter, quaintest. 1.** Agreeably curious, especially in an old-fashioned way: *a quaint old cottage.* **2.** Unfamiliar or unusual in character; odd: *The inhabitants of the island have quaint customs.* **3.** Inappropriate or illogical: *They fought the war out of a quaint sense of honor.* —See Synonyms at **strange.** [Middle English *queinte, cointe,* clever, skillfully made, from Old French *cointe,* expert, elegant, from Latin *cognitus,* past participle of *cognōscere,* to be acquainted with : *com-,* with + *gnōscere,* to know.] —**quaint·ly** *adv.* —**quaint·ness** *n.*

quake (kwāk) *intr.v.* **quaked, quaking, quakes. 1.** To shake or tremble with instability or shock: *The ground quaked.* **2.** To shiver or tremble, as with cold or strong emotion: *quaking with rage.* —See Synonyms at **shake.** ~*n.* **1.** An instance of quaking. **2.** An earthquake. [Middle English *quaken,* Old English *cwacian,* from Germanic *kwei-* (unattested), to shake.] —**quak·i·ly** *adv.* —**quak·y** *adj.*

Quak·er (kwā′kər) *n.* A member of the Society of Friends. Not used officially by the Friends. [From QUAKE, probably in allusion to the admonition of George Fox, founder of the Society, to "tremble at the word of the Lord."] —**Quak·er** *adj.* —**Quak·er·ism** *n.* —**Quak·er·ly** *adj. & adv.*

Quak·er-la·dies (kwā′kər-lā′dēz) *pl.n.* A plant, **bluets** (see).

quaking aspen *n.* A tree, the **aspen** (see).

quaking grass *n.* Any of several grass species of the genus *Briza,* having delicate, spreading panicles with ovoid spikelets. [Referring to its motion in wind.]

qual·i·fi·ca·tion (kwŏl′ə-fĭ-kā′shən) *n.* **1. a.** The act of qualifying. **b.** The condition of being qualified. **2.** Any quality, accomplishment, or ability that makes a person suitable for a particular position or task: *Despite her excellent qualifications she wasn't hired.* **3.** A condition or circumstance that must be met or complied with: *hadn't fulfilled the residence qualifications for graduation.* **4.** A restriction or modification: *an offer with a number of qualifications.*

qual·i·fied (kwŏl′ə-fīd′) *adj.* **1.** Having the appropriate qualifications for an office, position, or task. **2.** Limited, restricted, or modified: *gave qualified approval.* —**qual·i·fied·ly** (kwŏl′ə-fīd′lē, -fī′ĭd-lē) *adv.*

qual·i·fi·er (kwŏl′ə-fī′ər) *n.* **1.** One that qualifies or has qualified: *Five qualifiers proceeded to the final.* **2.** A preliminary round or heat in a contest or selection process. **3.** *Grammar.* A **modifier** (see).

qual·i·fy (kwŏl′ə-fī′) *v.* **-fied, -fying, -fies.** —*tr.* **1.** To describe by enumerating the characteristics or qualities of; characterize. **2.** To make competent or suitable for an office, position, or task. **3. a.** To declare competent or capable; certify. **b.** To make legally capable; license. **4.** To modify, limit, or restrict, as by giving exceptions. **5.** To make less harsh or severe; moderate: *qualified criticism.* **6.** *Grammar.* To modify the meaning of (a word or phrase). —*intr.* **1.** To be or to become qualified. **2.** To reach the later or final stages of a contest or selection process by competing successfully in earlier rounds. [French *qualifier,* from Medieval Latin *quālificāre,* to attribute a quality to : Latin *quālis,* of what kind (see **quality**) + *facere,* to make.]

qual·i·ta·tive (kwŏl'ə-tā'tĭv) *adj.* Of, pertaining to, or concerning quality: *made a purely qualitative assessment, taking no account of number or size.* [Late Latin *quālitātivus,* from Latin *quālitās,* QUALITY.] —**qual·i·ta·tive·ly** *adv.*

qualitative analysis *n.* Chemical determination of the constituents of a substance without regard to quantity. Compare **quantitative analysis.**

qual·i·ty (kwŏl'ə-tē) *n., pl.* **-ties. 1. a.** An inherent or distinguishing characteristic; property. **b.** A personal trait, especially a character trait; feature: *Her worst quality is her impatience.* **2.** The essential character of something; nature: *Mahogany has the quality of being durable.* **3. a.** Degree or grade of excellence: *Wine of low quality can ruin an otherwise elegant dinner.* **b.** Superiority of kind; excellence: *an intellect of unquestioned quality.* **5. a.** High social position. **b.** People of high social position. **6.** *Music.* Timbre, as determined by overtones: *The tenor's voice had a distinctive metallic quality.* **7.** *Phonetics.* The character of a vowel sound determined by the size and shape of the oral cavity and the amount of resonance with which the sound is produced. **8.** *Logic.* The positive or negative character of a proposition. —*adj.* Being of high quality; excellent: *quality goods; quality entertainment.* [Middle English *qualite,* from Old French, from Latin *quālitās* (stem *quālitāt-*), from *quālis,* of what kind.]
> **Synonyms:** attribute, character, property, trait.

quality control *n.* A system for ensuring the maintenance of proper standards, especially in manufactured goods, by means of measures including periodic random inspection.

quality factor *n.* The Q factor *(see).*

quality of life *n.* The degree of emotional, intellectual, or cultural satisfaction in one's everyday life as distinct from the degree of material comfort. Compare **standard of living.**

qualm (kwäm, kwôm) *n.* **1.** A feeling of misgiving, uneasiness, or doubt, especially over a matter of conscience. **2.** A sudden feeling of sickness, faintness, or nausea. [16th century : origin obscure.] —**qualm·ish** *adj.* —**qualm·ish·ly** *adv.*
> **Synonyms:** compunction, misgiving, reservation, scruple.

quamash. Variant of **camass.**

quan·da·ry (kwŏn'də-rē, -drē) *n., pl.* **-ries.** A state of uncertainty or perplexity; a dilemma. —See Synonyms at **predicament.** [16th century : origin obscure.]

quan·dong, quan·dang (kwŏn'dông') *n.* **1.** A shrubby Australian tree, *Santalum acuminatus,* that yields an edible fruit containing an edible seed. **2.** An Australian tree, *Elaeocarpus grandis,* that produces straw-colored, easily worked timber. [From a native Australian language.]

quant (kwŏnt) *n. British Regional.* A long pole used manually to propel a flat-bottomed boat, such as a punt, over shallow waterways. [Perhaps from Latin *contus,* from Greek *kontos,* pole for propelling a boat.] —**quant** *v.*

Quant (kwŏnt), **Mary** (1934–). British fashion designer. She opened her first boutique in 1957 with her husband, Alexander Plunket Greene, and by the 1960's had become one of the world's most influential designers.

quan·ta. Plural of **quantum.**

quan·tal (kwŏn'təl) *adj. Physics.* **1.** Of or pertaining to a quantum or a quantized system. **2.** Existing in only one of two possible states.

quan·ta·some (kwŏn'tə-sōm') *n. Botany.* One of the numerous granules located on the inner lamellar surface of a chloroplast. [Probably from Latin *quanta,* how many, plural of QUANTUM + -SOME.]

quan·tic (kwŏn'tĭk) *n. Mathematics.* A homogeneous polynomial having two or more variables, as in $x^3 + y^2x + y^3$. See **quadric, cubic, quartic.** [Latin *quantus,* how much + -IC.]

quan·ti·fi·er (kwŏn'tə-fī'ər) *n.* **1.** One that quantifies. **2.** *Grammar.* A modifier, such as *many* or *four,* indicating range, quantity, or application. **3.** *Logic.* An operator or symbol, indicating range, quantity, or application; especially, a *universal quantifier,* which indicates that every object of the kind specified is being referred to, and an *existential quantifier,* which indicates that at least one such object does actually exist.

quan·ti·fy (kwŏn'tə-fī') *tr.v.* **-fied, -fying, -fies. 1.** To determine or express the quantity of: *One cannot quantify the value of a human life.* **2.** *Logic.* To limit the quantity of (a term or proposition) by prefixing a quantifier such as *all, some,* or *none.* [Medieval Latin *quantificāre* : *quantus,* how great + *facere,* to make.] —**quan·ti·fi·a·ble** *adj.* —**quan·ti·fi·ca·tion** *n.*

quan·ti·ta·tive (kwŏn'tə-tā'tĭv) *adj.* **1. a.** Expressed or capable of expression as a quantity. **b.** Of, pertaining to, or susceptible of measurement. **c.** Of or pertaining to number or quantity. **2.** Pertaining to or based upon duration of sound rather than stress. Said especially of classical verse. [Medieval Latin *quantitātivus,* from Latin *quantitās,* QUANTITY.] —**quan·ti·ta·tive·ly** *adv.*

quantitative analysis *n.* Chemical determination of the amounts or proportions of constituents in a substance. Compare **qualitative analysis.**

quan·ti·ty (kwŏn'tə-tē) *n., pl.* **-ties.** *Abbr.* **qt., qty. 1. a.** A number or amount of something, either specified or indefinite. **b.** A considerable amount or number: *sell wholesale drugs in quanitity.* **c.** An exact amount or number. **2.** The measurable, countable, or comparable property or aspect of a thing. **3.** Something serving as the object of a mathematical operation. **4.** *Phonetics.* The length of a vowel or consonant sound expressed in terms of the time needed to produce it. **5.** *Logic.* The exact character of a proposition with respect to its universality, singularity, or particularity. **6.** *Physics.* An attribute that can be measured and assigned a value of a certain number of units. In this sense, also called "physical quantity." [Middle English *quantite,* from Old French, from Latin *quantitās* (stem *quantitāt-*), from *quantus,* how great.]

quantity surveyor *n.* A person who estimates, usually as a profession, the amounts and overall cost of the materials and labor needed in the construction of a building.

quan·tize (kwŏn'tīz') *tr.v.* **-tized, -tizing, -tizes.** *Physics.* **1.** To limit the possible values of (a magnitude or quantity) to a set of discrete values determined by quantum mechanical rules. **2.** To replace the dynamic variables of (a system) by the corresponding quantum mechanical operators in order to calculate the behavior of the system. [QUAN-T(UM) + -IZE.] —**quan·ti·za·tion** *n.*

Quan·trill (kwŏn'trĭl), **William Clarke** (1837–65). U.S. Confederate guerrilla leader. A schoolteacher turned thief and murderer, he led a group of men that sporadically supported the Confederacy during the Civil War. His wanton killing of civilians and war prisoners, particularly at Lawrence, Kansas, on August 21, 1863, earned him the epithet "bloodiest man in American history."

quan·tum (kwŏn'təm) *n., pl.* **-ta** (-tə). **1.** The quantity or amount of something. **2.** A specific portion of something. **3.** Something that may be counted or measured. **4.** *Physics.* A discrete, indivisible amount of some quantity, especially energy or angular momentum, by which a given system may change in any process. [Latin, neuter of *quantus,* how great.]

quantum chromodynamics *n. Physics.* Chromodynamics *(see).*

quantum electrodynamics *n. Physics.* The quantum-mechanical theory of the properties and interactions of charged elementary particles with each other and with electromagnetic radiation.

quantum gravitation *n. Physics.* A theory of gravitation in which interactions are caused by the exchange of particles (gravitons).

quantum jump *n.* **1.** *Physics.* The transition of an atomic or molecular system from one discrete energy level to another. It usually occurs with absorption or emission of radiation having energy equal to the difference between the two levels. **2.** Any abrupt change or step from one level or category to a quite different one, especially in knowledge or information. Also called "quantum leap."

quantum leap *n.* See **quantum jump** (sense 2).

quantum mechanics *n. Mathematics & Physics.* A formulation of the early ideas arising from quantum theory. It is used to interpret atomic and nuclear phenomena. See **wave mechanics, matrix mechanics, blackbody radiation.**

quantum number *n. Physics.* Any of a set of real numbers that individually characterize the properties and collectively specify the state of a particle or of a system that is quantized.

quantum state *n. Physics.* Any one of the possible states of a system described by quantum theory.

quantum statistics *n. Physics.* The use of statistics to determine the properties of large numbers of particles by calculating the distribution of the particles over possible quantum states. See **Fermi-Dirac statistics, Bose-Einstein statistics.**

quantum theory *n.* A mathematical theory of physical systems that was developed to account for several physical phenomena that could not be explained by classical mechanics. It postulates that a system can gain or lose energy only in discrete amounts (quanta). Further developments led to the theory of **wave-particle duality** *(see)* and were formalized in quantum mechanics.

quar. **1.** quarter. **2.** quarterly.

quar·an·tine (kwôr'ən-tēn', kwŏr'-) *n.* **1. a.** A period of time, originally lasting 40 days, during which a vehicle, a person, an animal, or goods suspected of carrying a contagious disease are detained at their port of entry under enforced isolation to prevent disease from entering a country. **b.** A place for such detention. **2.** Enforced isolation or restriction of free movement imposed to prevent a contagious disease from spreading. **3.** A condition of enforced isolation. —*tr.v.* **quarantined, -tining, -tines. 1.** To place in quarantine. **2.** To isolate politically or economically. [Italian *quarantina,* period of forty days, from *quaranta,* forty, from Latin *quadrāgintā.*]

quark (kwôrk, kwärk) *n. Physics.* Any of a hypothetical set of fermions having electric charges of magnitude one third or two thirds that of the electron, proposed (together with their antiparticles) as the fundamental units of baryons and mesons. [From a line in James Joyce's *Finnegans Wake,* "Three quarks for Muster Mark!"]

quar·rel¹ (kwôr'əl, kwŏr'-) *n.* **1.** An angry dispute; a disagreement; an argument. **2.** A cause for dispute or argument: *We have no quarrel with the findings.* —*intr.v.* **quarreled** or **-relled, -reling** or **-relling, -rels. 1.** To engage in a quarrel; argue angrily. **2.** To disagree; differ. **3.** To find fault with something; complain. —See Synonyms at **argue.** [Middle English, (cause for) complaint, from Old French, from Latin *querēla,* from *querī,* to complain.] —**quar·rel·er** *n.*

quarrel² *n.* **1.** A bolt for a crossbow. **2.** A small diamond-shaped or

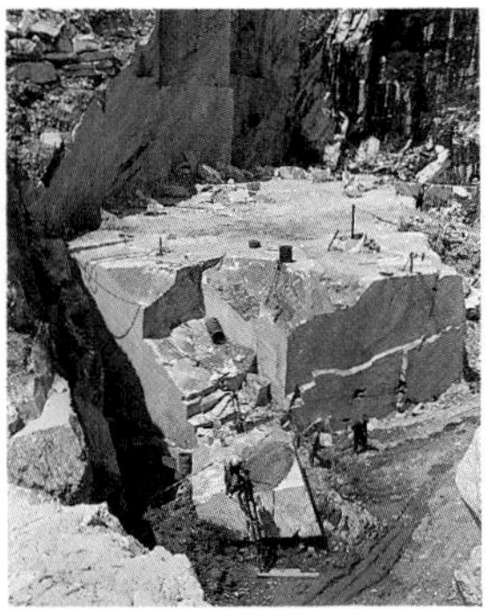

quarry *A quarry at Carrara in Italy, whose fine white marble has been prized by sculptors from Roman times to the present day. The Renaissance artist Michelangelo carved his statue of David from a single block of unflawed Carrara marble.*

square pane of glass in a latticed window. [Middle English *quarel,* from Old French, from Vulgar Latin *quadrellus* (unattested), diminutive of Late Latin *quadrus,* square.]

quar·rel·some (kwôr′əl-səm, kwŏr′-) *adj.* Tending to quarrel. —See Synonyms at **belligerent.**

quar·ri·on (kwôr′ē-ən, kwŏr′-) *n.* A parrot, the **cockatiel** *(see).* [Probably from an Australian native name.]

quar·ry[1] (kwôr′ē, kwŏr′ē) *n., pl.* **-ries. 1. a.** An animal that is hunted; prey. **b.** Such animals collectively; game. **2.** An object of pursuit. [Middle English *querre,* entrails of a beast given to the hounds, from Old French *cuiree,* variant of *co(u)ree,* from Vulgar Latin *corāta,* viscera, from Latin *cor,* heart.]

quarry[2] *n., pl.* **-ries. 1.** An open excavation or pit from which stone is obtained by digging, cutting, or blasting. **2.** A source from which material, such as information, can be extracted.
—*v.* **quarried, -rying, -ries.** —*tr.* **1.** To cut, dig, blast, or otherwise obtain (stone) from a quarry. **2.** To obtain (information) by long, careful searching. **3.** To use (land) as a quarry. —*intr.* To obtain material from or as if from a quarry. [Middle English *quarey, quarere,* from Old French *quarriere,* from *quarre* (unattested), "square stone," from Latin *quadrus,* square.] **—quar·ri·er** *n.*

quarry[3] *n., pl.* **-ries. 1.** A square or diamond shape. **2.** A pane of glass of this shape. [Variant of QUARREL (bolt).]

quart[1] (kwôrt) *n. Abbr.* **q., qt. 1. a.** A unit of volume or capacity in the U.S. Customary System, used in liquid measure, equal to 2 pints or .946 liter. **b.** A unit of volume or capacity in the U.S. Customary System, used in dry measure, equal to 2 pints or 1.101 liters. **c.** A unit of volume or capacity in the British Imperial System, used in liquid and dry measure, equal to 1.201 U.S. liquid quarts, 1.032 U.S. dry quarts, or 69.354 cubic inches. **2.** A container having a capacity of one quart. [Middle English, from Old French *quarte,* "fourth part (of a gallon)," from Latin *quārtus,* fourth.]

quart[2] (kärt) *n.* **1.** In card games like piquet, a sequence of four cards of one suit. **2.** Variant of **quarte.** [French *quarte,* fourth, QUARTE.]

quar·tan (kwôrt′n) *adj.* Occurring every fourth day, counting inclusively, or every 72 hours. Said of a fever.
—*n.* A recurrent malarial fever occurring every 72 hours. Also called "quartan malaria." [Middle English *quarteyne,* from Old French *quartaine,* from Latin *quārtāna (fēbris),* "quartan fever," from *quārtānus,* of the fourth, from *quārtus,* fourth.]

quarte, quart (kärt) *n.* The fourth regular position in fencing. [French, "fourth," "quart," from Old French. See **quart.**]

quar·ter (kwôr′tər) *n. Abbr.* **q., qr., quar. 1.** Any of four equal parts of something. **2.** One fourth of an hour; 15 minutes. **3.** A coin equal to one fourth of the dollar of the United States and Canada. **4. a.** One fourth of a year; three months: *Sales increased in the second quarter.* **b.** An academic term lasting for approximately three months. **5.** *Astronomy.* **a.** One fourth of the period of the moon's revolution around the earth. **b.** Either of two of the visible phases of the moon: the *first quarter,* from new moon until it approaches fullness, and the *third quarter,* from after fullness until it has disappeared in the sunrise. **6.** *Sports.* Any of four equal periods of playing time into which some games are divided: *The teams were tied when the last quarter ended.* **7.** A fourth of any of various units of weight or measure, as of a yard, a mile, a pound, or a hundredweight. **8.** *British.* A measure of grain equal to approximately eight bushels. **9. a.** Any of the four major divisions of the compass: north, south, east, or west. **b.** A fourth of the distance between any two of the 32 divisions of the compass. **10. a.** The general direction on either side of a ship located 45 degrees off the stern. **b.** Any of the four major divisions of the horizon as determined by the four points of the compass. **c.** A region or area of the earth thought of as falling in such a specified division of the compass. **11. a.** The upper portion of the after side of a ship, usually between the aftermost mast and the stern. **b.** The part of a yard between the slings and the yardarm. **12.** *Heraldry.* Any of four divisions of a shield. **13.** Any of the four limbs of the carcass of an animal, usually including the adjoining parts. **14.** Either side of a horse's hoof. **15.** The part of the side of a shoe between the heel and the vamp. **16.** *Plural.* A place of residence; specifically, the buildings or barracks housing military personnel. **17.** *Often* **quarters.** A proper or assigned station or place, as for officers and crew on a warship. **18.** *Often* **Quarter.** A district or section, as of a city, especially one characterized by a specified group of people or activity: *the Latin quarter; the financial quarter.* **19.** *Often* **quarters.** An unnamed person or group of persons, especially when considered as a source of something such as help or information: *got assistance from the highest quarters; no news from that quarter.* **20.** Mercy or clemency, especially when shown to an enemy: *gave no quarter and asked for none.*
—*v.* **quartered, -tering, -ters.** —*tr.* **1. a.** To cut or otherwise divide into four equal or equivalent parts. **b.** To quartersaw (a log). **2.** To divide or separate into a number of parts. **3.** To dismember (a human body) into four parts: *hanged, drawn, and quartered.* **4.** *Heraldry.* **a.** To divide (a shield) into four equal areas with vertical and horizontal lines. **b.** To place (a charge) in a quarter or quarters. **5. a.** To mark or place (holes, for example) a fourth of a circle apart. **b.** To fix (one machine part) at right angles to its connecting part. **6.** To provide (soldiers, for example) with lodgings. **7.** To traverse (an area of ground) laterally back and forth while slowly moving forward. Used especially of hunting dogs. —*intr.* **1.** To take up or be assigned lodgings. **2.** To traverse an area of ground by ranging over it from side to side.
—*adj.* **1.** Being one of four equal or equivalent parts. **2.** Being a fourth of a standard or usual value. [Middle English, from Old French *quartier,* from Latin *quārtārius,* from *quārtus,* fourth.]

quar·ter·age (kwôr′tər-ĭj) *n.* A monetary allowance, wage, or payment made or received quarterly.

quar·ter·back (kwôr′tər-băk′) *n. Football.* The backfield player whose position is behind the line of scrimmage and who usually calls the signals for the plays.
—*v.* **quarterbacked, -backing, -backs.** —*tr.* **1.** *Football.* To direct the offense of. **2.** To lead or direct the operations of: *quarterbacked the financing and organization of the new opera company.* —*intr.* To play quarterback.

quar·ter·bound (kwôr′tər-bound′) *adj.* Bound in material, such as leather, only along the spine and one quarter of the width of the adjoining part of the boards. Used of a book.

quarter day *n.* Any of the four days of the year regarded as the beginning of a new season or quarter, when most quarterly payments are due.

quar·ter-deck (kwôr′tər-dĕk′) *n.* The after part of the upper deck of a sailing ship, usually reserved for officers.

quar·ter·fi·nal (kwôr′tər-fī′nəl) *n.* In a competition or tournament, any of four matches constituting a round or stage whose winners go on to play in the semifinal round. **—quar·ter·fi·nal** *adj.*

quarter horse *n.* A strong saddle horse of a breed developed in the western United States. [Formerly trained for races of up to a quarter of a mile.]

quar·ter-hour, quar·ter hour (kwôr′tər-our′) *n.* **1.** Fifteen minutes. **2.** The point on a clock's face marking either 15 minutes after or 15 minutes before an hour.

quar·ter·ing (kwôr′tər-ĭng) *n. Heraldry.* **1.** The combining of different coats of arms on one shield, thereby showing the uniting of different families. **2. quarterings.** The coats of arms displayed in a quartering.

quar·ter·light (kwôr′tər-līt′) *n. British.* A small triangular window in the front of a car, next to the main side window.

quar·ter·ly (kwôr′tər-lē) *adj. Abbr.* **q., qr., quar. 1.** Occurring or appearing at regular intervals of three months: *a quarterly magazine; a quarterly payment.* **2.** Having four sections. Said of a heraldic shield.
—*n., pl.* **quarterlies.** *Abbr.* **q., qr., quar.** A publication issued regularly every three months.
—*adv.* **1.** *Heraldry.* In quarterings. **2.** At regular intervals of three months.

quar·ter·mas·ter (kwôr′tər-măs′tər, -mä′stər) *n. Abbr.* **Q.M. 1.** A military officer responsible for the food, clothing, and equipment of troops. **2.** A naval petty officer responsible for the navigation of a ship. [From QUARTER (residence).]

Quartermaster General *n. Abbr.* **Q.M.G.** A major general in the U.S. Army who is in command of a quartermaster corps.

quar·tern (kwôr′tərn) *n.* **1.** One fourth of something. **2.** *British.* A loaf of bread weighing about four pounds. [Middle English *quarteron,* from Old French, from *quartier,* QUARTER.]

quarter note *n. Music.* A note having one fourth the time value of a whole note. Also called "crotchet."

quar·ter-phase (kwôr′tər-fāz′) *adj. Electronics.* Two-phase.

quar·ter·saw (kwôr′tər-sô′) *tr.v.* **-sawed, -sawed** or **-sawn** (-sôn′), **-sawing, -saws.** To saw (a log) into quarters lengthwise along its axis.

quarter sessions *pl.n. Law.* **1.** In the United States, a local court with criminal jurisdiction and sometimes administrative functions that sits quarterly. **2.** A former British court that sat at least four times a year to try offenses and hear appeals.

quar·ter·staff (kwôr′tər-stăf′, -stäf′) *n., pl.* **-staves** (-stāvz′). A long wooden staff, formerly used as a weapon.

quar·ter·tone (kwôr′tər-tōn′) *n. Music.* Half a **semitone** *(see).*

quar·tet, quar·tette (kwôr-tĕt′) *n.* **1.** A musical composition for: **a.** Four singers. **b.** Four instruments, especially stringed instruments. **2.** A group of four performing musicians. **3.** A set of four persons or things. [French *quartette,* Italian *quartetto,* diminutive of *quarto,* fourth, from Latin *quārto.* See **quarto.**]

quar·tic (kwôr′tĭk) *adj. Mathematics.* Of or pertaining to the fourth degree; biquadratic.
—*n. Mathematics.* An algebraic equation of the fourth degree. [From Latin *quārtus,* fourth.]

quar·tile (kwôr′tīl′, -tĭl) *n. Statistics.* One of three values that mark the division of a frequency distribution into four parts, each containing a quarter of the whole group of items under consideration.
—*adj.* Of, pertaining to, or being a quartile. [Medieval Latin *quārtīlis,* of a quartile, from Latin *quārtus,* fourth. See **quarto.**]

quar·to (kwôr′tō) *n., pl.* **-tos.** *Abbr.* **q., Q., qto. 1. a.** The page size obtained by folding a whole sheet into four leaves. **b.** A book composed of pages of this size or folded in this way. Also written *4to, 4°.* **2.** A size of paper, 8 by 10 inches. [Latin *(in) quārto,* in quarter, from *quārtus,* fourth.] **—quar·to** *adj.*

quartz (kwôrts) *n.* **1.** A hard, crystalline, vitreous mineral form of silicon dioxide, SiO_2, found worldwide as a component of sandstone and granite or as pure crystals in such varieties as agate, chalcedony, chert, flint, opal, and rock crystal. It may be clear and transparent, as in rock crystal, or any of various colors, such as purple, as in amethyst, or yellow, as in citrine. **2.** Quartz glass.
—*adj.* **1.** Made of quartz. **2.** Of, pertaining to, or being a timepiece

that is regulated by electronic circuitry using a small quartz crystal to operate its mechanism and produce a high degree of accuracy: *a quartz watch.* [From German *Quarz,* from Middle High German *quarz,* from West Slavic *kwardy,* hard.] —**quartz·ose** (kwôrt'sōs') *adj.*

quartz crystal *n.* A small crystal of quartz accurately cut along certain axes so that it can be vibrated at a particular frequency, and used for its piezoelectric properties to produce an electric signal of constant known frequency.

quartz glass *n.* A pure silica glass, highly transparent to ultraviolet radiations.

quartz·if·er·ous (kwôrt-sif'ər-əs) *adj.* Containing quartz.

quartz·i·o·dine lamp (kwôrts'ī'ə-dīn', -dĭn, -dēn') *n.* A type of lamp, used especially for car headlights, having a quartz envelope containing inert gas with a small amount of iodine vapor and a tungsten filament. The iodine vapor improves the brightness of the lamp.

quartz·ite (kwôrt'sīt') *n.* A metamorphic rock resulting from the recrystallization of sandstone.

qua·sar (kwā'zär', -sär', -zər) *n. Astronomy.* A member of any of several classes of starlike objects having exceptionally large red shifts that are often emitters of radio frequency as well as visible radiation and have apparently immense speeds, energies, and distances from the earth. Also called "quasi-stellar object." [QUAS(I) + (STELL)AR.]

quash (kwŏsh) *tr.v.* **quashed, quashing, quashes. 1.** *Law.* To set aside or annul. **2.** To put down or suppress forcibly and completely. [Middle English *quassen,* from Old French *quasser, casser,* from Late Latin *cassāre,* from Latin *cassus,* empty, void.]

qua·si (kwā'zī', -sī', kwä'zē, -sē) *adv.* To some degree; almost or somewhat. Usually used in combination: *quasi-scientific literature.* ~*adj.* Resembling but not being the thing in question. Used in combination: *a quasi-victory.* [Latin *quasi,* as if : *quam,* than, how, as + *sī,* if.]

Qua·si·mo·do (kwä'zē-mō'dō), Salvatore (1901–68). Italian poet. Though his earlier work drew on an idyllic childhood in Sicily, his postwar writing, such as *Il Falso e Vero Verde* (1956), reflects concern over social issues. He was awarded the Nobel Prize in 1959.

qua·si-stel·lar object (kwä'zī-stĕl'ər, kwä'sī-, kwä'zē-, kwä'sē-) *n. Abbr.* **QSO** A quasar.

quasi-stellar radio source *n. Abbr.* **QSRS** *Astronomy.* A quasi-stellar object that is detected only by its radio emission.

quas·sia (kwŏsh'ə) *n.* **1. a.** A tree, *Quassia amara,* of tropical America, having bright scarlet flowers. **b.** The wood or bark of this tree. **2.** A bitter substance obtained from the wood and bark of this tree and related trees, used in medicine and as an insecticide. [New Latin, after Graman *Quassi,* 18th-century native of Surinam, who discovered its medicinal properties.]

qua·ter·nar·y (kwŏt'ər-nĕr'ē, kwə-tûr'nə-rē) *adj.* **1.** Consisting of four; in fours. **2.** *Chemistry.* **a.** Designating a compound having four alkyl groups connected to a nitrogen or phosphorus atom. **b.** Designating a compound consisting of four different atoms or radicals. **3. Quaternary.** *Geology.* Of, belonging to, or designating the geologic time, system of rocks, and sedimentary deposits of the second period of the Cenozoic era, from the end of the Tertiary (two million years ago) to the present, characterized by the appearance and development of human beings and including the Pleistocene and Holocene epochs. ~*n., pl.* **quaternaries. 1.** The number four. **2.** The member of a group that is fourth in order. **3. Quaternary.** *Geology.* The Quaternary period or system of deposits. [Middle English, set of four, from Latin *quaternārius,* consisting of four each, from *quaternī,* four each, from *quater,* four times.]

quaternary ammonium compound *n. Chemistry.* Any of a class of compounds containing an ion NR_4^+, where R is an organic group or a hydrogen atom.

qua·ter·ni·on (kwə-tûr'nē-ən) *n.* **1.** A set of four persons or items. **2.** *Mathematics.* An element of a system of four-dimensional vectors obeying laws similar to those of complex numbers. [Middle English, from Late Latin *quaterniō* (stem *quaterniōn-*), from Latin *quaternī,* four each. See **quaternary.**]

quat·rain (kwŏt'rān', kwŏ-trān') *n.* A stanza of verse having four lines that often rhyme alternately. [French, from Old French, from *quatre,* four, from Latin *quattuor.*]

quat·re·foil (kăt'ər-foil', kăt'rə-) *n.* **1.** A figure of a flower with four petals or a leaf with four leaflets, especially in heraldry. **2.** *Architecture.* An ornament or tracery with four foils or lobes. **3.** *Geometry.* A curve that has four lobes. [Middle English *quaterfoile,* set of four leaves : *quater-,* four, from Old French *quatre* + FOIL (leaf).]

quat·tro·cen·to (kwŏt'rō-chĕn'tō) *n.* The 15th-century period of Italian art and literature. [Italian, short for *(mil)quattro cento,* "(one thousand) four hundred."]

qua·ver (kwā'vər) *v.* **-vered, -vering, -vers.** —*intr.* **1.** To quiver, as from weakness or emotion; tremble. Used especially of the voice. **2.** To speak in a quivering voice. **3.** To produce a trill on a musical instrument or in singing. —*tr.* To utter or sing in a trilling or trembling voice. ~*n.* **1.** *Music. Chiefly British.* An **eighth note** (see). **2.** A quivering sound. **3.** A trill. [Middle English *quaveren,* frequentative of obsolete *quaven* (imitative), to tremble, from Germanic; akin to Low German *quabbeln,* to tremble.] —**qua·ver·ing·ly** *adv.* —**qua·ver·y** *adj.*

quay (kē, kā) *n.* A wharf or reinforced bank, such as one that juts

out from a harbor, where ships are loaded or unloaded. [Earlier *key,* Middle English *key, kay,* from Old French *chai, cay,* from Gaulish *caio,* rampart, retaining wall.]

quay·age (kē'ĭj, kā'-) *n.* **1.** A charge for the use of a quay. **2.** The space available for or on quays. **3.** Quays collectively.

quay·side (kē'sīd', kā'-) *n.* The area that runs alongside or forms a quay. —**quay·side** *adj.*

Que. Quebec (province).

quean (kwēn) *n.* **1.** *Scottish.* A young woman, especially one who is not married. **2.** An impudent or disreputable woman; especially, a prostitute. [Middle English *quen(e),* Old English *cwene,* woman, wife, from Germanic.]

quea·sy, quea·zy (kwē'zē) *adj.* **-sier, -siest** or **-zier, -ziest. 1. a.** Nauseated. **b.** Easily nauseated. **2.** Causing nausea; sickening. **3. a.** Causing uneasiness. **b.** Uneasy; troubled: *made queasy by the threat of war.* **4.** Easily troubled: *a queasy conscience.* [Middle English *coysy, qwesye,* perhaps originally "wounded," from Norman French, Old French *coisi* (unattested), akin to *coisier,* to injure.] —**quea·si·ly** *adv.* —**quea·si·ness** *n.*

Que·bec¹ (kwĭ-bĕk'). *Abbr.* **Que.** French **Qué·bec** (kā-bĕk'). Largest province in Canada, in the east of the country. Most of it is part of the Laurentian (or Canadian) Shield, a plateau of hard rock that was scoured by ice sheets and glaciers and is now rich in minerals and timber. Between this block and the Appalachian Mts. in the south lies the valley of the St. Lawrence River. Montreal is at the center of this rich agricultural strip, which provides cereals and dairy products. Originally a French colony known as New France or Canada (1534–1763), the province still retains French language and customs, and there is a strong separatist movement. Its capital is Quebec.

Quebec². Capital of Quebec province, Canada, at the confluence of the St. Lawrence and St. Charles rivers in the southeast of the country. A picturesque city, it is the hub of French Canadian culture. It is chiefly a distribution and manufacturing center with a wide range of industries including timber, printing, textiles, shipbuilding, and iron and steel production. Tourism is also important.

que·bra·cho (kā-brä'chō, kĭ-) *n., pl.* **-chos. 1.** Any of several South American trees having very hard wood; especially, *Aspidosperma quebracho-blanco,* whose bark is used in medicine, and *Schinopsis lorentzii,* whose wood yields tannin. **2.** The bark of any of these trees. [American Spanish, variant of *quiebrahacha,* "ax-breaker": *quiebra,* from *quebrar,* to break, from Latin *crepāre,* to rattle, crack + *hacha,* ax.]

Quech·ua, Kech·ua (kĕch'wə, -wä') *n., pl.* **-uas** or collectively **Quechua, Kechua. 1.** A member of a tribe of South American Indians originally constituting the ruling class of the Incan Empire. **2. a.** The language of the Quechua, also spoken by other Indian peoples of Peru, Ecuador, Bolivia, Chile, and Argentina. **b.** A language family consisting of the Quechua language. [Spanish, from *Quechuakkechúwa,* "plunderer."] —**Quech·uan** *n. & adj.*

queen (kwēn) *n. Abbr.* **qu. 1.** A female monarch or ruler. **2.** The wife or widow of a king. **3.** A woman or a thing personified as a woman who is eminent or supreme in a specified field or area: *a beauty queen. Paris is the queen of all cities.* **4.** *Abbr.* **Q** The most powerful piece in chess, able to move in any direction in a straight or diagonal line. **5.** A playing card bearing the figure of a queen, next above the jack and below the king in each suit. **6.** The fertile, fully developed female in a colony of social bees, ants, or termites. ~*v.* **queened, queening, queens.** —*tr.* **1.** To make (a woman) a queen. **2.** *Chess.* To raise (a pawn) to queen, when it has reached the far end of the board. —*intr.* **1.** To reign as queen. **2.** To act like a queen; domineer: *queens it over the whole family.* [Middle English *qu(e)ene,* Old English *cwēn,* woman, wife, queen, from Germanic.]

Queen Anne *n.* The style of English architecture and furniture typical of the reign of Queen Anne (1702–14).

Queen Anne's lace *n.* A widely distributed plant, *Daucus carota,* native to Eurasia, having finely divided leaves and flat clusters of small white flowers. Also called "wild carrot."

Queen Anne's War *n.* See **War of the Spanish Succession.**

Queen Char·lotte Islands (shär'lət). Group of islands off the coast of British Columbia, western Canada. Logging and fishing are the main occupations, and the native Indians are renowned for their canoe building. Masset in the north of Graham Island is the chief town.

queen consort *n., pl.* **queens consort.** The wife of a reigning king.

queen dowager *n.* The widow of a king.

Queen E·liz·a·beth Islands (ĭ-lĭz'ə-bəth). Also (until 1954) **Par·ry Islands** (păr'ē). The northern part of the Arctic Archipelago, which forms part of the Northwest Territories of Canada. The islands possess rich oil deposits, exploited since the early 1960's.

queen·ly (kwēn'lē) *adj.* **-lier, -liest. 1.** Of or resembling a queen. **2.** Pertaining to or befitting a queen. —**queen·li·ness** *n.*

Queen Maud Land (môd). Region of Antarctica between the Weddell Sea and Enderby Land. It was claimed by the Norwegian government in 1939.

queen mother *n.* A dowager queen who is the mother of the reigning monarch.

queen post *n.* Either of two upright supporting posts set vertically between the rafters and the tie beam at equal distances from the apex of a roof. Compare **king post.**

Queens (kwēnz). Borough of New York City, at the western end of Long Island. It is coextensive with Queen's County.

Queen's Bench *n. Abbr.* **Q.B.** See **King's Bench.**

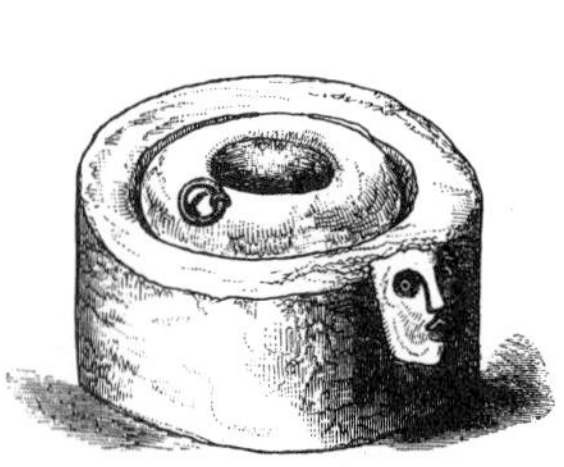

quern *Querns have been used for grinding grain into flour since before 5000 B.C. Early querns consisted simply of two stones rubbed together by hand. Rotary querns like this one date from Greek and Roman times. Grain poured into the central hollow of the revolving upper stone is channeled to the grinding surfaces and emerges as fine meal through holes in the fixed lower stone.*

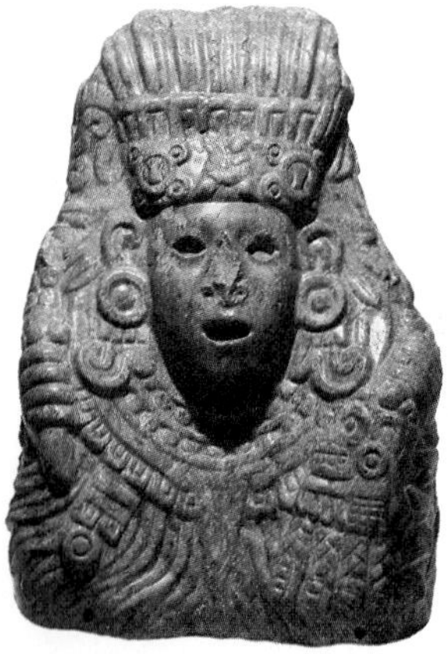

Quetzalcoatl *The Aztec god of civilization is thought to have had a historical counterpart in an early king of the Toltec people, who dominated Mexico before the Aztecs. The Aztecs believed Quetzalcoatl would one day return from the east to rule again, and when the Spanish conquistadors landed in 1519, their leader, Cortés, was welcomed as the god.*

Queens·ber·ry Rules (kwēnz'bĕr'ē) *pl. n.* **1.** A boxing code of fair play developed for boxing in 1867 by the eighth Marquis of Queensberry. **2.** A set of rules that prescribe fair play.

Queen's Counsel *n. Abbr.* **Q.C.** See **King's Counsel.**

Queen's County. See **Leix.**

queen·ship (kwēn'shĭp') *n.* **1.** The rank or state of being a queen. **2.** A noble or regal quality, as of a queen.

queen-size (kwēn'sīz') *adj.* Also **queen-sized** (-sīzd'). **1.** Relating to, used for, or being a bed approximately 60 iches by 80 inches in dimension: *queen-size sheets.* **2.** Extra large: *queen-size pantyhose.*

Queens·land (kwēnz'lănd', -lənd). Second-largest state of Australia, in the northeast of the country. It includes the adjacent islands in the Pacific Ocean and the Gulf of Carpentaria. The Great Barrier Reef runs along its eastern coastline, and the coastal plains give way to the high peaks of the Great Dividing Range. There are grasslands on the western hills and vast plains further west. Agriculture and manufacturing are both economically important, and there is also considerable mineral wealth, including copper, coal, gold, bauxite, uranium, oil, and gas. The first settlement, in 1824, was a penal colony. Brisbane is the capital.

queen's metal *n.* A form of britannia metal containing a small amount of zinc.

queen truss *n.* A building truss having queen posts.

queer (kwîr) *adj.* **queerer, queerest. 1.** Deviating from the expected or normal; strange: *a queer situation.* **2.** Odd or unconventional in behavior; eccentric. **3.** Of a questionable nature or character; suspicious. **4.** *Slang.* Fake; counterfeit. **5.** Feeling slightly unwell; queasy. —See Synonyms at **strange.**
~*tr.v.* **queered, queering, queers.** *Slang.* **1.** To ruin or spoil. **2.** To put into a bad position. [Perhaps from German *quer,* perverse, cross, from Middle High German *twerch, querch,* from Old High German *twerh, dwerah.* See **thwart.**] —**queer·ish** *adj.* —**queer·ly** *adv.* —**queer·ness** *n.*

que·le·a (kwē'lē-ə) *n.* A small African finch, *Quelea quelea,* with brown plumage and a red bill, that is a serious pest of grain crops. [New Latin, perhaps from Medieval Latin *qualea,* QUAIL.]

quell (kwĕl) *tr.v.* **quelled, quelling, quells. 1.** To put down forcibly; suppress: *quelled the riot.* **2.** To pacify; calm: *quelled her fears.* [Middle English *quellen,* to kill, destroy, Old English *cwellan,* from Germanic.]

Quemoy. See **Jinmen.**

quench (kwĕnch) *tr.v.* **quenched, quenching, quenches. 1.** To put out (a fire, for example); extinguish. **2.** To suppress; squelch: *Their disapproval quenched my enthusiasm.* **3.** To slake; satisfy: *Mineral water quenches the thirst.* **4.** To cool (hot metal) by thrusting into water or other liquid. **5.** To reduce (sparking or oscillation) in an electronic circuit. **6.** To suppress (luminescence, fluorescence, or electrical discharge, for example) by adding a deactivating agent. [Middle English *quenchen,* Old English *ācwencan.*] —**quench·a·ble** *adj.* —**quench·er** *n.*

Que·neau (kə-nō'), **Raymond** (1903–79). French novelist and poet. His bizarre, erudite humor, full of puns and surrealism, cloaked a profound pessimism.

que·nelle (kə-nĕl') *n.* A ball or dumpling of forcemeat, especially fish forcemeat, bound with eggs and poached in stock or water. [French.]

quer·ce·tin (kwûr'sĭ-tĭn) *n.* A yellow, powdered crystalline compound, $C_{15}H_{10}O_7$, synthesized or occurring as a glycoside in the rind and bark of numerous plants and used medicinally to treat abnormal capillary fragility. [Latin *quercētum,* oak forest, from *quercus,* oak.]

quer·ci·tron (kwûr'sĭ-trən, -trŏn', kwər-sĭt'rən) *n.* **1.** A tree, the **black oak** *(see).* **2. a.** The bright orange inner bark of the quercitron, from which a yellow dye is obtained. **b.** The dye obtained from this bark. [Latin *quercus,* oak + CITRON.]

que·rist (kwîr'ĭst) *n.* A person who asks questions; an inquirer. [From Latin *quaerere,* to seek, ask.]

quern (kwûrn) *n.* **1.** A hand-turned grain mill consisting of two stone wheels, one resting upon the other. **2.** A small hand mill for grinding spices. [Middle English *querne,* Old English *cweorn,* from Germanic.]

quer·u·lous (kwĕr'ə-ləs, kwĕr'yə-) *adj.* **1.** Given to complaining or fretting; peevish. **2.** Expressing a complaint or grievance; grumbling; fretful. [Latin *querulus,* from *querī,* to complain.] —**quer·u·lous·ly** *adv.* —**quer·u·lous·ness** *n.*

que·ry (kwîr'ē) *n., pl.* **-ries. 1.** A question; an inquiry. **2.** A doubt in the mind. **3.** *Abbr.* **q., qu.** A notation, usually a question mark, calling attention to an item to question its validity or accuracy.
~*tr.v.* **queried, -rying, -ries. 1.** To express doubt or uncertainty about; question. **2.** To put a question to (a person). **3.** To mark (an item) with a notation in order to question its validity or accuracy. —See Synonyms at **ask.** [Variant (influenced by INQUIRY) of earlier *quaere,* from Latin, imperative of *quaerere,* to seek, ask.] —**que·ri·er** *n.*

quest (kwĕst) *n.* **1.** The act or an instance of seeking or pursuing something; a search. **2.** In medieval romance, an expedition undertaken by a knight in order to perform some prescribed feat: *the quest for the Holy Grail.* **3.** *Archaic.* A jury of inquest. —**in quest of.** In pursuit of; seeking.
~*v.* **quested, questing, quests.** —*intr.* **1.** To make a search; go on a quest. **2.** To search for game. Used of a hunting dog. —*tr.* To search for; seek. [Middle English *queste,* from Old French, from Vulgar Latin *quaesita* (unattested), from Latin, feminine past participle of *quaerere,* to seek.] —**quest·er** *n.*

ques·tion (kwĕs'chən) *n. Abbr.* **q., qn., qu. 1. a.** An expression of inquiry that invites or calls for a reply. **b.** An interrogative sentence, phrase, or gesture. **2.** A subject or point open to controversy; an unsettled issue. **3.** A difficult matter, especially one conditioned by or considered in terms of a specified factor; problem: *a question of ethics.* **4.** A point or subject under discussion or being considered. **5. a.** A proposition brought up for consideration by an assembly. **b.** The act of bringing such a proposal to a vote. **6.** Uncertainty; doubt: *no question about its authenticity.* **7.** Possibility; chance: *no question of my giving in.* —**beg the question. 1.** To presuppose the conclusion or solution in one's argument. **2.** To equivocate. —**call into question.** To cast doubt upon. —**out of the question.** Not worth considering; impossible. —**pop the question.** *Informal.* To propose marriage.
~*v.* **questioned, -tioning, -tions.** —*tr.* **1.** To put a question to. **2.** To interrogate (a witness or suspect, for example). **3.** To express doubt about; dispute. **4.** To analyze carefully; examine. —*intr.* To ask questions. —See Synonyms at **ask.** [Middle English, from Old French, from Latin *quaestiō* (stem *quaestiōn-*), from *quaerere* (past participle *quaestus*), to seek, ask.] —**ques·tion·er** *n.* —**ques·tion·ing·ly** *adv.*

ques·tion·a·ble (kwĕs'chə-nə-bəl) *adj.* **1.** Open to doubt; uncertain; problematic. **2.** Of dubious morality or respectability. —See Synonyms at **doubtful.** —**ques·tion·a·bil·i·ty, ques·tion·a·ble·ness** *n.* —**ques·tion·a·bly** *adv.*

question mark *n.* **1.** A punctuation symbol (?) written at the end of a sentence or phrase to indicate a direct question. Also called "interrogation mark," "interrogation point," "interrogative." **2.** An unknown or uncertain factor: *The critic's reaction to the performance remained a question mark until the newspaper reached the newsstands.*

ques·tion·naire (kwĕs'chə-nâr') *n.* A printed form containing a set of questions, especially one addressed to a statistically significant number of subjects by way of gathering information, as in a survey. [French, from *questionner,* to question, from *question,* QUESTION.]

question time *n.* In Britain, a period during a parliamentary session when questions may be put to certain ministers concerning matters for which they are responsible.

Quet·ta (kwĕt'ə). Capital of Baluchistan province in Pakistan, situated on the main route north to Afghanistan via the Bolan Pass. It is an important trade center.

quet·zal (kĕt-säl', -săl') *n., pl.* **-zals** or **-zales** (-sä'lās, -săl'ās). **1.** A Central American bird, *Pharomacrus mocino,* having brilliant bronze-green and red plumage and, in the male, long, flowing tail feathers. **2.** *Abbr.* **Q a.** The basic monetary unit of Guatemala, equal to 100 centavos. See feature at **currency. b.** A coin worth one quetzal. [American Spanish, from Nahuatl *quetzalli,* tail feather.]

Quet·zal·co·a·tl (kĕt-säl'kō-ät'l, kĕt-săl'-). A god of the Toltecs and Aztecs, represented as a plumed serpent.

queue (kyo͞o) *n.* **1.** A line or file of people or vehicles waiting to do something, such as board a bus, or to receive attention in turn, as at a counter in a store. **2.** A long braid of real or artificial hair worn hanging down the back of the neck; a pigtail. **3.** *Computer Science.* A sequence of stored data or programs awaiting processing.
~*intr.v.* **queued, queuing, queues.** To join or wait in a queue. Often used with *up.* [French, tail, line, from Old French *coe, cue,* from Latin *cauda,* tail.]

Que·zon City (kā'zŏn'). City adjoining Manila on the island of Luzon, in the Philippines. It was the country's capital from 1948 to 1976.

Que·zon y Mo·li·na (kĕ-sôn' ē mô-lē'nä), **Manuel Luis** (1878–1944). Philippine statesman. A stalwart proponent of Filipino independence from the U.S., he served as resident commissioner for the Philippines in the U.S. House of Representatives (1909–16) and as a member of the Philippine senate (1916–35) before being elected the first president of the Philippine Commonwealth (1935).

quib·ble (kwĭb'əl) *intr.v.* **-bled, -bling, -bles. 1.** To make exaggerated distinctions or raise objections to unimportant details: *quibbling over trivialities.* **2.** *Archaic.* To make a pun.
~*n.* **1.** A petty distinction or minor objection. **2.** *Archaic.* A pun. [From obsolete *quib,* pun, perhaps from Latin *quibus,* dative and ablative plural of *quī,* who, which (used in legal documents and hence associated with quips and quibbles).]

quiche (kēsh) *n.* A rich custard, often with other ingredients, as cheese, bacon, or seafood, baked in an unsweetened pastry shell. [French, probably from German (dialectal) *Küche,* diminutive of *Kuchen,* cake, from Old High German *kuocho.*]

quick (kwĭk) *adj.* **quicker, quickest. 1.** Moving or functioning rapidly and energetically; speedy: *a quick worker.* **2.** Occupying a brief space of time: *a quick chat over lunch.* **3.** Understanding, thinking, or learning with speed and dexterity; intellectually sharp. **4.** Perceiving or responding with speed and sensitivity; keen. **5.** Done or occurring in a relatively short time: *a quick rise through the ranks.* **6.** Tending to react: *quick to attack her opponents.* **7.** *Archaic.* Pregnant. Used especially in the phrase *quick with child.* **8.** *Archaic.* Alive. —See Synonyms at **fast, nimble.**
~*n.* **1.** Sensitive or raw exposed flesh, as under the fingernails. **2.** The most personal and sensitive area of the emotions: *He felt cut to the quick.* **3.** The vital core of a thing; the essence. Used chiefly in the phrase *the quick of the matter.* **4.** *British.* Quickset.
~*adv.* **quicker, quickest.** Quickly; promptly.

~*interj.* Used to urge quick action or response. [Middle English *qui(c)ke,* swift, lively, alive, Old English *cwic(u),* living, alive, from Germanic.] **—quick•ly** *adv.* **—quick•ness** *n.*

Usage: *Quick* is occasionally used as an adverb in informal speech (especially in the imperative: *Come quick!*), but *quickly* is the preferred form in formal speech and writing.

quick assets *pl.n.* Liquid assets, including cash on hand and assets readily convertible to cash.

quick-change (kwĭk′chānj′) *n.* A performer, as an actor, who can quickly and adroitly change costumes and makeup, especially during a single performance.

quick•en (kwĭk′ən) *v.* **-ened, -ening, -ens.** *—tr.* **1.** To make more rapid; speed up; accelerate. **2.** To make alive; vitalize. **3.** To excite and stimulate; stir. *—intr.* **1.** To become more rapid. **2.** To show life; come or return to life: *"and the weak spirit quickens"* (T.S. Eliot). **3.** To reach the stage of pregnancy when the fetus can be felt to move. **—**See Synonyms at **speed.** **—quick•en•er** *n.*

quick-fire (kwĭk′fīr′) *adj.* Suggesting rapid gunfire: *quick-fire questions.*

quick-freeze (kwĭk′frēz′) *tr.v.* **-froze** (-frōz′), **-frozen** (-frō′zən), **-freezing, -freezes.** To freeze (food) by a process sufficiently rapid to retain natural flavor, nutritional value, or other properties.

quick•ie (kwĭk′ē) *n. Informal.* Something made, done, or consumed rapidly or hastily.

quick•lime (kwĭk′līm′) *n. Chemistry.* **Calcium oxide** *(see).* [So called because it is the first substance produced by heating limestone.]

quick march *n.* A march in quick time.

quick•sand (kwĭk′sănd′) *n.* A bed of loose sand and mud mixed with water forming a soft, shifting mass that yields easily to pressure and may suck down any denser object resting on its surface.

quick•set (kwĭk′sĕt′) *n. Chiefly British.* **1. a.** Cuttings or slips of a plant suitable for hedges. **b.** A single slip or cutting of such a plant. **2.** A hedge consisting of such plants. **—quick•set** *adj.*

quick•sil•ver (kwĭk′sĭl′vər) *n.* The element **mercury** *(see).*
~*adj.* Unpredictable; mercurial. [Middle English *quicksilver,* Old English *cwicseolfor* (translation of Latin *argentum vivum*) : QUICK ("living") + SILVER.]

quick•step (kwĭk′stĕp′) *n. Music.* A march for accompanying quick time.

quick-tem•pered (kwĭk′tĕm′pərd) *adj.* Easily aroused to anger.

quick time *n.* A military marching pace of 120 steps per minute.

quick-wit•ted (kwĭk′wĭt′ĭd) *adj.* Showing mental alertness and agility: *a quick-witted reply.* **—**See Synonyms at intelligent, shrewd. **—quick-wit•ted•ly** *adv.* **—quick-wit•ted•ness** *n.*

quid[1] (kwĭd) *n., pl.* **quid** or **quids.** *British Informal.* A pound sterling. [Probably from Latin *quid,* something, perhaps alluding to QUID PRO QUO; compare French *quibus,* "wherewithal."]

quid[2] *n.* A cut of something, as tobacco, to be chewed. [Middle English *quide,* cud, from Old English *cwidu.*]

quid•di•ty (kwĭd′ə-tē) *n., pl.* **-ties.** **1.** The real nature of a thing; the essence. **2.** A hairsplitting distinction; a quibble. [Medieval Latin *quidditās,* from Latin *quid,* what, something, anything.]

quid•nunc (kwĭd′nŭngk′) *n.* A nosy person; busybody. [Latin *quid nunc?* "What now?"]

quid pro quo (kwĭd prō kwō′) *n., pl.* **quid pro quos.** An equal exchange or substitution. [Latin, "something for something."]

qui•es•cent (kwī-ĕs′ənt, kwē-) *adj.* **1.** Inactive or still; dormant. **2.** *Medicine.* Designating a disease that is in an inactive or undetectable phase. **—**See Synonyms at **latent.** [Latin *quiēscēns* (stem *quiēscent-*), present participle of *quiēscere,* to be QUIET.] **—qui•es•cence** *n.* **—qui•es•cent•ly** *adv.*

qui•et (kwī′ĭt) *adj.* **-eter, -etest.** **1.** Making no noise; silent: *The students were quiet during the lecture.* **2.** Free of noise; hushed: *a quiet room.* **3.** Calm and unmoving; still: *quiet waters.* **4.** Free of turmoil and agitation; untroubled. **5.** Restful; soothing: *had a quiet cup of tea.* **6.** Characterized by tranquillity; serene. **7.** Not showy or garish; restrained: *a room decorated in quiet colors.* **—**See Synonyms at **calm, still.**
~*n.* The quality or condition of being quiet; silence; tranquillity. **—on the quiet.** In a surreptitious way; secretively.
~*v.* **quieted, -eting, -ets.** *—tr.* **1.** To cause to become quiet. **2.** *Law.* To make (a title) secure by freeing from all questions or challenges. *—intr.* To become quiet: *The child had been crying but soon quieted down.* **—**See Synonyms at **pacify.** [Middle English, from Old French, from Latin *quiētus,* from the past participle of *quiēscere,* to be quiet, be at rest, from *quiēs,* quiet.] **—qui•et•ly** *adv.* **—qui•et•ness** *n.*

qui•et•en (kwī′ĭ-tən) *v.* **-ened, -ening, -ens.** *Chiefly British. —tr.* To cause to be quiet. *—intr.* To become quiet. **—**See Synonyms at **pacify.**

qui•et•ism (kwī′ə-tĭz′əm) *n.* **1.** A form of Christian mysticism requiring passive contemplation and the joyful surrender of the will. **2.** A state of quiet and passivity. **—qui•et•ist** *adj. & n.* **—qui•et•is•tic** (kwī′ə-tĭs′tĭk) *adj.* **—qui•et•is•ti•cal•ly** *adv.*

quiet sun *n. Astronomy.* The sun at a time when there is very little sunspot activity.

qui•e•tude (kwī′ə-tōōd′, -tyōōd′) *n.* A condition of tranquillity. [Medieval Latin *quiētūdō,* from Latin *quiētus,* QUIET.]

qui•e•tus (kwī-ē′təs) *n.* **1.** Something that serves to suppress, check, or eliminate. **2.** Release from life; death. **3.** A final discharge, as of a duty or debt. [Medieval Latin *quiētus (est),* "(he is) discharged," from Latin *quiētus,* at rest, released, QUIET.]

quiff (kwĭf) *n. British.* **1.** A tuft of hair brushed up to a peak over the forehead and sometimes lacquered. **2.** A strand or curl of hair that falls on the forehead. [Origin unknown.]

quill (kwĭl) *n.* **1.** The hollow, stemlike main shaft of a feather. Also called "calamus." **2.** Any of the larger wing or tail feathers of a bird. **3.** A writing pen made from a quill. **4.** A plectrum for a stringed musical instrument of the clavichord type. **5.** A toothpick made from the stem of a feather. **6.** Any of the sharp hollow spines of a porcupine or hedgehog. **7.** A musical pipe having a hollow stem. **8.** A spindle or bobbin, originally a length of reed or cane, around which yarn is wound in weaving. **9.** A small roll of dried bark, especially cinnamon. **10.** In machinery, a hollow shaft that rotates on a solid shaft when gears are engaged.
~*tr.v.* **quilled, quilling, quills.** **1.** To wind (thread or yarn) onto a quill. **2.** To make or press small ridges in (fabric). [Middle English *quil(le),* akin to Middle Low German *quiele*†.]

quill•back (kwĭl′băk′) *n., pl.* **-backs** or collectively **quillback.** A North American freshwater fish, *Carpiodes cyprinus,* having one ray of the dorsal fin extending conspicuously beyond the others.

Quil•ler-Couch (kwĭl′ər-kōōch′), **Sir Arthur Thomas** (1863–1944). British critic and writer. He is best known as the editor of the *Oxford Book of English Verse* (1900) (under the pen name "Q").

quil•let (kwĭl′ĭt) *n. Archaic.* A verbal nicety or subtlety; a quibble. [Perhaps short for obsolete *quillity,* variant of QUIDDITY.]

quilt (kwĭlt) *n.* **1.** A bed coverlet or blanket made of two layers of fabric with a layer of cotton, wool, feathers, or down in between, all stitched firmly together, usually in a crisscross design. **2.** A thick protective cover similar to or suggestive of a quilt.
~*v.* **quilted, quilting, quilts.** *—tr.* **1.** To make into a quilt by stitching together (layers of fabric). **2.** To stitch like a quilt: *quilt a skirt.* **3.** To pad and stitch ornamentally. **4.** To sew between two layers of fabric. *—intr.* **1.** To make a quilt. **2.** To do quilted needlework. [Middle English *quilte,* from Old French *cuilte,* from Latin *culcita,* sack filled with feathers, mattress.]

quilt•ing (kwĭl′tĭng) *n.* **1.** Material used to make quilts. **2.** Quilted material.

Quim•per (kăɴ-pär′). Administrative center of Finistère department in Brittany, northwestern France. It is famous for its pottery and fine Gothic cathedral.

quin– *prefix.* Indicates cinchona or cinchona bark; for example, **quinidine.** [Spanish *quina,* cinchona bark, short for *quinaquina,* perhaps from Quechua.]

quin•a•crine hydrochloride (kwĭn′ə-krēn′) *n.* A bright-yellow, bitter, crystalline compound used primarily to treat malaria. Also *chiefly British* "mepacrine." [QUIN- + ACR(ID)INE.]

qui•na•ry (kwī′nə-rē) *adj.* **1.** Of, pertaining to, or based on the number five. **2.** Consisting of five things or parts. [Latin *quinārius,* from *quinī,* five each, distributive of *quinque,* five.]

qui•nate (kwī′nāt′) *adj.* Arranged in groups of five: *quinate leaflets.* [From Latin *quinī,* five each.]

quince (kwĭns) *n.* **1.** A tree, *Cydonia oblonga,* native to Asia, having white flowers and applelike fruit. **2.** The aromatic, many-seeded fruit of this tree, edible only when cooked. [Middle English *quynce,* plural of *quyn,* quince, from Old French *c(o)oin,* from Latin *cotōneum, cydōneum (mālum),* "Cydonian (apple)," from Greek *kudōnion,* from *Kudōnia,* Cydonia (Greek name of CANEA, Crete).]

quin•cunx (kwĭn′kŭngks′) *n.* An arrangement of five objects with one at each corner of a rectangle and one at the center. [Latin *quincunx* (stem *quincunc-*), five twelfths of a Roman coin (as denoted by five dots or dashes so arranged) : *quinque,* five + *uncia,* a twelfth part.] **—quin•cun•cial, quin•cunx•ial** (kwĭn-kŭn′shəl) *adj.* **—quin•cun•cial•ly** *adv.*

Quin•cy (kwĭn′zē, -sē), **Josiah** (1772–1864). U.S. politician, educator, and historian. As a U.S. congressman (1804–13), he bitterly opposed the accession of new territory and the country's involvement in the War of 1812. He also served as a Massachusetts senator, juror, and five-time mayor of Boston (1823–45) and wrote prolifically on the history of Harvard and Boston.

quin•dec•a•gon (kwĭn-dĕk′ə-gŏn′) *n. Geometry.* A polygon having 15 sides and 15 angles. [Irregularly from Latin *quindecim,* fifteen + -GON.] **—quin•de•cag•o•nal** (kwĭn′dĭ-kăg′ə-nəl) *adj.* **—quin•de•cag•o•nal•ly** *adv.*

quin•de•cen•ni•al (kwĭn′dĭ-sĕn′ē-əl) *adj.* **1.** Occurring once every 15 years. **2.** Lasting 15 years.
~*n.* A 15th anniversary. [Latin *quindecim,* fifteen + *annus,* year.] **—quin•de•cen•ni•al•ly** *adv.*

qui•nel•la (kwĭ-nĕl′ə, kē-) *n.* Also **qui•nie•la** (kē-nyĕl′ə). A system of betting in which the winning bettor must pick the first two finishers of a race but not necessarily in the correct sequence. [American Spanish, a lotterylike game.]

quin•i•dine (kwĭn′ə-dēn′) *n.* A colorless crystalline alkaloid, $C_{20}H_{24}N_2O_2$, resembling quinine and used in treating certain heart disorders and malaria. [QUIN- + -ID(E) + -INE.]

qui•nine (kwī′nīn′) *n.* **1.** A bitter, colorless, amorphous powder or crystalline alkaloid, $C_{20}H_{24}N_2O_2 \cdot 3H_2O$, derived from certain cinchona barks and used to treat malaria. **2.** Any of various compounds or salts of quinine. [QUIN- + -INE.]

quinine water *n.* A carbonated beverage flavored with quinine.

quin•oid (kwĭn′oid′) *n. Chemistry.* A substance resembling quinone in structure or physical properties. [QUIN(ONE) + -OID.]

qui•noi•dine (kwĭ-noi′dēn′, -dīn) *n.* A brownish-black mixture of alkaloids remaining after the extraction of crystalline alkaloids from cinchona bark, used as a substitue for quinine. [QUIN- + -OID + -INE.]

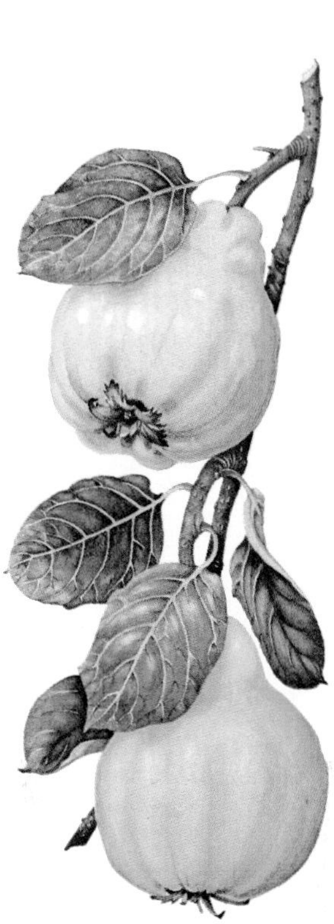

quince *A bushy, fast-growing fruit tree of the genus* Cydonia, *which is thought to have originated in central Asia. The fruit has a delicious smell, but is bitter and hard unless cooked. It was held sacred by the ancient Greeks and, according to a medieval Christian legend, was the forbidden fruit in the Garden of Eden.*

PRONUNCIATION KEY

ă, pat; ā, pay; âr, care;
ä, father, are; b, bib;
ch, church; d, deed; ĕ, pet;
ē, be; f, fife; g, gag; h, hat;
hw, which; ĭ, pit; ī, pie;
îr, pier; j, judge; k, kick;
l, lid, needle; m, mum;
n, no, sudden; ng, thing;
ŏ, pot; ō, toe; ô, paw, for;
oi, noise; ou, out; ŏŏ, book;
ōō, boot; p, pop; r, roar;
s, sauce; sh, ship, dish;
t, tight; th, thin, path;
th, this, bathe; ŭ, cut; ûr, fur;
v, valve; w, with; y, yes;
z, zebra, size; zh, vision;
ə, about, item, edible, gallop, circus, peaceful

IN FOREIGN WORDS:

à, *Fr.* ami; œ, *Fr.* feu, *Ger.* schön; ü, *Fr.* tu, *Ger.* über; KH, *Ger.* ich, *Scot.* loch; N, *Fr.* bon; y′, *Fr.* Compiègne

STRESS MARKS:

Primary stress: ′
in•cite′ (ĭn-sīt′)
Secondary stress: ′
in′sight′ (ĭn′sīt′)

quin·o·line (kwĭn′ə-lēn′, -lĭn) n. An aromatic organic base, C₉H₇N, having a pungent tarlike odor, synthesized or obtained from coal tar, and used as a preservative and in making antiseptics and dyes. [QUIN- + -OL + -INE.]

qui·none (kwĭ-nōn′, kwĭn′ōn′) n. Chemistry. Any of a class of aromatic compounds found widely in plants; especially, the yellow crystalline form, C₆H₄O₂, used in making dyes, in tanning hides, and in photography. [QUIN- + -ONE.]

quin·o·noid (kwĭn′ə-noid′, kwĭ-nō′noid′) adj. Chemistry. Of, containing, or resembling quinone, in structure or properties.

quin·qua·ge·nar·i·an (kwĭng′kwə-jə-nâr′ē-ən) n. A person 50 years old or between 50 and 60 years of age.
~adj. Of or characteristic of a quinquagenarian. [Latin quinquāgēnārius, consisting of fifty, from quinquāgēnī, fifty each, from quinquāginta, fifty.]

Quin·qua·ges·i·ma (kwĭng′kwə-jĕs′ə-mə) n. The Sunday before the beginning of Lent; the first day of Shrovetide. Also called "Quinquagesima Sunday." [Medieval Latin quinquāgēsima, from Latin, fiftieth, from quinquāginta, fifty.]

quinque– prefix. Indicates five; for example, **quinquefoliate.** [Latin quinque, five.]

quin·que·fo·li·ate (kwĭng′kwə-fō′lē-ĭt, -āt′) adj. Botany. Having five leaves, leaflets, or leaflike parts. [QUINQUE- + Latin folium, leaf, FOIL.]

quin·quen·ni·al (kwĭn-kwĕn′ē-əl, kwĭng-) adj. 1. Happening once every five years. 2. Lasting for five years.
~n. 1. A fifth anniversary. 2. A period of five years. —**quin·quen·ni·al·ly** adv.

quin·quen·ni·um (kwĭn-kwĕn′ē-əm, kwĭng-) n., pl. -**ums** or -**quennia** (-kwĕn′ē-ə). A period of five years. [Latin : QUINQUE- + annus, year.]

quin·que·va·lent (kwĭng′kwə-vā′lənt) adj. Chemistry. Pentavalent. —**quin·que·va·lence** n.

quin·sy (kwĭn′zē) n. Acute inflammation of the tonsils and surrounding tissue, often leading to the formation of an abscess. [Middle English quinesye, from Old French quinencie, from Medieval Latin quinancia, from Greek kunanchē, dog quinsy, sore throat : kuōn, hound + ankhein, to strangle.]

quint[1] (kwĭnt) n. In piquet and similar games, a sequence of five cards of the same suit in one hand. [French, from Latin quinta, feminine of quintus, fifth.]

quint[2] (kwĭnt) n. A quintuplet.

quin·tain (kwĭnt′n) n. 1. A post, or a target mounted on a post, to be tilted at. 2. The sport of tilting. [Middle English quintaine, from Old French, from Latin quintāna via, the fifth street in a Roman camp, supposedly used for military exercises, from quintānus, fifth in rank, from quintus, fifth.]

quin·tal (kwĭnt′l) n. Abbr. q., ql. 1. A unit of mass in the metric system equal to 100 kilograms (220 pounds). 2. A short hundredweight, 100 pounds (45.36 kilograms). [Middle English, from Old French, from Medieval Latin quintāle, from Arabic qintār, KANTAR.]

quin·tar (kĕn-tär′) n. Also **qin·dar·ka** (kĭn-där′kə). A monetary unit of Albania, equal to ¹⁄₁₀₀ of the lek. See feature at **currency.** [Albanian qintar.]

quinte (kănt, kănt) n. In fencing, the fifth in a series of eight parrying positions. [Old French, fifth.]

quin·tes·sence (kwĭn-tĕs′əns) n. 1. The pure, highly concentrated essence of something. 2. The purest or most typical example; embodiment: She was the quintessence of courtesy. 3. In ancient and medieval philosophy, the fifth and highest essence (after the four elements of earth, air, fire, and water), thought to be the substance of the heavenly bodies and latent in all things. [Middle English, from Old French quinte essence, from Medieval Latin quinta essentia (translation of Greek pemptē ousia, fifth essence) : Latin quinta, feminine of quintus, fifth + essentia, ESSENCE.]

quin·tes·sen·tial (kwĭn′tə-sĕn′shəl) adj. Of, pertaining to, of the nature of, or being a quintessence; purest or most typical. —**quin·tes·sen·tial·ly** adv.

quin·tet, quin·tette (kwĭn-tĕt′) n. 1. A group of five persons or things. 2. A musical composition for five voices or instruments. 3. A group of five musicians. [French quintette, from Italian quintetto, from quinto, fifth, from Latin quintus.]

quin·tile (kwĭn′tīl′, kwĭn′tl) n. 1. Astrology. The aspect of planets distant from each other by 72° or one fifth of the zodiac. 2. Statistics. The portion of a frequency distribution containing one fifth of the total sample. [From Latin quintus, fifth.]

Quin·til·ian (kwĭn-tĭl′yən, -ē-ən) (c. A.D. 35–c. 95). Roman rhetorician. Probably born in present-day Spain, he was educated in Rome and there spent most of his career as an orator, tutor, and author. His major work, the Institutio Oratorio, discusses the complete education and career of an orator from childhood to retirement.

quin·til·lion (kwĭn-tĭl′yən) n. 1. The cardinal number represented by 1 followed by 18 zeros, usually written 10¹⁸. 2. Chiefly British. The cardinal number represented by 1 followed by 30 zeros, usually written 10³⁰. [Latin quintus, fifth + (M)ILLION.] —**quin·til·lion** adj. —**quin·til·lionth** n. & adj.

quin·tu·ple (kwĭn-tōō′pəl, -tyōō′pəl, -tŭp′əl, kwĭn′tə-pəl) adj. 1. Consisting of or having five parts, members, or copies. 2. Multiplied by five; five times as much, as many, or as large.
~n. A fivefold amount or number.
~v. **quintupled, -pling, -ples.** —tr. To multiply or increase by five. —intr. To be multiplied fivefold. [French, from Late Latin quintuplex : Latin quintus, fifth + -plex, -fold.]

quin·tu·plet (kwĭn-tŭp′lĭt, -tōō′plĭt, -tyōō′plĭt, kwĭn′tə-plĭt) n. 1. A group or combination of five associated by common properties or behavior. 2. Any of five offspring born in a single birth. [From QUINTUPLE.]

quin·tu·pli·cate (kwĭn-tōō′plĭ-kĭt, kwĭn-tyōō′-) adj. 1. Multiplied by five; fivefold. 2. Being the fifth of a set of identical copies.
~n. 1. One of a set of five identical things. 2. A set of five copies.
~tr.v. (-kāt′) **quintuplicated, -cating, -cates.** 1. To make five copies of. 2. To multiply by five. [Late Latin quintuplicātus, from quintuplicāre, to make fivefold, from quintuplex, QUINTUPLE.]

quip (kwĭp) n. 1. A brief, witty remark delivered offhand. 2. A cleverly sarcastic remark; gibe. 3. A quibble. 4. Something that is curious or odd. —See Synonyms at **joke.**
~intr.v. **quipped, quipping, quips.** To make quips. [Earlier quippy, perhaps from Latin quippe, indeed, certainly (often used ironically), from quid, what.]

qui·pu (kē′pōō) n. A device consisting of variously colored and knotted cords attached to a base rope that was used by the Incas of Peru for calculating and recording. [Spanish quipo, from Quechua quipu.]

quire[1] (kwīr) n. Abbr. q., qr. 1. A set of 24 or sometimes 25 sheets of paper of the same size and stock; one twentieth of a ream. 2. Four sheets of paper folded to form 8 leaves, or 16 pages.
~tr.v. **quired, quiring, quires.** To fold or arrange in quires. [Middle English, from Old French quaer, set of four sheets, from Vulgar Latin quaternum (unattested), from Latin quaternī, set of four, from quater, four.]

quire[2] n. Archaic. A choir (see).

quirk (kwûrk) n. 1. A peculiarity of behavior; idiosyncrasy. 2. An unpredictable or unaccountable act or event: a quirk of fate. 3. A sudden sharp turn or twist. 4. A deceptive and cunning stratagem; subterfuge. 5. Architecture. A lengthwise groove on a molding between the convex upper part and the soffit. —See Synonyms at **eccentricity.** [16th century : origin obscure.] —**quirk·i·ly** adv. —**quirk·i·ness** n. —**quirk·y** adj.

quis·ling (kwĭz′lĭng) n. A traitor who serves as the puppet of the enemy occupying his country. [After Vidkun QUISLING.]

Quis·ling (kwĭz′lĭng), **Vidkun,** born Abraham Lauritz Jonsson (1887–1945). Norwegian politician. Forming the fascist National Union Party (1933), he went on to become minister president (1942) under the Nazi occupation. Following the Axis surrender (1945), he was tried and executed for treason.

quit (kwĭt) v. **quit** or **quitted** (kwĭt′ĭd), **quitting, quits.** —tr. 1. To end one's involvement with; leave: "You and I are on the point of quitting the theatre of our exploits" (Lord Nelson). 2. To give up; relinquish: quit his job. 3. To depart from; leave. 4. To discontinue; cease: Quit pestering me. 5. To rid oneself of by paying: quit a debt. 6. To conduct (oneself): Quit yourselves like adults. —intr. 1. To cease to perform. 2. To concede defeat; give up. 3. To leave a job.
~adj. Absolved of a duty, penalty, or obligation; free: quit of all concern for their safety. [Middle English quiten, to set free, release, from Old French quiter, from Medieval Latin quiētāre, to set free, quit, discharge, from Latin quiētus, freed, QUIET.]

quit·claim (kwĭt′klām′) n. Law. The transfer of a title, right, or claim to another.
~tr.v. **quitclaimed, -claiming, -claims.** To renounce all claim to (a possession or right). [Middle English quiteclaimen (verb), from Old French quiteclamer, "to declare free" : quite, free, QUIT + clamer, to CLAIM.]

quite (kwīt) adv. 1. To the greatest extent; completely: quite alone; not quite finished. 2. Actually; really: He's quite positive he'll get a raise. 3. To a degree; rather: The book is quite easy to understand. —**quite a** (or an). 1. Considerable. Used to qualify an indefinite noun: quite a few; quite a gap. 2. Informal. Exceptional; extraordinary: quite an establishment. —**quite something.** Informal. Something extraordinary or impressive.
~interj. Chiefly British. Used to indicate agreement. [Middle English, from adjective, "free," rid of, from Old French, from Latin quiētus, freed, QUIET.]

Usage: Many people have objected to the "weaker" senses of quite, where the word means "rather, somewhat" (It's quite warm today), preferring to restrict it to the more positive senses of "entirely" (quite certain) and "actually" (quite ill). However, the weaker sense is very widely used, especially in informal speech. Nowadays it is felt to be somewhat pedantic to criticize a phrase such as quite all right as containing a redundancy, or a phrase such as quite similar as containing a contradiction, and this kind of use will often be heard even in formal speech. Quite a(n), indicating indefinite quantity, is generally acceptable (Quite a large number stayed away); but when indicating extraordinary quality (quite a show), it is informal.

Qui·to (kē′tō). Capital of Ecuador and of Pichincha province. It is an educational, cultural, manufacturing, and political center and was the northern capital of the Inca empire.

quit·rent (kwĭt′rĕnt′) n. A rent paid by a freeman in lieu of services required of him by feudal custom. [Middle English quiterent : quite, free + rent, rent.]

quits (kwĭts) adj. Even with someone by payment or requital. —**call it quits.** To agree that something, such as a dispute or debt, is settled on both sides. [Middle English, "discharged," "paid up," from Medieval Latin quittus, QUIT.]

quit·tance (kwĭt′ns) n. 1. Release from a debt, obligation, or penalty. 2. A document or receipt certifying such a release. 3. Something given as requital or recompense; repayment. [Middle English *quitance*, from Old French, from *quiter*, to free, discharge a debt, QUIT.]

quit·ter (kwĭt′ər) *n. Informal.* One who gives up easily.

quit·tor (kwĭt′ər) *n.* An inflammation of the hoof cartilage of horses and other solid-hoofed animals, characterized by degeneration of hoof tissue, formation of a slough, and fistulous sores. [Middle English *quiture*, perhaps from Old French, decoction, from Latin *coctūra*, from *coquere* (past participle *coctus*), to cook.]

quiv·er[1] (kwĭv′ər) *v.* **-ered, -ering, -ers.** —*intr.* To shake with a slight rapid motion; tremble; vibrate. —*tr.* To cause to quiver. —See Synonyms at **shake.**
~*n.* The act or motion of quivering. [Middle English *quiveren*, perhaps from QUIVER (nimble).]

quiver[2] *n.* **1.** A portable case for arrows. **2.** A case full of arrows. [Middle English, from Norman French *quiveir* (unattested), Old French *cuivre*, from West Germanic.]

quiver[3] *adj. Archaic.* Nimble; brisk. [Middle English *quiver*, Old English *cwifer*-.]

quiv·er·ful (kwĭv′ər-fool′) *n., pl.* **-fuls. 1.** The amount held by a quiver. **2.** A large number: *a quiverful of children.*

qui vive (kē vēv′) *n.* Alert watchfulness or vigilance. Used chiefly in the phrase *on the qui vive.* [French, "(long) live who?" (a sentinel's challenge to determine the political sympathies of the person approaching).]

quix·ot·ic (kwĭk-sŏt′ĭk) *adj.* Also **quix·ot·i·cal** (-ĭ-kəl). Caught up in the romance of noble deeds or unreachable ideals; romantic, absent-minded, and unpractical. [After DON QUIXOTE.] —**quix·ot·i·cal·ly** *adv.* —**quix·o·tism** (kwĭk′sə-tĭz′əm) *n.*

quiz (kwĭz) *tr.v.* **quizzed, quizzing, quizzes. 1.** To question closely or repeatedly; interrogate. **2.** To test the knowledge of by posing questions. **3.** *British Archaic.* To poke fun at; mock. **4.** To look at questioningly or mockingly.
~*n., pl.* **quizzes. 1.** A short oral or written test of knowledge. **2.** *British.* A quiz show. **3.** A questioning or inquiry. **4.** A practical joke. **5.** An eccentric person. [18th century : origin obscure.] —**quiz·zer** *n.*

quiz show *n.* A radio or television program in which the knowledge of contestants is tested by questioning and usually rewarded with prizes.

quiz·mas·ter (kwĭz′măs′tər, -mä′stər) *n.* One who asks the contestants questions in a quiz show.

quiz program *n.* A quiz show.

quiz·zi·cal (kwĭz′ĭ-kəl) *adj.* **1.** Suggesting humorous or ironic puzzlement; questioning. **2.** Teasing; mocking: *"his face wore a somewhat quizzical, almost impertinent air"* (Lawrence Durrell). —**quiz·zi·cal·i·ty** (kwĭz′ĭ-kăl′ə-tē) *n.* —**quiz·zi·cal·ly** *adv.*

Qum. See **Qom.**

Qum·ran (koŏm-rän′). Village on the northwest coast of the Dead Sea in the part of Jordan occupied by Israel in 1967, thought to be the city of Salt mentioned in Joshua 15:62. It includes Khirbat Qumran, ruins left by a community of Essenes, a Jewish sect that flourished there from the mid-2nd century B.C. until A.D. 68, when it was finally destroyed by Vespasian's army. Remains of the sect's library, the Dead Sea Scrolls, were first found by local shepherds in 1947 in caves at Qumran.

quod (kwŏd) *n. British Slang.* Prison. [17th century : origin obscure.]

quod·li·bet (kwŏd′lə-bĕt′) *n.* **1.** A theological or philosophical argument, especially one presented or engaged in as an exercise. **2.** A usually humorous musical medley. [Middle English, scholastic debate, disputation, from Medieval Latin *quodlibetum*, from Latin *quodlibet*, what you please : *quod*, what + *libet*, it pleases, from *libēre*, to please.]

quoin, coign (koin, kwoin) *n.* **1. a.** An exterior angle of a wall or other masonry. **b.** A stone serving to form such an angle; a cornerstone. **2.** A keystone. **3.** *Printing.* A wedge-shaped block used to lock type in a chase. **4.** A wedge used to raise the level of a gun. ~*tr.v.* **quoined, quoining, quoins.** To provide, secure, or raise with a quoin or quoins. [Variant of COIN (corner).]

quoit (kwoit, koit) *n.* **1. quoits.** *Used with a singular verb.* A game in which flat rings of iron or rope are thrown at a stake, with points awarded for encircling it. **2.** One of the rings used in quoits. ~*tr.v.* **quoited, quoiting, quoits.** To throw in the manner of a quoit. [Middle English *coite*†.]

quok·ka (kwŏk′ə) *n.* A small, rare wallaby, *Setonix brachyurus,* occurring mainly on the islands off the coast of western Australia. [From a native Australian language.]

quon·dam (kwŏn′dəm, -dăm′) *adj.* That once was; former: *a quondam friend.* [Latin, "formerly," from *quom*, when.]

Quon·set (kwŏn′sĭt) *n.* A trademark for a prefabricated portable hut having a semicircular roof of corrugated metal that curves down to form walls.

quo·rum (kwôr′əm, kwōr′-) *n.* **1.** The minimum number of officers or members of a committee, organization, or assembly, usually a majority, who must be present for the valid transaction of business. **2.** A select group. [Middle English, a quorum of justices of the peace, from Latin texts of commissions reading *quorum vos . . . duos esse volumus,* "of whom we wish that you be . . . two," genitive plural of *quī,* who.]

quot. quotation.

quo·ta (kwō′tə) *n.* **1. a.** A share, as of goods to be distributed or work to be done, assigned to a group or to each member of a group; an allotment. **b.** A production assignment. **2.** A stipulated number, proportion, or amount, as of persons who may be admitted or of goods that may be imported: *import quotas.* [Medieval Latin, from Latin, feminine of *quotus,* of what number. See **quote.**]

quot·a·ble (kwō′tə-bəl) *adj.* Suitable for or worth quoting. —**quot·a·bil·i·ty** *n.* —**quot·a·bly** *adv.*

quo·ta·tion (kwō-tā′shən) *n. Abbr.* **quot. 1.** The act of quoting. **2.** A passage that is quoted. **3.** An estimate of costs or prices: *She gave me a quotation for painting the house.* **4.** *Commerce.* **a.** The quoting of current prices and bids for securities and goods. **b.** The prices or bids cited. —**quo·ta·tion·al** *adj.* —**quo·ta·tion·al·ly** *adv.*

quotation mark *n.* Either of a pair of punctuation marks used to mark the beginning and end of a passage attributed to another and repeated word for word. They appear in the form (" ") (double quotation marks) or (' ') (single quotation marks). Also called "inverted comma," "quote."

quote (kwōt) *v.* **quoted, quoting, quotes.** —*tr.* **1.** To repeat or copy the words of (another), usually with acknowledgment of the source. **2.** To cite or refer to for illustration or proof. **3.** To state (a price) for securities, goods, or services. —*intr.* To give a quotation, as from a book.
~*n. Informal.* **1.** A quotation. **2.** A quotation mark. [Middle English, to mark (chapters, references, or the like) with numbers, from Medieval Latin *quotāre*, from Latin *quotus,* of what number, from *quot,* how many.] —**quot·er** *n.*

quoth (kwōth) *tr.v. Archaic.* Uttered; said. Used only in the first and third persons, with the subject following: *"Quoth the raven 'Nevermore!'"* (Edgar Allan Poe). [Middle English *quoth,* Old English *cwæth,* he said, from *cwethan,* to say.]

quo·tha (kwō′thə) *interj. Archaic.* Used to express surprise or sarcasm, after quoting the word or phrase of another. [Contraction of *quoth he.*]

quo·tid·i·an (kwō-tĭd′ē-ən) *adj.* **1.** Recurring daily. Said especially of attacks of malaria. **2.** Everyday; commonplace. [Middle English *cotidien,* from Old French, from Latin *quotīdiānus,* from *quotīdiē,* each day : *quot,* how many, as many as + *diēs,* day.]

quo·tient (kwō′shənt) *n.* **1.** The quantity resulting from division of one quantity by another. **2.** *Informal.* The rate or proportion of a specified quality: *a high anxiety quotient among those with dangerous occupations.* [Middle English *quocient,* from Latin *quotiēns,* how many times, from *quot,* how many.]

qu·rush (koo′rəsh) *n., pl.* **qurush.** A monetary unit of Saudi Arabia, equal to ¹⁄₂₀ of the riyal. See feature at **currency.** [Arabic *quruš.*]

q.v. Which see. Used to indicate a cross-reference. [Latin *quod vide.*]

Q value *n. Physics.* The Q factor *(see).*

R

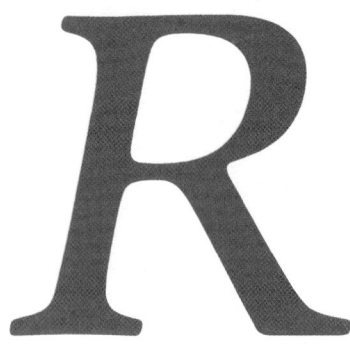

Ra *This bronze falcon head represents Ra, the ancient Egyptian sun god whose boat was believed to sail across the sky each day. It was thought to be towed back through the underworld each night. Since Ra was the supreme Egyptian deity, the pharaohs used "son of Ra" as one of their titles.*

rabbit *The rabbit is found in most parts of the world. Farmers consider it a serious pest, and myxomatosis—a disease affecting only rabbits and a few hares—was introduced in certain countries during the 1950's to control the rabbit population.*

r, R (är) *n., pl.* **r's** or **R's. 1.** The 18th letter of the modern English alphabet. See feature at **alphabet. 2.** Any of the speech sounds represented by this letter. **3.** The 18th in a series; 17th when *J* is omitted.

r, R, r., R. *Note:* As an abbreviation or symbol, *r* may be a small or a capital letter, with or without a period. Established forms or those generally preferred precede the definition. When no form is given, all four forms are in general use in that sense. **1. R** *Chemistry.* gas constant. **2. R.** rabbi. **3. R** *Chemistry.* radical. **4. r, R** radius. **5. r., R.** railroad; railway. **6. R** rand. **7. r.** range. **8. r.** rare. **9. R, R.** Réaumur (scale). **10. R.** rector. **11. R.** regiment. **12. R.** Regina. **13. R., r.** registered (trademark). **14. R.** regius. **15. R.** Republican (party). **16. r, R** resistance (electricity). **17. R** *Ecclesiastical.* response. **18. r.** retired. **19. R.** Rex. **20. r., R.** right. **21. r., R.** river. **22. r., R.** road. **23. r.** rod (unit of length). **24. R** roentgen (unit of radiation). **25. R** rook (in chess). **26. r., R.** rouble. **27. R.** royal. **28. r.** rubber (in card games). **29. r, r.** *Sports.* run. **30. r., R.** rupee. **31. R.** Rydberg constant.

Ra¹ (rä). Also **Re** (rā). The sun god, the supreme deity of the ancient Egyptians, represented as a man usually with the head of a hawk crowned with a solar disk and uraeus. [Egyptian *ra'.*]

Ra² The symbol for the element **radium.**

R.A. 1. rear admiral. **2.** *Astronomy.* right ascension. **3.** Royal Academy; Royal Academician. **4.** Royal Artillery.

R.A.A.F. Royal Australian Air Force.

Ra·bat (rä-bät'). Capital of Morocco, situated on the Atlantic Ocean at the mouth of the Bou Regreg estuary. There have been settlements here since ancient times, and it became a Muslim fortress (*c.* A.D. 700).

rabato. Variant of **rebato.**

Ra·baul (rə-boul'). Port in the northeast of the island of New Britain, Papua New Guinea. The town is surrounded by active volcanoes and was severely damaged by eruptions in 1937.

rab·bet (răb'ĭt) *n.* Also **re·bate** (rē'bāt', răb'ĭt). **1.** A cut or groove along or near the edge of a piece of wood that allows another piece to fit into it to form a joint. **2.** A joint made in this manner. —*v.* **rabbeted, -beting, -bets.** —*tr.* **1.** To cut a rabbet in. **2.** To join by a rabbet. —*intr.* To be joined by a rabbet. [Middle English *rabet,* from Old French *rabat,* a beating down, from *rabattre,* to beat down, reduce : *re-,* back + *abattre,* to beat down : *a-,* from Latin *ad-,* to + *battre,* to beat, from Latin *battuere.*]

rab·bi (răb'ī) *n., pl.* **-bis.** Also **rab·bin** (răb'ĭn). **1.** *Abbr.* **R.** The ordained spiritual leader of a Jewish congregation. **2.** Formerly, a person authorized to interpret Jewish law. [Hebrew *rabbī,* my master : *rabh,* great one + *-ī,* my.]

rab·bin·ate (răb'ĭn-āt') *n.* The office or function of a rabbi.

Rab·bin·ic (rə-bĭn'ĭk) *n.* The Hebrew language as used in the learned writings of the rabbis of the medieval period.

rab·bin·i·cal (rə-bĭn'ĭ-kəl) *adj.* Also **rab·bin·ic** (rə-bĭn'ĭk). Of, pertaining to, or characteristic of rabbis, or their views, learning, writings, or language. —**rab·bin·i·cal·ly** *adv.*

rab·bin·ism (răb'ĭn-ĭz'əm) *n.* Rabbinical teachings and traditions.

rab·bin·ist (răb'ĭn-ĭst) *n.* A strict observer of the Talmud and of rabbinical traditions. —**rab·bin·is·tic** (răb'ĭn-ĭs'tĭk) *n.*

rab·bit (răb'ĭt) *n., pl.* **-bits** or collectively **rabbit. 1.** Any of various long-eared, short-tailed, burrowing mammals of the family Leporidae, as the commonly domesticated Old World species *Oryctolagus cuniculus,* or the New World **cottontail** (*see*). **2.** Loosely, a hare. **3.** The fur of a rabbit or hare. **4.** A cheese dish, **Welsh rabbit** (*see*). —*intr.v.* **rabbited, -biting, -bits.** To hunt rabbits. [Middle English *rabet,* probably from Old French; akin to Walloon *robete,* diminutive of Flemish *robbe†.*] —**rab·bit·er** *n.*

rabbit ears *pl.n. Informal.* An indoor television antenna consisting of two usually adjustable rods connected to a base and swiveling apart at a V-shaped angle.

rabbit fever *n.* A disease, **tularemia** (*see*).

rab·bit·fish (răb'ĭt-fĭsh') *n., pl.* **-fishes** or collectively **rabbitfish. 1.** A fish, the *chimaera* (*see*); especially, the species *Chimaera monstrosa,* of European seas. Also called "ratfish." **2.** Any fish of the family Siganidae, of tropical Indo-Pacific waters, having a rounded, rabbitlike snout and spiny fins.

rabbit punch *n.* A chopping blow to the back of the neck.

rab·ble¹ (răb'əl) *n.* **1.** A tumultuous mob. **2.** A group of persons regarded with contempt: *a rabble of penniless aristocrats.* **3.** The lower classes. Used derogatorily, preceded by *the.* [Middle English *rabble†.*]

rab·ble² *n.* Also **rab·bler** (răb'lər). *Metallurgy.* **1.** An iron bar with one end bent like a rake, used to stir and skim molten iron in puddling. **2.** Any of various similar tools or mechanically operated devices used in roasting or refining furnaces. —*tr.v.* **rabbled, -bling, -bles.** *Metallurgy.* To stir or skim (molten iron) with a rabble. [French *râble,* fire shovel, from Old French *roable,* from Medieval Latin *rotābulum,* from Latin *rutābulum,* from *ruere†* (past participle *rutus*), to rake up.]

rab·ble·rous·er (răb'əl-rou'zər) *n.* One who incites a crowd to action or violence; a demagogue.

Ra·be·lais (răb'ə-lā'), **François** (*c.* 1494–1553). French humanist and satirist. A Franciscan, then a Benedictine monk, he studied medicine at Montpellier. His satirical tales attacked medieval scholasticism and superstition: the most popular are *Pantagruel* (1532) and *Gargantua* (1534). Despite his religious sincerity, his works are full of high-spirited vulgarity.

Rab·e·lai·si·an (răb'ə-lā'zē-ən, -zhən) *adj.* Pertaining to or characteristic of the works of Rabelais; broadly and lustily humorous.

ra·bi (rŭb'ē) *n.* **1.** In India and Pakistan, a crop that is harvested at the beginning of spring. Compare **kharif. 2.** In north India, the cool dry or winter season. [Urdu, spring crop, from Arabic *rabī',* spring.]

Ra·bi (rŭb'ē) *n.* Also **Ra·bi·a** (rə-bē'ə). Either the third or the fourth month of the Muslim calendar. See feature at **calendar.** [Arabic *rabī',* spring.]

Ra·bi (rä'bē), **Isidor Isaac** (1898–). U.S. physicist, born in Austria. He is particularly noted for his work on magnetic forces within the atom. He was awarded the Nobel Prize (1944).

rab·id (răb'ĭd) *adj.* **1.** Of or afflicted with rabies. **2.** Fanatical; extreme. **3.** Raging; uncontrollable: *rabid thirst.* [Latin *rabidus,* raving, from *rabere,* to rave.] —**rab·id·i·ty** (rə-bĭd'ə-tē, rā-), **rab·id·ness** *n.* —**rab·id·ly** *adv.*

ra·bies (rā'bēz) *n.* An acute, infectious, often fatal viral disease of most warm-blooded animals, especially wolves, cats, and dogs, that is transmitted to humans by the bite of infected animals. It affects the central nervous system and is characterized by convulsions and aversion to water. Also called "hydrophobia." [New Latin, from Latin *rabiēs,* rage, from *rabere,* to rave.] —**ra·bi·et·ic** (rā'bē-ĕt'ĭk) *adj.*

rac·coon, ra·coon (ră-kōōn') *n., pl.* **-coons** or collectively **raccoon** or **racoon. 1.** A carnivorous North American mammal, *Procyon lotor,* having grayish-brown fur, black, masklike facial markings, and a bushy, black-ringed tail. Also called "coon." **2.** The fur of this animal. **3.** Any of various similar or related animals. [Algonquian (Virginia) *aroughcoune, arathkone.*]

raccoon dog *n.* A wild dog, *Nyctereutes procyonoides,* of east Asia, having golden-brown hair and black eye patches like those of a raccoon.

race¹ (rās) *n.* **1. a.** A local geographic or global human population distinguished as a more or less distinct group by genetically transmitted physical characteristics. **b.** The division of mankind according to such characteristics: *discrimination on the grounds of race.* **2.** The human species as a whole: *the human race.* **3.** Any group of people united or classified together on the basis of common history, nationality, or geographic distribution. **4.** A genealogical line; a lineage; a family. **5.** Any group of people having a particular characteristic in common: *Gardeners are a patient, plodding race.* **6.** *Biology.* **a.** A plant or animal population that differs from others of the same species in one or more hereditary traits; a subspecies. **b.** A breed or strain, as of domestic animals. **7.** A distinctive quality. **8.** Sprightliness; style. —See Usage Note at **nation.** [French, group of people, generation, from Italian *razza†.*]

race[2] *n.* **1. a.** A competition of speed, such as in running or riding. **b. races.** A series of such competitions, especially in horse riding, held at a specific time on a regular course: *winning money at the races.* **2.** Any contest or pursuit of supremacy: *the race to be first in line.* **3. a.** Steady or rapid onward movement. **b.** *Archaic.* A steady onward movement, course, or span: *the sun's race.* **c.** *Archaic.* A human lifetime. **4. a.** A strong or swift current of water. **b.** The channel of such a current. **c.** An artificial channel built to transport water and utilize its energy. **5.** A groovelike part of a machine in which a moving part slides or rolls; especially, any of the rings holding the balls or rollers in a bearing. Also called "raceway." **6.** *Australian.* A fenced track for sheep or other livestock, especially one leading to a dip. **7.** *Aeronautics.* A **slipstream** *(see).*
~*v.* **raced, racing, races.** —*intr.* **1.** To compete in a contest of speed. **2.** To move rapidly or at top speed. **3.** To run too rapidly because of decreased resistance or a lighter load. Used of engines. —*tr.* **1.** To compete against in a contest of speed. **2.** To cause (an animal or vehicle) to compete in such a contest, especially habitually or professionally. **3.** To cause to move rapidly or at top speed. **4.** To cause (an engine with the gears disengaged, for example) to run too fast. [Middle English *ra(a)s,* from Old Norse *rās.*]

race[3] *n.* A root, especially of ginger. [Old French *rais, raiz,* root, from Latin *rādix* (stem *rādīc-*).]

race·card, race card (rās'kärd') *n. Chiefly British.* A printed list or program of horse races.

race·course (rās'kôrs') *n.* A course or track laid out for horse racing. Also called "racetrack."

race·horse (rās'hôrs) *n.* A horse bred and trained to race.

ra·ceme (rā-sēm', rə-) *n. Botany.* An inflorescence in which stalked flowers are arranged singly along a common main axis with the youngest at the top, as in the lily of the valley. [Latin *racēmus*†, stalk of a cluster of grapes, bunch of berries.]

race meeting *n. Chiefly British.* A series of races, usually horse races, held at a particular time and place.

ra·ce·mic (rā-sē'mĭk, -sĕm'ĭk, rə-) *adj.* Of or designating a chemical mixture containing equal quantities of dextrorotatory and levorotatory isomers so that it does not have a net optical activity. [French *racémique,* from Latin *racēmus,* RACEME.]

racemic acid *n.* An optically inactive form of tartaric acid, $C_4H_6O_6 \cdot H_2O$, that can be separated into dextrorotatory and levorotatory components and is sometimes found in grape juice during winemaking.

ra·ce·mi·form (rā-sē'mə-fôrm') *adj. Botany.* Resembling a raceme in form. [RACEME + -FORM.]

rac·e·mism (răs'ə-mĭz'əm, rā-sē'-) *n. Chemistry.* The condition of being racemic.

ra·ce·mize (rā'sə-mīz', răs'ə-) *v.* **-mized, -mizing, -mizes.** —*tr.* To convert (an optically active compound) into an optically inactive racemic mixture. —*intr.* To become racemic; change into a racemic mixture. —**rac·e·mi·za·tion** *n.*

rac·e·mose (răs'ə-mōs') *adj.* **1.** *Botany.* Designating any inflorescence in which the main axis continues to grow at the tip so that the oldest flowers are at the bottom and the youngest toward the tip. **2.** *Anatomy.* Having a structure of clustered parts. Said of glands. [Latin *racēmōsus,* full of clusters, from *racēmus,* RACEME.] —**rac·e·mose·ly** *adv.*

rac·er (rā'sər) *n.* **1.** One that takes part in races or is capable of great speed. **2.** Any of various fast-moving North American snakes of the genus *Coluber.*

race relations *pl.n.* Interaction and relationships between people of different races.

race riot *n.* A riot inspired by racial hatred or resentment, especially one resulting in a violent confrontation between groups of people of different races.

race suicide *n.* The gradual extinction of a people or race caused by the birth rate falling below the death rate as a result of a voluntary limitation on the number of children.

race·track (rās'trăk') *n.* **1.** A track, circuit, or course laid out for car racing, greyhound racing, or the like. **2.** A racecourse.

race·way (rās'wā') *n.* **1.** An artificial channel for transporting water. **2.** A racetrack. **3.** A machine **race** *(see).*

Ra·chel (rā'chəl). The second wife of Jacob and mother of his sons Joseph and Benjamin. Genesis 29–35. [Hebrew *rāḥēl,* "ewe."]

ra·chis (rā'kĭs) *n., pl.* **-chises** or **-chides** (rā'kə-dēz') *Biology.* A main axis or shaft, such as the main stem of an inflorescence, the shaft of a contour feather, or the spinal column. [New Latin, from Greek *rhakhis,* spine, backbone.] —**ra·chi·al** (rā'kē-əl) *adj.*

ra·chi·tis (rə-kī'tĭs) *n.* A childhood and infant disease, **rickets** *(see).* [New Latin, from Greek *rhakhitis,* disease of the spine : RACHIS + -ITIS.] —**ra·chit·ic** (rə-kĭt'ĭk) *adj.*

Rach·man·i·nov (răKH-mä'nə-nôf), **Sergei Vasilyevich** (1873–1943). Russian composer. A virtuoso pianist, he excelled at the interpretation of the late romantic composers; his own work is essentially a continuation of the genre. He left Russia (1917) to live in Switzerland and then in the United States.

ra·cial (rā'shəl) *adj.* **1.** Pertaining to or typical of a race or races, or an ethnic group or groups. **2.** Arising from or based upon differences between races or ethnic groups. —**ra·cial·ly** *adv.*

Ra·cine (rā-sēn'), **Jean** (1639–99). French playwright. The greatest tragedian of the French classical period, he wrote plays based on classical Greek and Roman themes, which include *Andromaque* (1667), *Britannicus* (1669), and *Phèdre* (1677). —**Ra·cin·i·an** *adj.*

ra·cism (rā'sĭz'əm) *n.* Also *chiefly British* **ra·cial·ism** (rā'shəl-ĭz'əm). **1.** The belief that certain races, especially one's own, are inherently superior to others. **2.** Discriminatory behavior or practices based on this view. —**rac·ist** *n. & adj.*

rack[1] (răk) *n.* **1.** A framework or stand for holding or displaying various articles, especially: **a.** A receptacle for livestock feed: *a hay rack.* **b.** A secure ledge for luggage. **c.** A series of hooks in a frame: *a hat rack.* **d.** A frame for holding bombs in an airplane. **e.** *Printing.* An upright framework for holding cases of type or galley proof. **f.** A triangular frame for arranging billiard balls at the start of a game. **2.** A toothed bar that meshes with another toothed structure, such as a pinion or gearwheel. **3.** An instrument of torture, consisting of a frame on which the victim's body is stretched. Often preceded by *the.* **4.** A state or cause of intense anguish. —**on the rack.** Under great strain or in anguish.
~*tr.v.* **racked, racking, racks. 1.** To place in or upon a rack. **2.** To torture by means of the rack. **3.** To torment; make suffer: *racked with pain.* **4.** To subject to stress or violent shaking. **5.** To strain with great effort; make heavy or taxing demands on: *racked his brain trying to remember.* **6.** To rack-rent. **7.** To move (a machine part) by use of a toothed rack. —**rack up.** *Slang.* To accumulate: *rack up points.* [Middle English *rekke, rakke,* probably from Middle Dutch *rec,* framework, *recken,* to stretch, from Germanic.] —**rack·er** *n.*

rack[2] *n.* A rapid, showy gait of a horse, in which each foot strikes the ground separately. Also called "single-foot."
~*intr.v.* **racked, racking, racks.** To go or move with this gait. [Perhaps of Arabic origin and akin to *rikwa,* easy-paced.]

rack[3], wrack (răk) *n.* A thin mass of wind-driven clouds.
~*intr.v.* **racked** or **wracked, racking** or **wracking, racks** or **wracks.** To be driven by the wind. Used of clouds. [Middle English *rak,* probably from Scandinavian, akin to Swedish *rak.*]

rack[4], wrack *n.* Destruction; decay. Now used only in the phrase *rack and ruin.* [Variant of WRACK (ruin).]

rack[5] *tr.v.* **racked, racking, racks.** To drain or draw off (wine or cider) from the dregs. [Middle English *rakken,* from Provençal *arracar,* from *raca*†, dregs, stems and husks of grapes.]

rack[6] *n.* **1.** A rib cut of lamb between the shoulder and the loin. **2.** A crown roast of lamb. [Perhaps from RACK (framework).]

rack and pinion *n.* A device for the conversion of rotary to linear motion, consisting of a pinion and a mated rack.

rack·et[1], rac·quet (răk'ĭt) *n.* **1.** A light bat with a long handle attached to a head consisting of a nearly elliptical hoop strung with a network of catgut, nylon, or silk, used in various ball games. **2.** A snowshoe resembling the head of a racket. [French *rachette, raquette,* from Italian *racchetta,* from dialectal Arabic *râḥet,* palm of the hand.]

racket[2] *n. Informal.* **1.** A clamor; an uproar; a din. **2. a.** A business that obtains money through fraud or extortion. **b.** An illegal or dishonest practice. **3.** *Slang.* Any business or job. **4.** A lively and often dissipated social life. —See Synonyms at **noise.**
~*intr.v.* **racketed, -eting, -ets.** To lead a lively and often dissipated social life. Often used with *about.* [16th century (clamor) : probably imitative.]

rack·et·eer (răk'ə-tîr') *n.* One engaged in an illegal business, especially a large-scale enterprise involving intimidation.
~*intr.v.* **racketeered, -eering, -eers.** To engage in an illegal business.

rack·et-press (răk'ĭt-prĕs') *n.* A frame usually consisting of two rigid pieces kept pressed together by a spring or screws and nuts, used to keep the head of a racket in shape.

rack·ets, rac·quets (răk'ĭts) *n. Used with a singular verb.* A game resembling squash, played on a four-walled court.

rack·et-tail (răk'ĭt-tāl') *n.* Any of various birds having a racket-shaped tail, especially certain hummingbirds and kingfishers.

rack·et·y (răk'ĭ-tē) *adj.* Noisy; raucous; rowdy.

Rack·ham (răk'həm), **Arthur** (1867–1939). British book illustrator. His graceful, ethereal style was best suited to fairy tales, such as *Peter Pan* (1906); among his other works is an edition of *A Christmas Carol* (1915).

rack railway *n.* A **cog railway** *(see).*

rack-rent (răk'rĕnt') *n.* An exorbitant rent.
~*tr.v.* **rack-rented, -renting, -rents.** To exact exorbitant rent for or from. [From RACK (to torture).] —**rack-rent·er** *n.*

ra·con (rā'kŏn') *n.* A radar beacon. [*Ra*dar beacon.]

rac·on·teur (răk'ŏn-tûr'; *French* rȧ-kôN-tœr') *n.* One who recounts stories and anecdotes with skill and wit. [French, from Old French, from *raconter,* to tell : *re-,* again + *aconter,* tell, count : *a-,* from Latin *ad-,* to + *co(u)nter,* to COUNT.]

racoon. Variant of **raccoon.**

racquet. Variant of **racket.**

rac·y (rā'sē) *adj.* **-ier, -iest. 1.** Full-flavored; piquant or pungent: *a racy wine.* **2.** Vigorous; lively: *a racy manner.* **3.** Humorous and slightly sexually improper; risqué. [From RACE (lineage, in the sense of a distinctive kind).] —**rac·i·ly** *adv.* —**rac·i·ness** *n.*

rad[1] (răd) *n. Physics.* A unit of energy absorbed from ionizing radiation, equal to 0.01 joule per kilogram of irradiated material. [Short for RADIATION.]

rad[2] **1.** radian. **2.** radiator.

rad. **1.** radical. **2.** radio. **3.** radius. **4.** radix.

RADA, R.A.D.A. In Britain, the Royal Academy of Dramatic Art.

ra·dar (rā'där) *n.* **1.** A method of detecting distant objects and determining their position, velocity, or other characteristics by analysis of very high frequency radio waves reflected from their surfaces.

raccoon Procyon lotor, *the raccoon (above), is a meat-eating mammal native to North America. It often hunts beside lakes and streams, searching with its hands underwater for clams and frogs—a habit that gave rise to a mistaken belief that it washes its food before eating it.*

PRONUNCIATION KEY
ă, pat; ā, pay; âr, care;
ä, father, are; b, bib;
ch, church; d, deed; ĕ, pet;
ē, be; f, fife; g, gag; h, hat;
hw, which; ĭ, pit; ī, pie;
îr, pier; j, judge; k, kick;
l, lid, needle; m, mum;
n, no, sudden; ng, thing;
ŏ, pot; ō, toe; ô, paw, for;
oi, noise; ou, out; o͝o, book;
o͞o, boot; p, pop; r, roar;
s, sauce; sh, ship, dish;
t, tight; th, thin, path;
th, this, bathe; ŭ, cut; ûr, fur;
v, valve; w, with; y, yes;
z, zebra, size; zh, vision;
ə, about, item, edible,
gallop, circus, peaceful

IN FOREIGN WORDS:
ȧ, *Fr.* ami; œ, *Fr.* feu, *Ger.* schön; ü, *Fr.* tu, *Ger.* über;
KH, *Ger.* ich, *Scot.* loch;
N, *Fr.* bon; y', *Fr.* Compiègne

STRESS MARKS:
Primary stress: '
in·cite' (ĭn-sīt')
Secondary stress: '
in'sight' (ĭn'sīt')

2. The equipment used in such detection. [*Radio detection and ranging.*]

radar astronomy *n.* The technique of investigating celestial objects in the solar system by reflecting radio waves off them and detecting and analyzing the reflected waves.

radar beacon *n.* A fixed device that sends or receives, amplifies, alters, and returns a radar signal, permitting a distant receiver to determine its bearing and sometimes its range. Also called "racon."

radar picket *n.* A ship or aircraft posted, usually during hostilities, to keep a radar watch for approaching aircraft.

ra·dar·scope (rā′där-skōp′) *n. Electronics.* The oscilloscope viewing screen of a radar receiver. [RADAR + (OSCILLO)SCOPE.]

Rad·cliffe (răd′klĭf′), **Ann,** born Ann Ward (1764–1823). British novelist. She pioneered the Gothic novel. Although her books, including *The Mysteries of Udolpho* (1794), were popular thrillers, they also had a notable influence on the romantic movement.

rad·dle¹ (răd′l) *tr.v.* **-dled, -dling, -dles.** To twist together or interweave. [Old French *rudelle, redelle,* rod twisted between upright stakes, perhaps from Middle High German *reidel.*]

raddle². Variant of **ruddle.**

rad·dled (răd′əld) *adj.* Worn-out, as by debauchery or general deterioration. Usually said of a person. [Probably alluding to the heavily rouged face of an old or debauched person. See **ruddle.**]

ra·di·al (rā′dē-əl) *adj.* **1. a.** Of, pertaining to, or arranged like rays or the radii of a circle. **b.** Radiating from or converging to a common center. **2.** Having or characterized by parts so arranged or so radiating: *a radial flower.* **3.** Moving or directed along a radius. **4.** *Anatomy.* Of, pertaining to, or near the radius or forearm: *the radial nerve.* **5.** Developing symmetrically about a central point. **6.** Radial-ply.
~*n.* **1.** A radial part, such as a ray, spoke, or radius. **2.** Any basal fin ray in a bony fish. **3.** A radial-ply tire. [Medieval Latin *radiālis,*

radial symmetry *A rose window in the basilica of St. Francis, in Assisi, Italy. Bisect the composition anywhere and each half will be a mirror image of the other.*

radar

"SEEING" THINGS OUT OF SIGHT

How objects are detected by bouncing radio waves

Radar enables objects like ships and aircraft to be detected and precisely located at long distances or in poor visibility. Radio waves are bounced off the object and the returning echo monitored.

The distance to the object is measured by the time taken for the radio waves to be reflected back to the radar aerial, and the location is indicated by the direction in which the aerial is pointing when the signal is received. This information is shown by light spots displayed on the scaled screen of a cathode-ray tube—the tube used in a television set.

Radar was developed in Britain in the 1930's from the ideas of the Italian radio pioneer Guglielmo Marconi. By the outbreak of World War II, a chain of radar stations along Britain's south and east coasts was capable of detecting aircraft more than 160 kilometers (100 miles) away. Now it can detect missiles up to 3,200 kilometers (2,000 miles) away and be used to locate typhoons and thunderstorms as well as help the police to catch speeding motorists.

AIR-TRAFFIC CONTROL *Approaching aircraft are shown by flight numbers on a radar screen and their positions located on a superimposed map.*

from Latin *radius,* rod, ray. See **radius.**] —**ra·di·al·ly** *adv.*

radial engine *n.* An internal-combustion engine, as formerly used in propeller-driven aircraft, with radially arrayed cylinders.

ra·di·al-ply (rā′dē-əl-plī′) *adj.* Designating a pneumatic tire in which the cords in the fabric casing are laid at approximately right angles to the center line of the tread. Compare **cross-ply.**

radial symmetry *n.* **1.** Symmetrical arrangement of constituents, especially of radiating parts, about a central point. **2.** *Biology.* The arrangement of the parts of an organism around a central axis such that a vertical cut through the axis in any plane produces two halves that are mirror images of each other. Compare **bilateral symmetry.**

ra·di·an (rā′dē-ən) *n. Abbr.* **rad** *Mathematics.* A unit of angular measure equal to the angle subtended at the center of a circle by an arc of length equal to the radius of the circle. It is equal to $360/_{2\pi}°$, approximately $57°17′44.6″$. [RADI(US) + -AN.]

ra·di·ance (rā′dē-əns) *n. Also* **ra·di·an·cy** (-ən-sē). **1.** The quality or state of being radiant. **2.** *Physics.* The radiant energy emitted per unit time in a given direction by a projected unit area of an emitting surface. Compare **irradiance.**

ra·di·ant (rā′dē-ənt) *adj.* **1.** Emitting heat or light. **2.** Consisting of or emitted as radiation: *radiant heat.* **3. a.** Filled with light; bright. **b.** Glowing or beaming, as with health or happiness. **4.** *Physics.* Designating photometric quantities that depend on energy measurements rather than on measurements of visible light: *radiant exitance.* In this sense, compare **luminous.** —See Synonyms at **bright.**
~*n.* **1.** An object or point from which light or heat rays are emitted. **2.** *Astronomy.* The apparent celestial origin of a meteoric shower. **3.** The part of a gas fire or other heater that gives out heat. [Latin *radiāns* (stem *radiant-*), present participle of *radiāre,* to RADIATE.] —**ra·di·ant·ly** *adv.*

radiant efficiency *n. Symbol* η_e *Physics.* A measure of the efficiency of a source of radiation, equal to the power it emits divided by the power consumed by the source.

radiant energy *n. Physics.* Energy transferred by radiation, especially by an electromagnetic wave.

radiant exitance *n. Symbol* M_e *Physics.* The radiant flux emitted from a surface per unit area at a given point.

radiant flux *n. Symbol* ϕ_e *Physics.* The rate of flow of energy as electromagnetic radiation.

radiant heat *n.* Heat transferred as radiation, especially as infrared radiation.

radiant intensity *n. Symbol* I_e *Physics.* The radiant flux per unit solid angle emitted from a given point.

ra·di·ate (rā′dē-āt′) *v.* **-ated, -ating, -ates.** —*intr.* **1.** To emit radiation. **2.** To issue or emerge in rays. **3.** To spread out or converge radially, in the manner of the spokes of a wheel. —*tr.* **1.** To emit (heat or light, for example). **2.** To diffuse or cause to go out from or as if from a center. **3.** To manifest in a glowing manner: *He radiated confidence.* **4.** To illuminate; light up.
~*adj.* (*also* -ət, -īt). **1.** *Botany.* Having rays, raylike parts, or ray flowers: *a radiate inflorescence.* **2.** *Biology.* Characterized by **radial symmetry** (*see*). **3.** Surrounded with rays. Said of a representation of a head, especially on a coin. [Latin *radiāre,* to emit beams, furnish with spokes, from *radius,* ray. See **radius.**]

ra·di·a·tion (rā′dē-ā′shən) *n.* **1.** The act or process of radiating. **2.** *Physics.* **a.** The emission of waves or particles. **b.** The propagating waves or particles, such as light, sound, radiant heat, or particles emitted by radioactivity. **3.** *Anatomy.* Radial arrangement of parts, as of a group of nerve fibers connecting different areas of the brain. **4.** *Biology.* A form of evolution, **adaptive radiation** (*see*).

radiation pattern *n. Electronics.* A diagram representing the strength of emission of electromagnetic radiation and its direction around a transmitting antenna.

radiation sickness *n.* Illness induced by ionizing radiation, ranging in severity from nausea, vomiting, headache, and diarrhea to loss of hair and teeth, reduction in red and white blood cell count, extensive hemorrhaging, sterility, and death.

ra·di·a·tive (rā′dē-ā′tĭv, -ə-tĭv) *adj. Physics.* Of or involving the emission of radiation, especially electromagnetic radiation.

ra·di·a·tor (rā′dē-ā′tər) *n.* **1. a.** A heating device consisting of a series of connected pipes or a flat structure containing ducts, through which hot water or steam can be circulated in a central-heating system. **b.** A similar portable device containing oil, which is heated electrically. **2.** A cooling device, as in automotive engines, through which water or other fluids circulate as a coolant. **3.** *Physics.* A body that emits radiation. **4.** A transmitting antenna.

rad·i·cal (răd′ĭ-kəl) *adj.* **1.** Arising from or going to a root or source. **2. a.** Affecting the basis of something; fundamental in its effect: *a radical revision of the procedure.* **b.** Broadly, having a profound or far-reaching effect: *radical reductions in staff levels.* **3.** Advocating or intended to effect fundamental or thoroughgoing changes, especially of economic and political structures. **4.** *Linguistics.* Of or designating a word root. **5.** *Botany.* Of, pertaining to, or growing from the root. **6.** *Medicine.* Designating treatment directed to the complete cure of a disease rather than simply to the relief of symptoms.
~*n.* **1.** One who advocates profound political, social, or other change. **2.** *Mathematics. Abbr.* **rad.** The root of a quantity as indicated by the radical sign. **3.** *Abbr.* **R** *Chemistry.* An atom or group of atoms with at least one unpaired electron. **4.** *Abbr.* **rad.** *Linguistics.* A word element, a **root** (*see*). [Middle English, of the root, fundamental, from Late Latin *rādīcālis,* having roots, from Latin *rādix* (stem *rādīc-*), root.] —**rad·i·cal·ly** *adv.* —**rad·i·cal·ness** *n.*

radical expression *n.* A mathematical expression or form in which radical signs appear.

rad·i·cal·ism (răd′ĭ-kə-lĭz′əm) *n.* **1.** The doctrines or practices of political or other radicals. **2.** The state or quality of being radical.

rad·i·cal·ize (răd′ĭ-kə-līz′) *tr.v.* **-ized, -izing, -izes.** To make radical or more radical, especially in political affairs. —**rad·i·cal·i·za·tion** *n.*

radical sign *n.* **1.** The sign $\sqrt{\ }$ placed before a quantity, indicating extraction of the root designated by a raised integral index. When extracting a square root, the index is customarily omitted. **2.** This sign together with a horizontal bar extending from its top to the end of the expression from which a root is to be extracted.

rad·i·cand (răd′ĭ-kănd′) *n.* The quantity under a radical sign: *3 is the radicand of* $\sqrt{3}$. [Latin *rādīcandum,* neuter gerundive of *rādīcāre,* to take root, from *rādix,* root. See **radical.**]

rad·i·ces. Alternate plural of **radix.**

rad·i·cle (răd′ĭ-kəl) *n.* **1.** *Botany.* The part of the plant embryo that develops into the primary root. **2.** *Anatomy.* A small structure resembling a root, such as a fibril of a nerve. [Latin *rādīcula,* diminutive of *rādix* (stem *rādīc-*), root.]

ra·di·i. Alternate plural of **radius.**

ra·di·o (rā′dē-ō) *n., pl.* **-os.** *Abbr.* **rad. 1.** The use of electromagnetic waves in the approximate frequency range from 10 kilohertz to 300,000 megahertz to transmit or receive electric signals without wires connecting the points of transmission and reception. **2.** Communication of audible signals, such as music, encoded in electromagnetic waves so transmitted and received. **3. a.** Transmission of programs for the public by this means; radio broadcasting as an industry or medium. **b.** Programs transmitted by radio: *The radio was interesting last night.* **4. a.** The equipment used to transmit radio signals; a transmitter. **b.** The equipment used to receive radio signals; a receiver. **c.** Equipment capable of both transmitting and receiving radio signals. **5.** A message sent by radio.
∼*adj.* **1.** Of, pertaining to, or sent by radio. **2.** Of, pertaining to, or designating oscillations of **radio frequency** *(see).*
∼*v.* **radioed, -oing, -os.** —*tr.* **1.** To transmit a message to, or communicate with, by radio. **2.** To broadcast by radio. —*intr.* To transmit a message by radio. [Short for RADIOTELEGRAPHY.]

radio- *prefix.* Indicates: **1.** Emission and propagation of radiation or radiant energy; for example, **radiometer. 2.** Radioactive; for example, **radiochemistry. 3.** Radio; for example, **radiotelephone.** [From RADIATION.]

ra·di·o·ac·tive (rā′dē-ō-ăk′tĭv) *adj. Physics.* Of or exhibiting radioactivity. —**ra·di·o·ac·tive·ly** *adv.*

radioactive dating *n.* Any method of determining the age of organic material, such as wood or fossils, using the decay rates of naturally occurring radioactive isotopes. See **carbon dating.**

radioactive decay *n.* See **decay** (sense 2).

radioactive series *n.* A group of nuclides related by a sequence of radioactive decay processes in which the heavier members of the group are transformed into successively lighter ones, the lightest being stable. Also called "decay chain."

ra·di·o·ac·tiv·i·ty (rā′dē-ō-ăk-tĭv′ə-tē) *n.* **1.** The spontaneous emission of radiation, either directly from unstable atomic nuclei or as a consequence of a nuclear reaction. **2.** The radiation so emitted, including alpha particles, nucleons, electrons, and gamma rays.

radio astronomy *n.* The study of celestial objects and phenomena by observation and analysis of emitted or reflected radio waves.

ra·di·o·au·tog·ra·phy (rā′dē-ō-ô-tŏg′rə-fē) *n.* **Autoradiography** *(see).*

radio beacon *n.* A fixed radio transmitter that broadcasts distinctive signals as a navigational aid.

radio beam *n.* A focused beam of radio signals transmitted by a radio beacon to guide aircraft or ships. Also called "beam."

ra·di·o·bi·ol·o·gy (rā′dē-ō-bī-ŏl′ə-jē) *n.* **1.** The study of the effects of radiation on living organisms. **2.** The use of radioactive tracers to study biological processes. —**ra·di·o·bi·o·log·i·cal** (rā′dē-ō-bī′ə-lŏj′ĭ-kəl) *adj.* —**ra·di·o·bi·o·log·i·cal·ly** *adv.* —**ra·di·o·bi·ol·o·gist** (rā′dē-ō-bī-ŏl′ə-jĭst) *n.*

radio cab *n.* A licensed taxi operating from a central unit to which customers can telephone to hire cabs. Also called "radio taxi."

ra·di·o·car·bon (rā′dē-ō-kär′bən) *n.* Radioactive carbon, especially **carbon 14** *(see).*

radiocarbon dating *n.* **Carbon dating** *(see).*

ra·di·o·chem·is·try (rā′dē-ō-kĕm′ĭs-trē) *n.* The chemistry of radioactive materials. —**ra·di·o·chem·i·cal** *adj.*

radio compass *n.* A navigational aid consisting of an automatic radio receiver that determines the transmission direction of incoming radio waves.

ra·di·o·el·e·ment (rā′dē-ō-ĕl′ə-mənt) *n.* Any naturally occurring or artificially produced radioactive element.

radio frequency *n. Abbr.* **RF 1.** The frequency of the waves transmitted by a specific radio station. **2.** Any frequency in the range within which radio waves can be transmitted, from about 10 kilohertz to about 300,000 megahertz. Radio frequency groups are: *very low frequency* (vlf), 10 to 30 kilohertz; *low frequency* (lf), 30 to 300 kilohertz; *medium frequency* (mf), 300 to 3,000 kilohertz; *high frequency* (hf), 3,000 to 30,000 kilohertz; *very high frequency* (vhf), 30 to 300 megahertz; *ultrahigh frequency* (uhf), 300 to 3,000 megahertz; *superhigh frequency* (shf), 3,000 to 30,000 megahertz; *extremely high frequency* (ehf), 30,000 to 300,000 megahertz.

ra·di·o·ge·nic (rā′dē-ō-jĕn′ĭk) *adj.* Caused by radioactivity. [RADIO- + -GENIC.]

ra·di·o·gram (rā′dē-ō-grăm′) *n.* **1.** A message transmitted by wireless telegraphy. **2.** A radiograph. **3.** *British.* A unit resembling a small cabinet and containing a radio and record player.

ra·di·o·graph (rā′dē-ō-grăf′, -gräf′) *n.* An image produced on a radiosensitive surface, such as a photographic film, by radiation other than visible light, especially x-rays passed through an object, or by photographing a fluoroscopic image. Also called "radiogram."
∼*tr.v.* **radiographed, -graphing, -graphs.** To make a radiograph of. [RADIO- + -GRAPH.]

ra·di·og·ra·phy (rā′dē-ŏg′rə-fē) *n.* Examination of the internal structure of a solid object by passing x-rays or gamma rays through it to produce a radiograph. The technique is used in industry and medicine. See **radiology.** —**ra·di·og·ra·pher** *n.* —**ra·di·o·graph·ic** (rā′dē-ō-grăf′ĭk) *adj.* —**ra·di·o·graph·i·cal·ly** *adv.*

radio ham *n.* A licensed amateur radio operator who broadcasts and receives radio messages on his own equipment, as a hobby.

ra·di·o·im·mu·no·as·say (rā′dē-ō-ĭm′yə-nō-ăs′ā, -ĭm-yōō′-) *n.* The technique of using radioactively labeled substances, particularly hormones, to measure the amounts of particular antibodies or hormones in the blood. [RADIO- + IMMUNE + ASSAY.]

radio interferometer *n.* A form of radio telescope in which two or more separate receiving antennae are connected to a single detector, information being obtained by analysis of the interference patterns produced by detected radio waves.

ra·di·o·i·so·tope (rā′dē-ō-ī′sə-tōp′) *n.* A naturally or artificially produced radioactive isotope of an element.

ra·di·o·lar·i·an (rā′dē-ō-lâr′ē-ən) *n.* Any of various marine protozoans of the order Radiolaria, having rigid siliceous skeletons and radiating spicules. [New Latin *Radiolaria,* from Late Latin *radiolus,* small sunbeam, diminutive of Latin *radius,* ray. See **radius.**]

ra·di·o·lo·ca·tion (rā′dē-ō-lō-kā′shən) *n.* The detection of distant objects by radar.

ra·di·ol·o·gy (rā′dē-ŏl′ə-jē) *n.* **1.** The use of ionizing radiation for radiotherapy and medical diagnosis; especially, the use of x-rays in medical radiography or fluoroscopy. **2.** Radioscopy. [RADIO- + -LOGY.] —**ra·di·o·log·i·cal** (rā′dē-ə-lŏj′ĭ-kəl) *adj.* —**ra·di·ol·o·gist** (rā′dē-ŏl′ə-jĭst) *n.*

ra·di·o·lu·cent (rā′dē-ō-lōō′sənt) *adj.* Allowing the passage of radiation, especially x-rays. [RADIO- + (TRANS)LUCENT.]

ra·di·om·e·ter (rā′dē-ŏm′ə-tər) *n.* Any of various devices for detecting or measuring radiation. See **Crookes radiometer.** [RADIO- + -METER.] —**ra·di·o·met·ric** (ra′dē-ō-mĕt′rĭk) *adj.* —**ra·di·om·e·try** (ra′dē-ŏm′ə-trē) *n.*

ra·di·o·nu·clide (rā′dē-ō-nōō′klīd′) *n.* A radioactive nuclide.

ra·di·o·paque (rā′dē-ō-pāk′) *adj.* Also **ra·di·o-o·paque** (rā′dē-ō-ō-pāk′). Absorbing, and therefore being opaque to, radiation, especially x-rays. Radiopaque substances are used, for example, in medical radiography as contrast media. [RADIO- + OPAQUE.]

ra·di·o·phone (rā′dē-ō-fōn′) *n.* A radiotelephone. —**ra·di·o·phon·ic** (rā′dē-ō-fŏn′ĭk) *adj.*

ra·di·o·pho·to·graph (rā′dē-ō-fō′tə-grăf′, -gräf′) *n.* Also **ra·di·o·pho·to** (-fō′tō). A photograph transmitted by radio waves, each image point being reproduced by a received electric impulse. —**ra·di·o·pho·tog·ra·phy** (rā′dē-ō-fə-tŏg′rə-fē) *n.*

ra·di·o·scope (rā′dē-ō-skōp′) *n.* A **fluoroscope** *(see).* [RADIO- + -SCOPE.]

ra·di·os·co·py (rā′dē-ŏs′kə-pē) *n.* The examination of the inner structure of opaque objects by x-rays or other penetrating radiation. Also called "radiology." [RADIO- + -SCOPY.] —**ra·di·o·scop·ic** (rā′dē-ō-skŏp′ĭk), **ra·di·o·scop·i·cal** (-ĭ-kəl) *adj.*

ra·di·o·sen·si·tive (rā′dē-ō-sĕn′sə-tĭv) *adj.* Sensitive to radiation. Said especially of certain forms of cancer.

ra·di·o·sonde (rā′dē-ō-sŏnd′) *n.* An instrument carried aloft, chiefly by balloon, to gather and transmit meteorological data.

radio source *n.* A celestial source of radio waves, such as a quasar or supernova remnant.

radio spectrum *n.* The entire range of electromagnetic communications frequencies, including those used for radio, radar, and television; the radio-frequency spectrum.

radio taxi *n.* A **radio cab** *(see).*

ra·di·o·tel·e·graph (rā′dē-ō-tĕl′ə-grăf′, -gräf′) *n.* **1.** The sending of messages by radiotelegraphy. **2.** A message sent by this means. —**ra·di·o·tel·e·graph** *v.* —**ra·di·o·tel·e·graph·ic** *adj.*

ra·di·o·te·leg·ra·phy (rā′dē-ō-tə-lĕg′rə-fē) *n.* **Wireless telegraphy** *(see).*

ra·di·o·tel·e·phone (rā′dē-ō-tĕl′ə-fōn′) *n.* A telephone in which audible communication is established by radio. Also called "radiophone," "wireless telephone." —**ra·di·o·tel·e·phon·ic** (rā′dē-ō-tĕl′ə-fŏn′ĭk) *adj.* —**ra·di·o·te·leph·o·ny** (rā′dē-ō-tə-lĕf′ə-nē) *n.*

radio telescope *n.* A sensitive, directional radio-antenna system used to detect and analyze radio waves from space.

ra·di·o·ther·a·py (rā′dē-ō-thĕr′ə-pē) *n.* The treatment of disease, particularly cancer, with radiation, especially by selective irradiation with x-rays or other ionizing radiation and by ingestion of radioisotopes.

ra·di·o·tho·ri·um (rā′dē-ō-thôr′ē-əm) *n.* A radioactive isotope of thorium with mass number 228.

radio wave *n.* A radio-frequency electromagnetic wave. Also called "Hertzian wave." See feature, next page.

radio window *n.* A region in the radio spectrum (10,000 to 40,000 megahertz) in which radio waves are not absorbed by the atmosphere or reflected by the ionosphere and can pass between earth and space.

rad·ish (răd′ĭsh) *n.* **1.** Any of various plants of the genus *Raphanus;*

radio telescope *Radio telescopes—like this one in West Germany—are used by astronomers to "listen" to the stars. Radio signals from space are reflected from a giant dish onto a central antenna and then analyzed to produce a radio map of the universe. Pulsars and quasars—celestial bodies that are powerful natural radio transmitters—were both first identified by radio astronomy.*

PRONUNCIATION KEY

ă, pat; ā, pay; âr, care;
ä, father, are; b, bib;
ch, church; d, deed; ĕ, pet;
ē, be; f, fife; g, gag; h, hat;
hw, which; ĭ, pit; ī, pie;
îr, pier; j, judge; k, kick;
l, lid, needle; m, mum;
n, no, sudden; ng, thing;
ŏ, pot; ō, toe; ô, paw, for;
oi, noise; ou, out; ŏŏ, book;
ōō, boot; p, pop; r, roar;
s, sauce; sh, ship, dish;
t, tight; th, thin, path;
th, this, bathe; ŭ, cut; ûr, fur;
v, valve; w, with; y, yes;
z, zebra, size; zh, vision;
ə, about, item, edible,
gallop, circus, peaceful

IN FOREIGN WORDS:

à, *Fr.* ami; œ, *Fr.* feu, *Ger.* schön; ü, *Fr.* tu, *Ger.* über; KH, *Ger.* ich, *Scot.* loch; N, *Fr.* bon; y′, *Fr.* Compiègne

STRESS MARKS:

Primary stress: ′
in·cite′ (ĭn-sīt′)
Secondary stress: ′
in′sight′ (ĭn′sīt′)

radio wave

SILENT SIGNALS IN THE EMPTY AIR

How radio waves send sounds around the world

A radio wave is an electromagnetic signal that travels at the speed of light and can be picked up by a receiving aerial similar to the one from which it was transmitted. Decoded, it reproduces the same sound waves that were converted by electricity into the electromagnetic signals at the transmitter.

The idea that such signals could exist was put forward in 1864 by the Scots physicist James Clerk Maxwell (1831–79). His theory of electromagnetism was proved correct in 1888, when a German physicist, Heinrich Hertz (1857–94), put an electric charge on two metal spheres, separated by a small gap. A few feet away he held another two spheres, also separated by a small gap. When a spark flashed between the two charged spheres, a similar spark flashed across the second gap. This was because the electric field produced a displacement current in empty space. This is the foundation of all radio communication. An elec-

tric charge moved rapidly up and down an aerial sets up a changing electric field. This sets up a changing magnetic field at right angles. The magnetic field sets up another changing electric field at right angles to itself, and so on. These changing waves travel at the speed of light. An aerial in their path has a current created in it matching that from the transmitter. Convert the current to sound waves, and you can hear sounds originated hundreds of miles away.

HOW SOUND TRAVELS FROM THE STUDIO TO THE LISTENER

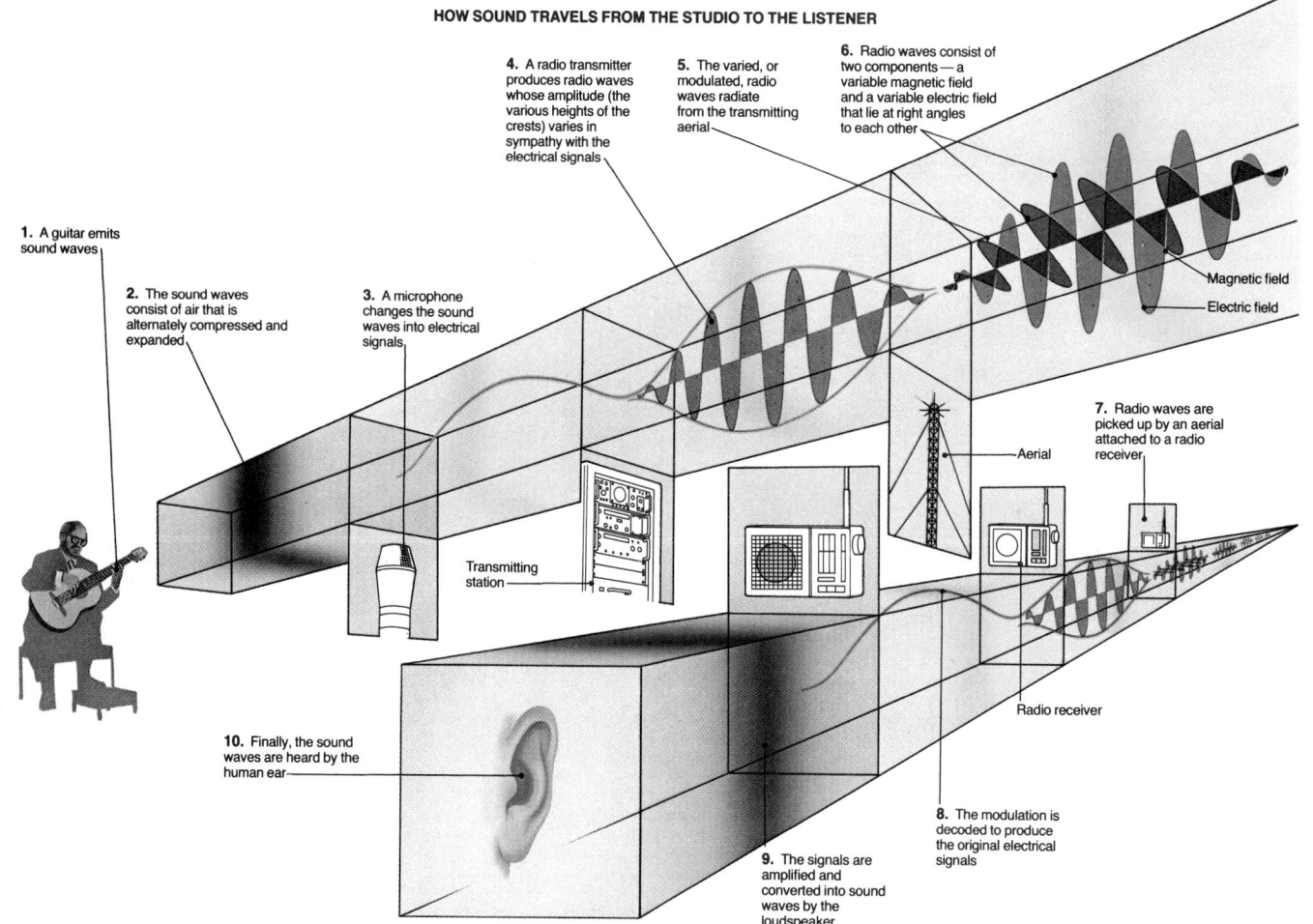

1. A guitar emits sound waves

2. The sound waves consist of air that is alternately compressed and expanded

3. A microphone changes the sound waves into electrical signals

4. A radio transmitter produces radio waves whose amplitude (the various heights of the crests) varies in sympathy with the electrical signals

5. The varied, or modulated, radio waves radiate from the transmitting aerial

6. Radio waves consist of two components — a variable magnetic field and a variable electric field that lie at right angles to each other

Magnetic field

Electric field

7. Radio waves are picked up by an aerial attached to a radio receiver

Aerial

Transmitting station

Radio receiver

8. The modulation is decoded to produce the original electrical signals

9. The signals are amplified and converted into sound waves by the loudspeaker

10. Finally, the sound waves are heard by the human ear

Radio waves are transmitted at the speed of light—about 299,800 kilometers (186,000 miles) a second. The lengths of the waves—that is, the distance from one crest to another—vary. Long-wave radio is transmitted at wavelengths of 1,000–2,000 meters, medium-wave at 187–577 meters, and short-wave at 10–100 meters. The frequency of the waves, measured in hertz after the

physicist who discovered them, is the number of waves that pass a stationary point in one second. The shorter the radio wave, the higher the frequency. Very high frequency bands (VHF) have wavelengths of 1–10 meters, and these are used for local TV and radio broadcasting. The term for thousands of cycles a second is kilohertz, and the term for millions of cycles a second is megahertz.

Radio waves can be sent around the world because they bounce back from a layer of the ionosphere that is about 90 kilometers (55 miles) above the earth. Because of the earth's curvature, they bounce back to a point hundreds of miles from where they were transmitted. The earth's surface bounces them back to the ionosphere, and so on around the world.

especially, *R. sativus*, having a thickened, edible root. **2.** The pungent root of this plant, eaten raw as an appetizer and in salads. [Middle English *radiche*, Old English *rædic*, from Latin *rādix* (stem *rādīc-*), root.]

ra·di·um (rā′dē-əm) *n. Symbol* **Ra** A rare brilliant-white, luminescent, highly radioactive metallic element having 16 isotopes of which radium 226 with a half-life of 1,622 years is the most common. It is used in cancer radiotherapy, as a neutron source for some research purposes, and as a constituent of luminescent paints. Atomic number 88, melting point 700°C, boiling point 1,737°C, valence 2. [New Latin, from Latin *radius*, ray (radium emits rays that penetrate opaque matter). See **radius**.]

radium therapy *n.* The use of radium in radiotherapy, especially in treating cancer.

ra·di·us (rā′dē-əs) *n., pl.* **-di·i** (-dē-ī′) *or* **-us·es.** **1.** *Abbr.* **R, r, rad. a.** A line segment that joins the center of a circle with any point on its circumference. **b.** A line segment that joins the center of a sphere

with any point on its surface. **c.** A line segment that joins the center of a closed figure, such as a polygon or ellipse, to a point on the circumference. **2.** The length of any such line segment. **3.** A measure of circular area or extent: *every family within a radius of 25 miles.* **4.** A measure of range of activity or influence. **5.** A radial part or structure, such as a mechanically pivoted arm or a spoke of a wheel. **6.** *Anatomy.* **a.** A long, prismatic, slightly curved bone, the shorter and thicker of the two forearm bones, located on the outer side of the ulna. **b.** A similar bone in many vertebrates. [Latin *radius*†, spoke of a wheel, ray.]

radius of curvature *n. Geometry.* The reciprocal of the curvature of a given curve at a given point.

radius vector *n.* **1.** *Mathematics.* **a.** A line segment that joins any variable point to the origin of polar or spherical coordinates. **b.** The length of such a line segment. **2.** *Astronomy.* A line segment that joins the center of a satellite to the focus of its orbit.

ra·dix (rā′dĭks) *n., pl.* **-dices** (rād′ə-sēz′, rā′də-) *or* **-dixes.** **1.** *Biology.*

A root or point of origin. **2.** *Abbr.* **rad.** *Mathematics.* The base of a system of numbers, as 2 is of the binary system and 10 is of the decimal system. [Latin *rādix,* root.]

radix point *n.* A **decimal point** *(see).*

Rad·nor·shire (răd′nər-shîr′, -shər). Former county of east-central Wales. A mountainous region, known for its sheep raising, it became part of the new county of Powys (1974).

ra·dome (rā′dōm′) *n.* A domelike protective housing for a radar antenna used especially in certain aircraft. [*radar* + *dome.*]

ra·don (rā′dŏn) *n. Symbol* **Rn** A colorless, radioactive, inert gaseous element formed by disintegration of radium. It is used as a radiation source in radiotherapy and to produce neutrons for research. Atomic number 86, atomic weight 222, melting point -71°C, boiling point -61.8°C, specific gravity (solid) 4, valence 0, half-life 3.823 days. [New Latin : RAD(IUM) + *-on,* suffix indicating inert gases.]

rad·u·la (răj′o͞o-lə) *n., pl.* **-lae** (-lē′). *Zoology.* In mollusks, a tonguelike organ bearing rows of horny teeth used for scraping up food and drawing it into the mouth. [New Latin, from Latin *rādula,* scraper, from *rādere,* to scrape.] **—rad·u·lar** *adj.*

Rae·burn (rā′bərn), **Sir Henry** (1756–1823). Scottish painter. He was known for his fashionable portraits, including those of Sir Walter Scott, David Hume, and James Boswell.

RAF, R.A.F. Royal Air Force.

raf·fi·a, raph·i·a (răf′ē-ə) *n.* **1.** An African palm tree, *Raphia ruffia,* having large leaves that yield a useful fiber. Also called "raffia palm." **2.** The fiber of these leaves, used for mats, baskets, and other products. [Malagasy.]

raf·fi·nose (răf′ə-nōs′) *n.* A white crystalline sugar, $C_{18}H_{32}O_{16}$, obtained from cottonseed meal and sugar beets. [French, from *raffiner,* to refine : *re-,* again + *affiner,* to refine : *a-,* to, from Latin *ad-* + *fin,* refined, from Old French, FINE.]

raff·ish (răf′ĭsh) *adj.* **1.** Vulgar; showy. **2.** Slightly disreputable; rakish. [Probably from dialectal *raff,* trash, from Middle English *raf.* See **raft** (amount).] **—raff·ish·ly** *adv.* **—raff·ish·ness** *n.*

raf·fle[1] (răf′əl) *n.* **1.** A lottery in which a number of persons buy chances on a prize. **2.** The disposing of an item as a prize in such a lottery.

—v. **raffled, -fling, -fles.** *—tr.* To dispose of in a raffle. Often used with *off.* *—intr.* To conduct or take part in a raffle. [Middle English *rafle,* a type of dice game, from Old French *raffle†,* act of snatching.] **—raf·fler** *n.*

raffle[2] *n.* Rubbish; debris. [Middle English, perhaps from Old French *ne rafle,* nothing at all.]

Raf·fles (răf′əlz), **Sir Thomas Stamford Bingley** (1781–1826). British colonial administrator. He is best known for his acquisition (1819) of Singapore for the East India Company, and his founding of the city there.

raf·fle·si·a (ră-flē′zhē-ə, -zē-ə) *n.* Any of various parasitic leafless plants of the tropical Asian genus *Rafflesia;* especially, *R. arnoldi,* having large flowers smelling of rotten meat and pollinated by carrion flies. [New Latin, after Sir Stamford RAFFLES.]

Ra·fi·nesque (rä-fē-nĕsk′) or **Ra·fi·nesque-Schmaltz** (-shmälts), **Constantine Samuel** (1783–1840). French and American naturalist, born in Turkey. A controversial and widely traveled ichthyologist and botanist, his thoughts on the origin of plant species presaged Darwin's theory of evolution.

raft[1] (răft, räft) *n.* **1.** A flat structure, typically made of planks, logs, or barrels, that floats on water and is used for transport or as a platform for swimmers. **2.** A **life raft** *(see).* **3.** A collection of floating ice, logs, or debris. **4.** In building, a layer of reinforced concrete used as a foundation to distribute the weight of a building, especially on subsiding ground.

—v. **rafted, rafting, rafts.** *—tr.* **1.** To convey on a raft. **2.** To make a raft from. *—intr.* To travel by raft. [Middle English *rafte,* from Old Norse *raptr,* beam, rafter.]

raft[2] *n. Informal.* A great number, amount, or collection; a lot. [Variant of Scottish *raff,* trash, from Middle English *raf,* perhaps from Scandinavian, akin to Old Norse *hreppa,* to catch, from Germanic *hrap-* (unattested).]

Raft (răft), **George** (1895–1980). U.S. actor. As a supporting actor he portrayed suave gangsters, shady nightclub owners, and other miscreants in several motion pictures, including *Scarface* (1932), before becoming a leading man in a few minor movies.

raft·er (răf′tər, räf′-) *n.* Any of the sloping beams that support a pitched roof. [Middle English *rafter,* Old English *ræfter,* from Germanic.]

rag[1] (răg) *n.* **1.** A scrap of cloth. **2.** Such scraps collectively, used, for example, as stuffing material or for pulp in papermaking. Also used adjectivally: *the rag content of a sheet of paper.* **3.** A scrap or fragment. **4.** *Slang.* A newspaper, especially one regarded as sensational or contemptible. **5. rags. a.** Threadbare or tattered clothing. **b.** *Informal.* Clothes. **6.** A jagged piece; a rough projection. **7.** The stringy central portion and membranous walls of citrus fruits. [Middle English *ragge,* probably back-formation from RAGGED.]

rag[2] *tr.v.* **ragged, ragging, rags.** *Slang.* **1.** To tease; taunt. **2.** To scold. **3.** *British.* To play a practical joke upon.

—n. British. A practical joke; a prank. [18th century : origin obscure.]

rag[3] *n.* **1.** A roofing slate with one rough surface. **2.** Any coarsely textured rock. [Middle English *ragghe†,* later associated with RAG (cloth).]

rag[4] *tr.v.* **ragged, ragging, rags.** To compose or play (a piece of music) in ragtime.

—n. A piece of music written in ragtime. [Short for RAGTIME.]

ra·ga (rä′gə) *n.* A traditional form in Hindu music, consisting of a theme that expresses some aspect of religious feeling and sets forth a tonal system on which variations are improvised within a prescribed framework of typical progressions, melodic formulas, and rhythmic patterns. [Sanskrit *rāga,* color, musical color.]

rag·a·muf·fin (răg′ə-mŭf′ĭn) *n.* A dirty or unkempt child. [After *Ragamoffyn,* demon in *Piers Plowman* (*c.* 1393), probably based on RAG (cloth).]

rag-and-bone man (răg′ən-bōn′) *n. Chiefly British.* A person who buys or gathers old clothes, furniture, and other junk, and sells it; a junkman.

rag·bag (răg′băg′) *n.* A jumbled collection; a mixture.

rag bolt *n.* A bolt having a jagged projection on the shank keeping it in place when driven in.

rag doll *n.* A doll made from or stuffed with scraps of cloth.

rage (rāj) *n.* **1. a.** Extreme, vehement anger; fury. **b.** A fit of anger. **2.** Furious intensity, as of a storm or disease. **3.** Burning desire or passion. **4.** *Informal.* A fad; a craze. —See Synonyms at **anger.** **—all the rage.** *Informal.* Very fashionable.

—intr.v. **raged, raging, rages.** **1.** To speak or act furiously. **2.** To move with great violence or intensity. **3.** To spread, prevail, or continue unchecked: *The epidemic raged.* [Middle English, from Old French, from Vulgar Latin *rabia* (unattested), from Latin *rabiēs,* madness, from *rabere,* to rave.]

rag·ged (răg′ĭd) *adj.* **1.** Tattered. **2.** Dressed in tattered or threadbare clothes. **3.** Unkempt or shaggy. **4.** Having a rough surface or edges; jagged. **5.** Uneven; sloppy; lacking smoothness or polish: *a ragged performance.* **6.** Harsh; rasping: *a ragged cry.* [Middle English, from Old Norse *roggvathr,* tufted, from *rogg†,* tuft of fur.] **—rag·ged·ly** *adv.* **—rag·ged·ness** *n.*

ragged robin *n.* A plant, *Lychnis flos-cuculi,* native to Eurasia, having reddish or white flowers with deeply lobed petals. Also called "cuckooflower." [From the ragged appearance of the petals.]

ra·gi (răg′ē) *n.* A grass, *Eleusine coracana,* of Africa and Asia, where it is cultivated for its edible grain. [Hindi *rāgī,* from Sanskrit, from Dravidian *rāki* (unattested).]

rag·lan (răg′lən) *n.* A loose coat, jacket, or sweater with slanted shoulder seams and with the sleeves extending in one piece to the neckline.

—adj. Having the shoulder seams extending diagonally from armhole to neckline: *a raglan sleeve.* [After Lord RAGLAN.]

Raglan, Fitzroy James Henry Somerset, 1st Baron (1788–1855). British field marshal. He lost an arm at Waterloo and rose to become military secretary to Wellington (1827–52) and commander of the British forces in the Crimean War.

ra·gout (ră-go͞o′) *n.* A rich stew of meat and vegetables. [French *ragoût,* from *ragoûter,* to renew the taste : *re-,* again + *a-,* from Latin *ad,* to + *goût,* taste, from Latin *gustus.*]

rag·tag (răg′tăg′) *n.* Rabble; riffraff. Also called "ragtag and bobtail."

—adj. Also **rag·gle-tag·gle** (răg′əl-tăg′əl). Low, coarse, and unkempt; ragged: *a ragtag army.* [RAG (scrap) + TAG.]

rag·time (răg′tīm′) *n.* A style of jazz characterized by elaborately syncopated rhythm in the melody and a steadily accented accompaniment. [Perhaps from *ragged time,* referring to the syncopation.]

rag trade *n. Informal.* The clothing trade. Preceded by *the.*

Ragusa. See **Dubrovnik.**

rag·weed (răg′wēd′) *n.* **1.** Any American plant of the genus *Ambrosia;* especially, *A. artemisiifolia* or *A. trifida,* whose profuse pollen is a chief cause of hay fever. Sometimes called "bitterweed." **2.** *Chiefly British.* The ragwort. [From the raggedness of the leaves.]

rag·worm (răg′wûrm′) *n.* A marine worm, the **clamworm** *(see).* [Referring to the raglike appearance of its appendages.]

rag·wort (răg′wûrt′, -wôrt′) *n.* Any of several plants of the genus *Senecio,* having yellow flowers; especially, *S. aureus,* the golden ragwort of eastern North America, and *S. jacobaea,* of Europe. [From the raggedness of the leaves.]

raid (rād) *n.* **1. a.** A sudden attack, such as one made by thieves for seizing something. **b.** A swift incursion, especially into hostile territory, to accomplish a specific task, such as the destruction of enemy installations. **2.** A sudden and forcible invasion by the police. **3.** A sudden act of seizing supplies or depleting resources: *a late-night raid on the refrigerator.* **4.** An attempt by speculators to drive stock prices down by selling.

—v. **raided, raiding, raids.** *—tr.* To make a raid on. *—intr.* To conduct or participate in a raid. [Middle English, Scottish dialect form of Old English *rād,* ROAD.] **—raid·er** *n.*

rail[1] (rāl) *n.* **1.** A bar or series of bars placed, usually horizontally, some distance above the ground and supported by vertical posts or a solid structure, as in a railing, balustrade, or fence. **2. a.** A bar or rod attached to a wall and used to hang objects from: *a picture rail.* **b.** A bar or rod on the side of a staircase used to hold on to for support or balance: *a hand rail.* **3.** A steel bar used, usually in pairs, as a track for a railroad, tramway, or the like. **4.** The railroad as a means of transportation: *We crossed Canada by rail.* **5.** A horizontal piece of wood in a door or in paneling.

—tr.v. **railed, railing, rails.** **1.** To supply with a rail or rails. **2.** To enclose or separate with a rail or rails. Usually used with *off* or *in.* [Middle English *raile,* from Old French *reille,* bar, from Latin *rēgula,* rod, straight piece of wood.]

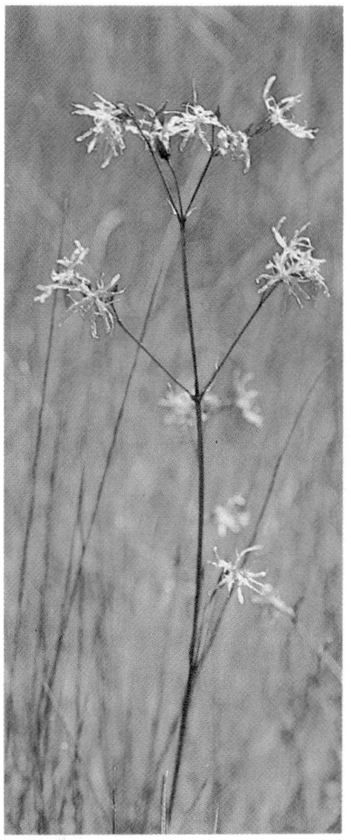

ragged robin *The wildflower* Lychnis flos-cuculi, *or ragged robin (above), is also called bachelor's-button, or cuckooflower. Country girls used to put several of them under an apron, naming them after local boys; the one that opened first told the girl whom she might marry. (The name bachelor's-button is also often applied to other flowers, such as carnations, cornflowers, and the common daisy.)*

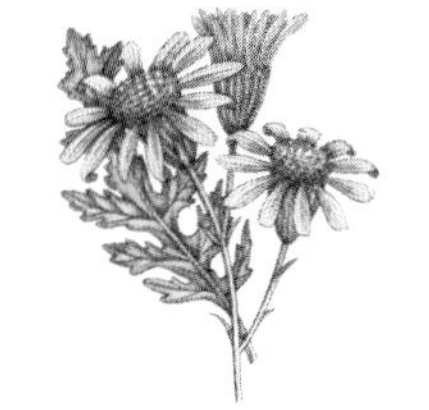

ragwort *A late-flowering relative of the daisy that gets its name from its ragged leaves. It is mildly poisonous.*

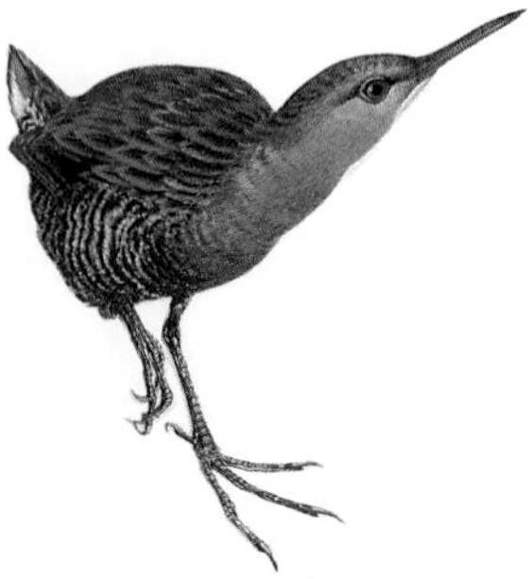

rail *There are more than 100 species of rail around the world. The water rail (above), which is native to Europe and Asia, is a marshland bird that seldom emerges from its cover among the reeds. It can often be detected by its hollow, squealing cry.*

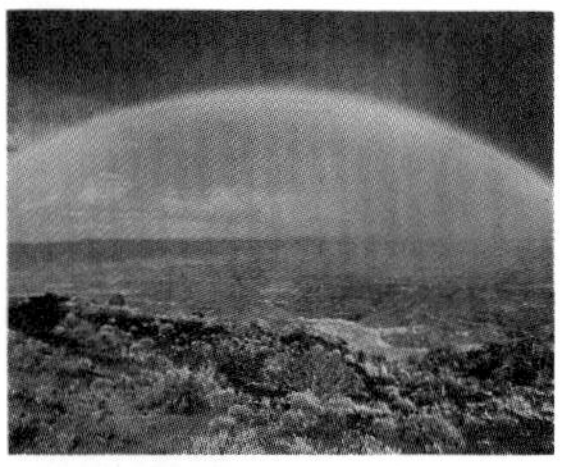

rainbow *The giant arc of a rainbow is created through refraction of the sun's rays by particles of water in the atmosphere, each droplet acting as a tiny prism.*

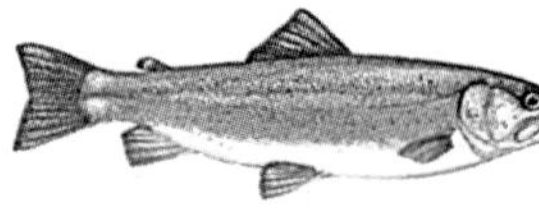

rainbow trout *Introduced into Europe from North America, the rainbow trout is a prized game fish. It grows fast, feeding at the surface largely on hovering insects, and a three-year-old specimen can be up to 500 millimeters (20 inches) long.*

rail[2] *n., pl.* **rails** or collectively **rail.** Any of various marsh birds of the family Rallidae, characteristically having brownish plumage and short wings adapted for only short flights. [Middle English *ra(i)le,* from Old French *raale,* from Old Northern French *raille,* Vulgar Latin *rasc(u)la* (unattested), perhaps imitative.]

rail[3] *intr.v.* **railed, railing, rails.** To use bitter, harsh, or abusive language. Used with *at* or *against.* [Middle English *railen,* from Old French *railler,* to mock, from Old Provençal *ralhar,* to scold, from Vulgar Latin *ragulāre* (unattested), to bray, from Late Latin *ragere*†, to neigh, roar.] **—rail·er** *n.*

rail·head (rāl′hĕd′) *n.* **1.** The farthest point on a railroad to which rails have been laid. **2.** *Military.* The section of a railroad where supplies are unloaded.

rail·ing (rā′lĭng) *n.* **1. a.** A banister, balustrade, or fence made of rails. **b.** The upper, horizontal part of a balustrade. **2.** Rails collectively. **3.** Material for making rails.

rail·ler·y (rā′lə-rē) *n., pl.* **-ies. 1.** Good-natured teasing or ridicule; banter. **2.** An instance of this. [French *raillerie,* from Old French *railler,* to RAIL (to use harsh language).]

rail·road (rāl′rōd′) *n. Abbr.* **r., R., Rwy., Ry. 1.** A road composed of parallel steel rails providing a track for locomotive-drawn trains and other rolling stock. **2.** The entire system of such track, together with the land, stations, rolling stock, and other property used in rail transport.
~tr.v. **railroaded, -roading, -roads. 1.** To transport by railroad. **2.** To supply (an area) with railroads. **3.** *Informal.* **a.** To pressure or coerce. Often used with *into*: *railroaded us into signing the contract.* **b.** To push or force hurriedly by exerting unfair pressure. Usually used with *through*: *They railroaded the bill through the state legislature.*

railroad flat *n.* An apartment in which the rooms are connected in a line, with windows at the front and rear.

rail-split·ter (rāl′splĭt′ər) *n.* One who splits logs or fences.

rail·way (rāl′wā′) *n.* **1.** A railroad. **2.** Any similar transport system using a fixed track: *a cable railway.* **3.** Any track on which wheeled equipment can move.

rai·ment (rā′mənt) *n. Archaic.* Clothing; garments. [Middle English *rayment,* short for obsolete *arrayment,* from Old French *araiement, araie,* an array, from *arayer,* to ARRAY.]

rain (rān) *n.* **1. a.** Water condensed from atmospheric vapor, falling to earth in drops. **b.** The descent of such water. **c.** A fall of such water; a rainstorm or shower. **d.** Rainy weather. **2.** The rapid falling of anything in large numbers or quantities. **3. rains.** The rainy season or seasonal rainfalls, as in certain tropical areas. **—rain or shine. 1.** Regardless of the weather. **2.** Under all circumstances.
~v. **rained, raining, rains.** *—intr.* **1.** To fall in drops of water from the clouds: *It rained every day.* **2.** To fall like rain. **3.** To release rain. *—tr.* **1.** To send or pour down. **2.** To offer, give, or deal out abundantly or forcefully: *His opponent rained blows on him.* **—rain out.** To postpone or cancel (a sports event) or other outdoor event because of rain. Often used in the passive. [Middle English *reyn, rain,* Old English *regn, rēn, regnian,* from Germanic.]

rain·bird (rān′bûrd′) *n.* Any of various birds, such as the green woodpecker, whose cry is said to indicate approaching rain.

rain·bow (rān′bō′) *n.* **1. a.** An arc of colors appearing in the sky opposite the sun as a result of the refractive dispersion of sunlight in drops of rain or mist. **b.** Any similar arc, as in a waterfall mist or graded display of colors. **2.** An illusory objective or hope: *chasing the rainbow of a quick fortune.* [Middle English *reinbowe,* Old English *rēnboga* : RAIN + BOW.]

rainbow bird *n.* A brightly colored Australian bee-eater, *Merops ornatus.*

rainbow trout *n.* A North American food fish, *Salmo gairdneri,* having a reddish longitudinal band and black spots.

rain check *n.* A ticket stub for an outdoor sports event entitling the holder to admission at a future date if the original event is canceled because of rain. **—take a rain check.** To postpone acceptance of an offer on the understanding that the offer may be taken up later.

rain·coat (rān′kōt′) *n.* A waterproof or water-resistant coat.

rain·drop (rān′drŏp′) *n.* A drop of rain.

Rai·ney (rā′nē), **Gertrude Malissa Nix Pridgett,** known as "Ma" (1886–1939). U.S. blues vocalist. Touring the South and Midwest with her song-and-dance partner and husband, William "Pa" Rainey, she was the first great black professional blues singer. She recorded nearly 100 songs and is remembered as the "mother of the blues."

rain·fall (rān′fôl′) *n.* **1.** A shower or fall of rain. **2.** *Meteorology.* The total quantity of water, as measured by a rain gauge, condensed or precipitated as rain, snow, hail, dew, hoar frost, rime, or sleet in a given area and time interval.

rain forest *n.* A dense evergreen forest occupying a tropical region with a large annual rainfall (over 100 inches).

rain gauge *n.* A device for measuring rainfall. Also called "pluviometer," "udometer."

Rai·nier III (rĕ-nyā′, rā-), **Prince de Monaco** (1923–). Ruling prince of Monaco (1949–). He succeeded his grandfather Louis II and relinquished many of his absolutist powers in 1962. He married the U.S. film star Grace Kelly in 1956.

Rai·nier, Mount (rā-nîr′, rā′nîr). Mountain in Mount Rainier National Park, in west-central Washington state. At 4,392 meters (14,408 feet), it is the highest peak in the Cascade Range.

rain·mak·er (rān′mā′kər) *n.* A person supposedly capable of producing rain by artificial or supernatural means.

rain·mak·ing (rān′mā′kĭng) *n.* **1.** The ceremony and rituals observed by a rainmaker. **2.** *Informal.* **Cloud seeding** *(see).*

rain·out (rān′out′) *n.* An outdoor event that is rained out.

rain·proof (rān′pro͞of′) *adj.* Impenetrable by rain. Said of coverings such as clothes or roofs. **—rain·proof** *v.*

Rains (rānz), **Claude** (1899–1967). U.S. actor; born in England. After a successful stage career in London, he moved to the U.S. (1926) where he portrayed several notable characters on film, especially the lead in *The Invisible Man* (1933) and the cynical yet kindhearted police chief in *Casablanca* (1943).

rain shadow *n.* A region with a relatively low rainfall, sheltered by adjacent high ground from prevailing, rain-bearing winds.

rain·spout (rān′spout′) *n.* A spout draining a roof gutter.

rain·storm (rān′stôrm′) *n.* A storm accompanied by rain.

rain tree *n.* A Central American tree, *Samarea saman,* widely planted as an ornamental in the tropics, having red-and-yellow flowers and leaflets that close when it starts to rain.

rain·wash (rān′wŏsh′) *n. Geology.* Decomposed rock and similar matter washed away by rain.

rain·wat·er (rān′wô′tər, -wŏt′ər) *n.* Water precipitated as rain, as opposed to well water or tapwater, with little dissolved mineral matter.

rain·wear (rān′wâr′) *n.* Waterproof clothing.

rain·y (rā′nē) *adj.* **-ier, -iest.** Characterized by, full of, or bringing rain. **—rain·i·ly** *adv.* **—rain·i·ness** *n.*

rainy day *n.* A time of need or trouble.

Rais (rā) or **Retz** (rĕts), **Gilles de** (1404–40). French marshal. A commander in the victorious campaigns of 1428–31 against the English, he later resorted to alchemy and witchcraft to finance his excessive lifestyle. He was tried and executed for murdering about 140 children and entered folklore as Bluebeard.

raise (rāz) *v.* **raised, raising, raises.** *—tr.* **1.** To move or cause to move upward or to a higher position; elevate; lift. **2. a.** To place or set upright; make erect. **b.** To cause to project or stand up or out. **c.** To cause (a blister, for example) to form. **3.** To erect or build. **4. a.** To cause to arise, appear, or exist. **b.** To awaken from or as if from death. **5.** To increase in size, quantity, or worth: *raise prices.* **6.** To increase in intensity, degree, strength, or pitch: *raise one's expectations.* **7.** To elevate in rank or dignity; promote. **8. a.** To grow or breed. **b.** To bring up; rear. **9.** To put forward for consideration. **10.** *Law.* To begin or set (a lawsuit) in operation. **11.** To express or utter (a cry or shout, for example). **12.** To bring about; cause; provoke: *raise a cheer.* **13.** To arouse or stir up: *raise a revolt.* **14.** To gather together; collect: *raise money.* **15.** To cause (dough) to puff up. **16.** To end or abandon (a siege, blockade, or the like). **17.** To remove or withdraw (an order). **18. a.** To increase (a poker bet). **b.** To bet more than (a preceding bettor in poker). **c.** To increase the bid of (one's bridge partner). **19.** *Nautical.* To bring (a shoreline or another ship, for example) into sight by approaching nearer. **20.** To establish radio contact with. **21.** To bring up the nap on the surface of (fabric). **22.** *Scottish.* To make angry; enrage. **23.** *Mathematics.* To multiply (a number) by a certain power or by itself a certain number of times: *4 raised to the power 3* *(4^3) equals 64.* *—intr.* To increase the stakes in poker or gambling. —See Synonyms at **lift.**
~n. **1.** An act of raising or increasing. **2.** An increase in salary. [Middle English *reisen, raisen,* from Old Norse *reisa.*] **—rais·er** *n.*

raised (rāzd) *adj.* **1.** Represented in relief, as a design might be; embossed. **2.** Leavened by yeast.

rai·sin (rā′zən) *n.* A sweet grape of several varieties, dried either in the sun or artificially. [Middle English *raisin,* from Old French, grape, from Latin *racēmus,* RACEME.]

rai·son d'ê·tre (rā-zôɴ dĕ′tr) *n., pl.* **raisons d'être** *(pronounced as singular).* Reason for being; point or justification for existing. [French.]

raj (räj) *n.* In India, dominion or sovereignty. **—the (British) Raj.** British rule in India. [Hindi *rāj,* reign, from Sanskrit *rājā,* from *rājati,* he rules.]

Raj·ab (rŭj′əb) *n.* The seventh month of the Muslim calendar. See feature at **calendar.** [Arabic.]

ra·jah, ra·ja (rä′jə) *n.* A prince, chief, or ruler in India and certain other eastern countries such as Malaysia. [Hindi *rājā,* from Sanskrit *rājan,* king.]

Ra·ja·sthan (rä′jə-stän′). State in northwestern India formed (1848) from a number of former principalities of Rajputana. It is divided into the Thar Desert in the west and the more fertile Deccan Plateau in the east. The two regions are separated by the Aravalli Mts., which yield salt, sandstone, marble, coal, mica, and gypsum. The state capital is Jaipur.

Raj·put, Raj·poot (räj′po͝ot) *n.* A member of a Hindu people claiming descent from the warlike and powerful rulers of northern India from the 8th to the 13th century.

rake[1] (rāk) *n.* **1.** A long-handled implement with a row of projecting teeth at its head, used to gather leaves or mown grass, or to loosen or smooth earth. **2.** Any similarly shaped implement, as for removing ashes from an oven or drawing betting chips across a table. **3.** Any of various toothed and often wheeled mechanical implements used for gathering hay, straw, or the like.
~v. **raked, raking, rakes.** *—tr.* **1.** To gather or move with or as if with a rake. **2.** To smooth, scrape, or loosen with a rake or similar implement. **3.** To search or examine thoroughly. **4.** To scrape; scratch; graze. **5.** To aim heavy gunfire along the length of. **6.** To direct one's gaze along the length of: *rake the horizon.* *—intr.* **1.** To

use a rake. **2.** To conduct a search. **—rake in.** To gain (money) in abundance. **—rake up.** To revive or bring to light: *rake up a scandal.* [Middle English *rake,* Old English *raca, racu.*] **—rak·er** *n.*

rake^{2} *n.* A profligate, sexually promiscuous man. [Short for RAKEHELL.]

rake^{3} *v.* **raked, raking, rakes.** *—intr.* To slant or incline from the vertical, as a ship's funnel does. *—tr.* To cause to lean or slant. *~n.* **1.** Inclination from the vertical or from the horizontal. **2.** A slope or slant; especially the slope from the back of a theater stage down to the front. **3.** The angle between the cutting edge of a tool and a plane perpendicular to the working surface to which the tool is applied. **4.** *Aeronautics.* The angle of inclination of an aircraft's wings. [17th century : probably akin to German *ragen*†, to project.]

rake·hell (rāk′hĕl′) *n. Archaic.* A rake; a roué.
~adj. Archaic. Dissolute; profligate. [Probably from the phrase, *to rake hell.*]

rake-off (rāk′ôf′) *n. Slang.* A percentage or share of the profits of an enterprise, especially one given or accepted as a bribe. [From the rake used by a croupier in a gambling house.]

rake's progress *n.* A continuous and dissolute decline; a descent into vice. [From William Hogarth's series of engravings, *A Rake's Progress* (1735).]

rak·i, rak·ee (răk′ē, rä′kē, rä′kə) *n.* A brandy of Turkey and the Balkan Peninsula, distilled from grapes or plums and flavored with anise. [Turkish *rāqī.*]

rak·ish^{1} (rā′kĭsh) *adj.* **1.** *Nautical.* Having a trim, streamlined appearance: *"We were schooner-rigged and rakish, with a long and lissom hull"* (John Masefield). **2.** Dashing; jaunty; smart. [From RAKE (to incline), from the raked masts on some fast pirate ships.] **—rak·ish·ly** *adv.* **—rak·ish·ness** *n.*

rakish^{2} *adj.* Characteristic of a roué or rake; debauched; dissolute. **—rak·ish·ly** *adv.* **—rak·ish·ness** *n.*

rale, râle (räl) *n.* An abnormal or pathological respiratory sound. [French *râle,* from *râler,* to make a rattling sound in the throat, from Old French, probably from Vulgar Latin *rasclāre* (unattested), to scrape.]

Ra·leigh (rô′lē, rŏl′ē). Capital of North Carolina, in the central part of the state. It is a political, cultural, trade, and industrial center.

Raleigh, Sir Walter (*c.* 1554–1618). British explorer, admiral, and writer. A favorite of Elizabeth I, he campaigned in Ireland and Cádiz, explored Guiana, colonized Virginia, and introduced tobacco and the potato to Europe. Found guilty of treason by James I, he was released for yet another expedition to Guiana and was executed after its failure. His literary output includes memoirs, poetry, and a history of the world.

ral·len·tan·do (răl′ən-tăn′dō; *Italian* räl′lĕn-tän′dō) *adv. Abbr.* **rall.** *Music.* So as to slacken gradually in tempo; ritardando. Used as a direction.
~n., pl. **rallentandos.** *Music.* A passage or movement performed with a gradual reduction in tempo. [Italian, slowing down, from *rallentare,* to relax : *re-* (intensifier) + *allentare,* to slow down, from Late Latin *allentāre* : Latin *ad-,* to + *lentus,* slow.] **—ral·len·tan·do** *adj.*

ral·line (răl′īn′, -ĭn) *adj.* Of, pertaining to, or belonging to the Rallidae, a family of birds containing the rails, crakes, and coots.

ral·ly^{1} (răl′ē) *v.* **-lied, -lying, -lies.** *—tr.* **1.** To call together for a common purpose; assemble. **2.** To reassemble and restore to order. **3.** To rouse or revive (one's strength, for example) from inactivity or decline. *—intr.* **1.** To meet for a common purpose. **2.** To join in a common effort or for a common purpose: *The workers rallied around to help.* **3.** To reassemble for a renewed effort, especially after being dispersed: *The brigade rallied for a final attack.* **4.** To recover abruptly from a setback or disadvantage. **5.** To show sudden improvement in health or spirits. **6.** *Finance.* To improve or rise after a fall. Said of stock market prices. **7.** In tennis and similar games, to exchange several strokes. —See Synonyms at **gather.**
~n., pl. **rallies.** **1.** An assembly, especially one intended to inspire enthusiasm for a cause. **2. a.** A reassembling, as of dispersed troops. **b.** The signal ordering this. **3.** A sharp improvement in health, vigor, or spirits. **4.** *Finance.* A notable rise in market prices and active trading after a decline. **5.** In tennis and similar games, an exchange of several strokes before one side scores a point. **6.** A race in which cars are driven over a fixed course with specific rules. [French *rallier,* from Old French *ralier* : *re-,* again + *alier,* to unite, ALLY.] **—ral·li·er** *n.*

rally^{2} *tr.v.* **-lied, -lying, -lies.** To tease good-humoredly; banter. [French *railler,* from Old French, to RAIL (abuse).] **—ral·li·er** *n.*

ram (răm) *n.* **1.** A male sheep. **2. Ram.** A constellation and sign of the zodiac, **Aries** *(see).* Preceded by *the.* **3.** Any of several devices used to drive, batter, or crush by forceful impact: **a.** A weapon, the **battering-ram** *(see).* **b.** The weight that drops in a pile driver or steam hammer. **c.** The plunger or piston of a force pump or hydraulic press. **4. a.** A projection on the prow of a warship, used to batter or cut into an enemy vessel. **b.** A ship having such a projection. **5.** A pump, a **hydraulic ram** *(see).*
~v. **rammed, ramming, rams.** *—tr.* **1.** To strike or drive against with a heavy impact; butt. **2.** To force, press, or drive down or into place. **3.** To cram; stuff. *—intr.* To crash; collide. [Middle English *ram,* Old English *ramm,* from Germanic *ramma-* (unattested).] **—ram·mer** *n.*

RAM (răm) *n.* Random-access memory.

Ra·ma (rä′mə) *n. Hinduism.* Any of three of the incarnations of Vishnu, regarded as heroes: Balarama, Parashurama, and especially Ramachandra. [Sanskrit *Rāma*†, dark-colored, black.]

Ra·ma·chan·dra (rä′mə-chŭn′drə) *n. Hinduism.* The seventh of Vishnu's incarnations and hero of the Hindu epic poem *Ramayana.* Also called "Rama."

Ram·a·dan, Ram·a·dhan (răm′ə-dän′) *n.* Also **Ram·a·zan** (răm′ə-zän′). **1.** The ninth month of the Muslim year, spent in fasting from sunrise to sunset. See feature at **calendar.** **2.** The fasting itself. [Arabic *Ramaḍān,* the hot month, from *ramaḍ,* dryness.]

Ra·ma·krish·na (rä′mə-krĭsh′nə) (1834–86). Hindu yogi and mystic. He is considered a leader of modern Hinduism.

Ra·man (rä′mən), **Sir Chandrasekhara Venkata** (1888–1970). Indian physicist. A specialist in spectroscopy, he discovered the Raman effect, for which he was awarded the Nobel Prize (1930).

Raman effect *n. Physics.* The alteration in frequency and random alteration in phase of light scattered in a material medium, used for investigating the structure of molecules. [After Sir C.V. RAMAN.]

Raman spectroscopy *n. Physics.* A form of spectroscopy for investigating the structure of molecules by analyzing the spectrum *(Raman spectrum)* of light scattered from a sample. [After Sir C.V. RAMAN.]

ra·mate (rā′māt′) *adj.* Having branches. [Latin *rāmus,* branch.]

Ra·ma·ya·na (rä-mä′yə-nə) *n.* A Sanskrit epic poem of ancient India, regarded as sacred by Hindus. It relates the adventures of Ramachandra. [Sanskrit *Rāmāyana* : *Rāma,* RAMA + *-ayana,* suffix meaning "pertaining to."]

ram·ble (răm′bəl) *intr.v.* **-bled, -bling, -bles.** **1.** To walk or wander aimlessly and for pleasure; stroll or roam. **2.** To follow an irregularly winding course of motion or growth. **3.** To speak or write with many digressions. —See Synonyms at **wander.**
~n. A leisurely stroll. [Probably from Middle Dutch *rammelen,* (of animals) to wander about in sexual heat, from *rammen,* to copulate with; akin to RAM.]

ram·bler (răm′blər) *n.* **1.** One who rambles. **2.** A person who takes long country walks, especially as a regular leisure pursuit. **3.** A variety of cultivated rose having weak stems that trail over the ground. In this sense, also called "rambler rose."

ram·bling (răm′blĭng) *adj.* **1.** Extended over an irregular area; sprawling: *a large, rambling Victorian house.* **2.** Lengthy and desultory; long-winded: *"By my rambling digressions, I perceive myself to be grown old"* (Benjamin Franklin). **—ram·bling·ly** *adv.*

Ram·bouil·let^{1} (räN-bo͞o-yā′). Town in the department of Yvelines, northern France, set in the forest of Rambouillet. Its famous chateau is the official summer residence of French presidents.

Ram·bouil·let^{2} (răm′bo͞o-lā; *French* räN-bo͞o-yā′) *n.* Any of a breed of merino sheep of French origin, raised for wool and meat. [After RAMBOUILLET.]

ram·bunc·tious (răm-bŭngk′shəs) *adj.* Boisterous; disorderly. [Probably variant of RUMBUSTIOUS.]

ram·bu·tan (răm-bo͞ot′ən) *n.* **1.** A tree, *Nephelium lappaceum,* of Southeast Asia, bearing edible, oval red fruit with soft spines. **2.** The fruit of this tree. [Malay *rambutan,* from *rambut,* hair, from the hairy covering of the fruit.]

Ra·meau (rä-mō′), **Jean Philippe** (1683–1764). French composer and critic. Although he was an organist, it is his orchestral works that display the greatest innovations. His opera-ballets include *Les Indes Galantes* (1735).

ram·e·kin, ram·e·quin (răm′ə-kĭn) *n.* **1.** A cheese preparation made with eggs, breadcrumbs, or pastry, baked and served in individual dishes. **2.** A small individual dish used for both baking and serving this. [French *ramequin,* from Middle Dutch *rameken,* diminutive of *ram,* cream, from Middle Low German *rōm(e).*]

ra·men·tum (rə-mĕn′təm) *n., pl.* **-ta** (-tə). Any of the brown scaly structures on the stems of fern fronds. [New Latin, from Latin *rādere,* to scrape + *-mentum,* -MENT.]

Ram·e·ses II (răm′ə-sēz′) or **Ram·ses** (răm′sēz), known as "Rameses the Great." (*c.* 1300-1224 B.C.). Egyptian king, best known for his great building. Most famous archaeological sites in Egypt bear evidence of his patronage. Known to the Greeks as Sesostris, he was probably the king connected with the Jewish exodus from Egypt.

ra·mi. Plural of **ramus.**

ram·ie (răm′ē) *n.* **1.** A woody Asian plant, *Boehmeria nivea,* having broad leaves. **2.** The flaxlike fiber from the stem of this plant, used in making fabrics and cordage. [Malay *rami.*]

ram·i·fi·ca·tion (răm′ə-fĭ-kā′shən) *n.* **1.** The act or process of branching out or dividing into branches. **2.** A branch or other subordinate part extending from a main body. **3.** An arrangement of branches or branching parts. **4.** A development or consequence growing out of and often complicating a problem, plan, or statement.

ram·i·form (răm′ə-fôrm′) *adj.* Branchlike or branching. [RAMUS + -FORM.]

ram·i·fy (răm′ə-fī′) *v.* **-fied, -fying, -fies.** *—tr.* To divide into or cause to extend in branches or branchlike parts. *—intr.* To branch out or become divided into branches. [French *ramifier,* from Medieval Latin *rāmificāre,* from Latin *rāmus,* branch.]

ra·min (rä-mēn′) *n.* **1.** Any of various trees of the genus *Gonystylus,* native to Southeast Asia; especially *G. bancanus,* valued for its light-colored hardwood. **2.** The wood of any such tree. [Malay.]

ram·jet (răm′jĕt′) *n.* **1.** A jet engine that compresses and heats its air intake for the fuel mixture by means of a specially shaped intake duct. It has no revolving parts and operates only at speed, requiring take-off assistance. **2.** An aircraft propelled by such an engine. Also called "athodyd."

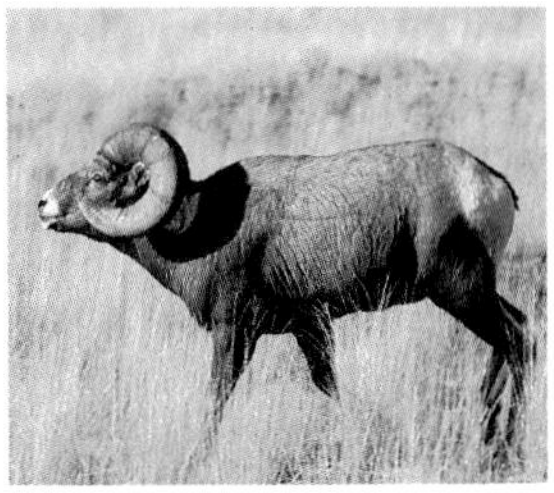

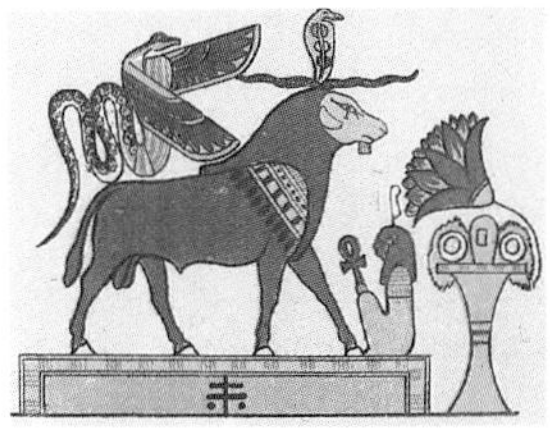

ram *Male sheep are known as rams. Above is a male bighorn, a wild sheep native to western North America. In ancient Egypt, the ram was believed to be the embodiment of the soul, and several ancient Egyptian gods are depicted with a ram's head. Below is the ram god of Mendes, a holy town in the Nile delta.*

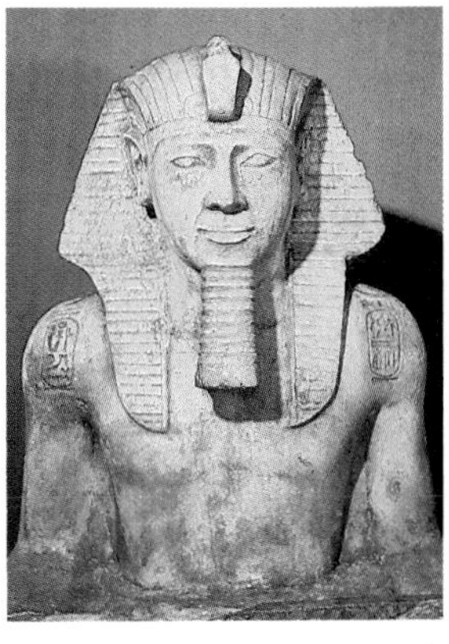

Rameses *The name of 12 kings of Egypt, of whom Rameses II was the most important. This statue of him was carved in about 1250 B.C.*

ra·mose (rā'mōs', rə-mōs') *adj.* Having many branches. [Latin *rāmōsus,* from *rāmus,* branch.]

ra·mous (rā'məs) *adj.* **1.** Of or resembling branches. **2.** Branching; ramose. [Latin *rāmōsus,* RAMOSE.]

ramp¹ (rămp) *n.* **1.** A sloping passage or roadway connecting different levels, as of a building or road. **2.** *Architecture.* A concave bend of a handrail where a sharp change in level or direction occurs, such as at a stair landing. **3.** A mobile staircase for entering and leaving an airplane. **4.** A sudden bump or change in level in a road surface, sometimes introduced deliberately to keep traffic to a low speed. **5.** A small platform straddling a cable, hosepipe, or the like and enabling vehicles to pass over it without touching it. **6.** A short upward projection from which a person or vehicle can be launched, as on a ski-jump or aircraft carrier. [French *rampe,* from *ramper,* to slope, creep, from Old French, to RAMP.]

ramp² *intr.v.* **ramped, ramping, ramps. 1.** To act threateningly or violently; rage. **2.** To assume a threatening stance. **3.** To stand in the rampant position. —*n.* The act of ramping. [Middle English *rampen,* from Old French *ramper,* to climb, rear up, from Frankish *rampōn* (unattested).]

ram·page (răm'pāj') *n.* A course of violent, frenzied, and destructive action or behavior. —**on the rampage.** Behaving violently and destructively. —*intr.v.* (răm-pāj') **rampaged, -paging, -pages.** To rush about wildly or violently; rage. [18th century (Scottish) : perhaps from RAMP (to rear up).] —**ram·pag·er** (răm-pā'jər) *n.*

ram·pa·geous (răm-pā'jəs) *adj.* Raging; frenzied: *"The hot rampageous horses of my will"* (W.H. Auden). —**ram·pa·geous·ly** *adv.* —**ram·pa·geous·ness** *n.*

ram·pant (răm'pənt) *adj.* **1.** Extending unchecked; unrestrained; widespread. **2.** Characterized by ungoverned vehemence and extravagance. **3.** Rearing or ramping on the hind legs. **4.** *Heraldry.* Rearing on the left hind leg with the forelegs raised, the right above the left, and usually with the head in profile. **5.** *Architecture.* Springing from a support or abutment higher at one side than at the other. Said of an arch or vault. [Middle English *rampaunt,* from Old French *rampant,* present participle of *ramper,* to climb, RAMP.] —**ram·pan·cy** *n.* —**ram·pant·ly** *adv.*

ram·part (răm'pärt') *n.* **1.** A fortification consisting of an elevation or embankment, often provided with a parapet. **2.** Anything that serves to protect or defend: *The cliff was a rampart against the ocean.* —See Synonyms at **bulwark.** —*tr.v.* **ramparted, -parting, -parts.** To protect or defend with or as if with a rampart. [French *rempart,* from *remparer,* to fortify : *re-* (intensifier) + *emparer,* to defend, fortify, from Provençal *antparar, amparar,* from Vulgar Latin *anteparāre* (unattested), to prepare for defense : Latin *ante-,* before + *parāre,* to prepare.]

ram·pike (răm'pīk') *n.* A standing dead tree or tree stump, especially one killed by fire. [Origin unknown.]

ram·pi·on (răm'pē-ən) *n.* **1.** A Eurasian plant, *Campanula rapunculus,* having clusters of bluish flowers and an edible root used in salads. **2.** Any of various similar plants of the genus *Phyteuma.* [Probably from Old French *raiponce,* from Medieval Latin *rapontium,* probably from Latin *rāpa, rāpum,* turnip, RAPE.]

ram·rod (răm'rŏd') *n.* **1.** A metal rod used to force the charge into a muzzleloading firearm. **2.** A rod used to clean the barrel of a firearm. **3.** A person who resembles a ramrod in inflexibility.

Ram·say (răm'zē), **Allan** (1713-84). Scottish portrait painter. He was court painter to George III. His portraits include George's wife, Queen Charlotte (National Portrait Gallery, London) and Jean-Jacques Rousseau (National Gallery, Edinburgh).

Ramsay, Sir William (1852-1916). Scottish chemist. Investigating a discovery made by his colleague, Baron Rayleigh, that atmospheric nitrogen seemed heavier than laboratory-prepared nitrogen, he discovered the inert gases argon (1894), helium (1895), neon, xenon, and krypton (1898). He and Rayleigh were awarded the Nobel Prize in 1904.

Ram·ses (răm'sēz'). See **Rameses II.**

ram·shack·le (răm'shăk'əl) *adj.* Likely to fall apart because of shoddy construction or lack of maintenance; rickety. [Back-formation from *ramshackled, ransackled,* from *ransackle,* frequentative of Middle English *ransaken,* to RANSACK.]

ram's horn *n. Judaism.* A shofar *(see).*

ram·son (răm'zən, -sən) *n.* **1.** A broad-leaved Eurasian garlic, *Allium ursinum,* having a bulbous root used in salads and relishes. **2.** The root of this plant. Usually used in the plural. [Middle English *ramsyn,* Old English *hramsan* (plural of *hramsa*), mistaken as singular.]

ram·til (răm'tĭl) *n.* An African plant, *Guizotia abyssinica,* grown for its oil-rich seeds. The seed is called "Niger seed." [Hindi *rāmtil* : Sanskrit *rāma,* dark (see **Rama**) + *tila†,* sesame.]

ram·u·lose (răm'yə-lōs') *adj.* Also **ram·u·lous** (-ləs). *Biology.* Having numerous small branches. [Latin *rāmulōsus,* from *rāmulus,* diminutive of *rāmus,* branch, RAMUS.]

ra·mus (rā'məs) *n., pl.* **-mi** (-mī). *Biology & Anatomy.* A branchlike part of a structure, such as a branch of a nerve fiber or a thin process projecting from a bone. [New Latin, from Latin, branch.]

ran. Past tense of **run.**

Ran (răn). *Norse Mythology.* The goddess of the sea who caught drowning persons in her net.

ranch (rănch) *n.* **1.** An extensive farm, especially one in the American West, on which large herds of cattle, sheep, or horses are raised.

2. Any large farm on which a particular crop or kind of animal is raised. **3.** A fish farm in the open sea for breeding migratory fish such as salmon. —*intr.v.* **ranched, ranching, ranches.** To work on or manage a ranch. [Mexican Spanish *rancho,* from Spanish, mess room, from Old Spanish *rancher, ranchar,* be billeted, from Old French *ranger,* to put in a line, from *renc,* line, row, from Frankish *hring* (unattested), ring.]

ranch·er (răn'chər) *n.* One who owns, manages, or works on a ranch.

ran·che·ro (răn-châr'ō) *n., pl.* **-ros.** *Southwestern U.S.* A rancher. [Mexican Spanish, from *rancho,* RANCH.]

ranch house *n.* **1.** The building on a ranch occupied by its owner or manager. **2.** A rectangular, one-story house with a low-pitched roof, a style common on Western ranches and in suburbs.

ranch·man (rănch'mən) *n., pl.* **-men** (-mĭn). A rancher.

ranch mink *n.* An American mink bred in captivity from Alaskan and Labrador strains for special pelt colors and qualities.

ran·cho (răn'chō) *n., pl.* **-chos.** *Southwestern U.S.* **1.** A hut or group of huts in which ranch workers live. **2.** A ranch. [Mexican Spanish, RANCH.]

ran·cid (răn'sĭd) *adj.* **1.** Stale or decomposed. Said of fats or oils. **2.** Having the disagreeable odor or taste of decomposed oils or fats; sour; rank. **3.** Disagreeable; mean-spirited; nasty: *a scowling, rancid old man.* [Latin *rancidus,* from *rancēre†,* to stink.] —**ran·cid·i·ty** (răn-sĭd'ə-tē), **ran·cid·ness** *n.*

ran·cor (răng'kər) *n.* Also *chiefly British* **ran·cour.** Bitter resentment; deep-seated ill will. [Middle English *rancour,* from Old French, from Late Latin *rancor* (stem *rancōr-*), rancidity, from *rancēre,* to stink. See **rancid.**] —**ran·cor·ous** (răng'kər-əs) *adj.* —**ran·cor·ous·ly** *adv.* —**ran·cor·ous·ness** *n.*

rand¹ (rănd, ränd) *n., pl.* **rand** or **rands. 1.** The basic monetary unit of the Republic of South Africa, equal to 100 cents. See feature at **currency. 2.** A note or coin worth one rand. [After the *Rand,* WITWATERSRAND.]

rand² (rănd, ränt, rŏnt) *n., pl.* **rands** or **rande** (-ə). *South African.* A ridge of hills or an extended area of high ground. [Afrikaans, from Dutch, strip, ridge, from Germanic *randa* (unattested), rim, edge.]

rand³ (rănd) *n.* A strip of leather inserted between the heel and sole of a shoe or boot. [Middle English, Old English, rim, margin, border, from Germanic.]

Rand (rănd), **Ayn** (1905-82). U.S. writer, born in Russia. In her many novels and plays and her controversial philosophical writings, she defended political conservatism and enlightened self-interest and denounced personal sacrifice for the common good, a view she called "Objectivism." *Anthem* (1938), *The Fountainhead* (1943), and *Introduction to Objectivist Epistomology* (1967) are among her major works.

ran·dan (răn'dăn) *n.* **1.** A type of boat designed to be rowed by three persons. **2.** The way of rowing this boat, in which the persons fore and aft use one oar each, and the person in the middle uses two. [19th century : origin obscure.]

R & D research and development.

Ran·dolph (răn'dŏlf'), **John,** also called "Randolph of Roanoke" (1773-1833). U.S. politician and orator. Serving 12 terms as U.S. representative from Virginia between 1799 and 1829 and as a U.S. senator from 1825 to 1827, he brought brilliant oratory skills, sporadic party support, and eccentric, sometimes demented behavior to national politics.

ran·dom (răn'dəm) *adj.* **1.** Having no specific pattern or objective; lacking causal relationships; haphazard. **2.** *Statistics.* **a.** Of or designating a phenomenon that does not produce the same outcome or consequences every time it occurs under identical circumstances. **b.** Of or designating an event having a relative frequency of occurrence that approaches a stable limit as the number of observations of the event increases to infinity. **c.** Of or designating a sample drawn from a population so that each member of the population has an equal chance to be drawn. **d.** Of or pertaining to a member of such a sample: *a random number.* —See Synonyms at **chance.** —**at random.** Without definite method or purpose; unsystematically: *They chose one man at random from the volunteers.* [Middle English *randoun,* from Old French *randon,* haphazard, from *randir,* to run, from Frankish *rant†* (unattested), a running.] —**ran·dom·ly** *adv.*

ran·dom-ac·cess (răn'dəm-ăk'sĕs') *adj. Computer Science.* Giving access directly to any required part of stored data: *a random-access computer memory.* Also called "direct access." Compare **sequential access.** See **read-write.**

ran·dom·ize (răn'də-mīz') *tr.v.* **-ized, -izing, -izes.** To make random, especially samples for scientific experimentation. —**ran·dom·i·za·tion** *n.*

random variable *n. Statistics.* A variable having numerical values determined by the results of a chance experiment. Also called "stochastic variable."

R and R rest and recreation.

ran·dy (răn'dē) *adj.* **-dier, -diest. 1.** Sexually aroused; lustful. **2.** Coarse and shrewish. —*n., pl.* **randies.** *Chiefly Scottish.* A shrewish woman. [Scottish, from *rand,* variant of RANT.] —**rand·i·ly** *adv.* —**rand·i·ness** *n.*

ranee. Variant of **rani.**

rang. Past tense of **ring.**

ran·ga·ti·ra (rŭng'gə-tîr'ə, răng'-) *n.* A Maori chief or noble person. [Maori.]

range (rānj) *n. Abbr.* **r. 1. a.** The extent of perception, knowledge, experience, or ability of someone or something. **b.** The area or sphere covered by or included in something; the scope: *Personal relations lie outside the range of sociology.* **c.** The limits within which something is valid or applicable; effective scope: *a long-range weather forecast; within the range of possibilities.* **2. a.** An amount or extent of variation: *a wide price range.* **b.** *Music.* The extent of pitch variation within the capacity of a voice or instrument. **c.** The limits between which a meter or other measuring instrument can be operated. **3. a.** The maximum or effective distance that can be traversed, as by bullets or by radiation. **b.** The distance to a target. **4.** The maximum distance that a ship or other vehicle can travel before exhausting its fuel supply. **5.** A place for shooting at targets. **6.** A testing area in which rockets and missiles are fired and flown. **7.** An extensive area of open land on which livestock wander and graze. **8.** The geographical region in which a particular kind of plant or animal normally lives or grows. **9.** The act of or opportunity for wandering or roaming over a large area: *gave free range to her imagination.* **10.** *Mathematics.* **a.** The totality of points in a set established by a **mapping** *(see).* Also called "codomain." Compare **domain. b.** The order of the highest nonzero determinant contained in a given matrix. **11.** *Statistics.* A measure of dispersion equal to the difference or interval between the smallest and largest of a set of quantities. **12.** A class, rank, or order. **13.** An extended group or series, especially of mountains. **14.** Any of a series of double-faced bookcases in a library stack room. **15.** A set of products or services of the same general type; a line: *a new range of sportswear.* **16.** A large cooking stove of a type usually heated by solid fuel and having one or more ovens, on which several foods can be cooked at the same time. **17.** The action or an act of ranging. **18.** *Geology.* A mineral belt.
~*v.* **ranged, ranging, ranges.** —*tr.* **1.** To arrange or dispose in a particular order, especially in rows or lines. **2.** To assign to a particular category; classify. **3.** To align (a gun or telescope, for example) with a target; train; sight. Usually used with *on.* **4.** To determine the distance of (a target). **5.** To move or travel over or through (a region), as in exploration. **6.** *Printing.* To set (lines of type) so that they are flush with the margin. **7.** *Nautical.* To uncoil (an anchor cable) on deck so that the anchor can descend easily. **8.** To turn (livestock) out onto a range to graze. —*intr.* **1.** To vary within specified limits: *"Joyce's humor ranges from subtle irony to boisterous horseplay"* (Richard Kain). **2.** To extend in a particular direction: *a river ranging to the east.* **3.** To extend in the same direction. **4.** To move over or through a given area as in exploration: *"his eye . . . ranged with delight over the treasures"* (Washington Irving). **5.** To roam or wander; rove. Used with *over.* **6.** To live or grow within a particular region. Used with *over.* **7.** To be capable of reaching a specified distance: *Our missiles range farther than theirs.* **8.** *Printing.* To lie flush at the margin. Used of lines of type. —See Synonyms at **wander.** [Middle English, series, line, from Old French *range, renge,* range, rank, from *renc, reng,* line, row, from Frankish *hring* (unattested), circle, ring.]

range finder *n.* Any of various optical, electronic, or acoustical instruments used to determine the distance of an object.

range light *n. Nautical.* **1.** Any of two or more lights used to guide a ship through a narrow channel at night. **2. range lights.** Two or more lights in a pattern on a powered vessel, used at night to indicate its course or size.

rang·er (rān′jər) *n.* **1.** A wanderer or rover. **2.** A person employed to patrol and guard a forest. **3.** A member of an armed troop assigned to patrol a region. **4. Ranger.** A member of a group of U.S. soldiers specially trained for making raids. Compare **commando. 5.** One of a cattle herd that grazes on a range.

rang·ing rod (rān′jĭng) *n.* A patterned pole used as a marker in surveying. Also called "ranging pole."

Ran·goon (răng-go͞on′). Capital and chief port of Burma. On the Rangoon River near its entrance into the Gulf of Martaban, it is the natural focus of Burma's transport network and the country's commercial and industrial center. The major exports are rice, cotton, timber, rubber, and petroleum products. Rangoon is dominated by the golden-spired Shwe Dagon Pagoda. It was severely damaged by an earthquake and tidal wave in 1930.

rang·y (rān′jē) *adj.* **-ier, -iest. 1.** Inclined to rove. **2.** Having slender, long limbs. **3.** Providing ample range; roomy.

ra·ni (rä′nē) *n., pl.* **-nis.** Also **ra·nee. 1.** The wife of a rajah. **2.** A reigning Hindu princess or queen. [Hindi *rānī,* from Sanskrit *rājñī,* feminine of *rājan,* king.]

Ran·jit Singh (rŭn′jĭt sĭng′), **Maharaja** (1780–1839). Sikh prince of the Punjab. After capturing Lahore (1799), he proclaimed himself maharajah and wrested control of the Punjab from the Afghans and Pathans, thus earning himself the title Lion of the Punjab.

rank[1] (răngk) *n.* **1. a.** A relative position in society. **b.** An official position or grade: *the rank of sergeant.* **c.** A relative position or degree of value in any graded scale: *"The critical power is of lower rank than the creative"* (Matthew Arnold). **d.** High or eminent station or position: *persons of rank.* **2.** A row, line, series, or range of people or things. **3.** *Military.* **a.** A line of soldiers, vehicles, or other military equipment standing side by side in close order. Compare **file. b. ranks.** The armed forces. **c. ranks.** Members of the armed forces excluding officers. Preceded by *the* or *other.* **4.** Any of the horizontal lines of squares on a chessboard. **5.** *Mathematics.* The number of rows of the greatest order determinant extracted from a given matrix. **6.** *Music.* A row or set of pipes in an organ that are controlled by the same stop. **7.** A place where taxis park while waiting to be hired. **—break ranks. 1.** *Military.* To fail to remain in line, especially during battle. **2.** To fail to support one's colleagues in a joint enterprise. **—close ranks.** To consolidate strength, as when under threat or attack. **—pull rank.** To use one's superior position to get one's way or gain an advantage.
~*v.* **ranked, ranking, ranks.** —*tr.* **1.** To place in a row or rows. **2.** To give a particular order or position to; classify. **3.** To outrank or take precedence over. —*intr.* **1.** To hold a particular rank or place: *rank first.* **2.** To hold a senior position or have authority or precedence. [Old French *ranc, renc,* rank, RANGE.]

rank[2] *adj.* **ranker, rankest. 1.** Growing profusely or with excessive vigor: *rank weeds.* **2.** Yielding a profuse, often excessive, crop; highly fertile: *rank earth.* **3.** Strong and offensive in odor or taste. **4.** Indecent; disgusting. **5.** Absolute; complete: *a rank amateur.* —See Synonyms at **flagrant.** [Middle English *rank,* Old English *ranc,* haughty, full-grown, overbearing, from Germanic.] **—rank·ly** *adv.* **—rank·ness** *n.*

Rank (răngk), **J(oseph) Arthur, 1st Baron** (1888–1972). British film producer and entrepreneur. A Methodist evangelist, he made his first secular motion picture in 1935. In 1946 he founded the Rank Organization and virtually controlled the British motion-picture industry, with a wide network of concerns covering every aspect of production and distribution.

Rank, Otto (1884–1939). Austrian psychologist. A protégé of Freud, though later renounced by him, he studied the psychiatric aspects of myth and creativity and also suggested that emotional disorders could be caused at the time of birth.

rank and file *pl.n.* **1.** The common soldiers of an army, excluding officers. **2.** Those who form the major portion of any group or organization, excluding the leaders and officers.

Ran·ke (răng′kə), **Leopold von** (1795–1886). German historian. He is best known for pioneering the modern methods of exhaustively analyzing source documents; his *History of the Latin and Teutonic Nations 1494–1535* (1824) and subsequent works on Prussian, French, English, Spanish, Italian, and Serbian history are regarded as the first examples of modern historical criticism.

rank·er (răng′kər) *n. British.* **1.** A soldier in the ranks. **2.** A commissioned officer who has risen from the ranks.

Ran·kin (răng′kĭn), **Jeanette** (1880–1973). U.S. feminist, pacifist, and legislator. Actively involved with the passage of woman suffrage in Montana, her home state, she was the first woman member of the U.S. House of Representatives (1916–18; 1940–42). An ardent pacifist, she is the only member of Congress to have voted against U.S. involvement in both World Wars.

Ran·kine scale (răng′kĭn) *n.* A scale of absolute temperature using Fahrenheit degrees, in which the freezing point of water is 491.69° and the boiling point of water is 671.69°. [After William J.M. *Rankine* (1820–72), Scottish physicist.]

rank·ing (răng′kĭng) *adj.* High-ranking; pre-eminent.
~*n.* A place or position on a usually specified scale: *has a high ranking on the tennis ladder.*

ran·kle (răng′kəl) *intr.v.* **-kled, -kling, -kles. 1.** To cause persistent irritation or resentment. **2.** *Archaic.* To become sore or inflamed; fester. [Middle English *ranclen,* from Old French *rancler, draoncler,* from *rancle, draoncle,* ulcer, festering sore, from Late Latin *dracunculus,* something twisted like a serpent, from Latin, diminutive of *dracō* (stem *dracōn-*), serpent.]

ran·sack (răn′săk′) *tr.v.* **-sacked, -sacking, -sacks. 1.** To search or examine (a room or box, for example) thoroughly, usually disordering the contents in the process. **2.** To search (a house or town, for example) for plunder; pillage. —See Synonyms at **rob.** [Middle English *ransaken,* from Old Norse *rannsaka,* search a house : *rann,* house, from Common Germanic *razn-* (unattested) + *-saka,* search.] **—ran·sack·er** *n.*

ran·som (răn′səm) *n.* **1.** The release of a person or property in return for payment of a stipulated price. **2.** The price or payment demanded or paid. **3.** *Theology.* A redemption from sin and its consequences. **—hold for** (or **to**) **ransom.** To confine or retain possession of (a person or property) until a stipulated price is paid.
~*tr.v.* **ransomed, -soming, -soms. 1.** To obtain the release of (a person or property) by paying a certain price. **2. a.** To hold captive or keep possession of while demanding such a payment. **b.** To release after receiving a ransom. **3.** *Theology.* To deliver from sin and its consequences. [Middle English *ransoun,* from Old French *rançon,* from Latin *redemptiō,* REDEMPTION.] **—ran·som·er** *n.*

Ran·som (răn′səm), **John Crowe** (1888–1974). U.S. poet and critic. He is best known for his critical work *The New Criticism* (1941). His collections of poetry include *Chills and Fever* (1924).

rant (rănt) *v.* **ranted, ranting, rants.** —*intr.* To speak or declaim in a violent, loud, or vehement manner. Often used in the phrase *rant and rave.* —*tr.* To exclaim with violence or extravagance.
~*n.* **1.** Violent, loud, or extravagant speech. **2.** *Chiefly Scottish.* Wild or uproarious merriment. [Probably from Dutch *ranten*†.] **—rant·er** *n.* **—rant·ing·ly** *adv.*

ran·u·la (răn′yə-lə) *n., pl.* **-lae** (-lē). A cyst on the underside of the tongue caused by obstruction of a duct or a salivary gland. [New Latin, from Latin, swelling in tongues of cattle, diminutive of *rāna*†, frog.]

ra·nun·cu·lus (rə-nŭng′kyə-ləs) *n., pl.* **-luses** or **-li** (-lī′). Any plant of the genus *Ranunculus,* including the buttercups, typically having yellow flowers. [New Latin, from Latin *rānunculus,* diminutive of *rāna*†, frog.]

PRONUNCIATION KEY

ă, pat; ā, pay; âr, care; ä, father, are; b, bib; ch, church; d, deed; ĕ, pet; ē, be; f, fife; g, gag; h, hat; hw, which; ĭ, pit; ī, pie; îr, pier; j, judge; k, kick; l, lid, needle; m, mum; n, no, sudden; ng, thing; ŏ, pot; ō, toe; ô, paw, for; oi, noise; ou, out; o͝o, book; o͞o, boot; p, pop; r, roar; s, sauce; sh, ship, dish; t, tight; th, thin, path; *th*, this, bathe; ŭ, cut; ûr, fur; v, valve; w, with; y, yes; z, zebra, size; zh, vision; ə, about, item, edible, gallop, circus, peaceful

IN FOREIGN WORDS:

à, *Fr.* ami; œ, *Fr.* feu, *Ger.* schön; ü, *Fr.* tu, *Ger.* über; KH, *Ger.* ich, *Scot.* loch; N, *Fr.* bon; y′, *Fr.* Compiègne

STRESS MARKS:

Primary stress: ′ in·cite′ (ĭn-sīt′)
Secondary stress: ′ in′sight′ (ĭn′sīt′)

rap¹ (răp) v. **rapped, rapping, raps.** —tr. **1.** To hit sharply and swiftly; strike: *rapped the table with his knuckles.* **2.** To utter sharply and abruptly. Used with *out.* —intr. **1.** To strike a quick, light blow or blows; knock. **2.** *Slang.* To talk freely and at length; chat. **3.** To improvise words and vocal sounds to an instrumental accompaniment. ~n. **1.** A quick, light blow or knock. **2.** A knocking or tapping sound. **3.** *Slang.* A talk, conversation, or discussion. **4.** *Slang.* **a.** A reprimand or censure. **b.** A legal sentence to serve in prison. **c.** Unpleasant consequences of wrongdoing, especially when one is not personally to blame. Used in the phrase *take the rap.* —**beat the rap.** *Slang.* To escape punishment or be acquitted of a charge. [Middle English *rappen,* akin to Norwegian *rappe,* Swedish *rappa,* (imitative).] —**rap·per** *n.*

rap² *n.* **1.** A counterfeit halfpenny passed in Ireland during the 18th century. **2.** *Informal.* The least bit: *I don't care a rap.* [Short for Irish Gaelic *ropaire†,* counterfeit halfpenny.]

ra·pa·cious (rə-pā′shəs) *adj.* **1.** Taking by force; plundering. **2.** Greedy; avaricious. **3.** Subsisting on live prey. Said especially of birds. [Latin *rapax* (stem *rapāc-*), from *rapere,* to seize.] —**ra·pa·cious·ly** *adv.* —**ra·pa·cious·ness, ra·pac·i·ty** (rə-păs′ə-tē) *n.*

rape¹ (rāp) *n.* **1. a.** The crime of forcing a female to submit to sexual intercourse. **b.** Such a crime committed against a male. **2.** The fact of having been raped. **3.** *Archaic.* The act of seizing and carrying off by force; abduction. **4.** Abusive or improper treatment; violation; profanation: *a rape of justice.* **5.** The act of plundering or despoiling a country or city, especially in war. ~v. **raped, raping, rapes.** —tr. **1.** To force (especially a female) to submit to sexual intercourse. **2.** *Archaic.* To seize and carry off by force. **3.** To plunder or pillage. —intr. To commit rape. [Middle English, from Old French *raper,* from Latin *rapere,* to seize.] —**rap·ist** *n.*

rape² *n.* A Eurasian plant, *Brassica napus,* cultivated for its seed, which yields a useful oil, and as fodder. Also called "colza." See **cole.** [Middle English, from Latin *rāpa, rāpum,* turnip.]

rape³ *n.* Often **rapes.** The refuse of grapes left after the extraction of the juice in wine making. [French *râpe,* grape stalk, from Old French, from *rasper,* to scrape off, RASP.]

rape oil *n.* The edible oil extracted from rapeseed, also used as a lubricant and in the manufacture of various products.

rape·seed (rāp′sēd′) *n.* The seed of the rape plant.

Raph·a·el¹ (răf′ē-əl, rä′fē-), born Raffaello Sanzio or Santi (1483–1520). Italian painter, one of the towering figures of the High Renaissance. He came to early prominence in Florence, but his most famous paintings were done in Rome, especially the great frescoes for the Stanza della Segnatura in the Vatican. Completed in 1511, they include *The School of Athens* and the *Triumph of Religion,* also called *Disputà.* In Rome, too, he painted what is considered his greatest altarpiece, the *Sistine Madonna* (1512), and many portraits. —**Raph·a·el·esque** *adj.*

Raph·a·el² (răf′ē-əl, rä′fē-). One of the archangels. [Hebrew *Rəphā′ēl,* "God has healed."]

ra·phe, rha·phe (rā′fē) *n. Biology.* A seamlike line or ridge between two similar parts, as in the scrotum, the coat of certain seeds, or the valves of a diatom. [New Latin, from Greek *rhaphē,* seam, from *rhaptein,* to sew.]

raphia. Variant of **raffia.**

ra·phide (rā′fīd) *n., pl.* **-phides** (răf′ə-dēz′). Also **ra·phis** (rā′fĭs), *pl.* **-phides.** *Botany.* Any of a bundle of needle-shaped crystals, composed chiefly of calcium oxalate, occurring in many plant cells. [Back-formation from *raphides,* plural, from New Latin, from Greek *rhaphis* (stem *rhaphid-*), needle, from *rhaptein,* to sew.]

rap·id (răp′ĭd) *adj.* **-ider, -idest. 1.** Moving, acting, or occurring with great speed; swift. **2.** Happening in a very short time: *a rapid change.* —See Synonyms at **fast.** ~n. Usually **rapids.** A fast-flowing section of a river usually caused by a steep descent in the riverbed. [Latin *rapidus,* hurrying, seizing, from *rapere,* to seize.] —**rap·id·ly** *adv.* —**ra·pid·i·ty** (rə-pĭd′ə-tē), **rap·id·ness** *n.*

Rap·i·dan (răp′ə-dăn′). River, c. 145 kilometers (90 miles) long, rising in northern Virginia in the Blue Ridge and flowing southeast and then northeast to the Rappahannock River.

Rapid City. City of southwestern South Dakota, on Rapid Creek near the Black Hills. It is the trade and transportation center of an extensive lumbering, ranching, and mining area.

rapid eye movement *n. Abbr.* **REM** Constant movement of the eyeballs behind the closed eyelids during **paradoxical sleep** *(see),* occurring when dreaming takes place.

rap·id-fire (răp′ĭd-fīr′) *adj.* **1.** Designed to fire shots in rapid succession. **2.** Marked by continuous, rapid occurrence: *rapid-fire questions.*

rapid transit *n.* An urban passenger-transportation system using elevated or underground trains or a combination of both.

ra·pi·er (rā′pē-ər, răp′yər) *n.* **1.** A long, slender, two-edged sword with a cuplike hilt, used in the 16th and 17th centuries. **2.** An 18th-century, lighter, sharp-pointed sword lacking a cutting edge and used only for thrusting. [French *rapière,* originally (espée) *rapière†,* rapier (sword).]

rap·ine (răp′ĭn) *n. Law.* Forcible seizure of another's property; plunder. [Middle English *rapyne,* from Old French *rapine,* from Latin *rapīna,* from *rapere,* to RAPE (seize).]

Rap·pa·han·nock (răp′ə-hăn′ək). River, 341 kilometers (212 miles)

rape Brassica napus, *or rape, has been cultivated since ancient times. The seed is pressed to yield edible oil, and the plant is used as cattle food. It is closely related to the mustard plant.*

long. It rises in the Blue Ridge Mts. of northern Virginia and flows generally southeast to Chesapeake Bay.

rap·pa·ree (răp′ə-rē′) *n.* **1.** A freebooting soldier of 17th-century Ireland. **2.** *Archaic.* A bandit or robber. [Irish Gaelic *rapaire,* short pike, either from English RAPIER or French *rapière,* RAPIER.]

rap·pee (ră-pē′) *n.* A strong snuff made from a dark, coarse tobacco. [French *râpé,* "grated" (tobacco), from *râper,* to grate, from Old French *rasper,* to RASP.]

rap·pel (ră-pĕl′) *n.* The act or method of descending from a mountainside or cliff by means of a double rope passed under one thigh and over the opposite shoulder, or through karabiners attached to a harness. ~*intr.v.* **rappelled, -pelling, -pels.** To descend from a steep height by rappel. [French, "recall," from Old French *rapel,* from *rapeler,* to summon, recall : *re-,* again + *apeler,* to summon, APPEAL.]

rap·pen (rä′pən) *n., pl.* **rappen.** A Swiss coin, the **centime** *(see).* [German *Rappen,* a raven, from Middle High German *rappe.*]

rap·port (rə-pôr′, -pōr′) *n.* A relationship; especially, one of mutual trust or emotional affinity. [French, from *rapporter,* to bring back, yield, from Old French *raporter* : *re-,* back, again + *aporter,* to bring, from Latin *apportāre* : *ad-,* to + *portāre,* to carry.]

rap·proche·ment (ră-prôsh-män′) *n.* **1.** A re-establishing of cordial relations, as between two countries. **2.** A state of reconciliation or

ARTIST OF THE HIGH RENAISSANCE

Master of inventiveness in gesture and grouping

Raphael (1483–1520) was a master of composition, and the grace and harmony of his paintings exemplify the ideals of the High Renaissance. He was the most assimilative genius of his age, absorbing and applying the techniques of both Leonardo da Vinci and Michelangelo without being an imitator of either.

The son of an Umbrian painter, Raphael trained with the painter Perugino, possibly in Perugia. At the age of 21 he moved to Florence. His *Madonna and Child* groups of this period reflect Leonardo's influence, particularly in their treatment of light and shade. Raphael went to Rome in 1508, commissioned by Pope Julius II to decorate a set of Vatican apartments; his frescoes in the Stanza della Segnatura include the outstanding *Disputà* and *School of Athens.* In 1514 he succeeded Bramante as architect of St. Peter's.

When Raphael died at the age of 37, his last painting, *The Transfiguration,* was unfinished and was completed by Giulio Romano, an assistant in his large and flourishing studio. Despite his short life, Raphael's influence on the work of succeeding ages is unparalleled in the history of art.

MADONNA DEL GRANDUCA *Raphael's Madonna paintings are noted for their serenity and tenderness of expression. This one in the Palazzo Pitti, Florence, dates from about 1505.*

of newly cordial relations. [French, from *rapprocher,* to bring together : *re-,* again + *approcher,* to approach, from Late Latin *appropriāre* : Latin *ad-,* to + *prope,* near.]
rap·scal·li·on (răp-skăl′yən) *n.* A rascal; a scamp. [Variant of obsolete *rascallion,* perhaps from RASCAL.]
rap session *n. Slang.* An informal discussion held by a group of people.
rap sheet *n. Informal.* A police arrest record.
rapt (răpt) *adj.* **1.** Transported with powerful emotion; enraptured. **2.** Deeply absorbed; engrossed. **3.** Expressing rapture: *a rapt expression on her face.* [Middle English, from Latin *raptus,* "seized," from the past participle of *rapere,* to seize.]
rap·tor (răp′tər) *n.* A bird of prey. [Latin, "one who seizes," from *raptus,* RAPT.]
rap·to·ri·al (răp-tôr′ē-əl, -tōr′ē-əl) *adj.* **1.** Subsisting by seizing prey; predatory. **2.** Adapted for the seizing of prey. Said of the feet of birds of prey. **3.** Of, pertaining to, or characteristic of birds of prey.
rap·ture (răp′chər) *n.* **1.** The state of being transported by a powerful emotion; great joy; ecstasy. **2.** *Often* **raptures.** An expression or utterance of great delight. **3.** *Archaic.* The transporting of a person from one place to another, especially to heaven. —See Synonyms at **ecstasy.**
~*tr.v.* **raptured, -turing, -tures.** *Archaic.* To enrapture. [Medieval Latin *raptūra,* "ecstasy," from Latin *raptus,* RAPT.]
rap·tur·ous (răp′chər-əs) *adj.* Expressing great joy or delight; ecstatic. —**rap·tur·ous·ly** *adv.* —**rap·tur·ous·ness** *n.*
ra·ra a·vis (râr′ə ā′vĭs) *n., pl.* **rara avises** or **rarae aves** (râr′ē ā′vēz). A rare or unique person or thing. [Latin, "rare bird."]
rare¹ (râr) *adj.* **rarer, rarest. 1.** *Abbr.* **r.** Infrequently occurring; uncommon; unusual. **2.** Highly valued owing to unusualness; special. **3.** Thin in density; rarefied. Said of gases. **4.** Of unusual excellence; exceptional: *a rare novel.* [Middle English, from Latin *rārus,* loose, thin, scarce, remarkable.] —**rare·ness** *n.*
rare² *adj.* **rarer, rarest.** Underdone so as to retain redness. Said of meat. [Variant of obsolete *rear,* half-cooked (originally of eggs) Middle English *rere,* Old English *hrēr.*] —**rare·ness** *n.*
rare·bit (râr′bĭt) *n.* A cheese dish, **Welsh rabbit** *(see).* [Folk-etymological variant of (WELSH) RABBIT.]
rare earth *n.* **1.** Any of various oxides of the rare-earth elements. **2.** Loosely, a rare-earth element.
rare-earth element (râr′ûrth′) *n.* Any of a group of metallic elements with atomic numbers from 57 to 71. Also called "rare earth," "lanthanide," "lanthanon." [Originally contrasted with the so-called "common-earth elements" (calcium, magnesium, and aluminum).]
rar·ee show (râr′ē) *n.* **1.** A **peepshow** *(see).* **2.** A street show. [From RARE (excellent).]
rar·e·fac·tion (râr′ə-făk′shən) *n.* Also **rar·e·fi·ca·tion** (-fĭ-kā′shən). **1.** The act or process of rarefying. **2.** The state of being rarefied. —**rar·e·fac·tive** *adj.*
rar·e·fied (râr′ə-fīd′) *adj.* **1.** Belonging or restricted to a small and select group; esoteric. **2.** Marked by a lofty or exalted style or quality: *a rarefied academic atmosphere.*
rar·e·fy (râr′ə-fī′) *v.* **-fied, -fying, -fies.** —*tr.* **1.** To make thin, less compact, or less dense. **2.** To purify or refine. —*intr.* To become thin, less dense, or purer. [Middle English *rarefien,* from Old French *rarefier,* from Latin *rārēfacere* : *rārus,* RARE + *facere,* to make.] —**rar·e·fi·a·ble** (râr′ə-fī′ə-bəl) *adj.*
rare gas *n. Chemistry.* An **inert gas** *(see).*
rare·ly (râr′lē) *adv.* **1.** Not often; seldom; infrequently: *"The truth is rarely pure and never simple"* (Oscar Wilde). **2.** In an unusual degree; exceptionally. **3.** With uncommon excellence.
Usage: The use of *ever* following *rarely* is commonly used for emphasis in informal speech *(I rarely ever go there),* but in formal contexts it is criticized as redundant. Generally acceptable are such combinations as *rarely if ever* and *rarely or never.* See also Usage note at **seldom.**
rare·ripe (râr′rīp′) *adj.* Ripening early.
~*n.* A fruit or vegetable that ripens early. [*Rare-,* variant (perhaps influenced by RARE, underdone) of RATHE.]
rar·ing (râr′ĭng) *adj. Informal.* Full of eagerness; enthusiastic. Followed by an infinitive: *We're raring to go.* [From dialectal *rare,* variant of REAR (to arouse, raise up).]
Rar·i·tan (răr′ĭ-tən). River, 137 kilometers (85 miles) long, rising in north-central New Jersey and flowing southeast to Raritan Bay, an arm of Lower New York Bay.
rar·i·ty (râr′ə-tē) *n., pl.* **-ties. 1.** Something that is especially valued because it is rare. **2.** The quality or state of being rare; infrequency of occurrence.
R.A.S. in Britain: **1.** Royal Agricultural Society. **2.** Royal Astronomical Society.
ras·bo·ra (răz-bôr′ə, -bōr′ə) *n.* Any of various tropical fishes of the genus *Rasbora,* of which several brightly colored species are kept in home aquariums. [From a native East Indian name.]
ras·cal (răs′kəl) *n.* **1.** An unscrupulous or dishonest person; a scoundrel. **2.** One who is playfully mischievous; a scamp. Often used affectionately or humorously, especially of children. **3.** *Archaic.* One belonging to the rabble.
~*adj. Archaic.* Of or suited to the rabble; base. [Middle English, from Old French *rascaille,* rabble, perhaps from Old Northern French *rasque* (unattested), dregs, mud, filth, from Vulgar Latin *rasica* (unattested), from Latin *rādere,* to scrape. Compare **rash** (eruption).] —**ras·cal·ly** *adj.*
ras·cal·i·ty (răs-kăl′ə-tē) *n., pl.* **-ties. 1.** The behavior or character of a rascal. **2.** A base or mischievous act.
rase. Variant of **raze.**
rash¹ (răsh) *adj.* **rasher, rashest. 1.** Acting without forethought or due caution; impetuous. **2.** Characterized by or resulting from ill-considered haste or boldness: *a rash decision.* —See Synonyms at **reckless.** [Middle English *rasch,* nimble, quick, eager, perhaps from Middle Dutch, *rasch;* probably cognate with RATHE.] —**rash·ly** *adv.* —**rash·ness** *n.*
rash² *n.* **1.** Any eruption of the skin in spots or blotches. **2.** An outbreak of many instances within a brief period: *a rash of defections to the other party.* [Possibly from obsolete French *rache,* from Old French *rasche,* scurf, from *raschier,* to scratch, from Vulgar Latin *rasciāre* (unattested), to scrape, from Latin *rādere* (past participle *rāsus*).]
rash·er (răsh′ər) *n.* A thin slice of bacon or ham to be fried or grilled. [16th century : origin obscure.]
Ras·mus·sen (räs′mo͝os-ən), **Knud Johan Victor** (1879–1933). Danish explorer and ethnologist. Of Eskimo descent, he spent much of his time in Arctic America studying the inhabitants and argued that the Eskimos and the Native Americans were descended from a common ancestor.
ra·so·ri·al (rə-zôr′ē-əl, rə-zōr′-, rə-sôr′-, rə-sōr′-) *adj.* Characteristically scratching the ground for food. Said of poultry. [Late Latin *rāsor,* "scraper," from Latin *rādere* (past participle *rāsus*), to scrape.]
rasp (răsp, räsp) *v.* **rasped, rasping, rasps.** —*tr.* **1.** To file or scrape with a rasp. **2.** To utter in a rough, grating tone. **3.** To irritate; grate upon (nerves or feelings). —*intr.* **1.** To grate; scrape harshly. **2.** To make a harsh, grating sound.
~*n.* **1.** A coarse file having abrasive, pointed projections. **2.** The act of filing with a rasp. **3.** A harsh, grating sound. [Middle English *raspen,* from Old French *rasper,* from Old High German *raspōn,* from Germanic *hrap-* (unattested), to snatch. See **raffle.**] —**rasp·er** *n.* —**rasp·ing·ly** *adv.* —**rasp·y** *adj.*
ras·pa·to·ry (răs′pə-tôr′ē, -tōr′ē) *n., pl.* **-ies.** A surgical instrument used for scraping the surface of a bone. [Medieval Latin *raspatorium* (unattested), or French *raspatoire,* from Old French *rasper, raspe,* RASP.]
rasp·ber·ry (răz′bĕr′ē, -bə-rē, räz′-) *n., pl.* **-ries. 1.** Any of various shrubby, usually prickly plants of the genus *Rubus,* bearing edible berries, such as *R. idaeus,* of Europe. **2.** The fruit of any of these plants, consisting of a mass of small, fleshy, usually red drupelets. **3.** Moderate to dark or purplish red. **4.** *Slang.* A derisive or contemptuous sound made by vibrating the extended tongue and the lips while exhaling. In this sense, also called "Bronx cheer." [From obsolete *raspis*† + BERRY.] —**rasp·ber·ry** *adj.*
Ras·pu·tin (răs-pyo͞o′tĭn), **Grigory Yefimovich,** born G.Y. Novykh (1872–1916). Russian monk and faith healer. A Siberian peasant, he preached and lived a religious life of "sinning in order to be forgiven." His relative success in treating the czarevich's hemophilia and his magnetic personality gained him great influence at the imperial court. He was murdered by nobles anxious to uphold the monarchy.
rasp·y (răs′pē) *adj.* **-ier, -iest.** Grating; harsh; rough.
Ras·ta·fa·ri·an, Ras Ta·fa·ri·an (răs′tə-fâr′ē-ən) *n.* A member of a cult of black nationalists, originating in Jamaica, that regard Ras Tafari, the former name of Ethiopian emperor **Haile Selassie** *(see),* as God. —**Ras·ta·fa·ri·an** *adj.* —**Ras·ta·fa·ri·an·ism** *n.*
ras·ter (răs′tər) *n. Electronics.* A pattern of lines produced by scanning an electron beam, as on a television screen. [German *Raster,* screen, from Latin *rastrum,* rake, from *rādere* (past participial stem *rās-*), to scrape.]
rat (răt) *n.* **1.** Any of various long-tailed rodents resembling, but larger than, mice; especially, any of the genus *Rattus,* such as the common black rat, *R. rattus.* See **brown rat. 2.** Any of various similar animals. **3.** *Slang.* A despicable, sneaky person, especially one who abandons his associates in time of trouble. **4.** *Slang.* A strikebreaker; a scab. **5.** *Slang.* One who informs on or betrays his associates. —**smell a rat.** *Slang.* To suspect that something underhand or treacherous is going on.
~*intr.v.* **ratted, ratting, rats. 1.** To hunt for or catch rats, especially with the aid of dogs. **2.** *Slang.* To desert or betray one's associates or friends. Used with *on.* [Middle English *rat,* Old English *ræt,* from Germanic *ratt-* (unattested).]
ra·ta (rä′tə) *n.* Either of two New Zealand trees of the genus *Metrosideros, M. robusta* or *M. lucida,* having hard, red wood.
rat·a·ble (rā′tə-bəl) *adj.* **1.** Capable of being rated, estimated, or appraised. **2.** *British.* Liable to assessment; taxable. —**rat·a·bil·i·ty, rat·a·ble·ness** *n.* —**rat·a·bly** *adv.*
rat·a·fi·a (răt′ə-fē′ə) *n.* Also **rat·a·fee** (-ə-fē′). **1.** A liqueur flavored with fruit kernels or almonds. **2.** A small macaroon flavored with almonds. [French, from West Indian French Creole.]
ratan. Variant of **rattan.**
rat·a·plan (răt′ə-plăn′) *n.* A tattoo, as of a drum, the hooves of a galloping horse, or machine-gun fire. [French (imitative).]
rat-a-tat-tat (răt′ə-tăt′tăt′) *n.* A series of short, sharp sounds, such as those made by knocking on a door. [Imitative.]
ra·ta·touille (răt-ə-to͞o′ē, rä-tä-, -twē) *n.* A vegetable stew made from tomatoes, peppers, eggplant, and squash. [French (dialect), from *touiller,* to stir.]
rat·bag (răt′băg′) *n. Chiefly British Slang.* An obnoxious person.
rat-bite fever (răt′bīt′) *n.* Either of two infectious diseases contract-

PRONUNCIATION KEY

ă, pat; ā, pay; âr, care;
ä, father, are; b, bib;
ch, church; d, deed; ĕ, pet;
ē, be; f, fife; g, gag; h, hat;
hw, which; ĭ, pit; ī, pie;
îr, pier; j, judge; k, kick;
l, lid, needle; m, mum;
n, no, sudden; ng, thing;
ŏ, pot; ō, toe; ô, paw, for;
oi, noise; ou, out; o͝o, book;
o͞o, boot; p, pop; r, roar;
s, sauce; sh, ship, dish;
t, tight; th, thin, path;
th, this, bathe; ŭ, cut; ûr, fur;
v, valve; w, with; y, yes;
z, zebra, size; zh, vision;
ə, about, item, edible,
gallop, circus, peaceful

IN FOREIGN WORDS:

à, *Fr.* ami; œ, *Fr.* feu, *Ger.* schön; ü, *Fr.* tu, *Ger.* über; KH, *Ger.* ich, *Scot.* loch; N, *Fr.* bon; y′, *Fr.* Compiègne

STRESS MARKS:

Primary stress: ′
in·cite′ (ĭn-sīt′)
Secondary stress: ′
in′sight′ (ĭn′sīt′)

ible from the bite of a rat: **1.** One arising from *Streptobacillus moniliformis* and characterized by skin inflammation, back and joint pains, headache, and vomiting. **2.** One arising from *Spirillum minus,* with ulceration at the site of the bite, a purplish rash, and recurrent fever. Also called "rat-bite disease."

rat-catch·er (răt′kăch′ər) *n.* A person who rids houses of rats or other vermin.

rat cheese *n.* Cheddar cheese.

ratch·et (răch′ĭt) *n.* **1.** A mechanism consisting of a pawl, or hinged catch, that engages the sloping teeth of a wheel or bar, permitting motion in one direction only. **2.** The pawl or bar of such a mechanism. **3.** The toothed wheel in such a mechanism. Also called "ratchet wheel." [French *rochet,* from Old French *rocquet,* head of a lance, from Frankish *rokko* (unattested), a distaff.]

rate[1] (rāt) *n.* **1. a.** A measured quantity, as of speed, cost, or value, calculated by its relation to some other quantity: *at the rate of 60 miles per hour; the birth rate.* **b.** A ratio that is fixed as a standard between two sums, quantities, or the like: *buying Canadian dollars at the current rate.* **2.** The speed at which something moves, changes, or progresses: *driving at a very dangerous rate.* **3.** The cost per unit of a commodity or service. **4.** A charge or payment calculated in relation to any particular sum or quantity: *paying high rates for electricity.* **5.** A specified level of relative quality. Used in combination: *first-rate; tenth-rate.* **6. rates.** In Great Britain, a tax on property assessed and levied by a local authority to pay for local services. **—at any rate. 1.** Whatever the case may be; anyway. **2.** At least.
~*v.* **rated, rating, rates.** —*tr.* **1.** To calculate the value of; appraise. **2.** To place in a particular rank or grade. **3.** To regard or account: *The play was rated a great success.* **4.** To value for purposes of taxation. **5.** To specify the performance limits of (a machine or firearm, for example). **6.** *Chiefly British Informal.* To think highly of: *I don't really rate this job.* **7.** *Informal.* To merit or deserve: *rate special treatment.* —*intr.* **1.** To be ranked in a particular class or grade. **2.** *Informal.* To have status, importance, or influence. —See Synonyms at **estimate.** [Middle English, from Old French, from Medieval Latin *rata,* calculated, fixed, from the feminine past participle of Latin *rērī,* to calculate.] **—rat·er** *n.*

rate[2] *tr.v.* **rated, rating, rates.** To berate angrily. [Middle English *raten,* perhaps from Old Norse *hrata.*]

ra·tel (rāt′l, rät′l) *n.* An animal, the **honey badger** *(see).* [Afrikaans *ratel*†.]

rate of exchange *n.* The ratio at which the unit of currency of one country may be or is exchanged for the unit of currency of another country. Also called "exchange rate."

rate·pay·er (rāt′pā′ər) *n. British.* One who is liable to pay rates.

rat·fink (răt′fĭngk′) *n. Slang.* A contemptible, obnoxious, or otherwise undesirable person. [RAT (to betray) + FINK.]

rat·fish (răt′fĭsh′) *n., pl.* **-fishes** or collectively **ratfish. 1.** A fish, *Hydrolagus affinis,* of Pacific waters, having a long, narrow tail. **2.** The **rabbitfish** *(see).*

Rat·haus (rät′hous′) *n. German.* A government or municipal building; a town hall.

Rath·bone (răth′bōn′), **Basil** (1892–1967). English actor, born in South Africa. As Mr. Murdstone in the film version of *David Copperfield* (1934) and as Errol Flynn's rival in a series of adventure movies, he usually played a villain until he was cast as Sherlock Holmes in *The Hound of the Baskervilles* (1940) and several sequels.

rathe (rāth, răth) *adj. Archaic & Poetic.* **1.** Appearing or ripening early in the year. **2.** Prompt; eager. [Middle English *rathe,* early, rapid, Old English *hræd, hræth,* from Germanic.]

Ra·the·nau (rä′tə-nou′), **Walter** (1867–1922). German industrialist and politician, one of the leading figures in the period of German reconstruction after World War I. As foreign minister (1922), he negotiated the Treaty of Rapallo with the U.S.S.R. He was assassinated by anti-Semites shortly afterward.

rath·er (răth′ər, rä′thər; rä′thûr′, rä′thûr′ *for sense 6*) *adv.* **1.** More readily; preferably: *I'd rather stay at home.* **2.** With more reason, logic, wisdom, or other justification. **3.** With more accuracy: *He's my friend, or rather he was my friend.* **4.** To a certain extent; somewhat: *rather nice.* **5.** On the contrary: *Locks are not for opening doors; rather, they are for keeping them firmly shut.* **6.** *Chiefly British.* Most certainly. Used as an emphatic affirmative reply. **7.** *Obsolete.* More quickly; earlier. [Middle English *rather,* Old English *hrathor,* comparative of *hrathe, hræth,* early, RATHE.]

Usage: *Rather* is usually preceded by *should* or *would* in expressing preference: *He would rather not go.* But *had* is equally acceptable: *I had rather be dead than be a slave.* In a contraction such as *he'd,* either *would* or *had* can be understood.

raths·kel·ler (rät′skĕl′ər, răt′-, răth′-) *n.* A restaurant in the style of the cellar of a German city hall that features the serving of beer. [Obsolete German, restaurant in the city hall basement: *Rat,* council + *Keller,* cellar, from Latin *cellarium.*]

rat·i·fi·ca·tion (răt′ə-fĭ-kā′shən) *n.* The action of officially and formally confirming something, such as a treaty or constitution.

rat·i·fy (răt′ə-fī′) *tr.v.* **-fied, -fying, -fies.** To give formal sanction to; approve and so make valid. —See Synonyms at **approve, confirm.** [Middle English *ratifien,* from Old French *ratifier,* from Medieval Latin *ratificāre* : Latin *ratus,* "fixed" (see **rate**) + *facere,* to make.] **—rat·i·fi·er** *n.*

rat·i·né (răt′ə-nā′) *n.* A loosely woven fabric with a coarse, knotted texture. [French, past participle of *ratiner*†, to adorn.]

rat·ing[1] (rā′tĭng) *n.* **1.** A place assigned on a scale; a standing. **2.** A classification according to specialty or proficiency, as of an armed serviceman. **3.** An evaluation of the financial status of a business or an individual: *has a very good credit rating.* **4.** A specified performance limit, as of capacity, range, or operational capability: *power rating.* **5.** The popularity of a television or radio program as estimated by a poll of segments of the audience. **6.** Any of the classes into which racing yachts are divided according to tonnage, dimensions, or the like. **7.** *British.* An enlisted man in the navy.

rating[2] *n.* A scolding.

ra·ti·o (rā′-shō, rā′shē-ō′) *n., pl.* **-tios. 1.** The relation in number between two similar magnitudes, determined by the number of times an object exists in one quantity as compared with the other: *the ratio of managerial staff to all employees.* **2.** *Mathematics.* The relative size of two quantities expressed as the quotient of one divided by the other: *The ratio of 7 to 4 is written 7:4 or 7/4.* **3.** The relative value of silver and gold in a currency system that is bimetallic. [Latin *ratiō,* computation, from *rērī* (past participle *ratus*), to consider.]

ra·ti·oc·i·nate (răsh′ē-ŏs′ə-nāt′) *intr.v.* **-nated, -nating, -nates.** To reason methodically and logically. [Latin *ratiōcinārе,* from *ratiō,* RATIO.] **—ra·ti·oc·i·na·tion** (răsh′ē-ŏs′ə-nā′shən) *n.* **—ra·ti·oc·i·na·tive** (răsh′ē-ŏs′ə-nā′tĭv) *adj.* **—ra·ti·oc·i·na·tor** *n.*

ra·tion (răsh′ən, rā′shən) *n.* **1.** *Often* **rations.** A fixed portion; especially, an amount of food, clothing, fuel, or the like, allotted to persons in military service or to civilians in times of scarcity. Also used adjectivally: *a ration book.* **2. rations.** Provisions. **3.** An allotted, deserved, or sufficient amount: *He's certainly used up his ration of goodwill.*
~*tr.v.* **rationed, -tioning, -tions. 1.** To supply with rations. **2. a.** To distribute in restricted allocations, as during wartime. **b.** To give sparingly, as if in rations. Often used with *out*: *The stern father rationed even his love out to his sons.* —See Usage note at **distribute.** [French, from Latin *ratiō* (stem *ratiōn-*), RATIO.]

ra·tion·al (răsh′ən-əl) *adj.* **1.** Having or exercising the ability to reason. **2.** Of sound mind; sane. **3.** Manifesting or based upon reason; logical. **4.** *Mathematics.* Designating an algebraic expression or equation in which no variable appears in an irreducible radical or with a fractional exponent. [Latin *ratiōnālis,* from *ratiō,* reason, RATIO.] **—ra·tion·al·ly** *adv.* **—ra·tion·al·ness** *n.*

ra·tion·ale (răsh′ə-năl′) *n.* **1.** The fundamental reasons for something; a logical basis. **2.** An exposition of principles or reasons. [Latin *ratiōnāle,* neuter of *ratiōnālis,* RATIONAL.]

rational horizon *n.* See **horizon** (sense 2b).

ra·tion·al·ism (răsh′ən-ə-lĭz′əm) *n.* **1.** *Theology.* **a.** The theory that the exercise of reason, rather than the acceptance of authority or spiritual revelation, provides the only valid basis for belief, and that reason is the prime source of spiritual truth. **b.** The rejection of religion on the grounds that it can have no logical or rational basis. **2.** In ethics, the theory that the exercise of reason provides the only valid basis for moral beliefs and rules of conduct. **3.** *Philosophy.* The theory, as exemplified in the philosophy of Descartes and Spinoza, that the exercise of reason, rather than empiricism, provides the only valid basis for and source of knowledge. Compare **empiricism. —ra·tion·al·ist** *n.* **—ra·tion·al·is·tic** (răsh′ən-ə-lĭs′tĭk) *adj.* **—ra·tion·al·is·ti·cal·ly** *adv.*

ra·tion·al·i·ty (răsh′ə-năl′ə-tē) *n., pl.* **-ties. 1.** The quality or condition of being rational. **2.** A rational belief or practice.

ra·tion·al·ize (răsh′ən-əl-īz′) *v.* **-ized, -izing, -izes.** —*tr.* **1.** To make conformable to reason; make rational. **2.** To interpret from a rational standpoint. **3.** *Psychology.* To devise self-satisfying but inadequate reasons for (one's behavior), especially while being unaware of unconscious motivation. **4.** *Mathematics.* To remove radicals without changing the value of (an expression) or roots of (an equation). **5.** *Chiefly British.* To bring modern, efficient methods to (an industry, for example). —*intr.* **1.** To think in a rational or logical way. **2.** *Psychology.* To rationalize one's behavior. **—ra·tion·al·i·za·tion** *n.* **—ra·tion·al·iz·er** *n.*

rational number *n.* Any number capable of being expressed as an integer or quotient of integers.

rat·ite (răt′īt′) *adj.* Designating any of a group of flightless birds having a flat breastbone without the keel characteristic of most flying birds and feathers lacking barbs.
~*n.* A ratite bird, such as the ostrich, emu, or kiwi. [New Latin *Ratitae* (group), from Latin *ratis,* raft (so named in allusion to the "keelless" sternum).]

rat kangaroo *n.* Any of various Australian marsupials of the subfamily Potoroinae, similar to kangaroos but having a long, ratlike face.

rat·line, rat·lin (răt′lĭn) *n. Nautical.* **1.** Any of the small ropes fastened horizontally to the shrouds of a ship and forming a ladder for going aloft. **2.** The rope used for this purpose.

RATO (rā′tō) rocket-assisted takeoff.

ra·toon, rat·toon (ră-to͞on′) *n.* A basal shoot sprouting from a plant such as the banana, pineapple, or sugar cane.
~*v.* **ratooned** or **rattooned, -tooning, -toons.** —*intr.* To produce or grow as a ratoon or ratoons. —*tr.* To propagate (a crop) from ratoons. [Spanish *retoño,* sprout, from *retoñar,* to sprout : *re-,* again + *otoñar,* to grow in the autumn, from *otoño,* autumn, from Latin *autumnus,* AUTUMN.]

rat race *n. Slang.* Ceaseless, hectic, and fiercely competitive activity, especially when involving a struggle for power or promotion: *As a merchant banker you can't avoid the rat race.*

PRONUNCIATION KEY

ă, pat; ā, pay; âr, care;
ä, father, are; b, bib;
ch, church; d, deed; ĕ, pet;
ē, be; f, fife; g, gag; h, hat;
hw, which; ĭ, pit; ī, pie;
îr, pier; j, judge; k, kick;
l, lid, needle; m, mum;
n, no, sudden; ng, thing;
ŏ, pot; ō, toe; ô, paw, for;
oi, noise; ou, out; o͝o, book;
o͞o, boot; p, pop; r, roar;
s, sauce; sh, ship, dish;
t, tight; th, thin, path;
th, this, bathe; ŭ, cut; ûr, fur;
v, valve; w, with; y, yes;
z, zebra, size; zh, vision;
ə, about, item, edible, gallop, circus, peaceful

IN FOREIGN WORDS:

à, *Fr.* ami; œ, *Fr.* feu, *Ger.* schön; ü, *Fr.* tu, *Ger.* über;
KH, *Ger.* ich, *Scot.* loch;
N, *Fr.* bon; y′, *Fr.* Compiègne

STRESS MARKS:

Primary stress: ′
in·cite′ (ĭn-sīt′)
Secondary stress: ′
in′sight′ (ĭn′sīt′)

rats (răts) *interj. Informal.* Used to express contemptuous disbelief or irritation.
rats·bane (răts′bān′) *n.* **1.** Rat poison. **2.** Arsenic trioxide.
rat snake *n.* Any of several nonvenomous, rodent-eating snakes such as those of the genera *Elaphe* and *Ptyas.*
rat-tail (răt′tāl′) *adj.* Also **rat·tailed** (-tāld′). **1.** Shaped like a rat's tail: *a rat-tail file.* **2.** Designating a spoon whose handle is prolonged like a tail along the back of the bowl.
~*n.* **1.** A fish, the **grenadier** *(see).* **2. a.** A horse's tail that is hairless. **b.** A horse with such a tail. **3.** A round file shaped like a rat's tail, used especially to widen holes in metal. In this sense also called "rat's tail."
rat-tail cactus *n.* A tropical American cactus, *Aporocactus flagelliformis,* having thin, creeping or hanging stems and brilliant crimson flowers.
rat·tan, ra·tan (ră-tăn′) *n.* **1.** Any of various climbing palms of the genera *Calamus, Daemonorops,* or *Plectomia,* of tropical Asia, having long, tough, slender stems. **2.** The stems of any of these palms, used to make wickerwork. **3.** A switch, stick, or cane made from such a stem. [Malay *rotan,* probably from *raut,* trim.]
rat·ter (răt′ər) *n.* **1.** A cat, dog, or person who catches and kills rats. **2.** *Slang.* A deserter, betrayer, or traitor.
Rat·ti·gan (răt′ĭ-gən), **Sir Terence Mervyn** (1911–77). British playwright. He first made his name with two farces, *French Without Tears* (1936) and *While the Sun Shines* (1943). Perhaps his best-known play is *The Winslow Boy* (1946).
rat·tle[1] (răt′l) *v.* **-tled, -tling, -tles.** —*intr.* **1.** To make or emit a quick succession of short, sharp sounds, as of pebbles being shaken in a container. **2.** To move with such sounds: *a train rattling along the track.* **3.** To talk rapidly and at length, usually without much serious content. Used with *on.* —*tr.* **1.** To cause to rattle. **2.** To utter or perform rapidly or effortlessly: *rattle off a list of names.* **3.** *Informal.* To disconcert; unnerve; fluster.
~*n.* **1.** A rapid succession of short, percussive sounds. **2.** A device for producing these sounds, such as a baby's toy. **3.** A rattling sound in the throat caused by obstructed breathing. **4.** The series of horny structures at the end of a rattlesnake's tail. **5.** Loud or rapid talk; babble. **6.** Idle or trivial chatter. **7.** An incessant talker. **8.** Any of several related European plants having a seed capsule that rattles, such as the red rattle, *Pedicularis palustris,* or the yellow rattle, *Rhinanthus minor.* [Middle English *ratelen,* from Middle Low German *rattelen,* akin to Middle High German *razzeln*†.]
rattle[2] *tr.v.* **-tled, -tling, -tles.** *Nautical.* To secure ratlines to (a rigging). Used with *down.* [Back-formation from *rattling,* variant of RATLINE.]
rat·tle·box (răt′l-bŏks′) *n.* Any of various plants or shrubs of the genus *Crotalaria,* having inflated pods in which the seeds rattle.
rat·tle·brain (răt′l-brān′) *n. Informal.* A talkative, foolish person. Also called "rattlehead," "rattlepate." —**rat·tle·brained** (răt′l-brānd′) *adj.*
rat·tler (răt′lər) *n.* **1.** One who or that which rattles. **2.** *Informal.* An outstanding example of something. **3.** *Informal.* A rattlesnake. **4.** *Informal.* A freight train.
rat·tle·snake (răt′l-snāk′) *n.* Any of various venomous New World snakes of the genera *Crotalus* and *Sistrurus,* having at the end of the tail a series of loosely attached, horny segments that can be vibrated to produce a rattling or buzzing sound.
rattlesnake flag *n.* Any of several flags bearing the motto "Don't Tread on Me" and a picture of a rattlesnake, used during the French and Indian War and the Revolutionary War.
rattlesnake plantain *n.* Any of various small orchids of the genus *Goodyera,* having mottled or striped leaves and spikes of whitish flowers. [From its leaves, which resemble a rattlesnake's skin.]
rat·tle·trap (răt′l-trăp′) *n. Informal.* A rickety, worn-out vehicle.
rat·tling (răt′lĭng) *adj. Informal.* **1.** Animated; brisk: *rattling conversation.* **2.** Very good.
~*adv. Informal.* Very; especially: *a rattling good yarn.*
rat·tly (răt′lē) *adj.* Rattling or apt to rattle; clattering.
rattoon. Variant of **ratoon.**
rat·trap (răt′trăp′) *n.* **1.** A trap for catching rats. **2.** A dilapidated or unsanitary dwelling.
rat·ty (răt′ē) *adj.* **-tier, -tiest. 1.** Of or characteristic of rats. **2.** Infested by rats. **3.** *Slang.* Dilapidated and shabby. **4.** *Slang.* Unkempt and dirty: *ratty hair.* **5.** *Chiefly British Slang.* Peevish; irritable. —**rat·ti·ly** *adv.* —**rat·ti·ness** *n.*
rau·cous (rô′kəs) *adj.* Rough-sounding and harsh. [Latin *raucus,* hoarse, harsh.] —**rau·cous·ly** *adv.* —**rau·cous·ness** *n.*
raun·chy (rôn′chē, rän′-) *adj.* **-chier, -chiest. 1.** *Informal.* **a.** Earthy; coarse; vulgar. **b.** Smutty; indecent. **2.** Marked by loud, driving rhythms. Said especially of rock music. [20th century : origin obscure.] —**raunch·i·ly** *adv.* —**raunch·i·ness** *n.*
Rausch·en·berg (rou′shən-bûrg′), **Robert** (1925–). U.S. painter and sculptor. He developed an individualistic style out of the collage and *objet trouvé* methods. One of his most notable works is *The Bed* (1955), which consists of his own bed, daubed with paint and hung vertically.
rau·wol·fi·a (rou-wŏŏl′fē-ə, rô-) *n.* Any of various tropical trees and shrubs of the genus *Rauwolfia;* especially, *R. serpentina,* of southeastern Asia. The root of this species is the source of alkaloid drugs such as reserpine, formerly used as tranquilizers but now used chiefly to treat high blood pressure. [New Latin, after Leonhard *Rauwolf* (died 1596), German botanist.]
rav·age (răv′ĭj) *v.* **-aged, -aging, -ages.** —*tr.* To destroy or despoil; devastate: *Invaders ravaged the countryside; a face ravaged by grief.* —*intr.* To cause destruction.
~*n.* **1.** The act or practice of ravaging. **2.** *Usually* **ravages.** Damage; destructive effects: *the ravages of disease.* [French, from Old French, from *ravir,* to RAVISH.] —**rav·ag·er** *n.*
rave[1] (rāv) *v.* **raved, raving, raves.** —*intr.* **1.** To speak wildly, irrationally, or incoherently: *raving like a madman.* **2.** To roar; rage. **3.** *Informal.* To speak with wild enthusiasm: *He raved about her looks.* **4.** To speak in an angry and vehement manner.
~*n.* **1.** The state or act of raving. **2.** *Informal.* A current fashion or trend. **3.** *Informal.* An extravagantly enthusiastic opinion or review.
~*adj. Informal.* Wildly enthusiastic: *rave reviews.* [Middle English *raven,* to be delirious, wander, from Old North French *raver*†.]
rave[2] *n.* A framework or rail attached to the side of a cart. [Variant of dialect *rathe*†.]
rav·el (răv′əl) *v.* **-eled, -eling, els.** Also *chiefly British* **-elled, -elling.** —*tr.* **1.** To separate the fibers or threads of (cloth, for example); unravel. Often used with *out.* **2.** To clarify by separating the aspects of. Often used with *out: "Must I ravel out my weaved-up folly"* (Shakespeare). **3.** To entangle or knot. **4.** To complicate or confuse. —*intr.* **1.** To become separated into component threads; unravel; fray. Used of cloth. **2.** To become entangled, knotted, or confused.
~*n.* **1.** A broken or frayed thread. **2.** A tangle or knot. [Dutch *rafelen,* to unravel, from obsolete Dutch *ravelen*†, to entangle.] —**rav·el·er** *n.*
Ra·vel (rə-vĕl′), **Maurice** (1875–1937). French composer, a leading figure of the so-called impressionist school. He is perhaps best known for his piano compositions, especially *Pavane pour une Infante Défunte* (1899) and *Le Tombeau de Couperin* (1917). He wrote two piano concertos, one for the left hand only (1931). His other major orchestral scores include the song cycle *Schéhérazade* (1903) and the ballet *Daphnis et Chloé* (1912).
rave·lin (răv′lĭn) *n.* A triangular, embanked salient outside the main ditch of a fortress. [French, from obsolete Italian *ravellino, rivellino,* perhaps from diminutive of *riva,* bank, from Latin *rīpa.*]
rav·el·ing (răv′əl-ĭng) *n.* Also *chiefly British* **rav·el·ling.** A thread or fiber that has become separated from a woven material.
rav·el·ment (răv′əl-mənt) *n. Archaic.* Confusion or entanglement.
ra·ven[1] (rā′vən) *n.* A large bird, *Corvus corax,* related to the crow, having black plumage and a croaking cry.
~*adj.* Black and shiny. [Middle English *raven,* Old English *hræfn,* from Germanic.]
rav·en[2] (răv′ən) *v.* **-ened, -ening, -ens.** —*tr.* **1.** To consume greedily; devour. **2.** To seek or seize (prey or plunder). —*intr.* **1.** To seek or seize prey or plunder. **2.** To eat ravenously; be voracious.
~*n.* Variant of **ravin.** [Old French *raviner,* ravage, seize by force, from Vulgar Latin *rapīnāre* (unattested), from Latin *rapīna,* rapine, from *rapere,* to seize.] —**rav·en·er** *n.*
rav·en·ing (răv′ən-ĭng) *adj.* **1.** Predatory; voracious. **2.** *Archaic.* Rabid. —**rav·en·ing·ly** *adv.*
Ra·ven·na (rə-vĕn′ə). Capital of Ravenna province in Emilia-Romagna, north-central Italy. It is an agricultural market and industrial center, connected to the Adriatic coast by canal. Ravenna rose to importance under the Romans and is famous for its colorful mosaics and its Roman and Byzantine buildings.
rav·en·ous (răv′ən-əs) *adj.* **1.** Extremely hungry; famished. **2.** Greedy; rapacious; voracious: *ravenous for power.* [Middle English, rapacious, from Old French *ravineux,* from *raviner,* to RAVEN.] —**rav·en·ous·ly** *adv.* —**rav·en·ous·ness** *n.*
ra·vi·gote (ră-vē-gôt′) *n.* A vinegar sauce spiced with minced onion, capers, and herbs, served with boiled meats or fish. [French, from *ravigoter,* to add new vigor : *re-,* again + *a-,* to, from Latin *ad-* + *vigueur,* vigor, from Latin *vigor,* VIGOR.]
rav·in, rav·en (răv′ən) *n. Poetic.* **1.** Plundering or pillage. **2.** Something taken as prey. **3.** The act or practice of preying. [Middle English *ravine,* from Old French, rapine, from Latin *rapīna,* from *rapere,* to seize.]
ra·vine (rə-vēn′) *n.* A deep, narrow cleft or gorge in the earth's surface, especially one worn by the flow of water. [French, mountain torrent, from Old French, rapine. See **ravin.**]
rav·ing (rā′vĭng) *adj.* **1.** Talking or behaving irrationally; wild: *a raving maniac.* **2.** *Informal.* Exciting admiration or notice: *a raving beauty.*
~*adv.* Used as an intensive: *raving mad.*
~*n. Often* **ravings.** Delirious, irrational speech. —**rav·ing·ly** *adv.*
ra·vi·o·li (răv′ē-ō′lē) *pl.n.* **1.** Small casings of pasta filled with chopped meat, cheese, or other ingredients and usually served with a sauce. **2.** *Used with a singular verb.* A dish consisting of ravioli. [Italian, plural of dialectal *raviolo,* diminutive of *rava,* turnip, from Latin *rāpa,* turnip.]
rav·ish (răv′ĭsh) *tr.v.* **-ished, -ishing, -ishes. 1.** To seize and carry away by force. **2.** To rape; deflower; violate. **3.** To enrapture. Usually used in the passive: *ravished by his charm.* [Middle English *ravisshen,* from Old French *ravir* (present stem *raviss-*), from Vulgar Latin *rapīre* (unattested), from Latin *rapere,* seize.] —**rav·ish·er** *n.* —**rav·ish·ment** *n.*
rav·ish·ing (răv′ĭsh-ĭng) *adj.* **1.** Entrancing; delightful. **2.** *Informal.* Extremely beautiful; gorgeous. —**rav·ish·ing·ly** *adv.*
raw (rô) *adj.* **1.** Uncooked: *raw meat.* **2.** Being in a natural condition; not subjected to manufacturing, refining, or finishing processes: *raw wool.* **3.** Untrained and inexperienced: *a raw recruit.* **4.** Recently finished; fresh: *raw plaster.* **5.** Having subcutaneous tis-

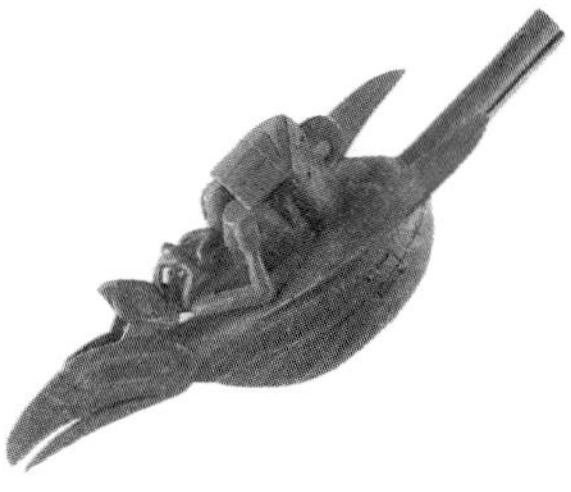

rattle *This rattle was used by a North American Indian shaman, or medicine man, as a charm to heal the sick. Made of wood in the shape of a bird, it is decorated with a human figure and a frog.*

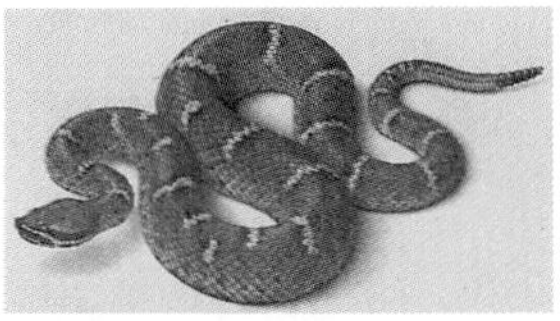

rattlesnake *There are about 30 species of rattlesnake, ranging in size from 300 millimeters (1 foot) to 2.5 meters (8 feet). All are pit vipers, so called because they are able to seek their prey in the dark by means of heat-sensitive pits near their nostrils.*

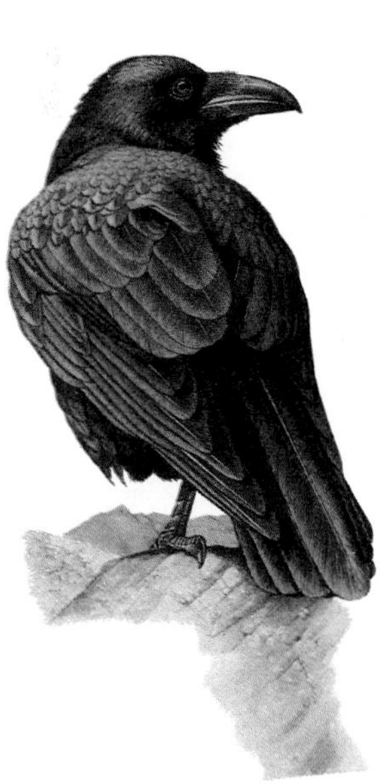

raven *The sinister appearance of these large coal-black crows gathering to feed on a carcass has given them an unsavory reputation. A small flock of ravens is kept at the Tower of London; legend has it that the Tower will fall if the birds leave.*

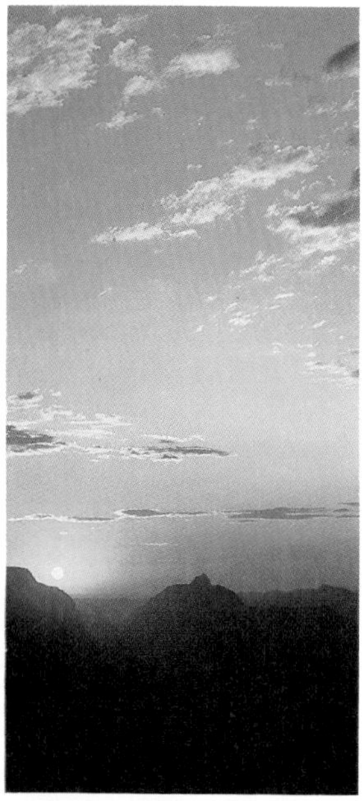

Rayleigh scattering *The changing colors of the sky at midday and dusk were first explained by the British physicist Lord Rayleigh (1842–1919). He discovered that light waves—like other types of electromagnetic radiation—are broken up, or scattered, as they pass through the air and that some wavelengths are scattered more than others. Which wavelengths dominate depends both on the size and on the number of molecules and particles through which the light passes. The size of the air molecules and dust particles in the earth's atmosphere has the effect of scattering wavelengths at the blue end of the sun's spectrum about five times more strongly than wavelengths at the red end—which is why the sky normally appears blue. At sunset and sunrise, however, when sunlight has to pass through a thicker layer of atmosphere, the greater number of molecules and particles in its path has the effect of absorbing the blue wavelengths—and allowing the redder colors in the spectrum to shine through.*

sue exposed: *a raw wound.* **6.** Penetratingly damp and cold. **7.** *Informal.* Cruel and unfair. **8.** Outspoken; crude. **9.** Undiluted; neat. Said of liquor. **10.** Not analyzed or modified. Said of statistics. **11.** Unhemmed or unfinished. Said of the edge of cloth. **—in the raw. 1.** In a crude or unrefined state. **2.** *Informal.* Nude; naked. **—on the raw.** On a sensitive area or topic: *Her comment about small men touched him on the raw.* [Middle English *raw,* Old English *hrēaw.*] **—raw·ly** *adv.* **—raw·ness** *n.*

raw·boned (rô′bōnd′) *adj.* Having a lean, gaunt frame with prominent bones. —See Usage note at **lean.**

raw·hide (rô′hīd′) *n.* **1.** The untanned hide of cattle or other animals. **2.** A whip or rope made of such hide.

ra·win·sonde (rā′wĭn-sŏnd′) *n.* A meteorological balloon tracked by a radio direction-finding instrument or radar and used for measuring wind speed in the upper atmosphere. [*Ra*dar + *win*d + radio *sonde.*]

Raw·lings (rô′lĭngz), **Marjorie Kinnan** (1896–1953). U.S. author. By giving up a career in journalism to live on a farm in the Florida backwoods, she became intimately acquainted with the lifestyle and people she wrote about in *The Yearling* (1938), her Pulitzer Prize winner, and several other novels and essays.

raw material *n.* **1.** *Often* **materials.** The natural products or basic materials on which manufacturing processes are carried out to give finished products. **2.** Somebody or something regarded as having the basic attributes or potential for a particular purpose.

raw sienna *n.* **1.** A brownish-yellow pigment made from untreated sienna. **2.** Brownish orange to light brown. Also called "sienna."

raw silk *n.* **1.** Untreated silk as reeled from the cocoon. **2.** Fabric woven from such silk.

ray[1] (rā) *n.* **1.** A thin line or narrow beam of radiation, especially of light. **2.** Any graphic or other representation of such a line. **3.** A slight trace or hint; a gleam: *a ray of hope.* **4.** *Geometry.* A straight line extending indefinitely from a point. **5.** Any structure having the form of lines extending from a point. **6.** *Botany.* A ray flower. **7.** *Zoology.* **a.** Any of the bony spines supporting the membrane of a fish's fin. **b.** Any of the arms of a starfish or related animal. *~v.* **rayed, raying, rays.** *—tr.* **1.** To send out as rays; emit. **2.** To decorate with rays or radiating lines. **3.** To cast rays upon; irradiate. *—intr.* To extend or issue forth in rays. Used of lines or light, for example. [Middle English, from Old French *rai,* from Latin *radius.* See **radius.**]

ray[2] *n.* Any of various marine cartilaginous fishes of the order Rajiformes (or Batoidei), having large, winglike, pectoral fins, horizontally flattened bodies, and narrow tails. See **electric ray.** [Middle English *raye,* from Old French *raie,* from Latin *raia*†.]

ray[3]. *Music.* Variant of **re.**

Ray (rā), **John** (*c.* 1627–1705). English pioneer naturalist. By using anatomy to distinguish specific plants and animals and establishing the category "species" as the basic unit of classification, he laid the foundation for the systematic classification of living things.

Ray, Man (1890–1976). U.S. artist. A founder of the Dadaist movement, he moved to Paris (1921) and experimented with surrealism. He later became a fashion photographer and filmmaker.

Ray, Satyajit (1921–). Indian film director, the most acclaimed of his generation. His motion pictures, such as *Pather Panchali* (1955) and *Distant Thunder* (1974), are notable for their realistic portrayal of everyday life and the artistic composition of their camera work.

Ray·burn (rā′bərn), **Samuel Taliaferro,** known as "Sam" (1882–1961). U.S. politician. Elected to the U.S. House of Representatives in 1912, he became speaker of the House in 1940 and held that position from 1940–46, 1949–53, and 1955–61. He was known for his homespun style and superb mastery of the legislative process.

ray flower *n.* Any of the flat, strap-shaped marginal flowers in the flower head of certain composite plants, such as the daisy. Also called "ray floret." Compare **disk flower.**

ray gun *n.* In science fiction, a weapon that emits rays that can paralyze, stun, kill, or vaporize.

Ray·leigh (rā′lē), **John William Strutt, 3rd Baron** (1842–1919). British physicist. He was awarded the 1904 Nobel Prize for his discovery, with Sir William Ramsay, of the inert gas argon. His son, **Robert John Strutt, 4th Baron Rayleigh** (1875–1947), developed the radiocarbon method of determining the age of rocks.

Rayleigh scattering *n.* The scattering of light waves by particles with dimensions much smaller than their wavelengths, resulting in angular separation of colors, and responsible for the reddish color of sunset and the blue of the sky. [Explained by Lord RAYLEIGH in 1871.]

ray·less (rā′lĭs) *adj.* **1.** Lacking rays: *a rayless flower.* **2.** Lacking light; gloomy: *a rayless dungeon.*

ray·on (rā′ŏn) *n.* **1.** Any of several similar synthetic textile fibers produced by forcing a cellulose solution through fine spinnerets and solidifying the resulting filaments. **2.** Any fabric made from such fibers. [From RAY (light).] **—ray·on** *adj.*

raze, rase (rāz) *tr.v.* **razed** or **rased, razing** or **rasing, razes** or **rases. 1.** To tear down or demolish; level to the ground. **2.** To erase. **3.** *Archaic.* To scrape; graze. —See Synonyms at **ruin.** [Middle English *rasen,* from Old French *raser,* from Vulgar Latin *rasāre* (unattested), from Latin *rādere* (past participle *rāsus*), to scrape.]

ra·zee (rā-zē′) *n., pl.* **-zees.** Formerly, a sailing ship made smaller by the removal of its upper deck or decks. *~tr.v.* **razeed, -zeeing, -zees.** To remove the upper deck or decks from (a sailing ship). [French *rasée,* from *raser,* to shave close.]

ra·zor (rā′zər) *n.* **1.** A sharp-edged cutting instrument, used especially for shaving the face. **2.** An instrument with electrically driven blades, used for shaving. *~tr.v.* **razored, -oring, -ors.** To use a razor on; shave or cut with a razor. [Middle English *raso(u)r,* from Old French *rasor,* from *raser,* to scrape, RAZE.]

ra·zor·back (rā′zər-băk′) *n.* **1.** A whale, the **rorqual** *(see).* **2.** A semiwild hog of the southeastern United States, having a narrow body with a ridged back. **3.** A sharp, ridged hill.

ra·zor·billed auk (rā′zər-bĭld′) *n.* A sea bird, *Alca torda,* of the northern Atlantic, having black-and-white plumage and a flattened, white-ringed bill. Also called "razorbill."

razor clam *n.* Any of various clams of the family Solenidae, characteristically having long, narrow shells.

razor cut *n.* A hairstyle produced by trimming the hair fairly short with a razor in layers so that it tapers toward the nape of the neck.

razor's edge *n.* **1.** A keen, sharp edge, as of a knife or mountain ridge. **2.** A thin dividing line: *the razor's edge of legality.* **3.** A critical or dangerous state of affairs. Used especially in the phrase *on the razor's edge.*

razz (răz) *n. Slang.* A derisive sound, a **raspberry** *(see).* *~tr.v.* **razzed, razzing, razzes.** *Slang.* To deride, heckle, or tease. [Short for *razzberry,* variant of RASPBERRY.]

raz·zi·a (răz′ē-ə) *n., pl.* **-zias.** A raid carried out for plunder or slaves, especially as formerly practiced by Muslims in North Africa. [French, from Arabic (Algerian) *gazīa,* from Arabic *gazwa.*]

raz·zle (răz′əl) *n. Slang.* **1.** A wild spree, especially a drinking spree. Used chiefly in the phrase *on the razzle.* **2.** A razzle-dazzle. [Shortened from RAZZLE-DAZZLE.]

raz·zle-daz·zle (răz′əl-dăz′əl) *n.* **1.** An exciting, glittering display, especially one intended to dazzle or impress, as in advertising. **2.** Ebullient energy; vigor. **3.** A razzle. [Reduplication of DAZZLE.]

razz·ma·tazz (răz′mə-tăz′) *n.* Also **razz·a·ma·tazz** (răz′ə-). Noisy excitement and show, especially when designed to impress or attract. [Variant of RAZZLE-DAZZLE.]

Rb The symbol for the element rubidium.

RBC red blood cell.

RBE *Physics.* relative biological effectiveness.

RBI, rbi *Baseball.* run batted in.

R.C. 1. Red Cross. **2.** reinforced concrete. **3.** Reserve Corps. **4.** Roman Catholic.

R.C.A. 1. Royal College of Art. **2.** Royal Canadian Academy. **3.** Radio Corporation of America.

R.C.A.F. Royal Canadian Air Force.

R.C.Ch. Roman Catholic Church.

R.C.M. Royal College of Music.

R.C.M.P. Royal Canadian Mounted Police.

R.C.N. Royal Canadian Navy.

R.C.P. Royal College of Physicians.

rcpt. receipt.

R.C.S. 1. Royal College of Science. **2.** Royal College of Surgeons.

rct. recruit.

R.C.V.S. Royal College of Veterinary Surgeons.

rd rod (unit of length).

rd. 1. road. **2.** round.

Rd. road.

R.D. rural delivery.

R.D.A. recommended daily allowance.

R.D.F. radio direction finder.

re[1], ray (rā) *n. Music.* A solmization syllable representing the second tone of the diatonic scale. [Middle English, from Medieval Latin. See **gamut.**]

re[2] (rē) *prep.* Concerning; in reference to; in the case of. Used in commercial or legal contexts. [Latin *rē,* from *rēs,* thing.]

Re The symbol for the element rhenium.

Re. Variant of **Ra** (Egyptian sun god).

re– *prefix.* Indicates: **1.** Restoration to a previous or improved condition or position; for example, **repay, rehouse, redecorate. 2.** Repetition of a previous action; for example, **reactivate.** ***Note:*** Many compounds other than those entered here may be formed with *re-.* In forming compounds *re-* is normally, in this dictionary, joined with the following element without space or hyphen: *reopen.* If the second element begins with *e,* it is preferable to separate it with a hyphen: *re-entry.* However, such compounds may often be found written solid and are indicated here as fully acceptable variants. If a compound resembling a familiar word is intended in a special sense, the hyphen is used to make the distinction: *re-creation,* meaning "creation anew." The hyphen may also be necessary to clarify an unusual nonce formation: *re-realignment,* or a compound that produces a series of three or more vowels: *re-aerify.* [Middle English *re-,* from Old French, from Latin *re-, red-,* in the following senses: 1. Back, as in **rebuke.** 2. Back to an earlier state or condition, as in **repair.** 3. Back in place, as in **remain.** 4. Backward, away, as in **refract.** 5. Again, repeatedly, in return for, as in **respond.** 6. Behind, as in **relinquish.** 7. Contrary, in the sense of negating, as in **repeal.** 8. Against, as in **reluctant.** 9. In response to, as in **requiem.** 10. As an intensive, as in **revere.**]

Re. rupee.

R.E. 1. real estate. **2.** Religious Education. **3.** Right Excellent. **4.** Royal Engineers.

're. Contraction of *are.*

reach (rēch) *v.* **reached, reaching, reaches.** *—tr.* **1.** To stretch out or put forth (a bodily part); extend. Often used with *out*: *reached*

her hand out to touch the ceiling. **2.** To touch or take hold of by extending some bodily part, especially the hand or something held therein: *Can you reach the table?* **3.** To get to, go as far as, or arrive at: *reach maturity; reach the end of a journey.* **4.** To communicate with; contact: *You can reach me at the office.* **5. a.** To extend as far as: *His property reached the edge of the forest.* **b.** To carry as far as: *His cry reached our ears.* **6.** To aggregate or amount to. **7.** *Informal.* To give or hand over to someone: *Reach me the sugar.* **8.** To hit or strike, especially in fencing or boxing. **9.** To make an impression on; affect: *reached the hearts of thousands.* —*intr.* **1.** To extend or thrust out something. **2.** To try to grasp, touch, or attain something: *reach for a gun; reach for the stars.* **3. a.** To extend in time or space: *His land reaches to the bottom of the hill.* **b.** To extend in influence or effect: *The effects of their policies reach throughout the land.* **4.** *Nautical.* To sail with the wind abeam.
~*n.* **1.** The act or an instance of reaching out. **2.** Power of or capacity for reaching, as: **a.** The extent or distance something can reach. **b.** The range or scope of influence or effect: *beyond the reach of the law.* **c.** The extent of one's ability to attain or achieve: *The larger model is beyond our reach.* **3.** An unbroken expanse of water, especially on a river or canal. **4. reaches.** A level, position, or grouping: *the upper reaches of the civil service.* **5.** A pole connecting the rear axle of a vehicle, such as a wagon, with the front. **6.** *Nautical.* The tack of a sailing vessel with the wind abeam. **7.** The stretch of water visible between bends in a river or channel. [Middle English *rechen,* Old English *ræcan,* from West Germanic *raikjan* (unattested).] **—reach·er** *n.*

Synonyms: *accomplish, achieve, attain, compass, gain.*

reach-me-down (rēch′mē-doun′) *n. Chiefly British.* Something of inferior quality through being secondhand or imitative.
~*adj. Chiefly British.* Secondhand; hand-me-down.

re·act (rē-ăkt′) *v.* **-acted, -acting, -acts.** —*intr.* **1.** To act in response or opposition to some former act or state. Used with *against, on,* or *upon.* **2. a.** To be affected or influenced by circumstances or events. **b.** *Medicine.* To be affected, especially adversely, by a drug, allergen, or the like. **3.** *Chemistry.* To undergo chemical change. —*tr. Chemistry.* To cause (substances) to undergo chemical change. [RE- + ACT, influenced by Medieval Latin *reagere* (past participle *reactus*), to react.]

re·ac·tance (rē-ăk′təns) *n. Symbol* **X** Opposition to the flow of alternating electric current caused by the inductance and capacitance in a circuit. See **impedance.**

re·ac·tant (rē-ăk′tənt) *n.* A substance participating in a chemical reaction; especially, a directly reacting substance present at the initiation of the reaction.

re·ac·tion (rē-ăk′shən) *n.* **1. a.** A response to a stimulus or former action; especially, a response indicating a person's feelings or views about something. **b.** Reciprocal action between two things. **2.** A reverse or opposing action. **3. a.** A tendency to revert to a former state. **b.** A tendency, as in art and especially politics, toward conservatism and opposition to progressive trends. **4.** A chemical change or transformation in which a substance decomposes, combines with other substances, or interchanges constituents with other substances. **5.** A **nuclear reaction** *(see).* **6.** A force produced in a system by an applied force, equal in magnitude to the applied force and acting in the opposite direction. **7. a.** The effect of a drug; especially, an adverse effect. **b.** The effect of a substance upon a person who is allergic to that substance. **c.** An adverse response by a person to such drugs or allergens. **8.** A period of depression, exhaustion, mental disorder, or the like, that occurs following shock or excessive exertion.

re·ac·tion·ar·y (rē-ăk′shə-nĕr′ē) *adj.* Also **re·ac·tion·ist** (-nĭst). Characterized by reaction; especially, opposing progressive trends or wishing to return to a former, outmoded state.
~*n., pl.* **reactionaries.** Also **re·ac·tion·ist.** An opponent of progress or liberalism.

reaction engine *n.* An engine that develops thrust by the expulsion of matter, especially ignited fuel gases. Also "reaction motor."

reaction time *n. Biology.* The time interval between the application of a stimulus and the detection of a response.

reaction turbine *n.* A type of turbine in which part of the torque is produced by pressure from fluid moving out of the rotating part.

re·ac·ti·vate (rē-ăk′tə-vāt′) *tr.v.* **-vated, -vating, -vates. 1.** To make active again. **2.** To restore the effectiveness or ability to function of. **—re·ac·ti·va·tion** (rē-ăk′tə-vā′shən) *n.*

re·ac·tive (rē-ăk′tĭv) *adj.* **1.** Tending to be responsive or to react to a stimulus. **2.** Characterized by reaction. **3.** *Chemistry & Physics.* Tending to participate in reactions. **4.** *Electricity.* Having electrical reactance.

reactive depression *n.* Mental depression that arises in response to unfavorable external circumstances without necessarily reflecting deep-seated personality or physiological problems.

re·ac·tor (rē-ăk′tər) *n.* **1.** A person or thing that reacts. **2.** *Electricity.* A circuit element, such as a coil, used to introduce reactance into a circuit. **3.** *Physics.* A **nuclear reactor** *(see).*

read (rēd) *v.* **read** (rĕd), **reading, reads.** —*tr.* **1.** To comprehend, take in the meaning of, or be able to convert into the intended sound (something written or printed) by looking at or, in the case of blind people, touching the characters or words and interpreting them. **2.** To utter or render aloud (something written or printed). **3.** To have the knowledge of (a language) necessary to understand printed or written material: *I can read Russian but I can't speak it.* **4. a.** To seek to interpret the true nature or meaning of (someone or something) through close scrutiny: *read the sky for signs of snow.* **b.** To ascertain the true thoughts, intent, or mood of: *He read her mind.* **5.** To interpret the signs or arrangement of: *read a map.* **6.** To ascribe a special meaning or interpretation, often mistakenly, to (something read, heard, experienced, or observed): *He read her tears as sadness, not joy. Don't read too much into what he says.* **7. a.** To foretell or predict (the future). **b.** To foretell the future by interpreting the arrangement of (lines on a hand or tea leaves, for example). **8.** To perceive, receive, or comprehend (a signal, message, or its sender): *I read you loud and clear.* **9.** *Chiefly British.* To be engaged in the study of: *read law at university.* **10.** To learn or get knowledge of from something written or printed: *He read that crime was rife.* **11.** To adopt or use in preference to another word or phrase in a doubtful or erroneous passage: *For "colour" read "color."* **12.** To indicate, register, or show: *The dial reads 0°.* **13.** To be interpreted as; mean: *The law reads that he is guilty.* **14.** To obtain or detect and transfer (information) from a computer storage device. **15.** To cause to be in a specified state by reading: *read me to sleep.* **16.** To interpret or be able to interpret (musical notation) and reproduce the appropriate notes. **17.** In various sports, to anticipate correctly (the moves or tactics of one's teammates or opponents). —*intr.* **1.** To read printed or written characters, as of words or music. **2.** To utter or render aloud the words that one is reading. **3.** To learn by reading. Used with *about* or *of*: *I read about it in the paper.* **4.** To have a particular wording: *The line reads thus.* **5.** To have a specified character or quality for the reader: *His poems read well.* **6.** To study: *reading for the bar.* **—read between the lines.** To perceive or detect a meaning or implication that is obscure or unexpressed. **—read up.** To acquire information or improve one's skill by reading or studying. Often used with *on.*
~*n.* **1.** The act or an instance of reading. **2.** Material suitable for reading or something to be read: *a good read.*
~*adj.* (rĕd). Informed by reading; learned. Used in combination: *well-read.* [Read (infinitive), read (past tense and past participle); Middle English *reden, redde, red,* Old English *rǣdan,* to advise, explain, read, *rædde, ræden,* from Germanic *rǣdhan* (unattested).]

Read (rēd), **Sir Herbert Edward** (1893–1968). British poet and literary and art critic. His first volume of poetry, *Naked Warriors,* appeared in 1919, his *Collected Poems* in 1966. He is more famous as a critic, for books such as *Art and Industry* (1934), *Art and Society* (1937), *Art and Alienation* (1967), *Form in Modern Poetry* (1932), and *Phases of English Poetry* (1950).

read·a·ble (rē′də-bəl) *adj.* **1.** Capable of being read easily; legible. **2.** Pleasurable or interesting to read. **—read·a·bil·i·ty** (rē′də-bĭl′ə-tē), **read·a·ble·ness** *n.* **—read·a·bly** *adv.*

Reade (rēd), **Charles** (1814–84). British novelist. His best-known work was *The Cloister and the Hearth* (1861).

read·er (rē′dər) *n.* **1.** One who reads, especially, a person who enjoys reading very much. **2.** A professional reciter of literary works. **3. a.** In the Roman Catholic Church, a **lector** *(see).* **b.** In the Episcopal and Anglican churches, a **lay reader** *(see).* **4.** A person employed by a publisher to read and evaluate manuscripts. **5.** A corrector of printers' proofs; a proofreader. **6.** *Chiefly British.* A senior university lecturer. **7.** A teaching assistant who reads and grades examination papers. **8. a.** A textbook of reading exercises designed as part of a course for people learning to read, especially for children. **b.** A literary anthology. **9.** A computer device for converting data from one form into another.

read·er·ship (rē′dər-shĭp′) *n.* **1.** The readers collectively or the total number of readers of a publication or publications. **2.** *Chiefly British.* The office or rank of a reader in a university.

read·i·ly (rĕd′ə-lē) *adv.* **1.** Promptly; quickly. **2.** Willingly. **3.** Easily; without difficulty or hindrance.

read·i·ness (rĕd′ē-nĭs) *n.* The quality or state of being ready or willing.

read·ing (rē′dĭng) *n.* **1.** The skill of being able to read. Also used adjectivally: *reading age.* **2.** Written or printed material. **3.** The act of rendering aloud written or printed matter. **4.** An official or public recitation of written material: *the reading of a will.* **5. a.** A personal interpretation or perception: *What's your reading of the situation?* **b.** A personal interpretation or appraisal of a text or passage. **6.** A specific form of a passage that can be understood in more than one way. **7.** The information indicated by a gauge or graduated instrument. **8.** In parliamentary procedure, the formal presentation of a bill to a legislative body at any of the stages of its passage.
~*adj.* Designed or used for reading: *a reading lamp.*

Read·ing (rĕd′ĭng). Administrative center of Berkshire, southern England, at the confluence of the Thames and Kennet rivers. It is an important railway junction.

re·ad·just (rē′ə-jŭst′) *v.* **-justed, -justing, -justs.** —*tr.* To adjust or arrange again. —*intr.* To adjust or adapt oneself, as to a new environment or changed circumstances. **—re·ad·just·er** *n.* **—re·ad·just·ment** *n.*

read-on·ly (rēd′ōn′lē) *adj. Computer Science.* Designating or pertaining to devices in which the information held cannot be changed: *a read-only memory.* Compare **random-access.**

read out *tr.v.* **1.** To read (a text, passage, or the like) aloud. **2.** To expel by proclamation from a social, political, or other group. **3.** To present a read-out of (computer data).

read-out (rēd′out′) *n.* Presentation of computer data, usually in digital form, from calculations or storage, often displayed on a screen. Compare **print-out.**

PRONUNCIATION KEY

ă, pat; ā, pay; âr, care;
ä, father, are; b, bib;
ch, church; d, deed; ĕ, pet;
ē, be; f, fife; g, gag; h, hat;
hw, which; ĭ, pit; ī, pie;
îr, pier; j, judge; k, kick;
l, lid, needle; m, mum;
n, no, sudden; ng, thing;
ŏ, pot; ō, toe; ô, paw, for;
oi, noise; ou, out; ŏŏ, book;
ōō, boot; p, pop; r, roar;
s, sauce; sh, ship, dish;
t, tight; th, thin, path;
th, this, bathe; ŭ, cut; ûr, fur;
v, valve; w, with; y, yes;
z, zebra, size; zh, vision;
ə, about, item, edible,
gallop, circus, peaceful

IN FOREIGN WORDS:

à, *Fr.* ami; œ, *Fr.* feu, *Ger.* schön; ü, *Fr.* tu, *Ger.* über; KH, *Ger.* ich, *Scot.* loch; N, *Fr.* bon; y′, *Fr.* Compiègne

STRESS MARKS:

Primary stress: ′
in·cite′ (ĭn-sīt′)
Secondary stress: ′
in′sight′ (ĭn′sīt′)

read-write (rēd′rīt′) *adj. Computer Science.* **1.** Of, pertaining to, or designating hardware or software enabling the transfer of information to and from a magnetic tape or disk: *a read-write head.* **2.** Designating a memory in which the information held may be altered or read at will. See **random-access.**

read·y (rĕd′ē) *adj.* **-ier, -iest. 1.** Prepared or available for service or action. **2.** Mentally disposed; willing: *He was ready to believe them.* **3.** Liable or about to do something. Used with an infinitive: *ready to leave.* **4.** Prompt in understanding or reacting: *a ready intelligence; a ready response.* **5.** Available: *ready money.* **—at the ready. 1.** In position for aiming and firing. Said of a rifle. **2.** In a position for immediate use or action.
~*tr.v.* **readied, readying, readies.** To cause to be ready. [Middle English *redy,* Old English *rǣde,* from Germanic *raidh-* (unattested), prepare.]

read·y-made (rĕd′ē-mād′) *adj.* **1.** Made to a set pattern rather than to individual specifications. Compare **made-to-order. 2.** Already existing and available for use: *a ready-made answer.* **3.** Unoriginal and commonplace: *ready-made prose.*
~*n.* **1.** Something that is ready-made. **2.** An ordinary object, such as a rubbish bin or pile of bricks, that is removed from its original surroundings and viewed as a work of art.

read·y-mix (rĕd′ē-mĭks′) *n.* **1.** A combination of ingredients sold in a form ready or nearly ready for use. **2.** Liquid concrete mixed before delivery to the site at which it is used.

read·y-to-wear (rĕd′ē-tə-wâr′) *adj.* Made to a set pattern; ready-made. Said of clothes.

re·af·firm (rē′ə-fûrm′) *tr.v.* **-firmed, -firming, -firms.** To affirm or assert again. **—re·af·fir·ma·tion** (rē′ăf-ər-mā′shən) *n.*

re·af·for·est (rē′ə-fôr′ĭst, -fŏr′ĭst) *tr.v.* **-ested, -esting, -ests.** *Chiefly British.* To reforest. **—re·af·for·es·ta·tion** *n.*

Rea·gan (rā′gən), **Ronald** (1911–). 40th U.S. president. After a career as an actor, he was elected governor of California (1966), a post he held for eight years. He was elected president of the United States in 1980 and was re-elected in 1984.

re·a·gent (rē-ā′jənt) *n.* Any substance used in a chemical reaction to detect, measure, examine, or produce other substances. [RE- + AGENT, after REACT.]

re·a·gin (rē-ā′jĭn) *n.* An antibody present in the blood of individuals allergic to a particular substance (allergen). Subsequent contact with the allergen provokes a reaction with the antibody that is responsible for the allergic response. [*Rea*gent + -IN.]

re·al[1] (rē′əl, rēl) *adj.* **1.** Being or occurring in fact or actuality; having verifiable existence: *Is that lake real or a mirage?* **2.** True and actual; not illusory or fictitious: *the real explanation.* **3.** Emphatically having all the attributes normally associated with the specified person or thing: *a real man.* **4.** Genuine and authentic; not artificial or spurious: *real gold.* **5.** *Philosophy.* Existing actually and objectively; not contingent. **6.** *Physics & Chemistry.* Designating a gas in which deviations from ideal gas behavior occur because of interactions between the constituent gas molecules. **7.** Of, pertaining to, or designating an image formed by light rays that converge in space. **8.** *Mathematics.* Of, pertaining to, or designating the nonimaginary part of a complex quantity. **9.** *Law.* Consisting of or pertaining to stationary or fixed property, such as buildings or land. Compare **personal. 10.** *Economics.* Valued according to current purchasing power rather than the nominal amount: *real incomes.* **11.** *Informal.* Used as an intensive: *a real idiot.* **—for real.** *Slang.* Not illusory or experimental; genuine and serious. **—the real.** The totality of actual, existing things, as opposed to imaginary things.
~*adv. Informal.* Very: *real sorry.* [Middle English, of real property or things, from Norman French, from Late Latin *reālis,* actual, real, from Latin *rēs,* thing.] **—real·ness** *n.*
Synonyms: *actual, authentic, concrete, existent, genuine, tangible, true, veritable.*

re·al[2] (rā-äl′) *n., pl.* **reals** or **-ales** (-ä′läs). A former Spanish silver monetary unit. [Spanish, from *real,* "royal," from Latin *rēgālis,* regal, from *rēx* (stem *rēg-*), king.]

re·al[3] (rā-äl′) *n., pl.* **reals** or **reis** (rās). Either of two former monetary units of Portugal and Brazil. [Portuguese, from *real,* "royal." See **real** (Spanish coin).]

real estate *n. Abbr.* **R.E.** Landed property, including all inherent natural resources and any manmade improvements established thereon. Also called "real property," "realty." **—re·al-es·tate** (rē′əl-ĕ-stāt′) *adj.*

real image *n. Optics.* An optical image formed by converging rays.

re·al·gar (rē-ăl′gär′, -gər) *n.* A soft orange or red arsenic ore, As_2S_2, used in fireworks, tanning, and as a pigment. [Middle English, from Medieval Latin, from Arabic *rajh al-ghār,* powder (of) the mine or cave.]

re·al·ism (rē′ə-lĭz′əm) *n.* **1.** Inclination toward literal truth rather than toward the abstract, romantic, or ideal. **2.** Inclination toward a pragmatic, practical, and material way of life rather than an idealistic or morally absolute one. **3.** *Often* **Realism.** In art and literature, a style favoring the representation of life or objects as they actually exist rather than romanticizing or idealizing them or presenting them in an abstract form. **4.** *Philosophy.* **a.** The doctrine that universal or general ideas and principles have an objective existence. Compare **nominalism. b.** The doctrine that the objects of perception exist independently of the perceiver. Compare **idealism. c.** Broadly, the view that theories, especially scientific or other explanatory theories, are objectively true or false.

re·al·ist (rē′ə-lĭst) *n.* **1.** One inclined to literal truth and pragmatism. **2.** A person who practices or believes in artistic or philosophical realism. Also used adjectivally: *a realist doctrine.*

re·al·is·tic (rē′ə-lĭs′tĭk) *adj.* **1.** Inclined toward the literal truth, as opposed to the abstract, romantic, or ideal. **2. a.** Closely resembling the object, scene, or person being represented; lifelike: *a realistic landscape.* **b.** Concerned with or seeking to represent what is objectively real, as in art or literature. **3.** Of or pertaining to philosophical realism. **4.** Practical-minded as opposed to idealistic; pragmatic: *Let's be realistic now and agree to at least a few of their demands.*

re·al·i·ty (rē-ăl′ə-tē) *n., pl.* **-ties. 1.** The quality or state of being actual or true. **2.** A person, entity, or event that is actual. **3.** The totality of all things possessing actuality, existence, or essence. **4.** That which exists objectively and in fact. **5.** *Philosophy.* The sum of all that is real, absolute, and unchangeable. **—in reality.** In actual fact.

re·al·i·za·tion (rē′ə-lə-zā′shən) *n.* **1.** The act or fact of realizing or the condition of being realized. **2.** The result of realizing.

re·al·ize (rē′ə-līz′) *v.* **-ized, -izing, -izes.** —*tr.* **1. a.** To comprehend completely or correctly: *realized the truth.* **b.** To become aware of; notice: *realized she was on the wrong road.* **2.** To make real or actualize (a plan or ambition, for example): *realize a dream.* **3.** To make or cause to appear realistic. **4.** To obtain or achieve, as gain or profit: *realize a return on an investment.* **5.** To bring in (a sum) as profit by sale. **6.** To convert (property) into money. **7.** *Music.* To complete or reconstruct in full (a part or harmonies, especially for a piece of baroque music) from the figured bass or **continuo** *(see).* **8.** *Phonetics.* To produce the sound of (a phoneme) in speech; articulate. —*intr.* To become conscious or aware of something. [French *réaliser,* from Old French *realiser,* from *real,* real, from Late Latin *reālis,* REAL.] **—re·al·iz·a·ble** *adj.* **—re·al·iz·er** *n.*

re·al·ly (rē′ə-lē, rē′lē) *adv.* **1.** In reality or fact. **2.** Truly; thoroughly: *a really perfect work.* **3.** Used as an intensive: *You really shouldn't have done it.*
~*interj.* Used to express mild surprise or incredulity.

realm (rĕlm) *n.* **1.** A kingdom. **2.** Any field, sphere, or province: *the realm of science.* [Middle English *realme, reaume,* from Old French, from Latin *regimen,* system of government, from *regere,* to rule.]

real number *n.* Any rational or irrational number. See **number.**

re·al·po·li·tik (rā-äl′pō′lĭ-tēk′) *n. Often* **Realpolitik.** A harshly realistic national policy having as its sole principle the advancement of the national interest. [German, "realistic politics."]

real presence *n. Theology.* The doctrine that Christ's actual body and blood are present in the Eucharist.

real property *n.* **Real estate** *(see).*

real tennis *n. Chiefly British.* **Court tennis** *(see).*

real time *n. Computer Science.* **1.** The actual time in which a physical process under computer study or control occurs. **2.** The time required for a computer to solve a problem, measured from the time data are fed in to the time a solution is received. **—real-time** (rē′əl-tīm′) *adj.*

re·al·tor (rē′əl-tər, -tôr′) *n. Often* **Realtor.** A real-estate agent affiliated with the National Association of Real Estate Boards.

re·al·ty (rē′əl-tē) *n., pl.* **-ties. Real estate** *(see).* [REAL + -TY.]

ream[1] (rēm) *n.* **1.** *Abbr.* **rm.** A quantity of paper, formerly 480 sheets, now 500 sheets or, in a printer's ream, 516 sheets. **2.** *Usually* **reams.** An extensive amount, as of paper or written or printed material: *wrote reams of verse.* [Middle English *rem(e),* from Old French *remme,* from Arabic *rizmah,* bundle.]

ream[2] *tr.v.* **reamed, reaming, reams. 1.** To form, shape, taper, or enlarge (a hole) with or as if with a reamer. **2.** To remove (material) by reaming. **3.** To squeeze the juice out of (fruit) with a reamer. [19th century : perhaps from Middle English *remen,* to make room, Old English *rȳman,* to widen.]

ream·er (rē′mər) *n.* **1.** One that reams. **2.** Any of various tools used to shape or enlarge holes. **3.** A utensil with a conical ridged projection rising from the middle of a bowl, used for extracting juice from citrus fruits.

reap (rēp) *v.* **reaped, reaping, reaps.** —*tr.* **1.** To cut (a crop) for harvest with a scythe, sickle, or reaper. **2.** To harvest (a crop so cut). **3.** To harvest a crop from. **4.** To obtain as a result of effort. —*intr.* **1.** To cut or harvest a crop. **2.** To obtain a return or reward. [Middle English *repen,* Old English *rīpan*†.]

reap·er (rē′pər) *n.* **1.** One who reaps. **2.** A machine for harvesting grain or pulse crops.

re·ap·por·tion (rē′ə-pôr′shən) *tr.v.* **-tioned, -tioning, -tions.** To distribute anew.

re·ap·por·tion·ment (rē′ə-pôr′shən-mənt) *n.* **1.** The act of reapportioning or the state of being reapportioned. **2.** The redistribution of representation in a legislative body; especially, the periodic reallotment of U.S. congressional seats according to changes in the census figures as required by the Constitution.

re·ap·prais·al (rē′ə-prā′zəl) *n.* A new or fresh appraisal or evaluation. **—re·ap·praise** *v.*

rear[1] (rîr) *n.* **1.** The hind part of something. **2.** The point or area farthest from the front of something. **3.** The part of a military deployment usually farthest from the fighting front. **4.** *Informal.* The buttocks. **—bring up the rear.** To be last, as in a line or race.
~*adj.* Of, at, or located in the rear. [Short for ARREAR.]

rear[2] *v.* **reared, rearing, rears.** —*tr.* **1.** To care for (a child or children) during the early stages of life; bring up. **2.** To lift upright; raise. **3.** To build; erect. **4.** To tend (growing plants or animals). —*intr.* **1.** To rise on the hind legs, as a horse does. Often used with *up.* **2.** To rise high in the air; tower. Often used with *up* or *over.* [Middle English *reren,* to lift up, raise, Old English *rǣran;* akin to RAISE.] —**rear·er** *n.*

rear admiral *n. Abbr.* **Rear Adm., R.A.** A naval officer ranking below a vice admiral and above a captain.

rear guard *n.* A detachment of troops that protects the rear of a military force. [Middle English *reregarde,* from Old French : *rere,* backward, behind, from Latin *retrō* + *garde,* GUARD.]

rear-guard (rîr'gärd') *adj.* **1.** Of or involving a rear guard. **2.** Done while in retreat from an advancing military, social, or other force: *fought rearguard actions against the invader.*

re·arm (rē-ärm') *v.* **-armed, -arming, -arms.** —*tr.* **1.** To arm again. **2.** To equip with better weapons. —*intr.* To arm oneself again. —**re·ar·ma·ment** (rē-är'mə-mənt) *n.*

rear·most (rîr'mōst') *adj.* Farthest in the rear; last.

re·ar·range (rē'ə-rānj') *tr.v.* **-ranged, -ranging, -ranges.** To change or restore the arrangement of. —**re·ar·range·ment** *n.*

rear-view mirror (rîr'vyōō') **1.** A small adjustable mirror centrally attached at the top or bottom of the windshield in a motor vehicle to allow the driver a view of what is directly behind. **2.** A similar mirror attached to the handlebar of a motorcycle or bicycle.

rear·ward¹ (rîr'wərd) *adj.* Directed toward or situated at the rear. ~*adv.* Also **rear·wards** (-wərdz). Toward, to, or at the rear. ~*n.* A position or place at the rear.

rear·ward² (rîr'wôrd') *n.* **1.** A position at the rear. **2.** The rear guard of an armed force. [Middle English *rerewarde,* from Norman-French : *rere,* behind, from Latin *retrō* + *warde,* guard, from Germanic.]

rea·son (rē'zən) *n.* **1.** The basis or motive for an action, decision, or conviction. **2.** A declaration or argument advanced to explain or justify an action, decision, or conviction: *She gave her reason for quitting.* **3.** An underlying fact or cause that provides a logical justification for a premise or occurrence. **4. a.** The power to think, judge, and draw logical conclusions. **b.** The intellect as opposed to emotions, feelings, instincts, or intuitions. **5.** Good judgment; sound sense; intelligence. **6.** A sound mental state; sanity. **7.** *Logic.* A premise, usually the minor premise, of an argument. —See Synonyms below and at **mind.** —See Usage note at **because, cause, why.** —**by reason of.** Because of. —**in** (or **within**) **reason.** Within the bounds of good sense or practicality. —**listen to reason.** To allow oneself to be persuaded by logical or sensible arguments. —**stand to reason.** To be logical or likely. Usually used impersonally: *It stands to reason that an athlete would be healthy.* —**with reason.** With good cause; justifiably. ~*v.* **reasoned, -soning, -sons.** —*intr.* **1.** To use the faculty of reason; think logically. **2.** To talk or argue logically and persuasively. **3.** To seek to persuade someone with reasons. Used with *with.* **4.** *Archaic.* To engage in conversation or discussion: *"Come . . . let us reason together"* (Isaiah 1:18). —*tr.* **1.** To determine, solve, or conclude by logical thinking. Often used with *out.* **2.** To seek to persuade (someone) with reasons. Used with *out of* or *into.* **3.** To discuss; debate. [Middle English *reisun,* from Old French, from Vulgar Latin *ratiōne* (unattested), from Latin *ratiō* (stem *ratiōn-*), calculation, judgment, reasoning, from *ratus,* past participle of *rērī,* to think, reason.] —**rea·son·er** *n.*

Synonyms: discernment, intuition, judgment, understanding.

rea·son·a·ble (rē'zən-ə-bəl) *adj.* **1.** Capable of reasoning; rational. **2.** Governed by or in accordance with reason or sound thinking. **3.** Within the bounds of common sense or normal expectations. **4.** Not excessive or extreme; fair; moderate. —**rea·son·a·bil·i·ty, rea·son·a·ble·ness** *n.* —**rea·son·a·bly** *adv.*

rea·soned (rē'zənd) *adj.* Having been well thought out; reasonable: *a reasoned argument.*

rea·son·ing (rē'zən-ĭng) *n.* **1.** The mental processes of one who reasons; especially, the drawing of conclusions or inferences from observation, facts, or hypotheses. **2.** The particular evidence or arguments used in this procedure.

re·as·sure (rē'ə-shŏŏr') *tr.v.* **-sured, -suring, -sures.** **1.** To restore confidence to. **2.** To assure again. **3.** To reinsure. —**re·as·sur·ance** *n.* —**re·as·sur·ing·ly** *adv.*

reata. Variant of **riata.**

Ré·au·mur, Re·au·mur (rā'ō-myŏŏr') *adj. Abbr.* **R, R., Réaum.** Designating or indicated on a temperature scale that registers the freezing point of water as 0° and the boiling point as 80°. [Introduced by René de RÉAUMUR.]

Réaumur, René Antoine Ferchault de (1683–1757). French physicist and natural philosopher, one of the leading figures of 18th-century science. He is best known for his invention of the alcohol thermometer (*c.* 1730) and the temperature scale named after him, but he also developed opaque glass and wrote a six-volume study of insects (1734–42).

reave¹ (rēv) *v.* **reft** (rĕft) or **reaved, reaving, reaves.** *Archaic.* —*tr.* **1.** To seize and carry off forcibly. **2.** To deprive; bereave. Used with *of.* —*intr.* To rob, plunder, or pillage. [Middle English *reven,* to plunder, Old English *rēafian.*]

reave² *tr.v.* **reft** (rĕft) or **reaved, reaving, reaves.** *Archaic.* To break or tear apart. [Middle English *reven,* variant (influenced by *riven,* RIVE) of REAVE (seize).]

Reb¹ (rĕb) *n. Sometimes* **reb.** *Informal.* A Confederate soldier in the Civil War. [Short for REBEL.]

Reb² *n.* A Jewish title of respect, approximately equivalent to "Mr." or "Sir," but used with the first name rather than the surname. [Yiddish, from Hebrew *rabbī,* my teacher, RABBI.]

re·bar·ba·tive (rē-bär'bə-tĭv) *adj.* Extremely unattractive; repellent. [French *rébarbatif,* from Old French *rebarber,* "to face beard to beard," face an enemy, hence, to be repellent : *re-,* back, against + *barbe,* beard, from Latin *barba.*]

re·bate¹ (rē'bāt') *n.* A deduction from an amount to be paid or a return of part of an amount already paid. ~*tr.v.* **rebated, -bating, -bates.** **1.** To deduct or return (an amount) from a payment or bill. **2.** *Archaic.* To dull or blunt (a weapon, for example). **3.** *Archaic.* To lessen; diminish. [Middle English *rebaten,* to deduct, subtract, from Old French *rabattre,* to beat down again, reduce : *re-,* again + *abattre,* to beat down : *a-,* to, from Latin *ad-* + *battre,* to beat, from Latin *battuere.*] —**re·bat·er** *n.*

rebate². Variant of **rabbet.**

re·ba·to (rĭ-bä'tō) *n., pl.* **-tos.** Also **ra·ba·to** (rə-bä'tō). A stiff, flaring collar of lace or other fabric, worn by both men and women in the early part of the 17th century. [Old French *rabat,* turndown collar, from *rabattre,* to turn down again, REBATE.]

re·bec, re·beck (rē'bĕk') *n.* A pear-shaped, two- or three-stringed musical instrument of medieval times, played with a bow. [Old French *rebec,* variant (influenced by *bec,* beak, because of the shape of the instrument) of *rebebe,* from Old Provençal *rebab,* from Arabic (dialectal) *rebāb.*]

Re·bec·ca, Re·bek·ah (rĭ-bĕk'ə). The wife of Isaac and the mother of Jacob and Esau. Genesis 24:1–67.

re·bel (rĭ-bĕl') *intr.v.* **-belled, -belling, -bels.** **1.** To refuse allegiance to and oppose by force an established government or ruling authority. Often used with *against.* **2.** To resist or defy any authority or generally accepted convention. **3.** To feel or express strong unwillingness or distaste: *rebelled at the unwelcome suggestion.* ~*n.* **reb·el** (rĕb'əl). **1.** A person who rebels or is in rebellion. **2.** A person who refuses to comply with accepted conventions. **3. Rebel.** A confederate soldier in the Civil War. Used chiefly by Union sympathizers. ~*adj.* **reb·el** (rĕb'əl). **1.** Of, pertaining to, or consisting of rebels. **2.** Rebellious; defiant. [Middle English *rebellen,* from Old French *rebeller,* from Latin *rebellāre,* to make war again : *re-,* again + *bellāre,* to make war, from *bellum,* war.]

re·bel·lion (rĭ-bĕl'yən) *n.* **1.** An uprising or organized opposition intended to change or overthrow an existing government or ruling authority. **2.** An act or show of defiance toward any authority or established convention. [Middle English, from Old French, from Latin *rebelliō* (stem *rebelliōn-*), from *rebellāre,* to REBEL.]

Synonyms: coup d'état, insurrection, mutiny, revolt, revolution, uprising.

re·bel·lious (rĭ-bĕl'yəs) *adj.* **1.** Participating in or inclined toward rebellion. **2.** Of or characteristic of a rebel. **3.** Resisting management or control; unruly. —See Usage note at **insubordinate.** —**re·bel·lious·ly** *adv.* —**re·bel·lious·ness** *n.*

Re·ber (rā'bər), **Grote** (1911–). U.S. astronomer. He built the world's first radio telescope in 1937 and has continued to play an active part in the development of subsequent telescopes.

re·bind (rē-bīnd') *tr.v.* **-bound** (-bound'), **-binding, -binds.** To bind again; especially, to put a new binding on (a book).

re·birth (rē-bûrth', rē'bûrth') *n.* **1.** A second or new birth; a reincarnation. **2.** A spiritual regeneration. **3.** A renaissance or revival.

re·bore (rē'bôr', -bōr') *n.* The process of drilling out the cylinder of an engine and fitting a slightly larger piston. ~*tr.v.* (rē-bôr', -bōr'), **rebored, -boring, -bores.** To give (an engine) a rebore.

re·born (rē-bôrn') *adj.* Born again; emotionally or spiritually revived or regenerated.

re·bound (rē-bound', rĭ-) *v.* **-bounded, -bounding, -bounds.** —*intr.* **1.** To spring or bounce back after hitting or colliding with something. **2.** To harm the person responsible for an act, especially an act of malice: *Their efforts to discredit me rebounded on them.* **3.** To re-echo; resound. **4.** To recover, as from a setback or disappointment. —*tr.* To cause to rebound. ~*n.* (rē'bound', rĭ-bound'). **1.** A springing or bounding back; a recoil. **2. a.** In basketball, a ball in the process of bouncing off the backboard after an unsuccessful shot. **b.** In soccer, hockey, and other games, a ball or puck that has rebounded, as off a goal post or goalkeeper. **3.** A quick recovery from a setback or disappointment. —**on the rebound. 1.** In the act of springing or bounding back. **2.** In reaction to disappointment, rejection, or depression: *marriage on the rebound.* [Middle English *rebounden,* from Old French *rebondir : re-,* again, back + *bondir,* to resound, BOUND (leap).]

re·bo·zo (rĭ-bō'sō) *n., pl.* **-zos.** A long scarf worn over the head and shoulders, especially by Mexican women. [Spanish, from *rebosar,* to muffle with a shawl.]

re·broad·cast (rē-brôd'kăst', -käst') *tr.v.* **-cast** or **-casted, -casting, -casts. 1.** To repeat the broadcast of (a program). **2.** To receive and send out (a broadcast) again. —**re·broad·cast** *n.*

re·buff (rĭ-bŭf') *n.* **1.** A blunt or abrupt repulsing or refusal, as to an offer of help or sympathy or to a person making unwelcome advances; a snub. **2.** Any abrupt setback to progress or action. ~*tr.v.* **rebuffed, -buffing, -buffs. 1.** To refuse or reject bluntly or contemptuously; snub. **2.** To repel or drive back. —See Synonyms at **refuse.** [Old French *rebuffer,* from Italian *ribuffare,* to scold, rebuff, from *ribuffo,* reprimand : *re-,* back, again, from Latin *re-* + *buffo,* puff, gust (imitative).]

re·build (rē-bĭld') *tr.v.* **-built** (-bĭlt'), **-building, -builds. 1.** To build again. **2.** To make extensive structural repairs to. **3.** To restore, as from a condition of ruin: *plans to rebuild the economy.*

re·buke (rĭ-byo͞ok′) *tr.v.* **-buked, -buking, -bukes.** To criticize or reprove sharply; reprimand. —See Synonyms at **admonish.**
∼*n.* A sharp reproof. [Middle English *rebuken,* from Old North French *rebuke;* akin to Old French *buchier,* to beat, chop down wood, from *busche,* log.]

re·bus (rē′bəs) *n., pl.* **-buses.** A riddle whose answer is depicted by symbols or pictures that suggest the sounds or give clues to the meanings of the words or syllables they represent. [Latin *rēbus,* by things, from *rēs,* thing.]

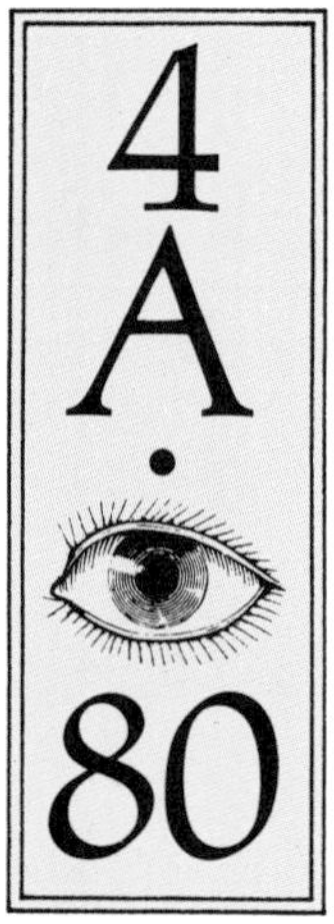

rebus *A picture taken from an early 20th-century children's book. The story attached to the puzzle explains that the rebus was designed by an ingenious beggar and set beside him in the street. Curious passersby then had to pay to discover its meaning. The solution: "For a period, I ate next to nothing."*

re·but (rĭ-bŭt′) *v.* **-butted, -butting, -buts.** —*tr.* **1.** To oppose or contradict by offering evidence or arguments, as in a legal case or a debate. **2.** *Archaic.* To repel. —*intr.* To present opposing evidence or arguments. [Middle English *rebuten,* from Old French *rebuter* : *re-,* again, back + *buter,* to BUTT.]

re·but·tal (rĭ-bŭt′l) *n.* The act of rebutting.

re·but·ter (rĭ-bŭt′ər) *n.* **1.** One that rebuts. **2.** *Law.* The defendant's answer to the plaintiff's surrejoinder.

rec (rĕk) *n. Informal.* A recreation ground.

rec. **1.** receipt. **2.** recipe. **3.** record; recorder; recording. **4.** recreation.

re·cal·ci·trant (rĭ-kăl′sə-trənt) *adj.* Stubbornly resistant to authority, domination, or guidance. —See Synonyms at **unruly.**
∼*n.* A recalcitrant person. [Latin *recalcitrāns* (stem *recalcitrant-*), present participle of *recalcitrāre,* to kick back : *re-,* back, again + *calcitrāre,* to kick, from *calx* (stem *calc-*), heel.] —**re·cal·ci·trance, re·cal·ci·tran·cy** *n.*

re·cal·esce (rē′kə-lĕs′) *intr.v.* **-esced, -escing, -esces.** To undergo recalescence. Used of a cooling metal.

re·ca·les·cence (rē′kə-lĕs′əns) *n. Metallurgy.* A sudden increase of heat in a cooling metal caused by an exothermic structural change. [Latin *recalescens* (stem *recalescent-*), present participle of *recalescere,* to grow warm again : *re-,* back, again + *calescere,* become warm, from *calēre,* to be warm.] —**re·ca·les·cent** *adj.*

re·call (rĭ-kôl′) *tr.v.* **-called, -calling, -calls.** **1.** To call back; ask or order to return. **2.** To summon back, as from a daydream or digression, to awareness of or concern with the subject or situation at hand. **3. a.** To remember or recollect. **b.** To cause to remember. **4.** To cancel, take back, or revoke. **5.** To request purchasers to return (defective goods, for example). **6.** To bring back; restore.
∼*n.* (rĭ-kôl′, rē′kôl′). **1.** The act of recalling or summoning back; especially, an official order to return. **2.** A signal, such as a bugle call, used to summon servicemen back to their posts. **3.** The ability to remember information or experiences. **4.** The act of revoking or canceling. **5.** *Computer Science.* A measure of the efficiency of an information retrieval system. **6. a.** A procedure by which a public official may be removed from office by special popular vote. **b.** The right to employ this procedure. **7.** A request by the manufacturer of a product for its return for necessary repairs or adjustments. —**re·call·a·ble** *adj.*

Ré·ca·mier (rā-kăm′ē-ə), **Jeanne Françoise Julie Adélaide,** born Julie Bernard (1777–1849). French society hostess. Through her beauty and wit she attracted many influential figures to her salon and was painted by David and Gérard.

re·cant (rĭ-kănt′) *v.* **-canted, -canting, -cants.** —*tr.* To make a formal retraction or disavowal of (a statement or belief to which one has previously committed oneself). —*intr.* To make a formal retraction or disavowal of a previous statement or previously held belief. [Latin *recantāre* : *re-,* back + *cantāre,* sing, chant, frequentative of *canere,* sing.] —**re·can·ta·tion** *n.* —**re·cant·er** *n.*

re·cap[1] (rē′kăp′) *tr.v.* **-capped, -capping, -caps.** **1.** To replace a cap or caplike covering on. **2.** To bond new rubber onto the tread and lateral surface of (a worn automobile tire).
∼*n.* (rē′kăp′). A tire thus reconditioned.

re·cap[2] (rē′kăp′) *tr.v.* **-capped, -capping, -caps.** *Informal.* To recapitulate.
∼*n. Informal.* A recapitulation. [Short for RECAPITULATE.]

re·ca·pit·u·late (rē′kə-pĭch′o͞o-lāt′) *v.* **-lated, -lating, -lates.** —*tr.* **1.** To repeat in concise form the main points of (a speech, discussion, or the like); sum up. **2.** *Biology.* To appear to repeat (the evolutionary stages of the species) during the embryonic development of the individual organism. —*intr.* To summarize the main points. [Late Latin *recapitulāre* : *re-,* back, again + *capitulāre,* to put under headings, from Latin *capitulum,* heading, small head, diminutive of *caput,* head.] —**re·ca·pit·u·la·tive** (rē′kə-pĭch′o͞o-lā′tĭv), **re·ca·pit·u·la·to·ry** (rē′kə-pĭch′o͞o-lə-tôr′ē, -tōr′ē) *adj.*

re·ca·pit·u·la·tion (rē′kə-pĭch′o͞o-lā′shən) *n.* **1.** The act or process of recapitulating. **2.** A summary or concise review. **3.** *Biology.* The apparent repetition of some evolutionary stages of the species during embryonic development. Also called "palingenesis." **4.** *Music.* The restatement of the exposition of a theme after its development, forming the final section of a movement in sonata form.

re·cap·tion (rē-kăp′shən) *n. Law.* The act of claiming and retaking that which has been wrongfully taken or detained, such as goods or a child. [RE- + CAPTION (seizure).]

re·cap·ture (rē-kăp′chər) *tr.v.* **-tured, -turing, -tures.** **1.** To capture again; retake or recover. **2.** To recall or revive the feeling or quality of: *an attempt to recapture that wonderful moment.* **3.** To acquire by the government procedure of recapture.
∼*n.* **1. a.** The act of recapturing. **b.** The condition of being recaptured. **2.** Anything recaptured. **3.** The lawful taking by a government of a fixed amount of the profits of a public-service company in excess of a stipulated rate of return.

re·cast (rē-kăst′) *tr.v.* **-cast, -casting, -casts.** **1.** To mold again: *recast a bell.* **2.** To set down or present (ideas, for example) in a new or different arrangement. **3.** To change the cast of (a theatrical production, film, or the like).
∼*n.* (rē′kăst′). **1.** The act or process of recasting. **2.** Something produced by recasting.

recd., rec'd. received.

re·cede (rē-sēd′) *tr.v.* **-ceded, -ceding, -cedes.** To cede back; yield or grant to one formerly in possession.

re·cede (rĭ-sēd′) *intr.v.* **-ceded, -ceding, -cedes.** **1.** To move back or away from a limit, point, or mark. **2.** To slope backward. **3.** To become or seem to become more distant. **4.** To become less; diminish. **5.** To withdraw or retreat from an agreement, stated position, or the like. **6. a.** To gradually cease to grow above the forehead or on the temples. Used of a man's hair. **b.** To move backward from the forehead. Used of a man's hairline. [Latin *recēdere,* to go back : *re-,* back, again + *cēdere,* to go.]

re·ceipt (rĭ-sēt′) *n. Abbr.* **rec., rcpt., rept., rec't, rect.** **1.** A written acknowledgment that a stipulated article, sum of money, or delivery of merchandise has been received. **2. a.** The act of receiving something. **b.** The fact of being received. **3.** *Usually* **receipts.** The quantity or amount of something received: *cash receipts.* **4.** *Archaic & Regional.* A recipe.
∼*tr.v.* **receipted, -ceipting, -ceipts.** **1.** To mark (a bill) as having been paid. **2.** To give or write a receipt for (money paid or goods delivered). [Middle English *receite,* from Old Northern French, from Medieval Latin *recepta,* from Latin *recipere* (past participle *receptus*), to take, RECEIVE.]

re·ceiv·a·ble (rĭ-sē′və-bəl) *adj.* **1.** Suitable for being received or accepted, especially as payment. **2.** Awaiting or requiring payment; due or collectable: *accounts receivable.*
∼*n.* **receivables.** Business assets represented by the total amount of accounts due for payment.

re·ceive (rĭ-sēv) *v.* **-ceived, -ceiving, -ceives.** —*tr.* **1. a.** To take or acquire (something given or offered). **b.** To take or accept (something delivered or transmitted, such as a letter or telephone call). **2.** To acquire knowledge of or information about: *receive bad news.* **3.** To have (a blessing or title, for example) bestowed on one. **4.** To meet with; experience: *receive sympathetic treatment.* **5.** To have inflicted or imposed on oneself: *receive a penalty.* **6.** To bear the weight or force of; support. **7.** To take or intercept the impact of (a blow, for example). **8.** To take in, hold, or contain. **9.** To admit as to a state or society: *receive new members.* **10.** To greet or welcome, especially in a formal manner. **11.** To perceive or acquire mentally: *receive a bad impression.* **12.** To accept as valid or regard with approval: *theories that are widely received.* **13.** To respond or react to in the specified way: *His suggestion was received with howls of derision.* **14.** To listen to and formally and authoritatively acknowledge: *receive an oath of allegiance.* **15.** To take (the sacraments). **16.** *Chiefly British.* To accept and pay for (goods known to be stolen), especially in order to resell them. **17.** To face (service), as in tennis. —*intr.* **1.** To acquire or get something; be a recipient. **2.** To admit or welcome guests or visitors. **3.** To partake of the Eucharist. **4.** *Electronics.* To convert incoming electrical or electromagnetic waves into visible or audible signals. **5.** *British.* To accept and pay for goods known to be stolen, especially in order to resell them. **6.** To be required to face and return the service, as in tennis. [Middle English *receiven,* from Old North French *receivre,* from Latin *recipere,* to take back, regain : *re-,* back, again + *capere,* to take.]

re·ceived (rĭ-sēvd′) *adj.* **1.** Generally accepted or believed. **2.** Conventional; clichéd: *received wisdom.*

Received Pronunciation *n. Abbr.* **R.P.** The form of English pronunciation based typically on that of the upper and upper-middle classes in England, having no characteristics peculiar to any region and generally accepted within England as a standard accent.

re·ceiv·er (rĭ-sē′vər) *n.* **1.** One who receives something; a recipient. **2.** An official appointed to receive and account for money due. **3.** *Law.* A person appointed by a court administrator to take into custody property or funds of others pending litigation, such as the property or funds of a person declared bankrupt or of unsound mind. **4.** One who knowingly buys or receives stolen goods. **5.** A receptacle intended for a specific purpose, as for collecting the products of distillation. **6.** *Electronics.* A device, such as a part of a radio, television set, or telephone, that receives incoming electrical or electromagnetic signals and converts them to perceptible forms.

re·ceiv·er·ship (rĭ-sē′vər-shĭp′) *n. Law.* **1.** The office or functions of a receiver. **2.** The state of being held in the custody of a receiver.

receiving end *n. Informal.* A position in which one is subjected directly to an unpleasant experience, especially criticism or abuse. Used chiefly in the phrase *on the receiving end.*

receiving order *n. Law.* A court order appointing a receiver to take custody of the property or funds of a debtor when an act of bankruptcy has been established.

re·cen·sion (rĭ-sĕn′shən) *n.* **1.** A critical revision of a text incorporating the most plausible elements found in varying sources. **2.** A text so revised. [Latin *recēnsiō* (stem *recēnsiōn-*), a reviewing, an enumeration, from *recēnsēre,* to survey again, review : *re-,* again, back + *cēnsēre,* to estimate, assess.]

re·cent (rē′sənt) *adj.* **1.** Of, belonging to, or occurring at a time immediately prior to the present. **2.** Modern; new. **3. Recent.** *Geology.* Of, belonging to, or designating the Holocene epoch.
∼*n.* **Recent.** *Geology.* The **Holocene** *(see)* epoch. Preceded by *the.* [Latin *recēns* (stem *recent-*), fresh, new.] —**re·cen·cy, re·cent·ness** *n.* —**re·cent·ly** *adv.*

re·cept (rē'sĕpt') *n.* A mental image formed from what is common to successive perceptions. [RE- + (CON)CEPT.]

re·cep·ta·cle (rĭ-sĕp'tə-kəl) *n.* **1.** Something that holds or contains; a container. **2.** *Botany.* **a.** The tip of a flower stalk, that bears and supports the floral organs. **b.** In certain seaweeds, the part of the blade that bears the reproductive structures. **3.** *Electricity.* A fitting connected to a power supply and equipped to receive a plug. [Latin *receptāculum,* from *receptāre,* to take again, frequentative of *recipere* (past participle *receptus*), to RECEIVE.]

re·cep·tion (rĭ-sĕp'shən) *n.* **1.** The act or process of receiving or accepting or of being received or accepted. **2. a.** A welcome, greeting, or acceptance: *a friendly reception.* **b.** A response or reaction: *Her speech got a very hostile reception.* **3.** A formal social function held to meet guests, as after a wedding, or entertain visitors, such as foreign dignitaries. **4.** *Electronics.* **a.** The action of receiving electrical or electromagnetic signals. **b.** The condition or quality of received signals. **5. a.** The place, as in an office or hospital, where clients or visitors are received and appointments made. **b.** The place in a hotel where guests register or make reservations. [Latin *receptiō* (stem *receptiōn-*), from *recipere* (past participle *receptus*), to RECEIVE.]

re·cep·tion·ist (rĭ-sĕp'shə-nĭst) *n.* A person employed, as in an office, hotel, or hospital, to receive callers or clients, answer the telephone, and deal with inquiries.

re·cep·tive (rĭ-sĕp'tĭv) *adj.* **1.** Capable of or qualified for receiving. **2.** Ready or willing to receive favorably. **3.** Quick to apprehend new ideas, impressions, or the like. **—re·cep·tive·ly** *adv.* **—re·cep·tiv·i·ty** (rē'sĕp-tĭv'ə-tē), **re·cep·tive·ness** *n.*

re·cep·tor (rĭ-sĕp'tər) *n. Anatomy.* A cell or group of cells specialized to sense or to receive stimuli.

re·cess (rē'sĕs', rĭ-sĕs') *n.* **1.** A temporary cessation of customary activities or proceedings, such as at the end of a legislative session: *the Easter recess.* **2.** The period of such cessation. **3.** *Usually* **recesses.** A remote, secret, or secluded place. **4.** *Anatomy.* An indentation or small hollow in an organ. **5.** An alcove.
~v. **recessed, -cessing, -cesses.** *—tr.* **1.** To place in a recess. **2.** To create or fashion a recess in. **3.** To suspend for a recess. *—intr.* To take a recess. [Latin *recessus,* from the past participle of *recēdere,* to RECEDE.]

re·ces·sion (rē-sĕsh'ən) *n.* The act of restoring possession to a former owner.

re·ces·sion (rĭ-sĕsh'ən) *n.* **1.** A decline in economic activity that is not as severe as a depression. **2.** The act of withdrawing or receding. **3.** The filing out of clergy and choir members after a church service. [Latin *recessiō* (stem *recessiōn-*), from *recessus,* RECESS.]

re·ces·sion·al (rĭ-sĕsh'ən-əl) *adj.* Of or pertaining to recession.
~n. A hymn that accompanies the exit of the clergy and choir after a service.

re·ces·sive (rĭ-sĕs'ĭv) *adj.* **1.** Tending to go backward or recede. **2.** *Genetics.* Of, pertaining to, or designating an allele that does not produce a phenotypic effect when paired with a dominant allele. Compare **dominant. 3.** *Phonetics.* Designating a stress that falls near the beginning of a polysyllabic word.
~n. Genetics. **1.** A recessive allele or trait. **2.** An organism having a recessive trait. **—re·ces·sive·ly** *adv.*

ré·chauf·fé (rā'shō-fā') *n.* **1.** Leftover food that is warmed up. **2.** Old material reworked or rehashed. [French, "warmed up," from *réchauffer,* to heat again, from Old French : *re-,* again, back + *chauffer,* to warm (see **chafe**).]

re·cher·ché (rə-shâr'shā') *adj.* **1.** Highly sought after; rare. **2.** Exquisite; refined. **3.** Familiar or known only to experts or connoisseurs. **4.** Overrefined; affected and forced. [French, past participle of *rechercher,* to search for, RESEARCH.]

re·chris·ten (rē-krĭs'ən) *tr.v.* **-ened, ening, ens. 1.** To christen again. **2.** To rename.

re·cid·i·vism (rĭ-sĭd'ə-vĭz'əm) *n.* A tendency to relapse into a former pattern of behavior; especially, a tendency to return to criminal habits. [From *recidivist,* from French *récidiviste,* relapser, from *récidiver,* to relapse, from Medieval Latin *recidīvāre,* from Latin *recidīvus,* a falling back, from *recidere,* fall back : *re-,* back, again + *cadere,* fall.] **—re·cid·i·vist** *n.* **—re·cid·i·vis·tic** (rĭ-sĭd'ə-vĭs'tĭk), **re·cid·i·vous** *adj.*

Re·ci·fe (rə-sē'fē) Capital of the state of Pernambuco in eastern Brazil. It is a busy port and industrial center.

recip. reciprocal; reciprocity.

rec·i·pe (rĕs'ə-pē) *n.* **1.** *Abbr.* **rec.** A formula for preparing a mixture or compound, especially in cooking or pharmacology, with a list of measured ingredients and often a set of directions for their use or application. **2.** *Symbol* ℞ A medical prescription. Not in current technical usage. **3.** A procedure or set of circumstances likely to lead to a specified end: *a recipe for disaster.* [Latin, "take," imperative of *recipere,* to take, RECEIVE.]

re·cip·i·ence (rĭ-sĭp'ē-əns) *n.* Also **re·cip·i·en·cy** (-ən-sē). The capacity to receive; receptivity.

re·cip·i·ent (rĭ-sĭp'ē-ənt) *adj.* Functioning as a receiver.
~n. **1.** One that receives or is receptive. **2.** *Medicine.* A person who receives blood or transplanted tissue from a donor. [Latin *recipiēns* (stem *recipient-*), present participle of *recipere,* to RECEIVE.]

re·cip·ro·cal (rĭ-sĭp'rə-kəl) *adj.* **1.** Performed or given in return: *a reciprocal present.* **2.** Interchanged, given, or owed by each of two parties to the other: *reciprocal funds.* **3.** Performed, experienced, or felt by both sides: *reciprocal hatred.* **4.** Equivalent or corresponding. **5.** *Grammar.* Expressing mutual action or relationship. Said of some verbs and compound pronouns. **6.** *Mathematics.* Of or pertaining to a quantity divided into 1.
~n. **1.** Anything that is reciprocal to something else; a converse or complement. **2.** *Mathematics.* The quotient of a specific quantity divided into 1. For example, the reciprocal of 7 is 1/7; the reciprocal of 2/3 is 3/2. [Latin *reciprocus,* alternating, returning.] **—re·cip·ro·cal·i·ty** (rĭ-sĭp'rə-kăl'ə-tē), **re·cip·ro·cal·ness** *n.* **—re·cip·ro·cal·ly** *adv.*

reciprocal ohm *n. Physics.* A **siemens** (*see*).

reciprocal pronoun *n. Grammar.* A pronoun or pronominal phrase expressing mutual action or relationship, such as *each other.*

re·cip·ro·cate (rĭ-sĭp'rə-kāt') *v.* **-cated, -cating, -cates.** *—tr.* **1.** To give or take mutually; interchange. **2.** To show or feel in response or return. **3.** To cause to move back and forth alternately. *—intr.* **1.** To move back and forth alternately. **2.** To give and take something mutually. **3.** To make a return for something given or done. **4.** To be complementary or equivalent. [Latin *reciprocāre,* to move back and forth, from *reciprocus,* RECIPROCAL.] **—re·cip·ro·ca·tive** (rĭ-sĭp'rə-kā'tĭv, -kə-tĭv) *adj.* **—re·cip·ro·ca·tor** *n.*

reciprocating engine *n.* An engine having a crankshaft turned by linearly reciprocating pistons.

re·cip·ro·ca·tion (rĭ-sĭp'rə-kā'shən) *n.* **1.** An alternating back-and-forth movement. **2.** The act or fact of reciprocating; a mutual giving or receiving; an interchange.

rec·i·proc·i·ty (rĕs'ə-prŏs'ə-tē) *n., pl.* **-ties.** *Abbr.* **recip. 1.** A reciprocal condition or relationship. **2.** A mutual or cooperative interchange of favors or privileges; especially, one constituting a commercial policy or trade agreement between two or more parties.

re·ci·sion (rĭ-sĭzh'ən) *n.* The act or an instance of rescinding; an annulment or cancellation. [Latin *recīsiō* (stem *recīsiōn-*), a cutting off, from *recīsus,* past participle of *recīdere,* to cut down : *re-,* back, back down, again + *caedere,* to cut.]

recit. *Music.* recitative.

re·cit·al (rĭ-sīt'l) *n.* **1.** A public reciting of poetry or prose. **2.** A retelling in detail; a narration. **3.** Something thus told. **4.** A performance of music or dance, especially by a soloist or small ensemble. **5.** *Law.* A preliminary part of a document setting out relevant facts. **—re·cit·al·ist** *n.*

rec·i·ta·tion (rĕs'ə-tā'shən) *n.* **1.** The act of reciting poetry or prose from memory, especially in a public performance. **2.** The material so recited. **3. a.** The oral delivery of prepared lessons by a pupil. **b.** The class period devoted to this.

rec·i·ta·tive[1] (rĕs'ə-tā'tĭv, rĭ-sī'tə-tĭv) *adj.* Pertaining to or having the character of a recital or recitation.

rec·i·ta·tive[2] (rĕs'ə-tə-tēv') *n.* Also **re·ci·ta·ti·vo** (rĕs'ə-tə-tē'vō; *Italian* rā'chē-tä-tē'vō) *pl.* **-vi** (-vē) or **-vos** (-vōz). *Abbr.* **recit. 1.** A musical style used in opera and oratorio, in which the text is declaimed in the rhythm of natural speech with slight melodic variation. **2.** A passage rendered in this form. [Italian *recitativo,* from *recitare,* to recite, from Latin *recitāre,* to RECITE.]

re·cite (rĭ-sīt') *v.* **-cited, -citing, -cites.** *—tr.* **1.** To repeat or utter aloud (something rehearsed or memorized), especially before an audience or teacher. **2.** To relate in detail. **3.** To list or enumerate. *—intr.* To deliver a recitation. [Middle English *reciten,* from Old French *reciter,* from Latin *recitāre,* to read out, cite again : *re-,* back, again + *citāre,* to CITE.] **—re·cit·er** *n.*

reck (rĕk) *v.* **recked, recking, recks.** *Archaic & Regional. —tr.* To take heed of; be concerned about: *He does not reck death. —intr.* To take heed; have caution. [Middle English *recken, recchen,* to be careful, to take care, Old English *reccan*†, *recan* (unattested).]

reck·less (rĕk'lĭs) *adj.* **1. a.** Heedless or careless. **b.** Headstrong; rash: *a reckless lover.* **2.** Having no regard for consequences; uncontrolled; wild: *a reckless driver.* [Middle English *recheles, reckeles,* Old English *rēcelēas.*] **—reck·less·ly** *adv.* **—reck·less·ness** *n.*
Synonyms: *adventurous, audacious, daring, foolhardy, precipitate, rash.*

reck·on (rĕk'ən) *v.* **-oned, -oning, -ons.** *—tr.* **1.** To count or compute: *reckon the amount due; reckoning time by the phases of the moon.* **2.** To consider as being; regard as: *I reckoned him a fool.* **3.** *Regional & Informal.* To think or suppose: *I reckon you're a stranger here. —intr.* **1.** To make a calculation; figure. Often used with *up.* **2.** To place reliance; depend. Used with *on* or *upon*: *reckon on financial aid.* **3.** To make allowance for a possibility; anticipate something. Used with *on* or *upon*: *I didn't reckon on your being here.* —See Synonyms at **calculate, consider. —reckon with. 1.** To come to terms or settle accounts with. **2.** To recognize as significant: *a force to be reckoned with.* **—reckon without.** To fail to take into account. [Middle English *reknen,* Old English *gerecenian,* to enumerate, from Germanic.]

reck·on·er (rĕk'ən-ər) *n.* **1.** One that reckons. **2.** A handbook of mathematical tables to facilitate computation.

reck·on·ing (rĕk'ən-ĭng) *n.* **1.** Computation. **2.** An itemized bill or statement of a sum due. **3.** The settlement of a bill or account. **4.** Calculation of the position of a ship, aircraft, or the like. **5.** Judgment of or retribution for past misdeeds. Used chiefly in the phrase *day of reckoning.*

re·claim (rē-klām') *tr.v.* **-claimed, -claiming, -claims. 1.** To make (marshland or desert, for example) suitable for cultivation or habitation, as by stabilizing, irrigating, or fertilizing. **2.** To procure (usable substances) from refuse or waste products. **3.** To turn (a person) from error, evil, or barbarism; reform. **4.** To demand or effect the return of. **5.** *Archaic.* To tame (a falcon, for example). **6.** To produce (land) by filling in an area previously submerged by

PRONUNCIATION KEY

ă, pat; ā, pay; âr, care; ä, father, are; b, bib; ch, church; d, deed; ĕ, pet; ē, be; f, fife; g, gag; h, hat; hw, which; ĭ, pit; ī, pie; îr, pier; j, judge; k, kick; l, lid, needle; m, mum; n, no, sudden; ng, thing; ŏ, pot; ō, toe; ô, paw, for; oi, noise; ou, out; ŏŏ, book; ōō, boot; p, pop; r, roar; s, sauce; sh, ship, dish; t, tight; th, thin, path; *th*, this, bathe; ŭ, cut; ûr, fur; v, valve; w, with; y, yes; z, zebra, size; zh, vision; ə, about, item, edible, gallop, circus, peaceful

IN FOREIGN WORDS:

à, *Fr.* ami; œ, *Fr.* feu, *Ger.* schön; ü, *Fr.* tu, *Ger.* über; KH, *Ger.* ich, *Scot.* loch; N, *Fr.* bon; y', *Fr.* Compiègne

STRESS MARKS:

Primary stress: '
in·cite' (ĭn-sīt')
Secondary stress: '
in'sight' (ĭn'sīt')

the sea. —See Usage note at **recover**, Synonyms at **save**.
~*n.* The act of reclaiming or condition of being reclaimed. [Middle English *reclamen,* to call back, from Old French *reclamer,* from Latin *reclāmāre,* to exclaim against : *re-,* back, against + *clāmāre,* to call out.] **—re·claim·a·ble** *adj.* **—re·claim·ant, re·claim·er** *n.*

rec·la·ma·tion (rĕk′lə-mā′shən) *n.* **1.** The act or process of reclaiming or condition of being reclaimed. **2.** A restoration, as to usefulness, or morality. [Old French, a protest, from Latin *reclāmātiō* (stem *reclamātiōn-*), cry of opposition, from *reclāmāre,* to RECLAIM.]

ré·clame (rā-kläm′) *n.* **1.** Public acclaim. **2.** A taste or flair for publicity. [French, publicity, from *réclamer,* to reclaim, from Old French *reclamer,* to RECLAIM.]

rec·li·nate (rĕk′lə-nāt′) *adj. Botany.* Bent or turned downward toward the base. Said especially of leaves and stems. [Latin *reclīnātus,* past participle of *reclīnāre,* to RECLINE.]

re·cline (rĭ-klīn′) *v.* **-clined, -clining, -clines.** *—tr.* To cause to assume a leaning or supine position. *—intr.* To lie back or down. [Middle English *reclinen,* from Old French *recliner,* from Latin *reclīnāre* : *re-,* back, again + *-clīnāre,* to bend.] **—rec·li·na·tion** (rĕk′lə-nā′shən) *n.* **—re·clin·er** *n.*

re·cluse (rĕk′lo͞os′, rĭ-klo͞os′) *n.* A person who withdraws from others to live in solitude and seclusion.
~*adj.* Withdrawn from the world; solitary. [Middle English *reclus(e),* from Old French, past participle of *reclure,* to shut up, from Latin *reclūdere,* to close off, unclose, open : *re-* (intensifier), again + *claudere,* to close.] **—re·clu·sion** (rĭ-klo͞o′zhən) *n.*

re·clu·sive (rĭ-klo͞o′sĭv, -zĭv) *adj.* **1.** Seeking or preferring seclusion or isolation. **2.** Providing seclusion: *a reclusive hut.*

rec·og·ni·tion (rĕk′əg-nĭsh′ən) *n.* **1.** The act of recognizing or state of being recognized, especially: **a.** An awareness that something perceived has previously been perceived by oneself. **b.** An acknowledgment, as of a claim or fact. **2.** Attention or favorable notice: *Her achievements won her general recognition.* **3.** An acknowledgment of the national status of a new government by another nation. [Latin *recognitiō* (stem *recognitiōn-*), from *recognōscere* (past participle *recognitus*), to RECOGNIZE.] **—re·cog·ni·tive, re·cog·ni·to·ry** (rĭ-kŏg′nə-tôr′ē, -tōr′ē) *adj.*

re·cog·ni·zance (rĭ-kŏg′nə-zəns, -kŏn′ə-zəns) *n.* **1.** *Law.* **a.** An obligation of record entered into before a court or magistrate by which a person binds himself to perform a particular act, such as to appear in court or pay a sum of money. **b.** A sum of money pledged to assure the performance of such an act. **2.** *Archaic.* A recognition. [Middle English *recognizance, reconissaunce,* recognition, from Old French *reconoissance,* from *reconoistre,* to RECOGNIZE.] **—re·cog·ni·zant** *adj.*

rec·og·nize (rĕk′əg-nīz′) *tr.v.* **-nized, -nizing, -nizes. 1.** To know or be aware that (something perceived) has been perceived by oneself before: *recognize a face.* **2.** To know or identify from past experience or knowledge: *recognize a red-winged blackbird.* **3. a.** To realize; comprehend and appreciate fully: *recognized the value of the discovery.* **b.** To perceive or acknowledge the validity or reality of: *recognize a demand.* **4.** To acknowledge the presence of; greet: *refused to recognize me in the street.* **5.** To give permission to (a person) to speak in a debate. Used especially of a chairman. **6.** To acknowledge or accept the national status of (a new government). **7.** To show approval or appreciation of: *recognize services rendered.* [Old French *reconoistre* (stem *reco(g)noiss-*), from Latin *recognōscere,* to know again : *re-,* again + *cognōscere,* to know : *co-,* with + *gnōscere,* become acquainted.] **—rec·og·niz·a·ble** (rĕk′əg-nī′zə-bəl) *adj.* **—rec·og·niz·a·bly** *adv.* **—rec·og·niz·er** *n.*

rec·og·nized (rĕk′əg-nīzd′) *adj.* Generally approved or acknowledged as meeting appropriate requirements: *a recognized brand of paint; a recognized art dealer.*

re·coil (rĭ-koil′) *intr.v.* **-coiled, -coiling, -coils. 1.** To spring back, as a gun does when fired. **2.** To shrink back, as in fear or repugnance: *She recoiled at the sight of the snake.* **3.** To harm the person responsible for an act, especially an act of malice. Used with *on* or *upon: Vice recoils upon the guilty men.*
~*n.* (rē′koil′, rĭ-koil′). **1.** The amount of space used by a gun as it recoils upon firing. **2.** The act or state of recoiling. [Middle English *recoilen, reculen,* from Old French *reculer* : *re-,* back, again + *cul,* backside, from Latin *cūlus.*] **—re·coil·er** *n.*
Synonyms: *blench, cower, cringe, flinch, quail, shrink.*

re·col·lect (rē′kə-lĕkt′) *tr.v.* **-lected, -lecting, -lects. 1.** To collect again. **2.** To calm or control (oneself).

rec·ol·lect (rĕk′ə-lĕkt′) *v.* **-lected, -lecting, -lects.** *—tr.* To recall to mind; remember. *—intr.* To have a recollection; remember. [Medieval Latin *recolligere* (past participle *recollectus*), to recall, from Latin, to gather again : *re-,* again + *colligere,* to gather, COLLECT.] **—rec·ol·lec·tive** *adj.* **—rec·ol·lec·tive·ly** *adv.*

rec·ol·lec·tion (rĕk′ə-lĕk′shən) *n.* **1.** The act or power of recollecting. **2.** Something recollected. —See Synonyms at **memory**.

re·com·bi·nant (rē-kŏm′bə-nənt) *n.* An individual in which genetic recombination has occurred.
~*adj.* Of, pertaining to, or characterized by genetic recombination. [RECOMBIN(E) + -ANT.]

recombinant DNA *n.* DNA prepared by laboratory manipulation in which genes from one species are combined with those of another species.

re·com·bi·na·tion (rē′kŏm-bə-nā′shən) *n.* The formation in an offspring of gene combinations not present in either of its parents.

re·com·mence (rē′kə-mĕns′) *v.* **-menced, -mencing, -mences.** To begin or commence again.

rec·om·mend (rĕk′ə-mĕnd′) *tr.v.* **-mended, -mending, -mends. 1.** To commend to the attention of another as reputable, worthy, or desirable. **2.** To make attractive or acceptable: *He has little to recommend him.* **3.** To counsel or advise (a particular course of action). **4.** *Archaic.* To commit to the charge of another: *recommended his soul to God.* [Middle English *recommenden,* from Medieval Latin *recommendāre* : Latin *re-,* again + *commendāre,* to COMMEND.] **—rec·om·mend·a·ble** *adj.* **—rec·om·mend·er** *n.*

rec·om·men·da·tion (rĕk′ə-mĕn-dā′shən) *n.* **1.** The act of recommending. **2.** Something that recommends; specifically, a favorable statement concerning a person's character or qualifications. **3.** Someone or something that is recommended. **—rec·om·men·da·to·ry** (rĕk′ə-mĕn′də-tôr′ē, -tōr′ē) *adj.*

re·com·mit (rē′kə-mĭt′) *tr.v.* **-mitted, -mitting, -mits. 1.** To commit again. **2.** To refer (a bill) to a committee again, for further consideration. **—re·com·mit·ment, re·com·mit·tal** *n.*

rec·om·pense (rĕk′əm-pĕns′) *tr.v.* **-pensed, -pensing, -penses. 1.** To reward or pay for services. **2. a.** To award compensation for (loss or damage, for example); make a return for. **b.** To award compensation to.
~*n.* **1.** Amends made for something, such as damage or loss. **2.** Payment in return for something given or done, such as services. [Middle English *recompensen,* from Old French *recompenser,* from Late Latin *recompensāre* : Latin *re-,* back, again + *compensāre,* to COMPENSATE.]

re·com·pose (rē′kəm-pōz′) *tr.v.* **-posed, -posing, -poses. 1.** To compose again. **2.** To restore to composure; calm. **—re·com·po·si·tion** (rē′kŏm-pə-zĭsh′ən) *n.*

re·con (rē′kŏn′) *n.* The smallest genetic unit that is capable of recombination. [*Recombination* + -ON.]

rec·on·cil·a·ble (rĕk′ən-sī′lə-bəl, rĕk′ən-sī′lə-bəl) *adj.* Capable of reconciliation or able to be reconciled. **—rec·on·cil·a·bil·i·ty, rec·on·cil·a·ble·ness** *n.* **—rec·on·cil·a·bly** *adv.*

rec·on·cile (rĕk′ən-sīl′) *tr.v.* **-ciled, -ciling, -ciles. 1.** To re-establish friendship between. **2.** To settle or resolve (a dispute, for example). **3.** To bring to acceptance or acquiescence: *reconcile oneself to defeat.* **4.** To make compatible or consistent. Often used with *to* or *with: reconcile my way of thinking with yours.* **5.** To purify (a consecrated place) in a special ceremony, after an act of desecration. [Middle English *reconcilen,* from Old French *reconcilier,* from Latin *reconciliāre* : *re-,* again + *conciliāre,* to CONCILIATE.] **—rec·on·cile·ment, rec·on·cil·i·a·tion** (rĕk′ən-sĭl′ē-ā′shən) *n.* **—rec·on·cil·er** *n.* **—rec·on·cil·i·a·to·ry** (rĕk′ən-sĭl′ē-ə-tôr′e, -tōr′ē) *adj.*

rec·on·dite (rĕk′ən-dīt′, rĭ-kŏn′dīt′) *adj.* **1.** Not easily understood; abstruse: *the recondite origin of life.* **2.** Concerned with abstruse or obscure subjects: *recondite scholarship.* **3.** Concealed; hidden. [Latin *reconditus,* past participle of *recondere,* to hide, put up again : *re-,* again + *condere,* bring together.] **—rec·on·dite·ly** *adv.* **—rec·on·dite·ness** *n.*

re·con·di·tion (rē′kən-dĭsh′ən) *tr.v.* **-tioned, -tioning, -tions. 1.** To restore by repairing, renovating, or rebuilding. **2.** To overhaul and restore to good working order.

re·con·nais·sance (rĭ-kŏn′ə-səns, -zəns) *n.* **1.** The process or activity of investigating or surveying. **2. a.** A preliminary survey made of a region to examine its terrain or to determine the disposition of enemy forces. **b.** A party making such a survey. [French, from Old French *reconoissance,* RECOGNIZANCE.]

re·con·noi·ter (rē′kə-noi′tər, rĕk′ə-) *v.* **-tered, -tering, -ters.** Also *chiefly British* **re·con·noi·tre, -tred, -tring, -tres.** *—tr.* To make a preliminary inspection of (an area or enemy positions, for example). *—intr.* To make a reconnaissance.
~*n.* An act of reconnoitering. [Obsolete French *reconnoître,* from Old French *reconoistre,* RECOGNIZE.] **—re·con·noi·ter·er** *n.*

re·con·sid·er (rē′kən-sĭd′ər) *v.* **-ered, -ering, -ers.** *—tr.* To consider (a decision, for example) again, with a view to possible revision. *—intr.* To consider a matter again and, especially, to come to a different decision. **—re·con·sid·er·a·tion** (rē′kən-sĭd′ə-rā′shən) *n.*

re·con·sti·tute (rē-kŏn′stĭ-to͞ot′, -tyo͞ot′) *tr.v.* **-tuted, -tuting, -tutes. 1.** To restore the constitution of (a concentrate or dried food, for example), as by the addition of water. **2.** To restore to existence or to an original condition; reconstruct. **—re·con·sti·tu·tion** (rē-kŏn′stə-to͞o′shən, -tyo͞o′shən) *n.*

re·con·struct (rē′kən-strŭkt′) *tr.v.* **-structed, -structing, -structs. 1.** To construct again; rebuild. **2. a.** To remake (something that is incomplete or damaged) guided by the available evidence: *reconstruct the orchestral score from the piano version.* **b.** To represent (an occurrence, such as a crime or historical event) in dramatic form on the basis of available evidence.

re·con·struc·tion (rē′kən-strŭk′shən) *n.* **1.** The act or result of reconstructing. **2. Reconstruction.** The period (1865–77) in the United States during which the states of the defeated Confederacy were administered directly by the federal government prior to their full readmission to the Union. **3.** *Finance.* **Reorganization** *(see).* **—re·con·struc·tive** *adj.*

re·con·vey (rē′kən-vā′) *tr.v.* **-veyed, -veying, -veys.** To convey back to a former owner or place. **—re·con·vey·ance** *n.*

rec·ord (rĕk′ərd) *n. Abbr.* **rec. 1. a.** An account made in an enduring form, especially in writing, that preserves the knowledge or memory of events or facts. **b.** The fact or condition of serving as such an account for future reference: *a newspaper of record.* **2.** Something on which such an account is made. **3.** *Often* **records.** Information or data on a particular subject collected and preserved: *look up parish records.* **4.** The known history of performance or achieve-

ment: *a fine war record.* **5.** The best performance known officially, as in a sport: *broke the world record.* **6.** *Law.* **a.** An account officially written and preserved as evidence or testimony. **b.** An account of judicial or legislative proceedings written and preserved as evidence. **c.** The documents or volumes containing such evidence. **7. a.** A disk with spiral grooves, designed to reproduce sound when played on a phonograph. **b.** A disk, spool, or cassette of magnetic tape on which sound or visual images have been registered for reproduction. **8.** Anything that provides a source of information about the past or preserves facts for reference: *Pop music is a record of contemporary youth culture.* **9.** An official report kept by the police of an individual's previous convictions. **10.** *Computer Science.* A small amount of data that is stored, processed, and retrieved as a single convenient unit. **—for the record.** For the sake of accuracy; as an official fact. **—off the record.** Confidentially or unofficially; not for publication. **—on record. 1.** Noted in official recordings of past facts or events: *the warmest summer on record.* **2.** Officially recorded or noted for public disclosure: *He is on record as having stated his acceptance of the new regime.*
~v. **re·cord** (rĭ-kôrd′), **-corded, -cording, -cords.** *—tr.* **1.** To set down for preservation in writing or other permanent form. **2.** To serve as a source of information about or as evidence of: *Her novel records a past way of life.* **3.** To register or indicate: *A thermometer records temperatures.* **4. a.** To register (a voice or piece of music, for example) in permanent form by mechanical or electrical means for reproduction. **b.** To perform (a piece of music, for example) that is to be registered in this way. *—intr.* To record something.
~adj. **rec·ord** (rĕk′ərd). *Abbr.* **rec.** Establishing a record: *a record crowd.* [Middle English *recorde,* from Old French *record,* from *recorder,* to record, from Latin *recordārī,* to remember, think over : *re-,* again + *cor* (stem *cord-*), mind, heart.]
rec·ord-break·ing (rĕk′ərd-brā′kĭng) *adj.* Establishing a new record: *a record-breaking time.*
re·cord·er (rĭ-kôr′dər) *n.* **1.** One that records, such as: **a.** An instrument for recording measurements. **b.** An official who records proceedings. **c.** A **tape recorder** *(see).* **2.** A flute, usually made entirely of wood, with eight fingerholes and a whistlelike mouthpiece, pitched in various ranges. Also called "English flute." **3.** *Law.* In England and Wales, a barrister or solicitor of at least ten years' standing who acts as a part-time municipal judge.
re·cord·ing (rĭ-kôr′dĭng) *n. Abbr.* **rec. 1.** A phonograph record or magnetic tape or wire upon which sound has been recorded. **2.** The sounds so recorded. **3.** The process of registering sound in a permanent form on a record or tape. **4.** A radio or television program that has been prerecorded.
Recording Angel *n.* An angel who supposedly registers the good and evil acts of every person.
recording studio *n.* See **studio** (sense 5).
record player *n.* A device for playing phonograph records, consisting of a single unit having a turntable, a pickup for converting vibrations of the needle into electrical signals, an amplifier, and one or more loudspeakers.
re-count (rē-kount′) *tr.v.* **-counted, -counting, -counts.** To count again.
~n. (rē′kount′, rē-kount′). An additional count; especially, a second count of votes cast in an election.
re·count (rĭ-kount′) *tr.v.* **-counted, -counting, -counts. 1.** To narrate the facts or details of. **2.** To enumerate. [Middle English *recounten,* from Old French *reconter* : *re-,* again, back + *conter, compter,* to relate, COUNT.] **—re·count·al** *n.*
re·coup (rĭ-ko͞op′) *v.* **-couped, -couping, -coups.** *—tr.* **1.** To receive or get back an equivalent for; make up for: *recoup the loss.* **2.** To return as an equivalent for; reimburse. **3.** *Law.* To deduct or withhold (part of something due) for a legally recognized reason. *—intr.* To regain a former favorable position. —See Usage note at **recover.** [Middle English *recoupen,* from Old French *recouper,* to cut back, retrench : *re-,* back + *couper,* to cut, strike, from *coup,* blow, COUP.] **—re·coup·a·ble** *adj.* **—re·coup·ment** *n.*
re·course (rē′kôrs′, -kōrs′, rĭ-kôrs′, -kōrs′) *n.* **1.** A turning or applying to a person or thing for aid or security: *have recourse to the courts.* **2.** One that is turned or applied to for aid or security: *His only recourse was the police.* **3.** *Law.* The right to demand payment from the endorser of a bill of exchange or other commercial paper when the first party liable fails to pay. —See Usage note at **resort.** [Middle English *recours,* from Old French, from Latin *recursus,* a running back, from *recurrere,* to run back : *re-,* again, back + *currere,* to run.]
re-cov·er (rē-kŭv′ər) *tr.v.* **-ered, -ering, -ers.** To cover again.
re·cov·er (rĭ-kŭv′ər) *v.* **-ered, -ering, -ers.** *—tr.* **1. a.** To get back or regain possession or control of (property). **b.** To retrieve; make up for: *recovered the time lost in the strike.* **2.** To restore (oneself) to a normal state, as after an illness or setback. **3.** To regain the use or enjoyment of: *recovered his health; land recovered from the sea.* **4.** *Law.* To gain as compensation by means of a favorable judgment in a civil lawsuit: *recover damages.* **5.** To derive (useful substances) from waste material. *—intr.* **1.** To regain a normal or usual condition or state, as of health or economic development. Often used with *from.* **2.** To receive a favorable judgment in a civil lawsuit. **3.** In swimming or rowing, to stretch the arm or oar forward in preparation for another stroke. [Middle English *recoveren,* from Old French *recoverer,* from Latin *recuperāre,* to RECUPERATE.] **—re·cov·er·a·ble** *adj.* **—re·cov·er·er** *n.*
Usage: *recover, reclaim, regain, recoup, retrieve. Recover* refers to the getting back of something lost. *Reclaim* applies both to the act of demanding the return of something and to the restoration of a thing to good condition. *Regain* suggests effort in getting back something lost or taken, usually a quality or status rather than an object. *Recoup* means getting back the equivalent of something lost or damaged. *Retrieve* pertains either to the physical recovery of a thing or to the repair or remedy of the consequences of an act.
re·cov·er·y (rĭ-kŭv′ə-rē) *n., pl.* **-ies. 1.** An act, instance, process, or duration of recovering; recuperation. **2.** A return to a normal condition. **3.** Something gained or restored in recovering. **4.** The obtaining of usable substances from unusable sources, such as waste material. **5.** *Law.* The process of recovering compensation, damages, or the like by a lawsuit. **6.** In fencing, the returning to an on guard position. **7.** In swimming or rowing, the action of recovering. **8.** In golf, a stroke to bring a ball out of a bunker or away from the rough.
recovery room *n.* A hospital room used for the care and observation of patients immediately after surgery.
rec·re·ant (rĕk′rē-ənt) *adj.* **1.** Unfaithful or disloyal to a belief, promise, or cause. **2.** Craven or cowardly.
~n. **1.** A faithless or disloyal person; an apostate. **2.** A coward. [Middle English *recreant,* from Old French, present participle of *recroire,* to yield, surrender, from Medieval Latin *recrēdere* : Latin *re-,* back, contrarily + *crēdere,* entrust, believe.] **—rec·re·ance, rec·re·an·cy** *n.* **—rec·re·ant·ly** *adv.*
re-cre·ate (rē′krē-āt′) *tr.v.* **-ated, -ating, -ates.** To reproduce (something that formerly existed); create anew. **—re-cre·a·tion** *n.*
rec·re·ate (rĕk′rē-āt′) *v.* **-ated, -ating, -ates.** *—tr.* To impart fresh life to; refresh mentally or physically. *—intr.* To take recreation; amuse oneself. [Latin *recreāre,* to create anew : *re-,* back, again + *creāre,* to CREATE.] **—rec·re·a·tive** (rĕk′rē-ā′tĭv) *adj.*
rec·re·a·tion (rĕk′rē-ā′shən) *n. Abbr.* **rec. 1.** Refreshment of one's mind or body through diverting activity. **2.** A form of relaxation or pleasurable exercise that fosters this. **—rec·re·a·tion·al** *adj.*
recreational vehicle *n.* A vehicle, as a camper or a motor home, used for pleasure traveling and recreation.
recreation ground *n. Chiefly British.* A piece of public land used for recreational activities, often equipped with swings, slides, and the like.
rec·re·ment (rĕk′rə-mənt) *n.* Waste matter; refuse; dross. [Latin *recrēmentum* : *re-,* back, again + *cernere,* to separate, sift.] **—rec·re·men·tal** (rĕk′rə-mĕn′təl) *adj.*
re·crim·i·nate (rĭ-krĭm′ə-nāt′) *v.* **-nated, -nating, -nates.** *—tr.* To accuse in return. *—intr.* To make an accusation against an accuser. [Medieval Latin *recrīmināre* : Latin *re-,* again, back + *crīmināre,* to accuse, from *crīmen,* accusation.] **—re·crim·i·na·tive** (rĭ-krĭm′ə-nā′tĭv), **re·crim·i·na·to·ry** (rĭ-krĭm′ə-nə-tôr′ē, -tōr′ē) *adj.* **—re·crim·i·na·tor** *n.*
re·crim·i·na·tion (rĭ-krĭm′ə-nā′shən) *n.* **1.** The act of recriminating, especially in a bitter way; mutual accusation. **2.** A bitter accusation, especially against an accuser; countercharge.
re·cru·desce (rē′kro͞o-dĕs′) *intr.v.* **-desced, -descing, -desces.** To break out anew after a dormant or inactive period. Used especially of something undesirable, such as a disease or state of discontent. —See Usage note at **return.** [Latin *recrūdēscere* : *re-,* again + *crūdēscere,* to get worse, from *crūdus,* harsh, raw.] **—re·cru·des·cence** *n.* **—re·cru·des·cent** *adj.*
re·cruit (rĭ-kro͞ot′) *v.* **-cruited, -cruiting, -cruits.** *—tr.* **1.** To enlist for military service. **2.** To strengthen or raise (an armed force) by enlistment. **3. a.** To obtain (new members or employees, for example). **b.** To supply with new members or employees. **4.** To enroll (another) in support of oneself or one's ideas: *"That's the struggle of humanity, to recruit others to your vision of what's real."* (Saul Bellow). **5.** To replenish. **6.** To renew or restore (health or vitality). *—intr.* **1.** To seek or enlist new members or recruits. **2.** To regain lost health or strength; recover: *"I believe the brain stands as much in need of recruiting as the body"* (Sterne).
~n. **1.** *Abbr.* **rct.** A newly enlisted member of a military force; especially, one of the lowest rank or grade. **2.** A new member of any organization or body. [Obsolete French dialectal *recrute,* new growth, from *recrue,* past participle of *recroître,* to grow again, from Latin *recrēscere* : *re-,* again + *crēscere,* to grow.] **—re·cruit·er** *n.* **—re·cruit·ment** *n.*
re·crys·tal·lize (rē-krĭs′tə-līz′) *v.* **-lized, -lizing, -lizes.** *—tr.* To dissolve (a substance) and then crystallize, especially so as to purify. *—intr.* **1.** To be recrystallized. **2.** To form new crystals or a crystal structure. Used of a deformed metal. **—re·crys·tal·li·za·tion** *n.*
rec't receipt.
rect. 1. receipt. **2.** rectangle; rectangular. **3.** rectified. **4.** rector; rectory.
rec·tal (rĕk′təl) *adj.* Pertaining to, near, or administered via the rectum. **—rec·tal·ly** *adv.*
rec·tan·gle (rĕk′tang′gəl) *n. Abbr.* **rect.** *Geometry.* A parallelogram with right angles. [Medieval Latin *rēctangulum* : Latin *rēctus,* right + *angulus,* ANGLE.]
rec·tan·gu·lar (rĕk-tăng′gyə-lər) *adj. Abbr.* **rect 1.** Having the shape of a rectangle. **2.** Having right angles. Said of a geometric figure, such as a spherical triangle. **3.** Having or pertaining to lines or planes that are mutually perpendicular: *a rectangular coordinate system.* **4.** Having a base that is a rectangle. Said of geometric solids. **—rec·tan·gu·lar·i·ty** (rĕk-tăng′gyə-lăr′ə-tē) *n.* **—rec·tan·gu·lar·ly** *adv.*
rectangular coordinate *n. Geometry.* A coordinate in a **Cartesian**

PRONUNCIATION KEY
ă, pat; ā, pay; âr, care;
ä, father, are; b, bib;
ch, church; d, deed; ĕ, pet;
ē, be; f, fife; g, gag; h, hat;
hw, which; ĭ, pit; ī, pie;
îr, pier; j, judge; k, kick;
l, lid, needle; m, mum;
n, no, sudden; ng, thing;
ŏ, pot; ō, toe; ô, paw, for;
oi, noise; ou, out; o͝o, book;
o͞o, boot; p, pop; r, roar;
s, sauce; sh, ship, dish;
t, tight; th, thin, path;
th, this, bathe; ŭ, cut; ûr, fur;
v, valve; w, with; y, yes;
z, zebra, size; zh, vision;
ə, about, item, edible,
gallop, circus, peaceful

IN FOREIGN WORDS:
à, *Fr.* ami; œ, *Fr.* feu, *Ger.* schön; ü, *Fr.* tu, *Ger.* über; KH, *Ger.* ich, *Scot.* loch; N, *Fr.* bon; y′, *Fr.* Compiègne

STRESS MARKS:
Primary stress: ′
in·cite′ (ĭn-sīt′)
Secondary stress: ′
in′sight′ (ĭn′sīt′)

coordinate system *(see)* that has the coordinate axes at right angles.

rectangular hyperbola *n. Geometry.* A hyperbola for which the two asymptotes are at right angles. It has an equation of the form $xy = e$ in Cartesian coordinates.

rec·ti·fi·er (rĕk′tə-fī′ər) *n.* **1.** A person or thing that rectifies. **2.** *Electricity.* A device, such as a diode, that converts alternating current to direct current. **3.** A worker who blends or dilutes whiskey or other alcoholic beverages. **4.** *Chemistry.* A condenser used to separate or purify.

rec·ti·fy (rĕk′tə-fī′) *tr.v.* **-fied, -fying, -fies. 1.** To set right; correct. **2.** To correct by calculation or adjustment. **3.** *Chemistry.* To refine or purify, especially by distillation. **4.** *Electricity.* To convert (alternating current) into direct current. **5.** To adjust (the proof of alcoholic beverages) by adding water or other liquids. —See Synonyms at **correct.** [Middle English *rectifien,* from Old French *rectifier,* from Medieval Latin *rēctificāre* : Latin *rēctus,* straight + *facere,* to make.] **—rec·ti·fi·a·ble** *adj.* **—rec·ti·fi·ca·tion** *n.*

rec·ti·lin·e·ar (rĕk′tə-lĭn′ē-ər) *adj.* Moving in, consisting of, bounded by, or characterized by a straight line or lines. [Late Latin *rēctilīneus* : *rēctus,* straight + *līnea,* LINE.] **—rec·ti·lin·e·ar·ly** *adv.*

rec·ti·tude (rĕk′tə-tōōd′, -tyōōd′) *n.* **1.** Moral uprightness. **2.** Rightness, as of intellectual judgment. **3.** Straightness. [Middle English, from Old French, from Late Latin *rēctitūdō,* from Latin *rēctus,* straight.]

rec·to (rĕk′tō) *n., pl.* **-tos.** The right-hand page of a book or front side of a leaf, as opposed to the **verso** *(see).* [Latin *rēctō (foliō),* on the right side of (a page), ablative of *rēctus,* right, straight.]

rec·tor (rĕk′tər) *n. Abbr.* **R., rect. 1.** A member of the clergy in charge of a parish in the Protestant Episcopal and Anglican churches. In former times, an Anglican rector owned the tithes from his parish. **2.** *Roman Catholic Church.* A priest appointed to be the administrative as well as spiritual head of a church or other institution such as a seminary or university. **3. a.** The principal of certain schools, colleges, and universities. **b.** In Scottish universities, a representative, often a prominent public figure, elected by the students to the governing body. [Latin *rēctor,* governor, from *rēctus,* past participle of *regere,* to rule.] **—rec·tor·ate** (rĕk′tə-rĭt) *n.* **—rec·to·ri·al** (rĕk-tôr′ē-əl, -tōr′ē-əl) *adj.*

rec·to·ry (rĕk′tə-rē) *n., pl.* **-ries.** *Abbr.* **rect. 1.** The house in which a rector lives. **2.** A rector's office.

rec·trix (rĕk′trĭks) *n., pl.* **rectrices** (rĕk′trə-sēz′, rĕk-trī′sēz) Any of the stiff main feathers of a bird's tail. [Latin, feminine of *rēctor,* governor (the feathers help regulate flight). See **rector.**]

rec·tum (rĕk′təm) *n., pl.* **-tums** or **-ta** (-tə). The portion of the large intestine extending from the sigmoid flexure of the colon to the anal canal. Also called "back passage." [New Latin *rectum (intestinum),* straight (intestine), from Latin *rēctus,* straight.]

rec·tus (rĕk′təs) *n., pl.* **-ti** (-tī). Any of various straight muscles, as of the abdomen, eye, neck, and thigh. [New Latin, from Latin *rēctus,* straight.]

re·cum·bent (rĭ-kŭm′bənt) *adj.* **1.** Lying down; reclining. **2.** Resting; idle. **3.** *Biology.* Resting upon the surface from which it arises: *a recumbent organ.* **4.** *Geology.* Designating or pertaining to a fold in a rock formation in which the strata in the fold lie almost parallel to those in the rest of the formation. —See Usage note at **prone.** [Latin *recumbēns* (stem *recumbent-*), present participle of *recumbere,* to lie down : *re-,* back, again + *-cumbere,* to lie.] **—re·cum·bence, re·cum·ben·cy** *n.* **—re·cum·bent·ly** *adv.*

re·cu·per·ate (rĭ-kōō′pə-rāt′, rĭ-kyōō′-) *v.* **-ated, -ating, -ates.** —*intr.* **1.** To return to health or strength; recover. **2.** To recover from financial loss. —*tr.* **1.** To restore to health or strength. **2.** To regain. [Latin *recuperāre* : RE- + *cup-,* from *capere,* to take.] **—re·cu·per·a·tion** *n.* **—re·cu·per·a·tive** (rĭ-kōō′pə-rā′tĭv, -pər-ə-tĭv, rĭ-kyōō′-), **re·cu·per·a·to·ry** (rĭ-kōō′pər-ə-tôr′ē, -tōr′ē, rĭ-kyōō′-) *adj.*

re·cu·per·a·tor (rĭ-kōō′pə-rā′tər, rĭ-kyōō′-) *n.* A heat exchanger using the waste heat from the flue gases of a furnace to heat the incoming air.

re·cur (rĭ-kûr′) *intr.v.* **-curred, -curring, -curs. 1.** To happen or come up again or repeatedly. **2.** To return to one's thoughts or attention: *a recurring nightmare.* **3.** To go back, as in thought, memory, or discourse. Used with *to.* **4.** *Mathematics.* To occur or be repeated an infinite number of times. Used of digits or groups of digits in a repeating decimal fraction. —See Usage note at **return.** [Latin *recurrere,* to run back : *re-,* back + *currere,* to run.] **—re·cur·rence** (rĭ-kûr′əns) *n.*

re·cur·rent (rĭ-kûr′ənt) *adj.* **1.** Occurring or appearing again or repeatedly; returning regularly. **2.** *Anatomy.* Running in a reverse direction. Said of arteries and nerves that turn back on themselves. **—re·cur·rent·ly** *adv.*

recurring decimal *n. Mathematics.* A repeating decimal *(see).*

recurrent fever *n.* **Relapsing fever** *(see).*

re·cur·sion (rĭ-kûr′zhən) *adj. Mathematics & Logic.* **1.** A repeated process or formula for generating or defining a series of terms, such as successive terms in a polynomial expression. Used adjectively. **2.** An expression generated in this way. [Late Latin *recursiō* (stem *recursiōn-*), a return, from Latin *recurrere* (past participle *recursus*), to RECUR.] **—re·cur·sive** (rĭ-kûr′sĭv) *adj.*

re·cur·vate (rĭ-kûr′vāt′, -vĭt) *adj.* Bent or curved backward. [Latin *recurvātus,* past participle of *recurvāre,* to RECURVE.]

re·curve (rē-kûrv′) *v.* **-curved, -curving, -curves.** —*tr.* To bend or curve backward or downward. —*intr.* To become recurved. [Latin *recurvāre* : *re-,* back, backward + *curvāre,* to curve, from *curvus,* CURVE.] **—re·cur·va·tion** (rē′kûr-vā′shən) *n.*

red currant *This fruit-bearing shrub was first cultivated in northwestern Europe, but the name comes partly from Greece. Red currants, like other currants, are so called because of the berries' similarity to the raisins of Corinth.*

rec·u·sant (rĕk′yə-zənt, rĭ-kyōō′-) *n.* **1.** A Roman Catholic who refused to attend the services of the Church of England between the reigns of Henry VIII and George II. **2.** A dissenter; a nonconformist. [Latin *recusāns* (stem *recusant-*), present participle of *recusāre,* to refuse : *re-,* contrary to, back + *causa,* CAUSE.] **—rec·u·san·cy** (rĕk′yə-zən-sē, rĭ-kyōō′zən-sē) *n.* **—rec·u·sant** *adj.*

re·cuse (rĭ-kyōōz′) *tr.v.* **-cused, -cusing, -cuses.** To challenge or object to (a judge or juror) on such grounds as his prejudice or lack of qualification. [Latin *recusāre,* to refuse. See **recusant.**]

re·cy·cle (rē-sī′kəl) *tr.v.* **-cled, -cling, -cles. 1.** To put or pass through a cycle again, as for further treatment. **2.** To start a different cycle in. **3. a.** To make new use of or to process for reuse (used and discarded objects and material). **b.** To extract useful materials from (rubbish, waste, or the like). **c.** To extract and reuse (useful substances found in waste). **—re·cy·cla·ble** *adj.*

red[1] (rĕd) *n.* **1.** Any of a group of colors that may vary in lightness and saturation, whose hue resembles that of fresh blood; the hue of the long-wavelength end of the spectrum; one of the additive or light primaries; one of the psychological primary hues, evoked in the normal observer by the long-wavelength end of the spectrum. See **primary color. 2.** A pigment or dye having or giving this hue. **3.** Something that has this hue, such as: **a.** Clothing or material: *She wore red.* **b.** A red ball used in some games, such as billiards, snooker, or croquet. **c.** One of the two colors on which bets may be placed in roulette and rouge-et-noir. **d.** A red light *(see).* **4.** *Often* **Red.** *Informal.* **a.** A Communist or radical revolutionary activist. **b.** A citizen of a Communist country. Often used derogatorily. **—in the red.** Having a debit rather than a credit balance; in debt. **—see red.** To become suddenly furious.
  ~*adj.* **redder, reddest. 1.** Having a color resembling that of blood. **2.** Reddish in color, or having parts that are reddish in color. Used in animal and plant names: *red fox; red oak.* **3. a.** Designating hair or an animal's coat having a color ranging from orange and copper-colored, to reddish brown. **b.** Having a coppery skin tone. **4.** Having a ruddy or flushed complexion, as from exertion or embarrassment. **5.** Bloodshot or red-rimmed. Said of eyes. **6.** Colored by the skins of the black grapes from which it is made. Said of wine. **7.** Involving or concerned with bloodshed or violence. **8.** *Often* **Red.** *Informal.* **a.** Radical or revolutionary in nature: *red political theories.* **b.** Of, pertaining to, or caused by revolution or revolutionaries: *red scare.* **c.** Communist or having a Communist government: *Red China.* **9.** Designating one of the three quark colors. The other two are blue and green. [Middle English *red, read,* Old English *rēad.*] **—red·ly** *adv.* **—red·ness** *n.*

red[2]. Variant of **redd.**

red. reduced; reduction.

re·dact (rĭ-dăkt′) *tr.v.* **-dacted, -dacting, -dacts. 1.** To draw up or draft (a proclamation or edict, for example). **2.** To make ready for publication; edit or revise. [Latin *redigere* (past participle *redactus*), to collect, drive back : *re-,* back + *agere,* to drive, do.] **—re·dac·tor** (rĭ-dăk′tər, -tôr′) *n.* **—re·dac·tion** (rĭ-dăk′shən) *n.*

red admiral *n.* A Eurasian and American butterfly, *Vanessa atalanta,* the wings of which are black with red and white markings.

red alert *n.* A state of readiness for an imminent danger, such as a natural disaster or enemy attack.

red algae *pl.n.* Algae of the division Rhodophyta, characteristically red or reddish in color and including dulse and similar seaweeds.

red-bait (rĕd′bāt′) *tr.v.* **-baited, -baiting, -baits.** To attack or denounce (a person or group) as Communist. **—red-bait·er** *n.* **—red-bait·ing** *n.*

red bark *n.* A form of cinchona that is reddish in color and has a high alkaloid content.

red beds *pl.n. Geology.* Sequences of red sedimentary rocks, especially sandstones or shales, formed in a highly oxidizing environment, the iron present being oxidized to red ferric oxide.

red·bird (rĕd′bûrd′) *n.* Any of various birds with red plumage, especially the cardinal.

red blood cell *n. Abbr.* **RBC.** An **erythrocyte** *(see).* Also called "red blood corpuscle."

red-blood·ed (rĕd′blŭd′ĭd) *adj. Informal.* Strong, brave, or virile.

red·breast (rĕd′brĕst′) *n.* **1.** Any of various birds with a red breast; especially the **robin** *(see).* **2.** A freshwater sunfish, *Lepomis auritus,* of eastern North America.

red·brick (rĕd′brĭk′) *adj.* Of or designating a British university dating from the late 19th century, especially as distinguished from Oxford or Cambridge, and from those founded since World War II.

Red Brigade *n.* A terrorist group formed in Italy in 1969 and committed to the abolition of capitalist society.

red·bud (rĕd′bŭd′) *n.* Any of several American shrubs or small trees of the genus *Cercis,* especially the **Judas tree** *(see).*

red·cap (rĕd′kăp′) *n.* A baggage porter, usually at a railroad station.

red carpet *n.* **1.** A carpet laid down for important visitors. **2.** Deferential or ceremoniously hospitable treatment.

red cedar *n.* **1.** An evergreen tree, *Juniperus virginiana,* of eastern North America. Also called "savin." **2.** A tall evergreen tree, *Thuya plicata,* of western North America. **3.** The reddish, aromatic, durable wood of this or of similar trees.

red cell *n.* An **erythrocyte** *(see).* Also called "red corpuscle."

Red China. An informal name for the People's Republic of **China.**

Red Cloud (1822–1909). U.S. Oglala Sioux Indian chief. Between 1865 and 1869 in a series of battles and guerrilla activities called Red Cloud's War, he forced the whites to abandon a series of garrisons in present-day Nebraska. After signing a treaty with the

United States (1869), he advocated peace and toured Washington, D.C., and other eastern cities.

red clover *n.* A Eurasian plant, *Trifolium pratense,* widely naturalized and planted as a forage or cover crop. It has leaflets in groups of three and globular heads of fragrant, rose-purple flowers.

red·coat (rĕd′kōt′) *n.* A British soldier during the American Revolution and the War of 1812.

red coral *n.* Any of various corals of the genus *Corallium,* having pinkish-red skeletons used to make jewelry and ornaments.

Red Crescent *n.* **1.** A branch of the Red Cross Society in a Muslim country. **2.** The emblem of such a branch.

Red Cross *n.* **1.** *Abbr.* **R.C.** An international organization, formed according to the terms of the Geneva Convention of 1864, for the care of the wounded, sick, and homeless in wartime and now also during and following natural disasters. Also officially called "Red Cross Society." **2.** Any national branch of this organization. **3.** The emblem of the organization, a Geneva cross or red Greek cross on a white background.

red currant *n.* **1.** Any of several shrubs of the genus *Ribes* that are cultivated for their small, acid-tasting, red fruits. **2.** The fruit of such a shrub, used to make jams and other preserves.

redd (rĕd) *tr.v.* **redd** or **redded, redding, redds.** Also **red, red, redding, reds.** *Regional.* To put in order; arrange. Used with *up.* [Middle English *redden,* probably variant of *ridden,* to RID.]

red deer *n.* A common Eurasian deer, *Cervus elaphus,* having a reddish-brown coat and many-branched antlers.

red·den (rĕd′n) *v.* **-dened, -dening, -dens.** —*tr.* To make red or redder. —*intr.* To become red; to become flushed or to blush.

red·dish (rĕd′ĭsh) *adj.* Mixed or tinged with red; somewhat red. **—red·dish·ness** *n.*

reddle. Variant of **ruddle.**

red-dog (rĕd′dôg′, -dŏg′) *v.* **-dogged, -dogging, -dogs.** *Football.* —*intr.* To charge across the line of scrimmage in an attempt to overwhelm the opposing quarterback before he can throw a pass. Used of linebackers and defensive backs. —*tr.* To charge (the passer) in this way.
∼*n.* The act or an instance of red-dogging.

red dwarf *n.* *Astronomy.* Any of a small class of mostly main-sequence stars that are generally cool and small.

rede (rēd) *tr.v.* **reded, reding, redes.** *Archaic.* **1.** To give advice to; counsel. **2.** To interpret; explain or tell.
∼*n.* *Archaic.* **1.** Advice or counsel. **2.** An interpretation or narration. [Middle English *reden,* to guide, direct, Old English *rǣdan.*]

re·dec·o·rate (rē-dĕk′ə-rāt′) *v.* **-rated, -rating, -rates.** —*tr.* To change the décor of, as by painting and renewing furnishings. —*intr.* To change the décor of a room, building, or the like. **—re·dec·o·ra·tion** (rē-dĕk′ə-rā′shən) *n.*

re·deem (rĭ-dēm′) *tr.v.* **-deemed, -deeming, -deems. 1. a.** To recover ownership of by paying a stipulated sum. **b.** To recover (pawned goods or mortaged land, for example) by payment. **2.** To pay off (a promissory note or loan, for example). **3.** To turn in (coupons or trading stamps, for example) and receive something in exchange. **4.** To fulfill (an oath, pledge, or promise). **5. a.** To convert (tokens or shares, for example) into cash. **b.** To convert (stocks, for example) into cash. **6.** To rescue or set free by paying a ransom. **7.** *Theology.* To save from a state of sinfulness and its consequences. **8.** To make up for; make amends for. **9.** To put (oneself) back in favor. —See Synonyms at **save.** [Middle English *redemen,* from Latin *redimere,* to buy back : *red-, re-,* back, again + *emere,* to take, buy.]

re·deem·a·ble (rĭ-dē′mə-bəl) *adj.* **1.** Capable of being converted into cash. Said, for example, of tokens or shares. **2.** Able to be repaid and thereby cancelled either at a fixed date or subject to notice. Said, for example, of bonds or debentures. **3.** Capable of being saved or redeemed.

re·deem·er (rĭ-dē′mər) *n.* **1.** One who redeems; a savior. **2. Redeemer.** Jesus Christ, who, in Christian belief, redeemed mankind from sinfulness by his death on the Cross.

re·deem·ing (rĭ-dē′mĭng) *adj.* Making up for or compensating for other faults or inadequacies: *He has one redeeming feature.*

re·de·fine (rē′dĭ-fīn′) *tr.v.* **-fined, -fining, -fines.** To define again, especially in a different way.

re·demp·tion (rĭ-dĕmp′shən) *n.* **1.** The act or an instance of redeeming or the condition of being redeemed. **2.** A recovery of something pawned or mortgaged; a repurchase. **3.** The payment of an obligation, such as a government's or corporation's payment of the value of its bonds. **4.** *Theology.* Salvation from sin through Christ's death on the Cross. **5.** Release from a danger or evil. **—beyond** (or **past**) **redemption.** No longer able to be saved, made good, or restored. [Middle English *redempcioun,* from Old French *redemption,* from Latin *redemptiō* (stem *redemptiōn-*), from *redimere* (past participle *redemptus*), to REDEEM.] **—re·demp·tion·al, re·demp·tive, re·demp·to·ry** (rĭ-dĕmp′tə-rē) *adj.*

re·demp·tion·er (rĭ-dĕmp′shən-ər) *n.* In Colonial America, an emigrant from Europe who paid for his voyage by serving as a bondservant for a stipulated period.

Re·demp·tor·ist (rĭ-dĕmp′tər-ĭst) *n.* A member of a Roman Catholic order, the Congregation of the Most Holy Redeemer, founded by St. Alphonsus de Liguori in 1732 to do missionary work. [Latin *redemptor,* redeemer.]

re·de·ploy (rē′dĭ-ploi′) *tr.v.* **-ployed, -ploying, -ploys. 1.** To move (military forces) from one combat zone to another. **2.** To assign new tasks to (workers). **—re·de·ploy·ment** *n.*

re·de·sign (rē′dĭ-zīn′) *tr.v.* **-signed, -signing, -signs.** To produce a new design for. **—re·de·sign** *n.*

re·de·vel·op (rē′dĭ-vĕl′əp) *v.* **-oped, -oping, -opes.** —*tr.* **1.** To develop (something) again. **2.** *Photography.* To tone or intensify (a developed negative) by a second developing process. **3.** To rebuild (an area, for example) according to new plans. —*intr.* To develop again. **—re·de·vel·op·er** *n.* **—re·de·vel·op·ment** *n.*

red·eye (rĕd′ī′) *n.* **1.** *Informal.* A danger signal on a railroad. **2.** *Slang.* Whiskey of an inferior grade. **3.** Any of several red-eyed fishes. **4.** *Slang.* A late-night or overnight flight.

red-faced (rĕd′fāst′) *adj.* Having a flushed face owing to embarrassment, anger, intoxication, or the like. **—red-faced·ly** *adv.*

red·fin (rĕd′fĭn′) *n.* Any of several small, freshwater fishes of the genus *Notropis,* such as *N. cornutus,* that have reddish fins and are often kept in aquariums.

red fir *n.* **1.** An evergreen coniferous tree, *Abies magnifica,* of California and Oregon, having reddish wood valued as timber. **2.** The wood of this tree, or of similar trees, such as the **Douglas fir** *(see).*

red fire *n.* Any of various combustible compounds, especially containing salts of lithium or strontium, that burn with a bright red flame and are used in flares and fireworks.

red·fish (rĕd′fĭsh′) *n., pl.* **-fishes** or collectively **redfish. 1.** A male salmon that has just spawned. Compare **blackfish. 2.** Any of several fishes that are reddish in color.

red fox *n.* Any of several foxes of the genus *Vulpes,* having reddish fur; especially, *V. vulpes,* of the Northern Hemisphere.

Red·ford (rĕd′fərd), **Robert** (1937–). U.S. actor and film director. His reputation as one of the biggest box-office stars was established in films such as *Butch Cassidy and the Sundance Kid* (1969), *The Candidate* (1972), *The Way We Were* (1973), *The Sting* (1973), and *All the President's Men* (1976). For the first film he directed, *Ordinary People,* he won an Academy Award as best director (1981).

red giant *n.* *Astronomy.* Any of a class of stars that are usually cool, very large, and are believed to be formed in the final stages of the evolution of certain stars.

Red·grave (rĕd′grāv′), **Sir Michael Scudamore** (1908–85). British actor. Beginning his stage career with the Liverpool Repertory Theatre in 1934, he went on to become one of the leading actors of his generation, especially in the plays of Shakespeare. His films include *The Lady Vanishes* (1938), *Dam Busters* (1954), and *Goodbye Mr. Chips* (1969). His daughters **Lynn** (1943–) and **Vanessa** and his son **Corin** (1939–) are all experienced stage and screen actors.

Redgrave, Vanessa (1937–). British actress. She won the *Evening Standard* award as best actress (1961) for her performances in *The Taming of the Shrew* and *As You Like It* with the Royal Shakespeare company. Her motion pictures include *Morgan* (1966), *Isadora* (1969), and *Julia* (1977), for which she won an Academy Award as best supporting actress.

red grouse *n.* A reddish-brown grouse, *Lagopus lagopus,* of British moorlands. Formerly called "moorcock."

Red Guard *n.* A member of a militant Chinese youth organization that denounced opposition to the **Cultural Revolution** *(see).*

red gum[1] *n.* **1.** Any of several Australian trees of the genus *Eucalyptus,* especially, *E. camaldulensis.* **2.** The hard, reddish wood of any of these trees.

red gum[2] *n.* A disease, **strophulus** *(see).*

red-hand·ed (rĕd′hăn′dĭd) *adj.* In the act of committing, or having just committed, a crime; in flagrante delicto: *caught red-handed.* **—red-hand·ed** *adv.* **—red-hand·ed·ly** *adv.*

red hat *n.* **1.** A large, red, tasseled hat presented to a newly created cardinal. It is never worn. **2.** This hat as a symbol of a cardinal's office.

red·head (rĕd′hĕd′) *n.* **1.** A person with red hair. **2.** A North American duck, *Aythya americana,* of which the male has black and gray plumage and a reddish head.

red heat *n.* **1.** The temperature of a red-hot substance. **2.** The physical condition of a red-hot substance.

red herring *n.* **1.** Something that draws attention away from the matter or issue at hand. **2.** A smoked herring having a reddish color. [From the use of red herring to give the scent in exercising hunting dogs.]

red-hot (rĕd′hŏt′) *adj.* **1.** Heated so as to emit red light (a temperature of about 500°C). **2.** Very hot. **3.** Heated, as with excitement, anger, or enthusiasm. **4.** New; very recent: *red-hot information.*
∼*n.* *Slang.* A **hot dog** *(see).*

re·di·a (rē′dē-ə) *n., pl.* **-diae** (-dē-ē′). A larva of parasitic flukes that gives rise to other rediae or to cercaria larvae. [New Latin, after Francesco *Redi* (1629–97), Italian naturalist.]

Red Indian *n.* A North American Indian.

red·in·gote (rĕd′ĭng-gōt′) *n.* **1.** A man's long double-breasted overcoat with a full skirt. **2.** A woman's full-length unlined coat or dress open down the front to show a dress or underskirt. [French, from English *riding coat.*]

red ink *n.* **1.** A financial loss in business. **2.** Deficit. [From the use of red ink to record debits in financial records.]

red·in·te·grate (rĭ-dĭn′tə-grāt′) *v.* **-grated, -grating, -grates.** —*tr.* To restore to a complete, whole, or harmonious state. —*intr.* *Psychology.* To undergo redintegration. [Middle English, from Latin *redintegrāre* : *red-,* RE- + *integrāre,* to INTEGRATE.]

red·in·te·gra·tion (rĭ-dĭn′tə-grā′shən) *n.* **1.** *Psychology.* The revival of a complete previous mental state due to recurrence of part of the complex of stimuli that gave rise to that previous mental state. **2.** The act or process or redintegrating.

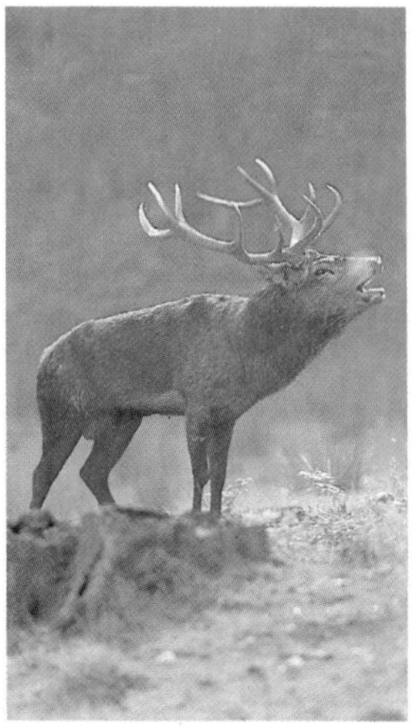

red deer *Native to the woodlands of Europe, Asia, and northwestern Africa, the red deer has long been hunted for both sport and food. The stags and hinds live separately except during the autumn breeding season. It is similar to, but smaller than, its North American counterpart, the wapiti.*

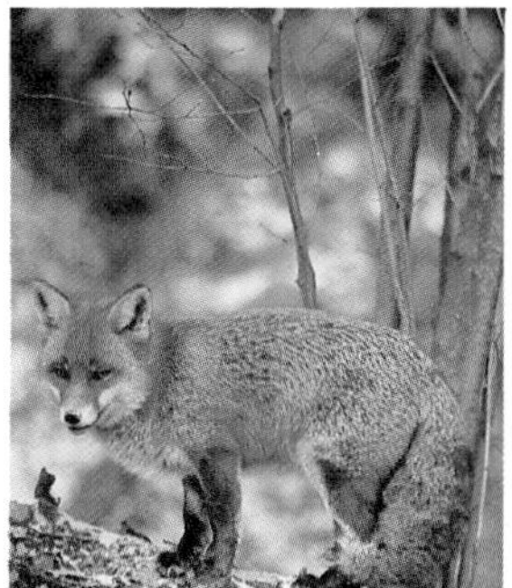

red fox *The red fox is the common fox of North America, Europe, and Asia. Adaptable in habits and diet, it manages to thrive even in towns and cities.*

redpoll *Redpolls are seed eaters and make their nests in pine, birch, and alder trees. The male redpoll (above) is distinguished by its red forehead and pink breast.*

redshank *For most of the year, redshanks are sociable birds, often gathering in large flocks on muddy open shores. But from mid-April to June, mating pairs retire to build their nests away from the flock in damp grassy areas or marshland. The birds breed in Europe and Asia, but most migrate during the northern winter, sometimes as far as India and South Africa.*

red squirrel *Of the 200 species of squirrel, the red and gray squirrels are the most common. The red squirrel shown above is a Eurasian species that lives mostly in pine woods.*

re·dis·trib·ute (rē′dĭs-trĭb′yŏŏt) *tr.v.* **-uted, -uting, -utes.** To distribute again in a different way; reallocate. **—re·dis·tri·bu·tion** (rē-dĭs′trĭ-byŏŏ′shən) *n.* **—re·dis·trib·u·tive** (rē′dĭs-trĭb′yə-tĭv) *adj.*

Red Jacket (*c.* 1756–1830). U.S. Seneca Indian leader. Although he fought along with the British during the American Revolution, he advocated peace with the United States when the war ended. Staunchly opposed to Christianity, he attempted to keep peace with whites while resisting their geographic and cultural encroachment.

red lead *n.* A bright-red powder, Pb₃O₄, used in paints, glass, pottery, and pipe-joint packing. Also called "minium."

red Leicester *n.* See **Leicester** (sense 2).

red-let·ter (rĕd′lĕt′ər) *adj.* Memorable: *a red-letter day.* [From the rubrication of feasts in church calendars.]

red light *n.* **1.** A red traffic light or other signal to stop. Also called "red." **2.** A danger signal.

red-light district (rĕd′līt′) *n.* A district containing many brothels.

red maple *n.* A medium-sized American maple, *Acer rubrum,* having reddish twigs and buds.

red meat *n.* Dark-colored meat, such as beef or lamb. Compare **white meat.**

red mulberry *n.* A tree, *Morus rubra,* of eastern and central North America, having irregularly lobed leaves and edible, blackberrylike fruit.

red mullet *n.* A goatfish (see).

red-neck (rĕd′nĕk′) *n.* **1.** *Slang.* A member of the white rural laboring class in the southern United States. **2.** *Offensive Slang.* A person who advocates a provincial, conservative, often bigoted sociopolitical attitude considered characteristic of a redneck. [Referring to the sunburned necks of laborers.]

re·do (rē′dŏŏ′) *tr.v.* **-did** (-dĭd′), **-done** (-dŭn′), **-doing, -does** (-dŭz′). **1.** To do again. **2.** To redecorate thoroughly; refurbish.

red ocher *n.* **1.** A natural red mixture of clay and iron oxide. See **ocher. 2.** A refined form of this mixture used as pigment.

red·o·lent (rĕd′ə-lənt) *adj.* **1.** Having or emitting fragrance; pleasantly odorous. **2.** Smelling. Used with *of: boatyards redolent of tar.* **3.** Evocative or reminiscent. Used with *of* or *with: music redolent of Mozart.* [Middle English, from Old French, from Latin *redolēns* (stem *redolent-*), present participle of *redolēre,* to emit an odor : *red-, re-,* in response, back + *olēre,* to smell.] **—red·o·lence, red·o·len·cy** *n.* **—red·o·lent·ly** *adv.*

Re·don (rə-dôn′), **Odilon** (1840–1916). French painter, lithographer, and etcher, regarded by the surrealists as one of their forerunners. He first gained notice by his eerie, dreamlike lithographs and was especially famous for his paintings of flowers.

red osier *n.* A North American shrub, *Cornus stolonifera,* often forming dense clumps and having red branches, white flowers, and bluish-white, berrylike fruit.

re·dou·ble (rē-dŭb′əl) *v.* **-bled, -bling, -bles.** *—tr.* **1.** To increase or intensify greatly: *redouble one's efforts.* **2.** To double. **3.** *Archaic.* To echo or re-echo. **4.** To double (a double) in bridge. *—intr.* **1.** To increase or intensify greatly: *Our efforts redoubled.* **2.** To be doubled; become twice as much or as great. **3.** *Archaic.* To echo; reverberate. **4.** To double a double in bridge.

re·doubt (rĭ-dout′) *n.* **1.** A small, often temporary defensive fortification, usually standing alone. **2.** Any defensive stronghold. **3.** Any place of refuge. [French *redoute,* from obsolete Italian *ridotta,* from Medieval Latin *reductus,* concealed place, from Latin, withdrawn, from the past participle of *redūcere,* withdraw : *re-,* back + *dūcere,* to lead.]

re·doubt·a·ble (rĭ-dou′tə-bəl) *adj.* **1. a.** Awesome; fearsome. **b.** Formidable. **2.** Worthy of respect or honor. [Middle English, from Old French *redoutable,* from *redouter,* to dread : *re-* (intensive) + *douter,* to fear, DOUBT.] **—re·doubt·a·bly** *adv.*

re·dound (rĭ-dound′) *intr.v.* **-dounded, -dounding, -dounds. 1.** To have an effect or consequence. **2.** To return, rebound, or recoil. Used with *on* on *upon.* **3.** *Archaic.* To contribute; accrue. [Middle English *redounden,* to abound, from Old French *redonder,* from Latin *redundāre,* to overflow : *red-, re-* (intensive) + *undāre,* to overflow, surge, from *unda,* wave.]

re·dox (rē′dŏks′) *n. Chemistry.* Oxidation-reduction (see). Also used adjectivally: *a redox reaction.* [*Red*uction of *ox*idation.]

red pepper *n.* **1.** A pimiento (see). **2.** Cayenne pepper (see).

red pine *n.* **1.** An evergreen timber tree, *Pinus resinosa,* of northeastern North America. **2.** A New Zealand coniferous tree, *Dacrydium cupressinum.* In this sense, also called "rimu."

Red Planet *n. Informal.* The planet **Mars** (see). Preceded by *the.*

red·poll (rĕd′pōl′) *n.* Any of several finches of the genus *Acanthis;* especially *A. flammea,* having brownish plumage and a red crown.

Red Poll *n.* Also **Red Polled** (pōld). Any of a breed of reddish, hornless cattle developed in England and raised for dairy and meat products.

re·draft (rē-drăft′, -dräft′) *tr.v.* **-drafted, -drafting, -drafts.** To make a new or revised version of (a written document, for example). *—n.* A second draft; a revision.

re·dress (rĭ-drĕs′) *tr.v.* **-dressed, -dressing, -dresses. 1.** To set right; remedy or rectify. **2.** To make amends for. **3.** To adjust (a balance, for example) so as to produce a condition of equality. **—See Synonyms at correct.** *—n.* (rĭ-drĕs′, rē′drĕs). **1.** Satisfaction or amends for wrong done; compensation. **2. a.** Correction or setting right. **b.** A means of rectification: *We had no redress.* **—See Synonyms at reparation.** [Middle English *redressen,* from Old French *redresser* : *re-,* back + *dresser,* to make straight, DRESS.] **—re·dress·a·ble, re·dress·i·ble**

adj. **—re·dress·al** *n.* **—re·dress·er, re·dres·sor** *n.*

Red River[1]. River, 1,175 kilometers (730 miles) long, rising in Yunnan province, southern China, and flowing southeast in deep, narrow gorges through northern Vietnam. It forms a great delta before its outlet on the Gulf of Tonkin. Silt rich in iron oxide gives the river its distinctive color.

Red River[2]. **1.** Also known as "Red River of the North." River, *c.* 500 kilometers (310 miles) long. It rises in northeastern South Dakota, flows north between Minnesota and North Dakota, and crosses into Manitoba, Canada, emptying into Lake Winnipeg. The river drains a rich wheat- and flax-growing area. **2.** River, 1,966 kilometers (1,222 miles) long, of the southwestern United States. Rising in the Texas Panhandle, it flows along the Texas-Oklahoma border, through Arkansas, and into Louisiana, where it joins the Mississippi River.

red salmon *n.* The **sockeye salmon** (see).

Red Sea. Sea running northwest from the Gulf of Aden to the Sinai Peninsula in Egypt, where it branches into the Gulf of Aqaba to the east and the Gulf of Suez to the west. It has been joined to the Mediterranean Sea by the Suez Canal since 1869 and is one of the world's major shipping routes, connecting Europe with the Far East and Australia. It is colored red at certain times of the year because of the reddish algae that appear in it.

red setter *n.* An **Irish setter** (see).

red·shank (rĕd′shăngk′) *n.* **1.** An Old World wading bird, *Tringa totanus,* having long red legs. **2.** A plant, **persicaria** (see).

red shift *n.* **1.** An increase apparent in the wavelength of radiation emitted by a receding celestial body as a consequence of the **Doppler effect** (see). Compare **blue shift. 2.** A similar increase in wavelength resulting from the presence of a high gravitational field. In this sense, also called "Einstein shift," "gravitational red shift." **—red-shift** (rĕd′shĭft′) *v.*

red-short (rĕd′shôrt′) *adj.* Brittle when red-hot. Said of iron or steel. **—red-short·ness** *n.*

---

red shift

MOVEMENT ALTERS WAVELENGTH

Why color is a clue to the movement of stars

Light from the stars changes color for the same reason that the whistle of a passing train changes pitch—because of a phenomenon known as the Doppler effect. Christian Doppler, the 19th-century Austrian physicist who first explained the phenomenon, showed that the wavelength of light or sound waves changes according to the movement of the wave source. Waves from a source moving toward an observer bunch up and become shorter; waves from a receding source are strung out, making them longer than normal. So the pitch of a train whistle rises as the train approaches, because higher sounds have shorter wavelengths, then drops as the train moves away.

Similarly, light from a star approaching the earth appears bluer than it should because lines in the spectrum of starlight have shifted toward the blue end of the spectrum. Conversely, light from a receding star appears redder than it should. Lines in the spectrum are shifted toward the red end, a phenomenon known as the red shift. Light from all the distant galaxies so far observed is red-shifted to a considerable degree, indicating that the galaxies are moving away from the earth at very high speeds, and thus that the universe as a whole is expanding.

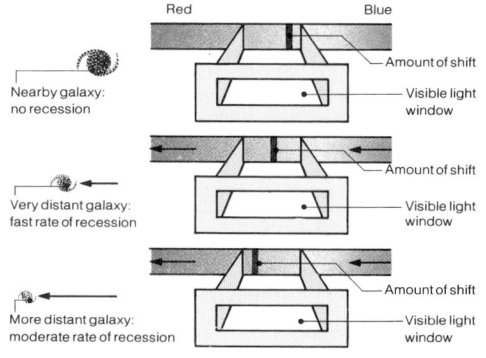

RECEIVING GALAXIES *As distant galaxies recede from the earth, their light shifts toward the red end part of the spectrum that is visible to the human eye (represented as the "visible light window" above). The amount of this shift shows how fast different galaxies are receding and what their present distance is from the earth.*

red snapper *n.* Any of several tropical and semitropical marine food fishes of the genus *Lutjanus,* having red or reddish bodies.

red spider *n.* Also **red spider mite.** A **spider mite** *(see).*

Red Spot *n. Astronomy.* A very large, reddish, variable oval patch (about 1,400 kilometers by up to 48,000 kilometers) occurring south of the equator in the atmosphere of the planet Jupiter. Also called "Great Red Spot."

red squill *n.* **1.** A plant, the **sea onion** *(see).* **2.** A powder prepared from the bulbs of this plant and used as a rat poison.

red squirrel *n.* **1.** A North American squirrel, *Tamiasciurus hudsonicus,* having reddish or tawny fur. **2.** A similar Eurasian squirrel, *Sciurus vulgaris.*

red·start (rĕd′stärt′) *n.* **1.** A small North American bird, *Setophaga ruticilla,* the male of which is black with orange markings on wings and tail. **2.** Any bird of the Eurasian genus *Phoenicurus;* especially, *P. phoenicurus,* of Europe, which has grayish plumage with a black throat and a red tail. [RED + obsolete *start,* tail, from Middle English *stert,* Old English *steort.*]

red tape *n.* Official requirements and procedures, such as the filling in of forms, considered as an obstructive bureaucratic device. [From the tape used to tie English governmental documents.]

red tide *n.* Ocean waters colored by the proliferation of red, one-celled, plantlike animals occurring in sufficient numbers to kill fish.

re·duce (rĭ-do͞os′, -dyo͞os′) *v.* **-duced, -ducing, -duces.** *—tr.* **1. a.** To lessen in extent, amount, number, degree, price, or other quality; diminish. **b.** To degrade or lower in rank, position, social circumstances, or the like. **2.** To gain control of, especially by conquest. **3.** To put in order or arrange systematically. **4.** To separate into components by analysis. **5.** To bring to a specified state or condition, as by simplification or transformation: *reduced him to tears.* **6.** To powder or pulverize. **7.** To cause (meat juices, for example) to thicken by evaporating excess water. **8.** *Chemistry.* **a.** To remove oxygen from (a compound), as in the smelting of metal ores. **b.** To add hydrogen to (a compound), as in hydrogenation reactions. **c.** To add electrons to (a compound, ion, or group), as in the change of ferric ions (Fe^{3+}) to ferrous ions (Fe^{2+}). **9.** *Mathematics.* To simplify the form of (an expression) without changing the value. **10.** To remove some of the silver from (an emulsion), forming a photographic image. **11.** To restore (a fracture or dislocation, or a fractured or displaced body part) to normal. *—intr.* **1. a.** To become diminished. **b.** To lose weight, as by dieting. **2.** To amount to or be viewable as something specified. Used with *to*: *The problem reduces to a question of time and money.* **3.** To thicken, especially by evaporation. Used of sauces and other liquids. **4.** *Chemistry.* To undergo reduction; lose oxygen or gain hydrogen or electrons. Used of chemical compounds. —See Synonyms at **decrease.** [Middle English *reducen,* to bring back, from Latin *redūcere* : *re-,* back, again + *dūcere,* to lead.] **—re·duc·i·bil·i·ty** (rĭ-do͞o′sə-bĭl′ĭ-tē, rĭ-dyo͞o′-) *n.* **—re·duc·i·ble** *adj.* **—re·duc·i·bly** *adv.*

re·duced (rĭ-do͞ost′, -dyo͞ost′) *adj.* **1.** Less in extent, amount, number, degree, price, or other quality: *at a reduced rate.* **2.** Less prosperous than formerly: *in reduced circumstances.*

re·duc·er (rĭ-do͞o′sər, -dyo͞o′sər) *n.* **1.** One that reduces. **2.** A chemical solution for reducing the density of photographic negatives or prints. **3.** A threaded cylinder for connecting pipes of different diameter.

reducing agent *n.* A substance that chemically reduces other substances.

re·duc·tase (rĭ-dŭk′tās′, -tāz′) *n.* Any enzyme that catalyzes biochemical reduction reactions. [REDUCT(ION) + -ASE.]

re·duc·ti·o ad ab·sur·dum (rĭ-dŭk′tē-ō ăd əb-sûr′dəm) *n.* **1.** Disproof of a proposition by showing the absurdity of its inevitable conclusion. **2.** Proof of a proposition by disproving its negation by means of reductio ad absurdum. **3.** The following through of a course or idea to absurdity. [Latin, "reduction to absurdity."]

re·duc·tion (rĭ-dŭk′shən) *n. Abbr.* **red. 1. a.** The act or process of reducing. **b.** The process or state of being reduced. **2. a.** The result of reducing. **b.** A reprographic copy of a picture, text, or the like, that is smaller than the original. **3.** The amount by which anything is lessened or diminished. **4.** The process of reducing or a chemical reaction in which something is reduced. Compare **oxidation. 5. a.** The cancelling of common factors in the numerator and denominator of a fraction. **b.** The converting of a fraction to its decimal equivalent. [Middle English *reduccion,* from Old French *reduction,* from Late Latin *reductiō* (stem *reductiōn-*), from Latin, from *redūcere,* to REDUCE.] **—re·duc·tion·al, re·duc·tive** *adj.*

reduction division *n. Biology.* **1.** The first meiotic division, in which the chromosome number is halved. **2. Meiosis** *(see).*

re·duc·tion·ism (rĭ-dŭk′shə-nĭz′əm) *n.* **1.** The systematic reduction of complicated information or objects to simple components. **2.** The theory or belief that a complex system can be understood completely on the basis of its simple constituents. **—re·duc·tion·ist** *n. & adj.*

re·dun·dan·cy (rĭ-dŭn′dən-sē) *n., pl.* **-cies.** Also **re·dun·dance** (-dəns). **1.** The condition or quality of being redundant, especially: **a.** Superfluity or excess. **b.** Unnecessary repetition. **2.** *Chiefly British.* **a.** Dismissal from a job by layoff or forced retirement. **b.** An instance of such job loss. **3.** Duplication or repetition of elements in electronic or mechanical equipment to provide alternative functional channels in case of failure. **4.** Repetition of parts or all of a message to circumvent transmission errors.

re·dun·dant (rĭ-dŭn′dənt) *adj.* **1.** Exceeding what is necessary or natural; superfluous. **2.** Needlessly repetitive; tautological. **3.** Copious or profuse. **4.** *Chiefly British.* Unemployed or about to be unemployed because of the elimination of one's job. [Latin *redundāns* (stem *redundant-*), present participle of *redundāre,* to overflow, run back : *red-, re-,* back + *undāre,* to overflow, from *unda,* wave.] **—re·dun·dant·ly** *adv.*

re·du·pli·cate (rĭ-do͞o′plə-kāt′, rĭ-dyo͞o′-) *v.* **-cated, -cating, -cates.** *—tr.* **1.** To repeat or redouble. **2.** *Linguistics.* **a.** To double (the initial syllable or all of a root word) to produce an inflectional or derivational form. **b.** To form (a new word) by doubling all or part of a word. *—intr.* To be doubled.
~adj. (rĭ-do͞o′plə-kĭt, rĭ-dyo͞o′-). **1.** Doubled. **2.** *Botany.* Having outward-curved margins: *reduplicate petals.* [Late Latin *reduplicāre* : Latin *re-,* again + *duplicāre,* to DUPLICATE.]

re·du·pli·ca·tion (rĭ-do͞o′plə-kā′shən, rĭ-dyo͞o′-) *n.* **1.** The act of reduplicating or the state of being reduplicated. **2.** A product or result of reduplicating. **3.** A word formed by or containing a reduplicated element. **4.** The added element in a word form that is reduplicated. **—re·du·pli·ca·tive** (rĭ-do͞o′plə-kā′tĭv) *adj.* **—re·du·pli·ca·tive·ly** *adv.*

re·du·vi·id (rĭ-do͞o′vē-ĭd, rĭ-dyo͞o′-) *n.* Any bloodsucking insect of the family Reduviidae. [New Latin *Reduviidae,* from Latin *reduvia, redivia,* hangnail, exuviae : *red-,* RE- + *-uvia,* from *-uere,* to put on.] **—re·du·vi·id** *adj.*

red water *n.* A disease of cattle caused by the protozoan *Babesia bovis* and characterized by the passage of red urine.

red whortleberry *n.* A shrub, the **cowberry** *(see).*

red·wing (rĕd′wĭng′) *n.* **1.** A **red-winged blackbird** *(see).* **2.** A European thrush, *Turdus iliacus,* having reddish feathers under the wings and a white eye stripe.

red-winged blackbird (rĕd′wĭngd′) *n.* A North American blackbird, *Agelaius phoeniceus,* the male of which has scarlet patches on the wings. Also called "redwing."

red·wood (rĕd′wo͝od′) *n.* **1.** A very tall evergreen coniferous tree, *Sequoia sempervirens,* of coastal and northern California. Compare **giant sequoia. 2.** The soft, reddish wood of this tree. **3.** Any of various woods of reddish color or yielding red dye.

Redwood National Park. Area, 22,761 hectares (56,201 acres), along the Pacific coast of northwestern California. Seals, sea lions, and birds live on the offshore rocks. Inland, there are stands of redwood, many of the trees more than 2,000 years old. The world's tallest tree (112 meters; 367 feet) is located in the park.

reebok. Variant of **rhebok.**

re·ech·o, re·ech·o (rē-ĕk′ō) *v.* **-oed, -oing, -oes.** *—intr.* **1.** To be repeated again and again by or as if by an echo. **2.** To resound or reverberate with or as if with repeated echoes. *—tr.* To echo back repeatedly.

reed (rēd) *n.* **1. a.** Any of various tall aquatic grasses having jointed, hollow stalks; especially, any of the genus *Phragmites,* such as *P. communis.* **b.** The stalk of any of these plants. **c.** A mass of reeds. **d.** Reeds collectively, especially for use as thatching material. **2.** A primitive wind instrument made of such a hollow stalk. **3.** *Music.* **a.** A flexible strip of cane or metal set into the mouthpiece of certain musical instruments to produce tone by vibrating in response to a stream of air. **b.** An instrument, such as an oboe or clarinet, fitted with a reed. **4.** A narrow, movable frame on a loom, fitted with reed or metal strips that separate the warp threads. **5.** *Architecture.* A reeding. **6.** An ancient Hebrew unit of length, equivalent to six cubits.
~tr.v. **reeded, reeding, reeds. 1.** To thatch with reed. **2.** *Architecture.* To decorate with reeding. [Middle English *rede, reod,* Old English *hrēod.*]

Reed (rēd), **Sir Carol** (1906–76). British film director, one of the most acclaimed of the post-World War II era. His most notable motion pictures were *The Third Man* (1949), *Our Man in Havana* (1959), *The Agony and the Ecstasy* (1965), and *Oliver!* (1968), the last of which won him an Academy Award.

Reed, John (1887–1920). U.S. journalist and poet. As a reporter in World War I he was in Petrograd during the October Revolution (1917), and recorded the experience in his famous book, *Ten Days That Shook the World* (1919), the best eyewitness account of the Bolshevik seizure of power. In 1919 he returned to the U.S.S.R., where he worked in the department of propaganda. He died of typhus and was buried in the Kremlin.

Reed (rēd), **Walter** (1851–1902). U.S. physician and army surgeon. In 1900, following an outbreak of yellow fever among army personnel in Cuba, he studied the disease and proved that it was transmitted by the *Aëdes aegypti* mosquito, a discovery that led to control of the disease.

reed·bed (rēd′bĕd′) *n.* A bed of reeds usually found in a marshy area.

reed·bird (rēd′bûrd′) *n.* The bobolink.

reed·buck (rēd′bŭk′) *n.* Any of several African antelopes of the genus *Redunca,* having incurved horns. Also called "nagor." [Translation of Afrikaans *rietbok.*]

reed grass *n.* A perennial Eurasian grass, *Glyceria maxima,* having tall erect stems and growing in rivers and ponds.

reed·ing (rē′dĭng) *n.* **1.** *Architecture.* A convex decorative molding having parallel strips resembling thin reeds. **2.** The indentations on the edge of a coin; milling.

reed·ling (rēd′lĭng) *n.* A bird, the **bearded reedling** *(see).*

reed mace *n.* A marsh plant, the **cattail** *(see).*

reed organ *n.* Any of various keyboard instruments in which vibrating reeds produce notes when acted upon by currents of air.

redstart *The European redstart,* Phoenicurus phoenicurus *(above), gets its name from its reddish tail;* steort *is an Old English word for tail. The birds nest in tree holes or in hollows on the ground in Europe and western Asia and migrate for the northern winter to tropical Africa. They feed mainly on insects.*

redwing *The European redwing,* Turdus iliacus *(above), is one of the smaller members of the thrush family; fully grown, it is about 21 centimeters (8¼ inches) long. It breeds in northern Europe and Asia, building nests of grass in trees, bushes, or on the ground and migrates as far as North Africa in winter.*

reed *Tall grasses have been used since prehistoric times to make clothing and domestic goods such as mats. The reed boat shown here is used by the Uru people of Lake Titicaca in South America.*

reed pipe *n.* An organ pipe with a reed that vibrates and produces a note when air is forced through it. Compare **flue pipe.**

reed stop *n.* A stop on an organ made up of reed pipes. Compare **flue stop.**

re-ed·u·cate, re·ed·u·cate (rē-ĕj′o͝o-kāt′) *tr.v.* **-cated, -cating, -cates. 1.** To educate again or anew; especially, to indoctrinate (criminals and political dissidents, for example) for purposes of rehabilitation. **2.** To retrain to function effectively, especially in a new working capacity. **—re-ed·u·ca·tion** (rē-ĕj′o͝o-kā′shən) *n.*

reed warbler *n.* A common European warbler, *Acrocephalus scirpaceus,* found chiefly around reedbeds and other marshy places.

reed·y (rē′dē) *adj.* **-ier, -iest. 1.** Full of reeds. **2.** Made of reeds. **3.** Resembling a reed especially in being slender or fragile. **4.** Having or designating a tone like that of a reed instrument; shrill or high-pitched. **—reed·i·ly** *adv.* **—reed·i·ness** *n.*

reef[1] (rēf) *n.* **1.** *Geology.* A strip or ridge of rocks, sand, or soil that rises to or near the surface of a body of water. **2.** A **coral reef** *(see).* **3.** In mining, a vein of ore. **4.** In Africa, the Precambrian gold-bearing conglomerates. —See Usage note at **shoal.** [Earlier *riff,* from Middle Dutch *rif,* ridge, perhaps from Old Norse, rib, ridge.] **—reef·y** *adj.*

reef[2] *n. Nautical.* A portion of a sail rolled and tied down to lessen the area exposed to the wind.

~*v.* **reefed, reefing, reefs.** —*tr.* **1.** To reduce the size of (a sail) by tucking in a part and tying it to or rolling it around a yard. **2.** To shorten (a topmast or bowsprit) by taking part in. —*intr.* To reduce the size of a sail by taking in reefs. [Middle English *riff,* from Old Norse *rif,* ridge, rib.]

reef·er[1] (rē′fər) *n.* **1.** One who reefs, such as a midshipman. **2.** A short, heavy, close-fitting, double-breasted jacket. In this sense also called "reefing jacket."

reef knot *Reef knots are used to make a long rope from two shorter ones. The Greeks and Romans were familiar with this knot; it is one of the few to be accurately depicted in ancient works of art.*

reefer[2] *n. Slang.* A marijuana cigarette. Not in current usage. [Perhaps from REEF (to roll up and shorten a sail).]

reef knot *n.* A **square knot** *(see),* especially one used to reef a sail.

reek (rēk) *v.* **reeked, reeking, reeks.** —*intr.* **1.** To give off or become permeated with a strong and unpleasant odor. **2.** To give off smoke, steam, or fumes. **3.** To be pervaded by something, especially of an unpleasant nature: *The whole business reeks of corruption.* —*tr.* **1.** To emit or exude (smoke or odors, for example). **2.** To process or treat by exposing to the action of smoke.

~*n.* **1.** A strong and offensive odor; a stench. **2.** Vapor; smoke; steam. [Middle English *reken,* Old English *rēocan,* from Germanic.] **—reek·er** *n.* **—reek·y** *adj.*

reel[1] (rēl) *n.* **1.** A cylinder, spool, or frame that turns on an axis and is used for winding rope, tape, or other flexible materials. **2.** Such a device attached to a fishing rod to let out or wind up the line. **3.** *Chiefly British.* A small spool around which sewing thread is wound. **4. a.** The wire, film, or other material wound on a reel. **b.** The quantity of such material wound on one reel.

~*tr.v.* **reeled, reeling, reels. 1.** To wind upon a reel. **2.** To wind or draw on a reel. Used with *in, out,* or *up*: *reel in a fish.* **3.** To recite rapidly and effortlessly. Used with *off.* [Middle English *reel,* Old English *hrēol*†.] **—reel·a·ble** *adj.*

reel[2] *v.* **reeled, reeling, reels.** —*intr.* **1.** To be thrown off balance or fall back: *He reeled under the blow.* **2.** To stagger, lurch, or sway, as from drunkenness. **3.** To go around and around in a whirling motion. **4.** To feel dizzy. —*tr.* To cause to reel.

~*n.* A staggering, swaying, or whirling movement. [Middle English *relen,* probably from REEL (spool).] **—reel·er** *n.*

reel[3] *n.* **1.** Any of various fast dances in 4/4 time, of Scottish origin. **2.** The music for a reel. [From REEL (whirl).]

re-e·lect, re·e·lect (rē′ĭ-lĕkt′) *tr.v.* **-lected, -lecting, -lects.** To elect to another term in office. **—re-e·lec·tion** *n.*

reel-to-reel (rēl′tə-rēl′) *adj.* Of, using, or designating magnetic tape that is wound onto one typically exposed reel from another: *reel-to-reel tape recorder.* Compare **cassette.**

re-en·act, re·enact (rē′ĭ-năkt′) *tr.v.* **-acted, -acting, -acts. 1.** To act out again (an earlier incident, for example). **2.** To enact (a law, for example) again or anew. **—re-en·act·ment** *n.*

re-en·trant, re·en·trant (rē-ĕn′trənt) *adj.* Pointing inward.

~*n.* **1.** A re-entrant angle or part. **2.** A marked indentation into a landform.

re-entrant angle *n.* An interior angle of a polygon greater than 180 degrees.

re-en·try, re·en·try (rē-ĕn′trē) *n., pl.* **-tries. 1.** The act of entering again or anew; a second or subsequent entry. **2.** *Law.* The recovery of possession of premises by the lessor under a right reserved in the lease or contract. **3.** In bridge and whist: **a.** The act of regaining the lead by taking a trick. **b.** The card that will take a trick and thus regain the lead. **4.** *Aerospace.* The return of a missile or spacecraft into the earth's atmosphere.

Reese (rēs), **Harold,** known as "Pee Wee" (1918–). U.S. baseball player. In 15 seasons with the Brooklyn Dodgers (1940–57) and 1 year with the Los Angeles Dodgers (1958), he played shortstop in 44 World Series games. He had a lifetime batting average of .269 and was inducted into the Baseball Hall of Fame in 1984.

reest (rēst) *intr.v.* **reested, reesting, reests.** *Chiefly Scottish.* To stop suddenly and refuse to budge; balk. Used of a horse. [Probably variant of Scottish *arreest,* to ARREST.] **—reest·y** *adj.*

reeve[1] (rēv) *n.* **1.** A high officer of local administration appointed by the Anglo-Saxon kings. **2.** In the later medieval period, a bailiff or steward of a manor. **3.** Any of various minor local officers. **4.** The elected president of a local council in some parts of Canada. [Middle English *reve, reeve,* Old English *(ge)rēfa,* from *rōf* (unattested), assembly.]

reeve[2] *tr.v.* **rove** (rōv) or **reeved, reeving, reeves.** *Nautical.* **1.** To pass (a rope or rod) through a hole, ring, pulley, or block. **2.** To fasten (a block, for example) by such a procedure. [Probably from Dutch *rēven,* to REEF (sail).]

reeve[3] *n.* A bird, the female **ruff** *(see).* [17th century.]

re-ex·am·ine, re·ex·am·ine (rē′ĭg-zăm′ĭn) *tr.v.* **-ined, -ining, -ines. 1.** To examine again or anew; review. **2.** *Law.* To question (one's own witness) again after cross-examination. Used of a lawyer. **—re-ex·am·i·na·tion** *n.*

re-ex·port, re·ex·port (rē-ĕk′spôrt, rē′ĭk-spôrt′) *tr.v.* **-ported, -porting, -ports.** To export (imported goods), often after processing.

~*n.* (rē-ĕk′spôrt). **1.** The act of re-exporting. **2.** Something re-exported. **—re-ex·por·ta·tion** *n.*

ref (rĕf) *n. Informal.* A referee at a sports event.

ref. 1. referee. **2.** reference; referred. **3.** refining. **4.** reformation; reformed. **5.** refunding.

re·face (rē-fās′) *tr.v.* **-faced, -facing, -faces. 1.** To renew or repair the surface of (a building, for example). **2.** To give a new facing to (a garment, for example).

re·fect (rĭ-fĕkt′) *tr.v.* **-fected, -fecting, -fects.** *Archaic.* To supply with food and drink. [Latin *reficere* (past participle *refectus*), to refresh : *re-,* again + *facere,* to make.]

re·fec·tion (rĭ-fĕk′shən) *n. Archaic.* **1.** Refreshment with food and drink. **2.** A light meal or repast. [Middle English *refeccioun,* from Old French *refection,* from Latin *refectiō* (stem *refectiōn-*), a restoring, from *reficere,* to refresh. See **refect.**]

re·fec·to·ry (rĭ-fĕk′tə-rē) *n., pl.* **-ries.** A room where meals are served, as in an institution such as a monastery or college. [Late Latin *refectōrium,* from Latin *reficere,* to REFECT.]

refectory table *n.* A long table with straight, heavy legs.

re·fer (rĭ-fûr′) *v.* **-ferred, -ferring, -fers.** —*tr.* **1.** To direct to a source for help or information: *refer a patient to a specialist.* **2.** To assign or attribute (an effect, for example) to some cause; ascribe responsibility for: *referred the cure to prayer.* **3.** To assign to or regard as belonging to a specified category, place, or time: *referred sharks to the fishes; referred dinosaurs to prehistoric times.* **4.** To submit (a matter in dispute) to an authority for arbitration, decision, or examination. **5.** To direct a person's attention to: *The administrator referred the matter to an assistant.* **6.** To return (a text, for example) to its originator for improvement. Used with *to,* or sometimes *back to,* in most senses. —*intr.* **1.** To pertain; concern; apply: *The tax laws refer to all residents.* **2.** To direct notice or attention; make reference: *The footnote refers to another book.* **3.** To have recourse, as for information or authority. Used with *to* in all senses. [Middle English *refer(r)en,* from Old French *referer,* from Latin *referre,* refer to, carry back : *re-,* back, again + *ferre,* to carry.] **—ref·er·a·ble** (rĕf′ər-ə-bəl, rĭ-fûr′ə-bəl) *adj.* **—re·fer·ral** (rĭ-fûr′əl) *n.* **—re·fer·rer** *n.*

Usage: In the general sense of "directing to a source," formal usage avoids the use of *refer back,* unless the implication is that a second act of reference is involved *(I referred him back to the passage he had mentioned earlier). Let me refer you to a good book on the subject* is the standard form, *back* being unnecessary.

ref·e·ree (rĕf′ə-rē′) *n. Abbr.* **ref. 1.** One to whom something is referred, as for settlement or decision; an arbitrator. **2.** *Sports.* An official supervising and judging play, as in boxing and football. **3. a.** One willing to testify to the ability or character of an applicant, especially for employment. **b.** One who carefully reads a new scientific or scholarly work to decide whether it should be published. **4.** *Law.* A judicial official to whom certain cases are referred for adjudication, especially in civil cases in which both parties agree to this procedure or in which complex documents must be analyzed. —See Synonyms at **judge.**

~*v.* **refereed, -reeing, -rees.** —*tr.* To judge or supervise as referee. —*intr.* To act as referee.

ref·er·ence (rĕf′ər-əns, rĕf′rəns) *n. Abbr.* **ref. 1.** The act of referring or the state of being referred. **2.** That to which something refers. **3.** Relation, connection, or correspondence: *with reference to your complaint.* **4. a.** A direction of attention: *many references to learned journals.* **b.** A naming of or allusion to a person, event, or situation. **5. a.** A note in a publication referring the reader to another passage or source. **b.** The passage or source so referred to. **c.** A mark, such as * or †, directing the reader to a footnote or other information. Also called "reference mark." **6.** *Law.* The submission of a case to a referee. **7. a.** A statement by one person attesting to another's ability, experience, character, or creditworthiness. **b.** Someone willing to provide such a testimonial. **8. a.** A source of information and facts: *works of reference.* Also used adjectivally: *a reference library.* **b.** The act of searching for information: *An almanac is useful for quick reference.* **9.** An object or activity taken as a norm; a standard: *using the dollar as a reference.* Also called "point of reference." —*tr.v.* **referenced, -encing, -ences. 1.** To furnish (a text or publication, for example) with references. **2.** To refer to or quote as a reference. **—ref·er·enc·er** *n.*

reference book *n.* **1.** A book, such as a dictionary or an encyclopedia, that is consulted for specific points of information, rather than read continuously. **2.** In South Africa, an identity document, recording domicile and employment records and other personal information, that all black adults are required to carry in white areas. In this sense, also called "pass," "passbook."

reference group *n. Sociology.* A group of people whose standards and behavior affect and are admired by a person not necessarily in the group.

ref·er·en·dum (rĕf'ə-rĕn'dəm) *n., pl.* **-dums** or **-da** (-də). **1. a.** The submission of a proposed public measure or actual statute to a direct popular vote. **b.** Such a vote. Compare **plebiscite**. **2.** The submission of any matter concerning a group to the direct vote of its members. **3.** A note from a diplomat to his government requesting instructions. [Latin, neuter gerundive of *referre,* to REFER.]

ref·er·ent (rĕf'ər-ənt, rĭ-fûr'ənt) *n.* **1.** One that is referred to; specifically, the object, event, or idea that a word, phrase, or sign represents. **2.** One that refers. **3.** *Logic.* The first term in a proposition, from which the relation proceeds; for example, in the sentence *Dogs like bones, dogs* is the referent. [Latin *referēns* (stem *referent-*), present participle of *referre,* REFER.] **—ref·er·ent** *adj.*

ref·er·en·tial (rĕf'ə-rĕn'shəl) *adj.* **1.** Of or constituting a reference. **2.** Full of references; allusive. **—ref·er·en·ti·al·i·ty** (rĕf'ə-rĕn-shē-ăl'ə-tē) *n.* **—ref·er·en·tial·ly** *adv.*

referred pain *n.* Pain felt in a part of the body other than the site of the disease or injury.

re·fill (rē-fĭl') *v.* **-filled, -filling, -fills.** *—tr.* To fill again. *—intr.* To become full again.
∼n. (rē'fĭl'). **1.** A product, such as an ink cartridge, intended to replace the used contents of a container. **2.** A second or subsequent filling.

re·fine (rĭ-fīn') *v.* **-fined, -fining, -fines.** *—tr.* **1.** To remove unwanted substances from; purify. **2.** To separate (crude oil, for example) into distinct substances. **3.** To remove by purifying. Used with *out* or *away.* **4.** To free from coarse characteristics; make more elegant, polished, or subtle. **5.** To improve, as by making more precise: *refine a theory.* *—intr.* **1.** To become free of impurities. **2.** To acquire polish or elegance. **3.** To use subtlety and precise distinctions in thought or speech. **4.** To make improvements, as by making something clearer or more precise. Used with *on* or *upon.* [RE- + FINE (verb).] **—re·fin·a·ble** *adj.* **—re·fin·er** *n.*

re·fined (rĭ-fīnd') *adj.* **1.** Free from coarseness or vulgarity; polite; genteel. **2.** Free of impurities; purified. **3.** Precise to a fine degree; subtle; exact.

re·fine·ment (rĭ-fīn'mənt) *n.* **1. a.** An act or process of refining. **b.** The state or quality of being refined. **2.** The result of refining; an improvement or elaboration. **3.** Fineness of thought, manners, or expression; polish; cultivation. **4.** A precise phrasing; a subtlety or subtle distinction. —See Usage note at **culture**.

re·fin·er·y (rĭ-fī'nə-rē) *n., pl.* **-ies.** An industrial plant for purifying a crude substance, such as petroleum, sugar, fat, or ore.

re·fin·ish (rē-fĭn'ĭsh) *tr.v.* **-ished, -ishing, -ishes.** To put a new finish on (furniture). **—re·fin·ish·er** *n.*

re·fit (rē-fĭt') *v.* **-fitted, -fitting, -fits.** *—tr.* To prepare and equip for further or additional use; especially, to modernize and re-equip (a ship, for example). *—intr.* To be made ready for further use.
∼n. (rē'fĭt', rē-fĭt'). **1.** An act or process of refitting, especially of a ship. **2.** A secondary or subsequent preparation of supplies and equipment. **—re·fit·ment** *n.*

refl. **1.** reflection; reflective. **2.** reflex; reflexive.

re·flate (rē-flāt') *v.* **-flated, -flating, -flates.** *Economics.* *—tr.* **1.** To increase (depressed prices) to desirable levels by the use of governmental monetary powers. **2.** To cause reflation in (a country's economy, for example). *—intr.* To cause reflation. Used of a government authority. Compare **deflate**.

re·fla·tion (rē-flā'shən) *n.* *Economics.* **1.** The act of reflating or the condition of being reflated. **2.** An increase of the money in circulation, effected by a government in order to increase consumer demand and thereby to stimulate the economy. **—re·fla·tion·a·ry** (rē-flā'shə-nĕr'ē) *adj.*

re·flect (rĭ-flĕkt') *v.* **-flected, -flecting, -flects.** *—tr.* **1.** To throw or bend back (heat, light, or sound, for example) from a surface. **2.** To form an image of; mirror. **3.** To manifest or express: *His work reflects intelligence.* **4.** *Mathematics.* To transform by reversing the sign of one coordinate. **5.** To consider; think: *He reflected that all was well.* **6.** To throw or bring (credit or discredit, for example) onto someone or something. **7.** *Archaic.* To bend back. *—intr.* **1.** To be thrown or bent back. Used especially of heat, light, or sound. **2. a.** To give back a likeness: *This surface reflects.* **b.** To become mirrored: *The statue reflected in the water.* **3.** To think, meditate, or consider seriously. Often used with *on* or *upon.* **4. a.** To bring blame or reproach. Used with *on* or *upon.* **b.** To cause the character of a person or thing to appear in a specified light. Used with *on* or *upon*: *The argument reflects badly on you.* [Middle English *reflecten,* from Old French *reflecter,* from Latin *reflectere,* to bend back : *re-,* back + *flectere,* to FLEX.]

re·flec·tance (rĭ-flĕk'təns) *n.* The ratio of the total radiant flux (as of light) reflected by a surface to the total falling on the surface. Compare **absorptance, transmittance.**

reflecting telescope *n.* An optical telescope in which the principal image-forming element is a parabolic or spherical mirror. Also called "reflector." Compare **refracting telescope.**

re·flec·tion (rĭ-flĕk'shən) *n.* Also *chiefly British* **re·flex·ion.** *Abbr.* **refl.** **1.** The act of reflecting or state of being reflected. **2.** Something reflected, such as light, radiant heat, sound, or an image. **3. a.** Concentration of the mind; careful consideration. **b.** A result of such consideration; a thought. **4. a.** An imputation of censure or discredit; reproach. Used chiefly in the phrase *cast reflections on* or *upon.* **b.** An expression, often discreditable, of the character of a person or thing. Used with *on* or *upon*: *a reflection on your honesty.* **5. a.** The act or an instance of bending back. **b.** *Anatomy.* A structure or part bent back upon itself. **6.** *Mathematics.* **a.** A transformation in which the sign of one coordinate is reversed. **b.** A symmetry relationship involving such a transformation. **—re·flec·tion·al** *adj.* **—re·flec·tion·less** *adj.*

reflection nebula *n.* A dark **nebula** *(see).*

re·flec·tive (rĭ-flĕk'tĭv) *adj. Abbr.* **refl.** **1. a.** Of, pertaining to, produced by, or resulting from reflection. **b.** Capable of or producing reflection. **2.** Meditative; pensive. —See Usage note at **pensive.** **—re·flec·tive·ly** *adv.* **—re·flec·tive·ness** *n.*

re·flec·tiv·i·ty (rē'flĕk-tĭv'ə-tē) *n., pl.* **-ties.** **1.** The quality of being reflective. **2.** The ability to reflect. **3.** *Physics.* The ratio of the intensity of the total radiation, as of light, reflected from a surface to the total falling on the surface.

re·flec·tor (rĭ-flĕk'tər) *n.* **1.** That which reflects. **2.** A surface that reflects radiation. **3.** A small red reflective disk or strip, usually attached to the rear of a vehicle to increase its visibility. **4.** A reflecting telescope. **5.** *Physics.* A layer of material placed around the core of a nuclear reactor to reflect neutrons back into the core.

re·flet (rə-flā') *n.* A lustrous or iridescent effect, as on pottery. [French, from Italian *riflesso,* reflection.]

re·flex (rē'flĕks') *adj. Abbr.* **refl.** **1.** *Physiology.* Of or designating an action or response performed without conscious control, such as a sneeze, blink, or hiccup. **2.** Of or designating any action or response performed unintentionally, automatically, or without deliberation: *a reflex response to danger; a reflex opposition to social change.* **3.** Reflected or directed back upon the source: *reflex thoughts; reflex effort.* **4.** Designating light that is reflected. **5.** Turned, thrown, or bent backward.
∼n. Abbr. **refl.** **1.** *Physiology.* A response to a stimulus performed without conscious control. **2.** *Psychology.* An automatic, instinctive, or mechanical response to a situation or other stimulus. **3. reflexes.** The ability to respond to outside influences, usually considered in terms of speed: *For karate you need fast reflexes.* **4.** Reflection or an image produced by reflection. **5.** A **reflex camera** *(see).* **6.** A linguistic form when viewed as descended from a usually specified earlier form; for example, *mother* and *fire* are reflexes of the Indo-European *māter* and *pūr* respectively.
∼tr.v. (rĭ-flĕks') **reflexed, -flexing, -flexes.** **1.** To bend, turn back, or reflect. **2.** To cause to undergo a reflex process. [Latin *reflexus,* past participle of *reflectere,* to REFLECT.]

reflex angle *n.* An angle greater than 180° and less than 360°.

reflex arc *n.* The neural path of a physiological reflex, the simplest form of which consists of a sensory neuron and a motor neuron linked in the brain or spinal cord by a synapse.

reflex camera *n.* A camera fitted with a mirror to reflect the exact focused image onto a coupled viewing screen.

re·flex·ive (rĭ-flĕk'sĭv) *adj.* **1.** Of or pertaining to a reflex. **2.** Directed back on itself: *"This is a sentence" is a reflexive expression.* **3.** *Abbr.* **refl.** *Grammar.* **a.** Of or designating a verb having an identical subject and direct object, such as *dressed* in the sentence *She dressed herself.* **b.** Designating the pronoun used as direct object of a reflexive verb, such as *herself* in *She dressed herself.* **4.** Designating or pertaining to a relation that is independent of the order of the terms. For example, equality is reflexive, for if $a = b$ then $b = a$. **5.** Automatic; unthinking: *a reflexive distrust of all authority.*
∼n. A reflexive verb or pronoun. **—re·flex·ive·ly** *adv.* **—re·flex·ive·ness, re·flex·iv·i·ty** (rē'flĕk-sĭv'ə-tē) *n.*

re·flex·ol·o·gy (rē'flĕk-sŏl'ə-jē) *n.* **1.** The study of reflexes. **2.** The practice of foot massage to treat ailments in all parts of the body.

ref·lu·ent (rĕf'lo͞o-ənt) *adj. Rare.* Flowing back; ebbing. [Latin *refluēns* (stem *refluent-*), present participle of *refluere,* flow back : *re-,* back + *fluere,* flow.] **—ref·lu·ence** *n.*

re·flux (rē'flŭks') *n.* **1.** The process or an act of flowing back; ebb. **2.** The pathological flow of liquid against its normal direction of movement, such as the flow of stomach contents into the esophagus. **3.** *Chemistry.* The process of refluxing. Also used adjectivally: *reflux extraction.*
∼tr.v. **refluxed, -fluxing, -fluxes.** *Chemistry.* To boil (a liquid) in a vessel attached to a condenser so that the liquid continuously condenses and runs back into the vessel. This process is used for extracting substances or carrying out reactions. [Middle English : RE- + FLUX.]

re·for·est (rē-fôr'ĭst, -fŏr'ĭst) *tr.v.* **-ested, -esting, -ests.** To replace or plant trees in (an area that was formerly a forest). Also *chiefly British* "reafforest." **—re·for·es·ta·tion** *n.*

re-form (rē-fôrm') *v.* **-formed, -forming, -forms.** *—tr.* To form again. *—intr.* To become formed again.

re·form (rĭ-fôrm') *v.* **-formed, -forming, -forms.** *—tr.* **1.** To improve, as by alteration, correction of error, or abolition of abuses and malpractices. **2.** To abolish (abuses or malpractices). **3.** To cause (a person) to abandon irresponsible or immoral practices. **4.** *Chemistry.* To change the structure of (hydrocarbons in petroleum) by heat and pressure, usually using catalysts, so as to produce hydrocarbons suitable for petrol. *—intr.* To abandon irresponsible or immoral practices. —See Synonyms at **correct.**
∼n. **1.** A change for the better; an improvement. **2.** The correction of abuses or evils. **3.** Action to improve social or economic conditions without radical or revolutionary change.
∼adj. Pertaining to or favoring reform: *a reform candidate for mayor.* [Middle English *reformen,* from Old French *reformer,* from Latin *refōrmāre* : *re-,* again, back + *fōrmāre,* to form, from *fōrma,*

PRONUNCIATION KEY

ă, pat; ā, pay; âr, care; ä, father, are; b, bib; ch, church; d, deed; ĕ, pet; ē, be; f, fife; g, gag; h, hat; hw, which; ĭ, pit; ī, pie; îr, pier; j, judge; k, kick; l, lid, needle; m, mum; n, no, sudden; ng, thing; ŏ, pot; ō, toe; ô, paw, for; oi, noise; ou, out; o͝o, book; o͞o, boot; p, pop; r, roar; s, sauce; sh, ship, dish; t, tight; th, thin, path; *th,* this, bathe; ŭ, cut; ûr, fur; v, valve; w, with; y, yes; z, zebra, size; zh, vision; ə, about, item, edible, gallop, circus, peaceful

IN FOREIGN WORDS:

à, *Fr.* ami; œ, *Fr.* feu, *Ger.* schön; ü, *Fr.* tu, *Ger.* über; KH, *Ger.* ich, *Scot.* loch; N, *Fr.* bon; y', *Fr.* Compiègne

STRESS MARKS:

Primary stress: ' **in·cite'** (ĭn-sīt')
Secondary stress: ' **in'sight'** (ĭn'sīt')

FORM.] —re·form·a·ble *adj.* —re·form·a·bil·i·ty *n.* —re·form·a·tive *adj.* —re·form·er *n.*

ref·or·ma·tion (rĕf′ər-mā′shən) *n. Abbr.* ref. 1. The act of reforming or the state of being reformed. 2. Reformation. The 16th-century movement that aimed at reforming Western Christianity, resulting in the separation of the Protestant churches from the Roman Catholic Church. —ref·or·ma·tion·al *adj.*

re·for·ma·to·ry (rĭ-fôr′mə-tôr′ē, -tōr′ē) *adj.* Serving or tending to reform.
~*n., pl.* reformatories. A penal institution for the discipline, reformation, and training of juvenile and first offenders. Also called "reform school." [REFORMAT(ION) + -ORY.]

re·formed (rĭ-fôrmd′) *adj. Abbr.* ref. 1. Improved in conduct or character. 2. Reformed. Of, pertaining to, or denoting the Protestant churches that follow the teachings of Calvin and Zwingli. 3. Reformed. Of, pertaining to, or designating Reform Judaism.

re·form·ism (rĭ-fôr′mĭz′əm) *n.* The advocacy of social or economic reform, especially in contrast to revolution. —re·form·ist *n.*

Reform Judaism *n.* A branch of Judaism introduced in the 19th century that endeavors to reconcile historical Judaism with modern life without requiring strict observance of traditional law. Compare Conservative Judaism, Orthodox Judaism.

re·fract (rĭ-frăkt′) *tr.v.* -fracted, -fracting, -fracts. 1. To deflect (light, for example) by refraction. 2. To measure the refractive power of (a lens, for example). [Latin *refringere* (past participle *refractus*), to break off : *re-*, away, backward + *frangere*, to break.]

refracting telescope *n.* A telescope in which the final image is produced entirely by lenses. Also called "refractor." Compare re·flecting telescope.

re·frac·tion (rĭ-frăk′shən) *n. Abbr.* refr. 1. *Physics.* The deflection of a propagating wave, as of light or sound, at the boundary between two mediums, or in a passage through a medium of nonuniform density, occurring when the speed of the wave is different in the different mediums or regions. 2. *Astronomy.* The apparent positional elevation of celestial objects caused by deflection of light entering the earth's atmosphere. 3. **a.** The capacity of the eye to refract light. **b.** The measurement of the angle through which an eye refracts light. —re·frac·tion·al *adj.*

re·frac·tive (rĭ-frăk′tĭv) *adj.* 1. Of or pertaining to refraction. 2. Causing refraction. Said especially of materials with a high refractive index, such as a diamond. —re·frac·tive·ly *adv.* —re·frac·tive·ness, re·frac·tiv·i·ty (rē′frăk-tĭv′ə-tē) *n.*

refractive index *n. Physics.* The ratio of the speed of light in a vacuum to the speed of light in the medium under consideration. Also called "index of refraction."

re·frac·tom·e·ter (rē′frăk-tŏm′ə-tər) *n.* Any of several optical instruments that measure indices of refraction. —re·frac·to·met·ric (rĭ-frăk′tə-mĕt′rĭk) *adj.* —re·frac·tom·e·try (rē′frăk-tŏm′ə-trē) *n.*

re·frac·tor (rĭ-frăk′tər) *n.* 1. One that refracts. 2. A refracting tele·scope (*see*).

re·frac·to·ry (rĭ-frăk′tə-rē) *adj.* 1. Obstinate; unmanageable. 2. Difficult to melt or work; resistant to heat. 3. Not responsive to treatment: *a refractory case of acne.* 4. *Physiology.* Designating the period following transmission of a nerve impulse during which a neuron will not respond to further stimulation. —See Synonyms at unruly.
~*n., pl.* refractories. 1. Any of various materials, such as alumina, silica, or magnesite, that do not significantly deform or change chemically at high temperatures. 2. *refractories.* Bricks of such materials and of various shapes used to line furnaces. [Earlier *refractary*, from Latin *refractārius*, from *refringere* (past participle *refractus*), to break off, REFRACT.] —re·frac·to·ri·ly *adv.* —re·frac·to·ri·ness *n.*

re·frain¹ (rĭ-frān′) *v.* -frained, -fraining, -frains. —*intr.* To hold oneself back; abstain. Used with *from.* —*tr. Archaic.* To restrain or hold back; curb. [Middle English *refreynen*, from Old French *refrener*, from Latin *refrēnāre*, hold back, bridle : *re-*, back + *frēnum*, bridle.] —re·frain·er *n.* —re·frain·ment *n.*

refrain² *n.* 1. **a.** A phrase or verse repeated at intervals throughout a song or poem, especially at the end of each stanza. **b.** Music for the refrain of a poem. 2. Loosely, a tune. 3. A repetitive utterance or theme. [Middle English *refreyn*, from Old French *refrain*, from *refraindre*, to echo, break off (a refrain "breaks off" to recur at intervals), from Vulgar Latin *refrangere* (unattested), from Latin *refringere*, to break off, REFRACT.]

re·fran·gi·ble (rĭ-frăn′jə-bəl) *adj.* Capable of being refracted. [New Latin *refrangibilis*, from *refrangere*, variant of Latin *refringere*, to REFRACT.] —re·fran·gi·bil·i·ty (rĭ-frăn′jə-bĭl′ə-tē), re·fran·gi·ble·ness *n.*

re·fresh (rĭ-frĕsh′) *v.* -freshed, -freshing, -freshes. —*tr.* 1. To revive (a person) with or as if with rest, food, or drink. 2. To make cool, clean, or damp; freshen. 3. To restore by some treatment: *refresh the paintwork.* 4. To renew by stimulation: *refresh one's memory.* —*intr.* 1. To take refreshment. 2. To become revived; reinvigorate. [Middle English *refresshen*, from Old French *refreschir, refreschier* : *re-*, again + *freis, fresche*, FRESH.]

re·fresh·er (rĭ-frĕsh′ər) *n.* One that refreshes.
~*adj.* Serving to reacquaint one with material previously studied: *a refresher course.*

re·fresh·ing (rĭ-frĕsh′ĭng) *adj.* 1. Serving to refresh. 2. Pleasantly new and different; unusual. —re·fresh·ing·ly *adv.*

re·fresh·ment (rĭ-frĕsh′mənt) *n.* 1. The act of refreshing or state of being refreshed; reinvigoration; revival. 2. Something that re-

freshes, such as food or drink. 3. **refreshments.** A light meal or snack and drinks.

re·frig·er·ant (rĭ-frĭj′ər-ənt) *adj.* 1. Cooling or freezing; refrigerating. 2. *Medicine.* Reducing fever.
~*n.* 1. A substance, such as air, ammonia, water, or carbon dioxide, used to produce refrigeration, either as the working substance of a refrigerator or by direct absorption of heat. 2. *Medicine.* Any agent used to produce cooling or reduce fever.

re·frig·er·ate (rĭ-frĭj′ə-rāt′) *tr.v.* -ated, -ating, -ates. 1. To cool or chill (a substance). 2. To preserve (food) by chilling. [Latin *refrigerāre* : *re-*, repeatedly, again + *frigerāre*, to make cool, from *frigus* (stem *frigor-*), cool.] —re·frig·er·a·tion (rĭ-frĭj′ə-rā′shən) *n.* —re·frig·er·a·tive (rĭ-frĭj′ə-rā′tĭv) *adj. & n.* —re·frig·er·a·to·ry (rĭ-frĭj′-ər-ə-tôr′ē, -tōr′ē) *adj.*

re·frig·er·a·tor (rĭ-frĭj′ə-rā′tər) *n.* An apparatus for reducing and maintaining the temperature of a chamber below the temperature of the external environment; especially, a kitchen appliance for cooling and storing foods. Also informally called "fridge."

re·frin·gent (rĭ-frĭn′jənt) *adj.* Of, pertaining to, or producing refraction; refractive. [Latin *refringēns* (stem *refringent-*), present participle of *refringere*, to REFRACT.]

reft. Alternate past tense and past participle of reave.

re·fu·el (rē-fyoo′əl) *v.* -eled, -eling, els or chiefly British -elled, -elling, -els. —*tr.* To supply again with fuel. —*intr.* To take on a fresh supply of fuel.

ref·uge (rĕf′yooj) *n.* 1. Protection or shelter, as from danger or hardship. 2. A place providing protection; a haven or sanctuary. 3. Anything to which one may turn for help, relief, or escape: *Silence was his only refuge.* —See Synonyms at shelter.
~*v.* refuged, -uging, -uges. *Archaic.* —*tr.* To give refuge to. —*intr.* To take refuge. [Middle English, from Old French, from Latin *refugium*, from *refugere*, flee back : *re-*, away, back + *fugere*, to flee.]

ref·u·gee (rĕf′yoo-jē′) *n.* A person who flees to find refuge; especially, one who escapes from invasion, oppression, or persecution, often to another country. [French *réfugié*, from the past participle of *réfugier*, to put in a refuge, from *refuge*, REFUGE.]

re·ful·gent (rĭ-fŭl′jənt) *adj.* Shining radiantly; brilliant; resplendent. [Latin *refulgēns* (stem *refulgent-*), present participle of *refulgēre*, to flash back : *re-*, back + *fulgēre*, to flash.] —re·ful·gence, re·ful·gen·cy *n.* —re·ful·gent·ly *adv.*

re·fund¹ (rĭ-fŭnd′, rē′fŭnd′) *v.* -funded, -funding, -funds. —*tr.* 1. To return or repay; give back. 2. To repay (a person); reimburse. —*intr.* To make repayment.
~*n.* (rē′fŭnd′). 1. A repayment of funds. 2. The amount repaid. [Middle English *refunden*, to pour back, from Old French *refunder*, from Latin *refundere* : *re-*, back + *fundere*, to pour.] —re·fund·er *n.* —re·fund·ment *n.*

re·fund² (rē-fŭnd′) *tr.v.* -funded, -funding, -funds. 1. To fund anew. 2. *Finance.* To pay back (a debt) with new borrowing; especially, to replace (a bond issue) with a new bond issue.

re·fur·bish (rē-fûr′bĭsh) *tr.v.* -bished, -bishing, -bishes. To make clean or fresh again; renovate. —re·fur·bish·ment *n.*

re·fus·al (rĭ-fyoo′zəl) *n.* 1. The act of refusing. 2. The opportunity to accept or reject; option: *He gave me first refusal.*

re·fuse¹ (rĭ-fyooz′) *v.* -fused, -fusing, -fuses. —*tr.* 1. To make known that one will not do, accept, give, or allow: *refused a second helping; refused permission for her to marry.* 2. To be unwilling and fail to jump (an obstacle). Used of a horse. —*intr.* To decline to do, accept, allow, or give something. [Middle English *refusen*, from Old French *refuser*, from Vulgar Latin *refūsāre* (unattested), from Latin *refundere* (past participle *refūsus*), to pour back. See refund.] —re·fus·er *n.*
Synonyms: decline, ignore, rebuff, reject, spurn.

ref·use² (rĕf′yoos) *n.* Anything discarded or rejected as useless or worthless; rubbish; waste matter.
~*adj.* Discarded or rejected as useless or worthless. [Middle English, something rejected, from Old French *refus*, refusal, from *refuser*, to REFUSE.]

re·fuse·nik (rĭ-fyooz′nĭk) *n.* A Soviet citizen whose application for a visa to emigrate has been refused. [REFUSE + -NIK.]

ref·u·ta·tion (rĕf′yoo-tā′shən) *n.* Also re·fu·tal (rĭ-fyoot′l). 1. The act of refuting. 2. Something that refutes.

re·fute (rĭ-fyoot′) *tr.v.* -futed, -futing, -futes. 1. To prove (a statement or argument) to be false or erroneous; disprove. 2. To prove (a person) to be wrong. —See Synonyms at deny. [Latin *refutāre*, rebut, drive back.] —re·fut·a·bil·i·ty (rĭ-fyoo′tə-bĭl′ə-tē, rĕf′yə-tə-) *n.* —re·fut·a·ble *adj.* —re·fut·a·bly *adv.* —re·fut·er *n.*
Usage: There is a widespread use of *refute* with the meaning "to deny," but it attracts criticism as it lacks the strong sense of "proof" that is inherent in the word.

reg (rĕg) *n.* A flat, stony desert, especially in the Sahara, where sheets of gravel and pebbles cover the surface. [Arabic.]

reg. 1. regent. 2. regiment. 3. region. 4. register; registered. 5. registrar. 6. registry. 7. regular; regularly. 8. regulation. 9. regulator.

Reg. 1. Regent. 2. Regina.

re·gain (rē-gān′) *tr.v.* -gained, -gaining, -gains. 1. To recover possession of; get back again. 2. To manage to reach again. —See Usage note at recover. —re·gain·er *n.*

re·gal¹ (rē′gəl) *adj.* 1. Pertaining to a king or queen; royal. 2. Belonging to or befitting a king or queen: *regal attire.* 3. Dignified; stately. [Middle English, from Old French, from Latin *rēgālis*, royal, from *rēx* (stem *rēg-*), king.] —re·gal·ly *adv.*

regal[2] *n.* A small, portable reed organ often used in dramatic works in the 16th and 17th centuries. [French *régale,* perhaps feminine of *régal,* REGAL.]

re·gale (rĭ-gāl′) *v.* **-galed, -gal·ing, -gales.** —*tr.* **1.** To delight or entertain; give pleasure to: *regaled us with folk songs.* **2.** To entertain sumptuously with food and drink; provide a feast for. —*intr.* To feast.
—*n. Obsolete.* **1.** A great feast; a sumptuous repast. **2.** A choice food or drink; a delicacy. **3.** Refreshment. [French *régaler,* from Old French *regaler,* from *regal,* REGAL.] **—re·gale·ment** *n.*

re·ga·li·a (rĭ-gāl′yə, -gā′lē-ə) *pl.n. Often used with a singular verb.* **1.** The emblems and symbols of royalty, such as the crown and scepter. **2.** The distinguishing symbols of any rank, office, order, or society. **3.** Magnificent attire; finery. [Medieval Latin *rēgālia,* plural of *rēgāle,* royal prerogative, from Latin, neuter of *rēgālis,* REGAL.]

re·gal·i·ty (rĭ-găl′ə-tē) *n., pl.* **-ties.** **1.** Royalty or sovereignty; kingship or queenship. **2.** A country or area under a monarch; a kingdom. **3.** The rights or privileges of a king or queen.

re·gard (rĭ-gärd′) *v.* **-gard·ed, -gard·ing, -gards.** —*tr.* **1.** To look upon or consider in a specified way: *I regard him as a fool.* **2.** To look at attentively; observe closely. **3.** To have great affection or admiration for: *She regards her father highly.* **4.** To relate to, concern, or refer to: *This item regards your question.* **5.** To consider or take account of. **6.** *Obsolete.* To take care of. —*intr.* **1.** To look; gaze. **2.** To give heed; pay attention. **—as regards.** Relating to; concerning. —See Synonyms at **consider.**
—*n.* **1.** Careful thought or attention; concern; heed: *He gives little regard to his appearance.* **2.** Respect, affection, or esteem: *He has won the regard of all.* **3.** A look or gaze. **4. regards.** Sentiments of respect or affection; good wishes: *send one's regards.* **5.** Reference or relation: *with regard to this case.* **6.** A particular point or respect: *I agree in this regard.* **7.** *Obsolete.* Appearance or aspect. [Middle English *regarden,* from Old French *regarder, reguarder,* to look at, regard : *re-,* back, back at + *guarder, garder,* to GUARD.]
Synonyms: *admiration, approbation, esteem.*
Usage: *Regard* is traditionally used as a singular in the phrase *in* (or *with*) *regard to* (not *in regards to*). *Regarding* and *as regards* are used in the same sense as "with reference to" but are not considered acceptable in formal English. In the same sense *with respect to* is acceptable, but *respecting* is not. • *Respects* is sometimes held preferable to *regards* in the sense of "particulars": *In some respects* (not *regards*) *the books are alike.*

re·gar·dant (rĭ-gär′dənt) *adj. Heraldry.* With the face turned backward in profile: *a lion regardant.* [Middle English, from Old French, from *regarder,* to REGARD.]

re·gard·ful (rĭ-gärd′fəl) *adj.* **1.** Showing regard; observant; heedful. Often used with *of.* **2.** Showing deference; respectful; considerate. **—re·gard·ful·ly** *adv.* **—re·gard·ful·ness** *n.*

re·gard·ing (rĭ-gär′dĭng) *prep.* In reference to; with respect to; concerning. —See Usage note at **regard.**

re·gard·less (rĭ-gärd′lĭs) *adj.* Heedless; unmindful. **—regardless of.** In spite of: *He bought it regardless of the price.*
—*adv.* In spite of everything; anyway. **—re·gard·less·ly** *adv.* **—re·gard·less·ness** *n.*

re·gat·ta (rĭ-gä′tə, -găt′ə) *n.* A boat race or series of boat races. [Italian (Venetian dialect) *regatta, regata*†, gondola race.]

regd. registered.

re·ge·late (rē′jə-lāt′, rē′jə-lāt′) *intr.v.* **-lat·ed, -lat·ing, -lates.** To undergo regelation. [RE- + Latin *gelāre,* to freeze.]

re·ge·la·tion (rē′jə-lā′shən) *n.* **1.** Successive melting and freezing of ice when pressure is applied and relaxed at the interface of two blocks of ice. **2.** The fusion of two blocks of ice by regelation.

re·gen·cy (rē′jən-sē) *n., pl.* **-cies.** **1.** The office, area of jurisdiction, or government of a regent or regents. **2.** A person or group selected to govern in place of a king or other ruler in the case of minority, absence, incompetence, or sickness. **3.** The period during which a regent governs, especially: **a. Regency.** In British history, the period 1811–20 during which George, Prince of Wales (later George IV) was regent for his father George III. **b. Regency.** In French history, the period 1715–23 during which Philippe, Duke of Orléans, was regent for the young Louis XV.
—*adj. Usually* **Regency.** Of, pertaining to, or characteristic of the style, especially in furniture, prevalent during the Regency periods in Britain and France.

re·gen·er·a·cy (rĭ-jĕn′ər-ə-sē) *n.* The state of being regenerated.

re·gen·er·ate (rĭ-jĕn′ə-rāt′) *v.* **-at·ed, -at·ing, -ates.** —*tr.* **1.** To reform or revitalize spiritually or morally. **2.** To form, construct, or create anew. **3.** *Biology.* To replace (a lost or damaged organ or part) by formation of new tissue. **4.** *Electronics.* To amplify (a signal in a radio receiver, for example) by positive feedback. —*intr.* **1.** To become formed or constructed again. **2.** To undergo spiritual conversion or rebirth. **3.** To effect regeneration.
—*adj.* (rĭ-jĕn′ər-ĭt). **1.** Spiritually or morally revitalized. **2.** Restored; refreshed; renewed. [Latin *regenerāre,* to reproduce : *re-,* again + *generāre,* to beget, GENERATE.] **—re·gen·er·a·ble** *adj.* **—re·gen·er·a·bly** *adv.* **—re·gen·er·a·tive** (rĭ-jĕn′ə-rā′tĭv, -ər-ə-tĭv) *adj.* **—re·gen·er·a·tive·ly** *adv.*

re·gen·er·a·tion (rĭ-jĕn′ə-rā′shən) *n.* **1.** The act or process of regenerating or the state of being regenerated. **2.** Spiritual or moral revival or rebirth. **3.** *Biology.* The regrowth of lost or destroyed parts or organs.

re·gen·er·a·tor (rĭ-jĕn′ə-rā′tər) *n.* One that regenerates.

Re·gens·burg (rā′gənz-bûrg′). Town in the state of Bavaria, West Germany. It is a commercial, industrial, and transport center. Dating from Roman times, it was the permanent seat of the Imperial Diet (1663–1806), and passed to Bavaria in 1810.

re·gent (rē′jənt) *n. Abbr.* **reg., regt., Regt.** **1.** One who rules during the minority, absence, or disability of a sovereign. **2.** *Archaic.* One acting as a ruler or governor. **3.** A person serving on a board that governs a state university or other educational institution or system. [Middle English, from Old French, ruling, from Medieval Latin *regēns* (stem *regent-*), from Latin, present participle of *regere,* to rule.] **—re·gent** *adj.*

regent bird *n.* An Australian bowerbird, *Sericulus chrysocephalus.*

reg·gae (rĕg′ā, rĕg′ē) *n.* A type of popular music originating in the West Indies with an insistent rhythm heavily accentuating the third beat of the bar. [20th century : of West Indian origin.]

Reg·gio di Ca·la·bri·a (răd′jō dē kä-lä′brē-ə). Seaport and industrial center in Calabria, southwestern Italy. Originally a Greek colony, it was taken by the Romans in 270 B.C.

Reggio nell'E·mi·lia (nĕl′ā-mē′lyä). Capital of the province of Reggio nell'Emilia in northern Italy on the Crostolo River. It lies on the ancient Via Emilia and is a commercial center for the surrounding rich agricultural area.

reg·i·cide (rĕj′ə-sīd′) *n.* **1.** The killing of a king. **2.** One who kills or helps to kill a king. [Latin *rēx* (stem *rēg-*), king + -CIDE.] **—reg·i·ci·dal** (rĕj′ə-sīd′l) *adj.*

re·gime, ré·gime (rā-zhēm′, rĭ-) *n.* **1. a.** A system of management or government. **b.** A government holding power; administration: *The new regime promised to hold elections.* **2.** A social system or pattern. **3.** A regimen. **4.** The pattern of seasonal fluctuation in a climate or in the volume of a river. **5.** *Informal.* The accepted way of doing or running things: *the new office regime.* [French *régime,* from Latin *regimen,* from *regere,* to rule.]

reg·i·men (rĕj′ə-mən, -mĕn′) *n.* **1.** A system of therapy: *a dietetic regimen.* **2.** A set of rules or prescribed procedure for regulating life or achieving some end. [Middle English, from Latin, REGIME.]

reg·i·ment (rĕj′ə-mənt) *n.* **1.** *Abbr.* **reg., regt., Regt.** A permanent military unit consisting of at least two battalions and sometimes other units and usually commanded by a colonel. **2.** A large, organized group. **3.** *Archaic.* Rule: *"the monstrous regiment of women"* (John Knox).
—*tr.v.* (rĕj′ə-mĕnt′), **regimented, -menting, -ments.** **1.** To organize or form into a regiment or regiments. **2.** To appoint to a regiment. **3.** To put into order; systematize. **4.** To force uniformity and discipline upon. [Middle English, from Old French, from Late Latin *regimentum,* from Latin *regere,* to rule.] **—reg·i·men·tal** (rĕj′ə-mĕn′təl) *adj.* **—reg·i·men·tal·ly** *adv.* **—reg·i·men·ta·tion** (rĕj′-ə-mĕn-tā′shən) *n.*

reg·i·men·tals (rĕj′ə-mĕn′təlz) *pl.n.* **1.** The uniform and insignia characteristic of a particular regiment. **2.** Military dress.

Re·gi·na[1] (rĭ-jī′nə) *n. Abbr.* **R., Reg.** The reigning British queen. Used as a title and signature on documents. [Latin.]

Regina[2]. Capital of Saskatchewan province, Canada, built on the Indian settlement of Wascana. It is a major agricultural center.

re·gion (rē′jən) *n. Abbr.* **reg.** **1.** Any large, usually continuous segment of a surface or space; an area. **2.** A large and indefinite portion of the earth's surface. **3.** A specific district or territory. **4.** A field of interest or activity; a sphere. **5.** A part of the earth characterized by distinctive animal or plant life: *birds of the Nearctic region.* **6.** An area of the body having natural or arbitrarily assigned boundaries: *the abdominal region.* **7.** Range; vicinity: *a price in the region of $5,000.* **8.** *Mathematics.* A **domain** (*see*). —See Synonyms at **area.** [Middle English *regioun,* kingdom, from Old French *region,* from Latin *regiō* (stem *regiōn-),* direction, boundary, from *regere,* to direct.]

re·gion·al (rē′jən-əl) *adj.* **1.** Of, pertaining to, or characteristic of a large geographic region. **2.** Of, pertaining to, or characteristic of a particular region or district; localized. **3.** Of, belonging to, or characteristic of a form of a language that is distributed in identifiable geographic areas and has identifiable phonetic, structural, and other differences from the standard form of the language; dialectal. **—re·gion·al·ly** *adv.*

regional ileitis *n. Medicine.* Inflammation, thickening, and ulceration of any part of the digestive tract, particularly the ileum. Also called "Crohn's disease."

re·gion·al·ism (rē′jən-ə-lĭz′əm) *n.* **1.** The political division of territory into partially autonomous regions. **2.** The theory or advocacy of such a political system. **3.** Attachment to one's native region. **4.** A feature, as of language, associated with a particular region. **5.** Interest in or depiction of regional characteristics and settings in art or literature.

re·gion·al·ize (rē′jən-ə-līz′) *tr.v.* **-ized, -iz·ing, -iz·es.** To divide into regions for administrative purposes; especially, to divide into partially autonomous administrative units. **—re·gion·al·i·za·tion** *n.*

ré·gis·seur (rā′zhē-sœr′) *n., pl.* **-seurs** (-sœr′). *French.* The director of a ballet.

reg·is·ter (rĕj′ĭ-stər) *n. Abbr.* **reg.** **1.** A formal or official recording of items, names, or actions. **2.** A book for such entries. **3.** An entry in a register. **4.** A device that automatically indicates a quantity or number. **5.** An adjustable, grill-like device through which heated or cooled air is released into a room. **6.** *Music.* **a.** The range of an instrument or voice. **b.** A part of such a range that has similar quality. **c.** A group of matched organ pipes; a stop. **7.** *Printing.* **a.** The alignment of printed lines for columns on both sides of a

Regency architecture *The Royal Pavilion at Brighton, England, was built between 1815 and 1823 by the Regency architect John Nash. Regency architecture combined oriental and French influences with classical Greek styles and was characterized by the use of delicate iron balconies, stucco plasterwork, and tall windows.*

page. **b.** The alignment of different color plates in the printing of a picture. **8.** *Computer Science.* A specific location in a storage device, especially one assigned to a particular operation.
~*v.* **registered, -tering, -ters.** —*tr.* **1.** To enter in a register; record officially; enroll. **2.** To indicate, as on an instrument or scale. **3.** To give outward signs of; express: *register emotions.* **4.** To cause (mail) to be officially recorded by payment of a fee. **5.** To cause to align or correspond. —*intr.* **1.** To place or cause placement of one's name in a register or on an official list: *We registered to vote.* **2.** To be indicated, as on an instrument or scale. **3.** To be shown or expressed. **4.** To create an impression on someone's mind. **5.** To be aligned; correspond. [Middle English *registre,* from Old French, from Medieval Latin *registrum, regest(r)um,* from Late Latin *regesta,* list, neuter plural past participle of Latin *regerere,* to bring back : *re-,* back + *gerere,* to bring, carry.] **—reg·is·ter·er** *n.* **—reg·is·tra·ble** (rĕj′ĭ-strə-bəl) *adj.*

registered mail *n.* **1.** Mail that is recorded by the post office when sent and at each point on its route so as to assure safe delivery. **2.** The postal service by which such mail is sent.

registered nurse *n. Abbr.* **R.N.** A trained nurse who has passed a state registration examination.

reg·is·trant (rĕj′ĭ-strənt) *n.* One who registers or is registered.

reg·is·trar (rĕj′ĭ-strär′, rĕj′ĭ-strär′) *n. Abbr.* **reg., regr. 1.** One who is in charge of registers or official records. **2.** *British.* An official in charge of a registry office, who is licensed to perform marriages. **3.** An officer in a college or university who keeps records of the enrollment and academic standing of students. **4.** An admitting officer in a hospital.

reg·is·tra·tion (rĕj′ĭ-strā′shən) *n.* **1.** A registering, as of voters or students. **2.** The number of persons registered; an enrollment. **3.** An entry in a register. **4.** A document certifying that one has registered. **5. a.** A selected combination of organ stops. **b.** The technique of selecting and adjusting organ stops.

registration number *n.* An assigned set of numerals and letters that identifies something that has been registered such as a motor vehicle or firearm.

reg·is·try (rĕj′ĭ-strē) *n., pl.* **-tries.** *Abbr.* **reg. 1.** Registration. **2.** A ship's registered nationality. **3.** A place for registering or where registers are kept.

registry office *n.* In Great Britain, an office where official records of births, marriages, and deaths are kept and where civil marriages are performed by a registrar.

re·gi·us professor (rē′jē-əs, -jəs) *n.* One holding a professorship established by royal bounty at any of certain older British universities. [Latin *rēgius,* royal, from *rēx* (stem *rēg-*), king + PROFESSOR.]

reg·let (rĕg′lĭt) *n.* **1.** *Architecture.* A narrow, flat molding. **2.** *Printing.* A flat piece of wood used to separate lines of type. [French *réglet,* from Old French *reglet,* from *regle,* rule, straight edge, from Latin *rēgula,* rule.]

reg·nal (rĕg′nəl) *adj.* Designating a specified year of a sovereign's reign calculated from the date of accession: *in her thirtieth regnal year.* [Medieval Latin *regnālis,* from Latin *rēgnum,* REIGN.]

reg·nant (rĕg′nənt) *adj.* **1. a.** Reigning; ruling. **b.** Ruling in one's own right and not merely as a consort: *Queen regnant.* **2.** Predominant. **3.** Widespread; prevalent. [Latin *regnāns* (stem *regnant-*), present participle of *regnāre,* to reign, from *rēgnum,* REIGN.]

reg·o·lith (rĕg′ə-lĭth′) *n.* Loose material, including soil, broken rock, volcanic ash, and glacial material, overlying the bedrock. Also called "mantle rock." [Greek *rhēgos,* blanket + -LITH.]

re·gorge (rē-gôrj′) *v.* **-gorged, -gorging, -gorges.** —*tr.* To disgorge. —*intr.* To flow back again. [French *regorger,* from Old French : *re-,* back + *gorger,* to gorge, from *gorge,* throat, GORGE.]

reg·o·sol (rĕg′ə-sŏl′) *n.* An unconsolidated azonal soil formed from alluvium or sands. [Greek *rhēgos,* blanket + Latin *solum,* soil.]

regr. registrar.

re·grate (rē-grāt′) *tr.v.* **-grated, -grating, -grates. 1.** Formerly, to purchase (goods, especially foodstuffs) in order to resell at a profit at or near the same marketplace. **2.** To retail or sell again (goods so purchased). [Middle English *regraten,* from Old French *regrater,* from *regratier* : perhaps *re-,* against + *grater,* to scratch, from Germanic.]

re·gress (rĭ-grĕs′) *intr.v.* **-gressed, -gressing, -gresses.** To go back; return to a previous condition or behavior pattern.
~*n.* (rē′grĕs′). **1.** Return or withdrawal. **2.** The act of reasoning from an effect to a cause. [Latin *regressus,* past participle of *regredī,* to go back : *re-,* back + *gradī,* to step, go.]

re·gres·sion (rĭ-grĕsh′ən) *n.* **1.** Reversion; retrogression. **2.** Relapse to a less perfect or developed state. **3.** *Psychology.* Reversion to a more primitive or less mature behavior pattern. **4.** *Statistics.* The tendency for the expected value of a random variable to approach more closely the mean value of its set than does the independent variable by means of which it was predicted.

re·gres·sive (rĭ-grĕs′ĭv) *adj.* **1.** Tending to return or revert. **2.** Characterized by regression or a tendency to regress. **3.** Designating taxation in which the rate lessens as the amount taxed increases. **—re·gres·sive·ly** *adv.* **—re·gres·sive·ness** *n.*

re·gret (rĭ-grĕt′) *tr.v.* **-gretted, -gretting, -grets. 1.** To feel disappointed, distressed, or repentant about. **2.** To feel sorrow or grief over; mourn.
~*n.* **1.** Distress, repentance, sorrow, or disappointment over a desire unfulfilled or an action performed or not performed. **2.** A sense of loss and longing for someone or something gone. **3.** *Often* **regrets.** An expression of grief or disappointment; especially, a courteous declining to accept an invitation. [Middle English *regretten,* from Old French *regreter,* to lament : perhaps *re-* (intensifier), again + Old Norse *grata,* to moan, sob.]
Synonyms: *grief, heartache, sorrow, woe.*

re·gret·ful (rĭ-grĕt′fəl) *adj.* Full of regret or sorrow. **—re·gret·ful·ly** *adv.* **—re·gret·ful·ness** *n.*

re·gret·ta·ble (rĭ-grĕt′ə-bəl) *adj.* Eliciting or deserving regret. —See Synonyms at **pathetic.**

regret·ta·bly (rĭ-grĕt′ə-blē) *adv.* **1.** In a regrettable manner. **2.** It is regrettable that: *Regrettably, the book won't be finished on time.*

re·group (rē-gro͞op′), *v.* **-grouped, -grouping, -groups.** —*intr.* To become an ordered group or formation again after dispersal or disordering: *We regrouped after the attack.* —*tr.* To cause to regroup.

regt., Regt. 1. regent. **2.** regiment.

reg·u·lar (rĕg′yə-lər) *adj. Abbr.* **reg. 1.** Customary, usual, or normal. **2.** Orderly, even, or symmetrical. **3.** Conforming to set procedure, principle, or discipline. **4.** Methodical; well-ordered. **5.** Occurring at fixed intervals; periodic. **6.** Constant; not varying. **7.** Formally correct; proper. **8.** Having the required qualifications for an occupation. **9.** Perfect; complete; thorough: *a regular villain.* **10.** *Informal.* Good; nice: *a regular guy.* **11.** *Botany.* Having similar and symmetrically arranged parts. **12.** *Grammar.* Belonging to a standard mode of inflection or conjugation. **13.** Belonging to a religious order and bound by its rules: *the regular clergy.* Compare **secular. 14.** *Geometry:* **a.** Having equal sides and equal angles. Said of polygons. **b.** Having faces that are congruent regular polygons with congruent polyhedral angles. Said of polyhedra. **15.** Belonging to or constituting the permanent army of a nation. **16.** Menstruating or defecating at normal intervals. **17.** In crystallography, having radial symmetry. —See Synonyms at **normal.**
~*n. Abbr.* **reg. 1.** A soldier belonging to a regular army. **2.** *Informal.* A habitual customer or patron. **3.** A member of the clergy or of a religious order. **4.** A loyal and dependable person. **5.** A clothing size designed for persons of average height. [Middle English *reguler,* under religious rule, from Old French, from Latin *rēgulāris,* containing rules, from *rēgula,* rule, ruler.] **—reg·u·lar·i·ty** (rĕg′yə-lăr′ə-tē) *n.* **—reg·u·lar·ly** *adv.*

reg·u·lar·ize (rĕg′yə-lə-rīz′) *tr.v.* **-ized, -izing, -izes.** To make regular; cause to conform. **—reg·u·lar·i·za·tion** *n.*

reg·u·late (rĕg′yə-lāt′) *tr.v.* **-lated, -lating, -lates. 1.** To control or direct according to a rule or procedure. **2.** To adjust in conformity to a specification or requirement. **3.** To adjust (a mechanism) for accurate and proper functioning. [Late Latin *rēgulāre,* from Latin *rēgula,* a rule.] **—reg·u·la·tive** (rĕg′yə-lā′tĭv, -lə-tĭv), **reg·u·la·to·ry** (-lə-tôr′ē, -tōr′-) *adj.*

reg·u·la·tion (rĕg′yə-lā′shən) *n. Abbr.* **reg. 1.** The act of regulating. **2.** A principle, rule, or law designed to control or govern behavior. **3.** A governmental order having the force of law. **4.** The ability of an embryo to continue normal development following injury to or alteration of a structure.
~*adj. Abbr.* **reg.** Prescribed in accordance with a rule or standard procedure: *a regulation uniform.*

reg·u·la·tor (rĕg′yə-lā′tər) *n. Abbr.* **reg. 1.** One that regulates. **2. a.** The mechanism in a watch by which its speed is governed. **b.** An accurate clock used as a standard for timing other clocks. **3. a.** A device to maintain uniform speed in a machine; a governor. **b.** A device to control the flow of gases, liquids, or electric current.

regulator gene *n.* A gene that controls the expression of an **operon** *(see).*

reg·u·lus (rĕg′yə-ləs) *n., pl.* **-li** (-lī′) or **-luses.** *Metallurgy.* **1.** The metallic part of a charge that sinks under the slag to the bottom of a furnace or crucible. **2.** A relatively impure product of various ores in smelting, **matte** *(see).* [Medieval Latin *rēgulus,* from Latin, a petty king (this metallic antimony combines readily with gold, the king of metals), diminutive of *rēx,* king.] **—reg·u·line** (rĕg′yə-lĭn, -līn′) *adj.*

Reg·u·lus (rĕg′yə-ləs) *n.* A bright triple star in the constellation Leo. Also called "Alpha Leonis."

Re·gu·lus (rĕg′yə-ləs), **Marcus Atilius** (died *c.* 250 B.C.). Roman general, hero of the First Punic War. Appointed consul in 267 B.C. and again in 256 B.C., he was captured by the Carthaginians in 255, and sent to sue for peace with the Roman senate; instead Regulus pleaded with the senate to reject the enemy's proposals.

re·gur·gi·tate (rē-gûr′jə-tāt′) *v.* **-tated, -tating, -tates.** —*intr.* **1.** To rush or surge back. **2.** To bring partially digested food back into the mouth to feed the young. Used especially of certain birds. —*tr.* **1.** To cause to pour back; especially, to vomit up (partially digested food). **2.** To bring (partially digested food) back into the mouth. Used especially of certain birds. **3.** To reproduce (facts, for example) in an unthinking fashion. [Medieval Latin *regurgitāre* : *re-,* back + Late Latin *gurgitāre,* to engulf, flood, from Latin *gurges,* a whirlpool.] **—re·gur·gi·ta·tion** *n.*

re·ha·bil·i·tate (rē′hə-bĭl′ə-tāt′) *tr.v.* **-tated, -tating, -tates. 1.** To restore (a delinquent person, for example) to useful life through education and therapy. **2.** To reinstate the good name of. **3.** To restore the former rank, privileges, or rights of. [Medieval Latin *rehabilitāre* : Late Latin *re-,* again + *habilitāre,* HABILITATE.] **—re·ha·bil·i·ta·tion** *n.* **—re·ha·bil·i·ta·tive** (rē′hə-bĭl′ə-tā′tĭv) *adj.*

re·hash (rē-hăsh′) *tr.v.* **-hashed, -hashing, -hashes.** To repeat, rework, or rewrite (old material) without significant alteration.
~*n.* (rē′hăsh′). A repeated or unoriginal account; a rehashing. [RE- + HASH (to chop over).]

re·hear (rē-hîr′) *tr.v.* **-heard** (-hûrd′), **-hearing, -hears. 1.** To hear

PRONUNCIATION KEY

ă, pat; ā, pay; âr, care;
ä, father, are; b, bib;
ch, church; d, deed; ĕ, pet;
ē, be; f, fife; g, gag; h, hat;
hw, which; ĭ, pit; ī, pie;
îr, pier; j, judge; k, kick;
l, lid, needle; m, mum;
n, no, sudden; ng, thing;
ŏ, pot; ō, toe; ô, paw, for;
oi, noise; ou, out; o͝o, book;
o͞o, boot; p, pop; r, roar;
s, sauce; sh, ship, dish;
t, tight; th, thin, path;
th, this, bathe; ŭ, cut; ûr, fur;
v, valve; w, with; y, yes;
z, zebra, size; zh, vision;
ə, about, item, edible,
gallop, circus, peaceful

IN FOREIGN WORDS:

à, *Fr.* ami; œ, *Fr.* feu, *Ger.* schön; ü, *Fr.* tu, *Ger.* über;
KH, *Ger.* ich, *Scot.* loch;
N, *Fr.* bon; y′, *Fr.* Compiègne

STRESS MARKS:

Primary stress: ′
in·cite′ (ĭn-sīt′)
Secondary stress: ′
in′sight′ (ĭn′sīt′)

again. **2.** *Law.* To give a second consideration to (a case).

re·hears·al (rĭ-hûr′səl) *n.* **1.** The act or an instance of practicing for a performance, especially for a public performance. **2.** A verbal repetition; a detailed enumeration: *a rehearsal of his woes.*

re·hearse (rĭ-hûrs′) *v.* **-hearsed, -hearsing, -hearses.** —*tr.* **1. a.** To practice (all or part of a play, concert, entertainment, or the like) in preparation for a public performance. **b.** To direct in rehearsal. **2.** To perfect or cause to perfect (an action) by repetition. **3.** To retell or recite. **4.** To list or enumerate. —*intr.* To practice all or part of a concert, entertainment, play, or the like. [Middle English *rehercen,* from Old French *rehercer,* to repeat, originally "to harrow again" : *re-,* again + *hercer,* to harrow, from *herce,* a harrow, from Latin *hirpex* (see **hearse**).] —**re·hears·er** *n.*

re·heat (rē-hēt′) *tr.v.* **-heated, -heating, -heats. 1.** To add fuel to (exhaust gas in a jet engine) in order to give further combustion and improve the power. **2.** To heat again.
~*n.* The process of reheating exhaust gases in a jet engine.

Re·ho·bo·am (rē′ə-bō′əm) *n. Often* **rehoboam.** A large wine bottle often used for champagne, holding about a gallon or somewhat more. [After *Rehoboam,* son of King Solomon (by analogy with JEROBOAM).]

re·house (rē-houz′) *tr.v.* **-housed, -housing, -houses.** To put or re-establish in a new, usually improved, dwelling or shelter.

Reich (rīk; *German* rīKH) *n.* The territory or government of a German empire or republic; specifically: the *First Reich,* the Holy Roman Empire (ninth century to 1806); the *Second Reich,* the German Empire (1871–1919); the Weimar Republic (1919–33); and the *Third Reich* (1933–45). [German, from Old High German *rīhhi,* realm.]

reichs·mark (rīks′märk′; *German* rīKHs′märk′) *n., pl.* **reichsmark** or **-marks.** *Abbr.* **RM.** A former monetary unit of Germany until 1948, having a value of 100 reichspfennigs. See **Deutsche mark.** [German : *Reichs,* genitive of REICH + MARK (money).]

reichs·pfen·nig (rīks′fĕn′ĭg; *German* rīKHs′pfĕn′ĭKH) *n.* A former bronze German coin, worth 1/100 of a reichsmark. See **pfennig.** [German : *Reichs,* genitive of REICH + PFENNIG.]

Reichs·tag (rīks′täg′; *German* rīKHs′täk′) *n.* **1.** The representative and legislative assembly of the German Empire (1871–1919) and of the Weimar Republic (1919–33). **2.** The building in Berlin in which the assembly met. [German : *Reichs,* genitive of REICH + *Tag,* council, diet, from *tagen,* to deliberate.]

re·i·fy (rē′ə-fī′, rā′-) *tr.v.* **-fied, -fying, -fies.** To regard or treat (an abstraction or ideal) as if concretely or materially existing. [Latin *rēs,* a thing + -FY.] —**re·i·fi·ca·tion** *n.* —**re·i·fi·er** *n.*

reign (rān) *n.* **1.** The exercise of sovereign power, as by a monarch. **2.** A period during which sovereignty is held. **3.** Dominance or widespread influence: *the reign of reason.*
~*intr.v.* **reigned, reigning, reigns. 1.** To exercise sovereign power. **2.** To hold the title of sovereign, but with limited authority. **3.** To be predominant or prevalent. [Middle English *rei(n)gne,* from Old French *reigne,* from Latin *rēgnum,* from *rēx* (stem *rēg-*), a king.]

reign·ing (rā′nĭng) *adj.* **1.** Currently exercising sovereign power. **2.** Currently holding a championship or other competitive title: *the reigning Miss World.*

Reign of Terror *n.* **1.** The period (1793–94) of the French Revolution during which thousands of persons were executed. **2. reign of terror.** Any period of widespread violence or intimidation.

Reik (rīk), **Theodor** (1888–1969). U.S. psychologist, born in Vienna. He was one of Freud's students and worked with him (1910–38), after which he settled in the United States.

re·im·burse (rē′ĭm-bûrs′) *tr.v.* **-bursed, -bursing, -burses. 1.** To repay: *He reimbursed his creditors.* **2.** To pay back or compensate (a person) for money spent, or losses or damages incurred. [RE- + obsolete *imburse,* to pay, to pocket money, from Old French *embourser* : EN- + *borser,* to obtain money, from *borse,* a purse, from Late Latin *bursa,* "oxhide," from Greek, hide, skin.] —**re·im·burs·a·ble** *adj.* —**re·im·burse·ment** *n.*

re·im·port (rē′ĭm-pôrt′, -pōrt′, rē-ĭm′pôrt′, -pōrt′) *tr.v.* **-ported, -porting, -ports.** To bring back into a country (goods made from raw materials originally exported from that country).
~*n.* (rē-ĭm′pôrt′, -pōrt′) **1.** The act of reimporting. **2.** Goods reimported. —**re·im·por·ta·tion** *n.*

re·im·pres·sion (rē′ĭm-prĕsh′ən) *n.* **1.** A second or subsequent impression. **2.** A reprinting of a book.

Reims (rēmz, răNs). *English* **Rheims** (rēmz). City in the department of Marne, in northeastern France on the Vesle River. It is a major marketing center for champagne wines. The site of the coronation of most French kings after Louis VII (1137), it has a fine Gothic cathedral. The German surrender was signed at Allied headquarters in Reims at the end of World War II (May 1945).

rein (rān) *n.* **1. a. reins.** A pair of long, narrow leather straps attached to the bit of a bridle and used by a rider or driver to control a horse or other animal. **b.** Any strap forming part of a harness, such as a bearing rein. **2. reins.** A harness used to control a young child. **3.** *Often* **reins.** A means of restraint, check, or guidance. **4.** *Often* **reins.** A means or instrument by which power is exercised: *the reins of government.* —**draw in the reins. 1.** To exert pressure on the reins. **2.** To slow or stop. —**give (free) rein to.** To release from restraints. —**keep a tight rein on.** To exercise close control over.
~*v.* **reined, reining, reins.** —*tr.* **1.** To check or hold back (a horse or other animal). Often used with *in, back,* or *up.* **2.** To guide or control. **3.** *Archaic.* To equip with reins. —*intr.* To control a horse or other animal with reins. Often used with *in, back,* or *up.* [Middle English *re(i)ne,* from Old French *re(s)ne,* from Vulgar Latin *retina* (unattested), from Latin *retinēre,* to RETAIN.]

re·in·car·nate (rē′ĭn-kär′nāt′) *tr.v.* **-nated, -nating, -nates.** To cause to be reborn in another body; incarnate again. Usually used in the passive: *believed he'd be reincarnated.*
~*adj.* (rē′ĭn-kär′nət). Reborn in another body; reincarnated. —**re·in·car·na·tion** (rē′ĭn-kär-nā′shən) *n.*

rein·deer (rān′dîr′) *n., pl.* **-deers** or collectively **reindeer.** A large deer, *Rangifer tarandus,* of arctic regions of the Old World and Greenland, having branched antlers in both sexes. It is identical to the caribou, but can be domesticated. [Middle English *reyndere,* from Old Norse *hreindyri* : *hreinn,* reindeer + *dyr,* deer.]

reindeer moss *n.* An erect, grayish, branching lichen, *Cladonia rangiferina,* of arctic regions, used as food by reindeer.

re·in·fec·tion (rē′ĭn-fĕk′shən) *n.* A second infection that follows recovery from a previous infection by the same causative agent.

re·in·force (rē′ĭn-fôrs′, -fōrs′) *tr.v.* **-forced, -forcing, -forces. 1.** To give more force or effectiveness to; strengthen; support. **2.** *Military.* To strengthen with additional manpower or equipment. **3.** To strengthen, as by adding extra support or padding. **4.** To increase in number. **5.** *Psychology.* To encourage by means of reinforcement. [RE- + *inforce,* variant of ENFORCE.]

reinforced concrete *n. Abbr.* **R.C.** Poured concrete containing steel bars or metal netting to increase its tensile strength. Also called "ferroconcrete."

re·in·force·ment (rē′ĭn-fôrs′mənt, -fōrs′mənt) *n.* **1.** The act or process of reinforcing, or the condition of being reinforced. **2.** Something that reinforces. **3.** *Often* **reinforcements.** Additional troops, vessels, or equipment sent to support a military action. **4.** *Psychology.* **a.** The occurrence or experimental introduction of an unconditioned stimulus along with a conditioned stimulus. **b.** The strengthening of a conditioned response by such means. **c.** The strengthening of an instrumental or operant conditioned response leading to satisfaction; reward. **d.** An event or condition that increases the likelihood that a given response will recur.

Rein·hardt (rīn′härt′), **Max** (1873–1943). Austrian stage actor, producer, and director. He managed his own theater in Berlin (1902–05); in 1919 he founded the *Grosse Schauspielhaus* and in 1920 the Salzburg Festival. In 1933 he fled Germany and settled in the United States. He was famous for his ambitious stage-setting and crowd scenes.

reins (rānz) *pl.n. Archaic.* **1.** The kidneys, loins, or lower back region. **2.** The seat of the affections and passions, which were formerly regarded as having their source in the kidneys and loins. [Middle English, from Old French, from Latin *rēnēs.* See **renal.**]

re·in·state (rē′ĭn-stāt′) *tr.v.* **-stated, -stating, -states. 1.** To restore to a previous condition or position. **2.** To bring back into use or existence. —**re·in·state·ment** *n.*

re·in·sure (rē′ĭn-shŏŏr′) *tr.v.* **-sured, -suring, -sures. 1.** To insure again. **2.** To insure by transferring in whole or in part a risk or contingent liability already covered under an existing contract. —**re·in·sur·ance** *n.* —**re·in·sur·er** *n.*

re·in·vest (rē′ĭn-vĕst′) *tr.v.* **-vested, -vesting, -vests.** To invest (capital or earnings) again. Used especially of receipts derived from securities. —**re·in·vest·ment** *n.*

reis. Alternate plural of **real** (Portuguese monetary unit).

re·is·sue (rē-ĭsh′ōō) *tr.v.* **-sued, -suing, -sues.** To issue again; make available again.
~*n.* **1.** A second or subsequent issue, as of a book altered in format or price. **2.** A reprinting of postage stamps from unchanged plates.

re·it·er·ate (rē-ĭt′ə-rāt′) *tr.v.* **-ated, -ating, -ates.** To say or do over again; repeat. [Latin *reiterāre* : *re-,* again + *iterāre,* ITERATE.] —**re·it·er·a·tion** (rē-ĭt′ə-rā′shən) *n.* —**re·it·er·a·tive** (rē-ĭt′ə-rā′tĭv, -ər-ə-tĭv) *adj.* —**re·it·er·a·tive·ly** *adv.*

reive (rēv) *intr.v.* **reived, reiving, reives.** *Chiefly Scottish.* To raid, rob, or plunder. [Variant of REAVE.] —**reiv·er** *n.*

re·ject (rĭ-jĕkt′) *tr.v.* **-jected, -jecting, -jects. 1.** To refuse to accept, recognize, or make use of; repudiate. **2.** To refuse to consider or grant; deny. **3.** To refuse affection or recognition to (a person). **4.** To discard as defective or useless; throw away. **5.** To spit out or vomit. **6.** To fail to accept (transplanted tissues or organs) owing to immunological incompatibility. —See Synonyms at **refuse.**
~*n.* (rē′jĕkt′). Something or someone that has been rejected as unsatisfactory or below standard. [Middle English *rejecten,* from Latin *rejicere* (past participle *rejectus*), to throw back : *re-,* back, away + *jacere,* to throw.] —**re·ject·er** *n.*

re·jec·tion (rĭ-jĕk′shən) *n.* **1.** The act or process of rejecting. **2.** The condition of being rejected. **3.** Something rejected.

re·jec·tor (rĭ-jĕk′tər) *n.* One that rejects; specifically, an electronic circuit that cuts out signals of a designated frequency range. Compare **acceptor.**

re·jig (rē-jĭg′) *tr.v.* **-jigged, -jigging, -jigs.** *Chiefly British.* **1.** To re-equip (a factory, workshop, or the like) with different machines or equipment; retool. **2.** *Informal.* To revise, rework, or rearrange. —**re·jig·ger** *n.*

re·joice (rĭ-jois′) *v.* **-joiced, -joicing, -joices.** —*intr.* **1.** To feel or be joyful. **2.** To possess or be lucky in possessing something. Used with *in*: *He rejoiced in the name of Herbert Sidebottom.* —*tr.* To fill with joy; gladden. [Middle English *rejoicen,* from Old French *rejoir* (stem *rejoiss-*) : *re-* (intensive) + *joir,* to be joyful, from Latin *gaudēre.*] —**re·joic·er** *n.*

reindeer *Reindeer, or caribou, are domesticated in Lapland and used as draft animals as well as for their meat, milk, and hides.*

re·joic·ing (rĭ-joi′sĭng) *n.* The feeling or expressing of joy or an instance of this; joyful celebration.
re·join[1] (rē′join′) *v.* **-joined, -joining, -joins.** —*tr.* **1.** To come again into the company of: *rejoined his regiment.* **2.** To join or put together again; reunite. —*intr.* To be or become joined again.
re·join[2] (rĭ-join′) *v.* **-joined, -joining, -joins.** —*tr.* To say as a reply. —*intr.* **1.** To respond; answer. **2.** *Law.* To answer a plaintiff's replication. [Middle English *rejoinen,* from Old French *rejoindre* : *re-,* back, again + *joindre,* to JOIN.]
re·join·der (rĭ-join′dər) *n.* **1.** An answer, especially in response to a reply. **2.** *Law.* A second pleading by a defendant, in answer to a plaintiff's replication. [Middle English *rejoyner,* from Old French *rejoindre* (substantive infinitive), to REJOIN (answer).]
re·ju·ve·nate (rĭ-jo͞o′və-nāt′) *tr.v.* **-nated, -nating, -nates.** **1.** To restore the youthful vigor or appearance of. **2.** To stimulate (a stream) to renewed erosive activity, as by a local uplift of land or an increase in precipitation. [RE- + Latin *juvenis,* a youth.] —**re·ju·ve·na·tion** (rĭ-jo͞o′və-nā′shən) *n.* —**re·ju·ve·na·tor** *n.*
re·ju·ve·nes·cence (rĭ-jo͞o′və-nĕs′əns) *n.* The act of making youthful again; rejuvenation. —**re·ju·ve·nes·cent** *adj.*
re·kin·dle (rē-kĭn′dəl) *v.* **-kindled, kindling, -kindles.** —*tr.* **1.** To relight. **2.** To revive or renew: *rekindle one's interest in books.* —*intr.* To be relit or revived.
rel. **1.** relating. **2.** relative; relatively. **3.** released. **4.** religion; religious.
re·lapse (rĭ-lăps′) *intr.v.* **-lapsed, -lapsing, -lapses.** **1.** To fall back into or revert to a former habit or state. **2.** To regress after partial recovery from illness. **3.** To slip back into bad ways; backslide. ~*n.* (rē′lăps′, rĭ-lăps′). The act or an instance of relapsing. [Latin *relapsus,* past participle of *relābī,* to slide back : *re-,* back + *lābī,* to slide.] —**re·laps·er** *n.*
relapsing fever *n.* Any of several infectious diseases characterized by chills and fever, and caused by spirochetes of the genus *Borrelia* transmitted by lice and ticks. Also called "recurrent fever."
re·late (rĭ-lāt′) *v.* **-lated, -lating, -lates.** —*tr.* **1.** To narrate or tell. **2.** To bring into logical or natural association. —*intr.* **1.** To have connection, relation, or reference. Used with *to: The pictures and maps relate to the text.* **2.** To form a mutually responsive relationship; interact: *The lonely boy couldn't relate to his classmates.* —See Synonyms at **join.** [Latin *relātus* (past participle of *referre,* to carry back, REFER) : *re-,* back + *-lātus,* "carried."] —**re·lat·er** *n.*
re·lat·ed (rĭ-lā′tĭd) *adj.* **1.** Connected; associated. **2.** Connected by kinship, marriage, or common origin. **3.** *Music.* Having a specified harmonic connection. —**re·lat·ed·ness** *n.*
re·la·tion (rĭ-lā′shən) *n.* **1.** A logical or natural association between two or more things; relevance of one to another; a connection: *the relation between smoking and heart disease.* **2.** The connection of people by blood or marriage; kinship. **3.** A person related to another by blood or marriage; a relative. **4.** The mode or way in which a person or thing is connected with another: *the relation of parent to child.* **5. relations.** The connections or associations drawing together persons, groups, or nations in personal, business, or diplomatic affairs. **6.** Reference; regard: *in relation to your query.* **7. a.** The act of telling or narrating. **b.** A narrative; an account. **8. relations.** Sexual intercourse.
re·la·tion·al (rĭ-lā′shən-əl) *adj.* **1.** Of or arising from kinship. **2.** Indicating or constituting relations. **3.** *Grammar.* Expressing a syntactic relation.
re·la·tion·ship (rĭ-lā′shən-shĭp′) *n.* **1.** The condition or fact of being related. **2.** Connection by blood or marriage; kinship. **3. a.** A particular kind of connection existing between people having dealings with one another: *I have a good working relationship with my boss.* **b.** A close emotional connection between two persons.
rel·a·tive (rĕl′ə-tĭv) *adj. Abbr.* **rel.** **1.** Having pertinence or relevance; connected; related. **2.** Considered in comparison with something else. **3.** Dependent upon or interconnected with something else for intelligibility or significance; not absolute. **4.** Referring to or qualifying an antecedent. **5.** *Grammar.* Designating a pronoun that introduces a relative clause and has reference to an antecedent. In the sentence *He who hesitates is lost,* the relative pronoun is *who.* Compare **demonstrative, interrogative.** **6.** *Music.* Having the same key signature. Said of major and minor scales and keys. **7.** *Physics & Chemistry.* Pertaining to or designating a physical quantity that is expressed as a ratio of the measured value to the value for some standard system: *relative density; relative humidity.*
~*n.* **1. a.** One related by kinship; a relation. **b.** One related by a common origin. **2.** One that is relative. **3.** *Grammar.* A relative term. [Middle English *relatif,* from Old French, from Late Latin *relātīvus,* from Latin *relātus.* See **relate.**] —**rel·a·tive·ly** *adv.* —**rel·a·tive·ness** *n.*
relative atomic mass *n. Symbol* A_r *Chemistry.* **Atomic weight** *(see).*
relative biological effectiveness *n. Abbr.* **RBE** *Physics.* A measure of the capacity of a specific ionizing radiation to produce a specific biological effect, usually expressed as the dose of a standard type of radiation relative to the dose of the ionization in question required to produce the effect.
relative clause *n. Grammar.* A dependent clause introduced by a relative pronoun. In the sentence *He who hesitates is lost,* the relative clause is *who hesitates.*
relative density *n. Symbol* **d** The density of a substance relative to the density of some standard substance; especially, **specific gravity** *(see).*
relative humidity *n. Abbr.* **r.h.** The ratio of the amount of water vapor in the air at a specific temperature to the maximum capacity of the air at that temperature. Compare **absolute humidity.**
relative majority *n.* The number of votes cast for a winning candidate that exceed those cast for the runner-up, when no one candidate receives more than 50 percent of all votes cast. Compare **absolute majority.**
relative permeability *n. Symbol* μ_r *Physics.* The ratio of the magnetic permeability of a given medium to that of free space (that is, to the magnetic constant).
relative permittivity *n. Symbol* ϵ_r *Physics.* The ratio of the electric permittivity of a given medium to that of free space (that is, to the electric constant). Also called "dielectric constant."
relative pitch *n.* **1.** The pitch of a tone as determined by its position in a scale. **2.** The ability to recognize or produce a tone by mentally establishing a relationship between its pitch and that of a recently heard tone. Compare **absolute pitch.**
rel·a·tiv·ism (rĕl′ə-tĭv-ĭz′əm) *n.* Any of various philosophical attitudes holding that moral value, knowledge, or truth is not absolute but relative, for example to an individual, historical circumstances, or a culture.
rel·a·tiv·ist (rĕl′ə-tĭv-ĭst) *n.* **1.** A proponent of relativism. **2.** A physicist specializing in the theories of relativity.
rel·a·tiv·is·tic (rĕl′ə-tĭv-ĭs′tĭk) *adj.* **1.** Of or pertaining to relativism. **2.** *Physics.* **a.** Of, pertaining to, or resulting from speeds that are approaching the speed of light: *relativistic increase in mass.* **b.** Of or pertaining to phenomena explicable by special or general relativity: *relativistic mechanics.*
rel·a·tiv·i·ty (rĕl′ə-tĭv′ə-tē) *n.* **1.** The quality or state of being relative. **2.** A state of dependence in which the existence, quality, or significance of one entity is determined by that of another. **3.** A theory of relative motion, space, and time developed by Albert Einstein in two parts. **Special relativity** (1905) deals with uniform motion at constant relative velocity, and is based on the principles that the speed of light is a constant, irrespective of the the motion of the observer, that physical laws are the same for all observers, and that mass and energy are equivalent. **General relativity** (published 1916) extends this to nonuniform (accelerated) motion, is applied particularly to gravitation, and introduces the principle that gravitational and inertial forces are equivalent.
re·la·tor (rĭ-lā′tər) *n.* One who relates or narrates.
re·lax (rĭ-lăks′) *v.* **-laxed, -laxing, -laxes.** —*tr.* **1.** To make lax or loose: *relax one's grip.* **2.** To make less severe, formal, or strict. **3.** To reduce in intensity; slacken. **4.** To relieve from effort or strain. —*intr.* **1.** To take one's ease; rest. **2.** To become lax or loose. **3.** To become less severe. **4.** To become less formal or tense. [Middle English *relaxen,* from Latin *relaxāre* : *re-,* back + *laxāre,* to loosen, from *laxus,* lax, loose.] —**re·lax·a·ble** *adj.* —**re·lax·er** *n.*
re·lax·ant (rĭ-lăk′sənt) *n.* A drug or therapeutic treatment that relaxes or relieves muscular or nervous tension.
~*adj.* Tending to relax or to relieve tension.
re·lax·a·tion (rē′lăk-sā′shən) *n.* **1. a.** The act of relaxing. **b.** The state of being relaxed. **2.** Refreshment of body or mind; recreation: *play golf for relaxation.* **3.** A loosening or slackening. **4.** A reduction in strictness or severity. **5.** *Physiology.* The return to normal length of inactive muscle or muscle fibers following contraction. **6.** *Physics.* The return or adjustment of a system to equilibrium following a small displacement or abrupt change. **7.** *Mathematics.* A numerical method in which the errors, or residuals, resulting from an initial approximation are reduced by succeeding approximations until all errors are within specific limits. —See Synonyms at **rest.** —**re·lax·a·tive** (rĭ-lăk′sə-tĭv) *adj. & n.*
relaxation time *n. Physics.* The time required for an exponential variable to decrease to $1/e$ (0.368) of its initial value.
re·laxed (rĭ-lakst′) *adj.* **1.** Free from strain or tension. **2.** Informal or easy-going in manner. —**re·lax·ed·ly** (rĭ-lăk′sĭd-lē) *adv.* —**re·laxed·ness** *n.*
re·lax·in (rĭ-lăk′sən) *n.* A female hormone secreted by the corpus luteum in the final stages of pregnancy that causes the cervix to dilate and relaxes the pelvic ligaments in childbirth. [RELAX + -IN.]
re·lay (rē′lā′) *tr.v.* **-laid** (-lād′), **-laying, -lays.** To lay again.
re·lay (rē′lā, rĭ-lā′) *n.* **1.** A crew of laborers who relieve another crew at work; a shift. **2.** A fresh team, as of horses or dogs, to relieve weary animals in a hunt, task, or journey. **3.** An act of passing something along from one person, group, or station to another. **4.** A relay race or any one of its lengths or laps. **5.** An automatic electromagnetic or electromechanical device that responds to a small current or voltage change by activating switches or other devices in an electric circuit.
~*tr.v.* **relayed, -laying, -lays.** **1.** To pass or send along by or as if by relay: *relay a message.* **2.** To supply with fresh relays. **3.** *Electronics.* To control or retransmit by means of a relay. **4.** *British.* To broadcast from a theater, concert hall, or the like via a transmitter. [Middle English *relai,* from Old French, from *relaier,* to relay, leave behind : *re-,* back + *laier,* to leave, variant of *laissier,* from Latin *laxāre,* to loosen, from *laxus,* lax, loose.]
relay race *n.* A race between two or more teams, in which each team member runs only a set part of the race, and then is relieved by another member of the team.
relay station *n.* An installation for receiving telecommunications signals and amplifying and retransmitting them.
re-lease (rē′lēs′) *tr.v.* **-leased, -leasing, -leases.** To lease again.
re·lease (rĭ-lēs′) *tr.v.* **-leased, -leasing, -leases.** **1.** To set free from confinement, restraint, or bondage; liberate. **2.** To free, unfasten,

PRONUNCIATION KEY

ă, pat; ā, pay; âr, care;
ä, father, are; b, bib;
ch, church; d, deed; ĕ, pet;
ē, be; f, fife; g, gag; h, hat;
hw, which; ĭ, pit; ī, pie;
îr, pier; j, judge; k, kick;
l, lid, needle; m, mum;
n, no, sudden; ng, thing;
ŏ, pot; ō, toe; ô, paw, for;
oi, noise; ou, out; o͝o, book;
o͞o, boot; p, pop; r, roar;
s, sauce; sh, ship, dish;
t, tight; th, thin, path;
th, this, bathe; ŭ, cut; ûr, fur;
v, valve; w, with; y, yes;
z, zebra, size; zh, vision;
ə, about, item, edible,
gallop, circus, peaceful

IN FOREIGN WORDS:

à, *Fr.* ami; œ, *Fr.* feu, *Ger.* schön; ü, *Fr.* tu, *Ger.* über; KH, *Ger.* ich, *Scot.* loch; N, *Fr.* bon; y′, *Fr.* Compiègne

STRESS MARKS:

Primary stress: ′
in·cite′ (ĭn-sīt′)
Secondary stress: ′
in′sight′ (ĭn′sīt′)

or let go of. **3.** To relieve from debt or obligation. **4. a.** To allow performance, sale, publication, distribution, or circulation of. **b.** To make known or available. **5.** To relinquish (a right or claim, for example). **6.** *Chemistry.* To free from chemical combination. —*n.* **1.** A deliverance; liberation. **2.** An authoritative discharge from an obligation or from prison. **3.** An unfastening or letting go of something caught or held fast. **4.** A device or catch for locking or releasing a mechanism. **5. a.** A freeing or issuing of something for general publication, use, or circulation: *the release of a new motion picture.* **b.** Something thus issued or released: *a press release; a record release.* **6.** *Law.* **a.** The relinquishment of a right, title, or claim to another. **b.** The document authorizing such a relinquishment. [Middle English *relesen,* from Old French *relessier, relaissier,* from Latin *relaxāre,* to RELAX.]

re·leas·er (rĭ-lē′sər) *n.* **1.** One that releases. **2.** *Zoology.* Any stimulus or combination of stimuli that elicits an instinctive behavioral pattern.

rel·e·gate (rĕl′ə-gāt′) *tr.v.* **-gated, -gating, -gates. 1.** To send or consign, especially to an obscure or inferior place, position, or condition. **2.** To assign to a class or category; classify. **3.** To refer or assign (a matter or task, for example) for decision or execution. **4.** To cast out; banish; exile. [Latin *relēgāre,* to send away : *re-,* back, away + *lēgare,* to send.] —**rel·e·ga·tion** *n.*

re·lent (rĭ-lĕnt′) *intr.v.* **-lented, -lenting, -lents.** To become softened or gentler in attitude, temper, or determination; go back on a harsh decision. —See Synonyms at **yield.** [Middle English *relenten,* from Medieval Latin *relentāre* (unattested) : *re-* (intensive), again + *lentāre,* soften, from Latin, bend, from *lentus,* pliable.]

re·lent·less (rĭ-lĕnt′lĭs) *adj.* **1.** Unyielding; pitiless: *relentless persecution.* **2.** Steady and persistent; unremitting: *the relentless advance of the tide.* —**re·lent·less·ly** *adv.* —**re·lent·less·ness** *n.*

rel·e·vant (rĕl′ə-vənt) *adj.* **1.** Related to the matter at hand; to the point; pertinent. **2.** Applicable to current social or political issues and affairs. **3.** *Linguistics.* Serving to distinguish one phoneme from others; distinctive. [Medieval Latin *relevāns* (stem *relevant-*), from Latin, present participle of *relevāre,* to lift up, RELIEVE.] —**rel·e·vance, rel·e·van·cy** *n.* —**rel·e·vant·ly** *adv.*

Synonyms: *apposite, apropos, apt, germane, material, pertinent.*

re·li·a·ble (rĭ-lī′ə-bəl) *adj.* Capable of being relied upon; trustworthy; dependable. —**re·li·a·bil·i·ty, re·li·a·ble·ness** *n.* —**re·li·a·bly** *adv.*

re·li·ance (rĭ-lī′əns) *n.* **1.** The act of relying. **2.** Confidence; dependence; trust. **3.** Something or someone depended on; a mainstay. —See Synonyms at **trust.**

re·li·ant (rĭ-lī′ənt) *adj.* Dependent; relying or trusting. Used with *on.* —**re·li·ant·ly** *adv.*

rel·ic (rĕl′ĭk) *n.* Also *archaic* **rel·ique** (rĕl′ĭk, rĭ-lēk′). **1.** Something that has survived the passage of time; especially, an object or custom whose original cultural environment has disappeared. **2.** *Biology.* A relict. **3.** Something cherished for its age or associations with a person, place, or event; a keepsake. **4.** An object of religious veneration; especially, an article reputed to be associated with a saint or martyr. **5.** Anything old, leftover, or remaining; a remnant. **6. relics.** The remains of a dead person; a corpse. —See Usage note at **remainder.** [Middle English *relik(e),* from Old French *relique,* from Late Latin *reliquia,* remains (especially of a martyr), from Latin, from *relinquere,* to leave behind, RELINQUISH.]

rel·ict (rĕl′ĭkt, rĭ-lĭkt′) *n.* **1.** *Biology.* An organism or species of an earlier time surviving in an environment that has undergone considerable change. **2.** *Rare.* A widow. —*adj.* *Geology.* Pertaining to something that has survived, such as structures or minerals after destructive processes. [Latin *relictus,* past participle of *relinquere,* to leave behind, RELINQUISH.]

re·lief (rĭ-lēf′) *n.* **1. a.** Ease from or lessening of pain or discomfort. **b.** Ease or lessening of a burden or something imposed, such as a levy: *tax relief.* **2. a.** Anything that lessens pain, discomfort, fear, anxiety, or the like. **b.** The feeling of buoyancy or well-being that immediately follows the removal or lessening of anxiety, pain, discomfort, or the like. **3.** Assistance, in the form of money or food, given to the needy, aged, or to the inhabitants of any disaster-stricken region. **4. a.** A release from a job, post, or duty, as of a sentinel. **b.** The person or group of persons taking over the duties of another. **5. a.** The projection of figures or forms from a flat background, or such a projection that is apparent only, as in painting. **b.** Any work of art featuring such projection. Also called "relievo." **6.** *Geography.* The variations in elevation of any area of the earth's surface. **7.** Distinction or prominence resulting from contrast: *Her dark hat brought her pallor into relief.* **8.** A diversion; a pleasant or amusing change: *light relief.* **9.** A bus, aircraft, ferry, or train that supplements or replaces an existing service. **10.** The act of raising a siege or blockade. **11.** *Law.* The obtaining of reparation or redress. **12.** In feudal law, a payment made by the heir of a deceased tenant to a lord for the privilege of succeeding to the tenant's estate. —**on relief.** Receiving government funds because of need or poverty. [Middle English, from Old French, from *relever,* to RELIEVE.]

relief map *n.* A map that depicts land elevations and sometimes water depths, as with contour lines, shading, or colors.

relief model *n.* A three-dimensional model of land configuration.

relief pitcher *n.* A baseball pitcher who replaces another pitcher during a game.

re·lieve (rĭ-lēv′) *tr.v.* **-lieved, -lieving, -lieves. 1.** To lessen or alleviate (something painful, oppressive, or distressing); ease: *Hypnotic*

HOW THINGS MOVE IN RELATION TO EACH OTHER
The theory that cast new light on the workings of the universe

The theory of relativity was proposed by Albert Einstein, the German-born mathematical physicist, early this century. It is based on the assumption that all motion is relative and that absolute rest is meaningless. That is, rest and motion do not exist by themselves—they depend on comparing one object with another.

For example, if a vehicle is traveling at 145 kilometers (90 miles) an hour toward another vehicle approaching it head on at 115 kilometers (70 miles) an hour, the velocity of the vehicles relative to each other is 260 kilometers (160 miles) an hour.

This relative velocity, however, applies to the two vehicles only in connection with each other. The velocity of the first vehicle relative to the earth is 145 kilometers (90 miles) an hour. Relative to the sun it is about 29,000 kilometers (18,000 miles) an hour. Einstein also put forward the ideas that mass and energy were equivalent and that time and space were inseparable—not independent concepts as had been previously supposed.

Einstein expounded his theory in two parts — the special theory of relativity (1905), which applies to observers or systems in uniform relative motion, and the general theory of relativity (1915), which deals also with observers in accelerated motion.

The special theory is developed from two principles: first, that the laws of natural phenomena are the same for all observers, and second, that the velocity of light is constant for all observers regardless of their own velocity. From these basic principles Einstein deduced that mass and energy are interchangeable and are related by the simple-sounding formula $E = mc^2$, where E is energy and m is mass and c is the speed of light.

The formula shows that a small mass can be converted into a huge amount of energy. This idea led to, among other things, the invention of the atom bomb and unlocked the secret of how the sun shines. Both processes are nuclear reactions in which a tiny amount of nuclear mass is liberated as light and heat.

Other findings of the special theory are that if a body moves at a high velocity relative to an observer, the observer sees that the length of the body has apparently contracted and that time for the body has slowed down.

These changes are significant only for speeds close to the speed of light. For example, if the body is a meter ruler with a clock strapped to it, the observer will measure the length of the ruler to be less than a meter and the clock will appear to be running slowly compared with the observer's clock. The observer will also see that the mass of the body increased with its velocity. For this reason it is impossible to travel faster than the speed of light, for at that speed mass becomes infinite.

In the general theory Einstein showed that the presence of massive bodies in space—or more specifically the presence of their gravitational fields—distorts space itself, so that the shortest distance between two points becomes a curve rather than a straight line. Light also is bent by the gravitational field of a massive body.

Many verifications of Einstein's theory have arisen in modern physics, especially in the fields of astrophysics and nuclear physics.

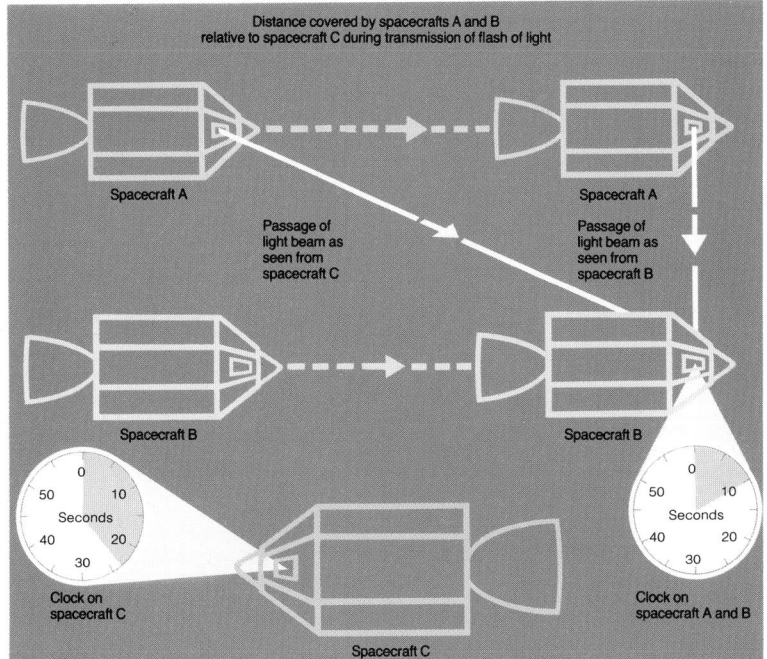

Distance covered by spacecrafts A and B relative to spacecraft C during transmission of flash of light

Spacecraft A

Spacecraft A

Passage of light beam as seen from spacecraft C

Passage of light beam as seen from spacecraft B

Spacecraft B

Spacecraft B

Clock on spacecraft C

Clock on spacecraft A and B

Spacecraft C

WHEN TIME SLOWS DOWN *Because the speed of all motion is relative to something else, time does not pass at the same rate for all observers. Consider, for instance, what happens when spacecrafts A and B, flying side by side, pass spacecraft C going in the opposite direction.*

If a flash of light is sent from A to B, it is seen by both craft as following a straight line, because neither craft is moving relative to the other. But seen from C the flash follows a diagonal line, from the position of A when the flash was emitted to the position of B when it was received.

This diagonal line is longer than the distance between spacecrafts A and B, and since the speed of light is constant, the time interval between emission and arrival must seem longer when viewed from C than from A or B. If A and B pass C at 90 percent of the speed of light, and the flash takes 10 seconds from A to B, to observers in C it will seem to take 23 seconds.

reliquary *A 13th-century French reliquary, decorated in enamel with angels in medallions. Reliquaries are used to store holy relics such as bones of saints.*

suggestion may relieve pain. **2.** To free from pain, anxiety, fear, or the like. **3. a.** To furnish assistance or aid to. **b.** To raise a siege or blockade of. **4.** To release (a person) from obligation or oppression, as by law or legislation. **5.** To free from a particular duty by providing or acting as a substitute. **6.** To make less oppressive, monotonous, or uniform: *"An explosive little laugh relieved the tension"* (F. Scott Fitzgerald). **7.** To make distinct or effective through contrast; set off: *A black sash relieves a white gown.* **8.** *Informal.* To rob; deprive: *I was relieved of my handbag.* **—relieve oneself.** To empty one's bowels or bladder. [Middle English *releven,* from Old French *relever,* relieve, raise again, from Latin *relevāre* : *re-,* again + *levāre,* to raise.] **—re·liev·a·ble** *adj.* **—re·liev·er** *n.*

Synonyms: *allay, alleviate, assuage, comfort, lighten, mitigate, soothe.*

relieving arch *n.* An arch built for reinforcement or to distribute weight more evenly.

re·lie·vo (rĭ-lē'vō) *n., pl.* **-vos.** Relief in art and architecture. [Italian *rilievo,* from *rilievare,* to emphasize, raise, from Latin *relevāre,* to RELIEVE.]

re·lig·ion (rĭ-lĭj'ən) *n. Abbr.* **rel., relig. 1.** The expression of man's belief in and reverence for a superhuman power or powers regarded as creating or governing the universe. **2.** Any personal or institutionalized system of beliefs or practices embodying this belief or reverence: *the Hindu religion.* **3.** The spiritual or emotional attitude of one who recognizes the existence of a superhuman power or powers. **4.** A cause, principle, or activity pursued with zeal or conscientious devotion: *A collector might make a religion of art.* **5.** The monastic way of life. **6.** *Archaic.* Sacred rites or practices. [Middle English *religioun,* from Old French *religion,* from Latin *religiō* (stem *religiōn-*), bond between man and the gods, perhaps from *religāre,* to bind back : *re-,* back + *ligāre,* to bind, fasten.]

re·lig·ion·ism (rĭ-lĭj'ə-nĭz'əm) *n.* Excessive or affected religious zeal. **—re·lig·ion·ist** *n.*

re·lig·i·ose (rĭ-lĭj'ē-ōs') *adj.* Excessively religious, particularly in an affected or sentimental manner. [From RELIGIOUS.]

re·lig·i·os·i·ty (rĭ-lĭj'ē-ŏs'ə-tē) *n., pl.* **-ties. 1.** The state of being religious. **2.** Excessive or affected piety.

re·lig·ious (rĭ-lĭj'əs) *adj. Abbr.* **rel. 1.** Of, pertaining to, or teaching religion. **2.** Adhering to or manifesting religion; pious; godly. **3.** Extremely scrupulous or conscientious. **4.** Pertaining to or belonging to an order taking vows of poverty, chastity, and obedience.

~n., pl. **religious.** *Abbr.* **rel.** A person belonging to a religious order, especially a monk or nun. [Middle English, from Old French, from Latin *religiōsus,* from *religiō,* RELIGION.] **—re·lig·ious·ly** *adv.* **—re·lig·ious·ness** *n.*

re·line (rē-līn') *tr.v.* **-lined, -lining, -lines. 1.** To make new lines on. **2.** To put a new lining in (a garment, for example).

re·lin·quish (rĭ-lĭng'kwĭsh) *tr.v.* **-quished, -quishing, -quishes. 1.** To retire from; give up; abandon. **2.** To put aside or desist from (something practiced, professed, or intended). **3.** To surrender; renounce. **4.** To let go or release (a grasp, for example). [Middle English *relinquysshen,* from Old French *relinquir* (stem *relinquiss-*), from Latin *relinquere,* to leave behind : *re-,* behind + *linquere,* to leave.] **—re·lin·quish·er** *n.* **—re·lin·quish·ment** *n.*

Synonyms: *cede, forgo, renounce, resign, surrender, waive, yield.*

rel·i·quar·y (rĕl'ə-kwĕr'ē) *n., pl.* **-ies.** A receptacle, such as a coffer or shrine, for keeping or displaying religious relics. [French *reliquaire,* from Medieval Latin *reliquiārium,* from *reliquia,* singular of Late Latin *reliquiae,* remains. See **relic.**]

re·liq·ui·ae (rĭ-lĭk'wĭ-ē') *pl.n.* Remains, especially of fossil organisms. [Latin.]

rel·ish (rĕl'ĭsh) *n.* **1.** An appetite for something; an appreciation or liking: *a relish for luxury.* **2. a.** Pleasure; zest. **b.** Anything that lends pleasure or zest. **3.** A spicy or savory condiment, such as pickles or chutney. **4.** The flavor of a food, especially when appetizing. **5.** A trace or suggestion of some pleasurable quality.

~v. **relished, -ishing, -ishes.** *—tr.* **1.** To enjoy; take pleasure in. **2.** To look forward to with eagerness: *I don't relish the prospect of working this weekend.* **3.** To like the flavor of. **4.** To give flavor to; spice. *—intr.* To have a pleasing or distinctive taste. —See Synonyms at **like.** [Alteration (through influence of -ISH) of obsolete *reles,* a taste, from Old French *reles,* variant of *relais,* something remaining, from *relaissier,* to leave behind, release, from Latin *relaxāre,* to loosen, RELAX.] **—rel·ish·a·ble** *adj.*

re·live (rē-lĭv') *v.* **-lived, -living, -lives.** *—tr.* To undergo again (an experience, for example), especially in the imagination.

re·lo·cate (rē-lō'kāt') *v.* **-cated, -cating, -cates.** *—tr.* To establish (one's home, a factory, or the like) in a new place. *—intr.* To become established in a new home, area, or place of business: *The company relocated in the suburbs.* **—re·lo·ca·tion** *n.*

re·lu·cent (rĭ-lo͞o'sənt) *adj.* Reflecting light; shining. [Latin *relūcēns* (stem *relūcent-*), present participle of *relūcēre,* to shine back : *re-,* back + *lūcēre,* to shine.]

re·luct (rĭ-lŭkt') *intr.v.* **-lucted, -lucting, -lucts.** *Archaic.* To show reluctance. [Latin *reluctārī,* to struggle against : *re-,* against + *luctārī,* to struggle.]

re·luc·tance (rĭ-lŭk'təns) *n.* Also **re·luc·tan·cy** (-tən-sē). **1.** The state of being reluctant; unwillingness. **2.** *Physics.* A magnetic quantity analogous to electric resistance and equal in a closed magnetic circuit to the ratio of magnetomotive force (analogous to voltage) to magnetic flux (analogous to current).

re·luc·tant (rĭ-lŭk'tənt) *adj.* **1.** Unwilling; averse: *reluctant to help.* **2.** Marked by unwillingness. **3.** *Archaic.* Offering resistance; opposing. [Latin *reluctāns* (stem *reluctant-*), present participle of *reluctārī,* to struggle against, RELUCT.] **—re·luc·tant·ly** *adv.*

rel·uc·tiv·i·ty (rĕl'ək-tĭv'ə-tē) *n., pl.* **-ties.** *Physics.* A measure of the resistance of a material to the establishment of a magnetic field within it, equal to the reciprocal of **magnetic permeability** *(see).* [*Reluctance* + *conductivity.*]

re·lume (rĭ-lo͞om') *tr.v.* **-lumed, -luming, -lumes.** *Poetic.* To make bright or clear again; illuminate again. [RE- + (IL)LUME.]

re·ly (rĭ-lī') *intr.v.* **-lied, -lying, -lies. 1.** To use unquestioningly for support, assistance, or the like; to have as one's main recourse; depend. Used with *on* or *upon.* **2.** To trust; have confidence. Used with *on* or *upon*: *rely on the children to behave.* [Middle English *relien,* to gather, rally, from Old French *relier,* from Latin *religāre,* to bind back : *re-,* back + *ligāre,* to fasten, to tie.]

Synonyms: *bank, count, depend, trust.*

rem (rĕm) *n. Physics.* The amount of ionizing radiation required to produce the same biological effect as one roentgen of high-penetration x-rays. [R(OENTGEN) E(QUIVALENT IN) M(AN).]

REM *n.* **Rapid eye movement** *(see).*

rem. remittance.

re·main (rĭ-mān') *intr.v.* **-mained, -maining, -mains. 1.** To continue in a specified condition, quality, or place. **2.** To stay or be left over after the removal, departure, loss, or destruction of others. **3.** To be left as still to be dealt with: *A cure remains to be found.* **4.** To endure or persist: *Despite therapy the pain remained.* —See Synonyms at **stay.** [Middle English *remaynen,* from Old French *remanoir, remaindre,* from Latin *remanēre,* to stay behind : *re-,* back in place + *manēre,* to stay.]

re·main·der (rĭ-mān'dər) *n.* **1.** Something that is left over after other parts have been taken away; the rest. **2.** *Mathematics.* **a.** In division, the dividend minus the product of the divisor and quotient. **b.** In subtraction, the **difference** *(see).* **3.** *Law.* An estate effective and enjoyable only after the termination of another estate created at the same time. **4.** A copy of a book remaining with a publisher after sales have fallen off, usually sold at a reduced price.

~adj. Remaining; leftover.

~tr.v. **remaindered, -dering, -ders.** To sell (books) as remainders. [Middle English *remaynder,* from Old French *remainder,* from *remaindre,* to REMAIN.]

Usage: *remainder, rest, residue, residuum, residuals, balance, remnant, leavings, tailings, remains, relic. Remainder,* the most general of these terms, is that which is left when something is taken away. *Rest* is used virtually interchangeably with *remainder* in its general meaning. *Residue* and *residuum* refer to what is left after something has undergone dissolution or diminution, as by combustion; also, both terms refer to what is left of an estate after probate costs and bequests have been satisfied. *Residuals* in modern usage refers to royalty payments made to artists on the remainder of the life of an artistic production after the original production or edition has run its course. *Balance* implies that which is left at a bank after withdrawals or the unpaid amount on a charge account. *Remnant* is any small piece or quantity remaining after the major part has been used. *Leavings* and *tailings* are the culls remaining after that which is valuable has been taken away: *the tailings of a gold mine. Remains* specifically refers to a corpse, although it also applies to monuments of the past. *Relic* is a treasured memento, cherished in memory of a person, event, or place.

re·mains (rĭ-māns') *pl.n.* **1.** All that is left after other parts have been taken away, used up, or destroyed. **2.** A corpse. **3.** The unpublished writings of a deceased author. **4.** Ancient ruins or fossils. —See Usage note at **remainder.**

re·make (rē-māk') *tr.v.* **-made** (-mād'), **-making, -makes.** To make anew; reconstruct.

~n. (rē'māk'). **1.** An instance of making anew. **2.** Something made again; a new version of something: *a remake of an old film.*

re·mand (rĭ-mănd') *tr.v.* **-manded, -manding, -mands. 1.** To send or order back. **2.** *Law.* To hold on bail or send back (a defendant in criminal proceedings) to prison, to another court, or to another agency for further proceedings. **—on remand.** Remanded on bail or in custody.

~n. **1.** The state of being remanded. **2.** The act of remanding. **3.** A person remanded. [Middle English *remaunden,* from Old French *remander,* from Late Latin *remandāre,* to send back word : Latin *re-,* back + *mandāre,* to send word.] **—re·mand·ment** *n.*

rem·a·nence (rĕm'ə-nəns) *n.* **1.** *Rare.* The state of remaining or enduring. **2.** *Physics.* The magnetic induction that remains in a material after removal of the magnetizing field. [Middle English *remanent,* remaining, from Latin *remanēns* (stem *remanent-*), present participle of *remanēre,* to REMAIN.] **—rem·a·nent** *adj.*

re·mark (rĭ-märk') *v.* **-marked, -marking, -marks.** *—tr.* **1.** To say or write briefly and casually as a comment. **2.** To take notice of; observe. *—intr.* To make a comment or observation. Used with *on* or *upon.* —See Synonyms at **see.**

~n. **1.** The act of noticing or observing; observation; mention: *a place worthy of remark.* **2.** A casual or brief expression of opinion; a comment. **3.** Variant of **remarque.** [French *remarquer* : RE- (intensive) + MARK.] **—re·mark·er** *n.*

re·mark·a·ble (rĭ-mär'kə-bəl) *adj.* **1.** Worthy of notice. **2.** Extraordinary; striking; uncommon. **—re·mark·a·ble·ness** *n.* **—re·mark·a·bly** *adv.*

re·marque, re·mark (rĭ-märk') *n.* **1.** A mark made in the margin of a plate in engraving to indicate its stage of development prior to

PRONUNCIATION KEY

ă, pat; ā, pay; âr, care; ä, father, are; b, bib; ch, church; d, deed; ĕ, pet; ē, be; f, fife; g, gag; h, hat; hw, which; ĭ, pit; ī, pie; îr, pier; j, judge; k, kick; l, lid, needle; m, mum; n, no, sudden; ng, thing; ŏ, pot; ō, toe; ô, paw, for; oi, noise; ou, out; o͝o, book; o͞o, boot; p, pop; r, roar; s, sauce; sh, ship, dish; t, tight; th, thin, path; *th,* this, bathe; ŭ, cut; ûr, fur; v, valve; w, with; y, yes; z, zebra, size; zh, vision; ə, about, item, edible, gallop, circus, peaceful

IN FOREIGN WORDS:

à, *Fr.* ami; œ, *Fr.* feu, *Ger.* schön; ü, *Fr.* tu, *Ger.* über; KH, *Ger.* ich, *Scot.* loch; N, *Fr.* bon; y', *Fr.* Compiègne

STRESS MARKS:

Primary stress: ' in·cite' (ĭn-sīt')
Secondary stress: ' in'sight' (ĭn'sīt')

completion. **2.** A print or proof from a plate carrying such a mark. [French, from *remarquer,* to REMARK.]

Re·marque (rə-märk´), **Erich Maria** (1898–1970). German-born U.S. novelist. From his experience in the trenches in World War I he drew the material for his first and most famous novel, *All Quiet on the Western Front* (1929).

re·match (rē´măch´, rē-măch´) *n. Sports.* A contest between opponents who have previously met each other in competition.

Rem·brandt (rĕm´brănt), born Rembrandt Harmenszoon van Rijn (1606–69). Dutch painter, generally regarded as the greatest master of the Dutch school. He worked in his native town of Leiden until c. 1632, thereafter chiefly in Amsterdam. Most of his early paintings were on religious and allegorical themes and display, in their mastery of light and shade, the influence of Caravaggio. In Amsterdam he established himself as the city's leading portrait painter. Among his most famous paintings are the group portraits, *The Shooting Company of Captain Frans Banning Cocq* (1642; known also as *The Night Watch*) and *The Syndics of the Cloth Guild* (1662). His series of self-portraits (1629–69) records the progress of his life with great perception. —**Rem·brandt·esque** *adj.*

re·me·di·a·ble (rĭ-mē´dē-ə-bəl) *adj.* Capable of being remedied. —**re·me·di·a·ble·ness** *n.* —**re·me·di·a·bly** *adv.*

re·me·di·al (rĭ-mē´dē-əl) *adj.* **1.** Supplying a remedy. **2.** Intended to correct something, such as a physical defect. **3.** Designating or pertaining to teaching methods intended to assist slow or backward pupils: *remedial classes.* —**re·me·di·al·ly** *adv.*

rem·e·dy (rĕm´ə-dē) *n., pl.* **-dies. 1.** Something, such as medicine or therapy, that relieves pain, cures disease, or corrects a disorder. **2.** Something that corrects an evil, fault, or error. **3.** *Law.* A legal means of preventing or correcting a wrong or enforcing a right. **4.** The allowance by a mint for deviation from the standard weight or quality of coins. ~*tr.v.* **remedied, -dying, -dies. 1.** To relieve or cure (a disease or disorder). **2.** To counteract or rectify (an error, wrong, or defect); set right. —See Synonyms at **correct.** [Middle English *remedie,* from Norman French, from Latin *remedium,* medicine : *re-,* again + *medērī,* to heal.] —**rem·e·di·less** *adj.*

re·mem·ber (rĭ-mĕm´bər) *v.* **-bered, -bering, -bers.** —*tr.* **1. a.** To bring back to the mind through an act of memory. **b.** To become aware of or think of again. **2.** To recall to the mind with effort or determination. **3.** To retain in the mind; keep carefully in memory: *remember a poem.* **4.** To keep (someone) in mind as worthy of affection, reward, or recognition: *He remembered her in his will.* **5.** To reward with a gift or tip. **6.** To mention (someone, usually oneself) to another as sending greetings: *Remember me to your mother.* **7.** *Archaic.* To remind. —*intr.* To have or use the faculty of memory. [Middle English *remembren,* from Old French *remembrer,* from Late Latin *rememorārī,* to remember again : *re-,* again + *memorārī,* to remind, from Latin *memor,* mindful.] —**re·mem·ber·a·ble** *adj.* —**re·mem·ber·er** *n.*

re·mem·brance (rĭ-mĕm´brəns) *n.* **1.** The act of remembering. **2.** The state of being remembered. **3.** Something serving to celebrate or honor the memory of a person or event; a memorial. **4.** The length of time over which one's memory extends. **5.** Something remembered; a reminiscence. **6.** A memento or souvenir. **7. remembrances.** Greetings. —See Synonyms at **memory.** [Middle English, from Old French, from *remembrer,* to REMEMBER.]

Remembrance Day *n.* **1.** In Great Britain, the Sunday nearest November 11, when those who died in both World Wars are honored. Also called "Remembrance Sunday." **2.** In Canada, November 11, a day similarly set aside to honor the war dead.

re·mem·branc·er (rĭ-mĕm´brən-sər) *n.* **1.** One that causes another to remember; a reminder. **2. Remembrancer. a.** An officer of the British judiciary responsible for collecting debts due to the Crown. In this sense, also called "King's (or Queen's) Remembrancer." **b.** An official who represents the City of London on ceremonial occasions, before parliamentary committees, and the like.

re·mex (rē´mĕks´) *n., pl.* **remiges** (rĕm´ə-jēz´). A quill or flight feather of a bird's wing. [New Latin, from Latin *rēmex* (stem *rēmig-*), oarsman : *rēmus,* oar + *agere,* to drive.] —**re·mig·i·al** (rĭ-mĭj´ē-əl) *adj.*

re·mind (rĭ-mīnd´) *tr.v.* **-minded, -minding, -minds.** To cause (someone) to remember or think. Used with *of,* an infinitive, or a clause: *The song reminded me of summer; Remind me to give you the address.* —**re·mind·er** *n.*

Rem·ing·ton (rĕm´ĭng-tən), **Eliphalet** (1793–1861). U.S. arms manufacturer. In 1816 he began making flintlock rifles, and in 1847 he manufactured the U.S. Navy's first breechloading rifle, the Jenks carbine. His Remington Arms Company became a major arms supplier to the U.S. government and, under his son **Philo** (1816–89), a major manufacturer of sewing machines and typewriters.

Remington, Frederic (1861–1909). U.S. Western painter, sculptor, and author. Educated in the fine arts, he traveled west, where he worked as a cowboy and spent his spare time traveling and creating his works, which capture the action and emotion of men working close to the land. "The Bronco Buster," a bronze sculpture, typifies his carefully detailed and highly popular works.

rem·i·nisce (rĕm´ə-nĭs´) *intr.v.* **-nisced, -niscing, -nisces.** To recollect and tell of past experiences or events. [Back-formation from REMINISCENT.]

rem·i·nis·cence (rĕm´ə-nĭs´əns) *n.* **1.** The act or process of recalling the past. **2.** A thing remembered; a memory. **3.** *Often* **reminis-**

Rembrandt

THE PASSING YEARS ARE CAPTURED IN HIS SELF-PORTRAITS
An artist who was fascinated by growing old

One of the greatest artists of all time, the Dutch painter Rembrandt van Rijn (1606–69) is noted for the vigor and realism of his work, particularly his portraits. His powers of observation and deep psychological insight are evident not only in his portraits but also in his striking religious paintings and landscapes.

All his life Rembrandt was fascinated with light and shade, and in many of his works a concentrated light falls on a central figure set in a shadowy background. Aging also fascinated him, and his many self-portraits record the gradual alteration of his features with a searching understanding and sincerity.

His success as a portrait painter began in 1632 with *The Anatomy Lesson of Dr. Tulp* and reached its peak in 1642 with his celebrated *Night Watch.* During this successful period, when he had many commissions and pupils, he married (1634) Saskia van Uylenborch, who brought him a good dowry and who appears in many of his works. She died in 1642.

Despite his wealth, extravagant living and waning popularity led him into financial difficulties and eventually bankruptcy (1656). But Rembrandt's powers remained undiminished; he continued teaching and in these difficult years produced works of insight, compassion, and technical mastery—such as *The Jewish Merchant* (1650) and *Old Jew in an Armchair* (1652). The self-portraits he had begun as a young man continued with ever greater depth of feeling and rank among the most tender expressions ever executed in paint.

MASTER OF THE PORTRAIT *Rembrandt's fascination with age drove him to paint a series of self-portraits that capture his development from a lively youth to a disillusioned old man. Here he is about 60.*

cences. A narration or account of past experiences. **4.** An event that brings to mind a similar, former event. —See Synonyms at **memory.** [Late Latin *reminiscentia.* See **reminiscent.**]

rem·i·nis·cent (rĕm´ə-nĭs´ənt) *adj.* **1.** Having the quality of or containing reminiscence or reminiscences. **2.** Inclined to engage in reminiscence: *What a reminiscent old man he is.* **3.** Tending to recall or suggest: *an evening reminiscent of happier times.* [Late Latin *reminiscens* (stem *reminiscent-*), present participle of *reminiscī,* to recollect : RE- + *min-,* from *mēns* (stem *ment-*), mind.] —**rem·i·nis·cent·ly** *adv.*

re·mise¹ (rĭ-mīz´) *tr.v.* **-mised, -mising, -mises.** *Law.* To relinquish a claim to; surrender by deed. [Middle English, from Old French,

remora *A marine fish with a suction pad on its head by which it attaches itself to sharks, whales, and turtles. It feeds mainly on the skin parasites of its carrier. There are about ten species, growing from 30 to 90 centimeters (1 to 3 feet) long.*

PRONUNCIATION KEY

ă, pat; ā, pay; âr, care; ä, father, are; b, bib; ch, church; d, deed; ĕ, pet; ē, be; f, fife; g, gag; h, hat; hw, which; ĭ, pit; ī, pie; îr, pier; j, judge; k, kick; l, lid, needle; m, mum; n, no, sudden; ng, thing; ŏ, pot; ō, toe; ô, paw, for; oi, noise; ou, out; o͝o, book; o͞o, boot; p, pop; r, roar; s, sauce; sh, ship, dish; t, tight; th, thin, path; *th*, this, bathe; ŭ, cut; ûr, fur; v, valve; w, with; y, yes; z, zebra, size; zh, vision; ə, about, item, edible, gallop, circus, peaceful

IN FOREIGN WORDS:

à, *Fr.* ami; œ, *Fr.* feu, *Ger.* schön; ü, *Fr.* tu, *Ger.* über; KH, *Ger.* ich, *Scot.* loch; N, *Fr.* bon; y', *Fr.* Compiègne

STRESS MARKS:

Primary stress: ′
in·cite′ (ĭn-sīt′)
Secondary stress: ′
in′sight′ (ĭn′sīt′)

from the feminine past participle of *remettre,* to remit, from Latin *remittere,* to REMIT.]

re·mise² (rĭ-mēz′) *n.* In fencing, a second thrust made after the first has failed.
~*intr.v.* **remised, -mising, -mises.** To make a remise. [French, from past participle of *remettre,* to put back. See **remit.**]

re·miss (rĭ-mĭs′) *adj.* **1.** Lax in attending to duty; negligent. **2.** Inclined to idleness; slack. [Middle English, from Latin *remissus,* slack, past participle of *remittere,* to REMIT.] **—re·miss·ly** *adv.* **—re·miss·ness** *n.*

re·mis·si·ble (rĭ-mĭs′ə-bəl) *adj.* Capable of being remitted or forgiven. **—re·mis·si·bil·i·ty** (rĭ-mĭs′ə-bĭl′ə-tē) *n.*

re·mis·sion (rĭ-mĭsh′ən) *n.* **1. a.** The act of remitting. **b.** The condition of being remitted. **2. a.** Release, as from a debt, penalty, or obligation. **b.** Forgiveness; pardon. **3.** A lessening of intensity or degree; an abatement; especially, a temporary abatement of the symptoms of a disease.

re·mit (rĭ-mĭt′) *v.* **-mitted, -mitting, -mits.** —*tr.* **1.** To send (money), as by mail. **2. a.** To cancel (a penalty or punishment). **b.** To pardon; forgive. **3.** To restore to an original condition; put back. **4. a.** *Law.* To refer (a case) back to a lower court for further consideration. **b.** To refer (a matter) back for further consideration to a committee, authority, or the like. **5.** To relax; slacken. **6.** To defer; postpone. —*intr.* **1.** To send money. **2.** To diminish; abate.
~*n.* (rē′mĭt). **1.** A case remitted to a lower court. **2. a.** A matter for further consideration by a committee or authority. **b.** An area of study or enquiry for a committee or authority. [Middle English *remitten,* from Latin *remittere,* to send back, release : *re-,* back + *mittere,* to send.] **—re·mit·ta·ble** *adj.*

re·mit·tal (rĭ-mĭt′l) *n.* Remission.

re·mit·tance (rĭ-mĭt′əns) *n. Abbr.* **rem. 1.** Money or credit sent to someone. **2.** The act of sending money or credit.

remittance man *n.* A person living abroad on funds sent from home, especially in former times.

re·mit·tent (rĭ-mĭt′ənt) *adj.* Characterized by temporary abatements in severity. Said especially of diseases.
~*n.* A remittent fever. **—re·mit·tence, re·mit·ten·cy** *n.* **—re·mit·tent·ly** *adv.*

re·mit·ter (rĭ-mĭt′ər) *n.* Also **re·mit·tor** (for sense 3). **1.** *Law.* The principle or act by which an individual holds property by a valid title dated prior to a defective title under which he at first held ownership. **2.** *Law.* The act of transferring a case for decision to another court, generally a lower one. **3.** One that remits.

rem·nant (rĕm′nənt) *n.* **1.** Something left over; a remainder. **2.** A leftover piece of fabric remaining after the rest has been used or sold. **3.** A surviving trace or vestige, as of a former condition. **4.** *Often* **remnants.** A small, remaining group of people. —See Usage note at **remainder.**
~*adj.* Remaining; leftover. [Middle English *remenant,* from Old French, present participle of *remanoir, remaindre,* to REMAIN.]

re·mod·el (rē-mŏd′l) *tr.v.* **-eled, -eling, -els** or *chiefly British* **-elled, -elling. 1.** To model again. **2.** To remake with a new structure or in a new style; reconstruct; renovate. **—re·mod·el·er** *n.*

remolade. Variant of **rémoulade.**

re·mon·e·tize (rē-mŏn′ə-tīz′, rē-mŭn′-) *tr.v.* **-tized, -tizing, -tizes.** To restore (silver, for example) to use as legal tender. **—re·mon·e·ti·za·tion** *n.*

re·mon·strance (rĭ-mŏn′strəns) *n.* **1.** The act of remonstrating. **2.** A speech or gesture of protest, opposition, or reproof; especially, a formal statement of public grievances.

re·mon·strant (rĭ-mŏn′strənt) *adj.* Characterized by remonstrance; expostulatory.
~*n.* **1.** One who remonstrates or signs a remonstrance. **2. Remonstrant. a.** Any of the Dutch Arminians who, in 1610, formally stated the grounds of their dissent from strict Calvinism. **b.** A member of the denomination founded by these dissenters.

re·mon·strate (rĭ-mŏn′strāt′, rĕm′ən-strāt′) *v.* **-strated, -strating, -strates.** —*tr.* To say or plead in protest, objection, or reproof. —*intr.* To make objections; argue or plead against some action: *remonstrate with one's superiors.* —See Synonyms at **object.** [Medieval Latin *remōnstrāre,* to demonstrate : Latin *re-,* completely + *monstrāre,* to show, from *monstrum,* an omen, a portent, from *monēre,* to warn.] **—re·mon·stra·tion** (rē′mŏn-strā′shən, rĕm′ən-) *n.* **—re·mon·stra·tive** (rĭ-mŏn′strə-tĭv) *adj.* **—re·mon·stra·tor** *n.*

re·mon·tant (rĭ-mŏn′tənt) *adj.* Blooming more than once during a season, as certain roses do.
~*n.* A remontant rose. [French, "rising again," from the present participle of *remonter,* to rise again, REMOUNT.]

rem·o·ra (rĕm′ər-ə) *n.* Any of several marine fishes of the family Echeneidae, having a sucking disk on the head with which they attach themselves to larger animals, ships, or other moving objects. Also called "suckerfish," "shark sucker." [Latin, "delay" (they were believed to be able to delay ships by sticking to them) : *re-,* back + *mora,* a delay.]

re·morse (rĭ-môrs′) *n.* **1.** Moral anguish arising from repentance for past misdeeds; bitter regret. **2.** *Obsolete.* Compassion. [Middle English, from Old French *remors,* from Medieval Latin *remorsus,* from Latin, a biting back, from the past participle of *remordēre,* to bite again : *re-,* again + *mordēre,* to bite.] **—re·morse·ful** *adj.* **—re·morse·ful·ly** *adv.* **—re·morse·ful·ness** *n.*

re·morse·less (rĭ-môrs′lĭs) *adj.* **1.** Having no pity or compassion; merciless. **2.** Very persistent; relentless. **—re·morse·less·ly** *adv.* **—re·morse·less·ness** *n.*

re·mote (rĭ-mōt′) *adj.* **-moter, -motest. 1. a.** Located far away; relatively distant in space: *Our hotel was remote from the city center.* **b.** Outlying; isolated; out-of-the-way: *a remote hamlet.* **2.** Distant in time: *the remote past.* **3. a.** Very slight or faint: *hadn't the remotest interest in what I was saying.* **b.** Having only a vague connection: *a cause very remote from everyday concerns.* **4.** Being distantly related by blood or marriage: *a remote descendant.* **5.** Distant in manner; aloof. **6.** Operating or controlled from a distance: *remote sensors.* **7.** Of, pertaining to, or designating computing devices or systems situated at some distance from the central computer that communicate with it usually by means of cables. —See Usage note at **distant.** [Latin *remōtus,* past participle of *removēre,* to move back or away : *re-,* back, away + *movēre,* to move.] **—re·mote·ly** *adv.* **—re·mote·ness** *n.*

remote control *n.* The direction of an activity, process, or machine from a distant point, as by radioed instructions or coded signals.

ré·mou·lade (rā′mo͞o-läd′) *n.* Also **re·mo·lade** (rā′mə-läd′). A piquant cold sauce for cold poultry, meat, and shellfish, made of mayonnaise with chopped pickles, capers, anchovies, and herbs. [French *rémoulade,* variant of Picard dialect *ramolas,* horseradish, variant of Latin *armoracea,* of Italic origin.]

re·mount (rē-mount′) *tr.v.* **-mounted, -mounting, -mounts. 1.** To mount again. **2.** To supply with fresh horses.
~*n.* (rē′mount′, rē-mount′). A fresh horse. [Middle English *remounten,* from Old French *remonter* : *re-,* again + *monter, munter,* to MOUNT.]

re·mov·a·ble (rĭ-mo͞o′və-bəl) *adj.* Capable of being removed. **—re·mov·a·bil·i·ty, re·mov·a·ble·ness** *n.* **—re·mov·a·bly** *adv.*

re·mov·al (rĭ-mo͞o′vəl) *n.* **1. a.** The act of removing. **b.** The fact of being removed. **2.** Relocation, as of a home or business. **3.** Dismissal, as from office.

re·move (rĭ-mo͞ov′) *v.* **-moved, -moving, -moves.** —*tr.* **1.** To move from a position occupied: *remove the dishes from the table.* **2.** To convey from one place to another: *removed the family to safety.* **3.** To take from one's person; doff: *remove one's hat.* **4.** To do away with; eliminate: *remove stains; removed his anxieties.* **5.** To dismiss from office. —*intr.* **1.** To change one's place of residence or business; move: *"In 1751, I removed from the country to the town"* (David Hume). **2.** *Poetic.* To depart; go away.
~*n.* **1.** The act of removing; a removal. **2.** The distance or degree of space, time, or status that separates persons or things: *"those who consider themselves to be at a safe remove from all the wretched"* (James Baldwin). **3.** A dish that succeeds another at a meal. [Middle English *removen,* from Old French *remouvoir,* from Latin *removēre,* to move back : *re-,* back + *movēre,* to move.] **—re·mov·er** *n.*

re·moved (rĭ-mo͞ovd′) *adj.* **1.** Distant in space, time, or nature; remote. **2.** Separated in relationship by a specified degree of descent: *My first cousin's child is my first cousin once removed.* **3.** *Archaic.* Succeeded by another dish at a meal: *fish removed by beef.* —See Usage note at **distant. —re·mov·ed·ly** (rĭ-mo͞o′vĭd-lē) *adj.* **—re·mov·ed·ness** *n.*

re·mu·da (rĭ-mo͞o′də) *n. Southwestern U.S.* A herd of horses from which ranch hands select their mounts. [American Spanish, change of horses, from Spanish, an exchange, from *remudar,* to exchange : *re-,* again, "in return" + *mudar,* to change, from Latin *mūtāre.*]

re·mu·ner·ate (rĭ-myo͞o′nə-rāt′) *tr.v.* **-ated, -ating, -ates. 1.** To pay (a person) for goods provided, services rendered, or losses incurred. **2.** To compensate for; make up for: *remunerate his efforts.* [Latin *remūnerāre* : *re-,* intensive + *mūnerāre,* to give, from *mūnus,* a gift.] **—re·mu·ner·a·bil·i·ty** (rĭ-myo͞o′nə-rə-bĭl′ə-tē) *n.* **—re·mu·ner·a·ble** *adj.* **—re·mu·ner·a·tor** *n.*

re·mu·ner·a·tion (rĭ-myo͞o′nə-rā′shən) *n.* **1.** An act of remunerating. **2.** That which remunerates; recompense; payment.

re·mu·ner·a·tive (rĭ-myo͞o′nə-rā′tĭv, -nər-ə-tĭv) *adj.* **1.** Likely to be well remunerated; profitable. **2.** Serving to remunerate. **—re·mu·ner·a·tive·ly** *adv.* **—re·mu·ner·a·tive·ness** *n.*

Re·mus (rē′məs). *Roman Mythology.* The twin brother of **Romulus** *(see).*

ren·ais·sance (rĕn′ə-säns′, -zäns′; *British* rĭ-nā′səns) *n.* **1.** A rebirth; a revival. **2. Renaissance. a.** The humanistic revival of classical art, literature, and learning that originated in Italy in the 14th century and later spread throughout Europe. **b.** The period of this revival (roughly 14th–16th century). **3.** *Sometimes* **Renaissance.** Any similar period of revived intellectual or artistic achievement or enthusiasm: *the Celtic Renaissance.*
~*adj.* **Renaissance. 1.** Of, pertaining to, or characteristic of the Renaissance or its artistic and intellectual works and styles. **2.** Of or designating the style of architecture and decoration prevalent during the Renaissance. [French, a rebirth, from Old French, from *renaistre* (present stem *renais-*), to be born again, from Latin *renascī* : *re-,* again + *nascī,* to be born.]

Renaissance man or **woman** *n.* A man or woman whose intellectual interests and achievements are wide-ranging; especially, one whose talents encompass both the arts and the sciences.

re·nal (rē′nəl) *adj.* Of, pertaining to, resembling, or in the region of the kidneys. [French *rénal,* from Late Latin *rēnālis,* from Latin *rēnēs*†, kidneys.]

renal dialysis *n.* **Hemodialysis** *(see).*

renal pelvis *n.* A small funnel-shaped cavity in the kidney in which urine collects before being discharged into the ureter. Also called "pelvis."

re·nas·cence (rĭ-năs′əns, -nā′səns) *n.* **1.** A new birth or life; a rebirth. **2.** A cultural revival; a renaissance.

THE FLOWERING OF EUROPEAN CULTURE

The civilization of ancient Rome inspires a new artistic movement

Renaissance is a French word meaning rebirth and is used to describe the developments in architecture, painting, and sculpture that began in Florence in the early 1400's and spread through Italy and across Europe by 1600. It was part of an intellectual movement that made man rethink his relationship with God and nature and stimulated scientific discoveries.

In the 14th century the Italian poet and writer Petrarch put forward the idea that since the fall of the Roman Empire, Italy had been in the Dark Ages, a period of decline and ignorance. If man could return to the styles and ideas of the Roman Empire there would be a new age of glory. Modern studies show that the Roman Empire was not the peak of human achievement and that the Dark Ages were not a cultural gap, but this myth achieved a strong hold on the Italian imagination. It stimulated the study of Roman art and civilization and led to the discovery of ancient Greek literature, philosophy, and science. This Greco-Roman revival led to a new Humanist movement that acknowledged man's feelings and aspirations without displacing God's importance.

The Renaissance saw the establishment of portraiture, frequently with landscape backgrounds, as an accepted art form. Portraiture developed through the patronage of the wealthy trading classes who were willing to pay for being immortalized in pictures. There was a new use of light and shade in painting to create the illusion of reality. The architect Brunelleschi calculated the mathematical rules governing perspective and these were eagerly adopted by painters.

The Italian Renaissance is divided into three periods. The Early Renaissance (1420–90) was marked by men such as Brunelleschi, the sculptor Donatello, and the painters Masaccio, Piero della Francesca, Botticelli, Mantegna, and Bellini. Brunelleschi revived the style of classical Roman architecture but adapted it to create a new harmony and style. Donatello gave his figures a new feeling of energy with minute details learned from studies of the human body. In painting the artists portrayed emotion, which added to the realism of their work.

In the High Renaissance (1490–1520), the architect Donato Bramante revised the designs for St. Peter's Basilica in classical style. Other artists of the time included Leonardo da Vinci and Raphael; they helped to perfect the realistic style of painting. The sculptor, painter, and architect Michelangelo worked from the end of the Early Renaissance into the Mannerist period (1520–1600). He could portray accurately the human body from any angle. Mannerism was an experimental period when artists began to assert their independence from classical ideas. It coincided with unease in the Roman Catholic Church as the rise of northern European Protestantism confronted it—the period known as the Reformation.

In northern Europe the Flemish painter Jan van Eyck was an early developer of oil paints and used vivid colors to paint reality in its smallest detail. Also in the Flemish school Hieronymus Bosch and Pieter Brueghel used realism to convey symbolic and sinister messages, and in Germany Albrecht Dürer portrayed the religious turmoil of the age.

BEGINNINGS OF RENAISSANCE PAINTING *The artist Masaccio (1401–28) is credited with the founding of Renaissance painting. His* Expulsion of Adam and Eve from Paradise *(left) is one of a series of frescoes in the Brancacci Chapel in Florence. It shows not only a more realistic sense of perspective but also portrays emotion in the characters. In contrast with the earlier International Gothic style, where figures were almost expressionless, his figures show the full horror of their fate. Masaccio employed the perspective rules of Brunelleschi. His frescoes served as examples to other painters throughout the next century.*

THE PERFECTION OF TECHNIQUE *Leonardo da Vinci (1452–1519) probably painted his* Ginevra de Benci *(above) as a wedding portrait in 1473–74. It conveys a melancholy mood, with the subject wearing an ambiguous expression and seeming to assess the viewer with critical eyes; perhaps the marriage was not of her choice. Apart from her face, all the light areas are small and irregular, and the spikiness of the leaves contrasts with the softness of her hair. The painting shows a considerable advance on the techniques of Masaccio 50 years earlier; technical progress in the 500 years since has been much slower.*

re·nas·cent (rĭ-năs′ənt, -nā′sənt) *adj.* Coming into being again; showing renewed growth or vigor. [Latin *renascēns* (stem *renascent-*), present participle of *renascī,* to be born again. See **renaissance.**]

ren·coun·ter (rĕn-koun′tər) *n. Archaic.* **1.** An unplanned meeting. **2.** A sudden encounter with an enemy.
∼*v.* **rencountered, -tering, -ters.** *Archaic.* —*tr.* To meet unexpectedly. —*intr.* To have an unexpected meeting. [French *rencontre,* from *rencontrer,* to have a (hostile) meeting : *re-,* again, against + *encontrer,* to ENCOUNTER.]

rend (rĕnd) *v.* **rent** (rĕnt) or **rended, rending, rends.** —*tr.* **1. a.** To tear or pull; wrench. **b.** To rip apart or into pieces; split. **2.** To remove forcibly; wrest. **3.** To penetrate and disturb as if by tearing: *Screams rent the silence.* **4.** To cause pain or distress to (the heart, for example). —*intr.* To burst; come apart. —See Synonyms at **tear.** [Middle English *renden,* Old English *rendan.*] —**rend·er** *n.*

ren·der (rĕn′dər) *tr.v.* **-dered, -dering, -ders. 1.** To submit or present for consideration, payment, or approval: *render a bill.* **2.** To give or make available: *render assistance.* **3.** To give what is due or proper: *asked much and rendered little.* **4.** To give in return or retribution: *render an apology for his rudeness.* **5.** To surrender or relinquish; yield. **6.** To represent, as in painting, writing, or music; depict in artistic form: *This poem renders precisely the pains of love.* **7.** To perform an interpretation of (a musical piece, for example). **8.** To express in another language or form; translate. **9.** To pronounce formally; hand down (a verdict, for example). **10.** To cause to become; make: *"This study renders men acute, inquisitive"* (Edmund Burke). **11.** To reduce, convert, or melt down (fat) by heating. **12.** To coat (brick, for example) with plaster or cement.
∼*n.* A payment in kind, services, or cash from a tenant to a feudal lord. [Middle English *rendren,* to give in return, relinquish, from Old French *rendre,* to give back, from Vulgar Latin *rendere* (unattested), variant of Latin *reddere* : *re-,* back + *dare,* to give.] —**ren·der·a·ble** *adj.* —**ren·der·er** *n.*

ren·der·ing (rĕn′dər-ĭng) *n.* A coat of plaster, cement, or the like covering a surface.

ren·dez·vous (rän′dā-vo͞o′, rän′də-) *n., pl.* **-vous** (-vo͞oz′). **1. a.** An arrangement or appointment to meet. **b.** A prearranged meeting place; especially, an assembly point for troops, ships, or spacecraft. **2.** The meeting itself. **3.** A popular gathering place.
∼*v.* **rendezvoused** (-vo͞od′), **-vousing** (-vo͞o′ĭng), **-vouses** (-vo͞oz′). —*tr.* To bring together (persons or military units) at a prearranged time and place. —*intr.* To meet together at a prearranged time and place. [Old French, from *rendez vous,* "present yourselves" : *rendez,* imperative of *rendre,* to RENDER + *vous,* you.]

ren·di·tion (rĕn-dĭsh′ən) *n.* **1.** The act of rendering. **2.** An interpretation of a musical score or dramatic piece. **3.** A performance of a musical or dramatic work. **4.** A translation, often interpretive. [Obsolete French, from Old French *rendre,* to give back, RENDER.]

ren·dzi·na (rĕn-jē′nə) *n.* A dark soil that develops under grass on limestone and chalk. [Russian, from Polish *redzina.*]

ren·e·gade (rĕn′ə-gād′) *n.* **1.** One who rejects a religion, cause, allegiance, or group for another; a deserter. **2.** An outlaw; a rebel.
∼*adj.* Of or like a renegade; treacherous. [Spanish *renegado,* from Medieval Latin *renegātus,* one who denies, renegade, from the past participle of *renegāre,* to deny : Latin *re-,* intensive + *negāre,* to deny.]

re·nege (rĭ-nĕg′, -nĭg′, -nēg′) *v.* **-neged, -neging, -neges.** —*intr.* **1.** To fail to carry out a promise or commitment: *renege on a contract.* **2.** In card games, to fail to follow suit when able and required by the rules to do so. —*tr. Obsolete.* To renounce; disown.
∼*n.* The act of reneging in card games. [Medieval Latin *renegāre,* to deny. See **renegade.**] —**re·neg·er** *n.*

re·ne·go·ti·ate (rē′nĭ-gō′shē-āt′) *tr.v.* **-ated, -ating, -ates.** To negotiate anew; especially, to revise the terms of (a contract) so as to limit or get back excess profits gained by the contractor. —**re·ne·go·ti·a·ble** *adj.* —**re·ne·go·ti·a·tion** *n.*

re·new (rĭ-no͞o′, -nyo͞o′) *v.* **-newed, -newing, -news.** —*tr.* **1.** To make new or as if new again; restore. **2.** To take up again; resume. **3.** To repeat so as to reaffirm: *renewed her promise of support.* **4.** To regain (spiritual or physical vigor); revive. **5. a.** To arrange for the extension of: *renew a contract.* **b.** To extend the period of loan of: *renew a library book.* **6.** To replenish. **7.** To bring into being again; re-establish. —*intr.* **1.** To become new again. **2.** To start again. **3.** To renew a contract, lease, or other agreement.

re·new·a·ble (rĭ-no͞o′ə-bəl, rĭ-nyo͞o′-) *adj.* **1.** Able to be renewed. **2.** Designating a commodity or resource, such as solar power or firewood, that is inexhaustible or replaceable by regrowth. —**re·new·a·bil·i·ty** (rĭ-no͞o′ə-bĭl′ə-tē, rĭ-nyo͞o′-) *n.*

re·new·al (rĭ-no͞o′əl, rĭ-nyo͞o′-) *n.* **1. a.** The act or an instance of renewing. **b.** The state of being renewed. **2.** Something renewed.

re·new·ed·ly (rĭ-no͞o′ĭd-lē, rĭ-nyo͞o′-) *adv.* Over again; anew.

Ren·frew·shire (rĕn′fro͞o-shîr′, -shər). Former county of west-central Scotland. In 1975 it became part of the Strathclyde Region.

Re·ni (rā′nē), **Guido** (1575–1642). Italian painter and engraver, forerunner of late 17th-century Roman classicism. He worked in Rome and his native Bologna. His best-known works are the *Crucifixion of St. Peter* (1605) and the *Aurora* fresco (1613–14).

reni–, reno– *prefix.* Indicates kidney or kidneys; for example, **reniform.** [Latin *rēnēs,* kidneys.]

ren·i·form (rĕn′ə-fôrm′, rē′nə-) *adj.* Shaped like a kidney: *a reniform leaf.* [RENI- + -FORM.]

ren·in (rĕn′ĭn) *n.* A protein-digesting enzyme, released by the kidneys in response to stress, that acts to raise blood pressure. [RENI- + -IN.]

re·ni·tent (rĕn′ə-tənt, rĭ-nī′tənt) *adj.* **1.** Resisting pressure; not pliant. **2.** Reluctant to yield or be swayed; recalcitrant. [Latin *renītens* (stem *renītent-*), present participle of *renītī,* to struggle against, resist : *re-,* back, against + *nītī,* to press forward, push.] —**ren·i·tence, ren·i·ten·cy** *n.*

Rennes (rĕn). Capital of Ille-et-Vilaine department, northwestern France. It is a railway junction and agricultural market center.

ren·net (rĕn′ĭt) *n.* **1.** The inner lining of the fourth stomach of calves and other young mammals. **2.** A dried extract made from the stomach lining of a ruminant, used to curdle milk. **3.** Rennin. [Middle English *rennet,* Old English *rynet* (unattested).]

ren·nin (rĕn′ĭn) *n.* A milk-coagulating enzyme produced by the stomach. It is an active constituent of rennet and is used in making cheeses and junkets. Also called "chymosin." [RENN(ET) + -IN.]

Re·no (rē′nō). City in western Nevada, on the Truckee River. Tourism is the major industry, and the city is noted for its short-term residency requirements for obtaining divorces.

Re·noir (rĕn′wär′), **Jean** (1894–1979). French film director. The son of the painter Auguste Renoir, he won great acclaim for the artistry of films such as *La Grande Illusion* (1937), *La Bête Humaine* (1938), and *La Règle du Jeu* (1939).

Renoir, Pierre Auguste (1841–1919). French impressionist painter. In the 1870's he began to exhibit at the impressionist salons. He developed the so-called rainbow palette, from which black was eliminated. Among his best-known paintings are *Le Moulin de la Galette* (1876) and *Les Parapluies* (1883). In the mid-1880's he developed a more classical manner, as in *Le Jugement de Paris* (*c.* 1914).

re·nounce (rĭ-nouns′) *v.* **-nounced, -nouncing, -nounces.** —*tr.* **1.** To give up (a title or activity, for example), especially by formal announcement. **2.** To reject; disown. —*intr.* **1.** In card games, to fail to follow suit because one does not hold a card of the required suit. **2.** *Law.* To give up a right. —See Synonyms at **relinquish.**
∼*n.* In card games: **1.** An act of renouncing. **2.** An opportunity to renounce. [Middle English *renouncen,* from Old French *renoncer,* from Latin *renūntiāre,* to bring back word, protest against, report : *re-,* back, against + *nūntiāre,* inform, from *nūntium,* message.] —**re·nounce·ment** *n.* —**re·nounc·er** *n.*

ren·o·vate (rĕn′ə-vāt′) *tr.v.* **-vated, -vating, -vates. 1.** To restore to an earlier, good condition; improve by repairing or remodeling. **2.** To impart new vigor to; revive. [Latin *renovāre* : *re-,* again + *novāre,* to make new, from *novus,* new.] —**ren·o·va·tion** (rĕn′ə-vā′shən) *n.* —**ren·o·va·tor** *n.*

re·nown (rĭ-noun′) *n.* **1.** The quality of being honored and acclaimed; celebrity. **2.** *Archaic.* Report; rumor. —See Synonyms at **fame.** [Middle English *renoun(e),* from Old French *renon, renom,* from *renomer,* to name again, make famous : *re-,* again, from Latin + *nomer,* to name, from Latin *nōmināre,* from *nōmen,* a name.]

re·nowned (rĭ-nound′) *adj.* Having renown; famous.

rent[1] (rĕnt) *n.* **1. a.** Payment, usually of an amount fixed by contract, made by one person or agency at stated regular intervals in return for the right to occupy or use the land or property of another. **b.** A similar payment made for the use of a facility or service provided by another, such as a telephone. **2.** *Economics.* **a.** The return derived from cultivated or improved land after deduction of all production costs. **b.** The revenue yielded by a piece of land in excess of that yielded by the poorest or least favorably located land, under equal market conditions.
∼*v.* **rented, renting, rents.** —*tr.* **1.** To obtain occupancy or use of (another's property, or a facility or service provided by another) in return for regular payments. **2.** To grant temporary occupancy or use of (one's own property or a service) in return for regular payments. Often used with *out.* —*intr.* To be rented or be available for renting: *The cottage rents for $100 a week.* [Middle English *rente,* income from property, from Old French, from Vulgar Latin *rendita* (unattested), from the feminine past participle of *rendere* (unattested), to RENDER.] —**rent·a·ble** *adj.*

rent[2]. Alternate past tense and past participle of **rend.**
∼*n.* **1.** An opening made by or as if by rending; a rip or gap. **2.** A breach of relations between people or groups; a rift.

rent-a-car (rĕnt′ə-kär′) *n.* **1.** A rented car. **2.** An agency that offers cars and vans for rent.

rent·al (rĕnt′l) *n.* **1.** An amount charged as rent. **2.** A list of tenants and rents. **3.** Property available for renting. **4.** The act of renting. **5.** An agency that rents something.
∼*adj.* Of, concerning, or available for rent.

rent control *n.* Governmental control and regulation of the amounts charged for rented housing.

rente (räNt) *n., pl.* **rentes** (*pronounced as singular*). *French.* **1.** Annual income, especially from government bonds; annuity. **2. a.** *Usually* **rentes.** The government bonds of various European countries, especially of France. **b.** The interest paid on these bonds.

rent·er (rĕn′tər) *n.* **1.** One who receives payment in exchange for the use of his property by another. **2.** One who pays rent for the use of another's property; a tenant.

rent-free (rĕnt′frē′) *adj.* Not subject to rent.
∼*adv.* Without having to pay or without paying rent.

ren·ti·er (räN-tyā′) *n. French.* One who derives an unearned income from rents or investments.

rent-roll (rĕnt′rōl′) *n.* **1.** A list of property, with the rent due and received from it. **2.** The income accruing from such property.

rent strike *n.* A collective refusal, for example by all the tenants in one building or area, to pay rent, usually as a form of protest or in order to bring rents down.

re·num·ber (rē-nŭm′bər) *tr.v.* **-bered, -bering, -bers.** To number again or in a different order.

re·nun·ci·a·tion (rĭ-nŭn′sē-ā′shən) *n.* **1.** The act or an instance of renouncing: *the renunciation of pleasures.* **2.** A declaration in which something is renounced. [Middle English, from Latin *renūntiātiō* (stem *renūntiātiōn-*) from *renūnitiāre,* to RENOUNCE.] **—re·nun·ci·a·tive** (rĭ-nŭn′sē-ā′tĭv, -sē-ə-tĭv) **re·nun·ci·a·to·ry** (rĭ-nŭn′sē-ə-tôr′ē, -tōr′ē) *adj.*

re·o·pen (rē-ō′pən) *v.* **-pened, -pening, -pens.** *—tr.* To open or take up again. *—intr.* To start again; resume.

re·or·der (rē-ôr′dər) *v.* **-dered, -dering, -ders.** *—tr.* **1.** To order again. **2.** To straighten out or put in order again. **3.** To rearrange. *—intr.* To order the same goods again.
~n. A further order of goods previously supplied.

re·or·gan·i·za·tion (rē-ôr′gə-nə-zā′shən) *n.* **1.** The act or process of organizing again or differently. **2.** *Finance.* A thorough alteration of the structure of a business enterprise, especially after a bankruptcy. In this sense, also called "reconstruction."

re·or·gan·ize (rē-ôr′gə-nīz′) *v.* **-ized, -izing, -izes.** *—tr.* To organize again or anew. *—intr.* To undergo or effect changes in organization. **—re·or·gan·iz·er** *n.*

re·or·i·en·tate (rē-ôr′ē-ən-tāt′) *tr.v.* **-tated, -tating, -tates.** **1.** To change the direction of; give a new orientation to. **2.** To change the general views or way of thinking of. **—re·or·i·en·ta·tion** *n.*

re·o·vi·rus (rē′ō-vī′rəs) *n.* Any of a group of spherical, RNA-containing viruses that are widely distributed in humans. They are found in the respiratory and digestive tracts but do not appear to cause disease. [*R*espiratory *e*nteric *o*rphan *virus.*]

rep¹, repp (rĕp) *n.* A ribbed or corded fabric of various materials, such as cotton, wool, or silk. [French *reps*†.]

rep² *n. Informal.* A representative.

rep³ *n. Physics.* A unit of absorbed radiation dose, equal to the absorbed dose in water that has been exposed to one roentgen. The rep has been largely replaced by the **rad** *(see).* [*R*oentgen + *e*quivalent + *p*hysical.]

rep⁴ *n. Informal.* **1.** A **repertory company** *(see).* **2. Repertory** *(see).*

rep. 1. repair. **2.** report. **3.** reporter. **4.** representative. **5.** reprint. **6.** republic.

Rep. 1. Representative. **2.** Republic. **3.** Republican (Party).

re·pack·age (rē′păk′ĭj) *tr.v.* **-aged, -aging, -ages.** To package again or anew; especially, to put in a new kind of package.

re·pair¹ (rĭ-pâr′) *tr.v.* **-paired, -pairing, -pairs. 1.** To restore to sound condition after damage or injury; mend. **2.** To set right; remedy: *repair an oversight.* **3.** To renew or revitalize. **4.** To make up for or compensate for (a loss or wrong, for example).
~n. Abbr. **rep. 1. a.** The work, act, or process of repairing: *beyond repair.* **b.** An instance of repairing. **2.** General condition after use or maintenance: *in good repair.* **3.** Something that has been repaired. [Middle English *repairen,* from Old French *reparer,* from Latin *reparāre* : *re-,* back (to an earlier state) + *parāre,* to put in order, prepare.] **—re·pair·a·ble** *adj.* **—re·pair·er** *n.*

repair² *intr.v.* **-paired, -pairing, -pairs. 1.** To betake oneself; go: *We all repaired to the restaurant.* **2.** To resort; go for help.
~n. Archaic. **1.** An act of going or sojourning. **2.** A place to which one goes frequently or habitually; a haunt. [Middle English *repairen,* to return, from Old French *repairer,* from Late Latin *repatriāre,* to REPATRIATE.]

re·pair·man (rĭ-pâr′măn′, -mən) *n., pl.* **-men** (-mĕn′, -mĭn). A man whose occupation is making repairs: *a bicycle repairman.*

re·pand (rĭ-pănd′) *adj. Botany.* Having a wavy margin: *a repand leaf.* [Latin *repandus,* bent back : *re-,* back, backwards + *pandus,* bent, turned, past participle of *pandere,* to spread.]

rep·a·ra·ble (rĕp′ər-ə-bəl) *adj.* Also **re·pair·a·ble** (rĭ-pâr′ə-bəl). Able to be repaired or made good. **—rep·a·ra·bil·i·ty** *n.* **—rep·a·ra·bly** *adv.*

rep·a·ra·tion (rĕp′ə-rā′shən) *n.* **1. a.** The act or process of repairing. **b.** The condition of being repaired. **2.** The act or process of making amends; expiation. **3.** Something done or paid to make amends; compensation. **4. reparations.** Compensation or remuneration required of a defeated nation for damage or injury during a war. [Middle English *reparacioun,* from Old French *reparation,* from Late Latin *reparātiō* (stem *reparātiōn-*), from Latin *reparāre,* to REPAIR.]
Synonyms: *amends, indemnity, redress, restitution.*

re·par·a·tive (rĭ-păr′ə-tĭv) *adj.* Also **re·par·a·to·ry** (rĭ-păr′ə-tôr′ē, -tōr′ē). **1.** Tending to repair. **2.** Of, pertaining to, or of the nature of reparations.

rep·ar·tee (rĕp′ər-tē′, -ər-tā′, -är-tē′, -är-tā′) *n.* **1.** A swift, witty reply; a ready or spirited retort. **2.** Witty and spirited conversation characterized by such replies. **3.** Skill in making such replies or conversation. —See Synonyms at **wit.** [French *repartie,* from *repartir,* to reply readily, from Old French, to depart again : *re-,* again + *partir,* to part, from Latin *partīre,* from *pars,* a part.]

re·par·ti·tion (rē′pär-tĭsh′ən) *n.* **1.** Distribution; apportionment. **2.** A partitioning again or in a different way.
~tr.v. **repartitioned, -tioning, -tions.** To partition again; redivide.

re·past (rĭ-păst′, -päst′) *n.* **1.** A meal or the food eaten or provided at a meal. **2.** *Obsolete.* Food; nourishment. [Middle English, from Old French, from *repaistre,* to feed, from Late Latin *repascere,* to feed again : Latin *re-,* again + *pascere,* to feed.]

re·pa·tri·ate (rē-pā′trē-āt′) *tr.v.* **-ated, -ating, -ates.** To return to the country of birth, citizenship, or ownership: *repatriate war refugees; repatriate the stolen statue.*
~n. (rē-pā′trē-ət, -āt′). Someone who has been repatriated. [Late Latin *repatriāre* : Latin *re-,* back + *patria,* native country.] **—re·pa·tri·a·tion** (rē-pā′trē-ā′shən) *n.*

re·pay (rĭ-pā′) *v.* **-paid** (-pād′), **-paying, -pays.** *—tr.* **1.** To pay back (money); refund. **2.** To pay (someone) back, either in return or in compensation. **3.** To make compensation for; make a return for. **4.** To make or do in return: *repay a call.* *—intr.* To make repayment or recompense. **—re·pay·a·ble** *adj.* **—re·pay·ment** *n.*

re·peal (rĭ-pēl′) *tr.v.* **-pealed, -pealing, -peals.** To revoke or rescind; withdraw or annul officially or formally: *Parliament repealed the law.* —See Synonyms at **nullify.**
~n. **1.** The act or process of repealing. **2. Repeal.** The repeal, effective in 1933, of the 18th Amendment to the U.S. Constitution, which prohibited alcoholic beverages. [Middle English *repelen,* from Norman French *repeler,* from Old French *rapeler* : *re-,* back, contrary + *apeler,* to APPEAL.] **—re·peal·a·ble** *adj.* **—re·peal·er** *n.*

re·peat (rĭ-pēt′) *v.* **-peated, -peating, -peats.** *—tr.* **1.** To utter or state again. **2.** To utter in duplication of another's utterance. **3.** To recite from memory. **4.** To pass on (something told in confidence) to another. **5.** To do, experience, or produce again. **6.** To manifest or express (oneself) in the same way or words: *History repeats itself.* *—intr.* **1.** To do or say something again. **2.** To occur more than once; recur. **3.** To strike the hour, half-hour, or quarter-hour, when a spring is pressed. Used of a watch or clock. **4.** To fire or be capable of firing several shots without being reloaded. Used of a gun. **5.** To commit the fraudulent offense of voting more than once in an election.
~n. **1.** The act of repeating. **2.** Something repeated; especially, a television or radio program that has been broadcast before. Also used adjectivally: *a repeat performance.* **3.** *Music.* **a.** A passage or section that is repeated. **b.** A sign usually consisting of a vertical pair of dots, indicating a passage to be repeated. **4. a.** A repeated or duplicate order for goods. **b.** The goods so ordered. [Middle English *repeten,* from Old French *repeter,* from Latin *repetere,* to go back to, seek again : *re-,* again + *petere,* to go to, seek.]

re·peat·ed (rĭ-pē′tĭd) *adj.* Said, done, or occurring again and again. **—re·peat·ed·ly** *adv.*

re·peat·er (rĭ-pē′tər) *n.* **1.** Someone or something that repeats. **2.** A watch or clock with a pressure-activated mechanism that strikes the hour and often the half-hour and quarter-hour. **3.** A repeating firearm. **4.** An electrical circuit in a transmission line for amplifying and retransmitting signals to compensate for power losses.

repeating decimal *n.* A decimal in which, after a certain digit, a pattern of one or more digits is repeated indefinitely, as in 1.5461616161. . . . Also called "circulating decimal," "recurring decimal."

repeating firearm *n.* A firearm capable of firing several times without reloading. Also called "repeater."

re·pel (rĭ-pĕl′) *v.* **-pelled, -pelling, -pels.** *—tr.* **1.** To drive back; ward off or keep away: *repel insects.* **2.** To offer successful resistance to; fight off: *repel an invasion.* **3.** To refuse to accept; reject: *repel an offer.* **4.** To turn away from; spurn. **5.** To cause aversion or distaste in: *His rudeness repels everyone.* **6.** To be resistant to; be incapable of absorbing or mixing with. **7.** To present an opposing force to; push back or away by a force: *Electric charges of the same sign repel each other.* *—intr.* **1.** To offer a resistant force to something. **2.** To cause aversion or distaste. [Middle English *repellen,* from Latin *repellere* : *re-,* back + *pellere,* to drive.] **—re·pel·ler** *n.*
Usage: *Repel* and *repulse* both have the physical sense of driving back or off. An invasion, for example, may be repelled or repulsed. *Repulse* may also apply to rebuffing or rejecting someone in a hostile or impolite manner *(I repulsed every attempt he made to get to know me),* but only *repel* is used in the sense of causing distaste or aversion to someone *(The picture repelled me).*

re·pel·lent (rĭ-pĕl′ənt) *adj.* **1.** Serving or tending to repel; capable of repelling something. **2.** Inspiring aversion or distaste; repulsive. **3.** Resistant or impervious to a specified substance. Often used in combination: *a water-repellent fabric.* —See Synonyms at **hateful.**
~n. Something that repels; especially: **1.** A substance used to repel insects. **2.** A substance or treatment for making a fabric or surface impervious or resistant to something. **—re·pel·lence, re·pel·len·cy** *n.*

re·pent¹ (rĭ-pĕnt′) *v.* **-pented, -penting, -pents.** *—intr.* **1.** To feel remorse or self-reproach for what one has done or failed to do; be contrite. **2.** To feel such remorse or regret for past conduct as to change one's mind regarding it. Used with *of: He repented of his severity.* **3.** To feel remorse or contrition for one's sins and to renounce sinful ways. *—tr.* **1.** To feel regret or self-reproach for. **2.** To change one's mind regarding (past conduct). [Middle English *repenten,* from Old French *repentir* : *re-,* in response to + *pentir,* to be sorry, from Vulgar Latin *penitīre* (unattested), to cause to repent, from Latin *paenitēre* (see **penitent**).] **—re·pent·er** *n.*

re·pent² (rē′pənt) *adj. Botany.* Creeping along the ground; prostrate. [Latin *rēpēns* (stem *rēpent-*), present participle of *rēpere,* to creep.]

re·pen·tance (rĭ-pĕn′təns) *n.* **1.** Remorse or contrition for past conduct or sin. **2.** The act or process of repenting.

re·pen·tant (rĭ-pĕn′tənt) *adj.* Characterized by or demonstrating repentance; penitent. **—re·pen·tant·ly** *adv.*

re·per·cus·sion (rē′pər-kŭsh′ən) *n.* **1.** An effect, influence, or result,

PRONUNCIATION KEY
ă, pat; ā, pay; âr, care;
ä, father, are; b, bib;
ch, church; d, deed; ĕ, pet;
ē, be; f, fife; g, gag; h, hat;
hw, which; ĭ, pit; ī, pie;
îr, pier; j, judge; k, kick;
l, lid, needle; m, mum;
n, no, sudden; ng, thing;
ŏ, pot; ō, toe; ô, paw, for;
oi, noise; ou, out; ŏŏ, book;
ōō, boot; p, pop; r, roar;
s, sauce; sh, ship, dish;
t, tight; th, thin, path;
th, this, bathe; ŭ, cut; ûr, fur;
v, valve; w, with; y, yes;
z, zebra, size; zh, vision;
ə, about, item, edible,
gallop, circus, peaceful

IN FOREIGN WORDS:
à, *Fr.* ami; œ, *Fr.* feu, *Ger.* schön; ü, *Fr.* tu, *Ger.* über;
KH, *Ger.* ich, *Scot.* loch;
N, *Fr.* bon; y′, *Fr.* Compiègne

STRESS MARKS:
Primary stress: ′
in·cite′ (ĭn-sīt′)
Secondary stress: ′
in′sight′ (ĭn′sīt′)

often indirect, produced by an event or action. **2.** A recoil, rebounding, or reciprocal motion after impact. **3.** A reflection, especially of sound; an echo. [Latin *repercussiō* (stem *repercussiōn-*), from *repercussus,* past participle of *repercutere,* to cause to rebound : *re-,* back + *percutere,* to PERCUSS.] **—re·per·cus·sive** *adj.*

rep·er·toire (rĕp′ər-twär′, -tôr′) *n.* Also **rep·er·to·ry** (rĕp′ər-tôr′ē, -tōr′ē). **1.** The stock of songs, plays, operas, or other pieces that a player or company is able to perform. **2.** The range or number of skills or special accomplishments of a particular person or group. [French *répertoire,* from Late Latin *repertōrium,* REPERTORY.]

rep·er·to·ry (rĕp′ər-tôr′ē, -tōr′ē) *n., pl.* **-ries. 1.** A repertoire. **2. a.** The performance of a number of different plays or other works by a company, usually in alternation. Also informally called "rep." **b.** A repertory company. **3.** A storehouse or other place where a stock of things is kept. **4.** Something stored in or as if in such a place; a stock or collection: *a repertory of photographic techniques.* [Late Latin *repertōrium,* from Latin *repertus,* past participle of *reperīre,* to find out, find again : *re-,* again + *parīre,* to produce, invent.] **—rep·er·to·ri·al** (rĕp′ər-tôr′ē-əl, -tōr′ē-əl) *adj.*

repertory company *n.* A company that presents and performs a number of different plays or other works during a season, usually in alternation. Also called "repertory," informally "rep."

rep·e·tend (rĕp′ə-tĕnd′, rĕp′ə-tĕnd′) *n.* **1.** A word, sound, or phrase that is repeated; a refrain. **2.** *Mathematics.* The digit or group of digits that repeats infinitely in a repeating decimal; for example, 61 in 1.54616161. . . . [Latin *repetendum,* neuter gerundive of *repetere,* to REPEAT.]

ré·pé·ti·teur (rā′pĕ-tē-tœr′) *n.* A coach for opera singers, ballet dancers, or other artists. [French.]

rep·e·ti·tion (rĕp′ə-tĭsh′ən) *n.* **1.** The act or process of repeating; the saying, doing, or producing of something again. **2.** A recitation or recital, especially of prepared or memorized material. **3.** Something repeated; a copy or reproduction. [Latin *repetītiō* (stem *repetītiōn-*), from *repetere,* to REPEAT.]

rep·e·ti·tious (rĕp′ə-tĭsh′əs) *adj.* Characterized by or filled with repetition, especially needless or tedious repetition. **—rep·e·ti·tious·ly** *adv.* **—rep·e·ti·tious·ness** *n.*

re·pet·i·tive (rĭ-pĕt′ə-tĭv) *adj.* Characterized by repetition; tending to repeat. **—re·pet·i·tive·ly** *adv.* **—re·pet·i·tive·ness** *n.*

re·phrase (rē-frāz′) *tr.v.* **-phrased, -phrasing, -phrases.** To phrase again; especially, to state in a new, clearer, or different way.

re·pine (rĭ-pīn′) *intr.v.* **-pined, -pining, -pines.** To be discontented or low in spirits; complain or fret. [RE- + PINE (to pain).]

repl. replacement.

re·place (rĭ-plās′) *tr.v.* **-placed, -placing, -places. 1. a.** To place again. **b.** To put back in place. **2.** To take or fill the place of; supplant or supersede. **3.** To be or provide a substitute for. **4.** To provide a new version of, especially by purchase: *replaced the broken lamp.* **—re·place·a·ble** *adj.* **—re·plac·er** *n.*

Synonyms: *displace, supersede, supplant.*

re·place·ment (rĭ-plās′mənt) *n. Abbr.* **repl. 1.** The act or process of replacing or of being replaced. **2.** One that replaces, such as a player who takes the place of an injured colleague in a team. **3.** *Chemistry.* A type of reaction in which one atom or group in a compound is replaced by another. **4.** *Geology.* A process in which one mineral is gradually replaced by another through deposition and removal.

re·plant (rē-plănt′, -plänt′) *tr.v.* **-planted, -planting, -plants. 1.** To plant something again, or in a new place. **2.** To supply with new plants: *replant a window box.* **3.** To reattach (a tooth or limb, for example) after separation from the body.

~n. (rē′plănt′, -plänt′). Something that has been replanted.

re·plant·a·tion (rē′plăn-tā′shən) *n.* **1.** The act of replanting or the condition of being replanted. **2.** Surgical reattachment of a bodily part that has been severed or separated.

re·play (rē-plā′) *tr.v.* **-played, -playing, -plays.** To play over again: *replay a match; replay a tape.*

~n. (rē′plā′). **1.** The act or process of replaying something. **2.** Something replayed; especially, a part of a television broadcast showing a particular sequence or piece of action, sometimes in slow motion.

re·plen·ish (rĭ-plĕn′ĭsh) *tr.v.* **-ished, -ishing, -ishes. 1.** To fill or make complete again; add a new stock or supply to: *replenish the larder.* **2.** To renew a supply of. [Middle English *replenisshen,* from Old French *replenir* (present stem *repleniss-*) : *re-,* again + *plenir,* to fill, from *plein,* full.] **—re·plen·ish·er** *n.* **—re·plen·ish·ment** *n.*

re·plete (rĭ-plēt′) *adj.* **1.** Plentifully supplied; abounding. Used with *with.* **2.** Filled to satiation; gorged. [Middle English *replet,* from Old French, from Latin *replētus,* past participle of *replēre,* to refill : *re-,* again + *plēre,* to fill.] **—re·plete·ness** *n.*

re·ple·tion (rĭ-plē′shən) *n.* **1.** The condition of being fully supplied or completely filled. **2.** A state of excessive fullness.

re·plev·i·a·ble (rĭ-plĕv′ē-ə-bəl) *adj.* Also **re·plev·is·a·ble** (rĭ-plĕv′ə-sə-bəl). *Law.* Capable of being recovered by replevin.

re·plev·in (rĭ-plĕv′ĭn) *n.* Also **re·plev·y** (-plĕv′ē). *Law.* **1.** An action to recover personal property unlawfully taken. **2.** The recovery of property by this action subject to the recoverer's willingness to have the matter settled finally in court. **3.** The writ or procedure by which the property is recovered.

~tr.v. **replevined, -ining, -ins.** *Law.* To replevy. [Middle English *replevyn,* from Norman French *replevine,* a pledge, from Old French *replevir,* to recover, "to pledge back" : *re-,* back + *plevir,* pledge, from Frankish *plegan* (unattested).]

re·plev·y (rĭ-plĕv′ē) *tr.v.* **-ied, -ying, -ies.** *Law.* To regain possession of (goods) by a writ of replevin.

~n. Law. Replevin. [Norman French *replevir,* from Old French. See **replevin.**]

rep·li·ca (rĕp′lĭ-kə) *n.* **1.** A copy or reproduction of a work of art, especially one made by the original artist. **2.** Any copy or close reproduction, especially one on a smaller scale. [Italian, from *replicare,* to repeat, from Latin *replicāre,* to REPLICATE.]

rep·li·cate (rĕp′lĭ-kāt′) *tr.v.* **-cated, -cating, -cates. 1.** To duplicate, copy, reproduce, or repeat. **2.** To fold over; bend (something) back upon itself.

~adj. (rĕp′lĭ-kət). Also **rep·li·cat·ed** (-kā′tĭd). Folded over or bent back upon itself: *a replicate leaf.* [Late Latin *replicāre,* to repeat, from Latin, to fold back : *re-,* back + *plicāre,* to fold.]

rep·li·ca·tion (rĕp′lĭ-kā′shən) *n.* **1.** A fold or a folding back. **2.** A reply; a response, especially to an answer. **3.** *Law.* The plaintiff's response to the defendant's answer or plea. **4.** An echo or reverberation. **5.** A copy or reproduction. **6.** The act or process of duplicating or reproducing something. **7.** The process by which exact copies of genetic material, such as DNA molecules, are produced.

re·ply (rĭ-plī′) *v.* **-plied, -plying, -plies.** *—intr.* **1.** To give an answer in speech or writing. **2.** To respond by some action or gesture: *She replied by shrugging her shoulders.* **3.** To echo. **4.** *Law.* To answer a defendant's plea. *—tr.* To say or give as an answer: *He replied that he was ill.* —See Synonyms at **answer.**

~n., pl. **replies. 1.** An answer in speech or writing. **2.** A response by action or gesture. **3.** *Law.* A plaintiff's speech or argument in answer to that of a defendant. [Middle English *replien,* from Old French *replier,* to fold back, reply, from Latin *replicāre,* to REPLICATE.] **—re·pli·er** *n.*

reply-paid (rĭ-plī′pād′) *adj.* With the reply prepaid by the sender. Said especially of a telegram.

re·po (rē′pō′) *n., pl.* **-pos.** *Informal.* A **repurchase agreement** *(see).* [Shortening and alteration of REPURCHASE AGREEMENT.]

re·point (rē-point′) *tr.v.* **-pointed, -pointing, -points.** To reset (bricks) in new mortar or cement; point (brickwork) again.

ré·pon·dez s'il vous plaît (rā-pôN-dā′ sēl vo͞o plā′). *Abbr.* **R.S.V.P.** *French.* Please reply. Used on formal invitations.

re·port (rĭ-pôrt′) *n. Abbr.* **rep., rept., rpt. 1.** An account that is prepared, presented, or delivered, usually in formal or organized form. **2.** A formal, detailed account of the proceedings or transactions of a group. **3.** *Usually* **reports.** *Law.* A published collection of authoritative accounts of court cases or of judicial decisions. **4.** Rumor or gossip; common talk: *According to report, they eloped.* **5.** Reputation; repute: *a man of bad report.* **6.** An explosive noise: *the sharp report of a rifle.* **7.** *Chiefly British.* An account and summary of a pupil's work, achievement, progress, and behavior at school.

~v. **reported, -porting, -ports.** *—tr.* **1.** To make or present an account of (an inquiry, for example), often officially, formally, or regularly. **2.** To relate or tell about: *reported the burglary to the police.* **3.** To write or provide an account or summary of for publication or broadcast: *report the news.* **4.** To submit or relate the results of considerations concerning: *The committee reported the bill.* **5.** To carry back and repeat to another. **6.** To complain about or denounce: *Report him to the principal.* *—intr.* **1.** To make a report. **2.** To serve as a reporter for a newspaper, broadcasting company, or other news medium. **3.** To present oneself: *report for duty.* **4.** To be accountable: *He reports directly to the chairman.* [Middle English, from Old French, from *reporter,* to carry back, from Latin *reportāre,* "to carry back" : *re-,* back + *portāre,* to carry.] **—re·port·a·ble** *adj.*

re·port·age (rĕp′ər-täzh′, rĭ-pôr′tĭj) *n.* **1.** The reporting of news or information of general interest. **2.** The style of such reporting. **3.** Writing that reports events; journalism.

re·port·ed·ly (rĭ-pôr′tĭd-lē, rĭ-pōr′-) *adv.* By report; supposedly.

reported speech *n.* **Indirect speech** *(see).*

re·port·er (rĭ-pôr′tər, rĭ-pōr′-) *n. Abbr.* **rep. 1.** A person who reports. **2.** A writer, investigator, or (especially on radio and television) presenter of news stories. **3.** A person authorized to write and issue official accounts of judicial or legislative proceedings. **—rep·or·to·ri·al** (rĕp′ər-tôr′ē-əl, -tōr′ē-əl, rē′pôr-, rē′pōr-) *adj.*

re·pose¹ (rĭ-pōz′) *n.* **1. a.** The act of resting; a rest. **b.** The state of being at rest; relaxation. **2.** Peace of mind; freedom from anxiety; composure. **3.** Calm; tranquillity. —See Synonyms at **rest.**

~v. **reposed, -posing, -poses.** *—tr.* **1.** To lay (oneself or part of one's body) down. **2.** To rest or relax (oneself). *—intr.* **1.** To lie at rest; relax. **2.** To lie or be supported by something. **3.** To lie dead: *repose in the grave.* [Middle English *reposen,* from Old French *reposer, repauser,* from Late Latin *repausāre* : *re-* (intensifier), again + *pausāre,* to rest, from Latin *pausa,* a stop, pause, from Greek *pausis,* from *pauein,* to stop.] **—re·pos·al** *n.* **—re·pos·er** *n.*

repose² *tr.v.* **-posed, -posing, -poses.** To place (faith or trust, for example): *The nation reposed its hopes in a single man.* [Middle English *reposen* : RE- + POSE (formed by analogy with Latin *repōnere,* to put back).]

re·pose·ful (rĭ-pōz′fəl) *adj.* Expressing repose; calm. **—re·pose·ful·ly** *adv.* **—re·pose·ful·ness** *n.*

re·pos·it (rĭ-pŏz′ĭt) *tr.v.* **-ited, -iting, -its.** To put away; store. [Latin *repōnere* (past participle *repositus*), to put back, replace : *re-,* back + *pōnere,* to place.] **—re·po·si·tion** (rē′pə-zĭsh′ən, rĕp′ə-) *n.*

re·pos·i·to·ry (rĭ-pŏz′ə-tôr′ē, -tōr′ē) *n., pl.* **-ries. 1.** A place where things may be put for safekeeping. **2.** A warehouse. **3.** A museum. **4.** A burial vault; a tomb. **5.** One that contains or is a store of something specified: *She was a repository of old family tales.* **6.** One who is entrusted with secrets or confidential information.

re·pos·sess (rē'pə-zĕs') *tr.v.* **-sessed, -sessing, -sesses. 1.** To take back possession of (property), as from someone who has not kept up installment payments. **2.** To give back possession to. **—re·pos·ses·sion** *n.*

re·pous·sé (rə-po͞o-sā') *adj.* **1.** Shaped or decorated with patterns in relief formed by hammering and pressing on the reverse side. Said especially of metal. **2.** Raised in relief.

~n. **1.** A repoussé design. **2.** The technique of hammering and pressing repoussé designs. [French, past participle of *repousser,* to push back, from Old French : *re-,* back + *pousser,* to PUSH.]

repp. Variant of **rep** (fabric).

repr. representing.

rep·re·hend (rĕp'rĭ-hĕnd') *tr.v.* **-hended, -hending, -hends.** To reprove; censure. —See Synonyms at **criticize.** [Middle English *reprehenden,* from Latin *reprehendere,* rebuke, hold back : *re-,* back + *prehendere,* to seize.]

rep·re·hen·si·ble (rĕp'rĭ-hĕn'sə-bəl) *adj.* Deserving of rebuke or censure; blameworthy. [Late Latin *reprehēnsibilis,* from Latin *reprehendere* (past participle *reprehēnsus*), to REPREHEND.] **—rep·re·hen·si·bil·i·ty, rep·re·hen·si·ble·ness** *n.* **—rep·re·hen·si·bly** *adv.*

rep·re·hen·sion (rĕp'rĭ-hĕn'shən) *n.* Rebuke; censure.

rep·re·sent (rĕp'rĭ-zĕnt') *tr.v.* **-sented, -senting, -sents. 1. a.** To stand for; symbolize. **b.** To indicate or communicate by signs or signals. **2.** To depict; portray. **3.** To present clearly to the mind. **4.** To point out forcefully: *represented the need for caution.* **5.** To describe or put forward (a person or thing) as an embodiment of some specified quality. **6. a.** To serve as the official and authorized delegate or agent for; act as a spokesperson for. **b.** To be present in the name of. **7.** To serve as an example of: *The class of mammals is represented by seven species in this museum.* **8.** To be the equivalent of. **9. a.** To stage (a play, for example); present; produce. **b.** To act the part or role of. —See Synonyms at **mean.** [Middle English *representen,* from Latin *repraesantāre,* show, bring back : *re-,* back, again + *praesentāre,* to PRESENT.] **—rep·re·sent·a·ble** *adj.* **—rep·re·sent·a·bil·i·ty** *n.*

rep·re·sen·ta·tion (rĕp'rĭ-zĕn-tā'shən, rĕp'rĭ-zən-) *n.* **1.** The act of representing or the state of being represented. **2.** That which represents. **3.** *Often* **representations. a.** An account or statement, as of facts, allegations, or arguments. **b.** An expostulation; a protest: *make representations to a higher authority.* **4.** A presentation or production, as of a play. **5.** The condition of serving as an official delegate, agent, or spokesman. **6.** The right or privilege of being represented by delegates having a voice in a governing or lawmaking body. **7.** *Law.* A statement of fact made by one party in order to induce another party to enter into a contract.

rep·re·sen·ta·tion·al (rĕp'rĭ-zĕn-tā'shən-əl, rĕp'rĭ-zən-) *adj.* Of or pertaining to representation, especially to realistic and naturalistic graphic representation in art, as opposed to abstraction.

rep·re·sen·ta·tion·al·ism (rĕp'rĭ-zĕn-tā'shən-ə-lĭz'əm, rĕp'rĭ-zən-) *n.* Also **rep·re·sen·ta·tion·ism** (-tā'shə-nĭz'əm) (for sense 1). **1.** *Philosophy.* A theory of perception that holds that since external objects are perceived through the mediation of the human mind, they can never be perceived directly as they really are, but only as representations of the "real" object. **2.** The practice and active support of representational art.

rep·re·sen·ta·tive (rĕp'rĭ-zĕn'tə-tĭv) *n. Abbr.* **rep., Rep. 1.** A person or thing serving as an example or type for others of the same classification; a typical instance. **2. a.** One qualified to serve as an authorized official delegate or agent. **b.** One present in the name of another person or body. **c.** One who travels around on behalf of a company, trying to obtain orders or customers. **3. a.** A member of a governmental body, usually legislative, chosen by popular vote. **b.** In the United States, a member of the U.S. House of Representatives or of the lower house of a state legislature.

~adj. **1.** Representing, depicting, portraying, or able to do so. **2.** Authorized to act as an official delegate or agent. **3.** Of, pertaining to, or characteristic of government by representation. **4.** Like or characteristic of others in the same class; typical. **—rep·re·sen·ta·tive·ly** *adv.* **—rep·re·sen·ta·tive·ness** *n.*

re·press (rĭ-prĕs') *tr.v.* **-pressed, -pressing, -presses. 1.** To hold back; restrain: *repress a laugh.* **2.** To suppress; quell: *repress a rebellion.* **3.** To control forcibly and oppressively; subjugate: *His parents repressed him in childhood.* **4.** *Psychology.* To force (memories, ideas, or fears, for example) into the subconscious mind. [Middle English *repressen,* from Latin *reprimere* (past participle *repressus*) : *re-,* back + *premere,* to press.] **—re·press·i·ble** *adj.* **—re·pres·sive** *adj.* **—re·pres·sive·ly** *adv.* **—re·pres·sive·ness** *n.*

re·pres·sion (rĭ-prĕsh'ən) *n.* **1. a.** The action of repressing. **b.** The state of being repressed. **2.** The unconscious exclusion of painful impulses, desires, or fears from the conscious mind.

re·pres·sor, re·press·er (rĭ-prĕs'ər) *n.* **1.** One that represses. **2.** *Biology.* A protein that prevents the synthesis of other proteins by interfering with the action of DNA.

re·prieve (rĭ-prēv') *tr.v.* **-prieved, -prieving, -prieves. 1.** To postpone or cancel the punishment of. **2.** To bring relief to.

~n. **1. a.** The postponement or cancellation of a punishment. **b.** A warrant for such a postponement or cancellation. **2.** Temporary relief, as from danger or pain. [Variant of earlier *reprive, repry,* from Middle English *repryen,* from Old French *reprendre* (past participle *repris*), to take back, from Latin *reprehendere,* to hold back, REPREHEND.] **—re·priev·a·ble** *adj.*

rep·ri·mand (rĕp'rə-mănd', -mänd') *tr.v.* **-manded, -manding, -mands.** To rebuke or censure severely. —See Synonyms at **admonish.**

~n. A severe or formal rebuke or censure. [French *reprimender,* from *reprimende,* a reprimand, ultimately from Latin *reprimenda,* neuter plural gerundive of *reprimere,* to REPRESS.]

re·print (rē'prĭnt') *n. Abbr.* **rep. 1.** Something that has been printed again; especially: **a.** A new or additional edition; a facsimile impression of an original. **b.** An offprint; a separately printed excerpt. **2.** A facsimile of a postage stamp printed after the original issue of the stamp has ceased.

~tr.v. (rē-prĭnt') **reprinted, -printing, -prints.** To print again; make a new copy or edition of. **—re·print·er** *n.*

re·pri·sal (rĭ-prī'zəl) *n.* **1.** Retaliation for an injury with the intent of inflicting at least as much injury in return. **2.** The forcible seizure of an enemy's goods or subjects in retaliation for inflicted injuries. **3.** An act or instance of any kind of retaliation. [Middle English *reprisail,* from Norman French *reprisaille,* from Medieval Latin *repraesālia,* contraction of *repraehensālia,* from Latin *reprehensus,* past participle of *reprehendere,* to REPREHEND.]

re·prise (rə-prēz') *n.* **1.** *Music.* A repetition of a phrase or verse; a return to an original theme. **2.** A repetition; a repeat.

~tr.v. **reprised, -prising, -prises.** *—tr.* To repeat; make a reprise of. [Middle English, from Old French, "a taking back," from the feminine past participle of *reprendre,* to take back, from Latin *reprehendere,* to REPREHEND.]

re·pro (rē'prō) *n., pl.* **-pros.** *Informal.* A **reproduction proof** *(see).*

re·proach (rĭ-prōch') *tr.v.* **-proached, -proaching, -proaches. 1.** To express displeasure with (a person) for something blameworthy; rebuke; censure. **2.** To bring shame upon; disgrace. —See Synonyms at **admonish.**

~n. **1.** Censure; rebuke; blame. **2.** That which causes rebuke or blame. **3.** Disgrace; shame. **—beyond reproach.** So good as to preclude any possibility of criticism. [Middle English *reprochen,* from Old French *reprochier,* from Vulgar Latin *repropiāre* (unattested), bring back near : Latin *re-,* back + *prope,* near.] **—re·proach·a·ble** *adj.* **—re·proach·a·ble·ness** *n.* **—re·proach·a·bly** *adv.* **—re·proach·er** *n.*

re·proach·ful (rĭ-prōch'fəl) *adj.* Expressing reproach or blame. **—re·proach·ful·ly** *adv.* **—re·proach·ful·ness** *n.*

rep·ro·bate (rĕp'rə-bāt') *n.* **1.** A morally unprincipled person; a scoundrel. **2.** *Theology.* One who is predestined to damnation.

~adj. **1.** Morally unprincipled; shameless. **2.** *Theology.* Rejected by God and without hope of salvation.

~tr.v. **reprobated, -bating, -bates. 1.** To disapprove of; condemn. **2.** *Theology.* To abandon to eternal damnation. [Late Latin *reprobātus,* past participle of *reprobāre,* to reprove : Latin *re-,* back, against + *probāre,* to test, PROVE.] **—rep·ro·ba·tion** (rĕp'rə-bā'shən) *n.*

re·pro·duce (rē'prə-do͞os', -dyo͞os') *v.* **-duced, -ducing, -duces.** *—tr.* **1.** To produce a counterpart, image, or copy of. **2.** *Biology.* To generate (offspring) by sexual or asexual means. **3.** To produce again or anew; re-create. **4.** To bring to mind again (a memory, for example). *—intr.* **1.** To generate offspring. **2.** To undergo copying. **—re·pro·duc·er** *n.* **—re·pro·duc·i·ble** *adj.*

re·pro·duc·tion (rē'prə-dŭk'shən) *n.* **1.** The act of reproducing or the condition of being reproduced. **2.** That which is reproduced, especially with reference to its faithfulness to an original: *disappointed by the poor quality of the sound reproduction.* **3.** A copy of a work of art, antique, or the like. Also used adjectivally: *reproduction furniture.* **4.** *Biology.* The sexual or asexual process by which organisms generate others of the same kind.

reproduction proof *n. Printing.* A proof of typeset material made for reproduction through a photographic process such as photo-offset lithography. Also informally called "repro."

re·pro·duc·tive (rē'prə-dŭk'tĭv) *adj.* **1.** Of or pertaining to reproduction. **2.** Tending to reproduce. **—re·pro·duc·tive·ly** *adv.* **—re·pro·duc·tive·ness** *n.*

re·pro·gram (rē-prō'grăm') *tr.v.* **-grammed** or **-gramed, -gramming** or **-graming, -grams.** To program again; especially, to supply (a computer) with new programs.

re·pro·graph·ics (rē'prə-grăf'ĭks) *n. Usually used with a singular verb.* **1.** The technique of reprography. **2.** The materials, equipment, and processes used in reprography.

re·prog·ra·phy (rĭ-prŏg'rə-fē) *n.* The process of reproducing, reprinting, or copying graphic material by mechanical, especially electronic, means. [REPRO(DUCE) + -GRAPHY.] **—rep·ro·graph·ic** (rĕp'rə-grăf'ĭk, rē'prə-) *adj.* **—rep·ro·graph·i·cal·ly** *adv.*

re·proof¹ (rĭ-pro͞of') *n.* An act or expression of reproving; a rebuke.

re·proof² (rē'pro͞of') *tr.v.* **-proofed, -proofing, -proofs. 1.** To make a new proof of (printed matter). **2.** To make resistant again, as by making heatproof or waterproof.

re·prove (rĭ-pro͞ov') *tr.v.* **-proved, -proving, -proves.** To rebuke for a fault or misdeed; scold. —See Synonyms at **admonish.** [Middle English *reproven,* from Old French *reprover,* from Late Latin *reprobāre,* REPROBATE.] **—re·prov·a·ble** *adj.* **—re·prov·er** *n.* **—re·prov·ing·ly** *adv.*

rept. 1. receipt. **2.** report.

rep·tant (rĕp'tənt) *adj. Biology.* Creeping or crawling. [Latin *reptāns* (stem *reptant-*), present participle of *reptāre,* to crawl, frequentative of *repere,* to crawl.]

rep·tile (rĕp'tĭl, -tīl') *n.* **1.** Any of various cold-blooded, usually egg-laying vertebrates of the class Reptilia, such as a snake, lizard,

PRONUNCIATION KEY

ă, pat; ā, pay; âr, care; ä, father, are; b, bib; ch, church; d, deed; ĕ, pet; ē, be; f, fife; g, gag; h, hat; hw, which; ĭ, pit; ī, pie; îr, pier; j, judge; k, kick; l, lid, needle; m, mum; n, no, sudden; ng, thing; ŏ, pot; ō, toe; ô, paw, for; oi, noise; ou, out; o͝o, book; o͞o, boot; p, pop; r, roar; s, sauce; sh, ship, dish; t, tight; th, thin, path; *th*, this, bathe; ŭ, cut; ûr, fur; v, valve; w, with; y, yes; z, zebra, size; zh, vision; ə, about, item, edible, gallop, circus, peaceful

IN FOREIGN WORDS:

à, *Fr.* ami; œ, *Fr.* feu, *Ger.* schön; ü, *Fr.* tu, *Ger.* über; KH, *Ger.* ich, *Scot.* loch; N, *Fr.* bon; y', *Fr.* Compiègne

STRESS MARKS:

Primary stress: '
in·cite' (ĭn-sīt')
Secondary stress: '
in'sight' (ĭn'sīt')

crocodile, turtle, or dinosaur, having an external covering of scales or horny plates, and breathing by means of lungs. **2.** A despicable or repulsive person.
~*adj.* **1.** Of, pertaining to, or characteristic of reptiles. **2.** Despicable; repulsive. **3.** *Archaic.* Creeping. [Middle English *reptil,* from Old French *reptile,* from Late Latin *reptile,* neuter of *reptilis,* creeping, from Latin *repere,* to creep.]

rep·til·i·an (rĕp-tĭl'ē-ən, -tĭl'yən) *adj.* **1.** Of or pertaining to reptiles. **2.** Resembling or characteristic of a reptile. **3.** Repulsive, contemptible, or devious.
~*n.* A reptile.

re·pub·lic (rĭ-pŭb'lĭk) *n. Abbr.* **rep., Rep., Repub. 1.** Any political order that is not a monarchy. **2. a.** A constitutional form of government, especially a democratic and representative one, in which the head of state is not a monarch, and supreme power is vested in the people or their elected representatives. **b.** A country having such a form of government. **3.** A particular republican administration constituting a stage in a country's political history: *the third republic.* **4.** Any group of people working freely and equally for the same cause: *the republic of letters.* **5.** An autonomous or partially autonomous political and territorial unit belonging to a sovereign federation; specifically, such a unit in the U.S.S.R. or Yugoslavia. [French *république,* from Latin *rēspūblica* : *rēs,* a thing, matter, affair + *pūblica,* feminine of *pūblicus,* PUBLIC.]

re·pub·li·can (rĭ-pŭb'lĭ-kən) *adj.* **1.** Of, pertaining to, or characteristic of a republic. **2.** In favor of the republic as a form of government. **3. Republican. a.** *Abbr.* **R., Rep., Repub.** Of, belonging to, or supporting the Republican Party of the United States. **b.** Of or supporting the government side in the Spanish Civil War.
~*n.* **1.** A person who favors the republic as a form of government.
2. Republican. A member or supporter of the Republican Party of the United States. **—re·pub·li·can·ism** *n.*

Republican calendar *n.* The **Revolutionary calendar** *(see).*

re·pub·li·can·ize (rĭ-pŭb'lĭ-kə-nīz') *tr.v.* **-ized, -izing, -izes.** To make republican. **—re·pub·li·can·i·za·tion** *n.*

Republican Party *n.* **1.** One of the two major political parties of the United States, organized in 1854 to oppose slavery. **2.** The Democratic-Republican Party, a former political party of the United States, organized in 1792 by Thomas Jefferson. See **Democratic Party.**

re·pub·li·ca·tion (rē'pŭb-lǐ-kā'shən) *n.* **1.** The act of republishing. **2.** That which is republished.

re·pub·lish (rē'pŭb'lĭsh) *tr.v.* **-lished, -lishing, -lishes. 1.** To publish anew or again. **2.** *Law.* To revive (a cancelled will, for example). **—re·pub·lish·er** *n.*

re·pu·di·ate (rĭ-pyōo'dē-āt') *tr.v.* **-ated, -ating, -ates. 1.** To reject emphatically as unfounded or unjust: *repudiated the accusation.* **2. a.** To refuse to recognize the validity or authority of: *repudiated the central government.* **b.** To refuse to pay. **3. a.** To disown (a son or a wife, for example). **b.** To refuse to have any dealings with. [Latin *repudiāre,* to reject, cast off, from *repudium,* a casting off.] **—re·pu·di·a·tive** (rĭ-pyōo'dē-ā'tĭv, -dē-ə-tĭv) *adj.* **—re·pu·di·a·tor** *n.*

re·pu·di·a·tion (rĭ-pyōo'dē-ā'shən) *n.* **1.** The act of repudiating or the state of being repudiated. **2.** The act of refusing to acknowledge a contract or debt.

re·pugn (rĭ-pyōon') *v.* **-pugned, -pugning, -pugns.** *Archaic.* **—***tr.* To oppose or resist. **—***intr.* To be opposed; conflict. [Middle English *repugnen,* from Old French *repugner,* from Latin *repugnāre,* to fight against : *re-,* against + *pugnāre,* to fight.]

re·pug·nance (rĭ-pŭg'nəns) *n.* Also **re·pug·nan·cy** (-nən-sē). **1.** Ex-

---

reptile

LIVING RELATIVES OF THE DINOSAURS

Reptiles were the first vertebrates to spend their lives on land

The Reptilia class includes the various groups of dinosaurs—the largest-known land animals—which have been extinct for some 65 million years. Four groups of reptiles survive today—snakes and lizards, crocodiles, turtles, and the primitive tuatara. All life on this planet began in the water and, over the long process of evolution, reptiles were the first vertebrates to adapt to living their entire life cycle on land. They evolved from primitive amphibians. Although some reptiles, crocodiles and turtles for example, have returned to live in the water, all reptiles breathe through lungs, not through gills. Newly born or freshly hatched reptiles do not pass through a period as aquatic larvae but are like miniature adults. They are cold-blooded creatures, and their behavior, not body function, is adapted to maintain them at an ideal temperature. They shun great heat or cold and bask in the sun for warmth.

LIZARD *The lizard (below) belongs to the order Squamata, whose members have scales covering the body. Some lizards can shed part of the tail if they are caught by a predator. Each vertebra has a preformed point at which to break. The new tail that grows is stumpy and formed around cartilage, not new bone.*

TUATARA *Most of this order, the Rhynchocephalia, is extinct and the tuatara (left), found only on islands off New Zealand, is the sole survivor. It is a small lizardlike creature, but its teeth are fused to the edges of its jaws—not set in sockets. The female lays up to 15 eggs that take 15 months to hatch.*

TURTLE *The marine turtles and the land tortoises compose the order Chelonia. The turtle (right) has flippers where the tortoise has feet. Turtles lay their eggs on land, but newly hatched young go straight to the sea to escape predators.*

CROCODILE *The order Crocodilia, the crocodiles, are the largest living reptiles and they live mainly in tropical rivers. Alligators, caymans, and gavials are of similar appearance to the crocodile, but the difference by which each can be recognized is in the number of teeth on each side of the jaw: crocodiles have 14 or 15, alligators and caymans between 17 and 22, and gavials between 27 and 29. The crocodile also differs in that one tooth on each side of its lower jaw sticks out when its mouth is closed. All are adapted to life in the water, with raised eyes and nostrils so that they can see and breathe almost submerged. Valves in their throats keep water out of the lungs as they dive.*

treme dislike or aversion. **2.** Contradiction; inconsistency.

re·pug·nant (rĭ-pŭg′nənt) *adj.* **1.** Offensive; distasteful; repulsive. **2.** Contradictory; inconsistent. [Middle English, from Old French, from Latin *repugnāns* (stem *repugnant-*), present participle of *repugnāre,* REPUGN.] **—re·pug·nant·ly** *adv.*

re·pulse (rĭ-pŭls′) *tr.v.* **-pulsed, -pulsing, -pulses. 1.** To drive back; repel. **2.** To spurn or reject with rudeness, coldness, or denial. —See Usage note at **repel.**
~n. **1.** The act of repulsing or the fact of being repulsed. **2.** Rejection; refusal. [Latin *repulsus,* past participle of *repellere,* to REPEL.] **—re·puls·er** *n.*

re·pul·sion (rĭ-pŭl′shən) *n.* **1.** The act of repulsing or the condition of being repulsed. **2.** Extreme aversion or dislike. **3.** *Physics.* A force that tends to increase the distance between two bodies having like magnetic poles or like electric charges.

re·pul·sive (rĭ-pŭl′sĭv) *adj.* **1.** Causing repugnance, extreme dislike, or aversion; disgusting. **2.** Tending to repel or drive off. **3.** *Physics.* Opposing in direction: *a repulsive force.* **—re·pul·sive·ly** *adv.* **—re·pul·sive·ness** *n.*

re·pur·chase agreement (rē-pûr′chĭs) *n.* A contract giving the seller of property the right or obligation to buy back the property under specified terms. Also called "repo."

rep·u·ta·ble (rĕp′yə-tə-bəl) *adj.* Having a good reputation; honorable; trustworthy: *buy from a reputable dealer.* **—rep·u·ta·bil·i·ty** *n.* **—rep·u·ta·bly** *adv.*

rep·u·ta·tion (rĕp′yə-tā′shən) *n.* **1.** The general estimation in which a person or thing is held by the public; what is known, said, or thought about a person. **2.** The state or fact of being highly thought of or having a good reputation. **3.** A specified character or trait ascribed to a person or thing: *a reputation for courtesy.* [Middle English *reputacion,* from Latin *reputātiō* (stem *reputātiōn-*), a reckoning, from *reputāre,* to consider, REPUTE.]

re·pute (rĭ-pyo͞ot′) *tr.v.* **-puted, -puting, -putes.** To consider, suppose, or regard. Usually used in the passive.
~n. **1.** Reputation. **2.** Good reputation. —See Synonyms at **fame.** [Middle English *reputen,* from Old French *reputer,* from Latin *reputāre,* to count over, consider : *re-,* over, again + *putāre,* to compute, consider.]

re·put·ed (rĭ-pyo͞o′tĭd) *adj.* Generally considered or supposed.

re·put·ed·ly (rĭ-pyo͞o′tĭd-lē) *adv.* According to what is generally believed or supposed.

req. 1. require; required. **2.** requisition.

re·quest (rĭ-kwĕst′) *tr.v.* **-quested, -questing, -quests. 1.** To ask for; express a desire for. **2.** To ask (a person) to do something.
~n. **1.** An expressed desire; an act of asking. **2.** That which is asked for. **—by request.** In response to an expressed desire. **—in request.** In great demand. **—on request.** When asked for.
~adj. Having been desired or demanded: *a request performance.* [Middle English, from Old French *requester,* from *requeste,* a request, from Vulgar Latin *requaesita* (unattested), from Latin *requīrere,* to seek again, REQUIRE.]

request stop *n.* A stop on a bus route at which one must signal to the driver if one wishes to be picked up or let off.

re·qui·em (rĕk′wē-əm, rē′kwē-) *n.* **1. Requiem.** *Roman Catholic Church.* **a.** A mass for a deceased person or persons. **b.** A musical composition for such a mass. **2.** Any hymn, composition, or service for the dead. [Middle English, from Latin (first word of the introit of the mass for the dead), accusative of *requiēs,* rest : *re-,* again + *quiēs,* rest.]

req·ui·es·cat (rĕk′wē-ĕs′kăt′, -kät′) *n.* A prayer for the repose of the souls of the dead. [Latin, "may he (or she) rest," from *requiescere,* to rest : *re-,* again + *quiescere,* to be quiet, rest, from *quiēs,* quiet, rest.]

re·quire (rĭ-kwīr′) *tr.v.* **-quired, -quiring, -quires. 1.** To have use for as a necessity; need: *Most plants require sunlight.* **2.** To ask or demand formally or authoritatively: *His presence was required in court.* **3.** To compel or oblige: *All students are required to attend classes.* **4.** To call for; demand as necessary or appropriate: *matters requiring our attention.* [Middle English *requiren,* from Old French *requerre,* from Vulgar Latin *requaerere* (unattested), from Latin *requīrere,* to seek again, search for, inquire : *re-,* again + *quaerere,* to seek, to ask.] **—re·quir·a·ble** *adj.* **—re·quir·er** *n.*

re·quired (rĭ-kwīrd′) *adj. Abbr.* **req. 1.** Needed; essential. **2.** Obligatory: *required reading.* —See Synonyms at **necessary.**

re·quire·ment (rĭ-kwīr′mənt) *n.* **1.** That which is required; something needed or wanted. **2.** Something obligatory; a prerequisite.

req·ui·site (rĕk′wə-zĭt) *adj.* Required; necessary; essential. —See Synonyms at **necessary.**
~n. Something needed, especially for a particular purpose; a necessity: *A visa is a requisite for travel to the Soviet Union.* [Middle English, from Latin *requīsītus,* past participle of *requīrere,* to REQUIRE.] **—req·ui·site·ly** *adv.* **—req·ui·site·ness** *n.*

req·ui·si·tion (rĕk′wə-zĭsh′ən) *n. Abbr.* **req. 1. a.** A formal written request for something that is needed. **b.** An order claiming something for official, especially military, use. **c.** The act of making such a request or claim. **2.** A necessity; a requirement. **3.** The condition of being needed or put into service: *All vehicles were in requisition during the war.* **4.** A formal request made by one government to another, demanding the return of a criminal.
~tr.v. **requisitioned, -tioning, -tions. 1.** To demand, as for military needs or in a time of emergency. **2.** To make demands of.

re·quit·al (rĭ-kwīt′l) *n.* **1.** The act of requiting. **2.** Return, as for an injury or for some friendly act.

re·quite (rĭ-kwīt′) *tr.v.* **-quited, -quiting, -quites. 1.** To make repayment or return for: *requite another's love.* **2.** To repay (a person): *requited the stranger for his help.* **3.** To avenge. [RE- + obsolete *quite,* variant of QUIT.] **—re·quit·a·ble** *adj.* **—re·quit·er** *n.*

rere·dos (rĕr′ĭ-dŏs′, rîr′-, rîr′dŏs′) *n.* **1.** A decorative screen or facing on the wall at the back of an altar. **2.** The back of an open hearth of a fireplace. [Middle English, from Old French *areredos* : *arere,* back, behind, from Vulgar Latin *ad retrō* (unattested) : Latin *ad,* to + *retrō,* backward + *dos,* back, from Latin *dorsum.*]

re·run (rē′rŭn′) *n.* The act or an instance of repeating a motion-picture presentation or a recorded television program.
~tr.v. (rē′rŭn′) **reran** (-răn′), **-run, -running, -runs.** To present a second production, broadcast, or showing of.

res. 1. research. **2.** reserve. **3.** residence; resident; resides; residing. **4.** resolution.

res adjudicata. Variant of **res judicata.**

re·sale (rē′sāl′, rē-sāl′) *n.* The selling again of a purchase. Also used adjectivally: *resale value.*

re·scind (rĭ-sĭnd′) *tr.v.* **-scinded, -scinding, -scinds.** To void; repeal. —See Synonyms at **nullify.** [Latin *rēscindere,* to cut off, abolish : *re-* (intensive) + *scindere,* to cut.] **—re·scind·a·ble** *adj.* **—re·scind·er** *n.* **—re·scind·ment** *n.*

re·scis·sion (rĭ-sĭzh′ən) *n.* The act of rescinding. [Late Latin *rescissiō* (stem *rescissiōn-*), from Latin *rēscissus,* past participle of *rēscindere,* RESCIND.]

re·scis·so·ry (rĭ-sĭz′ə-rē, -sĭs′ə-rē) *adj.* Pertaining to rescission or having the effect or power of rescinding. [Late Latin *rescissōrius,* from Latin *rēscissus,* past participle of *rēscindere,* RESCIND.]

re·script (rē′skrĭpt′) *n.* **1.** A formal decree or edict. **2.** An act of rewriting or something that is rewritten. **3.** In ancient Rome, a reply from the Roman emperor to a magistrate's query on a point of law. **4.** *Roman Catholic Church.* A response from the pope to a question regarding discipline or doctrine. [Latin *rēscriptum,* from the neuter past participle of *rēscrībere,* to write back or in reply : *re-,* back + *scrībere,* to write.]

res·cue (rĕs′kyo͞o) *tr.v.* **-cued, -cuing, -cues. 1.** To save, as from danger or imprisonment. **2.** *Law.* To take from legal custody by force. —See Synonyms at **save.**
~n. **1.** An act of freeing or saving. Also used adjectivally: *a rescue team.* **2.** *Law.* Removal from legal custody by force. [Middle English *rescuen,* from Old French *rescourre,* from Vulgar Latin *reexcutere* (unattested), to drive away, shake off : Latin *re-* (intensive) + *excutere,* to shake out or off : *ex,* out + *quatere,* to shake.] **—res·cu·a·ble** *adj.* **—res·cu·er** *n.*

re·search (rĭ-sûrch′, rē′sûrch′) *n. Abbr.* **res. 1.** Investigation or inquiry in order to gather new information or to collate what is already known about a subject, especially as a scholarly or scientific pursuit. Also used adjectivally: *a research grant.* **2.** Information gathered during such a course of investigation or inquiry.
~v. **researched, -searching, -searches.** *—intr.* To engage in or perform research. *—tr.* **1.** To study or investigate thoroughly. **2.** To carry out research for: *researching a new book.* [From obsolete French *recerche, recercher,* to seek out, to search again : *re-,* again + *cerch(i)er,* to SEARCH.] **—re·search·er** *n.*

re·seat (rē-sēt′) *tr.v.* **-seated, -seating, -seats. 1.** To fit (a valve, for example) in a new seating. **2.** To provide with a different or new seat or seats.

ré·seau, re·seau (rē-zō′, rĭ-zō′) *n., pl.* **-seaus** (-zōz′) or **-seaux** (*pronounced as singular*). **1.** A net or mesh foundation for lace. **2.** *Astronomy.* A reference grid of fine lines forming uniform squares on a photographic plate or print, used in locating stars and measuring planetary movements. **3.** In color photography, a mosaic screen of fine lines of three colors. [French, from Old French *reseuil,* diminutive of *raiz, roiz,* a net, from Latin *rētis, rēte.*]

re·sect (rĭ-sĕkt′) *tr.v.* **-sected, -secting, -sects.** To perform a resection of; cut off or pare down. [Latin *resectus,* past participle of *resecāre,* to cut off : *re-,* back, off + *secāre,* to cut.]

re·sec·tion (rĭ-sĕk′shən) *n.* The surgical removal of part of an organ or structure.

re·se·da (rĭ-sē′də) *n.* **1.** Any plant of the genus *Reseda,* which includes the mignonette. **2.** Grayish or dark green to yellow green or light olive. [New Latin, from Latin *resēda*†.] **—re·se·da** *adj.*

re·sem·blance (rĭ-zĕm′bləns) *n.* **1.** The condition or quality of resembling something; similarity in nature, form, or appearance; likeness. **2.** The extent to or manner in which something resembles something else. **3.** A point in which one thing or person resembles another; a likeness. —See Synonyms at **likeness.**

re·sem·ble (rĭ-zĕm′bəl) *tr.v.* **-bled, -bling, -bles.** To have a similarity to; be like. [Middle English *resemblen,* from Old French *resembler* : *re-* (intensifier) + *sembler,* to be like, from Latin *simulāre, similāre,* to imitate, from *similis,* like.] **—re·sem·bler** *n.*

re·sent (rĭ-zĕnt′) *tr.v.* **-sented, -senting, -sents.** To feel indignantly aggrieved at (an act, situation, or person). [From obsolete French *resentir,* to feel strongly : *re-* (intensive) + *sentir,* to feel, from Latin *sentīre.*]

re·sent·ful (rĭ-zĕnt′fəl) *adj.* Full of, characterized by, or inclined to feel resentment. **—re·sent·ful·ly** *adv.* **—re·sent·ful·ness** *n.*

re·sent·ment (rĭ-zĕnt′mənt) *n.* Indignation, bitterness, or ill will felt toward an act, situation, or person. —See Synonyms at **anger.**

re·ser·pine (rĭ-sûr′pĭn, -pēn′, rĕs′ər-pĭn, -pēn′) *n.* A white to yellowish powder, $C_{33}H_{40}N_2O_9$, isolated from the roots of certain species of rauwolfia, especially *Rauwolfia serpentina,* and used as a sedative

PRONUNCIATION KEY

ă, pat; ā, pay; âr, care; ä, father, are; b, bib; ch, church; d, deed; ĕ, pet; ē, be; f, fife; g, gag; h, hat; hw, which; ĭ, pit; ī, pie; îr, pier; j, judge; k, kick; l, lid, needle; m, mum; n, no, sudden; ng, thing; ŏ, pot; ō, toe; ô, paw, for; oi, noise; ou, out; o͝o, book; o͞o, boot; p, pop; r, roar; s, sauce; sh, ship, dish; t, tight; th, thin, path; *th,* this, bathe; ŭ, cut; ûr, fur; v, valve; w, with; y, yes; z, zebra, size; zh, vision; ə, about, item, edible, gallop, circus, peaceful

IN FOREIGN WORDS:

à, *Fr.* ami; œ, *Fr.* feu, *Ger.* schön; ü, *Fr.* tu, *Ger.* über; KH, *Ger.* ich, *Scot.* loch; N, *Fr.* bon; y′, *Fr.* Compiègne

STRESS MARKS:

Primary stress: ′ **in·cite′** (ĭn-sīt′)
Secondary stress: ′ **in′sight′** (ĭn′sīt′)

resin *A natural or synthetic substance used chiefly as a binding agent in the manufacture of paints and varnishes. Rosin—a dark, solid substance—is made from the resin of pine trees. The sap of the tree is milked into a container through cuts in the bark (above), then distilled to produce turpentine and rosin. Rosin is used on the bows of stringed musical instruments to increase the friction between the bow and the strings.*

PRONUNCIATION KEY

ă, pat; ā, pay; âr, care;
ä, father, are; b, bib;
ch, church; d, deed; ĕ, pet;
ē, be; f, fife; g, gag; h, hat;
hw, which; ĭ, pit; ī, pie;
îr, pier; j, judge; k, kick;
l, lid, needle; m, mum;
n, no, sudden; ng, thing;
ŏ, pot; ō, toe; ô, paw, for;
oi, noise; ou, out; o͝o, book;
o͞o, boot; p, pop; r, roar;
s, sauce; sh, ship, dish;
t, tight; th, thin, path;
th, this, bathe; ŭ, cut; ûr, fur;
v, valve; w, with; y, yes;
z, zebra, size; zh, vision;
ə, about, item, edible,
gallop, circus, peaceful

IN FOREIGN WORDS:

à, *Fr.* ami; œ, *Fr.* feu, *Ger.* schön; ü, *Fr.* tu, *Ger.* über;
KH, *Ger.* ich, *Scot.* loch;
N, *Fr.* bon; y', *Fr.* Compiègne

STRESS MARKS:

Primary stress: ′
in·cite′ (ĭn-sīt′)
Secondary stress: ′
in′sight′ (ĭn′sīt′)

and tranquilizer. [German *Reserpin,* from New Latin *Rauwolfia serpentina,* a species of snakeroot.]

res·er·va·tion (rĕz′ər-vā′shən) *n.* **1.** The act of reserving; a keeping back or withholding. **2.** Something that is kept back or withheld. **3. a.** A limiting qualification, condition, or exception. **b.** A misgiving or doubt: *has reservations about the aircraft's reliability.* **4.** A tract of land set apart by a government for a special purpose, as one in the United States for the use of a North American Indian people. **5. a.** An arrangement by which something, such as a restaurant table or a hotel accommodation, is secured in advance. **b.** That which is so secured. **c.** The record or promise of such an arrangement. **6.** *Law.* **a.** A clause in a conveyance retaining for the grantor a right or interest in the estate conveyed. **b.** The right or interest so retained. **7.** In the Christian Church, the practice of keeping consecrated hosts in a church after the celebration of the Eucharist. —See Synonyms at **qualm.**

re·serve (rĭ-zûrv′) *tr.v.* **-served, -serving, -serves. 1.** To keep back or save for future use or treatment or for a special purpose. **2. a.** To set apart for a particular person or use. **b.** To secure (a ticket or hotel room, for example) in advance; book. **3.** To keep or secure for oneself; retain: *I reserve the right to disagree.* **4.** To refrain from giving or expressing (judgment) immediately, especially in order to obtain further evidence. —See Synonyms at **keep.**

~n. Abbr. **res. 1.** Something kept back or saved for future use or a special purpose. **2.** The state of being kept back, set aside, or saved: *funds held in reserve.* **3.** A reservation, condition, or qualification: *accepted her story without reserve.* **4.** The keeping of one's feelings, thoughts, or affairs to oneself. **5.** Self-restraint in action or expression; reticence. **6.** Lack of enthusiasm; skeptical caution. **7.** An amount of capital held back from investment by a bank or a portion of profits not distributed by a company in order to meet probable or possible demands. **8.** An area of public land kept for a particular purpose: *a game reserve.* **9.** *Often* **reserves. a.** A fighting force kept uncommitted until strategic need arises. **b.** The part of a country's armed forces not on active duty but subject to call in an emergency. **10.** *Sports.* **a.** An extra member of a team kept in readiness in case any of the playing members should be injured or unable to play. **b. reserves.** The second or substitute team of a club. **11.** A reserve price.

~adj. Held in or forming a reserve: *a reserve supply of food.* [Middle English *reserven,* from Old French *reserver,* from Latin *reservāre,* to keep back : *re-,* back + *servāre,* to save, keep.] **—re·serv·a·ble** *adj.* **—re·serv·er** *n.*

reserve bank *n.* **1.** A central bank that holds the reserves of other banks. **2.** Any of the 12 main banks of the U.S. Federal Reserve System.

reserve currency *n.* Foreign currency that is kept in reserve by a government for the paying of international debts.

re·served (rĭ-zûrvd′) *adj.* **1.** Held in reserve; kept back or set aside. **2.** Not outgoing in manner or speech; undemonstrative; reticent. —See Synonyms at **humble. —re·serv·ed·ly** (rĭ-zûr′vĭd-lē) *adv.* **—re·serv·ed·ness** (-vĭd-nĭs) *n.*

Reserve Officers' Training Corps *n. Abbr.* **ROTC, R.O.T.C.** A U.S. military corps that trains college students for commission as officers upon graduation.

reserve price *n.* The price fixed and announced as the minimum at which property will be sold at an auction.

re·serv·ist (rĭ-zûr′vĭst) *n.* A member of a military reserve.

res·er·voir (rĕz′ər-vwär′, -vwôr′, -vôr′) *n.* **1.** A body of water collected and stored in a natural or artificial lake. **2.** A receptacle or chamber for storing a fluid. **3.** *Anatomy.* A **cisterna** *(see).* **4.** A large supply of something; a reserve: *a reservoir of gratitude.* [French *réservoir,* from *réserver,* to RESERVE.]

re·set (rē-sĕt′) *tr.v.* **-set, -setting, -sets. 1.** To set (a broken bone or printing type, for example) again. **2.** To change the setting of (a dial, for example); especially, to set (a counting device) back to zero or some other given value.

~n. (rē-sĕt′). **1.** An act of resetting. **2.** Something that is reset. **—re·set·ter** *n.*

res ges·tae (rās′ gĕs′tī′, rēz′ jĕs′tē) *pl.n.* **1.** Things done; deeds. **2.** *Law.* The facts of a case that are admissible in evidence. [Latin, things done.]

resh (rĕsh) *n.* The 20th letter of the Hebrew alphabet, corresponding to the letter *r* in English. See feature at **alphabet.** [Hebrew *rēsh,* from *rōsh,* "head."]

re·shuf·fle (rē-shŭf′əl) *tr.v.* **-fled, -fling, -fles. 1.** To shuffle again. **2.** To reorganize the allocation of positions or jobs within (a cabinet or board of directors, for example).

~n. An act of reshuffling; especially, a reshuffling of positions or jobs.

re·side (rĭ-zīd′) *intr.v.* **-sided, -siding, -sides. 1.** To live in a place for an extended or permanent period of time. **2.** To be inherently present; exist. Used with *in: the potential energy residing in flowing water.* **3.** To be vested. Used with *in: a power that resides in the Supreme Court.* [Middle English *residen,* from Old French *resider,* from Latin *residēre,* "to sit back," "remain sitting" : *re-,* back, back in place + *sedēre,* to sit.] **—re·sid·er** *n.*

res·i·dence (rĕz′ĭ-dəns) *n. Abbr.* **res. 1.** The place in which one lives; a dwelling; an abode. **2.** The act or a period of residing somewhere. **3. a.** A large house or mansion. **b.** A residency. **—in residence.** Living in or appointed to a particular place or institution in order to carry out a specified job or set of duties: *writer in residence.*

res·i·den·cy (rĕz′ə-dən-sē, -dĕn′sē) *n., pl.* **-cies. 1.** Residence. **2. a.** A protected state in which the powers of the protecting state are exercised by a resident representative; specifically, such a territory in India during the British Raj. **b.** The official residence of such a representative. **3.** A long-term engagement for a musical group to appear and play at a particular place. **4.** The period during which a physician receives advanced training in a medical specialty, usually at a certain hospital.

res·i·dent (rĕz′ə-dənt, -dĕnt′) *n. Abbr.* **res. 1.** One who resides in a particular place; a long-term or permanent inhabitant as opposed to a visitor. **2. a.** Formerly, the British representative of a governor general at an Indian native court. **b.** Formerly, a representative of the British government in a protected state. **3.** A nonmigratory bird or other animal. **4.** A physician serving a period of residency.

~adj. **1.** Dwelling in a particular place; residing. **2.** Living somewhere in connection with duty or work: *The summer camp has a resident naturalist.* **3.** Inherently present. **4.** Nonmigratory. Said of birds and other animals.

res·i·den·tial (rĕz′ə-dĕn′shəl) *adj.* **1.** Of, pertaining to, or involving residence: *a residential college.* **2.** Having residence; especially, residing in a place for occupational reasons: *a residential social worker.* **3.** Of, suitable for, or limited to private residences: *a residential neighborhood.*

res·i·den·ti·ar·y (rĕz′ə-dĕn′shē-ĕr′ē, -shə-rē) *adj.* **1.** Having a residence, especially an official one. **2.** Involving or required to live in an official residence.

~n., pl. **residentiaries. 1.** A resident. **2.** A member of the clergy required to live in an official residence.

re·sid·u·al (rĭ-zĭj′o͞o-əl) *adj.* **1.** Pertaining to or characteristic of a residue. **2.** Remaining as a residue. **3.** Persisting: *residual resentment.*

~n. **1.** The quantity left over at the end of a process; a remainder. **2.** *Statistics.* **a.** The difference between a given single value and the mean value of a number of observations. **b.** The difference between an observed value and the theoretical value. **3.** *Usually* **residuals.** Payment made to a performer, writer, or director for each repeat showing of a recorded television show or commercial. —See Usage note at **remainder.**

residual oil *n.* The low-grade oil products that remain after the distillation of petroleum.

re·sid·u·ar·y (rĭ-zĭj′o͞o-ĕr′ē) *adj.* **1.** Of, pertaining to, or constituting a residue. **2.** *Law.* Entitled to the residue of an estate.

res·i·due (rĕz′ə-do͞o′, -dyo͞o′) *n.* **1.** The remainder of something after removal of a part. **2.** Matter remaining after completion of any abstractive chemical or physical process, such as evaporation, combustion, distillation, or filtration; a residuum. **3.** *Law.* The remainder of a testator's estate after all claims, debts, and bequests are satisfied. Also called "residuum." **4.** *Geology.* Rock, soil, or the like produced by weathering of other rocks with associated removal of material. —See Usage note at **remainder.** [Middle English, from Old French *residu,* from Latin *residuum,* from *residuus,* remaining, from *residēre,* RESIDE.]

re·sid·u·um (rĭ-zĭj′o͞o-əm) *n.* **1.** Something remaining after removal of a part; a residue. **2.** *Law.* Residue. —See Usage note at **remainder.** [Latin, RESIDUE.]

re-sign (rē-sīn′) *tr.v.* **-signed, -signing, -signs.** To sign anew.

re·sign (rĭ-zīn′) *v.* **-signed, -signing, -signs.** *—tr.* **1.** To give over or submit (oneself); force (oneself) to acquiesce: *resigned herself to a long wait in line.* **2.** To give up (a job or position). **3.** To relinquish (a privilege, right, or claim). *—intr.* To give up one's job or office, especially by giving formal notice: *resign from the army.* —See Synonyms at **relinquish.** [Middle English *resignen,* from Old French *resigner,* from Latin *resignāre,* to unseal, resign : *re-,* back + *signāre,* to seal, sign, from *signum,* a mark, sign.] **—re·sign·er** *n.*

res·ig·na·tion (rĕz′ĭg-nā′shən) *n.* **1.** The act of resigning. **2.** An oral or written statement that one is resigning a position or office. **3.** Unresisting acceptance; passive submission. —See Synonyms at **patience.**

re·signed (rĭ-zīnd′) *adj.* Feeling or marked by resignation; acquiescent. **—re·sign·ed·ly** (rĭ-zī′nĭd-lē) *adv.*

re·sile (rĭ-zīl′) *intr.v.* **-siled, -siling, -siles. 1.** To draw back; recoil. **2.** To spring back; especially, to resume a prior position or form after being stretched or pressed. [Latin *resilīre,* to leap back, recoil : *re-,* back + *salīre,* to leap.]

re·sil·i·ence (rĭ-zĭl′yəns) *n.* Also **re·sil·ien·cy** (-yən-sē). **1.** The ability to recover quickly from illness, change, or misfortune; buoyancy. **2.** The property of a material that enables it to resume its original shape or position after being bent, stretched, or compressed; elasticity. **—re·sil·i·ent** *adj.* **—re·sil·i·ent·ly** *adv.*

res·in (rĕz′ĭn) *n.* **1.** Any of numerous clear to translucent, yellow or brown, solid or semisolid substances of plant origin, such as copal, rosin, and amber, obtained as exudations and used principally in lacquers, varnishes, synthetic plastics, and pharmaceuticals. **2.** Any of numerous similar polymerized synthetic materials or chemically modified natural resins including thermoplastic materials, such as polyvinyl, polystyrene, and polyethylene, and thermosetting materials, such as polyesters, epoxies, and silicones, that are used with fillers, stabilizers, pigments, and other components to form plastics.

~tr.v. **resined, -ining, -ins.** To treat or rub with a resin; apply resin to. [Middle English *resyn,* from Old French *resine,* from Latin *rēsīna,* from Greek *rhētinē*†.] **—res·in·ous** *adj.*

res·in·ate (rĕz′ə-nāt′) *tr.v.* **-ated, -ating, -ates.** To impregnate, permeate, or flavor with a resin.

resin canal *n.* A long intercellular channel found in certain conifers, such as pine, which is lined with glandular cells that secrete resin into the cavity. Also called "resin duct."

res·in·if·er·ous (rĕz′ə-nĭf′ər-əs) *adj.* Yielding resin.

res·in·oid (rĕz′ə-noid′) *adj.* Characteristic of, pertaining to, or containing resin.
~*n.* A resinoid synthetic, especially a thermosetting resin.

re·sist (rĭ-zĭst′) *v.* **-sisted, -sisting, -sists.** —*tr.* **1.** To strive or work against; fight off; oppose actively. **2.** To remain firm against the action or effect of; withstand: *resist rust.* **3.** To keep from giving in to or enjoying; abstain from: *could not resist a cake.* —*intr.* To offer resistance; act in opposition. —See Synonyms at **oppose.**
~*n.* A substance that can cover and protect a surface, as from corrosion. [Middle English *resisten,* from Latin *resistere,* to stand back, resist : *re-,* back, against + *sistere,* to place.] —**re·sist·er** *n.*

re·sis·tance (rĭ-zĭs′təns) *n.* **1.** The act or an instance of resisting, or the capacity to resist. **2.** Any force that tends to oppose or retard motion. **3.** The natural ability of the body to ward off disease. **4.** *Symbol* **r, R** *Electricity.* **a.** The opposition to the flow of electric current characteristic of a medium, substance, or circuit element. Also used adjectivally: *resistance loss.* **b.** A resistor. **5.** *Physics.* Any of various physical quantities analogous to electrical resistance, measuring such properties as opposition to sound. **6.** *Psychoanalysis.* A process in which the ego opposes the conscious recall of unpleasant experiences. **7.** *Often* **Resistance.** An underground organization engaged in a struggle for the national liberation of a country under military occupation. Also used adjectivally: *a resistance movement.*

resistance thermometer *n. Physics.* An accurate type of thermometer in which temperature is measured by determining the electrical resistance of a coil of thin wire, usually platinum.

resistance welding *n.* A method of welding by forcing two pieces of metal together and passing a high electric current across the junction, so as to heat the metals by the contact resistance at the junction.

re·sis·tant (rĭ-zĭz′tənt) *adj.* **1.** Showing or marked by resistance. **2.** Able to withstand the effects of something specified, such as heat or corrosion. Often used in combination: *rust-resistant.*

re·sist·i·ble (rĭ-zĭs′tə-bəl) *adj.* Capable of being resisted. —**re·sist·i·bil·i·ty** *n.* —**re·sist·i·bly** *adv.*

re·sis·tive (rĭ-zĭs′tĭv) *adj.* Capable of or tending toward resistance; resisting. —**re·sis·tive·ly** *adv.*

re·sis·tiv·i·ty (rē′zĭs-tĭv′ə-tē) *n.* **1.** The capacity for or tendency toward resistance. **2.** *Electricity.* The resistance per unit length of a substance with uniform unit cross-sectional area; the reciprocal of conductivity. Formerly called "specific resistance."

re·sist·less (rĭ-zĭst′lĭs) *adj. Archaic.* **1.** Incapable of being resisted. **2.** Powerless to resist. —**re·sist·less·ly** *adv.*

re·sis·tor (rĭ-zĭs′tər) *n.* An electric circuit element used to provide resistance. Also called "resistance."

res ju·di·ca·ta (rās jo͞o′dĭ-kä′tə, yo͞o′dĭ-kä′tə) *n.* Also **res ad·ju·di·ca·ta** (ăd-jo͞o′-, ăd-yo͞o′-) An adjudicated precedent in law that cannot be altered. [Latin, "thing decided."]

Res·nais (rə-nā′), **Alain** (1922–). French film director. His two most famous films, *Hiroshima, Mon Amour* (1959) and *Last Year in Marienbad* (1961), classed him as a member of the New Wave.

re·sole (rē-sōl′) *tr.v.* **-soled, -soling, -soles.** To put a new sole on (a shoe).

re·sol·u·ble (rĭ-zŏl′yə-bəl) *adj.* Capable of being resolved; resolvable. [Late Latin *resolūbilis,* from Latin *resolvere,* RESOLVE.] —**re·sol·u·bil·i·ty** (rĭ-zŏl′yə-bĭl′ə-tē), **re·sol·u·ble·ness** *n.*

res·o·lute (rĕz′ə-lo͞ot′) *adj.* **1.** Characterized by firmness or determination. **2.** Pursuing a fixed purpose; unwavering.
~*n.* Someone who is resolute. [Latin *resolūtus,* past participle of *resolvere,* to RESOLVE.] —**res·o·lute·ly** *adv.* —**res·o·lute·ness** *n.*

res·o·lu·tion (rĕz′ə-lo͞o′shən) *n. Abbr.* **res.** **1.** The state or quality of being resolute; firm determination. **2.** The act of resolving to do something. **3.** A course of action determined or decided upon. **4.** A formal statement of a decision or expression of opinion put before or adopted by an assembly. **5.** The action or process of separating or reducing something into its constituent parts: *the prismatic resolution of sunlight into its spectral colors.* **6.** *Medicine.* The subsiding or termination of an abnormal condition, as of a fever or inflammation. **7.** The act or process of finding a solution, as of a problem or puzzle. **8.** *Music.* **a.** The progression of a dissonant tone or chord to a consonant tone or chord. **b.** The tone or chord to which such a progression is made. **9.** *Physics.* The efficiency with which an instrument or technique can separate or distinguish the component parts of something; resolving power. —See Synonyms at **courage.**

re·sol·u·tive (rĭ-zŏl′yə-tĭv) *adj.* Having the power to disintegrate or dissolve something.

re·solv·a·ble (rĭ-zŏl′və-bəl) *adj.* Capable of being resolved; solvable. —**re·solv·a·bil·i·ty, re·solv·a·ble·ness** *n.*

re·solve (rĭ-zŏlv′) *v.* **-solved, -solving, -solves.** —*tr.* **1. a.** To make a firm decision about (a matter of controversy, for example); settle: *resolve a question.* **b.** To decide upon (a course of action); determine: *resolved to tell the truth.* **2.** To cause (a person) to reach a decision. **3.** To decide or express by formal vote. **4.** To separate (something) into constituent parts. **5.** To change or convert. Usually used reflexively: *His resentment resolved itself into resignation.* **6.** To find a solution to; solve. **7.** To remove or dispel (doubts or misunderstandings); clear up. **8.** To bring to a conclusion: *resolve a conflict.* **9.** *Medicine.* To reduce (an inflammation). **10.** *Music.* To cause (a note or chord) to progress from dissonance to consonance. **11.** *Chemistry.* To separate (a racemic compound or mixture) into its optically active constituents. **12.** *Optics.* **a.** To render visible and distinguish parts of (an image). **b.** To separate or distinguish (different lines) in a spectrum. **13.** *Mathematics.* To separate (a vector, for example) into coordinate components. **14.** *Obsolete.* To melt or dissolve (something). —*intr.* **1.** To reach a decision. Used with *on* or *upon*: *resolve on a plan of action.* **2.** To become separated or reduced to constituents. Used with *into.* **3.** *Music.* To undergo resolution. —See Synonyms at **decide.**
~*n.* **1.** Firmness of purpose; determination. **2.** A decision; a fixed purpose. **3.** A formal resolution made by a deliberative body. [Middle English *resolven,* to analyze, untie, solve, from Latin *resolvere,* to release, unbind, annul, resolve : *re-* (intensive), again + *solvere,* untie, release.] —**re·solv·er** *n.*

re·solved (rĭ-zŏlvd′) *adj.* Fixed in purpose; firmly determined; resolute. —**re·solv·ed·ly** (rĭ-zŏl′vĭd-lē) *adv.*

re·sol·vent (rĭ-zŏl′vənt) *adj.* **1.** Causing or capable of causing separation into constituents; solvent. **2.** Causing reduction in inflammation or swelling.
~*n.* A resolvent substance, especially: **1.** A solvent. **2.** A medicine that reduces inflammation or swelling.

resolving power *n. Physics.* A measure of the ability of an instrument to resolve optical images or spectra.

res·o·nance (rĕz′ə-nəns) *n.* **1.** The quality or condition of being resonant. **2.** *Physics.* **a.** The enhancement of the response of an electrical or mechanical system to a periodic driving force when the driving frequency is equal to the natural undamped frequency of the system. **b.** The condition of a system of subatomic particles in which the probability of a particular reaction, as for example nuclear capture of a neutron, is a maximum; the occurrence of a cross-section maximum. **c.** The event corresponding to such a maximum, especially the particle state so formed, having only a few possible modes of decay and characterized by a lifetime considerably longer than neighboring states. **3.** The intensification and prolongation of sound, especially of a musical note, produced by sympathetic vibration. **4.** *Medicine.* The sound produced by diagnostic percussion of the chest, abdomen, or other hollow organ. **5.** *Chemistry.* The phenomenon occurring in a chemical compound whereby its molecular structure can be represented by two or more conventional structures, the actual structure being regarded as a hybrid form of the representations. Used adjectivally: *a resonance hybrid.* **6.** *Phonetics.* The intensification of vocal tones during articulation, as by the air cavities of the mouth and nasal passages.

res·o·nant (rĕz′ə-nənt) *adj.* **1.** Of, pertaining to, or exhibiting resonance. **2.** Producing resonance: *resonant frequency excitation.* **3. a.** Strong and deep in tone; resounding: *a resonant voice.* **b.** Continuing to sound in the ears or memory. **4.** Having a prolonged, subtle, stimulating effect beyond the initial impact: *resonant Shakespearean verse.* [Latin *resonāns* (stem *resonant-*), present participle of *resonare,* to RESOUND.] —**res·o·nant·ly** *adv.*

resonant circuit *n.* An electrical circuit with inductance and capacitance chosen to produce a specific value of the natural frequency of the circuit. Also called "resonator."

res·o·nate (rĕz′ə-nāt′) *intr.v.* **-nated, -nating, -nates.** **1.** To exhibit resonance or resonant effects. **2.** To resound. [Latin *resonāre,* to RESOUND.] —**res·o·na·tion** *n.*

res·o·na·tor (rĕz′ə-nā′tər) *n.* **1.** A resonating system. **2.** A hollow chamber or cavity with dimensions chosen to permit internal resonant oscillation of electromagnetic or acoustical waves of specific frequencies. **3.** *Electronics.* **a.** Any of various microwave-generating tubes or devices containing such resonant chambers or cavities. **b.** A resonant circuit.

re·sorb (rē-sôrb′, -zôrb′) *v.* **-sorbed, -sorbing, -sorbs.** —*tr.* **1.** To absorb again. **2.** *Biology.* To dissolve and assimilate (bone tissue, for example). —*intr.* To be resorbed. [Latin *resorbēre* : *re-,* back + *sorbēre,* to suck.] —**re·sorp·tion** (rē-sôrp′shən, -zôrp′shən) *n.*

res·or·cin·ol (rə-zôr′sə-nôl′, -nōl′) *n.* Also **res·or·cin** (rə-zôr′sĭn). A white crystalline compound, $C_6H_4(OH)_2$, used to treat certain skin diseases and in dyes, resin adhesives, and pharmaceuticals. [RES(IN) + ORC(HIL) + -IN + -OL.]

re-sort (rē-sôrt′) *tr.v.* **-sorted, sorting, -sorts.** To sort again.

re·sort (rĭ-zôrt) *intr.v.* **-sorted, -sorting, -sorts.** **1.** To seek assistance, relief, or an expedient; have recourse. Used with *to*: *The government resorted to censorship of the press.* **2.** To go customarily or frequently; repair. Used with *to.*
~*n.* **1.** A place frequented by people for holidays or recreation: *a winter resort.* **2.** A customary or frequent going or gathering: *a popular place of resort.* **3.** A person or thing turned to for aid or relief: *a last resort.* **4.** The act of turning to a person or thing for aid or relief; recourse. [Middle English *resorten,* return, revert, from Old French *resortir,* to come out again, to resort : *re-,* again + *sortir,* to go out (see **sortie**).]

Usage: *Resort* and *recourse* are used in slightly different constructions in standard English: for example, *He resorted to force, He had recourse to force.* To *have resort to* is often heard, but the usage attracts criticism. Similarly, standard usage requires *as a last resort,* not *as a last recourse.*

re·sound (rĭ-zound′) *v.* **-sounded, -sounding, -sounds.** —*intr.* **1.** To be filled with sound; reverberate. **2.** To make a loud, long, or reverberating sound. **3.** To become famous, celebrated, or extolled. —*tr.* **1.** To send back (sound); re-echo. **2.** To extol; celebrate. [Middle English *resounen,* from Old French *resoner,* from Latin *resonāre,* to sound again, echo : *re-,* again + *sonāre,* to sound.]

re·sound·ing (rĭ-zoun′dĭng) *adj.* **1.** Resonating or reverberating; loud: *resounding applause.* **2.** Emphatic; decisive: *a resounding victory.* —**re·sound·ing·ly** *adv.*

re·source (rē′sôrs′, -sōrs′, -zôrs′, -zōrs′, rĭ-sôrs′, -sōrs′, -zôrs′, -zōrs′) *n.* **1.** Something that can be used for support or help: *The local library is a valuable resource.* **2.** An available supply that can be drawn upon when needed. **3.** The ability to deal effectively with a difficult or troublesome situation; initiative; capability. **4.** Any means of coping with a difficult situation. **5. a. resources.** The total means available for economic and political development, including such elements as mineral wealth, manpower, and armaments. **b. resources.** The total means available to a company for increasing production or profit, including such elements as plant, labor, and raw materials. **c.** Any such element considered individually. [French *ressource,* from Old French *ressourse,* relief, recovery, from *resourdre,* to rise again, from Latin *resurgere* : *re-,* again + *surgere,* to rise, SURGE.]

re·source·ful (rĭ-sôrs′fəl, rĭ-sōrs′-, rĭ-zôrs′-, rĭ-zōrs′-) *adj.* Capable of acting effectively or imaginatively, especially in a difficult situation or emergency. —**re·source·ful·ly** *adv.* —**re·source·ful·ness** *n.*

resp. **1.** respective; respectively. **2.** respiration.

re·spect (rĭ-spĕkt′) *tr.v.* **-spected, -specting, -spects. 1.** To acknowledge the basic integrity or worthiness of; esteem. **2.** To show consideration for; avoid violation of; treat with deference: *respect a neighbor's privacy.* **3.** *Archaic.* To relate or refer to.
—*n.* **1.** A feeling of deferential regard; esteem. **2.** The state of being regarded with honor or esteem. **3.** Willingness to show consideration or regard: *Have some respect for her feelings.* **4. respects.** Polite expressions of consideration or deference: *pay one's respects.* **5.** A particular aspect, feature, or detail: *The sisters are alike in many respects.* **6.** Relation; reference. Used chiefly in the phrases *in respect of* and *with respect to.* —See Usage note at **regard.** —**pay one's last respects.** To show signs of respect to a dead person before or at a funeral. [Latin *respectus,* past participle of *respicere,* to regard, look back : *re-,* back + *specere,* to look.] —**re·spect·ful** *adj.* —**re·spect·ful·ly** *adv.* —**re·spect·ful·ness** *n.*

re·spect·a·bil·i·ty (rĭ-spĕk′tə-bĭl′ĭ-tē) *n., pl.* **-ties. 1.** The quality, state, or characteristic of being respectable. **2.** Respectable members of a community.

re·spect·a·ble (rĭ-spĕk′tə-bəl) *adj.* **1.** Meriting respect or esteem; worthy. **2.** Conforming or tending to conform to conventionally accepted moral standards and behavior. **3.** Of moderately good quality: *a respectable day's work.* **4.** Considerable in amount, number, or size: *a respectable sum of money.* **5.** Of reasonable social standing; honest and decent. **6.** Having an acceptable appearance; presentable: *a respectable hat.* —**re·spect·a·ble·ness** *n.* —**re·spect·a·bly** *adv.*

re·spec·ter (rĭ-spĕk′tər) *n.* One who respects. —**no respecter of persons.** One who does not treat the powerful or rich with undue favor.

re·spect·ing (rĭ-spĕk′tĭng) *prep.* In relation to; concerning.

re·spec·tive (rĭ-spĕk′tĭv) *adj. Abbr.* **resp.** Belonging or pertaining to two or more persons or things regarded individually; particular: *"The two women stood by their respective telephones"* (Doris Lessing). —**re·spec·tive·ness** *n.*

re·spec·tive·ly (rĭ-spĕk′tĭv-lē) *adv. Abbr.* **resp.** Singly in the order designated or mentioned: *gave Paul and Anne a book and a record respectively.*

re·spell (rē-spĕl′) *tr.v.* **-spelled** or **-spelt** (-spĕlt′), **-spelling, -spells.** To spell again or in a new way, especially by using a phonetic alphabet.

Re·spi·ghi (rə-spē′gē), **Ottorino** (1879–1936). Italian composer. He wrote prolifically in almost every form, but little of his music is now performed, except for the symphonic poems *The Fountains of Rome* (1917) and *The Pines of Rome* (1924).

res·pi·ra·ble (rĕs′pər-ə-bəl, rĭ-spīr′-) *adj.* **1.** Suitable for breathing. **2.** Capable of or adapted for breathing. —**res·pi·ra·bil·i·ty** (rĕs′-pər-ə-bĭl′ĭ-tē, rĭ-spīr′-) *n.*

res·pi·ra·tion (rĕs′pə-rā′shən) *n. Abbr.* **resp. 1.** The act or process of inhaling and exhaling; breathing. **2.** The metabolic process by which an organism assimilates oxygen, oxidizes organic substances in the cells, with the release of energy, and releases carbon dioxide and other products of oxidation.

res·pi·ra·tor (rĕs′pə-rā′tər) *n.* **1.** An apparatus used in administering artificial respiration, such as an **iron lung** *(see).* **2.** A screenlike device worn over the mouth or nose, or both, to protect the respiratory tract.

res·pi·ra·to·ry (rĕs′pər-ə-tôr′ē, -tōr′ē, rĭ-spīr′ə-) *adj.* Of, pertaining to, affecting, or used in respiration.

respiratory distress syndrome *n.* A condition in newborn, especially premature, infants, in which the lungs are imperfectly expanded, leading to extreme difficulty in breathing. Also called "hyaline membrane disease."

re·spire (rĭ-spīr′) *v.* **-spired, -spiring, -spires.** —*intr.* **1.** To breathe in and out; inhale and exhale. **2.** To undergo the metabolic process of respiration. **3.** *Archaic.* To breathe easily again, as after a period of exertion or trouble. —*tr.* To inhale and exhale (air); breathe. [Middle English *respyren,* to breathe again, from Latin *respīrāre* : *re-,* again + *spīrāre,* to breathe.]

res·pite (rĕs′pĭt) *n.* **1. a.** A temporary cessation or postponement, usually of something disagreeable. **b.** An interval of rest or relief. **2.** The temporary suspension of a death sentence; a reprieve.
—*tr.v.* **respited, -piting, -pites. 1.** To provide with a period of temporary rest or relief. **2. a.** To grant (someone) a reprieve. **b.** To grant a reprieve from (a punishment or sentence). [Middle English *respit,* from Old French, from Latin *respectus,* a looking back, a refuge, from the past participle of *respicere,* to look back : *re-,* back + *specere,* to look.]

re·splen·dent (rĭ-splĕn′dənt) *adj.* Splendid or dazzling in appearance; brilliant. [Middle English, from Latin *resplendēns* (stem *resplendent-*), present participle of *resplendēre,* to shine brightly : *re-* (intensive) + *splendēre,* to shine.] —**re·splen·dence, re·splen·den·cy** *n.* —**re·splen·dent·ly** *adv.*

re·spond (rĭ-spŏnd′) *v.* **-sponded, -sponding, -sponds.** —*intr.* **1.** To make a reply; answer. **2.** To act in return or in answer. **3.** To react; especially, to react positively or cooperatively: *The patient responded well to the treatment.* —*tr.* To say in reply; answer. —See Synonyms at **answer.**
—*n.* **1.** *Architecture.* A pilaster supporting an arch. **2.** A chanted or sung response in a liturgy. [Latin *respondēre,* "to promise in return" : *re-,* back, in return + *spondēre,* to promise.] —**re·spon·der** *n.*

re·spon·dent (rĭ-spŏn′dənt) *adj.* **1.** Giving or given as a responsive. **2.** *Law.* Being a defendant.
—*n.* **1.** A person who responds. **2.** *Law.* A defendant, especially in a divorce suit. —**re·spon·dence, re·spon·den·cy** *n.*

re·sponse (rĭ-spŏns′) *n.* **1.** A reply or answer. **2.** Any act of responding; a reaction: *Public response has been overwhelming.* **3. a.** A reaction, such as that of an organism or mechanism, to a specific stimulus. **b.** A measure of this; for example, the ratio of the output signal of an electronic device to the input signal. **4.** *Abbr.* **R. a.** That which is spoken or sung by a congregation or choir in answer to the officiating minister or priest. **b.** A responsory. **5.** In the game of bridge, a bid made in reply to a partner's bid. [Middle English *respons,* from Old French, from Latin *responsum,* from past participle of *respondēre,* "to promise in return," RESPOND.]

re·spon·si·bil·i·ty (rĭ-spŏn′sə-bĭl′ĭ-tē) *n., pl.* **-ties. 1.** The state or fact of being responsible. **2.** A thing or person that one is answerable for; a duty, obligation, or burden. **3.** The power or ability to act without superior authority or guidance; the quality of being responsible.

re·spon·si·ble (rĭ-spŏn′sə-bəl) *adj.* **1. a.** Legally or ethically accountable for the care or welfare of another. **b.** Having control or authority over something; in charge: *She is responsible for sales.* **2.** Involving personal accountability or ability to act without guidance or superior authority. **3.** Being the source, explanation, or cause of something. Used with *for*: *He was responsible for the accident.* **4. a.** Capable of making moral, practical, or rational decisions on one's own and therefore answerable for one's behavior. **b.** Able to be trusted or depended upon; reliable. **5.** Based upon or characterized by good judgment or sound thinking. **6.** Having the means to pay debts or fulfill obligations. **7.** Required to render account; answerable. Used with *to*: *The cabinet is responsible to the president.* [From obsolete French, correspondent to, from Latin *respondēre,* to RESPOND.] —**re·spon·si·bly** *adv.*

***Synonyms:** accountable, answerable, liable.*

re·spon·sive (rĭ-spŏn′sĭv) *adj.* **1.** Answering or replying; responding. **2.** Readily reacting, as to suggestions, influences, stimuli, or efforts. **3.** Containing or using responses: *responsive liturgy.* —**re·spon·sive·ly** *adv.* —**re·spon·sive·ness** *n.*

re·spon·so·ry (rĭ-spŏn′sə-rē) *n., pl.* **-ries.** A chant or anthem recited or sung after a reading in a church service. Also called "response." [Middle English, from Late Latin *responsōria,* from Latin *respondēre* (past participle *responsus*), RESPOND.]

re·spon·sum (rĭ-spŏn′səm) *n., pl.* **-sa** (-sə). An answer by a rabbi to a question concerning Jewish law or its observance. [Latin, response.]

res pu·bli·ca (rās po͝ob′lĭ-kə) *n.* **1.** The state; the republic. **2.** The general public good or welfare. [Latin. See **republic.**]

rest[1] (rĕst) *n.* **1. a.** The act or state of ceasing from work, activity, or motion; quiet. **b.** A period during which someone is not required to work or something is not used: *gave the engine a rest.* **2.** Peace, ease, or refreshment resulting from sleep or the cessation of an activity. **3.** Sleep or quiet relaxation. **4.** The repose of death: *laid to rest.* **5.** Relief or freedom from disquiet or disturbance. **6.** Mental or emotional tranquillity. **7.** Termination or absence of motion. **8.** *Music.* **a.** An interval of silence corresponding to any of the possible time values within the measure. **b.** A mark or symbol indicating such a pause and its length. **9.** In prosody, a short pause in a line of verse; a caesura. **10.** A device used as a support or prop. Often used in combination: *a footrest.* **11.** In billiards, snooker, and similar games, a **bridge** *(see).* **12.** A place for lodging or shelter, especially for sailors or travelers. Often used in the name of a hotel, inn, or the like. —**at rest. 1.** In a state of rest or repose, especially: **a.** Asleep. **b.** Dead. **c.** Motionless. **2.** Free from anxiety or distress.
—*v.* **rested, resting, rests.** —*intr.* **1.** To refresh oneself by ceasing work or activity or by lying down, sleeping, or relaxing in some other manner. **2.** To cease temporarily from work, motion, or activity. **3.** To sleep. **4.** To be at peace or ease; be tranquil. **5.** To remain in a particular state; receive no further attention: *let the issue rest here.* **6.** To be supported; lie, lean, or sit. Used with *in, on, upon,* or *against.* **7.** To be imposed or vested as a responsibility or burden. Used with *on, upon,* or *with*: *The final decision rests with the chairman.* **8.** To depend or rely. Used with *on, upon,* or *with*: *His argument rests on a false assumption.* **9.** To be located or be in a specified place: *The last copy now rests in the British Museum.* **10.** To settle, fall, or be fixed: *His eyes rested on her.* **11.** To remain;

PRONUNCIATION KEY

ă, pat; ā, pay; âr, care;
ä, father, are; b, bib;
ch, church; d, deed; ĕ, pet;
ē, be; f, fife; g, gag; h, hat;
hw, which; ĭ, pit; ī, pie;
îr, pier; j, judge; k, kick;
l, lid, needle; m, mum;
n, no, sudden; ng, thing;
ŏ, pot; ō, toe; ô, paw, for;
oi, noise; ou, out; o͝o, book;
o͞o, boot; p, pop; r, roar;
s, sauce; sh, ship, dish;
t, tight; th, thin, path;
th, this, bathe; ŭ, cut; ûr, fur;
v, valve; w, with; y, yes;
z, zebra, size; zh, vision;
ə, about, item, edible,
gallop, circus, peaceful

IN FOREIGN WORDS:

à, *Fr.* ami; œ, *Fr.* feu, *Ger.* schön; ü, *Fr.* tu, *Ger.* über;
KH, *Ger.* ich, *Scot.* loch;
N, *Fr.* bon; y′, *Fr.* Compiègne

STRESS MARKS:

Primary stress: ′
in·cite′ (ĭn-sīt′)
Secondary stress: ′
in′sight′ (ĭn′sīt′)

linger. Used with *on* or *upon.* **12.** *Law.* To cease voluntarily the presentation of evidence in a case: *The defense rests.* —*tr.* **1. a.** To give rest or repose to; refresh by rest. **b.** To stop using, cultivating, or working. **2.** To place, lay, or lean for ease, support, or repose. **3.** To base or ground: *rested his conclusion on that fact.* **4.** To fix or direct (the eyes or gaze, for example). **5.** *Law.* To cease voluntarily the introduction of evidence in (a case). [Middle English *reste,* Old English *reste, ræst,* rest, resting place.] —**rest·er** *n.*

Synonyms: *comfort, ease, leisure, relaxation, repose.*

rest² *n.* **1.** That part which is left over after something has been removed; the remainder. **2.** *Used with a plural verb.* The ones remaining: *The rest are coming after the game.* —See Usage note at **remainder.**

~*intr.v.* **rested, resting, rests. 1.** To be or continue to be; remain: *rest easy.* **2.** *Obsolete.* To remain or be left over. [Middle English, from Old French *reste,* from *rester,* to remain, from Latin *restāre,* to keep back, stand firm : *re-,* back + *stāre,* to stand.]

rest³ *n.* A support for the butt of a lance on the side of a medieval breastplate, used when charging. [Middle English *(a)rest,* an arresting, from Old French, from *arester,* to ARREST.]

re·state (rē-stāt′) *tr.v.* **-stated, -stating, -states.** To state again or in a new form. —**re·state·ment** *n.*

res·tau·rant (rĕs′tər-ənt, -tə-ränt′) *n.* A place where meals are served, usually for payment, to the public. [French, "restorative," from *restaurer,* to restore, from Old French *restorer,* to RESTORE.]

res·tau·ra·teur (rĕs′tər-ə-tûr′) *n.* Also **res·taur·ant·eur** (-tə-rän-tûr′). The manager or owner of a restaurant or restaurants. [French, from *restaurer,* to restore. See **restaurant.**]

rest cure *n.* A complete rest from one's usual activities taken as part of a course of treatment, especially for nervous disorders.

rest energy *n. Physics.* The energy equivalent of the rest mass of a body, equal to the rest mass multiplied by the speed of light squared.

rest·ful (rĕst′fəl) *adj.* **1.** Giving tranquillity: *a restful atmosphere.* **2.** At rest; quiet. —See Synonyms at **comfortable.** —**rest·ful·ly** *adv.* —**rest·ful·ness** *n.*

rest·har·row (rĕst′hăr′ō) *n.* Any of several Old World plants of the genus *Ononis,* having tough, woody stems and roots, and pink, purplish, or yellow pealike flowers. [Middle English *(a)resten,* ARREST + HARROW (because its roots obstruct or "arrest" the harrow).]

rest home *n.* A place for the care of the elderly or frail.

rest·ing (rĕs′tĭng) *adj.* **1. a.** In a state of inactivity or rest. **b.** *Chiefly British.* Out of work. Said euphemistically of an actor. **2.** *Biology.* Dormant. Said especially of spores that germinate after a prolonged period.

resting cell *n. Biology.* A cell that is not actively in the process of dividing.

resting potential *n. Physiology.* The difference in charge that exists between the inside and outside of the cell membrane of a nonconducting nerve or muscle cell.

res·ti·tute (rĕs′tə-to͞ot′, -tyo͞ot′) *tr.v.* **-tuted, -tuting, -tutes.** To bring back to a former condition; restore. [Latin *restituere* (past participle *restitūtus*), to restore, set up again : *re-,* again + *statuere,* to set up, from *stāre,* to stand.]

res·ti·tu·tion (rĕs′tə-to͞o′shən, -tyo͞o′shən) *n.* **1.** The act of restoring to the rightful owner something that has been taken away, lost, or surrendered. **2.** The act of making good or compensating for loss, damage, or injury; indemnification; reparation. **3.** A return to or restoration of a previous state or position; for example, the return of a system to its original state after deformation. —See Synonyms at **reparation.**

res·tive (rĕs′tĭv) *adj.* **1.** Impatient or nervous under restriction, delay, or pressure; uneasy; restless. **2.** Difficult to control; refractory; unruly. **3.** Refusing to move; balky: *a restive horse.* [Middle English *restyffe,* unwilling to move, stationary, from Old French *restif,* from Vulgar Latin *restīvus* (unattested), remaining stationary, from Latin *restāre,* to keep back : *re-,* back + *stāre,* to stand.] —**res·tive·ly** *adv.* —**res·tive·ness** *n.*

rest·less (rĕst′lĭs) *adj.* **1.** Without quiet, repose, or rest: *a restless night.* **2.** Unable or unwilling to rest or relax: *a restless child.* **3.** Never still or motionless: *the restless sea.* **4.** Agitated or uneasy. —**rest·less·ly** *adv.* —**rest·less·ness** *n.*

rest mass *n.* The physical mass of a body that is at rest relative to the observer.

re·stock (rē-stŏk′) *tr.v.* **-stocked, -stocking, -stocks.** To stock again; furnish new stock for.

Res·ton (rĕs′tən), **James Barrett,** also known as "Scotty" (1909–). U.S journalist, born in Scotland. Associated with *The New York Times* since 1939, he began working in the London bureau and over the years held many positions, including executive editor (1968–69). He was awarded the Pulitzer Prize in 1945 and 1957.

res·to·ra·tion (rĕs′tə-rā′shən) *n.* **1.** The act of restoring or reinstating someone or something, or the state of being restored: *the restoration of the death penalty.* **2.** The repairing and refurbishing of furniture, buildings, or works of art to return them to something close to their original condition. **3.** That which has been restored, such as a renovated building. —**the Restoration. 1.** The return of Charles II to the British throne in 1660. **2. a.** The period between the return of Charles II and the Revolution of 1688. **b.** Loosely, the period from 1660 until the end of the 17th century. Also used adjectivally: *Restoration prose.*

Restoration comedy *n.* A genre of dramatic comedy characterized by social satire and wit that flourished especially during the period of the Restoration in England, from about 1660 until 1700.

re·stor·a·tive (rĭ-stôr′ə-tĭv, rĭ-stōr′-) *adj.* Tending to renew or restore something, such as health or strength.

~*n.* Something that restores or revives, such as a drug.

re·store (rĭ-stôr′, -stōr′) *tr.v.* **-stored, -storing, -stores. 1.** To bring back into existence or use; re-establish: *restore law and order.* **2.** To bring back to a previous, normal, or original condition, as by repair, cleaning, or reconstruction: *restore a work of art.* **3.** To put back in a prior position: *restore the emperor to the throne.* **4.** To give or bring back; make restitution of: *restore the stolen funds.* [Middle English *restoren,* from Old French *restorer,* from Latin *restaurāre* : *re-,* back + *instaurāre,* to renew.] —**re·stor·er** *n.*

re·strain (rĭ-strān′) *tr.v.* **-strained, -straining, -strains. 1. a.** To control; check; repress. **b.** To hold (a person) back; prevent. Used with *from*: *restrained them from going.* **2.** To deprive of freedom or liberty. **3.** To limit or restrict. [Middle English *restreynen,* from Old French *restraindre* (present stem *restrain-*), from Latin *restringere,* to RESTRICT.] —**re·strain·a·ble** *adj.*

Synonyms: *check, curb, inhibit, restrict.*

re·strained (rĭ-strānd′) *adj.* Showing or exercising restraint or self-restraint. —**re·strain·ed·ly** (rĭ-strā′nĭd-lē) *adv.*

re·strain·er (rĭ-strā′nər) *n.* A substance, often potassium bromide, added to photographic developer to reduce the fog on the film.

re·straint (rĭ-strānt′) *n.* **1.** The act of holding back or restraining. **2.** Loss or abridgment of freedom. **3.** Any influence that inhibits or restrains; a limitation. **4.** An instrument or means of controlling or restraining. **5. a.** Control or repression of feelings. **b.** Avoidance of excess, explicitness, or extravagance. [Middle English *restreinte,* from Old French *restrainte,* from the past participle of *restraindre,* RESTRAIN.]

restraint of trade *n.* Any action or condition that tends to prevent free competition in business, such as the creation of a monopoly or the limiting of a market.

re·strict (rĭ-strĭkt′) *tr.v.* **-stricted, -stricting, -stricts.** To hold down or keep within limits. —See Synonyms at **limit, restrain.** [Latin *restringere* (past participle *restrictus*), to bind back tight : *re-,* back + *stringere,* to bind.]

re·strict·ed (rĭ-strĭk′tĭd) *adj.* **1.** Subject to limits or restrictions. **2.** Not for general circulation; classified. Said of documents. **3.** Excluding or unavailable to certain groups, especially racial or religious minorities: *a restricted neighborhood.* —**re·strict·ed·ly** *adv.*

re·stric·tion (rĭ-strĭk′shən) *n.* **1.** The act of limiting or restricting. **2.** The state of being limited or restricted. **3.** Something that restricts; a limiting or restraining factor, condition, or regulation.

re·stric·tive (rĭ-strĭk′tĭv) *adj.* **1.** Tending or serving to restrict. **2.** *Grammar.* Designating a subordinate clause, phrase, or term considered to limit the application or reference of the word or word group that it modifies, thus being essential to the meaning of the sentence and usually not marked off by commas. In the sentence *People who read a great deal have large vocabularies,* the restrictive clause is *who read a great deal.* Compare **nonrestrictive.** —**re·stric·tive·ly** *adv.*

rest room *n.* A public lavatory.

re·struc·ture (rē-strŭk′chər) *tr.v.* **-tured, -turing, -tures.** To alter the structure or organization of: *The college restructured its curriculum.*

re·sult (rĭ-zŭlt′) *intr.v.* **-sulted, -sulting, -sults. 1.** To occur or exist as a consequence. Often used with *from.* **2.** To end in a particular way. Used with *in.* **3.** *Law.* To revert to a former owner owing to having been partially or ineffectually disposed of. Used of property. —See Synonyms at **follow.**

~*n.* **1.** The consequence of a particular action, operation, or course; outcome. **2.** A particular consequence. **3.** *Often* **results.** A positive or useful effect: *He may be stern but he certainly gets results.* **4.** *Often* **results.** An answer or finding arrived at through research or calculation: *published the results of the survey.* **5.** *Often* **results.** The final score, mark, or outcome of any encounter or endeavor involving competition: *football results; the election result.* —See Synonyms at **effect.** [Middle English *resulten,* from Medieval Latin *resultāre,* from Latin, to leap back, rebound : *re-,* back + *saltāre,* to leap, frequentative of *salīre,* to leap.]

re·sul·tant (rĭ-zŭl′tənt) *adj.* Issuing or following as a consequence or result.

~*n.* **1.** That which results; an outcome. **2.** *Mathematics & Physics.* A vector or vector quantity that results from the addition of two or more vectors, for example, a net force resulting from the simultaneous application of other component forces. Also used adjectivally: *resultant force; resultant velocity.*

re·sume (rĭ-zo͞om′) *v.* **-sumed, -suming, -sumes.** —*tr.* **1.** To continue after interruption or adjournment. **2.** To occupy or take again: *resume your seats.* **3.** To take on or take back again: *resume a gift.* —*intr.* To begin again after a pause or interruption: *The reader cleared her throat and then resumed.* [Middle English *resumen,* from Old French *resumer,* from Latin *resūmere,* to take up again : *re-,* again + *sūmere,* to take up.] —**re·sum·a·ble** *adj.*

rés·u·mé (rĕz′o͝o-mā′, rĕz′o͝o-mā′) *n.* **1.** A summing up; a summary. **2.** A summary of employment experience and personal information, submitted with a job application. [French, from the past participle of *résumer,* to RESUME.]

re·sump·tion (rĭ-zŭmp′shən) *n.* The act or an instance of resuming. [Middle English, from Old French, from Late Latin *resūmptiō* (stem *resūmptiōn-*), from Latin *resūmere,* RESUME.]

re·su·pi·nate (rĭ-so͞o′pə-nāt′, -nĭt) *adj. Biology.* Inverted or seemingly turned upside-down. [Latin *resupīnatus,* bent back, past participle of *resupīnāre*, to bend back : *re-*, back + *supīnus*, SUPINE.] —**re·su·pi·na·tion** (rĭ-sōō′pə-nā′shən) *n.*

re·su·pine (rē′sōō-pīn′, rĕs′ə-) *adj.* Lying on the back; supine. [Latin *resupīnus*, from *resupīnāre*. See resupinate.]

re·surge (rĭ-sûrj′) *intr.v.* **-surged, -surging, -surges.** **1.** To rise again; re-emerge to prominence or vitality. **2.** To sweep or surge back again. [Latin *resurgere* : *re-*, again + *surgere*, SURGE.]

re·sur·gent (rĭ-sûr′jənt) *adj.* Rising or tending to rise or emerge again; resurging. —**re·sur·gence** *n.*

res·ur·rect (rĕz′ə-rĕkt′) *v.* **-rected, -recting, -rects.** —*tr.* **1.** To bring back to life; raise from the dead. **2.** To bring back into practice, notice, or use. —*intr.* To rise from the dead; return to life. [Back-formation from RESURRECTION.]

res·ur·rec·tion (rĕz′ə-rĕk′shən) *n.* **1.** A rising from the dead or returning to life. **2.** The state of those who have returned to life. **3.** A returning or bringing back to practice, notice, or use; a revival. —**the Resurrection.** **1.** The rising again of Christ on the third day after the Crucifixion. **2.** The rising again of the dead at the Last Judgment. [Middle English *resurreccion,* from Old French *resurrection,* from Late Latin *resurrēctiō* (stem *resurrēctiōn-*), from Latin *resurgere* (past participle *resurrēctus*), to RESURGE.] —**res·ur·rec·tion·al** *adj.*

res·ur·rec·tion·ist (rĕs′ə-rĕk′shən-ĭst) *n.* Formerly, one who stole bodies from the grave in order to sell them for dissection.

resurrection plant *n.* Any of several plants that appear dead during dry periods and expand and continue to grow under moist conditions; especially, the **rose of Jericho** (*see*).

re·sus·ci·tate (rĭ-sŭs′ə-tāt′) *v.* **-tated, -tating, -tates.** —*tr.* To restore consciousness, vigor, or life to. —*intr.* To return to life or consciousness; revive. [Latin *resuscitāre,* to revive : *re-*, again + *suscitāre,* to raise, stir up : *sub-*, below, up from below + *citāre,* to set moving, from *citus,* quick, past participle of *ciēre, cīre,* to stir.] —**re·sus·ci·ta·ble** (rĭ-sŭs′ə-tə-bəl) *adj.* —**re·sus·ci·ta·tion** (rĭ-sŭs′ə-tā′shən) *n.* —**re·sus·ci·ta·tive** (rĭ-sŭs′ə-tā′tĭv, -ə-tə-tĭv) *adj.* —**re·sus·ci·ta·tor** *n.*

ret (rĕt) *tr.v.* **retted, retting, rets.** Also **rot** (rŏt), **rotted, rotting, rots.** To moisten or soak (flax or hemp, for example) to soften and separate the fibers by partial rotting. [Middle English *reten,* perhaps from Old Norse *reyta* (unattested), from Germanic *rutjan* (unattested), to ROT.]

ret. **1.** retain. **2.** retired. **3.** return; returned.

re·ta·ble (rē′tā′bəl) *n.* A structure forming the back of an altar, especially: **1.** An overhanging shelf for lights and ornaments. **2.** A frame enclosing carved or painted panels. [French, from Spanish *retablo,* from Medieval Latin *retabulum* (unattested), shortening of *retrōtabulum,* structure at the back of an altar : *retrō-,* back + *tabulum,* table, from Latin *tabula,* board, tablet (see table).]

re·tail (rē′tāl′) *n.* The sale of commodities in small quantities directly to the consumer.
—*adj.* Of, pertaining to, or engaged in the sale of goods in this way: *retail stores; retail prices.*
—*adv.* At retail; from a retailer.
—*v.* (rē′tāl′; rĭ-tāl′ *for sense 2*) **retailed, -tailing, -tails.** —*tr.* **1.** To sell in small quantities. **2.** To tell and retell (a story, especially gossip or scandal) in detail. —*intr.* To be sold at retail: *retails at about five dollars.* [Middle English *retaile,* "division," from Old French *retaille,* from *retailler,* to cut up : *re-* (intensive) + *tailler,* to cut (see tailor).] —**re·tail·er** (rē′tā′lər) *n.*

re·tain (rĭ-tān′) *tr.v.* **-tained, -taining, -tains.** **1. a.** To keep or hold in one's possession. **b.** To continue to have: *He retained their support.* **2.** To continue to adopt (a practice or name, for example); maintain: *The American edition retains the British spelling.* **3.** To keep or hold in a particular place, condition, or position: *The fleshy leaves of the cactus retain water.* **4.** To keep in mind; remember: *retained nothing of her childhood.* **5.** To hire (a lawyer) by the payment of a preliminary fee. **6.** To keep in one's service or pay. —See Synonyms at **keep.** [Middle English *reteinen,* from Old French *retenir,* from Latin *retinēre* : *re-,* back + *tenēre,* to hold.] —**re·tain·a·ble** *adj.* —**re·tain·ment** *n.*

retained object *n.* An object in a passive construction that is identical to the object in the corresponding active construction, such as *story* in *Susan was told the story by John.*

re·tain·er¹ (rĭ-tā′nər) *n.* **1.** A person or thing that keeps or retains. **2. a.** One who served in a noble household, as in the feudal period, but who ranked higher than a servant; an attendant. **b.** A domestic servant, especially one who has been with the same family for a long period of time. **3.** Any device, frame, or groove that restrains or guides something.

retainer² *n.* **1.** The act of retaining a lawyer or other adviser or the fact of being so retained. **2. a.** A preliminary fee paid to engage the services of a lawyer, consultant, or other professional. **b.** A regular fee paid to an outside consultant so that one may call upon his services when required. **3.** A fee paid to reserve rented accommodation or retain it during one's absence.

re·take (rē-tāk′) *tr.v.* **-took** (-tōōk′), **-taken** (-tā′kən), **-taking, -takes.** **1.** To take back or again. **2.** To photograph or film again.
—*n.* (rē′tāk′). **1.** A taking again. **2.** A scene or shot that has been or is to be filmed or photographed again. —**re·tak·er** *n.*

re·tal·i·ate (rĭ-tăl′ē-āt′) *v.* **-ated, -ating, -ates.** —*intr.* **1.** To return like for like; especially, to return evil for evil. **2.** To respond to aggression with another attack. —*tr.* To pay back (an injury) in kind. [Latin *retaliāre,* repay in kind : *re-,* back + *tāliō,* punishment in kind.] —**re·tal·i·a·tion** (rĭ-tăl′ē-ā′shən) *n.* —**re·tal·i·a·to·ry** (rĭ-tăl′ē-ə-tôr′ē, -tōr′ē) *adj.*

re·tard (rĭ-tärd′) *v.* **-tarded, -tarding, -tards.** —*tr.* To impede or delay; cause to proceed slowly. —*intr.* To become delayed. —See Synonyms at **delay, hinder.**
—*n.* **1.** Delay. **2.** *Music.* A slackening of tempo. [Middle English *retarden,* from Old French *retarder,* from Latin *retardāre* : *re-,* back, back in place + *tardāre,* to delay, from *tardus,* slow (see tardy).] —**re·tard·er** *n.*

re·tar·dant (rĭ-tär′dənt) *n.* Something that retards; specifically, a substance that slows down chemical reaction.
—*adj.* Causing retardation.

re·tar·date (rĭ-tär′dāt′, -dĭt) *n.* A mentally retarded person.

re·tar·da·tion (rē′tär-dā′shən) *n.* Also **re·tard·ment** (rē-tärd′mənt). **1.** The act of retarding. **2.** The condition of being retarded. **3.** The extent to which, or amount by which, something is retarded. **4.** *Psychology.* **Mental deficiency** (*see*).

re·tard·ed (rĭ-tär′dĭd) *adj.* Relatively slow or backward in mental or emotional development or in academic achievement.

retch (rĕch) *v.* **retched, retching, retches.** —*intr.* To try to vomit; heave. —*tr.* To vomit.
—*n.* The act or sound of this, usually involuntary. [Ultimately from Old English *hrǣcan,* to cough up phlegm, from Germanic (imitative).]

re·te (rē′tē) *n., pl.* **retia** (rē′tē-ə, rē′shə). An anatomical mesh or network, as of veins or nerves. [New Latin, from Latin *rēte,* a net.]

re·tell (rē-tĕl′) *tr.v.* **-told** (-tōld′), **-telling, -tells.** To relate or tell again.

re·tell·ing (rē-tĕl′ĭng) *n.* A new account or adaptation of an earlier story: *a retelling of a Greek myth.*

re·ten·tion (rĭ-tĕn′shən) *n.* **1.** The act of retaining. **2.** The condition of being retained. **3.** The capacity to remember; memory; remembrance. **4.** The ability to retain. **5.** *Pathology.* Involuntary withholding of normally eliminated bodily wastes or secretions. [Middle English *retencion,* from Old French, from Latin *retentiō* (stem *retentiōn-*), from *retinēre,* RETAIN.]

re·ten·tion·ist (rĭ-tĕn′shən-ĭst) *n.* One who favors the retention of something; especially, one who favors the retention of capital punishment.

re·ten·tive (rĭ-tĕn′tĭv) *adj.* Having the ability, tendency, or capacity to retain: *a retentive memory.* —**re·ten·tive·ness, re·ten·tiv·i·ty** (rē′tĕn-tĭv′ə-tē) *n.*

re·think (rē-thĭngk′) *v.* **-thought** (-thôt′), **-thinking, -thinks.** —*tr.* To consider or think through again, especially in order to resolve difficulties or with a view to changing one's opinion. —*intr.* To rethink something; think again.
—*n.* (rē′thĭngk′). An act of rethinking.

re·ti·ar·y (rē′shē-ĕr′ē) *adj.* Of, resembling, or forming a net or web. [From Latin *rēte,* net.]

ret·i·cent (rĕt′ə-sənt) *adj.* **1.** Characteristically silent or reluctant to speak; reserved in speech. **2.** Unwilling to make disclosures or give information. **3.** Restrained or reserved in style. [Latin *reticēns* (stem *reticent-*), present participle of *reticēre,* to keep silent : *re-* (intensive), again + *tacēre,* to be silent.] —**ret·i·cence** *n.* —**ret·i·cent·ly** *adv.*

ret·i·cle (rĕt′ĭ-kəl) *n.* A **graticule** (*see*). [Latin *rēticulum,* diminutive of *rēte,* net.]

re·tic·u·lar (rĭ-tĭk′yə-lər) *adj.* **1.** Netlike. **2.** Intricate; entangled. [New Latin *reticularis,* from Latin *rēticulum,* RETICLE.]

re·tic·u·late (rĭ-tĭk′yə-lĭt, -lāt′) *adj.* Resembling or forming a network: *reticulate veins of a leaf.*
—*v.* (rĭ-tĭk′yə-lāt′) **reticulated, -lating, -lates.** —*tr.* **1.** To make a net or network of. **2.** To mark with lines resembling a network. —*intr.* To form a net or network. [Latin *rēticulātus,* from *rēticulum,* RETICLE.]

re·tic·u·la·tion (rĭ-tĭk′yə-lā′shən) *n.* A network.

ret·i·cule (rĕt′ĭ-kyōōl′) *n.* **1.** A woman's handbag of a former type, often in the form of a pouch with a drawstring and originally made of a netted fabric. **2.** A **graticule** (*see*). [French *réticule,* from Latin *rēticulum,* RETICLE.]

re·tic·u·lo·cyte (rĭ-tĭk′yə-lō-sīt′) *n.* An immature red blood cell containing a network of filaments. [RETICUL(UM) + -CYTE.]

re·tic·u·lo·en·do·the·li·al system (rĭ-tĭk′yə-lō-ĕn′də-thē′lē-əl) *n.* The widely diffused bodily system comprising all phagocytic cells except the leukocytes. [From RETICUL(UM) + ENDOTHELIAL.]

re·tic·u·lum (rĭ-tĭk′yə-ləm) *n., pl.* **-la** (-lə). **1.** A netlike formation or structure; a network. **2.** *Zoology.* The second compartment of the stomach of ruminant mammals, lined with a membrane having honeycombed ridges. [Latin *rēticulum,* RETICLE.]

Re·tic·u·lum (rĭ-tĭk′yə-ləm) *n.* A constellation in the Southern Hemisphere near Dorado and Horologium. [Latin *rēticulum,* RETICLE.]

re·ti·form (rē′tə-fôrm′, rĕt′ə-) *adj.* Arranged like a net; reticulate. [Latin *rēte,* net + -FORM.]

ret·i·na (rĕt′n-ə) *n., pl.* **-nas** or **-nae** (-nē′). A delicate, multilayer, light-sensitive membrane lining the inner eyeball and connected by the optic nerve to the brain. [Middle English *rethina,* from Medieval Latin *retina,* from Latin *rēte,* net.]

ret·i·nal¹ (rĕt′n-əl) *adj.* Of, pertaining to, or constituting the retina.

ret·i·nal² (rĕt′n-ăl′, -ôl′) *n.* A crystalline retinal pigment, $C_{19}H_{27}CHO$, a component of **rhodopsin** (*see*). Also called "retinene." [Greek *rhētinē,* resin + -AL.]

ret·i·ni·tis (rĕt′n-ī′tĭs) *n. Pathology.* Inflammation of the retina. [RETIN(O)- + -ITIS.]

retino–, retin– *prefix.* Indicates the retina; for example, **retinitis, retinoscope.**

re·ti·nol (rĕt′n-ôl′, -ŏl′, -ōl′) *n.* **1. Rosin oil** *(see).* **2.** A derivative of **vitamin A** *(see).* [Greek *rhētinē,* resin + -OL.]

ret·i·no·scope (rĕt′n-ə-skōp′) *n.* An optical instrument for examining refraction of light in the eye. Also called "skiascope." [RETINO- + -SCOPE.]

ret·i·nos·co·py (rĕt′n-ŏs′kə-pē) *n.* Medical examination and analysis of the refractive properties of the eye. Also called "skiascopy." [RETINO- + -SCOPY.] **—ret·i·no·scop·ic** (rĕt′n-ə-skŏp′ĭk) *adj.*

ret·i·nue (rĕt′n-o͞o′, rĕt′n-yo͞o′) *n.* The attendants, aides, or retainers accompanying a person of importance or rank. [Middle English *retenue,* from Old French, from the feminine past participle of *retenir,* to RETAIN.]

re·tire (rĭ-tīr′) *v.* **-tired, -tiring, -tires.** *—intr.* **1.** To go away; depart, as for rest, seclusion, or shelter. **2.** To go to bed or to one's bedroom. **3.** To give up one's occupation, office, or business, so as to live at leisure on one's income, savings, or pension. **4.** To fall back; retreat. **5.** To withdraw from a competition or contest, as because of injury. *—tr.* **1.** To remove from office or active service. **2.** To lead back or away (troops, for example) from action; withdraw. **3.** To take out of circulation: *retire bonds.* **4.** In baseball, to put out (a batter or side): *The pitcher retired seven batters in a row.* [French *retirer* : *re-,* back + *tirer,* to draw (see **tier**).]

re·tired (rĭ-tīrd′) *adj. Abbr.* **r., ret. 1.** Withdrawn; secluded. **2.** Having given up one's job, business, or public life, usually because of age. **3.** Received by a person in retirement.

re·tir·ee (rĭ-tī′rē′, -tī′rē′) *n.* A person who has retired from an occupation, office, or business.

re·tire·ment (rĭ-tīr′mənt) *n.* **1.** The act of retiring. **2.** The condition of being retired, as from one's former occupation or office. **3.** Seclusion or privacy. **4.** A retreat; a place of seclusion. —See Synonyms at **solitude.**

retirement age *n.* The age at which workers generally retire; especially, the age at which a pension is payable.

re·tir·ing (rĭ-tī′rĭng) *adj.* **1.** Shy and modest; unobtrusive; reserved. **2.** At which one retires: *retiring age.* —See Synonyms at **humble, shy. —re·tir·ing·ly** *adv.*

re·tool (rē-to͞ol′) *tr.v.* **-tooled, -tooling, -tools. 1.** To fit out anew with tools; especially, to re-equip (a factory or workshop) for a different kind of production. **2.** To revise and reorganize.

retorsion. Variant of **retortion.**

re·tort[1] (rĭ-tôrt′) *v.* **-torted, -torting, -torts.** *—tr.* **1.** To return in kind; pay back. **2. a.** To reply; especially, to answer in a quick, sharp manner. **b.** To present a counterargument to. *—intr.* **1.** To make a retort. **2.** To retaliate. —See Synonyms at **answer.**
~n. **1.** A quick, incisive reply, especially one that turns the first speaker's words to his disadvantage. **2.** A counterargument. [Latin *retorquēre* (past participle *retortus*), to bend back : *re-,* back + *torquēre,* to bend, twist.] **—re·tort·er** *n.*

re·tort[2] (rĭ-tôrt′, rē′tôrt′) *n.* A closed laboratory vessel with an outlet tube, used for distillation, sublimation, or decomposition by heat. [French *retorte,* from Medieval Latin *retorta,* feminine of Latin *retortus,* "bent back" (the neck of the vessel is bent over), from *retorquēre,* to bend back, RETORT.]

re·tor·tion, re·tor·sion (rĭ-tôr′shən) *n.* Retaliation in kind by a state upon the citizens of another state. [RETORT + -ION, perhaps by analogy with CONTORTION.]

re·touch (rē-tŭch′) *tr.v.* **-touched, -touching, -touches. 1.** To add new details or touches to (make-up or a painting, for example), for correction or improvement. **2.** *Photography.* To improve or change (a negative or print) by adding details or removing flaws.
~n. (rē′tŭch′, rē-tŭch′). **1.** A detail changed or improved in a painting, photograph, or the like. **2.** A painting, photograph, or other work of art, that has been retouched. **3.** The act or art of altering or retouching.

re·trace (rē-trās′) *tr.v.* **-traced, -tracing, -traces. 1.** To trace back to the source or origin. **2.** To go back over (a route): *retrace one's steps.* **3.** To go back over in one's mind. **—re·trace·a·ble** *adj.*

re·tract (rĭ-trăkt′) *v.* **-tracted, -tracting, -tracts.** *—tr.* **1.** To take back or disavow (a statement, accusation, offer, or promise); **2.** To draw back or in: *The turtle retracted its head.* **3.** To withdraw or pull back (machinery, especially the undercarriage of an aircraft). **4.** *Phonetics.* **a.** To utter (a sound) with the tongue drawn back. **b.** To draw back (the tongue). *—intr.* **1.** To take back or disavow a statement, accusation, or the like. **2.** To be withdrawn or pulled back. **3.** To shrink or draw back. [Middle English *retracten,* from Old French *retracter,* from Latin *retractāre,* to handle again, frequentative of *retrahere* (past participle *retractus*), to draw back : *re-,* back, again + *trahere,* to draw.] **—re·tract·a·bil·i·ty** (rĭ-trăk′tə-bĭl′ə-tē) *n.* **—re·tract·a·ble, re·tract·i·ble** *adj.* **—re·trac·ta·tion** (rē′trăk-tā′shən) *n.* **—re·trac·tive** *adj.*

re·trac·tile (rĭ-trăk′tĭl) *adj.* Capable of being drawn back or in: *Cats have retractile claws.* **—re·trac·til·i·ty** (rē′trăk-tĭl′ə-tē) *n.*

re·trac·tion (rĭ-trăk′shən) *n.* **1.** The act of recanting or disavowing a statement, accusation, or the like. **2.** The act or power of drawing back or of being drawn back.

re·trac·tor (rĭ-trăk′tər) *n.* **1.** One that retracts. **2.** *Anatomy.* A muscle, as a flexor, that retracts an organ or part. **3.** *Medicine.* An instrument that holds back the edges of a wound or surgical incision.

re·tral (rē′trəl, rĕt′rəl) *adj.* **1.** *Biology.* At, close to, or toward the back. **2.** Backward; reverse. [Latin *retrō,* backward, behind.] **—re·tral·ly** *adv.*

re·tread (rē-trĕd′) *tr.v.* **-trod** (-trŏd′), **-trodden** (-trŏd′n), **-treading, -treads.** To tread (one's steps or route, for example) again.

re·tread (rē-trĕd′) *tr.v.* **-treaded, -treading, -treads.** To fit (a worn automobile tire) with a new tread.
~n. (rē′trĕd′). A retreaded tire.

re·treat (rĭ-trēt′) *n.* **1.** The act of retiring or withdrawing. **2.** A quiet, private, or secure place; a refuge. **3.** A period of seclusion, retirement, or solitude. **4. a.** The withdrawal of a military force from a dangerous position or from an enemy attack. **b.** The signal for such a withdrawal, made on a drum or trumpet. **5.** *Military.* A bugle call signaling the lowering of the flag at sunset. **6. a.** A period spent in spiritual renewal, as through prayer, contemplation, or spiritual reading. **b.** A place, such as a monastery, where such a period can be spent. **7.** An institution, often private, for the treatment of alcoholics, the mentally ill, or others in need of care. —See Synonyms at **shelter. —beat a retreat. 1.** *Military.* To give a signal for withdrawal of forces. **2.** To withdraw; flee.
~v. **retreated, -treating, -treats.** *—intr.* **1. a.** To withdraw or retire. **b.** To withdraw from a battle. Used of troops. **2.** To slope backward; recede. *—tr.* In chess, to move (a piece) back. [Middle English *retret,* from Old French *retrait,* from the past participle of *retraire,* to draw back, from Latin *retrahere,* to RETRACT.]

retort *Antoine Lavoisier, the 18th-century French chemist, used this retort in a famous experiment that demonstrated the presence of oxygen in the air. Any vessel used for the distillation or separation of substances is called a retort.*

re·trench (rĭ-trĕnch′) *v.* **-trenched, -trenching, -trenches.** *—tr.* **1.** To cut down or curtail (expenditure or costs). **2. a.** To delete (parts of a literary work). **b.** To shorten or abridge (a literary work). **3.** To deduct or remove. **4.** *Military.* To provide with a retrenchment. *—intr.* To curtail expenses; economize. [From obsolete French *retrencher,* from Old French *retrenchier* : *re-* (intensive), again + *trenchier,* to cut off (see **trench**).]

re·trench·ment (rĭ-trĕnch′mənt) *n.* **1.** The act or result of retrenching; especially, the cutting down of expenditure. **2.** *Military.* An inner line of defense, usually consisting of a trench and parapet.

re·tri·al (rē-trī′əl) *n.* A second trial, as of a legal case.

ret·ri·bu·tion (rĕt′rə-byo͞o′shən) *n.* **1.** Something given or demanded in repayment; especially, punishment or vengeance for a wrong or injury. **2.** *Theology.* Punishment or reward distributed in a future life according to performance in this one. [Middle English *retribucion,* from Old French *retribution,* from Late Latin *retribūtiō* (stem *retribūtiōn-*), from Latin *retribuere,* to pay back : *re-,* back + *tribuere,* to grant, pay (see **tribute**).]

re·trib·u·tive (rĭ-trĭb′yə-tĭv) *adj.* Also **re·trib·u·to·ry** (rĭ-trĭb′yə-tôr′ē, -tōr′ē). Of, involving, or characterized by retribution.

re·trib·u·ti·vism (rĭ-trĭb′yə-tĭ-vĭz′əm) *n.* The belief that criminals ought to be punished for the sake of vengeance rather than in order to prevent crime or rehabilitate the criminal. **—re·trib·u·ti·vist** *n.*

re·triev·al (rĭ-trē′vəl) *n.* **1.** An act or the process of retrieving. **2.** The possibility of repossession or restoration: *beyond retrieval.*

re·trieve (rĭ-trēv′) *v.* **-trieved, -trieving, -trieves.** *—tr.* **1.** To get back; regain. **2.** To revive; restore. **3. a.** To put right; rectify. **b.** To rescue, as from trouble or danger. **4.** To recall to mind; remember. **5.** To find and carry back; fetch. **6.** To manage to return (a difficult shot), as in tennis. **7.** *Computer Science.* To obtain (stored data) from a disk, tape, or other storage device. *—intr.* To find and bring back game. Used of a dog. —See Usage note at **recover.**
~n. The act of retrieving. [Middle English *retreven,* to find again, from Old French *retrover* : *re-,* again + *trover,* to find, perhaps from Vulgar Latin *tropāre* (unattested), to write, compose, from Latin *tropus,* trope, a manner of singing, a song, from Greek *tropos,* "a turning."] **—re·triev·a·bil·i·ty** *n.* **—re·triev·a·ble** *adj.* **—re·triev·a·bly** *adv.*

retriever *Several breeds of dogs have been trained as retrievers and used to pick up shot game. This is a black Labrador, a North American breed that was introduced to Europe by fishermen in the early 19th century.*

re·triev·er (rĭ-trē′vər) *n.* **1.** One that retrieves. **2.** A dog of any of several breeds developed and trained to retrieve game; especially, a golden retriever.

ret·ro (rĕt′rō) *n.* A **retrorocket** *(see).*

retro– *prefix.* Indicates: **1.** Backward or back; for example, **retrorocket. 2.** Situated behind; for example, **retrolental.** [Latin *retrō,* backward, behind.]

ret·ro·act (rĕt′rō-ăkt′) *intr.v.* **-acted, -acting, -acts. 1.** To act in opposition or reciprocally. **2.** To be retroactive in application. Used of a law or pay raise, for example.

ret·ro·ac·tion (rĕt′rō-ăk′shən) *n.* **1.** A retroactive action. **2.** An opposing or reciprocal action; a reaction.

ret·ro·ac·tive (rĕt′rō-ăk′tĭv) *adj.* **1.** Influencing or applying to a period prior to enactment: *retroactive laws.* **2.** Effective from a date in the past: *a retroactive pay increase.* [French *rétroactif,* from Latin *retroactus,* past participle of *retroagere,* to drive back : RETRO- + *agere,* to drive.] **—ret·ro·ac·tive·ly** *adv.* **—ret·ro·ac·tiv·i·ty** (rĕt′rō-ăk-tĭv′ə-tē) *n.*

ret·ro·cede (rĕt′rō-sēd′) *v.* **-ceded, -ceding, -cedes.** *—intr.* To go back; recede. *—tr.* To cede or give back; return. [Latin *retrōcēdere,* to go back : RETRO- + *cēdere,* to go.] **—ret·ro·ces·sion** (rĕt′rō-sĕsh′ən) *n.*

ret·ro·choir (rĕt′rō-kwīr′) *n.* The area behind the high altar in a cathedral or large church. [Medieval Latin *retrochorus* : RETRO- + CHOIR.]

ret·ro·flex (rĕt′rə-flĕks′) *adj.* Also **ret·ro·flexed** (rĕt′rə-flĕkst′). **1.** Bent, curved, or turned backward. **2.** *Phonetics.* Pronounced with the tip of the tongue turned back against the roof of the mouth.
~n. A retroflex consonant. [New Latin *retroflexus,* from Late

Latin *retrōflectere,* to bend back : RETRO- + Latin *flectere,* to bend, FLEX.] —**ret·ro·flex·ion, ret·ro·flec·tion** (rĕt′rə-flĕk′shən) *n.*

ret·ro·grade (rĕt′rə-grād′) *adj.* **1.** Moving or tending backward; retiring; retreating. **2.** Inverted or reversed, especially in order. **3. a.** Reverting to an earlier or inferior condition; declining or degenerating. **b.** Reversing or obstructing progress: *a retrograde decision.* **4.** *Astronomy.* **a.** Having or pertaining to orbital motion in an opposite direction to that of the earth around the sun. **b.** Having or pertaining to motion around a given planet in an opposite sense to the planet's orbital motion around the sun. **c.** Having an apparent clockwise rotation, resulting from the fact that the rotational period is greater than the orbital period. Said of a planet such as Venus. **d.** Having or designating an apparent backward motion on the celestial sphere, resulting from the fact that the orbital velocity around the sun is lower that that of the earth. ~*intr.v.* **retrograded, -grading, -grades. 1.** To move or seem to move backward. **2.** To decline; degenerate; deteriorate. [Middle English, from Latin *retrōgradus* : RETRO- + *gradus,* a step, grade.] —**ret·ro·gra·da·tion** (rĕt′rə-grā-dā′shən) *n.*

ret·ro·gress (rĕt′rə-grĕs′, rĕt′rə-grĕs′) *intr.v.* **-gressed, -gressing, -gresses. 1.** To return to an earlier, inferior, or less complex condition. **2.** To go or move backward. [Latin *retrōgradī* (past participle *retrōgressus*), to go backward : RETRO- + *gradī,* to step.] —**ret·ro·gres·sive** *adj.* —**ret·ro·gres·sive·ly** *adv.*

ret·ro·gres·sion (rĕt′rə-grĕsh′ən) *n.* **1.** The act or process of deteriorating or declining. **2.** *Biology.* A return to a less complex or more primitive state or stage.

ret·ro·ject (rĕt′rə-jĕkt′) *tr.v.* **-jected, -jecting, -jects.** To throw backward. Compare **project.** [RETRO- + *-ject,* as in PROJECT (verb).]

ret·ro·len·tal (rĕt′rō-lĕnt′l) *adj.* Behind a lens, especially the lens of the eye. [RETRO- + New Latin *lens* (stem *lent-*), LENS + -AL.]

ret·ro·rock·et (rĕt′rō-rŏk′ĭt) *n.* A rocket engine used to retard, arrest, or reverse the motion of an aircraft, missile, spacecraft, or other vehicle. Also called "braking rocket," "retro."

re·trorse (rĭ-trôrs′, rē′trôrs′) *adj.* Directed or turned backward or downward. Said especially of plant parts. [Latin *retrōrsus,* contraction of *retrōversus* : RETRO- + *versus,* "turned," past participle of *vertere,* to turn.] —**re·trorse·ly** *adv.*

ret·ro·spect (rĕt′rə-spĕkt′) *n.* A review, survey, or contemplation of things in the past. —**in retrospect.** Looking backward; reviewing the past: *In retrospect, life seems brief.* ~*v.* (rĕt′rə-spĕkt′, rĕt′rə-spĕkt′) **retrospected, -specting, -spects.** *Archaic.* —*intr.* **1.** To contemplate the past. **2.** To refer back. Used with *to.* —*tr.* To look back on or contemplate (things past). [Latin *retrōspectus,* past participle of *retrōspicere,* to look back at : RETRO- + *specere,* to look at.] —**ret·ro·spec·tion** (rĕt′rə-spĕk′shən) *n.*

ret·ro·spec·tive (rĕt′rə-spĕk′tĭv) *adj.* **1.** Looking back on, contemplating, or directed toward the past. **2.** Looking or directed backward. **3.** Applying to or influencing the past; retroactive. **4.** Of, pertaining to, or designating an exhibition showing the work of an artist or school over a period of years or a representative selection of an artist's work. ~*n.* A retrospective art exhibition. —**ret·ro·spec·tive·ly** *adv.*

re·trous·sé (rə-trōō-sā′, rĕ′trōō-sā′) *adj.* Turned up at the end. Said of a nose. [French, past participle of *retrousser,* to turn back, from Old French : *re-,* back + *trousser,* to TRUSS.]

ret·ro·ver·sion (rĕt′rō-vûr′zhən, -shən) *n.* **1.** A turning or tilting backward. **2.** The state of being turned or tilted backward. [Latin *retrōversus,* RETRORSE.]

re·try (rē-trī′) *tr.v.* **-tried, -trying, -tries.** To try (a law case) again.

ret·si·na (rĕt′sĭ-nə, rĕt-sē′nə) *n.* A resinated Greek wine. [Modern Greek, from Italian *resina,* resin, from Latin *rēsīna,* RESIN.]

re·turn (rĭ-tûrn′) *v.* **-turned, -turning, -turns.** —*intr.* **1.** To go or come back, as to an earlier condition or place. **2.** To revert in speech, thought, or practice. **3.** To recur; appear again: *Her cold has returned.* **4.** To answer; retort; respond. —*tr.* **1.** To send, put, give, or carry back: *return empty bottles to the store.* **2.** To give or send back in reciprocation: *return a compliment.* **3.** To produce or yield (profit or interest) as a result of labor, investment, or expenditure: *treasury bonds that returned 11%.* **4.** To reflect or send back (light or sound). **5. a.** To submit (a writ, report, or statement) to a judge or other person in authority. **b.** To render or deliver (a verdict). **c.** To declare to be as specified: *was returned not guilty.* **6.** To say in reply. **7.** To elect or re-elect, as to a legislative body. **8.** In card games, to respond to (a partner's lead) by leading the same suit. **9.** *Architecture.* To place (a wall molding or the like) at an angle to or turned away from the previous line of direction. **10.** In racket games and certain other sports, to hit, throw, or play (a ball) back: *struggled to return his opponent's serve.* ~*n.* *Abbr.* **ret. 1.** The act or state of going, coming, bringing, or sending back. **2. a.** Something that is brought or sent back, such as a defective or unsold article. **b.** Something that goes or comes back. **3.** A recurrence, as of a periodic occasion or event: *the annual return of spring.* **4. a.** Something exchanged for that received; a repayment. **b.** The repaying or reciprocating of something received. **5.** A reply; a response; an answer. **6. a.** The profit made on an exchange of goods or other commercial transaction. **b.** *Often* **returns.** A profit or yield, as from labor or investments. **c.** The profit per unit, as in the manufacturing of a particular product. **7.** A statement, report, or compilation of data, typically one of a formal or official character that is submitted to an appropriate authority, especially: **a.** A statement of a person's or corporation's income for tax purposes, or the form on which such a statement is made. **b.** *Usually*

returns. A report on the vote in an election: *Early returns showed the incumbent leading the challenger.* **8.** In card games, a lead that responds to the lead of one's partner. **9.** In racket games and certain other sports: **a.** The act of returning the ball to one's opponent. **b.** The ball so returned. **10.** *Football.* **a.** The act of running back the ball after a kickoff, punt, interception, or fumble. **b.** The yardage gained in a return. **11.** *Architecture.* **a.** The extension of a molding, projection, or other part at an angle (usually 90°) to the main part. **b.** A part of a building set at an angle to the façade. **12.** A channel, such as a pipe, carrying something back to its source. **13.** A round-trip ticket. **14.** *Law.* **a.** A report by a sheriff or other officer of the court showing how he has discharged a duty laid upon him. **b.** The bringing or sending back of a writ, subpoena, or other document, with a short written report on it, by a sheriff or other officer to the court from which it was issued. —**many happy returns (of the day).** Used as an expression of greetings or congratulations to a person on his or her birthday. ~*adj.* **1.** Of or for coming back: *the return voyage.* **2.** Given, sent, or done in reciprocation or exchange: *a return visit; a return blow.* **3.** Played or staged a second time, offering the original loser a chance to win: *a return boxing match.* **4. a.** Reversing or changing direction. **b.** Formed by a reversal or change in direction, as a bend in a road. **5.** *Chiefly British.* For travel to a destination and back again: *a return ticket.* [Middle English *reto(u)rnen,* from Old French *retorner,* from Vulgar Latin *retornāre* (unattested), to turn back : Latin *re-,* back + *tornāre,* to turn in a lathe, from *tornus,* lathe, from Greek *tornos.*] —**re·turn·er** *n.*

   Usage: **return, revert, recur, recrudesce.** *Return* denotes going back or coming back to a former place, position, or condition. *Revert* refers to returning to an earlier and less desirable condition. *Recur* applies to repeated occurrences of the same thing. *Recrudesce* is said of that which becomes active after a period of quiescence.

re·turn·a·ble (rĭ-tûr′nə-bəl) *adj.* **1. a.** Capable of being returned or brought back. **b.** Designating a bottle or other container that is returned when empty to the vender who refunds a deposit paid at the time of purchase. **2.** Legally required to be returned. ~*n.* A returnable bottle or container.

re·turn·ee (rĭ-tûr′nē′) *n.* Someone who has returned, as from a voyage or from exile.

re·tuse (rĭ-tōōs′, -tyōōs′) *adj.* Having a rounded or blunt apex with a shallow notch. Said chiefly of leaves. [Latin *retūsus,* past participle of *retundere,* to beat back : *re-,* back + *tundere,* to strike, beat.]

Retz. See Gilles de **Rais.**

Reu·ben¹ (rōō′bĭn). Jacob's eldest son, the ancestor of one of the tribes of Israel. Genesis 29:32. [Hebrew *Re'ū-bēn,* "behold, a son" (from Genesis 29:32) : *ra'u,* imperative plural of *ra'ah,* to behold, see + *ben,* son.]

Reuben² *n.* The tribe of Israel descended from Reuben.

re·u·ni·fy (rē-yōō′nĭ-fī′) *tr.v.* **-fied, -fying, -fies.** To make whole again; restore (especially a divided country) to a united state. —**re·u·ni·fi·ca·tion** (rē-yōō′nĭ-fĭ-kā′shən) *n.*

re·un·ion (rē-yōōn′yən) *n.* **1.** The act of reuniting. **2.** The state of being reunited. **3.** A gathering of the members of a group, such as a family, who have been separated.

Ré·u·nion (rē-yōōn′yən, rā-). One of the Mascarene Islands, east of Madagascar in the Indian Ocean. It is an overseas department of France. It consists mainly of one active and several extinct volcanoes, with settlement and cultivation in the coastal lowlands. Sugar, molasses, and rum are the main exports. St. Denis is the capital and chief port. See map at **Indian Ocean.**

re·u·nite (rē′yōō-nīt′) *v.* **-nited, -niting, -nites.** —*tr.* To bring together again. —*intr.* To come together again. [Medieval Latin *reūnīre* : *re-,* again + *ūnīre,* from Late Latin, to UNITE.]

Reu·ter (roi′tər), **Paul Julius, Baron von,** born Israel Beer Josaphat (1816–99). German industrialist, the founder of Reuter's Telegraph Company. In 1849 he began his own small pigeon-post service in Germany. Two years later he settled in London and opened a news office. By 1858 he had succeeded in having his foreign telegrams published by the English press. He eventually built up worldwide cable connections.

Reu·ther (rōō′thər), **Walter Philip** (1907–70). U.S. labor leader. Associated with the United Automobile Workers since 1935 and serving as their president from 1946 until his death, he became president of the Congress of Industrial Organization in 1952 and was instrumental in the merging of the AFL-CIO (1955).

rev (rĕv) *n. Informal.* **1.** A revolution, as of an engine. **2.** A revolution per minute. ~*v.* **revved, revving, revs.** *Informal.* —*tr.* To increase the speed of (an engine). Often used with *up.* —*intr.* To operate at an increased speed. Often used with *up.*

rev. 1. revenue. **2.** reverse; reversed. **3.** review; reviewed. **4.** revise; revision. **5.** revolution. **6.** revolving.

Rev. 1. Revelation (New Testament). **2.** Reverend (title).

re·val·o·rize (rē-văl′ə-rīz′) *tr.v.* **-rized, -rizing, -rizes.** To establish a new value for (currency, assets, or the like). [Back-formation from *revalorization,* from French : RE- + VALORIZATION.] —**re·val·o·ri·za·tion** *n.*

re·val·u·ate (rē-văl′yōō-āt′) *tr.v.* **-ated, -ating, -ates.** Also **re·val·ue** (-văl′yōō), **-ued, -uing, -ues.** To give a new value to (currency), especially an increased value. Compare **devaluate.** —**re·val·u·a·tion** (rē-văl′yōō-ā′shən) *n.*

re·vamp (rē-vămp′) *tr.v.* **-vamped, -vamping, -vamps. 1.** To patch up or restore; renovate. **2.** To revise or reconstruct (a manuscript, for example). **3.** To vamp (a shoe or boot) anew. ~*n.* The act, process, or result of revamping.

re·vanch·ism (rĭ-vănch′ĭz′əm) *n.* A foreign policy motivated by a desire to regain territory that was lost to an enemy. [French *revanche,* revenge, from *revancher,* to revenge, from Old French *revencher,* to REVENGE.] —**re·vanch·ist** *n. & adj.*

rev counter *n. Informal.* An instrument for counting the rate at which an engine is revolving; a tachometer.

Revd Reverend.

re·veal[1] (rĭ-vēl′) *tr.v.* **-vealed, -vealing, -veals. 1.** To divulge or disclose; make known. **2.** To bring to view; expose; show. **3.** To make known by divine or supernatural means, as through revelation. Used of God. [Middle English *revelen,* from Old French *reveller,* from Latin *revēlāre,* to unveil, reveal : *re-,* back, back to a prior condition + *vēlāre,* to veil, from *vēlum,* a veil.] —**re·veal·a·ble** *adj.* —**re·veal·er** *n.* —**re·veal·ment** *n.*
     Synonyms: betray, disclose, divulge, expose, impart.

re·veal[2] *n. Architecture.* The internal, vertical side of a recess or opening, as of a doorway or window. [From obsolete *revale,* to lower, from Old French *revaler* : RE- + *avaler,* to lower (see vail).]

revealed religion *n.* Religion that is based on ideas or beliefs gained through revelation by God rather than through natural reasoning.

re·veal·ing (rĭ-vēl′ĭng) *adj.* **1.** Significant; telling. **2.** Showing or telling something not known or seen before: *a revealing conversation; a revealing dress.* —**re·veal·ing·ly** *adv.*

re·veil·le (rĕv′ə-lē) *n.* **1.** The sounding of a bugle early in the morning to awaken and summon persons in a military camp or garrison. **2.** The first military formation of the day. [French *réveillez,* imperative of *réveiller,* to rouse, awaken, from Old French *reveiller* : *re-,* again + *veiller,* to rouse, from Latin *vigilāre,* to watch, from *vigil,* awake.]

rev·el (rĕv′əl) *intr.v.* **-eled, -eling, -els** or *chiefly British* **-elled, -elling, -els. 1.** To take great pleasure or delight. Used with *in: revels in gossip.* **2.** To engage in uproarious festivities; make merry. ~*n. Often* **revels.** A noisy, festive occasion. [Middle English *revelen,* from Old French *reveller,* to make noise, "to rebel," from Latin *rebellāre,* to REBEL.] —**rev·el·er** *n.*

rev·e·la·tion (rĕv′ə-lā′shən) *n.* **1.** An act of revealing or something revealed; especially, a dramatic disclosure of something not previously known or realized. **2.** Something that reveals unexpected qualities or provides fresh understanding. **3.** *Theology.* A manifestation of divine will or truth. [Middle English, from Old French, from Late Latin *revēlātiō* (stem *revēlātiōn-*), from Latin *revēlāre,* REVEAL.] —**rev·e·la·tion·al** *adj.*

Rev·e·la·tion (rĕv′ə-lā′shən) *n. Abbr.* **Rev.** *Also* **Revelations.** The last book in the New Testament, attributed to St. John. Also called the "Apocalypse," the "Revelation of St. John the Divine."

rev·e·la·tion·ist (rĕv′ə-lā′shən-ĭst) *n.* One who believes in divine revelation.

rev·el·ry (rĕv′əl-rē) *n., pl.* **-ries.** Boisterous merrymaking. —**rev·el·rous** *adj.*

rev·e·nant (rĕv′ə-nənt) *n.* **1.** One that returns after an absence. **2.** One who returns after death; a ghost. [French, from the present participle of *revenir,* to return, from Latin *revenīre* : *re-,* again, back + *venīre,* to come.]

re·venge (rĭ-vĕnj′) *tr.v.* **-venged, -venging, -venges. 1.** To inflict punishment in return for (injury or insult); retaliate. **2.** To seek or take vengeance for (oneself or another person). ~*n.* **1.** Vengeance; retaliation. **2.** The act of taking vengeance. **3.** A desire for revenge; vindictiveness. **4.** An opportunity for, or instance of, getting back at an opponent for an earlier reversal or defeat. [Middle English *revengen,* from Old French *revenger, revencher,* from Late Latin *revindicāre,* to avenge : Latin *re-* (intensive), again + *vindicāre,* to VINDICATE.]

re·venge·ful (rĭ-vĕnj′fəl) *adj.* Desiring revenge. —*See Synonyms at* **vindictive.** —**re·venge·ful·ly** *adv.* —**re·venge·ful·ness** *n.*

rev·e·nue (rĕv′ə-nōō, -nyōō) *n. Abbr.* **rev. 1.** The income of a government from all sources appropriated for the payment of public expenses. **2.** Yield from property or investment; income. **3.** A single source of income. **4.** A government department set up to collect public funds. Also used adjectively: *a revenue officer.* [Middle English, return, return to place, from Old French, from the feminine past participle of *revenir,* to return, from Latin *revenīre* : *re-,* back, again + *venīre,* to come.]

rev·e·nu·er (rĕv′ə-nōō′ər, -nyōō′ər) *n.* **1.** A government revenue agent. **2.** A small motorboat formerly used in patrols to catch smugglers.

revenue tariff *n.* A tariff imposed to raise public funds rather than to affect trade.

re·ver·ber·ate (rĭ-vûr′bə-rāt′) *v.* **-ated, -ating, -ates.** —*intr.* **1.** To re-echo; resound. **2.** To be repeatedly reflected. **3.** To rebound or recoil; redound. —*tr.* **1.** To re-echo (a sound). **2.** To reflect (heat or light) repeatedly. [Latin *reverberāre,* to cause to rebound : *re-,* back + *verberāre,* to whip, lash, from *verbera,* whips, rods.] —**re·ver·ber·a·tion** (rĭ-vûr′bə-rā′shən) *n.* —**re·ver·ber·ant, re·ver·ber·a·tive** (rĭ-vûr′bə-rā′tĭv) *adj.* —**re·ver·ber·a·tor** *n.*

reverberation pedal *n.* On a piano, the "loud pedal" or **sustaining pedal** (*see*).

reverberation time *n.* The time taken for a sound in a room to diminish in intensity by 60 decibels, used as a measure of the acoustic properties of the room.

re·ver·ber·a·to·ry (rĭ-vûr′bə-rə-tôr′ē, -tōr′ē) *adj.* Of, pertaining to, or causing reverberation. ~*n.* A reverberatory furnace.

reverberatory furnace *n.* A furnace for smelting metals in which the fuel and the ore are separated and the heat is reflected onto the ore by a curved roof. Also called "reverberatory."

re·vere (rĭ-vîr′) *tr.v.* **-vered, -vering, -veres.** To regard with awe, great respect, or devotion; venerate. [Latin *reverērī* : *re-* (intensive), again + *verērī,* to respect, feel awe of.] —**re·ver·er** *n.*
     Synonyms: adore, idolatrize, idolize, venerate, worship.

Re·vere (rĭ-vîr′), **Paul** (1735–1818). U.S. Revolutionary hero. On April 18, 1775, he went on his famous ride to Lexington, celebrated in a poem by Longfellow, to warn the people of Massachusetts that a British expedition was advancing toward Lexington.

rev·er·ence (rĕv′ər-əns) *n.* **1.** A feeling of profound awe and respect and often of love; veneration. **2.** An act of showing respect; especially, an obeisance. **3.** The state of being revered. **4.** *Archaic & Irish.* **Reverence.** A title of respect for a clergyman. Preceded by *His* or *Your.* —See Synonyms at **honor.** ~*tr.v.* **reverenced, -encing, -ences.** To regard with reverence.

rev·er·end (rĕv′ər-ənd) *adj.* **1.** Deserving of reverence. **2.** Pertaining to or characteristic of the clergy; clerical. **3. Reverend.** *Abbr.* **Rev., Revd** Designating a member of the clergy: *the Reverend John Smith.* ~*n. Informal.* A cleric or minister. [Middle English, from Old French, from Latin *reverendus,* gerundive of *reverērī,* REVERE.]

Reverend Mother *n.* A title of or form of address for the superior of a convent.

rev·er·ent (rĕv′ər-ənt) *adj.* Feeling or expressing reverence. [Middle English, from Latin *reverēns* (stem *reverent-*), present participle of *reverērī,* REVERE.] —**rev·er·ent·ly** *adv.*

rev·er·en·tial (rĕv′ə-rĕn′shəl) *adj.* Showing reverence: *a reverential tone of voice.* —**rev·er·en·tial·ly** *adv.*

rev·er·ie (rĕv′ər-ē) *n.* **1. a.** Absent-minded musing; daydreaming. **b.** A daydream: *a reverie of years long past.* **2.** *Music.* A piece of music evoking a dreamy state. **3.** *Archaic.* A fantastic or deluded notion. [Middle English, from Old French, from *rever†,* to dream.]

re·vers (rĭ-vîr′, -vâr′) *n., pl.* **revers** (-vîrz′, -vârz′). A part of a garment, such as a lapel, turned back to show the reverse side. [French, from Old French, REVERSE.]

re·ver·sal (rĭ-vûr′səl) *n.* **1.** The act or an instance of reversing. **2.** The state of being reversed. **3.** An unfavorable change: *a reversal of fortune.* **4.** *Law.* A changing or setting aside, as of a lower court's decision by an appellate court.

re·verse (rĭ-vûrs′) *adj. Abbr.* **rev. 1. a.** Turned backward in position, direction, or order; opposite; contrary. **b.** Upside-down, back to front, or inverted. **2.** Moving or acting in a manner contrary to the usual: *a reverse snobbery that admires the lowly.* **3.** Causing backward movement: *reverse gear.* **4.** *Printing.* Having the black and white areas reversed. ~*n. Abbr.* **rev. 1.** The opposite or contrary of something. **2. a.** The back or rear of something. **b.** The side of a coin not carrying the principal design. Compare **obverse. 3.** A change to an opposite position, condition, or direction. **4.** A change in fortune from better to worse; a setback. **5. a.** A mechanism for reversing movement, as a gear in a motor vehicle. **b.** The reverse position or operating condition of such a mechanism. —**in reverse. 1.** In the contrary direction, order, or position. **2.** In a direction or manner contrary to the usual: *discrimination in reverse.* ~*v.* **reversed, -versing, -verses.** —*tr.* **1. a.** To turn to the opposite direction or tendency. **b.** To cause to move in a direction opposite to the normal one: *reverse a car.* **2.** To turn inside out or upside-down. **3.** To exchange the positions of; transpose. **4.** To cause to be completely different or opposite in character or effect: *reversed their policy on wage restraint.* **5.** *Law.* To revoke or annul (a decision or decree). **6.** To cause (the charge for a telephone call) to be paid by the recipient. —*intr.* **1. a.** To turn or move in the opposite direction. **b.** To move backward. **2.** To reverse the action of an engine. [Middle English *revers,* from Old French, from Latin *reversus,* past participle of *revertere,* REVERT.] —**re·verse·ly** *adv.* —**re·vers·er** *n.*

re·verse-charge call (rĭ-vûrs′ chärj′) *n. Chiefly British.* A collect telephone call.

reversed fault *n. Geology.* A fault in which older beds on one side of the fault plane are thrust over younger beds on the other side as a result of compression. Also called "reverse fault."

reverse tran·scrip·tase (trăn-skrĭp′tās, -tāz) *n.* An enzyme that allows synthesis of DNA.

re·ver·si (rĭ-vûr′sē) *n.* A game played on a checkerboard with counters that are colored differently on each side. These are turned over when captured and become the captor's pieces. [French. See **reverse.**]

re·vers·i·ble (rĭ-vûr′sə-bəl) *adj.* **1.** Capable of being reversed or revoked or of returning to a former state. **2.** *Chemistry & Physics.* Capable of successively assuming or producing either of two states: *a reversible reaction.* **3.** In thermodynamics, pertaining to or occurring by processes that are at thermodynamic equilibrium: *a reversible electric cell.* **4.** Patterned, woven, or finished so that either side may be worn or used as the outer side: *a reversible coat.* ~*n.* A reversible item of clothing. —**re·vers·i·bil·i·ty, re·vers·i·ble·ness** *n.* —**re·vers·i·bly** *adv.*

re·ver·sion (rĭ-vûr′zhən) *n.* **1.** A return to a former condition, belief, or practice. **2.** A turning away or in the opposite direction. **3.** *Genetics.* **Atavism** (*see*). **4.** *Law.* **a.** The return of an estate or an interest in it to the grantor or his heirs after the grant has expired. **b.** The estate thus returned. **c.** The right to succeed to such an estate. **5.** The right or expectation of obtaining or succeeding to something at a future time. **6.** The sum payable by an insurance company on an insured person's death.

re·ver·sion·ar·y (rĭ-vûr′zhə-nĕr′ē) *adj. Law.* Also **re·ver·sion·al** (-zhən-əl). Of or connected with the reversion of an estate.

re·ver·sion·er (rĭ-vûr′zhən-ər) *n. Law.* A person entitled to receive an estate in reversion.

re·vert (rĭ-vûrt′) *intr.v.* **-verted, -verting, -verts. 1.** To return to a former, often less desirable condition, practice, subject, or belief. **2.** *Law.* To return to the former owner or his heirs. Used of money or property. **3.** *Biology.* To return to a simpler or more primitive form or condition. Used of organisms, organs, and the like. —See Usage note at **return.** [Middle English *reverten,* from Old French *revertir,* from Latin *revertere,* to turn back : *re-,* back + *vertere,* to turn.] —**re·vert·er** *n.* —**re·vert·i·ble** *adj.* —**re·ver·tive** *adj.*

re·vest (rē-vĕst′) *tr.v.* **-vested, -vesting, -vests.** To vest (power or possession, for example) once again in a person or agency. [Middle English *revesten,* to dress (in ecclesiastical garments), from Old French *revestir,* from Late Latin *revestīre,* to clothe again : Latin *re-,* again + *vestīre,* to clothe, from *vestis,* clothes.]

re·vet (rĭ-vĕt′) *v.* **-vetted, -vetting, -vets.** —*tr.* To face (a wall of earth) with a layer of stone or other suitable material. —*intr.* To construct a revetment. [French *revêtir,* from Old French *revestir,* to clothe again. See **revest.**]

re·vet·ment (rĭ-vĕt′mənt) *n.* **1.** A facing, as of masonry, used to support an embankment, wall, or the like. **2.** A barricade against explosives.

re·view (rĭ-vyōō′) *v.* **-viewed, -viewing, -views.** —*tr.* **1.** To look over, study, or examine again. **2.** To consider retrospectively; look back on. **3.** To examine with an eye to criticism or correction. **4.** To write or give a critical report on (a book or artistic production). **5.** *Law.* To examine (an action or verdict), especially in a higher court, in order to correct possible errors. **6.** To subject to a formal inspection, especially a military inspection. —*intr.* **1.** To go over or re-examine material. **2.** To act as a reviewer, especially for a newspaper or magazine.

—*n. Abbr.* **rev. 1.** A re-examination or reconsideration. **2.** A retrospective view or survey. **3.** An inspection or examination for the purpose of evaluating something. **4.** A published report or essay giving a critical estimate, as of an artistic work or performance. **5.** A periodical publication devoted primarily to such reports. **6.** A formal military inspection. **7.** *Law.* An examination of an action or verdict, especially by a higher court, in order to correct possible errors. **8.** An entertainment, a **revue** *(see).* [From obsolete French *revoir* (past participle *reveu*), to see again, look over : *re-,* again, over + *voir,* to see, from Latin *vidēre.*] —**re·view·a·ble** *adj.*

re·view·al (rĭ-vyōō′əl) *n.* The act or an instance of reviewing.

re·view·er (rĭ-vyōō′ər) *n.* One who reviews; specifically, a critic writing for a newspaper or magazine.

re·vile (rĭ-vīl′) *v.* **-viled, -viling, -viles.** —*tr.* To denounce with abusive language; rail against. —*intr.* To use abusive language. —See Synonyms at **malign, scold.** [Middle English *revilen,* from Old French *reviler* : *re-* (intensive), again + *vil,* VILE.] —**re·vile·ment** *n.* —**re·vil·er** *n.* —**re·vil·ing·ly** *adv.*

re·vis·al (rĭ-vī′zəl) *n.* The act of revising; revision.

re·vise (rĭ-vīz′) *v.* **-vised, -vising, -vises.** —*tr.* **1.** To change or modify: *revise an earlier opinion.* **2.** To prepare a newly edited version of (a text). **3.** *Chiefly British.* To review (academic work), especially in preparation for an examination. —*intr.* To make revisions. —See Synonyms at **correct.**

—*n.* (rē′vīz′, rĭ-vīz′). *Abbr.* **rev.** *Printing.* A proof made from an earlier proof on which corrections have been made. [Latin *revīsere,* to look back : *re-,* again, back + *vīsere,* look at, from *vidēre* (past participle *vīsus*), to see.] —**re·vis·a·ble** *adj.* —**re·vis·er** *n.*

Revised Standard Version *n. Abbr.* **R.S.V.** A modern American revision (1946–57) of the American Standard edition of the English Bible, in the King James tradition.

Revised Version *n. Abbr.* **R.V., Rev. Ver.** A revision of the King James Version of the Bible, prepared by a committee of scholars from Britain and the United States (1870–84).

re·vi·sion (rĭ-vĭzh′ən) *n. Abbr.* **rev. 1.** The act or procedure of revising. **2.** The result of revising; a corrected or new version. —**re·vi·sion·al, re·vi·sion·ar·y** (rĭ-vĭzh′ə-nĕr′ē) *adj.*

re·vi·sion·ism (rĭ-vĭzh′ə-nĭz′əm) *n.* **1.** A policy of modification or change, especially of a political or religious doctrine. **2.** *Often* **Revisionism.** A recurrent tendency within the Communist movement to revise Marxist theory in such a way as to provide justification for a retreat from the original doctrine. Often used derogatorily. —**re·vi·sion·ist** *n. & adj.*

re·vis·it (rē-vĭz′ĭt) *tr.v.* **-ited, -iting, -its.** To visit again.

—*n.* A second or repeated visit. —**re·vis·i·ta·tion** *n.*

re·vi·so·ry (rĭ-vī′zə-rē) *adj.* Of, pertaining to, effecting, or having the power of revision.

re·vi·tal·ize (rē-vīt′l-īz′) *tr.v.* **-ized, -izing, -izes.** To impart new life or vigor to; restore the vitality of. —**re·vi·tal·i·za·tion** *n.*

re·viv·al (rĭ-vī′vəl) *n.* **1.** The act of reviving or the condition of being revived. **2. a.** A restoration to use, acceptance, activity, or vigor after a period of obscurity or quiescence. **b.** A return to use or fashion, as of former styles, manners, or activities: *the Gothic Revival.* **3.** A new presentation of an old play, motion picture, ballet, or other theatrical work. **4.** A reawakening of faith or interest in religion. **5.** An evangelistic meeting or series of meetings for the purpose of reawakening religious faith, often characterized by impassioned preaching and public declarations of faith.

re·viv·al·ism (rĭ-vī′və-lĭz′əm) *n.* **1.** The spirit or activities characteristic of religious revivals. **2.** A movement or tendency to revive practices or ideas of an earlier time.

re·viv·al·ist (rĭ-vī′və-lĭst) *n.* **1.** A person who promotes or leads religious revivals. **2.** A person who revives practices or ideas of an earlier time. —**re·viv·al·ist, re·viv·al·is·tic** *adj.*

re·vive (rĭ-vīv′) *v.* **-vived, -viving, -vives.** —*tr.* **1.** To bring back to life or consciousness; resuscitate. **2.** To impart new health, vigor, or spirit to: *The nap revived me.* **3.** To restore to use, currency, activity, or notice: *revive an old custom.* **4.** To restore the validity or effectiveness of. **5.** To renew in the mind; recall. **6. a.** To put on a new production of (a stage work). **b.** To present (an old motion picture) again. **7.** To bring back (a former artistic style, for example) into popularity or fashion. —*intr.* **1.** To return to life or consciousness. **2.** To regain health, vigor, or good spirits. **3.** To return to use, currency, or notice; flourish again. **4.** To return to validity, effectiveness, or operative condition. [Middle English *reviven,* from Old French *revivre,* from Late Latin *revīvere* : Latin *re-,* again + *vīvere,* to live.] —**re·viv·er** *n.*

re·viv·i·fy (rē-vĭv′ə-fī′) *tr.v.* **-fied, -fying, -fies.** To impart new life to. [French *revivifier,* from Late Latin *revīvificāre* : *re-,* again + *vīvificāre,* to VIVIFY.] —**re·viv·i·fi·ca·tion** (rē-vĭv′ə-fĭ-kā′shən) *n.*

rev·i·vis·cence (rĕv′ə-vĭs′əns) *n.* A return to life or vigor; a revival. [Late Latin *reviviscentia,* from Latin *reviviscere,* "to start to live again," ultimately from *vivere,* to live.] —**rev·i·vis·cent** *adj.*

rev·o·ca·ble, re·vok·a·ble (rĕv′ə-kə-bəl, rĭ-vō′-) *adj.* Capable of being revoked. —**rev·o·ca·bil·i·ty, rev·o·ca·ble·ness** *n.* —**rev·o·ca·bly** *adv.*

rev·o·ca·tion (rĕv′ə-kā′shən) *n.* The act of revoking, or the condition of being revoked; cancellation; repeal. —**rev·o·ca·to·ry** (rĕv′ə-kə-tôr′ē, -tōr′ē) *adj.*

re·voke (rĭ-vōk′) *v.* **-voked, -voking, -vokes.** —*tr.* To void or annul by recalling, withdrawing, or reversing; cancel; rescind: *revoke a decree.* —*intr.* In card games, to fail to follow suit when one is required and able to do so. —See Synonyms at **nullify.**

—*n.* In card games, an act of revoking; a failure to follow suit. [Middle English *revoken,* from Old French *revoquer,* from Latin *revocāre,* to call back : *re-,* back + *vocāre,* to call.] —**re·vok·er** *n.*

re·volt (rĭ-vōlt′) *v.* **-volted, -volting, -volts.** —*intr.* **1.** To institute or take part in a rebellion against authority, especially that of the state; rebel or mutiny. **2.** To be affected by or turn away in disgust or revulsion. Used with *against, at,* or *from.* —*tr.* To fill with disgust or abhorrence; repel.

—*n.* **1.** An uprising against state authority; a rebellion. **2.** Any act of protest or rejection: *a citizen's revolt against high taxes.* **3.** The state of a person or persons in rebellion: *be in revolt.* —See Synonyms at **rebellion.** [French *révolter,* from Italian *rivoltare,* from Vulgar Latin *revolvitāre* (unattested), from Latin *revolvere,* to roll back, REVOLVE.] —**re·volt·er** *n.*

re·volt·ing (rĭ-vōl′tĭng) *adj.* **1.** Causing disgust; repulsive; abhorrent. **2.** *Informal.* Nasty; disagreeable. —**re·volt·ing·ly** *adv.*

rev·o·lute (rĕv′ə-lōōt′) *adj. Botany.* Rolled back on the undersurface from the tip or margins, as some leaves are. [Latin *revolūtus,* past participle of *revolvere,* to roll back, REVOLVE.]

rev·o·lu·tion (rĕv′ə-lōō′shən) *n. Abbr.* **rev. 1.** A sudden political overthrow brought about from within a given system, especially: **a.** A forcible substitution of rulers or of ruling groups: *a palace revolution.* **b.** Seizure of state power by the militant vanguard of a subject class or nation. —See Synonyms at **rebellion. 2.** Activity aimed at overthrowing a government or social system. **3.** A recognizably momentous change in any situation, field, or sphere of activity: *the revolution in physics.* **4. a.** Orbital motion around a point, especially as distinguished from axial rotation: *the earth's revolution around the sun.* **b.** A turning or rotational motion around an axis. **c.** A single complete cycle of such orbital or axial motion. [Middle English *revolucioun,* from Old French *revolution,* from Late Latin *revolūtiō* (stem *revolūtiōn-*), from Latin *revolvere* (past participle *revolūtus*), REVOLVE.]

rev·o·lu·tion·ar·y (rĕv′ə-lōō′shə-nĕr′ē) *adj.* **1.** Of, pertaining to, or bringing about a political or social revolution. **2.** Characterized by or resulting in radical change: *a revolutionary discovery.* **3.** Completely original or new and disruptive of the old: *a revolutionary approach to public relations.* **4.** Moving in circles; revolving. **5. Revolutionary. a.** Of or pertaining to any of various revolutions, especially the French Revolution. **b.** Of or pertaining to the activities or period of the American Revolution.

—*n., pl.* **revolutionaries.** Also **rev·o·lu·tion·ist** (-nĭst). One who advocates or fights in a revolution.

Revolutionary calendar *n.* The calendar introduced in France on October 24, 1793, by the National Convention and abolished under Napoleon on December 31, 1805. It reckoned time from September 22, 1792, the date of the founding of the First Republic, and divided the year into ten months. Also called "Republican calendar."

Revolutionary War *n.* The **American Revolution** *(see).*

rev·o·lu·tion·ize (rĕv′ə-lōō′shə-nīz′) *tr.v.* **-ized, -izing, -izes. 1.** To bring about a radical change in; alter extensively or drastically. **2.** To cause (a country) to undergo a political, industrial, or social revolution. **3.** To imbue with revolutionary principles. —**rev·o·lu·tion·iz·er** *n.*

re·volve (rĭ-vŏlv′) *v.* **-volved, -volving, -volves.** —*intr.* **1.** To orbit a

central point: *Planets, asteroids, and comets revolve around the sun.*
2. To turn on an axis; rotate. **3.** To recur in cycles or at periodic intervals. **4.** To have a central theme or concern; center: *The discussion revolved around politics.* —*tr.* **1.** To cause to revolve. **2.** To think over (a problem); ponder or reflect on. —See Synonyms at **turn.** [Middle English *revolven*, from Latin *revolvere*, to roll back : *re-*, back + *volvere*, to roll.] —**re·volv·a·ble** *adj.*

re·volv·er (rĭ-vŏl'vər) *n.* **1.** A pistol having a revolving cylinder with several cartridge chambers. **2.** One that revolves.

revolving credit *n.* **1.** *Finance.* A bank credit that can be drawn on either for a limited total amount that is renewable as soon as it is paid back or a limited amount at any one time, with no limit on the number of times. **2.** A form of credit made available to customers of a retail shop, whereby they are allowed a constant stipulated amount of credit in return for regular payment to the shop.

revolving door *n.* A door having several partitions attached to a central axis on which it turns, thus keeping out drafts.

revolving fund *n.* *Finance.* A fund of money from which loans or investments are made, which is kept at a constant level by repayment of the loans with interest or by the returns from the investments that it finances.

Rev·son (rĕv'sən), **Charles** (1906–75). U.S. cosmetics tycoon. With $300 in capital and some experience as a nail-polish salesman, he founded a cosmetics company called Revlon with his two brothers and a chemist (1932). Under his leadership the company expanded and diversified and at the time of his death manufactured 3,000 products and had annual sales of more than $600 million.

re·vue, re·view (rĭ-vyōō') *n.* An entertainment consisting of sketches, songs, and dances, often satirizing current events, trends, and personalities. [French, from Old French, past participle of *revoir*, to REVIEW.]

re·vul·sion (rĭ-vŭl'shən) *n.* **1.** A sudden and strong change or reaction in feeling; especially, a feeling of violent disgust or loathing. **2.** A withdrawing or turning away from something. **3.** *Medicine.* Treatment of a diseased part or organ by diverting the blood to another part of the body, as by counterirritation. [Latin *revulsiō* (stem *revulsiōn-*), from *revellere* (past participle *revulsus*), to pull back or away : *re-*, back + *vellere*, to pull, tear.]

re·vul·sive (rĭ-vŭl'sĭv) *n. Medicine.* A substance that produces revulsion. [REVULS(ION) + -IVE.] —**re·vul·sive** *adj.*

Rev. Ver. Revised Version (of the Bible).

re·ward (rĭ-wôrd') *n.* **1. a.** Something given or received in recompense for worthy behavior or a service rendered. **b.** Requital or retribution for harm done. **2.** Money offered for some special service, such as the return of a lost article or the capture of a criminal. **3.** A satisfying return or result; a profit. —See Synonyms at **bonus.** ~*tr.v.* **rewarded, -warding, -wards. 1.** To bestow a reward on. **2.** To give a reward because of or in return for: *They rewarded his bravery with a medal.* **3.** To satisfy or gratify: *Her patience was rewarded.* [Middle English *rewarden*, to heed, regard, reward, from Norman French *rewarder*, "to look at" : *re-* (intensive) + *warder*, to watch over, from Germanic.] —**re·ward·er** *n.*

re·ward·ing (rĭ-wôr'dĭng) *adj.* Worthwhile or gratifying: *a rewarding experience.* —**re·ward·ing·ly** *adv.*

re·wind (rē-wīnd') *tr.v.* **-wound** (-wound'), **-winding, -winds.** To wind again or anew. ~*n.* (rē'wīnd'). The act or process of rewinding something, such as film or tape. —**re·wind·er** *n.*

re·wire (rē-wīr') *tr.v.* **-wired, -wiring, -wires.** To provide with new wiring.

re·word (rē-wûrd') *tr.v.* **-worded, -wording, -words.** To state, express, or compose again using different words.

re·work (rē-wûrk') *tr.v.* **-worked, -working, -works. 1.** To work over again; revise or rewrite. **2.** To use (a theme or metaphor, for example) in a new or different context, often in an altered form. **3.** To subject to a repeated or new process.

re·write (rē-rīt') *tr.v.* **-wrote** (-rōt'), **-written** (-rĭt'n), **-writing, -writes.** To write again, especially in a different form. ~*n.* (rē'rīt'). Something that has been rewritten. —**re·writ·er** *n.*

rex (rĕks) *n., pl.* **rexes. 1.** A genetic variation, as of a domestic rabbit, in which the guard hairs of the fur are very short or lacking. **2.** Any of a breed of domestic cats having no guard hairs and very short, curly underfur. [From French *castorrex*, a breed of rabbit, from Latin *castor*, beaver + *rēx*, king.]

Rex (rĕks) *n. Abbr.* **R.** The reigning king. Used as a title and signature on documents. [Latin *rēx*, king.]

Rex·roth (rĕks'rŏth'), **Kenneth** (1905–82). U.S. poet, painter, and critic. Providing a link between the modernist poets such as Ezra Pound and the beat-generation poets such as Allen Ginsberg, he combined sensitive imagery with strong social concerns. His poetry, artwork, and criticism helped broaden the audience for contemporary art.

Rey·kja·vik or **Rey·kja·vik** (rā'kyə-vēk') Capital and chief port of Iceland, on Faxaflói Bay in the southwest of the country. The center of the cod-fishing industry, it is the commercial and industrial hub of Iceland.

Rey·nard (rā'nərd, -närd', rĕn'ərd) *n.* The fox, as personified in folklore and fable.

Reyn·olds (rĕn'əldz), **Sir Joshua** (1723–92). British painter, the first president of the Royal Academy. He was the leading painter of his day and one of the most important in the history of English painting. In the course of his lifetime he painted more than 2,000 historical subjects and portraits.

Reynolds number *n. Physics.* A dimensionless number characterizing the type of flow in a fluid, used especially in the study of the effects of viscosity and velocity control in fluid systems. [After Osborne *Reynolds* (1842–1912), British physicist.]

Re·za Shah Pah·la·vi (rā'zə shä pä'lə-vē'), born Reza Khan (1877–1944). Iranian soldier, shah of Iran from 1925 to 1941. In 1935 he officially changed the name of Persia to its older name, Iran, He did much to modernize Iranian life, but in 1941 Soviet and British forces occupied Iran and forced him to abdicate in favor of his son Muhammad Reza Shah.

RF radio frequency.

R factor *n* A genetic element in bacteria that gives them immunity or resistance to antibiotics and is transmitted from one bacterium to another by conjugation. [Resistance *factor.*]

RFD, R.F.D. rural free delivery.

Rh 1. The symbol for the element rhodium. **2.** rhesus. See **Rh factor.**

r.h. 1. relative humidity. **2.** right hand.

rhab·do·man·cy (răb'də-măn'sē) *n.* Divination by means of a wand or a rod, especially in searching for underground water or ores. [Late Greek *rhabdomanteia* : *rhabdos*, rod + -MANCY.] —**rhab·do·man·cer** *n.*

rhab·do·my·o·ma (răb'dō-mī-ō'mə) *n., pl.* **-mas** or **-mata** (-mə-tə). *Pathology.* A benign tumor in striated muscular fibers. [New Latin, from Greek *rhabdos*, rod + MYOMA.]

rhab·do·vi·rus (răb'də-vī'rəs) *n.* Any of a group of RNA-containing plant and animal viruses that include the rabies virus. [Greek *rhabdos*, rod + VIRUS.]

Rhad·a·man·thine (răd'ə-măn'thĭn, -thīn') *adj.* Of or characteristic of Rhadamanthus; especially, rigorously and uncompromisingly adhering to the letter of the law.

Rhad·a·man·thus (răd'ə-măn'thəs). *Greek Mythology.* The judge of the dead in the underworld.

Rhae·ti·a (rē'shē-ə, -shə). An ancient Alpine Roman province that included portions of modern Switzerland and Austria. —**Rhae·ti·an** *adj. & n.*

Rhae·to-Ro·man·ic (rē'tō-rō-măn'ĭk) *adj.* Also **Rhae·to-Ro·mance** (-rō-măns'). Of or belonging to a group of closely related Romance dialects spoken in southern Switzerland, northern Italy, and the Tyrol. ~*n.* Also **Rhae·to-Ro·mance.** These dialects considered as a distinct Romance language.

rhaphe. Variant of **raphe.**

rhap·sod·ic (răp-sŏd'ĭk) *adj.* Also **rhap·sod·i·cal** (-ĭ-kəl). **1.** Of, resembling, or characteristic of a rhapsody. **2.** Impassioned or enthusiastic; ecstatic. —**rhap·sod·i·cal·ly** *adv.*

rhap·so·dist (răp'sə-dĭst) *n.* Also **rhap·sode** (-sōd'). **1.** In ancient Greece, a reciter of epic poetry, especially of the works of Homer. **2.** A person who uses extravagantly enthusiastic or impassioned language.

rhap·so·dize (răp'sə-dīz') *v.* **-dized, -dizing, -dizes.** —*intr.* To express oneself in an immoderately enthusiastic manner. —*tr.* To recite in the manner of a rhapsody.

rhap·so·dy (răp'sə-dē) *n., pl.* **-dies. 1. a.** Exalted or excessively enthusiastic expression of feeling in speech or writing. **b.** *Often* **rhapsodies.** An extravagant expression of enthusiasm. **2.** In ancient Greece, an epic poem, or a portion of one, suitable for uninterrupted recitation. **3.** A literary work written in an impassioned or exalted style. **4.** *Music.* A composition that is free or irregular in form, often improvisatory in character, and typically has a melodic content based on folk tunes. [Latin *rhapsōdia*, from Greek *rhapsōidia*, from *rhapsōidos*, "weaver of songs," rhapsodist : *rhaptein*, to sew together + *ōidē*, song.]

rhat·a·ny (răt'n-ē) *n., pl.* **-nies. 1.** Either of two South American shrubs, *Krameria triandra* or *K. argentea*, having thick, fleshy roots. **2.** The dried root of either of these plants, formerly used as an astringent. Also called "krameria." [Spanish *ratania*, from Quechua *ratánya*.]

rhbdr. rhombohedron.

rhe·a (rē'ə) *n.* Any of several flightless South American birds of the genus *Rhea*, resembling the ostrich but somewhat smaller and having three toes instead of two. [New Latin *Rhea*, arbitrarily named after RHEA.]

Rhe·a (rē'ə). *Greek Mythology.* One of the Titans, the wife of Cronos and mother of Zeus.

rhe·bok, ree·bok (rē'bŏk') *n.* An antelope, *Pelea capreolus*, that is found in southern Africa and has brownish-gray hair. [From Dutch *reebok*, ROEBUCK.]

Rhee (rē), **Syngman** (1875–1965). Korean politician, president of South Korea (1948–60). After World War II he was a key figure in the administration of American-occupied South Korea, and in 1948 he became the first president of the Republic of Korea. He was re-elected in 1952, 1956, and 1960, but in May 1960 he was forced from office by public demonstrations and went into exile in Hawaii.

Rheims. See **Reims.**

Rhein. See **Rhine.**

Rheinland-Pfalz. See **Rhineland-Palatinate.**

rhe·mat·ic (rĭ-măt'ĭk) *adj.* **1.** Of or pertaining to word formation. **2.** Derived from or pertaining to a verb. [Greek *rhēmatikos*, from *rhēma*, word, verb.]

Rhen·ish (rĕn'ĭsh) *adj.* Of or pertaining to the river Rhine or the lands bordering on it. ~*n.* **Rhine wine** (see).

rhe·ni·um (rē'nē-əm) *n. Symbol* **Re** A rare dense silvery-white me-

rhea The large flightless rhea resembles the ostrich and is native to South America. It is the male bird that builds the nest and incubates the eggs.

rhesus monkey *A reddish-brown species of macaque found in Southeast Asia and considered sacred in some parts of India. One of the most widely used research animals, the rhesus monkey was important in the discovery of the Rh, or rhesus, factor in human blood.*

rhinoceros *A hoofed mammal found in Africa and Asia, the rhinoceros is chiefly solitary and lives on leaves and grass. Some of its five species have a single horn, but others—such as the African black (above)—have two.*

tallic element with a very high melting point. It is used for electrical contacts and with tungsten for high-temperature thermocouples. Atomic number 75, atomic weight 186.2, melting point 3,180°C, boiling point 5,627°C, specific gravity 21.02, valences 1, 2, 3, 4, 5, 6, 7. [New Latin, from Latin *Rhēnus,* the RHINE.]

rheo– *prefix.* Indicates a flow or current; for example, **rheology.** [From Greek *rheos,* current, stream, from *rhein,* to flow.]

rhe·o·base (rē′ō-bās′) *n.* The weakest nerve impulse that is needed to produce a response in a tissue.

rhe·ol·o·gy (rē-ŏl′ə-jē) *n.* The study of the deformation and flow of matter. [RHEO- + -LOGY.] **—rhe·o·log·i·cal** (rē′ə-lŏj′ĭ-kəl) *adj.* **—rhe·ol·o·gist** *n.*

rhe·om·e·ter (rē-ŏm′ə-tər) *n.* An instrument for measuring the flow of viscous liquids, as of blood. [RHEO- + -METER.]

rhe·o·stat (rē′ə-stăt′) *n.* A continuously variable electrical resistor used to regulate current, typically having a coil of wire with a sliding contact. [RHEO- + -STAT.] **—rhe·o·stat·ic** *adj.*

rhe·o·tax·is (rē′ə-tăk′sĭs) *n.* The movement of an organism in response to a current, usually of water. [RHEO- + -TAXIS.] **—rhe·o·tac·tic** *adj.*

rhe·sus baby (rē′səs) *n.* A baby affected by **hemolytic disease** *(see).*

rhesus factor *n.* **Rh factor** *(see).*

rhesus monkey *n.* A brownish macaque monkey, *Macaca mulatta,* of India, used extensively in biological experimentation. [New Latin *rhesus,* arbitrarily from Latin *Rhēsus,* name of a mythological king of Thrace.]

rhe·tor (rē′tôr′, -tər) *n.* **1.** A teacher of rhetoric in ancient Greece or Rome. **2.** An orator. [Middle English, from Medieval Latin *rēthor,* from Greek *rhētōr.*]

rhet·o·ric (rĕt′ər-ĭk) *n. Abbr.* **rhet. 1.** The study of the elements used in literature and public speaking, such as content, structure, cadence, and style. **2.** The art of oratory, especially the persuasive use of language to influence the thoughts and actions of listeners. **3. a.** Affectation, grandiloquence, or insincerity in speech or writing. **b.** Speech or writing that is impressive or persuasive, but often insincere or empty. [Middle English *rethorik,* from Old French *rethorique,* from Latin *rhētorica,* from Greek *rhētorikē (tekhnē),* "rhetorical (art)," from *rhētorikos,* rhetorical, from *rhētōr,* RHETOR.]

rhe·tor·i·cal (rĭ-tôr′ĭ-kəl, rĭ-tŏr′-) *adj.* **1.** Concerned primarily with style or effect; showy, inflated, or insincere. **2.** Of or pertaining to rhetoric; oratorical. **—rhe·tor·i·cal·ly** *adv.*

rhetorical question *n.* A question to which no answer is required or expected, or to which only one answer may be made.

rhet·o·ri·cian (rĕt′ə-rĭsh′ən) *n.* **1.** An expert in or teacher of rhetoric. **2.** An eloquent speaker or writer. **3.** One given to verbal extravagance.

rheum (ro͞om) *n.* A watery or thin mucous discharge from the eyes or nose. [Middle English *reume,* from Old French, from Latin *rheuma,* from Greek, stream, humor of the body, rheum, from *rhein,* to flow.] **—rheum·y** *adj.*

rheu·mat·ic (ro͞o-măt′ĭk) *adj.* Of, pertaining to, or afflicted with rheumatism.
~*n.* **1.** A person suffering from rheumatism. **2. rheumatics.** *Informal.* Pains due to rheumatism. [Middle English *rewmatyk,* from Latin *rheumaticus,* troubled with rheum, from Greek *rheumatikos,* subject to rheum, from *rheuma,* stream, body humor, RHEUM.]

rheumatic fever *n.* A severe disease occurring chiefly in children as a complication of streptococcal infection of the throat, characterized by fever and painful inflammation of the joints, and frequently resulting in permanent damage to the valves of the heart.

rheu·mat·ick·y (ro͞o-măt′ĭ-kē) *adj. Informal.* Suffering from stiffness or pain in the joints, such as that caused by rheumatism.

rheu·ma·tism (ro͞o′mə-tĭz′əm) *n.* Any of several disorders, such as fibrositis and rheumatoid arthritis, that affect the muscles, tendons, joints, or bones, and are characterized by discomfort and disability. [Latin *rheumatismus,* rheum, catarrh, from Greek *rheumatismos,* from *rheumatizesthai,* to suffer from a flux, from *rheuma,* stream, flux, RHEUM.]

rheu·ma·toid (ro͞o′mə-toid′) *adj.* Of, resembling, or afflicted with rheumatism. **—rheu·ma·toi·dal·ly** *adv.*

rheumatoid arthritis *n.* A chronic disease marked by stiffness and inflammation of the membranes of the joints, weakness, loss of mobility, and deformity.

rheumatoid factor *n.* An antibody present in the blood serum of many patients with rheumatoid arthritis that can be a means of diagnosing the disease.

rheu·ma·tol·o·gy (ro͞o′mə-tŏl′ə-jē) *n.* The branch of medicine concerned with the diagnosis and treatment of rheumatic diseases. [RHEUMAT(ISM) + -LOGY.] **—rheu·ma·tol·o·gist** *n.*

Rh factor *n.* Any of several antigens on the surface of red blood cells of Rh positive blood that induce adverse reactions with blood cells that lack these antigens (Rh negative cells). Also called "rhesus factor." [First discovered in the blood of RHESUS MONKEYS.]

rhi·nal (rī′nəl) *adj.* Of or pertaining to the nose; nasal.

Rhine (rīn). *German* **Rhein.** *French* **Rhin** (răN). *Dutch* **Rijn.** Longest river in western Europe, *c.* 1,320 kilometers (820 miles) long. Its two principal headwaters, the Vorder Rhine and Hinter Rhine, rise in the Swiss Alps and join near Chur to form the Rhine proper. The Rhine carries more traffic than any other waterway in the world. The chief commodities that are transported are iron ore, coal, petroleum, sand, gravel, and steel products. Canals link the river with the Meuse, Rhône-Saône, Marne, and Danube valleys, thus forming a comprehensive waterway network.

Rhine·land (rīn′lănd′, -lənd). A historic region in modern West Germany, consisting of those areas adjoining the Rhine.

Rhine·land-Pa·lat·i·nate (rīn′lănd′pə-lăt′n-āt′, -ĭt). *German* **Rhein·land-Pfalz** (rīn′länt-pfäls′). State in West Germany. It consists of forested uplands intersected by fertile river valleys, the chief rivers being the Rhine and the Moselle. The cultivation of vines is widespread, and some of Germany's best-known wines are produced here. The state is nevertheless heavily industrialized. Mainz is the capital.

rhi·nen·ceph·a·lon (rī′nĕn-sĕf′ə-lŏn′, -lən) *n., pl.* **-la** (-lə). The olfactory region of the brain, in the cerebrum. [RHIN(O)- + ENCEPHALON.] **—rhi·nen·ce·phal·ic** (rī′nĕn-sə-făl′ĭk) *adj.*

rhine·stone (rīn′stōn′) *n.* A colorless, artificial gem of paste or glass, often with facets that sparkle in imitation of diamond. [Translation of French *caillou du Rhin;* originally made at Strasbourg, France.]

Rhine wine *n.* **1.** Any of several typically white wines produced in the Rhine valley. **2.** Any similar light, dry wine produced elsewhere. Also called "Rhenish."

rhi·ni·tis (rī-nī′tĭs) *n.* Inflammation of the nasal mucous membranes, as occurs in the common cold. [New Latin : RHIN(O)- + -ITIS.]

rhi·no¹ (rī′nō) *n., pl.* **-nos.** *Informal.* A rhinoceros.

rhino² *n. British Slang.* Money; cash. Not in current usage. [17th century : origin obscure.]

rhino–, rhin– *prefix.* Indicates nose or nasal; for example, **rhinoscopy, rhinitis.** [Greek *rhis*† (stem *rhin-*), nose.]

rhi·noc·er·os (rī-nŏs′ər-əs) *n., pl.* **-oses** or collectively **rhinoceros.** Any of several large, thick-skinned, herbivorous mammals of the family Rhinocerotidae, of Africa and Asia, having one or two upright horns on the snout. An example is the one-horned Indian rhinoceros, *Rhinoceros unicornis.* [Middle English *rinoceros,* from Latin *rhīnocerōs,* from Greek *rhinokerōs,* "nose-horned" : RHINO- + *keras,* horn.] **—rhi·noc·e·rot·ic** (rī-nŏs′ə-rŏt′ĭk) *adj.*

rhinoceros beetle *n.* Any of several scarabaeid beetles having one or more horns on the head, such as *Oryctes rhinoceros,* a pest of oriental coconut palms.

rhinoceros bird *n.* The **oxpecker** *(see).*

rhi·nol·o·gy (rī-nŏl′ə-jē) *n.* The anatomy, physiology, and pathology of the nose. [RHINO- + -LOGY.] **—rhi·nol·o·gist** *n.*

rhi·no·plas·ty (rī′nō-plăs′tē, -nə-) *n.* Plastic surgery of the nose. [RHINO- + -PLASTY.] **—rhi·no·plas·tic** *adj.*

rhi·nos·co·py (rī-nŏs′kə-pē) *n.* Examination of the nasal passages. [RHINO- + -SCOPY.]

rhi·no·vi·rus (rī′nō-vī′rəs) *n* Any of a group of RNA-containing viruses that cause the common cold and other infections of the respiratory tract.

rhizo–, rhiz– *prefix.* Indicates a root; for example, **rhizomorphous, rhizoid.** [Greek *rhiza,* root.]

rhi·zo·bi·um (rī-zō′bē-əm) *n., pl.* **-bia** (-bē-ə). Any of various nitrogen-fixing bacteria of the genus *Rhizobium* that form nodules on the roots of leguminous plants such as clover and beans. [New Latin *Rhizobium* : RHIZO- + Greek *bios,* life.]

rhi·zo·carp (rī′zō-kärp′) *n.* **1.** A plant having persistent roots but stems and leaves that die down at the end of each growing season. **2.** A plant that produces subterranean flowers and fruit. [RHIZO- + -CARP.] **—rhi·zo·car·pous** *adj.*

rhi·zo·ceph·a·lan (rī′zō-sĕf′ə-lən) *n.* Any of various small aquatic crustaceans of the order Rhizocephala that are parasitic on other crustaceans. [New Latin *Rhizocephala,* "root-headed ones" (from the rootlike processes extending from the limbless body) : RHIZO- + *-cephala,* from *-cephalus,* -CEPHALOUS.] **—rhi·zo·ceph·a·lous** *adj.*

rhi·zo·gen·ic (rī′zō-jĕn′ĭk) *adj.* Also **rhi·zo·ge·net·ic** (-jə-nĕt′ĭk), **rhi·zog·e·nous** (rī-zŏj′ə-nəs). *Botany.* Giving rise to roots: *rhizogenic tissue.* [RHIZO- + -GENIC.]

rhi·zoid (rī′zoid′) *adj.* Rootlike.
~*n.* **1.** A slender, rootlike filament by which mosses, liverworts, and ferns attach to the substratum and absorb nourishment. **2.** A rootlike extension of the thallus of a fungus. [RHIZ(O)- + -OID.] **—rhi·zoi·dal** *adj.*

rhi·zome (rī′zōm′) *n. Botany.* A rootlike, usually horizontal stem growing under or along the ground, and sending out roots from its lower surface and leaves or shoots from its upper surface. Also called "rootstock," "rootstalk." [New Latin *rhizoma,* from Greek *rhizōma,* mass of roots of a tree, from *rhizousthai,* to take root, from *rhiza,* root.] **—rhi·zom·a·tous** (rī-zŏm′ə-təs, -zō′mə-təs) *adj.*

rhi·zo·morph (rī′zō-môrf′) *n.* A rootlike part, such as the threadlike structure in certain fungi, consisting of strands of hyphae. [RHIZO- + -MORPH.]

rhi·zo·mor·phous (rī′zō-môr′fəs) *adj. Botany.* Having the form of a root. [RHIZO- + -MORPHOUS.]

rhi·zoph·a·gous (rī-zŏf′ə-gəs) *adj.* Feeding on roots. [RHIZO- + -PHAGOUS.]

rhi·zo·pod (rī′zō-pŏd′) *n.* Any protozoan of the class Rhizopoda, such as an amoeba, characteristically moving and taking in food by means of pseudopodia. [New Latin *Rhizopoda,* "root-footed" (from its rootlike pseudopodia) : RHIZO- + -POD.] **—rhi·zop·o·dan** (rī-zŏp′ə-dən) *adj. & n.* **—rhi·zop·o·dous** *adj.*

rhi·zo·pus (rī′zō-pəs) *n.* Any of various often destructive fungi of the genus *Rhizopus,* such as *R. nigricans,* the common bread mold. [New Latin, "one having rootlike feet" (from its rhizoids) : RHIZO- + Greek *pous,* foot (see **-pod**).]

rhi·zo·sphere (rī′zə-sfîr′) *n.* The soil immediately surrounding the root system of a plant.

rhi·zot·o·my (rī-zŏt′ə-mē) *n., pl.* **-mies.** Surgical severance of spinal nerve roots to relieve severe pain or muscle spasm. [RHIZO- + -TOMY.]

Rh negative *adj.* Lacking an **Rh factor** *(see).*

rho (rō) *n.* The 17th letter in the Greek alphabet written P, ρ. Transliterated in English as *rh* or *r.* See feature at **alphabet.** [Greek *rhō,* perhaps shortened from *rhōs,* head, of Semitic origin, akin to Hebrew *rēsh, rōsh,* "head," RESH.]

rho·da·mine (rō′də-mēn′) *n.* Any of several synthetic red to pink dyes. [RHOD(O)- + AMINE (the dyes are prepared from aminophenol).]

Rhode Island (rōd). *Abbr.* **R.I.** State in New England, northeastern United States. It is the smallest state in the Union, but one of the most densely populated. Manufacturing is the chief industry, metalwares, textiles, and plastics being the main products. Fishing and tourism are important, and the state's resorts include Newport. Providence is the capital.

Rhode Island Red *n.* A domestic fowl of an American breed having dark reddish-brown feathers and producing brown eggs.

Rhodes (rōdz). Largest island in the Greek Dodecanese group, lying off the southwestern coast of Turkey. The interior is mountainous, but the island has fertile coastal strips and valleys where wheat, tobacco, cotton, olives, vines, oranges, and vegetables are grown. Tourism is also economically important. Rhodes, the capital, was founded in 408 B.C. and was the site of the Colossus of Rhodes, one of the Seven Wonders of the World, which was destroyed (*c.* 244 B.C.) by an earthquake.

Rhodes, Cecil John (1853–1902). British industrialist and imperialist. In 1870 he went to South Africa and a year later staked a claim in the Kimberley diamond fields. In 1880 he founded the De Beers Mining Company, and he organized the British South Africa Company in 1889, thus gaining a virtual monopoly over mining in South Africa. In 1890 he became prime minister of the Cape Colony, but was forced to resign (1896) after being implicated in the Jameson Raid of 1895. He spent the rest of his life developing Rhodesia (Zimbabwe). He left a large fortune, most of which he willed to public causes such as the Rhodes scholarships.

Rhodesia. See **Zimbabwe.** —**Rho·de·sian** *adj. & n.*

Rho·de·sia and Ny·as·a·land (rō-dē′zhə; nī-ăs′ə-lănd′). From 1953 to 1963 a federation in central Africa consisting of the self-governing colony of Southern Rhodesia (now Zimbabwe) and the British protectorates of Northern Rhodesia (now Zambia) and Nyasaland (now Malawi).

Rhodesian man *n.* An extinct species of man, with a low forehead and massive brow ridges, whose fossil remains were found in central Zambia (formerly Northern Rhodesia), now classified as *Homo sapiens rhodesiensis.*

Rhodesian ridgeback *n.* A large dog of a breed developed in Africa, having short, yellowish-tan hair that forms a ridge along the back. Also called "ridgeback."

Rhodes scholarship *n.* A scholarship available to students from the United States and certain other countries to study at Oxford University. —**Rhodes scholar** *n.*

rho·di·um (rō′dē-əm) *n. Symbol* **Rh** A hard, durable, silvery-white metallic element that is used to form high-temperature alloys with platinum and is plated on other metals to produce a durable corrosion-resistant coating. Atomic number 45, atomic weight 102.905, melting point 1,966°C, boiling point 3,727°C, specific gravity 12.41, valences 2, 3, 4, 5, 6. [New Latin, "rose red" (from the color of its compounds), from Greek *rhodon,* rose.]

rhodo-, rhod- *prefix.* Indicates rose or rose-red; for example, **rho·dolite.** [Greek *rhodon,* rose.]

rho·do·chro·site (rō′də-krō′sīt′) *n.* A naturally occurring impure form of manganese carbonate, $MnCO_3$, light-pink to rose-red in color with a pearly or vitreous luster, used as a manganese ore. [German *Rhodochrosit :* RHODO- + Greek *khrōsis,* coloring, from *khrōs, khroos,* color, skin + -ITE.]

rho·do·den·dron (rō′də-dĕn′drən) *n.* Any of various evergreen shrubs of the widely cultivated genus *Rhododendron,* of the North Temperate Zone, having clusters of variously colored flowers. See **azalea.** [New Latin, from Latin, from Greek, "rose tree" : RHODO- + Greek *dendron,* tree.]

rho·do·lite (rō′də-līt′) *n.* A rose-red or pink variety of garnet, used as a gem. [RHODO- + -LITE.]

rho·do·nite (rō′də-nīt′) *n.* A pink to rose-red mineral, essentially $MnSiO_3$, used as an ornamental stone. Also called "manganese spar." [German *Rhodonit :* Greek *rhodon,* rose + -ITE.]

rho·dop·sin (rō-dŏp′sĭn) *n.* The light-sensitive pigment in the retinal rods of the eyes, consisting of opsin and retinal. Also called "visual purple." [RHODO- + Greek *opsis,* sight + -IN.]

rhomb. Variant of **rhombus.**

rhom·ben·ceph·a·lon (rŏm′bĕn-sĕf′ə-lŏn′, -lən) *n.* The portion of the embryonic brain from which the metencephalon, myelencephalon, and subsequently the cerebellum, pons, and medulla oblongata develop. Also called "hindbrain." [New Latin : RHOMB(US) + ENCEPHALON.]

rhom·bic (rŏm′bĭk) *adj.* 1. Having the shape of a rhombus. 2. *Crystallography.* Orthorhombic *(see).*

rhom·bo·he·dron (rŏm′bō-hē′drən) *n., pl.* **-drons** or **-dra** (-drə). *Abbr.* **rhbdr.** A prism with six faces, each a rhombus. [New Latin : RHOMBUS + -HEDRON.] —**rhom·bo·he·dral** *adj.*

rhom·boid (rŏm′boid′) *n.* 1. A parallelogram with unequal adjacent sides. 2. Either of two muscles in the upper part of the back. ~*adj.* Having a shape like a rhomboid. [Greek *rhomboeidēs :* RHOMBUS + -OID.] —**rhom·boi·dal** (rŏm-boid′l) *adj.*

rhom·bus (rŏm′bəs) *n., pl.* **-buses** or **-bi** (-bī′). Also **rhomb** (rŏm). An equilateral parallelogram. [Latin, from Greek *rhombos,* bull-roarer, magic wheel, rhombus.]

rhon·chus (rŏng′kəs) *n., pl.* **-chi** (-kī′). A coarse sound somewhat like snoring, usually caused by secretion in the bronchial tube. [Late Latin, snoring, from Greek *rhonkhos, rhonkos.*] —**rhon·chal, rhon·chi·al** (rŏng′kē-əl) *adj.*

Rhône (rōn). Also **Rhone.** Major European river, *c.* 800 kilometers (500 miles) long. It issues from the Rhône Glacier in the Swiss Alps and flows through Lake Geneva, then southward through France to the Mediterranean. The river is important for hydroelectric power, and its valley south of Lyon is noteworthy for its excellent vineyards. The Rhône-Saône valley is a main north-south communications route. South of Lyon the river is navigable, and an extensive canal system links it with other major rivers.

rho·tic (rō′tĭk) *adj. Phonetics.* 1. Pertaining to, designating, or speaking a variety of English in which the consonant sound (r) has not been lost before a consonant sound or pause. 2. Designating a consonant sound that is a variety of (r). [From the Greek letter RHO.]

r.h.p. rated horsepower.

Rh positive *adj.* Containing an **Rh factor** *(see).*

rhu·barb (rōō′bärb′) *n.* 1. Any of several plants of the genus *Rheum,* characterized by large, long-stalked leaves; especially, *R. rhaponticum,* the common garden rhubarb, having long, green or reddish, acid leafstalks that are edible when cooked and sweetened. Also called "pieplant." 2. The dried, bitter-tasting rhizome and roots of *R. palmatum* or *R. officinale,* of central Asia, used as a laxative. 3. *Slang.* A heated discussion, quarrel, or fight. ~*interj.* Used to convey an indistinct mumbling sound, as for background noise in a play. [Middle English *rubarbe,* from Old French *r(e)ubarbe,* probably from Medieval Latin *reubarb(ar)um,* probably alteration of *rha barbarum,* barbarian rhubarb : Late Latin *rha,* rhubarb, from Greek *rha, rhēon,* probably from *Rha,* former name of the Volga, on whose banks rhubarb was grown, + Latin *barbarus,* BARBAROUS.]

rhumb (rŭm, rŭmb) *n.* 1. A rhumb line. 2. Any of the points of the mariner's compass. [Earlier *rumb,* from Old Spanish *rumbo* and Old French *rumb,* modifications (influenced by Latin *rhombus,* RHOMBUS) of Middle Dutch *ruum, rume,* room, space.]

rhumba. Variant of **rumba.**

rhum·ba·tron (rŭm′bə-trŏn′) *n. Electronics.* A **cavity resonator** *(see).* [RHUMBA (rumba) + -TRON (alluding to the rhythmical variations of the waves).]

rhumb line *n.* 1. An imaginary line that cuts all the earth's meridians at a given constant angle. Also called "loxodrome," "loxodromic curve." 2. The course of a ship following such a line; a course sailed using a constant compass bearing.

rhyme (rīm) *n.* Also *archaic* **rime.** 1. Correspondence of terminal sounds of words or of lines of verse. See **assonance, consonance, feminine rhyme, masculine rhyme.** 2. A poem or verse having a regular correspondence of sounds, especially at the ends of lines: *a nursery rhyme.* 3. Poetry or verse of this kind. 4. A word that corresponds with another in terminal sound, such as *night* and *fight,* and *baboon* and *harpoon.* ~*v.* **rhymed, rhyming, rhymes.** Also *archaic* **rimed, riming, rimes.** —*intr.* 1. To form a rhyme; correspond in sound: *Death rhymes with breath.* 2. To compose rhymes or verse. 3. To make use of rhymes in composing verse. —*tr.* 1. To put into rhyme or compose with rhymes. 2. **a.** To use (a word or words) as a rhyme or rhymes. **b.** To pronounce as a rhyme. [Middle English *rime, ryme,* from Medieval Latin *rithmus,* variant of Latin *rhythmus,* RHYTHM.]

rhym·er (rī′mər) *n.* One who composes verse, especially of inferior quality. —See Synonyms at **poet.**

rhyme royal *n.* A stanza form consisting of seven lines in iambic pentameter with the first line rhyming with the third, the second with the fourth and fifth, and the last two with each other.

rhyme·ster (rīm′stər) *n.* One who makes up light verse that rhymes. —See Synonyms at **poet.**

rhym·ing slang (rī′mĭng) *n. British.* A type of humorous slang in which a word is replaced by a word or words that rhyme with it; for example, *brown bread* meaning *dead,* and *mince pies* meaning *eyes,* are instances of rhyming slang. Often only the first element is used, as *plates* (meaning *feet*) from *plates of meat.*

rhyn·cho·ce·phal·i·an (rĭng′kō-sə-fāl′yən) *adj.* Of or belonging to the Rhynchocephalia, an order of lizardlike reptiles of which only one species, the tuatara, is extant. ~*n.* A rhynchocephalian reptile. [New Latin *Rhynchocephalia :* Greek *rhunkhos,* snout, bill, beak + CEPHAL(O)- + -IA.]

rhy·o·lite (rī′ə-līt′) *n.* A fine-grained extrusive, acid igneous rock, the mineralogical equivalent of granite, consisting largely of quartz, feldspar, and often mica. [German *Rhyolit :* irregularly from Greek *rhuax,* stream (of lava), from *rhein,* to flow + -ITE.] —**rhy·o·lit·ic** (rī′ə-lĭt′ĭk) *adj.*

rhythm (rĭth′əm) *n.* 1. **a.** Any kind of movement characterized by the regular recurrence of strong and weak elements: *the rhythm of the tides.* **b.** Action characterized by a smooth, regular, settled movement: *The crowd put the tennis player off his rhythm.* 2. Non-random variation, especially uniform or regular variation, of any

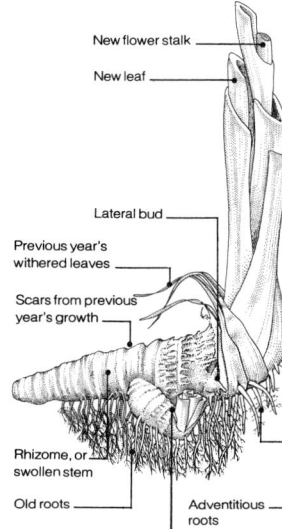

New flower stalk
New leaf
Lateral bud
Previous year's withered leaves
Scars from previous year's growth
Rhizome, or swollen stem
Old roots
New branch rhizome
Adventitious roots

rhizome *Plants that spread by means of underground stems, or rhizomes, include all the grasses and the iris shown above. Rhizomes burrow horizontally through the soil, storing food in winter and in spring throwing out new shoots above and roots below.*

quantity or condition characterizing a process, as in the body. **3.** *Music.* **a.** The part of music concerned with patterns of sound based on such elements as accent and tempo. **b.** A specified kind of this rhythm: *a waltz rhythm.* **4. a.** The metrical flow of sound with a regulated pattern of long and short, or accented and unaccented syllables, best exemplified in poetry or verse. **b.** A specified kind of such a metrical flow: *sprung rhythm.* **5.** In painting, sculpture, and other visual arts, a regular or harmonious pattern created by lines, forms, and colors. [French *rhythme,* from Latin *rhythmus,* from Greek *rhuthmos,* recurring motion, rhythm, akin to *rhein,* to flow.]
     Synonyms: *beat, cadence, meter.*

rhythm and blues *n. Abbr.* **R & B.** An urban form of blues using electrically amplified instruments, developed in the United States in the 1940's.

rhyth·mi·cal (rĭth′mĭ-kəl) *adj.* Also **rhyth·mic** (-mĭk). Pertaining to or characterized by rhythm; especially, recurring with measured regularity. —**rhyth·mi·cal·ly** *adv.*

rhyth·mics (rĭth′mĭks) *n. Used with a singular verb.* The study of rhythm.

rhyth·mist (rĭth′mĭst) *n.* One who is expert in or has a keen sense of rhythm.

rhythm method *n.* A birth-control method that is dependent on the avoidance of sexual intercourse during the ovulatory phase of the menstrual cycle.

rhythm section *n.* The members of a musical band or group, such as the drummer and bass guitarist, that supply the rhythm.

rhy·ton (rī′tŏn′) *n.* In ancient Greece, a drinking vessel or horn tapering to a hole in the bottom through which the wine could run. [Greek *rhuton,* from *rhutos,* flowing, from *rhein,* to flow.]

RI Rhode Island (used with a Zip Code).

R.I. **1.** Rhode Island. **2.** King and Emperor [Latin *Rex et Imperator*]. **3.** Queen and Empress [Latin *Regina et Imperatrix*].

ri·a (rē′ə) *n.* A long narrow sea inlet, caused by flooding of a narrow valley , which unlike a fiord deepens toward the sea, and is typically found in southwestern Ireland and northwestern Spain. [Spanish, "river mouth."]

Riad. See **Riyadh.**

ri·al¹ (rē-ôl′, -äl′) *n.* **1. a.** The basic monetary unit of Iran, equal to 100 dinars. **b.** A coin worth one rial. **2.** The basic monetary unit of Saudi Arabia, equal to 100 halalas or 20 quirsh. **3.** The basic monetary unit of Yemen, equal to 100 fils. See feature at **currency.** [Persian, from Arabic *riyāl,* from Spanish *real,* REAL (coin).]

rial². Variant of **riyal.**

ri·al-o·man·i (rē′ôl-ō-mä′nē) *n.* The basic monetary unit of Oman, equal to 1,000 baizas.

ri·al·to (rē-ăl′tō, rä-äl′-) *n., pl.* **-tos. 1.** An exchange or trading center. **2.** A theater district. [After the *Rialto,* Venice, an island forming the center of the city.]

ri·a·ta, re·a·ta (rē-ä′tə) *n.* A lariat; lasso. [Spanish *(la) reata,* (the) lasso, LARIAT.]

rib (rĭb) *n.* **1. a.** Any of the long, curved bones occurring in 12 pairs in humans and extending from the spine to or toward the breastbone and enclosing the heart and lungs. **b.** A similar bone in most other vertebrates. **2.** Any part or piece considered similar to a rib and serving to shape or support: *the rib of an umbrella.* **3.** A cut of meat enclosing one or more ribs. **4.** Any of the curved members attached to the keel of a boat and extending upward and outward to form the framework of the hull. **5.** Any of the formed transverse pieces along the length of an airplane wing used to establish shape. **6.** *Architecture.* **a.** An arch or a projecting arched member of a vault. **b.** Any of the curved pieces of an arch. **7. a.** A knitting stitch formed by working alternate plain and purl on one row, reversing this order on the next, and so on. **b.** The evenly ridged pattern formed by this. **c.** Material knitted in rib, usually found at the collar, waist, and neck of a woolen garment. **8.** *Botany.* Any of the main veins of a leaf or similar organ. **9.** A ridge of a mountain. **10.** *Mining.* A vein of ore.
     ~*tr.v.* **ribbed, ribbing, ribs. 1.** To shape, support, or provide with a rib or ribs. **2.** To work in rib: *Rib 30 rows, then cast off.* **3.** To make with ridges or raised markings. **4.** *Informal.* To tease or make fun of. [Middle English *rib(be),* Old English *rib(b),* from Germanic.]

rib·ald (rĭb′əld) *adj.* Characterized by or indulging in vulgar, lewd, coarse humor. —See Synonyms at **coarse.**
     ~*n.* A ribald person. [Middle English *ribaud,* retainer of low rank, lewd person, rascal, blasphemer, from Old French *ribauld, ribaut,* from *riber,* to be wanton, from Old High German *rīban,* to be in heat, copulate, "to rub."]

rib·ald·ry (rĭb′əl-drē) *n., pl.* **-ries.** Ribald language or joking.

rib·and (rĭb′ənd) *n. Archaic.* A ribbon, especially one used as a decoration. [Middle English, from Old French *riban,* probably from a Germanic compound of BAND.]

rib·band (rĭb′ănd, -ənd, -ən) *n.* A length of flexible wood or metal used to hold the ribs of a ship in place while the exterior planking or plating is being applied. [RIB + BAND (strip).]

Rib·ben·trop (rĭb′ən-trŏp′), **Joachim von** (1893–1946). German politician. In 1938 Hitler made him foreign minister, and he played a major role in the negotiation of the German-Soviet nonaggression pact of 1939. He remained foreign minister until Hitler's death in 1945. He was convicted of war crimes at Nuremberg and hanged.

rib·bing (rĭb′ĭng) *n.* **1.** Ribs collectively. **2.** An arrangement of ribs, as in a boat. **3.** Knitted rib. **4.** *Informal.* An instance of teasing.

rib·bon (rĭb′ən) *n.* **1.** A narrow strip or band of fine fabric, such as satin or velvet, finished at the edges and used for trimming or tying.

2. Anything resembling a ribbon, such as a measuring tape. **3. ribbons.** Tattered or ragged strips: *a dress torn to ribbons.* **4.** An inked strip of cloth used for making the impression of typed characters, as in a typewriter. **5.** A band of colored cloth signifying an award, as of a military decoration or membership in an order. **6. ribbons.** *Informal.* Reins for driving horses.
     ~*tr.v.* **ribboned, -boning, -bons. 1.** To decorate or tie with ribbons. **2.** To tear into ribbons or shreds. [Middle English *riban,* variant of RIBAND.]

ribbon development *n. British.* Land development marked by continuous building along a road leading away from a town and not having a natural social center.

rib·bon-fish (rĭb′ən-fĭsh′) *n., pl.* **-fishes** or collectively **ribbonfish.** Any of several marine fishes, chiefly of the genus *Trachipterus,* having long, narrow, compressed bodies. See **oarfish.**

ribbon snake *n.* A nonvenomous North American snake, *Thamnophis sauritus,* having yellow or reddish stripes along the body.

ribbon worm *n.* A nemertean *(see).*

rib cage *n.* The enclosing structure formed by the ribs and the bones to which they are attached.

Ri·be·ra (rē-bĕr′ə), **José de,** also known as "Lo Spagnoletto" (*c.* 1591–1652). Spanish painter. He studied in Rome (*c.* 1613–14) where he came under the influence of Caravaggio. In 1616 he settled in Naples. He painted both religious and secular subjects.

ri·bo·fla·vin (rī′bō-flā′vĭn) *n.* A crystalline orange-yellow pigment, $C_{17}H_{20}O_6N_4$, that is part of the vitamin B complex, being essential for carbohydrate metabolism. It is found in milk, leafy vegetables, fresh meat, and egg yolks, and produced synthetically. Also called "lactoflavin," "vitamin B₂," "vitamin G." [RIBO(SE) + FLAVIN.]

ri·bo·nu·cle·ase (rī′bō-nōō′klē-ās, -nyōō′-, -āz) *n. Abbr.* **RNAase.** Any of various enzymes that promote the hydrolysis of RNA.

ri·bo·nu·cle·ic acid (rī′bō-nōō′klē-ĭk, -nyōō′-) *n.* See **RNA.** [RIBO(SE) + NUCLEIC ACID.]

ri·bose (rī′bōs′) *n.* A pentose sugar, $C_5H_{10}O_5$, occurring as a component of RNA and certain coenzymes. [German *Ribon(säure),* a tetrahydroxyl acid from which ribose is obtained : *Ribon-,* arbitrary alteration of English *arabinose,* ribose : (GUM) ARAB(IC) + -IN + -OSE + *Säure,* acid.]

ribosomal RNA *n. Abbr.* **rRNA.** The RNA that forms a constituent of ribosomes.

ri·bo·some (rī′bə-sōm′) *n.* Any of numerous spherical cytoplasmic particles, consisting of RNA and protein, that are the sites of protein synthesis in the cell. [RIBO(SE) + -SOME (body).] —**ri·bo·so·mal** *adj.*

rib·wort (rĭb′wûrt′, -wôrt′) *n.* A weedy plant, *Plantago lanceolata,* having lancelike, ribbed leaves and a dense spike of small whitish flowers.

Ri·car·do (rĭ-kär′dō), **David** (1772–1823). English political economist, one of the chief founders of the so-called classical school of economists. His most important work, *Principles of Political Economy and Taxation* (1817), supported the law of supply and demand in a free market.

Ric·ci (rē′chē), **Matteo** (1552–1610). Italian Jesuit missionary. He was a missionary in India (1578) and settled in China in 1583. His reports of life in China were the first knowledgeable accounts of Chinese life received by the West.

rice (rīs) *n.* **1.** A cereal grass, *Oryza sativa,* that is cultivated extensively in warm climates and is a staple food throughout the world. **2.** The starchy edible seed of this grass.
     ~*tr.v.* **riced, ricing, rices.** To sieve (food) to the consistency of rice. [Middle English *rys, ryce,* from Old French *ris,* from Italian *riso,* from Latin *oryza,* from Greek *oruzon, oruza,* from East Iranian *vrīz-* (unattested), akin to Sanskrit *vrīhi†.*]

Rice (rīs), **Elmer,** born Elmer Reizenstein (1892–1967). U.S. playwright and novelist. He graduated from New York Law School (1912), but soon turned to writing. Rice wrote both comedies and dramas, including *The Adding Machine* (1923), *We, the People* (Pulitzer Prize winner, 1929), and *Dream Girl* (1945).

rice·bird (rīs′bûrd′) *n.* **1.** *Southern U.S.* The bobolink *(see).* **2.** Any of various birds that frequent rice fields, such as the Java sparrow.

rice paper *n.* A thin, edible paper made chiefly from the pith of the rice-paper tree.

rice-pa·per tree (rīs′pā′pər) *n.* A shrub or small tree, *Tetrapanax papyriferum,* of eastern Asia, grown as a source of fiber for rice paper.

ric·er (rī′sər) *n.* A kitchen utensil used for ricing soft foods by extrusion through small holes.

ri·cer·car (rē′chär-kär′) *n.* Also **ri·cer·ca·re** (-kär′ā). A musical composition developing a basic theme, similar to a fugue.

rice weevil *n.* A small, destructive insect, *Sitophilus oryzae,* that infests stored grain and cereal products.

rich (rĭch) *adj.* **richer, richest. 1.** Possessing great wealth; owning much money, goods, or land. **2.** Composed of rare or valuable materials; made with fine or elaborate craftsmanship; costly: *a rich brocade.* **3.** Of great worth; valuable. **4.** Elaborate or sumptuous: *a rich feast.* **5.** Plentiful; abundant; ample. **6.** Abundantly or copiously supplied. Used with *in* or *with: rich in tradition.* **7.** Abounding in natural resources: *a rich land.* **8.** Producing or yielding much; abundant: *a rich harvest.* **9.** Of or designating food that contains a large or excessive proportion of tasty, fatty ingredients, such as eggs, butter, or cream: *a rich sauce.* **10.** Pleasing and satisfying to the senses, owing to a quality such as fullness, mellowness, or intensity: *a rich tenor voice; a rich blue.* **11.** Containing a large proportion of fuel to air. Said of a fuel mixture. **12.** *Informal.* Full of amusement; satisfyingly funny: sometimes used ironically: *That's rich!* [Middle English *riche,* originally powerful, great, partly from Old French *riche,* from Frankish *rīki* (unattested), and partly from Old English *rīce.*] —**rich·ly** *adv.* —**rich·ness** *n.*

Rich·ard I (rĭch′ərd), known as "Coeur de Lion" or "the Lion-Hearted" (1157–99). King of England (1189–99), third son and successor of Henry II. He set out on the Third Crusade in 1190 and gained, by a treaty with Saladin, access for Christians to Jerusalem. He was captured by Leopold V of Austria in 1192, handed over to Emperor Henry VI, and ransomed in 1194. He was in England in 1194, before returning to France, where he was slain in a minor engagement.

Richard II (1367–1400). King of England (1377–99), son of the Black Prince and successor to his grandfather, Edward III. At the age of 14 he made a heroic appearance before the rebels taking part in the Peasants' Revolt (1381), placating them with promises of concessions that were immediately revoked. From 1386 until the end of his reign he was at odds with the baronial opposition in Parliament, and his rule became increasingly authoritarian.

Richard III (1452–85). King of England (1483–85), younger brother of Edward IV and last of the Yorkist kings. When Edward IV died in 1483, Richard seized his two sons, including the rightful heir, Edward V, and imprisoned them in the Tower of London. Richard was then crowned king. The two princes were murdered in the Tower, possibly on Richard's orders. In 1485 Richard was slain at the Battle of Bosworth Field.

Richard Roe *n.* A name used in legal proceedings to designate a fictitious or unidentified person. See **John Doe.**

Rich·ards (rĭch′ərdz), **I(vor) Armstrong** (1893–1979). British literary critic and grammarian. In the 1920's he collaborated with Charles Ogden in the formulation of Basic English, publishing with him *The Foundations of Aesthetics* (1921) and *The Meaning of Meaning* (1923).

Rich·ard·son (rĭch′ərd-sən), **Henry Hobson** (1838–86). U.S. architect. Born in Louisiana, he graduated from Harvard, then studied in Paris and worked in New York City. In 1878 he moved his office to Boston. The city and the surrounding area have many distinguished works designed by him, including Trinity Church in Copley Square.

Richardson, Sir Ralph David (1902–83). British stage and film actor. He is noted for his strong characterization in classic roles as well as in contemporary works, such as Pinter's *No Man's Land* (1975).

Richardson, Samuel (1689–1761). English novelist. He worked as a printer until the age of 50, when he began to write his first work, *Pamela* (1740). It was written in the form of a series of letters, as were its successors, *Clarissa Harlowe* (1747–48) and *The History of Sir Charles Grandison* (1753–54).

Richardson, Tony (1928–). English film director. He established his reputation in the 1950's with a series of films in the then prevailing mood of social realism, *Look Back in Anger* (1958), *A Taste of Honey* (1961), and *The Loneliness of the Long Distance Runner* (1962). His other films include *Tom Jones* (1962).

Riche·lieu (rĕsh′lōō, rē-shə-lyœ′), **Armand Jean du Plessis, Duc de** (1585–1642). French prelate and statesman, chief minister of Louis XIII, known as Cardinal Richelieu. He worked devotedly to strengthen the authority of the monarchy, suppressing numerous conspiracies by the nobles and directing France during the Thirty Years' War (1618–48). He founded the French Academy in 1635.

Richelieu River. River, *c.* 120 kilometers (75 miles) long, flowing from the northern end of Lake Champlain, near the New York-Quebec border, across southern Quebec to the St. Lawrence River. It is a link in the waterway connecting the Hudson and St. Lawrence rivers.

rich·en (rĭch′ən) *tr.v.* **-ened, -ening, -ens.** To make rich.

rich·es (rĭch′ĭz) *pl.n.* **1.** Abundant wealth. **2.** Valuable or precious possessions. [Middle English *riches, richesse,* wealth (taken as a plural), from Old French, from *riche,* powerful, RICH.]

Rich·ler (rĭch′lər), **Mordecai** (1931–). Canadian writer. His comic novels are predominantly concerned with Jewish themes and include *The Apprenticeship of Duddy Kravitz* (1959), *The Incomparable Atuk* (1963), and *Cocksure* (1968).

rich·ly (rĭch′lē) *adv.* **1.** In a rich way or manner. **2.** In full measure; thoroughly: *richly rewarded.*

Rich·mond (rĭch′mənd). Capital of Virginia, on the James River. It is a port exporting coal and tobacco and it manufactures tobacco products and chemicals. Settled in 1637, it was capital of the Confederacy during the Civil War.

Rich·ter scale (rĭk′tər) *n.* A logarithmic scale ranging from 1 to 10, used to express the magnitude of an earthquake. [After Charles F. *Richter* (1900–86), U.S. seismologist.]

Richt·ho·fen (rĭkʜt′hō-fən), **Manfred, Baron von,** known as "the Red Baron" (1892–1918). German pilot. During World War I he was credited with shooting down 80 enemy aircraft, making him the leading ace of the war. He was killed in action in 1918.

ri·cin (rī′sĭn, rĭs′ĭn) *n.* A highly poisonous protein extracted from castor-oil beans and used as a biochemical reagent. [Latin *ricinus*†, castor-oil plant.]

ri·cin·o·le·ic acid (rĭs′ĭn-ō-lē′ĭk) *n.* An unsaturated fatty acid, $C_{18}H_{34}O_3$, prepared from castor oil and used in making soaps and in textile finishing. [Latin *ricinus,* castor-oil plant (see **ricin**) + OLEIC.]

rick¹ (rĭk) *n.* A stack of hay, straw, or similar material, especially when covered or thatched for protection from the weather.

~*tr.v.* **ricked, ricking, ricks.** To pile in ricks. [Middle English *reke,* Old English *hrēac,* akin to Old Norse *hraukr*†.]

rick² *tr.v.* **ricked, ricking, ricks.** *British.* To sprain, strain, or pull (one's back, for example).

~*n.* A sprain or similar injury. [Middle English *wricken,* from Middle Low German *wricken*†, to sprain.]

Rick·en·back·er (rĭk′ĭn-băk′ər), **Edward Vernon** known as "Eddie" (1890–1973). U.S. World War I ace and businessman. An automobile racer and daredevil, he was assigned to the 94th Aero Pursuit Squadron in World War I. He downed 26 enemy aircraft on the Western Front, becoming the most decorated American combat pilot in the war.

rick·ets (rĭk′ĭts) *n. Used with a singular verb.* A deficiency disease resulting from a lack of vitamin D, characterized by defective bone growth, and occurring chiefly in children. Also called "rachitis." [Variant of RACHITIS.]

rick·ett·si·a (rĭ-kĕt′sē-ə) *n., pl.* **-siae** (-sī-ē′). Any of various microorganisms, mostly of the genus *Rickettsia,* carried as parasites by ticks, fleas, and lice. Transmitted to humans, they cause diseases such as typhus, Q fever, and trench fever. [After Howard T. *Ricketts* (1871–1910), U.S. pathologist.] —**rick·ett·si·al** *adj.*

rick·et·y (rĭk′ĭt-ē) *adj.* **-ier, -iest. 1.** Likely to break or fall apart; shaky. **2.** Feeble with age; infirm. **3.** Of, having, or resembling rickets. [From RICKETS.] —**rick·et·i·ness** *n.*

rick·ey (rĭk′ē) *n., pl.* **-eys.** A drink of soda water, lime juice, and usually gin. [20th century : origin obscure.]

Rick·o·ver (rĭk′ō′vər), **Hyman George** (1900–86). U.S. admiral, born in Russia. Convinced of the practicality of nuclear-powered submarines, he worked unceasingly on the technical development and military acceptance of the *Nautilus,* the world's first atomic naval craft. He was also a critic of the American educational system.

rick·rack, ric·rac (rĭk′răk′) *n.* A flat, narrow braid in zigzag form, used as a trimming. [Reduplication of RACK (to torture).]

rick·shaw, rick·sha (rĭk′shô′) *n.* A small two-wheeled oriental carriage drawn by one or two men. Also called "jinricksha." [Short for JINRICKSHA.]

ric·o·chet (rĭk′ə-shā′, -shĕt′) *intr.v.* **-cheted** (-shād′) or **-chetted** (-shĕt′ĭd), **-cheting** (-shā′ĭng) or **-chetting** (-shĕt′ĭng), **-chets.** To rebound at least once from a surface or surfaces. Used of a projectile, such as a bullet.

~*n.* An instance of such deflection. [French *ricochet*†.]

ri·cot·ta (rē-kôt′tä) *n.* An Italian cottage cheese made from the whey drained from other cheeses made with sheep's milk. [Italian, from Latin *recocta,* feminine past participle of *recoquere,* to cook again : *re-,* again + *coquere,* to cook.]

ric·tus (rĭk′təs) *n.* **1. a.** The expanse of an open mouth, a bird's beak, or similar structure. **b.** A gaping grimace. **2.** A cleft, split, or gap. [Latin *rictus,* from the past participle of *ringī*†, to gape.] —**ric·tal** *adj.*

rid (rĭd) *tr.v.* **rid** or **ridded, ridding, rids.** To free from something objectionable or undesirable: *Let me rid your mind of fear.* —**get rid of.** To dispose of. [Middle English *rud(d)en, rid(d)en,* from Old Norse *rythja* (past participle *ruddr*), from Germanic *rudjan* (unattested).] —**rid·der** *n.*

rid·dance (rĭd′əns) *n.* A welcome removal of or deliverance from something. —**good riddance.** Used to express relief at the removal or prospect of the removal of an unwanted person or thing. [RID + -ANCE.]

rid·den (rĭd′n). Past participle of **ride.**

~*adj.* Dominated; oppressed. Usually used in combination: *disease-ridden; cliché-ridden.*

rid·dle¹ (rĭd′l) *tr.v.* **-dled, -dling, -dles. 1.** To pierce with numerous holes; perforate. **2.** To put through a coarse sieve. **3.** To permeate and thereby weaken or damage: *riddled with errors.*

~*n.* A coarse sieve for separating and grading materials such as gravel: *a potato riddle.* [Middle English *rid(d)len,* to sift, from *riddil,* sieve, Old English *hriddel, hridder.*] —**rid·dler** *n.*

riddle² *n.* **1.** A question or statement requiring one to puzzle over it to answer or understand; conundrum. **2.** Something perplexing; an enigma.

~*v.* **riddled, -dling, -dles.** —*tr.* To solve or explain (a riddle). —*intr.* **1.** To solve or propound riddles. **2.** To speak in riddles. [Middle English *redel(es), ridil,* Old English *rædelse,* from *rædan* (unattested), to READ.] —**rid·dler** *n.*

Rid·dle (rĭd′l), **Nelson** (1921–85). U.S. composer, conductor, and arranger. A big-band trombone player in the 1940's, he was the NBC staff arranger (1947–50) and became a highly successful Hollywood composer. Among his many works are the theme from *The Untouchables* (1959) and the Academy-Award-winning score for *The Great Gatsby* (1974).

ride (rīd) *v.* **rode** (rōd), **ridden** (rĭd′n), **riding, rides.** —*intr.* **1.** To sit on, control, and be conveyed by an animal or a machine: *riding sidesaddle on the horse.* **2.** To be conveyed or transported, as in a vehicle, boat, or aircraft: *ride in a bus.* **3.** To travel over a surface: *This car rides well.* **4.** To lie at anchor. Used of a ship. **5.** To seem to be floating in space: *a star riding in the sky.* **6.** To progress effortlessly; be swept along as if by some relentless force: *rode to power on a surge of patriotism.* **7.** *Archaic.* To carry a rider or support something in a particular manner. **8.** To lie over something; overlap. Used especially of bones. **9.** To work or move from the proper place. Used with *up: shorts that ride up.* **10.** To continue undisturbed by any action: *We let the problem ride.* —*tr.* **1.** To sit

rickshaw *A traditional hand-pulled rickshaw in Calcutta, India. Modern rickshaws are often modified tricycles, which are pedaled rather than pulled.*

on, control, and be transported by: *ride a bike.* **2.** To be supported or carried upon. **3.** To travel over, along, or through: *ride the roads.* **4.** To rest upon by overlapping; overlie. **5.** To take part in or do by riding: *He rode his last race.* **6.** To control or dominate. **7.** To cause to ride, as by taking on one's shoulders: *riding his son on his back.* **8.** To keep (a vessel) at anchor. **9.** *Informal.* To tease or ridicule. **—ride for a fall.** To court danger or disaster. **—ride herd on.** To keep watch or control over. **—ride high.** To be elated, as from success. **—ride out.** To withstand or survive successfully. **—ride roughshod over.** To take a course of action without regard for the feelings, opinions, or welfare of.
~*n.* **1.** An excursion or journey by any means of conveyance, as on horseback, in a car, or on a boat. **2.** A path made for riding on horseback, especially through woodlands. **3.** At amusement parks or similar places, any of various entertainments in which persons ride for pleasure or excitement. **4.** An experience of a specified type to which one is subjected: *The committee gave the minister a rough ride.* **—take for a ride.** *Informal.* To deceive or swindle. [Ride, rode, ridden; Middle English *riden, rad* (or *rod*), *riden,* Old English *rīdan, rād, riden* (unattested), from Germanic.]

Ri·deau Canal (rē-dō′). Canal, 203 kilometers (126 miles) long, in southern Ontario, Canada, connecting the Ottawa River at Ottawa with Lake Ontario at Kingston. The canal, which has 47 locks, was built along the course of the Rideau River in 1826–32.

rid·er (rī′dər) *n.* **1.** One who or that which rides; especially, one who rides horses. **2.** *riders.* Material, such as iron plates, added to a ship's frame to strengthen it. **3.** A clause, usually having little relevance to the main issue, added to a document, such as a congressional bill. **4.** An amendment or addition, as to a document or statement: *The jury added a rider to the verdict.* **5.** A small weight that can slide along an arm of a chemical balance, used to make small changes to the balancing weight. **6.** *Mathematics.* A problem that can be posed arising from a theorem, especially in geometry. **7.** *Mining & Geology.* A thin seam lying over a thicker seam.

ridge (rĭj) *n.* **1.** The long, narrow upper section or crest of something: *ridge of a wave.* **2.** A long, narrow land elevation; a long hill or chain of mountains. **3.** A long, narrow, or crested part of the body: *the ridge of the nose.* **4.** The horizontal line that is formed by the juncture of two sloping planes; especially, the line formed by the surfaces of a roof. **5.** Any narrow raised strip, as in cloth or on ploughed land. **6.** *Meteorology.* An area of high pressure extending from the center of an anticyclone and separating two low-pressure regions.
~*v.* **ridged, ridging, ridges.** —*tr.* To mark with, form into, or provide with ridges. —*intr.* To form ridges. [Middle English *rigge,* back, ridge, Old English *hrycg,* from Germanic.] **—ridg·y** *adj.*

ridge·back (rĭj′băk′) *n.* A dog, a **Rhodesian ridgeback** (see).

ridge·ling, ridg·ling (rĭj′lĭng) *n.* In veterinary medicine, a male animal, such as a horse, with one or two undescended testicles. Also called "rig." [Obsolete *ridgel,* probably "(animal) with testes near the back," from RIDGE.]

ridge·pole (rĭj′pōl′) *n.* **1.** A horizontal beam at the ridge of a roof, to which the rafters are attached. **2.** The horizontal pole at the top of a tent. Also called "ridge beam," "ridge piece."

ridge·way (rĭj′wā′) *n. British.* A road, track, or other path along the top of a hill or range of hills.

Ridg·way (rĭj′wā), **Matthew Bunker** (1895–). U.S. army officer. He led America's first major airborne assault, the attack on Sicily in 1943, and participated in the Normandy invasion and the Battle of the Bulge (1944). He held high-ranking positions during and after the Korean War, including chief of staff of the army (1953–55).

rid·i·cule (rĭd′ə-kyōōl′) *n.* **1.** Words or actions intended to evoke contemptuous laughter at or feelings toward a person or thing. **2.** Subjection to such a contemptuous attitude.
~*tr.v.* **ridiculed, -culing, -cules.** To deride, mock, or make fun of. [French *ridicule,* from Latin *rīdiculum,* joke, jest, from *rīdiculus,* laughable, RIDICULOUS.] **—rid·i·cul·er** *n.*
Synonyms: *deride, gibe, mock, taunt, twit.*

ri·dic·u·lous (rĭ-dĭk′yə-ləs) *adj.* Deserving or inspiring ridicule; absurd or preposterous; silly or laughable. —See Synonyms at **foolish.** [Latin *rīdiculōsus, rīdiculus,* laughable, from *rīdēre†,* to laugh.] **—ri·dic·u·lous·ly** *adv.* **—ri·dic·u·lous·ness** *n.*

rid·ing¹ (rī′dĭng) *n.* The action or skill of one who rides on horseback.
~*adj.* Pertaining to, used in, or worn for riding: *a riding school; riding boots.*

riding² *n.* **1.** Formerly, one of the three administrative divisions of Yorkshire, England: North Riding, East Riding, and West Riding. **2.** Any similar administrative division; specifically, in Canada, a parliamentary constituency. [Middle English *riding,* Old English *thrithing* (unattested), from Old Norse *thrithjungr,* third part, from *thrithi,* third.]

riding habit *n.* The costume worn by a horseback rider.

riding lamp *n.* A lamp or light hung on a boat, ship, or other vessel, that is at anchor.

Rie·fen·stahl (rē′fən-shtäl′), **Leni** (1902–). German film director and photographer. In her youth she made pro-Nazi films, including *Triumph of the Will* (1934) and *The Olympic Games* (1936), covering the Berlin Olympics. Her later works include photographic studies of Sudanese peoples, among them *Last of the Nuba* (1973).

ri·el (rē-ĕl′) *n.* The basic monetary unit of Kampuchea, equal to 100 sen. See feature at **currency.**

Ri·el (rē-ĕl′), **Louis** (1844–85). French-Canadian rebel. As leader of

the métis in Western Canada, he attempted to halt the encroachment of English-speaking settlers. As a result of his rebellion the province of Manitoba was established (1870). During a similar uprising in Saskatchewan he was captured, tried for treason, and hanged.

Rie·mann (rē′män′), **Georg Friedrich Bernhard** (1826–66). German mathematician, a pioneer of non-Euclidean geometry. After 1851 he developed an approach, now known as Riemannian geometry, by which a generalized space was studied without a prior framework for calculating distances between points. His work influenced Einstein's theory of relativity.

Rie·mann·i·an geometry (rē-män′ē-ən) *n.* A non-Euclidean geometry based on the postulate that there are no parallel lines. Also called "elliptic geometry." [After G. F. B. RIEMANN.]

Ries·ling (rēs′lĭng) *n.* **1.** A sweet or dry white wine with a light, flowery bouquet produced especially in Germany and Alsace. **2.** The type of grape used in the making of this wine. [German, earlier *Rüssling†.*]

ri·fam·pi·cin (rī-făm′pə-sən) *n.* An antibiotic active against various infections, used chiefly to treat tuberculosis. [From *rifamycin,* earlier *rifomycin* (replication *i*nhibiting *f*ungus + -MYCIN), its source + *ampicillin* (to which it is comparable in efficacy).]

rife (rīf) *adj.* **rifer, rifest. 1.** Frequently or commonly happening or appearing; widespread; prevalent. **2.** Abundant; numerous. **3.** Abounding; full. Used with *with: That department is rife with incompetents.* —See Synonyms at **prevailing.** [Middle English *rif, ryfe,* Old English *rȳfe,* probably from Old Norse *rifr,* acceptable.]

riff (rĭf) *n.* In jazz and rock music, a short rhythmic phrase repeated constantly. [20th century : origin obscure.]

Riff (rĭf) *n.* A member of a Berber people of the Rif country in northern Morocco, Africa.

rif·fle (rĭf′əl) *n.* **1.** The act of shuffling cards. **2.** *Mining.* **a.** The sectional stone or wood bottom lining of a sluice, arranged to trap mineral, especially gold, particles. **b.** A groove or block in such a lining. **3. a.** A rocky shoal or sandbar lying just below the surface of a waterway. **b.** A stretch of choppy water caused by such a shoal or sandbar; a rapid.
~*v.* **riffled, -fling, -fles.** —*tr.* **1.** To shuffle (playing cards) by holding part of a pack in each hand and raising up the edges before releasing them to fall alternately in one stack. **2.** To thumb through (the pages of a book, for example). —*intr.* **1.** To shuffle cards. **2.** To thumb through pages. **3.** To become choppy. [Perhaps blend of RUFFLE (disturb) and RIPPLE.]

rif·fler (rĭf′lər) *n.* A file with curved ends suitable for scraping. [Old French *rifloir,* from *riflert,* to scratch, file.]

riff·raff (rĭf′răf′) *n.* **1.** Worthless or disreputable persons. **2.** Rubbish; trash. [Middle English *riffe raffe, rif and raf,* one and all, from Old French *rif et raf : rifler,* to file (see **riffler**) + *raffe,* a sweeping, from Middle High German *raffen,* to snatch (see **raffle**).]

ri·fle¹ (rī′fəl) *n.* **1.** A firearm with a rifled bore designed to be fired from the shoulder. **2.** An artillery piece or naval gun that has been rifled. **3. rifles.** Troops armed with rifles.
~*tr.v.* **rifled, -fling, -fles.** To cut spiral grooves within (a gun barrel, for example) to improve the accuracy of the projectile's flight. [Originally "spiral groove," from *rifle,* to cut spiral grooves, from Old French *rifler,* to file. See **riffler.**]

rifle² *tr.v.* **-fled, -fling, -fles. 1. a.** To ransack with intent to steal. **b.** To plunder; pillage. **2.** To rob; strip bare: *rifle a safe.* [Middle English *riflen,* from Old French *rifler,* to scratch, file, plunder. See **riffler.**] **—ri·fler** *n.*

ri·fle·bird (rī′fəl-bûrd′) *n.* Any of several birds of paradise of the genus *Ptiloris,* of Australia and New Guinea. [From its cry.]

ri·fle·man (rī′fəl-mən) *n., pl.* **-men** (-mĭn). **1.** A soldier equipped with a rifle. **2.** One expert in firing a rifle. **3.** A New Zealand wren, *Acanthisitta chloris.*

rifle range *n.* An area set aside for shooting practice at targets, using rifles.

ri·fle·ry (rī′fəl-rē) *n.* The art and practice of marksmanship.

ri·fling (rī′flĭng) *n.* Spiral grooves cut inside a gun barrel.

rift¹ (rĭft) *n.* **1.** A narrow fissure, cleft, or chink, as in rock. **2.** A break in friendly relations.
~*v.* **rifted, rifting, rifts.** —*intr.* To split open; burst; break. —*tr.* To cause to split open or break. [Middle English *rift, ryft,* from Scandinavian, akin to Danish *rift,* breach.]

rift² *n.* **1.** A shallow area in a waterway. **2.** The backwash of a wave that has broken upon a beach. [Probably variant of *riff,* dialectal variant of REEF.]

rift valley *n.* A long, narrow depression in the earth's surface formed when the land sinks between two fairly parallel faults.

rig¹ (rĭg) *tr.v.* **rigged, rigging, rigs. 1.** To fit out or provide (an aircraft, for example) with equipment. **2. a.** To equip (a ship) with sails, shrouds, and yards. **b.** To fit (sails, shrouds, and the like) to masts and spars. **3.** *Informal.* To dress, clothe, or adorn: *rigged out in her best dress.* **4.** To make, construct, or erect, often in haste or in a makeshift manner. Often used with *up.* **5.** To manipulate dishonestly for personal gain: *rig a competition.*
~*n.* **1.** The arrangement of masts, spars, and sails on a sailing vessel: *a square rig.* **2. a.** Any special equipment or gear for a particular purpose. **b.** A citizens' band receiver and transmitter. **3.** The installation and apparatus used for drilling oil and gas wells. **4.** A truck. **5.** A vehicle with one or more horses harnessed to it. [Middle English *riggen,* probably from Scandinavian, akin to Norwegian *rigga.*]

rig[2] *n.* A **ridgeling** *(see).*

Ri·ga (rē′gə). City and port in western U.S.S.R., on the Gulf of Riga, an inlet of the Baltic Sea. It is capital of the Latvian S.S.R. A member of the Hanseatic League from 1282, it passed to Poland (1581), Sweden (1621), and Russia (1710) and was capital of the independent state of Latvia (1919–40).

rig·a·doon (rĭg′ə-do͞on′) *n.* **1.** A lively jumping quickstep for one couple. **2.** Music for this dance, usually in rapid duple time. [French *rigaudon, rigodon,* said to have been invented by a famous dancing master of Marseille named *Rigaud.*]

rigamarole. Variant of **rigmarole.**

rig·a·to·ni (rĭg′ə-tō′nē) *n.* Large, ribbed, macaroni tubes, slightly curved and cut into short lengths. [Italian, plural of *rigato,* past participle of *rigare,* to draw a line, corrugate, from *riga,* line, from Germanic.]

Ri·gel (rī′jəl) *n.* A bright double star in the constellation Orion. [Arabic *rijl,* (Orion's) foot.]

rig·ger[1] (rĭg′ər) *n.* **1.** One who rigs, specifically: **a.** One who fits rigging to sailing ships. **b.** One who assembles or aligns aircraft parts or parachutes. **c.** One who works with hoisting tackle, cranes, pulleys, and scaffolds. **d.** One who works on an oil rig. **2.** A protective scaffold set up against a building under construction.

rigger[2] *n.* A metal bracket attached to the side of a racing or rowing boat that supports an oarlock.

rig·ging (rĭg′ĭng) *n.* **1.** The system of ropes, chains, and tackle used to support and control the masts, sails, and yards of a sailing vessel. **2.** Any system of gear for a specific task.

right (rīt) *adj.* **righter, rightest.** *Abbr.* **R., r., rt. 1.** In accordance with or conformable to justice, law, morality, or similar principle: *right action.* **2.** In accordance with fact, reason, or truth; correct: *the right answer.* **3.** Fitting, proper, or appropriate: *the right one for the job.* **4.** Most favorable, desirable, or convenient: *the right time to act.* **5.** In a satisfactory state or condition; in good order: *I'll put it right in a moment.* **6.** Mentally sound or normal; sane: *in one's right mind.* **7.** Physically normal or healthy; well: *Are you feeling quite right?* **8.** Intended to be worn facing outward or toward an observer: *the right side of cloth.* **9.** *Archaic.* Genuine; not spurious. **10. a.** Designating, belonging to, or located on the side of the body to the east when the subject is facing north. **b.** Designating or located on the corresponding side of anything that can be considered to have a front: *the bird's right wing.* **c.** Designating or located on that side of anything which an observer directly facing it perceives to be on or toward his right side. **11.** *Often* **Right.** Of or tending toward the political right. **12.** *Geometry.* **a.** Formed by or in reference to a line or plane that is perpendicular to another line or plane. **b.** Having the axis perpendicular to the base. Said of solids: *right cone.* **13.** *Archaic.* Straight; uncurved; direct: *a right line.*
~*n.* **1.** That which is just, morally good, legal, proper, or fitting: *Two wrongs don't make a right.* **2. a.** The right side or direction: *My house is on the right.* **b.** That which is on or toward the right side or direction. **3.** *Often* **Right. a.** The individuals and groups pursuing generally conservative or reactionary political policies, in opposition to broadly egalitarian or socialist policies. **b.** Support for such policies measured in terms of an imaginary political continuum: *moving further to the right.* **4.** *Boxing.* The right hand or a blow given by the right hand. **5.** That which is due to anyone by law, tradition, or nature: *She was given her rights.* **6.** A just or legal claim or title. **7.** *Finance.* **a.** A shareholder's privilege of buying additional shares in a company at a special price, usually at par or at a price below the current market value. **b.** *Often* **rights.** A privilege of subscribing for a particular stock or bond. **—by right** or **rights.** Justly; properly. **—in one's own right.** By virtue of one's own position, efforts, or achievements. **—to rights.** In a satisfactory or orderly condition: *set the place to rights.*
~*adv.* **1.** In a straight line; directly; straight. Often used with *to, into,* or *through*: *He went right to the heart of the matter.* **2.** Properly; suitably; conveniently; well: *The suit doesn't fit right.* **3.** Exactly; just: *It happened right over there.* **4.** Immediately: *She will be right down.* **5.** Completely; thoroughly; quite: *The wind blew right through him.* **6.** According to law, morality, or justice. **7.** Accurately; correctly. **8.** On or toward the right side or direction. **9. a.** *Archaic.* Extremely: *He answered right well.* **b.** *Regional.* Very; thoroughly: *had a right good time.* **10.** Very. Used in certain titles: *the Right Reverend; Right Honorable.*
~*v.* **righted, righting, rights.** —*tr.* **1.** To put in or restore to an upright or proper position: *They righted their boat.* **2.** To put in order or set right; correct. **3.** To make reparation or amends for; redress: *right a wrong.* —*intr.* To regain an upright position.
~*interj.* Used to indicate assent, agreement, or comprehension. **—right on.** *Slang.* Used to express enthusiastic approval or agreement. [Middle English *riht, right,* Old English *riht.*] **—right·er** *n.* **—right·ness** *n.*
Synonyms: *birthright, franchise, perk, prerogative, privilege, title.*

right angle *n.* An angle formed by the perpendicular intersection of two straight lines; an angle of 90 degrees. **—at right angles.** Forming such an angle.

right-an·gled (rīt′ăng′gəld) *adj.* Forming or containing one or more right angles: *a right-angled triangle.*

right ascension *n. Abbr.* **R.A.** The angular distance of a celestial body or point on the celestial sphere, measured eastward from the vernal equinox along the celestial equator to the hour circle of the body or point and expressed in degrees or in hours.

right away *adv.* Without hesitation; immediately.

right·eous (rī′chəs) *adj.* **1.** Meeting accepted standards of what is right and just; morally right; virtuous. **2.** Having justification or good reason: *righteous anger.* —See Synonyms at **moral.** [Middle English *rightwise, ryghtuous,* Old English *rihtwīs* : *riht,* RIGHT + *wīs,* WISE (way).] **—right·eous·ly** *adv.* **—right·eous·ness** *n.*

right·ful (rīt′fəl) *adj.* **1.** Right or proper; just. **2.** Having a just or proper claim: *Return this dog to its rightful owner.* **3.** Held or owned by just or proper claim: *This dog is my rightful property.* **—right·ful·ly** *adv.* **—right·ful·ness** *n.*

right-hand (rīt′hănd′) *adj.* **1.** Of or located on the right side. **2.** Directed toward the right side: *a right-hand turn.* **3.** Of, for, or done by the right hand. **—right-hand·er** *n.*

right-hand·ed (rīt′hăn′dĭd) *adj.* **1.** Using the right hand more easily or skillfully than the left. **2.** Done with the right hand. **3.** Made to be used by the right hand. **4.** Turning or spiraling from left to right; clockwise. **—right-hand·ed·ly** *adv.* **—right-hand·ed·ness** *n.*

right-hand man *n.* One who is indispensable.

right·ism (rīt′ĭz′əm) *n. Sometimes* **Rightism.** Reactionary or conservative political activities or ideas. **—right·ist** *adj.* & *n.*

right·ly (rīt′lē) *adv.* **1.** With correctness or certainty: *I can't rightly say when I'll come.* **2. a.** Uprightly; with honesty. **b.** Justifiably: *She was rightly angered.* **3.** Properly; suitably.

right-mind·ed (rīt′mīn′dĭd) *adj.* Having principles and views based on what is considered to be right. **—right-mind·ed·ness** *n.*

right of asylum *n.* The right of receiving asylum.

right off *adv.* Right away; immediately. **—right off the bat.** Right away; at once.

right of search *n. Law.* The right of a warring nation to stop any neutral vessel on the high seas and search it for contraband.

right of way *n.* **1.** *Law.* **a.** The right to pass over property owned by another party. **b.** The path or thoroughfare on which such passage is made. **2.** The strip of land over which facilities such as highways, railroads, or power lines are built. **3.** The customary or legal right of a person, vessel, or vehicle to pass in front of another.

right-to-life (rīt′tə-līf′) *adj.* Of, relating to, or advocating laws that forbid abortion on demand; antiabortion. **—right-to-lif·er** *n.*

right whale *n.* Any of several whalebone whales of the Balaenidae family, characterized by a large head and absence of a dorsal fin.

right wing *n.* **1.** The political right. **2.** A division holding relatively conservative views within a larger political group. **—right-wing** (rīt′wĭng′) *adj.* **—right-wing·er** *n.*

rig·id (rĭj′ĭd) *adj.* **1.** Not bending; inflexible. **2.** Not moving; fixed. **3.** Rigorous; severe: *a rigorous examination.* **4.** Scrupulously strict; undeviating: *a rigid point of view.* —See Synonyms at **stiff.** [French *rigide,* from Latin *rigidus,* from *rigēre,* to be stiff.] **—rig·id·ly** *adv.* **—rig·id·ness** *n.*

ri·gid·i·ty (rĭ-jĭd′ə-tē) *n., pl.* **-ties. 1.** The state or quality of being rigid; stiffness; inflexibility. **2.** An instance of being rigid.

rigidity modulus *n. Symbol* ζ *Physics & Engineering.* A modulus of elasticity measuring the response of a material to torsion or other shear, given by the ratio of the shear stress to the shear strain. Also called "shear modulus."

rig·ma·role (rĭg′mə-rōl′) *n.* Also **rig·a·ma·role** (-ə-mə-rōl′). **1.** Confused, rambling, or incoherent speech or writing; nonsense. **2.** A complicated and petty set of procedures. [Alteration of obsolete *ragman roll,* list, catalogue (in Middle English referring to a written roll used in a game of chance), of obscure origin.]

rig·or (rĭg′ər) *n.* Also *British* **rig·our. 1.** Strictness or severity, as in temperament, action, or judgment. **2.** A harsh or trying circumstance; hardship. **3.** A severe or cruel act. **4.** *Medicine.* An attack of shivering or trembling with a sensation of coldness that marks the start of a fever. **5.** *Physiology.* A state of rigidity in living tissues or organs, as caused by shock, that prevents response to stimuli. **6.** *Obsolete.* Stiffness or rigidity. [Middle English, from Latin *rigor,* stiffness, severity, from *rigēre,* to be stiff.]

rig·or·ism (rĭg′ə-rĭz′əm) *n.* Severity or strictness in conduct, judgment, or practice; especially, in Roman Catholic theology, the stance that the rigorous or strict course is to be preferred in doubtful matters of conscience. **—rig·or·ist** *n.* **—rig·or·is·tic** *adj.*

rigor mor·tis (rĭg′ər môr′tĭs) *n.* Muscular stiffening following death, due to chemical change in the tissues. [Latin, "the stiffness of death."]

rig·or·ous (rĭg′ər-əs) *adj.* **1.** Characterized by or acting with rigor; rigid and severe. **2.** Full of rigors; trying; harsh: *a rigorous climate.* **3.** Demanding or characterized by strict accuracy or observance of standards: *rigorous tests.* —See Synonyms at **burdensome. —rig·or·ous·ly** *adv.* **—rig·or·ous·ness** *n.*

Rig-Ve·da (rĭg-vā′də, -vē′də) *n.* The most ancient collection of Hindu sacred verses. [Sanskrit *ṛigveda* : *ṛic* (stem *ṛig-*), "praise," hymn + *veda,* "knowledge," sacred writing, Veda.]

Riis (rēs), **Jacob August** (1849–1914). U.S. journalist and reformer, born in Denmark. As a reporter for New York newspapers, he photographed and wrote about the horrid living conditions in the city slums. These stories and his several books, including *Children of the Tenements* (1903), led to improvements in inner-city housing and education.

Ri·je·ka (rē-yĕk′ə). *Italian* **Fiu·me** (fyo͞o′mā). Yugoslavia's largest port, in the northwestern part of the country. An Italian force seized it from the Hungarians in 1919, and it was formally awarded to Italy by a treaty of 1924. In 1947 it was transferred to Yugoslavia.

Rijn. See **Rhine.**

PRONUNCIATION KEY
ă, **pat**; ā, **pay**; âr, **care**;
ä, **father**, are; b, **bib**;
ch, **church**; d, **deed**; ĕ, **pet**;
ē, be; f, **fife**; g, **gag**; h, **hat**;
hw, **which**; ĭ, **pit**; ī, **pie**;
îr, **pier**; j, **judge**; k, **kick**;
l, lid, needle; m, **mum**;
n, no, sudden; ng, **thing**;
ŏ, pot; ō, **toe**; ô, **paw**, **for**;
oi, **noise**; ou, **out**; o͝o, **book**;
o͞o, **boot**; p, **pop**; r, **roar**;
s, sauce; sh, **ship**, **dish**;
t, tight; th, **thin**, **path**;
th, **this**, bathe; ŭ, **cut**; ûr, **fur**;
v, valve; w, **with**; y, yes;
z, zebra, size; zh, vision;
ə, about, item, edible,
gallop, circus, peaceful

IN FOREIGN WORDS:
à, *Fr.* **ami**; œ, *Fr.* **feu**, *Ger.* **schön**; ü, *Fr.* **tu**, *Ger.* **über**;
KH, *Ger.* **ich**, *Scot.* **loch**;
N, *Fr.* bon; y′, *Fr.* **Compiègne**

STRESS MARKS:
Primary stress: ′
in·cite′ (ĭn-sīt′)
Secondary stress: ′
in′sight′ (ĭn′sīt′)

rijs·ta·fel (rīs′tä′fəl) *n.* A Dutch-Indonesian meal of rice served with piquant side dishes of meat and vegetables.
Riks·mål (rēks′mōl) *n.* **Bokmål** *(see).*
rile (rīl) *tr.v.* **riled, riling, riles. 1.** To vex; anger; irritate. **2.** To stir up (liquid). [Variant of ROIL.]
rile·y (rī′lē) *adj.* **1.** Riled; upset. **2.** Roiled; turbid.
Ri·ley (rī′lē), **James Whitcomb** (1849–1916). U.S. poet. In his many whimsical, sentimental poems he captured the regional dialect and mood of his homestate Indiana. He was called "The Hoosier Poet," and his works originally appeared in newspapers and later were collected in books such as *The Old Swimmin' Hole and 'Leven More Poems* (1883).
Ril·ke (ril′kə), **Rainer Maria** (1875–1926). Austrian poet, born in Prague. His verse is marked by a strain of mystic lyricism, in collections including *The Book of Hours* (1905), *Sonnets to Orpheus* (1923), and *The Duino Elegies* (1923).
rill (rĭl) *n.* Also **rille** (for sense 2). **1.** A small brook; rivulet. **2.** Any of various long, narrow, straight depressions on the moon's surface. [Dutch *ril* or Low German *rille.*]
rill·et (rĭl′ĭt) *n.* A small rill.
rim (rĭm) *n.* **1.** The border, edge, or margin of an object, especially one that is circular. **2.** The circular outer part of a wheel furthest from the axle; specifically, the circular metal structure around which a tire is fitted. —See Synonyms at **border.**
~*tr.v.* **rimmed, rimming, rims. 1.** To furnish with a rim; put a rim around; border. **2.** *Sports.* To roll around the rim of (a hole, basket, or cup) without falling in. Used of a ball. [Middle English *rime, rym,* Old English *rima,* from Germanic *rimō* (unattested).]
Rim·baud (răm-bō′, răN-), **(Jean Nicolas) Arthur** (1854–91). French poet. His stormy relationship with Verlaine is alluded to in the prose poem *Une Saison en Enfer* (1873). Rimbaud gave up writing at 19 and lived an adventurous life in Europe, the Near East, and North Africa, dying in Marseille at the age of 37.
rime¹ (rīm) *n.* Granular ice formed from supercooled fog droplets accumulating on the windward side of trees and other objects.
~*tr.v.* **rimed, riming, rimes.** To cover with or as if with rime. [Middle English *rim,* Old English *hrīma,* from Germanic *hrīmaz* (unattested), hoarfrost.] —**rim·y** *adj.*
rime². Variant of **rhyme.**
rime riche (rēm rēsh′) *n., pl.* **rimes riches** *(pronounced as singular).* Rhyme using words or parts of words that are pronounced identically but have different meanings, for example, *write-right* or *port-deport.* [French, "rich rhyme."]
Ri·mi·ni (rĭm′ə-nē). Popular Adriatic resort in Emilia-Romagna, Italy. It has many Roman and medieval remains.
Rimini, Francesca da. See **Francesca da Rimini.**
ri·mose (rī′mōs, rī-mōs′) *adj.* Full of chinks, cracks, or crevices. [Latin *rīmōsus,* from *rīma,* cleft, crevice, fissure.] —**ri·mose·ly** *adv.* —**ri·mos·i·ty** (rī-mŏs′ə-tē) *n.*
rim·ple (rĭm′pəl) *n.* A fold; wrinkle.
~*v.* **-pled, -pling, -ples.** —*tr.* To wrinkle; rumple. —*intr.* To form wrinkles or creases. [Middle English *rymple* from Old English *hrympel.*]
Rim·sky-Kor·sa·kov (rĭm′skē-kôr′sə-kôf′, -kôv′), **Nikolai Andreyevich** (1844–1908). Russian composer. His music often incorporates Russian folk themes; his many operas include *The Snow Maiden* (1881), and he is especially remembered for his orchestral piece *Scheherezade* (1888).
ri·mu (rē′mo͞o) *n.* A tree, the **red pine** *(see).* [Maori.]
rind (rīnd) *n.* A tough outer covering, such as bark, the skin of some fruits, or the surface layer on cheese or bacon. [Middle English *rinde,* Old English *rind(e).*]
rin·der·pest (rĭn′dər-pĕst′) *n.* An acute, contagious viral disease, chiefly of cattle, characterized by ulceration of the intestinal tract. Also called "cattle plague." [German *Rinderpest* : *Rinder,* plural of *Rind,* ox, cow, from Old High German *(h)rind* + *Pest,* pestilence, plague, from Latin *pestis,* PEST.]
Rine·hart (rīn′härt′), **Mary Roberts** (1876–1958). U.S. author. She first began writing short stories in 1903, and her first mystery, *The Circular Staircase,* was published in 1908. Her many popular books include *The Yellow Room* (1945) and *A Light in the Window* (1948).
rin·for·zan·do (rēn′fôr-tsän′dō) *adv. Music.* With a sudden increase of emphasis. Used as a direction. [Italian, present participle of *rinforzare,* to reinforce : *ri-,* from Latin *re-,* again + *inforzare,* from Old French *enforcier,* to ENFORCE.]
ring¹ (rĭng) *n.* **1.** Any circular object, form, or arrangement with an empty circular center: *blew smoke rings; a ring of bystanders.* **2.** A small circular band, generally made of precious metal, often set with jewels, and worn on a finger: *a wedding ring.* **3.** Any circular band used for carrying, holding, or containing something: *a napkin ring.* **4.** An electric element, gas burner, or the like, used as a source of heat, especially for cooking. **5.** A circular movement or course, as in dancing. **6.** An enclosed, usually circular area in which exhibitions, sports, or contests take place: *a circus ring.* **7. a.** A rectangular arena set off by stakes and ropes, in which boxing or wrestling contests are held. **b.** The sport of boxing. Preceded by *the.* **8. a.** An enclosed area in which bets are placed at a racetrack. **b.** Bookmakers collectively. **9. a.** An exclusive group of persons acting privately or illegally to advance their own interests, as in business or politics. **b.** A group of dealers illegally agreeing not to bid against each other at an auction, so as to achieve a lower sale price for a lot which is then reauctioned among themselves. **10. a.** A circular strip of bark removed from a tree trunk or branch to inhibit or stop growth. **b.** *Botany.* An **annual ring** *(see).* **11.** A field of contenders in a contest: *an unknown candidate entering the ring.* **12.** *Geometry.* The planar area between two concentric circles; an annulus. **13.** Any of the turns comprising a spiral or helix. **14.** *Chemistry.* A group of atoms chemically bound in a manner graphically representable as a circular form. Also called "closed chain." —**run rings round.** *Informal.* To show far greater skill than.
~*v.* **ringed, ringing, rings.** —*tr.* **1.** To surround with a ring; encircle. **2.** To form into a ring or rings, as by cutting. **3.** To ornament or supply with a ring or rings. **4.** To remove a circular strip of bark around the circumference of (a tree trunk or branch) in order to kill it or retard its growth; ring-bark. **5.** To put a ring in the nose of (a pig, bull, or other animal). **6.** To hem in (cattle or other animals) by riding in a circle around them. **7.** To toss a ring over (a peg) in a game. **8.** To put a ring around the leg of (a bird) for subsequent identification. —*intr.* **1.** To form a ring or rings. **2.** To move, run, or fly in a spiral or circular course. [Middle English *ring,* Old English *hring,* from Germanic.]
ring² *v.* **rang** (răng), **rung** (rŭng), **ringing, rings.** —*intr.* **1.** To give forth a clear, resonant sound when caused to vibrate. **2.** To cause a bell or bells to sound. **3. a.** To sound a bell in order to summon someone. **b.** To make a telephone call: *I'll ring later.* **4.** To have a sound or character suggestive of a specified quality: *a perception that rings true.* **5.** To be filled with sound; resound. **6.** To persist vividly in the mind: *his plea still ringing in my ear.* **7.** To hear a persistent humming or buzzing: *ears ringing from the blast.* —*tr.* **1.** To cause (a bell, chimes, or the like) to ring. **2.** To produce (a sound) by or as if by ringing. **3. a.** To announce, proclaim, or signal by or as if by ringing. **b.** To summon or usher in in this way. Used with *in* or *out*: *ring in the new year.* **4.** To telephone (someone). Often used with *up.* **5.** To test (a coin, for example) for quality by the sound it produces when struck against something. —**ring a bell.** *Informal.* To arouse a memory: *The name doesn't ring a bell.* —**ring up. 1.** To make a telephone call. **2.** To record (a price) on a cash register.
~*n.* **1.** The sound created by a bell or other sonorous, vibrating object. **2.** Any loud sound, especially one that is repeated or continued. **3.** A telephone call. **4.** A suggestion of a particular quality: *Her offer has a suspicious ring.* **5.** A set of bells. **6.** An act or instance of sounding a bell. [Middle English *ringen,* Old English *hringan.* Rang, rung; Middle English *rang, rungen,* analogous formations to verbs such as SING.]
ring-bark (rĭng′bärk′) *tr.v.* **-barked, -barking, -barks.** To ring (a tree trunk or branch).
ring-billed gull (rĭng′bĭld′) *n.* A North American gull, *Larus delawarensis,* having a black ring around its bill.
ring binder *n.* A booklike file with two or more circular clasps inside the spine that can be opened to allow loose leaves to be inserted.
ring·bolt (rĭng′bōlt′) *n.* A bolt having a ring fitted through an eye at its head.
ring·bone (rĭng′bōn′) *n.* A bony growth on the fetlock, pastern, or coffin bone of a horse's foot, usually causing lameness. [It tends to spread around a horse's foot like a ring.]
ring·dove (rĭng′dŭv′) *n.* **1.** An Old World pigeon, *Streptopelia risoria,* having black markings forming a half circle on the neck. **2.** The **wood pigeon** *(see).*
ringed (rĭngd) *adj.* **1.** Wearing a ring or rings. **2.** Encircled or surrounded by bands or rings. **3.** Having ringlike markings.
rin·gent (rĭn′jənt) *adj. Biology.* Having gaping liplike parts, as the corolla of some flowers or the shells of certain bivalves do. [Latin *ringēns* (stem *ringent-*), present participle of *ringī,* to open wide the mouth, gape. See **rictus.**]
ring·er¹ (rĭng′ər) *n.* **1.** One that rings. **2.** A horseshoe or quoit thrown so that it encircles the peg.
ringer² *n.* **1.** One that sounds a bell or chime. **2.** *Informal.* A person who bears a striking resemblance to another. **3.** *Slang.* A contestant entered dishonestly into a competition.
Ring·er's solution (rĭng′ərz) *n.* A solution of the chlorides of sodium, potassium, and calcium, used to maintain living tissues and organs in vitro and to treat dehydration. [After Sydney *Ringer* (1835–1910), British physician.]
ring finger *n.* The third finger of the hand, especially the left hand, as counted from the forefinger.
ring·git (rĭng′gĭt) *n.* The basic monetary unit of Malaysia, equal to 100 sen. See feature at **currency.**
ring·hals (rĭng′hăls′) *n., pl.* **ringhals.** Also **rink·hals** (rĭngk′-). An African snake, *Haemachates haemachatus,* that spits venom. Also called "spitting cobra," "spitting snake." [Afrikaans *ringhals, rinkals,* "ring-necked" : *ring,* ring, circle, from Middle Dutch *rinc* + *hals,* neck, from Middle Dutch.]
ring·lead·er (rĭng′lē′dər) *n.* A person who leads others, especially in unlawful or improper activities.
ring·let (rĭng′lĭt) *n.* **1.** A spirally curled lock of hair. **2.** A small circle or ring. **3.** Any of various butterflies of the family Satyridae having brownish wings marked with white rings. —**ring·let·ed** *adj.*
Ring·ling (rĭng′lĭng), **Charles** (1863–1926). U.S. circus owner. With his brothers **Albert** (1852–1916), **Otto** (1858–1911), **Alfred** (1861–1919), and **John** (1866–1936), he formed a song-and-dance troop (1882) that through his deft management and business acquisitions evolved into The Ringling Brothers and Barnum & Bailey Circus (1907).

PRONUNCIATION KEY

ă, pat; ā, pay; âr, care;
ä, father, are; b, bib;
ch, church; d, deed; ĕ, pet;
ē, be; f, fife; g, gag; h, hat;
hw, which; ĭ, pit; ī, pie;
îr, pier; j, judge; k, kick;
l, lid, needle; m, mum;
n, no, sudden; ng, thing;
ŏ, pot; ō, toe; ô, paw, for;
oi, noise; ou, out; o͝o, book;
o͞o, boot; p, pop; r, roar;
s, sauce; sh, ship, dish;
t, tight; th, thin, path;
th, this, bathe; ŭ, cut; ûr, fur;
v, valve; w, with; y, yes;
z, zebra, size; zh, vision;
ə, about, item, edible,
gallop, circus, peaceful

IN FOREIGN WORDS:

à, *Fr.* ami; œ, *Fr.* feu, *Ger.* schön; ü, *Fr.* tu, *Ger.* über;
KH, *Ger.* ich, *Scot.* loch;
N, *Fr.* bon; y′, *Fr.* Compiègne

STRESS MARKS:

Primary stress: ′
in·cite′ (ĭn-sīt′)
Secondary stress: ′
in′sight′ (ĭn′sīt′)

ring·mas·ter (rĭng′măs′tər, -mäs′tər) *n.* A person in charge of the performances in a circus ring.

Ring Nebula *n.* A planetary nebula in the constellation Lyra. [From its resemblance to a smoke ring.]

ring-necked pheasant (rĭng′nĕkt′) *n.* A widely distributed bird, *Phasianus colchicus,* native to the Old World, the male of which has brightly colored plumage and a white ring around the neck.

ring ousel *n.* A European thrush, *Turdus torquatus,* of mountainous regions, the male of which is black with a white neck band.

ring·side (rĭng′sīd′) *n.* **1.** The area or seats immediately outside an arena or ring, as at a boxing match. **2.** Any place providing a close view of a spectacle. Also used adjectivally: *ringside seats.*

ring·tail (rĭng′tāl′) *n.* **1.** An animal with ringlike markings on its tail; especially, the **cacomistle** (*see*). Also called "ring-tailed cat." **2.** Any of various Australian phalangers with prehensile tails.

ring-tailed (rĭng′tāld′) *adj.* **1.** Having a tail with ringlike markings. **2.** Having a tail that curls to form a ring.

ring·worm (rĭng′wûrm′) *n.* Any of a number of contagious skin diseases caused by several related fungi, and characterized by ring-shaped, scaly, itching patches on the skin.

rink (rĭngk) *n.* **1.** An area surfaced with smooth ice for skating, hockey, or curling. **2.** A smooth floor suited for roller-skating. **3.** A building that houses a surface prepared for skating. **4.** A section of a bowling green large enough for play. **5.** A team of players in quoits, bowling, or curling. [Middle English (Scottish) *rinc,* jousting area, perhaps from Old French *renc, ranc,* row, range, RANK.]

rinkhals. Variant of **ringhals.**

rink·y-dink (rĭng′kē-dĭngk′) *adj. Slang.* **1.** Old-fashioned. **2.** Insignificant. [Origin unknown.]

rinse (rĭns) *tr.v.* **rinsed, rinsing, rinses.** **1.** To wash lightly with water. **2.** To remove (soap, dirt, or impurities) from clothing or hair, for example, by rinsing in clean water. —*n.* **1.** The act or an instance of rinsing. **2.** The water or other solution used in this process. **3. a.** A cosmetic solution used in conditioning or tinting the hair. **b.** A hairstyle treated with such a solution. [Middle English *ryncen,* from Old French *rincer, raincier†.*] —**rins·er** *n.*

Ri·o de Ja·nei·ro (rē′ō dē jə-nâr′ō, dā zhə-). Chief seaport and former capital of Brazil, on Guanabara Bay in the southeastern part of the country. Brazil's second-largest city, it is backed by towering mountains, the most spectacular of which are Sugar Loaf and Corvocado, which is surmounted by a colossal statue of Christ. A tourist center, the city has magnificent beaches, including the famous Copacabana. It is also a cultural, financial, commercial, manufacturing, and transport center.

Ri·o Grande (rē′ō grănd′). River in the southern United States. Rising in the San Juan Mts. of southwestern Colorado, it flows 3,035 kilometers (1,885 miles) south, then southeast, to the Gulf of Mexico. For much of its length it forms the border between the United States and Mexico.

ri·ot (rī′ət) *n.* **1.** A wild or turbulent disturbance created by a large number of people. **2.** *Law.* A violent disturbance of the public peace by three or more persons assembled for a common private purpose. Also used adjectivally: *riot police.* **3.** An unrestrained outbreak, as of laughter or passions. **4.** A wild profusion, as of colors. **5. a.** Unrestrained merrymaking; revelry. **b.** *Archaic.* Debauchery. **6.** *Slang.* An irresistibly funny person or thing. **7.** In hunting, the following by a hound of the scent of the wrong prey. —**run riot.** **1.** To move or act with wild abandon. **2.** To grow luxuriantly or abundantly. —*v.* **rioted, -oting, -ots.** —*intr.* **1.** To take part in a riot. **2.** To live wildly or engage in uncontrolled revelry. —*tr.* To waste (money or time) in wild or wanton living. Used with *away* or *out.* [Middle English *riot(e),* debauchery, revel, riot, from Old French *ri(h)ot(e),* from *r(u)ihoter†,* to quarrel.] —**ri·ot·er** *n.*

Riot Act *n.* **1.** A law, enacted in England in 1715, providing that if 12 or more persons unlawfully assemble and disturb the public peace, they must disperse upon proclamation or be considered guilty of felony. **2. riot act.** Any severe or forceful warning or reproach. Used chiefly in the phrase *read the riot act.*

ri·ot·ous (rī′ət-əs) *adj.* **1.** Of, pertaining to, or resembling a riot. **2.** Taking part in or inciting to riot or uproar. **3.** Uproarious; boisterous. **4.** Dissolute; profligate. **5.** Abundant or luxuriant: *a riotous growth.* —**ri·ot·ous·ly** *adv.* —**ri·ot·ous·ness** *n.*

rip¹ (rĭp) *v.* **ripped, ripping, rips.** —*tr.* **1.** To cut or tear apart roughly or energetically; slash: *ripped open the parcel.* **2.** To remove by cutting or tearing roughly: *ripped the bandage off her leg.* **3.** To split or saw (wood) along the grain. **4.** *Informal.* To produce, display, or exclaim suddenly. Used with *out: ripped out a gun; ripped out a vicious oath.* —*intr.* **1.** To become torn or split apart. **2.** *Informal.* To move quickly or violently. **3.** *Informal.* To make a vehement verbal attack. Used with *into: ripped into her opponent's record.* —**let rip.** To give full vent to one's feelings: *let rip and told him what she thought of him.* —See Synonyms at **tear.** —*n.* **1.** A torn or split place, especially along a seam; a tear. **2.** The act of ripping. [Middle English *rippen†.*] —**rip·per** *n.*

rip² *n.* **1.** A stretch of broken water in a river, estuary, or tidal channel. **2.** A **rip current** (*see*). [Perhaps from RIP (the act of tearing).]

rip³ *n. Archaic.* **1.** A dissolute person. **2.** An old or worthless horse. [Perhaps shortened variant of REPROBATE.]

R.I.P. rest in peace [Latin *requiescat in pace*].

ri·par·i·an (rĭ-pâr′ē-ən) *adj.* **1.** Of, on, or pertaining to the bank of a river. **2.** Designating a right due to an owner of riparian land, for example a right to fish. —*n.* One who owns riparian land. [Latin *rīpārius,* from *rīpa,* bank, shore.]

rip·cord (rĭp′kôrd′) *n.* **1.** A cord pulled to release the pack of a parachute. **2.** A cord pulled to release gas from a balloon.

rip current *n.* A current of water disturbed by an opposing current, especially in tidal waters, or by passage over an irregular bottom. Also called "rip," "riptide."

ripe (rīp) *adj.* **riper, ripest.** **1.** Fully developed or mature; especially, ready for harvesting or consumption: *ripe pears.* **2.** Resembling matured fruit, as in fullness: *a ripe figure.* **3.** Sufficiently advanced in preparation or ageing to be used: *ripe cheese.* **4.** Thoroughly matured, as by study or experience; seasoned: *ripe judgment.* **5.** Advanced in years: *the ripe old age of 85.* **6.** Fully developed; prepared to do or undergo something; ready: *ripe for picking.* **7.** Sufficiently advanced; opportune. Said of time. [Middle English *ripe,* Old English *rīpe.*] —**ripe·ly** *adv.* —**ripe·ness** *n.*

rip·en (rī′pən) *v.* **-ened, -ening, -ens.** —*tr.* To make ripe; cause to mature. —*intr.* To become ripe; mature. —**rip·en·er** *n.*

ri·pi·e·no (rĭ-pyä′nō) *n. Music.* A passage in which the whole orchestra plays. [Italian, "full."]

Rip·ley (rĭp′lē), **George** (1802–80). U.S. minister, scholar, and literary critic. A Boston Unitarian minister (1826–41), he was involved with the New England Transcendentalist movement, founded and contributed to the *Dial* (1840–44), and participated in the communal living experiment at Brook Farm (1841–47).

Ripley, Robert LeRoy (1893–1949). U.S. cartoonist. A New York sports cartoonist in search of material, he one day sketched athletes who had performed unusual feats (1918). He continued to publicize extraordinary events and oddities in a syndicated cartoon series called "Believe It or Not," a radio show, and several books.

rip off *tr.v. Slang.* **1.** To exploit, swindle, cheat, or defraud. **2.** To steal: *ripped off a case of whiskey.* **3.** To steal from; rob: *Shoplifters ripped off the store.*

rip-off (rĭp′ôf′, -ŏf′) *n. Slang.* **1. a.** An act of exploitation or overcharging. **b.** Something that is overpriced. **2.** A theft.

Rip·on (rĭp′ən). City in central Wisconsin, settled in 1844. Its industrial products include washing machines and canned foods. The city was the site of a political meeting (1854) that led to the formation of the Republican Party.

ri·poste, ri·post (rĭ-pōst′) *n.* **1.** In fencing, a quick thrust given after parrying an opponent's lunge. **2.** A quick, retaliatory action or retort. —*intr.v.* **riposted, -posting, -postes.** To make a riposte. [French, from Italian *risposta,* answer, feminine past participle of *rispondere,* to answer, from Latin *respondēre,* to RESPOND.]

rip·ping (rĭp′ĭng) *adj. British Informal.* Wonderful; splendid. Not in current usage.

rip·ple¹ (rĭp′əl) *v.* **-pled, -pling, -ples.** —*intr.* **1.** To form or display little undulations or waves on the surface, as on disturbed water. **2. a.** To flow with such undulations or waves on the surface. **b.** To have a movement resembling rippling water: *rippling muscles.* **3.** To rise and fall gently in tone or volume: *Laughter rippled.* —*tr.* To cause to form small waves or undulations. —*n.* **1.** A slight wave or undulation. **2.** Anything resembling such undulations in appearance: *ripples in the fabric.* **3.** A sound that gently rises and falls. **4.** *Electronics.* A small alternating, usually undesirable signal superimposed on an otherwise constant signal. **5.** A small rapid. [17th century (verb) : origin obscure.] —**rip·pler** *n.* —**rip·pling·ly** *adv.* —**rip·ply** *adj.*

ripple² *n.* A comblike, toothed instrument for removing seeds from flax and other fibers. —*tr.v.* **rippled, -pling, -ples.** To remove seeds from (flax or other fibers) with a ripple. [Middle English *rip(e)len,* to remove seeds, from Germanic, akin to Middle Low German *repelen.*]

rip·plet (rĭp′lĭt) *n.* A little wave or ripple.

rip·rap (rĭp′răp′) *n.* **1.** A loose assemblage of broken stones erected in water or on soft ground as a foundation. **2.** The broken stones used for this. —*tr.v.* **riprapped, -rapping, -raps.** **1.** To construct a riprap in or upon. **2.** To strengthen with a riprap. [Reduplication of RAP (to strike).]

rip-roar·ing (rĭp′rôr′ĭng, -rō′rĭng) *adj. Informal.* Noisy, lively, and exciting. [RIP + (UP)ROAR(IOUS).]

rip·saw (rĭp′sô′) *n.* A coarse-toothed handsaw for cutting wood along the grain.

rip·snort·er (rĭp′snôr′tər) *n. Slang.* A person or thing remarkable for strength, intensity, or excellence. —**rip·snort·ing** *adj.*

rip tide *n.* A **rip current** (*see*).

Rip·u·ar·i·an (rĭp′yoo-âr′ē-ən) *adj.* Of or designating a group of Franks who lived along the Rhine, near Cologne, in the fourth century. —**Rip·u·ar·i·an** *n.* [Medieval Latin *Ripuārius†.*]

Rip Van Winkle (rĭp′ văn wĭng′kəl) *n.* One who is completely unaware of current trends and conditions. [After a character who slept for 20 years in a tale (1819) by Washington Irving.]

rise (rīz) *v.* **rose** (rōz), **risen** (rĭz′ən), **rising, rises.** —*intr.* **1.** To assume a standing position after lying, sitting, or kneeling. **2.** To get out of bed, especially after a night's rest. **3.** To move from a lower to a higher position; ascend. **4.** To increase in height or level: *The lake rose after the rain.* **5.** To appear above the horizon: *The sun rises in the east.* **6.** To extend upward; be prominent: *The tower rose above the hill. The cliff rises to 200 feet.* **7.** To slant or slope upward: *Fields rose above the river.* **8.** To originate; come into existence: *a storm rising in the north.* **9.** To be built or erected. **10.** To appear at the surface of the water. Used of fish. **11.** To puff up or become larger during cooking or as a result of leavening: *Bread dough rises in a warm place.* **12.** To become stiff and erect: *Hackles rose.* **13.** To increase in quantity, value, or price: *rising prices.* **14. a.** To increase in intensity, force, pitch, or prominence: *The temperature rises in summer.* **b.** To register an increase: *The index rose sharply.* **15.** To attain a higher status: *rose in her esteem.* **16. a.** To become apparent to the mind or senses: *Fears rose to haunt him.* **b.** To become elated: *Her spirits rose.* **17.** To uplift oneself to meet a demand: *rose to the challenge.* **18.** To return to life. **19.** To rebel. Often used with *up.* **20.** To close a session of an official assembly; adjourn. *—tr.* **1.** To cause to rise. **2.** *Nautical.* To cause (a distant object at sea) to become visible above the horizon by advancing closer.

~n. **1.** The act of rising; an ascent. **2.** The degree of elevation or ascent; an upward slope. **3.** The appearance of the sun or other heavenly body above the horizon. **4.** An increase in height, as of the level of water. **5.** A gently sloping hill or elevation. **6.** An origin, beginning, or source: *the rise of a river.* **7.** *British.* An increase in salary or wages. **8.** The emergence of a fish seeking food or bait at the water's surface. **9.** An increase in price, worth, quantity, or degree. **10.** An increase in intensity, volume, or pitch. **11.** Elevation in social status, prosperity, or importance. **12.** The height of a flight of stairs or of a single step. **—get a rise out of.** *Slang.* To provoke or tease (someone) successfully. **—give rise to.** To give occasion or opportunity to: *give rise to doubt.* [Rise, rose, risen; Middle English *risen, ros, risen,* Old English *rīsan, rās, risen.* (*Rās* and *risen* are attested only in compounds.)]

Synonyms: *ascend, climb, mount, soar.*

ris·er (rī′zər) *n.* **1.** A person who rises, especially from sleep: *a late riser.* **2.** The vertical part of a stair step.

ris·i·bil·i·ty (rĭz′ə-bĭl′ə-tē) *n., pl.* **-ties. 1.** The ability or tendency to laugh. **2. risibilities.** A sense of the ludicrous or amusing. **3.** Laughter; hilarity.

ris·i·ble (rĭz′ə-bəl) *adj.* **1.** Capable of laughing or inclined to laugh. **2.** Pertaining to or used in laughter. **3.** Apt to excite laughter; ludicrous; laughable. [Late Latin *rīsibilis,* from Latin *rīdēre* (past participle *rīsus*), to laugh. See **ridiculous.**] **—ris·i·bly** *adv.*

ris·ing (rī′zĭng) *adj.* **1.** Ascending, sloping upward, or advancing: *rising ground.* **2.** Approaching maturity or prominence; emerging: *the rising generation; a rising young actress.*

~n. **1.** An uprising; a revolt. **2.** A prominence or projection. **3.** The leaven or yeast used to make dough rise in baking.

~adv. Almost or approaching a specified age.

rising damp *n.* Damp that enters a building through the foundations, rising up the walls by capillary action.

risk (rĭsk) *n.* **1.** The possibility of suffering harm or loss; danger: *There is the risk we won't return.* **2.** A factor, element, or course involving uncertain danger; a hazard: *The stormy weather is a risk we shall have to take.* **3.** *Insurance.* **a.** The danger or probability of loss to the insurer. **b.** The amount that the insurance company stands to lose. **c.** A person or thing considered with respect to the possibility of loss to an insurer: *a poor risk.* —See Synonyms at **danger.**

~tr.v. **risked, risking, risks. 1.** To expose to a chance of loss or damage; hazard. **2.** To incur the risk of: *risking death.* **3.** To take the risk arising from: *I'll risk staying another hour.* [French *risque(r),* from Italian *risco*†, danger, from *riscare*†, to run into danger.] **—risk·er** *n.*

risk capital *n. British.* Money invested in an enterprise subject to risk, such as a new business venture.

risk·y (rĭs′kē) *adj.* **-ier, -iest.** Accompanied by or involving risk or danger; hazardous. **—risk·i·ness** *n.*

Ri·sor·gi·men·to (rē-sôr′jē-mĕn′tō) *n.* The period of or the movement for the liberation and political unification of Italy, beginning about 1750 and lasting until 1870. [Italian, "resurrection," from *risorgere,* to resurrect, from Latin *resurgere,* to rise again : *re-,* again + *surgere,* to rise. See **surge.**]

ri·sot·to (rē-sôt′ō, rĭ-sŏt′ō) *n.* An Italian dish of rice cooked in stock with grated cheese or vegetables and seasonings, often served with chopped meat or seafood. [Italian, from *riso,* rice.]

ris·qué (rĭs-kā′) *adj.* Suggestive of or bordering on indelicacy or impropriety: *a risqué joke.* [French, from the past participle of *risquer,* to RISK.]

ris·sole (rĭ-sōl′, rē-sôl′) *n.* A small ball or cake that is made with a minced meat or fish mixture coated with breadcrumbs and egg, and usually fried. [French, from Old French *roissole,* from (unattested) Vulgar Latin *russeola (pasta),* "reddish (pastry)," from the feminine of Late Latin *russeolus,* diminutive of Latin *russeus,* reddish, from *russus,* red.]

ris·so·lé (rē-sô-lā′) *adj.* Browned by frying. [French, past participle of *rissoler,* to brown by deep frying, from *rissole,* RISSOLE.]

ri·tar·dan·do (rē′tär-dän′dō) *adv. Abbr.* **rit., ritard.** *Music.* Gradually slowing in tempo. Used as a direction. [Italian, from Latin *retardandum,* gerund of *retardāre,* to RETARD.]

rite (rīt) *n.* **1.** The prescribed or customary form for conducting a religious or other solemn ceremony: *the rite of baptism.* **2.** A ceremonial act or series of acts: *fertility rites.* **3.** *Often* **Rite.** The liturgy of a Christian church, especially one of the historical forms of the Eucharistic service: *the Anglican Rite.* **4.** *Often* **Rite.** A branch or division of the Christian church as determined by specific liturgy and law: *Catholics of the Latin Rite.* **5.** Any formal practice, custom, or procedure. [Middle English *ryte,* from Latin *rītus.*]

rite of passage *n.* A ceremony, as in a primitive society, that marks a person's change of status, for example at puberty or on marriage; broadly, any ritual or ceremony that marks a transition in the life of an individual.

ri·tor·nel·lo (rē′tôr-nĕl′ō) *n., pl.* **-li** (-lē) or **-los.** *Music.* **1.** An instrumental interlude recurring between verses in a vocal work. **2.** A passage for full orchestra in a baroque concerto grosso. **3.** An instrumental interlude in early 17th-century opera. [Italian, a refrain, diminutive of *ritorno,* return, from *ritornare,* to return, from Vulgar Latin *retornāre* (unattested), to RETURN.]

rit·u·al (rĭch′o͞o-əl) *n.* **1.** The prescribed form or order of conducting a religious or solemn ceremony. **2.** A body of ceremonies or rites. **3.** A book of rites or ceremonial forms. **4. a.** A ceremonial act or a series of such acts. **b.** The performance of such acts. **5.** Any habitual detailed method of procedure: *the ritual of household chores.*

~adj. **1.** Of or characterized by a rite or rites. **2.** Performed as a rite or ritual: *a ritual fire dance.* [Latin *rītuālis,* from *rītus,* RITE.] **—rit·u·al·ly** *adv.*

rit·u·al·ism (rĭch′o͞o-ə-lĭz′əm) *n.* **1.** The study, practice, or observance of ritual. **2.** Insistence upon or adherence to ritual.

rit·u·al·ist (rĭch′o͞o-əl-ĭst) *n.* **1.** An authority on or student of ritual. **2.** A person who practices or advocates the observance of ritual.

rit·u·al·is·tic (rĭch′o͞o-əl-ĭs′tĭk) *adj.* Pertaining to, characterized by, or devoted to ritual or ritualism. **—rit·u·al·is·ti·cal·ly** *adv.*

rit·u·al·ize (rĭch′o͞o-ə-līz′) *v.* **-ized, -izing, -izes.** *—intr.* To engage in or practice ritualism. *—tr.* **1.** To make into or convert to ritual. **2.** To impose a ritual on. **—rit·u·al·i·za·tion** *n.*

ritz·y (rĭt′sē) *adj.* **-ier, -iest.** *Informal.* Elegant; luxurious and fashionable. [From the *Ritz* hotels founded by César *Ritz* (1850–1918), Swiss hotelier.]

riv·age (rĭv′ĭj) *n. Archaic.* A coast, shore, or bank. [Middle English, from Old French, from *rive,* bank, shore, from Latin *rīpa.*]

ri·val (rī′vəl) *n.* **1.** A person who attempts to equal or surpass another, or who pursues the same object as another; a competitor: *They were rivals for the same job.* **2.** One that equals or almost equals another in some respect. —See Synonyms at **opponent.**

~adj. Acting as or being a rival; competing.

~v. **rivaled, -valing, -vals.** Also *chiefly British* **-valled, -valling.** *—tr.* **1.** To attempt to equal or surpass. **2.** To be the equal of; be a match for: *"rivalled the beauties of the best Grecian architecture"* (Henry Fielding). *—intr. Archaic.* To be a competitor or rival; compete. Used with *with.* [Latin *rīvālis,* "one using the same brook as another," rival, from *rīvus,* brook.]

Synonyms: *compete, emulate, vie.*

ri·val·ry (rī′vəl-rē) *n., pl.* **-ries. 1.** The act or an instance of competing or emulating. **2.** The state or condition of being a rival.

rive (rīv) *v.* **rived, rived** or **riven** (rĭv′ən), **riving, rives.** *Archaic. —tr.* **1.** To rend or tear apart. **2.** To break into pieces, as by a blow; cleave or split asunder. **3.** To break or distress (the heart or spirit, for example). *—intr.* To be or become broken or split. [Middle English *riven,* from Old Norse *rīfa.*]

riv·er (rĭv′ər) *n.* **1.** *Abbr.* **R., r., riv.** A large natural stream of water flowing toward an ocean, lake, or other body of water. **2.** Any stream or abundant flow resembling this: *rivers of milk.* **—sell down the river.** To betray or deceive. **—up the river.** *Slang.* In or to prison. [Middle English, from Norman French *rivere,* river bank, river, from Vulgar Latin *rīpāria* (unattested), feminine of Latin *rīpārius,* on a bank, from *rīpa,* bank.]

Ri·ver·a (rĭ-vĕr′ə), **Diego** (1886–1957). Mexican artist. His murals celebrate the struggle for independence and draw inspiration from his socialist beliefs, exalting the Indian peasantry at the expense of the ruling classes.

river basin *n.* See **basin** (sense 5).

riv·er·bed (rĭv′ər-bĕd′) *n.* The area covered or once covered by water, between the banks of a river.

riv·er·boat (rĭv′ər-bōt′) *n.* A boat suitable for use on a river.

river horse *n. Informal.* The **hippopotamus** *(see).*

riv·er·ine (rĭv′ər-īn′, -ĭn) *adj.* **1.** Pertaining to or resembling a river. **2.** Located on or inhabiting the banks of a river; riparian.

Riv·ers (rĭv′ərz), **Larry** (1923–). U.S. artist. In many of his complex, often fragmentary works, including *The History of the Russian Revolution* (1965), he combines the bold brushwork of abstract expressionism with the realistic commercial images associated with pop art.

riv·er·side (rĭv′ər-sīd′) *n.* The bank of a river.

~adj. On or close to a bank of a river.

riv·et (rĭv′ĭt) *n.* A metal bolt or pin, having a head on one end, used to fasten metal plates or other objects together by inserting the shank through a hole in each piece and hammering down the plain end so as to form a new head.

~tr.v. **riveted, -eting, -ets. 1.** To fasten or secure with or as if with a rivet. **2.** To hammer the headless end of (a bolt, pin, or similar device) so as to form a head and fasten something. **3.** To fasten or secure firmly; fix. **4.** To engross; grip: *riveted by the scene.* [Middle English *ryvette,* from Old French *rivet*†, to fix.] **—riv·et·er** *n.*

riv·et·ing (rĭv′ĭt-ĭng) *adj.* Completely absorbing the attention; fascinating.

Riv·i·er·a (rĭv′ē-âr′ə). **1.** The coastal region stretching along the Mediterranean Sea from Hyères in southeastern France to La Spezia, Italy, that includes the fashionable resorts of Cannes, Monte Carlo, Nice, and St. Tropez. **2. riviera.** Any resort area extending

PRONUNCIATION KEY

ă, pat; ā, pay; âr, care;
ä, father, are; b, bib;
ch, church; d, deed; ĕ, pet;
ē, be; f, fife; g, gag; h, hat;
hw, which; ĭ, pit; ī, pie;
îr, pier; j, judge; k, kick;
l, lid, needle; m, mum;
n, no, sudden; ng, thing;
ŏ, pot; ō, toe; ô, paw, for;
oi, noise; ou, out; o͝o, book;
o͞o, boot; p, pop; r, roar;
s, sauce; sh, ship, dish;
t, tight; th, thin, path;
th, this, bathe; ŭ, cut; ûr, fur;
v, valve; w, with; y, yes;
z, zebra, size; zh, vision;
ə, about, item, edible,
gallop, circus, peaceful

IN FOREIGN WORDS:

à, *Fr.* ami; œ, *Fr.* feu, *Ger.* schön; ü, *Fr.* tu, *Ger.* über; KH, *Ger.* ich, *Scot.* loch; N, *Fr.* bon; y′, *Fr.* Compiègne

STRESS MARKS:

Primary stress: ′
in·cite′ (ĭn-sīt′)
Secondary stress: ′
in′sight′ (ĭn′sīt′)

along a coastline and usually having a mild climate. [Italian, "shore," from Vulgar Latin *rīpāria* (unattested). See **river**.]

ri·vi·ère (rē-vyâr′) *n.* A necklace of diamonds or other precious stones, generally in one strand. [French, short for *rivière de diamants*, "stream of diamonds," from Old French *rivere*, RIVER.]

riv·u·let (rĭv′yə-lĭt) *n.* A small brook or stream; streamlet. [Earlier *rivelet*, probably from Italian *rivoletto*, diminutive of *rivolo*, small stream, from Latin *rīvulus*, diminutive of *rīvus*, brook, stream.]

Ri·yadh or **Ri·ad** (rē-yäd′). Capital of Saudi Arabia. Situated in an oasis in Nejd province, of which it is capital, it was once a walled town. The impact of the country's oil wealth has made it a commercial center with much modern architecture.

ri·yal (rē-ôl′, -äl′) *n.* The basic monetary unit of Qatar, equal to 100 dirhams. See feature at **currency**. [Arabic *riyāl*, from Spanish *real*, REAL (coin).]

Riz·zio (rĭt′sē-ō, rēt′sē-ō′), **David** (*c.* 1533–66). Italian musician and confidant of Mary Queen of Scots. First entering the queen's service as a musician, he later became her trusted secretary and helped arrange her marriage to Lord Darnley. He was stabbed to death by the 4th Earl of Morton and several other Scotsmen.

RK galaxy (är′kā′) *n.* A ring galaxy composed of a ring structure with a large bright knot of incandescent material on the ring itself.

RM reichsmark.

rm. **1.** ream. **2.** room.

rms root mean square.

R.M.S. **1.** Railway Mail Service. **2.** Royal Mail Service. **3.** Royal Mail Steamer.

Rn The symbol for the element radon.

R.N. **1.** registered nurse. **2.** Royal Navy.

RNA *n.* A nucleic acid occurring in all living cells, consisting of a single-stranded chain of alternating phosphate and ribose units with the bases adenine, guanine, cytosine, and uracil bonded to the ribose. RNA occurs in several forms, mostly in the cytoplasm, and has an essential role in protein syntheses. See **messenger RNA**, **ribosomal RNA**, **transfer RNA**. [*Ribonucleic acid*.]

RNAase *n.* **Ribonuclease** (see).

ro. rood (measure).

roach¹ (rōch) *n., pl.* **roaches** or collectively **roach**. **1.** A freshwater

game fish, *Rutilus rutilus*, of northern Europe, having reddish fins. **2.** Any of various similar or related fishes, such as some North American sunfishes. [Middle English *roche*, from Old French *roche†.*]

roach² *n.* **1.** An insect, the **cockroach** (see). **2.** *Slang.* The butt or filter, usually homemade, of a marijuana cigarette.

roach³ *n.* *Nautical.* The upward curvature of the bottom edge of a square sail intended to prevent chafing. [18th century : origin obscure.]

Roach (rōch), **Hal** (1892–). U.S. film director. His film company produced comedies featuring Harold Lloyd, Laurel and Hardy, and others, and he directed films such as *Fraternally Yours* (1933) and *Of Mice and Men* (1940).

roach clip *n.* A device used to hold the butt of a marijuana cigarette.

road (rōd) *n.* *Abbr.* **Rd.**, **rd.**, **R.**, **r.** **1. a.** An open way, generally public, for the passage of vehicles, persons, and animals. Used as part of certain street names: *Old Mill Road*. **2.** A course or path: *the road to success*. **3.** A passage or tunnel in a mine. **4.** A railroad. **5.** *Usually* **roads**. *Nautical.* A **roadstead** (see). **—hit the road.** *Informal.* To begin a journey. **—one for the road.** A last drink before setting out. **—on the road. 1.** On tour. Said especially of a theatrical company. **2.** Traveling or moving around, especially as a salesman. [Middle English *rood, rode*, riding, journey, Old English *rād*.] See feature, next page.

road·bed (rōd′bĕd′) *n.* **1. a.** The foundation upon which the ties, rails, and ballast of a railroad are laid. **b.** A layer of ballast directly under the ties. **2.** The foundation and surface of a road.

road·block (rōd′blŏk′) *n.* **1.** An obstruction across a road set up, as by the police or army, for purposes of detection, security, or defense. **2.** An obstruction in a road, as rocks or a fallen tree. **3.** Something, as a situation or condition, that prevents further progress toward an accomplishment.

road hog *n.* *Informal.* A driver who drives inconsiderately and selfishly, often keeping his vehicle near the middle of the road.

road·hold·ing (rōd′hōld′ĭng) *n.* *Chiefly British.* The ability of a motor vehicle to retain its grip or hold on a surface without skidding.

roach *A widespread and common freshwater fish growing to about 35 centimeters (14 inches). Roach are fished for food in eastern Europe, but are used mainly as game fish elsewhere.*

---

river

THE WINDING ROUTE TO THE SEA
How a river changes the face of the countryside

A river is a natural flowing stream of water that cuts its own course through the land until it reaches the sea, a lake, or another river. On its way, it constantly changes the landscape. Most rivers have their sources in mountains or uplands and are fed by rain or melting snow. They begin as torrents, channeling a downward route through the rock or soil. Each particle a river removes, whether a grain of sand or a boulder, adds to its cutting power and wears away its course.

In the mountains the river course is known as the torrent stage. It cuts steep, V-shaped valleys, litters the bed with boulders, and plunges over waterfalls. These are formed where hard rock adjoins soft rock. The soft rock is worn away faster, leaving a sudden, vertical plunge, often many feet deep. As the river pours out of the high ground into its valley stage, the water moves more smoothly, and other streams join it as tributaries. Swollen by the extra flood, the river widens and

the sides of its valley become shallower.

As it reaches the flatlands of the coastal plain or lakeside, the river begins to loop, or meander, often changing course. Though flowing quietly, it still reshapes the country, depositing silt among the eddies of inner bends, to create gentle, often muddy, banks, and eating away the outer banks. Large quantities of soil carried from the upper reaches build up as mudflats and sandbanks at its estuary.

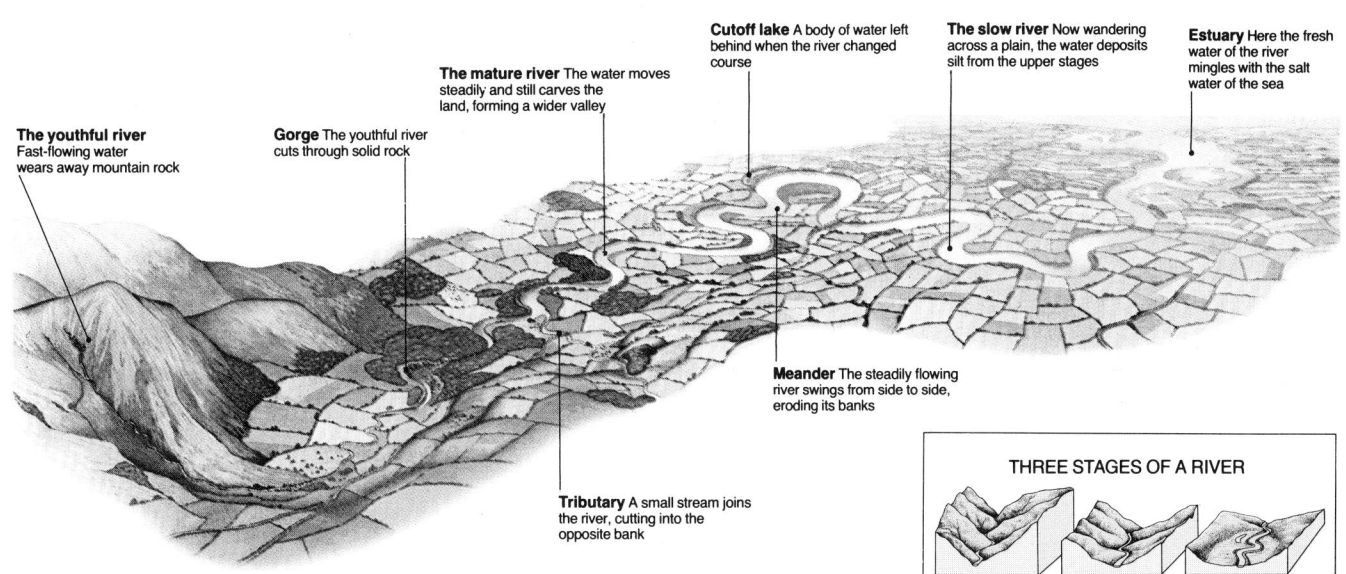

The youthful river Fast-flowing water wears away mountain rock

Gorge The youthful river cuts through solid rock

The mature river The water moves steadily and still carves the land, forming a wider valley

Cutoff lake A body of water left behind when the river changed course

The slow river Now wandering across a plain, the water deposits silt from the upper stages

Estuary Here the fresh water of the river mingles with the salt water of the sea

Meander The steadily flowing river swings from side to side, eroding its banks

Tributary A small stream joins the river, cutting into the opposite bank

THREE STAGES OF A RIVER

The fast-flowing torrent reach of a river cuts a steep-sided, V-shaped valley. In the mid, or valley, stage, the V starts to open out, until in the final stage the river takes a constantly changing course across flat country to the sea.

ANATOMY OF A RIVER *In its upper stages the torrent is often strong enough to move boulders and the river flow is broken and turbulent—rushing at differing speeds around and over obstacles. At the wider, valley stage most rivers are deeper and navigable, and freshwater fish feed and breed among the eddies and the vegetation at*

the water's edge. On the flatlands near its mouth, the river deposits mud and silt, often creating new and rich stretches of farmland, called alluvial plains. Some rivers form a delta at their mouths—a tract of land built up from deposited sediment, through which the river diverges into a number of channels on its course to the sea.

road·house (rōd'hous') *n.* An inn, restaurant, or nightclub situated on a road, especially in the countryside.

road·ie (rōd'ē) *n., pl.* **-ies.** A person who is responsible for the traveling arrangements of a pop group on tour, and who supervises their instruments and equipment. Also called "road manager."

road metal *n.* Crushed or broken stone, cinders, or similar material used in the construction and repair of roads and roadbeds.

road·run·ner (rōd'rŭn'ər) *n.* A swift-running, crested bird, *Geococcyx californianus,* of southwestern North America, having streaked, brownish plumage and a long tail.

road sense *n.* The ability to use public roads and negotiate traffic safely.

road show *n.* A touring entertainment, especially one given by pop groups or similar artists.

road·side (rōd'sīd') *n.* The area bordering on a road.

---

road

4,000 YEARS OF ROAD BUILDING

The ribbons of stone and asphalt that speeded up travel

Paved roads for wheeled vehicles were constructed as early as the third millennium B.C. in Egypt, Mesopotamia, and China, but Darius the Great, ruler of the Persian Empire (521–486 B.C.), built the first imperial road system. Roads connecting the provinces with the several capital cities ensured rapid communications for his army and messengers. The Romans later built a network of paved roads to link cities and forts across their empire.

As the ancient empires declined, their roads fell into disrepair and it was not until the 18th century in Europe that military requirements led to a revival of road building by governments. A subsequent expansion of trade, accompanied by an increase in wheeled traffic, influenced governments to encourage interest in scientific road building. Pierre Tresaguet (1716–96), inspired by the archeology of classical civilizations, introduced into France construction methods similar to those of the Romans. Thomas Telford (1757–1834) introduced Tresaguet's methods into Britain, and both Telford and John McAdam (1756–1836) improved upon his technique.

When, during the 20th century, automobiles with rubber tires raised intolerable levels of dust from crushed-stone road surfaces, a wearing surface of tar was laid on the top of a macadam (McAdam) road and called a tarmacadam, or tarmac, road. Concrete was first used during the 1920's to pave Italian roadways.

ROMAN *The road was founded on compacted earth covered with pebbles set in mortar. This was overlaid with a hard filling that was cambered (curved) and sometimes paved with stone slabs.*

MACADAM *A cambered foundation of compacted earth formed the base of the road. It was covered with two 4-inch courses of stones and a wearing surface of pebbles that the steel wheels of horse-drawn wagons and coaches gradually crushed and smoothed to a fine dust.*

MODERN *Today's super highways have a thick subbase of pebbly material, a base layer of concrete, a layer of tar or rolled asphalt, and a wearing course of rolled asphalt. The hard shoulder is asphalted.*

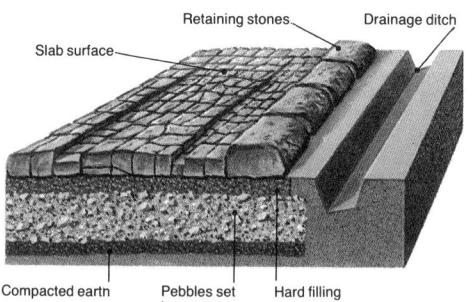

Retaining stones — Drainage ditch
Slab surface
Compacted earth — Pebbles set in mortar — Hard filling

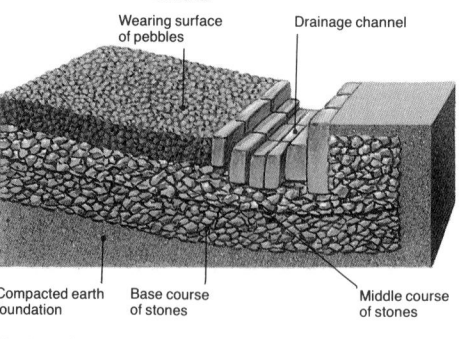

Wearing surface of pebbles — Drainage channel
Compacted earth foundation — Base course of stones — Middle course of stones

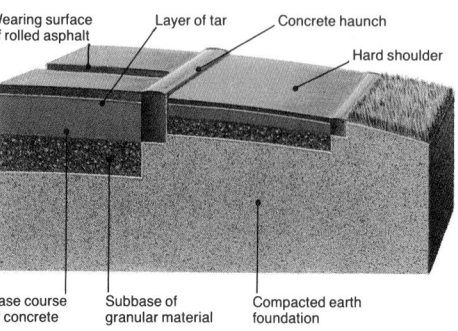

Wearing surface of rolled asphalt — Layer of tar — Concrete haunch
Hard shoulder
Base course of concrete — Subbase of granular material — Compacted earth foundation

---

road·stead (rōd'stĕd') *n. Nautical.* A sheltered, offshore anchorage area for ships. Also called "roads."

road·ster (rōd'stər) *n.* **1.** An open car having no back seats and usually a luggage compartment in the rear. **2.** A horse for riding on a road.

road test *n.* **1.** A test designed to assess the performance and roadworthiness of a vehicle by driving it on a road. **2.** A test of a person's driving ability as a requirement for a driver's license. **—road-test** (rōd'tĕst') *v.*

road·way (rōd'wā') *n.* A road, especially the part over which vehicles travel.

road·work (rōd'wûrk') *n.* Outdoor long-distance running, especially as part of an athlete's training.

road·worth·y (rōd'wûr'thē) *adj.* Fit to be driven on a public road. Said of a motor vehicle. **—road·worth·i·ness** *n.*

roam (rōm) *v.* **roamed, roaming, roams.** *—intr.* To move or travel without purpose or plan; rove; wander. *—tr.* To wander over or through. **—See Synonyms at wander.**
~*n.* The act of roaming. [Middle English *roment*.] **—roam·er** *n.*

roan (rōn) *adj.* **1.** Having a chestnut *(strawberry roan),* bay *(red roan),* or black *(blue roan)* coat thickly sprinkled with white or gray hairs. Said chiefly of horses. **2.** Made or prepared from a soft, flexible sheepskin leather.
~*n.* **1.** The characteristic coloring of a roan horse. **2.** A roan horse or other animal. **3.** Roan leather, often treated to resemble morocco, and used in bookbinding. [Old French *roant*.]

Ro·a·noke Island (rō'ə-nōk'). Island off the coast of North Carolina and the site of the first English colonies in North America. They were founded at the instigation of Sir Walter Raleigh (1585, 1587), but by 1591 all the colonists had disappeared, perhaps killed by Indians or disease.

roar (rôr) *v.* **roared, roaring, roars.** *—intr.* **1.** To utter a loud, deep, prolonged sound, especially in distress, rage, or excitement. **2.** To utter a loud, harsh, growling sound, like that characteristic of a lion. **3.** To laugh loudly or excitedly. **4.** To make or produce a harsh, loud noise or din: *the wind roaring in the trees.* **5.** To move or operate with a loud noise: *roared through the town on motorbikes.* **6.** To breathe with a rasping sound. Used of a horse. *—tr.* **1.** To utter or express with a deep, loud, and prolonged sound. **2.** To bring (oneself) into a specified state by roaring: *The crowd roared itself hoarse.*
~*n.* **1.** A loud, deep sound or cry, as of a person in distress or rage. **2.** The loud, deep cry characteristic of a lion. **3.** A loud, prolonged noise, such as that produced by waves, motorbikes, or gunfire. **4.** A loud burst of laughter. [Middle English *roren, raren,* Old English *rārian* (imitative).] **—roar·er** *n.*

roar·ing (rôr'ĭng) *adj. Informal.* Very lively or successful; thriving: *a roaring trade.*
~*adv. Informal.* Extremely; very: *roaring drunk.*

roast (rōst) *v.* **roasted, roasting, roasts.** *—tr.* **1.** To cook (meat, for example), as: **a.** With dry heat, especially with fat in an oven. **b.** By direct exposure to dry heat, as over an open fire or in hot ashes. **2.** To prepare (coffee beans, for example) for use by heating. **3.** To dry, brown, or parch by exposing to heat. **4.** To expose to great or excessive heat. **5.** *Metallurgy.* To heat (ores) in a furnace in order to dehydrate, purify, or oxidize. **6.** *Informal.* To criticize or ridicule harshly. *—intr.* **1.** To cook meat or other food in an oven. **2.** To undergo roasting. **3.** *Informal.* To feel extremely hot.
~*n.* **1.** Something roasted. **2.** A cut of meat suitable or prepared for roasting. **3.** The act or process of roasting.
~*adj.* Roasted: *roast chicken.* [Middle English *rosten,* from Old French *rostir,* probably from Old High German *rōsten,* from *rōst,* grate, gridiron, from Germanic *raust* (unattested).]

roast·er (rōs'tər) *n.* **1.** One that roasts. **2.** A special dish or apparatus for roasting. **3.** Something fit for roasting, such as a chicken.

rob (rŏb) *v.* **robbed, robbing, robs.** *—tr.* **1.** To take property from (a place, person, or persons) illegally, by using or threatening to use violence or force; commit robbery against: *robbed by muggers; robbed a bank.* **2.** To deprive (a person) of something belonging, desired, or legally due by any unjust procedure: *rob a person of his reputation.* **3.** To deprive of something important, essential, or desirable: *robbed the joke of its point.* *—intr.* To commit or engage in robbery. [Middle English *robben,* from Old French *rober,* from Germanic.] **—rob·ber** *n.*
Synonyms: *burgle, filch, loot, pilfer, plunder, ransack, steal, thieve.*

rob·a·lo (rŏb'ə-lō, rō'bə-) *n., pl.* **-los** or collectively **robalo.** Any of various chiefly tropical marine food and aquarium fishes of the family Centropomidae, such as the **snook** (see). [Spanish *róbalo,* probably modification of *lobaro* (unattested), from *lobo,* wolf, "wolflike fish," from Latin *lupus.*]

Robbe-Gril·let (rŏb-grē-yā'), **Alain** (1922–). French novelist. He is an exponent of the "new novel," about which he has written in *Vers un Nouveau Roman* (1964). His novels include *Jealousy* (1957), in which the action is presented through the clinically detached prose of an observer who neither speaks nor appears in person.

robber baron *n.* **1.** A feudal lord who robbed travelers passing through his domain. **2.** One of the American industrial or financial magnates of the latter 19th century who became wealthy by unethical means, such as exploitation of labor or political connections.

robber crab *n.* A large Indo-Pacific crab, *Birgo latus,* that feeds on coconuts broken open with its pincers. Also called "coconut crab."

robber fly *n.* Any of various predatory flies of the family Asilidae, characteristically having long, bristly legs.

rob·ber·y (rŏb′ər-ē) *n., pl.* **-ies. 1.** The act of unlawfully taking the property of another by the use of force or intimidation. **2.** An instance of this.

Robbia, della. See **della Robbia.**

Rob·bins (rŏb′ĭnz), **Harold** (1916–). U.S. novelist. A prolific and highly popular author, he won critical acclaim for his early works, including *Never Love a Stranger* (1948), and continued to write popular but less critically accepted works such as *The Betsy* (1971) and *The Lonely Lady* (1976).

Robbins, Jerome (1918–). U.S. choreographer. Trained as a dancer, he staged his first ballet in 1944 and later won fame for creating the dance sequences in hit musicals such as *West Side Story* (1957) and *Fiddler on the Roof* (1964).

robe (rōb) *n.* **1.** A long, loose, flowing outer garment, especially: **a.** An official garment worn on formal occasions to show office or rank, as by a judge or high church official. **b.** A dressing gown or bathrobe. **2. robes.** *Archaic.* Clothes in general; dress. **3.** A blanket or covering made of fur, cloth, or other material: *a lap robe.*
—*v.* **robed, robing, robes.** —*tr.* To clothe or dress in or as if in a robe or robes. —*intr.* To put on a robe or robes. [Middle English, from Old French, from Vulgar Latin *rauba* (unattested), "clothes taken away as booty," robe, from Germanic; akin to ROB.]

Rob·ert I (rŏb′ərt), known as "Robert the Bruce" (1274–1329). King of Scotland (1306–29). He seized the crown in 1306 and gradually extended his control over Scotland. In 1314 he won effective independence from England by his victory at Bannockburn, formally acknowledged by England in the Treaty of Northampton (1328).

Rob·erts (rŏb′ərts), **Oral** (1918–). U.S. evangelist. A preacher and faith healer, he has reached millions of people through his faith-healing tours and his popular radio and television programs. He also has published numerous religious books and pamphlets and founded Oral Roberts University (1963).

Robe·son (rōb′sən), **Paul** (1898–1976). U.S. actor and singer. He won fame playing the title role in Eugene O'Neill's *Emperor Jones* (1925), further establishing his reputation in *Showboat* (1928), in which he sang "Ol' Man River," a song with which he is especially associated. In 1943 he played the title role in a record-breaking New York run of *Othello.*

Robes·pierre (rōbz′pîr, -pē-âr′), **Maximilien François Marie Isidore de** (1758–94). French revolutionary leader. A radical lawyer, he became an early member of the Jacobin Club. The chief architect of the Reign of Terror, Robespierre was famous for his austere and incorruptible character. He introduced laws permitting the confiscation of property and arrest of suspected traitors. A reaction to these measures led to his arrest and execution.

rob·in (rŏb′ĭn) *n.* **1.** A small North American songbird, *Turdus migratorius.* Also called "American robin." **2.** A similar Eurasian songbird, *Erithacus rubecula,* having an orange breast and a brown back. **3.** Any of various birds resembling a robin. [Middle English, from Old French, from the name *Robin.*]

Robin Goodfellow. See **Puck.**

Rob·in Hood (rŏb′ĭn hŏŏd) *n.* Legendary English outlaw. He is first mentioned in *Piers Plowman* (*c.* 1377), and ballads concerning his exploits became popular in the following centuries. Though he may have been an entirely mythical folk hero, various historical prototypes have been suggested, including a 12th-century Earl of Huntingdon and a disinherited follower of Simon de Montfort.

ro·bin·i·a (rə-bĭn′ē-ə, rō-) *n.* Any tree of the genus *Robinia;* especially, the **false acacia** *(see).* [New Latin, after Jean *Robin* (died 1629), French botanist.]

Rob·in·son (rŏb′ĭn-sən), **Edward G.,** born Emmanuel Goldenberg (1893–1973). U.S. film actor, born in Romania. He made his reputation in gangster films such as *Little Caesar* (1930) and *Kid Galahad* (1937) and later played character parts, as in *Double Indemnity* (1944) and *The Cincinatti Kid* (1965).

Robinson, Edwin Arlington (1869–1935). U.S. poet. In his finely structured and sometimes seemingly pessimistic poetry, he created stark psychological sketches of a variety of characters. He earned Pulitzer prizes for *Collected Poems* (1921), *The Man Who Died Twice* (1924), and *Tristram* (1927).

Robinson, Jack Roosevelt, known as "Jackie" (1919–72). U.S. baseball player. The first black player in major-league baseball, he was a second baseman for the Brooklyn Dodgers from 1947 to 1956. Renowned for his daring base running, he had a lifetime batting average of .311 and was inducted into the Baseball Hall of Fame in 1962.

Robinson, Sugar Ray, born Walker Smith (1920–). U.S. boxer. He was six times world champion, once as a welterweight (1946–51) and five times as a middleweight (1951–60).

Robinson, (William) Heath (1872–1944). British cartoonist and book illustrator. He is especially remembered for his humorous drawings of fantastic inventions collected in *Absurdities* (1934) and other volumes.

Robinson Cru·soe (krōō′sō) *n.* The hero of Daniel Defoe's novel *Robinson Crusoe* (1719), a shipwrecked sailor who lived for years on a small tropical island.

ro·bo·rant (rŏb′ər-ənt) *adj.* Restoring vigor or strength.
—*n.* A roborant drug; a tonic. [Latin *rōborāns* (stem *rōborant-*), present participle of *rōborāre,* to strengthen, from *rōbur,* strength.]

ro·bot (rō′bət, -bŏt′) *n.* **1.** An externally manlike mechanical device capable of performing human tasks or behaving in a human manner. **2.** Any machine or device that works automatically or by remote control; especially, a machine in a factory that can be programmed to perform a variety of different tasks normally done by humans. Also called "automaton." **3.** A person who works mechanically without original thought. **4.** *South African.* A set of traffic lights. [Czech, in Karel Čapek's play *R.U.R. (Rossum's Universal Robots),* 1920, from *robota,* compulsory labor, drudgery.] —**ro·bot·ism** *n.* —**ro·bot·is·tic** *adj.*

robot bomb *n.* **1.** A small, explosive-carrying, jet-propelled gyroscopically guided missile. Also called "V-1," "buzz bomb," "flying bomb." **2.** A **guided missile** *(see).*

ro·bot·ics (rō-bŏt′ĭks) *n.* The science of the designing, building, and application of robots. [ROBOT + -ICS.]

robot pilot *n.* An **automatic pilot** *(see).*

Rob Roy (rŏb roi), born Robert Macgregor (1671–1734). Scottish clan chief and cattle dealer. He was outlawed (1712) for failing to pay his debts and began a career of banditry that lasted until his arrest in 1722. He was pardoned in 1727. Sir Walter Scott's novel *Rob Roy* (1818) was based on his career.

ro·bust (rō-bŭst′, rō′bŭst) *adj.* **1.** Full of health and strength; vigorous. **2.** Powerfully built; sturdy. **3.** Requiring or suited to physical strength or endurance: *robust work.* **4.** Boisterous; rough. **5.** Marked by richness and fullness; full-bodied: *a robust wine.* **6.** Down-to-earth; straightforward: *a robust intellect.* —See Synonyms at **healthy.** [Latin *rōbustus,* oaken, from *rōbur, rōbus,* oak, strength.] —**ro·bust·ly** *adv.* —**ro·bust·ness** *n.*

roc (rŏk) *n.* A legendary bird of prey of enormous size and strength. [From Spanish *rocho,* from Arabic *rukhkh,* from Persian *rukh*†.]

ro·caille (rō-kī′, rō-) *n.* The light, shell-like, curving decoration used in rococo architecture. [French, "rockwork," from Old French *roche,* ROCK.]

roc·am·bole (rŏk′əm-bōl′) *n.* **1.** A European plant, *Allium scorodoprasum,* having a garliclike bulb. **2.** The bulb of this plant, used as a seasoning. [French, from German *Rockenbolle,* "distaff bulb" : *Rocken,* distaff, from Old High German *rocko* + *Bolle,* bulb, from Old High German *bolla,* ball.]

Ro·cham·beau (rō′shăm′bō′), **Jean Baptiste Donatien de Vimeure, Comte de** (1725–1807). French army officer. A veteran of several European wars, he came to the United States with 6,000 French troops to fight for American independence (1780). In 1781 he helped defeat the British at Yorktown, the last major battle of the war.

Roche (rōsh), **Mazo de la** (1885–1961). Canadian novelist. She wrote 15 novels about the Whiteoak family of Jalna, the first of which was *Jalna* (1927).

Rochelle, La. See **La Rochelle.**

Ro·chelle powder (rô-shĕl′) *n.* A cathartic, **Seidlitz powder** *(see).*

Rochelle salt *n.* A colorless efflorescent crystalline compound, $KNaC_4H_4O_6 \cdot 4H_2O$, used in making mirrors, in electronics, and as a laxative. [After LA ROCHELLE.]

roche mou·ton·née (rôsh mōō-tô-nā′) *n., pl.* **roches moutonnées** (*pronounced as singular*). A glacially molded mass of rock, worn smooth on the upstream side by abrasion, the downstream side being rough as a result of the plucking action of the ice. Also called "sheepback." [French, "fleecy rock."]

Roch·es·ter[1] (rŏch′ĕs-tər). City of southeastern Minnesota. The city produces varied manufactured goods, such as electronic equipment and foodstuffs, but is best known for the Mayo Clinic, established here in 1889.

Rochester[2]. Port of New York State, on the Genesee River on the south side of Lake Ontario. It is a port of entry and has diverse manufactures.

Rochester, John Wilmot, 2nd Earl of (1647–80). British poet. A wit and libertine at the court of Charles II, he is especially remembered for his satirical writings, which include *A Satire Against Mankind* (1675), and for his amorous poems.

roch·et (rŏch′ĭt) *n.* A ceremonial vestment made of linen or lawn, worn by bishops and other church dignitaries. [Middle English, from Old French, from Frankish *rok* (unattested), coat.]

rock[1] (rŏk) *n.* **1.** Any relatively hard naturally formed mass of mineral or petrified matter; stone. **2. a.** A relatively large body of such material, as a cliff or peak. **b.** A relatively small piece or fragment of such material; a stone. **3.** *Geology.* Any naturally formed mineral mass or aggregate that constitutes a significant part of the earth's crust. **4.** A person or thing suggestive of a mass of stone in stability, solidity, or strength: *St. Peter was the rock upon which the church was built.* **5.** *Usually* **rocks.** *Slang.* Money. **6.** *Slang.* A large gem, especially a diamond. **7.** *Chiefly British.* A kind of hard candy, usually peppermint-flavored, and produced as a brightly colored stick. —**on the rocks. 1.** *Informal.* In a state of destruction or ruin: *Their marriage is on the rocks.* **2.** Without money; bankrupt. **3.** Served over ice cubes without water or a mixer. —**the Rock. 1.** *Informal.* The Rock of **Gibraltar** *(see).* **2.** *Slang.* **Alcatraz** *(see).* [Middle English *rokke,* from Old Northern French *roque,* variant of Old French *roche,* from Medieval Latin *rocca*†.]

rock[2] *v.* **rocked, rocking, rocks.** —*intr.* **1.** To move back and forth or from side to side, especially gently or rhythmically: *The boat rocked on the waves.* **2.** To sway violently, as from a blow or shock; shake. **3.** To be washed and panned in a cradle or rocker. Used of ores. **4.** To dance to rock'n'roll music. —*tr.* **1.** To sway back and forth or from side to side; especially, to soothe or lull to sleep: *rocked the baby in his arms.* **2.** To cause to shake or sway violently. **3.** To disturb or distress deeply; shock: *The scandal rocked the town.* **4.** To wash or pan (ore) in a cradle or rocker. **5.** In mezzotint en-

roadrunner *The poor flight of the roadrunner gives this bird its name since it is most often seen running along roads or across open land. A relative of the cuckoo, it is found in southwestern North America and feeds on lizards, snakes, and insects.*

robin *Many birds of the thrush family found throughout the world are called robins. The American robin is the largest, while the European robin,* Erithacus rubecula *(above)—which grows to about 14 centimeters (5½ inches)—frequently becomes very tame.*

graving, to roughen (a copper plate) with various rockers and roulettes. —See Synonyms at **swing.**
~*n.* **1.** The act of rocking. **2.** A rocking motion. **3.** **Rock 'n' roll** *(see).* **4.** **Rock music** *(see).* [Middle English *rokken,* Old English *roccian,* perhaps from Germanic *rukk-* (unattested).] —**rock·ing·ly** *adv.*

rock·a·bil·ly (rŏk′ə-bĭl′ē) *n.* A form of rock music combining elements of country music and rhythm and blues. [*Rock* music + hill*billy.*]

rock-and-roll. Variant of **rock 'n' roll.**

rock bass *n.* **1.** A freshwater food fish, *Ambloplites rupestris,* of eastern and central North America. **2.** Any of various similar or related fishes.

rock bottom *n.* The lowest level; the absolute bottom: *Prices have reached rock bottom.* —**rock-bot·tom** (rŏk′bŏt′əm) *adj.*

rock-bound (rŏk′bound′) *adj.* Hemmed in by or bordered with rocks: *a rock-bound lake.*

rock candy *n.* Sugar in the form of large, hard, clear crystals.

Rock Cornish hen *n.* A small fowl of a breed developed by crossing white Plymouth Rock and Cornish strains, and used especially as a roasting chicken. Also called "Cornish hen."

rock crystal *n.* Transparent colorless quartz.

rock dove *n.* A bird, *Columba livia,* native to Europe but widely distributed elsewhere, having gray plumage with iridescent neck markings. It is the ancestor of the common domestic pigeon. Also called "rock pigeon."

Rock·e·fel·ler (rŏk′ə-fĕl′ər). U.S. family, including **John Davison** (1839-1937), a business magnate who amassed great wealth through the Standard Oil Company and spent about half his fortune on philanthropic works. His son, **John Davison, Jr.** (1874-1960) continued the family's philanthropic efforts and had five sons: **John Davison, III** (1906-78), a family businessman and philanthropist; **Nelson** (1908-79), a Republican politician who served as governor of New York (1959-73) and U.S. vice president (1974-77); **Laurance** (1910-), a conservationist; **Winthrop** (1912-73), governor of Arkansas (1966-70); and **David** (1915-), a banking executive. **John Davison, IV,** known as "Jay" (1937-), was governor of West Virginia (1977-85).

rock·er (rŏk′ər) *n.* **1.** Any of various mechanical devices or parts that operate with a rocking motion. **2.** A rocking chair. **3.** A rocking horse. **4.** Either of the two curved pieces upon which a cradle, rocking chair, or similar device rocks. **5.** *Mining.* A cradle for washing or panning ores. **6.** A small steel plate with a curved, toothed edge, used to roughen a copper plate for a mezzotint. **7.** An ice skate with a curved blade. **8.** *Sometimes* **Rocker.** In Britain, especially in the 1960's, a youth belonging to a gang of motorcyclists, typically having slicked-back hair and wearing a leather jacket, and often in conflict with **mods** *(see).* —**off one's rocker.** *Slang.* Out of one's mind; crazy.

rocker arm *n.* A pivoted lever, as in an internal-combustion engine, used to transfer cam or pushrod motion to a valve stem.

rock·er·y (rŏk′ər-ē) *n., pl.* **-ies.** A small-scale rock garden, usually forming part of a larger garden.

rock·et¹ (rŏk′ĭt) *n.* **1. a.** Any device propelled by ejection of matter, especially by the high-velocity ejection of the gaseous combustion products produced by internal ignition of solid or liquid fuels, used for launching a spacecraft or as a signal. **b.** A rocket engine. **2. a.** A weapon carrying an explosive or other warhead, and using rocket power. **b.** An incendiary weapon with a rounded hollow warhead filled with explosives and formerly fired from a ship. **3.** A firework for aerial display that rises vertically, then explodes and sprays a shower of colored stars. Also called "skyrocket."
~*v.* **rocketed, -eting, -ets.** —*intr.* **1.** To move or fly directly and swiftly, as a rocket does. **2.** To rise rapidly or unexpectedly: *Prices rocketed.* —*tr.* **1.** To assault with rockets. **2.** To carry by means of a rocket. [French *roquette,* from Italian *rocchetto,* diminutive of *rocca,* ROCK (referring to cylindrical shape of firework).]

rocket² *n.* **1.** A plant, *Eruca sativa,* native to Eurasia, having yellowish-white flowers and leaves that are sometimes used in salads. **2.** Any of several related plants, especially one of the genera *Sisymbrium,* such as *S. irio* (London rocket), *Cakile* (sea rocket), or *Diplotaxis* (wall rocket). [French *roquette,* from Italian *ruchetta,* diminutive of *ruca,* from Latin *ērūca,* "caterpillar," plant with downy stems, perhaps from *er,* hedgehog.]

rock·et·eer (rŏk′ə-tîr′) *n.* A person who designs, launches, studies, or pilots rockets.

rocket engine *n.* An engine that propels, especially one that propels spacecraft or aircraft, by means of rockets.

rocket motor *n.* A rocket engine, especially one using solid propellants.

rock·et·ry (rŏk′ĭt-rē) *n.* The science and technology of rocket design, construction, and flight.

rock·et·sonde (rŏk′ĭt-sŏnd′) *n.* Recording equipment adapted for use on a rocket, and used for observation in the upper atmosphere.

rock·fish (rŏk′fĭsh′) *n., pl.* **-fish** or collectively **rockfish. 1.** Any of various fishes living among rocks. **2.** Any of various fishes, chiefly of the genus *Sebastodes,* of Pacific waters. **3.** The **striped bass** *(see).*

rock flour *n.* Pulverized rock produced, for example, along the faces of a moving fault or during movement of a glacier.

rock garden *n.* A rocky area in which plants especially adapted to such terrain are cultivated.

rock hound *n.* **1.** One who specializes in geology. **2.** One who collects rocks and minerals as a hobby. —**rock·hound·ing** *n.*

rocking horse *A "safety," or "swing," rocking horse, a type first made in the 1870's and in common use from 1900 onward.*

Rockies. See **Rocky Mountains.**

rock·ing chair (rŏk′ĭng) *n.* A chair mounted on rockers or springs, so that the sitter may rock on it.

rocking horse *n.* A toy horse large enough for a child to ride, mounted on rockers or springs.

rock·ling (rŏk′lĭng) *n., pl.* **-lings** or collectively **rockling.** Any of various small marine fishes of the family Gadidae, of North Atlantic coastal waters, having barbels around the mouth. [ROCK (stone) + LING (fish).]

rock lobster *n.* The **spiny lobster** *(see).*

rock maple *n.* **1.** A tree, the **sugar maple** *(see).* **2.** The tough, close-grained wood of the sugar maple.

rock music *n.* A form of popular music that became established in the late 1950's, growing out of various types of U.S. folk music, such as blues and gospel, and that is characterized by strong repetitive rhythms. Also called "rock."

Rock·ne (rŏk′nē), **Knute Kenneth** (1888-1931). U.S. football coach, born in Norway. In 13 seasons as head coach of the University of Notre Dame football team (1918-31) he won 105 games, lost 12, and tied 5. He revolutionized the sport through his use of offensive strategies based on speed and agility instead of brute force.

rock 'n' roll, rock-and-roll (rŏk′ən-rōl′) *n.* Popular music combining elements of rhythm and blues with country and western music, and having a heavily accented beat. Also called "rock."

rock oil *n. Chiefly British.* **Petroleum** *(see).*

rock·oon (rŏ-kōōn′) *n.* A rocket carrying scientific instruments to study the upper atmosphere that is carried to a certain height by balloon, then fired. [*Rock*et + ball*oon.*]

rock pigeon *n.* The **rock dove** *(see).*

rock plant *n.* Any plant adapted for growing among rocks or in rocky ground.

rock python *n.* The **amethystine python** *(see).*

rock-ribbed (rŏk′rĭbd′) *adj.* **1.** Having rocks or rock outcroppings. **2.** Stern and unyielding.

rock-rose (rŏk′rōz′) *n.* Any of various plants or shrubs of the genus *Helianthemum* and related genera, having roselike yellow, white, or reddish flowers, and often cultivated as garden ornamentals.

rock salmon *n. British.* Any of various coarse fish, such as the dogfish, that are used as food.

rock salt *n.* A mineral form of common salt (sodium chloride). Also called "halite."

rock samphire *n.* A plant, **samphire** *(see).*

rock-shaft (rŏk′shăft′, -shäft′) *n.* A shaft that oscillates or rocks upon its bearings, but does not revolve.

Rock·well (rŏk′wĕl′), **Norman** (1894-1978). U.S. artist and illustrator. Perhaps best known for his numerous *Saturday Evening Post* cover illustrations, he depicted the sentimental side of American life in his hundreds of characteristic paintings. His illustrations of the Four Freedoms (1943) are among his most popular works.

rock-work (rŏk′wûrk′) *n.* Ornamental stonework, as in a rock garden or rockery.

rock·y¹ (rŏk′ē) *adj.* **-ier, -iest.** **1.** Consisting of, containing, or abounding in rock or rocks. **2.** Resembling or suggesting rock; firm or hard; tough; unyielding. **3.** Marked by obstructions or difficulties: *the rocky road to success.* —**rock·i·ness** *n.*

rock·y² *adj.* **-ier, -iest.** **1.** Unsteady; unstable; shaky. **2.** *Informal.* Weak, dizzy, or nauseous. —**rock·i·ness** *n.*

Rocky Mountain goat *n.* The **mountain goat** *(see).*

Rocky Mountain National Park. Area, 1,049 square kilometers (405 square miles), of central Colorado, northwest of Denver. It is a scenic resort region along the Continental Divide, with many high, snow-capped peaks.

Rocky Mountains. Also **Rock·ies** (rŏk′ēz). Mountain system of western North America, forming the Continental Divide. It extends 4,800 kilometers (3,000 miles) from the northern Mexican border to the Yukon, but is sometimes considered to include its continuation through the Yukon to Alaska. It rises to 4,399 meters (14,431 feet) at Mt. Elbert and in its extended form to 6,050 meters (19,850 feet) at Mt. Logan.

Rocky Mountain sheep *n.* The **bighorn** *(see).*

Rocky Mountain spotted fever *n.* An acute infectious disease caused by a microorganism, *Rickettsia rickettsii,* and transmitted by ticks. It is characterized by muscular pains, high fever, and skin eruptions and is endemic throughout North America. Also called "spotted fever."

ro·co·co (rə-kō′kō, rō′kə-kō′) *n.* **1.** A style of art, developed from the baroque, that originated in France (about 1720) and soon spread throughout Europe; especially, this style used in architecture and decoration, characterized by elaborate, profuse designs of scrolls and curves intended to produce a delicate effect. **2.** *Music.* The style immediately following the baroque in Europe (about 1726 to 1775).
~*adj.* **1.** Of or in rococo style. **2.** Profuse or elaborate; overdone; florid: *rococo writing.* [French, fanciful alteration of ROCAILLE.]

rod (rŏd) *n.* **1.** A straight, thin piece or bar of metal, wood, or other material: *a curtain rod.* **2.** A shoot or stem cut from, or growing as part of, a woody plant. **3.** A stick, or a bundle of sticks, used for beating, as for punishment. **4.** A **fishing rod** *(see).* **5.** A wand or staff symbolizing power or authority. **6.** Power or dominion, especially of a tyrannical nature: *"under the rod of a cruel slavery."* (John Henry Newman). **7.** A metal bar in a machine: *a piston rod.* **8.** A measuring stick. **9.** A **leveling rod** *(see).* **10.** A **lightning rod** *(see).* **11.** A **divining rod** *(see).* **12.** *Abbr.* **rd, r.** A linear measure equal to 5.5 yards, 16.5 feet, or 5.03 meters. Also called "pole," *British* "perch." **b.** A square rod, equal to 30.25 square yards. **13.** *Anatomy.* Any of various rod-shaped cells in the retina that contain the pigment rhodopsin and are sensitive to dim light. Compare **cone.** **14.** Any elongated microorganism; especially, a bacterium. **15.** *Slang.* A pistol or revolver. [Middle English *rodd,* Old English *rodd.*]

rode. Past tense of **ride.**

ro·dent (rōd'ənt) *n.* Any of various mammals of the order Rodentia, such as a mouse, rat, squirrel, or beaver, characterized by large, continuously growing incisors adapted for gnawing or nibbling. ~*adj.* **1.** Gnawing. **2.** Of or pertaining to rodents. [New Latin *Rodentia,* from Latin *rōdēns* (stem *rōdent-*), present participle of *rōdere,* to gnaw.]

ro·dent·i·cide (rō-děn'tĭ-sīd') *n.* An agent used to kill rodent pests. [RODENT + -CIDE.]

rodent ulcer *n.* A malignant tumor of the face, especially the lips

and nostrils, that destroys the underlying muscle and bone.

ro·de·o (rō'dē-ō', rō-dā'ō) *n., pl.* **-os. 1.** A cattle roundup. **2.** An enclosure for keeping cattle that have been rounded up. **3.** A public entertainment including riding broncos, lassoing, and similar displays. [Spanish, from *rodear,* to surround, from Latin *rotāre,* to ROTATE.]

Rodg·ers (rŏj'ərz), **Richard Charles** (1902–79). U.S. composer. He collaborated with the librettist Lorenz Hart (1895–1943) on *Pal Joey* (1940) and other musicals, but is especially remembered for those he produced with Oscar Hammerstein II, including *Oklahoma!* (1943), *South Pacific* (1949), *The King and I* (1951), and *The Sound of Music* (1959).

Ro·din (rō-dăn'), **(François) Auguste René** (1840–1917). French sculptor. He first exhibited at the Paris Salon in 1877 and later won an immense reputation for the originality of his compositions, which recall Michelangelo in their sense of tragic grandeur. His controversial public commissions included *The Burghers of Calais*

---

rococo

A FRENCH ART STYLE OF CHARM AND ELEGANCE
Avoiding pomposity with scrolls and frills

During the early 18th century French patrons and artists reacted against the massiveness and pomposity of the baroque style and adopted a lighter, smaller-scale style that came to be known as rococo.

Rococo—originally a term of abuse applied to overelaborate works—was coined later in the century, probably by combining the French *rocaille* (rock) and *coquille* (shell), both of which were favorite rococo motifs. It was primarily a decorative style, predominantly

French, but also adopted in southern Germany, where the style was mainly used in churches. Art historians generally regard it as an aspect of, rather than a successor to, the baroque style.

Rococo was characterized by a profusion of ornate scrolls and curves and was first used in metalwork and interior decoration. French architects, furniture makers, and artists adopted it and used it to transform the courts of northern Europe and Russia. French art-

ists—chiefly Antoine Watteau, François Boucher, and Jean Fragonard—created a new genre of rococo painting: charming, wistful, lightweight, and sometimes mildly erotic, in which courtiers dally in leafy gardens with pretty, gaily dressed young ladies.

Both baroque and rococo styles were superseded in the second half of the 18th century when discoveries in classical art inspired a passion for a new style, neoclassicism, which lasted well into the 19th century.

MEISSEN FIGURES *In this Meissen porcelain of 1770, a shepherd and sleeping shepherdess, her breast exposed, form a scene that reflects the French taste for pastoral fantasy.*

HEAVEN'S GATES *The ornate ceiling of the Wieskirche at Steingaden, Bavaria, typifies the German religious use of the rococo style, which in France was purely secular.*

THE SWING *Fragonard's painting of 1768 or 1769 is considered to express the essence of rococo art, which was by then already in decline. The flirtatious young girl on the swing, her silk and lace dress billowing around her, kicks off her slipper above her lover's head, allowing him a delectable glimpse of leg and petticoat. Fragonard was a virtuoso who could turn his hand instantly to accord with different tastes—in this case the romanticized eroticism demanded by his client.*

(1894) and an effigy of Balzac in his dressing gown. His most ambitious work was the *Gates of Hell*, on which he worked from the 1880's until his death.

rod·o·mon·tade (rŏd′ə-mŏn-tād′, -täd′) *n.* **1.** *Often* **rodomontades.** Pretentious boasting or bragging; bluster. **2.** A pretentious boast. ~*adj.* Pretentiously boastful or bragging. ~*intr.v.* **rodomontaded, -tading, -tades.** To boast or brag; bluster; rant. [French, from obsolete Italian *rodomontada,* from *rodomonte,* braggart, after *Rodomonte,* a boastful Moorish king in the epics *Orlando Innamorato* (1487) and *Orlando Furioso* (1516).]

roe¹ (rō) *n.* **1.** The egg-laden ovary of a fish. Also called "hard roe." **2.** The egg mass of certain crustaceans, such as the lobster. **3.** Soft

---

Rodin

THE SCULPTOR OF THE 19TH CENTURY

A new realism inspired by classical art

François Auguste Rodin (1840–1917) was the most influential sculptor of the 19th century. Taking his inspiration from Renaissance artists and classical Greek sculptors, he sculpted his figures with a vivid sense of realism by placing them in convincing postures and giving them an appearance of movement.

Rodin, who was born in Paris, produced his first important work in bronze, called *Bronze Age,* in 1877. This male figure was so lifelike that some people thought it was cast from a living model. In 1880 he began his major life's work, called the *Gates of Hell,* which was inspired by Dante's poem *The Inferno.* It was never finished but it provided ideas for several of his most famous pieces, including *The Kiss, The Thinker, Eve,* and *The Old Courtesan.*

Rodin often stimulated the imagination of his audience by leaving part of the stone unsculptured, so giving the impression that his figure had recently emerged. His work was a bridge between classical and modern styles and inspired Brancusi, Maillol, and the sculptures of Matisse.

MONUMENT TO BALZAC *Rodin's statue of Balzac was finished in 1898 but rejected by the committee that commissioned it. It was erected in the boulevard Raspail, Paris, in 1939.*

---

roe (see). [Middle English *roof, roughe, row,* from Middle Low German or Middle Dutch *roge.*]

roe² *n., pl.* **roes** or collectively **roe.** A **roe deer** (see).

roe·buck (rō′bŭk′) *n.* A male roe deer.

roe deer *n.* A small Eurasian deer, *Capreolus capreolus,* having a brownish coat and short, branched antlers in the male. Also called "roe." [*Roe,* Middle English *ro, ra(a),* Old English *rā, rāha,* from Germanic.]

roent·gen, rönt·gen (rĕnt′gən, rŭnt′-) *n.* Symbol **R** An obsolete unit of radiation dosage equal to the quantity of ionizing radiation that will produce one electrostatic unit of electricity in one cubic centimeter of dry air at 0°C and standard atmospheric pressure. See **rad.** [After Wilhelm Konrad ROENTGEN.]

Roent·gen or **Rönt·gen** (rĕnt′gən), **Wilhelm Konrad** (1845–1923). German physicist. He discovered x-rays and developed x-ray photography, revolutionizing medical diagnosis, and was awarded the first Nobel Prize for physics (1901).

roentgen equivalent man *n.* See **rem.**

roent·gen·ize (rĕnt′gən-īz′, rŭnt′-) *tr.v.* **-ized, -izing, -izes.** To subject to the action of x-rays. —**roent·gen·i·za·tion** *n.*

roent·gen·o·gram (rĕnt′gə-nə-grăm′, rŭnt′-) *n.* Also **roent·gen·o·graph** (-grăf′). A photograph made with x-rays.

roent·gen·ol·o·gy (rĕnt′gə-nŏl′ə-jē, rŭnt′-) *n.* Radiology with x-rays. —**roent·gen·o·log·ic** (rĕnt′gən-ə-lŏj′ĭk), **roent·gen·o·log·i·cal** *adj.* —**roent·gen·o·log·i·cal·ly** *adv.* —**roent·gen·ol·o·gist** *n.*

Roentgen ray *n.* An **x-ray** (see).

Roeth·ke (rĕt′kē, rĕth′-), **Theodore** (1908–63). U.S. poet. A professor of English at several universities, he wrote mostly short, lyrical poems that displayed his remarkable control of the language. His works were published in several collections, including his Pulitzer Prize winner *The Waking* (1953).

ro·ga·tion (rō-gā′shən) *n.* **1.** *Usually* **rogations.** A solemn prayer or supplication, especially as chanted during the rites of the Rogation Days. **2.** A law proposed by a tribune or consul to the people of ancient Rome for acceptance or rejection. [Middle English *rogacioun,* from Latin *rogātiō* (stem *rogātiōn-*), from *rogāre,* to ask, supplicate.] —**ro·ga·tion·al** *adj.*

Rogation Days *pl.n. Ecclesiastical.* The three days preceding Ascension Day, designated as days of special prayer.

rog·a·to·ry (rŏg′ə-tôr′ē, -tōr′ē) *adj. Law.* **1.** Requesting information, especially with proper authorization: *rogatory letters.* **2.** Empowered to carry out investigations: *a rogatory commission.* [French *rogatoire,* from Medieval Latin *rogātōrius,* from Latin *rogāre,* to ask, supplicate.]

rog·er (rŏj′ər) *interj. Often* **Roger. 1.** Used in telecommunications to indicate that a message has been received and understood. **2.** *Slang.* Used to express agreement or understanding. ~*n. Often* **Roger.** The **Jolly Roger** (see). [From the name *Roger,* in signaling code representing *R* and (message) *received.*]

Rog·ers (rŏj′ərz), **Ginger,** born Virginia McMath (1911–). U.S. actress and entertainer. She is best remembered for her partnership with Fred Astaire in a number of 1930's film musicals, including *Top Hat* (1935), *Follow the Fleet* (1936), and *Shall We Dance* (1937).

Rogers, Robert (1731–95). U.S. soldier and frontiersman. During the French and Indian Wars he and his troops, called Rogers' Rangers, conducted daring raids and ambushes. After the war, however, Rogers' greed and illegal dealings lost him respect and several jobs. He published two fanciful accounts of frontier life, moved to England to escape his debts, and died there in poverty.

Rogers, William Penn Adair, known as "Will" (1879–1935). U.S. humorist and actor. In Broadway shows, a syndicated newspaper column, several movies, such as *A Connecticut Yankee* (1931), and numerous books, he delighted millions with his wry, homespun humor. He was killed in a plane accident with aviator Wiley Post.

Rog·et (rō-zhā′), **Peter Mark** (1779–1869). British philologist. A physician and secretary of the Royal Society, he was the author of the *Thesaurus of English Words and Phrases* (1852), which has appeared in many subsequent editions.

rogue (rōg) *n.* **1.** An unprincipled and dishonest person; a scoundrel. **2.** A person who is playfully mischievous; a rascal or scamp. Used humorously. **3.** *Archaic.* A wandering beggar; a vagrant or vagabond. **4.** A vicious and solitary animal; especially, an elephant separated from its herd. **5.** An organism, especially a cultivated plant, that shows an undesirable variation from a standard. ~*v.* **rogued, roguing, rogues.** —*tr.* **1.** To defraud. **2. a.** To remove (diseased or abnormal specimens) from a group, as of plants of the same variety. **b.** To remove such specimens from (a field, for example). —*intr.* To remove undesired plant specimens. ~*adj.* **1.** Vicious and solitary. Said of an animal. **2.** Taking an independent and often rebellious stance; maverick: *a rogue trade union.* **3.** Defective. Said especially of a new motor vehicle. [16th century (cant) : origin obscure.]

ro·guer·y (rō′gər-ē) *n., pl.* **-ies. 1.** Behavior characteristic of a rogue; trickery. **2.** An unprincipled or dishonest act. **3.** A mischievous act.

rogues' gallery *n.* **1.** A collection of photographs of criminals maintained in police files and used for making identifications. **2.** Broadly, any collection of people of some particular, usually disreputable type, such as criminals.

ro·guish (rō′gĭsh) *adj.* **1.** Dishonest or unprincipled. **2.** Playfully mischievous. —**ro·guish·ly** *adv.* —**ro·guish·ness** *n.*

Röhm (rœm), **Ernst** (1887–1934). German soldier and politician. He took part in the Munich putsch (1923) and in 1930 was appointed chief of staff of the Sturmabteilung, or Brown Shirts, a uniformed branch of the Nazi Party. Under Röhm the S.A. became a paramilitary force that threatened to rival the authority of the regular army. In 1934 Hitler had Röhm and other leaders of the organization executed.

roil (roil) *v.* **roiled, roiling, roils.** —*tr.* **1.** To make (a liquid) muddy or cloudy by stirring up sediment. **2.** To displease or disturb; irritate; vex. —*intr.* To be in a state of turbulence or agitation. [Perhaps from Old French *ruiler,* to mix mortar, from Late Latin *regulāre,* to REGULATE.]

roil·y (roi′lē) *adj.* **-ier, -iest. 1.** Muddy; cloudy. **2.** Agitated.

roist·er (rois′tər) *intr.v.* **-ered, -ering, -ers. 1.** To engage in boisterous merrymaking; revel noisily. **2.** To behave in a blustering manner; swagger. [Probably from Old French *rustre,* churl, boor, alteration of *ruste,* rude, rough, churlish, from Latin *rūsticus,* RUSTIC.] —**roist·er·er** *n.* —**roist·er·ous** *adj.* —**roist·er·ous·ly** *adv.*

Ro·land (rō′lənd). A legendary hero, nephew of Charlemagne, killed in battle at Roncesvalles (778).

role, rôle (rōl) *n.* **1.** A character or part to be played by an actor in a dramatic production. **2.** The behavior expected of or associated with an individual or group in society, as determined by social position, sex, or other factors. **3.** A function or position: *your role as a journalist.* [French *rôle,* from Old French *rol(l)e,* roll (on which a part is written), from Medieval Latin *ro(tu)lus, ro(tu)la,* roll of parchment, from Latin *rotulus,* small wheel. See **roll.**]

role model *n.* An individual who serves as a model in a particular behavioral role for another individual to emulate.

role-play·ing (rōl′plā′ĭng) *n.* **1.** The usually subconscious adoption of behavior or attitudes felt to be characteristic of a given position in society. **2.** The taking on of another's position and psychological perspective, usually in order to evaluate responses to likely situations or problems, especially as a training method for social workers and others or as a technique in psychotherapy. —**role-play** *v.*

role reversal *n.* The adoption of a social role opposite to that normally taken by the subject.

rolf (rôlf, rōlf, rôf) *tr.v.* **rolfed, rolfing, rolfs.** To administer rolfing to. —**rolf·er** *n.*

Rolfe (rōlf, rôlf), **John** (1585–1622). English colonist in Virginia. In 1612 he began the cultivation of tobacco, which soon became the staple crop of the colony. He was married to Pocohontas in 1614 and traveled with her to England in 1616. After her death he returned to Virginia, where he was probably massacred by native tribesmen.

rolf·ing (rôl′fĭng, rōl′-, rôf′-) *n.* Deep massage designed to relieve muscular and emotional tension and to reorientate the body to the force of gravity. [After Ida *Rolf* (1897–1979), U.S. physiotherapist.]

roll (rōl) *v.* **rolled, rolling, rolls.** —*intr.* **1.** To move forward along a surface by revolving on an axis or by repeatedly turning over. **2.** To travel or be moved on wheels or rollers. **3.** To travel or be carried in a vehicle: *rolled past the cornfields in the car.* **4. a.** To move or flow with an undulating rhythm: *The waves rolled toward the shore.* **b.** To be carried on a stream. **5. a.** To operate: *The presses began to roll.* **b.** *Informal.* To get underway; proceed: *The political campaign is ready to roll.* **6.** To go by; elapse. Used with *on, away,* or *by*: *The hours rolled on.* **7.** To recur periodically; progress as in cycles. Sometimes used with *around*: *Summer has rolled around again.* **8.** To move in a periodic revolution, as does a planet in its orbit. **9.** To turn and twist from side to side: *The puppy rolled in the mud.* **10.** To rotate: *His eyes rolled with fright.* **11.** To turn around or revolve on or as on an axis. **12.** To extend or appear to extend in gentle rises and falls: *rolling hills.* **13.** To move or rock from side to side. Used of a ship. Compare **pitch. 14.** To walk with a swaying, unsteady motion. **15.** To form the shape of a ball or cylinder. Often used with *up*: *The caterpillar rolled up.* **16.** To become flattened by or as if by pressure applied by a roller. **17.** To make a deep, prolonged, surging sound. Said especially of thunder. **18.** To make a sustained, trilling sound, as do certain birds. **19.** To wander; travel around: *rolling from town to town.* —*tr.* **1.** To cause to move forward along a surface by revolving on an axis, or by repeatedly turning over. **2.** To move or push along on or as if on wheels or rollers: *roll the plane out of the hangar.* **3.** To impel or send onward in a steady, undulating motion: *The sea rolls its waves onto the sand.* **4.** To impart a swaying, rocking motion to: *Heavy seas rolled the ship.* **5.** To cause to turn around or rotate: *roll one's eyes.* **6.** To pronounce or utter with a trill: *You must roll your "r's" when speaking Spanish.* **7.** To utter or emit in full, sonorous tones. **8.** To beat (a drum) with a continuous series of short blows. **9. a.** To wrap (something) around and around upon itself or around something else. Often used with *up*: *roll up a scroll.* **b.** To form (oneself) into a ball, as a hedgehog does. **10. a.** To envelop or enfold in a covering: *roll laundry in a sheet.* **b.** To shape into a ball or cylinder, as by rubbing between the hands or turning over and over: *rolled a cigarette; rolled snow into a ball.* **11.** To spread, compress, or flatten by applying pressure with a roller: *roll out dough.* **12.** *Printing.* To apply ink to (type) with a roller or rollers. **13.** To cause (a film camera, for example) to operate. **14.** To throw (dice) in craps or other games. **15.** *Slang.* To rob (a drunken, sleeping, or otherwise helpless person). —See Synonyms at **turn.** —**roll in. 1.** To arrive in large numbers; pour in. **2.** *Informal.* To arrive at one's destination: *rolled in late again.* **3.** *Informal.* To abound in; be plentifully supplied with: *rolling in money.* —**roll one's own.** *Slang.* To make one's own cigarettes.

~*n.* **1.** The act or an instance of rolling. **2. a.** Anything rolled up in the form of a cylinder: *a roll of carpet.* **b.** A length of leather or other material that may be wound up, with pockets for storing toiletries, tools, or other useful objects. **3.** A quantity of something, such as cloth or wallpaper, rolled into a cylinder, often considered as a unit of measure. **4.** A piece of parchment or paper bearing an inscription that may be or is rolled up; a scroll. **5.** A register or catalogue. **6.** A list of names of persons belonging to a given group: *call the roll.* **7.** A mass of something in cylindrical or rounded form: *a roll of tobacco.* **8. a.** A small rounded portion of bread: *a dinner roll.* **b.** A pastry made by rolling up dough on which a filling has been spread: *a jelly roll.* **c.** Any food that is prepared by rolling up, especially by wrapping pastry around a filling: *a sausage roll.* **9.** A rolling, swaying, or rocking motion or gait. **10.** A gentle swell or undulation of a surface: *the roll of the plains.* **11.** A deep reverberation or rumble. **12.** A rapid succession of short sounds: *the roll of a drum.* **13.** A trill: *the roll of her "r's."* **14.** A resonant, rhythmical flow of words. **15.** A roller; especially, a cylinder on which to roll something up or with which to flatten something. **16.** *Architecture.* A volute on a Corinthian or Ionic capital. **17.** A gymnastic movement in which the body performs a complete turn on itself, normally head over heels. **18.** A maneuver in which an airplane makes a single, complete rotation about its longitudinal axis without changing direction or losing altitude. **19.** *Slang.* Money; especially, a wad of paper money. —**strike off the rolls.** To deprive of membership, especially membership of a professional body after malpractice; expel. [Middle English *rol(l)en,* from Old French *rol(l)er,* from Vulgar Latin *rotulāre* (unattested), from Latin *rotulus, rotula,* small wheel, from *rota,* wheel.]

Rol·land (rô-läɴ′), **Romain** (1866–1944). French novelist, biographer, dramatist, and man of letters. His varied works include *Jean Christophe* (1904–12), a 10-volume novel about a German musical genius. He was awarded the Nobel Prize for literature in 1915.

roll·a·way (rōl′ə-wā′) *adj.* Set upon rollers for easy moving and storing: *a rollaway bed.*

roll·back (rōl′băk′) *n.* A reduction of prices or wages to a previous lower level by governmental action or direction.

roll bar, roll-bar (rōl′bär′) *n.* A strong steel frame reinforcing the roof of a car for protection in case the car should roll over, found especially in cars used for race events.

roll call *n.* **1.** The reading aloud of a list of names of people, as in a classroom or barracks, to determine who is absent. **2.** The time fixed for such a reading.

roll-call vote (rōl′kôl′) *n.* **1.** A procedure of voting in a legislative assembly or other body, in which each member votes when his name is called from the roll. **2.** An instance of such a voting procedure.

rolled gold (rōld) *n. Chiefly British.* Filled gold.

rolled oats *n. Used with a singular or plural verb.* **1.** Flakes produced by simultaneously heating and flattening hulled oat grains between rollers. **2.** A breakfast cereal made by simmering such flakes in water or milk.

rolled-steel joist (rōld′stēl′) *n.* An **RSJ** *(see).*

roll·er (rō′lər) *n.* **1.** One that rolls. **2.** Any of various cylindrical devices, specifically: **a.** A small, spokeless wheel, such as that of a roller skate or caster. **b.** An elongated cylinder upon which something is wound, such as a window blind or roll of foil. **c.** A heavy cylinder used to perform leveling or crushing operations. **d.** *Printing.* A cylinder, usually of hard rubber, used to ink the type before the paper is impressed. **e.** A cylinder of wire mesh, foam rubber, or other material around which a strand of hair is wound to produce a soft curl or wave. **f.** A device for spreading paint, consisting of a revolving cylinder of foam rubber or fiber fitted to a bracket and handle. **g.** A small steel cylinder in a roller bearing. **h.** Any of a set of revolving cylinders along which heavy objects may be rolled. **3.** A long, rolled bandage. **4.** A heavy, swelling wave that breaks on the coast. **5.** Any of various birds of the family Coraciidae, mostly of warm regions of the Old World, having bright-blue wings, stocky bodies, and hooked bills, and noted for their aggressiveness. **6.** A tumbler pigeon of a breed that somersaults during flight. **7.** A **steamroller** *(see).*

roller bearing *n.* A bearing using rollers to reduce friction between machine parts.

roller coaster *n.* A steep, sharply banked, elevated railway with small open passenger cars, operated as a fairground attraction.

roller derby *n.* A relay race on roller skates; especially, a type of race run on an oval track with two teams of skaters often involving aggressive tactics.

roller skate *n.* A skate having four small wheels instead of a runner, for skating on pavements and hard, smooth surfaces.

roll·er-skate (rō′lər-skāt′) *intr.v.* **-skated, -skating, -skates.** To skate on roller skates. —**roller skater** *n.*

roller towel *n.* A long towel with its ends sewn together that is hung from a roller.

Rolle's theorem (rôlz, rōlz) *n.* A theorem in mathematics stating that if a curve is continuous, has two x-intercepts, and has a tangent at every point between the intercepts, at least one of these tangents is parallel to the x-axis. [After Michel *Rolle* (d. 1719).]

roll film *n.* Photographic film rolled on a spool.

rol·lick (rŏl′ĭk) *intr.v.* **-licked, -licking, -licks.** To behave or move in a carefree, frolicsome manner; romp.

~*n.* A carefree escapade; a lark. [Probably a blend of ROMP or ROLL and FROLIC.] —**rol·lick·some, rol·lick·y** *adj.*

rol·lick·ing (rŏl′ĭk-ĭng) *adj.* Carefree and high-spirited; boisterous. —**rol·lick·ing·ly** *adv.*

roe deer *A small Eurasian deer that barks like a dog when alarmed. Both sexes are almost tailless and the male's antlers are very short.*

PRONUNCIATION KEY

ă, pat; ā, pay; âr, care;
ä, father, are; b, bib;
ch, church; d, deed; ĕ, pet;
ē, be; f, fife; g, gag; h, hat;
hw, which; ĭ, pit; ī, pie;
îr, pier; j, judge; k, kick;
l, lid, needle; m, mum;
n, no, sudden; ng, thing;
ŏ, pot; ō, toe; ô, paw, for;
oi, noise; ou, out; ŏŏ, book;
ōō, boot; p, pop; r, roar;
s, sauce; sh, ship, dish;
t, tight; th, thin, path;
th, this, bathe; ŭ, cut; ûr, fur;
v, valve; w, with; y, yes;
z, zebra, size; zh, vision;
ə, about, item, edible,
gallop, circus, peaceful

IN FOREIGN WORDS:

à, *Fr.* ami; œ, *Fr.* feu, *Ger.* schön; ü, *Fr.* tu, *Ger.* über; KH, *Ger.* ich, *Scot.* loch; ɴ, *Fr.* bon; y′, *Fr.* Compiègne

STRESS MARKS:

Primary stress: ′
in·cite′ (ĭn-sīt′)
Secondary stress: ′
in′sight′ (ĭn′sīt′)

roll·ing (rō'lĭng) *adj.* Progressive; developing or increasing with time: *rolling devolution.*

rolling hitch *n. Nautical.* A hitch for tying the end of one rope to a spar or the middle of another rope. The knot jams when tension is applied.

rolling mill *n.* **1.** A factory in which metal is rolled into sheets, bars, or other forms. **2.** A machine used for rolling metal.

rolling pin *n.* A smooth cylinder usually of wood and with a handle at each end, used for rolling out pastry or dough.

rolling stock *n.* The locomotives, freight cars, and other wheeled vehicles used on a railroad.

rolling stone *n.* A wanderer or person of restless or unsettled habits.

Rolling Stones. British rock group, in the vanguard of the 1960's revolution in popular music. It consisted originally of Mick Jagger (1943–), Brian Jones (1942–69), Keith Richard (1943–), Charlie Watts (1941–), and Bill Wyman (1936–). Its many hit records include the singles *Satisfaction* and *Honky Tonk Woman.*

roll·mops (rōl'mŏps') *n., pl.* **rollmops.** Also **roll·mop,** *pl.* **-mops.** A marinated fillet of herring sometimes wrapped around a gherkin or onion, and served as an hors d'oeuvre. [German *Rollmops* : *rollen,* to ROLL + *Mops,* pug dog.]

roll on *tr.v.* To apply or put on by means of a rolling action.

roll-on (rōl'ŏn') *n.* A liquid deodorant applied by a revolving ball in the mouth of a container. Also used adjectivally: *a roll-on deodorant.*

roll-on roll-off *adj.* **1.** Designating a ferry or other ship designed so that large or heavy vehicles can drive on and drive off. **2.** Of, pertaining to, or designating systems of transport operating in this way: *roll-on roll-off cargo.*

roll·o·ver (rōl'ō'vər) *n.* **1.** The act or process of rolling over. **2.** An accident in which a motor vehicle overturns.

Rolls (rōlz), **Charles Stewart** (1877–1910). British car manufacturer. In 1906 he merged his firm with that of car designer Henry Royce to form Rolls Royce Ltd., subsequently one of the world's most prestigious car manufacturers. Rolls was also an aviation pioneer. He died in an air crash.

roll-top desk (rōl'tŏp') *n.* A desk fitted with a flexible, sliding lid made of parallel slats. Also called "roll top."

roll up *intr.v.* **1.** *Informal.* To arrive, especially in a vehicle. **2.** To pile up or increase; become progressively larger. —*tr.v.* **1.** *Military.* To drive (the enemy's flank or line) around and back on itself. **2.** To pile up or increase.

roll-up (rōl'ŭp') *n.* **1.** *British Informal.* A cigarette put together by the smoker with a cigarette paper and tobacco. **2.** *Australian.* A gathering or assembly of people.

roll·way (rōl'wā') *n.* A surface along which cylinders or objects on rollers may be moved.

ro·ly-po·ly (rō'lē-pō'lē) *adj.* Short and plump; pudgy. —*n., pl.* **roly-polies.** **1.** A roly-poly person. **2.** *Chiefly British.* A pudding made by rolling up jam or fruit in pastry dough and cooking it. Also called "roly-poly pudding." [Perhaps from ROLL + POLL (head).]

ROM (rŏm) *n. Computer Science.* A read-only memory.

rom. roman (printing type).

Rom. **1.** Roman. **2.** Romance (language). **3.** Romania; Romanian. **4.** Romans (New Testament).

Roma. See **Rome.**

Ro·ma·gna (rō-mä'nyə). Historic region of north-central Italy, bordering on the Adriatic Sea. It was the center of Byzantine rule in Italy (540–751). The region was donated to the papacy by Pepin the Short (754) and Charlemagne (774), but was not effectively incorporated into the Papal States until the early 1500's. It is now part of Emilia-Romagna.

Ro·ma·ic (rō-mā'ĭk) *n.* Modern vernacular Greek. [Modern Greek *Rhōmaikos,* from Greek, Roman (especially, of the eastern Roman Empire at Byzantium), from *Rhōmē, Rhōma,* Rome, from Latin *Rōma,* ROME.] —**Ro·ma·ic** *adj.*

ro·maine (rō-mān') *n.* A variety of lettuce, *Lactuca sativa longifolia,* having long crisp leaves forming a slender head. Also called "cos," "cos lettuce." [French, from the feminine of *Romain,* Roman, from Old French, ROMAN.]

ro·ma·ji (rō'mä-jē) *n.* The Roman alphabet as used to transliterate Japanese. [Japanese, from *Roman.*]

ro·man (rō'mən) *n. Abbr.* **rom.** *Sometimes* **Roman.** The most common style of type, characterized by upright letters having serifs and vertical lines thicker than horizontal lines. This definition is printed in roman. Compare **italic.** —*adj. Abbr.* **rom.** *Sometimes* **Roman.** Of, set in, or printed in roman. [It represents the style used in ancient Roman inscriptions and manuscripts.]

Ro·man (rō'mən) *adj. Abbr.* **Rom.** **1.** Of, pertaining to, derived from, or characteristic of Rome and its people, especially ancient Rome. **2.** Of, in, pertaining to, or characteristic of the Latin language. **3.** Of or pertaining to the Roman Catholic Church. **4.** Of or designating an architectural style developed by the ancient Romans, characterized by great, round arches and barrel vaults, masonry construction, and classical orders as decorative features. —*n. Abbr.* **Rom.** **1.** A native, resident, or citizen of Rome, especially ancient Rome. **2.** The Italian language as spoken in Rome. **3.** A member of the Roman Catholic Church. [Middle English *Roman* and *Romain,* respectively from Old English *Rōman,* a Roman, and

Old French *Romain,* Roman, a Roman, both from Latin *Rōmānus,* from *Rōma,* ROME.]

ro·man à clef (rō-män' ä klĕ') *n., pl.* **romans à clef** (-mänz'-, *or pronounced as singular*). *French.* A novel in which actual persons, events, or places are depicted in fictional guise. [Literally, "novel with key."]

Roman alphabet *n.* **1.** The alphabet evolved by the ancient Romans from that of the Greeks by way of the Etruscan alphabet, consisting of 23 letters upon which are founded the modern western European alphabets. Also called "Latin alphabet." **2.** Any of the modern alphabets derived from this.

Roman calendar *n.* A lunar calendar used by the ancient Romans until it was superseded by the **Julian calendar** *(see)* in 46 B.C. It consisted of ten months and in each month designated the day of the new moon as the **calends** *(see),* the day of the full moon as the **ides** *(see),* and the ninth day before the ides as the **nones** *(see).* Dates were calculated backward from these three points.

Roman candle *n.* A firework consisting of a tube from which streams of sparks are ejected. [Originated in Italy.]

Roman Catholic *adj. Abbr.* **R.C., Rom. Cath.** Of, designating, belonging to, or pertaining to the Roman Catholic Church. —*n.* A member of the Roman Catholic Church.

Roman Catholic Church *n. Abbr.* **R.C.Ch.** The Christian church recognizing the primacy of the see of Rome and the authority of the Pope and characterized by a hierarchical structure of bishops and priests in which doctrinal and disciplinary authority are dependent upon apostolic succession. Also called "Catholic Church," "Church of Rome."

Roman Catholicism *n.* The doctrines, practices, and institutions of the Roman Catholic Church. Also called "Catholicism."

ro·mance (rō-măns', rō'măns) *n.* **1.** A long, medieval narrative in prose or verse, telling of the adventures of chivalric heroes. **2. a.** Any long, fictitious tale of heroes and extraordinary or mysterious events, usually set in a distant time and place. **b.** Any sequence of real events resembling such a tale in excitement, nobility, or idealized love. **3.** The class of literature of such tales. **4.** A quality suggestive of the adventure, mystery, and idealized exploits found in such tales. **5.** A novel, story, or film dealing with a love affair, especially in a sentimental fashion. **6.** The class or style of fictional works about idealized love. **7. a.** A love affair; especially, a short-lived but passionately idealistic attachment of two young people. **b.** Love or romantic involvement, especially when idealized. **c.** A strong, usually short-lived attachment or enthusiasm. **8.** Inclination toward love, adventure, or mystery; romantic spirit. **9.** A fictitiously embellished account or explanation. **10.** A short, lyrical song or instrumental piece. —*v.* **romanced, -mancing, -mances.** —*intr.* **1.** To invent, write, or recount tales of adventure, nobility, or love. **2.** To tell extravagant and exaggerated lies. **3.** To think or behave in a romantic manner. —*tr. Informal.* To behave romantically toward; woo. [Middle English *roma(u)ns, roma(u)nce,* French, work written in French, from Old French *romanz, romant,* from Vulgar Latin *Rōmānicē* (unattested), in the vernacular (as opposed to *Latinē,* in Latin), from Latin *Rōmānicus,* Roman, made in Rome, from *Rōmānus,* ROMAN.] —**ro·manc·er** *n.*

Ro·mance (rō-măns', rō'măns) *adj. Abbr.* **Rom.** Of, designating, or belonging to any of the languages that developed from Latin, the principal ones being French, Italian, Portuguese, Romanian, and Castilian Spanish and Catalan. —*n.* The Romance languages. [From ROMANCE (French, "the Roman tongue").]

Roman Empire. **1.** The lands governed by the ancient Romans. In A.D. 395 it was divided into the Eastern Roman Empire or **Byzantine Empire** and the **Western Roman Empire.** **2.** The government of Rome and its lands from 27 B.C by Augustus and the later emperors. **3.** Any empire held to be a successor of the Roman Empire, such as the Byzantine Empire or Holy Roman Empire.

Ro·man·esque (rō'mən-ĕsk') *adj.* **1.** Of, pertaining to, or designating a transitional style of European architecture prevalent from the 9th to the 12th century, and characterized by rounded arches, massive vaulting, and thick walls. See Norman. **2.** Of, pertaining to, or designating the styles in art prevalent in this period. —*n.* The Romanesque style. [From ROMAN.]

ro·man-fleuve (rō-män'flœv') *n., pl.* **romans-fleuves** (*pronounced as singular*). *French.* A long novel, often in many volumes, chronicling the history of an individual, family, or community. Also called "saga novel." [Literally, "river-novel" (because the development of its plot is now rapid, now slow, like the flow of a river), coined by Romain Rolland.]

Roman holiday *n.* **1.** A time of enjoyment derived from the suffering of others. **2.** Any savage and spectacular entertainment reminiscent of the staged public battles of Roman gladiators. [So called from the gladiatorial contests of the ancient Romans.]

Ro·ma·ni·a or **Ru·ma·ni·a** or **Rou·ma·ni·a** (rō-mā'nē-ə, -nyə, rōō-). *Abbr.* **Rom.** Republic of southeastern Europe. It is dominated by the Carpathian Mts., with the Transylvanian uplands to the northwest and lower Danubian plains in the southeast. Romania achieved rapid industrial expansion during the 1960's and 1970's, and machinery, chemicals, consumer goods, agricultural produce, oil, and gas are major exports. The country was formed by the union of Walachia and Moldavia (1861) and achieved independence in 1878. After World War II it became a Soviet satellite, but under President Nicolae Ceauşescu, it has since 1967 pursued an

Romanesque

ART INSPIRED BY RELIGION
A rich combination of styles

Romanesque was the art style that began in France and northern Italy in the late 9th century and spread across Europe to reach its peak in the 11th and early 12th centuries; after this it began to develop into the Gothic style. It was expressed mainly through architecture, with the characteristics—derived from Roman architecture—of thick walls and semicircular arches supported by squat cylindrical columns. The development of the cross vault enabled builders to give churches stone ceilings rather than the traditional wooden roofs, which were subject to the risk of fire.

Throughout the political chaos of the Dark Ages in Europe, the Church had been the guardian of learning. With the return of a degree of stability in the 10th century, there was a rise in the number of monasteries and an increase in church building. The monastery of Cluny, north of Lyons in France, was particularly influential. Its third head, Abbot Hugh, was a builder who toured Europe and advised on the plans of over 1,000 buildings. The second abbey church of Cluny, built by his predecessor, inspired copies throughout Europe, including Durham Cathedral. After 1066 Romanesque was spread through England by the Normans who also took it to Sicily and southern Italy.

Romanesque artists decorated the new churches with sculptures, frescoes, illuminated gospels, and missals (books containing the Mass). They drew on many styles, including Roman, Byzantine, Islamic, and barbarian sources.

PISA CATHEDRAL *This Romanesque building in Italy, begun in 1063, is faced with gray-green and white marble and mosaic inlays. The façade consists of tiers of arcades ascending into the gable. There is an elliptical dome at the crossing point of the nave and transepts.*

---

increasingly independent course. Area, 237,500 square kilometers (91,699 square miles). Population 22,100,000. Capital, Bucharest.

Ro·ma·ni·an, Ru·ma·ni·an (rō-mā′nē-ən, -nyən, rōō-) *adj.* Of or pertaining to Romania, its people, or their language. ~*n.* **1.** A native or inhabitant of Romania. **2.** The Romance language of the Romanians.

Ro·man·ic (rō-măn′ĭk) *adj.* **1.** Of or derived from the ancient Romans or their language. **2.** Of or pertaining to the Romance languages. ~*n.* Romance. [Latin *Rōmānicus,* from *Rōmānus,* ROMAN.]

Ro·man·ism (rō′mən-ĭz′əm) *n.* **1.** Roman Catholicism. Usually used derogatorily. **2.** Admiration for the spirit of ancient Rome.

Ro·man·ist (rō′mən-ĭst) *n.* **1. a.** A Roman Catholic. **b.** A member of the Church of England who favors Catholic ritual. **2.** A student of or authority on Roman law, culture, and institutions. ~*adj.* **1.** Of, belonging to, or designating the Roman Catholic Church. **2.** Favoring Catholic ritual.

Ro·man·ize (rō′mən-īz′) *v.* **-ized, -izing, -izes.** —*tr.* **1.** To convert (a person) to Roman Catholicism. **2.** To make (a ritual, for example) Roman Catholic in character. **3.** To make Roman in character: *Our laws were Romanized.* **4.** To write or transliterate (a language, for example) into the Roman alphabet. —*intr.* **1.** To be converted to Roman Catholicism. **2.** To adopt Roman Catholic practices. —**Ro·man·i·za·tion** *n.*

Roman law *n.* The system of laws of ancient Rome, upon which the legal systems of many countries are based. See **civil law.**

Roman nose *n.* A nose with a high, prominent bridge.

Roman numeral *n.* One of the numerals formed with letters of the Roman alphabet used as numerical symbols by the ancient Romans and still used today in certain formal contexts. In this system I stands for 1, V for 5, X for 10, L for 50, C for 100, D for 500, and M for 1000. Compare **Arabic numeral.**

Ro·ma·no (rə-mä′nō, rō-) *n.* A hard, dry Italian cheese similar to but sharper than Parmesan. [Italian, Roman, from Latin *Romanus.*]

Ro·ma·nov or **Ro·ma·noff** (rō-mä′nəf, rō′mə-nôf′). Family name of the imperial dynasty (1613–1917) in Russia. The line began with the accession of Czar Michael and ended with the abdication of Nicholas II during the Russian Revolution.

Ro·mans (rō′mənz) *n.* Used with a singular verb. *Abbr.* **Rom.** A book of the New Testament, an epistle of Saint Paul to the Christians of Rome.

Ro·mansch, Ro·mansh (rō-mănsh′, rō-mänsh′) *n.* The Rhaeto-Romanic dialects spoken in eastern Switzerland and in neighboring parts of Italy. [Romansch *Ruman(t)sch, Roman(t)sch,* "Roman," "Romance language," from Vulgar Latin *Rōmānicē* (unattested), in the Roman manner, in the Roman tongue. See **romance.**]

Roman snail *n.* A large snail, *Helix pomatia,* that is the more commonly used edible species.

ro·man·tic (rō-măn′tĭk) *adj.* **1. a.** Of, pertaining to, designating, characterized by, or evoking feelings of love, especially of a passionate or sentimental nature: *romantic lighting.* **b.** Given or inclined to such feelings or thoughts: *a romantic young girl.* **2.** Of or pertaining to a sexual relationship. **3. a.** Of or pertaining to a literary romance. **b.** Characteristic of the atmosphere or mood of such romances; idealistic, heroic, exciting, and noble. **4.** Imaginative but impractical: *romantic notions.* **5.** Not based on fact; fictitious. **6.** *Often* **Romantic.** Of or characteristic of romanticism in the arts. ~*n.* **1.** A person whose mind and emotions are oriented toward love, adventure, or high ideals; a romantic person. **2.** A person who enjoys the artistic products of romanticism more than those of other movements and styles. **3.** *Often* **Romantic.** A writer or other artist creating works of art in the style or spirit of romanticism; especially, one who lived in the romantic era. [French *romantique,* from Old French *romant, romanz,* ROMANCE.] —**ro·man·ti·cal·ly** *adv.*

ro·man·ti·cism (rō-măn′tə-sĭz′əm) *n.* **1.** *Often* **Romanticism.** A literary and artistic movement originating in Europe toward the end of the 18th century that sought to assert the validity of subjective experience and to escape from the prevailing subordination of content and feeling to classical forms. Also called "Romantic Movement." **2.** The spirit and attitudes characteristic of this movement. —**ro·man·ti·cist** *n.*

ro·man·ti·cize (rō-măn′tə-sīz′) *v.* **-cized, -cizing, -cizes.** —*tr.* **1.** To make romantic in style or character. **2.** To consider or portray in an often inappropriately romantic way: *Don't romanticize bank robbery.* —*intr.* **1.** To think or speak in a romantic way; fantasize. **2.** To act in a romantic way; flirt. **3.** To render the account of some event more interesting; exaggerate.

Rom·a·ny, Rom·ma·ny (rŏm′ə-nē, rō′mə-) *n., pl.* **-nies** or collectively **Romany** or **Rommany. 1.** A Gypsy. **2.** The Indic language of the Gypsies. ~*adj.* Of or pertaining to the Gypsies, their culture, or their language. [Romany *romani,* plural of *romano,* gypsy, from *rom,* man, husband, gypsy man, from Sanskrit *ḍomba, ḍoma,* man of a low caste of musicians, from Dravidian.]

ro·maunt (rō-mänt′) *n. Archaic.* A medieval romance in verse or prose. [Middle English, from Old French *romant, romanz,* ROMANCE.]

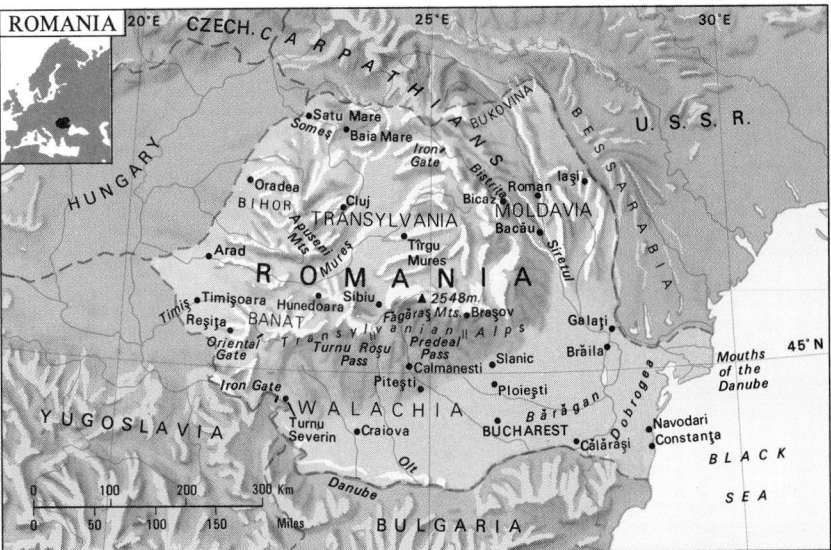

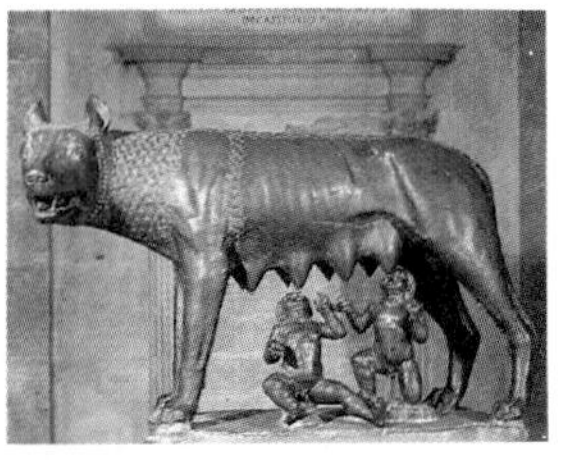

Romulus and Remus *These legendary twins were abandoned at birth but, as this fifth-century Roman statue shows, they were suckled and reared by a wolf.*

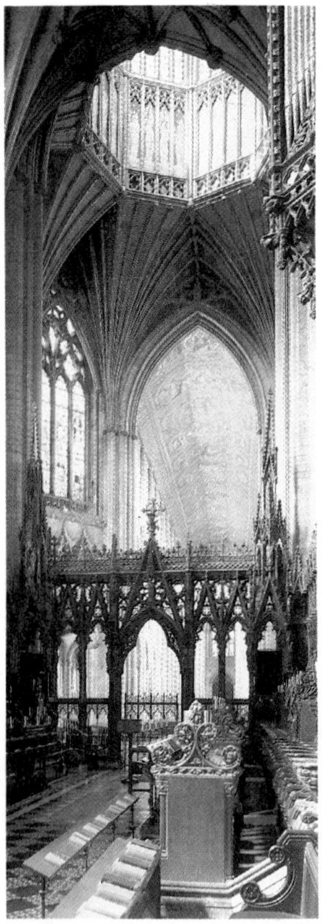

rood screen *The choir is separated from the nave in many churches by the rood screen, which rises from the floor to a beam that was called the rood (cross) beam.*

Rom·bauer (rŏm′bou′ər), **Irma von Starkloff** (1877–1962). U.S. cookery expert. Her now famous cookbook, *Joy of Cooking*, began as a collection of recipes for her son and daughter. First published privately in 1931, it has undergone numerous revisions and sold millions of copies.

Rom. Cath. Roman Catholic.

Rome[1] (rōm). *Italian* **Ro·ma** (rō′mə, -mä) Capital of Italy and of the Latium region, known as the Eternal City. On the Tiber River, it is built on and around seven hills and was founded, according to legend, by Romulus on the Palatine hill (753 B.C.). Once the center of the Roman Empire, it has many ancient remains, including the Forum and Colosseum. Rome fell to the Goths in the 5th century and to the Byzantines in A.D. 552 and was later sacked by the Arabs (846) and Normans (1084). Gradually it came under papal control, its fortunes following those of the papacy until it was annexed to Italy (1870). During the Renaissance it was a flourishing art center, and it is rich in buildings and works of art of the period. Rome became Italy's capital in 1871. It is also a cultural, tourist, and manufacturing center.

Rome[2]. **1.** The ancient Roman kingdom, republic, and empire. **2.** The Roman Catholic Church or Roman Catholicism.

Ro·me·o (rō′mē-ō) *n., pl.* **-os.** An ardent male lover. [After the tragic hero of Shakespeare's *Romeo and Juliet.*]

Rom·ish (rō′mĭsh) *adj.* Of or pertaining to the Roman Catholic Church.

Rom·mel (rŏm′əl), **Erwin** (1891–1944). German general, nicknamed "the Desert Fox," famous for his desert campaigns of World War II. In 1941 he was made commander in chief of the newly formed Afrika Korps. Following victories at Tobruk and Benghazi (1942), he invaded Egypt, but was forced to withdraw after the Battle of El Alamein (1942) and was recalled to Europe in 1943. He was implicated in the July Plot (1944) to assassinate Hitler and apparently committed suicide when his complicity was discovered.

Rom·ney (rŏm′nē), **George** (1734–1802). British portrait painter. A Lancashire cabinetmaker's son, he trained under an itinerant artist and later became a commercial portrait painter. In 1762 he moved to London, where he acquired a fashionable clientele.

romp (rŏmp) *intr.v.* **romped, romping, romps. 1.** To play or frolic boisterously. **2.** To win a race or contest easily. **3.** To proceed easily or effortlessly. Often used with *about* or *along.*
—*n.* **1.** An occasion of lively, merry play; a frolic. **2.** *Archaic.* One who sports and frolics, especially a girl. **3.** An easy win. [Variant of RAMP (to rage).]

romp·er (rŏm′pər) *n.* **1.** One who romps; especially, a young child. **2. rompers.** A baby's one-piece playsuit, usually with short legs.

Ro·mu·lo (rŏm′yōō-lō′), **Carlos Pena** (1899–1985). Filipino soldier, educator, journalist, and diplomat. Noted for his support of the Allies during the Japanese invasion and occupation of the Philippines (1941–45), he accompanied Douglas MacArthur on his historic return to the islands in 1945.

Rom·u·lus (rŏm′yə-ləs). *Roman Mythology.* The son of Mars and a vestal virgin, who, with his twin brother **Remus,** was abandoned as an infant to die but was suckled by a she-wolf. He later killed Remus and founded Rome in 753 B.C.

Romulus Au·gus·tu·lus (ô-gŭs′tə-ləs) (born *c.* A.D. 460). The last Roman emperor of the West (475–76). As a youth he was deposed by the German ruler Odoacer, who spared his life. He died in retirement at an unknown date.

Ron·ces·valles (rŏn′sə-vălz′). *French* **Ronce·vaux** (rôɴs-vō′). Mountain pass and village of Navarre, northern Spain. It was the site of the defeat and massacre of the rear guard of Charlemagne's army, under Roland, by the Saracens (778).

rond de jambe (rôɴ′ də zhôɴb′) *n., pl.* **ronds de jambe** *(pronounced as singular).* In ballet, a circular movement of the leg from below the knee, executed either in the air or on the ground.

ron·deau (rŏn′dō, rŏn-dō′) *n., pl.* **-deaux** (-dōz, -dōz′) **1.** A lyrical poem of French origin having 13, or sometimes 10, lines with two rhymes throughout and with the opening phrase repeated twice as a refrain. Also called "roundel." **2.** *Music.* **a.** An originally monophonic medieval song of the trouvères or troubadours. **b.** An early rondo. [French, variant of RONDEL.]

ron·del (rŏn′dəl, -dĕl) *n.* A rondeau that usually has 14 lines. Also called "roundel." [Middle English, from Old French, "small circle" (from the repetition of the first lines at the end of the poem), from *ronde, rounde,* ROUND.]

ron·de·let (rŏn′də-lĕt) *n.* A short rondeau having five or seven lines and one refrain in one stanza. [Old French, diminutive of RONDEL.]

ron·do (rŏn′dō, rŏn-dō′) *n., pl.* **-dos.** A musical composition having a refrain that occurs at least three times in its original key. [Italian *rondò,* from French *rondeau,* RONDEAU.]

ron·dure (rŏn′jər) *n.* *Archaic.* Something circular or gracefully rounded. [Old French *rondeur,* from *rond, rounde,* ROUND.]

rone (rōn) *n.* *Scottish.* A gutter or drainpipe on a house. [19th century : origin obscure.]

ron·nel (rŏn′əl) *n.* **1.** A solid, light-brown compound, $C_8H_8Cl_3O_3PS$, used as an insecticide, especially against flies and cockroaches. **2. Ronnel.** A trademark for ronnel outside the United States. [From *Ronnel,* a non-U.S. trademark.]

Ron·sard (rôɴ-sär′), **Pierre de** (1524–85). French lyric poet. His love poems are his most highly regarded works, among them *Les Amours* (1552) and *Sonnets pour Hélène* (1578).

röntgen. Variant of **roentgen.**

Röntgen, Wilhelm. See Wilhelm **Roentgen.**

roo, 'roo (rōō) *n.* *Australian Informal.* A kangaroo. [Shortening.]

rood (rōōd) *n.* **1.** A cross or crucifix, especially: **a.** One representing the cross on which Christ was crucified. **b.** One surmounting a rood screen in a medieval church. **2.** *Archaic.* The cross on which Christ was crucified. **3.** *Abbr.* **ro.** A British Imperial unit of length that varies from 5½ to 8 yards. **4.** *Abbr.* **ro.** A British Imperial unit of area usually equal to ¼ acre or 40 square rods. [Middle English *ro(o)d,* Old English *rōd,* rod, cross.]

rood arch *n.* An arch in a church, between the choir and the nave.

rood beam *n.* A beam in a church across the entrance to the choir, where it supports the rood and usually forms the head of the rood screen.

rood loft *n.* A gallery above a rood screen.

rood screen *n.* An ornamented wooden or stone altar screen, usually surmounted by a crucifix, separating the choir of a church from the nave.

roof (rōōf, rŏŏf) *n.* **1.** An exterior surface and its supporting structures on the top of a building. **2.** The top covering of anything. **3.** Anything resembling or compared to a roof, such as the sky or overhead foliage. **4.** *Anatomy.* The upper covering structure of any part of the body: *roof of the mouth.* **5.** The highest point; summit: *the roof of the world.* **—a roof over one's head.** Somewhere to live. **—go through** or **hit the roof.** *Slang.* To lose one's temper suddenly. **—raise the roof.** *Informal.* **1.** To be extremely noisy and boisterous. **2.** To complain loudly and bitterly.
—*tr.v.* **roofed, roofing, roofs.** To furnish or cover with a roof. Often used with *in* or *over.* [Middle English *ro(o)f,* Old English *hrōf.*]

roof·er (rōō′fər, rŏŏf′ər) *n.* One who makes or repairs roofs.

roof garden *n.* A garden on a flat roof of a building.

roof·ing (rōō′fĭng, rŏŏf′ĭng) *n.* **1.** The act of constructing a roof. **2.** A roof of a building. **3.** Materials used in building a roof.

roof·less (rōōf′lĭs, rŏŏf′lĭs) *adj.* **1.** Lacking a roof. **2.** Having no home or shelter; homeless.

roof rack *n.* *Chiefly British.* A metal rack fixed to the top of a motor vehicle for carrying luggage or other objects.

roof·top (rōōf′tŏp′, rŏŏf′-) *n.* The upper surface of a roof of a building.

roof·tree (rōōf′trē′, rŏŏf′-) *n.* A long horizontal beam extending along the ridge of a roof; a ridgepole.

rook[1] (rŏŏk) *n.* **1.** A crowlike Old World bird, *Corvus frugilegus,* with white patches at the base of its bill, that nests in colonies near the tops of trees. **2.** *Slang.* A swindler; especially, one who cheats when gambling.
—*tr.v.* **rooked, rooking, rooks.** *Slang.* To swindle, especially by overcharging or by cheating when gambling. [Middle English *rok, ruke,* Old English *hrōc.*]

rook[2] *n.* *Abbr.* **R** A chess piece that may move in a straight line over any number of empty squares in a rank or file. Also called "castle." [Middle English *rok(e),* from Old French *roc(k),* from Arabic *rukh,* from Persian *rukh*†.]

rook·er·y (rŏŏk′ər-ē) *n., pl.* **-ies. 1. a.** A place where rooks nest and breed. **b.** A colony of rooks or their nests. **2. a.** The breeding ground of certain other birds and animals, such as seals. **b.** A colony of such birds or animals. **3.** *Informal.* A crowded tenement.

rook·ie (rŏŏk′ē) *n.* *Slang.* **1.** An untrained recruit, especially in an army. **2.** Any inexperienced person. [Alteration of RECRUIT (influenced by the bird ROOK).]

room (rōōm, rŏŏm) *n.* *Abbr.* **rm. 1.** Space that is or may be occupied by something; open space: *a desk that takes up too much room.* Sometimes used in combination: *shelf-room.* **2.** An area or part inside a building enclosed by a floor, a ceiling, and walls. **3.** The people present in such an area: *The whole room was amazed.* **4. rooms.** Living quarters; lodgings. **5.** Scope; opportunity. Used with *for* or *to*: *room for error.* **—make room.** To make more space available, usually by giving way or removing something.
—*intr.v.* **roomed, rooming, rooms.** To occupy a room; lodge. [Middle English *roum,* Old English *rūm.*]

room and board *n.* Lodging and meals either earned or provided.

room divider *n.* A partition dividing up a room.

room·er (rōō′mər, rŏŏm′ər) *n.* A lodger.

room·ful (rōōm′fŏŏl′, rŏŏm′-) *n., pl.* **-fuls. 1.** As much or as many as a room will hold. **2.** The number of people in a room.

room·ing house (rōō′mĭng, rŏŏm′ĭng) *n.* A house where lodgers may rent rooms.

room·mate (rōōm′māt′, rŏŏm′-) *n.* A person with whom one shares a room or an apartment.

room service *n.* **1.** A service in a hotel attending to guests' requirements, especially for refreshments, in their rooms. **2.** The staff providing this service.

room temperature *n.* A comfortable living temperature inside a room: *serve the cheese at room temperature.*

room·y (rōō′mē, rŏŏm′ē) *adj.* **-ier, -iest.** Having plenty of room; spacious; large. **—room·i·ly** *adv.* **—room·i·ness** *n.*

Roo·ney (rōō′nē), **Mickey** (1920–). U.S. actor. Primarily known for his acting as a child and young man in such memorable motion pictures as *Huckleberry Finn* (1939) and *National Velvet* (1944). He has also performed on stage and television.

Roo·se·velt (rō′zə-vĕlt′, rōz′vĕlt′, -vəlt, rōō′-), **(Anna) Eleanor** (1884–1962). U.S. diplomat, author, and political figure. The niece of Theodore Roosevelt, she married Franklin D. Roosevelt, a distant cousin, in 1905. During her husband's presidency (1933–45), she became the most highly respected and influential first lady to date. As a delegate to the United Nations (1945–53, 1961–62), she was an outspoken advocate of human rights. Among her many writings are *This I Remember* (1949) and *On My Own* (1958).

Roosevelt, Franklin Delano (1882–1945). 32nd U.S. president (1933–45). His political career was interrupted in 1921 when he was crippled by polio, but he went on to become governor of New York (1929–32). As president he fulfilled his promise of a New Deal for the American people by initiating relief programs, measures to aid employment and assist industrial and agricultural recovery from the Depression. He was the only U.S. president to be re-elected three times (1936, 1940, 1944).

Roosevelt, Theodore (1858–1919). 26th U.S. president (1901–09). As president he won, through forceful diplomacy, a concession to build the Panama Canal (1903). His foreign policy exemplified his principle "speak softly and carry a big stick," and in 1906 he won the Nobel Peace Prize for his mediation in the Russo-Japanese War.

roost (ro͞ost) *n.* **1.** A perch on which domestic fowls or other birds rest or sleep. **2.** A place with perches for fowls or other birds. **3.** A place for temporary rest or sleep. **—come home to roost.** To recoil unpleasantly upon the doer: *His corrupt practices came home to roost.* **—rule the roost.** To be in charge; be in a dominant position.
~v. **roosted, roosting, roosts.** *—intr.* **1.** To rest or sleep on a perch or roost. **2.** To settle down for the night. *—tr.* To supply with a roost or put to roost. [Middle English *rooste,* Old English *hrōst.*]

roost·er (ro͞os′tər) *n.* **1. a.** The adult male of the common domestic fowl; a cock. **b.** The adult male of various other birds. **2.** A pugnacious and cocky person.

root¹ (ro͞ot, ro͝ot) *n.* **1. a.** The usually underground portion of a plant that serves as support, draws water and mineral ions from the surrounding soil, and in some plants stores food. **b.** Any similar underground plant part, such as a rhizome, corm, or tuber. **c.** Any of numerous small, hairlike growths that serve to attach and support plants such as the ivy and other vines. **2.** *Anatomy.* **a.** The embedded part of an organ or structure such as a hair or tooth. **b.** The point of emergence of a nerve from the spinal cord, consisting of a bundle of nerve fibers. **3. a.** Any base or support. **b.** A part of an object by which it is attached to a base or larger object: *the root of a propeller.* **4.** Any base or support. **5.** An essential part or element; a basic core or fundamental nature: *strikes at the roots of our democracy.* **6.** A primary source or cause; origin: *Love of money is the root of all evil.* Also used adjectivally: *the root cause.* **7.** An antecedent or ancestor. **8.** An emotional or psychological attachment or historical association with a particular place or society: *His roots are in New England.* **9.** *Linguistics.* **a.** In etymology, a word or word element from which other words are formed. **b.** In morphology, a base to which prefixes and suffixes may be added. Also called "radical." **10.** *Mathematics.* **a.** A number that when multiplied by itself a specified number of times forms a product equal to a given number: *a fourth root of 16 is 2.* **b.** A number or quantity that when substituted for the variable satisfies the polynomial equation $f(x)=0$. See **function. c.** A **multiple root** *(see).* **11.** *Music.* **a.** The note from which a chord is built. **b.** The first or lowest note of a triad or chord. —See Synonyms at **origin. —put down roots.** To settle; become established, as by taking up permanent residence in a place. **—take root. 1.** To put out roots and grow. **2.** To become fixed, established, or recognized.
~v. **rooted, rooting, roots.** *—intr.* **1.** To grow a root or roots. **2.** To become firmly established, settled, or entrenched. *—tr.* **1.** To cause to put out roots and grow. **2.** To implant by or as if by the roots; fix: *stood rooted to the spot.* **3.** To pull or dig up by or as if by the roots. Used with *up* or *out.* **4.** To eliminate; remove totally. Used with *out: root out abuses.* [Middle English *rot(e),* Old English *rōt,* from Old Norse.] **—root·er** *n.*

root² *v.* **rooted, rooting, roots.** *—tr.* **1.** To dig (the ground, for example) with or as with the snout or nose. **2.** To bring to light or turn up by searching. Often used with *out: rooted out dark secrets from his past.* *—intr.* **1.** To dig in the ground with or as with the snout or nose. Used chiefly of pigs. **2.** To search about or rummage for something. Often used with *about* or *around.* [Alteration (influenced by ROOT of a plant) of earlier *wroot,* Middle English *wroten,* Old English *wrōtan.*] **—root·er** *n.*

root³ *intr.v.* **rooted, rooting, roots.** To give encouragement or support, especially to a team or contestant. Used with *for.* [Perhaps from ROOT (to dig with the snout).] **—root·er** *n.*

Root (ro͞ot), **Elihu** (1845–1937). U.S. lawyer and public official. A highly regarded New York lawyer, he served as U.S. secretary of war (1899–1903), secretary of state (1905–09), and senator (1909–13). He received the Nobel Peace Prize in 1912 for his efforts to re-establish friendly relations with Latin America and Japan.

root·age (ro͞o′tĭj, ro͝ot′ĭj) *n.* **1.** A system or growth of roots. **2.** Establishment or fixing by or as if by roots.

root·ball (ro͞ot′bôl′, ro͝ot′-) *n.* The tightly packed mass of roots and soil produced by a plant grown in a container.

root beer *n.* A carbonated soft drink made from extracts of the roots of several plants.

root canal *n.* The pulp-filled cavity in a root of a tooth.

root cap *n. Botany.* A thimble-shaped mass of cells that covers and protects the tip of a growing root.

root cellar *n.* A cellar, usually covered with earth, used for the storage of root crops and other vegetables.

root·ed (ro͞o′tĭd, ro͝ot′-) *adj.* Deep-seated or deeply felt.

root hair *n. Botany.* A thin, hairlike outgrowth of a plant root that absorbs water and minerals from the soil.

root knot *n.* A disease of plants caused by a nematode and characterized by protuberant enlargements on the roots.

root·less (ro͞ot′lĭs, ro͝ot′-) *adj.* **1.** Having no roots: *a rootless tooth.* **2.** Not belonging to any particular place or society: *the rootless refugees in a strange country.* **—root·less·ly** *adv.* **—root·less·ness** *n.*

root·let (ro͞ot′lĭt, ro͝ot′-) *n.* A small root or division of a root.

root mean square *n. Abbr.* **rms** The square root of the arithmetic mean of the squares of a set of numbers.

root mean square deviation *n. Statistics.* **Standard deviation** *(see).*

root·stalk (ro͞ot′stôk′, ro͝ot′-) *n.* A plant part, a **rhizome** *(see).*

root·stock (ro͞ot′stŏk′, ro͝ot′-) *n.* **1.** A rootlike underground stem, such as a **rhizome** *(see).* **2.** A root or part of a root used as a stock for grafting. **3.** A source or origin.

root vegetable *n.* A vegetable, such as a carrot or beet, that is grown for its edible root.

root·y (ro͞o′tē, ro͝ot′ē) *adj.* **-ier, -iest. 1.** Full of roots. **2.** Consisting of or resembling roots. **—root·i·ness** *n.*

rope (rōp) *n.* **1. a.** Flexible, heavy cord of twisted fibers, wire, or other material. **b.** A section of such cord. **c.** Any strand or other object resembling a rope, especially one consisting of braided or wound material. **2.** A cord with a noose at one end for hanging a person. **3.** Death by hanging. Preceded by *the.* **4. ropes.** Several cords strung between poles to enclose a boxing ring. Preceded by *the.* **5.** Any string of items attached in one line by twisting or braiding: *a rope of onions.* **6. ropes.** The special procedures, details, or conditions of a field of activity: *learning the ropes.* **7.** A sticky glutinous formation of stringy matter in a liquid. **—on the ropes.** *Informal.* Nearing total collapse, defeat, or ruin.
~v. **roped, roping, ropes.** *—tr.* **1.** To tie or fasten with or as with rope. **2.** To enclose, mark off, or divide with a rope. Usually used with *off.* **3.** To join or connect (mountaineers) securely with a rope. Used with *up: The guide roped the party up.* **4.** To catch with a rope. **5.** *Informal.* To trick or deceive. Usually used with *in.* *—intr.* **1.** To become ropy and sticky. **2.** In mountaineering, to tie oneself to the other climbers. Used with *up.* [Middle English *rop(e),* Old English *rāp.*] **—rop·er** *n.*

rope ladder *n.* A flexible ladder made from two ropes linked by rungs.

rope·walk (rōp′wôk′) *n.* **1.** A long, usually covered path or alley where ropes are made. **2.** A long, narrow building containing a ropewalk.

rope·way (rōp′wā′) *n.* A system of overhead cables and supporting towers used to transport goods or passengers in containers or cabins suspended from the cables, as at a ski resort.

rope yarn *n.* The fibers of hemp, nylon, or other material from which rope is made.

rop·y (rō′pē) *adj.* **-ier, -iest. 1.** Resembling a rope or ropes. **2.** *British Informal.* Of poor or inferior quality. **3.** Forming sticky glutinous strings or threads. **—rop·i·ly** *adv.* **—rop·i·ness** *n.*

roque (rōk) *n.* A difficult form of croquet played on a hard court. [Alteration of CROQUET.]

Roque·fort (rōk′fərt) *n.* A French cheese made from ewes' and goats' milk and containing a blue mold, *Penicillium roqueforti.* [After *Roquefort*-sur-Soulzon, village in southeastern France.]

roqu·e·laure (rŏk′ə-lôr, rŏk′lôr, -lōr) *n.* A man's knee-length cloak popular during the 18th and early 19th centuries. [After the Duc de *Roquelaure* (1656–1738), French marshal.]

ro·quet (rō-kā′, -kā) *v.* **-queted, -queting, -quets.** *—tr.* In croquet: **1.** To cause one's ball to strike (another player's ball). **2.** To strike (another ball). Used of a ball. *—intr.* In croquet, to strike another player's ball with one's own.
~n. The act of roqueting. [Arbitrarily formed from CROQUET.]

ror·qual (rôr′kwəl) *n.* Any of several whalebone whales of the genus *Balaenoptera,* having longitudinal grooves on the throat and a small, pointed dorsal fin. Also called "finback," "razorback." [French, from Norwegian *rørhval,* from Old Norse *reytharhvalr* : *reythr,* rorqual, "red whale" (from its red streaks), from *rauthr,* red + *hvalr,* whale.]

Ror·schach test (rôr′shäk′, -shäKH′) *n. Psychology.* A type of projective test of personality in which a subject's interpretations of ten abstract inkblot designs are analyzed as a measure of emotional and intellectual functioning and integration. [Devised by Hermann *Rorschach* (1884–1922), Swiss psychiatrist.]

Ro·sa (rō′zə), **Salvator** (1615–73). Italian painter, born near Naples. He developed a distinctive preoccupation with wild landscapes and battle scenes. He was also a poet, actor, and musician.

ro·sa·ceous (rō-zā′shəs) *adj.* **1.** *Botany.* Of or belonging to the Rosaceae, the plant family that includes the roses. **2.** Resembling the flower of a rose. [New Latin *Rosaceae,* from Latin *rosāceus,* made of roses : ROSE + -ACEOUS.]

ros·an·i·line (rō-zăn′ə-lĭn) *n.* Also **ros·an·i·lin** (-lĭn). A brownish-red crystalline organic compound, $C_{20}H_{19}N_3$, derived from aniline and used in the manufacture of dyes. [ROSE (flower) + ANILINE.]

ro·sa·ry (rō′zə-rē) *n., pl.* **-ries. 1.** *Roman Catholic Church.* **a.** A form of devotion to the Virgin Mary, consisting of a recitation of any of three sets of five decades each of the Ave Maria, each decade preceded by a Lord's Prayer, ending with a Gloria Patri, and commemorating an event in the life of Christ or Our Lady. See **mystery. b.** A string of beads on which these prayers are counted. **2.** Similar beads used by other religious groups. [Middle English, from Medieval Latin *rosārium,* from Latin, rose garden, from *rosa,* ROSE.]

rosary pea *n.* A woody vine, *Abrus precatorius,* of tropical Asia,

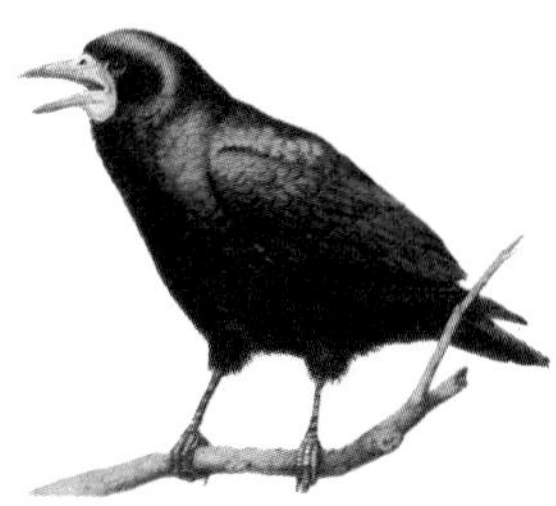

rook Corvus frugilegus, *the common rook of Europe and Asia, is among the most sociable of birds. It feeds in flocks, mainly on insects in the soil, and nests in large rookeries high up in tall trees. Some rookeries may contain as many as 9,000 pairs, and the birds' incessant cawing has given rise to the collective names by which they are sometimes known—a clamor or a parliament of rooks.*

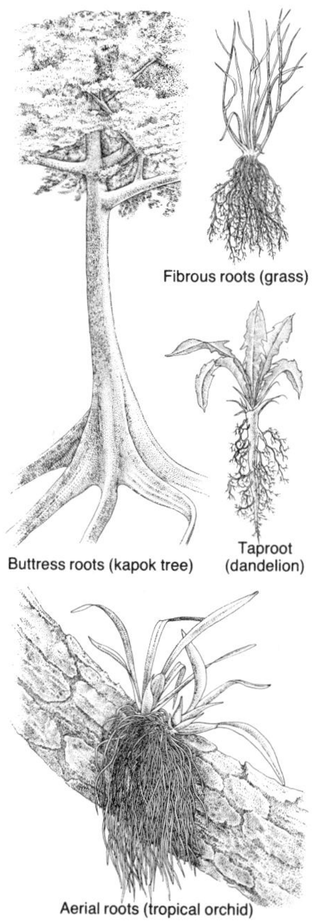
Fibrous roots (grass)
Buttress roots (kapok tree)
Taproot
(dandelion)
Aerial roots (tropical orchid)

root *Aboveground roots include buttress roots, which help to support tree trunks, and aerial roots, which absorb moisture from the air. The two major types of underground roots are fibrous roots—masses of slender tendrils of roughly equal size—and taproots—large central roots through which the plant draws the bulk of its water supply.*

having scarlet, black-spotted, poisonous seeds that are used as beads. Also called "Indian licorice," "jequirity bean."

Ros·com·mon (rŏs-kŏm′ən). County of Connacht province, north-central Republic of Ireland. Bounded by the Shannon River in the east, it is largely boggy and has several lakes. Its county town is also called Roscommon.

rose¹ (rōz) *n.* **1.** Any of numerous shrubs or vines of the genus *Rosa,* usually having prickly stems, compound leaves, and variously colored, often fragrant flowers. **2.** The flower of any of these plants, occurring in a wide variety of colors, such as pink, red, yellow, and white. **3.** Any of various plants related to or resembling the rose. **4.** A dark pink to purplish pink, to moderate red or purplish red. **5.** *Usually* **roses.** A rosy color of the cheeks. **6.** An ornament resembling a rose in form; a rosette. **7.** A perforated nozzle for spraying water from a hose or watering can. **8. a.** A form of gem cut, marked by a flat base and a faceted, hemispheric upper surface. **b.** A diamond so cut. **9.** A **rose window** (see). **10.** A **compass rose** (see). *~adj.* Rose-colored. [Middle English *rose,* Old English *rose, rōse,* from Latin *rosa.*]

rose². Past tense of **rise.**

Rose (rōz), **Billy** (1899-1966). U.S. showman and song writer. The composer and lyricist of more than 50 hit songs, including "It's Only a Paper Moon" and "Me and My Shadow," he produced many musicals, such as *Crazy Quilt* (1931) and *Carmen Jones* (1943), and owned several popular nightclubs.

ro·sé (rō-zā′) *n.* A pink, light wine, traditionally made from red grapes from which the skins are removed during fermentation. [French "pink," from Old French *rose,* rosy, a rose, from Latin *rosa,* ROSE.]

rose apple *n.* An East Indian tree, *Eugenia jambos,* cultivated in the tropics for its edible fruit and ornamental flowers.

ro·se·ate (rō′zē-ĭt, -āt′) *adj.* **1.** Rose-colored. **2.** Cheerful; optimistic; rosy. [Latin *roseus,* from *rosa,* ROSE.] —**ro·se·ate·ly** *adv.*

Ro·seau (rō-zō′). Capital of Dominica, in the Windward Islands of the West Indies. It is on the southwestern coast of the island.

rose-bay (rōz′bā′) *n.* **1.** Any of several shrubs of the genus *Rhododendron;* especially, *R. maximum,* of northeastern North America, having large, glossy leaves and clusters of white or pink flowers. This species is also called "great laurel." **2.** A shrub, the **oleander** (see). **3.** *Chiefly British.* A plant, the **willow herb** (see).

rose-breast·ed grosbeak (rōz′brĕs′tĭd) *n.* A North American bird, *Pheucticus ludovicianus,* the male of which is black and white with a rose-red patch on the breast.

rose-bud (rōz′bŭd′) *n.* The bud of a rose.

rose-bush (rōz′boÍosh′) *n.* A shrub that bears roses.

rose campion *n.* A widely naturalized European plant, *Lychnis coronaria,* that is covered with white, woolly down and has rose-red flowers. Also called "dusty miller."

rose chafer *n.* A long-legged gray beetle, *Macrodactylus subspinosus,* that causes damage to garden plants, especially roses. Also called "rose beetle."

rose-col·ored (rōz′kŭl′ərd) *adj.* **1.** Having the color rose. **2.** Seeing or seen in an optimistic light. —**rose-colored glasses.** An optimistic viewpoint: *sees life through rose-colored glasses.*

rose geranium *n.* A woody plant, *Pelargonium graveolens,* having rose-pink flowers and fragrant leaves used for flavoring and in perfumery.

rose-hip (rōz′hĭp′) *n.* The fruit of the rose, a **hip** (see).

ro·selle (rō-zĕl′) *n.* A tropical Old World plant, *Hibiscus sabdariffa,* with yellow flowers. Its immature floral bracts are used to make jelly and beverages. [Origin uncertain.]

rose-mar·y (rōz′mâr′ē) *n., pl.* **-ies.** An aromatic evergreen shrub, *Rosmarinus officinalis,* native to southern Europe but widely cultivated, having light-blue flowers and grayish-green leaves that are used in cooking and perfume manufacture. [Middle English, alteration (influenced by ROSE and MARY) of *rosmarine,* from Latin *rōs marīnus,* "sea dew" : *rōs,* dew + *marīnus,* of the sea, from *mare,* sea.]

rose moss *n.* **1.** Any moss of the genus *Rhodobryum;* especially, *R. roseum,* characterized by conspicuous terminal leaf rosettes. **2.** A garden plant, **portulaca** (see).

Ro·sen·berg (rō′zən-bûrg′), **Julius** (1918-53). U.S. government weapons inspector who helped to transmit nuclear secrets to the Russian vice consul in New York. He was executed with his wife, **Ethel** (1915-53). They were the first U.S. civilians to be executed for espionage.

rose of Jericho *n.* A fernlike desert plant, *Anastatica hierochuntica,* that forms a tight ball when dry and unfolds and blooms under moist conditions. Also called "resurrection plant."

rose of Sharon *n.* **1.** A tall shrub, *Hibiscus syriacus,* having large reddish, purple, or white flowers. Also called "althea." **2.** A shrubby plant, *Hypericum calycinum,* native to Eurasia, having evergreen leaves and yellow flowers. Also called "St. Johnswort."

ro·se·o·la (rō-zē′ə-lə, rō′zē-ō′lə) *n.* Any red skin rash, such as that associated with measles. [New Latin, diminutive of Latin *roseus,* rosy, from *rosa,* ROSE.]

rose pink *n.* A light purplish pink to moderate or strong pink. —**rose-pink** *adj.*

rose quartz *n.* A pinkish quartz used as a gemstone.

rose-root (rōz′roÍot′, -roÍot′) *n.* A plant, *Sedum roseum,* of the Northern Hemisphere, having fleshy leaves and greenish-yellow or purple flowers.

Roses, Wars of the *pl.n.* A sporadic dynastic war (1455-85) in England between the supporters of the House of York (white rose) and of the House of Lancaster (red rose) for possession of the English crown.

Ro·set·ta stone (rō-zĕt′ə) *n.* A basalt tablet now in the British Museum, inscribed with a decree of Ptolemy V of 196 B.C. in Greek, Egyptian hieroglyphics, and demotic characters, that was discovered in 1799 near the town of Rosetta (*Arabic* Rashid), Egypt, and provided the key to the decipherment of hieroglyphics.

ro·sette (rō-zĕt′) *n.* **1.** An ornament or badge made of ribbon or silk that is gathered into a shape resembling a rose and is used to decorate clothing or worn in the buttonhole of civilian dress to indicate the possession of certain medals or honors. **2.** Any roselike marking or formation, such as one of the clusters of spots on a leopard's fur. **3.** *Architecture.* A painted, carved, or sculptured ornament in a stylized circular pattern resembling a rose. **4.** *Botany.* A circular cluster of leaves or other plant parts. [French, "small rose," from Old French, from *rose,* rose, from Latin *rosa,* ROSE.]

Rose-wall (rōz′wôl), **Kenneth Ronald** (1934–). Australian tennis player. In an outstanding career, he took most major titles, but as a British professional from 1956 he was barred at Wimbledon until 1968 and never took the Wimbledon singles title.

rose-wa·ter (rōz′wô′tər) *n.* A fragrant preparation made by steeping or distilling rose petals in water, used in cosmetics and in cooking.

rose window *n.* A circular window, usually of stained glass, with radiating tracery in the form of a rose.

rose-wood (rōz′woÍod′) *n.* **1.** Any of various tropical or semitropical trees, chiefly of the genus *Dalbergia,* having hard reddish or dark wood with a strongly marked grain. **2.** The wood of any of these trees, used in cabinetmaking.

Rosh Ha·sha·nah (rōsh hə-shä′nə, rōsh) *n.* The Jewish New Year, a solemn occasion celebrated on the first or first and second of Tishri (usually late September or early October). [Hebrew *rōsh hasshānāh,* beginning of the year : *rōsh,* head + *hash-shānāh,* the year.]

Ro·si·cru·cian (rō′zə-kroÍo′shən, rŏz′ə-) *n.* **1.** A member of a secret religious organization active in the 17th and 18th centuries and claiming to have esoteric and magical knowledge. **2.** A member of a modern international fraternity, the Rosicrucian Order, supposedly descended from the Rosicrucians and devoted to the application of esoteric religious doctrine to modern life. [Medieval Latin *(Frater) Rosae Crucis,* translation of the German name (Friar) Christian *Rosenkreutz,* supposed founder of the society in the 15th century.] —**Ro·si·cru·cian** *adj.* —**Ro·si·cru·cian·ism** *n.*

ros·in (rŏz′ĭn) *n.* A translucent yellowish to dark-brown resin derived from the sap of various pine trees and used to increase sliding friction on the bows of certain stringed instruments and in a wide variety of manufactured products, including varnishes, inks, linoleum, and soldering compounds. Also called "colophony." *~tr.v.* **rosined, -ining, -ins.** To coat or rub with rosin. [Middle English *rosyn, rosine,* variants of RESIN.] —**ros·in·y** *adj.*

rosin oil *n.* A white to brown viscous liquid obtained by fractional distillation of rosin and used in lubricants, electrical insulation, and printing inks. Also called "retinol," "rosinol."

ros·in·weed (rŏz′ĭn-wēd′) *n.* Any of several North American plants of the genus *Silphium* and related genera, having a resinous juice; especially the **compass plant,** the **cup plant,** and the **gum plant** (*all of which see*).

Ros·kil·de (rôs′kĭl-ə). Town of eastern Denmark, on the Roskilde Fjord. It was the Danish capital until 1443, and its cathedral (begun in the 12th century) has many royal tombs.

Ross (rôs), **Betsy Griscom** (1752-1836). U.S. patriot and legendary maker of the first American flag. According to tradition, in June 1776, she was asked by George Washington to make a flag for the country that would declare independence the following month. After a brief discussion, Washington sketched a design and she proceeded to sew America's first starred and striped flag.

Ross, Harold Wallace (1892-1951). U.S. publisher and editor. The first editor of the *New Yorker* magazine, established in 1925, he set the humorous tone and demanded the literary and journalistic excellence that contributed to the publication's success.

Ross, Sir James Clark (1800-62). British polar explorer. He explored the Arctic with his uncle, Sir John Ross, discovering the north magnetic pole in 1831. On a voyage to the Antarctic (1839-43), he discovered the sea later named after him.

Ross, Sir John (1777-1856). British naval officer and explorer. In his second and most successful Arctic expedition (1829-33), he discovered and explored parts of the present-day Northwest Territories and located the magnetic north pole (1831).

Ross, Sir Ronald (1857-1932). English physician and medical researcher. While studying malaria in India, he discovered that the disease was transmitted by the *Anopheles* mosquito. For his role in combating malaria he received a Nobel Prize in 1902.

Ross and Crom·ar·ty (krŏm′ər-tē). Former county of northern Scotland. It included Lewis in the Outer Hebrides, which became part of the Western Isles (1975), and a part of the mainland that was absorbed into the Highland Region (1975).

Ros·sel·li·ni (rŏs′ə-lē′nē), **Roberto** (1906-77). Italian film director. With De Sica he pioneered the neorealist school of cinema, characterized by informal camera techniques and concern with the underprivileged. His films include *Rome, Open City* (1945), describing conditions in Rome under the German occupation.

Ros·set·ti (rō-zĕt′ē), **Christina Georgina** (1830-94). British poet, the sister of Dante Gabriel Rossetti. Her first publication, *Goblin*

Market and Other Poems, appeared in 1862, and a posthumous volume, *New Poems,* was published in 1896.

Rossetti, Dante Gabriel (1828–82). British painter and poet. He was a leading member of the Pre-Raphaelite Brotherhood that he helped found (1848) with Millais and Holman Hunt. His paintings include many portraits of Elizabeth Siddal, whom he married in 1860 and who died two years later of an overdose of laudanum. He buried the manuscripts of many early poems in his wife's coffin, but later disinterred them and published them as *Poems* (1870).

Ross Ice Shelf. A mass of floating ice, the largest in the world, at the head of the Ross Sea on the Pacific coastline of Antarctica. Its estimated size ranges from 496,000 to 540,000 square kilometers (192,000 to 208,000 square miles).

Ros·si·ni (rô-sē′nē), **Gioacchino Antonio** (1792–1868). Italian composer. He established his reputation with a series of 36 operas, all written in the space of 19 years. They include *Tancredi* (1813), *The Barber of Seville* (1816), and *William Tell* (1829).

Ross Island. Island in the Ross Sea, Antarctica. It is the site of Mt. Terror and the active volcano Mt. Erebus.

Ross Sea. Area of the South Pacific Ocean lying east of Victoria Land, Antarctica.

Ros·tand (rô-stäN′), **Edmond** (1868–1918). French playwright. He is chiefly remembered for the verse drama *Cyrano de Bergerac* (1897), a chivalric comedy based loosely on the 17th-century French writer and adventurer of that name.

ros·tel·late (rŏs′tə-lāt′, -lĭt) *adj.* Having a rostellum. [New Latin *rostellatus,* from ROSTELLUM.]

ros·tel·lum (rŏs-tĕl′əm) *n., pl.* **-tella** (-tĕl′ə). *Biology.* A small, beaklike part, such as a projection on the stigma of an orchid, a tubular mouth part on some insects, or the hooked projection on the head of a tapeworm. [New Latin, from Latin, diminutive of *rostrum,* beak, ROSTRUM.] **—ros·tel·lar** *adj.*

ros·ter (rŏs′tər) *n.* A plan or list showing the order in which each member of an organization, military unit, or other group becomes liable for a particular duty.
~*tr.v.* **rostered, -tering, -ters.** To place on a roster. [Dutch *rooster,* gridiron, list (on a ruled sheet), from Middle Dutch, gridiron, from *roosten,* to roast, from *roost,* gridiron, from Germanic *raust* (unattested). See **roast.**]

Ros·tock (rŏs′tŏk). Industrial port of East Germany, on the Baltic Sea. It was an important member of the Hanseatic League (14th century) and has many medieval remains.

Ros·tov (rŏs′tŏv). Also **Ros·tov-on-Don** (-ŏn-dŏn′). Industrial port in southeastern European U.S.S.R. It is on the Don River near the Sea of Azov and is a cultural and scientific center.

Ros·tow (rŏs′tou′), **Walt Whitman** (1916–). U.S. economist. One of America's foremost economists, he served as President Kennedy's special assistant for national security affairs. He wrote several important works, including *The Stages of Economic Growth* (1960), in which he coined Kennedy's campaign slogan "the New Frontier."

Ros·tro·po·vich (rŏs′trə-pō′vĭch), **Mstislav Leopoldovich** (1927–). Russian cellist, noted for his outstanding range of tone. He traveled widely in the West after 1947 and had works written for him by Prokofiev, Shostakovich, and Britten. In 1975 he left the U.S.S.R.

ros·trum (rŏs′trəm) *n., pl.* **-trums** or **-tra** (-trə) (the only form for sense 2). **1.** A dais, platform, or similar raised place used, for example, by public speakers or conductors. **2.** *Often* **rostra.** In ancient Rome, the speakers' platform in the Forum, which was decorated with the prows of captured enemy ships. **3.** *Biology.* A beaklike or snoutlike projection. [Latin, beak, ship's prow.] **—ros·tral** (rŏs′trəl) *adj.* **—ros·trate** (rŏs′trāt′) *adj.*

ros·y (rō′zē) *adj.* **-ier, -iest. 1.** Having the characteristic pink or red color of a rose. **2.** Flushed with a healthy glow. **3.** Optimistic or giving cause for optimism. **—ros·i·ly** *adv.* **—ros·i·ness** *n.*

rosy pastor *n.* A bird, the **pastor** *(see).*

rot[1] (rŏt) *v.* **rotted, rotting, rots.** —*intr.* **1.** To undergo decomposition, especially organic decomposition; decay. **2.** To disappear or fall by decaying. Used with *off* or *away.* **3.** To undergo moral or intellectual decay; become decadent or degenerate. **4.** To waste away, as from neglect or inactivity. —*tr.* To cause to decompose, deteriorate, or decay. —See Synonyms at **decay.**
~*n.* **1.** The process of rotting or the condition of being rotten. **2.** A condition of degeneration or decline: *brought in a new director in an attempt to stop the rot.* **3. Athlete's foot** *(see).* **4.** Any of several plant diseases characterized by the breakdown of tissue and caused by various bacteria, fungi, or other microorganisms. See **dry rot, wet rot. 5.** *Archaic.* Any disease causing the decay of flesh. **6.** *Informal.* Foolish talk; nonsense.
~*interj.* Used to express contempt or impatience, especially in reaction to foolish talk. [Middle English *roten, rotyen,* Old English *rotian,* from Germanic *rutjan* (unattested).]

rot[2]**.** Variant of **ret.**

rot. rotating; rotation.

ro·ta (rō′tə) *n., pl.* **-tas. 1.** *Chiefly British.* A roster, especially one regulating unofficial activities: *a rota for driving the children to school.* **2. Rota.** The supreme court of the Roman Catholic Church, called in full the Sacred Roman Rota and functioning as a court of final appeal, especially in cases regarding the dissolution of marriages. [Latin, wheel.]

Ro·tar·i·an (rō-târ′ē-ən) *n.* A member of a Rotary Club.

ro·ta·ry (rō′tə-rē) *adj.* **1.** Of, pertaining to, causing, or characterized by rotation, especially rotation around an axis. **2.** Operating by means of a rotary part or parts: *a rotary mower.*
~*n., pl.* **rotaries. 1.** A part or device that rotates around an axis. **2.** A **traffic circle** *(see).* [Medieval Latin *rotārius,* from Latin *rota,* wheel.]

Rotary Club *n.* Any club belonging to Rotary International, an organization pledged to give service to the community.

rotary engine *n.* An engine, such as a turbine, in which power is supplied directly to vanes or other rotary parts.

rotary harrow *n.* A harrow, consisting of a series of freely turning wheels rimmed with spikes. Also called "rotary hoe."

rotary plow *n.* A plow having a series of hoes arranged on a revolving power-driven shaft. Also called "rotary tiller."

rotary press *n.* A printing press having a cylinder to which curved plates are attached so that, when revolving, they will print onto a continuous roll of paper.

ro·tate (rō′tāt′) *v.* **-tated, -tating, -tates.** —*intr.* **1.** To turn or spin on an axis. **2.** To proceed in sequence; alternate. —*tr.* **1.** To cause to rotate. **2.** To plant or grow (crops) in a fixed order of succession. **3.** To perform in a fixed order of succession; alternate. —See Synonyms at **turn.**
~*adj. Botany.* Having radiating parts; wheel-shaped. [Latin *rotāre,* to revolve, from *rota,* wheel.] **—ro·tat·a·ble** *adj.*

ro·ta·tion (rō-tā′shən) *n. Abbr.* **rot. 1.** Motion in which the path of every point in the moving object is a circle or circular arc centered on a specific axis, especially on an internal axis: *the axial rotation of the earth.* **2.** A single complete cycle of such motion; a revolution. **3.** *Geometry.* A coordinate transformation consisting of an angular displacement, or successive angular displacements, of coordinate axes with the origin remaining fixed. **4. a.** A regularly recurring sequence: *The chairmanship goes to each member in strict rotation.* **b.** The use or application of a planned sequence, as in the growing of crops. **—ro·ta·tion·al** *adj.*

ro·ta·tive (rō′tə-tĭv) *adj.* **1.** Of, pertaining to, causing, or characterized by rotation. **2.** Characterized by or occurring in alternation or succession. **—ro·ta·tive·ly** *adv.*

ro·ta·tor (rō′tā′tər) *n.* **1.** One that rotates. **2.** Any of several muscles that effect rotation of a part of the body.

ro·ta·to·ry (rō′tə-tôr′ē, -tōr′ē) *adj.* **1.** Of, pertaining to, causing, or characterized by rotation. **2.** Occurring or proceeding in alternation or succession.

ROTC, R.O.T.C. Reserve Officers' Training Corps.

rote[1] (rōt) *n.* **1.** Memorization by means of repetition and with little or no comprehension: *learn by rote.* **2.** Mechanical routine; unthinking repetition. [Middle English *rote*†.]

rote[2] *n.* A medieval stringed instrument. [Middle English, from Old French, from Germanic.]

ro·te·none (rō′tə-nōn′) *n.* A white crystalline compound, $C_{23}H_{22}O_6$, extracted from the roots of derris and cubé and used as an insecticide. [Japanese *rōten,* derris plant + -ONE.]

rot·gut (rŏt′gŭt′) *n. Slang.* Alcoholic drink of a very inferior kind.

Roth·er·mere (rŏth′ər-mîr), **Harold Sydney Harmsworth, 1st Viscount** (1868–1940). British newspaper magnate and politician. The younger brother of Lord Northcliffe, he assisted in the founding and purchase of several papers, and was air minister (1917–18). He acquired the *Daily Mirror* (1914) from his brother and bought the *Daily Mail* (1922) after Northcliffe's death.

Rothe·say (rŏth′sē, -sā). Port and capital of the Isle of Bute, western Scotland. Incorporated into Strathclyde Region (1975), it is a tourist center and fishing town.

Roth·ko (rŏth′kō), **Mark,** born Marcus Rothkovich (1903–70). In the late 1940's and early 1950's he produced a series of large, abstract canvases employing horizontal bands of color with blurred edges. *Number 10* (1950) is characteristic of his style.

Roth·schild (rŏth′chīld′, rŏs′-). A German banking family. The Rothschild bank was founded at Frankfurt by **Meyer Amschel Rothschild** (1743–1812). His eldest son took over the Frankfurt business, and four younger sons set up branches in Vienna, London, Naples, and Paris. All the founding members were created Austrian barons, and the family won international fame by negotiating major loans to European governments.

ro·ti (rō′tē) *n.* A flat, usually circular, piece of unleavened bread, similar to a chapatti. [Hindi, bread.]

ro·ti·fer (rō′tə-fər) *n.* Any of various minute, multicellular aquatic organisms of the phylum Rotifera, having at the anterior end a wheellike ring of cilia used for feeding and locomotion. Also called "wheel animalcule." [New Latin *Rotifera* : Latin *rota,* wheel (see **rotate**) + -FER.] **—ro·tif·er·al** (rō-tĭf′ər-əl), **ro·tif·er·ous** *adj.*

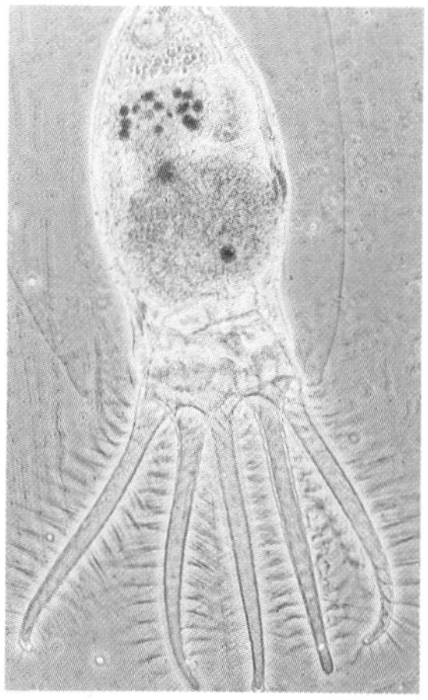

rotifer *These minute and almost transparent freshwater animals are members of the taxonomic class Rotifera—so called because they have a wheellike ring of microscopic tentacles or cilia (seen here from the side) with which they propel themselves through the water and gather food particles.*

ro·tis·se·rie (rō-tĭs′ə-rē) *n.* **1.** A cooking device equipped with a rotating spit on which meat or other food is roasted. **2.** A shop or restaurant specializing in meats roasted in this way. [French *rôtisserie,* from Old French *rostisserie,* from *rostir* (present stem *rostiss-*), to ROAST.]

rot·l (rŏt′l) *n.* Any of various units of weight used in countries bordering on the eastern Mediterranean, varying in amount from about half a kilogram to two and a half kilograms (one to five pounds). [Arabic *raṭl, riṭl,* perhaps altered by metathesis from Greek *litra.* See **litre.**]

ro·to·gra·vure (rō′tə-grə-vyo͝or′, -grā′vyər) *n.* **1.** An intaglio printing process in which letters and pictures are transferred from an etched copper cylinder to a web of paper, plastic, or similar material in a rotary press. **2.** Printed material, such as a newspaper section, produced by this process. [Latin *rota,* wheel + GRAVURE.]

ro·tor (rō'tər) n. **1.** A rotating part of a mechanical device; especially, the moving part of an electric motor or generator. Compare **stator. 2.** An assembly of rotating horizontal airfoils, such as that of a helicopter. **3.** The rotating part of the distributor in an internal-combustion engine. In this sense, also called "rotor arm." [Short for ROTATOR.]

rotor ship n. A ship propelled by one or more tall cylindrical rotors operated by wind power.

ro·to·till (rō'tə-tĭl') tr.v. **-tilled, -tilling, -tills.** To turn over with a rotary plow: *rototill the garden.* [Back-formation from ROTO-TILLER.]

Ro·to·till·er (rō'tə-tĭl'ər) n. A trademark for a rotary cultivator.

rot·ten (rŏt'n) adj. **-tener, -tenest. 1.** In a state of putrefaction or decay; decomposed. **2.** Having a foul odor resulting from or suggestive of decay; putrid. **3.** Made weak or unsound by rot. **4.** Morally corrupt or despicable. **5.** *Informal.* Very bad; wretched, as by being: **a.** Disagreeable; unpleasant: *had a rotten time.* **b.** Unkind: *a rotten thing to do.* **c.** Unwell. **d.** Ashamed: *felt a bit rotten about letting them down.* **e.** Inferior; of a poor standard: *a rotten actor.* [Middle English *roten, rotin,* from Old Norse *rotinn,* from Germanic *ruteno-* (unattested), akin to *rutjan* (unattested), to ROT.] **—rot·ten·ly** adv. **—rot·ten·ness** n.

rotten borough n. In England prior to the Parliamentary reform of 1832, a constituency entitled to send a representative to Parliament despite having hardly any voters. Compare **pocket borough.**

rot·ten·stone (rŏt'n-stōn') n. A friable variety of tripoli, the product of decomposed siliceous limestone, used for polishing.

rot·ter (rŏt'ər) n. *Chiefly British Informal.* An objectionable or despicable person. [ROT + -ER.]

Rot·ter·dam (rŏt'ər-dăm'). Seaport and industrial city of South Holland province, western Netherlands. It lies on the Nieuwe Maas River near its mouth on the North Sea and is a major world port and the heart of the largest conurbation in the Netherlands. The city's inner port is connected to the Hook of Holland, its outer port, by the New Waterway (constructed 1866–90). Adjoining Europoort, built in the 1960's, the port handles mostly petroleum. Rotterdam is also the main seaport for the heavily industrialized Ruhr district of West Germany. The city's industries include shipbuilding, petrochemicals, engineering, paper, and foodstuffs.

Rott·wei·ler (rŏt'wī'lər, rôt'vī'-) n. A dog of an ancient German breed, having a stocky body, a short black coat, and tan face markings. [Originally bred in *Rottweil,* town in southwestern Germany.]

ro·tund (rō-tŭnd') adj. **1.** Rounded; plump. **2.** Sonorous in delivery or grandiloquent in style. —See Synonyms at **fat.** [Latin *rotundus,* round.] **—ro·tund·ly** adv. **—ro·tund·i·ty** (rō-tŭn'də-tē), **ro·tund·ness** n.

ro·tun·da (rō-tŭn'də) n. A circular building, hall, or room, especially one with a dome. [Italian *rotonda,* from Latin *rotunda,* feminine of *rotundus,* round.]

ro·tu·ri·er (rō-tü-ryā') n. A person of low rank; a commoner. [French, from Old French, from *roture,* newly broken land, obligation to a lord for land, hence, a commoner, from Vulgar Latin *ruptūra,* from Latin, a RUPTURE.]

Rou·ault (rōō-ō'), **Georges Henri** (1871–1958). French artist. Apprenticed to a glazier in his youth, he worked on stained-glass windows and retained as an artist a fondness for flat areas of luminous color enclosed by strong, dark outlines. His works include *The Clown* (1905) and a series of 58 prints, *Miserere* (1916–27).

rou·ble, ru·ble (rōō'bəl) n. *Abbr.* **r., R. 1.** The basic monetary unit of the U.S.S.R., equal to 100 kopeks. **2.** A coin or note worth one rouble. See feature at **currency.** [Russian *rubl',* "silver bar," from Old Russian, "bar," "block," from *rubiti,* to cut up, build, from Balto-Slavic *romb-* (unattested).]

rouche. Variant of **ruche.**

rou·é (rōō-ā') n. A debauched and dissipated man; a profligate. [French, "broken on the wheel," completely tired, from the past participle of *rouer,* to break on the wheel, from Medieval Latin *rotāre,* to turn, from Latin, to ROTATE.]

Rou·en (rōō-äɴ'). Capital of Seine-Maritime department, northern France. On the Seine River, it is a port handling trade for Paris. It is also a cultural and industrial center. Once the capital of Normandy, it was held by England between 1419 and 1449. It has fine Gothic architecture, including a cathedral (12th–15th century).

rouge (rōōzh) n. **1.** A red or pink cosmetic for coloring the cheeks. **2.** A reddish powder, chiefly ferric oxide, used to polish metals or glass.

~v. **rouged, rouging, rouges.** —tr. To put rouge on; color with rouge. —intr. To use rouge as a cosmetic. [French, from Old French, red, from Latin *rubeus.*]

rouge et noir (rōōzh' ä nwär') n. A gambling card game played at a table marked with two red and two black diamond-shaped spots, on which bets are placed. Also called "trente et quarante." [French, "red and black."]

Rou·get de Lisle (rōō-zhā' də lēl'), **Claude Joseph** (1760–1836). French soldier and songwriter. While stationed in Strasbourg during the French Revolution, he composed the music and lyrics for the only song he ever wrote, "La Marseillaise" (1792), first adopted as the French national anthem in 1795.

rough (rŭf) adj. **rougher, roughest. 1.** Having an uneven surface; full of bumps, ridges, or other irregularities; not smooth. **2.** Rugged, uneven, or uncultivated. Said of land. **3.** Coarse, shaggy, or uneven in texture: *a rough bearskin.* **4.** Characterized by violent motion; turbulent; agitated: *rough waters.* **5.** Severely inclement;

stormy; tempestuous: *rough weather.* **6.** Characterized by rowdy, unruly, or boisterous behavior: *a rough neighborhood.* **7. a.** Marked by lack of care, gentleness, or consideration; harsh or brutal: *rough treatment.* **b.** Lacking amenities or comforts: *a rough hotel.* **8.** Lacking refinement; uncouth; unmannerly. **9. a.** Produced, performed, or dispensed without attention to precision, elaboration, or completeness: *a rough translation; rough justice.* **b.** Tentative or approximate: *a rough idea of the cost.* **c.** Used in doing work of a preliminary kind: *a rough draft.* **d.** *Informal.* Of low quality; substandard. **10.** Harsh to the ear. **11.** Harsh or sharp to the taste: *a rough wine.* **12.** In a natural state: *rough diamonds.* **13.** Requiring physical strength rather than intelligence; unskilled: *rough work.* **14.** *Informal.* Difficult, unpleasant, or unfair. **15.** *Informal.* Unwell: *feeling a bit rough.*

~n. **1.** Uneven or overgrown ground. **2.** The part of a golf course left unmown and uncultivated, as distinguished from the fairway and the greens. **3.** A rough, disagreeable, or difficult aspect or condition: *took the rough with the smooth.* **4.** Something in an unfinished or hastily worked-out state. **5.** A rough, unruly, or violent person; hooligan. **—in the rough.** In a crude or unfinished state.

~tr.v. **roughed, roughing, roughs. 1.** To make rough; roughen. **2.** To subject to rough treatment or physical violence. Used with *up.* **3.** To prepare or indicate in a rough or unfinished form: *rough in the illustrations for a book.* **—rough it.** To get along without the usual comforts: *rough it on a camping trip.*

~adv. In a rough manner; roughly: *slept rough.* [Middle English *ruch, r(o)ugh,* Old English *rūh.*] **—rough·er** n. **—rough·ly** adv. **—rough·ness** n.

Synonyms: jagged, rugged, scabrous, uneven.

rough·age (rŭf'ĭj) n. **1.** Any rough or coarse material. **2.** The relatively coarse, indigestible parts of certain foods and fodder that contain cellulose and stimulate peristalsis; dietary fiber.

rough-and-read·y (rŭf'ən-rĕd'ē) adj. Rough or crude but effective or usable.

rough-and-tum·ble (rŭf'ən-tŭm'bəl) adj. Characterized by roughness and disregard for order or rules.

~n. **1.** A disorderly scuffle. **2.** A rough-and-tumble quality: *enjoyed the rough-and-tumble of a game of football.*

rough breathing n. **1.** An aspirate sound in ancient Greek like that of the letter *h* in English. **2. a.** The mark (ʽ) placed over initial sounds in Greek to indicate a preceding aspirate. **b.** This mark in Modern Greek as an orthographic feature.

rough·cast (rŭf'kăst', -käst') n. **1.** A coarse plaster used for outside wall surfaces. Also called "slapdash." **2.** A rough, preliminary model or form.

~tr.v. **roughcast, -casting, -casts. 1.** To plaster (a wall, for example) with roughcast. **2.** To shape or work into a rough or preliminary form. **—rough·cast·er** n.

rough-dry (rŭf'drī') tr.v. **-dried, -drying, -dries.** To dry (something laundered) without ironing or smoothing out.

~adj. Laundered but not ironed.

rough·en (rŭf'ən) v. **-ened, -ening, -ens.** —tr. To make rough. —intr. To become rough.

rough·hew (rŭf'hyōō') tr.v. **-hewed** or **-hewn** (-hyōōn'), **-hewing, -hews. 1.** To hew or shape (timber or stone, for example) roughly, without finishing. **2.** To make in rough form; roughcast.

rough·house (rŭf'hous') n. Rowdy, uproarious play or behavior.

~v. **roughhoused, -housing, -houses.** —intr. To engage in boisterous or rowdy activity. —tr. To handle or treat roughly, usually in fun.

rough-leg·ged hawk (rŭf'lĕg'ĭd) n. A buzzard, *Buteo lagopus,* having dark plumage and whitish feathers covering the legs.

rough·neck (rŭf'nĕk') n. **1.** A rough, pugnacious man. **2.** A worker on an oil rig.

rough·rid·er (rŭf'rī'dər) n. **1.** A skilled rider of little-trained horses, especially one who breaks horses for riding. **2. Roughrider.** A member of the 1st U.S. Volunteer Cavalry regiment under Theodore Roosevelt in the Spanish-American War.

rough·shod (rŭf'shŏd') adj. Shod with horseshoes having projecting nails or points to prevent slipping.

roul. *Philately.* roulette.

rou·lade (rōō-läd') n. **1.** A musical embellishment consisting of a rapid run of several notes sung to one syllable. **2.** A slice of meat rolled around a filling and cooked. [French, "a rolling," from *rouler,* to roll, from Old French *roller,* to ROLL.]

rou·leau (rōō-lō') n., pl. **-leaux** (-lōz') or **-leaus. 1.** A small roll, especially of coins wrapped in paper. **2.** A roll or fold of ribbon used for piping. [French, from Old French *rolel,* diminutive of *rol(l)e,* a roll, from Latin *rotulus,* small wheel. See **roll.**]

rou·lette (rōō-lĕt') n. **1.** A gambling game played with a shallow bowl enclosing a rotating disk that has numbered slots alternately colored red and black, the players betting on which slot, or which color, a small ball will come to rest in. **2.** A small, toothed disk of tempered steel attached to a handle and used to make rows of dots, slits, or perforations, as in engraving or on a sheet of postage stamps. **3.** *Abbr.* **roul.** *Philately.* Any of the short consecutive incisions made between individual stamps in a sheet for easy separation. Compare **perforation. 4.** *Geometry.* A curve, such as a cycloid or epicycloid, that is generated by the motion of a point on one curve as it rolls along another.

~tr.v. **rouletted, -letting, -lettes.** To mark or divide with a roulette. [French, from Old French, from *rouelle,* from Late Latin *rotella,* diminutive of Latin *rota,* a wheel.]

rotunda *The domed cylinder of the Radcliffe Camera, a rotunda in Oxford, England. The building was designed by the 18th-century architect James Gibbs.*

Roumania. See **Romania.**
Roumelia. See **Rumelia.**
round¹ (round) *adj. Abbr.* **rd.** **1.** Spherical; globular; ball-shaped. **2.** Circular or circular in cross-section. **3. a.** Having a curved edge or surface; not flat or angular: *a round arch.* **b.** Full; plump: *round cheeks.* **4.** Formed or articulated with the lips assuming an oval shape: *a round vowel.* **5.** Whole or complete; full; entire: *a round dozen.* **6. a.** Expressed or designated as a whole number or integer; not fractional; integral. **b.** Adjusted so as to express an exact number in an approximate, more convenient form: *That's a thousand dollars in round figures.* **c.** Approximate; rough; not exact: *a round estimate.* **7.** Large; ample; considerable: *a round sum.* **8. a.** Fully characterized or drawn; substantial; developed: *The novel lacks round characters.* **b.** Brought to a satisfying perfection; finished: *a round, polished writing style.* **9. a.** Sonorous; full in tone. **b.** Full-bodied; satisfying: *a round taste.* **10.** Brisk; rapid; smart: *a round pace.* **11.** Outspoken; candid; blunt. **12.** Made with full force; unrestrained: *a round thrashing.*
—*n.* **1.** The state of being round. **2.** Something round, as a circle, disk, globe, or ring; a curved or rounded form or part. **3.** A rung or crossbar, as on a ladder or chair. **4.** The part of the thigh on a beef animal between the rump and shank, considered as a piece of meat. **5.** A distinct set, group, or session: *a round of negotiations.* **6.** Movement around a circle or about an axis. **7.** A round dance. **8.** A complete course, succession, or series, often ending at the starting point: *a round of parties.* **9.** *Often* **rounds. a.** A course of customary or prescribed actions, duties, or places: *the daily round; a sentry's rounds.* **b.** A set of calls or visits for a particular purpose: *a doctor's rounds; delivery rounds.* **10.** A complete range or extent. **11. a.** Drinks for a group of people, bought at one time: *I'll buy a round.* **b.** One's turn to buy these drinks: *It's my round.* **12.** A single outburst of applause or cheering. **13. a.** A single shot or volley from a gun or guns. **b.** Ammunition for a single shot. **14.** A rounded slice of bread. **15.** *Archery.* A specified number of arrows shot from a specified distance to a target. **16. a.** An interval of play in various games and sports that occupies a specific time, comprises a certain number of plays, or allows each player a turn. **b.** A playing of all the holes in golf. **17.** *Music.* A short, rhythmical canon in which each part enters in unison at equal time intervals. —**go** (or **make**) **the rounds.** To be widely circulated. —**in the round.** **1.** With the stage in the center of the audience: *theater in the round.* **2.** Not attached to a background; freestanding. Said of sculpture.
—*v.* **rounded, rounding, rounds.** —*tr.* **1.** To make round. **2.** To pronounce with rounded lips; labialize. **3.** To lessen in angularity; fill out; make plump. **4.** To bring to completion or perfection; finish. **5.** To make a complete circuit of; go or pass around. **6.** To make a turn about or to the other side of: *rounded a bend in the road.* **7.** To encompass; surround. **8.** To move or cause to proceed in a circular course. **9.** To bring (a number) to the nearest whole or round number. Used with *up* or *down.* —*intr.* **1.** To become round. **2.** To take a circular course; complete or partially complete a circuit. **3.** To turn about, as on an axis; reverse. **4.** To become curved, filled out, or plump. Often used with *out.* —**round off. 1.** To express (a number) approximately or only to a specified number of decimals. **2.** To bring or come to completion or perfection: *round off the meal with dessert.* —**round on.** To attack suddenly; turn on angrily. —**round up. 1.** To seek out and bring together; gather. **2.** To herd (cattle) together from various places.
—*adv.* Around.
—*prep.* **1.** Around. **2.** From the beginning to the end of; throughout: *a plant that grows round the year.* —See Usage note at **about.** [Middle English, from Old French *ronde,* from Latin *rotundus.*] —**round·ness** *n.*
round² *tr.v.* **rounded, rounding, rounds.** *Archaic.* To say in a whisper. [Middle English *r(o)unen,* Old English *rūnian.*]
round·a·bout (round′ə-bout′) *adj.* Indirect; oblique; circuitous: *in a roundabout way.*
—*n. Chiefly British.* **1.** A merry-go-round. **2.** A traffic circle.
round angle *n.* An angle of 360°.
round clam *n.* The quahog *(see).*
round dance *n.* **1.** A folk dance performed with the dancers arranged in a circle. **2.** A ballroom dance performed with circular movements around the room. Also called "round."
round·ed (roun′dĭd) *adj.* **1.** Made round; shaped in a circle or sphere. **2.** Pronounced with the lips shaped ovally; labialized. **3.** Complete; balanced.
roun·del (roun′dəl) *n.* **1.** A curved form; especially: **a.** A semicircular panel, window, or recess. **b.** *Heraldry.* A circular design or symbol. **2.** In poetry: **a.** A **rondel** *(see).* **b.** A **rondeau** *(see).* **c.** An English variation of the rondeau, consisting of three triplets with a refrain after the first and third. [Middle English, from Old French *rondel,* "small circle," RONDEL.]
roun·de·lay (roun′də-lā′) *n.* **1.** A poem or song with a regularly recurring refrain. **2.** A dance in a circle; a round dance. [Old French *rondelet,* diminutive of *rondel,* RONDEL.]
round·er (roun′dər) *n.* **1.** One that rounds; specifically, a tool for rounding corners and edges. **2.** One who makes rounds, such as a watchman. **3.** A complete circuit, made without stopping, of all the bases in rounders. **4.** *Informal.* A dissolute or dishonest person.
round·ers (roun′dərz) *n. Used with a singular verb. Chiefly British.* A ball game played with a rounded bat or stick between two teams, usually of nine players, in which members of the batting side successively attempt to hit the ball and run around all the bases with-

out stopping before the ball is retrieved, thus scoring rounders.
round game *n.* Any game in which players play individually, as opposed to in teams or with partners.
round hand *n.* A style of handwriting in which the letters are rounded and full, rather than angular.
Round·head (round′hĕd′) *n.* A member or supporter of the Parliamentary or Puritan party during the English Civil War (1642-49). Used as a term of derision by the Royalists in reference to the Puritans' close-cropped hair. Compare **Cavalier.**
round·house (round′hous′) *n.* **1.** A circular building for housing and repairing locomotives, having radial tracks converging on a large turntable. **2.** A cabin on the after part of the quarter-deck of a ship. **3.** *Slang.* A punch or swing delivered with a sweeping side-arm movement.
round·ish (roun′dĭsh) *adj.* Rather round. —**round·ish·ness** *n.*
round·let (round′lĭt) *n.* A little circle or a small circular object. [Middle English *roundelet,* from Old French *rondelet,* diminutive of *rondel,* small circle, RONDEL.]
round·ly (round′lē) *adv.* **1.** In the form of a circle or sphere. **2.** In a forceful manner; bluntly; candidly. **3.** Fully; thoroughly.
round robin *n.* **1.** A petition or protest on which the signatures are arranged in the form of a circle in order to conceal the order of signing. **2.** A letter sent among members of a group, often with comments added by each person in turn. **3.** A tournament in which each contestant is matched against every other contestant. **4.** An extended sequence.
round-shoul·dered (round′shōl′dərd) *adj.* Having the shoulders bent forward and drooping and the upper back rounded.
rounds·man (roundz′mən) *n., pl.* **-men** (-mĭn). **1.** A police officer in charge of several patrolmen. **2.** *British.* One who makes rounds, such as a deliveryman.
Round Table *n.* **1.** The table of King Arthur, made circular in order to avoid disputes about precedence among his knights. **2.** King Arthur and his knights as a group. **3. round table.** A conference or discussion with several participants all on an equal footing.
round-the-clock (round′thə-klŏk′) *adj.* Also **a·round-the-clock** (ə-round′-). Throughout the entire day and night; continuous. —**round the clock** *adv.*
round trip *n.* A trip from one place to another and back again, usually over the same route.
round·up (round′ŭp′) *n.* **1. a.** The herding together of cattle for inspection, branding, or shipping. **b.** The cattle that are herded together. **c.** The cowboys and horses employed in such herding. **2.** Any similar gathering up, as of persons under suspicion by the police. **3.** A summing up; summation; résumé.
round·worm (round′wûrm′) *n.* A nematode *(see).*
roup (ro͞op) *n.* An infectious disease of poultry and pigeons characterized by inflammation and discharge from the mouth and eyes. [16th century : origin obscure.]
rouse (rouz) *v.* **roused, rousing, rouses.** —*tr.* **1.** To cause to come out of a state of slumber, calmness, complacency, apathy, or depression. **2. a.** To excite, as to anger or action; spur. **b.** To provoke (an emotion): *roused her fury.* **3.** To startle (game) from a covert or lair. —*intr.* **1.** To awaken, as from sleep, repose, or unconsciousness. **2.** To stir; become active. **3.** To rise or start from cover, as game birds do. —See Synonyms at **provoke.** [Originally "to startle (game) from cover," Middle English *rowsen†,* to shake feathers or body.] —**rous·er** *n.*
rouse·a·bout (rous′ə-bout′) *n. Australian & New Zealand.* A person who works on a sheep station, especially during the shearing season; a farmhand. Also called "roustabout." [Variant of ROUST-ABOUT.]
rous·ing (rou′zĭng) *adj.* **1.** Inducing excitement or enthusiasm; stirring: *a rousing sermon.* **2.** Active; lively; vigorous: *a rousing march tune.* —**rous·ing·ly** *adv.*
Rous sarcoma (rous) *n.* A malignant tumor that can be produced on chickens by inoculation with the specific viral causative agent *(Rous sarcoma virus).* [After Francis Peyton *Rous* (1879-1970), U.S. pathologist.]
Rous·seau (ro͞o-sō′), **Henri,** also known as "Le Douanier" (1844-1910). French primitive painter. A collector of tolls, he retired at 41 to take up painting full time. His early work was mocked for its naive style and apparently inept draughtsmanship. However, a few artists, including Picasso, were impressed by his work. His paintings include the apocalyptic *War* (1894), jungle scenes such as *The Snake Charmer* (1907), and group portraits such as *The Cart of Père Juniet* (1908).
Rousseau, Jean Jacques (1712-78). French philosopher, born in Geneva. Rousseau held that mankind is essentially good but corrupted by society, and his novel *The New Héloïse* (1761) proposed spiritual refreshment through a return to nature. In his major political work, *On the Social Contract* (1762), he argued that individuals surrendered their natural rights to society and that these should find expression through the general will.
Rous·sil·lon (ro͞o-sē-yôn′). A small region and former province of southern France, bordering on Spain along the Pyrenees and on the Mediterranean. Wine, fruit, and olives are the chief products of this fertile and densely populated region, which also has a tourist industry. The region was settled by the Romans (*c.* 121 B.C.) and later passed to the Visigoths, the Arabs, the Carolingians, the Spaniards, and the French (1642).
roust (roust) *tr.v.* **rousted, rousting, rousts.** To force or drive out, especially out of bed. [Alteration of ROUSE.]

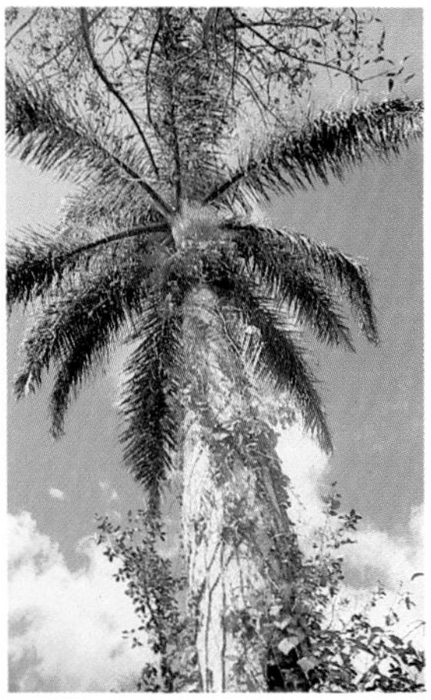

royal palm *One of about 2,600 species of palm, the royal palm is native to tropical and subtropical America. It grows to a height of about 30 meters (100 feet).*

PRONUNCIATION KEY

ă, pat; ā, pay; âr, care;
ä, father, are; b, **bib**;
ch, **church**; d, **deed**; ĕ, pet;
ē, be; f, **fife**; g, **gag**; h, **hat**;
hw, **which**; ĭ, pit; ī, pie;
îr, pier; j, **judge**; k, **kick**;
l, lid, needle; m, **mum**;
n, no, sudden; ng, **thing**;
ŏ, pot; ō, toe; ô, paw, for;
oi, noise; ou, **out**; o͝o, **book**;
o͞o, boot; p, **pop**; r, roar;
s, sauce; sh, **ship**, **dish**;
t, tight; th, **thin**, **path**;
th, this, bathe; ŭ, cut; ûr, **fur**;
v, valve; w, with; y, yes;
z, zebra, size; zh, vision;
ə, about, item, edible, gallop, circus, peaceful

IN FOREIGN WORDS:

à, *Fr.* ami; œ, *Fr.* feu, *Ger.* schön; ü, *Fr.* tu, *Ger.* über; KH, *Ger.* ich, *Scot.* loch; N, *Fr.* bon; y', *Fr.* Compiègne

STRESS MARKS:

Primary stress: ′
in·cite′ (ĭn-sīt′)
Secondary stress: ′
in′sight′ (ĭn′sīt′)

roust·a·bout (rous′tə-bout′) *n.* **1.** A deck or wharf laborer, especially on the Mississippi River. **2.** A laborer in a circus. **3.** A laborer employed for temporary or unskilled jobs, as in an oil field. **4.** *Australian & New Zealand.* A **rouseabout** *(see).* [ROUST + ABOUT.]

rout¹ (rout) *n.* **1.** A disorderly retreat or flight following defeat. **2.** An overwhelming defeat. **3.** A disorderly crowd of persons; boisterous mob; rabble. **4.** A public disturbance; a riot. **5.** *Archaic.* A company of people or animals, especially of knights or wolves. **6.** *Archaic.* A large evening party.
~*tr.v.* **routed, routing, routs.** **1.** To put to disorderly flight or retreat. **2.** To defeat overwhelmingly. —See Synonyms at **defeat.** [Middle English *route,* troop, disorderly crowd (influenced by French *deroute,* defeat), from Old French, dispersed group, troop, from Vulgar Latin *rupta* (unattested), from Latin *rumpere* (past participle *ruptus*), to break.]

rout² *v.* **routed, routing, routs.** —*intr.* **1.** To dig for food with the snout; root. **2.** To search; poke around; rummage. —*tr.* **1.** To dig up with the snout. **2.** To expose to view or uncover. **3.** To hollow, scoop, or gouge out. **4.** To fetch, force, or drive out after searching. Often used with *out.* **5.** To cut grooves or shapes in (wood, metal, or the like). Often used with *out.* [Variant of ROOT (to dig up).]

route (ro͞ot, rout) *n. Abbr.* **rte. 1.** A road, course, or way for travel from one place to another. **2.** A regular way taken from one place to another; a customary line of travel. **3.** *Medicine.* The means by which a drug is introduced into the body: *the intravenous route.* —See Synonyms at **way.**
~*tr.v.* **routed, routing, routes. 1.** To send along; forward. **2.** To schedule or dispatch on a particular route: *The travel agency routed them to Paris by way of Luxembourg.* [Middle English, from Old French, from unattested Vulgar Latin *rupta (via),* "broken or beaten (way)." See **rout** (retreat).]

route·march, route march (ro͞ot′märch′) *n.* A long and hard march by soldiers in training. —**route·march** *v.*

rout·er¹ (ro͞o′tər, rou′tər) *n.* One that routes.

rout·er² (rou′tər) *n.* One that routs; specifically, a machine tool for cutting grooves or shapes.

rou·tine (ro͞o-tēn′) *n.* **1.** A prescribed and detailed course of action to be followed regularly; a standard procedure. **2.** A set of customary and often mechanically performed procedures or activities. **3. a.** A particular sequence of dance steps. **b.** A set piece of entertainment, especially in a nightclub or theater. **4.** A particular kind of behavior or activity, especially for effect. **5.** A computer program, or part of a program, for performing a particular task. —See Synonyms at **method.**
~*adj.* **1.** In accordance with established procedure. **2.** Habitual; regular. **3.** Lacking in interest or originality. [French, from Old French, from ROUTE (beaten path).] —**rou·tine·ly** *adv.* —**rou·tin·ism** *n.* —**rou·tin·ist** *n.*

rou·tin·ize (ro͞o-tē′nīz′) *tr.v.* **-ized, -izing, -izes. 1.** To establish a routine for. **2.** To reduce to a routine. —**rou·tin·iz·a·tion** *n.*

roux (ro͞o) *n., pl.* **roux** (ro͞oz, ro͞o). A mixture of flour and butter or other fat, heated together and used as a basis for many sauces. [French *(beurre) roux,* browned (butter), from *roux,* reddish brown, from Old French *rous,* from Latin *russus,* red.]

rove¹ (rōv) *v.* **roved, roving, roves.** —*intr.* **1.** To wander about at random, especially over a wide area; roam. **2.** To move or look around without settling: *his gaze roved around the room.* —*tr.* To roam or wander over or through. —See Synonyms at **wander.**
~*n.* An act of roaming; a ramble. [Middle English *roven,* (in archery) to shoot at a random mark (sense influenced by ROVER, a pirate), probably from Scandinavian, akin to Icelandic *rāfa,* to wander, loiter.]

rove² *tr.v.* **roved, roving, roves. 1.** To card (wool). **2.** To stretch and twist (fibers) before spinning; ravel out.
~*n.* A slightly twisted and extended fiber or sliver. [18th century : origin obscure.]

rove³. Alternate past tense and past participle of **reeve.**

rove⁴ *n.* A metal ring or small plate over which the end of a rivet is flattened. [Old Norse *ró.*]

rove beetle *n.* Any of numerous beetles of the family Staphylinidae, often found in decaying matter and having slender bodies and short wing covers. [Perhaps from ROVE (to wander about).]

rov·er¹ (rō′vər) *n.* **1.** One who roves; wanderer; nomad. **2. a.** In croquet, a ball that has gone through all the hoops but has not hit the winning peg. **b.** A player of such a ball. **3.** *Archery.* A mark selected by chance. [Middle English, from *roven,* to shoot at a random mark. See **rove** (to wander about).]

rover² *n.* **1.** A pirate. **2.** A pirate vessel. [Middle English, from Middle Dutch *rōver,* robber, from *rōven,* to rob.]

rov·ing (rō′vĭng) *adj.* **1.** Wandering or having a tendency to wander or roam. **2.** Not limited to a specific area or sphere of activity: *a roving commission; a roving ambassador.*

row¹ (rō) *n.* **1. a.** A horizontal linear arrangement or array. **b.** A line of things or people placed or occurring side by side. **2.** A line of adjacent seats, as in a theater, auditorium, or classroom. **3.** A street flanked by a continuous line of buildings on one or both sides. **4.** *Mathematics.* A horizontal line of quantities in a determinant or matrix.
~*tr.v.* **rowed, rowing, rows.** To place in a row. [Middle English *raw,* Old English *rāw, rǣw.*]

row² *v.* **rowed, rowing, rows.** —*intr.* **1.** To propel a boat with or as if with oars. **2.** To race in rowing boats as a sport. —*tr.* **1.** To propel (a boat) with or as if with oars. **2.** To carry in or on a boat propelled by oars. **3.** To propel or convey in a manner resembling rowing. **4.** To employ (a specified number of oars or oarsmen). **5.** To pull (an oar) as part of a racing crew. **6.** To race against by rowing.
~*n.* **1.** An act of rowing. **2.** A trip or excursion in a row boat. [Middle English *rowen,* Old English *rōwan.*] —**row·er** *n.*

row³ (rou) *n.* **1.** A boisterous disturbance or quarrel; brawl. **2.** Noise; clamor; uproar. **3.** A loud or strong protest; trouble. Used chiefly in the phrases *make a row* or *kick up a row.*
~*intr.v.* **rowed, rowing, rows.** To take part in a row. [18th century (slang) : origin obscure.]

R.O.W. 1. right of way. **2.** Rights of Women.

row·an (rou′ən) *n.* A small, deciduous tree, *Sorbus aucuparia,* native to Europe, having clusters of white flowers and orange-red berries. Also called "mountain ash." [Of Scandinavian origin, akin to Old Norse *reynir.*]

row·boat (rō′bōt′) *n.* A small boat propelled by oars.

row·dy (rou′dē) *n., pl.* **-dies.** A rough, disorderly person.
~*adj.* **rowdier, -diest.** Disorderly; rough. [Probably from ROW (quarrel).] —**row·di·ly** *adv.* —**row·di·ness, row·dy·ism** *n.*

row·el (rou′əl) *n.* **1.** A sharp-toothed wheel inserted into the end of the shank of a spur. **2.** A disk of leather or other material with a central hole that is inserted beneath the skin of a horse in order to drain an abscess, for example.
~*tr.v.* **roweled** or **-elled, -eling** or **-elling, -els.** To spur; urge with a rowel. [Middle English *rowelle,* from Old French *roele,* from Late Latin *rotella,* diminutive of Latin *rota,* a wheel.]

row·en (rou′ən) *n.* A second crop of hay in a season; an aftermath. [Middle English *rewayn,* from Old Northern French, Old French *regaïn* : *re-,* again + *gaïn,* rowen, from *gaaignier,* to till, "to obtain food," "gain."]

row house *n.* One of a series of identical houses situated side by side and joined by common walls.

rowing machine *n.* An exercise apparatus resembling the bottom and sides of a rowing boat with oars and a sliding seat.

Row·land·son (rō′lənd-sən), **Thomas** (1756–1827). British caricaturist. He delighted particularly in satirizing grossness and sensuality in crowded social scenes. His *Tour of Dr. Syntax* (1812–21) was especially popular, and he also illustrated works by Sterne, Smollett, Swift, and Goldsmith.

row·lock (rō′lŏk′) *n. Chiefly British.* An **oarlock** *(see).*

Rowse (rous), **Alfred Leslie** (1903–). British historian and man of letters. He is especially known as a scholar of the Tudor period, which he has described in *The Elizabethan Renaissance.*

Rox·burgh·shire (rŏks′bûr-ə-shîr′, -shər). Former county of southern Scotland. Incorporated into the Borders Region (1975), it is largely hilly sheep pastureland.

roy·al (roi′əl) *adj. Abbr.* **R. 1.** Of or pertaining to a king, queen, or other monarch. **2.** Of the rank of a king or queen. **3.** Of, pertaining to, or designating the family of a monarch. **4.** Issued or performed by a monarch. **5.** Founded, chartered, or authorized by a monarch. **6.** Befitting a king; stately; majestic. **7.** Superior in size or quality. **8.** Magnificent; first-rate: *a royal welcome.*
~*n.* **1.** A sail set on the royal mast. **2.** A paper size, 20 by 25 inches for printing, 19 by 24 inches for writing. **3.** *Informal.* A member of a royal family. **4.** A stag having antlers with at least 12 branches. Also called "royal stag." [Middle English *roial,* from Old French, from Latin *rēgālis,* from *rēx* (stem *rēg-*), king.] —**roy·al·ly** *adv.*

Royal Academy of Arts *n.* An art society founded in 1768 by George III to support and encourage the visual arts in Britain by instruction and the holding of exhibitions. The number of academicians is limited to 40.

Royal Air Force *n. Abbr.* **R.A.F.** The air force of the United Kingdom.

royal blue *n.* Deep to strong blue. —**roy·al-blue** *adj.*

Royal British Legion *n.* An organization providing assistance for former servicemen and servicewomen. Also called "British Legion."

Royal Canadian Mounted Police *n. Abbr.* **R.C.M.P.** The Canadian federal police force. Also called "Mounties."

royal fern *n.* A deep-rooted fern, *Osmunda regalis,* of worldwide distribution, having tall, upright fronds.

royal flush *n.* The highest hand attainable in poker, consisting of the five highest cards of one suit.

Royal Highness *n.* A title of or form of address for a member of a royal family. Used with *His, Her,* or *Your.*

roy·al·ism (roi′əl-ĭz′əm) *n.* Support of or adherence to the principles of rule by a monarch.

roy·al·ist (roi′əl-ĭst) *n.* **1.** A supporter of a monarch or of the principle of monarchy. **2. Royalist. a.** An Englishman loyal to Charles I; a Cavalier. **b.** A Colonial American loyal to British rule; a Tory. —**roy·al·ist, roy·al·is·tic** *adj.*

royal jelly *n.* A nutritious substance secreted in the pharyngeal glands of worker bees, serving as food for the young larvae and as the only food for those that develop into queen bees.

Royal Marines *n.* A corps of troops serving on land, sea, or in the air, administered by the Royal Navy but having ranks corresponding to those of the army.

roy·al·mast (roi′əl-măst′, -məst′) *n.* Also **royal mast.** The small mast immediately above the topgallant mast.

Royal Navy *n. Abbr.* **R.N.** The navy of the United Kingdom.

royal palm *n.* Any of several palm trees of the genus *Roystonea,* mostly from the West Indies; especially, *R. regia,* having a tall, naked trunk surmounted by a large tuft of pinnate leaves.

royal penguin *n.* A crested penguin, *Eudyptes schlegeli,* having white cheeks and throat, found on Macquarie Island, off Tasmania.

royal poinciana *n.* A tropical and semitropical tree, *Delonix regia,* native to Madagascar, having clusters of large scarlet and yellow flowers and long pods. Also called "flamboyant."

royal purple *n.* A moderate or strong violet to deep purple or dark reddish purple. —**roy·al·pur·ple** (roi′əl-pûr′pəl) *adj.*

Royal Society *n. Abbr.* **R.S.** The oldest and most prestigious British scientific society, incorporated by royal charter in 1662 by Charles II.

roy·al·ty (roi′əl-tē) *n., pl.* **-ties. 1. a.** A king, queen, or other person of royal lineage. **b.** Monarchs and their families collectively. **2.** The lineage or rank of a king or queen. **3.** The power, status, or authority of monarchs. **4.** Royal quality or bearing. **5.** A right or prerogative of the crown, as that of receiving a percentage of the proceeds from mines in the royal domain. **6. a.** The granting of a right by a sovereign to a business enterprise or individual to exploit natural resources. **b.** The payment for such a right. **7. a.** A share paid to an author or composer out of the proceeds resulting from the sale or performance of his work. **b.** A share in the proceeds paid to an inventor or proprietor for the right to use his invention or services.

Royce (rois), **Sir (Frederick) Henry** (1863–1933). British car designer and manufacturer. Working in Manchester, he founded the engineering firm of Royce Ltd. (1884), later merging it with the company of Charles Rolls to form Rolls Royce Ltd. (1906). Royce designed the first of the famous Silver Ghost cars in the same year.

Royce, Josiah (1855–1916). U.S. educator and philosopher. While substituting for William James at Harvard (1882), he began a lifelong association with that university. He made significant contributions to the fields of logic, mathematics, religion, and metaphysics. Among his many important works are *The Spirit of Modern Philosophy* (1892) and *The Problem of Christianity* (1913).

roz·zer (rŏz′ər) *n. British Slang.* A policeman. [19th century : origin obscure.]

R.P., RP 1. Received Pronunciation. **2.** Reformed Presbyterian. **3.** Regius Professor.

r.p.m. revolutions per minute.

R.P.O. Railway Post Office.

r.p.s. revolutions per second.

rpt. report.

R.Q. respiratory quotient.

RR railroad.

R.R. 1. railroad. **2.** Right Reverend (title). **3.** rural route.

–rrhagia *suffix. Pathology.* Indicates an abnormal or excessive flow or discharge; for example, **menorrhagia.** [New Latin, from Greek, from *rhēgnunai,* to burst forth.]

–rrhea, -rrhoea *suffix. Pathology.* Indicates a flow or discharge; for example, **seborrhea, amenorrhea.** [Middle English *-ria,* from Late Latin *-rrhoea,* from Greek *-rrhoia,* from *rhoia,* a flowing, flux, from *rhein,* to flow.]

RR Lyrae variable *n. Astronomy.* A type of pulsating variable star characterized by periods that range from several hours to about one day and having absolute magnitudes close to 0.6.

rRNA *n.* **Ribosomal RNA** *(see).*

RRP retailers' recommended price.

R.S. 1. recording secretary. **2.** right side. **3.** Royal Society.

R.S.F.S.R. Russian Soviet Federative Socialist Republic.

RSJ *n.* A rolled-steel joist: a steel beam, usually an H- or I-beam, used in building construction.

R.S.V. Revised Standard Version (of the Bible).

r.s.v.p., R.S.V.P. répondez s'il vous plaît (English *please reply*).

rt. right.

rte. route.

Rt. Hon. Right Honorable (title).

Rt. Rev. Right Reverend (title).

Ru The symbol for the element ruthenium.

rub (rŭb) *v.* **rubbed, rubbing, rubs.** —*tr.* **1.** To apply pressure and friction to (a surface), manually or mechanically. **2.** To clean, polish, or manipulate by applying pressure and friction. **3.** To apply firmly and with friction upon a surface. **4.** To move (an object or objects) against another or each other repeatedly and with friction. **5.** To cause to become worn, chafed, or irritated. **6.** To remove or erase. Used with *out, off,* or *away.* —*intr.* **1.** To exert pressure and friction on something. **2.** To move along in contact with a surface; graze or scrape. **3.** To become worn or chafed from friction. **4.** To be removed by pressure and friction. Used with *off* or *out.* —**rub elbows** (or **shoulders**). To mix or socialize closely. —**rub it in.** To remind someone repeatedly of some mistake, shortcoming, or failure. —**rub off.** To be communicated or transferred; be infectious: *Her enthusiasm rubbed off on me.* —**rub out.** *Slang.* To murder. —**rub the wrong way.** *Informal.* To arouse hostility or irritation in; antagonize.

—*n.* **1.** An act of rubbing. **2.** An unevenness on a surface. **3.** An act or remark wounding to the feelings; a rebuke or sarcasm. **4.** Difficulty: *"Aye, there's the rub"* (Shakespeare). [Middle English *rubben,* perhaps from Middle Low German *rubben†*.]

Rub al Kha·li (rōōb′ äl KHä′lē). Vast desert area in southern Saudi Arabia. [Arabic, "Empty Quarter."]

ru·basse (rōō-băs′, -bäs′) *n.* A dark red variety of quartz containing iron oxide. [French *rubace,* from Old French *rubi, rubis,* RUBY.]

ru·ba·to (rōō-bä′tō) *n., pl.* **-tos.** *Music.* Variation of tempo within a phrase or measure without altering its length.

—*adj.* Characterized by rubato. [Italian, *(tempo) rubato,* "stolen (time)," from the past participle of *rubare,* to rob, from Germanic.]

rub·ber[1] (rŭb′ər) *n.* **1.** A light-cream to dark-amber amorphous, elastic, solid polymer of isoprene, $(C_5H_8)_n$, generally prepared by coagulation and drying of the milky sap, or latex, of various tropical plants, especially the **rubber tree** *(see).* Also called "caoutchouc," "India rubber." **2.** Any of various materials made from natural rubber by curing, vulcanizing, adding pigment, and otherwise modifying for use in a wide variety of manufactured products including electric insulation, elastic bands and belts, tires, and containers. **3.** Any of numerous synthetic elastic materials of varying chemical composition, with properties similar to those of natural rubber. **4.** *Slang.* A condom. **5. a.** One who rubs. **b.** One who gives a massage; a masseur or masseuse. **6.** Something used for rubbing or erasing; specifically, an eraser made of rubber.

—*adj.* Made of or pertaining to rubber.

rubber[2] *n. Abbr.* **r. 1.** In bridge, whist, and other games and sports, a series of games of which two out of three or three out of five must be won to terminate the play. **2.** The game that breaks a tie and ends such a series. [17th century (in bowls) : origin obscure.]

rubber band *n.* An elastic loop of natural or synthetic rubber, used to hold papers or objects together. Also called "elastic," "elastic band."

rub·ber-base paint (rŭb′ər-bās′) *n.* **Latex paint** *(see).*

rubber bullet *n.* A projectile, considered less dangerous than a conventional bullet, that is fired to wound or deter, as in riot control.

rubber cement *n.* A solution of rubber in a volatile solvent, used as an adhesive.

rubber check *n.* A check returned by a bank because of insufficient funds in the account on which it is drawn.

rub·ber·ize (rŭb′ər-īz′) *tr.v.* **-ized, -izing, -izes.** To coat, treat, or impregnate with rubber.

rub·ber·neck (rŭb′ər-nĕk′) *n. Slang.* A gawking tourist or sightseer. —*intr.v.* **rubbernecked, -necking, -necks.** *Slang.* **1.** To look about or survey with unsophisticated wonderment or curiosity. **2.** To sightsee.

rubber plant *n.* **1.** Any of several tropical plants yielding sap that can be coagulated to form crude rubber. **2.** A plant, *Ficus elastica,* that has large, glossy, leathery leaves and is popular as a house plant. It grows as a tall tree in its native India and Malaysia.

rubber stamp *n.* **1.** A piece of rubber affixed to a handle and bearing raised characters, used to make ink impressions of names, dates, and the like. **2.** A person or body that gives perfunctory approval or endorsement of a policy without assessing its merit. **3.** A perfunctory authorization or endorsement.

rub·ber-stamp (rŭb′ər-stămp′) *tr.v.* **-stamped, -stamping, -stamps. 1.** To mark with the imprint of a rubber stamp. **2.** To endorse, vote for, or approve without question or deliberation.

rubber tree *n.* A tree, *Hevea braziliensis,* native to tropical America but widely cultivated throughout the tropics, yielding a milky juice, or latex, that is a major source of commercial rubber.

rub·ber·y (rŭb′ər-ē) *adj.* Of or like rubber; elastic; resilient.

rub·bing (rŭb′ĭng) *n.* A representation of a raised or indented surface made by placing paper over the surface and rubbing the paper gently with a marking agent such as charcoal or chalk.

rub·bish (rŭb′ĭsh) *n.* **1.** Something discarded as refuse; debris; litter. **2.** Worthless material. **3.** Foolish talk or writing; nonsense. [Middle English *robishe, robys, robous,* from Norman French *robbous,* plural of *robel* (unattested), RUBBLE.] —**rub·bish·y** *adj.*

rub·ble (rŭb′əl) *n.* **1.** Fragments of rock or masonry crumbled by natural or manmade forces. **2. a.** Irregular fragments or pieces of rock used in masonry. **b.** The masonry made with such rocks. In this sense, also called "rubblework." [Middle English *robyl,* from Norman French *robel* (unattested), from Old French *robe,* booty; see **robe.**] —**rub·bly** *adj.*

rub down *tr.v.* **1.** To clean and dry (oneself, or a horse, for example) by rubbing vigorously. **2.** To massage.

rub·down (rŭb′doun′) *n.* **1.** An energetic massage of the body. **2.** An act or instance of cleaning or drying by rubbing.

rube (rōōb) *n. Slang.* An unsophisticated country fellow; rustic. [Probably from *Rube,* nickname for *Reuben.*]

ru·be·fa·cient (rōō′bə-fā′shənt) *adj.* Producing redness and warmth of the skin.

—*n.* A substance that irritates the skin, causing redness, and often used as a counterirritant. [Latin *rubefaciēns* (stem *rubefacient-*), present participle of *rubefacere,* to redden : *rubeus,* red, reddish + *facere,* to make.] —**ru·be·fac·tion** (rōō′bə-făk′shən) *n.*

Rube Gold·berg (rōōb gōld′bûrg′) *adj.* Of, pertaining to, or being a contrivance that brings about by complicated means what apparently could be accomplished simply. [After Reuben (*Rube*) L. *Goldberg* (1883–1970), inventor of such contrivances.]

ru·bel·la (rōō-bĕl′ə) *n.* A disease, German measles *(see).* [New Latin, from Latin, feminine of *rubellus,* reddish, from *rubeus,* red, reddish.]

ru·bel·lite (rōō′bə-līt′) *n.* A pink or red variety of tourmaline used as a gemstone. [Latin *rubellus,* reddish (see **rubella**) + -ITE.]

Ru·bens (rōō′bənz), **Peter Paul** (1577–1640). Flemish baroque painter. Appointed court painter (1609) to the Archduke Albert, he set up a studio in Antwerp and, aided by assistants, produced many paintings, often with religious, historical, or allegorical themes. *An Allegory of War and Peace* (1629) is among examples of his grand style, while *The Straw Hat* (1622-25) shows his more tender and intimate portraiture. He was knighted by Charles I of England

rubber tree *Natural rubber is made from the milky juice, or latex, of this tropical tree, which is native to South America. The latex is extracted by tapping the tree, as seen here on a Borneo plantation.*

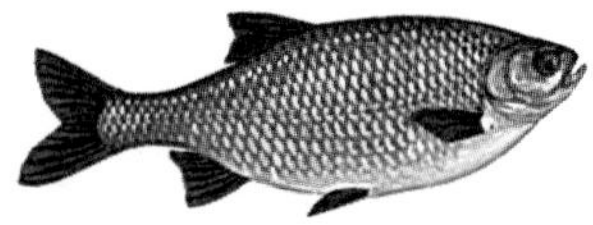

rudd *Found in both still and flowing water, the rudd is a favorite target for anglers in Europe; it is also fished commercially in eastern Europe.*

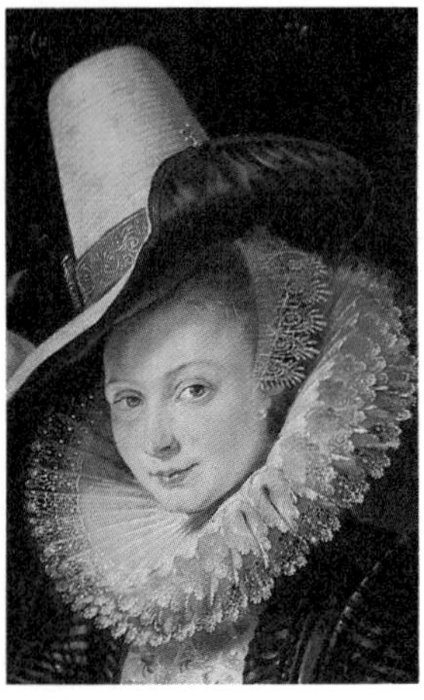

ruff *Isabella Brant wearing a ruff; a detail from a painting by Rubens, who married her in 1609.*

(1629), who commissioned him to paint the ceiling of the Banqueting House in Whitehall. **—Ru·ben·esque** *adj.*

ru·be·o·la (ro͞o′bē-ō′lə, ro͞o-bē′ə-lə) *n.* See **measles** (sense 1). [New Latin, neuter plural diminutive of Latin *rubeus,* red.] **—ru·be·o·lar** *adj.*

ru·bes·cent (ro͞o-bĕs′ənt) *adj.* Reddening. [Latin *rubescēns* (stem *rubescent-*), present participle of *rubescere,* to grow red, inchoative of *rubēre,* to be red.] **—ru·bes·cence** *n.*

Ru·bi·con (ro͞o′bĭ-kŏn). A small river of northern Italy rising just north of San Marino and flowing northeast to the Adriatic Sea. Caesar's crossing of it with his army in 49 B.C. constituted an illegal entry into Italy and thereby initiated civil war. **—cross** (or **pass**) **the Rubicon.** To embark on an undertaking from which one cannot turn back.

ru·bi·cund (ro͞o′bə-kənd) *adj.* Having or showing a healthy rosiness; ruddy. [Latin *rubicundus,* from *rebēre,* to be red.] **—ru·bi·cun·di·ty** (ro͞o′bə-kŭn′də-tē) *n.*

ru·bid·i·um (ro͞o-bĭd′ē-əm) *n. Symbol* **Rb** A soft, silvery-white alkali-metal element that ignites spontaneously in air and reacts violently with water. It is used in photocells and in the manufacture of vacuum tubes. Atomic number 37, atomic weight 85.47, melting point 38.89°C, boiling point 688°C, specific gravity (solid) 1.532, valences 1, 2, 3, 4. [New Latin, from Latin *rubidus,* red (from the red lines in its spectrum).]

ru·bid·i·um-stron·ti·um dating (ro͞o-bĭd′ē-əm-strŏn′chē-əm, -tē-əm) *n.* A method of dating rocks and minerals by measuring the amount of the isotope strontium 87 present as a result of the radioactive decay of rubidium 87. It is used for ages up to 10^9 (a billion) years.

ru·big·i·nous (ro͞o-bĭj′ə-nəs) *adj.* Rust-colored; reddish-brown. [Latin *rūbīginōsus,* from *rūbīgo, rōbīgo,* rust.]

Ru·bik's cube (ro͞o′bĭks) *n.* Also **Rubik cube.** A puzzle consisting of a cube with each face made up of nine smaller colored cubes joined by internal connections so that the faces can be rotated. The test of skill is to rearrange the puzzle so that each face has a different single color, starting from a position in which each face is randomly made up of different colors. [After Ernő *Rubik,* 20th-century Hungarian teacher of architecture.]

Ru·bin·stein (ro͞o′bən-stīn′), **Anton Grigoryevich** (1829–94). Russian composer and pianist. Of German-Jewish extraction, he was, in his time, considered a rival to Liszt. He helped found (1862) the St. Petersburg Conservatoire.

Rubinstein, Artur or **Arthur** (1887–1982). Polish-born U.S. pianist. Performing in public by the time he was 11 years old, he went on to acquire an international reputation for his interpretations of the works of Chopin. He became a U.S. citizen in 1946.

ru·bi·ous (ro͞o′bē-əs) *adj.* Having the color of a ruby; red.

ruble. Variant of **rouble.**

ru·bric (ro͞o′brĭk) *n.* **1.** A part of a manuscript or book, such as a title, heading, or initial letter, that appears in decorative red lettering or is in some other way distinguished from the rest of the text. **2.** A title or heading of a statute or chapter in a code of law, originally written or printed in red. **3.** A name for a class or category; a title. **4.** *Ecclesiastical.* A direction in a missal, hymnal, or other liturgical book. **5.** Any brief, authoritative rule or direction. **6.** A short commentary or explanation covering a broad subject. **7.** *Archaic.* Red ocher. [Middle English *rubrike,* from Old French *rubriche,* from Latin *rubrīca (terra),* "red earth," "red ocher," from *ruber,* red.] **—ru·bri·cal** *adj.*

ru·bri·cate (ro͞o′brə-kāt′) *tr.v.* **-cated, -cating, -cates. 1.** To arrange, write, or print as a rubric. **2.** To provide with rubrics. **3.** To establish rules for. [Late Latin *rubrīcāre,* from *rubrīca,* RUBRIC.] **—ru·bri·ca·tor, ru·bri·ca·tion** *n.*

ru·bri·cian (ro͞o-brĭsh′ən) *n.* A person learned in the rubrics of ecclesiastical ritual.

ru·by (ro͞o′bē) *n., pl.* **-bies. 1.** A deep-red transparent form of corundum, highly valued as a precious stone. **2.** Something made from a ruby, as a watch bearing. **3.** A dark or deep red to deep purplish red.
~*adj.* Of or having the color of rubies. [Middle English, from Old French *rubi,* from Medieval Latin *rubīnus (lapis),* "red stone," from Latin *rubeus,* red.]

ruby silver *n.* A mineral, **pyrargyrite** *(see).*

ruby spinel *n.* A red form of **spinel** *(see)* used as a gemstone.

ru·by-throat·ed hummingbird (ro͞o′bē-thrōt′ĭd) *n.* A small bird, *Archilochus colubris,* of eastern North America, having metallic-green upper plumage and, in the male, a brilliant red throat.

ruche, rouche (ro͞osh) *n.* A ruffle, gather, or pleat of lace, muslin, or other fine fabric used for trimming women's garments.
~*tr.v.* **ruched, ruching, ruches.** To decorate with ruches. [French, beehive, frill (pleated like a straw beehive), from Old French *ruche,* bark of a tree, beehive made of barks, from Medieval Latin *rūsca,* from Gaulish *rūska* (unattested), akin to Old Irish *rūsc*†, bark.]

ruch·ing (ro͞o′shĭng) *n.* **1.** Ruches collectively. **2.** Fabric for ruches.

ruck[1] (rŭk) *n.* **1.** A large number mixed together; a jumble. **2.** The multitude of ordinary people. [Middle English *ruke*†, heap, stack.]

ruck[2] *v.* **rucked, rucking, rucks.** —*tr.* **1.** To make a fold in; crease. Often used with *up.* **2.** To disturb or irritate. Often used with *up.* —*intr.* **1.** To become creased. **2.** To become irritated.
~*n.* A crease or pucker, as in cloth. [Ultimately from Old Norse *hrukka,* wrinkle, crease.]

ruck·sack (rŭk′săk′, ro͝ok′-) *n.* A bag with straps fitting around the shoulders, worn on the back and often supported by a light frame, used by hikers or travelers for carrying equipment, supplies, or the like. [German *Rucksack* : *Rücken,* back, from Old High German *hrukki* + *Sack,* sack, from Old High German *sac,* from Latin *saccus,* SACK.]

ruck·us (rŭk′əs) *n. Informal.* A noisy disturbance; commotion. [Probably RUC(TION) + (RUMP)US.]

ruc·tion (rŭk′shən) *n. Informal.* A riotous disturbance; noisy quarrel. [19th century : origin obscure.]

ru·da·ce·ous rock (ro͞o-dā′shəs) *n.* A sedimentary rock composed of fragments of disintegrated rock material 2 millimeters (0.08 inch) or more in diameter. [New Latin, from Latin *rūdus,* rubble + -ACEOUS.]

rud·beck·i·a (rŭd-bĕk′ē-ə) *n.* Any plant of the genus *Rudbeckia,* native to North America but widely cultivated for their showy, yellow, daisylike flowers. See **black-eyed Susan.** [New Latin, after Olaus *Rudbeck* (1630–1702), Swedish botanist.]

rudd (rŭd) *n.* A European freshwater fish, *Scardinius erythrophthalmus,* having a brownish body and red fins. [Probably from obsolete *rud,* a ruddy color. See **ruddle.**]

rud·der (rŭd′ər) *n.* **1.** A vertically hinged plate mounted at the stern of a vessel for directing its course. **2.** A similar structure at the tail of an aircraft, used for effecting horizontal changes in course. **3.** Anything that controls direction; a guide. [Middle English *rother, rodyr,* Old English *rōther,* steering oar.]

rud·der·post (rŭd′ər-pōst′) *n.* The vertical shaft of a rudder, allowing it to pivot when the tiller or steering gear is operated. Also called "rudderstock."

rud·dle (rŭd′l) *n.* Also **red·dle** (rĕd′l), **rad·dle** (răd′l). Red ocherous iron ore, an earthy variety of hematite, used in dyeing and marking.
~*tr.v.* **ruddled, -dling, -dles.** Also **red·dle, rad·dle.** To dye or mark with red ocher: *ruddle sheep.* [Diminutive of obsolete *rud,* a ruddy color, Middle English *rud(d)e,* Old English *rudu.*]

rud·dle·man (rŭd′l-mən) *n., pl.* **-men** (-mĭn). A man who sells ruddle, or red ocher.

rud·dock (rŭd′ək) *n. British Regional.* The Old World robin. [Middle English *ruddok,* Old English *rudduc* : *rudu* (see **ruddle**) + *-uc,* -OCK.]

rud·dy (rŭd′ē) *adj.* **-dier, -diest. 1.** Having a healthy, reddish color. **2.** Reddish; rosy. **3.** *British Informal.* Used as an intensive. [Middle English *rudie,* Old English *rudig,* from *rudu,* red color.] **—rud·di·ly** *adv.* **—rud·di·ness** *n.*

ruddy duck *n.* A North American duck, *Oxyura jamaicensis,* having stiff, pointed tail feathers and, in the male, brownish-red upper plumage and a black-and-white head.

rude (ro͞od) *adj.* **ruder, rudest. 1.** Ill-mannered; uncivil; discourteous. **2.** Lacking the graces of civilized life; unrefined; uncouth. **3.** Lowly; humble: *a rude thatched hut.* **4.** Primitive; uncivilized. **5.** Formed without skill or precision; makeshift; crude: *made a rude shelter.* **6.** Approximate; rough: *"the height of the cliffs thus affording a rude measure of the age of the streams"* (Charles Darwin). **7.** Vigorous; robust. **8. a.** Harsh; severe: *rude winters.* **b.** Violent and upsetting: *a rude shock.* **9.** Discordant: *"rude harsh-sounding rhymes"* (Shakespeare). [Middle English, from Old French, from Latin *rudis,* rough, raw, akin to *rūdus*†, broken stone.] **—rude·ly** *adv.* **—rude·ness** *n.*

ru·der·al (ro͞o′də-rəl) *adj. Botany.* Growing in rubbish, poor land, or waste places.
~*n. Botany.* A ruderal plant. [New Latin *rūderālis,* from Latin *rūdera,* ruins, rubbish, plural of *rūdus*†, broken stone.]

ru·di·ment (ro͞o′də-mənt) *n.* **1.** *Often* **rudiments.** A fundamental element, principle, or skill, as of a field of learning. **2.** *Often* **rudiments.** Something in an incipient or undeveloped form; beginnings: *the rudiments of social behavior in children.* **3.** *Biology.* An initial group of cells which gives rise to a structure; a vestige. [French, from Latin *rudīmentum,* beginning (formed after *elementum,* ELEMENT), from *rudis,* RUDE.]

ru·di·men·ta·ry (ro͞o′də-mĕn′tər-ē) *adj.* Also **ru·di·men·tal** (-təl). **1.** Of, pertaining to, or involving basic facts or principles that must be learned first; elementary. **2.** In the earliest stages of development; incipient. **3.** *Biology.* Imperfectly or incompletely developed; vestigial: *a rudimentary organ.* **—ru·di·men·ta·ri·ly** *adv.* **—ru·di·men·ta·ri·ness** *n.*

Ru·dolf I (ro͞o′dŏlf′), also known as Rudolph of Hapsburg (1218–91). German king. In 1273 he became the first Hapsburg to be elected Holy Roman Emperor. His conquest of Austria and the surrounding territories formed the power base for his descendants until 1918.

rue[1] (ro͞o) *v.* **rued, ruing, rues.** —*tr.* To feel remorse or sorrow because of; regret; repent. —*intr.* To feel remorse or sorrow; be penitent or regretful.
~*n. Archaic.* Sorrow; regret. [Middle English *ruen,* Old English *hrēowan,* to make penitent, distress.] **—ru·er** *n.*

rue[2] *n.* An aromatic Eurasian plant of the genus *Ruta;* especially, *R. graveolens,* having evergreen leaves that yield an acrid, volatile oil formerly used in medicine. Formerly called "herb-of-grace." [Middle English, from Old French, from Latin *rūta,* from Greek *rhutē.*]

rue·ful (ro͞o′fəl) *adj.* **1.** Inspiring pity or compassion. **2.** Causing, feeling, or expressing sorrow or regret. **3.** Expressive of a faintly sardonic regret; wry. **—rue·ful·ly** *adv.* **—rue·ful·ness** *n.*

ru·fes·cent (ro͞o-fĕs′ənt) *adj. Botany.* Tinged with red. [Latin *rūfēscēns* (stem *rūfēscent-*), present participle of *rūfēscere,* to become reddish, from *rūfus,* reddish.] **—ru·fes·cence** *n.*

ruff[1] (rŭf) *n.* **1.** A stiffly starched, frilled, or pleated circular collar of lace, muslin, or other fine fabric worn by men and women especially in Europe in the 16th and 17th centuries. **2.** A distinctive collarlike projection around the neck, as of feathers on a bird or of fur on a mammal. **3. a.** A Eurasian sandpiper, *Philomachus pugnax,* the male of which has collarlike, erectile feathers around the neck during the breeding season. **b.** The male of this bird. The female is called a "reeve." [Short for RUFFLE (frill).] —**ruffed** *adj.*

ruff² *n.* In card games: **1.** The playing of a trump card when one cannot follow suit. **2.** An old game resembling whist.
—*v.* **ruffed, ruffing, ruffs.** In card games: —*tr.* To trump. —*intr.* To play a trump. [Old French *roffle,* name of a card game, earlier *ronfle,* probably from Italian *ronfa,* perhaps alteration of *trionfa,* "triumph," trump card, from Latin *triumphus,* TRIUMPH.]

ruff³, ruffe (rŭf) *n.* A European freshwater fish, *Acerina cernua,* related to the perches. Also called "pope." [Middle English *ruf, ruffe,* sea bream, perhaps from *ruch, r(o)wgh,* ROUGH (from its rough scales).]

ruffed grouse *n.* A chickenlike North American game bird, *Bonasa umbellus,* having mottled brownish plumage. Also called "partridge."

ruf·fi·an (rŭf′ē-ən, rŭf′yən) *n.* **1.** A tough, violent man. **2.** A thug or gangster. [French *rufien, ruf(f)ian,* from Italian *ruffiano,* pander, "filthy or scabby person," from *roffia, ruffia,* scab, filth, probably from Germanic.] —**ruf·fi·an, ruf·fi·an·ly** *adj.* —**ruf·fi·an·ism** *n.*

ruf·fle¹ (rŭf′əl) *n.* **1.** A strip of frilled or closely pleated fabric used for trimming or decoration. **2.** Something resembling such trimming, as a bird's ruff. **3.** A slight discomposure; an agitation. **4.** An irregularity in smoothness; a slight disturbance. **5.** A low continuous beating of a drum that is not as loud as a roll.
—*v.* **ruffled, -fling, -fles.** —*tr.* **1.** To disturb the smoothness or regularity of; ripple: *Wind ruffled the surface of the water.* **2.** To pleat or gather (fabric) into a ruffle. **3.** To erect (the feathers). Often used with *up.* **4.** To discompose; fluster. **5.** To flip through (the pages of a book). **6.** To beat a ruffle on (a drum). **7.** To shuffle (cards). —*intr.* **1.** To become irregular or rough. **2.** To flutter. **3.** To become flustered. [Middle English *ruffelen†.*]

ruffle² *intr.v.* **-fled, -fling, -fles.** To behave arrogantly or roughly; swagger. [Middle English *ruffelen†.*] —**ruf·fler** *n.*

ru·fous (rōō′fəs) *adj. Zoology.* Reddish brown. [Latin *rūfus,* red, reddish.]

rug (rŭg) *n.* **1.** A piece of heavy fabric used to cover a portion of a floor. **2.** An animal skin used as a floor covering. **3.** *Chiefly British.* A blanket or piece of thick, warm fabric or fur used as a coverlet or wrap. [Probably from Scandinavian; akin to Swedish *rugg,* ruffled hair, and to Old Norse *rogg,* tuft. See **rugged.**]

ru·ga (rōō′gə) *n., pl.* **-gae** (-gē, -gī′). *Biology & Anatomy.* A fold, crease, or wrinkle, as in the lining of the stomach. [Latin *rūga,* fold.]

Rug·by (rŭg′bē). Town of Warwickshire, central England, an important railway junction and manufacturing center.

Rugby football (rŭg′bē) *n.* Also **rugby.** Either of two types of British football in which players on two competing teams may kick, dribble, or run with the ball. Forward passing, substitution of players, and timeouts are not allowed. *Rugby Union* is a strictly amateur game, played between two teams of 15 players. Also called "rugger" in Great Britain. *Rugby League* is both amateur and professional and is played between two teams of 13 players. [After *Rugby School,* in RUGBY, where it originated.]

rug·ged (rŭg′ĭd) *adj.* **1.** Having a rough, irregular surface. **2.** Having strong features marked with furrows or wrinkles. **3.** Austere; stern. **4.** Demanding great effort, ability, or endurance. **5.** Lacking culture or polish. **6.** Vigorous; sturdy; hardy. —See Synonyms at **rough.** [Middle English, shaggy, probably from Scandinavian; akin to Old Norse *rögg,* tuft, from Germanic *rawwō* (unattested).] —**rug·ged·ly** *adv.* —**rug·ged·ness** *n.*

rug·ger (rŭg′ər) *n. British.* Rugby Union. See **Rugby football.**

ru·gose (rōō′gōs) *adj.* Also **ru·gous** (rōō′gəs), **ru·gate** (-gāt′). **1.** Having many wrinkles or creases. **2.** *Botany.* Having a rough and ridged surface, as certain prominently veined leaves do. [Latin *rūgōsus,* creased, from *rūga,* fold.] —**ru·gose·ly** *adv.* —**ru·gos·i·ty** (rōō-gŏs′ə-tē) *n.*

Ruhr (rōōr). A major industrial region of the world, in West Germany. It comprises the valley of the Ruhr River, which rises in Sauerland and flows west to the Rhine at Duisburg, and the Lippe valley to the north. The Ruhr provides most of West Germany's coal and nearly half its electricity supply. Raw materials are imported via Rotterdam and the Rhine, and the region's products include iron, steel, chemicals, and glass.

ru·in (rōō′ĭn) *n.* **1.** Total destruction or disintegration, rendering something formless, useless, or valueless. **2.** The cause of such destruction: *A single flaw is the ruin of a diamond.* **3.** *Often* **ruins.** A condition of total destruction or collapse. **4.** *Often* **ruins.** The remains of something destroyed, disintegrated, or decayed. **5.** A person whose physical or mental capacities have been destroyed. **6. a.** The loss or severe impairment of one's health, position, or honor. **b.** The cause of such loss.
—*v.* **ruined, -ining, -ins.** —*tr.* **1.** To destroy or demolish; reduce to ruin or disintegrate. **2.** To harm, damage, or spoil irreparably. **3.** To reduce to poverty or bankruptcy. **4.** *Archaic.* To deprive of chastity. —*intr. Archaic.* To fall into ruin. [Middle English *ruine,* from Old French, from Latin *ruīna,* "fall," from *ruere,* to fall, crumble.] —**ru·in·a·ble** *adj.* —**ru·in·er** *n.*

Synonyms: damage, demolish, destroy, devastate, raze, wreck.

ru·in·a·tion (rōō′ĭ-nā′shən) *n.* **1. a.** The act of ruining. **b.** The condition of being ruined. **2.** The cause of ruin.

ru·in·ous (rōō′ĭ-nəs) *adj.* **1.** Causing or apt to cause ruin; destructive. **2.** Falling to ruin; dilapidated or decayed. —**ru·in·ous·ly** *adv.* —**ru·in·ous·ness** *n.*

Ruis·dael (rīz′däl′, rīs′-), **Jacob van** (*c.* 1628–82). Dutch artist. Possibly the greatest Dutch landscape painter, he composed baroque, tranquil works that proved profoundly influential on Western European landscape painting. See feature, next page.

rule (rōōl) *n.* **1. a.** Governing power or its possession or use; authority; control: *under the rule of Henry VIII.* **b.** The period of time that such authority lasts: *the nineteen-year rule of Henry VIII.* **2.** An authoritative direction for conduct or procedure, specifically: **a.** Any of the regulations governing procedure in a legislative body. **b.** A principle of conduct observed by the members of a group. **c.** A regulation observed by the players in a game, sport, or contest. **3.** A code of principles for the conduct of religious services or activities. **4.** An established standard or habit of behavior. **5.** Something that generally prevails or obtains. **6.** A standard method or procedure for solving a class of mathematical problems. **7.** *Law.* A court order limited in application to a specific case. **b.** A subordinate regulation governing a particular matter. **8.** A straightedged measuring or drawing device; a ruler. **9.** *Printing.* **a.** A thin, straight line used to make a border or to separate columns. **b.** A dash used as a punctuation mark: *an em rule; an en rule.* **c.** A thin metal strip of various widths and designs, used to print rules. **10.** The discipline and regulations under which a religious order lives: *the Benedictine rule.* —**as a rule.** Usually; normally.
—*v.* **ruled, ruling, rules.** —*tr.* **1.** To exercise control over; govern. **2.** To dominate by powerful influence; hold sway over. **3.** To keep within proper limits; restrain. **4.** To decide or declare as a judgment; decree. **5. a.** To mark with straight parallel lines: *ruled notepaper.* **b.** To mark (a straight line), as with a ruler. —*intr.* **1.** To exercise authority; be in control or command. **2.** To formulate and issue a decree or decision. —**rule out. 1.** To make impossible. **2.** To exclude as a possibility; dismiss. —See Synonyms at **decide.** [Middle English *reule, reule,* from Old French, from Latin *rēgula,* straight stick, ruler, rule, pattern.] —**rul·a·ble** *adj.*

ruled surface (rōōld) *n.* A surface, such as a cone or a cylinder, generated by the motion of a straight line.

rule of thumb *n.* A useful principle with wide application, not intended to be strictly accurate. [From the use of the thumb in measuring.]

rul·er (rōō′lər) *n.* **1.** One that rules or governs; especially, a sovereign. **2.** A straightedged strip, as of wood or metal, for drawing straight lines and measuring lengths.

rul·ing (rōō′lĭng) *adj.* Exercising control or dominion; predominant.
—*n.* **1.** An authoritative or official decision. **2.** A ruled line or ruled lines.

rum¹ (rŭm) *n.* **1.** An alcoholic drink distilled from fermented molasses or sugar cane. **2.** Intoxicating beverages. [17th century : perhaps shortened from *rumbullion†.*]

rum² *adj.* Also **rum·my** (rŭm′ē). *British Informal.* Odd; strange. [16th century (cant) : originally "fine," "lively," perhaps from Romany *rom,* man.]

Rum. See **Byzantine Empire.**

Rumania. See **Romania.**

Rumanian. Variant of **Romanian.**

rum·ba, rhum·ba (rŭm′bə, rōōm′-, rōōm′-) *n.* **1.** A complex syncopated dance that originated among black Cubans. **2.** A modern ballroom adaptation of this dance. **3.** A piece of music composed in the rhythm of this dance. [American Spanish, from *rumbo,* carousel, from Spanish, pomp, perhaps extended use of *rumbo,* bearing, rhumb line, from Middle Dutch *rume.*]

rum baba *n.* A *baba (see).*

rum·ble (rŭm′bəl) *v.* **-bled, -bling, -bles.** —*intr.* **1.** To make a continuous, deep, heavy, reverberating sound, as thunder does. **2.** To move or proceed with such a sound. **3.** *Slang.* To engage in a gang fight. —*tr.* **1.** To utter with a rumbling sound. **2.** To polish or mix (metal parts) in a tumbling box.
—*n.* **1.** A continuous, deep, heavy, rolling sound. **2.** A **tumbling box** *(see).* **3.** A luggage compartment or servant's seat in the rear of a carriage or of an early automobile. **4.** *Slang.* A gang fight. [Middle English *romblen,* probably from Middle Dutch *rommelen* (imitative).] —**rum·bler** *n.* —**rum·bling·ly** *adv.* —**rum·bly** *adj.*

rumble seat *n.* An uncovered passenger seat that opens out from the rear of an automobile.

rum·bus·tious (rŭm-bŭs′chəs) *adj.* Lively and noisy; boisterous. [Probably variant of ROBUSTIOUS.]

Ru·me·li·a or **Rou·me·li·a** (rōō-mē′lē-ə). The possessions of the former Ottoman Empire in the Balkan Peninsula, including Macedonia, Albania, and Thrace.

ru·men (rōō′mĕn) *n., pl.* **-mina** (-mə-nə) or **-mens.** The first division of the stomach of a ruminant animal, in which food is partly digested before being regurgitated for further chewing. [Latin *rūmen†,* throat, gullet.]

Rum·ford (rŭm′fərd), **Benjamin Thompson, Count** (1753–1814). British scientist and diplomat, born in the U.S. colonies. After serving as an administrator in America, Britain, and France, he became a minister of the elector of Bavaria. His observations of the elector's artillery growing hot with sustained firing helped him establish, on his return to England, the motive theory of heat.

ru·mi·nant (rōō′mə-nənt) *n.* Any of various hoofed, even-toed, usu-

Ruisdael

AN EARLY MASTER OF LANDSCAPE

The forces of nature loom over man in the paintings of Ruisdael

The flowering of Dutch baroque art that followed the Netherlands' declaration of independence in 1581 from Spain was dominated by Rembrandt van Rijn (1606-69), but also produced important painters working in a variety of genres—religious subjects, landscapes, still lifes, architectural scenes, and everyday life and people. Of these, Jacob van Ruisdael (*c.* 1628-82) is acknowledged as the greatest landscapist. He was born at Haarlem into an artistic family that included his uncle and teacher, Salomon van Ruysdael (*c.* 1600-70).

In Ruisdael's drawings and most famous paintings, man and his efforts are all but overwhelmed by the majestic yet ominous presence of nature. Beginning with an early preoccupation with trees, Ruisdael's subjects broadened to encompass sylvan scenes, waterfalls, seascapes, beaches and dunes, old castles and ruins, riverscapes, and views of the Dutch countryside and North Sea towns.

NATURE ABOVE ALL *Many Dutch baroque painters delighted in celebrating scenes of bustling, joyful human activity. Ruisdael, by contrast, found his inspiration in the dwarfing of man's efforts—evidenced in his best-known paintings and engravings, including such masterworks as* The Jewish Graveyard, The Cornfield, *and at left,* The Windmill at Wijk—*by the grandeur of land, sky, and horizons receding beyond humanity's reach.*

The German romantic writer Johann Goethe (1749-1832) found in Ruisdael's painting a distinctive poetic vision of man's transient place and modest stature in nature's grander cycle of death and rebirth.

It was only after traveling across the majestic landscapes of Germany, then returning to settle in the teeming cosmopolitan city of Amsterdam, that the young Ruisdael began to explore the theme of nature's preeminence that would bring out the full range of his own artistic powers.

ally horned mammals of the suborder Ruminantia, such as cattle, sheep, goats, deer, and giraffes, characteristically having a stomach divided into four compartments, and chewing a cud consisting of regurgitated, partially digested food.
~*adj.* **1.** Characterized by the chewing of cud. **2.** Of or belonging to the Ruminantia. **3.** Meditative; contemplative. [Latin *rūmināns* (stem *rūminant-*), present participle of *rūmināri,* to chew cud, RUMINATE.]
ru·mi·nate (rōō'mə-nāt') *v.* **-nated, -nating, -nates.** —*intr.* **1.** To chew cud. **2.** To meditate at length; muse. Often used with *on* or *upon.* —*tr.* To meditate or reflect on. [Latin *rūmināri,* from *rūmen,* RUMEN.] —**ru·mi·nat·ing·ly, ru·mi·na·tive·ly** *adv.* —**ru·mi·na·tive** *adj.* —**ru·mi·na·tor** *n.* —**ru·mi·na·tion** (rōō'mə-nā'shən) *n.*
rum·mage (rŭm'ĭj) *v.* **-maged, -maging, -mages.** —*tr.* **1.** To search thoroughly by handling, turning over, or disarranging the contents of. **2.** To discover by searching thoroughly. Used with *up* or *out.* —*intr.* To make a thorough, energetic search.
~*n.* **1.** An act of rummaging; a thorough search among a number of things. **2.** A confusion of miscellaneous articles. [Originally "arrangement of cargo in a ship's hold," odds and ends, from Anglo-French *rumage* (unattested), variant of Old French *arrumage,* from *arrumer,* to put in a ship's hold : *a-,* from Latin *ad-,* to, at + *run,* ship's hold, from Middle Dutch *ruim,* ROOM.] —**rum·mag·er** *n.*
rummage sale *n.* **1.** A sale of unclaimed or excess goods, as at a warehouse or docks. **2.** A sale of secondhand miscellaneous objects, contributed by donors usually to raise money for a charity.
rum·mer (rŭm'ər) *n.* A large drinking glass. [Perhaps from German *Römer,* from Dutch *roemer,* "glass for drinking toasts," from *roemen,* to praise, extol.]
rum·my¹ (rŭm'ē) *n.* A card game, played in many variations, in which the object is to get sets of three or more cards of the same denomination or suit. [20th century : origin obscure.]
rummy² *n., pl.* **-mies.** *Slang.* A drunkard.
rummy³. *British Slang.* Variant of **rum** (odd).
ru·mor (rōō'mər) *n.* Also *Chiefly British* **ru·mour. 1.** Unverified information of uncertain origin usually spread by word of mouth; gossip; hearsay. **2.** An instance of this; a current but unverified report or assertion.
~*tr.v.* **rumored, -moring, -mors.** Also *chiefly British* **ru·mour, -moured, -mouring, -mours.** To spread or tell by rumor. [Middle English *rumo(u)r,* from Old French, from Latin *rūmor.*]

ru·mor·mon·ger (rōō'mər-mŭng'gər, -mŏng'gər) *n.* One who spreads rumors.
rump (rŭmp) *n.* **1.** The fleshy hindquarters of an animal. **2.** A cut of beef or veal from this part. **3.** The human buttocks. **4.** The part of a bird's back nearest the tail. **5.** The part that remains after the removal or departure of a larger, more valuable, or more important part; a worthless, insignificant, or unrepresentative remnant. **6.** A legislature having only a small part of its original membership and so unrepresentative or lacking authority. **7. Rump.** The **Rump Parliament** *(see).* [Middle English *rumpe,* from Scandinavian, akin to Danish *rumpe†,* buttocks.]
rum·ple (rŭm'pəl) *v.* **-pled, -pling, -ples.** —*tr.* To wrinkle, tousle, or form into folds or creases. —*intr.* To become rumpled.
~*n.* An uneven fold; an irregular or untidy crease. [Obsolete *rumple* (noun), from Middle Dutch *rompelen, rumpelen,* from *rompe,* wrinkle.] —**rum·ply** *adj.*
Rump Parliament *n.* The part of the **Long Parliament** *(see)* that remained after Pride's Purge (1648) until dismissed by Cromwell (1653). It was recalled (1659), but again disbanded at the restoration of Charles II (1660). Also called "Rump."
rum·pus (rŭm'pəs) *n.* A noisy clamor. [18th century : probably fanciful coinage.]
rumpus room *n.* A room for play and parties.
rum·run·ner (rŭm'rŭn'ər) *n.* **1.** One who illegally transports liquor across a border. **2.** A boat used for this purpose.
Rum·sey (rŭm'zē), **James** (1743-92). U.S. inventor. At the urging of his business associate George Washington, he demonstrated his unfinished steam-powered boat that was propelled by jets of water forced from the stern (1787). Despite his other inventions, including improved saw and grist mills, he was unable to raise the funds necessary to complete the steamboat project.
run (rŭn) *v.* **ran** (răn), **run, running, runs.** —*intr.* **1. a.** To move on foot at a pace faster than the walk and in such a manner that both feet leave the ground during each stride. **b.** To move at a gait faster than the canter; gallop. Used of a horse. **2.** To retreat rapidly; flee: *turn and run.* **3.** To move freely and without restraint: *children running about in the park.* **4.** To move or roll forward, as if out of control: *The car ran down the hill and into a wall.* **5.** To make a short, quick trip or visit: *run down to the store.* **6. a.** To swim rapidly: *A trout took the fly and ran upstream.* **b.** To shoal or migrate inshore or upstream, especially prior to spawning. **7.** To move or act quickly or hurriedly: *Her eye ran down the list.* **8.** To have fre-

quent recourse: *always running to the doctor.* **9.** To take part in a race. **10.** To compete for elected office; stand: *running for congress.* **11.** To finish a race in a specified position: *He ran second.* **12. a.** To be in operation: *The car's engine is running.* **b.** To be powered in the specified way: *runs on unleaded gasoline.* **13.** To provide regular transport from one place to another; ply: *The ferry runs every hour.* **14.** *Nautical.* To sail or steer before the wind or on a specified course: *run before the storm; run into port.* **15.** To operate or progress in the specified way in relation to a schedule: *Tonight's programs are running an hour late. All the trains ran on time last month.* **16.** To flow in a steady stream, as fluids or loose particles do. **17.** To melt and flow: *Tin must be hot for the solder to run.* **18.** To flow and spread, as dyes in a fabric sometimes do: *The colors ran.* **19.** To be wet; flow with liquid; stream: *The street ran with blood.* **20.** To discharge liquid or reach a specified state by discharging liquid: *left the hot water running. The well has run dry.* **21.** To discharge pus or mucus: *a running sore; a running nose.* **22.** To surge, as waves or the tides do: *A heavy surf was running.* **23.** To extend in space; stretch or reach: *a line running down the middle of the road. The pipes run under the floorboards.* **24.** To spread or climb. Used of a creeping plant. **25.** To spread rapidly: *A rumor ran through the crowd.* **26.** To impress itself persistently on one's consciousness: *a tune running through my head all day.* **27.** To unravel along a line: *Her stocking ran.* **28.** To continue to have legal force; remain valid: *The lease has two years to run.* **29.** To continue to be performed or shown. Used of a play or film. **30.** To pass: *Days ran into weeks.* **31.** To persist or recur: *Gout runs in the family.* **32.** *Law.* To be concurrent: *Fishing rights run with ownership of the land.* **33. a.** To accumulate or accrue. **b.** To become payable: *Your note runs, with interest, to June 1st.* **34.** To be expressed in a given way: *His reasoning ran thus.* **35.** To tend or incline: *His tastes run to the macabre.* **36.** To vary or range in quality, price, size, proportion, or the like: *House prices were running high.* **37.** To come into or out of a specified condition: *We ran into debt.* —*tr.* **1. a.** To traverse on foot at a pace faster than the walk: *run the entire distance.* **b.** To cause (a horse) to move at a gait faster than the canter. **2.** To allow to move without restraint: *He runs his sheep on hill pasture.* **3.** To do or accomplish by or as if by running: *run errands.* **4.** To hunt or pursue: *Wolves ran the sheep in the night.* **5.** To bring to a specified condition by or as if by running: *ran himself into the ground.* **6.** To cause to pass, move, or go lightly or quickly: *ran his fingers over the keyboard; ran a comb through her hair.* **7.** To compel to leave: *They ran him out of town.* **8. a.** To compete in (a race). **b.** To cause to compete in or as if in a race: *She ran two horses in the Derby.* **c.** To cause (a race) to take place. **9.** To present or nominate for elective office: *They ran him for mayor.* **10.** To compete in a given manner against: *She ran them a close second.* **11.** To cause to move or progress freely: *Run up the jib now.* **12.** To cause to function; operate: *He ran his engine.* **13.** To convey or transport: *Run me into town.* **14.** To cause to ply: *They don't run the ferries here in winter.* **15.** To cause (a boat or car, for example) to move on a specified course: *ran our boat into a cove; ran the car into a tree.* **16. a.** To smuggle: *run rifles.* **b.** To evade and pass through (a blockade, for example). **17.** To move swiftly down or through: *run the rapids.* **18. a.** To cause to flow: *run water into a bathtub.* **b.** To fill (a bathtub) with water. **19.** To emit or flow with: *The fountains ran wine.* **20. a.** To melt, fuse, or smelt (metal). **b.** To mold or cast (molten metal): *run gold into ingots.* **21.** To cause to extend in a specified way: *run a road into the hills.* **22.** To mark or trace on a surface: *run a pencil line between two points.* **23.** To sew with a continuous line of stitches: *run a seam.* **24.** To cause to unravel along a line: *ran her stocking.* **25.** To cause to penetrate: *She ran a pin into her thumb.* **26.** To cause to continue being shown or performed: *They ran the film for a month.* **27.** To publish in a periodical: *They're running a special feature on European cookery.* **28.** To cause or allow (an account, for example) to accumulate. **29.** To expose oneself or be subjected to (risk, for example). **30.** To have (a fever) as a symptom. **31.** To score (balls or points) consecutively in billiard games: *run 15 balls.* **32.** To carry out or perform (a test or experiment, for example). **33. a.** To be the manager or proprietor of: *runs a cocktail lounge.* **b.** To be in charge of; conduct, control, or direct: *What a way to run a business!* **34.** To unite or combine: *We ran two companies into one.* **—run across.** To meet or find by chance. **—run after.** **1.** To pursue; chase. **2.** *Informal.* To seek the company or attentions of. **—run away with.** **1. a.** To make off with. **b.** To elope with. **2.** To cause to lose control; get the better of: *His ambition ran away with him.* **3.** To win (an election or competition) by a large margin. **4.** To form (an impression or opinion) too hastily: *Don't run away with the idea that it'll be easy.* **—run for it.** To attempt to escape. **—run into.** **1.** To meet by chance. **2.** To encounter; be faced with: *ran into difficulties.* **3.** To collide with. **4.** To reach as far as; add up to: *The cost could run into millions.* **—run over.** **1.** To knock down or drive over, as in a car. **2.** To overflow. **3.** To examine, review, or rehearse. **4.** To extend beyond.

∼*n.* **1. a.** A pace faster than the walk. **b.** A gait faster than the canter. **2. a.** An act of running. **b.** A running race: *a cross-country run.* **c.** An act of running away; a bolt: *made a run for it.* **3. a.** A distance covered by or as if by running. **b.** The time taken to cover it: *a two minute run from the station.* **4.** A quick trip or visit, especially by car: *a run into town.* **5.** *Cricket.* **a.** A successful act of running from one popping crease to the other by both batsmen. **b.** The point so scored. **6.** *Baseball.* An act of successfully completing a circuit of the bases and returning to home plate. **7.** The distance a golf ball rolls after hitting the ground. **8.** A migration of fish inshore or upstream, especially prior to spawning: *the shad run.* **9.** Unrestricted freedom or use: *I had the run of their library.* **10.** A stretch or period of riding, as in a race or to hounds. **11.** A track or slope along or down which something can travel: *a ski run.* **12. a.** A journey between points on a scheduled or regular route. **b.** The distance so covered. **c.** The time taken to cover this distance. **13. a.** A continuous period of operation, as by a machine or factory. **b.** The production achieved during such a period. **14.** The final approach of a military aircraft to its target: *a bombing run.* **15.** A transit of smuggled goods. **16. a.** A movement or flow, as of fluid or sand. **b.** The duration of such a flow. **c.** The amount of such a flow. **17.** A pipe or channel through which something flows: *a mill run.* **18.** A small, fast-flowing stream or brook. **19.** *Mining.* A fall or slide, as of sand or mud. **20.** A continuous length or extent of something: *a ten-foot run of tubing.* **21.** *Mining.* A vein or seam, as of ore or rock. **22.** The direction, configuration, or lie of something: *the run of the grain in leather.* **23.** A trail or burrow made or frequented by animals: *a rabbit run.* **24. a.** An outdoor enclosure for domestic animals or poultry. **b.** *Australian.* A large stretch of grazing land. **25.** A length of unraveled stitches, as in a stocking. **26.** An unbroken series or sequence: *a run of dry summers.* **27.** An unbroken sequence of theatrical performances. **28.** *Music.* A rapid sequence of notes; a roulade. **29. a.** Urgent and heavy demand for a product. **b.** Urgent and heavy demand by depositors, creditors, or the like: *a run on the bank.* **c.** Pressure on a currency caused by widespread selling. **30. a.** In certain games, a continuous set or sequence, as of playing cards in one suit. **b.** A successful sequence of shots or points. **31.** A sustained state or condition: *a run of good luck.* **32.** A trend or tendency: *the run of events.* **33.** The average type, group, or category; majority: *The broad run of voters want him to win.* **—a run for one's money.** **1.** Strong competition. **2.** A degree of satisfaction or enjoyment derived from an expenditure of money or effort. **—in the long run.** In the final analysis or outcome. **—on the run.** **1. a.** In rapid retreat. **b.** In hiding, as a fugitive might be. **2.** Hurrying busily from place to place. **—the runs.** *Slang.* Diarrhea.

∼*adj.* **1.** In a liquid state; melted. **2.** Poured into a mold while liquid: *run metal.* **3.** Drained; extracted: *run honey.* **4.** Smuggled: *run liquor.* [Run, ran, run; Middle English *runnen, ran, runnen,* Old English *rinnan* (but influenced by the past participle), *ran(n), gerunnen,* reinforced by Old Norse cognate verb *rinna.*]

run·a·bout (rŭn′ə-bout′) *n.* **1. a.** A usually small car used for short journeys. **b.** A light aircraft. **c.** A small motorboat. **2.** A vagabond or wanderer.

run·a·gate (rŭn′ə-gāt′) *n.* *Archaic.* **1.** A renegade or deserter. **2.** A vagabond. [Variant of RENEGADE (influenced by RUN).]

run-a·round (rŭn′ə-round′) *n.* **1.** *Informal.* Deception, evasion, or delaying tactics. Used chiefly in the phrase *give someone the runaround.* **2.** *Printing.* Type set in a column narrower than the body of the text, as on either side of a picture.

run·a·way (rŭn′ə-wā′) *n.* **1.** One that runs away, such as a fugitive or a horse that has bolted. **2.** An act of running away.

∼*adj.* **1.** Escaping or having escaped. **2.** Of or done by running away. **3.** Easily won, as a victory in a race. **4.** Completely out of control: *a runaway train; runaway inflation.*

run·back (rŭn′băk′) *n.* *Football.* **1.** The act of returning a kickoff, punt, or intercepted forward pass. **2.** The distance covered in a runback.

run·ci·ble spoon (rŭn′sə-bəl) *n.* A three-pronged fork, such as a pickle fork, curved like a spoon and having a cutting edge. [*Runcible,* a nonsense word coined by Edward LEAR.]

run·ci·nate (rŭn′sə-nāt′, -nĭt) *adj.* *Botany.* Having saw-toothed divisions directed backward: *runcinate leaves.* [Latin *runcinātus,* past participle of *runcināre,* to plane, from *runcina,* carpenter's plane (formerly taken also to mean a saw), from Greek *rhukanē*†.]

run down *intr.v.* **1.** To lose power and stop working: *The battery has run down.* **2.** To grow gradually weaker; suffer a loss of health or vigor. —*tr.v.* **1. a.** To pursue and capture. **b.** To find by diligent searching; track down: *ran down the source of the trouble.* **2.** To hit with a moving vehicle. **3.** To disparage; denigrate. **4.** To review: *ran down the list once more.* **5.** *Baseball.* To put out a runner after trapping him between two bases.

run-down (rŭn′doun′) *n.* **1.** A summary or résumé. **2.** *Baseball.* A play in which a runner is put out when he is trapped between bases.

∼*adj.* (rŭn-doun′). **1. a.** In poor physical condition; weak or exhausted. **b.** In a poor state of repair; dilapidated. **2.** Unwound and not running.

Rund·stedt (ro͝ont′stĕt′, -shtĕt), **Karl Rudolf Gerd von** (1875–1953). German general. Recognized by both the Allies and Axis powers as one of Nazi Germany's ablest commanders, he participated in the invasions of France (1940) and Russia (1941) and the Battle of the Bulge (1944).

rune (ro͞on) *n.* **1.** Any of the letters of an alphabet used by ancient Germanic peoples, especially by the Scandinavians and Anglo-Saxons. **2.** Any poem, riddle, or the like written in runic characters. **3.** Any character or symbol supposed to have magical powers or significance. **4.** A Finnish poem or canto. [In sense 4, from Finnish *runo.* In other senses, Middle English *roun, rune,* secret writing, rune, from Old Norse *rūn* (unattested).]

rung¹ (rŭng) *n.* **1. a.** A rod or bar forming a step of a ladder. **b.** Anything resembling this. **2.** A crosspiece supporting the legs or back of a chair. **3.** A point or level in a hierarchy or similar series of

PRONUNCIATION KEY

ă, pat; ā, pay; âr, care;
ä, father, are; b, bib;
ch, church; d, deed; ĕ, pet;
ē, be; f, fife; g, gag; h, hat;
hw, which; ĭ, pit; ī, pie;
îr, pier; j, judge; k, kick;
l, lid, needle; m, mum;
n, no, sudden; ng, thing;
ŏ, pot; ō, toe; ô, paw, for;
oi, noise; ou, out; o͝o, book;
o͞o, boot; p, pop; r, roar;
s, sauce; sh, ship, dish;
t, tight; th, thin, path;
th, this, bathe; ŭ, cut; ûr, fur;
v, valve; w, with; y, yes;
z, zebra, size; zh, vision;
ə, about, item, edible,
gallop, circus, peaceful

IN FOREIGN WORDS:

à, *Fr.* ami; œ, *Fr.* feu, *Ger.* schön; ü, *Fr.* tu, *Ger.* über;
KH, *Ger.* ich, *Scot.* loch;
N, *Fr.* bon; y′, *Fr.* Compiègne

STRESS MARKS:

Primary stress: ′
in·cite′ (ĭn-sīt′)
Secondary stress: ′
in′sight′ (ĭn′sīt′)

ascending stages. **4.** *Nautical.* Any of the spokes or handles on a ship's steering wheel. [Middle English *rung, rong,* Old English *hrung,* akin to Old High German *runga,* Gothic *hrugga*†.]
rung². Past tense and past participle of **ring.**
ru·nic (rōō'nĭk) *adj.* **1.** Consisting of, inscribed with, or written in runes. **2.** Made in the ornate interlacing style characteristic of rune-bearing monuments. **3.** Having a cryptic or magical significance.
run in *tr.v.* **1.** To insert or include as something extra. **2.** *Printing.* To make (a body of text) solid without a paragraph or other break. **3.** *Slang.* To take into legal custody. **4.** To run (an engine or car) for a certain period at low speed when new so that engine parts in contact become smooth.
run-in (rŭn'ĭn') *n.* **1.** A quarrel; an argument; a fight. **2.** *Printing.* Matter added to a text.
~*adj.* (rŭn-ĭn'). Added or inserted in text.
run·let (rŭn'lĭt) *n.* A rivulet. [Diminutive of RUN (stream).]
run·nel (rŭn'əl) *n.* **1.** A rivulet; a brook. **2.** A narrow channel or course, as for water. **3.** On a beach, a long narrow hollow between two shingle ridges running parallel to the coastline. [Middle English *rynel,* Old English *rynel,* from *rinnan,* to run, flow.]
run·ner (rŭn'ər) *n.* **1.** One that runs, as: **a.** One that competes in a race. **b.** A messenger or errand boy. **2.** An agent or collector, as for a bank or brokerage house. **3.** One who solicits business for others. **4.** A smuggler or a vessel engaged in smuggling. **5.** An antique dealer who has no retail outlet but acts as a go-between for other dealers. **6.** A device in or on which a mechanism slides or moves, as: **a.** The blade of a skate. **b.** Either of the pieces of wood or metal on which a sled runs. **c.** The supports on which a drawer slides. **7.** A long narrow carpet. **8.** A long narrow tablecloth. **9.** A channel along which molten metal is poured into a mold; a gate. **10. a.** A slender, creeping stem that puts forth roots and shoots either from nodes along its length or at the tip. **b.** A plant, such as the strawberry, having such a stem. **c.** A twining vine.
runner bean *n.* The **scarlet runner** *(see).*
run·ner-up (rŭn'ər-ŭp') *n.* One that takes second place in a race, competition, or election.
run·ning (rŭn'ĭng) *n.* **1.** The act or sport of one that runs. **2. a.** The act or skill of managing something. **b.** The act or process of operating something. Also used adjectivally: *high running costs.* **—in** (or **out of**) **the running.** Still in (or no longer in) serious contention, as in a race or other competitive situation.
~*adj.* **1.** Performed while running: *a running jump.* **2.** Intended for the use of runners: *a running track; running shoes.* **3.** Piped and supplied by taps: *running water.* **4.** Continuous: *a running battle.* **5.** Describing events as they happen: *a running commentary.*
~*adv.* Consecutively: *four years running.*
running board *n.* A narrow footboard extending under and beside the doors of some cars and other vehicles.
running gear *n.* **1.** The working parts of a car, locomotive, or other vehicle. **2.** Running rigging.
running hand *n.* A type of handwriting done rapidly without lifting the pen from the paper.
running head *n. Printing.* A title printed at the top of every page or every other page. Also called "running headline," "running title."
running knot *n.* A **slipknot** *(see).*
running light *n.* **1.** Any of several lights on a boat or ship kept lighted between dusk and dawn. **2.** Any of several similar lights on an aircraft; a navigation light.
running mate *n.* **1.** A horse used as a pacemaker for another horse of the same stable. **2.** The candidate or nominee for the lesser of two closely associated political offices, such as the vice-presidency.
running rigging *n.* The part of a ship's rigging that comprises the ropes with which sails are raised, lowered, or trimmed and booms and gaffs are operated. Also called "running gear."
running stitch *n.* Any of a series of small, even stitches.
run·ny (rŭn'ē) *adj.* **-nier, -niest. 1.** Inclined to run or flow. **2.** Discharging mucus. Said of the nose.
Run·ny·mede (rŭn'ē-mēd'). A meadow on the south bank of the Thames, near Egham, Surrey, where King John signed the Magna Carta in 1215. [Middle English *Runimede,* "meadow on the council island" : Old English *Rūnīeg,* council island : *rūn,* secret, secret council + *īeg, īg,* ISLAND + *mede,* MEAD (meadow).]
run off *intr.v.* **1.** To run away, abscond, or elope. **2.** To flow off or drain away. *—tr.v.* **1.** To cause to flow off or drain away. **2.** To decide (a contest or competition) by a run-off. **3.** To produce (a copy), as with a printing or duplicating machine.
run-off (rŭn'ôf', -ŏf') *n.* **1. a.** The overflow of a fluid from a container. **b.** The amount of precipitation that reaches streams and rivers and flows away to the sea. **2.** Eliminated waste products from manufacturing processes. **3.** A final round or contest to decide the winner in the event of a tie.
run-of-the-mill (rŭn'əv-*th*ə-mĭl') *adj.* Ordinary; not special. —See Synonyms at **average.** [From *run of (the) mill,* products of a mill that are not graded for quality.]
run on *intr.v.* **1.** To continue on and on. **2.** To talk at length and without a break. *—tr.v. Printing.* To continue (a text) without a formal break.
run-on (rŭn'ŏn', -ôn') *n. Printing.* Matter that is appended or added without a formal break.
run out *intr.v.* **1.** To become completely used up. Used of a supply or allocation of something. **2.** To exhaust one's supply of something. Often used with *of.* **3.** To become void, especially through the passage of time or an omission: *The insurance policy had run out.* *—tr.v.* To put out by force; compel to leave: *ran him out of town.*
runt (rŭnt) *n.* **1.** An undersized animal; especially, the smallest animal of a litter. **2.** A person of small stature. [16th century : origin obscure.] **—runt·i·ness** *n.* **—runt·ish, runt·y** *adj.*
run through *tr.v.* **1.** To pierce, as with a sword. **2.** To use up (money, for example) wastefully; fritter away. **3.** To examine, review, or rehearse quickly.
run-through (rŭn'thrōō') *n.* A complete but rapid review or rehearsal of something, such as a theatrical work.
run up *tr.v.* **1.** *Informal.* To make quickly by sewing. **2.** To raise (a flag) on a flagpole. **3.** *Informal.* To allow (a debt, for example) to accumulate.
run-up (rŭn'ŭp') *n.* An often sudden and rapid increase: *a run-up in interest rates.*
run·way (rŭn'wā') *n.* **1.** A strip of level ground, usually paved, on which aircraft take off and land. **2.** A path, channel, or track over which something runs. **3.** A chute down which logs are skidded. **4.** A narrow walkway extending from a stage into an auditorium. **5.** A narrow track in a bowling lane on which balls are returned after they are bowled. **6.** A smooth ramp for wheeled vehicles.
Run·yon (rŭn'yən), **(Alfred) Damon** (1884–1946). U.S. writer. From his experiences as a journalist of New York low life, he wrote many popular stories in collections such as *Guys and Dolls* (1931), later the subject for a hit musical of the same name.
ru·pee (rōō-pē', rōō'pē) *n. Abbr.* **Re., r., R. 1. a.** The basic monetary unit of India, equal to 100 paise. **b.** The basic monetary unit of Nepal, equal to 100 paisa or pice. **c.** The basic monetary unit of Pakistan, equal to 100 paisa. **d.** The basic monetary unit of Sri Lanka, the Seychelles, and Mauritius, equal to 100 cents. **e.** The basic monetary unit of the Maldives, equal to 100 laris. **2.** A coin or note worth one rupee. See feature at **currency.** [Hindi *rupaīyā,* from Sanskrit *rūpya,* wrought silver, from *rūpa*†, shape, image.]
Ru·pert's Land (rōō'pərtz). The Canadian territory granted the Hudson's Bay Company in 1670, most of which was incorporated in the Northwest Territories after its purchase by Canada in 1869.
ru·pi·ah (rōō-pē'ä) *n., pl.* **rupiah** or **-ahs. 1.** The basic monetary unit of Indonesia, equal to 100 sen. **2.** A note worth one rupiah. See feature at **currency.** [Hindi *rupaīyā,* RUPEE.]
rup·ture (rŭp'chər) *n.* **1. a.** The act of breaking open or bursting. **b.** The state of being broken open or burst. **2.** A break in friendly relations between individuals or nations. **3.** *Pathology.* **a.** A **hernia** *(see),* especially of the groin or intestines. **b.** A tear in bodily tissue.
~*v.* **ruptured, -turing, -tures.** *—tr.* **1.** To break open; burst. **2.** To cause a break in (friendly relations). **3.** To cause to suffer a hernia. *—intr.* To undergo or suffer a rupture. —See Synonyms at **break.** [Middle English *ruptur,* from Old French *rupture,* from Latin *ruptūra,* from *rumpere* (past participle *ruptus*), to break.] **—rup·tur·a·ble** *adj.*
ru·ral (rōōr'əl) *adj.* **1.** Of, pertaining to, or characteristic of the country as opposed to the city; rustic. **2.** Of or pertaining to people who live in the country. **3.** Of or pertaining to farming; agricultural. [Middle English, from Old French, from Latin *rūrālis,* from *rūs* (stem *rūr-*), country.] **—ru·ral·ism** *n.* **—ru·ral·ist** *n.* **—ru·ral·i·ty** (rōō-răl'ə-tē) *n.* **—ru·ral·ly** *adv.*
Synonyms: *arcadian, bucolic, pastoral, rustic, sylvan.*
rural dean *n.* In the Church of England, a clergyman who supervises the running of a number of parishes.
rural free delivery *n. Abbr.* **R.F.D., RFD** Free government delivery of mail in rural areas.
Ru·ri·ta·ni·a (rōōr'ə-tā'nē-ə) *n.* An imaginary central European kingdom used as a setting for tales of romance, adventure, and suspense. [After the setting of Anthony Hope's novels *The Prisoner of Zenda* (1894) and *Rupert of Hentzau* (1898).] **—Ru·ri·ta·ni·an** *adj.*
Rus. Russia; Russian.
ruse (rōōz) *n.* An action meant to confuse or mislead; a clever trick. —See Synonyms at **artifice.** [Middle English, detour of a hunted animal, from Old French, from *ruser,* to repulse, detour. See **rush** (to dash off).]
rush¹ (rŭsh) *v.* **rushed, rushing, rushes.** *—intr.* **1.** To move, act, or proceed with great speed and vigor. **2.** To act or proceed with impetuous haste: *rushed into marriage.* **3.** To make a sudden or swift attack or charge. Used with *on* or *upon.* **4.** *Football.* To move the ball by running rather than passing. *—tr.* **1.** To cause to move, act, or proceed with unusual haste or vigor: *Medical supplies were rushed to the scene.* **2.** To pressure into hasty action. **3.** To perform with great haste. **4.** To attack swiftly and suddenly. **5.** To attempt to impress or seek the favor of.
~*n.* **1.** The act of rushing; a sudden forward motion or turbulent movement. **2.** An eager, often competitive movement of people in pursuit of some object: *a rush for the best seats; a gold rush.* **3.** Urgency; need for haste: *There's no rush.* **4.** A sudden attack; an onslaught. **5.** *Football.* An attempt to move the ball by running with it. **6.** A great flurry of activity or press of business: *the usual last-minute rush.* **7.** *Slang.* A sudden, pleasurable rushing sensation induced by taking certain drugs. **8.** *Often* **rushes.** The first, unedited print of a scene in a motion picture.
~*adj.* Requiring or marked by haste or urgency: *a rush job.* [Middle English *russhen,* from Norman French *russher,* variant of Old French *ruser,* to repulse, from Latin *recusāre,* to object to (in Vulgar Latin, "to repel") : *re-,* back + *causārī,* to plead, give as a reason, from *causa,* CAUSE.] **—rush·er** *n.*
rush² *n.* **1.** Any of various grasslike marsh plants of the genus *Jun-*

PRONUNCIATION KEY

ă, pat; ā, pay; âr, care;
ä, father, are; b, bib;
ch, church; d, deed; ĕ, pet;
ē, be; f, fife; g, gag; h, hat;
hw, which; ĭ, pit; ī, pie;
îr, pier; j, judge; k, kick;
l, lid, needle; m, mum;
n, no, sudden; ng, thing;
ŏ, pot; ō, toe; ô, paw, for;
oi, noise; ou, out; ŏŏ, book;
ōō, boot; p, pop; r, roar;
s, sauce; sh, ship, dish;
t, tight; th, thin, path;
th, this, bathe; ŭ, cut; ûr, fur;
v, valve; w, with; y, yes;
z, zebra, size; zh, vision;
ə, about, item, edible,
gallop, circus, peaceful

IN FOREIGN WORDS:

à, *Fr.* ami; œ, *Fr.* feu, *Ger.* schön; ü, *Fr.* tu, *Ger.* über; KH, *Ger.* ich, *Scot.* loch; N, *Fr.* bon; y', *Fr.* Compiègne

STRESS MARKS:

Primary stress: '
in·cite' (ĭn-sīt')
Secondary stress: '
in'sight' (ĭn'sīt')

cus, having pliant, hollow, or pithy stems and clusters of small, brownish flowers. **2.** Any of various similar, usually aquatic plants. **3.** The stem of a rush, used in making baskets, mats, and chair seats. [Middle English *rush, rish,* Old English *rysc.*]

Rush (rŭsh), **Benjamin** (1745–1813). U.S. physician, politician, author, and educator. A member of the Second Continental Congress and a signer of the Declaration of Independence, he used his political and academic position to propound many liberal causes, notably the humane treatment of the mentally handicapped and the abolition of slavery.

rush hour *n.* Either of the two periods in the day when most people are traveling to or from work. **—rush-hour** (rŭsh'our') *adj.*

rush·light (rŭsh'līt') *n.* A candle consisting of a rush wick in tallow. Also called "rush candle."

Rush·more, Mount (rŭsh'môr'). Peak, 1,708 meters (5,600 feet) high, in the Black Hills of southwestern South Dakota. The northeastern face has gigantic busts of presidents Washington, Jefferson, Lincoln, and Theodore Roosevelt, carved (1927–41) by Gutzon Borglum and his son Lincoln. The sculptures are included in Mt. Rushmore National Memorial.

rush·y (rŭsh'ē) *adj.* **-ier, -iest. 1.** Resembling or characteristic of rushes; rushlike. **2.** Abounding in rushes: *a rushy marsh.*

rusk (rŭsk) *n.* **1.** A light, soft-textured sweetened biscuit. **2.** Sweet raised bread dried and browned in an oven. [Spanish and Portuguese *rosca†,* a coil, twisted roll.]

Rus·kin (rŭs'kĭn), **John** (1819–1900). English art critic. He developed a philosophy in which art, morality, economics, and religion are interrelated. His ideas are expressed in works such as *The Stones of Venice* (1851–53) and *Sesame and Lilies* (1865).

Rus·sell (rŭs'əl), **Bertrand Arthur William, 3rd Earl** (1872–1970). British philosopher. In his *Principia Mathematica* (1910–13) he attempted to show that mathematics was an extension of logic. He later developed interests in social morality, epistemology, languages, and education. He was a prominent pacifist in World War I and II. In 1950 he was awarded the Nobel Prize for literature.

Russell, Ken (1927–). British film and television director. His films, such as *Women in Love* (1969), *The Music Lovers* (1970), *Mahler* (1974), and *Valentino* (1977) are notable for their use of spectacular visual effects.

Russell, Lillian (1861–1922). U.S. entertainer. With a clear soprano voice suited for opera and musical comedy, she attained stardom in 1881 in *The Great Mogul.* She performed in numerous productions in America and England, led a flamboyant, highly publicized life, and wrote beauty articles for two Chicago newspapers.

Russell Cave National Monument. Area of 124 hectares (310 acres) in northeastern Alabama. The cave contains archaeological evidence of nearly continuous human habitation from *c.* 6000 B.C. to A.D. 1650.

Russell diagram *n. Astronomy.* A **Hertzsprung-Russell diagram** *(see).*

rus·set (rŭs'ĭt) *n.* **1.** Moderate to deep reddish brown. **2.** A coarse reddish-brown to brown homespun cloth. **3.** An eating apple with a rough reddish-brown skin. [Middle English, from Old French *rousset,* from *rous,* red, from Latin *russus.*] **—rus·set** *adj.*

Rus·sia (rŭsh'ə). *Abbr.* **Rus. 1.** See **Russian Soviet Federative Socialist Republic. 2.** See **Union of Soviet Socialist Republics.**

Rus·sian (rŭsh'ən) *n. Abbr.* **Rus., Russ. 1. a.** A native or inhabitant of the U.S.S.R. **b.** A native or inhabitant of the Russian Soviet Federative Socialist Republic. **c.** A native or inhabitant of the former Russian Empire. **2.** One who is of Russian descent. **3.** The Slavic language of the Russian people that is the official language of the U.S.S.R.
~adj. **1.** Of or pertaining to Russia, its people, or their language. **2.** Loosely, of or pertaining to the U.S.S.R., especially when considered as a political power.

Russian dressing *n.* Mayonnaise with chili sauce, chopped pickles, and pimientos.

Russian Orthodox Church *n.* **1.** An independent branch of the Eastern Orthodox Church in Russia headed by the Patriarch of Moscow. **2.** A branch of this church outside Russia.

Russian Revolution *n.* **1.** The seizure of the central organs of state power in Petrograd by the Bolsheviks under the leadership of Lenin on November 7, 1917 (October 25, Old Style). Also called "October Revolution." **2.** The entire sequence of events in Russia that began with the overthrow of czarism by the uprising of March 1917 (the *February Revolution),* continued with the removal of the provisional government and the inauguration of socialist revolution led by the Bolsheviks, and ended with the defeat of counterrevolution in the civil war (1918–22).

Russian roulette *n.* **1.** An act of bravado, traditionally done as a wager, in which a person spins the cylinder of a revolver loaded with one bullet, aims the muzzle at his head, and pulls the trigger. **2.** Any exceptionally hazardous or foolhardy venture.

Russian Soviet Federative Socialist Republic. Formerly **Russian Soviet Federated Socialist Republic.** *Abbr.* **R.S.F.S.R.** The largest constituent republic of the U.S.S.R. It stretches from the Baltic Sea to the Pacific Ocean and from the Arctic Ocean to the Black Sea. It covers approximately 76 percent of the country and has 52 percent of its people. More than 80 percent of the republic's inhabitants are Russian. It includes 16 autonomous soviet socialist republics and accounts for about 70 percent of the country's total agricultural and manufacturing output. Moscow is the capital.

Russian thistle *n.* A red-stemmed, prickly plant, *Salsola kali tenui-*

folia, native to Asia, that is a troublesome weed in western North America.

Russian wedding ring *n.* A ring consisting of three interlaced loops, each made of a different type of gold.

Russian wolfhound *n.* A dog, the **borzoi** *(see).*

Russo– *prefix.* Indicates Russia; for example, **Russophilia.** [From RUSSIA.]

Rus·so-Jap·a·nese War (rŭs'ō-jăp'ə-nēz', -nēs') *n.* A war (1904–05) between Russia and Japan arising out of their conflicting interests in Manchuria and resulting in defeat for Russia.

Rus·so·phil·i·a (rŭs'ə-fĭl'ē-ə) *n.* Interest in or enthusiasm for Russia, its culture, people, government, or language. [RUSSO- + -PHILIA.] **—Rus·so·phile** (rŭs'ə-fīl', -fĭl) *n.*

Rus·so·pho·bi·a (rŭs'ə-fō'bē-ə) *n.* Dislike or fear of Russia or its policies. [RUSSO- + -PHOBIA.] **—Rus·so·phobe** (rŭs'ə-fōb') *n.*

rust (rŭst) *n.* **1.** Any of various powdery or scaly reddish-brown or reddish-yellow hydrated ferric oxides formed on iron and steel by low-temperature oxidation in the presence of water. **2.** Any of various metallic coatings, especially oxides, formed by corrosion. **3.** A stain or coating resembling iron rust. **4.** Any deterioration of ability or character resulting from inactivity or neglect. **5.** *Botany.* **a.** Any of various parasitic fungi of the order Uredinales that are injurious to a wide variety of plants, including cereals. **b.** A plant disease caused by such fungi, characterized by reddish or brownish spots on leaves, stems, and other parts. **6.** A strong reddish brown. *~v.* **rusted, rusting, rusts.** *—intr.* **1.** To become corroded; form rust. **2.** To deteriorate or degenerate through inactivity or neglect. **3.** To become the color of rust. **4.** To develop a disease caused by a

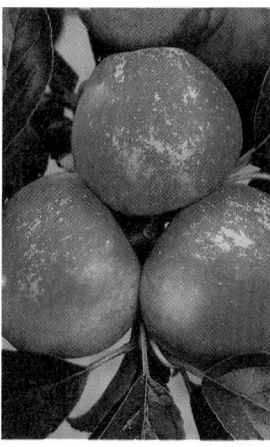

russet *Most of this group of dessert apple varieties are related to a crab apple,* Malus sylvestris mitis. *This variety is "Rosemary russet."*

Russian Revolution

THREE UPHEAVALS THAT BROUGHT LENIN TO POWER

War provides the catalyst for the Bolshevik revolution

The revolution that put the Bolshevik party into power in Russia came after the age-old tyranny of czardom had disintegrated; it was the third in a sequence of three. The revolution of 1905 broke out after government troops had fired on demonstrators in St. Petersburg (now Leningrad), who were weary of the Russo-Japanese War. In its wake came a parliament (Duma) elected by popular vote for the first time. However the Duma's authority was soon dissipated by the czar, and Russia drifted into World War I, a conflict that would break the backbone of the czarist regime.

Military defeat, heavy losses, and poor leadership at the front, coupled with famine and administrative chaos at home, intensified the pressure. To make matters worse, Czar Nicholas II had made himself commander in chief of the army, thereby assuming total responsibility for military reversals. The February Revolution (1917) was an explosion of riots and strikes that

eventually forced the czar to abdicate. A provisional government, dominated by Kerensky, sought to continue the war but received little support. Mass desertion at the front followed and the army was by now ripe for revolution. The German government, intent on sabotaging Russia's war effort, helped Lenin and other Bolsheviks to return from exile in Switzerland by providing them with a sealed train to cross Europe.

In October 1917 Lenin and his associates engineered Bolshevik leadership of soviets (councils of workers and soldiers) whose "Red Guards" stormed the headquarters of the provisional government in the Winter Palace at St. Petersburg and seized power. Local Bolsheviks established control of soviets in other key cities, taking Russia out of the war and into a Communist revolution. But their triumph was far from complete, for a bloody three-year civil war was to follow.

MAN OF THE PEOPLE *Lenin roused the workers and soldiers by advocating actions that were simplified into powerful slogans such as "All power to the Soviets" and "Peace, Land, Bread."*

rye *This cereal, which will grow even in poor soil, is cultivated mainly for animal fodder. Flour made from it produces a dark bread—the black bread of eastern Europe—and it is sometimes used in place of barley in whiskey distilling.*

rust fungus. —*tr.* **1.** To corrode or subject (a metal) to rust formation. **2.** To impair or spoil by misuse, inactivity, and the like. —*adj.* Rust-colored. [Middle English *rust,* Old English *rūst.*] —**rust·a·ble** *adj.* —**rust·less** *adj.*

rus·tic (rŭs′tĭk) *adj.* **1.** Of, pertaining to, or characteristic of country life. **2. a.** Charmingly simple and unsophisticated. **b.** Lacking refinement or polish; uncouth. **3.** Made of rough tree branches: *rustic furniture.* **4.** Having a rough surface with deep or chamfered joints. Said of masonry. —See Synonyms at **rural.** —*n.* **1.** A rural person. **2.** A crude, coarse, or simple person. [Middle English *rustyk,* from Old French *rustique,* from Latin *rūsticus,* from *rūs,* country.] —**rus·ti·cal·ly** *adv.* —**rus·tic·i·ty** (rŭs-tĭs′ə-tē) *n.*

rus·ti·cate (rŭs′tĭ-kāt′) *v.* **-cated, -cating, -cates.** —*intr.* **1.** To go to or live in the country. **2.** To lead a simple, rustic life. —*tr.* **1.** To send to the country. **2.** To impart a rustic character to. **3.** *British.* To suspend (a student) from a university or school. **4.** To construct (masonry) in the rustic style. [Latin *rūsticārī,* from *rūsticus,* RUSTIC.] —**rus·ti·ca·tion** *n.* —**rus·ti·ca·tor** *n.*

rus·tle (rŭs′əl) *v.* **-tled, -tling, -tles.** —*intr.* To move with soft whispering sounds. —*tr.* To cause to make such sounds. —*n.* A soft whispering sound: *The gentle rustle of a silken gown.* [Middle English *rustlen, rustelen,* akin to Frisian *russelje,* Dutch *ridselen* (imitative).] —**rus·tler** *n.* —**rus·tling·ly** *adv.*

rustle² *v.* **-tled, -tling, -tles.** —*tr.* To steal (cattle or other livestock). —*intr.* **1.** To steal livestock. **2.** *Informal.* To act or proceed energetically; hustle. —**rustle up.** To prepare or produce, especially hastily or in an improvised fashion. [Probably from RUSTLE (to move with soft sounds).] —**rus·tler** *n.*

rust·proof (rŭst′prŏŏf′) *adj.* Specially treated so as to be incapable of rusting. —**rust·proof** *v.*

rust·y (rŭs′tē) *adj.* **-ier, -iest. 1.** Covered with or affected by rust; corroded. **2.** Consisting of or produced by rust. **3.** Rust-colored. **4.** Working or operating stiffly or incorrectly because of or as if because of rust. **5.** Weakened or impaired by neglect, disuse, or lack of practice. —**rust·i·ly** *adv.* —**rust·i·ness** *n.*

rut¹ (rŭt) *n.* **1.** A sunken track or groove made by the passage of vehicles. **2.** A fixed, monotonous routine of thought or action. —*tr.v.* **rutted, rutting, ruts.** To furrow. [Old French *rote, route,* way, ROUTE.]

rut² *n.* **1.** A cyclically recurring condition of sexual excitement and reproductive activity in male mammals, such as deer. **2.** The comparable condition of female mammalian sexual activity; estrus. —*intr.v.* **rutted, rutting, ruts.** To be in rut. [Middle English *rutte,* from Old French *rut, ruit,* "bellowing (of stags in rut)," from Late Latin *rūgitus,* from Latin *rūgīre,* to roar.]

ru·ta·ba·ga (rŏŏ′tə-bā′gə, rŏŏt′ə-, rŏŏ′tə-bā′gə) *n.* **1.** A plant, *Brassica napobrassica,* native to Eurasia, having a thick, bulbous root used as food and livestock feed. **2.** The edible root of this plant. Also called "swede," "Swedish turnip." [Swedish (dialectal) *rotabagge,* "baggy root" : *rot,* root, from Old Norse *rōt* + *bagge,* from Old Norse *baggi,* BAG.]

ruth (rŏŏth) *n. Archaic.* **1.** Compassion or pity. **2.** Sorrow; misery; grief. [Middle English *ruthe, rewthe,* from *rewen,* to rue, from Old English *hrēowan.*]

Ruth¹ (rŏŏth). In the Old Testament, a Moabite widow who went to Bethlehem where she later married Boaz.

Ruth² *n.* A book of the Old Testament in which the story of Ruth is told.

Ruth, George Herman, known as "Babe" (1895–1948). U.S. baseball player. In six seasons with the Boston Red Sox and 15 seasons with the New York Yankees, he hit 714 home runs, played in 10 World Series, was among the first inductees into the Baseball Hall of Fame (1936), and held a total of 54 major league records, including most career home runs, most home runs in one season, and most runs batted in.

Ru·the·ni·a (rŏŏ-thē′nē-ə). Region of eastern Europe, in western Ukraine west of the Carpathian Mts. Part of it constituted a province of Czechoslovakia (1918–39), and all of it was annexed by the U.S.S.R. in 1945. [Medieval Latin, Russia, from *Rut(h)enī,* Russians, from Russian *Rusin,* from Old Russian *Rus′,* "Norsemen."]

Ru·the·ni·an (rŏŏ-thē′nē-ən) *n.* **1.** A member of a group of Ukrainians living in Ruthenia. **2.** A Ukrainian dialect spoken by these people. —**Ru·the·ni·an** *adj.*

ru·then·ic (rŏŏ-thĕn′ĭk, -thē′nĭk) *adj. Chemistry.* Of or pertaining to ruthenium. Said especially of a compound that contains ruthenium with a high valence.

ru·then·i·ous (rŏŏ-thē′nē-əs) *adj. Chemistry.* Of or pertaining to ruthenium. Said especially of a compound that contains ruthenium with a low valence.

ru·the·ni·um (rŏŏ-thē′nē-əm) *n. Symbol* **Ru** A hard white acid-resistant metallic element found in platinum ores. It is used to harden platinum and palladium for jewelry and in alloys for nonmagnetic wear-resistant instrument pivots and electrical contacts. Atomic number 44, atomic weight 101.07, melting point 2,250°C, boiling point 3,900°C, specific gravity 12.41, valences 1, 2, 3, 4, 5, 6, 7, 8. [New Latin; discovered in the Ural Mountains in Russia, from

Medieval Latin *Ruthenia,* Russia. See **Ruthenia.**]

ruth·er·ford (rŭth′ər-fərd) *n.* A unit of radioactivity equal to the quantity of radioactive material that undergoes one million disintegrations per second. [After Ernest RUTHERFORD.]

Rutherford, Ernest, 1st Baron (1871–1937). New Zealand-born British scientist. He classified radiation into alpha, beta, and gamma types; his finding that alpha radiation consists of positive charged helium atoms led to his discovery (1906) of the atomic nucleus. He was awarded the Nobel Prize for chemistry (1908).

Rutherford, Dame Margaret (1892–1972). British actress. Starting her film career in 1936, she appeared in more than 40 films, mostly comedies, in parts characterized by a uniquely British eccentricity. In *Murder She Said* (1962) and its sequels, she played Agatha Christie's detective, Miss Marple.

ruth·er·for·di·um (rŭth′ər-fôr′dē-əm, -fŏr′-) *n.* The element **unnilquadium** *(see).* Not in current technical usage. [After Ernest RUTHERFORD.]

ruth·ful (rŏŏth′fəl) *adj. Archaic.* **1.** Full of or causing sorrow. **2.** Compassionate. —**ruth·ful·ly** *adv.* —**ruth·ful·ness** *n.*

ruth·less (rŏŏth′lĭs) *adj.* Having or showing no compassion, pity, or leniency; merciless. —See Synonyms at **cruel.** —**ruth·less·ly** *adv.* —**ruth·less·ness** *n.*

ru·ti·lant (rŏŏ′tə-lənt) *adj. Archaic.* Having a reddish glow or gleam. [Middle English *rutilaunt,* from Latin *rutilāns* (stem *rutilant-*), from *rutilāre,* to make reddish, from *rutilus,* reddish.]

ru·tile (rŏŏ′tĭl, -tēl, -tīl) *n.* The lustrous red, reddish-brown, yellowish, or black natural mineral form of titanium dioxide, TiO_2, used as a gemstone, as a source of titanium, and in paints and fillers. [German *Rutil,* from Latin *rutilus,* reddish. See **rutilant.**]

Rut·land (rŭt′lənd). Former county of central England. Absorbed into Leicestershire (1974) despite local opposition, it was the smallest county of England. Its county town was Oakham.

rut·tish (rŭt′ĭsh) *adj.* Lustful; libidinous.

rut·ty (rŭt′ē) *adj.* **-tier, -tiest.** Full of ruts. —**rut·ti·ness** *n.*

Ru·wen·zo·ri Mountains (rŏŏ′ən-zôr′ē, -zōr′ē). Mountain range between Uganda and Zaire, central Africa. Extending from Lake Albert to Lake Edward, the range rises to 5,120 meters (16,798 feet) at Mt. Ngaliema (Mt. Stanley). The peaks are snow-capped and are thought to be Ptolemy's Mountains of the Moon.

R.V. Revised Version (of the Bible).

Rwan·da (rŏŏ-än′də). Small republic of central Africa. It is chiefly mountainous with part of Lake Kivu to the west and the volcanic Virunga Mts. in the northwest. Densely populated, it was a refuge in the days of the slave trade and was administered with Burundi by Belgium as Ruanda-Urundi from 1919 until independence (1962). There has been sporadic violence between the two main ethnic groups, the Hutu and Tutsi, since 1959. A poor, predominantly agricultural country, Rwanda relies on exports of coffee and tea, but its considerable mineral resources are now being developed. Area, 26,338 square kilometers (10,169 square miles). Population, 4,800,000. Capital, Kigali. See map at **Tanzania.**

Rwy., Ry. railway.

Rx (är′ĕks′) *n.* A medical prescription. [Alteration of ℞, symbol used in prescriptions, abbreviation of Latin *recipe,* imperative of *recipere,* to take.]

-ry. Variant of **-ery.**

ryd·berg (rĭd′bûrg′) *n.* A unit of energy, the **hartree** *(see).* [After Johannes Robert *Rydberg* (1854–1919), Swedish physicist.]

Rydberg constant *n. Physics. Symbol* **R.** A constant used in formulae for series of lines in atomic spectra, equal to $1.09737 \times 10^7 \mathrm{m}^{-1}$.

rye¹ (rī) *n.* **1.** A widely cultivated cereal grass of the genus *Secale,* the seeds of which are valued as grain. **2.** The grain of this plant, used in making flour and whiskey and for livestock feed. **3.** Rye bread. **4.** Rye whiskey. [Middle English *rye, ruge,* Old English *ryge.*]

rye² *n.* A male Gypsy. [Romany *rai,* from Sanskrit *rājan,* king.]

Rye (rī). Market town and resort of East Sussex, southeastern England. It is one of the Cinque Ports, but silt deposits have moved the coastline 3 kilometers (2 miles) from the town.

rye bread *n.* Bread made partially or entirely from rye flour.

rye grass *n.* Any of several pasture or meadow grasses of the genus *Lolium,* native to Eurasia, some species of which are cultivated for forage.

rye whiskey *n.* Whiskey distilled from rye.

Ryle (rīl), **Sir Martin** (1918–84). British astronomer. He was best known for pioneering the technique of setting up a line of two or more radio telescopes and using the earth's rotation to multiply their effective aperture. In 1974 he shared with Antony Hewish (1924–) the Nobel Prize for physics.

ry·ot (rī′ət) *n.* A peasant or tenant farmer in India. [Hindi *ra′īyat,* from Arabic *ra′īyah,* herd, peasants, from *ra′ā,* pasture.]

Ryu·kyu Islands (ryŏŏ′kyŏŏ′). Island group of the west Pacific Ocean. Forming an arc between Kyushu Island (Japan) and Taiwan, they were seized from China by Japan (1879) and were occupied by the United States from 1945, returning to Japan in 1953 and 1972. Okinawa is the main island. See map at **Japan.**

s, S (ĕs) *n., pl.* **s's** or **S's. 1.** The 19th letter of the modern English alphabet. See feature at **alphabet. 2.** Any of the speech sounds represented by this letter. **3.** Anything shaped like the letter S. **4.** The 19th in a series; 18th when *J* is omitted.

s, S, s., S. *Note:* As an abbreviation or symbol, *s* may be a small or a capital letter, with or without a period. Established forms or those generally preferred precede the definition. When no form is given, all four forms are in general use in that sense. **1. S.** Sabbath. **2. S.** saint. **3. S.** Saturday. **4. S.** Saxon. **5. s., S.** school. **6. s., S.** sea. **7. s** second (unit of time). **8. s** second of arc. **9. s.** see. **10. s.** semi-. **11. S.** September. **12. s.** shilling. **13. S.** *Medicine.* signature. **14. S.** signor; signore. **15. s.** singular. **16. s.** sire. **17. s.** sister. **18. s.** small. **19. s., S.** society. **20. s.** son. **21. south**; southern. **22. s** stere. **23. S** *Physics.* strangeness. **24. s.** substantive. **25. S** The symbol for the element sulfur. **26. S.** Sunday.

–s¹ *suffix.* Indicates the plural form, for which it is used in most nouns not ending in a sibilant (such as *s* or *sh*), an affricate (such as *ch*), or a postconsonantal *y*; for example, **charms, toys.** Compare **-es** (in nouns). [Middle English *-es, -s,* Old English *-as,* nominative and accusative plural ending of some nouns.]

–s² *suffix.* Indicates the third person singular form of the present indicative, for which it is used in most verbs not ending in a sibilant, an affricate, or a postconsonantal *y*; for example, **takes, runs.** Compare **-es** (in verbs). [Middle English *-es,* Old English *-es, -as.*]

–s³ *suffix.* **1.** Used in the formation of certain adverbs; for example, **unawares. 2.** Used to form adverbs indicating regular repetition of an action; for example, *mornings* he takes the train or *nights* as in *She works nights.* [In Middle and Old English the genitive singular ending *-es* was used to form adverbs from some nouns and adjectives.]

–'s¹ *suffix.* Indicates the possessive case, for which it is used in singular nouns, in some pronouns, and in irregularly formed plural nouns; for example, **nation's, somebody's, men's.** [Middle and Old English *-es,* genitive singular ending.]

–'s² *suffix.* Indicates the plural form in abbreviations, numbers, or symbols used as nouns; for example, **MA's, D.T.'s, 1960's, A's.** [From -s (plural suffix).]

–'s³ *suffix.* **1.** Is: *She's here.* **2.** Has: *He's been eating.* **3.** Us: *Let's go.* **4.** Does: *What's it mean?*

s.a. without date [Latin *sine anno*].

S.A. 1. Salvation Army. **2.** South Africa. **3.** South America. **4.** South Australia. **5.** Sturmabteilung.

Saa·nen (sä'nən, zä'-) *n.* A dairy goat of a breed developed in Switzerland, having a white, short-haired coat and no horns. [After *Saanen,* a town in southwestern Switzerland.]

Saar·brück·en (zär-brōōk'ən, -brü'kən, sär-). Capital of Saarland, southwestern West Germany. On the Saar River near the French border, it is the industrial center of the Saar coal fields.

Saa·ri·nen (sär'ə-nən, -nĕn'), **Eero** (1910–61). Finnish-born U.S. architect. His innovative designs include the General Motors Technical Center at Warren, Michigan, and the Trans World Airlines terminal at Kennedy Airport in New York City.

Saar·land (zär'länd', sär'-, zär'länt'). State of southwestern West Germany, bordered by Luxembourg and France. With rich coal deposits, it has heavy industries, including iron and steel and metal goods and also glass and textiles. A German-speaking border territory, Saarland became the Saar Territory, administered by France under the League of Nations (1919). After a plebiscite, the territory became the German province of Saarland (1935). It was part of the French zone of occupied Germany in 1945 and joined a customs union with France (1948). A referendum (1955) rejected plans for an autonomous, neutral state, and the area gained its present status (1957). Saarbrücken is the capital.

Sab. Sabbath.

sab·a·dil·la (săb'ə-dĭl'ə, -dē'ə) *n.* **1.** A tropical American plant, *Schoenocaulon officinale,* having poisonous seeds used in insecticides. **2.** The dry, ripe seeds of this plant. [Spanish *cebadilla,* diminutive of *cebada,* barley, from *cebo,* feed, from Latin *cibus,* food, probably of non-Indo-European origin.]

Sa·bah (sä'bä', -bə). State of Malaysia, on the island of Borneo. It was the British protectorate of North Borneo after 1882 and joined the Federation of Malaysia (1963). Sabah produces rubber, copra, cocoa, rice, and wood and has oil and copper resources.

Sab·a·oth (săb'ā-ōth', sə-bā'ōth') *pl.n.* Hosts; armies: *the Lord of Sabaoth.* Romans 9:29; James 5:4. [Latin *Sabaōth,* from Greek, from Hebrew *ṣəbhā'oth,* from *ṣābhā',* host, army.]

sa·ba·yon (sä'bä-yôn') *n.* A dessert sauce, **zabaglione** *(see).* [French, from Italian *zabaione,* ZABAGLIONE.]

sab·bat (săb'ət, sä-bä') *n.* The **witches' Sabbath** *(see).* [French, "Sabbath," from Latin *sabbatum,* SABBATH.]

Sab·ba·tar·i·an (săb'ə-târ'ē-ən) *n.* **1.** A person who observes Saturday as the Sabbath, as in Judaism and some sects of Christianity. **2.** A person who believes in strict observance of the Sabbath. ~*adj.* Of the Sabbath or Sabbatarians. [Late Latin *sabbatārius,* from Latin *sabbatum,* SABBATH.] —**Sab·ba·tar·i·an·ism** *n.*

Sab·bath (săb'əth) *n. Abbr.* **S., Sab. 1.** Saturday, taken as the seventh day of the week, named in the Ten Commandments as the day of rest and worship and observed as such by the Jews and some Christian sects. **2.** Sunday, taken as the first day of the week, observed as the day of rest by most Christian churches. [Middle English *sabat(h),* from Old English *sabat* and Old French *sab(b)at,* both from Latin *sabbatum,* from Greek *sabbaton,* from Hebrew *shabbāth,* from *shābhath,* to rest.]

sab·bat·i·cal (sə-băt'ĭ-kəl) *adj.* Also **sab·bat·ic** (-ĭk). **1.** Of, pertaining to, or appropriate to the Sabbath as the day of rest. **2.** Of or pertaining to a sabbatical year: *took a sabbatical leave.* ~*n.* **sabbatical.** A sabbatical year. [Late Latin *sabbaticus,* from Greek *sabbatikos,* from *sabbaton,* SABBATH.]

sabbatical year *n.* **1.** *Often* **Sabbatical year.** A year during which land remained fallow, observed every seven years by the ancient Jews. **2.** A leave of absence, often with pay, usually granted every seventh year, as to a college professor, for travel, research, or rest.

Sa·bel·li·an (sə-bĕl'ē-ən) *n.* **1.** An extinct division of the subfamily of Italic Indo-European languages, including ancient Aequian, Sabine, and Volscian. **2.** A member of any of the Sabellian-speaking peoples of ancient Italy, including the Sabines and the Samnites. [Latin *Sabellus†,* Sabine.] —**Sa·bel·li·an** *adj.*

sa·ber (sā'bər) *n.* Also *chiefly British* **sa·bre. 1.** A heavy cavalry sword with a one-edged, slightly curved blade. **2. a.** A fencing sword having a tapering two-edged blade and a guard that covers the back of the hand. **b.** The art of fencing with the saber. ~*tr.v.* **sabered, sabering sabers.** Also *chiefly British* **sabred, sabring, sabres.** To strike, wound, or kill with a saber. [French, earlier *sable,* from German *Sabel, Säbel,* from Hungarian *szablya* or Polish *szabla.*]

sa·ber-toothed tiger (sā'bər-tōōtht') *n.* Any of various extinct cats of the Oligocene to the Pleistocene epoch, especially one of the larger members of the genus *Smilodon,* characterized by long upper canine teeth.

sa·bin (sā'bĭn) *n.* A unit of acoustic absorption equivalent to the absorption by one square foot of a surface that absorbs all incident sound. [After W.C.W. *Sabine* (1868–1919), U.S. physicist.]

Sa·bine (sā'bīn') *n.* **1.** A member of an ancient tribe of central Italy, conquered and assimilated by the Romans in 290 B.C. **2.** The Sabellian language of this people. [Middle English *Sabyn,* from Latin *Sabīnus†.*] —**Sa·bine** *adj.*

Sa·bin vaccine (sā'bĭn) *n.* A live but nonvirulent form of the polio virus taken orally to immunize against poliomyelitis. [After Albert Bruce *Sabin* (1906–), U.S. microbiologist.]

sa·ble (sā'bəl) *n.* **1. a.** A carnivorous mammal, *Martes zibellina,* of northern Europe and Asia, having soft, dark fur. **b.** The highly valued pelt or fur of this animal. **2.** The similar fur of other species of martens; especially, the fur of the American marten, *Martes americana.* In this sense, also called "American sable." **3. a.** The color black, especially in heraldry. **b. sables.** Black garments worn in mourning. **4.** A grayish yellowish brown. ~*adj.* **1.** Made of or trimmed with sable fur. **2.** Of the color of sable fur. **3. a.** Of the color black, as in heraldry or mourning.

b. Dark; somber. [Middle English, from Old French, from Medieval Latin *sabelum,* from Slavic, akin to Russian *sobol†.*]

sable antelope *n.* A large African antelope, *Hippotragus niger,* having a usually dark coat and backward-curving horns.

sa·bot (să-bō', săb'ō) *n.* **1.** A shoe carved from a single piece of wood, worn in several European countries. **2.** A wooden-soled sandal or shoe having a leather upper. [French, from Old French, perhaps blend of *savate,* shoe, akin to Spanish *zapáto,* shoe, perhaps of Oriental origin + *bot, bote,* BOOT.]

sab·o·tage (săb'ə-täzh') *n.* **1.** The deliberate damaging of property or disruption of procedure carried out, as by enemy agents or dissatisfied workers, with the intention of obstructing productivity or normal functioning. **2.** Treacherous action intended to defeat or frustrate an endeavor; deliberate subversion.
~*tr.v.* **sabotaged, -taging, -tages.** To commit sabotage against. [French, from *saboter,* "to clatter shoes," work clumsily, deliberately wreck, from SABOT.]

sab·o·teur (săb'ə-tûr') *n.* A person who commits sabotage. [French, from *saboter,* to work clumsily, SABOTAGE.]

sa·bra (sä'brə) *n.* A native-born Israeli. [Modern Hebrew *sābrāh,* "prickly pear," a plant widespread in the Negev.]

sabre. *Chiefly British.* Variant of **saber.**

sab·u·lous (săb'yə-ləs) *adj.* Gritty; sandy. [Latin *sabulōsus,* from *sabulum,* coarse sand.] —**sab·u·los·i·ty** (săb'yə-lŏs'ə-tē) *n.*

sac (săk) *n.* A pouchlike part in a plant or animal, sometimes filled with fluid. [French, a bag, from Latin *saccus,* SACK.]

Sac·a·ja·we·a (săk'ə-jə-wē'ə) (*c.* 1788-1812). U.S. Indian guide. Along with her husband, a French-Canadian trapper, she accompanied Meriwether Lewis and William Clark on their westward expedition (1804-06). She was able to procure horses and safe passage for the explorers from her people, the Shoshone Indians of the northwest.

sac·cate (săk'āt') *adj.* Shaped like or having a pouch or sac. [New Latin *saccatus,* from Latin *saccus,* a bag, SACK.]

sac·cha·rase (săk'ə-rās', -rāz') *n.* An enzyme, **invertase** (*see*). [SACCHAR(O)- + -ASE.]

sac·cha·rate (săk'ə-rāt') *n.* A salt or ester of saccharic acid. [SACCHAR(IC ACID)- + -ATE.]

sac·char·ic acid (sə-kăr'ĭk) *n.* A white crystalline acid, COOH(CHOH)4COOH, formed by the oxidation of glucose. [SACCHAR(O)- + -IC.]

sac·cha·ride (săk'ə-rīd') *n.* Any of a series of compounds of carbon, hydrogen, and oxygen in which the atoms of the latter two elements are in the ratio of 2:1, especially sugars and other carbohydrates containing the group $C_6H_{10}O_5$. [SACCHAR(O)- + -IDE.]

sac·char·i·fy (sə-kăr'ə-fī', să-) *tr.v.* **-fied, -fying, -fies.** Also **sac·cha·rize** (săk'ə-rīz') **-rized, -rizing, -rizes.** To convert (starch, for example) into sugar. [SACCHAR(O)- + -FY.] —**sac·char·i·fi·ca·tion** (sə-kăr'ə-fĭ-kā'shən) *n.*

sac·cha·rim·e·ter (săk'ə-rĭm'ə-tər) *n.* **1.** A polarimeter that indicates the concentration of sugar in a solution. **2.** An instrument that determines the sugar content of a fermenting sample from carbon dioxide measurements. [SACCHAR(O)- + -METER.]

sac·cha·rin (săk'ər-ĭn) *n.* A white crystalline powder, $C_7H_5NO_3S$, having a taste about 500 times sweeter than cane sugar, used as a calorie-free sweetener. [SACCHAR(O)- + -IN.]

sac·cha·rine (săk'ər-ĭn, -rēn', -ə-rīn') *adj.* **1.** Of, pertaining to, or characteristic of sugar or saccharin; sweet. **2.** Ingratiatingly or cloyingly sweet: *a saccharine smile.* [SACCHAR(O)- + -INE.] —**sac·cha·rine·ly** *adv.* —**sac·cha·rin·i·ty** (săk'ə-rĭn'ə-tē) *n.*

saccharo-, sacchar- *prefix.* Indicates sugar; for example, **saccharometer, saccharide, saccharin.** [Latin *saccharum,* sugar, from Greek *sakkharon,* from Pali *sakkharā,* from Sanskrit *śarkarā,* gravel, SUGAR.]

sac·cha·roid (săk'ə-roid') *adj.* Also **sac·cha·roi·dal** (săk'ə-roid'l). Designating rocks and minerals having a granular structure similar to that of loaf sugar. [SACCHAR(O)- + -OID.]

sac·cha·rom·e·ter (săk'ə-rŏm'ə-tər) *n.* A hydrometer that determines the amount of sugar in a solution from relative density measurements. [SACCHARO- + -METER.]

sac·cha·ro·my·cete (săk'ə-rō-mī'sēt') *n.* Any of various yeast fungi, especially of the genus *Saccharomyces,* many of which ferment sugar. [SACCHARO- + -MYCETE.]

sac·cha·rose (săk'ə-rōs', -rōz') *n.* A sugar, **sucrose** (*see*). [SACCHAR(O)- + -OSE.]

Sac·co (săk'ō), **Nicola** (1891-1927). U.S. anarchist, born in Italy. Immigrating to Massachusetts in 1908, he became involved with socialist movements. In 1921 he was convicted along with Bartolomeo Vanzetti of murder, although the evidence was circumstantial. Despite outcries from Italian-Americans, the two were sentenced to death and executed. In 1977, after reviewing the case, Massachusetts governor Michael Dukakis pardoned the pair.

sac·cu·late (săk'yə-lāt', -lĭt) *adj.* Also **sac·cu·lat·ed** (-lā'tĭd), **sac·cu·lar** (-lər). **1.** Formed of or divided into a series of saclike dilations or pouches. **2.** Possessing a saccule or saccules. [New Latin *sacculus,* SACCULE + -ATE.]

sac·cule (săk'yōōl) *n.* Also **sac·cu·lus** (săk'yə-ləs) *pl.* **-li** (-lī'). **1.** A small sac. **2.** The smaller of two membranous sacs in the vestibule of the labyrinth of the ear. [New Latin *sacculus,* from Latin, diminutive of *saccus,* bag, SACK.]

sac·er·do·tal (săs'ər-dōt'l, săk'-) *adj.* **1.** Of or pertaining to priests or the priesthood; priestly. **2.** Of or pertaining to sacerdotalism. [Middle English, from Old French, from Latin *sacerdōtālis,* from *sacerdōs* (stem *sacerdōt-*), a priest.] —**sac·er·do·tal·ly** *adv.*

sac·er·do·tal·ism (săs'ər-dōt'l-īz'əm, săk'-) *n.* The belief that ordained priests are invested with supernatural powers and are the indispensable mediators between God and man.

sa·chem (sā'chəm) *n.* **1.** The chief of a tribe or confederation among some North American Indian peoples. Also called "sagamore." **2.** Any of the high officials of the Tammany Society. [Narraganset *sâchim,* "chief," from Proto-Algonquian *saakimaawa* (unattested). See also **sagamore.**]

sa·cher torte (sä'kər tôrt', zä'KHər tôr'tə) *n.* A rich chocolate cake filled with jam and coated with chocolate icing. [German *Sachertorte* : *Sacher,* surname of a family of 19th- and 20th-century hotel owners + TORTE.]

sa·chet (să-shā') *n.* **1.** A small bag or packet containing perfumed powder and used to scent clothes, as in trunks or closets. **2.** A small sealed packet containing a quantity of a product, such as shampoo or dried yeast, that is enough for use on a single occasion. [French, from Old French, a small bag, diminutive of *sac,* a bag, from Latin *saccus,* SACK.]

Sachs (zäks, säks), **Hans** (1494-1576). German poet and dramatist. A cobbler by trade, he became a Meistersinger of Nuremberg. Though much of his vast output of songs seems dull by modern standards, his shorter plays and verse anecdotes still amuse. His life inspired Wagner's opera *Die Meistersinger von Nürnberg* (1868).

Sachsen. See **Saxony.**

sack¹ (săk) *n.* Also **sacque** (for sense 2). **1.** *Abbr.* **sk. a.** A large bag of strong, coarse material for holding objects in bulk. **b.** The contents of such a bag. **c.** The amount a sack will hold. **2.** A short, loose-fitting garment for women and children. **3.** *Slang.* Dismissal from employment: *His boss finally gave him the sack.* **4.** *Slang.* A bed, mattress, or sleeping bag. **5.** *Baseball.* A base. —**hit the sack.** *Informal.* To go to bed.
~*tr.v.* **sacked, sacking, sacks. 1.** To place in a sack. **2.** *Slang.* To discharge from employment. —**sack out.** *Slang.* To go to sleep. [Middle English *sack, sak,* Old English *sæcc, sacc,* from Latin *saccus,* from Greek *sakkos,* from Semitic; akin to Hebrew *śaq,* sack, sackcloth.]

sack² *tr.v.* **sacked, sacking, sacks.** To loot or pillage (a captured city, for example).
~*n.* **1.** The looting or pillaging of a captured town. **2.** Plunder; loot. [French (*mettre à*) *sac,* (to put in) a sack, to plunder, from Italian *sacco,* bag, from Latin *saccus,* SACK.]

sack³ *n.* Any of various light, dry, strong wines from Spain and the Canary Islands that were imported to England in the 16th and 17th centuries. [16th-century (*wyne*) *seck,* from Old French (*vin*) *sec,* dry (wine), from Latin *siccus,* dry.]

sack·but (săk'bŭt') *n.* A medieval musical instrument resembling the trombone. [French *saquebute, saqueboute,* "hooked lance" : *saquer, sachier†,* to pull, draw + *bouter,* to push, thrust against, from Common Romance *bottāre* (unattested), from Germanic.]

sack·cloth (săk'klôth', -klŏth') *n.* **1.** Sacking. **2. a.** A rough cloth of camel's hair, goat hair, hemp, cotton, or flax. **b.** Garments made of this cloth, worn as a symbol of mourning or penitence.

sack·ing (săk'ĭng) *n.* A coarse, stout woven cloth, as of jute or hemp, used for making sacks.

Sack·ville-West (săk'vĭl-wĕst'), **Victoria Mary,** known as "Vita" (1892-1962). English author. In her many novels, including *The Edwardians* (1930) and *All Passion Spent* (1931), she wrote primarily about life in Kent, where she spent much of her life.

sa·cral¹ (sā'krəl) *adj.* Of, near, or pertaining to the sacrum. [New Latin *sacralis,* from SACRUM.]

sacral² *adj.* Pertaining to sacred rites or observances. [Latin *sacer* (stem *sacr-*), SACRED.]

sac·ra·ment (săk'rə-mənt) *n.* **1.** Any of various religious rites considered to have been instituted or observed by Jesus as a visible sign of inner grace or a means of achieving grace. In the Roman Catholic and Eastern Churches these rites include baptism, confirmation, the Eucharist, matrimony, holy orders, penance, and the Sacrament of the Sick. **2.** *Often* **Sacrament. a.** The Eucharist. **b.** The consecrated elements of the Eucharist; especially, the bread or Host. **3.** Something considered to have sacred or mystical significance; a spiritual symbol or bond. [Middle English, from Old French *sacrement,* from Latin *sacrāmentum,* from Latin, oath, solemn obligation, from *sacrāre,* to consecrate, from *sacer* (stem *sacr-*), SACRED.]

sac·ra·men·tal (săk'rə-měn'təl) *adj.* **1.** Pertaining to, of the nature of, or used in a sacrament. **2.** Having the force and sacred character of a sacrament: *a sacramental obligation.*
~*n.* Any rite, action, or sacred object instituted by some Christian churches for use in worship. —**sac·ra·men·tal·ly** *adv.*

sac·ra·men·tal·ism (săk'rə-měn'tə-lĭz'əm) *n.* **1.** The doctrine that observance of the sacraments is necessary for salvation and that such participation can confer grace. **2.** Emphasis upon the efficacy of a sacramental. —**sac·ra·men·tal·ist** *n.*

sac·ra·men·tar·i·an (săk'rə-měn-târ'ē-ən) *n. Often* **Sacramentarian.** A person who regards the sacraments, especially the Eucharist, as merely visible symbols and not as inherently efficacious or as being a corporeal manifestation of Christ.
~*adj.* **1.** *Often* **Sacramentarian.** Of or pertaining to sacramentarians. **2.** Of or pertaining to sacramentalism or sacramentalists. —**sac·ra·men·tar·i·an·ism** *n.*

Sac·ra·men·to (săk'rə-měn'tō). Capital of California, in the north-central part of the state. On the Sacramento River, it was founded as Fort Sutter (1839) and expanded with the gold rush of 1848. It

sable antelope *The plains of Africa are the home of this black-skinned antelope. Like its northern fur-bearing namesake, the sable, it has been hunted—but for its curved and ringed horns rather than its skin.*

became the state capital (1854) and terminus of the Pony Express (1860). It has a deep-water port connected to the Pacific by the Suisun Canal.

Sacrament of the Sick *n. Roman Catholic Church.* A sacrament in which a priest anoints and prays for a sick person, especially one in danger of death. Also called "extreme unction."

sa·crar·i·um (sə-krâr'ē-əm) *n., pl.* **-ia** (-ē-ə). **1.** The sanctuary or sacristy of a church. **2.** In the Roman Catholic Church, a **piscina** *(see).* [Medieval Latin *sacrārium,* from Latin, a place for keeping holy things, from *sacer,* SACRED.]

sa·cred (sā'krĭd) *adj.* **1.** Dedicated, consecrated, or set apart for the worship of a deity. **2.** Dedicated or devoted exclusively to a single use, purpose, or person. **3.** Worthy of reverence or respect; venerable: *the sacred teachings of Buddha.* **4.** Of or pertaining to religious objects, rites, or practices. **5.** Earnest, serious, and grave; solemn: *upheld her sacred duty.* [Middle English, from the past participle of *sacren,* to consecrate, from Old French *sacrer,* from Latin *sacrāre,* from *sacer* (stem *sacr-*), dedicated, holy, sacred.] **—sa·cred·ly** *adv.* **—sa·cred·ness** *n.*

Sacred College *n.* The **College of Cardinals** *(see).*

sacred cow *n.* A person, idea, institution, or object regarded as immune from reasonable criticism. [Referring to the veneration of cows as sacred by Hindus.]

sacred mushroom *n.* Any of various mushrooms, such as those of the species *Psilocybe* and *Amanita,* that are ritually eaten for their hallucinogenic effects in various parts of the world.

sac·ri·fice (săk'rə-fīs') *n.* **1. a.** The act of offering something to a deity in propitiation or homage; especially, the ritual slaughter of an animal or person. **b.** The victim offered in this way. **2. a.** The forfeiture of something highly valued, as an idea, object, or friendship, for the sake of one considered to have a greater value or claim. **b.** Something so forfeited. **3. a.** The relinquishment of something at less than its presumed value. **b.** Something so relinquished. **c.** A loss so sustained. **4.** *Baseball.* A sacrifice hit. **~** *v.* **sacrificed, -ficing, -fices.** *—tr.* **1.** To offer as a sacrifice to a deity. **2.** To forfeit (something of value) for something considered to have a greater value or claim. **3.** To sell or give away at a loss. **4.** In chess, to allow one's opponent to capture (a piece) without the loss of an equivalent piece, as for tactical reasons. *—intr.* **1.** To make or offer a sacrifice. **2.** *Baseball.* To make a sacrifice hit. [Middle English, from Old French, from Latin *sacrificium* : *sacer,* holy, SACRED + *facere,* to do, make.] **—sac·ri·fic·er** *n.*

sacrifice fly *n. Baseball.* A fly ball enabling a runner to score after it is caught by a fielder.

sacrifice hit *n. Baseball.* A bunt that allows a runner to advance a base while the batter is retired.

sac·ri·fi·cial (săk'rə-fĭsh'əl) *adj.* Of, pertaining to, of the nature of, or being a sacrifice: *a sacrificial lamb.* **—sac·ri·fi·cial·ly** *adv.*

sacrificial anode *n. Metallurgy.* A piece of electropositive metal, such as magnesium or zinc, connected by a wire to a steel structure and buried in the ground to inhibit corrosion of the steel. [The magnesium corrodes instead of (sacrifices itself for) the steel.]

sac·ri·lege (săk'rə-lĭj) *n.* **1.** The misuse, theft, desecration, or profanation of something consecrated to a deity. **2.** An act of gross disrespect toward something regarded as sacred: *thought it a sacrilege to put ketchup on filet mignon.* [Middle English, from Old French, from Latin *sacrilegium,* from *sacrilegus,* one who steals sacred things : *sacer,* SACRED + *legere,* to gather, pluck, steal.] **—sac·ri·le·gist** (săk'rə-lē'jĭst) *n.*

sac·ri·le·gious (săk'rə-lē'jəs, -lĭj'əs) *adj.* **1.** Disrespectful or irreverent toward something regarded as sacred; impious. **2.** Guilty of sacrilege. **—See Synonyms at profane. —sac·ri·le·gious·ly** *adv.* **—sac·ri·le·gious·ness** *n.*

sa·cring bell (sā'krĭng) *n.* A bell rung at the elevation of the Host in the Mass. [Middle English *sacringe belle* : *sacringe,* gerund of *sacren,* to consecrate (see **sacred**) + BELL.]

sac·ris·tan (săk'rĭ-stən) *n.* Also **sa·crist** (sā'krĭst, săk'rĭst). **1.** A person in charge of a sacristy. **2.** A sexton. [Middle English, from Medieval Latin *sacristānus,* from *sacrista,* "one in charge of sacred vessels," from Latin *sacer* (stem *sacr-*), SACRED.]

sac·ris·ty (săk'rĭ-stē) *n., pl.* **-ties.** A room in a church housing the sacred vessels and vestments; a vestry. [French *sacristie,* from Medieval Latin *sacristia,* from *sacrista,* SACRISTAN.]

sac·ro·il·i·ac (săk'rō-ĭl'ē-ăk', să'krō-) *adj. Anatomy.* Of, pertaining to, or affecting the sacrum and ilium and their articulation or associated ligaments. **~** *n.* The sacroiliac joint or region. [SACR(UM) + ILI(UM) + -AC.]

sac·ro·lum·bar (săk'rō-lŭm'bər, -bär') *adj.* Of, pertaining to, or affecting the sacrum and the lumbar region. [SACR(UM) + LUMBAR.]

sac·ro·sanct (săk'rō-săngkt') *adj.* Being or regarded as being sacred and inviolable. [Latin *sacrōsanctus,* consecrated with religious ceremonies : *sacrō,* by a sacred rite, ablative of *sacrum,* a holy thing, religious rite, from *sacer,* SACRED + *sanctus,* past participle of *sancīre,* to consecrate.] **—sac·ro·sanc·ti·ty** (săk'rō-săngk'tə-tē) *n.*

sa·crum (sā'krəm, săk'rəm) *n., pl.* **sacra** (sā'krə, săk'rə). A triangular bone consisting in humans of five fused vertebrae and forming the posterior section of the pelvis. [New Latin, from Late Latin *(os) sacrum* (translation of Greek *hieron osteron,* "sacred bone," because it was used in sacrifice), from Latin, a sacred thing, from *sacer,* SACRED.]

sad (săd) *adj.* **sadder, saddest.** **1.** Affected or characterized by sorrow or unhappiness. **2.** Expressive of sorrow or unhappiness.

3. Causing sorrow or gloom; depressing. **4.** Deplorable; sorry: *a sad state of affairs.* **5.** Dark-hued; somber. [Middle English *sad,* grave, sad, full (of something), Old English *sæd,* sated, weary, from Germanic.] **—sad·ly** *adv.* **—sad·ness** *n.*

Synonyms: *dejected, depressed, desolate, doleful, downcast, melancholy, miserable, sorrowful, wretched.*

Sa·dat (sə-dăt', -dät'), **Muhammad Anwar el-** (1918-81). Egyptian politician who succeeded to the presidency on Nasser's death (1970). He is best remembered for his dramatic visit to Israel and his attempts to initiate a lasting settlement between the two countries. For this he was awarded the Nobel Peace Prize jointly with Menachem Begin (1978). He was assassinated by Muslim fundamentalists.

sad·den (săd'n) *v.* **-dened, -dening, -dens.** *—tr.* To make sad. *—intr.* To grow sad.

saddhu. Variant of **sadhu.**

sad·dle (săd'l) *n.* **1.** A leather seat for a rider, secured on an animal's back by a girth. **2.** The padded part of a driving harness fitting over a horse's back. **3.** The part of an animal's back upon which a saddle is placed. **4.** Something resembling or suggestive of a saddle in position, function, or shape, as: **a.** The seat of a bicycle, motorcycle, or similar vehicle. **b.** A cut of meat, especially lamb or mutton, consisting of part of the backbone and both loins. **c.** The lower part of a male fowl's back. **d.** A saddle-shaped depression in the ridge of a hill; a col. **e.** A ridge between two peaks. **f.** The clitellum of an earthworm. **5.** *Geometry.* A saddle-shaped surface. **—in the saddle.** In a position of control or dominance. **~** *v.* **saddled, -dling, -dles.** *—tr.* **1.** To put a saddle on (a horse, for example). **2.** To load or burden; encumber: *saddled with ten children.* **3.** To impose (a burdensome responsibility) upon another: *She saddled her debts on him.* *—intr.* **1.** To saddle a horse. **2.** To get into a saddle. Often used with *up.* [Middle English *sadel,* Old English *sadol,* from Germanic.]

sad·dle·back (săd'l-băk') *n.* **1.** A rare New Zealand songbird, *Philesturnus carunculatus,* having black plumage with a brown back patch and orange wattles. **2.** A **saddle roof** *(see).*

sad·dle·bag (săd'l-băg') *n.* A bag or pouch, usually one of a pair, hung across the back of an animal behind the saddle or over the rear wheel of a bicycle or motorcycle.

sad·dle·bill (săd'l-bĭl') *n.* A tropical African stork, *Ephippiorhynchus senegalensis,* having black and white plumage and a large red bill with a black band around the middle. Also called "jabiru."

sad·dle·bow (săd'l-bō') *n.* The arched upper front part of a saddle; a pommel. [Middle English *sadelbowe,* Old English *sadulboga* : SADDLE + BOW (arch).]

sad·dle·cloth (săd'l-klôth', -klŏth') *n.* A cloth placed between a saddle and a horse's back to prevent rubbing.

saddle horse *n.* A horse bred or schooled for riding.

sad·dler (săd'lər) *n.* One who makes, repairs, or sells saddles and other riding equipment.

saddle roof *n.* A roof having a gable at each end connected by a ridge. Also called "saddleback."

sad·dler·y (săd'lə-rē) *n., pl.* **-ies.** **1.** Saddles, harnesses, and other equipment for horses; tack. **2.** A shop selling such equipment. **3.** The craft or business of a saddler.

saddle shoe *n.* A flat casual shoe, often white, having a band of leather in a contrasting color across the instep.

saddle soap *n.* A preparation containing mild soap and neat's-foot oil, used for cleaning and softening leather.

saddle sore *n.* **1.** A sore on a horse's back caused by an improperly fitted saddle. **2.** A sore on a rider caused by saddle chafing.

saddle stitch *n.* **1.** A simple running stitch used primarily as ornament on the edges of clothing and accessories and usually done in a thread contrasting in color with the fabric. **2.** *Bookbinding.* A stitch used in sewing through the leaves of a book at the fold lines. **—sad·dle-stitch** (săd'l-stĭch') *v.*

sad·dle·tree (săd'l-trē') *n.* The frame of a saddle.

Sad·du·cee (săj'ə-sē', săd'yə-) *n.* A member of a Jewish sect of the 2nd century B.C. through the 1st century A.D. that retained the older interpretation of the written Mosaic law against the oral tradition, and denied the resurrection of the dead. Compare **Pharisee.** [Middle English *Saducee,* Old English *Sadducēas* (plural), from Late Latin *Saddūcaeus,* from Late Greek *Saddoukaios,* from Hebrew *Ṣəddūqī,* probably "descendant of *Ṣādōq,*" Zadok, "righteous," high priest of Israel in King David's time (II Samuel 8:17).] **—Sad·du·ce·an** (săj'ə-sē'ən) *adj.* **—Sad·du·cee·ism** *n.*

sa·de, sa·dhe (sā'də, -dē) *n.* Also **tsa·de** (tsä'də, -dē). The 18th letter of the Hebrew alphabet. See feature at **alphabet.** [Hebrew *ṣadhe.*]

Sade (säd), **Donatien Alphonse François, Comte de,** known as "Marquis de Sade" (1740-1814). French novelist. While imprisoned during the 1780's and 1790's for prohibited sexual practices, he wrote several pornographic fantasies, whose preoccupation with sexual violence led to the term "sadism."

sad·hu, sad·dhu (sä'dōō) *n.* A Hindu ascetic holy man. [Sanskrit *sādhu,* from adjective, "straight," right, holy, from Indo-Iranian *sādh* (unattested).]

sad·i·ron (săd'ī'ərn) *n.* A heavy flatiron having points at both ends and a removable handle. [SAD (in the obsolete sense "heavy") + IRON.]

sa·dism (sā'dĭz'əm, săd'ĭz'-) *n.* **1.** *Psychology.* An abnormal condition in which a person derives sexual gratification from inflicting pain and humiliation on others. **2.** Delight in cruelty. **3.** Extreme

sage grouse *During courtship, the male sage grouse spreads its long tail feathers into a spiky fan (above). Sage grouse live in the Western sagebrush plains, where they feed on insects, berries, and shoots.*

saiga *This antelope of the dry, cold steppes of Eurasia has a large downward-pointing nose that may help to warm the air it breathes and minimize water loss.*

cruelty. [After Comte Donatien de SADE.] **—sa·dist** *n.* **—sa·dis·tic** (sə-dĭs′tĭk) *adj.* **—sa·dis·ti·cal·ly** *adv.*

sa·do·mas·o·chism (sā′dō-măs′ə-kĭz′əm, -măz′ə-kĭz′əm, săd′ō-) *n.* The combination of sadism and masochism in one person, marked by the gaining of pleasure from both inflicting and submitting to pain. [SAD(ISM) + MASOCHISM.] **—sa·do·mas·o·chist** *n.* **—sa·do·mas·o·chis·tic** (sā′dō-măs′ə-kĭs′tĭk, -măz′ə-kĭs′tĭk, săd′ō-) *adj.*

sad sack *n. Informal.* An extremely inept or clumsy person.

Sa·far, Sa·phar (sə-fär′) *n.* The second month of the Muslim calendar. See feature at **calendar.** [Arabic.]

sa·fa·ri (sə-fä′rē) *n., pl.* **-ris. 1.** An overland expedition, especially for hunting or observing wild animals in Africa. **2.** The people, animals, and equipment of a safari. **3.** *Informal.* A journey or trip: *a sightseeing safari.* [Arabic *safarī*, a journey, from *safara,* to travel, set out.] **—sa·fa·ri** *v.*

safari suit *n.* An outfit consisting of a loose, shirtlike jacket with a belt and pleated pockets and matching trousers or skirt.

safe (sāf) *adj.* **safer, safest. 1.** Free from harm or injury; unhurt: *safe and sound after their ordeal.* **2. a.** Free from the threat of harm or danger: *I covered the shrub with netting so the berries would be safe from hungry birds.* **b.** Affording protection against harm or danger: *a safe harbor.* **c.** Unable or unlikely to cause harm or danger: *a safe drug.* **3.** Free from the risk of loss or failure: *a safe investment.* **4.** *Baseball.* Having reached a base without being put out, as a batter or base runner.

~n. **1.** A metal container, usually having a lock, used for storing valuables. **2.** A repository for protecting stored items, especially a cooled compartment for perishable foods. **3.** *Slang.* A condom. [Middle English *sauf,* from Old French, from Latin *salvus,* healthy, uninjured, safe.] **—safe·ly** *adv.* **—safe·ness** *n.*

safe-con·duct (sāf-kŏn′dŭkt) *n.* **1.** An official document or an escort assuring unmolested passage, as through enemy territory. **2.** The protection afforded by a safe-conduct.

safe·crack·er (sāf′krăk′ər) *n.* A criminal who breaks into safes in order to steal. **—safe·crack·ing** *n.*

safe-de·pos·it box (sāf′dĭ-pŏz′ĭt) *n.* A fireproof metal box, usually in a bank vault, for the safe storage of valuables, as important documents or jewelry.

safe·guard (sāf′gärd′) *n.* **1.** One that serves as a protection or precaution, as: **a.** A mechanical device or technical improvement designed to prevent accidents. **b.** A protective stipulation, as in a contract. **2.** A safe-conduct.

~tr.v. **safeguarded, -guarding, -guards.** To keep safe or secure, as from danger or attack; protect. —See Synonyms at **defend.**

safe house *n.* A place affording safe conditions for clandestine activities, as: **1.** One used by intelligence officers, as for the debriefing of a person seeking political asylum. **2.** One in which an escaped prisoner, especially a prisoner of war, may seek refuge.

safe·keep·ing (sāf′kē′pĭng) *n.* The act of keeping safe or the state of being kept safe; protection.

safe·light (sāf′līt′) *n.* A lamp having one or more color filters capable of permitting moderate darkroom illumination without exposure of photosensitive film or paper.

safe·ty (sāf′tē) *n., pl.* **-ties. 1.** Freedom from or prevention of danger, risk, or injury. **2.** Any of various devices designed to prevent accidents, especially a lock on a firearm preventing accidental firing. Also called "safety catch." **3.** *Football.* **a.** A play in which a member of the offensive team downs the ball, willingly or unwillingly, behind his own goal line, resulting in two points for the defensive team. **b.** Either of two defensive backs, usually positioned closest to the goal line they defend. **4.** *Slang.* A condom.

~adj. Contributing to or insuring safety; protective.

safety belt *n.* A **seat belt** *(see).*

safety curtain *n.* A fireproof curtain or screen lowered between the stage and the auditorium in a theater when no performance is taking place to contain any possible outbreak of fire.

safety factor *n.* A **factor of safety** *(see).*

safety film *n.* Nonflammable photographic film.

safety fuse *n.* A slow-burning fuse used for detonating an explosive from a safe distance.

safety glass *n.* Glass that has been toughened, reinforced, or otherwise modified so as to diminish the risk of breakage or to reduce the risk of injury should breakage occur. The main types either have a laminated structure including a wire or plastic sheet (*laminated glass*) or are tempered so that they will break into small pieces without sharp edges (*toughened glass*).

safety helmet *n.* A reinforced hat made of plastic or metal that is worn especially by workers on building sites.

safety lamp *n.* A miner's lamp with a protective wire gauze surrounding the flame to prevent ignition of flammable gases.

safety match *n.* A match that can be lighted only by being struck against a chemically prepared friction surface.

safety net *n.* **1.** A net held above the ground to break a person's fall, especially one used for circus performers, as acrobats. **2.** An arrangement or measure that provides a guarantee, especially of financial security.

safety pin *n.* **1.** A pin in the form of a clasp, having a sheath to cover and hold the point when the pin is closed. **2.** A pin that prevents the premature or accidental detonation of an explosive device such as a bomb or grenade.

safety razor *n.* A razor in which the blade is fitted into a holder with guards to prevent cutting of the skin.

safety valve *n.* **1.** A valve in a pressure container, as in a steam boiler, that automatically opens when pressure reaches a dangerous level. **2.** An outlet for the release of an excess, as of emotion.

saf·flow·er (săf′lou′ər) *n.* **1.** A plant, *Carthamus tinctorius,* native to Asia, having orange flowers that yield a dyestuff and seeds that are the source of an oil used in cooking, cosmetics, paints, and medicine. **2.** The dried flowers of this plant. **3.** Any of the products of this plant. [Earlier *safflore,* from Dutch *saffloer* or German *Safflor,* from Old French *saffleur,* from obsolete Italian *saffiore*†.]

saf·fron (săf′rən) *n.* **1. a.** A plant, *Crocus sativus,* native to the Old World, having purple or white flowers with orange stigmas. **b.** The dried stigmas of this plant, used to color foods and as a cooking spice and a dyestuff. **c.** Any of various similar or related plants, such as the autumn crocus. **2.** A moderate orange-yellow to moderate orange. [Middle English *saffran,* from Old French *safran,* from Medieval Latin *safranum,* from Arabic *za'farān.*] **—saf·fron** *adj.*

saf·ra·nine (săf′rə-nēn′, -nĭn) *n.* Also **saf·ra·nin** (-nĭn). Any of a family of dyes based on phenazine, used in the textile industry and as a biological stain. [French *safran,* SAFFRON + -INE.]

saf·role (săf′rōl′) *n.* A colorless or pale-yellow oily liquid, $C_{10}H_{10}O_2$, derived from oil of sassafras and other essential oils and used in flavorings, perfume, and soap. [French *safran,* SAFFRON + -OLE.]

sag (săg) *v.* **sagged, sagging, sags.** *—intr.* **1.** To sink, curve, or bulge downward, as from pressure, weight, or slackness. **2.** To hang loosely or unevenly; droop. **3.** To diminish in firmness, strength, or vigor; weaken: *Morale is sagging.* **4.** To decline in value or price. **5.** *Nautical.* To drift to leeward. *—tr.* To cause to sag or curve in the middle.

~n. **1.** The act, degree, or extent of sagging. **2.** A sunken place or area; depression. **3.** A decline, as in price or value. **4.** *Nautical.* A drift to leeward. [Middle English *saggen,* from Middle Low German *sacken,* to settle, ultimately of Scandinavian origin.]

sa·ga (sä′gə) *n.* **1.** An Icelandic prose narrative of the 12th and 13th centuries recounting historical and legendary events and exploits. **2.** A long, heroic narrative, as a novel or series of novels relating the history of a family. **3.** A series of events, usually occurring over a relatively long time: *the saga of Arctic exploration.* [Old Norse, a story, legend; akin to SAW (saying).]

sa·ga·cious (sə-gā′shəs) *adj.* Possessing or showing sound judgment and keen perception; wise. —See Synonyms at **shrewd.** [From Latin *sagāx* (stem *sagāc-*), quick-witted.] **—sa·ga·cious·ly** *adv.* **—sa·ga·cious·ness** *n.*

sa·gac·i·ty (sə-găs′ə-tē) *n.* The quality of being sagacious; wisdom.

sag·a·more (săg′ə-môr′, -mōr′) *n.* **1.** A subordinate chief among the Algonquian Indians of North America. **2.** A North American Indian chief, a **sachem** *(see).* [Eastern Abnaki *sàkama,* from Proto-Algonquian *saakimaawa* (unattested). See also **sachem.**]

Sa·gan (sā′gən), **Carl** (1934–). U.S. astronomer and author. Primarily known for his research on the probability of extraterrestrial life, he contributed to the Mariner and Viking space missions and has written on a wide variety of scientific topics in books such as *Intelligent Life in the Universe* (1966) and *The Dragons of Eden* (1977), a Pulitzer Prize winner.

Sa·gan (sä-gäN′), **Françoise,** pen name of Françoise Quoirez (1935–). French novelist and playwright. Her work generally deals with sexual ennui among prosperous, middle-class characters. Her works include the popular success *Bonjour Tristesse* (1954).

saga novel *n.* A **roman-fleuve** *(see).*

sage[1] (sāj) *n.* A person, usually an elderly man, who is venerated for his experience, judgment, and wisdom.

~adj. **sager, sagest. 1.** Having, proceeding from, or showing wisdom and calm judgment; judicious: *Ask your grandmother for her advice; she's a sage old woman.* **2.** *Obsolete.* Serious; solemn: *"a sage Requiem"* (Shakespeare). [Middle English, from Old French, from Vulgar Latin *sapius* (unattested), from Latin *sapere,* to be sensible, be wise.] **—sage·ly** *adv.* **—sage·ness** *n.*

sage[2] *n.* **1. a.** Any of various plants and shrubs of the genus *Salvia*; especially, *S. officinalis,* having aromatic grayish-green leaves used as a cooking herb. **b.** The leaves of this plant. **2.** Sage green. [Middle English *sauge,* from Old French *sauge,* from Latin *salvia,* "the healing plant," from *salvus,* healthy, safe.]

sage·brush (sāj′brŭsh′) *n.* Any of several aromatic American plants of the genus *Artemisia*; especially, *A. tridentata,* a shrub of arid regions of western North America, having silver-green leaves and large clusters of small white flowers.

sage green *n.* A grayish green. **—sage-green** (sāj′grēn′) *adj.*

sage grouse *n.* A bird, *Centrocercus urophasianus,* of western North America, the male of which has long, pointed tail feathers that can be spread in a fan during courtship displays.

sag·gar, sag·ger (săg′ər) *n.* **1.** A protective casing of fire clay in which delicate ceramic articles are fired. **2.** Clay used to make saggars.

~tr.v. **saggared, -garing, -gars.** To place or bake in a saggar. [Perhaps a contraction of SAFEGUARD.]

Sa·git·ta (sə-jĭt′ə) *n.* A constellation in the Northern Hemisphere near Aquila and Cygnus. [Latin *sagitta*†, Sagitta, arrow.]

sag·it·tal (săj′ə-təl) *adj.* **1.** Of or like an arrow or arrowhead. **2.** *Anatomy.* Of or designating the suture uniting the two parietal bones of the skull. **3.** *Zoology & Anatomy.* Of or designating the vertical plane that divides the body of a symmetrical animal into right and left halves. [Latin *sagitta*†, arrow.] **—sag·it·tal·ly** *adv.*

Sag·it·tar·i·us (săj′ə-târ′ē-əs) *n.* **1.** A constellation in the Southern Hemisphere near Scorpius and Capricornus. **2. a.** The ninth sign of the **zodiac** *(see).* Also called "Archer." **b.** One born under this sign.

[Middle English, from Latin *sagittārius,* an archer, Sagittarius, from *sagitta†,* arrow.]

sag·it·tate (săj′ə-tāt′) *adj. Botany.* Having the shape of an arrowhead: *sagittate leaves.* [Latin *sagitta†,* arrow.]

sa·go (sā′gō) *n.* A powdery starch from the trunk of the sago palm that is used to thicken foods and stiffen textiles. [Malay *sāgū.*]

sago palm *n.* Any of various tropical Asian palm trees, especially of the genus *Metroxylon,* that yield sago.

sa·gua·ro (sə-gwä′rō, sə-wä′-) *n., pl.* **-ros. 1.** A very large cactus, *Carnegiea gigantea,* of the southwestern United States and northern Mexico, having upward-curving branches, white flowers, and edible red fruit. **2.** The fruit of this cactus. [Mexican Spanish.]

Saguaro National Monument. Area covering 31,457 hectares (78,644 acres) in southeastern Arizona, set aside to preserve the giant saguaros and other desert species found there.

Sa·hap·tin (sə-hăp′tĭn) *n., pl.* **-tins** or collectively **Sahaptin.** Also **Sha·hap·tin** (shə-). **1.** A member of a North American Indian people of Idaho, Washington, and Oregon. **2.** The language of this people.

Sa·ha·ra (sə-hâr′ə, -hä′rə). The largest desert in the world, covering *c.* 9,065,000 square kilometers (3,500,000 square miles) of North Africa. It extends from the Atlantic Ocean to the Red Sea and merges with the Sahel to the south. It has one of the harshest climates in the world, and much of it averages less than 125 millimeters (5 inches) of rain a year, has a daily temperature range of up to 30°C (86°F), and is swept by sandstorms. Stone deserts and tracts of bare rock and gravel cover some 70 percent of the Sahara, and sand dunes another 15 percent. Desert peoples include the Tuareg of the central mountains, those of largely Negroid descent in the Tibesti Massif, and people of mixed Berber and Arab origin. Of the Sahara's traditional inhabitants, some 60 percent farm in the oases, both natural ones and those irrigated by water pumped from great depths. The rest rely on the herding of goats, camels, and sheep. The desert is rich in minerals, including deposits of oil, gas, phosphates, manganese, zinc, iron ore, and salt. **—Sa·ha·ran** *adv.*

Sa·hel (sə-hāl′, -hēl′). Semidesert and dry grassland region fringing the south of the Sahara. It stretches across eight countries from Senegal eastward into Sudan. In the late 1960's and throughout the 1970's it suffered drought, with 12 consecutive years when the rainfall was below normal.

sa·hib (sä′ĭb) *n.* In India, a title of respect equivalent to *master* or *sir.* Used especially for European colonials. [Hindi *ṣāḥib,* master, lord, from Arabic, friend, companion, master.]

said (sĕd). Past tense and past participle of **say.**
~ *adj. Law.* Named or mentioned before; aforementioned.

sai·ga (sī′gə) *n.* A Eurasian antelope, *Saiga tatarica,* having a stubby, proboscislike nose. [Russian *saĭga,* from Chagatai *saigak.*]

Saigon. See **Ho Chi Minh City.**

sail (sāl) *n.* **1.** A length of triangular or rectangular fabric, as canvas, attached to a ship or boat to catch the wind and propel it. **2.** A sailing vessel. **3. a.** Sails collectively. **b.** Sailing vessels collectively. **4.** A trip or voyage in a sailing vessel. **5.** Something, as the blade of a windmill, resembling a sail in form or function.
~ *v.* **sailed, sailing, sails.** —*intr.* **1.** To move across the surface of water, especially by means of a sail. **2.** To travel by water in a vessel. **3.** To start out on a voyage or journey. **4.** To operate a sailing craft, especially for sport. **5.** To glide smoothly and easily: *skiers sailing down the slopes.* —*tr.* **1.** To navigate or manage (a vessel). **2.** To voyage upon or across (a body of water): *sail the Pacific.* **—sail into.** To attack or criticize vigorously. [Middle English *sail(le),* Old English *segl,* from Germanic *seglam* (unattested).]

sail·boat (sāl′bōt′) *n.* A boat propelled partly or wholly by sail.

sail·cloth (sāl′klôth′, -klŏth′) *n.* A strong fabric, as cotton canvas, suitable for making sails or tents.

sail·fish (sāl′fĭsh′) *n., pl.* **-fishes** or collectively **sailfish.** Any of various large marine fishes of the genus *Istiophorus,* with a spearlike upper jaw and a large, saillike dorsal fin.

sail·ing (sā′lĭng) *n.* **1.** The sport of sailing a vessel, especially a sailboat. **2.** The skill to operate and navigate a vessel; navigation. **3.** The departure or time of departure from a port.

sail·or (sā′lər) *n.* **1.** One who serves in a navy or works on a ship; especially, an ordinary seaman. **2.** One who travels by water. **3.** A low-crowned straw hat with a flat top and flat brim. [Variant of earlier *sailer,* from SAIL (verb).] **—sail·or·ly** *adj.*

sain·foin (sān′foin′, săn′-) *n.* A plant, *Onobrychis viciaefolia,* native to Eurasia, that has compound leaves and pink or white flowers and is often used as fodder. [French, from Old French, from Medieval Latin *sānum faenum,* "wholesome hay" : Latin *sānum, sānus,* healthy, whole + *faenum, fēnum,* hay.]

saint (sānt) *n.* **1.** *Abbr.* **S., St.** *Theology.* **a.** A person recognized, especially by canonization, as being entitled to public veneration and capable of interceding for people on earth. **b.** A person who has died and gone to heaven. **c. Saint.** A member of any of various religious groups; especially, a **Latter-Day Saint** *(see).* **2.** A very charitable, unselfish, or patient person.
~ *tr.v.* **sainted, sainting, saints.** To name, recognize, or venerate as a saint; canonize. [Middle English, from Old French, from Latin *sanctus,* sacred, from the past participle of *sancīre,* to sanctify.]

Saint. Entries not found under **Saint** may appear at **St.** Biographies of saints appear at the name of the individual saint; for example, for **Saint Paul,** see **Paul.**

Saint Ag·nes' Eve (ăg′nĭs, -nĭ-sĭz) *n.* The night of January 20th, when, according to legend, a woman will dream of her future husband. [After St. *Agnes* (died A.D. 304), Christian child martyr who was beheaded for refusing to marry.]

Saint Andrew's cross *n.* A cross shaped like the letter X.

Saint Anthony's cross *n.* A tau cross *(see).*

Saint Bernard *n.* A large, strong dog of a breed developed in Switzerland, having a thick brown and white coat and originally used by monks of the hospice of St. Bernard in the Swiss Alps to help patrol the snow-covered region for travelers in distress.

saint·dom (sānt′dəm) *n.* The condition or quality of being a saint.

Sainte-Beuve (săɴt-bœv′), **Charles Augustin** (1804–69). French writer. He is best known for his criticism, wide-ranging in interest, which encouraged the romantic movement.

saint·ed (sān′tĭd) *adj.* **1.** Being a saint; canonized. **2.** Of saintly character; holy.

Saint El·mo's fire (ĕl′mōz) *n.* A visible electric discharge emanating from a pointed object, as the mast of a ship or wing of an airplane, during an electrical storm. [After St. *Elmo* (died A.D. 303), patron saint of sailors.]

Saint-Ex·u·pé·ry (săɴ′tĕg-zü-pā-rē′), **Antoine de** (1900–44). French writer. His novels and his famous children's book, *Le Petit Prince* (1943), were inspired by his career as a pilot, particularly on the mail routes of North Africa and South America. He died on an air force mission in World War II.

Saint-Gau·dens (sānt-gô′dənz), **Augustus** (1848–1907). U.S. sculptor, born in Ireland. Brought to New York City as an infant and apprenticed to a cameo cutter at the age of 13, he studied art in New York, Paris, and Rome. Noted for his vivid, naturalistic memorials, he sculpted statues of David Farragut (1878–81), Abraham Lincoln (1887), and numerous other works.

Saint George's cross *n.* A red cross on a white background, as used in the British flag.

---

sail

COMBINING SAILS TO HARNESS THE POWER OF THE WIND
The triangular sail that revolutionized seagoing

Wind power has been used to drive sailing vessels since at least 3000 B.C., when Egyptian trading ships used square sails to supplement their oarsmen when the wind was behind them. The wind's energy was trapped in this way almost unaltered for 4,000 years. The square sail receives wind only from the rear, but can be angled to obtain maximum thrust. Sailing was revolutionized in the 9th century A.D. by the lateen sail, probably invented by Arab seamen. This triangular sail, slung fore and aft from the masthead on a loose-fitted boom, could accept the wind on either side. Some of its effectiveness was due to a principle unknown to its inventors—air passing over the leading edge of a billowing sail creates a vacuum in front of the sail, drawing it forward in the same way an airplane wing is lifted. The resulting airflow increases a ship's speed. The combination of lateen sails with square sails on three-masted ships, adopted by the British, Dutch, and Portuguese in the 15th and 16th centuries, was probably the crucial development that launched the great age of sail and exploration.

In the early 18th century the triangular headsail was introduced on large vessels. The steering wheel was being installed in ships by then and the greater degree of control it gave made it safer to sail close to the wind at speed, as the triangular headsails allowed.

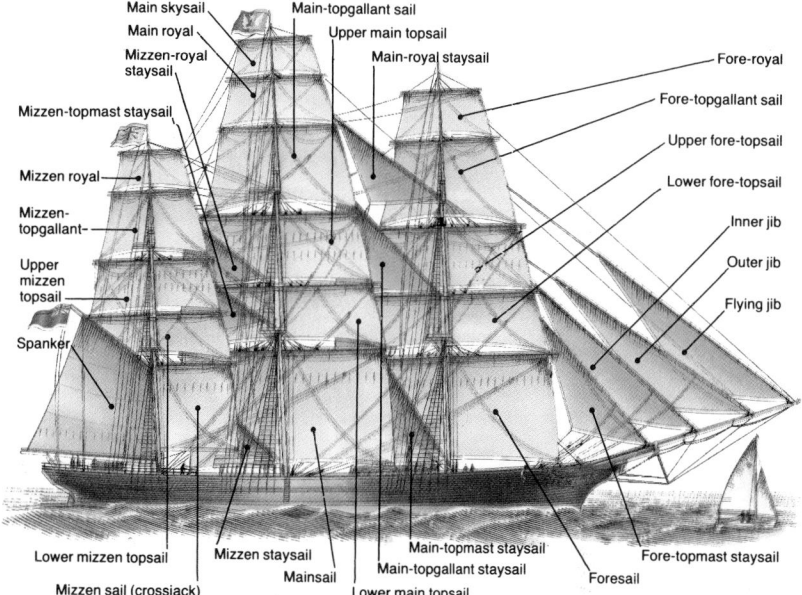

FULL-RIGGED SAILING SHIP *Once the lateen sail had been combined with the square sail, the might of the wind had been harnessed by man. Great ships, fitted with this typical clipper rigging, a mass of sails, masts, and shrouds, could race along with large cargoes for thousands of miles at speeds of about 15 knots (about 17 miles an hour), occasionally reaching 20 knots (just over 23 miles an hour).*

saint·hood (sānt'hŏŏd') n. **1.** The status, character, or condition of being a saint. **2.** Saints collectively.

Saint John (jŏn). City and port in New Brunswick, eastern Canada, at the mouth of the Saint John River. Founded by the French as a trading post (1635), it became the eastern terminus of the Canadian Pacific Railway. It has an ice-free port.

Saint John's wort (jŏnz) n. **1.** Any of various plants of the genus *Hypericum,* having yellow, five-petaled flowers with many stamens. **2.** A shrubby plant, the **rose of Sharon** (see). [After *Saint John* the Baptist; the plants were formerly gathered on St. John's Eve for magical and medicinal use.]

Saint-Just (săn'-zhüst'), **Louis Antoine Léon de** (1767–94). French politician and soldier. He was the Committee of Public Safety's military supervisor and led the French at Fleurus (1794), but was executed with Robespierre that same year.

Saint Lau·rent (săn' lô-rän'), **Yves** (1936–). French fashion designer. Becoming Dior's assistant at the age of 17, he eventually succeeded him but lost control of the fashion house in 1960. He subsequently founded (1962) his own house and has become one of the most important designers in the world.

saint·ly (sānt'lē) adj. **-lier, -liest.** Resembling, pertaining to, or befitting a saint. **—saint'li·ness** n.

Saint Nicholas. Santa Claus (see).

Saint Patrick's Day n. March 17, observed in honor of St. Patrick, the patron saint of Ireland.

saint·pau·li·a (sānt-pô'lē-ə) n. A plant, the **African violet** (see). [New Latin, after W. von *Saint Paul-Illaire* (died 1910), German soldier who discovered it.]

Saint-Saëns (săn-säns'), **(Charles) Camille** (1835–1921). French composer and critic. The lighthearted orchestral suite *Carnival of the Animals* (1922) is still his most popular work. As a critic, he championed Liszt, Wagner, and Berlioz. He wrote 12 operas, of which the most famous is *Samson and Delilah* (1877), 5 symphonies, and 5 piano concertos.

saint's day n. A day nominated by the church for the commemoration of a particular saint.

Saint-Si·mon (săn'sē-môn'), **Claude Henri de Rouvroy, Comte de** (1760–1825). French political philosopher. He envisaged an industrial state run by technocrats, in which poverty would be abolished and religion replaced by rationalism. His ideas greatly influenced the development of socialism, particularly in France.

Saint-Simon, Louis de Rouvroy, Duc de (1675–1755). French courtier and writer. His *Mémoires* for the years 1694 to 1723 provide a personal view of the court of Louis XIV.

Saint Val·en·tine's Day (văl'ən-tīnz') n. February 14, on which valentines are traditionally exchanged.

Sa·ïs (sā'ĭs). Ancient Egyptian city on the Nile delta; a capital of Lower Egypt in the 7th and 6th centuries B.C.

saith (sĕth, sā'ĭth). Archaic. Third person singular present indicative of **say.**

saithe (sāth, sāth) n. The **coalfish** (see). [Old Norse *seithr.*]

Sai·va (sī'və, shī'-) n. In Hinduism, a member of the cult of the god Shiva. [Sanskrit *śaiva-,* belonging to Shiva, from *śivaḥ,* Shiva.]

sake¹ (sāk) n. **1.** Purpose, motive, or end: *a quarrel only for the sake of argument.* **2.** Advantage; good: *for the sake of her health.* **3.** Personal benefit or interest; welfare: *for his own sake.* [Middle English *sake,* contention, lawsuit, guilt (the phrase "for the sake of" probably originated in legal usage), Old English *sacu,* lawsuit, from Germanic *sakō* (unattested), charge, accusation.]

sa·ke², sa·ki (sä'kĕ, -kē) n. A Japanese alcoholic drink made from fermented rice. [Japanese, "alcohol."]

sa·ker (sā'kər) n. A southern Eurasian falcon, *Falco cherrug,* having brown plumage and often trained for falconry. [Middle English *sagre,* from Old French *sacre,* from Arabic *şaqr.*]

Sa·kha·lin (săk'ə-lēn'). Island off the coast of the extreme eastern U.S.S.R., between the Sea of Okhotsk and the Sea of Japan. Sakhalin was colonized by Russia and Japan in the 18th and 19th centuries and was under joint control until 1875 and later from 1905 to 1945. The island has valuable coal and iron deposits.

Sa·kha·rov (sä'kə-rôf', -rŏv'), **Andrei Dimitrievich** (1921–). Soviet physicist. After working on nuclear power in the 1940's and 1950's, he became an outspoken critic of his government's part in the arms race. He was exiled to Gorky. In 1975 he was awarded the Nobel Peace Prize.

sa·ki¹ (sä'kē, săk'ē) n. Any small South American monkey belonging to either of two genera, *Pithecia* or *Chiroptes,* and having curly hair and a long, bushy tail. [French, from Tupi *saqi.*]

saki². Variant of **sake** (liquor).

Saki. See H.H. Munro.

Sakkara. See Saqqara.

Sakta. Variant of **Shakta.**

Sakti. Variant of **Shakti.**

sal (săl) n. Salt. Used chiefly in compounds: *sal volatile.* [Latin *sāl.*]

sa·laam (sə-läm') n. **1.** A Muslim salutation or ceremonial greeting performed by bowing low while placing the right palm on the forehead. **2.** In the East, a respectful or ceremonial greeting. ~v. **salaamed, -laaming, -laams.** —tr. To greet with a salaam. —intr. To perform a salaam. [Arabic *salām,* "peace" (part of *assalām 'alaikum,* "peace to you").]

sal·a·ble, also **sale·a·ble** (sā'lə-bəl) adj. **1.** Offered or suitable for sale. **2.** Easily sold. **—sal·a·bil·i·ty** (sā'lə-bĭl'ə-tē) n.

sa·la·cious (sə-lā'shəs) adj. **1.** Stimulating to the sexual imagination; especially, morbidly appealing to lust: *salacious writing.*

salamander *Giant salamanders —native to China and Japan—can grow to about 1.5 meters (5 feet) in length. The smaller European type (above) is sometimes called the fire salamander, from an old belief that it could withstand flames.*

2. Lustful; lecherous. [Latin *salāx* (stem *salāc-*), fond of leaping (said of male animals), lustful, from *salīre,* to leap.] **—sa·la·cious·ly** adv. **—sa·la·cious·ness, sa·lac·i·ty** (sə-lăs'ə-tē) n.

sal·ad (săl'əd) n. **1.** A cold dish typically consisting of green, leafy raw vegetables, such as lettuce, often with radish, cucumber, tomato, tossed with a dressing. **2.** A cold dish of chopped fruit, vegetables, meat, fish, eggs, or other food, usually prepared with a dressing, as mayonnaise. **3.** A course consisting of salad. **4.** A green vegetable, especially lettuce, or an herb eaten raw or used in salad. [Middle English *salade,* from Old French, from Provençal *salada,* from Vulgar Latin *salāta* (unattested), from the feminine past participle of *salāre* (unattested), to salt, from Latin *sāl,* salt.]

salad bar n. A counter in a restaurant from which customers may serve themselves various salad ingredients and dressings.

salad burnet n. A short perennial plant, *Sanguisorba minor,* with compound leaves sometimes used in salads and petalless flowers borne in round heads.

salad days pl.n. A time of youth, innocence, and inexperience. [From Shakespeare: "my salad days when I was green in judgment, cold in blood" (*Antony and Cleopatra,* Act 1, scene 5).]

salad dressing n. A sauce, as of mayonnaise or oil and vinegar, served on salad.

Sal·a·din (săl'ə-dĭn) (c. 1137–93). Kurdish general and Sultan of Egypt. As a vizier he conquered Egypt (1169), founded a dynasty (1175), conquered Syria, and took Jerusalem (1187), thereby precipitating the Third Crusade. He became renowned throughout Islam and Christendom for his chivalry and generosity to the poor of all faiths.

Sal·a·man·ca (săl'ə-măng'kə). Capital of Salamanca province in central Spain, on the Tormes River. Conquered by Hannibal (220 B.C.), it prospered as a cultural center following the founding of its university (1230), which is the oldest in Spain. The city's many historic sites include the old university buildings, a 12th-century cathedral, and a fine 18th-century plaza.

sal·a·man·der (săl'ə-măn'dər) n. **1.** Any of various small, lizardlike amphibians of the order Caudata, having porous, scaleless skin and four legs that are often weak or rudimentary. **2. a.** A mythical creature, generally resembling a lizard, once thought capable of living in or withstanding fire. **b.** In the theory of Paracelsus, an elemental spirit supposed to live in fire. **3.** An object, such as a poker, used in fire or capable of withstanding heat. **4.** Metallurgy. A mass of solidified material, largely metallic, left in a blast-furnace hearth. **5.** A portable stove, especially one used to heat or dry buildings under construction. [Middle English *salamandre,* from Old French, from Latin *salamandra,* from Greek *salamandra†.*] **—sal·a·man·drine** (săl'ə-măn'drĭn) adj.

sa·la·mi (sə-lä'mē) n. A highly spiced and salted sausage, either hard or soft in consistency, that originated in Italy. [Italian, plural of *salame,* "salted pork," from *salare,* to salt, from Vulgar Latin *salāre* (unattested). See **salad.**]

Sal·a·mis (săl'ə-mĭs). Greek island in the Aegean Sea west of Athens. The Battle of Salamis (480 B.C.) was a major Greek naval victory over the Persians. It was fought in the narrow straits that separate the island from the coast of Attica, allowing the Greeks' smaller ships to overcome the Persians' superior numbers.

sal ammoniac n. A chemical, **ammonium chloride** (see). [Middle English *sal armoniak,* from Medieval Latin *sāl armōniacus,* from Latin *sāl ammōniacus* : SAL + AMMONIAC.]

sal·a·ried (săl'ə-rēd, săl'rēd) adj. Earning or yielding a regular salary: *a salaried worker; a salaried job.*

sal·a·ry (săl'ə-rē, săl'rē) n., pl. **-ries.** A fixed amount of money, usually for nonmanual services, paid to a person on a regular, often weekly or monthly basis. Compare **wage.** [Middle English *salarie,* from Norman French, from Old French *salaire,* from Latin *salārium,* originally "money given to Roman soldiers to buy salt," from *salārius,* of salt, from *sāl,* salt.]

Sa·la·zar (săl'ə-zär', sä'lə-), **Antonio de Oliveira** (1889–1970). Portuguese politician. Following a military coup, he twice served as finance minister (1926, 1928) and in 1932 became prime minister. His financial policies stabilized the country but repressed opposition, and his attempts to retain Portugal's colonies led to many wars and much international criticism. His dictatorship lasted until 1968.

sal·chow (săl'kôf', -kō', -kou') n. A jump in figure skating performed by taking off from the back inside edge of one skate, making a complete turn in the air, and landing on the back outside edge of the other skate. [After Ulrich *Salchow* (1877–1949), Swedish skater.]

sale (sāl) n. **1. a.** The exchange of goods or services for an amount of money or its equivalent. **b.** The act or an instance of selling. **2.** An opportunity for selling or being sold; demand. **3.** Availability for purchase: *a store where pets are for sale; furniture on sale.* **4.** A selling of goods to the highest bidder; an auction. **5.** A special disposal of goods at lowered prices, especially a seasonal one held to clear stock. **6. sales. a.** Activities and transactions entailed in the selling and marketing of goods or services: *She's head of sales.* Also used adjectivally: *a sales conference.* **b.** Gross receipts of a business. [Middle English *sale,* Old English *sala,* from Old Norse.]

saleable. Variant of **salable.**

Sa·lem¹ (sā'ləm). City of northeastern Massachusetts, on an inlet of Massachusetts Bay. Salem was the site of the witchcraft trials of 1692, and its port was a center for the China trade and a privateering base in the American Revolution and the War of 1812. Its many historical landmarks, including the House of Seven Gables immortalized by Nathaniel Hawthorne, are tourist attractions.

Salem². Capital of Oregon, in the northwestern part of the state on the Willamette River. Founded (1840–41) by Methodist missionaries, it became the capital of Oregon Territory in 1851 and remained the capital when Oregon became a state in 1859.

sal·ep (săl'əp, sə-lĕp') *n.* A starchy meal ground from the dried roots of various Old World orchids of the genera *Orchis* and *Eulophia*, used for food and formerly as a medicine. [French or Spanish, from Turkish *sālep*, from Arabic *saḥleb*, variant of *khasyu aththa'lab*, "the fox's testicles," a kind of orchid.]

sal·er·a·tus (săl'ə-rā'təs) *n.* Sodium or potassium bicarbonate used as a leavening agent; baking soda. [New Latin *sal aeratus*, "aerated salt."]

Sa·ler·no (sə-lûr'nō, -lĕr'nō). Port in Campania, southwestern Italy, capital of Salerno province. Originally a Roman colony, the town came under Norman rule after 1076. During the Norman period a magnificent cathedral was founded, and Salerno won fame for its medical school, around which one of Europe's earliest universities developed.

sales check *n.* A slip of paper given by a store to a customer as a record or receipt of a purchase or sale.

sales·clerk (sālz'klûrk') *n.* A person employed to sell goods in a store.

sales·girl (sālz'gûrl') *n.* A saleswoman.

Sa·le·sian (sə-lē'zhən, sā-) *n.* A member of the Society of St. Francis of Sales, a Roman Catholic order founded in Turin in 1845 and dedicated chiefly to education and missionary work. —**Sa·le·sian** *adj.*

sales·la·dy (sālz'lā'dē) *n., pl.* **-dies.** A saleswoman.

sales·man (sālz'mən) *n., pl.* **-men** (-mĭn). A man employed to sell merchandise in a store or in a designated territory.

sales·man·ship (sālz'mən-shĭp') *n.* **1.** The work or occupation of a salesman. **2.** Skill or ability in selling, as by persuasive speaking.

sales·per·son (sālz'pûr'sən) *n.* A salesman or saleswoman.

sales·room (sālz'rōōm', -rŏŏm') *n.* A room in which articles to be sold and especially auctioned are put on display.

sales talk *n.* Argument or persuasive speaking intended to induce a person to purchase a product or service or accept an idea or suggestion. Also called "sales pitch."

sales tax *n.* A tax levied as a percentage of the retail price of goods that is collected by the retailer.

sales·wom·an (sālz'wŏŏm'ən) *n., pl.* **-women** (-wĭm'ĭn). A woman employed to sell merchandise in a store or in a designated territory.

sali– *prefix.* Indicates salt; for example, **salimeter.** [Latin *sāl* (stem *sali-*), salt.]

Sa·li·an (sā'lē-ən, sāl'yən) *n.* A member of a tribe of Franks who settled in the Rhine region of the Netherlands in the 4th century A.D. [Late Latin *Saliī†*, the Salian Franks.] —**Sa·li·an** *adj.*

sal·ic (săl'ĭk) *adj.* Pertaining to or designating minerals, such as quartz and the feldspars, containing large amounts of silica and alumina. [S(ILICA) + AL(UMINA) + -IC.]

Sa·lic (să'lĭk, săl'ĭk) *adj.* Also **Sa·lique** (sā'lĭk, săl'ĭk, sā-lēk', sā-). **1.** Of or pertaining to the Salians. **2.** Of or pertaining to the Salic law or to the legal code of the Salians. [Old French *salique*, from Medieval Latin *Salicus*, from Late Latin *Saliī†*, the Salian Franks.]

sal·i·cin (săl'ə-sĭn) *n.* A bitter glucoside, $C_{13}H_{18}O_7$, obtained mainly from the bark of poplar and willow trees and formerly used as an analgesic and antipyretic. [French *salicine* : Latin *salix* (stem *salic-*), willow + -IN.]

Salic law A law, thought to derive from the code of laws of the Salians, prohibiting a woman from succession to the throne.

sa·lic·y·late (sə-lĭs'ə-lāt', -lĭt, săl'ə-sĭl'ĭt) *n.* A salt or ester of salicylic acid. [SALICYL(IC ACID) + -ATE.]

sal·i·cyl·ic acid (săl'ə-sĭl'ĭk) *n.* A white crystalline acid, $C_7H_6O_3$, used in making aspirin, as a preservative, and in the external treatment of certain skin conditions such as eczema. [French *salicyle*, the radical of salicylic acid : SALIC(IN) + -YL.]

sal·i·cyl·ism (săl'ə-sĭl'ĭz'əm, sə-lĭs'ə-lĭz'-) *n.* Poisoning caused by an overdose of a drug such as aspirin containing salicylic acid, characterized by headache, dizziness, vomiting, collapse, and, in many cases, kidney failure. [SALICYL(IC ACID) + -ISM.]

sa·li·ence (sā'lē-əns, săl'yəns) *n.* Also **sa·li·en·cy** (sā'lē-ən-sē, săl'yən-). **1.** The quality or condition of being salient. **2.** A pronounced feature or part; highlight.

sa·li·ent (sā'lē-ənt, săl'yənt) *adj.* **1.** Projecting or jutting beyond a line or surface; protruding: *a salient angle.* **2.** Strikingly conspicuous; prominent: *the salient point in her lecture.* **3.** *Zoology.* Springing; jumping: *salient tree toads.*

~*n.* **1.** The part of a battle line, trench, fortification, or other military defense that projects closest to the enemy. **2.** A projecting angle or part. [Latin *saliēns* (stem *salient-*), present participle of *salīre*, to leap, jump.] —**sa·li·ent·ly** *adv.* —**sa·li·ent·ness** *n.*

sa·li·en·tian (sā'lē-ĕn'shən) *n.* An amphibian of the order Salientia (formerly Anura or Batrachia), which includes the frogs and toads. Also called "anuran." [New Latin *Salientia*, from Latin, neuter plural of *saliēns*, leaping, SALIENT.]

Sa·lie·ri (sä-lyâr'ē, säl-) **Antonio** (1750–1825). Italian composer. A teacher of Beethoven, Schubert, and Liszt, he became (1788) composer to the imperial court of Austria. He was more popular (but less talented) than his rival, Mozart, who accused him of trying to poison him.

sa·lif·er·ous (sə-lĭf'ər-əs) *adj.* Containing or yielding salt. [SALI- + -FEROUS.]

sal·i·fy (săl'ə-fī') *tr.v.* **-fied, -fying, -fies. 1.** To form or convert into a salt, as by chemical combination. **2.** To mix or impregnate with a salt. [French *salifier* : SALI- + -FY.] —**sal·i·fi·a·ble** *adj.* —**sal·i·fi·ca·tion** *n.*

sa·lim·e·ter (sə-lĭm'ə-tər) *n. Chemistry.* A specially graduated hydrometer that indicates directly the percentage of a salt in a salt solution. [SALI- + -METER.] —**sal·i·met·ric** (săl'ə-mĕt'rĭk) *adj.* —**sa·lim·e·try** (sə-lĭm'ə-trē) *n.*

sa·li·na (sə-lī'nə, -lē'nə) *n.* A salt marsh, spring, pond, or lake. [Spanish, from Latin *salīnae*, salt pits, from *salīnus*, SALINE.]

sa·line (sā'lēn, -lĭn') *adj.* **1.** Of, pertaining to, or containing salt; salty. **2.** Of or pertaining to mineral salts having the characteristics of common salt.

~*n.* **1.** Any salt of the alkali or alkaline-earth metals, used in medicine as a cathartic. **2.** A saline solution, especially one that is isotonic with blood and is used in medicine. In this sense, also called "physiological saline." [Middle English *salyne*, from Latin *salīnus*, from *sāl*, salt.] —**sa·lin·i·ty** (sə-lĭn'ə-tē) *n.*

Sal·in·ger (săl'ən-jər) **J(erome) D(avid)** (1919–). U.S. author. He achieved recognition for his novel about adolescence, *Catcher in the Rye* (1951). His other works concentrate mainly on the lives and times of the Glass family; these stories include *Raise High the Roofbeam, Carpenters,* and *Seymour: An Introduction* (1963).

sal·i·nom·e·ter (săl'ə-nŏm'ə-tər) *n.* Any of various instruments, especially a salimeter, used to measure the amount of salt in a solution. [SALIN(E) + -METER.] —**sal·i·no·met·ric** (săl'ə-nə-mĕt'rĭk) *adj.* —**sal·i·nom·e·try** (săl'ə-nŏm'ə-trē) *n.*

Salique. Variant of Salic.

Salis·bur·y¹ (sôlz'bĕr'ē, -brē). City in Wiltshire, southeastern England, at the confluence of the Avon and Wylye rivers. Its cathedral (1220–58) is a magnificent example of early English architecture, with the tallest spire in England (123 meters; 404 feet). The town, a market center, attracts many tourists.

Salisbury². See Harare.

Salisbury Plain. Chalk plateau in Wiltshire, north of Salisbury in southern England. The area is rich in prehistoric remains, which include the megalithic monument of Stonehenge.

Sa·lish (sā'lĭsh) *n.* Also **Sa·lish·an** (-lĭ-shən). **1.** A family of North American Indian languages of the northwestern United States and British Columbia. **2.** The Indians speaking languages of the Salish family. —**Sa·lish·an** *adj.*

sa·li·va (sə-lī'və) *n.* The watery, tasteless liquid mixture of salivary and oral mucous gland secretions that lubricates chewed food, moistens the oral walls, and contains the enzyme ptyalin, which functions in the predigestion of starches. [Latin *salīva†*.]

sal·i·vary (săl'ə-vĕr'ē) *adj.* **1.** Of, pertaining to, or producing saliva. **2.** Of or pertaining to a salivary gland.

salivary gland *n.* A gland that secretes saliva; especially, any of three pairs of large glands, the parotid, submandibular, and sublingual, the secretions of which enter the mouth and mingle in saliva.

sal·i·vate (săl'ə-vāt') *v.* **-vated, -vating, -vates.** —*intr.* To secrete or produce saliva. —*tr.* To produce excessive salivation in (a person or animal). [Latin *salīvāre*, to spit out, from *salīva*, SALIVA.]

sal·i·va·tion (săl'ə-vā'shən) *n.* **1.** The act or process of secreting saliva. **2.** An abnormally abundant flow of saliva.

Salk (sôlk, sôk), **Jonas Edward** (1914–). U.S. microbiologist. In 1954 he developed a vaccine against poliomyelitis, a dread disease that had struck more than 50,000 and killed some 3,300 people the preceding year. Mass inoculation of schoolchildren proved by the end of 1955 that the vaccine was effective on a wide scale.

Salk vaccine *n.* A vaccine made from a deactivated virus, used to immunize actively against poliomyelitis. [After Jonas SALK.]

sal·let (săl'ĭt) *n.* A light medieval helmet, sometimes fitted with a visor and with a piece at the back to protect the neck. [Middle English *sal(l)et*, from Old French *salade*, from Old Italian *celata*, perhaps from Vulgar Latin *caelāta* (unattested), from Latin, feminine past participle of *caelāre*, to engrave (as on the metal of a helmet), from *caelum*, chisel.]

sal·low¹ (săl'ō) *adj.* **-lower, -lowest.** Of a pale, sickly yellowish hue or complexion.

~*tr.v.* **sallowed, -lowing, -lows.** To make sallow. [Middle English *salowe*, Old English *salo*, dusky, from Germanic.] —**sal·low·ish** *adj.* —**sal·low·ly** *adv.* —**sal·low·ness** *n.*

sallow² *n.* Any of several of the broader-leaved European willows, especially the three common species *Salix caprea, S. cinerea,* and *S. aurita.* [Middle English *salwe,* Old English *sealh,* from Germanic.]

Sal·lust (săl'əst), Latin name Gaius Sallustius Crispus (c. 86–34 B.C.). Roman politician and historian. He became governor of Numidia, but resigned after being implicated in corruption. He then turned to historical writing, producing his well-known accounts of the Catilinarian conspiracy and the Jugurthine War.

sal·ly¹ (săl'ē) *intr.v.* **-lied, -lying, -lies. 1.** To rush or leap forth suddenly; especially, to issue suddenly from a defensive or besieged position to make an attack upon an enemy. **2.** To set out on a trip or excursion: *sallied forth to see the world.*

~*n., pl.* **sallies. 1.** A sudden rush forward; a leap. **2.** An assault from a defensive position; a sortie. **3.** A sudden emergence, as from rest to action or from silence to comment; an outburst. **4.** A quick witticism or bantering remark; a quip. **5.** A venturing forth; an excursion or jaunt. —See Synonyms at joke. [Old French *saillie*, a sally, from the feminine past participle of *salir, saillir,* to leap or rush forward, from Latin *salīre,* to leap.]

sally² *n. Chiefly British.* The woolen covering of the end of a bell-

salmon *Salmo salar (above) is the Atlantic salmon; several other species are native to the Pacific. Salmon spend most of their lives at sea, but they return to rivers to spawn. Pacific salmon die after spawning; the Atlantic salmon, however, often returns to the sea and spawns again in a year or two.*

salsify *The long, fleshy white root of this vegetable plant has an oysterlike flavor.*

rope. [Perhaps from SALLY, referring to the sudden movement of the bell.]

Sal·ly Lunn (săl′ē lŭn′) *n.* A round, light tea cake similar to a muffin. [Perhaps from the name of a girl who sold them in Bath, England, about 1800.]

sal·ma·gun·di (săl′mə-gŭn′dē) *n.* **1.** A salad of chopped meat, anchovies, eggs, and onions, often arranged in rows on lettuce and served with vinegar and oil. **2.** A mixture or assortment; a potpourri. [French *salmigondis, salmigondin*†.]

sal·mi, sal·mis (săl′mē) *n.* A highly spiced dish consisting of a roasted game bird minced and stewed in wine. [French *salmis,* short for *salmigondis,* SALMAGUNDI.]

salm·on (săm′ən, să′mən) *n., pl.* **-mons** or collectively **salmon. 1. a.** Any of various large food and game fishes of the genera *Salmo* and *Oncorhynchus,* of northern waters, characteristically swimming from salt to fresh water to spawn and having delicate pinkish flesh. **b.** *Australian.* Any of various similar unrelated fishes, such as the barramunda. **2.** Salmon pink. [Middle English *samoun, salmon,* from Norman French, from Old French *saumon,* from Latin *salmo* (stem *salmon-*), probably akin to *salīre,* to leap.] **—salm·on** *adj.*

salm·on·ber·ry (săm′ən-bĕr′ē, să′mən-) *n., pl.* **-ries. 1.** A prickly shrub, *Rubus spectabilis,* of western North America, bearing fragrant reddish flowers. **2.** The edible salmon-colored raspberrylike fruit of the salmonberry.

sal·mo·nel·la (săl′mə-nĕl′ə) *n., pl.* **-nellae** (-nĕl′ē) or **-nellas** or **-nella. 1.** Any of various rod-shaped bacteria of the genus *Salmonella,* many of which are pathogenic. **2.** Salmonellosis. [New Latin, after Daniel E. *Salmon* (1850–1914), U.S. veterinarian.]

sal·mo·nel·lo·sis (săl′mə-nĕ-lō′sĭs) *n.* Food poisoning caused by salmonella. [SALMONELL(A) + -OSIS.]

salm·o·noid (săm′ə-noid′, săl′mə-) *adj.* **1.** Resembling or characteristic of a salmon. **2.** Of or belonging to the family Salmonidae, which includes the salmon, trout, and whitefishes.
~n. A salmonoid fish.

salmon pink *n.* A yellowish pink.

salmon trout *n.* Any of various salmonlike fish, especially the sea trout.

sal·ol (săl′ôl′, -ōl′) *n.* A white crystalline powder, $C_{13}H_{10}O_3$, derived from salicylic acid and used in the manufacture of plastics and sun-tan oils and medicinally as an analgesic and antipyretic. [Originally a trademark : SAL(ICYLIC ACID) + -OL.]

Sa·lo·me (sə-lō′mē, săl′ə-mā′). Daughter of Herodias and niece of Herod Antipas, who granted her the head of John the Baptist in return for her dancing. Matthew 14:6-11.

sa·lon (sə-lŏn′, săl′ŏn′, să-lôɴ′) *n.* **1.** A large room, as a drawing room, used for receiving and entertaining guests, as one in a French mansion. **2.** A periodic gathering of social, artistic, or intellectual distinction customarily held at the residence of a well-known person. **3.** A hall or gallery for the exhibition of works of art. **4.** *Often* **Salon.** Any of various exhibitions of works by living artists held annually in France. **5.** A commercial establishment offering a product or service related to fashion: *a beauty salon; a dress salon.* [French, from Italian *salone,* augmentative of *sala,* a hall, room, from Germanic.]

Salonika. See **Thessaloniki.**

sa·loon (sə-lo͞on′) *n.* **1.** A large room or hall for receptions, public entertainment, or exhibitions. **2. a.** A large, comfortable social lounge for passengers on a ship. **b.** The officers' dining and social room on a cargo ship. **3.** *Chiefly British.* A sedan automobile. **4.** A place where alcoholic drinks are sold and drunk; tavern. [French *salon,* SALON.]

sa·loop (sə-lo͞op′) *n.* A hot drink, formerly used medicinally, made from salep, sassafras, or similar aromatic herbs. [Variant of SALEP.]

Salop. See **Shropshire.**

salp (sălp) *n.* Also **sal·pa** (săl′pə). Any of various free-swimming primitive chordates of the genus *Salpa,* of warm seas, having a translucent, somewhat flattened, keglike body. [New Latin *salpa,* from Latin, a kind of stockfish, from Greek *salpē*†.] **—sal·pi·form** (săl′pə-fôrm′) *adj.*

sal·pi·glos·sis (săl′pə-glŏs′ĭs) *n.* Any of various plants of the genus *Salpiglossis,* especially those grown as garden ornamentals for their showy, variously colored tubular flowers. [New Latin, "trumpet-tongue," irregularly from Greek *salpinx* (stem *salping-*), trumpet + *glōssa,* tongue.]

sal·pin·gec·to·my (săl′pĭn-jĕk′tə-mē) *n., pl.* **-mies.** The surgical removal of a Fallopian tube. [New Latin *salpinx* (stem *salping-*), SALPINX + -ECTOMY.]

sal·pin·gi·tis (săl′pĭn-jī′tĭs) *n.* *Pathology.* Inflammation of a Fallopian or Eustachian tube. [New Latin *salpinx* (stem *salping-*), SALPINX + -ITIS.]

sal·pinx (săl′pĭngks) *n., pl.* **salpinges** (săl-pĭn′jēz). **1.** The Fallopian tube. **2.** The Eustachian tube. [New Latin, from Greek *salpinx*†, trumpet.] **—sal·pin·gi·an** (săl-pĭn′jē-ən, -jən) *adj.*

sal·sa (säl′sə) *n.* **1.** A type of music of Latin-American origin, combining elements of rock and jazz. **2.** A dance performed to this music. [American Spanish, from Spanish, SAUCE.]

sal·si·fy (săl′sə-fē, -fī′) *n.* **1.** A plant, *Tragopogon porrifolius,* native to Europe, having grasslike leaves, purple flowers, and an edible taproot. **2.** The oyster-flavored root of this plant, eaten as a vegetable. Also called "vegetable oyster," "oyster plant." [French *salsifis,* from obsolete Italian *salsifica*†.]

sal soda *n.* A hydrated sodium carbonate used as a general cleanser.

salt (sôlt) *n.* **1.** A colorless or white crystalline solid, chiefly sodium chloride, extensively used as a food seasoning and preservative. **2.** A chemical compound formed by replacing all or part of the hydrogen atoms of an acid with one or more metal ions or other positive ions from a base. **3.** *Often* **salts.** Any of various mineral salts used as a laxative or cathartic, as **Epsom salts** or **Glauber's salts** *(both of which see).* **4. salts. Smelling salts** *(see).* **5.** An element that gives flavor, piquancy, or zest. **6.** Sharp, lively wit; pungency of expression. **7.** *Informal.* A sailor, especially when old or experienced. **8.** A saltshaker or saltcellar. **—salt of the earth.** A very small group of persons regarded as being admirable and worthy of imitation. **—with a grain of salt.** With reservations concerning truth or accuracy; skeptically. **—worth one's salt.** Worthy of continued support or sustenance: *Any plumber worth his salt could repair that leak.*
~adj. **1.** Tasting of, containing, or filled with salt; salty. **2.** Preserved in salt or a salt solution. **3. a.** Flooded with sea water. **b.** Found in or near such a flooded area: *salt grasses.* **4.** Sharp or pungent.
~tr.v. **salted, salting, salts. 1.** To add salt to; treat, season, or sprinkle with salt. **2.** To cure or preserve by treating with salt or a salt solution. **3.** To provide salt for (deer or cattle, for example). **4.** To add zest or liveliness to; season: *salt a lecture with anecdotes.* **5.** To give an appearance of value to by fraudulent means; especially, to place valuable minerals in (a mine, for example) for the purpose of deceiving. **—salt away.** To put aside (money, for example); save. **—salt out.** To separate (a dissolved substance) by adding a salt to the solution to increase the number of ions. [Middle English *salt,* Old English *sealt.*] **—salt·ish** *adj.* **—salt·ness** *n.*

SALT (sôlt) *n.* Strategic Arms Limitation Talks.

salt-and-pep·per (sôlt′ən-pĕp′ər) *adj.* Pepper-and-salt.

sal·tant (săl′tənt, sôl′-) *adj.* Jumping or dancing. [Latin *saltāns* (stem *saltant-*), present participle of *saltāre,* to leap, frequentative of *salīre* (past participle *saltus*), to jump.]

sal·ta·rel·lo (săl′tə-rĕl′ō, sôl′-) *n., pl.* **-rellos** or **-relli** (-rĕl′ē). **1.** A lively Italian dance with a skipping step at the beginning of each measure. **2.** Music for this dance, generally in triple or sextuple time. [Italian, from *saltare,* to leap, from Latin *saltāre.* See **saltant.**]

sal·ta·tion (săl-tā′shən, sôl-) *n.* **1.** The act of leaping, jumping, or dancing. **2.** An abrupt, discontinuous movement, transition, or development. **3.** *Biology.* Abrupt variation within a species, usually caused by mutation. [Latin *saltātiō* (stem *saltātiōn-*), from *saltātus,* past participle of *saltāre,* to leap. See **saltant.**]

sal·ta·to·ri·al (săl′tə-tôr′ē-əl, -tōr′ē-əl, sôl′-) *adj.* **1.** Of or relating to leaping or dancing. **2.** *Zoology.* Adapted for or characterized by leaping.

sal·ta·to·ry (săl′tə-tôr′ē, -tōr′ē, sôl′-) *adj.* **1.** Of, pertaining to, or adapted for leaping or dancing. **2.** Proceeding by leaps, hops, or abrupt movements. [Latin *saltātōrius,* from *saltātus,* past participle of *saltāre,* to leap. See **saltant.**]

salt·box (sôlt′bŏks′) *n.* A frame house with two stories in front and one in back and a roof with a long rear slope.

salt cake *n.* Impure sodium sulfate, used in making paper pulp, soaps and detergents, glass, ceramic glazes, and dyes.

salt·cel·lar (sôlt′sĕl′ər) A small dish for holding and dispensing salt. [Variant (influenced by CELLAR) of Middle English *salt saler* : SALT + *saler,* saltcellar, from Old French *saliere,* from Latin *salārius,* of salt, from *sāl,* salt.]

salt dome *n.* *Geology.* A dome-shaped formation in stratified rock with a core of salt. Oil and gas are often found in association with salt domes.

salt·er (sôl′tər) *n.* **1.** A person who manufactures or sells salt. **2.** A person who treats meat, fish, or other foods with salt.

salt·ern (sôl′tərn) *n.* **1.** A building or place of salt manufacture; a saltworks. **2.** A series of saltwater pools producing salt by natural evaporation. [Ultimately from Old English *sealtærn, sealtern* : *sealt,* SALT + *ærn, ern,* house.]

salt flat *n.* A wide, flat stretch of country that has very salty soil owing to the evaporation of a body of water formerly present.

salt glaze *n.* A glaze given to stoneware by burning salt in the kiln when the ware is fired. **—salt-glaze** (sôlt′glāz′) *v.*

salt grass *n.* Any of various grasses, such as those of the genus *Distichlis,* that grow in salt marshes and alkaline regions.

sal·ti·grade (săl′tĭ-grād′, sôl′-) *adj.* Adapted for or proceeding by leaping. Said of certain insects and spiders. [New Latin *Saltigradae,* former designation for saltigrade spiders : Latin *saltus,* a leap, from the past participle of *salīre,* to leap + *gradī,* to step.]

sal·tine (sôl-tēn′) *n.* A thin, crisp cracker sprinkled with coarse salt.

sal·tire (săl′tīr′, sôl′-) *n.* *Heraldry.* An ordinary in the shape of a St. Andrew's cross, formed by the crossing of a bend and a bend sinister. [Middle English *sawturoure, sawtire,* from Old French *sau(l)toir,* originally a cross-shaped stile that kept cattle from straying but that people could jump over, from *sau(l)ter,* to jump, from Latin *saltāre.* See **saltant.**]

Salt Lake City. Capital of Utah, in the north-central part of the state near the Great Salt Lake. Founded by a party of Mormons led by Brigham Young, it is today the headquarters of the Mormon Church.

salt lick *n.* **1.** A natural deposit of exposed salt that animals lick. **2.** A block of salt or an artificial medicated saline preparation set out for cattle, sheep, or deer to lick.

salt marsh *n.* Low coastal grassland frequently inundated by the tide. Also called "salt meadow," "marsh."

Sal·ton Sea (sôl′tən). Shallow salt lake, 958 square kilometers (370 square miles), in southeastern California. It was formed by the flooding of the Colorado River (1905-06) into Salton Sink, a depression c. 71 meters (232 feet) below sea level.

salt pan n. **1.** A depression in the ground from which sea water evaporates to leave a salt deposit. **2.** A large vessel used to make salt by evaporating sea water.

salt·pe·ter (sôlt′pē′tər) n. Also chiefly British **salt·pe·tre.** **1.** Potassium nitrate (see). **2.** Sodium nitrate (see). [Variant of earlier salpetre, from Middle English, from Old French, from Medieval Latin salpetra, probably "salt rock" (so called because it appears as a saltlike crust on rocks) : Latin sāl, salt + petra, rock, from Greek.]

salt·shak·er (sôlt′shā′kər) n. A container with a perforated top for sprinkling table salt.

sal·tus (săl′təs, sôl′-) n., pl. **-tuses.** A sudden break in a sequence, as in the logical steps in an argument. [Latin, "leap."]

salt·wa·ter (sôlt′wô′tər, -wŏt′ər) adj. Of, pertaining to, consisting of, or inhabiting salt water.

salt·works (sôlt′wûrks′) pl.n. Used with a singular or plural verb. A place where salt is manufactured commercially.

salt·wort (sôlt′wûrt′, -wôrt′) n. **1.** Any of several plants of the genus Salsola; especially, S. kali, native to the Old World, having stiff, prickly leaves and growing on sandy seashores. Also called "glasswort," "kali." **2.** A plant, the **sea milkwort** (see).

salt·y (sôl′tē) adj. **-ier, -iest. 1.** Pertaining to, containing, or seasoned with salt. **2.** Suggestive of the sea or sailing life. **3. a.** Piquant. **b.** Witty and pungent; racy. —**salt·i·ly** adv. —**salt·i·ness** n.

sa·lu·bri·ous (sə-loo′brē-əs) adj. Conducive or favorable to health or well-being; wholesome: a salubrious climate. [Latin salubris, from salus, health.] —**sa·lu·bri·ous·ly** adv. —**sa·lu·bri·ous·ness, sa·lu·bri·ty** (sə-loo′brə-tē) n.

sa·lu·ki (sə-loo′kē) n., pl. **-kis.** A tall, slender dog of an ancient breed developed in Arabia and Egypt, having a smooth, silky, variously colored coat. [Arabic salūqīy, (dog) of Salūq, an ancient southern Arabian city.]

sal·u·tar·y (săl′yə-tĕr′ē) adj. **1.** Effecting or intended to effect an improvement; beneficially corrective: salutary advice. **2.** Favorable or conducive to health or recovery; wholesome or curative. [Middle English, Old French salutaire, from Latin salūtāris, of health, from salus (stem salūt-), health.] —**sal·u·tar·i·ly** (săl′yə-târ′ə-lē) adv. —**sal·u·tar·i·ness** n.

sal·u·ta·tion (săl′yə-tā′shən) n. **1. a.** A polite expression of greeting or good will. **b.** A gesture of greeting, as a bow or a kiss. **2.** Words of greeting, such as Dear Sir in a letter or Ladies and Gentlemen in a speech. [Middle English salutacioun, from Latin salūtātiō (stem salūtātiōn-), from salūtātus, past participle of salūtāre, to SALUTE.]

sa·lu·ta·to·ri·an (sə-loo′tə-tôr′ē-ən, -tōr′ē-ən) n. The student, usually the one ranking second highest in the class, who delivers the salutatory at graduation exercises.

sa·lu·ta·to·ry (sə-loo′tə-tôr′ē, -tōr′ē) n., pl. **-ries.** An opening or welcoming address. —adj. Of, pertaining to, or expressing a salutation.

sa·lute (sə-loot′) v. **-luted, -luting, -lutes.** —tr. **1.** To greet or address with an expression of welcome, good will, or respect. **2.** To recognize (a military superior) with a gesture prescribed by regulations, as by raising the hand to the cap. **3.** To honor formally and ceremoniously. **4.** To express appreciative acknowledgment of; commend. —intr. To perform a salute. —n. **1.** An act, gesture, or expression of welcome, honor, respect, or courteous recognition: They stood in silence as a salute to his courage. **2.** An act of respect toward a military superior performed by raising the outstretched hand to the cap. **3.** A formal military display of honor or greeting, as the firing of cannon. [Middle English saluten, from Latin salūtāre, to preserve, salute, wish health to, from salus (stem salūt-), health, safety.] —**sa·lut·er** n.

sal·va·ble (săl′və-bəl) adj. Capable of being saved or salvaged. [Late Latin salvāre, to save, SALVAGE.]

Sal·va·dor (săl′və-dôr′). Formerly **São Sal·va·dor** (soun săl′vä-dôr′) or **Ba·hi·a** (bä-ē′ə). Seaport and capital of Bahia state, northeastern Brazil. It is a major industrial center. Founded by the Portuguese in 1549, it was the capital of Portuguese America until 1763.

Sal·va·do·ri·an (săl′və-dôr′ē-ən, -dōr′ē-ən) n. Also **Sal·va·do·ran** (-dôr′ən, -dōr′ən). A native or inhabitant of El Salvador. —**Sal·va·do·ri·an** adj.

sal·vage (săl′vĭj) tr.v. **-vaged, -vaging, -vages. 1.** To save (a ship, for example) from loss or destruction. **2.** To save (discarded or damaged material) for further use. **3.** To save or retrieve from disaster or loss: salvage the project; managed to salvage a few orders. —n. **1. a.** The rescue of a ship, its crew, or its cargo from fire or shipwreck. **b.** The ship, crew, or cargo rescued. **c.** Compensation given for aid in such a rescue. **2. a.** The act of saving imperiled property from loss. **b.** Property so saved. **c.** Material thus saved that can be sold or used. [French, the act of saving, from Old French salver, to save, from Late Latin salvāre, from Latin salvus, preserved, unharmed, safe.] —**sal·vage·a·ble** adj. —**sal·vag·er** n.

Sal·var·san (săl′vər-săn′) n. A former trademark for an arsenic compound, **arsphenamine** (see). [German.]

sal·va·tion (săl-vā′shən) n. **1. a.** Preservation or deliverance from evil or difficulty. **b.** A source, means, or cause of salvation. **2. a.** The deliverance of man or his soul from the power or penalty of sin; redemption. **b.** Christian Science. The realization of the supremacy of Life, Truth, and Love, carrying with it the destruction of the illusions of sin, sickness, and death. [Middle English, from Old French, from Late Latin salvātiō (stem salvātiōn-), from salvāre, to save, SALVAGE.] —**sal·va·tion·al** adj.

Salvation Army n. Abbr. **S.A.** An international evangelical and charitable organization founded in 1865 by William Booth.

sal·va·tion·ist (săl-vā′shə-nĭst) n. **1.** Usually **Salvationist.** A member of the Salvation Army. **2.** An evangelist.

salve¹ (săv, säv) n. **1.** An analgesic or medicinal ointment. **2.** Something that soothes or heals; balm. —tr.v. **salved, salving, salves. 1.** To soothe as if with salve; appease. **2.** To dress (a wound or sore) with salve. [Middle English salf, salve, Old English salf, sealf, from Germanic.]

salve² (sălv) tr.v. **salved, salving, salves.** To save (a ship, for example) from danger, loss, or destruction. [Back-formation from SALVAGE.]

sal·ver (săl′vər) n. A tray or platter, often made of or plated with silver, used to serve food or drinks or present calling cards. [French salve (influenced by platter), a tray for presenting food (to the king), from Spanish salva, originally "foretasting of food to detect poison," from salvar, to foretaste food or drink, "to save," from Late Latin salvāre, to save, SALVAGE.]

sal·vi·a (săl′vē-ə) n. Any of various plants and shrubs of the genus Salvia; especially, S. splendens, native to South America and widely cultivated for its showy scarlet flowers. [New Latin, from Latin, "the healing plant," SAGE.]

sal·vo¹ (săl′vō) n., pl. **-vos** or **-voes. 1.** A simultaneous discharge of firearms. **2. a.** The simultaneous release of a rack of bombs or rockets, as from an aircraft. **b.** The projectiles thus released. **3.** A sudden outburst: a salvo of cheers; a salvo of applause. **4.** A salute; tribute: salvos of praise from reviewers. [Earlier salve, salva, from Italian salva, salute, volley, from Latin salvē, hail, imperative of salvēre, to be in good health, from salvus, safe, well.]

salvo² n., pl. **-vos. 1.** A reservation, as in a document; a proviso. **2.** A means, as an excuse or evasion, of saving face or allaying a guilty conscience. [From the first word of such Medieval Latin phrases as salvō iure, with (someone's) right kept safe.]

sal vo·la·ti·le (săl′ və-lăt′l-ə) n. **1.** A solution used to make smelling salts that consists of ammonium carbonate and aromatic oils dissolved in alcohol and aqueous ammonia. Also called "spirits of ammonia." **2. Ammonium carbonate** (see). [New Latin, "volatile salt."]

sal·vor (săl′vər, -vôr′) n. A person or ship involved in salvaging a ship or cargo at sea. [From SALVE (to salvage).]

Salz·burg (sôlz′bûrg′, sälz′-, sälz′-, zälts′boorg′). Capital of Salzburg state, Austria, on the Salzach River near the West German border. It is one of Austria's main tourist centers, and its many historic buildings include the 11th-century fortress of Hohensalzburg and a fine 17th-century cathedral. Mozart was born in the city, and a music festival is held annually. Originally a Celtic settlement and then a Roman trading post, Salzburg developed in the 8th century around a Benedictine monastery. For nearly a thousand years after c. 800 it was governed by its autocratic archbishops.

SAM (săm) n. A surface-to-air missile.

Sam. Samuel (Old Testament).

sam·a·ra (săm′ər-ə, sə-mâr′ə, -mä′rə) n. Botany. A winged, one-seeded fruit that does not split open, as that of the ash or sycamore. Also called "key," "key fruit." [New Latin, from Latin samara†, seed of the elm.]

Samara. See Kuybyshev.

Sa·ma·ri·a¹ (sə-mâr′ē-ə). Region of the Middle East, now in Israel and Jordan. In ancient times it was the center of Palestine, between Galilee in the north and Judah in the south.

Samaria². Hill city in ancient Palestine, now a village in Jordan (occupied by the Israelis in 1967). It was built by King Omri as the capital of the Northern Kingdom (Israel) in the early 9th century B.C., but later fell to Sargon of Assyria (721 B.C.). Its people were deported to Babylon, and foreign settlers, many from Syria and Mesopotamia, were brought in. Most of these non-Jewish settlers adopted Judaism, but recognized only the Pentateuch, causing hostility with the Jews. Samaria was destroyed by John Hyrcanus (one of the Maccabees) in 120 B.C. and restored by Herod the Great. It has Roman remains, and excavations in the 20th century have revealed remnants of Omri's palace.

Sa·mar·i·tan (sə-măr′ĭ-tən, -mâr′ĭ-tən) n. **1.** A native or inhabitant of Samaria. **2. a. Samaritans.** An organization for helping those in a state of emotional distress and suicidal despair. **b.** A member of this organization. **3.** A Good Samaritan (see). —adj. Of or pertaining to Samaria or to Samaritans.

sa·mar·i·um (sə-mâr′ē-əm, -măr′ē-əm) n. Symbol **Sm** A silvery or pale-gray metallic rare-earth element found in monazite and bastnaesite and used as a dopant for laser materials, in infrared absorbing glass, and as a neutron absorber in certain nuclear reactors. Atomic number 62, atomic weight 150.35, melting point 1,072°C, boiling point 1,900°C, specific gravity (approximately) 7.50, valences 2, 3. [New Latin : SAMAR(SKITE) + -IUM.]

Sam·ar·kand (săm′ər-kănd′). City in Uzbek S.S.R., south-central U.S.S.R. A key station on the ancient Silk Road, it was taken by the Arabs (712) and became a great center of Islamic culture. Pillaged by Genghis Khan (1220), it became prominent again from 1365 as the royal city of the Mongol ruler Tamerlane. The Russians conquered the city in 1868.

Sa·mar·ra (sə-mär′ə). City in central Iraq, on the Tigris River. From 836 to 892 it replaced Baghdad as the capital of the Abbassid

sampler *A sampler by Hannah Taylor, made in 1774 in Newport, Rhode Island. Samplers were so called because they were used to display a variety, or "sample," of stitches.*

samurai *As the warrior caste of feudal Japan, the samurai were the only class permitted to bear arms. This armor was made for the Akita family in about 1741.*

caliphs, and it is today an important center of pilgrimage for Shiite Muslims.

sa·mar·skite (sə-mär′skīt′, săm′ər-) *n.* A black mineral oxide with red-brown streaks that is a source of several rare-earth elements. [After Colonel von *Samarski,* 19th-century Russian mine official.]

sam·ba (săm′bə, säm′-) *n.* **1.** A dance that originated in Africa and was modified in Brazil as a ballroom dance. **2.** Music in 4/4 time for dancing the samba.
∼*intr.v.* **sambaed, -baing, -bas.** To dance the samba. [Portuguese, of African origin.]

sam·bal (säm-bäl′) *n.* A sharp, spicy, and vinegary sauce or chutney of raw vegetables or fruit, used as a relish, especially with curry. [Malay, condiment.]

sam·bar, sam·bur (săm′bər, säm′-) *n.* A large deer, *Cervus* (*or Rusa*) unicolor, of southeastern Asia, having a reddish-brown coat and three-pronged antlers. [Hindi *sābar, sāmbar,* from Sanskrit *śambara*†.]

Sam Browne belt (săm′ broun′) *n.* A belt worn as part of a military or police uniform, having a shoulder strap that runs diagonally across the chest. [Modeled after the sword belt invented by Sir *Sam*uel James *Browne* (1824–1901), British general who, having lost his left arm, could not support his sword with his left hand.]

same (sām) *adj.* **1.** Being the very one; not different; identical: *went to the same school.* **2.** Exhibiting close similarity with another; being alike in every or almost every respect: *We were both wearing the same dress.* **3.** Conforming absolutely; unaltered; unchanged. Often used with *as*: *playing according to the same rules as before.* **4.** Being the one previously mentioned or indicated; aforesaid: *This same man turned out to be my old school friend.*
∼*pron.* **1.** Someone or something identical with or similar to another: *Let's do the same as we did last week.* **2.** The person or thing previously mentioned or described. **—all the same. 1.** In spite of all; nonetheless. **2.** Of no importance; of little significance: *It's all the same to me what we do.* **—just the same.** Nevertheless.
∼*adv.* In the identical way. Preceded by *the: He walks the same as his father.* [Middle English, from Old Norse *samr.*]
Synonyms: *equal, equivalent, identical, selfsame.*

sa·mekh (sä′mĕk′) *n.* The 15th letter of the Hebrew alphabet. See feature at **alphabet**. [Hebrew *sāmekh.*]

same·ness (sām′nĭs) *n.* **1.** The condition of being the same; identity. **2.** A lack of variety or change; monotony.

sam·foo, sam·fu (săm′fo͞o′) *n.* A type of loose suit consisting of a jacket and trousers that is worn by Chinese women, especially in Southeast Asia. [Cantonese *saam foo,* "shirt and trousers."]

Sa·mi·an (sā′mē-ən) *adj.* Of or pertaining to the island of Samos or its inhabitants.
∼*n.* A native or inhabitant of Samos.

Samian ware *n.* A type of pottery produced in southern Gaul in the first three centuries A.D. and commonly found in Roman sites in Britain. [From the type of earth, similar to that found in SAMOS.]

sam·iel (səm-yĕl′) *n.* A wind, **simoom** *(see).* [Turkish *samyeli* : *sam,* poisonous + *yel,* wind.]

sam·i·sen (săm′ĭ-sĕn′) *n.* A Japanese musical instrument that resembles a banjo, has a very long neck and three strings, and is played with a plectrum. [Japanese, "three-stringed" : *sami,* three + *sen,* string.]

sam·ite (săm′īt′, sā′mīt′) *n.* A heavy silk fabric, often interwoven with gold or silver, worn in the Middle Ages. [Middle English *samit,* from Old French, from Medieval Latin *examitum,* from Medieval Greek *hexamiton,* from Greek *hexamitos,* of six threads : HEXA- (six) + *mitos,* thread of the warp.]

sa·miz·dat (sä′mēz-dät′) *n.* **1. a.** The secret printing and distribution of literature that has been officially banned by the government in the U.S.S.R. **b.** The literature produced by this system. **2.** An underground press. [Russian, from *sam,* self + *izdatel'stvo,* publisher, from *izdat',* to publish (*iz,* out + *dat',* to give).]

sam·let (săm′lĭt) *n.* A young salmon. [Blend of SALMON + -LET.]

Sam·nite (săm′nīt′) *n.* **1.** In ancient Italy, a member of a people, related to the Sabines, who inhabited Samnium. **2.** The Oscan language spoken by this people. **—Sam·nite** *adj.*

Sam·ni·um (săm′nē-əm). An ancient region of south-central Italy that was eventually absorbed into the Roman commonwealth in the 3rd century B.C., after a series of wars against Rome.

Sa·mo·a (sə-mō′ə). Mainly volcanic archipelago in the South Pacific. Discovered by the Dutch in 1722, the tropical islands were disputed by the United States, Britain, and Germany in the 19th century, and there were rivalries among native chiefs. Finally a treaty of 1899 assigned the smaller eastern group of islands to the United States and the western group to Germany. See **American Samoa, Western Samoa.**

Sa·mo·an (sə-mō′ən) *adj.* Of or pertaining to Samoa, its Polynesian inhabitants, or their language.
∼*n.* **1.** A native or inhabitant of Samoa. **2.** The Polynesian language of Samoa.

Sa·mos (sā′mŏs′). Greek island in the Aegean Sea, lying close to mainland Turkey. In the 7th century B.C. it became an important Greek commercial center, reaching its cultural zenith under the 6th-century tyrant Polycrates. Pythagoras was born here. Held by Persia (522–479 B.C.), Athens, Sparta, Rome, Byzantium, and Genoa, Samos fell to the Ottoman Turks in 1475. It was restored to Greece in 1912. The island is fertile and produces citrus fruit, grapes, olives, and tobacco.

Sam·o·set (săm′ə-sĕt′, sə-mŏs′ĭt) (died *c.* 1653). U.S. Indian chief. Having learned a few English words from Englishmen fishing off the coast of what is now Maine, he surprised the Pilgrims at Plymouth Plantation with his friendly greeting, "Welcome, Englishmen" (1621). He was the first Indian to sell land to the Pilgrims (1625).

Sam·o·thrace (săm′ō-thrās′). *Modern Greek* **Sam·o·thrá·ki** (sä′mə-thrä′kē). Mountainous Greek island in the northern Aegean Sea. It was a center of worship in ancient times. The statue *Winged Victory* (now in the Louvre, Paris), dating back to the 4th century B.C., was found here in 1863.

sam·o·var (săm′ə-vär′) *n.* A metal urn of Russian origin that has a spigot and a heating device inside to boil water for tea. [Russian, "self-boiler" : *samo-,* self + *varit',* to boil, cook, probably from Old Church Slavonic *variti.*]

Sam·o·yed, Sam·o·yede (săm′ə-yĕd′, -oi-ĕd′) *n.* **1.** A member of a Ural-Altaic people inhabiting the tundra lands of the northeastern European Soviet Union and northwestern Siberia. **2.** A branch of the Uralic family of languages represented by four living languages spoken by the Samoyeds. **3.** A dog of a breed originally developed in northern Eurasia, having a thick, long white coat. [Russian *samoed,* from Lapp *Sāme-Āednàma,* "of Lapland."] **—Sam·o·yed·ic** (săm′ə-yĕd′ĭk, săm′oi-) *adj.*

samp (sămp) *n.* **1.** A coarse hominy. **2.** A boiled porridge made from samp. [Narraganset *nasàump,* corn mush.]

sam·pan (săm′păn′) *n.* Any of various flat-bottomed skiffs, usually propelled by oars, used on the waterways of the Orient. [Chinese *sān bǎn,* "three board."]

sam·phire (săm′fīr′) *n.* **1.** Any of several Old World plants of coastal areas, especially: **a.** *Crithmum maritimum,* having fleshy divided leaves and small yellow flowers. Also called "rock samphire." **b.** *Inula crithmoides,* having linear fleshy leaves and yellow daisylike flowers. Also called "golden samphire." **2.** A plant, the **glasswort** *(see).* [Variant (perhaps influenced by earlier *camphire,* camphor) of earlier *sampere,* from Old French *(herbe de) Saint Pierre,* "Saint Peter's herb."]

sam·ple (săm′pəl, säm′-) *n.* **1.** A portion, piece, entity, or segment regarded as representative of a whole or of a group; a specimen. Also used adjectivally: *a sample copy; a sample question.* **2.** *Statistics.* A set of elements drawn from and analyzed to estimate the characteristics of a population. In this sense, also called "sampling." —See Synonyms at **example**.
∼*tr.v.* **sampled, -pling, -ples.** To take a sample of; especially, to evaluate or examine by a sample. [Middle English, short for Old French *essample,* EXAMPLE.]

sam·pler (săm′plər, säm′-) *n.* **1.** One that takes, appraises, or analyzes a sample, as a machine for testing food products. **2.** A piece of cloth embroidered with various designs or mottoes so as to show the skill of the sewer.

sam·pling (săm′plĭng, säm′-) *n.* **1.** *Statistics.* A sample. **2.** The process of selecting a sample.

sampling distribution *n.* The distribution of a statistic, such as occurs when a number of sample means are calculated for a given population.

sampling gate *n.* A circuit that produces an output only when first activated by a preliminary pulse.

sam·sa·ra (səm-sä′rə) *n.* **1.** In Hinduism, the eternal cycle of birth, suffering, death, and rebirth. **2.** In Buddhism, the world and existence as experienced by unenlightened beings, characterized by insubstantiality, impermanence, and the endless round of birth, old age, disease, and death. [Sanskrit *saṁsāra,* "a passing through" : *sam,* together, completely + *sarati,* it runs, it flows.]

Sam·son[1] (săm′sən). An Israelite judge of extraordinary strength, betrayed to the Philistines by Delilah. Judges 14–16. [Hebrew *Shimshōn,* "like the sun," from *shemesh,* sun.]

Samson[2] *n.* A man of great physical strength. [After SAMSON.]

Sam·u·el[1] (săm′yo͞o-əl). A Hebrew judge and prophet of the 11th century B.C.

Samuel[2] *n. Abbr.* **Sam.** Either of two books, I and II Samuel, of the Old Testament.

sam·u·rai (săm′ə-rī′, săm′yə-) *n., pl.* **samurai** or **-rais. 1.** The military aristocracy of feudal Japan. **2.** A professional warrior belonging to the samurai. [Japanese, "warrior."]

Sa·n'a or **Sa·naa** (sä-nä′). Capital of Yemen. It lies in the center of the country on a high plain (2,210 meters; 7,250 feet). A walled city celebrated in the early Islamic period, it has many fine buildings, chief of which is the Great Mosque.

San An·dre·as Fault (săn′ ăn-drā′əs). Fracture in the earth's crust running along the coast of California. More than 960 kilometers (600 miles) long, it is a fault where two of the earth's tectonic plates are moving slowly past each other in the horizontal plane. At irregular intervals the immense strain is released in tremors and earthquakes, such as the major earthquake that devastated San Francisco in 1906.

San An·to·ni·o (săn′ ăn-tō′nē-ō′). City in south-central Texas, on the San Antonio River. A Catholic mission was founded here in 1718, and its chapel, the Alamo, was the site of a famous Mexican attack (1836) during the struggle for Texan independence. Its ruins are now a major tourist attraction. The city is also an important military center.

san·a·tive (săn′ə-tĭv) *adj.* Able to cure or heal; curative. [Middle English, from Old French *sanatif* or Late Latin *sānātīvus,* from *sānāre,* to cure, from *sānus,* sound, SANE.]

san·a·to·ri·um (săn′ə-tôr′ē-əm, -tōr′ē-əm) *n., pl.* **-ums** or **-toria** (-tôr′ē-ə, -tōr′ē-ə). Also **san·a·tar·i·um** (-târ′ē-əm) *pl.* **-ums** or **-taria** (-târ′-

San Andreas Fault

THE CRACK THAT DIVIDES SAN FRANCISCO
Displaced orange trees reveal movements in the earth's crust

The San Andreas fault system, which runs along the coast of California, is one of the few places in the world where the meeting of two plates of the lithosphere, formed from the earth's crust and upper mantle, is visible. The Pacific plate to the west of the fault is drifting northwestward past the slower-moving North American plate. In the process a narrow strip of the California coast is gradually being sheared off from the mainland. Every so often, the plates bind, but the underground pressures causing them to move continue, making the boundary rock bend and tense. Eventually it gives under the accumulated strain, causing an earthquake.

San Francisco straddles the San Andreas Fault and is therefore at risk from earthquakes. The worst in living memory happened just before dawn on April 18, 1906. Buildings collapsed and fires roared through the city unchecked, because water mains had burst. Ten square kilometers (4 square miles) were devastated and almost 700 people died. The city was rebuilt, but it could be destroyed again unless a way is found of preventing earthquakes. Prediction is still far from reliable and methods of control are in their infancy. For the time being the worst effects of earthquakes can be avoided by careful siting of communities and the construction of shock-resistant buildings.

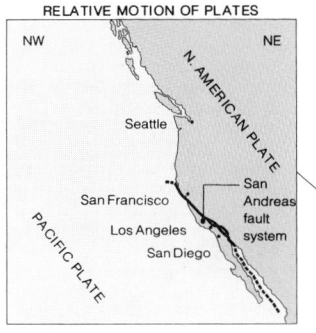

RELATIVE MOTION OF PLATES

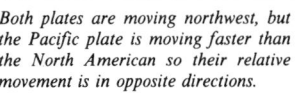

Both plates are moving northwest, but the Pacific plate is moving faster than the North American so their relative movement is in opposite directions.

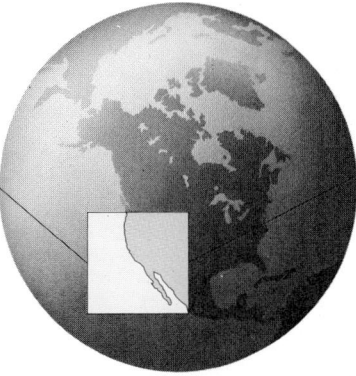

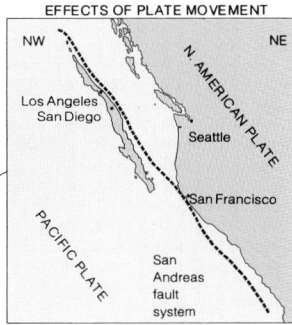

EFFECTS OF PLATE MOVEMENT

If the San Andreas Fault continues to slip at its present rate, in 50 million years Los Angeles will be an island off the west coast of Canada.

FAULT IN AN ORANGE GROVE *An aerial photograph shows the displacement of trees in a Californian orange grove. The earthquake of 1940 in the Imperial Valley of southeastern California shifted* the two sides of this subfault of the San Andreas system 3 meters (10 feet). It is now stationary, but the main fault is moving irregularly at an average of a few inches a year.

ĕ-ə). **1.** An institution for the treatment of chronic diseases, such as tuberculosis, or for medically supervised convalescence. **2.** A sanitarium. **3.** *British.* A building or part of a building at a college or boarding school reserved for those who are sick. [New Latin, from Late Latin *sānātōrium,* neuter of *sānātōrius,* from Latin *sānātus,* past participle of *sānāre,* to heal, from *sānus,* healthy, SANE.]

san·be·ni·to (săn′bə-nē′tō) *n., pl.* **-tos. 1.** A yellow garment with a Saint Anthony's cross on its front and back, worn by a penitent under the Spanish Inquisition. **2.** A black garment similar to a sanbenito but with painted flames and devils on it, worn by an impenitent at an auto-da-fé. [Spanish *sambenito,* after *San Benito,* Saint BENEDICT (from its resemblance to the Benedictine scapular).]

San Ber·nar·di·no (săn bûr′nər-dē′nō). City of southern California, at the foot of the San Bernardino Mts., part of the Coast Range extending for *c.* 95 kilometers (60 miles). The city produces varied manufactures and is the gateway to the resort and recreational areas of the mountains.

San·cho Pan·za (săn′chō păn′zə, sän′chō pän′zə). The down-to-earth squire in Cervantes' *Don Quixote.*

sanc·ti·fy (săngk′tə-fī′) *tr.v.* **-fied, -fying, -fies. 1.** To reserve for sacred use; consecrate. **2.** To make holy; purify. **3.** To give religious sanction or legitimacy to: *sanctify a marriage.* **4.** To make productive of holiness or blessing. [Middle English *sanctifien,* from Old French *sanctifier,* from Late Latin *sanctificāre* : Latin *sanctus,* holy, sacred, from the past participle of *sancīre,* to consecrate + *facere,* to make.] **—sanc·ti·fi·ca·tion** *n.* **—sanc·ti·fi·er** *n.*

sanc·ti·mo·ni·ous (săngk′tə-mō′nē-əs) *adj.* Making a pretense of sanctity, piety, or righteousness; hypocritically virtuous and high-minded. [Latin *sanctimōnia,* sanctity (from *sanctus,* sacred + *mōnia,* -MONY) + -OUS.] **—sanc·ti·mo·ni·ous·ly** *adv.* **—sanc·ti·mo·ni·ous·ness, sanc·ti·mo·ny** (săngk′tə-mō′nē) *n.*

sanc·tion (săngk′shən) *n.* **1.** Authoritative permission or approval that makes a course of action valid: *received her parents' sanction to rent her own apartment.* **2.** Support or encouragement, as from pub-

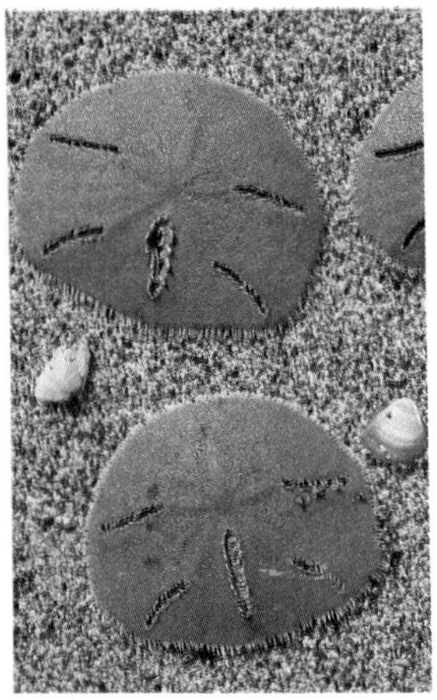

sand dollar *Found on sandy ocean beds throughout the world, sand dollars are flat, circular sea urchins belonging to the scientific order Exocycloida.*

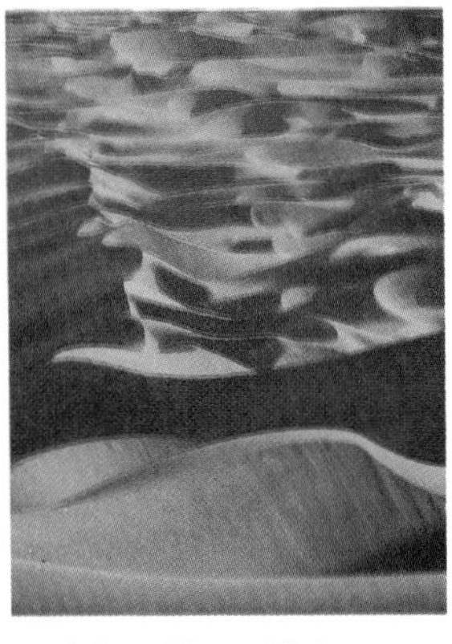

sand dune *The world's largest areas of sand dunes are in deserts. These huge wind-shaped dunes are on the arid coastal strip of Peru near the Atacama Desert, the driest region in the world.*

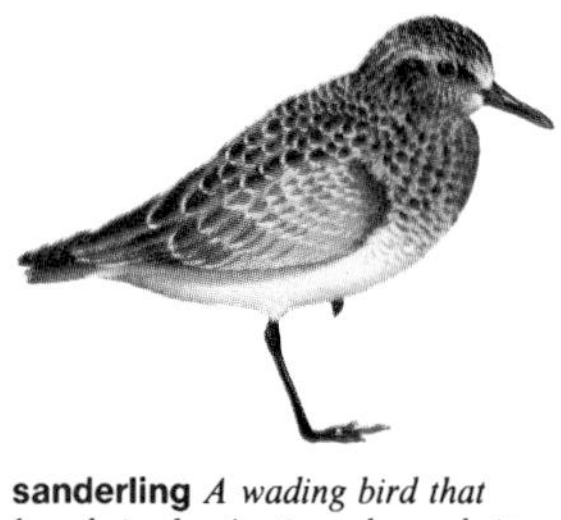

sanderling *A wading bird that breeds in the Arctic and spends its winter in flocks along the shores of southern Europe. It feeds on tiny sea creatures along the water's edge.*

lic opinion or established custom. **3.** A penalty for noncompliance with a law or decree. **4.** A penalty, specified or in the form of moral pressure, that acts to ensure compliance or conformity. **5.** A consideration, influence, or principle that dictates an ethical choice. **6.** A coercive measure adopted usually by several nations acting together against a nation violating international law. **7.** A law or decree, especially an ecclesiastical decree.
~*tr.v.* **sanctioned, -tioning, -tions. 1.** To grant authority or permission for; legitimize or ratify. **2.** To approve, support, or encourage: *a practice sanctioned by the frequency of its occurrence.* —See Synonyms at **approve.** [French, from Latin *sanctiō* (stem *sanctiōn-*), an ordaining, a sanction, from *sanctus,* sacred. See **sanctify.**]

sanc·ti·ty (săngk′tə-tē) *n., pl.* **-ties. 1.** Saintliness, holiness, or godliness. **2.** The quality or condition of being considered hallowed or sacred; inviolability. **3.** Anything considered sacred. [Middle English *saunctite,* from Old French *saincteté,* from Latin *sanctitās* (stem *sanctitāt-*), from *sanctus,* sacred. See **sanctify.**]

sanc·tu·ar·y (săngk′cho͞o-ĕr′ē) *n., pl.* **-ies. 1.** A sacred place, such as a church, temple, or mosque. **2.** The most holy part of a sacred place, such as the area around the altar in a church. **3.** A church or other sacred place in which fugitives formerly were safe from arrest or punishment. **4.** Immunity from arrest or punishment afforded by or as if by taking refuge in a sanctuary: *sought sanctuary at the French embassy in Prague.* **5.** A place of refuge or asylum. **6.** A reserved area in which wildlife is protected from hunting or other molestation. —See Synonyms at **shelter.** [Middle English *sanctuarie,* from Old French *saintuarie,* from Late Latin *sanctuārium,* from Latin *sanctus,* sacred. See **sanctify.**]

sanc·tum (săngk′təm) *n., pl.* **-tums** or **-ta** (-tə). **1.** A sacred or holy place. **2.** A private place, as a room or study, where one is free from disturbance. [Latin, neuter of *sanctus,* sacred. See **sanctify.**]

sanctum sanc·to·rum (săngk-tôr′əm, -tōr′əm) *n.* **1.** The **holy of holies** *(see).* **2.** An inviolably private place; sanctum. [Late Latin, "the holy of holies" (translation of Greek *to hagion tōn hagiōn,* translation of Hebrew *qōdesh ha-qqodashīm*).]

Sanc·tus (săngk′təs) *n.* **1.** The hymn of praise that culminates the Preface in many eucharistic liturgies. **2.** A musical setting of this. [Middle English, from Medieval Latin, first word of the hymn, from Late Latin, "holy" (first word of the hymn sung by the angels in Isaiah 6:3), from Latin. See **sanctify.**]

sand (sănd) *n.* **1. a.** Loose, granular, gritty particles of worn or disintegrated rock, especially quartz, finer than gravel and coarser than dust. **b.** *Often* **sands.** A tract or stretch of land, as a beach or desert, covered with this material. **c.** The sand in an hourglass. **2. sands.** Moments of allotted time or duration: *"The sands are number'd that make up my life"* (Shakespeare). **3.** *Slang.* Grit; courage. **4.** A light grayish brown to yellowish gray. **—built on sand.** Based on a foundation that is insecure or uncertain.
~*tr.v.* **sanded, sanding, sands. 1.** To sprinkle or cover with or as if with sand: *sanded the icy road.* **2.** To polish or scrape with sand or sandpaper. **3.** To mix or adulterate with sand. [Middle English *sand,* Old English *sand,* from Germanic *sandam, sandaz* (unattested).]

Sand (sănd, sänd, säɴd), **George,** pen name of Amandine Aurore Lucie Dupin, Baroness Dudevant (1804–76). French writer. She married Casimir Dudevant in 1822, and her first novel, *Indiana,* which was a plea for feminine independence, was published in 1832, a year after she had left her husband and gone to live with Jules Sandeau. She wrote many successful novels, including *La Mare au Diable* (1846). Alfred de Musset and Frédéric Chopin were among her lovers.

san·dal[1] (săn′dəl) *n.* **1.** A light shoe consisting of a sole fastened to the foot by thongs or straps. **2.** A light slipper or low-cut shoe fastened to the foot by an ankle strap. **3.** A strap or band for fastening a low shoe or slipper on the foot. **4.** A rubber overshoe cut very low and covering little more than the sole of the shoe. [Middle English *sandalie,* from Latin *sandalium,* from Greek *sandalion,* diminutive of *sandalon,* sandal.]

sandal[2] *n.* Sandalwood. [Middle English, from Old French, from Medieval Latin *sandalum, santalum,* from Greek *santalon, sandanon,* probably from Sanskrit *candanaḥ.*]

san·dal·wood (săn′dəl-wo͝od′) *n.* **1. a.** Any of several Asian or Australasian evergreen trees of the genus *Santalum*; especially, *S. album,* having aromatic yellowish heartwood that is used in cabinetmaking and wood carving and that yields an oil used in perfumery. Also called "sandal." **b.** The wood of this tree or of similar trees. **2.** Any of various trees similar to the sandalwood, especially *Pterocarpus santalinus,* the dark-red wood of which yields a dye. **3.** A light to moderate or grayish brown.

san·da·rac, san·da·rach (săn′də-răk′) *n.* **1.** A tree, *Tetraclinis articulata* (or *Callitris quadrivalvis*), of northern Africa, having wood yielding a brittle, translucent resin used in varnishes. **2.** The resin of this tree. [Latin *sandaraca,* red pigment, beebread, from Greek *sandarak(h)ē,* (red pigment derived from) realgar.]

sand·bag (sănd′băg′) *n.* **1.** A bag filled with sand, used in piles to form protective walls, as against flooding or gunfire, or as a ballast in a balloon or boat. **2.** A small, narrow bag partially filled with sand, used as a weapon.
~*tr.v.* **sandbagged, -bagging, -bags. 1.** To put sandbags in, on, or around as a means of protection. **2. a.** To hit with a sandbag. **b.** To force by crude means; coerce.

sand·bank (sănd′băngk′) *n.* A bank of sand in a sea or river formed by currents and often exposed at low tide.

sand·bar (sănd′bär′) *n.* An offshore shoal of sand built up by the action of waves or currents.

sand·blast (sănd′blăst′, -bläst′) *n.* **1.** A blast of air or steam carrying sand at high speed to etch glass or to clean stone or metal surfaces. **2.** A machine used to apply such a blast.
~*tr.v.* **sandblasted, -blasting, -blasts.** To apply a sandblast to for the purpose of cleaning or engraving. **—sand·blast·er** *n.*

sand-blind (sănd′blīnd′) *adj. Archaic.* Partially blind; dim-sighted. [Middle English *sand-blind,* Old English *sāmblind* (unattested) : *sām-,* half + BLIND.] **—sand-blind·ness** *n.*

sand·box (sănd′bŏks′) *n.* **1.** A small shaker containing sand to be sprinkled on wet ink. **2.** A box on a locomotive containing sand for sprinkling on icy rails. **3.** A boxlike enclosure filled with sand for children to play in.

sandbox tree *n.* A tropical American tree, *Hura crepitans,* having a spiny trunk and woody seed capsules that split explosively when ripe. [So called because the capsules were formerly used to hold sand for drying ink.]

Sand·burg (sănd′bûrg′, săn′-), **Carl** (1878–1967). U.S. poet and biographer. His verses, usually dealing with the common man and the American experience, were published in numerous collections, including his Pulitzer Prize winner, *Cornhuskers* (1918). He also won a Pulitzer (1940) for the last volume of his biography of Abraham Lincoln.

sand-cast (sănd′kăst′, -käst′) *tr.v.* **-cast, -casting, -casts.** To make (a casting) by pouring molten metal into a mold made of sand.

sand crack *n.* A fissure in the side of a horse's hoof, often causing lameness.

sand dab *n.* A food fish of the genus *Citharichthys,* of Pacific waters, related to and resembling the flounders.

sand dollar *n.* Any of various thin, circular echinoderms, especially *Echinarachnius parma,* of sandy ocean bottoms of the northern Atlantic and Pacific.

sand dune *n.* A **dune** *(see).*

sand eel *n.* The **sand lance** *(see).*

sand·er (săn′dər) *n.* **1.** One that spreads sand. **2.** One that sands surfaces; especially, a machine with an abrasive-covered disk or belt, used for smoothing, polishing, or refinishing.

san·der·ling (săn′dər-lĭng) *n.* A small shore bird, *Crocethia* (or *Calidris*) *alba,* having predominantly gray and white plumage. [Perhaps from SAND + -LING.]

sand flea *n.* **1.** Any of various small crustaceans, such as the sand hopper, living on sandy beaches. **2.** A flea, the **chigoe** *(see).*

sand fly *n.* Any of various small biting flies of the genus *Phlebotomus,* of tropical areas, some of which transmit diseases.

sand glass *n.* An instrument, such as an hourglass, that measures time by the trickling of sand.

sand grouse *n.* Any of various sandy-colored pigeonlike birds of the genera *Pterocles* and *Syrrhaptes,* of arid and semiarid regions of the Old World.

san·dhi (săn′dē, sän′-) *n. Linguistics.* The modification of the sound of a morpheme because of its position in certain phonetic contexts; for example, the difference between the pronunciation of *the* in *the house* and in *the other house* is an instance of sandhi. [Sanskrit *saṁdhi,* "a placing together" : *sam,* together + *dadhāti,* he places.]

sand·hog (sănd′hôg′, -hŏg′) *n.* A laborer who works inside a caisson, as in the construction of underwater tunnels.

sand hopper *n.* The **beach flea** *(see).*

Sand·hurst (sănd′hûrst′). Village in Berkshire, south-central England. It is the site of the Royal Military Academy (founded 1790).

San Di·e·go (săn′ dē-ā′gō). City and seaport in southern California, on San Diego Bay. The city has an oceanographic institute, a major naval and marine base, and shipbuilding, aviation, and aerospace industries.

sand lance *n.* Any of several small marine fishes of the genus *Ammodytes,* having a slender body with a forked tail fin and often burrowing in coastal sand or shingle. Also called "launce," "sand launce," "sand eel."

sand lizard *n.* A light-brown to grayish European lizard, *Lacerta agilis,* the male of which has bright green underparts.

sand·man (sănd′măn′) *n.* A character in fairy tales and folklore who puts children to sleep by sprinkling sand in their eyes.

sand painting *n.* **1.** A ceremonial design of the Navajo Indians made by trickling fine colored sand onto a base of neutral sand. **2.** The art of making such designs.

sand·pa·per (sănd′pā′pər) *n.* Paper coated on one side with sand or other abrasive material, used for smoothing.
~*tr.v.* **sandpapered, -pering, -pers.** To rub with sandpaper.

sand·pi·per (sănd′pī′pər) *n.* Any of various small wading birds of the family Scolopacidae, usually having a long, straight bill.

San·dring·ham (săn′drĭng-əm). Village in Norfolk, in eastern England. Sandringham House, with its estate, has been a country residence of English royalty since 1863.

sand smelt *n.* A widely distributed fish of the genus *Atherina,* closely related to the gray mullet and found in inshore waters.

sand·stone (sănd′stōn′) *n.* Variously colored sedimentary rock composed predominantly of sandlike quartz grains cemented by lime, silica, or other materials.

sand·storm (sănd′stôrm′) *n.* A strong wind, especially in a desert, carrying clouds of sand through the air.

sand table *n.* A table on which a relief model of a town or terrain is built out of sand for the study of military tactics.

sand trap *n.* A hazard on a golf course consisting of a depression filled with sand. Also called "bunker."
sand viper *n.* Any of various snakes of sandy areas, especially the **horned viper** *(see).*
sand·wich (sănd′wĭch, săn′wĭch) *n.* **1.** Two or more slices of bread with meat, cheese, jam, or other filling placed between them. **2.** Something resembling a sandwich.
~*tr.v.* **sandwiched, -wiching, -wiches. 1.** To insert between two things of another type. **2.** To fit with difficulty between two other things; make room or time for: *sandwich a meeting between lunch and leaving the office.* [After the 4th Earl of SANDWICH.]
Sand·wich (sănd′wĭch, săn′-). Market town in Kent, southeastern England. It was one of the original Cinque Ports, but its harbor later silted up and it now lies some 3 kilometers (2 miles) from the sea. Sandwich is a tourist resort.
Sandwich, John Montagu, 4th Earl of (1718–92). The earl was a habitual gambler. His consumption of cold beef placed between slices of bread during one of his gambling sessions is said to have given rise to the word *sandwich.*
sandwich board *n.* Either of two large boards bearing advertising placards, hinged at the top by straps for hanging on a carrier's shoulders.
sandwich compound *n.* A type of chemical compound, such as ferrocene, in which a metal atom or ion is sandwiched between two parallel organic rings.
Sandwich Islands. See **Hawaii.**
sandwich man *n.* A man hired to carry a sandwich board.
sand·worm (sănd′wûrm′) *n.* Any of various segmented worms, especially of the genera *Nereis* and *Arenicola,* generally inhabiting coastal mud or sand and often used as fishing bait.
sand·wort (sănd′wûrt′, -wôrt′) *n.* Any of numerous low-growing plants of the genera *Arenaria, Minuartia,* and *Moehringia,* having small, usually white flowers.
sand·y (săn′dē) *adj.* **-ier, -iest. 1.** Covered with, consisting of, or containing a high proportion of sand: *sandy soil.* **2.** Like sand, as in being unstable. **3. a.** Of the color of sand; yellowish red. **b.** Having hair of this color. **—sand·i·ness** *n.*
sand yacht *n.* A vehicle with wheels and sails, designed to be propelled across flat stretches of sand, as on a beach, by the wind. **—sand yachting** *n.*
Sandy Hook. Low, sandy peninsula in northeastern New Jersey, at the entrance to lower New York Bay. The region was first explored by Henry Hudson's seafarers in 1609.
sane (sān) *adj.* **saner, sanest. 1.** Mentally healthy; of sound mind. **2.** Having or showing sound judgment; reasonable; rational. [Latin *sānus,* sound, whole, healthy.] **—sane·ly** *adv.* **—sane·ness** *n.*
San Fer·nan·do Valley (săn′ fər-năn′dō). Fertile valley in southwestern California. The valley was first entered by European explorers in 1769. Part of it is within the city limits of Los Angeles.
San·for·ized (săn′fə-rīzd′) *adj.* Being a trademark for fabrics preshrunk by a patented mechanical process before being made into clothing so as to minimize later shrinkage.
San Fran·cis·co (săn′ frən-sĭs′kō). Major city and seaport in western California, on a peninsula between San Francisco Bay and the Pacific Ocean, which are linked by the strait known as the Golden Gate. Founded as a Spanish mission in 1776, it boomed during the California gold rush of 1848 and further expanded after the opening of the transcontinental railroad (1869). Lying on the San Andreas fault, it was partially destroyed in an earthquake and fire in 1906 and has been subject to lesser tremors at irregular intervals. The city is the financial center of the West Coast and also serves a prosperous agricultural and mining region. Among its famous sights are the Golden Gate Bridge, the municipal cable car system, and the island of Alcatraz. **—San Fran·cis·can** *adj. & n.*
sang. Past tense of **sing.**
san·ga·ree (săng′gə-rē′) *n.* A cold drink usually made of wine, often Madeira, and grated nutmeg. [Spanish *sangría,* "a bleeding," from *sangre,* blood, from Latin *sanguis.* See **sanguine.**]
Sang·er (săng′ər), **Frederick** (1918–). British biochemist. He determined the order of amino acids in the insulin molecule and was awarded the Nobel Prize for chemistry in 1958 and 1980.
Sanger, Margaret Higgins (1883–1966). U.S. social reformer. A New York nurse who had witnessed the problems stemming from unwanted pregnancies and self-induced abortions, she devoted herself to campaigning for birth control. She published numerous periodicals and founded the organization (1929) that later became the Planned Parenthood Federation (1942).
sang-froid (säN-frwä′) *n.* Composure; imperturbability. —See Synonyms at **equanimity.** [French, "cold blood."]
san·gri·a (săng-grē′ə, săn-) *n.* A cold drink made of red wine mixed with brandy, sugar, fruit juice, and soda water. [Spanish *sangría,* "bleeding," from *sangre,* blood, from Latin *sanguis.* See **sanguine.**]
san·gui·nar·i·a (săng′gwə-nâr′ē-ə) *n.* A plant, the **bloodroot** *(see).* [New Latin, from Latin *sanguinarius,* bloody, from *sanguis* (stem *sanguin-*), blood.]
san·gui·nar·y (săng′gwə-nĕr′ē) *adj.* **1.** Accompanied by bloodshed and carnage. **2.** Bloodthirsty. **3.** Consisting of or stained with blood. [Latin *sanguinārius,* of blood, from *sanguis* (stem *sanguin-*), blood.] **—san·gui·nar·i·ly** (săng′gwə-nâr′ə-lē) *adv.*
san·guine (săng′gwĭn) *adj.* **1. a.** Of the color of blood; red. **b.** Ruddy; florid. Said of the complexion. · **2. a.** *Archaic.* Having blood as the dominant humor in terms of medieval physiology. See **humor. b.** Having the courageous or passionate temperament and ruddy complexion formerly thought to be characteristic of one dominated by this humor. **3.** Eagerly optimistic; cheerful. [Middle English *sanguin,* from Old French, from Latin *sanguineus,* of blood, bloody, from *sanguis*† (stem *sanguin-*), blood.] **—san·guine·ly** *adv.* **—san·guine·ness, san·guin·i·ty** (săng-gwĭn′ə-tē) *n.*
san·guin·e·ous (săng-gwĭn′ē-əs) *adj.* **1. a.** Pertaining to or involving blood or bloodshed. **b.** Bloodthirsty; sanguinary. **2.** Blood-red. **3.** Cheerful; optimistic; sanguine. [Latin *sanguineus,* SANGUINE.]
san·guin·o·lent (săng-gwĭn′ə-lənt) *adj.* Of, mixed with, or tinged with blood. [Latin *sanguinolentus,* full of blood, from *sanguis* (stem *sanguin-*), blood. See **sanguine.**]
San·he·drin (săn-hē′drĭn, -hĕd′rĭn, săn-) *n.* The highest judicial and ecclesiastical council of the ancient Jewish nation, composed of from 70 to 72 members. Also called "Great Sanhedrin." [Hebrew *sanhedhrīn,* from Greek *sunedrion,* a council, from *sunedros,* sitting within council : SYN- (together) + *hedra,* a seat, a sitting.]
san·i·cle (săn′ĭ-kəl) *n.* Any of various plants of the genus *Sanicula,* having clusters of small, greenish-white or pale pink flowers and reputedly having medicinal value as an astringent. [Middle English, from Old French, from Medieval Latin *sanicula,* probably from Latin *sānus,* healthy, SANE (because the plant was once thought to have healing powers).]
sa·ni·es (sā′nē-ēz′) *n.* A thin, fetid, greenish fluid consisting of serum and pus discharged from a wound, ulcer, or fistula. [Latin *saniēs*†.] **—sa·ni·ous** (sā′nē-əs) *adj.*
san·i·tar·i·um (săn′ə-târ′ē-əm) *n., pl* **-ums** or **-ia** (-ē-ə). **1.** A health resort. **2.** A sanatorium.
san·i·tar·y (săn′ə-tĕr′ē) *adj.* **1.** Of, pertaining to, or used for the preservation of health. **2.** Free from dirt and infection; hygienic. [French *sanitaire,* from Latin *sānitās,* health, SANITY.] **—san·i·tar·i·ly** (săn′ə-târ′ə-lē) *adv.*
sanitary engineer *n.* An engineer specializing in the maintenance of services and conditions conducive to the preservation of public health. **—sanitary engineering** *n.*
sanitary napkin *n.* A usually disposable pad of absorbent material worn to absorb menstrual flow.
san·i·ta·tion (săn′ə-tā′shən) *n.* **1.** The formulation and application of measures designed to protect public health. **2.** The disposal of sewage and refuse. [From SANITARY.]
san·i·tize (săn′ə-tīz′) *tr.v.* **-tized, -tizing, -tizes. 1.** To make sanitary. **2.** To make innocuous or inoffensive.
san·i·ty (săn′ə-tē) *n.* **1.** The condition of having sound mental health; saneness. **2.** Soundness of judgment or reason. [Middle English *sanite,* from Old French, from Latin *sānitās* (stem *sānitāt-*), health, sanity, from *sānus,* healthy, SANE.]
San Joa·quin Valley (săn′ wô-kēn′). Rich, irrigated agricultural area in central California. It produces grapes, asparagus, tomatoes, celery, nuts, rice, alfalfa, corn, sugar beets, dairy products, cattle, hogs, sheep, and poultry.
San Jo·se (săn′ hō-zā′). City in western California. It is an important center for fruit canning and wine production and also has some light industry.
San Jo·sé (săn′ hō-zā′). Capital of Costa Rica, in the center of the country. Founded in 1738, it became the capital in 1823. The city lies on a temperate upland plateau and is a center for coffee processing and distribution.
San Jose scale *n.* A destructive scale insect, *Aspidiotus perniciosus,* that does considerable damage to fruit trees and fruit-bearing plants. [After SAN JOSE, California.]
San Juan (săn hwän′, wän′). Capital and chief port of Puerto Rico, on the northeastern coast of the island. Developed by the Spaniards after 1533, the city was taken by U.S. troops in 1898. San Juan is a tourist center, with industries that include food processing and machinery manufacturing.
San Juan Islands. Archipelago of 172 islands in northwestern Washington State, east of Vancouver Island. The islands were discovered and named *c.* 1790 by Spanish explorers. Some of the smaller islands are privately owned.
sank. Past tense of **sink.**
San·khya (säng′kyə) *n.* A system of Hindu philosophy based on the distinction between spirit and matter. [Sanskrit *sāṁkhya-,* "based on calculation," from *saṁkhyā-,* calculation, from *saṁkhyāti*†, he counts up.]
San Ma·ri·no (săn′ mə-rē′nō, săn′). Small republic in the Apennine Mts. of central Italy. Traditionally said to have been founded in the 4th century, it became a city-state whose independence was recognized by the pope in 1631. In 1862 it joined a customs union with Italy, and a treaty of mutual friendship was signed in 1897. The main agricultural products are wine, cereals, and cattle. Tourism and ceramics are among the chief industries. Area, 61 square kilometers (24 square miles). Population, 19,000. Capital, San Marino. See map at **Italy.**
San Mar·tín (săn′ mär-tēn′, sän′), **José de** (1778–1850). South American soldier and statesman, born in Argentina. He devoted himself to the struggle of South American countries to throw off the authority of Spain and played a major part in freeing Chile (1817–18) and Peru (1821).
san·nup (săn′əp) *n.* A married male North American Indian. [From a Massachuset word akin to Eastern Abnaki *sénape,* "man."]
san·nya·si (sŭn-yä′sē) *n.* Also **san·nya·sin** (-sĭn). An ascetic Hindu holy man or mendicant. [Hindi and Urdu, from Sanskrit *saṁnyāsin,* setting aside : *sam,* together + *ni,* down + *as,* throw.]
San Re·mo (săn rē′mō, rā′-, sän). City in Liguria, northwestern

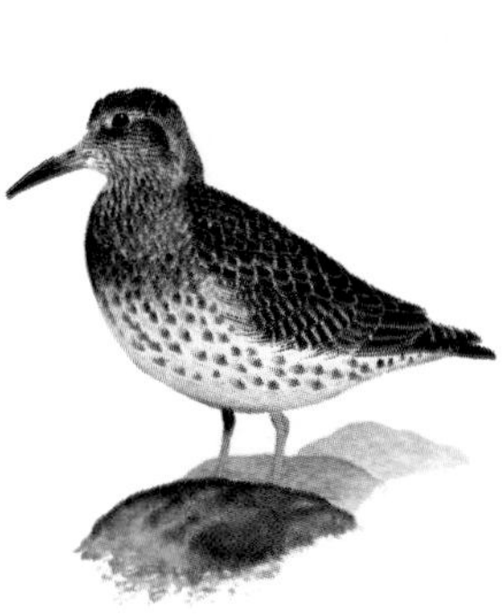

sandpiper *Found mainly in the Northern Hemisphere, the wading sandpiper is a relative of the dunlin. It lives chiefly on rocky shores, feeding on insects and other invertebrates, and has a shrill piping call. This is the purple sandpiper.*

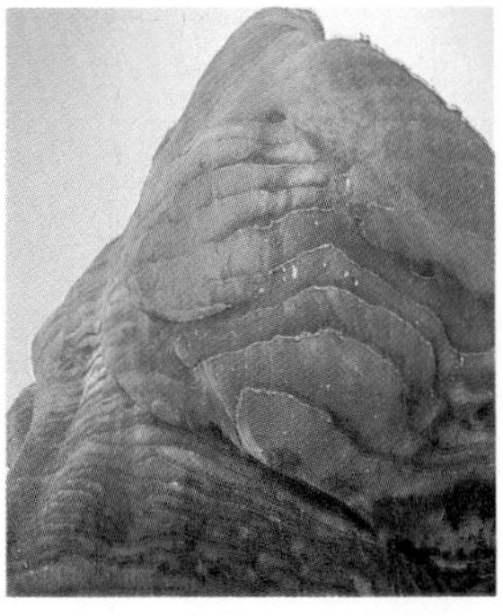

sandstone *This variously colored soft sedimentary rock is generally formed from quartz crystals.*

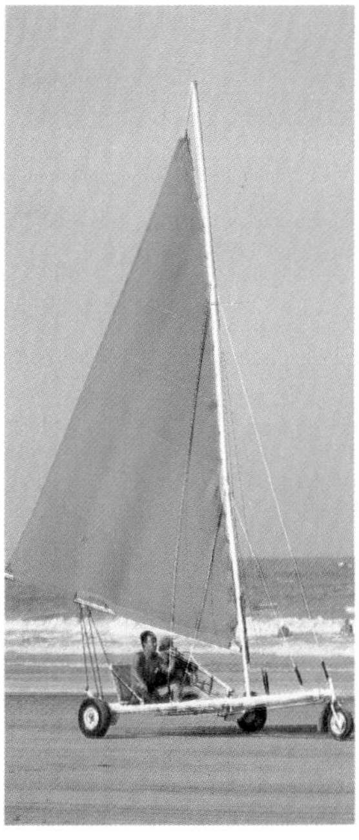

sand yacht *An ingenious recreational vehicle, seen here on a beach near Malindi, Kenya.*

Italy, on the Ligurian Sea and the Italian Riviera. It is a fashionable resort and a major flower market.

sans (sănz) *prep.* Without. [Middle English *saunz, san(s),* from Old French *san(s), sen(s),* from Vulgar Latin *sene* (unattested), from Latin *sine* (influenced by Latin *absentiā,* in the absence of).]

San Sal·va·dor (săn săl'və-dôr'). Capital of El Salvador, in the interior of the country. Founded in 1528 on high volcanic slopes, it has been repeatedly damaged by severe earthquakes. Its products include textiles, cigars, and processed food.

San Salvador Island. Formerly **Wat·ling Island** (wŏt'lĭng). Island in the Bahamas group of the West Indies. It was the first landfall (1492) of Columbus during his first voyage to the Americas.

sans-cu·lotte (sănz'kyōo-lŏt') *n., pl.* **sans-culottes. 1.** An extreme republican during the French Revolution. **2.** A revolutionary extremist. [French *sans-culotte,* "without breeches" (the revolutionaries wore pantaloons instead of the kneebreeches worn by members of the upper classes) : SANS + CULOTTES.] —**sans-cu·lot·tic** (sănz'kyōo-lŏt'ĭk *adj.* —**sans-cu·lot·tism** (-ĭz'əm) *n.*

San Se·bas·tián (săn' sə-băs'chən, săn' sĕb'äs-chän'). Coastal resort and capital of Guipúzcoa province, northern Spain, on the Bay of Biscay. Overlooked by the fortress of Castillo de la Mota, the city was the summer residence of the Spanish court. It has fishing, paper, and steel industries.

san·se·vie·ri·a (săn'sə-vîr'ē-ə) *n.* Any of various tropical Old World plants of the genus *Sansevieria,* having thick, lance-shaped leaves and often cultivated as a house plant. Also called "mother-in-law's tongue." [New Latin, after Raimondo di Sangro (1710–71), Prince of *San Severo,* Italy.]

San·skrit (săn'skrĭt) *n. Abbr.* **Skr., Skt. 1.** An ancient language of India, belonging to the Indic branch of the Indo-Iranian subfamily of Indo-European languages, of which it is the oldest known member. It is the language of the Vedas and of Hinduism. **2.** The literary language of ancient and medieval India, classical Sanskrit, the grammar of which was fixed by Indian grammarians before the 4th century B.C. [Sanskrit *saṃskṛta,* put together, well-formed, refined : *saṃ,* together + *kṛ,* to make.] —**San·skrit·ist** *n.*

San·skrit·ic (săn-skrĭt'ĭk) *adj.* **1.** Designating or belonging to a large group of Indian languages and dialects, both ancient and modern, such as Hindi, Pali, Bengali, and Punjabi. **2.** Of, relating to, or written in Sanskrit.

—*n.* The Sanskritic group of languages.

sans ser·if (săn sĕr'ĭf) *n.* A typeface without serifs. Also called "Gothic."

San·ta An·na or **San·ta An·a** (săn'tə ăn'ə, săn'tə ä'nə), **Antonio López de** (1794–1876). Mexican general and statesman. As president of Mexico (1833–36) he tried to crush the Texan revolt at the Alamo (1836) but was defeated and captured at San Jacinto (1836). He was made dictator in 1841, deposed in 1845, and recalled in 1846, only to be driven from Mexico City by the U.S. Army before being exiled in 1848. He was recalled once more to be president (1853–55) before being exiled again; returning at last to Mexico City in 1874 to die in poverty.

San·ta Bar·ba·ra (săn'tə bär'bər-ə, bär'brə). City of southern California, on the Pacific Ocean. It is a residential and resort city with many recreational facilities; it also has electronics and aerospace research and development firms and an orchid industry.

San·ta Cat·a·li·na (săn'tə kăt'l-ē'nə). Also **Cat·a·li·na Island.** Island off the coast of Huntington Beach in southern California. It is a popular resort spot, with a picturesque, irregular coastline dotted with coves and beaches.

San·ta Claus (săn'tə klôz') *n.* The personification of the spirit of Christmas, usually represented as a jolly, fat old man with a white beard and a red suit. Also called "Saint Nicholas." [Variant of Dutch dialectal *Sante Klaas,* unexplained shortening of *Sint Nicolaes,* Saint Nicholas.]

San·ta Fe (săn'tə fā'). Capital of New Mexico, in the north-central part of the state, on the Santa Fe River. It was founded at the terminus of the Santa Fe Trail. Surviving examples of Spanish colonial architecture include the governor's palace (1610). Santa Fe is a market center and a major tourist resort noted for its Indian and Mexican crafts.

San·ta Fé (săn'tä fā'). River port on the Salado River in northeastern Argentina, capital of Santa Fé province. Founded in 1573, it is the center of a grain-growing and stock-rearing area. Its port was opened to oceangoing ships in 1911.

San·ta Fe Trail (săn'tə fā'). Caravan route of the western United States, extending *c.* 1,255 kilometers (780 miles) from Independence, Missouri, southwest to Santa Fe, New Mexico. Starting in 1821, annual wagon caravans made the 40- to 60-day trip over the trail, returning after a 4- to 5-week stay in Santa Fe. The railroad replaced the trail in 1880.

Santa Isabel. See **Malabo.**

San·ta Mon·i·ca (săn'tə mŏn'ĭ-kə). City in southern California, on Santa Monica Bay. It has varied manufactures but is known primarily for its spectacular beach.

San·tan·der (săn'tän-dĕr'). Port and capital of Santander province in northern Spain, on the Bay of Biscay. A major port for the Americas in colonial days, it is now an important tourist center, and its industries include fishing and fish processing, shipbuilding, and ironworking. Nearby are the famous caves of Altamira, with prehistoric paintings.

San·ta·ya·na (săn'tə-yä'nä), **George** (1863–1952). Spanish-born philosopher. He moved to the United States in 1872 and earned a degree at Harvard, where he lectured for a time before returning to Europe. He wrote verse and novels as well as many works of philosophy, including the series *Realms of Being* (1927–40).

San·ti·a·go (săn'tē-ä'gō). Capital of Chile and of Santiago province. It is on the Mapocho River, and was founded by the Spanish conquistador Pedro de Valdivia in 1541. Greater Santiago contains nearly a third of Chile's population and produces half the nation's total industrial output.

Santiago de Com·po·ste·la (də kŏm'pə-stĕl'ə). City in Galicia, northwestern Spain. Its Romanesque cathedral is reputedly built over the tomb of St. James (*Santiago* in Spanish), patron saint of Spain. Santiago has been one of the most important centers of pilgrimage in Europe since the 9th century.

Santiago de Cu·ba (kyōo'bə). Seaport and capital of Oriente province in southern Cuba. It is Cuba's second-largest city and has a major cathedral and a university. On July 26, 1953, Fidel Castro began his revolt here by leading a guerrilla attack on the army barracks.

San·to Do·min·go (săn'tō də-mĭng'gō). Formerly (1936–1961) **Ciu·dad Tru·jil·lo** (sē'ōō-dåd' trōō-hē'ō, -hē'yō). Capital and chief port of the Dominican Republic, on the southern coast at the mouth of the Ozama River. It is the oldest continuously inhabited settlement established by Europeans in the Western Hemisphere, having been founded by Bartholomew Columbus, brother of Christopher, in 1496. Its cathedral (1514) is the oldest in the New World. The city has been the country's capital since 1844 and is a major manufacturing and tourist center.

san·ton·i·ca (săn-tŏn'ĭ-kə) *n.* **1.** A wormwood, *Artemisia maritima* (or *A. cina*), of the Old World, having flowers that yield santonin. **2.** The dried unopened flowers of this plant. [New Latin, from Latin *(herba) santonica,* from the feminine of *santonicus,* of the *Santoni,* a people of Aquitania.]

san·to·nin (săn'tə-nĭn) *n.* A colorless crystalline compound, $C_{15}H_{18}O_3$, obtained from species of wormwood, especially santonica, and used as a vermifuge. [SANTON(ICA) + -IN.]

Santorini. See **Thíra.**

San·tos (săn'təs, săn'tōōsh'). Seaport of São Paulo state, southeastern Brazil. It is the world's largest coffee-exporting port and also a fashionable residential and resort area.

Saône (sōn). River, 431 kilometers (268 miles) long, rising in the Vosges Mts. of eastern France and flowing generally southwest to join the Rhône River at Lyon. It is an important transportation link between Paris and Marseilles.

São Pau·lo (souɴ pou'lōō). Largest city in Brazil and capital of São Paulo state. It was founded on the Tiete River by Portuguese Jesuits in 1554. Independence from Portugal was proclaimed here in 1822. The spread of coffee growing in the state stimulated rapid expansion of the city after the 1880's, and the metropolis is the biggest financial, commercial, and industrial center in South America.

São Salvador. See **Salvador.**

São To·mé and Prín·ci·pe (tə-mā'; prēn'sē-pə). Small country consisting of four islands off the coast of West Africa in the Gulf of Guinea. The two main islands (São Tomé and Principe) and the islets of Pedras Tinhosas and Rôlas make up the group. The archipelago was discovered by the Portuguese in 1471 and proclaimed a colony of Portugal (1522). The Dutch held the islands from 1641 until 1740, when the archipelago was recovered by the Portuguese, who ruled the islands until their independence (1975). The economy is almost entirely agricultural, and cocoa, coffee, palm oil, and bananas are exported. Area, 964 square kilometers (372 square miles). Population, 85,000. Capital, São Tomé. See map at **Cameroon.**

sap¹ (săp) *n.* **1. a.** The watery fluid that circulates through a plant, carrying food and other substances to the tissues. **b.** Any plant juice or fluid. **2.** Any essential bodily fluid. **3.** Health and energy; vitality. **4.** *Slang.* A weak, foolish, or gullible person. **5.** A club or bludgeon; blackjack.

—*tr.v.* **sapped, sapping, saps.** To hit or knock out with a sap. [Middle English *sap,* Old English *sæp.*] —**sap·less** *adj.*

sap² *n.* A tunnel that extends to a point underneath an enemy's fortifications.

—*v.* **sapped, sapping, saps.** —*tr.* **1.** To undermine the foundations of (a fortification). **2.** To deplete or weaken gradually or insidiously. —*intr.* To dig a sap. [Earlier *sappe,* trench, from French *sappe,* "an undermining," or Old Italian *zappat.*]

sap·a·jou (săp'ə-jōō, -zhōō') *n.* A monkey, the **capuchin** (see). [French, from Tupi.]

sapanwood. Variant of **sappanwood.**

sa·pe·le (sə-pē'lē) *n.* **1.** Any of several West African trees of the genus *Entandrophragma,* yielding a hard, dark wood resembling mahogany. **2.** The wood of such a tree used in furniture making. [West African name.]

Saphar. Variant of **Safar.**

sap·head (săp'hĕd') *n. Slang.* A fool. —**sap·head·ed** *adj.*

sa·phe·na (sə-fē'nə) *n., pl.* **-nae** (-nē). Either of two large superficial veins on the inner and outer sides of the leg and foot. [Middle English, from Medieval Latin, from Arabic *ṣāfin.*] —**sa·phe·nous** *adj.*

sap·id (săp'ĭd) *adj.* **1.** Having a distinctive, usually pleasant flavor; savory. **2.** Pleasing to the mind; engaging. [Latin *sapidus,* tasty, from *sapere,* to taste, savor.] —**sa·pid·i·ty** (să-pĭd'ə-tē) *n.*

sa·pi·ent (sā'pē-ənt) *adj.* Having wisdom; wise. [Middle English, from Old French, from Latin *sapiēns* (stem *sapient-*), present parti-

ciple of *sapere,* to taste, to have good taste, to be sensible or wise.]
—**sa·pi·ence** *n.* —**sa·pi·ent·ly** *adv.*

Sa·pir (sə-pîr′), **Edward** (1884–1939). U.S. anthropologist and linguist, born in Germany. He was a professor at the University of Chicago (1925–31) and then at Yale. He is renowned for his studies of the languages of the American Indians of the Northwest and for his interest in the ways in which language shapes thought.

sap·ling (săp′lĭng) *n.* **1.** A young tree. **2.** A youth. **3.** A greyhound less than one year old. [SAP (juice) + -LING.]

sap·o·dil·la (săp′ə-dĭl′ə, -dē′yə) *n.* **1.** An evergreen tree, *Achras zapota,* of tropical America, having latex that yields chicle. **2.** The edible russet fruit of this tree. Also called "naseberry." [Spanish *zapotillo,* diminutive of *zapote,* sapodilla fruit, from Nahuatl *tzapotl.*]

sap·o·na·ceous (săp′ə-nā′shəs) *adj.* Having the qualities of soap. [New Latin *saponaceus* : Latin *sāpō* (stem *sāpōn-*), soap + -ACEOUS.] —**sap·o·na·ceous·ness** *n.*

sap·o·na·ted (săp′ə-nā′tĭd) *adj.* Combined or treated with a soap. [Latin *sāpō* (stem *sāpōn-*), soap.]

sa·pon·i·fi·ca·tion (sə-pŏn′ə-fĭ-kā′shən) *n. Chemistry.* The hydrolysis of an ester by an alkali, producing a free alcohol and an acid salt; especially, alkaline hydrolysis of fats to make soap.

sa·pon·i·fy (sə-pŏn′ə-fī′) *v.* **-fied, -fy·ing, -fies.** *Chemistry.* —*tr.* **1.** To convert (an ester) by saponification. **2.** To convert (fats) into soap. —*intr.* To undergo saponification. [French *saponifier* : Latin *sāpō* (stem *sāpōn-*), soap.] —**sa·pon·i·fi·a·ble** *adj.* —**sa·pon·i·fi·er** *n.*

sap·o·nin (săp′ə-nĭn) *n.* Any of various plant glucosides that form soapy colloidal solutions when mixed and agitated with water, used in detergents, synthetic sex hormones, foaming agents, and emulsifiers. [French *saponine* : Latin *sāpō* (stem *sāpōn-*), soap + -IN.]

sap·o·nite (săp′ə-nīt′) *n.* An amorphous, hydrous silicate of aluminum and magnesium occurring as a soaplike mass in the cavities of certain rocks, such as diabase. [Swedish *saponit* : Latin *sāpō* (stem *sāpōn-*), soap + -ITE.]

sa·por (sā′pər, -pôr′) *n.* A quality perceptible to the sense of taste. [Middle English, from Latin *sapor,* taste, from *sapere,* to taste.] —**sap·o·rif·ic** (săp′ə-rĭf′ĭk), **sa·po·rous** (sā′pər-əs, săp′ər-) *adj.*

sap·pan·wood, sap·an·wood (să-păn′wood′, săp′ən-) *n.* **1.** A tree, *Caesalpinia sappan,* of tropical Asia, having wood that yields a red dye. **2.** The wood of this tree. [Malay *sapang* + WOOD.]

sap·per (săp′ər) *n.* **1.** A soldier skilled in sapping. **2.** A military engineer who lays, detects, and disarms mines.

Sap·phic (săf′ĭk) *adj.* **1.** Of or pertaining to the Greek poet Sappho. **2. a.** Designating a verse meter of 11 syllables with a dactyl at the third foot. **b.** Designating a stanza of three lines in such meter followed by a shorter line of a dactyl and spondee. **3.** *Usually* **sapphic.** Of or pertaining to lesbianism.
~*n.* A Sapphic meter, line, stanza, or poem.

sap·phire (săf′īr′) *n.* **1.** Any of several relatively pure forms of corundum, especially a blue form used as a gemstone. **2.** A corundum gem. **3.** The deep blue color of a gem sapphire.
~*adj.* Having the color of a blue sapphire. [Middle English *saphir, safir,* from Old French *safir,* from Latin *sapphīrus,* from Greek *sappheiros;* perhaps akin to Sanskrit *śanipriya,* "precious to the planet Saturn" : *Śani†,* the planet Saturn + *priya-,* precious.]

sap·phi·rine (săf′ə-rīn′, -rēn′, să-fīr′ĭn) *adj.* Of or resembling sapphire.
~*n. Mineralogy.* A rare light blue or green aluminum-magnesium silicate mineral.

sap·phism (săf′ĭz′əm) *n.* Lesbianism. [After SAPPHO, referring to her supposed homosexuality.]

Sap·pho (săf′ō) (c. 612–580 B.C.). Greek lyric poet. She lived on Lesbos, and her passionate poetry appears to have been directed at her coterie of female admirers. Only fragments of her work have survived, but it was ranked very highly by the ancients.

Sap·po·ro (sə-pôr′ō, -pōr′ō). City in Japan, capital of the island of Hokkaido. It is a popular winter resort with an annual festival in which giant figures of carved ice are displayed.

sap·py (săp′ē) *adj.* **-pi·er, -pi·est. 1.** Full of sap; juicy. **2.** Vital; vigorous. **3.** *Slang.* Silly or foolish. —**sap·pi·ly** *adv.* —**sap·pi·ness** *n.*

sa·pre·mi·a, sa·prae·mi·a (sə-prē′mē-ə) *n.* Septicemia (see).

sapro-, sapr- *prefix.* Indicates dead or decaying material; for example, **saprophyte, sapremia.** [Greek, from *sapros,* rotten, putrid, akin to *sēpein,* to rot. See *septic.*]

sap·robe (săp′rōb′) *n.* An organism that derives its nourishment from nonliving or decaying organic matter. [SAPRO- + Greek *bios,* life.] —**sa·pro·bic** (să-prō′bĭk) *adj.* —**sa·pro·bi·cal·ly** *adv.*

sap·ro·gen·ic (săp′rə-jĕn′ĭk) *adj.* Also **sa·prog·e·nous** (sə-prŏj′ə-nəs). **1.** Producing decay or putrefaction: *saprogenic bacteria.* **2.** Resulting from decay or putrefaction. [SAPRO- + -GENIC.] —**sap·ro·ge·nic·i·ty** (săp′rə-jə-nĭs′ə-tē) *n.*

sap·ro·lite (săp′rə-līt′) *n.* Clay, silt, or other remnants remaining in the site of a disintegrated rock. [SAPRO- + -LITE.]

sap·ro·pel (săp′rə-pĕl′) *n.* An organic sludge that accumulates on the beds of lakes or seas. It consists of the decomposed remains of aquatic organisms, mainly algae. [SAPRO- + Greek *pēlos,* clay, mud.] —**sap·ro·pel·ic** (săp′rə-pĕl′ĭk, -pē′lĭk) *adj.*

sa·proph·a·gous (să-prŏf′ə-gəs) *adj.* Feeding on decaying matter. [SAPRO- + -PHAGOUS.]

sap·ro·phyte (săp′rə-fīt′) *n. Biology.* A living organism, such as a fungus or bacterium, that lives on and derives its nourishment from dead or decaying organic matter. [SAPRO- + -PHYTE.] —**sap·ro·phyt·ic** (săp′rə-fĭt′ĭk) *adj.*

sap·ro·zo·ic (săp′rə-zō′ĭk) *adj.* **1.** Pertaining to or designating nutrition by absorption of dissolved organic materials, as in protozoans and some fungi. **2.** Feeding on dead or decaying organic matter. [SAPRO- + -ZOIC.]

sap·wood (săp′wood′) *n.* Newly formed living wood that lies just inside the bark of a tree or woody plant, is actively involved in food and water transport, and is lighter in color than the heartwood. Also called "alburnum."

Saq·qa·ra or **Sak·ka·ra** (sə-kä′rə). Historical site near the village of Saqqara in lower Egypt. It lies close to the site of the ancient city of Memphis, and its most prominent monument is the stone-built stepped pyramid of King Zoser.

sar·a·band, sar·a·bande (săr′ə-bănd′) *n.* **1.** A stately court dance of the 17th and 18th centuries, in slow triple time. **2.** Music for the saraband. [French, from Spanish *zarabanda†.*]

Sar·a·cen (săr′ə-sən) *n.* **1.** A member of a pre-Islamic nomadic people of the Syrian-Arabian deserts. **2.** An Arab. **3.** A Muslim of the time of the Crusades. [Middle English, from Old French *Saracin,* from Late Latin *Saracēnus,* from Late Greek *Sarakēnos,* probably from Arabic *sharqīyīn,* "Easterners," from *sharq,* sunrise, east, from *shāraqa,* to rise.] —**Sar·a·cen, Sar·a·cen·ic** (săr′ə-sĕn′ĭk) *adj.*

Saragossa. See **Zaragoza.**

Sa·rah (sâr′ə). The wife of Abraham and mother of Isaac. Genesis 7:15. [Hebrew *Sārāh,* "princess."]

Sa·ra·je·vo (să′rə-yā′vō, săr′ə-). Industrial city in central Yugoslavia. It is the capital of the republic of Bosnia and Hercegovina. In 1914 Archduke Francis Ferdinand, heir apparent to the throne of Austria-Hungary, was assassinated here by Gavrilo Princip, a Serbian nationalist, an event that precipitated World War I.

sa·ran (sə-răn′) *n.* Any of various thermoplastic resins derived from vinyl compounds and used to make packaging films, corrosion-resistant pipes, fittings, and bristles and as a fiber in various heavy textiles. [From the trademark *Saran.*]

Sar·a·nac Lakes (săr′ə-năk′). Three lakes in a resort region of northeastern New York State, known as Upper Saranac, Middle Saranac, and Lower Saranac. They are linked by the Saranac River, which flows from the Lower Saranac northeast to Lake Champlain.

sarape. Variant of **serape.**

Sar·a·so·ta (săr′ə-sō′tə). City of southwestern Florida, on Sarasota Bay, an inlet of the Gulf of Mexico. It is a yachting and fishing resort, with varied light industry. The city is the winter home of the Ringling Brothers and Barnum & Bailey Circus and the site of the Circus Hall of Fame.

Sar·a·to·ga Springs (săr′ə-tō′gə). Resort city of eastern New York State. Famed for its carbonated mineral waters, the village became a health and pleasure resort after the American Revolution. During the 19th century it was one of the most popular social and sporting centers in America.

Saratoga trunk *n.* A large traveling trunk with a rounded lid. [After SARATOGA SPRINGS.]

Sa·ra·wak (sə-rä′wäk). State of Malaysia on the northwestern coast of the island of Borneo. It has a mountainous interior and a swampy coastal plain where rubber, pepper, and rice are grown. It is rich in oil, its main export.

sar·casm (sär′kăz′əm) *n.* **1.** A sharply mocking or contemptuously ironic remark intended to wound another. **2.** A kind of ironic wit that typically uses statements or implications pointedly opposite or irrelevant to the meaning that the speaker wishes to convey. **3.** The use of sarcasm. —See Synonyms at **wit.** [French *sarcasme,* from Greek *sarkasmos,* from *sarkazein,* "to tear flesh," bite the lips in rage, speak bitterly, from *sarx* (stem *sark-*), flesh.]

sar·cas·tic (sär-kăs′tĭk) *adj.* **1.** Characterized by or full of sarcasm. **2.** Given to using sarcasm. [French *sarcastique,* from *sarcasme,* SARCASM.] —**sar·cas·ti·cal·ly** *adv.*

Usage: **sarcastic, ironic, caustic, satirical, sardonic.** These adjectives apply to language or remarks that are bitter, cutting, or derisive. *Sarcastic* and *ironic* both pertain to a form of expression in which meanings are conveyed obliquely. *Sarcastic* suggests taunting and ridicule; *ironic* suggests a milder and subtler form of mockery. *Caustic* can apply to any expression that is mocking or ironic in a harsh or cutting way. *Satirical* refers to expression that seeks to expose wrong or folly to ridicule, often by means of sarcasm or irony. *Sardonic* can describe both the content and the manner of expression and implies scorn or mockery overlaid with cynicism.

sarce·net, sarse·net (sär′snĭt) *n.* A fine, soft silk cloth. [Middle English *sarsenet,* from Norman French *sarzinett,* perhaps diminutive of *(drap) Sarzin,* Saracen (cloth), from Latin *Saracēnus,* SARACEN.]

sarco-, sarc- *prefix.* Indicates flesh; for example, **sarcoma, sarcophagus.** [Greek *sarx* (stem *sark-*), flesh.]

sar·co·carp (sär′kə-kärp′) *n. Botany.* The fleshy pulp surrounding the seed of a drupaceous fruit such as a peach or plum. [French *sarcocarpe* : SARCO- + -CARP.]

sar·coid (sär′koid′) *adj.* Pertaining to or resembling flesh.
~*n.* A fleshy tumor. [Greek *sarkoeidēs* : SARC(O)- + -OID.]

sar·co·ma (sär-kō′mə) *n., pl.* **-mas** or **-mata** (-mə-tə). A malignant tumor arising from nonepithelial connective tissues, such as muscle, blood, or fat. [New Latin, from Greek *sarkōma,* fleshy excrescence : *sarkoun,* to make fleshy, from *sarx* (stem *sark-*), flesh + -OMA.] —**sar·co·ma·toid** (sär-kō′mə-toid′), **sar·co·ma·tous** (-təs) *adj.*

sar·co·ma·to·sis (sär-kō′mə-tō′sĭs) *n. Pathology.* A condition characterized by the formation of numerous sarcomas in the body. [New Latin : *sarcoma* (stem *sarcomat-*), SARCOMA + -OSIS.]

sar·co·mere (sär′kə-mîr′) *n.* A contractile unit in a striated muscle fibril. [SARCO- + -MERE.]

sar·coph·a·gus (sär-kŏf′ə-gəs) *n., pl.* **-gi** (-jī′) or **-guses.** A stone coffin, often inscribed or decorated with sculpture. [Latin *sarcophagus (lapis),* "flesh-eating (stone)," from Greek *(lithos) sarkophagos* : SARCO- + -PHAGOUS.]

sar·co·plasm (sär′kə-plăz′əm) *n.* The cytoplasm of striated muscle fibers occurring between the muscle fibrils. [SARCO- + -PLASM.] —**sar·co·plas·mic** (sär′kə-plăz′mĭk) *adj.*

sar·cop·tic mange (sär-kŏp′tĭk) *n.* Mange that is caused by the mite *Sarcoptes scabiei.* [From New Latin *Sarcoptes,* genus name : SARCO- + Greek *koptein,* to cut.]

sar·cous (sär′kəs) *adj.* Of, pertaining to, or consisting of flesh or muscle. [Greek *sarx* (stem *sark-*), flesh.]

sard (särd) *n.* A clear or translucent deep orange-red to brownish red chalcedony. [French *sarde,* from Latin *sarda,* perhaps variant of Greek *sardion,* "the Sardian stone," from *Sardeis,* SARDIS.]

sardar. Variant of **sirdar.**

sar·dine (sär-dēn′) *n.* **1.** Any of various small or half-grown edible herrings or related fishes of the family Clupeidae; especially, a young pilchard, frequently canned in oil. **2.** Any of numerous small, silvery freshwater or marine fishes that are unrelated to the sardine but are similarly processed. [Middle English *sardeyn,* from Old French *sardine,* from Latin *sardīna,* from Greek *sardinos,* possibly from *Sardō,* SARDINIA.]

Sar·din·i·a (sär-dĭn′ē-ə). Island in the Mediterranean. It is largely mountainous, its chief agricultural area being the fertile Campidano plain in the southwest. Cereals, olives, and vines are grown, and sheep and goats are raised. Sardinia is rich in minerals, including zinc, lead, coal, and copper.

Sar·din·i·an (sär-dĭn′ē-ən) *n.* **1.** A native or inhabitant of Sardinia. **2.** A Romance language spoken in Sardinia. —**Sar·din·i·an** *adj.*

Sar·dis (sär′dĭs). Also **Sar·des** (-dēz′). Capital of ancient Lydia, now a small village in western Turkey. When Lydia was absorbed into the Persian Empire following the defeat of Croesus (*c.* 550 B.C.), Sardis remained the provincial capital of Asia Minor. It later became an early center of Christianity. Excavations of the site have yielded the earliest known coins, dating from *c.* 700 B.C.

sar·don·ic (sär-dŏn′ĭk) *adj.* Scornful or mocking, especially in a cynical way. —See Usage note at **sarcastic.** [French *sardonique,* from Latin *Sardonius (rīsus),* bitter (laugh), from Late Greek *Sardonios,* Sardinian, alteration (influenced by Latin *herba Sardonia,* "Sardinian herb," a poisonous plant supposed to distort the face of the eater) of *sardanios,* bitter, scornful.] —**sar·don·i·cal·ly** *adv.* —**sar·don·i·cism** (sär-dŏn′ə-sĭz′əm) *n.*

sar·don·yx (sär-dŏn′ĭks, sär′də-nĭks′) *n.* A variety of chalcedony with alternating brown and white bands. [Middle English *sardonix,* from Latin *sardonyx,* from Greek *sardonux* : probably *sardion,* SARD + *onux,* ONYX.]

sar·gas·so (sär-găs′ō) *n.* A seaweed, **gulfweed** (*see*). [Portuguese *sargaço†.*]

Sar·gas·so Sea (sär-găs′ō). Large area of the North Atlantic between latitudes 20° and 35°N and longitudes 30° and 70°W. Ocean currents sweep clockwise around it, leaving its center relatively still. The sea is named after the floating seaweed *Sargassum bacciferum,* found here in abundance.

sarge (särj) *n. Informal.* Sergeant.

Sar·gent (sär′jənt), **John Singer** (1856–1925). U.S. portrait painter. He is famous for his portraits and water colors, including his celebrated World War I landscape *Gassed* (1918).

Sar·gon (sär′gŏn′, -gən). King of Assyria (722–705 B.C.), founder of the last major Assyrian dynasty. He continued his predecessor's war against the northern Jewish kingdom of Israel (later known as Samaria) and destroyed it (721), taking many Israelite captives.

sa·ri (sä′rē) *n., pl.* **-ris.** An outer garment, worn as traditional dress chiefly by Hindu women, consisting of a length of lightweight cloth with one end wrapped about the waist to form a skirt and the other draped over the shoulder or covering the head. [Hindi *sārī,* from Sanskrit *śāṭī,* "cloth," sari.]

sark (särk) *n. Chiefly Scottish.* A shirt. [Middle English *serk,* from Old Norse *serkr,* from Germanic.]

Sark (särk). One of the Channel Islands and part of the bailiwick of Guernsey. Sark comprises Great Sark and Little Sark, connected by a narrow isthmus called the Coupée. Created a seigneury by Elizabeth I, the island is still ruled in a semifeudal manner by a seigneur or dame.

Sar·ma·ti·a (sär-mā′shē-ə, -shə). An ancient region in eastern Europe, between the Vistula and the Volga in present-day Poland and the U.S.S.R.

sar·men·tose (sär-mĕn′tōs′) *adj.* Also **sar·men·tous** (-təs). *Botany.* Having slender, prostrate stems or runners that root at intervals, as the strawberry does. [Latin *sarmentōsus,* full of twigs, from *sarmentum,* twig, from *sarpere,* to cut off, prune.]

Sar·noff (sär′nôf′), **David** (1891–1971). U.S. businessman, born in Russia. He gained renown as the first telegraph operator to intercept distress signals from the *Titanic* (1912). Later, as president of the Radio Corporation of America (RCA), he played a major role in the development of television, founding the National Broadcasting Company (NBC) and pioneering the use of color transmission.

sa·rod (sə-rōd′) *n.* An Indian musical instrument that resembles a lute and has two sets of strings. [Hindi.]

sa·rong (sə-rông′, -rŏng′) *n.* A skirt consisting of a length of brightly colored cloth wrapped about the waist that is worn by both men and women of the Malay Archipelago and the Pacific islands. [Malay, sheath, covering, sarong.]

sa·ros (sä′rŏs′) *n.* A cycle of 6,585.32 days during which solar and lunar eclipses occur at regular intervals in the same sequence. [Greek, from Babylonian *šāru,* 3,600 (years); the modern use is apparently based on a misinterpretation of the original cycle as one of 18.5 years.]

Sa·roy·an (sə-roi′ən), **William** (1908–81). U.S. writer. He achieved success as a short-story writer with *The Daring Young Man on the Flying Trapeze* (1934). He also produced novels and plays.

sar·rus·o·phone (sə-rōō′zə-fōn′, -rūs′ə-fōn′) *n.* A brass wind instrument that has a double reed and is played like a bassoon. [After *Sarrus,* 19th-century French bandmaster who invented it (1856).] —**sar·rus·o·phon·ist** *n.*

sar·sa·pa·ril·la (săs′pə-rĭl′ə, sär′spə-) *n.* **1. a.** The dried roots of any of several tropical American plants of the genus *Smilax,* especially *S. aristolochiaefolia,* of Mexico, used as a flavoring and formerly as an emetic and to treat psoriasis. **b.** A sweet soft drink flavored with sarsaparilla. **2.** Either of two North American plants, *Aralia hispida* or *A. nudicaulis,* having clusters of small white flowers. [Spanish *zarzaparrilla* : *zarza,* bramble, from Arabic *sharaṣ,* thorny plant + *parrilla,* diminutive of *parra†,* vine.]

sar·sen (sär′sən) *n.* A sandstone boulder of the Tertiary period that is found mainly on the chalk lands of southern England. [17th century : from earlier *Sardens, Saracen's stones,* probably from SARACEN.]

sarsenet. Variant of **sarcenet.**

Sarto, Andrea del. See **Andrea del Sarto.**

sar·to·ri·al (sär-tôr′ē-əl, -tōr′ē-əl) *adj.* **1.** Of or pertaining to a tailor or tailoring. **2.** Of or pertaining to clothing or fashion, especially men's clothing or fashion. **3.** *Anatomy.* Of or pertaining to the sartorius. [Latin *sartor,* a tailor. See **sartorius.**] —**sar·to·ri·al·ly** *adv.*

sar·to·ri·us (sär-tôr′ē-əs, -tōr′ē-əs) *n.* A flat, narrow thigh muscle, the longest of the human body, crossing the front of the thigh obliquely from the hip to the inner side of the tibia. [New Latin *sartorius (musculus),* "tailor's muscle" (because it enables one to sit in a cross-legged position like a tailor at work), from Latin *sartor,* a tailor, from *sartus,* past participle of *sarcīre,* to mend.]

Sar·tre (sär′trə), **Jean-Paul** (1905–80). French philosopher and writer. A friend of Simone de Beauvoir and a Marxist sympathizer, he was a founder and leading exponent of the existentialist school. His work includes novels such as the *Roads to Freedom* trilogy (1945–49), philosophical essays such as *Being and Nothingness* (1943), and many plays, including *In Camera* (1944). In 1964 he refused the Nobel Prize for literature, for "personal reasons."

sash[1] (săsh) *n.* A band or ribbon worn about the waist, as for ornament, or over the shoulder as a symbol of rank. [Earlier *shash,* from Arabic *shāsh,* muslin.]

sash[2] *n.* A frame in which the panes of a window or door are set; especially, either of the two movable frames in a sash window. ~*tr.v.* **sashed, sashing, sashes.** To furnish with a sash. [Variant of earlier *shashes* (plural), from French *châssis,* a frame, CHASSIS.]

sa·shay (să-shā′) *intr.v.* **-shayed, -shaying, -shays.** *Informal.* **1. a.** To flounce and sway. **b.** To glide. **2.** To perform the chassé in dancing. ~*n. Informal.* An excursion; a sally. [Variant of CHASSÉ.]

sa·shi·mi (sä-shē′mē) *n.* A Japanese dish consisting of very thin slices of raw fish. [Japanese.]

sash window *n.* A window consisting of a fixed frame enclosing two movable sashes set in grooves one above the other so that they can slide up and down.

sa·sin (sä′sĭn, săs′ĭn) *n.* The **blackbuck** (*see*).

Sas·katch·e·wan[1] (să-skăch′ə-wän′, -wən). *Abbr.* **Sask.** Province of south-central Canada. Its southern prairies provide two-thirds of Canada's wheat, and the province is also rich in minerals, including uranium, copper, zinc, coal, potash, oil, and natural gas. The area was under the control of the Hudson's Bay Company (1670–1869) and became a province in 1905. Regina is the capital.

Saskatchewan[2]. River in central Canada. It is formed by the confluence of the North and South Saskatchewan rivers just east of Prince Albert, and flows east to Lake Winnipeg. The Qu'Appelle and Gardiner dams are major elements in the South Saskatchewan River project for hydroelectric power and irrigation.

sas·ka·toon (săs′kə-tōōn′) *n.* A shrub, *Amelanchier alnifolia,* of northwestern North America, having white flowers and edible dark-purple fruit. [Cree *misāskwatomin,* saskatoon berry : *misāskwat,* saskatoon willow + *-min,* berry.]

Sas·ka·toon (săs′kə-tōōn′). City in central Saskatchewan, Canada. Founded in 1883 on the South Saskatchewan River, it is a major rail junction and distribution center for a large agricultural area.

sass (săs) *n. Informal.* Impertinent, disrespectful speech; backtalk. ~*tr.v.* **sassed, sassing, sasses.** *Informal.* To talk impudently to; answer back. [Back-formation from SASSY (impudent).]

sas·sa·by (săs′ə-bē) *n., pl.* **-bies** or collectively **sassaby.** An African antelope, *Damaliscus lunatus,* having curved, ridged horns. [Bantu (Tswana) *tshêsêbê.*]

sas·sa·fras (săs′ə-frăs′) *n.* **1. a.** A North American tree, *Sassafras albidum,* having irregularly lobed leaves and aromatic bark. **b.** The dried root bark of this tree, used as flavoring and as a source of a volatile antiseptic oil containing camphor, safrole, and pinene. **2.** Any of various other trees with aromatic bark, as the Australian species *Doryphora sassafras* and *Atherosperma moschatum.* [New Latin, from Spanish *sasafrás†.*]

Sas·sa·nid (săs′ə-nĭd) *n., pl.* **-nids** or **Sassanidae** (sə-săn′ə-dē). Also **Sas·sa·ni·an** (sə-sā′nē-ən). A member of the dynasty of Persian kings ruling from the 3rd to the middle of the 7th century A.D. [Medieval Latin *Sassanidae* (plural), from *Sassan*, grandfather of Ardashir I, founder of the dynasty.] **—Sas·sa·nid** *adj.*

Sas·se·nach (săs′ə-năk′, -năKH′) *n. Chiefly Scottish.* An English person. Used derogatorily. [Irish *Sasanach*, from *Sasan-*, Saxon, from Late Latin *Saxonēs*, SAXON(s).] **—Sas·se·nach** *adj.*

Sas·soon (să-sōōn′), **Siegfried** (1886-1967). British poet and writer. He served in the army with distinction in Palestine and France until 1917, when disgust at the course of World War I led him to make a public refusal to serve further. His work includes *War Poems* (1919) and several largely autobiographical novels.

sass·wood (săs′wŏŏd′) *n.* A tree, the **sassy** (*see*).

sas·sy[1] (săs′ē) *adj.* **-sier, -siest.** *Informal.* **1.** Impudent. **2.** Jaunty. [Variant of SAUCY.] **—sas·si·ly** *adv.* **—sas·si·ness** *n.*

sassy[2] *n., pl.* **-sies.** A tree, *Erythrophloeum guineense*, of western Africa, having bark that yields a poison. Also called "sasswood." [Probably of African origin.]

sas·tru·ga (sə-strōō′gə) *n., pl.* **-gi** (-gē). Also **zas·tru·ga** (zə-). A long, wavelike ridge of snow formed by the wind and found on the polar plains. [Russian *zastruga*, groove : *za*, by + *struga*, deep place.]

sat. Past tense and past participle of **sit.**

Sat. Saturday.

Sa·tan (sāt′n) *n.* In Judaism and Christianity, the chief adversary of God and mankind; the Devil. [Middle English, Old English, from Late Latin *Satān*, from Greek *Satan*, from Hebrew *śāṭān*, devil, adversary, from *śāṭan*, to accuse.]

sa·tang (sə-tăng′) *n., pl.* **satang.** A coin equal to ¹/₁₀₀ of the baht of Thailand. See feature at **currency.** [Thai *satān*.]

sa·tan·ic (sə-tăn′ĭk) *adj.* Also **sa·tan·i·cal** (-ĭ-kəl). **1.** Pertaining to or suggestive of Satan or Satanism. **2.** Profoundly cruel or evil; fiendish. **—sa·tan·i·cal·ly** *adv.*

Sa·tan·ism (sāt′n-ĭz′əm) *n.* **1.** Worship of Satan, especially in the form of a travesty of Christian ritual. **2. satanism.** Evil or satanic practices or tendencies. **—Sa·tan·ist** *n.*

satch·el (săch′əl) *n.* A small bag, often having a shoulder strap and used, especially by schoolchildren, for carrying articles such as clothing and books. [Middle English *sachel*, from Old French, from Latin *saccellus*, diminutive of *saccus*, a bag, SACK.]

sate[1] (sāt) *tr.v.* **sated, sating, sates.** **1.** To indulge (a person, an appetite, or a desire) fully. **2.** To indulge to excess; glut. **—See** Synonyms at **satiate.** [Probably variant (influenced by SATIATE) of obsolete *sade*, Middle English *sad(d)en*, Old English *sadian*.]

sate[2]. *Archaic.* Past tense of **sit.**

sa·teen (să-tēn′) *n.* A cotton fabric with a satin weave and a glossy sheen. [Variant of SATIN (influenced by VELVETEEN).]

sat·el·lite (săt′l-īt′) *n.* **1.** *Astronomy.* A relatively small body orbiting a planet; a moon. **2.** *Aerospace.* A man-made object designed to orbit a celestial body, as the earth or moon. Also called "artificial satellite." **3.** One who attends a powerful dignitary. **4.** One that is dependent on another, as: **a.** A subservient follower. **b.** A nation that is dominated politically by another. **c.** A small town, such as a suburb, that is economically dependent on a larger neighboring town or city. [French, from Latin *satelles* (stem *satellit-*), an attendant, escort, probably from Etruscan *śatnal*.]

sa·tem (sä′təm) *adj.* Of, pertaining to, or constituting the group of those Indo-European languages in which the velar *k* of primitive Indo-European became *s* and the labiovelar *kw* became *k*. Compare **centum.** [Avestan *satam*, hundred (an arbitrarily chosen word whose initial sound illustrates the sound change).]

Sa·ti (sä′tē) *n. Hinduism.* The goddess Devi as a self-sacrificing mother.

sa·tia·ble (sā′shə-bəl) *adj.* Capable of being satiated. [Latin *satiābilis*, from Latin *satiāre*, to SATIATE.] **—sa·tia·bil·i·ty** (sā′shə-bĭl′ə-tē), **sa·tia·ble·ness** *n.* **—sa·tia·bly** *adv.*

sa·ti·ate (sā′shē-āt′) *tr.v.* **-ated, -ating, -ates.** **1.** To gratify to excess; surfeit. **2.** To satisfy (an appetite or desire) fully; sate. *~adj.* (-ĭt). Filled to satisfaction; satiated. [From Latin *satiāre*, from *satis*, sufficient, enough.] **—sa·ti·a·tion** *n.*

Synonyms: glut, gorge, sate, surfeit.

Sa·tie (sä-tē′), **Erik**, born Alfred Erik Leslie-Satie (1866-1925). French composer, chiefly of piano works and ballets, noted for his eccentricity and humor. He used simplicity of technique to achieve surreal effects, as in the *Gymnopédies* (1888).

sa·ti·e·ty (sə-tī′ə-tē) *n.* **1.** The condition of being full to satisfaction. **2.** The condition of being gratified beyond the point of satisfaction; surfeit. [Obsolete French *societé*, from Latin *satietās* (stem *satie-tāt-*), sufficiency, from *satis*, sufficient, enough.]

sat·in (săt′n) *n.* A smooth fabric, as of silk, rayon, or nylon, with a glossy face and a dull back. *~adj.* **1.** Made of satin. **2.** Resembling satin, as in texture or appearance. [Middle English, from Old French, from Arabic; possibly ultimately from Chinese.]

sat·i·net, sat·i·nette (săt′n-ĕt′) *n.* A thin satin or an imitation satin, such as a blend of cotton and silk or cotton and wool. [French, from Old French, diminutive of SATIN.]

sat·in-flow·er (săt′n-flou′ər) *n.* **1.** A European plant, *Stellaria holostea*, with white flowers. **2.** A plant, *Godetia grandiflora*, of California, having showy red-blotched flowers.

sat·in·pod (săt′n-pŏd′) *n.* A plant, **honesty** (*see*).

satin stitch *n.* An embroidery stitch worked in close parallel lines to give a smooth finish.

satin weave *n.* A basic weave construction with the interlacing of the threads so arranged that the face of the cloth is covered with warp yarn or filling yarn and no twill line is distinguishable.

sat·in·wood (săt′n-wŏŏd′) *n.* **1. a.** A tree, *Chloroxylon swietenia*, of southern Asia, having hard, yellowish, close-grained wood. **b.** The wood of this tree, used in cabinetwork. **2. a.** Any of several other trees having similar wood. **b.** The wood of any of these trees.

sat·in·y (săt′n-ē) *adj.* Lustrous and smooth like satin.

sat·ire (săt′īr′) *n.* **1.** A dramatic or literary work or performance in which irony, derision, caricature, or wit is used to expose folly or wickedness, especially by ridiculing aspects of and personalities in contemporary society. **2.** The branch of entertainment or art, especially literature, comprising such works. **3.** The use of derisive wit

---

satellite

TRANSMITTERS IN ORBIT
Relaying signals and monitoring the weather

Artificial satellites for communications purposes can relay television programs, telephone calls, telex, computer data, and printed matter. They operate by receiving radio signals from the earth, amplifying them, and transmitting them to other points on earth. Such satellites must orbit hundreds of miles above the earth; at low levels their range would be severely limited by the earth's curvature.

Weather satellites record information on cloud, snow, ice cover, and temperature, and transmit it by infrared TV pictures. They are particularly vital for giving advance warning of hurricanes and other storm systems, and their information, shared internationally, has led to the saving of lives and property that has more than repaid their cost.

The first weather satellites, code named Tiros, were launched in 1960 by the United States. Tiros was followed by increasingly involved series in many different orbits: ESSA (Environmental Science Services Administration) satellites, the Nimbus series, and the National Oceanic and Atmospheric Administration series (NOAA). Another series in geostationary orbits—that is, maintaining position above the same point of the earth—provide permanent monitoring of selected areas. Most of these are U.S. satellites, but the U.S.S.R. has its own series, Meteor.

In the 1970's three other U.S. satellites, Landsats (originally called Earth Resources and Technology satellites), were placed in orbits that scan the whole earth every 18 days, and can stay in operation indefinitely. Landsats use both still and TV cameras and work in four wavelengths, each revealing a different type of information—on forest cover, crops, water and air pollution, and marine resources.

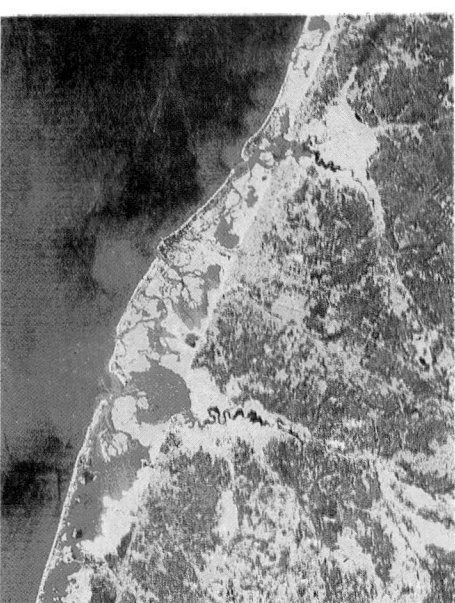

DEVELOPMENT AID *Computer-aided photography by a U.S. satellite provides information on land cover to help in making decisions about land development. Different colors indicate different features: red areas show urban complexes; green, forest land; and blue, marsh areas and water. The deeper the intensity of the color, the more concentrated is the feature.*

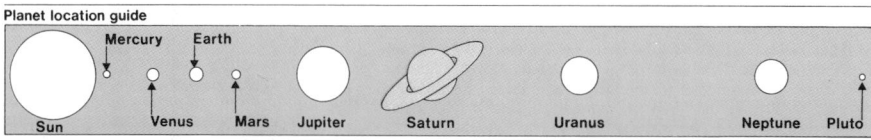

saturated *Ethane (C₂H₆)—a colorless, odorless gas—is known as a saturated compound; its atoms are linked only by single bonds (upper drawing). Unsaturated compounds—such as the flammable gas ethene, or ethylene, C₂H₄ (lower drawing)—contain double or triple bonds and combine with other chemicals more readily than saturated compounds. Ethane and ethylene are both used in the manufacture of plastics.*

or irony to attack or ridicule folly, stupidity, or wickedness. —See Synonyms at **caricature.** [French, from Latin *satira, satura,* satire, medley, mixture, mixed fruits, from the feminine of *satur,* full of food, sated.]

sa·tir·i·cal (sə-tĭr′ĭ-kəl) *adj.* Also **sa·tir·ic** (-tĭr′ĭk). Constituting, characteristic of, or inclined to the use of satire. —See Usage note at **sarcastic.** —**sa·tir·i·cal·ly** *adv.* —**sa·tir·i·cal·ness** *n.*

sat·i·rist (săt′ər-ĭst) *n.* **1.** A writer of satirical works. **2.** One who uses or tends to use satire.

sat·i·rize (săt′ə-rīz′) *tr.v.* **-rized, -rizing, -rizes.** To ridicule or attack by means of satire.

sat·is·fac·tion (săt′ĭs-făk′shən) *n.* **1.** The fulfillment or gratification of a desire, need, or appetite. **2.** Pleasure or contentment, as that derived from the gratification of a desire or from a personal achievement or attainment: *gets a lot of satisfaction from her work.* **3.** Reparation in the form of penance for sin; atonement. **4.** Compensation for injury or loss, as to one's honor or reputation; reparation. **5.** A source of gratification. **6.** Assurance; certainty.

sat·is·fac·to·ry (săt′ĭs-făk′tə-rē) *adj.* **1.** Giving satisfaction; sufficient to meet a demand or requirement; adequate: *a satisfactory reason.* **2.** Warranting some pleasure; gratifying. **3.** Serving to atone for sin. —**sat·is·fac·to·ri·ly** *adv.* —**sat·is·fac·to·ri·ness** *n.*

sat·is·fy (săt′ĭs-fī′) *v.* **-fied, -fying, -fies.** —*tr.* **1.** To gratify the need, desire, or expectation of. **2.** To fulfill (a need or desire). **3.** To relieve of doubt or question; assure. **4.** To suffice to dispel (a doubt or question). **5.** To fulfill or discharge (an obligation, contract, or debt). **6.** To discharge an obligation to (a creditor). **7.** To conform to the requirements of (a standard or rule, for example). **8.** To make reparation to (a wronged party). **9.** *Mathematics.* To fulfill the conditions of (a theorem, equation, or the like). —*intr.* To give satisfaction. [Middle English *satisfien,* from Old French *satisfier,* from Latin *satisfacere* : *satis,* sufficient, enough + *facere,* to do, make.] —**sat·is·fi·er** *n.* —**sat·is·fy·ing·ly** *adv.*

sa·to·ri (sä-tôr′ē, -tōr′ē, sə-) *n.* A state of spiritual enlightenment sought in Zen Buddhism. [Japanese, "insight."]

sa·trap (sā′trăp′, săt′răp′) *n.* **1.** A governor of a province in ancient Persia. **2.** Any colonial governor or subordinate ruler. [Middle English *satrape,* from Old French, from Latin *satrapēs,* from Greek, from Old Persian *khshathrapāvan,* "protector of the country" : *khshathra-,* province, country + *-pāvan,* protector.]

sa·trap·y (sā′trə-pē, săt′rə-) *n., pl.* **-ies.** **1.** The territory or sphere under the rule of a satrap. **2.** The office of satrap. **3.** The period of rule of a satrap. [French *satrapie,* from Latin *satrapia,* from Greek *satrapeia,* from *satrapēs,* SATRAP.]

sat·su·ma (săt-sōō′mə, săt′sə-) *n.* **1. a.** A variety of the small citrus tree *Citrus reticulata,* native to Japan, grown widely for its sweet mandarinlike fruit. **b.** The fruit of this tree, having a loose orange rind and segmented pulp. **2. Satsuma.** A fine yellow Japanese porcelain ware. [After *Satsuma,* former province of Kyushu, Japan.]

sat·u·rant (săch′ər-ənt) *n.* A substance used to saturate a solution. [Latin *saturāns* (stem *saturānt-*), present participle of *saturāre,* to SATURATE.] —**sat·u·rant** *adj.*

sat·u·rate (săch′ə-rāt′) *tr.v.* **-rated, -rating, -rates.** **1.** To wet thoroughly; fill with moisture. **2.** To steep, imbue, or impregnate thoroughly: *"The recollection was saturated with sunshine"* (Vladimir Nabokov). **3.** To fill to capacity or beyond; surfeit; sate. **4.** *Chemistry.* **a.** To cause (a solution) to be saturated. **b.** To cause (a compound) to be saturated. **5.** *Military.* To subject (a target) to heavy bombardment with the aim of totally destroying enemy defenses. —*adj.* (-rĭt). Saturated. [Latin *saturāre,* to fill, satiate, from *satur,* full of food, sated.] —**sat·u·ra·bil·i·ty** (săch′ər-ə-bĭl′ə-tē) *n.* —**sat·u·ra·ble** (săch′ər-ə-bəl) *adj.* —**sat·u·ra·tor** *n.*

sat·u·rat·ed (săch′ə-rā′tĭd) *adj.* **1.** Unable to hold or contain more of a substance; full. **2.** *Chemistry.* **a.** Containing all the solute that can normally be dissolved at a given temperature. Said of a solution. **b.** Containing all the vapor, as water vapor, that can normally

---

Saturn

A GASEOUS GIANT AND ITS MYSTERIOUS RINGS

The complex of icy circles seen by Voyager space probes

Saturn, one of the outer planets of the Solar System and second in size only to Jupiter, is visible to the naked eye as a bright, yellowish star. Saturn's overall density is less than that of water, and it probably has a rocky core surrounded by layers of liquid hydrogen, which are in turn overlaid by a gaseous atmosphere—the actual surface that we can see. The cloud tops are very cold, at a temperature of about −180°C (−292°F). But the core must be hot since Saturn radiates more energy than it receives from the Sun.

The main glory of Saturn is its magnificent system of rings, visible with a small telescope, which are composed of icy particles. There are two main rings, separated by a gap known as Cassini's Division, and various less conspicuous rings. The Voyager space probes have shown that the rings are very complex and are made up of thousands of individual thin rings separated by gaps.

Saturn has a wealth of satellites; nine were known before the flights of the Pioneer and Voyager space probes, and today at least 20 are known. Most of them are comparatively small, but there is one large satellite, Titan, which is 5,800 kilometers (3,600 miles) in diameter—bigger than the planet Mercury. Titan has a dense atmosphere composed chiefly of nitrogen, with considerable quantities of methane. On Titan's surface, hidden by a reddish photochemical smog, there may be cliffs of solid methane, rivers of liquid methane, and a methane drizzle from the clouds.

Planet location guide

Sun   Mercury   Venus   Earth   Mars   Jupiter   Saturn   Uranus   Neptune   Pluto

VOYAGER'S VIEW OF SATURN *Color pictures sent back to the earth by Voyager 2 revealed among the yellow and pastel hues of the planet's surface many dark and light bands in both hemispheres. The contrasts are believed to be caused by Saturn's weather system. Three of Saturn's moons—Tethys, Dione, and Rhea—show as bright spots below Saturn, and Tethys casts its shadow on the planet.*

SATURN'S RINGS *Computer-enhanced color pictures of Saturn's rings record differences that may be caused by chemical variations from one part to another. The lumps of icy material that make up the rings range from the size of a house down to that of coins. The outermost ring contains two strands twisted around each other and this braided effect is believed to be caused by Saturn's magnetic field.*

be present at a given temperature. Said of a gas. **c.** Having all available valence bonds filled. Said especially of organic compounds. **3.** *Geology.* Of or designating minerals that can crystallize from magmas even in the presence of excess silica. **4.** In a state of saturation. Said of a color. **5.** Soaked with moisture; drenched.

sat·u·ra·tion (săch'ə-rā'shən) *n.* **1. a.** The act or process of saturating. **b.** The condition of being saturated. **2.** *Physics.* A state of a ferromagnetic substance in which an increase in applied magnetic field strength does not produce an increase in magnetic field strength. **3.** *Chemistry.* The state of a compound or solution that is fully saturated. **4.** *Meteorology.* A condition in which air at a specific temperature contains all the moisture vapor possible without precipitating; 100 percent relative humidity. **5.** Vividness of hue; degree of difference of a color from a gray of the same lightness or brightness. **6.** *Military.* The striking of a target with so many missiles that it is totally destroyed. Also used adjectivally: *saturation bombing.* **7.** The flooding of a market with all of a commodity that consumers can purchase.

saturation point *n.* **1.** *Chemistry.* The point at which a substance will receive no more of another substance in solution. **2.** The point at which no more can be absorbed, assimilated, or incorporated.

saturation zone *n.* The layers of rock below the water table that are saturated with water.

Sat·ur·day (săt'ər-dē, -dā') *n. Abbr.* **S., Sat.** The day of the week following Friday; the first day of the weekend. [Middle English *Saterday,* Old English *Sæterdæg,* short for *sæternesdæg,* "Saturn's day" : *Sætern, Saturnus,* SATURN + *dæg,* DAY.]

Saturday night special *n. Informal.* A cheap handgun.

Sat·urn¹ (săt'ərn). The Roman god of agriculture, identified with the Greek god Cronus. [Middle English *Saturnus, Satourn,* Old English *Saturnus,* from Latin *Saturnus,* Saturn (the god), Saturn (the planet), probably of Etruscan origin.]

Sat·urn² *n.* **1.** The sixth planet from the sun and the second-largest in the Solar System, having an equatorial diameter of about 74,000 miles, or 119,000 kilometers, a mass 95 times that of Earth, and an orbital period of 29.5 years at a mean distance from the sun of about 886,000 miles, or 1,425,000 kilometers. It has nine major and numerous minor satellites and is encircled by a system of rings composed of many small, solid icy bodies. **2.** In alchemy, the element lead.

sat·ur·na·li·a (săt'ər-nā'lē-ə, -nāl'yə) *pl.n.* **1. Saturnalia.** The ancient Roman seven-day festival of Saturn, which began on December 17 and was marked by wild revelry. **2.** *Used with a singular verb.* An occasion or period of unrestrained or orgiastic revelry and licentiousness. [Latin *saturnālia,* the festival of Saturn, from the neuter plural of *Saturnālis,* Saturnian, from *Saturnus,* SATURN.] **—sat·ur·na·li·an** *adj.*

Sa·tur·ni·an (sə-tûr'nē-ən) *adj.* **1.** Of or pertaining to the planet Saturn or to its supposed astrological influence. **2.** *Archaic.* Of or pertaining to the god Saturn or to the golden age of his reign.

sa·tur·ni·id (sə-tûr'nē-ĭd) *n.* Any of various often large and colorful moths of the mainly tropical family Saturniidae. [New Latin *Saturniidae,* from *Saturnia* (type genus), from Latin *Saturnia,* daughter of SATURN.] **—sa·tur·ni·id** *adj.*

sat·ur·nine (săt'ər-nīn') *adj.* **1.** Having or showing the temperament of one born under the supposed astrological influence of the planet Saturn. **2. a.** Gloomy, taciturn, or sullen in disposition. **b.** Scornfully mocking; sarcastic: *a saturnine laugh.*

sat·urn·ism (săt'ər-nĭz'əm) *n. Pathology.* **Lead poisoning** *(see).* [Middle English *saturne,* from Medieval Latin *sāturnus,* lead, from Latin *Sāturnus,* SATURN + -ISM.]

sa·tya·gra·ha (sə-tyä'grə-hə) *n.* Often **Satyagraha.** The policy of nonviolent resistance initiated in India by Mahatma Gandhi as a means of pressing for political reform. [Sanskrit *satyāgraha,* "insistence on truth" : *satya,* truth, from *sat, sant,* existing, true + *āgraha,* the act of holding firmly, insistence : *ā,* to + *grbhṇāti,* he seizes.]

sat·yr (săt'ər, sā'tər) *n.* **1.** *Greek Mythology.* Any of a class of manlike woodland gods or demons often having the pointed ears, legs, and short horns of a goat. **2.** A lecher. **3.** A man afflicted with satyriasis. **4.** Any of various butterflies of the family Satyridae, having brown wings marked with eyelike spots. [Middle English, from Latin *satyrus,* from Greek *saturos†.*] **—sa·tyr·ic** (sā-tîr'ĭk, sə-, sā-), **sa·tyr·i·cal** (-ĭ-kəl) *adj.*

sat·y·ri·a·sis (săt'ə-rī'ə-sĭs, sā'tə-) *n.* Abnormally strong sexual drive in the heterosexual male. Compare **nymphomania.** [Late Latin, from Greek. See **satyr, -iasis.**]

satyr play *n.* A comic drama in a burlesque style, having a chorus of satyrs, traditionally staged following a series of tragic plays at ancient Greek dramatic festivals. See **tetralogy.**

sauce (sôs) *n.* **1.** A flavorful soft or liquid dressing or relish, often cooked, served as an accompaniment to food. **2.** Stewed fruit, served with other foods or eaten as a dessert. **3.** *Regional.* Vegetables; greens. **4.** Something that adds zest, flavor, or piquancy to something else. **5.** *Informal.* Impudence; sauciness. **6.** *Slang.* Alcoholic liquor.
~*tr.v.* **sauced, saucing, sauces. 1.** To season or flavor with sauce. **2.** To add piquancy or zest to. **3.** *Informal.* To be impertinent or impudent to. [Middle English, from Old French, from Latin *salsa,* feminine of *salsus,* salted, from the past participle of *sallere,* to salt, from *sāl,* salt.]

sauce béarnaise *n.* **Béarnaise sauce** *(see).*

sauce béchamel *n.* **Béchamel sauce** *(see).*

sauce-boat (sôs'bōt') *n.* A low, boat-shaped vessel with a wide lip at one end and a handle at the other end, used chiefly for serving gravies and sauces.

sauce bordelaise *n.* **Bordelaise sauce** *(see).*

sauce-box (sôs'bŏks') *n. Informal.* An impertinent person.

sauce-pan (sôs'păn') *n.* A cooking pan of medium depth with a handle and usually a lid.

sau·cer (sô'sər) *n.* **1.** A small, shallow dish having a slight circular depression in the center for holding a cup. **2.** An object similar in shape to a saucer. [Middle English, sauce dish, from Old French *saussier,* from *sausse, sauce,* SAUCE.]

sauc·y (sô'sē) *adj.* **-ier, -iest. 1.** Impertinent or disrespectful; impudent. **2.** Piquant; pert. **3.** Risqué; racy. **—sauc·i·ly** *adv.* **—sauc·i·ness** *n.*

Sa·ud (sä-ōōd', soud), born Saud ibn Abd al-Aziz (1902-69). King of Saudi Arabia (1953-64). He was deposed by his brother Faisal following his failure to deal with the difficulty of using his country's wealth from oil to modernize a conservative nation.

Sau·di A·ra·bi·a (sou'dē ə-rā'bē-ə, sô'dē, sä-ōō'dē). Kingdom in southwestern Asia. The country, covering most of the Arabian Peninsula, was founded in 1932 by Ibn Saud, a descendant of the puritanical Wahhabi Muslim rulers of the 18th century. The rulers of the country are the guardians of the holiest shrines of Islam at Mecca and Medina, which attract hundreds of thousands of pilgrims annually. Saudi Arabia is mostly desert and includes the world's largest continuous sand area—the Rub al Khali, or Empty Quarter. Only Asir in the southwest and the various oases are cultivated. Food and consumer goods are imported on a lavish scale made possible by the country's enormous wealth in oil. The country is the world's greatest exporter of oil and possesses a significant proportion of the world's proven reserves. Area, 2,149,690 square kilometers (830,000 square miles). Population, 8,400,000. Capital, Riyadh. **—Sau·di, Sau·di A·ra·bi·an** *adj. & n.*

sau·er·bra·ten (sou'ər-brä'tən) *n.* A pot roast of beef that has been marinated in vinegar, water, wine, and spices before being cooked. [German : *sauer,* sour + *Braten,* roast meat.]

sau·er·kraut (sou'ər-krout') *n.* Chopped or shredded cabbage that is salted and fermented in its own juice. [German *Sauerkraut* : *sauer,* sour + *Kraut,* cabbage.]

sau·ger (sô'gər) *n.* A small North American freshwater fish, *Stizostedion canadense,* having a spiny dorsal fin. [Origin unknown.]

Saul (sôl). First king of Israel (11th century B.C.), proclaimed by Samuel; succeeded by David. [Hebrew *Shā-ul,* "asked for."]

Sault Sainte Ma·rie Canals (sōō' sānt' mə-rē'). Also **Soo Canals** (sōō). Two ship canals by-passing the rapids on the St. Marys River between Lake Superior and Lake Huron. The Canadian canal has one lock; the U.S. canal, which can accommodate larger ships, has four locks. Although closed by ice in the winter, the canals are among the busiest in the world and are a vital link in the Great Lakes Waterway. The cities of Sault Sainte Marie, Ontario, and Sault Sainte Marie, Michigan, lie opposite each other on the banks of the canals.

sau·na (sou'nə, sô'-) *n.* **1.** A steam bath in which the steam is usually produced by pouring water over heated rocks. **2.** A room for taking a sauna. [Finnish.]

saun·ter (sôn'tər) *intr.v.* **-tered, -tering, -ters.** To walk at a leisurely pace; stroll.

satyr *Half man and half goat, the satyr of Greek mythology is mischievous, drunken, and lecherous. This 2,000-year-old Roman sculpture shows a satyr's head with its pointed goatlike ears and budding horns.*

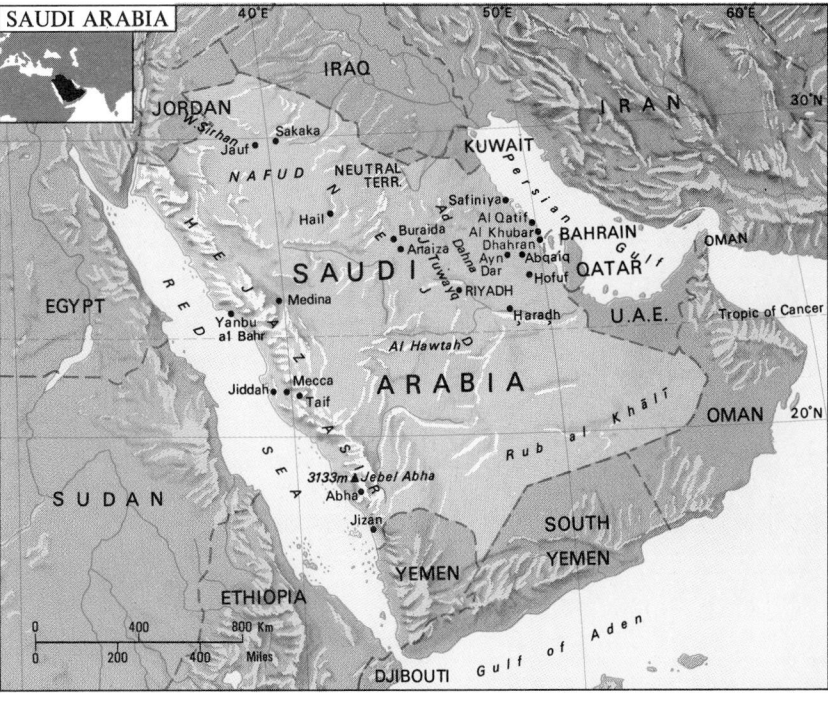

~*n.* A leisurely pace; a stroll. [Probably Middle English *santeren†*, to muse.]

saur–, sauro– *prefix.* Indicates lizardlike; for example, **sauropod**. [New Latin *saurus*, lizard, from Latin, from Greek *saurost†*.]

–saur, –saurus *suffix.* Indicates a lizardlike creature; for example, **brontosaurus**. [New Latin *saurus*, lizard. See **saur–**.]

sau·rel (sôr′əl, sô-rĕl′) *n.* **1.** A marine fish, *Trachurus trachurus*, of eastern Atlantic waters. **2.** The **jack mackerel** *(see).* [French, from New Latin *saurus*, horse mackerel, lizard, from Greek *saurost†*.]

sau·ri·an (sôr′ē-ən) *n.* Any of various reptiles of the suborder Sauria, which includes the true lizards.
~*adj.* Of, belonging to, or characteristic of the Sauria. [New Latin *Sauria*, from *saurus*, lizard. See **saur–**.]

sau·ro·pod (sôr′ə-pŏd′) *n.* Any of various large semiaquatic herbivorous dinosaurs of the suborder Sauropoda, of the Jurassic and Cretaceous periods. [New Latin *Sauropoda* : SAUR- + -POD.] —**sau·ro·pod, sau·rop·o·dous** (sô-rŏp′ə-dəs) *adj.*

sau·ry (sôr′ē) *n., pl.* **-ries.** Any of several offshore marine fishes of the family Scomberesocidae, related to the needlefishes. [New Latin *saurus*, saury, lizard. See **saur–**.]

sau·sage (sô′sĭj) *n.* A seasoned and finely chopped meat that is usually stuffed into a cylindrical casing, as a prepared animal intestine, and cooked or cured. [Middle English *sausige*, from Old North French *saussiche*, from Late Latin *salsīcia*, from *salsīcius*, prepared by salting, from *salsus*, salted. See **sauce**.]

sausage dog *n. British Informal.* A dachshund.

sau·té (sō-tā′, sô-) *tr.v.* **-téed, -téing, -tés.** To fry lightly in fat in a shallow, open pan.
~*n.* Sautéed food.
~*adj.* Sautéed. [French, "tossed (in a pan)," from the past participle of *sauter*, to leap, from Old French, from Latin *saltāre*, frequentative of *salīre* (past participle *saltus*), to leap.]

Sau·terne, Sau·ternes (sō-tûrn′, -târn′, sô-) *n.* A sweet white wine. [French, from *Sauternes*, a commune in southwestern France.]

sau·vi·gnon (sō′vēn-yōN′) *n.* A variety of white grape widely used for making white wine. [French, of obscure origin.]

sav·age (săv′ĭj) *adj.* **1.** Not domesticated; wild; untamed. **2.** Not civilized; in a primitive state. **3.** Ferocious; fierce. **4.** Vicious or merciless; brutal: *savage cuts in spending.* **5.** Lacking polish or manners; rude. **6.** Rugged; desolate: *savage terrain.*
~*n.* **1.** A primitive or uncivilized person. **2.** A brutal, fierce, or vicious person. **3.** A rude person; a boor.
~*tr.v.* **savaged, -aging, -ages.** **1.** To attack violently. **2.** To bite or maul ferociously. [Middle English *sauvage*, from Old French, from Vulgar Latin *salvāticus* (unattested), from Latin *silvāticus*, of the woods, wild, from *silva*, woods, forest. See **sylvan**.] —**sav·age·ly** *adv.* —**sav·age·ness** *n.*

sav·age·ry (săv′ĭj-rē) *n., pl.* **-ries.** **1.** The condition or quality of being savage. **2.** A cruel or barbarous action.

sa·van·na, sa·van·nah (sə-văn′ə) *n.* A flat, treeless grassland of tropical or subtropical regions. [Earlier *zavana*, from Spanish, from Taino *zabana*.]

Sa·van·nah¹ (sə-văn′ə). City of southeastern Georgia, a port of entry on the Savannah River. The city is a major rail, fishing, shipping, and industrial center. Founded in 1733, it was the last city conquered during Gen. William T. Sherman's march to the sea in the Civil War. Many beautiful old churches, homes, and public buildings remain.

Savannah². River, 505 kilometers (314 miles) long, flowing southeast to the Atlantic Ocean along the South Carolina-Georgia border. Savannah, Georgia, is the head of navigation for oceangoing ships.

sa·vant (să-vänt′, -väN′) *n.* A learned, scholarly person. [French, from the present participle of *savoir*, to know, from Vulgar Latin *sapēre* (unattested), from Latin *sapere*, to be sensible, be wise.]

sav·a·rin (săv′ər-ĭn) *n.* A yeast-leavened cake baked in a ring-shaped mold and moistened with liqueur or fruit syrup and often served with a filling, as of fruit, in the center. [After Anthelme Brillat-*Savarin* (1755-1826), French writer and gourmet.]

save¹ (sāv) *v.* **saved, saving, saves.** —*tr.* **1.** To deliver or preserve from disaster, harm, danger, or loss. **2.** To keep in a safe, intact condition; safeguard. **3.** To prevent or reduce the waste, loss, or expenditure of: *Save energy—insulate your home.* **4.** To keep for future use or enjoyment; store. Often used with *up.* **5.** To treat with care in order to prevent fatigue, wear, or damage; spare: *Save your legs and travel by bus.* **6.** To make unnecessary; obviate: *This will save you an extra trip.* **7.** *Theology.* To deliver from sin or its consequences; redeem. **8.** *Sports.* **a.** To prevent an opponent from scoring or winning, especially in hockey. **b.** *Baseball.* To preserve (a victory) by protecting a team's lead. Said of a relief pitcher. —*intr.* **1.** To avoid wasting, losing, or spending something, especially habitually; be economical: *drove slowly to save on gasoline.* **2.** To accumulate money or goods for future use. **3.** To preserve a person or thing from harm or loss.
~*n.* **1.** An act that prevents an opponent from scoring. **2.** *Baseball.* The successful protection by a relief pitcher of a team's lead. [Middle English *saven, salven,* from Old French *sauver,* from Late Latin *salvāre,* from Latin *salvus,* safe.] —**sav·a·ble, save·a·ble** *adj.* —**sav·a·ble·ness** *n.*

Synonyms: *deliver, reclaim, redeem, rescue.*

save² *prep.* With the exception of; except; but: *all save one.*
~*conj.* **1.** Were it not; except. Used with *that.* **2.** *Archaic.* Unless. [Middle English *save, sa(u)f,* from Old French *sa(u)f, salf,* from

Latin *salvō,* without injury or prejudice to, except, ablative singular of *salvus,* safe, sound, healthy.]

save-all (sāv′ôl′) *n.* Any device or contrivance that prevents the waste, damage, or loss of something, or that catches the waste products of a process for further use in manufacture.

sav·e·loy (săv′ə-loi′) *n.* A highly seasoned smoked pork sausage. [Variant of obsolete French *cervelat,* from Italian *cervellato,* from *cervello,* brain (the sausage is sometimes made from the brain of pigs), from Latin *cerebellum,* diminutive of *cerebrum,* brain.]

sav·er (sā′vər) *n.* **1.** One that saves; especially, a person who saves money regularly. **2.** Something that prevents loss, waste, or expenditure. Usually used in combination: *money-saver; time-saver.*

sav·in, sav·ine (săv′ĭn) *n.* **1.** An evergreen Eurasian shrub, *Juniperus sabina,* the young shoots of which yield an oil formerly used medicinally. **2.** Any of several similar or related shrubs or trees; especially, the **red cedar** *(see).* [Middle English *savin,* from Old English *safīne* and Old French *savine,* both from Latin *(herba) Sabīna,* "Sabine (plant)," from *Sabīnus,* SABINE.]

sav·ing (sā′vĭng) *adj.* **1.** Serving to redeem; compensating: *A sense of humor was his saving grace.* **2.** Making, expressing, or containing a reservation; qualifying: *a saving clause.*
~*n.* **1.** Preservation or rescue from harm, danger, or loss. **2.** Avoidance of excess expenditure; economy. **3.** A reduction in expenditure or cost. **4.** **savings.** Sums of money saved. **5.** Something that is saved. **6.** *Law.* An exception or reservation.
~*prep.* With the exception of.
~*conj.* Except; save.

savings account *n.* An account that draws interest at a bank.

savings bank *n.* A bank that receives and invests the savings of private depositors and pays interest on the deposits.

sav·ior (săv′yər) *n.* Also *chiefly British* **sav·iour.** **1.** A person who rescues someone or something from dire circumstances. **2.** **Savior.** Christ. [Middle English *saviour, sauveur,* from Old French *sauveour,* from Late Latin *salvātor,* from *salvāre,* to SAVE.]

sa·voir-faire (săv′wär-fâr′) *n.* The ability to say and do the right thing in any situation; social adroitness. —See Synonyms at **tact.** [French, "knowing how to do."]

sa·voir-vi·vre (săv′wär-vē′vrə) *n.* The ability to live with taste and elegance. [French, "knowing how to live."]

Sav·o·na·ro·la (săv′ə-nə-rō′lə), **Girolamo** (1452-98). Italian religious reformer. A Dominican friar, he gained a vast popular following with his fervent preaching, which enabled him to lead a revolt that turned the Medici family out of Florence in 1494. He became the virtual ruler of Florence, but after criticizing Pope Alexander VI he was excommunicated in 1497 and later executed.

sa·vor (sā′vər) *n.* Also *chiefly British* **sa·vour.** **1.** The taste or smell of something. **2.** A specific taste or smell. **3.** A distinctive or typical quality. **4.** The power or quality of exciting interest; zestfulness. —See Synonyms at **smell.**
~*v.* **savored, -voring, -vors.** Also *chiefly British* **savoured, -vouring, -vours.** —*intr.* **1.** To have a particular savor: *The kitchen savored of fresh bread.* **2.** To have an implication or suggestion; smack: *savors of corruption.* —*tr.* **1.** To impart a flavor or scent to. **2.** To taste, smell, or experience with appreciation and enjoyment; relish. [Middle English *savour,* from Old French, from Latin *sapor,* taste, savor, from *sapere,* to taste, savor.] —**sa·vor·er** *n.* —**sa·vor·less** *adj.* —**sa·vor·ous** *adj.*

sa·vor·y¹ (sā′və-rē) *adj.* Also *chiefly British* **sa·voury.** **1.** Appetizing to the taste or smell. **2.** Piquant, pungent, or salty to the taste; not sweet. **3.** Morally respectable; inoffensive.
~*n., pl.* **savories.** Also *chiefly British* **savouries.** A dish of pungent taste, as anchovies on toast, sometimes served in Britain as an hors d'oeuvre or instead of a dessert. [Middle English *savory, savure,* from Old French *savoure,* from the past participle of *savourer,* to savor, from Late Latin *sapōrāre,* from Latin *sapor,* SAVOR.] —**sa·vor·i·ly** *adv.* —**sa·vor·i·ness** *n.*

savory² *n., pl.* **-ies.** **1.** Either of two aromatic herbs, *Satureja hortensis* or *S. montana,* native to the Old World. The former species is also called "summer savory" and the latter "winter savory." **2.** The leaves of either of these plants, used as seasoning. [Middle English *saverey,* variant (perhaps influenced by SAVORY) of Old English *sætherie,* from Latin *satureia†.*]

sa·voy cabbage (sə-voi′) *n.* A variety of cabbage with crinkled leaves and a compact head. [After SAVOY, where it was cultivated.]

Sa·voy (sə-voi′). Region on the French-Italian border in the western Alps, ruled by the House of Savoy from the 11th century. Savoy grew to include Nice in France and Piedmont in Italy and became a duchy in 1416. The House of Savoy gained control of Sardinia in 1713, and Savoy, with Piedmont and the island of Sardinia, formed the kingdom of Sardinia. Genoa was added in 1815. On the unification of Italy in 1860, French Savoy was ceded to France. Today Savoy comprises mainly the French departments of Haute-Savoie and Savoie. Chambéry is the chief city.

Sa·voy·ard (sə-voi′ärd′, săv′oi-ärd′, săv′wä-yär′) *n.* **1.** A native or inhabitant of Savoy. **2.** A dialect of French spoken in Savoy. **3.** A performer in or enthusiastic admirer of Gilbert and Sullivan operas, most of which were first staged at London's Savoy Theatre.
~*adj.* Of or pertaining to Savoy, its inhabitants, or their dialect.

sav·vy (săv′ē) *intr.v.* **-vied, -vying, -vies.** *Slang.* To understand or know; comprehend.
~*adj.* **-vier, -viest.** *Slang.* Practical and perceptive.
~*n. Slang.* Practical understanding or knowledge; common sense.

[From Spanish *sabe (usted),* (you) know, from *saber,* to know, from Latin *sapere,* to be sensible, be wise.]

saw¹ (sô) *n.* **1.** A tool, usually portable and either hand-operated or power-operated, having a thin metal blade or disk with a sharp-toothed edge, used for cutting wood, metal, or other hard materials. **2.** A powered disk tool lacking teeth, used for cutting metal. **3.** A fixed machine for the operation of a saw or series of saws.
~*v.* **sawed, sawed** or **sawn** (sôn), **sawing, saws.** —*tr.* **1.** To cut with a saw. **2.** To produce or shape with a saw. —*intr.* **1.** To use a saw. **2.** To cut or be cut with or as if with a saw. **3.** To make movements like those used in sawing: *sawed at the ball with the bat.* [Middle English *sawe,* Old English *sagu.*]

saw² *n.* A familiar saying, especially one worn out through repetition. **—See Synonyms at saying.** [Middle English *sawe,* Old English *sagu,* speech, talk, from Germanic *sagō* (unattested); akin to SAGA.]

saw³. Past tense of **see** (to perceive with the eyes).

saw·bill (sô′bĭl′) *n.* A duck, the **merganser** *(see).*

saw·bones (sô′bōnz′) *n. Slang.* A physician, especially a surgeon.

saw·dust (sô′dŭst′) *n.* The small particles of wood that fall from a wooden object as a result of sawing.

sawed-off (sôd′ôf′, -ŏf′) *adj.* **1.** Having one edge sawed off: *a sawed-off shotgun.* **2.** *Slang.* Shorter than average.

saw·fish (sô′fĭsh′) *n., pl.* **-fishes** or collectively **sawfish.** Any of various marine fishes of the genus *Pristis,* related to the rays and skates and having a bladelike snout with teeth along both sides.

saw·fly (sô′flī′) *n., pl.* **-flies.** Any of various destructive insects, chiefly of the family Tenthredinidae, the females of which have sawlike ovipositors used for cutting into plant tissue to deposit eggs.

saw grass *n.* Any of several grasses or sedges, especially *Cladium jamaicense,* having leaves with minutely toothed margins.

saw·horse (sô′hôrs′) *n.* A rack or trestle used to support a piece of wood being sawed.

saw log *n.* A log large enough for sawing into boards.

saw·mill (sô′mĭl′) *n.* **1.** A plant where timber is machine-cut into boards. **2.** A large machine for sawing timber.

sawn. Alternate past participle of **saw** (to cut with a saw).

sawn-off (sôn′ôf′, -ŏf′) *adj. British.* Sawed-off.

saw palmetto *n.* Any of several low-growing, prickly palms of the genus *Sabal,* of the southeastern United States.

saw set *n.* An instrument used to deflect the teeth of a saw by bending each tooth slightly, alternate teeth being bent in the same direction.

saw-toothed (sô′to͞otht′) *adj.* Having teeth resembling the teeth of a saw; serrate.

saw-whet owl (sô′hwĕt′) A small brown and white owl, *Aegolius acadicus,* of western North America, lacking ear tufts. [From the resemblance of its call to the sound made in sharpening a saw.]

saw·yer (sô′yər) *n.* **1.** One employed at sawing wood, as in a sawmill. **2.** Any of several longicorn beetles having larvae that bore holes in wood. [Middle English *sawier,* from *sawen,* to SAW.]

sax (săks) *n. Informal.* A saxophone.

Sax. Saxon; Saxony.

saxe blue (săks) *n.* A light grayish blue. [French *Saxe,* SAXONY.]

sax·horn (săks′hôrn′) *n.* Any of a family of valved brass wind instruments resembling the bugle and having a full, even tone and wide range. [Invented (1845) by Adolphe *Sax* (1814-94), Belgian musical instrument maker.]

sax·ic·o·lous (săk-sĭk′ə-ləs) *adj.* Also **sax·ic·o·line** (-līn′). Growing on or living among rocks. [Latin *saxum,* rock + -COLOUS.]

sax·i·frage (săk′sĭ-frĭj, -frāj′) *n.* Any of numerous plants of the genus *Saxifraga,* of temperate regions, having small flowers and leaves often forming a basal rosette. [Middle English, from Old French, from Late Latin *saxifraga (herba),* "rock-breaking (herb)" (because it grows in rock crevices), from Latin *saxifragus* : *saxum,* rock + *frangere* (stem *frag-*), to break.]

Sax·on (săk′sən) *n. Abbr.* **S., Sax. 1.** A member of a West Germanic people that inhabited northern Germany and invaded England in the 5th and 6th centuries with the Angles and Jutes. See **Anglo-Saxon. 2.** A native or inhabitant of Saxony. **3.** The West Germanic language or dialect spoken by any of the Saxon peoples. **4.** The Germanic elements present in English as distinguished from the French and Latin elements. **5.** An Englishman as distinguished from an Irishman, a Welshman, or a Scot.
~*adj.* **1.** Of or pertaining to the Saxons or their language. **2.** Of Anglo-Saxon origin. **3.** Of or pertaining to Saxony, the German Saxons, or their language. [Middle English, from Old French, from Late Latin *Saxō* (stem *Saxon-*), from Greek *Saxones* (plural), from West Germanic *Saxon-* (unattested), probably from Germanic *sahsam* (unattested), knife (perhaps considered as their typical weapon); compare Old English *Seaxan,* Saxon, and *seax,* knife, tool, from Germanic *sahsam* (unattested).]

Saxon blue *n.* A dye made from indigo dissolved in a sulfuric acid solution. [After SAXONY, where it originated.]

sax·o·ny, Sax·o·ny (săk′sə-nē) *n.* **1.** A high-grade wool fabric originally made from the wool of sheep raised in Saxony. **2.** A fine soft woolen fabric similar in weave to tweed.

Sax·o·ny (săk′sə-nē). *Abbr.* **Sax.** *German* **Sach·sen** (zăk′sən). Area of northern Germany and the original home of the Saxons. Conquered by Charlemagne in the 8th century, it became a duchy after his death. The area was frequently divided after 1180 and re-formed in various ways, moving generally southeastward. The dukes became electors of the Holy Roman Empire (1356) and made Dresden their capital. Raised to kingship (1806), the elector lost half his territory to Prussia (1815). This province of Prussia later became part of East Germany (1949). The kingdom of Saxony was part of the German Empire (1871–1918) and, as the state of Saxony, part of prewar Germany. This too became part of East Germany (1949).

sax·o·phone (săk′sə-fōn′) *n.* A wind instrument with a single-reed mouthpiece, a usually curved conical metal bore, and finger keys that is made in a variety of sizes. [Invented (1846) by Adolphe *Sax.* See **saxhorn.**] **—sax·o·phon·ist** *n.*

sax·tu·ba (săks′to͞o′bə, -tyo͞o′bə) *n.* A large bass saxhorn. [SAX(HORN) + TUBA.]

say (sā) *v.* **said** (sĕd), **saying, says** (sĕz). —*tr.* **1.** To utter aloud; pronounce; speak. **2.** To express in words; state; declare. **3.** To state (an opinion, for example) with positive assurance or conviction. **4.** To repeat or recite: *say grace.* **5.** To report or maintain; allege: *They say she's won.* **6.** To estimate or suppose; assume: *Let's say that you're right.* **7.** To describe as being; classify: *Her father is said to be very sick.* **8.** To express or convey; communicate: *What is the artist saying in this painting?* **9.** To indicate; show: *When I woke, the clock said midnight.* **10.** To adduce in favor or defense of something: *There's a lot to be said for the system.* **11.** To state by way of instruction: *He said to start without him if he was late.* —*intr.* To make a statement or express an opinion. **—go without saying.** To be so self-evident as to need no justification or explanation. **—not to say.** Perhaps in fact; indeed: *seemed unwelcoming, not to say hostile.* **—that is to say.** In other words; meaning.
~*n.* **1.** A turn or chance to speak. **2.** What one has to say; one's opinion. **3.** The right or power to influence a decision; voice: *They want to have a say in the matter.*
~*adv.* **1.** Approximately: *There were, say, 500 people present.* **2.** For instance: *a woodwind, say an oboe.*
~*interj.* Used to gain the attention of someone. [Say, said (past tense and past participle); Middle English *seggen* (later *sayen*), *saide,* Old English *secgan, sægde* (past tense), *(ge)sægd* (past participle).] **—say·er** *n.*

Say·ers (sā′ərz), **Dorothy Leigh** (1893–1957). British novelist and translator. She is best known for her detective stories, usually featuring Lord Peter Wimsey, the gentlemanly amateur investigator who made his first appearance in *Whose Body?* (1923). For the last 20 years of her life she concentrated on religious books and drama, particularly her cycle of radio plays, *The Man Born to Be King.*

say·ing (sā′ĭng) *n.* **1.** An adage; a maxim. **2.** A word of wit or wisdom; mot.
Synonyms: *adage, aphorism, epigram, maxim, motto, proverb, saw.*

say-so (sā′sō′) *n., pl.* **-sos.** *Informal.* **1.** An unsupported statement or assurance. **2.** An authoritative assertion; a dictum. **3.** The right of final decision; authority.

say·yid (sä′yĭd) *n.* A Muslim claiming descent from Muhammad. Used as a title of respect. [Arabic, "lord."]

Sb The symbol for the element antimony [Latin *stibium*].

S.B. Bachelor of Science.

'sblood (zblŭd) *interj. Archaic.* Used as an oath. [Contraction of *God's blood.*]

Sc The symbol for the element scandium.

SC South Carolina (used with a Zip Code).

sc. 1. scene. **2.** scilicet. **3.** scruple (weight). **4.** sculpsit.

Sc. Scotch; Scots; Scottish.

s.c. *Printing.* small capital.

S.C. 1. Signal Corps. **2.** South Carolina.

scab (skăb) *n.* **1. a.** The crustlike material that covers a healing wound. **b.** A small patch of such material. **2.** Scabies or mange in domestic animals or livestock. **3. a.** Any of various plant diseases caused by fungi or bacteria and resulting in crustlike spots on fruit, leaves, or roots. **b.** A spot or the spots caused by such a disease. **4.** *Informal.* **a.** A worker who refuses to join a labor union. **b.** An employee who works while others are on strike; a strikebreaker. Also used adjectivally: *scab labor.* **5.** *Informal.* A low or contemptible person.
~*intr.v.* **scabbed, scabbing, scabs. 1. a.** To form a scab. **b.** To become covered with a scab. **2.** *Informal.* To take a job held by a worker on strike; act as a scab. [Middle English *scabbe,* from Old Norse *skabb.*]

scab·bard (skăb′ərd) *n.* A sheath or container for a weapon such as a dagger or sword.
~*tr.v.* **scabbarded, -barding, -bards.** To put into or furnish with a scabbard. [Middle English *scauberc,* from Norman French *escaubers* (plural) : probably Old High German *scār,* scissors, sword + *-berc,* protection, from *bergan,* to protect.]

scabbard fish *n.* Any of several narrow-bodied marine fishes of the family Trichiuridae; especially, *Lepidopus caudatus,* of Mediterranean waters. [From its narrow, sheathlike body.]

scab·ble (skăb′əl) *tr.v.* **-bled, -bling, -bles.** To work or dress (stone) to a stage prior to that of fine tooling. [Earlier *scapple,* Middle English *scaplen,* from Old French *eschapler,* "to cut off," dress timber : *es-,* from Latin *ex-,* off + *chapler,* to cut, from Late Latin *capulāre.*]

scab·by (skăb′ē) *adj.* **-bier, -biest. 1.** Having, consisting of, or covered with scabs or something resembling scabs. **2.** Suffering from scabies. **3.** *Informal.* Low; mean; vile: *a scabby trick.* **—scab·bi·ly** *adv.* **—scab·bi·ness** *n.*

sca·bies (skā′bēz′) *n., pl.* **scabies. 1.** A contagious skin disease that is caused by a mite, *Sarcoptes scabiei,* and characterized by intense

Meadow saxifrage
Saxifraga granulata

Rue-leaved saxifrage
Saxifraga tridactylites

Starry saxifrage
Saxifraga stellaris

Mossy saxifrage
Saxifraga hypnoides

Yellow saxifrage
Saxifraga aizoides

Purple saxifrage
Saxifraga oppositifolia

saxifrage *Most saxifrages are mountain plants that root in cracks between the rocks. It was once thought that saxifrage roots could penetrate rock, and the name means "rock breaking."*

scabious *The male stamens of these meadow and garden flowers jut above the broad heads like pins, giving the plant a second common name: pincushion flower. The plant was named scabious because its juice was once thought to be a cure for the skin complaint scabies.*

scale *The scale-covered skin of the water python,* Liasis fuscus.

scallop *The twin-shelled scallop filters its food from seawater on the ocean bed. It detects predators, such as starfish, by means of a row of tiny eyes along its mantle—and escapes by clapping its shell shut, jetting itself away from danger.*

itching. **2.** A disease in animals, especially sheep, that is similar to scabies. [Latin *scabiēs,* roughness, scurf, itch, from *scabere,* to scratch.] **—sca·bi·et·ic** (skā'bē-ĕt'ĭk) *adj.*

sca·bi·ous[1] (skā'bē-əs, skăb'ē-) *adj.* **1.** Of or pertaining to scabies. **2.** Having scabs. [Latin *scabiōsus,* scabby, from SCABIES.]

sca·bi·ous[2] (skā'bē-əs) *n.* Any of various plants of the genera *Knautia, Succisa,* or *Scabiosa*; especially, *Knautia arvensis* and *Scabiosa columbaria,* having opposite leaves and blue compound flower heads. See **devil's bit.** [Middle English *scabiose,* from Medieval Latin *scabiōsa (herba),* "(herb) for scabies," from Latin, feminine of *scabiōsus,* SCABIOUS.]

scab·rous (skăb'rəs, skā'brəs) *adj.* **1.** Roughened with small projections; rough to the touch; scaly. **2.** Difficult to handle tactfully; thorny. **3.** Indelicate or salacious; indecent: *a scabrous novel.* —See Synonyms at **rough.** [Latin *scabrōsus,* rough, from *scaber,* rough, scurfy.] **—scab·rous·ly** *adv.* **—scab·rous·ness** *n.*

scad (skăd) *n., pl.* **scads** or collectively **scad. 1.** Any of several marine fishes of the family Carangidae, related to the jacks and pompanos. **2.** The **horse mackerel** *(see).* [17th century : origin obscure.]

scads (skădz) *pl.n. Informal.* A large number or amount: *scads of people.* [19th century : origin obscure.]

scaf·fold (skăf'əld, -ōld') *n.* **1.** A raised wooden framework or platform. **2.** A platform for the execution of condemned prisoners. Usually preceded by *the.* **3.** Scaffolding.
~*tr.v.* **scaffolded, -folding, -folds.** To provide or support with scaffolding. [Middle English, from Old North French *escafaut,* variant of Old French *eschafaud,* from *chafaud,* scaffold, from Vulgar Latin *catafalicum* (unattested), CATAFALQUE.] **—scaf·fold·er** *n.*

scaf·fold·ing (skăf'əl-dĭng, skăf'ōl'-) *n.* **1.** A temporary platform or system of platforms, usually made of planks and tubular metal poles, used by workmen when constructing, repairing, or cleaning a building. **2.** The materials for scaffolding.

sca·glio·la (skăl-yō'lə) *n.* Plasterwork in imitation of ornamental marble, consisting of ground gypsum and glue colored with marble or granite dust. [Italian, diminutive of *scaglia,* scale, chip, small piece of marble, from Germanic.]

sca·lar (skā'lər) *n.* A quantity, such as mass, length, or time, completely described by a number on an appropriate scale. Scalars have magnitude but not direction. Compare **vector.** [Latin *scālāris,* of a staircase, from *scālae,* stairs, SCALE.] **—sca·lar** *adj.*

sca·la·re (skə-lâr'ē, -lä'rē) *n.* See **angelfish** (sense 2). [New Latin, "ladderlike" (from its parallel stripes), from Latin, neuter of *scālāris,* of a staircase, from *scālae,* stairs, SCALE.]

sca·lar·i·form (skə-lăr'ə-fôrm') *adj. Biology.* Ladderlike; having rungs: *scalariform xylem vessels.* [New Latin *scalariformis* : Latin *scālāris,* of a ladder (see **scalar**) + -FORM.]

scalar product *n.* The numerical product of the lengths of two vectors and the cosine of the angle between them. Also called "dot product," "inner product." Compare **vector product.**

scal·a·wag, scal·la·wag (skăl'ə-wăg') *n.* Also **scal·ly·wag** (skăl'ē-wăg'). **1.** *Informal.* A reprobate; rascal. **2.** A white Republican Southerner during Reconstruction. [Origin unknown.]

scald[1] (skôld) *v.* **scalded, scalding, scalds.** —*tr.* **1.** To burn with or as if with hot liquid or steam. **2.** To subject to or treat with boiling water, especially: **a.** To blanch or partly cook (food) in boiling water. **b.** To sterilize (instruments, for example). **3.** To heat (a liquid) almost to the boiling point. —*intr.* To be or become scalded.
~*n.* **1.** A burn or injury caused by scalding. **2. a.** A superficial discoloration on fruit, vegetables, leaves, or tree trunks caused by sudden exposure to intense sunlight or the action of gases. **b.** A disease of some cereal grasses, caused by a fungus of the genus *Rhynchosporium.* [Middle English *scalden,* from Old North French *escalder,* from Late Latin *excaldāre,* to wash in hot water : Latin *ex-,* to bring into a certain condition + *cal(i)da,* hot water, from the feminine of *calidus,* warm.]

scald[2]. 1. Variant of **skald. 2.** Variant of **scall.**

scald·ing (skôl'dĭng) *adj.* **1.** Burning hot to the touch or taste. **2.** Cutting; biting: *a scalding review.*

scale[1] (skāl) *n.* **1. a.** Any of the small, flattened, hard plates characteristically forming the external covering of fishes, reptiles, and certain mammals. **b.** A similar part, such as any of the minute structures overlapping to form the covering on the wings of butterflies and moths. **2.** *Pathology.* A dry, thin flake of epidermis shed from the skin. **3.** A small, thin, platelike piece of anything that flakes off from a surface. **4.** *Botany.* Any of various thin, often overlapping parts, such as any of the protective rudimentary leaves covering the buds of certain trees, or a membranous bract. **5. a.** A scale insect. **b.** A plant disease or infestation caused by scale insects. **6. a.** A flaky oxide film formed on a metal, as on iron, heated to high temperatures. **b.** A flake of rust. **7.** A coating of calcium carbonate formed inside boilers, kettles, and similar hot-water devices in hard-water regions; fur.
~*v.* **scaled, scaling, scales.** —*tr.* **1.** To clear or strip of scale or scales. **2.** To remove in layers or scales. **3.** To cover with scales; cause incrustation to form on. —*intr.* **1.** To come off in layers or scales; flake. **2.** To become covered with incrustation. [Middle English, from Old French *escale,* "shell," "husk," from Germanic.]

scale[2] *n.* **1.** A system of ordered marks at fixed intervals used as a reference standard in measurement. **2.** An instrument or device bearing such marks. **3. a.** The proportion used in determining the relationship of a representation to that which it represents. Also used adjectivally: *a scale drawing.* **b.** A calibrated line, as on a map or architectural plan, to indicate such a proportion. **4.** A progressive classification, as of size, amount, importance, or rank: *a salary scale; the social scale.* **5.** A relative level or degree: *entertain on a lavish scale.* Also used adjectivally in combination: *a small-scale exporter.* **6.** *Mathematics.* A system of notation in which the value of numbers is determined by their place relative to the fixed constant of the system: *decimal scale.* **7.** *Music.* An ascending or descending series of tones proceeding by a particular scheme of intervals and varying in pitch arrangement and interval size. In this sense, see **chromatic, diatonic. —to scale.** According to or in a uniform proportion or ratio.
~*v.* **scaled, scaling, scales.** —*tr.* **1.** To climb up to the top of or over with or as if with a ladder, rope, or other device. **2.** To draw or reproduce in accordance with a particular proportion or scale. **3.** To adjust according to a proportion; regulate. **4.** To increase or decrease the size or importance of in fixed proportions. Used with *up* or *down.* —*intr.* **1.** To go up; climb; ascend. **2.** To ascend in steps or stages. [Middle English, ladder, graduation, from Late Latin *scāla,* ladder, from Latin *scālae,* stairs.]

scale[3] *n.* **1.** *Often* **scales.** Any instrument or machine for weighing: *bathroom scales.* **2.** Either of the pans, trays, or dishes of a balance. **—turn** (or **tip**) **the scales. 1.** To exercise a decisive effect. **2.** To amount in weight to; weigh. Used with *at.*
~*v.* **scaled, scaling, scales.** —*tr.* To weigh with scales. —*intr.* To have as a weight. [Middle English, from Old Norse *skāl,* bowl, scale of a balance.]

scale·board (skāl'bôrd', -bōrd') *n.* **1.** Thin sheets of wood used as a veneer or a backing for pictures, mirrors, and the like. **2.** A wooden strip used for aligning hand-set type.

scale insect *n.* Any of various destructive sucking insects of the family Coccidae, the females of which secrete and remain under waxy scales on plant tissue.

scale leaf *n.* A membranous, often small modified leaf, such as one that protects flower buds.

scale moss *n. Botany.* Any of various leafy liverworts of the order Jungermanniales.

sca·lene (skā'lēn', skā-lēn') *adj.* **1.** Having unequal sides. Said of geometric figures, especially triangles. **2.** *Anatomy.* Designating or pertaining to the scalenus. [Late Latin *scalēnus,* from Greek *skalēnos,* uneven.]

sca·le·nus (skə-lē'nəs, skā-) *n., pl.* **-ni** (-nī'). Any one of four paired muscles in the neck, responsible for bending the neck and for raising the top two ribs during inhalation. Also called "scalene muscle." [New Latin. See **scalene.**]

scal·er (skā'lər) *n.* **1.** An electronic circuit that records the aggregate of a specific number of signals that occur too rapidly to be recorded individually. **2.** A dental instrument used for removing tartar from teeth.

Scales (skālz) *pl.n.* The constellation and sign of the zodiac **Libra** *(see).* Preceded by *the.*

Scal·i·ger (skăl'ə-jər), **Julius Caesar** (1484–1558). Italian scholar. He wrote commentaries on classical texts, the most famous being *Poetice* (1561). This analysis of Aristotelian theories of tragedy inspired later generations of French dramatists.

scall (skôl) *n.* Also **scald** (skôld). A scaly eruption of the skin or scalp. Not in current technical usage. [Middle English *scalle,* from Old Norse *skalli,* a bald head.]

scal·lion (skăl'yən) *n.* **1.** A young onion before the enlargement of the bulb. Also called "green onion." **2.** Any of several similar onionlike plants, such as a leek or shallot. [Middle English *scalo(u)n,* from Norman French, from Vulgar Latin *escalōnia* (unattested), from Latin *Ascalōnia (caepa),* "Ascalonian (onion)," from *Ascalō,* Ascalon, ancient port in southern Palestine.]

scal·lop (skŏl'əp, skăl'-) *n.* Also **scol·lop** (skŏl'-), **es·cal·lop** (ĕ-skŏl'-əp, ĕ-skăl'-) (for sense 5). **1.** Any of various marine bivalve mollusks of the family Pectinidae, having fan-shaped shells with a radiating fluted pattern. **2.** The edible adductor muscle of a scallop. **3.** A scallop shell, or a similarly shaped dish, used for baking and serving seafood. **4.** Any of a series of variously curved projections forming an ornamental border, as on fabrics or lace. **5.** A thin, boneless slice of meat.
~*tr.v.* **scalloped, -loping, -lops.** Also **scollop, escallop** (for senses 2, 3). **1.** To design or border (material or part of a garment, for example) with scallops. **2.** To bake in a scallop shell or in a casserole with milk or a sauce and often with breadcrumbs. **3.** To cut (meat) into scallops. [Middle English *scalop,* from Old French *escalope,* shell, probably from Germanic.] **—scal·lop·er** *n.*

scallywag. Variant of **scalawag.**

sca·lop·pi·ne, sca·lop·pi·ni (skăl'ə-pē'nē, skä'lə-) *pl.n.* **1.** Small, thin slices of veal or other meat, especially when cooked in a sauce of wine or tomatoes and seasonings. **2.** *Used with a singular verb.* A dish of scaloppine. [Italian *scaloppine,* plural of *scaloppina,* diminutive of *scaloppa,* fillet of meat, from Old French *escalope,* shell (the fillets are served curled like shells). See **scallop.**]

scalp (skălp) *n.* **1.** *Anatomy.* The skin covering the top of the human head. **2.** The scalp with attached hair, formerly cut or torn from an enemy as a battle trophy by certain North American Indians. **3.** Any trophy of victory. **4.** *Informal.* The profit made by a ticket scalper.
~*tr.v.* **scalped, scalping, scalps. 1.** To cut or tear the scalp from. **2.** *Informal.* To defeat, especially in a humiliating or spectacular manner. **3. a.** To buy and resell (securities and commodities) to make a small but quick profit. **b.** *Informal.* To buy and resell (tick-

ets) at inflated prices. **c.** To take advantage of or cheat (a customer, for example) by selling at inflated prices. [Middle English, probably from Scandinavian; akin to Old Norse *skalpr,* sheath, "shell."] —**scalp·er** *n.*

scal·pel (skăl′pəl, skăl-pĕl′) *n.* A small straight knife with a very thin, sharp, sometimes removable blade, used especially in surgery and dissection. [Latin *scalpellum,* diminutive of *scalper,* knife, from *scalpere,* to cut, scratch.]

scalp lock *n.* A long lock of hair left on the shaven head by certain North American Indians as a challenge to an enemy.

scal·y (skā′lē) *adj.* **-ier, -iest. 1.** Covered or partially covered with scales or scale. **2.** Shedding scales; flaking. **3.** *Slang.* Mean; despicable. —**scal·i·ness** *n.*

scaly anteater *n.* A mammal, the **pangolin** *(see).*

scam (skăm) *n. Informal.* A fraudulent business operation; a swindle. [20th century : origin obscure.]

scam·mo·ny (skăm′ə-nē) *n., pl.* **-nies. 1.** A plant, *Convolvulus scammonia,* of the eastern Mediterranean region, having large roots formerly used as a purgative. **2.** A resinous preparation made from the roots of this plant. [Middle English *scamonie,* from Latin *scammōnea,* from Greek *skammōnia†.*]

scamp¹ (skămp) *n.* **1.** A rogue; rascal. **2.** A mischievous or prankish youngster. [Originally "highwayman," "robber," from obsolete *scamp,* to slip away, bolt, probably from Middle Dutch *schampen,* from Old French *escamper,* to SCAMPER.]

scamp² *tr.v.* **scamped, scamping, scamps.** To perform in a careless or perfunctory way. [Probably a blend of SCANT and SKIMP.] —**scamp·er** *n.*

scam·per (skăm′pər) *intr.v.* **-pered, -pering, -pers.** To run or go hurriedly or playfully.
~*n.* A hasty or playful run or departure. [Flemish *scamperen,* to decamp, from Old French *escamper,* from Vulgar Latin *excampāre* (unattested) : Latin *ex-,* out of, away + *campus,* field (see **camp**).] —**scam·per·er** *n.*

scam·pi (skăm′pē) *n., pl.* **scampi.** A dish consisting of shrimp cooked in a garlic and butter sauce. [Italian, plural of *scampo,* a kind of lobster.]

scan (skăn) *v.* **scanned, scanning, scans.** —*tr.* **1.** To examine or consider in close detail; scrutinize. **2.** To look over (a wide area) quickly but thoroughly, as from one end to another. **3.** To analyze (verse) into metrical feet and rhythm patterns. **4.** *Electronics.* **a.** To move a finely focused beam of light or electrons in a systematic pattern over (a surface) in order to reproduce, or sense and subsequently transmit, an image. **b.** To move a radar beam over (a sector of sky) in search of a target. **c.** *Computer Science.* To search (a series of punched cards or a magnetic tape) automatically for specific data. **d.** *Medicine.* To examine (a part of the body) using a scanner. **5.** To look over or leaf through hastily. —*intr.* **1.** To analyze verse into metrical feet. **2.** To conform to a metrical pattern. Used of verse. **3.** *Electronics.* To undergo electronic scanning. **4.** To use a scanner to examine a part of the body. —See Synonyms at **see.**
~*n.* An act or instance of scanning. [Middle English *scannen,* from Late Latin *scandere,* "to analyze the rising and falling rhythm in verses," from Latin, to climb.] —**scan·na·ble** *adj.*

Scand. Scandinavia; Scandinavian.

scan·dal (skăn′dəl) *n.* **1.** Any act or set of circumstances that brings about disgrace or offends accepted standards of morality or propriety; a public disgrace. **2.** The reaction caused by such an act or set of circumstances; outrage; shame. **3.** Any talk damaging to the character; malicious gossip. **4.** Damage to reputation or character caused by offensive or grossly improper behavior; disgrace. **5.** One whose conduct brings about disgrace or defamation. —See Synonyms at **disgrace.**
~*tr.v.* **scandaled** or **-dalled, -daling** or **-dalling, -dals.** *Archaic.* To spread scandal about; defame. [French *scandale,* from Late Latin *scandalum,* from Greek *skandalon,* trap, snare, stumbling block.]

scan·dal·ize (skăn′də-līz′) *tr.v.* **-ized, -izing, -izes.** To shock the moral sensibilities of. —**scan·dal·iz·er** *n.*

scan·dal·ous (skăn′də-ləs) *adj.* **1.** Causing scandal; shocking; offensive. **2.** Containing defamatory or libelous material. —**scan·dal·ous·ly** *adv.* —**scan·dal·ous·ness** *n.*

scandal sheet *n.* A newspaper or other periodical that habitually prints stories of a sensational or defamatory nature.

scan·dent (skăn′dənt) *adj. Botany.* Climbing: *a scandent vine.* [Latin *scandēns* (stem *scandent-*), present participle of *scandere,* to climb.]

scan·di·a (skăn′dē-ə) *n.* **Scandium oxide** *(see).* [From SCANDIUM.]

Scan·di·an (skăn′dē-ən) *adj.* Scandinavian. [Latin *Scandia,* variant of *Scandinavia,* SCANDINAVIA.] —**Scan·di·an** *n.*

Scan·di·na·vi·a (skăn′də-nā′vē-ə) *n. Abbr.* **Scand.** Region of northern Europe. Strictly it is the peninsula comprising the kingdoms of Norway and Sweden, but culturally it also takes in Denmark. Finland, Iceland, and the Faeroe Islands are often included.

Scan·di·na·vi·an (skăn′də-nā′vē-ən, -nāv′yən) *n. Abbr.* **Scand. 1.** A native or inhabitant of Scandinavia. **2.** The North Germanic languages. —**Scan·di·na·vi·an** *adj.*

Scandinavian Peninsula. The peninsula in northwestern Europe comprising Norway and Sweden.

scan·di·um (skăn′dē-əm) *n. Symbol* **Sc** A silvery-white, very lightweight metallic element found in various rare minerals. An artificially radioactive isotope of it is used as a tracer in oil-well and pipeline studies. Atomic number 21, atomic weight 44.956, melting point 1,539°C, boiling point 2,727°C, specific gravity 2.992, valence 3. [New Latin, from Latin *Scandia,* ancient name for Scandinavia, where it was discovered.] —**scan·dic** *adj.*

scandium oxide *n.* A white amorphous powder, Sc_2O_3, used as a source of scandium and in the manufacture of ceramics. Also called "scandia."

scan·ner (skăn′ər) *n.* One that scans, specifically: **1.** An electronic device providing a visual representation on a cathode-ray screen of the distribution of a radioactive compound in a given system, as the human body. **2.** A device that transmits or receives a radar signal within a predetermined solid angle. See **optical scanner.**

scan·ning (skăn′ĭng) *n.* Any of various electronic or optical techniques by which images or recorded information are sensed for subsequent modification, integration, or transmission. Also used adjectively: *a scanning device.*

scanning electron microscope *n.* An electron microscope capable of forming a three-dimensional image on a cathode-ray screen by means of a focused beam of electrons that is scanned across the object to be viewed; the image is formed both by the electrons that the object scatters and by the secondary electrons produced.

scan·sion (skăn′shən) *n.* **1.** The analysis of verse into metrical feet and rhythm patterns. **2.** The way a line or verse scans. [Late Latin *scansiō* (stem *scansiōn-*), from Latin, a climbing, from *scandere* (past participle *scansus*), to climb.]

scan·so·ri·al (skăn-sôr′ē-əl, -sōr′ē-əl) *adj. Zoology.* Adapted to or specialized for climbing. [Latin *scansōrius,* from *scandere* (past participle *scansus*), to climb.]

scant (skănt) *adj.* **scanter, scantest. 1.** Deficient in quantity or amount; meager; inadequate. **2.** Being only just, or just short of, a specified measure: *a scant three miles.* **3.** Inadequately supplied. Used with *of: scant of breath.* —See Synonyms at **meager.**
~*tr.v.* **scanted, scanting, scants. 1.** To provide with an inadequate portion or allowance; skimp. **2.** To limit, as in amount or share; stint. **3.** To reduce the size or amount of; cut down. **4.** To treat inadequately or neglectfully. [Middle English, from Old Norse *skamt,* neuter of *skammr,* short.] —**scant·ly** *adv.* —**scant·ness** *n.*

scant·ling (skănt′lĭng, -lĭn) *n.* **1.** A small piece of timber, usually one having a cross section no more than five inches square. **2.** Such pieces of timber collectively. **3.** The dimensions of building materials such as stone or timber, especially in breadth and thickness. **4.** *Usually* **scantlings.** *Nautical.* The dimensions of the structural parts of a vessel, such as its frames, plates, and girders. **5.** A very small amount. [Alteration of obsolete *scantlon,* Middle English *scantilon,* carpenter's gauge, dimension, from Old French *escantillon, eschandillon,* probably from Vulgar Latin *scandilia* (unattested), measure, scale, from Latin *scandere,* to climb.]

scant·y (skăn′tē) *adj.* **-ier, -iest. 1.** Barely sufficient or adequate. **2.** Deficient in extent or degree; small; insufficient. —See Synonyms at **meager.** —**scant·i·ly** *adv.* —**scant·i·ness** *n.*

Scap·a Flow (skăp′ə flō′) Sheltered stretch of sea in the Orkney Islands, northern Scotland. It was the base of the British home fleet in both World Wars.

scape¹ (skāp) *n.* **1.** *Botany.* A leafless flower stalk growing from a basal rosette of leaves. **2.** A similar stalklike part, such as a feather shaft or a segment of an insect's antenna. **3.** *Architecture.* The shaft of a column. [Latin *scāpus†,* stalk.]

scape² *Archaic.* A variant of **escape.**

-scape *suffix.* Indicates scene or view; for example, **seascape.** [Back-formation from LANDSCAPE.]

scape·goat (skāp′gōt′) *n.* **1.** A live goat over whose head Aaron confessed all the sins of the children of Israel and which was sent into the wilderness symbolically bearing their sin on the Day of Atonement. Leviticus 16. **2.** A person or group made to bear the blame for others or unjustly regarded as being responsible for hardship or disaster.
~*tr.v.* **scapegoated, -goating, -goats.** To make a scapegoat of. [(E)SCAPE + GOAT (improper translation of Hebrew *azāzel,* probably "goat for Azazel" (desert demon), misconstrued as *ēz-ōzēl,* "goat that escapes.")]

scape·grace (skāp′grās′) *n.* An unprincipled or incorrigible person; rascal. [(E)SCAPE + GRACE.]

scaph·oid (skăf′oid′) *adj.* Boat-shaped.
~*n. Anatomy.* See **navicular** (sense 2). [New Latin *scaphoides,* from Greek *skaphoeidēs* : *skaphē,* tub, boat + -OID.]

scaph·o·pod (skăf′ə-pŏd′) *n. Zoology.* A **tooth shell** *(see).* [New Latin *scaphopoda* : Greek *skaphos,* boat + -POD.]

scap·o·lite (skăp′ə-līt′) *n.* Any of a series of variously colored mineral silicates of aluminum, calcium, and sodium. Also called "wernerite." [French : Latin *scāpus,* stalk, SCAPE (from its prismatic crystals) + -ITE.]

sca·pose (skā′pōs′) *adj. Botany.* Resembling or consisting of a scape.

scap·u·la (skăp′yə-lə) *n., pl.* **-las** or **-lae** (-lē′). **1.** *Anatomy.* Either of two large, flat, triangular bones forming the back part of the shoulder. Also called "shoulder blade." **2.** The corresponding bone in other vertebrates. [Latin, shoulder blade, shoulder.]

scap·u·lar (skăp′yə-lər) *n.* Also **scap·u·lar·y** (-lĕr′ē) *pl.* **-ies. 1.** A monk's sleeveless outer garment hanging from the shoulders and sometimes having a cowl. **2.** Two pieces of cloth joined by strings and worn under the clothing about the shoulders as a badge or token of affiliation to certain religious orders, or as a sacramental. **3.** Any of the feathers covering the shoulder of a bird.
~*adj. Anatomy.* Of or pertaining to the shoulder or scapula. [Mid-

scarab *Regarded by the ancient Egyptians as a symbol of resurrection and immortality, the scarab, or dung beetle (above), is native to Mediterranean countries. The Egyptian god of dawn, Khepera, was conventionally portrayed as a scarab. Khepera is shown below receiving the sun in a detail from the Papyrus of Anhai, painted in about 1150 B.C.*

dle English *scapulare,* from Medieval Latin *scapulāre, scapulārium,* "shoulder cloak," from Latin *scapula,* shoulder, SCAPULA.]

scar[1] (skär) *n.* **1.** A mark left on the skin or other tissue following the healing of a surface injury or wound. **2.** Any impression or sign of damage caused by or remaining as evidence of mental or physical injury. **3.** *Botany.* A mark indicating a former attachment, as of a leaf to a stem. **4.** A mark, dent, or other blemish made by use, motion, or contact.
~*v.* **scarred, scarring, scars.** —*tr.* To mark with or as if with a scar. —*intr.* To form a scar. [Middle English *(e)scare,* from Old French *esc(h)are,* scab, from Late Latin *eschara,* from Greek *eskhara*†, hearth, scab caused by burning.]

scar[2] *n.* Also *Scottish* **scaur** (skär, skôr). *Geology.* A bare rock face, especially in northern England, where it indicates a limestone cliff. [Middle English *skerre,* from Old Norse *sker,* low reef.]

scar·ab (skăr′əb) *n.* Also **scar·a·bae·us** (skăr′ə-bē′əs) *pl.* **-uses** or **-baei** (-bē′ī′). **1.** Any scarabaeid beetle; especially, *Scarabaeus sacer,* regarded as sacred by the ancient Egyptians. **2.** A representation of a scarab beetle, especially one cut from a stone or gem, used in ancient Egypt as a talisman and a symbol of the soul. [Latin *scarabaeus*†.]

scar·a·bae·id (skăr′ə-bē′ĭd) *n.* Any of the numerous beetles of the family Scarabaeidae, including the chafers and dung beetles. [New Latin *Scarabaeidae,* from Latin *scarabaeus,* SCARAB.] —**scar·a·bae·id, scar·a·bae·oid** (skăr′ə-bē′oid′), **scar·a·boid** (skăr′ə-boid′) *adj.*

Scar·a·mouch, Scar·a·mouche (skăr′ə-mo͞osh′, -mo͞och′, -mouch′) *n.* A stock character in old Italian comedy and pantomime, depicted as a boastful, cowardly braggart or buffoon. [French *Scaramouche,* from Italian *Scaramuccia,* jocular use of *scaramuccia,* SKIRMISH.]

Scar·bor·ough (skär′bûr′ō, -bər-ə). Seaside resort of North Yorkshire, in northeastern England. There are remains of a 4th-century Roman signaling station above the town.

scarce (skârs) *adj.* **scarcer, scarcest. 1.** Uncommonly or infrequently seen or found. **2.** Insufficient to meet a demand or requirement; not plentiful or abundant. —**make oneself scarce.** *Informal.* To leave hurriedly or surreptitiously.
~*adv.* Hardly; scarcely. [Middle English *scars,* from Norman French *escars,* from Vulgar Latin *excarpsus* (unattested), "picked," "choice," hence "rare," variant of Latin *excerptus,* past participle of *excerpere,* to pick out, select : *ex-,* out + *carpere,* to pick, pluck.] —**scarce·ness** *n.*

scarce·ly (skârs′lē) *adv.* **1.** By a small margin; just barely. **2.** Almost not; hardly. **3.** Certainly not.
Usage: Because *scarcely* has the force of a negative its use with another negative word in the same clause is disapproved in formal English. *We could scarcely hear it* is preferable to *We couldn't scarcely hear it,* and *They departed with scarcely a word* is preferable to *They departed without scarcely a word.* The use of *when* or, less often, *before* rather than *than* with a following clause is also preferred: *Scarcely had he entered when the telephone rang.*

scar·ci·ty (skâr′sə-tē) *n., pl.* **-ties. 1.** An insufficient amount or supply; shortage. **2.** Infrequency of appearance or occurrence; rarity.

scare (skâr) *v.* **scared, scaring, scares.** —*tr.* **1.** To startle with fear; frighten; alarm; terrify. **2.** To force or drive by frightening. Used with *away, off, out,* or other adverbs. **3.** *Informal.* To cause to be in a specified state by frightening: *It scared him silly.* —*intr.* To become frightened. —See Synonyms at **frighten.** —**scare up.** *Informal.* To gather or prepare hurriedly; improvise.
~*n.* **1.** A condition or sensation of sudden fear. **2.** A general state of alarm, especially when exaggerated or groundless; a panic. **3.** Something that causes unreasonable or exaggerated alarm. Also used adjectivally: *scare stories.* [Middle English *skerren,* from Old Norse *skirra,* from *skjarr,* shy, timid, from North Germanic *skerza-* (unattested).] —**scar·er** *n.* —**scar·ing·ly** *adv.*

scare·crow (skâr′krō′) *n.* **1.** An object, usually a crude figure of a man, set up in a field to scare birds away from crops. **2.** Something frightening but not inherently dangerous. **3.** A person resembling a scarecrow, especially in being shabbily dressed or very thin.

scared·y-cat (skâr′dē-kăt′) *n. Informal.* One who is timid or easily scared.

scarf[1] (skärf) *n., pl.* **scarves** (skärvz) or **scarfs. 1.** A piece of cloth worn about the neck, shoulders, or head. **2.** A narrow cloth strip used on the surface of a bureau or table. [Probably from Old North French *escarpe,* sash, sling.]

scarf[2] *n., pl.* **scarfs. 1.** A joint made by cutting and notching the ends of two timbers and strapping or bolting them together to make a continuous piece. Also called "scarf joint." **2.** The end of a timber notched in this fashion. **3.** A cut made into the body of a whale in order to remove the blubber.
~*tr.v.* **scarfed, scarfing, scarfs. 1.** To join by means of a scarf joint. **2.** To cut a scarf in. [Middle English *skarf*†.]

scarf·skin (skärf′skĭn′) *n.* The epidermis or outermost layer of skin.

scar·i·fi·ca·tor (skăr′ə-fĭ-kā′tər) *n.* A surgical instrument with several spring-operated lancets, used for skin scarification.

scar·i·fy (skăr′ə-fī′) *tr.v.* **-fied, -fying, -fies. 1.** To make superficial incisions in (the skin), as when vaccinating. **2.** To break up the surface of (topsoil, for example). **3.** To wound with severe criticism. **4.** *Botany.* To slit or soften the outer coat of (seeds) to speed germination. [Middle English *scarifien,* to make incisions on the bark of a tree, from Old French *scarifier,* from Late Latin *scarīficāre,* variant of Latin *scarīfāre,* from Greek *skariphasthai,* to scratch an outline, sketch, from *skariphos,* stylus.] —**scar·i·fi·ca·tion** *n.* —**scar·i·fi·er** *n.*

scar·i·ous (skâr′ē-əs) *adj.* Also **scar·i·ose** (-ōs′). *Botany.* Thin, membranous, and dry: *scarious bracts.* [New Latin *scariosus*†.]

scar·la·ti·na (skär′lə-tē′nə) *n.* **Scarlet fever** *(see).* [New Latin, from Italian *(febbre) scarlattina,* scarlet (fever), diminutive of *scarlatto,* SCARLET.] —**scar·la·ti·noid** (skär′lə-tē′noid′) *adj.*

Scar·lat·ti (skär-lä′tē), **Domenico** (1685–1757). Italian composer, son of the prolific composer **Alessandro Scarlatti** (1660–1725). He was a virtuoso harpsichordist, and his numerous works for the instrument were influential in the development of keyboard music generally and of the sonata form.

scar·let (skär′lĭt) *n.* **1.** A strong to vivid red or reddish orange. **2.** Clothing or cloth of the color scarlet. [Middle English, from Old French *escarlate*†.] —**scar·let** *adj.*

scarlet fever *n.* An acute contagious disease caused by a hemolytic streptococcus, occurring mainly in children, and characterized by a scarlet skin rash and high fever. Also called "scarlatina."

scarlet pimpernel *n.* See **pimpernel.**

scarlet runner *n.* A climbing bean plant, *Phaseolus coccineus,* native to tropical America, having scarlet flowers and long pods containing edible seeds. Also called "runner bean."

scarlet tanager *n.* A New World bird, *Piranga olivacea,* of which the male has bright scarlet plumage with a black tail and wings.

scarp (skärp) *n.* **1.** A steep slope; cliff. **2.** A steep slope at the outer edge of a fortification.
~*tr.v.* **scarped, scarping, scarps.** To cut or make into a steep slope. [Italian *scarpa,* probably from Gothic *skarpō* (unattested), pointed object.]

Scar·ron (skä-rôN′), **Paul** (1610–60). French writer. Though he was a noted dramatist, his best-known work is the burlesque epic and novel *Le Roman Comique* (1651–57).

scar tissue *n.* A dense, often hard layer of connective tissue formed over a healing wound or cut.

scarves. Alternate plural of **scarf.**

scar·y (skâr′ē) *adj.* **-ier, -iest.** *Informal.* Frightening; alarming.

scat[1] (skăt) *intr.v.* **scatted, scatting, scats.** *Informal.* To go away hastily; leave at once. Usually used in the imperative. [Perhaps short for SCATTER.]

scat[2] *n.* A type of jazz singing consisting of the improvisation and repetition of meaningless syllables sung to a melody. Also used adjectivally: *a scat singer.*
~*intr.v.* **scatted, scatting, scats.** To sing scat. [Perhaps imitative.]

scat[3] *n.* Any of several fishes of the genus *Scatophagus,* of tropical Asia and adjacent areas; especially, *S. argus,* having a flat, rounded, spotted or striped body, and popular as an aquarium fish. [Shortened from New Latin *Scatophagus,* from Greek *skatophagos,* SCATOPHAGOUS.]

scat[4] *n. Often* **scats.** The excremental dropping of an animal, especially an animal being hunted. [Greek *skōr* (stem *skat-*).]

scathe (skāth) *tr.v.* **scathed, scathing, scathes. 1.** To criticize severely. **2.** To harm or injure severely, especially by fire or heat; wither; sear.
~*n.* Harm; injury. [Middle English *skathen,* from Old Norse *skadha.*] —**scathe·ful** *adj.*

scath·ing (skā′thĭng) *adj.* **1.** Extremely severe or harsh; bitterly denunciatory: *scathing criticism.* **2.** Harmful or painful; injurious. —**scath·ing·ly** *adv.*

scato- *prefix.* Indicates feces or excrement; for example, **scatology.** [Greek *skato-,* from *skōr* (stem *skat-*), dung, ordure.]

sca·tol·o·gy (skə-tŏl′ə-jē, skā-) *n.* **1.** The study of fecal excrement, as in medicine or paleontology. **2.** An obsession with excrement or excretory functions. **3.** Preoccupation with obscenity, as in literature. [SCATO- + -LOGY.] —**scat·o·log·ic** (skăt′l-ŏj′ĭk), **scat·o·log·i·cal** *adj.* —**sca·tol·o·gist** *n.*

sca·toph·a·gous (skə-tŏf′ə-gəs, skā-) *adj.* Feeding on dung, as a beetle or fly. [Greek *skatophagos* : SCATO- + -PHAGOUS.]

scat·ter (skăt′ər) *v.* **-tered, -tering, -ters.** —*tr.* **1.** To cause to separate and go in various directions; disperse. **2. a.** To distribute widely or loosely by or as if by sprinkling or throwing or dropping randomly. **b.** To cover or strew (a surface) by scattering. **3.** *Physics.* To deflect (radiation or particles). —*intr.* **1.** To separate and go in several directions; disperse. **2.** To appear, occur, or fall over a wide area and at widely spaced intervals.
~*n.* **1.** The act of scattering. **2.** The condition or extent of being scattered. **3.** Something that is scattered. [Middle English *scateren,* probably variant of *schateren,* to SHATTER.] —**scat·ter·er** *n.*

scat·ter·brained (skăt′ər-brănd′) *adj. Informal.* Lacking in power of concentration or attention; forgetful, disorganized, or thoughtless. —**scat·ter·brain** *n.*

scat·ter·good (skăt′ər-go͝od′) *n.* A spendthrift.

scat·ter·ing (skăt′ər-ĭng) *n.* **1.** A sparse distribution or irregular occurrence of something: *a scattering of applause.* **2.** *Physics.* The dispersal of a beam of particles or of radiation into a range of directions resulting from physical interactions.
~*adj.* Placed at intervals or occurring irregularly.

scatter rug *n.* A small rug for carpeting a part of the floor. Also called "throw rug."

scaup (skôp) *n., pl.* **scaups** or collectively **scaup.** Either of two diving ducks, *Aythya marila* or *A. affinis,* having predominantly black and white plumage. Also called "scaup duck." [Perhaps from Scottish *scaup,* variant of SCALP (rare sense "bed of mussels"), because these ducks feed on shellfish.]

scaur. *Scottish.* Variant of **scar** (rock).

scav•enge (skăv′ənj) *v.* **-enged, -enging, -enges.** —*tr.* **1.** To collect and remove refuse from; clean up. **2.** To search through (rubbish, discarded matter, or the like) for reusable material, such as food. **3.** To collect (reusable material) by searching. **4.** To expel (exhaust gases) from a cylinder of an internal-combustion engine. **5.** *Metallurgy.* To clean (molten metal) by chemically removing impurities. —*intr.* To act as a scavenger; especially, to search through discarded material for edible or useful things. [Back-formation from SCAVENGER.]

scav•en•ger (skăv′ən-jər) *n.* **1.** An organism that feeds on dead animal flesh or other decaying organic matter. **2.** One who scavenges. **3.** *Chemistry.* A substance added to a mixture to remove impurities or to counteract the undesirable effects of other constituents. **4.** *Metallurgy.* A metal added to a molten metal or alloy that acts, by combining with oxygen or nitrogen, to remove impurities. [Alteration of earlier *scavager,* Middle English *skawager,* toll collector, from street cleaner, from Norman French *scawager,* from *scawage,* a toll levied on foreign merchants, from Flemish *scawen,* to look at, SHOW.]

sce•nar•i•o (sĭ-nâr′ē-ō′, sĭ-när′-, sĭ-năr′-) *n., pl.* **-os. 1.** An outline of the plot of a dramatic or literary work. **2.** A **screenplay** *(see).* **3.** An outline of an imagined chain of events; a possible state of affairs or course of action. [Italian, "scenery," from Late Latin *scaenārius,* of the stage, from Latin *scaena,* stage, SCENE.]

sce•nar•ist (sĭ-nâr′ĭst, sĭ-när′-, sĭ-năr′-) *n.* A writer of scenarios.

scend, send (sĕnd) *intr.v.* **scended** or **sended, scending** or **sending, scends** or **sends.** *Nautical.* To rise upward or plunge downward on a wave or swell.
∼*n.* The rising and falling movement of a ship on a wave or swell. [Probably alteration of SEND.]

scene (sēn) *n.* **1.** A locality as seen by a viewer; view. **2. a.** The surroundings and place where an action or event occurs: *The police arrived at the scene of the accident.* **b.** Such a place or setting marked by a specified feature or characteristic: *The road was a scene of carnage following the accident.* **3.** *Abbr.* **sc.** The place in which the action of a play, film, novel, or other narrative occurs; setting; locale. **4.** *Abbr.* **sc.** A subdivision of an act in a dramatic presentation in which the setting is fixed and the time continuous. **5.** *Abbr.* **sc.** A shot or series of shots in a film constituting a unit of continuous related action. **6.** The scenery and properties for a dramatic presentation. **7.** *Archaic.* A theater stage. **8.** A real or fictitious episode, especially when described. **9.** A public display of passion or temper. **10.** *Slang.* **a.** A place or realm of a particular activity or interest: *The battle for promotion has livened up the football scene.* **b.** A given situation: *a bad scene.* **—behind the scenes. 1.** Backstage. **2.** In private. **—set the scene.** To describe the events leading up to, or the surrounding location of, a particular scene or event. **—steal the scene.** To draw favorable attention to oneself and away from others. [French *scène,* from Old French *scene,* stage, from Latin *scaena,* stage, theater, from Greek *skēnē*†, "tent."]

scen•er•y (sē′nə-rē) *n., pl.* **-ies. 1.** The overall appearance of the natural surroundings of an area, especially when considered aesthetically; the landscape. **2.** Painted backdrops and similar properties on a theatrical stage.

sce•nic (sē′nĭk) *adj.* **1.** Of, pertaining to, or having picturesque natural landscapes: *a scenic route.* **2.** Of or pertaining to theatrical scenery. **3.** Representing an event, piece of action, or the like. Said of a work of art. **—sce•ni•cal•ly** *adv.*

scent (sĕnt) *n.* **1.** A distinctive odor or smell, especially a pleasant one. **2.** A perfume. **3.** An odor left by the passing of an animal. **4. a.** The trail of a hunted animal or fugitive. **b.** Any trail, set of clues, or the like that may be followed. **5. a.** The sense of smell. **b.** The power of following a trail, set of clues, or the like. **6.** A hint of something imminent; suggestion. **—**See Synonyms at **smell.**
∼*v.* **scented, scenting, scents.** —*tr.* **1.** To perceive or identify by the sense of smell. **2.** To suspect or detect as if by smelling: *scent danger.* **3.** To perfume. —*intr.* To hunt by means of the sense of smell. Used of hounds. [Middle English *sent,* from *senten,* to smell, scent, from Old French *sentir,* from Latin *sentīre,* to feel.]

scent gland *n.* A specialized exocrine gland in many mammals that secretes a strong-smelling substance.

scep•ter (sĕp′tər) *n.* Also *chiefly British* **scep•tre. 1.** A staff held by a sovereign on ceremonial occasions as an emblem of authority. **2.** Sovereign office or power.
∼*tr.v.* **sceptered, -tering, -ters.** Also *chiefly British* **sceptred, -tring, -tres.** To invest with royal authority. [Middle English *(s)ceptre,* from Old French, from Latin *scēptrum,* from Greek *skēptron*†, "staff," "stick."]

sceptic. Variant of **skeptic.**

sceptical. Variant of **skeptical.**

scepticism. Variant of **skepticism.**

sceptre. *Chiefly British.* Variant of **scepter.**

sch. school.

Scha•den•freu•de (shäd′n-froi′də) *n.* A feeling of pleasure caused by another's unhappiness or misfortune; malicious delight. [German : *Schade,* harm + *Freude,* joy.]

schav (shäv) *n.* A chilled soup made with sorrel, onions, lemon juice, eggs, and sugar and served with sour cream. [Polish *szczaw,* sorrel, akin to Russian *ščavel*†.]

sched•ule (skĕj′o͞ol, -əl; *British* shĕd′yo͞ol) *n.* **1.** A written list or statement, usually in tabular form, as: **a.** A listing of rates or prices. **b.** An agenda. **c.** A timetable, as for buses or trains. **2.** A program of forthcoming events or appointments. **3.** A production plan allotting work to be done and specifying deadlines. **4.** A supplementary statement of details appended to a document.
∼*tr.v.* **scheduled, -uling, -ules. 1.** To enter on a schedule. **2.** To make up a schedule for. **3.** To plan or appoint for a certain time or date. [Middle English *cedule, sedule,* slip of parchment or paper, short note, from Old French *cedule,* from Late Latin *schedula,* diminutive of Latin *scheda, scida,* papyrus leaf, from Greek *skhedē.*]

schee•lite (shā′līt′) *n.* A variously colored natural form of calcium tungstate, $CaWO_4$, found in igneous rocks and used as a source of tungsten. [After Karl Wilhelm *Scheele* (1742–86), Swedish chemist.]

Sche•her•a•za•de (shə-hĕr′ə-zä′də, -zäd′). The fictional narrator of the tales in *The Arabian Nights.*

Scheldt (skĕlt). *French* **Es•caut** (ĕ-skō′). *Dutch* **Schel•de** (skĕl′də). River in northwestern Europe. Rising in Aisne department, France, it flows 435 kilometers (270 miles) through Belgium and the port of Antwerp to join the North Sea in the Netherlands via the West Scheldt estuary (Westerschelde). The river was cut off from its East Scheldt outlet (Oosterschelde) by dikes built in the 19th century. The Scheldt is navigable for most of its length and connects with the Belgian and Dutch canal systems.

scat *A brightly colored fish found in salt and fresh water along the coasts of Asia and Indonesia.*

sche•ma (skē′mə) *n., pl.* **-mata** (-mə-tə). **1.** A summarized or diagrammatic representation of something; outline. **2.** A pattern or structure, especially of a logical proof or argument. [German *Schema,* from Greek *skhēma,* form. See **scheme.**]

sche•mat•ic (skē-măt′ĭk) *adj.* Pertaining to or in the form of a scheme or schema; diagrammatic.
∼*n.* A structural or procedural diagram, especially of an electrical or mechanical system. **—sche•mat•i•cal•ly** *adv.*

sche•ma•tism (skē′mə-tĭz′əm) *n.* The patterned disposition or arrangement of constituents within a given system.

sche•ma•tize (skē′mə-tīz′) *tr.v.* **-tized, -tizing, -tizes.** To form into, or express by means of, a scheme or schema. [Greek *skhēmatizein,* to give a form to, from *skhēma,* form, manner. See **scheme.**] **—sche•ma•ti•za•tion** *n.*

scheme (skēm) *n.* **1.** A systematic plan of action. **2.** An orderly combination of related or successive parts or things; system. **3.** An underhand or secret plan; plot; intrigue. **4.** A visionary plan. **5.** A chart, diagram, or outline of a system or object. **6.** *Scottish.* A housing estate, especially a council estate.
∼*v.* **schemed, scheming, schemes.** —*tr.* **1.** To contrive a plan or scheme for. **2.** To plot. —*intr.* To make plans, especially secret or devious ones. [Latin *schēma,* form, figure, manner, from Greek *skhēma.*] **—schem•er** *n.*

schemozzle. Variant of **shemozzle.**

Sche•nec•ta•dy (skə-nĕk′tə-dē). City of eastern New York State, on the Mohawk River. Founded in 1661, the city prospered after the opening of the Erie Canal (1820's) and the building of the railroads (1830's).

scher•zan•do (skĕrt-sän′dō) *adv. Music.* In a playful or sportive manner. Used as a direction to the performer.
∼*n., pl.* **scherzandos.** *Music.* A scherzando passage or movement. [Italian, gerund of *scherzare,* to joke, from *scherzo,* joke, SCHERZO.] **—scher•zan•do** *adj.*

scher•zo (skĕrt′sō) *n., pl.* **-zos** or **-zi** (-sē). *Music.* A lively movement commonly in 3/4 time. [Italian, joke, from Middle High German *scherz,* from *scherzen,* to joke, leap with joy.]

Schia•pa•rel•li (skăp′ə-rĕl′ē), **Elsa** (*c.* 1890–1973). Italian-born French fashion designer. She did much to make Paris the world center of fashion design.

Schiaparelli, Giovanni Virginio (1835–1910). Italian astronomer. He is best known for his discovery of linear markings on the surface of Mars, which he thought were water channels. His theory that Mercury and Venus rotate on their axes as they travel around the sun, so that they always have the same side facing the sun, was not refuted until the 1960's.

Schick test (shĭk) *n.* A test of susceptibility to diphtheria in which diphtheria toxin is injected into the skin. A red patch indicates the absence of antibodies and therefore the need for immunization. [After Béla *Schick* (1877–1967), U.S. pediatrician.]

Schiff's reagent (shĭfs) *n.* An aqueous solution of rosaniline and sulfurous acid used to test for the presence of aldehydes, which oxidize the reduced form of the dye rosaniline back to its original magenta color. [After Hugo *Schiff* (1834–1915), German chemist.]

schil•ler (shĭl′ər) *n.* A lustrous, almost metallic sheen on certain minerals caused by internal reflections from microscopic inclusions. [German *Schiller,* iridescence, from Middle High German *schilher,* iridescent taffeta, from *schilhen,* to wink, blink, from Old High German *scilihen.*]

Schil•ler (shĭl′ər), **Johann Christoph Friedrich von** (1759–1805). German poet and dramatist. His historical plays include *Wallenstein* (1798–99), *Maria Stuart* (1800), and *Wilhelm Tell* (1804); he also wrote a study of aesthetics. He is an important figure in the romantic movement.

schil•ling (shĭl′ĭng) *n.* **1.** The basic monetary unit of Austria, equal to 100 gröschen. See feature at **currency. 2.** A coin worth one schilling. [German *Schilling,* from Middle High German *schillinc,* from Old High German *skilling,* from Germanic *skillingaz* (unattested), SHILLING.]

schip•per•ke (skĭp′ər-kē, -kə) *n.* A small dog of a breed developed in Belgium, having a dense, long, black coat. [Flemish, "little skipper" (it is often trained as a watchdog on a boat), from *schipper,* skipper, from Middle Dutch, from *schip,* ship.]

PRONUNCIATION KEY

ă, pat; ā, pay; âr, care; ä, father, are; b, bib; ch, church; d, deed; ĕ, pet; ē, be; f, fife; g, gag; h, hat; hw, which; ĭ, pit; ī, pie; îr, pier; j, judge; k, kick; l, lid, needle; m, mum; n, no, sudden; ng, thing; ŏ, pot; ō, toe; ô, paw, for; oi, noise; ou, out; o͝o, book; o͞o, boot; p, pop; r, roar; s, sauce; sh, ship, dish; t, tight; th, thin, path; *th*, this, bathe; ŭ, cut; ûr, fur; v, valve; w, with; y, yes; z, zebra, size; zh, vision; ə, about, item, edible, gallop, circus, peaceful

IN FOREIGN WORDS:

à, *Fr.* ami; œ, *Fr.* feu, *Ger.* schön; ü, *Fr.* tu, *Ger.* über; KH, *Ger.* ich, *Scot.* loch; N, *Fr.* bon; y′, *Fr.* Compiègne

STRESS MARKS:

Primary stress: ′ in•cite′ (ĭn-sīt′)
Secondary stress: ′ in′sight′ (ĭn′sīt′)

schism (sĭz′əm, skĭz′-) *n.* **1.** A separation or division into hostile, opposing groups or factions; especially, a formal breach of union within a Christian church. **2.** The offense of attempting to promote or perpetuate such a split within a church or religious group. **3.** A body or sect that has brought about, or is the result of, a separation or division. [Middle English *(s)cisme,* from Old French, from Late Latin *schisma,* from Greek *skhisma,* a split, division, from *skhizein,* to split.] **—schis·mat·ic** (sĭz-măt′ĭk, skĭz′-) *n. & adj.* **—schis·mat·i·cal·ly** *adv.*

schist (shĭst) *n.* Any of various medium- to coarse-grained metamorphic rocks composed of parallel layers, which are often wavy and flaky. [French *schiste,* from Latin *(lapis) schistos,* "fissile (stone)," from Greek *skhistos (lithos),* talc, from *skhizein,* to split.] **—schis·tose** (shĭs′tōs′), **schis·tous** (shĭs′təs) *adj.* **—schis·tos·i·ty** (shĭ-stŏs′ə-tē) *n.*

schis·to·some (shĭs′tə-sōm′) *n.* Any of several chiefly tropical trematode worms of the genus *Schistosoma,* many of which are parasitic in the blood of humans and other mammals. Also called "blood fluke." [New Latin *Schistosoma,* "cleft body" : Greek *skhistos,* cleft, from *skhizein,* to split + -SOME (body).]

schis·to·so·mi·a·sis (shĭs′tō-sō-mī′ə-sĭs) *n.* Any of various generally tropical diseases caused by infestation with schistosomes. Also called "bilharziasis," "bilharzia." [New Latin : *Schistosoma,* SCHISTOSOME + -IASIS.]

schiz·o (skĭt′sō) *adj. Slang.* Schizophrenic.
~*n., pl.* **schizos.** *Slang.* A schizophrenic person.

schizo-, schiz- *prefix.* Indicates division, split, or cleavage; for example, **schizophrenia, schizont.** [New Latin, from Greek *skhizo-,* from *skhizein,* to split.]

schiz·o·carp (skĭz′ə-kärp′, skĭt′sə-) *n.* A dry fruit that splits at maturity into two or more closed carpels, each usually containing one seed, as in the mallow. [SCHIZO- + -CARP.] **—schiz·o·car·pic** (skĭz′ə-kär′pĭk, skĭt′sə-), **schiz·o·car·pous** (-kär′pəs) *adj.*

schiz·o·gen·e·sis (skĭz′ō-jĕn′ə-sĭs, skĭt′sō-) *n. Biology.* Reproduction by fission. [New Latin : SCHIZO- + -GENESIS.] **—schiz·o·ge·net·ic** (skĭz′ō-jə-nĕt′ĭk, skĭt′sō-) *adj.*

schi·zog·o·ny (skĭ-zŏg′ə-nē, skĭt-sŏg′-) *n. Biology.* Reproduction by multiple asexual fission, characteristic of many protozoans. [New Latin *schizogonia* : SCHIZO- + -GONY.] **—schi·zog·o·nous, schiz·o·gon·ic** (skĭz′ə-gŏn′ĭk, skĭt′sə-) *adj.*

schiz·oid (skĭt′soid′) *adj.* **1.** Characteristic of, tending to, or resembling schizophrenia. **2.** Loosely, marked by extremes of mood or temperament.
~*n.* A schizoid person. [SCHIZ(O)- + -OID.]

schiz·o·my·cete (skĭz′ō-mī′sēt′, -mī-sēt′, skĭt′sō-) *n.* Any of numerous single-celled microorganisms of the class Schizomycetes, which includes the bacteria. [New Latin *Schizomycetes,* "fission fungi" (from their multiplying by fission) : SCHIZO- + -MYCETE.] **—schiz·o·my·ce·tous** (skĭz′ō-mī-sē′təs, skĭt′sō-) *adj.*

schiz·ont (skĭz′ŏnt′, skĭt′sŏnt′) *n.* A protozoan cell produced by schizogony in the life cycle of a sporozoan. [SCHIZO- + -*ont,* being, from Greek *ōn* (stem *ont-*), present participle of *einai,* to be.]

schiz·o·phre·ni·a (skĭt′sə-frē′nē-ə, -frĕn′ē-ə) *n.* Any of a group of psychotic conditions characterized by withdrawal from reality and accompanied by highly variable affective, behavioral, and intellectual disturbances. Formerly called "dementia praecox." [New Latin, "split mind" : SCHIZO- + -PHRENIA.] **—schiz·o·phren·ic** (skĭt′sə-frĕn′ĭk) *adj. & n.*

schiz·o·phyte (skĭz′ə-fīt′, skĭt′sə-) *n.* Any of various single-celled or simple colonial organisms of the division Schizophyta, including bacteria and the blue-green algae, reproducing asexually, usually by fission. [New Latin *Schizophyta* : SCHIZO- + -PHYTE.] **—schiz·o·phyt·ic** (skĭz′ə-fīt′ĭk, skĭt′sə-) *adj.*

schiz·o·pod (skĭz′ə-pŏd′) *n.* Any of various shrimplike crustaceans of the orders Euphausiacea and Mysidacea (formerly included in the single order Schizopoda). [New Latin *Schizopoda,* "split-footed ones" (from the splitting of the thoracic limbs) : SCHIZO- + -POD.] **—schiz·op·o·dous** (skĭ-zŏp′ə-dəs) *adj.*

schiz·o·thy·mi·a (skĭt′sə-thī′mē-ə) *n.* Schizoid behavior that resembles schizophrenia in the tendency to withdrawal and introversion but remains within the limits of normality. [New Latin, "split spirit" : SCHIZO- + -THYMIA.] **—schiz·o·thy·mic** (skĭt′sə-thī′mĭk) *adj.*

schiz·y (skĭt′sē) *adj.* **-i·er, -i·est.** *Slang.* Schizoid. [Shortening and alteration of SCHIZOID.]

Schle·gel (shlā′gəl), **August Wilhelm von** (1767–1845). German critic and translator. Best known for his translations of the works of Shakespeare, he also translated other foreign authors and contributed critical work to the romantic movement.

Schlegel, (Carl Wilhelm) Friedrich von (1772–1829). German writer and critic. A Sanskrit scholar, he was a leader of the romantic movement, formulating its aims and publishing his poetry and philosophy in the magazine *Das Athenäum.*

schle·miel (shlə-mēl′) *n. Slang.* An unlucky and habitual bungler; dolt. [Yiddish, perhaps from Hebrew *Shelūmīel,* character in the Bible.]

schlep (shlĕp) *v.* **schlepped, schlepping, schleps.** *Slang.* **—***tr.* To carry clumsily or with difficulty; lug. **—***intr.* **1.** To carry something clumsily. **2.** To move slowly or laboriously.
~*n. Slang.* **1.** An arduous journey. **2.** A clumsy or stupid person. **3.** A boring event or period of time. [Yiddish *shleppen,* to drag, trail, from Middle Low German *slēpen.*]

Schles·in·ger (shlĕs′ĭn-jər), **Arthur Meier** (1888–1965). U.S. histo-

rian and professor. His influential scholarly works included *The Rise of the City, 1878–1898* (1933) and *New Viewpoints in American History* (1922), essays on American historiography. His son **Arthur Meier, Jr.** (1917–), also a historian and professor, served as a political adviser to President John F. Kennedy. Among his many books are *The Age of Jackson* (1945) and *A Thousand Days* (1965), both Pulitzer Prize winners.

Schlesinger, John Richard (1926–). British theater and film director. His films, often dourly naturalistic, include *Billy Liar* (1963), *Midnight Cowboy* (1969), and *Sunday Bloody Sunday* (1970).

Schles·wig (shlĕs′wĭg). Former duchy on the Jutland peninsula, northern Europe, to the north of the Eider River. The greater part of it is now incorporated in the West German state of Schleswig-Holstein.

Schles·wig-Hol·stein (shlĕs′wĭg-hōl′stīn′). State of West Germany. It comprises most of the two former duchies of Schleswig and Holstein. These were inherited by the Danish royal house in 1460. Centuries of conflict ensued as the Danes periodically sought to make them part of Denmark, while their predominantly German populations resisted or sought union with German states, later the German Confederation. Eventually (1866) Prussia annexed both duchies. The northern part of Schleswig was awarded to Denmark after a plebiscite (1920), and it now forms the Danish county of Sønderjylland (South Jutland). Schleswig-Holstein is a low-lying, largely fertile area. There are good harbors along the coast and tourist resorts on offshore islands. The port of Kiel is the state capital.

Schlie·mann (shlē′män), **Heinrich** (1822–90). German archaeologist. Retiring from business (1863), he began to excavate for Homer's Troy at Hissarlik in Turkey. His carelessness and determination to prove the existence of the city somewhat devalued the veracity of his results. From Troy, he went on to excavate most of the sites of Mycenaean Greece.

schlie·ren (shlîr′ən) *pl.n.* **1.** *Geology.* Irregular tabular bodies occurring as essential components of plutonic rock but differing in structure or composition from the principal mass. **2.** *Physics.* Regions of a transparent medium, as of a flowing gas, that exhibit densities different from that of the bulk of the medium. [German *Schlieren,* plural of *Schliere,* streak, from dialectal German *Schlier,* "slimy mass," from Middle High German *slier,* mud, slime.]

schli·ma·zel (shlĭ-mä′zəl) *n. Slang.* An extremely unlucky or inept person; a habitual failure. [Yiddish, "bad luck."]

schlock (shlŏk) *n. Slang.* Something, as merchandise, creative artifacts, or entertainment, that is meretricious or of obviously inferior quality. [Yiddish, "broken merchandise," perhaps from German *Schlag,* a blow, from Middle High German *slac,* from Old High German *slag.*] **—schlock, schlock·y** *adj.*

schmaltz, shmalz (shmälts) *n.* **1.** *Informal.* Excessive sentimentality, especially in art or music. **2.** *Informal.* Excessively profuse flattery or praise. **3.** Animal fat used as food, especially chicken fat. [Yiddish *shmalts,* "melted fat," from Middle High German *smalz,* from Old High German.] **—schmaltz·y** *adj.*

Schmidt (shmĭt), **Helmut** (1918–). German politician. A member of the Social Democratic Party, he was minister of defense (1969–72) and minister of finance (1972–74). From 1974 to 1982 he was federal chancellor.

Schmidt telescope *n.* A reflecting telescope consisting of a concave spherical mirror and a transparent plate of glass at its center of curvature, used to offset spherical aberration, coma, and astigmatism. [After Bernhard *Schmidt* (1879–1935), Swedish-born German astronomer, who invented it.]

schmo, schmoe (shmō) *n., pl.* **schmoes.** Also **shmo** *pl.* **shmoes.** *Slang.* A dull or stupid person. [Yiddish *shmok,* from Slovene *šmok.*]

schmuck (shmŭk) *n. Slang.* A clumsy or stupid person; oaf. [Yiddish *schmuck,* "penis," from German *Schmuck,* ornament, from Middle Low German *smuck.*]

schnap·per (shnăp′ər, snăp′-) *n. Australian.* See **snapper** (sense 3). [Pseudo-German spelling of SNAPPER (fish).]

schnapps (shnäps, shnăps) *n., pl.* **schnapps.** Any of various strong alcoholic liquors. [German *Schnaps,* from Low German *snaps,* mouthful, from *snappen,* to snap, from Middle Low German, SNAP.]

schnau·zer (shnou′zər, shnout′sər) *n.* A dog of a breed developed in Germany, having a wiry gray or black coat and a blunt muzzle. [German *Schnauzer,* from *Schnauze,* snout.]

schnit·zel (shnĭt′səl) *n.* A thin cutlet of veal coated with bread crumbs and fried lightly in butter. [German *Schnitzel,* diminutive of *Schnitz,* slice, from Middle High German *sniz.*]

Schnitz·ler (shnĭts′lər), **Arthur** (1862–1931). Austrian playwright and novelist. His work portrays Viennese café society. His best-known work, *Reigen* (1900), also known as *La Ronde,* met with such controversy for its sexual explicitness that he forbade it to be performed until 50 years after his death.

schnook (shnŏŏk) *n. Slang.* A stupid or easily victimized person; dupe. [Yiddish *shnok.*]

schnor·rer (shnôr′ər, shnōr′-) *n. Slang.* One who takes advantage of the generosity of friends; parasite; sponger. [Yiddish, from *schnorren,* to beg (while playing a pipe or harp), from Middle High German *snurren,* to hum, whirr.]

schnoz·zle (shnŏz′əl) *n. Slang.* The nose. [Probably alteration (influenced by NOZZLE) of Yiddish *shnoitsl,* diminutive of *shnoits,* snout, from German *Schnauze.*]

schol·ar (skŏl′ər) *n.* **1. a.** A learned or erudite person. **b.** A specialist in some given branch of the humanities. **2. a.** One who studies;

especially, a school pupil. **b.** One considered in the light of his ability to learn: *a poor scholar.* **3.** A student who holds a scholarship. [Middle English *scoler,* from Old French *escoler,* from Late Latin *scholāris,* of a school, from Latin *schola,* SCHOOL.]

schol·ar·ly (skŏl′ər-lē) *adj.* Pertaining to, characteristic of, or befitting scholars or scholarship. **—schol·ar·li·ness** *n.*

schol·ar·ship (skŏl′ər-shĭp′) *n.* **1.** The methods, qualities, and attainments of a scholar; learning; erudition. **2.** Existing knowledge resulting from scholarly research in a particular field. **3. a.** An award of financial aid to a student or pupil, usually gained through competitive examination, that is given by a fund or endowment set up for such a purpose. **b.** The position of a student or pupil who has won such an award. **—See Synonyms at knowledge.**

scho·las·tic (skə-lăs′tĭk) *adj.* **1.** Of or pertaining to schools, scholars, or education. **2.** *Usually* **Scholastic.** Pertaining to or characteristic of the medieval Schoolmen or Scholasticism: *Scholastic theology.* **3.** Pedantic; dogmatic.
~*n.* **1.** *Usually* **Scholastic.** A Schoolman. **2.** A dogmatist; pedant. **3.** A formalist in art. **4.** A Jesuit student at a scholasticate, between the novitiate and the priesthood. [Latin *scholasticus,* from Greek *skholastikos,* academic, from *skholazein,* to study, attend lectures, from *skholē,* school.] **—scho·las·ti·cal·ly** *adv.*

scho·las·ti·cate (skə-lăs′tə-kāt′, -kĭt) *n. Roman Catholic Church.* **1.** An institution where Jesuit scholastics undergo a period of general study before beginning their theological studies and entering the priesthood. **2. a.** A scholastic. **b.** The status or period of being a scholastic. [New Latin *scholasticātus,* from Latin *scholasticus,* SCHOLASTIC.]

scho·las·ti·cism (skə-lăs′tə-sĭz′əm) *n.* **1.** *Usually* **Scholasticism.** The dominant theological and philosophical school of medieval western Europe, based on the authority of the Latin Fathers and of Aristotle and his commentators. **2. a.** Close adherence to the traditional doctrines of a school or religious order. **b.** Pedantry.

scho·li·ast (skō′lē-ăst′) *n.* Any of the ancient commentators who annotated the classical authors. [Late Greek *skholiastēs,* from *skholiazein,* to comment on, from *skholion,* SCHOLIUM.]

scho·li·um (skō′lē-əm) *n., pl.* **-ums** or **-lia** (-lē-ə). **1.** An explanatory note or commentary, as on a Greek or Latin text. **2.** A note amplifying a proof or process, as in mathematics. [New Latin, from Greek *skholion,* diminutive of *skholē,* lecture, SCHOOL.]

Schön·berg (shœn′bĕrk′, shûrn′bûrg′), **Arnold** (1874-1951). Austrian composer and teacher. His style is usually characterized as atonal, a term he disliked. An example is *Pierrot Lunaire* (1912), a set of recitations with chamber accompaniment. He immigrated to the United States in 1933 to escape Nazi persecution.

school¹ (skool) *n. Abbr.* **s., S., sch. 1.** An institution for the instruction or education of children or young people. **2.** An institution within a college or university for instruction in a specialized field: *medical school.* **3.** Any institution that provides instruction, especially of a practical or technical nature: *a driving school; drama school.* **4.** The pupils and sometimes the teachers of a school. **5.** The building or group of buildings housing a school, in which instruction is given or in which pupils work and live. **6.** A college or university. **7.** The process of being educated; especially, formal education comprising a planned series of courses over a number of years. **8.** A session or period of instruction at a school: *went swimming before school.* **9.** A group of persons, especially intellectuals or artists, whose thought, work, or style demonstrates some common influence or unifying belief. **10.** A class of people distinguished by shared values, opinions, or principles: *a politician of the old school.* **11.** The education provided by a set of circumstances or experiences. **12.** The prescribed regulations and drill instructions applying to individuals or to a unit of an army or navy.
~*tr.v.* **schooled, schooling, schools. 1.** To instruct; educate. **2.** To train; discipline. **—See Synonyms at teach.** [Middle English *scole,* Old English *scōl,* from Medieval Latin *scōla,* from Latin *schola,* leisure, school, from Greek *skholē,* leisure (devoted to learning), lecture, school.]

school² *n.* A large group of aquatic animals, especially fish, swimming together; a shoal.
~*intr.v.* **schooled, schooling, schools.** To swim in, or form into, a school. [Middle English *scole,* from Middle Dutch *schōle,* troop, group.]

school board *n.* A local board that oversees public schools.

school·book (skool′book′) *n.* A textbook for use in school.

school·boy (skool′boi′) *n.* A boy attending school.

school bus *n.* A publicly or privately owned vehicle that is used for taking schoolchildren to and from school or school-related activities.

school·child (skool′chīld′) *n., pl.* **-children** (-chĭl′drən). A child attending school.

school committee *n.* A school board.

school district *n.* A limited area within a state often comprising several towns that functions as the administrative unit of a public-school system.

school·girl (skool′gûrl′) *n.* A girl attending school.

school·house (skool′hous′) *n.* A building used as a school, especially in a rural area.

school·ing (skool′lĭng) *n.* **1.** Instruction or training given at school; especially, a program of formal education. **2.** The training of a horse or of a horse and rider in dressage.

school·man (skool′mən) *n., pl.* **-men** (-mĭn). **1.** *Often* **Schoolman.** A philosopher or theologian of a medieval university; an adherent of

Scholasticism. **2.** A professional teacher or scholar.

school·marm (skool′märm′) *n. Also* **school·ma'am** (-mäm′, -măm′). *Informal.* **1.** A woman schoolteacher, especially one who is pedantic, old-fashioned, or a priggish disciplinarian. **2.** A woman who resembles a schoolmarm, as in being priggish. [Dialectal *marm,* variant of *ma'am,* MADAM.] **—school·marm·ish** *adj.*

school·mas·ter (skool′măs′tər, -mä′stər) *n.* **1.** A male teacher or headmaster. **2.** A reddish-brown food fish, the snapper *Lutjanus apodus,* of the tropical Atlantic and the Gulf of Mexico.

school·mate (skool′māt′) *n.* A school companion or associate.

school·mis·tress (skool′mĭs′trĭs) *n.* **1.** A woman teacher. **2.** A headmistress of a school.

school·room (skool′room′, -room′) *n.* A classroom.

school·teach·er (skool′tē′chər) *n.* One who teaches in a school below the college level.

school·work (skool′wûrk′) *n.* Lessons done at school or assigned as homework.

school year *n.* The period of a year that constitutes a complete annual session of school.

schoo·ner (skoo′nər) *n.* **1.** A ship with two or more masts, all of which are fore-and-aft-rigged, the mainmast being abaft of and taller than the foremast. **2.** A large beer glass, generally holding a pint or more. **3.** A prairie schooner *(see).* [18th century : origin obscure.]

Scho·pen·hau·er (shō′pən-hou′ər), **Arthur** (1788-1860). German philosopher. Rejecting the theories of Hegel, he held that primordial reality—the will to live—is irrational and that attempts to understand the world rationally are doomed to failure. His major work was the *The World as Will and Idea* (1818).

schorl (shôrl) *n.* A black, opaque variety of tourmaline. [German *Schörl†.*] **—schor·la·ceous** (shôr-lā′shəs) *adj.*

schot·tische (shŏt′ĭsh, shŏ-tēsh′) *n.* **1.** A German round dance in ²/₄ time, resembling a slow polka. **2.** A piece of music for this dance. [German *Schottische,* short for *(der) schottische (Tanz),* (the) Scottish (dance).]

Schrö·ding·er (shrœ′dĭng-ər), **Erwin** (1887-1961). Austrian physicist. He won the Nobel Prize (1933) for his work on the development of the quantum theory. He left Austria after the Nazi Anschluss.

Schrödinger wave equation *n. Physics.* A partial differential equation, fundamental to wave mechanics, describing the behavior of a particle in a potential, based on the de Broglie hypothesis of wave-particle duality. Also called "wave equation."

Schu·bert (shoo′bərt), **Franz Peter** (1797-1828). Austrian composer. In addition to his 600 songs, which established the tradition of the German lied, his genius for the lyrical is evident in his eight surviving symphonies and his many other instrumental works. **—Schu·bert·i·an** (shō-bûr′tē-ən, -bär′tē-ən) *adj.*

Schulz (shoolts), **Charles Monroe** (1922-). U.S. cartoonist. The creator of the *Peanuts* comic strip, he has enjoyed international success with characters such as Charlie Brown, Lucy, Linus, Schroeder, and Snoopy. There have also been *Peanuts* books, television specials, and a musical, *You're a Good Man, Charlie Brown* (1967).

Schu·man (shoo′män′), **Robert** (1886-1963). French statesman. He was prime minister (1947-48) and president of the Assembly of the European Economic Community (1958-60). While foreign minister (1948-53), he prepared the Schuman Plan that led to the establishment of the European Coal and Steel Community.

Schu·mann (shoo′män′, -mən), **Robert Alexander** (1810-56). German composer. One of the earliest composers of the romantic movement, he started by writing for the piano only but later composed songs and orchestral and instrumental works.

Schurz (shoorts), **Carl** (1829-1906). U.S. politician and editor, born in Germany. He immigrated to the United States in 1852 and immediately turned his attention to politics. After serving as a Union general in the Civil War, he became a U.S. senator (1869-75). He was noted for his oratory and influence on the Republican Party.

schuss (shoos) *intr.v.* **schussed, schussing, schusses.** To make a fast straight run in skiing.
~*n.* **1.** A straight, steep course for skiing. **2.** The act of skiing such a course. [German *Schuss,* shot, from Middle High German *schuz,* from Old High German *scuz.*]

schuss·boom·er (shoos′boo′mər) *n.* One who schusses.

Schutz·staf·fel (shoots′shtä′fəl) *n., pl.* **-feln** (-fəln). *German.* The **SS** *(see).* [German, "defense squadron."]

Schuy·ler (skī′lər), **Philip John** (1733-1804). U.S. Revolutionary general and politician. A wealthy New York landowner, he was a member of the Second Continental Congress (1775-77) and commander of the New York region during the Revolution. He was a strong supporter of the ratification of the Constitution.

schwa (shwä, shvä) *n.* **1.** A vowel sound that in English occurs in many unstressed syllables, as the sound of *a* in *alone* or *e* in *linen.* Also called "indeterminate vowel." **2.** The symbol (ə) used to represent a schwa. [German *Schwa,* from Hebrew *shəwā′,* probably from *shaw′,* emptiness.]

Schwaben. See **Swabia.**

Schwann (shvän), **Theodor** (1810-82). German physiologist. He developed cell theory, showing that animals are formed of cells.

Schwann cell (shvän, shwän) *n.* A cell responsible for the formation of a myelin sheath around certain nerve fibers. [After Theodor SCHWANN.]

Schwarz·wald (shvärts′vält′). Also **Black Forest**. Highland region of southwestern West Germany, extensively forested. It stretches from the Swiss border northward to the Main River.

Schweit·zer (shwīt′sər, shvīt′-), **Albert** (1875–1965). German-born French missionary. From 1913 he ran a hospital in the Gabon village of Lambaréné, financed by his organ recitals of the music of Bach. His books include *The Quest for the Historical Jesus* (1906). He was awarded the Nobel Peace Prize (1952).

Schweiz. See **Switzerland**.

sci. science; scientific.

sci·a·gram, ski·a·gram (skī′ə-grăm′) n. Also **sci·a·graph** (-grăf′, -gräf′). A picture or photograph made up of shadows or outlines. [Greek *skia*, shadow + -GRAM.]

sci·ag·ra·phy, ski·ag·ra·phy (skī-ăg′rə-fē) n. The art or technique of making sciagrams. [SCIA(GRAM) + -GRAPHY.]

sci·am·a·chy, ski·am·a·chy (skī-ăm′ə-kē) n. Fighting with shadows or imaginary enemies. [Greek *skiamakhia* : *skia*, shadow + *-makhia*, -fighting.]

sci·at·ic (sī-ăt′ĭk) adj. **1.** *Anatomy*. Of or pertaining to the **ischium** *(see)*. **2.** Of or pertaining to sciatica. [French *sciatique*, from Late Latin *(i)sc(h)iaticus*, variant of Latin *ischiadicus*, from Greek *iskhiadikos*, from *iskhion*, hip joint, ISCHIUM.]

sci·at·i·ca (sī-ăt′ĭ-kə) n. Neuralgia of the sciatic nerve, characterized by pain down the back of the leg, often caused by pressure from a slipped disk. [Middle English, from Medieval Latin *sciatica (passiō)*, "suffering in the hip," from Late Latin *sciaticus*, SCIATIC.]

sciatic nerve n. *Anatomy*. A sensory and motor nerve originating in the sacral plexus and running through the pelvis and down the leg.

sci·ence (sī′əns) n. Abbr. **sci. 1.** Learning or study concerned with demonstrable truths or observable phenomena, and characterized by the systematic application of scientific method. **2.** Such learning or study concerned with the phenomena of the physical universe; any or all of the natural sciences: *the biological sciences.* **3.** Any branch of knowledge conducted according to scientific method: *forensic science.* **4.** Any methodological activity, discipline, or study. **5.** Any skill or technique that may be developed through systematic learning: *the science of drawing.* **6.** Knowledge, especially when gained through experience. **7.** **Christian Science** *(see)*. [Middle English, knowledge, learning, from Old French, from Latin *scientia*, from *sciēns* (stem *scient-*), present participle of *scīre*, to know.]

science fiction n. Abbr. **SF** A literary or cinematic genre in which fantasy, typically based on speculative scientific discoveries and developments, forms an element of the plot or background; especially, imaginative work based on prediction of future scientific discoveries, environmental changes, space travel, and life on other planets. —**sci·ence-fic·tion** (sī′əns-fĭk′shən) adj.

sci·en·ter (sī-ĕn′tər) adv. *Law.* Deliberately or knowingly. [Latin, from *scīre*, to know.]

sci·en·tial (sī-ĕn′shəl) adj. **1.** Of or producing knowledge or science. **2.** Having knowledge or skill.

sci·en·tif·ic (sī′ən-tĭf′ĭk) adj. Abbr. **sci. 1.** Of, pertaining to, or used in science. **2.** Broadly, having or appearing to have an exact, objective, factual, systematic, or methodological basis. [Medieval Latin *scientificus*, "producing knowledge" : Latin *scientia*, knowledge, SCIENCE + -FIC.] —**sci·en·tif·i·cal·ly** adv.

scientific method n. The totality of principles and processes regarded as characteristic of or necessary for scientific investigation, generally taken to include rules for concept formation, conduct of observations and experiments, and validation of hypotheses by observations or experiments.

sci·en·tism (sī′ən-tĭz′əm) n. **1.** The theory that investigational methods used in the natural sciences should be applied in all fields of inquiry. **2.** The application of quasi-scientific techniques or justifications to unsuitable subjects or topics. —**sci·en·tis·tic** (sī′ən-tĭs′tĭk) adj.

sci·en·tist (sī′ən-tĭst) n. **1.** A student of or expert in a science, especially one or more of the natural sciences. **2. Scientist.** A Christian Scientist.

Sci·en·tol·o·gy (sī′ən-tŏl′ə-jē) n. A trademark for the church and religious system founded by L. Ron Hubbard (1922–86) and based on his writings and system of **Dianetics** *(see)*. [Latin *scientia*, knowledge, SCIENCE + -LOGY.] —**Sci·en·tol·o·gist** n.

sci–fi (sī′fī′) n. *Informal.* Science fiction.

scil·i·cet (sĭl′ĭ-sĕt′, skē′lĭ-kĕt′) adv. Abbr. **sc., scil., ss** That is to say; namely. Used when introducing an explanation of an obscure or ambiguous part of a text or when supplying a missing word. [Latin, short for *scīre licet*, "it is permitted to know," it is evident, of course, namely : *scīre*, to know + *licet*, third person singular present tense of *licēre*, to be allowed (see **leisure**).]

scil·la (sĭl′ə) n. Any bulbous plant of the genus *Scilla*. See **squill** (sense 1). [New Latin, from Greek *skilla*, SQUILL.]

Scil·ly Islands (sĭl′ē). Archipelago in the northeastern Atlantic, lying *c.* 40 kilometers (25 miles) off the southwestern tip of mainland England and forming part of the county of Cornwall. Five of the 140 islands are inhabited. Hugh Town, on St. Mary's Island, is the chief town and administrative center.

scim·i·tar (sĭm′ə-tər, -tär′) n. A curved Oriental sword with an edge on the convex side. [French *cimeterre*, from Italian *scimitarra*, from Persian *šimšīr†*.]

scin·tig·ra·phy (sĭn-tĭg′rə-fē) n. A technique used in medical diagnosis, in which the distribution of a radioactive tracer in a part of the body is measured by a scintillation counter. See **scintiscan**. [SCINTI(LLATION) + -GRAPHY.]

scin·til·la (sĭn-tĭl′ə) n. A minute amount; trace. [Latin, spark.]

scin·til·late (sĭn′tə-lāt′) v. **-lated, -lating, -lates.** —intr. **1.** To throw off sparks; flash. **2.** To sparkle or shine. **3.** To be animated and witty. —tr. To give off (sparks or flashes). —See Synonyms at **flash**. [Latin *scintillāre*, from *scintilla*, spark.] —**scin·til·lant** adj. —**scin·til·lat·ing·ly** adv.

scin·til·la·tion (sĭn′tə-lā′shən) n. **1.** The action of scintillating. **2.** A spark; flash. **3.** *Astronomy*. Rapid variation in the light of a celestial body caused by turbulence in the earth's atmosphere; a twinkling. **4.** *Physics*. A flash of light produced in certain media by absorption of an ionizing particle or photon.

scintillation counter n. A device for detecting and counting scintillations produced by ionizing radiation.

scin·til·la·tor (sĭn′tə-lā′tər) n. *Physics*. A substance that scintillates when hit by high-energy particles or photons.

scin·ti·scan (sĭn′tĭ-skăn′) n. A diagram of the distribution of radiation produced when the body is scanned using the technique of scintigraphy. [SCINTI(GRAPHY) + SCAN.]

sci·o·lism (sī′ə-lĭz′əm) n. A pretentious attitude of scholarship; superficial knowledgeability. [Late Latin *sciolus*, smatterer, diminutive of *scius*, knowing, from *scīre*, to know + -ISM.] —**sci·o·list** n. —**sci·o·lis·tic** (sī′ə-lĭs′tĭk) adj.

sci·o·man·cy (sī′ə-măn′sē) n. Divination by the apparent consulting of ghosts. [Late Latin *sciomantia*, from Greek *skia*, shade, ghost + -MANCY.] —**sci·o·man·cer** n. —**sci·o·man·tic** (sī′ə-măn′tĭk) adj.

sci·on (sī′ən) n. **1.** A descendant, heir, or young member of a family. **2.** A detached shoot or twig containing buds from a woody plant and used in grafting. [Middle English, from Old French *ciun*, *cion*, twig, sprout, from Germanic.]

Scip·i·o¹ (skĭp′ē-ō′, sĭp′-), full name Publius Cornelius Scipio Aemilianus Africanus Minor (*c.* 185–129 B.C.). Roman general. In the Third Punic War he was responsible for the final destruction of Carthage (146 B.C.).

Scipio², full name Publius Cornelius Scipio Africanus Major (234–183 B.C.). Roman general. In 204 he invaded North Africa and ended the Second Punic War by defeating Hannibal in 202.

sci·re fa·ci·as (sī′rē fā′shē-əs, fā′shəs) n. *Law.* **1.** A writ requiring the party against whom it is issued to appear and show cause why a judicial record should not be enforced, repealed, or annulled. **2.** A judicial proceeding under such a writ. [Latin *scīre facias*, "you are to cause (him) to know" (phrase commonly used in the writ) : *scīre*, to know + *facias*, second person singular present subjunctive of *facere*, to make, do.]

scirocco. Variant of **sirocco**.

scir·rhus (skĭr′əs, sĭr′-) n., pl. **scirrhi** (skĭr′ī′, sĭr′ī′) or **-rhuses**. A hard cancerous growth. [New Latin, from Greek *skirros, skiros†*, hard.] —**scir·rhous, scir·rhoid** (skĭr′oid′, sĭr′-) adj.

scis·sel (sĭs′əl, sĭz′-) n. The scrap metal left when disks are punched out of a sheet of metal. [French *cisaille*, "clippings," from *cisailler*, to clip.]

scis·sile (sĭs′əl, -īl′) adj. Capable of being cut or split easily. [French, from Latin *scissilis*, from *scindere* (past participle *scissus*), to cut. See **scission**.]

scis·sion (sĭzh′ən, sĭsh′-) n. The act of cutting or severing; division; fission. [French, from Late Latin *scissiō* (stem *scissiōn-*), from Latin *scindere* (past participle *scissus*), to cut.]

scis·sor (sĭz′ər) tr.v. **-sored, -soring, -sors.** To cut or clip with scissors or shears.

scis·sors (sĭz′ərz) pl.n. Used with a singular or plural verb. **1.** A cutting implement consisting of two blades, each with a loop handle, joined by a swivel pin that allows the cutting edges to be opened and closed. Also called "pair of scissors." **2.** A movement in certain sports, as: **a.** In wrestling, a hold in which the legs are locked about the head or body of the opponent. **b.** A movement of the legs, as in swimming, jumping, or gymnastics, that suggests the opening and closing of scissors. [Middle English *sisoures*, from Old French *cisoires*, from Medieval Latin *cīsōria*, plural of Late Latin *cīsōrium*, cutting instrument, from Latin *caedere* (past participle *caesus*, in compounds *-cīsus*), to cut.]

scis·sor·tail (sĭz′ər-tāl′) n. A bird, *Muscivora forficata*, of the southwestern United States, Mexico, and Central and South America, having a long, forked tail. Also called "scissor-tailed flycatcher."

sci·u·rine (sī′ə-rīn′, sī-yŏŏr′īn′) adj. **1.** Of, pertaining to, or belonging to the rodent family Sciuridae, which includes the squirrels and marmots. **2.** Resembling a squirrel. [Latin *sciūrus*, squirrel, from Greek *skiouros*, "shadow tail," squirrel (*skia*, shadow + *oura*, tail) + -INE.] —**sci·u·rine** n.

sci·u·roid (sī′ə-roid′, sī-yŏŏr′oid′) adj. **1.** Resembling or characteristic of a squirrel; sciurine. **2.** *Botany*. Similar in shape to a squirrel's tail; bushy and curved. [Latin *sciūrus*, SQUIRREL + -OID.]

sclaff (sklăf) v. **sclaffed, sclaffing, sclaffs.** *Golf.* —intr. To scrape or strike the ground with the club behind the ball before hitting it. —tr. **1.** To strike (the ground) with the club before hitting the ball. **2.** To hit (a ball) in this way. ~n. A golf stroke made in this manner. [Scottish, to strike with a flat surface (imitative).] —**sclaff·er** n.

scle·ra (sklîr′ə) n. Also **scle·rot·ic** (sklə-rŏt′ĭk), **scle·rot·i·ca** (sklə-rŏt′ĭ-kə). The tough, white, fibrous outer envelope of tissue covering all of the eyeball except the cornea. [New Latin, from Greek *sklēros*, hard.] —**scle·ral** adj.

scler·e·id (sklĕr′ē-ĭd) n. Any of various cells (except fibers) that make up sclerenchyma. [Greek *sklēros*, hard.]

scle·ren·chy·ma (sklə-rĕng′kə-mə) n. Supportive or protective plant tissue consisting of thick-walled, usually lignified cells. [New Latin : SCLER(O)- + -ENCHYMA.] —**scle·ren·chym·a·tous** (sklîr′ən-kĭm′ə-təs) adj.

scle·rite (sklîr′īt′) n. Any of the hard outer plates forming part of the exoskeleton of an arthropod, especially an insect. [SCLER(O)- + -ITE.]

scle·ri·tis (sklə-rī′tĭs) n. Also **scle·ro·ti·tis** (sklîr′ə-tī′tĭs). Inflammation of the sclera. [New Latin : SCLER(O)- + -ITIS.] —**scle·rit·ic** (sklə-rĭt′ĭk) adj.

sclero-, scler– prefix. Indicates: **1.** Hardness; for example, **scleroderma, sclerite. 2.** Of or affecting the sclera; for example, **sclerotomy, scleritis.** [New Latin, from Greek *sklēros*, hard.]

scle·ro·der·ma (sklîr′ō-dûr′mə) n. Pathological thickening and hardening of the skin or other connective tissue. [New Latin : SCLERO- + -DERMA.]

scle·ro·der·ma·tous (sklîr′ō-dûr′mə-təs) adj. **1.** Characterizing or afflicted with scleroderma. **2.** Zoology. Having an outer covering of hard plates or bony scales.

scle·roid (sklîr′oid′) adj. Biology. Hard or hardened; indurated. [SCLER(O)- + -OID.]

scle·ro·ma (sklə-rō′mə) n., pl. **-mata** (-mə-tə). An abnormally hard patch of skin or mucous membrane. [New Latin, from Greek *sklērōma*, hardening, from *sklēroun*, to harden, from *sklēros*, hard.]

scle·rom·e·ter (sklə-rŏm′ə-tər) n. An instrument used to determine relative hardness of solids, especially minerals and metals, by measurement of the pressure required on a standard diamond stylus to achieve penetration. [SCLERO- + -METER.]

scle·ro·phyll (sklîr′ə-fĭl′) n. Any woody plant with leathery, evergreen leaves that are specialized to reduce water loss. [SCLERO- + -PHYLL.]

scle·ro·pro·tein (sklîr′ō-prō′tēn, -tē-ĭn) n. Any of a large class of proteins, such as keratin, elastin, and collagen, found in skeletal and connective tissue. Also called "albuminoid."

scle·rosed (sklə-rōzd′, -rōst′) adj. **1.** Affected with sclerosis; hardened. **2.** Lignified. [From SCLEROSIS.]

scle·ro·sis (sklə-rō′sĭs) n., pl. **-ses** (-sēz′). **1. a.** Pathology. A thickening or hardening of a body part, as of an artery or the spinal cord, especially from tissue overgrowth or disease. **b.** A disease characterized by sclerosis. See **arteriosclerosis, atherosclerosis, multiple sclerosis. 2.** Botany. The hardening of an outer cell wall by formation or deposit of lignin. [Middle English *sclirosis*, from Medieval Latin *sclīrōsis*, from Greek *sklērōsis*, hardening, from *sklēroun*, to harden, from *sklēros*, hard.] —**scle·ro·sal** adj.

scle·rot·ic (sklə-rŏt′ĭk) adj. **1.** Affected or characterized by sclerosis. **2.** Anatomy. Of or pertaining to the sclera. ~n. Variant of **sclera.** [New Latin *scleroticus*, from SCLEROSIS and SCLERA.]

sclerotica. Variant of **sclera.**

sclerotitis. Variant of **scleritis.**

scle·ro·ti·um (sklə-rō′shē-əm) n., pl. **-tia** (-shē-ə). A dense mass of branching filaments, or hyphae, in certain fungi, containing stored food and capable of remaining dormant for long periods. [New Latin, from Greek *sklērotēs*, hardness, from *sklēros*, hard.] —**scle·ro·tial** (sklə-rō′shəl) adj.

scler·o·ti·za·tion (sklĕr′ə-tĭ-zā′shən) n. The process by which the cuticle of an insect is hardened by the cross linkage of chitin protein molecules. [Greek *sklērotēs*, hardness (from *sklēros*, hard) + -IZATION.] —**scler·o·tized** (sklĕr′ə-tīzd′) adj.

scle·rot·o·my (sklə-rŏt′ə-mē) n., pl. **-mies.** Surgical incision into the sclera. [SCLERO- + -TOMY.]

scle·rous (sklîr′əs) adj. Hardened; toughened; bony. [Greek *sklēros*, hard.]

scoff¹ (skôf, skŏf) intr.v. **scoffed, scoffing, scoffs.** To jeer or mock; speak derisively. Often used with *at.* ~n. An expression of derision or scorn; a jeer. [Middle English *scoffen*, from *scof*, mockery, probably from Scandinavian, akin to Danish *skof*, jest.] —**scoff·er** n. —**scoff·ing·ly** adv.

scoff² v. **scoffed, scoffing, scoffs.** —tr. To eat (food) quickly and greedily. —intr. To eat greedily. [Variant of dialectal *scaff*, associated with Afrikaans *schoff*, Dutch *schoft*, a quarter of a day, hence, a meal.]

scoff·law (skôf′lô′, skŏf′-) n. One who habitually violates the law or fails to answer court summonses.

scold (skōld) v. **scolded, scolding, scolds.** —tr. To reprimand harshly or noisily. —intr. To find fault angrily or persistently. ~n. A person who persistently nags or criticizes. [Middle English *scalden, scolden,* from *scald, scold,* ribald or abusive person, perhaps from Old Norse *skāld,* poet.] —**scold·er** n. —**scold·ing·ly** adv.

Synonyms: berate, nag, revile, upbraid.

scold·ing (skōl′dĭng) n. A sharp or rude reprimand.

scol·e·cite (skŏl′ə-sīt′, skō′lə-) n. A white zeolite mineral, CaAl₂Si₃ O₁₀·3H₂O, consisting of monoclinic crystals. [Greek *skōlēx* (stem *skōlek-*), worm (from its appearance).]

sco·lex (skō′lĕks′) n., pl. **-lices** (-lə-sēz′). The anterior end of a tapeworm, having suckers or hooklike parts that serve as organs of attachment to the host. [New Latin, from Greek *skōlēx*, worm.]

sco·li·o·sis (skō′lē-ō′sĭs, skŏl′ē-) n. Also **sco·li·o·ma** (skō′lē-ō′mə, skŏl′ē-). Abnormal lateral curvature of the spine. [New Latin, from Greek *skiliōsis*, crookedness, from *skolios*, crooked.] —**sco·li·ot·ic** (skō′lē-ŏt′ĭk, skŏl′ē-) adj.

scollop. Variant of **scallop.**

scol·o·pen·drid (skŏl′ə-pĕn′drĭd) n. Any of various centipedes of the family Scolopendridae, which includes some large, poisonous,

tropical species. [New Latin *Scolopendridae,* from Latin *scolopendra,* millipede, from Greek *skolopendra†.*] —**scol·o·pen·drid, scol·o·pen·drine** (skŏl′ə-pĕn′drĭn′, -drĭn) adj.

scom·broid (skŏm′broid′) adj. Of or belonging to the suborder Scombroidei, which includes marine fishes such as the mackerel. ~n. A scombroid fish. [New Latin *Scombroidei,* from Latin *scomber,* mackerel, from Greek *skombros†.*]

sconce¹ (skŏns) n. A small earthwork or fort for defense. [Dutch *schans,* from Middle High German *Schanze,* fortification originally made of latticework, from Italian *scanso,* defense, from *scansare,* to turn off, ward off, from Vulgar Latin *excampsāre* (unattested) : Latin *ex-,* out + *campsāre,* to turn around, sail by, from Greek *kamptein* (aorist stem *kamps-*), to bend, curve, turn.]

sconce² n. **1.** A decorative wall bracket for candles or lights. **2.** A flattened candlestick that has a handle. **3. a.** The head or skull. **b.** Sense or wit. [Middle English, from Old French *esconse,* lantern, hiding place, from Medieval Latin *(a)sconsa,* from Latin *absconsus,* past participle of *abscondere,* to hide away : *(ab)s-,* away + *condere,* to hide.]

scone (skōn, skŏn) n. A small, rich pastry or quick bread, often triangular in shape, that is sometimes baked on a griddle. [Short for Dutch *schoonbrood,* fine white bread, from Middle Dutch *schoonbroot,* from *schoon,* beautiful, bright, white + *broot,* bread.]

Scone (skōōn). Village in central Scotland, now in Tayside Region. Pictish and Scottish kings were crowned in Old Scone until 1651. Early kings sat on the Stone of Scone (or Stone of Destiny), but it was captured by the English (1297) and is now incorporated into the coronation chair in Westminster Abbey, London.

scoop (skōōp) n. **1.** A shovellike utensil, usually having a deep, curved dish and short handle, used for taking up and transferring loose material such as grain or sugar. **2.** A long-handled utensil with a round bowl, especially one for liquids; a ladle. **3.** An implement for bailing water from a boat. **4.** A narrow, spoon-shaped instrument for surgical extraction in cavities or cysts. **5. a.** A thick-handled kitchen utensil for dispensing balls of ice cream, mashed potatoes, or the like, usually having a sweeping band in the dish that is levered by the thumb to free the contents. **b.** A portion gathered in such a scoop. **6.** The bucket or shovel of a steam shovel or dredge. **7.** A scooping movement or action; a sweep. **8.** A wide hole or bowl-shaped cavity. **9.** Informal. A large, sudden profit, especially one gained through speculation. **10.** Informal. A usually sensational story acquired by luck or initiative and reported by a paper in advance of its competitors. ~tr.v. **scooped, scooping, scoops. 1.** To take up or dip into with or as if with a scoop; spoon. **2.** To hollow out or excavate; form by digging. Used with *out.* **3.** To gather or collect swiftly and unceremoniously; grab. Used with *up.* **4.** Informal. To forestall or outmaneuver (a competitor), especially in acquiring and publishing an important news story. **5.** To make (a large profit) suddenly or by luck. **6.** In hockey, golf, or the like, to hit (the ball) from underneath so that it rises steeply. [Middle English, from Middle Low German and Middle Dutch *schōpe.*] —**scoop·er** n.

scoot (skōōt) intr.v. **scooted, scooting, scoots.** To go speedily; dart or scurry off; hurry. ~n. A darting or scurrying off; a hurried departure. [Probably from Scandinavian, akin to Old Norse *skjōta,* to shoot, throw, push.]

scoot·er (skōō′tər) n. **1.** A child's vehicle consisting of a long footboard between two small end wheels, the front wheel being controlled by an upright steering handle. **2.** A **motor scooter** (see). [From SCOOT.]

scop (skŏp) n. A bard or minstrel of Anglo-Saxon England. [Middle English *scop(e),* Old English *scop,* from Germanic.]

scope (skōp) n. **1.** Range of perceptions or mental activity. **2.** Breadth or opportunity to function or extend; outlet. **3. a.** The area covered by a given activity or subject. **b.** Agreed or stipulated limits of application or treatment. **4.** The length or sweep of a mooring cable. **5.** Informal. A microscope, periscope, telescope, or the like. [Originally "something aimed at," "purpose," from Italian *scopo,* from Greek *skopos,* watcher, goal, aim.]

-scope suffix. Indicates an instrument for observing or detecting; for example, **oscilloscope, telescope, microscope.** [Latin *-scopium,* from Greek *-skopion,* from *skopein,* to see.]

Scopes (skōps), **John Thomas** (1901–70). U.S. teacher. Charged with violating a Tennessee statute that prohibited the teaching of evolution, he became the central, albeit reluctant focus of a famous court battle (July 1925). The proceedings, dubbed the Monkey Trial, were a public circus, complete with famous legal protagonists (William Jennings Bryan and Clarence Darrow) and scores of journalists (including the acerbic H.L. Mencken). Scopes was found guilty, but his conviction was later overturned on a technicality.

sco·pol·a·mine (skō-pŏl′ə-mēn′, -mĭn) n. A thick, syrupy, colorless alkaloid, C₁₇H₂₁NO₄, extracted from such plants as henbane and used as a mydriatic, smooth-muscle relaxant, sedative, and truth serum. Also called "hyoscine." [German *Scopolamin* : New Latin *Scopolia,* genus of plants from which the alkaloid is extracted, named after Giovanni Scopoli (1723–88), Italian naturalist + -AMINE.]

sco·po·phil·i·a (skō′pə-fĭl′ē-ə) n. Also **scop·to·phil·i·a** (skŏp′tə-). The derivation of sexual pleasure from viewing sexual organs or erotic scenes; voyeurism. [New Latin : Greek *skopein,* to see + -PHILIA.]

scop·u·la (skŏp′yə-lə) n., pl. **-lae** (-lē′). A dense, brushlike tuft of hairs, as on the legs of certain spiders. [Late Latin *scōpula,* diminutive of Latin *scopa*†, twigs, broom.] —**scop·u·late** (skŏp′yə-lāt′) *adj.*

-scopy *suffix.* Indicates viewing, examining, or observing; for example, **microscopy, telescopy**. [Greek *-skopia,* from *skopein,* to look into, behold.]

scor·bu·tic (skôr-byo͞o′tĭk) *adj.* Related to, resembling, or suffering from scurvy. [New Latin *scorbuticus,* from Late Latin *scorbūtus,* scurvy, from Russian *skrobota,* "scratch," from *skrest′,* to scratch, scrape.] —**scor·bu·ti·cal·ly** *adv.*

scorch (skôrch) *v.* **scorched, scorching, scorches.** —*tr.* **1.** To burn slightly so as to alter the color or taste. **2.** To wither or parch with intense heat; char. **3.** To subject to severe censure or anger; excoriate. —*intr.* **1.** To become scorched or singed. **2.** *British Informal.* To move at a very fast pace. —See Synonyms at **burn.**
~*n.* **1.** A slight or surface burn. **2.** A discoloration caused by heat. Also used adjectivally: *a scorch mark.* **3.** Brown spotting on plant leaves caused especially by fungi, heat, or lack of water. [Middle English *scorchen, scorcnen,* perhaps from Old Norse *skorpna,* to shrivel.] —**scorch·ing·ly** *adv.*

scorch·er (skôr′chər) *n.* **1.** One that scorches. **2.** *Informal.* An extremely hot day.

scorch·ing (skôr′chĭng) *adj. Informal.* **1.** Very hot. Said of the weather. **2.** Biting; scathing: *scorching criticism.*
~*adv.* Used as an intensive: *scorching hot.* —**scorch·ing·ly** *adv.*

score (skôr, skōr) *n., pl.* **scores** or **score** (for sense 7). **1.** A notch or incision made by or as if by a sharp instrument. **2.** An evaluative record, usually numerical, of any competitive event: *keeping score.* **3. a.** The total number of points, goals, or the like made by each competitor or side in a contest, either finally or at a given stage. **b.** The number of points, goals, or the like attributed to any one competitor or team. **c.** The act of scoring a point, goal, or the like. **4.** A result, usually expressed numerically, of a test or examination. **5. a.** An amount due, as on a customer's account. **b.** A harbored grievance; grudge: *I have a score to settle with him.* **6.** A ground; a reason: *I've no grudge against her on that score.* **7.** A group of 20 items. Sometimes used in combination: *threescore years and ten.* **8. scores.** Large numbers. **9.** The written form of a musical composition for orchestral or vocal parts, either complete or for a particular instrument or voice. **10.** The music composed for a musical or film. **11.** *Informal.* **a.** A surprising or significant gain. **b.** The act of buying illicit drugs. **c.** A successful robbery. **d.** A sexual conquest. —**know the score.** *Informal.* To be aware of the true facts of a situation.
~*v.* **scored, scoring, scores.** —*tr.* **1. a.** To mark with lines, notches, or incisions. **b.** To make lines, notches, or incisions on (a surface). **2.** To cancel or eliminate by or as if by superimposing lines. Used with *out.* **3.** In cooking, to mark the surface of (meat, for example) with cuts that are usually parallel. **4. a.** To gain (a point or points) in a game or contest: *scored a goal in the last minute.* **b.** To achieve or win in total: *had scored 300 by the end of play.* **5.** To count as or be worth: *A try scores four points.* **6.** To keep a record of (a debt or offense, for example). **7.** To achieve or gain (a success or advantage, for example). **8.** To evaluate and assign a mark to. **9.** *Music.* **a.** To orchestrate or arrange (music) for a particular instrument or voice. **b.** To compose music for (a film, for example). **10.** To criticize cuttingly; berate. **11.** *Informal.* To be successful in obtaining (something, especially an illicit drug): *score heroin.* —*intr.* **1.** To make a point in a game or contest. **2.** To keep the score of a game or contest. **3.** *Informal.* **a.** To achieve a purpose or advantage, often at another's expense. **b.** To succeed in obtaining illicit drugs. **c.** To succeed in having sexual relations with someone. [Middle English *scor,* Old English *scoru* (attested only in plural *scora*), twenty, from Old Norse *skor,* notch, twenty.]

score·board (skôr′bôrd′, skōr′bōrd′) *n.* A large board, used especially in sports, that records and displays a score.

score·card (skôr′kärd′, skōr′-) *n.* **1.** A printed card enabling a spectator to identify players and record the progress of a game. **2.** A small card used by an individual player, as in golf, to record his own performance.

score·keep·er (skôr′kē′pər, skōr′-) *n.* An official who records the score throughout a game or competition.

score·less (skôr′lĭs, skōr′-) *adj.* Having no point scored: *a scoreless game.*

sco·ri·a (skôr′ē-ə, skōr′-) *n., pl.* **scoriae** (skôr′ē-ē′, skōr′-). **1.** *Geology.* Rough fragments of burnt, basic lava, darker and more cindery than pumice. Also called "cinders," "slag." **2.** *Metallurgy.* The refuse of a smelted metal or ore; slag. [Middle English, slag, dross, from Latin *scōria,* from Greek *skōria,* from *skōr,* excrement.] —**sco·ri·a·ceous** (skôr′ē-ā′shəs, skōr′-) *adj.*

sco·ri·fy (skôr′ə-fī′, skōr′-) *tr.v.* **-fied, -fying, -fies.** To separate (an ore) into scoria and a precious metal. [SCORI(A) + -FY.] —**sco·ri·fi·ca·tion** *n.* —**sco·ri·fi·er** *n.*

scorn (skôrn) *n.* **1.** Contempt or disdain, as felt toward a person or thing considered despicable or inferior. **2.** An object of scorn or contempt. **3.** An expression of scorn; derision.
~*v.* **scorned, scorning, scorns.** —*tr.* **1.** To consider or treat as contemptible or unworthy. **2.** To reject with derision. —*intr.* To express contempt. [Middle English *scornen, schornen,* to despise, from Old French *escharnir,* from Vulgar Latin *escarnīre* (unattested), from Germanic *skarnjan* (unattested).] —**scorn·er** *n.* —**scorn·ful** *adj.* —**scorn·ful·ly** *adv.* —**scorn·ful·ness** *n.*

scor·pae·noid (skôr-pē′noid′) *adj.* Of or belonging to the suborder Scorpaenoidei, which includes the scorpion fishes and gurnards.
~*n.* A scorpaenoid fish. [New Latin *Scorpaenoidei* : *Scorpaena* (genus), from Latin, a fish, from Greek *skorpaina,* feminine of *skorpios,* a sea fish, SCORPION + *-oidei,* plural of Latin *-oidēs,* -OID (likeness).]

Scor·pi·o (skôr′pē-ō′) *n.* **1.** The eighth sign of the **zodiac** *(see).* Also called "Scorpion." **2.** One born under this sign. **3.** Variant of **Scorpius.** [Latin, scorpion.]

scor·pi·oid (skôr′pē-oid′) *adj.* **1.** Pertaining to or resembling a scorpion. **2.** *Botany.* Curved or curled like the tail of a scorpion: *a scorpioid inflorescence.* [Greek *skorpioeidēs,* scorpionlike : *skorpios,* SCORPION + -OID.]

scor·pi·on (skôr′pē-ən) *n.* **1.** Any of various arachnids of the order Scorpionida, of warm, dry regions, having a segmented body and an erectile tail tipped with a venomous sting. **2.** Any of various similar arachnids, such as the **whip scorpion** *(see).* **3. Scorpion. a.** The constellation **Scorpius** *(see).* **b.** A sign of the zodiac, **Scorpio** *(see).* **4.** A type of whip usually thought to have been armed with knotted cords or steel spikes. [Middle English *scorpioun,* from Old French *scorpion,* from Latin *scorpiō* (stem *scorpiōn-*), from Greek *skorpios*†.]

scorpion fish *n.* Any of numerous small, often brilliantly colored marine fishes of the family Scorpaenidae, having poisonous spines in the dorsal fin in most species.

scorpion fly *n.* Any insect of the order Mecoptera, having in the male of most species a curved genital structure that resembles the sting of a scorpion.

scorpion grass *n.* The **forget-me-not** *(see).*

Scor·pi·us (skôr′pē-əs) *n.* Also **Scor·pi·o** (-pē-ō′). A constellation in the Southern Hemisphere near Libra and Sagittarius. It contains the star Antares. Also called "Scorpion." [New Latin, from Latin *scorpius, scorpiō,* SCORPION.]

scor·zo·ne·ra (skôr′zə-nîr′ə) *n.* Any of several Eurasian plants of the genus *Scorzonera,* similar and related to the salsify; especially, the Mediterranean species *S. hispanica,* the roots of which are eaten as a vegetable. [Italian, from *scorzone,* a poisonous snake, alteration of Medieval Latin *curtio*† (stem *curtiōn-*), poisonous snake; the plant was perhaps used as an antidote.]

Scot (skŏt) *n.* **1.** A native or inhabitant of Scotland. **2.** A member of the ancient Gaelic tribe that migrated to the northern part of Britain from Ireland in about the 6th century A.D. —See Usage note at **Scotch.** [Middle English, from Old English (attested in plural, *Scottas*), from Late Latin *Scottus*†.]

Scot. Scotch; Scotland; Scottish.

scot and lot (skŏt) *n.* A municipal tax formerly levied in Great Britain on the members of a community proportionate to their ability to pay. —**pay scot and lot.** To pay in full; settle all obligations. [Middle English *scot,* tax, contribution, partly from Old Norse *skot* and partly from Old French *escot,* from Frankish *skot* (unattested).]

scotch[1] (skŏch) *tr.v.* **scotched, scotching, scotches. 1.** To put an abrupt and decisive end to; crush; stifle: *scotch a rumor.* **2.** To cut or score; scratch. **3.** To injure so as to render harmless; cripple.
~*n.* **1.** A surface cut or abrasion; a gash or scratch. **2.** A line drawn on the ground, such as one used in playing hopscotch. [Middle English *scocchen,* from Norman French *escocher,* to cut a notch : *es-,* from Latin *ex-* (intensifier) + Old French *coche,* notch, from Vulgar Latin *cocca*† (unattested).]

scotch[2] *tr.v.* **scotched, scotching, scotches.** To hold (a wheel or log, for example) with a wedge to prevent rolling or slipping.
~*n.* A block or wedge used as a prop behind or under a wheel or other object likely to roll. [Perhaps variant of *scatch,* stilt, from Old French *escache,* "wooden leg," from Frankish *skakkja* (unattested), from *skakan* (unattested), to run fast, from Germanic *skakan* (unattested), to SHAKE.]

Scotch (skŏch) *n. Abbr.* **Sc., Scot. 1.** *Used with a plural verb.* The people of Scotland; the Scots. **2.** The English language as used in Scotland; Scots. **3.** Scotch whisky.
~*adj.* **1.** Of or pertaining to the people, language, or culture of Scotland. **2.** Tight with money; frugal. [Contraction of SCOTTISH.]
Usage: The people of Scotland are variously referred to as *Scotsmen* and *Scotswomen,* with *Scots* being used as a more informal and neutral term. *Scotchman/woman* are forms sometimes heard outside of Scotland, but many people find them mildly offensive. *The Scottish* is a generally acceptable collective term. Of the corresponding adjectives, *Scotch,* though fairly common, is now used chiefly of products originating in or associated with Scotland *(Scotch whisky, Scotch broth, Scotch wool). Scottish* is used most frequently when the sense of "located in or pertaining to Scotland" is referred to *(Scottish universities, Scottish newspapers);* and *Scots* is most commonly used of people.

Scotch broth *n.* A nourishing soup made from vegetables, pearl barley, and stock.

Scotch catch *n. Music.* A sixteenth note on the beat followed by a dotted eighth note, a figure often found in Scottish dance music. Also called "Scotch snap."

Scotch egg *n.* A cold snack consisting of a hard-boiled egg wrapped in sausage meat that is coated with bread crumbs and deep-fried.

Scotch-I·rish (skŏch′ī′rĭsh) *adj.* Of, relating to, or characteristic of the people of northern Ireland who are of Scottish descent, especially those who immigrated to America.

Scotch·man (skŏch′mən) *n., pl.* **-men** (-mĭn). A male Scot. —See Usage note at **Scotch.**

Scotch mist *n.* **1.** A dense, wet mist. **2.** A **mizzle** *(see).*

Scotch pine *n.* **1.** A Eurasian pine tree, *Pinus sylvestris,* having prickly cones and needlelike leaves, and valued for its timber. **2.** The wood of this tree.

Scotch tape *n.* A trademark for a cellulose adhesive tape.

Scotch terrier *n.* A Scottish terrier *(see).*

Scotch whisky *n.* Whiskey distilled in Scotland from malted barley, and often blended with grain spirit.

Scotch·wom·an (skŏch'wŏŏm'ən) *n., pl.* **-women** (-wĭm'ĭn). A female Scot. —See Usage note at **Scotch.**

sco·ter (skō'tər) *n.* Any of several dark-colored marine diving ducks of the genera *Oidemia* and *Melanitta,* of northern coastal areas. Sometimes called "coot." [Perhaps related to Old Norse *skoti,* shooter, and *skjōta,* to shoot (from its swiftness).]

scot-free (skŏt'frē') *adv.* **1.** Without having to pay; free from obligation. **2.** Without incurring any penalty; unpunished. [Middle English *scot,* tax. See **scot and lot.**] —**scot-free** *adj.*

sco·tia (skō'shə) *n.* A hollow concave molding at or near the base of a column. [Latin, from Greek *skotia,* from *skotos,* darkness (referring to the shadow produced by the cavity).]

Sco·tia (skō'shə). *Poetic.* Scotland. [Medieval Latin, from Late Latin *Scottus,* Scotsman, Irishman. See **Scot.**]

Sco·tism (skō'tĭz'əm) *n.* The scholastic philosophy of Joannes **Duns Scotus** *(see).* —**Sco·tist** *n.*

Scot·land (skŏt'lənd). *Abbr.* **Scot.** Country in northwestern Europe. It is part of the United Kingdom and occupies the northern part of the island of Great Britain. The population is concentrated in the heavily industrialized Central Lowlands, which occupy the valleys of the Clyde and Forth rivers between the Southern Uplands and the Highlands of the north. The Scots themselves were emigrants from Ireland, who together with the native Picts and with emigrants from Scandinavia had formed a kingdom by the 9th century. Frequent wars with England ended when the two crowns were united (1603) under James I of England (James VI of Scotland). Tourism is a major industry, and the discovery of North Sea oil has brought new prosperity to some parts of the country. Area, 78,749 square kilometers (30,405 square miles). Population, 5,100,000. Capital, Edinburgh.

Scotland Yard *n.* **1.** The headquarters of the London Metropolitan Police, formerly housed at New Scotland Yard on the Thames embankment, now at Broadway, Victoria. **2.** The London Metropolitan Police, especially the Criminal Investigation Department (C.I.D.). Also officially called "New Scotland Yard" and informally "the Yard."

scot·o·bi·ot·ic (skŏt'ō-bī-ŏt'ĭk) *adj.* Capable of thriving in darkness. [Geeek *skotos,* darkness + BIOTIC.]

sco·to·ma (skə-tō'mə) *n., pl.* **-mas** or **-mata** (-mə-tə). An area of pathologically diminished vision within the visual field. [New Latin, from Medieval Latin, dim sight, from Greek *skotōma,* dizziness, vertigo, from *skotoun,* to darken, from *skotos,* darkness.]

sco·to·pi·a (skə-tō'pē-ə) *n.* The ability of the eyes to adapt to dim light. [New Latin : Greek *skotos,* darkness (see **scotoma**) + -OPIA.] —**sco·to·pic** (skə-tō'pĭk, -tŏp'ĭk) *adj.*

Scots (skŏts) *adj. Abbr.* **Sc.** Scottish. —See Usage note at **Scotch.** ~*n.* Any of the dialects of English spoken in Scotland.

Scots·man (skŏts'mən) *n., pl.* **-men** (-mĭn). A male Scot. —See Usage note at **Scotch.**

Scots·wom·an (skŏts'wŏŏm'ən) *n., pl.* **-women** (-wĭm'ĭn). A female Scot. —See Usage note at **Scotch.**

Scott (skŏt), **Dred** (c. 1795-1858). American slave. Taken by his master from a slave state to a free state and then to a territory where slavery was prohibited by the Missouri Compromise, he sued for his freedom. In 1857 the U.S. Supreme Court ruled against Scott, declaring that the Missouri Compromise was unconstitutional because Congress had no power to prohibit slavery in the territories.

Scott, Robert Falcon (1868-1912). British Antarctic explorer. On his second expedition to Antarctica (1910-12) he attempted to be the first to reach the South Pole, but discovered that Roald Amundsen had beaten him to it by a month. On the return journey, he and his four companions died of exposure.

Scott, Sir Walter (1771-1832). Scottish novelist and poet. His romantic ballads did much to popularize the history and folklore of Scotland. His historical novels, beginning with *Waverley* (1814), influenced the development of the form.

Scott, Winfield (1786-1866). U.S. general. He became a hero for his victories in the War of 1812 and his bold strategy in the Mexican War. However, as Union commander at the outset of the Civil War, he urged caution and was forced to resign after the disastrous first Battle of Bull Run (1861).

Scot·ti·cism (skŏt'ə-sĭz'əm) *n.* An idiom or other expression characteristic of Scottish English.

Scot·tie, Scot·ty (skŏt'ē) *n., pl.* **-ties.** **1.** A Scotsman. **2.** A Scottish terrier.

Scot·tish (skŏt'ĭsh) *adj. Abbr.* **Sc., Scot.** Of, pertaining to, or characteristic of Scotland, its people, or its language. ~*n.* **1.** Any of the dialects of English spoken in Scotland. **2.** *Used with a plural verb.* The people of Scotland. —See Usage note at **Scotch.**

Scottish deerhound *n.* A deerhound *(see).*

Scottish Gaelic *n.* The Gaelic language of the Scottish Highlanders. Also called "Erse."

Scottish rite *n.* A ceremonial rite in a Masonic system.

Scottish terrier *n.* A terrier of a breed originating in Scotland, having a heavy-set body, short legs, a blunt muzzle, and a dark,

wiry coat. Also called "Scotch terrier," "Scottie," and formerly "Aberdeen terrier."

scoun·drel (skoun'drəl) *n.* A villain; a rogue. [16th century : origin obscure.] —**scoun·drel·ly** *adj.*

scour[1] (skour) *v.* **scoured, scouring, scours.** —*tr.* **1. a.** To clean, polish, or wash by scrubbing vigorously, usually with an abrasive. **b.** To remove by scrubbing. **2.** To remove dirt or grease from (cloth or fibers) by means of a detergent. **3.** To clear (an area) of someone or something undesirable. **4.** To clear (a channel or pipe) by removing obstructions or flushing with water. **5.** To cause (livestock) to purge their bowels. **6.** *Geology.* To erode by the action of a strong current. —*intr.* **1.** To scrub something in order to clean or polish it. **2.** To have diarrhea. Used of livestock. ~*n.* **1.** A scouring action or effect. **2.** A place that has been scoured, as by flushing with water. **3.** A cleansing agent for wool or other cloth or fibers. **4.** *Usually* **scours.** Diarrhea in livestock. [Middle English *scouren,* from Middle Dutch *scūren,* from Old French *escurer,* from Late Latin *excūrāre,* to clean out : Latin *ex-,* out + Late Latin *cūrāre,* to clean, from Latin, to take care of, from *cūra,* care, cure.] —**scour·er** *n.*

scour[2] *v.* **scoured, scouring, scours.** —*tr.* **1.** To range over (an area) quickly and energetically. **2.** To search through or over thoroughly. —*intr.* **1.** To range over or about an area, especially in a search. **2.** To move swiftly; scurry; run. [Middle English *scouren,* perhaps from Old Norse *skȳra,* to rush in.]

scourge (skûrj) *n.* **1.** A whip used to inflict punishment. **2.** Any means of inflicting severe suffering, vengeance, or punishment. **3.** A cause of widespread affliction, as pestilence or war might be. ~*tr.v.* **scourged, scourging, scourges.** **1.** To flog. **2.** To chastise severely; excoriate. **3.** To afflict with severe or widespread suffering; devastate. [Middle English, from Old French *escorge,* from *escorgier,* to whip, from Vulgar Latin *excorrigiāre* (unattested) : Latin *ex-* (intensive) + *corrigia,* thong, shoelace, "whip," from Celtic.] —**scourg·er** *n.*

scouring rush *n.* Any of several species of horsetail; especially, *Equisetum hyemale,* having rough-ridged stems formerly used for scouring utensils.

scour·ings (skour'ĭngz) *pl.n.* **1.** The refuse that remains after scouring grain. **2.** Dregs; scum.

scouse (skous) *n.* Also **scous·er** (skou'sər) (for sense 1a). **1.** *British.* **a.** A native of Liverpool. **b.** *Often* **Scouse.** The dialect of English spoken in Liverpool. **2.** Lobscouse *(see).* [Shortened from LOBSCOUSE (dish particularly associated with Liverpool).]

scout[1] (skout) *n.* **1. a.** A person, aircraft, or ship dispatched from a main body to gather information, as about the terrain or enemy ahead. **b.** The action so performed; a reconnoitering. **2.** A person employed to discover and recruit persons with talent, as in sports or entertainment: *a talent scout.* **3.** *Usually* **Scout. a.** A member of the Boy Scouts. **b.** A member of the Girl Scouts. **4.** *British.* A person employed by a college, especially one at Oxford University, to clean students' rooms. **5.** An individual; person: *He's a good scout.* ~*v.* **scouted, scouting, scouts.** —*tr.* To spy upon or explore carefully in order to obtain information. —*intr.* **1.** To act as a scout, especially as a scout for talent. **2.** To search or look. Often used with *about* or *around.* [Middle English *scoute,* from Old French *escoute,* "listener," spy, from *escouter,* to listen, from Vulgar Latin *ascultāre* (unattested), variant of Latin *auscultāre.*] —**scout·er** *n.*

scout[2] *v.* **scouted, scouting, scouts.** —*tr.* To reject contemptuously; dismiss with disdain or derision. —*intr.* To scoff. Used with *at.* [Probably from Scandinavian; akin to Old Norse *skúta, skúti,* mockery, taunt.]

Scout Association *n.* A worldwide organization of young men and boys, founded in England in 1908, for developing character, practical skills, and self-reliance.

scout·ing (skou'tĭng) *n.* The activities of the Boy Scouts or Girl Scouts.

scout·mas·ter (skout'măs'tər, -mä'stər) *n.* The adult leader in charge of a troop of Boy Scouts.

scow (skou) *n.* A large flat-bottomed boat with square ends, used chiefly for transporting cargo. [Dutch *schouw,* ferryboat, from Middle Dutch *scoude, scouwe,* akin to Old Saxon *skaldan†,* to push a boat from the shore.]

scowl (skoul) *n.* A look of anger, sullenness, or strong disapproval. ~*intr.v.* **scowled, scowling, scowls.** To lower or contract the brows in an expression of anger, disapproval, or bitterness; frown angrily. [Middle English *scoulen,* probably from Scandinavian; akin to Danish *skule†,* to scowl.] —**scowl·er** *n.* —**scowl·ing·ly** *adv.*

SCP single-cell protein.

SCR silicon-controlled rectifier.

scr. scruple (unit of weight).

scrab·ble (skrăb'əl) *v.* **-bled, -bling, -bles.** —*intr.* **1.** To scrape or grope about frenetically with or as if with the hands or claws. Often used with *about* or *around.* **2.** To struggle, especially in a frantic or confused manner. **3.** To make hasty, disordered markings; scribble. —*tr.* **1.** To make or obtain by scraping or scratching. **2.** To scribble on. **3.** To make scrabbling movements on or with. ~*n.* **1.** The act or an instance of scrabbling. **2.** A scribble; a doodle. **3.** A confused fight or struggle. [Middle Dutch *schrabbelen,* frequentative of *schrabben,* to scrape.]

Scrab·ble (skrăb'əl) *n.* A trademark for a board game in which players build words with small lettered blocks.

scrag (skrăg) *n.* **1.** A bony or scrawny person or animal. **2.** A piece of inferior bony meat, especially from a neck of lamb. **3.** *Informal.* The human neck. —*tr.v.* **scragged, scragging, scrags.** *Informal.* **1.** To wring the neck of; kill by strangling. **2.** To seize and manhandle roughly. [Variant of obsolete *crag(ge)*, neck, throat, Middle English *crag, crage*, from Middle Dutch *crāghe.*]

scrag·gly (skrăg′lē) *adj.* **-glier, -gliest.** Ragged; irregular; untended or unkempt. [From SCRAG.]

scrag·gy (skrăg′ē) *adj.* **-gier, -giest. 1.** Bony and lean; scrawny. **2.** Jagged; ragged; rough. —**scrag·gi·ly** *adv.* —**scrag·gi·ness** *n.*

scram (skrăm) *intr.v.* **scrammed, scramming, scrams.** *Slang.* To leave a scene at once; go abruptly. Often used in the imperative. —*n.* A rapid shutting down of a nuclear reactor, especially in an emergency. [Short for SCRAMBLE.]

scram·ble (skrăm′bəl) *v.* **-bled, -bling, -bles.** —*intr.* **1.** To move or climb hurriedly, especially on the hands and knees. **2.** To struggle urgently, as with competitors, in order to get something: *All scrambled for the best seat.* **3.** *Military.* To take off with all possible haste, as to intercept enemy aircraft. **4.** To ride a motorcycle across rough terrain, especially in a race. —*tr.* **1.** To mix or throw together confusedly. **2.** To gather together in a hurried or disorderly fashion. Often used with *up.* **3.** To cook (beaten eggs) until of a firm but soft consistency. **4.** *Electronics.* To distort or garble (a signal) so as to render it unintelligible without a special receiver. **5.** *Military.* To cause (aircraft) to scramble. —*n.* **1.** The act or an instance of scrambling. **2.** An arduous hike over rough terrain. **3.** An unceremonious scuffle for something. **4.** A motorcycle race across rough terrain. [Imitative; compare dialectal *scamble*†, to struggle for, and *cramble*†, to crawl.]

scrambled eggs *pl.n.* **1.** Eggs or an egg beaten and cooked until of a firm but soft consistency. **2.** *Informal.* The gold braid worn on the bill of the cap of a high-ranking officer in the armed forces.

scram·bler (skrăm′blər) *n.* **1.** One that scrambles. **2.** An electronic device that scrambles telecommunication signals to make them unintelligible to an eavesdropper. **3.** A motorcycle with thick ridged tires and strong suspension, designed for riding across rough terrain; a trail bike.

scram·jet (skrăm′jĕt′) *n.* A ramjet airplane engine that burns fuel in the supersonic airstream produced by the plane after reaching supersonic speeds by conventional means. [S(UPERSONIC) + C(OM-BUSTION) + RAMJET.]

Scran·ton (skrăn′tən). City of northeastern Pennsylvania, in a mountainous region on the Lackawanna River. It is the commercial and industrial center of an anthracite-coal area, although mining decreased after World War II. Varied manufactures are produced.

scrap¹ (skrăp) *n.* **1. a.** A small detached piece or bit; fragment. **b.** A shred; particle. **2.** An unincorporated fragment of writing. **3. scraps.** Leftover and unwanted bits of food. **4.** Material left over or discarded as refuse; especially, metal suitable for reprocessing. **5. scraps.** Crisp pieces of rendered animal fat; cracklings. —*tr.v.* **scrapped, scrapping, scraps. 1.** To break down into parts for disposal or salvage. **2.** To discard as useless or worthless. [Middle English, from Old Norse *skrap*, trifles, remains.]

scrap² *n. Informal.* A fight; scuffle. [Perhaps variant of SCRAPE.] —**scrap** *v.* —**scrap·per** *n.*

scrap·book (skrăp′bŏŏk′) *n.* A book with blank pages for the mounting and preserving of pictures, clippings, or the like.

scrape (skrāp) *v.* **scraped, scraping, scrapes.** —*tr.* **1.** To rub, scratch, or grate roughly over or against (a surface). **2.** To draw (a sharp or abrasive object) forcefully over a surface. **3.** To clean, abrade, or smooth by drawing a sharp edge or rough instrument over, especially repeatedly. **4.** To remove (an outer layer or adherent matter) by scraping. **5.** To injure the surface of by rubbing against something rough or sharp. **6.** To amass or produce with difficulty. Used with *together* or *up*: *scrape up some cash.* —*intr.* **1.** To come into sliding, abrasive contact. **2.** To rub or move with a harsh grating noise. **3.** To draw the foot backward along the floor when bowing. **4.** To scrimp; be very thrifty. **5.** To proceed or manage precariously or with difficulty; succeed narrowly. Usually used with *along* or *through*: *She scraped through the test.* —*n.* **1.** The act of scraping. **2.** The sound of scraping. **3.** An abrasion on the skin. **4.** *Informal.* **a.** An embarrassing predicament. **b.** A fight; scuffle. [Middle English *scrapen*, from Old Norse *skrapa* or Middle Dutch *schrapen.*]

scrap·er (skrā′pər) *n.* **1.** One that scrapes. **2.** A tool for scraping off paint or other adherent matter.

scrap·er·board (skrā′pər-bôrd′, -bōrd′) *n.* A board covered with white clay and a black surface layer that is scraped away to produce white line drawings.

scrap heap *n.* **1.** A pile or heap of waste material. **2.** A place for discarding useless or worthless material.

scra·pie (skrā′pē, skrăp′ē) *n.* A virus disease of sheep marked by progressive degeneration of the central nervous system. [From SCRAPE.]

scrap·ing (skrā′pĭng) *n.* **1.** Often **scrapings.** Something that is scraped, or left to be scraped. **2.** The sound made by something being scraped.

scrap·ple (skrăp′əl) *n.* A mixture of ground pork and cornmeal that is set in a mold and then sliced and fried. [Diminutive of SCRAP (bit).]

scrap·py¹ (skrăp′ē) *adj.* **-pier, -piest.** Composed of scraps; fragmentary or disjointed. —**scrap·pi·ly** *adv.* —**scrap·pi·ness** *n.*

scrap·py² *adj.* **-pier, -piest.** *Informal.* Quarrelsome; contentious. —**scrap·pi·ly** *adv.* —**scrap·pi·ness** *n.*

scratch (skrăch) *v.* **scratched, scratching, scratches.** —*tr.* **1.** To make a thin, shallow cut or mark on (a surface) with a sharp instrument. **2.** To draw something abrasive, especially the nails, across (the skin) to relieve itching. **3. a.** To scrape or graze on an abrasive surface: *scratched my hand on the brambles.* **b.** To scrape or abrade (a surface). **4. a.** To form (words or pictures, for example) by scratching. **b.** To write or draw hurriedly or haphazardly. **5.** To strike out or cancel (a word, name, or passage) by or as if by drawing lines through. Often used with *out.* **6.** To withdraw (an entry) from a contest. —*intr.* **1.** To use the nails or claws to dig, scrape, or wound. **2. a.** To draw something abrasive, especially the nails, across the skin to relieve itching. **b.** To produce a chafing or itching sensation. **3.** To make a harsh, scraping sound. **4.** To claw and scrape the ground searching for food, as hens do. **5.** To withdraw from a contest. **6.** In billiards, to make a scratch. **7.** To get along or manage with difficulty, especially in making a living. Often used with *along.* —**scratch together** (or **up**). To assemble or put together haphazardly or with difficulty. —*n.* **1. a.** An act of scratching, as to relieve irritation. **b.** A linelike mark produced by scratching. **c.** A slight wound resembling a line or series of lines. **2.** A mark or scribble hastily made. **3.** A sound made by scratching, as on a phonograph record. **4.** *Sports.* **a.** A starting line for a race. **b.** A line formerly drawn across a prize ring at which the boxers began each round. **c.** The starting time or position or initial score of a competitor who has no handicap or allowance. **5.** A contestant who has been withdrawn or who has withdrawn from a contest. **6.** In billiards: **a.** A shot that results in a penalty, as when the cue ball falls into a pocket or jumps the cushion. **b.** A fluke or chance shot. **7.** Poultry feed. **8.** *Slang.* Money. —**from scratch.** From the very beginning. —**up to scratch.** *Informal.* **1.** Meeting the requirements or standards. **2.** In fit condition. —*adj.* **1.** Done haphazardly or by chance. **2.** Assembled hastily or at random. **3.** *Sports.* Without handicap or allowance. [Middle English, probably blend of *scrat, scratten*†, and *cratch, cracchen*†, both meaning "to scratch."] —**scratch·er** *n.*

scratch hit *n. Baseball.* A batted ball that is not squarely struck or cleanly fielded but is counted as a hit.

scratch test *n.* A test for allergy performed by scratching the skin and applying an allergen to the wound.

scratch·y (skrăch′ē) *adj.* **-ier, -iest. 1.** Characterized by or consisting of scratches. **2.** Making a harsh, scratching noise: *a scratchy record.* **3.** Irregular; uneven: *played a scratchy stroke.* **4.** Harsh and irritating: *a scratchy fabric.* —**scratch·i·ly** *adv.* —**scratch·i·ness** *n.*

scrawl (skrôl) *v.* **scrawled, scrawling, scrawls.** —*tr.* To write hastily or illegibly. —*intr.* To write in a sprawling, irregular way. —*n.* **1.** Irregular, often illegible handwriting. **2.** Something, such as a note, written hastily or illegibly. [Perhaps from obsolete *scrawl*, to gesticulate.] —**scrawl·er** *n.* —**scrawl·y** *adj.*

scraw·ny (skrô′nē) *adj.* **-nier, -niest.** Unattractively thin and bony; skinny. —See Usage note at **lean.** [Variant of dialectal *scranny*, probably from Scandinavian; compare Norwegian *scran*, shriveled.] —**scraw·ni·ness** *n.*

scream (skrēm) *v.* **screamed, screaming, screams.** —*intr.* **1.** To utter a long, loud, piercing cry, as of pain. **2.** To make or move with a loud, piercing sound: *Jet planes screamed through the air.* **3.** To speak or write in a heated, hysterical manner. **4.** To be conspicuous or obvious: *dressed in screaming colors.* **5.** To laugh wildly or uncontrollably. —*tr.* **1.** To utter or say in a screaming voice. **2.** To cause to be in a specified state by screaming: *screamed herself sick.* —*n.* **1.** A long, loud, piercing cry or sound. **2.** *Slang.* Someone or something hilariously or ridiculously funny. [Middle English *scremen*, from Old Norse *skræma.*]

    Synonyms: screech, shriek.

scream·er (skrē′mər) *n.* **1.** One that screams. **2.** *Slang.* Something that evokes screams of laughter. **3.** *Slang.* A sensational headline. **4.** Any of several large aquatic birds of the family Anhimidae, of South America, having a harsh, resonant call.

scream·ing·ly (skrē′mĭng-lē) *adv.* So as to produce uproarious, uncontrolled laughter: *screamingly funny.*

scree (skrē) *n.* **1.** Loose rock debris, usually comprising coarse, angular fragments. Also called "talus." **2.** A slope of this at the base of a steep incline or cliff. [Back-formation from *screes* (plural), contraction of *screethes* (unattested), from Old Norse *skrīdha*, landslide, from Germanic *skrīth-* (unattested).]

screech (skrēch) *n.* **1.** A high-pitched, harsh, piercing cry; a shriek. **2.** A sound resembling this. —*v.* **screeched, screeching, screeches.** —*tr.* To say or utter in or as if in a screeching voice. —*intr.* **1.** To utter a high-pitched, strident sound, as in pain or fright. **2.** To make a prolonged, shrill, grating noise. —See Synonyms at **scream.** [Earlier *scritch*, Middle English *scrichen*, from Old Norse *skraekja* (imitative).] —**screech·er** *n.* —**screech·y** *adj.*

screech owl *n.* **1.** Any of various small owls of the genus *Otus*; especially, *O. asio*, of North America, having a whistlelike call. Compare **hoot owl. 2.** Any owl having a screeching call.

screed (skrēd) *n.* **1. a.** A long, monotonous harangue or piece of writing. **b.** Often **screeds.** Any lengthy piece of writing, such as a letter. **2. a.** A strip of wood, plaster, or metal placed on a wall or horizontal surface as a guide for the even application of plaster or concrete. **b.** A layer or strip of material used to level off a horizon-

screamer *During the breeding season or when alarmed, the cry of a single screamer—a wading bird of South America—can be heard up to about 3 kilometers (2 miles) away. This is the crested screamer.*

tal surface, such as a floor. **c.** A smooth, final surface, as of concrete, applied to a floor. **3.** *Scottish.* A rent; a tear. [Middle English, probably variant of SHRED.]

screen (skrēn) *n.* **1. a.** A movable device, especially a framed construction such as a hinged or sliding room divider, designed to divide, conceal, or protect. **b.** A decorative partition, as one in a church. **2.** Anything that serves to divide, conceal, or protect. **3. a.** A coarse sieve used for sifting out fine particles, as of sand, gravel, or coal. **b.** A system for appraising and selecting personnel. **4.** An insertion of framed wire or plastic mesh used in windows and doors to keep out insects. **5.** The white or silver surface upon which a picture is projected for viewing. **6.** The motion-picture industry. Preceded by *the.* **7.** *Electronics.* **a.** The electrode placed between the anode and the control grid in a tetrode valve. Also called "screen grid." **b.** The phosphorescent surface upon which the image is formed in a cathode-ray tube. **8.** *Printing.* A glass plate marked off with crossing lines, placed before the lens of a camera when photographing for halftone reproduction. **9.** A body of troops or ships sent in advance of or surrounding a larger body in order to protect or warn of attack. **10.** *Meteorology.* A white-painted wooden box with louvered sides that stands 1.25 meters (4 feet) above the ground and in which meteorological instruments are kept so that readings unaffected by strong winds and direct sunshine may be taken.
~*tr.v.* **screened, screening, screens. 1. a.** To provide with a screen. **b.** To divide or separate with a screen. Often used with *off.* **2. a.** To conceal from view. **b.** To protect, guard, or shield. **3. a.** To sift or sift out by means of a sieve or screen. **b.** To interview or examine (applicants or candidates, for example) systematically in order to determine suitability. **4.** To show (a film, for example) on a screen. **5.** To test or examine, as for the presence of disease. **—**See Synonyms at **hide.** [Middle English *screne,* from Old French *escren,* from Middle Dutch *scherm,* shield.] **—screen·er** *n.*

screen·ing (skrē'nĭng) *n.* **1. screenings.** Refuse, such as waste coal, separated out by a screen. **2.** The mesh material used to make door or window screens. **3.** A presentation of a motion picture.

screening test *n.* A program of diagnostic tests, such as mass x-rays or cervical smears, carried out as a routine on a large section of the population.

screen memory *n. Psychology.* A memory of something that is unconsciously used to repress recollection of an associated but distressing event.

screen·play (skrēn'plā') *n.* The script for a film, including camera directions and descriptions of scenes. Also called "scenario."

screen-print (skrēn'prĭnt') *tr.v.* **-printed, -printing, -prints.** To print using the silk-screen process. **—screen-print·er** *n.*

screen-print·ing (skrēn'prĭn'tĭng) *n.* The **silk-screen process** *(see).*

screen test *n.* A brief filmed sequence made to test the ability of an aspiring actor or actress. **—screen-test** (skrēn'tĕst') *v.*

screen·writer (skrēn'rī'tər) *n.* A writer of screenplays.

screw (skro͞o) *n.* **1. a.** A cylindrical rod incised with one or more helical or advancing spiral threads, such as a lead screw or worm screw. **b.** The tapped collar or socket that receives this. **2.** A metal pin with incised thread or threads, having a broad slotted head so that it can be driven as a fastener by turning it with a screwdriver, especially: **a.** A tapered and pointed wood screw. **b.** A cylindrical and flat-tipped machine screw. **3.** A device having helical form, such as a corkscrew. **4.** A **propeller** *(see).* **5.** A twist or turn of or as if of a screw. **6.** *British Slang.* Salary; wages. **7.** *British.* A small twisted paper packet, as of tobacco. **8.** *British Slang.* An old broken-down horse. **9.** *Chiefly British Slang.* A stingy or crafty bargainer. **10.** *Slang.* A prison guard. **11.** *Usually* **screws. a.** A former instrument of torture, a **thumbscrew** (sense 2) *(see).* **b.** Any means of coercion or intimidation. Used chiefly in the phrase *put the screws on* or *to.* **12.** In billiards, snooker, or the like: **a.** The curving or backward motion of the cue ball hit just below and to one side of the center. **b.** A stroke imparting such motion to the cue ball. **—have a screw loose.** *Slang.* **1.** To behave in an eccentric or whimsical manner. **2.** To be insane.
~*v.* **screwed, screwing, screws.** *—tr.* **1.** To drive or tighten (a screw). **2. a.** To fasten, tighten, or attach by or as if by means of a screw. **b.** To attach (a tapped or threaded fitting or cap) by twisting into place. Used with *on* or *in.* **c.** To rotate (a part) on a threaded axis. **3. a.** To contort (one's face). Often used with *up.* **b.** To twist or crumple (paper, for example). Often used with *up.* **4.** *Slang.* To take unfair advantage of; cheat or exploit. **5.** To use force or pressure to obtain. **6.** To give (a ball) a curving or backward motion, as in billiards or snooker. *—intr.* **1.** To turn or twist. Used with *around.* **2. a.** To become attached by means of screw threads. Used with *into, on,* or *to.* **b.** To be capable of such attachment. **—screw out of.** *Slang.* To deprive of something due or expected: *screwed him out of his raise.* [Middle English *skrewe,* from Old French *escroue,* originally "screw socket," from West Germanic *scrūva* (unattested), from Latin *scrōfa,* sow (probably because screw threads coil like a sow's tail, and perhaps influenced in sense by Latin *scrobis,* ditch, pudenda, hence, in Vulgar Latin, screw socket).] **—screw·er** *n.* **—screw·like** *adj.*

screw·ball (skro͞o'bôl') *n.* **1.** *Baseball.* A pitched ball curving in the direction opposite to a normal curve ball. **2.** *Slang.* An eccentric, impulsively whimsical, or irrational person.
~*adj. Slang.* Odd; eccentric; zany.

screw bean *n.* **1.** A mesquite, *Prosopis pubescens,* of the southwestern United States, having compound leaves, tiny yellowish-white flowers, and twisted pods used as fodder. **2.** The pod of this tree.

screw cap *n.* A cap that screws onto the threaded mouth of a container, such as a bottle, jar, or the like.

screw·driv·er (skro͞o'drī'vər) *n.* **1.** A tool used for turning screws. **2.** A cocktail of vodka and orange juice.

screw eye *n.* A wood screw with an eyelet in place of a head.

screw jack *n.* A **jackscrew** *(see).*

screw log *n. Nautical.* A **patent log** *(see).*

screw pine *n.* A plant, the **pandanus** *(see).*

screw propeller *n.* A **propeller** *(see).*

screw thread *n.* **1.** The continuous helical groove on a screw or on the inner surface of a nut. **2.** One complete turn of a screw thread.

screw up *tr.v.* **1.** *Informal.* To muster or summon up: *screwed up my courage.* **2.** *Slang.* To make a mess of; bungle. **3.** *Slang.* To make neurotic and anxious. *—intr.v. Slang.* To fail in an undertaking as a result of bungling.

screw-up (skro͞o'ŭp') *n. Slang.* **1.** One who screws up; bungler. **2.** A blunder; bungle.

screw·worm (skro͞o'wûrm') *n.* The parasitic larva of the screwworm fly, which can cause injury or death to livestock.

screwworm fly *n.* A blue-green fly, *Cochliomyia hominivorax,* of the New World, that breeds in the living tissue of mammals, having penetrated chiefly through open wounds.

screw·y (skro͞o'ē) *adj.* **-ier, -iest.** *Slang.* **1.** Eccentric; crazy. **2.** Ludicrously odd, unlikely, or inappropriate. **—screw·i·ness** *n.*

Scri·a·bin (skrē-ä'bĭn), **Alexandr** (1872–1915). Russian composer. He is noted for works for the keyboard that include chords on the interval of the fourth.

scrib·ble¹ (skrĭb'əl) *v.* **-bled, -bling, -bles.** *—tr.* **1.** To write hurriedly without heed to legibility or grammatical form. **2.** To cover with scribbled writing or meaningless marks. **3.** To draw hurriedly or carelessly. *—intr.* To write or draw in a hurried, careless way.
~*n.* **1.** Careless, hurried writing or drawing. **2.** Meaningless marks and lines. [Middle English *scriblen,* from Medieval Latin *scrībillāre,* frequentative of Latin *scrībere,* to write.]

scribble² *tr.v.* **-bled, -bling, -bles.** To card (wool or cotton) coarsely. [Probably from Low German and akin to SCRUB (to rub hard).]

scrib·bler (skrĭb'lər) *n.* **1.** One who scribbles. **2.** A very minor or untalented author.

scribe (skrīb) *n.* **1.** A public clerk or secretary, especially in ancient times. **2.** A professional copyist of manuscripts and documents, as in ancient or medieval times. **3.** A writer or journalist. Usually used humorously. **4.** A scriber. **5.** In ancient times, a scholar or teacher of the Jewish law.
~*v.* **scribed, scribing, scribes.** *—tr.* To mark or produce with a scriber. *—intr.* To work as a scribe. [Middle English, from Latin *scrība,* official writer, clerk, scribe, from *scrībere,* to write.] **—scrib·al** *adj.*

scrib·er (skrī'bər) *n.* A sharply pointed tool used for marking lines on wood, metal, ceramic, or the like.

scrim (skrĭm) *n.* **1.** A durable, loosely woven cotton or linen fabric used for curtains, upholstery lining, or in industry. **2.** A similar fabric used in the theater for creating special effects of light or atmosphere. [18th century : origin obscure.]

scrim·mage (skrĭm'ĭj) *n.* **1.** A rough and confused struggle; a tussle. **2.** *Football.* **a.** The contest between two teams from the time the ball is snapped back until it becomes out of play. **b.** A team's practice session. **3.** In Rugby football, a scrum. Not in current usage. **—line of scrimmage.** *Football.* An imaginary line across the field on which the ball rests and at which the teams line up for a new play.
~*intr.v.* **scrimmaged, -maging, -mages.** To engage in a football scrimmage. [Alteration of *scrimish,* obsolete variant of SKIRMISH.]

scrimp (skrĭmp) *v.* **scrimped, scrimping, scrimps.** *—intr.* To economize severely. Often used with *on* or in the phrase *scrimp and save.* *—tr.* **1.** To be excessively sparing with or of. **2.** To cut or make too small or scanty. [Perhaps of Scandinavian origin.] **—scrimp·i·ness** *n.* **—scrimp·y** *adj.*

scrim·shaw (skrĭm'shô') *v.* **-shawed, -shawing, -shaws.** *—tr.* To decorate (whale ivory, bone, or shells) with intricate carvings or designs. *—intr.* To produce such work.
~*n., pl.* **scrimshaws** or collectively **scrimshaw. 1.** A bone or ivory article so fashioned. **2.** The art of producing such articles. [19th century (nautical use) : origin obscure.]

scrip¹ (skrĭp) *n.* **1.** A small scrap of paper, especially one with writing, such as a list or a schedule. **2.** Paper money issued for temporary emergency use. [Alteration of SCRIPT (influenced by SCRAP).]

scrip² *n. Finance.* **1.** A provisional certificate entitling the holder to a fractional share of stock or of other jointly owned property. **2.** Such certificates collectively. [Short for *subscription (receipt),* receipt for portion of a loan.]

scrip³ *n. Archaic.* A wallet, small satchel, or bag. [Middle English *scrippe,* from Old French *escreppe,* variant of Old North French *escarpe,* "pilgrim's knapsack." See **scarf.**]

scrip issue *n. Finance.* An issue of shares made by a company free of charge to existing shareholders. Also called "bonus issue."

Scripps (skrĭps). Family of U.S. newspaper editors and publishers. **James Edmund** (1835–1906) owned a number of Detroit papers; his half-brother **Edward Wyllis** (1854–1926) founded his first newspaper in 1878, organized the first major U.S. chain of newspapers (1895), and established the United Press International (1907), becoming a pioneer in the use of syndication. His son **Robert Paine** (1895–1938) joined with Roy Wilson Howard (1883–1964) to reor-

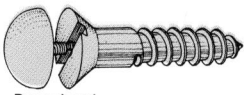

Dome head
Round head
Raised head
Phillips head
Length
Gauge
Countersunk
screw *A spirally threaded fastener pin that bites into the surrounding material as it is driven in.*

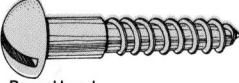

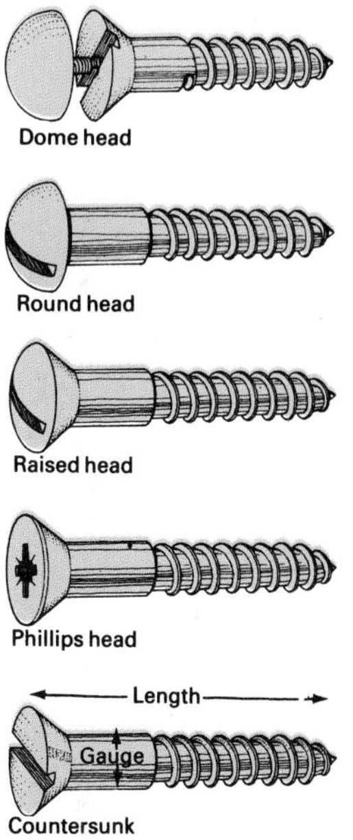

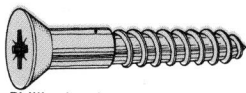

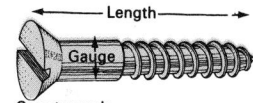

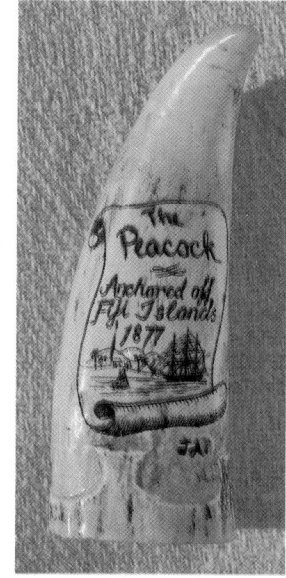

scrimshaw *Usually carved on whalebone or ivory, scrimshaw is the traditional art of the seafarer. This sperm-whale tooth records part of a 19th-century voyage.*

ganize the papers into the vast Scripps-Howard chain. Edward and his half-sister **Ellen Browning** (1836-1932), also involved in the newspaper business, founded (1901) a marine biology station in San Diego that later became the Scripps Institution of Oceanography.

scrip·sit (skrĭp′sĭt). *Latin.* He (or she) wrote (it). Placed after the author's name on a manuscript.

script (skrĭpt) *n.* **1. a.** Handwriting as distinguished from print. **b.** A style of writing with cursive characters. **c.** A particular system of writing: *cuneiform script.* **2. a.** A type that imitates handwriting. **b.** Matter printed with this type. **3.** *Law.* An original document as distinguished from a copy. **4.** The text of a play, broadcast, or motion picture; especially, a copy of a text used by a director or performer. **5.** *British.* An examinee's written paper.
~*tr.v.* **scripted, scripting, scripts.** To write a script for (a motion picture or broadcast): *Perelman scripted several Marx Brothers movies.* [Middle English *skript,* from Old French *escript,* from Latin *scriptum,* from *scriptus,* past participle of *scrībere,* to write.]

Script. Scriptural; Scriptures.

scrip·to·ri·um (skrĭp-tôr′ē-əm, -tōr′ē-əm) *n., pl.* **-riums** or **-toria** (-tôr′ē-ə, -tōr′ē-ə). A room in a monastery set aside for the copying, writing, or illuminating of manuscripts and records. [Medieval Latin, from Latin *scrībere* (past participle *scrīptus*), to write.]

scrip·tur·al (skrĭp′chər-əl) *adj.* **1.** Of or pertaining to writing. **2.** Scriptural. *Abbr.* **Script.** Of, pertaining to, based upon, or contained in the Scriptures. —**scrip·tur·al·ly** *adv.*

Scrip·ture (skrĭp′chər) *n.* **1.** *Often* **Scriptures.** *Abbr.* **Script. a.** A sacred writing or book; especially, the **Holy Scripture** *(see).* **b.** A passage from such a writing or book. **2.** *scripture.* A statement regarded as authoritative and definitive, such as a code of regulations. [Middle English, from Late Latin *scrīptūra,* from Latin, act of writing, from *scrībere* (past participle *scrīptus*), to write.]

script·writ·er (skrĭpt′rī′tər) *n.* A person who writes copy to be used by an announcer, performer, or director in a film or broadcast.

scriv·en·er (skrĭv′ə-nər, skrĭv′nər) *n. Archaic.* **1.** A professional copyist; a scribe. **2.** A notary. [Middle English *scriveiner,* from *scrivein,* scribe, from Old French *escrevein,* from Vulgar Latin *scrībānem* (unattested), accusative of *scrība,* SCRIBE.]

scro·bic·u·late (skrō-bĭk′yə-lĭt, -lāt′) *adj. Biology.* Marked with many shallow depressions, grooves, or pits. [Latin *scrobiculus,* diminutive of *scrobis,* trench.]

scrod (skrŏd) *n.* A young cod or haddock, especially one split and boned for cooking. [Possibly from obsolete Dutch *schrood,* shred.]

scrof·u·la (skrŏf′yə-lə) *n.* Tuberculosis of the lymph nodes, a now rare condition chiefly affecting children and characterized by running sores in the neck region. Also called "King's evil," "struma." [Middle English *scrophulas* (plural), from Medieval Latin *scrōfulae,* swelling of the glands, "small sows," from Latin *scrōfa,* sow (probably after Greek *khoirades,* scrofula, from *khoiras,* like a pig's back).]

scrof·u·lous (skrŏf′yə-ləs) *adj.* **1.** Pertaining to, affected with, or resembling scrofula. **2.** Morally degenerate; corrupt. —**scrof·u·lous·ly** *adv.* —**scrof·u·lous·ness** *n.*

scroll (skrōl) *n.* **1. a.** A roll of parchment, papyrus, or the like. **b.** An ancient book or volume written on a scroll. **2.** A list of names. **3.** Ornamentation resembling a partially unrolled scroll of paper, especially: **a.** The volute in Ionic and Corinthian capitals. **b.** The curved head on an instrument of the violin family. **c.** *Heraldry.* A ribbon inscribed with a motto.
~*tr.v.* **scrolled, scrolling, scrolls.** **1.** To inscribe on a scroll. **2.** To roll up into a scroll. **3.** To ornament with a scroll or scrolls. [Middle English *scrowle,* variant (influenced by *rowle,* a roll) of *scrow,* from Old French *escro(u)e,* strip of parchment, from Frankish *skrōda* (unattested), piece, shred.]

scroll saw *n.* A hand or power saw with a narrow ribbonlike blade for cutting curved or irregular shapes. See **fretsaw, jigsaw.**

scroll·work (skrōl′wûrk′) *n.* Embellishment with a scroll motif; especially, ornamentation executed in wood with a scroll saw.

Scrooge (skrōōj) *n. Often* **scrooge.** A mean-spirited, miserly person; a skinflint. [After Ebenezer *Scrooge,* a miserly character in *A Christmas Carol* by Charles Dickens.]

scro·tum (skrō′təm) *n., pl.* **-ta** (-tə) or **-tums.** The external sac of skin enclosing the testes in most mammals. [Latin *scrōtum.*] —**scro·tal** (skrōt′l) *adj.*

scrounge (skrounj) *v.* **scrounged, scrounging, scrounges.** *Informal.* —*tr.* **1.** To sponge; cadge. **2.** To obtain by salvaging or foraging; round up. —*intr.* **1.** To obtain something by cadging or sponging. **2.** To forage about in an effort to acquire something at no cost. [Variant of dialectal *scrunge†,* to steal.] —**scroung·er** *n.*

scrub[1] (skrŭb) *v.* **scrubbed, scrubbing, scrubs.** —*tr.* **1.** To rub hard, as with a brush, soap, and water, in order to clean. **2.** To remove (dirt or stains) by such rubbing. **3.** To cleanse (a gas) in a scrubber. **4.** *Informal.* To cancel or abandon. —*intr.* To clean or wash something by hard rubbing. —**scrub up** To wash the hands and arms thoroughly before an operation. Used of a surgeon.
~*n.* An act of scrubbing. [Middle English *scrobben,* from Middle Low German or Middle Dutch *schrobben, schrubben.*]

scrub[2] *n.* **1.** Vegetation characterized by straggly, stunted trees, shrubs, or brushwood. **2.** A growth or tract of stunted vegetation. Sometimes used in combination: *scrubland.* **3.** A domestic animal of inferior breeding or poor appearance. **4.** An undersized or insignificant person. **5.** *Australian.* Remote rural areas. Preceded by *the.* **6.** *Sports.* A player not in the first team.
~*adj.* **1.** Undersized, stunted, or inferior. **2.** Made up of or partici-

pated in by scrubs: *a scrub team.* [Middle English, probably of Scandinavian origin.]

scrub·ber (skrŭb′ər) *n.* **1.** One that scrubs. **2.** An apparatus for removing impurities from a gas.

scrub brush *n.* A brush with strong, stiff bristles used for doing heavy cleaning jobs. Also called "scrubbing brush."

scrub bird *n.* Either of two rare Australian birds of the genus *Atrichornis,* having brown plumage and long, pointed tails.

scrub·by (skrŭb′ē) *adj.* **-bier, -biest. 1.** Covered with or consisting of scrub or underbrush. **2.** Small; straggly; stunted. **3.** Shabby or paltry; wretched. —**scrub·bi·ness** *n.*

scrub fowl *n.* A megapode *(see).*

scrub oak *n.* Any of several shrubby or small oaks, such as *Quercus ilicifolia,* of eastern North America.

scrub pine *n.* Any of several small, straggling pine trees, such as *Pinus virginiana,* of the eastern United States.

scrub typhus *n.* An acute infectious disease common in southeastern Asia and the western Pacific, caused by a parasitic microorganism, *Ricksettsia tsutsugamushi,* and transmitted by a mite. Also called "tsutsugamushi disease," "Japanese river fever."

scrub wallaby *n.* A small wallaby, the **pademelon** *(see).*

scrub·wom·an (skrŭb′wōōm′ən) *n., pl.* **-women** (-wĭm′ĭn). A woman hired to clean; charwoman.

scruff (skrŭf) *n.* The back of the neck; the nape. [Variant of obsolete *scuff,* perhaps from Old Norse *skoft,* hair on the head.]

scruf·fy (skrŭf′ē) *adj.* **-fier, -fiest.** Shabby; untidy. [From obsolete *scruff,* scurf.]

scrum (skrŭm) *n.* A formation in Rugby football: **1.** A *set scrum,* in which the two sets of forwards must interlock together against each other, the ball is thrown in, and the opposing hookers try to kick the ball backward out to their own team. **2.** A *loose scrum,* in which the players join together in the struggle to win the ball during play. Also called "scrummage" and formerly "scrimmage."
~*intr.v.* **scrummed, scrumming, scrums.** To engage in or form a scrum. Often used with *down.* [Shortened from SCRUMMAGE.]

scrum half *n.* **1.** In Rugby football, the player who throws the ball into a set scrum. **2.** The position of this player in a team.

scrum·mage (skrŭm′ĭj) *n.* In Rugby football, a scrum.
~*intr.v.* **scrummaged, -maging, -mages.** To engage in a scrum. [Alteration of SCRIMMAGE.] —**scrum·mag·er** *n.*

scrump·tious (skrŭmp′shəs) *adj. Informal.* **1.** Delicious. **2.** Splendid; delightful. [Perhaps alteration of SUMPTUOUS.]

scrunch (skrŭnch, skrōōnch) *v.* **scrunched, scrunching, scrunches.** —*tr.* **1.** To crush or crunch. **2.** To crumple or squeeze. Often used with *up.* —*intr.* To move with or make a crunching sound: *scrunching along the gravel path.*
~*n.* A crunching sound. [Alteration of CRUNCH.]

scru·ple (skrōō′pəl) *n.* **1.** *Often* **scruples.** A feeling of doubt or uncertainty as to whether a course of action is ethically right or justifiable; a dictate of conscience. **2.** *Abbr.* **sc., scr.** A unit of apothecary weight equal to 20 grains. **3.** A minute part or amount. —See Synonyms at **qualm.**
~*intr.v.* **scrupled, -pling, -ples.** To hesitate through the demands of conscience or principle. [French *scrupule,* from Latin *scrūpulus,* small sharp stone, small weight, scruple, from *scrūpus†,* rough stone.]

scru·pu·lous (skrōō′pyə-ləs) *adj.* **1.** Having scruples; principled. **2.** Very conscientious and exacting; punctilious. —See Synonyms at **meticulous.** [Middle English, from Latin *scrūpulōsus,* from *scrūpulus,* SCRUPLE.] —**scru·pu·los·i·ty** (skrōō′pyə-lŏs′ə-tē), **scru·pu·lous·ness** *n.* —**scru·pu·lous·ly** *adv.*

scru·ta·ble (skrōō′tə-bəl) *adj.* Comprehensible through scrutiny. [Medieval Latin *scrūtabilis,* searchable, from Latin *scrūtārī,* to search. See **scrutiny.**]

scru·ti·nize (skrōōt′n-īz′) *tr.v.* **-nized, -nizing, -nizes.** To examine or observe with great care; inspect minutely or critically. —**scru·ti·niz·er** *n.* —**scru·ti·niz·ing·ly** *adv.*

scru·ti·ny (skrōōt′n-ē) *n., pl.* **-nies. 1.** A close, careful examination or study; a critical, sustained look. **2.** Close observation; surveillance. **3.** *British.* An official examination of the votes cast in an election. [Middle English, from Latin *scrūtinium,* from *scrūtārī,* to search, examine (originally said of ragpickers), "to rummage in a heap of rubbish," from *scrūta,* rubbish.]

scry (skrī) *intr.v.* **scried, scrying, scries.** To see or predict the future by means of a crystal ball. [Aphetic variant of DESCRY.]

scu·ba (skōō′bə) *n.* An apparatus containing compressed air used for underwater breathing. [*S*elf-*c*ontained *u*nderwater *b*reathing *a*pparatus.]

scuba diver *n.* One who uses scuba gear in underwater swimming. —**scuba dive** *v.* —**scuba diving** *n.*

scud (skŭd) *intr.v.* **scudded, scudding, scuds. 1.** To run or skim along swiftly and easily. **2.** *Nautical,* To run before a gale with little or no sail set.
~*n.* **1.** The act of scudding. **2. a.** A ragged mass of cloud driven along by the wind at a lower level than the main cloud layer. **b.** A sudden light shower or gust of wind. [Perhaps variant of SCUT (rabbit's tail, hence "run like a rabbit").]

scu·do (skōō′dō) *n., pl.* **-di** (-dē). A former monetary unit and coin of Italy and Sicily. [Italian, "shield," from Latin *scūtum.*]

scuff (skŭf) *v.* **scuffed, scuffing, scuffs. 1.** To scrape or drag the feet while walking; shuffle. **2.** To become scratched or scraped with wear: *These shoes scuff easily.* —*tr.* To scrape or scratch the surface of (shoes, for example) with use.

~*n.* **1.** The sound or act of scuffing. **2.** A worn or rough spot resulting from scuffing. **3.** A flat, backless slipper. [Imitative.]

scuf·fle[1] (skŭf′əl) *intr.v.* **-fled, -fling, -fles. 1.** To fight or struggle confusedly at close quarters. **2. a.** To shuffle. **b.** To go or move about in a hurried and confused manner.
~*n.* **1.** A rough, disorderly struggle at close quarters. **2.** The action or sound of scuffling. —See Synonyms at **conflict.** [Probably from Scandinavian; akin to Old Norse *skūfa,* to push.] **—scuf·fler** *n.*

scuffle[2] *n.* A type of hoe manipulated by pushing rather than pulling. Also called "scuffle hoe." [Dutch *schoffel,* from Middle Dutch *schoffel, schuffel,* shovel.]

scull (skŭl) *n.* **1.** A long oar twisted from side to side over the stern of a boat to propel it. **2.** Either of a pair of short-handled oars used by a single rower. **3.** A small, light boat for sculling, especially a racing boat.
~*v.* **sculled, sculling, sculls.** —*tr.* To propel (a boat) with a scull or sculls. —*intr.* To use a scull or sculls to propel a boat. [Middle English *sculle*†.] **—scull·er** *n.*

scul·ler·y (skŭl′ə-rē) *n., pl.* **-ies.** A small room adjoining a kitchen in which dishwashing and other kitchen chores are done. [Middle English, from Norman French *squillerie,* Old French *escuelerie,* from *escuelier,* keeper of dishes, from *escuele,* dish, from Vulgar Latin *scūtella* (unattested), variant (influenced by Latin *scūtum,* SCUTUM) of Latin *scutella,* salver, diminutive of *scutra*†, platter.]

scul·lion (skŭl′yən) *n. Archaic.* **1.** A servant employed to do menial tasks in a kitchen. **2.** A despicable or contemptible person. [Middle English *sculyon,* probably from Old French *escovillon,* dishcloth, diminutive of *escouve,* broom, from Latin *scopa.* See **scopula.**]

sculp. sculpsit; sculpture.

scul·pin (skŭl′pĭn) *n., pl.* **-pins** or collectively **sculpin.** Any of various marine and freshwater fishes of the family Cottidae, of northern waters, having a large, flattened head and prominent spines. Also called "bullhead." [Perhaps variant of obsolete *scorpene,* from Latin *scorpaena,* sea scorpion. See **scorpaenoid.**]

sculp·sit (skŭlp′sĭt). *Latin. Abbr.* **sc., sculp., sculpt.** He (or she) sculptured (it). Placed after the artist's name.

sculpt (skŭlpt) *v.* **sculpted, sculpting, sculpts.** —*tr.* To sculpture. —*intr.* To be a sculptor. [French *sculpter, sculper,* from Latin *sculpere,* to carve. See **sculpture.**]

sculpt. sculpsit.

sculp·tor (skŭlp′tər) *n.* **1.** One who sculptures; especially, an artist who works in stone, metal, or other hard or plastic material. **2. Sculptor.** A constellation in the Southern Hemisphere near Cetus and Phoenix. Also called "Sculptor's Workshop." [Latin, from *sculpere* (past participle *sculptus*), to carve. See **sculpture.**]

sculp·tress (skŭlp′trĭs) *n.* A woman who sculptures.

sculp·ture (skŭlp′chər) *n. Abbr.* **sculp. 1.** The art or practice of shaping figures or designs, as by carving wood, chiseling marble, modeling clay, or casting in metal. **2. a.** A work of art created in this manner. **b.** Such works collectively. **3.** Ridges, indentations, or other markings, as on a shell, formed by natural processes.
~*v.* **sculptured, -turing, -tures.** —*tr.* **1.** To fashion (stone, bronze, wood, or the like) into a three-dimensional figure. **2.** To represent in sculpture. **3.** To ornament with sculpture. **4.** To give sculptural shape or contour to, as by erosion. —*intr.* To make sculptures. [Middle English, from Latin *sculptūra,* from *sculpere* (past participle *sculptus*), to carve.] **—sculp·tur·al** *adj.* **—sculp·tur·al·ly** *adv.*

sculp·tur·esque (skŭlp′chə-rĕsk′) *adj.* Suggestive of sculpture; having the qualities of sculpture. **—sculp·tur·esque·ly** *adv.* **—sculp·tur·esque·ness** *n.*

scum (skŭm) *n.* **1.** A filmy layer of extraneous or impure matter that forms on or rises to the surface of a liquid or body of water. **2.** The refuse or dross of molten metals. **3.** Any refuse or worthless matter. **4.** *Informal.* An element of society or an individual regarded as being vile or worthless.
~*v.* **scummed, scumming, scums.** —*tr.* To remove the scum from; skim. —*intr.* To become covered with scum. [Middle English *scume, scome,* from Middle Dutch *schūm,* from Germanic *skūma-* (unattested), cover.] **—scum·mer** *n.* **—scum·my** *adj.*

scum·ble (skŭm′bəl) *tr.v.* **-bled, -bling, -bles.** In painting and drawing, to soften the colors or outlines of by covering with a film of opaque or semiopaque color or by rubbing.
~*n.* **1.** The effect produced by scumbling. **2.** Material used for scumbling. [Probably frequentative of SCUM.]

scun·cheon (skŭn′chən) *n. Architecture.* The inside vertical face of a door or window frame. [Middle English, from Old French *escoinson* (French *écoinçon*), a beveled inside edge.]

scun·ner (skŭn′ər) *n.* A strong dislike; aversion. [Middle English *skunner*†.]

scup (skŭp) *n., pl.* **scups** or collectively **scup.** A food fish, *Stenotomus chrysops,* of western Atlantic waters, related to and resembling the porgies. [Short for Narraganset *mishcùp.*]

scup·per[1] (skŭp′ər) *n.* **1.** *Nautical.* An opening in the side of a ship at deck level to allow water to run off. **2.** Any opening for draining off water, as on a building. [Middle English *skopper,* perhaps from Old French *escopir,* to spit (imitative).]

scupper[2] *tr.v.* **-pered, -pering, -pers.** *Chiefly British Slang.* **1.** To overwhelm or massacre. **2.** To ruin or destroy. [19th century (military use) : origin obscure.]

scup·per·nong (skŭp′ər-nông′, -nŏng′) *n.* **1.** A grape, the **muscadine** *(see)*; especially, a cultivated variety having sweet, yellowish fruit. **2.** A sweet wine made from such grapes. [After the *Scuppernong* River, North Carolina.]

scurf (skûrf) *n.* **1.** Scaly or shredded dry skin, as in dandruff. **2.** Any loose, scaly crust coating a surface, especially of a plant. [Middle English *scurf, scorf,* Old English *scurf,* variant (probably influenced by Old Norse *skurfōttr,* scurfy) of *sceorf, sceorfan,* to gnaw.] **—scurf·i·ness** *n.* **—scurf·y** *adj.*

scur·ril·i·ty (skə-rĭl′ə-tē) *n., pl.* **-ties. 1.** The quality of being scurrilous. **2.** A scurrilous remark or piece of writing.

scur·ri·lous (skûr′ə-ləs) *adj.* **1.** Given to the use of vulgar, obscene, or abusive language. **2.** Coarse, obscene, or abusive. [Latin *scurrīlis,* buffoonlike, jeering, from *scurra,* buffoon, perhaps from Etruscan.] **—scur·ri·lous·ly** *adv.* **—scur·ri·lous·ness** *n.*

scur·ry (skûr′ē) *intr.v.* **-ried, -rying, -ries. 1.** To go with light running steps; hurry; scamper. **2.** To flurry or swirl about.
~*n., pl.* **scurries. 1.** The act or noise of scurrying. **2.** A light whirling movement; flurry. **3.** A short run or race on horseback. [Probably short for HURRY-SCURRY.]

scur·vy (skûr′vē) *n.* A disease caused by deficiency of vitamin C, characterized by spongy and bleeding gums, bleeding under the skin, and extreme weakness.
~*adj.* **scurvier, -viest.** Mean; worthless; contemptible. [From SCURF (but used later to render like-sounding French *scorbut,* the skin disease, from Medieval Latin *scorbūtus.* See **scorbutic**).] **—scur·vi·ly** *adv.* **—scur·vi·ness** *n.*

scurvy grass *n.* A plant, *Cochlearia officinalis,* of northern regions, having bitter foliage, formerly used to cure scurvy.

scut (skŭt) *n.* A stubby erect tail, such as that of a hare, rabbit, or deer. [Middle English *scut*†, hare.]

scu·tage (skyōō′tĭj) *n.* In feudal times, a tax paid in lieu of military service. [Middle English, from Medieval Latin *scūtāgium,* "shield money," from Latin *scūtum,* shield, SCUTUM.]

scu·tate (skyōō′tāt′) *adj.* **1.** *Zoology.* Covered with bony plates or scales. **2.** *Botany.* Round in shape like a buckler or shield. [New Latin *scutatus,* from Latin *scūtātus,* equipped with a shield, from *scūtum,* shield, SCUTUM.]

scutch (skŭch) *tr.v.* **scutched, scutching, scutches.** To separate the valuable fibers of (flax or other textile material) from the woody parts by beating.
~*n.* An implement for scutching. [Obsolete French *escoucher,* from Old French *escousser,* from Vulgar Latin *excussāre* (unattested), frequentative of Latin *excutere* (past participle *excussus*), to shake out : *ex-,* out + *quatere,* to shake.] **—scutch·er** *n.*

scutch·eon (skŭch′ən) *n.* **1.** Variant of **escutcheon. 2.** A shield-shaped object, such as a scute.

scutch grass *n.* **1. Bermuda grass** *(see).* **2. Couch grass** *(see).*

scute (skyōōt) *n. Zoology.* A horny, chitinous, or bony external plate or scale, as on the shell of a turtle. [New Latin, SCUTUM.]

scu·tel·late (skyōō-tĕl′ĭt, skyōōt′l-āt′) *adj.* Also **scu·tel·lat·ed** (skyōōt′l-ā′tĭd) (for sense 1). **1.** *Zoology.* **a.** Covered with bony plates or scales. **b.** Having a scutellum. **2.** *Botany.* Shaped like a shield or platter. [From SCUTELLUM.]

scu·tel·la·tion (skyōōt′l-ā′shən) *n.* An arrangement or covering of scales, as on a bird's leg.

scu·tel·lum (skyōō-tĕl′əm) *n., pl.* **-tella** (-tĕl′ə). **1.** *Zoology.* A shield-like bony plate or scale, as on the thorax of some insects. **2.** *Botany.* Any of several shield-shaped structures, such as the cotyledon of a grass. [New Latin, diminutive of SCUTUM.]

scu·ti·form (skyōō′tə-fôrm′) *adj.* Shield-shaped: *scutiform leaves.* [New Latin *scutiformis* : Latin *scūtum,* SCUTUM + -FORM.]

scut·ter (skŭt′ər) *intr.v.* **-tered, -tering, -ters.** *British Informal.* To scurry. [Variant (influenced by SCATTER) of SCUTTLE (to run).]

scut·tle[1] (skŭt′l) *n.* **1.** A small opening or hatch with a movable lid in the deck, side, wall, or roof of a ship or in the roof, wall, or floor of a building. **2.** The lid or hatch for this.
~*tr.v.* **scuttled, -tling, -tles. 1.** To cut or open a hole or holes in (a ship's hull). **2. a.** To sink (a ship) by this means. **b.** To sink (a ship) by opening the seacocks. **3.** *Informal.* **a.** To scrap; discard. **b.** To undermine; sabotage. [Middle English *skottell,* from obsolete French *escoutille,* from Spanish *escotilla,* diminutive of *escota,* opening in a garment, "seam," probably from Gothic *skaut,* seam, hem.]

scuttle[2] *n.* **1.** A metal pail for carrying coal. **2.** A shallow open basket for carrying vegetables, flowers, grain, or the like. [Middle English *scutel,* Old English *scutel,* ultimately from Latin *scutella,* salver. See **scullery.**]

scuttle[3] *intr.v.* **-tled, -tling, -tles.** To run with short hurried movements; scurry. [Variant of dialectal *scuddle,* frequentative of SCUD.] **—scut·tle** *n.*

scut·tle·butt (skŭt′l-bŭt′) *n.* **1.** A drinking fountain on a ship. **2.** *Archaic.* A cask on a ship used to hold the day's supply of drinking water. **3.** *Slang.* Gossip; rumor. [SCUTTLE (hatch) + BUTT (cask).]

scu·tum (skyōō′təm) *n., pl.* **-ta** (-tə). **1.** *Zoology.* A bony, calcareous, chitinous, or horny scale or plate, as on certain barnacles and on the thorax of an insect. **2. Scutum.** *Astronomy.* A constellation in the equatorial region of the southern sky near Sagittarius and Serpens Cauda. [Latin *scūtum,* shield.]

scuz·zy (skŭz′ē) *adj.* **-zier, -ziest.** *Slang.* Dirty; grimy. [Origin unknown.]

Scyl·la (sĭl′ə). A headland on the Italian side of the Strait of Messina, opposite the whirlpool Charybdis, personified by Homer as a female sea monster who devoured sailors. **—between Scylla and Charybdis.** In a position where avoidance of one danger exposes one to destruction by another.

scy·phis·to·ma (sī-fĭs′tə-mə) *n., pl.* **-mae** (-mē) or **-mas.** A seden-

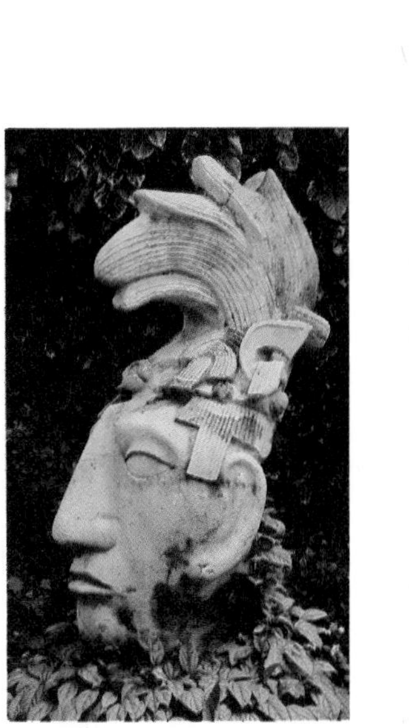

sculpture *A carved Aztec head protrudes from a cloak of encroaching vegetation. The Aztecs dominated central Mexico from the 12th century until the Spanish Conquest in the 16th century.*

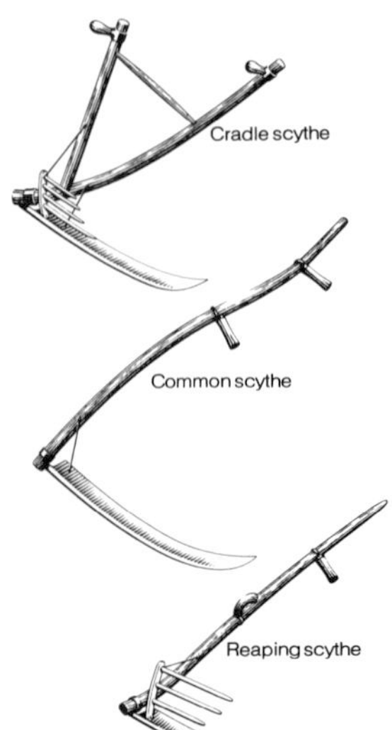

scythe *Until the invention of faster mechanical cutters and lawn mowers in the 19th century, scythes were the main tools used for cutting hay and grass and for harvesting cereal crops.*

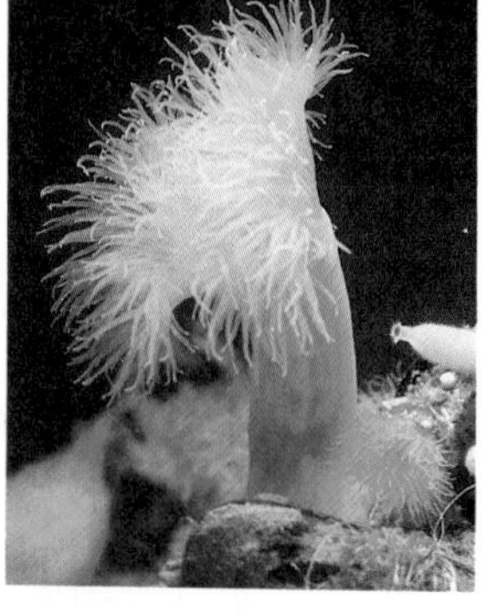

sea anemone *Found throughout the world, the flowerlike sea anemone feeds on fish and other sea creatures, stunning its prey with stinging tentacles. There are over 1,000 species, some of which can grow to 1.5 meters (5 feet) across.*

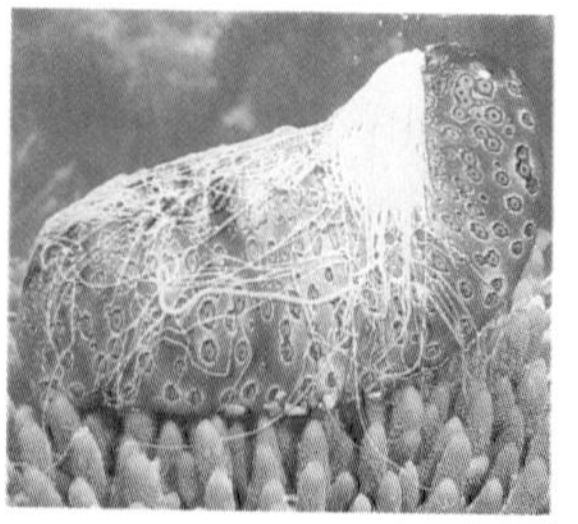

sea cucumber *Although it gets its name from its resemblance to a plant, the sea cucumber is actually an animal. When alarmed, some species—like the warm-water type shown here—exude sticky filaments to confuse or trap an attacker. Others can expel their own intestines, then grow a new set.*

tary polyplike form in the life cycle of scyphozoans that gives rise to free-swimming medusoid forms. [New Latin, from Greek *skuphos,* cup + *stoma,* mouth.]

scy·pho·zo·an (sī′fə-zō′ən) *n.* Any of various marine coelenterates of the class Scyphozoa, including the jellyfishes. [New Latin *Scyphozoa,* "cuplike creatures" : Greek *skuphos,* cup + -ZOA.] **—scy·pho·zo·an** *adj.*

scythe (sīth) *n.* An implement consisting of a long, curved single-edged blade with a long, bent handle, used for mowing or reaping. *~tr.v.* **scythed, scything, scythes.** To cut with or as if with a scythe. [Middle English *sithe, sythe,* Old English *sīthe,* from Germanic.]

Scyth·i·a (sĭth′ē-ə, sĭth′-). An ancient region of Asia and southeastern Europe north of the Black Sea.

Scyth·i·an (sĭth′ē-ən, sĭth′-) *n.* **1.** A member of the ancient nomadic people inhabiting Scythia. **2.** The extinct Iranian language of these people. **—Scyth·i·an** *adj.*

SD South Dakota (used with a Zip Code).

s.d. **1.** sine die. **2.** *Statistics.* standard deviation.

S.D. **1.** *Statistics.* standard deviation. **2.** special delivery.

S.Dak. South Dakota.

SDP Social Democratic Party.

S.D.R., S.D.R.s special drawing rights (from the International Monetary Fund).

Se The symbol for the element selenium.

SE southeast; southeastern.

sea (sē) *n.* **1.** *Abbr.* **s., S. a.** The continuous body of salt water covering most of the earth's surface; especially, this body regarded as a geophysical entity distinct from earth and sky. Usually preceded by *the.* **b.** A tract of water within an ocean, such as the North Sea. **c.** A relatively large body of salt water completely or partly landlocked, such as the Caspian Sea. **d.** A body of fresh water, such as the Sea of Galilee. **2.** *Sometimes* **seas.** The condition of the ocean's surface with regard to its course, flow, swell, or turbulence: *a high sea.* **3.** Something that suggests the sea in extent or quantity. **4.** Seafaring as a way of life. **5.** A lunar **mare** *(see).* **—at sea. 1.** On the open waters of the ocean. **2.** At a loss; perplexed. **—go to sea. 1.** To become a sailor. **2.** To set out on an ocean voyage. **—put (out) to sea.** To leave port. [Middle English *se(e),* Old English *sæ,* from Common Germanic *saiwa-* (unattested).]

sea anchor *n. Nautical.* A drag, usually in the form of a canvas-covered conical frame, floating behind a vessel to prevent drifting or to maintain a heading into the wind. Also called "drag anchor," "drift anchor," "drogue."

sea anemone *n.* Any of numerous flowerlike marine coelenterates of the order Actiniaria.

sea bass *n.* Any of various marine food fishes of the genus *Centropristes* and related genera; especially, *C. striatus,* of coastal Atlantic waters of the United States. Also called "sea perch."

sea·bed (sē′bĕd′) *n.* The floor of the sea or the ocean.

Sea·bee (sē′bē′) *n.* A member of one of the U.S. Navy's construction battalions, established to build naval aviation bases. [Alteration of *cee bee,* from the initials of *C*onstruction *B*attalion.]

sea bird *n.* A bird, such as a petrel or albatross, that frequents the sea, especially far from shore.

sea biscuit *n.* **Hardtack** *(see).*

sea·board (sē′bôrd′, -bōrd′) *n.* **1.** The seacoast. **2.** Land near the sea. [SEA + BOARD (obsolete sense "border").] **—sea·board** *adj.*

sea·borne (sē′bôrn′, -bōrn′) *adj.* **1.** Conveyed by sea; transported by ship. **2.** Carried on or over the sea.

sea bread *n.* **Hardtack** *(see).*

sea bream *n.* Any of various marine food fishes of the family Sparidae; especially, *Pagellus centrodontus,* of European waters, and *Archosargus rhomboidalis,* of western Atlantic coastal waters.

sea breeze *n.* A cool breeze blowing inland from the sea, especially during the day.

sea buckthorn *n.* A Eurasian coastal shrub, *Hippophae rhamnoides,* having narrow leaves, greenish flowers, and orange fruits.

sea butterfly *n.* A marine organism, a **pteropod** *(see).*

sea·coast (sē′kōst′) *n.* Land bordering the sea.

sea·cock (sē′kŏk′) *n.* A valve through which water can be let into or pumped out of the interior of a ship.

sea cow *n.* **1.** Any of several marine mammals of the order Sirenia, such as a manatee or dugong. **2.** Any of several other aquatic animals, such as a walrus.

sea cucumber *n.* Any of various cucumber-shaped echinoderms of the class Holothuroidea. See **trepang.**

sea dog *n.* A sailor with long experience of the sea.

sea·dog (sē′dôg′, -dŏg′) *n.* A **fogbow** *(see).*

sea duck *n.* Any of various diving ducks, such as the eider or scoter, of coastal areas.

sea eagle *n.* Any of various fish-eating eagles or similar birds, such as the bald eagle or the osprey.

sea ear *n.* A mollusk, the **ormer** *(see).*

sea elephant *n.* The **elephant seal** *(see).*

sea fan *n.* Any of various yellowish to reddish fan-shaped corals of the genus *Gorgonia.*

sea·far·er (sē′fâr′ər) *n.* A sailor or mariner.

sea·far·ing (sē′fâr′ĭng) *n.* **1.** Travel by sea. **2.** The calling of a sailor. *~adj.* **1.** Following a life at sea. **2.** Traveling by sea.

sea feather *n.* Any of several anthozoans of the family Pennatulidae, having a featherlike shape.

sea·food (sē′fo͞od′) *n.* Edible fish and shellfish from the sea.

sea·fowl (sē′foul′) *n.* **1.** A sea bird. **2.** Sea birds collectively.

sea·front (sē′frŭnt′) *n.* A strip of land at the very edge of the sea, especially when part of a town.

sea·girt (sē′gûrt′) *adj.* Surrounded by the sea.

sea·go·ing (sē′gō′ĭng) *adj.* **1.** Designed or used for ocean voyages. **2.** Seafaring.

sea gooseberry *n.* A marine organism of the genus *Pleurobrachia,* having two tentacles and a round, iridescent body. [From its round, berrylike shape.]

sea green *n.* Moderate bluish green. **—sea-green** *adj.*

sea gull *n.* A gull, especially any appearing near coastal areas.

sea holly *n.* An Old World plant, *Eryngium maritimum,* growing on seashores and having prickly leaves and blue or purplish flowers.

sea horse *n.* **1.** Any small marine fish of the genus *Hippocampus,* characteristically swimming in an upright position, and having a prehensile tail, a horselike head, and a body covered with bony plates. **2.** Loosely, a walrus. **3.** A mythical animal, half fish and half horse, ridden by Neptune and other sea gods.

Sea Island cotton *n.* **1.** A species of cotton, *Gossypium barbadense,* native to tropical America and widely cultivated for its fine, long-staple fibers. **2.** The fibers or fabric derived from this plant. [After the *Sea Islands* off South Carolina and Georgia, where it was originally cultivated.]

sea kale *n.* A European plant, *Crambe maritima,* having cabbagelike leaves and young shoots that are edible.

sea king *n.* A piratical Scandinavian chief of the early Middle Ages.

seal[1] (sēl) *n.* **1. a.** A die or signet having a raised or incised emblem, used to stamp an impression upon a receptive substance such as wax or lead. **b.** The impression made. **c.** The design or emblem itself, belonging exclusively to the user: *the king's seal.* **d.** A small disk or wafer of wax, lead, or paper bearing such an imprint and affixed to a document to prove authenticity or to seal it. **2.** Any act, event, or sign that is regarded as a confirmation or guarantee. **3.** An adhesive agent such as wax, paraffin, or putty used to close or secure something or to prevent seepage of moisture or air. **4.** A device or fluid in a drainpipe preventing the upward passage of gas. **5.** An airtight closure. **6.** A small decorative paper sticker: *a Christmas seal.* **—set one's seal on. 1.** To impart something of one's personal character to: *set her seal on the magazine.* **2.** To approve; endorse. **—set the seal on. 1.** To sanction in a formal or authoritative way. **2.** To bring to an end, especially in an appropriate manner. **—under seal of.** In confidence or secrecy on specified grounds: *under seal of confession.*
~tr.v. **sealed, sealing, seals. 1.** To affix a seal to so as to prove authenticity or attest to accuracy, quality, or conformity to an appropriate standard. **2. a.** To close with or as if with a seal: *seal an envelope; seal one's lips.* **b.** To close hermetically. **c.** To make fast or fill up as with plaster or cement. **d.** To give a protective coating to (a porous surface, for example). **3.** To grant, certify, or designate under seal or authority. **4.** To establish or determine irrevocably. **5.** To settle or agree upon; confirm: *sealed the bargain.* **6.** To provide (a road) with a hard surface. **—seal off.** To close off or enclose (a road or area) so as to prevent entry or exit. [Middle English, from Norman French, Old French, from Latin *sigillum,* seal, diminutive of *signum,* sign.] **—seal·a·ble** *adj.*

seal[2] *n.* **1.** Any of various aquatic, fish-eating mammals of the families Phocidae *(earless seals)* and Otariidae *(eared seals),* having a sleek, torpedo-shaped body and limbs that are modified into paddlelike flippers. **2.** The pelt or fur of a seal, especially a fur seal. **3.** Leather made from the hide of a seal.
~intr.v. **sealed, sealing, seals.** To hunt seals. [Middle English *selch, seel,* Old English *seolh,* from Germanic.]

sea lamprey *n.* A common marine lamprey, *Petromyzon marinus.*

sea lane *n.* An established course along which sea traffic moves, as when leaving or entering port.

seal·ant (sē′lənt) *n.* A sealing agent.

sea lavender *n.* Any of several salt-marsh plants of the genus *Limonium,* having clusters of small lavender or pinkish flowers.

sea lawyer *n. Slang.* An argumentative or fault-finding sailor.

sealed-beam (sēld′bēm′) *adj.* Designating a motor vehicle headlight in which the lens is sealed to the prefocused reflector in order to maintain a vacuum in the lamp cavity.

sea legs *pl.n. Informal.* The ability to walk on board ship with steadiness, especially in rough seas.

seal·er[1] (sē′lər) *n.* **1.** One that seals. **2.** An undercoat of paint or varnish used to size a surface. **3.** An officer who inspects, tests, and certifies weights and measures.

sealer[2] *n.* A person or ship engaged in seal hunting.

seal·er·y (sē′lə-rē) *n., pl.* **-ies.** A place where seals are hunted.

sea lettuce *n* Any of several green seaweeds of the genus *Ulva,* having thin, irregularly shaped fronds sometimes used as food.

sea level *n.* The level of the ocean's surface; especially, the **mean sea level** *(see).*

sea lily *n.* Any of various marine crinoids having a flowerlike body supported by a long stalk.

seal·ing wax (sē′lĭng) *n.* A resinous preparation of shellac, turpentine, a filler, and a dye that is soft and fluid when heated but solidifies upon cooling, used to seal letters, jars, or other objects.

sea lion *n.* Any of several seals of the family Otariidae, having distinct external ears, especially *Zalophus californianus,* of the northern Pacific.

seal point *n.* A type of Siamese cat having dark brown ears, muzzle, paws, and tail.

UNCHANGING ZONES AND CURRENTS IN THE EVER-MOVING SEA

Life in the different layers of the sea's depths

Although seawater circulates ceaselessly between the poles and the equator and its surface is continuously disturbed by the pull of the moon and the wind, it is not consistent in temperature but varies greatly from place to place and from top to bottom. It is forced by the shape of landmasses and the ocean bed into a number of vast currents and drifts, all of which have an effect on climate.

The best-known current is the Gulf Stream, which carries water warmed by the tropical sun almost to Newfoundland, beyond which it widens and branches. One branch is the North Atlantic Drift, which warms

the northwestern shores of Europe in winter. All currents have a typical but remarkable integrity because seawater at a certain temperature and density does not easily mingle with different seawater around it. Some seawater may have been carried along in the same current for centuries—never mixing with the water that surrounds it.

Just as the sea maintains differences at the surface, so different layers are maintained from top to bottom in the warmer seas. The euphotic zone, the upper 200 meters (656 feet), is aerated and sunlit enough for minute plant and animal life, such as algae and plankton,

to flourish. They are the first link in the food chain that sustains all sea creatures.

Besides the algae and plankton, the euphotic zone holds a concentration of sea creatures of greater size. There are both carnivores and herbivores and they are predominantly either colorless or blue—the best camouflage in the sea.

The bathyal zone, below the euphotic zone, contains carnivores and creatures that live off the dead matter that sinks down from above. In the total darkness of the depths, the variety of living things decreases as does the food dropping from above.

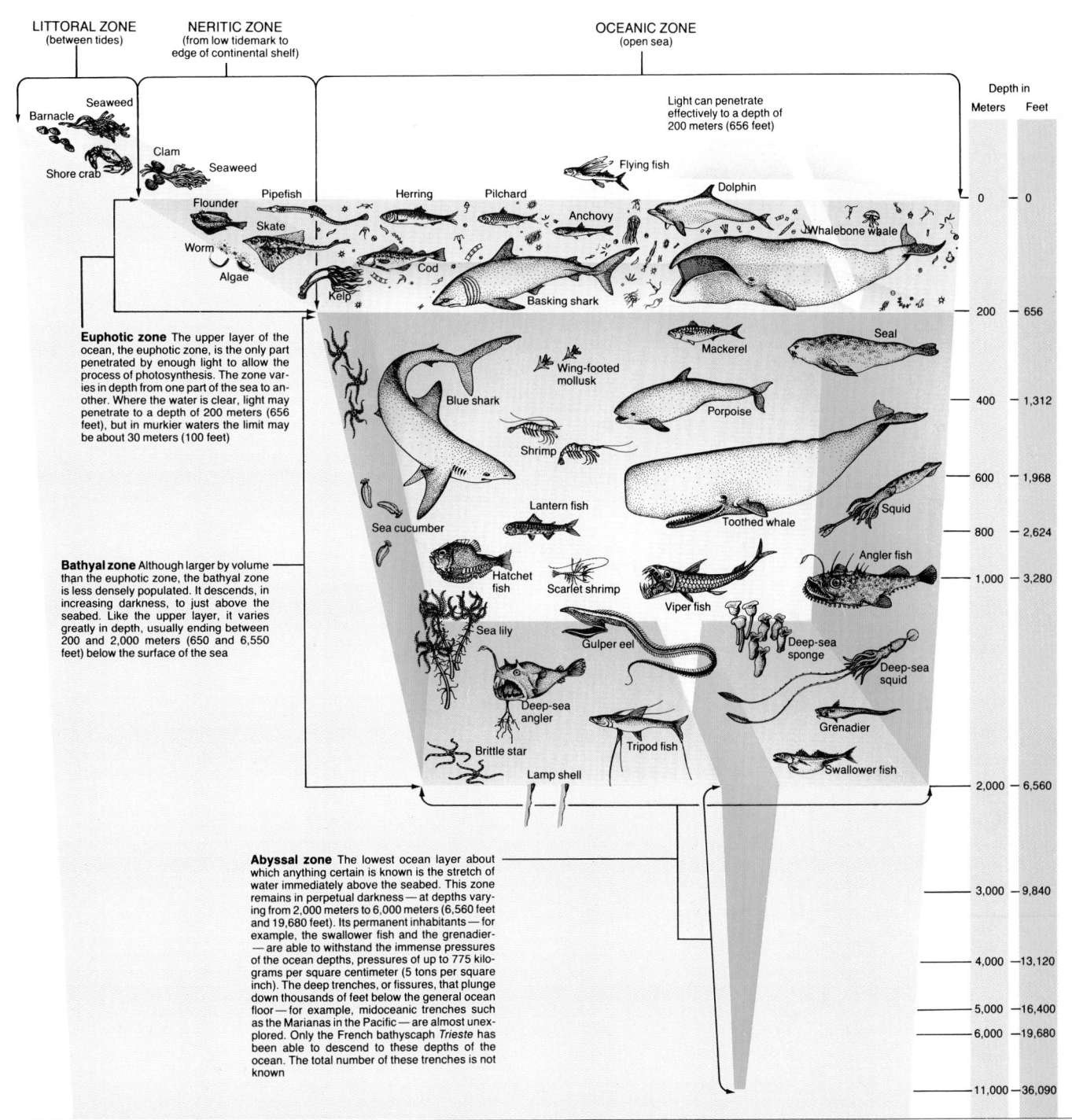

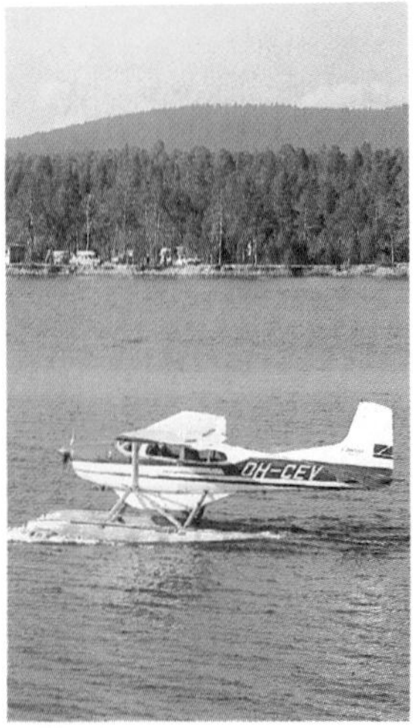

seaplane *Seaplanes are most widely used in thickly forested regions such as Canada and the Scandinavian countries where open water provides an abundance of ready-made landing strips. This plane operates in northern Finland.*

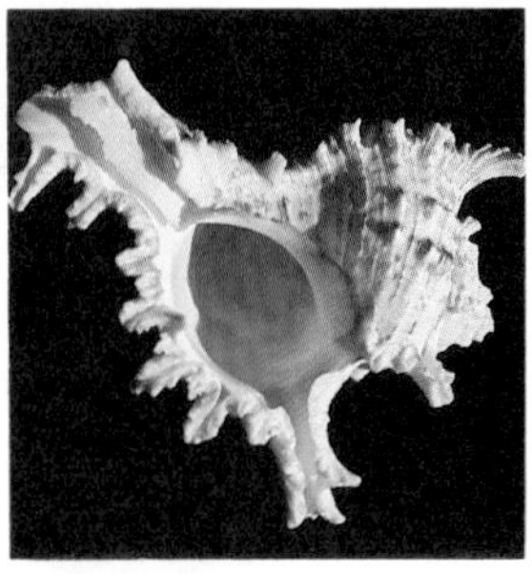

seashell *The hard outer shell that protects the soft boneless body of many marine mollusks. There are about 80,000 species of mollusk, though not all produce shells. This elaborate Pacific shell was found on a beach in California.*

seal ring *n.* A finger ring bearing a seal.

seal·skin (sēl'skĭn') *n.* **1.** The pelt or fur of a fur seal, especially the underfur. **2.** A garment made of this skin. **—seal·skin** *adj.*

Sea·ly·ham terrier (sē'lē-hăm', -ē-əm) *n.* A terrier of a breed developed in Wales, having a wiry white coat, a long head, and short legs. [Originally bred at *Sealyham,* Dyfed, Wales.]

seam (sēm) *n.* **1. a.** A line of junction formed by sewing together two pieces of material along their edges. **b.** A similar line, ridge, or groove made by fitting, joining, or lapping together two sections along their edges. **c.** A suture or scar, as left on the skin after surgery. **2.** Any line across a surface, such as a crack, fissure, or wrinkle. **3.** A thin layer or stratum, as of coal or rock. **—bursting at the seams.** Overcrowded or too full.
~*v.* **seamed, seaming, seams.** —*tr.* **1.** To fasten or join with or as if with a seam. **2.** To mark with a groove, wrinkle, scar, or other seamlike line. **3.** In knitting, to form ridges in by purling. —*intr.* To crack open; become fissured or furrowed. [Middle English *se(e)m,* Old English *sēam,* from Germanic.] **—seam·er** *n.*

sea·man (sē'mən) *n., pl.* **-men** (-mĭn). **1.** A mariner or sailor. **2.** *Abbr.* **S** *U.S. Navy.* An enlisted man ranking above seaman apprentice and below petty officer. **3.** In the British Navy and certain other navies, a sailor ranking below a petty officer.

seaman apprentice *n. U.S. Navy.* An enlisted man ranking above a seaman recruit and below a seaman.

seaman recruit *n. U.S. Navy.* An enlisted man of the lowest rank.

sea·man·ship (sē'mən-shĭp') *n.* Skill in managing or navigating a boat or ship.

sea·mark (sē'märk') *n.* **1.** A landmark visible from the sea, used as a guide in navigation. **2.** The mark along a coastline indicating the upper tidal limits.

sea mew *n.* Any of various gulls frequenting coastal areas, especially *Larus canus,* of Europe.

sea mile *n.* A former unit of length equal to 6,000 feet or 1,000 fathoms. Compare **nautical mile.**

sea milkwort *n.* A fleshy plant, *Glaux maritima,* of shores and brackish marshes, having pink flowers. Also called "saltwort."

seam·less (sēm'lĭs) *adj.* **1.** Without seams; woven without a seam: *seamless stockings.* **2.** Having a steady or rhythmic flow; harmonious: *seamless prose.* **—seam·less·ness** *n.*

sea·mount (sē'mount') *n.* A submerged submarine mountain rising at least 1,000 meters (3,300 feet) above the ocean floor.

sea mouse *n.* Any of various segmented marine worms of the genus *Aphrodite*; especially, *A. aculeata,* having a flattened elliptical body with overlapping scales covered by long hairs.

seam·stress (sēm'strĭs) *n.* A woman who sews, especially for a living.

seam·y (sē'mē) *adj.* **-ier, -iest. 1.** Having, marked with, or showing a seam or seams. **2.** Unattractively or unpleasantly rough and raw; sordid: *the seamy side of life.* **—seam·i·ness** *n.*

Sean·ad Éir·eann (săn'ăd âr'ĭn) *n.* The Senate, or upper house of parliament, in the Republic of Ireland. [Irish *seanad,* senate, from Latin *senātus,* SENATE + *Éireann,* of Ireland.]

sé·ance (sā'äns') *n.* **1.** A meeting of persons to receive messages from or communicate with the spirits of the dead. **2.** A meeting, session, or sitting. [French, "a sitting," from Old French, from *seoir,* to sit, from Latin *sedēre,* to sit.]

sea onion *n.* A plant, *Urginea maritima,* of the Mediterranean area, cultivated for its bulb that yields a powder used medicinally and as a rat poison. Also called "sea squill," "red squill."

sea otter *n.* A large marine otter, *Enhydra lutris,* of northern Pacific coasts, formerly hunted for its soft dark-brown coat.

sea parrot *n.* A bird, the **puffin** *(see).*

sea pen *n.* Any of various marine anthozoans of the families Stylatulidae and Funiculinidae. [From its resemblance to a quill pen.]

sea perch *n.* A fish, the **sea bass** *(see).*

sea pink *n.* See **thrift,** a plant (sense 3).

sea·plane (sē'plān') *n.* An aircraft equipped with floats for landing on or taking off from a body of water.

sea·port (sē'pôrt', -pōrt') *n.* A harbor or town having facilities for seagoing ships.

sea power *n.* **1.** A nation having naval strength. **2.** Naval strength.

sea purse *n.* A **mermaid's purse** *(see).*

sea·quake (sē'kwāk') *n.* An earthquake under the sea floor.

sear[1] (sîr) *v.* **seared, searing, sears.** —*tr.* **1.** To make withered; dry up or shrivel. **2.** To char, scorch, or burn the surface of with or as if with a hot instrument. —*intr.* To become withered or dried up; shrivel. —See Synonyms at **burn.**
~*n.* Any condition, such as a scar, produced by searing. [Middle English *seren,* Old English *sēarian,* from *sēar,* withered.]

sear[2] *n.* The catch in a gunlock that keeps the hammer half-cocked or fully cocked. [Probably from Old French *serre,* grasp, lock, from *serrer,* to grasp. See **serried.**]

sea raven *n.* A large sculpin, *Hemitripterus americanus,* of the western Atlantic.

search (sûrch) *v.* **searched, searching, searches.** —*tr.* **1.** To make a thorough examination of (a place, building, or receptacle, for example) in order to find something; look over; explore. **2.** To make a careful examination or investigation of; probe: *search one's conscience.* **3.** To make a thorough check of (a legal document or records, for example); scrutinize: *search a title.* **4.** To examine the person or personal effects of in order to find something concealed, especially as part of a police procedure. **5.** To come to know by investigation; learn. Used with *out.* **6.** To probe (a wound) so as to remove a foreign body. **7.** *Military.* To penetrate every part of (an area), as with gunfire. —*intr.* To conduct a thorough investigation; seek. Often used with *for.* **—search me.** *Informal.* Used to indicate that one is perplexed or unable to answer a question.
~*n.* **1.** An act of searching; an investigation, examination, or probe. **2.** The exercise of **right of search** *(see).* [Middle English *serchen,* from Norman French *sercher,* Old French *cerchier,* "to go around," from Late Latin *circāre,* from Latin *circus,* circle.] **—search·a·ble** *adj.* **—search·er** *n.*

search·ing (sûr'chĭng) *adj.* Penetrating; keen: *a searching gaze.* **—search·ing·ly** *adv.*

search·light (sûrch'līt') *n.* **1.** An apparatus containing a light source and a reflector for projecting a bright beam of approximately parallel rays of light. **2.** The beam of light so projected.

search party *n.* A group of persons who make a search, as for a missing person or a fugitive.

search warrant *n.* A warrant giving legal authorization to a police officer to make a search.

sear·ing (sîr'ĭng) *adj.* **1.** Scorching. **2.** Intense; withering.

Searle (sûrl), **Ronald William Fordham** (1920–). British cartoonist. His popular grotesque draughtsmanship combines wickedness with humor.

sea robin *n.* Any of various marine fishes of the family Triglidae, having extremely long pectoral fins with fingerlike rays.

sea room *n.* Space at sea adequate for maneuvering a ship.

sea·scape (sē'skāp') *n.* A view or picture of the sea. [SEA + -SCAPE.]

sea scorpion *n.* Any of various marine fishes of the family Cottidae, having a tapering body and a large bony or spiny head.

Sea Scout *n.* A member of a program designed to train Boy Scouts in seamanship.

sea serpent *n.* A large snakelike or dragonlike legendary marine animal.

sea·shell (sē'shĕl') *n.* The calcareous shell of a marine mollusk or similar marine organism.

sea·shore (sē'shôr', -shōr') *n.* **1.** Land immediately adjoining the sea. **2.** *Law.* Ground lying between high-water and low-water marks; foreshore.

sea·sick·ness (sē'sĭk'nĭs) *n.* Nausea and vomiting provoked by the motion of a vessel at sea. **—sea·sick** *adj.*

sea·side (sē'sīd') *n.* **1.** The seashore. **2.** Any coastal area as a place of resort or recreation. Also used adjectivally: *a seaside hotel.*

sea slug *n.* Any of various shell-less marine gastropods of the suborder Nudibranchia. Also called "nudibranch."

sea snail *n.* Any of various small marine fishes of the family Liparidae, especially *Liparis liparis,* having a soft, tadpole-shaped body with a ventral sucker.

sea snake *n.* Any of various venomous tropical marine snakes of the family Hydrophidae, chiefly of the Pacific and Indian oceans.

sea·son (sē'zən) *n.* **1. a.** Any of the four equal divisions of the year, spring, summer, autumn, and winter, indicated by the passage of the sun through an equinox or solstice and derived from the apparent north-south movement of the sun caused by the fixed direction of the earth's axis in solar orbit. **b.** Any division of the year, rainy or dry, in tropical climates. **2.** A recurrent period that is characterized by certain occupations, events, festivities, or crops: *the flu season; the Christmas season.* **3. a.** The time of year during which a tourist resort is at its busiest: *It's quieter out of season.* **b.** The time of year, especially formerly, when fashionable society assembled in a place for a period of intense social activity: *the London season.* **4.** A suitable, natural, or convenient time. **5.** Any period of time. **6.** The period of year during which a certain activity may legally take place, such as the hunting of a certain species of animal. **—in season. 1.** Available or ready for eating or other use. **2.** Legally permitted to be hunted or fished during a stipulated time. **3.** At the right moment; opportunely. **4.** In heat. Said of animals. **—out of season. 1.** Not available or ready for eating or hunting. **2.** Not at the right or proper moment; inopportunely.
~*v.* **seasoned, -soning, -sons.** —*tr.* **1.** To improve or enhance the flavor of (food) by adding salt, spices, or other flavorings. **2.** To add zest, piquancy, or interest to. **3.** To dry (timber) until it is usable; cure. **4.** To render competent through trial and experience. **5.** To accustom; inure. **6.** To moderate; temper. —*intr.* To become seasoned. [Middle English *sesoun,* from Old French *seson,* from Latin *satiō* (stem *satiōn-*), act of sowing (in Vulgar Latin, "sowing time"), from *serere* (past participle *satus*), to sow, plant.]

sea·son·a·ble (sē'zə-nə-bəl) *adj.* **1.** In keeping with the time or the season: *very seasonable weather.* **2.** Occurring or performed at the proper time; timely. **—sea·son·a·bly** *adv.*

sea·son·al (sē'zə-nəl) *adj.* Of or dependent upon a particular season: *seasonal variations in employment.* **—sea·son·al·ly** *adv.*

sea·son·er (sē'zə-nər, sēz'nər) *n.* **1.** One that uses seasonings. **2.** Seasoning.

sea·son·ing (sē'zə-nĭng) *n.* **1.** Anything used to flavor food, especially salt and pepper. **2.** The act or process by which something, such as timber, is seasoned.

Sea·speak (sē'spēk') *n.* An international maritime language, based on simplified English, enabling communication of essential messages between mariners of different nations.

sea spider *n.* Any of various marine arachnids of the class Pycnogonida, having long legs and a relatively small body.

sea squill *n.* A plant, the **sea onion** *(see).*

sea squirt *n.* Any of various sedentary marine animals of the class Ascidiacea. [It squirts water when disturbed.]

seat (sēt) *n.* **1.** Something that may be sat upon, such as a chair, bench, or the like. **2.** A place in which one may sit; especially, a place in which one is entitled to sit, as by the purchase of a ticket. **3.** The part of something on which one rests in sitting. **4. a.** The buttocks. **b.** That part of a garment covering the buttocks. **5. a.** A part serving as the base of something. **b.** The surface or part upon which another part sits or rests. **6. a.** The place where anything is or is held to be located or based: *the seat of the emotions.* **b.** A center of authority; capital: *the seat of government.* **7.** A place of abode or residence; especially, a large house that is part of an estate. **8. a.** Membership in an official or controlling body, as of a board of directors. **b.** Membership or the right of membership in a legislative body, obtained by election, appointment, or inheritance. **c.** *Chiefly British.* A constituency for parliament. **9.** The manner in which one sits and grips the saddle on a horse: *She has a good seat.* —*tr.v.* **seated, seating, seats. 1. a.** To place in or on a seat. **b.** To cause or assist to sit down. **2.** To have or provide seats for: *We can seat 300.* **3.** To repair or replace the seat of (a chair or pair of trousers, for example). **4.** To install in a position of authority or eminence. **5.** To fix firmly in place. [Middle English *sete,* from Old Norse *sæti,* from Germanic.]

sea tangle *n.* Any of various brown seaweeds, especially of the genus *Laminaria.*

seat belt *n.* A safety strap to secure the occupant of a seat in a vehicle or aircraft. Also called "safety belt."

seat·ing (sē′tĭng) *n.* **1.** The arrangement or provision of seats in a room, auditorium, or the like. **2.** The member or part upon or within which another part is seated. **3.** Material for upholstering seats.

SEATO (sē′tō) Southeast Asia Treaty Organization.

sea·train (sē′trān′) *n.* A seagoing vessel capable of carrying a train of railroad cars.

sea trout *n.* **1.** Any of several trouts or similar fishes that live in the sea but migrate to fresh water to spawn. **2.** Any of several marine fishes of the genus *Cynoscion,* especially the **weakfish** *(see).*

Se·at·tle (sē-ăt′l). City in west-central Washington State, on Puget Sound. It is the largest city in the Pacific Northwest, a commercial, transportation, and industrial hub, and a major port of entry. Recreational areas abound in and around the city.

sea urchin *n.* Any of various echinoderms of the class Echinoidea, having a soft body enclosed in a round, spiny casing.

sea wall *n.* An embankment to prevent erosion of a shoreline.

sea walnut *n.* Any of several ctenophores of the genus *Mnemiopsis* and related genera, having a translucent, ovoid body with lengthwise ridges and rows of hairlike cilia.

sea·ward (sē′wərd) *adv.* Also **sea·wards** (-wərdz). Toward the sea. —**sea·ward** *adj.*

sea·ware (sē′wâr′) *n.* Seaweed that has been cast ashore and is collected for use as fertilizer. [SEA + *ware,* seaweed, Middle English *ware,* Old English *wār.*]

sea·way (sē′wā′) *n.* **1.** A sea route. **2.** An inland waterway for ocean shipping. **3.** A ship's progress through the water; headway. **4.** A rough sea.

sea·weed (sē′wēd′) *n.* **1.** Any of numerous marine algae, such as a kelp, rockweed, or gulfweed. **2.** Any of various other marine plants.

sea wormwood *n.* A wormwood, *Artemisia maritima,* of the Old World, having flowers that yield **santonin** *(see).*

sea·wor·thy (sē′wûr′thē) *adj.* Designating a vessel that is fit to sail or make a sea voyage. —**sea·wor·thi·ness** *n.*

sea wrack *n.* Any material cast ashore, especially seaweed.

se·ba·ceous (sĭ-bā′shəs) *adj. Physiology.* **1.** Of, pertaining to, or resembling fat or sebum; fatty. **2.** Secreting fat or sebum. [Latin *sēbāceus* : *sēbum,* tallow (see **sebum**) + -ACEOUS.]

sebaceous gland *n.* Any of various glands in the dermis of the skin that open into a hair follicle and produce and secrete sebum.

se·bac·ic acid (sĭ-bā′sĭk) *n.* A white crystalline acid, $C_{10}H_{18}O_4$, used in the manufacture of certain synthetic resins and fibers, various plasticizers, and polyester rubbers. Also called "decanedioic acid." [*Sebacic,* from SEBACEOUS (because originally obtained from melted suet).]

Se·bas·tian (sə-băs′chən), **Saint** (3rd century A.D.). Roman martyr. Believed to have been an officer of the Praetorian Guard, he was executed by a squad of archers. Other legends allege that he survived and was beaten to death by Diocletian.

Sebastopol. See **Sevastopol.**

sebi-, sebo- *prefix.* Indicates fat or fatty material; for example, **sebiferous, seborrhoea.** [New Latin, from Latin *sēbum,* tallow. See **sebum.**]

se·bif·er·ous (sĭ-bĭf′ər-əs) *adj.* Producing or secreting fatty, oily, or waxy matter; sebaceous. [SEBI- + -FEROUS.]

seb·or·rhe·a, seb·or·rhoe·a (sĕb′ə-rē′ə) *n.* A disease of the sebaceous glands characterized by excessive secretion of sebum or an alteration in its quality, resulting in an oily coating, crusts, or scales on the skin. [SEBO- + -RRHEA.] —**seb·or·rhe·al, seb·or·rhe·ic** *adj.*

se·bum (sē′bəm) *n.* The oily secretion of the sebaceous glands, which protects the skin from desiccation. Also called "smegma." [Latin *sēbum*†, tallow.]

sec¹ (sĕk) *adj.* **1.** Dry. Said of wines. **2.** Somewhat sweet. Said of champagne. Compare **brut.** [French.]

sec² *n. Informal.* A second or moment: *Just a sec!*

sec³ 1. secant. **2.** second (unit of time). **3.** second (unit of angular measure).

SEC Securities and Exchange Commission.

sec. 1. secondary. **2.** secretary. **3.** sector.

se·cant (sē′kənt, -kănt′) *n. Abbr.* **sec 1.** In geometry: **a.** A straight line intersecting a curve at two or more points. **b.** The straight line drawn from the center through one end of a circular arc and intersecting the tangent to the other end of the arc. **2.** In trigonometry: **a.** The reciprocal of the cosine of an angle. **b.** For an acute angle, the ratio of the hypotenuse to the side of a right-angled triangle adjacent to the acute angle. [French *(ligne) secante,* "cutting line," from Latin *secāns* (stem *secant-*), present participle of *secāre,* to cut.]

sec·co (sĕk′ō) *n., pl.* **-cos.** The art or an example of painting on dry plaster. Compare **fresco.** [Italian, "dry," from Latin *siccus.*]

se·cede (sĭ-sēd′, sē′-) *intr.v.* **-ceded, -ceding, -cedes.** To withdraw formally from membership in an organization, association, or alliance. [Latin *sēcēdere,* to go away : *sē,* apart + *cēdere,* to go.]

se·cern (sĭ-sûrn′) *tr.v.* **-cerned, -cerning, -cerns. 1.** *Rare.* To discern as separate; distinguish. **2.** *Physiology.* To secrete. Used of a gland or follicle. [Latin *sēcernere,* to separate : *sē,* apart + *cernere,* to separate, discern.] —**se·cern·ment** *n.*

se·ces·sion (sĭ-sĕsh′ən) *n.* **1.** The act or an instance of seceding. **2.** *Usually* **Secession.** The withdrawal of 11 Southern states from the Federal Union in 1860–61, precipitating the Civil War. [Latin *sēcessiō* (stem *sēcessiōn-*), from *sēcēdere* (past participle *secessus*), SECEDE.] —**se·ces·sion·al** *adj.*

se·ces·sion·ism (sĭ-sĕsh′ə-nĭz′əm) *n.* The policy of those maintaining the right of secession. —**se·ces·sion·ist** *adj.* & *n.*

sech hyperbolic secant.

se·clude (sĭ-klo͞od′) *tr.v.* **-cluded, -cluding, -cludes. 1.** To remove or set apart from others; place in solitude. **2.** To screen from view; make private. [Middle English *secluden,* to shut off, keep away, from Latin *sēclūdere* : *sē,* apart + *claudere,* to shut.]

se·clud·ed (sĭ-klo͞o′dĭd) *adj.* **1.** Removed or remote from others; solitary. **2.** Screened from view; hidden or private. —**se·clud·ed·ly** *adv.* —**se·clud·ed·ness** *n.*

se·clu·sion (sĭ-klo͞o′zhən) *n.* **1. a.** The act of secluding. **b.** The state of being secluded. **2.** A secluded place or abode. —See Synonyms at **solitude.** [Medieval Latin *sēclūsiō* (stem *sēclusiōn-*), from Latin *sēclūdere* (past participle *sēclūsus*), SECLUDE.]

se·clu·sive (sĭ-klo͞o′sĭv, -zĭv) *adj.* Fond of, seeking, or tending to seclusion. —**se·clu·sive·ly** *adv.* —**se·clu·sive·ness** *n.*

sec·o·bar·bi·tal (sĕk′ō-bär′bĭ-tôl′) *n.* A barbiturate, $C_{12}H_{18}N_2O_3$, that is used as a sedative and hypnotic in the form of its sodium salt. [*Seconal,* a trademark for secobarbital + BARBITAL.]

sec·ond¹ (sĕk′ənd) *n.* **1.** *Abbr.* **s, sec** *Symbol* ″ **a.** A unit of time equal to 1/60 of a minute. **b.** The SI unit of time equal to the duration of 9,192,631,770 periods of the radiation produced by the transition between two hyperfine levels in the ground state of cesium-133. **2.** *Informal.* A brief lapse of time; moment. **3.** *Abbr.* **s, sec** *Symbol* ″ *Geometry.* A unit of angular measure equal to 1/60 of a minute of arc. —See Synonyms at **moment.** [Middle English *seconde,* unit in geometry, from Old French, from Medieval Latin *(pars minūta) secunda,* "second (small part)" (after the second sexagesimal division), from Latin, feminine of *secundus,* SECOND (in number).]

second² *adj.* **1. a.** Coming next after the first in order, place, rank, time, or quality. **b.** Graded or judged to be between the first and third grades or levels. **2. a.** Repeating an initial instance; another: *a second chance.* **b.** Alternate: *every second year.* **c.** Similar to or evoking the memory of a specified person or event from the past: *a second Hitler.* **3.** Inferior to another; subordinate: *second to none.* **4.** *Music.* **a.** Having a lower pitch. **b.** Singing or playing a part having a lower range. **c.** Singing or playing a part subordinate to the principal one. **5.** Designating the next-to-lowest forward gear, as in a motor vehicle or bicycle.

—*n.* **1.** The ordinal number two in a series. **2.** One that is next in order, place, time, or quality after the first. **3.** An article of merchandise that is imperfect in some way. **4.** The official attendant of a contestant in a duel or boxing match. **5.** *Music.* **a.** The interval between consecutive notes on the diatonic scale. **b.** A note separated by this interval from another note. **c.** A combination of two such notes in notation or in harmony. **d.** The second part, instrument, or voice in a harmonized composition. **6.** An utterance of endorsement of a proposal or nomination, as in debating procedure. **7.** The next-to-lowest forward gear, as in a motor vehicle or bicycle, having the second-highest ratio. **8. seconds.** *Informal.* A second helping of food.

—*tr.v.* **seconded, -onding, -onds. 1.** To attend (a duelist, for example) as an aide or assistant. **2.** To promote or encourage; reinforce. **3.** To endorse (a motion or nomination) as a required preliminary to discussion or vote.

—*adv.* **1.** In the second order, place, or rank. **2.** But for one other; save one. Sometimes used in combination: *the second-highest peak.* [Middle English, from Old French, from Latin *secundus,* following, coming next.]

se·cond³ (sĭ-kŏnd′, sĕk′ənd) *tr.v.* **-conded, -conding, -conds.** *British.* **1.** To transfer (an employee) temporarily to another department, branch, or task. **2.** *Military.* To remove (an officer) from service with a view to transferral to another post, such as a staff or nonregimental post. [French *en second,* in second rank (or position).]

Second Advent *n.* The **Second Coming** *(see).*

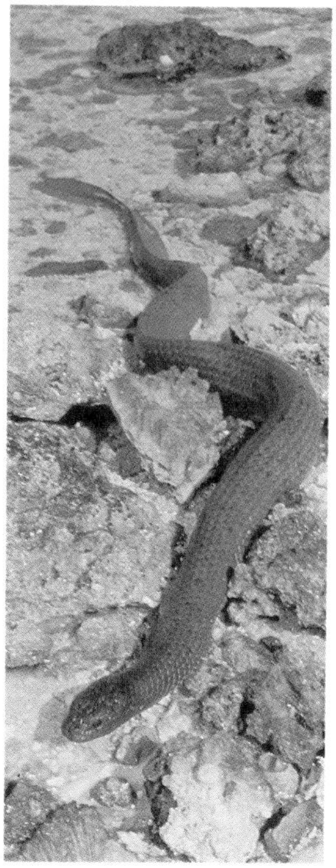

sea snake *The powerful venom of this tropical marine reptile is used to stun or paralyze the fish on which it feeds.*

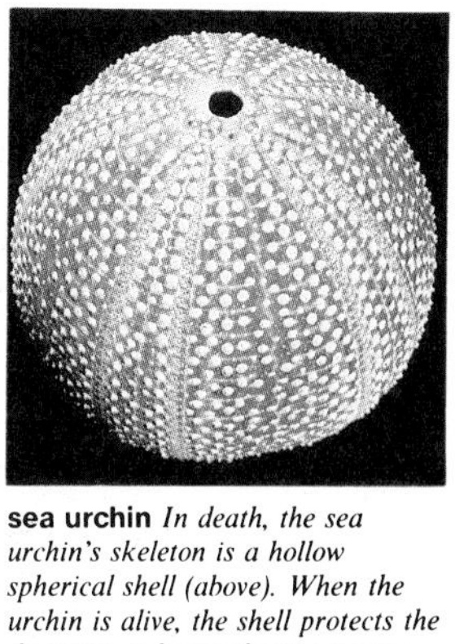

sea urchin *In death, the sea urchin's skeleton is a hollow spherical shell (above). When the urchin is alive, the shell protects the digestive and reproductive organs, and the outside is covered with spines and with five bands of tubular feet. When the animal dies, the spines and feet drop off, leaving a pattern of white scars. Sea urchins, some species of which are edible, are found worldwide.*

sec·on·dar·y (sĕk′ən-dĕr′ē) *adj. Abbr.* **sec. 1. a.** One step removed from the first; of the second rank; not primary. **b.** Inferior; lesser. **2.** Derived from what is primary or original: *a secondary source.* **3.** Of, pertaining to, or designating the shorter flight feathers projecting along the inner part of the edge of a bird's wing. **4.** *Electricity.* Having an induced current that is generated by an inductively coupled primary. Said of a circuit or coil. **5.** *Chemistry.* **a.** Designating a compound in which two hydrogen atoms have been replaced by a metal, radical, or alkyl group. **b.** Designating an organic compound having a functional group attached to a carbon that is attached to one hydrogen and two other groups. **6.** *Geology.* Resulting from changes in the pre-existing minerals. **7.** Of, pertaining to, or designating education received at secondary school. **8.** Designating an industry that uses the raw materials gathered by a primary industry and processes or manufactures products from them. **9.** *Linguistics.* Having been derived from a word that was itself derived from another word, such as *hauntingly,* from *haunting,* from *haunt.* **10.** *Botany.* Designating plant growth of a type caused by activity of the cambium and resulting in an increase in the width of stems and branches.
~*n., pl.* **secondaries. 1.** One that acts in an auxiliary, subordinate, or inferior capacity. **2.** Any of the shorter flight feathers projecting along the inner part of the edge of a bird's wing. **3.** *Electricity.* A coil or circuit having an induced current. **4.** *Astronomy.* A body that orbits a primary; a satellite. **5.** A secondary color. [Middle English, from Latin *secundārius,* from *secundus,* SECOND.] —**sec·on·dar·i·ly** *adv.* —**sec·on·dar·i·ness** *n.*

secondary battery *n. Electricity.* A **storage battery** (*see*).

secondary cell *n.* A rechargeable electric cell that converts chemical energy into electrical energy by a reversible chemical reaction. Also called "storage cell." Compare **primary cell.**

secondary color *n.* A color produced by mixing two primary colors in approximately equal proportions.

secondary depression *n.* A small, concentrated area of low atmospheric pressure on the margin of a main depression.

secondary electron *n.* An electron produced in secondary emission.

secondary emission *n. Physics.* The emission of electrons from the surface of a substance bombarded by electrons or ions.

secondary school *n.* Any school providing education for young people, usually between the ages of 11 and 18, after primary school but preceding college or an occupation.

secondary sex characteristic *n.* Any of various anatomical, physiological, or behavioral characteristics, such as voice quality, abundance of facial hair, or breast development, that first appear in humans at puberty and differentiate between the sexes without having a direct reproductive function. Also called "secondary sexual characteristic."

secondary stress *n.* A stress weaker than a primary stress, but stronger than a tertiary or weak stress. Also called "secondary accent." Compare **primary stress, tertiary stress.**

second base *n. Baseball.* **1.** The base across the diamond from home plate, to be touched second by a runner. **2.** The position played by a second baseman.

second baseman *n. Baseball.* The infielder who is positioned near and usually to the first-base side of second base.

second best *n.* One that is slightly or just below the best, as in quality, value, or importance.

sec·ond-best (sĕk′ənd-bĕst′) *adj.* Next to the best.

second childhood *n.* Senility; dotage.

second class *n.* **1.** The group or class that is next below the first or highest, as in quality, rank, or value. **2.** The class on a train or other means of transport ranking next below first class.

sec·ond-class (sĕk′ənd-klăs′, -kläs′) *adj.* **1. a.** In the rank or class that is next below the first or best. **b.** Inferior; second-rate. **c.** Socially, economically, or politically disadvantaged: *a second-class citizen.* **2.** Of, pertaining to, or designating travel accommodations ranking below the highest or first class. **3.** Of, pertaining to, or designating a class of U.S. and Canadian mail consisting of newspapers and periodicals. —**second-class** *adv.*

Second Coming *n.* The return of Christ as judge upon the last day. Also called "Second Advent," "parousia."

second cousin *n.* See **cousin.**

sec·ond-de·gree burn (sĕk′ənd-də-grē′) *n.* A burn that damages underlying skin tissue. Not in current technical usage.

Second Empire *n.* **1.** The French empire and government of Napoleon III. **2.** The period of Napoleon III's reign (1852–70).
~*adj.* Of, resembling, or pertaining to the ornate style of furniture and architecture developed in the Second Empire.

second estate *n. Often* **Second Estate.** The aristocracy, especially as distinguished from other classes. See **first estate, third estate, fourth estate.**

second fiddle *n.* **1.** A secondary role. **2.** One who plays a secondary role.

sec·ond-gen·er·a·tion (sĕk′ənd-jĕn′ə-rā′shən) *adj.* Pertaining or belonging to a generation whose grandparents were original immigrants: *second-generation Americans.*

second growth *n.* Trees that cover an area after the removal of the original forest growth as by cutting or fire.

sec·ond-guess (sĕk′ənd-gĕs′) *v.* **-guessed, -guessing, -guesses.** —*tr.* **1.** To criticize (a decision) after the outcome is known. **2.** To anticipate the moves of; outwit. —*intr.* To criticize a decision in retrospect. —**sec·ond-guess·er** *n.*

second hand[1] *n.* The hand of a timepiece that marks the seconds.

second hand[2] *n.* An intermediary person or source. Usually preceded by *at: heard at second hand.*

sec·ond-hand, sec·ond-hand (sĕk′ənd-hănd′) *adj.* **1.** Previously used or owned by another; not new. **2.** Dealing in previously used goods. **3.** Obtained or derived from another; not original. —**second-hand, second-hand** *adv.*

sec·ond-in-com·mand (sĕk′ənd-ĭn-kə-mănd′) *n., pl.* **seconds-in-command.** The person next in authority to someone in charge; especially, a military officer ranking second to a commanding officer.

second lieutenant *n.* An officer in the U.S. Army, Air Force, or Marine Corps of the lowest commissioned grade, ranking below a first lieutenant.

sec·ond·ly (sĕk′ənd-lē) *adv.* In the second place; second. Used chiefly to introduce a second enumerated point.

second mate *n.* The officer on a merchant ship ranking below the first mate. Also called "second officer."

second mortgage *n.* A mortgage on property that is already mortgaged and that has a claim secondary to the first mortgage.

second nature *n.* An acquired personal disposition, tendency, or habit so long practiced as to seem innate.

se·con·do (sā-kôn′dō) *n., pl.* **-di** (-dē). *Music.* **1.** The second part in a concert piece; especially, the lower part in a piano duet. **2.** One who performs such a part. [Italian, "second," from Latin *secundus,* SECOND (next).]

second person *n. Grammar.* The form of a pronoun, verb, or verb inflection used in referring to the person or persons addressed; for example, *you* and *shall* in *you shall not enter.*

sec·ond-rate (sĕk′ənd-rāt′) *adj.* Not of the best quality; mediocre; inferior. —**sec·ond-rat·er** *n.*

second reading *n.* The intermediate stage in the enactment of a law in a legislative body, especially: **1.** In the United States, the debate and vote on a bill, sometimes with amendments, after a committee has reported on it. **2.** In Britain, the debate and vote on a bill's general features.

Second Republic *n.* **1.** The French republic and government from 1848 to 1852. **2.** The period of this republic's existence.

second sight *n.* The ability to perceive future or remote events or things; clairvoyance.

sec·ond-sto·ry man (sĕk′ənd-stôr′ē, -stōr′ē) *n.* A burglar adept at entering through upstairs windows.

sec·ond-strike (sĕk′ənd-strīk′) *adj.* Designating, based on, or employing nuclear weapons capable of retaliating after an initial enemy attack: *a second-strike force; second-strike capability.*

sec·ond-string (sĕk′ənd-strĭng′) *adj.* **1.** Designating or pertaining to a reserve player or team. **2.** Second-rate; inferior.

second thought *n. Usually* **second thoughts.** A revised opinion on a matter, especially when it has previously been considered too quickly.

second wind *n.* Renewed energy or ability to function, as after fatigue or breathlessness through exertion.

Second World *n..* The countries of the Soviet bloc, especially as an economic and political group. See **First World.**

Second World War. See **World War II.**

se·cre·cy (sē′krə-sē) *n.* **1.** The fact or condition of being secret or hidden. **2.** The ability to keep secrets. **3.** A tendency to be secretive or to conceal things. [Middle English, variant of *secretee,* from *secre(t),* SECRET.]

se·cret (sē′krĭt) *adj.* **1.** Kept from general knowledge or view; kept hidden. **2.** Tending not to disclose information; discreet. **3.** Operating in a clandestine or confidential manner. **4.** Not visibly expressed or acknowledged. **5.** Not frequented; secluded. **6.** Known or shared only by the initiated: *secret rites.* **7.** Beyond ordinary understanding; mysterious. **8.** Of, pertaining to, or containing information whose secrecy is important to national security.
~*n.* **1.** Something kept hidden from others or known only to oneself or to a few. **2.** Something that remains beyond understanding or explanation; a mystery. **3.** A factor or element needed to achieve a particular end or state: *the secret of her success.* **4.** *Secret.* A variable prayer said after the Offertory and before the Preface in the liturgy of the Mass. —**in secret.** In a manner or place not known to others; in secrecy. [Middle English *secre(t),* from Old French, from Latin *sēcrētus,* separate, out of the way, secret, from the past participle of *sēcernere,* to put apart, separate : *sē,* apart + *cernere,* to separate.] —**se·cret·ly** *adv.*
Synonyms: clandestine, covert, furtive, stealthy, surreptitious, underhand.

secret agent *n.* A spy.

se·cret·a·gogue (sə-krē′tə-gôg′, -gŏg′) *n. Physiology.* An agent that stimulates glandular secretion. [SECRET(E) + -AGOGUE.]

sec·re·tar·i·at (sĕk′rə-târ′ē-ĭt) *n.* **1. a.** A department of an international or public organization that administers and executes the organization's decisions and programs under the direction of a secretary-general or secretary. **b.** The premises or staff of such a department. **2.** The office of secretary. **3.** A group of secretaries in a company or other organization.

sec·re·tar·y (sĕk′rə-tĕr′ē) *n., pl.* **-ies.** *Abbr.* **sec., secy. 1. a.** A person employed to handle correspondence, keep files, and do clerical work for an individual or company. **b.** An officer who keeps records of meetings and legal transactions and is responsible for the day-to-day business of a club, society, or similar organization. **2.** *Often* **Secretary.** An official presiding over an administrative department of state. **3.** A diplomatic officer assisting an ambassador or minister. **4.** A desk with a small bookcase on top. [Middle English *secretarie,* from Medieval Latin *sēcrētārius,* confidential officer, secretary, from Latin *sēcrētus,* SECRET.] **—sec·re·tar·i·al** *adj.*

secretary bird *n.* A large southern African bird of prey, *Sagittarius serpentarius.* [The quills on its crest resemble quill pens.]

sec·re·tar·y-gen·er·al (sĕk′rə-tĕr′ē-jĕn′ər-əl) *n., pl.* **secretaries-general.** *Sometimes* **Secretary-General.** A principal administrative officer, as in certain political parties or international bodies: *the secretary-general of NATO.*

secretary of state *n., pl.* **secretaries of state.** *Often* **Secretary of State. 1.** The foreign minister of the United States. **2.** A British minister who heads any of several government departments.

se·crete¹ (sĭ-krēt′) *tr.v.* **-creted, -creting, -cretes.** To generate and separate out (a substance) from cells or bodily fluids. [Back-formation from SECRETION.] **—se·cre·tor** *n.*

secrete² *tr.v.* **-creted, -creting, -cretes. 1.** To conceal. **2.** To appropriate (money, for example) secretly. —See Synonyms at **hide.** [From obsolete *secret,* to conceal, keep secret, from SECRET.]

se·cre·tin (sĭ-krē′tĭn) *n.* A hormone secreted in the duodenum to stimulate the flow of pancreatic juice. [SECRET(ION) + -IN.]

se·cre·tion (sĭ-krē′shən) *n.* **1.** The process of secreting a substance, especially one that is not a waste, from blood or cells. **2.** A substance so secreted. [Latin *sēcrētiō* (stem *sēcrētiōn-*), separation, from *sēcernere,* to separate. See **secret.**]

se·cre·tive (sē′krə-tĭv, sĭ-krē′tĭv) *adj.* **1.** Tending not to disclose information; uncommunicative. **2.** Secretory. **—se·cre·tive·ly** *adv.* **—se·cre·tive·ness** *n.*

se·cre·tor (sĭ-krē′tər) *n.* A person in whose saliva and other body fluids the A or B antigens determining blood group can be detected.

se·cre·to·ry (sĭ-krē′tə-rē) *adj.* Pertaining to or performing the function of secretion.

secret police *n.* A police force, operating largely in secrecy and often with illegal methods, serving to control dissidents and ensure the security of the state.

secret service *n.* **1.** A government agency pursuing intelligence and counterintelligence activities. **2.** The activities of such an agency. **3. Secret Service.** The branch of the U.S. Treasury Department concerned with the protection of the president, other leading public figures, and their families, and with the suppression of counterfeiting. In this sense, preceded by *the.*

sect (sĕkt) *n.* **1.** A group of people forming a distinct unit within a larger group by virtue of certain refinements or distinctions of belief or practice. **2. a.** A breakaway religious body; especially, one regarded as extreme, intolerant, or exclusive by the larger group from which it has separated. **b.** Any religious denomination, especially one regarded as exclusive or outlandish. **3.** Any small faction united by common interests or beliefs: *a Maoist sect.* [Middle English *secte,* from Old French, from Latin *secta,* "following," from *sectus,* archaic past participle of *sequī,* to follow.]

sect. sector.

-sect *suffix.* **1.** Indicates cut or divide; for example, **trisect, bisect. 2.** Indicates cut or divided; for example, **pinnatisect.** [Latin *sectus,* past participle of *secāre,* to cut.]

sec·tar·i·an (sĕk-târ′ē-ən) *adj.* **1.** Pertaining to, characteristic of, or involving a sect or faction or its members. **2.** Adhering or confined to the dogmatic views of a sect.
∼n. **1.** A member of a sect. **2.** One characterized by bigoted adherence to a factional viewpoint. **—sec·tar·i·an·ism** *n.* **—sec·tar·i·an·ize** *v.*

sec·ta·ry (sĕk′tə-rē) *n., pl.* **-ries. 1.** A sectarian. **2.** A dissenter from an established church; specifically, a Protestant nonconformist in the 17th and 18th centuries. [Medieval Latin *sectārius,* from Latin *secta,* SECT.]

sec·tile (sĕk′tĭl, -tīl′) *adj.* Capable of being cut or severed smoothly by a knife. [Latin *sectilis,* from *secāre,* to cut.] **—sec·til·i·ty** (sĕk-tĭl′ə-tē) *n.*

sec·tion (sĕk′shən) *n.* **1. a.** Any of several component or constituent parts or groups; a portion. **b.** A part separated from a main body by or as if by cutting. **2.** Any division or grouping within an organized whole: *the accounts section.* **3.** A subdivision of a written work. **4.** A division of a statute or legal code. **5.** A grouping in an orchestra or band, consisting of members who play the same type of instrument. **6.** In printing, a **signature** *(see).* **7.** The act or process of separating or cutting; especially, the surgical separation of tissue. **8.** A thin slice, as of tissue, suitable for microscopic examination. **9.** A segment of a fruit, especially a citrus fruit. **10.** The representation of a solid object as it would appear if cut by an intersecting plane, so that the internal structure is displayed. **11.** In geometry, the planar configuration formed by the intersection of a solid by a plane. Also called "plane section." **12.** A district or area with some particular characteristic. **13.** A land unit of one square mile. **14. a.** A portion of a railroad track maintained by a single crew. **b.** An area in a sleeping car containing an upper and lower berth. **15.** *Military.* **a.** An army tactical unit smaller than a platoon and larger than a squad. **b.** A unit of vessels or aircraft within a division. **16. a.** A character (§) used in printing to mark the beginning of a section. **b.** This character used as the fourth in a series of reference marks for footnotes. In both senses, also called "section mark." **—in section.** In the view revealed by taking a section.
∼tr.v. **sectioned, -tioning, -tions. 1.** To separate or divide into parts. **2.** To separate (tissue) surgically. **3.** To cut so as to reveal a section. [French, from Latin *sectiō* (stem *sectiōn-*), a cutting, from *sect-,* past participial stem of *secāre,* to cut.]

-section *suffix.* Indicates the act or process of dividing or cutting; for example, **vivisection.** [From SECTION.]

sec·tion·al (sĕk′shən-əl) *adj.* **1.** Pertaining to or characteristic of a particular section: *sectional prejudice in society.* **2.** Composed of or divided into component sections.
∼n. A piece of furniture made up of sections that can be used separately or together. **—sec·tion·al·ly** *adv.*

sec·tion·al·ism (sĕk′shən-ə-lĭz′əm) *n.* Excessive devotion to sectional interests. **—sec·tion·al·ist** *n. & adj.*

sec·tion·al·ize (sĕk′shən-ə-līz′) *tr.v.* **-ized, -izing, -izes. 1.** To divide into sections, especially into geographical sections. **2.** To make sectional in nature or outlook. **—sec·tion·al·i·za·tion** *n.*

sec·tor (sĕk′tər, -tôr′) *n. Abbr.* **sec., sect. 1.** In geometry, the portion of a circle bounded by two radii and one of the intercepted arcs. **2.** A measuring instrument consisting of two graduated arms hinged together at one end. **3.** *Military.* **a.** A division of a defensive position for which one unit is responsible. **b.** A division of an offensive position; a zone of action. **4.** A part or division of something, such as a specialized field of activity or interest: *the public sector of the economy.*
∼tr.v. **sectored, -toring, -tors.** To divide into sectors. [Late Latin, from Latin, cutter, from *secāre,* to cut.] **—sec·tor·al, sec·tor·i·al** (sĕk-tôr′ē-əl, -tōr′ē-əl) *adj.*

sec·u·lar (sĕk′yə-lər) *adj.* **1.** Of or pertaining to temporal rather than to spiritual matters; worldly. **2.** Not pertaining to or concerned with religion or a religious body: *secular schools.* **3.** Advocating or characterized by secularism: *a secular outlook.* **4.** Not following monastic vows or living in a religious community. Said of the clergy. Compare **regular. 5.** Occurring or observed once in an age or century. **6.** Lasting for centuries.
∼n. **1.** A secular clergyman. **2.** A layman. [Middle English *seculer,* from Old French, from Latin *saeculāris,* from *saeculum*†, generation, age.] **—sec·u·lar·ly** *adv.*

sec·u·lar·ism (sĕk′yə-lə-rĭz′əm) *n.* **1.** Religious skepticism or indifference. **2.** The view that religious considerations should be excluded from civil affairs or public education. **—sec·u·lar·ist** *n.* **—sec·u·lar·is·tic** *adj.*

sec·u·lar·i·ty (sĕk′yə-lăr′ə-tē) *n., pl.* **-ties. 1.** The condition or quality of being secular. **2.** Something secular.

sec·u·lar·ize (sĕk′yə-lə-rīz′) *tr.v.* **-ized, -izing, -izes. 1.** To transfer from ecclesiastical or religious to civil or lay use or ownership. **2.** To draw away from religious influences or orientation; make worldly. **3.** To lift the monastic rules from (a cleric); make secular. **—sec·u·lar·i·za·tion** *n.* **—sec·u·lar·iz·er** *n.*

secular parallax *n. Astronomy.* The continuously increasing angular displacement in the position of stars resulting from the motion of the sun through space. See **parallax.**

se·cund (sē′kŭnd′, sĭ-kŭnd′) *adj. Botany.* Arranged on or turned to one side of an axis. [Latin *secundus,* following, second.]

sec·un·dines (sĕk′ən-dīnz′, sĭ-kŭn′dīnz) *pl.n. Physiology.* The **afterbirth** *(see).* [Late Latin *secundīnae,* from Latin *secundus,* second, following. See **secund.**]

se·cure (sĭ-kyo͝or′) *adj.* **-curer, -curest. 1.** Free from danger or risk of loss or escape; safe. **2.** Free from fear or doubt; not anxious or unsure. **3. a.** Not likely to fail or give way; stable; strong. **b.** Well-fastened. **4.** Assured; certain; guaranteed. **5.** *Archaic.* Careless or overconfident.
∼v. **secured, -curing, -cures.** *—tr.* **1.** To guard from danger or risk of loss; specifically, to fortify or consolidate (a military position). **2.** To make firm or tight; fasten. **3.** To make certain; guarantee; ensure. **4. a.** To guarantee payment to (a creditor). **b.** To guarantee payment of (a loan, for example) with a pledge. **5.** To confine or lock up. **6.** To get possession of; acquire; procure. **7.** To bring about; effect. *—intr.* To become or make oneself safe. Used with *against.* [Latin *sēcūrus,* "without care" : *sē,* without + *cūra,* care.] **—se·cur·a·ble** *adj.* **—se·cure·ly** *adv.* **—se·cure·ment** *n.* **—se·cure·ness** *n.* **—se·cur·er** *n.*

Securities and Exchange Commission *n. Abbr.* **SEC** A U.S. governmental agency that supervises the issue and exchange of securities so as to protect investors against malpractice.

se·cu·ri·ty (sĭ-kyo͝or′ə-tē) *n., pl.* **-ties. 1.** The state of being secure; especially: **a.** Freedom from risk or danger. **b.** Freedom from doubt, anxiety, or fear. **2.** Anything that gives or assures safety. **3.** Something deposited or given as assurance of the fulfillment of an obligation; pledge. **4.** One who undertakes to guarantee the obligation of another; surety. **5. a.** A document that guarantees the right of the holder to repayment, as of a debt or claim. **b. securities.** Broadly, investments in the form of stocks, shares, and bonds. **6. a.** Measures adopted to thwart theft, espionage, escape, or attack. **b.** An organization or department entrusted with such operations. [Middle English *securite,* from Latin *sēcūritās* (stem *sēcūritāt-*), from *sēcūrus,* SECURE.]

security blanket *n.* **1.** A blanket or other familiar object carried about by a child to give a feeling of security. **2.** Something that dispels anxiety.

security clearance *n.* **1.** The investigation of persons or groups to ensure that they are not a security risk, before allowing them access to confidential information or to people or places requiring protection. **2.** The permission or clearance subsequently granted.

Security Council *n.* The permanent peace-keeping organ of the

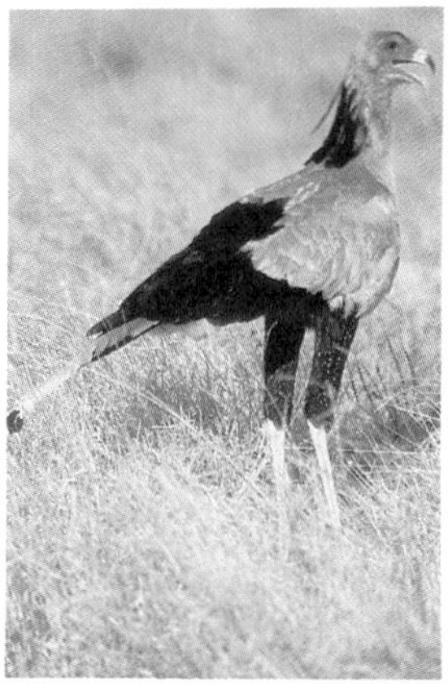

secretary bird *Snakes, mice, and lizards are the main prey of the secretary bird, which hunts on foot in the African savanna. The bird was named because of the quills on its crest—like the quill pens 18th-century male secretaries pushed into the backs of their wigs.*

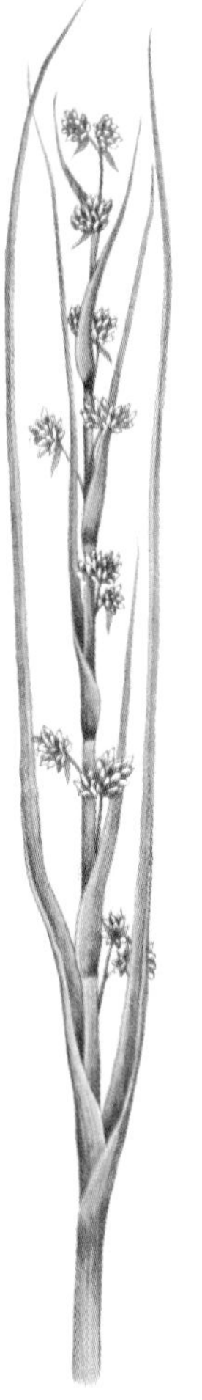

sedge *Related to the grass family, sedge is a rushlike plant with a solid and usually three-sided stem. It grows in bogs and marshes.*

United Nations, composed of 5 permanent members and 10 elected members.
security risk *n.* **1.** A government servant or candidate for government service thought to be a danger to national security because of dissident political beliefs, liability to blackmail, or unreliability of character. **2.** Any person thought likely to be disloyal.
secy. secretary.
se·dan (sĭ-dăn′) *n.* **1.** A sedan chair. **2.** A closed automobile having two or four doors and a front and rear seat. [Perhaps obscurely from Vulgar Latin *sedda* (unattested), variant of Latin *sella,* seat, chair.]
sedan chair *n.* A portable enclosed chair for one person, fashionable in Britain in the 17th and 18th centuries, having poles front and rear and carried by two men. Also called "sedan."
se·date¹ (sĭ-dāt′) *adj.* Serenely deliberate in character or manner; composed; collected. —See Synonyms at **serious.** [Latin *sēdātus,* past participle of *sēdāre,* to settle, calm, compose, from *sedēre,* to sit.] **—se·date·ly** *adv.* **—se·date·ness** *n.*
sedate² *tr.v.* **-dated, -dating, -dates.** To administer a sedative to (a patient). [Back-formation from SEDATIVE.]
se·da·tion (sĭ-dā′shən) *n.* **1.** The reduction of stress or excitement by administration of a sedative. **2.** The calm relaxed condition induced by a sedative.
sed·a·tive (sĕd′ə-tĭv) *adj.* Having a soothing, calming, or tranquilizing effect.
~n. A sedative agent or drug. [Middle English, from Medieval Latin *sēdātīvus,* from *sedāre,* to calm, settle; see **sedate** (adjective).]
sed·en·tar·y (sĕd′n-tĕr′ē) *adj.* **1.** Characterized by or requiring much sitting: *a sedentary job.* **2.** Accustomed to sitting or to taking little exercise. **3.** Remaining in one area; not migratory: *sedentary birds.* **4.** Seated or in a sitting posture: *a sedentary statue.* **5.** *Zoology.* Attached to a surface and not free-moving. Said of a barnacle, for example. [French *sédentaire,* from Latin *sedentārius,* from *sedēns* (stem *sedent-*), present participle of *sedēre,* to sit.] **—sed·en·tar·i·ly** *adv.* **—sed·en·tar·i·ness** *n.*
Se·der (sā′dər) *n., pl.* **-ders** or **Sedarim** (sĭ-där′ĭm). *Sometimes* **seder.** *Judaism.* The feast commemorating the exodus of the Israelites from Egypt, celebrated on the first evening or first two evenings of Passover. [Hebrew *sēdher,* "order," "arrangement."]
se·de·runt (sə-dîr′ənt, -dĕr′-) *n. Scottish.* **1.** A session or sitting, especially of an ecclesiastical assembly. **2.** The people present at such a session. **3.** Any session of talking or drinking. [Latin, "they (the persons named below) sat," from *sedēre,* to sit.]
sedge (sĕj) *n.* Any of numerous plants of the family Cyperaceae, especially of the genus *Carex,* resembling grasses but having solid rather than hollow stems and often found near water. [Middle English *segge,* Old English *secg,* from Germanic.] **—sedg·y** *adj.*
sedge warbler *n.* A small bird, *Acrocephalus schoenobaenus,* commonly found near water, having a brown streaked plumage.
se·di·li·a (sə-dē′lē-ə) *pl.n. Singular* **sedile** (-lē). *Usually used with a plural verb.* The seats or set of seats, generally three, in the sanctuary of a church for the use of the celebrant and his ministers. [Latin *sedīlia,* plural of *sedīle,* seat, from *sedēre,* to sit.]
sed·i·ment (sĕd′ə-mənt) *n.* **1.** Material that settles to the bottom of a liquid; dregs; lees. **2.** Material comprising weathered particles of pre-existing rock, or particles of chemical or organic origin, deposited by wind, water, or glacial ice. [French, from Latin *sedimentum,* a settling, from *sedēre,* to sit, settle.]
sed·i·men·ta·ry (sĕd′ə-mĕn′tə-rē, -mĕn′trē) *adj.* **1.** Of, containing, resembling, or derived from sediment. **2.** *Geology.* Of, designating, or pertaining to rocks formed from sediment.
sed·i·men·ta·tion (sĕd′ə-mən-tā′shən, sĕd′ə-mĕn-) *n.* The act or process of depositing sediment; especially, the process of forming sedimentary rocks.
sed·i·men·tol·o·gy (sĕd′ə-mən-tŏl′ə-jē, sĕd′ə-mĕn′-) *n.* The study of the classification and origin of sedimentary rocks and associated geological deposits. [SEDIMENT + -LOGY.] **—sed·i·men·to·log·i·cal** (sĕd′ə-mən′tə-lŏj′ĭ-kəl, -mĕn′-) *adj.* **—sed·i·men·tol·o·gist** *n.*
se·di·tion (sĭ-dĭsh′ən) *n.* **1.** Conduct or language inciting to rebellion against the authority of the state. **2.** *Archaic.* An insurrection; rebellion. [Middle English *sedicioun,* from Old French *sedition,* from Latin *sēditiō* (stem *sēditiōn-*), "a going apart," separation : *sē, sēd,* apart + *itiō,* act of going, from *īre* (past participle *itus*), to go.]
se·di·tious (sĭ-dĭsh′əs) *adj.* **1.** Of, resembling, or characterized by sedition. **2.** Engaged in or inclined to sedition. —See Usage note at **insubordinate.** **—se·di·tious·ly** *adv.* **—se·di·tious·ness** *n.*
se·duce (sĭ-do͞os′, -dyo͞os′) *tr.v.* **-duced, -ducing, -duces.** **1. a.** To lead (a person) away from duty or proper conduct. **b.** Broadly, to entice into wrongful behavior; corrupt. **2.** To induce to have sexual intercourse with one. **3. a.** To persuade or beguile. Often used with *into.* **b.** To win over; attract. —See Synonyms at **lure.** [Middle English *seduisen,* from Old French *seduire* (present stem *seduis-*), from Latin *sēdūcere,* to lead away : *sē,* apart + *dūcere,* to lead.] **—se·duce·a·ble, se·duc·i·ble** *adj.* **—se·duc·er** *n.*
se·duc·tion (sĭ-dŭk′shən) *n.* Also *archaic* **se·duce·ment** (sĭ-do͞os′mənt, sĭ-dyo͞os′-). **1.** The act of seducing or the condition of being seduced. **2.** Something that seduces or has the qualities to seduce to wrongdoing; temptation. **3.** *Often* **seductions.** Something that attracts; an enticement. [French *séduction,* from Latin *sēductiō* (stem *sēductiōn-*), from *sēdūcere* (past participle *sēductus),* SEDUCE.]
se·duc·tive (sĭ-dŭk′tĭv) *adj.* Tending to seduce; alluring; beguiling. **—se·duc·tive·ly** *adv.* **—se·duc·tive·ness** *n.*
se·duc·tress (sĭ-dŭk′trĭs) *n.* A woman who seduces.
sed·u·lous (sĕj′o͞o-ləs) *adj.* **1.** Diligent; assiduous. **2.** Deliberate and industrious; painstaking: *sedulous flattery.* —See Usage note at **busy.** [Latin *sēdulus,* diligent, zealous, from *sē dolō,* "without guile," hence with zeal : *sē,* without + *dolus,* guile.] **—se·du·li·ty** (sĭ-do͞o′lə-tē, sĭ-dyo͞o′-), **sed·u·lous·ness** *n.* **—sed·u·lous·ly** *adv.*
se·dum (sē′dəm) *n.* Any of numerous rock plants of the genus *Sedum,* having thick, fleshy leaves and clusters of starlike flowers. See **orpine, stonecrop.** [Latin *sedum*†, houseleek.]
see¹ (sē) *v.* **saw** (sô), **seen** (sēn), **seeing, sees.** *—tr.* **1.** To perceive with the eye. **2.** To realize or come to know by seeing: *saw that the driver was in difficulties.* **3.** To have a mental image of; visualize. **4.** To understand; comprehend. **5.** To regard in a particular way; view: *sees things differently now.* **6. a.** To imagine; believe possible: *I don't see him as a teacher.* **b.** To consider as likely: *I can see her getting angry when she finds out.* **7.** To foresee. **8.** To know through first-hand experience; undergo: *He saw some service in North Africa.* **9.** To be characterized by, be the occasion of, or bring forth: *Her long reign saw the heyday of colonialism.* **10.** To find out; ascertain: *See if he's ready.* **11.** *Abbr.* **s.** To refer to; read: *See page xi of the Introduction.* **12.** To discern; recognize: *saw the snags right away.* **13. a.** To meet socially, especially often or regularly. **b.** To visit socially or for consultation: *see a doctor.* **c.** To receive, as for consultation. **14.** To find attractive: *What do you see in him?* **15.** To watch or view as a spectator or tourist: *seeing the sights of London.* **16.** To escort; attend: *saw them home.* **17.** To make sure; take care: *See that it gets done right away.* **18.** To learn, as by reading or hearing on the radio: *I see that the airline strike has been called off.* **19.** In card games: **a.** To match (a bet). **b.** To match the bet of (another player). *—intr.* **1. a.** To have the power to see objects. **b.** To exercise that power. **c.** To perceive things with any of the senses, as if by the power of sight: *see with one's fingers.* **2.** To understand; comprehend. **3.** To consider; think a matter over: *Let's see, which should we take?* **4.** To have foresight: *We can see only to the end of the year.* **—see about. 1.** To attend to. **2.** To investigate. **—see here.** Used to demand a more reasonable attitude. **—see off.** To be present to wish good-by to (a person leaving on a journey). **—see through.** To understand the true character or nature of. **—see to.** To attend to. **—see you.** *Informal.* Used as a farewell. [See, saw, seen; Middle English *se(e)n, sauh, seyen,* Old English *sēon, seah* (plural *sāwon*), *gesewen.*]
Synonyms: *behold, contemplate, descry, discern, espy, note, notice, observe, perceive, remark, scan, survey, view.*
see² *n.* **1.** The official seat, center of authority, jurisdiction, or office of a bishop. **2.** A diocese. [Middle English, from Norman French *se, sed,* from Vulgar Latin *sedem* (unattested), from Latin *sēdem,* accusative of *sēdes,* "seat," "residence."]
See·beck effect (sē′bĕk′, zā′-) *n.* The production of an electric current in a circuit consisting of two wires of different metals joined at their ends, when the junctions so formed are maintained at different temperatures. Compare **Peltier effect.** [After Thomas *Seebeck* (1770–1831), German physicist.]
seed (sēd) *n.* **1.** A fertilized and ripened plant ovule containing an embryo and its food source. **2.** The hard, seedlike fruit of certain plants, such as grasses. **3.** Broadly, any propagative part of a plant, such as a tuber or spore. **4.** Seeds collectively. **5.** Anything resembling a seed in size or shape. **6.** A source or beginning; germ. **7.** *Formal.* Offspring; progeny. **8.** *Archaic.* Sperm; semen. **9.** A **seed oyster** *(see).* **10.** A small crystal added to a supersaturated solution or a supercooled liquid to cause crystallization. **11.** *Sports.* A seeded player. **—go** (or **run**) **to seed. 1.** To pass into the seed-bearing stage. **2.** To become weak or devitalized; deteriorate. **—in seed.** Bearing seeds. Said of a plant.
~v. **seeded, seeding, seeds.** *—tr.* **1.** To plant seeds in (land); sow. **2.** To plant in soil. **3.** To remove the seeds from (fruit). **4. a.** To add a small crystal to (a supersaturated solution or a supercooled liquid) to cause crystallization. **b.** To sprinkle (a supercooled cloud) with particles, as of silver iodide, in order to produce rain by condensation and precipitation. **5.** *Sports.* **a.** To arrange (the drawing for positions in a tournament) so that the more skilled contestants meet only in the later rounds. **b.** To rank (a contestant) in this way. *—intr.* **1.** To sow seed. **2.** To produce or shed seed. [Middle English *seed, seid,* Old English *sǣd.*] **—seed·less** *adj.* **—seed·like** *adj.*
seed bank *n.* A place for storing plant seeds at low temperatures.
seed·bed (sēd′bĕd′) *n.* **1.** A piece of land prepared for seeding. **2.** A place favorable to the development of something.
seed cake *n.* A sweet cake containing aromatic seeds, usually caraway seeds.
seed capsule *n.* The part of a fruit surrounding the seeds; the pericarp. Also called "seed case."
seed coat *n.* The outer protective covering of a seed; the testa.
seed corn *n.* Cereal grain that is kept or sold for sowing.
seed·er (sē′dər) *n.* **1.** A machine or implement used for planting seeds. **2.** A machine used to remove the seeds from fruit.
seed fern *n.* Any seed-bearing fernlike plant of the extinct group Pteridospermae. Also called "pteridosperm."
seed leaf *n. Botany.* See **cotyledon** (sense 1).
seed·ling (sēd′lĭng) *n.* A young plant that develops by germination of a seed.
seed money *n.* Money needed or provided to start a new project.
seed oyster *n.* A young oyster; especially, one suitable for transplanting to another bed. Also called "seed."
seed pearl *n.* A very small, often imperfect, pearl.

seed plant *n.* A seed-bearing plant; a spermatophyte.
seed·pod (sēd′pŏd) *n.* See **pod** (fruit).
seed potato *n.* A small potato tuber used for planting.
seeds·man (sēdz′mən) *n., pl.* **-men** (-mĭn). A dealer in seed.
seed·y (sē′dē) *adj.* **-ier, -iest. 1.** Having many seeds. **2.** Shabby-looking; disreputable in appearance. **3.** Tired or sick; out of sorts. **—seed·i·ly** *adv.* **—seed·i·ness** *n.*
See·ger (sē′gər), **Peter,** known as "Pete" (1919–). U.S. folk singer. A left-wing activist and crucial figure in the revival of national interest in folk music, he influenced many younger performers, including Joan Baez. Among his well-known songs are "Where Have All the Flowers Gone" and "If I Had a Hammer."
see·ing (sē′ĭng) *conj.* Inasmuch as; in view of the fact that. Often used with *that.*
Seeing Eye *n.* A trademark for a dog trained to lead a blind person.
seek (sēk) *v.* **sought** (sôt), **seeking, seeks.** *—tr.* **1.** To try to locate or discover; search for. **2.** To endeavor to obtain or reach. **3.** To move to; go to or toward: *Water seeks its own level.* **4.** To ask for; request: *seek professional advice.* **5.** To try; endeavor. Used with an infinitive: *sought to persuade them.* **6.** *Archaic.* To explore. *—intr.* To make a search or investigation. Often used with *after* or *for.* **—seek out.** To search determinedly for and find. [Seek, sought, sought; Middle English *seken, so(u)hte, soht,* Old English *sēcan, sōhte, sōht.*] **—seek·er** *n.*
seel (sēl) *tr.v.* **seeled, seeling, seels.** To stitch closed the eyes of (a falcon, for example). [Middle English *silen,* from Old French *ciller,* from Medieval Latin *ciliāre,* from Latin *cilium,* eyelid.]
seem (sēm) *intr.v.* **seemed, seeming, seems. 1.** To give the impression of being; appear. **2.** To appear, according to one's perception of the situation: *I can't seem to get the story straight.* **3.** To appear to be so; be evident: *It seems you object to the plan.* **4.** To appear to exist: *There seems no reason to postpone it.* [Middle English *semen,* to beseem, seem, from Old Norse *sœma,* to conform to, honor, from *sœmr,* fitting.]

Usage: Constructions like *can't seem* and *won't seem,* followed by an infinitive, are common in speech and informal writing: *I can't seem to find the key; He won't seem to learn.* They have sometimes attracted criticism, however, usually on the grounds that auxiliary verbs such as *can't/won't* apply to the main verb, and should not be made to apply to *seem.* Formal English would prefer alternative constructions, such as *do not seem able, seems that he won't.*

seem·ing (sē′mĭng) *adj.* Apparent, but usually not real; ostensible. *~n.* Outward appearance; semblance. **—seem·ing·ly** *adv.* **—seem·ing·ness** *n.*
seem·ly (sēm′lē) *adj.* **-lier, -liest. 1.** Conforming to accepted standards of conduct and good taste; proper; suitable. **2.** *Archaic.* Of pleasing appearance; handsome.
~adv. In a seemly manner. [Middle English *semely, semeliche,* from Old Norse *sœmiligr,* from *sœmr,* fitting.] **—seem·li·ness** *n.*
seen. Past participle of **see.**
seep (sēp) *intr.v.* **seeped, seeping, seeps. 1.** To pass slowly through small openings or pores; ooze. **2.** To become gradually diffused: *The news seeped out.*
~n. **1.** A spot where water or petroleum oozes out of the ground. **2.** A seepage. [Perhaps variant of dialectal *sipe,* from Middle English *sipen,* Old English *sipian.*]
seep·age (sē′pĭj) *n.* **1.** The act or process of seeping or oozing; leakage. **2.** A quantity of something that has seeped.
seer¹ (sîr, sē′ər) *n.* **1.** One that sees; specifically, someone able to see into the future; a clairvoyant. **2.** Someone possessing spiritual insight; a sage. [Middle English, from *seen,* to SEE.]
seer² (sîr) *n.* Any of several varying Indian units of weight; especially, a unit of weight equivalent to one kilogram (2.2 pounds). [Hindi *ser.*]
seer·ess (sîr′ĭs) *n.* A woman who is a seer or clairvoyant.
seer·suck·er (sîr′sŭk′ər) *n.* A light, thin fabric, generally cotton or rayon, with a crinkled surface and often a striped pattern. [Hindi *sirsakar,* from Persian *shīr-o-shakar,* "milk and sugar" : *shīr,* milk, from Avestan *khshīra,* perhaps from Dravidian + *shakar,* sugar, akin to Sanskrit *śarkāra,* SUGAR.]
see·saw, see-saw (sē′sô′) *n.* **1.** A long plank balanced on a central fulcrum so that, with a person sitting on either end, one end goes up as the other goes down. Also called "teeter," "teeter-totter." **2.** The act or game of riding a seesaw. **3.** A back-and-forth or up-and-down movement. Also used adjectivally: *a seesaw motion.* **4.** An alternation between two situations or positions.
~intr.v. **seesawed** or **see-sawed, -sawing, -saws. 1.** To play on a seesaw. **2.** To move back and forth or up and down. **3.** To alternate or oscillate. [Reduplication of SAW (to cut), from the up-and-down movement of sawing.]
seethe (sē*th*) *v.* **seethed, seething, seethes.** *—intr.* **1.** To churn and foam as if boiling. Used of a liquid. **2.** To move in agitated confusion. **3.** To be violently excited or agitated. Often used with *with*: *seething with fury.* **4.** *Archaic.* To come to a boil. *—tr. Archaic.* **1.** To boil. **2.** To soak; steep. [Middle English *sethen,* Old English *sēothan.*] **—seethe** *n.*
see-through, see·through (sē′thrōō′) *adj.* Partially or completely transparent.
Se·fer·is (sə-fĕr′ēs), **George,** pen name of Georgios Seferiadis (1900–71). Greek poet. A diplomat by profession, he was hailed as the poet of the future on the publication of such works as *Strophé* (1931). He won the Nobel Prize for literature (1963).
seg·ment (sĕg′mənt) *n.* **1.** Any of the parts into which something is or can be divided. **2.** In geometry, a portion of a figure cut off by a line or plane; especially: **a.** The area bounded by a chord and the arc of a curve subtended by the chord. **b.** The portion of a curve between any two points on the curve. **c.** The portion of a sphere bounded by two parallel planes intersecting or tangent to the sphere. **3.** *Biology.* A clearly differentiated, repeated subdivision of an organism or part, such as a metamere.
~v. (sĕg-mĕnt′) **segmented, -menting, -ments.** *—tr.* To divide into segments. *—intr.* To become divided into segments. [Latin *segmentum,* from *secāre,* to cut.] **—seg·men·tal** (sĕg-mĕnt′l), **seg·men·tar·y** (sĕg′mən-tĕr′ē) *adj.* **—seg·men·tal·ly** *adv.*
seg·men·ta·tion (sĕg′mən-tā′shən) *n.* **1.** Division into segments. **2.** *Biology.* See **cleavage** (sense 4). **3.** *Zoology.* **Metameric segmentation** *(see).*
segmentation cavity *n. Biology.* A **blastocoel** *(see).*
se·gno (sā′nyō) *n., pl.* **-gni** (-nyē). *Music.* A notational sign; especially, the sign marking the beginning or end of a repeat. [Italian, sign, from Latin *signum.*]
se·go (sē′gō) *n., pl.* **-gos.** The succulent, edible bulb of the sego lily. [Of Ute origin.]
sego lily *n.* A plant, *Calochortus nuttallii,* of western North America, having showy flowers. [*Sego,* from Paiute.]
Se·go·vi·a (sə-gō′vē-ə). Capital of Segovia province, central Spain. Built on a hill above the Eresma River, it is still supplied from the river by a Roman aqueduct.
Segovia, Andrés (1894–). Spanish guitarist. Segovia stimulated new interest in the guitar as an instrument for serious music through his arrangements of Bach, Handel, and others.
Se·grè (sə-grā′), **Emilio Gino** (1905–). Italian-born U.S. physicist. In 1937 he produced the first artificial element, technetium. He discovered antiprotons with Owen Chamberlain (1955), and they were jointly awarded the 1959 Nobel Prize for physics.
seg·re·gate (sĕg′rə-gāt′) *v.* **-gated, -gating, -gates.** *—tr.* **1.** To separate or isolate from others or from a main body or group. **2.** To enforce the separation of (a race, class, or minority) from the rest of society. **3.** To divide (a society or community) along racial lines. *—intr.* **1.** To become separated from a main body or mass. **2.** To practice a policy of racial segregation. **3.** *Genetics.* To undergo segregation. [Latin *sēgregāre,* "to separate from the flock" : *sē,* apart + *grex* (stem *greg-*), flock.] **—seg·re·ga·tive** *adj.* **—seg·re·ga·tor** *n.*
seg·re·gat·ed (sĕg′rə-gā′tĭd) *adj.* **1.** Practicing or characterized by segregation, especially along racial lines. **2.** Restricted to the members of one race or other group: *a segregated school.* **3.** Providing separate facilities or divided for members of different races or other groups: *segregated buses.*
seg·re·ga·tion (sĕg′rə-gā′shən) *n.* **1.** The act or process of segregating or the condition of being segregated. **2.** The policy and practice of imposing separation of races, as in schools, housing, and industry; especially, discriminatory practices against nonwhites in a society dominated by whites. **3.** *Genetics.* The separation into different gametes of paired alleles in meiosis.
seg·re·ga·tion·ist (sĕg′rə-gā′shən-ĭst) *n.* One who advocates or practices a policy of racial segregation. **—seg·re·ga·tion·ist** *adj.*
se·gue (sĕg′wā′, sā′gwā′) *n. Music.* An uninterrupted transition from one movement or piece of music to another. Also used as a direction to proceed to the next movement without a pause.
~intr.v. **segued, -gueing, -gues.** To make a transition directly from one section or theme, as of music, to another. [Italian, "it follows," from *sequire,* to follow, from Latin *sequī.*]
se·gui·di·lla (sĕg′ə-dē′yä) *n.* **1.** A Spanish stanza form of four to seven short verses. **2.** A lively Spanish dance. **3.** The music for this dance, in triple time. [Spanish, from *seguida,* "sequence," from the feminine past participle of *seguir,* to follow, from Vulgar Latin *sequere* (unattested), from Latin *sequī,* to follow.]
sei·cen·to (sā-chĕn′tō) *n.* The 17th century, especially with regard to the Italian literature and art of the period. [Italian *(mil) seicento,* (one thousand) six hundred : *sei,* six, from Latin *sex* + *cento,* hundred, from Latin *centum.*]
seiche (sāsh) *n.* A vibration of the surface of lakes, bays, channels, or inland seas as a result of seismic or atmospheric disturbances. [Swiss French *seiche†.*]
sei·del (sīd′l, zīd′l) *n.* A beer mug. [German, from Middle High German *sīdel,* from Latin *situla,* bucket.]
Seid·litz powder (sĕd′lĭts) *n. Sometimes* **Seidlitz powders.** A cathartic consisting of Rochelle salts, sodium bicarbonate, and tartaric acid. Also called "Rochelle powder." [So called because it has laxative properties similar to those of the spring water of *Seidlitz,* the German name of Sedlice, village in Bohemia.]
seign·eur (sān-yər′) *n.* **1.** Formerly, a feudal lord or landowner, especially in France. **2.** Formerly in Canada, the landlord of a large estate subdivided into smaller holdings. **3.** The hereditary civil head of government of the island of Sark. [French, from Old French, from Vulgar Latin *senior.* See **seignior.**] **—seign·eur·i·al** *adj.*
seign·eur·y, seign·eur·ie (sān′yə-rē) *n., pl.* **-ies. 1.** The power, status, estate, or house of a seigneur. **2.** The official designation of the island of Sark.
seign·ior (sān-yôr′, sān′yôr′) *n.* A man of rank; specifically, a feudal lord. [Middle English *seignour,* from Old French *seigneur,* from Medieval Latin *senior,* from Latin, older, comparative of *senex,* old.] **—sei·gnio·ri·al** (sān-yôr′ē-əl) *adj.*
seign·ior·age (sān′yər-ĭj) *n.* A profit or revenue taken from the minting of coins, usually by means of the difference between the

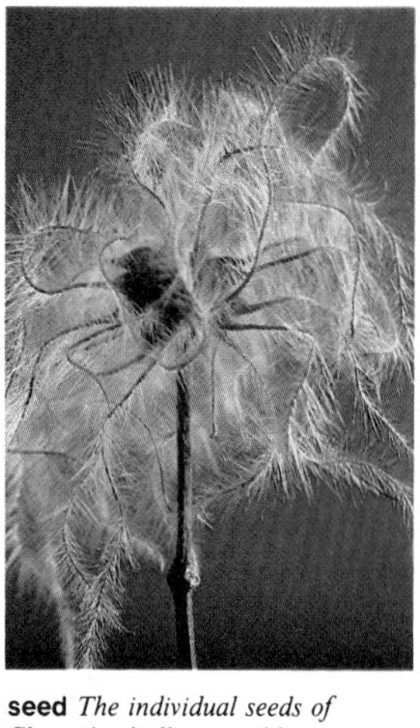

seed *The individual seeds of* Clematis vitalba, *or old-man's-beard, are attached to the hairy plumes that give the plant its name. The seeds are spread by the wind.*

PRONUNCIATION KEY
ă, pat; ā, pay; âr, care; ä, father, are; b, bib; ch, church; d, deed; ĕ, pet; ē, be; f, fife; g, gag; h, hat; hw, which; ĭ, pit; ī, pie; îr, pier; j, judge; k, kick; l, lid, needle; m, mum; n, no, sudden; ng, thing; ŏ, pot; ō, toe; ô, paw, for; oi, noise; ou, out; ŏŏ, book; ōō, boot; p, pop; r, roar; s, sauce; sh, ship, dish; t, tight; th, thin, path; *th*, this, bathe; ŭ, cut; ûr, fur; v, valve; w, with; y, yes; z, zebra, size; zh, vision; ə, about, item, edible, gallop, circus, peaceful

IN FOREIGN WORDS:
à, *Fr.* ami; œ, *Fr.* feu, *Ger.* schön; ü, *Fr.* tu, *Ger.* über; KH, *Ger.* ich, *Scot.* loch; N, *Fr.* bon; y′, *Fr.* Compiègne

STRESS MARKS:
Primary stress: ′ **in·cite′** (ĭn-sīt′)
Secondary stress: ′ **in′sight′** (ĭn′sīt′)

value of the bullion used and the face value of the coin. [Middle English *seigneurage,* duty imposed by a lord as his prerogative, from Old French, from *seigneur,* SEIGNIOR.]

seign·ior·y (sān′yə-rē) *n., pl.* **-ies. 1.** The estate of a feudal lord; a manor. **2.** The authority and power of a feudal lord.

seine (sān) *n.* A large fishing net made to hang vertically in the water by weights at the lower edge and floats at the top. ∼*v.* **seined, seining, seines.** —*intr.* To fish with a seine. —*tr.* To fish for or catch with a seine. [Middle English *seine,* Old English *segne,* from West Germanic *sagina* (unattested), from Latin *sagēna,* from Greek *sagēnē*†.]

Seine (sĕn). River of northern France, rising in the Langres Plateau. It flows *c.* 770 kilometers (480 miles), passing through Paris and reaching the English Channel at Le Havre. The Seine channel is dredged to allow oceangoing vessels to reach Rouen.

seise. *Law.* Variant of **seize.**

seisin. Variant of **seizin.**

seism (sī′zəm) *n.* An **earthquake** *(see).* [Greek *seismos,* from *seiein,* to shake.]

seis·mic (sīz′mĭk) *adj.* Of, subject to, or caused by an earthquake or a natural or manmade earth vibration. [SEISM(O)- + -IC.] —**seis·mi·cal·ly** *adv.* —**seis·mic·i·ty** (sīz-mĭs′ə-tē) *n.*

seismic wave *n.* A vibration emitted by an earthquake or a manmade explosion.

seis·mism (sīz′mĭz′əm) *n.* The collective phenomena involved in earthquakes. [SEISM(O)- + -ISM.]

seismo-, seism– *prefix.* Indicates earthquake; for example, **seismograph, seismism.** [Greek *seismos,* SEISM.]

seis·mo·gram (sīz′mə-grăm′) *n.* The record of an earth tremor made by a seismograph. [SEISMO- + -GRAM.]

seis·mo·graph (sīz′mə-grăf′, -gräf′) *n.* An instrument for automatically detecting and recording the intensity, direction, and duration of any movement of the ground, especially that caused by an earthquake or manmade explosion. [SEISMO- + -GRAPH.] —**seis·mog·ra·pher** (sīz-mŏg′rə-fər) *n.* —**seis·mo·graph·ic** *adj.* —**seis·mog·ra·phy** *n.*

seis·mol·o·gy (sīz-mŏl′ə-jē) *n.* The geophysical science of earthquakes and of the mechanical properties of the earth's interior. [SEISMO- + -LOGY.] —**seis·mo·log·ic** (sīz′mə-lŏj′ĭk), **seis·mo·log·i·cal** *adj.* —**seis·mo·log·i·cal·ly** *adv.* —**seis·mol·o·gist** *n.*

seis·mom·e·ter (sīz-mŏm′ə-tər) *n.* A detecting device that receives seismic waves. [SEISMO- + -METER.] —**seis·mo·met·ric** (sīz′mə-mĕt′rĭk), **seis·mo·met·ri·cal** *adj.*

seis·mo·scope (sīz′mə-skōp′) *n.* An instrument that indicates the occurrence or time of occurrence of a seismic wave. [SEISMO- + -SCOPE.] —**seis·mo·scop·ic** (sīz′mə-skŏp′ĭk) *adj.*

seisor. *Law.* Variant of **seizor.**

sei whale (sā) *n.* A widely distributed, dark blue rorqual, *Balaenoptera borealis,* valued for its whalebone. [Partial translation of Norwegian *sei-val* : *sei,* coalfish + *val,* whale.]

seize (sēz) *v.* **seized, seizing, seizes.** Also **seise** (for sense 5c). **seised, seising, seises.** —*tr.* **1.** To grasp suddenly and forcibly; lay hold of; clutch or grab. **2.** To grasp with the mind; comprehend. **3.** To have a sudden and overpowering effect upon; possess or overwhelm. **4.** To take into custody; make a prisoner of; arrest. **5. a.** To take quick and forcible possession of; capture. **b.** To take possession of by legal authority or process; confiscate. **c.** *Law.* To put in legal possession, as of an estate or other property. Used chiefly in the passive with *of.* **6.** To avail oneself eagerly and immediately of (an opportunity). **7.** *Nautical.* To bind with turns of small line. —*intr.* **1.** To take up or lay hold eagerly or forcibly. Used with *on* or *upon.* **2. a.** To cohere or fuse with another part as a result of high pressure or temperature, restricting or preventing further motion. Often used with *up.* **b.** To come to a halt. Used with *up*: *The talks seized up.* [Middle English *saisen, seisen,* from Old French *seisir, saisir,* from Gallo-Latin *sacīre* (unattested), to claim, from Germanic.] —**seiz·a·ble** *adj.*

sei·zin, sei·sin (sē′zĭn) *n.* *Law.* Legal possession of a freehold estate. [Middle English, from Norman French *sesine,* Old French *seisine,* from *seisir,* to SEIZE.]

seiz·ing (sē′zĭng) *n.* *Nautical.* A binding of larger lines made with multiple turns of smaller line.

sei·zor, sei·sor (sē′zər, -zôr′) *n.* *Law.* One that takes seizin.

sei·zure (sē′zhər) *n.* **1.** The act or an action of seizing or the state of being seized. **2.** A sudden paroxysm, such as an epileptic convulsion or heart attack.

se·jant (sē′jənt) *adj.* *Heraldry.* In a sitting position with forepaws extended to the ground: *a lion sejant.* [Variant of *seant,* from Old French, present participle of *seoir,* to sit, from Latin *sedēre.*]

Sejm (sām) *n.* The unicameral legislative body of the Polish People's Republic. [Polish, "assembly."]

se·la·chi·an (sĭ-lā′kē-ən) *adj.* Of or belonging to the order Selachii, which includes the sharks and rays. ∼*n.* A member of the Selachii. [New Latin *Selachii,* from Greek *selakhē,* plural of *selakhos*†, cartilaginous fish.]

sel·a·gi·nel·la (sĕl′ə-jə-nĕl′ə) *n.* Any of numerous fernlike, usually prostrate plants of the genus *Selaginella,* having small scalelike leaves and bearing spores in cones. [New Latin, from Latin *selāgō*† (stem *selāgin-*), plant resembling the savin.]

se·lah (sē′lə) *n.* A Hebrew word of unknown meaning often marking the end of a verse in the Psalms and thought to be a term indicating a pause or rest. [Hebrew *selāh.*]

---

seismograph

MEASURING EARTHQUAKES
Needles to detect the earth's faintest jolt

The needle of a delicate seismograph can pick up and define any movement in the ground, detecting and recording its direction, duration, and intensity. All earthquakes, however faint, emit shock waves, known as seismic waves, which radiate in all directions. These waves trigger the movement of the seismograph needle, and a pen fixed to its head traces the movement on a graph.

Modern seismographs consist of a rigid frame, with a weight suspended from a horizontal boom. Shock waves jolt the frame but the weight remains still, and the needle fixed to the weight traces the relative motion of the frame. The size of the shock waves, indicating the size of the earthquake, is measured on a scale created by an American, Charles F. Richter, in 1935. The scale is logarithmic; in it, a shock magnitude of 8, for example, is 10 times greater than 7, and 100 times greater than 6.

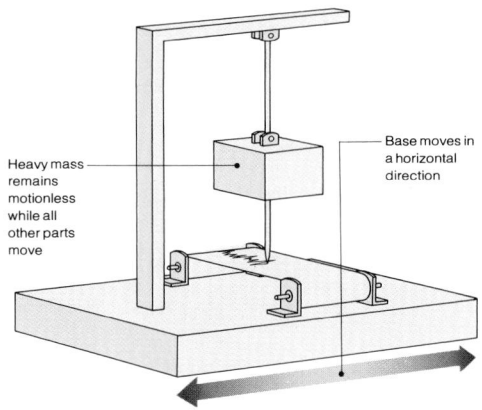

HORIZONTAL MOVEMENT *Shock waves radiating vertically or horizontally can be measured by a seismograph. This one, with its weight held on a pendulum and the needle pointing down, records horizontal movement in the earth.*

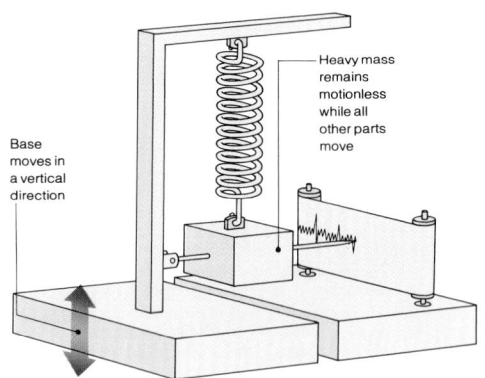

VERTICAL MOVEMENT *In this seismograph, the weight is suspended from the rigid boom by a spring, and the needle and pen are held horizontally. The base holding the boom will jolt vertically and the pen will record vertical movement.*

---

sel·dom (sĕl′dəm) *adv.* Not often; infrequently; rarely. ∼*adj.* *Archaic.* Infrequent; rare. [Middle English *selden, seldom,* Old English *seldan,* from Common Germanic *seldo-* (unattested).] —**sel·dom·ness** *n.*
   Usage: Acceptable idioms include *seldom if ever* and *seldom or never,* but not *seldom or ever* or *seldom ever,* though the latter pair are sometimes encountered in informal speech. See also **rarely.**

se·lect (sĭ-lĕkt′) *v.* **-lected, -lecting, -lects.** —*tr.* To choose from among several; take in preference; pick out. —*intr.* To make a choice or selection; choose. —See Synonyms at **choose.** ∼*adj.* **1.** Singled out in preference; chosen; picked out. **2.** Of special value or quality; choice. **3.** Open to or made up of a limited number of people, especially those of high social or economic status: *select company.* [Latin *sēligere* (past participle *sēlectus*), to choose out : *sē,* apart + *legere,* to choose.] —**se·lect·ness** *n.*

se·lec·tee (sĭ-lĕk′tē′) *n.* One who is selected, especially for military service.

se·lec·tion (sĭ-lĕk′shən) *n.* **1. a.** The act of selecting or the fact of being selected; choosing; choice. **b.** That which is selected. **2.** A carefully chosen or representative collection of persons or things. **3.** A range of items of the same kind, as of goods for sale: *a good selection of wines.* **4.** *Biology.* A process that favors or induces the survival and perpetuation of one kind of organism in competition with others. See **natural selection.** —See Synonyms at **choice.** [Latin *sēlectiō* (stem *sēlectiōn*-). See **select.**]

se·lec·tive (sĭ-lĕk′tĭv) *adj.* **1.** Of or characterized by selection or discrimination; tending to select or empowered to select: *selective import controls.* **2.** Careful in selecting; fastidious; particular. **3.** *Electronics.* Capable of rejecting frequencies other than those selected or tuned. —**se·lec·tive·ly** *adv.* —**se·lec·tive·ness** *n.*

selective service *n.* A system for calling up individuals for compulsory military service.

se·lec·tiv·i·ty (sĭ-lĕk′tĭv′ə-tē) *n.* **1.** The state or quality of being selective. **2.** *Electronics.* The degree to which an electronic receiver or other circuit is selective.

se·lect·man (sĭ-lĕkt′mən) *n., pl.* **-men** (-mĭn). A member of a board of town officers chosen annually in New England communities to manage local affairs.

se·lec·tor (sĭ-lĕk′tər) *n.* **1.** One that selects. **2.** A device forming part of an automatic telephone switching system that connects one circuit to one or more other circuits.

sel·e·nate (sĕl′ə-nāt′) *n.* A salt or ester of selenic acid. [From SELENIUM.]

Se·len·e (sə-lē′nē) *n.* The Greek goddess of the moon. [Greek *selēnē,* moon.]

se·len·ic acid (sĭ-lĕn′ĭk, -lē′nĭk) *n.* A highly corrosive, hygroscopic, white solid acid with composition H_2SeO_4. [From SELENIUM.]

sel·e·nif·er·ous (sĕl′ə-nĭf′ə-rəs) *adj.* Containing selenium: *seleniferous soil.*

sel·e·nite (sĕl′ə-nīt′) *n.* Gypsum in the form of colorless clear crystals. [Latin *selēnītēs,* from Greek *selēnītēs (lithos),* "moon (stone)" (because its brightness supposedly waxed and waned with the moon), from *selēnē,* moon.]

se·le·ni·um (sĭ-lē′nē-əm) *n. Symbol* **Se** A nonmetallic element, red in powder form, black in vitreous form, and metallic gray in crystalline form, resembling sulfur and obtained primarily as a by-product of electrolytic copper refining. It is widely used in rectifiers, as a semiconductor, and in xerography, and certain forms exhibit photovoltaic and photoconductive action, making it useful in photocells, photographic exposure meters, and solar cells. Atomic number 34, atomic weight 78.96, melting point (of gray selenium) 217°C, boiling point (gray) 684.9°C, specific gravity (gray) 4.79, (vitreous) 4.28, valence 2, 4, or 6. [New Latin, from Greek *selēnē,* moon (named by analogy to a related element, tellurium, from Latin *tellus,* earth).]

selenium cell *n.* A photoconductive cell consisting of an insulated selenium strip between two suitable electrodes.

sel·e·nod·e·sy (sĕl′ə-nŏd′ĭ-sē) *n.* The study or mapping of the physical characteristics of the moon, such as its exact shape, size, and gravity; lunar geodesy. [Greek *selēnē,* moon + (GEO)DESY.] —**sel·e·nod·e·sist** *n.* —**se·le·no·det·ic** (sĕl′ə-nə-dĕt′ĭk) *adj.*

se·le·no·dont (sə-lē′nə-dŏnt′) *adj.* Having crescent-shaped ridges on the crowns of the teeth, as in deer do.
~*n.* A selenodont mammal. [Greek *selēnē,* moon + -ODONT.]

sel·e·nog·ra·phy (sĕl′ə-nŏg′rə-fē) *n.* The study of the physical features of the moon. [New Latin *selenographia* : Greek *selēnē,* moon + -GRAPHY.] —**sel·e·nog·ra·pher, sel·e·nog·ra·phist** *n.* —**se·le·no·graph·ic** (sĕl′ə-nə-grăf′ĭk), **sel·e·no·graph·i·cal** *adj.* —**se·le·no·graph·i·cal·ly** *adv.*

sel·e·nol·o·gy (sĕl′ə-nŏl′ə-jē) *n.* The astronomical study of the moon. [Greek *selēnē,* moon + -LOGY.] —**sel·e·no·log·i·cal** (sĕl′ə-nə-lŏj′ĭ-kəl) *adj.* —**sel·e·nol·o·gist** *n.*

se·le·no·mor·phol·o·gy (sə-lē′nō-môr-fŏl′ə-jē) *n.* The study of the surface and landscape of the moon. [Greek *selēnē,* moon + MORPHOLOGY.]

sel·e·no·sis (sĕl′ə-nō′sĭs) *n.* Selenium poisoning.

se·le·nous acid (sĭ-lē′nəs, sĕl′ə-) *n.* Also **se·le·ni·ous acid** (sĭ-lē′nē-əs). A transparent, colorless crystalline acid, H_2SeO_3, used as a chemical reagent. [From SELENIUM.]

Se·leu·ci·a (sə-lōō′shē-ə). Ancient city of Mesopotamia, on the Tigris southeast of modern Baghdad. It was the eastern capital of the Seleucid empire.

Se·leu·cid (sĭ-lōō′sĭd). A Hellenistic dynasty founded by Seleucus I after the death of Alexander. It ruled in Babylonia from 312 B.C. and in Syria from 301 B.C. to 64 B.C. —**Se·leu·cid, Se·leu·ci·dan** *adj.*

self (sĕlf) *n., pl.* **selves** (sĕlvz). **1.** The total, essential, or particular being of one person; the individual. **2.** The qualities of one person distinguishing him from another; a person's typical personality or character: *not his usual cheerful self.* **3.** An individual's consciousness of his own being or identity; subjectivity; ego. **4.** One's own interests, welfare, or advantage; selfish concerns.
~*pron.* Myself, yourself, himself, or herself: *a living wage for self and family.*
~*adj.* **1.** *Obsolete.* Same or identical. **2. a.** Uniform throughout. Said of a color. **b.** Self-colored. **3.** Homogeneous, as in color, design, or material; matching. Said especially of clothes: *a self belt.* [Middle English *se(o)lf, silf,* noun, pronoun, and adjective, Old English *self, silf.*]

self- *prefix.* Indicates: **1.** Oneself or itself; for example, **self-correcting, self-perpetuating. 2.** Of the self, oneself, or itself; for example, **self-control, self-government, self-knowledge. 3.** With regard to oneself; for example, **self-assurance, self-interest. 4.** By, by means of, or relying solely upon, oneself; for example, **self-appointed, self-educated, self-help. 5.** Acting on or directed toward oneself or itself; for example, **self-addressed, self-pity. 6.** In oneself or itself; inherently; for example, **self-contradictory, self-evident. 7.** Autonomous, automatic, or automatically; for example, **self-propelled, self-winding.** *Note:* Many compounds other than those entered here may be formed with *self*-. When *self*- is joined with a word that can stand alone, it is joined by a hyphen: *self-deception.* In the rare cases when *self*- is joined with a form that cannot stand alone as a word, it is joined without space or hyphen: *selfhood.* [Middle English, Old English, from SELF.]

self-a·base·ment (sĕlf′ə-bās′mənt) *n.* Degradation or humiliation of oneself, especially because of feelings of guilt or inferiority.

self-ab·ne·ga·tion (sĕlf′ăb′nĭ-gā′shən) *n.* The setting aside of self-interest for the sake of others or for a belief or principle. —**self-ab·ne·gat·ing** *adj.*

self-a·buse (sĕlf′ə-byōōs′) *n.* **1.** Criticism of oneself or one's abilities. **2.** Masturbation.

self-act·ing (sĕlf′ăk′tĭng) *adj.* Capable of acting or working automatically.

self-ac·tu·al·ize (sĕlf′ăk′chōō-ə-līz′) *intr.v.* **-ized, -izing, -izes.** To achieve one's full potential. —**self-ac·tu·al·i·za·tion** *n.* —**self-ac·tu·al·iz·er** *n.*

self-ad·dressed (sĕlf′ə-drĕst′) *adj.* Addressed to oneself.

self-ag·gran·dize·ment (sĕlf′ə-grăn′dĭz-mənt) *n.* The act or practice of enhancing one's own importance, power, or reputation. —**self-ag·gran·diz·ing** *adj.*

self-an·neal·ing (sĕlf′ə-nē′lĭng) *adj.* Designating those metals, such as lead and tin, that do not harden as a result of cold-working.

self-an·ni·hi·la·tion (sĕlf′ə-nī′ə-lā′shən) *n.* **1.** Self-destruction. **2.** A loss of self-awareness, as in a mystical state.

self-ap·point·ed (sĕlf′ə-poin′tĭd) *adj.* Designated or chosen by oneself rather than by due authority; unsanctioned and usually ill-qualified: *a self-appointed authority on English grammar.*

self-as·ser·tion (sĕlf′ə-sûr′shən) *n.* Forceful assertion of one's own personality, wishes, claims, or views. —**self-as·ser·tive** *adj.* —**self-as·ser·tive·ly** *adv.*

self-as·sured (sĕlf′ə-shōōrd′) *adj.* Having or showing confidence and sureness. —**self-as·sur·ance** *n.*

self-a·ware (sĕlf′ə-wâr′) *adj.* Aware of one's own personality or individual qualities. —**self-a·ware·ness** *n.*

self-cen·tered (sĕlf′sĕn′tərd) *adj.* Engrossed in oneself and one's affairs. —**self-cen·tered·ly** *adv.* —**self-cen·tered·ness** *n.*

self-col·ored (sĕlf′kŭl′ərd) *adj.* **1.** In the natural or original color. **2.** Of only one color.

self-com·mand (sĕlf′kə-mănd′) *n.* Full presence of mind; self-control.

self-con·fessed (sĕlf′kən-fĕst′) *adj.* According to one's own admission; avowed.

self-con·fi·dence (sĕlf′kŏn′fə-dəns) *n.* Confidence in oneself or one's abilities. —**self-con·fi·dent** *adj.* —**self-con·fi·dent·ly** *adv.*

self-con·scious (sĕlf′kŏn′shəs) *adj.* **1.** Conscious to the point of discomfort or embarrassment of one's appearance or manner; socially ill at ease. **2.** Having or showing an excessive concern for one's impact upon others; unnatural or contrived: *a very self-conscious style of poetry.* **3.** Aware of oneself or one's own being, actions, or thoughts. —See Synonyms at **shy.** —**self-con·scious·ly** *adv.* —**self-con·scious·ness** *n.*

self-con·tained (sĕlf′kən-tānd′) *adj.* **1.** Constituting a complete and independent unit: *a self-contained apartment.* **2. a.** Not dependent on others; self-sufficient. **b.** Keeping to oneself; reserved.

self-con·tent (sĕlf′kən-tĕnt′) *n.* Also **self-con·tent·ment** (sĕlf′kən-tĕnt′mənt). Satisfaction, especially complacent satisfaction, with oneself and one's condition. —**self-con·tent·ed** *adj.* —**self-con·tent·ed·ly** *adv.*

self-con·tra·dic·tion (sĕlf′kŏn′trə-dĭk′shən) *n.* **1.** The act, state, or fact of contradicting oneself or itself. **2.** An idea or statement containing contradictory elements. —**self-con·tra·dic·to·ry** (sĕlf′kŏn′trə-dĭk′tə-rē) *adj.*

self-con·trol (sĕlf′kən-trōl′) *n.* Control of one's emotions, desires, or actions by one's own will. —**self-con·trolled** *adj.*

self-cor·rect·ing (sĕlf′kə-rĕk′tĭng) *adj.* Correcting its or one's own mistakes; especially, designating a typewriter with a mechanism facilitating correction of typing errors.

self-crit·i·cal (sĕlf′krĭt′ĭ-kəl) *adj.* Critical of oneself; watchful for one's own faults and weaknesses. —**self-crit·i·cal·ly** *adv.* —**self-crit·i·cism** *n.*

self-de·cep·tion (sĕlf′dĭ-sĕp′shən) *n.* Also **self-de·ceit** (sĕlf′dĭ-sēt′). The act of deceiving oneself or the state of being deceived by oneself. —**self-de·cep·tive** *adj.*

self-de·feat·ing (sĕlf′dĭ-fē′tĭng) *adj.* Conflicting with or going against one's or its own purposes or welfare.

self-de·fense (sĕlf′dĭ-fĕns′) *n.* **1.** The act or skill of defending oneself against physical attack. **2.** Defense of what belongs to oneself, as of one's rights or beliefs. **3.** *Law.* The right to protect oneself against violence or threatened violence with whatever force or means are reasonably necessary. —**self-de·fen·sive** *adj.*

self-de·ni·al (sĕlf′dĭ-nī′əl) *n.* Sacrifice of one's own comfort or gratification; restraint of one's natural desires. —See Synonyms at **absti-**

nence. **—self·de·ny·ing** *adj.* **—self·de·ny·ing·ly** *adv.*

self·dep·re·cat·ing (sĕlf'dĕp'rĭ-kā'tĭng) *adj.* Tending to undervalue oneself and one's abilities. **—self·dep·re·cat·ing·ly** *adv.* **—self·dep·re·ca·tion** *n.*

self·de·struct (sĕlf'dĭ-strŭkt') *n.* A mechanism forming part of a missile or other device that enables it to destroy itself under predetermined circumstances or on command. Also used adjectivally: *a self-destruct mechanism.*
~ *intr.v.* **self·destructed, -structing, -structs.** To destroy itself, especially automatically.

self·de·struc·tive (sĕlf'dĭ-strŭk'tĭv) *adj.* Marked by an impulse or tendency to harm or kill oneself. **—self·de·struc·tion** *n.* **—self·de·struc·tive·ly** *adv.* **—self·de·struc·tive·ness** *n.*

self·de·ter·mi·na·tion (sĕlf'dĭ-tûr'mə-nā'shən) *n.* **1.** Determination of one's own fate or course of action without compulsion; free will. **2.** Freedom of a people or area to determine its own political status and alignment; independence.

self·dis·ci·pline (sĕlf'dĭs'ə-plĭn) *n.* Training and control of one's impulses and conduct, usually for personal improvement.

self·dis·cov·er·y (sĕlf'dĭ-skŭv'ə-rē) *n.* The act or process of achieving understanding or knowledge of oneself.

self·doubt (sĕlf'dout') *n.* A lack of faith or confidence in oneself. **—self·doubt·ing** *adj.*

self·ed·u·cat·ed (sĕlf'ĕj'ə-kā'tĭd) *adj.* Educated by one's own efforts, not by formal instruction. **—self·ed·u·ca·tion** *n.*

self·ef·fac·ing (sĕlf'ĭ-fā'sĭng) *adj.* Not drawing attention to oneself; modest or shy. **—self·ef·face·ment** *n.*

self·em·ployed (sĕlf'ĕm-ploid') *adj.* Earning one's livelihood directly from one's own trade or business, not as an employee.

self·es·teem (sĕlf'ə-stēm) *n.* Pride in oneself; self-respect.

self·ev·i·dent (sĕlf'ĕv'ə-dənt) *adj.* Requiring no proof or explanation. **—self·ev·i·dence** *n.* **—self·ev·i·dent·ly** *adv.*

self·ex·am·i·na·tion (sĕlf'ĭg-zăm'ə-nā'shən) *n.* **1.** Careful, introspective consideration of one's own thoughts, feelings, or motives. **2.** Examination of one's own body for medical reasons; especially, examination by a woman of her breasts as a precaution against cancer.

self·ex·cit·ed (sĕlf'ĭk-sī'tĭd) *adj.* *Electricity.* **1.** Designating an oscillator that provides its own energy source. **2.** Designating an electrical machine in which the current that excites the magnetic field is generated by the machine itself.

self·ex·plan·a·to·ry (sĕlf'ĭk-splăn'ə-tôr'ē, -tōr'ē) *adj.* Needing no explanation; obvious in meaning.

self·ex·pres·sion (sĕlf'ĭk-sprĕsh'ən) *n.* Expression of one's own personality, feelings, or ideas, as through speech or art.

self·fer·ti·li·za·tion (sĕlf'fûr'tə-lə-zā'shən) *n.* Fertilization by sperm from the same animal, as in some hermaphrodites, or by pollen from the same flower. See **autogamy**. **—self·fer·ti·lized, self·fer·ti·liz·ing, self·fer·tile** *adj.*

self·ful·fill·ing (sĕlf'fŏŏl-fĭl'ĭng) *adj.* **1.** Achieving self-fulfillment. **2.** Achieving fulfillment as a result of having been predicted or expected: *a self-fulfilling prophecy.*

self·ful·fill·ment (sĕlf'fŏŏl-fĭl'mənt) *n.* Fulfillment of oneself.

self·gov·ern·ment (sĕlf'gŭv'ərn-mənt) *n.* **1.** Political independence; autonomy. **2.** *Archaic.* Self-control. **—self·gov·erned, self·gov·ern·ing** *adj.*

self·hard·en·ing (sĕlf'härd'n-ĭng) *adj.* Of, designating, or pertaining to materials, such as certain steels, that harden without special treatment.

self·heal (sĕlf'hēl') *n.* Any of several plants reputed to have healing powers; especially, *Prunella vulgaris,* a plant native to Europe, having violet-blue flowers. Also called "heal-all," "all-heal."

self·help (sĕlf'hĕlp') *n.* The act or an instance of helping or providing for oneself without assistance from others. Also used adjectivally: *a self-help project.*

self·hood (sĕlf'hŏŏd') *n.* **1.** The state of having a distinct identity; individuality. **2.** The fully developed self; achieved personality. **3.** Self-centeredness. [Translation of German *Selbheit.*]

self·im·age (sĕlf'ĭm'ĭj) *n.* One's mental concept of oneself or one's position in relation to others; how one sees oneself.

self·im·por·tance (sĕlf'ĭm-pôr'təns) *n.* Excessively high opinion of one's own importance or station; pomposity; conceit. **—self·im·por·tant** *adj.* **—self·im·por·tant·ly** *adv.*

self·im·posed (sĕlf'ĭm-pōzd') *adj.* Imposed by oneself on oneself; voluntarily assumed or endured.

self·im·prove·ment (sĕlf'ĭm-prōōv'mənt) *n.* Improvement of one's condition through one's own efforts.

self·in·clu·sive (sĕlf'ĭn-klōō'sĭv, -zĭv) *adj.* **1.** Enclosing or including itself. **2.** Whole or complete in itself.

self·in·duced (sĕlf'ĭn-dōōst', -dyōōst') *adj.* **1.** Induced by oneself or itself; willfully acquired or brought on. **2.** *Electricity.* Produced by self-induction.

self·in·duct·ance (sĕlf'ĭn-dŭk'təns) *n.* *Electricity.* The ratio of the electromotive force produced in a circuit by self-induction to the rate of change of current producing it. It is expressed in henries. Also called "coefficient of self-induction."

self·in·duc·tion (sĕlf'ĭn-dŭk'shən) *n.* The generation by a changing current of an electromotive force in the same circuit that tends to counteract such change. **—self·in·duc·tive** *adj.*

self·in·dul·gence (sĕlf'ĭn-dŭl'jəns) *n.* Excessive indulgence of one's own appetites, desires, or attitudes. **—self·in·dul·gent** *adj.* **—self·in·dul·gent·ly** *adv.*

self·in·flict·ed (sĕlf'ĭn-flĭk'tĭd) *adj.* Inflicted or imposed upon one-

self-heal *Prunella vulgaris, also known as heal-all. It is widespread and was formerly thought to be of value in the treatment of a sore throat.*

self: *a self-inflicted punishment.* **—self·in·flic·tion** *n.*

self·in·ter·est (sĕlf'ĭn'trĭst, -ĭn'tər-ĭst) *n.* **1.** Personal advantage or interest; selfish motive or gain. **2.** Pursuit of or excessive regard for such advantage or interest. **—self·in·ter·est·ed** *adj.*

self·ish (sĕl'fĭsh) *adj.* **1.** Concerned chiefly or only with one's own welfare, pleasure, or advantage, without regard for the well-being of others; egoistic. **2.** Arising from, characterized by, or showing such concern: *a selfish whim.* **—self·ish·ly** *adv.* **—self·ish·ness** *n.*

self·jus·ti·fy·ing (sĕlf'jŭs'tə-fī'ĭng) *adj.* **1.** Making excuses for one's behavior. **2.** Automatically arranging type to fill a full line.

self·knowl·edge (sĕlf'nŏl'ĭj) *n.* Knowledge of one's own nature, abilities, and limitations; insight into oneself.

self·less (sĕlf'lĭs) *adj.* Without concern for oneself; unselfish. **—self·less·ly** *adv.* **—self·less·ness** *n.*

self·liq·ui·dat·ing (sĕlf'lĭk'wə-dā'tĭng) *adj.* **1.** Designating a loan advanced to finance the purchase or production of goods that can be quickly converted into cash. **2.** Producing a return equal to the sum invested to create or maintain it: *a self-liquidating toll-bridge project.*

self·load·ing (sĕlf'lō'dĭng) *adj.* Automatically ejecting the shell and chambering the next round from the magazine; automatic or semi-automatic. Said of a firearm.

self·lock·ing (sĕlf'lŏk'ĭng) *adj.* Locking automatically when shut.

self·love (sĕlf'lŭv') *n.* The instinct or desire to promote one's own well-being; regard for or love of self. **—self·lov·ing** *adj.*

self·made (sĕlf'mād') *adj.* **1.** Having achieved success purely by one's own efforts: *a self-made man.* **2.** Made by oneself or itself.

self·mail·er (sĕlf'mā'lər) *n.* A folder that can be mailed without being enclosed in an envelope. **—self·mail·ing** *adj.*

self·mas·ter·y (sĕlf'măs'tə-rē) *n.* Self-command.

self·per·pet·u·at·ing (sĕlf'pər-pĕch'ōō-ā'tĭng) *adj.* Having the power to renew or perpetuate itself indefinitely.

self·pit·y (sĕlf'pĭt'ē) *n.* Pity for oneself, especially of an exaggerated or self-indulgent kind. **—self·pit·y·ing** *adj.* **—self·pit·y·ing·ly** *adv.*

self·pol·li·na·tion (sĕlf'pŏl'ə-nā'shən) *n.* The transfer of pollen from an anther to a stigma of the same flower. **—self·pol·li·nat·ed, self·pol·li·nat·ing** *adj.*

self·por·trait (sĕlf'pôr'trĭt, sĕlf'pōr'-, -trāt') *n.* A pictorial or literary portrait of oneself created by oneself.

self·pos·ses·sion (sĕlf'pə-zĕsh'ən) *n.* Full command of one's faculties, feelings, and behavior, especially in difficult circumstances; presence of mind; poise. **—self·pos·sessed** *adj.*

self·pres·er·va·tion (sĕlf'prĕz'ər-vā'shən) *n.* **1.** Protection of oneself from harm or destruction. **2.** The instinct for such individual preservation; the innate desire to stay alive.

self·pro·claimed (sĕlf'prō-klāmd', -prə-) *adj.* So called by oneself; self-styled.

self·pro·pelled (sĕlf'prə-pĕld') *adj.* Containing its own means of propulsion. Said of a vehicle, for example.

self·re·al·i·za·tion (sĕlf'rē'ə-lə-zā'shən) *n.* The complete development or fulfillment of one's own potential.

self·re·cord·ing (sĕlf'rĭ-kôr'dĭng) *adj.* Automatically recording its own functions or operations. Said of a machine or instrument.

self·re·gard (sĕlf'rĭ-gärd') *n.* **1.** Consideration of oneself or one's interests. **2.** Self-respect.

self·reg·u·lat·ing (sĕlf'rĕg'yə-lā'tĭng) *adj.* Regulating itself automatically.

self·re·li·ance (sĕlf'rĭ-lī'əns) *n.* Reliance upon one's own capabilities, judgment, or resources. **—self·re·li·ant** *adj.* **—self·re·li·ant·ly** *adv.*

self·re·proach (sĕlf'rĭ-prōch') *n.* The act or habit of blaming or finding fault with oneself. **—self·re·proach·ful** *adj.* **—self·re·proach·ful·ly** *adv.*

self·re·spect (sĕlf'rĭ-spĕkt') *n.* Due respect for oneself and one's personal worth. **—self·re·spect·ing** *adj.*

self·re·straint (sĕlf'rĭ-strānt') *n.* Restraint of one's emotions, desires, or inclinations; self-control.

self·right·eous (sĕlf'rī'chəs) *adj.* Piously sure of one's righteousness. **—self·right·eous·ly** *adv.* **—self·right·eous·ness** *n.*

self·right·ing (sĕlf'rī'tĭng) *adj.* Able to right itself when overturned: *a self-righting boat.*

self·ris·ing flour (sĕlf'rī'zĭng) *adj.* A commercially produced mixture of flour and leavening.

self·rule (sĕlf'rōōl') *n.* Self-government.

self·sac·ri·fice (sĕlf'săk'rə-fīs') *n.* Sacrifice of one's personal interests or well-being for the sake of others or for a cause. **—self·sac·ri·fic·ing** *adj.*

self·same (sĕlf'sām') *adj.* Exactly identical; the very same. **—See** Synonyms at **same.** [Middle English *selve same* : *self,* SELF (obsolete sense "same") + SAME.] **—self·same·ness** *n.*

self·sat·is·fac·tion (sĕlf'săt'ĭs-făk'shən) *n.* Satisfaction, especially complacent satisfaction, with oneself or one's own accomplishments. **—self·sat·is·fied** *adj.*

self·seal·ing (sĕlf'sē'lĭng) *adj.* Able to be sealed without the application of moisture: *a self-sealing envelope.*

self·seed·ed (sĕlf'sē'dĭd) *adj.* Self-sown.

self·seek·ing (sĕlf'sē'kĭng) *n.* The determined pursuit of one's own ends or interests. **—self·seek·er** *n.* **—self·seek·ing** *adj.*

self·serv·ice (sĕlf'sûr'vĭs) *adj.* Designating a retail commercial enterprise in which the customers serve themselves and pay a cashier.

self·serv·ing (sĕlf'sûr'vĭng) *adj.* Serving one's own interests, especially without consideration for the needs or interests of others.

self·sown (sĕlf'sōn') *adj.* Growing from seed dispersal by natural means rather than sown by man; self-seeded. Said of plants.

self-start·er (sĕlf'stär'tər) *n.* **1.** A device for starting an engine, a **starter** *(see).* **2.** A person with initiative.

self-stud·y (sĕlf'stŭd'ē) *n.* A form of study in which the student is to a large extent responsible for his own instruction. Also used adjectivally: *a self-study course.*

self-styled (sĕlf'stīld') *adj.* As characterized by oneself, often without right or justification: *a self-styled author.*

self-suf·fi·cient (sĕlf'sə-fĭsh'ənt) *adj.* **1.** Able to provide for oneself without the help of others; not dependent on others. **2.** Having undue confidence; smug or overbearing. **—self-suf·fi·cien·cy** *n.*

self-sup·port (sĕlf'sə-pôrt', -pōrt') *n.* The act of or capacity for supporting oneself, especially financially, without the help of others. **—self-sup·port·ed, self-sup·port·ing** *adj.*

self-taught (sĕlf'tôt') *adj.* Having taught oneself without formal instruction or the help of others.

self-will (sĕlf'wĭl') *n.* Willfulness, especially in satisfying one's own desires or adhering to one's own opinions. **—self-willed** *adj.*

self-wind·ing (sĕlf'wīn'dĭng) *adj.* Having a mechanism that does not need winding. Said of watches in which the spring is wound by a weight activated by the movement of the wearer's hand.

self-worth (sĕlf'wûrth) *n.* Self-esteem.

Sel·juk (sĕl'jōŏk', sĕl-jōŏk') *n.* A member of any of several Turkish dynasties ruling over central and western Asia from the 11th to the 13th century. [Turkish, after *Seljūk,* the reputed eponymous ancestor.] **—Sel·juk** *adj.*

Sel·kirk (sĕl'kûrk). Also **Sel·kirk·shire** (-shîr', -shər). A former county of southern Scotland, now part of the Borders Region. Its administrative center was Selkirk, a royal burgh on Ettrick Water.

Selkirk, Alexander (1676-1721). Scottish sailor whose experiences inspired Defoe's *Robinson Crusoe.* In 1704 he was marooned on the uninhabited island of Juan Fernández. He was discovered there in 1709.

sell (sĕl) *v.* **sold** (sōld), **selling, sells.** *—tr.* **1.** To exchange or deliver for money or its equivalent, as goods, services, or property; dispose of for a price. **2.** To deal in; offer for sale as one's business: *sells computers.* **3.** To give up or surrender, often treacherously or dishonorably, in exchange for a price or reward: *witches who had sold themselves to Satan.* **4.** To promote the sale of; cause to be sold: *Publicity sold that product.* **5. a.** To convince of the worth or desirability of something. Used with *on: He's completely sold on the idea.* **b.** To convince someone of the worth or desirability of (an idea or product, for example): *tried to sell their policy to the electorate.* **6.** To achieve sales of: *has already sold half a million copies in hardback.* **7.** *Informal.* To cheat or dupe. *—intr.* **1.** To exchange ownership for money or its equivalent; engage in selling goods or services. **2.** To be sold or be on sale. **3.** To attract prospective buyers; be popular on the market: *an item that sells well.* **4.** To be approved of; gain acceptance. **—sell a bill of goods.** To take unfair advantage of. **—sell down the river.** To betray the trust or faith of. **—sell off.** To get rid of by selling, often at reduced prices; deplete. **—sell short. 1.** *Finance.* To contract for the sale of securities or commodities one expects to own at a later date and on more advantageous terms. **2.** To undervalue (oneself or another); fail to appreciate the worth of. *—n.* **1.** The act of selling. **2.** A sales presentation of a specified type. See **hard sell, soft sell. 3.** *Slang.* A hoax or swindle. [Sell, sold, sold; Middle English *sellen, sold,* Old English *sellan, sealde, seald,* to give, betray, sell.] **—sell·a·ble** *adj.*

sell·er (sĕl'ər) *n.* **1.** A person who sells; a salesperson or vender. **2.** An item that sells in a particular manner: *a best seller.*

Sel·lers (sĕl'ərz), **Peter** (1925-80). British comic actor, noted for the brilliance and variety of his characterizations. He won fame in the 1950's radio series *The Goon Show* and established an international reputation in films such as *Dr. Strangelove* (1963) and the *Pink Panther* series (1963-77).

sellers' market *n. Economics.* A market condition characterized by relatively high prices, occurring when the supply of commodities falls short of market demand. Compare **buyers' market.**

sell·ing point (sĕl'ĭng) *n.* A particularly attractive aspect, as of a product or idea, that is stressed in order to promote its sale.

sell out *tr.v.* **1.** To sell the whole of (one's stock). **2.** To sell (one's share in a business). **3.** To betray (a cause, a principle, or a colleague), especially for the sake of gain: *sold out his artistic principles.* *—intr.v.* **1.** To sell the whole of one's stock. **2.** To sell one's share in a business. **3.** To betray one's principles, colleagues, or other loyalties.

sell·out (sĕl'out') *n.* **1.** A betrayal. **2.** An event for which all the tickets are sold. **3.** One who has betrayed principles or a cause.

sel·syn (sĕl'sĭn) *n.* A device for the instantaneous transmission and reception, from a generator to a motor, of the angular movement of rotating parts. Also called "synchro." [SEL(F) + SYN(CHRONOUS).]

selt·zer (sĕlt'sər) *n.* **1.** A natural effervescent spring water of high mineral content. **2.** Such water artificially prepared and containing carbon dioxide. Also called "seltzer water." [German *Selterser (Wasser),* "(water) of Nieder Selters," a district near Wiesbaden, West Germany, locality of the springs.]

sel·vage, sel·vedge (sĕl'vĭj) *n.* **1.** The edge of a fabric woven so that it will not unravel; especially, an ornamental fringe at either end of an oriental carpet. **2.** Any edge similar to this, usually a tapelike one. **3.** The edge plate of a lock with a slot for a bolt. [Middle English : *selve, self,* SELF + *egge,* EDGE (after obsolete Dutch *selfegghe*).]

selves. Plural of **self.**

Selz·nick (sĕlz'nĭk), **David Oliver** (1902-65). U.S. film producer. He established his reputation as a producer with films such as *David Copperfield* (1935) and *A Star is Born* (1937). His production of *Gone With the Wind* (1939) became one of the world's greatest box-office successes.

sem. seminary.

se·man·teme (sī-măn'tēm') *n.* An irreducible linguistic unit of meaning. [SEMANT(IC) + -EME.]

se·man·tic (sə-măn'tĭk) *adj.* **1.** Pertaining to meaning in language. **2.** Of, pertaining to, or according to the science of semantics. [Greek *sēmantikos,* significant, from *sēmainein,* to signify, show by a sign, from *sēma,* sign.]

se·man·ti·cist (sə-măn'tə-sĭst) *n.* A specialist in semantics.

se·man·tics (sə-măn'tĭks) *n. Used with a singular verb.* **1.** *Linguistics.* The study or science of meaning in language forms, particularly with regard to its historical change. **2.** *Logic.* The study of relationships between signs and symbols and what they represent. **3.** Subtleties in meaning. Often used derogatorily.

sem·a·phore (sĕm'ə-fôr', -fōr') *n.* **1.** Any visual signaling apparatus with flags, lights, or mechanically moving arms, as on a railroad. **2.** A visual system of sending information by means of two flags, one in each hand, using an alphabetic code based on the positions of the signaler's arms. ~*v.* **semaphored, -phoring, -phores.** *—tr.* To send (a message) by semaphore. *—intr.* To signal with a semaphore. [Greek *sēma,* sign + -PHORE.] See feature, next page.

se·ma·si·ol·o·gy (sī-mā'sē-ŏl'ə-jē) *n.* Semantics, especially the study of semantic development. [Greek *sēmasia,* meaning, from *sēmainein,* to signify, mean (see **semantic**) + -LOGY.] **—se·ma·si·o·log·i·cal** (sī-mā'sē-ə-lŏj'ĭ-kəl) *adj.* **—se·ma·si·ol·o·gist** *n.*

se·mat·ic (sī-măt'ĭk) *adj.* Serving as a warning or signal of danger, particularly to predators. Said especially of the coloring of certain animals. [Greek *sēma* (stem *sēmat-*), sign.]

sem·bla·ble (sĕm'blə-bəl) *adj.* Appearing real; apparent. ~*n. Archaic.* Something that closely resembles something else. [Middle English, from Old French, from *sembler,* to resemble, seem, from Latin *similāre, simulāre,* to SIMULATE.] **—sem·bla·bly** *adv.*

sem·blance (sĕm'bləns) *n.* **1.** An outward or token appearance. **2.** A representation or resemblance. **3.** The barest trace; a modicum. [Middle English, from Old French, from *semblant,* present participle of *sembler,* to resemble, seem. See **semblable.**]

se·mé (sə-mā') *adj. Heraldry.* Having a design embellished with small, delicate figures, as a lacing of stars or flowers. [French, past participle of *semer,* to sow, scatter, from Latin *sēmināre,* from *sēmen,* seed.]

semeiology. Variant of **semiology.**

semeiotic. Variant of **semiotic.**

se·meme (sē'mēm') *n.* The meaning expressed by a morpheme. [SE-M(ANTIC) + -EME.]

se·men (sē'mən) *n.* **1.** The viscous whitish fluid that is ejaculated from the male reproductive organs of animals and transports spermatozoa. **2.** Sperm. [Middle English, from Latin *sēmen,* "seed."]

se·mes·ter (sə-mĕs'tər) *n.* One of two divisions of 15 to 18 weeks each on an academic year. [German *Semester,* from Latin *(cursus) sēmēstris,* "(period) of six months" : *sex,* six + *mēnsis,* month.]

sem·i (sĕm'ē, sĕm'ī) *n., pl.* **semis.** *Informal.* A semitrailer.

semi– *prefix. Abbr.* **s.** Indicates: **1.** Partly, partially, or incompletely; for example, **semiaquatic, semiliterate. 2.** Half of; for example, **semicircle. 3.** Occurring twice within a particular period of time; for example, **semimonthly.** *Note:* Many compounds other than those entered here may be formed with *semi-.* In this dictionary, in forming compounds, *semi-* is normally joined with the following element without space or hyphen: *semiannual.* However, many users prefer the hyphenated form, especially if the second element begins with a capital letter or with *i: semi-Americanized, semi-idle.* [Latin *sēmi-.*]

sem·i·ab·stract (sĕm'ē-ăb-străkt', -ăb'străkt') *adj.* Of or relating to an art form characterized by recognizable but stylized subject matter. **—sem·i·ab·strac·tion** *n.*

sem·i·an·nu·al (sĕm'ē-ăn'yōō-əl, sĕm'ī-) *adj.* Happening or issued twice a year. **—sem·i·an·nu·al·ly** *adv.*

sem·i·a·quat·ic (sĕm'ē-ə-kwăt'ĭk, sĕm'ī-) *adj.* Adapted for living or growing in or near water; not entirely aquatic.

sem·i·ar·id (sĕm'ē-ăr'ĭd, sĕm'ī-) *adj.* Designating regions often found in continental interiors, that are transitional between savannah grassland and the desert, having relatively low rainfall and scrubby vegetation with coarse grasses; partly arid.

sem·i·au·to·mat·ic (sĕm'ē-ô'tə-măt'ĭk, sĕm'ī-) *adj.* **1.** Partially automatic. **2.** Having an automatic reloading mechanism but requiring a pull of the trigger for each shot; autoloading. Said of a firearm. Compare **automatic.** **—sem·i·au·to·mat·ic** *n.*

sem·i·au·ton·o·mous (sĕm'ē-ô-tŏn'ə-məs, sĕm'ī-) *adj.* Partially self-governing; especially, having powers of self-government within a larger organization or structure.

sem·i·breve (sĕm'ē-brēv', sĕm'ī-) *n. British.* A **whole note** *(see).*

sem·i·cir·cle (sĕm'ē-sûr'kəl) *n.* **1.** A half of a circle as divided by a diameter. **2.** An object or arrangement of objects or people in the shape of a half-circle. **—sem·i·cir·cu·lar** (sĕm'ī-sûr'kyə-lər) *adj.*

semicircular canal *n.* One of the three tubular and looped structures in the labyrinth of the inner ear, together functioning in the maintenance of a sense of balance and orientation.

sem·i·civ·i·lized (sĕm′ē-sĭv′ə-līzd′, sĕm′ī-) *adj.* Partly civilized.
sem·i·co·lon (sĕm′ī-kō′lən) *n.* A mark of punctuation (;) indicating a degree of separation intermediate in value between the comma and the period.
sem·i·con·duc·tor (sĕm′ē-kən-dŭk′tər, sĕm′ī-) *n.* Any of various solid crystalline substances, such as germanium or silicon, having electrical conductivity greater than insulators but less than good conductors.

---

semaphore

ONE OF THE FIRST SIGNALING SYSTEMS
Arms that point out messages

Semaphore is a visual signaling system using different positions of movable arms to represent letters, numbers, or other information. It is known that the Greeks and Romans used flags and torches, especially on hilltops and towers, for military communications. The invention of the telescope in the early 1600's extended the range of visual signaling.

In 1794 a French engineer, Claude Chappe, invented a system which was used in the Napoleonic wars whereby messages were conveyed over a route of 144 miles in two minutes.

Today, the U.S. Navy uses semaphore flags for short-range signaling by and to ships.

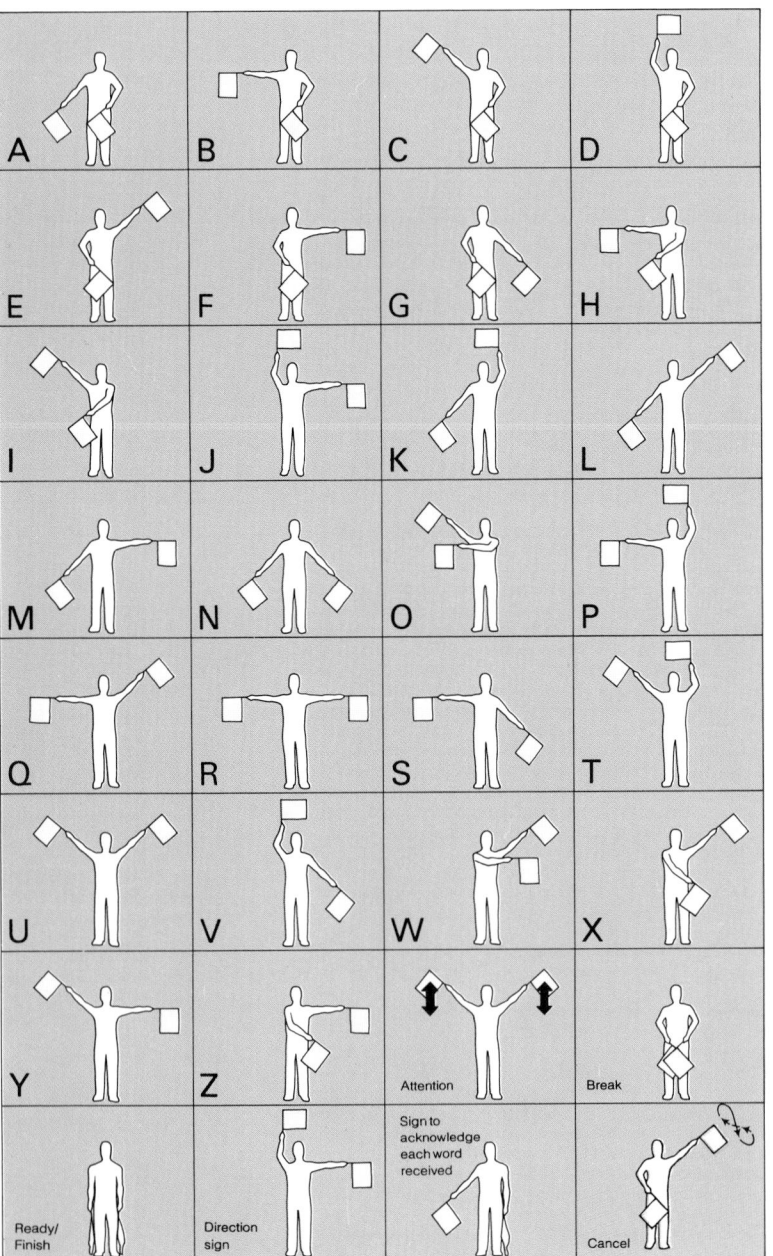

SEMAPHORE ALPHABET *Signals can be sent by arm movements, with or without flags, as well as by machine. The receiver may be in front of or behind the signaler, so the direction sign—with left arm horizontal—is given first to show which way the signs are to be read.*

---

sem·i·con·scious (sĕm′ē-kŏn′shəs, sĕm′ī-) *adj.* Half-conscious; not fully conscious or aware. —**sem·i·con·scious·ly** *adv.* —**sem·i·con·scious·ness** *n.*
sem·i·des·ert (sĕm′ē-dĕz′ərt, sĕm′ī-) *n.* A semiarid area. —**sem·i·des·ert** *adj.*
sem·i·de·tached (sĕm′ē-dĭ-tăcht′, sĕm′ī-) *adj.* Attached to another building on one side only. Said of either of a pair of houses joined by a common wall. —**sem·i·de·tached** *n.*
sem·i·di·am·e·ter (sĕm′ē-dī-ăm′ə-tər, sĕm′ī-) *n.* The apparent angular radius of a celestial body when viewed as a disk from Earth.
sem·i·di·ur·nal (sĕm′ē-dī-ûr′nəl, sĕm′ī-) *adj.* **1.** Of, pertaining to, occurring, or performed during a half-day. **2.** Occurring or coming approximately once every 12 hours, as the tides do. **3.** Designating the arc described by a celestial body between its meridian passage and its points of rising or setting.
sem·i·dome (sĕm′ē-dōm′, sĕm′ī-) *n.* A roof covering a semicircular space; half a dome.
sem·i·el·lip·ti·cal (sĕm′ē-ĭ-lĭp′tĭ-kəl, sĕm′ī-) *adj.* Having the form or shape of half of an ellipse, especially when divided along the major axis.
sem·i·fi·nal (sĕm′ē-fī′nəl, sĕm′ī-) *n.* **1.** One of the two competitions of the next to the last round in an elimination tournament. **2.** A match, competition, or other event that precedes the final event. —**sem·i·fi·nal** *adj.* —**sem·i·fi·nal·ist** *n.*
sem·i·flu·id (sĕm′ē-flōō′ĭd, sĕm′ī-) *adj.* Also **sem·i·flu·id·ic** (sĕm′-ē-flōō-ĭd′ĭk). Intermediate in flow properties between solids and liquids; highly viscous. —**sem·i·flu·id** *n.* —**sem·i·flu·id·i·ty** (sĕm′-ē-flōō-ĭd′ə-tē) *n.*
sem·i·for·mal (sĕm′ē-fôr′məl, sĕm′ī-) *adj.* Being or appropriate for a somewhat formal occasion: *semiformal dining; semiformal attire.*
sem·i·group (sĕm′ē-grōōp′) *n. Algebra.* A nonempty set with an associative binary multiplication.
sem·i·liq·uid (sĕm′ē-lĭk′wĭd, sĕm′ī-) *adj.* Intermediate in properties, especially flow properties, between liquids and solids. —*n.* A semiliquid substance.
sem·i·lit·er·ate (sĕm′ē-lĭt′ər-ĭt, sĕm′ī-) *adj.* **1.** Having achieved an elementary level of literacy. **2.** Having limited knowledge or understanding, as of a technical subject.
sem·i·log·a·rith·mic (sĕm′ē-lôg′ə-rĭth′mĭk, sĕm′ī-) *adj.* **1.** Having one logarithmic and one arithmetic scale: *semilogarithmic graph paper.* **2.** Characteristic of a relationship expressed using such scales.
sem·i·lu·nar (sĕm′ē-lōō′nər, sĕm′ī-) *adj.* Also **sem·i·lu·nate** (-lōō′nāt′). Shaped like a half-moon; crescent.
semilunar bone *n. Anatomy.* The **lunate bone** *(see).*
semilunar valve *n.* Either of two crescent-shaped valves, each having three cusps, located in the aorta and in the pulmonary artery and preventing blood from flowing back into the heart.
sem·i·month·ly (sĕm′ē-mŭnth′lē, sĕm′ī-) *adj.* Occurring or issued twice a month. —*n., pl.* **semimonthlies.** A semimonthly publication. —*adv.* Twice monthly; at half-monthly intervals. —See Usage note at **bi-.**
sem·i·nal (sĕm′ə-nəl) *adj.* **1.** Of, relating to, or containing semen or seed. **2.** Highly influential in an original way; constituting or providing a basis for further development. [Middle English, from Old French, from Latin *sēminālis,* from *sēmen* (stem *sēmin-*), seed, SEMEN.] —**sem·i·nal·ly** *adv.*
sem·i·nar (sĕm′ə-när′) *n.* **1. a.** A small group, usually of advanced students, engaged in original research and meeting regularly, under the guidance of a professor, to exchange and discuss their views and findings. **b.** A course of study so pursued. **c.** A scheduled meeting of such a group. **2.** A meeting for an exchange of ideas on a particular topic; conference. [German *Seminar,* from Latin *sēminārium,* seed plot, nursery. See **seminary.**]
sem·i·nar·i·an (sĕm′ə-nâr′ē-ən) *n.* Also **sem·i·nar·ist** (sĕm′ə-nâr′ĭst, -nə-rĭst). A seminary student.
sem·i·nar·y (sĕm′ə-nĕr′ē) *n., pl.* **-ies.** *Abbr.* **sem. 1.** A place of education, especially: **a.** A theological school for the training of priests, ministers, or rabbis. **b.** *Archaic.* A private secondary school for girls. **2.** A place or environment in which something is developed or nurtured. [Middle English, seed plot, place for cultivation, nursery garden, from Latin *sēminārium,* garden, seed plot, nursery, from *sēminārius,* of seeds, from *sēmen* (stem *sēmin-*), seed.]
sem·i·na·tion (sĕm′ə-nā′shən) *n. Rare.* The dispersal or production of seed. [Latin *sēminātiō* (stem *sēminātiōn-*), propagation, from *sēminātus,* past participle of *sēmināre,* to sow, from *sēmen* (stem *sēmin-*), seed.]
sem·i·nif·er·ous (sĕm′ə-nĭf′ər-əs) *adj. Biology.* **1.** Conveying or producing semen: *the seminiferous tubules of the testis.* **2.** Bearing seed. [Latin *sēmen* (stem *sēmin-*), SEMEN + -FEROUS.]
Sem·i·nole (sĕm′ə-nōl′) *n., pl.* **-noles** or collectively **Seminole. 1.** A member of a Muskhogean-speaking North American Indian people, now living chiefly in Oklahoma. **2.** The language of this people. [Creek *simanóli, simalóni,* from American Spanish *cimarrón,* wild, runaway. See **maroon** (to abandon).] —**Sem·i·nole** *adj.*
sem·i·no·mad (sĕm′ē-nō′măd′, sĕm′ī-) *n.* One of a people whose living habits are largely nomadic but who plant some crops. —**sem·i·no·mad·ic** (sĕm′ē-nō-măd′ĭk) *adj.*
sem·i·of·fi·cial (sĕm′ē-ə-fĭsh′əl, sĕm′ī-) *adj.* Having some official authority or sanction. —**sem·i·of·fi·cial·ly** *adv.*
se·mi·ol·o·gy, se·mei·ol·o·gy (sē′mē-ŏl′ə-jē, sē′mī-, sĕm′ē-, sĕm′ī-) *n.* **1.** The science dealing with signs, sign language, or systems of signaling. **2.** *Medicine.* See **symptomatology** (sense 1). [New Latin

semaeologia : Greek *sēmeion,* mark, sign, from *sēma,* sign, signal + -LOGY.]

se·mi·ot·ic, se·mei·ot·ic (sē'mē-ŏt'ĭk, sē'mī-, sĕm'ē-, sĕm'ī-) *adj.* **1.** Of or relating to semiotics. **2.** *Medicine.* Relating to symptomatology. [Greek *sēmeiōtikos,* observant of signs, from *sēmeioun,* to mark, give signals, note, from *sēmeion,* sign. See **semiology.**]

se·mi·ot·ics, se·mei·ot·ics (sē'mē-ŏt'ĭks, sē'mī-, sĕm'ē-, sĕm'ī-) *n. Used with a singular verb.* **1.** The study of all forms of human communicative behavior, especially of signs and symbols. **2.** See **symptomatology** (sense 1). **—se·mi·o·ti·cian** (sē'mē-ə-tĭsh'ən) *n.*

sem·i·pal·mate (sĕm'ē-păl'māt', sĕm'ī-) Also **sem·i·pal·mat·ed** (-mā'tĭd). Having partial or reduced webbing between the toes, as some wading birds do.

sem·i·par·a·site (sĕm'ē-păr'ə-sīt', sĕm'ī-) *n. Biology.* A **hemiparasite** *(see).* **—sem·i·par·a·sit·ic** (sĕm'ē-păr'ə-sĭt'ĭk) *adj.* **—sem·i·par·a·sit·ism** *n.*

sem·i·per·me·a·ble (sĕm'ē-pûr'mē-ə-bəl, sĕm'ī-) *adj.* **1.** Partially permeable. **2.** Of or relating to a natural or artificial membrane that is permeable to some molecules in a mixture or solution but not to all. See **osmosis.**

sem·i·po·lar bond (sĕm'ē-pō'lər) *n. Chemistry.* A **coordinate bond** *(see).*

sem·i·por·ce·lain (sĕm'ē-pôr'sə-lĭn, -pôr'-, sĕm'ī-) *n.* Any of several glazed ceramic wares resembling porcelain but having little or no translucency.

sem·i·pre·cious (sĕm'ē-prĕsh'əs, sĕm'ī-) *adj.* Designating stones of less value than precious stones, such as the topaz.

sem·i·pri·vate (sĕm'ē-prī'vĭt, sĕm'ī-) *adj.* Shared with usually one to three other hospital patients: *a semiprivate room.*

sem·i·pro (sĕm'ē-prō', sĕm'ī-) *adj. Informal.* Semiprofessional. **—sem·i·pro** *n.*

sem·i·pro·fes·sion·al (sĕm'ē-prə-fĕsh'ən-əl, sĕm'ī-) *adj.* **1.** Taking part in a sport or other activity for pay, but not on a full-time basis. **2.** Composed of or engaged in by semiprofessional players. *~n.* A semiprofessional person.

sem·i·qua·ver (sĕm'ē-kwā'vər) *n. Chiefly British. Music.* A **sixteenth note** *(see).*

Se·mir·a·mis (sə-mîr'ə-mĭs). The legendary founder of Babylon.

sem·i·rig·id (sĕm'ē-rĭj'ĭd, sĕm'ī-) *adj.* **1.** Moderately rigid. **2.** Having some rigid components.

sem·i·round (sĕm'ē-round', sĕm'ī-) *adj.* Having a round side and a flat side. **—sem·i·round** *n.*

sem·i·skilled (sĕm'ē-skĭld', sĕm'ī-) *adj.* Possessing or requiring some skills or training, but less than those required for specialized work.

sem·i·sol·id (sĕm'ē-sŏl'ĭd, sĕm'ī-) *adj.* Intermediate in properties, especially in rigidity, between solids and liquids. *~n.* A semisolid substance, such as a stiff dough or firm gelatin.

Sem·ite (sĕm'īt') *n.* Also **Shem·ite** (shĕm'īt'). A member of a people of Caucasian stock comprising chiefly Jews and Arabs but in ancient times also including Babylonians, Assyrians, Phoenicians, and others of the eastern Mediterranean area. [New Latin *semita,* from Late Latin *Sēm,* Shem (traditional ancestor of the Semites), from Greek, from Hebrew *Shem.*]

Se·mit·ic (sə-mĭt'ĭk) *adj.* **1.** Of, pertaining to, or designating a subfamily of the Afro-Asiatic family of languages including Arabic, Hebrew, Ethiopic, Amharic, and Aramaic. **2.** Of, pertaining to, or designating any of the people who speak a Semitic language; especially, the Jewish or Arabic peoples. *~n.* **1.** The Semitic subfamily of languages. **2.** Any one of these languages.

Se·mit·ics (sə-mĭt'ĭks) *n. Used with a singular verb.* The study of the history, languages, and cultures of the Semitic peoples.

Sem·i·tism (sĕm'ə-tĭz'əm) *n.* **1.** A Semitic word, idiom, or characteristic. **2.** A policy of favoring Jewish interests.

Sem·i·to-Ha·mit·ic (sĕm'ə-tō'hă-mĭt'ĭk) *n.* A family of languages, **Afro-Asiatic** *(see).* **—Sem·i·to-Ha·mit·ic** *adj.*

sem·i·tone (sĕm'ē-tōn', sĕm'ī-) *n. Music.* The smallest interval normally used in Western music, equal to half a tone in the standard diatonic scale. Also called "half step," "half tone." **—sem·i·ton·ic** (sĕm'ē-tŏn'ĭk, sĕm'ī-) *adj.*

sem·i·trail·er (sĕm'ē-trā'lər, sĕm'ī-) *n.* A trailer with wheels at the rear only, the forward end being supported by the towing vehicle.

sem·i·trans·par·ent (sĕm'ē-trăns-pâr'ənt, -pâr'-, sĕm'ī-) *adj.* Not completely transparent.

sem·i·trop·i·cal (sĕm'ē-trŏp'ĭ-kəl, sĕm'ī-) *adj.* Partly tropical; subtropical.

sem·i·vow·el (sĕm'ī-vou'əl) *n. Phonetics.* A speech sound that from the articulatory viewpoint is a vowel but that functions as a consonant in the sound system of a particular language; for example, (w) and (y) in English are semivowels. Also called "glide."

sem·i·week·ly (sĕm'ē-wēk'lē, sĕm'ī-) *adj.* Issued or happening twice a week. *~n., pl.* **semiweeklies.** A semiweekly publication. *~adv.* Twice weekly. **—See Usage note at bi-.**

sem·o·li·na (sĕm'ə-lē'nə) *n.* The gritty, coarse particles of wheat left after the finer flour has passed through the bolting machine, used for making pasta. [Variant of Italian *semolino,* diminutive of *semola,* bran, from Latin *simila,* fine flour. See **simnel.**]

sem·pi·ter·nal (sĕm'pī-tûr'nəl) *adj.* Eternal; perpetual. [Middle English, from Old French *sempiternel,* from Late Latin *sempiternālis,* from Latin *sempiternus : semper,* always + *aeternus,* eternal.] **—sem·pi·ter·ni·ty** (sĕm'pī-tûr'nə-tē) *n.*

sem·pli·ce (sĕm'plĭ-chā') *adv. Music.* Simply; plainly. Used as a direction. [Italian, from Latin *simplex* (stem *simplic-*), simple.] **—sem·pli·ce** *adj.*

sem·pre (sĕm'prā) *adv. Music.* In the same manner throughout. Used as a direction. [Italian, "always," from Latin *semper.*]

semp·stress (sĕmp'strĭs, sĕm'-) *n. Rare.* A seamstress. [Variant of SEAMSTRESS.]

sen (sĕn) *n., pl.* **sen. 1. a.** A former monetary unit equal to ¹/₁₀₀ of the yen of Japan. **b.** A monetary unit equal to ¹/₁₀₀ of the dollar of Brunei. **c.** A monetary unit equal to ¹/₁₀₀ of the rupiah of Indonesia. **d.** A monetary unit equal to ¹/₁₀₀ of the riel of Kampuchea. **e.** A monetary unit equal to ¹/₁₀₀ of the dollar or ringgit of Malaysia. See feature at **currency. 2.** A coin worth one sen. [Japanese, from Chinese (Mandarin) *qián,* money, coin.]

sen., Sen. 1. senate; senator. **2.** senior.

se·nar·i·us (sə-nâr'ē-əs) *n., pl.* **-narii** (-nâr'ē-ī'). A Greek or Latin verse consisting of six feet. [Latin *sēnārius,* from adjective, SENARY.]

sen·ar·mon·tite (sĕn'är-mŏn'tīt') *n.* A white or grayish mineral, Sb_2O_3, that occurs in cubic crystalline form. [After Henri de *Sénarmont* (died 1862), French mineralogist.]

sen·a·ry (sĕn'ə-rē) *adj.* Of or pertaining to the number six; having six things or parts. [Latin *sēnārius,* from *sēnī,* six each, from *sex,* six.]

sen·ate (sĕn'ĭt) *n. Abbr.* **sen., Sen. 1.** An assembly or council of citizens having the highest deliberative and legislative functions in a government, especially: **a. Senate.** The upper house of Congress in the United States, to which two members are elected from each state. **b. Senate.** The upper house in the bicameral legislature of many U.S. states. **c. Senate.** The upper legislative house in Australia, Canada, France, and other countries. **d.** The supreme council of state of the ancient Roman republic and, nominally, of the empire. **2.** The building or hall in which a senate meets. **3.** The governing body of some universities, composed of faculty members and sometimes student representatives. [Middle English *senat,* from Old French, from Latin *senātus,* from *senex,* old, an old man, an elder.]

sen·a·tor (sĕn'ə-tər) *n. Often* **Senator.** *Abbr.* **Sen., sen.** A member of a senate. **—sen·a·tor·ship** *n.*

sen·a·to·ri·al (sĕn'ə-tôr'ē-əl, -tōr'ē-əl) *adj.* **1.** Of, concerning, or befitting a senator or a senate. **2.** Composed of senators.

senatorial courtesy *n.* The custom in the U.S. Senate of refusing to confirm a Presidential appointment to office opposed by both senators from the state of the appointee or by the senior senator of the President's party.

senatorial district *n.* A territorial district from which a senator is elected.

se·na·tus con·sul·tum (sə-nä'tōōs kōn-sōōl'tōōm, sə-nä'təs kən-sŭl'təm) *n., pl.* **senatus consulta** (-sōōl'tə, -sŭl'tə). *Latin.* A decree of the ancient Roman senate.

send¹ (sĕnd) *v.* **sent** (sĕnt), **sending, sends.** *—tr.* **1. a.** To cause to be conveyed to a destination by an intermediary: *sent his reply by telegram.* **b.** To express for conveyance: *She sends her love.* **2.** To cause or order to go, especially: **a.** To direct to go on a mission or errand. **b.** To enable or arrange for (someone) to go: *sent all their children to private schools.* **c.** To command or request to depart; dismiss: *Send the guard away.* **d.** To direct or require to go or be taken; consign: *sent them to prison.* **e.** To cause to go or move in a specified way or direction: *The rain sent them hurrying indoors.* **f.** To direct (a person) to a source of information; refer. **3. a.** To give off; emit (heat or smoke, for example). Often used with *forth* or *out.* **b.** To produce; cause to grow: *sending forth new roots.* **4.** To direct or propel with force: *an explosion that sent glass flying everywhere.* **5.** To cause to take place or befall; bestow or inflict: *a punishment sent by the gods.* **6. a.** To put or drive into some state or condition: *The news sent him into a rage.* **b.** *Slang.* To transport with delight; carry away. *—intr.* To dispatch a messenger or message. Often used with *out: send out for Chinese food.* **—send away for.** To order by mail. **—send down.** *British.* To suspend or dismiss from a university. **—send for. 1.** To order. **2.** To summon. **—send packing.** *Informal.* To dismiss summarily or abruptly. [Send, sent, sent; Middle English *senden, sente, sent,* Old English *sendan, sende, sended.*] **—send·er** *n.*

send². Variant of **scend.**

sen·dal (sĕn'dl) *n.* A light, thin silk used in the Middle Ages. [Middle English *cendal,* from Old French, obscurely akin to Greek *sindōn†,* a fine linen cloth.]

send off *tr.v.* **1.** *Sports.* To order (a player) to leave the field because of a serious violation of the rules. **2.** To give a send-off to.

send-off (sĕnd'ôf', -ŏf') *n.* **1.** A demonstration of affection and good wishes for one about to leave on a journey or to begin a new undertaking. **2.** A start given to someone or something.

send up *tr.v.* **1.** To satirize or make fun of, especially by mimicry or parody. **2.** *Informal.* To send to prison.

send-up (sĕnd'ŭp') *n.* An amusing imitation or parody.

se·ne (sā'nā) *n., pl.* **sene.** A monetary unit of Western Samoa equal to ¹/₁₀₀ of a tala. [Samoan, from CENT.]

Sen·e·ca¹ (sĕn'ĭ-kə) *n., pl.* **-cas** or collectively **Seneca. 1.** A member of an Iroquoian-speaking North American Indian people formerly inhabiting western New York. **2.** The language of this people.

Seneca². Latin name Marcus Annaeus Seneca; known as "the Elder" (c. 55 B.C.–A.D. 39). Roman writer on rhetoric. His works include the *Controversiae,* a series of imaginary legal cases that illustrate various approved methods of oratorical presentation.

Seneca³. Latin name Lucius Annaeus Seneca; known as "the

Younger" (*c.* 4 B.C.–A.D. 65). Roman writer, philosopher, and politician. The son of Seneca the Elder, he was tutor to the young Nero and became one of the emperor's chief advisers on his accession. He produced several works of moral philosophy advocating stoicism and also wrote nine tragedies. Seneca was forced to commit suicide for alleged conspiracy against Nero.

Seneca Falls. Village of west-central New York State, in the Finger Lakes region. Settled *c.* 1787, it was the home of Amelia Bloomer and Elizabeth Cady Stanton. The first women's rights convention in the United States was held here in 1848.

Seneca Lake. Largest, 174 square kilometers (67 square miles) of the Finger Lakes in west-central New York State. It is surrounded by a farming and resort region.

se•nec•ti•tude (sĭ-nĕk'tə-to͞od', -tyo͞od') *n.* Old age. [Medieval Latin *senectitūdō,* from Latin *senectūs,* from *senex,* old.]

sen•e•ga (sĕn'ə-gə) *n.* The dried root of a North American plant, *Polygala senega,* used as an expectorant. [Variant of SENECA.]

Sen•e•gal (sĕn'ə-gôl'). A river of western Africa. Formed by the confluence of the Bafing and Bakoy rivers, both of which rise in the Fouta Djallon in northern Guinea, it flows 1,690 kilometers (1,050 miles) to the Atlantic at St. Louis in Senegal.

Senegal. A state of West Africa, which takes its name from the Senegal River. Consisting mainly of lowland plains it has important phosphate and iron-ore deposits. Because of the Sahel droughts of the 1970's, groundnuts, which accounted for more than three quarters of the country's total exports, now account for only a quarter. Fishing and tourism are increasingly important. Senegal is one of West Africa's most industrialized countries, producing textiles, beer, foodstuffs, tobacco, and cement. By 1887 the French had conquered all of Senegal. It gained independence in 1960, but maintains close ties with France. In 1981 it joined with Gambia to form the Confederation of Senegambia. Area, 196,722 square kilometers (75,934 square miles). Population, 5,500,000. Capital, Dakar. See map at **West African States.**

se•nes•cence (sĭ-nĕs'əns) *n.* The state associated with advancing age of an organism or part, usually characterized by a reduced capacity to repair and maintain tissues. **—se•nes•cent** *adj.*

sen•e•schal (sĕn'ə-shəl) *n.* An official in a royal or noble medieval household in charge of domestic arrangements and the administration of servants; a steward. [Middle English, from Old French, from Medieval Latin *siniscalcus,* from Germanic.]

sen•gi (sĕng'gē) *n., pl.* **sengi.** A unit of money equal to 1/10,000 of the zaire of Zaire. See feature at **currency.**

se•nile (sē'nīl', sĕn'īl') *adj.* **1.** Pertaining to, characteristic of, or proceeding from old age. **2.** Exhibiting senility. **3.** *Geology.* Worn away nearly to the base level, as at the end of an erosion cycle. [French *sénile,* from Latin *senīlis,* from *senex* (stem *sen-*), old.] **—se•nile•ly** *adv.*

senile dementia *n.* Progressive deterioration of mental faculties in old age. See **presenile dementia.**

se•nil•i•ty (sĭ-nĭl'ə-tē) *n.* **1.** The state of being senile. **2.** Mental and physical deterioration with old age.

sen•ior (sēn'yər) *adj. Abbr.* **Sr., sr., Sen., sen., Snr. 1.** More advanced in age. Used especially after a name to denote the older of two persons who share the same name, such as a father and son: *Douglas Fairbanks, Sr.* **2. a.** Pertaining to or having a high or higher rank: *senior levels of management.* **b.** Above others in terms of length of service or appointment. **3.** Of, designating, or intended for older or more advanced students or pupils.
—*n.* A senior person, especially: **1.** One who is older: *He is three years my senior.* **2.** A final-year student in high school or college. [Latin, comparative of *senex,* old.]

senior citizen *n.* A person of or over the age of retirement.

Usage: The phrase *senior citizen* is now widely used as a euphemism for "elderly person," especially in the fields of politics and advertising. While many people find it unobjectionable, the phrase has attracted criticism on the grounds that it lacks any real meaning, and that it distracts people's attention from the problems involved in society's care (or lack of care) of the aged.

senior high school *n.* A high school usually comprising grades 10, 11, and 12.

sen•ior•i•ty (sēn-yôr'ə-tē, -yŏr'ə-tē) *n., pl.* **-ties. 1.** The state of being older or higher in rank. **2.** Precedence of position; especially, precedence over others of the same rank by reason of a longer span of service.

sen•i•ti (sĕn'ə-tē) *n., pl.* **seniti.** A unit of money equal to 1/100 of the pa'anga of Tonga. See feature at **currency.**

sen•na (sĕn'ə) *n.* **1.** Any of various plants of the genus *Cassia,* having compound leaves and usually yellow flowers. **2.** The dried leaves or pods of *C. angustifolia* or *C. acutifolia,* used medicinally as a cathartic. [New Latin, from Arabic *sanā'.*]

Sen•nach•er•ib (sə-năk'ər-ĭb') (died 681 B.C.). King of Assyria (704–681). The son of Sargon II, he is especially remembered for his building works, which included the restoration of Nineveh.

sen•net¹ (sĕn'ĭt) *n.* A call on a trumpet or cornet signaling the ceremonial exits and entrances of actors in Elizabethan drama. [Perhaps variant of SIGNET.]

sennet² *n.* Any of several barracudas, especially *Sphyraena borealis,* of western Atlantic waters. [Origin obscure.]

Sen•nett (sĕn'ĭt), **Mack,** born Michael Sinott (1884–1960). U.S. film producer and director, born in Canada. His many slapstick films include the Keystone comedies (1912–16).

sen•night, se'n•night (sĕn'īt') *n. Archaic.* A week. [Middle English *seoveniht, sennet,* Old English *seofon nihta* : *seofon,* SEVEN + *nihta,* plural of *niht,* NIGHT.]

sen•nit (sĕn'ĭt) *n.* **1.** *Nautical.* Braided cordage formed by plaiting several strands of rope fiber or similar material. **2.** Plaited straw, grass, or palm leaves for making hats. [17th century : origin obscure.]

sen•o•pi•a (sĕn-ō'pē-ə) *n.* Improvement of near vision sometimes occurring in the aged because of swelling of the crystalline lens in incipient cataract. [Latin *senex,* old + -OPIA.]

se•ñor (sān-yôr') *n., pl.* **señores** (sān-yôr'ās). *Abbr.* **Sr. 1.** The Spanish title of courtesy for a man, equivalent to the English *Mr.* or *sir.* It may be used alone or prefixed to a name. **2.** A Spanish or Spanish-speaking man.

se•ño•ra (sān-yôr'ä) *n., pl.* **señoras** (sān-yôr'äs). *Abbr.* **Sra. 1.** The Spanish title of courtesy for a married woman, equivalent to the English *Mrs.* or *madam.* It may be used alone or prefixed to a name. **2.** A Spanish or Spanish-speaking woman.

se•ño•ri•ta (sān'yō-rē'tä) *n., pl.* **-tas** (-täs). *Abbr.* **Srta. 1.** The Spanish title of courtesy for an unmarried young woman or a girl, equivalent to the English *Miss.* It may be used alone or prefixed to a name. **2.** A Spanish or Spanish-speaking unmarried woman or girl.

sen•sate (sĕn'sāt') *adj.* Perceived by the senses. [Late Latin *sēnsātus,* gifted with sense, from Latin *sēnsus,* SENSE.] **—sen•sate•ly** *adv.*

sen•sa•tion (sĕn-sā'shən, sən-) *n.* **1. a.** A perception associated with stimulation of a sense organ or with a specific bodily condition: *the sensation of heat.* **b.** The faculty to feel or perceive; physical sensibility: *He had little sensation left in his leg.* **2.** An emotional state that is hard to define but is associated with particular conditions or circumstances: *a strange sensation of relief.* **3. a.** A condition of intense public interest and excitement. **b.** An event, person, or object causing such public excitement. [Medieval Latin *sēnsātiō* (stem *sēnsātiōn-*), from Late Latin *sēnsātus,* SENSATE.]

sen•sa•tion•al (sĕn-sā'shən-əl, sən-) *adj.* **1.** Of or pertaining to sensation. **2.** Arousing or intended to arouse strong curiosity, interest, or reaction, especially by exaggerated or lurid details. **3.** Outstanding; wonderful. **—sen•sa•tion•al•ly** *adv.*

sen•sa•tion•al•ism (sĕn-sā'shən-əl-ĭz'əm, sən-) *n.* **1. a.** The use of sensational matter or methods, as in writing, art, or politics. **b.** Sensational subject matter. **c.** Interest in or the effect of such subject matter. **2.** *Philosophy.* The theory that sensation is the only source of knowledge. Also called "sensualism." **3.** The ethical doctrine that feeling is the only criterion of good. **—sen•sa•tion•al•ist** *n.* **—sen•sa•tion•al•is•tic** *adj.*

sense (sĕns) *n.* **1.** Any of the animal functions of hearing, sight, smell, touch, and taste. **2.** The faculty of external perception exemplified by these functions. **3. senses.** The faculties of sensation as means of providing physical gratification and pleasure. **4. a.** Intuitive or acquired perception or ability to make appropriate judgments: *a good sense of timing.* **b.** A capacity to appreciate or understand: *a sense of humor.* **c.** A vague feeling, impression, or presentiment: *a sense of impending trouble.* **d.** Recognition or awareness of moral issues and their relevance to one's own conduct: *a sense of duty.* **5. a.** *Usually* **senses.** One's normal conscious or rational state: *Come to your senses.* **b.** A capacity for sound practical judgments; common sense: *hasn't got an ounce of sense.* **c.** The quality of being consistent with good judgment: *There's no sense in waiting.* **6. a.** Import; point; intended meaning. **b.** Lexical meaning. **c.** The meaning of a word in a particular context. **7.** The prevailing view; consensus. **—make sense. 1.** To be coherent or intelligible. **2.** *Informal.* To be practical or advisable. —See Synonyms at **meaning, mind.**
—*tr.v.* **sensed, sensing, senses. 1.** To become aware of, often on the basis of intuition rather than explicit information; perceive. **2.** To detect something automatically: *sense radioactivity.* **3.** *Informal.* To grasp; understand. [Latin *sēnsus,* the faculty of perceiving, from the past participle of *sentīre,* to perceive by senses, to feel.]

sense datum *n.* A basic unanalyzable experience resulting from the stimulation of a sense organ.

sense•less (sĕns'lĭs) *adj.* **1.** Without sense or meaning; meaningless. **2.** Foolish; lacking sense: *a senseless boy.* **3.** Insensate; unconscious. **—sense•less•ly** *adv.* **—sense•less•ness** *n.*

sense organ *n.* A specialized organ or structure, such as the eye, the stimulation of which initiates a process of sensory perception.

sense perception *n.* Perception by the bodily senses.

sen•si•bil•i•ty (sĕn'sə-bĭl'ə-tē) *n., pl.* **-ties. 1.** The ability to feel or perceive. **2. a.** Keen intellectual or aesthetic perception: *the sensibility of a painter to color.* **b.** The capacity for sensitive emotional response, as to the feelings of another; sensitiveness. **3.** *Often* **sensibilities. a.** Receptiveness to impression, whether pleasant or unpleasant; acuteness of feeling. **b.** Acute susceptibility to emotional influences; oversensitiveness. **4.** *Botany.* The susceptibility of plants to environmental influences.

sen•si•ble (sĕn'sə-bəl) *adj.* **1.** Perceptible by the senses or by the mind. **2.** Readily perceived; appreciable. **3.** Having the faculty of sensation; able to feel or perceive. **4.** Having a perception of something; cognizant; aware. **5.** Acting with or showing good sense: *a sensible choice.* **6.** Practical and unpretentious: *sensible shoes.* —See Usage note at **sensitive.** [Middle English, from Old French, from Latin *sēnsibilis,* from *sēnsus,* SENSE.] **—sen•si•ble•ness** *n.* **—sen•si•bly** *adv.*

sensible horizon *n.* See **horizon** (sense 2a).

sen•sil•lum (sĕn-sĭl'əm) *n., pl.* **-silla** (-sĭl'ə). An epithelial sense organ consisting of one cell or several cells. [New Latin, diminutive

PRONUNCIATION KEY

ă, pat; ā, pay; âr, care; ä, father, are; b, bib; ch, church; d, deed; ĕ, pet; ē, be; f, fife; g, gag; h, hat; hw, which; ĭ, pit; ī, pie; îr, pier; j, judge; k, kick; l, lid, needle; m, mum; n, no, sudden; ng, thing; ŏ, pot; ō, toe; ô, paw, for; oi, noise; ou, out; o͝o, book; o͞o, boot; p, pop; r, roar; s, sauce; sh, ship, dish; t, tight; th, thin, path; *th*, this, bathe; ŭ, cut; ûr, fur; v, valve; w, with; y, yes; z, zebra, size; zh, vision; ə, about, item, edible, gallop, circus, peaceful

IN FOREIGN WORDS:

à, *Fr.* ami; œ, *Fr.* feu, *Ger.* schön; ü, *Fr.* tu, *Ger.* über; KH, *Ger.* ich, *Scot.* loch; N, *Fr.* bon; y', *Fr.* Compiègne

STRESS MARKS:

Primary stress: ′ in•cite′ (ĭn-sīt′)
Secondary stress: ′ in′sight′ (ĭn′sīt′)

of Medieval Latin *sensus,* sense organ, from Latin, *sense.*]

sen·si·tive (sĕn′sə-tĭv) *adj.* **1.** Capable of perceiving with a sense or senses. **2.** Responsive to and readily affected by external conditions or emotional stimulation: *a sensitive part of the body; a sensitive child.* **3.** Susceptible to the attitudes, feelings, or circumstances of others; acutely or sympathetically aware. **4. a.** Easily upset. **b.** Quick to take offense; touchy. **5.** Easily irritated: *sensitive skin.* **6.** Readily altered by the action of some agent: *sensitive to light.* **7.** Registering very slight differences or changes of condition. Said of an instrument. **8.** Unusually susceptible to external conditions and tending to fluctuate. Said of stock market prices. **9. a.** Dealing with classified information, usually involving national security: *a sensitive post in the State Department.* **b.** Liable to arouse controversy or strong feelings: *a sensitive issue.* [Middle English, from Old French *sensitif,* from Medieval Latin *sēnsitīvus,* from Latin *sēnsus,* SENSE.] **—sen·si·tive·ly** *adv.* **—sen·si·tive·ness** *n.*

Usage: *Sensitivity* can be used as the noun relating to any of the senses of *sensitive,* but *sensitiveness* is the form usually employed for the personal tendency to be offended easily or to react readily to criticism. *Sensitive* should also be clearly distinguished from *sensible, sensual,* and *sensuous. Sensitive* refers primarily to the delicate nature of someone's feelings (*he's very sensitive about that issue*); *sensible* emphasizes one's conscious awareness of something (*he was sensible that a lot remained to be done*); *sensual* applies specifically to gratification of the physical senses, especially those associated with sexual activity (*sensual pleasures*); *sensuous* refers to satisfaction of any of the senses, especially through the aesthetic enjoyment of nature, art, and so on (*sensuous colors/music*).

sensitive plant *n.* **1.** A woody tropical American plant, *Mimosa pudica,* having leaflets and stems that fold and droop when touched. **2.** Any of various similar plants, such as *Cassia nictitans,* of eastern North America.

sen·si·tiv·i·ty (sĕn′sə-tĭv′ə-tē) *n., pl.* **-ties. 1.** The quality or condition of being sensitive. **2.** *Electronics.* The minimum input signal required to produce a specific output signal. **3.** *Photography.* The degree of response of a plate or film to light, especially to light of a particular wavelength. —See Usage note at **sensitive.**

sen·si·tize (sĕn′sə-tīz′) *v.* **-tized, -tizing, -tizes.** —*tr.* **1.** To make sensitive. **2.** *Photography.* To make (a film or plate) sensitive to light, especially to light of a specific wavelength. —*intr.* To become sensitive. **—sen·si·ti·za·tion** *n.* **—sen·si·tiz·er** *n.*

sen·si·tom·e·ter (sĕn′sə-tŏm′ə-tər) *n.* A device used for measuring the sensitivity of photographic film to light. [SENSIT(IVE) + -METER.] **—sen·si·tom·e·try** *n.*

sen·sor (sĕn′sər, -sôr′) *n.* A device, such as a photoelectric cell, that receives and responds to a signal or stimulus. [Latin *sēnsus,* SENSE.]

sen·so·ri·mo·tor (sĕn′sə-rē-mō′tər) *adj.* Of, pertaining to, or combining the functions of the sensing and motor activities. Said of nerves. [*sensory* + *motor.*]

sen·so·ri·um (sĕn-sôr′ē-əm, sĕn-sōr′-) *n., pl.* **-ums** or **-soria** (-sôr′ē-ə, -sōr′ē-ə). **1.** The part of the brain that receives and correlates the impressions conveyed from various sensory areas. **2.** The entire sensory system. [Late Latin *sēnsōrium,* organ of sensation, from Latin *sēnsus,* SENSE.]

sen·so·ry (sĕn′sə-rē) *adj.* Also **sen·sor·i·al** (sĕn-sôr′ē-əl, sĕn-sōr′-). **1.** Of or pertaining to the senses or sensation. **2.** Transmitting impulses from sense organs to nerve centers; afferent.

sensory deprivation *n.* A situation in which a subject undergoes complete deprivation of sensory stimulation, so that his physical and psychological reactions may be observed.

sen·su·al (sĕn′shōō-əl) *adj.* **1.** Pertaining to or affecting any of the senses or a sense organ; sensory. **2. a.** Pertaining to, consisting in, or excessively fond of the gratification of the physical appetites, especially sexual appetites. **b.** Suggesting sexuality or a sensual disposition; voluptuous. **c.** Carnal rather than spiritual or intellectual; worldly. —See Synonyms at **sensuous.** —See Usage note at **sensitive.** [Middle English, from Latin *sēnsuālis,* from *sēnsus,* SENSE.] **—sen·su·al·ly** *adv.* **—sen·su·al·ness** *n.*

sen·su·al·ism (sĕn′shōō-əl-ĭz′əm) *n.* **1.** Sensuality. **2.** The ethical doctrine that the pleasures of the senses are the highest good. **3.** *Philosophy.* **Sensationalism** *(see).* **—sen·su·al·ist** *n.* **—sen·su·al·is·tic** *adj.*

sen·su·al·i·ty (sĕn′shōō-ăl′ə-tē) *n., pl.* **-ties. 1.** The quality or state of being sensual. **2.** Excessive devotion to sensual pleasures.

sen·su·al·ize (sĕn′shōō-ə-līz′) *tr.v.* **-ized, -izing, -izes.** To make sensual. **—sen·su·al·i·za·tion** *n.*

sen·su·ous (sĕn′shōō-əs) *adj.* **1.** Pertaining to or derived from the senses. **2.** Having qualities that appeal to the senses, especially on an aesthetic level. **3.** Readily susceptible to influences perceived by the senses; highly appreciative of the pleasures of sensation. —See Usage note at **sensitive.** [Latin *sēnsus,* SENSE + -OUS.] **—sen·su·ous·ly** *adv.* **—sen·su·ous·ness** *n.*

Synonyms: *epicurean, luxurious, sensual, sybaritic.*

sent. Past tense and past participle of **send.**

sen·tence (sĕn′təns) *n.* **1.** A complete and independent grammatical unit comprising a word or a group of words, and usually consisting of at least one subject with its predicate, containing a finite verb or verb phrase; for example, *The door is open* and *Go!* are sentences. **2. a.** A judicial decision of what punishment is to be inflicted on a convicted person. **b.** The punishment so meted out. **3.** *Archaic.* An opinion; especially, one given formally after deliberation. **4.** *Archaic.* An aphorism.

~*tr.v.* **sentenced, -tencing, -tences. 1.** To pass sentence upon (a convicted person). **2.** To cause to undergo something undesirable; condemn. [Middle English, opinion, judgment, thought, from Old French, from Latin *sententia,* a way of thinking, opinion, from *sentīre,* to feel.] **—sen·ten·tial** (sĕn-tĕn′shəl) *adj.* **—sen·ten·tial·ly** *adv.*

sen·tenc·er (sĕn′tən-sər) *n.* One that pronounces sentence.

sen·ten·tious (sĕn-tĕn′shəs) *adj.* **1.** Terse, pithy, and aphoristic in expression. **2.** Fond of using maxims. **3.** Given to pompous moralizing. [Latin *sententiōsus,* full of meaning, from *sententia,* opinion, SENTENCE.] **—sen·ten·tious·ly** *adv.* **—sen·ten·tious·ness** *n.*

sen·tience (sĕn′shəns, -shē-əns, -tē-əns) *n.* Also **sen·tien·cy** (sĕn′shən-sē, -shē-ən-sē, -tē-ən-sē). **1.** The quality or state of being sentient; consciousness. **2.** Feeling as distinguished from perception or thought.

sen·tient (sĕn′shənt, -shē-ənt, -tē-ənt) *adj.* Having the power of sensation; conscious.

~*n.* A sentient being. [Latin *sentiēns* (stem *sentient-*), present participle of *sentīre,* to feel.] **—sen·ti·ent·ly** *adv.*

sen·ti·ment (sĕn′tə-mənt) *n.* **1. a.** A thought, attitude, or general mental disposition modified or colored by emotion: *a certain amount of anti-American sentiment.* **b.** *Often* **sentiments.** An opinion about a specific matter; view. **2.** The emotional import of a passage, work of art, or the like, as distinguished from the form of expression. **3. a.** Susceptibility to delicate or refined feeling. **b.** An expression of this, especially in art or literature. **4.** Excessive susceptibility to such feeling; emotion that borders on mawkishness. —See Synonyms at **opinion.** [Middle English *sentement,* from Old French, from Medieval Latin *sentīmentum,* from Latin *sentīre,* to feel.]

sen·ti·men·tal (sĕn′tə-mĕn′tl) *adj.* **1. a.** Characterized by, influenced by, or exhibiting delicate or refined feeling. **b.** Affectedly or extravagantly emotional; mawkish. **2.** Based on or influenced by emotional considerations rather than reason: *kept the ring for sentimental reasons.* **3.** Appealing to the sentiments, especially to romantic feelings: *sentimental music.* **—sen·ti·men·tal·ly** *adv.*

sen·ti·men·tal·ism (sĕn′tə-mĕnt′l-ĭz′əm) *n.* **1.** A predilection for the sentimental. **2.** An idea or expression marked by excessive sentiment. **—sen·ti·men·tal·ist** *n.*

sen·ti·men·tal·i·ty (sĕn′tə-mĕn-tăl′ə-tē) *n., pl.* **-ties. 1.** The condition or quality of being excessively or affectedly sentimental. **2.** Any expression of this.

sen·ti·men·tal·ize (sĕn′tə-mĕnt′l-īz′) *v.* **-ized, -izing, -izes.** —*tr.* To be sentimental about or impart a sentimental quality to. —*intr.* To behave in a sentimental manner. **—sen·ti·men·tal·i·za·tion** *n.*

sen·ti·nel (sĕnt′n-əl) *n.* One that keeps guard; a sentry.

~*tr.v.* **sentineled, -neling, -nels.** Also *chiefly British* **-nelled, -nelling. 1.** To watch over as a sentinel. **2.** To provide with a sentinel. **3.** To post as a sentinel. [French *sentinelle,* from Italian *sentinella,* perhaps from *sentire,* to perceive, watch, from Latin *sentīre,* to perceive, feel.]

sen·try (sĕn′trē) *n., pl.* **-tries. 1.** A guard, especially a soldier posted at some spot to prevent the passage of unauthorized persons. **2.** The duty of a sentry; a watch. [Perhaps short for obsolete *centrinell,* variant of SENTINEL.]

sentry box *n.* A small shelter for a sentry at his post.

sentry palm *n.* The **kentia palm** *(see).*

Seoul (sōl). The capital of South Korea. The capital of Korea since 1392, it became the capital of South Korea after the partition of the country in 1948. It suffered severe damage during the Korean War. Its economy is supported by cotton, flour, paper, and chemical manufacturing and by engineering.

se·pal (sē′pəl) *n.* One of the usually green segments forming the calyx of a flower. Compare **petal.** [French *sépale,* from New Latin *sepalum* : *sepa,* sepal, variant of Greek *skepē*†, covering + (PET)AL, misnamed by N.J. de Necker (died 1790), who combined the terms petal and sepal, not distinguishing between the corolla and calyx.] **—se·palled, se·paled, sep·a·lous** (sĕp′ə-ləs) *adj.*

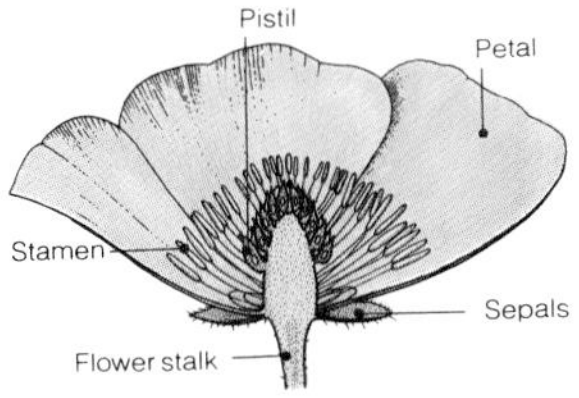

sepal *The sepals on a plant—as in the meadow buttercup shown here in cross section—are the protective casing that encloses and shelters the flower in bud. They fold back as the petals unfurl. The flower's reproductive organs are in the center: the pollen-producing stamens; and the pistils containing the embryonic seeds that are fertilized by pollen.*

se·pal·oid (sē′pə-loid′, sĕp′ə-) *adj.* Also **se·pal·ine** (-līn′, -lĭn). Resembling or characteristic of a sepal.

-sepalous *suffix.* Indicates sepals of a certain type or number; for example, **polysepalous.**

sep·a·ra·ble (sĕp′ər-ə-bəl, sĕp′rə-) *adj.* Capable of being separated. [French *séparable* or Latin *sēparābilis,* from *sēparāre,* to SEPARATE.] **—sep·a·ra·bil·i·ty** *n.* **—sep·a·ra·bly** *adv.*

sep·a·rate (sĕp′ə-rāt′) *v.* **-rated, -rating, -rates.** —*tr.* **1. a.** To set apart; disunite or disjoin. **b.** To occupy the space or time between; keep or cause to be apart: *separates the ancient and modern parts of the city.* **c.** To space apart. **2.** To differentiate or discriminate between; distinguish. **3.** To remove from a compound or complex whole; isolate, extract, or sort into constituent elements. **4.** To part (a married couple) by decree. **5.** To terminate a contractual relationship with; discharge. —*intr.* **1.** To become disconnected or severed; come apart. **2.** To withdraw or secede. **3.** To part company; disperse. **4.** To cease living together in a conjugal relationship. **5.** To become divided into components or parts.

~*adj.* (sĕp′ər-ĭt, sĕp′rĭt). **1.** Set apart from the rest; not connected; disjoined. **2.** Existing as a distinct and independent entity: *on three separate occasions.* **3.** Dissimilar; peculiar to oneself or itself: *went their separate ways.* **4.** Not shared; individual. **5.** *Archaic.* Withdrawn from others; solitary; isolated.

~*n.* (sĕp′ər-ĭt, sĕp′rĭt). A garment, such as a skirt, jacket, or pair of slacks, that may be purchased separately and worn in various combinations with other garments. Usually used in the plural. [Middle English *separaten,* from Latin *sēparāre* (past participle *sēparātus*) :

sē, apart + *parāre*, to make ready, prepare.] —**sep·a·rate·ly** *adv.* —**sep·a·rate·ness** *n.*

    Synonyms: *diverge, divide, divorce, part, sever, sunder.*

sep·a·ra·tion (sĕp'ə-rā'shən) *n.* **1. a.** The act or process of separating. **b.** The state of being separated. **2.** The place where a division or parting occurs. **3.** An interval or space that separates; a gap. **4. a.** *Law.* An agreement or court decree terminating the conjugal relationship of a husband and wife. See **judicial separation. b.** Discharge, as from employment or military service.

sep·a·ra·tist (sĕp'ər-ə-tĭst, sĕp'rə-tĭst, sĕp'ə-rā'tĭst) *n.* Also **sep·a·ra·tion·ist** (sĕp'ə-rā'shə-nĭst). One who secedes or advocates separation, as from an established church or political unit; a secessionist. —**sep·a·ra·tism** *n.* —**sep·a·ra·tist, sep·a·ra·tis·tic** *adj.*

sep·a·ra·tive (sĕp'ə-rā'tĭv, sĕp'ər-ə-tĭv, sĕp'rə-tĭv) *adj.* Tending to separate or causing separation.

sep·a·ra·tor (sĕp'ə-rā'tər) *n.* **1.** One that separates. **2.** A device for separating cream from milk.

Se·phar·di (sə-fär'dē) *n., pl.* **-dim** (-dĭm). A member of one of the two main divisions of Jews; a Spanish or Portuguese Jew or a descendant from one of these. Compare **Ashkenazi.** [Modern Hebrew *Səphāradhī*, Spaniard, from *Səphāradh*, Spain.] —**Se·phar·dic** *adj.*

se·pi·a (sē'pē-ə) *n.* **1.** A dark-brown ink or pigment originally prepared from the secretion of the cuttlefish. **2. a.** A drawing or picture done in this pigment. **b.** A photograph in a brown tint. **3.** Dark grayish yellowish brown to dark or moderate olive brown. ~*adj.* **1.** Of the color sepia. **2.** Done in sepia. [Italian *seppia*, from Latin *sēpia*, cuttlefish, dark-brown pigment prepared from its secretion, from Greek, akin to *sēpein*, to rot. See **septic.**]

se·pi·o·lite (sē'pē-ə-līt') *n. Mineralogy.* See **meerschaum** (sense 1). [German *Sepiolith* : Greek *sēpion*, cuttlebone, from *sēpia*, cuttlefish (see **sepia**) + -LITE.]

se·poy (sē'poi') *n.* Formerly, a native of India serving as a soldier under European, especially British, command. [Perhaps from Portuguese *sipae*, from Urdu *sipāhī*, from Persian, from *sipāh*, army, from Old Persian *spādat†*.]

sep·pu·ku (sĕ-pōō'kōō, sĕp'pōō-kōō) *n. Japanese.* **Hara-kiri** *(see).* [Japanese, "to cut open the stomach."]

sep·sis (sĕp'sĭs) *n.* **1.** The presence of pus-forming microorganisms in the blood or tissues. **2.** *Archaic.* A putrefactive process in the body. [New Latin, from Greek *sēpsis*, putrefaction, from *sēpein*, to make rotten. See **septic.**]

sept (sĕpt) *n.* A division of a tribe or clan, especially in medieval Ireland or Scotland. [Perhaps variant of SECT.]

Sept. September.

sep·ta. Plural of **septum.**

sep·tal (sĕp'təl) *adj.* Of or pertaining to a septum.

sep·tar·i·um (sĕp-târ'ē-əm) *n., pl.* **-ia** (-ē-ə). An irregular polygonal system of calcite-filled cracks occurring in certain rock concretions. [New Latin : SEPT(I)- (partition) + -ARIUM.] —**sep·tar·i·an** *adj.*

sep·tate (sĕp'tāt') *adj.* Having a septum or septa. [New Latin *septatus*, from SEPTUM.]

Sep·tem·ber (sĕp-tĕm'bər) *n. Abbr.* **S., Sept.** The ninth month of the year, according to the Gregorian calendar. September has 30 days. See feature at **calendar.** [Middle English *Septembre*, from Old French, from Latin *September*, the seventh month (of the Roman calendar), from *septem*, seven.]

sep·te·nar·i·us (sĕp'tə-nâr'ē-əs) *n., pl.* **-narii** (-nâr'ē-ī). A Greek or Latin verse consisting of seven feet. [Latin *septēnārius*, SEPTENARY.]

sep·te·nar·y (sĕp'tə-nĕr'ē) *adj.* Of, pertaining to, or based on the number seven. ~*n., pl.* **septenaries.** A set or group of seven. [Latin *septēnārius*, from *septēnī*, seven each, from *septem*, seven.]

sep·ten·ni·al (sĕp-tĕn'ē-əl) *adj.* **1.** Occurring every seven years. **2.** Lasting for or containing seven years. [Latin *septennium*, period of seven years, from *septennis*, of seven years : *septem*, seven + *annus*, year.] —**sep·ten·ni·al·ly** *adv.*

sep·ten·tri·on (sĕp-tĕn'trē-ŏn', -ən) *n. Archaic.* The north; northern regions. [Middle English *septemtrioun*, from Old French *septentrion*, from Latin *septentriōnēs*, "seven plow oxen," northern constellation : *septem*, seven + *triōnēs*, plow oxen.] —**sep·ten·tri·o·nal** (sĕp'tĕn'trē-ə-nəl) *adj.*

sep·tet, sep·tette (sĕp-tĕt') *n.* **1.** A group of seven. **2.** *Music.* **a.** A composition for seven voices or instruments. **b.** The musicians performing such a composition. [German *Septett*, from Latin *septem*, seven.]

septi-¹ *prefix.* Indicates seven; for example, **septilateral.** [Latin, from *septem*, seven.]

septi-², sept– *prefix.* Indicates partition or septum; for example, **septarium, septifragal.** [From SEPTUM.]

sep·tic (sĕp'tĭk) *adj.* **1.** Of, pertaining to, characterized by, or of the nature of sepsis. **2.** Causing sepsis; putrefactive. [Latin *sēpticus*, putrefying, septic, from Greek *sēptikos*, from *sēptos*, rotten, from *sēpein†*, to make rotten.] —**sep·tic·i·ty** (sĕp-tĭs'ə-tē) *n.*

sep·ti·ce·mi·a (sĕp'tĭ-sē'mē-ə) *n. Botany.* A systemic disease caused by pathogenic organisms or their toxins in the bloodstream. Also called "blood poisoning," "sapremia." [New Latin : Latin *sēpticus*, SEPTIC + -EMIA.] —**sep·ti·ce·mic** (sĕp'tĭ-sē'mĭk) *adj.*

sep·ti·ci·dal (sĕp'tĭ-sīd'l) *adj. Botany.* Splitting along the junctions of the carpels. Said of a seed capsule. [SEPTI- (partition) + *-cidal*, from -CIDE.] —**sep·ti·ci·dal·ly** *adv.*

septic tank *n.* A sewage disposal tank in which a continuous flow of waste material is decomposed by anaerobic bacteria.

sep·tif·ra·gal (sĕp-tĭf'rə-gəl) *adj. Botany.* Characterized by the breaking apart of fruits along natural dividing walls. [From SEPTI- (partition) + Latin *frangere*, to break.]

sep·ti·lat·er·al (sĕp'tə-lăt'ər-əl) *adj.* Seven-sided. [SEPTI- (seven) + LATERAL.]

sep·til·lion (sĕp-tĭl'yən) *n.* **1.** The cardinal number represented by 1 followed by 24 zeros, usually written 10²⁴. Called in British usage "quadrillion." **2.** In British usage, the cardinal number represented by 1 followed by 42 zeros, usually written 10⁴². [French : SEPTI- (seven) + (MI)LLION.] —**sep·til·lion** *adj.* —**sep·til·lionth** *n. & adj.*

sep·tu·a·ge·nar·i·an (sĕp'chōō-ə-jə-nâr'ē-ən, sĕp'tōō-) *adj.* **1.** Being seventy years old or between seventy and eighty years old. **2.** Of or like someone of this age. ~*n.* A person of seventy or between seventy and eighty years of age. [Latin *septuāgēnārius*, noun and adjective, from *septuāgēnī*, seventy each, from *septuāgintā*, seventy. See **Septuagint.**]

Sep·tu·a·ges·i·ma (sĕp'chōō-ə-jĕs'ə-mə, sĕp'tōō-) *n.* The third Sunday before Lent. Also called "Septuagesima Sunday." [Middle English *Septuagesime*, from Old French, from Late Latin *septuāgēsima*, feminine of *septuāgēsimus*, seventieth, from *septuāgintā*, seventy. See **Septuagint.**]

Sep·tu·a·gint (sĕp'chōō-ə-jĭnt', sĕp'tōō-) *n. Abbr.* **LXX.** A Greek translation of the Old Testament made in the third century B.C. [Latin *septuāgintā*, seventy, "the Seventy," designation of the 70 or 72 Jewish scholars who, according to an unhistorical tradition, completed the translation in 72 days on the island of Pharos : *septem*, seven + *-gintā*, decimal suffix, ten times.]

sep·tum (sĕp'təm) *n., pl.* **-ta** (-tə). **1.** A thin partition or membrane between two cavities or soft masses of tissue in a plant or animal. **2.** In filamentous organisms, a cell wall at right angles to the length of the filament. [Latin *sēptum*, *saeptum*, partition, from *sēpīre*, *saepīre*, to surround with a hedge, from *sēpes*, *saepes†*, hedge.]

sep·tu·ple (sĕp-tōō'pəl, sĕp-tyōō'-) *adj.* **1.** Consisting of or having seven parts, members, or copies. **2.** Multiplied by seven; seven times as much, as many, or as large. ~*n.* A sevenfold amount or number. ~*v.* **septupled, -pling, -ples.** —*tr.* To multiply or increase by seven. —*intr.* To be multiplied sevenfold. [Late Latin *septuplus*, sevenfold : Latin *septem*, seven + *-plex*, -fold.]

sep·ul·cher (sĕp'əl-kər) *n.* Also *chiefly British* **sep·ul·chre. 1.** A burial vault. **2.** A receptacle for sacred relics, especially in an altar. ~*tr.v.* **sepulchered, -chering, -chers.** Also *chiefly British* **sepul·chre, -chred, -chring, -chres.** To place in a sepulcher; inter. [Middle English *sepulcre*, from Old French, from Latin *sepulcrum*, from *sepultus*, past participle of *sepelīre*, to bury.]

se·pul·chral (sə-pŭl'krəl) *adj.* **1.** Of or pertaining to a sepulcher. **2.** Suggestive of the grave; gloomy. —**se·pul·chral·ly** *adv.*

seq. **1.** sequel. **2.** the following. [Latin *sequēns.*]

seqq. the following (ones). [Latin *sequentes, sequentia.*]

se·qua·cious (sĭ-kwā'shəs) *adj.* **1.** *Archaic.* Disposed to follow others in a slavish, unquestioning way. **2.** Following in logical sequence and regularity. [Latin *sequāx* (stem *sequāc-*), pursuing, sequacious, from *sequī*, to follow.] —**se·qua·cious·ly** *adv.* —**se·quac·i·ty** (sĭ-kwăs'ə-tē) *n.*

se·quel (sē'kwĕl) *n. Abbr.* **seq. 1.** Anything that follows; a continuation. **2.** A film, play, or literary work complete in itself but continuing the narrative of an earlier work. **3.** A result or consequence. —See Synonyms at **effect.** [Middle English *sequele*, from Old French *sequelle*, from Latin *sequēla*, from *sequī*, to follow.]

se·que·la (sĭ-kwĕl'ə) *n., pl.* **-lae** (-lē). Something that follows; especially, a pathological condition or the various complications resulting from a disease. [Latin *sequēla*, SEQUEL.]

se·quence (sē'kwəns) *n.* **1.** A following of one thing after another; succession. **2.** An order of succession. **3.** A related or continuous series. **4.** Three or more playing cards in consecutive order; a run. **5.** A series of single shots in a film, so edited as to constitute an aesthetic or dramatic unit; an episode. **6.** *Music.* A melodic or harmonic pattern successively repeated at different pitches, with or without a key change. **7.** *Roman Catholic Church.* A hymn read or sung between the gradual and the gospel. **8.** *Mathematics.* An ordered set of quantities, as x, 2x², 3x³, 4x⁴. **9.** A subsequent or consequent event or development. —See Synonyms at **series.** [Middle English, from Late Latin *sequentia*, from Latin *sequēns* (stem *sequent-*), present participle of *sequī*, to follow.]

se·quenc·er (sē'kwən-sər, -kwĕn'-) *n.* **1.** A device for sorting information into a predetermined order for data processing. **2.** An electronic device that sets into a predetermined order a sequence of operations. [SEQUENC(E) + -ER.]

se·quent (sē'kwənt) *adj.* **1.** Following in order or time; subsequent. **2.** Following as a result; consequent. ~*n.* That which follows, in sequence or in consequence. [Latin *sequēns.* See **sequence.**]

se·quen·tial (sĭ-kwĕn'shəl) *adj.* **1.** Forming a sequence or characterized by ordered sequence, as of notes or units. **2.** Sequent. —**se·quen·ti·al·i·ty** (sĭ-kwĕn'shē-ăl'ĭ-tē) *n.* —**se·quen·tial·ly** *adv.*

sequential access *n.* A method of obtaining information from a computer file by reading through it from the start. Compare **random access.**

se·ques·ter (sĭ-kwĕs'tər) *v.* **-tered, -tering, -ters.** —*tr.* **1.** To remove or set apart; segregate. **2.** *Law.* To take temporary possession of (property) as security against legal claims. **3.** To requisition or confiscate, especially by legal authority. **4.** To isolate or withdraw into seclusion. Usually used reflexively or in the passive: *to sequester oneself; a sequestered spot.* —*intr. Chemistry.* To undergo seques-

tration. [Middle English, from Late Latin *sequestrāre,* to separate, give up for safekeeping, from Latin *sequester,* depository.]
se·ques·trant (sĭ-kwĕs′trənt) *n.* A chemical that promotes sequestration. [From SEQUESTER.]
se·ques·trate (sĭ-kwĕs′trāt′) *tr.v.* **-trated, -trating, -trates. 1.** *Law.* To seize. **2.** *Archaic.* To set apart. [Late Latin *sequestrāre,* to SEQUESTER.] **—se·ques·tra·tor** (sē′kwĕs-trā′tər, sĭ-kwĕs′trā-tər) *n.*
se·ques·tra·tion (sē′kwĕs-trā′shən) *n.* **1.** The act of sequestering or state of being sequestered; segregation or separation. **2.** *Law.* **a.** Seizure of property. **b.** A writ authorizing seizure of property. **3.** *Chemistry.* The inhibition or prevention of normal ion behavior by combination with added materials; especially, the prevention of metallic ion precipitation from solution by formation of a coordination complex with a phosphate.
se·ques·trum (sĭ-kwĕs′trəm) *n., pl.* **-tra** (-trə). A dead bone fragment that has separated from healthy bone. [New Latin, from Latin, deposit, "something separated," from *sequester,* depository.]
se·quin (sē′kwĭn) *n.* **1.** A small shiny ornamental disk, often sewn on cloth; a spangle. **2.** A gold coin of the Venetian Republic. In this sense, also called "zecchino." [French, from Italian *zecchino,* from *zecca,* the mint, from Arabic *sikkah,* coin die.] **—se·quinned, se·quined** *adj.*
se·quoi·a (sĭ-kwoi′ə) *n.* Any very large evergreen tree of the genus *Sequoia,* which includes the **redwood** and the **giant sequoia** *(both of which see).* [New Latin, after SEQUOYA.]
Sequoia National Park. Area of 156,680 hectares (386,863 acres) in east-central California. The park includes 35 groves of giant sequoias, spectacular mountains such as Mt. Whitney, the highest point in the contiguous United Sates, and deep canyons. The Gen. Sherman Tree, the largest sequoia, is thought to be 3,500 years old.
Se·quoy·a or **Se·quoy·ah** (sĭ-kwoi′ə) (*c.* 1770–1843). U.S. Cherokee leader and scholar. A silversmith and trader in Georgia, he created the Cherokee syllabary, compiling a table of more than 80 characters to record the sounds of the language as written words. Over the years he taught thousands of his people to read and write.
se·ra. Alternate plural of **serum.**
sé·rac (sə-răk′, sā-) *n.* An ice pinnacle between intersecting crevasses in an icefall in a glacier. [Swiss French, piece of white cheese (which the ice resembles), perhaps from Latin *serum,* whey.]
se·ra·glio (sĭ-răl′yō, -räl′yō) *n., pl.* **-glios. 1.** A large harem. **2.** A sultan's palace. [Italian *serraglio,* probably from Turkish *serai*†, a palace, lodging, from Persian.]
se·ra·pe, sa·ra·pe (sə-rä′pē) *n.* A woolen cloak or poncho worn by Latin-American men. [Mexican Spanish *sarape*†.]
ser·aph (sĕr′əf) *n., pl.* **-aphs** or **seraphim** (sĕr′ə-fĭm). **1.** A celestial being having three pairs of wings. Isaiah 6:2. **2.** One of the nine orders of angels. See **angel.** [Back-formation from plural *seraphim,* from Middle English *seraphin,* Old English *seraphin,* from Late Latin *seraphim, seraphin,* from Hebrew *Śərāphīm,* plural of *śārāph.*] **—se·raph·ic** (sĭ-răf′ĭk) *adj.* **—se·raph·i·cal·ly** *adv.*
Se·ra·pis (sĭ-rā′pĭs) *n.* A god combining features of Egyptian and Greek deities, whose worship became widespread in the ancient world from the Hellenistic period onward.
Serb (sûrb) *n.* A Serbian. [Serbo-Croatian *Srb*†.] **—Serb** *adj.*
Ser·bi·a (sûr′bē-ə). *Abbr.* **Serb.** Largest constituent republic of Yugoslavia, in the northeast of the country. Largely mountainous in the west and south, it descends to the fertile Danubian plain in the north. It has large mineral deposits and is also the country's main agricultural producer. Settled by the Serbs in the 7th century A.D., it was established as an independent kingdom in the 12th century but was subsequently held by the Turks (1389–1829). After World War I the Kingdom of the Serbs, Croats, and Slovenes was proclaimed (1918) but was later renamed Yugoslavia (1929). In 1946 Serbia became a constituent republic of Yugoslavia under the new constitution.
Ser·bi·an (sûr′bē-ən) *n.* **1.** A member of a southern Slavic people that is the dominant ethnic group of Serbia. **2.** A Serbo-Croatian. **—Ser·bi·an** *adj.*
Ser·bo-Cro·a·tian (sûr′bō-krō-ā′shən) *n.* The Slavonic language of the Serbs and Croats of Yugoslavia, usually written in Cyrillic letters in Serbia and in Roman letters in Croatia. Also called "Croatian."
~adj. Of or pertaining to this language or those who speak it.
sere¹ (sîr) *adj.* Withered; dry. [Middle English *sere,* Old English *sēar.*]
sere² *n.* The entire sequence of ecological communities successively occupying an area. [From SERIES.]
ser·e·nade (sĕr′ə-nād′, sĕr′ə-nād′) *n.* **1. a.** A musical performance given outdoors in the evening, especially, one given by a lover for his sweetheart. **b.** A piece of music so performed. **2.** An instrumental form comprising characteristics of the suite and the sonata.
~v. **serenaded, -nading, -nades.** *—tr.* To perform a serenade for. *—intr.* To perform a serenade. [French *sérénade,* from Italian *serenata,* evening serenade, from *sereno,* serene (influenced in meaning by *sera,* evening), from Latin *serēnus,* SERENE.] **—ser·e·nad·er** *n.*
ser·en·dip·i·ty (sĕr′ən-dĭp′ə-tē) *n.* The faculty of making fortunate and unexpected discoveries by accident. [Coined (1754) by Horace Walpole after the characters in the fairy tale *The Three Princes of Serendip* (that is, Sri Lanka), who made such discoveries.] **—ser·en·dip·i·tous** *adj.*
se·rene (sĭ-rēn′) *adj.* **1.** Unruffled; tranquil; dignified. **2.** Unclouded; fair; bright. **3.** *Often* **Serene.** August. Used as part of a title of respect for certain royal personages: *His Serene Highness.* —See Synonyms at **calm.** [Latin *serēnus,* serene, bright, clear.] **—se·rene·ly** *adv.* **—se·rene·ness** *n.*
Ser·en·get·i (sĕr′ən-gĕt′ē). Plain and wildlife preserve on the southeast shore of Lake Victoria, Tanzania. It covers *c.* 14,500 square kilometers (5,600 square miles) and is noted for its wildlife.
se·ren·i·ty (sĭ-rĕn′ə-tē) *n., pl.* **-ties. 1.** The state or quality of being serene; dignified calm; quiet. **2.** Clearness, brightness, and stillness, as of the air and sky. —See Synonyms at **equanimity.**
serf (sûrf) *n.* **1.** A person in a condition bordering on slavery, especially a member of the lowest feudal class in medieval Europe, bound to the land and subject to the control of a lord. **2.** Anyone in a state of servitude or oppression. [Old French, from Latin *servus,* slave.] **—serf·dom** *n.*
serge (sûrj) *n.* A twilled cloth of worsted or worsted and wool, often used for suits. [Middle English *sarge, serge,* from Old French, from Vulgar Latin *sārica* (unattested), from Latin *sērica (lāna),* (wool) of the Seres (a people), that is, silk, from Greek *sērikos,* of silk, originally "pertaining to the Seres." See **silk.**]
ser·geant (sär′jənt) *n.* Also *chiefly British* **ser·jeant** (for senses 2, 3). *Abbr.* **Sgt. 1. a.** Any of several ranks of noncommissioned officers in the U.S. Army, Air Force, or Marine Corps. **b.** One holding any of these ranks. **2. a.** The rank of police officer next below a captain, lieutenant, or inspector. **b.** One holding this rank. **3.** A **sergeant at arms** *(see).* [Middle English *sergeaunte, sergant,* from Old French *sergent,* from Latin *serviēns* (stem *servient-*), present participle of *servīre,* to serve, from *servus,* slave, servant.] **—ser·gean·cy, ser·geant·ship** *n.*
sergeant at arms *n.* An officer appointed to keep order within an organization, such as a legislative, judicial, or social body. Also called "sergeant."
sergeant first class *n. Abbr.* **Sfc.** A noncommissioned officer next below master sergeant in the U.S. Army.
sergeant major *n. Abbr.* **Sgt. Maj., S.M. 1.** A noncommissioned officer serving as chief administrative assistant of a headquarters unit of the U.S. Army, Air Force, or Marine Corps. **2.** *Chiefly British.* A noncommissioned officer of the highest rank. **3.** A fish, *Abudefduf saxatilis,* of warm seas, having a flattened body with dark vertical stripes.
se·ri·al (sîr′ē-əl) *adj.* **1.** Of, forming, or arranged in a series. **2.** Published or produced in installments, as a novel might be. **3.** Pertaining to such publication or production. **4.** *Music.* Designating or pertaining to music based on a series of intervals chosen by the composer, especially on a 12-tone row, rather than on the diatonic scale. **5.** *Computer Science.* Designating or pertaining to a system of computer operation in which processing is carried out sequentially. In this sense compare **parallel.**
~n. A literary or dramatic work published or produced in installments. [From SERIES.] **—se·ri·al·ly** *adv.*
se·ri·al·ize (sîr′ē-əl-īz′) *tr.v.* **-ized, -izing, -izes.** To write, publish, or produce in serial form. **—se·ri·al·i·za·tion** *n.*
serial number *n.* A number that is one of a series, used for identification, as of a machine or banknote, for example.
se·ri·ate (sîr′ē-āt′, -ĭt) *adj.* Arranged or occurring in a series or in rows. [From SERIES.] **—se·ri·ate·ly** *adv.*
se·ri·a·tim (sîr′ē-ā′təm, sĕr′-) *adv.* One after another; in a series. [Medieval Latin, from Latin *seriēs,* SERIES.]
se·ri·ceous (sĭ-rĭsh′əs) *adj. Biology.* Covered with soft, silky hairs. [Late Latin *sēriceus,* from *sēricus,* of Seres. See **serge.**]
ser·i·cin (sĕr′ə-sən) *n.* A viscous, gelatinous protein that forms on the surface of raw-silk fibers. [Latin *sēricus,* silken, of Seres (see **serge**) + -IN.]
ser·i·cul·ture (sîr′ə-kŭl′chər) *n.* The production of raw silk and the breeding of silkworms for this purpose. [French *sériculture* : Latin *sēricus,* silken, of Seres (see **serge**) + CULTURE.] **—ser·i·cul·tur·al** *adj.* **—ser·i·cul·tur·ist** *n.*
ser·i·e·ma (sĕr′ī-ē′mə) *n.* Either of two cranelike South American birds, *Cariama cristata* or *Chunga burmeisteri,* having a tuftlike crest at the base of the bill. [Tupi *seriema, çariama,* "crested."]
se·ries (sîr′ēz) *n., pl.* **series. 1.** A number of things, events, or people having some common characteristic and following one another in order of their occurrence in space or time. **2.** A set of publications, typically in a uniform format, having some common theme or feature: *a series of phrase books.* **3. a.** *Sports.* A number of games played one after the other by the same opposing teams. **b.** *Baseball.* The **World Series** *(see).* **4.** A group of thematically connected performances; especially, a set of radio or television programs featuring the same fictional characters in a succession of self-contained episodes. **5.** A group of objects related in terms of their composition, structure, or properties: *the paraffin series.* **6.** *Mathematics.* A finite or sequentially ordered infinite set of terms expressed in the form $x_1 + x_2 + x_3 + \ldots\ldots$ where x_i is a real or complex number. **7.** *Grammar.* A succession of coordinate elements in a sentence. **8.** An arrangement of electrical components such that the current flows through each in turn. Compare **parallel. 9.** *Geology.* A subdivision of a system that represents the rocks formed during an epoch. [Latin *seriēs,* from *serere,* to join.]
Synonyms: *chain, progression, sequence, string, succession, train.*
series circuit *n.* An electrical circuit connected so that current passes through each circuit element in turn without branching. See **parallel** (sense 7).
se·ries-wound (sîr′ēz-wound′) *adj.* Designating an electric motor or dynamo with its armature circuit and field circuit connected in series with the external circuit. Compare **shunt-wound.**

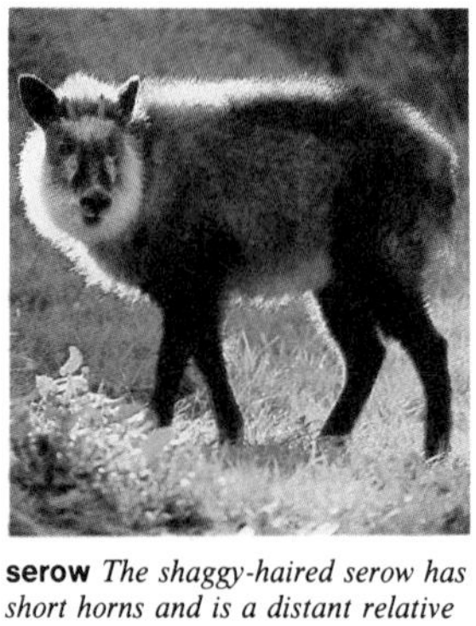

serow *The shaggy-haired serow has short horns and is a distant relative of the mountain goat. It lives in the hill forests of eastern Asia.*

ser·if (sĕr′ĭf) *n. Printing.* A fine line finishing off the main strokes, as at the top and bottom of *M* or ending the cross stroke of *T.* [Perhaps from Dutch *schreef,* line, from Middle Dutch *scrēve.*]

ser·i·graph (sĕr′ə-grăf′, -gräf′) *n.* A print made by the silk-screen process. [Latin *sēri(cum),* SILK + -GRAPH.] **—se·rig·ra·phy** (sə-rĭg′rə-fē) *n.*

ser·in (sĕr′ən) *n.* Any of several Old World finches of the genus *Serinus,* having yellowish streaked plumage. See **canary.** [French, from Old French, perhaps from Old Provençal *serena,* bee-eater, from Latin *sīrēn,* a kind of bird, from *Sīrēn,* SIREN.]

ser·ine (sĕr′ēn′) *n.* An amino acid, $C_3H_7NO_3$, that is a common constituent of many proteins. [SER(ICIN) + -INE.]

se·rin·ga (sə-rĭng′gə) *n.* **1.** **Syringa** *(see).* **2.** Any of several rubber trees of the Brazilian genus *Hevea.*

se·ri·o·com·ic (sîr′ē-ō-kŏm′ĭk) *adj.* Combining serious and comic characteristics. [SERIO(US) + COMIC.]

se·ri·ous (sîr′ē-əs) *adj.* **1.** Grave in character or manner; responsible. **2.** Said, done, or acting in earnest; marked by sincerity or commitment. **3.** Concerned with important rather than trivial matters. **4.** Requiring or employing considerable thought, effort, or concentration: *serious music.* **5.** Causing anxiety; critical; dangerous. **6.** Not to be taken lightly; of considerable significance, gravity, or effect: *serious damage.* —See Synonyms at **critical.** [Middle English *seryous,* from Old French *serieux,* from Late Latin *sēriōsus,* from Latin *sērius.*] **—se·ri·ous·ly** *adv.* **—se·ri·ous·ness** *n.*

Synonyms: *earnest, grave, sedate, sober, solemn, staid.*

serjeant *Chiefly British.* Variant of **sergeant.**

Ser·kin (sûr′kĭn), **Rudolf** (1903–). U.S. pianist, born in Austria-Hungary. He made his debut in Vienna at the age of 12 and first appeared in the United States in 1936. Concentrating on the works of Bach, Mozart, Beethoven, Schubert, and Brahms, he is known for his energy and classical clarity.

ser·mon (sûr′mən) *n.* **1.** A religious discourse delivered as part of a church service. **2.** Any discourse or speech; especially, a lengthy and tedious reproof or exhortation. [Middle English *sermun,* from Norman French, from Latin *sermō* (stem *sermōn-*), a speaking, a discourse.] **—ser·mon·ic** (sûr-mŏn′ĭk) *adj.*

ser·mon·ize (sûr′mə-nīz′) *v.* **-ized, -izing, -izes.** *—tr.* To preach to. *—intr.* To deliver, or speak as though delivering, a sermon. **—ser·mon·iz·er** *n.*

Sermon on the Mount *n.* A discourse of Jesus, delivered on the Mount of Olives. Matthew 5–7.

sero– *prefix.* Indicates serum, as **serology.** [From SERUM.]

se·rol·o·gy (sĭ-rŏl′ə-jē) *n.* The medical study of serum. [SERO- + -LOGY.] **—ser·o·log·ic** (sîr′ə-lŏj′ĭk), **ser·o·log·i·cal** *adj.* **—se·rol·o·gist** *n.*

se·ro·sa (sĭ-rō′sə, -zə) *n., pl.* **-sas** or **-sae** (-sē′). A **serous membrane** *(see).* [New Latin, feminine of *serosus,* SEROUS.]

se·ro·ther·a·py (sîr′ō-thĕr′ə-pē) *n.* Treatment of disease by administration of a serum or antitoxin. Also called "serum therapy." [SERO- + THERAPY.]

ser·o·tine (sĕr′ə-tīn′) *adj.* Also **se·rot·i·nous** (sĭ-rŏt′ə-nəs), **se·rot·i·nal** (-nəl). *Biology.* Late in developing or blooming.
~*n.* A European insectivorous bat, *Eptesicus serotinus.* [Latin *sērōtinus,* late, from *sērō,* late, from *sērus,* late.]

se·ro·to·nin (sîr′ə-tō′nĭn, sĕr′-) *n.* An organic compound, $C_{10}H_{12}N_2O$, found in animal and human tissue, especially the brain, blood serum, and gastric mucosa, and capable of raising the body temperature, contracting smooth muscle, and changing behavior. Also called "hydroxytryptamine." [SERO- + TON(IC) + -IN.]

se·ro·type (sîr′ə-tīp′, sĕr′-) *n.* A subspecific category of microorganisms, distinguished by having the same serological activity. Also called "serological type." [*Sero*logical *type.*]

se·rous (sîr′əs) *adj.* Containing, secreting, or resembling serum. [New Latin *serosus,* from SERUM.]

serous cavity *n.* A body cavity lined with serous membrane.

serous membrane *n.* A thin membrane lining a closed bodily cavity. Also called "serosa."

se·row (sə-rō′) *n.* Any of several goatlike antelopes of the genus *Capricornis,* of mountainous regions of eastern Asia, having short horns and a dark coat. [Lepcha *să-ro,* Tibetan goat.]

Ser·pens (sûr′pənz, -pĕnz′) *n.* A constellation in the equatorial region of the northern sky, made up of two parts: *Serpens Cauda,* the "tail," and *Serpens Caput,* the "head," both near Hercules and Ophiuchus. Also called the "Serpent." [Latin *serpēns,* SERPENT.]

ser·pent (sûr′pənt) *n.* **1.** A snake, especially a large one. **2.** *Often* **Serpent.** The creature that tempted Eve; Satan. Genesis 3. **3.** A sly or treacherous person. **4.** A kind of firework that writhes while burning. **5.** *Music.* A deep-toned wind instrument of serpentine shape, used principally in the 18th century. **6.** **Serpent.** The constellation Serpens. [Middle English, from Old French, from Latin *serpēns* (stem *serpent-*), "crawling thing," from the present participle of *serpere,* to crawl, creep.]

ser·pen·tine (sûr′pən-tēn′, -tīn′) *adj.* **1.** Of or resembling a serpent, as in form or movement; sinuous. **2.** Subtle, sly, and treacherous.
~*n.* A greenish, brownish, or spotted mineral, $Mg_6(Si_4O_{10})(OH)_8$, used as a source of magnesium and in architecture as a decorative stone. [Middle English, from Old French *serpentin,* from Late Latin *serpentīnus,* from Latin *serpēns,* SERPENT.]

ser·pi·go (sər-pī′gō) *n.* A spreading skin eruption or lesion, such as ringworm. [Middle English, from Medieval Latin *serpīgo,* from Latin *serpere,* to creep.] **—ser·pig·i·nous** (sər-pĭj′ə-nəs) *adj.*

ser·ra·nid (sə-rā′nĭd, -răn′ĭd) *n.* Also **ser·ra·noid** (sĕr′ə-noid′), **ser·ran** (sĕr′ən). Any of various fishes belonging to the family Serranidae, which includes the sea basses and groupers. [New Latin *Serranidae,* from *Serranus* (genus), from Latin *serra,* saw (perhaps from its serrated dorsal fin). See **serrate.**] **—ser·ra·nid, ser·ra·noid** *adj.*

ser·rate (sĕr′āt′, -ĭt) *adj.* Also **ser·rat·ed** (-rā′tĭd). **1.** Having notched, toothlike projections. **2.** Having the edge or margin notched with toothlike projections: *serrate leaves.*
~*tr.v.* (sə-rāt′, sĕr′āt′) **serrated, -rating, -rates.** To provide or mark with notched, toothlike projections. [Latin *serrātus,* saw-shaped, from Latin *serra*†, saw.]

ser·ra·tion (sĕ-rā′shən) *n.* **1.** The state of being serrate. **2.** A series or set of teeth or notches. **3.** A single such tooth or notch.

ser·ried (sĕr′ēd) *adj.* Pressed together in rows; in close order: "*Troops in serried ranks assembled*" (W.S. Gilbert). [From past participle of obsolete *serry,* to press together, from Old French *serré,* past participle of *serrer,* to close, from Vulgar Latin *serrāre* (unattested), from Latin *sērāre,* to fasten with a bolt, from *sera,* lock.]

ser·ru·late (sĕr′yə-lĭt, -lāt′, sĕr′ə-) *adj.* Also **ser·ru·lat·ed** (-lā′tĭd). Having small, toothlike notches along the edge; minutely serrate. [New Latin *serrulatus,* from Latin *serrula,* diminutive of *serra,* saw. See **serrate.**]

ser·tu·lar·i·an (sûr′cho͞o-lâr′ē-ən, sûr′tə-lâr′-) *n.* Any of various colonial hydroids of the genus *Sertularia,* having stalkless polyps arranged in pairs on a long, branching stem. [New Latin *Sertularia,* from Latin *sertula,* diminutive of *serta,* melilot, garland, from the feminine past participle of *serere,* to join, entwine.]

se·rum (sîr′əm) *n., pl.* **-rums** or **sera** (sîr′ə). **1.** The clear yellowish fluid obtained upon separating blood into its solid and liquid components. Also called "blood serum." **2.** The fluid from the tissues of immunized animals, used especially as an antitoxin. **3.** Any watery fluid from animal tissue, as is found in edema. **4.** **Whey** *(see).* [Latin, whey, serum.]

serum albumin *n.* The main protein fraction of blood serum that is involved in maintaining osmotic pressure, and that is used in the treatment of shock.

serum globulin *n.* A protein fraction of blood serum chiefly containing antibodies.

serum hepatitis *n.* See **hepatitis.**

serum sickness *n.* An allergic reaction, such as a skin eruption, vomiting, or fever, that may follow injection of serum.

serv. **1.** servant. **2.** service.

serum therapy *n.* **Serotherapy** *(see).*

ser·val (sûr′vəl, sər-väl′) *n.* A long-legged wild cat, *Felis serval,* of Africa, having a yellowish coat with black spots. [French, from Portuguese *(lobo) cerval,* deerlike (wolf), from *cervo,* deer, from Latin *cervus.*]

ser·vant (sûr′vənt) *n. Abbr.* **serv. 1.** One that serves another or others. **2.** Someone privately employed to perform domestic services. **3.** Someone publicly employed to perform services, as for a government. **—your humble** (or **obedient**) **servant.** Used chiefly in letters as a conventional expression of politeness. [Middle English, from Old French, from the present participle of *servir,* to SERVE.]

serve (sûrv) *v.* **served, serving, serves.** *—tr.* **1.** To be a servant to or of; work for (an employer or company, for example): *served the firm for 30 years.* **2. a.** To prepare and offer (food or drink): *serve tea.* **b.** To place food or drink before (someone); wait on. **c.** To assist the celebrant during (Communion or Mass). **3. a.** To meet the requirements of; provide with something useful or needed: *a bus serving the rural areas; served the public for 100 years.* **b.** To supply (goods or services) to customers. **4.** To be useful or adequate for fulfilling (a need or purpose); suffice for: *not quite big enough, but it will serve the purpose.* **5.** To be of assistance to; promote the interests of; aid: *serving the national interest.* **6.** To perform or complete (a stipulated term), as in prison, elective office, or an apprenticeship. **7.** To fight or undergo military service for: *served his country in two World Wars.* **8.** To give homage and obedience to. **9. a.** To treat in a specified, usually unpleasant way; requite: *It will serve her right.* **b.** To perform a function for in a specified way; avail: *if my memory serves me well.* **10.** To copulate with. Used of male animals. **11.** To be used in common by: *One phone serves the whole office.* **12.** To enable (a cannon, for example) to keep firing: *serve the guns.* **13.** *Law.* **a.** To deliver or present (a legal writ or summons). **b.** To present such a writ to. **14.** To put (the ball or shuttlecock) in play in games such as tennis or badminton. **15.** To bind (a rope) with fine cord or wire. *—intr.* **1.** To be employed as a servant. **2. a.** To do military service: *served in the Navy.* **b.** To perform or discharge an official duty; hold office: *served under four presidents.* **3. a.** To be of service or use; function: *serve as a reminder.* **b.** To be reliable or safe: *if memory serves.* **c.** To function so as to produce a specified effect: *a repressive measure that merely served to increase opposition to the government.* **4.** To meet requirements or needs; satisfy; suffice: "*'Tis not so deep as a well . . . but 'twill serve*" (Shakespeare). **5.** To wait at table; provide people with food or drink: *Shall I serve?* **6.** To put a ball or shuttlecock into play in games such as tennis or badminton. **7.** To assist the celebrant during Mass or a Communion service.
~*n.* In many games played on a court: **1.** The manner or act of serving. **2.** One's turn or right to serve which, in tennis, lasts throughout a game. **3.** *Tennis.* The game in which a particular player serves: *lost her serve.* [Middle English *serven,* from Old French *servir,* from Latin *servīre,* from *servus,* slave.]

serv·er (sûr′vər) *n.* **1.** One that serves. **2.** Something used in serving food or drink, such as a tray or utensil. **3.** An attendant to the celebrant at a Communion service or Mass. **4.** The player who serves, as in tennis or badminton.

serv·ice (sûr′vĭs) *n. Abbr.* **serv. 1.** The occupation, condition, or duties of a servant. **2.** Employment in duties or work for another; especially, such employment for a government. **3.** A branch or department of an organization or government, together· with its employees: *the diplomatic service.* **4.** Any branch of the armed forces of a nation. **5. a.** Useful work or duty performed by a person or thing: *has done good service.* **b.** The condition of being used for the performance of work: *Some of the old planes are still in service.* **6. a.** The action of helping others; assistance: *if I may be of service.* **b.** An act of helping others; a favor: *did us all a great service.* **7.** Power to control or make use of some resource; disposal: *My staff is at your service.* **8. a.** Installation, maintenance, or repairs provided or guaranteed by a dealer or manufacturer. **b.** A regularly performed inspection and carrying out of repairs, as of a car or other machine, for the purpose of routine maintenance. **9.** *Often* **services.** Work done for others as an occupation or business: *needed the services of a good accountant.* **10.** An organization or system providing the public with something useful or necessary: *a taxi service; an answering service.* **11.** A nonmaterial commodity produced by human labor, especially as distinguished from a manufactured product. **12. a.** A meeting for public worship. **b.** A particular religious rite: *the burial service.* **13.** The act or manner of serving food, attending to customers, or the like: *fast, friendly service.* **14.** A set of dishes or utensils: *a silver tea service.* **15.** The act, manner, turn, or right of serving in racket games; a serve. **16.** Copulation by a male animal with a female. **17.** *Law.* The serving of a writ or summons. **18.** Any material, such as cord, used in binding or wrapping rope. *~adj.* **1.** Concerned with the provision of services rather than the production of goods: *service industries.* **2.** Not for use by the general public; reserved for employees, deliveries, or the like: *a service entrance.* **3.** Of or pertaining to the armed forces. *~tr.v.* **serviced, -icing, -ices. 1.** To perform routine maintenance on so as to ensure effective operation: *service a car.* **2.** To provide with services. **3.** To copulate with. Used of a male animal. **4.** To meet the interest payments on (a loan). [Middle English *servis(e)*, from Old French *service*, from Latin *servitium*, servitude, slavery, from *servus*, slave.]

Serv·ice (sûr′vĭs), **Robert William** (1874–1958). Canadian author, born in England. He immigrated to Canada in the 1890's, working in British Columbia and at White Horse in the Yukon. His vivid writing about life in the Klondike brought him enormous popularity. He is best known for his verse "The Shooting of Dan McGrew."

serv·ice·a·ble (sûr′vĭs-ə-bəl) *adj.* **1.** Ready or suitable for service; useful or usable. **2.** Able to give good service; long-wearing. —**serv·ice·a·bil·i·ty, serv·ice·a·ble·ness** *n.* —**serv·ice·a·bly** *adv.*

service area *n.* An area adjoining a highway in which garage facilities, restaurants, and restrooms are provided.

serv·ice·ber·ry (sûr′vĭs-bĕr′ē, sär′vĭs-) *n., pl.* **-ries. 1.** The fruit of the service tree. **2.** The **shadbush** *(see),* or one of its fruit. [SERVICE (TREE) + BERRY.]

service break *n.* A game won during an opponent's serve, as in tennis.

service cap *n.* A visored flat-topped military cap.

service charge *n.* **1.** A charge added to a customer's bill, as at a restaurant, to pay for service. **2.** An additional charge for a service for which there is often already a basic fee.

service line *n. Sports.* A boundary line, as in tennis or handball, that must not be overstepped in serving.

serv·ice·man (sûr′vĭs-măn′, -mən) *n., pl.* **-men** (-mĕn′, -mĭn). **1.** A male member of the armed forces. **2.** A man whose work is the maintenance and repair of equipment.

service mark *n.* A device that identifies a service offered to the public, as by an airline or insurance company.

service module *n.* The part of the third stage of an Apollo spacecraft containing the rocket motor, fuel supply, and various service facilities, which is jettisoned prior to reentry into the earth's atmosphere.

service road *n.* A narrow road running parallel to a main road to provide access to houses, shops, and the like, along its length.

service station *n.* **1.** A **filling station** *(see).* **2.** A place where services can be obtained, as repair, maintenance, or replacement of electrical or mechanical devices.

serv·ice tree (sûr′vĭs, sär′-) *n.* Either of two Old World trees, *Sorbus domestica* or *S. torminalis,* having clusters of white flowers and brownish, edible fruit. [Middle English *serves,* plural of *serve,* Old English *syrfe,* from Vulgar Latin *sorbea* (unattested), from Latin *sorbus†.*]

serv·ice·wom·an (sûr′vĭs-wŏom′ən) *n., pl.* **-women** (-wĭm′ĭn). A female member of the armed forces.

ser·vi·ette (sûr′vē-ĕt′) *n.* A table napkin. [French, from Old French, towel, napkin, from *servir,* to SERVE.]

ser·vile (sûr′vəl, -vīl′) *adj.* **1.** Slavish in character or attitude; obsequious; submissive. **2.** Of or suitable to a slave or servant: *"freed from servile bands"* (John Bunyan). —See Synonyms at **obedient.** [Middle English, from Latin *servīlis,* from *servus,* slave.] —**ser·vile·ly** *adv.* —**ser·vile·ness, ser·vil·i·ty** (sər-vĭl′ə-tē) *n.*

serv·ing (sûr′vĭng) *n.* An individual portion or helping of food or drink. *~adj.* Pertaining to or used for serving: *a serving spoon.*

ser·vi·tor (sûr′və-tər, -tôr′) *n. Archaic.* A servant; an attendant.

[Middle English, from Old French, from Latin *servītor,* from Latin *servīre,* to SERVE.] —**ser·vi·tor·ship** *n.*

ser·vi·tude (sûr′və-tōod′, -tyōod′) *n.* **1.** Submission to the control, will, or political domination of another; slavery. **2.** Forced labor imposed as a punishment for crime: *penal servitude.* **3.** *Law.* A right that grants use of another's property for certain purposes. [Middle English, from Old French, from Latin *servitūdō,* from *servus,* slave.]

Synonyms: bondage, slavery.

ser·vo·mech·a·nism (sûr′vō-mĕk′ə-nĭz′əm) *n.* A feedback system that consists of a sensing element, an amplifier, and a servomotor, and is used in the automatic control of a mechanical device. Also called "servo." [SERVO(MOTOR) + MECHANISM.]

ser·vo·mo·tor (sûr′vō-mō′tər) *n.* An electric motor or hydraulic piston that supplies power to a servomechanism. Also called "servo." [French *servo-moteur* : *servo-,* from Latin *servus,* slave + French *moteur,* MOTOR.]

ses·a·me (sĕs′ə-mē) *n.* **1.** A plant, *Sesamum indicum,* of tropical Asia, bearing small, flat seeds used as food and as a source of oil. **2.** The seeds of this plant. Also called "benne." [Latin *sēsamum, sīsamum,* from Greek *sēsamon, sēsamē,* of Semitic origin; akin to Arabic *simsim,* Akkadian *shamashshamu.*]

ses·a·moid (sĕs′ə-moid′) *adj.* Of or designating a small bone, such as the kneecap, that develops in a tendon. [Greek *sēsamoeidēs,* shaped like a sesame seed : SESAME + -OID.] —**ses·a·moid** *n.*

Se·so·tho (sĭ-sōō′tōo) *n.* The dialect of **Sotho** *(see)* spoken in Lesotho. Formerly called "Basuto."

sesqui- *prefix.* Indicates one and a half; for example, **sesquicentennial.** [Latin, from *semisque* (unattested), one-half more : *sēmis,* half + *-que* (enclitic), and.]

ses·qui·car·bon·ate (sĕs′kwə-kär′bə-nāt′) *n.* A mixed salt consisting of a carbonate and a hydrogen carbonate, such as sodium sesquicarbonate, $NaCO_3NaHCO_3$.

ses·qui·cen·ten·ni·al (sĕs′kwə-sĕn-tĕn′ē-əl) *adj.* Of or pertaining to a period of 150 years. *~n.* A 150th anniversary or its celebration. [SESQUI- + CENTENNIAL.]

ses·qui·pe·da·li·an (sĕs′kwə-pə-dā′lē-ən) *adj.* **1.** Long and ponderous; polysyllabic. **2.** Given to using long words. *~n.* A long word. [Latin *sesquipedalis,* of a foot and a half in length : SESQUI- + *pes* (stem *ped-*), foot.]

ses·sile (sĕs′ĭl′, -əl) *adj.* **1.** *Botany.* Stalkless and attached directly at the base: *sessile leaves.* **2.** *Zoology.* Permanently attached or fixed; not free-moving. [Latin *sessilis,* of sitting, low (said of plants), from *sessus,* past participle of *sedēre,* to sit.]

sessile oak *n.* An oak, the **durmast** *(see).*

ses·sion (sĕsh′ən) *n.* **1. a.** A meeting of a legislative or judicial body for the purpose of transacting business. **b.** A series of such meetings. **c.** The term or period during which such meetings are held. **2.** The part of a year or of a day during which a school holds classes. **3.** A group of people assembled for a common purpose or with a common interest: *a gossip session.* **4.** A court of criminal jurisdiction in the United States. **5. a.** Any period of time devoted to a specific activity. **b.** A period of time spent singing or playing and recording music in a studio; a recording session. **6.** The ruling body of a Presbyterian church. *~adj.* Designating a professional musician who provides instrumental or vocal accompaniment during recording sessions for other people's records: *a session guitarist.* [Middle English *sessioun,* a session, a sitting, from Old French *session,* from Latin *sessiō* (stem *sessiōn-*), from *sessus,* past participle of *sedēre,* to sit.] —**ses·sion·al** *adj.* —**ses·sion·al·ly** *adv.*

Ses·sions (sĕsh′ənz), **Roger Huntington** (1896–1985). U.S. composer. His early work shows the influence of Stravinsky, but with *Violin Sonata* (1953) he began to introduce serialism into his work.

ses·terce (sĕs′tərs) *n.* A silver or bronze coin of ancient Rome, equivalent to ¼ of a denarius. [Latin *sestertius,* (coin) worth two and a half (asses) (i.e., two plus a half of a third ass) : *sēmis,* a half + *tertius,* a third.]

ses·ter·ti·um (sĕs-tûr′shē-əm) *n., pl.* **-tia** (-shē-ə). A money of account in ancient Rome, equivalent to 1,000 sesterces. [Latin *(mille) sestertium,* (a thousand) sesterces, from the genitive plural of *sestertius,* SESTERCE.]

ses·tet (sĕs-tĕt′) *n.* A stanza constituting the last six lines of a sonnet. Compare **octet.** [Italian *sestetto,* from *sesto,* sixth, from Latin *sextus.*]

ses·ti·na (sĕs-tē′nə) *n.* An originally Provençal verse form consisting of six six-line stanzas and a three-line envoi, repeating the end words of the first stanza in the other five stanzas according to an elaborate pattern. [Italian, from *sesto,* sixth, from Latin *sextus.*]

set[1] (sĕt) *v.* **set, setting, sets.** *—tr.* **1.** To put or cause to be situated in a specified place or position: *Set the box on the table.* **2.** To put (a broken or dislocated bone) into a position that will restore a proper and normal state. **3. a.** To adjust according to a standard: *set one's watch by the station clock.* **b.** To adjust to a specified point or calibration: *set the alarm for six o'clock.* **4.** To fix (the hair) in position while wet so as to achieve a particular style. **5.** To arrange scenery upon (a theater stage) or in (a television or motion-picture studio). **6. a.** To put (a precious stone, for example) in a setting; mount. **b.** To apply jewels to; stud. **7. a.** To arrange (type or filmset characters) preparatory to printing; compose. **b.** To transpose (text) into filmset characters or type. **8.** To place in a sitting position; seat: *set the child on his knee.* **9. a.** To put (a hen) on eggs for the purpose of hatching them. **b.** To put (eggs) beneath a hen or in an incubator.

10. To bring into or cause to be in a specified condition or relation: *Her wealth sets her apart from others.* **11.** To cause to be taken into account so as to offset or compensate for something else; balance: *set these losses against tax.* **12.** To cause to take up a hostile position or attitude; pit (one person) against another. **13.** To focus (one's hopes or attention, for example) toward a particular purpose. **14.** To put into a rigid position showing defiance or determination: *set one's jaw.* **15. a.** To put an edge or point on (a cutting instrument). **b.** To adjust (a saw) by deflecting the teeth. **16.** To prepare for effective use or action, as: **a.** To make (a table) ready for a meal. **b.** To make (a trap) ready to operate. **17.** To detail or assign to a particular duty, task, or station: *set them to work cleaning up.* **18.** To allot or prescribe (a task). **19.** To determine, fix, or assign: *set a date.* **20.** To establish (a record). **21.** To present as a model for emulation: *set an example.* **22.** To provide (a scene or story) with a specified background in space and time: *a novel set in 18th-century England.* **23.** To compose music to fit (a given text). **24.** To cause (a liquid or a soft substance) to become firm or solid. **25.** To incite to make an attack: *set his dogs on us.* **26.** To point to the location of (game) by holding a fixed attitude. Used of a hunting dog. **27.** *Horticulture.* To produce, as after pollination: *set seed.* **28.** To sink (a nail) so that its head lies below the surrounding surface. —*intr.* **1.** To go down toward and below the horizon. Used of the sun or any other heavenly body. **2.** To diminish or decline; wane. **3.** To sit on eggs. Used of a hen. **4.** To solidify, harden, or congeal. **5.** To embark upon a journey. Used with *out, forth,* or *off.* **6.** To become restored to a normal state; knit. Used of a broken bone. **7.** To have or follow a specified course or direction. Used of a wind, current, or the like. **8.** *Horticulture.* To mature or develop, as after pollination. **9.** To point to the position of game by holding a fixed attitude. Used of a hunting dog. **10.** *Regional.* To sit. **—set about.** To start or begin doing. **—set against. 1.** To compare; weigh. **2.** To make unfriendly or hostile to. **—set aside. 1.** To separate and reserve for a special purpose or later consideration. **2.** To dismiss or discard. **3.** To declare invalid or void; annul. **—set down. 1.** To put into written or printed form; record. **2.** To regard or consider: *set him down as a sneak.* **3.** To attribute: *set the error down to inexperience.* **4.** To land (an aircraft), especially in abnormal circumstances. **—set forth.** To make known or propound (plans or ideas, for example). **—set in.** To begin to happen and become established: *Infection set in.* **—set out. 1.** To display for exhibition or sale. **2.** To describe or expound; put forward in detail. **3.** To lay out (a room, town, or garden, for example); plan. **4.** To plant out (seedlings, for example).

~*adj.* **1.** Fixed or prescribed by authority, agreement, or convention: *set mealtimes.* **2.** Consisting of or offering a fixed number and combination of dishes for one price: *a set menu.* **3.** Fixed, rigid, or unmoving: *a set smile.* **4.** Clichéd or stereotyped: *set phrases.* **5.** Rigid and unchanging in disposition: *set in one's ways.* **6.** Holding resolutely to a particular attitude or intention: *set on going; dead set against it.* **7.** Ready for action: *get set.*

~*n.* **1. a.** The act or process of setting. **b.** The condition resulting from setting. **2.** A permanent firming or hardening of a substance, as by cooling. **3.** The manner in which something is positioned. **4.** The carriage or bearing of a part of the body. **5.** An inclination or tendency, as of the mind or character, in a particular direction. **6.** The direction or course of wind or water. **7.** An act of styling the hair by setting it: *a shampoo and set.* **8.** A seedling, slip, or cutting that is ready for planting. **9.** Variant of **sett. —set eyes on.** To catch sight of; see. **—set foot in.** To enter. **—set foot on.** To step onto. **—set one's heart on.** To be determined to do something. **—set (or put) one's house in order.** To arrange one's affairs. **—set one's sights on.** To have as a goal. **—set someone straight.** To correct a person by informing accurately. **—set store by.** To regard as valuable or worthwhile. [Set (infinitive, past tense, past participle); Middle English *setten, sette,* to cause to sit, place, Old English *settan, sette, sett.*]

set[2] *n.* **1.** A group of persons, things, or circumstances that belong together by virtue of similarities, as in appearance, character, or function, especially: **a.** A group of persons who associate with each other and share a common lifestyle and common interests: *the jet set.* **b.** A group of related objects having the same or a similar function and often used together in a particular activity: *a chess set; a set of wine glasses.* **c.** A group of situations, events, or the like considered collectively or as forming a whole: *a set of lectures.* **2.** A part of a program or a session of music, typically popular music or jazz, performed at one time: *played a relaxed set.* **3. a.** A basic configuration of dancers, as in a country dance or a square dance. **b.** The series of movements constituting such a dance. **4. a.** The scenery constructed for a dramatic performance. **b.** The area, as in a studio or on location, in which a motion picture is filmed. **5.** An apparatus that receives radio or television signals; a receiver. **6.** *Mathematics & Logic.* A collection or group specified in such a way that, given any object, it can be determined whether that object does or does not belong to that collection or group: *the empty set; the set of positive integers.* **7.** In tennis and other games, a group of games constituting one division or unit of a match. —See Synonyms at **circle.** [Middle English *sette,* sect, set, from Old French, from Latin *secta,* SECT (later confused with *set,* to place, taken as "a group or number set together").]

se·ta (sē′tə) *n., pl.* **setae** (sē′tē′). *Biology.* **1.** A stiff hair, bristle, or bristlelike growth or organ. **2.** *Botany.* The stalk that bears the capsule in mosses. [New Latin, from Latin *sēta, saeta*†, bristle.] **—se·tal** *adj.*

se·ta·ceous (sĭ-tā′shəs) *adj.* **1.** Having or consisting of bristles; bristly. **2.** Resembling a bristle or bristles; bristlelike. [New Latin *setaceus* : SET(A) + -ACEOUS.]

set back *tr.v.* **1.** To impede the progress or advance of. **2.** *Informal.* To cost (a person) a specified amount.

set·back (sĕt′băk′) *n.* **1.** An unanticipated or sudden check in progress; a reverse. **2. a.** A steplike recession in a wall. **b.** Any of a series of such recessions in the rise of a tall building.

set chisel *n.* A chisel with a cutting edge on a tapered shaft; a cold chisel.

Seth (sĕth). The third son of Adam. Genesis 4:25.

se·tif·er·ous (sĭ-tĭf′ər-əs) *adj.* Also **se·tig·er·ous** (-tĭj′ər-əs). Setose. [From Latin *seta,* bristle + -FEROUS.]

se·ti·form (sē′tə-fôrm′) *adj.* Having the shape of a seta or bristle. [SET(A) + -FORM.]

set·line (sĕt′līn′) *n.* A long fishing line towed by a boat and supporting many smaller lines bearing baited hooks. Also "trawl," "trawl line."

set off *tr.v.* **1.** To show to best advantage; enhance by contrast. **2.** To cause to explode. **3. a.** To cause (sudden or hurried activity); spark off: *set off a wave of selling.* **b.** To cause (a person) to start some activity: *set him off on one of his boring stories.*

set·off (sĕt′ôf′) *n.* **1.** Anything that has the effect of enhancing something else, especially by contrast. **2.** Anything that offsets or compensates for something else. **3. a.** A counterclaim. **b.** The settlement of a debt by a debtor's establishing such a claim against the creditor. **4.** See **offset** (sense 3).

Se·ton (sēt′n), **Saint Elizabeth Ann Bayley,** known as "Mother Seton" (1774–1821). U.S. religious leader. A widow with five young children, she was converted to Catholicism in 1805. She opened the first Catholic free school and a college for women in Maryland in 1809 and founded the order known as the Sisters of Charity. She was the first native-born American to be canonized (1974).

se·tose (sē′tōs′) *adj.* Bristly or bristlelike; setaceous. [Latin *sētōsus,* from *sēta,* bristle, SETA.]

set piece *n.* **1.** An often brilliantly executed artistic or literary work, or part of a work, characterized by a formal pattern. **2.** A realistic piece of stage scenery constructed to stand by itself. **3.** An elaborate firework display that forms a pattern. **4.** A carefully planned and executed operation, especially a military operation.

set point *n.* A point that, if won, wins a set, as in tennis.

set·screw (sĕt′skro͞o′) *n.* **1.** A screw, often without a head, used to hold two parts in a position relative to each other without motion. **2.** A screw used to regulate the tension of a spring.

set square *n.* A device used in technical drawing consisting of a flat sheet, usually of plastic or wood, in the shape of a right-angle triangle, used to draw vertical lines in conjunction with a T-square and also to construct angles of 30°, 45°, and 60°.

sett, set (sĕt) *n.* **1.** A badger's burrow. **2.** A small square or rectangular block, usually made of granite, used especially formerly as a paving stone. **3. a.** A square section in a tartan pattern. **b.** The pattern itself. **4.** An adjustment made to the reeds in a loom so as to weave a particular pattern.

set·tee (sĕ-tē′) *n.* **1.** A long wooden bench with a high back. **2.** A small sofa. [Perhaps variant of SETTLE (bench).]

set·ter (sĕt′ər) *n.* **1.** One that sets. **2.** A dog of any of several long-haired breeds, originally trained to indicate the presence of game by crouching in a set position.

set theory *n.* The study of the mathematical properties of sets.

set·ting (sĕt′ĭng) *n.* **1.** The context or surroundings in which an event, story, or the like is set. **2.** A mounting, as for a jewel. **3.** The scenery constructed for a theatrical, motion-picture, or television performance. **4.** Music composed or arranged to fit a text. **5.** Any of the positions in which a machine or instrument can be set. **6.** The cutlery, glassware, and the like for one person at table. **7.** The descent of the sun or other celestial body below the horizon.

set·tle (sĕt′l) *v.* **-tled, -tling, -tles.** —*tr.* **1.** To place, dispose, or establish in a desired position; especially, to place (oneself) in a comfortable position. **2.** To put in order; arrange in a final or satisfactory form. **3.** To reach decisive agreement regarding (a course of action, for example); decide on. **4.** To conclude or resolve (a dispute, for example). **5.** To decide (a lawsuit) by mutual agreement of the involved parties, usually without court action: *settled the affair out of court.* **6. a.** To cause to take up residence in a place. **b.** To colonize or otherwise provide (a place) with inhabitants or settlers. **7.** To fix or establish in a more or less permanent and unvarying form: *a settled life.* **8.** To cause to become less disturbed or agitated; restore calmness or quiet to: *settle one's stomach.* **9.** To pay or pay back (what is owing): *settle an account; a few old scores to settle.* **10. a.** To cause to come to rest, sink, or become compact. **b.** To cause (a liquid) to become clear by forming a sediment. **11.** *Law.* To secure or assign (property or title, for example) to another by a legal settlement. Used with *on* or *upon.* —*intr.* **1.** To discontinue moving and come to rest in one place. **2.** To subside gradually; shift to a lower level. **3.** To sink and become more compact: *The dust settled.* **4. a.** To become clear. Used of liquids. **b.** To be separated from a solution or mixture as a sediment. **5.** To become less agitated or restless; regain calmness or composure. Often used with *down.* **6.** To take up permanent residence. **7.** To reach a decision; determine. Used with *on, upon,* or *with.* **8.** To decide a lawsuit by mutual agreement: *settled out of court.* **9.** To pay what is

PRONUNCIATION KEY

ă, pat; ā, pay; âr, care;
ä, father, are; b, bib;
ch, church; d, deed; ĕ, pet;
ē, be; f, fife; g, gag; h, hat;
hw, which; ĭ, pit; ī, pie;
îr, pier; j, judge; k, kick;
l, lid, needle; m, mum;
n, no, sudden; ng, thing;
ŏ, pot; ō, toe; ô, paw, for;
oi, noise; ou, out; o͝o, book;
o͞o, boot; p, pop; r, roar;
s, sauce; sh, ship, dish;
t, tight; th, thin, path;
th, this, bathe; ŭ, cut; ûr, fur;
v, valve; w, with; y, yes;
z, zebra, size; zh, vision;
ə, about, item, edible, gallop, circus, peaceful

IN FOREIGN WORDS:

à, *Fr.* ami; œ, *Fr.* feu, *Ger.* schön; ü, *Fr.* tu, *Ger.* über; KH, *Ger.* ich, *Scot.* loch; N, *Fr.* bon; y′, *Fr.* Compiègne

STRESS MARKS:

Primary stress: ′
in·cite′ (ĭn-sīt′)
Secondary stress: ′
in′sight′ (ĭn′sīt′)

owing. Often used with *up.* —See Synonyms at **decide.** **—settle down. 1.** To begin living a more ordered life, as by marrying or taking a permanent job. **2.** To apply one's attention purposefully and diligently. **—settle for.** To accept in spite of incomplete satisfaction. **—settle in. 1.** To become comfortably adapted to a new environment or situation. **2.** To help (someone) to settle in.
∼n. A long wooden bench with a high back, often including storage space beneath the seat. [Middle English *setlen,* to place in order, seat, Old English *setlan,* from *setl,* seat.]
set·tle·ment (sĕt′l-mənt) *n.* **1.** The act or process of settling. **2. a.** The establishment of a new population in a place. **b.** A newly colonized region. **3.** A small community, especially in a thinly populated or newly settled area. **4.** An understanding or agreement by which differences are resolved. **5. a.** An arrangement or legal instrument by which property is settled on a person. **b.** Property thus transferred. **6.** A welfare center providing community services in a deprived inner city area. Also called "settlement house." **7.** Slow sinking, as of a wall or building, due to subsidence.
set·tler (sĕt′l-ər, sĕt′lər) *n.* One that settles; especially, a person who settles in a new and previously uncolonized region.
set·tlings (sĕt′l-ĭngz, sĕt′lĭngz) *pl.n.* Sediment; dregs.
set to *intr.v.* **1.** To begin working actively or eagerly. **2.** To begin fighting.
set-to (sĕt′to͞o′) *n., pl.* **-tos.** A brief but usually heated fight or contest.
set up *tr.v.* **1.** To place in a raised or upright position; erect or elevate. **2.** To establish in a position of power: *set up a dictator.* **3.** To cause or produce: *set up a howl.* **4.** To restore or improve the health and well-being of. **5.** To establish; found. **6.** To establish (a person) in business by providing capital, equipment, and the like. **7.** To put forward or propose. **8.** To put (especially oneself) forward, often without justification, as having some quality: *sets himself up as an expert on wine.* **9.** To create conditions favorable for the scoring of (a goal, try, or the like). **10.** *Informal.* To provide (drinks) for a person or group. **11.** *Informal.* To arrange for (someone) to be discovered in incriminating or embarrassing circumstances. *—intr.v.* To start in business: *has set up as a decorator.*
set·up (sĕt′ŭp′) *n. Informal.* **1.** The way in which anything operates or is constituted or arranged. **2.** Physical make-up; physique. **3.** *Usually* **set·ups.** *Informal.* The ingredients and mixers necessary for serving a variety of alcoholic drinks. **4.** A situation prearranged to place someone in an incriminating or embarrassing position. **5.** A task, undertaking, or contest prearranged so that it is accomplished or won without any real difficulty.
Seu·rat (sə-rä′), **Georges Pierre** (1859–91). French painter, the founder of pointillism. Developing the impressionist concerns with light and atmosphere, he evolved a distinctive technique for rendering appearances through innumerable dots of pure color, which produced a number of masterpieces, including *Une Baignade* (1884) and *La Grande Jatte* (1886).
Seuss (so͞os), **Dr.** See Theodor Seuss **Geisel.**
Se·vas·to·pol (sə-văs′tə-pôl′). *English* **Se·bas·to·pol** (-băs′-). Seaport in the Crimea, in southwestern U.S.S.R. It became the main base of the Russian Black Sea fleet (1804). It was twice captured after prolonged sieges: 322 days (1854–55) by the Allies in the Crimean War and 250 days (1941–42) by the Germans in World War II.
sev·en (sĕv′ən) *n.* **1. a.** The cardinal number that is one more than six. **b.** A symbol representing this, such as 7, VII, or vii. **2.** A set made up of seven persons or things. **3. a.** The seventh in a series. **b.** A playing card marked with seven pips. **4.** Seven parts: *cut in seven.* **5.** A size, as in clothing, designated as seven. **6.** Seven hours after midnight or midday. [Middle English *seven,* Old English *seofon.*] **—sev·en** *adj & pron.*
seven deadly sins *pl.n.* The sins of pride, lust, envy, anger, covetousness, gluttony, and sloth. Also called "cardinal sins." See feature, next page.
sev·en·fold (sĕv′ən-fōld′) *adj.* **1.** Consisting of seven parts or members. **2.** Having seven times as many or as much. **—sev·en·fold** *adv.*
seven seas *pl.n.* All the oceans of the world.
Seven Sisters *pl.n. Astronomy.* The **Pleiades** *(see).*
sev·en·teen (sĕv′ən-tēn′, sĕv′ən-tēn′) *n.* **1. a.** The cardinal number that is one more than 16. **b.** A symbol representing this, such as XVII. **2.** A set made up of 17 persons or things. **3.** The seventeenth in a series. [Middle English *seventene,* Old English *seofontīne* : SEVEN + -TEEN.] **—sev·en·teen** *adj. & pron.*
sev·en·teenth (sĕv′ən-tēnth′, sĕv′ən-tēnth′) *n.* **1.** The ordinal number 17 in a series. Also written 17th. **2.** One of 17 equal parts. **—sev·en·teenth** *adj. & adv.*
sev·en·teen-year locust (sĕv′ən-tēn-yîr′) *n.* A cicada of the genus *Magicicada,* of the eastern United States, which as a nymph remains underground for 17 or sometimes 13 years.
sev·enth (sĕv′ənth) *n.* **1.** The ordinal number seven in a series. Also written 7th. **2.** One of seven equal parts. **3.** *Music.* **a.** A note that is on the seventh diatonic degree with respect to another given note. **b.** The interval encompassing two such notes. **c.** A chord consisting of a note together with its third, fifth, and seventh. In this sense, also called "seventh chord." **—sev·enth** *adj. & adv.*
Sev·enth-Day Adventist (sĕv′ənth-dā′) *n.* A member of a sect of Adventism distinguished chiefly for its observance of the Sabbath on Saturday. See **Adventist.**
seventh heaven *n.* **1.** The furthest of the concentric spheres containing the stars and comprising the dwelling place of God and the angels in the Muslim and cabbalist systems. **2.** A state of great joy and satisfaction.
sev·en·ti·eth (sĕv′ən-tē-ĭth) *n.* **1.** The ordinal number 70 in a series. Also written 70th. **2.** One of 70 equal parts. **—sev·en·ti·eth** *adj. & adv.*
sev·en·ty (sĕv′ən-tē) *n., pl.* **-ties. 1. a.** The cardinal number that is 10 more than 60. **b.** A symbol representing this, such as 70 or LXX. **2.** A set made up of 70 persons or things. **3.** The seventieth in a series. **4. seventies. a.** The range of numbers from 70 to 79 considered as a range of age, price, temperature, or the like. **b.** *Often* **Seventies.** The years numbered 70 to 79 in a century. In this sense, also used adjectivally: *a well-known seventies group.* **—sev·en·ty** *adj. & pron.*
sev·en-up (sĕv′ən-ŭp′) *n.* A card game originally requiring seven points to win. Also called "all fours," "pitch."
Seven Wonders of the World *pl.n.* The **wonders of the ancient world** *(see).*
sev·en-year itch (sĕv′ən-yîr′) *n.* A tendency towards infidelity that is supposed to develop after seven years of marriage.
sev·er (sĕv′ər) *v.* **-ered, -ering, -ers.** *—tr.* **1.** To divide or separate into parts; keep apart or make distinct. **2.** To cut or break off forcibly; remove by cutting. **3.** To break off (a relationship, for example); dissolve. *—intr.* **1.** To become cut or broken apart. **2.** To divide; separate or go apart. —See Synonyms at **separate, tear.** [Middle English *severen,* from Norman French *severer,* from Vulgar Latin *sēperāre* (unattested), from Latin *sēparāre,* to SEPARATE.] **—sev·er·a·ble** (sĕv′ər-ə-bəl) *adj.*
sev·er·al (sĕv′ər-əl) *adj.* **1.** More than two but not many; of an indefinitely small number. **2.** Single; distinct. **3.** Respectively different; diverse; various. **4.** *Law.* Pertaining separately to each party involved.
∼pron. Several persons or things; a few. [Middle English *severall,* separate, distinct, from Norman French *several,* from Medieval Latin *sēparālis,* from Latin *sēpār,* separate, from *sēparāre,* to SEPARATE.] **—sev·er·al·ly** *adv.*
sev·er·ance (sĕv′ər-əns) *n.* **1.** The act or process of severing, division, or separation. **2.** The condition of being severed.
severance pay *n.* A sum of money usually based on length of employment for which an employee is eligible upon termination.
se·vere (sə-vîr′) *adj.* **-verer, -verest. 1.** Having or showing a harsh, unsparing, and inflexible disposition in one's treatment of or attitude toward others; stern; strict. **2.** Adhering to or based on stringent and exacting rules or standards: *severe discipline.* **3.** Grave and austere in appearance, manner, or temperament; forbidding. **4.** Extremely plain and unadorned, as in dress or style; sober and restrained. **5.** Causing intense pain or distress; hard; grievous: *a severe winter; severe depression.* **6.** Extremely difficult to perform or accomplish; arduous. [French *severe,* from Latin *sevērus.*] **—se·vere·ly** *adv.* **—se·vere·ness, se·ver·i·ty** (sə-vĕr′ə-tē) *n.*
Synonyms: *ascetic, austere, exacting, stern, strict.*
Sev·ern (sĕv′ərn). Britain's longest river. It rises on the northeastern slopes of Plynlimmon and flows for 340 kilometers (211 miles) through the Vale of Powys and to the Bristol Channel via an exceptionally long estuary; the tidal bore can reverse the flow of the river as far up as Gloucester.
Severnaya Dvina. See **Dvina, Northern.**
Se·ve·rus (sə-vîr′əs), full name Lucius Septimius Severus (A.D. 146–211). Roman emperor (193–211), born in Roman North Africa. He restored order to the empire after a turbulent period and consolidated the eastern frontier. He died at York while planning a major campaign into Scotland.
Se·vier (sə-vîr′), **John** (1745–1815). U.S. soldier, frontiersman, and politician. He was instrumental in winning the Revolutionary Battle of Kings Mountain (1780) and after the war became governor (1785–88) of the self-proclaimed state of Franklin. The region later became the state of Tennessee, with Sevier as its first governor.
Sé·vi·gné (sā-vē-nyā′), **Marie de Rabutin-Chantal, Marquise de** (1626–96). French writer. A widow from the age of 25, she is remembered for her prolific correspondence. Her letters, including many to her daughter, radiate lively wit and understanding and vividly depict aristocratic life in the age of Louis XIV.
Se·ville (sə-vĭl′). *Spanish* **Se·vi·lla** (sə-vē′lyä). A port of southwestern Spain, the capital of Sevilla province. It was an important Moorish stronghold and center of culture and learning (712–1248) and prospered as the main port for the Spanish colonies in the New World from 1492 until eclipsed by Cádiz in the late 18th century.
Seville orange *n.* **1.** A citrus tree, *Citrus aurantium,* that bears bitter oranges, used to make marmalade. **2.** The fruit of this tree. Also called "bitter orange." [After SEVILLE where it is cultivated.]
Sè·vres (sĕv′rə) *n.* A fine porcelain made in Sèvres, northern France. Also called "Sèvres ware."
sew (sō) *v.* **sewed, sewn** (sōn) or **sewed, sewing, sews.** *—tr.* **1.** To make, repair, or fasten using a needle and thread. **2.** To close, enclose, or attach by means of stitches. *—intr.* To work with a needle and thread or with a sewing machine. **—sew up.** *Informal.* **1.** To bring (a business deal) to a successful close. **2.** To gain control of. [Middle English *sewen,* Old English *seowian.*]
sew·age (so͞o′ĭj) *n.* Liquid and solid waste carried off with ground water in sewers or drains. [SEW(ER) + -AGE.]
Sew·all Wright effect (so͞o′əl) *n.* **Genetic drift** *(see).* [After *Sewall Wright* (1889–), U.S. geneticist and statistician.]
Sew·ard (so͞o′ərd), **William Henry** (1801–72). U.S. statesman.

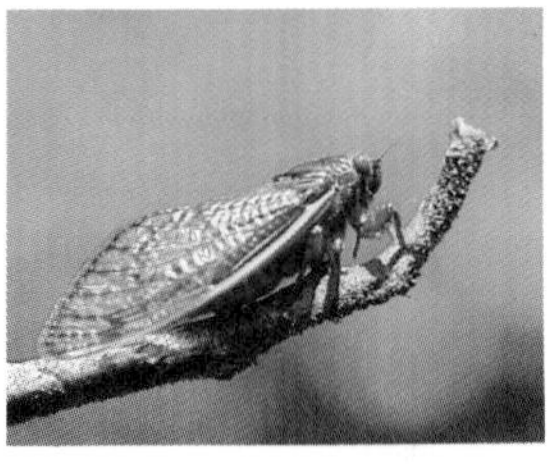

seventeen-year locust *This sap-sucking cicada of North America gets its name because its nymphs live for up to 17 years before metamorphosing into the winged adult form (above). The nymphs feed underground on the sap of tree roots.*

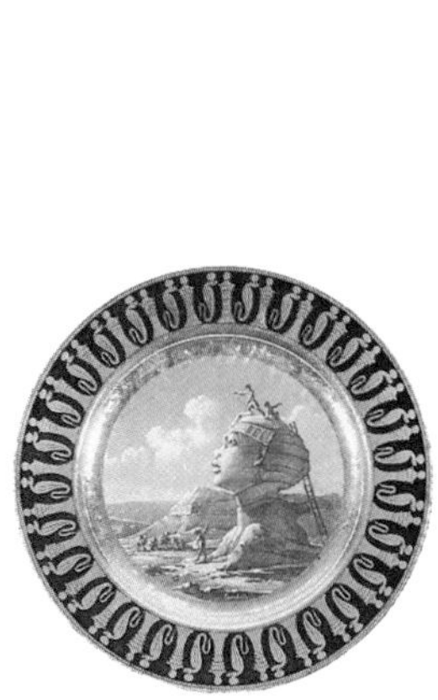

Sèvres plate *Porcelain ware that takes its name from the suburb of Paris where it has been manufactured since 1756. This example is* The Sphinx *from the "Egyptian Service" painted by Swebach-Desfontaines in 1811.*

seven deadly sins

VICES FATAL TO SPIRITUAL PROGRESS
Root causes of both venial and mortal sins

The list of the seven deadly sins, Pride *(Superbia),* Envy *(Invidia),* Anger *(Ira),* Sloth *(Accidie),* Covetousness *(Avaricia),* Gluttony *(Gula),* and Lust *(Luxuria),* came into being among the monastic communities of desert saints in Egypt in late Greco-Roman times. Not to be confused with mortal sins, which are specific kinds of sinful action, the seven deadly sins are the unhealthy moral states that if left unremedied are bound to lead to sinful acts. These seven pernicious states of mind were likened to the seven nations of Canaan overcome by Israel. Late in the sixth century, Gregory the Great popularized the list in the West. Leading the seven is Pride, the rebellion of the individual against God, considered as the source of all the others. The list has been criticized, because it occurs neither in the Bible nor in the writings of major Church fathers before Gregory, and also because it is arbitrary and incomplete—where, for example, are fear and lack of faith? Use of the list has been largely dropped by Christian churches, yet the seven deadly sins live on in the cultural consciousness, as well as in the spiritual discourse of everyday people. A florid procession of the seven forms a high point in Spenser's *Faerie Queen,* and the list occurs in many other classic authors, including Dante, Shakespeare, and Burns. The outstanding treatment of the seven deadly sins in English literature is in Chaucer's *Canterbury Tales,* in the magnificent sermon that concludes the book.

GRAPHIC PAINTINGS *The seven deadly sins have been a favorite theme of artists. The tabletop above, painted by Hieronymus Bosch, uses the cartwheel design much favored in his time to illustrate virtues and vices. Each division is devoted to a particular sin and at the hub is the all-seeing eye of God. Within it is Christ above a Latin inscription meaning "Beware, the Lord sees."*

Elected to the U.S. Senate in 1848, he became known for his fiery opposition to slavery, coining the term "irrepressible conflict" to describe the antagonism between freedom and slavery. As secretary of state (1861–69), he negotiated the purchase of Alaska from the Russians in 1867—a bargain long known as "Seward's Folly."

Sew·ell (sōō′əl), **Anna** (1820–78). British author of the children's classic *Black Beauty* (1877). Partially crippled from childhood, she wrote her one novel, set in the form of the autobiography of a horse, to expose the maltreatment of animals in her day.

sew·er[1] (sōō′ər) *n.* An artificial, usually underground conduit for carrying off sewage or rainwater. [Middle English *sewer,* from Norman French *sever(e),* from Vulgar Latin *exaquāria* (unattested) : Latin *ex-,* out of + *aqua,* water.]

sew·er[2] (sōō′ər) *n.* A medieval servant who supervised the serving of meals. [Middle English *sewer,* from Norman French *asseour,* from Old French *asseoir,* to cause to sit (seating of guests was a sewer's responsibility), from Latin *assidēre,* to sit down : *ad-,* to + *sedēre,* to sit.]

sew·er[3] (sō′ər) *n.* One that sews.

sew·er·age (sōō′ər-ij) *n.* **1.** A system of sewers. **2.** The removal of waste materials by means of a sewer system. **3.** Sewage.

sew·ing (sō′ing) *n.* **1.** The act, skill, or hobby of one who sews. **2.** An article that is or is to be worked on with needle and thread; needlework.

sewing circle *n.* A group of women who meet regularly for the purpose of sewing, often for charitable causes.

sewing machine *n.* A machine that sews, often having additional attachments for special stitching.

sewn. Past participle of **sew.**

sex (sĕks) *n.* **1. a.** The sum of properties by which organisms are classified according to their reproductive functions. **b.** Either of two divisions, designated *male* and *female,* of this classification. **2.** Males or females collectively. **3.** The condition or character of being male or female; the physiological, functional, and psychological differences that distinguish the male and the female. **4.** The sexual urge or instinct or sexual desire as it manifests itself in behavior. **5.** Sexual intercourse. **6.** The genitalia.
~*tr.v.* **sexed, sexing, sexes.** To determine the sex of. [Middle English, from Old French *sexe,* from Latin *sexus*†.]

sex– *prefix.* Indicates six; for example, **sexpartite.** [Latin *sex,* six.]

sex·a·ge·nar·i·an (sĕk'sə-jə-nâr'ē-ən) *adj.* **1.** Being sixty years old or between sixty and seventy years old. **2.** Of or like someone of this age.
~*n.* A person of sixty or between sixty and seventy years of age. [Latin *sexāgēnārius,* from *sexāgēnī,* sixty each, from *sexāgintā,* sixty : SEX- + *-gintā,* ten times.]

Sex·a·ges·i·ma (sĕk'sə-jĕs'ə-mə) *n.* The second Sunday before Lent. Also called "Sexagesima Sunday." [Late Latin *sexāgēsima,* sixtieth (day before Easter), from Latin, feminine of *sexāgēsimus,* sixtieth, from *sexāgintā,* sixty. See **sexagenarian.**]

sex·a·ges·i·mal (sĕk'sə-jĕs'ə-məl) *adj.* Relating to or based upon the number 60. [From Latin *sexāgēsimus,* sixtieth, from *sexāgintā,* sixty. See **sexagenarian.**]

sex appeal *n.* Attractiveness that arouses sexual desire; the possession of qualities that are sexually attractive.

sex·cen·te·nar·y (sĕk'sĕn'tə-nĕr'ē) *adj.* Pertaining to 600 or to a 600-year period.
~*n., pl.* **sexcentenaries.** A 600th anniversary or its commemoration. [From Latin *sexcentēnī,* six hundred each : SEX- + *centēnī,* a hundred each, from *centum,* hundred.]

sex chromosome *n.* Either of a pair of chromosomes, usually designated X or Y, that combine to determine the sex of an individual. In humans, XX results in a female and XY in a male. See **X chromosome, Y chromosome.**

sex·en·ni·al (sĕk-sĕn'ē-əl) *adj.* **1.** Occurring every six years. **2.** Of or for six years. [Latin *sexennium,* (period of) six years : SEX- + *annus,* year.] **—sex·en·ni·al·ly** *adv.*

sex hormone *n.* Any of various animal hormones, such as estrogen and androgen, affecting the growth or function of the reproductive organs and the development of secondary sex characteristics.

sex·ism (sĕk'sĭz'əm) *n.* **1.** Discrimination based on sex; expecially, prejudice against the female sex. **2.** Any arbitrary stereotyping of males and females on the basis of their gender. [SEX + -ISM, after RACISM.] **—sex·ist** *adj.* & *n.*

sex·less (sĕks'lĭs) *adj.* **1.** Lacking sexual characteristics; asexual; neuter. **2.** Arousing or exhibiting no sexual interest or desire. **—sex·less·ly** *adv.* **—sex·less·ness** *n.*

sex linkage *n.* The condition in which a gene responsible for a specific phenotypic trait is located on a sex chromosome, usually on the X chromosome but not on the Y chromosome, resulting in sexually dependent inheritance of the trait.

sex-linked (sĕks'lĭngkt') *adj.* **1.** Carried by a sex chromosome, especially an X chromosome. Said of genes. **2.** Broadly, sexually determined. Said especially of inherited traits.

sex object *n.* One who is valued, or is portrayed as having value, purely for her or his sexual attributes.

sex·ol·o·gy (sĕk-sŏl'ə-jē) *n.* The study of human sexual behavior. [SEX + -LOGY.] **—sex·o·log·ic** (sĕk'sə-lŏj'ĭk), **sex·o·log·i·cal** *adj.* **—sex·ol·o·gist** *n.*

sex·par·tite (sĕks-pär'tīt') *adj.* Composed of or divided into six parts. [SEX- + PARTITE.]

sex·pot (sĕks'pŏt') *n. Informal.* A strikingly sexy person.

sext (sĕkst) *n.* **1.** The fourth of the seven **canonical hours** *(see).* **2.** The time of day set aside for this prayer, usually the sixth hour, or noon. [Middle English *sexte,* from Latin *sexta (hora),* sixth (hour), from the feminine of *sextus,* sixth.]

Sex·tans (sĕks'tənz) *n.* A constellation in the equatorial region of the sky near Leo and Hydra. Also called the "Sextant." [New Latin, SEXTANT.]

sex·tant (sĕks'tənt) *n.* **1.** An instrument used in navigation for measuring the altitudes of celestial bodies and hence determining the position of the observer. **2. Sextant.** The constellation Sextans. [New Latin *sextans* (stem *sextant-*), from Latin, a sixth part (the instrument has an arc graduated in sixths of a circle).]

sex·tet (sĕks-tĕt') *n.* **1. a.** A group of six vocalists or musicians. **b.** A musical composition written for six performers. **2.** Any group of six persons or things. [Respelling of SESTET, after Latin *sex,* six.]

sex·tile (sĕks'tīl') *adj.* Designating the position of two celestial bodies when they are 60 degrees apart. [Latin *sextīlis,* one sixth (of a circle), from *sextus,* sixth.]

sex·til·lion (sĕks-tĭl'yən) *n.* **1.** The cardinal number represented by 1 followed by 21 zeros, usually written 10^{21}. **2.** In British usage, the cardinal number represented by 1 followed by 36 zeros, usually written 10^{36}. [French : SEX- + -(M)ILLION.] **—sex·til·lion** *adj.* **—sex·til·lionth** *n.* & *adj.*

sex·to·dec·i·mo (sĕks'tō-dĕs'ə-mō') *n., pl.* **-mos. 1.** The page size of a book composed of printer's sheets folded into 16 leaves or 32 pages. **2.** A book composed of pages of this size. Also called "sixteenmo." Also written *16 mo, 16°.* [Latin *sextōdecimō,* ablative of *sextusdecimus,* a sixteenth : *sextus,* sixth + *decimus,* tenth, from *decem,* ten.] **—sex·to·dec·i·mo** *adj.*

sex·ton (sĕks'tən) *n.* A church officer responsible for the care and upkeep of the church, its furnishings and vestments, the churchyard, and sometimes for bell-ringing or gravedigging. [Middle English *segerstone, sexton,* from Norman French *segerstaine,* from Medieval Latin *sacristānus,* SACRISTAN.]

Sex·ton (sĕks'tən), **Anne** (1928–74). U.S. poet. In numerous poems noted for their irony and lyric intensity, she examined her own attempts to deal with emotional illness and mental breakdowns. In 1966 she won a Pulitzer Prize for her volume *Live or Die.* Her death, at age 46, was apparently a suicide.

sexton beetle *n.* The **burying beetle** *(see).*

sex·tu·ple (sĕk-sto͞o'pəl, -styo͞o'-, -stŭp'əl, sĕk'stŭp'əl) *adj.* **1.** Consisting of or having six parts, members, or copies. **2.** Multiplied by six; six times as much, as many, or as large.
~*n.* A sixfold amount or number.
~*v.* **sextupled, -pling, -ples.** —*tr.* To multiply or increase by six. —*intr.* To be multiplied sixfold. [Medieval Latin *sextuplus,* irregularly (influenced by *quintuplus,* QUINTUPLE) from Latin *sex,* six.] **—sex·tu·ply** *adv.*

sex·tu·plet (sĕk-stŭp'lĭt, -sto͞o'plĭt, -styo͞o'-, sĕk'stŭp'lĭt) *n.* **1.** One of six offspring delivered at one birth. **2.** A collection or set of six similar persons or things; a sextet. **3.** *Music.* A set of six equal notes to be performed in the time normally given for four notes of the same value. [SEXTU(PLE + TRI)PLET.]

sex·tu·pli·cate (sĕk-sto͞o'plĭ-kĭt, -styo͞o'-) *adj.* **1.** Six times as many or as much; sixfold. **2.** Sixth in a group or set.
~*n.* One of six similar things. [SEXTU(PLE + DU)PLICATE.] **—sex·tu·pli·cate·ly** *adv.* **—sex·tu·pli·ca·tion** *n.*

sex·u·al (sĕk'sho͞o-əl) *adj.* **1.** Pertaining to, affecting, or associated with sex, the sexes, or the sex organs and their functions. **2.** Implying or symbolizing erotic desires or activities. **3.** Having a sex or sexual organs. **4.** Of, pertaining to, or designating reproduction involving the union of male and female gametes. [From Late Latin *sexuālis,* from Latin *sexus,* SEX.] **—sex·u·al·ly** *adv.*

sexual intercourse *n.* **1.** Copulation between a man and a woman, involving the insertion of the erect penis into the vagina. **2.** Intercourse between two or more individuals involving genital stimulation. Also called "intercourse."

sexual reproduction *n.* Reproduction involving the union of male and female gametes.

sex·u·al·i·ty (sĕk'sho͞o-ăl'ə-tē) *n.* **1.** The condition of being characterized and distinguished by sex. **2.** Concern or preoccupation with sex. **3.** The quality of possessing a sexual character or potency. **4.** The condition of having sexual feelings and desires of a certain kind; a particular sexual nature.

sexual selection *n.* A Darwinian adjunct of natural selection hypothesizing the selection by females of characteristics involved in male courtship displays and combat and hence the retention of such characteristics in future generations.

sex·y (sĕk'sē) *adj.* **-ier, -iest.** *Informal.* Arousing or intended to arouse sexual desire or interest.

Sey·chelles (sā-shĕl', -shĕlz'). A republic of the northwestern Indian Ocean, comprising an archipelago of *c.* 85 coral or volcanic islands, northeast of Madagascar. It was discovered by Vasco da Gama (1502), settled by the French (1770's), and seized by the British (1794). The Seychelles became an independent republic within the Commonwealth in 1976. Its economy rests on tropical produce, particularly copra and cinnamon, and, increasingly, on tourism and fishing. Mahé is the largest island, with more than 60 percent of the population. Area, 278 square kilometers (107 square miles). Population, 63,000. Capital, Victoria (on Mahé). See map at **Indian Ocean.**

Sey·fert galaxy (sē'fərt, sī'-) *n.* Any of a number of spiral galaxies with an exceptionally bright nucleus. [After Carl K. *Seyfert* (1911–60), U.S. astronomer.]

Sey·mour (sē'môr', -mōr'), **Jane** (*c.* 1509–37). English noblewoman, the third wife of Henry VIII and the mother of Edward VI. A lady-in-waiting to Anne Boleyn, she married Henry in 1536 soon after Anne's execution. She died shortly after providing the king with his only male heir.

sez (sĕz). *Nonstandard.* Variant of **says.**

SF science fiction.

sfer·ics (sfîr'ĭks, sfĕr'-) *n.* Also **spherics.** *Used with a singular verb.* **1.** The study of atmospherics, especially using electron detectors. **2. Atmospherics** *(see).* [Short for ATMOSPHERICS.]

sfor·zan·do (sfôr-tsän'dō) *adv.* Also **for·zan·do** (fôr-). *Abbr.* **sf., sfz.** Suddenly and strongly accented. Used as a musical direction.
~*n.* Also **for·zan·do.** A sforzando note or chord. [Italian, gerund of *sforzare,* to use force : *s-,* from Latin *ex-,* out of + *forzare,* to force, from Vulgar Latin *fortiāre* (unattested), from *fortia* (unattested), FORCE.] **—sfor·zan·do** *adj.*

S.G. solicitor general.

sgd. signed.

sgraf·fi·to (zgrä-fē'tō) *n., pl.* **-fiti** (-fē'tē). **1.** Decoration, as on a wall or piece of pottery, produced by scratching through a surface of plaster or glazing to reveal a different color beneath. **2.** Something decorated in this way. [Italian, from the past participle of *sgraffire,* to scratch, from *sgraffio,* a scratch, from *sgraffiare,* to produce sgraffito : *s-,* from Latin *ex-,* out of + *graffiare,* to scratch (see **graffito**).]

's Gravenhage. See **Hague, The.**

PRONUNCIATION KEY

ă, pat; ā, pay; âr, care;
ä, father, are; b, bib;
ch, church; d, deed; ĕ, pet;
ē, be; f, fife; g, gag; h, hat;
hw, which; ĭ, pit; ī, pie;
îr, pier; j, judge; k, kick;
l, lid, needle; m, mum;
n, no, sudden; ng, thing;
ŏ, pot; ō, toe; ô, paw, for;
oi, noise; ou, out; o͝o, book;
o͞o, boot; p, pop; r, roar;
s, sauce; sh, ship, dish;
t, tight; th, thin, path;
th, this, bathe; ŭ, cut; ûr, fur;
v, valve; w, with; y, yes;
z, zebra, size; zh, vision;
ə, about, item, edible,
gallop, circus, peaceful

IN FOREIGN WORDS:

à, *Fr.* ami; œ, *Fr.* feu, *Ger.* schön; ü, *Fr.* tu, *Ger.* über;
KH, *Ger.* ich, *Scot.* loch;
N, *Fr.* bon; y', *Fr.* Compiègne

STRESS MARKS:

Primary stress: '
in·cite' (ĭn-sīt')
Secondary stress: '
in'sight' (ĭn'sīt')

Sgt. sergeant.

Sgt. Maj. sergeant major.

sh (sh) *interj.* Used to urge silence.

sh. **1.** share. **2.** sheet. **3.** shilling.

Shaan·xi or **Shan-si** or **Shen-si** (shän′sē′). Province in north-central China, to the south of the Huang He. It is crossed by the Wei River valley, one of the earliest cultural and political centers of northern China and today a rich agricultural region and the most densely populated part of the province. Since the 1960's Shaanxi has developed industrially. Xi'an is the capital.

Sha·ban, shaa·ban (shə-bän′) *n.* The eighth month of the year on the Muslim calendar. See feature at **calendar.** [Arabic *sha'bān.*]

Shab·bat (shä-bät′, shä′bəs) *n., pl.* **-batim** (-bä′tim, -bô′sīm). The Jewish Sabbath. [Hebrew *shabbāth,* SABBATH.]

shab·by (shăb′ē) *adj.* **-bier, -biest. 1.** Threadbare; worn-out. **2.** Wearing worn-out clothes; seedy. **3.** Dilapidated; in poor repair. **4.** Despicable; mean. **5.** Unfair. [Obsolete *shab,* a scab, from Middle English *schab(be),* Old English *sceabb,* from Old Norse *skabbr* (unattested). See **scab.**] **—shab·bi·ly** *adv.* **—shab·bi·ness** *n.*

Shabuoth. Variant of **Shavuot.**

shack (shăk) *n.* A small, crudely built cabin; shanty. **—shack up** *Slang.* **1.** To live, room, or stay at a place: *I'm shacking up with my cousin until I find a place.* **2.** To live in sexual intimacy with another person while unmarried. [Short for Mexican Spanish *jacal,* from Aztec *xacatti,* thatched cabin.]

shack·le (shăk′əl) *n.* **1.** A metal fastening, usually one of a pair, for encircling and confining the ankle or wrist of a prisoner or captive; fetter; manacle. **2.** Any of several devices, such as a clevis, used to fasten or couple. **3.** Anything that confines or restrains. *—tr.v.* **shackled, -ling, -les. 1.** To put shackles on; fetter. **2.** To fasten or connect with a shackle. **3.** To restrict; confine; hamper. [Middle English *schackle,* Old English *sceacel,* fetter, from Germanic *skakulo-* (unattested).] **—shack·ler** *n.*

Shack·le·ton (shăk′əl-tən), **Sir Ernest Henry** (1874–1922). British Antarctic explorer. In 1907–09 he led an expedition that came within 161 kilometers (100 miles) of the South Pole. On a second expedition Shackleton's ship *Endurance* became icebound and he made a gruelling journey to South Georgia to get help. He died on South Georgia, leading his third expedition (1921–22).

shad (shăd) *n., pl.* **shads** or collectively **shad. 1.** Any of several food fishes of the genus *Alosa,* related to the herrings but atypical in swimming to estuaries or up streams from marine waters to spawn. **2.** Broadly, any of various unrelated silvery fishes. [Middle English *shad,* Old English *sceadd†.*]

shad·ber·ry (shăd′bĕr′ē) *n., pl.* **-ries.** The fruit of the shadbush.

shad·bush (shăd′bŏosh′) *n.* Any of various North American shrubs or trees of the genus *Amelanchier,* having white flowers and edible blue-black or purplish fruit. Also called "shadblow," "serviceberry," "Juneberry." [So called because the flowers bloom at about the same time shad appear in U.S. rivers.]

shad·dock (shăd′ək) *n.* **1.** A tropical tree, *Citrus maxima* (or *C. grandis*), closely related to the grapefruit. **2.** The edible yellow, pear-shaped fruit of this tree. Also called "pomelo," "pompelmous." [After Captain *Shaddock,* commander of an East India Company ship, who took the seed to Jamaica in 1696.]

shade (shād) *n.* **1.** Light diminished in intensity as a result of the interception of the rays; comparative darkness. **2.** Cover or shelter from the sun provided by an object's interception of its rays. **3.** A place or area sheltered from the sun. **4.** Any of various devices, such as a lampshade, used to reduce or screen light or heat. **5. shades.** *Slang.* Sunglasses. **6.** Relative obscurity or inconspicuousness. **7. shades.** Dark shades occurring at dusk: *shades of evening.* **8.** The part of a picture or photograph depicting darkness or shadow. **9.** The degree to which a color is mixed with black or is decreasingly illuminated; gradation of darkness. **10.** A color that resembles a standard color but is slightly different in saturation, hue, or luminosity: *a shade of red.* **11.** A slight difference or variation; nuance. **12.** A small amount; trace; jot. **13.** A disembodied spirit; ghost. **14. shades.** *Informal.* Reminders; echoes: *seeing her again roused shades of the past.*
—v. **shaded, shading, shades.** *—tr.* **1.** To screen from light or heat. **2.** To obscure or darken. **3. a.** To represent the effect of shade in (a picture). **b.** To produce gradations of light or color in (a picture). **c.** To cover in (part of a picture) with fine pencil lines, brushstrokes, or the like. **4.** To change or vary by slight degrees: *shade the meaning.* *—intr.* To change gradually or imperceptibly, as from one state or color into another. Often used with *off.*
—adj. Providing or intended to provide shade: *a shade tree.* [Middle English *schade,* Old English *sceadu, scead.*]

shad·ing (shā′dĭng) *n.* **1.** Screening against light or heat. **2.** The lines or other marks used in a sketch, engraving, or painting to represent gradations of light or color. **3.** Any small variation, gradation, or difference.

shad·ow (shăd′ō) *n.* **1.** An area that is not, or is only partially, irradiated or illuminated because of the interception of radiation by an opaque object between the area and the source of radiation. **2.** The rough image of the intervening object, especially the umbral image, that delimits the shaded area. **3.** An imperfect, insubstantial, or delusive imitation; a semblance. **4. shadows.** The darkness following sunset. **5.** Gloom or unhappiness or an influence that causes such feeling. **6.** A shaded area in a picture or photograph. **7.** A mirrored image or reflection. **8.** A phantom; ghost. **9.** One who constantly follows another around, such as: **a.** A constant

companion. **b.** A detective. **10.** A faint indication; premonition. **11.** A vestige; remnant. **12.** An insignificant portion or amount; a slight trace. **13.** Shelter; protection. **14.** An influence that dominates or overshadows: *grew up in his brother's shadow.*
—adj. Belonging to a shadow cabinet and acting as the counterpart in opposition to a particular member of the government.
—tr.v. **shadowed, -owing, -ows. 1.** To cast a shadow upon; shade. **2.** To make gloomy or dark; cloud. **3.** To represent vaguely, mysteriously, or prophetically. **4.** To follow after, especially in secret; trail. [Middle English *schadow,* Old English *sceaduwe,* oblique case of *sceadu,* SHADE.] **—shad·ow·er** *n.*

shad·ow·box (shăd′ō-bŏks′) *intr.v.* **-boxed, -boxing, -boxes.** To spar with an imaginary opponent, as in training.

shadow cabinet *n.* The members of the main opposition party in the British Parliament who act as spokesmen for their party on the issues dealt with by their ministerial counterparts in government, and who are expected to hold positions in the cabinet when their party is returned to power.

shad·ow·graph (shăd′ō-grăf′, -gräf′) *n.* An image produced by casting a shadow on a screen.

shadow play *n.* A play presented by casting shadows of puppets or actors on a screen.

shad·ow·y (shăd′ō-ē) *adj.* **-ier, -iest. 1.** Resembling a shadow; insubstantial; unreal. **2.** Full of shadows; dark; shady. **3.** Barely perceptible; indistinct; dim. **—See Usage note at dark. —shad·ow·i·ness** *n.*

Sha·drach (shăd′răk). A Hebrew captive who miraculously escaped death in Nebuchadnezzar's fiery furnace. Daniel 3.

shad·y (shā′dē) *adj.* **-ier, -iest. 1.** Full of shade; shaded. **2.** Providing shade. **3. a.** Of dubious character or honesty. **b.** Legally or morally questionable. **—See Synonyms at dishonest. —See Usage note at dark. —shad·i·ly** *adv.* **—shad·i·ness** *n.*

Shaf·fer (shăf′ər), **Peter** (1926–). British playwright. His works include *Equus* (1973) and the historical dramas *The Royal Hunt of the Sun* (1964) and *Amadeus* (1979).

shaft¹ (shăft, shäft) *n.* **1.** The long, narrow stem or body of a spear or arrow. **2.** A spear, arrow, or the like. **3.** Something suggestive of an arrow in appearance or effect: *shafts of satire.* **4.** *Slang.* Harsh, unfair treatment. **5.** A ray or beam of light. **6.** The handle of any of various tools or implements. **7.** The rib of a feather. **8.** *Anatomy.* **a.** The midsection of a long bone; the diaphysis. **b.** The section of a hair projecting from the surface of the body. **c.** Any elongated cylindrical body part. **9.** The section of a column or pillar between the capital and base. **10.** One of two parallel poles between which an animal is harnessed. **11.** *Machinery.* A long, generally cylindrical bar, especially one that rotates and transmits power: *a drive shaft.* [Middle English *shaft,* Old English *sceaft,* from Germanic *skaftaz* (unattested).]

shaft² *n.* **1.** A long, narrow passage sunk into the earth; a tunnel. **2.** A vertical passage housing an elevator. **3.** A duct or conduit for the passage of air, as for ventilation or heating.

Shaftes·bur·y (shăfts′bĕr′ē, -bə-rē), **Anthony Ashley Cooper, 1st Earl of** (1621–83). English politician, the father of the Whig Party. Shaftesbury joined the Parliamentarians in early 1644, during the English Civil War, and was appointed to official posts in 1648–49 by Cromwell's government. In 1654 he withdrew his support from Cromwell and took part in the restoration of Charles II in 1660. In 1667 he became one of the five ministers in the so-called cabal (after the initials of the five leaders) administration, rising to be Lord Chancellor as the Earl of Shaftesbury in 1672. Dismissed from office in the following year, he organized an oppositon faction, which was the origin of the Whig Party.

shaft·ing (shăf′tĭng, shäf′-) *n.* **1.** A system of shafts, as in a mechanical device, for transmitting motion or power. **2.** Material from which shafts are made.

shag¹ (shăg) *n.* **1.** A tangle or mass, especially of rough, matted hair. **2. a.** A coarse long nap, as on some woolen cloth. **b.** Cloth having such a nap. **3.** Coarse shredded tobacco.
—tr.v. **shagged, shagging, shags. 1.** To make shaggy; roughen. **2.** *Baseball.* To chase and catch (fly balls) in batting practice. [Middle English *shagge* (unattested), Old English *sceacga,* beard, from Germanic *skag-* (unattested).] **—shag** *adj.*

shag² *n.* A dance step of the 1930's consisting of a hop on each foot in alternation. [20th century : origin obscure.] **—shag** *v.*

shag³ *n.* A marine bird, of the genus *Phalacrocorax* (*P. aristotelis*) which also includes the cormorants. The mature bird is black and has a short crest and yellow beak. [Perhaps from its shaggy crest.]

shag·bark (shăg′bärk′) *n.* A North American hickory tree, *Carya ovata,* having shaggy bark, compound leaves, and edible nuts with a hard shell. Also called "shellbark."

shag·gy (shăg′ē) *adj.* **-gier, -giest. 1.** Having, covered with, or resembling long, rough hair or wool. **2.** Bushy and matted. **3.** Poorly groomed; unkempt. **—shag·gi·ly** *adv.* **—shag·gi·ness** *n.*

shag·gy-dog story (shăg′ē-dôg′, -dŏg′) *n.* A long, drawn-out anecdote with an absurd or anticlimactic punch line.

shaggy mane *n.* An edible ink cap fungus, *Coprinus comatus,* having a long white stalk and a grayish-white flaking cap. Also called "shaggy cap."

shaggy parasol *n.* A basidiomycete fungus, *Lepiota rhacodes,* having a broad, pale brown cap covered in brown scales.

sha·green (shə-grēn′) *n.* **1.** The rough hide of a shark or ray, covered with numerous bony denticles, and used as an abrasive and as leather. **2.** Leather with a granular surface, prepared from the skins

shag *In spring the shag's erect crest distinguishes it from its larger relative, the cormorant. Both birds dive for fish in deep coastal waters and nest on remote cliffs.*

of various animals. [From French *chagrin,* "rough hide." See **chagrin.**] **—sha·green** *adj.*

shag·pile (shăg′pīl′) *n.* A long shaglike or soft pile on a carpet.

shah (shä) *n.* The monarch of certain lands of the Middle East, especially, formerly, Iran. [Persian *shāh,* from Old Persian *khshāyathiya.*]

Shahaptin. Variant of **Sahaptin.**

Shah Ja·han or **Je·han** (jə-hän′) (1592–1666). Mogul emperor of India (1628–58), who brought the Mogul Empire to its golden age. A noted patron of the arts, he was also a great builder and had the Taj Mahal erected. He was deposed by his son Aurangzeb.

Shahn (shän), **Benjamin,** known as "Ben" (1898–1969). U.S. artist, born in Lithuania. His uniquely personal style of realism was first apparent in a series of 23 gouaches (1931–32) about the Sacco-Vanzetti trial. He was also noted for his urban paintings, graphics, and book illustrations.

shai·tan, shei·tan (shī-tän′) *n.* **1.** *Often* **Shaitan, Sheitan.** *Islam.* Satan; the Devil. **2.** An evil spirit; a fiend. [Arabic *shaiṭān,* from Hebrew *śāṭān,* SATAN.]

Sha·ka (shä′kə) (*c.* 1787–1828). Chief of the Zulu (1816–28) who made the Zulu state the strongest in southern Africa. An outstanding war leader, he built a disciplined and highly successful army.

shake (shāk) *v.* **shook** (shŏŏk), **shaken** (shā′kən), **shaking, shakes.** *—tr.* **1.** To cause to move to and fro with short jerky movements. **2.** To cause to quiver or tremble; vibrate or rock: *A severe tremor shook the ground.* **3.** To cause to stagger or waver; upset; unsettle. **4.** To remove or dislodge by jerky movements: *shake the dust out.* **5.** To bring to a specified condition by or as if by jerky movements: *shook her out of her complacency.* **6.** To disturb or agitate; unnerve. Often used with *up.* **7.** To brandish or wave: *shake one's fist.* **8.** To clasp (hands or another's hand) in greeting or leave-taking or as a sign of agreement. **9.** To free oneself from; get rid of. Usually used with *off.* **10.** *Music.* To trill (a note). **11.** To rattle and mix (dice) before casting. **12.** To make unstable; weaken: *His convictions were shaken.* **13.** *Australian Slang.* To rob; steal. *—intr.* **1.** To move to and fro in short jerky movements. **2.** To tremble, as from cold or in anger. **3.** To totter or waver; become unsteady. **4. a.** *Music.* To trill. **b.** To change pitch rapidly or tremulously because of emotion. Used of the voice. **5.** To shake hands.

∼n. **1.** An act of shaking. **2.** A trembling or quivering movement. **3.** *Informal.* An earthquake. **4.** A fissure in rock. **5.** A crack in timber caused by wind or frost. **6.** *Music.* A trill. **7.** A drink in which the ingredients are mixed by shaking: *a milk shake.* **8.** *Informal.* An instant; moment: *She'll be here in two shakes.* **—no great shakes.** *Informal.* Unexceptional; ordinary; mediocre. **—the shakes.** *Informal.* **1.** The chill accompanying intermittent fever. **2.** Uncontrollable trembling, especially as a symptom of alcoholism or metal poisoning. [Shake, shook, shaken; Middle English *schaken, schook, schaken,* Old English *sceacan, sceōc, sceacen,* from Germanic *skakan* (unattested).] **—shak·a·ble, shake·a·ble** *adj.*

Synonyms: *quake, quiver, shiver, shudder, tremble, wobble.*

shake down *intr.v. Informal.* **1.** To put together hurriedly, or settle down on, a makeshift bed. **2.** To settle down or settle in comfortably. *—tr.v. Informal.* **1.** To extort money from. **2.** To make a thorough search of. **3.** To subject to a shakedown cruise.

shake·down (shāk′doun′) *n. Informal.* **1.** A hastily made up resting place; a makeshift bed. **2.** An extortion of money by blackmail or other means. **3.** A thorough search of a place or person. **4.** A period of appraisal followed by adjustments to improve efficiency or functioning.

∼adj. Informal. Designed to test the performance of a ship or airplane and familiarize the crew with the operation: *a shakedown cruise.*

shak·er (shā′kər) *n.* **1.** One that shakes. **2.** A container used for shaking something out: *a salt shaker.* **3.** A container used to mix or blend by shaking: *a cocktail shaker.*

Shak·er (shā′kər) *n.* A member of a millenarian religious sect originating in England in 1747, practicing communal living and observing celibacy. [From the former custom of dancing with shaking movements during ceremonies.]

Shake·speare or **Shak·spere** (shāk′spîr), **William** (1564–1616). English dramatist and poet, the greatest writer in English literature. He was born at Stratford-upon-Avon, the son of a tradesman, was educated at the free grammar school, and in 1582 married Anne Hathaway. By 1592 he had established a reputation in London both as an actor and a playwright. His first play, *Henry VI* (in three parts), dates from 1590–91, while his first major poem, *Venus and Adonis,* appeared in 1593 and was dedicated to his patron, the Earl of Southampton. Shakespeare's prolific dramatic output for the open-air Globe Theatre includes such historical plays as *Julius Caesar* and *Henry V* (1598–1600) and such comedies as *As You Like It* and *Twelfth Night* (1598–1600). His tragedies begin with *Romeo and Juliet* (1594–5) and include *Hamlet* (1600–01), *Othello* (1604–05), *King Lear* (1605), and *Macbeth* (1605–06). Shakespeare's later fantasy plays *The Winter's Tale* (*c.* 1610) and *The Tempest* (*c.* 1611) were written for an indoor theater at Blackfriars. The first collected edition of his works, known as the First Folio, contained 36 plays and was published posthumously in 1623.

Shake·spear·e·an, Shake·spear·i·an (shāk-spîr′ē-ən) *adj.* Of, pertaining to, or like Shakespeare, his works, or his style.

∼n. A scholar of Shakespeare or his works.

Shakespearean sonnet *n.* The sonnet form used by Shakespeare, composed of three quatrains and a final couplet with the rhyme pattern *abab cdcd efef gg,* and retaining the break or pause in theme that falls between the octave and sestet in earlier sonnet forms. Also called "Elizabethan sonnet," "English sonnet."

shake up *tr.v. Informal.* To reorganize or rearrange drastically.

shake-up (shāk′ŭp′) *n. Informal.* A thorough or drastic reorganization, as in the personnel of a business or government.

shak·ing palsy (shā′kĭng) *n.* **Parkinson's disease** *(see).*

shak·o (shăk′ō, shā′kō) *n., pl.* **-os** or **-oes.** A stiff, cylindrical military dress hat with a metal plate in front, a short visor, and a plume. [French *schako,* from Hungarian *csákó,* from *csákó (süveg),* pointed (cap), from *csák,* peak, from German *Zacken,* point, from Middle High German *zacke.*]

Shak·ta (shäk′tə) *n.* Also **Sak·ta** (säk′tə). A member of a Hindu sect that worships Shakti. [Sanskrit *śākta,* from *śakti,* SHAKTI.] **—Shak·tism** *n.* **—Shak·tist** *n.*

Shak·ti (shŭk′tē, shäk′-). Also **Sak·ti** (sŭk′tē, säk′-). *Hinduism.* **1.** The female principle, especially as personified by the wife of the god Shiva. **2.** The personification of nature and generative power. [Sanskrit *śakti,* from *śaknōti,* is strong.]

shak·y (shā′kē) *adj.* **-ier, -iest. 1.** Trembling or quivering; tremulous; shaking. **2.** Unsteady or unsound; weak: *a shaky table.* **3.** Not to be depended upon; insecure. **—shak·i·ly** *adv.* **—shak·i·ness** *n.*

shale (shāl) *n.* A sedimentary rock produced from clay, which has a fine-grained structure in well-defined narrow strata 0.1 to 0.4 millimeter (0.004 to 0.016 inch) thick. [Probably from German *Schale,* from Old English *sc(e)alu.* See **scale.**]

shale oil *n.* A fuel oil obtained from oil shales.

shall (shăl) *v.* past **should** (shŏŏd) or *archaic* **shouldst** (shŏŏdst) or **shouldest** (shŏŏd′ĭst) for second person singular, present **shall** or *archaic* **shalt** (shălt) for second person singular. Used as an auxiliary followed by a simple infinitive or, in reply to a question or suggestion, with the infinitive understood. It can indicate: **1.** In the first person singular or plural, simple futurity: *I shall be twenty-eight tomorrow.* **2.** In the second and third persons: **a.** Determination or promise: *Your services shall be rewarded.* **b.** Inevitability: *That day shall come.* **c.** Command: *Thou shalt not kill.* **d.** Compulsion, with the force of *must,* in statutes, deeds, and other legal documents: *The penalty shall not exceed two years in prison.* **3.** *Formal.* In all persons, indefinite futurity, in conditional clauses and in clauses expressing doubt, anxiety, or desire: *If you shall ever change your opinion, come to me again.* [Shall, shalt, should; Middle English *schal, schalt, scholde,* Old English *sceal, scealt, sceolde.*]

Usage: In formal writing, as indicated above, *shall* is employed in the first person to indicate futurity: *I shall leave tomorrow.* In the second and third persons, the same sense of futurity is expressed by *will: He will come this afternoon.* Use of the auxiliaries *shall* and *will* is reversed when the writer wants to indicate such conditions as determination, promise, obligation, command, compulsion, permission, or inevitability; *will* is then employed in the first person and *shall* in the second and third. Thus, *I will leave tomorrow* (meaning, "I am determined, or obligated, or compelled, or fated to leave"). *He shall come this afternoon* likewise can express any of the conditions enumerated, such as promise, permission, command, or compulsion. Such, at least, are the rules of traditional grammar. However, these distinctions are only rarely observed in American English, even in formal writing. In general usage, *will* is widely employed in all three persons to indicate futurity: *We will be in New York next week. Shall* is largely neglected, except in some interrogatives, such as *Shall we go? Where shall we take our vacation this year?* and in a few set phrases: *We shall overcome. Will,* in all three persons, is employed more often than *shall* in expressing any of the forms of emphatic futurity. In speech, the degree of stress of the auxiliary verb is usually more indicative of the intended meaning than the choice of *shall* or *will.* In writing, a condition other than mere futurity is often expressed more clearly by an alternative to *shall* or *will,* such as *must* or *have to* (indicating determination, compulsion, or obligation) or by use of an intensifying word, such as *certainly* or *surely,* with *shall* or *will.* Informally, contractions such as *I'll, we'll,* and *you'll* are generally employed without distinction between the functions of *shall* and *will* as formally defined.

shal·loon (shă-lōōn′) *n.* A lightweight wool or worsted twill fabric, used chiefly for coat linings. [French *chalon,* after *Châlons*-sur-Marne, France.]

shal·lop (shăl′əp) *n.* An open boat fitted with oars, sails, or both. [French *chaloupe,* from Dutch *sloep,* SLOOP.]

shal·lot (shə-lŏt′, shăl′ət) *n.* **1.** A plant, *Allium ascalonicum,* closely related to the onion, cultivated for its edible bulb that divides into smaller sections. **2.** The mildly flavored bulb of this plant, used in cookery. [Obsolete *eschalot,* from obsolete French *eschalotte,* from Old French *eschaloigne,* from Vulgar Latin *iscalōnia* (unattested), from Latin *Ascalōnia (caepa),* (onion) of Ascalon. See **scallion.**]

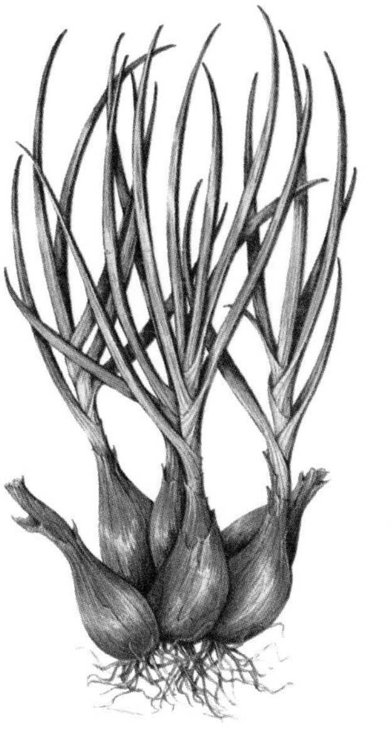

shallot *A small onionlike bulb that grows in clusters.*

shal·low (shăl′ō) *adj.* **-lower, -lowest. 1. a.** Measuring little from bottom to top or surface; not deep. **b.** Gently sloping or curved; not steep. **2.** Lacking depth, as in intellect, character, or significance: *shallow criticism.* —See Synonyms at **superficial.**

∼n. Usually **shallows.** A shallow part of a body of water; a shoal.

∼v. **shallowed, -lowing, -lows.** *—tr.* To make shallow. *—intr.* To become shallow. [Middle English *schalowe,* akin to Old English *sceald,* shallows. See **shoal.**] **—shal·low·ly** *adv.* **—shal·low·ness** *n.*

sha·lom (shä-lōm′, shə-) *interj.* Used as a greeting or farewell. [Hebrew, *shālōm,* peace.]

sha·lom a·lei·chem (shô′ləm ə-lā′KHəm, -kəm, shō′-) *interj.* Used as a greeting or farewell. [Hebrew *shālôm 'alēkhem,* peace be with you.]

shalt. *Archaic.* Second person singular present tense of **shall.**

sham (shăm) *n.* **1.** Something false or empty purporting to be genuine; a spurious imitation. **2.** The quality of deceitfulness; empty pretense. **3.** A person who assumes a false character; impostor. **4.** *Archaic.* A decorative cover made to simulate an article of household linen and used over or in place of it: *a pillow sham.* —*adj.* Not genuine; fake, pretended, or counterfeit. —*v.* **shammed, shamming, shams.** —*tr.* To simulate; feign. —*intr.* To assume a false appearance or character; dissemble. [Perhaps dialectal variant of SHAME.] —**sham·mer** *n.*

sha·man (shä′mən, shā′-, shăm′ən) *n.* **1.** A priest of shamanism. **2.** A medicine man among certain North American Indians. [German *Schamane,* from Russian *shaman,* from Tungus *šaman,* from Tocharian *ṣamāne,* from Prakrit *samaṇa,* from Sanskrit *śramaṇás†,* "ascetic."]

sha·man·ism (shä′mə-nĭz′əm, shā′-, shăm′ə-) *n.* **1.** The religious practices of certain peoples of northern Asia who believe that good and evil spirits pervade the world and can be summoned or heard through inspired priests acting as mediums. **2.** Any similar form of spiritualism, such as that practiced among certain North American Indian tribes. —**sha·man·ist** *n.* —**sha·man·is·tic** *adj.*

Sha·mash (shä′mäsh). The sun-god of Assyro-Babylonian religion, worshiped as the author of justice and compassion. [Akkadian, "sun," akin to Hebrew *shémesh.*]

sham·ble (shăm′bəl) *intr.v.* **-bled, -bling, -bles.** To walk in an awkward, lazy, or unsteady manner, shuffling the feet. —*n.* A shambling walk; a shuffling gait. [From earlier *shamble,* ungainly, perhaps from *shamble legs,* probably referring to legs which were ungainly like those of a meat table. See **shambles.**]

sham·bles (shăm′bəlz) *n. Used with a singular verb.* **1.** A scene or condition of complete disorder or ruin: *left the room in a shambles.* **2.** A place or scene of bloodshed or carnage. **3.** *Archaic.* A meat market or slaughterhouse. [From plural of earlier *shamble,* table for display or sale of meat, Middle English *shamel,* Old English *sc(e)amul,* table, from West Germanic *skamel* (unattested), from Latin *scamellum,* diminutive of *scamnum,* bench.]

shame (shăm) *n.* **1.** A painful emotion caused by a strong sense of guilt, embarrassment, unworthiness, or disgrace. **2.** Capacity for such a feeling: *Have you no shame?* **3.** A person or thing that brings dishonor, disgrace, or condemnation. **4.** A condition of disgrace or dishonor; ignominy. **5.** A great disappointment or an occasion for pity or regret. —See Synonyms at **disgrace.** —**put to shame. 1.** To fill with shame; disgrace. **2.** To outdo thoroughly; surpass. —*tr.v.* **shamed, shaming, shames. 1.** To cause to feel shame. **2.** To bring dishonor or disgrace upon. **3.** To force by making ashamed. Used with *into* or *out of: He was shamed into an apology.* —*interj.* **1.** Used to express strong disapproval. **2.** *South African.* Used to express sympathy or tender admiration. [Middle English *s(c)hame,* Old English *sc(e)amu,* from Germanic *skamô.*]

shame·faced (shăm′fāst′) *adj.* **1.** Indicative of shame; ashamed: *a shamefaced explanation.* **2.** Extremely modest or shy; bashful. [Variant (influenced by FACE) of earlier *shamefast,* from Middle English *sham(e)fast,* Old English *sceamfæst* : *sceamu,* SHAME + *fæst,* FAST (firm), as if held firm by shame.] —**shame·fac·ed·ly** (shăm′fā′sĭd-lē) *adv.* —**shame·fac·ed·ness** *n.*

shame·ful (shăm′fəl) *adj.* **1.** Bringing or deserving shame; disgraceful; indecent. **2.** *Archaic.* Full of shame; shamefaced; ashamed. —**shame·ful·ly** *adv.* —**shame·ful·ness** *n.*

shame·less (shăm′lĭs) *adj.* **1.** Not subject to the restraint of shame; impudent or immodest; brazen. **2.** Done without shame: *a shameless lie.* —**shame·less·ly** *adv.* —**shame·less·ness** *n.*

Synonyms: *barefaced, bold, brash, brazen, forward, impudent, unblushing.*

sham·mes (shä′məs) *n., pl.* **shammosim** (shä-mô′sĭm). *Judaism.* **1.** A sexton in a synagogue. Also called "beadle." **2.** The candle used to light the other eight candles of the Chanukah Menorah. [Yiddish *shames,* from Hebrew *shammāsh,* from Aramaic *shəmmāsh,* to serve.]

shammy. Variant of **chamois.**

sham·poo (shăm-pōō′) *n., pl.* **-poos. 1.** Any of various liquid or cream preparations of soap or detergent used to wash the hair and scalp. **2.** Any of various cleaning agents, as for rugs, upholstery, or cars. **3.** An act of washing or cleaning with shampoo. —*v.* **shampooed, -pooing, -poos.** —*tr.* To wash or clean with shampoo. —*intr.* To wash the hair with shampoo. [From Hindi *chāmpo,* from *chāmpnā,* massage, press, mark.]

sham·rock (shăm′rŏk′) *n.* Any of several plants, such as a trefoil, medick, clover, or wood sorrel, having compound leaves with three small leaflets, considered the national emblem of Ireland. [From Irish *seamrog,* diminutive of *seamar,* clover, from Old Irish *semar†.*]

sha·mus (shä′məs, shā′-) *n. Slang.* A policeman or private detective. [Perhaps variant of SHAMMES.]

Shan (shän, shăn) *n.* **1.** A member of a group of Mongoloid tribes living in Burma, Thailand, and southern China. **2.** The northern Tai language spoken by these tribes. —**Shan** *adj.*

Shan·dong (shän′dŏong′) or **Shan·tung** or **Shan-tung** (shän′tŭng′). Densely populated maritime province of northeastern China. It is crossed by the lower Huang He and the Grand Canal and has mountains in the east and center, where the sacred Tai Shan mountains reach 1,500 meters (5,000 feet). The lowlands are highly fertile, but with low, unreliable rainfall, famines have been frequent. Settled by Chinese farmers since earliest times, Shandong became a province under the Ming dynasty.

shan·dy·gaff (shăn′dē-găf′) *n.* A drink of beer mixed with lemonade, ginger ale, or ginger beer. Also called "shandy." [19th century : origin obscure.]

Shang (shäng) *n.* A Chinese dynasty (*c.* 1525–1027 B.C.). Its capital was Yin, present-day Anyang.

shang·hai (shăng-hī′) *tr.v.* **-haied, -haiing, -hais. 1.** *Informal.* To kidnap (a man) for compulsory service aboard a ship, especially after rendering him insensible. **2.** *Slang.* To trick or coerce (a person) into some action. [After SHANGHAI, from the former custom of kidnaping sailors to man ships going to that city.]

Shang·hai or **Shang-hai** (shäng-hī′). Largest city in China, lying within, but independent of, the eastern province of Jiangsu, on the Huangpu River at its confluence with the Chang Jiang (Yangtze) estuary. One of the world's leading seaports, it is also the most important industrial center in China. Its commercial and industrial importance dates from 1842, when the Treaty of Nanking opened the port to western trade. In the 19th century much of the city was ceded to Britain (1843) and the United States (1862), the two cessions being merged into the International Settlement in 1863. The French maintained a separate cession (1849). Great Britain and the United States gave up their claims during World War II and France withdrew in 1946. Shanghai is surpassed only by Beijing as a leading educational and cultural center of China.

Shan·gri-la (shăng′grĭ-lä′) *n.* An imaginary, remote paradise on earth; utopia. [After *Shangri-La,* the imaginary land in *Lost Horizon* (1933) by James Hilton (1900–54).]

shank (shăngk) *n.* **1.** *Anatomy.* The part of the human leg between the knee and ankle or the corresponding part in other vertebrates. **2.** The whole leg of a human being. **3.** A cut of meat from the leg of an animal. **4.** The long, narrow part of a nail or pin. **5.** A stem, stalk, or similar part. **6.** The stem of an anchor. **7.** The long shaft of a fishhook. **8.** That part of a tobacco pipe between the bowl and stem. **9.** The shaft of a key. **10.** The narrower section of a spoon's handle. **11. a.** The narrow part of a shoe's sole under the instep. **b.** A piece of metal or other material used to reinforce or shape this part. **12.** The ring or other projection on the back of some buttons by which they are sewn to the cloth. **13. a.** The part of a drill or other tool that connects the functioning head to the handle. **b.** See **tang** (sense 4b). **14.** Any of various long-legged wading birds of the genus *Tringa;* especially, the redshank and greenshank. **15. a.** The latter part of a period of time. **b.** The earlier or best part of a period of time: *the shank of the evening.* [Middle English *shanke,* Old English *sc(e)anca.*]

Shan·kar (shän′kär′), **Ravi** (1920–). Indian sitar player who has stimulated appreciation of Indian classical music throughout the Western world.

shank·piece (shăngk′pēs′) *n.* An arch support inserted into the shank of a shoe.

shanks' mare *n. Informal.* One's own legs as a means of transportation: *go on shanks' mare.*

Shan·non (shăn′ən). Chief river of the Republic of Ireland and the longest river in the British Isles, *c.* 390 kilometers (240 miles) long. It rises in northwest Cavan and flows south to Limerick, where it broadens into a long, wide estuary that empties into the Atlantic.

Shansi. See **Shaanxi** and **Shanxi.**

shan't (shănt, shänt). Contraction of *shall not.*

shan·tung (shăn′tŭng′) *n.* **1.** A heavy silk fabric with a rough, nubby surface, made of spun wild silk. **2.** An imitation of this fabric, made of rayon or cotton. [Manufactured in SHANDONG.]

Shantung or **Shan-tung.** See **Shandong.**

shan·ty (shăn′tē) *n., pl.* **-ties.** A roughly built or ramshackle cabin; a shack. [19th century (originally from use of houses of Irish immigrants) : perhaps from Irish *sean tig,* "old house" : *sean,* old + *tig,* house, from Old Irish *tech.*]

shan·ty·man (shăn′tē-mən, -măn′) *n., pl.* **-men** (-mĭn, -měn′). A man who lives in a shanty; especially, a lumberjack.

shan·ty·town (shăn′tē-toun′) *n.* A town or district of a town consisting of ramshackle huts or shanties.

Shan·xi or **Shan·si** (shän′sē′). Strategic province of northeast China. Much of it is a high plateau cut by the Fen He, a tributary of the Huang He. With fertile loess soils, Shansi was part of the Chinese heartland. Its low rainfall is now offset by irrigation and reforestation. Taiyuan is the capital.

shape (shāp) *n.* **1.** The outline or characteristic surface configuration of a thing; a contour; a form. **2.** The contour of a person's body; a figure. **3.** Developed, definite, or proper form. **4.** Any form or condition in which something can exist or appear; an embodiment. **5.** Assumed or false appearance; guise. **6.** An imaginary or ghostly form; a phantom. **7. a.** Something used to give or determine form, such as a mold or pattern. **b.** Something formed by a pattern or set in a mold. **8.** *Informal.* Condition as regards health, efficiency, state of repair, or the like: *an athlete in good shape.* —See Synonyms at **form.** —*v.* **shaped, shaped** or *archaic* **shapen** (shā′pən), **shaping, shapes.** —*tr.* **1.** To give a particular form to. **2.** To cause to conform to a particular form or pattern; modify; adapt to fit. **3.** To plan and supervise. —*intr.* **1.** *Informal.* To take a definite form; develop. Often used with *into* or *up.* **2.** *Informal.* To proceed or develop in a satisfactory or desirable manner. Used with *up: After a bad start, the team shaped up.* [Middle English, Old English *(ge)sceap.*]

SHAPE (shāp). Supreme Headquarters Allied Powers, Europe.
shaped (shāpt) *adj.* **1.** Formed by shaping: *shaped clay.* **2.** Having the shape of or possessing a similar shape to something specified. Often used in combination: *egg-shaped.*
shape•less (shāp′lĭs) *adj.* **1.** Having no distinct shape. **2.** Lacking symmetrical or attractive form; not shapely. **—shape•less•ly** *adv.* **—shape•less•ness** *n.*
shape•ly (shāp′lē) *adj.* **-lier, -liest.** Having a pleasing or attractive shape; well-proportioned. **—shape•li•ness** *n.*
Shap•ley (shăp′lē), **Harlow** (1885–1972). U.S. astronomer. A bold thinker, he worked at Mt. Wilson Observatory (1914–21) and then at Harvard Observatory, specializing in photometry and spectroscopy and devoting particular study to the structures of the universe. Most of his theories are widely accepted today.
shard (shärd) *n.* Also **sherd** (shûrd). **1.** A piece of broken pottery; a **potsherd** *(see).* **2.** A fragment of a brittle substance, as of glass or metal. **3.** *Zoology.* A tough sheath; especially, the outer wing covering of a beetle. [Middle English *sherd,* Old English *sceard.*]
share¹ (shâr) *n.* **1.** A part or portion belonging to, distributed to, contributed by, or owed by a person or group. **2.** An equitable, reasonable, or full amount. **3.** *Abbr.* **sh., shr.** Any of the equal parts into which the capital stock of a company is divided. **—go shares.** To be involved equally or jointly, as in a business venture. **—on shares.** With each individual concerned taking a share, usually equal, of any profit or loss. Used of an enterprise.
~*v.* **shared, sharing, shares.** —*tr.* **1.** To divide and parcel out in shares; apportion. **2.** To participate in, use, or experience in common with others. —*intr.* To have or take a part or share. **—share and share alike.** To share equally; have equal shares. [Middle English *share,* division, share, Old English *scearu,* division or fork of the body, tonsure.] **—shar•er** *n.*
Synonyms: partake, participate.
share² *n.* A plowshare. [Middle English *shaar,* Old English *scēar.*]
share•crop•per (shâr′krŏp′ər) *n.* A tenant farmer who gives a share of his crop to the landlord in lieu of rent. **—share•crop** *v.*
share•hold•er (shâr′hōl′dər) *n.* A person or institution that owns or holds a share or shares in a company.
sharif. Variant of **sherif.**
shark (shärk) *n.* **1.** Any of numerous chiefly marine, sometimes large and voracious fishes of the order Pleurotremata, having a cartilaginous skeleton and tough skin covered with small, toothlike scales. **2. a.** A ruthless, greedy, or dishonest person; a swindler. **b.** A vicious usurer. **3.** *Slang.* A person with unusually great skill in some field of activity: *She's a shark at poker.*
~*intr.v.* **sharked, sharking, sharks.** To live by fraud, trickery, or usury. [16th century : origin obscure.]
shark•skin (shärk′skĭn′) *n.* **1.** A shark's skin. **2.** Leather made from a shark's skin. **3.** A rayon and acetate fabric having a smooth, somewhat shiny surface.
shark sucker *n.* A **remora** *(see).*
sharp (shärp) *adj.* **sharper, sharpest. 1.** Having a thin, keen edge or a fine, acute point; suitable for or capable of cutting or piercing: *a sharp knife.* **2.** Having an acute edge or point; not rounded or blunt; peaked: *a sharp nose.* **3.** Abrupt or acute; not gradual; sudden. **4.** Clear or marked; distinct. **5.** Shrewd; astute. **6.** Artful; underhand. **7.** Vigilant; alert. **8.** Brisk; vigorous. **9. a.** Harsh; biting; acrimonious. **b.** Stinging; bitter; pungent: *a sharp taste.* **c.** Bitterly cold. **10.** Fierce or impetuous; violent. **11. a.** Intense; severe. **b.** Painful. **12.** Sudden and shrill. **13.** Composed of hard, angular particles: *sharp sand.* **14.** *Music.* **a.** Raised in pitch by a semitone. **b.** Above the proper pitch. **c.** Having the key signature in sharps. Compare **flat. 15.** *Phonetics.* Voiceless. Said of a consonant. **16.** Attractively stylish; snappy: *a sharp dresser.*
~*adv.* **1.** In a sharp manner. **2.** Punctually; exactly. **3.** *Music.* Above the true or proper pitch.
~*n.* **1. a.** A musical note raised one semitone above its normal pitch. **b.** A sign (#) indicating this. Compare **flat. 2.** A slender sewing needle with a very fine point. **3.** *Informal.* A sharper.
~*v.* **sharped, sharping, sharps.** *Music.* —*tr.* To raise by a semitone. —*intr.* To sound above the proper pitch. [Middle English *s(c)harp,* Old English *scearp.*] **—sharp•ly** *adv.* **—sharp•ness** *n.*
Synonyms: acute, keen.
sharp•en (shär′pən) *v.* **-ened, -ening, -ens.** —*tr.* To make sharp or sharper. —*intr.* To become sharp or sharper. **—sharp•en•er** *n.*
sharp end *n. Informal.* The point of direct action, confrontation, or decision-making.
sharp•er (shär′pər) *n.* One who deals dishonestly with others; especially, a gambler who cheats.
sharp-eyed (shärp′īd′) *adj.* **1.** Having keen eyesight. **2.** Keenly perceptive or observant; alert.
sharp•ie (shär′pē) *n.* **1.** A long, narrow, flat-bottomed fishing boat used in New England, having a center board and one or two masts, each rigged with a triangular sail. **2.** *Informal.* An alert or quick-witted person. [From SHARP.]
sharp•shoot•er (shärp′shōō′tər) *n.* An expert marksman.
sharp-tongued (shärp′tŭngd′) *adj.* Harsh, critical, or sarcastic.
shash•lik, shash•lick (shäsh-lĭk′, shäsh′lĭk) *n.* A dish consisting of marinated cubes of mutton or veal, grilled or roasted on a spit, often with slices of eggplant, onion, and tomato; shish kebab. [Russian *shashlyk,* of Turkic origin.]
Shas•ta, Mount (shăs′tə). Volcanic peak, 4,320 meters (14,162 feet) high, in the Cascade Range in northern California. It was discovered *c.* 1827 and has long been dormant except for sulfurous springs near the top.
Shasta daisy *n.* A cultivated variety of *Chrysanthemum* (or *Leucanthemum) maximum,* of the Pyrenees, having large, white, daisylike flowers. [After MT. SHASTA.]
Shatt al Ar•ab (shăt′ ăl är′əb). Tidal river flowing for *c.* 195 kilometers (121 miles) into the northern end of the Persian Gulf and formed by the confluence of the Tigris and Euphrates rivers. It is navigable as far up as Basra, the chief port of Iraq.
shat•ter (shăt′ər) *v.* **-tered, -tering, -ters.** —*tr.* **1.** To cause to break or burst suddenly into pieces, as with a violent blow. **2.** To damage seriously; disable; ruin. **3.** To disturb or severely upset. **4.** *Informal.* To tire completely; exhaust. —*intr.* To break into pieces; smash or burst. —See Synonyms at **break.**
~*n.* **1.** The act of shattering. **2.** *Usually* **shatters.** A splintered or fragmented condition. [Middle English *schateren,* akin to SCATTER.]
shat•ter•proof (shăt′ər-prōōf′) *adj.* **1.** Designed to resist shattering. **2.** Designed to break into small, round granules rather than sharp, jagged pieces.
shave (shāv) *v.* **shaved, shaved** or **shaven** (shā′vən), **shaving, shaves.** —*tr.* **1.** To remove the beard or other body hair from. **2.** To cut (the beard, for example) at the surface of the skin with a razor. Often used with *off.* **3.** To crop, trim, or mow closely. **4.** To remove thin slices from: *shave a wooden board.* **5.** To cut into thin slices; shred: *shave cheese.* **6.** To come close to or graze in passing. **7.** *Informal.* To take off or away. —*intr.* To remove one's own beard or hair with a razor.
~*n.* **1.** The act, process, or result of shaving. **2.** A thin slice or scraping; a shaving. **3.** Any of various tools used for shaving. [Middle English *shaven,* to scrape, shave, Old English *sceafan.*]
shav•er (shā′vər) *n.* **1. a.** A person who shaves. **b.** An electric or mechanical device used to shave, especially an electric razor. **2.** *Informal.* A young person, especially a boy.
Sha•vi•an (shā′vē-ən) *adj.* Of or characteristic of George Bernard Shaw or his works: *Shavian wit.*
~*n.* An admirer or disciple of George Bernard Shaw. [From *Shavius,* pseudo-Latin form of the name *Shaw.*]
shav•ing (shā′vĭng) *n.* A thin slice; a sliver: *wood shavings.*
~*adj.* Used in or for shaving the face: *a shaving mirror.*
Sha•vu•ot, Sha•bu•oth (shə-vōō′ōt, -ōth′, -əs) *n.* A Jewish holiday commemorating the revelation of the Law on Mount Sinai and the celebration of the wheat festival in ancient times, observed on the sixth and seventh of Sivan. Also called "Feast of Weeks," "Pentecost." [Hebrew *shābhū'ōth,* from *shābhūa',* week.]
Shaw (shô), **Artie,** born Arthur Arshawsky (1910–). U.S. jazz clarinetist, composer, and band leader. After 1935 he headed various bands organized around his virtuosity on the clarinet.
Shaw, George Bernard (1856–1950). Irish dramatist and writer. He established a reputation in London as a controversial music and theater critic and an idiosyncratic spokesman for socialism. Shaw was a founder of the Fabian Society (1884) and an early enthusiast of Wagner and Ibsen. He won further recognition through his many plays, often satirical in theme, which include *Man and Superman* (1905), *Pygmalion* (1912), and *St. Joan* (1924). His prolific writings on social, political, and religious issues include *The Intelligent Woman's Guide to Socialism and Capitalism* (1928). He was awarded the Nobel Prize for literature in 1925.
Shaw, Henry Wheeler, pen name "Josh Billings" (1818–85). U.S. humorist. After a varied life as a farmer, explorer, coal miner, and real estate dealer, he began (1860) to write humorous sketches in a broad rural dialect. His lectures and books, including the annual *Farmer's Allminax* (1869–80) brought him enormous popularity.
shawl (shôl) *n.* A square or oblong piece of cloth, knitted fabric, or the like worn especially by women as a covering for the head, neck, and shoulders.
~*tr.v.* **shawled, shawling, shawls.** To cover with a shawl. [Earlier *shal, shaul,* from Urdu, from Persian *shāl*.]
shawm (shôm) *n.* Any of various early double-reed wind instruments, forerunners of the modern oboe. [Middle English *schallemele, schalme,* from Old French *chalemel,* from Vulgar Latin *calamellus* (unattested), diminutive of Latin *calamus,* reed, from Greek *kalamos.*]
Shawn (shôn), **Edwin Myers,** known as "Ted" (1891–1972). U.S. dancer and choreographer. While studying ballet to recover full use of his legs after a bout of diphtheria, he decided to make dancing his career. In 1914 he married Ruth St. Denis and together they founded the Denishawn School of Dancing. Many of his works were based on Indian themes and motifs.
Shaw•nee (shô-nē′) *n., pl.* **-nees** or collectively **Shawnee. 1.** A member of an Algonquian-speaking North American Indian people, formerly living in the Tennessee Valley and adjacent areas, now surviving in Oklahoma. **2.** The language of this people.
Shaw•wal (shə-wäl′) *n.* The tenth month of the year in the Muslim calendar. See feature at **calendar.** [Arabic *Shawwāl.*]
Shays (shāz), **Daniel** (*c.* 1747–1825). U.S. Revolutionary soldier and insurrectionist. Settling in western Massachusetts after the war, he found economic conditions dreadful and the state legislature unwilling to listen to the pleas of himself and his fellow farmers. The resulting armed conflict (1786–87) was led by several men, but is known to history as Shays's Rebellion. Although condemned to death for his actions, Shays was later pardoned and lived the rest of his life quietly in New York State.
she (shē) *pron.* The third person singular pronoun in the nominative

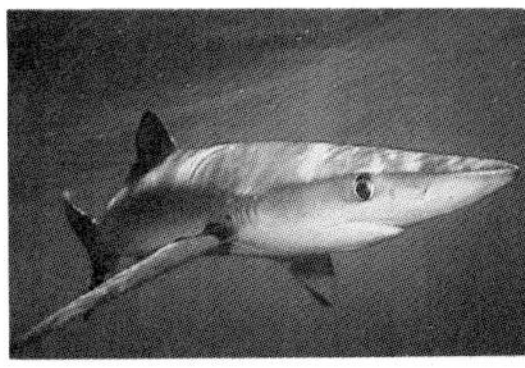

shark *The blue shark (above) is a native of tropical and temperate waters of all seas.*

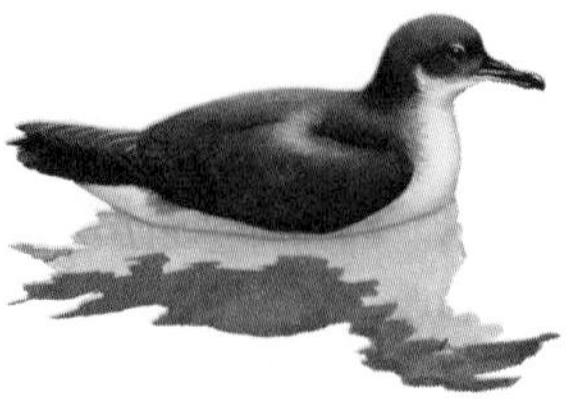

shearwater *In its long flights, this seabird skims the crests of waves and appears to shear the water. Shearwaters are capable of flying vast distances; Manx shearwaters, such as the one shown here, have been known to fly nearly 5,000 kilometers (3,000 miles) in 12 days.*

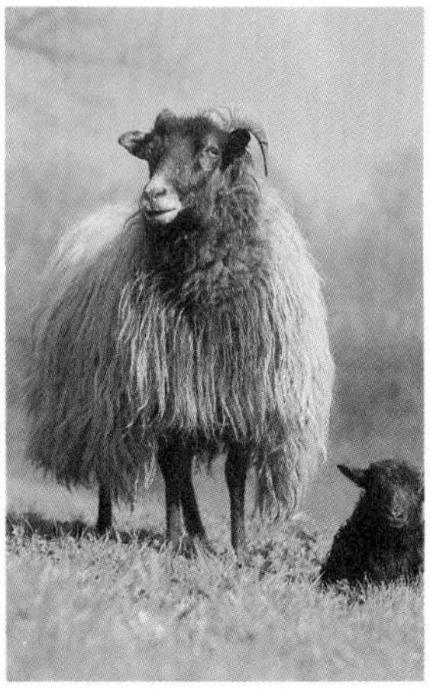

sheep *Six species of wild sheep live in Asia and North America. None has the long woolly coat characteristic of many domestic sheep, such as the German breed shown here.*

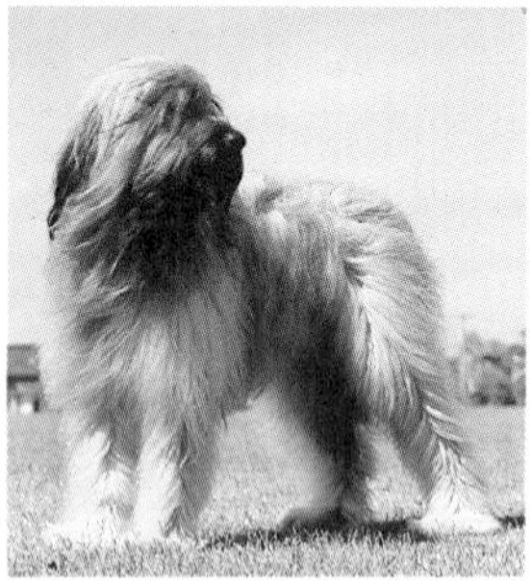

sheepdog *Dogs have been used by shepherds for centuries to help control flocks. This is a Briard, one of an old breed of sheepdogs from the Brie district of France.*

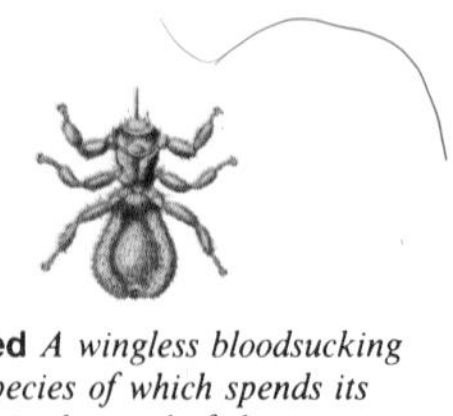

sheep ked *A wingless bloodsucking fly, one species of which spends its whole life in the wool of sheep, on whose blood it feeds. Full-grown larvae are produced one at a time, and they begin the metamorphosis to adult form almost immediately.*

case, feminine gender. **1.** Used to represent the female person, animal, or other being last mentioned or implied. **2.** Used traditionally of certain objects and institutions such as ships, cars, and nations. *∼n.* A female animal or person. Often used in combination: *a she-cat. Is the dog a she or a he?* —See Usage note at **me.** [Middle English *s(c)ho, s(c)he,* Old English *sēo,* she (Old English *hēo,* she, remained in Middle English dialects but only appears in Modern English HER).]

shea (shē, shā) *n.* The **shea tree** (*see*).

shea butter *n.* A whitish or yellowish fat obtained from the nut of the **shea tree** *(see),* used as food and for making soap and candles.

sheaf (shēf) *n., pl.* **sheaves** (shēvz). **1.** A bundle of cut stalks of grain or similar plants, usually laid lengthwise and bound with straw or twine. **2.** Any gathering or collection of articles, especially papers, held or bound together. **3.** An archer's quiver of arrows. *∼tr.v.* **sheafed, sheafing, sheafs.** To bind into a sheaf. [Middle English *sheef, shefe,* Old English *scēaf.*]

shear (shîr) *v.* **sheared** or *archaic* **shore** (shôr, shōr), **shorn** (shôrn, shōrn) or **sheared, shearing, shears.** *—tr.* **1.** To remove (fleece, hair, or the like) by cutting or clipping with a sharp instrument. **2.** To remove the hair or fleece from. **3.** To cut with or as if with shears. **4.** To strip, divest, or deprive of something: *laws that sheared the king of his power.* **5.** To cause to break or fracture, especially as a result of shearing strain. *—intr.* **1.** To use shears or a similar cutting tool. **2.** To move or proceed by or as if by cutting. Used with *through*: *The little craft sheared through the waves.* **3.** *Physics.* To become deformed by forces tending to produce a shearing strain. **4.** To break or fracture, especially as a result of shearing strain.
∼n. **1.** The act, process, or result of shearing. **2.** Something cut off by shearing. **3.** A shearing. Used to indicate a sheep's age: *a two-shear ram.* **4.** *Physics.* **a.** An applied force or system of forces that tends to produce a shearing strain. Also called "shear stress," "shearing stress." **b.** Shearing strain. **5.** Any device for cutting material by means of a knife blade. [Shear, shore, shorn; Middle English *sc(h)eren, share, shorn,* Old English *sceran, scǣron* (third person plural), *scoren.*] **—shear·er** *n.*

shearing strain *n.* A condition in or deformation of an elastic body caused by forces that tend to produce an opposite but parallel sliding motion of the body's planes.

shear legs *n.* Also **sheer·legs** (shîr′lĕgz′). An apparatus used to lift heavy weights, consisting of two or more spars joined at the top and spread at the base, the tackle being suspended from the top. Also called "shears," "sheers."

shear·ling (shîr′lĭng) *n.* **1.** A year-old sheep that has been shorn once. **2.** The skin of such a sheep, or of any newly shorn sheep, tanned and with the wool on. [Middle English *scherling* : *scheren,* to SHEAR + -LING.]

shear modulus *n.* A **rigidity modulus** (*see*).

shear pin *n.* A replaceable pin placed in a machine in such a position that it will shear and arrest the movement of the machine if the stress exceeds a predetermined value.

shears (shîrz) *pl.n.* **1.** Large-sized scissors. **2.** Any of various other implements or machines that cut with scissorlike action. **3.** *Used with a singular verb.* A lifting crane, a **shear legs** *(see).* [Middle English *s(c)here* (singular), scissors, Old English *scēara* (plural).]

shear·wa·ter (shîr′wô′tər, -wŏt′ər) *n.* Any of various oceanic birds of the family Procellariidae, especially of the genus *Puffinus,* having long wings and a hooked bill. See **Manx shearwater.** [From its habit of skimming close to the water.]

sheat·fish (shēt′fĭsh′) *n., pl.* **-fishes** or collectively **sheatfish.** A large freshwater catfish, *Silurus glanis,* of Eurasia. [Variant of obsolete *sheath-fish* : SHEATH (probably from its shell-like covering or its sheathlike shape) + FISH.]

sheath (shēth) *n., pl.* **sheaths** (shē*th*z, shēths). **1.** A case for the blade of a knife, sword, or similar instrument. **2.** Any of various coverings applied like or resembling a sheath. **3.** *Biology.* An enveloping structure or part, such as the tubular base of a leaf surrounding a stem. **4.** A close-fitting dress, usually having a straight skirt and no belt. **5.** A protective covering for an electric cable. **6.** A condom. [Middle English *s(c)hethe,* Old English *scēath, scǣth.*]

sheath·bill (shēth′bĭl′) *n.* Either of two shore birds, *Chionia alba* or *C. minor,* of Antarctic regions, having white plumage and a horny covering on the base of the bill.

sheathe (shē*th*) *tr.v.* **sheathed, sheathing, sheathes.** **1.** To insert into or provide with a sheath. **2.** To retract into a sheath or sheaths: *sheathed its claws.* **3.** To encase in sheathing. **—sheath·er** *n.*

sheath·ing (shē′*th*ĭng) *n.* **1.** A layer of boards or of other wood or fiber materials applied to the outer studs, joists, and rafters of a building to strengthen the structure and serve as a base for an exterior weatherproof cladding. **2.** An exterior covering, usually metal, on the underwater part of a ship's hull, to protect against marine growths. **3.** The action of providing sheathing for something.

sheath knife *n.* A knife having a fixed blade and fitting into a sheath.

shea tree (shā, shē) *n.* An African tree, *Butyrospermum parkii,* having fruit containing oily seeds that yield an edible fat called shea butter. Also called "shea." [From Bambara *si.*]

sheave[1] (shēv) *tr.v.* **sheaved, sheaving, sheaves.** To bind into a sheaf or sheaves; gather; collect.

sheave[2] (shĭv) *n.* A wheel with a grooved rim, especially one used as a pulley. [Middle English *shive, sheve,* Old English *scīfe* (unattested).]

sheaves (shēvz *for sense 1,* shĭvz *for sense 2*). **1.** Plural of **sheaf.** **2.** Plural of **sheave.**

She·ba (shē′bə). Biblical name for an ancient region of southern Arabia, encompassing present-day Yemen and the Hadhramaut region of South Yemen. On the trade route between India and Africa, it became a region of great wealth at its height in the 6th and 5th centuries B.C.

Sheba, Queen of. A queen who came from southern Arabia to test the wisdom of King Solomon. I Kings 10:1.

she·bang (shĭ-băng′) *n. Informal.* A situation, organization, contrivance, or set of facts or things. Used chiefly in the phrase *the whole shebang.* [19th century : origin obscure.]

Shebat. Variant of **Shevat.**

she·been (shĭ-bēn′) *n. Chiefly Irish & South African.* A place where alcohol is sold and drunk illegally. [Anglo-Irish *síbín;* akin to *séibe,* mugful.]

shed[1] (shĕd) *v.* **shed, shedding, sheds.** *—tr.* **1.** To pour forth or cause to pour forth: *shed a tear.* **2.** To send forth; diffuse or radiate: *shed light; shed confidence.* **3.** To repel without allowing penetration: *A duck's feathers shed water.* **4.** To lose by a natural process: *"He was a middle-aged child that had never shed its baby fat"* (Truman Capote). *—intr.* **1.** To lose a natural growth or covering, especially fur, by a natural process: *Cats tend to shed if their fur is not brushed.* **2.** To pour forth, fall off, or drop out: *All the leaves have shed.*
∼n. An elevation in the earth's surface from which water flows in two directions; a watershed. [Shed, shed (past tense and past participle); Middle English *sheden, schede, scheden,* shed, divide, Old English *scēadan, scēad, sceādon,* to divide.]

shed[2] *n.* **1.** A small, usually low, structure, either freestanding or attached to a larger structure, serving for storage or shelter. **2.** A large structure, often open on all sides, for storage, locomotive repair, sheepshearing, shelter, or the like. [Earlier *shadde,* perhaps specialized use of SHADE.]

she'd (shēd). **1.** Contraction of *she had.* **2.** Contraction of *she would.*

shed·der (shĕd′ər) *n.* One that sheds by a natural process, such as a long-haired animal, a crab, or a lobster.

she-dev·il (shē′dĕv′əl) *n.* A malicious or cruel woman.

sheen (shēn) *n.* **1.** A smooth, glossy shine on a surface. **2.** Glistening brightness; radiance. **3.** *Poetic.* Splendid attire. [From obsolete *sheen,* beautiful, bright, Old English *sciene, scēne.*]

Sheen (shēn), **Fulton John** (1895–1979). U.S. Roman Catholic prelate. Ordained in 1919, he became a bishop in 1951. Beginning in 1930, he won a wide audience with his radio and television broadcasts. Bishop Sheen was known for his strong stands against communism, materialism, and birth control and his advocacy of prayer in public schools.

sheep (shēp) *n., pl.* **sheep.** **1.** Any of various usually horned, ruminant mammals of the genus *Ovis;* especially, the domesticated species *O. aries,* raised in many breeds for its wool, edible flesh, or skin. **2.** The skin of a sheep or leather made from it. **3.** One who is meek, submissive, or easily led. **—separate the sheep from the goats.** To distinguish or discriminate between the worthy and the unworthy. [Middle English *she(e)p,* Old English *scē(a)p,* from West Germanic *skǣpa* (unattested).]

sheep·back (shēp′băk′) *n. Geology.* **Roche moutonnée** *(see).*

sheep·cote (shēp′kōt′, -kŏt′) *n.* A sheepfold. [Middle English *shepcote* : SHEEP + COTE.]

sheep dip *n.* **1.** Any of various liquid disinfectants used to destroy parasites in the wool of sheep prior to shearing. **2.** A deep trough containing a disinfectant in which sheep are dipped.

sheep·dog (shēp′dôg′, -dŏg′) *n.* A dog trained to guard and herd sheep. See **Old English sheepdog, Shetland sheepdog.**

sheep·fold (shēp′fōld′) *n.* A pen for sheep.

sheep·herd·er (shēp′hûr′dər) *n.* One who herds a large flock of sheep in open range; shepherd.

sheep·ish (shē′pĭsh) *adj.* **1.** Embarrassed or bashful, as by consciousness of a fault: *a sheepish grin.* **2.** Resembling a sheep in meekness or stupidity. **—sheep·ish·ly** *adv.* **—sheep·ish·ness** *n.*

sheep ked *n.* A wingless parasitic fly, *Melophagus ovinus,* that feeds chiefly on sheep.

sheep laurel *n.* An evergreen shrub, *Kalmia angustifolia,* of eastern North America, having rose-pink flowers and poisonous foliage.

sheep's eyes *pl.n.* Bashful, amorous glances.

sheep·shank (shēp′shăngk′) *n.* A knot used to shorten a line.

sheeps·head (shēps′hĕd′) *n.* A food fish, *Archosargus probatocephalus,* of American Atlantic waters, having dark, vertical markings. [From the resemblance of its teeth to those of a sheep.]

sheep·shear·ing (shēp′shîr′ĭng) *n.* **1.** The act of shearing sheep. **2. a.** The time or season when sheep are sheared. **b.** The festivities held at this time. **—sheep·shear·er** *n.*

sheep·skin (shēp′skĭn′) *n.* The skin of a sheep either tanned with the fleece left on or in the form of leather or parchment.

sheep's sorrel *n.* A sorrel, *Rumex acetosella,* common on dry heaths and acid soils.

sheep tick *n.* A tick, *Ixodes ricinus,* parasite on many mammals and birds, which carries the virus causing louping ill in sheep and cattle.

sheer[1] (shîr) *v.* **sheered, sheering, sheers.** *—intr.* To swerve or deviate from a course. Usually used with *away* or *off.* *—tr.* To cause to swerve or deviate. Usually used with *away* or *off.*
∼n. **1.** A swerving or deviating course. **2.** *Nautical.* **a.** The upward

curve, or the amount of upward curve, of the longitudinal lines of a ship's hull as viewed from the side. **b.** The position in which a ship is placed to enable it to keep clear of a single bow anchor. [Perhaps a variant of SHEAR.]

sheer² *adj.* **sheerer, sheerest. 1.** Thin, fine, and transparent; diaphanous: *sheer curtains; sheer chiffon.* **2.** Not mixed or blended with anything; undiluted; pure: *sheer luck.* **3.** Perpendicular or nearly perpendicular; steep: *sheer rocks; a sheer drop.*
∼*adv.* **1.** Perpendicularly or nearly perpendicularly. **2.** Absolutely; outright. [Perhaps Middle English *schir,* bright, shining, Old English *scīr.*] **—sheer·ly** *adv.* **—sheer·ness** *n.*

sheerlegs, sheers. Variants of **shear legs.**

sheet¹ (shēt) *n. Abbr.* **sh. 1.** A rectangular piece of linen, cotton, or similar material serving as a basic article of bedding, commonly used in pairs, one above and one below the body of the sleeper. **2.** A broad, thin, usually rectangular mass or piece of any material, such as paper, metal, glass, or plywood. **3.** A broad, flat, continuous surface or expanse: *a sheet of rain.* **4.** A newspaper; especially, a tabloid: *a scandal sheet.* **5.** *Geology.* A broad, relatively thin deposit or layer of igneous or sedimentary rock. **6.** The large block of stamps printed by a single impression of a plate before the individual stamps have been separated. **7. a.** A piece of paper. **b.** A piece of paper printed and folded ready to be bound as pages in a book.
∼*v.* **sheeted, sheeting, sheets.** *—tr.* To cover with, wrap in, or provide with a sheet or sheets. *—intr.* To fall in sheets, as heavy rain does. [Middle English *s(c)hete,* cloth, Old English *scēte.*]

sheet² *n. Nautical.* A rope or chain attached to one or both of the lower corners of a sail, serving to move or extend it. **—three sheets to the wind.** *Slang.* Drunk.
∼*intr.v.* **sheeted, sheeting, sheets.** *Nautical.* To extend in a certain direction. Used of the sheets of a sail. [Middle English *s(c)hete,* Old English *scēata,* corner of a sail.]

sheet anchor *n.* **1.** A large extra anchor intended for use in emergency. **2.** A person or thing that can be turned to in time of emergency, especially one that can be relied on if all else fails.

sheet bend *n.* A knot in which one rope or piece of string is made fast to the bight of another. Also called "weaver's hitch" "weaver's knot."

sheet glass *n.* Molten glass drawn into a wide sheet which, after annealing and hardening, is cut into required lengths.

sheet·ing (shē′tĭng) *n.* Any material, such as metal or cloth, in the form of or used to make a sheet.

sheet lightning *n.* Lightning that appears as a broad, sheetlike illumination, caused by diffusion of a lightning flash by a thunder cloud.

sheet metal *n.* Metal that has been rolled into a sheet thinner than plate but thicker than foil.

sheet music *n.* Music printed on unbound sheets of paper.

Sheet·rock (shēt′rŏk′) *n.* A trademark for a kind of plasterboard.

sheets (shēts) *pl.n. Nautical.* The spaces at the bow (the *bow sheets*) and stern (the *stern sheets*) of an open rowing boat that are not occupied by oarsmen.

Shef·field (shĕf′ēld). Industrial city in South Yorkshire, northern England, at the confluence of the Don River and four tributaries. Since the 14th century it has been the most important center for cutlery manufacture in the country. It is also a leading center for silver and for heavy steel manufacture.

sheik, sheikh (shēk, shāk) *n.* **1.** A Muslim religious official. **2.** The leader of an Arab family, village, or tribe. [Arabic *shaikh,* old man, from *shākha,* to be old.]

sheik·dom (shēk′dəm, shāk′-) *n.* The area ruled by a sheik.

sheitan. Variant of **shaitan.**

shek·el (shĕk′əl) *n.* **1.** The basic monetary unit of Israel, equal to 100 new agora. See feature at **currency. 2. a.** Any of several ancient units of weight; especially, an ancient Hebrew unit equal to about half an ounce. **b.** A gold or silver coin equal in weight to one of these units; especially, the chief silver coin of the Hebrews. **3. shekels.** *Slang.* Cash; money. [Hebrew *sheqel,* from *shāqal,* to weigh.]

She·ki·nah (shĭ-kē′nə) *n.* A visible manifestation of the divine presence as described in Jewish theology. [Hebrew *shəkhīnāh,* from *shākhan,* to dwell.]

shel·drake (shĕl′drāk′) *n., pl.* **-drakes** or collectively **sheldrake. 1.** Any of various large Old World ducks of the genus *Tadorna;* especially, *T. tadorna,* having predominantly black and white plumage. Also called "shelduck." **2.** Any of several other ducks. [Middle English *sheldedrake* : *sheld-,* variegated, perhaps of Low German origin, akin to Middle Dutch *schillede* + DRAKE (duck).]

shel·duck (shĕl′dŭk′) *n.* See **sheldrake** (sense 1).

shelf (shĕlf) *n., pl.* **shelves** (shĕlvz). **1.** A flat, usually rectangular structure of a rigid material, such as wood, glass, or metal, fixed at right angles to a wall or other vertical surface and used to hold or store objects. **2.** The contents or capacity of such a structure. **3.** Anything resembling such an object, such as a balcony or a ledge of rock. **4.** A **continental shelf** *(see).* **5.** *Mining.* Bedrock. **—on the shelf. 1.** In a state of disuse; put aside. **2.** *Informal.* **a.** Unemployed. **b.** Out of circulation. **c.** Retired. [Middle English *shelf(e),* perhaps from Middle Low German *schelf.*]

shelf ice *n.* An extension of glacial ice into coastal waters that is in contact with the bottom near the shore but not toward the outer edge.

shelf life *n.* The amount of time that something, such as a drug or packaged food, may be stored without deteriorating.

shell (shĕl) *n.* **1. a.** The usually hard outer covering that encases certain organisms such as mollusks, certain insects, and turtles. **b.** A similar outer covering on an egg, fruit, or nut. **2.** The material composing such a covering. **3.** Anything resembling such a covering, especially: **a.** A framework, case, or exterior, as of a building, motor vehicle, or machine. **b.** A thin layer of pastry. **c.** The hull of a ship. **d.** The external part of the ear. **e.** A long, narrow racing boat propelled by oarsmen. **4. a.** A projectile or piece of ammunition; especially, the hollow tube containing explosives used to propel such a projectile. **b.** A metal or cardboard case, containing the charge, primer, and shot, fired from a shotgun; a cartridge. **5. a.** An attitude or manner adopted to mask one's true feelings. **b.** *Informal.* A state of shyness or reserve: *brought her out of her shell.* **6.** *Physics.* **a.** Any of the set of hypothetical spherical surfaces centered on the nucleus of an atom that contain the orbits of electrons having the same principal quantum number. **b.** All the electrons in an atom that have the same principal quantum number. **c.** Any of a set of groupings of nucleon energy states in a nucleus, or of nucleons occupying such states, in which the binding energies of states differ from one another by much less than from the binding energies of states in another grouping.
∼*v.* **shelled, shelling, shells.** *—tr.* **1. a.** To remove the shell of. **b.** To remove from a shell, pod, or the like. **2.** To separate (grains, kernels of corn, or the like) from the ear, husk, or cob. **3.** To fire artillery shells at; bombard. *—intr.* To shed or become free of a shell. **—shell out.** *Informal.* To pay or hand out (money). [Middle English *shell,* Old English *scell, scill.*] **—shell·er** *n.* **—shell·y** *adj.* See feature, next page.

she'll (shēl, shĭl). Contraction of *she will* or *she shall.*

shel·lac (shə-lăk′) *n.* **1.** A purified resin formed into thin yellow or orange flakes or buttons and widely used in varnishes, paints, stains, inks, and sealing wax. **2.** A thin varnish made by dissolving shellac in denatured alcohol, used as a wood coating.
∼*tr.v.* **shellacked, -lacking, -lacs. 1.** To apply shellac to. **2.** *Slang.* To deal blows to; batter. **3.** *Slang.* To defeat decisively. [SHEL(L) + LAC (lacquer), translation of French *laque en écailles,* lac (melted) in thin plates.]

shell·back (shĕl′băk′) *n.* A veteran sailor; especially, one who has crossed the equator. [Referring to a sailor hardened by experience.]

shell·bark (shĕl′bärk′) *n.* A tree, the **shagbark** *(see).*

Shel·ley (shĕl′ē), **Mary Wollstonecraft,** born Mary Godwin. (1797–1851). British novelist, the daughter of the feminist writer Mary Wollstonecraft and the philosopher William Godwin and the wife of Percy Bysshe Shelley. She ran away with Shelley in 1814 and married him two years later. She is famous as the author of *Frankenstein, or the Modern Prometheus* (1818).

Shelley, Percy Bysshe (1792–1822). British poet. In 1811 he was expelled from Oxford University for circulating an atheist pamphlet; in 1813 *Queen Mab,* a poem that virulently attacked the monarchy, church, and other established institutions, was privately printed. His works include the verse dramas *The Cenci* (1819) and *Prometheus Unbound* (1820) and several odes, among them *To the West Wind* and *To a Skylark.*

shell·fire (shĕl′fīr′) *n.* The firing of artillery projectiles at, or their reception in, a target area.

shell·fish (shĕl′fĭsh′) *n., pl.* **-fishes** or collectively **shellfish.** Any aquatic animal having a shell or shell-like exoskeleton, as a mollusk or crustacean, especially those having edible flesh.

shell·flow·er (shĕl′flou′ər) *n.* **1.** A tall plant, *Molucella laevis,* native to Asia, having tiny flowers and conspicuous green calyxes. Also called "bells of Ireland." **2.** A tall plant, *Alpina speciosa,* native to tropical Asia, having showy, variously colored flowers. [From the shell-like appearance of the flowers.]

shell pink *n.* Pinkish white to strong yellowish pink, including grayish and light yellowish pinks. **—shell-pink** (shĕl′pĭngk′) *adj.*

shell·proof (shĕl′pro͞of′) *adj.* Able to withstand shellfire.

shell shock *n.* Any of various usually acute, often hysterical neuroses originating in trauma suffered under fire in modern warfare. **—shell-shocked** (shĕl′shŏkt′) *adj.*

shel·ter (shĕl′tər) *n.* **1. a.** Something that provides cover or protection, as from the weather or bombardment. **b.** The cover or protection so provided. **2.** A refuge; a haven. **3.** The state of being covered or protected.
∼*v.* **sheltered, -tering, -ters.** *—tr.* To provide cover or protection for. *—intr.* To take cover; find refuge. **—shel·ter·er** *n.*
Synonyms: *asylum, cover, haven, refuge, retreat, sanctuary.*

shel·tered (shĕl′tərd) *adj.* **1.** Protected or overprotected from harm or harsh realities: *a sheltered life.* **2.** Providing special facilities or supervision for the semi-independent elderly or disabled.

shelter tent *n.* A small tent usually formed of two or more pieces of waterproof material. Also called "pup tent."

shel·tie, shel·ty (shĕl′tē) *n. pl.* **-ties. 1.** A **Shetland pony** *(see).* **2.** A **Shetland sheepdog** *(see).* [Norse *sjalti,* Shetland pony, Shetlander, from Old Norse *Hjalti,* Shetlander, from *Hjaltland,* Shetland, probably from *hjalt,* hilt, from Germanic *heltaz* (unattested), HILT.]

shelve (shĕlv) *v.* **shelved, shelving, shelves.** *—tr.* **1.** To place or arrange on a shelf or shelves. **2.** To put away as though on a shelf; put aside; postpone: *"as usual, Dixon shelved this question"* (Kingsley Amis). **3.** To cause to retire from service; dismiss. **4.** To furnish with shelves. *—intr.* To slope gradually; incline. [From SHELVES.]

shelves. Plural of **shelf.**

shelv·ing (shĕl′vĭng) *n.* **1.** Shelves collectively. **2.** Material for shelves.

Shem (shĕm). The eldest son of Noah. Genesis 5:32.

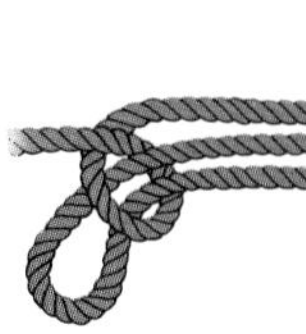

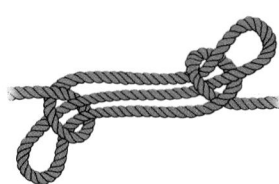

sheepshank *A knot used to shorten a rope.*

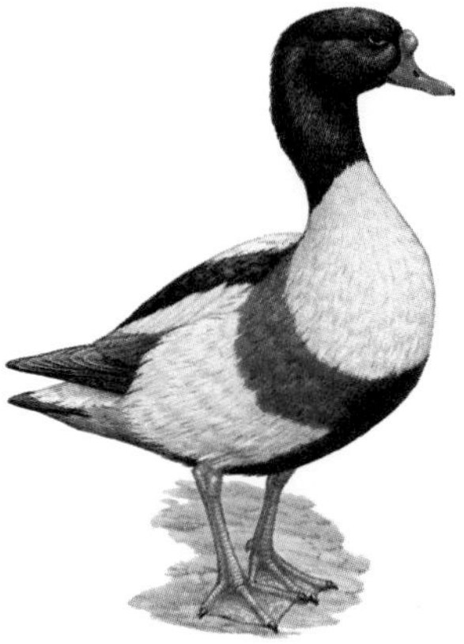

sheldrake *The large waterfowl known as the sheldrake—this is a male bird—is native to Europe and parts of Asia, and feeds on water snails, shellfish, insects, and fish. It frequently nests in rabbit burrows on sand dunes.*

PRONUNCIATION KEY

ă, pat; ā, pay; âr, care;
ä, father, are; b, bib;
ch, church; d, deed; ĕ, pet;
ē, be; f, fife; g, gag; h, hat;
hw, which; ĭ, pit; ī, pie;
îr, pier; j, judge; k, kick;
l, lid, needle; m, mum;
n, no, sudden; ng, thing;
ŏ, pot; ō, toe; ô, paw, for;
oi, noise; ou, out; o͝o, book;
o͞o, boot; p, pop; r, roar;
s, sauce; sh, ship, dish;
t, tight; th, thin, path;
th, this, bathe; ŭ, cut; ûr, fur;
v, valve; w, with; y, yes;
z, zebra, size; zh, vision;
ə, about, item, edible, gallop, circus, peaceful

IN FOREIGN WORDS:

à, *Fr.* ami; œ, *Fr.* feu, *Ger.* schön; ü, *Fr.* tu, *Ger.* über; KH, *Ger.* ich, *Scot.* loch; N, *Fr.* bon; y′, *Fr.* Compiègne

STRESS MARKS:

Primary stress: ′
in·cite′ (ĭn-sīt′)
Secondary stress: ′
in′sight′ (ĭn′sīt′)

NATURE'S OWN COATS OF ARMOR
The remains of tiny creatures decorate the seashore

The shells found on the seashores of the world are the hard outer skeletons of soft-bodied animals known as mollusks. They consist largely of calcium carbonate, which is secreted by glands contained in a fleshy part of the mollusk known as the mantle. These glands also produce the exquisite colors with which the shells are tinted. Shells, in all their variety of shapes and sizes, are built up in three layers—a horny outer layer, a chalky middle layer, and a glossy inner layer.

Shell-bearing mollusks are mostly univalves or bi-valves. Univalves have one spiral shell shaped like a cone or a bowl. They include snails, cowries, periwinkles, abalones, and whelks. Bivalves have a pair of flattish shells and include oysters, clams, mussels, scallops, and shipworms.

The two shells of bivalves may be the same size (as in mussels), of unequal size (as in scallops), or extremely small in relation to the animal's body (as in shipworms, which have a pair of small shells at the front end of a long wormlike body). Many bivalve shells have a thick lining of nacre—mother-of-pearl.

Although hundreds of different species of mollusk are found on beaches, every beach—whether sandy or rocky, sheltered or exposed—has its own characteristic inhabitants and so is able to produce a fascinating variety of shells.

The best time to collect shells is at low tide, when more beach is exposed. It is especially good during the spring tides, which occur for a few days every two weeks at the time of a full or new moon.

SOME COMMON SHELLS, AND WHERE THEY ARE FOUND

Abalone (univalve)
Haliotis tuberculata
80 – 100 millimeters
(3 – 4 inches)
Lives on and under stones

Edible periwinkle (univalve)
Littorina littorea
15 – 40 millimeters (½ – 1½ inches)
Found on rocks and beneath seaweed

Humpback cowrie
(univalve)
Cypraea mauritiana
70 – 110 millimeters (2¾ – 4⅜ inches)
Lives on rocks

Pullet carpet shell (bivalve)
Venerupis pullastra
40 – 65 millimeters (1½ – 2½ inches)
Found in sand and muddy gravel

Great scallop, or escallop (bivalve)
Pecten maximus
70 – 160 millimeters (2¾ – 6¼ inches)
Lives in coarse sand

Giant clam (bivalve)
Tridacna gigas
Up to 1.2 meters (4 feet)
Lives on coral reefs in pools

Horse mussel (bivalve)
Modiolus modiolus
180 – 220 millimeters (7 – 8⅔ inches)
Lives among brown seaweed

Curved razor (bivalve)
Ensis ensis
80 – 130 millimeters
(3 – 5 inches)
Lives in sand

Grooved razor (bivalve)
Solen marginatus
130 millimeters (5 inches)
Lives in sandy mud

Queen scallop (bivalve)
Chlamys opercularis
40 – 90 millimeters (1½ – 3½ inches)
Lives in coarse sand and gravel

Queen conch (univalve)
Strombus gigas
150 – 300 millimeters
(6 – 12 inches)
Found in sand and
muddy sand

Common whelk (univalve)
Buccinum undatum
50 – 100 millimeters (2 – 4 inches)
Found in muddy gravel, sand, and on
rocky shores

Common otter shell (bivalve)
Lutraria lutraria
100 – 130 millimeters (4 – 5 inches)
Lives in sand and sandy mud

Prickly cockle (bivalve)
Cardium echinata
65 millimeters (2½ inches)
Lives in sand and muddy sand

Sand gaper, or old maid (bivalve)
Mya arenaria
120 – 150 millimeters (4¾ – 6 inches)
In clay, sand, and sandy mud

Argonaut, or paper nautilus (univalve)
Argonauta nodosa
150 – 180 millimeters (6 – 7 inches)
Found on rocks on seafloor

Common limpet (univalve)
Patella vulgaris
20 – 50 millimeters (¾ – 2 inches)
Lives on rocks

Smooth buckle, or spindle shell (univalve)
Neptunea antiqua
130 millimeters (5 inches)
Lives in sand and mud

Shemite. Variant of **Semite.**

she•moz•zle, sche•moz•zle (shĭ-mŏz′əl) *n.* **1.** A muddle; a state of chaos. **2.** An uproar; a noisy row. [Yiddish.]

Shen•an•do•ah National Park (shĕn′ən-dō′ə). Area, 78,324 hectares (193,537 acres), extending *c.* 129 kilometers (80 miles) along the crest of the Blue Ridge Mts. in northern Virginia. The park is heavily forested, with numerous streams and waterfalls.

Shenandoah Valley. Part of the Great Appalachian Valley in Virginia, between the Allegheny Mts. to the west and the Blue Ridge Mts. to the east. In the Civil War (1861–65) the valley was the scene of several of Stonewall Jackson's campaigns.

she•nan•i•gans (shə-năn′ĭ-gənz) *pl.n. Informal.* **1.** Prankishness; mischief. **2.** Treachery; deceit. [19th century : origin obscure.]

Shensi. See **Shaanxi.**

Shen•yang or **Shen-yang** (shŭn′yäng′). Formerly **Muk•den** (mo͝ok′dən). City in northeastern China, the capital of Liaoning province. The fourth-largest city in China, it is the center of a highly developed industrial region. The city fell to the Japanese in the Russo-Japanese War (1904–05). It was here also that the Mukden, or Manchurian, Incident took place (1931), when the Japanese used an explosion on the railway as an excuse to occupy the city and begin the occupation of Manchuria.

she-oak (shē′ōk′) *n.* Any of various Australian trees of the genus *Casuarina,* such as the **beefwood** *(see).* See **casuarina.** [SHE (used in the obsolete sense of a lesser plant) + OAK.]

she•ol (shē′ōl′) *n.* **1.** Hell. **2. Sheol.** A place described in the Old Testament as the abode of the dead. [Hebrew *shəōl.*]

Shep•ard (shĕp′ərd), **Alan Bartlett, Jr.** (1923–). U.S. astronaut. On May 5, 1961, he became the first American in space. He also commanded the Apollo 14 mission to the Moon in 1971.

shep•herd (shĕp′ərd) *n.* **1.** One who herds, guards, and cares for sheep. **2.** One who cares for a group of people, as a priest or teacher.
~*tr.v.* **shepherded, -herding, -herds.** To herd, guard, or care for as or in the manner of a shepherd. [Middle English *sheepherde,* Old English *scēaphirde* : *scēap,* SHEEP + *hirde,* HERD (herdsman).]

shepherd dog *n.* A sheepdog.

shep•herd•ess (shĕp′ər-dĭs) *n.* A woman shepherd.

shepherd's pie *n.* A dish of minced beef or lamb with gravy, topped by a layer of mashed potatoes.

shep•herd's-purse (shĕp′ərdz-pûrs′) *n.* A common weed, *Capsella bursa-pastoris,* having small white flowers and flat, heart-shaped fruit. [From its pouchlike pods.]

shepherd's weatherglass *n.* A plant, the **pimpernel** *(see).*

Sher•a•ton (shĕr′ə-tən) *adj.* Of or designating a style of English furniture originated by Thomas Sheraton, and characterized by straight lines and graceful proportions.

Sheraton, Thomas (1751–1806). British furniture designer. His four-volume *Cabinet-Maker and Upholsterer's Drawing Book* (1791–94) provides an elegant and influential survey of contemporary taste.

sher•bet (shûr′bĭt) *n.* **1.** A sweet-flavored water ice to which milk, egg white, or gelatin has been added. Also called "sorbet." **2.** *British.* **a.** A beverage made of sweetened, diluted fruit juice. **b.** A powder eaten as a sweet and used to make effervescent drinks. **3.** A stemmed glass in which desserts are served. [Turkish *sherbet* and Persian *sharbat,* from Arabic *sharbah,* drink, from *shariba,* to drink. See also **syrup, shrub.**]

sherd. Variant of **shard.**

Sher•i•dan (shĕr′ə-dən), **Philip Henry** (1831–88). U.S. Union general. An outstanding fighter with a flair for leadership, he was known for his daring and bravery in the Chattanooga (1836) and Wilderness (1864) campaigns. After his victory at Five Forks (April 1, 1865), he cut off the Confederate retreat at Appomattox, forcing the surrender of Robert E. Lee.

Sheridan, Richard Brinsley Butler (1751–1816). British dramatist and politician, born in Ireland. He is known for his comedies of manners, especially *The Rivals* (1775) and *The School for Scandal* (1777). Elected an M.P. in 1780, he became an outstanding Whig orator and was treasurer of the navy (1806–07).

she•rif, sha•rif (shə-rēf′) *n.* **1. a.** A descendant of the prophet Muhammad through his daughter Fatima. **b.** The title of certain Arab princes claiming such descent. **2.** The chief magistrate of Mecca. Also called "grand sherif." **3.** A Moroccan prince or ruler. [Arabic *sharīf,* "noble," from *sharafa,* to be highborn.]

sher•iff (shĕr′ĭf) *n.* **1.** The chief executive of the courts of superior jurisdiction in a U.S. county; the chief law-enforcement officer in a county. **2.** In England and Wales, the chief officer of the Crown in every county, whose powers are now mainly ceremonial. **3.** In Scotland, a judge presiding over a *sheriff court* (roughly equivalent to an English county court and the middle tier of a Crown Court). [Middle English *shir(r)eve, shirrif,* Old English *scīrgerēfa* : *scīr,* SHIRE + *gerēfa,* officer, REEVE.]

Sher•lock Holmes (shûr′lŏk′ hōmz′). English detective with superb powers of observation and deduction, a central character in stories and novels by Sir Arthur Conan Doyle.

Sher•man (shûr′mən), **Roger** (1721–93). U.S. Revolutionary patriot. A member of the Continental Congress and the Constitutional Convention, he helped draft—and signed—the Declaration of Independence, the Articles of Confederation, and the Constitution. He also signed the Articles of Association (1774) and is the only person who signed all four of these crucial state documents.

Sherman, William Tecumseh (1820–91). Union general in the Civil War. As commander of all Federal forces in the west after 1864, he helped secure Union victory by his capture of Atlanta and march through the Carolinas (1864–65).

Sher•pa (shûr′pə) *n., pl.* **-pas** or collectively **Sherpa.** A member of a Tibetan people living in northern Nepal.

sher•ry (shĕr′ē) *n., pl.* **-ries.** **1.** A fortified Spanish wine ranging from very dry to sweet, and usually drunk as an aperitif. **2.** A similar wine made outside Spain. [Earlier *sherris,* "wine of Jerez," from *Xeres,* older form of JEREZ.]

Sher•wood (shûr′wo͝od′), **Robert Emmet** (1896–1955). U.S. playwright. A highly successful author, he won four Pulitzer Prizes—three for plays: *Idiot's Delight* (1936), *Abe Lincoln in Illinois* (1939), and *There Shall Be No Night* (1941); and one for his memoir, *Roosevelt and Hopkins* (1949), based on the papers of Harry Hopkins (1890–1946).

Sherwood Forest. Ancient royal forest, mainly in Nottinghamshire, central England, famous as the scene of Robin Hood's exploits. Today only parts of it remain.

she's (shēz). **1.** Contraction of *she is.* **2.** Contraction of *she has.*

Shet•land (shĕt′lənd) *adj.* Of or from the Shetland Islands.
~*n.* **1.** A fine, loosely twisted yarn made from the wool of Shetland sheep and used for knitting and weaving. Also called "Shetland wool." **2.** A garment, especially a sweater, made of this wool.

Shetland Islands. Also **Shet•lands** (shĕt′ləndz). The most northerly part of Britain, comprising *c.* 100 islands off northern Scotland. They lie northeast of the Orkney Islands and constitute the county of Shetland or Zetland. The largest of them are Mainland, Yell, Unst, Fetlar, and Whalsey, and 19 are inhabited. The poor soil supports some crops, chiefly oats and barley, but the main economic activities are the raising of sheep, cattle, and Shetland ponies, fishing, and tourism. The islands are noted for their wool, knitwear, and knitted lace. Under Norse rule from the late 9th century, the Shetland Islands were annexed to the Scottish crown in 1472. Lerwick on Mainland is the administrative center.

Shetland pony *n.* A small, compactly built pony of a breed originating in the Shetland Islands. Also called "sheltie."

Shetland sheepdog *n.* A dog of a breed developed in the Shetland Islands, having a rough coat and resembling a small collie. Also called "sheltie."

She•vat (shə-vät′) *n.* Also **She•bat** (-bät′, -vät′). The fifth month of the Hebrew calendar. See feature at **calendar.** [Hebrew *shəbhāt.*]

shew (shō) *v.* **shewed, shewing, shews.** *Archaic.* To show.

shew•bread, show•bread (shō′brĕd′) *n.* The 12 loaves of blessed, unleavened bread placed every Sabbath in the sanctuary of the Tabernacle by the ancient Hebrew priests. Exodus 25:20. Leviticus 24:5-9. [16th century (Tindale) : translating German *Schaubrot,* from Hebrew *lĕchem pānim,* "bread of presence" (that is, the bread left in the presence of God in the temple).]

shf, SHF superhigh frequency.

Shi•ah, Shi•a (shē′ə) *n.* **1.** The principal minority sect of Islam, composed of the followers of Ali, the cousin and son-in-law of Muhammad, who regard the heirs of Ali as the legitimate successors to the Prophet and reject the other caliphs and the Sunnite legal and political institutions. Compare **Sunni.** **2.** A **Shiite** *(see).*
~*adj.* Shiite. [Arabic *shī'ah,* following (of Ali), from *shā'a,* to follow, accompany.]

shib•bo•leth (shĭb′ə-lĭth, -lĕth′) *n.* **1.** A password, phrase, custom, or usage that reliably distinguishes the members of one group or class from another. **2.** A slogan, catchword, or saying, especially one distinctive of a particular group. [Hebrew *shibbōleth,* an ear of corn, stream (password used by the Gileadites in the Bible, Judges 12:6).]

shield (shēld) *n.* **1.** An article of protective armor made of metal or other rigid material carried on the forearm to ward off blows or missiles. **2.** A means of defense; protection. **3.** Something resembling a shield in shape, such as a trophy or badge. **4. a.** Something such as a protective plate that screens off potentially dangerous machinery or equipment. **b.** *Military.* A steel sheet attached to a gun to protect the gunners from small-arms fire. **5.** *Zoology.* A protective plate or similar hard outer covering. **6.** *Heraldry.* A design or drawing of a shield on which a coat of arms is displayed. **7.** *Physics.* A mass of material, such as lead or cement, that encloses a nuclear reactor in order to reduce the amount of radiation that escapes into the surrounding area. **8.** *Geology.* A **craton** *(see).*
~*v.* **shielded, shielding, shields.** —*tr.* **1.** To protect or defend with or as if with a shield; guard. **2.** To cover up; conceal. —*intr.* To act or serve as a shield or safeguard. —See Synonyms at **defend.** [Middle English *shild, sheld,* Old English *scild, sceld.*] **—shield•er** *n.*

shield•bug (shēld′bŭg′) *n.* Any of numerous flattened, shield-shaped, plant-eating insects.

shield fern *n.* Either of two large tufted ferns, *Polystichum aculeatum* or *P. setiferum,* having round, shield-shaped indusia (spore-protecting coverings). Also called "buckler fern."

Shield of David *n.* A symbol of Judaism, the **Star of David** *(see).*

shiel•ing (shē′lĭng) *n. Scottish.* A shepherd's hut. [Scottish *shiel,* shed, hut, Middle English *schele, shale,* probably from Scandinavian; akin to Old Norse *skjol,* shelter, hut.]

shift (shĭft) *v.* **shifted, shifting, shifts.** —*tr.* **1.** To move or transfer from one place or position to another. **2.** To exchange for or replace with something similar in quality or kind; switch. **3.** To change (gears) in an automobile. **4.** *Linguistics.* To alter phonetically or as part of a systematic change. —*intr.* **1.** To change position, direction, place, form, or the like. **2. a.** To provide for one's

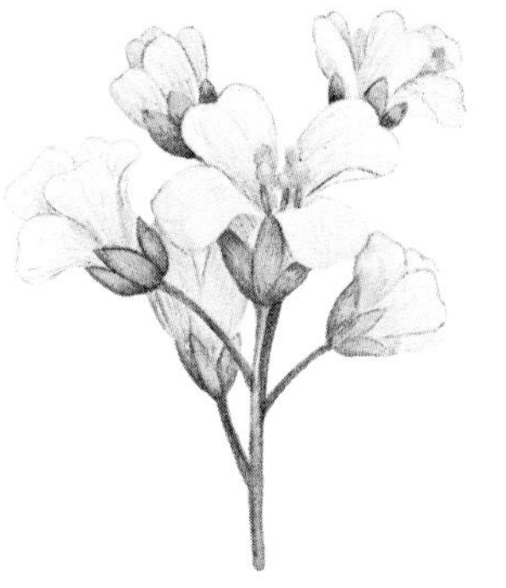

shepherd's-purse *A weed that thrives in all kinds of soil. The tiny white flowers are self-pollinating, and the pods, like wallets, open to shower seeds.*

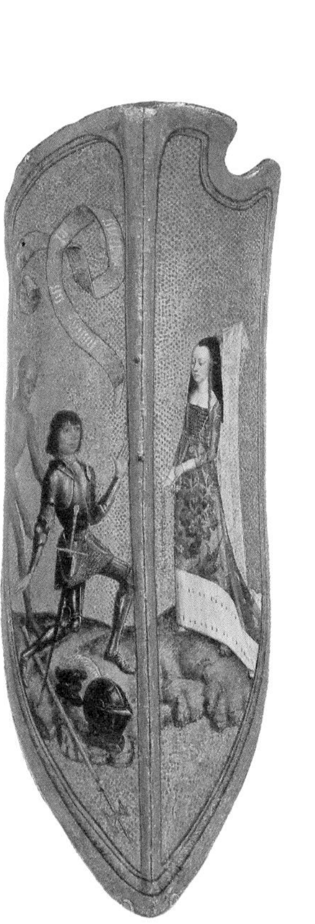

shield *This 15th-century Flemish shield was made for a medieval tournament. It represents a courtly love scene: the knight kneeling before his lady is vowing: "Vous ou la Mort" ("You or Death"), and it is possible that the figures are actual portraits. The socket at the top of the gilded wooden shield was designed to hold a lance.*

needs; get along; manage: *I can shift for myself.* **b.** To get along by resourceful or evasive means. **3.** To change gears, as when driving an automobile.

~*n.* **1.** A change, transference, or displacement from one individual, position, or configuration to another. **2.** A change of direction or form. **3. a.** A group of workers who work for a particular period, and are replaced by the next group. **b.** The working period or time of such a group: *The night shift ends at six.* **4.** *Music.* A change of the position of the hand in playing the violin or another instrument. **5.** *Linguistics.* **a.** A systematic change of the phonetic or phonemic structure of a language. **b. Functional shift** *(see).* **6. a.** A woman's dress hanging straight from the shoulders. Also called "chemise." **b.** A woman's undergarment; a slip; a chemise. **7.** An ingenious, evasive, or fraudulent expedient; a trick. **8.** In football, a lateral movement of the offensive backfield from one formation to another just before the ball is put into play. [Middle English *shiften,* to arrange, apportion, change, Old English *sciftan,* to arrange, from Germanic *skip-* (unattested).] **—shift•er** *n.*

shift•less (shĭft′lĭs) *adj.* **1.** Showing a lack of ambition or purpose; lazy. **2.** Showing a lack of resourcefulness or efficiency; not capable. [From SHIFT (archaic sense "resourcefulness").] **—shift•less•ly** *adv.* **—shift•less•ness** *n.*

shift•y (shĭf′tē) *adj.* **-ier, -iest. 1.** Tricky; crafty. **2.** Suggesting craft, guile, or deceitfulness; furtive. **3.** Full of expedients; resourceful. **—shift•i•ly** *adv.* **—shift•i•ness** *n.*

shi•gel•la (shĭ-gĕl′ə) *n., pl.* **-gellae** (-gĕl′ē). Any bacterium of the genus *Shigella,* some species of which cause dysentery in humans. [New Latin, after K. *Shiga* (1870–1957), Japanese bacteriologist who discovered it.]

shih-tzu (shē′tso͞o′) *n.* A small long-haired dog of a breed originating in Tibet, resembling a terrier or pekingese. [Chinese, "lion."]

Shi•ism, Shi'•ism (shē′ĭz′əm) *n.* The religion or doctrines of the **Shiah** *(see).*

Shi•ite, Shi'•ite (shē′īt′) *n.* A member of the **Shiah** *(see)* branch of Islam. Also called "Shiah." **—Shi•ite, Shi•it•ic** (shē-ĭt′ĭk) *adj.*

shi•ka•ree, shi•ka•ri (shĭ-kä′rē) *n. Anglo-Indian.* A big-game hunting guide. [Hindi, from Persian *shikārī,* from *shikār,* hunting, from Middle Persian *shkār*†.]

Shi•ko•ku (shĭ-kō′ko͞o). Smallest of the four main islands of Japan. It covers 18,770 square kilometers (7,247 square miles) and lies across the Inland Sea from Kyushu and Honshu.

shik•sa, shik•se, shick•sa (skĭk′sə) *n.* **1.** A non-Jewish girl or young woman. Usually used derogatorily. **2.** A Jewish girl or young woman who fails to live up to traditional Jewish teachings or practices. Usually used derogatorily. [Yiddish *shikse,* feminine of *sheygets,* from Hebrew *sheqeṣ,* blemish.]

shill (shĭl) *n.* One who works as a decoy, as in a confidence game, by posing as a customer or an innocent bystander.

~*intr.v.* **shilled, shilling, shills.** To act as a shill. [Probably short for *shillabert,* decoy, impostor.]

shil•le•lagh, shil•la•lah (shə-lā′lē, -lə) *n.* A club or cudgel, especially one of oak or blackthorn. [Such clubs were originally made in *Shillelagh,* town in County Wicklow, Ireland.]

shil•ling (shĭl′ĭng) *n. Abbr.* **s., sh. 1.** Formerly, a coin equal to $^1/_{20}$ of the pound of the United Kingdom, the Republic of Ireland, and a number of former British dominions. **2.** The basic monetary unit of Kenya, Somalia, Tanzania, and Uganda, equal to 100 cents. See feature at **currency. 3.** *Printing.* A **virgule** *(see).* [Middle English *shilling,* Old English *scilling,* from Germanic *skillingaz* (unattested).]

shil•ly-shal•ly (shĭl′ē-shăl′ē) *intr.v.* **-lied, -lying, -lies. 1.** To put off acting; hesitate or waver. **2.** To idle or dawdle.

~*adj.* Hesitant; vacillating.

~*n., pl.* **shilly-shallies.** Procrastination; hesitation.

~*adv.* In a hesitant manner; irresolutely. [Originally in phrases such as *stand* (or *go*), *shill I? shall I?,* reduplication of *shall I?*] **—shil•ly-shal•li•er** *n.*

Shi•loh (shī′lō). Ancient village of central Palestine, west of the Jordan River on the east slope of Mt. Ephraim. It was a meeting place and sanctuary for the Israelites; the Ark of the Covenant was kept here until its capture by the Philistines.

Shiloh National Military Park. Area in southwestern Tennessee, set aside to commemorate the Civil War Battle of Shiloh (or Pittsburg Landing), fought on April 6–7, 1862. The battle was one of the bloodiest contests of the war, with casualties of more than 10,000 on each side.

shim (shĭm) *n.* A thin, often tapered piece of metal, wood, stone, or other material, inserted as a leveler or filter between parts or materials or between a piece of furniture and the floor.

~*tr.v.* **shimmed, shimming, shims.** To make (parts) fit by inserting a shim or shims. [18th century : origin obscure.]

shim•mer (shĭm′ər) *intr.v.* **-mered, -mering, -mers.** To shine with a soft tremulous or flickering light. —See Usage note at **flash.**

~*n.* A flickering or tremulous light; a glimmer. [Middle English *schimeren,* Old English *scimerian, scimrian,* from Germanic; akin to SHINE.] **—shim•mer•y** *adj.*

shim•my (shĭm′ē) *n., pl.* **-mies. 1.** A dance popular in the 1920's, characterized by rapid shaking of the body. Also called "shimmy shake." **2.** Abnormal vibration or wobbling, as in the chassis of a car. **3.** *Regional.* A chemise.

~*intr.v.* **shimmied, -mying, -mies. 1.** To vibrate or wobble. **2.** To shake the body in or as if in dancing the shimmy. [Short for *shimmy-shake,* perhaps "to shake one's chemise," from *shimmy,* alteration of CHEMISE.]

shin¹ (shĭn) *n.* **1.** *Anatomy.* **a.** The front part of the leg below the knee and above the ankle. **b.** The front of the tibia. **2.** A cut of meat from the lower part of the foreleg in beef cattle, as opposed to the upper foreleg or shank.

~*v.* **shinned, shinning, shins.** —*tr.* **1.** To climb (a rope or pole, for example) by gripping and pulling alternately with the hands and legs. Usually used with *up.* **2.** To kick or hit in the shins. —*intr.* To climb something by shinning it. Usually used with *up.* [Middle English *shine,* Old English *sinu.*]

shin² (shĭn, shēn) *n.* The 22nd letter in the Hebrew alphabet. See feature at **alphabet.** [Hebrew *shīn,* variant of *shēn,* tooth (from the shape of the letter).]

Shi•nar (shī′när′). The Biblical name for an ancient country on the lower courses of the Tigris and Euphrates. Genesis 10:10.

shin•bone (shĭn′bōn′) *n. Anatomy.* The **tibia** *(see).*

shin•dig (shĭn′dĭg′) *n. Slang.* **1.** A noisy party or celebration. Also called "shindy." **2.** A shindy. [Probably an alteration of SHINDY.]

shin•dy (shĭn′dē) *n., pl.* **-dies.** *Slang.* **1.** A commotion; a row; an uproar. Also called "shindig." **2.** A shindig. [Alteration of SHINTY.]

shine (shīn) *v.* **shone** (shōn) or **shined, shining, shines.** —*intr.* **1.** To emit light; be radiant; beam. **2.** To reflect light; glint or glisten. **3.** To distinguish oneself in some sphere; excel: *shine at tennis.* **4.** To become clearly apparent. —*tr.* **1.** To aim or cast the beam or glow of: *Shine the torch over here.* **2.** To make glossy or bright by polishing: *shined his shoes.*

~*n.* **1.** Brightness; radiance; luster. **2.** An act of shining something: *gave her shoes a shine.* **3.** Fair weather. Used in the phrase *rain or shine.* **—take a shine to.** *Informal.* To like spontaneously. [Shine, shone (past tense); Middle English *shinen, schon,* Old English *scīnan, scān* (past singular). The past participle *shone* is formed in Modern English from the past tense *shone.*]

shin•er (shī′nər) *n.* **1.** One that shines. **2.** *Slang.* A black eye. **3. a.** Any of numerous small, often silvery North American freshwater fishes of the family Cyprinidae, especially one of the genus *Notropis.* **b.** Any of various other small silvery fishes, especially the mackerel.

shin•gle¹ (shĭng′gəl) *n.* **1.** A thin oblong piece of wood, asbestos, or other material, laid in overlapping rows to cover the roofs and sides of houses. **2.** A woman's close-cropped layered haircut. **3.** *Informal.* A small signboard, as one indicating a doctor's office.

~*tr.v.* **shingled, -gling, -gles. 1.** To cover (a roof or building) with shingles. **2.** To cut (a woman's hair) short and in layers so that the hair is full out at the back of the head and tapers in to the nape of the neck. [Middle English *scincle, scingle,* from Latin *scindula,* variant of *scandula,* a roofing shingle, from *scandere,* to ascend.] **—shin•gler** *n.*

shingle² *n.* **1.** Gravel consisting of rounded, water-worn stones of various sizes, often found on beaches. **2.** A stretch of shore covered with such gravel. [16th century : origin obscure.] **—shin•gly** *adj.*

shingle³ *tr.v.* **-gled, -gling, -gles.** To hammer the slag out of (puddled iron) during the manufacture of wrought iron. [French *cingler,* from German *zängeln,* from *Zange,* TONG(S).]

shin•gles (shĭng′gəlz) *pl.n. Used with a singular or plural verb. Pathology.* An infection caused by chickenpox viruses and characterized by skin eruptions along the routes of cutaneous nerves on one side of the body, often accompanied or followed by severe neuralgia. The virus may remain latent within the body between outbreaks. Also called "herpes zoster," "zoster." [Middle English, from Medieval Latin *cingulus,* from Latin *cingulum,* girdle, from *cingere,* to gird.]

shin•ny¹ (shĭn′ē) *v.* **-nied, -nying, -nies.** *Informal.* —*intr.* To climb by shinning. —*tr.* To climb (a rope, for example) by shinning.

shinny² *n.* Also **shin•ty** (shĭn′tē). **1.** A simple form of hockey played by schoolboys. **2.** The curved stick used in this game. [Probably from *shin ye, shin t'ye,* "shin to you," a cry used in the game.]

shin•plas•ter (shĭn′plăs′tər, -pläs′tər) *n.* **1.** A note of paper currency issued privately; especially, such a note devalued by lack of backing or by inflation. **2.** *Australian.* A promissory note used in the outback as currency. [From the comparison of such notes to cheap brown paper used in plasters for sore legs.]

Shin•to (shĭn′tō) *n.* Also **Shin•to•ism** (-ĭz′əm). The indigenous religion of Japan, marked by the veneration of nature spirits and of ancestors. [Japanese *shintō,* "the way of the gods" : *shin,* from Chinese *shén,* god(s) + *tō,* for *do,* way, from Mandarin Chinese *dào,* way.] **—Shin•to•ist** *n. & adj.*

shin•y (shī′nē) *adj.* **-ier, -iest.** Having a surface that reflects light, as: **1.** Glossy; glistening: *shiny satin.* **2.** Bright; polished: *shiny shoes.* **3.** Clear; shining: *shiny-eyed.* **4.** Worn away so as to appear smooth and glossy. Said of fabric. **—shin•i•ness** *n.*

ship (shĭp) *n.* **1.** Any vessel of considerable size adapted for deep-water navigation and powered by wind or engines. **2.** A three-masted sailing vessel with square mainsails on all masts. **3.** *Maritime Law.* A vessel intended for marine transport, without regard to form, rig, or means of propulsion. **4.** A ship's company. **5.** A spaceship or airship. **—dress ship.** To display the ensign, signal flags, and bunting on a ship.

~*v.* **shipped, shipping, ships.** —*tr.* **1.** To place or take on board a ship. **2. a.** To send or transport. **b.** *Informal.* To dispatch to a specified destination. **3.** To bring into a vessel; especially, to lift (oars) from the water and place inside the boat without removing them from the rowlocks. **4.** To take in (water) over the side. **5.** To set (a mast or rudder, for example) in place for use. —*intr.* **1.** To go or travel by means of a ship. **2.** To hire oneself out or enlist for

PRONUNCIATION KEY

ă, pat; ā, pay; âr, care;
ä, father, are; b, bib;
ch, church; d, deed; ĕ, pet;
ē, be; f, fife; g, gag; h, hat;
hw, which; ĭ, pit; ī, pie;
îr, pier; j, judge; k, kick;
l, lid, needle; m, mum;
n, no, sudden; ng, thing;
ŏ, pot; ō, toe; ô, paw, for;
oi, noise; ou, out; o͝o, book;
o͞o, boot; p, pop; r, roar;
s, sauce; sh, ship, dish;
t, tight; th, thin, path;
th, this, bathe; ŭ, cut; ûr, fur;
v, valve; w, with; y, yes;
z, zebra, size; zh, vision;
ə, about, item, edible, gallop, circus, peaceful

IN FOREIGN WORDS:

à, *Fr.* ami; œ, *Fr.* feu, *Ger.* schön; ü, *Fr.* tu, *Ger.* über;
KH, *Ger.* ich, *Scot.* loch;
N, *Fr.* bon; y', *Fr.* Compiègne

STRESS MARKS:

Primary stress: ′
in•cite′ (ĭn-sīt′)
Secondary stress: ′
in′sight′ (ĭn′sīt′)

service on a ship. [Middle English *s(c)hip,* Old English *scip.*]

-ship *suffix.* Indicates: **1.** The quality or condition of; for example, **friendship, scholarship. 2.** The status, rank, or office of; for example, **professorship, authorship. 3.** The art or skill of; for example, **penmanship, leadership.** [Middle English *-s(c)hip(e),* Old English *-scipe.*]

ship·board (shĭp′bôrd′, -bōrd′) *n. Obsolete.* The side of a ship. **—on shipboard.** On board a ship.
∼*adj.* Occurring on board a ship: *a shipboard romance.*

ship·build·ing (shĭp′bĭl′dĭng) *n.* The industry or occupation of constructing ships. **—ship·build·er** *n.*

ship canal *n.* A canal deep enough for ships. Also called "shipway."

ship chandler *n.* A person who deals in equipment for ships.

ship fever *n.* **Typhus** *(see),* especially as it formerly occurred on overcrowded ships.

ship·load (shĭp′lōd′) *n.* **1.** The cargo or passengers carried by a ship. **2.** A capacity cargo for a ship.

ship·man (shĭp′mən) *n., pl.* **-men** (-mĭn). *Archaic.* **1.** A sailor. **2.** A shipmaster.

ship·mas·ter (shĭp′măs′tər, -mäs′tər) *n.* The master or captain of a ship.

ship·mate (shĭp′māt′) *n.* A sailor serving on the same ship as another; a fellow sailor.

ship·ment (shĭp′mənt) *n. Abbr.* **shpt. 1.** The act of sending or transporting goods. **2.** A quantity of goods or cargo transported.

ship of the line *n.* Formerly, a warship large enough to take a position in the line of battle.

ship·per (shĭp′ər) *n.* A person or company that consigns or receives goods for shipping; a shipping agent.

ship·ping (shĭp′ĭng) *n.* **1.** The act or business of transporting goods, especially by ship. **2.** The body of ships belonging to one port, industry, or country, often referred to in aggregate tonnage. **3.** Ships collectively.

shipping clerk *n.* A person employed to manage the shipment or receipt of goods.

shipping lane *n.* A regular or prescribed route for ships.

ship-rigged (shĭp′rĭgd′) *adj. Nautical.* Rigged as a ship, with three or more masts and square sails.

ship's biscuit *n.* A type of bread, **hardtack** *(see).*

ship·shape (shĭp′shāp′) *adj.* Neatly arranged; orderly; tidy. [Originally, "arranged in a manner befitting a ship" (said of rigging).] **—ship·shape** *adv.*

ship's papers *pl.n.* The documents giving details of ownership, nationality, destination, or the like that international law requires a ship to carry and be able to provide on demand for inspection.

ship-to-shore (shĭp′tə-shôr′, -shōr′) *adj.* In operation between a ship and the shore. Said of a radio system. **—ship-to-shore** *adv.*

ship·way (shĭp′wā′) *n.* **1.** The structure supporting a ship during construction or in dry dock. **2.** A **ship canal** *(see).*

ship·worm (shĭp′wûrm′) *n.* Any of various wormlike marine mollusks of the genera *Teredo* and *Bankia,* having rudimentary shells with which they bore into wood, often doing extensive damage.

ship·wreck (shĭp′rĕk′) *n.* **1.** The destruction of a ship, as by storm or collision. **2.** The remains of a wrecked ship. **3.** Complete failure or ruin: *the shipwreck of all our hopes.*
∼*tr.v.* **shipwrecked, -wrecking, -wrecks. 1.** To cause (a ship or its passengers) to suffer shipwreck. **2.** To ruin utterly. [Earlier *shipwrack,* Middle English *shipwrak,* Old English *scipwræc,* cargo thrown overboard to lighten a ship in danger : SHIP + *wræc,* thing driven by the sea, WRACK.]

ship·wright (shĭp′rīt′) *n.* A skilled worker, such as a carpenter, employed in the construction or maintenance of ships.

ship·yard (shĭp′yärd′) *n.* A place where ships are built or repaired.

Shi·raz (shĭ-räz′). City in southwestern Iran, the capital of Fars province. It has been a leading commercial and administrative town since the 8th century. It is noted especially for its metalwork, wines, and carpets.

shire (shīr) *n.* Any of the counties of the United Kingdom. Used chiefly in combination: *Lancashire.* [Old English *scir*†.]

shire horse *n.* A large, powerful draft horse of a breed originating in the shires of Lincoln, Cambridge, or Huntingdon.

shirk (shûrk) *v.* **shirked, shirking, shirks.** *—tr.* To put off or avoid discharging (work or duties). *—intr.* To avoid work or duty.
∼*n.* A person who avoids work or duty. Also called "shirker." [From obsolete *shirk,* parasite, rogue, probably from German *Schurke,* scoundrel, perhaps from Old High German *(fiur)-scurgo,* "fire stirrer," stoker, hence devil (as an infernal stoker), from *scurigen,* to poke.]

Shir·ley poppy (shûr′lē) *n.* A variety of the field poppy having scarlet, pink, or salmon single or double flowers. [After *Shirley* Vicarage, Croydon, Surrey, England, where it was first grown.]

shirr (shûr) *tr.v.* **shirred, shirring, shirrs. 1.** To gather (cloth) into decorative parallel rows using fine elastic thread. **2.** To cook (eggs) by baking unshelled in molds.
∼*n.* A decorative gathering of cloth into parallel rows. Also called "shirring." [19th century : origin obscure.]

shirt (shûrt) *n.* A garment for the upper part of the body, especially a man's, typically made of light fabric and having a collar, long or short sleeves, and a buttoned front opening. **—keep one's shirt on.** *Slang.* To remain calm or patient. **—lose one's shirt.** *Slang.* To lose everything one has or owns. [Middle English *sherte, scurte,* Old English *scyrte;* akin to Old Norse *skyrta* (whence SKIRT), from Germanic *skurt-* (unattested), SHORT.]

shirt·ing (shûr′tĭng) *n.* Fabric suitable for making shirts.

shirt·sleeve (shûrt′slēv′) *n.* A sleeve of a shirt.
∼*adj.* Also **shirt·sleeved** (shûrt′slēvd′) **1.** Dressed informally, without a coat or jacket: *shirtsleeve spectators.* **2.** Calling for the removal of coats or jackets: *shirtsleeve weather.* **3.** Informal and direct: *shirtsleeve negotiations.*

shirt·tail (shûrt′tāl′) *n.* **1.** The part of a shirt that extends below the waist, especially in the back. **2.** Something that is small, inadequate, or of little value.
∼*adj.* **1.** Very young or immature: *shirttail kids.* **2.** Of small size or little value; puny.

shirt·waist (shûrt′wāst′) *n.* **1.** A woman's tailored shirt, with details copied from men's shirts. **2.** A woman's dress with the bodice styled like a tailored shirt.

shish ke·bab (shĭsh′ kə-bŏb′, -băb′) *n.* Also **shish ke·bob, shish ka·bob** (-bŏb′). A dish consisting of pieces of seasoned marinated meat cooked on skewers, often over charcoal. Also called "kebab," "kebob." [Turkish *şiş kebabiu* : *şiş,* skewer + *kebap,* roast meat.]

shit·tim·wood (shĭt′əm-wo͝od′) *n.* **1.** A tree, probably a species of acacia, that was a source of a wood mentioned frequently in the Bible. Also called "shittah tree." **2.** The wood of this tree, used to make the ark of the Tabernacle. Exodus 25:10. [Hebrew *shiṭṭīm,* plural of *shiṭṭāh,* related to Egyptian *sont,* acacia.]

shiv (shĭv) *n. Slang.* A knife or razor, especially when considered as a weapon. [Romany *chiv*†, "blade."]

shi·va, shi·vah (shĭv′ə) *n. Judaism.* A seven-day period of formal mourning observed after the funeral of a close relative. [Yiddish, from Hebrew *shiv'āh,* seven.]

Shi·va (shē′və). Also **Si·va** (shē′və, sē′-) *Hinduism.* The god of destruction and reproduction, a member of the Hindu triad along with Brahma and Vishnu. [Sanskrit *Śiva,* "the auspicious (one)," from *siva,* auspicious, dear.] **—Shi·va·ism** *n.* **—Shi·va·ist** *n.*

shivaree. Variant of **charivari.**

shiv·er[1] (shĭv′ər) *v.* **-ered, -ering, -ers.** *—intr.* **1.** To shudder or shake, as from cold or excitement; tremble. **2.** To quiver or vibrate, as by the force of wind. *—tr. Nautical.* To cause (a sail) to flutter in the wind. **—**See Synonyms at **shake.**
∼*n.* **1.** An act of shivering; a tremble. **2.** *Often* **shivers.** A tingling sensation caused by fear, excitement, or the like: *It sent shivers up my spine.* [Middle English *shiveren,* earlier *chiveren,* perhaps alteration of *chevelen,* to shiver, originally "to chatter" (used of teeth), from Old English *ceafl,* the jaw.]

shiver[2] *v.* **-ered, -ering, -ers.** *—intr.* To break into fragments or splinters; shatter. *—tr.* To cause to break into fragments. **—**See Synonyms at **break.** [Middle English, from *scivre,* fragment, perhaps of Low German origin, akin to Middle Low German *schever.*]

shiv·er·y[1] (shĭv′ər-ē) *adj.* **1.** Trembling, as from cold or fear. **2.** Making one shiver with cold or fear; chilling.

shivery[2] *adj.* Easily broken; brittle.

Shko·dër (shkō′dər). City in Albania, capital of Shkodër province. It is the manufacturing and cultural center of northern Albania.

S.H.M. simple harmonic motion.

shmo. Variant of **schmo.**

shoal[1] (shōl) *n.* **1.** A shallow area in any body of water. **2.** An elevation of the bottom of a body of water, constituting a hazard to navigation; a sandbank or sandbar.
∼ *v.* **shoaled, shoaling, shoals.** *—intr.* To become shallow. *—tr.* **1.** To make shallow. **2.** To come or sail into a shallower area of (water): *The ship shoaled water.*
∼*adj.* Having little depth; shallow. [Middle English *schald, sholde,* originally "shallow," Old English *sc(e)ald,* from Germanic *skaldaz* (unattested).] **—shoal·y** *adj.*

Usage: *shoal, reef, bar, bank.* These nouns have reference to elevations of ground under water. A *shoal* is an elevation coming close to but not above the surface of the water. The term is also applied to the shallow area thus formed. A *reef* is a ridge, usually of rock or coral, extending near or slightly above the low-tide mark. A *bar* is a ridge, usually of sand, near the surface and often exposed at low water. A *bank* in this comparison is a large, totally submerged plateau of mud or sand that is not a danger to shipping.

shoal[2] *n.* **1.** A large group; a crowd. **2.** A school of fish or other marine animals.
∼*intr.v.* **shoaled, shoaling, shoals.** To come together in a shoal. [Probably from Middle Dutch or Middle Low German *schōle.* See **school** (of fish).]

shoat, shote (shōt) *n.* A young pig just after weaning. [Middle English *shote,* probably Low German origin, akin to West Flemish *schote.*]

shock[1] (shŏk) *n.* **1.** A violent collision or impact; a heavy blow. **2.** Something that jars the mind or emotions as if with a violent, unexpected blow. **3.** The disturbance of function, equilibrium, or emotional and mental state caused by such a blow. **4.** *Pathology.* A generally temporary state of massive physiological reaction to bodily damage or emotional trauma, usually characterized by a cold sweat, marked loss of blood pressure, and the depression of vital processes such as respiration. **5.** The sensation and muscular spasm caused by an electric current passing through the body or through a bodily part. **6. Shock therapy** *(see).*
∼*v.* **shocked, shocking, shocks.** *—tr.* **1.** To strike with great surprise and agitation. **2.** To fill with a powerful feeling of disgust, incredulity, or horror; outrage; scandalize. **3.** To induce a state of

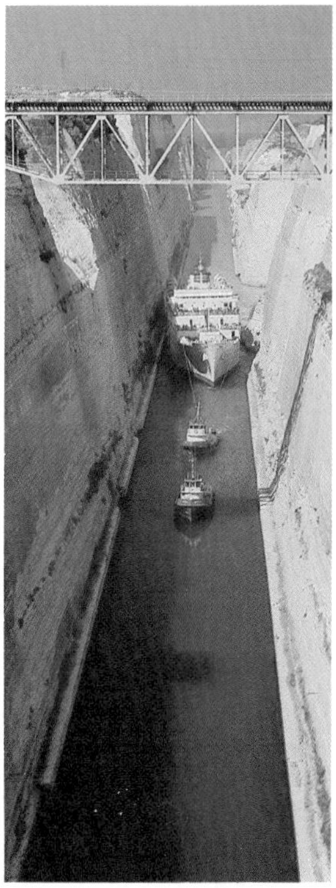

ship canal *A manmade canal large enough to carry oceangoing vessels. Some—such as the St. Lawrence Seaway—link the sea to inland ports. Others—such as the Corinth Canal shown here—link two seas. The canal, which is 6.4 kilometers (4 miles) long, cuts through the Isthmus of Corinth in Greece to join the Ionian Sea and the Aegean Sea.*

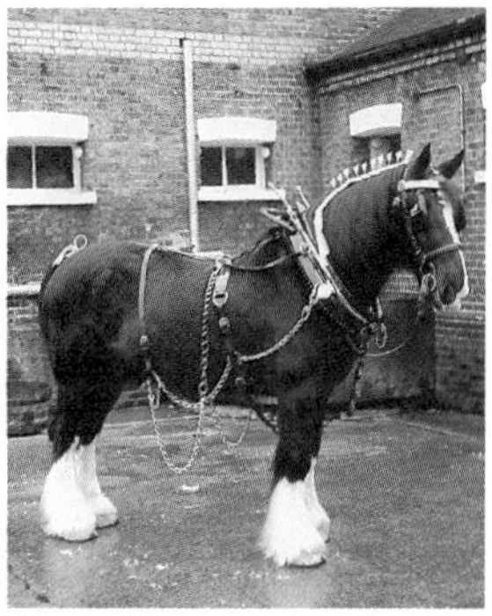

shire horse *These large English-bred horses are still used as draft horses on farms in some parts of the country. But they are more often seen at shows in decorative livery, as here. Shires usually have a white blaze and white "feathered" feet, and can be up to 17.3 hands tall at the shoulder—almost 1.8 meters (6 feet).*

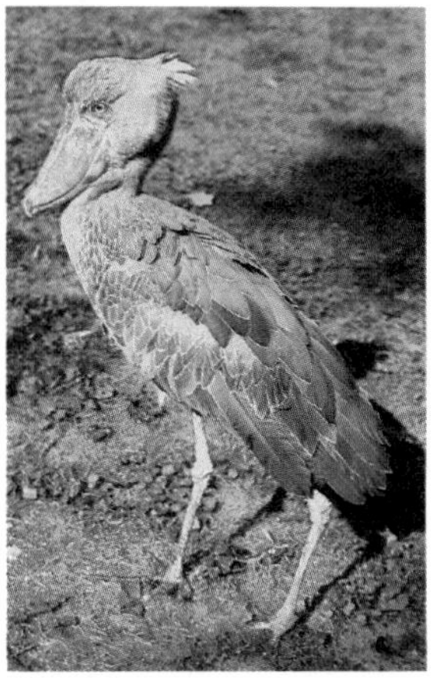

shoebill *The capacious beak of the shoebill, also known as the shoe-billed stork, helps the bird to forage for lungfish, frogs, and baby crocodiles in the swamps of East Africa where it lives.*

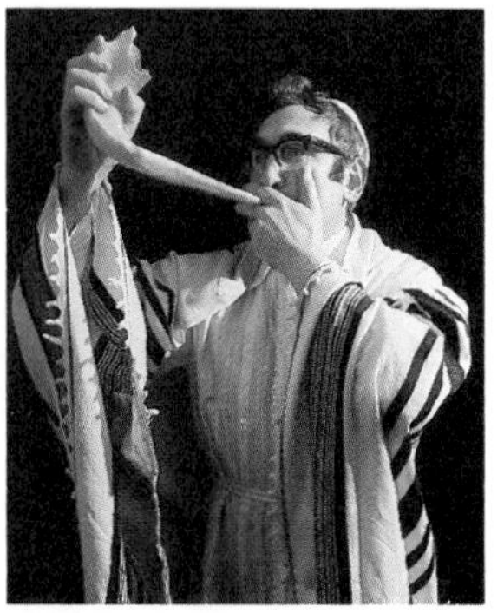

shofar *An ancient Hebrew instrument made from a ram's horn and used originally to sound a warning or summons. Today it is used ceremonially at Jewish religious festivals.*

shock in (a person). **4.** To subject (an animal or person) to an electric shock. *—intr.* **1.** To be susceptible to shock. **2.** *Archaic.* To come into contact violently, as in battle; collide. [French *choc,* from *choquer†,* to strike (with fear).] **—shock•a•ble** *adj.*

shock[2] *n.* A number of sheaves of corn stacked upright in a field for drying.
~tr.v. **shocked, shocking, shocks.** To gather (sheaves of corn) into shocks. [Middle English *shokke,* probably from Middle Dutch or Middle Low German *schok,* shock, group of sixty, akin to Old Saxon *scok†.*]

shock[3] *n.* A thick, shaggy, heavy mass: *a shock of hair.*
~adj. Thick and shaggy. [Perhaps from SHOCK (stack).]

shock absorber *n.* Any of various devices used to absorb mechanical shocks; especially, a hydraulically damped coupling used to absorb impulsive forces generated by the contact of the wheels of a motor vehicle with irregular road surfaces.

shock•er (shŏk′ər) *n.* One that startles, shocks, or horrifies; especially, a sensational story or novel.

shock-head•ed (shŏk′hĕd′ĭd) *adj.* Having thick, shaggy hair.

shock•ing (shŏk′ĭng) *adj.* **1.** Highly disturbing emotionally. **2.** Highly offensive; indecent or distasteful. **3.** Very vivid or intense in tone or color. **4.** *Informal.* Nasty; very bad. **—shock•ing•ly** *adv.*

Shock•ley (shŏk′lē), **William Bradford** (1910–). U.S. physicist, born in England. He directed U.S. naval research into antisubmarine warfare during World War II, and in 1948 developed the transistor jointly with John Bardeen (1908–) and Walter Houser Brattain (1902–). The three were awarded the 1956 Nobel Prize in physics for their work.

shock•proof (shŏk′pro͞of′) *adj.* Able to withstand the effects of collisions or blows.

shock stall *n. Aeronautics.* Air resistance on an aircraft when it is close to the speed of sound that may lead to stalling.

shock therapy *n.* The inducing of shock by electric current or drugs, sometimes causing convulsions, as a therapy for mental illness. Also called "shock," "shock treatment."

shock treatment *n.* **1.** Shock therapy. **2.** Any brutally direct approach to a problem.

shock troops *pl.n. Military.* Highly experienced and capable soldiers specially trained to lead attacks.

shock tube *n. Physics.* A long tube in which a shock wave can be produced for spectroscopic investigation of radicals and excited molecules formed by the high temperature of the wave.

shock wave *n.* A large-amplitude compression wave, such as that produced by an explosion or by supersonic motion of a body in a medium.

shod•dy (shŏd′ē) *n., pl.* **-dies. 1.** Wool fibers obtained by shredding unfelted woolen or worsted rags or worn garments. **2.** Yarn, fabric, or garments made from or containing such recycled wool fibers. **3.** Inferior or imitation goods; cheap, derivative material.
~adj. **shoddier, -iest. 1.** Transparently imitative or inferior. **2.** Of poor quality or workmanship; trashy. **3.** Made of or containing shoddy or other inferior material. [19th century : of obscure (dialectal) origin.] **—shod•di•ly** *adv.* **—shod•di•ness** *n.*

shoe (sho͞o) *n., pl.* **shoes** or *archaic* **shoon** (sho͞on). **1.** A durable covering for the human foot; especially, either of a matched pair made of leather or similar material reaching about to the ankle and having a rigid sole and a heel of variable height. **2.** A horseshoe. **3.** A part or device placed at an end, foot, or bottom, especially: **a.** A strip of metal fitted onto the bottom of a sled runner. **b.** A skid placed under the wheel of a vehicle to retard its motion. **c.** A metal or rubber rim or casing protecting the bottom end of a walking stick, cane, or the like. **4.** The part of a brake that presses against the wheel or drum to retard its motion. **5.** The sliding contact plate on an electric train or tram that conducts electricity from the third rail. **6.** An oblong box used for holding and dealing cards in some gambling card games in which several packs of cards are used. **—fill someone's shoes.** To take the place of; succeed (another). **—in someone's shoes.** In someone else's position or predicament: *I wouldn't want to be in his shoes.*
~tr.v. **shod** (shŏd), **shod** or **shodden** (shŏd′n), **shoeing, shoes. 1.** To furnish or fit with shoes. **2.** To cover with a wooden or metal guard to protect against wear. [Middle English *sho(o),* Old English *scōh,* from Germanic *skōhaz* (unattested).]

shoe•bill (sho͞o′bĭl′) *n.* A tall wading bird, *Balaeniceps rex,* native to swampy regions of eastern tropical Africa, and having slaty plumage, long black legs, a stubby neck, and a large shoelike bill with a hook on the upper mandible.

shoe•horn (sho͞o′hôrn′) *n.* A curved implement, often of horn or smooth metal, inserted at the heel to help slip on a shoe.
~tr.v. **shoehorned, -horning, -horns.** To squeeze into an insufficient space.

shoe•lace (sho͞o′lās′) *n.* A string or cord used for lacing and fastening a shoe.

shoe•mak•er (sho͞o′mā′kər) *n.* A person who makes or repairs shoes and boots as an occupation. **—shoe•mak•ing** *n.*

sho•er (sho͞o′ər) *n.* A person who shoes horses; a blacksmith.

shoe•string (sho͞o′strĭng′) *n.* **1.** A shoelace. **2.** A small sum of money; barely adequate funds: *living on a shoestring.*
~adj. **1.** Having or using a barely adequate amount, especially of money. **2.** Cut to or in the shape of a shoestring; long and slender: *shoestring potatoes.*

shoe•tree (sho͞o′trē′) *n.* A foot-shaped form inserted into a shoe when it is not being worn to preserve its shape.

sho•far, sho•phar (shō′fär′, -fər) *n., pl.* **-fars** or **shofroth** (shō-frōt′, -frōth′), **-phars** or **shophroth.** *Judaism.* A trumpet made of a ram's horn, blown for warning, summoning, and ritual purposes by the ancient Hebrews, and now sounded in the synagogue at Rosh Hashanah and Yom Kippur. [Hebrew *shōphār,* "ram's horn."]

sho•gun (shō′gŭn′, -go͞on′) *n.* Any of a line of military leaders of Japan who, until 1867, exercised absolute rule under the nominal leadership of the emperor. [Japanese *shōgun,* "general," from Chinese *jiāng jūn : jiāng,* to lead, command + *jūn,* army.]

sho•gun•ate (shō′gən-ĭt, -āt′) *n. Sometimes* **Shogunate.** The government of a shogun.

sho•ji (shō′jē) *n., pl.* **shoji** or **-jis.** A translucent paper screen forming a sliding door or partition in a Japanese house. [Japanese *shōji,* from Chinese *zhàngzi.*]

Sho•lem A•lei•chem (shô′ləm ə-lā′KHəm), pen name of Sholem Yakov Rabinowitz (1859–1916). Russian writer, known for his Yiddish tales, which are celebrated for their homespun wisdom. He settled in the United States at the outbreak of World War I.

Sho•lo•khov (shô′lə-kôf′, -kôv′), **Mikhail Alexandrovich** (1905–). Russian novelist. The four-part novel by which he is best known was published in English as *And Quiet Flows the Don* (1934) and *The Don Flows Home to the Sea* (1940); the work spans the pre- and post-revolutionary periods and has been acclaimed in the U.S.S.R. as an outstanding example of socialist realism. Sholokhov was awarded the 1965 Nobel Prize for literature.

Sho•na (shŏn′ə) *n., pl.* **-nas** or collectively **Shona.** Also **Ma•sho•na** (mə-shŏn′ə), *pl.* **-nas** or collectively **Mashona. 1.** A member of any of various closely related groups of southern African people, living chiefly in Zimbabwe. **2.** The Bantu language of this people. **—Sho•na** *adj.*

shone. Past tense and past participle of **shine.**

shoo (sho͞o) *interj.* Used to scare away animals or birds.
~v. **shooed, shooing, shoos.** *—tr.* To drive or scare away, as by crying "shoo." *—intr.* To cry "shoo." [Middle English *schowe* (imitative).]

shoo•fly (sho͞o′flī′) *n., pl.* **-flies. 1.** A child's rocker having the seat built between two sides cut in the shape of an animal. **2.** *Slang.* An undercover police officer who checks on the performance and honesty of other police officers. [SHOO + FLY (insect).]

shoofly pie *n.* A pie with a filling of molasses and brown sugar and a buttery, sprinkled topping.

shoo-in (sho͞o′ĭn) *n. Informal.* A contestant or candidate who seems certain of winning.

shook[1] (sho͝ok) *n.* **1.** A set of parts for assembling a barrel or packing case. **2.** A shock of grain. [18th century : origin obscure.]

shook[2]. Past tense of **shake.**

shook-up (sho͝ok′ŭp′) *adj. Slang.* Emotionally upset.

shoon. *Archaic.* Plural of **shoe.**

shoot (sho͞ot) *v.* **shot** (shŏt), **shooting, shoots.** *—tr.* **1.** To hit, wound, or kill with a missile fired from a weapon; especially, to kill with a bullet. **2.** To fire or let fly (a missile) from a weapon. **3.** To discharge or fire (a weapon). **4.** To cause to move directly and swiftly by or as if by a sudden release of tension. **5.** To send forth swiftly or dartingly: *She shot a look of contempt at him.* **6.** To pass over or through swiftly: *shoot the rapids.* **7.** To cover (country) in hunting for game. **8.** To record in photographs or on film. **9.** To put forth; begin to grow or produce; generate. Used especially of a plant. **10.** To pour, empty out, or discharge down or as if down a chute. **11.** To variegate with streaks or threads of a different color: *a black coat shot with gray.* **12.** In golf, to make (a specified number of strokes). **13.** *Sports.* **a.** To move or propel (a ball), as by hitting or kicking, toward a goal. **b.** To score (a goal). **c.** To play (golf, craps, or pool). **14.** To slide into or out of a fastening: *shoot a door bolt.* **15.** To measure the altitude of with a sextant or other instrument: *shoot a star.* **16.** *Informal.* To inject (a drug) by means of a hypodermic needle. *—intr.* **1.** To discharge a missile from a weapon. **2.** To discharge fire; go off. **3.** To move swiftly, as if discharged from a weapon; dart: *shot past in a car; Pain shot through his leg.* **4.** To protrude; extend; project. **5.** To hunt game with a weapon: *shoot in the marshes.* **6.** To put forth new growth; germinate; sprout. **7. a.** To take pictures; film. **b.** To start filming. **8.** To propel a ball, as by kicking or hitting, toward the goal. **9.** To aim; strive: *shoot for the top of her profession.* **10.** To begin questioning someone. Used in the imperative. **—shoot down. 1.** To bring down (an aircraft, for example) by hitting and damaging with a missile. **2.** *Informal.* **a.** To ruin the plans, hopes, or aspirations of. **b.** To show (a plan or idea, for example) to be impractical or invalid. **—shoot up. 1.** *Informal.* **a.** To grow or get taller rapidly. **b.** To rise or increase rapidly. **2.** *Informal.* To hit many times with shot or other projectiles. **3.** *Informal.* To terrorize (an area) by lawless, wild shooting. **4.** *Slang.* To inject (a narcotic drug) directly into a vein.
~n. **1.** The motion or movement of something that is shot; a forward or upward advance. **2. a.** The young growth arising from a germinating seed; a sprout. **b.** A bud or young leaf on a plant. **3.** Any new growing part. **4.** A narrow and swift or turbulent section of a stream; a rapid. **5.** An inclined channel through which something, such as timber, can be shot; chute. **6. a.** A party or expedition engaged in shooting game. **b.** Land where game may be shot. **7.** *Informal.* The launching of a rocket or similar missile. **8.** An act of or occasion for filming. **9.** In rowing, the interval between strokes. [Middle English *shoten,* past *shote,* past participle *shote(n),* Old English *scēotan, scēat* (past singular), *scoten.*]

shoot•er (sho͞o′tər) *n.* **1.** One that shoots. **2.** *Slang.* A firearm.

shooting gallery *n.* An enclosed target range for shooting practice or competition.

shooting iron *n. Informal.* A firearm, such as a pistol.

shooting script *n.* A script giving details of camerawork, including the order in which sequences are to be shot.

shooting star *n.* **1.** A briefly visible meteor *(see).* **2.** Any of several North American plants of the genus *Dodecatheon,* having nodding flowers with reflexed petals.

shooting stick *n.* A type of walking stick opening into a seat at one end, typically used by spectators at races.

shoot-out (shoot′out′) *n.* A confrontation in which armed opponents fire guns at one another.

shop (shŏp) *n.* **1.** A place, such as a building or room, where retail goods or certain services can be obtained. **2.** A workshop for the manufacture or repair of machinery: *a machine shop.* **3.** *Informal.* **a.** Any commercial or industrial establishment. **b.** A business or other similar activity: *set up shop; close up shop.* **4.** A home workshop. **5. a.** A schoolroom equipped with tools and machinery for instruction in the manual arts. **b.** The manual arts as a technical science or course of study. —**talk shop.** To talk about one's business or occupation, especially to the exclusion of other topics. ~*v.* **shopped, shopping, shops.** —*intr.* **1.** To visit shops for the purpose of looking for and buying goods. Often used with *for.* **2.** To search for something with the intention of acquiring it. —*tr. British Slang.* To betray to the police. —**shop around. 1.** To investigate the different prices and quality of competing goods or services before deciding on a purchase. **2.** To investigate a number of possibilities before deciding on a course of action. [Middle English *shoppe,* Old English *sceoppa,* booth, stall, from Germanic *skupp-* (unattested).]

shop floor *n.* **1.** The area, in a factory for example, where manual workers, as opposed to management, operate. **2.** These workers, especially when organized as a union. —**shop-floor** *adj.*

shophar. Variant of **shofar.**

shop·keep·er (shŏp′kē′pər) *n.* An owner or manager of a shop.

shop·lift·er (shŏp′lĭf′tər) *n.* One who steals goods on display in a shop. —**shop·lift** *v.* —**shop·lift·ing** *n.*

shop·per (shŏp′ər) *n.* One who buys goods at shops; a customer.

shopping bag *n.* A strong bag with handles, designed for carrying a shopper's purchases.

shopping center *n.* A group of shops and stores forming a central retail market within a given rural or suburban area.

shopping mall *n.* **1.** An urban shopping area limited to pedestrians. **2.** A shopping center with stores facing an enclosed walkway for pedestrians.

shop steward *n.* A union member chosen by fellow workers to represent them in their dealings with the management.

shop·talk (shŏp′tôk′) *n.* Talk or conversation concerning one's business or occupation.

shop·worn (shŏp′wôrn′) *adj.* **1.** Worn, frayed, tarnished, or otherwise defective from being on display in a store. **2.** Worn-out; exhausted. **3.** Trite; hackneyed: *shopworn anecdotes.*

sho·ran (shôr′ăn′, shōr′-) *n.* A relatively short-range radar navigation system by which a ship or aircraft can determine its position with high precision by measuring the times required for a radio signal to reach each of two ground stations of known position and to return. [*Sho*rt *ra*nge *n*avigation.]

shore¹ (shôr, shōr) *n.* **1.** The land along the edge of an ocean, sea, lake, or river. **2.** Land: *set foot on shore.* **3.** *Often* **shores.** A country: *When will you see these shores again?* ~*v.tr.* **shored, shoring, shores.** To put or set on shore. [Middle English, from Middle Dutch and Middle Low German *schore*†.]

shore² *tr.v.* **shored, shoring, shores.** To prop up or support with or as if with an inclined timber. Usually used with *up.* ~*n.* A beam or timber propped against a ship, wall, or other structure as a temporary support. [Middle English, *shoren,* from Middle Dutch *schoren*†.]

shore³ *Archaic.* Past tense of **shear.**

shore bird *n.* Any of various birds, such as the sandpiper, plover, or snipe, that frequent the shores of coastal or inland waters.

shore leave *n.* **1.** Permission granted to a sailor to spend time ashore. **2.** The amount of time so allowed.

shore·line (shôr′līn′, shōr′-) *n.* The line marking the edge of a body of water.

shor·ing (shôr′ĭng, shōr′-) *n.* A system of shores or props used for supporting something.

shorn. Alternate past participle of **shear.**

short (shôrt) *adj.* **shorter, shortest. 1.** Having little length; not long: *a short corridor; short arms.* **2.** Having little height; not tall; low: *Jockeys must be short.* **3.** Having a small extent in time; brief. **4.** Not attaining that which is required; inadequate; insufficient: *in short supply.* **5.** Lacking the required length, extent, or amount: *a plank two inches short.* **6.** Lacking; inadequately supplied with something: *I would lend you some money, but I'm short.* **7.** Not lengthy; concise; succinct: *short and to the point.* **8.** *Finance.* **a.** Not owning the stocks or commodities one is selling. **b.** Pertaining to or designating a sale of stocks or goods not yet owned by the seller, but which the seller must produce to meet the terms of a contract. **9.** Lacking in retentiveness: *a short memory.* **10.** Rudely brief; abrupt; curt. **11.** Containing shortening; crisp; friable: *short pastry.* **12.** In prosody, designating a syllable that is of relatively brief duration in classical verse and unstressed in English verse. **13.** *Phonetics.* **a.** Designating a particular pronunciation of the letters for the vowel sounds, such as the sound of (ă) in *pan,* of (ĕ) in *pen,* of (ĭ) in *pin,* of (ŏ) in *pond,* of (oo) in *put,* and of (ŭ) in *putt,* as distinguished from the sound of (ā) in *pane,* of (ē) in *penal,* of (ī) in *pine,* of (ō) in *post,* and of (oo) in *poop.* **b.** Designating a speech sound of relatively brief duration, as opposed to the same or similar sound of relatively long duration. —**in short.** To sum up concisely. —**short of. 1.** Not equivalent to; less than: *something short of a mile.* **2.** Lacking a sufficient amount of: *short of breath.* **3.** Without reaching an extreme; almost including: *took every step short of mining his back garden.* **4.** Except for; apart from: *Short of buying a car, I don't know how I'll get in to work.* —**short on.** Lacking in: *short on ideas.* ~*adv.* **1.** Abruptly; suddenly: *stop short.* **2.** Rudely; crossly. **3.** Concisely. **4.** Without owning what one is selling: *sell short.* —**caught** (or **taken**) **short.** Unexpectedly lacking what is necessary. —**fall short.** To fail to meet expectations or requirements. ~*n.* **1.** Anything that is short, especially: **a.** A briefly articulated or unaccented syllable. **b.** A short vowel. **c.** A short sale, or a person who sells short. **d. shorts.** Short trousers extending to the knee or above. **e. shorts.** Men's underpants. **f.** A short motion-picture. **short subject** *(see).* **2. shorts.** A by-product of wheat processing, consisting of bran mixed with coarse meal or flour. **3. a.** A short circuit. **b.** A malfunction caused by a short circuit. **4.** *Baseball.* A shortstop. ~*v.* **shorted, shorting, shorts.** —*tr.* **1.** To cause a short circuit in. **2.** *Informal.* To give (a person) less than is right or proper; short-change. —*intr.* To short-circuit. [Middle English *short,* Old English *sceort,* from Germanic *skurtaz* (unattested).] —**short·ish** *adj.* —**short·ness** *n.*

short account *n.* The account of a person who sells short.

short·age (shôr′tĭj) *n.* A deficiency in amount; a deficit.

short-arm (shôrt′ärm′) *adj.* Designating a blow in which the arm is kept in a bent position rather than punched out straight.

short·bread (shôrt′brĕd′) *n.* A type of rich, crumbly biscuit made with flour, sugar, and butter.

short·cake (shôrt′kāk′) **1.** A dessert consisting of a cake made with rich biscuit dough, split and filled with strawberries or other fruit, and topped with cream. **2.** A type of rich semisweet biscuit, similar to shortbread.

short·change (shôrt′chānj′) *tr.v.* **-changed, -changing, -changes. 1.** To give less change than is due. **2.** *Informal.* To swindle, cheat, or trick. —**short·chang·er** *n.*

short circuit *n.* An accidentally established low-resistance connection between two points in an electric circuit that bypasses the load and causes an excessive current to flow. Also called "short."

short-cir·cuit (shôrt′sûr′kĭt) *v.* **-cuited, -cuiting, -cuits.** —*tr.* **1.** To cause to have a short circuit. **2.** To avoid; bypass. **3.** *Informal.* To stop the progress of; impede; block. —*intr.* To become affected with a short circuit.

short·com·ing (shôrt′kŭm′ĭng) *n.* A deficiency or flaw.

short covering *n.* The buying of securities, stocks, or commodities to make provision for a short sale.

short cut *n.* **1.** A quicker, more direct route than the customary one. **2.** Any means of speeding up a process: *Becoming famous is a short-cut to getting your book published.*

short-dat·ed (shôrt′dā′tĭd) *adj. Finance.* Designating gilt-edged securities redeemable after a time less than five years away. Compare **long-dated, medium-dated.**

short-day (shôrt′dā′) *adj.* Designating or producing plants that will flower only when exposed to periods of daylight of less than 12 hours: *short-day seeds.* Compare **long-day.**

short division *n.* A division of one number by another, usually no more than two digits, without writing out the remainders.

short·en (shôrt′n) *v.* **-ened, -ening, -ens.** —*tr.* **1.** To make short or shorter. **2.** To take in (a sail) so that less canvas is exposed to the wind. **3.** To cause to come down or decrease: *shortened the odds.* **4.** To add shortening to (dough) so as to produce a crumbly texture. —*intr.* **1.** To become short or shorter. **2.** To decrease; lessen.

shortened form *n.* An abbreviated form of a polysyllabic word, as *auto* for *automobile.*

short·en·ing (shôrt′nĭng, shôrt′n-ĭng) *n.* A fat, such as butter, lard, or vegetable oil, used to make cake or pastry light or flaky.

short·fall (shôrt′fôl′) *n.* **1.** A failure to attain a required amount or level; a shortage; a deficiency. **2.** The amount by which a supply falls short of expectation, need, or demand.

short·hand (shôrt′hănd′) *n.* **1. a.** A system of rapid handwriting employing symbols to represent words, phrases, and letters; stenography. **b.** The handwriting itself. **2.** Any system, form, or instance of abbreviated or formulaic reference: *"The classical error is to regard a scientific law as only a shorthand for its instances"* (Jacob Bronowski). —**short·hand** *adj.*

short-hand·ed (shôrt′hăn′dĭd) *adj.* Lacking the usual or necessary number of workmen, employees, or assistants.

short-haul (shôrt′hôl′) *adj.* Involving or designating the transport of goods or passengers over short distances.

short·horn (shôrt′hôrn′) *n.* Any of a breed of beef or dairy cattle originating in northern England and having short, curved horns. Also called "Durham."

short hundredweight *n.* See **hundredweight** (sense 1).

shor·tie, shor·ty (shôr′tē) *n. Informal.* A short person or thing. ~*adj. Informal.* Short in length: *a shortie jacket.*

short·leaf pine (shôrt′lēf′) *n.* A pine, *Pinus echinata,* that has short, flexible leaves and is common in the southern United States.

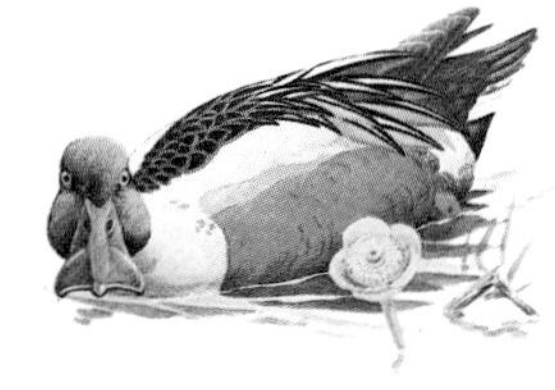

shoveler *Named for its spadelike bill, the shoveler uses the beak as a sieve, straining weeds and insects from the water in ponds and lakes. Unlike most dabbling ducks, the shoveler rarely upends its body to pick up food under the water, but it may dive when alarmed. The birds breed in North America, Europe, and Asia, and some migrate for part of the year to Central America and southern Africa.*

short-lived (shôrt′līvd′, -lĭvd′) *adj.* Living or lasting only a short time; ephemeral.
short·ly (shôrt′lē) *adv.* **1.** In a short time; soon; presently. **2.** In a few words; concisely. **3.** Abruptly or curtly.
short order *n.* Food quickly prepared and served, as in a diner. **—short-or·der** *adj.*
short-range (shôrt′rānj′) *adj.* Of or having a limited range in distance or time: *a short-range forecast.*
short shrift *n.* **1.** Summary and unsympathetic treatment or dismissal. **2.** *Archaic.* The short space of time granted a condemned prisoner for his confession before execution.
short sight *n.* Myopia.
short·sight·ed (shôrt′sī′tĭd) *adj.* **1.** Suffering from myopia; nearsighted. **2.** Lacking foresight. **3.** Resulting from a lack of foresight. **—short·sight·ed·ly** *adv.* **—short·sight·ed·ness** *n.*
short-spo·ken (shôrt′spō′kən) *adj.* Given to shortness or abruptness in manner or speech; curt.
short·stop (shôrt′stŏp′) *n. Baseball.* **1.** The field position between second and third bases. **2.** The player who occupies this position.
short story *n.* A short piece of prose fiction typically concentrating on a single situation or character.
short subject *n.* A brief motion picture often shown between showings of longer motion pictures. Also called "short."
short-tem·pered (shôrt′tĕm′pərd) *adj.* Easily moved to anger.
short-term (shôrt′tûrm′) *adj.* **1.** Lasting or extending for a relatively short period of time: *short-term effects.* **2.** Payable or reaching maturity within a relatively short time: *a short-term loan.*
short ton *n. Abbr.* **s.t.** See **ton** (sense 1b).
short-waist·ed (shôrt′wā′stĭd) *adj.* Having or being of less than average length from shoulders to waist: *a short-waisted dress.*
short wave *n. Abbr.* **sw** An electromagnetic wave with wavelength in the short-wave region.
short-wave (shôrt′wāv′) *adj. Abbr.* **sw 1.** Having a wavelength in the range 10 to 100 meters. **2.** Capable of receiving or transmitting at such wavelengths.
short-wind·ed (shôrt′wĭn′dĭd) *adj.* **1.** Having shortness of breath; easily winded. **2.** Not discursive; brief: *a short-winded speech.*
shorty. Variant of **shortie.**
Sho·sho·ne, Sho·sho·ni (shō-shō′nē) *n., pl.* **-nes** or collectively **Shoshone, -nis** or collectively **Shoshoni. 1.** A member of a Uto-Aztecan-speaking North American Indian people, formerly occupying parts of the American West. **2.** The language of this people.
Sho·sho·ne·an (shō-shō′nē-ən) *n.* An Indian linguistic group in western North America, comprising most of the Uto-Aztecan languages found in the United States. **—Sho·sho·ne·an** *adj.*
Shoshone Falls. Cascade, 65 meters (212 feet) high, flowing over a rim 275 meters (900 feet) wide in the Snake River of southern Idaho. The falls have been reduced by irrigation projects upstream.
Shos·ta·ko·vitch (shŏs′tə-kō′vĭch), **Dmitri Dmitrievich** (1906–75). Russian composer, one of the most prolific and most widely acclaimed of the 20th century. He wrote in all forms but is perhaps best known for his 15 symphonies and his chamber music.
shot[1] (shŏt) *n., pl.* **shots** or **shot** (for sense 2). **1.** A firing or discharge of a weapon, such as a gun or bow. **2. a.** Tiny pellets, especially made of lead, discharged from a shotgun in one charge. **b.** Any of these pellets. **c.** A projectile, such as an iron ball, fired from a cannon, for example. **3.** In certain games, such as soccer, billiards, golf, or tennis, a hit or kick of the ball. **4.** One who shoots, considered with regard to the accuracy of his aim: *a good shot.* **5.** The distance over which something is shot; range. **6.** An attempt to hit or land on something with a missile or rocket: *a moon shot.* **7.** *Informal.* An attempt, guess, or opportunity: *had a shot at making the team.* **8.** The heavy metal ball that an athlete throws in the shot-put. **9.** *Mining.* A charge of explosives used in blasting. **10. a.** A photograph or one in a series of photographs. **b.** A single cinematic view or take. **11.** *Informal.* A hypodermic injection. **12.** *Informal.* A drink of liquor, especially a jigger. **13.** *Nautical.* A unit designating chain length, in the United States equal to 15 fathoms, in Great Britain 12½ fathoms. **—like a shot.** Quickly; in an instant. **—shot in the arm.** Something that revives or stimulates: *a shot in the arm for the industry.* **—shot in the dark.** A wild guess. *~tr.v.* **shotted, shotting, shots.** To load or weight with shot. [Middle English *shot,* Old English *sceot.*]
shot[2] *adj.* **1.** Of changeable, variegated, or iridescent color. Said of fabric having different-colored warp and weft. **2.** *Informal.* Worn-out; ruined; exhausted.
shot[3]**.** Past tense and past participle of **shoot.**
shote. Variant of **shoat.**
shot·gun (shŏt′gŭn′) *n.* A shoulder-held firearm that fires multiple pellets through a smooth bore.
shotgun wedding *n.* A wedding that one or both of the partners are forced to enter into, especially as a consequence of the woman becoming pregnant. Also called "shotgun marriage." [Alluding to the bride's father or relatives armed to force the groom to marry.]
shot hole *n.* A hole drilled into rock or other material into which an explosive charge is inserted for blasting.
shot-put (shŏt′po͝ot′) *n.* **1.** An athletic event in which the contestants attempt to throw or put a shot or heavy ball as far as possible. **2.** One such throw. **—shot-put·ter** *n.*
shott (shŏt) *n.* Also **chott** (chŏt). **1.** A shallow intermittent salt lake or salt marsh in a hot desert. **2.** The depression or hollow occupied by such a salt lake or salt marsh.
shot·ten (shŏt′n) *adj.* **1.** Having recently spawned and being thus less desirable as food. Said of fish, especially herring. **2.** *Archaic.* Of no value; worthless. [Archaic past participle of SHOOT (specialized sense "to spawn").]
should (sho͝od). Past tense of **shall,** but more often used as an auxiliary verb indicating: **1.** Obligation; duty; necessity: *They should tell him the bad news.* **2.** Anticipation of a probable occurrence; expectation: *They should arrive at noon.* **3.** Condition; contingency of one condition upon another: *Should he so much as move, shoot him dead.* **4.** Moderation of the directness or bluntness of a request or statement: *I should like to query that figure.* **5.** An implication of the unusual or surprising: *Who should I bump into in the street but my ex-husband!* **6.** *Informal.* An ironic negative, asserting the negative in a positive way: *With his talent, he should worry* (meaning *should not worry*) *about winning!*

Usage: In traditional grammar the rules governing the use of *should* and *would* were based on the rules governing the use of *shall* and *will.* In modern times and especially in American usage, these rules have been greatly eroded, even more in the case of *should* and *would* than in the case of *shall* and *will.* Either *should* or *would* is now used in the first person to express conditional futurity: *If I had known that, I should* (or *would*) *have made a different reply.* But in the second and third persons only *would* is used: *If he had known that, he would have made a different reply. Would* cannot always be substituted for *should,* however. *Should* is used in all three persons in a conditional clause: *if I* (or *you* or *he*) *should decide to go. Should* is also used in all three persons to express duty or obligation (the equivalent of *ought to*): *I* (or *you* or *he*) *should go.* On the other hand, *would* is used to express volition or promise: *I agreed that I would do it.* Either *would* or *should* is possible as an auxiliary with *like, be inclined, be glad, prefer,* and related verbs: *I would* (or *should*) *like to call your attention to an oversight.* Here *would* is more common in American usage than *should. Should have* is sometimes incorrectly written *should of* by writers who have mistaken the source of the spoken contraction *should've.* See also Usage notes at **shall, ought.**

shoul·der (shōl′dər) *n.* **1.** *Anatomy.* **a.** The part of the human body between the neck and upper arm. **b.** The joint connecting the arm with the trunk. **2.** The corresponding part of an animal. **3. shoulders. a.** The two shoulders and the area of the back between them. **b.** This area of the back considered as the part to bear burdens. **4.** The forequarter of some animals. **5.** The part of a garment that covers the shoulder. **6.** The angle between the face and the flank of a bastion in fortifications. **7.** *Printing.* The extended flat surface on the body of type beyond the letter or character. **8.** A cut of meat, as lamb, consisting of the top part of the foreleg. **9. a.** The edge or ridge running on either side of a main road. **b.** Any projection or slope that resembles a shoulder in shape. **—rub shoulders with.** *Informal.* To meet or associate with. **—shoulder to shoulder.** United in a common cause or effort. **—straight from the shoulder.** With utter frankness.
~v. **shouldered, -dering, -ders.** *—tr.* **1.** To carry (a burden, for example) on or as on the shoulders; bear or support; assume. **2.** To push (one's way) through with or as if with the shoulder. **3.** To apply force to with or as if with the shoulder. *—intr.* To push with the shoulder or shoulders. [Middle English *shulder,* Old English *sculdor,* from Germanic *skuldra-* (unattested).]
shoulder bag *n.* A handbag or traveling bag that is supported by means of a long strap passing over the shoulder.
shoulder blade *n.* The **scapula** *(see).*
shoulder girdle *n.* The **pectoral girdle** *(see).*
shoulder patch *n.* A military identification patch worn on the upper portion of the sleeve, as to designate one's unit.
shoulder strap *n.* **1.** A strap attached to the shoulder of a military uniform to show rank. **2.** A strap that fits over the shoulder, such as one that supports a garment.
should·n't (sho͝od′ənt). Contraction of *should not.*
shouldst (sho͝odst). Also **should·est** (sho͝od′ĭst). *Archaic.* Second person singular past tense of **shall.** Used with *thou.*
shout (shout) *n.* A loud, vigorous cry, often expressing strong emotion or a command.
~v. **shouted, shouting, shouts.** *—tr.* To utter with a shout. *—intr.* **1.** To utter a loud cry; yell. **2.** To speak or laugh loudly. **—shout down.** To overwhelm or silence by shouting loudly. [Middle English *shouten*†.] **—shout·er** *n.*
shove (shŭv) *v.* **shoved, shoving, shoves.** *—tr.* **1.** To cause to move with a sudden push or thrust. **2.** To push roughly or rudely; jostle. **3.** *Informal.* To put or place somewhere. *—intr.* To push rudely or roughly or with sudden force. **—shove off. 1.** To set a beached boat afloat. **2.** *Informal.* To leave. Often used in the imperative. *~n.* The act of shoving; especially, a rude push. [Middle English *sho(u)ven,* Old English *scūfan,* from Germanic.] **—shov·er** *n.*
shov·el (shŭv′əl) *n.* **1.** A tool with a handle and a somewhat flattened scoop for picking up earth, coal, or other materials. **2.** A large mechanical device for heavy digging or excavation, usually a jawed scoop suspended from a boom or crane. **3.** *Informal.* A shovel hat.
~v. **shoveled, -eling, -els** or *chiefly British* **-elled, -elling, -els.** *—tr.* **1.** To dig into or move with a shovel. **2.** To clear or make (a path, for example) with a shovel. **3.** To convey roughly or in large quantities, as with a shovel: *shoveled cake into her mouth.* *—intr.* To dig or work with a shovel. [Middle English *shovel,* Old English *scofl,* from Germanic.]
shovelboard. Variant of **shuffleboard.**

PRONUNCIATION KEY

ă, pat; **ā**, pay; **âr**, care; **ä**, father, are; b, bib; ch, church; d, deed; **ĕ**, pet; **ē**, be; f, fife; g, gag; h, hat; hw, which; **ĭ**, pit; **ī**, pie; **îr**, pier; j, judge; k, kick; l, lid, needle; m, mum; n, no, sudden; ng, thing; **ŏ**, pot; **ō**, toe; **ô**, paw, for; oi, noise; ou, out; **o͝o**, book; **o͞o**, boot; p, pop; r, roar; s, sauce; sh, ship, dish; t, tight; th, thin, path; *th*, this, bathe; **ŭ**, cut; **ûr**, fur; v, valve; w, with; y, yes; z, zebra, size; zh, vision; **ə**, about, item, edible, gallop, circus, peaceful

IN FOREIGN WORDS:

à, *Fr.* ami; **œ**, *Fr.* feu, *Ger.* schön; **ü**, *Fr.* tu, *Ger.* über; KH, *Ger.* ich, *Scot.* loch; N, *Fr.* bon; **y′**, *Fr.* Compiègne

STRESS MARKS:

Primary stress: ′
in·cite′ (ĭn-sīt′)
Secondary stress: ′
in′sight′ (ĭn′sīt′)

shov•el•er (shŭv′ə-lər) *n.* Also *chiefly British* **shov•el•ler.** **1.** One who works with a shovel. **2.** A widely distributed duck, *Anas clypeata*, having a long, broad bill.
shov•el•ful (shŭv′əl-fo͝ol′) *n., pl.* **-fuls.** The amount a shovel will hold.
shovel hat *n.* A stiff, broad-brimmed, low-crowned hat, turned up at the sides and projecting in front, formerly worn by some clergymen. Also informally called "shovel."
shov•el•head (shŭv′əl-hĕd′) *n.* A shark, *Sphyrna tiburo,* of Atlantic and Pacific waters.
shov•el•nose (shŭv′əl-nōz′) *n.* A sturgeon, *Scaphirhynchus platorynchus*, of the Mississippi River, having a broad, flat snout. Also called "shovelnose sturgeon."
shov•el-nosed (shuv′əl-nōzd′) *adj.* Having a broad, flattened snout, bill, or head.
show (shō) *v.* **showed, shown** (shōn) or **showed, showing, shows.** —*tr.* **1. a.** To cause or allow to be seen; make visible: *a white carpet shows the dirt; showed her talent.* **b.** To present to the view of: *She showed me her operation scar.* **c.** To exhibit or present to the public: *Which film is being shown at the Plaza?* **d.** To present (an animal of a recognized breed) for judging in a competitive exhibition. **2.** To conduct; guide: *Show me around your garden.* **3. a.** To point out; demonstrate. **b.** To make clear; prove. **c.** To teach by practical demonstration: *Show me how to knit.* **4. a.** To manifest; reveal. **b.** To indicate; register. **5.** To grant; confer; bestow: *showed great devotion to the cause.* **6.** *Law.* To plead; allege: *show cause.* —*intr.* **1.** To be or become visible or evident: *If you're nervous, it certainly doesn't show.* **2.** To appear: *His face showed red.* **3.** To be exhibited; run: *The movie will show for three days.* **4.** *Informal.* To make an appearance; show up. **5.** *Sports.* To finish third or better for betting purposes. —**show for.** To have as evidence of gain, as from a course of action: *nothing to show for my efforts.* —**show up. 1.** To expose or reveal (faults, flaws, or the like). **2.** To be clearly or ultimately visible: *The white shows up well against the dark background.* **3.** *Informal.* To put in an appearance; arrive. **4.** *Informal.* To cause to feel shame or inferiority.
∼*n.* **1.** The act of showing or revealing. **2.** A display; a manifestation; a demonstration: *a show of force.* **3.** An outward appearance; a semblance: *A show of kindness concealed her diabolical motives.* **4.** A striking appearance or display; a spectacle. **5.** A pompous or ostentatious display: *It's all done for show.* **6. a.** A public exhibition or competition: *a flower show.* **b.** An entertainment such as a play or film: *a television show.* **7. a.** A trace; an indication. **b.** In obstetrics, a discharge of blood occurring at the start of labor. **8.** *Informal.* Any affair or undertaking: *Who is supposed to be running this show?* **9.** *Informal.* An attempt or try; an effort: *put up a bad show.* **10.** *Sports.* Third place or better for betting purposes: *win, place, and show.* —**show of hands.** A raising of hands among the members of a group so that a vote may be taken.
∼*adj.* Of, in, or used for a show or shows. [Middle English *shewen, showen,* to look at, cause to look at, show, Old English *scēawian,* to look at, see, from Germanic.] —**show•er** (shō′ər) *n.*
Synonyms: *display, exhibit, expose, flaunt, parade.*
show bill *n.* An advertising poster.
show biz *n. Slang.* Show business.
show•boat (shō′bōt′) *n.* A river steamboat having a troupe of actors and a theater on board for performances on the river.
showbread. Variant of **shewbread.**
show business *n.* The entertainment business, especially that part of it concerned with theater and motion pictures.
show•case (shō′kās′) *n.* **1.** A display case or cabinet, as in a shop or museum. **2.** A setting in which something is displayed to advantage: *The war was a showcase for the effectiveness of tanks.*
∼*tr.v.* **showcased, -casing, -cases.** To display prominently and to advantage: *The vehicle showcased the actor's talents.*
show•down (shō′doun′) *n.* **1.** *Informal.* A confrontation that forces a disputed issue to a conclusion. **2.** In card games such as poker, the laying down of the players' hands of cards for the purpose of determining the winner.
show•er (shou′ər) *n.* **1.** A brief fall of rain, hail, snow, or sleet. **2.** Any brief or sudden fall resembling a spray or shower: *a meteor shower.* **3.** An abundant flow; an outpouring: *a shower of abuse.* **4.** A stream of elementary particles resulting from the impact of a high-energy particle, especially a cosmic-ray particle, on a target particle. **5.** A party held to honor and present gifts to someone, especially a bride-to-be. **6. a.** A bath in which water is sprayed onto the bather by means of a device, usually situated overhead. **b.** A device so used to spray water, usually having a nozzle through which fine jets of water can pass. **c.** A room or cubicle equipped for such baths. Also called "shower bath."
∼*v.* **showered, -ering, -ers.** —*tr.* **1.** To sprinkle; spray. **2. a.** To bestow on abundantly: *showered her with gifts.* **b.** To present in abundance: *showered gifts on her.* —*intr.* **1.** To fall or pour down in a shower. **2.** To have a shower bath. [Middle English *shour,* Old English *scūr,* from Germanic.] —**show•er•y** *adj.*
show•girl (shō′gûrl′) *n.* A chorus girl.
show•ing (shō′ĭng) *n.* **1.** A performance, as in a competition or test of skill: *a poor showing.* **2.** A presentation of evidence, facts, or figures: *On the present showing he will pass easily.*
show•jump•ing (shō′jŭm′pĭng) *n.* A horseriding competition in which competitors must complete a course of fences and obstacles and are judged on the number of errors committed and sometimes on time taken. —**show•jump•er** *n.*
show•man (shō′mən) *n., pl.* **-men** (-mĭn). **1.** A theatrical producer. **2.** A person who displays a flair for showiness or the dramatic. —**show•man•ship** *n.*
shown. Past participle of **show.**
show off *tr.v.* To display in such a way as to invite admiration. —*intr.v. Informal.* To behave like a show-off.
show-off (shō′ôf′, -ŏf′) *n. Informal.* **1.** The act of showing off. **2.** One who self-confidently displays his talent or ability, especially to an excessive degree.
show•piece (shō′pēs′) *n.* **1.** An exhibition piece. **2.** Something that is exemplary of its kind.
show•place (shō′plās′) *n.* A place that is visited for its beauty, excellence, or historical interest.
show•room (shō′ro͞om′, -ro͝om′) *n.* A room in which goods are on display.
show stopper *n. Informal.* **1.** A person or event, such as a theatrical act, that receives enthusiastic applause and so causes a short interruption in the proceedings. **2.** Broadly, anything that receives instant and enthusiastic admiration or approval.
show trial *n.* A public judicial trial that is primarily designed to serve the propaganda needs of a regime.
show•y (shō′ē) *adj.* **-ier, -iest. 1.** Making a conspicuous display; striking: *showy flowers.* **2.** Displaying brilliance and virtuosity of ability or performance. **3.** Ostentatious; gaudy; flashy. —See Synonyms at **ornate.** —**show•i•ly** *adv.* —**show•i•ness** *n.*
shpt. shipment.
Shqiperi. See **Albania.**
shr *Finance.* share.
shrank. Alternate past tense of **shrink.**
shrap•nel (shrăp′nəl) *n. Military.* **1. a.** An antipersonnel projectile containing metal balls, fused to explode in the air above enemy troops. **b.** These projectiles collectively. **2.** Shell fragments from any high-explosive shell. [After Henry *Shrapnel* (1761–1842), British artillery officer who invented it.]
shred (shrĕd) *n.* **1.** A long, thin, irregular strip cut or torn off. **2.** A small amount; a particle; a scrap: *not a shred of evidence.*
∼*tr.v.* **shredded** or **shred, shredding, shreds.** To cut or tear into shreds: *a machine that shreds paper.* [Middle English *shrede,* Old English *scrēade.*] —**shred•der** *n.*
shrew (shro͞o) *n.* **1.** Any of various small, chiefly insectivorous mammals of the family Soricidae, having a long, pointed nose and small, often poorly developed eyes. Sometimes called "shrewmouse." **2.** A woman with a violent, scolding, or nagging temperament; a scold. [Middle English *shrewe* (unattested), Old English *scrēawa.*]
shrewd (shro͞od) *adj.* **shrewder, shrewdest. 1.** Having or showing keen insight; sharp; astute: *a shrewd political commentator.* **2.** Having experience, cleverness, and cunning, especially in practical affairs: *a shrewd businessman.* —See Synonyms at **clever.** [Middle English *shrewed(e),* wicked, dangerous, serious, from SHREW (evil person).] —**shrewd•ly** *adv.* —**shrewd•ness** *n.*
Synonyms: *astute, quick-witted, sagacious.*
shrew•ish (shro͞o′ĭsh) *adj.* Like a shrew in temperament; ill-tempered; nagging. —**shrew•ish•ly** *adv.* —**shrew•ish•ness** *n.*
shrew mole *n.* Any of several shrewlike moles of the family Talpidae; especially, *Neurotrichus gibbsi,* of western North America, or *Uropsilus soricipes,* of eastern Asia.
shriek (shrēk) *n.* **1.** A shrill outcry; a high-pitched scream; a screech. **2.** Any sound suggestive of a shriek.
∼*v.* **shrieked, shrieking, shrieks.** —*intr.* **1.** To utter a shriek. **2.** To make a shrill sound similar to a shriek: *"the winds shriek through the clouds"* (Ezra Pound). —*tr.* To utter with a shriek. —See Synonyms at **scream.** [Middle English *shriken* (imitative), probably from Old Norse *skrækja.*] —**shriek•er** *n.*
shriev•al•ty (shrē′vəl-tē) *n.* The office, tenure, or jurisdiction of a sheriff. —**shriev•al** *adj.*
shrift (shrĭft) *n. Archaic.* **1.** The act of shriving. **2.** Confession to or absolution given by a priest. [Middle English *shrift(e),* Old English *scrift,* from *scrīfan,* to SHRIVE.]
shrike (shrīk) *n.* Any of various carnivorous birds of the family Laniidae, having a hooked bill, and often impaling its prey on sharp-pointed thorns or barbs of wire fencing. Some species are also called "butcherbird." [Probably from Middle English *shrik* (unattested), from Old English *scrīc,* thrush (imitative).]
shrill (shrĭl) *adj.* **shriller, shrillest. 1.** High-pitched and piercing. **2.** Producing a sharp, high-pitched tone or sound. **3.** Insistently nagging or sharp in tone: *shrill attacks on the government.*
∼*v.* **shrilled, shrilling, shrills.** —*tr.* To utter in a shrill manner; scream; shriek. —*intr.* To produce a shrill cry or sound. [Middle English *shrille,* from *shrillen,* to shriek, perhaps from Scandinavian; akin to Norwegian *skrylla.*] —**shrill•ness** *n.* —**shril•ly** *adv.*
shrimp (shrĭmp) *n., pl.* **shrimps** or collectively **shrimp. 1. a.** Any of various small, slender-bodied, chiefly marine decapod crustaceans of the order Crangon, many species of which are edible. **b.** Any of various similar unrelated crustaceans. **2.** *Informal.* A diminutive or unimportant person.
∼*intr.v.* **shrimped, shrimping, shrimps.** To fish for shrimps. [Middle English *shrimpe,* pigmy, shrimp, perhaps of Low German origin; akin to Middle Low German *schrempen,* to shrink, wrinkle.]
shrimp plant *n.* A shrubby plant, *Beloperone guttata,* having inconspicuous flowers borne between shrimplike reddish bracts.
shrine (shrīn) *n.* **1.** A container or receptacle for sacred relics; a reliquary. **2.** The tomb of a saint or other venerated person. **3.** A

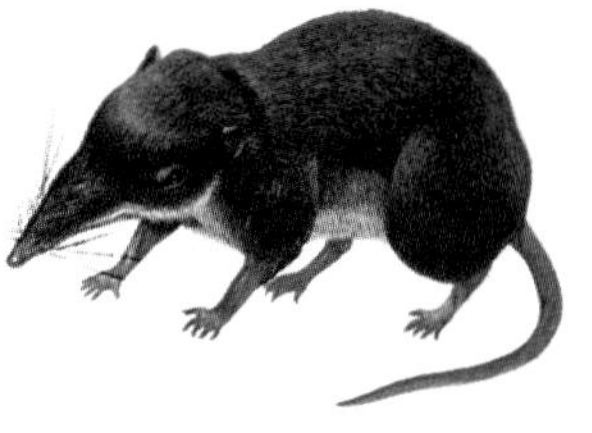

shrew *Although shrews are the smallest mammals, they have big appetites: some species have to eat their own body weight in food every day and will resort to cannibalism. Their main defense against predators —a foul-smelling secretion—deters carnivorous mammals, but not birds of prey. This is the greater white-toothed shrew,* Crocidura russula.

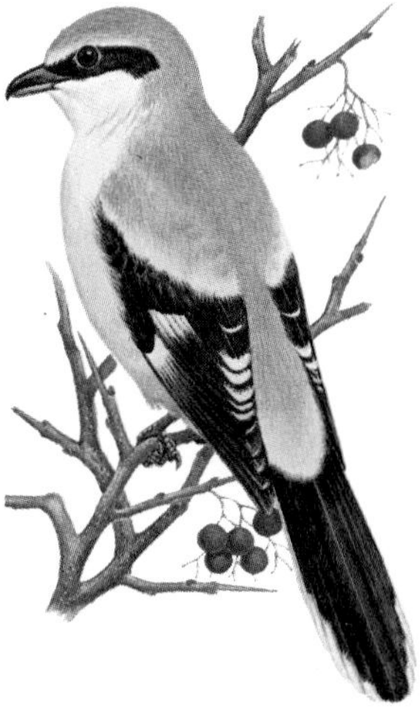

shrike *Found in North America, Eurasia, and Africa, the shrike supplements its diet of insects with small birds, catching and killing them with its talons in midflight. From its habit of then impaling the corpses on thornbushes, it is also called the butcherbird. This is the great gray shrike.*

PRONUNCIATION KEY

ă, pat; ā, pay; âr, care;
ä, father, are; b, bib;
ch, church; d, deed; ĕ, pet;
ē, be; f, fife; g, gag; h, hat;
hw, which; ĭ, pit; ī, pie;
îr, pier; j, judge; k, kick;
l, lid, needle; m, mum;
n, no, sudden; ng, thing;
ŏ, pot; ō, toe; ô, paw, for;
oi, noise; ou, out; o͝o, book;
o͞o, boot; p, pop; r, roar;
s, sauce; sh, ship, dish;
t, tight; th, thin, path;
th, this, bathe; ŭ, cut; ûr, fur;
v, valve; w, with; y, yes;
z, zebra, size; zh, vision;
ə, about, item, edible,
gallop, circus, peaceful

IN FOREIGN WORDS:

à, *Fr.* ami; œ, *Fr.* feu, *Ger.* schön; ü, *Fr.* tu, *Ger.* über; KH, *Ger.* ich, *Scot.* loch; N, *Fr.* bon; y', *Fr.* Compiègne

STRESS MARKS:

Primary stress: ′
in·cite′ (ĭn-sīt′)
Secondary stress: ′
in′sight′ (ĭn′sīt′)

site hallowed by a venerated object or its associations.
~*tr.v.* **shrined, shrining, shrines.** To enshrine. [Middle English *shrin(e),* box, chest, reliquary, Old English *scrīn,* from Latin *scrīnium*†, box, bookcase.]

shrink (shrĭngk) *v.* **shrank** (shrăngk) or **shrunk** (shrŭngk), **shrunk** or **shrunken** (shrŭng′kən), **shrinking, shrinks.** —*intr.* **1.** To draw together or constrict from heat, moisture, or cold; contract. Used especially of fabrics. **2.** To become reduced in amount or value; dwindle. **3.** To draw back, as through shyness. **4.** To be reluctant; flinch: *shrank from the task of leading the charge.* —*tr.* To cause to constrict. —See Synonyms at **contract, decrease, recoil.**
~*n.* **1.** A shrinking or shrinkage. **2.** *Slang.* A psychiatrist or psychoanalyst. [Shrink, shrank, shrunk; Middle English *shrinken, shrank* (also *shrunk*), *shrunken,* Old English *scrincan, scranc* (plural *scruncon*), *(ge)scruncen.*] —**shrink·a·ble** *adj.* —**shrink·er** *n.*
Usage: This verb has two past tenses, *shrank* and *shrunk,* the former being more common. The past participle form is *shrunk. Shrunken* is occasionally used in this way, but generally this form is restricted to adjectival use *(a shrunken figure).*

shrink·age (shrĭng′kĭj) *n.* **1.** The act or process of shrinking. **2.** A reduction or depreciation, as in value. **3.** The amount of weight lost by livestock, as during shipment, before being marketed.

shrinking violet *n. Informal.* A shy or retiring person.

shrink wrapping *n.* A transparent form-fitting plastic wrapping, especially of polyethylene or polyvinyl chloride, used to protect a commodity from dust, moisture, and abrasion. Also called "shrink package."

shrink-wrap (shrĭngk′răp′) *tr.v.* **-wrapped, -wrapping, -wraps.** To enclose (an article) in shrink wrapping.

shrive (shrīv) *v.* **shrove** (shrōv) or **shrived, shriven** (shrĭv′ən) or **shrived, shriving, shrives.** *Archaic.* —*tr.* **1.** To hear the confession of and give absolution to (a penitent). **2.** To obtain absolution for (oneself) by confessing and doing penance. —*intr.* **1.** To make or go to confession. **2.** To hear confessions. [Shrive, shrove, shriven; Middle English *shriven, shrove, shriven,* Old English *scrīfan, scrāf* (past singular), *scrifen(e),* from West Germanic *skrīban* (unattested), to write, "prescribe (penance)," from Latin *scrībere,* to write.] —**shriv·er** *n.*

shriv·el (shrĭv′əl) *v.* **-eled, -eling, -els** or *chiefly British* **-elled, -elling, els.** —*intr.* **1.** To shrink and wrinkle, often in drying. Often used with *up.* **2.** To lose vitality; become wasted. —*tr.* To cause to become shriveled. [Perhaps from Old Norse *skrīfla* (unattested), to wrinkle.]

Shrop·shire (shrŏp′shîr′, -shər). Formerly **Sal·op** (săl′əp). A county of western England, on the Welsh border. It is predominantly agricultural, with plains to the north and east of the Severn River, and hills to the southwest. Shrewsbury is the county town.

shroud (shroud) *n.* **1.** A cloth used to wrap a body for burial; a winding sheet. **2.** Something that conceals, protects, or screens: *a shroud of darkness.* **3.** One of a set of ropes or wire cables stretched from the masthead to a vessel's sides to support the mast. **4.** A similar support for a chimney or comparable structure. **5.** One of the ropes connecting the harness and canopy of a parachute.
~*v.* **shrouded, shrouding, shrouds.** —*tr.* **1.** To wrap (a corpse) in burial clothing. **2.** To envelop; screen; hide. **3.** *Archaic.* To shelter; protect. —*intr. Archaic.* To take cover; find shelter. [Middle English *sc(h)rud,* garment, clothing, Old English *scrūd,* from Germanic.]

shroud-laid (shroud′lād′) *adj.* Designating a rope made from four strands twisted to the right, usually around a core.

Shrove·tide (shrōv′tīd′) *n.* The three days, Shrove Sunday, Shrove Monday, and Shrove Tuesday, preceding Ash Wednesday. [Middle English *schroftyde* : *schrof-,* "shriving," irregularly from *schrov-,* past stem of *shriven,* SHRIVE + *tyde, tid(e),* TIDE (time).]

Shrove Tuesday (shrōv) *n.* The day before Ash Wednesday.

shrub¹ (shrŭb) *n.* A woody plant of relatively low height, distinguished from a tree by having several stems rather than a single trunk; a bush. [Middle English *schrubbe,* Old English *scrybb.*]

shrub² *n.* A drink made from fruit juice, sugar, and a spirit such as rum or brandy. [Arabic *shurb,* a drink, from *shariba,* to drink. See also **sherbet, syrup.**]

shrub·ber·y (shrŭb′ə-rē) *n., pl.* **-ies.** **1.** A group or planting of shrubs. **2.** Shrubs collectively.

shrub·by (shrŭb′ē) *adj.* **-bier, -biest.** **1.** Consisting of, planted with, or covered with shrubs. **2.** Of or resembling a shrub; shrublike. —**shrub·bi·ness** *n.*

shrubby veronica *n.* A plant, **hebe** *(see).*

shrug (shrŭg) *v.* **shrugged, shrugging, shrugs.** —*tr.* To raise (the shoulders) as a gesture of doubt, disdain, or indifference. —*intr.* To make this gesture. —**shrug off. 1.** To minimize the importance of. **2.** To get rid of without trouble: *shrug off a cold.*
~*n.* **1.** An act of shrugging. **2.** A woman's short jacket or sweater, open down the front. [Middle English *shruggen*†.]

shrunk. Past participle and alternate past tense of **shrink.**

shrunken. Alternate past participle of **shrink.**

shtick (shtĭk) *n. Slang.* A characteristic talent or act of an entertainer. [Yiddish, probably from Middle High German *stich,* a thrust, puncture, from Old High German *stih.*]

shuck (shŭk) *n.* The outer covering of something, such as a pea pod, corn husk, or oyster shell.
~*tr.v.* **shucked, shucking, shucks.** **1.** To remove the husk or shell from. **2.** *Informal.* To cast off (clothing, for example). [17th century : origin obscure.] —**shuck·er** *n.*

shucks (shŭks) *interj.* Used to express disappointment, disgust, or annoyance. [From SHUCK ("thing of no value").]

shud·der (shŭd′ər) *intr.v.* **-dered, -dering, -ders.** **1.** To tremble or shiver convulsively, as from fear, cold, or aversion. **2.** To vibrate; quiver: *The engine shuddered to a halt.* —See Synonyms at **shake.**
~*n.* A convulsive shiver, as from fear or cold. [Middle English *shoddren, shudren,* from Middle Low German *schōderen.*] —**shud·der·ing·ly** *adv.*

shuf·fle (shŭf′əl) *v.* **-fled, -fling, -fles.** —*tr.* **1.** To move (the feet) in short dragging movements along the floor or ground while walking or dancing. **2.** To move back and forth or from one place to another. **3.** To mix together or otherwise handle (papers, for example) in a disordered, haphazard fashion. **4.** To put aside or conceal hastily; cover up: *Important issues were quickly shuffled off.* **5.** To mix together (playing cards, for example) to change the order of arrangement. —*intr.* **1.** To move by shuffling one's feet. **2.** To dance the shuffle. **3.** To shift about from side to side. **4.** To act in a shifty or deceitful manner; equivocate. **5.** To shuffle playing cards.
~*n.* **1.** The act or an instance of shuffling. **2.** A dance in which the feet scrape along the floor at each step. **3.** An evasive or deceitful action; a dodge. **4. a.** The act of mixing cards. **b.** A player's turn to do this. [Probably from Low German *schüffeln,* to walk clumsily, shuffle cards.] —**shuf·fler** *n.*

shuf·fle·board (shŭf′əl-bôrd′, -bōrd′) *n.* Also **shov·el·board** (shŭv′əl-). **1.** A game in which disks are pushed or slid along a smooth, level surface toward numbered squares with a pronged cue. **2.** The surface on which this game is played. [Alteration (influenced by SHUFFLE) of earlier *shove-board* : SHOVE + BOARD.]

shul (sho͞ol, sho͝ol) *n.* A synagogue. [Yiddish.]

shun (shŭn) *tr.v.* **shunned, shunning, shuns.** To avoid (a person, group, or thing) deliberately and consistently; keep away from. —See Synonyms at **escape.** [Middle English *shun(n)en,* Old English *scunian*†, to avoid, be afraid, abhor.] —**shun·ner** *n.*

shun·pike (shŭn′pīk′) *n.* A side road taken to avoid the tollgates on a turnpike. —**shun·pik·er** *n.*

shunt (shŭnt) *n.* **1.** The act or an instance of shunting. **2.** A railroad switch. **3.** A low-resistance connection between two points in an electric circuit that forms an alternative path for a portion of the current. Also called "by-pass." **4.** *Medicine.* A passage through which blood passes from one part or organ to another. It may be created by surgery or occur as a congenital abnormality.
~*v.* **shunted, shunting, shunts.** —*tr.* **1.** To turn or move (something) aside or onto another course. **2.** To move or switch (a train or car) from one track to another. **3.** *Electricity.* To provide or divert (current) by means of a shunt. **4.** To evade or avoid (a task, for example) by refusing or putting aside. **5.** *Informal.* To transfer to a different position or task, usually a less demanding or important one. —*intr.* **1.** To move or turn aside. **2.** To move from one track to another. Used of a train. **3.** *Electricity.* To become diverted by means of a shunt. Used of a circuit. [Middle English *shunten,* to flinch, shy, run away, perhaps from *shun(n)en,* SHUN.]

shunt·er (shŭn′tər) *n.* A railroad locomotive used in shunting rather than in pulling trains on journeys.

shunt-wound (shŭnt′wound′) *adj.* Of or designating a direct-current motor or generator in which the field coil is connected in parallel with the armature so that the same voltage appears across each. Compare **series-wound.**

shush (shŭsh, sho͝osh) *interj.* Used to express a demand for silence.
~*tr.v.* **shushed, shushing, shushes.** To demand silence from by saying "shush": *"Simon shushed him quickly as though he had spoken too loudly in church"* (William Golding). [Imitative.]

shut (shŭt) *v.* **shut, shutting, shuts.** —*tr.* **1. a.** To move (a door, lid, or valve, for example) into closed position over or within an opening. **b.** To bring (something that extends or opens out) into a folded or compact state: *shut the book.* **2.** To block passage or access to; close: *shut the garage.* **3.** To fasten or secure with a lock, catch, or latch. Often used with *up.* **4.** To deny (someone) access to a place; bar: *She was shut out of her house.* **5.** To keep from leaving a place; confine: *I was shut in the cellar.* **6.** To cause to reject or ignore: *shut his mind to criticism.* **7.** To catch in something being closed: *shut my sleeve in the door.* **8.** To close (a business establishment). Often used with *up.* —*intr.* **1.** To become shut; close. **2.** To admit of being shut: *The door shuts easily now that you've oiled the hinges.* —**shut up.** *Informal.* **1.** To silence (a person). **2.** To be or become silent: *I'll have my say and then I'll shut up.*
~*n.* **1.** The line of connection between welded pieces of metal. **2.** *Archaic.* The act or time of closing or shutting.
~*adj.* Closed. [Middle English *shutten,* originally a West Midland form of *shitten, shetten,* Old English *scyttan.*]

shut down *tr.v.* **1. a.** To cause (an industrial plant, for example) to close. **b.** To stop the operation of (a machine, for example). **2.** To put a check on or stop to. —*intr.v.* To stop working; close. Used of a factory, machine, or the like.

shut·down (shŭt′doun′) *n.* **1.** A temporary or permanent closing of an industrial plant. **2.** The failure or intentional cessation of operation of any apparatus or equipment.

Shute (sho͞ot), **Nevil,** born Nevil Shute Norway (1899–1960). British novelist, who lived in Australia after 1950. His many internationally popular novels include *A Town Like Alice* (1950) and *On the Beach* (1957).

shut·eye (shŭt′ī′) *n. Slang.* Sleep.

shut-in (shŭt′ĭn′) *n.* An invalid.
~*adj.* Confined to a house or hospital, as by illness.

shut off *tr.v.* **1.** To stop or prevent from flowing or working: *shut off the water supply.* **2.** To separate or isolate.

shut·off (shŭt'ôf', -ŏf') *n.* **1.** A device that shuts something off. **2.** A stoppage or interruption.

shut out *tr.v.* **1.** To forbid access to; bar; exclude. **2.** To keep from being seen: *shut out the view of the gasworks.*

shut·out (shŭt'out') *n.* **1.** A lockout (see). **2.** *Sports.* A game in which one side is kept from scoring.

shut·ter (shŭt'ər) *n.* **1.** One that shuts. **2.** A hinged window cover, usually made of wood and fitted with louvers, and used to exclude light but not necessarily air. **3.** Any of the movable louvers on a pipe organ, controlled by pedals, that open and close the swell box. **4.** A mechanical device that opens and shuts the lens aperture of a camera to expose a plate or film. **5.** A similar device in a motion-picture projector that enables an image to be thrown onto the screen only when the film is momentarily stationary. ~*tr.v.* **shuttered, -tering, -ters.** To furnish or close with a shutter or shutters.

shut·ter·bug (shŭt'ər-bŭg') *n. Slang.* An enthusiastic amateur photographer.

shut·tle (shŭt'l) *n.* **1.** A device used in weaving to carry the woof thread back and forth between the warp threads. **2.** A device for holding the thread in tatting, in netting, and in a sewing machine. **3. a.** A train, bus, or aircraft making short, frequent trips to and fro between two points. Also used adjectivally: *a shuttle service.* **b.** A space shuttle. **4.** The act of shuttling. ~*v.* **shuttled, -tling, -tles.** *—intr.* To go, move, or travel back and forth by or as if by a shuttle. *—tr.* To move or transport by or as if by a shuttle. [Middle English *schutylle,* Old English *scytel,* dart.]

shut·tle·cock (shŭt'l-kŏk') *n.* **1.** A small rounded piece of cork or similar material with a crown of feathers, used in the games of badminton and battledore. Also called "bird," "birdie." **2.** The game of battledore. ~*tr.v.* **shuttlecocked, -cocking, -cocks.** To send or bandy back and forth like a shuttlecock. [SHUTTLE + COCK (bird).]

shuttle diplomacy *n.* Diplomatic negotiations conducted by an intermediary from a neutral country who travels frequently between the disputant nations.

shy¹ (shī) *adj.* **shier** or **shyer, shiest** or **shyest. 1.** Easily startled; timid. Said especially of an animal. **2.** Nervous in company; unsure of oneself; reserved. **3.** Distrustful; wary; cautious. **4.** *Informal.* Not having paid an amount due, as one's ante in poker. **5.** *Informal.* Short; lacking: *Eleven is one shy of a dozen.* **6.** Reluctant to engage in or associate with a specified thing, activity, or group. Usually used in combination: *work-shy.* ~*intr.v.* **shied, shying, shies. 1.** To move suddenly, as if startled: *The horse shied at the noise.* **2.** To draw back, as through fear or caution: *He shied away from responsibility.* ~*n., pl.* **shies.** A sudden movement, as from fright; a start. [Middle English *schey,* timid, Old English *scēoh,* from Germanic *skiuhwaz* (unattested).] **—shy·er** *n.* **—shy·ly** *adv.* **—shy·ness** *n.*

Synonyms: bashful, coy, demure, diffident, modest, retiring, self-conscious, timid.

shy² *v.* **shied, shying, shies.** *—tr.* To throw with a swift sideways motion. *—intr.* To throw something in this manner. ~*n., pl.* **shies. 1.** A quick throw; a fling. **2.** *Informal.* A gibe; a sneer. **3.** *Informal.* An attempt; a try. [Earliest senses, "to take sudden fright," "shrink," "flinch," probably from SHY (timid).]

Shy·lock (shī'lŏk') *n.* A heartless, exacting creditor. [After *Shylock,* the ruthless usurer in Shakespeare's *Merchant of Venice* (1596).]

shy·ster (shī'stər) *n. Slang.* A person given to unethical or unscrupulous practices, especially in business, law, or politics. [From German *Scheisser,* one who defecates, from *scheissen,* to defecate + -STER.]

si (sē) *n. Music.* The former name for *ti* (see).

Si The symbol for the element silicon.

SI International System of measurement. See **SI unit.** [French *Système international.*]

si·al (sī'ăl') *n.* The silicon- and alumina-rich rocks that form the earth's continental upper crust. Compare **sima.** [S*i*lica + *al*umina.] **—si·al·ic** (sī-ăl'ĭk) *adj.*

si·al·a·gogue, si·al·o·gogue (sī-ăl'ə-gôg', -gŏg') *n. Medicine.* Any drug or agent that stimulates the flow of saliva. [New Latin *sialagōgus,* from Greek *sialon,* saliva + -AGOGUE.] **—si·al·a·gog·ic** (sī-ăl'-ə-gŏj'ĭk), **si·al·o·gog·ic** *adj.*

Siam. See **Thailand.**

si·a·mang (sē'ə-măng') *n.* A large black gibbon, *Symphalangus syndactylus* (or *Hylobates syndactylus*), of Sumatra and the Malay Peninsula, having an inflatable throat sac and webbing joining the second and third toes. [Malay.]

Si·a·mese (sī'ə-mēz', -mēs') *adj.* Thai. ~*n., pl.* **Siamese. 1.** A Thai (see). **2.** The language, Thai (see).

Siamese cat *n.* A short-haired cat of a breed developed in the Orient, having blue eyes and a pale fawn or gray coat, often with darker ears, face, tail, and feet.

Siamese fighting fish *n.* A small, often brightly colored freshwater fish, *Betta splendens,* native to tropical Asia and popular in home aquariums.

Siamese twin *n.* Either of a pair of twins born with their bodies joined together. [After Chang and Eng (1811–74), joined twins born in *Siam.*]

Sian. See **Xi'an.**

sib (sĭb) *n.* **1. a.** A blood relation; a kinsman. **b.** Relatives collec-

tively. **2.** A brother or sister; a sibling. **3.** A plant that is the product of a self-pollination, especially one in a group of plants that are mainly the products of cross-pollinations. Also called "sibling." ~*adj.* Related by blood; akin. Used with *to.* [Middle English *sib(be),* Old English *sibb.*]

Sib·bald's rorqual (sĭb'əldz) *n.* The blue whale *(see).* [After Sir Robert *Sibbald* (1641–1722), Scottish scientist and physician.]

Si·be·li·us (sĭ-bā'lē-əs, sĭ-bāl'yəs), **Jean Julius Christian** (1865–1957). Finnish composer, the most famous of his country. Often looked upon as a nationalist composer, he is best known popularly for the symphonic tone poem *Finlandia* (1900). He also wrote seven symphonies and a violin concerto.

Si·be·ri·a (sī-bîr'ē-ə). Vast geographical region of the U.S.S.R., stretching from the Urals in the west to the Pacific Ocean in the east and from the Arctic Ocean south to the Mongolian border. About two fifths of the region is covered in forest. Most of the population lives in the southwest, which is now one of the most densely industrialized parts of the U.S.S.R., owing largely to the Kuznetsk Basin, rich in coal and iron deposits. Petroleum and natural gas fields are also exploited in the western lowlands, and huge hydroelectric stations are located on the Angara River at Irkutsk and Bratsk. **—Si·be·ri·an** *adj. & n.*

Siberian husky *n.* A husky of a breed from northeastern Asia.

sib·i·lant (sĭb'ə-lənt) *adj.* **1.** Producing a hissing sound. **2.** *Phonetics.* Characterized by the sound of (s) or (sh). ~*n. Phonetics.* **1.** A speech sound that suggests hissing, such as (s), (sh), (z), or (zh). **2.** A sibilant consonant. [Latin *sībilāns* (stem *sībilant-*), present participle of *sībilāre,* to hiss, whistle, SIBILATE.] **—sib·i·lance, sib·i·lan·cy** *n.* **—sib·i·lant·ly** *adv.*

sib·i·late (sĭb'ə-lāt') *v.* **-lated, -lating, -lates.** *—intr.* To utter a hissing sound; hiss. *—tr.* To pronounce with a hissing sound. [Latin *sībilāre,* to hiss, whistle.] **—sib·i·la·tion** *n.*

sib·ling (sĭb'lĭng) *n.* **1.** One of two or more persons having one or normally both parents in common; a brother or sister. **2.** A self-pollinated plant; a sib. [Middle English *siblyng,* Old English *sibling* : SIB + -LING.]

sib·yl (sĭb'əl) *n.* **1.** Any of various women regarded as oracles or prophetesses in the ancient world. **2. a.** A prophetess. **b.** A witch; a sorceress. [Middle English *Sibile, Sybylle,* from Old French *Sibile, Sebile,* from Latin *Sibylla,* from Greek *Sibulla†.*] **—sib·yl·line** (sĭb'-ə-līn', -lēn'), **si·byl·ic** (sĭ-bĭl'ĭk) *adj.*

sic¹ (sĭk, sēk) *adv.* Thus; so. Used in written texts to indicate that a surprising or dubious word, phrase, or fact is not a mistake and is to be read as it stands. [Latin *sīc.*]

sic², sick (sĭk) *tr.v.* **sicced, siccing, sics** or **sicked, sicking, sicks. 1.** To urge to attack or chase. **2.** To set upon or chase. Used only in the imperative, as a command to a dog. [Dialectal variant of SEEK.]

Sic. Sicilian; Sicily.

sic·ca·tive (sĭk'ə-tĭv) *n.* A substance added to paints and some medicines to promote drying; a drier. [Latin *siccātīvus,* drying, from *siccāre,* to dry, from *siccus,* dry.] **—sic·ca·tive** *adj.*

sice. Variant of **syce.**

Si·chuan (sĕch'wän'). Also **Sze·chwan** (sĕch'-). Province in southwestern China, lying to the east of Tibet. The capital is Chengdu. It forms a natural geographical region, being entirely ringed by mountains. It is China's leading producer of rice and is also important for its sugar cane, cotton, and cattle farming.

Sicilies, the Two. See **Two Sicilies, the.**

Sic·i·ly (sĭs'ə-lē). *Abbr.* **Sic.** Italian **Si·ci·lia** (sē-chē'lyə). Region of southern Italy, consisting mainly of the island of Sicily, separated from the extreme southwestern tip of the mainland by the narrow Strait of Messina. The region also includes the Egadi, Lipari, and Pelagian island groups and the islands of Pantelleria and Ustica. The main island is the largest in the Mediterranean. It is almost entirely hilly and mountainous, the highest point being Mt. Etna, an active volcano. Palermo is the capital. **—Si·cil·ian** *adj. & n.*

sick¹ (sĭk) *adj.* **sicker, sickest. 1. a.** Not in normal health physically or psychologically; ill; unwell. **b.** Nauseated, queasy. **c.** Wishing or forced to vomit. **2.** Of or for sick persons: *sick leave.* **3. a.** Morbid or macabre; unwholesome; in deliberately bad taste: *a sick joke.* **b.** Culturally ailing or unsound; rotten; decadent: *a sick society.* **4.** *Informal.* **a.** Deeply distressed; chagrined; upset: *felt sick at losing the game.* **b.** Disgusted; revolted. **c.** Weary; tired. Usually used with *of: sick of it all.* **d.** Pining; longing: *sick for home.* **5.** In need of repairs. Said of a ship. **6.** Unable to produce a profitable yield of crops, especially as a result of excessive cultivation of a single crop. [Middle English *sēk,* Old English *sēoc,* from Germanic *siukaz* (unattested).] **—sick·ish** *adj.*

Synonyms: ill, indisposed, poorly, unwell.

sick². Variant of **sic** (to urge to attack).

sick·bay (sĭk'bā') *n.* An area, as on a ship, used as a hospital or infirmary.

sick·bed (sĭk'bĕd') *n.* A sick person's bed.

sick call *n. Military.* **1. a.** The daily line-up of personnel requiring medical attention. **b.** The signal announcing this. **2.** A call made by a doctor to a sick person.

sick·en (sĭk'ən) *v.* **-ened, -ening, -ens.** *—tr.* To make sick; fill with nausea or revulsion. *—intr.* To become sick or show signs of sickness. **—sick·en·er** *n.*

sick·en·ing (sĭk'ə-nĭng) *adj.* **1.** Causing sickness or nausea. **2.** Revolting or disgusting; loathsome. **3.** *Informal.* Very annoying or disagreeable. **—sick·en·ing·ly** *adv.*

Siamese cat *Originally from Southeast Asia, the Siamese breed of domestic cat is characterized by pointed ears, a long tail, and blue eyes.*

sick headache *n.* **1.** A headache accompanied by nausea. **2.** An attack of migraine.

sick·le (sĭk′əl) *n.* An implement having a semicircular blade attached to a short handle, for cutting grain or tall grass. ∼*tr.v.* **sickled, -ling, -les.** To cut with a sickle. [Middle English *sikel,* Old English *sicol, sicel,* from West Germanic, from Vulgar Latin *sicila* (unattested), variant of Latin *sēcula.*]

sick leave *n.* Leave of absence given because of sickness.

sick·le-bill (sĭk′əl-bĭl′) *n.* Any of several birds having sharply curved bills; especially, *Falculea palliata,* of Madagascar.

sickle cell *n.* An abnormal crescent-shaped red blood cell.

sickle cell anemia *n.* A hereditary anemia characterized by the presence of oxygen-deficient sickle-shaped red blood cells, episodic pain, and leg ulcers.

sick·ly (sĭk′lē) *adj.* **-lier, -liest. 1.** Prone to sickness; ailing. **2.** Of, caused by, or associated with sickness: *a sickly pallor; a sickly shade of green.* **3.** Conducive to ill health; unhealthy. **4.** Inducing vomit; nauseating; sickening: *sickly, rich food.* **5.** Mawkish; weak. ∼*adv.* In a sick manner. ∼*tr.v.* **sicklied, -lying, -lies.** *Archaic.* To make sickly, as in color. —**sick·li·ness** *n.*

sick·ness (sĭk′nĭs) *n.* **1.** The condition of being sick; illness. **2.** A disease; a malady. **3.** Nausea.

sick·room (sĭk′rōōm′, -rŏŏm′) *n.* A room occupied by a sick person.

sic pas·sim (sĭk păs′ĭm, sēk pä′sĭm) *adv.* Thus everywhere. Used in textual annotation to indicate that a term or idea is to be found throughout the work cited. [Latin.]

Sid·dons (sĭd′nz), **Sarah Kemble** (1755–1831). British actress, the most illustrious member of the theatrical Kemble family. From 1785, when she first played Lady Macbeth, to 1812, when she gave her last performance in the same role, she was acknowledged as the finest Shakespearean actress of her day.

sid·dur (sĭd′ŏŏr′, sĭd′ər) *n., pl.* **siddurim** (sĭd′ə-rēm′) or **-durs.** A Jewish prayer book containing prayers for the various days of the year. Compare **machzor.** [Hebrew *siddūr,* "order," "arrangement (of prayers)," from *siddēr,* to arrange.]

side (sīd) *n.* **1.** *Geometry.* **a.** A line bounding a plane figure. **b.** A surface bounding a solid figure. **2.** A surface of an object; especially, a surface joining a top and bottom: *Hold the box by its sides.* **3.** A surface of an object that extends more or less perpendicularly from an observer standing in front of it: *the side of the mountain.* **4.** Either of the two surfaces of a flat object, such as a piece of paper. **5. a.** The area to the left or right of the observer, or of an axis: *played on the left side of the field.* **b.** The left or right half of the trunk of a human or the corresponding part of an animal body: *a side of mutton.* **6.** The space immediately next to someone or something: *stood at her side.* Often used in combination: *roadside.* **7.** One of two or more contrasted parts or places within an area, identified by its location with respect to a center: *the north side of the park.* **8. a.** An area separated from another area by some intervening line, barrier, or other feature: *on this side of the Atlantic.* **b.** That which comes before some dividing line: *this side of madness.* **9. a.** One of two or more opposing groups, teams, or sets of opinions. **b.** A sports team. **c.** One of the positions maintained in a dispute or debate: *He always takes her side in arguments.* **10.** A distinct aspect or quality: *the cruel side of her nature.* **11.** A line of descent: *my aunt on my mother's side.* **12.** *British Slang.* Arrogance or affected superiority: *has got too much side.* **13.** In certain games, such as billiards, tennis, or table tennis, a spin imparted to the ball by a sideways motion of the bat or cue, usually causing a variation in the ball's movement. **—on the side.** *Informal.* **1.** In addition to a main activity, occupation, or arrangement, often with a suggestion of illegality: *was making a bit of money on the side.* **2.** Served as a side dish. **—put to** (or **on**) **one side.** To set apart from the main subject under consideration. **—side by side.** Next to each other; close together. **—split one's sides.** To be convulsed with laughter. **—take sides.** To associate oneself with a faction, contested opinion, or cause. ∼*adj.* **1.** Located on a side: *a side chapel.* **2.** From or to one side; oblique: *a side view.* **3.** Minor; incidental: *a side interest.* **4.** In addition to the main part; supplementary: *a side benefit.* ∼*v.* **sided, siding, sides.** *—intr.* To align oneself. Used with *with* or *against:* *sided with Peter against Paul.* *—tr.* **1.** To agree with; support. **2.** To be positioned next to. **3.** To provide sides or siding for: *side a barn.* [Middle English *side,* Old English *sīde,* from Germanic.]

side arm *n.* A small weapon carried at the side or waist, such as a sword or pistol.

side·arm (sīd′ärm′) *adj. Baseball.* Thrown with or marked by a sweep of the arm between shoulder and hip height: *a sidearm curve ball.*

side·band (sīd′bănd′) *n.* Either of the two bands of frequencies, one just above and one just below a carrier frequency, that result from modulation of a carrier wave.

side·board (sīd′bôrd′, -bōrd′) *n.* A piece of dining-room furniture originally for holding dishes of food and usually having drawers and shelves for storing tableware.

side·burns (sīd′bûrnz′) *pl.n.* Growths of hair or whiskers down the sides of a man's face in front of the ears. Also *chiefly British* "sideboards." [Alteration of *burnsides,* from Ambrose E. *Burnsides* (1824–81), U.S. Civil War general who wore them.]

side·car (sīd′kär) *n.* **1.** A one-wheeled car for a single passenger, attached to the side of a motorcycle. **2.** A cocktail combining

---

brandy, an orange-flavored liqueur, and lemon juice.

side chain *n. Chemistry.* A radical, group, or chain of atoms attached to a carbon atom in the main chain of an organic molecule or to the cyclic nucleus of such a molecule.

sid·ed (sī′dĭd) *adj.* Having sides usually of a specified number or kind. Used in combination: *straight-sided.*

side dish *n.* A small dish, as of salad, served with a main course.

side-dress (sīd′drĕs′) *tr.v.* **-dressed, -dressing, -dresses.** To treat (plants) by placing fertilizer near their roots, on or in the soil.

side drum *n.* A small double-headed snare drum, traditionally worn at the side by soldiers.

side effect *n.* A peripheral or secondary effect; especially, an undesirable secondary effect of a drug or therapy.

side issue *n.* An issue that is not directly relevant to the main point under consideration.

side·kick (sīd′kĭk′) *n. Informal.* A close friend or associate. [Earlier *sidekicker,* perhaps from *kicker* (in draw poker), an unmatched card held with a pair or three of a kind for purposes of bluffing or improving the hand.]

side·light (sīd′līt′) *n.* **1.** A light coming from the side. **2.** *Nautical.* Either of two lights, red to port, green to starboard, shown by ships at night. **3.** Incidental information.

side·line (sīd′līn′) *n.* **1. a.** A line along either of the two sides of a playing court or field, marking its limits. **b. sidelines.** The space outside such limits, occupied by spectators. **c. sidelines.** The position or point of view of those who observe and do not participate in some activity. **2.** A subsidiary line of merchandise. **3.** An activity pursued in addition to one's regular occupation. ∼*tr.v.* **sidelined, -lining, -lines.** To remove or keep (a player) from active participation, as in athletic contests.

side·ling (sīd′lĭng) *adj.* **1.** Directed to one side; oblique. **2.** Sloping. ∼*adv.* Obliquely; sideways. [Middle English *sideling* : SIDE + -LING (adverbial suffix).]

side·long (sīd′lông′, -lŏng′) *adj.* Directed to one side; sideways. ∼*adv.* On, from, or toward the side; obliquely; sideways. [Alteration of SIDELING.]

side·man (sīd′măn′) *n., pl.* **-men** (-mĕn′). An instrumentalist in a jazz band who is not the leader or a featured soloist.

si·de·re·al (sī-dîr′ē-əl) *adj.* **1.** Of, pertaining to, or concerned with the stars or constellations; stellar. **2.** Measured or determined in relation to the stars: *sidereal time.* [Latin *sīdereus,* from *sīdus* (stem *sīder-*), constellation.]

sidereal day *n.* The time required for a complete rotation of the earth, measured as the interval between two successive transits of a star over the same meridian, or 23 hours, 56 minutes, 4.09 seconds of solar time.

sidereal hour *n.* A 24th part of a sidereal day.

sidereal month *n.* See **month** (sense 3).

sidereal time *n.* Time based upon the axial and orbital rotation of the earth with reference to the background of stars.

sidereal year *n.* The time required for one complete revolution of the earth about the sun, relative to the fixed stars, or 365.256 mean solar days.

sid·er·ite (sīd′ə-rīt′) *n.* **1.** An impure yellowish-brown iron carbonate mineral. **2.** An iron meteorite. [SIDER(O)- + -ITE.] —**sid·er·it·ic** (sīd′ə-rīt′ĭk) *adj.*

sidero–, sider– *prefix.* Indicates iron; for example, **siderolite, siderosis.** [Greek *sidēros†,* iron.]

side road *n.* A road that joins and is subsidiary to a main road.

sid·er·o·lite (sīd′ər-ə-līt′) *n.* A meteorite that contains iron, nickel, silicon, magnesium, and small amounts of other elements. [SIDERO- + -LITE.]

sid·er·o·sil·i·co·sis (sīd′ə-rō-sīl′ĭ-kō′sĭs) *n.* A lung disease caused by excessive inhalation of dust containing silica and iron oxide.

sid·er·o·sis (sīd′ə-rō′sĭs) *n.* A chronic disease of the lungs caused by excessive inhalation of dust containing iron oxide or iron particles. [SIDER(O)- + -OSIS.] —**sid·er·ot·ic** (sīd′ə-rŏt′ĭk) *adj.*

sid·er·o·stat (sīd′ər-ə-stăt′) *n.* An optical system consisting of a rotating clock-driven mirror that reflects light from a celestial body in a relatively fixed direction to a fixed telescope or other bulky instrument. [Latin *sīdus* (stem *sīder-*), constellation (see **sidereal**) + -STAT.] —**sid·er·o·stat·ic** (sīd′ər-ə-stăt′ĭk) *adj.*

side·sad·dle (sīd′săd′l) *n.* A saddle designed so that a woman can sit with both legs on one side of the horse. ∼*adv.* On or as if on a sidesaddle.

side show *n.* **1.** A small show offered in addition to the main attraction, as at a circus. **2.** A diverting incident or spectacle.

side·slip (sīd′slĭp′) *intr.v.* **-slipped, -slipping, -slips.** To slip or skid to one side. ∼*n.* **1.** A sideways skid, as of a motor vehicle. **2.** *Aviation.* Movement sideways and downward along the lateral axis as the result of banking too steeply, or caused deliberately in order to reduce altitude steeply without gaining speed.

side·spin (sīd′spĭn′) *n.* A rotary motion that spins a ball horizontally.

side·split·ting (sīd′splĭt′ĭng) *adj.* Causing convulsions of laughter. —**side·split·ting·ly** *adv.*

side step *n.* A step to one side, as in dancing or to avoid something.

side·step (sīd′stĕp′) *v.* **-stepped, -stepping, -steps.** *—intr.* **1.** To step aside. **2.** To dodge an issue or responsibility. *—tr.* **1.** To step out of the way of (an opponent in a sports match, for example). **2.** To evade (an issue, for example); skirt. —**side·step·per** *n.*

side street *n.* A relatively minor street, usually providing access to

---

residential areas rather than serving as a main thoroughfare.

side stroke *n.* A swimming stroke in which a person swims on one side and thrusts the arms forward and downward alternately while performing a scissors kick with the legs.

side·swipe (sīd′swīp′) *tr.v.* **-swiped, -swiping, -swipes.** To strike along the side in passing: *skidded and sideswiped a parked car.* ~*n.* **1.** A glancing blow on or along the side. **2.** A caustic remark made in the course of other comments.

side·track (sīd′trăk′) *tr.v.* **-tracked, -tracking, -tracks. 1.** To divert from a main issue or course. **2.** To delay action on: *sidetrack a bill in Congress.* **3.** To transfer to a railroad siding. ~*n.* **1.** An instance of sidetracking. **2.** A railroad siding.

side-valve (sīd′vălv′) *adj.* Designating an internal-combustion engine with the inlet and outlet valves located within the cylinder block rather than the cylinder head. Compare **overhead valve.**

side·walk (sīd′wôk′) *n.* A walk or raised path along the side of a street for pedestrians; pavement.

sidewalk artist *n.* An artist who draws pictures, usually with chalk, on a sidewalk surface as a means of acquiring money from passers-by. Also *British* "pavement artist."

side·ward (sīd′wərd) *adj.* Moving or directed toward one side. ~*adv.* Also **side·wards** (-wərdz). Toward or from one side.

side·ways (sīd′wāz′) *adv.* Also **side·way** (-wā′), **side·wise** (-wīz′). **1.** Toward one side; in a sideward direction. **2.** From one side. **3.** Presenting the side instead of the front or back. ~*adj.* Also **side·way, side·wise.** Toward or from one side.

side wheel *n.* A paddle wheel on the side of a steamboat. **—side-wheel** *adj.* **—side-wheel·er** *n.*

side·wind·er (sīd′wīn′dər) *n.* **1.** A small rattlesnake, *Crotalus cerastes,* of the southwestern United States and Mexico, that moves by a distinctive sideways looping motion of its body. **2.** *Slang.* A dangerous or treacherous character. **3.** A powerful blow by the fist delivered from the side. **4.** *Military.* A short-range supersonic air-to-air missile.

sid·ing (sī′dĭng) *n.* **1.** A short section of railroad track connected to a main track either to provide access, as to a factory or mine, or to provide storage space for rolling stock. **2.** Material, such as planks or shingles, used for surfacing the outside of a building.

si·dle (sīd′l) *intr.v.* **-dled, -dling, -dles. 1.** To move sideways; edge along. **2.** To move in a nervous, furtive manner: *sidled into the office late.* **3.** To make advances in a fawning manner. ~*n.* A sidelong step or movement. [Back-formation from SIDELING and SIDELONG.] **—si·dling·ly** *adv.*

Sid·ney or **Syd·ney** (sĭd′nē), **Sir Philip** (1554–86). English poet, critic, soldier, and courtier. His most important works are a collection of pastoral idylls, *Arcadia*; a sonnet sequence, *Astrophel and Stella*; and two essays of criticism, *The Defence of Poesie* and *An Apology for Poetry* (all published posthumously).

Si·don (sīd′n). Ancient Phoenician seaport on the Mediterranean coast, occupying the site of present-day Saida in Lebanon. It was one of the oldest Phoenician trading centers, famous for its glass and purple dyes.

siege (sēj) *n.* **1.** The surrounding and blockading of a town or fortress by an army intent on capturing it. **2.** A prolonged attempt to break the resistance of a person or group, as by force or psychological pressure: *The siege began when the police surrounded the terrorist hideout.* **3.** *Obsolete.* **a.** A seat. **b.** A seat of rule. **—lay siege to.** To begin a siege against. ~*tr.v.* **sieged, sieging, sieges.** To lay siege to; besiege. [Middle English *sege,* from Old French, "seat," from Vulgar Latin *sedicum* (unattested), from *sedicāre* (unattested), "to seat oneself," from Latin *sedēre,* to be seated.]

Sieg·fried (sēg′frēd′). The hero of the first part of the **Nibelungenlied** *(see)* and other medieval epics. [German, from Old High German *Sigifrith* : *sigu, sigo,* victory + *fridu,* peace.]

sie·mens (sē′mənz) *n., pl.* **siemens.** The SI unit of electrical conductance equal to the conductance of a device that has a resistance of one ohm. Formerly called "mho," "reciprocal ohm." [After Ernst Werner von SIEMENS.]

Siemens (sē′mənz, zē′-), **Ernst Werner von** (1816–92). German electrical engineer. He installed the first telegraph line between Frankfurt and Berlin in 1848–49 and the first lines in Russia in 1850. With his brothers **Wilhelm** (1823–83) and **Karl** (1829–1906), he went on to install lines between India and Europe, as well as across the Atlantic. The Siemens unit of electrical conductance is named after him.

Si·en·a (sē-ĕn′ə). City in north-central Italy, the capital of Siena province. In the 13th and 14th centuries it boasted the finest painters in Italy. The city is rich in fine architecture. The Palio festival, with its horse race through the streets of the town center, is held twice each summer. **—Si·en·ese** *n. & adj.*

Sien·kie·wicz (shĕn-kā′vĭch), **Henryk** (1846–1916). Polish novelist. Although he is most widely known for his historical novel *Quo Vadis?* (1895), his critical reputation rests on his trilogy dealing with Poland's struggle for national liberation, *With Fire and Sword* (1883), *The Deluge* (1886), and *Pan Michael* (1888). He was awarded the Nobel Prize for literature in 1905.

si·en·na (sē-ĕn′ə) *n.* **1.** A special clay containing iron and manganese oxides, used as a pigment for oil and water-color painting. **2. Raw sienna** *(see).* **3. Burnt sienna** *(see).* [From *terra-sienna,* from Italian *terra di Sienna,* "earth of SIENA."]

si·er·ra (sē-ĕr′ə) *n.* **1.** A rugged range of mountains having an irregular or serrated profile. **2.** Any of several mackerellike fishes of the genus *Scomberomorus,* of tropical seas. [Spanish, "a saw," from Latin *serra.* See **serrate.**] **—si·er·ran** (sē-ĕr′ən) *adj.*

Si·er·ra Le·one (sē-ĕr′ə lē-ōn′). Republic on the western coast of Africa. Although the economy is predominantly agricultural, the country has an important mining industry, with diamonds, bauxite, and titanium accounting for *c.* 70 percent of the country's exports by value. Freetown was founded as a British colony for ex-slaves in 1787, and thereafter British control was gradually extended into the interior, over which a protectorate was proclaimed in 1896. The country gained its independence in 1961. Area, 71,740 square kilometers (27,699 square miles). Population, 3,500,000. Capital, Freetown. See map at **West African States.**

Sierra Ma·dre (mä′drə). Chief mountain system of Mexico, comprising three principal ranges: the Sierra Madre Oriental, running roughly parallel to the coast of the Gulf of Mexico; the Sierra Madre Occidental, running parallel to the Pacific Coast; and the Sierra Madre del Sur, a continuation of the latter range, running south from Guadalajara. The two highest peaks, Orizaba and Popocatépetl, are both above 5,000 meters.

Sierra Ne·va·da[1] (nə-vä′də). Chief mountain range in southern Spain, in the Granada region, extending for *c.* 100 kilometers (60 miles) parallel to the Mediterranean coast. It contains the highest peak in Spain, Mulhacén, which rises to 3,485 meters (11,424 feet).

Sierra Nevada[2]. Range in eastern California containing the highest peak in the United States (excluding Alaska), Mt. Whitney, which rises to 4,420 meters (14,494 feet).

si·es·ta (sē-ĕs′tə) *n.* A short sleep or rest, usually taken after the midday meal, especially in hot countries. [Spanish, from Latin *sexta (hora),* sixth (hour after sunrise), noon, from *sextus,* sixth.]

sieve (sĭv) *n.* Any meshwork, especially a utensil of wire mesh or closely perforated metal, used for straining, sifting, or separating. ~*tr.v.* **sieved, sieving, sieves.** To pass through a sieve; sift. [Middle English *sive,* Old English *sife.*]

sieve tube *n.* A series of cells joined end to end, with pores in their connecting walls, forming a tube through which nutrients are conducted in vascular plants.

si·fa·ka (sĭ-fä′kə) *n.* Either of two Madagascan primates, *Propithecus diadema* or *P. verreauxi,* that are related to lemurs and have long, often brightly colored fur. [From Malagasy.]

sift (sĭft) *v.* **sifted, sifting, sifts.** —*tr.* **1.** To put through a sieve or other straining device in order to separate the fine from the coarse particles. **2.** To apply by scattering with a sieve: *Sift icing sugar on the cake.* **3.** To separate by or as if by using a sieve; screen. **4.** To examine closely and carefully: *sift the evidence.* —*intr.* **1.** To sift something. **2.** To fall through or as if through a sieve: *White light sifted through the spreading cedar tree.* **3.** To make a careful and critical examination. Used with *through.* [Middle English *siften,* Old English *siftan.*] **—sift·er** *n.*

sift·ing (sĭf′tĭng) *n.* **1. siftings.** Material removed or separated with or as if with a sieve. **2.** *Computer Science.* An internal sorting technique in which data are displaced to permit the insertion of new data.

sig. 1. signal. **2.** signature. **3.** signor; signore.

Sig. 1. signor; signore. **2.** *Medicine.* signature.

sigh (sī) *v.* **sighed, sighing, sighs.** —*intr.* **1.** To exhale audibly in a long, deep breath, as from sorrow, weariness, or relief. **2.** To produce a similar sound: *willows sighing in the wind.* **3.** To feel yearning, longing, or grief; mourn. —*tr.* **1.** To express with or as if with an audible exhalation. **2.** *Archaic.* To lament; mourn. ~*n.* An act or a sound of sighing. [Middle English *sighen,* probably altered from *siken* (weak past tense *sighte*), Old English *sīcan,* from West Germanic *sīk-* (unattested).]

sight (sīt) *n.* **1.** The ability to see; the faculty of vision: *Surgeons saved her sight.* **2.** The act or fact of seeing. **3.** The field or range of one's vision: *Get out of my sight!* **4.** The way in which one sees and evaluates experience; a point of view; an estimation: *In his sight she was perfect.* **5.** Something that is seen; an object of vision; a view: *The garden is a lovely sight.* **6.** Something worth seeing; an attraction or spectacle: *the sights of London.* **7.** *Informal.* Something unsightly: *Her hair was a sight.* **8. a.** A device used to assist aim by guiding the eye, as on a firearm or surveying instrument. **b.** *Often* **sights.** An aim or observation taken with such a device: *A rabbit came into his sights.* **c. sights.** An aim; a goal; an ambition: *set his sights on promotion.* **9.** *Informal.* A considerable amount; a lot: *a sight more than what he's earning.* **—at first sight. 1.** Immediately; at once: *love at first sight.* **2.** Without a close examination; according to initial impressions. **—at (or on) sight.** As soon as seen: *Shoot on sight.* **—catch sight of.** To manage to see; glimpse. **—in sight. 1.** Able to be seen. **2.** Coming closer; approaching: *The end is in sight.* **—know by sight.** To recognize (a person) by his appearance rather than by his name or any other personal detail. **—lose sight of.** To allow to be neglected or remain unconsidered: *mustn't lose sight of our objectives.* **—out of sight.** *Slang.* Incredible; marvelous. **—sight for sore eyes.** Something pleasurable to behold; a welcome sight. **—sight unseen.** Without seeing the object in question: *bought the car sight unseen.* ~*tr.v.* **sighted, sighting, sights. 1.** To see or observe within one's field of vision: *sight land.* **2.** To observe or take a sight of with an instrument: *sight a target.* **3.** To adjust the sights of (a rifle, for example). **4.** To provide with sights. **5.** To take aim with (a firearm). [Middle English *si(g)ht,* Old English *sihth, gesiht,* eyesight, vision, thing seen.]

sight draft *n.* A draft or bill payable upon demand or presentation. Also called "sight bill."

sight·ed (sī′tĭd) *adj.* **1.** Having sight; not blind. **2.** Having eyesight of a specified kind. Used in combination: *short-sighted.*

sight gag *n.* A comic effect that depends on something seen rather than on words.

sight·less (sīt′lĭs) *adj.* **1.** Blind. **2.** Invisible. **—sight·less·ly** *adv.* **—sight·less·ness** *n.*

sight·ly (sīt′lē) *adj.* **-lier, -liest.** Pleasing to see; handsome.

sight-read (sīt′rēd′) *v.* **-read** (-rĕd′), **-reading, -reads.** *—tr.* To read or perform (music, for example) at first sight without preparation. *—intr.* To read or perform something at sight. **—sight-read·er** *n.*

sight rule *n.* An **alidade** *(see).*

sight·see·ing (sīt′sē′ĭng) *n.* The act or pastime of touring places of interest. **—sight·see** *v.* **—sight·se·er** *n.*

sig·il (sĭj′əl, sĭg′-) *n.* **1.** A seal; a signet. **2.** A supposedly magical sign or image. [Latin *sigillum,* diminutive of *signum,* SIGN.]

sigill. seal. [Latin *sigillum.*]

sig·lum (sĭg′ləm) *n., pl.* **-gla** (-lə). A letter, especially an initial, used for identification. [From Late Latin *sigla* (plural), perhaps from *singula,* neuter plural of *singulus,* single.]

sig·ma (sĭg′mə) *n.* **1.** The 18th letter in the Greek alphabet, written Σ,σ. Transliterated in English as *S, s.* See feature at **alphabet. 2.** *Physics. Symbol* Σ. Any of three elementary particles in the baryon family. [Greek, from Semitic, akin to Hebrew *sāmekh,* SAMEK.] **—sig·mate** (sĭg′māt′) *adj.*

sig·moid (sĭg′moid′) *adj.* Also **sig·moi·dal** (sĭg-moid′l). **1.** Having the shape of the letter S. **2.** Of or pertaining to the sigmoid colon. [Greek *sigmoeidēs* : SIGMA + -OID.]

sigmoid colon *n. Anatomy.* An S-shaped bend in the final part of the colon between the descending section and the rectum. Also called "sigmoid flexure."

sig·moid·o·scope (sĭg-moi′də-skōp′) *n.* An instrument equipped with a light that is inserted into the anus in order to inspect the rectum and sigmoid colon. [SIGMOID + -SCOPE.] **—sig·moid·os·co·py** (sĭg′moi-dŏs′kə-pē) *n.*

sign (sīn) *n., pl.* **signs** or **sign** (for sense 7 only). **1.** Something that points to the presence or existence of a fact, condition, or quality not immediately evident; an indication: *"Her silence . . . is a sign that she has a weapon"* (J. P. Donleavy). **2.** An action or gesture used to convey an idea, command, desire, or information: *blew a kiss as a sign of her affection.* **3.** A board, poster, or placard displayed in a public place to advertise or to convey information or a direction: *a road sign; a stop sign.* **4.** A conventional figure or device that stands for a word, phrase, or operation; especially, a symbol, as in mathematics or musical notation: *the plus and minus signs.* **5.** *Medicine.* Any bodily manifestation that indicates the presence of a malfunction or disease to an observer but is not apparent to the patient. Compare **symptom. 6.** A portentous incident or event; especially, something that indicates a supernatural existence. **7.** An indicator, such as a spoor or scent, of the presence or trail of an animal: *deer sign.* **8.** A trace or vestige: *no sign of life.* **9.** *Astrology.* Any of the 12 divisions of the zodiac, each named after a constellation and represented by a symbol. Also called "sign of the zodiac."
~*v.* **signed, signing, signs.** *—tr.* **1.** To affix one's signature to: *signed the letter.* **2.** To write (one's signature). **3.** To approve, authorize, or ratify by affixing a signature, seal, or other mark: *signed the petition.* **4.** To engage by obtaining a signature on a contract: *sign a new player.* **5.** To relinquish or transfer (title or ownership, for example) to another by signature. Used with *away, off,* or *over.* **6.** To express or signify with a sign; signal. **7.** To express in sign language. **8.** To make a mark with a sign; especially, to consecrate with the sign of the cross. *—intr.* **1.** To make a sign or signs; signal. **2.** To communicate by sign language. **3.** To write one's signature. **—sign in.** To sign one's signature in a book upon arriving at a destination. **—sign off. 1.** In broadcasting, to announce the end of transmission, as at the end of the day. **2.** To end a letter, as with a signature or a message of affection. **—sign on. 1.** In broadcasting, to announce the beginning of transmission, as at the start of the day. **2.** To join or enlist; sign up: *signed on as a midshipman.* **3.** To engage the services of; employ. **—sign out.** To sign one's signature in a book before leaving to go elsewhere. **—sign up. 1.** To join or enlist; sign on. **2.** To engage the services of; employ: *signed up two players.* [Middle English *signe,* from Old French, from Latin *signum,* distinctive mark or figure, seal, signal.]
***Synonyms:** badge, indication, mark, symptom, token.*

Si·gnac (sēn-yäk′), **Paul** (1863–1935). French neoimpressionist painter and theoretician, a disciple of Georges Seurat. He painted mainly landscapes and marines, like the *Port of St. Tropez* (1916). He was an exponent of pointillism.

sig·nal (sĭg′nəl) *n. Abbr.* **sig. 1. a.** A sign, gesture, mechanical device, or other indicator serving as a means of communication: *Tears are a signal of grief. The railroad signal was green.* **b.** A message communicated by such means: *The commander sent the signal to advance.* **2.** That which is the occasion for or incites action: *The execution was the signal for mass protests.* **3.** *Electronics.* An impulse or fluctuating electric quantity, such as voltage, current, or electric field strength, the variations of which represent coded information. **4.** The sound, image, or message transmitted or received in telegraphy, telephony, radio, television, or radar.
~*adj.* **1.** Out of the ordinary; remarkable; conspicuous: *a signal feat.* **2.** Used or acting as a signal: *a signal flare.*
~*v.* **signaled, -naling, -nals** or *chiefly British* **-nalled, -nalling, -nals.** *—tr.* **1.** To make a signal or signals to (a person or thing); communicate with by signals: *signaled her to stop her car.* **2.** To relate or make known, as by signals; herald: *Gunfire signaled the start of the battle.* *—intr.* To make a signal or signals. [French, from Old French *s(e)ignal,* from Medieval Latin *signāle,* from Latin *signālis,* of a sign, from *signum,* SIGN.] **—sig·nal·er** *n.*

Signal Corps *n.* The branch of the U.S. Army that handles communications.

sig·nal·ize (sĭg′nə-līz′) *tr.v.* **-ized, -izing, -izes. 1.** To make remarkable or conspicuous. **2.** To point out particularly.

sig·nal·ly (sĭg′nə-lē) *adv.* Conspicuously; noticeably; especially.

sig·nal·man (sĭg′nəl-mən, -măn′) *n., pl.* **-men** (-mĭn, -mĕn′). **1.** One whose job it is to operate railroad signals. **2.** A soldier trained to communicate by signals. In this sense, also called "signaler."

sig·nal·ment (sĭg′nəl-mənt) *n.* A detailed description of the appearance of a person, as for police files. [French *signalement,* from *signaler,* to mark out, describe, from *signal,* SIGNAL.]

signal-to-noise ratio (sĭg′nəl-tə-noiz′) *n.* The ratio of the amplitude of the signal in an electronic device to the amplitude of the noise in that device.

sig·na·to·ry (sĭg′nə-tôr′ē, -tōr′ē) *adj.* Bound by signed agreement. ~*n., pl.* **signatories.** A person or nation that has signed a treaty or other document. [Latin *signātōrius,* from *signāre,* to mark, affix one's seal to, from *signum,* SIGN.]

sig·na·ture (sĭg′nə-cho͝or′) *n. Abbr.* **sig. 1. a.** The name of a person as written by himself, especially to approve a document. **b.** The act of signing one's name. **2.** Any sign that indicates the presence or activity of a person, group, or thing: *The robbery bore the signature of a professional.* **3.** *Music.* **a.** A **key signature** *(see).* **b.** A **time signature** *(see).* **4.** In printing: **a.** A group of printed pages, most commonly 16 or 32, folded from a single sheet, that is bound together with others to make up a book. Also called "section." **b.** A letter, number, or symbol placed at the bottom of the first page of such a group of printed pages of a book as a guide to the proper sequence of the sheets in binding. **5.** *Abbr.* **S., Sig.** That part of a medical prescription giving the doctor's instructions to the patient. **6.** An identifying tune, design, or logo. [Medieval Latin *signātura,* from Latin *signāre,* to mark with a sign, from *signum,* SIGN.]

sign·board (sīn′bôrd′, -bōrd′) *n.* A board that bears a sign giving information.

sign·er (sī′nər) *n.* **1.** One that signs. **2.** A person skilled in sign language, especially as an interpreter for the deaf.

sig·net (sĭg′nĭt) *n.* **1.** A small seal; especially, an official seal used on a document. **2.** The impression made with such a seal.
~*tr.v.* **signeted, -neting, -nets.** To mark or endorse with a signet. [Middle English, from Old French, diminutive of *signe,* SIGN.]

signet ring *n.* A finger ring bearing a signet or set of initials.

sig·nif·i·cance (sĭg-nĭf′ĭ-kəns) *n.* Also **sig·nif·i·can·cy** (-kən-sē). **1.** The state or quality of being significant; meaning. **2.** Importance; consequence: *an event of great significance.* **3.** Implied or underlying meaning: *I understand the words, but not their real significance.* —See Synonyms at **importance, meaning.**

sig·nif·i·cant (sĭg-nĭf′ĭ-kənt) *adj.* **1.** Having or expressing a meaning; meaningful. **2.** Having or expressing a covert meaning: *She darted me a significant glance.* **3.** Important; notable; valuable. [Latin *significāns* (stem *significant-*), present participle of *significāre,* to SIGNIFY.] **—sig·nif·i·cant·ly** *adv.*

significant figures *pl.n. Mathematics.* The digits of the decimal form of a number beginning with the digit farthest to the left and higher than zero and extending to the right to include all digits warranted by the accuracy of measuring devices used to obtain the numbers or to include a specific number of digits after rounding up or down. Also called "significant digits."

sig·ni·fi·ca·tion (sĭg′nə-fĭ-kā′shən) *n.* **1.** Intended meaning; sense. **2.** The act or process of signifying. —See Synonyms at **meaning.**

sig·nif·i·ca·tive (sĭg-nĭf′ĭ-kā′tĭv) *adj.* **1.** Indicative; significant. **2.** Signifying; symbolic.

sig·ni·fy (sĭg′nə-fī′) *v.* **-fied, -fying, -fies.** *—tr.* **1.** To serve as a sign or symbol of; betoken; denote. **2.** To make known; indicate: *signified her approval with a gesture.* *—intr.* To have meaning or importance. —See Synonyms at **mean** (convey sense). [Middle English *signifien,* from Old French *signifier,* from Latin *significāre* : *signum,* SIGN + *facere,* to make.] **—sig·ni·fi·er** *n.*

sign language *n.* A system of communication by means of hand gestures, used especially by deaf people.

sign manual *n., pl.* **signs manual.** A person's signature; especially, the signature of a monarch at the top of a royal decree.

sign of the cross *n.* A gesture describing the form of a cross, made in token of faith in Christ or as an invocation of blessing or divine protection; especially, such a gesture of the right hand from the forehead to the breast and then from the left to the right shoulder.

sign of the zodiac *n. Astrology.* A **sign** *(see).*

si·gnor (sēn-yôr′, -yōr′) *n., pl.* **signori** (sēn-yôr′ē, -yōr′ē) or **-gnors.** Also **si·gnior.** *Abbr.* **S., sig., Sig. 1.** The Italian title of courtesy for a man, used before a surname and equivalent to the English *Mr.* **2.** In an Italian-speaking country, a gentleman. [See **signore.**]

si·gno·ra (sēn-yôr′ə, -yōr′ə) *n., pl.* **signore** (sēn-yôr′ē, -yōr′ē) or **-ras.** The Italian title of courtesy for or form of address to a married woman, equivalent to the English *Mrs.* or *madam.* [See **signore.**]

si·gno·re (sēn-yôr′ā, -yōr′ā) *n., pl.* **signori** (sēn-yôr′ē, -yōr′ē). *Abbr.* **S., sig., Sig. 1.** The Italian form of address to a man, equivalent to the English *sir.* **2.** In an Italian-speaking country, a gentleman. [Italian, from Latin *senior,* older, SENIOR.]

PRONUNCIATION KEY

ă, pat; ā, pay; âr, care;
ä, father, are; b, bib;
ch, church; d, deed; ĕ, pet;
ē, be; f, fife; g, gag; h, hat;
hw, which; ĭ, pit; ī, pie;
îr, pier; j, judge; k, kick;
l, lid, needle; m, mum;
n, no, sudden; ng, thing;
ŏ, pot; ō, toe; ô, paw, for;
oi, noise; ou, out; o͝o, book;
o͞o, boot; p, pop; r, roar;
s, sauce; sh, ship, dish;
t, tight; th, thin, path;
th, this, bathe; ŭ, cut; ûr, fur;
v, valve; w, with; y, yes;
z, zebra, size; zh, vision;
ə, about, item, edible, gallop, circus, peaceful

IN FOREIGN WORDS:

à, *Fr.* ami; œ, *Fr.* feu, *Ger.* schön; ü, *Fr.* tu, *Ger.* über; KH, *Ger.* ich, *Scot.* loch; N, *Fr.* bon; y′, *Fr.* Compiègne

STRESS MARKS:

Primary stress: ′
in·cite′ (ĭn-sīt′)
Secondary stress: ′
in′sight′ (ĭn′sīt′)

sign language

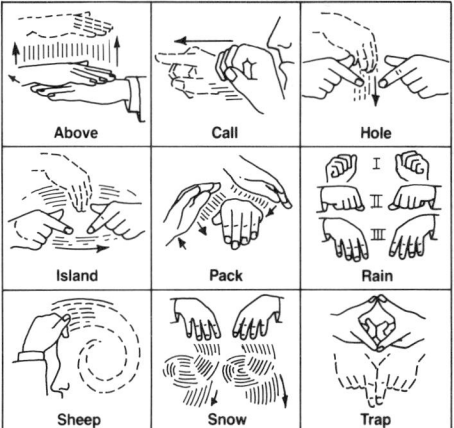
si·gno·ri·na (sēn'yô-rē'nə) *n., pl.* **-ne** (-nā) or **-nas.** The Italian title of courtesy for or form of address to an unmarried woman, equivalent to the English *Miss.* [Italian, diminutive of SIGNORA.]

sign·post (sīn'pōst') *n.* **1.** A post supporting a sign. **2.** Anything that serves as an indication, sign, or guide.

Sig·urd (sĭg'ŏord', -ərd). *Norse Mythology.* The hero who slew the dragon Fafnir. He corresponds to Siegfried of the *Nibelungenlied.*

Si·ha·nouk (sē'ə-nŏok'), **Prince (Samdech Preah) Norodom** (1922-). Former king of Cambodia. He was elected king in 1941 and abdicated in March 1955 to become prime minister and minister of foreign affairs in the following October. In 1960 he was elected head of state, a position that he held until he was deposed by a right-wing faction that opposed his policy of allowing the Vietcong troops to use Cambodian territory. He was restored to power in 1975 when the Khmer Republic was overthrown, but resigned in 1976. In 1979 he was made a special envoy of the Khmer Rouge to the United Nations.

Sikh (sēk) *n.* An adherent of Sikhism.
~*adj.* Of or pertaining to the Sikhs or Sikhism. [Hindi, from Sanskrit *śiṣya,* "disciple," from *śikṣati,* he helps, pays homage, learns, serves, desiderative of *śaknōti,* he can, is able to do.]

Sikh·ism (sē'kĭz'əm) *n.* The doctrines and practices of a monotheistic religious sect that broke away from orthodox Hinduism in the 16th century. Its members live chiefly in northern India.

Si Kiang. See Xi Jiang.

Sik·kim (sĭk'ĭm). State of northern India. It was formerly a constitutional monarchy (controlled by India), but was incorporated into India in 1975. Almost the entire state lies within the eastern Himalayas. Most of the people are subsistence farmers, but spices and tea are grown for sale. The capital is Gangtok. —**Sik·kim·ese** *n.*

si·lage (sī'lĭj) *n.* Fodder prepared by storing and fermenting green forage plants in a silo or pit. [Alteration (influenced by SILO) of ENSILAGE.]

si·lane (sī'lān') *n.* Any of a class of silicon hydrides with the general formula Si_nH_{2n+2}. They are similar to the alkanes and are named by the number of silicon atoms in the molecule (as *disilane,* Si_2H_6). [*Silicon* + -ANE.]

sild (sĭld) *n.* Any of various small Norwegian herrings, especially when canned or otherwise prepared for eating. [Norwegian.]

si·lence (sī'ləns) *n.* **1.** The condition or quality of being or keeping silent; avoidance of speech or noise. **2.** The absence of sound; stillness. **3.** A period of time without communication by word or noise: *two minutes' silence.* **4.** Refusal or failure to speak out.
~*tr.v.* **silenced, -lencing, -lences. 1.** To make silent or bring to silence. **2.** To curtail the expression of; suppress. [Middle English, from Old French, from Latin *silentium,* from *silēre,* to be silent.]

si·lenc·er (sī'lən-sər) *n.* **1.** One that silences. **2.** A device in the exhaust system of an internal-combustion engine, especially one fitted to a motor vehicle, in which the sound is deadened by making the exhaust gases pass through a system of baffle plates. **3.** A device attached to the muzzle of a firearm to muffle the report.

si·lent (sī'lənt) *adj.* **1. a.** Making no sound or noise; quiet. **b.** Free of all sound. **2.** Not disposed to speak; taciturn. **3.** Unable to speak; mute. **4.** Refusing or failing to give information or an opinion: *remained silent on the matter.* **5.** Not voiced or expressed; tacit: *silent declarations of love.* **6.** Inactive or undisturbed; quiescent: *a silent volcano.* **7.** Having no phonetic value; unpronounced; for example, the letter *b* in *subtle* is silent. **8.** Having no sound track: *a silent film.* —See Synonyms at **still.**
~*n.* A silent film. [Latin *silēns* (stem *silent*-), present participle of *silēre,* to be silent.] —**si·lent·ly** *adv.* —**si·lent·ness** *n.*

silent butler *n.* A small receptacle with a handle and a hinged cover, used for collecting ashes and crumbs.

silent partner *n.* One who makes financial investments in a business enterprise but does not participate in its management. Also *chiefly British* "sleeping partner."

si·le·nus (sī-lē'nəs) *n., pl.* **-ni** (-nī). *Greek Mythology.* Any of various minor woodland deities or spirits and companions of Dionysus.

Si·le·nus (sī-lē'nəs). *Greek Mythology.* A satyr, the foster father of Bacchus.

si·le·sia (sī-lē'zhə, -shə) *n.* A thin, light, twilled cotton fabric used for linings. [After SILESIA, where it was first produced.]

Si·le·sia (sī-lē'zhə). Region of east-central Europe, extending along the foot of the Sudeten Mts. and the western Carpathians and into the Oder valley. Most of it now lies in Poland, with the rest in Czechoslovakia and East Germany. The area is mainly agricultural land and forest, but the south forms one of Europe's main coal-mining and manufacturing regions. —**Si·le·sian** *n. & adj.*

sil·hou·ette (sĭl'ŏo-ĕt') *n.* **1.** A representation of the outline of something, especially a person's profile, usually filled in with black or another solid color. **2.** The shadow image or outline of something, such as one produced on a white, illuminated screen by an object interposed between the screen and the source of light.
~*tr.v.* **silhouetted, -etting, -ettes.** To represent or cause to be seen as a silhouette. [French, short for *portrait à la silhouette,* after Étienne de Silhouette (1709-67), French controller-general known for his parsimony (such portraits were inexpensive).]

sil·i·ca (sĭl'ĭ-kə) *n.* A white or colorless crystalline compound, SiO_2, occurring abundantly as quartz, sand, flint, agate, and many other minerals, and used to manufacture a wide variety of materials, notably glass and concrete. Also called "silicon dioxide." [New Latin, from Latin *silex* (stem *silic*-), flint.]

silica gel *n.* Amorphous silica that resembles white sand and is used as a drying and dehumidifying agent, a catalyst and catalyst carrier, an anticaking agent in cosmetics, and in chromatography.

sil·i·cate (sĭl'ĭ-kāt', -kĭt) *n.* Any of numerous compounds containing silicon, oxygen, and a metallic or organic radical, occurring in most rocks except limestone and dolomite and forming the basis of common glass and bricks. [SILIC(A) + -ATE.]

si·li·ceous (sī-lĭsh'əs) *adj.* Containing, resembling, pertaining to, or consisting of silica. [Latin *siliceus,* of flint, from *silex,* flint.]

silici-, silic- *prefix.* Indicates silica or silicon; for example, **siliciferous, silicide.** [From SILICA.]

si·lic·ic (sī-lĭs'ĭk) *adj.* Pertaining to, resembling, or derived from silica or silicon. [SILIC- + -IC.]

silicic acid *n.* A jellylike substance, $SiO_2 \cdot nH_2O$, produced when sodium silicate solution is acidified and used for the same purposes as silica gel.

sil·i·cide (sĭl'ə-sīd') *n.* A compound of silicon with another element or radical. [SILIC(I)- + -IDE.]

sil·i·cif·er·ous (sĭl'ə-sĭf'ər-əs) *adj.* Bearing, producing, or in partial combination with silica. [SILICI- + -FEROUS.]

si·lic·i·fy (sī-lĭs'ə-fī') *v.* **-fied, -fying, -fies.** —*tr.* To convert into silica. —*intr.* To be converted into silica. [SILICI- + -FY.] —**si·lic·i·fi·ca·tion** (sī-lĭs'ə-fī-kā'shən) *n.*

sil·i·cle (sĭl'ĭ-kəl) *n.* Also **si·lic·u·la** (sī-lĭk'yə-lə). *Botany.* A short, flat siliqua, such as the fruit of the plant honesty. [Latin *silicula,* diminutive of *siliqua,* seed pod, SILIQUA.]

sil·i·con (sĭl'ĭ-kən, -kŏn') *n. Symbol* **Si** A nonmetallic element occurring extensively in the earth's crust in silica and silicates, having both an amorphous and a crystalline allotrope, and used in combination with other materials in glass, semiconducting devices, concrete, brick, refractories, pottery, and silicones. Atomic number 14, atomic weight 28.086, melting point 1,410°C, boiling point 2,355°C, specific gravity 2.33, valence 4. [From SILICA.]

silicon carbide *n.* A bluish-black crystalline compound, SiC, one of the hardest known substances, used as an abrasive and heat-

silkworm *A woman employed in a spinning factory in China sorts the cocoons produced by the silkworm. The worms—the larvae of* Bombyx mori, *a species of moth—feed on the leaves of the mulberry tree.*

silverfish *Flour, paper, and cloth are the favorite foods of the silverfish, a wingless insect that lives in damp, cool places.*

refractory material, and in single crystals as a semiconductor, especially in high-temperature applications.

silicon chip *n.* A chip based on a silicon wafer, used in microprocessors.

sil·i·con-con·trolled rectifier (sĭl'ĭ-kən-kən-trōld') *n. Abbr.* **SCR.** An electronic device consisting of a four-layer chip of semiconducting material in which the anode-cathode current is controlled by the signal applied to a third electrode, called the gate.

silicon dioxide *n. Chemistry.* **Silica** *(see).*

sil·i·cone (sĭl'ĭ-kōn') *n.* Any of a group of semi-inorganic polymers based on the structural unit R_2SiO, where R is an organic group, characterized by thermal stability, water repellence, and physiochemical inertness. They are used in adhesives, lubricants, protective coatings, paints, electrical insulation, synthetic rubber, and prosthetic replacements for bodily parts. Compare **siloxane.** [SILIC(I)- + -ONE.]

sil·i·co·sis (sĭl'ĭ-kō'sĭs) *n.* Fibrosis of the lungs caused by long-term inhalation of silica dust and resulting in a chronic shortness of breath. [New Latin : SILIC(I)- + -OSIS.]

si·li·qua (sĭl'ĭ-kwə, sĭ-lē'kwə) *n.* Also **si·lique** (sĭ-lēk'). A long pod that is divided by a membranous partition and splits at both seams, characteristic of fruit of the mustards and related plants. [French, from Latin *siliqua*†, pod.] **—sil·i·quous** (sĭl'ə-kwəs), **sil·i·quose** (sĭl'ə-kwōs') *adj.*

silk (sĭlk) *n.* **1.** The fine, lustrous fiber produced by certain insect larvae and spiders; especially, fiber produced by a silkworm to form its cocoon. **2.** Thread or fabric made from this fiber. **3. a.** A garment made from this fabric, such as a gown. **b. silks.** Brightly colored silk garments used to identify a jockey or harness driver. **4.** Any silky, filamentous material, such as the styles forming a tuft on an ear of corn.
~adj. Of, resembling, or pertaining to silk.
~intr.v. **silked, silking, silks.** To develop silk. Used of corn. [Middle English *silk, selk,* Old English *sioloc, seolec,* from Late Latin *sericum* (noun), Latin *sericus* (adjective), from *seres,* from Greek *Sēres,* an oriental people (probably originally meaning "the silk people"), from Chinese *sī,* silk. See also **serge, sericeous.**]

silk cotton *n.* A silky fiber, such as kapok, attached to the seeds of certain trees.

silk-cot·ton tree (sĭlk'kŏt'n) *n.* Any of several trees of the family Bombacaceae; especially, *Ceiba pentandra,* native to tropical America, cultivated for its leathery fruit containing the fiber **kapok** *(see).*

silk·en (sĭl'kən) *adj.* **1.** Made of silk. **2.** Resembling silk in texture or appearance; smooth and lustrous: *silken hair.* **3.** Delicately pleasing or caressing in effect: *a silken voice.* **4.** Wearing silk.

silk hat *n.* A man's silk-covered top hat.

Silk Road. Ancient trade route between China and the Mediterranean, linking China to the Roman Empire. Its length was *c.* 6,400 kilometers (4,000 miles). It was the route followed by Marco Polo on his historic trip to Cathay.

silk-screen process (sĭlk'skrēn') *n.* A method of producing a stencil for printing in which a design is imposed upon a screen of silk or other fine fabric that is coated with an impermeable substance on areas to be left blank. Ink is forced through the cloth onto the printing surface. Also called "screen printing."

silk·worm (sĭlk'wûrm') *n.* Any of various caterpillars that produce silk cocoons; especially, the larva of a Chinese moth, *Bombyx mori,* that spins a cocoon of fine, lustrous fiber that is the source of commercial silk.

silk·y (sĭl'kē) *adj.* **-ier, -iest. 1.** Resembling silk; soft and smooth; lustrous. **2.** Made of silk; silken. **3.** Having long, silklike hairs or a silky covering: *a silky leaf.* **4.** Ingratiatingly smooth; seductive. **—silk·i·ly** *adv.* **—silk·i·ness** *n.*

silky oak *n.* A tree, *Grevillea robusta,* native to Australia, having divided leaves and showy clusters of orange flowers.

sill (sĭl) *n.* **1.** The horizontal member, often of wood or stone, that bears the upright portion of a frame; especially, the base of a window or door frame. **2.** The horizontal member at the base of a window protruding beyond the frame. **3.** *Geology.* A relatively thin sheet of igneous rock intruded between beds of other rock. [Middle English *sille, selle,* Old English *syll(e),* threshold, sill.]

sillabub. Variant of **syllabub.**

sil·li·man·ite (sĭl'ĭ-mə-nīt') *n.* A gray, brown, or green mineral, Al_2SiO_5, that occurs in metamorphic rocks. [After Benjamin *Silliman* (1779–1864), U.S. chemist.]

Sil·li·toe (sĭl'ĭ-tō'), **Alan** (1928–). British novelist, one of the leading figures in the kitchen-sink movement of the 1950's and 1960's. His two most famous novels of working-class life, *Saturday Night and Sunday Morning* (1958) and *The Loneliness of the Long Distance Runner* (1959), were both made into successful films.

Sills (sĭlz), **Beverly,** born Belle Silverman (1929–). U.S. coloratura soprano. She made her debut with the New York City Opera in 1955 and became its general director in 1979.

sil·ly (sĭl'ē) *adj.* **-lier, -liest. 1.** Showing a lack of good sense; unreasoning; foolish. **2.** Showing a lack of or disregard for intelligence; fatuous. **3.** *Informal.* Semiconscious; dazed: *knocked me silly.* **4.** *Archaic.* Innocent; harmless; helpless.
~n., pl. **sillies.** *Informal.* A silly person. —See Synonyms at **foolish.** [Middle English, "pitiable," originally variant of *seely,* happy, blessed, Old English *gesǣlig.*] **—sil·li·ly** *adv.* **—sil·li·ness** *n.*

sil·ly-bil·ly (sĭl'ē-bĭl'ē) *n., pl.* **-billies.** *Informal.* A silly person. Used affectionately or humorously.

si·lo (sī'lō) *n., pl.* **-los. 1. a.** A tall, cylindrical, airtight structure in which fodder is stored. **b.** A pit dug for the same purpose. **2.** *Military.* A sunken missile shelter with facilities either for lifting the missile to a launch position or for launching from underground.
~tr.v. **siloed, -loing, -los.** To store in a silo. [Spanish, from Latin *sirus,* from Greek *siros*†, pit for the storage of grain.]

si·lox·ane (sĭ-lŏk'sān') *n.* Any of a class of organic or inorganic chemical compounds of silicon, oxygen, and usually carbon and hydrogen, based on the structural unit R_2SiO, where R is CH_3, H, C_2H_5, or a more complex group. Compare **silicone.** [*Sil*icon + *ox*ygen + -ANE.]

silt (sĭlt) *n.* A sedimentary material consisting of fine mineral particles intermediate in size between sand and clay.
~v. **silted, silting, silts.** *—intr.* To become filled with silt. Usually used with *up.* *—tr.* To fill with silt. Usually used with *up.* [Middle English *cylte,* probably from Scandinavian, akin to Danish and Norwegian *sylt,* salt marsh.] **—sil·ta·tion** (sĭl-tā'shən) *n.*

silt·stone (sĭlt'stōn') *n.* A sandstone formed from consolidated silt.

Si·lu·res (sĭl'yə-rēz', sĭ-lo͝or'ēz) *pl.n.* A people described by the Roman historian Tacitus as occupying southwestern Britain at the time of the Roman invasion.

Si·lu·ri·an (sĭ-lo͝or'ē-ən, sī-) *adj.* **1.** Of, belonging to, or designating the geological time or system of rocks of the third period of the Paleozoic era, characterized by the appearance of land plants. **2.** Of or pertaining to the Silures or their culture.
~n. Geology. The Silurian period or system of rocks. Preceded by *the.* [After the SILURES, the rocks having been first identified in the part of Wales supposed to have been inhabited by them.]

si·lu·rid (sĭ-lo͝or'ĭd, sī-) *adj.* Of or belonging to the family Siluridae, which includes various freshwater catfishes of Europe and Asia.
~n. A silurid fish. [New Latin *Siluridae,* from Latin *silurus,* a large freshwater fish, probably the sheatfish, from Greek *silouros.*]

silva. Variant of **sylva.**

silvan. Variant of **sylvan.**

sil·ver (sĭl'vər) *n.* **1.** *Symbol* **Ag** A lustrous white, ductile, malleable metallic element, occurring both uncombined and in ores such as argentite, having the highest thermal and electrical conductivity of the metals. It is highly valued for jewelry, tableware, and other ornamental use, and is widely used in coinage, photography, dental and soldering alloys, electrical contacts, and printed circuits. Atomic number 47, atomic weight 107.870, melting point 960.8°C, boiling point 2,212°C, specific gravity 10.50, valences 1, 2. See **sterling silver. 2.** This metal as a commodity or medium of exchange. **3.** Coins made of this metal or a metal similar in color. **4. a.** Tableware, especially cutlery, and other domestic articles made of or plated with this metal. **b.** Any tableware. **5.** Lustrous light gray to white. **6.** *Photography.* A silver salt, especially silver nitrate, used to sensitize paper. **7.** A silver medal.
~adj. **1.** Made of, containing, or coated with silver. **2.** Of, pertaining to, or based on silver: *the silver standard.* **3.** Having a lustrous medium-gray color: *silver hair.* **4.** Having a sonorous, ringing sound. **5.** Eloquent; persuasive: *a silver tongue.* **6.** Of or designating a 25th anniversary: *a silver jubilee.*
~v. **silvered, -vering, -vers.** *—tr.* **1.** To cover, plate, or adorn with silver or a similar lustrous substance, usually by chemical reduction of silver nitrate solution or by deposition of an evaporated metal film in vacuum. **2.** To cause to resemble silver: *Moonlight silvered the waves.* **3.** To coat (photographic paper) with a film of silver nitrate or other silver salt. *—intr.* To become silvery. [Old English *siolfor, seolfor,* Common Germanic *silubhra-*† (unattested).]

silver age *n. Classical Mythology.* The second of the great periods of the world's history, characterized by the diminishing awareness and practice of morality and religion. Compare **golden age, iron age.**

silver birch *n.* A Eurasian birch tree, *Betula pendula,* having silvery-white, peeling bark.

silver bromide *n.* A pale-yellow powder, AgBr, that darkens on exposure to light, and is used as the light-sensitive component on ordinary photographic films and plates.

silver certificate *n.* A paper money bill formerly issued as legal tender by the U.S. government in representation of deposited silver bullion.

silver chloride *n.* A white granular powder, AgCl, that darkens on exposure to light and is used in photography and optics.

silver-eye (sĭl'vər-ī') *n.* An Australian songbird, the **white-eye** *(see).*

silver fir *n.* Any of various coniferous trees of the genus *Abies,* the leaves of which have a silvery undersurface. See **fir.**

sil·ver·fish (sĭl'vər-fĭsh') *n., pl.* **-fishes** or collectively **silverfish. 1.** A silvery, wingless insect, *Lepisma saccharina,* that often causes extensive damage to bookbindings, starched clothing, and similar material. **2.** Any of various fishes having silvery scales, such as a variety of the goldfish *Carassius auratus.*

silver fox *n.* **1.** A variety of the red fox in a color phase in which it has black fur tipped with white. **2.** The fur of this animal.

silver iodide *n.* A pale yellow powder, AgI, that darkens on exposure to light and is used in artificial rainmaking, in photography, and as an antiseptic.

silver medal *n.* A medal awarded for achieving second place in a race or similar competition.

sil·vern (sĭl'vərn) *adj. Poetic.* Like silver; silvery.

silver nitrate *n.* A poisonous, colorless crystalline compound, $AgNO_3$, that darkens when exposed to light in the presence of organic matter and is used in photography, mirror manufacturing, hair dyeing, silver-plating, and as an external medicine.

silver plate *n.* **1.** Tableware or other household articles made of metal plated with silver. **2.** The thin layer of silver used to plate such articles.

sil·ver-plate (sĭl′vər-plāt′) *tr.v.* **-plated, -plating, -plates.** To cover (a base metal or article) with a thin layer of silver.

sil·ver·point (sĭl′vər-point′) *n.* **1.** A sketching process using a silver-tipped stylus and specially prepared paper. **2.** The stylus used in this process.

silver salmon *n.* The **coho salmon** (see).

silver screen *n.* **1.** *Informal.* Motion pictures collectively. Preceded by *the.* **2.** A screen used for showing a film.

sil·ver·side (sĭl′vər-sīd′) *n.* Also **sil·ver·sides** (-sīdz′). Any of various marine and freshwater fishes of the family Atherinidae, having a silvery band along each side.

sil·ver·smith (sĭl′vər-smĭth′) *n.* A person who makes, repairs, or replates articles of silver or silver plate. **—sil·ver·smith·ing** *n.*

silver standard *n.* A monetary standard under which a fixed quantity of silver constitutes the basic unit of currency.

sil·ver-tongued (sĭl′vər-tŭngd′) *adj.* Fluent and persuasive in speech; eloquent.

sil·ver·ware (sĭl′vər-wâr′) *n.* Articles, especially cutlery, made of or plated with silver.

sil·ver·weed (sĭl′vər-wēd′) *n.* **1.** A plant, *Potentilla anserina,* having yellow flowers and leaves that often have silvery hairs. **2.** Any of various twining shrubs of the genus *Argyreia* of southeastern Asia, having purple flowers and silvery leaves.

sil·ver·y (sĭl′və-rē) *adj.* **1.** Like silver in color or luster. **2.** Having a clear, ringing sound. **3.** Containing or coated with silver. **—sil·ver·i·ness** *n.*

sil·vi·cul·ture (sĭl′vĭ-kŭl′chər) *n.* The care and cultivation of forest trees; forestry. [French : Latin *silva, sylva,* forest, SILVA + CULTURE.] **—sil·vi·cul·tur·al** *adj.* **—sil·vi·cul·tur·ist** *n.*

si·ma (sī′mə) *n.* The lower layer of the earth's outer crust, rich in silica and magnesium, that underlies the **sial** (see). [German *Sima* : New Latin *si*lica + *ma*gnesium.]

Sim·chath To·rah (sĭm′ĸнäs tôr′ə, tōr′ə). A Jewish holiday celebrated on the 23rd day of Tishri, marking the end of the cycle of reading the Torah, and coinciding with the last day of Succoth. [Hebrew *shimḥath tōrāh,* "rejoicing over the Law" : *śimḥath,* inflectional form of *śimḥāh,* joy, merriment, from *śāmaḥ,* he rejoiced + TORAH.]

Si·me·non (sē-mə-nôn′), **Georges Joseph Christian** (1903–). Belgian novelist and short-story writer. His first work was published in 1922, and during the next 14 years he produced over 1,500 short stories, writing under more than a dozen pseudonyms. The first novel introducing his famous detective, Inspector Maigret, was published in 1931. He has published 212 novels, including 80 in the Maigret series.

Sim·e·on (sĭm′ē-ən). **1.** In the Old Testament, the second son of Jacob and Leah and the name of the tribe of Israel descended from him. Genesis 29:33. **2.** The man who, upon seeing the infant Jesus, spoke the Nunc Dimittis. Luke 2:25–35.

Simeon Sty·li·tes (stī-lī′tēz), **Saint** (c. 390–459 A.D.). Syrian monk. He entered a monastery near Aleppo, but was forced to leave it and became a hermit. He then spent 40 years on a high column, from c. 420, and thus became the first-known Christian stylite, or "column-dweller."

sim·i·an (sĭm′ē-ən) *adj.* Also **sim·i·ous** (-əs). Pertaining to, characteristic of, or resembling an ape or monkey.
~*n.* An ape or monkey. [Latin *sīmia,* ape, perhaps from *sīmus,* snub-nosed, from Greek *simos,* bent upwards, snub-nosed.]

sim·i·lar (sĭm′ə-lər) *adj.* **1.** Showing some resemblance; related in appearance or nature; alike though not identical. **2.** *Geometry.* Designating figures having corresponding angles equal and corresponding line segments proportional. [French *similaire,* from Latin *similis,* like.] **—sim·i·lar·ly** *adv.*

Usage: Similar is an adjective only, and is not used adverbially in standard English. *X is similar to Y* is acceptable, but *X works similar to Y* is nonstandard.

sim·i·lar·i·ty (sĭm′ə-lăr′ə-tē) *n., pl.* **-ties. 1.** The condition or quality of being similar; resemblance. **2.** A respect in which persons or things are similar. **—See Synonyms at likeness.**

sim·i·le (sĭm′ə-lē) *n.* A figure of speech in which two different things are compared, the comparison usually being made explicit by being introduced with *like* or *as;* for example, *"saw the crowd race away like scattered sheep"* (Saki). Compare **metaphor.** [Latin, neuter of *similis,* SIMILAR.]

si·mil·i·tude (sĭ-mĭl′ə-tōōd′, -tyōōd′) *n.* **1.** Similarity. **2.** Something closely resembling another; a counterpart; a double. **3.** A simile, allegory, or parable. **—See Synonyms at likeness.** [Middle English, from Old French, from Latin *similitūdo,* from *similis,* SIMILAR.]

Sim·la (sĭm′lə). City in northwestern India, capital of Himachal Pradesh state. Situated in the foothills of the Himalayas, its pleasant climate made it a popular holiday and health resort, and it was India's summer capital from 1865 to 1939.

Sim·men·tal (sĭm′ən-täl′, zĭm′-). Any of a breed of European cattle reared for milk, meat, and as draft animals, having a reddish or yellowish coat. **—Sim·men·tal** *adj.*

sim·mer (sĭm′ər) *v.* **-mered, -mering, -mers.** *—intr.* **1.** To cook gently just below or at the boiling point. **2.** To be filled with barely controlled anger or resentment; seethe. *—tr.* To cook (something) just below or at the boiling point. **—simmer down. 1.** To reduce the liquid volume of by boiling slowly. **2.** To become calm after excitement or anger.

~*n.* The state or process of simmering. [Earlier *simper,* Middle English *simperen* (imitative).]

sim·nel (sĭm′nəl) *n.* **1.** *Chiefly British.* A rich fruitcake, often covered with marzipan, traditionally eaten at Eastertide. Also called "simnel cake." **2.** A crisp bread made of fine wheat flour. [Middle English *simenel,* from Old French, from Latin *simila,* fine flour, or Greek *semidalis,* perhaps from Semitic, akin to Akkadian *samīdu.* See also **semolina.**]

si·mo·le·on (sĭ-mō′lē-ən) *n. Slang.* A dollar. [Origin unknown.]

Si·mon (sī′mən), **(Marvin) Neil** (1927–). U.S. playwright. Beginning in 1948 as a television writer for Phil Silvers, Jackie Gleason, and Sid Caesar, he wrote his first comedy, *Come Blow Your Horn,* in 1960. Since then he has had an almost unbroken string of successes characterized by eccentric characters and rapid-fire comedic lines.

si·mo·ni·ac (sī-mō′nē-ăk′, sĭ-) *n.* One who practices simony. **—si·mo·ni·a·cal** (sī′mə-nī′ə-kəl, sĭm′ə-) *adj.* **—si·mo·ni·a·cal·ly** *adv.*

Si·mon·i·des of Ce·os (sī-mŏn′ĭ-dēz; sē′ŏs) (6th–5th century B.C.). Greek poet. Although only fragments of his work exist, he is considered one of the finest Greek poets, noted especially for his epitaphs on the slain warriors at Marathon and Thermopylae. He is the first Greek poet known to have accepted commissions.

Si·mon Ma·gus (sī′mən mā′gəs). Samaritan sorcerer of the 1st century A.D.; converted to Christianity.

Simon Peter. See Saint **Peter.**

si·mon-pure (sī′mən-pyoor′) *adj.* Genuine; thoroughgoing; real. [From the *real Simon Pure,* after *Simon Pure,* a character who is impersonated by a rival in Susanna Centlivre's play *A Bold Stroke for a Wife* (1717).]

si·mo·ny (sī′mə-nē, sĭm′ə-) *n.* The buying or selling of ecclesiastical pardons, offices, or emoluments. [Middle English *simonie,* from Old French, from Late Latin *sīmōnia,* after *Simon* Magus, a Samaritan who offered money to the Apostles Peter and John for the power of conferring the Holy Ghost on whomsoever he wished. Acts 8:18–19.] **—si·mo·nist** *n. & adj.*

Simon Ze·lo·tes (zē-lō′tēz). Christian leader of the 1st century A.D. and one of the Twelve Apostles.

si·moom (sĭ-moom′) *n.* Also **si·moon** (-moon′). A strong hot sand-laden wind of the Sahara and Arabian deserts. Also called "samiel." [Arabic *samūm,* "poisonous," from *samma,* "he poisoned," from *sam,* poison, from Aramaic *sammā,* drug, poison.]

simp (sĭmp) *n. Slang.* A simpleton; a fool. [From SIMPLE.]

sim·pa·ti·co (sĭm-pä′tĭ-kō′, -pät′ĭ-kō′) *adj. Informal.* **1.** Of like mind or temperament; compatible. **2.** Having attractive qualities; likeable. [Italian, from *simpatia,* sympathy, from Latin *sympathīa,* SYMPATHY.]

sim·per (sĭm′pər) *v.* **-pered, -pering, -pers.** *—intr.* To smile in a silly, coy, self-conscious manner. *—tr.* To express with a silly or coy smile.
~*n.* A silly or self-conscious smile. [Scandinavian, akin to Danish dialectal *simper†.*] **—sim·per·er** *n.* **—sim·per·ing·ly** *adv.*

sim·ple (sĭm′pəl) *adj.* **-pler, -plest. 1.** Having or composed of one thing or part only; not combined or compound: *a simple device.* **2.** Not involved or complicated; easy: *"All that was intricate and false; the truth was simple"* (W. H. Auden). **3.** Without additions or modifications; bare; mere: *the simple facts.* **4.** Without embellishment; not ornate or adorned: *a simple black dress.* **5.** Not elaborate, elegant, or luxurious: *a simple dwelling.* **6.** Not affected; unassuming or unpretentious: *simple manners.* **7.** Not guileful or deceitful; sincere. **8.** Humble or lowly in condition or rank: *a simple peasant.* **9.** Ordinary or common: *not migraine, just a simple headache.* **10.** Not important or significant; trivial. **11. a.** Having or manifesting little sense or intellect; stupid. **b.** Mentally subnormal. **12.** *Biology.* Having no divisions or subdivisions; not compound: *a simple leaf.* **13.** *Chemistry.* Consisting of only one compound; not complex or mixed: *a simple salt.* **14.** *Music.* Without figuration or ornamentation: *simple harmony.* **—See Synonyms at naive.**
~*n. Archaic.* **1.** A fool; a simpleton. **2.** A person of humble birth or condition. **3.** A medicinal plant or the medicine obtained from it. [Middle English, from Old French, from Latin *simplus.*]

simple fraction *n.* A fraction in which both the numerator and the denominator are integers. Also called "common fraction."

simple fracture *n.* See **fracture.**

simple fruit *n. Botany.* A fruit developed from a single pistil that may consist of one carpel or several united carpels.

simple harmonic motion *n. Abbr.* **S.H.M.** *Physics.* A periodic motion that can be described as a sinusoidal function of time; specifically, the motion of a particle that obeys the equation $x = A\cos(kt + \phi)$, where x is the displacement of the particle from the origin at any time t, A is the maximum displacement, ϕ is the initial phase or angular displacement at $t = 0$, and k is a constant equal to 2π times the frequency of the oscillation.

simple interest *n.* Interest paid only on the original principal, not on the interest accrued. Compare **compound interest.**

simple machine *n.* A device for changing the magnitude or direction of a force, a **machine** (see).

simple microscope *n.* A microscope having one lens or lens system, such as a magnifying glass or hand lens.

sim·ple-mind·ed (sĭm′pəl-mīn′dĭd) *adj.* **1.** Not sophisticated; artless. **2.** Stupid or silly. **3.** Mentally subnormal. **—sim·ple-mind·ed·ly** *adv.* **—sim·ple-mind·ed·ness** *n.*

simple pendulum *n.* A **pendulum** (see).

simple sentence *n.* A sentence having no coordinate or subordinate clauses; for example, *I jumped.* Compare **complex sentence.**

Simple Simon n. Informal. A foolish fellow; a simpleton. [After the title character of a nursery rhyme.]

simple sugar n. A monosaccharide (see).

simple tense n. Grammar. A tense in which the verb is expressed without an auxiliary; for example, the simple past tense of "go," I went, as opposed to the perfect (or present perfect) tense, I have gone. Compare **compound tense.**

simple time n. Music. A time in which each beat in the bar is divisible into two. Compare **compound time.**

sim·ple·ton (sĭm′pəl-tən) n. A silly person; a fool. [SIMPLE + -ton, "town" (as in surnames derived from place names).]

sim·plex (sĭm′plĕks′) adj. Designating a system of telegraphy in which only one message can be sent in either direction at one time. Compare **duplex, multiplex.** —n. A simplex system. [Latin simplex, simple, single.]

sim·plic·i·ty (sĭm-plĭs′ə-tē) n., pl. **-ties.** The state or quality of being simple, especially: **1.** Absence of complexity, adornment, or artificiality. **2.** Lack of good sense or intelligence; foolishness. [Middle English symplicite, from Old French, from Latin simplicitās, from simplex, simple.]

sim·pli·fy (sĭm′plə-fī′) tr.v. **-fied, -fying, -fies.** To make simple or simpler; render less complex or intricate. [French simplifier, from Medieval Latin simplificāre : Latin simplus, SIMPLE + facere, to make.] —**sim·pli·fi·ca·tion** (sĭm′plə-fĭ-kā′shən) n. —**sim·pli·fi·er** n.

sim·plis·tic (sĭm-plĭs′tĭk) adj. Showing a tendency to oversimplify an issue or problem by ignoring complexities or complications: Increasing jail terms is a simplistic approach to crime. —**sim·plism** (sĭm′plĭz′əm) n. —**sim·plis·ti·cal·ly** adv.

Sim·plon Pass (sĭm′plŏn′). Pass in the Lepontine Alps, southern Switzerland, at an altitude of 2,010 meters (6,590 feet). It is crossed by a railroad connecting Brig in Switzerland with Iselle in Italy through the Simplon Tunnel, which runs for 19.8 kilometers (12.3 miles) and is the longest in the world.

sim·ply (sĭm′plē) adv. **1.** In a simple manner; plainly. **2.** Merely; only: I left simply to avoid her. **3.** Absolutely; altogether: a simply marvelous film. **4.** Speaking frankly; candidly: You are, quite simply, inadequate for this job.

Simp·son Desert (sĭmp′sən). Uninhabited, arid wilderness in central Australia, lying mainly in Northern Territory, but extending slightly into Queensland and South Australia. It occupies c. 145,000 square kilometers (56,000 square miles).

sim·u·la·crum (sĭm′yə-lā′krəm) n., pl. **-cra** (-krə). Also archaic **sim·u·la·cre** (-kər), pl. **-cres.** **1.** An image or representation of something. **2.** An unreal or false semblance of something. [Latin, from simulāre, to SIMULATE.]

sim·u·lar (sĭm′yə-lər, -lär′) n. Archaic. One that simulates. —adj. Archaic. Simulated; sham.

sim·u·late (sĭm′yə-lāt′) tr.v. **-lated, -lating, -lates.** **1. a.** To have or take on the appearance, form, or sound of; imitate. **b.** To make so as to resemble the real or genuine thing: simulated diamonds. **2.** To make a pretense of; feign: simulate an interest. **3.** To imitate or create the conditions of, as for an experiment or for training. —See Synonyms at **imitate, pretend.** —adj. (sĭm′yə-lĭt, -lāt′). Archaic. Simulated; assumed; pretended. [Latin simulāre, from similis, SIMILAR.] —**sim·u·la·tive** (sĭm′yə-lā′tĭv, -lə-tĭv) adj. —**sim·u·lant** (sĭm′yə-lənt) adj. & n.

sim·u·la·tion (sĭm′yə-lā′shən) n. **1.** The act or process of simulating. **2.** An imitation. **3.** The assumption of a false appearance; a feigning or pretending. **4.** A process for studying or finding a solution for a problem or for calculating the effects of a course of action, by representing it in mathematical terms, especially using a computer.

sim·u·la·tor (sĭm′yə-lā′tər) n. One that simulates; especially, an apparatus that generates test conditions approximating actual or operational conditions.

si·mul·cast (sī′məl-kăst′, -kăst′, sĭm′əl-) tr.v. **-casted, -casting, -casts.** To broadcast simultaneously by radio and television. —n. A broadcast so transmitted. [Simultaneous + broadcast.]

si·mul·ta·ne·ous (sī′məl-tā′nē-əs, sĭm′əl-) adj. **1.** Happening, existing, or done at the same time. **2.** Mathematics. Collectively restricting the values of a set of variables: simultaneous equations. —See Synonyms at **contemporary.** [Formed by analogy with INSTANTANEOUS from Latin simul, at the same time.] —**si·mul·ta·ne·i·ty, si·mul·ta·ne·ous·ness** n. —**si·mul·ta·ne·ous·ly** adv.

sin¹ (sĭn) n. **1.** A transgression of a religious or moral law, especially when deliberate. **2.** Theology. A condition of estrangement from God resulting from a transgression of His known will. **3.** Any course of action regarded as shameful or deplorable: The way they treat that dog is a sin. —**live in sin.** To cohabit as wife and husband without being married. —intr.v. **sinned, sinning, sins. 1.** To commit a sinful act; violate a religious or moral law. **2.** To commit an offense or violation; do wrong. Usually used with against. [Middle English sinne, sunne, Old English syn(n).]

sin² (sēn) n. The 21st letter of the Hebrew alphabet. See feature at **alphabet.** [Hebrew śin, variant of šin, "tooth," SHIN (letter).]

sin³ sine.

Si·nai (sī′nī′). Triangular peninsula forming the northeastern part of Egypt and providing a land bridge between Africa and Asia. It lies between the Suez Canal and the Gulf of Suez on the west and Israel and the Gulf of Aqaba on the east. Mt. Sinai, of sacred importance in the Jewish, Christian, and Islamic traditions, has usually been identified with Mt. Musa in the southern mountainous region of the peninsula. Sinai has rich deposits of manganese and petroleum and has been of central strategic significance in the Arab-Israeli hostilities since 1956.

sin·an·thro·pus (sĭ-năn′thrə-pəs, sĭ-, sī′năn-thrō′pəs, sĭn′ăn-) n. An extinct humanlike primate, Sinanthropus pekinensis, known as Peking man. It is now designated as Homo erectus. [New Latin Sinanthropus, "Chinese human" : SIN(O)- + -ANTHROPUS.]

sin·a·pism (sĭn′ə-pĭz′əm) n. A mustard plaster. [French sinapisme, from Late Latin sināpismus, from Greek sinapismos, use of a mustard plaster, from sinapizein, to apply a mustard plaster, from sinapi, mustard, related to earlier napu, probably from Egyptian.]

Si·na·tra (sə-nä′trə), **Frank,** born Francis Albert Sinatra (1915–). U.S. popular singer and screen actor. After World War II he began a long and successful film career, appearing in such films as On The Town (1949) and Guys and Dolls (1955). He won an Academy Award as best supporting actor for his performance in From Here to Eternity (1953).

since (sĭns) adv. **1.** From a time in the past up to the present; from then until now. Often preceded by ever: She arrived last week and has been here ever since. **2.** At a time between a past time or event and the present; between then and now. **3.** At some past time; before now; ago: long since forgotten. —prep. **1.** During the time following: She has not been home since Easter. **2.** Continuously throughout the time following: up since seven. —conj. **1.** During the time after which: She hasn't been home since she graduated. **2.** Continuously from the time when: She hasn't spoken since she sat down. **3.** As a result of the fact that; inasmuch as. [Middle English sin(ne)s, contraction of sithen(es), Old English siththan, "after that."]

sin·cere (sĭn-sîr′) adj. **-cerer, -cerest. 1.** Not feigned or affected; true: sincere indignation. **2.** Presenting no false appearance; not hypocritical; honest: a sincere believer. **3.** Archaic. Pure; unadulterated. [Latin sincērus, clean, pure, genuine, honest.] —**sin·cere·ly** adv. —**sin·cere·ness** n.

Synonyms: heartfelt, natural, unaffected, unfeigned, wholehearted.

sin·cer·i·ty (sĭn-sĕr′ə-tē, -sîr′ə-tē) n., pl. **-ties. 1.** The quality or condition of being sincere; sincereness. **2.** A sincere feeling or expression.

sin·ci·put (sĭn′sə-pət) n., pl. **-puts** or **sincipita** (sĭn-sĭp′ə-tə). Anatomy. **1.** The upper half of the cranium, especially the anterior portion above and including the forehead. **2.** The forehead. [Latin, from earlier sēmicaput (unattested) : SEMI + caput, head.] —**sin·cip·i·tal** (sĭn-sĭp′ə-təl) adj.

Sin·clair (sĭn-klâr′), **Upton Beall** (1878–1968). U.S. novelist. His first novel, The Jungle (1906), exposed the unsanitary conditions in the Chicago stockyards and helped form the wave of public protest that led to reform legislation. He won a Pulitzer Prize for Dragon's Teeth in 1942.

Sind (sĭnd). Province of southeastern Pakistan, bordering on the Arabian Sea and on India to the south and east. It occupies the lower Indus Valley. The capital is Karachi. The leading industrial center in this chiefly agricultural province is Hyderabad.

Sin·dhi (sĭn′dē) n., pl. **-dhis** or collectively **Sindhi. 1.** A member of the predominantly Muslim people of Sind. **2.** The Indic language of Sind. —**Sin·dhi** adj.

sine (sīn) n. Abbr. **sin 1.** The ordinate of the endpoint of an arc of a unit circle centered at the origin of a Cartesian coordinate system, the arc being of length x and measured counterclockwise from the point $(1, 0)$ if x is positive, or clockwise if x is negative. **2.** In a right-angled triangle, the function of an acute angle that is the ratio of the opposite side to the hypotenuse. [Medieval Latin sinus, "fold of a garment" (mistranslation of Arabic jayb, chord of an arc, sine, through confusion with Arabic jayb, fold of a garment), from Latin, curve, fold, hollow. See **sinus.**]

si·ne·cure (sī′nə-kyŏōr′, sĭn′ə-) n. **1.** An office, position, or charge that is remunerated but requires little or no work. **2.** An ecclesiastical benefice not involving any of the spiritual duties of a parish. [Medieval Latin (beneficium) sine cūrā, (benefice) without care (of souls) : sine, without + cūrā, ablative of cūra, cure, care.] —**si·ne·cur·ism** n. —**si·ne·cur·ist** n.

sine curve (sīn) n. The graph of the equation $y = \sin x$. Also called "sinusoid."

si·ne di·e (sī′nē dī′ē, sē′nā dē′ā) adv. Abbr. **s.d.** Indefinitely: The legislature was adjourned sine die. [Latin, "without a day (fixed)".]

si·ne qua non (sĭn′ā kwä nŏn′, sī′nē kwä nŏn′) n. An essential element or condition. [Latin, "without which not."]

sin·ew (sĭn′yōō) n. **1.** A tendon. **2.** Vigorous strength; muscular power. **3.** Often **sinews.** The source or mainstay, as of vitality or strength. [Middle English sin(e)we, sen(e)ue, Old English sinu, seonu, from Germanic.]

sine wave (sīn) n. Physics. A waveform with an amplitude variation that can be expressed as the sine or cosine of a linear function of time or space or both.

sin·ew·y (sĭn′yōō-ē) adj. **1.** Like or consisting of sinews. **2.** Lean and muscular. **3.** Strong; vigorous.

sin·fo·ni·a (sĭn′fə-nē′ə) n., pl. **-nias** or **-nie** (-nē′ā′). Music. **1.** A usually extended symphonic work in sonata form. **2.** An orchestral overture, especially to an 18th-century Italian opera. [Italian, symphony.]

sin·fo·niet·ta (sĭn′fən-yĕt′ə) n., pl. **-tas.** Music. **1.** A symphony that is shorter in length than usual or that uses a small orchestra. **2.** A small symphony orchestra, especially a string orchestra. [Italian, diminutive of SINFONIA.]

sin·ful (sĭn′fəl) *adj.* Marked by or full of sin; wicked. **—sin·ful·ly** *adv.* **—sin·ful·ness** *n.*

sing (sĭng) *v.* **sang** (săng) or **sung** (sŭng), **sung, singing, sings.** *—intr.* **1.** To utter a series of words or sounds in musical tones. **2. a.** To perform songs for an audience, especially as a profession. **b.** To render a song or songs to an accompaniment. Used with *to: sing to the guitar.* **3. a.** To make noises that are melodious or sound like music. Used chiefly of birds. **b.** To give or have the effect of melody; lilt. **4.** To produce musical sounds when played. **5.** To make a high whine or hum. **6.** To be filled with a buzzing sound. Used chiefly of the ears or head. **7. a.** To proclaim or extol something in verse. **b.** To relate a tale in a song. Used with *of: sang of ancient heroes.* **8.** *Slang.* **a.** To give information or evidence against someone; inform. **b.** To confess to a crime. *—tr.* **1.** To utter (a song or lyrics, for example) with musical inflections of the voice. **2.** To intone; chant. **3.** To proclaim or extol, often in verse: *sings your praises.* **4.** To bring to a specified state by singing: *Sing me to sleep.* **—sing out. 1.** To sing loudly. **2.** To shout out. *~n.* **1.** The act of singing. **2.** A gathering of people for group singing. [Middle English *singen, sang, sungen,* Old English *singan, sang* (past singular), *sungen.*] **—sing·a·ble** *adj.*

sing. singular.

Sin·ga·pore (sĭng′gə-pôr′, -pōr′, sĭng′ə-). Independent republic lying off the southern tip of the Malay Peninsula. In addition to the main island of Singapore it includes some 60 smaller islands. A major commercial center with a large shipping and shipbuilding industry, Singapore has one of the highest standards of living in Southeast Asia. It is highly industrialized, with petroleum products, electronics, and rubber accounting for half its exports. Tourism is also important. Three quarters of the population is Chinese. In 1963 Singapore joined the Federation of Malaysia but withdrew two years later to become an independent republic. Area, 581 square kilometers (224 square miles). Population, 2,400,000. Capital, Singapore.

singe (sĭnj) *tr.v.* **singed, singeing, singes. 1.** To burn superficially; scorch. **2.** To burn the ends of. **3.** To burn off the feathers or bristles of by subjecting briefly to flame. —See Synonyms at **burn.** *~n.* A burn that is superficial. [Middle English *sengen,* Old English *sencgan,* from Germanic.] **—sing·er** (sĭn′jər) *n.*

sing·er (sĭng′ər) *n.* **1.** A person who sings, especially a trained or professional vocalist. **2.** A poet, especially in ancient or medieval times. **3.** A songbird.

Sing·er (sĭng′ər), **Isaac Bashevis** (1904–). U.S. novelist and short-story writer, born in Poland. He has published such collections as *Gimpel the Fool and Other Stories* (1961) and *A Crown of Feathers* (1973). He was awarded the Nobel Prize for literature in 1978.

Singer, Isaac Merritt (1811–75). U.S. inventor and manufacturer. In 1851 he patented a sewing machine capable of making continuous stitches. Although he lost (1856) an infringement suit to Elias Howe, who had earlier patented the needle and type of lockstitch used in Singer's machine, he continued to improve his machine and his company long dominated the market.

Singhalese. Variant of **Sinhalese.**

sin·gle (sĭng′gəl) *adj.* **1. a.** Not accompanied by another or others; solitary. **b.** Even one, not to mention others. Used with a negative: *Not a single person offered to help.* **2.** Consisting of one form or part; not double or multiple. **3.** One throughout; undiversified; uniform. **4.** Separate from others; distinct; individual: *every single day.* **5.** Designed to accommodate or be sufficient for one person: *a single bed.* **6. a.** Unmarried. **b.** Of or associated with the state of being unmarried: *living in single bliss.* **7.** Without a partner: *a single parent.* **8.** *Botany.* Having only one rank or row of petals: *a single flower.* **9.** One-against-one: *single combat.* *~n.* **1.** A separate unit; an individual. **2.** Something, such as a room or bed, intended for use by one person. **3.** An unmarried person. **4.** A one-dollar bill. **5.** In baseball, a **one-base hit** *(see).* **6.** In cricket, a single run. **7.** A small phonograph record, often with only one piece of music or track on each side, usually to be played at 45 revolutions per minute. Also called "forty-five." **b.** A piece of music or track on one side of such a record. **8.** See **singles.** *~v.* **singled, -gling, -gles.** *—tr.* **1.** To choose or distinguish from among others. Used with *out.* **2.** *Baseball.* To cause (a runner) to score or advance by making a one-base hit. *—intr. Baseball.* To make a one-base hit. [Middle English *sengle,* from Old French, from Latin *singulus.*] **—sin·gle·ness** *n.*

   Synonyms: *individual, sole, solitary, unique.*

sin·gle-act·ing (sĭng′gəl-ăk′tĭng) *adj.* Designating a steam engine or pump in which the pistons are pressurized on one side only. Compare **double-acting.**

sin·gle-ac·tion (sĭng′gəl-ăk′shən) *adj.* Having a hammer that must be cocked by hand after each shot. Said of a firearm.

sin·gle-blind (sĭng′gəl-blĭnd′) *adj.* Pertaining to or designating an experimental procedure, such as one to test reactions to medicinal drugs, in which the experimenters know the composition of the test items and control substances but the subjects do not. Compare **double-blind.**

single bond *n. Chemistry.* A type of chemical bond formed by one pair of shared electrons.

sin·gle-breast·ed (sĭng′gəl-brĕs′tĭd) *adj.* Closing with a narrow overlap and a single row of fasteners. Said of a coat or jacket.

SINGAPORE — 104° E — MALAYSIA — 1° 30′ N — Johor — Strait — Kranji — SINGAPORE — 177m — Changi — Bukit Timah — Tuas — SINGAPORE — Strait of Singapore — INDONESIA — 0 10 Km — 0 10 Miles

sin·gle-cell protein (sĭng′gəl-sĕl′) *n.* A protein produced by a mass of cells that have been cultured from a single cell.

single crochet *n.* A crochet stitch, the **slipstitch** *(see).*

single cross *n. Genetics.* A first-generation hybrid produced by a cross between two inbred lines.

single entry *n.* A system of bookkeeping in which a business keeps only a single account showing amounts due and amounts owed. Compare **double entry. —sin·gle-en·try** (sĭng′gəl-ĕn′trē) *adj.*

single file *n.* A line of people, animals, or things standing or moving one behind the other. Also called "Indian file." *~adv.* In single file.

sin·gle-foot (sĭng′gəl-foŏt′) *n.* A horse's gait, the **rack** *(see).* *~intr.v.* **single-footed, -footing, -foots.** To go at this gait.

sin·gle-hand·ed (sĭng′gəl-hăn′dĭd) *adj.* **1.** Working or done without help; unassisted. **2.** Designed for use with one hand. **3.** Having or using only one hand. **—sin·gle-hand·ed, sin·gle-hand·ed·ly** *adv.* **—sin·gle-hand·ed·ness** *n.*

sin·gle-heart·ed (sĭng′gəl-här′tĭd) *adj.* Characterized by sincerity and dedication: *a single-hearted belief in family cohesiveness.* **—sin·gle-heart·ed·ly** *adv.* **—sin·gle-heart·ed·ness** *n.*

single knot *n.* An overhand knot *(see).*

sin·gle-lens reflex (sĭng′gəl-lĕnz′) *adj. Abbr.* **SLR** Designating a form of reflex camera in which the lens through which light enters the camera to expose the film also serves to illuminate the viewfinder screen after the light has been reflected by a retractable viewfinder mirror. *~n.* A single-lens reflex camera.

sin·gle-mind·ed (sĭng′gəl-mīn′dĭd) *adj.* **1.** Having one overriding purpose or opinion. **2.** Steadfast. **—sin·gle-mind·ed·ly** *adv.* **—sin·gle-mind·ed·ness** *n.*

sin·gle-phase (sĭng′gəl-fāz′) *adj.* Producing, carrying, or powered by a single alternating voltage.

sin·gles (sĭng′gəlz) *n. Used with a singular verb.* A match, as in tennis, between two players only.

singles bar *n.* A bar used mostly by single people, especially with the aim of pairing off.

sin·gle-space (sĭng′gəl-spās′) *v.* **-spaced, -spacing, -spaces.** *—tr.* To type (copy) without leaving a blank line between the lines of print. *—intr.* To type copy without line spaces.

sin·gle-stick (sĭng′gəl-stĭk′) *n.* **1.** A one-handed fencing stick fitted with a hand guard. Also called "backsword." **2.** The art, sport, or exercise of fencing with such a stick.

sin·glet (sĭng′glĭt) *n.* **1.** *Chiefly British.* **a.** A man's sleeveless undershirt. **b.** A sleeveless vest worn for running or other sports. **2.** *Physics.* A multiplet with a single member. **3.** *Chemistry.* A single, shared electron in a chemical bond. [From *single* (in sense 1, referring to an unlined garment), after DOUBLET.]

single tax *n.* A system by which all revenue is derived from a tax on one object, especially on land.

sin·gle·ton (sĭng′gəl-tən) *n.* **1.** A playing card that is the only one of its suit in a player's hand. **2.** An individual as distinguished from a pair or group. [From *single* (by analogy with SIMPLETON).]

sin·gle-tongu·ing (sĭng′gəl-tŭng′ĭng) *n.* The articulation of notes on a wind instrument by repeatedly moving the tongue against the upper teeth or alveolar ridge as if to pronounce a *t.* Compare **double-tonguing, triple-tonguing. —sin·gle-tongue** *v.*

sin·gle·tree (sĭng′gəl-trē′) *n.* A **whiffletree** *(see).*

sin·gly (sĭng′glē) *adv.* **1.** Without company or help; alone. **2.** One by one; individually.

Sing Sing (sĭng′ sĭng′). Prison in Ossining, southeastern New York State, on the Hudson River.

sing·song (sĭng′sông′, -sŏng′) *n.* **1.** Verse characterized by mechanical regularity of rhythm and rhyme. **2.** Enunciation marked by a monotonously repetitive rise and fall in pitch. **3.** *Chiefly British.* An informal session of singing or a meeting to sing.

~adj. Characterized by a repetitive rise-and-fall tone.

sin·gu·lar (sĭng′gyə-lər) *adj.* **1.** Being only one; separate; individual. **2. a.** Remarkable; extraordinary; rare. **b.** Deviating strongly from a norm; peculiar; odd. **3.** *Abbr.* **s., sing.** *Grammar.* Of, pertaining to, or being the grammatical number denoting a single person or thing or several considered as a single unit. Compare **plural. 4.** *Logic.* Of or pertaining to the specific as distinguished from the general; individual. —See Synonyms at **strange.**

~n. Abbr. **s., sing.** *Grammar.* The singular number, a form denoting it, or a word having a singular number. [Middle English *singuler,* solitary, single, from Old French, from Latin *singulāris,* from *singulus,* SINGLE.] **—sin·gu·lar·ly** *adv.* **—sin·gu·lar·ness** *n.*

sin·gu·lar·i·ty (sĭng′gyə-lăr′ə-tē) *n., pl.* **-ties. 1.** The condition or quality of being singular. **2.** A trait marking out a person or thing as distinct from others; a peculiarity. **3.** Something uncommon or unusual. **4.** *Physics.* A point in space-time at which there is an infinite density of matter, theoretically the ultimate fate of matter within the event horizon of a black hole. A singularity without an event horizon is a **naked singularity** *(see).*

sin·gu·lar·ize (sĭng′gyə-lə-rīz′) *tr.v.* **-ized, -izing, -izes.** To make conspicuous; distinguish from others. **—sin·gu·lar·i·za·tion** *n.*

sin·gul·tus (sĭng-gŭl′təs) *n.* A hiccup *(see).* [Latin.]

sinh hyperbolic sine.

Sin·ha·lese (sĭn′hə-lēz′, -lēs′) *n., pl.* **Sinhalese.** Also **Sin·gha·lese** (sĭng′gə-), *pl.* **Singhalese. 1.** A member of a people constituting the major portion of the population of Sri Lanka. **2.** The Indic language of this people.

~adj. Also **Sin·gha·lese.** Of or pertaining to the Sinhalese or their language. [Sanskrit *sinhalam,* Sri Lanka.]

Si·ni·cism (sī′nə-sĭz′əm, sĭn′ə-) *n.* A custom or trait peculiar to the Chinese. [Medieval Latin *Sinicus,* Chinese, from Late Latin *Sinae,* the Chinese. See **Sino-.**]

sin·is·ter (sĭn′ĭ-stər) *adj.* **1. a.** Suggesting an evil force or motive: *a sinister smile.* **b.** Evil or base. **2.** Presaging trouble; ominous. **3.** On the left side; left. **4.** *Heraldry.* On the left of the bearer and hence on the right of the observer. Compare **dexter.** [Middle English *sinistre,* from Old French, from Latin *sinister*†, left, on the left, hence evil, unlucky (in augury the left side being regarded as inauspicious).] **—sin·is·ter·ly** *adv.* **—sin·is·ter·ness** *n.*

sin·is·tral (sĭn′ĭ-strəl) *adj.* **1.** Of, facing, or situated on the left side. **2.** Left-handed. Compare **dextral. 3.** *Zoology.* Designating or pertaining to a gastropod shell that has its aperture to the left when facing the observer with the apex upward. **—sin·is·tral·ly** *adv.*

sin·is·trorse (sĭn′ĭ-strôrs′, sĭn′ĭ-strôrs′) *adj.* Growing upward in a spiral that turns from right to left: *a sinistrorse vine.* Compare **dextrorse.** [New Latin *sinistrorsus,* turned toward the left : SINISTER (left) + *versus,* past participle of *vertere,* to turn.] **—sin·is·trorse·ly** *adv.*

sin·is·trous (sĭn′ĭ-strəs) *adj. Archaic.* Sinister; ill-omened. **—sin·is·trous·ly** *adv.*

Si·nit·ic (sĭ-nĭt′ĭk, sī-) *n.* The branch of Sino-Tibetan that comprises Chinese. **—Si·nit·ic** *adj.*

sink (sĭngk) *v.* **sank** (săngk) or **sunk** (sŭngk), **sunk, sinking, sinks.** *—intr.* **1.** To descend beneath the surface or to the bottom of a liquid or soft substance; especially, to cease to float through lack of buoyancy: *The ship sank.* **2.** To move to a lower level; go down slowly or in stages. **3.** To appear to move downward or below the horizon. **4.** To slope downward; incline. **5.** To pass into a worsened physical condition; approach death. **6. a.** To become weaker, quieter, or less forceful: *Her voice sank and died away.* **b.** To fall down or give way, as through weakness or fatigue: *sank into a chair.* **7.** To diminish, as in value or amount. **8. a.** To suffer a loss of morale, spirit, or vitality. Used with *in* or *into*: *sank into a deep depression.* **b.** To be depressed or dismayed: *My heart sank.* **c.** To decline, as in morality or reputation. Used with *in* or *into*: *sank into anonymity.* **9.** To penetrate or cut through something. Used with *in* or *into*: *The blade sank in.* **10.** *Informal.* To penetrate or be absorbed by the mind. Used with *in* or *into*: *The message finally sank in.* **11.** To seep or be soaked up. Used with *in* or *into.* **12.** To become hollowed or shrunken. Used of the cheeks. *—tr.* **1.** To cause to descend beneath the surface; especially, to cause (a vessel) to lose buoyancy and cease to float. **2.** To cause or allow to fall; drop or lower. **3. a.** To force into the ground: *sink piles into a riverbed.* **b.** To cause to cut through or penetrate: *sank her fork into the steak.* **4.** To dig or drill (a mine or well) in the earth. **5.** To degrade; debase the character or reputation of. **6.** To cause to diminish, as in value or price. **7.** To suppress; hide; conceal: *sink our differences for the sake of appearances.* **8.** To cause to fail or suffer a reverse: *could sink the whole project.* **9.** To invest (money). Used with *in* or *into.* **10.** To lose (part or all of an investment). **11.** To pay off (a debt). **12.** To cause (a ball) to enter a target in games such as golf, billiards, or basketball. **13.** *Informal.* To defeat, as in a game. **—sink or swim.** To succeed through one's own efforts or else fail completely.

~n. **1.** A water basin fixed to a wall or floor and having a drainpipe and generally a piped supply of water. **2.** A cesspool. **3.** A **sinkhole** *(see).* **4.** In thermodynamics, the part of a system from which heat or, more generally, energy is removed from the system. **5.** Any place regarded as an abode of wickedness and corruption. [Middle English *sinken, sank, sunken,* Old English *sincan, sanc* (past singular), *suncen.*] **—sink·a·ble** *adj.* **—sink·age** (sĭng′kĭj) *n.*

Usage: The past tense of this verb is most commonly *sank,* though *sunk* is often heard, especially informally. The past participle is *sunk; sunken* is only adjectival *(sunken treasure).*

sink·er (sĭng′kər) *n.* **1.** One that sinks. **2.** A weight used for sinking fishing lines, nets, or the like. **3.** *Slang.* A doughnut. **4.** *Baseball.* A fastball that sinks as it approaches the plate.

sink·hole (sĭngk′hōl′) *n.* **1.** A natural depression in a land surface communicating with a subterranean passage, generally occurring in limestone regions and formed by solution or by collapse of a cavern roof. **2.** A natural hole or hollow in limestone or chalk into which surface water disappears.

Sinkiang Uighur Autonomous Region. See **Xinjiang Uigur Zizhiqu.**

sinking fund *n.* A fund accumulated over a period and invested for the paying off of a public or corporate debt.

sin·less (sĭn′lĭs) *adj.* Free from or without sin or guilt. **—sin·less·ly** *adv.* **—sin·less·ness** *n.*

sin·ner (sĭn′ər) *n.* One who sins; especially, a reprobate.

sinnet. Variant of **sennit.**

Sinn Fein (shĭn′ fān′) *n.* An Irish nationalist organization founded in about 1905 that constitutes the political branch of the **I.R.A.** *(see)* and is dedicated to the political and economic independence of a united Ireland. It split into the **Official** and **Provisional** wings *(both of which see)* after a similar split in the I.R.A. in 1969. [Irish Gaelic *sinn féin,* "we ourselves."] **—Sinn Fein·er** (shĭn′ fā′nər) *n.* **—Sinn Fein·ism** (fā′nĭz′əm) *n.*

Sino– *prefix.* Indicates Chinese; for example, **Sinophile.** [French, from Late Latin *Sinae,* the Chinese, from Greek *Sinai,* from Arabic *Sīn,* China, from Chinese (Mandarin) *Qín,* dynastic name of the country. See also **China.**]

si·no·a·tri·al node (sī′nō-ā′trē-əl) *n.* A group of specialized cells in the wall of the right atrium of the heart that initiates the heartbeat. Also called "pacemaker." [*Sino-,* from Latin *sinus,* cavity + ATRIAL.]

Si·no·logue (sī′nə-lôg′, -lŏg′, sĭn′ə-) *n.* A student of Sinology. [French *sinologue* : SINO- + -LOGUE.]

Si·nol·o·gy (sī-nŏl′ə-jē, sĭ-nŏl′-) *n.* The study of Chinese language, literature, or civilization. [French *sinologie* : SINO- + -LOGY.] **—Si·no·log·i·cal** (sī′nə-lŏj′ĭ-kəl, sĭn′ə-) *adj.* **—Si·nol·o·gist** *n.*

Si·no·phile (sī′nə-fīl′, sĭn′ə-) *n.* One who admires the Chinese and Chinese culture. [SINO- + -PHILE.] **—Si·no·phile** *adj.*

Si·no-Ti·bet·an (sī′nō-tĭ-bĕt′n, sĭn′ō-) *n.* A linguistic group that includes the Sinitic and Tibeto-Burman families. **—Si·no-Ti·bet·an** *adj.*

sin·ter (sĭn′tər) *n.* **1.** *Geology.* A crust of porous silica, deposited by a hot spring or geyser. **2.** A mass formed by sintering.

~v. **sintered, -tering, -ters.** *—tr.* To weld together (metallic powder, for example) partially and without melting. *—intr.* To form a homogeneous mass by heating without melting. [German *Sinter,* iron dross, from Old High German *sintar.*]

Sin·tra (sēn′trə). *Formerly* **Cin·tra.** Town in the Estremadura region of western Portugal, near the Atlantic coast just west of Lisbon. It was a Moorish center until 1147.

sin·u·ate (sĭn′yo͞o-ĭt, -āt′) *adj.* Also **sin·u·at·ed** (-ā′tĭd). Having a wavy indented margin. Said of a leaf. [Latin *sinuātus,* past participle of *sinuāre,* to bend, wind, from *sinus,* a bend, curve, fold. See **sinus.**] **—sin·u·ate·ly** *adv.* **—sin·u·a·tion** (sĭn′yo͞o-ā′shən) *n.*

sin·u·os·i·ty (sĭn′yo͞o-ŏs′ə-tē) *n., pl.* **-ties. 1.** The quality of being sinuous. **2.** A bending or curving shape or movement.

sin·u·ous (sĭn′yo͞o-əs) *adj.* **1.** Supple and lithe in movement. **2.** Characterized by many curves or turns; winding. **3.** Devious and intricate. [Latin *sinuōsus,* from *sinus,* a bend, curve, fold. See **sinus.**] **—sin·u·ous·ly** *adv.* **—sin·u·ous·ness** *n.*

si·nus (sī′nəs) *n.* **1.** A depression or cavity formed by a bending or curving. **2.** *Anatomy.* **a.** Any of various air-filled cavities in the cranial bones, especially one communicating with the nostrils. **b.** A wide channel for the passage of blood, especially venous blood. **3.** *Pathology.* A fistula or channel to a suppurating cavity. **4.** *Botany.* A notch or indentation between lobes of a leaf or corolla. [Latin *sinus*†, a bend, curve, fold, hollow.]

si·nus·i·tis (sī′nə-sī′tĭs) *n.* Inflammation of a sinus membrane, especially in the nasal region.

si·nus·oid (sī′nə-soid′, sī′nyə-) *n.* **1.** *Mathematics.* A **sine curve** *(see).* **2.** *Anatomy.* A minute blood vessel occurring in such organs as the liver and adrenal gland. [Medieval Latin *sinus,* sine, from Latin, a curve + -OID.] **—si·nus·oid·al** (sī′nə-soid′l, sī′nyə-) *adj.*

sinusoidal projection *n.* An equal-area map projection in which the standard parallel is the equator, the other parallels of latitude are drawn as horizontal lines spaced at true intervals, and the meridians of longitude, apart from the standard meridian (usually the prime meridian), are drawn as sine curves.

Sion. Variant of **Zion.**

Siou·an (so͞o′ən) *n.* A large North American Indian language family spoken from Lake Michigan to the Rocky Mountains and southward to Arkansas by many peoples, including the Omaha, Iowa, Winnebago, Sioux, and Crow groups. **—Siou·an** *adj.*

Sioux (so͞o) *n., pl.* **Sioux** (so͞o, so͞oz). **1.** A member of any of the various groups of Siouan-speaking North American Indian peoples, formerly occupying parts of the Great Plains in the Dakotas, Minnesota, and Nebraska. **2.** Any Siouan language. See **Dakota. —Sioux** *adj.*

Sioux City. City in northwestern Iowa, at the junction of the Big Sioux and Floyd rivers with the Missouri. It is a shipping, trade, and industrial center for an extensive agricultural and livestock area.

PRONUNCIATION KEY

ă, pat; ā, pay; âr, care;
ä, father, are; b, bib;
ch, church; d, deed; ĕ, pet;
ē, be; f, fife; g, gag; h, hat;
hw, which; ĭ, pit; ī, pie;
îr, pier; j, judge; k, kick;
l, lid, needle; m, mum;
n, no, sudden; ng, thing;
ŏ, pot; ō, toe; ô, paw, for;
oi, noise; ou, out; o͝o, book;
o͞o, boot; p, pop; r, roar;
s, sauce; sh, ship, dish;
t, tight; th, thin, path;
th, this, bathe; ŭ, cut; ûr, fur;
v, valve; w, with; y, yes;
z, zebra, size; zh, vision;
ə, about, item, edible,
gallop, circus, peaceful

IN FOREIGN WORDS:

à, *Fr.* ami; œ, *Fr.* feu, *Ger.* schön; ü, *Fr.* tu, *Ger.* über;
KH, *Ger.* ich, *Scot.* loch;
N, *Fr.* bon; y′, *Fr.* Compiègne

STRESS MARKS:

Primary stress: ′
in·cite′ (ĭn-sīt′)
Secondary stress: ′
in′sight′ (ĭn′sīt′)

Sioux Falls. City of southeastern South Dakota, on the Big Sioux River. It was settled in 1856, abandoned in 1862 because of Indian raids, and resettled in 1865 after the establishment of Fort Dakota. Sioux Falls is the largest city in the state.

sip (sĭp) v. **sipped, sipping, sips.** —tr. To drink delicately and in small quantities: *She sipped the hot tea.* —intr. To drink in sips. ~n. 1. The act of sipping. 2. A small quantity of liquid sipped. [Middle English *sippen*, probably of Low German origin; akin to Low German *sippen*, to sip.]

si·phon, sy·phon (sī′fən) n. 1. A pipe or tube fashioned or deployed in an inverted U shape and filled until atmospheric pressure is sufficient to force a liquid from a reservoir in one end of the tube over a barrier higher than the reservoir and out of the other end. 2. A bottle from which soda water can be dispensed under pressure. 3. *Zoology.* A tubular organ, especially of aquatic invertebrates such as squids, by which water is taken in or expelled. ~v. **siphoned** or **syphoned, -phoning, -phons.** —tr. 1. To draw off or convey through a siphon: *siphoned gasoline from her tank.* 2. To divert (money, for example) for another purpose. Used with *off.* —intr. To pass through a siphon. [French, from Latin *sīphō, sīphōn*, from Greek *siphōn†*, pipe, tube.] —**si·phon·al** (sī′fə-nəl), **si·phon·ic** (sī-fŏn′ĭk) *adj.*

si·phon·o·phore (sī-fŏn′ə-fôr′, -fōr′, sī′fə-nə-) n. Any of various colonial marine coelenterates of the order Siphonophora, which includes the Portuguese man-of-war : Latin *sīphō(n)*, tube, SIPHON + New Latin *-phora*, neuter plural of *-phorus*, -PHOROUS.]

si·phon·o·stele (sī-fŏn′ə-stēl′, sī′fə-nə-stē′lē) n. A vascular tube surrounding the pith in the stems of certain plants. [SIPHON + STELE (vascular tissue).] —**si·phon·o·ste·lic** (sī-fŏn′ə-stē′lĭk) *adj.*

si·phun·cle (sī′fŭng′kəl) n. *Zoology.* 1. A tubelike structure in the body of a shelled cephalopod, such as a chambered nautilus, extending through each chamber of the shell. 2. A dorsal tube in an aphid, secreting a waxy fluid. Formerly called "nectary." [Latin *sīphunculus*, diminutive of *sīphō, sīphōn*, tube, SIPHON.]

sip·pet (sĭp′ĭt) n. A small piece of toast or fried bread soaked in gravy or other juice and often served as a garnish on soups or stews. [*Sip*, alteration of SOP + -ET.]

Si·quei·ros (sē-kyâr′ōs′), **David Alfaro** (c. 1898–1974). Mexican muralist. One of Mexico's best-known and most original artists, he created dramatic works that reflected his commitment to revolutionary protest. His major works include murals at the Palace of Fine Arts (1945–50) and the National University (1952–56) in Mexico City.

sir (sûr) n. 1. **a.** A respectful or polite form of address for a man. **b. Sir.** A conventional form used instead of a man's name at the opening of a letter. 2. **Sir.** A title of honor used before the first name or the full name of baronets and knights. 3. *Obsolete.* A form of address used with a noun indicating a man's profession, rank, or the like. Sometimes used humorously or derogatorily: *"Sir boy, now let me see your archery"* (Shakespeare). 4. *Archaic.* A gentleman of rank. [Middle English, variant of SIRE.]

Siracusa. See **Syracuse.**

sir·dar, sar·dar (sûr′där′, sər-där′) n. A person of rank in India or Pakistan. [Hindi *sardār*, from Persian : *sar*, head + *dār*, possession, from Old Persian, from *dar-*, to hold, possess.]

sire (sīr) n. 1. A father or forefather. 2. *Abbr.* **s.** The male parent of an animal, especially a domesticated mammal such as a horse. 3. *Archaic.* **Sire.** A title or form of address for a nobleman, especially for a king. ~tr.v. **sired, siring, sires.** 1. To procreate as the father; beget. Used especially of a domesticated mammal. 2. To give rise to; originate. [Middle English, from Old French, from Vulgar Latin *seior* (unattested), variant of Latin *senior*, older, from *senex*, old.]

si·ren (sī′rən) n. 1. *Often* **Siren.** *Greek Mythology.* Any of a group of sea nymphs who, by their sweet singing, lured sailors to destruction on the rocks surrounding their island. 2. A dangerously seductive woman; a temptress. 3. A device in which compressed air or steam is driven against a rotating perforated disk to create a loud, penetrating whistle, wailing, or other sound as a signal or warning. 4. Any instrument producing a similar sound as a signal or warning. 5. Any of several North American amphibians of the family Sirenidae, having an eellike body and no hind limbs. ~adj. Suggesting the effect of the mythological sirens; bewitching. [Middle English *ser(e)yne, siren*, from Old French *sereine*, from Late Latin *sīrēna*, from Latin *Sīrēn*, from Greek *Seirēn*.]

si·re·ni·an (sī-rē′nē-ən) n. Any herbivorous aquatic mammal of the order Sirenia, including the manatee and the dugong. ~adj. Of or belonging to the Sirenia. [New Latin *Sīrēnia* (order), from Latin *Sīrēn*, SIREN.]

Sir·i·us (sĭr′ē-əs) n. A star in the constellation Canis Major. It appears as the brightest star in the sky and is approximately 8.7 light years distant from Earth. Also called "Canicula," "Dog Star." [Latin, from Greek *Seirios*, from *seirios†*, burning, glowing.]

sir·loin (sûr′loin′) n. A cut of beef from the upper part of the loin between the rump and the porterhouse. [Earlier *surloyn(e)*, from Old French *surlonge* : *sur*, above, from Latin *super* + *longe, loigne*, loin, from Latin *lumbus*.]

si·roc·co (sə-rŏk′ō) n., pl. **-cos.** Also **sci·roc·co** (shə-), pl. **-cos.** 1. A hot, humid south or southeast wind of southern Italy, Sicily, and the Mediterranean islands, originating in the Sahara as a dry, dusty wind but becoming moist as it passes over the Mediterranean. 2. A warm or hot southerly wind, especially one moving toward a low

barometric pressure center. [Italian, from Arabic *sharuq*, "east (wind)," from *sharaqa*, (the sun) rose.]

sir·rah (sĭr′ə) n. *Archaic.* Fellow. Used as a contemptuous form of address. [Probably alteration of Middle English SIRE (sir).]

sir·ree, sir·ee (sə-rē′) n. *Informal.* Sir. Used after *yes* or *no* for emphasis.

Sir Rog·er de Cov·er·ley (sər rŏj′ər də kŭv′ər-lē) n. An English country dance performed by an unspecified number of couples initially facing each other in a long line. [After the fictitious character in a series of essays by Addison and Steele in the *Spectator.*]

sirup. Variant of **syrup.**

sir·vente (sîr-vänt′) n., pl. **-ventes** (-vänt′, -vänts′). Also **sir·ven·tes** (-vēn′təs), pl **sirventes** (*pronounced as singular*). A form of lyric verse used by the Provençal troubadours to satirize political, social, or moral themes. [French, from Provençal *sirventes*, from *sirvent, servent*, servant, from Latin *serviēns* (stem *servient-*), present participle of *servīre*, to serve, from *servus*, servant.]

sis (sĭs) n. *Informal.* Sister.

si·sal (sī′səl, -zəl) n. 1. A fleshy plant, *Agave sisalana*, native to Mexico, widely cultivated for its large leaves that yield a stiff fiber used for cordage and rope. 2. **a.** The fiber of this plant. **b.** The fiber of certain similar or related plants. [Mexican Spanish, after *Sisal*, town in Yucatán, Mexico.]

sis·kin (sĭs′kĭn) n. Any of several small birds of the family Fringillidae, especially: 1. *Carduelis spinus*, of Eurasia, having yellow and black plumage. 2. *Carduelis pinus*, the pine siskin of North America, a dark, streaked finch with yellow patches on the wings and tail. [Middle Dutch *sīseken*, formed as diminutive of Middle Low German *sīsek*, of Slavic origin.]

Sis·ley (sĭs′lē, sē-slē′), **Alfred** (c. 1840–99). French painter of English parentage. Influenced by Monet in his selection of colors, he painted lyrical, almost wistful landscapes that show a strong concern for composition and balance. He is considered a leading figure of the impressionist movement.

sis·si·fied (sĭs′ĭ-fīd′) *adj. Informal.* Womanish; effeminate. Said of a male.

sis·sy (sĭs′ē) n., pl. **-sies.** Also *British* **cis·sy.** 1. An effeminate or weak boy or man; a milksop. 2. A timid or cowardly person. [From *sis*, diminutive for SISTER.] —**sis·sy** *adj.*

sissy bar n. *Informal.* A narrow bar that rises like an inverted U from behind the seat of a motorcycle or bicycle and that supports the driver or a passenger.

sis·ter (sĭs′tər) n. 1. *Abbr.* **s.** A female having the same mother and father as another person (*full sister*), having one parent in common with another person (*half sister*), having one parent in common with another person by marriage rather than by blood (*stepsister*), or having a shared mother and father after adoption (*adoptive sister*). 2. A female who shares a common ancestry, allegiance, character, or purpose with another or others, especially: **a.** A kinswoman. **b.** A female fellow member, as of a labor union. **c.** A female who shares feminist beliefs, principles, and aspirations. **d.** A fellow woman, friend, or companion. 3. *Informal.* A girl or woman. Used as a form of direct address. 4. **Sister.** *Abbr.* **Sr.** A member of a religious order of women; a nun. **b.** A title or form of address for such a person. 5. *British.* **a.** The nurse in charge of a hospital ward. **b.** A title or form of address for such a person. 6. One identified as female and closely related to another. ~adj. Standing in the relationship of a sister; related by or as if by sisterhood: *sister souls.* [Middle English *suster, sister*, Old English *sweostor, swuster.*]

sis·ter·hood (sĭs′tər-hŏŏd′) n. 1. The state or relationship of being a sister or sisters. 2. The quality of being sisterly. 3. A society of women; especially, a religious society of women. 4. **a.** The feminist movement. **b.** Feminists collectively.

sis·ter-in-law (sĭs′tər-ĭn-lô′) n., pl. **sisters-in-law.** 1. The sister of one's wife or husband. 2. The wife of one's brother. 3. The wife of the brother of one's spouse.

sis·ter·ly (sĭs′tər-lē) *adj.* Characteristic of or befitting a sister or sisters. ~adv. As a sister. —**sis·ter·li·ness** n.

Sis·tine (sĭs′tēn′, sĭ-stēn′) *adj.* Also **Six·tine** (sĭk′stēn′, -stīn′). 1. Of or concerning any of the popes named Sixtus. 2. Of or pertaining to the Sistine Chapel in the Vatican, built for Pope Sixtus IV. [Italian *sistino*, from New Latin *sixtinus*, from the name *Sixtus*.]

sis·troid (sĭs′troid′) *adj.* Lying between the convex sides of two curves. Compare **cissoid.** [SISTR(UM) + -OID.]

sis·trum (sĭs′trəm) n., pl. **-trums** or **-tra** (-trə). An ancient Egyptian musical instrument consisting of a thin metal frame with rods or loops that rattle. [Middle English, from Latin, from Greek *seistron*, from *seiein*, to shake.]

Sis·y·phe·an (sĭs′ĭ-fē′ən) *adj.* 1. Of or pertaining to Sisyphus. 2. **sisyphean.** Endless and to no avail: *sisyphean labors.*

Sis·y·phus (sĭs′ĭ-fəs). *Greek Mythology.* A cruel king of Corinth who because of disrespect to Zeus was condemned forever to roll a huge stone up a hill in Hades, only to have it roll down again on nearing the top.

sit (sĭt) v. **sat** (săt) or *archaic* **sate** (săt), **sat, sitting, sits.** —intr. 1. To rest with the body supported upon the buttocks and the torso vertical. 2. To rest with the hindquarters lowered onto a supporting surface. Used of animals. 3. To perch. Used of birds. 4. To cover eggs for hatching; brood. 5. To be situated; lie. 6. To take and maintain a position for an artist or photographer; pose. 7. **a.** To occupy a seat in an official capacity as a judge or as a member of a deliberative body: *sits on the executive committee.* **b.** To be in session. Used of a deliberative or judicial body. **8.** To remain inactive or unused. **9.** To lie or rest in a specified manner: *sat uneasily on the edge of the chair.* **10.** To affect one with or as if with a burden; weigh. Used with *on* or *upon*: *Official duties sat heavily on her.* **11. a.** To fit, fall, or hang in a specified manner. Used of clothing: *That dress sits well on her.* **b.** To be agreeable to one; please: *Arrogance does not sit well with him.* **12.** To lie, rest, or belong in a specified place: *The cookie jar sat on the top shelf.* **13.** To blow from a particular direction. Used of the wind. **14.** To baby-sit or keep watch over an invalid. **15.** *Chiefly British.* To take an examination: *sitting for her finals.* —*tr.* **1.** To cause to sit; to seat. Often used reflexively: *Sit yourself over there.* **2.** To keep one's seat upon (a horse or other animal): *learning how to sit a horse.* **3.** *Chiefly British.* To take (an examination), as for a degree. **—sit back.** To relax; not concern or worry oneself: *Sit back and enjoy the film.* **—sit on** (or **upon**). *Informal.* **1.** To suppress or delay publication of (information, news, or a decision, for example). **2.** To rebuke sharply; reprimand. **—sit out. 1.** To stay until the end of: *sit out a speech.* **2.** To remain seated throughout; take no part in (a dance or game, for example). **3.** To lean out over the side of a small sailing vessel with the back toward the water when sailing close to the wind, so as to keep the boat level. **—sit tight.** *Informal.* To be patient and await the next move. **—sitting pretty.** *Informal.* In an advantageous or favorable position. **—sit up. 1.** To sit straight or erect. **2.** To stay up later than one's customary bedtime. **3.** To become suddenly alert or attentive.

∼*n.* An act, instance, or period of sitting. [Sit, sat (past); Middle English *sitten, sat(e),* Old English *sittan, sæt* (plural *sǣton*). Sat (past participle); Middle English *sat,* adopted from the past tense *sat(e)* and replacing the regular *seten,* Old English *(ge)seten.*]

si·tar (sĭ-tär′) *n.* A Hindu stringed instrument made of seasoned gourds and teak and having a track of 20 metal frets with 3 to 7 main playing strings above and 13 sympathetic resonating strings below. [Hindi *sitār,* "three-stringed" : Persian *si,* three + *tār,* string, from Avestan *tąthra-* (unattested).] **—si·tar·ist** *n.*

sit·com (sĭt′kŏm′) *n. Informal.* A **situation comedy** *(see).* **—sit·com** *adj.*

sit down *intr.v.* To seat oneself; take a seat. —*tr.v.* To seat (oneself or another).

sit-down (sĭt′doun′) *adj.* Served to and eaten by people seated at a table. Said of a meal: *a sit-down dinner.*

∼*n.* **1.** A work stoppage in which the workers refuse to leave their place of employment pending agreement. Also called "sit-down strike," "sit-in." **2.** A protest demonstration, a **sit-in** *(see).*

site (sīt) *n.* **1.** The place or plot of land where something was, is, or is to be situated, especially a place where construction work is taking place. **2.** The place or setting of an event.

∼*tr.v.* **sited, siting, sites.** To situate or locate on a site: *siting a power plant.* [Middle English, from Old French, from Latin *situs,* place, locality, from *situs,* past participle of *sinere*†, to allow (to remain in a place), hence lay, put.]

sith (sĭth) *conj. Archaic.* Since. [Middle English *sith(th)e,* Old English *siththa, siththan,* SINCE.] **—sith** *adv. & prep.*

sit in *intr.v.* **1.** To participate in a sit-in. **2.** To take the place of an absent person: *sat in for me at the meeting.* **3.** To be present as an observer or guest: *sat in on the meeting.*

sit-in (sĭt′ĭn′) *n.* **1.** A protest demonstration, as for civil rights, in which participants seat themselves in an appropriate place and refuse to move until their objectives are considered. Also called "sit-down." **2.** A work stoppage, a **sit-down** *(see).*

Sit·ka (sĭt′kə). Town on Baranof Island, in the Alexander Archipelago of Alaska. From 1867 to 1900 it was the capital of Alaska.

Sitka National Historical Park. Area in southeastern Alaska, near Sitka, set aside to commemorate a decisive battle between the Tlingit Indians and Russian settlers in 1804 in which the Russians defeated the native tribesmen.

Sitka spruce *n.* A North American spruce tree, *Picea sitchensis,* that is an important source of softwood.

si·tol·o·gy (sī-tŏl′ə-jē) *n.* The science of foods, nutrition, and diet. [Greek *sitos*†, food, grain + -LOGY.]

si·tos·ter·ol (sī-tŏs′tə-rôl′, -rōl′, sĭ-) *n.* Any of various sterols extracted from soya beans for the preparation of medicines, such as synthetic steroid hormones, and cosmetics. [Greek *sitos,* food + STEROL.]

sit·tel·la (sĭ-tĕl′ə) *n.* Any of various Australian birds of the genus *Neositta,* some species of which use small twigs to draw out of concealment the grubs on which they feed. Also called "tree-runner." [New Latin, diminutive of Latin *sitta,* nuthatch.]

sit·ter (sĭt′ər) *n.* **1.** One that sits; especially, one who sits for an artist or photographer. **2.** A baby sitter. **3.** A brooding hen.

sit·ting (sĭt′ĭng) *n.* **1.** The act or position of one that sits. **2.** A period during which one is seated and occupied with a single activity, such as posing for a portrait or reading a book. **3.** A term or session, as of a legislature or court. **4.** A time at which a meal is served, typically one of several such periods allocated in order to make full use of limited facilities. **5. a.** An act or period of incubation of eggs by a bird. **b.** The number of eggs under a brooding bird.

Sitting Bull (*c.* 1834–90). North American chief. He led the Indian forces during the Sioux war against the U.S. Army (1876–77), defeating Gen. George A. Custer's cavalry at the Battle of the Little Bighorn (1876).

sitting duck *n. Informal.* An easy target or victim. Also called "sitting target."

sitting room *n.* A living room in a private house.

sit·u·ate (sĭch′o͞o-āt′) *tr.v.* **-ated, -ating, -ates. 1.** To place in a certain spot or position; locate. **2.** To place under particular circumstances or in a given condition.

∼*adj.* (sĭch′o͞o-ĭt, -āt′). *Archaic.* Situated. [Medieval Latin *situāre,* to put, place, from *situs,* place, SITE.]

sit·u·a·tion (sĭch′o͞o-ā′shən) *n.* **1.** A place or position in which something is situated; a location. **2.** A position or status with regard to conditions and attendant circumstances; especially, a person's financial position or status. **3.** A combination of circumstances at a given moment; a state of affairs. **4.** A critical or problematic combination of circumstances. **5.** A position of employment; a post. —See Synonyms at **state.** [Middle English, from Medieval Latin *situātiō* (stem *situātiōn-*), from *situāre,* to SITUATE.] **—sit·u·a·tion·al** *adj.*

situation comedy *n.* **1.** A kind of comedy in which the humor is derived from the reactions of a regular cast of characters to unusual situations, such as misunderstandings or embarrassing coincidences. **2.** A radio or television series using this type of comedy. In this sense, also called "sitcom."

si·tus (sī′təs) *n., pl.* **situs.** Position; especially, the normal position of a bodily organ. [Latin *situs,* place, SITE.]

Sit·well (sĭt′wəl), **Dame Edith Louisa** (1887–1964). British poet, biographer, and critic. One of the most famous literary eccentrics of the 20th century, she wrote *English Eccentrics* in 1933, by which time she had already established a reputation for her poetry, written in the obscure manner of the French symbolists. Her brother, **Sir Osbert** (1892–1969), was a poet, novelist, and short-story writer.

sitz bath (sĭts, zĭts) *n.* A type of bath in which one bathes in a sitting position. [Partial translation of German *Sitzbad* : *Sitz,* a sitting, from Old High German *siz,* from *sizzen,* to sit + *Bad,* bath.]

sitz·krieg (sĭts′krēg′, zĭts′-) *n.* A war in which very little actual fighting takes place; a nonaggressive war. [German, "sitting war."]

sitz·mark (sĭts′märk′, zĭts′-) *n.* A hollow made in the snow by a skier falling backward. [Partial translation of German *Sitzmarke* : *Sitz,* a sitting + *Marke,* mark.]

SI unit (ĕs′ī′) *n.* Any of the units that form part of the Système international d'unités, used for all scientific purposes. The seven base units are the meter, kilogram, second, ampere, kelvin, candela, and mole; the radian and the steradian are treated as supplementary units. All other units are derived from these units.

Siva. Variant of **Shiva.**

Si·van (sĭv′ən) *n.* The ninth month of the Hebrew year. See feature at **calendar.** [Hebrew *Sīwān,* from Assyro-Babylonian *Simānu,* possibly related to Persian *Sefend,* an Iranian deity.]

six (sĭks) *n.* **1. a.** The cardinal number that is one more than five. **b.** A symbol representing this, such as 6, VI, or vi. **2.** A set made up of six persons or things. **3. a.** The sixth in a series. **b.** A playing card marked with six pips. **4.** Six parts: *cut into six.* **5.** A size, as in clothing, designated as six. **6.** Six hours after midnight or midday. **7.** Something having six parts, units, or members, especially a motor vehicle having six cylinders. **—at sixes and sevens.** *Informal.* In a state of confusion or disorder. **—six of one and half a dozen of the other.** A merely nominal difference; a situation in which neither choice is clearly preferable. [Middle English *six, sex,* Old English *s(i)ex, six.*] **—six** *adj. & pron.* **—six·fold** *adj. & adv.*

six-gun (sĭks′gŭn′) *n.* A **six-shooter** *(see).*

Six Nations. See **Iroquois.**

six-pack (sĭks′păk′) *n.* A pack of six cans of a drink, especially beer or a soft drink.

six·pence (sĭks′pəns) *n.* **1.** A British coin worth six old pennies or half a shilling (2.5 new pence), no longer in circulation. **2.** The sum of six British old pennies.

six·pen·ny (sĭks′pə-nē; sĭks′pĕn′ē *for sense 3*) *adj.* **1.** Valued at, selling for, or worth sixpence (2.5 new pence). **2.** Of little worth; cheap; paltry. **3.** Designating a nail of a certain size, generally two inches.

six-shoot·er (sĭks′sho͞o′tər) *n. Informal.* A six-chambered revolver. Also called "six-gun."

six·teen (sĭk-stēn′) *n.* **1. a.** The cardinal number that is one more than 15. **b.** A symbol representing this, such as 16 or XVI. **2.** A set made up of 16 persons or things. **3.** The 16th in a series. **4.** A size, as in clothing, designated as 16. [Middle English *sixtene,* Old English *sixtȳne* : SIX + -TEEN.] **—six·teen** *adj. & pron.*

six·teen·mo (sĭk-stēn′mō) *n., pl.* **-mos. Sextodecimo** *(see).*

six·teenth (sĭk-stēnth′) *n.* **1.** The ordinal number 16 in a series. **2.** Any of 16 equal parts. **—six·teenth** *adj. & adv.*

sixteenth note *n. Music.* A note having 1/16 the time value of a whole note. Also *chiefly British* "semiquaver."

sixth (sĭksth) *n.* **1.** The ordinal number six in a series. **2.** One of six equal parts. **3.** *Music.* **a.** An interval of six degrees in a diatonic scale. **b.** A tone separated by this interval from a given tone. **c.** The harmonic combination of two tones separated by this interval. **d.** The sixth tone of a scale; the submediant. **—sixth** *adj. & adv.*

sixth sense *n.* A power of perception seemingly independent of and additional to the five senses.

six·ti·eth (sĭk′stē-ĭth) *n.* **1.** The ordinal number 60 in a series. **2.** Any of 60 equal parts. **—six·ti·eth** *adj. & adv.*

Sixtine. Variant of **Sistine.**

six·ty (sĭk′stē) *n., pl.* **-ties. 1. a.** The cardinal number that is ten more than 50. **b.** A symbol representing this, such as 60 or LX. **2.** A set

PRONUNCIATION KEY

ă, pat; ā, pay; âr, care; ä, father, are; b, bib; ch, church; d, deed; ĕ, pet; ē, be; f, fife; g, gag; h, hat; hw, which; ĭ, pit; ī, pie; îr, pier; j, judge; k, kick; l, lid, needle; m, mum; n, no, sudden; ng, thing; ŏ, pot; ō, toe; ô, paw, for; oi, noise; ou, out; o͝o, book; o͞o, boot; p, pop; r, roar; s, sauce; sh, ship, dish; t, tight; th, thin, path; *th*, this, bathe; ŭ, cut; ûr, fur; v, valve; w, with; y, yes; z, zebra, size; zh, vision; ə, about, item, edible, gallop, circus, peaceful

IN FOREIGN WORDS:

à, *Fr.* ami; œ, *Fr.* feu, *Ger.* schön; ü, *Fr.* tu, *Ger.* über; KH, *Ger.* ich, *Scot.* loch; N, *Fr.* bon; y', *Fr.* Compiègne

STRESS MARKS:

Primary stress: ′ in·cite′ (ĭn-sīt′)
Secondary stress: ′ in′sight′ (ĭn′sīt′)

made up of 60 persons or things. **3.** The 60th in a series. **4.** A size, as in clothing, designated as 60. **5. sixties. a.** The range of numbers from 60 to 69, considered as a range of age, price, temperature, or the like. **b.** The years numbered 60 to 69 in a century. Also used adjectively: *sixties music.* —**six·ty** *adj. & pron.*

six·ty-fourth note (sĭk′stē-fôrth′, -fōrth′) *n. Music.* A note having 1/64 the time value of a whole note. Also *chiefly British* "hemidemi-semiquaver."

siz·a·ble, size·a·ble (sī′zə-bəl) *adj.* Of considerable size; fairly large. —**siz·a·ble·ness** *n.* —**siz·a·bly** *adv.*

size¹ (sīz) *n.* **1.** The physical dimensions, proportions, magnitude, or extent of something. **2.** Any of a series of graduated categories of dimension by which articles for sale are classified. **3.** Considerable extent, amount, or dimensions: *grown to quite a size.* **4.** Qualities or status with reference to relative importance or the capacity to meet certain requirements: *of no great size in her field.* **5.** The actual state of affairs or truth of the matter: *That's about the size of it.* —**cut down to size.** *Informal.* **1.** To reduce the self-importance of. **2.** To reduce to manageable proportions. —**try (out) for size.** *Informal.* To test; give a preliminary trial to.
~*tr.v.* **sized, sizing, sizes. 1.** To arrange, classify, or distribute according to size. **2.** To make, cut, or shape to a required size. —**size up. 1.** *Informal.* To make an estimate or form a judgment of: *sized up the stranger with a frank gaze.* **2.** To meet certain specifications or requirements: *applicants who fail to size up.* [Middle English *syse,* fixed amount, assize, from Old French *sise,* short for *assise,* ASSIZE.]

size² *n.* Any of several gelatinous or glutinous substances usually made from glue, wax, or clay and used as a glaze or filler for porous materials such as paper, cloth, or wall surfaces. Also called "sizing."
~*tr.v.* **sized, sizing, sizes.** To treat or coat with size or a similar substance. [Middle English *cyse, syse,* probably a specialized use of SIZE (dimension).] —**siz·y** *adj.*

sized (sīzd) *adj.* Having a particular or specified size. Often used in combination: *medium-sized.*

siz·ing (sī′zĭng) *n.* A glaze or filler; size.

siz·zle (sĭz′əl) *intr.v.* **-zled, -zling, -zles. 1.** To make the hissing sound characteristic of frying fat. **2.** *Informal.* To seethe with anger or indignation. **3.** *Informal.* To be extremely hot.
~*n.* A hissing sound. [Imitative.]

siz·zler (sĭz′lər) *n. Informal.* A very hot day.

S.J. Society of Jesus.

Sjæl·land (shĕl′än′). *English* **Zea·land** (zē′lənd). Denmark's largest island, lying off the extreme southwestern coast of Sweden. Low-lying and fertile, the island is the site of Copenhagen.

sk. sack.

Skag·er·rak (skăg′ə-răk′). Strait separating Norway and Denmark, linking the North Sea and the Baltic Sea by way of the Kattegat and extending for *c.* 240 kilometers (150 miles). Here the British and German fleets engaged in the Battle of Jutland (1916).

skald, scald (skôld, skäld) *n.* An ancient Scandinavian poet; a bard. [Old Norse *skáld.*] —**skald·ic** *adj.*

Skar·a Brae (skăr′ə brā′). Stone Age village on the western coast of Mainland, Orkney, Scotland, dating from *c.* 2000 B.C.–1500 B.C. It is perhaps the most completely preserved settlement of its kind in Europe.

skat (skät) *n.* **1.** A card game for three persons played with 32 cards, from the sevens up to and including the aces. **2.** One of the combinations of cards occurring in this game. [German *Skat,* from Italian *scarto,* a discarded card, from *scartare,* to reject, discard : *s-,* negative prefix, from Latin *ex-,* out of + *carta,* card, from Latin *charta,* leaf of papyrus (see **card**).]

skate¹ (skāt) *n.* **1. a.** A shoe or boot having a runner fixed to its sole, enabling the wearer to glide easily over ice; an ice skate. **b.** The bladelike metal runner of an ice skate. **2.** A roller skate (*see*).
~*intr.v.* **skated, skating, skates.** To glide or move along on or as if on skates. [Mistaken as singular of earlier *scates,* from Dutch *schaats,* a skate, from Old North French *escace,* stilt, from Frankish *skakkja* (unattested), from *skakan* (unattested), to run fast. See **scotch** (block).]

skate² *n.* Any of various marine cartilaginous fishes of the family Rajidae, having a flattened body with the pectoral fins forming winglike lateral extensions; a large ray. [Middle English *scate,* from Old Norse *skata†.*]

skate·board (skāt′bôrd′, -bōrd′) *n.* An elongated oval or oblong board having a set of four roller-skate wheels mounted under it, designed to be ridden standing up.
~*intr.v.* **skateboarded, -boarding, -boards.** To ride on a skateboard, using one's feet and weight to propel oneself and change direction. —**skate·board·er** *n.* —**skate·board·ing** *n.*

skat·er (skā′tər) *n.* **1.** One who skates. **2.** An insect, the **water strider** (*see*).

skating rink *n.* An ice rink (*see*).

skat·ole, skat·ol (skăt′ōl′, skā′tōl′) *n.* A white crystalline organic compound, C₉H₉N, having a strong fecal odor, found naturally in feces, beets, and coal tar and used as a fixative in the manufacture of perfume. [Greek *skōr* (stem *skat-*), dung + -OLE.]

skean (shkēn) *n.* A type of double-edged dagger formerly used in Ireland and Scotland. [Gaelic *sgian,* knife.]

ske·dad·dle (skĭ-dăd′l) *intr.v.* **-dled, -dling, -dles.** *Informal.* To run off or leave hastily.
~*n. Informal.* A hurried retreat. [19th century : origin obscure.]

skeet (skēt) *n.* A variety of trapshooting in which clay targets are thrown from traps to simulate birds in flight and are fired at from

different stations by the shooter. [Ultimately from Old Norse *skjóta,* to shoot.]

skeg (skĕg) *n.* **1.** A timber that connects the keel and the sternpost of a ship. **2.** An arm extending to the rear of the keel to support the rudder and protect the propeller. **3.** A series of timbers attached to the stern of a small boat, serving as a keel to keep the boat on course. [Dutch *scheg(ge),* from Old Norse *skegg,* beard, projection.]

skein (skān) *n.* **1.** A length of thread or yarn wound in a loose, elongated coil. **2.** Something like or suggestive of this; a tangle. **3.** A flock of geese or similar birds in flight. [Middle English *skeyne,* from Old French *escaigne†.*]

skel·e·tal (skĕl′ə-təl) *adj.* Pertaining to, forming, or resembling a skeleton. —**skel·e·tal·ly** *adv.*

skeletal muscle *n.* A striated muscle (*see*).

skel·e·ton (skĕl′ə-tən) *n.* **1. a.** The internal vertebrate structure composed of bone and cartilage that protects and supports the soft organs, tissues, and parts. **b.** The hard external supporting and protecting structure in many invertebrates and certain vertebrates, such as turtles; the exoskeleton. **2.** A supporting structure or essential framework, as of a building. **3.** A bare outline or sketch. **4.** *Informal.* A very thin or emaciated person or animal. **5.** A scandalous or humiliating fact that is kept secret from others. Used chiefly in the phrases *skeleton in the closet* and *family skeleton.*
~*adj.* **1.** Of or resembling a skeleton. **2.** Having or consisting only of an outline, essential parts, or the smallest practicable number: *a skeleton staff.* [New Latin, from Greek, neuter of *skeletos,* dried up, withered.]

skel·e·ton·ize (skĕl′ə-tə-nīz′) *tr.v.* **-ized, -izing, -izes. 1.** To create an outline of or framework for. **2.** To reduce to a minimum.

skeleton key *n.* A key with a large portion of the bit filed away so that it can open different locks. Also called "passkey."

skep (skĕp) *n.* **1.** A beehive, especially one made of straw. **2.** A large straw or wickerwork basket. [Middle English *skep(pe),* Old English *sceppe,* the quantity held by a skep, from Old Norse *skeppa†,* basket.]

skep·tic, scep·tic (skĕp′tĭk) *n.* **1.** One who doubts or disagrees; especially, one who instinctively or habitually questions assertions or generally accepted conclusions. **2.** One inclined to skepticism in religious matters. **3. a.** Often **Skeptic.** An adherent of a philosophical school of skepticism. **b. Skeptic.** A member of an ancient Greek school of philosophical skepticism, especially that of Pyrrho of Elis. [Latin *Scepticus,* singular of *Sceptici,* followers of Pyrrho, from Greek *Skeptikoi,* from *skeptesthai,* to examine, consider.]

skep·ti·cal, scep·ti·cal (skĕp′tĭ-kəl) *adj.* **1.** Doubting; questioning. **2.** Pertaining to or characteristic of skeptics or skepticism. —**skep·ti·cal·ly** *adv.*

skep·ti·cism, scep·ti·cism (skĕp′tə-sĭz′əm) *n.* **1.** A doubting or questioning attitude or state of mind; dubiety. **2.** The philosophical doctrine that absolute knowledge is impossible and that inquiry must be a process of doubting in order to acquire approximate or relative certainty. **3.** Doubt or disbelief of religious tenets, especially those of Christianity. —See Synonyms at **uncertainty.**

sker·ry (skĕr′ē) *n., pl.* **-ries.** A small, sometimes rocky island. [Orkney dialect, from Old Norse *sker,* SCAR (crag).]

sketch (skĕch) *n.* **1.** A hasty or undetailed drawing or painting, often done as a preliminary study. **2.** A brief, general account or presentation; an outline. **3. a.** A brief, light, or informal short story, essay, or other literary composition. **b.** A short, usually humorous scene or play in a revue or variety show. **c.** *Music.* A brief composition, especially for the piano. **4.** *Informal.* An amusing person.
~*v.* **sketched, sketching, sketches.** —*tr.* **1.** To make a rough drawing or sketch of. **2.** To outline; describe briefly. Often used with *out* or *in.* —*intr.* To make a sketch or sketches. [Dutch *schets* or German *Skizze,* from Italian *schizzo,* from *schizzare,* to sketch, from Vulgar Latin *schediāre,* from Latin *schedius,* hastily put together, from Greek *skhedios,* impromptu.] —**sketch·er** *n.*

sketch·book (skĕch′bŏŏk′) *n.* **1.** A pad consisting of sheets of paper used for sketching. **2.** A book of literary sketches.

sketch·y (skĕch′ē) *adj.* **-ier, -iest. 1.** Resembling a sketch; giving only an outline. **2.** Incomplete; slight; vague. —**sketch·i·ly** *adv.* —**sketch·i·ness** *n.*

skew (skyōō) *v.* **skewed, skewing, skews.** —*intr.* **1.** To take an oblique course or direction. **2.** To look obliquely or sideways. —*tr.* **1.** To turn or place at an angle. **2.** To give a bias to; distort.
~*adj.* **1.** Placed or turned to one side; asymmetrical. **2.** Distorted or biased in meaning or effect. **3.** Having a part that diverges, as from a straight line or a right angle, as in gearing. **4. a.** *Geometry.* Neither parallel nor intersecting. Said of straight lines in space. Compare **parallel. b.** *Statistics.* Not symmetrical about the mean. Said of distributions.
~*n.* An oblique or slanting movement, position, or direction. [Middle English *skewen,* to skew, escape, from Old North French *eskuer,* from Germanic *skiuhwan* (unattested). See **eschew.**] —**skew·ness** *n.*

skew arch *n. Architecture.* An arch whose line is not at right angles to the abutments.

skew·back (skyōō′băk′) *n. Architecture.* Either of two inset abutments sloped to support a segmental arch.

skew·bald (skyōō′bôld′) *adj.* Having spots or patches of white and a color other than black on its coat: *a skewbald horse.* Compare **piebald.**
~*n.* A horse with this coloring. [From earlier *skued†* + BALD.]

skew·er (skyōō′ər) *n.* **1.** A long metal or wooden pin used to secure

meat during cooking or to hold pieces of meat and vegetables during broiling. **2.** Any of various picks or rods having a similar function or shape.
~*tr.v.* **skewered, -ering, -ers.** To hold together or pierce with or as if with a skewer. [Variant of dialectal *skiver*†.]
ski (skē) *n., pl.* **skis. 1.** Either of a pair of long, flat runners of wood, metal, or other material that curve upward in front and can be attached to a boot for gliding or traveling over snow. **2.** A **water-ski** *(see).*
~*adj.* Of, pertaining to, or associated with skiing: *a ski resort.*
~*v.* **skied, skiing, skis.** —*intr.* To glide or travel on skis, especially as a sport. —*tr.* To travel over on skis. [Norwegian *ski(d)*, from Old Norse *skīth*, ski, snowshoe.] —**ski·er** *n.* —**ski·ing** *n. & adj.*
skiagram. Variant of **sciagram.**
skiagraphy. Variant of **sciagraphy.**
skiamachy. Variant of **sciamachy.**
ski·a·scope (skī′ə-skōp′) *n. Optometry.* A **retinoscope** *(see).* [Greek *skia*, shadow + -SCOPE.]
ski·as·co·py (skī-ăs′kə-pē) *n. Optometry.* **Retinoscopy** *(see).*
ski binding *n.* An attachment on a ski used to secure the ski to the skier's boot.
ski·bob (skē′bŏb′) *n.* A bicyclelike vehicle with two small skis instead of wheels, used for traveling downhill over snow by a rider wearing miniature skis for balance. [SKI + BOB(SLED).] —**ski·bob·ber** *n.* —**ski·bob·bing** *n.*
skid (skĭd) *n.* **1.** An act or state of sliding or slipping over a surface, often uncontrollably and sideways. **2. a.** A plank, log, or timber, usually one of a pair, used as a support or as a track for sliding or rolling heavy objects. **b.** A small platform for stacking merchandise to be moved or temporarily stored. **c.** One of several logs or timbers forming a skid road. **3. skids.** *Nautical.* A wooden framework attached to the side of a ship to prevent damage, as when unloading. **4.** A shoe or drag applying pressure to a wheel to brake a vehicle. **5.** A runner in the landing gear of certain aircraft. —**on the skids.** *Slang.* On a downward path to ruin, failure, or depravity. —**put the skids under.** *Slang.* To hasten the failure of.
~*v.* **skidded, skidding, skids.** —*intr.* **1.** To lose traction and slip or slide sideways while moving. Used chiefly of a vehicle. **2.** To slide without revolving. Said of a wheel that does not turn while a vehicle is in motion. **3.** *Aviation.* To move sideways in a turn because of insufficient banking. —*tr.* **1.** To brake (a wheel) with a skid. **2.** To haul on a skid or skids. [17th century : origin obscure.]
skid fin *n.* An upright auxiliary airfoil formerly placed above the upper wing in biplanes to increase lateral stability.
skid road *n.* **1.** A track made of logs laid transversely, spaced about five feet apart, and used to haul logs to a loading platform or a mill. **2. a.** *Western U.S.* An area of a town often occupied by loggers. **b.** *Slang.* Skid row.
skid row *n. Slang.* A squalid area of a town where derelicts, vagrants, and destitute alcoholics gather. [Variant (influenced by ROW) of SKID ROAD.]
skied. 1. Past tense and past participle of **ski. 2.** Past tense and past participle of **sky.**
skiey. Variant of **skyey.**
skiff (skĭf) *n. Nautical.* An open boat with a flat or rounded bottom having a pointed bow and a square stern and propelled by oars, sail, or motor. [French *esquif*, from Italian *schifo*.]
skif·fle (skĭf′əl) *n.* Folk or country music played by performers using unconventional or improvised instruments, especially percussion instruments such as bottles, jugs, or washboards. Also used adjectively: *a skiffle band.* [Probably imitative.]
ski·jor·ing (skē′jôr′ĭng, -jōr′ĭng) *n.* A sport in which a skier is drawn over ice or snow by a horse or vehicle. [Norwegian *skikjøring* : SKI + *kjøring*, driving, from *kjøre*, to drive, from Old Norse *keyra*.] —**ski·jor·er** *n.*
ski jump *n.* **1.** A jump or leap made by a skier. **2.** A steep slope ending in a high ramp overhanging a slope, used for such a jump. **3.** A ramp used to assist the takeoff of a jump jet. —**ski-jump** (skē′jŭmp′) *v.* —**ski-jump·er** *n.*
ski lift *n.* Any of various power-driven conveyors, usually with attached towing bars, suspended chairs, or gondolas, used to carry skiers to the top of a trail or slope.
skill (skĭl) *n.* **1.** The capacity to accomplish successfully something requiring special knowledge or ability; proficiency. **2.** An art, trade, or technique acquired through training or experience, particularly one requiring use of the hands or body. **3.** *Obsolete.* Understanding. —See Synonyms at **ability.** [Middle English *skil(e)*, reason, skill, from Old Norse *skil.*]
skilled (skĭld) *adj.* **1.** Having or showing skill; expert: *a skilled mechanic.* **2.** Having or requiring specialized ability or training, especially in a trade or craft: *a skilled occupation.* —See Synonyms at **proficient.**
skil·let (skĭl′ĭt) *n.* **1.** A frying pan. **2.** *Chiefly British.* A long-handled stewing pan or saucepan sometimes having legs. [Middle English *skelet*, probably from *skele*, pail, from Scandinavian, akin to Old Norse *skjóla.*]
skill·ful (skĭl′fəl) *adj.* Also *chiefly British* **skil·ful. 1.** Possessing or exercising skill; able; expert. **2.** Characterized by, showing, or requiring skill. —See Synonyms at **proficient.** —**skill·ful·ly** *adv.* —**skill·ful·ness** *n.*
skim (skĭm) *v.* **skimmed, skimming, skims.** —*tr.* **1.** To remove floating matter from (a liquid). **2.** To remove (floating matter, especially scum or cream) from a liquid. **3.** To coat or cover with or as

skimmer *Trailing its long lower bill in the water, a skimmer swoops across a lake, scooping up fish as it flies. The birds live in large flocks on the fringes of lakes and rivers in Asia and Africa.*

if with a thin layer, as of scum or ice. **4. a.** To hurl across and close to the surface of water, ice, or the like, so as to bounce: *skimming stones.* **b.** To glide or pass quickly and lightly over. **5.** To read or glance through quickly or superficially; peruse hastily: *skimmed the newspaper as he breakfasted.* —*intr.* **1.** To move or pass swiftly and lightly over or near a surface; glide; graze. **2.** To give a quick and superficial reading, scrutiny, or consideration. Used with *over* or *through.* **3.** To become coated with a thin layer: *The cocoa skimmed over as it cooled.*
~*n.* **1.** The act of skimming. **2.** Something that has been skimmed, such as skim milk. **3.** A thin layer or film. [Middle English *skymen*, from Old French *escumer*, from *escume*, foam, from Old High German *scūm.*]
ski mask *n.* A knitted mask that covers the head and has openings for the mouth and eyes, worn especially by skiers in cold or windy weather.
skim·mer (skĭm′ər) *n.* **1.** One that skims. **2.** A flat utensil, usually perforated and resembling a ladle, used in skimming liquids. **3.** A wide-brimmed hat with a flat shallow crown. **4.** Any of several chiefly tropical coastal birds of the genus *Rynchops*, having long narrow wings and a long bill with a longer lower mandible for skimming the water's surface for food.
skim·mi·a (skĭm′ē-ə) *n.* A shrub of the genus *Skimmia*, native to southern and southeastern Asia but grown elsewhere for its ornamental foliage and red berries. [New Latin, from Japanese *mijama-skimmi.*]
skim milk *n.* Also **skimmed milk.** Milk from which the cream has been removed.
skim·ming (skĭm′ĭng) *n. Often* **skimmings.** Matter that has been skimmed off a liquid.
ski·mo·bile (skē′mō-bēl′) *n.* A snowmobile *(see).*
skimp (skĭmp) *v.* **skimped, skimping, skimps.** —*tr.* **1.** To do hastily, carelessly, or with poor material. **2.** To be extremely sparing with; scrimp. —*intr.* To be very or unduly thrifty. Usually used with *on: skimp on the budget.*
~*adj.* Scanty; skimpy. [Perhaps a variant of SCRIMP.]
skimp·y (skĭm′pē) *adj.* **-ier, -iest. 1.** Inadequate in size, fullness, or amount; scanty. **2.** Unduly thrifty; stingy; niggardly. —See Synonyms at **meager.** —**skimp·i·ly** *adv.* —**skimp·i·ness** *n.*
skin (skĭn) *n.* **1.** The tissue forming the external, protective covering of the body of a vertebrate. It consists of an outer **epidermis** and an inner **dermis** *(both of which see).* Also used adjectively: *a skin graft.* **2.** An animal pelt, especially the comparatively pliable pelt of a small or young animal. Often used in combination: *pigskin; sheepskin.* **3.** Anything resembling skin in function or appearance; any outer layer, accretion, or protection, such as the rind of fruit, the surface film on boiled milk, or the plating on a ship or rocket. **4.** A container for liquid made of animal skin. **5.** *Often* **skins.** *Slang.* A drum. —**by the skin of one's teeth.** By the smallest margin; very closely; scarcely or barely. —**get under someone's skin. 1.** To anger or irritate. **2.** To be or become an obsession to. —**have a thick (or thin) skin.** To be unperturbed (or easily hurt) by criticism or insults. —**jump out of one's skin.** To be suddenly very startled or frightened. —**no skin off someone's nose.** *Informal.* Being a matter that does not adversely affect one. —**save one's skin.** To escape harm or avoid death.
~*v.* **skinned, skinning, skins.** —*tr.* **1.** To remove skin from; flay or peel: *skin a rabbit.* **2.** To cover with or as if with skin. Often used with *over.* **3.** To remove or peel off (skin or any outer covering). **4.** *Slang.* To fleece; swindle. **5.** To bruise, cut, or scrape the skin or surface of: *skinned her knee while playing.* —*intr.* To become covered with or as if with skin. Often used with *over.* [Middle English, from Old Norse *skinn.*]
skin-deep (skĭn′dēp′) *adj.* Superficial or shallow.
~*adv.* Shallowly; to a superficial degree.
skin-dive (skĭn′dīv′) *intr.v.* **-dived, -diving, -dives.** To engage in skin diving.
skin diving *n.* Underwater swimming, exploration, or fishing in which the diver is equipped with goggles, flippers, and a snorkel or other breathing device. —**skin diver** *n.*
skin drag. Skin friction *(see).*
skin effect *n.* The tendency of electric current density in a conductor carrying alternating current to be greater at the surface than at the center, producing an increase in resistance.
skin flick *n. Slang.* A motion picture containing pornographic nudity. Also called "nudie."
skin-flint (skĭn′flĭnt′) *n.* A miser; a niggard. [From the notion that one would go so far as to try to skin a flint for money.]
skin friction *n.* Friction caused by a fluid crossing the surface of bodies, such as rockets, moving at high speeds. Also called "skin drag."
skin graft *n.* A surgical graft of skin from one part of the body to another or from one individual to another. —**skin grafting** *n.*
skin-head (skĭn′hĕd′) **1.** *Slang.* A person whose head is shaved. **2.** A young British working-class tough with close-cropped hair.
skink (skĭngk) *n.* Any of numerous, mainly tropical, smooth, shiny lizards of the family Scincidae, having a cylindrical body and short or rudimentary legs. [Latin *scincus*, from Greek *skinkos*†.]
skinned (skĭnd) *adj.* Having skin, especially of a specified kind. Used in combination: *fair-skinned.*
skin·ner (skĭn′ər) *n.* A person who flays, dresses, or sells animal skins.
Skin·ner (skĭn′ər), **B(urrhus) F(rederic)** (1904–). U.S. psycholo-

skin

THE BODY'S PROTECTIVE TISSUE
Microscopic structures that are vital to life

Skin is the perfect protective wrapper for the body. Elastic and waterproof, no more than 0.3 millimeter (one hundredth of an inch) thick, it keeps moisture out and also prevents the body—which is, as a whole, about 60 percent water—from drying out. It acts as a barrier against dirt and germs and provides a tough, resilient cover that withstands bumps and knocks. The skin also supplies much of the body's vitamin D, manufacturing it from sunlight.

Skin is made up of two main layers: the epidermis, the fine outer layer, only 0.1 millimeter (¹⁄₂₅₀ inch) thick, and the dermis, the relatively thick underlayer.

The outermost part of the epidermis consists of flat, dead cells that are constantly worn away by friction. The lower epidermis is made up of rapidly dividing cells that, every few weeks, build 1.59 square meters (17 square feet) of new skin to replace worn surface layers. Fingernails and toenails grow from actively dividing skin cells at the nail bases.

All the skin's vital structures are in the dermis. Among them are millions of receptors sensitive to touch, pain, cold, and warmth. In the more sensitive areas—the fingertips and lips—there are as many as 200 touch receptors to every square centimeter (0.16 square inch). Less sensitive areas, such as the shoulders, have about four to each square centimeter. Blood vessels and sweat glands control body temperature. When the body is cold, blood vessels contract, reducing blood flow; when it is hot, they dilate and the sweat glands excrete moisture, which evaporates and cools the body.

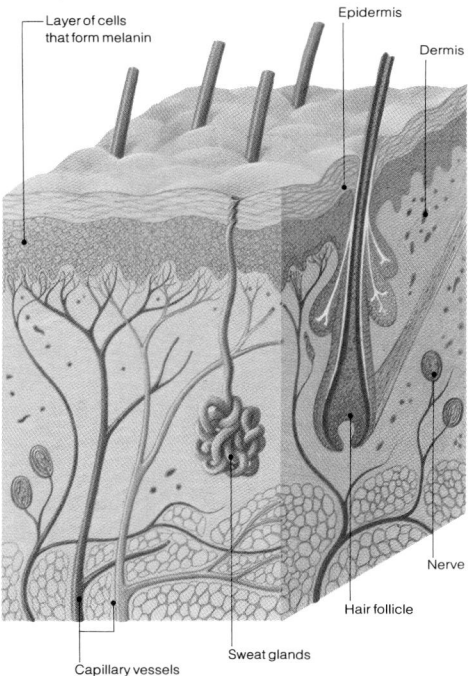

Layer of cells that form melanin
Epidermis
Dermis
Nerve
Hair follicle
Sweat glands
Capillary vessels

INSIDE THE SKIN *Embedded in the skin are sweat glands, hair follicles, and capillary vessels that control the blood supply. Each hair has a separate muscle that raises it on end and an oil gland that helps to keep the skin waterproof, supple, and germ-resistant. Between the two main layers of skin, a layer of cells that form melanin pigment controls skin color.*

gist, the foremost representative of the behaviorist school. His first important publication was *The Behavior of Organisms* (1938); his most influential has been *Beyond Freedom and Dignity* (1971).
Skinner, Cornelia Otis (1901-79). U.S. actress and author. She first appeared on stage in 1921, with a theatrical company managed by her father, **Otis** (1858-1942). Best known for her one-woman shows and original monologues, she collaborated with Emily Kimbrough on the lighthearted memoir *Our Hearts Were Young and Gay* (1942).
Skinner box *n.* A box used in laboratories to study learning behavior in animals. It is fitted with levers that the animal, usually a rat, can press to obtain a reward or avoid a painful stimulus. [After B.F. SKINNER.]

skin·ny (skĭn′ē) *adj.* **-nier, -niest.** Very thin or slender; especially, unattractively thin. —See Usage note at **lean. —skin·ni·ness** *n.*
skin·ny-dip (skĭn′ē-dĭp′) *intr.v.* **-dipped, -dipping, -dips.** *Informal.* To swim in the nude. —**skin·ny-dip·per** *n.*
skin-pop (skĭn′pŏp′) *tr.v.* **-popped, -popping, -pops.** *Slang.* To inject (a narcotic drug, for example) beneath the skin rather than into a vein. —**skin-pop·ping** *n.*
skin test *n.* A test for an allergy or infectious disease that is performed by means of a **patch test** *(see),* a **scratch test** *(see),* or an injection beneath the skin of an allergen or extract of the disease-causing organism.
skin·tight (skĭn′tīt′) *adj.* Fitting or clinging closely to the skin. Said of clothes.
skip¹ (skĭp) *v.* **skipped, skipping, skips.** —*intr.* **1.** To bound or trip lightly, especially by taking two steps at a time with each foot; hop and step; caper. **2.** To bounce over or be deflected from a surface; skim or ricochet. **3.** To pass from point to point omitting or disregarding what intervenes. Often used with *through.* **4.** To be promoted in school beyond the next regular class or grade. **5.** *Informal.* To leave hastily; abscond: *She skipped off somewhere.* —*tr.* **1.** To leap or jump lightly over. **2.** To pass over, omit, or disregard: *skipped the first page.* **3.** To cause to ricochet or skim. **4.** To fail to attend: *skip classes.* **5.** To be promoted beyond (the next class or grade). **6.** *Informal.* To leave hastily or secretly: *has skipped the country.* —**skip it.** *Informal.* To abandon or forget a subject, topic, or the like. Used in the imperative.
~*n.* **1.** A leaping or jumping movement; especially, a gait in which hops and steps alternate. **2.** A passing over or omission. [Middle English *skippen†.*]
skip² *n. Informal.* A skipper, as of a boat or sports team. Used as a form of address. [Short for SKIPPER (master of a ship).]
skip distance *n.* The smallest separation between a transmitter and a receiver that permits radio signals of a specific frequency to travel from one to the other by reflection from the ionosphere.
skip·jack (skĭp′jăk′) *n., pl.* **-jacks** or collectively **skipjack. 1.** Any of several tropical or subtropical marine food fishes of the genus *Euthynnus;* especially, *E. pelamis,* related to and resembling the tuna. Also called "skipjack tuna." **2.** Any of various other fishes, as certain herrings. **3.** The **click beetle** *(see).* [Originally "a fop" : SKIP (to bound) + JACK (fellow).]
ski pole *n.* Either of a pair of light poles usually made of metal and pointed at the lower ends, used by skiers to assist in turning and to gain momentum. Also called "ski stick."
skip·per¹ (skĭp′ər) *n.* **1.** The master of a ship, especially of a small one. **2.** The captain of an airplane or other aircraft. **3.** *Informal.* The captain of a side in sports.
~*tr.v.* **skippered, -pering, -pers.** To act as the skipper of. [Middle English *skypper,* from Middle Dutch *schipper,* from *schip,* ship.]
skipper² *n.* **1.** One that skips. **2.** Any of numerous butterflies of the families Hesperiidae and Megathymidae, having a hairy, mothlike body and a darting flight pattern. **3.** Any of several marine fishes; especially, a saury, *Cololabis saira,* of Pacific waters.
skirl (skûrl) *v.* **skirled, skirling, skirls.** —*intr.* **1.** To produce the shrill, piercing tone of the chanter pipe of a set of bagpipes. **2.** To produce music. Used of bagpipes. —*tr.* To play (music) on the bagpipes.
~*n.* **1.** The shrill sound made by the bagpipes. **2.** Any shrill, piercing sound. [Middle English *skirlen, skrillen,* probably of Scandinavian origin; akin to Norwegian dialectal *skrylla.*]
skir·mish (skûr′mĭsh) *n.* **1.** A minor encounter in war between small bodies of troops, often unconnected with or at a distance from the main operations. **2.** Any minor or preliminary conflict or dispute.
~*intr.v.* **skirmished, -mishing, -mishes.** To engage in a skirmish: *only skirmished with enemy patrols.* [Middle English *skirmisshe, skarmuch,* from Old French *eskermir* (present stem *eskirmiss-*), to fight with the sword, from Germanic.]
skirr (skûr) *v.* **skirred, skirring, skirrs.** —*intr.* To move or fly rapidly, especially with a whirring sound. Used with *away, off,* or other adverbs. —*tr.* To search through; scour. [Perhaps variant of SCOUR (to hurry).]
skir·ret (skûr′ĭt) *n.* An Old World plant, *Sium sisarum,* having a sweetish, edible root. [Middle English *skirwhite,* variant (influenced by *skir,* bright, and *whit,* white) of Old French *eschervi,* probably a variant of *carvi,* caraway, from Arabic *alkarawyā,* CARAWAY.]
skirt (skûrt) *n.* **1.** That part of a garment, such as a dress or coat, that hangs from the waist down. **2.** A separate garment hanging from the waist and worn by women and girls. **3. a.** One of the leather flaps hanging from the side of a saddle. **b.** The lower outer section of a rocket vehicle. **c.** A hanging part around the base of a hovercraft or certain racing cars. **4.** A cloth trimming that hangs in pleats or folds from the bottom edge of a piece of furniture. **5.** A border, margin, or outer edge. **6. skirts.** The edge or outskirts, as of a town. **7.** *Slang.* A woman or girl. **8.** A cut of beef from the lower flank.
~*v.* **skirted, skirting, skirts.** —*tr.* **1.** To lie along, form the border of, or surround; bound. **2.** To move or pass around rather than across or through: *The pilot changed course to skirt the hurricane.* **3.** To evade or elude (a topic of conversation, for example) by circumlocution: *skirt a touchy topic.* —*intr.* To be near or move along the edge or border of something. [Middle English, from Old Norse *skyrta,* SHIRT.]
skirt·ing (skûr′tĭng) *n.* **1.** Fabric used for skirts. **2.** A border or

skink *Some of these shiny-scaled lizards are legless burrowers. The sandfish, for instance, which is a type of skink, spends much of its life underground. This species, which does have legs, is native to Australia.*

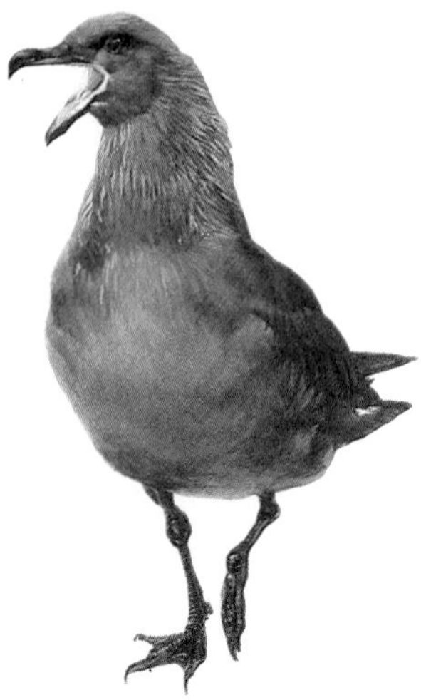

skua *An ocean-going bird that lives in the regions around both poles. It is a skillful flyer and often harries other fishing birds to make them disgorge their catch, which the skua will frequently retrieve before the fish hits the water.*

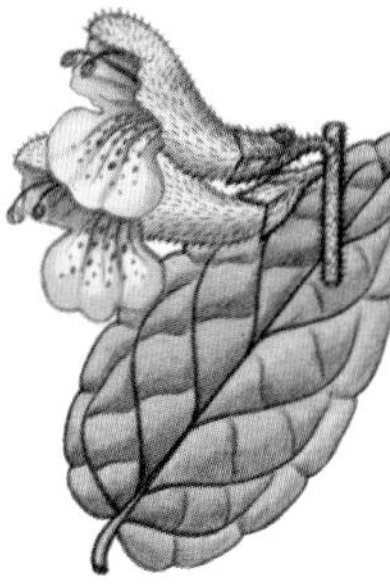

skullcap *A square-stemmed plant with a pouchlike flower, the skullcap grows in marshes. Native to the New World, the plant was used as a sedative by American Indians—it has antispasmodic properties.*

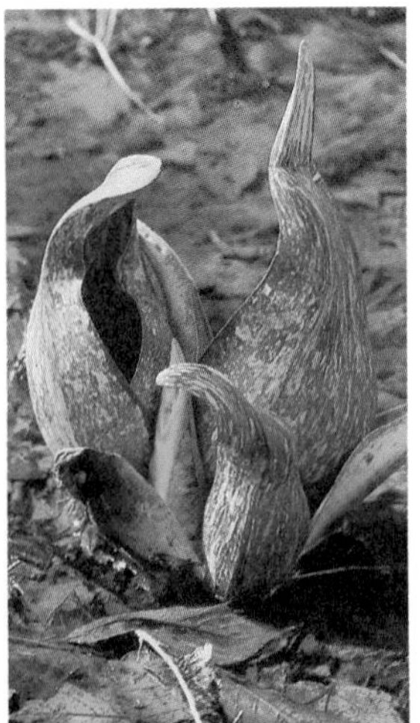

skunk cabbage *The veined leaves of* Symplocarpus foetidus *(above) are preceded by hooded flowers that have a pungent scent. The plant is a native of swamplands in the eastern United States.*

edge. **3.** *Chiefly British.* A molding that runs around the base of an interior wall; baseboard.

skirting board *n. Chiefly British.* A **baseboard** *(see).*

ski run *n.* A slope or course, usually marked, down which skiers ski.

ski stick *n.* A **ski pole** *(see).*

skit (skĭt) *n.* **1.** A short, usually comic theatrical sketch. **2.** A short humorous or satirical piece of writing. [Perhaps from Old Norse; akin to *skjóta,* to SHOOT.]

ski touring *n.* Cross-country skiing for pleasure rather than competition. **—ski tourer** *n.*

ski tow *n.* A type of ski lift in which skiers cling to a continuous rope as they are hauled up a slope.

skit·ter (skĭt′ər) *v.* **-tered, -tering, -ters.** *—intr.* **1.** To skip, scamper, or move lightly or rapidly along a surface; dart; flit. **2.** To fish by drawing a lure or baited hook over the surface of the water with a skipping movement. *—tr.* To cause to skitter. [Frequentative of dialectal *skite,* to run rapidly, shoot about.]

skit·ter·y (skĭt′ə-rē) *adj.* Nervous; skittish.

skit·tish (skĭt′ĭsh) *adj.* **1.** Excitable or nervous. **2. a.** Extremely lively or frivolous in action or character. **b.** Undependable or fickle. **3.** Shy, coy, or timid. [Middle English, perhaps ultimately from Old Norse *skjóta,* to shoot, shoot about.] **—skit·tish·ly** *adv.* **—skit·tish·ness** *n.*

skit·tle (skĭt′l) *n. Chiefly British.* **1. skittles.** *Used with a singular verb.* A game in which a wooden ball is bowled with the aim of knocking down nine pins. **2.** One of the pins used in this game. **—all beer and skittles.** Nothing but pleasure and enjoyment. [17th century : origin obscure.]

skive (skīv) *tr.v.* **skived, skiving, skives.** To shave or cut off the surface of (leather or rubber); pare. [Ultimately from Old Norse *skīfa,* to slice.]

skiv·er (skī′vər) *n.* **1.** A soft, thin leather split off the outside of sheepskin and used especially for bookbinding. **2.** A person who skives leather. **3.** A knife or other cutting device used in skiving.

Skiv·vies (skĭv′ēz). A trademark for underwear.

skoal, skol (skōl) *interj.* Used as a drinking toast. [Norwegian and Danish *skaal* and Swedish *skål,* from Old Norse *skāl,* drinking cup.]

Skop·je (skôp′yə). City in southern Yugoslavia, the capital of Macedonia, on the Vardar River. After its capture by the Turks in 1392 and until the fall of Constantinople in 1453, it was the most important Turkish city in Europe. Much of the city was destroyed by an earthquake in 1963.

Skr., Skt. Sanskrit.

sku·a (skyo͞o′ə) *n.* **1.** A predatory gull-like sea bird, *Catharacta skua,* of northern regions, having brownish plumage. **2.** *British.* A related bird, the **jaeger** *(see).* [New Latin, from Faroese *skūvur,* Old Norse *skūfr*†, tassel.]

skulk (skŭlk) *intr.v.* **skulked, skulking, skulks. 1.** To lurk; lie in hiding. **2.** To move about stealthily or furtively. **3.** *Chiefly British.* To evade work or obligations.

~n. One who skulks. [Middle English *skulken,* from Scandinavian; akin to Danish *skulke*†.] **—skulk·er** *n.*

skull (skŭl) *n.* **1.** The framework of the head of vertebrates, made up of the bones of the **cranium** *(see)* and face. **2.** The skull as a symbol of death. **3.** The head, especially regarded as the seat of thought or intelligence. Often used derogatorily: *can't get it into your thick skull.* [Middle English *schulle, skulle*†.]

skull and crossbones *n. Used with a singular or plural verb.* A representation of a human skull above two long crossed bones, a symbol of death once used by pirates, especially on their flags, and now often used as a warning label on poisons.

skull·cap (skŭl′kăp′) *n.* **1. a.** A light, close-fitting, brimless cap sometimes worn indoors. **b.** A similar cap worn by Roman Catholic prelates and by male Jews. **2.** Any of various plants of the genus *Scutellaria,* having clusters of two-lipped, helmet-shaped flowers. **3.** *Anatomy.* The **calvaria** *(see).*

skull·dug·ger·y, skul·dug·ger·y (skŭl-dŭg′ə-rē) *n. Informal.* Crafty deception or trickery. [From earlier (Scottish) *sculduddery*†, wantonness.]

skunk (skŭngk) *n.* **1.** Any of several small, carnivorous New World mammals of the genus *Mephitis* and related genera; especially, *M. mephitis,* having a bushy tail and black fur with white markings and ejecting an unpleasant-smelling secretion from glands near the anus. **2.** *Slang.* A mean or despicable person.

~tr.v. **skunked, skunking, skunks.** *Slang.* **1.** To defeat overwhelmingly, especially by keeping from scoring in a game. **2.** To cheat, as by failing to pay. [Massachuset *squnck,* from Proto-Algonquian *shekākwa* (unattested) : *shek-* (unattested), to urinate + *-ākw-* (unattested), small mammal.]

skunk cabbage *n.* **1.** An ill-smelling swamp plant, *Symplocarpus foetidus,* of eastern North America, having minute flowers enclosed in a mottled greenish or purplish spathe. **2.** A similar plant, *Lysichitum americanum,* of western North America. Also called "skunkweed."

sky (skī) *n., pl.* **skies. 1. a.** The upper atmosphere, appearing as a hemisphere above the earth. **b.** The apparent hemispherical dome, as seen from the earth's surface, upon which the celestial bodies seem to move; it appears blue in the daytime and almost black at night. **2.** The highest level or degree of something; the ultimate: *reaching for the sky.* **3.** The celestial or heavenly regions. **4.** *Often* **skies. a.** The appearance of the upper air: *blue skies.* **b.** The climate or weather as indicated by the sky. **—praise to the skies.** To praise in an extravagantly enthusiastic way.

~tr.v. **skied, skying, skies. 1.** To hit or throw (a ball, for example) high in the air. **2.** To hang (a painting, for example) high up on a wall above the line of vision, especially in an exhibition. [Middle English, cloud, sky, from Old Norse *sky̅,* cloud, from Common Germanic *skewja-* (unattested).]

sky blue *n.* Light to pale blue. **—sky-blue** (skī′blo͞o′) *adj.*

sky·borne (skī′bôrn′, -bōrn′) *adj.* Airborne.

sky·dive (skī′dīv′) *intr.v.* **-dived, -diving, -dives.** *Sports.* To jump from an aircraft, performing various maneuvers before pulling the ripcord of one's parachute. **—sky·div·er** *n.* **—sky·div·ing** *n.*

Skye (skī). Largest and most northerly island of the Inner Hebrides, off western Scotland. It is part of the Highland Region and is *c.* 80 kilometers (50 miles) long. Bonnie Prince Charlie took refuge here in 1746 after his defeat at Culloden Moor.

Skye terrier *n.* A small terrier of a breed native to the Isle of Skye, having a long, low body, short legs, and shaggy hair.

sky·ey, ski·ey (skī′ē) *adj.* **1.** Of or from the skies: *skyey influences.* **2.** Blue like the sky. **3.** Lofty.

sky-high (skī′hī′) *adv.* **1.** At or to an exceptionally high level: *The price of real estate has gone sky-high.* **2.** In a lavish or enthusiastic manner. **3.** In pieces or to pieces; apart: *blew it sky-high.*

~adj. **1.** High up in the air. **2.** Exorbitantly high.

sky·jack (skī′jăk′) *tr.v.* **-jacked, -jacking, -jacks.** To hijack (an aircraft, especially one in flight) through the use or threat of force. [SKY + (HI)JACK.] **—sky·jack·er** *n.*

sky·lark (skī′lärk′) *n.* An Old World bird, *Alauda arvensis,* having brownish plumage and noted for its singing while in flight.

~intr.v. **skylarked, -larking, -larks.** To frolic or have fun.

sky·light (skī′līt′) *n.* An overhead window admitting daylight.

sky·line (skī′līn′) *n.* **1.** The line along which the surface of the earth and sky appear to meet; the horizon. **2.** An outline, as of a group of buildings or a mountain range, seen against the sky.

sky pilot *n. Slang.* A clergyman, especially a service chaplain.

sky·rock·et (skī′rŏk′ĭt) *n.* A firework, a **rocket** *(see).*

~intr.v. **skyrocketed, -eting, -ets.** To rise rapidly or suddenly, as in amount, position, or reputation.

sky·sail (skī′səl, -sāl′) *n.* A small square sail above the royal in a square-rigged vessel.

sky·scrap·er (skī′skrā′pər) *n.* A very tall building.

sky·ward (skī′wərd) *adj.* Moving or going toward the sky.

~adv. Also **sky·wards** (-wərdz). Toward the sky.

sky wave *n.* A radio wave transmitted from one point on the earth's surface and received at another point after reflection by the ionosphere. Also called "ionospheric wave." Compare **ground wave.**

sky·way (skī′wā′) *n.* **1.** An airline route; air lane. **2.** An elevated highway.

sky·writ·ing (skī′rī′tĭng) *n.* **1.** The process of writing in the sky by releasing a visible vapor from a flying aircraft. **2.** The letters or words thus formed. **—sky·writ·er** *n.*

s.l. without place. Used in book cataloguing. [Latin *sine loco.*]

slab¹ (slăb) *n.* **1.** A broad, flat, somewhat thick piece, as of cake, stone, or cheese. **2.** An outside piece cut from a log when squaring it to make planks. **3.** *Baseball.* The piece of rubber on which the pitcher stands.

~tr.v. **slabbed, slabbing, slabs. 1.** To make or shape into a slab or slabs. **2.** To cover or pave with slabs. **3.** To dress (a log) by cutting slabs. [Middle English *s(c)labbe*†.]

slab² *adj. Archaic.* Viscous. Used in the phrase *thick and slab.* [Probably of Scandinavian origin; akin to Danish *slab,* mud.]

slab-sid·ed (slăb′sī′dĭd) *adj. Informal.* **1.** Having flat sides. **2.** Tall and slim; lanky; lean.

slack¹ (slăk) *adj.* **1.** Not lively or moving; slow; dull; sluggish. **2.** Not active or busy; lacking in work. **3.** Not tense or taut; loose. **4.** Lacking firmness; weak; relaxed: *a slack grip.* **5.** *Informal.* Lacking in diligence; idle or negligent. **6.** Flowing or blowing with little speed. Said of the wind or tide. **7.** *Phonetics.* Lax.

~v. **slacked, slacking, slacks.** *—tr.* **1.** To slacken. **2.** To be remiss about. *—intr.* To be or become slack. **—slack off.** To decrease in activity or intensity; fall off; abate.

~n. **1.** A loose or slack part or portion of something, such as a rope or sail. **2.** A period of little activity; a lull. **3. a.** A cessation of movement in a current of air or water. **b.** An area of still water. **4. slacks.** A pair of trousers for casual wear.

~adv. In a slack manner. [Middle English *slak,* Old English *slæc.*] **—slack·ly** *adv.* **—slack·ness** *n.*

slack² *n.* A mixture of coal fragments, coal dust, and dirt that remains after screening coal. [Middle English *sleck,* probably from Middle Dutch *slacke.*]

slack³ *n. Chiefly British.* **1.** A small dell or hollow. **2.** A bog; a morass. **3.** A depression between lines of sand dunes along a coast or in a desert. [Middle English *slak,* from Old Norse *slakki*†.]

slack·en (slăk′ən) *v.* **-ened, -ening, -ens.** *—tr.* **1.** To make slower; slow down. **2.** To make less vigorous, intense, firm, or severe. **3.** To reduce the tension or tautness of; loosen. *—intr.* **1.** To slow down. **2.** To become slacker in some way, as by growing less energetic, active, firm, or strict. **3.** To become less tense or taut; loosen. In all senses, often used with *off.*

slack·er (slăk′ər) *n.* A person who shirks work or responsibility.

slack water *n.* **1.** The period at high or low tide when there is no visible flow of water. **2.** An area in a sea or river unaffected by currents; still water.

slag (slăg) *n.* **1.** The vitreous mass left as a residue by the smelting of metallic ore. Also called "cinder." **2.** Volcanic refuse, **scoria**

(see). **3.** A mixture of coal dust, shale, and other waste mineral matter produced during coal mining.
∼*v.* **slagged, slagging, slags.** —*tr.* To change into slag. —*intr.* To form slag; become slaglike: *The ore slags as it cools.* [Middle Low German *slagge,* perhaps from *slagen,* to strike (alluding to fragments of rock).] —**slag·gy** *adj.*

slag heap *n.* A large mound consisting of slag deposited as a waste product from coal-mining operations.

slain. Past participle of **slay.**

slake (slāk) *v.* **slaked, slaking, slakes.** —*tr.* **1.** To quench; allay; satisfy: *slake one's thirst.* **2.** To lessen the force or activity of; moderate: *slaking his anger.* **3.** To cool or refresh by moistening. **4.** To combine (lime) chemically with water or moist air. —*intr.* To undergo a slaking process; crumble or disintegrate. Used of lime. [Middle English *slaken,* to lessen, Old English *slacian,* from *slæc,* SLACK (loose).]

slaked lime *n. Chemistry.* **Calcium hydroxide** *(see).*

sla·lom (slä′ləm) *n.* **1.** Skiing in a zigzag course. **2.** A race, especially a skiing race, along a zigzag course, usually marked with poles. [Norwegian, "sloping path" : *sla(d)*†, sloping + *lom, lâm,* path.] —**sla·lom** *v.*

slam[1] (slăm) *v.* **slammed, slamming, slams.** —*tr.* **1.** To shut (a door or window, for example) with force and loud noise. **2.** To put, throw, or otherwise forcefully move so as to produce a loud noise. **3.** To hit or strike with great force. **4.** *Slang.* To criticize harshly; attack verbally. **5.** *Informal.* To beat easily and by a wide margin. **6.** To operate (brakes) suddenly and forcefully. Used with *on.* —*intr.* **1.** To close or swing into place with force so as to produce a loud noise: *Don't let the door slam.* **2.** To hit something with force; crash. **3.** To enter or leave a place violently or angrily: *slammed out of the house.*
∼*n.* **1.** A forceful closing or other movement that produces a loud noise. **2.** The noise so produced. **3.** *Slang.* A harsh criticism. **4.** A long, powerful hit in baseball. [Perhaps from Scandinavian, akin to Old Norse *slam(b)ra,* to strike at.]

slam[2] *n.* In bridge, whist, or other card games derived from these, the winning of all the tricks *(grand slam)* or all but one *(little slam)* during the play of one hand. [17th century: origin obscure.]

slam-bang (slăm′băng′) *adv.* **1.** Loudly and violently. **2.** Recklessly.

s.l.a.n. without place, year, or name. Used in book cataloguing. [Latin *sine loco, anno, vel nomine.*]

slan·der (slăn′dər) *n.* **1.** *Law.* The utterance of defamatory statements that are injurious to the reputation or well-being of a person. Compare **libel. 2.** A malicious statement or report.
∼*tr.v.* **slandered, -dering, -ders.** To utter damaging or defamatory reports about. —See Synonyms at **malign.** [Middle English *s(c)laundre,* from Old French *esclandre,* variant of *escandle,* from Latin *scandalum,* SCANDAL.] —**slan·der·er** *n.* —**slan·der·ous** *adj.* —**slan·der·ous·ly** *adv.*

slang (slăng) *n.* **1.** A kind of informal vocabulary used in place of standard terms for added vividness, spontaneity, or humor and typically consisting of ephemeral coinages and figures of speech. **2.** Language peculiar to a group; argot or jargon.
∼*v.* **slanged, slanging, slangs.** —*tr. Chiefly British.* To direct abusive language at (somebody); insult. —*intr.* **1.** To use slang. **2.** *Chiefly British.* To use abusive or insulting language. [18th-century : origin obscure.] —**slang·i·ly** *adv.* —**slang·i·ness** *n.* —**slang·y** (slăng′ē) *adj.*

slant (slănt, slänt) *v.* **slanted, slanting, slants.** —*tr.* **1.** To give an oblique direction to. **2.** To present (information) so as to give it a particular bias, as by emphasizing certain facts. —*intr.* **1.** To incline or move obliquely. **2.** To have a bias. Used with *toward.*
∼*n.* **1. a.** A sloping direction, plane, or course; an incline. **b.** Slope; obliquity. **2.** A particular bias, emphasis, or point of view.
∼*adj.* Slanting or sloping. [Earlier *slent,* from Middle English *slenten*†, from Old Norse *sletta,* to throw.] —**slant·ing·ly** *adv.*

slant·wise (slănt′wīz′, slänt′-) *adv.* Also **slant·ways** (-wāz′). At a slant or slope; obliquely.
∼*adj.* Slanting; oblique.

slap (slăp) *n.* **1. a.** A smacking blow made with the open hand or with any flat thing. **b.** The sound so made. **2.** An injury, as to one's pride; a rebuff or rebuke. Used chiefly in the phrase *a slap in the face.*
∼*v.* **slapped, slapping, slaps.** —*tr.* **1.** To strike with a flat object, especially the palm of the hand. **2.** To put or place with a slapping sound: *"He took a clipping from his wallet and slapped it on the bar"* (Nathanael West). **3.** To set or apply in an emphatic manner: *slapped a tax on eggs.* **4.** To put or place carelessly or in a hurried manner: *slap a few pictures on the wall.* —*intr.* To strike or beat with the force and sound of a slap. —**slap down. 1.** To put (a person) down; rebuff or reprimand. **2.** To put a stop to; squelch; suppress.
∼*adv. Informal.* Directly and with force. [Low German *slapp* (imitative).] —**slap·per** *n.*

slap·dash (slăp′dăsh′) *adj.* Acting or done hastily or carelessly.
∼*adv.* In a reckless, haphazard manner.
∼*n.* **1.** Careless or hasty work. **2. Roughcast** *(see).*

slap·hap·py (slăp′hăp′ē) *adj.* **-pier, -piest.** *Slang.* **1.** Dazed, silly, or incoherent from or as if from blows to the head. **2.** Reckless or casual in a jolly, cheerful manner.

slap·jack (slăp′jăk′) *n.* **1.** A pancake. **2.** A simple card game. [SLAP + (FLAP)JACK.]

slap·stick (slăp′stĭk′) *n.* **1.** Comedy characterized by boisterous farce and broad visual humor. Also used adjectivally. **2.** A paddle designed to produce a loud whacking sound, formerly used in farces to simulate the sound of a heavy blow.

slash (slăsh) *v.* **slashed, slashing, slashes.** —*tr.* **1.** To cut or form by violent sweeping strokes. **2.** To lash violently with sweeping strokes. **3.** To make a gash or gashes in. **4.** To cut a slit or slits in (a garment) to reveal the lining: *a slashed sleeve.* **5.** To criticize sharply: *a slashing attack.* **6.** To reduce or curtail drastically: *Profits were slashed.* —*intr.* To make violent and sweeping strokes with or as if with a sharp instrument. —See Synonyms at **tear.**
∼*n.* **1.** A sweeping stroke made with a sharp instrument: *a slash with a machete.* **2.** A cut or other injury made by such a stroke; a gash; a slit. **3.** An ornamental slit in a fabric or article of clothing. **4. a.** Branches and other residue left on a forest floor after the cutting of timber. **b.** *Often* **slashes.** Wet or swampy ground overgrown with bushes and trees. **5.** *Printing.* A **virgule** *(see).* [Middle English *slaschen,* perhaps from Old French *esclaschier, esclachier,* to break (imitative).] —**slash·er** *n.*

slat (slăt) *n.* **1.** A narrow strip of metal or wood, as in a Venetian blind. **2.** A movable auxiliary airfoil running along the leading edge of the wing of an aircraft. **3. slats.** *Slang.* The ribs.
∼*tr.v.* **slatted, slatting, slats.** To provide or make with slats. [Middle English *s(c)lat,* from Old French *esclat,* splinter, fragment, from *esclater*†, to splinter.]

slatch (slăch) *n. New England.* **1.** A momentary lull between breaking waves, favorable for launching a boat. **2.** A lull in a high windstorm. [Variant of SLACK (lull).]

slate (slāt) *n.* **1.** A fine-grained metamorphic rock that splits into thin, smooth-surfaced layers. **2. a.** A piece of slate cut for use as a roofing tile. **b.** A piece of slate or similar material used, especially formerly, as a writing tablet. **3.** A list of the candidates of a political party running for various offices. **4.** A dark gray to purplish gray. **5.** A record of past performance or activity. —**start with a clean slate** or **wipe the slate clean.** To overlook past failures and make a fresh start.
∼*tr.v.* **slated, slating, slates. 1.** To cover (a roof, for example) with slates. **2.** To put on a list of candidates. **3.** To designate or destine: *"I was slated to amass wealth beyond the dreams of avarice"* (S.J. Perelman). [Middle English *s(c)late,* from Old French *esclate,* feminine of *esclat,* fragment, splinter. See **slat.**] —**slat·y** *adj.*

slate blue *n.* Grayish blue to dark bluish gray. —**slate-blue** (slāt′blo͞o′) *adj.*

slat·er (slā′tər) *n.* **1.** One employed to lay slate roofs. **2.** Any of several small isopod crustaceans; especially, a woodlouse.

Sla·ter (slā′tər), **Samuel** (1768–1835). U.S. inventor and manufacturer, born in England. Since it was illegal to export cloth-making machines from England, he memorized the complicated plans for a textile mill and duplicated the machinery and methods at a mill in Rhode Island (1790–93), launching the U.S. textile industry.

slath·er (slăth′ər) *tr.v.* **-ered, -ering, -ers.** *Informal.* **1.** To use great amounts of; lavish. **2. a.** To spread thickly with. **b.** To spread thickly.
∼*n.Often* **slathers.** *Slang.* A great amount; lots: *slathers of money.* [19th century : origin obscure.]

slat·ing (slā′tĭng) *n.* **1.** The act, process, or occupation of laying slates. **2.** Slates collectively, used as a building material.

slat·tern (slăt′ərn) *n.* A woman who is untidy or slovenly in person or habits; a slut. [Perhaps variant of dialectal *slattering,* present participle of *slatter*†, to spill awkwardly.]

slat·tern·ly (slăt′ərn-lē) *adj.* **1.** Slovenly; untidy. **2.** Characteristic of or befitting a slattern. —See Synonyms at **sloppy.** —**slat·tern·li·ness** *n.*

slaugh·ter (slô′tər) *n.* **1.** The killing of animals for food. **2.** The killing of a large number of persons; carnage; massacre.
∼*tr.v.* **slaughtered, -tering, -ters. 1.** To kill (animals) for food; butcher. **2. a.** To kill in large numbers; massacre. **b.** To kill in a violent or brutal manner. **3.** *Informal.* To defeat easily. [Middle English *slau(g)hter,* probably from Old Norse *slātr,* butchered meat.] —**slaugh·ter·er** *n.* —**slaugh·ter·ous** *adj.*

slaugh·ter·house (slô′tər-hous′) *n.* **1.** A place where animals are butchered; an abattoir. **2.** A scene of massacre or carnage.

Slav (släv) *n.* A member of any of the Slavic-speaking peoples of eastern Europe. [Middle English *Sclave,* from Medieval Latin *S(c)lavus,* from Late Greek *Sklabos*†.]

Slav. Slavic.

slave (slāv) *n.* **1.** One who is legally bound in servitude to a person or household to perform labor. **2.** One who is submissive to or hopelessly in the power of a particular person or influence: *a slave to her eating habits.* **3.** One whose condition is likened to that of slavery, as through having to work extremely hard or under duress. **4.** A machine or component that is controlled, powered, or fed information by another machine or component. Also used adjectivally: *a slave cylinder.*
∼*intr.v.* **slaved, slaving, slaves.** To work like a slave; drudge. Often used with *away.* [Middle English *sclave,* from Old French *esclave,* slave, from Medieval Latin *sclavus,* from *Sclavus,* SLAV (the Slavs were reduced to slavery by conquest).]

slave driver *n.* **1.** A severely exacting employer or supervisor. **2.** An overseer of slaves at work.

slav·er[1] (slăv′ər) *intr.v.* **-ered, -ering, -ers. 1.** To slobber. **2.** To fawn; drivel. Often used with *over.*
∼*n.* **1.** Saliva drooling from the mouth. **2.** Slobbering flattery or

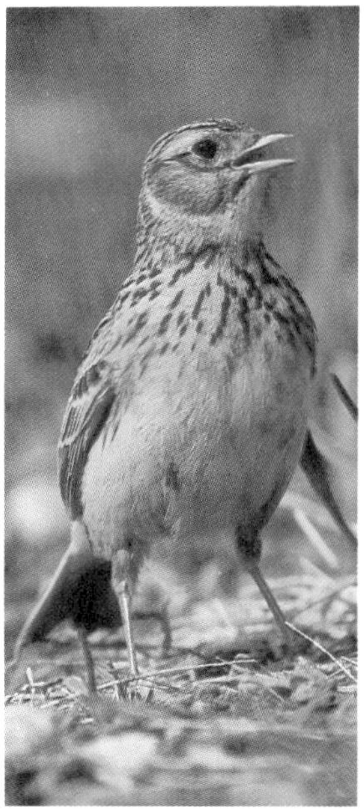

skylark *The male skylark marks out its territory by singing a clear, warbling song while hovering high in the air. Found throughout Europe, Asia, and North Africa, the skylark is considered a delicacy in some countries.*

PRONUNCIATION KEY

ă, pat; ā, pay; âr, care; ä, father, are; b, bib; ch, church; d, deed; ĕ, pet; ē, be; f, fife; g, gag; h, hat; hw, which; ĭ, pit; ī, pie; îr, pier; j, judge; k, kick; l, lid, needle; m, mum; n, no, sudden; ng, thing; ŏ, pot; ō, toe; ô, paw, for; oi, noise; ou, out; o͝o, book; o͞o, boot; p, pop; r, roar; s, sauce; sh, ship, dish; t, tight; th, thin, path; *th*, this, bathe; ŭ, cut; ûr, fur; v, valve; w, with; y, yes; z, zebra, size; zh, vision; ə, about, item, edible, gallop, circus, peaceful

IN FOREIGN WORDS:

à, *Fr.* ami; œ, *Fr.* feu, *Ger.* schön; ü, *Fr.* tu, *Ger.* über; KH, *Ger.* ich, *Scot.* loch; N, *Fr.* bon; y', *Fr.* Compiègne

STRESS MARKS:

Primary stress: ′ in·cite′ (ĭn-sīt′) Secondary stress: ′ in′sight′ (ĭn′sīt′)

drivel. [Middle English *slaveren,* probably from Old Norse *slafra.*]

slav·er² (slā′vər) *n.* **1.** A ship engaged in slave traffic. **2.** A person who traffics in slaves. **—slav·ing** *n.*

slav·er·y (slā′və-rē, slāv′rē) *n., pl.* **-ies. 1.** Bondage to a master or household as a slave. **2.** A mode of production in which slaves constitute the principal work force. **3.** The condition of being subject or addicted to a particular influence. **4.** A condition of subjection likened to that of a slave: *wage slavery.* **—See Synonyms at servitude.**

Slave State. 1. Any of the states of the Union in which slavery was legal before the Civil War, including Alabama, Arkansas, Delaware, Florida, Georgia, Kentucky, Louisiana, Maryland, Mississippi, Missouri, North Carolina, South Carolina, Tennessee, Texas, and Virginia. **2. slave state.** A country under totalitarian rule.

slave trade *n.* Traffic in slaves; specifically, that of black Africans to America.

slav·ey (slā′vē) *n., pl.* **-eys.** A household servant, especially one who is overworked.

Slav·ic (slä′vĭk) *adj. Abbr.* **Slav.** Of or pertaining to the Slavs or their languages or cultures.

~*n. Abbr.* **Slav.** A branch of the Indo-European language family, divided into East Slavic, South Slavic, and West Slavic.

slav·ish (slā′vĭsh) *adj.* **1.** Pertaining to or characteristic of a slave; servile. **2.** Pertaining to or characteristic of the institution of slavery; oppressive. **3.** Blindly dependent on or imitative of something: *a slavish copy of the original.* **4.** Extremely laborious or difficult. **—slav·ish·ly** *adv.* **—slav·ish·ness** *n.*

Slav·ism (slä′vĭz′əm) *n.* Anything peculiar to or characteristic of the Slavs or the Slavic languages.

Sla·vo·ni·a (slə-vō′nē-ə). Historic region in northern Yugoslavia, between the Drava and Sava rivers. A Slavic state was established here in the 7th century. It was later ruled by Hungary (three times), Turkey, and Austria. It has been part of Yugoslavia since 1918.

Sla·von·ic (slə-vŏn′ĭk) *n.* Slavic. **—Sla·von·ic** *adj.*

Slav·o·phile (slä′və-fīl′) *n.* Also **Slav·o·phil** (-fĭl′). **1.** A person who admires the Slavs. **2.** *Sometimes* **slavophile.** In 19th-century Russia, one who advocated the supremacy of Slavic, especially Russian, culture. [SLAV + -PHILE.] **—Slav·o·phile, Slav·o·phil** *adj.* **—Sla·voph·i·lism** (slə-vŏf′ə-lĭz′əm) *n.*

slaw (slô) *n.* Coleslaw *(see).*

slay (slā) *tr.v.* **slew** (slōō) or **slayed** (for sense 2), **slain** (slān) or **slayed** (for sense 2), **slaying, slays. 1.** To kill violently, as in battle. **2.** *Slang.* To overwhelm, as with admiration, laughter, or love: *Her jokes slay me.* [Slay, slew, slain; Middle English *slen(en), slew, slayn,* Old English *slēan, slōh, slǣgen.*] **—slay·er** *n.*

Usage: The usual past-tense form of this verb is *slew;* the usual past participle is *slain.* But in informal speech *slayed* is often used for both past tense and past participle in the sense "overwhelm": *The comedian slayed the audience.*

S.L.B.M. submarine-launched ballistic missile.

sld. 1. sailed. **2.** sealed.

sleave (slēv) *tr.v.* **sleaved, sleaving, sleaves.** To separate or disentangle (a twisted mass of threads, for example).

~*n.* A tangled or knotted thread. [Middle English *sleven* (unattested), Old English *slǣfan,* to cut, cut up, akin to *-slīfan,* to splice. See **sliver.**]

sleave silk *n.* Raw untwisted silk; floss, as for embroidery.

sleaze (slēz) *n. Informal.* **1.** Squalidness or disreputableness; sleaziness. **2.** A sleazy person. [Back-formation from SLEAZY.]

slea·zy (slē′zē) *adj.* **-zier, -ziest. 1.** Having a sordid, squalid, or disreputable character: *a sleazy restaurant.* **2.** Flimsy or thin. Said of fabric. **3.** Made of low-quality materials; shoddy. [17th century : origin obscure.] **—slea·zi·ly** *adv.* **—slea·zi·ness** *n.*

sled (slĕd) *n.* **1.** A vehicle mounted on low runners, drawn by work animals, used for carrying people or loads over ice and snow; sledge. **2.** A light wooden frame on runners, used by children for coasting over snow or ice.

~*v.* **sledded, sledding, sleds.** *—tr.* To carry or convey on a sled. *—intr.* To travel on a sled. [Middle English *sledde,* from Middle Low German.] **—sled·der** *n.*

sled·ding (slĕd′ĭng) *n.* **1.** The act of using a sled for hauling, transportation, or sport. **2.** The weather or snow conditions in which one uses a sled. **3.** *Informal.* Progress; going: *The sledding gets tougher every year in this business.*

sledge (slĕj) *n.* A vehicle on low runners drawn by horses, dogs, or other work animals and used for transporting loads across ice and snow.

~*v.* **sledged, sledging, sledges.** *—tr.* To convey on a sledge. *—intr.* To travel on a sledge. [Dutch (dialectal) *sleeds,* from Middle Dutch *sleedse.*]

sledge·ham·mer (slĕj′hăm′ər) *n.* A long, heavy hammer, often wielded with both hands, used for driving wedges and posts and for other heavy work.

~*tr.v.* **sledgehammered, -mering, -mers.** To strike with or as if with such a hammer.

~*adj.* Ruthlessly severe; crushing. [Middle English *sleg(g)e,* Old English *slecg* + HAMMER.]

sleek (slēk) *adj.* **sleeker, sleekest. 1. a.** Smooth and lustrous as if polished; glossy. **b.** Smooth, shiny, and healthy-looking. Said of hair or of the coat or fur of an animal. **2.** Appearing well-fed or well-groomed; prosperous-looking; thriving. **3.** Polished or smooth in behavior, especially in an unctuous way; slick.

~*tr.v.* **sleeked, sleeking, sleeks. 1.** To make sleek; smooth or polish. **2. a.** To make calm or free from agitation. **b.** To cause to appear in a favorable light; gloss over. Used with *over.* [Variant of SLICK.] **—sleek·ly** *adv.* **—sleek·ness** *n.*

sleep (slēp) *n.* **1. a.** A natural, periodically recurring physiological state of rest, characterized by relative physical and nervous inactivity, unconsciousness, and lessened responsiveness to external stimuli. See **paradoxical sleep, orthodox sleep. b.** A period of this form of rest: *had a long sleep after her exertions.* **c.** A similar condition of inactivity, such as unconsciousness, dormancy, or hibernation. **2.** *Botany.* **Nyctinasty** *(see).* **3.** Death. Often used euphemistically. **—go to sleep. 1.** To fall asleep. **2.** To become numb because of pressure on a bodily part. Used chiefly of limbs. **—put to sleep.** To kill (an animal) humanely.

~*v.* **slept** (slĕpt, slēp), **sleeping, sleeps.** *—intr.* **1.** To be in the state of sleep or to fall asleep. **2.** To be in a condition resembling sleep, such as hibernation, dormancy, or inattentiveness. **3.** To have sexual intercourse. Used with *with* or *together.* **4.** To be dead. Often used euphemistically. *—tr.* **1. a.** To pass (time) by sleeping. **b.** To get rid of by sleeping: *went home to sleep his hangover off.* **2.** To provide (a certain number of people) with accommodation for sleeping: *a bed that sleeps two.* **—sleep around.** *Informal.* To be sexually promiscuous. **—sleep in. 1.** To sleep at one's place of employment: *The housekeeper sleeps in.* **2.** To sleep past one's usual hour of waking. **—sleep on.** To give (a matter) long consideration, especially by delaying one's decision until the next day. **—sleep out. 1.** To sleep at one's own home rather than at one's place of work. **2.** To sleep outdoors. [Middle English *slepe,* from Old English *slēp.*]

sleep·er (slē′pər) *n.* **1.** A person or animal that sleeps. **2.** A sleeping car or compartment on a railroad train. **3.** Any of various usually small marine and freshwater fishes of the tropical family Eleotridae, related to the gobies. **4.** *Chiefly British.* A heavy beam used as a support for rails in a railroad track; crosstie. **5.** *British.* A thin ring, usually of gold, worn in a pierced ear in order to keep the hole open when earrings are not being worn. **6.** A person who is planted as a spy for future use. **7.** *Informal.* One that achieves unexpected recognition or success, such as a racehorse, book, or motion picture. **8.** An earmarked unbranded calf.

sleep-in (slēp′ĭn′) *adj.* Being one who lives where employed: *a sleep-in cook.*

sleeping bag *n.* A large, warmly lined bag, often zippered, in which a person can sleep outdoors.

sleeping car *n.* A railroad car providing berths for sleeping.

sleeping partner *n. Chiefly British.* A silent partner *(see).*

sleeping pill *n.* A sedative or hypnotic drug in the form of a pill or capsule used to relieve insomnia.

sleeping sickness *n.* **1.** An often fatal, endemic infectious disease of man and animals in tropical Africa, caused by either of two protozoans of the genus *Trypanosoma,* transmitted by the tsetse fly, and characterized by fever and lethargy. Also called "African trypanosomiasis." **2.** *Pathology.* **Encephalitis lethargica** *(see).*

sleep·less (slēp′lĭs) *adj.* **1.** Without sleep; wakeful; restless; unquiet. **2.** Never sleeping or resting; always alert or active. **—sleep·less·ly** *adv.* **—sleep·less·ness** *n.*

sleep·walk·ing (slēp′wô′kĭng) *n.* Walking while asleep or in a sleeplike condition. Also called "noctambulation," "noctambulism," "somnambulism." **—sleep·walk** *v.* **—sleep·walk·er** *n.*

sleep·y (slē′pē) *adj.* **-ier, -iest. 1.** Ready for or needing sleep; drowsy. **2.** Sluggish, inattentive, or lethargic; dull. **3.** Inducing sleep; soporific. **4.** Quiet and without activity: *a sleepy little town.* **—sleep·i·ly** *adv.* **—sleep·i·ness** *n.*

sleep·y·head (slē′pē-hĕd′) *n. Informal.* **1.** A drowsy or sleepy person. **2.** A slow or dull person.

sleet (slēt) *n.* A mixture of rain and snow or melting snow.

~*intr.v.* **sleeted, sleeting, sleets.** To shower sleet. [Middle English *slete,* Old English *slēte* (unattested).] **—sleet·y** *adj.*

sleeve (slēv) *n.* **1.** The part of a garment that covers all or a part of the arm. **2.** Any encasement or shell into which a piece of equipment fits. **3.** A **sleeve coupling** *(see).* **4.** A paper or cardboard envelope for storing a phonograph record; jacket. **—laugh up one's sleeve.** To be secretly amused, especially over the discomfiture of another. **—up one's sleeve.** Hidden but ready to be used when needed; in reserve. [Middle English *slefe, sleve,* Old English *slīf, slēf.*] **—sleeve·less** *adj.*

sleeve board *n.* A small ironing board used for ironing sleeves.

sleeve coupling *n.* A thin steel cylinder uniting two lengths of shafting or pipe. Also called "sleeve."

sleeved (slēvd) *adj.* Having a sleeve or sleeves, especially of a specified kind. Often in combination: *short-sleeved.*

sleev·ing (slē′vĭng) *n.* Flexible plastic tubing into which bare wires are inserted for insulation in electrical and electronic equipment.

sleigh (slā) *n.* A light vehicle mounted on runners for use on snow or ice, having one or more seats and usually drawn by a horse.

~*intr.v.* **sleighed, sleighing, sleighs.** To ride in or drive a sleigh. [Dutch *slee,* from *slede,* from Middle Dutch *slēde.*] **—sleigh·er** *n.*

sleight (slīt) *n.* **1.** Deftness; dexterity. **2. a.** Cunning; trickery. **b.** A skillful trick or deception; a stratagem. [Middle English *sle(i)ght,* from Old Norse *slœgdh,* from *slœgr,* sly.]

sleight of hand *n.* **1.** Tricks or feats, as in conjuring, performed so quickly that their manner of execution cannot be observed; legerdemain. **2.** Skill in performing sleight of hand. **3. a.** Cunning deception or sophistry. **b.** An act of cunning deception or sophistry. **—sleight-of-hand** (slīt′əv-hănd′) *adj.*

slen·der (slĕn′dər) *adj.* **-derer, -derest. 1.** Having little width in proportion to height or length; elongated. **2.** Gracefully slim; willowy: *"She was slender as a willow shoot is slender—and equally graceful, equally erect"* (Frank Norris). **3.** Spare or small in amount or extent; meager: *slender wages.* **4.** Having little force, justification, or foundation; limited: *only a slender chance of success.* [Middle English *s(c)lendre*†.] **—slen·der·ly** *adv.* **—slen·der·ness** *n.*

slen·der·ize (slĕn′də-rīz′) *v.* **-ized, -izing, -izes.** *—intr.* To become slender or more slender. *—tr.* **1.** To make slender or more slender. **2.** To cause to appear slender. Used especially of a garment.

slept. Past tense and past participle of **sleep.**

sleuth (slo͞oth) *n.* **1.** A detective. **2.** A **sleuthhound** *(see).*

~*v.* **sleuthed, sleuthing, sleuths.** *—tr.* To track or follow. *—intr.* To act as a detective. [Short for SLEUTHHOUND.]

sleuth·hound (slo͞oth′hound′) *n.* **1.** A dog used for tracking or pursuing, as a bloodhound. Also called "sleuth." **2.** A detective. [Middle English : *sleuth,* track of an animal, from Old Norse *slōdh*† + HOUND.]

slew[1], slue (slo͞o) *n. Informal.* A large amount or number; a lot: *a whole slew of awards.* [Irish Gaelic *sluagh,* from Old Irish *slúag, slóg.*]

slew[2]. Past tense of **slay.**

slew[3]. Variant of **slough** (mud-filled hollow).

slew[4]. Variant of **slue** (to twist).

slice (slīs) *n.* **1.** A thin, flat, or wedge-shaped piece cut from a larger object. **2.** A portion or share. **3. a.** A knife with a broad, thin, flexible blade, used for cutting and serving food. **b.** A similar implement for spreading printing ink. **c.** A wide serving spatula. **4.** *Sports.* **a.** A stroke that causes a ball to deviate to the right if the player is right-handed or to the left if the player is left-handed. **b.** The course followed by such a ball.

~*v.* **sliced, slicing, slices.** *—tr.* **1.** To cut or divide into slices. **2.** To cut or remove from a larger piece. Often used with *off* or *away.* **3.** To cut through or across with or as if with a knife. **4.** To divide into portions or shares; parcel out. **5.** To spread, work at, or clear away with a bladed tool such as a slice bar. **6.** *Sports.* To hit (a ball) with a slice. *—intr.* **1.** To cut with or as if with a knife; pass cleanly or effortlessly: *The wind sliced through us.* **2.** *Sports.* To slice a ball. [Middle English *s(c)lice,* slice, splinter, from Old French *esclice,* from *esclicer,* to reduce to splinters, from West Germanic *slītjan* (unattested), from Germanic *slītan* (unattested), to SLIT.] **—slice·a·ble** *adj.* **—slic·er** *n.*

slice bar *n.* An iron tool with a flat, broad end used to loosen and clear out clinkers from furnace grates.

slice of life *n.* A vividly realistic portrayal, as in drama or literature, of a segment of real life. **—slice-of-life** (slīs′əv-līf′) *adj.*

slick (slĭk) *adj.* **slicker, slickest. 1.** Deftly executed; neat. **2.** Superficially attractive or skillful but without real quality; glib. **3.** Shrewd; wily. **4.** Smooth and slippery as if covered with ice.

~*n.* **1.** A smooth or slippery surface or area. **2.** An **oil slick** *(see).* **3.** Any of various implements, especially a chisel, used for smoothing and polishing. Also called "slick chisel." **4.** A racing-car tire with a smooth tread. **5.** A magazine printed on glossy, high-quality paper, featuring articles and fiction of popular appeal but small literary merit. Compare **pulp.**

~*tr.v.* **slicked, slicking, slicks.** To make (hair, for example) sleek, smooth, or glossy. [Middle English *slike,* perhaps from Old English *slice* (unattested).]

slick·en·side (slĭk′ən-sīd′) *n.* A polished and striated rock surface caused by one rock mass sliding over another in a fault plane. [Dialectal *slicken,* glossy, variant of SLICK + SIDE.]

slick·er (slĭk′ər) *n.* **1.** *Informal.* A stylish, sophisticated person: *a city slicker.* **2.** *Informal.* A cheat; a swindler. **3.** A glossy raincoat, especially one made of oilskin.

slide (slīd) *v.* **slid** (slĭd), **sliding, slides.** *—intr.* **1.** To move in smooth, continuous contact with a surface. **2.** To move or pass smoothly and quietly; glide. **3.** To pass gradually into a new, often less desirable state; drift: *slid into a life of crime.* **4.** To go unattended or unacted upon: *Let it slide.* **5.** To lose one's balance or intended direction on a slippery surface. **6.** To undergo a gradual decline. *—tr.* **1.** To cause to slide. **2.** To place quietly and unobtrusively: *slid his hand into the drawer.*

~*n.* **1.** A sliding movement, action, or progression: *a further slide in stock prices.* **2.** A smooth surface or track for sliding: *a toboggan slide.* **3.** A playground apparatus for children to slide down, typically consisting of a smooth metal chute mounted by means of a ladder. **4.** A part or mechanism that operates by sliding, as a sliding seat in a rowing boat or the U-shaped section of tube on a trombone that is moved to produce different pitches. **5.** An image on a transparent celluloid plate for use with a viewer or projector. **6.** A small glass plate for mounting specimens to be examined under a microscope. **7.** An avalanche of rock or soil. **8.** *Music.* **a.** A **portamento** *(see).* **b.** An ornament consisting of two grace notes approaching the main note. [Slide, slid, slid; Middle English *sliden, slydde, slide,* Old English *slīdan, -slād, -sliden.*] **—slid·er** *n.*

slide guitar *n.* **1.** A style of guitar playing, **bottleneck** *(see).* **2.** A guitar played in the bottleneck style.

slid·er (slī′dər) *n.* **1.** Someone or something that slides. **2.** *Baseball.* A fast curve ball that breaks only slightly.

slide rule *n.* A device consisting essentially of two logarithmically scaled rules mounted to slide along each other so that multiplication, division, and sometimes more complex calculations can be reduced to the mechanical equivalent of addition or subtraction.

slide valve *n.* A valve that slides back and forth over ports in the cylinder wall of a steam engine, permitting the intake and outflow of steam to move the piston.

sliding scale *n.* A scale in which indicated prices, taxes, or wages vary in accordance with some other factor, such as wages with the cost-of-living index or medical fees with a patient's income.

slight (slīt) *adj.* **slighter, slightest. 1.** Small in size, degree, or amount; meager. **2.** Of small importance; inconsiderable; trifling. **3.** Slender or frail; delicate: *a slight figure.*

~*tr.v.* **slighted, slighting, slights. 1.** To treat with disdain or discourteous indifference; snub. **2.** To fail to give sufficient consideration or attention to; treat as unimportant.

~*n.* An act of pointed disrespect or discourtesy. [Middle English *sl(e)ight,* smooth, slight, from Old Norse *slēttr,* smooth, sleek.] **—slight·ness** *n.*

slight·ing (slī′tĭng) *adj.* Constituting or conveying a slight; disparaging; disrespectful. **—slight·ing·ly** *adv.*

slight·ly (slīt′lē) *adv.* **1.** To a small degree or extent; somewhat. **2.** In a slight or delicate way: *She is slightly built.*

Sli·go (slī′gō). County in the northwest of the Republic of Ireland. Sligo's Atlantic coastline is indented and much of the interior is mountainous. Beef and dairy farming are the chief occupations of the people. The county town is called Sligo.

slily. Variant of **slyly.**

slim (slĭm) *adj.* **slimmer, slimmest. 1.** Small in girth or thickness in proportion to height or length: *a slim volume.* **2.** Pleasantly thin; slender: *a slim build.* **3.** Small in quality or amount; scant; meager.

~*v.* **slimmed, slimming, slims.** *—tr.* To reduce in volume or amount. Often used with *down: slim down the defense budget.* *—intr.* **1.** To become slim. **2.** *British.* To diet for the purpose of losing weight. [Dutch, small, inferior, from Middle Dutch *slim,* slanting, bad.] **—slim·ly** *adv.* **—slim·ness** *n.*

slime (slīm) *n.* **1. a.** Viscous mud. **b.** Any substance having a runny or glutinous consistency, especially when considered unpleasant or offensive. **2.** A mucous substance secreted by certain animals, such as fish or slugs.

~*v.* **slimed, sliming, slimes.** *—tr.* **1.** To smear with slime. **2.** To remove slime from (fish to be canned, for example). *—intr.* To become slimy. [Middle English *slim(e),* Old English *slīm,* akin to Latin *limus,* mud.]

slime mold *n.* Any of various fungi of the class Myxomycetes, having a vegetative body consisting of a slimy, motile, multinucleate mass of protoplasm. Also called "slime fungus," "myxomycete," "mycetozoan."

slim·y (slī′mē) *adj.* **-ier, -iest. 1.** Consisting of or resembling slime; viscous. **2.** Covered with or exuding slime. **3.** Vile; disgusting; foul. **—slim·i·ly** *adv.* **—slim·i·ness** *n.*

sling[1] (slĭng) *n.* **1. a.** A weapon consisting of a looped strap with which a stone is whirled and then let fly. **b.** A slingshot. **2.** A looped rope, strap, or chain for supporting, cradling, or hoisting something, especially: **a.** A strap used to carry a rifle over the shoulder. **b.** *Nautical.* A rope or chain for supporting a yard. **c.** *Nautical.* An arrangement, as of looped ropes or nets, for supporting cargo that is being transferred. **d.** A band suspended from the neck to support an injured arm or hand. **e.** A baglike device made of soft material, equipped with straps and worn over the back or chest and used for carrying a baby. **3.** An act of slinging.

~*tr.v.* **slung** (slŭng), **slinging, slings. 1.** To hurl from or as if from a sling; fling. **2.** To carry or support by means of a sling: *with his rifle slung over his shoulder.* **3.** To move by means of a sling; raise or lower in a sling. **4.** To cause to hang loosely or freely; let swing. —See Synonyms at **throw.** [Middle English, perhaps from Middle Low German *slinge.*] **—sling·er** (slĭng′ər) *n.*

sling[2] *n.* A drink of brandy, whiskey, or gin, sweetened and usually lemon-flavored. See **gin sling.** [18th century : origin obscure.]

sling·back (slĭng′băk′) *n.* An open-backed shoe held in place by a strap above the heel.

sling·shot (slĭng′shŏt′) *n.* A Y-shaped stick with an elastic strap attached to the prongs, used for flinging small stones.

slink (slĭngk) *v.* **slunk** (slŭngk), **slinking, slinks.** *—intr.* To move in a quiet, furtive manner; sneak: *"Back to the thicket slunk/The guilty Serpent"* (Milton). *—tr.* To give birth to prematurely. Used especially of a cow.

~*n.* **1.** An animal, especially a calf, born prematurely. **2.** The flesh or skin of a slink.

~*adj.* Born prematurely. [Middle English *slynken,* Old English *slincan.*] **—slink·ing·ly** *adv.*

slink·y (slĭng′kē) *adj.* **-ier, -iest. 1.** Of feline sleekness and grace. **2.** Soft, close-fitting, and usually glamorous. Said of women's clothing. **3.** *Informal.* Stealthy; furtive. **—slink·i·ness** *n.*

slip[1] (slĭp) *v.* **slipped, slipping, slips.** *—intr.* **1.** To move lightly and smoothly; glide. **2.** To move or pass swiftly, stealthily, or imperceptibly: *The years slipped by.* **3. a.** To slide unexpectedly and by accident; lose one's balance. **b.** To slide out of place; shift position. **c.** To escape, as from a fastening or grip. **4.** To get away completely; escape; be lost: *let chances slip by.* **5.** To be said unintentionally, as through lack of discretion: *let slip that he'd got a raise.* **6.** To put on or take off clothing quickly or smoothly. Used with *into* or *out of.* **7.** To fall below a usual or prescribed standard; decline or deteriorate. **8. a.** To make a mistake. **b.** To fall into error; lapse. **9.** To slide sideways; sideslip. Used of an aircraft. **10.** To fail to engage. Used of the clutch of a motor or vehicle. *—tr.* **1.** To cause to move in a smooth, easy, or sliding motion. **2.** To place, insert, or introduce smoothly. **3.** To put on or remove (clothing) quickly or smoothly. Used with *on* or *off.* **4.** To free oneself or itself from; get loose from: *The drifting vessel had slipped its moorings.* **5.** To pass out of (one's memory or attention) so as to be forgotten or unnoticed: *It slipped my mind.* **6.** To bring forth (young) prematurely. Used of an animal. **7.** To unleash or free (a dog or hawk, for example). **8.** To undo or unfasten: *slip the knot.* **9.** To dislocate (a bone), or suffer displacement of (an intervertebral disk). **10.** *Informal.* To give inconspicuously or surreptitiously: *slipped the speaker a note.* **11.** In knitting, to pass (a stitch) from one needle to the other without working it. **—slip one over on.** *Informal.* To hoodwink; trick.

~n. **1.** An act of slipping, sliding, or falling. **2. a.** An error in judgment or procedure; a fault or deviation. **b.** A slight mistake or oversight in speech or writing: *a slip of the pen.* **3. a.** A **slipway** *(see).* **b.** A space for a ship between two docks or wharves. **4.** A woman's loose, sleeveless undergarment serving as a lining for a dress or skirt. **5.** A pillowcase. **6.** A leash allowing quick release of the dog. **7.** The difference between a vessel's actual speed through water and the speed at which the vessel would move if the screw were propelling against a solid. **8.** The difference between optimal and actual output in a mechanical device. **9.** *Geology.* **a.** A smooth crack at which rock strata have moved relative to each other. **b.** A small fault. **10.** Movement between two parts where none should exist, as between the clutch plates of a motor vehicle. **11.** *Aviation.* The sliding movement of an aircraft in certain attitudes of the craft. See **sideslip. 12.** *Geology.* Relative movement along a fault plane. —See Synonyms at **error. —give someone the slip.** *Informal.* To escape or elude. [Middle English *slippen,* to slip, slip away, probably from Middle Low German.]

slip[2] *n.* **1.** A part of a plant cut or broken off for grafting or planting; a scion or cutting. **2.** Any long, narrow piece; a strip. **3.** A youthful, slender person: *a slip of a girl.* **4.** A small piece of paper; especially, a small form or list: *a sales slip.* **5. a. slips.** *Chiefly British.* The area along the sides of the gallery in a theater. **b.** A narrow pew in a church. **6.** *Chiefly British.* A galley proof.

~tr.v. **slipped, slipping, slips.** To make a slip from (a plant or plant part). [Middle English *slippe*†, a strip.]

slip[3] *n.* Thinned potter's clay used for decorating or coating ceramics. [Middle English *slyppe,* a soft mass, curds, mud, Old English *slypa,* slime.]

slip·case (slĭp′kās′) *n.* An open-ended protective box for a book.

slip·cov·er (slĭp′kŭv′ər) *n.* A fitted removable cover of cloth or other fabric for a piece of upholstered furniture.

~v. **slipcovered, -ering, -ers.** To provide with a slipcover.

slip·knot (slĭp′nŏt′) *n.* **1.** A knot made with a loop so that it slips easily along the rope or cord around which it is tied. Also called "running knot." **2.** A knot made so that it can readily be untied by pulling one free end.

slip-on (slĭp′ŏn′, -ôn′) *adj.* Designed to be easily put on or taken off: *a slip-on blouse.*

~n. A slip-on garment or shoe.

slip·o·ver (slĭp′ō′vər) *adj.* Designed to be put on or taken off over the head.

~n. A slipover garment, such as a sweater.

slip·page (slĭp′ĭj) *n.* **1.** A slipping. **2.** The amount or extent of slipping. **3.** Loss of motion or power due to slipping.

slipped disk *n.* Protrusion of the inner pulp of an intervertebral disk through its fibrous wall, causing pressure on adjacent nerves and resulting in sciatica or back pain.

slip·per (slĭp′ər) *n.* **1.** A light, low slip-on shoe for indoor wear, usually having an upper made of soft material. **2.** A light slip-on shoe for dancing or evening wear.

slipper orchid *n.* Any of various tropical orchids of the genus *Paphiopedilum* and related genera, having slipper-shaped flowers.

slip·per·wort (slĭp′ər-wûrt′, -wôrt′) *n.* A plant, the **calceolaria** *(see).*

slip·per·y (slĭp′ə-rē) *adj.* **-ier, -iest. 1.** Causing or tending to cause sliding or slipping, as a waxed, greasy, or wet surface may. **2.** Tending to slip or slide, as from one's grasp or from a position of being secured. **3.** Elusive; evasive; untrustworthy: *a slippery customer.* [Perhaps coined by Miles Coverdale (1535) to translate German *schlipfferig,* based on dialectal *slipper, from* Middle English *sli(p)per,* Old English *slipor.*] **—slip·per·i·ly** *adv.* **—slip·per·i·ness** *n.*

slippery elm *n.* A tree, *Ulmus rubra,* of eastern North America, having twigs and leaves with a mucilaginous, aromatic juice formerly used medicinally.

slip·py (slĭp′ē) *adj.* **-pier, -piest.** *Informal.* **1.** Slippery. **2.** *Chiefly British.* Quick; nimble; alert. Often used in the phrase *look slippy.*

slip ring *n.* A metal ring mounted on a rotating part of a machine to provide a continuous electrical connection through brushes on stationary contacts.

slip-sheet (slĭp′shēt′) *n.* *Printing.* A blank sheet of paper slipped between newly printed sheets to prevent offsetting.

~tr.v. **slip-sheeted, -sheeting, -sheets.** *Printing.* To insert blank sheets between (printed sheets).

slip·shod (slĭp′shŏd′) *adj.* **1.** Made or done carelessly and unsystematically. **2.** Slovenly in appearance; shabby; seedy. [Originally "wearing slippers or loose shoes" : SLIP + SHOD.]

slip·slop (slĭp′slŏp′) *n.* **1.** *Archaic.* Sloppy, unappetizing food; slops. **2.** Trivial or sentimental talk or writing; twaddle. [Reduplication of SLOP.]

slip·stitch (slĭp′stĭch′) *n.* **1.** A stitch used wherever stitching must be invisible, as on hems and facings, made by picking up one or two threads of fabric and then passing the needle diagonally through the hem edge. **2.** The basic chain stitch used for edgings in crochet. In this sense also called "single crochet." **—slip·stitch** *v.*

slip-stream (slĭp′strēm′) *n.* **1.** The turbulent flow of air driven backward by the propeller or propellers of an aircraft. Also called "race." **2.** The stream of air behind any fast-moving object.

~intr.v. **slip-streamed, -streaming, -streams.** In cycling or motor racing, to drive in the slip-stream of another vehicle as a way of maintaining a high speed while conserving energy or fuel.

slip up *intr.v.* *Informal.* To make a mistake; blunder.

slip-up (slĭp′ŭp′) *n.* *Informal.* An error or oversight; a mistake.

slip·way (slĭp′wā′) *n.* A sloping incline leading down to the water on which ships are built or repaired. Also called "slip."

slit (slĭt) *n.* A long, narrow, usually straight cut, tear, or opening.

~tr.v. **slit, slitting, slits. 1.** To make a long, narrow incision in. **2.** To cut lengthwise into strips; split. —See Synonyms at **tear.**

~adj. Having or resembling a slit: *slit eyes; a slit skirt.* [Middle English *slitte,* perhaps from Old English *geslit,* a tearing, akin to *slītan,* to slit, from Germanic *slītan* (unattested).]

slith·er (slĭ*th*′ər) *v.* **-ered, -ering, -ers.** *—intr.* **1.** To slip and slide, as on a loose or uneven surface. **2.** To move along by gliding, as a snake does. *—tr.* To cause to slither.

~n. A slithering movement or gait. [Middle English *slideren,* Old English *slid(o)rian,* frequentative of *slīdan,* to SLIDE.] **—slith·er·y** *adj.*

slit trench *n.* A narrow, shallow trench dug during combat for the protection of a single soldier or a small group.

sliv·er (slĭv′ər; *also* slī′vər *for sense 2*) *n.* **1.** A sharp, slender piece cut, split, or broken off; a splinter. **2.** A continuous strand of loose wool, flax, or cotton, ready for drawing and twisting.

~v. **slivered, -ering, -ers.** *—tr.* To split, cut, or form into slivers. *—intr.* To become split into slivers. [Middle English *slivere,* from *slyven,* to split, Old English *-slīfan*† (unattested). See **sleave.**]

sli·vo·vitz (slĭv′ə-vĭts′) *n.* A dry, colorless plum brandy. [Serbo-Croatian *šljivovica,* from *šljiva,* plum.]

Sloan (slōn), **John French** (1871–1951). U.S. painter, etcher, and engraver. Working first in Philadelphia and then in New York City, he was a skilled artist and gifted teacher whose works included nudes, portraits, and city scenes such as *McSorley's Bar, Bleecker Street on Saturday Night,* and *Spring in Washington Square.*

Sloane (slōn), **Sir Hans** (1660–1753). English physician and botanist. He was secretary to the Royal Society (1693–1712) and president of the Royal College of Physicians (1719–35). He was also the founder of the Botanic Garden at Chelsea Manor.

slob (slŏb) *n.* *Informal.* An obnoxious, uncouth, or slovenly person. [Irish *slab,* mud, probably from Scandinavian; akin to Old Danish *slab,* mud.]

slob·ber (slŏb′ər) *v.* **-bered, -bering, -bers.** *—intr.* **1.** To let saliva dribble from the mouth; slaver; drool. **2.** To spill food from the mouth while eating or drinking. **3.** To indulge in mawkish sentimentality in speech or writing. *—tr.* To wet or smear with or as if with saliva or food dribbled from the mouth.

~n. **1.** Saliva or liquid running from the mouth; drivel; slaver. **2.** Driveling, oversentimental speech or writing. [Middle English *sloberen,* perhaps of Low German origin, akin to Low German *slubberen* (imitative).] **—slob·ber·er** *n.* **—slob·ber·y** *adj.*

sloe (slō) *n.* **1.** A shrub, the **blackthorn** *(see).* **2.** The tart, blue-black, plumlike fruit of this shrub. [Middle English *slo(o),* Old English *slā(h).*]

sloe-eyed (slō′īd′) *adj.* **1.** Having dark, blue-black eyes. **2.** Having slanted eyes.

sloe gin *n.* A liqueur made by steeping sloes in gin.

slog (slŏg) *v.* **slogged, slogging, slogs.** *—tr.* To strike powerfully, wildly, or unskillfully, as in boxing. *—intr.* **1.** To walk with a slow, plodding gait: *The old nag slogged along.* **2.** To work doggedly; toil. Often used with *at* or *away.*

~n. **1. a.** Hard, unremitting work. **b.** A spell of this. **2.** A long, exhausting march or hike. **3.** A powerful swipe or blow. [19th century : origin obscure.] **—slog·ger** *n.*

slo·gan (slō′gən) *n.* **1.** A phrase expressing the aims or nature of an enterprise or organization; motto. **2.** A catch phrase used in advertising or promotion. **3.** A battle cry, as formerly used by a Scottish clan. [Earlier (Scottish) *slog(g)orne,* from Gaelic *sluagh-ghairm* : *sluagh,* host, army + *gairm,* shout, cry.]

slo·gan·eer (slō′gə-nîr′) *n.* One that invents or uses slogans. *—intr.v.* **sloganeered, -eering, -eers.** To invent or use slogans.

sloop (slo͞op) *n.* *Nautical.* A single-masted, fore-and-aft-rigged sailing boat with a single headsail set from the forestay. Compare **cutter.** [Dutch *sloep(e)*†.]

sloop of war *n.* A small, armed vessel larger than a gunboat, carrying guns on one deck only.

slop[1] (slŏp) *n.* **1.** Liquid spilled or splashed. **2.** Soft mud or slush. **3.** Unappetizing, watery food or soup. **4.** *Usually* **slops.** Waste food used to feed pigs or other animals; swill. **5.** *Usually* **slops.** Liquid or semiliquid waste, such as: **a.** Liquid household refuse. **b.** Human excreta. **c.** Beer spilled while being drawn from a barrel. **d.** Mash remaining after the process of alcohol distillation. **6.** Repulsively effusive writing or speech.

~v. **slopped, slopping, slops.** *—intr.* **1.** To spill, splash, or overflow. **2.** To heave to and fro within a container. Usually used with *about* or *around.* **3.** To move in an awkward or slovenly manner as if plodding through mud: *"he slopped along in broken slippers, hands in pockets, whistling"* (Alan Sillitoe). *—tr.* **1.** To spill (liquid). **2.** To

PRONUNCIATION KEY

ă, pat; ā, pay; âr, care;
ä, father, are; b, bib;
ch, church; d, deed; ĕ, pet;
ē, be; f, fife; g, gag; h, hat;
hw, which; ĭ, pit; ī, pie;
îr, pier; j, judge; k, kick;
l, lid, needle; m, mum;
n, no, sudden; ng, thing;
ŏ, pot; ō, toe; ô, paw, for;
oi, noise; ou, out; o͝o, book;
o͞o, boot; p, pop; r, roar;
s, sauce; sh, ship, dish;
t, tight; th, thin, path;
th, this, bathe; ŭ, cut; ûr, fur;
v, valve; w, with; y, yes;
z, zebra, size; zh, vision;
ə, about, item, edible, gallop, circus, peaceful

IN FOREIGN WORDS:

à, *Fr.* ami; œ, *Fr.* feu, *Ger.* schön; ü, *Fr.* tu, *Ger.* über;
KH, *Ger.* ich, *Scot.* loch;
N, *Fr.* bon; y', *Fr.* Compiègne

STRESS MARKS:

Primary stress: ′
in·cite′ (ĭn-sīt′)
Secondary stress: ′
in′sight′ (ĭn′sīt′)

spill liquid upon. **3.** To dish out or serve unappetizingly or clumsily. **4.** To feed slops to (animals). [Middle English *sloppe,* a muddy place, probably Old English *sloppe* (unattested).]

slop[2] *n.* **1. slops.** Articles of clothing and bedding issued to sailors from a ship's stores. **2. slops.** Short, full trousers or breeches worn by men in the 16th century. **3.** A loose outer garment, such as a smock or overalls. **4. slops.** *Chiefly British.* Cheap, ready-made garments. [Middle English *sloppe,* a kind of garment, perhaps Old English *(ofer)slop,* surplice.]

slope (slōp) *v.* **sloped, sloping, slopes.** —*intr.* **1.** To incline upward or downward; lie on a slant. **2.** To follow a sloping course; ascend or descend at an angle. **3.** *Informal.* To go or walk steadily; travel. Usually used with *off.* —*tr.* **1.** To cause to slope. **2.** *Military.* To bring (a rifle) into a sloping position resting on the shoulder. Used chiefly in the command *slope arms.*

∼*n.* **1.** Any inclined line, surface, plane, position, or direction. **2.** A stretch of ground forming a natural or artificial incline: *ski slopes.* **3.** Any deviation from the horizontal. **4.** The amount or degree of such deviation. **5.** *Mathematics.* The rate at which an ordinate of a point on a line on a plane containing the line changes with respect to a change in its abscissa. [Middle English *slope,* sloping, short for *aslope,* perhaps Old English *āslopen* (unattested), past participle of *āslūpan,* to slip away : *ā-,* away + *slūpan,* to slip.] **—slop·er** *n.* **—slop·ing·ly** *adv.*

slop·py (slŏp′ē) *adj.* **-pier, -piest. 1.** Wet, slushy, or muddy. **2.** Watery and unappetizing: *a sloppy stew.* **3.** Spotted or splashed with liquid or slop. **4.** *Informal.* Untidy or unsystematic; messy. **5.** *Informal.* Careless; slipshod. **6.** *Informal.* Oversentimental; slushy. **—slop·pi·ly** *adv.* **—slop·pi·ness** *n.*

Synonyms: *blowzy, frowzy, slatternly, slovenly, unkempt, untidy.*

sloppy joe *n.* Ground cooked meat in a usually spicy sauce served on a bun.

slop·work (slŏp′wûrk′) *n.* **1.** The manufacture of cheap, ready-made clothes. **2.** Such clothes. **3.** Any work of inferior quality.

slosh (slŏsh) *v.* **sloshed, sloshing, sloshes.** —*tr.* **1.** To pour or splash (a liquid). **2.** To stir or agitate in a liquid: *slosh clothes in water.* **3.** *British Informal.* To hit or punch heavily. —*intr.* **1.** To splash or flounder in water or another liquid. **2.** To move with a lapping sound or motion; gurgle: *Water sloshed around in the basin.*

∼*n.* **1.** Slush. **2.** The sound of splashing liquid. **3.** *British Informal.* A punch or blow. [Variant of SLUSH.] **—slosh·y** *adj.*

sloshed (slŏsht) *adj. Slang.* Drunk.

slot[1] (slŏt) *n.* **1.** A long, narrow groove, opening, or notch, as for receiving coins in a vending machine. **2.** A gap between a main and an auxiliary airfoil to provide space for airflow and facilitate the smooth passage of air over the wing. **3.** A place in a program schedule, sequence, hierarchy, or organization; niche.

∼*v.* **slotted, slotting, slots.** —*tr.* **1.** To cut or make a slot or slots in. **2.** To place or fit in or as if in a slot. —*intr.* To fit into a slot. [Middle English, indentation running down the middle of the breast, from Old French *esclot*†.]

slot[2] *n.* The track or trail of an animal, especially a deer. [Old French *esclot,* horse's hoofprint, probably from Old Norse *slōdh,* animal's track. See **sleuthhound.**]

sloth (slōth, slôth, slŏth) *n.* **1.** Aversion to work or exertion; laziness; indolence. **2.** Any of various shaggy, slow-moving, arboreal mammals of the family Bradypodidae, of tropical America, including: **a.** Any member of the genus *Bradypus.* Also called "ai." **b.** Any member of the genus *Choloepus.* Also called "unau." [Middle English *slowthe,* from *slow,* SLOW.]

sloth bear *n.* A bear, *Melursus ursinus,* of south-central Asia, having a long snout and dark, shaggy hair.

sloth·ful (slōth′fəl, slôth′-, slŏth′-) *adj.* Lazy; indolent; sluggish. **—sloth·ful·ly** *adv.* **—sloth·ful·ness** *n.*

slot machine *n.* **1.** A vending machine having a slot or slots into which coins are inserted in order to operate it. **2.** A coin-operated gambling machine, typically with drums bearing symbols that spin independently, money being paid out if the pictures are aligned in certain combinations when the drums come to rest.

slouch (slouch) *v.* **slouched, slouching, slouches.** —*intr.* **1.** To sit, stand, or walk with an awkward, drooping posture; assume an excessively relaxed position. **2.** To droop or hang down. —*tr.* To cause to slouch.

∼*n.* **1.** A slouching movement, posture, or position. **2.** An ungainly, lazy, or incompetent person. [16th century : origin obscure.] **—slouch·i·ly** *adv.* **—slouch·i·ness** *n.* **—slouch·y** *adj.*

slouch hat *n.* A soft hat with a broad, flexible brim.

slough[1] (slo͞o, slou) *n.* Also **slew** (slo͞o), **slue** (slo͞o) (for sense 2). **1. a.** A depression or hollow, usually filled with mud. **b.** A stagnant inlet, backwater, marsh, or bog. **2.** A state of deep despair or degradation. [Middle English *slo(g)h,* Old English *slōh, slō(g).*] **—slough·i·ness** *n.* **—slough·y** *adj.*

slough[2] (slŭf) *n.* **1.** The dead outer skin shed by a snake or amphibian. **2.** *Medicine.* Dead tissue separated from a living structure. **3.** Broadly, anything that can be shed, such as an outer layer.

∼*v.* **sloughed, sloughing, sloughs.** —*intr.* **1.** To be cast off or shed; come off. **2.** To shed a slough. **3.** *Medicine.* To separate from surrounding tissue. Used of dead tissue. —*tr.* **1.** To shed; throw off. **2.** To get rid of; discard as undesirable or unfavorable. Often used with *off.* [Middle English *slugh(e), slouh,* perhaps of Low German origin, akin to Low German *slu(we),* husk, shell, from Common Germanic *slūhwō* (unattested).]

slough of despond (slou, slo͞o) *n.* A state of depression or despair. [After a place in Bunyan's *Pilgrim's Progress* (1678).]

Slo·vak (slō′văk′, -väk′) *n.* Also **Slo·vak·i·an** (slō-vä′kē-ən, -văk′ē-ən). **1.** A member of a Slavic people living in Slovakia. **2.** The West Slavic language of these people, closely related to Czech. **—Slo·vak, Slo·vak·i·an** *adj.*

Slo·vak·i·a (slō-vä′kē-ə, -văk′ē-ə). Easternmost of the three natural regions that make up Czechoslovakia. The Slovak Socialist Republic is one of the two equal constituent republics of the country. Mining, shipbuilding, and metal processing are highly developed industries. Nearly 90 percent of the population is of Slovak stock. Bratislava is the capital.

slov·en (slŭv′ən) *n.* One who is careless and untidy in personal appearance or work. [Middle English *sloveyn,* perhaps from Middle Dutch *sloff*†, negligent.]

Slo·vene (slō′vēn′) *n.* **1.** A native or inhabitant of Slovenia. **2.** The South Slavic language spoken in Slovenia.

∼*adj.* Of or pertaining to Slovenia, the Slovenes, or their language.

Slo·ve·ni·a (slō-vē′nē-ə, -vēn′yə). Constituent republic of Yugoslavia, lying mainly in the Julian Alps and the Karst plateau in the north of the country. The capital is Ljubljana. It is the richest and most industrialized part of Yugoslavia. **—Slo·ve·ni·an** *n. & adj.*

slov·en·ly (slŭv′ən-lē) *adj.* **-lier, -liest. 1.** Having the habits or appearance of a sloven. **2.** Showing qualities associated with a sloven, especially: **a.** Untidy; messy. **b.** Careless; marked by negligence; slipshod: *a slovenly piece of work.* —See Synonyms at **sloppy.** **—slov·en·li·ness** *n.* **—slov·en·ly** *adv.*

slow (slō) *adj.* **slower, slowest. 1. a.** Not moving or able to move quickly; proceeding at a low speed: *a slow boat.* **b.** Marked by a low speed or tempo: *a slow waltz.* **2. a.** Taking or requiring a long time: *the slow job of making bread.* **b.** Taking more time than is necessary: *a slow worker.* **c.** Made or achieved over a long period of time; gradual: *a slow recovery.* **3.** Registering a time or rate behind or below the correct one: *a slow clock.* **4. a.** Lacking in promptness or willingness: *slow to accept; a slow response.* **b.** Not easily aroused; not precipitate: *slow to anger.* **5.** Sluggish; inactive: *Business was slow.* **6.** *Informal.* Lacking in interest; boring: *a slow film.* **7.** Mentally dull; obtuse: *a slow student.* **8. a.** Only moderately warm; low: *a slow oven.* **b.** Burning without strength: *a slow flame.* **9.** Not conducive to fast movement. Said of a sports surface: *a slow track.* —See Synonyms at **stupid.**

∼*adv.* **slower, slowest.** In a slow manner; slowly.

∼*v.* **slowed, slowing, slows.** —*tr.* To make slow or slower. Often used with *up* or *down.* —*intr.* To become slow or slower; go or act slowly or more slowly. Often used with *up* or *down*: *The doctor told him to slow up for the sake of his health.* —See Synonyms at **delay.** [Middle English *slow, slaw,* Old English *slāw,* from Germanic *slǣwaz* (unattested).] **—slow·ly** *adv.* **—slow·ness** *n.*

Usage: *Slow* and *slowly* are both adverbs. *Slow* is more often encountered in speech and dialogue, in commands and exhortations (*Drive slow*), and where forcefulness is otherwise sought. In general, *slowly* is preferred in written usage, especially formal usage, when it accommodates the sense desired as well as *slow.* Sense and established idiom are the main factors in determining a choice. Often *slow* and *slowly* are interchangeable. But *slow* is the established idiomatic form with certain senses of common verbs: *This watch runs slow* (loses time); *Trains are running slow* (behind schedule); *Go slow* or *Take it slow* (figuratively, proceed on a course of action in a deliberate manner).

slow·down (slō′doun′) *n.* **1.** A slackening of pace. **2.** An intentional slowing down of production or service by labor or management.

slow match *n.* A fuse that burns slowly and is used to set off explosives.

slow motion *n.* **1.** A motion-picture technique in which the action shown appears to be slower than the original action because the sequence is projected at a slower speed than that at which it was filmed. **2.** A rate of action that is slower than normal. **—slow-mo·tion** (slō′mō′shən) *adj.*

slow neutron *n.* A **thermal neutron** *(see).*

slow-pitch (slō′pĭch′) *n.* A form of softball in which there are ten players to a team, base stealing is not permitted, and pitches, in order to be legal, must travel in an arc from three to ten feet high. Also called "slow-pitch softball."

slow·poke (slō′pōk′) *n. Informal.* One who is excessively slow in action or movement.

slow virus *n.* Any infectious virus that has a long incubation period in the body before symptoms of disease appear.

slow-wit·ted (slō′wĭt′ĭd) *adj.* Slow to comprehend; dull; stupid. **—slow-wit·ted·ly** *adv.* **—slow-wit·ted·ness** *n.*

slow·worm (slō′wûrm′) *n.* A limbless European lizard, *Anguis fragilis,* having a smooth, snakelike body. Also called "blindworm." [Middle English *slowurm,* Old English *slāwyrm* : *slā,* perhaps "slime" + *wyrm,* WORM.]

SLR single-lens reflex (camera).

slub (slŭb) *tr.v.* **slubbed, slubbing, slubs.** To draw out and twist (a sliver of silk or other textile fiber) in preparation for spinning.

∼*n.* **1.** A soft, thick nub in yarn that is either an imperfection or purposely set for a desired effect. **2.** A slightly twisted roll of fiber, as of silk or cotton.

∼*adj.* Having an uneven, irregular appearance. Said of material. [18th century : origin obscure.]

sludge (slŭj) *n.* **1.** Mud, mire, or ooze covering the ground or forming a deposit, as on a riverbed. **2.** Slushy matter or sediment such as that precipitated by the treatment of sewage or collected in a

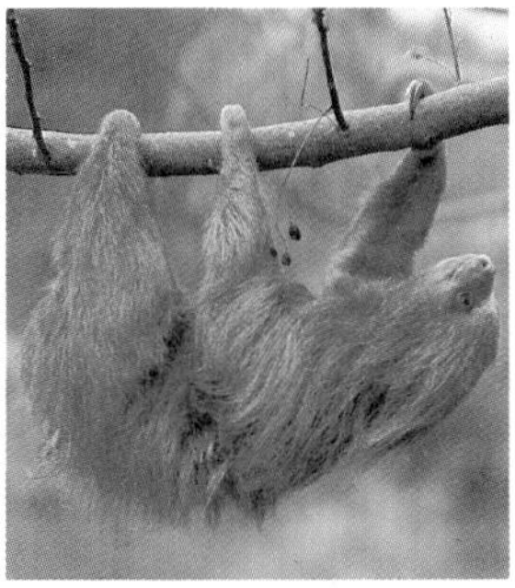

sloth *The toes of the two-toed sloth (above)—there are two on the forefeet and three on the hind limbs—are large claws that enable the animal to hang from tree branches. It is native to South America and lives on the fruit and leaves of trees, spending so much time upside-down that its fur grows in the opposite direction from that of other animals.*

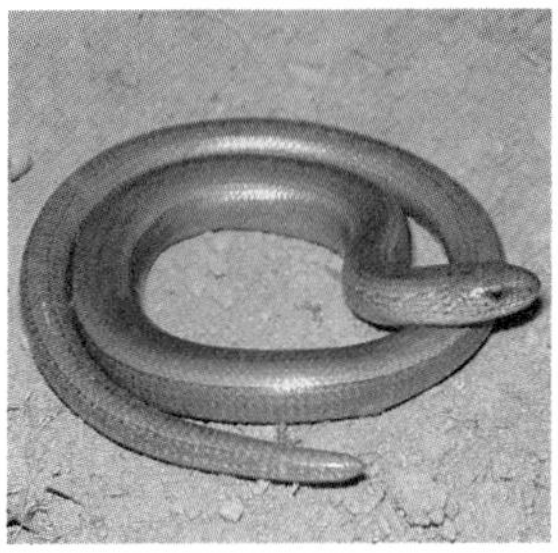

slowworm *Although the slowworm resembles a snake, it is actually a legless lizard and is not venomous. It is found mostly in European forests and lives on slugs, worms, and caterpillars.*

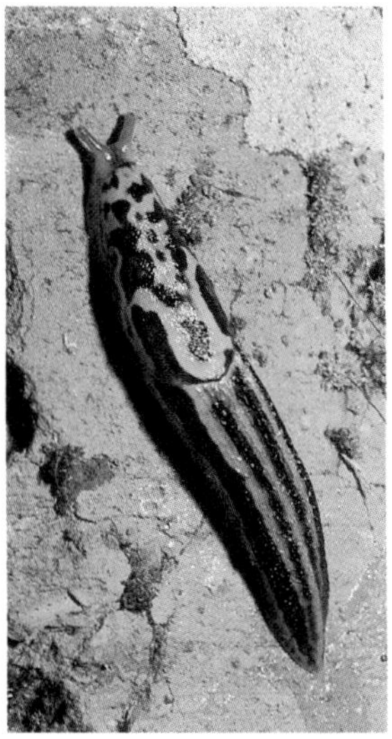

slug *Slugs, which are relatives of the snail, have no shell. They live in damp places all over the world and feed mostly on plants.*

PRONUNCIATION KEY

ă, pat; ā, pay; âr, care; ä, father, are; b, bib; ch, church; d, deed; ĕ, pet; ē, be; f, fife; g, gag; h, hat; hw, which; ĭ, pit; ī, pie; îr, pier; j, judge; k, kick; l, lid, needle; m, mum; n, no, sudden; ng, thing; ŏ, pot; ō, toe; ô, paw, for; oi, noise; ou, out; o͝o, book; o͞o, boot; p, pop; r, roar; s, sauce; sh, ship, dish; t, tight; th, thin, path; *th*, this, bathe; ŭ, cut; ûr, fur; v, valve; w, with; y, yes; z, zebra, size; zh, vision; ə, about, item, edible, gallop, circus, peaceful

IN FOREIGN WORDS:

à, *Fr.* ami; œ, *Fr.* feu, *Ger.* schön; ü, *Fr.* tu, *Ger.* über; KH, *Ger.* ich, *Scot.* loch; N, *Fr.* bon; y', *Fr.* Compiègne

STRESS MARKS:

Primary stress: ′
in·cite′ (ĭn-sīt′)
Secondary stress: ′
in′sight′ (ĭn′sīt′)

boiler. **3.** Finely broken or half-formed ice on a body of water. [Perhaps alteration of dialectal *slutch,* mire.] **—sludg·y** *adj.*

slue¹, slew (slo͞o) *v.* **slued, sluing, slues** or **slewed, slewing, slews.** *—tr.* **1.** To turn or twist (something) sideways. **2.** To twist (a mast or boom) around on its axis. *—intr.* To turn, twist, move, or skid to the side.
∼n. **1.** The act of sluing. **2.** The position to which something has slued. [18th century : origin obscure.]

slue². Variant of **slew** (a large number).

slue³. Variant of **slough** (backwater).

slug¹ (slŭg) *n.* **1.** A round bullet or pellet, as used in an air gun. **2.** *Informal.* A swig or shot of liquor. **3.** A lump of metal or glass ready to be processed. **4.** *Printing.* **a.** A strip of type metal, less than type-high, used for spacing. **b.** A line of cast type in a single strip of metal. **c.** A compositor's type line of identifying marks or instructions. **5.** *Physics.* A unit of mass equal to the mass accelerated at the rate of one foot per second per second when acted upon by a force of one pound weight. Also called "geepound." **6.** A small metal disk for use in a coin-operated machine, especially one used illegally. [Probably from SLUG (animal).]

slug² *n.* **1.** Any of various terrestrial gastropod mollusks of the family Limacidae and other genera, having an elongated body with no shell. **2.** The smooth, soft larva of certain insects, especially the sawfly. Also called "slugworm." **3.** *Informal.* A lazy person; a sluggard. [Middle English *slugge,* slow person or animal, probably from Scandinavian; akin to Norwegian (dialectal) *slugg.*]

slug³ *tr.v.* **slugged, slugging, slugs.** To strike heavily, especially with the fist.
∼n. A hard, heavy blow, as with the fist or a baseball bat. [Perhaps from SLUG (round bullet).]

slug·a·bed (slŭg′ə-bĕd′) *n.* One inclined to stay in bed out of laziness. [SLUG (sluggard) + ABED.]

slug·fest (slŭg′fĕst′) *n. Slang.* A fight marked by a vicious exchange of blows.

slug·gard (slŭg′ərd) *n.* A slothful, lazy person; an idler. [Middle English *sluggart,* probably from *sluggen,* to be lazy, from Scandinavian; akin to Swedish (dialectal) *slugga.*] **—slug·gard·ly** *adj.* **—slug·gard·ness** *n.*

slug·ger (slŭg′ər) *n.* **1.** One that slugs, as a boxer who swings out with his fists. **2.** A baseball player who hits many home runs or runs batted in.

slug·gish (slŭg′ĭsh) *adj.* **1.** Displaying little movement or activity; slow; inactive. **2.** Lacking in alertness, vigor, or energy; dull or lazy. **3.** Slow to perform or respond to treatment or stimulation. [Middle English, perhaps from *sluggen,* to be lazy. See **sluggard.**] **—slug·gish·ly** *adv.* **—slug·gish·ness** *n.*

sluice (slo͞os) *n.* **1.** An artificial structure equipped with a valve or gate and used for holding back or regulating the flow of a body of water. **2.** The body of water so regulated or held back. **3.** The valve or gate used in a sluice. Also called "sluice gate," "sluice valve." **4.** A channel or drain, especially one for carrying off excess water. Also called "sluiceway." **5.** A long inclined trough, as for carrying logs or for washing gold ore.
∼v. **sluiced, sluicing, sluices.** *—tr.* **1. a.** To flood or drench by means of a sluice. **b.** To pour or splash water over or upon. **c.** To wash with a sudden flow of water; flush. Often used with *out* or *away.* **2.** To draw off or let out by a sluice. **3.** To send (logs) down a sluice. **4.** To wash (gold ore) in a sluice. *—intr.* To flow out from or as if from a sluice. [Middle English *scluse,* from Old French *excluse,* from Gallo-Roman *exclūsa* (unattested), from the feminine past participle of Latin *exclūdere,* to shut out, EXCLUDE.]

slum (slŭm) *n.* A heavily populated urban area characterized by poor housing and squalor.
∼intr.v. **slummed, slumming, slums.** To visit a slum or any place considered inferior to one's usual environment, as from curiosity. [19th century : origin obscure.]

slum·ber (slŭm′bər) *v.* **-bered, -bering, -bers.** *—intr.* **1.** To sleep or doze. **2.** To be dormant or quiescent. *—tr.* To pass (time) in sleep. Often used with *away.*
∼n. **1.** *Often* **slumbers.** Sleep: *was awakened from her slumbers.* **2.** A state of inactivity or dormancy. [Middle English *slum(b)eren,* perhaps frequentative of *slumen,* to doze, probably from *slume,* sleep, Old English *slūma.*] **—slum·ber·er** *n.* **—slum·ber·ing·ly** *adv.*

slum·ber·ous (slŭm′bər-əs) *adj.* **1.** Sleepy; drowsy. **2. a.** Suggestive of or like sleep. **b.** Peaceful; tranquil. **3.** Causing or inducing sleep; soporific. **—slum·ber·ous·ly** *adv.* **—slum·ber·ous·ness** *n.*

slumber party *n.* An overnight party in which guests, usually teenage girls, wear nightclothes, socialize, and sometimes sleep.

slum·gul·lion (slŭm′gŭl′yən, slŭm-gŭl′-) *n.* A watery meat stew. [Earlier *slum,* slime, perhaps from German *Schlamm,* mud, from Middle High German *slam* + *gullion*†.]

slum·lord (slŭm′lôrd′) *n. Informal.* A profiteering landlord of slum property.

slump (slŭmp) *intr.v.* **slumped, slumping, slumps.** **1.** To fall or sink suddenly and heavily; plump; collapse. **2.** To decline suddenly; suffer a slump. **3.** To droop, as in sitting or standing; slouch.
∼n. A sudden falling off or decline, as in interest, prices, or business. [17th century ("to sink in a bog") : perhaps from Scandinavian; akin to Norwegian *slumpa,* to fall, Low German *slump,* bog.]

slung. Past tense and past participle of **sling** (to hurl).

slung·shot (slŭng′shŏt′) *n.* A small, heavy weight attached to a thong, used as a weapon.

slunk. Past tense and past participle of **slink.**

slur (slûr) *tr.v.* **slurred, slurring, slurs.** **1.** To pass over lightly or carelessly; treat without due consideration. Often used with *over.* **2.** To pronounce (words or sounds) indistinctly. **3.** To speak slightingly of; disparage; slander. **4.** *Music.* **a.** To glide over (a series of notes) smoothly without a break. **b.** To mark with a slur. **5.** *Printing.* To blur or smudge.
∼n. **1. a.** A disparaging remark; an aspersion. **b.** A blot or stain, as on one's reputation. **2.** A slurred utterance or manner of speech. **3.** *Music.* **a.** A curved line connecting notes on a score to indicate that they are to be played or sung legato. **b.** A passage played or sung in this manner. **4.** *Printing.* A smeared or blurred impression. [Middle English *sloor, slore,* mud, perhaps from Middle Dutch; compare Low German *slūren,* Middle Dutch *sloren,* to drag.]

slurp (slûrp) *v.* **slurped, slurping, slurps.** *—tr.* To eat or drink in a noisy manner. *—intr.* To eat or drink something noisily. [Dutch *slurpen,* to slurp, lap, from Middle Dutch *slorpen.*] **—slurp** *n.*

slur·ry (slûr′ē) *n., pl.* **-ries.** A thin mixture of a liquid, especially water, and a finely divided substance, such as cement, plaster of Paris, or clay particles. [Middle English *slory,* probably akin to *sloor,* mud. See **slur.**]

slush (slŭsh) *n.* **1.** Partially melted snow or ice. **2.** Soft mud; mire. **3.** Refuse grease or fat from a ship's galley. **4.** Maudlin speech or writing; sentimental drivel.
∼v. **slushed, slushing, slushes.** *—tr.* **1.** To splash or soak with slush. **2.** To fill (joints in masonry) with mortar. Usually used with *up.* *—intr.* **1.** To walk or proceed through slush. **2.** To make a splashing or slushy sound. [17th century : origin obscure.] **—slush·i·ness** *n.* **—slush·y** *adj.*

slush fund *n.* A contingency fund; especially, one kept by a political group to finance corrupt practices such as bribing public officials. [From SLUSH (sense 3), alluding to greasing as bribery.]

slut (slŭt) *n.* **1.** A slovenly, dirty woman; a slattern. **2. a.** A woman of loose morals. **b.** A prostitute. [Middle English *slutte*†.] **—slut·tish** *adj.* **—slut·tish·ly** *adv.* **—slut·tish·ness** *n.*

sly (slī) *adj.* **slier** or **slyer, sliest** or **slyest.** **1.** Stealthily clever; crafty; cunning. **2.** Secretive rather than open; underhand; deceitful. **3.** Playfully mischievous; roguish; arch. **—on the sly.** Secretively or surreptitiously. [Middle English *sli, sleih,* from Old Norse *slœgr,* cunning, clever, "able to strike," from *slōg-,* past stem of *slā,* to strike.] **—sly·ly, sli·ly** *adv.* **—sly·ness** *n.*
Synonyms: *artful, crafty, cunning, foxy, tricky, wily.*

sly·boots (slī′bo͞ots′) *n. Informal.* A sly person.

slype (slīp) *n. Architecture.* A covered passage, especially one between the transept and chapter house of a cathedral. [Probably from Middle Flemish *slijpen,* to slip.]

Sm The symbol for the element samarium.

s.m. sadomasochism; sadomasochistic.

S.M. sergeant major.

smack¹ (smăk) *v.* **smacked, smacking, smacks.** *—tr.* **1.** To strike, as with the flat of the hand, heartily and noisily. **2.** To make a sound by pressing together (the lips) and opening them again quickly. **3.** To move or place with force, causing a smacking sound: *smacked the money on the bar.* *—intr.* To make or give a smack.
∼n. **1.** A sharp blow or slap. **2.** The loud, sharp sound of smacking. **3.** A noisy kiss.
∼adv. **1.** With a smack: *fell smack on her head.* **2.** Directly; right: *went smack against the rules.* [Middle Low German or Middle Dutch *smacken* (imitative).]

smack² *n.* **1. a.** A distinctive flavor or taste. **b.** A suggestion or trace. **2.** A small amount; a smattering. **3.** *Slang.* Heroin.
∼intr.v. **smacked, smacking, smacks.** **1.** To have a distinctive taste. Used with *of.* **2.** To give an indication; suggest. Used with *of*: *smacks of foul play.* [Middle English, Old English *smæc.*]

smack³ *n.* A single-masted boat, such as a sloop, used chiefly in fishing. [Dutch *smak,* from Middle Dutch *smacke*†.]

smack·er (smăk′ər) *n.* **1.** A loud kiss. **2.** A resounding blow. **3.** *Slang.* A dollar.

smack·ing (smăk′ĭng) *adj.* **1.** Given with a smacking sound: *a smacking kiss.* **2.** Brisk; vigorous; spanking: *a smacking breeze.*

small (smôl) *adj.* **smaller, smallest.** *Abbr.* **s.** **1.** Little or relatively little; of less than usual or average size, number, quantity, magnitude, or extent: *a small house; a small portion of pie.* **2.** Limited in importance or significance; trivial. **3.** Limited in degree, scope, or intensity: *paid small attention; had small hope.* **4.** Lacking position, influence, or status; minor. **5.** Engaged in commercial or other activity on a relatively limited scale: *small businesses.* **6.** Unpretentious; modest. **7.** Not fully grown; very young. **8.** Showing littleness of mind or character; petty: *very small of him to object.* **9.** Belittled; humiliated: *made him feel small.* **10.** Designating a letter written or printed in lower case. **11.** Soft; low: *a small voice.*
∼adv. **1.** In small pieces: *Cut it up small.* **2.** In a small manner.
∼n. **1.** A small, slender part: *the small of the back.* **2. smalls.** *British Informal.* Small items of laundry, such as underclothes. [Middle English *smal(l),* Old English *smæl.*] **—small·ness** *n.*
Synonyms: *diminutive, infinitesimal, little, minuscule, minute, tiny.*

small arm *n.* A firearm small enough to be carried in the hand.

small beer *n.* **1.** Weak or bad beer. **2.** Someone or something of little consequence. [Popularized by Shakespeare's "To suckle fools and chronicle small beer" (*Othello*).]

small calorie *n.* A **calorie** *(see).*

small capital *n. Abbr.* **s.c.** A letter having the form of a capital letter but being lower in height; for example, the words SMALL CAPITALS are printed in small capitals.

small change *n.* **1.** Coins of low denomination. **2.** Something of little value or significance.

small circle *n.* In geometry, a circle on the surface of a sphere with a radius that is not a radius of the sphere. Compare **great circle.**

small·clothes (smôl′klōthz′, -klōz′) *pl.n.* Men's close-fitting knee breeches worn in the 18th century.

small fry *pl.n.* **1.** Young or small fish. **2.** Young, unimportant, or insignificant persons or things.

small·hold·er (smôl′hōl′dər) *n. Chiefly British.* One who owns or rents a smallholding.

small·hold·ing (smôl′hōl′dĭng) *n. Chiefly British.* An area of agricultural land smaller than an average farm.

small hours *pl.n.* The early hours of the morning before dawn.

small intestine *n.* The part of the intestine in which digestion is completed, extending from the pylorus to the cecum and consisting of the duodenum, the jejunum, and the ileum.

small-mind·ed (smôl′mīn′dĭd) *adj.* Having or characterized by a narrow, petty, or selfish attitude; lacking breadth of sympathy or interest. **—small-mind·ed·ly** *adv.* **—small-mind·ed·ness** *n.*

small·mouth bass (smôl′mouth′) *n.* A North American freshwater food and game fish, *Micropterus dolomieui.*

small·pox (smôl′pŏks′) *n.* An infectious disease, now eradicated, caused by a virus and characterized by widespread pimples that blister and form pockmarks. Also called "variola."

small print *n.* **Fine print** *(see).*

small-scale (smôl′skāl′) *adj.* **1.** Small or limited in scope, range, or extent. **2.** Having a small scale. Said of a map.

small·sword (smôl′sôrd′, -sōrd′) *n.* A lightweight, tapering sword used, especially in former times, for fencing.

small talk *n.* Casual, light, or trivial conversation.

small-time (smôl′tīm′) *adj. Informal.* Insignificant or unimportant; minor: *a small-time comedian.* **—small-tim·er** *n.*

smalt (smôlt) *n.* A deep-blue paint and ceramic pigment produced by pulverizing a glass made of silica, potash, and cobalt oxide. [French, from Italian *smalto,* from Germanic; akin to SMELT.]

smalt·ite (smôl′tīt′) *n.* Also **smalt·ine** (smôl′tĭn, -tēn′). A white to silver-gray mineral arsenide of cobalt and nickel, usually with some iron present. It is an important ore of cobalt. [Originally *smaltine,* from French : SMALT + -INE.]

sma·rag·dite (smə-răg′dīt′) *n.* A fibrous, green amphibole mineral occurring in rocks such as eclogite. [French, from Latin *smaragdus,* a kind of precious stone. See **emerald.**]

smarm (smärm) *intr.v.* **smarmed, smarming, smarms.** *British Informal.* To behave in an unctuous or ingratiating way; gush. [19th century (dialectal) : origin obscure.]

smarm·y (smär′mē) *adj.* **-ier, -iest.** *Informal.* **1.** Sleek. **2.** Gushingly or unctuously flattering. **—smarm·i·ness** *n.*

smart (smärt) *intr.v.* **smarted, smarting, smarts. 1. a.** To cause a sharp, usually superficial stinging pain, as an acrid liquid or a slap may. **b.** To be the source of such a pain, as a wound may. **c.** To feel such a pain. **2.** To suffer acutely, as from mental distress, wounded feelings, or remorse: *smarting from wounded pride.* **3.** To suffer or pay a heavy penalty. Usually used with *for.*

~n. Sharp mental or physical pain.

~adj. **smarter, smartest. 1. a.** Characterized by sharp, quick thought; bright. **b.** Amusingly or impertinently clever; witty: *a smart answer.* **2.** Characterized by sharp, quick movement, especially: **a.** Forceful; stinging: *a smart slap.* **b.** Brisk; energetic: *a smart pace.* **3.** Characterized by or involving astuteness or shrewdness. **4.** Neat, fresh, and spruce, as in dress or appearance. **5.** Associated with or consisting of persons of fashion and sophistication; fashionable. **—See Synonyms at intelligent.**

~adv. In a smart manner: *play it smart.* [Middle English *smarten, smerten,* Old English *smeortan.*] **—smart·ly** *adv.* **—smart·ness** *n.*

smart al·eck (ăl′ĭk) *n. Informal.* One who shows off his cleverness in a self-assertive and arrogant way. [SMART + *Aleck,* nickname for *Alexander.*] **—smart-al·eck·y** (smärt-ăl′ĭ-kē) *adj.*

smart·en (smärt′n) *v.* **-ened, -ening, -ens.** *—tr.* **1.** To improve in appearance or stylishness; spruce up. Usually used with *up.* **2.** To make brighter or quicker: *smarten the pace.* *—intr.* To make oneself smart or smarter. Usually used with *up.*

smart money *n.* **1.** Compensation beyond the value of actual harm, awarded by juries in cases of gross negligence or willful misconduct. **2.** Money gambled or invested by experienced gamblers or those having privileged information.

smart·weed (smärt′wēd′) *n.* A plant, the **water pepper** *(see).*

smash (smăsh) *v.* **smashed, smashing, smashes.** *—tr.* **1.** To break into pieces suddenly, noisily, and violently; shatter: *smashed the glass.* **2. a.** To throw or dash (something) violently so as to shatter or crush: *smashed the vase against the wall.* **b.** To strike with a heavy blow; batter: *smashed the door in.* **3.** To hit (a ball or shuttlecock) with an aggressive overhead stroke. **4.** To crush or destroy completely; ruin. **5.** To break up; put an end to: *smash a criminal gang.* *—intr.* **1.** To move or be moved suddenly into violent contact with another object: *smashed into a wall.* **2.** To break into pieces, as from a violent blow or collision. **3.** To smash a ball or shuttlecock. **4.** To become wrecked or destroyed. **5.** To go bankrupt. Often used with *up.* **—See Synonyms at break.**

~n. **1. a.** The act or sound of smashing. **b.** The condition of having been smashed. **2. a.** Total defeat, destruction, or ruin. **b.** Financial failure; bankruptcy. **3.** A collision or crash. **4.** An aggressive overhead stroke, as in tennis or badminton. **5.** *Informal.* A resounding success. **6.** A drink made of mint, sugar, soda water, and alcoholic liquor, usually brandy.

~adj. Informal. Of, pertaining to, or being a resounding success: *a smash hit.*

~adv. With a sudden, violent crash. [Imitative; perhaps blend of SMACK and CRASH.]

smashed (smăsht) *adj. Slang.* Intoxicated; drunk.

smash·er (smăsh′ər) *n.* **1.** One that smashes. **2.** *British Informal.* One that is outstandingly fine or attractive.

smash·ing (smăsh′ĭng) *adj. Informal.* Extraordinarily or unusually impressive, fine, or attractive; wonderful; admirable.

smash·up (smăsh′ŭp′) *n.* **1.** A total collapse or defeat. **2.** A serious collision between vehicles; a crash.

smat·ter (smăt′ər) *v.* **-tered, -tering, -ters.** *—tr.* **1.** To speak (a language) without fluency. **2.** To study or approach superficially; dabble in. *—intr.* To have a superficial knowledge; dabble.

~n. A smattering. [Middle English *smat(e)ren* (probably imitative).] **—smat·ter·er** *n.*

smat·ter·ing (smăt′ər-ĭng) *n.* **1.** A fragmented or superficial knowledge. **2.** A small amount or number; a scattering. [From SMATTER.]

smear (smîr) *v.* **smeared, smearing, smears.** *—tr.* **1. a.** To spread or daub with a sticky, greasy, or dirty substance. **b.** To spread or daub (a sticky, greasy, or dirty substance) on a surface. **2.** To stain or blur by or as if by smearing. **3.** To stain or attempt to destroy the reputation of; vilify. *—intr.* To be or become smeared.

~n. **1.** A mark made by smearing; a spot; a blot. **2.** A substance to be spread on a surface; especially, a substance or preparation placed on a slide for microscopic examination. **3.** A malicious, unsubstantiated charge made in an attempt to destroy someone's reputation; slander. Also used adjectivally: *a smear campaign.* [Middle English *smeren,* to anoint, cover, daub, Old English *smierwan, smerian.*] **—smear·y** *adj.*

smear test *n.* A **Pap test** *(see).*

smec·tic (smĕk′tĭk) *adj. Chemistry.* Of, pertaining to, or designating one of the two types of anisotropic melts characteristic of a liquid crystal, in which the molecules are linearly oriented in a planar arrangement. Compare **nematic.** [Greek *smēktikos,* cleansing, detergent, from *smēkhein,* to cleanse (referring to the soapy consistency of such substances).]

smeg·ma (smĕg′mə) *n.* **1. Sebum** *(see).* **2.** The sebaceous substance secreted under the foreskin. [Greek *smēgma* (stem *smēgmat-*), detergent, from *smēkhein,* to cleanse (referring to the soaplike consistency).] **—smeg·mat·ic** (smĕg-măt′ĭk) *adj.*

smell (smĕl) *v.* **smelled** or **smelt** (smĕlt), **smelling, smells.** *—tr.* **1.** To perceive the scent of (something) by means of the olfactory nerves. **2. a.** To sense the presence of by or as if by the olfactory nerves; detect: *smelled danger ahead.* **b.** To find or discover by smelling. Used with *out.* *—intr.* **1.** To use the sense of smell; perceive the scent of something. **2.** To have or emit an odor, often of a specified kind: *doesn't smell fresh; smells of old socks.* **3.** To be suggestive; smack of something. Used with *of*: *smells of dishonesty.* **4.** To have or emit an unpleasant odor; stink. **5.** To appear to be dishonest; suggest evil or corruption. **—smell a rat.** *Slang.* To suspect that something is amiss.

~n. **1.** The sense by which odors are perceived; the olfactory sense. **2. a.** That quality of something that can be perceived by the olfactory sense; odor; scent. **b.** An unpleasant odor. **3.** The act or an instance of smelling. **4.** A distinctive or pervasive quality; an aura: *the smell of corruption.* [Middle English *smellen, smullen*†.]

Synonyms: *aroma, bouquet, fragrance, odor, perfume, savor, scent, stench, stink.*

Usage: *Smell* in the intransitive sense "to emit an odor" is modified by an adjective: *The flowers smell good* (not *well*) or *bad* (not *badly*) or *sweet* (not *sweetly*). The adjective in such constructions may in turn be modified by an adverb: *smells unbelievably bad.* An adverb may also occur in *smells of* constructions: *smells strongly of garlic. Smell* in the intransitive sense "to emit an unpleasant odor; stink" is modified by an adverb: *The fish smells disgustingly* (indicating degree of foul smell, in constrast with *smells disgusting,* which merely specifies an odor).

smelling salts *pl.n.* Any of several preparations based on spirits of ammonia, sniffed as a restorative after dizziness and fainting.

smell·y (smĕl′ē) *adj.* **-ier, -iest.** *Informal.* Having an unpleasant or offensive odor. **—smell·i·ness** *n.*

smelt[1] (smĕlt) *v.* **smelted, smelting, smelts.** *—tr.* **1.** To extract the metallic constituents from (ore) by melting. **2.** To extract (metal) from ore in this way. *—intr.* To melt or fuse. Used of ores. [Middle Low German *smelten.*]

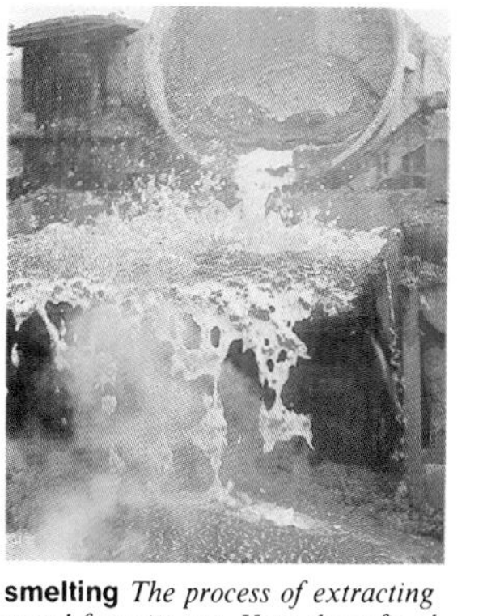

smelting *The process of extracting metal from its ore. Here the refined metal is being poured into troughs to cool.*

smelt[2] *n., pl.* **smelts** or collectively **smelt. 1.** Any of various small marine and freshwater food fishes of the family Osmeridae; especially, *Osmerus eperlanus,* of Europe. Also called "sparling." **2.** The sand smelt, *Atherina presbyter.* [Middle English, Old English *smelt, smylt.*]

smelt[3]**.** Alternate past tense and past participle of **smell.**

smelt·er (smĕl′tər) *n.* Also **smelt·er·y** (smĕl′tə-rē), *pl.* **-ies** (for sense 1b). **1. a.** An apparatus for smelting, usually a furnace. **b.** An establishment for smelting. **2.** A person engaged in the smelting industry.

Sme·ta·na (smĕt′n-ə), **Bedřich** (1824–84). Czech composer. He played a leading part in the founding of the Czech national opera (1862) and was its principal conductor until 1874. His most famous works are the opera *The Bartered Bride* (1866), the tone poem *Ma*

Vlast (1879), and two string quartets both called *From My Life* (1876, 1882).

smew (smyo͞o) *n.* A small, crested Old World duck, *Mergellus albellus,* having a narrow bill and white and black plumage in the male. [17th century : origin obscure.]

smid·gen, smid·gin (smĭj′ən) *n. Informal.* A very small quantity or portion; a bit. [Probably alteration of dialectal *smitch,* particle.]

smi·lax (smī′lăks′) *n.* **1.** Any plant of the genus *Smilax,* which mainly comprises climbing vines. The dried roots of certain species are also called "sarsaparilla." **2.** A vine, *Asparagus asparagoides,* that is popular as a floral decoration. [New Latin, from Latin *smīlax,* a kind of oak, smilax, bindweed, from Greek *smilax†.*]

smile (smīl) *n.* **1.** A facial expression characterized by an upward curving of the corners of the mouth, typically expressing pleasant feelings such as amusement, affection, or approval, but sometimes arising from bitterness, cynicism, or derision. **2.** A pleasant or favorable disposition or aspect. ~*v.* **smiled, smiling, smiles.** —*intr.* **1.** To have or form a smile. **2. a.** To express approval or beneficence. Often used with *upon* or *on.* **b.** To regard with detached amusement or patient resignation. Often used with *at: smiled at misfortune.* —*tr.* **1.** To express with a smile. **2.** To act upon or change with or as if with a smile: *She smiled away her cares.* [Middle English *smilen,* perhaps from Scandinavian, akin to Swedish *smila.*] —**smil·er** *n.* —**smil·ing·ly** *adv.*

Smiles (smīlz), **Samuel** (1812-1904). British writer, the most famous popularizer of the Victorian ethic of self-improvement and hard work, especially in *Self-Help* (1859) and *Thrift* (1875).

smirch (smûrch) *tr.v.* **smirched, smirching, smirches.** **1.** To soil, stain, or dirty, as with grime. **2.** To dishonor or defame. ~*n.* Something that smirches; a blot, smear, or stain. [Middle English *smorchen†.*]

smirk (smûrk) *intr.v.* **smirked, smirking, smirks.** To smile in a self-conscious, knowing, or self-satisfied manner. ~*n.* A knowing, self-satisfied smile. [Middle English *smirken,* Old English *smearcian,* to smile.] —**smirk·er** *n.* —**smirk·ing·ly** *adv.*

smite (smīt) *v.* **smote** (smōt) or *archaic* **smit** (smĭt), **smitten** (smĭt′n) or **smit** or **smote, smiting, smites.** —*tr.* **1.** To strike heavily with or as if with the hand, a tool, a weapon, or the like. **2.** To attack, damage, or destroy by or as if by blows. **3. a.** To affect, as with disease; afflict: *smitten with plague.* **b.** To strike down in retribution; chasten or chastise. Used of God. **c.** To affect sharply with deep feeling: *smitten with love.* —*intr.* To strike or beat: *smote upon the oaken door.* [Smite, smote or smit, smitten; Middle English *smiten, smot* or *smite, smitten,* Old English *smītan, smiton* (plural) or *smāt* (singular), *smiten.*] —**smit·er** *n.*

smith (smĭth) *n.* **1.** A metalworker; especially, one who works metal when it is hot and malleable. Often used in combination: *silversmith; goldsmith.* **2.** A blacksmith (see). **3.** A person who makes or creates something specified. Used in combination: *a wordsmith; a songsmith.* [Middle English, Old English.]

Smith (smĭth), **Adam** (1723-90). Scottish economist and moral philosopher. He came to prominence with his *Theory of Moral Sentiments* (1759), but is best known for his great work of political economy, *An Inquiry into the Nature and Causes of the Wealth of Nations* (1776), which laid the foundations of classical free-market economic theory.

Smith, Alfred Emanuel, known as "the Happy Warrior" (1873-1944). U.S. politician. Prominent in New York State Democratic politics, he held a variety of positions before becoming governor for four terms (1919-20 and 1923-28). In 1928 he won the Democratic nomination for the presidency but was decisively defeated by Herbert Hoover.

Smith, Bessie (*c.* 1894-1937). U.S. jazz singer. She was known as the Empress of the Blues, thanks to her recordings in the 1920's with leading jazz musicians such as Louis Armstrong.

Smith, Ian Douglas (1919-). Rhodesian politician. He formed the Rhodesian Front Party in 1961 to campaign for Southern Rhodesia's independence from Great Britain. In 1964 he became prime minister of Rhodesia, and in 1965 he unilaterally declared its independence. In 1970 his rebel regime proclaimed Rhodesia a republic. For the next decade his white supremacist party fought a losing battle against black guerrilla forces.

Smith, John (*c.* 1580-1631). English adventurer, colonist, explorer, and author. He arrived in Virginia with the first English settlers in May 1607 and soon became leader of the struggling colony. Captured by Indians, he claimed to have escaped death through the intervention of Chief Powhatan's daughter Pocahontas. Smith's maps and accounts of his explorations in Virginia and New England were invaluable to later explorers and colonists.

Smith, Joseph (1805-44). U.S. religious leader, founder of the Mormon Church, officially called the Church of Jesus Christ of Latter-day Saints. He alleged that a vision had shown him the hiding place of sacred tablets, which he unearthed in 1827 and transcribed in the *Book of Mormon* (1830). The following year he founded his new church at Fayette, New York. In 1844 he was arrested with his brother on charges of treason and conspiracy and was murdered by a mob at the prison in Carthage, Illinois.

Smith, Kate, born Kathryn Elizabeth Smith (*c.* 1907-86). U.S. entertainer. She began singing before audiences as a child but did not become a full-time singer until 1930. Her radio and television programs were enormously popular, but she is probably best known for her rendition of Irving Berlin's "God Bless America."

Smith, Margaret Chase (1897-). U.S. politician. She worked as a teacher and a newspaperwoman before being elected to fill a seat in the U.S. House of Representatives vacated by the death of her husband (1940). She is the first woman to serve in both the House (1940-49) and the U.S. Senate (1949-73).

Smith, Walter Wellesley, known as "Red" (1905-82). U.S. journalist. Long considered the dean of American sportswriters, he was, after 1954, the most widely syndicated columnist in the country. His literate and amusing column earned him a Pulitzer Prize in 1976.

smith·er·eens (smĭth′ə-rēnz′) *pl.n. Informal.* Fragments or splintered pieces; bits: *The dish broke into smithereens.* [Perhaps from Irish *smidirín,* diminutive of *smiodar†,* small fragment.]

smith·er·y (smĭth′ə-rē) *n., pl.* **-ies.** **1.** The occupation or craft of a smith. **2.** A smithy.

Smith·son (smĭth′sən), **James** (1765-1829). British chemist and mineralogist. He was elected to the Royal Society at the age of 22 and endowed the Smithsonian Institution in his will.

smith·son·ite (smĭth′sə-nīt′) *n.* A white or yellow to brown mineral, chiefly zinc carbonate ($ZnCO_3$), used as a source of zinc. Also called "dry-bone ore." [After James Smithson.]

smith·y (smĭth′ē, smĭth′ē) *n., pl.* **-ies.** A blacksmith's workshop; a forge. [Middle English *smithy,* from Old Norse *smidhja.*]

smock (smŏk) *n.* **1.** A loose shirtlike outer garment worn, as by artists, to protect the clothes while working. **2.** A similar garment, usually knee-length and often decorated with smocking, as worn formerly by farm laborers. Also called "smock frock." **3.** A loose dress gathered in below the bust rather than at the waist, worn especially by pregnant women. ~*tr.v.* **smocked, smocking, smocks.** To decorate (fabric) with smocking. [Middle English *smok,* women's undergarment, smock, Old English *smoc.*]

smock·ing (smŏk′ĭng) *n.* Needlework decoration accomplished by stitching small regularly spaced gathers into a honeycomb or diamond-shaped pattern.

smock mill *n.* A type of windmill in which the top part only, rather than the entire body, turns in the wind.

smog (smŏg, smôg) *n.* Fog that has become mixed and polluted with smoke. [Blend of SMOKE and FOG.] —**smog·gy** *adj.*

smoke (smōk) *n.* **1.** Small particles of carbonaceous matter in the air, resulting mainly from the incomplete combustion of organic material such as wood or coal. **2.** A suspension of particles in a gaseous medium. **3.** Something insubstantial, unreal, or transitory. **4. a.** An act of smoking a form of tobacco. **b.** *Informal.* Tobacco in a form that can be smoked; especially, a cigarette. **5.** A grayish blue to dark gray. **6. Smoke.** *British Slang.* London. **7.** A substance used to produce a smoke screen. ~*v.* **smoked, smoking, smokes.** —*intr.* **1. a.** To emit smoke or a smokelike substance. **b.** To emit smoke excessively. **2. a.** To draw in and exhale smoke from a cigarette, cigar, pipe, or the like. **b.** To do this habitually. —*tr.* **1.** To draw in and exhale the smoke of (burning tobacco, for example). **2.** To preserve or cure (meat or fish) by exposure to the smoke of burning wood. **3.** To fumigate. **4.** To expose (glass) to smoke in order to darken or change its color. —**smoke out.** **1.** To force out of a place of hiding or concealment by the use of smoke. **2.** To detect and bring to public view; expose; reveal. [Middle English, Old English *smoca.*]

smoke bomb *n.* A bomb that is designed to give out thick smoke upon exploding, used especially to provide cover or concealment.

smoke detector *n.* An alarm device that automatically detects the presence of smoke.

smoke-dried (smōk′drīd′) *adj.* Cured in smoke. Said of fish or meat.

smoked rubber *n.* A crude, raw form of natural rubber made by coagulating latex with acid and drying sheets of it over wood fires.

smokeho. Variant of **smoko.**

smoke·house (smōk′hous′) *n.* A structure in which meat or fish is cured with smoke.

smoke·jack (smōk′jăk′) *n.* A device for turning a roasting spit in a chimney, activated by the current of rising gases.

smoke·less (smōk′lĭs) *adj.* Emitting little or no smoke.

smokeless powder *n.* A propellant charge composed mainly of nitrocellulose, which produces little or no smoke, used in projectiles and small artillery rockets.

smok·er (smō′kər) *n.* **1.** One that smokes. **2.** A railroad car, or a section of one, in which smoking is permitted. Also called "smoking car." **3.** An informal social gathering for men.

smoke screen *n.* **1.** A mass of dense artificial smoke used to conceal military areas or operations from an enemy. **2.** Any action or statement used to conceal plans or intentions.

smoke·stack (smōk′stăk′) *n.* A large chimney through which combustion vapors, gases, and smoke are discharged.

smoke tree *n.* Either of two trees, *Cotinus coggygria,* of Eurasia, or *C. obovatus,* of the southern United States, having plumelike clusters of small yellowish flowers. [The flower clusters resemble puffs of smoke.]

smoking jacket *n.* A man's evening jacket, often made of a fine fabric, elaborately trimmed, and usually worn at home.

smok·y (smō′kē) *adj.* **-ier, -iest.** **1.** Emitting smoke profusely. **2.** Full of smoke. **3.** Resembling or suggestive of smoke, especially in taste or color. **4.** Darkened, stained, or discolored by smoke. —**smok·i·ly** *adv.* —**smok·i·ness** *n.*

smoky quartz *n.* A mineral, **cairngorm** (see).

smol·der, smoul·der (smōl′dər) *intr.v.* **-dered, -dering, -ders.** **1.** To

burn or smoke slowly without flame. **2.** To exist in a hidden or suppressed state. **3.** To manifest repressed emotion such as anger or hatred: *eyes smoldering with revenge.*
~n. **1.** A smoldering fire. **2.** Smoke from a smoldering fire. [Middle English *smolderen,* from *smolder,* smolder.]

Smo·lensk (smō-lĕnsk′). City in the Russian S.F.S.R., western U.S.S.R., on the Dnieper River. An important trade center from the 9th century, it was held briefly by Poland (1611–54), France (1812), and Germany (1941–43). It is today a major railway junction with engineering and textile industries.

Smol·lett (smŏl′ĭt), **Tobias George** (1721–71). Scottish novelist, one of the founders of the English novel. Among his works are *Peregrine Pickle* (1751) and *Humphry Clinker* (1771).

smolt (smōlt) *n.* A young salmon at the stage at which it turns silvery and migrates from fresh water to the sea. [Middle English, obscurely related to Old English *smelt,* SMELT (fish).]

smooch (smo͞och) *intr.v.* **smooched, smooching, smooches.** *Slang.* To kiss.
~n. Slang. A kiss. [Alteration of *smouch,* to kiss.]

smooth (smo͞o*th*) *adj.* **smoother, smoothest. 1. a.** Having a surface free from irregularities, roughness, or projections; even: *a smooth lawn.* **b.** Free from hair or bristles; soft. **2.** Having a surface whose roughness or projections have been worn level by use: *smooth tires.* **3. a.** Having a fine, uniform consistency or texture; not lumpy: *smooth custard.* **b.** Free from harshness or acidity: *a smooth white wine.* **4. a.** Having an even or gentle motion: *a smooth drive.* **b.** Having flowing regularity: *smooth rhythm.* **5.** Having no obstructions or difficulties: *a smooth operation.* **6.** Having or showing an unruffled temperament; serene. **7.** Not harsh or coarse in sound; mellifluous. **8. a.** Polite and affable; polished. **b.** Excessively or suspiciously suave; plausible; persuasive: *a smooth talker.* **9.** *Phonetics.* Not aspirated. —See Synonyms at **level, suave.**
~v. **smoothed, smoothing, smoothes.** *—tr.* **1.** To make (something) even, level, unwrinkled, or the like. Sometimes used with *out* or *down*: *smoothed down his hair.* **2. a.** To rid of obstructions, hindrances, difficulties, or the like: *smooth the way for a settlement.* **b.** To remove (obstructions or difficulties): *smooth away a problem.* **3.** To soothe or alleviate; make calm. Sometimes used with *over*: *smoothed over hurt feelings.* **4.** To make less harsh or crude; refine. *—intr.* To become smooth.
~n. **1.** A smooth part or surface. **2.** The act of smoothing. [Middle English *smoth(e),* Old English *smōth*; akin to Old Saxon *smōthi*†.] **—smooth·er** *n.* **—smooth·ly** *adv.* **—smooth·ness** *n.*

smooth·bore (smo͞o*th*′bôr′, -bōr′) *adj.* Having an unrifled barrel. Said of a firearm.
~n. Also **smooth bore.** A firearm having no rifling.

smooth breathing *n.* **1.** The symbol (ʼ) written over some initial vowels in classical Greek to indicate that they are not aspirated. **2.** The absence of aspiration so indicated.

smooth·en (smo͞o′*th*ən) *v.* **-ened, -ening, -ens.** *—tr.* To make smooth. *—intr.* To become smooth.

smooth hound *n.* A **hound shark** *(see).*

smooth·ie (smo͞o′*th*ē) *n. Informal.* One who is smooth and charming, sometimes excessively so, as when socializing with members of the opposite sex.

smooth muscle *n.* The unstriated involuntary muscle of the internal organs, as of the intestine, bladder, and blood vessels, excluding the heart.

smooth snake *n.* A small common European snake, *Coronella austriaca,* whose young hatch immediately from newly laid eggs.

smooth-talk (smo͞o*th*′tôk′) *tr.v.* **-talked, -talking, -talks.** *Informal.* To speak to in an ingratiating and persuasive manner.

smor·gas·bord (smôr′gəs-bôrd′, -bōrd′) *n.* A meal consisting of a number of varied dishes, such as salads, cheeses, and pâté, served buffet-style. [Swedish *smörgåsbord* : *smörgås,* (open-faced) sandwich, bread and butter : *smör,* butter, from Old Norse *smör, smjör,* fat + *gås,* goose, piece of butter, from Old Norse *gās* + *bord,* table, from Old Norse *bordh.*]

smote. Past tense and alternate past participle of **smite.**

smoth·er (smŭ*th*′ər) *v.* **-ered, -ering, -ers.** *—tr.* **1. a.** To suffocate (a person or animal) by depriving of air. **b.** To deprive (a fire) of the oxygen necessary for it to burn. **2.** To conceal, suppress, or hide: *smothered a yawn; smothered the report.* **3.** To cover (a foodstuff) thickly with another foodstuff: *smothered the steak with onions.* **4.** To overwhelm, as with kisses or affection. *—intr.* **1.** To suffocate. **2.** To be concealed, stifled, or suppressed.
~n. **1.** Something that smothers, as a dense cloud of smoke or dust or a spray of spume. **2.** A disordered mass of things. **3.** A smoldering or smoky condition. [Middle English *smotheren, smortheren,* from *smorther,* a smother, from Old English *smorian*†, to suffocate, smother.] **—smoth·er·y** *adj.*

smoulder. Variant of **smolder.**

smudge (smŭj) *v.* **smudged, smudging, smudges.** *—tr.* **1.** To make a small, dirty mark on. **2.** To smear or blur (writing, for example). **3.** To fill (an orchard or other planted area) with dense smoke from a smudge pot in order to prevent damage from insects or frost. *—intr.* **1.** To make a smudge, as with dirt, soot, or ink. **2.** To become smudged.
~n. **1.** A dirty mark, blotch or smear. **2.** A smoky fire used as a protection against insects or frost. [Middle English *smogen*†.] **—smudg·i·ly** *adv.* **—smudg·i·ness** *n.* **—smudg·y** *adj.*

smudge pot *n.* A receptacle in which oil or other smoky fuel is burned, as to protect an orchard from insects or frost or to indicate wind direction.

smug (smŭg) *adj.* **smugger, smuggest.** Pleased with oneself; complacent; self-satisfied. [Probably from Low German *smuck,* neat, smooth, sleek, from Middle Low German, from *smucken,* to adorn.] **—smug·ly** *adv.* **—smug·ness** *n.*

smug·gle (smŭg′əl) *v.* **-gled, -gling, -gles.** *—tr.* **1.** To import or export without paying lawful customs charges or duties. **2.** To bring in or take out illicitly or by stealth. **3.** To place in concealment; hide. Often used with *away.* *—intr.* To engage in smuggling. [Earlier *smuckle,* from Low German *smukkelen, smuggeln* and Dutch *smokkelen.*] **—smug·gler** *n.*

smut (smŭt) *n.* **1. a.** A particle or flake of soot or dirt. **b.** A dirty mark or smudge made by soot, smoke, or dirt. **2.** Obscenity or obscene matter for reading or viewing. **3. a.** Any of various plant diseases, particularly affecting cereals, caused by fungi of the order Ustilaginales and producing black, powdery masses of spores on the affected parts. **b.** A fungus causing such a disease.
~v. **smutted, smutting, smuts.** *—tr.* **1.** To blacken or smudge, as with smoke or grime. **2.** To affect (a plant) with smut. **3.** To free (grain, for example) from smut. *—intr.* To become affected with smut, as a plant. [Perhaps from Low German *smutt*†.] **—smut·ti·ly** *adv.* **—smut·ti·ness** *n.* **—smut·ty** *adj.*

smutch (smŭch) *tr.v.* **smutched, smutching, smutches.** To soil, stain, or besmirch.
~n. A stain or spot of dirt. [Perhaps alteration of SMUDGE.]

Smuts (smŭts), **Jan Christiaan** (1870–1950). South African statesman. He was a lawyer and political journalist before becoming a general in the second Anglo-Boer War (1899–1902). He later became prime minister of the Union of South Africa (1919–24, 1939–48). He was an early proponent of the British Commonwealth and a prime mover in the formation of The League of Nations. Later he drafted the preamble to the declaration of human rights that was included in the charter of the United Nations.

Smyrna. See **Izmir.**

Sn The symbol for the element tin. [Latin *stannum.*]

snack (snăk) *n.* **1.** A hurried or light meal. **2.** A small amount of food eaten between meals.
~intr.v. **snacked, snacking, snacks.** To eat a hurried or light meal. [Middle English *snake,* a bite, from *snaken,* to bite.]

snack bar *n.* A café or counter where light meals are served.

snaf·fle (snăf′əl) *n.* A bit for a horse, consisting of two bars jointed at the center. Also called "snafflebit."
~tr.v. **snaffled, -fling, -fles. 1.** *British Informal.* To take, seize, or steal. **2.** To put a snaffle on or control with a snaffle. [16th century; origin obscure.]

sna·fu (snă-fo͞o′) *adj. Slang.* In a state of complete confusion.
~tr.v. **snafued, -fuing, -fus.** *Slang.* To make chaotic or confused.
~n., pl. **snafus.** *Slang.* Any chaotic or confused situation. [*S*ituation *n*ormal: *a*ll *f*ouled *u*p.]

snag (snăg) *n.* **1.** Any rough, sharp, or jagged protuberance, such as: **a.** A tree or part of a tree that protrudes above the surface in a body of water and is hazardous to shipping. **b.** The stump of a broken off branch. **c.** An unaligned or broken tooth; a snaggletooth. **2.** A break, pull, or tear in a fabric that has been caught on a snag. **3.** An obstacle or difficulty, especially one that is unforeseen or hidden. —See Synonyms at **obstacle.**
~tr.v. **snagged, snagging, snags. 1. a.** To hinder, obstruct, or impede by or as if by a snag. **b.** To tear or catch on a snag. **2.** To free or clear of snags. **3.** *Informal.* To catch unexpectedly and quickly: *snagged the long fly ball.* [Probably from Scandinavian, akin to Old Norse *snagi*†, peg.] **—snag·gy** *adj.*

snag·gle·tooth (snăg′əl-to͞oth′) *n., pl.* **-teeth** (-tēth′). A tooth that is broken or out of alignment. [From dialectal *snaggled,* snaggletoothed, from SNAG.] **—snag·gle·toothed** *adj.*

snail (snāl) *n.* **1.** Any of numerous aquatic or terrestrial mollusks of the class Gastropoda, characteristically having a spirally coiled shell, a broad retractile foot, and a distinct head. **2.** A slow-moving or lazy person. [Middle English, Old English *snæg(e)l, sneg(e)l.*]

snail's pace *n.* A very slow pace or rate of progress.

snake (snāk) *n.* **1.** Any of various scaly, legless, sometimes venomous reptiles of the suborder Serpentes, having a long, tapering, cylindrical body. **2. Snake.** The constellation **Hydra** *(see).* **3.** A treacherous person. **4.** A long, highly flexible metal wire used for cleaning drains. **5.** *Economics.* The concept of fixing the value of currencies to each other within narrow limits, so that on a graph the values of these currencies appear as parallel lines, despite fluctuation with other currencies.
~v. **snaked, snaking, snakes.** *—tr.* To follow (a course) in the manner of a snake. *—intr.* To move with a sinuous, snakelike motion. [Middle English, Old English *snaca.*] See feature, next page.

Snake (snāk). River in the northwestern United States. It rises in Yellowstone National Park, Wyoming, and flows 1,670 kilometers (1,038 miles) westward to join the Columbia River near Pasco, Washington. The largest and deepest of its many gorges is Hell's Canyon, *c.* 160 kilometers (100 miles) long and reaching a maximum depth of *c.* 2,410 meters (*c.* 7,900 feet).

snake·bird (snāk′bûrd′) *n.* Any of several long-necked, long-billed birds of the genus *Anhinga,* such as the **water turkey** *(see).* [From its elongated, snakelike neck.]

snake·bite (snāk′bīt′) *n.* **1.** The bite of a snake. **2.** Poisoning resulting from the bite of a venomous snake.

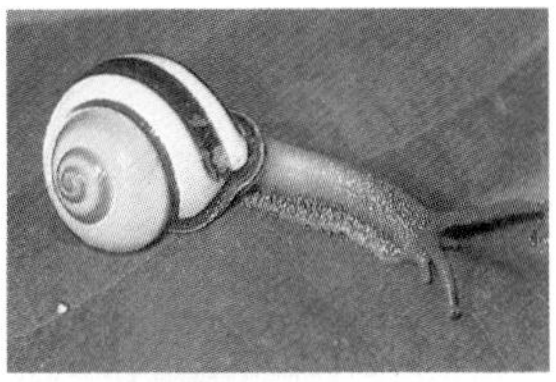

snail *Snails are found throughout the world on land and in the sea. Land snails are usually most active at night or in wet weather and feed on vegetation and sometimes small dead animals, such as slugs. This striped snail is native to New Guinea.*

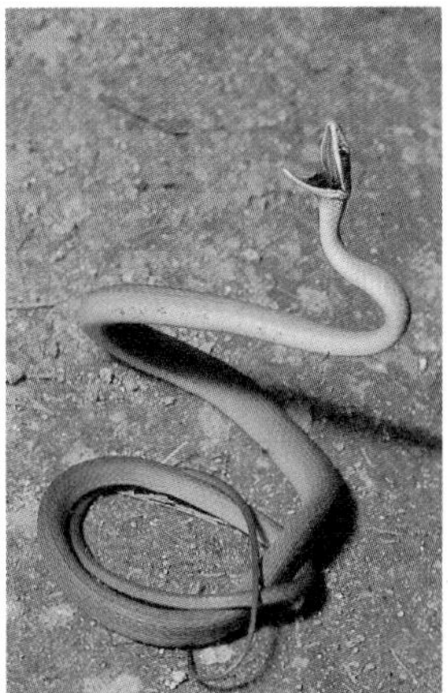

snake Opheodrys aestivus, *the rough green snake, lives on spiders and insects and is native to Mexico and the southern and eastern United States. Like many snakes, it rears up when alarmed.*

snake

THE REPTILE THAT MEN FEAR

The deaf snake that responds to the charmer's music

Snakes have no external ear openings and are, as far as we know, completely deaf to sounds in the air, but they react to vibrations passing through the ground. When they sway to the piping of a snake charmer, they are mimicking the movements of the charmer himself.

Snakes are reptiles and there are 2,500 species of them divided into 11 families or main types. Only two whole families—cobras, which include sea snakes, and vipers—are venomous enough to

poison man, but individual species of other families have venom fatal to man—the boomslang of the Colubridae family in Africa, for example. Other snakes produce enough poison to kill small animals.

All snakes are carnivorous. They have jawbones loosely attached to the skull so they can swallow their prey whole—an African snake with a neck the width of a man's finger can swallow a hen's egg.

POISONOUS SNAKES
The venomous cobra (right) and mamba have short fangs at the front of the mouth and inject poison as they bite to kill. The viper family have long, tubular fangs, and some species are so deadly that they need only to strike a victim once for the poison to squirt through those fangs and take its very rapid effect.

KILLING WITHOUT POISON *Although not poisonous, the python, boa (above), and anaconda can be dangerous because they are constrictors. To kill they wrap themselves around their prey and squeeze it to death. A python has been known to swallow a leopard, and anacondas can grow to more than 11 meters (36 feet) long.*

snake charmer *The snake cannot hear the sound of the flute but is "charmed" by the instrument's to-and-fro movement.*

snake charmer *n.* An entertainer who uses rhythmic music and bodily movements to control a snake.
snake dance *n.* **1.** A dance performed as part of a biennial religious ceremony of the Hopi Indians, in which the dancers carry live rattlesnakes in their mouths. **2.** An informal procession of persons who join hands and move forward in a zigzag line.
snake fence *n.* A worm fence *(see).*
snake fly *n.* Any of various predatory insects of the family Raphidiidae, having an elongated, snakelike neck.
snake·head (snāk′hĕd′) *n.* A plant, the **turtlehead (see).**
snake in the grass *n.* A false friend or lurking danger.
snake mackerel *n.* A fish, the **escolar** *(see).*
snake·mouth (snāk′mouth′) *n., pl.* **-mouths** (-mouthz′). An orchid, *Pogonia ophioglossoides,* of eastern North America, having a solitary rose-purple flower with a fringed lip.
snake oil *n.* Any liquid falsely represented as having medicinal properties and usually hawked at a carnival or fair.
snake pit *n. Slang.* A mental institution.
snake plant *n.* Any of several tropical Old World plants of the genus *Sansevieria,* having narrow, rigid, often mottled leaves and widely cultivated as a house plant.
snake·root (snāk′rōōt′, -rŏŏt′) *n.* Any of various plants having roots or rhizomes reputed to cure snakebite.
snakes·head (snāks′hĕd′) *n.* A plant, the **fritillary (see).**
snake·skin (snāk′skĭn′) *n.* The skin of a snake, especially when prepared as leather.
snake·stone (snāk′stōn′) *n.* **1.** A small stone or piece of porous substance reputed to cure snakebite. **2.** A whetstone.
snake·weed (snāk′wēd′) *n.* Any of various plants reputed to cure snakebite.
snak·y (snā′kē) *adj.* **-ier, -iest. 1.** Pertaining to or characteristic of snakes. **2.** Having the form or movement of a snake; serpentine. **3.** Overrun with snakes. **4.** Treacherous; sly. **—snak·i·ly** *adv.* **—snak·i·ness** *n.*
snap (snăp) *v.* **snapped, snapping, snaps.** *—intr.* **1.** To make a brisk, sharp, cracking sound. **2.** To break suddenly with such a sound. **3.** To give way abruptly under pressure or tension: *The weight of responsibility made her nerves snap.* **4.** To bring the jaws briskly together, often with a clicking sound; bite or attempt to bite.

Often used with *at.* **5.** To snatch or grasp eagerly. Often used with *up* or *at.* **6.** To speak abruptly or irritably. Often used with *at.* **7.** To move swiftly and smartly: *snap to attention.* **8.** To open or close with a click: *The lock snapped shut.* *—tr.* **1.** To snatch at with or as if with the teeth; bite. **2.** To cause to come apart or break with a snapping sound. **3.** To utter abruptly or irritably: *snapped out an order.* **4. a.** To cause to emit a snapping sound: *snap a whip.* **b.** To cause to move into place or close with a snapping sound. **5.** To pick up or get hold of quickly and avidly: *snapped up a bargain.* **6. a.** To take (a photograph). **b.** To take a photograph of. **7.** *Sports.* To center (a football). **—snap back.** To recover quickly. **—snap out of it.** *Informal.* To throw off something, such as a bad mood, by making a conscious effort.
—n. **1.** A sudden, sharp, cracking sound or the action producing such a sound. **2.** A sudden breaking of something brittle, such as a twig. **3.** A clasp, catch, or other fastening device that operates with a snapping sound. **4.** A sudden attempt to bite, snatch, or grasp. **5. a.** The sound produced by rapid movement of the second finger pressed down from the tip of the thumb to its base. **b.** The act of producing this sound. **6.** A curt or irritable retort or manner of speech: *answered me with a snap.* **7.** A thin, crisp cooky: *a ginger snap.* **8.** *Informal.* Briskness, liveliness, or energy. **9.** A brief spell of cold weather. **10.** A snapshot. **11.** *Informal.* An effortless task. **12.** In football, the passing of the ball from a center to a back that initiates play.
—adj. **1.** Made, done, or brought about on the spur of the moment, with little warning or consideration: *a snap decision; a snap election.* **2.** Fastening with a snap. **3.** *Informal.* Simple; easy.
—adv. With a snap. [Partly from Middle Low German or Middle Dutch *snappen,* to seize, speak hastily; partly imitative.]
snap bean *n.* A bean, such as the **string bean** *(see),* cultivated for its unripe, crisp pods.
snap-brim (snăp′brĭm′) *n.* A hat having a flexible brim, usually turned down in front and up at the back.
snap·drag·on (snăp′drăg′ən) *n.* Any of several plants of the genera *Antirrhinum* or *Misopates;* especially, *A. majus,* of the Mediterranean region, having clusters of two-lipped, variously colored flowers. [From a fanciful likening of the flower to a dragon's mouth.]
snap fastener *n.* A small two-part metal device for holding edges together, consisting of a stud that snaps into a corresponding socket. Also *chiefly British* "press-stud."
snap·per (snăp′ər) *n., pl.* **snappers** or collectively **snapper** (for senses 2, 3, and 4). **1.** One that snaps. **2.** Any of numerous widely distributed marine fishes of the family Lutjanidae. **3.** A large, red carnivorous Australian fish of the genus Pagrosomus. Also called "schnapper." **4.** A snapping turtle.
snapping beetle *n.* The **click beetle** *(see).*
snapping turtle *n.* Any of several New World freshwater turtles of the family Chelydridae; especially, *Chelydra serpentina* or *Macrochelys temmincki,* of North America, having a rough shell and powerful hooked jaws.
snap·pish (snăp′ĭsh) *adj.* **1.** Liable to snap or bite, as a dog might be. **2.** Liable to speak sharply or curtly; irritable; curt. **—snappish·ly** *adv.* **—snap·pish·ness** *n.*
snap·py (snăp′ē) *adj.* **-pier, -piest. 1.** *Informal.* Lively or energetic; brisk. **2.** *Informal.* Smart or chic in appearance. **3.** Snappish. **—make it snappy.** *Informal.* To be quick; hurry up. **—snap·pi·ly** *adv.* **—snap·pi·ness** *n.*
snap ring *n.* In mountaineering, an oval-shaped or pear-shaped steel ring that is snapped to the eye of a piton and through which a rope is run.
snap roll *n.* An aerial maneuver in which an aircraft is put through a sharp roll of 360 degrees about its longitudinal axis.
snap·shot (snăp′shŏt′) *n.* An informal photograph taken with a small hand-held camera.
snare¹ (snâr) *n.* **1.** A trapping device, often consisting of a noose, used for capturing birds and small animals. **2.** Anything that serves to entangle, trap, or catch out the unwary. **3.** A surgical instrument with a wire loop controlled by a mechanism in the handle, used to remove growths, such as tumors and polyps.
—tr.v. **snared, snaring, snares. 1.** To trap (an animal) with a snare. **2.** To entrap or ensnare. [Middle English, Old English *sneare,* from Old Norse *snara.*] **—snar·er** *n.*
snare² *n.* **1.** Any of the wires or cords stretched across the lower skin of a snare drum to increase reverberation. **2.** A snare drum. [Probably from Middle Dutch, string.]
snare drum *n.* A small double-headed drum having a snare or snares stretched across the lower head to increase reverberation.
snarl¹ (snärl) *v.* **snarled, snarling, snarls.** *—intr.* **1.** To growl viciously while baring the teeth. **2.** To speak angrily or threateningly. *—tr.* To utter with anger or hostility.
—n. **1.** A vicious growl. **2.** Any vicious or hostile utterance or expression. [From obsolete *snar,* to snarl, from Middle Low German *snarren.*] **—snarl·er** *n.* **—snarl·ing·ly** *adv.* **—snarl·y** *adj.*
snarl² *n.* **1.** A tangled mass, as of hair or yarn. **2.** Any confused, complicated, or tangled situation.
—v. **snarled, snarling, snarls.** *—intr.* To become tangled or confused. *—tr.* **1.** To tangle or knot (hair or yarn, for example). **2.** To bring into a confused or tangled condition. Often used with *up: Traffic was snarled up at the lights.* [Middle English *snarle;* perhaps akin to SNARE (trap).] **—snarl·er** *n.* **—snarl·y** *adj.*
snatch (snăch) *v.* **snatched, snatching, snatches.** *—tr.* **1.** To grasp or seize abruptly or violently: *snatched her handbag.* **2.** To take, get,

or obtain hurriedly, unexpectedly, or improperly: *snatch a bite to eat; snatched a goal in the closing minutes.* **3.** To rescue or save opportunely: *snatched from death.* —*intr.* To seize or grasp, or attempt to seize or grasp. Used with *at: snatched at the chance.*
∼*n.* **1.** The act or an action of snatching; a quick grasp or grab. **2.** A brief period of time: *slept in snatches.* **3.** A small amount; a bit or fragment: *a snatch of dialogue.* **4.** In weightlifting, a lift in which one raises the weight from the floor to above one's head in one movement. **5.** *Slang.* A kidnaping. [Middle English *snacchen, snecchen*†, to make a sudden gesture.] —**snatch·er** *n.*

snatch block *n. Nautical.* A block that can be opened on one side to receive the looped part of a rope.

snatch·y (snăch'ē) *adj.* **-ier, -iest.** Occurring in snatches; intermittent; spasmodic.

snaz·zy (snăz'ē) *adj. Slang.* **-zier, -ziest.** Smooth, fashionable, or flashy. [Perhaps a blend of SNAPPY and JAZZY.]

Snead (snēd), **Samuel Jackson,** known as "Sam" (1912–). U.S. golfer. He won three PGA championships (1942, 1949, 1951) and three Masters tournaments (1949, 1952, 1954). His powerful tee shots earned him the nickname "Slammin' Sammy."

sneak (snēk) *v.* **sneaked** or *informal* **snuck** (snŭk), **sneaking, sneaks.** —*intr.* **1.** To go or move in a quiet, stealthy way; slink: *sneaked out of the meeting.* **2.** To behave in a furtive or cowardly manner. —*tr.* **1.** To move, give, take, or put in a quiet, stealthy manner: *sneak a chocolate into one's mouth.* **2.** *Informal.* To steal.
∼*n.* **1.** One who sneaks; a stealthy, cowardly, or underhand person. **2.** The act or an instance of sneaking, as a quiet, stealthy movement.
∼*adj.* Acting with or involving secrecy, stealth, or surprise: *a sneak attack.* [Of dialectal origin, perhaps ultimately akin to Old English *snīcan,* to crawl, Old Norse *snīkja*†.]

sneak·er (snē'kər) *n.* **1.** One who sneaks. **2.** A canvas shoe with a soft rubber sole.

sneak·ing (snē'kĭng) *adj.* **1.** Acting in a stealthy, furtive way. **2.** Unavowed; secret: *a sneaking affection.* **3.** Gradually growing or persistent: *a sneaking suspicion.* —**sneak·ing·ly** *adv.*

sneak preview *n.* A single public showing of a film prior to its general release, usually as an addition to an announced program.

sneak thief *n.* A burglar who enters without breaking in.

sneak·y (snē'kē) *adj.* **-ier, -iest.** Furtive, underhand, or deceitful. —**sneak·i·ly** *adv.* —**sneak·i·ness** *n.*

sneer (snîr) *n.* **1.** A scornful facial expression characterized by a slight raising of one corner of the upper lip. **2.** Any contemptuous facial expression, sound, or statement.
∼*v.* **sneered, sneering, sneers.** —*tr.* To utter with a sneer or in a sneering manner. —*intr.* **1.** To assume a sneer to express a scornful, contemptuous, or derisive attitude: *sneered at his amateur efforts.* **2.** To speak or write in a scornful, contemptuous, or derisive manner. [16th century : perhaps from Low Dutch *sneere*†.] —**sneer·er** *n.* —**sneer·ful** *adj.* —**sneer·ing·ly** *adv.*

sneeze (snēz) *intr.v.* **sneezed, sneezing, sneezes.** To expel air forcibly from the mouth and nose in an explosive, spasmodic, involuntary action resulting from irritation, as from dust, in the nose. —**sneeze at.** *Informal.* To dismiss lightly; consider as of little worth. Used in negative statements: *an offer not to be sneezed at.*
∼*n.* An instance of sneezing. [Middle English *snesen,* misreading of obsolete *fnesen,* Old English *fnēosan* (unattested), from Old Norse *fnȳsa* (imitative).] —**sneez·er** *n.* —**sneez·y** *adj.*

sneeze·weed (snēz'wēd') *n.* **1.** Any of several North American plants of the genus *Helenium,* having yellow, rayed flowers. **2.** The **sneezewort** *(see).*

sneeze·wort (snēz'wûrt', -wôrt') *n.* A plant, *Achillea ptarmica,* native to Europe, having loosely clustered, daisylike white flowers. Also called "sneezeweed." [The dried leaves were used to induce sneezing.]

snell (snĕl) *n.* A length of fine, threadlike material, such as monofilament or gut, that connects a fishhook to a heavier line; a leader [Origin unknown.]

Snell's Law (snĕlz) *n. Physics.* The principle that in refraction of a light ray at a boundary between two mediums, the sine of the angle of incidence divided by the sine of the angle of refraction at the boundary is a constant for the given mediums. [After Willebrord *Snell* (1591–1626), Dutch physicist.]

snib (snĭb) *tr.v.* **snibbed, snibbing, snibs.** *Chiefly Scottish & Canadian* To latch (a door). [Origin obscure.]

snick (snĭk) *tr.v.* **snicked, snicking, snicks.** To make a cut, incision, or notch in.
∼*n.* A small cut, notch, or incision. [Perhaps from SNICKERSNEE, or perhaps from Scandinavian; compare Old Norse *snikka,* to whittle.]

snick·er (snĭk'ər) *n.* Also **snig·ger** (snĭg'ər) (for sense 1). **1.** A snide, slightly stifled laugh. **2.** A whinny.
∼*intr.v.* **snickered, -ering, -ers.** Also **sniggered, -gering, -gers** (for sense 1). **1.** To utter a partly stifled laugh. **2.** To whinny. [Imitative.] —**snick·er·ing·ly** *adv.*

snick·er·snee (snĭk'ər-snē') *n.* A large knife resembling a sword. Used humorously. [Earlier *stick or snee,* a fight with knives : Dutch *steken,* to stick, stab, from Middle Dutch + *snijden,* to cut, from Middle Dutch *snīden.*]

snide (snīd) *adj.* **snider, snidest. 1.** Derogatory in a malicious, superior way; sarcastic. **2.** Fake; counterfeit. [19th century : origin obscure.] —**snide·ly** *adv.* —**snide·ness** *n.*

sniff (snĭf) *v.* **sniffed, sniffing, sniffs.** —*intr.* **1.** To inhale a short, audible breath through the nose, as in smelling something or stopping one's nose from running. **2.** To indicate ridicule, contempt, or doubt by or as if by sniffing. Often used with *at.* —*tr.* **1.** To inhale (a powdered drug, for example) forcibly through the nose. **2.** To smell or try to smell by sniffing. **3.** To perceive or detect by or as if by sniffing. **4.** To utter contemptuously with or as if with a sniff.
∼*n.* **1.** An instance or the sound of sniffing. **2.** Anything that is sniffed or perceived by sniffing; a faint odor; a whiff. [Middle English *sniffen* (imitative).]

snif·fle (snĭf'əl) *intr.v.* **-fled, -fling, -fles.** To breathe audibly through a congested nose, as when crying or suffering from a cold.
∼*n.* **1.** An act or sound of sniffling. **2. sniffles.** *Informal.* A condition, such as a head cold, accompanied by sniffles. Preceded by *the.* [Frequentative of SNIFF.]

snif·fy (snĭf'ē) *adj.* **-fier, -fiest.** *Informal.* Disposed to showing arrogance or contempt; haughty; disdainful.

snif·ter (snĭf'tər) *n.* **1.** A pear-shaped glass with a narrow top used in serving brandy and other aromatic liquors. **2.** *Slang.* A small amount of an alcoholic drink. [From dialectal *snifter,* to sniff, perhaps from Scandinavian; compare Middle Swedish *snypta,* Middle Danish *snyfte.*]

snigger. Variant of **snicker.**

snip (snĭp) *v.* **snipped, snipping, snips.** —*tr.* To cut, clip, or separate in a short, quick stroke or strokes with scissors or shears. —*intr.* To cut or clip with short, quick strokes.
∼*n.* **1.** An act of snipping or the sound produced by snipping. **2. a.** A small cut made with scissors or shears. **b.** A small piece cut or clipped off. **3.** *Slang.* **a.** Something accomplished without difficulty. **b.** *British.* A bargain. **4. snips.** Small hand shears used in cutting sheet metal. Also called "tinsnips." **5.** *Informal.* A small, insignificant person or thing, especially one that is irritating. [Low German or Dutch *snippen,* to snap (imitative).]

snipe (snīp) *n., pl.* **snipe** or **snipes. 1.** Any of various long-billed wading birds of the genus *Capella;* especially, the common, widely distributed species *C. gallinago.* **2.** Any of various similar or related birds. **3.** A shot or gunshot from a concealed place.
∼*intr.v.* **sniped, sniping, snipes. 1.** To shoot snipe. **2.** To shoot at individuals from a concealed place. Often used with *at.* **3.** To direct snide, carping criticism, especially from a safe position. Often used with *at.* [Middle English, perhaps from Old Norse *(mȳri)snīpa*†, (moor) snipe.]

snipe fish *n.* Any fish of the family Macrorhamphosidae, having a long snout.

snipe fly *n.* Any of various two-winged predatory flies of the family Rhagionidae.

snip·er (snī'pər) *n.* One who shoots at people from a concealed place, especially a marksman detailed to pick off enemy soldiers.

snip·pet (snĭp'ĭt) *n.* A small piece; a fragment. [Diminutive of SNIP.]

snip·py (snĭp'ē) *adj.* **-pier, -piest.** *Informal.* **1.** Impertinent; saucy. **2.** Fragmentary.

snitch (snĭch) *v.* **snitched, snitching, snitches.** *Slang.* —*tr.* To steal (something, especially something of little value). —*intr.* To turn informer. Usually used with *on.*
∼*n. Slang.* **1.** A thief. **2.** An informer. **3.** The nose. [17th century (in the sense, a fillip on the nose) : origin obscure.] —**snitch·er** *n.*

sniv·el (snĭv'əl) *intr.v.* **-eled, -eling, -els** or *chiefly British* **-elled, -elling, -els. 1.** To cry or weep with sniffling. **2.** To speak or whine tearfully. **3.** To run at the nose. **4.** To sniffle.
∼*n.* **1.** The act or an instance of sniffling or sniveling. **2.** Nasal mucus. [Middle English *snevelen,* Old English *snyflan* (unattested), akin to *snyflung, snofl,* mucus.] —**sniv·el·er** *n.*

snob (snŏb) *n.* **1.** One who overvalues rank and status and despises his supposed inferiors. **2.** An arrogant or affected person who strives to flatter, imitate, or associate with people of higher status or prestige. **3.** One who has or affects refined or esoteric tastes in cultural matters and who despises anything that does not match these standards. [Obsolete *snob,* person of the lower classes, from dialectal *snob,* cobbler.]

snob·ber·y (snŏb'ə-rē) *n., pl.* **-ies.** Snobbish behavior.

snob·bish (snŏb'ĭsh) *adj.* Of, characteristic of, befitting, or resembling a snob; pretentious. —**snob·bish·ly** *adv.* —**snob·bish·ness** *n.*

snob·bism (snŏb'ĭz'əm) *n.* Snobbery; snobbishness.

Sno-Cat (snō'kăt') *n.* A trademark for a type of snowmobile.

snood (sno͞od) *n.* **1.** A small netlike cap worn by women to keep the hair in place. **2.** A headband or fillet.
∼*tr.v.* **snooded, snooding, snoods.** To hold (the hair) in place with a snood. [Middle English (unattested), Old English *snōd*†.]

snook (sno͝ok, sno͞ok) *n., pl.* **snooks** or collectively **snook.** Any of several chiefly marine fishes of the family Centropomidae; especially, *Centropomus undecimalis,* of warm Atlantic waters. Also called "robalo." [Dutch *snoek,* pike, from Middle Dutch *snoec*†.]

snook·er (sno͝ok'ər) *n.* A game played on a billiard table with 15 red balls and 6 others of different colors, each becoming, in a fixed order, the object ball that must be hit into one of the side pockets by the cue ball, which is white.
∼*tr.v.* **snookered, -ering, -ers.** To put in a difficult position; prevent from succeeding; thwart. [19th century : origin obscure.]

snoop (sno͞op) *intr.v.* **snooped, snooping, snoops.** *Informal.* To pry into the private affairs of others, especially by prowling about.
∼*n. Informal.* One who snoops. [Dutch *snoepen,* to eat on the sly.] —**snoop·er** *n.*

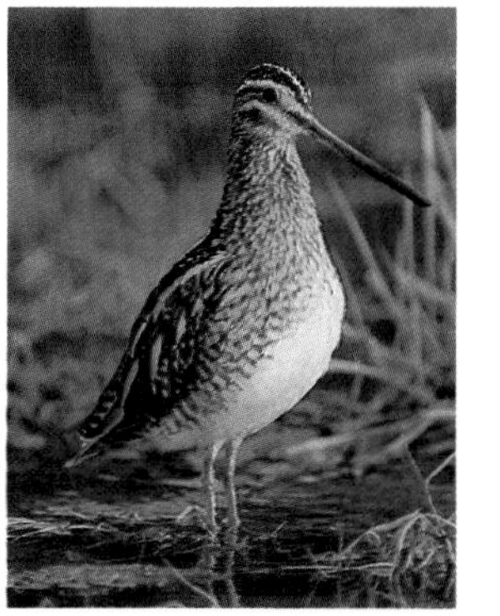

snipe *The long bill of this shore bird—which is found in warm and temperate regions around the world—enables it to forage for worms, beetles, and grubs among reeds and grasses along the water's edge. The species shown here is the common snipe,* Gallinago gallinago.

PRONUNCIATION KEY

ă, pat; ā, pay; âr, care; ä, father, are; b, bib; ch, church; d, deed; ĕ, pet; ē, be; f, fife; g, gag; h, hat; hw, which; ĭ, pit; ī, pie; îr, pier; j, judge; k, kick; l, lid, needle; m, mum; n, no, sudden; ng, thing; ŏ, pot; ō, toe; ô, paw, for; oi, noise; ou, out; o͝o, book; o͞o, boot; p, pop; r, roar; s, sauce; sh, ship, dish; t, tight; th, thin, path; *th,* this, bathe; ŭ, cut; ûr, fur; v, valve; w, with; y, yes; z, zebra, size; zh, vision; ə, about, item, edible, gallop, circus, peaceful

IN FOREIGN WORDS:

à, *Fr.* ami; œ, *Fr.* feu, *Ger.* schön; ü, *Fr.* tu, *Ger.* über; KH, *Ger.* ich, *Scot.* loch; N, *Fr.* bon; y', *Fr.* Compiègne

STRESS MARKS:

Primary stress: ' **in·cite'** (ĭn-sīt')
Secondary stress: ' **in'sight'** (ĭn'sīt')

snorkel

A SIMPLE DEVICE THAT OPENS A NEW WORLD
Using a snorkel is an introduction to fabulous underwater sights

Snorkeling is an easy and inexpensive way to begin to explore the underwater world. The snorkel is an open tube fitted with a mouthpiece at one end. Face immersed, a swimmer paddles along the surface peering down into the water through a transparent, watertight mask and breathing through the mouthpiece of the snorkel whose other end is above the water. Most snorkelers also use rubber foot fins, which aid in buoyancy and increase swimming speed. The word snorkel was used for the ventilation tube

of World War II German submarines: it drew in fresh air and allowed expulsion of fumes from the sub's internal-combustion engines, almost the exact mechanical analogy of what it does for human beings.

Although the snorkel alone does not permit the extended deep dives possible with compressed air tanks, experienced snorkelers by holding their breath can stay under for a couple of minutes at depths down to 100 feet. Such feats, however, are quite dangerous.

ADVENTURE *Many discoveries await the snorkeler but perhaps the most thrilling is the coral reef and the fantastic colors and shapes of its denizens. The snorkel shown has two safety features: its upper U bend keeps water out on a rough day, while the wire basket keeps objects from blocking the tube.*

snowberry *This garden shrub—originally native to North America, but which now grows wild in Europe, too—thrives in any soil and does not mind shade. Its large white berries, ignored by birds, can last all winter long.*

snoop·y (snōō′pē) *adj.* **-ier, -iest.** *Informal.* Tending to snoop; prying. —See Usage note at **curious.**

snoot (snōōt) *n. Slang.* The nose. [Variant of SNOUT.]

snoot·y (snōō′tē) *adj.* **-ier, -iest.** *Informal.* Snobbish or aloof; haughty. [20th century : origin obscure.]

snooze (snōōz) *intr.v.* **snoozed, snoozing, snoozes.** *Informal.* To take a light nap; doze.
~*n. Informal.* A brief light sleep. [18th century (cant) : origin obscure.]

Sno·qual·mie Falls (snō-kwŏl′mē). A waterfall about 82 meters (270 feet) high on the Snoqualmie, a river flowing about 72 kilometers (45 miles) through west-central Washington.

snore (snôr, snōr) *intr.v.* **snored, snoring, snores.** To breathe through both nose and mouth while sleeping, making snorting noises caused by the vibration of the soft palate.
~*n.* An instance of snoring or the noise produced by snoring. [Middle English *snoren,* to snort (probably imitative).] —**snor·er** *n.*

snor·kel (snôr′kəl) *n.* **1.** A retractable vertical tube in a submarine, containing air-intake and exhaust pipes for the engines and for ventilation and permitting extended periods of submergence at periscope depth. **2.** A breathing apparatus used by skin divers, consisting of a long tube held in the mouth.
~*intr.v.* **snorkeled, -keling, -kels** or *chiefly British* **-kelled, -kelling, -kels.** To swim under water using a snorkel. [German *Schnorchel,* from (dialectal) German, snout, from *schnarchen,* to snore, from Middle High German *snarche(l)n.*]

Snor·ri Stur·lu·son (snôr′ē stûr′lə-sən) (1178-1241). Icelandic chieftain and historian. His works include *Heimskringla,* a series of sagas, and the Younger, or Prose, *Edda.*

snort (snôrt) *v.* **snorted, snorting, snorts.** —*intr.* **1. a.** To exhale forcefully and noisily through the nostrils, as a horse does. **b.** To inhale forcefully through the nose or mouth and produce a vibratory snoring noise from the soft palate. **2.** To express scorn, ridicule, or contempt with or as if with a snort. **3.** *Informal.* To emit a loud outburst of laughter. **4.** *Slang.* To inhale a powdered drug, as cocaine. —*tr.* **1.** To express with a snort. **2.** To eject from the nostrils with or as if with a snort. **3.** *Slang.* To inhale (a powdered drug, such as cocaine) through the nose.
~*n.* **1.** The act or sound of snorting. **2.** *Slang.* **a.** An alcoholic drink, especially when swallowed in one gulp. **b.** The inhalation of a powdered drug. [Middle English *snorten* (imitative).]

snort·er (snôr′tər) *n.* **1.** One that snorts. **2.** *Informal.* Anything that is outstanding, as in size, appearance, or severity.

snot (snŏt) *n. Slang.* **1.** Nasal mucus; phlegm. **2.** A nasty or contemptible person. [Middle English *snot(te),* from Low German or from Old English *gesnot;* akin to SNOUT.]

snot·ty (snŏt′ē) *adj.* **-tier, -tiest.** *Slang.* **1.** Dirtied with nasal mucus. **2. a.** Nasty; unpleasant. **b.** Snooty; self-important.

snout (snout) *n.* **1.** The projecting nose, jaws, or front part of an animal's muzzle. **2.** A similar extended front part of the head in

certain insects, such as weevils. **3.** A spout, nozzle, or similar projection likened to a snout. **4.** *Slang.* The human nose. [Middle English *sn(o)ute,* probably from Middle Dutch *snūt(e).*]

snout beetle *n.* A **weevil** (see).

snow (snō) *n.* **1. a.** Solid precipitation in the form of small white or translucent ice crystals of various shapes originating in the atmosphere as frozen particles of water vapor. **b.** A mass of fallen snow lying on the ground: *children playing in the snow.* **2. a.** Anything resembling snow, such as frozen carbon dioxide. **b.** The white specks on a television screen resulting from weak reception. **3.** A fall of snow. **4.** *Slang.* Cocaine or heroin in powdered form.
~*v.* **snowed, snowing, snows.** —*intr.* To fall as snow. —*tr.* **1.** To cover, shut off, or close in with snow. Used with *in, over, under,* or *up.* **2.** *Slang.* To overwhelm with insincere talk, especially with flattery. —**snow under.** To overwhelm, especially with work. [Middle English *snawe, snow,* Old English *snāw.*]

Snow (snō), **C(harles) P(ercy), Baron** (1905-80). British novelist, noted for his interest in the "two cultures" of science and the humanities. His long, semiautobiographical novel sequence *Strangers and Brothers* includes such works as *The Masters* (1951) and *The Corridors of Power* (1964). He became a senior civil servant and parliamentary secretary in the ministry of technology (1964-66).

snow·ball (snō′bôl′) *n.* **1.** A mass of soft, wet snow packed into a ball that can be thrown, as in play. **2.** Any of several plants or shrubs having rounded clusters of white flowers, especially a cultivated variety of *Viburnum opulus.*
~*v.* **snowballed, -balling, -balls.** —*intr.* **1.** To throw snowballs. **2.** To grow rapidly and uncontrollably, as in size or significance, like a snowball rolling down snow. —*tr.* To throw snowballs at.

snowball tree *n.* The cultivated variety of the guelder rose, having ball-like clusters of sterile flowers.

snow·bell (snō′bĕl′) *n.* Either of two shrubs, *Styrax grandifolia* or *S. americana,* of the southeastern United States, having bell-shaped white flowers.

snow·ber·ry (snō′bĕr′ē) *n., pl.* **-ries.** Any of various shrubs of the genus *Symphoricarpos;* especially, *S. rivularis,* having small pinkish flowers and white berries.

snow·bird (snō′bûrd′) *n.* **1.** Any of several birds, such as the junco, seen mainly in winter conditions. **2.** Any white or partly white bird, such as the snow bunting.

snow blindness *n.* Usually temporary conjunctivitis and deteriorated vision caused by sunlight reflected from snow or ice. —**snow-blind** (snō′blīnd′) *adj.*

snow·blink (snō′blĭngk′) *n.* A white glow in the sky reflected from snowfields.

snow·bound (snō′bound′) *adj.* Confined in one place by heavy snow; snowed in.

snow·broth (snō′brôth′, -brŏth′) *n.* Melted snow; slush.

snow bunting *n.* A bird, *Plectrophenax nivalis,* of northern regions, having black and white plumage in the male.

snow·bush (snō′bŏŏsh′) *n.* Also **snow·brush** (-brŭsh′). A shrub, *Ceanothus velutinus,* of western North America, having large clusters of small white flowers.

snow·cap (snō′kăp′) *n.* A cap of snow, as on a mountaintop. —**snow·capped** *adj.*

snow chain *n.* A linked metal covering for a tire, used for improved traction on snowy or icy surfaces. Also called "tire chain."

Snow·don (snōd′n). Highest peak in Wales, in northwestern Gwynedd in the Snowdon Range. The summit rises to 1,085 meters (3,560 feet). The scenic surrounding area has been a part of the Snowdonia National Park since 1951.

Snowdon, Anthony Charles Robert Armstrong-Jones, Earl of (1930-). British photographer. He married Princess Margaret in 1960. They were divorced in 1978.

snow·drift (snō′drĭft′) *n.* A bank of snow heaped up by the wind.

snow·drop (snō′drŏp′) *n.* Any of several bulbous plants of the genus *Galanthus,* native to Eurasia; especially, *G. nivalis,* having solitary, nodding white flowers that bloom early in spring.

snowdrop tree *n.* Any of several trees or shrubs of the genus *Halesia;* especially *H. carolina,* of the southeastern United States, having drooping, bell-shaped white flowers. Also called "silver-bell tree."

snow·fall (snō′fôl′) *n.* **1.** The amount of snow that falls during a given period or in a given area. **2.** A fall of snow.

snow fence *n.* A fence composed of thin upright slats used to prevent snow from drifting, as onto roads or walks.

snow·field (snō′fēld′) *n.* A large, permanently snow-covered area.

snow·flake (snō′flāk′) *n.* **1.** An aggregation of ice crystals falling as a single flake of snow. **2.** Any of several bulbous plants of the genus *Leucojum,* native to Europe, having white or whitish flowers.

snow goose *n.* A goose, *Chen hyperborea,* that breeds in northern regions, having white plumage with black wing tips.

snow job *n. Slang.* An effort to overwhelm or deceive with insincere talk, especially flattery.

snow leopard *n.* A large feline mammal, *Uncia uncia,* of the highlands of central Asia, having long, thick, whitish fur with dark markings. Also called "ounce."

snow line *n.* **1.** The lower altitudinal boundary of a permanently snow-covered area, such as the snowcap of a mountain. **2.** The fluctuating latitudinal boundaries around the polar regions marking the extent of snow cover.

snow·man (snō′măn′) *n., pl.* **-men** (-mĕn′). A figure, usually intended to resemble a man, made of shaped masses of snow.

snow·mo·bile (snō′mō-bēl′) *n.* Any of several motor vehicles for traveling on snow; especially, a small vehicle with skilike runners in front and tanklike treads. Also called "skimobile," *chiefly British* "ski-scooter." [SNOW + (AUTO)MOBILE.]

snow mold *n.* A plant disease affecting turf, forage grasses, and cereals, caused by the fungus *Fusarium nivale* and occurring after snow or during prolonged cold weather.

Snow Mountains. The collective name for the mountain ranges extending over 644 kilometers (400 miles) through central New Guinea, including the Nassau and Orange ranges. Highest elevation, Mt. Carstensz, 4,999 meters (16,400 feet).

snow-on-the-mountain (snō′ŏn-*thə*-moun′tən, snō′ôn-) *n.* A widely cultivated plant, *Euphorbia marginata,* of central North America, having white-margined leaves and showy white bracts.

snow pea *n.* **1.** A variety of pea, *Pisum sativum,* with edible pods. **2.** The pod of the snow pea. In both senses, also called "sugar pea."

snow pellets *pl.n.* **Graupel** *(see).*

snow plant *n.* A saprophytic plant, *Sarcodes sanguinea,* of the mountains of western North America, having a fleshy, scaly, reddish stalk and scarlet flowers.

snow·plow (snō′plou′) *n.* **1.** Any plowlike device or vehicle used to remove snow, as from roads and railway tracks. **2.** A skiing maneuver in which the toes are turned inward so that the skis meet in a V shape, enabling the skier to slow down or stop.

snow·shed (snō′shĕd′) *n.* A roofing built over portions of a railroad track to protect them from snowslides.

snow·shoe (snō′sho͞o′) *n.* A racket-shaped frame containing interlaced leather strips that can be attached to the foot to facilitate walking on deep snow.
~*intr.v.* **snowshoed, -shoeing, -shoes.** To go or walk on snowshoes. **—snow·sho·er** (snō′sho͞o′ər) *n.*

snowshoe rabbit *n.* A hare, *Lepus americanus,* of northern North America, having large, heavily furred feet and fur that is white in winter and brown in summer. Also called "snowshoe hare," "varying hare."

snow·storm (snō′stôrm′) *n.* A storm marked by heavy snowfall and high winds; a blizzard.

snow·suit (snō′so͞ot′) *n.* A child's zippered winter coverall.

snow-white (snō′hwīt′) *adj.* White as snow.

snow·y (snō′ē) *adj.* **-ier, -iest. 1.** Abounding in snow; covered with or characterized by snow. **2.** Resembling or suggestive of snow; white; pure. **—snow·i·ly** *adv.* **—snow·i·ness** *n.*

Snowy Mountains. Mountain range in the Australian Alps of New South Wales, southeastern Australia. Mt. Kosciusko, Australia's highest mountain, is among its peaks.

snr., Snr. senior.

snub (snŭb) *tr.v.* **snubbed, snubbing, snubs. 1.** To treat with scorn or contempt; slight by ignoring or behaving coldly toward. **2.** To reprove or stop short in a sharp, cutting manner; rebuke. **3. a.** To check suddenly the movement of (a rope or cable running out) by turning it about a post. **b.** To secure (a vessel or animal, for example) in this manner.
~*n.* **1.** A deliberate slight or affront. **2.** A sudden checking, as of a rope or cable running out.
~*adj.* Short and slightly flattened at the tip. Said of a nose. [Middle English *snubben,* to rebuke, from Old Norse *snubba.*] **—snub·ber** *n.*

snub-nosed (snŭb′nōzd′) *adj.* **1.** Having a short nose with a slightly flattened tip. **2.** Having a very short barrel: *a snub-nosed pistol.*

snuck. *Informal.* Past tense and past participle of **sneak.**

snuff¹ (snŭf) *v.* **snuffed, snuffing, snuffs.** *—tr.* **1.** To inhale through the nose; sniff. **2.** To sense, perceive, or examine by or as if by smelling. *—intr.* To snort or sniff.
~*n.* An act of snuffing or the sound produced in snuffing; a sniff. [Probably from Middle Dutch *snuffen.*]

snuff² *n.* The charred portion of a candlewick.
~*tr.v.* **snuffed, snuffing, snuffs. 1.** To cut off the charred portion of (a candlewick). **2.** To extinguish (a candle or lamp, for example), especially by smothering the flame. Often used with *out.* **3.** To put a sudden end to; destroy. Usually used with *out.* **4.** *Slang.* To kill. [Middle English *snoffe*† (noun).]

snuff³ *n.* **1.** A preparation of finely pulverized tobacco that can be drawn up into the nostrils by inhaling. **2.** The quantity of this inhaled at a single time; a pinch of snuff. **3.** Any powdery substance, such as a medicine, taken by inhaling. **—up to snuff.** *Informal.* **1.** Normal in health; fit. **2.** As good as usual or as expected; up to standard.
~*intr.v.* **snuffed, snuffing, snuffs.** To take snuff. [Dutch *snuf,* short for *snuf(tabak),* (tobacco) for snuffing, from Middle Dutch *snuffen,* to SNUFF.]

snuff·box (snŭf′bŏks′) *n.* A small, often highly decorative box with a hinged lid that is used for carrying snuff in the pocket.

snuff·er¹ (snŭf′ər) *n.* One who uses snuff.

snuffer² *n.* **1.** A small hollow cone with a handle, used to snuff out candles. **2. snuffers.** An instrument resembling a pair of shears that is used for cutting the snuff from or for extinguishing candles.

snuf·fle (snŭf′əl) *v.* **-fled, -fling, -fles.** *—intr.* **1.** To breathe noisily, as through a congested nose or when crying; to sniffle. **2.** To talk whiningly or nasally; snivel. *—tr.* To utter in a snuffling tone or express by means of a snuffle.
~*n.* **1.** An act or the sound of snuffling. **2. snuffles.** *Informal.* A condition, such as a head cold, accompanied by snuffles. Preceded by *the.* [Probably from Low German or Dutch *snuffelen.*] **—snuf·fler** *n.*

snug (snŭg) *adj.* **snugger, snuggest. 1.** Comfortably sheltered from the cold and the weather; cozy. **2.** Small but well arranged; compact: *a snug apartment.* **3. a.** Closely secured and well built; especially, adequately protected against bad weather. Said of a ship. **b.** Seaworthy. **4.** Close-fitting. Said of a garment. **5.** Providing adequate means for a relatively comfortable life: *a snug income.* —See Synonyms at **comfortable.**
~*tr.v.* **snugged, snugging, snugs. 1.** To make snug or secure. **2.** *Nautical.* To prepare (a vessel) to weather a storm, as by taking in sail or securing movable gear. Often used with *down.*
~*n. Chiefly British.* A small, enclosed or private bar in a public house or inn. [16th century (a nautical term meaning neat, trim) : perhaps from Scandinavian; akin to Old Norse *snöggr,* "close-cropped."] **—snug, snug·ly** *adv.* **—snug·ness** *n.*

snug·ger·y (snŭg′ə-rē) *n., pl.* **-ies.** *Chiefly British.* **1.** A snug position or place. **2.** A snug.

snug·gle (snŭg′əl) *v.* **-gled, -gling, -gles.** *—intr.* To lie or press close together; nestle or cuddle. Often used with *together, with,* or *up.* *—tr.* To draw close or hold closely, as for comfort or in affection; hug. [Frequentative of SNUG (verb).]

so¹ (sō) *adv.* **1. a.** In the manner described, shown, expressed, implied, or indicated; thus: *"She became his loyal friend and remained so to the end"* (Constantine Fitzgibbon). **b.** In such a manner: *The table was so arranged that I sat next to him.* **2. a.** To the amount or degree expressed or understood; in such quantity or to such an extent: *He was so weary that he fell.* **b.** To a certain degree or limit: *so far, so good. I can only do so much.* **c.** To the same degree or extent: *not quite so hot as yesterday.* **3.** To a great extent or degree; very or very much: *so kind of you to come; loved her so.* **4.** Because of the reason given; consequently; as a result: *He was weary and so he fell.* **5.** In the same way; also; likewise: *You were on time and so was I.* **6.** Then; apparently. Used in expressing astonishment, disapproval, or sarcasm: *So you think you've got troubles?* **7.** In truth; indeed: *"Your button's undone." "So it is!"* **—so as to.** In order to: *started early so as to avoid the rush.* **—so there.** The decision is final. Used to add force to expressions of defiance or refusal: *Well, I'm going to do it anyway, so there!*
~*adj.* **1.** True; factual: *It is so.* **2.** Perfectly ordered or arranged. Usually used in the phrase *just so.*
~*conj.* **1.** With the purpose or reason that; in order that. Usually used with *that: I stopped so that you could catch up.* **2.** With the result or consequence that: *He agreed, so they went ahead.*
~*pron.* **1.** That; this; the same as has already been implied or specified: *I don't think so. Did he say so?* **2.** Approximately that quantity, amount, or number: *another ten minutes or so.*
~*interj.* Used to express surprise or comprehension. [Middle English *so, s(w)a,* Old English *swā.*]

Usage: *So* used as a conjunction is generally followed by *that* when it introduces a clause stating purpose or reason *(He stayed a day longer so that he could avoid the traffic),* but the *that* is often dropped in informal contexts. In the expression of result or consequence the use of *so* without *that* is more widely acceptable *(The traffic was very heavy, so he stayed a day longer),* though some stylists prefer alternative constructions (such as *and therefore he stayed a day longer*). See also Usage note at **as.**

so². *Music.* Variant of **sol.**

So. south; southern.

s.o. seller's option.

soak (sōk) *v.* **soaked, soaking, soaks.** *—tr.* **1.** To make thoroughly wet or saturated; drench; wet through. **2. a.** To immerse in liquid, often for a prolonged period; steep. **b.** To remove or draw out by immersion. Usually used with *out: soak out blood stains.* **3.** To absorb (liquid) through pores or interstices. Usually used with *up.* **4.** *Informal.* To take in eagerly or effortlessly as if by absorption; absorb or assimilate. Used with *up: soaking up the sun; soak up facts.* **5.** *Informal.* **a.** To drink (alcohol), especially to excess. **b.** To make (a person) drunk. **6.** *Slang.* To charge or tax excessively; force to pay too much. *—intr.* **1.** To be immersed until thoroughly saturated. **2.** To penetrate or permeate; seep. Often used with *in, into, through,* or *away.* **3.** *Slang.* To drink to excess.
~*n.* **1.** The act or process of soaking or the condition of being soaked. **2.** *Slang.* A drunkard. [Middle English *soken,* Old English *socian,* akin to *sūcan,* to SUCK.] **—soak·er** *n.*

soak·age (sō′kĭj) *n.* **1.** The process of soaking or the condition of being soaked. **2.** The amount of liquid that soaks into or through an object or seeps out of it.

so-and-so (sō′ən-sō′) *n., pl.* **-sos. 1.** A person or thing left unspecified. **2.** *Informal.* A very unpleasant person. Used euphemistically in place of various unsavory epithets: *He's a real so-and-so.* Also used adjectivally: *her so-and-so father.*

soap (sōp) *n.* **1.** A cleansing agent, manufactured in bars, granules, flakes, or liquid form, consisting of a mixture of the sodium salts of various fatty acids made from natural oils and fats. Compare **detergent. 2.** *Chemistry.* A mixture of metallic salts of long-chain fatty acids, especially: **a.** One containing sodium salts (a *hard soap*). **b.** One containing potassium salts (a *soft soap*). **3.** *Slang.* Flattery. **4.** *Slang.* Money, especially money used for bribery. **5.** *Informal.* A soap opera. **—no soap.** *Slang.* **1.** Not possible or permissible. **2.** Without success; futile: *tried to talk him out of it, but no soap.*
~*tr.v.* **soaped, soaping, soaps.** To treat or cover with soap. [Middle English *sope, saip,* Old English *sāpe.*]

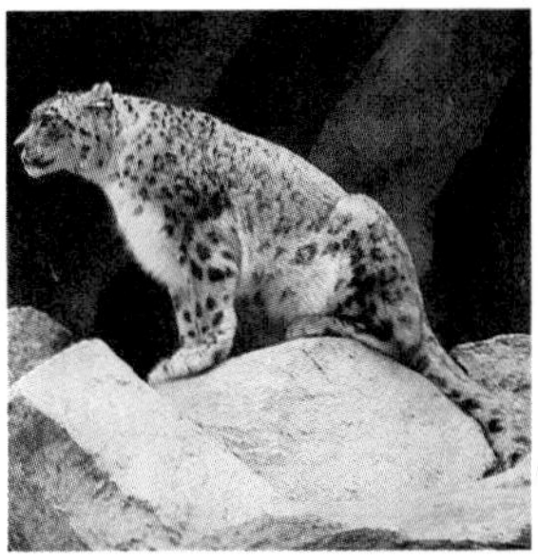

snow leopard *Sheep, goats, and marmots are the chief prey of the snow leopard, which lives at altitudes of up to 6,000 meters (20,000 feet) in the mountains of central Asia. The snow leopard hunts at night and is capable of leaping 9 meters (30 feet) in a single bound.*

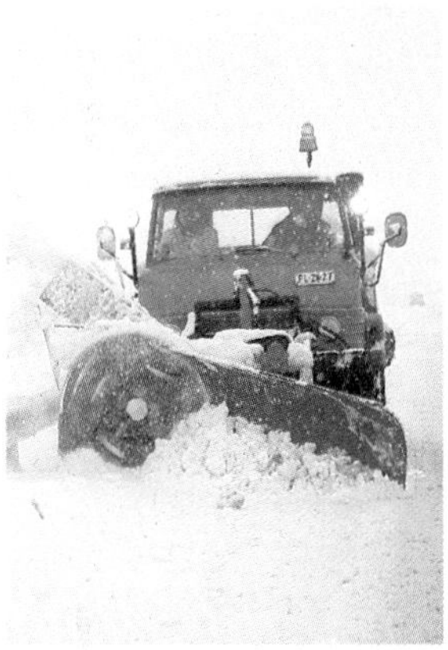

snowplow *A modern snowplow in operation. Alongside its blade is a powerful blower to hurl the snow clear of the road.*

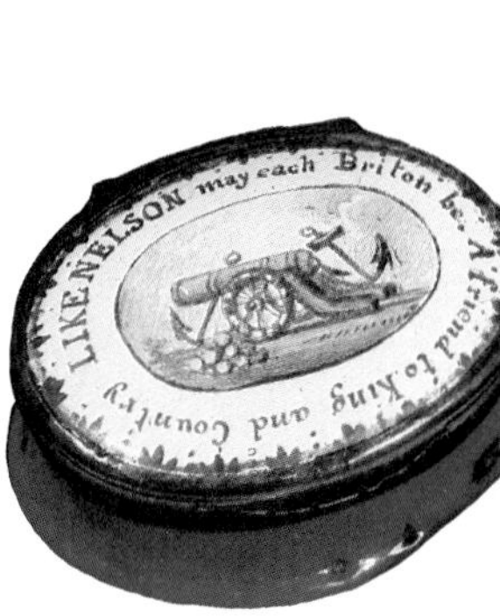

snuffbox *One of the souvenir enameled snuffboxes made to commemorate the death of the British admiral Lord Nelson at the Battle of Trafalgar in 1805.*

soap·bark (sōp′bärk′) *n.* **1.** A tree, *Quillaja saponaria,* of western South America, having bark used as soap and as a source of saponin. **2.** The bark of this tree. **3.** Any of several other trees or shrubs having similar bark.

soap·ber·ry (sōp′bĕr′ē) *n., pl.* **-ries. 1.** Any of various chiefly tropical New World trees of the genus *Sapindus,* having pulpy fruit that lathers like soap. **2.** The fruit of any of these trees.

soap·box, soap box (sōp′bŏks′) *n.* **1.** A box or crate in which soap is packed. **2.** A temporary platform for making an impromptu or nonofficial public speech. **3.** A child's crude motorless vehicle made of a wooden box mounted on a wheeled frame. ~*adj.* Of or pertaining to oratory or an orator characterized by ranting, fanaticism, or eccentricity. —**soap·box·er** *n.*

soap bubble *n.* **1.** A bubble formed from soapy water. **2.** Anything beautiful but transient, insubstantial, or illusory.

soap opera *n.* A daytime radio or television serial drama characterized by stock characters and situations, romance, sentimentality, and melodrama. [Many were originally sponsored by soap companies.]

soap plant *n.* **1.** A plant, *Chlorogalum pomeridianum,* of California, having small white flowers and a bulbous root formerly used as soap. **2.** Any of several other plants having parts used as soap.

soap·stone (sōp′stōn′) *n.* Steatite *(see).* [From its soapy texture.]

soap·suds (sōp′sŭdz′) *pl.n.* Lather or foam from soapy water.

soap·wort (sōp′wûrt′, -wôrt′) *n.* A Eurasian plant, *Saponaria officinalis,* with pale pink flowers, the leaves and stems of which make a lather when rubbed together. Also called "bouncing Bet."

soap·y (sō′pē) *adj.* **-i·er, -i·est. 1.** Containing or consisting of soap; covered or filled with soap. **2.** Pertaining to or resembling soap. **3.** *Slang.* Unctuous; flattering in an oily way. —**soap·i·ly** *adv.* —**soap·i·ness** *n.*

soar (sôr, sōr) *intr.v.* **soared, soaring, soars. 1. a.** To fly upward or rise high into the air; climb swiftly or powerfully. **b.** To rise steeply; be at a great height. **2.** To fly or glide high in the air without visibly moving the wings. **3.** *Aviation.* To glide while maintaining altitude. **4.** To rise suddenly above a normal or usual level; increase greatly. **5.** To rise to an exalted level; be inspired: *My heart soared.* —See Synonyms at **rise.** ~*n.* **1.** The act of soaring. **2.** The altitude or scope attained in soaring. [Middle English *soren,* from Old French *esorer,* from Vulgar Latin *exaurāre* (unattested) : Latin *ex-,* out of + *aura,* the air, a breeze, from Greek, a breeze.] —**soar·er** *n.* —**soar·ing·ly** *adv.*

Soa·res (swär′ĭsh), **Mário Alberto** (1924–). Portuguese politician. Frequently imprisoned for his political views, he was eventually exiled (1970), but returned after a coup (1974) and as leader of the Socialist Party became prime minister (1976–78). He resigned in 1980.

so·a·ve (sō-ä′vā) *n.* A dry white Italian table wine. [Italian, "sweet," from Latin *suāvis,* pleasing.]

sob (sŏb) *v.* **sobbed, sobbing, sobs.** —*intr.* **1.** To weep aloud with convulsive gasping and sniffling; cry uncontrollably. **2.** To make a sound resembling that of sobbing. —*tr.* **1.** To utter with sobs. **2.** To put or bring (oneself) into a specified condition by sobbing: *sob oneself to sleep.* —See Synonyms at **cry.** ~*n.* An act of sobbing or the sound produced in sobbing; a short, audible catch of the breath. [Middle English *sobben,* to catch breath, probably imitative and of Low German origin; akin to Dutch dialectal *sabben†,* to suck.] —**sob·bing·ly** *adv.*

s.o.b. *Slang.* son of a bitch.

So·bat (sō′bät). A river flowing 320 kilometers (205 miles) from southwestern Ethiopia to the White Nile in southeastern Sudan.

so·be·it (sō-bē′ĭt) *conj. Archaic.* Provided that; if it be so that.

so·ber (sō′bər) *adj.* **-berer, -berest. 1.** Habitually sparing in the use of alcohol; temperate. **2.** Not intoxicated. **3.** Having or showing an earnest, dignified disposition; serious or grave. **4.** Plain or subdued; not garish or gay. Said of clothes or colors. **5.** Without frivolity, excess, exaggeration, or speculative imagination: *sober facts.* **6.** Characterized by self-control or sanity; reasonable; rational. —See Synonyms at **serious.** ~*v.* **sobered, -bering, -bers.** —*tr.* To make sober: *a sobering experience.* —*intr.* To become sober. Often used with *up.* [Middle English *sobre,* from Old French, from Latin *sōbrius.*] —**so·ber·ly** *adv.* —**so·ber·ness** *n.*

so·ber·sides (sō′bər-sīdz′) *n., pl.* **sobersides.** *Informal.* A serious, sedate person.

So·bran·je (sə-brän′yə) *n.* The Bulgarian national assembly. [Bulgarian, "assembly."]

so·bri·e·ty (sə-brī′ə-tē) *n.* **1.** Seriousness or gravity, as in manner or approach. **2.** Absence of drunkenness. [Middle English, from Old French *sobrieté* or Latin *sōbrietās,* from *sōbrius,* SOBER.]

so·bri·quet (sō′brĭ-kā′, sō′brĭ-kā′) *n.* Also **sou·bri·quet** (sōō′brĭ-kā′, sōō′brĭ-kā′). **1.** An affectionate or humorous nickname. **2.** An assumed name. [French *sobriquet,* earlier *soubriquet†* (originally "a tap under the chin").]

sob sister *n.* **1.** A journalist, especially a woman, employed as a writer or editor of sob stories. **2.** A sentimental and ineffective person who seeks to do good.

sob story *n.* **1.** A tale of personal hardship or misfortune intended to arouse pity **2.** A maudlin plea given as an explanation or rationalization.

soc., Soc. **1.** socialist. **2.** society.

soc·age (sŏk′ĭj) *n.* Feudal tenure of land by a tenant not a knight, in return for agricultural or other nonmilitary services or for pay-

ment. [Middle English *sokage,* from *soke,* SOKE.] —**soc·ag·er** *n.*

so-called (sō′kôld′) *adj.* Designated thus or known by this term. Often used to imply that the thing or person so designated does not merit the term: *a so-called paradise.*

Usage: So-called is written thus when it precedes a noun and the noun is not enclosed in quotation marks, even when sarcasm is intended: *these so-called friends.* An alternative construction is *these "friends." So called* without a hyphen may be used in still another alternative: *these friends, so called.*

soc·cer (sŏk′ər) *n.* The most common international type of football, in which two teams of 11 players each play on a rectangular field with net goals at either end, maneuvering a round ball by kicking, heading, or by using any part of the body except the arms and hands in attempts to score points by getting the ball into the opposing team's goal. Also *chiefly British* "association football," "football." [Shortening and alteration of *association football.*]

So·chi (sō′chē). A port and health resort of the Soviet Union, in the southwest on the Black Sea.

so·cia·bil·i·ty (sō′shə-bĭl′ə-tē) *n., pl.* **-ties. 1.** The disposition or quality of being sociable. **2.** An instance of being sociable.

so·cia·ble (sō′shə-bəl) *adj.* **1.** Pleasant, friendly, and enjoying good company. **2.** Providing occasion for conversation and conviviality. ~*n.* A **social** *(see).* [French, from Latin *sociābilis,* from *sociāre,* to join, to share, from *socius,* partner.] —**so·cia·ble·ness** *n.* —**so·cia·bly** *adv.*

so·cial (sō′shəl) *adj.* **1. a.** Living or tending to live together in communities. **b.** Of, pertaining to, or characteristic of the activities of and the relations among human beings living in a community. **c.** Of or pertaining to human society and its modes of organization: *social classes.* **2.** Living in an organized group or similar close aggregate: *social insects.* **3.** In Greek and Roman history, involving allies or members of a confederacy. **4.** Of or pertaining to fashionable or polite society: *social graces.* **5.** Fond of the company of others; sociable. **6. a.** Intended for convivial activities. **b.** Engaged in only in convivial circumstances rather than habitually: *social drinking.* **7.** Pertaining to or occupied with matters affecting human welfare: *a social worker.* **8.** Growing thickly in clumps, often covering a large area. Said of plant species. ~*n.* An informal social gathering, as of the members of a club or church congregation. Also called "sociable." [From French or Latin *sociālis,* of companionship, from *socius,* companion, partner.]

social anthropology *n.* The branch of anthropology dealing with communal relationships and social customs and beliefs in human societies, especially primitive societies.

social class. See **class** (sense 3).

social climber *n.* One striving to become a member of a higher social class.

social contract *n.* **1.** A theory of the ideal basis of political rule, advanced by political philosophers such as Hobbes, Locke, and especially Rousseau, holding that government must rest on the consent of the governed, who freely give up certain individual rights and liberties in exchange for the advantages of having an organized government. **2.** A reciprocal system in which individuals or organizations give up certain freedoms in exchange for the benefits a government can bestow.

social credit *n.* **1.** An economic and political theory, formulated by the British engineer C.H. Douglas, holding that every person in a society should be paid dividends from the profits of industry and commerce. **2.** **Social Credit.** A Canadian political party advocating this theory. —**Social Crediter** *n.*

Social Darwinism *n.* The application of some aspects of the Darwinian theory of biological evolution to the history and development of human society.

social democracy. *n.* A political theory advocating a gradual advance toward socialism through democratic means. —**social democrat** *n.*

Social Democratic Party *n. Abbr.* **SDP** A British political party of the center, founded in 1981 chiefly by ex-members of the Labour Party, believing in a mixed economy and strongly committed to Britain's membership in the European Economic Community.

social disease *n.* **1.** Venereal disease. Used euphemistically. **2.** A disease occurring especially among particular social classes predisposed to it by a given set of living or working conditions.

social engineering *n.* The attempt to adjust or manage institutional arrangements or patterns of behavior in a society by applying the principles of social science. —**social engineer** *n.*

social insurance *n.* A national system of insurance, as against sickness, unemployment, or disability, usually financed jointly by employers, employees, and the government.

so·cial·ism (sō′shə-lĭz′əm) *n.* **1.** A social system in which the means of producing and distributing goods are owned collectively and political power is exercised by the whole community. **2.** The theory or practice of those who support such a social system. **3.** In Marxist-Leninist theory, the building, under the dictatorship of the proletariat, of the material base for communism, a transitional stage between capitalism and communism.

so·cial·ist (sō′shə-lĭst) *n.* **1.** An advocate of socialism. **2.** *Abbr.* **soc.** Often **Socialist.** A member of a socialist party. ~*adj.* **1.** Of, promoting, or practicing socialism. **2.** **Socialist.** Of, belonging to, or constituting a socialist party.

so·cial·is·tic (sō′shə-lĭs′tĭk) *adj.* Of, advocating, or tending toward socialism. —**so·cial·is·ti·cal·ly** *adv.*

Socialist Party *n.* Any of certain political parties advocating socialism to be achieved by democratic process; specifically, an American party growing out of an earlier Socialist Labor Party and achieving its greatest electoral support in the presidential election of 1912.

socialist realism *n.* An official Marxist theory of art, strongly held and propagated in the Soviet Union and other Communist countries, holding that the purpose of any art is to promote socialism.

so·cial·ite (sō′shə-līt′) *n.* One prominent in fashionable society.

so·cial·i·ty (sō′shē-ăl′ə-tē) *n., pl.* **-ties. 1. a.** The state or quality of being sociable; sociability. **b.** An instance of sociableness. **2.** The tendency to form communities and societies.

so·cial·ize (sō′shə-līz′) *v.* **-ized, -izing, -izes.** —*tr.* **1.** To fit for companionship with others; train or bring up so as to be well adapted, as in attitude or manners, for life in society. **2.** To place under government or group ownership or control; establish on a socialistic basis. **3.** To convert or adapt to the needs of society. —*intr.* To take part in social relationships or social activities. —**so·cial·i·za·tion** *n.* —**so·cial·iz·er** *n.*

socialized medicine *n.* The provision of medical and hospital care for all at a nominal cost by means of government regulation of health services and subsidies derived from taxation.

so·cial·ly (sō′shə-lē) *adv.* **1.** In a social manner; with regard to social relations: *socially inept.* **2.** With regard to society: *socially important.* **3.** By society: *socially acceptable behavior.*

social mobility *n.* The movement of individuals from one social class to another, especially from a lower class to a higher one.

social psychology *n.* The branch of psychology concerned with the relationships among individuals and groups.

social realism *n. Sometimes* **Social Realism.** A movement in painting, literature, and other arts rejecting romanticism and concentrating on the realistic portrayal of contemporary political, economic, and social conditions.

social register *n.* A directory listing persons of social prominence in the community.

social science *n.* **1.** The study of society and of individual relationships in and to society, generally regarded as including sociology, psychology, anthropology, economics, political science, and history. **2.** Any of these disciplines. —**social scientist** *n.*

social security *n.* **1.** The provision by the government of financial and other assistance to those in need, such as the unemployed, the elderly, and the disabled. **2.** The economic assistance provided by social security: *living on social security.*

social service *n.* **1. a.** *Often* **social services.** Services and facilities that are government-funded and usually controlled by national or local government, such as health care, education, and social work. **b.** The staff of these services and facilities. **2.** Social work.

social studies *pl.n.* A course of study, often taught in schools, that includes sociology, geography, history, and politics.

social work *n.* The provision of welfare work, assistance, and advice to those in need, as the poor, the aged, and those with domestic and emotional problems. —**social worker** *n.*

so·ci·e·tal (sə-sī′ə-təl) *adj.* Of or pertaining to the structure, organization, or functioning of society. —**so·ci·e·tal·ly** *adv.*

so·ci·e·ty (sə-sī′ə-tē) *n., pl.* **-ties.** *Abbr.* **s., S., soc., Soc. 1. a.** The totality of social relationships among human beings. **b.** A group of human beings broadly distinguished from other groups by mutual interests, participation in characteristic relationships, shared institutions, and a common culture. **c.** The institutions and culture of a distinct self-perpetuating group. **2. a.** The rich, privileged, and fashionable social class. **b.** A particular sector of a community or population marked by shared customs and aspirations: *polite society; middle-class society.* **3. a.** Companionship; company. **b.** Participation in social or communal activity: *He doesn't care much for society.* **4.** *Biology.* A colony or community of organisms, usually of the same species. **5.** An organization of people associated on the basis of common aims, beliefs, interests, or occupations.

~*adj.* Of, for, or characteristic of fashionable society: *a society ball.* [From Old French *societe,* from Latin *societās* (stem *societāt-*), fellowship, union, society, from *socius,* companion.]

So·ci·e·ty Islands (sə-sī′ə-tē) Group of volcanic and coral islands in the central South Pacific, part of French Polynesia. They comprise the Windward Islands, including Tahiti and the Leeward Islands.

Society of Friends *n.* A Christian sect founded in about 1650 in England by George Fox. It rejects ritual, formal sacraments, a formal creed, a priesthood, and violence. Also known informally as "Quakers."

Society of Jesus *n. Abbr.* **S.J.** The Jesuits (*see*).

So·cin·i·an (sō-sĭn′ē-ən) *n.* An adherent of a sect holding unitarian views, including denial of the divinity of Jesus. [New Latin *Socinianus,* after Laelius and Faustus *Socinus,* 18th-century Italian theologians.] —**So·cin·i·an** *adj.* —**So·cin·i·an·ism** *n.*

socio– *prefix.* Indicates: **1.** Society; for example, **sociometry.** **2.** Social; for example, **socioeconomic.** [From French, from Latin *socius,* companion.]

so·ci·o·bi·ol·o·gy (sō′sē-ō-bī-ŏl′ə-jē, sō′shē-) *n.* The study of the social organization of animal species and its relationship to human social evolution. —**so·ci·o·bi·o·log·i·cal** (sō′sē-ō-bī′ə-lŏj′ĭ-kəl, sō′shē-) *adj.* —**so·ci·o·bi·o·log·i·cal·ly** *adv.* —**so·ci·o·bi·ol·o·gist** (sō′sē-ō-bī-ŏl′ə-jĭst, sō′shē-) *n.*

so·ci·o·ec·o·nom·ic (sō′sē-ō-ĕk′ə-nŏm′ĭk, -ē′kə-nŏm′ĭk, sō′shē-) *adj.* Of, based on, or influenced by a combination of social and economic considerations.

THE OFFICIAL AESTHETICS OF THE SOVIET UNION

In Communist countries literature and the arts serve the state's ideals

By 1932 the Russian Revolution was 15 years old, and dictator Joseph Stalin (1879–1953) was unhappy with his country's artists and writers. Many of them were using forms of expression that baffled the masses. The remedy came in 1934, blessed by the brand-new Union of Soviet Writers. Called socialist realism, it has dominated Soviet arts and literature ever since.

Realism was taken to mean an objective rendering of life. However, objectivity was suspended when portraying life and aspirations that fit Marxist ideals.

Central to socialist realism is the "positive hero," who single-mindedly overcomes danger and personal misfortune to make the ideals of the Revolution come true. Similar aesthetic doctrines prevail in Soviet-bloc nations and in Communist China, where Mao Zedong (1893–1976) proclaimed that "Revolutionary art and literature should create all kinds of characters on the basis of actual life and help the masses to push history forward."

Socialist realism insists that artists not only express the aims and ideals of the people as defined by Marxism, but also create in forms that are easily understood by the masses. Those two criteria are evident in this 1937 painting by Sergei V. Gerasimov of a picnic at a collective farm in the Soviet Union. The same standards apply to writing, film, and all creative expression.

so·ci·o·lin·guis·tics (sō′sē-ō-lĭng-gwĭs′tĭks, sō′shē-) *n. Used with a singular verb.* The study of language in the context of its use in a particular society and of the social and cultural factors that influence it. —**so·ci·o·lin·guis·tic** *adj.*

so·ci·ol·o·gy (sō′sē-ŏl′ə-jē, sō′shē-) *n.* The study of human social behavior; especially, the study of the origins, organization, institutions, and development of human society. [French *sociologie* : SOCIO- + -LOGY.] —**so·ci·o·log·ic** (sō′sē-ə-lŏj′ĭk, sō′shē-), **so·ci·o·log·i·cal** *adj.* —**so·ci·o·log·i·cal·ly** *adv.* —**so·ci·ol·o·gist** (sō′sē-ŏl′ə-jĭst, sō′shē-) *n.*

so·ci·om·e·try (sō′sē-ŏm′ə-trē, sō′shē-) *n.* The quantitative study of relationships between individuals in groups and populations; especially, the study and measurement of preferences.

so·ci·o·po·lit·i·cal (sō′sē-ō-pə-lĭt′ĭ-kəl, sō′shē-) *adj.* Of, based on, or influenced by a combination of social and political considerations.

so·ci·o·re·li·gious (sō′sē-ō-rĭ-lĭj′əs, sō′shē-) *adj.* Both social and religious.

sock¹ (sŏk) *n., pl.* **socks** (for all senses) or **sox** (for sense 1). **1.** A short stocking reaching a point between the ankle and the knee. **2. a.** A light shoe worn by comic actors in ancient Greek and Roman plays. Compare **buskin. b.** Comic drama; comedy. **3.** A **windsock** (*see*).

~*tr.v.* **socked, socking, socks.** To provide with socks. —**sock away.** *Informal.* To put aside (money); save. —**sock in.** To close to air traffic: *fog that socked in the airport.* [Middle English *socke,* Old English *socc,* a kind of light shoe, from Latin *soccus,* probably from Greek *sukkhos†.*]

sock² *v.* **socked, socking, socks.** *Slang.* —*tr.* To hit or strike forcefully; punch. —*intr.* To deliver a blow. —**sock it to someone.** *Slang.* **1.** To impress (someone) forcefully. **2.** To attack vigorously.

~*n. Slang.* A hard blow or punch. [18th century : origin obscure.]

sock·dol·a·ger, sock·dol·o·ger (sŏk-dŏl′ə-jər) *n. Slang.* **1.** A conclusive blow or remark. **2.** Something outstanding. [Perhaps a fanciful blend of SOCK (blow) and DOXOLOGY.]

sock·et (sŏk′ĭt) *n.* **1.** An opening or cavity that acts as the receptacle for an inserted part: *a light-bulb socket.* **2.** Any of various devices

into which something is inserted, especially: **a.** An electrical power point in which a plug or light bulb fits. **b.** A recessed piece of metal used, in conjunction with a bar or wrench, to turn bolts or nuts. **3. a.** The hollow part of a joint that receives the end of a bone. **b.** A hollow or concavity into which a part, such as the eye, fits.
~*tr.v.* **socketed, -eting, -ets.** To furnish with or insert into a socket. [Middle English *soket,* spearhead shaped like a plowshare, socket, from Norman French *soket,* diminutive of Old French *soc,* plowshare, probably of Celtic origin.]

sock·eye salmon (sŏk′ī′) *n.* A salmon, *Oncorhynchus nerka,* of northern Pacific coastal waters. Also called "red salmon." [By folk etymology from Salish *sukkegh.*]

so·cle (sō′kəl) *n.* A plain low block or plinth serving as a pedestal, as for a vase or a column, or supporting a wall. [French *socle,* from Italian *zoccolo,* "wooden shoe," from Latin *socculus,* diminutive of *soccus,* a light shoe. See sock (stocking).]

soc·man (sŏk′mən) *n., pl.* **-men** (-mĭn). Also **soke·man** (sōk′-), *pl.* **-men.** A tenant holding land under the system of socage. [Medieval Latin *sokemannus* : Old English *sōcn,* SOKE + *mann,* MAN.]

Soc·ra·tes (sŏk′rə-tēz′) (c. 469–399 B.C.). Greek philosopher. He initiated a question-and-answer method of teaching as a means of achieving self-knowledge. He argued that virtue is knowledge, vice is ignorance, and no one wittingly does wrong. His stance led to his being charged with atheism and corrupting the minds of youth. He was sentenced to death and drank hemlock, dying in the presence of his pupils. His theories have survived through the writings of Plato, his most important pupil.

So·crat·ic (sō-krăt′ĭk) *adj.* Also **So·crat·i·cal** (-ĭ-kəl). Of, pertaining to, or characteristic of Socrates or his philosophical methods of instruction and argument.
~*n.* An adherent of the teachings of Socrates. —**So·crat·i·cal·ly** *adv.* —**So·crat·i·cism** (sō-krăt′ə-sĭz′əm) *n.*

Socratic irony *n.* Pretended ignorance, used by Socrates as a method of instruction or to reveal inconsistencies in the arguments of an opponent. Also called "irony."

Socratic method *n.* A philosophical procedure used by Socrates as a form of instruction, using repeated and pointed questioning to elicit truths assumed to be innate in all rational beings.

sod (sŏd) *n.* **1.** A section of grass-covered surface soil held together by matted roots; turf. **2.** The ground, especially when covered with grass.
~*tr.v.* **sodded, sodding, sods.** To cover with sod. [Middle English *sod(de),* from Middle Low German or Middle Dutch *sode,* akin to Old Frisian *sāda†.*]

so·da (sō′də) *n.* **1. a.** Any of various forms of sodium carbonate, especially **washing soda** (see). **b.** Loosely, chemically combined sodium. **2. a.** **Soda water** (see). **b.** Any carbonated soft drink; pop. **3.** A beverage made from soda water, ice cream, and sometimes flavoring. **4.** In faro, the card turned face up at the beginning of the game. [Medieval Latin *soda†,* perhaps from *sodānum,* glasswort (a plant used to treat headaches), from Arabic *sudā,* headache, from *sada'a,* to split.]

soda ash *n.* Crude anhydrous **sodium carbonate** (see), used especially as an industrial chemical.

soda biscuit *n.* **1.** A breadlike biscuit leavened with baking soda. **2.** A soda cracker.

soda bread *n.* Bread made with baking soda, cream of tartar, and soured milk.

soda cracker *n.* A thin, usually square cracker leavened slightly with baking soda and sometimes salted.

soda fountain *n.* **1.** An apparatus with faucets for dispensing soda water and other soft drinks. **2.** A counter serving soft drinks, ice-cream dishes, and other snacks.

soda jerk *n. Slang.* One who works at a soda fountain. [Short for *soda jerker.*]

soda lime *n.* A mixture of calcium oxide and sodium or potassium hydroxide, used as a drying agent and carbon dioxide absorbent.

so·da·list (sō′də-lĭst, sō-dăl′ĭst) *n.* A member of a sodality.

so·da·lite (sō′də-līt′) *n.* A blue-white vitreous mineral, essentially 3(NaAlSiO₄)·NaCl, found in igneous rocks.

so·dal·i·ty (sō-dăl′ə-tē) *n., pl.* **-ties.** **1.** A society or association; especially, in the Roman Catholic Church, a devotional or charitable society. **2.** Brotherhood; fellowship. [From Latin *sodālitās,* fellowship, brotherhood, from *sodālis,* fellow, intimate.]

soda niter *n. Chemistry.* **Sodium nitrate** (see).

soda pop *n. Informal.* A carbonated soft drink; pop.

soda water *n.* Effervescent water charged under pressure with purified carbon dioxide gas, used as a beverage or mixer. Also called "carbonated water," "soda."

sod·den (sŏd′n) *adj.* **1.** Thoroughly soaked; saturated. **2.** Soggy and heavy from improper cooking; doughy. **3.** Bloated and dulled, especially from overindulgence in drink. **4.** *Archaic.* Boiled.
~*v.* **soddened, -dening, -dens.** —*tr.* To make sodden; saturate. —*intr.* To become sodden. [Middle English, Old English *soden,* from the past participle of *sethen, sēothan,* to SEETHE.] —**sod·den·ly** *adv.* —**sod·den·ness** *n.*

Sod·dy (sŏd′ē), **Frederick** (1877–1956). British chemist and physicist. With Lord Rutherford he put forward the theory of atomic disintegration. His discovery that certain elements possessing the same chemical properties differed in their nuclear mass *(Soddy's law)* laid the foundation of the isotope theory. He was awarded a Nobel Prize for his work on radioactivity in 1921.

so·di·um (sō′dē-əm) *n. Symbol* **Na** A soft, light, extremely malleable silver-white metallic element that reacts explosively with water. It is naturally abundant in combined forms, especially in common salt, and is present in a wide variety of industrially important compounds. Atomic number 11, atomic weight 22.99, melting point 97.8°C, boiling point 892°C, specific gravity 0.968, valence 1. [New Latin : SOD(A) + -IUM.]

sodium ammonium phosphate *n.* A colorless, odorless crystalline compound, NaNH₄HPO₄·4H₂O, used as an analytical reagent.

sodium benzoate *n.* The sodium salt of benzoic acid, C₆H₅COONa, used as a food preservative, antiseptic, and intermediate in dye manufacture, and in the production of pharmaceuticals. Also called "benzoate of soda."

sodium bicarbonate *n.* A white crystalline compound, NaHCO₃, with a slightly alkaline taste, used in making effervescent salts and beverages, artificial mineral water, baking soda, pharmaceuticals, and in fire extinguishers. Also called "baking soda," "bicarbonate of soda," and informally "bicarb."

sodium borate *n.* A crystalline compound, Na₂B₄O₇·10H₂O, used in the manufacture of glass, detergents, and pharmaceuticals. Also called "borax."

sodium carbonate *n.* A compound used in the manufacture of sodium bicarbonate, sodium nitrate, glass, ceramics, detergents, and soap, chiefly used as a white powder (Na₂CO₃, sal soda) or a white crystalline decahydrate (Na₂CO₃·IOH₂O, washing soda).

sodium chlorate *n.* A colorless crystalline compound, NaClO₃, used as a bleaching and oxidizing agent and in explosives.

sodium chloride *n.* A colorless crystalline compound, NaCl, used in the manufacture of chemicals and as a food preservative and seasoning. Also called "common salt," "salt."

sodium cyanide *n.* A poisonous white crystalline compound, NaCN, used in extracting gold and silver from ores and in dye manufacture.

sodium cyclamate *n.* A soluble white crystalline powder, C₆H₁₁NHSO₃Na, 30 times as sweet as sugar and formerly a major constituent of low-calorie sweetening agents.

sodium dichromate *n.* A red-orange crystalline compound, Na₂Cr₂O₇·2H₂O, used as an oxidizing agent.

sodium glutamate *n.* **Monosodium glutamate** (see).

sodium hydrosulfite *n.* A yellowish powder, (NAO)₂S₂O₄·2H₂O, used as a bleaching and reducing agent. Also called "hydrosulfite," "sodium hyposulfite," "sodium dithionite."

sodium hydroxide *n.* A strongly alkaline compound, NaOH, used in the manufacture of chemicals and soaps and in petroleum refining. Also called "caustic soda," "lye."

sodium hypochlorite *n.* An unstable salt, NaOCl, usually stored in solution and used as a fungicide and an oxidizing bleach.

sodium hyposulfite *n.* **1. Sodium hydrosulfite** (see). **2. Sodium thiosulfate** (see).

sodium nitrate *n.* A white crystalline compound, NaNO₃, used in solid rocket propellants and in the manufacture of explosives and tobacco. Also called "niter," "saltpeter," "soda niter," "Chile saltpeter," "caliche."

sodium pen·to·bar·bi·tal (pĕn′tə-bär′bə-tôl′, -tōl′) *n.* **Pentobarbital sodium** (see).

sodium pen·to·thal (pĕn′tə-thôl′, -thōl′) *n. Chemistry.* **Thiopental sodium** (see).

sodium perborate *n.* A white odorless crystalline compound, NaBO₂·H₂O₂·3H₂O, used as a mild alkaline oxidizing agent in dentifrices, as a deodorant, and as an industrial reagent.

sodium peroxide *n.* A yellowish-white powder, Na₂O₂, employed industrially as an oxidizing and bleaching agent and medically as a germicide, antiseptic, and disinfectant.

sodium phosphate *n.* Any of the three sodium salts of phosphoric acid, NaH₂PO₄, Na₂HPO₄, and Na₃PO₄, widely used in industry, pharmaceutical manufacturing, medicine, and chemistry.

sodium propionate *n.* A clear crystalline compound, C₂H₅COONa, capable of retarding the growth of molds and bacteria and used to prevent food spoilage.

sodium silicate *n.* Any of various water-soluble silicate glass compounds used as a preservative for eggs, in plaster and cement, and in various purification and refining processes. Also called "liquid glass," "soluble glass," "water glass."

sodium sulfate *n.* A white crystalline compound, Na₂SO₄, used to manufacture paper, glass, dyes, and pharmaceuticals.

sodium sulfide *n.* A hygroscopic yellow compound, Na₂S, used as a metal ore reagent and in photography, engraving, and printing.

sodium sulfite *n.* A white crystalline or powdered compound, Na₂SO₃, used in preserving foods, silvering mirrors, developing photographs, and making dyes.

sodium thiosulfate *n.* A white crystalline compound, Na₂S₂O₃·5H₂O, used as a photographic fixing agent and as a bleach. Also called "hypo," "hyposulfite," "sodium hyposulfite."

so·di·um-va·por lamp (sō′dē-əm-vā′pər) *n.* An electric lamp containing a small amount of sodium and neon gas, used in generating yellow light for lighting streets and highways.

Sod·om¹ (sŏd′əm). City of ancient Palestine, possibly located south of the Dead Sea, which, with nearby Gomorrah, was destroyed by "brimstone and fire from the Lord" (Genesis 19:24).

Sodom², **sodom** *n.* A place of exceptional wickedness or depravity. [After SODOM (city).]

sod·om·ite (sŏd′ə-mīt′) *n.* A person who practices sodomy. [Middle English, from Old French, from Late Latin, from Greek *Sodomitēs,* inhabitant of SODOM.]

Sodomite *n.* An inhabitant of Sodom.

sod·om·ize (sŏd′ə-mīz′) *tr.v.* **-ized, -izing, -izes.** To practice sodomy on.

sod·o·my (sŏd′ə-mē) *n.* **1.** Anal copulation of one male with another. **2.** Anal or oral copulation with a member of the opposite sex. **3.** Copulation with an animal. [Middle English, from Medieval Latin *sodomia,* from Late Latin *peccatum sodomiticum,* the sin of SODOM, (city).]

so·ev·er (sō-ĕv′ər) *adv.* At all; in any way. Used to generalize or emphasize a word or phrase, usually in combination, as with *how, what, when,* or *where:* "Space to breathe, how short soever" (Ben Jonson). [SO + EVER.]

so·fa (sō′fə) *n.* A long upholstered seat with a back and arms. [Originally a raised dais with carpets and cushions, ultimately from Arabic *suffah;* perhaps akin to Hebrew *sapāh,* carpet, divan.]

sofa bed *n.* A sofa whose seat unfolds to form a bed.

so·far (sō′fär′) *n.* A system for determining a position at sea, especially that of lost survivors, by the sound ranging of the explosion of an underwater charge by three widely separated shore stations. [*Sound fixing and ranging.*]

sof·fi·o·ne (sŏf′ē-ō′nĕ, -nä, sō′fē-) *n., pl.* **soffioni** (-nē). A jet of steam or other vapor that issues from the ground in a volcanic region. [Italian, augmentative form of *soffio,* a puff, from *soffiare,* to blow, from Latin *sufflare,* to blow upon.]

sof·fit (sŏf′ĭt) *n.* The underside of a structural component, such as a beam, arch, staircase, or cornice. [French *soffite,* from Italian *soffito, soffitta,* from Vulgar Latin *suffīctus* (unattested), from Latin *suffīxus,* "something fastened beneath." See **suffix**.]

So·fi·a (sō′fē-ə, sō-fē′ə). Bulgarian **So·fi·ya** (sō′fē-yä). Capital of Bulgaria, in the country's western mountains. It is Bulgaria's chief industrial, communications, cultural, and commercial center. Its monuments include the ruined 7th-century church of St. Sofia.

S. of Sol. Song of Solomon (Old Testament).

soft (sôft, sŏft) *adj.* **softer, softest. 1. a.** Offering little resistance; easily molded, cut, or worked; malleable; not hard. **b.** Yielding readily to pressure or weight; not firm. **c.** Marked by wet or sodden ground: *The going was soft.* **2.** Marked by or done with relatively little force; light: *a soft tap with a hammer.* **3. a.** Smooth or fine to the touch; not harsh or coarse. **b.** Lacking sharpness or acidity; bland; mellow. **4.** Not loud or strident; low-toned. **5.** Not brilliant or glaring; subdued: *soft lights.* **6.** Not sharply drawn or delineated: *soft contours.* **7.** Gentle; agreeable; mild; balmy: *soft weather; a soft breeze.* **8.** Having or showing a mild, gentle, or sympathetic disposition, as: **a.** Not stern or rigorous; lenient: *too soft on offenders.* **b.** Adopting a moderate rather than an aggressive approach or position: *a soft socialist.* **c.** Easily moved; compassionate. **d.** Easily swayed; yielding; compliant. **9. a.** Tender; affectionate: *soft glances.* **b.** Amorously inclined; infatuated. Used with *on.* **10. a.** Lacking powers of endurance or exertion, especially as a result of prolonged ease or self-indulgence; weak; not robust. **b.** Out of condition; flabby. **11.** *Informal.* Simple; feeble-minded: *soft in the head.* **12.** *Military.* Lacking protection against bombs, missiles, or rockets: *a soft target.* **13.** Soft-core: *a soft pornography.* **14.** *Finance.* **a.** Designating a loan issued on very favorable terms. **b.** Fluctuating and tending to decline; not firm. Said of prices on a market. **c.** Not backed by bullion or by government credit and so not readily exchangeable for other currencies. Said of a currency. **15.** Having low dissolved mineral content. Said of water. **16. a.** Sibilant rather than guttural, as *c* in *certain* and *g* in *gem.* **b.** Voiced and weakly articulated: *a soft consonant.* **c.** Palatalized, as certain consonants in Slavic languages are. **17.** *Physics.* **a.** Of low penetrating power. Said of radiation. **b.** Having a relatively high pressure. Said of a vacuum. **18.** *Informal.* Easy: *a soft job.* —*n.* A soft object or part. —*adv.* In a soft manner; gently. [Middle English *soft(e),* agreeable, pleasant, Old English *sōfte, sēfte,* from Germanic *samfti-* (unattested).] —**soft′ly** *adv.* —**soft′ness** *n.*

sof·ta (sôf′tə, sŏf′-) *n.* A Muslim student of theology and religious law. [Turkish, from Persian *sōkhta,* "aflame, burning" (devoted to learning).]

soft·ball (sôft′bôl′, sŏft′-) *n.* **1.** A variation of baseball played on a smaller diamond with a larger, softer ball that is pitched underhand. **2.** The ball used.

soft-boiled (sôft′boild′, sŏft′-) *adj.* **1.** Boiled in the shell to a soft consistency. Said of an egg. **2.** *Informal.* Soft-hearted; lenient.

soft clam *n.* The soft-shell clam *(see).*

soft coal *n.* Bituminous coal *(see).*

soft-core (sôft′kôr′, -kōr′, sŏft′-) *adj.* Intended to be sexually titillating but not explicit; not hard-core: *soft-core pornography.*

soft·cov·er (sôft′kŭv′ər, sŏft′-) *n.* **1.** A paperback. **2.** A paperback format. Also used adjectively: *a softcover edition.*

soft drink *n.* A nonalcoholic, usually carbonated drink.

soft drug *n.* A drug, such as marijuana, that is considered to be less damaging to the health than a hard drug.

soft·en (sô′fən, sŏf′ən) *v.* **-ened, -ening, -ens.** —*tr.* To make less severe or softer. —*intr.* To become soft or softer. —**soften up. 1.** To weaken the defenses and reduce the morale of (an enemy), as by bombardment prior to full-scale attack. **2.** To cajole, flatter, or otherwise reduce the resistance of (a potential customer, for example). —**soft′en·er** *n.*

soft-finned (sôft′fĭnd′, sŏft′-) *adj. Zoology.* Having fins supported by flexible cartilaginous rays. Compare **spiny-finned.**

soft focus *n.* A slightly blurred photographic effect, usually obtained by setting a lens slightly out of focus.

soft fruit *n. Chiefly British.* Soft, stoneless fruit such as raspberries, blackberries, and strawberries.

soft goods *pl.n.* See **dry goods** (sense 2).

soft grass *n.* A downy grass, *Holcus mollis,* found on acid soils.

soft hail *n.* A form of hail, **graupel** *(see).*

soft·head (sôft′hĕd′, sŏft′-) *n.* A foolish or feeble-minded person; a simpleton.

soft·head·ed (sôft′hĕd′ĭd, sŏft′-) *adj.* Lacking judgment, realism, or firmness: *a softheaded concession.* —**soft·head·ed·ly** *adv.*

soft·heart·ed (sôft′här′tĭd, sŏft′-) *adj.* Easily moved; tender; merciful. —**soft·heart·ed·ly** *adv.* —**soft·heart·ed·ness** *n.*

soft landing *n.* The landing of a space vehicle on a celestial body in such a way as to prevent damage or destruction.

soft-lin·er (sôft′lī′nər, sŏft′-) *n.* One that takes a moderate or flexible position, especially on a political issue.

soft-mouthed shark (sôft′mouthd′, sŏft′-) *n.* A **hound shark** *(see).*

soft palate *n.* The movable fold, consisting of muscular fibers enclosed in mucous membrane, that is suspended from the rear of the hard palate and closes off the nasal cavity from the oral cavity during swallowing or sucking.

soft paste, soft-paste (sôft′pāst′, sŏft′-) *n.* Any of various ceramics containing frit or refined clay.

soft pedal *n.* A pedal on a piano operating a mechanism that softens or mutes the sound.

soft-ped·al (sôft′pĕd′l, sŏft′-) *tr.v.* **-aled, -aling, -als** or chiefly British **-alled, -alling, -als. 1.** To soften or mute the tone of (a piano) by depressing the soft pedal. **2.** *Informal.* To make less emphatic or obvious; moderate; play down.

soft rock *n.* A style of rock'n'roll characterized by the predominance of melody and minimal use of electronic modulations.

soft roe *n.* The spermatozoa or testes of a fish; milt.

soft rot *n.* Any of various bacterial plant diseases characterized by watery disintegration of the tissues. Compare **dry rot.**

soft sciences *pl.n. Informal.* The social sciences as opposed to the physical sciences.

soft sell *n. Informal.* A subtly persuasive, unaggressive method of selling or advertising. Compare **hard sell.**

soft-shell (sôft′shĕl′, sŏft′-) *adj.* Also **soft-shelled** (-shĕld′). Having a soft, brittle, or unhardened shell.

soft-shell clam *n.* A common edible clam, *Mya arenaria,* having a thin, elongated shell. Also called "gaper," "soft clam."

soft-shell crab *n.* A marine crab before its shell has hardened after molting.

soft-shelled turtle *n.* Any of various freshwater turtles of the family Trionychidae, having a flat carapace covered with leathery skin.

soft-shoe (sôft′shōō′, sŏft′-) *adj.* Of or pertaining to a type of tap dancing performed without metal taps on the shoes.

soft shoulder *n.* A border of soft earth or grass running along the edge of a road.

soft soap *n.* **1.** A fluid or semifluid soap. **2. Green soap** *(see).* **3.** *Informal.* Flattery; cajolery.

soft-soap (sôft′sōp′, sŏft′-) *tr.v.* **-soaped, -soaping, -soaps.** *Informal.* To cajole or flatter. —**soft-soap′er** *n.*

soft sore *n.* A chancroid *(see).*

soft-spo·ken (sôft′spō′kən, sŏft′-) *adj.* **1.** Speaking with a soft or gentle voice. **2.** Smooth; suave; ingratiating.

soft spot *n.* **1.** A place in one's heart or affections; a tender or sentimental feeling. **2.** In the skull of an infant, either of the points of juncture of the sagittal and lambdoid or the sagittal, coronal, and frontal sutures; the **fontanelle** *(see).*

soft touch *n. Informal.* A person who is easily persuaded to donate or lend money.

soft·ware (sôft′wâr′, sŏft′-) *n.* **1.** Written or printed data, such as programs, routines, and symbolic languages, essential to the operation of computers. **2.** Documents containing information on the operation and maintenance of computers, such as manuals, circuit diagrams, and flow charts. Compare **hardware, firmware.** [Coined after HARDWARE ("the machines").]

soft water *n.* Water containing little or no dissolved salts of calcium or magnesium, especially water containing less than 85.5 parts per million of calcium carbonate. Compare **hard water.**

soft·wood (sôft′wŏŏd′, sŏft′-) *n.* **1.** The wood of a coniferous tree. **2.** A coniferous tree. Compare **hardwood.**

soft·y (sôf′tē, sŏf′-) *n., pl.* **-ies.** *Informal.* A weak, effeminate, or sentimental person.

Sog·di·an (sŏg′dē-ən) *n.* **1.** A member of an ancient Iranian people who inhabited Sogdiana. **2.** Their extinct Iranian language. —**Sog·di·an** *adj.*

Sog·di·a·na (sŏg′dē-ā′nə). An ancient region of central Asia and a province of the Persian Empire.

sog·gy (sŏg′ē) *adj.* **-gier, -giest. 1.** Saturated or sodden with moisture; soaked. **2.** Lacking spirit; dull. **3.** Humid; sultry. [From dialectal *sog†,* a marsh.] —**sog·gi·ly** *adv.* —**sog·gi·ness** *n.*

Sog·ne Fjord (sông′nə). The longest, 180 kilometers (112 miles), and deepest, to 1,220 meters (to 4,081 feet), of the Norwegian fjords, on the west coast, north of Bergen.

So·ho¹ (sō′hō). District of central London, England, in the City of Westminster. A haunt of foreign émigrés in the 17th century, Soho is known today for its restaurants, theaters, cinemas, nightclubs, and sex shops.

Soho². District of southwestern New York City, south of Houston

soil

THE THIN FERTILE LAYER ABOVE THE BEDROCK
How living things and weathering create soil from rock

The layer of earth that covers much of the world's land surface began as rock. The exposed surface of this has been weathered into increasingly fine particles of rubble. The process exposes minerals that react with chemicals in the atmosphere and in the bodies of dead organisms, such as insects. The reactions transform the rubble into a detritus that is fertile enough to be colonized by living organisms and that is recognized as soil.

Different soils have different structures but a highly productive agricultural or garden soil will have four main layers, called Horizons. A-Horizon is the topsoil, which should be rich in the humus formed from decayed plant material,

such as fallen leaves and deciduous plants. This topsoil is alive with microorganisms that break down dead plant and animal matter and also with soil invertebrates—beetles and mites feeding upon the microorganisms. Vertebrates, such as lizards, mice, and moles, also stir up the soil.

B-Horizon, which is the coarser layer below the rich 150 millimeters (6 inches) or so of topsoil, is also permeated and enriched by the excrement of burrowing worms and centipedes. This may be 600-900 millimeters (2-3 feet) thick. The subsoil below it—C-Horizon—usually holds the water table; a permanently saturated soil layer that is largely infertile. Beneath this is the solid bedrock of D-Horizon.

Arrow indicates direction and depth of the leaching of soil chemicals by the action of water

A-Horizon Dark-colored layer of decaying leaves, twigs, and animal remains mixed with weathered rock particles, such as quartz and clay. In it there is intense biological activity, ranging from insects and worms to rodents and plant roots. Most soluble chemicals have been leached or washed out by rainwater into lower layers

B-Horizon Chiefly fine particles of rock but little organic matter, dead or alive. In regions of low rainfall this layer will contain some soluble chemicals. Where rainfall is high, however, soluble materials are washed down into the layer below. In tropical zones even the silica is dissolved out, allowing remaining iron oxides to give the soil a reddish-brown color

C-Horizon The subsoil lying below the soil proper (A- and B-horizons). This layer consists of broken and partly decayed fragments from the solid rock layer lying below it, together with clay particles and soluble materials washed down from layers above

D-Horizon Solid rock, known as the bedrock. The bedrock may be igneous, sedimentary, or metamorphic

Street, noted for its galleries, cafés, and artists' lofts.
soi·di·sant (swä′dē-zäN′) *adj.* Self-styled; so-called: *a soi-disant magician.* [French.]
soi·gné, soi·gnée (swän-yā′) *adj.* **1.** Showing sophisticated elegance; fashionable: *a soigné little café.* **2.** Well-groomed; polished. [French, from the past participle of *soigner*, to take care of, from Medieval Latin *soniare.*]
soil¹ (soil) *n.* **1.** The top layer of the earth's surface, suitable for the growth of plant life. **2.** A particular kind of earth or ground: *sandy soil.* **3.** Country; territory; region: *native soil.* **4.** Land, usually with agricultural or rural connotations: *a man of the soil.* **5.** A place or condition favorable to growth; breeding ground. [Middle English, from Norman French, from Latin *solium*, seat (influenced in meaning by *solum*, base, ground).]
soil² *v.* **soiled, soiling, soils.** —*tr.* **1.** To make dirty, particularly on the surface; begrime; smudge. **2.** To disgrace; tarnish: *It soiled his reputation.* **3.** To pollute with sin; defile. —*intr.* To become dirty, stained, or tarnished.

~*n.* **1. a.** The state of being soiled. **b.** A stain or discoloration caused by dirt and grime. **2.** Moral stain. **3.** Filth, sewage, or refuse matter. **4.** Manure, especially human feces, used as fertilizer. [Middle English *soilen*, from Old French *souiller, suill(i)er*, from Vulgar Latin *suculāre* (unattested), from Latin *suculus, sucula*, diminutives of *sūs*, pig.]
soil³ *tr.v.* **soiled, soiling, soils. 1.** To feed (livestock) with soilage. **2.** To purge (livestock) by feeding with green food. [Perhaps from obsolete *soil*, to manure, from SOIL (manure).]
soil·age (soi′lĭj) *n.* Green crops cut for feeding penned livestock.
soil pipe *n.* A drain pipe that carries off waste from a plumbing fixture, especially a toilet.
soil profile *n.* See profile (sense 5b).
soil·ure (soil′yər) *n.* **1.** Soiling or the condition of being soiled. **2.** A blot, stain, or smudge.
soi·ree, soi·rée (swä-rā′) *n.* A party of other social gathering held in the evening, often one featuring a musical or literary recital. [French *soirée*, from *soir*, evening, from Latin *sērum*, late hour, neuter of *sērus*, late.]
Sois·sons (swä-sôN′). A city of France, in the north on the Aisne River. It was almost destroyed by German bombardment in World War I.
so·journ (sō′jûrn′, sō-jûrn′) *intr.v.* **-journed, -journing, -journs.** To stay for a time; reside temporarily.
~*n.* A temporary stay; a brief residence. [Middle English *sojournen*, from Old French *sojorner*, from Vulgar Latin *subdiurnāre* (unattested) : Latin *sub-*, during, under + Late Latin *diurnum*, day, from Latin *diurnus*, daily, from *diēs*, day.] —**so·journ·er** *n.*
soke (sōk) *n.* **1.** In early English law, the right of local jurisdiction, generally one of the feudal rights of lordship. **2.** The district over which such jurisdiction was exercised. [Middle English, from Medieval Latin *sōca*, from Old English *sōcn*, inquiry, right of local jurisdiction, from Germanic *sōkniz* (unattested), akin to SEEK.]
sokeman. Variant of socman.
sol¹ (sōl) *n.* Also **so** (sō). *Music.* **1.** The syllable used to represent the fifth tone of a diatonic scale. **2.** The tone G. [Middle English, from Medieval Latin, from *solve*, "purge" (imperative), occurring in a hymn to Saint John the Baptist (see gamut), from Latin, from *solvere*, to loosen, SOLVE.]
sol² (sōl) *n.* **1.** A former monetary unit of France, equal to 12 deniers. **2.** An old French coin of this value. [Middle English, from Old French, from Latin *solidus*, SOLIDUS.]
sol³ (sōl) *n., pl.* **soles** (sō′lās). **1.** The basic monetary unit of Peru, equal to 100 centavos. See feature at currency. **2.** A coin or note worth one sol. [Spanish, "sun" (depicted on the coin), from Latin *sōl.*]
sol⁴ (sôl, sōl) *n. Chemistry.* A colloidal dispersion of a solid in a liquid medium. [Short for HYDROSOL.]
Sol (sōl, sôl) *n.* The sun personified. [Middle English, from Latin *sōl.*]
sol. solicitor.
so·la. **1.** Feminine of solus. **2.** A plural of solum.
sol·ace (sōl′ĭs) *n.* Also **sol·ace·ment** (-mənt). **1.** Comfort in sorrow, misfortune, or distress; consolation. **2.** That which furnishes comfort or consolation.
~*tr.v.* **solaced, -acing, -aces. 1.** To comfort, cheer, or console, as in trouble or sorrow. **2.** To allay or assuage. [Middle English *solas*, from Old French, from Latin *sōlācium, sōlātium*, from *sōlārī*, to comfort, console.] —**sol·ac·er** *n.*
so·lan (sō′lən) *n. Archaic.* A gannet, *Morus bassanus*, of northern Atlantic coastal regions. Also called "solan goose." [Middle English *soland* : probably Old Norse *sūlaf*, gannet, pillar + *önd*, duck.]
so·lan·der (sə-lăn′dər) *n.* A book-shaped box used to protect a book, library materials such as maps, or botanical specimens. It may be hinged or may have two parts, one sliding into the other. Also called "solander case." [After Daniel C. *Solander* (1736–1782), Swedish botanist.]
so·la·nine (sō′lə-nēn′, -nĭn) *n.* A bitter poisonous alkaloid, $C_{45}H_{73}NO_{15}$, derived from potato sprouts, tomatoes, and nightshade, formerly used to treat epilepsy. [French : Latin *sōlānum*, nightshade, from *sōl*, sun + -INE]
so·la·num (sə-lā′nəm, -lä′nəm, -lăn′əm) *n.* A plant of the genus *Solanum*, which includes the potato, eggplant, and certain nightshades. [New Latin, from Latin, nightshade.]
so·lar (sō′lər) *adj.* **1.** Of, pertaining to, or proceeding from the sun: *solar rays.* **2.** Utilizing or operated by energy derived from the sun: *solar heating.* **3.** Determined or measured with respect to the sun. [Middle English, from Latin *sōlāris*, from *sōl*, sun.]
solar battery *n.* A system consisting of a large number of connected solar cells.
solar cell *n.* A semiconductor device that converts the energy of sunlight into electric energy.
solar constant *n.* The amount of solar radiation perpendicularly impinging on a surface of unit area at a distance of one astronomical unit from the sun in a unit interval of time, having an average value of 1,388 watts per square meter.
solar day *n.* The interval between two successive meridian passages of the sun.
solar eclipse *n.* An **eclipse** *(see)* of the sun.
solar flare *n.* A temporary outburst of solar gases from a small area of the sun's surface, a source of intense radiation.
solar furnace *n.* A parabolic reflector that focuses solar radiation at a point to obtain high temperatures (up to 4,000°C).

solar cell

FROM SUNLIGHT TO ELECTRICITY
Solar cells are useful in space—but much less so on earth

Solar cells, which convert sunlight directly into electricity, were first produced in 1954. Such cells are made from silicon, a semiconductor, in which a photon, or "packet" of light, can initiate a flow of electrons, producing an electric current. The flow is small, and many cells must be joined together to produce an appreciable current. Cells are no more than about 15 percent efficient and are expensive. But they are also reliable, have no moving parts, and consume no fuel, all of which makes them ideal sources of energy for satellites. More efficient cells may be developed, but they are unlikely to be widely used on earth for one reason: their power supply—sunlight—is highly variable, and their output is correspondingly erratic.

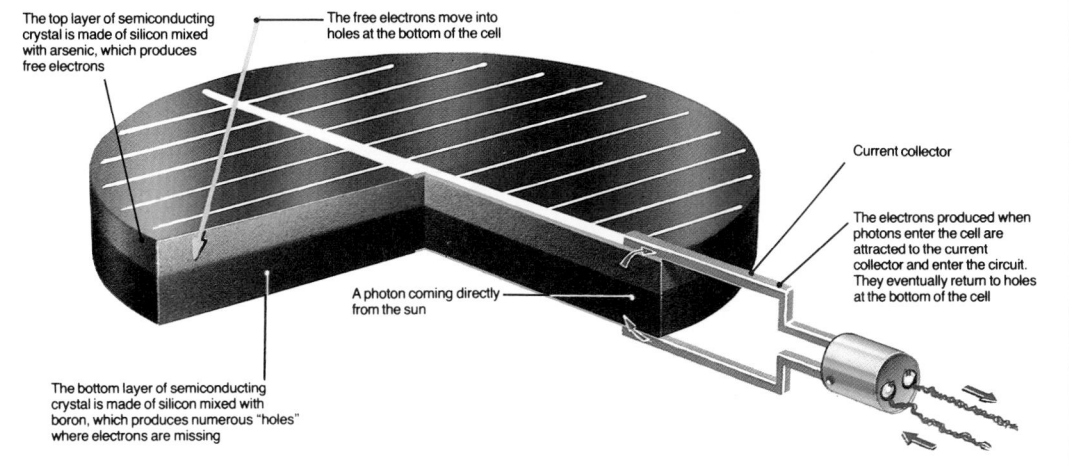

The top layer of semiconducting crystal is made of silicon mixed with arsenic, which produces free electrons

The free electrons move into holes at the bottom of the cell

Current collector

The electrons produced when photons enter the cell are attracted to the current collector and enter the circuit. They eventually return to holes at the bottom of the cell

A photon coming directly from the sun

The bottom layer of semiconducting crystal is made of silicon mixed with boron, which produces numerous "holes" where electrons are missing

solar house *n.* A house having large quantities of heat-absorbing material behind large glass areas, designed to supplement or replace conventional heating methods.

so·lar·im·e·ter (sō′lə-rĭm′ə-tər) *n.* An instrument used to measure the flux of solar radiation through a surface. Also called "pyranometer." [SOLAR + -METER.]

so·lar·i·um (sō-lâr′ē-əm) *n., pl.* **-laria** (-lâr′ē-ə) or **-iums.** **1.** A room, gallery, or glassed-in porch exposed to the sun, as in a hospital. **2.** A room or establishment with apparatus for artificial suntanning. [Latin *sōlārium,* sundial, terrace, balcony, from *sōl,* sun.]

so·lar·ize (sō′lə-rīz′) *v.* **-ized, -izing, -izes.** —*tr.* To expose (photographic film) briefly to the sun after developing and develop again so as to reverse some tones and increase highlights. —*intr.* To be overexposed. Used of photographic film. —**so·lar·i·za·tion** *n.*

solar month *n.* See **month** (sense 5).

solar plexus *n.* The large network of sympathetic nerves and ganglia located in the peritoneal cavity behind the stomach and having branching tracts that supply nerves to the abdominal viscera. [From the branching ganglia resembling the sun's rays.]

solar power *n.* Power or energy obtained by direct conversion of radiation from the sun, either by its heating effect or by use of photoelectric cells to generate electricity. See feature, next page.

Solar System *n.* Often **solar system.** The sun together with the nine planets, asteroids, comets, and all other celestial bodies that orbit the sun. See feature, page 1581.

solar wind *n.* The flow of charged particles from the sun, affecting the earth's magnetic field and causing the aurora.

solar year *n.* A **tropical year** *(see).*

so·la·ti·um (sō-lā′shē-əm) *n., pl.* **-tia** (-shē-ə). *Law.* Compensation for damage to the feelings as distinct from financial loss or physical suffering. [Late Latin *sōlātium,* SOLACE.]

sold. Past tense and past participle of **sell.**

sol·dan (sōl′dən, sōl′-) *n. Archaic.* A sultan. [Middle English *soldan, soudan,* from Old French, from Arabic *sulṭān,* SULTAN.]

sol·der (sŏd′ər, sô′dər) *n.* **1.** Any of various fusible alloys used to join metallic parts when applied in the melted state to the solid metal. The two types are *soft solder,* which contains tin and lead and often flux and is used for electrical connections, and *hard solder,* which is an alloy of copper and zinc used for brazing. **2.** Anything that joins or cements.
—*v.* **soldered, -dering, -ders.** —*tr.* **1.** To unite or repair with solder. **2.** To serve as a bond between; join closely. —*intr.* To be capable of being soldered. Used of metals. [Middle English *souldour, soudur,* from Old French *soudure, soldure,* from *souder, solder,* to solder, from Latin *solidāre,* to make solid, from *solidus,* SOLID.] —**sol·der·er** *n.*

soldering iron *n.* A copper tip held in a handle, usually heated electrically and used for applying soft solder.

sol·dier (sōl′jər) *n.* **1.** One who serves in an army. **2.** A private or a noncommissioned officer as distinguished from a commissioned officer. **3.** An active and loyal follower or worker. **4.** A sexually undeveloped form of certain ants and termites, which have the jaws specialized to serve as fighting weapons.
—*intr.v.* **soldiered, -diering, -diers. 1.** To be or serve as a soldier.

2. To make a show of working or feign illness in order to avoid work; shirk or malinger. [Middle English *souldeour,* mercenary, from Old French *soud(i)er, soldier,* from *soulde,* pay, from Latin *solidus,* SOLIDUS.]

soldier beetle *n.* Any of various carnivorous beetles of the family Cantharidae and especially of the genera *Cantharis* and *Rhagonycha,* commonly seen on flowers.

sol·dier·ly (sōl′jər-lē) *adj.* Befitting a good soldier.

soldier of fortune *n.* One who serves in a military capacity wherever there may be profit or adventure; a mercenary.

sol·dier·y (sōl′jə-rē) *n., pl.* **-ies. 1.** Soldiers collectively. **2.** A body of soldiers. **3.** The military profession.

sole¹ (sōl) *n.* **1.** The undersurface of the foot. **2.** The undersurface of a shoe, sock, or boot. **3.** The part on which something rests while standing, especially: **a.** The bottom surface of a plow. **b.** The bottom surface of the head of a golf club.
—*tr.v.* **soled, soling, soles. 1.** To furnish (a shoe or boot) with a sole. **2.** *Golf.* To put the sole of (a club) on the ground, as in preparing to make a stroke. [Middle English, from Old French *sole,* from Vulgar Latin *sola* (unattested), from Latin *solea,* sandal, from *solum,* bottom, ground, sole of the foot.]

sole² *adj.* **1.** Being the only one; existing or functioning without another or others; only. **2.** Of or pertaining to only one individual or group; exclusive: *The court has the sole right to decide.* **3.** *Law.* Single or unmarried. **4.** *Archaic.* Solitary. —See Synonyms at **single.** [Middle English *soul(e), sole,* unmarried, alone, from Old French, from Latin *sōlus,* alone, single.]

sole³ *n., pl.* **sole** or **soles. 1.** Any of various chiefly marine flatfishes of the family Soleidae, related to and resembling the flounders; especially, the European species *Solea solea,* the Dover sole, valued as a food fish. **2.** Any of various other flatfishes, such as the lemon sole. [Middle English, from Old French, sole (fish), SOLE (of the foot), from the shape of the fish.]

sol·e·cism (sŏl′ə-sĭz′əm, sō′lə-) *n.* **1.** A nonstandard usage or grammatical construction. **2.** A violation of etiquette; an instance of bad manners or incorrect behavior. **3.** An impropriety, mistake, or incongruity. [From Latin *soloecismus,* from Greek *soloikismos,* from *soloikos,* speaking incorrectly, referring to the corrupt Attic dialect spoken by Athenian colonists at *Soloi,* in Cilicia.] —**sol·e·cist** *n.* —**sol·e·cis·tic** (sŏl′ə-sĭs′tĭk, sō′lə-) *adj.*

sole·ly (sōl′lē, sō′lē) *adv.* **1.** Alone; singly. **2.** Entirely; exclusively.

sol·emn (sŏl′əm) *adj.* **1.** Deeply earnest; serious; grave: *a solemn voice.* **2.** Of impressive and serious nature: *a solemn occasion.* **3.** Performed with full ceremony: *a solemn high Mass.* **4.** Invoking the force of religion; sacred: *a solemn vow.* **5.** Gloomy; somber. —See Synonyms at **serious.** [Middle English *solem(p)ne,* from Old French, from Latin *sollemnis,* stated, established, appointed.] —**sol·emn·ly** *adv.* —**sol·emn·ness** *n.*

so·lem·ni·ty (sə-lĕm′nə-tē) *n., pl.* **-ties. 1.** The condition or quality of being solemn; gravity; seriousness. **2.** A solemn proceeding or observance, as of a religious feast.

sol·em·nize (sŏl′əm-nīz′) *tr.v.* **-nized, -nizing, -nizes. 1.** To celebrate or observe (a religious occasion, for example) with formal ceremonies or rites. **2.** To perform with formal ceremony: *solemnize*

solar power

DIRECT USE OF THE SUN'S ENERGY
Home heating and electricity from solar power

The sun pours out energy at a phenomenal rate but only a minute fraction of it fuels life on earth—and so indirectly provides us with fossil fuels. If solar energy could be used directly, it would exceed all our present needs many thousands of times over. As resources decline, research into solar power is intensifying.

There are many ways of harnessing solar power indirectly—through winds, tides, fossil fuels, and differences in ocean temperatures. But direct uses of solar energy involve just two main methods. In thermal methods the sun's heat is collected to heat water. The commonest system is the solar panel water heater shown below; another system uses mirrors to focus the sun's rays. In nonthermal methods, solar cells produce electricity directly from sunlight. Such cells are vital for spacecraft, but too inefficient and expensive for commercial use on earth.

SOLAR POWER STATION *In this power station near Mt. Etna in Sicily, mirrors on the ground follow the sun and focus its rays on a tower-top collector, which heats water to generate electricity.*

PRINCIPLES BEHIND THE SOLAR PANEL

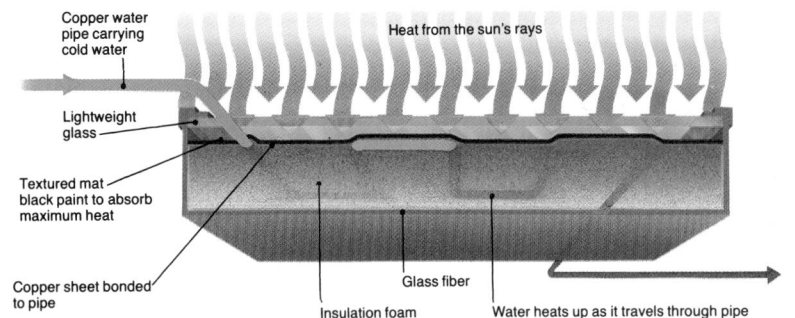

Copper water pipe carrying cold water

Heat from the sun's rays

Lightweight glass

Textured mat black paint to absorb maximum heat

Copper sheet bonded to pipe

Glass fiber

Insulation foam

Water heats up as it travels through pipe

The principles of the domestic solar-powered water heater are extremely simple: water is heated as it flows through tubes in a flat container that is set to face the sun. Efficiency depends partly on the rate of water flow and insulation, but principally on the climate. In some places solar panels can provide all domestic hot water and central heating.

a marriage. **3.** To make serious or grave. —See Synonyms at **observe.** —**sol·em·ni·za·tion** *n.*

so·le·noid (sō′lə-noid′) *n.* **1.** A cylindrical coil of wire used to produce an axial magnetic field by a flow of electric current. **2.** An assembly consisting essentially of such a coil and a metal core free to slide along the coil axis under the influence of the magnetic field, often used as a switch, as in connecting the battery to the starter motor in a motor vehicle. [From French *solénoïde,* from Greek *sōlēnoeidēs,* pipe-shaped, grooved, tubular : *sōlēn†,* channel, pipe + -OID.] —**so·le·noid·al** (sō′lə-noid′l) *adj.* —**so·le·noid·al·ly** *adv.*

So·lent, The (sō′lənt). Strait in the English Channel, separating the Isle of Wight from the coast of Hampshire in southern England.

sole·plate (sōl′plāt′) *n.* The undersurface of a clothes iron.

sol-fa (sōl-fä′) *n. Music.* **1.** The set of syllables *do, re, mi, fa, sol, la,* and *ti,* used to represent the tones of the scale. **2.** The use of the sol-fa syllables. ~*v.* **sol-faed, -faing, -fas.** —*intr.* To use the sol-fa syllables. —*tr.* To sing using the sol-fa syllables. [SOL (note) + FA.]

sol·fa·ta·ra (sōl′fə-tär′ə) *n.* A volcanic fissure that gently emits sulfurous vapors and water vapor. [Italian *Solfatara,* name of a sulfurous volcano near Naples, from *solfo,* SULFUR.] —**sol·fa·ta·ric** (sōl′fə-tär′ĭk) *adj.*

sol·feg·gi·o (sōl-fĕj′ē-ō′, -fĕj′ō) *n.* Also **sol·fège** (sōl-fĕzh′, sōl-). *Music.* **1.** The study and use of the sol-fa syllables to train the ear and voice, using a fixed system in which the lowest tone is always C. **2.** A singing exercise using the sol-fa syllables. [Italian, from *solfeggiare,* "to sol-fa," from *solfa,* sol-fa : SOL (note) + *fa,* FA.]

sol·fe·ri·no (sōl′fə-rē′nō, sōl′-) *n.* A moderate purplish red. [From a dye discovered in the year of the Battle of *Solferino* (1859). Compare **magenta.**] —**sol·fe·ri·no** *adj.*

so·lic·it (sə-lĭs′ĭt) *v.* **-ited, -iting, -its.** —*tr.* **1.** To seek to obtain by persuasion, entreaty, or formal application: *solicit votes; solicit customers.* **2.** To petition (a person) persistently; importune: *solicited the neighbors for donations.* **3.** To entice or incite (a person) to action, particularly to an immoral or illegal action. **4.** To approach or accost (a person) with an offer of sexual services. —*intr.* **1.** To make an earnest or urgent request or petition for something desired. **2.** To approach someone with an offer of sexual services. [Middle English *soliciten,* to disturb, fill with concern, from Old French *solliciter,* from Latin *sollicitāre,* to disturb, agitate, from *sollicitus,* SOLICITOUS.] —**so·lic·i·ta·tion** (sə-lĭs′ĭ-tā′shən) *n.*

so·lic·i·tor (sə-lĭs′ĭ-tər) *n. Abbr.* **sol. 1.** One who solicits, as for a business or charity. **2.** The chief law officer of some cities, towns, or government departments. **3.** *British.* A lawyer who advises clients on legal matters and prepares a client's case for a barrister to represent the client in court. A solicitor may represent a client as an advocate but only in certain lower courts. Compare **barrister.** —See Usage note at **lawyer.**

solicitor general *n., pl.* **solicitors general. 1.** A law officer assisting an attorney general. **2.** The chief law officer in a state not having an attorney general. **3. Solicitor General.** In the United Kingdom, a Crown law officer ranking below the Attorney-General (in England, Wales, and Northern Ireland) or below the Lord Advocate (in Scotland).

so·lic·i·tous (sə-lĭs′ĭ-təs) *adj.* **1.** Anxious and concerned; apprehensive. **2.** Taking or showing great care; meticulous or attentive. **3.** Full of desire; eager. —See Synonyms at **thoughtful.** [From Latin *sollicitus,* thoroughly moved, agitated : *sollus,* whole, entire + *citus,* past participle of *ciēre,* to put in motion, move.] —**so·lic·i·tous·ly** *adv.* —**so·lic·i·tous·ness** *n.*

so·lic·i·tude (sə-lĭs′ĭ-tōōd′, -tyōōd′) *n.* **1.** The state of being solicitous or concerned. **2. a.** Anxiety; concern. **b.** That which causes anxiety or concern. —See Synonyms at **anxiety.**

sol·id (sŏl′ĭd) *adj.* **1.** Of definite shape and volume; not liquid or gaseous. **2.** Not hollowed out or having internal spaces; consisting of solid matter throughout: *a solid block of wood.* **3.** Being the same substance throughout: *solid gold.* **4. a.** Of or pertaining to three-dimensional geometric figures: *solid geometry.* **b.** Having three dimensions: *a solid configuration.* **5. a.** Without gaps or openings; continuous: *a solid line of people.* **b.** Without breaks or interruptions: *three solid weeks.* **6.** Of good quality and substance; well-made: *solid foundations.* **7.** Having a close rather than loose consistency; hard and firm: *solid rock.* **8.** Substantial; satisfying: *a solid meal.* **9.** Sound; well-grounded; concrete: *solid facts.* **10.** Financially sound. **11.** Reputable and dependable: *a solid citizen.* **12.** Sensible, reliable, and consistent, but without brilliance or excellence; steady: *a solid worker.* **13.** Written or printed without a hyphen or space. Said of compound words. **14.** *Printing.* Without leads between the lines. **15. a.** Acting together; unanimous: *a solid voting bloc.* **b.** Firmly united: *a solid marriage.* **16.** *Geology.* Not superficial. ~*n.* **1.** A substance that is neither liquid nor gaseous, the atoms being packed more closely than in a liquid or gas; a solid substance. **2.** A geometric figure having three dimensions. **3. solids.** Solid, rather than liquid, food. [Middle English *solide,* whole, solid, from Old French, from Latin *solidus.*] —**sol·id·ly** *adv.* —**sol·id·ness** *n.*

solid angle *n.* An angle subtended at a point by a surface, measured in steradians with respect to the area delimited on the unit sphere centered on that point by the locus of points of intersection of the sphere with the lines joining the point to the perimeter of the surface. Compare **polyhedral angle.**

sol·i·dar·i·ty (sŏl′ə-dăr′ə-tē) *n., pl.* **-ties. 1.** A feeling or quality of fellowship, arising from a union of interests, aspirations, or sympathies among members of a group: *the solidarity felt by members of a labor union.* **2.** The unity and firmness that results from such fellowship: *The solidarity of the party led to its success.*

sol·i·dar·y (sŏl′ə-dĕr′ē) *adj.* Characterized by solidarity; united. [French *solidaire,* from *solide,* SOLID.]

solid fuel *n.* **1.** Fuel, such as wood, coal, or coke, that is solid rather than liquid or gaseous. Also used adjectivally: *a solid-fuel heating system.* **2.** A solid propellant in a rocket.

so·lid·i·fy (sə-lĭd′ə-fī′) *v.* **-fied, -fying, -fies.** —*tr.* **1.** To make solid, compact, or hard. **2.** To make strong or united. —*intr.* To become solidified. —**so·lid·i·fi·ca·tion** *n.*

so·lid·i·ty (sə-lĭd′ə-tē) *n., pl.* **-ties. 1.** The condition or property of being solid. **2.** Soundness, as of judgment, moral character, or finances; stability. **3.** Something that is solid.

solid of revolution *n.* A volume generated by the rotation of a plane figure about an axis in its plane.

solid propellant *n.* A rocket propellant in solid form, combining both fuel and oxidizer in the form of a compact, cohesive grain.

solid solution *n. Chemistry.* A homogeneous crystalline structure in which one or more types of atoms or molecules may be partly substituted for the original atoms and molecules without changing the crystal structure.

sol·id-state (sŏl′ĭd-stāt′) *adj.* **1.** Characteristic of or pertaining to the physical properties of solid materials, especially to the electromagnetic, thermodynamic, and structural properties of crystalline solids. **2.** Based on or consisting chiefly or exclusively of semiconducting materials, components, and related devices: *solid-state audio equipment; solid-state watches.*

sol·i·dus (sŏl′ĭ-dəs) *n., pl.* **-di** (-dī′). **1.** A diagonal mark (/); a virgule *(see).* **2.** An ancient Roman coin used until the fall of the Byzantine Empire. [Middle English, from Latin, from adjective, SOLID.]

sol·i·fid·i·an (sŏl′ĭ-fĭd′ē-ən) *n.* A person who believes that faith alone is sufficient to ensure salvation. [From New Latin *solifidius :*

Solar System

THE FAMILY OF THE SUN

A few large objects and thousands of small ones form patterns that suggest their origins

The Solar System consists of the Sun itself, nine planets, almost four dozen satellites, thousands of small, rocky asteroids, and an uncounted number of comets. The Sun makes up some 99.9 percent of the Solar System's mass, and most of the remaining 0.1 percent is taken up by the giant planet Jupiter.

The planets fall into two groups. The terrestrial planets are small, dense, and close to the Sun. They are separated by a belt of asteroids from the giant planets, which have gaseous surfaces and relatively small solid cores, most of their globes being liquid. The exception is Pluto, a frozen world with an orbit so eccentric that it is sometimes nearer the Sun than Neptune (as it is now, for a 20-year period, 1979–99).

The planets, revolving in elliptical orbits that are nearly circular, are held to the Sun by gravity. The closer they are to the Sun, the faster they must move to counteract the Sun's greater pull. Mercury travels around the Sun in 88 days, moving at 48 kilometers (30 miles) a second. Pluto's year is 248 Earth years, and it moves at three miles a second.

THE SOLAR SYSTEM

Planet	Mean distance from the Sun million kilometers	million miles
Mercury	57.9	36
Venus	108.2	67
Earth	149.6	93
Mars	227.9	141.6
Jupiter	778.3	483.6
Saturn	1,427	886.7
Uranus	2,869.6	1,783
Neptune	4,496.6	2,794
Pluto	5,900	3,666

A FLAT, ORDERED SYSTEM *Taken as a whole, the Solar System's most noticeable feature is its flatness. All planets are in the same plane. Moreover, all orbit in the same direction. This suggests that the solar family condensed out of a revolving cloud of gas and dust. Several aggregations of matter came together, the biggest of them being the Sun.*

The Sun would have driven off the lighter-weight materials, including hydrogen and helium, from the inner planets—hence their density compared with the gaseous outer ones. This theory also suggests the notion that planetary formation would be a common result of the formation of any star.

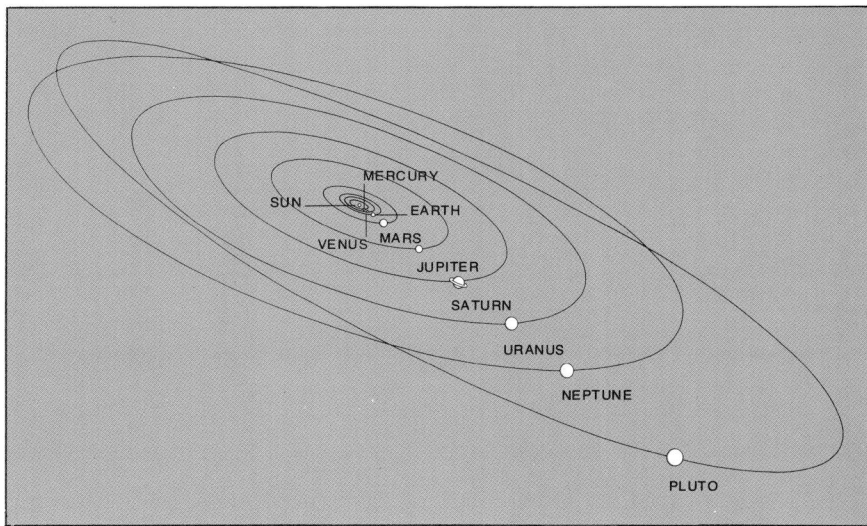

Latin *sōlus*, alone + *fidēs*, faith.] —**sol·i·fid·i·an·ism** *n.*
so·li·fluc·tion (sŏ′lə-flŭk′shən) *n.* The downhill flow of surface deposits saturated with thaw water, as soil or clay, over a slope that is still frozen. [Latin *solum*, soil + FLUXION.]
so·lil·o·quize (sə-lĭl′ə-kwīz′) *v.* **-quized, -quizing, -quizes.** —*intr.* To utter or deliver a soliloquy. —*tr.* To put into the form of a soliloquy. —**so·lil·o·quist** (sə-lĭl′ə-kwĭst), **so·lil·o·quiz·er** *n.*

so·lil·o·quy (sə-lĭl′ə-kwē) *n., pl.* **-quies. 1.** A literary or dramatic form of discourse in which a character talks to himself or reveals his thoughts in the form of a monologue without addressing a listener. **2.** The act of speaking to oneself in or as if in solitude. [From Late Latin *sōliloquium* : Latin *sōlus,* alone + *loquī,* to speak.]
sol·ip·sism (sŏl′əp-sĭz′əm, sō′ləp-) *n. Philosophy.* **1.** The theory that the self is the only thing that can be known and verified. **2.** The

theory or view that the self is the only reality. Compare **objectivism**. [Latin *sōlus*, alone + *ipse*†, self + -ISM.] —**sol·ip·sist** *n.* —**sol·ip·sis·tic** (sŏl′əp-sĭs′tĭk, sō′ləp-) *adj.*

sol·i·taire (sŏl′ə-târ′) *n.* **1.** A diamond or other gemstone set alone, as in a ring. **2.** A game for one person played on a special board in which marbles or pegs are arranged in slots in a pattern, the object being to remove each marble or peg, save one, by jumping others over them. **3.** Any of a number of card games played by one person, in which the cards must be matched up in certain combinations. [French, from Old French, solitary, from Latin *sōlitārius*, SOLITARY.]

sol·i·tar·y (sŏl′ə-tĕr′ē) *adj.* **1. a.** Existing, living, or going without others; alone. **b.** Avoiding the company of others; not gregarious. **2.** Happening, done, or made alone. **3.** Remote; secluded; unfrequented: *a solitary retreat.* **4.** Having no companions; lonely. **5.** Single; sole. **6.** *Zoology.* Not living in groups or organized colonies: *solitary wasps.* —See Synonyms at **single**. ~*n.*, *pl.* **solitaries. 1.** A person who lives alone; a recluse. **2.** *Informal.* Solitary confinement. [Middle English, from Latin *sōlitārius*, from *sōlus*, alone.] —**sol·i·tar·i·ly** (sŏl′ə-târ′ə-lē) *adv.* —**sol·i·tar·i·ness** (sŏl′ə-tĕr′ē-nĭs) *n.*

solitary confinement *n.* The confinement of a prisoner in a cell in which he is isolated from all others.

sol·i·tude (sŏl′ə-tŏod′, -tyŏod′) *n.* **1.** The state of being alone or remote from others; isolation. **2.** A lonely or secluded place. [Middle English, from Old French, from Latin *sōlitūdo*, from *sōlus*, alone.]

Synonyms: isolation, retirement, seclusion.

sol·ler·et (sŏl′ə-rĕt′) *n.* A steel shoe made of overlapping plates, forming a part of a suit of armor. [Old French, diminutive of *soller*, shoe, from Medieval Latin *subtēlāris*, from Late Latin *subtēl*, hollow of the foot : Latin *sub-*, under + *tālus*, ankle (see **talus**).]

sol·mi·za·tion (sŏl′mə-zā′shən) *n.* *Music.* A system of using syllables to name the tones of the scale, as in **sol-fa** *(see)*. [French *solmisation*, from *solmiser*, to sol-fa : SOL (note) + MI.]

soln solution.

so·lo (sō′lō) *n.*, *pl.* **-los. 1.** A musical composition or passage for an individual voice or instrument, with or without accompaniment. **2.** A performance or endeavor accomplished by a single individual, as an airplane flight in which the pilot is unaccompanied. **3.** Any of various card games in which one player singly opposes others, as *solo whist*, in which each player plays independently rather than as one of a pair. ~*adj.* **1.** Composed, arranged for, or performed by a single voice or instrument. **2.** Made or done by a single individual. ~*adv.* Unaccompanied; alone. ~*intr.v.* **soloed, -loing, -los.** To perform alone; especially, to fly an airplane without a companion or instructor. [Italian, from Latin *sōlus*, alone.]

so·lo·ist (sō′lō-ĭst) *n.* One who performs a solo or solos.

Sol·o·mon (sŏl′ə-mən) (*c.* 973–*c.* 933 B.C.) King of Israel. Succeeding his father, David, he built the Temple of Jerusalem. The Bible attributes great wisdom to him.

Solomon Islands. Also **Sol·o·mons** (sŏl′ə-mənz). Country comprising part of the Solomon Islands group in the southwestern Pacific. There are six main islands, Choiseul, New Georgia, Santa Isabel, Guadalcanal, Malaita, and San Cristobal, and many smaller islands and groups. (Bougainville and Buka, the northernmost islands, are part of Papua New Guinea). Most of the islands are mountainous and wooded, and the chief products are timber, copra, and coconuts. A British protectorate was established over most of them by 1899. They witnessed fierce fighting in World War II, notably at Guadalcanal (1942–43). The Solomons became an independent state in 1978. Area, 28,446 square kilometers (10,983 square miles). Population, 220,000. Capital, Honiara (on Guadalcanal). See map at **Pacific Ocean.**

Solomon's seal *n.* **1.** A six-pointed star or hexagram, like a Star of David, supposed to possess mystical powers and sometimes used as a charm or amulet. **2.** Any of several plants of the genus *Polygonatum*, having paired drooping greenish-white flowers. [The plant is probably so called from the seallike markings on the root stocks.]

so·lon (sō′lən) *n.* A wise lawgiver. [After SOLON.]

So·lon (sō′lən) (*c.* 638–559 B.C.). Athenian lawgiver and poet. His reforms preserved a class system based on wealth, but ended privilege by birth. The political franchise was extended, and serfdom was effectively abolished by outlawing the use of an individual's freedom as security for debt. The reforms were controversial, but became the basis of Greek law.

so long *interj.* *Informal.* Good-by.

sol·stice (sŏl′stĭs, sōl′-) *n.* **1.** *Astronomy.* Either of two times of the year when the sun has no apparent northward or southward motion, at the most northern or most southern point of the ecliptic. In the Northern Hemisphere, the summer solstice, when the sun is in the zenith at the tropic of Cancer, occurs about June 21 or 22; the winter solstice, when the sun is over the tropic of Capricorn, occurs about December 21 or 22. The solstices are reversed in the Southern Hemisphere. **2.** A highest point; culmination. [Middle English, from Old French, from Latin *sōlstitium* : *sōl*, sun + *sistere* (past participial stem *stit-*), to stand.] —**sol·sti·tial** (sŏl-stĭsh′əl, sōl-) *adj.*

Sol·ti (shōl′tē), **Sir Georg** (1912–). Hungarian-born British conductor. He has been musical director of the Royal Opera Covent Garden (1961–71) and conductor of the Chicago Symphony Orchestra.

sol·u·bil·i·ty (sŏl′yə-bĭl′ə-tē) *n.*, *pl.* **-ties. 1.** The quality or condition of being soluble. **2.** The maximum amount of a substance that can be dissolved in a given amount of solvent, usually expressed as the mass or volume of solute in a unit mass or volume of solvent at a given temperature.

sol·u·bi·lize (sŏl′yə-bə-līz′) *tr.v.* **-lized, -lizing, -lizes.** To make (substances such as fats and lipids, which are not appreciably soluble under standard conditions) soluble in water by the action of a detergent or similar agent.

sol·u·ble (sŏl′yə-bəl) *adj.* **1.** Capable of being dissolved; especially, having a high solubility. **2.** Capable of being solved or explained. [Middle English, from Old French, from Late Latin *solūbilis*, from *solvere*, to loosen.] —**sol·u·ble·ness** *n.* —**sol·u·bly** *adv.*

soluble glass *n.* *Chemistry.* **Sodium silicate** *(see).*

soluble RNA *n.* *Abbr.* **sRNA** *Genetics.* **Transfer RNA** *(see).*

so·lum (sō′ləm) *n.*, *pl.* **-la** (-lə) or **-lums.** The surface layers of a soil profile in which topsoil formation occurs. [New Latin, from Latin, base, foundation. See **sole** (of a shoe).]

so·lus (sō′ləs) *adj. & adv.* *Feminine* **so·la** (-lə). Alone; by oneself. Used especially in stage directions. [Latin, alone.]

sol·ute (sŏl′yŏot′) *n.* *Chemistry.* A substance dissolved in another substance, usually the component of a solution present in the lesser amount. Compare **solvent.** [From Latin *solūtus*, past participle of *solvere*, to loosen.] —**sol·ute** *adj.*

so·lu·tion (sə-lŏo′shən) *n.* **1.** *Abbr.* **soln** A homogeneous mixture of two or more substances, retaining its constitution in subdivision to molecular volumes, displaying no settling, and having various possible proportions of the constituents, which may be solids, liquids, gases, or intercombinations. **2.** The process of forming such a mixture. **3.** The state of being dissolved. **4.** The method or process of solving a problem. **5.** The answer to or disposition of a problem. **6.** *Law.* The payment of a claim or debt or the discharging of an obligation. **7.** The action of separating or breaking up; a dissolution. **8.** *Mathematics.* A number or function or set of numbers or functions that yield a true statement when substituted in a given equation. [Middle English, from Old French, from Latin *solūtiō* (stem *solūtiōn-*), from *solūtus*. See **solute**.]

solution set *n.* *Logic & Mathematics.* A **truth set** *(see).*

So·lu·tre·an, So·lu·tri·an (sə-lŏo′trē-ən) *adj.* *Anthropology.* Of or relating to an Upper Paleolithic culture in Europe that succeeded the Aurignacian and was characterized by improved flint implements and stylized symbolic forms of art. [After *Solutré*, a village in France.]

solv·a·ble (sŏl′və-bəl, sôl′-) *adj.* Capable of being solved. —**solv·a·bil·i·ty** (sŏl′və-bĭl′ə-tē, sôl′-), **solv·a·ble·ness** *n.*

sol·va·tion (sŏl-vā′shən, sôl-) *n.* Any of a class of chemical reactions, such as the formation of hydrated copper sulfate in aqueous solution, in which solvent molecules combine with ions of the solvent. Compare **solvolysis.** [SOLV(ENT) + -ATION.]

Sol·vay process (sŏl′vā′) *n.* A process used to manufacture sodium carbonate from salt, ammonia, carbon dioxide, and limestone. [Invented by Ernest Solvay (1838–1922), Belgian chemist.]

solve (sŏlv, sôlv) *tr.v.* **solved, solving, solves. 1.** To find a solution to; answer; explain. **2.** To work out a correct solution to (a mathematical problem). [Middle English *solven*, to loosen, unbind, from Latin *solvere*.] —**solv·er** *n.*

sol·vent (sŏl′vənt, sôl′-) *adj.* **1.** Able to meet financial obligations. **2. a.** Capable of dissolving another substance. **b.** Causing or promoting dissolution or disintegration. ~*n.* **1.** *Chemistry.* **a.** The component of a solution that is present in excess or that undergoes no change of state. **b.** A liquid capable of dissolving another substance. Compare **solute.** **2.** Something that weakens, loosens, or dissipates. [Latin *solvēns* (stem *solvent-*), present participle of *solvere*, to loosen. See **solve**.] —**sol·ven·cy** (sŏl′vən-sē, sôl′-) *n.*

sol·vol·y·sis (sŏl-vŏl′ə-sĭs, sôl-) *n.* Any of a class of ionic chemical reactions, such as hydrolysis, in which solute and solvent react to form other products. Compare **solvation.** [SOLV(ENT) + -LYSIS.]

Sol·way Firth (sŏl′wā′). Inlet of the Irish Sea, between the coast of Cumbria in England and Dumfries and Galloway Region in Scotland. There is a tidal bore.

Sol·zhe·nit·syn (sŏl′zhə-nēt′sĭn, sôl′-), **Alexandr Isayevich** (1918–). Russian writer. For criticizing Stalin he was sentenced to labor camps and exile in Siberia (1945–56), and works like *One Day in the Life of Ivan Denisovich* (1962) describe the experience. *The Gulag Archipelago*, published only outside the U.S.S.R., is a history of the labor camp system. He was awarded the Nobel Prize for literature in 1970 and expelled from the U.S.S.R. in 1974.

so·ma¹ (sō′mə) *n.*, *pl.* **-mata** (-mə-tə) or **-mas.** *Biology.* The body of an organism, exclusive of the germ cells. [New Latin, from Greek.]

soma² *n.* **1.** An intoxicating drink prepared from the juice of an unidentified plant, used in Vedic rituals in ancient India. **2.** The plant from which this drink was prepared. [Sanskrit *sōma.*]

So·ma·li (sō-mä′lē, sə-), *n.*, *pl.* **-lis** or collectively **Somali. 1.** A member of one of a group of Hamitic tribes of Somaliland. **2.** The Cushitic language of the Somali. **3.** A native or inhabitant of Somalia. —**So·ma·li** *adj.*

So·ma·li·a (sə-mä′lē-ə, -mäl′yə). Country in East Africa. It is hot and arid, and one of the world's poorest states. The population is chiefly Muslim and largely nomadic. Livestock rearing is the main occupation, but farming and fishing are being developed. Livestock, bananas, and plantains are exported. The state was created (1960) from former British and Italian possessions in Somaliland. The armed forces seized power (1969), establishing a revolutionary

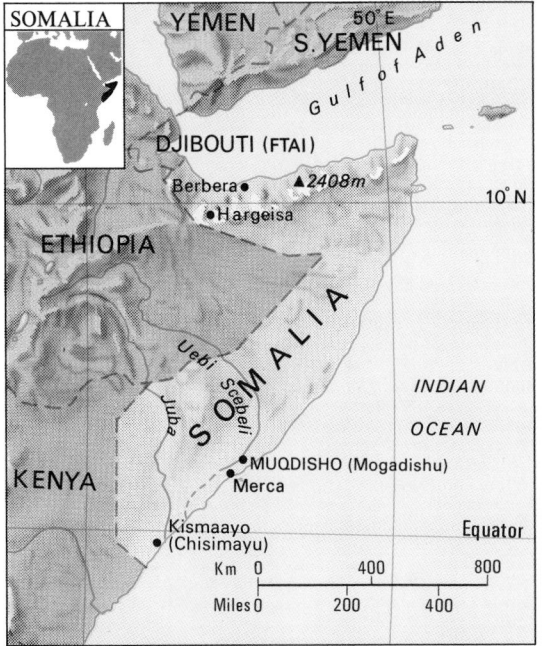

SOMALIA

YEMEN 50°E
S.YEMEN
Gulf of Aden
DJIBOUTI (FTAI)
Berbera• ▲2408m
•Hargeisa 10°N
ETHIOPIA
Uebi Scebeli
SOMALIA
INDIAN
OCEAN
Juba
KENYA
•MUQDISHO (Mogadishu)
•Merca
Kismaayo
(Chisimayu) Equator
Km 0   400   800
Miles 0   200   400

council. In 1977, Somalia invaded the Ogaden border region of Ethiopia to support Somali guerrillas. Although formal withdrawal took place in 1978, guerrilla activities persisted. Many Somali Ethiopians fled to Somalia, and in 1981 some 25 percent of people in Somalia were refugees. Area, 637,657 square kilometers (246,201 square miles). Population, 3,600,000. Capital, Mogadishu.

So·ma·li·land (sə-mäʹlē-lănd′). Region of northeastern Africa. It is now divided between Djibouti, Ethiopia, and Somalia. The area is peopled mainly by Somali nomads, converted to Islam in the 7th to 10th centuries. Its strategic value after the opening of the Suez Canal (1869) led to European colonization in the 19th century. French Somaliland became the French Territory of the Afars and Issas (1967) and gained independence as Djibouti (1977). Italian Somaliland and the Somali-speaking part of Ethiopia (Ogaden) became a province of Italian East Africa (1936). This was taken by British forces in World War II. Italian Somaliland was made the U.N. Trust Territory of Somalia under Italian control (1950). The British returned Ogaden to Ethiopia, and Italy granted the trust territory internal self-government as Somalia (1956). British Somaliland and Somalia combined as the independent state of Somalia (1960).

so·mat·ic (sə-mătʹĭk) adj. 1. Of or pertaining to the body, especially as distinguished from a bodily part, the mind, or the environment; physical. 2. Of or pertaining to the wall of the body cavity, especially as distinguished from the head, limbs, or viscera. 3. Of or pertaining to the soma or to somatoplasm. [From Greek sōmatikos, from sōma, body, SOMA.] —**so·mat·i·cal·ly** adv.

somatic cell n. Any cell other than a germ cell.

somato– prefix. Indicates body; for example, **somatology**. [From Greek sōma (stem sōmat-), body.]

so·ma·to·gen·ic (sō′mə-tə-jĕnʹĭk, sō-măt′ə-) adj. Arising within the body in response to environmental stimuli on somatic cells. [SOMATO- + -GENIC.]

so·ma·tol·o·gy (sō′mə-tŏlʹə-jē) n. 1. The physiological and anatomical study of the body. 2. Physical anthropology (see). [SOMATO- + -LOGY.] —**so·ma·to·log·i·cal** (sō′mə-tə-lŏjʹĭ-kəl, sō-măt′ə-) adj.

so·ma·to·plasm (sō′mə-tə-plăzʹəm, sō-măt′ə-) n. 1. The entirety of specialized protoplasm, other than germ plasm, constituting the body. 2. The protoplasm of a somatic cell. [SOMATO- + -PLASM.]

so·ma·to·pleure (sō′mə-tə-plʊorʹ, sō-măt′ə-) n. A complex sheet of embryonic cells in certain vertebrates, formed by association of part of the mesoderm with the ectoderm and developing as the internal body wall. [SOMATO- + PLEURA.]

so·ma·to·tro·phin (sō′mə-tə-trōʹfĭn, sō-măt′ə-) n. **Growth hormone** (see). [SOMATO- + Greek trophē, nourishment (from trephein, to feed) + -IN.]

so·ma·to·type (sō′mə-tə-tīpʹ, sō-măt′ə-) n. The morphological type of a human body; physique. See endomorph, mesomorph, ectomorph. —**so·ma·to·typ·ic** (sō′mə-tə-tĭpʹĭk, sō-măt′ə-) adj.

som·ber, som·bre (sŏmʹbər) adj. Also archaic **som·brous** (-brəs). 1. a. Gloomy or shadowy; dim. b. Dark in color; dull: "A city takes on that sombre garb of grey" (Theodore Dreiser). 2. Melancholy; dismal. [French, from Old French, shade, from Vulgar Latin subombrāre (unattested), to shade : Latin sub-, under + umbra, shade.]

som·bre·ro (sŏm-brârʹō) n., pl. **-ros**. A broad-brimmed Spanish or Mexican hat of felt or straw. [Spanish, hat, from sombra, shade, from Vulgar Latin subombrāre. See somber.]

some (sŭm) adj. 1. Being an unspecified or unknown thing or things: some people from the office. Some fool laughed. 2. Being an unspecified quantity, part, or number: I'll have some cake. 3. Being an appreciable amount; considerable: some way to go yet. 4. Being at least a little or a small amount of something: You might give me some idea. 5. Remarkable or impressive: That was some party! 6. Being no person or thing of the specified kind at all. ~pron. 1. An unspecified amount or part but not all: Can I have some? 2. Certain unspecified people or things: Some like it hot. ~adv. 1. Approximately; about: some 30 years ago. 2. Informal. To a certain degree: wants to think about it some more. [Middle English som(e), Old English sum, one, a certain one.]

–some[1] suffix. Indicates: 1. Being or tending to be; for example, **burdensome**. 2. Likely or inclined to; for example, **quarrelsome**, **tiresome**. 3. Tending or likely to produce; for example, **awesome**. [Middle English -som, Old English -sum.]

–some[2] suffix. Indicates body; for example, **chromosome**. [New Latin -soma, from Greek sōma.]

–some[3] suffix. Indicates a group of. Used with numerals; for example, **threesome**. [Middle English -sum, from sum, som, SOME.]

some·bod·y (sŭmʹbŏd′ē, -bŭd′ē, -bə-dē) pron. An unspecified or unknown person; someone. ~n., pl. **somebodies**. Informal. A person of importance.

some·day (sŭmʹdā′) adv. At some time in the future.

Usage: Someday and sometime express future time indefinitely. This sense can also be conveyed by some day and some time. The two-word forms are always used when some is an adjective modifying and specifying a more particular day or time (used as nouns): We'll succeed someday. Come sometime. Let's meet sometime (or some time) when your schedule permits. Come some day (not someday) soon. Choose some day (not someday) that is not so busy. Sometime is also used in the sense "occasional" but is criticized because it allows confusion with the meaning "former": He's a musician and sometime composer.

some·how (sŭmʹhou′) adv. In a way not specified, understood, or known.

some·one (sŭmʹwŭn′, -wən) pron. Some person; somebody.

some·place (sŭmʹplās′) adv. Informal. Somewhere.

som·er·sault, sum·mer·sault (sŭmʹər-sôlt′) n. Also archaic **som·er·set, sum·mer·set** (-sĕt′). 1. An acrobatic feat in which the body rolls in a complete circle, heels over head, either along the ground or in midair. 2. Loosely, any complete reversal, as of sympathies or opinions. ~intr.v. **somersaulted** or **summersaulted**, **-saulting**, **-saults**. Also archaic **somerset, summerset**, **-setted**, **-setting**, **-sets**. To execute a somersault. [From Old French sombresau(l)t, variant of sobresault, from Old Provençal sobresaut (unattested) : sobre-, over, above, from Latin suprā + saut, leap, from Latin saltus, leap.]

Som·er·set (sŭmʹər-sĕt′). Also **Som·er·set·shire** (-shĭr′, -shər). County in southwestern England. It borders the British Channel and comprises a lowland plain flanked by the uplands of Exmoor, the Quantocks, the Blackdown Hills, and the Mendips. Dairy and fruit farming are important, and the county is famous for its cider. Cheddar Gorge and the ancient Arthurian site of Glastonbury are among its tourist attractions. Taunton is the county town.

some·thing (sŭmʹthĭng) pron. 1. An undetermined or unspecified thing. 2. A certain quantity, part, number, or quality: There's something of her mother about her. I know something of French literature. 3. Used as a substitute for a name, word, or thing that has been forgotten or is not known: She's something in publishing. 4. A thing, amount, or achievement of at least some value; a little more or better than nothing: managed to salvage a few bits of furniture, which was something. 5. A person, thing, event, or achievement that is impressive or important: That's really something! —**make something of**. 1. To cause trouble over. 2. To do well with; make effective or profitable use of. —**something of**. In some way; to some extent: It's something of a mystery. ~adv. 1. Rather; to some extent: She sounds something like me. 2. To a great degree. Used with an adjective to form an adverbial phrase: messed it up something awful.

something else pron. Slang. Something spectacular or impressive.

some·time (sŭmʹtīm′) adv. 1. At an indefinite or unstated time. 2. At an indefinite time in the future. 3. Archaic. Sometimes. 4. Archaic. Formerly. —See Usage note at **someday**. ~adj. 1. Having been at some prior time; former: a sometime secretary. 2. Informal. Occasional. —See Usage note at **someday**.

some·times (sŭmʹtīmz′) adv. 1. On some occasions; at times; now and then. 2. Obsolete. At some prior time; once; formerly.

some·way (sŭmʹwā′) adv. Also **someways** (-wāz′). Informal. In some way or another; somehow.

some·what (sŭmʹhwŏt′, -wŏt′, sŭm-hwŏtʹ, -wŏtʹ) adv. To some extent or degree; rather. ~pron. Some amount, part, or degree; something. Usually used with of: He is somewhat of a fool.

some·where (sŭmʹhwâr′, -wâr′) adv. 1. At, in, or to a place not specified or known; some place. 2. At or to some unspecified point in time, amount, or degree. Usually used with in or about. —**get** (or **go**) **somewhere**. To achieve something or make progress. ~n. An unknown or unspecified place.

so·mite (sōʹmīt′) n. 1. Zoology. A body segment, a **metamere** (see). 2. Embryology. One of the segmental masses of mesoderm in the vertebrate embryo, occurring in pairs along the notochord. [SOM(A) + -ITE.] —**so·mit·ic** (sō-mĭtʹĭk) adj.

Somme (sŏm, sŭm). River in northern France. It rises in the Aisne department and flows west through Amiens and Abbeville to the

English Channel. It is 243 kilometers (152 miles) long. The World War I Battle of the Somme (1916) was one of the bloodiest engagements in history and the first in which tanks were used.

som·nam·bu·late (sŏm-năm′byə-lāt′) *intr.v.* **-lated, -lating, -lates.** To walk while asleep. **—som·nam·bu·la·tion** *n.*

som·nam·bu·lism (sŏm-năm′byə-lĭz′əm) *n.* Sleepwalking. **—som·nam·bu·list** *n.* **—som·nam·bu·lis·tic** (sŏm-năm′byə-lĭs′tĭk), **som·nam·bu·lar** (sŏm-năm′byə-lər) *adj.*

somni–, somn– *prefix.* Indicates sleep; for example, **somnifacient, somnambulate.** [From Latin *somnus,* sleep.]

som·ni·fa·cient (sŏm′nə-fā′shənt) *adj.* Tending to produce sleep; hypnotic. [SOMNI- + -FACIENT.]

som·nif·er·ous (sŏm-nĭf′ər-əs) *adj.* Also **som·nif·ic** (-nĭf′ĭk). Inducing sleep. [From Latin *somnifer:* SOMNI- + -FEROUS.]

som·no·lence (sŏm′nə-ləns) *n.* Drowsiness; sleepiness.

som·no·lent (sŏm′nə-lənt) *adj.* **1.** Drowsy; sleepy. **2.** Inducing or tending to induce sleep; soporific. [Middle English *sompnolent,* from Old French, from Latin *somnolentus,* from *somnus,* sleep.] **—som·no·lent·ly** *adv.*

So·mo·za (sō-mō′sä, sə-mō′zə), family of Nicaraguan political leaders, including **Anastasio Somoza Garcia** (1896-1956), who became the head of Nicaragua's army (1933), deposed President Juan Bautista Sacasa (1936), assumed the presidency, and ruled for 20 years. He was assassinated in 1956, at which time his son, **Luis Somoza Debayle** (1922-67), became president and served until 1963. His brother **Anastasio Somoza Debayle** (1925-80) was elected president in 1967 and employed the aggressive leadership used by his father. Anastasio's tumultuous presidency (1967-72, 1974-79) brought violent uprisings against his government. He resigned in 1979 and was assassinated in exile.

son (sŭn) *n. Abbr.* **s. 1.** A male offspring. **2.** Any male descendant. **3. a.** An adopted male child. **b.** A son-in-law. **4.** A male person associated with or considered as a product of something such as a place, activity, or cause: *sons of toil.* **5.** A young man. Used as a familiar term of address. **6. Son.** The second person of the Trinity, Christ. [Middle English *son(e),* Old English *sunu.*]

so·nant (sō′nənt) *adj. Phonetics.* Voiced.
~*n. Phonetics.* **1.** A voiced speech sound. **2.** A syllabic consonant; a sonorant. [Latin *sonāns* (stem *sonānt-*), present participle of Latin *sonāre,* to sound.]

so·nar (sō′när′) *n.* **1.** A system using transmitted and reflected acoustic waves to detect and locate submerged objects. **2.** An apparatus using such a system, as in a submarine. [*So*und *na*vigation *r*anging.]

so·na·ta (sə-nä′tə) *n.* A musical composition, as for the piano, violin, or other instrument, consisting of three or four independent movements varying in key, mood, and tempo. [Italian, from the feminine past participle of *sonare,* to sound, from Latin *sonāre.*]

sonata form *n.* A musical form consisting of three sections, the exposition, development, and recapitulation, often followed by a coda.

son·a·ti·na (sŏn′ə-tē′nə) *n.* A sonata with shorter movements than the typical sonata. [Italian, diminutive of SONATA.]

sonde (sŏnd) *n.* A device, such as a **radiosonde** (*see*), launched into the atmosphere for making meteorological or other observations. [French. See **sound** (to measure water).]

Sond·heim (sŏnd′hīm′), **Stephen** (1930-). U.S. composer and lyricist. Beginning his Broadway career by writing the lyrics for *West Side Story* (1957), he composed music and wrote acerbic lyrics for several successful productions, including *A Funny Thing Happened on the Way to the Forum* (1962), *Follies* (1971), and *Sweeney Todd* (1979). He won a Pulitzer Prize (1985) for *Sunday in the Park with George.*

sone (sōn) *n.* A subjective unit of loudness equal to the loudness of a pure tone having a frequency of 1,000 hertz at 40 decibels above the listener's threshold of hearing. [From Latin *sonus,* a sound.]

son et lu·mi·ère (sôn′ ā lüm-yâr′) *n.* A theatrical entertainment given at night in a historic, usually outdoor setting, using recorded sound, lighting, and other effects to present the history of the place. [French, sound and light.]

song (sông, sŏng) *n.* **1.** A usually brief musical composition consisting of words set to music, written or adapted for singing. **2.** The act or art of singing. **3.** A melodious utterance, such as a bird call. **4. a.** Poetry; verse. **b.** A lyric poem or ballad. **5.** *Informal.* A small amount of money: *picked it up for a song.* [Middle English *song, sang,* Old English *sang.*]

Song, Sung (sŏong). Chinese dynasty (960-1279). Under its rule China achieved one of its highest levels of culture and prosperity.

Song, Mei-ling (1897-). Wife of Nationalist Chinese president Jiang Jieshi (Chiang Kai-shek) and sister of T.V. Song. Educated in the United States, she introduced her husband to Western culture and publicized his cause in the West.

Song, Qing-Ling, also known as "Soong" or "Sung Ch'ing-ling" (1892-1981). Chinese politician. The sister of T.V. Song, she married the Nationalist leader Sun Zhong-shan (Sun Yat-sen) and became an active member of the movement. In modern China she has been honored as a link between the original revolutionary movement and the present Communist regime.

Song, T.V., born Sung Tzu-Wen (1894-1971). Chinese financier and politician. He financed the Guomindang (Nationalist) Party of Sun Zhong-shan (Sun Yat-sen) and established (1924) the Central Bank of China at Canton. He held various offices in the Guomindang governments and as foreign affairs minister negotiated (1945)

the Sino-Soviet treaty of friendship. In 1949 he left China for the United States.

song and dance *n.* **1.** A theatrical performance, as in vaudeville, that combines singing and dancing. **2.** *Slang.* **a.** An overelaborate effort to explain or justify. **b.** An elaborate story or explanation intended to mislead or deceive.

song·bird (sông′bûrd′, sŏng′-) *n.* A bird, especially one of the order Passeriformes, having a melodious song or call.

song·ful (sông′fəl, sŏng′-) *adj.* Melodious; tuneful.

Song of Solomon. *Abbr.* **S. of Sol.** A book of the Old Testament consisting of a dramatic love poem traditionally attributed to Solomon. Also called "Canticle of Canticles," "Song of Songs."

song sparrow *n.* A North American songbird, *Melospiza melodia,* having streaked brownish plumage.

song·ster (sông′stər, sŏng′-) *n.* **1.** One that sings. **2.** A writer of songs or verses.

song thrush *n.* An Old World songbird, *Turdus philomelos,* having brown upper plumage and a spotted breast. Formerly also called "mavis," "throstle."

song·writ·er (sông′rī′tər, sŏng′-) *n.* One who writes lyrics or composes tunes, or both, for songs, especially popular songs.

son·ic (sŏn′ĭk) *adj.* **1.** Of or relating to audible sound: *a sonic wave.* **2.** Having a speed approaching or being that of sound in air, approximately 332 meters per second (738 miles per hour) at sea level. [From Latin *son(us),* sound + -IC.]

sonic barrier *n.* The large increase in aerodynamic drag that acts on an aircraft as it approaches the speed of sound. Also called "sound barrier."

sonic boom *n.* A loud transient explosive sound caused by the shock wave preceding an aircraft traveling at supersonic speeds.

son-in-law (sŭn′ĭn-lô′) *n., pl.* **sons-in-law.** The husband of one's daughter.

son·net (sŏn′ĭt) *n.* A 14-line poem usually in iambic pentameter and often made up either of a stanza of eight lines (an octet) followed by one of six lines (a sestet), or, in the Shakespearean form, three sets of four lines followed by a couplet, embodying the statement and the resolution of a single theme. [French, from Italian *sonetto,* from Old Provençal *sonet,* diminutive of *son,* song, from Latin *sonus,* sound.]

son·net·eer (sŏn′ə-tîr′) *n.* **1.** A composer of sonnets. **2.** An inferior poet.

son·ny (sŭn′ē) *n., pl.* **-nies.** A little boy or young man. Used as a familiar form of address. [Diminutive of SON.]

son of a gun *n., pl.* **sons of guns.** *Informal.* A man regarded with the admiring approval of his fellows, often because of his macho qualities; a rogue. Often used as a term of address.

So·no·ra (sə-nôr′ə, -nōr′ə). State of northwestern Mexico, on the Gulf of California south of Arizona. It played a key role in the Mexican Revolution against Spain (1910). Its capital is Hermosillo.

so·no·rant (sə-nôr′ənt, sə-nōr′-, sŏn′ər-) *n. Phonetics.* **1.** Any of a class of phonemes, such as (1), (r), (n), and (m), articulated without friction, being vocalic or consonantal in function according to context. **2.** Either of the semivowels (w) and (y). [SONOR(OUS) + -ANT.]

so·nor·i·ty (sə-nôr′ə-tē, sə-nōr′-) *n., pl.* **-ties. 1.** The quality or state of being sonorous; resonance. **2.** A sound.

so·no·rous (sə-nôr′əs, sə-nōr′-, sŏn′ər-) *adj.* **1.** Having or producing sound. **2.** Having or producing a full, deep, or rich sound. **3.** Rich and impressive, as in style or delivery; grandiloquent. [Latin *sonōrus,* from *sonor,* sound, from *sonāre,* to sound.] **—so·no·rous·ly** *adv.*

son·sy, son·sie (sŏn′sē) *adj. Chiefly Scottish.* **1.** Plump. Used appreciatively. **2.** Cheerful. **3.** Bringing good luck. [Gaelic *sonas,* good luck, from *sona,* lucky.]

Soo Canals. See Sault Sainte Marie Canal.

Soochow. See Suzhou.

soon (sōon) *adv.* **sooner, soonest. 1.** Within a short time; not long after the present time or the time in question. **2.** Without delay or hesitation; quickly; promptly: *came as soon as he got our message; the sooner the better.* **3.** Before the usual or appointed time; early. **4.** *Obsolete.* Immediately. **—as soon.** Willingly; by preference: *I'd as soon stay at home.* **—no sooner.** Immediately or immediately after. Used with *than.* **—sooner or later.** Inevitably. **—would sooner.** Would prefer to; would rather: *would sooner die than marry him.* [Middle English *sone, soon(e),* Old English *sōna,* from Germanic *scænō* (unattested).]

Usage: *No sooner* is generally followed by *than* in constructions such as *No sooner had she come in than the phone rang,* though *when* is a common alternative in informal speech.

soon·er (sōo′nər) *n. Slang.* **1.** A person who settled homestead land in the early West before it was officially made available, in order to have first choice of location. **2. Sooner.** A native or resident of Oklahoma. [From SOON.]

soot (sŏot, sŭt, sōot) *n.* A fine dispersion of black particles, chiefly carbon, produced by the incomplete combustion of coal, oil, wood, or other fuels.
~*tr.v.* **sooted, sooting, soots.** To cover or smudge with soot. [Middle English *so(o)t,* Old English *sōt.*]

sooth (sōoth) *adj. Archaic.* **1.** True; truthful. **2.** Soft; soothing.
~*n. Archaic.* Truth; reality. [Middle English *so(o)th,* Old English *sōth.*] **—sooth·ly** *adv.*

soothe (sōoth) *v.* **soothed, soothing, soothes. —***tr.* **1.** To calm; mollify; placate. **2.** To reduce the intensity of (pain or emotions, for example); assuage; alleviate. **—***intr.* To bring comfort, composure, or relief. —See Synonyms at **relieve**. [Middle English *sothen*, to show to be true, Old English *sōthian*, from *sōth*, truth, SOOTH.] —**sooth·er** *n.* —**sooth·ing·ly** *adv.* —**sooth·ing·ness** *n.*

sooth·fast (sōōth′făst′, -fäst′) *adj. Archaic.* **1.** Truthful; honest. **2.** True; real. [Middle English *sothfast*, Old English *sōthfæst* : *sōth*, SOOTH + *fæst*, FAST (firm).]

sooth·say (sōōth′sā′) *intr.v.* **-said** (-sĕd′), **-saying, -says** (-sĕz′). To foretell future events; predict; prophesy. [Back-formation from SOOTHSAYER.]

sooth·say·er (sōōth′sā′ər) *n.* One who claims to predict future events; prophet; seer. [Middle English *sothsayer* : *soth*, SOOTH + *sayer*, one who says, from *sayen*, to SAY.]

soot·y (sōōt′ē, sōō′tē, sŭt′ē) *adj.* **-i·er, -i·est. 1.** Covered with soot. **2.** Of or producing soot. **3.** Black or dark like soot.

sooty mold *n.* **1.** A fungal growth of mycelium and sooty spores on the surface of a leaf. **2.** Any of various epiphytic fungi, such as species of *Cladosporium*, producing such growths.

sooty tern *n.* An oceanic bird, *Sterna fuscata*, mainly from tropical Atlantic regions, having dark upper plumage.

sop (sŏp) *v.* **sopped, sopping, sops.** —*tr.* **1.** To dip, soak, or drench in a liquid; saturate. **2.** To take up by absorption. Usually used with *up.* —*intr.* To be or become thoroughly soaked or saturated. —*n.* **1.** A bit of bread or other food soaked in a liquid. **2.** Something, especially something of little value, offered in order to gain the favor or mollify the feelings of the recipient. [From Middle English *soppe*, dipped bread, Old English *sopp*.]

SOP standard operating procedure.

sop. soprano.

soph·ism (sŏf′ĭz′əm) *n.* **1.** A plausible but fallacious argument. **2.** Deceptive or fallacious argumentation; sophistry. [Middle English *sophime*, from Old French *sophi(s)me*, from Latin *sophisma*, from Greek, acquired skill, clever device, from *sophizesthai*, to play subtle tricks. See **sophist**.]

soph·ist (sŏf′ĭst) *n.* **1. Sophist.** Any of a class of ancient Greek philosophers active during the second half of the 5th century B.C. who specialized in providing instruction in ethics and the art of public speaking and came to be disparaged for their oversubtle, self-serving reasoning. **2.** A scholar or thinker, especially one skillful in devious argumentation. [From Latin *sophistēs*, from Greek, expert, deviser, from *sophizesthai*, to play subtle tricks, from *sophos*†, skilled, clever.]

so·phis·tic (sə-fĭs′tĭk) *adj.* Also **so·phis·ti·cal** (-tĭ-kəl). **1.** Of, pertaining to, or characteristic of sophists, especially the Sophists of ancient Greece. **2.** Marked by sophistry; fallacious or specious. —**so·phis·ti·cal·ly** *adv.*

so·phis·ti·cate (sə-fĭs′tĭ-kāt′) *v.* **-cated, -cating, -cates.** —*tr.* **1.** To cause to become less natural or simple; especially, to make less naive and more worldly-wise. **2.** To make less true, genuine, or honest; corrupt, pervert, or adulterate. **3.** To make more complex; refine. —*intr.* To use sophistry. —*n.* (sə-fĭs′tĭ-kĭt) A sophisticated person. [From Medieval Latin *sophisticāre*, from Latin *sophisticus*, sophistic, from Greek *sophistikos*, from *sophistēs*, SOPHIST.] —**so·phis·ti·ca·tion** *n.* —**so·phis·ti·ca·tor** *n.*

so·phis·ti·cat·ed (sə-fĭs′tĭ-kā′tĭd) *adj.* **1. a.** Having acquired worldly knowledge; lacking natural simplicity or naiveté. **b.** Having acquired worldly refinement; urbane; cultured. **2.** Complex or complicated; elaborate. **3.** Suitable for or appealing to the tastes of sophisticated people. —**so·phis·ti·cat·ed·ly** *adv.*

soph·is·try (sŏf′ə-strē) *n., pl.* **-tries. 1.** A plausible but misleading or fallacious argument. **2.** Plausible but fallacious argumentation; faulty reasoning.

Soph·o·cles (sŏf′ə-klēz′) (*c.* 495-406 B.C.). Greek dramatist. Together with Euripides and Aeschylus, he was one of the three greatest dramatists of ancient Greece. Of more than 100 plays written by him only 7 survive. These include *Ajax*, probably the earliest; *Oedipus Rex*, considered his masterpiece; *Antigone*; and *Oedipus at Colonus*. —**Soph·o·cle·an** (sŏf′ə-klē′ən) *adj.*

soph·o·more (sŏf′ə-môr′, -mōr′) *n.* A second-year student in a four-year American college or high school. Also used adjectivally: *a sophomore year*. [Greek *sophos*, wise + Greek *mōros*, foolish.]

soph·o·mor·ic (sŏf′ə-môr′ĭk, -mōr′ĭk, -mŏr′ĭk) *adj.* **1.** Of or characteristic of a sophomore. **2.** Immature and overconfident. —**soph·o·mor·i·cal·ly** *adv.*

So·phy, So·phi (sō′fē) *n., pl.* **-phies.** A title formerly given to kings of Persia. [Persian *Safī*, surname of a ruling Persian dynasty (1500-1736), from Arabic *Safī-ud-din*, "purity of religion."]

-sophy *suffix.* Indicates knowledge or a system of thought; for example, *theosophy.* [From Greek *sophia*, wisdom, and *sophos*, wise. See **sophist**.]

so·por (sō′pər, -pôr′) *n.* An abnormally deep sleep; stupor. [Latin *sopor*, sleep.]

sop·o·rif·er·ous (sŏp′ə-rĭf′ər-əs, sō′pə-) *adj.* Inducing sleep; soporific. [From Latin *soporifer* : SOPOR + -FEROUS.] —**sop·o·rif·er·ous·ly** *adv.* —**sop·o·rif·er·ous·ness** *n.*

sop·o·rif·ic (sŏp′ə-rĭf′ĭk) *adj.* **1.** Inducing or tending to induce sleep. **2.** Drowsy. —*n.* A sleep-inducing drug. [SOPOR + -FIC.]

sop·ping (sŏp′ĭng) *adj.* Soaked thoroughly; drenched. —*adv.* Used as an intensive: *sopping wet.*

sop·py (sŏp′ē) *adj.* **-pi·er, -pi·est. 1.** Soaked; sopping. **2.** *Informal.* Oversentimental in a silly way. —**sop·pi·ness** *n.*

so·pra·ni·no (sō′prä-nē′nō, sŏp′rä-) *n., pl.* **-nos.** A musical instrument, as a recorder, that is higher in pitch than the soprano of its family. [Italian, diminutive of SOPRANO.]

so·pra·no (sə-prăn′ō, -prä′nō) *n., pl.* **-os** or **-prani** (-prä′nē). *Abbr.* **sop.** *Music.* **1.** The highest natural human voice, found in some women and in young boys. **2.** A singer having such a voice. **3.** A part for such a voice in four-part harmony. **4.** The tonal range characteristic of a soprano. **5.** The highest-pitched musical instrument in certain families of instruments. —*adj.* Of, pertaining to, for, or in the range of a soprano: *a soprano saxophone.* [Italian, from *sopra*, above, from Latin *suprā*.]

sorb¹ (sôrb) *tr.v.* **sorbed, sorbing, sorbs.** To take up and hold, as by absorption. [Back-formation from ABSORB.]

sorb² *n.* **1.** Any of several Old World trees of the genus *Sorbus* or related genera, such as the white beam or the rowan. **2.** The fruit of such a tree. In this sense, also called "sorb apple." [French *sorbe*, from Latin *sorbus*, SERVICE (tree).]

Sorb (sôrb) *n.* A Wend (see). [German *Sorbe*, perhaps variant of *Serbe*, Serb, from Serbian *Srb*, SERB.]

sor·be·fa·cient (sôr′bə-fā′shənt) *adj.* Bringing about absorption. —*n.* A drug that either causes or facilitates absorption. [From Latin *sorbēre*, to absorb + -FACIENT.]

sor·bet (sôr′bĭt) *n.* **1.** See **sherbet** (sense 1). **2.** A water ice made with fruit juice or fruit purée. [French, from Italian *sorbetto*, from Turkish *sherbet*, SHERBET.]

Sor·bi·an (sôr′bē-ən) *n.* **1.** A Wend (see). **2.** Wendish (see). [From SORB.] —**Sor·bi·an** *adj.*

sor·bic acid (sôr′bĭk) *n.* A white crystalline solid, $C_6H_8O_2$, found in the berries of the mountain ash and also synthesized, used as a food preservative and fungicide. [From SORB (tree).]

sor·bi·tol (sôr′bĭ-tôl′, -tōl′) *n.* A white sweet crystalline alcohol, $C_6H_8(OH)_6$, found in certain fruits and manufactured from sucrose for use as an artificial sweetener and raw material for making ascorbic acid and some plastics. [SORB (tree) + -ITOL.]

sor·bose (sôr′bōs′) *n.* A white crystalline sugar, $C_6H_{12}O_6$, used in the manufacture of ascorbic acid. [SORB (tree) + -OSE.]

sor·cer·er (sôr′sər-ər) *n.* One who practices sorcery; a wizard or magician. [Middle English *sorser*, from Old French *sorcier*, from Vulgar Latin *sortiārius* (unattested), caster of lots, from *sors* (stem *sort-*), lot, chance.]

sor·cer·ess (sôr′sər-ĭs) *n.* A woman who practices sorcery.

sor·cer·y (sôr′sə-rē) *n.* The use of supernatural powers to produce supernatural effects, especially through the assistance of evil spirits; witchcraft; black magic. —See Synonyms at **magic**. [Middle English *sorcerie*, from Old French, from *sorcier*, SORCERER.] —**sor·cer·ous** *adj.* —**sor·cer·ous·ly** *adv.*

sor·did (sôr′dĭd) *adj.* **1.** Filthy or dirty; foul: *a sordid sewer.* **2.** Depressingly squalid; wretched: *sordid shantytowns.* **3.** Morally degraded; vile; despicable: *sordid betrayal.* **4.** Exceedingly mercenary; grasping; selfish. [French *sordide*, from Latin *sordidus*, from *sordēre*, to be dirty.] —**sor·did·ly** *adv.* —**sor·did·ness** *n.*

sor·di·no (sôr-dē′nō) *n., pl.* **-ni** (-nē). Also **sor·dine** (sôr′dēn′, sôr-dēn′). A mute for a musical instrument. [Italian, from *sordo*, deaf, mute, from Latin *surdus*.]

sore (sôr, sōr) *adj.* **sorer, sorest. 1.** Causing physical pain, as from injury or disease; aching or tender: *a sore foot.* **2.** Feeling physical pain; hurting: *sore all over from the fall.* **3.** Causing or involving hardship, misery, or distress; grievous: *sore need.* **4.** Causing embarrassment, irritation, or the like: *a sore subject.* **5.** Full of distress; grieved; sorrowful. **6.** *Informal.* Angered; annoyed. —*adv. Archaic.* Sorely. —*n.* **1.** An open wound or ulcer on the skin or a mucous membrane. **2.** Any source of pain, distress, or irritation. [Middle English *sar, sor*, Old English *sār*.] —**sore·ness** *n.*

so·re·di·um (sə-rē′dē-əm) *n., pl.* **-dia** (-dē-ə). A type of asexual spore produced by certain lichens, consisting of a few algal cells enclosed in fungal hyphae. [New Latin, irregularly from Greek *sōros*, heap, pile.]

sore·head (sôr′hĕd′, sōr′-) *n. Informal.* A person who is easily offended, annoyed, or angered.

sore·ly (sôr′lē, sōr′-) *adv.* **1.** Severely; painfully; grievously. **2.** Extremely; greatly: *His skill was sorely needed.*

Sor·en·sen (sôr′ən-sən), **Theodore Chaikin** (1928–). U.S. author and public official. He served as a special counsel to Presidents John F. Kennedy and Lyndon B. Johnson (1961–64) and has written several works on political topics, including *Decision-Making in The White House* (1963) and *The Kennedy Legacy* (1969).

sore throat *n.* Any of various inflammations of the tonsils, pharynx, or larynx characterized by pain in swallowing.

sor·ghum (sôr′gəm) *n.* **1.** An Old World grass of the genus *Sorghum*; especially, *S. vulgare*, several varieties of which are widely cultivated as grain and forage or as a source of syrup. **2.** Syrup made from the juice of this plant. [New Latin, from Italian *sorgo*, perhaps from Vulgar Latin *syricum (grāmen)* (unattested), Syrian (grass), from Latin *Syricum*, SYRIAN.]

sor·go, sor·gho (sôr′gō) *n., pl.* **-gos** or **-ghos.** Any of various sorghums cultivated as a source of syrup. [Italian *sorgo*, SORGHUM.]

sor·i·cine (sôr′ə-sēn′, sōr′-, sŏr′-) *adj.* Of or belonging to the family Soricidae, which includes the shrews. [From Latin *sōricīnus*, from *sōrex* (stem *sōric-*), shrew, akin to Greek *hurax*, HYRAX.]

so·ri·tes (sō-rī′tēz′) *n., pl.* **sorites.** *Logic.* A form of argument in which a series of incomplete syllogisms is so arranged that the predicate of each premise forms the subject of the next. [Latin *sōrītēs*, from Greek *sōreitēs*, from *sōros*, heap, pile.]

sorrel *This widely distributed grassland plant flowers in summer and autumn. It is shown here growing among buttercups. The plant is used in cooking for soup and salad greens. Slightly toxic, it also figures in a variety of herbal remedies.*

so·ro·ral (sə-rôr′əl, -rōr′əl) *adj.* Of, pertaining to, or like a sister; sisterly. [From Latin *soror,* sister.]

so·ror·ate (sə-rôr′ĭt, -rōr′ĭt) *n.* The custom of marriage of a man to his wife's sister or sisters, usually after the first wife has died or proved sterile. [From Latin *soror,* sister.]

so·ror·i·cide (sə-rôr′ə-sīd′, sə-rōr′-) *n.* **1.** The killing of one's sister. **2.** One who kills a sister. [Medieval Latin *sororicidium* : Latin *soror,* sister + -CIDE.] **—so·ror·i·cid·al** (sə-rôr′ə-sīd′l, sə-rōr′-) *adj.*

so·ror·i·ty (sə-rôr′ə-tē, sə-rōr′-) *n., pl.* **-ties. 1.** A sisterhood. **2.** A social club for women students, as at a university. Compare **fraternity.** [From Medieval Latin *sorōritās,* from Latin *soror,* sister.]

so·ro·sis (sə-rō′sĭs) *n., pl.* **-ses** (-sēz′). *Botany.* A fleshy composite fruit, such as a pineapple, formed from an enlarged spike or perianth. [From Greek *sōros,* heap.]

sorp·tion (sôrp′shən) *n. Chemistry.* **1.** The process of sorbing. **2.** The state of being sorbed. [Back-formation from ABSORPTION and ADSORPTION.]

sor·rel¹ (sôr′əl, sŏr′-) *n.* **1.** Any of several plants of the genus *Rumex,* having acid-flavored leaves sometimes used as salad greens; especially, *R. acetosella,* a widely naturalized species native to Eurasia. **2.** Any of various plants of the genus *Oxalis. See* **wood sorrel.** [Middle English *sorel,* from Old French *surele,* from *sur,* sour, from Germanic.]

sorrel² *n.* **1.** Brownish orange to light brown. **2.** A horse of this color. [Middle English *sorelle,* sorrel-colored, from Old French *sorel,* from *sor,* red-brown, from Germanic.]

Sor·ren·to (sə-rĕn′tō). City of Campania, southern Italy, on the Sorrento Peninsula separating the Gulf of Salerno from the Bay of Naples. It is a popular tourist center and summer resort.

sor·row (sŏr′ō, sôr′ō) *n.* **1.** Mental anguish or suffering, especially because of injury or loss; sadness. **2.** Something that causes such suffering; misfortune. **3.** The expression of such suffering; grieving. —See Synonyms at **regret.**
~*intr.v.* **sorrowed, -rowing, -rows.** To feel or display sorrow; grieve. [Middle English *sorge, sorow,* Old English *sorh, sorg,* anxiety, sorrow.] **—sor·row·er** *n.*

sor·row·ful (sŏr′ō-fəl, -ə-fəl, sôr′-) *adj.* Causing, feeling, or expressing sorrow; mournful. —See Synonyms at **sad. —sor·row·ful·ly** *adv.* **—sor·row·ful·ness** *n.*

sor·ry (sŏr′ē, sôr′ē) *adj.* **-rier, -riest. 1. a.** Feeling sympathy, pity, or distress; sorrowful. **b.** Feeling regret or penitence. Often used to express apology: *I am sorry to be late.* **2.** Inspiring a mixture of pity and scorn; pitiful; deplorable: *a sorry sight.* **3.** Worthless or inferior; contemptible; paltry: *a sorry attempt at apology.* **4.** Causing sorrow or grief; sad; distressing.
~*interj.* Used to express apology or to ask someone to repeat what he has just said. [Middle English *sary, sory,* Old English *sārig,* painful, sad.] **—sor·ri·ly** *adv.* **—sor·ri·ness** *n.*

sort (sôrt) *n.* **1.** A particular class or kind of persons or things grouped together on the basis of some common characteristic. **2.** The character or nature of something; type; quality. **3.** Something that approximates to a certain, often inadequate degree to the specific thing: *a job of a sort; lives in a sort of a penthouse.* **4.** *Informal.* A person: *a good sort.* **5.** Manner; way. **6.** *Usually* **sorts.** *Printing.* One of the characters in a font of type. —See Synonyms at **type. —of sorts. 1.** Of a mediocre or inferior kind. **2.** Of one kind or another. **—out of sorts.** *Informal.* **1.** Somewhat ill; slightly sick. **2.** In a bad mood; irritable; cross. **—sort of.** *Informal.* Somewhat; rather.
~*v.* **sorted, sorting, sorts.** —*tr.* **1.** To arrange according to class, kind, or size; classify. **2.** To separate from others: *sort out the wheat from the chaff.* **3.** To clarify by going over mentally: *tried to sort out her feelings.* **4.** *Scottish Informal.* To repair; restore to working order. —*intr.* To be in harmony; fit in; agree. Used with *with.* [Middle English, from Old French *sorte,* probably from Common Romance *sorta* (unattested), "kind," from Latin *sors* (stem *sort-*), lot, fortune.] **—sort·a·ble** *adj.* **—sort·er** *n.*

Usage: The numerical status of *sort of* and *kind of* when used with a plural noun has long been a source of controversy. Constructions such as *These sort of problems need to be solved* attract criticism on the ground that the singular noun requires a singular modifier. In defense of the construction (which has literary precedent going back to Shakespeare), some argue that the modifer *these/those* is used because of the collective plural sense of the whole noun phrase: *These (sort of) problems need to be solved.* However, many people prefer to avoid the problem altogether, using instead such constructions as *Problems of this sort . . .*

sor·tie (sôr′tē, sôr-tē′) *n.* **1.** A sally by besieged forces upon the besiegers. **2.** A single flight of an aircraft on a combat mission.
~*intr.v.* **sortied, -tieing, -ties.** To go on a sortie. [French, "a going out," from past participle of *sortir*†, to go out.]

sor·ti·lege (sôr′tl-ĭj) *n.* The act or practice of foretelling the future by drawing lots. [Middle English, from Old French, from Medieval Latin *sortilegium,* from *sortilegus,* diviner : Latin *sors* (stem *sort-*), lot + *legere,* to read.]

sor·ti·tion (sôr-tĭsh′ən) *n.* The drawing of lots, as in the selection of candidates for office. [Latin *sortitiō* (stem *sortitiōn-*), from *sortīrī,* to cast lots, from *sors,* lot.]

so·rus (sôr′əs, sōr′-) *n., pl.* **sori** (sôr′ī′, sōr′ī′). *Botany.* **1.** A cluster of spore cases borne by ferns on the undersides of the fronds. **2.** A similar structure in certain fungi and lichens. [New Latin, from Greek *sōros,* heap.]

S O S (ĕs′ō-ĕs′, ĕs′ō-ĕs′) *n.* **1.** The letters represented by the radiotelegraphic signal •••–––•••, used internationally as a distress signal, particularly by ships and aircraft. **2.** Any call or signal for help.

so-so (sō′sō′) *adj. Informal.* Neither very good nor very bad; mediocre; passable. —See Synonyms at **average.**
~*adv. Informal.* Indifferently; tolerably; passably.

sos·te·nu·to (sō′stə-no͞o′tō) *adv. Abbr.* **sost.** *Music.* In a sustained or prolonged manner. Used as a direction.
~*n., pl.* **sostenutos** or **-ti** (-tē). *Abbr.* **sost.** *Music.* A passage played or sung in this manner. [Italian, past participle of *sostenere,* to SUSTAIN.] **—sos·te·nu·to** *adj.*

sot (sŏt) *n.* A chronic drunkard. [Middle English *sot,* a fool, Old English *sott,* from Medieval Latin *sottius*†.]

so·te·ri·ol·o·gy (sō-tîr′ē-ŏl′ə-jē) *n.* The theological doctrine of salvation as effected by Christ. [Greek *sōtērion,* deliverance, from *sōtēr,* savior, from *sōzein,* to save, from *saos,* safe + -LOGY.] **—so·te·ri·o·log·ic** (sō-tîr′ē-ə-lŏj′ĭk), **so·te·ri·o·log·i·cal** *adj.*

So·thic (sō′thĭk, sŏth′ĭk) *adj.* **1.** Designating the ancient Egyptian year, consisting of 365¹/₄ days. **2.** Designating a cycle consisting of 1,461 years of 365 days in the ancient Egyptian calendar. [Greek *Sōthis,* the star Sirius, which appeared on the eastern horizon at sunrise when the year commenced.]

So·this (sō′thĭs) *n.* Sirius, the Dog Star. [Greek *Sōthis,* the Egyptian, the star Sirius. See **Sothic.**]

So·tho (sō′tō) *n., pl.* **-thos** or collectively **Sotho. 1.** A group of Bantu languages spoken in Lesotho, Botswana, and South Africa. **2.** A member of a Sotho-speaking people. **3.** The dialect of Sotho spoken in Lesotho. In this sense, also called "Sesotho."

sot·tish (sŏt′ĭsh) *adj.* **1.** Stupefied from or as if from drink. **2.** Tending to drink excessively; drunken. **—sot·tish·ly** *adv.*

sot·to vo·ce (sŏt′ō vō′chē) *adv.* **1.** Very softly; especially, so as not to be overheard; in an undertone. **2.** *Music.* Very softly. Used as a direction. [Italian, "under the voice."]

sou (so͞o) *n.* **1.** A former French coin of very low value. **2.** A very small amount of money. [French, back-formation from Old French *sous,* plural of *sout,* from Latin *solidus,* SOLIDUS.]

Sou. southern.

sou·brette (so͞o-brĕt′) *n.* **1. a.** A saucy, coquettish, and intriguing lady's maid in comedies or comic opera. **b.** An actress or singer taking such a part. **2.** Any flirtatious or frivolous young woman. [French, from Provençal *soubreto,* feminine of *soubret,* coy, from *sobrar,* to be above, from Latin *superāre,* from *super,* above.]

soubriquet. Variant of **sobriquet.**

sou·chong, soo·chong (so͞o′chông′, -shông′) *n.* One of several varieties of black tea native to China and adjacent regions. [Chinese *xiăo zhŏng,* small kind.]

souf·fle (so͞o′fəl) *n. Medicine.* A blowing sound heard through a stethoscope, as that caused by the movement of blood through the blood vessels. [French, from *souffler,* to blow, ultimately from Latin *sufflāre* : *suf-,* SUB- + *flāre,* to blow.]

souf·flé (so͞o-flā′) *n.* A light, fluffy baked dish made with egg yolks and beaten egg whites combined with various other ingredients and served as a main dish or sweetened as a dessert.
~*adj.* Also **souf·fléed** (-flād′). Made light and puffy by beating or cooking. [French, from the past participle of *souffler,* to blow, puff up. See **souffle.**]

sough (sŭf, sou) *intr.v.* **soughed, soughing, soughs.** To make a soft murmuring or rustling sound: *a gentle soughing wind.*
~*n.* A deep, soft murmuring sound, as of the wind or a gentle surf. [Middle English *swoghen,* Old English *swōgan.*]

sought. Past tense and past participle of **seek.**

sought-af·ter (sôt′ăf′tər, -äf′tər) *adj.* In great demand; highly regarded.

soul (sōl) *n.* **1.** The animating and vital principle in humankind credited with the faculties of thought, action, and emotion and conceived as forming an immaterial entity distinguished from but temporally coexistent with the body. **2.** *Theology.* The spiritual nature of man considered in relation to God, regarded as immortal, separable from the body at death, and susceptible to happiness or misery in a future state. **3.** The disembodied spirit of a dead human being. **4. Soul.** *Christian Science.* God. **5.** The vital, central part or feature of something. **6.** A human being: *a village of 200 souls.* **7.** A person considered as the perfect embodiment of some quality; personification. **8.** A person considered as an inspiring force; a prime mover. **9.** The emotional nature in humankind as distinguished from the mind or intellect. **10.** Depth and sincerity of feeling or the ability to convey this effectively. **11. a.** A capacity for intense and uninhibited emotional feeling, especially considered as a characteristic quality of black American culture. **b.** Soul music. [Middle English *soul,* Old English *sāwol,* from Common Germanic *saiwalō* (unattested).]

soul brother *n. Slang.* A fellow black male.

soul food *n.* Food that belongs to the traditional diet of blacks in the southern United States.

soul·ful (sōl′fəl) *adj.* Full of or expressing deep feeling; profoundly emotional. **—soul·ful·ly** *adv.* **—soul·ful·ness** *n.*

soul·less (sōl′lĭs) *adj.* **1.** Devoid of sensitivity or the capacity for deep feeling. **2.** Devoid of human qualities; depressingly impersonal: *a big soulless office.* **—soul·less·ly** *adv.* **—soul·less·ness** *n.*

soul mate *n.* A person with whom one shares a deep empathy in terms of disposition, point of view, or sensitivity.

soul music *n.* Music derived from black American gospel music with elements of rhythm and blues, characterized by emotional fervor and earthiness.

soul-search·ing (sōl'sûr'chǐng) n. The penetrating examination of oneself and one's motives, convictions, and feelings.

soul sister n. Slang. A fellow black female.

sound¹ (sound) n. **1. a.** A vibratory disturbance characterized by longitudinal waves in the pressure and density of a fluid, or in the elastic strain in a solid, with frequency in the approximate range between 20 and 20,000 hertz, and capable of being detected by the organs of hearing. **b.** Loosely, such a disturbance of any frequency. **2. a.** The sensation stimulated in the organs of hearing by such a disturbance. **b.** Such sensations collectively. **3.** A distinctive auditory effect produced by a particular cause: the sound of the whistle. **4.** The distance over which something can be heard; earshot: within sound of cannon fire. **5. a.** An articulation made by the vocal apparatus. **b.** The distinctive character of such an articulation. For example, bear and bare have the same sound. **6.** A mental impression conveyed; import; implication: I don't like the sound of that. **7.** Auditory material that is recorded, as for a film or television program. **8.** A style of popular music associated with a particular place, person, or the like: the Motown sound. **9.** Archaic. Rumor; report. ~v. **sounded, sounding, sounds.** —intr. **1.** To make or give forth a sound. **2. a.** To produce a particular effect when heard: Your engine sounds very noisy. **b.** To present a particular impression; seem to be: That argument sounds reasonable. It sounds as if we've lost. —tr. **1.** To cause to give forth or produce a sound. **2.** To summon, announce, or signal by a sound: sound a warning. **3.** To articulate (a speech sound); pronounce. **4.** To make known; celebrate. **5.** To examine (a bodily organ or part) by causing to emit sound; auscultate. —**sound off. 1.** To count cadence when marching in military formation. **2.** Informal. To express one's opinions, complaints, or prejudices in a loud, vigorous tone. [Middle English sun, soun, from Old French son, from Latin sonus.]

sound² adj. **sounder, soundest. 1.** Free from defect, decay, or damage; in good condition. **2.** Free from disease or injury; healthy: sound in body and mind. **3.** Having a firm basis; solid; substantial: a sound foundation. **4.** Financially secure or stable; reliable: a sound economy. **5. a.** Founded on valid reasoning; free from misapprehension or logical flaws; sensible and cogent: a sound observation. **b.** Marked by or showing common sense and good judgment; level-headed: sound advice. **c.** Marked by or showing impressive breadth of learning; well-versed. **6.** Thorough; severe: a sound thrashing. **7.** Deep and unbroken; undisturbed: a sound sleep. **8.** Free from moral defect; upright; honorable. **9.** Worthy of confidence; trustworthy. **10.** Compatible with an accepted point of view; orthodox, especially in a theological sense. **11.** Law. Legally valid. —See Synonyms at **healthy, valid.** ~adv. Deeply: sound asleep. [Middle English sund, Old English gesund.] —**sound·ly** adv. —**sound·ness** n.

sound³ n. **1.** A long, relatively wide body of water, wider than a strait or a channel, connecting larger bodies of water. **2.** A long, wide ocean inlet. **3.** The air bladder of a fish. [Middle English sound, sound, swimming, Old English sund, swimming.]

sound⁴ v. **sounded, sounding, sounds.** —tr. **1.** To measure the depth of (water), especially by means of a weighted line; fathom. **2.** To try to find out the attitudes or intentions of, especially by indirect questioning. Usually used with out. **3.** Surgery. To probe (a bodily cavity) with a sound. —intr. **1.** To measure depth. **2.** To dive swiftly downward. Used of a whale or fish. ~n. Surgery. An instrument used to examine bodily cavities. [Middle English sounden, from Old French sonder, from sonde, a sounding line, probably from Old English sund-, from sund, sea.] —**sound·a·ble** adj.

sound barrier n. The **sonic barrier** (see).

sound box n. A hollow chamber in the body of a musical instrument, such as a violin, that intensifies the resonance of the tone.

sound camera n. A motion-picture camera equipped to record sound and image synchronously.

sound effects pl.n. Imitative sounds, as of thunder or an explosion, produced artificially for use in a film, play, or other performance. Also called "effects."

sound·er (soun'dər) n. One that sounds; specifically, a device for making soundings of the sea.

sound·ing¹ (soun'dǐng) n. **1.** The act of one that sounds. **2.** An environmental probe for scientific observation. **3.** Often **soundings. a.** The measurement of the depth of water, as by a hand line or by sonic or ultrasonic means. **b.** A measured depth of water. **c.** Water shallow enough for depth measurements to be taken by a hand line.

sound·ing² adj. **1.** Emitting a full sound; resonant. **2.** Having a rich or impressive sound but little significance; high-sounding.

sounding balloon n. A **ballon sonde** (see).

sounding board n. **1.** A thin board forming the upper portion of the resonant chamber in a musical instrument, such as a violin or piano, and serving to increase resonance. Also called "sound board." **2.** A dome or other structure suspended behind or over a pulpit or platform to reflect the speaker's voice to the audience. **3.** Any person or group whose reactions to an idea, opinion, or point of view will serve as a measure of its effectiveness or acceptability. **4.** Any device or agency serving to spread or popularize an idea or point of view.

sounding lead n. The metal weight at the end of a sounding line.

sounding line n. A line marked at intervals of fathoms and weighted at one end, used to determine the depth of water.

sounding rocket n. A rocket used to make observations anywhere within the earth's atmosphere.

sound·less (sound'lǐs) adj. Having or making no sound; silent. —**sound·less·ly** adv. —**sound·less·ness** n.

sound·proof (sound'proof') adj. Not penetrable by audible sound. ~tr.v. **soundproofed, -proofing, -proofs.** To make soundproof.

sound ranging n. The electronic location of a sound source, as of enemy weapons, by checking time intervals indicated by microphones of known position.

sound stage n. A room or studio, usually soundproof, used for the production of motion pictures.

sound system n. A set of equipment for playing back recorded sound that usually consists of a record deck, amplifier, speakers, and often a cassette player and radio.

sound·track (sound'trăk') n. **1.** The narrow strip at one side of a motion picture that carries the sound recording. **2.** A recording of the music featured in a motion picture.

sound wave n. A wave of sound.

soup (soop) n. **1.** A liquid food prepared from meat, fish, or vegetable stock with various other ingredients added, served either hot or cold. **2.** Slang. Anything suggestive of the consistency of soup, especially: **a.** Dense fog. **b.** Nitroglycerine. —**in the soup.** Informal. In trouble; having difficulties. —**soup up.** Informal. **1.** To increase the power or speed potential of (an engine). **2.** To improve; make more effective. [French soupe, from Old French, broth, sop, from Late Latin suppa, from Germanic.]

soup·çon (soop-sôn', soop'sôn') n. A very small amount; a trace; a touch. [French, SUSPICION.]

soup kitchen n. A place where food is offered free or at very low cost to the needy.

soup·spoon (soop'spoon') n. A spoon with a rounded bowl, used for eating soup.

soup·y (soo'pē) adj. **-ier, -iest. 1.** Having the consistency or appearance of soup. **2.** Foggy. **3.** Informal. Inordinately sentimental.

sour (sour) adj. **sourer, sourest. 1.** Having a taste characteristic of that produced by acids; sharp, tart, or tangy, as lemons are. **2.** Made acid or rancid by fermentation: sour milk. **3.** Having the characteristics of fermentation or rancidity; tasting or smelling of decay. **4.** Bad-tempered and morose; peevish: a sour temper. **5. a.** Disagreeable; unpleasant. **b.** Not up to the expected or usual ability or quality; bad: His pitching went sour. **6.** Designating soil that is excessively acid and damaging to crops. **7.** Containing an excess of sulfur compounds. Said of gasoline. ~n. **1.** The sensation of sour taste, one of the four primary tastes. **2.** Something that is sour. **3.** A mixed drink made especially with whiskey, lime or lemon juice, sugar, and sometimes soda water. ~v. **soured, souring, sours.** —tr. To make sour: "Continued adversity had soured Johnson's temper" (T.B. Macaulay). —intr. To become sour. [Middle English so(u)r, Old English sūr, from Germanic.] —**sour·ly** adv. —**sour·ness** n.

sour·ball (sour'bôl') n. A round piece of hard, tart candy.

source (sôrs, sōrs) n. **1.** A spring, lake, or other body of water at which a stream or river originates. **2. a.** The place or thing from which something originates; the starting point: the source of their quarrel. **b.** That from which something comes or is derived: a source of income; alternative sources of energy. **c.** One that causes, creates, or initiates something: a source of continual annoyance. **3.** A person or place that supplies information. Also used adjectivally: a source book. **4.** A book, document, or other record supplying primary or firsthand information. **5.** The electrode in a field-effect transistor from which the majority carriers flow into the interelectrode region. **6.** In thermodynamics, the part of a system at which heat, or more generally energy, is added to the system. In this sense, compare **sink.** —See Synonyms at **origin.** ~tr.v. **sourced, sourcing, sources. 1.** To give the source of (a quotation, for example). **2.** To obtain (materials) from a producer: sourcing steel from Germany. [Middle English sours, source, from Old French sourse, from the feminine past participle of sourdre, to rise, from Latin surgere, to SURGE.]

source language n. A language from which a translation into another language is made. Compare **target language.**

source program n. A computer program as written in the original programming language for conversion into machine language by the computer.

sour cherry n. **1.** A tree, Prunus cerasus, native to Eurasia, having white flowers and tart red fruit. **2.** The edible fruit of this tree.

sour cream n. A smooth, thick cream, artificially soured by the use of lactic acid bacteria, widely used as an ingredient in soups, salads, and various meat dishes.

sour·dough (sour'dō') n. **1.** Sour fermented dough used as leaven in making bread. **2.** Slang. An old-time settler or prospector, especially in Alaska and northwestern Canada.

sour grapes n. A disparaging attitude toward something that one secretly wants or admires but cannot attain. [From Aesop's fable of the fox that, unable to reach the grapes it wants, decides that they are unripe.]

sour mash n. **1.** A mixture of new mash and mash from a preceding run used to distill certain malt whiskeys. **2.** The whiskey distilled from this mash.

sour·puss (sour'poos') n. Informal. A person with a habitually gloomy or sullen expression or attitude. [SOUR + PUSS (face).]

sour·sop (sour'sŏp') n. **1.** A tropical American tree, Annona muri-

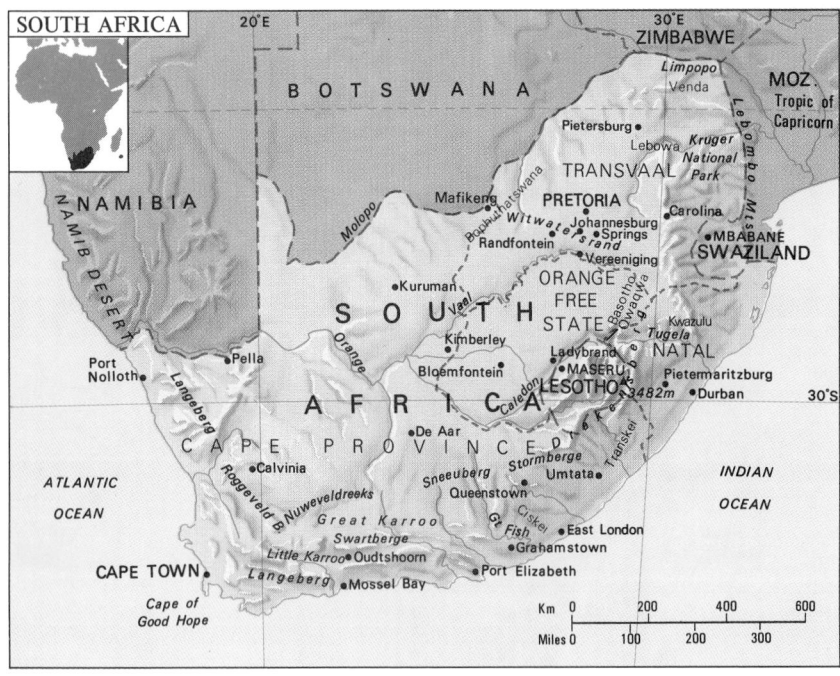

SOUTH AFRICA

---

cata, bearing spiny fruit with tart, edible pulp. **2.** The fruit of this tree.

Sou·sa (sōō′zə, -sə), **John Philip** (1854–1932). American bandmaster and composer. He wrote comic operas, as well as marches such as *Liberty Bell, Washington Post March,* and *Stars and Stripes Forever.*

sou·sa·phone (sōō′zə-fōn′, sōō′sə-) *n.* A large brass wind instrument similar to the tuba, having a flaring bell. [After John Philip Sousa.]

souse¹ (sous) *v.* **soused, sousing, souses.** —*tr.* **1.** To plunge in a liquid. **2.** To make soaking wet; drench. **3.** To steep in a mixture, as in pickling. **4.** *Slang.* To make intoxicated. —*intr.* To become immersed or soaking wet.
~*n.* **1.** The act or process of sousing. **2. a.** Food steeped in pickle; especially, the feet, ears, and head of a pig. **b.** The liquid used in pickling; brine. **3.** *Slang.* A drunkard. [Middle English *sousen,* to souse, to pickle, from *souse,* pickled meat, from Old French *sous, souz,* from Old Saxon *sultia,* Old High German *sulza,* brine.]

souse² *v.* **soused, sousing, souses.** *Archaic.* —*tr.* To pounce upon; attack. —*intr.* To swoop down, as an attacking hawk does. Used with *on* or *upon.* [Middle English *souce,* swooping motion, perhaps variant of *sours,* SOURCE.]

souslik. Variant of **suslik.**

sou·tache (sōō-tăsh′) *n.* A narrow flat braid in a herringbone effect, used for trimming and embroidery. [French, from Hungarian *sujtás.*]

sou·tane (sōō-tän′, -tăn′) *n.* A cassock worn by Roman Catholic priests. [French, from Italian *sottana,* garment worn under (religious vestments), from *sotto,* under, from Latin *subtus,* beneath, from *sub,* under.]

south (south) *n. Abbr.* **s, S, s., S., So., Sth. 1. a.** The direction along a meridian to the right of an observer facing in the direction of the earth's rotation; the direction to the right as one faces the rising sun. **b.** The cardinal point on the mariner's compass 180° clockwise from north. **2.** An area or region lying in this direction. **3.** *Often* **South. a.** One of the four positions at 90° intervals that lies in the south, points north, and stands at right angles to west and east. **b.** In games such as bridge and mahjong, a player who occupies or is said to occupy this position. **4. South. a.** The southern or Antarctic part of the earth. **b.** In the United States, the states lying south of Pennsylvania and east of the Mississippi.
~*adj.* **1.** To, toward, of, facing, or in the south. **2.** Coming from or originating in the south. Said of a wind. **3. South.** Officially or conventionally designating the southern part of a country, continent, or other geographic area: *South America.*
~*adv.* In, from, or toward the south. [Middle English *south,* Old English *sūth.*]

South Africa *Abbr.* **S.A.** Southernmost, richest, and most industrialized country of Africa. Its narrow coastal plains rise sharply to interior plateaus, flanked by the Drakensberg Mts. in the east. Desert areas in the northwest include part of the Kalahari. The population consists chiefly of Bantu-speaking Africans (67 percent), with a ruling white minority (19 percent), Asians (3 percent), and others of mixed race (11 percent). The country has immense mineral resources, including gold, diamonds, chrome, platinum, phosphates, copper, iron, and coal. Mining accounts for some 13 percent of the country's production, manufacturing 24 percent, and agriculture 8 percent. Manufactures include steel and other metals, machinery,

chemicals, and textiles. Only about 12 percent of the land is arable, but 74 percent is suited to grazing, and South Africa is noted for citrus fruits, apples, grapes, wines, cereals, cotton, beef, and wool. Forestry, fishing, and fish processing are also important. With no oil deposits, and because of Middle Eastern conflicts and embargos, South Africa now produces 47 percent of its oil from coal. Johannesburg is the main industrial center and Durban the chief port. The Portuguese were the first Europeans to reach South Africa (1488). Dutch settlers arrived in the 17th century, and Britain eventually gained formal possession of the Cape (1814). Europeans from the Cape met the first African peoples at the Great Fish River, and the first major conflict between them occurred in 1781. Hostility between British and Dutch settlers (known as Boers or Afrikaners) led to the Greak Trek (1835–43), a migration of Boers from the Cape who founded Natal, Orange Free State, and Transvaal. Britain seized Natal (1843), but the other two territories became Boer republics. After the Anglo-Boer Wars (1880–81, 1899–1902) the British and former Boer territories were combined as the Union of South Africa (1910). In 1961 this became an independent republic and withdrew from the Commonwealth. Its ruling National Party's policy of apartheid, which provides for separate development of ethnic groups, has led to internal opposition and the hostility of many nations. Four black homelands have been granted independence: Transkei (1976), Bophuthatswana (1977), Venda (1979), and Ciskei (1980). However, they are not recognized by other countries. A new constitution approved by referendum (1983) gave limited political rights to Asians and those of mixed race. South Africa also administers Namibia. Area, 1,221,037 square kilometers (471,445 square miles). Population, 23,800,000. Capitals, Pretoria (seat of government); Cape Town (seat of legislature); Bloemfontein (seat of judiciary).

South African *n.* A native or inhabitant of the Republic of South Africa, especially one of European descent. —**South African** *adj.*

South America. *Abbr.* **S.A.** A division of the Americas. It is the world's fourth-largest continent. —**South American** *adj. & n.*

South·amp·ton (south-hămp′tən, sou-thămp′-). City and major port in Hampshire, southern England, at the head of Southampton Water. Britain's largest passenger port, Southampton also has considerable freight trade and industries that include ship and yacht building, marine engineering, electronics, and aircraft.

Southampton, Henry Wriothesley, 3rd Earl of (1573–1624). English soldier and statesman. He was a patron of the Elizabethan poets, especially Shakespeare, who dedicated *Venus and Adonis* (1593) and *Rape of Lucrece* (1594) to him; several of the sonnets are probably addressed to him.

South Australia *Abbr.* **S.A.** State in south-central Australia, much of which is inhospitable terrain, with deserts, mountains, salt lakes, and swampland. Agriculture, which produces cereals, vines, sheep, and livestock, is confined mostly to the Murray River area in the extreme southeast. There are valuable mineral deposits in the state; iron ore, salt, gypsum, coal, and natural gas. Adelaide, the capital, is the chief industrial center.

south·bound (south′bound′) *adj.* Going toward the south.

south by east *n. Abbr.* **SbE** The direction, or point on the mariner's compass, halfway between due south and south-southeast. It is 168° 45′ east of due north. —**south by east** *adj. & adv.*

south by west *n. Abbr.* **SbW** The direction, or point on the mariner's compass, halfway between due south and south-southwest. It is 168° 45′ west of due north. —**south by west** *adj. & adv.*

South Car·o·li·na (kăr′ə-lī′nə). *Abbr.* **S.C.** State in the southeastern United States. Extensive coastal lowlands rise to inland plateaus that flank the Appalachian Mts. Traditionally known for its cotton and tobacco plantations, the state is also extensively forested and manufactures furniture, wood pulp, and paper. Other important industries include textiles and chemicals. Columbia is the capital. —**South Car·o·lin·i·an** (kăr′ə-lĭn′ē-ən) *adj. & n.*

south celestial pole *n. Astronomy.* The **South Pole** (see).

South China Sea. Arm of the western Pacific Ocean, lying off Southeast Asia and partially enclosed by Taiwan, the Philippines, and Borneo. It is subject to violent typhoons.

South Da·ko·ta (də-kō′tə). *Abbr.* **S.Dak.** State in north-central United States. It is bisected by the Missouri River, with fertile prairies to the east. The Great Plains to the west include the Black Hills and also the Badlands in the south. Gold and other minerals are mined, but the state's main products are cereals, soybeans, flax, and livestock. Pierre is the capital. —**South Da·ko·tan** *adj. & n.*

South Dev·on (dĕv′ən) *n.* Any of a breed of red English cattle reared for milk and meat. [SOUTH + DEVON, breed of cattle.]

South·down (south′doun′) *n.* Any of a breed of small, hornless sheep of English origin, having dense, short, fine-textured wool. [From the *South Downs* in southern England.]

South Downs. See **Downs, North and South.**

south·east (south-ēst′, sou-ēst′) *n. Abbr.* **SE 1.** The direction, or point on the mariner's compass, halfway between south and east. It is 135° east of due north. **2.** *Sometimes* **Southeast.** The part of any country or region lying in this direction.
~*adj.* **1.** Situated, toward, facing, or in the southeast. **2.** Coming from the southeast. Said of a wind.
~*adv.* In, from, or toward the southeast. —**south·east·ern** *adj.*

Southeast Asia. Subcontinent comprising the 10 modern states of Burma, Thailand, Laos, Kampuchea, Vietnam, Malaysia, Singapore, Brunei, Indonesia, and the Philippines. It covers 3 percent of the world's land area and has 8 percent of its people. The mainland is traversed by part of the Alpine-Himalayan mountain belt, which continues in the island arcs of the East Indies. Several major fertile valleys cross the area, including those of the Irrawaddy and Mekong. The region is the wettest of the major land areas, its equatorial lowlands having *c.* 3,000 millimeters (120 inches) of rain a year and temperatures averaging 27°C (81°F). Elsewhere there is a pronounced dry season. Rain forests with rich wildlife once covered much of the region, and they still provide 18 percent of the world's hardwoods. Soils are generally poor, but farming is important except in Singapore; Southeast Asia produces more than 19 percent of the world's rice and 27 percent of its cassava. Commercial products include rice, palm oil, cane sugar, coffee, natural rubber, and copra. The region is rich in minerals. It accounts for more than 50 percent of the world's tin, and Singapore has a thriving import-export trade. Southeast Asia has some of the world's poorest countries, including Kampuchea and Laos.

Southeast Asia Treaty Organization. *Abbr.* **SEATO** The signatories to the Southeast Asian Collective Defense Treaty of 1954: Australia, France, New Zealand, Pakistan, the Philippines, Thailand, the United Kingdom, and the United States. The organization was abolished in June 1977.

south·east by east *n. Abbr.* **SEbE** The direction, or point on the mariner's compass, halfway between southeast and east-southeast. It is 123° 45′ east of due north. **—southeast by east** *adj. & adv.*

southeast by south *n. Abbr.* **SEbS** The direction, or point on the mariner's compass, halfway between southeast and south-southeast. It is 146° 15′ east of due north. **—southeast by south** *adj. & adv.*

south·east·er (south-ē′stər, sou-ē′-) *n.* A storm or wind blowing from the southeast.

south·east·er·ly (south-ē′stər-lē, sou-ē′-) *adj.* **1.** Toward or in the southeast. **2.** Coming from the southeast. Said of a wind. ~*n., pl.* **-lies.** A storm or wind blowing from the southeast. **—south·east·er·ly** *adv.*

south·east·ward (south-ēst′wərd, sou-ēst′-) *adj.* Situated toward or facing the southeast. ~*n.* **1.** A direction or point toward the southeast. **2.** A region or part situated in or toward the southeast. ~*adv.* Also **south·east·wards** (-wərdz). Toward the southeast. **—south·east·ward·ly** *adj. & adv.*

south·er (sou′thər) *n.* A strong wind coming from the south.

south·er·ly (sŭth′ər-lē) *adj.* **1.** Situated in or toward the south. **2.** Coming from the south. Said of a wind. ~*n., pl.* **southerlies.** A storm or wind blowing from the south. **—south·er·ly** *adv.*

southerly burst·er (bûr′stər) *n.* A strong dry wind bringing exceptionally low temperatures to New South Wales, Australia, when a mass of polar air pulled northward behind a low bursts into warmer areas.

south·ern (sŭth′ərn) *adj. Abbr.* **s, S, s., S., So., Sou. 1.** Situated toward, in, or facing the south. **2.** Coming from the south. Said of a wind. **3.** Native to or growing in the south. **4.** *Often* **Southern.** Of, pertaining to, or characteristic of southern regions or the South. [Middle English *southerne*, Old English *sūtherne.*]

Southern Alps. Mountain range in New Zealand, forming the backbone of South Island. It contains Mt. Cook, 3,763 meters (12,346 feet), the country's highest peak.

Southern Bug. See **Bug** (Ukraine).

Southern Cross *n.* A constellation, **Crux** *(see).*

Southern Crown *n.* A constellation, **Corona Australis** *(see).*

south·ern·er (sŭth′ər-nər) *n.* **1.** A native or inhabitant of the south. **2.** *Often* **Southerner.** A native or inhabitant of the southern United States.

Southern Hemisphere. The half of the earth lying south of the equator.

southern lights *pl.n.* The **aurora australis** *(see).*

south·ern·most (sŭth′ərn-mōst′) *adj.* Farthest south.

south·ern·wood (sŭth′ərn-wŏŏd′) *n.* A woody plant, *Artemisia abrotanum,* native to southern Europe, having finely divided grayish aromatic foliage. Also called "old man."

Sou·they (sou′thē, sŭth′ē), **Robert** (1774–1843). English poet and historian. He was one of the Lake Poets, a pioneer of the romantic movement, and a friend of Coleridge and Wordsworth. In 1813 he became poet laureate.

South Gla·mor·gan (glə-môr′gən). Since 1974 a county in southern Wales, formed from southern Glamorgan and parts of Monmouthshire. The eastern part of the county is dominated by the industrial centers of Cardiff and Barry, while the west consists of arable lowlands. Cardiff, the administrative center, is also the capital of Wales.

south·ing (sou′thĭng) *n.* **1.** The difference in latitude between two positions as a result of a movement to the south. **2.** Progress toward the south. **3.** *Astronomy.* A south declination.

South Island. Also **Middle Island.** The larger but less populous of the two main islands of New Zealand. The principal cities are Christchurch and Dunedin. Much of the southwestern part of the island is taken up by the Fiordland National Park.

South Korea. See **Korea, South.**

south·paw (south′pô′) *n. Informal.* **1.** A left-handed player, especially a left-handed baseball pitcher. **2.** A left-handed person. ~*adj. Informal.* Left-handed.

South Pole *n.* **1.** The southern end of the earth's axis of rotation. **2.** The celestial zenith of the heavens as viewed from the south ter-

restrial pole. Also called "south celestial pole." **3. south pole.** The south-seeking **magnetic pole** *(see)* of a magnet.

south·ron (sŭth′rən, south′-) *n.* **1.** *Chiefly Scottish. Often* **Southron.** A person who lives in the south, especially an Englishman. **2.** A native or inhabitant of the American South. Used by the Confederate side in the Civil War. ~*adj. Chiefly Scottish.* Southern and especially English. [Middle English (Scottish), variant of *southren, southerne,* SOUTHERN.]

South Seas. Area of the Pacific Ocean generally considered to include the central Pacific, the South Pacific, and the southwestern Pacific. Early explorers referred to the entire Pacific Ocean as the South Seas.

South Slavic *n.* The southern division of the Slavic languages, consisting of Old Church Slavonic, Bulgarian, Macedonian, Serbo-Croatian, and Slovene.

south·south·east (south′south-ēst′, sou′sou-ēst′) *n. Abbr.* **SSE** The direction, or point on the mariner's compass, halfway between due south and southeast. It is 157° 30′ east of due north. ~*adj.* Situated toward, facing, or in this direction. ~*adv.* In, from, or toward this direction.

south·south·west (south′south-wĕst′, sou′sou-wĕst′) *n. Abbr.* **SSW** The direction, or point on the mariner's compass, halfway between due south and southwest. It is 157° 30′ west of due north. ~*adj.* Situated toward, facing, or in this direction. ~*adv.* In, from, or toward this direction.

South·um·bri·an (sou-thŭm′brē-ən) *n.* A native or inhabitant of the northern part of the Anglo-Saxon kingdom of Mercia. **—South·um·bri·an** *adj.*

south·ward (south′wərd, sŭth′ərd) *adj.* Situated toward, facing, or in the south. ~*n.* **1.** A direction toward the south. **2.** A region situated in or toward the south. ~*adv.* Also **south·wards** (south′wərdz, sŭth′ərdz). Toward the south. **—south·ward·ly** *adj. & adv.*

south·west (south-wĕst′, sou-wĕst′) *n. Abbr.* **SW 1.** The direction, or point on the mariner's compass, halfway between south and west. It is 135° west of due north. **2.** *Sometimes* **Southwest.** The part of any country or region lying in this direction. **3. Southwest.** A region of the southwestern United States generally considered to include New Mexico, Arizona, Texas, California, Nevada, Utah, and Colorado. ~*adj.* **1.** To, toward, of, facing, or in the southwest. **2.** Coming from the southwest. Said of a wind. ~*adv.* In, from, or toward the southwest. **—south·west·ern** *adj.*

South-West Africa. See **Namibia.**

southwest by south *n. Abbr.* **SWbS** The direction, or point on the mariner's compass, halfway between southwest and south-southwest. It is 146° 15′ west of due north. **—southwest by south** *adj. & adv.*

southwest by west *n. Abbr.* **SWbW** The direction, or point on the mariner's compass, halfway between southwest and west-southwest. It is 123° 45′ west of due north. **—southwest by west** *adj. & adv.*

south·west·er (south-wĕs′tər, sou-wĕs′-) *n.* A storm or wind from the southwest.

south·west·er·ly (south-wĕs′tər-lē, sou-wĕs′-) *adj.* **1.** Toward or in the southwest. **2.** Coming from the southwest. Said of a wind. ~*n., pl.* **southwesterlies.** A storm or wind blowing from the southwest. **—south·west·er·ly** *adv.*

south·west·ward (south-wĕst′wərd, sou-wĕst′-) *adj.* Situated toward, facing, or in the southwest. ~*n.* **1.** A direction toward the southwest. **2.** A region or part situated in or toward the southwest. ~*adv.* Also **south·west·wards** (-wərdz). Toward the southwest. **—south·west·ward·ly** *adj. & adv.*

South Yemen. Poor desert country in the southwest of the Arabian Peninsula, southwestern Asia. The Hadhramaut valley is its only fertile area, yet 70 percent of the people make a living from the land, producing millet, wheat, cotton, sheep, and goats. Aden's oil refinery accounts for more than 80 percent of exports, crude petroleum being the main import. The port of Aden was annexed by Britain (1839), and it was a British protectorate (1882–1914). Britain negotiated treaties with other rulers in the area, and the 17 sultanates combined in the Federation of South Arabia (1959). This was taken over by forces of the National Liberation Front during a civil war (1967). Britain withdrew, and the Southern Yemen People's Republic was proclaimed. It became the only Arab Marxist nation (1969) but receives development aid from both East and West. Area, 332,968 square kilometers (128,526 square miles). Population, 2,000,000. Capital, Aden. See map at **Yemen.**

South Yorkshire (yôrk′shĭr′, -shər). Metropolitan county in northern England. It was formed (1974) from parts of the former West Riding of Yorkshire and Nottinghamshire and the county boroughs of Barnsley, Doncaster, Rotherham, and Sheffield.

Sou·tine (sōō-tēn′), **Chaim** (1894–1943). French artist, born in Lithuania. His style is a vivid and turbulent expressionism; he is noted for his portraits. His works include *Choirboys* (1927) and *The Old Actress* (1924).

sou·ve·nir (sōō′və-nîr′) *n.* Something serving as a token of remembrance, as of a place, occasion, or experience; memento. [French, "memory," from *souvenir,* to recall, from Latin *subvenīre,* to come to mind : *sub-,* up to + *venīre,* to come.]

sou'·west·er (sou-wĕs′tər) *n.* **1.** A waterproof hat, worn especially

space shuttle

BACK AND FORTH TO OUTER SPACE
A replacement for expensive rockets

On April 14, 1981, the American space shuttle *Columbia* landed on a runway in the Mojave Desert in California. Slowing to a halt it looked much like an ordinary airplane. In fact, it had been rocketed from Cape Canaveral, Florida, two days earlier and since then had orbited in space with a crew of two astronauts. *Columbia* was the first reusable spacecraft to be launched.

A space shuttle consists of a winged craft, or orbiter, the size of a DC-9 airliner, which is launched by reusable solid-fuel rocket boosters and a large external fuel tank. It is designed to launch satellites into space and to carry on board scientists who will be able to carry out experiments in the weightless conditions of space. Once its space mission has ended, it reenters the atmosphere to return to earth and land on a runway. During this reentry, it is not a powered craft and it relies on its gliding ability to make a safe touchdown. By 1986 a fleet of 4 space shuttles had flown 24 successful missions.

On January 28, 1986, *Challenger*, a seasoned veteran of the fleet, was embarking on its 10th mission when it exploded shortly after takeoff, killing all crew members and passengers aboard. The disaster, which was later determined to have resulted from structural flaw, caused the suspension of all shuttle missions, thus delaying indefinitely plans to orbit a manned space station by the mid-1990's.

LIFT-OFF *The space shuttle is dwarfed by its external fuel tank flanked by the rocket boosters, which will fall away at a height of 45 kilometers (28 miles). The boosters land in the sea to be recovered later, but the fuel tank is discarded.*

sow thistle *A tall-growing plant of the genus* Sonchus, *resembling the dandelion.*

by sailors, with a broad brim at the back to protect the neck. Also called "nor'wester." **2.** A southwester.

sov. sovereign (coin).

sov·er·eign (sŏv′ər-ən, sŏv′rən) *n.* Also **sov·ran** (sŏv′rən) (for sense 1). **1.** The head of state in a monarchy; a king or queen; a monarch. **2.** *Abbr.* **sov.** A former British gold coin having a nominal value of one pound. ~*adj.* Also **sovran**. **1.** Self-governing; independent: *a sovereign state.* **2.** Having supreme rank or power. **3.** Paramount; supreme. **4. a.** Of superlative quality or efficacy: *a sovereign remedy.* **b.** Unmitigated: *sovereign contempt.* [Middle English *souverein,* from Old French, from Vulgar Latin *superānus* (unattested), from Latin *super,* above.] **—sov′er·eign·ly** *adv.*

sov·er·eign·ty (sŏv′ər-ən-tē, sŏv′rən-) *n., pl.* **-ties. 1. a.** Supremacy of authority or rule, especially as exercised by the sovereign body in a state. **b.** The right to exercise such authority. **2.** Royal rank, authority, or power. **3.** The condition of political independence and self-government. **4.** A sovereign territory.

so·vi·et (sō′vē-ĕt′, sŏv-yĕt′, sŏv′ē-ĕt′) *n.* **1.** In the U.S.S.R., any of the popularly elected legislative assemblies existing at local, regional, and national levels, organized on the basis of the workers', soldiers', and peasants' councils of the revolutionary period. See **Supreme Soviet. 2. Soviets.** The people and government of the Soviet Union. ~*adj.* **1. Soviet.** Of or pertaining to the Union of Soviet Socialist Republics. **2.** Of or pertaining to a soviet. [Russian *sovet,* "council," from Old Russian *suvĕtu.*]

so·vi·et·ize, So·vi·et·ize (sō′vē-ĭ-tīz′, sŏv′ē-) *tr.v.* **-ized, -izing, -izes. 1.** To cause to come under Soviet control. **2.** To bring into line with the cultural, economic, or political norms of the U.S.S.R. **—so·vi·et·i·za·tion** *n.*

Soviet Union. See **Union of Soviet Socialist Republics.**

sov·khoz (sŏf-kôz′, -КНôz′) *n., pl.* **-khozy** (-kô′zē, -КНô′zē). A large state-owned farm in the U.S.S.R. that pays wages to its workers. [Russian, shortened from *sovetskoe khozyaistvo,* soviet economy.]

sow¹ (sō) *v.* **sowed, sown** (sōn) or **sowed, sowing, sows.** —*tr.* **1.** To scatter or plant (seed) over or in the ground for growing. **2.** To plant seed in (land). **3. a.** To implant and cause to arise; introduce: *sow doubts.* **b.** To disseminate; cause to spread: *sow rebellion.* **4.** To strew or cover with anything; spread thickly. —*intr.* To scatter seed for growing. [Middle English *sowen, sawan,* Old English *sāwan.*] **—sow·er** *n.*

sow² (sou) *n.* **1.** An adult female pig. **2. a.** A channel that conducts molten iron to the molds in a pig bed. **b.** The mass of metal solidified in such a channel or mold. [Middle English *sow(e),* Old English *sugu.*]

So·we·to (sə-wē′tō, sō-). Group of black African townships southwest of Johannesburg, South Africa. In June 1976, following the introduction of the compulsory use of Afrikaans for instruction in schools, students rioted in Soweto. Some 200 people were killed, and more than 1,000 were wounded. Unrest continues to this day. [*South Western Townships.*]

sow thistle *n.* Any of various plants of the genus *Sonchus;* especially, *S. oleraceus,* native to Europe, having prickly leaves and yellow flowers. Also called "milk thistle."

sox. Alternate plural of **sock** (sense 1).

soy (soi) *n.* **1.** The soybean. **2.** A salty brown liquid condiment made by fermenting soybeans in brine. [Japanese *shō-yu,* from Chinese *shi-yu* : *shi,* salted beans + *yu,* oil.]

soy·bean (soi′bēn′) *n.* **1.** A leguminous Asiatic plant, *Glycine max,* widely cultivated for forage and for its nutritious, edible seeds. **2.** The seed of the soybean.

sp. 1. special. **2.** specialist. **3.** species. **4.** specific. **5.** spelling.

Sp. Spain; Spanish.

s.p. *Genealogy.* without issue. [Latin *sine prole.*]

S.P. starting price.

spa (spä) *n.* **1.** A mineral spring. **2.** A resort area having mineral springs. [After *Spa,* Belgium.]

Spaak (späk), **Paul Henri** (1899–1972). Belgian statesman. He was the first president of the United Nations Assembly (1946) and of the Assembly of the Council of Europe (1949). He was also secretary-general of NATO (1957–61).

Spaatz (späts, späts), **Carl** (1891–1974). U.S. Air Force general. One of the America's first military pilots, he became chief of the Army Air Forces (1941) and commanded the daylight bombing of Germany (1944). In 1947 he became chief of staff of the Air Force when it was established as a separate branch of the services.

space (spās) *n.* **1. a.** A set of elements or points satisfying given geometric postulates: *a non-Euclidean space.* **b.** The infinite three-dimensional extent in which all matter exists. **2.** The expanse beyond the earth's atmosphere in which the solar system, stars, and galaxies exist; the universe. **3. a.** A measurable interval or extent existing between two or more points or bounded by limits in three dimensions: distance, area, or volume. **b.** Such an interval or extent considered as being unoccupied; unfilled space: *clear a space in the cupboard; wide open spaces.* **c.** An amount of room available or designated for a particular purpose: *a parking space; used a smaller size of type to save space.* **4.** A period or interval of time. **5.** *Music.* Any of the intervals between the lines of a staff. **6.** *Printing.* Any of the blank pieces of type or other means used for separating words or characters. **7.** Any of the intervals during the telegraphic transmission of a message when the key is open or not in contact.

8. Broadcast time or blank space in a publication that is available for advertisers.
~*tr.v.* **spaced, spacing, spaces. 1.** To place or arrange with spaces between. **2.** To separate or keep apart. [Middle English, time interval, from Old French *espace,* from Latin *spatium†,* space, distance.] **—spac·er** *n.*

space age *n.* The period, starting in the middle of the 20th century, when humans have been able to explore space.
~*adj.* Also **space-age** (spās'āj'). Extremely modern in design; based on or suggestive of the technology used in spacecraft.

space biology *n.* See **exobiology** (sense 2).

space capsule *n.* See **capsule** (sense 6).

space charge *n.* An electric charge in a vacuum or region of low gas pressure, as in an electronic valve or vacuum tube, carried by a stream of electrons or ions.

space·craft (spās'krăft', -kräft') *n., pl.* **spacecraft.** A vehicle designed to be launched into space. Also called "spaceship."

spaced-out (spāst'out') *adj. Slang.* **1.** Elated or stupefied as a result of taking a narcotic or hallucinogenic drug; high. **2.** Dazed or lacking concentration.

space flight *n.* A flight of a vehicle into space.

space heater *n.* A heater, especially a portable free-standing one, used to heat an enclosed area.

space lattice *n.* Any of the 14 possible geometric arrangements of points in three-dimensional space at which the components of a crystal may occur. Also called "Bravais lattice."

space·less (spās'lĭs) *adj.* Having no spatial limits.

space·man (spās'măn') *n., pl.* **-men** (-měn'). **1.** Someone who travels in outer space; an astronaut. **2.** In science fiction, one who comes to Earth from outer space.

space medicine *n.* The medical science of the biological, physiological, and psychological effects of space flight upon humans.

space·port (spās'pôrt', -pōrt') *n.* An installation for testing and launching spacecraft.

space probe *n.* A spacecraft carrying instruments designed to explore the physical properties of outer space or of celestial bodies other than Earth. Also called "probe."

space science *n.* **1.** Any of several scientific disciplines, such as exobiology, that study phenomena occurring in the upper atmosphere, in space, or on celestial bodies other than Earth. **2.** Disciplines related to or dealing with the problems of space flight.

space·ship (spās'shĭp') *n.* A spacecraft *(see).*

space shuttle *n.* A space vehicle designed to transport astronauts between Earth and an orbiting space station.

space sickness *n.* Any of various ailments affecting humans during or as a result of space flight.

space station *n.* A large manned satellite designed for permanent orbit around Earth and used for scientific research, military reconnaissance, or as an assembly point for long-range spacecraft.

space suit *n.* A protective pressure suit having an independent air supply and other devices designed to permit the wearer relatively free movement in space.

space-time (spās'tīm') *n.* The four-dimensional continuum of one temporal and three spatial coordinates, in which any event or physical object is located. Also called "space-time continuum."

space walk *n.* An excursion by an astronaut outside a spacecraft in space; extravehicular activity. **—space walker** *n.*

space writer *n.* A writer, especially a journalist, paid according to the amount of space his material occupies in print.

spacial. Variant of **spatial.**

spac·ing (spā'sĭng) *n.* **1.** The action or result of arranging with intervening spaces. **2.** A temporal or spatial interval, typically one forming part of a regular arrangement; space.

spa·cious (spā'shəs) *adj.* **1.** Providing or having much space or room; roomy; extensive. **2.** Expansive in range or scope; allinclusive. [Middle English, *spacios* or Latin *spatiōsus;* see **space, -ous.**] **—spa·cious·ly** *adv.* **—spa·cious·ness** *n.*

spade¹ (spād) *n.* **1.** A sturdy digging tool having a long thick handle and a heavy, flat iron blade that can be pressed into the ground with the foot. **2.** Any of various digging or cutting tools resembling the spade. **3.** *Military.* A sharp metal piece at the back of a guncarriage trail that embeds into the ground to retard the backward motion of the carriage during recoil. **—call a spade a spade.** To speak frankly and directly.
~*tr.v.* **spaded, spading, spades.** To dig or cut with a spade. [Middle English *spade,* Old English *spadu.*] **—spad·er** *n.*

spade² *n.* **1.** The black symbol appearing on one of the four suits of playing cards, in the shape of an inverted heart with a short stalk at the fissure of the two lobes. **2.** A card bearing this symbol. [Italian *spada,* "broad sword" (from its flat, broad shape), from Latin *spatha,* spatula, from Greek *spathē,* broad blade.]

spade·fish (spād'fĭsh') *n., pl.* **-fishes** or collectively **spadefish.** Any of several marine food fishes of the family Ephippidae, especially the genus *Chaetodipterus.* [From their flat, spade-shaped bodies.]

spades *n. Used with a singular or plural verb.* One of the four suits of playing cards identified by the symbol of a spade.

spade·work (spād'wûrk') *n.* The usually dull and arduous preparatory work necessary to a project or activity.

spa·dix (spā'dĭks) *n., pl.* **spadices** (spā'dĭ-sēz'). *Botany.* A clublike spike bearing minute flowers, usually enclosed within a sheathlike spathe, as in the calla and the jack-in-the-pulpit. [Latin *spādīx,* broken-off palm branch, from Greek *spadix;* akin to Greek *spasmos,* SPASM.] **—spa·di·ceous** (spā-dĭsh'əs) *adj.*

spa·ghet·ti (spə-gĕt'ē) *n.* **1.** A pasta in the form of long, solid strings that are cooked by boiling. **2.** *Electricity.* A slender tube of insulating material into which bare wire is inserted, especially in radio circuits. [Italian, plural diminutive of *spago†,* string.]

spa·ghet·ti·ni (spăg'ə-tē'nē) *n.* A form of pasta that is thinner than spaghetti. [Italian, diminutive of SPAGHETTI.]

spaghetti Western *n.* A low-budget Western film made by the Italian film industry.

spa·gyr·ic (spə-gĭr'ĭk) *adj.* Of or pertaining to alchemy; alchemical. [New Latin *spagiricus†,* coined by Paracelsus.]

Spain (spān). *Abbr.* **Sp.** Country occupying much of the Iberian Peninsula, southwestern Europe. Most of it is a high plateau, the Meseta, that is broken by mountain ranges and great river valleys. Spain is industrializing steadily; 25 percent of its workers are in manufacturing, and 17 percent in agriculture and fishing. With few fossil fuel resources, the country has an ambitious nuclear program and is a major uranium producer. The chief exports are fruits and vegetables, chemicals, engineering goods, footwear and leather goods, textiles, wine, olive oil, fish, and cork. Tourism is very important, with more than 35 million visitors a year. Spain, the ancient Roman province of Hispania, eventually emerged as a nation with the expulsion of its last Moorish conquerors (1492) and the joining of the kingdoms of Aragon and Castile (1497). The next two centuries were a golden age, during which a vast empire was built. However, most of this was lost in the 19th century, when the New World colonies gained independence. Spain remained neutral in both world wars. After elections (1931) a republic was declared, but a bitter civil war (1936–39) brought the dictator Gen. Francisco Franco to power. Following Franco's death (1975), Juan Carlos, grandson of the last king, became head of state, and the Spaniards endorsed a parliamentary monarchy in a referendum (1978). Area, 504,782 square kilometers (194,846 square miles). Population, 37,400,000. Capital, Madrid. See map, next page.

spake. *Archaic.* Past tense of **speak.**

Spalato. See **Split.**

spall (spôl) *n.* A chip or fragment from a piece of stone or ore.
~*v.* **spalled, spalling, spalls.** —*tr.* To break up into chips or fragments. —*intr.* To chip or crumble. [Middle English *spalle†.*]

spal·la·tion (spô-lā'shən) *n.* A nuclear reaction in which many particles are ejected from an atomic nucleus by an incident particle of sufficiently high energy. [SPALL + -ATION.]

Spam (spăm) *n.* A trademark for a type of canned processed meat made mainly from ham.

span¹ (spăn) *n.* **1.** The full extent of space or time between two extremities: *the span of a bridge; a short life span.* **2.** The distance between the tips of an aircraft's wings. **3.** The section between two intermediate supports of a bridge. **4.** The length of time during or over which something functions effectively: *a child's attention span.* **5.** A former unit of measure equal to the length of the fully extended hand from the tip of the thumb to the tip of the little finger, generally considered as nine inches.
~*tr.v.* **spanned, spanning, spans. 1.** To measure by or as if by the fully extended hand. **2.** To encircle with the hand or hands in or as if in measuring. **3.** To reach or extend over or across (an extent in space or time): *a career that spanned 40 years.* **4.** To form a span over; bridge. [Middle English *span(ne),* short interval, distance, Old English *span(n).*]

span² *n.* **1.** *Nautical.* A stretch of rope made fast at either end. **2.** A pair of animals, especially horses or oxen matched in size, strength, or color, driven together. [Middle Dutch *span,* from *spannen,* to unite.]

span³. *Archaic.* Past tense and past participle of **spin.**

Span. Spanish.

Span·dau (spän'dou', shpän'-). Industrial district of West Berlin, Germany, surrounding the canal port at the confluence of the Havel and Spree rivers. Its old fortress is a prison where the Nazi war criminal Rudolf Hess is detained.

span·drel, span·dril (spăn'drəl) *n. Architecture.* **1.** The triangular space between the left or right exterior curve of an arch and the rectangular framework surrounding it. **2.** The space between two adjacent arches and the horizontal molding or cornice above them. [Middle English *spaundrell,* perhaps diminutive of Norman French *spaund(e)re,* from Old French *espandre,* to spread out, expand, from Latin *expandere,* to EXPAND.]

spang (spăng) *adv.* Precisely; squarely; firmly: *landed spang in the middle of the street.* [20th century : origin obscure.]

span·gle (spăng'gəl) *n.* **1.** A small, often circular piece of sparkling metal or plastic that may be sewn on clothing for decoration; a sequin. **2.** Any small sparkling object, drop, or spot.
~*v.* **spangled, -gling, -gles.** —*tr.* To adorn or cause to sparkle by covering with or as if with spangles: *"the network of lights spangled the long, straight streets"* (Alec Waugh). —*intr.* To sparkle in the manner of spangles. [Middle English *spangele,* diminutive of *spange,* perhaps from Middle Dutch, buckle.] **—span·gly** *adj.*

Span·iard (spăn'yərd) *n.* A native or inhabitant of Spain.

span·iel (spăn'yəl) *n.* **1.** Any of several breeds of small to medium-sized dogs, originally bred as sporting dogs and usually having drooping ears, short legs, and a silky, wavy coat. **2.** An obsequious or servile person. [Middle English *spaynel,* from Old French *espaignol,* "Spanish," from Vulgar Latin *spāniōlus* (unattested), from Latin *Hispāniōlus,* from *Hispānia,* SPAIN.]

Span·ish (spăn'ĭsh) *adj. Abbr.* **Sp., Span.** Of or pertaining to Spain, its inhabitants, or their language or culture.

~*n. Abbr.* **Sp., Span. 1.** The Romance language of Spain and Spanish America. **2.** *Used with a plural verb.* The people of Spain.

Spanish America. The parts of America inhabited mostly by Spanish-speaking people and including: **1.** South America, excepting Brazil, Guyana, Surinam, and French Guiana. **2.** Central America, excepting Belize. **3.** Mexico, Cuba, Puerto Rico, and the Dominican Republic.

Span·ish-A·mer·i·can (spăn'ĭsh-ə-mĕr'ĭ-kən) *adj.* **1.** Of or pertaining to the countries or people of Spanish America. **2.** Of or pertaining to people of Spanish descent residing in the United States.
~*n.* **1.** A native or inhabitant of a Spanish-American country. **2.** A person of Spanish descent who lives in the United States.

Spanish-American War *n.* The war between Spain and the United States in 1898, as a result of which Spain ceded Puerto Rico, the Philippine Islands, and Guam to the United States and abandoned all claim to Cuba, which became independent in 1902.

Spanish Armada *n.* A fleet sent against England by Philip II of Spain in 1588, considered invincible but defeated and subsequently destroyed by storms. Also called "Armada."

Spanish bayonet *n.* Any of several New World plants of the genus *Yucca*; especially, *Y. aloifolia,* having a tall, woody stem, stiff, pointed leaves, and a large cluster of white flowers, or the similar species *Y. filamentosa,* which is also called "Adam's needle."

Spanish cedar *n.* **1.** Any of several tropical American trees of the genus *Cedrela*; especially, *C. odorata,* having reddish, aromatic wood. **2.** The wood of this tree.

Spanish chestnut *n.* **1.** A tree, *Castanea sativa,* of the Mediterranean area, bearing edible nuts. **2.** The nut of this tree. Sometimes called "marron."

Spanish flu *n.* A form of influenza that broke out in pandemic proportions in 1918 and caused millions of deaths. [Perhaps so called after a great epidemic in 1557, which appears to have begun in Spain.]

Spanish fly *n.* **1.** A European blister beetle, *Lytta vesicatoria.* **2.** A preparation, **cantharides** *(see),* produced from these beetles.

Spanish Guinea. See **Equatorial Guinea.**

Spanish Inquisition. The state tribunal of the Roman Catholic Church instituted in Spain in 1480 to suppress heresy and infamous for its ruthless methods. It was abolished in 1834.

Spanish mackerel *n.* Any of various marine food fishes of the genus *Scomberomorus*; especially, a commercially important species, *S. maculatus,* of American Atlantic coastal waters.

Spanish Main. 1. In the 16th and 17th centuries, the Spanish pos-

sessions in the coastal regions of northern South America between Panama and the Orinoco River. **2.** Those parts of the Caribbean traversed by Spanish ships in colonial times.

Spanish Mo·roc·co (mə-rŏk'ō). A former Spanish colony on the northern coast of Morocco, part of Morocco since 1956.

Spanish moss *n.* An epiphytic plant, *Tillandsia usneoides,* growing on trees of the southeastern United States and tropical America, having gray, threadlike stems drooping in long, matted clusters.

Spanish Neth·er·lands (nĕth'ər-ləndz). The southern part of the Netherlands, which remained under Spanish Hapsburg rule when the Dutch Netherlands won independence in 1648. In 1714 it passed to the Austrian Hapsburgs, and as the Austrian Netherlands it declared its independence as Belgium in 1789.

Spanish omelet *n.* **1.** An omelet served with a sauce of tomatoes, onions, and green peppers. **2.** An omelet made by frying chopped vegetables, such as onions, tomatoes, green peppers, and potatoes, before adding the beaten eggs.

Spanish onion *n.* A mild-flavored, yellow-skinned onion, probably derived from *Allium fistulosum.*

Spanish paprika *n.* A mild seasoning made from pimientos.

Spanish rice *n.* A dish consisting of rice, tomatoes, spices, chopped onions, and green peppers.

Spanish Sahara. See **Western Sahara.**

spank (spăngk) *v.* **spanked, spanking, spanks.** —*tr.* To slap on the buttocks with a flat object or with the open hand, especially as punishment. —*intr.* To move briskly or spiritedly.
~*n.* A slap on the buttocks. [Perhaps imitative.]

spank·er (spăng'kər) *n.* **1.** *Nautical.* A quadrilateral gaff sail set abaft the after mast of a square-rigged sailing ship. Also called "driver." **2.** *Informal.* Something of exceptional quality or remarkable appearance.

spank·ing (spăng'kĭng) *adj.* **1.** *Informal.* Exceptional of its kind in size, strength, quality, or, especially, smartness. **2.** Moving quickly and smartly; brisk; lively: *set off at a spanking pace.*
~*adv.* Very; exceedingly: *spanking new* [17th century : origin obscure.]

span·ner (spăn'ər) *n.* **1.** One that spans. **2.** *Chiefly British.* A wrench, adjustable wrench, or the like. **3.** A **measuring worm** *(see).* [German *Spanner,* from *spannen,* to stretch, tighten, from Old High German *spannan.*]

span-new (spăn'nōō', -nyōō') *adj. Regional.* Entirely new. [Middle English *spannewe,* partial translation of Old Norse *spānnȳr : spānn,* chip + *nȳr,* new.]

span roof *n.* A roof that has two equal sloping sides.

span·worm (spăn′wûrm′) *n.* A **measuring worm** *(see).* [From SPAN (to bind).]

spar[1] (spär) *n.* **1.** *Nautical.* A wooden or metal pole used as a mast, boom, yard, or bowsprit, or in any other way to support rigging. **2.** A similar pole used as part of a crane or derrick. **3.** *Aeronautics.* A principal structural member in an aircraft wing that runs from tip to tip or from root to tip.
∼*tr.v.* **sparred, sparring, spars. 1.** To supply with spars. **2.** *Archaic.* To fasten with a bolt. [Middle English *sparre,* rafter, pole, from Old French *esparre* or from Old Norse *sperra,* beam, both from Germanic.]

spar[2] *intr.v.* **sparred, sparring, spars. 1. a.** To box without exerting oneself to the full, as in a training session. **b.** To fight in any matched and generally indecisive contest. **2.** To bandy words about in argument; dispute. **3.** To fight by striking with the feet and spurs. Used of cocks.
∼*n.* **1.** The act of sparring. **2.** A boxing match. **3.** A cockfight. [Middle English *sparren,* to thrust or strike rapidly, Old English *sperran*†, to strike.]

spar[3] *n.* **1.** Any of various bright, nonmetallic, readily cleavable minerals with a vitreous luster, such as feldspar. **2.** A fragment of such a mineral. **3.** An ornament made of spar. [Low German, from Middle Low German; akin to Old English *spærf*†, gypsum.]

Spar, SPAR (spär) *n.* A member of the women's reserve of the U.S. Coast Guard. [Contraction of Latin *semper paratus,* "always prepared," the motto of the U.S. Coast Guard.]

spa·rax·is (spə-răk′sĭs) *n., pl.* **sparaxis.** Any plant of the South African genus *Sparaxis,* related to the iris and having colorful flowers. [New Latin, from Greek, retching.]

spar deck *n.* A light upper deck of a ship.

spare (spâr) *v.* **spared, sparing, spares.** —*tr.* **1. a.** To treat mercifully; deal with leniently. **b.** To refrain from harming or destroying. **2.** To save or relieve from enduring (something unpleasant): *Spare us the gory details.* **3.** To refrain from using or applying; use with restraint. **4.** To give or grant out of one's resources; afford: *Can you spare ten minutes?* —*intr.* **1.** To be frugal. **2. a.** To be merciful or lenient. **b.** To refrain or forbear.
∼*adj.* **sparer, sparest. 1. a.** Not in immediate or regular use but ready when needed. **b.** In excess of what is needed; extra: *spare cash.* **c.** Free for other use; unoccupied: *spare time.* **2. a.** Economical; meager. **b.** Thin or lean. —See Synonyms at **meager** and Uusage note at **lean** (thin).
∼*n.* **1.** A replacement, such as a spare tire, reserved for future use. **2.** *Bowling.* **a.** The act of knocking down all ten pins with two successive rolls of the ball by a single player. **b.** The score so made. [Middle English *sparen,* to leave unharmed, show mercy, Old English *sparian,* from Germanic *sparōjan* (unattested).] —**spare·ly** *adv.* —**spare·ness** *n.* —**spar·er** *n.*

spare·ribs (spâr′rĭbz′) *pl.n.* A cut of pork consisting of the ribs with most of the meat trimmed off. [By folk etymology from Middle Low German *ribbespēr* : *rebbe,* rib + *spēr,* spit.]

spare tire *n.* **1.** An extra tire carried for emergencies with a motor vehicle. **2.** *Informal.* A roll of flab around the middle of the body.

sparge (spärj) *tr.v.* **sparged, sparging, sparges. 1.** To spray or sprinkle with moisture. **2.** To introduce air or gas into (a liquid).
∼*n.* A sprinkle. [Probably from Latin *spargere,* to sprinkle.] —**sparg·er** *n.*

spar·id (spăr′ĭd, spâr′-) *adj.* Also **spar·oid** (-oid′). Of or belonging to the family Sparidae, which includes the bream, the porgies, and similar fishes.
∼*n.* Also **sparoid.** A member of the Sparidae. [New Latin *sparidae* : *Sparus* (genus), from Latin, gilthead, from Greek *sparos*† + -ID.]

spar·ing (spâr′ĭng) *adj.* **1.** Economical; frugal: *sparing in her use of words.* **2.** Scanty; not profuse: *a sparing application.* **3.** Forbearing; lenient. —**spar·ing·ly** *adv.* —**spar·ing·ness** *n.*
Synonyms: economical, frugal, thrifty.

spark[1] (spärk) *n.* **1.** An incandescent particle, especially: **a.** One thrown off from a burning substance. **b.** One resulting from friction. **c.** One remaining in an otherwise extinguished fire; an ember. **2.** A glistening particle of something, such as metal. **3. a.** A flash of light; especially, a flash produced by electric discharge. **b.** A short pulse or discharge of electric current. **4.** A trace or suggestion, as: **a.** A quality or feeling with latent potential; a seed: *the spark of genius.* **b.** An animating or activating factor: *the spark of revolt.* **5. sparks.** *Used with a singular verb. Informal.* A ship's radio operator. **6.** *Electricity.* **a.** The luminous phenomenon resulting from a disruptive discharge through an insulating material. **b.** The discharge itself, especially as occurring in an internal-combustion engine. **7.** A small diamond or other gem.
∼*v.* **sparked, sparking, sparks.** —*intr.* **1.** To give off sparks. **2.** To operate correctly by producing a spark. Used of the ignition system of an internal-combustion engine. —*tr.* **1.** To set in motion; activate; provoke. Usually used with *off*: *sparked off a strike.* **2.** To rouse to action. —See Usage note at **flash.** [Middle English *sparke,* Old English *spearca, spærca*; akin to Middle Dutch *sparke*†.] —**spark·er** *n.*

spark[2] *n.* **1.** A young dandy. **2.** A lover; a suitor.
∼*v.* **sparked, sparking, sparks.** —*tr.* To court or woo. —*intr.* To play the suitor. [Perhaps of Scandinavian origin.]

Spark (spärk), **Muriel Sarah** (1918–). British novelist, poet, and critic. Among her works, noted for their black humor, are *The Ballad of Peckham Rye* (1960), *The Prime of Miss Jean Brodie* (1961), and *Territorial Rights* (1979).

spark arrester *n.* **1.** A device to keep sparks from escaping, as at a chimney opening. **2.** A device to control electric sparking at a point where a circuit is made or broken.

spark chamber *n.* A device consisting of electrically charged parallel metal plates in a chamber filled with inert gas, used to detect and measure charged elementary particles as they pass from one plate to another, leaving a trail of sparks.

spark coil *n.* An induction coil used to produce a spark, as in an internal-combustion engine.

spark gap *n.* A gap in an otherwise complete electric circuit across which a discharge occurs at some prescribed voltage.

spar·kle (spär′kəl) *intr.v.* **-kled, -kling, -kles. 1.** To give off sparks. **2.** To give off or reflect flashes of light; glitter. **3.** To be witty and animated. **4.** To perform brilliantly; shine. **5.** To effervesce. —See Usage note at **flash.**
∼*n.* **1.** A small spark or gleaming particle. **2.** A glittering appearance. **3.** Animation; vivacity. **4.** Effervescence. [Middle English *sparklen,* frequentative of *sparken,* to SPARK.]

spar·kler (spär′klər) *n.* **1.** One that sparkles. **2.** A firework on a piece of wire held in the hand that burns down gradually and gives off a shower of sparks. **3.** *Informal.* A diamond.

sparkling wine *n.* Any of various effervescent, usually white wines, as champagne, produced by a process that involves fermentation in the bottle.

spark plug *n.* Also *British* **sparking plug. 1.** A device inserted in the head of an internal-combustion-engine cylinder that ignites the fuel mixture by means of an electric spark. **2.** *Informal.* A person who gives impetus or energy to a project or endeavor.

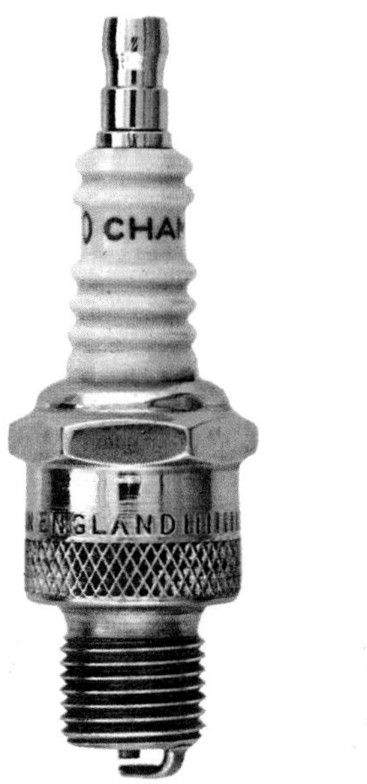
spark plug *The electrical terminal that produces the spark to ignite the gas-air mixture in an internal-combustion engine.*

spark·plug (spärk′plŭg′) *tr.v.* **-plugged, -plugging, -plugs.** *Informal.* To give impetus to (a project, for example); energize.

spark transmitter *n.* *Electronics.* A now obsolete radio transmitter using a discharge across a spark gap to create a signal.

spark·y (spär′kē) *adj.* **-ier, -iest.** Animated; lively.

spar·ling (spär′lĭng) *n.* **1.** A fish, the European **smelt** *(see).* **2.** A young herring. [Middle English *sperlinge,* from Old French *esperlinge,* from Germanic.]

sparoid. Variant of **sparid.**

sparring partner *n.* **1.** A boxer who fights with another in training bouts. **2.** A partner in a friendly contest or dispute.

spar·row (spăr′ō) *n.* **1.** Any of various small New World birds of the genera *Spizella, Zonotrichla, Melospiza,* and other closely related genera within the family Fringillidae, having grayish or brownish plumage. **2.** Any of several similar or related birds, such as the common **house sparrow** *(see).* [Middle English *sparowe,* Old English *spearwa,* from Germanic.]

spar·row·grass (spăr′ō-grăs′, -gräs′) *n.* Also **spar·ry·grass** (spăr′ē-). *Regional.* Asparagus. [By folk etymology from ASPARAGUS.]

sparrow hawk *n.* **1.** A small North American falcon, *Falco sparverius,* that hunts small birds and mammals. **2.** Any of various small hawks of the genus *Accipiter,* which prey on small birds and mammals; especially, *A. nisus,* of Europe and Asia.

sparrow hawk *There are 23 species of sparrow hawk, and sparrows are only one of the small birds that these swift-flying predators hunt. The Levant sparrow hawk (above), however, feeds mainly on lizards and grasshoppers.*

sparse (spärs) *adj.* **sparser, sparsest.** Growing or distributed at widely spaced intervals; not dense: *a sparse crop.* —See Synonyms at **meager.** [Latin *sparsus,* past participle of *spargere,* to strew, scatter.] —**sparse·ly** *adv.* —**sparse·ness, spar·si·ty** (spär′sə-tē) *n.*

Spar·ta (spär′tə). City-state of ancient Greece. Founded in *c.* 1000 B.C., it became one of the most powerful city-states, renowned for its dedication to military discipline. The Spartans defeated the Athenians in the Peloponnesian Wars (431–404 B.C.), but finally fell to the Macedonians in the 4th century B.C. The modern settlement of Sparta was founded close by in the mid-19th century.

Spar·ta·cus (spär′tə-kəs) (died 71 B.C.). Thracian gladiator. He raised an army of slaves that terrorized Roman Italy for two years (73–71). He was finally defeated and killed by Crassus.

spar·tan (spärt′n) *adj.* **1. Spartan.** Of or pertaining to Sparta or its people. **2.** Resembling the Spartans in fortitude or self-discipline; rigorous; austere. **3.** Frugal: *a spartan existence.*
∼*n.* **1. Spartan.** A citizen of Sparta. **2.** Someone of spartan character. —**Spar·tan·ism** *n.*

spar varnish *n.* A waterproof varnish.

spasm (spăz′əm) *n.* **1.** A sudden, involuntary contraction of a muscle or group of muscles. **2.** Any sudden burst of energy, activity, or emotion. [Middle English *spasme,* from Old French, from Latin *spasmus,* from Greek *spasmos,* from *span*†, to draw, pull.]

spas·mod·ic (spăz-mŏd′ĭk) *adj.* **1.** Pertaining to, affected by, or having the character of a spasm; convulsive. **2.** Happening intermittently; fitful: *spasmodic rifle fire.* **3.** Jerky; disjointed: *spasmodic prose.* **4.** Occurring suddenly and violently: *spasmodic fury.* [New Latin *spasmodicus,* from Greek *spasmodikos,* from *spasmos,* SPASM.] —**spas·mod·i·cal·ly** *adv.*

Spas·sky (spăs′kē, spä′skē), **Boris Vasilievich** (1937–). Russian chess player. He was U.S.S.R. Grand Master, International Grand Master, and World Chess Student champion and U.S.S.R. and World Chess Champion (1969–72).

spas·tic (spăs′tĭk) *adj.* **1.** Pertaining to or characterized by spasms; continuously convulsing or contracting. **2.** Caused by spasms or spastic paralysis.
∼*n.* **1.** A person suffering from muscular spasms. **2.** A person suffering from spastic paralysis. [Latin *spasticus,* from Greek *spastikos,* from *span,* to pull, draw. See **spasm.**] —**spas·ti·cal·ly** *adv.* —**spas·tic·i·ty** (spă-stĭs′ĭ-tē) *n.*

spastic paralysis *n.* A chronic pathological condition involving weakness of the limbs with exaggerated tendon reflexes and muscular spasms. It is a common result of cerebral palsy.

spat¹. Past tense and past participle of **spit** (to eject saliva).

spat² (spăt) *n., pl.* **spat** or **spats.** An oyster or similar bivalve mollusk in the larval stage, especially when it settles to the bottom and begins to develop a shell.
~*intr.v.* **spatted, spatting, spats.** To spawn. Used of oysters and similar mollusks. [17th century : origin obscure.]

spat³ *n.* A cloth or leather gaiter covering the shoe upper and the ankle and fastening under the shoe with a strap. [Short for earlier SPATTERDASH.]

spat⁴ *n.* **1.** A brief, petty quarrel. **2.** *Informal.* A slap or smack. **3.** A spattering sound, as of raindrops.
~*v.* **spatted, spatting, spats.** —*intr.* **1.** To engage in a brief, petty quarrel. **2.** To strike with a light spattering sound; slap. —*tr. Informal.* To slap. [Probably imitative.]

spate (spāt) *n.* **1.** A sudden flood, rush, or outpouring: *a spate of angry words.* **2.** *Chiefly British.* **a.** A flash flood. **b.** A freshet resulting from a downpour of rain or melting of snow. **c.** A sudden heavy fall of rain. [Middle English *spate†.]*

spathe (spāth) *n. Botany.* A leaflike organ that encloses or spreads from the base of the spadix of certain plants, such as the jack-in-the-pulpit or the calla. [Latin *spatha,* broad flat instrument, from Greek *spathē,* broad blade.] —**spa·tha·ceous** (spā-thā′shəs, -thā′shəs), **spa·those** (spā′thōs′, -thōs′) *adj.*

spath·ic (spăth′ĭk) *adj.* Having good cleavage. Said of minerals. [From obsolete *spath,* spar, from German *Spat(h),* from Middle High German *spat.]*

spa·tial, spa·cial (spā′shəl) *adj.* Of, pertaining to, involving, or having the nature of space. [Latin *spatium,* SPACE.] —**spa·ti·al·i·ty** (spā′shē-ăl′ə-tē) *n.* —**spa·tial·ly** *adv.*

spa·ti·o·tem·po·ral (spā′shē-ō-těm′pər-əl) *adj.* **1.** Of, pertaining to, or existing in both space and time. **2.** Of or relating to space-time. [Latin *spatium,* SPACE + TEMPORAL.] —**spa·ti·o·tem·po·ral·ly** *adv.*

spat·ter (spăt′ər) *v.* **-tered, -tering, -ters.** —*tr.* **1.** To scatter (a liquid substance) in drops or small splashes. **2.** To spot, splash, or soil. **3.** To strike like a shower: *A handful of pebbles spattered the window.* **4.** To sully the reputation of; defame. —*intr.* **1.** To throw off drops or small splashes; splatter. **2.** To fall with a splash.
~*n.* **1.** The act of spattering. **2.** A spattering sound. **3.** A drop or splash of something spattered; a spot or stain. [Perhaps a frequentative of Dutch *spatten,* from Middle Dutch (perhaps imitative).]

spat·ter·dash (spăt′ər-dăsh′) *n.* A legging formerly worn as a protection from splashes, as of mud. [SPATTER + DASH, to break.]

spat·ter·work (spăt′ər-wûrk′) *n.* The reproduction of designs by spattering color over a stencil.

spat·u·la (spăch′ə-lə) *n.* **1.** A small implement having a broad, flat, flexible blade that is used to spread or mix a semisolid substance such as icing, plaster, or paint. **2.** *Medicine.* An implement with a flat, blunt blade used to press down the tongue, to spread ointments, or to transfer powders. [Latin *spat(h)ula,* diminutive of *spatha,* blade, broad sword, from Greek *spathē.]* —**spat·u·lar, spat·u·lous** *adj.*

spat·u·late (spăch′ə-lĭt) *adj.* Shaped like a spatula: *spatulate leaves.*

spav·in (spăv′ĭn) *n.* Either of two diseases affecting the hock joint of horses: *bog spavin,* an infusion of lymph that enlarges the joint, and *bone spavin,* a bony deposit that stiffens the joint. [Middle English *spaveyne,* from Old French *espavin†.]* —**spav·ined** *adj.*

spawn (spôn) *n.* **1.** The eggs of aquatic animals such as bivalve mollusks, fishes, and amphibians. **2.** Offspring occurring in numbers; brood. **3.** A person regarded as the issue of some usually undesirable parent or family: *the spawn of the devil.* **4.** The product or outcome of something. **5.** Fragments of mycelia used to start a mushroom culture.
~*v.* **spawned, spawning, spawns.** —*intr.* **1.** To deposit eggs; produce spawn. **2.** To produce offspring in numbers like spawn. —*tr.* **1.** To produce (spawn). **2.** To give birth to. Usually used derogatorily of human beings. **3.** To give rise to; engender. **4.** To plant with mycelia. [Middle English *spawne,* from *spawnen,* to spawn, from Norman French *espaundre,* to shed roe, from Old French *espandre,* to shed, spread, from Latin *expandere,* to spread out, EXPAND.]

spawn·er (spô′nər) *n.* A female fish, especially at spawning time.

spawning bed *n.* A nest made on the bed of a stream by fish such as salmon or trout for depositing spawn and milt.

spay (spā) *tr.v.* **spayed, spaying, spays.** To excise the ovaries of (a female animal). [Middle English *spayen,* from Old French *espeer,* to cut with a sword, from *espee,* sword, from Latin *spatha,* broad sword, from Greek *spathē.]*

S.P.C.A. Society for the Prevention of Cruelty to Animals.

S.P.C.C. Society for the Prevention of Cruelty to Children.

speak (spēk) *v.* **spoke** (spōk) or *archaic* **spake** (spāk), **spoken** (spō′kən) or *archaic* **spoke, speaking, speaks.** —*intr.* **1.** To utter words as ordinary speech; talk. **2. a.** To engage in discussion; converse; talk. Also used with an adverb to convey the speaker's attitude toward the message in such phrases as *strictly speaking, to speak frankly.* **b.** To acknowledge another; be on friendly social terms: *They are no longer speaking.* **3.** To deliver an address or lecture; make a speech. **4.** To convey a message: *Actions speak louder than words.* **5.** To be expressive. **6.** To emit a report on firing: *"Our cannons speak and the enemy's now open in full chorus"* (Ambrose Bierce). **7. a.** To make communicative sounds. **b.** To give an impression of speaking: *teach a dog to speak for a bone.* **8.** To be relevant or comprehensible: *Modern art does not always speak to modern man.* —*tr.* **1.** To articulate in a speaking voice. **2.** To converse in or be able to converse in (a language). **3. a.** To express aloud; declare; tell. **b.** To express without words: *His eyes spoke love.* **c.** To communicate in print or writing. **4.** To reveal; show to be. **5.** *Nautical.* To hail and communicate with (another vessel) at sea. —**so to speak.** That is to say; as it were. —**speak for. 1.** To speak on behalf of; represent. **2.** To claim: *This ticket is spoken for.* —**speak for itself.** To be self-evident. —**speak of.** To refer to. —**speak out** (or **up**). **1.** To speak more clearly or louder. **2.** To speak without hesitation or fear: *spoke up for human rights.* —**speak well for.** To express or indicate something favorable about. —**to speak of.** Worthy of mention or discussion. [Speak, spake, spoken; Middle English *speken, spake, spoken,* Old English *specan, spǣc, gespecen.* Past tense *spoke* was formed on analogy with BREAK, BROKE, BROKEN.] —**speak·a·ble** *adj.*
Synonyms: chatter, converse, discourse, gossip, talk.

speak·eas·y (spēk′ē′zē) *n., pl.* **-ies.** A bar selling alcoholic drinks illegally, especially one in the United States during the period of Prohibition.

speak·er (spē′kər) *n.* **1.** One who speaks. Often used in combination: *English-speakers.* **2.** One who delivers a public speech. **3.** *Often* **Speaker.** The presiding officer of a legislative assembly. **4.** A loudspeaker (*see*).

Speaker of the House *n.* The presiding officer of the U.S. House of Representatives.

speak·ing (spē′kĭng) *adj.* **1.** Of, pertaining to, or involving speech: *within speaking distance.* **2.** Inhabited largely by speakers of a specified language. Used in combination: *English-speaking countries.* **3.** Expressive or telling; eloquent. —**on speaking terms.** Sufficiently acquainted or friendly to allow conversation.

speaking tube *n.* A tube or pipe formerly used for speaking from one room or building to another.

spear (spîr) *n.* **1.** A weapon consisting of a long shaft with a sharply pointed head. **2.** A shaft with a sharp point and barbs for spearing fish. **3.** A spearman. **4.** A slender stalk, as of asparagus.
~*v.* **speared, spearing, spears.** —*tr.* **1.** To pierce with or as if with a spear. **2.** To catch (a football, for example) with a thrust of the arm. —*intr.* **1.** To stab with or as if with a spear. **2.** To sprout like a spear. [Middle English *spere,* Old English *spere.]* —**spear·er** *n.*

spear·fish (spîr′fĭsh′) *n., pl.* **-fishes** or collectively **spearfish.** Either of two large marine game fishes, *Tetrapturus angustirostris* or *T. belone,* having the upper jaw elongated into a spearlike projection.

spear·head (spîr′hĕd′) *n.* **1.** The sharpened head of a spear. **2. a.** The vanguard in a military thrust. **b.** A person or group seen as the driving force in a given action or endeavor.
~*tr.v.* **spearheaded, -heading, -heads.** To be the leader or leaders of (a drive or an attack).

spear·man (spîr′mən) *n., pl.* **-men** (-mĭn). A soldier armed with a spear.

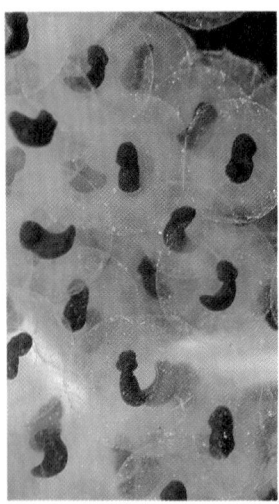

spawn *Fish and amphibians that disperse eggs and sperm into the water to be fertilized are said to spawn; the fertilized eggs are then called spawn. Here embryos of the common frog (Rana temporaria) can be seen developing.*

---

spear

THE WEAPON OF THE HUNTER
Primitive man invented the spear

The spear is one of the earliest man-made weapons, developed from primitive man's use of the stick. With a point hardened by fire, it could be thrust or thrown to bring down animals in the hunt. Stone tips were being fitted to spears 47,000 years ago in the Dordogne, France, but it was in the Bronze Age (from 3000 B.C.) and the Iron Age (from 1200 B.C.) that the spear became a prime weapon. Metalworkers shaped spearheads that were not only ornate but efficient killing weapons. The medieval bill had a hooked blade and spearhead combined and was the forerunner of the pike, which could be set into the ground to repel cavalry.

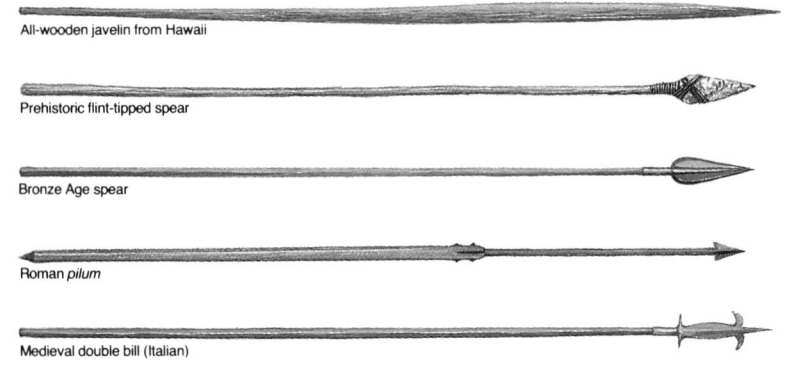

All-wooden javelin from Hawaii

Prehistoric flint-tipped spear

Bronze Age spear

Roman *pilum*

Medieval double bill (Italian)

SIMPLE AND DEADLY *The basic design of the spear remained unchanged for centuries; only in the composition of the tip did major differences appear. All-wooden javelins took on a tapered shape for balance in throwing. The earliest stone tips slowly gave way to flint, which could be chipped and sharpened with more precision. The Bronze Age introduced spearheads of far greater strength and sharpness; stronger still were such iron spears as the Roman pilum, which could either be thrown or used for thrusting. A later development, the bill, added one or two hooked blades to the spearhead.*

spear·mint (spîr′mĭnt′) *n.* An aromatic plant, *Mentha spicata,* native to Europe, having clusters of small purplish flowers and yielding an oil widely used as flavoring. [Perhaps so called from the sharpness of the leaf.]
spear side *n.* The male side of a family. Compare **distaff side.**
spear·wort (spîr′wûrt′, -wôrt′) *n.* Any of several plants related to the buttercup; especially, *Ranunculus flammula,* native to Eurasia, having lance-shaped leaves and yellow flowers.
spec *n. Often* **specs.** *Informal.* A specification.
~*tr.v.* **specced** or **spec'd, speccing** or **spec'ing, specs.** *Informal.* To write specifications for. [Shortening of SPECIFICATION.]
spec. 1. special. **2.** speculation.
spe·cial (spĕsh′əl) *adj. Abbr.* **sp., spec. 1.** Surpassing what is common or usual; exceptional. **2. a.** Distinct among others of a kind; singular. **b.** Primary: *their special concern.* **3.** Peculiar to a specific person or thing; particular. **4.** Having a limited or specific function, application, or scope. **5.** Esteemed; close: *special friends.* **6.** Additional; extra: *a special holiday flight.* **7.** *Informal.* Exceptionally fine: *She's pretty special.*
~*n. Abbr.* **sp., spec. 1.** Something arranged, issued, or made for a particular purpose or occasion. **2. a.** A featured attraction, such as a reduced price: *a special on shrimp.* **b.** A dish specially featured on a menu. **3.** A single television production that features a specific work, a given topic, or a particular performer. [Middle English, from Old French *especial,* from Latin *speciālis,* special, of a particular kind, from *speciēs,* kind, SPECIES.] **—spe·cial·ly** *adv.*
Usage: *Special* and *specially* have wider application than *especial* and *especially.* In the senses that it shares with *especial,* the adjective *special* is now much more commonly used. *Especial* is increasingly rare and is used chiefly to stress pre-eminence or outstanding quality: *a work of especial ingenuity.* The adverb *especially,* on the other hand, has not been similarly displaced by *specially. Specially* is used with reference to a particular purpose: *specially trained; specially arranged. Especially* is used in the sense of "particularly" or "pre-eminently": *He's especially talented. Jones especially is implicated. Prudence is the best policy, especially now.*
special act *n.* A legislative act that applies only to a particular person or area.
special court-martial *n., pl.* **special courts-martial.** A court-martial consisting of at least three officers for trying intermediate offenses.
special delivery *n.* The delivery of a piece of mail, for an additional charge, by a special messenger rather than by scheduled delivery. **—spe·cial-de·liv·er·y** (spĕsh′əl-dĭ-lĭv′ə-rē, -lĭv′rē) *adj.*
special drawing rights *pl.n. Abbr.* **S.D.R., S.D.R.s.** Rights accorded to certain member countries of the International Monetary Fund to draw on the Fund's reserves.
special effects *pl.n.* Illusory effects used in motion pictures and taped television shows that are created by techniques such as animation or 3-D photography.
Special Forces *pl.n.* A division of the U.S. Army composed of soldiers specially trained in guerrilla fighting.
special handling *n.* The handling of fourth-class or parcel-post mail as first-class mail for an extra charge.
spe·cial·ism (spĕsh′ə-lĭz′əm) *n.* **1.** Confinement or limitation to some field of study or occupation. **2.** A field of specialization.
spe·cial·ist (spĕsh′ə-lĭst) *n. Abbr.* **sp. 1.** One who has devoted himself to a particular branch of study or research. **2.** A doctor specializing in a particular field of medicine. **3.** Any of several enlisted ranks in the U.S. Army that correspond to those of corporal through sergeant first class. **—spe·cial·is·tic** (spĕsh′ə-lĭs′tĭk) *adj.*
spe·ci·al·i·ty (spĕsh′ē-ăl′ə-tē) *n., pl.* **-ties. 1.** A distinguishing mark or feature; a special characteristic; a peculiarity. **2. specialities.** Special points of consideration; details; particulars. **3.** *Chiefly British.* Something at which one is particularly adept or for which one makes special provision; a specialty.
spe·cial·i·za·tion (spĕsh′ə-lə-zā′shən) *n.* **1.** The action of specializing or the process of becoming specialized. **2.** An area in which one specializes.
spe·cial·ize (spĕsh′ə-līz′) *v.* **-ized, -izing, -izes.** —*intr.* **1.** To train or employ oneself in a special study, field, or activity. **2.** *Biology.* To develop so as to become adapted to a specific environment or function. —*tr.* **1.** To make more specific or particular. **2.** To give a particular character or function to. **3.** *Biology.* To adapt by specialization.
special pleading *n.* **1.** *Law.* A plea asserting new or special matter to offset the opposing party's allegations, as an alternative to direct denial. **2.** A presentation of an argument that emphasizes only a favorable or a single aspect of the question at issue.
special relativity *n. Physics.* The early part of the theory of **relativity** *(see),* dealing with uniform motion.
special session *n.* An extraordinary session of a court or of a legislative body.
special sort *n.* A special printing character not normally forming part of a particular font. Also called "peculiar."
spe·cial·ty (spĕsh′əl-tē) *n., pl.* **-ties. 1.** *Law.* A special contract or agreement, especially a deed, kept under seal. **2.** A special pursuit, occupation, service, product, or the like. **3.** An aspect of medicine to which physicians confine their practice after certification of special knowledge by examination. **4.** A special feature or characteristic; peculiarity.
spe·ci·a·tion (spē′sē-ā′shən, spē′shē-) *n. Biology.* The evolutionary process by which new species are formed. [SPECI(ES) + -ATION.]
spe·cie (spē′shē, -sē) *n.* Minted money; coin. **—in specie. 1.** In coin. **2.** *Law.* In kind; in the same kind or shape. [Latin *(in) specie,* (in) kind, from the ablative of *speciēs,* kind, SPECIES.]
specie point *n. Finance.* The **gold point** (sense 1) *(see).*
spe·cies (spē′shēz, -sēz) *n., pl.* **species.** *Abbr.* **sp. 1.** *Biology.* **a.** A fundamental category of taxonomic classification, ranking after a genus, and consisting of organisms capable of interbreeding. **b.** A group of organisms belonging to such a category, represented in taxonomic nomenclature by a Latin adjective or epithet following a genus name. **2.** The human race. Preceded by *the.* **3.** *Logic.* A class of individuals or objects grouped by virtue of their common attributes and assigned a common name; a division subordinate to a genus. **4.** A kind, variety, or type. **5.** *Roman Catholic Church.* **a.** The outward appearance or form of the Eucharistic elements that is retained after their consecration. **b.** Either of the consecrated elements of the Eucharist. [Latin *speciēs,* appearance, likeness, a particular kind, from *specere,* to look at.]
specif. specifically.
spec·i·fi·a·ble (spĕs′ə-fī′ə-bəl) *adj.* Capable of being specified.
spe·cif·ic (spə-sĭf′ĭk) *adj. Abbr.* **sp. 1.** Explicitly designated; particular; definite. **2.** Pertaining to, characterizing, or distinguishing a species. **3.** Special, distinctive, or unique, as a quality or attribute may be. **4.** Intended for, applying to, or acting upon a particular thing. **5.** Designating a disease produced by a particular microorganism or condition. **6. a.** Designating a customs charge levied upon goods by unit or weight rather than according to value. **b.** Designating a commodity rate applicable to the transport of a single commodity between named points. **7.** *Physics.* **a.** Designating an extensive physical quality per unit mass: *specific heat capacity.* **b.** Designating a property of a substance per unit mass, length, area, or volume. **c.** Designating a property of a substance divided by the same property of a standard reference substance: *specific gravity.*
~*n.* **1.** *Often* **specifics.** A specific factor, such as a quality, statement, requirement, or attribute: *discussing specifics.* **2.** *Medicine.* A remedy intended for some particular ailment or disorder. [Medieval Latin *specificus,* from Latin *speciēs,* kind, SPECIES.] **—spe·cif·i·cal·ly** *adv.* **—spec·i·fic·i·ty** (spĕs′ə-fĭs′ə-tē) *n.*
-specific *suffix.* Indicates confined in effect, relevance, or scope to what is specified; for example, **job-specific, sex-specific.**
spec·i·fi·ca·tion (spĕs′ə-fĭ-kā′shən) *n. Abbr.* **spec. 1. a.** An act of specifying. **b.** A precisely stated requirement. **2. a.** *Often* **specifications.** A detailed and exact statement of particulars; especially, a statement prescribing materials, dimensions, and instructions for something to be built, installed, or manufactured. **b.** A single item or article that has been specified. **3.** An exact written description of an invention by an applicant for a patent.
specific gravity *n. Abbr.* **sp gr** The ratio of the mass of a solid or liquid to the mass of an equal volume of air or hydrogen under prescribed conditions of temperature and pressure.
specific heat capacity *n.* The amount of heat required to raise the temperature of unit mass of substance by unit interval of temperature under prescribed conditions, usually either at constant volume or constant temperature. It is measured in joules per kilogram per kelvin (SI units) or calories per gram per degree Celsius (c.g.s. units). Formerly called "specific heat."
specific impulse *n.* A performance measure for rocket propellants, equal to units of thrust per unit weight of propellant consumed per unit time. Also called "specific thrust."
specific performance *n. Law.* A remedy awarded by a court requiring the terms of a contract to be fulfilled where damages are insufficient.
specific resistance *n. Electricity.* **Resistivity** *(see).* Not in current technical usage.
specific volume *n.* The volume of unit mass of a substance; the reciprocal of density.
spec·i·fy (spĕs′ə-fī′) *tr.v.* **-fied, -fying, -fies. 1.** To state explicitly, especially as a definite requirement. **2.** To include in a specification. [Middle English *specifien,* from Old French *specifier,* from Medieval Latin *specificāre,* from *specificus,* SPECIFIC.]
spec·i·men (spĕs′ə-mən) *n.* **1.** An individual, item, or part seen as representative of a class, genus, or whole; an example. Also used adjectivally: *a specimen copy.* **2.** A sample, as of tissue, blood, or urine, used for medical or scientific analysis and diagnosis. **3.** An object or organism selected and presented as part of a collection or series: *showed me his finest specimen.* **4.** *Informal.* A person of a specified, usually unpleasant type: *an unsavory specimen.* —See Synonyms at **example.** [Latin *specimen,* mark, token, example, from *specere,* to look at.]
spe·ci·os·i·ty (spē′shē-ŏs′ə-tē) *n., pl.* **-ties. 1.** The state or quality of being specious. **2.** A specious person or thing.
spe·cious (spē′shəs) *adj.* **1.** Seemingly fair, attractive, sound, or true but actually not so; deceptive: *a specious resemblance.* **2.** Having the ring of truth or plausibility but actually fallacious: *a specious argument.* [Middle English, attractive, fair, from Latin *speciōsus,* good-looking, from *speciēs,* outward appearance, from *specere,* to look at.] **—spe·cious·ly** *adv.* **—spe·cious·ness** *n.*
speck (spĕk) *n.* **1.** A small spot, mark, or discoloration. **2.** A very small bit of something; particle.
~*tr.v.* **specked, specking, specks.** To mark with specks; spot; speckle. [Middle English *specke,* Old English *specca*†.]
speck·le (spĕk′əl) *n.* A speck or small spot; especially, a natural dot of color occurring in large numbers on skin, plumage, or foliage.

spearwort *This member of the buttercup family flourishes in damp soil, growing large yellow flowers on long stems.*

PRONUNCIATION KEY
ă, pat; ā, pay; âr, care;
ä, father, are; b, bib;
ch, church; d, deed; ĕ, pet;
ē, be; f, fife; g, gag; h, hat;
hw, which; ĭ, pit; ī, pie;
îr, pier; j, judge; k, kick;
l, lid, needle; m, mum;
n, no, sudden; ng, thing;
ŏ, pot; ō, toe; ô, paw, for;
oi, noise; ou, out; ŏŏ, book;
ōō, boot; p, pop; r, roar;
s, sauce; sh, ship, dish;
t, tight; th, thin, path;
th, this, bathe; ŭ, cut; ûr, fur;
v, valve; w, with; y, yes;
z, zebra, size; zh, vision;
ə, about, item, edible,
gallop, circus, peaceful

IN FOREIGN WORDS:
à, *Fr.* ami; œ, *Fr.* feu, *Ger.* schön; ü, *Fr.* tu, *Ger.* über; KH, *Ger.* ich, *Scot.* loch; N, *Fr.* bon; y′, *Fr.* Compiègne

STRESS MARKS:
Primary stress: ′
in·cite′ (ĭn-sīt′)
Secondary stress: ′
in′sight′ (ĭn′sīt′)

PRONUNCIATION KEY

ă, pat; ā, pay; âr, care;
ä, father, are; b, bib;
ch, church; d, deed; ĕ, pet;
ē, be; f, fife; g, gag; h, hat;
hw, which; ĭ, pit; ī, pie;
îr, pier; j, judge; k, kick;
l, lid, needle; m, mum;
n, no, sudden; ng, thing;
ŏ, pot; ō, toe; ô, paw, for;
oi, noise; ou, out; o͝o, book;
o͞o, boot; p, pop; r, roar;
s, sauce; sh, ship, dish;
t, tight; th, thin, path;
th, this, bathe; ŭ, cut; ûr, fur;
v, valve; w, with; y, yes;
z, zebra, size; zh, vision;
ə, about, item, edible,
gallop, circus, peaceful

IN FOREIGN WORDS:

à, *Fr.* ami; œ, *Fr.* feu, *Ger.* schön; ü, *Fr.* tu, *Ger.* über; KH, *Ger.* ich, *Scot.* loch; N, *Fr.* bon; y', *Fr.* Compiègne

STRESS MARKS:

Primary stress: ′
in·cite′ (ĭn-sīt′)
Secondary stress: ′
in′sight′ (ĭn′sīt′)

~*tr.v.* **speckled, -ling, -les.** To mark with or as if with speckles. [Middle English *spakle,* perhaps of Middle Low German origin.]

speckled trout *n.* The **brook trout** *(see).*

specs (spĕks) *pl.n. Informal.* Glasses; spectacles.

spec·ta·cle (spĕk′tə-kəl) *n.* **1.** A public performance or display, especially a lavish visual entertainment. **2. a.** An object of interest; a marvel or curiosity. **b.** An object or scene considered regrettable: *made a spectacle of himself.* **3. a.** Something seen or able to be seen. **b.** The sight of something: *"We pleased ourselves with the spectacle of Dublin's commerce"* (James Joyce). **4. spectacles. a.** A pair of glasses. **b.** Something resembling glasses in shape or function. [Middle English, from Old French, from Latin *spectāculum,* from *spectāre,* frequentative of *specere,* to look at.]

spec·ta·cled (spĕk′tə-kəld) *adj.* **1.** Wearing spectacles. **2.** Having markings suggesting spectacles. Said of animals.

spec·tac·u·lar (spĕk-tăk′yə-lər) *adj.* **1.** Of the nature of a spectacle; visually impressive. **2.** Striking or remarkable; dramatic: *a spectacular suggestion.*
~*n.* An entertainment, such as a film or television program, with lavish visual presentation. **—spec·tac·u·lar·i·ty** (spĕk′tăk-yə-lăr′ə-tē) *n.* **—spec·tac·u·lar·ly** *adv.*

spec·tate (spĕk′tāt′) *intr.v.* **-tated, -tating, -tates.** *Informal.* To be present as a spectator. [Back-formation from SPECTATOR.]

spec·ta·tor (spĕk′tā′tər) *n.* **1.** One who attends and views a show, sports match, or other event. **2.** An observer of any event; eyewitness; onlooker. [Latin *spectātor,* from *spectāre,* look at. See **spectacle.**]

spectator sport *n.* A sport that attracts large numbers of people who watch it rather than participate in it.

spec·ter (spĕk′tər) *n.* Also *chiefly British* **spec·tre. 1.** A ghost; phantom; apparition. **2.** Something fearful that has no reality. **3.** A mental image of something unpleasant: *the specter of final exams.* [French, from Latin *spectrum,* appearance, image. See **spectrum.**]

spec·tra. Plural of **spectrum.**

spec·tral (spĕk′trəl) *adj.* **1.** Of or resembling a specter; ghostly. **2.** Of, pertaining to, or produced by a spectrum. **—spec·tral·i·ty** (spĕk-trăl′ə-tē), **spec·tral·ness** *n.* **—spec·tral·ly** *adv.*

spectral line *n. Physics.* A discrete peak of intensity in a spectrum; especially, one of the visible dispersed images of the slit through which light enters the collimator of a spectroscope, produced by light of a single wavelength.

spectral type *n.* Any of several methods of classifying stars according to their observed spectra. See **Harvard classification.**

spectro– *prefix.* Indicates spectrum; for example, **spectrograph, spectroscope.** [From SPECTRUM.]

spec·tro·bo·lom·e·ter (spĕk′trō-bə-lŏm′ə-tər) *n. Physics.* A bolometer combined with a spectroscope for investigating how the intensity of a source of radiant energy varies over the range of wavelengths emitted.

spec·tro·gram (spĕk′trə-grăm′) *n. Physics.* A graph or photograph of a spectrum. [SPECTRO- + -GRAM.]

spec·tro·graph (spĕk′trə-grăf′, -gräf′) *n. Physics.* **1.** A spectroscope equipped to photograph spectra. **2.** A spectrogram. [SPECTRO- + -GRAPH.] **—spec·tro·graph·ic** (spĕk′trə-grăf′ĭk) *adj.* **—spec·tro·graph·i·cal·ly** *adv.* **—spec·trog·ra·phy** (spĕk-trŏg′rə-fē) *n.*

spec·tro·he·li·o·gram (spĕk′trə-hē′lē-ō-grăm′) *n. Physics.* A photograph of the sun taken in a narrow wavelength band centered on a selected wavelength.

spec·tro·he·li·o·graph (spĕk′trə-hē′lē-ō-grăf′, -gräf′) *n. Physics.* An instrument used to make spectroheliograms. **—spec·tro·he·li·o·graph·ic** (spĕk′trə-hē′lē-ō-grăf′ĭk) *adj.*

spec·tro·he·li·o·scope (spĕk′trə-hē′lē-ō-skōp′) *n. Physics.* An instrument used to observe solar radiation. **—spec·tro·he·li·o·scop·ic** (spĕk′trə-hē′lē-ō-skŏp′ĭk) *adj.*

spec·trol·o·gy (spĕk-trŏl′ə-jē) *n.* The study of specters.

spec·trom·e·ter (spĕk-trŏm′ə-tər) *n. Physics.* A spectroscope equipped with calibrated scales for measuring the positions of spectral lines. [SPECTRO(SCOPE) + -METER.] **—spec·tro·met·ric** (spĕk′trə-mĕt′rĭk) *adj.* **—spec·trom·e·try** (spĕk-trŏm′ə-trē) *n.*

spec·tro·pho·tom·e·ter (spĕk′trə-fō-tŏm′ə-tər) *n. Physics.* An instrument used to determine the distribution of energy in a spectrum of luminous radiation. **—spec·tro·pho·to·met·ric** (spĕk′trə-fō′tō-mĕt′rĭk), **spec·tro·pho·to·met·ri·cal** *adj.* **—spec·tro·pho·tom·e·try** (spĕk′trə-fō-tŏm′ə-trē) *n.*

spec·tro·scope (spĕk′trə-skōp′) *n. Physics.* Any of various instruments for resolving and observing or recording spectra. [SPECTRO- + -SCOPE.] **—spec·tro·scop·ic** (spĕk′trə-skŏp′ĭk), **spec·tro·scop·i·cal** *adj.* **—spec·tro·scop·i·cal·ly** *adv.*

spectroscopic analysis *n. Physics.* The analysis of a spectrum to determine characteristics of its source, such as the analysis of the optical spectrum of an incandescent body to determine its composition or motion.

spec·tros·co·py (spĕk-trŏs′kə-pē) *n. Physics.* The study of spectra, especially the experimental observation of spectra. [SPECTRO- + -SCOPY.] **—spec·tros·co·pist** *n.*

spec·trum (spĕk′trəm) *n., pl.* **-tra** (-trə) or **-trums. 1.** *Physics.* The distribution of a characteristic of a physical system or phenomenon, especially: **a.** The distribution of energy emitted by a radiant source, as by an incandescent body, arranged in order of wavelengths. **b.** The distribution of atomic or subatomic particles in a system, as in a magnetically resolved molecular beam, arranged in order of masses. Also called "mass spectrum." **c.** A graphic or photographic representation of any such distribution. **2. a.** The complete range of electromagnetic radiation arranged in order of frequency or wavelength. Also called "electromagnetic spectrum." **b.** The complete range of colors as dispersed from light. **3. a.** A range of values of a quantity or set of related quantities. **b.** A broad sequence or range of related qualities, ideas, or activities: *the whole spectrum of 20th-century thought.* [Latin, appearance, image, form, from *specere,* to look at.]

spec·u·lar (spĕk′yə-lər) *adj.* Of, resembling, produced by, or aided by a mirror or speculum. **—spec·u·lar·ly** *adv.*

spec·u·late (spĕk′yə-lāt′) *intr.v.* **-lated, -lating, -lates. 1.** To conjecture on a given subject or situation without knowing all the facts. **2.** To engage in the buying or selling of a commodity with an element of risk on the chance of large profit. —See Synonyms at **conjecture.** [Latin *speculārī,* to spy out, watch, observe, from *specula,* watchtower, from *specere,* to look at.] **—spec·u·lat·or** *n.*

spec·u·la·tion (spĕk′yə-lā′shən) *n. Abbr.* **spec. 1. a.** The act of speculating; consideration of or conjecture about some subject or idea. **b.** A conclusion, opinion, or theory reached by speculating. **2. a.** Engagement in risky business transactions on the chance of quick or considerable profit. **b.** An instance of commercial speculating. **3.** A card game in which players buy trumps from each other on a chance of getting the highest trump dealt.

spec·u·la·tive (spĕk′yə-lə-tĭv, -lā′tĭv) *adj.* **1.** Of, characterized by, or based upon contemplative speculation; conjectural or theoretical in nature rather than pragmatic or realistic. **2. a.** Given to or spent in speculation or conjecture. **b.** Seeming to speculate: *a speculative gaze.* **3. a.** Engaging in, given to, or involving financial speculation. **b.** Involving chance; risky. **—spec·u·la·tive·ly** *adv.* **—spec·u·la·tive·ness** *n.*

speculative philosophy *n.* Philosophy that is theoretical or transcendent rather than demonstrative or empirical.

spec·u·lum (spĕk′yə-ləm) *n., pl.* **-la** (-lə) or **-lums. 1.** A mirror or polished metal plate used as a reflector in optical instruments. **2.** An instrument for dilating the opening of a body cavity, especially the vagina, for medical examination. **3.** *Biology.* **a.** A bright patch of color on the wings of certain birds, especially ducks. Also called "mirror." **b.** A transparent spot on the wings of some butterflies or moths. [Latin, mirror, from *specere,* to look at.]

speculum metal *n.* An alloy of copper, tin, and other metals that takes a high polish and is used in mirrors and reflectors.

sped. Past tense and past participle of **speed.**

speech (spēch) *n.* **1. a.** The faculty or act of speaking; utterance of articulate sounds. **b.** The faculty or act of expressing or describing thoughts, feelings, or perceptions in words. **2. a.** That which is spoken; an utterance. **b.** A line or set of lines spoken by a character in a dramatic work. **3.** Conversation; vocal communication. **4. a.** A talk or public address. **b.** A printed copy of an address. **5.** A person's habitual manner or style of speaking. **6.** The language or dialect of a nation or region. **7.** The sounding of a musical instrument. **8.** The study of oral communication, speech sounds, and vocal physiology. **9.** *Archaic.* Rumor. [Middle English *speche,* Old English *spēc, sprǣc.*]

speech community *n.* All the speakers of a particular language or dialect, whether located in one area or scattered.

speech defect *n.* A defect in speaking, such as a lisp or stammer, having a physiological or psychological cause.

speech·i·fy (spē′chə-fī′) *intr.v.* **-fied, -fying, -fies.** To make a speech, especially a pompous one; orate. **—speech·i·fi·ca·tion** (spē′chə-fī-kā′shən) *n.* **—speech·i·fi·er** *n.*

speech·less (spēch′lĭs) *adj.* **1.** Lacking the faculty of speech; dumb. **2.** Temporarily unable to speak, as through astonishment. **3.** Refraining from speech; silent. **4.** Unexpressed or inexpressible in words: *speechless admiration.* —See Synonyms at **dumb.** **—speech·less·ly** *adv.* **—speech·less·ness** *n.*

speech-read·ing (spēch′rē′dĭng) *n.* **Lip-reading** *(see).*

speech pathology *n.* **1.** The study of speech defects and disabilities and methods of correcting them. **2. Speech therapy** *(see).* **—speech pathologist** *n.*

speech therapy *n.* The practice or profession of dealing with speech defects and disabilities. Also called "speech pathology." **—speech therapist** *n.*

speed (spēd) *n.* **1.** *Mathematics & Physics.* The rate or a measure of the rate of motion, especially: **a.** *Average speed,* or the distance traveled divided by the time of travel. **b.** *Instantaneous speed,* the limit of this quotient as the time of travel becomes vanishingly small; the first derivative of distance with respect to time. **c.** The magnitude of a **velocity** *(see).* **2.** A rate of performance; swiftness of action. **3.** The act or state of moving rapidly; rapidity; swiftness. **4.** A transmission gear or set of gears in a motor vehicle or bicycle. **5.** A rate of rotation, especially that of a record turntable, usually expressed in revolutions per minute or other unit time. **6.** *Photography.* **a.** A numerical expression of the sensitivity of a film, plate, or paper to light. **b.** The capacity of a lens to accumulate light at an appropriate aperture. See **f-stop. c.** The length of time required or permitted for a camera shutter to open and admit light. **7.** *Slang.* An amphetamine taken to increase energy, reduce fatigue, or produce euphoria. **8.** *Archaic.* Prosperity, success, or luck.
~*v.* **sped** (spĕd) or **speeded, speeding, speeds.** —*tr.* **1. a.** To hasten. **b.** To send or dispatch with speed or haste. **2. a.** To increase the speed or rate of; accelerate. Often used with *up.* **b.** To set the speed of (a machine). **3. a.** To wish Godspeed to. **b.** *Archaic.* To help to succeed or prosper; aid. **c.** To further, promote, or expedite (a matter or legal action). Often used with *along.* —*intr.* **1. a.** To go

or move rapidly. **b.** To drive fast; exceed a traffic speed limit. **2.** To pass quickly. Used of time. **3.** To move, perform, or happen at a faster rate; accelerate. Usually used with *up.* **4.** *Obsolete.* **a.** To prove successful; prosper. **b.** To get along; fare. [Middle English *sped(e),* success, prosperity, speed, from Old English *spēd, spēd.*]
Synonyms: *accelerate, expedite, hasten, hurry, precipitate, quicken.*

speed·ball (spēd′bôl′) *n. Slang.* An intravenous dose of cocaine and heroin or morphine.

speed·boat (spēd′bōt′) *n.* A fast motorboat.

speed·er (spē′dər) *n.* One that speeds; especially, a driver who exceeds a legal or safe speed.

speed limit *n.* The maximum speed legally permitted on a given stretch of road.

speed·om·e·ter (spē-dŏm′ə-tər) *n.* An instrument for measuring and indicating speed.

speed-read·ing (spēd′rē′dĭng) *n.* A method of reading rapidly by assimilating several words or phrases at a glance or by skimming. **—speed-read** *v.* **—speed-read·er** *n.*

speed·ster (spēd′stər) *n.* **1.** A speeder. **2.** A fast vehicle, usually a sports car.

speed trap *n.* A stretch of road on which the speed of vehicles is secretly checked by police using electronic or other devices.

speed·way (spēd′wā′) *n.* **1.** A racecourse for automobiles or motorcycles. **2.** A road designed for fast-moving traffic.

speed·well (spēd′wĕl′) *n.* Any of various plants of the genus *Veronica,* having clusters of small, usually blue flowers.

speed·y (spē′dē) *adj.* **-ier, -iest. 1.** Characterized by rapid motion; swift. **2.** Accomplished or arrived at without delay; prompt; quick. —See Synonyms at **fast. —speed·i·ly** *adv.* **—speed·i·ness** *n.*

speer, speir (spîr) *v.* **speered** or **speired, speering** or **speiring, speers** or **speirs.** *Scottish. —intr.* To ask questions. *—tr.* To ask; inquire. [Middle English, from Old English *spyrian,* to seek; akin to SPOOR.]

Speer (shpâr, spîr), **Albert** (1905–81). German architect and Nazi politician. As Adolf Hitler's personal architect (1933–45), he was awarded several commissions, including the design of the parade grounds of the Nuremberg party congress (1936).

spe·le·ol·o·gy (spē′lē-ŏl′ə-jē) *n.* **1.** The study of the physical, geologic, and biological aspects of caves. **2.** The exploration of caves. [Latin *spēleum,* cave, from Greek *spēlaion*† + -LOGY.] **—spe·le·o·log·i·cal** (spē′lē-ə-lŏj′ĭ-kəl) *adj.* **—spe·le·ol·o·gist** *n.*

spell[1] (spĕl) *v.* **spelled** or **spelt** (spĕlt), **spelling, spells.** *—tr.* **1.** To name or write in order the letters constituting (a word or part of a word). **2.** To be the ordered letters of; form (a word). **3.** To mean; be a sign of: *That tone of voice spells trouble. —intr.* To form a word or words correctly by naming the letters. **—spell out. 1.** *Informal.* To make explicit and understandable: *He didn't need to spell out his threat.* **2.** To spell slowly, letter by letter, especially when trying to read or decipher. [Middle English *spellen,* to read out, from Old French *espelir, espeller,* from Germanic.] **—spell·a·ble** *adj.*

spell[2] *n.* **1.** A word or formula used to work magic. **2.** Compelling attraction; fascination. **3.** A bewitched state; trance. [Middle English *spell,* discourse, Old English *spel(l),* story, fable.]

spell[3] *n.* **1.** A short, indefinite period of time. **2.** *Informal.* A period characterized by some specified condition, such as weather, activity, or illness: *a dry spell; a dizzy spell.* **3.** A short period of work; shift: *a spell at the helm.* **4.** *Australian.* A period or interval of rest. **5.** *Informal.* A short distance.
~v. **spelled, spelling, spells.** *—tr.* **1.** To relieve (a person) from work temporarily by taking a turn. **2.** To allow to rest a while. [Perhaps from Middle English *spelen,* to relieve at work, Old English *spelian*†, to substitute.]

spell·bind (spĕl′bīnd′) *tr.v.* **-bound** (-bound′), **-binding, -binds.** To put or hold under or as if under a spell; enthrall; enchant.

spell·bind·er (spĕl′bīn′dər) *n.* One that holds others spellbound.

spell·bound (spĕl′bound′) *adj.* Entranced; fascinated.

spell·er (spĕl′ər) *n.* **1.** One who spells words, usually in a specified manner. **2.** An elementary textbook to teach spelling.

spellican. Variant of **spillikin.**

spell·ing (spĕl′ĭng) *n. Abbr.* **sp. 1. a.** The forming of words with letters in an accepted order; orthography. **b.** The art or study of orthography. **c.** A person's ability to spell. **2.** The way in which a word is spelled.

spelling bee *n.* A contest in which competitors are eliminated as they fail to spell a given word correctly.

spelling pronunciation *n.* The pronunciation of a word based on the way in which it is spelled, as (fôr′hĕd′) rather than (fôr′ĭd) for the word "forehead."

Spell·man (spĕl′mən), **Francis Joseph** (1889–1967). U.S. prelate. Elevated to archbishop of New York in 1939, he remained politically and theologically conservative throughout his tenure. His efficient administration of the New York diocese doubled the number of parishioners and made possible the building of many churches, schools, and hospitals.

spelt[1] (spĕlt) *n.* A hardy wheat, *Triticum spelta,* from which many cultivated wheats are derived. [Probably from Middle Dutch *spelte.*]

spelt[2]. Alternate past tense and past participle of **spell** (to form words).

spel·ter (spĕl′tər) *n.* Impure zinc, especially in the form of ingots, slabs, or plates. [Obscurely akin to Middle Dutch *speauter*†; akin to Old French *peautre,* PEWTER.]

spe·lun·ker (spĭ-lŭng′kər, spē′lŭng′kər) *n.* One who explores and studies caves. [From obsolete *spelunk,* cave, from Middle English, from Latin *spelunca,* from Greek *spēlunx*; akin to Greek *spēlaion.* See **speleology.**] **—spe·lun·king** *n.*

spen·cer[1] (spĕn′sər) *n. Nautical.* A **trysail** *(see).* [Perhaps from the surname *Spencer.*]

spencer[2] *n.* **1.** A short double-breasted overcoat worn by men in the early 19th century. **2.** A close-fitting waist-length jacket formerly worn by women. **3.** A short-sleeved woman's vest. [After George *Spencer,* 2nd Earl Spencer (1758–1834).]

Spen·cer (spĕn′sər), **Herbert** (1820–1903). English philosopher. One of the most influential philosophers of Victorian England, he advocated the theory of evolution and believed that the individual is superior to society and that science is superior to religion. His best-known work, *The Synthetic Philosophy,* was completed in 1896.

Spencer Gulf. Inlet of the Indian Ocean, on the southern coast of Australia between Eyre Peninsula to the west and Yorke Peninsula to the east.

Spen·ce·ri·an·ism (spĕn-sîr′ē-ə-nĭz′əm) *n.* The system of logical positivism developed by Herbert Spencer and setting forth the idea that evolution is the mechanistic passage from the simple, indefinite, and incoherent to the complex, definite, and coherent. Also called "synthetic philosophy."

spend (spĕnd) *v.* **spent** (spĕnt), **spending, spends.** *—tr.* **1.** To pay out (money). **2.** To use, concentrate, or devote. Often used with *on*: *spending his energy on pleasures.* **3.** To use up, consume, or expend: *The gale spent its force.* **4.** To pass (time) in a specified manner or place. **5. a.** To throw away; waste; squander. **b.** To sacrifice. *—intr.* **1.** To pay out money. **2.** *Obsolete.* To be exhausted or consumed. [Spend, spent, spent; Middle English *spenden, spente, spent,* partly from Old English *spendan,* from Latin *expendēre,* to EXPEND, and partly from Old French *despendre,* to dispend, squander.] **—spend·a·ble** *adj.*

spend·er (spĕn′dər) *n.* One that spends money in a specified way: *a big spender.*

Spen·der (spĕn′dər), **Stephen** (1909–). English poet and critic. He was a leading member of a group of socialist poets in the 1930's and fought with the Republicans in the Spanish Civil War. Much of his work is characterized by imagery of an industrialized society.

spending money *n.* Cash for small personal needs.

spend·thrift (spĕnd′thrĭft′) *n.* One who squanders money; a prodigal spender.
~adj. Wasteful or extravagant. [SPEND + THRIFT (accumulated wealth).]

Speng·ler (spĕng′lər, shpĕng′-), **Oswald** (1880–1936). German philosopher. He argued that civilizations and cultures are subject to the same cycle of growth and decay as human beings. His chief work, *The Decline of the West* (1918–22), reflects the pessimistic atmosphere in Germany after World War I.

Spen·ser (spĕn′sər), **Edmund** (*c.* 1552–99). English poet. He is known chiefly for his allegorical epic romance *The Faerie Queen* (1590–96). His other works include the pastoral *Shepherd's Calendar* (1579) and the lyrical marriage poem *Epithalamion* (1595).

Spen·se·ri·an sonnet (spĕn-sîr′ē-ən) *n.* A sonnet comprising three interlocking quatrains and a couplet with the rhyme pattern *abab bcbc cdcd ee.* [After Edmund SPENSER.]

Spenserian stanza *n.* A stanza consisting of eight lines of iambic pentameter and a final alexandrine, rhymed *ababbcbcc,* used by Edmund Spenser in *The Faerie Queene.*

spent (spĕnt). Past tense and past participle of **spend.**
~adj. **1.** Consumed; used up; expended: *a spent bullet.* **2.** Depleted of energy, force, or strength; exhausted; worn out.

sperm[1] (spûrm) *n.* **1.** A male gamete or reproductive cell, a **spermatozoon** *(see).* **2.** The male fluid of fertilization, **semen** *(see).* [Middle English *sperme,* from Old French *esperme,* from Late Latin *sperma,* seed, sperm, from Greek *sperma.*]

sperm[2] *n.* The sperm whale or a substance associated with it, such as spermaceti or sperm oil. [Short for SPERMACETI.]

sperm–, spermi–, spermo– *prefix.* Indicates: **1.** Sperm; for example, **spermicidal. 2.** Seed; for example, **spermophile.** [Greek *sperma,* seed.]

–sperm *suffix. Botany.* Indicates a seed; for example, **gymnosperm.** [From SPERM (semen).]

sper·ma·ce·ti (spûr′mə-sē′tē, -sĕt′ē) *n.* A white, waxy substance consisting of various esters of fatty acids, obtained from the head of the sperm whale and used for making candles, ointments, and cosmetics. [Middle English, from Medieval Latin *spermacētī,* "sperm of the whale" : Late Latin *sperma,* SPERM + Latin *cētī,* genitive of *cētus,* whale (see **cetacean**).]

sper·ma·ry (spûr′mə-rē) *n., pl.* **-ries.** An organ in which male gametes are formed, especially in invertebrate animals. [New Latin *spermarium,* from Late Latin *sperma,* SPERM.]

sper·ma·the·ca (spûr′mə-thē′kə) *n.* A receptacle in certain female invertebrates, especially insects, in which spermatozoa are stored before fertilization takes place. [New Latin : Late Latin *sperma,* SPERM + THECA.] **—sper·ma·the·cal** *adj.*

sper·mat·ic (spûr-măt′ĭk) *adj.* **1. a.** Of, pertaining to, or resembling spermatozoa; spermous. **b.** Carrying or containing spermatozoa. **2.** Pertaining to a spermary or to a testis. [Late Latin *spermaticus,* from Greek *spermatikos,* from *sperma* (stem *spermat-*), SPERM.]

spermatic cord *n.* A cordlike structure consisting of the vas def-

speedboat *The first speedboats were designed in France in about 1900 and used specially adapted car engines. Speedboat racing became popular internationally, and speeds rose from about 30 kilometers (20 miles) per hour in 1903 to the present-day speeds of around 160 kilometers (100 miles) per hour.*

speedwell *A roadside plant that, according to folklore, speeds the traveler well. The bright-blue blossoms of the* Veronica officinalis, *shown above, are a common summer sight. Speedwell tea, brewed from the dried plant, was once used as a substitute for ordinary tea. Herbalists use it as a cough remedy.*

erens and its accompanying arteries, veins, nerves, and lymphatic vessels. It passes from the abdominal cavity through the inguinal canal and down into the scrotum to the back of the testicle, which is suspended in the scrotum by this structure.

spermatic fluid *n.* The male fluid of fertilization, **semen** *(see).*

sper·ma·tid (spûr′mə-tĭd) *n.* Any of four haploid cells formed from a spermatocyte during meiosis in the male that develop into spermatozoa without further division. [SPERMAT(O)- + -ID.]

sper·ma·ti·um (spûr-mā′shē-əm) *n., pl.* **-tia** (-shē-ə). *Botany.* A nonmotile, sporelike structure in red algae and certain fungi, generally acting as a male gamete. [New Latin, from Greek *spermation,* diminutive of *sperma* (stem *spermat-*), SPERM.] —**sper·ma·ti·al** *adj.*

spermato-, spermat– *prefix.* Indicates: **1.** Sperm; for example, **spermatogonium, spermatid. 2.** Seed; for example, **spermatophyte.** [Late Latin *sperma* (stem *spermat-*), SPERM.]

sper·mat·o·cyte (spûr-măt′ə-sīt′, spûr′mə-tə-) *n.* A diploid cell that is converted by meiotic division into four spermatids during spermatogenesis. [SPERMATO- + -CYTE.]

sper·mat·o·gen·e·sis (spûr′măt′ə-jĕn′ə-sĭs, spûr′mə-tə-) *n.* The generation of spermatozoa from spermatogonia in the testis by meiosis and spermiogenesis. [New Latin : SPERMATO- + -GENESIS.] —**sper·mat·o·ge·net·ic** (spûr′măt′ə-jə-nĕt′ĭk, spûr′mə-tə-jə-nĕt′ĭk), **sper·mat·o·gen·ic** (spûr′măt′ə-jĕn′ĭk, spûr′mə-tə-) *adj.*

sper·mat·o·go·ni·um (spûr′măt′ə-gō′nē-əm, spûr′mə-tə-) *n., pl.* **-nia** (-nē-ə). Any of the cells of the gonads in male animals that are the progenitors of spermatocytes. [New Latin : SPERMATO- + -GONIUM.] —**sper·mat·o·go·ni·al** *adj.*

sper·ma·toid (spûr′mə-toid′) *adj.* Resembling sperm. [SPERMAT(O)- + -OID.]

sper·mat·o·phore (spûr-măt′ə-fôr′, -fōr′, spûr′mə-tə-) *n.* An extruded mass or capsule of spermatozoa in certain animals, such as some mollusks, insects, and amphibians. [SPERMATO- + -PHORE.] —**sper·ma·toph·o·ral** (spûr′mə-tŏf′ər-əl) *adj.*

sper·mat·o·phyte (spûr-măt′ə-fīt′, spûr′mə-tə-) *n. Botany.* Any plant of the division Spermatophyta, which includes all seed-bearing plants and is divided into angiosperms and gymnosperms. [New Latin *Spermatophyta* : SPERMATO- + -PHYTE.] —**sper·mat·o·phyt·ic** (spûr-măt′ə-fĭt′ĭk, spûr′mə-tə-) *adj.*

sper·mat·or·rhe·a (spûr-măt′ə-rē′ə, spûr′mə-tə-rē′ə) *n.* Involuntary seminal discharge without orgasm. [New Latin : SPERMATO- + -RRHEA.]

sper·mat·o·zo·id (spûr-măt′ə-zō′ĭd, spûr′mə-tə-) *n. Botany.* A ciliated male gamete produced in an antheridium; an antherozoid. [SPERMATOZO(ON) + -ID.]

sper·mat·o·zo·on (spûr-măt′ə-zō′ŏn, spûr′mə-tə-zō′ən) *n., pl.* **-zoa** (-zō′ə). A fertilizing gamete of a male animal, usually a long nucleated cell with a thin, motile tail. It is produced in the testis by spermatogenesis. Also called "sperm," "sperm cell," "zoosperm." [New Latin : SPERMATO- + -ZOON.] —**sper·mat·o·zo·al, sper·mat·o·zo·an,** **sper·mat·o·zo·ic** *adj.*

sperm bank *n.* A place where sperm is stored for use in artificial insemination.

sperm count *n.* An estimation of the number of spermatozoa in a specimen of semen, used as an indication of male fertility.

spermi–, spermo– Variants of **sperm-.**

sper·mi·cide (spûr′mĭ-sīd′) *n.* A usually chemical agent that kills spermatozoa. [SPERMI- + -CIDE.] —**sper·mi·cid·al** (spûr′mĭ-sīd′l) *adj.*

sper·mine (spûr′mĕn′) *n.* A crystalline compound, $C_{10}H_{26}N_4$, found as a phosphate in semen, yeast, and certain body tissues.

sper·mi·o·gen·e·sis (spûr′mē-ə-jĕn′ə-sĭs) *n.* The transformation of a spermatid into a spermatozoon. [New Latin : *spermium,* spermatozoon, probably from SPERM + -GENESIS.]

sper·mo·go·ni·um (spûr′mə-gō′nē-əm) *n., pl.* **-nia** (-nē-ə). *Botany.* A hollow structure in which spermatia are formed, as in certain fungi. [SPERMO- + -GONIUM.]

sperm oil *n.* A yellow, waxy oil, obtained chiefly from the head of the sperm whale and used as an industrial lubricant.

sperm·o·phile (spûr′mə-fīl′) *n.* Any of various North American ground squirrels of the genus Citellus. [New Latin *spermophilus,* "fond of seed" : SPERMO- + -PHILE.]

sper·mous (spûr′məs) *adj.* Spermatic.

sperm whale *n.* A toothed whale, *Physeter catodon,* having a very large head with cavities containing sperm oil and spermaceti and a long, narrow, toothed lower jaw. Also called "cachalot."

Sper·ry (spĕr′ē), **Elmer Ambrose** (1860–1930). U.S. engineer and inventor. Although he received over 400 patents for products ranging from mining machinery to electric automobiles, he is primarily recognized for the invention of the gyrocompass, a nonmagnetic navigational aid, and the gyroscopic stabilizer, both of which made water and air travel significantly safer.

sper·ry·lite (spĕr′ĭ-līt′) *n.* A white platinum mineral, essentially $PtAs_2$, occurring in the form of cube-shaped crystals. [After F.L. *Sperry,* 19th-century Canadian mineralogist.]

spes·sar·tite (spĕs′ər-tīt′) *n.* A brownish type of garnet used as a gemstone, consisting of a silicate of aluminum and manganese, usually with small amounts of iron. [French, from *Spessart,* mountain range in Germany.]

spew (spyoo) *v.* **spewed, spewing, spews.** Also *archaic* **spue, spued, spuing, spues.** —*tr.* **1.** To vomit or spit out through the mouth. **2.** To throw out or send forth with force or vigor. Often used with *forth* or *out: spewing out insults.* —*intr.* **1.** To vomit. **2.** To be thrown out or sent forth with force or vigor. Often used

with *forth* or *out: Lava spewed forth from the crater.* —*n.* Also *archaic* **spue.** Something that is spewed; vomit. [Middle English *spewen,* Old English *spīwan* and *spīowan.*]

Spey (spā). River in northeastern Scotland, rising in the Mondhliath Mts. and flowing *c.* 170 kilometers (105 miles) into the North Sea. Its rapid, unnavigable waters are noted for salmon.

sp gr specific gravity.

sphag·num (sfăg′nəm) *n.* **1.** Any of various mosses of the genus Sphagnum, whose decomposed remains form peat. **2.** A mass of these plants, used for potting plants and for surgical dressings. Also called "bog moss," "peat moss." [New Latin, from Latin *sphagnos,* a kind of moss, from Greek *sphagnos†.*] —**sphag·nous** *adj.*

sphal·er·ite (sfăl′ə-rīt′) *n.* A yellow, brown, black, or white zinc ore, essentially ZnS with some cadmium and iron. Also called "blende," "zinc blende." [German *Sphalerit* : Greek *sphaleros,* slippery, from *sphallein†,* to trip + -ITE.]

sphene (sfēn) *n.* A titanium ore, chiefly $CaTiSiO_5$. Also called "titanite." [French *sphène,* from Greek *sphēn,* wedge.]

sphe·nic (sfē′nĭk) *adj.* Wedge-shaped. [SPHEN(O)- + -IC.]

spheno-, sphen– *prefix.* Indicates wedge-shaped; for example, **sphenogram, sphenodon.** [Greek *sphēn,* wedge.]

sphe·no·don (sfē′nə-dŏn′, sfēn′ə-) *n.* A reptile, the **tuatara** *(see).* [SPHEN(O)- + -ODON.]

sphe·no·gram (sfē′nə-grăm′, sfēn′ə-) *n.* A cuneiform character. [SPHENO- + -GRAM.]

sphe·noid (sfē′noid′) *n.* The **sphenoid bone** *(see).* —*adj.* Also **sphe·noid·al** (sfē-noid′l). **1.** Wedge-shaped. **2.** Of or pertaining to the sphenoid bone. [New Latin *sphenoides,* from Greek *sphēnoeidēs* : SPHEN(O)- + -OID.]

sphenoid bone *n.* A compound bone with winglike projections, situated at the base of the skull. Also called "sphenoid."

spher·al (sfîr′əl) *adj.* **1.** Of, pertaining to, or having the shape of a sphere; spherical. **2.** Symmetrical.

sphere (sfîr) *n.* **1.** *Geometry.* **a.** A three-dimensional surface all points of which are equidistant from a fixed point. **b.** A figure or solid bounded by such a surface. **2.** Any object or figure resembling a sphere; a globe; a ball. **3.** A planet, star, or other heavenly body. **4.** The sky, appearing as a hemisphere to an observer: *the sphere of the heavens.* **5.** In ancient astronomy, any of a series of concentric, transparent, revolving globes on whose transparent surfaces the moon, sun, planets, and stars were thought to be fixed. **6. a.** The environment in which one exists, acts, or has influence; range; domain. **b.** Any area of activity or interest; field. **7.** One's social stratum, rank, or position. —*tr.v.* **sphered, sphering, spheres. 1.** To form into a sphere. **2.** To put in or as if in a sphere. **3.** To surround or encompass. [Middle English *spere, sphere,* from Old French *espere,* from Latin *sphaera, sphēra,* ball, globe, from Greek *sphaira†.*]

-sphere *suffix.* Indicates: **1.** The shape of a sphere; for example, **bathysphere. 2.** A globular surrounding mass; for example, **ionosphere.** [From SPHERE.]

sphere of influence *n.* An area of the world dominated politically or economically by one country.

spher·i·cal (sfîr′ĭ-kəl, sfĕr′-) *adj.* Also **spher·ic** (sfîr′ĭk, sfĕr′-). **1. a.** Having the shape of a sphere; globular. **b.** Having a shape approximating that of a sphere. **2.** Of or pertaining to a sphere or spheres. **3.** Of or pertaining to heavenly bodies; celestial. —**spher·i·cal·i·ty** (sfîr′ĭ-kăl′ə-tē, sfĕr′-), **spher·i·cal·ness** *n.* —**spher·i·cal·ly** *adv.*

spherical aberration *n.* An optical defect of refracting and reflecting spherical surfaces in which light rays from one axial point, falling on the surface at different distances from the optical axis, do not come to a common focus.

spherical angle *n.* An angle formed at the intersection of the arcs of two great circles of a sphere.

spherical astronomy *n.* The branch of astronomy dealing with positions on the celestial sphere.

spher·i·cal-co·or·di·nate system (sfîr′ĭ-kəl-kō-ôr′də-nĭt, -nāt′, sfĕr′-) *n.* A three-dimensional system for locating points in space by means of a radius vector and two angles measured from the center of a sphere with respect to two arbitrary, fixed, perpendicular directions.

spherical excess *n.* The difference between the sum of the angles of a spherical triangle and the sum of the angles of a plane triangle.

spherical geometry *n.* The geometry of circles, angles, and figures on the surface of a sphere. Also called "spherics."

spherical polygon *n.* Any part of a spherical surface that is bounded by arcs of three or more great circles.

spherical triangle *n.* A triangle the three sides of which are arcs of intersecting great circles.

spherical trigonometry *n.* The modified form of trigonometry applied to spherical triangles. Also called "spherics."

sphe·ric·i·ty (sfĭr-ĭs′ə-tē, sfĕr′-) *n.* **1.** The state of being spherical. **2.** The extent to which a surface is spherical.

spher·ics (sfîr′ĭks, sfĕr′-) *n. Used with a singular verb.* **1. a.** Spherical geometry *(see).* **b.** Spherical trigonometry *(see).* **2.** Variant of **sferics.**

sphe·roid (sfîr′oid′, sfĕr′-) *n.* A spherelike body that is generated by revolving an ellipse around one of its axes. [Late Latin *sphaeroīdēs,* from Greek *sphaeroeidēs* : SPHERE + -OID.] —**sphe·roi·dal, sphe·roi·dal** *adj.* —**sphe·roi·dal·ly** *adv.* —**sphe·roi·dic·i·ty** (sfîr′oi-dĭs′ə-tē, sfĕr′-) *n.*

sphe·rom·e·ter (sfîr-ŏm′ə-tər) *n.* An instrument for measuring the curvature of a surface, such as that of a sphere or cylinder. [SPHER(E) + -METER.]

spher·ule (sfĭr′ool, -yool, sfĕr′-) *n.* A miniature sphere or spherical body. [Late Latin *sphaerula,* diminutive of Latin *sphaera,* SPHERE.] **—spher·u·lar** (sfĭr′yə-lər, sfĕr′-) *adj.*

spher·u·lite (sfĭr′ə-līt′, -yə-līt′, sfĕr′-) *n.* A small, usually spheroidal crystalline body having a radiating structure and found in obsidian and other silicic lava flows. [SPHERUL(E) + -ITE.] **—spher·u·lit·ic** (sfĭr′ə-lĭt′ĭk, -yə-lĭt′ĭk, sfĕr′-) *adj.*

sphinc·ter (sfĭngk′tər) *n.* A ringlike muscle that normally maintains constriction of a bodily passage or orifice and that relaxes as required by normal physiological functioning. [Late Latin, from Greek *sphinktēr,* that which binds tight, from *sphingein†,* to bind tight.] **—sphinc·ter·al** *adj.*

sphin·go·my·e·lin (sfĭng′gō-mī′ə-lĭn) *n.* A compound that contains sphingosine, phosphoric acid, choline, and a fatty acid group, found in the myelin sheath of nerves. [Greek *sphingein†,* to draw tight + MYELIN.]

sphin·go·sine (sfĭng′gō-sēn′, -sĭn) *n.* A long-chain organic compound occurring as a constituent of certain phospholipids in the brain. [Greek *sphingos-,* from *sphingein†,* hold fast, bind, draw tight + -INE.]

sphinx (sfĭnks) *n., pl.* **sphinxes** or **sphinges** (sfĭn′jēz′). **1.** *Greek Mythology.* Usually **Sphinx.** A winged monster having the head of a woman and the body of a lion that destroyed all who could not answer its riddle. **2. a.** *Usually* **Sphinx.** The huge stone statue having a lion's body and a man's head at Al Giza in Egypt. **b.** Any Egyptian figure having a lion's body and the head of a man, ram, or hawk. **3.** Any enigmatic person. [Middle English *spynx,* from Latin *Sphinx,* from Greek, perhaps from *sphingein†,* to draw tight, but dialectal variants, *Phix* and *Bix,* suggest perhaps a deity from Mount *Phikion* in Boeotia.]

sphinx moth *n.* The hawk moth (*see*).

sphra·gis·tics (sfră-jĭs′tĭks) *n. Used with a singular verb.* The study of engraved seals and signets. [French *sphragistique,* from Late Greek *sphragistikos,* from Greek *sphragist†,* seal, signet.]

sphyg·mic (sfĭg′mĭk) *adj. Physiology.* Pertaining to the pulse. [Greek *sphugmikos,* from *sphugmos,* pulsation, from *sphuzein†,* to throb.]

sphygmo-, sphygm– *prefix.* Indicates the pulse; for example, **sphygmograph, sphygmoid.** [Greek *sphugmos,* pulsation. See **sphygmic.**]

sphyg·mo·gram (sfĭg′mə-grăm′) *n.* A record or tracing produced by a sphygmograph. [SPHYGMO- + -GRAM.]

sphyg·mo·graph (sfĭg′mə-grăf′, -gräf′) *n.* An instrument for recording the character and variations of the arterial pulse. [SPHYGMO- + -GRAPH.]

sphyg·moid (sfĭg′moid′) *adj. Physiology.* Resembling a pulse; pulselike. [SPHYGM(O)- + -OID.]

sphyg·mo·ma·nom·e·ter (sfĭg′mō-mə-nŏm′ə-tər) *n.* Also **sphyg·mom·e·ter** (sfĭg-mŏm′ə-tər). An instrument for measuring blood pressure in the arteries. [SPHYGMO- + MANOMETER.]

spi·ca (spī′kə) *n., pl.* **-cae** (-kē) or **-cas.** A bandage applied in overlapping opposite spirals to immobilize a digit or limb. [Latin *spīca,* "point," ear of grain (from the resemblance of the V-shaped bandage to the V-shaped spikelets on an ear of grain).]

Spi·ca (spī′kə) *n.* The brightest star in the constellation Virgo, 210 light-years distant from Earth. [Latin *spīca,* "point," ear of grain. See **spica.**]

spi·cate (spī′kāt′) *adj. Botany.* Having or forming a spike. [Latin *spīcātus,* from the past participle of *spīcāre,* to provide with spikes, from *spīca,* ear of grain, SPIKE.]

spic·ca·to (spĭ-kä′tō) *adj. Music.* Performed with a bowing technique in which the bow is made to bounce slightly off the string. ~*adv. Music.* With a spiccato technique. Used as a direction. ~*n., pl.* **spiccatos.** *Music.* A spiccato technique or passage. [Italian, from the past participle of *spiccare†,* to separate.]

spice (spīs) *n.* **1.** Any of various aromatic and pungent vegetable substances, such as cinnamon or nutmeg, used to flavor foods or beverages. **2.** These substances collectively. **3.** Something that adds zest, flavor, or excitement. **4.** A pungent aroma; perfume. ~*tr.v.* **spiced, spicing, spices. 1.** To season with spices. **2.** To add zest or excitement to. Often used with *up.* [Middle English, from Old French *espice,* from Late Latin *speciēs,* goods, spices, from Latin, appearance, kind, SPECIES.]

spice·ber·ry (spīs′bĕr′ē) *n., pl.* **-ries.** Any of various plants or shrubs having spicy berries, such as the wintergreen.

spice·bush (spīs′boosh′) *n.* An aromatic shrub, *Lindera benzoin,* of eastern North America, having clusters of small, early-blooming yellow flowers. Also called "benjamin bush."

Spice Islands. See **Moluccas.**

spic·er·y (spī′sə-rē) *n., pl.* **-ies. 1.** Spices collectively. **2.** The aromatic quality of spices. **3.** *Obsolete.* A place where spices are stored.

spick-and-span, spic-and-span (spĭk′ən-spăn′) *adj. Informal.* **1.** Neat and clean; spotless. **2.** Brand-new; fresh. [Short for obsolete *spick and spannew : spick,* probably from Dutch *spikspelldernieuw, -splinternieuw,* "spike-splinter new" + SPAN-NEW.]

spic·ule (spĭk′yool) *n.* Also **spic·u·la** (-yə-lə) *pl.* **-lae** (-lē′). **1.** A small needlelike structure or part; especially, any of the silicate or calcium carbonate growths supporting the soft tissue of certain invertebrates, especially sponges. **2.** *Astronomy.* Any of the innumerable hairlike eruptions of hot gas from the sun's chromosphere.

[Latin *spīculum,* SPICULUM.] **—spic·u·lar, spic·u·late** (spĭk′yə-lĭt, -lāt′) *adj.*

spic·u·lum (spĭk′yə-ləm) *n., pl.* **-la** (-lə). A spicule or similar needlelike structure. [Latin *spīculum,* diminutive of *spīca,* point.]

spic·y (spī′sē) *adj.* **-ier, -iest. 1. a.** Containing or flavored with spice. **b.** Having the characteristics of spice, such as flavor and aroma. **2. a.** Piquant; pungent. **b.** Lively, keen, or spirited. **3.** Slightly scandalous; risqué. **—spic·i·ly** *adv.* **—spic·i·ness** *n.*

spi·der (spī′dər) *n.* **1. a.** Any of numerous arachnids of the order Araneae, having eight legs, a body divided into a cephalothorax and an abdomen, and several spinnerets that produce silk used to make nests, cocoons, or webs for trapping insects. **b.** Any of various similar arachnids. **2.** One that is similar to a spider, as in appearance, character, or movement. **3.** A cast-iron frying pan with a long handle, originally equipped with short legs. **4.** A trivet. **5.** Any of var-

---

spider

SPINNERS OF GOSSAMER THREADS

Spiders are found throughout the world

Spiders are found all over the world, from mountaintops to dark caves—there are 30,000 different species. All hatch from eggs and most live for about a year.

All spiders—both male and female—produce silk from a group of spinnerets at the end of the body, but not all spin webs. The silk—about 0.005 millimeter (1/5000 inch) in diameter—can be sticky or dry and is used in various ways by the spider. Some spin webs with it, wanderers leave a silk trail behind them like an anchor line, some make their homes of silk, and young spiders migrate on the gossamer threads that act like parachutes to disperse them over long distances. Spiders that make sticky webs to catch their prey spin dry cross threads on which to approach the prey so that they do not get stuck themselves.

All spiders feed on insects, although the tropical bird-eating spiders also prey on hummingbirds. The bird eaters include the giant tarantula, which grows up to 90 millimeters (3½ inches) across the body. The European aquatic species feed mainly on fish and lizards and other small creatures.

Some, such as the wolf spider, capture their prey by running and pouncing on them, and the spitting spider spits two lines of sticky thread to enwrap them. But however the victims are caught, they are all stabbed by the spider's fangs, which inject a poison. Although the poison is quickly fatal to the spider's prey, only a few species, such as the North American black widow, are dangerous to man. The courtship of spiders typically consists of various elaborate displays, with the male dancing frantically, touching the female, or vibrating her web in a special way. But contrary to popular belief, very few females devour the males after mating. If a male dies soon after mating it is usually from exhaustion or starvation.

DIVING FOR PREY *The European fisher-spider begins to eat a minnow after catching it underwater. Tiny hairs covering the spider trap enough air to allow it to make a 45-minute dive.*

spider crab *Like spiders, spider crabs have long legs in proportion to their bodies. Some species of this marine scavenger are a mere 10 millimeters across (less than half an inch). But some have a spread of up to 4 meters (13 feet).*

spinnaker *A yacht with two brightly colored spinnakers running before the wind.*

spinning wheel *The spinning wheel, which was probably invented in India, was introduced to Europe during the Middle Ages. The wheel, operated by a treadle, turns the spindle that twists the loose fibers into thread.*

ious machines or devices with limbs radiating from a central point. [Middle English *spither, spithre,* Old English *spīthra.*]

spider crab *n.* Any of various crabs, especially of the family Majidae, having long legs and a relatively small body.

spi·der·flow·er (spī′dər-flou′ər) *n.* The **cleome** *(see).*

spi·der-hunt·ing wasp (spī′dər-hŭn′tĭng) *n.* Any of various wasps of the family Pompilidae, which catch spiders by paralyzing them with their poisonous sting.

spider lily *n.* Any of various chiefly tropical American plants of the genus *Hymenocallis,* having narrow leaves and clusters of white flowers.

spider mite *n.* Any of various mites of the family Tetranychidae, such as *Tetranychus urticae,* that feed on plants and are serious pests of fruit trees and other crop plants. Also called "red spider," "red spider mite."

spider monkey *n.* Any of several tropical American monkeys of the genus *Ateles,* having long legs and a long, prehensile tail.

spider orchid *n.* Any of several European orchids of the genus *Ophrys,* having broad-lipped flowers. [Referring to the velvety spiderlike lip of the flowers.]

spider plant *n.* Any of several plants of the genus *Chlorophytum*; especially, the South African species *C. elatum,* which has narrow, green and white leaves and is commonly grown as a house plant. [From the fancied resemblance of the leaves to a spider's legs.]

spi·der·wort (spī′dər-wûrt′, -wôrt′) *n.* Any of various New World plants of the genus *Tradescantia*; especially, *T. virginiana,* which has blue or purple flowers and is grown as a house plant.

spi·der·y (spī′də-rē) *adj.* **1.** Resembling or suggesting a spider. **2. a.** Resembling a spider's legs; long and slender: *spidery penstrokes.* **b.** Resembling a spider's web; especially, very fine and meshlike. **3.** Infested with spiders.

spie·gel·ei·sen (spē′gə-lī′zən) *n.* An alloy of iron with approximately 15 to 30 percent manganese and small quantities of carbon and silicon, used in the Bessemer process. Also called "spiegel." [German *Spiegeleisen,* "mirror-iron" : *Spiegel,* mirror, from Old High German *spiagal,* from Medieval Latin *spēglum,* from Latin *speculum,* SPECULUM + *Eisen,* iron, from Old High German *īsan, īsarn.*]

spiel (spēl) *n. Slang.* **1.** A voluble story or speech usually intended to persuade. **2.** Talk that is considered glib or tedious: *gave us his usual spiel about morale.*
~*v.* **spieled, spieling, spiels.** *Slang.* —*intr.* To talk at length or extravagantly. —*tr.* To say or utter at length or extravagantly. [German *Spiel,* "play," from Old High German *spil,* from Germanic *spillōn* (unattested), to play.] **—spiel·er** *n.*

Spiel·berg (spēl′bûrg′), **Steven** (1947–). U.S. film director and producer. One of the most commercially successful directors of all time, he has entertained and thrilled millions of filmgoers with *Jaws* (1975), *Close Encounters of the Third Kind* (1977), *Raiders of the Lost Ark* (1981), *E.T.* (1982), and other films that display his storytelling genius and his ability to create and sustain suspense.

spif·fy (spĭf′ē) *adj.* **-fier, -fiest.** *Slang.* Smart in appearance or dress; stylish. [19th century : origin obscure.] **—spif·fi·ness** *n.*

spig·ot (spĭg′ət) *n.* **1.** The vent plug of a cask. **2.** A wooden tap placed in the bunghole of a cask. **3.** A short projection on a component, such as a pipe, designed to fit into a hole or slot in a mating part. [Middle English, perhaps from Latin *spiculum,* diminutive of *spicum,* variant of *spīca,* SPICA.]

spike[1] (spīk) *n.* **1. a.** A long, thick, sharp-pointed piece of wood or metal. **b.** A heavy nail. **2. a.** A sharp-pointed projection along the top of a fence. **b.** A sharp metal projection set in the sole or the sole and heel of an athletic shoe for grip. **3. spikes. a.** A pair of athletic shoes with spikes. **b.** Shoes with spike heels. **4.** *Slang.* A hypodermic needle. **5. a.** A peak on a graph, especially one showing a maximum, as of voltage. **b.** An occurrence producing a peak on a graph. **6.** An unbranched antler of a young deer. **7.** A small young mackerel. **8.** The act of spiking a ball.
~*tr.v.* **spiked, spiking, spikes. 1.** To secure or provide with a spike. **2.** To impale, pierce, or injure with or on a spike. **3.** To disable (a muzzleloading gun) by driving a spike into the vent. **4.** To put an end to; block: *spike a plot.* **5.** *Slang.* To add alcoholic liquor to (a drink). **6. a.** To drive (a volleyball) into the opposing court at a steep downward angle. **b.** To slam (a football) to the ground after scoring a touchdown or making a big play. [Middle English *spyk,* probably from Middle Dutch *spiker*; akin to SPOKE.]

spike[2] *n.* **1.** An ear of grain. **2.** *Botany.* A usually elongated, racemose inflorescence with stalkless or nearly stalkless flowers arranged along an axis, as in the foxglove. [Middle English *spik,* from Latin *spīca,* point, ear of grain.]

spike heel *n.* A very high thin heel on a woman's dress shoe.

spike lavender *n.* A lavender plant, *Lavandula latifolia,* of southern Europe, yielding an oil used in perfumes and paints. [From SPIKE (inflorescence).]

spike·let (spīk′lĭt) *n. Botany.* A small or secondary spike; especially, one of those forming the inflorescence of grasses or similar plants.

spike·nard (spīk′närd′) *n.* **1.** An aromatic plant, *Nardostachys jatamansi,* of India, having rose-purple flowers. Also called "nard." **2.** A costly ointment of the ancient world, probably prepared from this plant. Also called "nard." **3.** A North American plant, *Aralia racemosa,* having small, greenish flowers and an aromatic root. [Middle English, from Medieval Latin *spīca nardi,* spike of a nard (translation of Greek *nardostakhus*) : Latin *spīca,* SPIKE + *nardus,* NARD.]

spik·y (spī′kē) *adj.* **-ier, -iest. 1.** Having a projecting sharp point or points. **2.** Resembling a spike, especially in shape. **3.** Irritable; ill-tempered. **—spik·i·ly** *adv.* **—spik·i·ness** *n.*

spile (spīl) *n.* **1.** A post used as a foundation; a pile. **2.** A wooden plug; a bung. **3.** A spout used in taking sap from a tree.
~*tr.v.* **spiled, spiling, spiles.** To support, plug, or tap with a spile. [Perhaps from Middle Dutch or Middle Low German *spile,* bar.]

spil·i·kins, spil·li·kins (spĭl′ĭ-kənz) *n. Used with a singular verb.* See **jackstraw** (sense 1).

spill[1] (spĭl) *v.* **spilled** or **spilt** (spĭlt), **spilling, spills.** —*tr.* **1.** To cause or allow (a substance) to run or fall out of a container, especially accidentally. **2.** To shed (blood). **3. a.** To let the wind out of (a sail). **b.** To relieve the pressure of (wind) on a sail. **4.** To eject or cause to fall: *The horse spilled his rider.* **5.** *Informal.* To divulge. —*intr.* **1.** To run or fall out of a container, especially accidentally. **2.** To spread out or flow as if spilled: *The audience started to spill out of the theater.* **3.** To escape from a sail. Used of the wind. **—spill the beans.** *Informal.* To divulge all.
~*n.* **1.** An act of spilling. **2.** That which is spilled. **3.** A fall, as from a horse. **4.** A spillway. [Middle English *spillen,* to destroy, kill, shed (blood), spill, Old English *spillan.*] **—spill·er** *n.*

spill[2] *n.* **1.** A piece of wood or rolled paper used to light a fire. **2.** A small peg used as a plug; a spile. [Probably from Middle Low German or Middle Dutch *spile.*]

spill·age (spĭl′ĭj) *n.* **1.** An act or the process of spilling. **2.** That which is spilled; the amount spilled.

Spil·lane (spə-lān′), **Mickey** (1918–). U.S. author. The creator of the fictional hard-boiled detective Mike Hammer, he wrote a series of popular detective novels, including *I, the Jury* (1947) and *One Lonely Night* (1951), that emphasized violence and sex.

spill·way (spĭl′wā′) *n.* A channel for water overflow, as from a reservoir. Also called "spill."

spilth (spĭlth) *n.* Spillage. [From SPILL.]

spin (spĭn) *v.* **spun** (spŭn) or *archaic* **span** (spăn), **spinning, spins.** —*tr.* **1.** To draw out and twist (fibers) into thread. **2.** To form (thread or yarn) in this manner. **3. a.** To form (a thread, web, or cocoon, for example) by extruding viscous filaments. Used chiefly of spiders and caterpillars. **b.** To produce (synthetic yarn) by extruding chemical substances. **4.** To draw out and twist in a manufacturing process: *spin glass into threads.* **5.** To narrate from memory or invent from one's imagination. Used chiefly in the phrase *spin a yarn.* **6.** To cause to rotate; turn around or twirl. **7.** To turn on a lathe, usually into a round shape. **8.** To cause (an aircraft) to dive in a spin. **9.** To fish (a river, for example) using a spinner. —*intr.* **1.** To make thread or yarn by the drawing out and twisting of fibers. **2.** To form a thread, web, or cocoon by extruding viscous filaments. **3.** To rotate rapidly; whirl. **4.** To seem to be whirling, as from dizziness; reel: *The news set my head spinning.* **5.** To ride or drive rapidly. Usually used with *along.* **6.** To fish with a spinner. **7.** To dive in a spin. Used of an aircraft. **—spin out. 1.** To prolong or draw out (a story or task, for example). **2.** To pass (time): *spun out the rest of the afternoon.* **3.** To cause (a sum of money) to last a long time. —See Synonyms at **turn.**
~*n.* **1.** The act of spinning. **2.** A swift whirling motion. **3.** *Informal.* A state of mental confusion. **4.** *Informal.* A short excursion in or on a vehicle. **5. a.** The flight condition of an aircraft in a nose-down, spiraling, stalled descent. **b.** Any sudden, swift, or steep descending movement. **6.** A rotating motion imparted to a ball by a sports player. **7.** *Physics.* **a.** The intrinsic angular momentum of an elementary particle. **b.** The total angular momentum of an atomic nucleus. **c.** A nonnegative integral or half-integral quantum number that specifies the value of such momenta in units of Planck's constant divided by 2π. **8.** *Australian Informal.* A stroke of fortune of a specified kind: *a bad spin.* [Spin, spun, spun; Middle English *spinnen, spon* (plural), *spunne,* Old English *spinnan, spunnon* (plural), *gespunnen.*]

spi·na bif·i·da (spī′nə bĭf′ĭ-də, bī′fə-) *n.* A condition, present at birth, in which part of the spinal cord protrudes through a gap in the backbone. It may result in paralysis and incontinence and be associated with **hydrocephalus** *(see).* [New Latin, bifid spine.]

spin·ach (spĭn′ĭch) *n.* **1.** A widely cultivated plant, *Spinacia oleracea,* native to Asia, having succulent, edible leaves. **2.** The leaves of this plant, eaten as a vegetable. [Probably from Middle Dutch *spinaetse,* from Old French *espinache,* from Medieval Latin *spinachia,* from Arabic *'isfānāk,* from Persian *ispānāk.*]

spi·nal (spī′nəl) *adj.* **1.** Of, pertaining to, or situated near the spine or spinal cord; vertebral. **2.** Resembling a spine or spinous part.
~*n.* A spinal anesthetic. **—spi·nal·ly** *adv.*

spinal anesthesia *n.* **1.** Anesthesia in part of the body produced by injecting an anesthetic substance (*spinal anesthetic*) into the spinal canal. **2.** *Pathology.* Loss of sensation in part of the body because of injury to or disease of the spinal cord.

spinal canal *n.* The canal formed by the successive openings in the vertebrae through which the spinal cord and its membranes pass. Also called "vertebral canal."

spinal column *n.* The series of articulated vertebrae extending from the base of the skull to the base of the trunk or the end of the tail, encasing the spinal cord and forming the supporting axis of the body; the backbone. Also called "spine," "vertebral column."

spinal cord *n.* The part of the central nervous system contained within the spinal canal and continuous at its cranial end with the medulla oblongata of the brain.

spinal meningitis *n. Pathology.* **Cerebrospinal meningitis** (see).

spin·dle (spĭnd'l) *n.* **1. a.** A notched stick for spinning fibers into thread by hand. **b.** A pin or rod holding a bobbin or spool upon which thread is wound on a spinning wheel or spinning machine. **2.** Any of various slender mechanical parts that revolve or serve as axes for larger revolving parts, as in a lock or on an axle. **3.** *Biology.* A group of fibers extending from one end of a cell to the other, formed during mitosis and meiosis and along which the chromosomes are distributed. **4.** Any slender, tapering rod or rodlike piece. **5.** A measure or yarn of varying length. **6.** A turned, usually decorative vertical support of a handrail. —*v.* **spindled, -dling, -dles.** —*tr.* To impale or perforate on the spike of a spindle: *Do not fold, spindle, or mutilate this card.* —*intr.* To grow into a thin, elongated, or weakly form. Used especially of a plant. [Middle English *spindel*, rod of a spinning wheel, Old English *spinel*.]

spin·dle-legs (spĭnd'l-lĕgz') *pl.n.* Also **spin·dle-shanks** (-shăngks'). **1.** Long, thin legs. **2.** *Used with a singular verb.* A tall, lanky person with long, thin legs. —**spin·dle-legged** *adj.*

spindle side *n.* The **distaff side** (see).

spindle tree *n.* Any of various shrubs or trees of the genus *Euonymus,* many species of which have pink or orange fruits. [So called because the wood is often used to make spindles.]

spin·dling (spĭnd'lĭng) *adj.* Spindly. —*n.* A spindly plant or animal.

spin·dly (spĭnd'lē) *adj.* **-dlier, -dliest.** Slender, long, and usually weak-looking.

spin·drift (spĭn'drĭft') *n.* Wind-blown sea spray. Also called "spoondrift." [Variant of SPOONDRIFT.]

spin-dry·er, spin-dri·er (spĭn'drī'ər) *n.* A machine that extracts moisture from wet laundry by spinning it around rapidly. Also called "spinner." —**spin-dry** *v.*

spine (spĭn) *n.* **1.** The spinal column of a vertebrate. **2.** Any of various pointed projections or appendages of animals, such as a quill on a porcupine. **3.** *Botany.* A sharp-pointed projection arising from the stem of a plant. **4.** *Anatomy.* A sharp projection arising from a bone. **5.** The vertical back of a book to which the pages are attached and which normally bears the title on the outside. **6. a.** Strength of character. **b.** A main support or prop. **7.** A sharp-backed hill, mountain, or ridge. [Middle English, from Old French *espine,* from Latin *spīna,* thorn, prickle, spine.] —**spined** *adj.*

spine-chill·er (spĭn'chĭl'ər) *n.* A book, film, or other work that arouses a pleasurably terrifying thrill. —**spine-chill·ing** *adj.*

spi·nel (spə-nĕl') *n.* A mineral, magnesium aluminum oxide, $MgAl_2O_4$. Spinels show a range of colors, depending on any additional elements present, and some are used as gemstones. [Italian *spinella,* diminutive of *spina,* thorn (from its sharply pointed crystals), from Latin *spīna.*]

spine·less (spĭn'lĭs) *adj.* **1.** Lacking a vertebral column. **2.** Having no spiny projections. **3.** Lacking in courage, strength of character, or will power. —**spine·less·ly** *adv.* —**spine·less·ness** *n.*

spi·nes·cent (spī-nĕs'ənt) *adj. Biology.* **1.** Having a spine or spines. **2.** Having or tending toward the form of a spine. [Late Latin *spīnescēns* (stem *spīnescent-*), present participle of *spīnescere,* to grow thorny, from Latin *spīna,* thorn, SPINE.] —**spi·nes·cence** *n.*

spin·et (spĭn'ĭt) *n.* **1.** A small harpsichord with a single keyboard. **2.** A small, compact upright piano. [French *espinette,* from Italian *spinetta,* virginal, spinet, diminutive of *spina,* thorn, SPINE (referring to the plucking of the strings).]

spi·nif·er·ous (spī-nĭf'ər-əs) *adj.* Also **spi·nig·er·ous** (-nĭj'ər-əs). Spine-bearing; spiny. Said especially of plants. [Latin *spīnifer* : Latin *spīna,* thorn, SPINE + -FEROUS.]

spi·ni·fex (spī'nə-fĕks') *n.* **1.** Any of various chiefly Australian grasses of the genus *Spinifex,* growing in arid regions and having spiny leaves or seeds. **2.** Any of various Australian grasses of the genus *Triodia,* having spiny leaves. Also called "porcupine grass." [New Latin : SPIN(E) + Latin *-fex,* "maker."]

spin·na·ker (spĭn'ə-kər) *n.* A large triangular sail set on a spar that swings out opposite the mainsail, used on racing yachts when running before the wind. [Probably from *Sphinx,* name of the first yacht to carry a spinnaker sail, in about 1866; perhaps influenced by *spanker.*]

spin·ner (spĭn'ər) *n.* **1.** One that spins. **2.** An angler's lure that spins rapidly. **3.** A spin-dryer. **4.** A fairing fitted over the hub of the propeller in some aircraft. **5.** A device consisting of a dial and an arrow that is spun to indicate the next move in certain board games.

spin·ner·et (spĭn'ə-rĕt') *n.* **1.** A structure in spiders and certain insect larvae, containing passages through which silky filaments are secreted. **2.** A device for making rayon, nylon, and other synthetic fibers, consisting of a plate pierced with holes through which plastic material is extruded in filaments. [SPINNER + -ET.]

spin·ney (spĭn'ē) *n., pl.* **-neys.** *Chiefly British.* A small grove; copse. [Old French *espinei,* thicket, from Vulgar Latin *spīnēta* (unattested), from Latin *spīnētum,* thorn hedge, from *spīna,* thorn.]

spin·ning (spĭn'ĭng) *n.* **1.** The process of making fibrous or viscous material into yarn or thread. **2.** The act or technique of angling with a light rod and line, drawing a rotating lure through the water to imitate the movement of a small fish or insect.

spinning frame *n.* A machine that draws and twists fibers into yarn and winds it onto spindles.

spinal cord

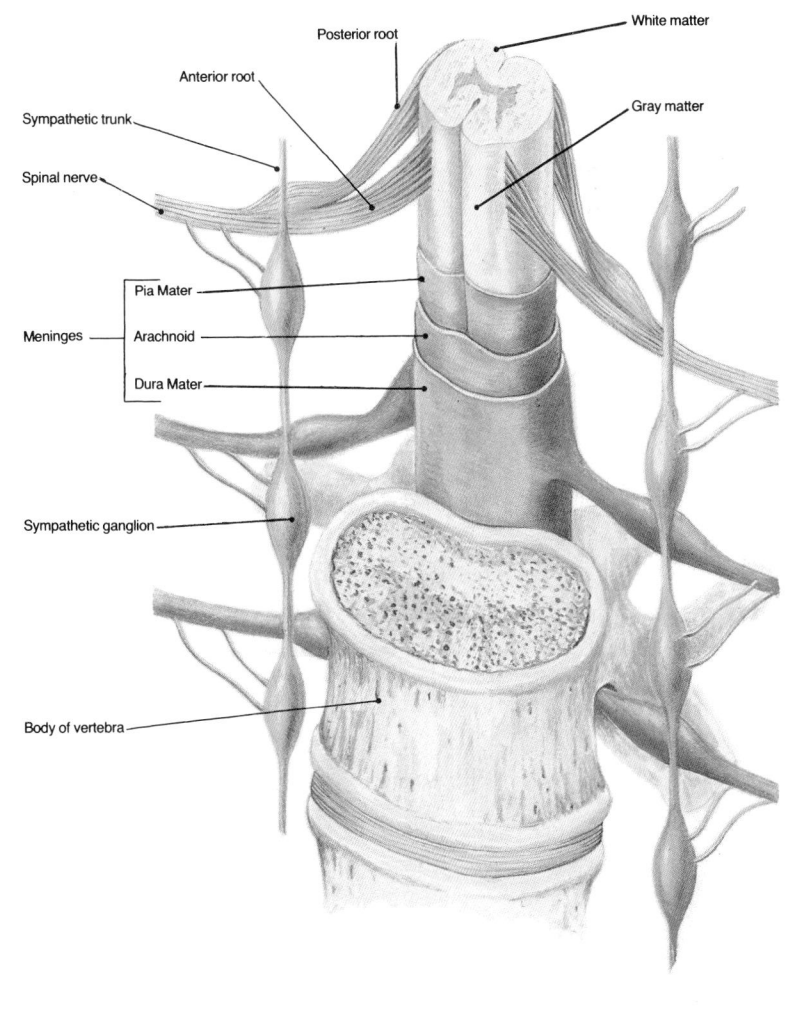

MAN'S INTERNAL TELEGRAPH SYSTEM
The spinal cord carries messages to and from the brain

The central nervous system, man's internal communications network, consists of the brain and spinal cord (shown below). The brainstem is the connecting link. Nerve fibers that make up the spinal cord transmit to the brain information about touch, position, pain, and temperature, and carry back instructions to muscles to react.

The spinal cord consists of gray cells and white nerve fibers that float in a protective cerebrospinal fluid, held in by tough membranes called meninges and surrounded by the bony structure of the spinal column. The gray matter surrounding the central canal consists of nerve cell bodies from which axons, the nerve fibers, relay impulses outward. Bundles of axons, forming the white matter, conduct these impulses to

the brain. Synapses are the points of contact between axons and branching dendrites, which transmit incoming impulses to the cell bodies.

Nerve fibers radiate from the spinal cord to the muscles and skin. Sensory fibers enter the back of the cord bringing messages from body tissues; motor fibers leaving the front of the cord take instructions to the tissues. The muscle receptors, which can detect tension and pressure from regions as distant as the toes, fingertips, and tongue, all send messages to the brain via the spinal cord. The messages travel in a series of electrical impulses. The ganglion sorts them out and sends them up the right channel to the brain for analysis and decision. Impulses in motor nerves then instruct the muscles.

Posterior root · White matter · Anterior root · Gray matter · Sympathetic trunk · Spinal nerve · Pia Mater · Meninges · Arachnoid · Dura Mater · Sympathetic ganglion · Body of vertebra

spinning jenny *n.* An early spinning machine having several spindles.

spinning mule *n.* A type of spinning machine, a **mule** (sense 4) (see).

spinning wheel *n.* An apparatus for making yarn or thread, comprising a foot- or hand-driven wheel and a single spindle.

spi·node (spī'nōd') *n. Mathematics.* See **cusp** (sense 3). [Latin *spīna,* spine + NODE.]

spin off *tr.v.* **1.** To throw off while rotating at high speed. **2.** To establish or produce as a spin-off.

spin-off (spĭn'ôf', -ŏf') *n.* **1.** A usually useful object or result obtained incidentally through pursuing a different object or result. **2.** Something derived from an earlier work, especially a television show starring a character who had a popular minor role in an earlier show.

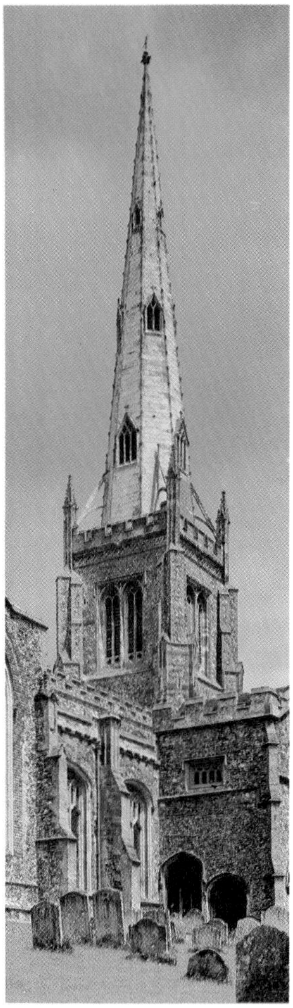

spire *Thaxted Church, Essex, England. A spire in the Perpendicular style.*

PRONUNCIATION KEY

ă, pat; ā, pay; âr, care;
ä, father, are; b, bib;
ch, church; d, deed; ĕ, pet;
ē, be; f, fife; g, gag; h, hat;
hw, which; ĭ, pit; ī, pie;
îr, pier; j, judge; k, kick;
l, lid, needle; m, mum;
n, no, sudden; ng, thing;
ŏ, pot; ō, toe; ô, paw, for;
oi, noise; ou, out; o͝o, book;
o͞o, boot; p, pop; r, roar;
s, sauce; sh, ship, dish;
t, tight; th, thin, path;
th, this, bathe; ŭ, cut; ûr, fur;
v, valve; w, with; y, yes;
z, zebra, size; zh, vision;
ə, about, item, edible, gallop, circus, peaceful

IN FOREIGN WORDS:

à, *Fr.* ami; œ, *Fr.* feu, *Ger.* schön; ü, *Fr.* tu, *Ger.* über; KH, *Ger.* ich, *Scot.* loch; N, *Fr.* bon; y', *Fr.* Compiègne

STRESS MARKS:

Primary stress: ′ **in·cite′** (ĭn-sīt′)
Secondary stress: ′ **in′sight′** (ĭn′sīt′)

spi·nose (spī′nōs′) *adj.* Bearing spines; spiny. Said especially of plants. [Latin *spīnōsus,* from *spīna,* thorn, SPINE.] **—spi·nose·ly** *adv.* **—spi·nos·i·ty** (spī-nŏs′ə-tē) *n.*

spi·nous (spī′nəs) *adj.* **1.** Resembling a spine or thorn. **2.** Having spines or similar projections; spiny.

spinous process *n.* The rearward projection from the arch of a vertebra.

Spi·no·za (spĭ-nō′zə), **Baruch** or **Benedict de** (1632–77). Dutch philosopher. His controversial pantheistic doctrine advocated an intellectual love of God. His best-known work is his *Ethics* (1677).

spin·ster (spĭn′stər) *n.* **1.** A woman who has remained single beyond the conventional age for marrying. **2.** A woman whose occupation is spinning. [Middle English *spinnester* : *spinnen,* to SPIN + -STER.] **—spin·ster·hood** *n.* **—spin·ster·ish** *adj.*

spin·thar·i·scope (spĭn-thăr′ə-skōp′) *n.* A device for observing individual scintillations produced by ionizing radiation, with the aid of a tube with a magnifying lens at one end and a phosphorescent screen and a speck of a radioactive salt at the other. [Greek *spintharis*†, spark + -SCOPE.] **—spin·thar·i·scop·ic** (spĭn-thăr′ə-skŏp′ĭk) *adj.*

spin·ule (spĭn′yo͞ol) *n.* A small spine or thorn. [Latin *spīnula,* diminutive of *spīna,* thorn, SPINE.]

spin·u·lose (spĭn′yə-lōs′) *adj.* Also **spi·nu·lous** (spī′nyə-ləs). **1.** Having spinules. **2.** Shaped like a spinule.

spin·y (spī′nē) *adj.* **-ier, -iest. 1.** Bearing or covered with spines, thorns, or similar stiff projections. **2.** Shaped like a spine. **3.** Difficult; troublesome. **—spin·i·ness** *n.*

spiny anteater *n.* A mammal, the **echidna** *(see).*

spin·y-finned (spī′nē-fĭnd′) *adj.* Having fins supported by sharp, spiny, inflexible rays. Said of some fishes. Compare **soft-finned.**

spiny lobster *n.* Any of various edible marine decapod crustaceans of the family Palinuridae, having a spiny carapace and lacking the large pincers characteristic of true lobsters. Also called "langouste," "rock lobster," and sometimes "crayfish."

spir·a·cle (spĭr′ə-kəl, spī′rə-) *n.* **1.** *Zoology.* A respiratory aperture, such as: **a.** Any of several tracheal openings in the exoskeleton of an insect or spider. **b.** A small respiratory opening behind the eye of cartilaginous fishes, such as sharks, rays, and skates. **c.** The blowhole of a cetacean. **2.** *Geology.* A small volcanic vent formed by gases in a lava flow. **3.** Any opening through which air is admitted and expelled. [Latin *spīrāculum,* a breathing hole, from *spīrāre,* to breathe.] **—spi·rac·u·lar** (spī-răk′yə-lər, spĭ-), **spi·rac·u·late** (spī-răk′yə-lĭt, -lāt′, spĭ-) *adj.*

spi·ral (spī′rəl) *n.* **1. a.** The locus in a plane of a point moving around a fixed center at a monotonically increasing or decreasing distance from the center. **b.** The three-dimensional locus of a point moving parallel to and about a central axis at a constant or continuously varying distance; a helix. **2.** Something having the form of such a curve: *spirals of smoke.* **3.** A continuously accelerating increase or decrease, often of related factors: *the wage-price spiral.* ~*adj.* Of or resembling a spiral; coiled or helical: *a spiral staircase.* ~*v.* **spiraled** or **-ralled, -raling** or **-ralling, -rals.** —*intr.* **1.** To take a spiral form or course. **2.** To rise or fall at a steady rate. —*tr.* To cause to spiral. [Medieval Latin *spīrālis,* from Latin *spīra,* coil, SPIRE (spiral).] **—spi·ral·ly** *adv.*

spiral binding *n.* A binding for notebooks and booklets in which a cylindrical spiral of wire or plastic is passed through a row of punched holes at the edge of each sheet.

spiral galaxy *n.* A galaxy having a nucleus and spiral arms consisting mainly of gas, dust, and stars. Formerly called "spiral nebula."

spiral of Archimedes *n.* The locus of a point moving toward or away from a central point at a constant speed along a line rotating around that central point at a constant speed. Its spiral has the equation $r = a\theta$, where a is a constant.

spi·rant (spī′rənt) *n.* *Phonetics.* A **fricative** *(see).* [Latin *spīrāns* (stem *spīrant-*), present participle of Latin *spīrāre,* to breathe.] **—spi·rant** *adj.*

spire¹ (spīr) *n.* **1.** A structure that tapers upward to a point; especially, a steeple. **2.** The top part or point of something that tapers upward; a pinnacle. **3.** A slender, tapering shoot or stem, such as a newly sprouting blade of grass. **4.** Any slender, tapering object. ~*v.* **spired, spiring, spires.** —*tr.* To provide with a spire or spires. —*intr.* To rise taperingly, like a spire. [Middle English *spir(e),* slender stalk, Old English *spīr.*]

spire² *n.* **1. a.** A spiral. **b.** A single turn of a spiral; whorl. **2.** *Zoology.* The area farthest from the aperture and nearest the apex on a coiled gastropod shell. [French, from Latin *spīra,* a coil, twist, spire, from Greek *speira.*]

spi·re·a, spi·rae·a (spī-rē′ə) *n.* Any of various plants or shrubs of the genus *Spiraea,* having clusters of small white or pink flowers and often cultivated as garden ornamentals. [Latin *spīraea,* meadowsweet, from Greek *speiraia,* from *speira,* coil, SPIRE.]

spire·let (spīr′lĭt) *n.* *Architecture.* See **flèche** (sense 1).

spi·reme (spī′rēm′) *n.* *Biology.* **1.** The tangle of filaments that appears at the beginning of the prophase stage of meiosis or mitosis. **2.** Any of these filaments. [German *Spirem,* from Greek *speirēma,* coil, from *speira,* coil, SPIRE.]

spi·rif·er·ous (spī-rĭf′ər-əs) *adj.* Having a spire, a spiral structure, or spiral parts. [SPIR(E) + -FEROUS.]

spi·ril·lum (spī-rĭl′əm) *n., pl.* **-rilla** (-rĭl′ə). **1.** Any of various flagellated aerobic bacteria of the genus *Spirillum,* having an elongated spiral form. *S. minus* causes rat-bite fever. **2.** Any spiral-shaped bacterium. Compare **bacillus, coccus.** [New Latin, diminutive of Latin *spīra,* SPIRE (spiral).]

spir·it (spĭr′ĭt) *n.* **1.** That which is traditionally believed to be the vital principle or animating force within living beings, often contrasted with nonliving matter. **2. a. Spirit.** The Holy Spirit. **b.** *Christian Science.* God. **3.** Any supernatural being or power, such as: **a.** A ghost. **b.** One regarded as able to enter and take control of a person. **4.** That which is traditionally regarded as the nonmaterial essence or true nature of an individual, especially: **a.** The intangible, spiritual core of a person; the soul. **b.** The essential and activating principle of a person; the will. **5.** A person as characterizd by a specified quality: *a free spirit.* **6.** An inclination or tendency of a specified kind: *a remark made in a spirit of friendliness.* **7. a.** *Often* **spirits.** One's mood or emotional state: *in high spirits.* **b. spirits.** A particular mood or emotional state characterized by vigor and animation. **8.** An attitude or frame of mind: *take a remark in the spirit in which it was intended.* **9.** Liveliness; vigor; mettle. **10.** Strong loyalty or dedication: *team spirit.* **11.** The predominant mood or quality of an occasion or period: *the spirit of the age.* **12.** The real sense or significance of something: *the spirit of the law rather than the letter.* **13.** *Often* **spirits.** An alcohol solution of an essential or volatile substance. **14. spirits.** A distilled alcoholic liquor, such as gin, whiskey, or rum. **—in (the) spirit.** In the mind or the imagination. **—in** (or **out of**) **spirits.** In a cheerful (or gloomy) state of mind. **—the Spirit.** The Holy Spirit. ~*tr.v.* **spirited, -iting, -its. 1.** To carry off mysteriously or secretly. Used with *away* or *off.* **2.** To impart courage, animation, or determination to; stimulate; encourage. [Middle English, from Norman French, from Latin *spīritus,* breath, breath of a god, inspiration, from *spīrāre,* to breathe.]

spir·it·ed (spĭr′ĭ-tĭd) *adj.* **1.** Full of or characterized by animation, vigor, or courage: *a spirited debate.* **2.** Having a specified mood or nature. Used in combination: *high-spirited.* **—spir·it·ed·ly** *adv.* **—spir·it·ed·ness** *n.*

spirit gum *n.* A glue used to attach false beards and mustaches to the face. It consists of a gum dissolved in ether or alcohol.

spir·it·ism (spĭr′ĭ-tĭz′əm) *n.* Spiritualism. **—spir·it·ist** *n.* **—spir·it·is·tic** (spĭr′ĭ-tĭs′tĭk) *adj.*

spirit lamp *n.* A lamp burning methylated spirits or some other alcohol-based fuel.

spir·it·less (spĭr′ĭt-lĭs) *adj.* Lacking energy, courage, or enthusiasm. **—spir·it·less·ly** *adv.* **—spir·it·less·ness** *n.*

spirit level *n.* See **level** (sense 7a).

spir·i·to·so (spĭr′ĭ-tō′sō, -zō) *adv.* *Music.* In a spirited or lively manner. Used as a direction. [Italian, spirited.] **—spir·i·to·so** *adj.*

spir·it·ous (spĭr′ĭ-təs) *adj.* **1.** Spirituous. **2.** *Archaic.* Refined; pure.

spir·it·rap·ping (spĭr′ĭt-răp′ĭng) *n.* Supposed communication from the dead through messages rapped out on a table or a similar surface. **—spir·it·rap·per** *n.*

spirits of ammonia *n.* *Used with a singular verb.* **Sal volatile** *(see).*

spirits of salt *n.* *Used with a singular verb.* **Hydrochloric acid** *(see).* No longer in technical usage.

spirits of turpentine *n.* *Used with a singular verb.* Refined turpentine.

spirits of wine *n.* *Used with a singular verb.* Also **spirit of wine.** Rectified ethanol.

spir·i·tu·al (spĭr′ĭ-cho͞o-əl) *adj.* **1.** Of, pertaining to, consisting of, or having the nature of spirit or a spirit; not tangible or material. **2.** Of, concerned with, or affecting the soul. **3.** Of, from, or pertaining to God; divine. **4.** Of or belonging to a church or religious organization; ecclesiastical. **5.** Of, pertaining to, or having highly developed or refined qualities of mind or sensibility. **6.** Linked by or sharing a deep intellectual or emotional affinity: *his spiritual heir.* **7.** Pertaining to or having the nature of spirits; supernatural. ~*n.* **1. a.** A religious folk song of black American origin. **b.** Any work composed in imitation of a black spiritual. **2.** *Usually* **spirituals.** Religious, spiritual, or ecclesiastical matters. **3.** The realm of the spirit. [Middle English, from Old French *spirituel,* from Latin *spīrituālis.* See **spirit, -al.**] **—spir·i·tu·al·ly** *adv.* **—spir·i·tu·al·ness** *n.*

spir·i·tu·al·ism (spĭr′ĭ-cho͞o-ə-lĭz′əm) *n.* **1. a.** The belief that the dead communicate with the living, usually through a medium. **b.** The practices or doctrines of those holding such a belief. **2.** Any philosophy, doctrine, or religion emphasizing the spiritual rather than the material; especially, any doctrine holding that spirit is the prime or only aspect of reality. Compare **materialism. —spir·i·tu·al·ist** *n.* **—spir·i·tu·al·is·tic** (spĭr′ĭ-cho͞o-ə-lĭs′tĭk) *adj.*

spir·i·tu·al·i·ty (spĭr′ĭ-cho͞o-ăl′ə-tē) *n., pl.* **-ties. 1. a.** The state, quality, or fact of being spiritual. **b.** Attachment to or involvement in religious matters. **2.** Ecclesiastics collectively; the clergy. **3.** *Often* **spiritualities.** Something belonging to the church or to an ecclesiastic, such as property or revenue. [Middle English, from Old French *spiritualite,* from Late Latin *spīrituālitās.* See **spiritual, -ity.**]

spir·i·tu·al·ize (spĭr′ĭ-cho͞o-ə-līz′) *tr.v.* **-ized, -izing, -izes. 1.** To impart a spiritual nature to; refine. **2.** To invest with or treat as having a spiritual sense or meaning. **—spir·i·tu·al·i·za·tion** *n.* **—spir·i·tu·al·iz·er** *n.*

spir·i·tu·al·ty (spĭr′ĭ-cho͞o-əl-tē) *n., pl.* **-ties.** Spirituality.

spir·i·tu·el, spir·i·tu·elle (spĭr′ĭ-cho͞o-ĕl′, spē′rē-to͞o-ĕl′, -tü-ĕl′) *adj.* Having or showing a refined and witty mind or nature. [French, "spiritual."]

spir·i·tu·ous (spĭr′ĭ-cho͞o-əs) *adj.* **1.** Having the nature of or containing alcohol; alcoholic. **2.** Distilled as contrasted with fermented. **—spir·i·tu·os·i·ty** (spĭr′ĭ-cho͞o-ŏs′ə-tē), **spir·i·tu·ous·ness** *n.*

spirit varnish *n.* See **varnish** (sense 1b).
spir·ket·ing (spûr′kĭ-tĭng) *n. Nautical.* **1.** Deck planking near the sides of a ship. **2.** The inside planking fitted above the waterways in a wooden ship. [From obsolete *spirket†*, the space between the side or floor timbers of a ship.]
spiro-[1] *prefix.* Indicates spiral or coiled form; for example, **spirochete.** [Latin *spīra,* coil, SPIRE.]
spiro-[2] *prefix.* Indicates respiration or breathing; for example, **spirograph.** [Latin *spīrāre,* to breathe.]
spi·ro·chete, spi·ro·chaete (spī′rə-kēt′) *n.* Any of various slender, nonflagellated, twisted bacteria of the order Spirochaetales, many of which are pathogenic, causing syphilis, relapsing fever, yaws, and other diseases. [New Latin *Spirochaeta* (genus) : SPIRO- (coil) + CHAETA.] **—spi·ro·che·tal** (spī′rə-kēt′l) *adj.*
spi·ro·che·to·sis (spī′rə-kē-tō′sĭs) *n.* Any of various diseases, such as syphilis, caused by a spirochete. [New Latin : SPIROCHET(E) + -OSIS.]
spi·ro·graph (spī′rə-grăf′, -gräf′) *n.* An instrument for registering the depth and rapidity of respiratory movements. [SPIRO- (breathing) + -GRAPH.] **—spi·ro·graph·ic** (spī′rə-grăf′ĭk) *adj.* **—spi·rog·ra·phy** (spī-rŏg′rə-fē) *n.*
spi·ro·gy·ra (spī′rə-jī′rə) *n.* Any of various green, filamentous freshwater algae of the genus *Spirogyra,* having chloroplasts in spirally twisted bands. [New Latin : SPIRO- (coil) + Greek *guros,* ring.]
spi·roid (spī′roid′) *adj.* Resembling a spiral. [New Latin *spiroides,* from Greek *speiroeidēs* : *speira,* SPIRE + -OID.]
spi·rom·e·ter (spī-rŏm′ə-tər) *n.* An instrument for measuring the volume of air entering and leaving the lungs. [SPIRO- (breathing) + -METER.] **—spi·ro·met·ric** (spī′rə-mĕt′rĭk) *adj.* **—spi·rom·e·try** (spī-rŏm′ə-trē) *n.*
spi·ro·no·lac·tone (spə-rō′nō-lăk′tōn′, spī-rŏn′ə-) *n.* A synthetic steroid drug that inhibits the action of the hormone aldosterone and is used mainly as a diuretic. [SPIRO- + *-no-* (infix) + LACTONE.]
spirt. Variant of **spurt** (sense 1).
spir·u·la (spĭr′ə-lə, -yə-lə) *n., pl.* **-lae** (-lē′). Any small cephalopod mollusk of the genus *Spirula*; especially, *S. peronii,* having a coiled internal shell. [Late Latin *spīrula,* small twisted cake or cracknel, diminutive of Latin *spīra,* coil, SPIRE.]
spir·y (spīr′ē) *adj.* **-ier, -iest.** Resembling a spire in shape.
spit[1] (spĭt) *n.* **1.** Saliva, especially when expectorated; spittle. **2.** The act or an instance of expectorating. **3.** Something resembling saliva, such as the frothy secretion of certain insects. **4.** A brief, scattered fall of rain or snow. **5.** A spitting image.
~v. **spat** (spăt) or **spit, spitting, spits.** *—tr.* **1.** To eject from the mouth. Often used with *out.* **2. a.** To eject as if by spitting. **b.** To utter in a violent, contemptuous, or angry manner. Often used with *out*: *spit out an insult.* *—intr.* **1.** To eject saliva from the mouth. **2.** To express contempt or hostility by or as if by spitting. **3.** To make a hissing or sputtering noise. **4.** To rain or snow in light, scattered drops or flakes. **—spit it out.** *Informal.* To say what one is thinking without further delay; speak up. [*Spit, spat,* Middle English *spitten,* Old English *spittan.*]
spit[2] *n.* **1.** A slender, pointed rod on which meat is impaled for roasting in front of or over a fire. **2.** A narrow ridge of sand or shingle extending into a body of water or across a bay.
~tr.v. **spitted, spitting, spits.** To impale on or as if on a spit. [Middle English *spit(e),* Old English *spitu.*]
spit·al (spĭt′l) *n. Archaic.* **1.** A hospital; especially, one for the poor or for those suffering from contagious diseases. **2.** A wayside shelter. [Variant of obsolete *spittle,* shortened variant of HOSPITAL.]
Spit·al·fields (spĭt′l-fēldz′). District in London belonging originally to the spital or rest home of St. Mary's Priory. Formerly a silk-weaving center, it has a famous wholesale market for flowers, fruits, and vegetables.
spit and polish *n. Used with a singular verb.* Close attention paid to cleanliness, smart appearance, and ceremonial, especially in the armed forces.
spit·ball (spĭt′bôl′) *n.* **1.** A piece of paper chewed and shaped into a lump for use as a projectile. **2.** *Baseball.* An illegal pitch in which the ball is moistened on one side with spit. In this sense, also called "spitter."
spite (spīt) *n.* **1.** Malicious ill will prompting an urge to hurt, annoy, or humiliate another. **2.** An instance of such feeling. **—in spite of.** Regardless of; despite.
~tr.v. **spited, spiting, spites.** **1.** To show spite toward. **2.** To thwart out of spite. [Middle English, insult, ill will, short for Old French *despit.* See **despite.**]
spite·ful (spīt′fəl) *adj.* Filled with, prompted by, or showing spite; malicious. —See Synonyms at **vindictive.** **—spite·ful·ly** *adv.* **—spite·ful·ness** *n.*
spit·fire (spĭt′fīr′) *n.* A quick-tempered or highly excitable person, especially a girl or woman.
spit·ter (spĭt′ər) *n.* **1.** One that spits. **2.** *Baseball.* See **spitball** (sense 2). **3.** A young deer with unbranched horns.
spitting cobra *n.* The **ringhals** *(see).*
spitting image *n.* A perfect, usually physical likeness or counterpart. [Perhaps from the phrase *the very spit of,* an exact likeness, as if the image has been "spat out."]
spitting snake *n.* The **ringhals** *(see).*
spit·tle (spĭt′l) *n.* **1.** Spit; saliva. **2.** The frothy liquid secreted by spittlebugs; cuckoo spit; frog spit. [Middle English *spetil,* Old English *spātl.*]
spit·tle·bug (spĭt′l-bŭg′) *n.* Any of various insects of the family Cercopidae, the nymphs of which form frothy masses of liquid on plant stems. Also called "spittle insect," "froghopper."
spit·toon (spĭ-to͞on′) *n.* A bowl-shaped, usually metal vessel for spitting into. Also called "cuspidor." [SPIT + *-oon,* as in such words as BALLOON and DOUBLOON.]
spitz (spĭts) *n.* A dog of a breed originating in Germany, having a long, thick, usually white coat and a tail curled over the back. [German *Spitz,* from *spitz,* "pointed" (from its pointed muzzle), from Old High German *spizzi.*]
spiv (spĭv) *n. British Slang.* **1.** A petty swindler or black marketeer. **2.** A flashily dressed and disreputable-looking man. [From dialectal *spiff†*, dandy.] **—spiv·vy** *adj.*
splanch·nic (splăngk′nĭk) *adj.* Of or pertaining to the viscera. [Greek *splankhnikos,* of the bowels, from *splankhna,* inward parts.]
splash (splăsh) *v.* **splashed, splashing, splashes.** *—tr.* **1.** To dash or scatter (a liquid) about in flying masses. **2.** To dash liquid upon; wet or soil by splashing. **3.** To cause to splash: *He splashed his oar in the water.* **4.** To make (one's way) through liquid so as to dash or scatter it. **5.** To display (a story, poster, or photograph) prominently. *—intr.* **1.** To cause a liquid to fly in scattered masses. **2.** To fall into or move through liquid with this effect. Often used with *about* or *around.* **3.** To move, spill, or fly about in scattered masses.
~n. **1.** The act, an instance, or a sound of splashing. **2.** A flying mass of liquid or semiliquid substance. **3.** A mark or patch produced by or as if by scattered liquid or semiliquid substance: *a splash of light.* **4.** A striking though often short-lived impression; a stir. Used chiefly in the phrase *make a splash.* **5.** A small amount of liquid: *Coffee? Just a splash.*
~adv. With a splash. [Alteration of PLASH (to splash).] **—splash·er** *n.*
splash·board (splăsh′bôrd′, -bōrd′) *n.* **1.** A structure that protects a vehicle from splashes of mud or water. **2.** A screen on a boat to keep water from splashing on the deck. **3.** A board for closing a spillway or sluice.
splash down *intr.v.* To make a splashdown. Used of a missile or spacecraft.
splash·down (splăsh′doun′) *n.* The landing of a missile or spacecraft in a body of water.
splash·y (splăsh′ē) *adj.* **-ier, -iest.** **1.** Making or liable to make splashes. **2.** Covered with splashes of color. **3.** *Informal.* Showy; ostentatious. **—splash·i·ly** *adv.* **—splash·i·ness** *n.*
splat[1] (splăt) *n.* A slat of wood, such as one in the middle of a chair back. [From obsolete *splat,* to spread out flat.]
splat[2] *n.* A slapping noise.
~adv. With a splat. [Imitative.]
splat·ter (splăt′ər) *v.* **-tered, -tering, -ters.** *—tr.* To cause to spatter or splash. *—intr.* To spatter or splash.
~n. A splash of liquid. [Perhaps a blend of SPLASH and SPATTER.]
splay (splā) *adj.* **1.** Spread out; broad. **2.** Turned outward. **3.** Clumsy; awkward.
~n. **1.** Expansion; spread. **2.** *Architecture.* Either of two side walls of a window or other opening that forms an oblique rather than a right angle to the main wall.
~v. **splayed, splaying, splays.** *—tr.* **1.** To spread (the limbs, for example) out or apart, especially clumsily. Usually used with *out.* **2.** To make the edges of (a window or other aperture) slant or slope out; bevel. **3.** To dislocate (a bone). Used of an animal. *—intr.* **1.** To be spread out or apart. **2.** To slant or slope. Usually used with *out.* [Middle English *splayen,* to spread out, short for *displayen,* to DISPLAY.]
splay·foot (splā′fo͝ot′) *n., pl.* **-feet** (-fēt′). **1.** A physical deformity characterized by abnormally flat and turned-out feet. **2.** A foot or feet of this kind. **—splay·foot·ed** *adj.*
spleen (splēn) *n.* **1.** A large, dark-red organ situated below and behind the stomach and containing lymphoid tissue. It forms lymphocytes and antibodies and helps to remove worn-out red blood cells and foreign particles from the bloodstream. **2.** A homologous organ or tissue in other vertebrates. Also called "milt." **3.** *Obsolete.* **a.** This organ considered as the seat of mirth. **b.** Merriment. **c.** Caprice; whim. **4.** *Archaic.* **a.** This organ considered as the seat of melancholy. **b.** Melancholy. **5.** Ill temper and malice. Used chiefly in the phrase *vent one's spleen.* [Middle English *splen(e),* from Old French *esplen,* from Latin *splēn,* from Greek.] **—spleen·y** *adj.*
spleen·ful (splēn′fəl) *adj.* Ill-tempered, irritable, or spiteful. [The spleen was once thought of as the seat of negative emotions.] **—spleen·ful·ly** *adv.*
spleen·wort (splēn′wûrt′, -wôrt′) *n.* Any of various ferns of the genus *Asplenium,* having featherlike, often evergreen fronds. [So called because it was thought to cure spleen disorders.]
splen·dent (splĕn′dənt) *adj.* **1.** Shining or lustrous; brilliant. **2.** Celebrated; illustrious. [Middle English, from Latin *splendēns* (stem *splendent-*), present participle of *splendēre,* to shine.]
splen·did (splĕn′dĭd) *adj.* **1.** Magnificent; grand. **2.** Imposing by reason of showiness. **3.** Glorious; illustrious. **4.** Gleaming with light or color; radiant. **5.** Very good or satisfying: *had a splendid evening.* [French *splendide,* from Latin *splendidus,* from *splendēre,* to shine.] **—splen·did·ly** *adv.* **—splen·did·ness** *n.*
splen·dif·er·ous (splĕn-dĭf′ər-əs) *adj.* Splendid. [Middle English, from Medieval Latin *splendiferus* : SPLENDOR + -FEROUS.] **—splen·dif·er·ous·ly** *adv.* **—splen·dif·er·ous·ness** *n.*
splen·dor (splĕn′dər) *n.* Also *British* **splen·dour.** **1.** The state or quality of being splendid. **2.** Something splendid. **3.** *Heraldry.* The sun depicted with rays and a human face. [Middle English *splen-*

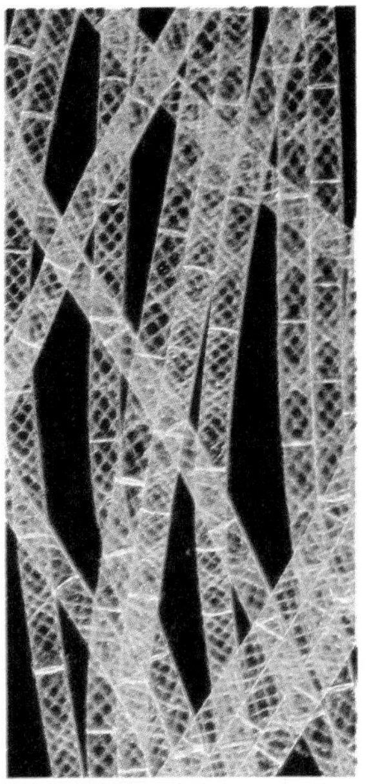
spirogyra *A genus of filamentlike green algae (here magnified 22 times) that carries chlorophyll in spirals. Up to 60 centimeters (2 feet) long, clusters of the filaments are sometimes called mermaid's tresses.*

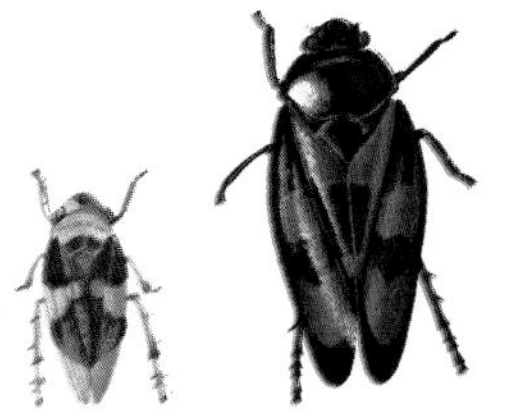
spittlebug *The larvae of some species of spittle insects, or froghoppers, decorate hedges in spring with a frothy secretion. The sticky fluid is blown out to deter predators and reduce water loss from the insect's body. These two adult insects—shown here twice life size—are the common spittlebug,* Philaenus spumarius *(left), whose larvae do produce a frothy secretion, and the larger* Cercopsis vulnerata, *which does not.*

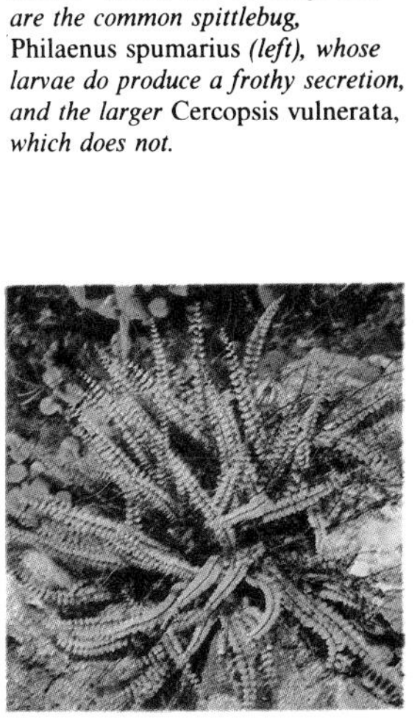
spleenwort *A genus of 650 species of evergreen ferns. This is the maidenhair spleenwort,* Asplenium trichomanes.

dure, from Old French *splendeur,* from Latin *splendour,* from *splendēre,* to shine.] **—splen·dor·ous, splen·drous** (splĕn′drəs) *adj.*

sple·nec·to·my (splĭ-nĕk′tə-mē) *n., pl.* **-mies.** The surgical removal of the spleen.

sple·net·ic (splĭ-nĕt′ĭk) *adj.* Also **sple·net·i·cal** (-nĕt′ĭ-kəl). **1.** Of or pertaining to the spleen. **2.** Ill-tempered, irritable, or spiteful. **3.** *Archaic.* Melancholy.
—n. An ill-humored person. [Late Latin *splēnēticus,* from Latin *splēn,* SPLEEN.] **—sple·net·i·cal·ly** *adv.*

splen·ic (splĕn′ĭk) *adj.* Of, in, near, or pertaining to the spleen.

sple·ni·tis (splĭ-nī′tĭs) *n.* Inflammation of the spleen.

sple·ni·us (splē′nē-əs) *n., pl.* **-nii** (-nē-ī′). Either of two muscles of the back of the neck, extending from the backbone to the skull, that rotate and extend the head and neck. [New Latin, from Latin *splēnium,* patch, plaster, spleenwort, from Greek *splēnion,* from *splēn,* SPLEEN.] **—sple·ni·al** *adj.*

spleno-, splen- *prefix.* Indicates spleen; for example, **splenitis.** [Greek *splēno-,* from *splēn,* spleen.]

sple·no·meg·a·ly (splē′nō-mĕg′ə-lē) *n.* Enlargement of the spleen.

splice (splīs) *tr.v.* **spliced, splicing, splices. 1. a.** To join (film or wire, for example) at the ends, usually with an adhesive. Often used with *to* or *together.* **b.** To join (ropes) by interweaving strands. **2.** To join (pieces of wood) by overlapping and binding or bolting. **3.** *Informal.* To unite in marriage. Usually used in the passive.
—n. **1.** A joint made by splicing. **2.** The place where parts have been spliced. [Probably from Middle Dutch *splissen.*] **—splic·er** *n.*

spline (splīn) *n.* **1. a.** Any of a series of projections on a shaft that fit into slots on a mating part, enabling one to drive the other. **b.** A slot or groove receiving such a projection. **2.** A wooden or metal strip; especially, one that fits into a groove at the edge of one board to join it to another.
—tr.v. **splined, splining, splines.** To cut splines into. [18th century : origin obscure.]

splint (splĭnt) *n.* **1.** A thin piece, as of wood, split off from a larger piece; a splinter. **2.** Any rigid device used to prevent motion of a joint or the ends of a fractured bone. **3.** A thin, flexible wooden strip, such as one used in weaving baskets and chair bottoms. **4.** A plate or strip of metal, such as one used in making armor. **5.** A bony enlargement of the cannon bone or splint bone of a horse.
—tr.v. **splinted, splinting, splints.** To support or restrict with or as if with a splint. [Middle English *splent, splint,* small strip of metal, splint, from Middle Low German or Middle Dutch *splinte.*]

splint bone *n.* Either of two small metacarpal or metatarsal bones in horses or related animals, on each side of the cannon bone.

splin·ter (splĭn′tər) *n.* **1.** A sharp, slender piece, as of wood, bone, glass, or metal, split or broken off from a main body. **2.** A group, as a political faction, that has broken away from a parent group. Also used adjectivally: *a splinter group.*
—v. **splintered, -tering, -ters.** *—intr.* **1.** To split or break into sharp, slender pieces. **2.** To split or break into parts; shatter. **3.** To break away from a parent group. *—tr.* To cause to splinter. **—**See Synonyms at **break.** [Middle English, from Middle Dutch.] **—splin·ter·y** *adj.*

split (splĭt) *v.* **split, splitting, splits.** *—tr.* **1. a.** To divide sharply or cleanly, especially into lengthwise sections or into two parts of approximately equal size. **b.** To separate from a whole. Often used with *off.* **2.** To break, burst, or rip apart with force; rend. **3.** To separate (persons or groups); disunite. Often used with *up.* **4.** To divide and share among people. **5.** To separate into layers, components, or parts. Often used with *up.* **6.** *Slang.* To depart from; leave. **7.** To mark (a vote or ballot) in favor of candidates from different parties. *—intr.* **1. a.** To become separated into parts; especially, to divide lengthwise. **b.** To be separated from a whole. Often used with *off.* **2.** To become broken or ripped apart, especially as a result of internal pressure. **3. a.** To become divided or part company as a result of discord or disagreement. **b.** To end a relationship; especially, to separate or divorce. Used with *up.* **4.** To divide or share something with others. **5.** *Slang.* To depart. **—**See Synonyms at **break, tear. —split hairs.** To make trivial distinctions; quibble.
—n. **1.** The act or result of splitting. **2.** A gap, rift, or cleft. **3.** A piece split off from a larger whole; splinter. **4.** A breach or rupture in a group; schism. **5.** A split strip of flexible wood or other material used in basketmaking. **6.** *Informal.* **a.** A bottle of an alcoholic or carbonated beverage half the usual size. **b.** A drink of half the usual quantity. **7. a.** A dessert of sliced fruit, ice cream, and toppings: *a banana split.* **b.** Something made up of two or more different constituents or ingredients. **8.** *Often* **splits.** An acrobatic feat in which the legs are stretched out in opposite directions at right angles to the trunk. **9.** A single thickness of a hide split into layers. **10.** In ten-pin bowling, an arrangement of pins left standing after the first bowl with one or more intermediate pins knocked down.
—adj. **1.** Divided or separated; *split loyalties.* **2.** Fissured longitudinally; cleft. [Dutch *splitten,* from Middle Dutch.] **—split·ter** *n.*

Split (splĭt). *Italian* **Spa·la·to** (spä′lə-tō′). City on the Dalmatian coast, in Croatia, Yugoslavia. It has been a major Adriatic port since the early Middle Ages and is a cultural, market, tourist, and manufacturing center. It was held by Venice (1420–1797) and by Austria until 1918.

split ends *pl.n.* A condition of damaged hair in which the ends of individual hairs have a tendency to split.

split infinitive *n. Grammar.* An infinitive verb form with an element, usually an adverb, interposed between *to* and the verb form.
Usage: The split infinitive, as in *to officially propose,* is not a grammatical error, and it has ample precedent in literature. It nevertheless attracts strong criticism among those who feel that *to* and the following verb form a unit that should not be separated. The split infinitive is most acceptable when it expresses a given meaning in the clearest and most concise way: *We expect our output to more than double next year.* It is also considered better to split an infinitive than to place an adverb in such a way that ambiguity or stiltedness results. Rewriting the sentence *I want to really help them* as either *I want really to help them* or *I want to help them really* makes it unclear whether *really* modifies *want* or *help.*

split-lev·el (splĭt′lĕv′əl) *adj.* Having the floor levels of adjoining rooms separated by about half a story.
—n. A split-level house.

split pea *n.* A pea dried and split and used for cooking in soups and stews or as a vegetable.

split personality *n.* **1.** A form of hysteria in which an individual manifests two or more relatively distinct identities. **2.** Such an individual. **3.** Loosely, **schizophrenia** *(see).*

split pin *n.* A strong, metal pin with two arms that can be bent outward, used for holding wheels on axles and the like.

split rail *n.* A fence rail split lengthwise from a log.

split ring *n.* A usually metal ring consisting of two spiral turns pressed flat together, between which keys or other objects may be slid on or off.

split-screen (splĭt′skrēn′) *adj.* Of or designating a cinematic technique in which two or more images are projected simultaneously onto different parts of the same screen. **—split screen** *n.*

split second *n.* An instant; a flash.

split-second (splĭt′sĕk′ənd) *adj.* **1.** Performed in a very short space of time. **2.** Requiring or showing great precision and accuracy.

split shift *n.* A working shift split into several periods by an interval considerably longer than a lunch break.

split·ting (splĭt′ĭng) *adj.* **1.** Acute; piercing. **2.** Extremely painful.

splotch (splŏch) *n.* An irregularly shaped stain, spot, or discolored area.
—tr.v. **splotched, splotching, splotches.** To mark with a splotch or splotches. [Perhaps a blend of SPOT + BLOTCH.] **—splotch·y** *adj.*

splosh (splŏsh) *n.* A splash. [Imitative.] **—splosh** *v.*

splurge (splûrj) *v.* **splurged, splurging, splurges.** *—intr.* **1.** To indulge in an extravagant expense or luxury: *went out and splurged on champagne and caviar.* **2.** To be showy or ostentatious. *—tr.* To spend extravagantly or wastefully.
—n. **1.** An extravagant display. **2.** An extravagant spending spree. [19th century : origin obscure.]

splut·ter (splŭt′ər) *v.* **-tered, -tering, -ters.** *—intr.* **1.** To make a spitting sound. **2.** To speak incoherently, as when confused or angry. *—tr.* To utter or express hastily and incoherently.
—n. **1.** A spluttering noise. **2.** Spluttering talk. [Perhaps alteration (influenced by SPLASH) of SPUTTER.] **—splut·ter·er** *n.*

Spock (spŏk), **Benjamin McLane** (1903–). U.S. pediatrician. He had a great influence on child care through his book *Baby and Child Care* (1946), which he revised in 1979.

Spode (spōd) *n.* A trademark for porcelain or chinaware of fine quality.

spod·u·mene (spŏd′yə-mēn′) *n.* A greenish to pinkish or lilac mineral, essentially $LiAlSi_2O_6$, used as a source of lithium and in transparent varieties as a gemstone. [French *spodumène,* from Greek *spodoumenos,* present participle of *spodousthai,* to be burned to ashes (because the mineral becomes ash-gray when exposed to flame), from *spodos*†, wood ashes.]

spoil (spoil) *v.* **spoiled** or **spoilt** (spoilt), **spoiling, spoils.** *—tr.* **1.** To impair the value or quality of; damage or ruin. **2. a.** To harm the character of (a child, for example) by overindulgence. **b.** To pamper; coddle. **3.** To make dissatisfied. Used with *for: spoiled him for the old life.* **4.** *Archaic.* **a.** To plunder; despoil. **b.** To take by force. *—intr.* **1.** To become tainted, rotten, or otherwise unfit for use; decay. Used especially of food. **2.** *Archaic.* To pillage. **—**See Synonyms at **decay, pamper. —spoil for.** To be eager for; crave. Used chiefly in the phrase *be spoiling for a fight.*
—n. **1.** *Usually* **spoils.** Goods or property seized from a victim after a conflict, especially after a military victory. **2. spoils.** Incidental benefits reaped by a winner. **3.** *Archaic.* The act of plundering; spoliation. **4.** Refuse material removed from an excavation. [Middle English *spoilen,* to despoil, plunder, from Old French *espoillier,* from Latin *spoliāre,* from *spolium,* hide torn from an animal, booty.]

spoil·age (spoi′lĭj) *n.* **1.** The condition or process of becoming spoiled; damage or decomposition. **2.** Material that has been spoiled. **3.** Waste caused by spoiling.

spoil·er (spoi′lər) *n.* **1.** One who seizes spoils or booty. **2.** One that causes spoilage; a corrupting agent. **3.** A long, narrow hinged plate on the upper surface of an aircraft wing, raised to reduce lift or speed. **4.** An air deflector on either end of a motor vehicle used to prevent the wheels from lifting off the road at high speeds. **5.** A candidate for office whose chances of winning are slight but who may garner enough votes to prevent one of the leading candidates from winning.

spoil·sport (spoil′spôrt′, -spōrt′) *n.* One who mars the pleasures of others, often by inappropriate prudence.

spoils system *n.* The practice after an election of rewarding loyal supporters of the winning candidates and party with appointive public offices. Compare **merit system.**

Spo·kane (spō-kăn′). City of eastern Washington. It is a commercial, transportation, and industrial center for an area that has irri-

PRONUNCIATION KEY

ă, pat; ā, pay; âr, care;
ä, father, are; b, bib;
ch, church; d, deed; ĕ, pet;
ē, be; f, fife; g, gag; h, hat;
hw, which; ĭ, pit; ī, pie;
îr, pier; j, judge; k, kick;
l, lid, needle; m, mum;
n, no, sudden; ng, thing;
ŏ, pot; ō, toe; ô, paw, for;
oi, noise; ou, out; ŏŏ, book;
ōō, boot; p, pop; r, roar;
s, sauce; sh, ship, dish;
t, tight; th, thin, path;
th, this, bathe; ŭ, cut; ûr, fur;
v, valve; w, with; y, yes;
z, zebra, size; zh, vision;
ə, about, item, edible,
gallop, circus, peaceful

IN FOREIGN WORDS:

à, *Fr.* ami; œ, *Fr.* feu, *Ger.* schön; ü, *Fr.* tu, *Ger.* über;
KH, *Ger.* ich, *Scot.* loch;
N, *Fr.* bon; y′, *Fr.* Compiègne

STRESS MARKS:

Primary stress: ′
in·cite′ (ĭn-sīt′)
Secondary stress: ′
in′sight′ (ĭn′sīt′)

gated farms, cattle ranches, and mining industries. A trading fort was established here in 1810, but settlement did not begin until the 1870's.

spoke[1] (spōk) *n.* **1.** Any of the rods or braces that connect the hub and the rim of a wheel. **2.** Any of the handles that project from the rim of a ship's steering wheel. **3.** A rung of a ladder.
~*tr.v.* **spoked, spoking, spokes. 1.** To equip with spokes. **2.** To impede (a wheel) by inserting a rod. [Middle English *spake, spoke,* Old English *spāca.*]

spoke[2]. Past tense and *archaic* past participle of **speak.**

spo·ken (spō'kən). Past participle of **speak.**
~*adj.* **1.** Uttered; expressed orally. **2.** Speaking or using speech in a specified manner or voice. Used in combination: *soft-spoken.* **—spoken for.** Reserved or engaged.

spoke·shave (spōk'shāv') *n.* A **drawknife** *(see).*

spokes·man (spōks'mən) *n., pl.* **-men** (-mĭn). A person chosen or authorized to speak on behalf of another or others. [*Spokes,* possessive case of *spoke,* "speaking," from *spoke,* archaic past participle of SPEAK + MAN.]

spokes·per·son (spōks'pûr'sən) *n.* A spokesman or spokeswoman. [SPOKES(MAN) + PERSON.]

spokes·wom·an (spōks'wŏŏm'ən) *n., pl.* **-women** (-wĭm'ĭn). A woman who speaks on behalf of another or others. [SPOKES(MAN) + WOMAN.]

spo·li·a·tion (spō'lē-ā'shən) *n.* **1.** The act of despoiling or plundering; especially, the seizure of neutral vessels at sea by a belligerent power in time of war. **2.** *Law.* The intentional alteration or destruction of a document so as to invalidate it as evidence. [Middle English *spoliacioun,* from Latin *spoliātiō* (stem *spoliātiōn-*), from *spoliāre,* to despoil. See **spoil.**] **—spo·li·a·tor** (spō'lē-ā'tər) *n.*

spon·da·ic (spŏn-dā'ĭk) *adj.* Of, pertaining to, or consisting of spondees. [French *spondaïque,* from Late Latin *spondaicus, spondiācus,* from Greek *spondeiakos,* from *spondeios,* SPONDEE.]

spon·dee (spŏn'dē') *n.* A metrical foot in poetry consisting of two long or stressed syllables. [Middle English *sponde,* from Old French *spondee,* from Latin *spondeum,* from Greek *spondeios (pous),* "(meter) used at a libation," from *spondē,* libation.]

spon·dy·li·tis (spŏn'də-lī'tĭs) *n.* Inflammation of the joints of the vertebrae. [New Latin : Greek *spondulos, sphondulos*†, vertebra + -ITIS.]

sponge (spŭnj) *n.* **1.** Any of numerous primitive, chiefly marine invertebrate animals of the phylum Porifera, characteristically having a porous body supported by a skeleton composed of fibrous material or siliceous or calcareous spicules, and often forming colonies. **2. a.** The light, fibrous, absorbent skeleton of certain of these organisms. **b.** A piece of such a skeleton, used for bathing, cleaning, and other purposes. **3.** Any of various substances having spongelike qualities, such as certain forms of plastics, rubber, or cellulose. **4.** A porous metal used to absorb gases: *a platinum sponge.* **5.** A gauze pad used to absorb blood and other fluids, as in surgery and wound dressing. **6.** Dough that is leavened or in the process of being leavened. **7.** Any of various light cakes, such as sponge cake. **8. a.** A wash or rub with a sponge. **b.** A sponge bath. **9.** *Informal.* A sponger. **—throw** (or **toss**) **in the sponge.** *Informal.* To give up; admit defeat.
~*v.* **sponged, sponging, sponges.** *—tr.* **1.** To moisten, wipe, or clean with a sponge. Often used with *down* or *off.* **2.** To wipe out; erase. **3.** To absorb or soak up. Often used with *up.* **4.** *Informal.* To obtain free by imposing on another's generosity: *sponge a meal.* *—intr.* **1.** To fish for sponges. **2.** *Informal.* To live by imposing on the generosity of others. Often used with *off* or *on.* [Middle English *spo(u)ng(e),* Old English *sponge,* from Latin *spongia,* from Greek *sphongos,* sponge, from the same Mediterranean origin as FUNGUS.]

sponge bath *n.* A washing of the body with a sponge or cloth, without immersion.

sponge cake *n.* A very light, porous cake made of flour, sugar, beaten eggs, and flavoring and containing no shortening.

sponge cloth *n.* A loosely woven cloth, usually of cotton.

sponge finger *n. British.* A small sponge cake shaped like a finger; a lady finger.

sponge mushroom *n.* A **morel** (mushroom) *(see).*

spong·er (spŭn'jər) *n.* **1.** A person or boat that gathers sponges. **2.** *Informal.* A person who sponges on others; a parasite.

sponge rubber *n.* A soft, porous rubber used in toys, cushions, gaskets, and weather stripping, and as a vibration dampener.

spon·gin (spŭn'jĭn) *n.* A fibrous protein that forms the skeletal structure of some sponges. [German *Spongin* : Latin *spongia,* SPONGE + -IN.]

spon·gi·o·blast (spŭn'jē-ə-blăst', -bläst') *n.* Any of the embryonic epithelial cells that give rise to the neuroglia cells. [Latin *spongia,* SPONGE + -BLAST.] **—spon·gi·o·blast·ic** (spŭn'jē-ə-blăs'tĭk) *adj.*

spon·gi·o·cyte (spŭn'jē-ə-sīt') *n.* A neuroglia cell. [Latin *spongia,* SPONGE + -CYTE.]

spon·go·coel (spŏng'gə-sēl') *n. Zoology.* The central cavity of a sponge that opens to the outside by way of the osculum. [SPONG(E) + -COEL.]

spong·y (spŭn'jē) *adj.* **-ier, -iest. 1.** Like a sponge, especially in elasticity, absorbency, or porousness. **2.** Full of small holes. **3.** Soft and wet. **—spong·i·ness** *n.*

spon·son (spŏn'sən) *n.* **1.** Any of several structures that project from the side of a ship or tank; especially, a gun platform. **2.** An air-filled projection on the hull of a seaplane, canoe, or other vessel, giving greater stability. [19th century : origin obscure.]

spon·sor (spŏn'sər) *n.* **1.** A person or group that assumes responsibility for another person or group, as during a period of apprenticeship. **2.** A person or group that pledges financial support to or promotes an activity or organization. **3.** A legislator who proposes and urges the adoption of a bill. **4.** One who presents a candidate for baptism or confirmation; a godparent. **5.** A business enterprise that pays for or subsidizes a broadcast, concert, sports event, or the like, usually in return for advertising time or space.
~*tr.v.* **sponsored, -soring, -sors.** To act as a sponsor for. [Latin, from *spondēre,* to make a solemn pledge.] **—spon·so·ri·al** (spŏn-sôr'ē-əl, -sōr'ē-əl) *adj.* **—spon·sor·ship** *n.*

spon·ta·ne·i·ty (spŏn'tə-nē'ə-tē) *n., pl.* **-ties. 1.** The condition or quality of being spontaneous. **2.** Spontaneous behavior, impulses, or movements.

spon·ta·ne·ous (spŏn-tā'nē-əs) *adj.* **1.** Happening, arising, or performed without apparent external cause; self-generated. **2.** Voluntary and impulsive; unpremeditated: *spontaneous applause.* **3.** Unconstrained and unstudied in manner or characteristic behavior. **4.** Growing without cultivation or human labor; indigenous. Said of plants. —See Synonyms below and at **voluntary.** [Late Latin *spontāneus,* from Latin *sponte,* of one's own accord, out of free will.] **—spon·ta·ne·ous·ly** *adv.* **—spon·ta·ne·ous·ness** *n.*
Synonyms: automatic, impulsive, instinctive, involuntary.

spontaneous abortion *n.* A **miscarriage** (sense 2) *(see).*

spontaneous combustion *n.* Ignition of a material, such as powdered coal or hay, without an external source of heat, caused by slow oxidation of the material, producing a rise in temperature.

spontaneous generation *n. Biology.* The origination of live organisms from nonliving matter, once thought to explain the appearance of maggots in rotting meat. Compare **primordial soup.** See **abiogenesis.**

spon·toon (spŏn-tōōn') *n.* A short pike carried by subordinate infantry officers in the 18th and early 19th centuries. [French *sponton,* from Italian *spuntone,* from *spuntare,* to blunt, remove the point : *s-,* from Latin *ex-* (removal) + *punto,* point, from Latin *punctum,* from *pungere,* to pierce.]

spoof (spōōf) *n.* **1.** A good-humored hoax. **2.** A gentle satirical imitation; a light parody. —See Synonyms at **caricature.**
~*v.* **spoofed, spoofing, spoofs.** *—tr.* **1.** To deceive. **2.** To do a spoof of; satirize gently. *—intr.* To do a spoof. [From *Spoof,* a trademark for a card game characterized by nonsense and hoaxing.] **—spoof·er** *n.*

spook (spōōk) *n. Informal.* **1.** A ghost; specter. **2.** A spy.
~*v.* **spooked, spooking, spooks.** *Informal. —tr.* **1.** To haunt. **2.** To frighten; especially, to startle and cause sudden or violent activity among (cattle, for example). *—intr.* To become frightened. [Dutch, from Middle Dutch *spoocke,* akin to Middle Low German *spōk*†.] **—spook·ish** *adj.*

spook·y (spōō'kē) *adj.* **-ier, -iest.** *Informal.* **1.** Ghostly; eerie; unnatural. **2.** Easily startled; skittish; nervous. **—spook·i·ly** *adv.* **—spook·i·ness** *n.*

spool (spōōl) *n.* **1.** A wood, metal, plastic, or cardboard cylinder upon which wire, thread, film, magnetic tape, or string is wound. It usually has a head or rim at each end and a hole through the center. **2.** The amount of thread or other material on a particular spool. **3.** Anything similar to a spool in shape or function.
~*v.* **spooled, spooling, spools.** *—tr.* To wind on a spool. Often used with *up.* *—intr.* To be wound on a spool. Often used with *up.* [Middle English *spole, spule,* from Old French *espole,* from Middle Dutch *spoele,* akin to Old High German *spuolo*†.]

spoon (spōōn) *n.* **1. a.** A utensil consisting of a small, shallow bowl on a handle, used in preparing, serving, or eating food. **b.** A spoonful. **2.** Something similar to a spoon or its bowl, especially: **a.** A shiny, curved metallic fishing lure. Also called "spoon bait." **b.** A paddle or oar with a curved blade. **3.** A golf club with more loft than a brassie. **—born with a silver spoon in one's mouth.** Born into wealthy or privileged circumstances.
~*v.* **spooned, spooning, spoons.** *—tr.* **1.** To lift, scoop up, or carry (food, for example) with or as if with a spoon. Often used with *out* or *up.* **2.** To shove or scoop (a ball) into the air, as in golf. *—intr.* **1.** To fish with a spoon lure. **2.** To give a ball an upward scoop, as in golf. **3.** *Informal.* To show affection by kissing, caressing, or talking amorously. [Middle English *spo(o)n,* Old English *spōn,* chip of wood.]

spoon·bill (spōōn'bĭl') *n.* **1.** Any of several long-legged wading birds, mainly of the genus *Platalea,* of tropical and subtropical regions, having a long, flat bill with a broad, spatulate tip. **2.** Any of various broad-billed ducks, such as the shoveler. **3.** The **paddlefish** *(see).*

spoon·drift (spōōn'drĭft') *n.* **Spindrift** *(see).* [Obsolete *spoon*†, to drive back and forth (said of a boat) + DRIFT.]

spoon·er·ism (spōō'nə-rĭz'əm) *n.* A usually unintentional transposition of the initial sounds of two or more words, as in *Let me sew you to your sheet* for *Let me show you to your seat.* [After the Rev. William A. *Spooner* (1844–1930), English scholar and warden of New College, Oxford, noted for such slips.]

spoon·feed (spōōn'fēd') *tr.v.* **-fed** (-fĕd'), **-feeding, -feeds. 1.** To feed (a baby, for example) with a spoon. **2. a.** To present (information, lessons, or the like) in such a thoroughgoing manner as to make any independent thought or effort on the part of the recipient unnecessary. **b.** To present with information in such a manner. **3.** To mollycoddle; pamper.

spoon·ful (spōōn'fŏŏl') *n., pl.* **-fuls.** The amount a spoon will hold.

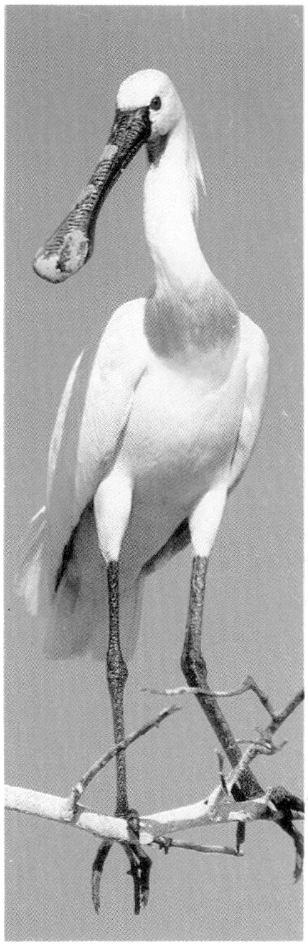

spoonbill *The long-legged spoonbill uses its wide, flat bill to fish for crustaceans on the muddy bottoms of lakes and lagoons. Spoonbills are found worldwide in tropical and subtropical regions.*

spoor (spŏŏr) n. The track, trail, or footprint of an animal, especially a wild animal. —See Synonyms at **trace**.
~v. **spoored, spooring, spoors.** —tr. To track by following a spoor. —intr. To track an animal by its spoor. [Afrikaans, from Middle Dutch spo(o)r.]

Spor·a·des (spôr'ə-dēz'). Two groups of Greek islands in the southeastern Aegean Sea. The southern group includes the Dodecanese.

spo·rad·ic (spô-răd'ĭk, spō-) adj. **1.** Occurring at irregular intervals in time; occasional. **2.** Appearing singly or at widely scattered localities; isolated in occurrence: a sporadic disease. —See Synonyms at **periodic**. [Medieval Latin sporadicus, from Greek sporadikos, isolated, scattered, from sporas, scattered, dispersed.] —spo·rad·i·cal·ly adv. —spo·rad·i·cal·ness n.

spo·ran·gi·um (spô-răn'jē-əm, spō-) n., pl. **-gia** (-jē-ə). An asexual spore-bearing structure in certain plants, such as fungi, mosses, and ferns. [New Latin : SPOR(O)- + Greek angeion, vessel, container (see angiology).] —spo·ran·gi·al adj.

spore (spôr, spōr) n. **1.** An asexual, usually single-celled reproductive organ characteristic of nonflowering plants such as fungi, mosses, or ferns. **2.** A similar structure formed by or involved in sexual reproduction in some other organisms. **3.** A microorganism, such as a bacterium, in a dormant or resting state.
~intr.v. **spored, sporing, spores.** To produce or carry spores. [New Latin spora, from Greek, a sowing, seed.] —spo·ra·ceous (spə-rā'shəs, spō-) adj.

spore case n. A sporangium or other structure containing spores.

spo·ri·cide (spôr'ə-sīd', spōr'-) n. An agent that kills spores. —spo·ri·cid·al (spôr'ə-sīd'l, spōr'-) adj.

sporo-, spori-, spor- prefix. Indicates spore; for example, sporocarp, sporangium. [New Latin spora, spore, from Greek, a sowing, seed.]

spo·ro·carp (spôr'ə-kärp', spōr'-) n. Botany. **1.** A multicellular structure in which spores are formed in aquatic ferns. **2.** An ascocarp (see). [SPORO- + -CARP.]

spo·ro·cyst (spôr'ə-sĭst', spōr'-) n. Biology. **1.** A protective case containing the spores of sporozoan protozoans. **2.** A saclike larval stage in many trematode worms, from which redia larvae are produced. [SPORO- + -CYST.]

spo·ro·cyte (spôr'ə-sīt', spōr'-) n. Biology. A cell that produces haploid spores during meiosis. [SPORO- + -CYTE.]

spo·ro·gen·e·sis (spôr'ə-jĕn'ə-sĭs, spōr'-) n. The production or formation of spores. [SPORO- + -GENESIS.] —spo·rog·e·nous (spə-rŏj'ə-nəs, spō-) adj.

spo·ro·go·ni·um (spôr'ə-gō'nē-əm, spōr'-) n., pl. **-nia** (-nē-ə). A stalked structure in mosses and liverworts that produces asexual spores. [New Latin : SPORO- + -GONIUM.]

spo·rog·o·ny (spô-rŏg'ə-nē, spō-) n. The production of sporozoites by multiple fission of the zygote, characteristic of sporozoan protozoans. [SPORO- + -GONY.]

spo·ro·phore (spôr'ə-fôr', spōr'ə-fōr') n. A spore-bearing structure, especially in fungi. [SPORO- + -PHORE.]

spo·ro·phyll (spôr'ə-fĭl', spōr'-) n. A leaf or leaflike organ in mosses, ferns, and the like that bears sporangia. [SPORO- + -PHYLL.]

spo·ro·phyte (spôr'ə-fīt', spōr'-) n. **1.** The spore-producing phase in plants that reproduce by alternation of generations. **2.** An individual plant in this phase. Compare **gametophyte**. [SPORO- + -PHYTE.] —spo·ro·phyt·ic (spôr'ə-fĭt'ĭk, spōr'-) adj.

-sporous suffix. Indicates having a specified number or kind of spores; for example, homosporous. [SPOR(E) + -OUS.]

spo·ro·zo·an (spôr'ə-zō'ən, spōr'-) n. Any of numerous parasitic protozoans of the class Sporozoa, such as the malaria parasite, many of which have complex reproductive processes. [New Latin Sporozoa : SPORO- + -ZOA.] —spo·ro·zo·an adj.

spo·ro·zo·ite (spôr'ə-zō'īt', spōr'-) n. A sporozoan that has been formed by sporogony and is ready to penetrate a new host cell. [SPOROZO(AN) + -ITE.]

spor·ran (spôr'ən, spōr'-) n. A leather or fur pouch worn hanging on the belt at the front of the kilt in Highland dress. [Scottish Gaelic sporan, from Late Latin bursa, bag, from Greek, leather.]

sport (spôrt, spōrt) n. **1.** A game or other activity, usually providing exercise and pleasure and involving competition. **2.** Sports collectively. **3.** Any pleasurable pastime; diversion; recreation. **4. a.** Light mockery; raillery; jest: a remark made in sport. **b.** An object of mockery. **5.** One at the mercy of or controlled by external forces: a sport of fate. **6.** Informal. A cheerful or good-natured person. **7.** Informal. A person who shows sportsmanlike qualities to a specified extent: a poor sport. **8.** Informal. A person who lives a merry, extravagant life. **9.** Australian. Used as an informal term of address. **10.** Genetics. An organism that shows a marked change from the parent stock; a mutation. **11.** Archaic. Amorous dalliance; flirting.
~v. **sported, sporting, sports.** —intr. **1.** To play happily; frolic. **2.** To joke or trifle. Often used with with. **3.** To mutate. —tr. To display or show off: His shoes sported pink laces.
~adj. Also **sports** (spôrts, spōrts). **1.** Of, relating to, or used in sports: sports equipment. **2.** Suitable for casual or informal use: a sport shirt. [Middle English sporten, to amuse, divert, short for disporten, to DISPORT.] —sport·ful adj. —sport·ful·ly adv. —sport·ful·ness n.

sport·ing (spôr'tĭng, spōr'-) adj. **1.** Used in, appropriate for, or pertaining to hunting, racing, and other sports. **2.** Showing sportsmanship. **3.** Of or associated with gambling. —sport·ing·ly adv.

sporting chance n. Informal. A fair chance of success.

spor·tive (spôr'tĭv, spōr'-) adj. **1.** Playful; frolicsome. **2.** Pertaining to or interested in sports. **3.** Archaic. Amorous; wanton. —spor·tive·ly adv. —spor·tive·ness n.

sports car n. A small car, usually with two seats, having a low center of gravity and often a folding or removable roof. Its steering and suspension are designed for precise control at high speeds on curving roads.

sports·cast (spôrts'kăst', -käst', spōrts'-) n. A radio or television broadcast of a sports event or of sports news. [SPORTS + (BROAD)CAST.] —sports·cast·er n.

sports·man (spôrts'mən, spōrts'-) n., pl. **-men** (-mĭn). **1. a.** One who participates actively in sports, especially outdoor sports. **b.** One who participates in hunting, angling, or similar outdoor pursuits. **2.** One who abides by the rules of a contest, plays fair, and accepts victory or defeat graciously.

sports·man·like (spôrts'mən-līk', spōrts'-) adj. Also **sports·man·ly** (-lē). Of, like, or befitting a good sportsman.

sports·man·ship (spôrts'mən-shĭp', spōrts'-) n. The qualities and conduct of a good sportsman; fair play and abidance by the rules.

sports medicine n. Medicine dealing with the diseases and injuries resulting from participation in sports.

sports·wear (spôrts'wâr', spōrts'-) n. **1.** Clothes designed to be worn for sporting activities. **2.** Clothes designed for comfort and casual wear.

sports·wom·an (spôrts'wŏŏm'ən, spōrts'-) n., pl. **-women** (-wĭm'ĭn). A woman who is active in sports.

sport·y (spôr'tē, spōr'-) adj. **-i·er, -i·est.** Informal. **1.** Of or appropriate to sports or participation in sports. **2.** Interested or taking part in sports. **3.** Casual in style. Used of clothes. **4.** Dashing; flashy. —sport·i·ly adv. —sport·i·ness n.

spor·u·late (spôr'yə-lāt', spōr'-) intr.v. **-lated, -lating, -lates.** To produce or release spores, especially by multiple cell fission. [New Latin sporula, diminutive of spora, SPORE.] —spor·u·la·tion n.

spot (spŏt) n. **1. a.** A particular place of relatively small and definite limits: a holiday spot. **b.** A place noted for a specified feature or activity: a trouble spot; a favorite night spot. **2.** A mark on a surface differing in color from the surroundings and usually of round or irregular shape; especially, a stain or blot. **3.** A position; location: X marks the spot. **4.** Informal. A situation, especially a difficult or embarrassing one; predicament: in a tight spot. **5.** A brief amount of advertising time on a radio or television program. **6.** An amount of time allocated to a performer or entertainer. **7.** A personal defect or blemish, often affecting one's reputation. **8.** An edible marine fish, Leiostomus xanthurus, of North American Atlantic waters, having a dark spot above each pectoral fin. **9.** Chiefly British Informal. A small amount; bit: a spot of tea. **10.** Informal. A spotlight. **11.** A colored dot or other shape, such as a heart, on a playing card, domino, or dice, used to distinguish suit, value, or the like. **12.** In billiards: **a.** The white ball that is distinguished by a black spot. Also called "spot ball." **b.** The player using this ball. —change one's spots. To change one's character, usually for the better. Usually used in the negative. —hit the spot. Informal. To be just what is needed; be quite satisfying. —on the spot. **1.** Without delay; at once. **2.** At the scene of action. **3.** In a responsible, difficult, or delicate position; under pressure.
~v. **spotted, spotting, spots.** —tr. **1.** To cause a spot or spots to appear upon, especially: **a.** To soil with spots. **b.** To decorate with spots; dot. **2.** To place in a particular location; situate precisely. **3.** To locate or identify; discern. **4.** Sports. To yield as a handicap: spotted her opponent six points. —intr. **1.** To become marked or be susceptible to marking with spots. **2.** To cause a discoloration; make a stain. **3.** To act as a spotter.
~adj. **1.** Paid for or delivered immediately: spot sales. **2.** Paid immediately on delivery: spot cash. **3.** Presented between major radio or television programs: a spot announcement. [Middle English spot(te), perhaps of Low German origin; akin to Middle Dutch spotte, from Common Germanic sput- (unattested).] —spot·ta·ble adj.

spot check n. An inspection or investigation that is carried out at random or limited to a few instances.

spot-check (spŏt'chĕk') v. **-checked, -checking, -checks.** —tr. To subject to a spot check. —intr. To make a spot check.

spot height n. A precise point the height of which above sea level has been accurately measured and indicated on a map.

spot·less (spŏt'lĭs) adj. **1.** Perfectly clean. **2.** Free from blemish; impeccable. —spot·less·ly adv. —spot·less·ness n.

spot·light (spŏt'līt') n. **1.** A strong beam of light that illuminates only a small area, used especially to center attention on a stage actor. **2.** A lamp that produces such a light. Also called "spot." **3.** Public notoriety or prominence. **4.** Any artificial source of light with a strongly focused beam, as on a motor vehicle.
~tr.v. **-lighted** or **-lit** (-lĭt'), **-lighting, -lights.** **1.** To illuminate with a spotlight. **2.** To focus attention on.

spot·ted (spŏt'ĭd) adj. **1.** Marked and stained with spots. **2.** Patterned with spots. **3.** Blemished; stained.

spotted fever n. **1.** Any of various often fatal infectious diseases, such as typhus and Rocky Mountain spotted fever, caused by Rickettsiae, that are transmitted by ticks and mites and are characterized by skin eruptions. **2.** An epidemic form of **cerebrospinal meningitis** (see).

spotted hyena n. An African hyena, Crocuta crocuta, with a spotted coat. Also called "laughing hyena."

spot·ter (spŏt'ər) n. **1.** One that looks for, locates, and usually reports something, especially: **a.** A military or civil-defense lookout. **b.** *Informal.* A person hired to detect dishonest acts by employees, as in a bank. **2.** *Sports.* **a.** One who identifies players on the field, as for a radio or television announcer. **b.** One who is responsible for watching and guarding a performer during practice to prevent injury, as in gymnastics or water-skiing.

spot·ty (spŏt′ē) *adj.* **-tier, -tiest. 1.** Having or marked with spots; spotted. **2.** Lacking consistency of quality; uneven. **—spot·ti·ly** *adv.* **—spot·ti·ness** *n.*

spot-weld (spŏt′wĕld′, -wĕld′) *tr.v.* **-welded, -welding, -welds.** To join (two metal sheets, wires, or the like) by one or more small welds created by electrically generated heat and pressure.
∼*n.* A weld so formed. **—spot-weld·er** *n.*

spous·al (spou′zəl, -səl) *adj.* Of or pertaining to marriage.
∼*n. Usually* **spousals.** Marriage. [Variant of ESPOUSAL.]

spouse (spous, spouz) *n.* One's marriage partner; a husband or wife.
∼*tr.v.* (spouz, spous) **spoused, spousing, spouses.** *Archaic.* To marry; wed. [Middle English *sp(o)use,* from Old French *(e)spous,* from Latin *spōnsus,* betrothed (person), betrothal, from *spondēre,* to make a solemn pledge, betroth.]

spout (spout) *v.* **spouted, spouting, spouts.** *—intr.* **1.** To gush forth in a rapid stream or in spurts. Often used with *out.* **2.** To discharge a liquid or other substance continuously or in spurts. **3.** *Informal.* To speak volubly and tediously. *—tr.* **1.** To cause to flow or spurt out. **2.** *Informal.* To utter pompously and volubly.
∼*n.* **1.** A tube, mouth, funnel, or pipe through which liquid or material such as grain is released or discharged, such as the mouth of a teapot or roof drainpipe. **2.** A continuous stream of liquid or material such as grain. [Middle English *spouten,* perhaps from Middle Dutch *spouten, spoiten.*] **—spout·er** *n.*

spp. species (plural).

S.P.Q.R. The Senate and the People of Rome. [Latin *Senatus Populusque Romanus.*]

S.P.R. Society for Psychical Research.

sprach·ge·fühl (shpräkʜ′gə-fül′) *n.* A feeling for language; an ear for the idiomatically correct or appropriate. [German, "language feeling."]

sprag (språg) *n.* **1. a.** A piece of wood or metal wedged beneath a wheel or between spokes to keep a vehicle from rolling down a slope. **b.** A pointed stake lowered at an angle into the ground from a vehicle to prevent movement. **2.** A prop to support a mine roof. [Perhaps of Scandinavian origin.]

sprain (sprān) *n.* **1.** A painful wrenching or laceration of the ligaments of a joint. **2.** The condition resulting from such an injury.
∼*tr.v.* **sprained, spraining, sprains.** To cause a sprain in (a joint). [17th century : perhaps from Old French *espraindre,* to squeeze out, strain, from Vulgar Latin *expremere* (unattested), variant of Latin *exprimere,* to press out : *ex-,* out + *premere,* to press.]

sprang. Past tense of **spring.**

sprat (sprăt) *n.* **1.** A small marine food fish, *Clupea sprattus,* of northeastern Atlantic waters. Also called "brisling." **2.** Broadly, any of various similar fish, such as a young herring. [Earlier *sprot,* Middle English *sprotte,* Old English *sprott,* akin to Middle Low German or Middle Dutch *sprot*†.]

sprawl (sprôl) *v.* **sprawled, sprawling, sprawls.** *—intr.* **1.** To sit or lie with the body and limbs spread out awkwardly. Often used with *out.* **2.** To spread out in a straggling or disordered fashion, as handwriting, a town, or a crowd might. *—tr.* To cause to spread out in a straggling or disordered fashion.
∼*n.* **1.** A sprawling position or posture. **2.** Haphazard growth or extension outward, especially that resulting from new housing on the outskirts of a town: *urban sprawl.* [Middle English *sprewlen, spraulen,* Old English *sprēawlian.*] **—sprawl·er** *n.*

spray[1] (sprā) *n.* **1. a.** Water or other liquid moving in a mass of dispersed droplets, as from a wave. **b.** Something resembling this, such as a cluster of small flying objects. **2. a.** A fine jet of liquid discharged from an atomizer or a pressurized container. **b.** Such a container. **c.** Any of numerous commercial products, including paints, cosmetics, and insecticides, dispensed in this way.
∼*v.* **sprayed, spraying, sprays.** *—tr.* **1.** To disperse (a liquid) in a mass or jet of droplets. **2.** To apply (a liquid) in the form of a spray. **3.** To apply a spray to (a surface). **4.** To shoot out small projectiles at: *sprayed them with machine-gun fire.* *—intr.* **1.** To discharge sprays of liquid. **2.** To move in the form of a spray. [Originally, "to sprinkle," from Middle Dutch *spraeyen*†.] **—spray·er** *n.*

spray[2] *n.* **1.** A small branch bearing buds, flowers, or berries. **2.** An ornament or other object resembling this in shape or design. [Middle English, Old English *spræg*† (unattested).]

spray-dry (sprā′drī′) *tr.v.* **-dried, -drying, -dries.** To dehydrate (milk, for example) into a powder form by spraying into hot air.

spray gun *n.* A gunlike device that forces liquid through a nozzle so that it emerges as a spray.

spray-on (sprā′ŏn′, -ôn′) *adj.* Applied as a spray from a pressurized container: *spray-on deodorant.*

spread (sprĕd) *v.* **spread, spreading, spreads.** *—tr.* **1.** To broaden or open to a fuller extent or width; stretch. Often used with *out*: *spread sail. He spread out the map.* **2.** To make wider the gap between; move farther apart. **3. a.** To distribute over a surface in a layer; apply: *spread jam.* **b.** To cover with a thin layer. **4.** To extend over a considerable area or period of time; distribute widely. **5.** To cause to become widely known; disseminate. **6. a.** To prepare (a table) for eating; set. **b.** To arrange (food or a meal) on a table. *—intr.* **1.** To be extended or enlarged. **2.** To become distributed or widely dispersed; increase in range of occurrence. **3.** To become known over a wider area; be disseminated. **4.** To become distributed in a thin layer: *Margarine spreads easily.* **5.** To become separated; be forced farther apart. **6.** To be displayed or revealed. Often used with *out*: *The valley spread out before us.*
∼*n.* **1. a.** The act of spreading; extension; dispersion. **b.** Diffusion; dissemination, as of news. **2. a.** An open area of land; expanse. **b.** A ranch or farm. **3.** The extent or limit to which something is or can be spread over time or space; range. **4.** A cloth covering for a bed, table, or the like. **5.** *Informal.* An abundant meal laid out on a table. **6.** A pastelike food to be spread on bread or crackers. **7. a.** The facing pages of a book, magazine, or newspaper with related matter extending across the fold. **b.** An article or advertisement running across two or more columns. **8.** An increase in size of the hips and waist: *middle-age spread.* **9.** A gap between two points. **10.** A difference, as between a buying and selling price. **11.** The wingspan of an aircraft.
∼*adj.* **1.** Extended; expanded. **2.** Flat and shallow. Said of a gem. **3.** *Phonetics.* **a.** Extended to form a long, narrow opening. Said of the lips. **b.** Articulated with spread lips. Said of a vowel. [Middle English *spred(d)en,* Old English *sprǣdan* (only in compounds, such as *tō-sprǣdan*).] **—spread·a·ble** *adj.*

spread eagle *n.* **1. a.** A figure of an eagle with wings and legs spread. **b.** The emblem on the Great Seal of the United States. **2.** A posture or design resembling a spread eagle, especially a figure performed with the skates heel to heel in ice skating.

spread-ea·gle (sprĕd′ē′gəl) *adj.* Also **spread-ea·gled** (-gəld). With the arms and legs stretched out. **2.** *Informal.* Full of patriotic or jingoistic rhetoric.
∼*v.* **spread-eagled, -gling, -gles.** *—tr.* **1.** To place in a spread-eagle position, especially as a means of punishment. **2.** To defeat or knock out. *—intr.* **1.** To make a grandiloquent, patriotic speech. **2.** To perform a spread eagle in ice skating.

spread·er (sprĕd′ər) *n.* One that spreads, specifically: **1.** A butter knife. **2.** An implement for scattering fertilizer or seed. **3.** A device, such as a bar, for keeping wires or stays apart.

spread-on-im·pact bullet (sprĕd′ŏn-ĭm′păkt′, sprĕd′ôn-) *n.* A **dum-dum bullet** *(see).*

sprech·ge·sang (shprĕkʜ′gə-zäng′) *n.* A technique of vocal production halfway between speaking and singing. [German, "speaking song."]

spree (sprē) *n.* **1.** A gay, lively outing. **2.** A period or bout of unrestrained overindulgence in some activity: *a buying spree; a drinking spree.* [Perhaps alteration of Scottish *spreath,* cattle raid, from Irish Gaelic *sprēidh,* from Latin *praeda,* booty.]

Spree (shprā). River, *c.* 400 kilometers (250 miles) long, rising in southeastern East Germany and flowing generally north through the Spree Forest to Berlin and its juncture with the Havel River at Spandau.

sprig (sprĭg) *n.* **1. a.** A small shoot or twig together with its leaves and flowers. **b.** An ornament or motif resembling this. **2.** A small brad without a head. **3.** *Informal.* A young person.
∼*tr.v.* **sprigged, sprigging, sprigs. 1.** To decorate with a design of sprigs. **2.** To remove a sprig or sprigs from (a bush or tree). **3.** To fasten with a small headless brad. [Middle English *sprigg(e)*†.] **—sprig·ger** *n.*

sprigged (sprĭgd) *adj.* Designating a fabric or material decorated with a design of sprigs: *sprigged muslin.*

spright·ly (sprīt′lē) *adj.* **-lier, -liest.** Buoyant or animated; full of life. —See Synonyms at **nimble.**
∼*adv.* With briskness; gaily. [*Spright,* variant of SPRITE + -LY.] **—spright·li·ness** *n.*

spring (sprĭng) *v.* **sprang** (sprăng) or **sprung** (sprŭng), **sprung, springing, springs.** *—intr.* **1.** To move upward, forward, or in a specified manner in a single quick motion; leap: *He sprang over the fence.* **2.** To appear or emerge suddenly. Often used with *up.* **3.** To move suddenly on or as if on a spring: *The door sprang shut.* **4.** To arise from a source; develop; issue. Often used with *from.* **5.** To become warped, bent, or cracked. Used of wood. **6.** To move out of place; come loose, as a machine part may. **7.** To explode. Used of a mine. *—tr.* **1.** To cause to leap, dart, or come forth suddenly. **2.** To jump over; vault. **3.** To actuate or cause to move on or as if on a spring: *spring a bolt.* **4.** To explode (a mine). **5.** To cause to warp, bend, or crack, as by force. **6.** To develop or present unexpectedly: *spring a surprise; sprang a leak.* **7.** To provide with a spring or springs. **8.** *Slang.* To cause to be released from prison.
∼*n.* **1.** An elastic device, such as a coil of wire, that regains its original shape after being compressed or extended. **2.** An actuating force or factor; a motive. **3. a.** The quality of elasticity; resilience. **b.** Energy; healthy bounce: *a spring in one's step.* **4.** The act or an instance of springing; especially, a jump or leap. **5.** A flock of teal. **6.** The return to normal shape after removal of stress; recoil. **7.** A natural fountain or flow of water from the earth's surface. **8.** A source, origin, or beginning. **9. a.** The season of the year, occurring between winter and summer, during which the weather becomes warmer and plants revive, extending from the vernal equinox to the summer solstice, and popularly considered to comprise March, April, and May in the Northern Hemisphere, and September, October, and November in the Southern Hemisphere. **b.** Any time of growth or youth. **10.** *Architecture.* The point where an arch or vault rises up from its support. Also called "springing." **11.** A warping, bending, or cracking, such as that caused by excessive force.

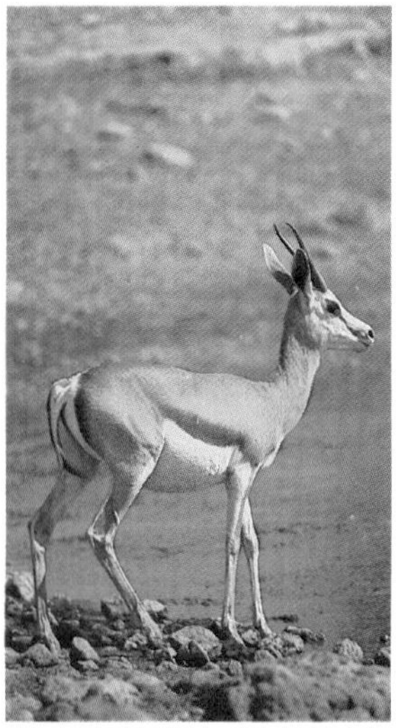

springbok *When alarmed, this southern African antelope flees in bounding leaps up to 3 meters (10 feet) high—a habit from which it gets its name. The national emblem of South Africa, the springbok once roamed the region in herds of up to a million animals; but it is now rare.*

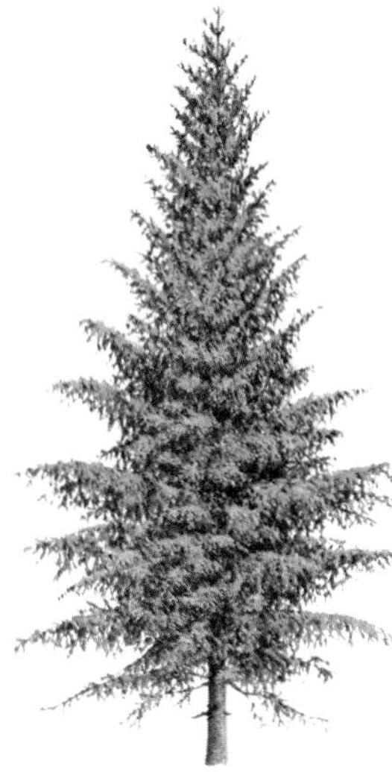

spruce *This group of fast-growing conifers is widely cultivated commercially for making paper.*

~*adj.* **1.** Of or acting like a spring. **2.** Having or supported by springs. **3.** Coming from a spring: *spring water.* **4.** Of, occurring in, or characteristic of the season of spring. **5.** Sown in the spring. Said of a crop. [Spring, sprang, sprung; Middle English *springen, sprang, sprungen,* Old English *springan, sprang* (past singular), *sprungen.*]

spring balance *n.* A device for weighing relatively small objects, consisting of a coiled spring, to the free end of which the object to be weighed is attached so that the spring extends. The amount of the extension is read off on a scale calibrated in units of weight.

spring beauty *n.* Any of several plants of the genus *Claytonia;* especially, *C. virginica,* of eastern North America, having narrow leaves and white or pinkish flowers.

spring·board (sprĭng′bôrd′, -bōrd′) *n.* **1.** A flexible board mounted on a fulcrum and having one end secured, used by gymnasts to gain momentum. **2.** A **diving board** *(see).* **3.** Anything that lends impetus to or helps to launch an activity, career, or the like.

spring·bok (sprĭng′bŏk′) *n., pl.* **-boks** or collectively **springbok.** Also **spring·buck** (-bŭk′) *pl.* **-bucks** or collectively **springbuck.** A small brown and white antelope, *Antidorcas marsupialis,* of southern Africa, able to leap high into the air. [Afrikaans : *spring,* to SPRING, from Middle Dutch *springen* + *bok,* male deer, BUCK.]

spring chicken *n.* **1.** A young chicken, especially one from two to ten months old, having tender meat. **2.** *Informal.* A young or naive person: *You're no spring chicken.*

spring-clean (sprĭng′klēn′) *v.* **-cleaned, -cleaning, -cleans.** —*tr.* To clean (a house, for example) thoroughly and comprehensively, especially at the end of the winter. —*intr.* To spring-clean a room or house. **—spring-clean·ing** *n.*

springe (sprĭnj) *n.* A device for snaring small game, made by attaching a noose to a branch under tension.

~*v.* **springed, springeing** or **springing, springes.** —*tr.* To trap with a springe; ensnare. —*intr.* To prepare a springe. [Middle English *sprenge, springe,* Old English *sprencg* (unattested).]

spring·er (sprĭng′ər) *n.* **1.** One that springs. **2.** A springer spaniel. **3.** A cow about to give birth. **4.** *Architecture.* **a.** The point where an arch is supported by a wall or column. **b.** The bottom stone of an arch resting on this point.

springer spaniel *n.* A dog of either of two breeds, the English and the Welsh springer spaniels, having drooping ears and a silky brown and white coat, and originally used for flushing game.

spring fever *n.* The feelings of languor, rejuvenation, or yearning that may affect people at the advent of spring.

Spring·field[1] (sprĭng′fēld′). Capital of Illinois, in the central part of the state on the Sangamon River. In a rich agricultural and coal region, it is a governmental, commercial, medical, and insurance center. Abraham Lincoln lived here from 1837 to 1861 and was instrumental in having Springfield named capital in 1839.

Springfield[2]. City of southwestern Massachusetts, on the Connecticut River. The city has insurance, chemical, plastic, metallurgical, paper, and printing industries. It was settled in 1636 by Puritans. Basketball was invented here in 1891 by Dr. James Naismith (1861–1939).

Springfield[3]. City of southwestern Missouri, in a resort area of the Ozark Mts. It is the industrial, trade, and shipping center of a rich area producing dairy products, livestock, poultry, grain, and fruit. The city also has varied manufactures.

Springfield rifle *n.* A magazine-fed breech-loading bolt-action .30-caliber rifle. Also called "Springfield." [First made at the former U.S. Armory at SPRINGFIELD, Massachusetts.]

spring-form pan (sprĭng′fôrm′) *n.* A round baking pan with a high rim that can be expanded and removed from the base by releasing a spring. Also called "spring form."

spring·haas (sprĭng′häs′) *n.* A nocturnal African rodent, *Pedetes capensis,* resembling a small kangaroo. [Afrikaans, "spring hare."]

spring·halt (sprĭng′hôlt′) *n.* A **stringhalt** *(see).* [Alteration of STRINGHALT.]

spring·head (sprĭng′hĕd′) *n.* A source, as of a stream.

spring·house (sprĭng′hous′) *n.* A small room or building constructed over a spring and used to keep food cool.

spring·ing (sprĭng′ĭng) *n. Architecture.* A **spring** (sense 10) *(see).*

spring·let (sprĭng′lĭt) *n.* A small spring of water; a rill.

spring-load·ed (sprĭng′lō′dĭd) *adj.* Secured or returned to position by means of a spring.

spring lock *n.* A lock in which the bolt shoots automatically by means of a spring.

spring onion *n.* A small, immature onion with a small bulb and long green leaves, usually eaten raw in salads.

spring peeper *n.* A small, brownish tree frog, *Hyla crucifer,* of eastern North America, having a shrill, high-pitched call.

spring roll *n. Chiefly British.* An **egg roll** *(see).*

spring·tail (sprĭng′tāl′) *n.* Any of various small wingless insects of the order Collembola, having abdominal appendages that act as springs to catapult them through the air.

spring tide *n.* **1.** The tide generally having the greatest rise and fall, occurring at or shortly after the new moon and full moon of each month, when the sun, moon, and earth are approximately aligned. Compare **neap tide. 2.** Any flood or rush, as of emotion.

spring·time (sprĭng′tīm′) *n.* **1.** The season of spring. Also called "springtide." **2.** The earliest or most enthusiastic period.

spring·wood (sprĭng′wo͝od′) *n.* Young, usually soft wood that lies directly beneath the bark and develops in early spring. Compare **summerwood.**

spring·y (sprĭng′ē) *adj.* **-ier, -iest.** Resilient; elastic. **—spring·i·ly** *adv.* **—spring·i·ness** *n.*

sprin·kle (sprĭng′kəl) *v.* **-kled, -kling, -kles.** —*tr.* **1.** To scatter or release (water or sand, for example) in drops or small amounts. **2.** To scatter drops or small amounts upon. **3.** To distribute or intersperse in random fashion. —*intr.* **1.** To scatter small drops or particles of something. **2.** To fall or rain in small or infrequent drops.

~*n.* **1.** The act or an instance of sprinkling. **2.** A light, sparse rainfall. **3.** A small amount; a sprinkling. [Middle English *sprenklen,* probably from Middle Dutch *sprenkelen.*]

sprin·kler (sprĭng′klər) *n.* One that sprinkles, specifically: **1.** An outlet on a sprinkler system. **2.** A device attached to a hose or watering can for sprinkling water onto grass and other plants.

sprinkler system *n.* A fire-extinguishing system consisting of a network of water pipes equipped to release water, usually automatically, at temperatures above a predetermined limit.

sprin·kling (sprĭng′klĭng) *n.* A small amount or quantity, especially when tossed or sparsely distributed.

sprint (sprĭnt) *n.* **1.** A short race run or swim at top speed. **2.** A short burst of great activity.

~*v.* **sprinted, sprinting, sprints.** —*intr.* To run or swim at top speed. —*tr.* To cover (a specified distance) by sprinting. [Of Scandinavian origin.] **—sprint·er** *n.*

sprit (sprĭt) *n.* **1.** A pole extending diagonally across a fore-and-aft sail from the lower part of the mast to the peak of the sail. **2.** A **bowsprit** *(see).* [Middle English *spret(te), spryt(t),* Old English *sprēot,* pole.]

sprite (sprīt) *n.* **1.** A small or elusive supernatural being; an elf or pixie. **2.** Someone resembling a sprite in smallness or delicacy. [Middle English *spr(e)it,* from Old French *esp(i)rit,* from Latin *spīritus,* SPIRIT.]

sprit·sail (sprĭt′səl, -sāl′) *n.* A sail extended by a sprit.

sprock·et (sprŏk′ĭt) *n.* **1.** A wheel rimmed with toothlike projections to engage the links of a chain in a drive system. Also called "sprocket wheel." **2.** Any one of these projections. **3.** A cylinder with a toothed rim that engages in the perforations in a film to pull it through a camera or projector. [16th century : origin obscure.]

sprout (sprout) *v.* **sprouted, sprouting, sprouts.** —*intr.* **1.** To begin to grow; give off shoots or buds. **2.** To grow or develop quickly. Often used with *up.* —*tr.* To cause to grow or sprout.

~*n.* **1.** A young plant growth, such as a bud or shoot. **2.** Something resembling or suggestive of a sprout. **3. sprouts. Brussels sprouts** *(see).* **4.** *Informal.* A young person. [Middle English *spruten,* Old English *sprūtan.*]

sprouting broccoli *n.* See **broccoli.**

spruce[1] (spro͞os) *n.* **1.** Any of various coniferous evergreen trees of the genus *Picea,* such as the **Norway spruce** *(see),* having needlelike foliage, drooping cones, and soft wood often used for paper pulp. **2.** Any of various similar or related trees. **3.** The wood of any of these trees. [Short for *Spruce fir,* "Prussian fir," from Middle English *Spruce,* alteration of *Pruce,* from Old French, from Medieval Latin *Prussia,* PRUSSIA.]

spruce[2] *adj.* **sprucer, sprucest.** Neat or dapper in appearance.

~*v.* **spruced, sprucing, spruces.** —*tr.* To make spruce; dress neatly. Usually used with *up.* —*intr.* To make oneself spruce. Used with *up.* [Perhaps from *Spruce,* Prussia, Prussian leather (from the fineness of the leather).] **—spruce·ly** *adv.* **—spruce·ness** *n.*

spruce beer *n.* A slightly fermented beverage made with an extract of spruce needles and twigs with sugar or molasses.

spruce pine *n.* A tree, the **black spruce** *(see).*

sprue[1] (spro͞o) *n.* A chronic, chiefly tropical disease characterized by diarrhea, emaciation, and anemia, due to deficient absorption of food in the small intestine. [Dutch *spruw,* from Middle Dutch *sprouwe,* akin to Middle Low German *sprūwe*†.]

sprue[2] *n.* **1.** A channel leading to or from a mold. **2.** Metal or plastic that solidifies in a sprue. [19th century : origin obscure.]

sprung. Past participle and alternate past tense of **spring.**

sprung rhythm *n.* A forcefully accented verse rhythm in which each foot has a stressed syllable followed by an irregular number of unstressed syllables. [Coined by Gerard Manley HOPKINS.]

spry (sprī) *adj.* **sprier** or **spryer, spriest** or **spryest.** Active, vigorous, and healthy: *a spry octogenarian.* —See Synonyms at **nimble.** [Perhaps from Scandinavian, akin to Swedish dialectal *sprygg,* active.] **—spry·ly** *adv.* **—spry·ness** *n.*

spud (spŭd) *n.* **1.** A sharp tool resembling a spade for rooting or digging out weeds. **2.** *Informal.* A potato.

~*tr.v.* **spudded, spudding, spuds. 1.** To remove (weeds, for example) with a spud. **2.** To begin drilling (an oil well). [Middle English *spudde*†, short knife.]

spue. *Archaic.* Variant of **spew.**

spume (spyo͞om) *n.* Foam or froth, especially on the sea.

~*intr.v.* **spumed, spuming, spumes.** To froth or foam. [Middle English, from Old French *(e)spume,* from Latin *spūma.*] **—spu·mous, spum·y** *adj.*

spu·mo·ne, spu·mo·ni (spo͞o-mō′nē) *n.* An Italian ice cream with layers of different colors or flavors, containing candied fruit or nuts. [Italian, from *spuma,* foam, from Latin *spūma,* SPUME.]

spun. Past tense and past participle of **spin.**

spun glass *n.* **1. Fiber glass** *(see).* **2.** Fine blown glass having delicate, often spiral threading or filigree.

spunk (spŭngk) *n.* **1.** Tinder such as touchwood. **2.** *Informal.* Spirit;

pluck. [Scottish Gaelic *spong,* tinder, sponge, from Latin *spongia,* SPONGE.]

spunk·y (spŭng′kē) *adj.* **-ier, -iest.** *Informal.* Spirited. **—spunk·i·ly** *adv.* **—spunk·i·ness** *n.*

spun silk *n.* A yarn made from short-fibered silk and silk waste, often mixed with cotton.

spun sugar *n.* Sugar spun into a confectionary fluff. Also called "cotton candy."

spun yarn *n.* A lightweight line made of several rope yarns loosely wound together, used for seizings on board ship.

spur (spûr) *n.* **1.** Either of a pair of spikes or spiked wheels attached to a rider's heels and used to urge the horse forward. **2.** An incentive or goad; stimulus. **3.** A spurlike attachment or projection, such as: **a.** A spinelike projection on the leg of some birds. **b.** A climbing iron; a crampon. **c.** A gaff attached to the leg of a gamecock. **d.** A short or stunted branch of a tree. **4.** A lateral ridge projecting from a mountain or mountain range. **5.** An oblique reinforcing prop or stay of timber or masonry. **6.** A **spur track** *(see).* **7.** *Botany.* A tubular extension of the corolla or calyx of a flower, as in a larkspur. **—on the spur of the moment.** On impulse or without preparation. **—win one's spurs.** To gain distinction, especially for the first time.
∼*v.* **spurred, spurring, spurs.** —*tr.* **1.** To urge (a horse) on by the use of spurs. **2.** To incite; prompt; stimulate. Often used with *on.* **3.** To put spurs on. —*intr.* To ride quickly, as by spurring a horse. [Middle English *spore, spure,* Old English *spora, spura.*]

spurge (spûrj) *n.* Any of various plants of the genus *Euphorbia,* characteristically having milky juice and small flowers that in some species are surrounded by showy bracts. [Middle English, from Old French *(e)spurge,* "purge" (certain species were formerly used as purgatives), from *espurgier,* to purge, from Latin *expurgāre* : *ex-,* away + *purgāre,* to purge, purify.]

spur gear *n.* A gear with teeth radially arrayed on the rim parallel to its axis. Also called "spur wheel."

spurge laurel *n.* A low-growing shrub, *Daphne laureola,* native to southern Europe but widely cultivated for ornament, having glossy evergreen leaves and small yellowish-green flowers. Also called "daphne."

spu·ri·ous (spyo͝or′ē-əs) *adj.* **1. a.** Lacking authenticity or validity, especially in essence or origin; false. **b.** Not genuine; counterfeit. **2.** Illegitimate; bastard. **3.** *Botany.* Similar in appearance but unlike in structure or function. Said of plant parts that superficially resemble other parts. [Late Latin *spurius,* false, from Latin, illegitimate, perhaps from Etruscan; akin to *spurcus,* dirty, impure.] **—spu·ri·ous·ly** *adv.* **—spu·ri·ous·ness** *n.*

spurn (spûrn) *v.* **spurned, spurning, spurns.** —*tr.* **1.** To reject or refuse disdainfully; scorn. **2.** *Archaic.* **a.** To kick at disdainfully. **b.** To tread on; trample. —*intr.* To refuse something contemptuously. —See Synonyms at **refuse.**
∼*n.* **1.** A contemptuous rejection. **2.** *Archaic.* A kick or shove. [Middle English *spurnen, spornen,* Old English *spurnan, spornan.*] **—spurn·er** *n.*

spur-of-the-mo·ment (spûr′əv-*th*ə-mō′mənt) *adj.* Made, done, or occurring without planning or forethought.

spurred (spûrd) *adj.* **1.** Wearing spurs. **2.** *Biology.* Having a spur or spurs: *spurred flowers.*

spur·ry, spur·rey (spûr′ē) *n., pl.* **-ries** or **-reys.** Any of several weedy, low-growing plants of the genera *Spergula* or *Spergularia;* especially, *Spergula arvensis,* native to Europe, having whorled leaves and small white flowers. [Dutch *spurrie,* from Middle Dutch *sporie, speurie,* probably from Medieval Latin *spergula.*]

spur·ri·er (spûr′ē-ər) *n.* A maker of spurs. [Middle English *sporior,* from *spore,* SPUR.]

spurt (spûrt) *n.* Also **spirt** (for sense 1). **1.** A sudden and forcible gush or outburst, as of water or emotion. **2.** Any sudden outbreak or short burst of energy or activity.
∼*v.* **spurted, spurting, spurts.** Also **spirt, spirted, spirting, spirts** (for sense 1). —*intr.* **1.** To flow suddenly; gush. Often used with *out.* **2.** To make a short burst of effort. —*tr.* To force out in a burst; squirt. [Earlier *spirt, sprit,* to sprout, Middle English *sprutten,* Old English *spryttan.*]

spur track *n.* A short side track that connects with the main track of a railroad system. Also called "spur."

spur wheel *n.* A **spur gear** *(see).*

sput·nik (spŭt′nĭk, spo͝ot′-) *n.* Any of the artificial Earth satellites launched by the U.S.S.R., especially *Sputnik 1,* the first artificial satellite to orbit the Earth, launched October 4, 1957. [Russian *sputnik (zemlyi),* "fellow traveler (of Earth)" : *s-,* for *so,* with + *put′,* path, way + *-nik,* agent noun suffix.]

sput·ter (spŭt′ər) *v.* **-tered, -tering, -ters.** —*intr.* **1.** To throw out small particles in short bursts, often with spitting sounds. **2.** To make sporadic spitting sounds. **3.** To speak in a hasty or confused fashion; stammer. **4.** *Physics.* To cause the atoms of a solid to be removed from its surface by bombardment with ions in a discharge tube. —*tr.* **1.** To throw out (food particles, for example) in short bursts, often with spitting sounds. **2.** To utter in a hasty or confused fashion. **3.** *Physics.* **a.** To coat (a solid surface) with metal atoms by sputtering. **b.** To coat (a solid surface) by sputtering.
∼*n.* **1.** The act of sputtering. **2.** The sound of sputtering. **3.** The particles that are emitted during sputtering. **4.** Hasty or confused utterances. [Dutch *sputteren* (imitative).] **—sput·ter·er** *n.*

spu·tum (spyo͞o′təm) *n., pl.* **-ta** (-tə). **1.** Saliva spat from the mouth. **2.** Matter, including saliva, mucus from the respiratory tract, and foreign material, coughed up and spat out. [Latin *spūtum,* from *spūtus,* past participle of *spuere,* to spit.]

Spuy·ten Duy·vil Creek (spīt′n dī′vəl). Tidal channel, now a ship canal, in New York City. It is *c.* 1.6 kilometers (1 mile) long, separates the tip of Manhattan Island from the mainland, and connects the Hudson and Harlem rivers.

spy (spī) *n., pl.* **spies. 1. a.** A clandestine agent employed by a state to obtain intelligence relating to its potential or actual enemies at home or abroad. **b.** An agent employed by a business organization to obtain secret information relating to its competitors. **2.** One who secretly watches another or others. **3.** The act of watching covertly or secretly.
∼*v.* **spied, spying, spies.** —*tr.* **1. a.** To observe (a place or situation) carefully and secretly and gain information. Used with *out: spy out the land.* **b.** To discover by careful and secret observation. Used with *out.* **2.** To catch sight of; see. —*intr.* **1. a.** To observe secretly and closely. Often used with *on, into,* or *upon.* **b.** To engage in espionage. **2.** To investigate; pry. Used with *into: spying into their activities.* [Middle English *spie,* from Old French *espie,* from *espier,* to spy, watch, from Frankish *spehōn* (unattested).]

spy·glass (spī′glăs′, -gläs′) *n.* **1.** A small telescope. **2. spyglasses.** Binoculars.

spy·hole (spī′hōl′) *n.* A peephole, especially one set in a front door to permit scrutiny of any callers.

sq. 1. sequence. **2.** square. **3.** the following.

Sq. 1. Squadron. **2.** Square. Used in street names.

Sqn. Ldr. squadron leader.

squab (skwŏb) *n.* **1.** A young, unfledged pigeon. **2.** A short, fat person. **3.** A soft cushion. **4.** A couch; sofa.
∼*adj.* **1.** Newly hatched or unfledged. **2.** Short and fat; squat. [17th century : perhaps from Scandinavian, akin to Swedish dialectal *sqvabb*†, fat flesh, soft mass.] **—squab·by** *adj.*

squab·ble (skwŏb′əl) *intr.v.* **-bled, -bling, -bles.** To engage in a minor but noisy quarrel; bicker. —See Synonyms at **argue.**
∼*n.* A trivial but noisy quarrel. [Imitative, probably from Scandinavian; akin to Swedish dialectal *sqvabbel,* to quarrel (imitative).] **—squab·bler** *n.*

squad (skwŏd) *n.* **1.** A small group of persons working or acting together. **2.** *Military.* The smallest unit of personnel, used especially as a drill formation. **3.** A group of sportsmen from whom a team is selected. [French *escouade,* variant of *escadre,* from Italian *squadra,* SQUARE.]

squad car *n.* A police patrol car connected by radiotelephone with headquarters. Also called "cruiser," "patrol car," "prowl car."

squad·ron (skwŏd′rən) *n. Abbr.* **Sq. 1. a.** A group of naval vessels assigned to a particular task. **b.** A basic subdivision of a fleet. **2.** An armored or cavalry unit consisting of two to four troops, a headquarters, and certain auxiliary units. **3.** An air force unit, subordinate to a wing and consisting of two or more flights. It is the basic tactical unit. [Italian *squadrone,* "square formation (of troops)," from *squadra,* SQUAD.]

squadron leader *n. Abbr.* **Sqn. Ldr.** An officer in the British air force and certain other air forces ranking below a wing commander and above a flight lieutenant.

squa·lene (skwā′lēn′) *n.* A natural unsaturated aliphatic hydrocarbon, $C_{30}H_{50}$, found in human sebum and other fatty deposits, that is an intermediate in the biosynthesis of cholesterol. [New Latin *Squalus,* genus of sharks (squalene is found in the liver oil of sharks), from Latin *squalus,* a sea fish + -ENE.]

squal·id (skwŏl′ĭd) *adj.* **1.** Dirty or wretched in appearance. **2.** Morally repulsive; sordid. —See Synonyms at **dirty.** [Latin *squālidus,* from *squālēre,* to be filthy, from *squālus*†, scabby, filthy.] **—squa·lid·i·ty** (skwŏ-lĭd′ə-tē), **squal·id·ness** *n.* **—squal·id·ly** *adv.*

squall (skwôl) *n.* **1. a.** A sudden, brief burst of wind, lasting longer than a gust, and often accompanied by rain. **b.** A sudden increase in wind speed by 8 meters per second (16 knots) or more to at least 11 meters per second (22 knots) and lasting for at least one minute. **2.** *Informal.* A disturbance or commotion. **3.** A loud yell.
∼*intr.v.* **squalled, squalling, squalls. 1.** To blow strongly for a brief period. **2.** To scream or cry harshly and loudly. [Probably from Scandinavian, akin to Swedish and Norwegian *skval,* splash, akin to Old Norse *skvala,* SQUEAL.] **—squall·er** *n.* **—squall·y** *adj.*

squall line *n.* A zone of squalls and other violent changes in weather, marking the replacement of a warm air current by cold air.

squal·or (skwŏl′ər) *n.* The state or quality of being squalid. [Latin, from *squālēre,* to be filthy. See **squalid.**]

squa·ma (skwā′mə) *n., pl.* **-mae** (-mē′). **1.** *Biology.* A scale or scalelike structure. **2.** A thin plate of bone. [Latin *squāma*†, scale.] **—squa·mate** (skwā′māt′) *adj.*

squa·ma·tion (skwə-mā′shən) *n.* **1.** The condition of being scaly or of forming scales. **2.** An arrangement of scales, as on a fish.

squa·mo·sal (skwə-mō′səl, -zəl) *n.* The squamous part of the temporal bone. [Latin *squāmōsus,* SQUAMOUS.] **—squa·mo·sal** *adj.*

squa·mous (skwā′məs) *adj.* Also **squa·mose** (-mōs′). **1.** Covered with, formed of, or resembling scales; scaly. **2.** Of or designating epithelium consisting of flat, scalelike cells. **3.** Of or designating the portion of the temporal bone that forms part of the side of the cranium. [Latin *squāmōsus,* from *squāma*†, scale.] **—squa·mous·ly** *adv.* **—squa·mous·ness** *n.*

squamous cell *n.* An epithelial cell that is flat and scaly.

squa·mu·lose (skwăm′yə-lōs′) *adj.* Having or consisting of minute scales; minutely scaly. Said especially of plants. [New Latin *squāmula,* diminutive of Latin *squāma*†, scale.]

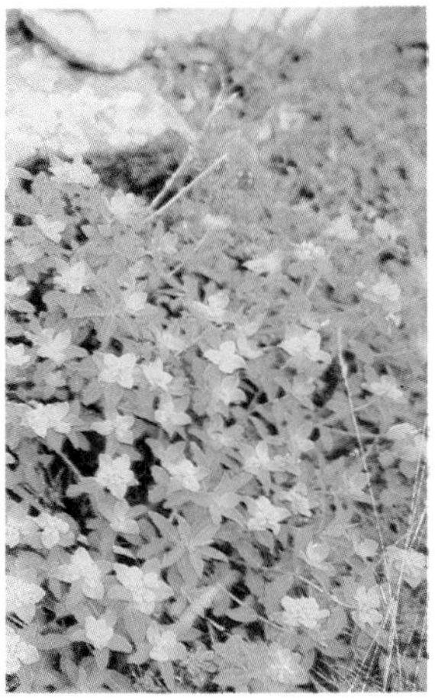

spurge *Petty spurge* (Euphorbia peplus) *has a milky white juice in its stems and leaves that can make horses and cows ill or even kill them. The oily juice from the seeds was once used medicinally as a purgative; hence the name "spurge." In Africa a member of the spurge family was used to make poison for the tips of arrows.*

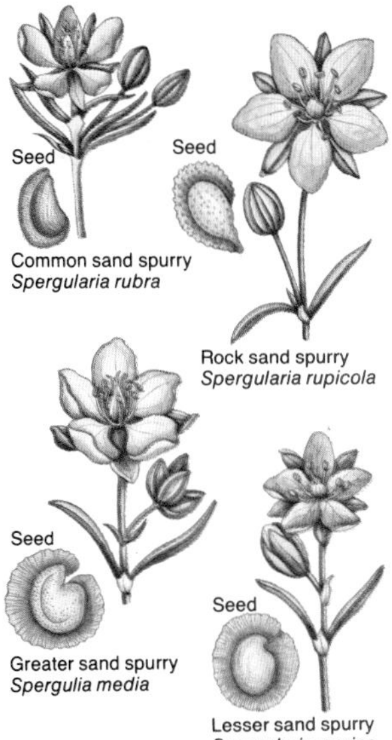
Seed
Seed
Common sand spurry
Spergularia rubra
Rock sand spurry
Spergularia rupicola
Seed
Seed
Greater sand spurry
Spergulia media
Lesser sand spurry
Spergularia marina

spurry *A herb with thin, succulent leaves. It grows well in sandy or rocky soil.*

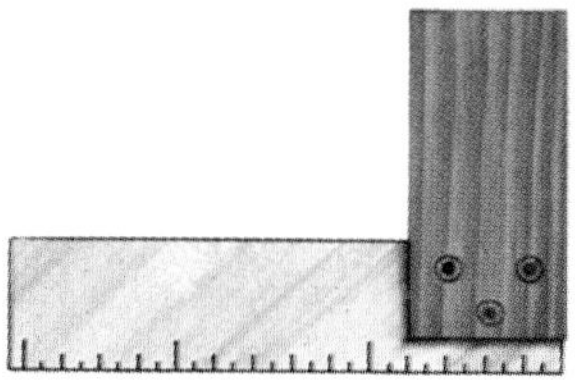

square *A straightedged, right-angled instrument used by carpenters and metalworkers to check that joints and surfaces are true.*

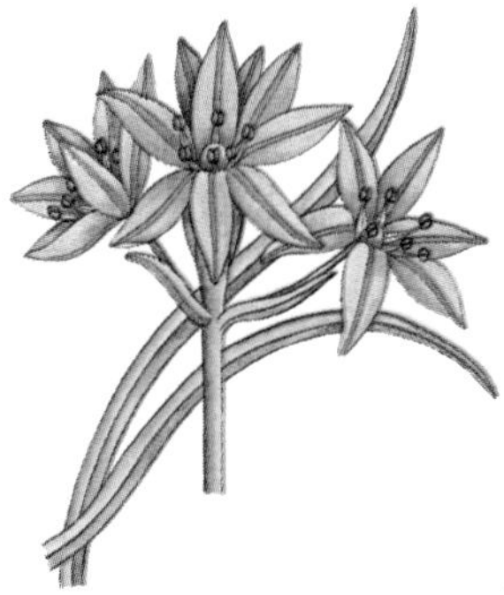

squill *A wiry little plant with long leaves that grows on the sides of cliffs. This is the spring squill,* Scilla verna.

squan·der (skwŏn′dər) *tr.v.* **-dered, -dering, -ders. 1.** To spend wastefully or extravagantly. **2.** *Obsolete.* To scatter; disperse.
∼*n.* Extravagant expenditure; prodigality. [16th century : origin obscure.] **—squan·der·er** *n.* **—squan·der·ing·ly** *adv.*

Squan·to (skwŏn′tō) (died 1622). U.S. Indian and friend of the Plymouth Colony Pilgrims. Captured as a young man by Capt. Thomas Hunt, he was sold as a slave in Spain, but soon escaped, made his way to England, and joined an expedition to the New World (1619). Back in his homeland, he befriended the Pilgrims soon after they settled Plymouth (1620). He taught them about growing corn, showed them fertile fish grounds, and probably participated in the first Thanksgiving celebration.

square (skwâr) *n. Abbr.* **sq. 1.** A rectangle having four equal sides and four right angles. **2.** Any object, shape, arrangement, design, or the like having this form, such as: **a.** A square scarf. **b.** Any of the small square spaces constituting the surface of a chessboard. **c.** A military drill area within a barracks. **d.** An open, usually four-sided public area in a town, often having a central garden or grass and trees, sometimes including the surrounding buildings. **3. a.** A T-shaped or L-shaped instrument for drawing or testing right angles. **b.** A **try square** *(see).* **4.** The product of a number or quantity multiplied by itself. **5.** *Archaic.* A standard, rule, or pattern. **6.** *Informal.* One characterized by conventional or old-fashioned attitudes, appearance, or the like. **—back to square one.** Back to the very beginning, having made no progress. **—on the square. 1.** At right angles. **2.** Honestly and openly. **—out of square.** Not at a precise right angle.
∼*adj.* **squarer, squarest.** *Abbr.* **sq. 1.** Having four equal sides and four right angles. **2.** Forming a right angle. **3. a.** Designating an area equal to a square whose edge is of a specified length: *a square foot.* **b.** Designating a square having edges of a specified length. Used after the noun: *a foot square.* **4. a.** Being at right angles to something. **b.** Set at right angles to the mast and keel. Said of the yards of a square-rigged ship. **5.** Approximately square or rectangular in cross section: *a square house.* **6.** Characterized by blocklike solidity or sturdiness. **7.** Honest; direct: *a square answer.* **8.** Just; equitable: *a square deal.* **9.** Orderly; neat. **10.** Paid-up; settled. **11.** *Sports.* Even; tied. **12.** *Informal.* Rigidly conventional or old-fashioned. **—square peg in a round hole.** A misfit.
∼*v.* **squared, squaring, squares.** *—tr.* **1.** To make square or rectangular in shape. **2.** To test for conformity to a desired plane, straight line, or right angle. **3.** To divide into squares. Often used with *off.* **4.** To bring into conformity or agreement. **5.** To set straight or at right angles: *square one's cap.* **6.** To pay or settle: *square a debt.* **7.** *Sports.* **a.** To even the score of; tie with. **b.** To level (the score, for example). **8.** To multiply (a number or quantity) by itself. **9.** *Informal.* **a.** To bribe. **b.** To arrange, usually corruptly; fix. *—intr.* **1.** To be at right angles. **2.** To agree or conform; balance. **3.** To settle a bill or debt. Often used with *up.* **—square away. 1.** To square the yards of a sailing vessel. **2.** To put away or in order. **—square off.** To assume a fighting stance. **—square up to.** To face or confront resolutely.
∼*adv.* **1.** At right angles. **2.** In a square shape. **3.** Solidly. **4.** Directly; straight. **5.** In an honest manner; straightforwardly. [Middle English, from Old French *esquare,* from Vulgar Latin *exquadra* (unattested), from *exquadrāre* (unattested), to square : Latin *ex-* (intensive) + *quadrāre,* to square, from *quadrus,* a square.] **—square·ly** *adv.* **—square·ness** *n.* **—squar·er** *n.* **—squar·ish** *adj.*

square bracket *n.* Either of two symbols, [or]. See **bracket** (sense 4.b.).

square dance *n.* **1.** A dance in which sets of four couples form squares. **2.** Any of various similar group dances of rural origin.

square-dance (skwâr′dăns′, -däns′) *intr.v.* **-danced, -dancing, -dances.** To perform a square dance. **—square-dancer** *n.*

square knot *n.* A common double knot with the loose ends parallel to the standing parts. Also called "reef knot."

square matrix *n. Mathematics.* A matrix in which there are equal numbers of rows and columns.

square meal *n.* A substantial, satisfying, and nourishing meal.

square measure *n.* A system of units used in measuring area.

square number *n.* A number that is the square of an integer: *1, 4, 9, and 16 are square numbers.*

square rig *n.* A sailing-ship rig with sails of rectangular cut set approximately at right angles to the keel line from horizontal yards. **—square-rigged** (skwâr′rĭgd′) *adj.*

square-rig·ger (skwâr′rĭg′ər) *n.* A square-rigged vessel.

square root *n.* A divisor of a quantity that when squared gives the quantity: *4 is the square root of 16.*

square sail *n.* A four-sided sail bent to a yard set athwart the mast.

square wave *n.* A rectangular-shaped waveform that alternates between two fixed values for equal periods of time.

squar·rose (skwăr′ōs′, skwär′-) *adj.* **1.** *Biology.* Having rough or spreading hairs or scalelike projections. **2.** *Botany.* Spreading or curved backward at the tip: *squarrose bracts.* [Latin *squarrōsus,* alteration (influenced by Latin *squāma,* scale) of *escharōsus* (unattested), scabby, from Greek *eskhara,* hearth, scab, SCAR.]

squash[1] (skwŏsh, skwôsh) *v.* **squashed, squashing, squashes.** *—tr.* **1. a.** To beat, squeeze, or flatten to a compressed shape or a pulp; crush. **b.** To press or squeeze tightly. Often used with *in* or *into.* **2.** To put down or suppress; quash. **3.** To silence (a person), as with crushing words. *—intr.* **1. a.** To be crushed or flattened. **b.** To exert pressure; squeeze. Used with *in* or *into.* **2.** To move with a squelching sound.
∼*n.* **1. a.** An act or sound of squashing. **b.** The state of being squashed. **2.** A crush; a crowded condition. **3.** *Chiefly British.* A citrus-based soft drink. **4.** A racket game played with a hard rubber ball in a closed wall court between two players. [Old French *esquasshe,* from Vulgar Latin *exquassāre* (unattested) : Latin *ex-* (intensive) + *quassāre,* to shatter, frequentative of *quatere,* to shake.] **—squash·er** *n.*

squash[2] *n.* **1.** Any of various plants of the genus *Cucurbita,* having a marrowlike, fleshy, edible fruit with a hard rind. **2.** The fruit of such a plant, used as a vegetable. [Short for *isquoutersquash,* from Massachuset *askōōtasquash* : *askōt-* (unidentified root) + Proto-Algonquian *aškw-,* plant + *-ash,* inanimate plural ending.]

squash·y (skwŏsh′ē, skwô′shē) *adj.* **-ier, -iest. 1.** Easily squashed. **2.** Marshy; boggy. **—squash·i·ly** *adv.* **—squash·i·ness** *n.*

squat (skwŏt) *v.* **squatted, squatting, squats.** *—intr.* **1.** To crouch close to the ground with the weight of the body resting on the heels and with the knees bent. **2.** To live in an unoccupied dwelling or settle on unoccupied land without legal claim. *—tr.* To put (oneself) in a crouching or squatting posture.
∼*adj.* **squatter, squattest. 1.** Seated in a squatting position. **2.** Short and thick; low and broad.
∼*n.* **1.** A squatting or crouching posture. **2.** The act of squatting or crouching. **3.** The place occupied by a squatter. [Middle English *squatten,* to flatten, hence to squat, from Old French *esquatir* : *es-,* from Latin *ex-* (intensive) + *quatir,* to press flat, from Vulgar Latin *coactīre* (unattested), to press together, from Latin *cogere* (past participle *coāctus*), to drive together : *com-,* together + *agere,* to drive.]

squat·ter (skwŏt′ər) *n.* **1.** One who lives in an unoccupied dwelling or settles on unoccupied land without legal claim. **2.** One who occupies a piece of public land in order to acquire title to it.

squaw (skwô) *n.* A North American Indian woman. [Massachuset *squa, eshqua,* from Proto-Algonquian *ethkwēwa* (unattested), "woman."]

squawk (skwôk) *v.* **squawked, squawking, squawks.** *—intr.* **1.** To utter a harsh scream; screech. **2.** *Informal.* To make a loud or angry protest. *—tr.* To utter with or as if with a squawk.
∼*n.* **1.** A loud screech. **2.** *Informal.* A loud or insistent protest. [Imitative.] **—squawk·er** *n.*

squaw·root (skwô′ro͞ot′, -ro͝ot′) *n.* A plant, *Conopholis americana,* of eastern North America, that has yellowish flowers and a stem covered with brownish scales and is parasitic on the roots of oaks and other trees.

squeak (skwēk) *n.* **1.** A brief, thin, shrill cry or sound, such as that made by a mouse or an unoiled metal hinge. **2.** *Informal.* An escape. Used chiefly in the phrases *a close squeak* or *a narrow squeak.*
∼*v.* **squeaked, squeaking, squeaks.** *—intr.* **1.** To utter or make a squeak. **2.** To pass or win by a slight margin. Used with *through* or *by.* **3.** *Informal.* To turn informer; squeal. *—tr.* To utter in a squeaky voice. [Middle English *squeken* (imitative); akin to Old Norse *skvakka,* to croak.] **—squeak·er** *n.*

squeak·y (skwē′kē) *adj.* **-ier, -iest. 1.** Characterized by squeaking tones: *a squeaky voice.* **2.** Tending to squeak: *squeaky shoes.* **—squeak·i·ly** *adv.* **—squeak·i·ness** *n.*

squeal (skwēl) *n.* **1.** A shrill, high-pitched cry, as of fear or surprise. **2.** A similar high-pitched sound, such as that made by tires against a road surface when a car brakes suddenly.
∼*v.* **squealed, squealing, squeals.** *—intr.* **1.** To utter or produce a squeal. **2.** *Slang.* To betray a friend or a secret; turn informer. **3.** *Informal.* To complain or protest shrilly. *—tr.* To utter or produce with a squeal. [Middle English *squelen* (imitative); akin to Old Norse *skvala,* to shriek.] **—squeal·er** *n.*

squea·mish (skwē′mĭsh) *adj.* **1. a.** Easily nauseated or sickened. **b.** Nauseated: *felt squeamish at the sight of blood.* **2.** Easily shocked or disgusted. **3.** Excessively fastidious or scrupulous. [Middle English *squaymisch,* variant of *squaymous,* from Norman French *escoymos*†.] **—squea·mish·ly** *adv.* **—squea·mish·ness** *n.*

squee·gee (skwē′jē′) *n.* **1.** A T-shaped implement having a crosspiece edged with rubber or leather, used to remove water from a surface such as a window. **2.** A similar implement or a rubber roller used in printing and photography.
∼*tr.v.* **squeegeed, -geeing, -gees.** To wipe or smooth with a squeegee. [Probably from *squeege,* to press, alteration of SQUEEZE.]

squeeze (skwēz) *v.* **squeezed, squeezing, squeezes.** *—tr.* **1. a.** To press hard upon or together; compress. **b.** To press (someone's hand or arm) gently, as in affection: *squeezed her hand.* **2.** To exert pressure on, as by way of extracting liquid: *squeeze an orange.* **3. a.** To extract by applying pressure: *squeeze juice from a lemon.* **b.** To extract or produce under pressure or with difficulty. Often used with *out: squeezed a confession out of the suspects.* **4.** To extract by dishonest means; extort. **5.** To obtain room or passage for by pushing or exerting pressure; cram; force: *squeezed himself into the crowded elevator.* **6.** To oppress with exacting or exorbitant demands. **7.** To find time or space for; manage to fit in. **8.** *Bridge.* To force (an opponent) to use a potentially winning card in a trick he cannot take. *—intr.* **1.** To give way under pressure. **2.** To exert pressure. **3.** To force one's way, as through a crowd.
∼*n.* **1.** An act or instance of squeezing. **2. a.** A handclasp. **b.** A brief embrace. **3.** A crowded situation; a crush: *a tight squeeze.* **4.** A small amount squeezed out of something: *a squeeze of lemon juice.* **5. a.** *Informal.* A squeeze play. **b.** Financial pressure caused by shortages or narrowing economic margins. **6.** *Informal.* An act of blackmailing: *put the squeeze on his old employer.* **7.** A forced discard of a potentially winning card in bridge. [Earlier *squease,*

intensive form of *quease,* to press, Middle English *queysen,* Old English *cwȳsan.*] **—squeez·er** *n.*

squeeze play *n.* **1.** *Baseball.* A play in which the batter attempts to bunt so that a runner on third base may score. **2.** *Informal.* Pressure exerted to obtain a concession or achieve a goal.

squelch (skwĕlch) *v.* **squelched, squelching, squelches.** *—intr.* To make or move with a splashing, squashing, or sucking sound. *—tr.* **1.** To crush by or as if by trampling; suppress; squash. **2.** *Informal.* To put down or silence, as with a crushing remark. *—n.* **1.** An act of squelching. **2.** A sound made by squelching. **3.** An electric circuit that cuts off a radio receiver when the signal is too weak for reception of anything but noise. [Imitative.] **—squelch·er** *n.* **—squelch·y** *adj.*

squib (skwĭb) *n.* **1. a.** A small firecracker. **b.** A broken firecracker that burns but does not explode. **2.** A brief, satirical piece of writing, such as a lampoon. *—v.* **squibbed, squibbing, squibs.** *—intr.* **1.** To write or publish a squib. **2.** To set off a squib. *—tr.* To attack or lampoon with squibs. [Probably imitative.]

squid (skwĭd) *n., pl.* **squids** or collectively **squid.** Any of various marine cephalopod mollusks of the genera *Loligo, Rossia,* and related genera, having a usually elongated body, ten arms surrounding the mouth, a vestigial internal shell, and a pair of triangular or rounded fins. Compare **octopus.** *—intr.v.* **squidded, squidding, squids.** To fish with squid as bait. [17th century : origin obscure.]

squif·fy (skwĭf'ē) *adj. Slang.* Slightly drunk or intoxicated. [19th century : origin obscure.]

squig·gle (skwĭg'əl) *n.* A small wiggly mark or scrawl. *—intr.v.* **squiggled, -gling, -gles. 1.** To form a squiggle or squiggles. **2.** To squirm and wriggle. [Imitative.] **—squig·gly** *adj.*

squill (skwĭl) *n.* **1.** Any of several bulbous plants of the genus *Scilla,* native to Eurasia, having narrow leaves and bell-shaped blue, white, or pink flowers. Also called "scilla." Compare **sea onion. 2.** The dried inner scales of the bulbs of the sea onion, used as rat poison and formerly as a cardiac stimulant and expectorant. [Middle English, from Latin *squilla, scilla,* from Greek *skilla*†.]

squil·la (skwĭl'ə) *n., pl.* **-las** or **squillae** (skwĭl'ē). Any of various burrowing marine crustaceans of the order Stomatopoda, and especially of the genus *Squilla,* having a pair of jointed grasping appendages. Also called "mantis shrimp." [New Latin *Squilla,* type genus, from Latin *squilla*†, shrimp, prawn.]

squinch (skwĭnch) *n.* A quarter-spherical segment of masonry vaulting or corbeling thrown across the upper inside corners of a square tower as the transition to a circular or octagonal superstructure. [Variant of obsolete *scunch,* short for SCUNCHEON.]

squint (skwĭnt) *v.* **squinted, squinting, squints.** *—intr.* **1.** To look with the eyes partly open, as when concentrating. **2.** To look or glance sideways or obliquely. **3.** To have an indirect or implicit tendency. **4.** To suffer from **strabismus** *(see). —tr.* **1.** To cause (the eyes) to squint. **2.** To close (the eyes) partly. *—n.* **1.** An instance of squinting. **2.** An inclination; tendency. **3.** Strabismus *(see).* **4.** *British Informal.* A glance, view, or look: *Take a squint at it.* **5.** A hagioscope *(see). —adj.* **1.** Not straight; oblique; askew. **2.** Affected with strabismus. [Short for ASQUINT.] **—squint·er** *n.*

squint-eyed (skwĭnt'īd') *adj.* **1.** Having strabismus. **2.** With squinting eyes. **3.** Looking askance.

squire (skwīr) *n.* **1.** An English country gentleman, especially one who is the chief landowner in a particular district. **2.** Formerly, a young nobleman attendant upon and ranked next below a knight in the feudal hierarchy. **3.** A judge or other local dignitary. **4.** A man who attends or escorts a woman. **5.** *British.* Used as an informal or familiar term of address for a man. *—tr.v.* **squired, squiring, squires.** To attend as a squire or escort. [Middle English *squier, esquier,* from Old French *esquier, escuier,* "shield-bearer," from Late Latin *scūtārius,* from Latin *scūtum,* a shield.]

squire·ar·chy, squir·ar·chy (skwīr'är'kē) *n., pl.* **-chies.** Squires collectively; especially, the section of society made up of landed proprietors having considerable political power. **—squire·arch** *n.* **—squire·arch·al, squire·arch·i·cal** *adj.*

squirm (skwûrm) *intr.v.* **squirmed, squirming, squirms. 1.** To twist about in a wriggling motion; writhe. **2.** To feel or show signs of humiliation or embarrassment. *—n.* An act of squirming or a squirming movement; a wriggle. [Perhaps imitative (associated with WORM).] **—squirm·er** *n.* **—squirm·y** *adj.*

squir·rel (skwûr'əl, skwŭr'əl) *n.* **1.** Any of various arboreal rodents of the genus *Sciurus* and related genera, usually with gray or reddish-brown fur and a long, flexible, bushy tail. See **gray squirrel, red squirrel. 2.** Any of various related animals of the family Sciuridae, such as the **ground squirrel** or the **flying squirrel** *(both of which see).* **3.** The fur of a squirrel. [Middle English *squyrel,* from Norman French *esquirel,* from Vulgar Latin *scūriolus* (unattested), diminutive of *scūrius* (unattested), variant of Latin *sciūrus,* squirrel, from Greek *skiouros,* "shadow-tail" : *skia,* shadow + *oura,* tail.]

squirrel cage *n.* **1.** A cage consisting of a number of bars fitted to the circumference of circular end plates. The cage can be mounted to enable it to rotate as a small animal inside the cage runs in a direction perpendicular to its axis. **2.** The rotor of an induction motor *(a squirrel-cage motor)* having copper bars arranged in the

shape of a squirrel cage. **3.** An electric fan with long narrow blades arranged like the bars in a squirrel cage.

squirrel corn *n.* A low-growing North American plant, *Dicentra canadensis,* having finely divided leaves, cream-colored flowers, and tubers resembling grains of corn.

squir·rel·fish (skwûr'əl-fish', skwŭr'-) *n., pl.* **-fishes** or collectively **squirrelfish.** Any of various fishes of the genus *Holocentrus* and related genera, of warm marine waters, having large eyes and a usually reddish body.

squir·rel·ly (skwûr'ə-lē, skwŭr'-) *adj. Slang.* Eccentric; crazy.

squirrel monkey *n.* Either of two tropical American monkeys, *Saimiri sciureus* or *S. örstedii,* having short, thick fur and a long, nonprehensile tail.

squir·rel-tail grass (skwûr'əl-tāl', skwŭr'-) *n.* A European grass, *Hordeum marinum,* that grows in salt marshes and has bushy spikelets.

squirrel *There are about 250 species of squirrels, found almost worldwide. Most feed by day, living on a diet of nuts and seeds. This is the California ground squirrel, Citellus beecheyi.*

squirt (skwûrt) *v.* **squirted, squirting, squirts.** *—intr.* **1.** To be ejected in a thin swift stream. Used of a liquid. **2.** To eject liquid in a thin swift stream. *—tr.* **1.** To eject (liquid) in a thin swift stream. **2.** To soak or wet with liquid so ejected. *—n.* **1.** The act of squirting. **2.** A device, such as a syringe, used to squirt. **3.** A squirted stream of liquid. **4.** *Informal.* **a.** An insignificant but impudent person. **b.** A youngster; kid. [Middle English *squirten, swirten,* of Low German origin; akin to Low German *swirtjen* (imitative).] **—squirt·er** *n.*

squirt gun *n.* A toy gun designed to squirt a stream of water.

squirting cucumber *n.* A hairy vine, *Ecballium elaterium,* of the Mediterranean region, having fruit that when ripe discharges its seeds and juice explosively.

squish (skwĭsh) *v.* **squished, squishing, squishes.** *Informal. —tr.* To squash or compress noisily. *—intr.* To emit or move with a sound like that of soft mud being compressed. *—n. Informal.* A squashy sound, as of mud being compressed. [Alteration of SQUASH.] **—squish·y** *adj.*

sr steradian.

Sr The symbol for the element strontium.

sr. senior.

Sr. 1. senior (after a surname). **2.** señor. **3.** sister (religious).

Sra. señora.

Sri Lan·ka (srē läng'kə, shrē). Formerly **Cey·lon** (sĭ-lŏn'). Island republic in the Indian Ocean, off southeastern India. Its central highlands are surrounded by coastal lowlands and swamps. With few natural resources apart from its fertile land, Sri Lanka is heavily dependent on the export of tropical products, especially tea, rubber, and coconuts. Rice is the chief import. Tourism is expanding rapidly. Some 72 percent of the inhabitants are Buddhist Sinhalese, and 21 percent are Hindu Tamils of southern Indian stock; conflict between them has recurred in recent years. The island's spices attracted the Arabs (12th and 13th centuries) and the Portuguese, Dutch (1658), and British, who conquered the island (1796–1815) and made it a colony (1802). Ceylon gained independence (1948) and became the Republic of Sri Lanka (1972). A new constitution was adopted in 1978. Area, 65,610 square kilometers (25,325 square miles). Population, 14,900,000. Capital, Colombo. **—Sri Lan·kan** *adj & n.*

Sri·na·gar (srē-nŭg'ər). One of the capitals of Jammu and Kashmir, northwestern India. The city lies on the river Jhelum and is noted for its mosques, gardens, palaces, fort, and its many canals.

sRNA *n.* **Transfer RNA** *(see).*

S.R.O. standing room only.

Srta. señorita.

ss scilicet.

SS (ĕs-ĕs', ĕs'-) *n.* An elite military section of the Nazi party whose functions included the policing of the rest of the German army and

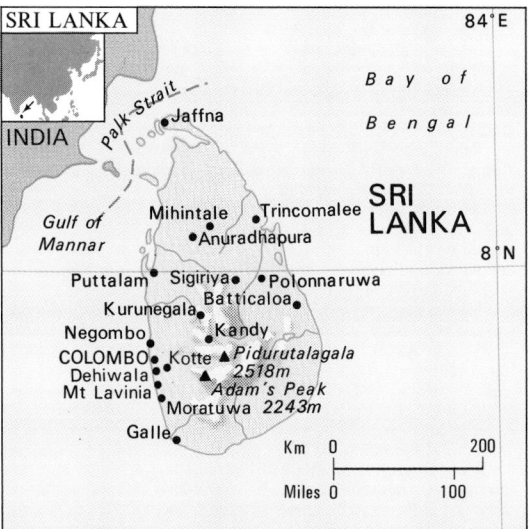

SRI LANKA map showing Palk Strait, Jaffna, Bay of Bengal, INDIA, Gulf of Mannar, Mihintale, Anuradhapura, Trincomalee, SRI LANKA, Puttalam, Sigiriya, Polonnaruwa, Kurunegala, Batticaloa, Negombo, Kandy, COLOMBO, Kotte, Pidurutalagala 2518m, Dehiwala, Mt Lavinia, Adam's Peak 2243m, Moratuwa, Galle. 84°E, 8°N. Km 0 200, Miles 0 100.

squirrel monkey *Eating mainly fruit and insects, the small squirrel monkey is found in the rain forests of Central and South America in groups of up to 500 animals.*

stack *In geological terms, a stack is a pillar of rock shaped by the eroding power of waves. This red sandstone stack is at Ladram Bay, Devon, England.*

stadium *The ancient Greek stadium at Delphi, used for athletic competitions and chariot races. The stadium was built in the second century* A.D.

the protecting of Hitler's person. [German, abbreviation of SCHUTZSTAFFEL.]
SS **1.** steamship. **2.** saints. **3.** most holy. [Latin, *sanctissimus.*]
S.S. **1.** steamship. **2.** social security. **3.** Sunday school.
SSA Social Security Administration.
SSE south-southeast.
SSM surface-to-surface missile.
ssp. subspecies.
S.S.R. Soviet Socialist Republic.
SSS Selective Service System.
SST supersonic transport.
SSW south-southwest.
st. **1.** stanza. **2.** state. **3.** statute. **4.** stet. **5.** stitch. **6.** stone. **7.** street. **8.** strophe.
-st. Variant of **-est** (verb inflection).
St. **1.** saint. **2.** statute. **3.** strait. **4.** street.
s.t. short ton.
sta. **1.** station. **2.** stationary.
stab (stăb) *v.* **stabbed, stabbing, stabs.** *—tr.* **1.** To pierce or wound with or as if with a pointed weapon. **2.** To plunge (a weapon or instrument) into something. *—intr.* **1.** To lunge with or as if with a pointed weapon. Often used with *at.* **2.** To inflict a wound in this way.
∼n. **1.** A thrust made with a pointed instrument or weapon. **2. a.** A wound inflicted by stabbing. **b.** A sharp, localized pain. **3.** *Informal.* An attempt; try; effort: *had a stab at skating.* **—stab in the back.** A treacherous attack; a betrayal. [Middle Scots, to wound with a pointed weapon.] **—stab·ber** *n.*
Sta·bat Ma·ter (stä′bät mä′tər, stä′bät mā′tər) *n.* **1.** A medieval Latin hymn on the sorrows of the Virgin Mary at the Crucifixion. **2.** A musical setting for this hymn. [Latin, "the mother was standing" (opening words of the hymn).]
sta·bile (stā′bĭl, stā′bīl′) *adj.* Immobile; stable; unchangeable.
∼n. (stā′bēl′). An abstract sculpture, usually of sheet metal, with no moving parts. [Latin *stabilis,* STABLE.]
sta·bil·i·ty (stə-bĭl′ə-tē) *n., pl.* **-ties.** **1.** The condition or quality of being stable, as: **a.** Resistance to sudden change, dislodgment, or overthrow. **b.** Constancy of character, emotional state, or purpose; steadfastness. **c.** Reliability; dependability. **2.** The ability of an object, such as a ship or an aircraft, to maintain equilibrium or resume its original position after displacement, as by the sea or strong winds. **3.** A vow committing a Benedictine monk to one monastery for life.
sta·bi·lize (stā′bə-līz′) *v.* **-lized, -lizing, -lizes.** *—tr.* **1.** To make stable. **2.** To maintain the stability of. *—intr.* To become stable. **—sta·bi·li·za·tion** *n.*
sta·bi·liz·er (stā′bə-lī′zər) *n.* **1.** One that stabilizes. **2.** *Nautical.* A device in a ship or boat, such as a gyroscopically controlled fin, used to prevent excessive rolling. **3.** *Aeronautics.* Any airfoil used to stabilize an aircraft in flight. **4.** *Chemistry.* A substance that renders or maintains a solution, mixture, suspension, or state resistant to chemical change.
sta·ble[1] (stā′bəl) *adj.* **-bler, -blest.** **1. a.** Resistant to sudden change of position or condition; not liable to change or fluctuation: *a stable personality; a stable economy.* **b.** Maintaining equilibrium; self-restoring. **2.** *Physics.* Having no known mode of decay; indefinitely long-lived. Said of certain elementary particles. **3.** Lasting or likely to last for a long time. **4.** *Chemistry.* Not easily decomposed or otherwise modified chemically. **5.** Consistently dependable or reliable. [Middle English, from Old French *estable,* from Latin *stabilis,* standing firm.] **—sta·ble·ness** *n.* **—sta·bly** *adv.*
stable[2] *n.* **1. a.** A building for the shelter and feeding of domestic animals, especially horses and cattle. **b.** The animals lodged in such a building collectively. **2. a.** All of the racehorses belonging to a single owner or racing establishment. **b.** The personnel employed to look after and train such a collection of racehorses. **3.** A group under common ownership, authority, training, management, or the like: *boxers from the same stable.*
∼v. **stabled, stabling, stables.** *—tr.* To put or keep (an animal) in a stable. *—intr.* To live or be kept in a stable. [Middle English, from Old French *estable,* from Latin *stabulum,* "standing place," enclosure, stable.]
sta·ble·boy (stā′bəl-boi′) *n.* A man or boy who is employed in a stable to look after horses.
stable fly *n.* A fly, *Stomoxys calcitrans,* that sucks the blood of humans and domestic animals.
sta·ble·mate (stā′bəl-māt′) *n.* **1.** A horse kept in the same stable as another. **2.** A member of a stable.
sta·bling (stā′blĭng) *n.* **1.** Stables collectively. **2.** Accommodation in a stable for animals.
stablish. *Archaic.* Variant of **establish.**
stac·ca·to (stə-kä′tō) *adj.* **1.** *Music. Abbr.* **stacc.** Performed with a crisp, sharp attack to simulate rests between successive notes. Often used as a direction. **2.** Composed of abrupt, distinct, emphatic parts or sounds: *staccato machine-gun fire.*
∼n., pl. **staccatos** or **-ti** (-tē). **1.** *Music.* A staccato passage or movement. **2.** An abrupt, staccato manner or sound. [Italian, past participle of *(di)staccare,* to detach, from Old French *destach(i)er.* See **detach.**] **—stac·ca·to** *adv.*
stack (stăk) *n.* **1.** A large, usually conical pile of straw or fodder arranged for outdoor storage. **2.** Any orderly pile, especially one arranged in layers. **3.** A group of three or more unslung rifles supporting each other with their butts on the ground and forming a cone. **4. a.** A chimney or flue. **b.** A group of chimneys. **5.** A vertical exhaust pipe, as on a ship or locomotive. **6.** Several rows of bookshelves forming one structure; a bookcase. **7.** *Usually* **stacks.** The area of a library, usually inaccessible to the public, in which books are stored on shelves. **8.** An English measure of coal or cut wood equal to 3.06 cubic meters (108 cubic feet). **9.** An arrangement of aircraft circling an airport at prescribed levels, awaiting instructions to land. **10.** *Geology.* A free-standing column of rock in the sea that has been separated from the coast by erosion. **11.** *Computer Science.* A temporary storage area in a computer memory. **12.** *Often* **stacks.** *Informal.* A large amount or quantity: *stacks of work to get through.*
∼v. **stacked, stacking, stacks.** *—tr.* **1.** To arrange in a stack; pile. **2.** To load with stacks of some material. **3.** To cheat by prearranging the order of (playing cards, for example); rig. **4.** To direct (two or more aircraft) to circle at different heights above an airport while waiting to land. *—intr.* To circle an airport in a stack. Used of aircraft. **—stack up.** **1.** To add up or total. **2.** To measure up or equal. [Middle English *stak, sta(ke),* from Old Norse *stakkr,* haystack, from Germanic.] **—stack·er** *n.*
stac·te (stăk′tē) *n.* A spice used by the ancient Jews in making incense. Exodus 30:34. [Latin *stactē,* from Greek *staktē,* from the feminine of *staktos,* oozing, distilling, from *stazein,* to ooze.]
stad·dle (stăd′l) *n.* A foundation or supporting framework; especially, a stone platform upon which hay or straw is stacked to protect it from vermin. [Middle English *stathel,* Old English *stathol.*]
stad·hold·er (stăd′hōl′dər) *n.* Also **stadt·hold·er** (stăt′-). **1.** Formerly, a governor or viceroy in a province of the Netherlands. **2.** Formerly, the chief magistrate of the United Provinces of the Netherlands. [Partial translation of Dutch *stadhouder,* translation of Latin *locum tenens,* "(one) holding the place (of another)," lieutenant : *stad,* place, from Middle Dutch *stad, stat* + *houder,* holder.] **—stad·hold·er·ate** *n.*
stad·i·a system (stā′dē-ə) *n.* A method of surveying in which distances are determined at one pointing only of the telescopic instrument, this having two parallel lines, *stadia hairs,* used to intercept intervals on a calibrated rod with bold graduation marks, a *stadia rod.* Also called "stadia tacheometry." [Italian, probably from Latin, plural of STADIUM (measure of length) + SYSTEM.]
sta·di·um (stā′dē-əm) *n., pl.* **-dia** (-dē-ə) or **-diums** (for sense 3). **1.** In ancient Greece, a course on which races were held, usually semicircular and having tiers of seats for spectators. **2.** An ancient Greek measure of distance, based on the length of such a course and probably equal to about 185 meters (607 feet). **3.** A large, often unroofed structure in which sporting events are held. **4.** A stage in the progress of something, such as a disease. [Middle English, measure of distance, from Latin, from Greek *stadion,* alteration of *spadion,* racetrack (particularly the racetrack of this length at Olympia), from *span,* to draw, pull. See **spasm.**]
Staël (stäl), **Madame de,** born Anne Louise Germaine Necker (1766–1817). French novelist, critic, and literary patron. Although her novelistic efforts have largely been forgotten, it was the ideas contained in her other writings, particularly *Letters on the Works and the Character of J.J. Rousseau* (translated 1789), that made her famous and helped form the bridge between the waning neoclassical philosophy and the emerging romanticism.
staff[1] (stăf, stäf) *n., pl.* **staffs** (except sense 4) or **staves** (stāvz) (except sense 3). **1. a.** A stick or cane carried as an aid or support in walking or climbing. **b.** A thick stick used as a weapon; a cudgel. **c.** A pole upon which a flag is displayed. **d.** A rod, baton, or the like carried as a symbol of authority. **2.** A rule or similar graduated stick used for testing or measuring, as in surveying. **3. a.** A group of assistants responsible to a manager or other person of authority. **b.** A group of military officers who serve a commanding officer but do not participate in combat and have no authority to command. **c.** The personnel who are employed to perform a specified job or task: *the nursing staff of a hospital.* **d.** The employees of a company, institution, or the like. **4.** *Music.* The set of horizontal lines and their intermediate spaces upon which notes are written or printed. In this sense, also called "stave." **5.** Figuratively, anything that is a staple or support: *My memories are the staff of my old age.*
∼tr.v. **staffed, staffing, staffs.** To provide with a staff of employees. [Middle English *staf,* Old English *stæf,* stick, rod.]
staff[2] *n.* A building material that resembles stucco, composed of plaster of Paris and fiber and used especially as a wall covering over the skeleton of temporary buildings. [Probably from German *staffieren,* to dress, trim, adorn, from Middle Low German *stafferen, stofferen,* from Old French *estoffer,* to STUFF.]
staff officer *n.* A commissioned military officer who holds a position on the staff of a commander.
staff of life *n.* A staple or necessary food, especially bread.
Staf·ford·shire (stăf′ərd-shîr′, -shər). County in central England. The county has important industrial areas, with the famous Potteries district in the north. Its county town is Stafford.
Staffordshire bull terrier *n.* A dog of a breed developed in England, having a short, variously colored coat, a stocky body, and widely set forelegs. Also called "Staffordshire terrier."
staff sergeant *n.* **1.** A noncommissioned army officer of the rank above a sergeant and below a sergeant first class. **2.** A noncommissioned air force officer of the rank above an airman first class and below a technical sergeant. **3.** A noncommissioned marine corps officer of the rank above a sergeant and below a gunnery sergeant.

staff tree *n.* Any of various dicotyledonous, shrubby plants of the genus *Celastrus,* which includes the bittersweet.

stag (stăg) *n.* **1.** The adult male of various deer, especially the red deer. **2.** An animal, especially a pig, castrated after reaching sexual maturity. **3.** A man who attends a social affair without escorting a woman. **4.** A social affair for men only.
~*adj.* **1.** For or attended by men only: *a stag party.* **2.** *Informal.* Pornographic: *stag films.* **3.** Unaccompanied by someone of the opposite sex: *stag women.* **—go stag.** To attend a dance or party without a companion of the opposite sex. [Middle English *stag(ge),* Old English *stagga.*]

stag beetle *n.* Any of numerous large beetles of the family Lucanidae, having long, powerful, antlerlike mandibles.

stage (stāj) *n.* **1.** Any raised and level floor or platform. **2. a.** The raised platform upon which theatrical performances are presented. **b.** Any area in which actors perform. **c.** The acting profession or the world of theater. Preceded by *the.* **3.** The scene or setting of an event or series of events. **4.** A platform on a microscope on which slides to be viewed are mounted. **5.** A workman's scaffold. **6.** A resting place on a journey, especially one providing overnight accommodations. **7.** The distance between stopping places on a journey; a leg of a journey: *proceeded by easy stages.* **8.** A stagecoach. **9.** A level or story of a building. **10.** The height of the surface of a river or other fluctuating body of water in relation to some datum: *at flood stage.* **11. a.** A level, degree, or period of time in the course of a process; a step in development: *a larval stage.* **b.** A moment or point in the course of an action or series of events: *At this early stage it is hard to see who will win.* **12.** *Aerospace.* One of two or more successive propulsion units of a rocket vehicle that fires after the preceding one has been jettisoned. See **multistage rocket. 13.** *Geology.* A subdivision of a series representing rock formed during an age. **14.** *Electronics.* An element or group of elements in a complex arrangement of parts; especially, a single tube or transistor and its accessory components in an amplifier. **—set the stage for.** To prepare or pave the way for.
~*v.* **staged, staging, stages.** *—tr.* **1. a.** To exhibit, present, or perform on or as if on a stage: *stage a boxing match.* **b.** To produce or direct (a theatrical performance). **2.** To arrange and carry out: *stage an invasion.* *—intr.* To be adaptable to or suitable for theatrical presentation. [Middle English, from Old French *estage,* from Vulgar Latin *staticum* (unattested), "standing place," position, from Latin *stāre,* to stand.]

stage business *n.* In the theater, **business** (sense 9) *(see).*

stage·coach (stāj′kōch′) *n.* A four-wheeled horse-drawn vehicle formerly used to transport mail, parcels, and passengers.

stage·craft (stāj′krăft′, -kräft′) *n.* The practice of or skill in theatrical techniques such as directing, writing, or producing.

stage direction *n.* An instruction in the text of a play that prescribes how a certain part of the play should be acted or presented.

stage door *n.* A door at the back or side of a theater admitting the actors, technicians, and other staff.

stage effect *n.* A special effect used on stage to simulate, by means of taped sounds and lighting, conditions such as thunder or wind.

stage fright *n.* Acute fear or nervousness felt by a person at the prospect of or while performing before an audience.

stage·hand (stāj′hănd′) *n.* A person employed in a theater to shift scenery, adjust lighting, or the like.

stage left *n.* The area of the stage to the left of a centrally placed actor facing the audience.

stage-man·age (stāj′măn′ĭj) *tr.v.* **-aged, -aging, -ages. 1.** To serve as overall supervisor of the stage and actors for (a theatrical production). **2.** To manipulate or contrive from behind the scenes. **—stage manager** *n.* **—stage management** *n.*

stag·er (stā′jər) *n.* One who possesses the wisdom of long experience: *an old stager.*

stage right *n.* The area of the stage to the right of a centrally placed actor facing the audience.

stage-struck (stāj′strŭk′) *adj.* Enthralled with the stage or with hopes of becoming an actor.

stage whisper *n.* **1.** The conventional whisper of an actor, intended to be heard by the audience. **2.** Any whisper intended to be overheard.

stagey. Variant of **stagy.**

stag·fla·tion (stăg-flā′shən) *n.* *Economics.* A condition in which a high rate of price and wage inflation is coupled with stagnant consumer demand and high unemployment. [*Stag*nation + in*flation.*] **—stag·fla·tion·ar·y** (stăg-flā′shə-nĕr′ē) *adj.*

stag·ger (stăg′ər) *v.* **-gered, -gering, -gers.** *—intr.* **1.** To move or stand unsteadily, as if under a great weight; totter. **2.** To lose strength or confidence; waver. *—tr.* **1.** To cause to totter, sway, or reel. **2. a.** To cause to lose confidence, have doubts, or hesitate. **b.** To overwhelm with emotion or surprise. **3.** To place regularly in oblique lines on or as if on alternating sides of a middle line; set in a zigzag row or rows: *theater seats staggered for clear viewing.* **4.** To arrange in alternating or overlapping time periods: *Examinations were staggered to prevent congestion of the hall.*
~*n.* **1.** The act of staggering; a tottering, swaying, or reeling motion. **2.** A staggered pattern, arrangement, or order. [Alteration of Middle English *stakeren,* from Old Norse *stakra,* frequentative of *staka,* to push, cause to stumble.] **—stag·ger·er** *n.*

stag·ger·bush (stăg′ər-bo͝osh′) *n.* A shrub, *Lyonia mariana,* of the eastern United States, having poisonous foliage.

stag·ger·ing (stăg′ər-ĭng) *adj.* Astonishing; amazing: *got through a staggering amount of work.* **—stag·ger·ing·ly** *adv.*

stag·gers (stăg′ərz) *n.* *Used with a singular verb.* **1.** Any of various diseases marked by vertigo, confusion, and weakness. **2.** Any of various diseases of the nervous system in animals; especially, a cerebrospinal disease in horses in which the animal loses coordination, staggers, and often falls. In this sense, also called "blind staggers."

stag·horn fern (stăg′hôrn′) *n.* Any of several tropical epiphytic ferns of the genus *Platycerium,* having large divided fronds that resemble antlers.

stag·hound (stăg′hound′) *n.* A large hound used to hunt deer.

stag·ing (stā′jĭng) *n.* **1.** A temporary platform; scaffold. **2. a.** The business of running stagecoaches as an enterprise. **b.** Travel by stagecoach. **3. a.** The process of producing and directing a dramatic work. **b.** A particular production of a dramatic work. **4.** The act of jettisoning a stage of a multistage rocket.

staging area *n.* A place where troops and equipment are assembled before moving out on a mission or other military operation.

stag·nant (stăg′nənt) *adj.* **1.** Not moving or flowing; without a current; motionless. **2.** Foul from standing still; polluted; stale. **3. a.** Lacking liveliness or briskness; inactive; sluggish. **b.** Lacking growth; not developing. [Latin *stagnāns* (stem *stagnant-*), present participle of *stagnāre,* to be stagnant, from *stagnum,* pond, swamp.] **—stag·nan·cy** *n.* **—stag·nant·ly** *adv.*

stag·nate (stăg′nāt′) *intr.v.* **-nated, -nating, -nates.** To be or become stagnant. [Latin *stagnāre.* See **stagnant.**] **—stag·na·tion** *n.*

stag party *n.* A party for men only, held especially for a prospective bridegroom a short time before his wedding. Compare **hen party.**

stag·y, stage·y (stā′jē) *adj.* **-ier, -iest.** Having a theatrical character or quality; especially, artificial and affected. **—stag·i·ly** *adv.* **—stag·i·ness** *n.*

staid (stād) *adj.* **1.** Steady, reserved, and often priggish in style, manner, or behavior; sober. **2.** Fixed; permanent. —See Synonyms at **serious.** [From *staid,* obsolete past participle of STAY.] **—staid·ly** *adv.* **—staid·ness** *n.*

stain (stān) *v.* **stained, staining, stains.** *—tr.* **1.** To discolor, soil, or spot. **2.** To bring into disrepute; taint; tarnish. **3.** To color (glass, for example) with a coat of penetrating liquid dye or tint. **4.** To color (specimens for the microscope) with a dye in order to heighten contrast between different structures, as of tissue. *—intr.* To produce or receive discolorations.
~*n.* **1.** A stained spot or smudge, as from foreign matter like blood or gravy. **2.** A blemish upon one's moral character, personality, or reputation. **3.** A liquid substance applied especially to wood that penetrates the surface and imparts a rich color. **4.** A colored solution used for staining microscopic specimens. [Middle English *steynen,* short for *disteynen,* to deprive of color, stain, from Old French *desteindre,* from Vulgar Latin *distingere* (unattested) : Latin *dis-* (reversal) + *tingere,* to dye.] **—stain·a·bil·i·ty** *n.* **—stain·a·ble** *adj.* **—stain·er** *n.*

stained glass *n.* Glass colored by mixing pigments inherently in the glass, by fusing colored metallic oxides onto the glass, or by painting and baking transparent colors on the glass surface. **—stained-glass** (stānd′glăs′, -gläs′) *adj.* See feature, next page.

stain·less (stān′lĭs) *adj.* **1.** Without stain or blemish. **2.** Resistant to stain or corrosion. **—stain·less·ly** *adv.*

stainless steel *n.* Any of various steels alloyed with sufficient chromium to resist corrosion or rusting associated with exposure of ordinary steel to water and moist air. **—stain·less-steel** (stān′lĭs-stēl′) *adj.*

stair (stâr) *n.* **1.** *Usually* **stairs.** A series or flight of steps; a staircase. **2.** One of a flight of steps. [Middle English *steir(e), stair(e),* Old English *stǣger.*]

stair·case (stâr′kās′) *n.* A flight or series of flights of steps and a supporting structure connecting separate levels.

stair·way (stâr′wā′) *n.* A flight of stairs; a staircase.

stair·well (stâr′wĕl′) *n.* A vertical shaft around which a staircase has been built.

stake[1] (stāk) *n.* **1.** A piece of wood or metal sharpened at one end for driving into the ground, or used as a marker, a fence pole, or a tent peg. **2. a.** A vertical post to which an offender was formerly bound for execution by burning. **b.** Execution by burning at the stake. Preceded by *the.* **3.** A vertical post secured at the edge of a platform, as on a truck to stop the load from sliding off. **—pull up stakes.** To conclude one's affairs and move on.
~*tr.v.* **staked, staking, stakes. 1.** To indicate the location or limits of with or as if with stakes. Often used with *out*: *stake out a claim.* **2. a.** To fasten or secure with a stake or stakes. **b.** To support with a stake or stakes. **3.** To tether or tie to a stake. [Middle English *stake,* Old English *staca.*]

stake[2] *n.* **1.** *Often* **stakes. a.** Money or property risked in a wager or gambling game. **b.** The reward or prize, such as money, awarded to the winner of a contest or race, especially a horse race. **c.** A race offering a reward or prize to the winner; especially, a horse race in which money is contributed by the horse owners equally to make up the prize. **2.** A share or interest in any enterprise, especially a financial share. **3.** *Informal.* A **grubstake** *(see).* **—at stake.** In question; at risk; involved.
~*tr.v.* **staked, staking, stakes. 1.** To gamble or risk; hazard. **2.** To provide working capital for; finance. [Perhaps originally "something placed on a post as wager in a game," from STAKE (post).]

stake out *tr.v.* **1.** To assign (a police officer, for example) to an area in order to conduct surveillance. **2.** To conduct a stakeout of.

PRONUNCIATION KEY

ă, pat; ā, pay; âr, care;
ä, father, are; b, bib;
ch, church; d, deed; ĕ, pet;
ē, be; f, fife; g, gag; h, hat;
hw, which; ĭ, pit; ī, pie;
îr, pier; j, judge; k, kick;
l, lid, needle; m, mum;
n, no, sudden; ng, thing;
ŏ, pot; ō, toe; ô, paw, for;
oi, noise; ou, out; o͝o, book;
o͞o, boot; p, pop; r, roar;
s, sauce; sh, ship, dish;
t, tight; th, thin, path;
th, this, bathe; ŭ, cut; ûr, fur;
v, valve; w, with; y, yes;
z, zebra, size; zh, vision;
ə, about, item, edible,
gallop, circus, peaceful

IN FOREIGN WORDS:

à, *Fr.* ami; œ, *Fr.* feu, *Ger.* schön; ü, *Fr.* tu, *Ger.* über; KH, *Ger.* ich, *Scot.* loch; N, *Fr.* bon; y′, *Fr.* Compiègne

STRESS MARKS:

Primary stress: ′
in·cite′ (ĭn-sīt′)
Secondary stress: ′
in′sight′ (ĭn′sīt′)

stake·out (stāk'out') *n.* Surveillance of an area, building, or person, especially by the police.

Sta·kha·nov·ite (stə-kä'nə-vīt') *n.* A Soviet worker whose exceptional diligence and zeal earn him high government esteem. [After Alexei *Stakhanov* (1905–77), Russian miner who set a productivity record in 1935 that was taken as a model.] —**Sta·kha·nov·ism** (stə-kä'nə-vĭz'əm) *n.*

sta·lac·tite (stə-lăk'tīt', stăl'ək-) *n.* A cylindrical or conical deposit, usually of calcite or aragonite, projecting downward from the roof of a cavern as a result of the dripping of mineral-rich water. Compare **stalagmite.** [New Latin *stalactites,* from Greek *stalaktos,* dripping, verbal adjective from *stalassein†,* to drip.] —**sta·lac·ti·form** (stə-lăk'tə-fôrm') *adj.* —**stal·ac·tit·ic** (stăl'ăk-tĭt'ĭk, stə-lăk'-), **stal·ac·tit·i·cal** *adj.*

sta·lag (stä'läg, stăl'ăg') *n.* A German prisoner-of-war camp; especially, one for noncommissioned officers and privates. [German *Stalag,* short for *Stammlager,* "base camp" : *Stamm,* a base, stem + *Lager,* a camp, sleeping place.]

sta·lag·mite (stə-lăg'mīt', stăl'əg-) *n.* A cylindrical or conical deposit, usually of calcite or aragonite, projecting upward from the floor of a cavern as a result of the dripping of mineral-rich water. Compare **stalactite.** [New Latin *stalagmites,* from Greek *stalagmos,*

a dropping, from *stalassein†,* to drip. See **stalactite.**] —**stal·ag·mit·ic** (stăl'ăg-mĭt'ĭk, stə-lăg'-), **stal·ag·mit·i·cal** *adj.*

St. Al·bans (ôl'bənz). City of Hertfordshire, southeastern England. The site of the Roman town of Verulamium, it has many Roman remains, including an amphitheater, a mosaic pavement, and a hypocaust. Saint Alban was martyred here (*c.* A.D. 303).

stale¹ (stāl) *adj.* **staler, stalest. 1.** Having lost freshness, effervescence, or palatability; flat or dry. **2.** Lacking in originality or spontaneity; trite: *a stale joke.* **3.** Impaired in efficacy, strength, or motivation, as from constant repetition of an activity. **4.** *Law.* Having lost legal efficacy or force through lack of exercise or action: *a stale claim.* —See Synonyms at **trite.**
~*v.* **staled, staling, stales.** —*tr.* To make stale. —*intr.* To become stale. [Middle English, old enough to clear, well-aged (said of alcoholic drink), from Old French *estale,* not moving, from *estaler,* to halt, from *estal,* a fixed place, from Frankish *stal* (unattested), position.] —**stale·ly** *adv.* —**stale·ness** *n.*

stale² *intr.v.* **staled, staling, stales.** To urinate. Used of horses and camels.
~*n.* Urine of horses or camels. [Middle English *stalen,* from Germanic; akin to Middle Low German *stallen.*]

stale·mate (stāl'māt') *n.* **1.** *Chess.* A position in which a player cannot make a legal move. **2.** A situation in which further action by either of two opponents is impossible; a deadlock.
~*tr.v.* **stalemated, -mating, -mates.** To bring into a stalemate. [Obsolete *stale,* stalemate, from Middle English, from Old French *estal* (see **stale**) + MATE (checkmate).]

Sta·lin (stä'lĭn, stăl'ĭn), **Joseph Vissarionovich,** born Joseph Vissarionovich Dzhugashvili (1879–1953). Soviet statesman. He was one of the main architects of the U.S.S.R., becoming leader (1927) and premier (1941). In his search for supreme power, he exiled Trotsky (1929), purged the government and army, forced the collectivization of agriculture, and embarked on a policy of industrialization. He triumphed as a leader during World War II and attended the conferences at Tehran (1943), Yalta (1945), and Potsdam (1945). His rule was officially denounced in the U.S.S.R. in 1956.

Stalingrad. See **Volgograd.**

Sta·lin·ism (stä'lə-nĭz'əm, stăl'ə-) *n.* The bureaucratic and authoritarian exercise of state power and mechanistic application of Marxist-Leninist principles associated with Stalin's leadership, especially in the U.S.S.R. and the socialist states of central Europe. —**Sta·lin·ist** *n.* & *adj.*

stalk¹ (stôk) *n.* **1. a.** The main stem of a herbaceous plant. **b.** A stem or similar structure that supports a plant part such as a flower, flower cluster, or leaf. **2.** Any slender or elongated support or structure. [Middle English *stalk(e),* probably diminutive of *stale,* ladder rung, handle, from Old English *stalu.*] —**stalk·y** *adj.*

stalk² *v.* **stalked, stalking, stalks.** —*intr.* **1.** To walk with a stiff, haughty, or angry gait: *stalked off in a huff.* **2.** To move threateningly or menacingly: *Pestilence stalked through the land.* **3.** To track game. —*tr.* **1.** To pursue by tracking stealthily. **2.** To traverse (a place or area) threateningly or menacingly. [Middle English *stalken,* Old English *(be)stealcian,* to walk cautiously, from Germanic; akin to STEAL.] —**stalk·er** *n.*

stalk·ing-horse (stô'kĭng-hôrs') *n.* **1. a.** A horse trained to conceal the hunter while stalking. **b.** A canvas screen made in the figure of a horse, used for similar concealment. **2.** Anything used to cover one's true feelings, plans, or purpose; a decoy. **3.** Any sham candidate put forward to conceal the candidacy of another or to divide the opposition.

stall (stôl) *n.* **1. a.** A compartment for one domestic animal in a barn or shed. **b.** A parking space for an automobile. **2. a.** A small compartment, booth, or cubicle. **b.** A booth from which a trader can sell his goods. **3. a.** An enclosed seat in the chancel or choir of a church, especially one reserved for a clergyman. **b.** A pew in a church. **4.** *Chiefly British.* **a.** A seat in the front part of a theater. **b.** The area on the bottom level of a theater toward the front. **5.** A protective sheath, as a **fingerstall** *(see).* **6.** A sudden, unintended loss of power in an engine. **7.** The condition in which a decrease in an aircraft's speed or an increase in the angle of the airfoil to the forward direction of the aircraft causes a sudden fall in lift and may cause loss of control and a sharp decrease in altitude. **8.** *Informal.* A ruse or delaying tactic.
~*v.* **stalled, stalling, stalls.** —*tr.* **1.** To put or lodge (an animal) in a stall. **2.** To maintain (an animal) in a stall for fattening. **3.** To check the motion or progress of; bring to a standstill. **4.** To evade or put off by employing delaying tactics. Often used with *off: stall off creditors.* **5.** To cause (an engine) accidentally to stop running. **6.** To cause (an aircraft) to go into a stall. —*intr.* **1.** To live or be lodged in a stall. Used of an animal. **2.** To stick fast in mud or snow. **3.** To come to a standstill. **4.** To employ delaying tactics to postpone action or to evade pressing circumstances. **5.** To stop running from mechanical failure. Used of an engine. **6.** To lose forward speed causing a stall. Used of an aircraft. [Middle English *stal(l),* Old English *steall,* standing place, stable.]

stall-feed (stôl'fēd') *tr.v.* **-fed** (-fĕd'), **-feeding, -feeds.** To lodge and feed (an animal) in a stall for the purpose of fattening.

stalling angle *n.* The angle between the chord of an airfoil and the undisturbed air flow at which a stall occurs. Also called "critical angle," "stall angle."

stal·lion (stăl'yən) *n.* An adult male horse that has not been castrated. [Middle English *stalo(u)n,* from Old French *estalon,* from Germanic.]

---

stained glass

WINDOWS GLAZED WITH COLOR

The modern revival of a medieval art form

From the beginning of the second millennium, while the massiveness of Romanesque architecture gave way in Europe to the airiness of Gothic, the craft of making stained-glass windows blossomed into an art form. Biblical scenes and figures were portrayed in windows created to open men's minds to an appreciation of God's light. Pictures were formed from colored glass pieces of various shapes held in grooved lead strips, with iron frames (armatures) as dividing panels to give the window rigidity.

Medieval glass-making techniques were largely haphazard. Color, produced by the beechwood ash added as a catalyst, depended for its shade on the composition of the mix and the conditions in which it was melted. Accurate control was impossible in the crude medieval

furnace. Yet the blue and red 13th-century glass of cathedrals such as Chartres in France and York in England, irregular in thickness and full of impurities, has a jewel-like luminosity never since reproduced. The red was in fact flashed—a thin red strip was fused onto clear glass—because coloring it while molten made it too dark.

In the 14th century, techniques improved to give finer glass and a wider variety of colors and shades. Yellow was produced by staining clear glass with silver salts. Developments in the 15th century included techniques for producing two or three colors on one piece of glass. In later centuries, stained glass gave way to enamel-painted pictures on clear glass, and the art of making stained-glass pictures declined, not to be revived until the 20th century.

ROMANESQUE WINDOW *The oldest complete stained-glass window, in Augsburg Cathedral in Germany, dates from the 11th century. It portrays five Old Testament figures, Hosea, David, and Daniel (above), Moses, and Jonas. Brown, gold, green, and white are predominant in medieval German glass.*

ABSTRACT ART *20th-century artists have revived the glory of stained-glass windows. This window (right), by Georg Meistermann, is in the south aisle of St. Mary's Church, Cologne-Kalk, Germany.*

stal·wart (stôl′wərt) *adj.* **1.** Having physical strength; robust. **2.** Resolute; uncompromising. —See Synonyms at **strong.**
∼*n.* One who is stalwart; especially, one who actively supports a cause or organization, such as a political party. [Middle English (Scottish dialect) variant of *stalworth, stalwurth,* Old English *stælwierthe,* serviceable : *stæl,* place + *wierthe, weorth,* worth.] —**stal·wart·ly** *adv.* —**stal·wart·ness** *n.*

sta·men (stā′mən) *n., pl.* **-mens** or **stamina** (stā′mə-nə, stăm′ə-). The pollen-producing reproductive organ of a flower, usually consisting of a filament supporting an anther. [Latin *stāmen,* thread of the warp, stamen.]

stam·i·na[1] (stăm′ə-nə) *n.* The physical or mental strength required to resist or withstand disease, fatigue, or hardship; endurance. [Latin, plural of *stāmen,* thread of the warp, thread of human life.]

sta·mi·na[2]**.** Alternate plural of **stamen.**

stam·i·nal[1] (stăm′ə-nəl) *adj.* Pertaining to, showing, or producing stamina.

sta·mi·nal[2] (stā′mə-nəl, stăm′ə-) *adj.* Pertaining to a stamen or stamens.

stam·i·nate (stăm′ə-nĭt, -nāt′) *adj. Botany.* **1.** Having a stamen or stamens. **2.** Bearing stamens but lacking pistils.

stam·i·node (stăm′ə-nōd′, stā′mə-) *n.* Also **stam·i·no·di·um** (stăm′ə-nō′dē-əm, stā′mə-) *pl.* **-dia** (-dē-ə). *Botany.* A sterile functionless stamen. [New Latin *staminodium,* from Latin *stāmen,* STAMEN.]

stam·i·no·dy (stăm′ə-nō′dē, stā′mə-) *n.* The transformation of a plant part, such as a petal or sepal, into a stamen. [New Latin *stamen* (stem *stamin-*) + -ODE + -Y.]

stam·mel (stăm′əl) *n.* **1.** *Obsolete.* A coarse, red woolen cloth formerly used for undergarments. **2.** *Archaic.* The bright red color of this cloth.
∼*adj. Obsolete.* Red. [Probably variant of *stamin,* Middle English *stamyn,* from Latin *stāminea,* feminine of *stāmineus,* made of threads, from *stāmen,* thread of the warp.]

stam·mer (stăm′ər) *v.* **-mered, -mering, -mers.** —*intr.* To intrude involuntary pauses or repetitions, especially of initial consonants, into one's speaking, either because of a speech disorder or through tension, fear, or the like. —*tr.* To utter with a stammer.
∼*n.* An instance or habit of stammering. [Middle English *stameren,* Old English *stamerian,* from Germanic.] —**stam·mer·er** *n.* —**stam·mer·ing·ly** *adv.*

stamp (stămp) *v.* **stamped, stamping, stamps.** —*tr.* **1.** To bring down (the foot) forcibly upon a hard surface. **2.** To bring the foot down upon (an object or surface) forcibly. **3.** To bring into a specified condition by or as if by thrusting downward forcibly with the foot: *stamped the sand smooth.* **4.** To form or cut out by application of a mold, form, or die. **5.** To imprint or impress with a mark, design, or seal. **6.** To impress forcibly or permanently: *Her face was stamped on his mind.* **7.** To affix an adhesive stamp to (an envelope, for example). **8.** To identify, characterize, or reveal: *stamps the painting as being fake.* —*intr.* **1.** To thrust the foot forcibly downward. **2.** To walk with forcible, heavy steps. —**stamp out.** To eradicate; destroy. —See Usage note at **stomp.**
∼*n.* **1.** The act of stamping. **2. a.** An implement or device used to impress, cut out, or shape something to which it is applied. **b.** The impression or shape thus formed. **3.** A mark, design, or seal the impression of which on a piece of paper indicates payment of a fee, ownership, approval, completion, or the like. **4. a.** A small piece of gummed paper sold by a government for attachment to an article that is to be mailed; a postage stamp. **b.** Any similar piece of gummed paper issued for a specified purpose, such as indicating that a tax has been paid by an individual. **5.** Any identifying or characterizing mark or impression: *bears the stamp of originality.* **6.** Characteristic nature or quality; class; kind: *Women of her stamp are one in a hundred.* [Middle English *stampen,* Old English *stampian* (unattested), to pound, stamp.]

stamp duty *n.* A tax put on certain legal documents, such as deeds or conveyances, and certified by a piece of paper that bears an authorized stamp.

stam·pede (stăm-pēd′) *n.* **1.** A sudden headlong rush of startled animals, especially cattle or horses. **2.** A sudden headlong rush of a crowd of people. **3.** Any precipitous mass movement.
∼*v.* **stampeded, -peding, -pedes.** —*intr.* To participate in a stampede. —*tr.* To cause to stampede. [Mexican Spanish *estampida,* from Spanish, uproar, crash, "a stamping or pounding," from *estampar,* to pound, stamp, from Germanic.] —**stam·ped·er** *n.*

stamping ground *n.* One's customary environment or favorite gathering place.

stamp mill *n.* **1.** A machine that crushes ore. **2.** A building in which ore is crushed.

stance (stăns) *n.* **1.** The posture or position of a standing person or animal; especially, the position assumed by an athlete or sportsman directly before action. **2.** An emotional or intellectual attitude or position. [French, from Italian *stanza,* STANZA.]

stanch, staunch (stônch, stŏnch) *tr.v.* **stanched, stanching, stanches** or **staunched, staunching, staunches. 1. a.** To stop or check (the flow of a bodily fluid, especially blood). **b.** To stop or check the flow of (a bodily fluid, especially blood). **c.** To check the flow of blood from (a wound). **2.** To stop or check (an outflow or loss); stem: *stanched the flow of foreign investment out of the country.*
∼*adj.* Variant of **staunch.** [Middle English *staunchen,* to stop from flowing, from Old French *estanch(i)er,* from Vulgar Latin *stancāre* (unattested), from *stancus*† (unattested), dried.] —**stanch·er** *n.*

stan·chion (stăn′chən, -shən) *n.* **1.** An upright pole, post, or support. **2.** A framework consisting usually of two vertical bars, used to secure cattle in a stall.
∼*tr.v.* **stanchioned, -chioning, -chions. 1.** To build stanchions for; equip with stanchions. **2.** To confine (cattle) by means of stanchions. [Middle English *stanchon,* from Old French *estanchon,* from *estanc(h)e,* a stay, prop, from Latin *stāre.*]

stand (stănd) *v.* **stood** (stŏŏd), **standing, stands.** —*intr.* **1. a.** To maintain an upright position on the feet. **b.** To be placed in or maintain an erect position upon a base, support, or bottom. **2. a.** To rise to a standing position. Often used with *up.* **b.** To assume a standing position in a manner specified: *stand straight; stand to one side.* **3.** To point or set. Used of a gun dog. **4.** To measure a specified height when in a standing position: *stands five feet tall.* **5. a.** To remain stable, upright, or intact: *hardly a house left standing after the earthquake.* **b.** To remain valid, effective, or unaltered: *The agreement still stands.* **6.** To maintain a position, attitude, or course: *stand firm.* **7. a.** To be expressed as or show a specified figure or amount. Used with *at: Your balance stands at $500.* **b.** To occupy a specified position or level on or as if on a scale; rank: *Her reputation stands high. He stands third in the class.* **8.** To be in a position offering the likelihood or expectation of loss or gain: *stood to lose a fortune.* **9.** To be in a particular or specified state, condition, or situation: *stands corrected; stands in awe of him.* **10.** To act in the specified capacity or perform the specified function: *stand surety; stand guard.* **11.** To be situated or placed: *The castle stood on a hill.* **12. a.** To remain in a stationary position: *the train now standing at the platform.* **b.** To remain in a state of inactivity: *machinery standing idle.* **13.** To remain without flowing or being disturbed; be stagnant. **14.** *Chiefly British.* To be a candidate for public office: *will stand in the next election.* **15.** To take or hold a particular course or direction; steer: *a ship standing to windward.* —*tr.* **1.** To cause to stand; place upright. **2. a.** To resist or endure without yielding or without sustaining damage; withstand: *stand the siege; can't stand the strain.* **b.** To tolerate; put up with; bear: *can't stand the sight of him.* **3. a.** To be subjected to; undergo: *stand trial.* **b.** To submit to and emerge successfully from: *an argument that will not stand close examination.* **4.** *Informal.* To pay the cost for; treat: *stand someone to a drink.* —See Synonyms at **bear.** —**stand a chance.** To have a chance, as of gaining or accomplishing. —**stand down. 1.** *Law.* To leave the witness stand after giving testimony. **2.** *Chiefly British.* To withdraw, retire, or resign, as from a position of office or authority. **3.** *Chiefly British.* **a.** To go off duty. Used of a member of the armed forces. **b.** To be taken off duty. —**stand for. 1. a.** To signify; indicate. **b.** To represent; symbolize. **2.** To be a supporter or advocate of: *stands for freedom of the press.* **3.** *Informal.* To tolerate; endure; put up with. —**stand on. 1.** To depend on. **2.** To be strict in the observance of; insist on: *Don't stand on ceremony.* **3.** In navigation, to maintain the same course or tack. —**stand one's ground.** To hold one's position, as against attack. —**stand on one's own (two) feet.** To be independent and responsible for oneself. —**stand over. 1.** To keep close surveillance on or watch closely, especially in a threatening manner. **2.** To hold over or be held over; postpone. —**stand to.** *British.* **1.** To take up positions in readiness for action. Used of soldiers. **2.** To cause (soldiers) to stand to.
∼*n.* **1.** The act of standing. **2.** A ceasing of work or activity; standstill; halt. **3.** A stop on a theatrical, concert, or other performance tour. **4.** The place or spot where a person stands. **5.** A booth, stall, or counter for the display of goods for sale. **6.** A parking space reserved for taxis. **7.** An act of or position for defense or resistance, especially when desperate or decisive in a campaign: *made a final stand at the river.* **8.** A stance or opinion one is prepared to uphold: *take a stand.* **9.** *Usually* **stands.** The bleachers at a playing field or stadium. **10.** A small rack, prop, or table for holding any of various articles: *a music stand; a bedside stand.* **11.** A group or growth of tall plants or trees: *a stand of pine.* **12.** A witness stand. [Stand, stood (past tense); Middle English *standen, sto(o)d,* Old English *standan, stōd* (past singular).] —**stand·er** *n.*

stan·dard (stăn′dərd) *n. Abbr.* **std. 1.** A flag, banner, or ensign, especially: **a.** The ensign of a chief of state, nation, or city. **b.** A pole topped with an emblem or flag of an army, especially one raised formerly in battle to indicate the rallying point for the soldiers of one side. **c.** The flag of a mounted military regiment. **2. a.** An acknowledged measure of comparison for quantitative or qualitative value; criterion; norm. **b.** An object that under stated conditions defines, represents, or records the magnitude of a unit. **3.** The set proportion by weight of gold or silver to alloy metal prescribed for use in coinage. **4.** The commodity or commodities used to back a monetary system. **5. a.** A degree or level of requirement, excellence, or attainment. **b.** *Usually* **standards.** A requirement of moral conduct. **6.** *Chiefly British.* A class or level in a primary school. **7.** A pedestal, stand, or base. **8.** *Botany.* **a.** The large upper petal of the flower of a sweet pea or related plant. **b.** Any of the narrow, upright petals of an iris. **9.** A shrub or small tree that through grafting or training has a single stem of limited height with a crown of leaves and flowers at its apex. —See Synonyms at **ideal.**
∼*adj.* **1. a.** Serving as or conforming to a standard of measurement or value. **b.** Of a normal, familiar, and commonly used kind: *a standard type of plug.* **c.** Well known and widely accepted as an authority: *a standard atlas.* **d.** Of average but not exceptional quality: *a standard grade of beef. The acting and production were pretty standard.* **e.** Supplied automatically as an ordinary part or feature

stalactites and stalagmites *Limestone-rich water dripping into a cave forms stalactites on the cave's roof and stalagmites on its floor. Pillars are formed when the two meet. The large stalagmite shown here is in Somerset, England. It is called the Witch of Wookey after a local legend that a witch was turned to stone in the cave.*

stallion *A male horse. This is an English draft breed.*

of a product. **2.** *Linguistics.* Conforming to usage, as in pronunciation, vocabulary, and grammatical construction, that is widely regarded as acceptable and typically associated with educated speakers of a language: *standard English.* —See Synonyms at **normal.** [Middle English, from Norman French *estaundart,* Old French *estendart,* flag marking a place for rallying, from *estendre,* to EXTEND.]

stan·dard-bear·er (stăn′dərd-bâr′ər) *n.* **1.** One who bears the colors of a military unit. **2.** One who is in the vanguard, as of a political or religious movement.

stan·dard-bred (stăn′dərd-brĕd′) *n.* One of an American breed of horses developed for harness racing.

standard candle *n.* In optics, a **candela** *(see).*

standard cell *n.* A voltaic cell that produces a constant known electromotive force, enabling it to be used as a method of calibrating electrical measuring instruments.

standard deviation *n. Abbr.* **s.d., S.D.** *Symbol* σ, s *Statistics.* **1.** The square root of the **variance** *(see).* **2.** A statistic used as a measure of dispersion in a distribution, the square root of the arithmetic average of the squares of the deviations from the mean. In this sense, also called "root mean square deviation."

standard gauge *n.* A railroad track having a width of 56$\frac{1}{2}$ inches. —**stan·dard-gauge** (stăn′dərd-gāj′) *adj.*

stan·dard·ize (stăn′dər-dīz′) *tr.v.* **-ized, -izing, -izes. 1.** To cause to conform to a standard. **2.** To evaluate by comparison with a standard. —**stan·dard·i·za·tion** *n.*

standard of living *n.* The quality of material comfort as enjoyed by a country, an individual, or a section of society; especially, this quality as gauged by statistical surveys of the number and type of consumer goods per household. Compare **quality of life.**

standard operating procedure *n.* An established procedure to be followed for a given operation or situation.

standard time *n.* The time in any of 24 time zones, usually the mean solar time at the central meridian of each zone. In the continental United States, there are four standard time zones: Eastern (E.S.T., E.T.), using the 75th meridian; Central (C.S.T., C.T.), using the 90th meridian; Mountain (M.S.T., M.T.), using the 105th meridian; and Pacific (P.S.T., P.T.), using the 120th meridian.

stand by *intr.v.* **1.** To be available and ready for action if needed. **2.** To remain inactive; refrain from intervening: *couldn't just stand by and see him swindled.* **3.** To wait for something, such as a broadcast transmission, to begin again. —*tr.v.* **1.** To aid; support. **2.** To keep or maintain (one's word, policy, or promise).

stand·by (stănd′bī′) *n., pl.* **-bys. 1.** One that can always be depended upon. **2.** That which is kept in readiness to fill a need: *Baked beans are a good standby to feed hungry mouths.* —**on standby.** Ready and waiting.
  ~*adj.* **1.** Kept in reserve for use when needed: *a standby generator.* **2.** Issued or available only immediately prior to a journey: *a standby air ticket.* **3.** Of, pertaining to, or waiting for an aircraft on which one can travel with a standby ticket: *standby passengers.*
  ~*adv.* Using a standby ticket: *flew standby to New York.*

stand·ee (stăn-dē′) *n.* One using standing room.

stand in *intr.v.* To act as a stand-in.

stand·in (stănd′ĭn′) *n.* **1.** One who substitutes for an actor during lights and camera adjustments or in hazardous stunts. **2.** Any person who acts as a substitute.

stand·ing (stăn′dĭng) *n.* **1. a.** Status with respect to credit, rank, or reputation. **b.** High reputation; esteem. **2.** Length of time; duration: *a friendship of long standing.*
  ~*adj.* **1.** Remaining upright; erect. **2.** Made or performed from a standing or stationary position: *a standing jump.* **3. a.** Remaining valid or unchanged: *a standing arrangement.* **b.** Well-established and familiar: *a standing joke.* **4.** Not flowing; stagnant.

standing army *n.* A permanent army of paid soldiers.

standing crop *n. Ecology.* The total number of living organisms in a particular area or at a particular level of a food chain at a given time, usually expressed in terms of **biomass** *(see).*

standing order *n.* An order or operating instruction held to be in force until specifically altered or withdrawn, especially a regulation relating to military or parliamentary procedure.

standing ovation *n.* An ovation in which those applauding stand.

standing room *n.* Space in which to stand, as in a public place or vehicle where all seats are filled.

standing stone *n.* A large, upright stone or slab of stone, usually found in ancient henge monuments.

standing wave *n.* A wave in which the amplitude of the resultant of a transmitted and a reflected wave is stationary in time and in which some of the energy of the transmitted wave is absorbed by the reflecting boundary. Also called "stationary wave."

Stan·dish (stăn′dĭsh), **Miles** or **Myles** (c. 1584-1656). English Pilgrim colonist in America. A soldier of fortune hired by the English Pilgrims to accompany them on their voyage to the New World (1620), he emerged as a leader in the difficult early years of the colony. He was the first colonist to learn the Indian languages and established a lasting peace with the Indians.

stand off *intr.v.* **1.** To keep apart; remain aloof. **2.** To maintain a distance from something; avoid. **3.** *Nautical.* To take or maintain a course away from shore. —*tr.v.* **1.** To prevent from advancing; drive back. **2.** To put off; evade.

stand·off (stănd′ôf′, -ŏf′) *n.* A standoff insulator.

stand·off (stănd′ôf′, -ŏf′) *n.* **1.** A tie, as in a contest; a draw. **2.** An effect that neutralizes or counterbalances.

standoff insulator *n.* An insulator used to support a conductor a specified distance from a surface.

stand-off·ish (stănd-ô′fĭsh, -ŏf′ĭsh) *adj.* Coldly reserved; aloof.

stand oil *n.* A drying oil, such as linseed or tung, heated with minimum oxidation until thickened and used in oil enamel paints.

stand out *intr.v.* **1.** To protrude; stick out. **2.** To be conspicuous, distinctive, or prominent. **3.** To hold out; maintain support or opposition. Used with *for* or *against: stand out against a verdict.* **4.** *Nautical.* To take or maintain a course away from shore.

stand·out (stănd′out′) *n.* One that is outstanding or excellent.

stand·pipe (stănd′pīp′) *n.* **1.** A large vertical pipe into which water is pumped in order to produce a desired pressure. **2.** A vertical pipe with a tap erected outdoors, as for use when a domestic supply is interrupted.

stand·point (stănd′point′) *n.* A position from which things are considered or judged; a point of view. [Translation of German *Standpunkt.*]

St. An·drews (sānt ăn′drōoz). Coastal resort of Fife Region, eastern Scotland. It was once the ecclesiastical capital of Scotland and has the country's oldest university (1411). Its Royal and Ancient Club (1754) is a renowned golfing center.

stand·still (stănd′stĭl′) *n.* A condition in which activity or progress has ceased; a halt: *Work came to a standstill.*

stand up *intr.v.* To remain unimpaired or prove valid or satisfactory when subjected to testing conditions: *stood up to long wear.* —*tr.v. Informal.* To fail to keep an appointment with (a person). —**stand up for.** To side with; defend. —**stand up to.** To face up to; confront fearlessly. —**stand up with.** To act as best man or maid of honor for.

stand-up (stănd′ŭp′) *adj.* **1.** Erect; upright: *a stand-up collar.* **2.** Taken or performed while standing: *a stand-up supper.* **3.** Designating a fist fight confined largely to heavy blows with little maneuvering. **4.** Designating or practicing a style of comic performance done solo and without stage properties.

Stan·ford-Bi·net scale (stăn′fərd bĭ-nā′) *n.* A revision of the **Binet-Simon scale** *(see)* used in one form or another since 1916. Also called "Stanford-Binet test," "Stanford Revision of the Binet scale." [Prepared at *Stanford* University, California.]

stang. *Obsolete.* Past tense of **sting.**

stan·hope (stăn′hōp′) *n.* A light open horse-drawn vehicle with one seat and two wheels. [Designed by the Reverend Fitzroy *Stanhope* (1787-1864), English clergyman.]

Stan·i·slav·sky (stăn′ə-slăv′skē, -släf′skē), **Konstantin Sergeyevitch Alexeyev** (1863-1938). Russian actor, producer, and director. He cofounded (1898) the Moscow Art Theater, where he devised a system of acting in which actors develop their own conception of their roles.

stank. Past tense of **stink.**

Stanley. See **Port Stanley.**

Stan·ley (stăn′lē), **Sir Henry Morton,** born John Rowlands (1841-1904). British journalist and explorer. He found (1871) the lost explorer David Livingstone at Lake Tanganyika and explored (1874-77) Equatorial Africa. He founded (1879) the Congo Free State for Leopold II of Belgium.

stan·na·ry (stăn′ə-rē) *n., pl.* **-ries.** A place or region where tin is mined. [Medieval Latin *stannāria,* neuter plural of Late Latin *stannum,* tin. See **stannic.**]

stan·nic (stăn′ĭk) *adj.* Of or containing tin, especially with valence 4. [Probably from French *stannique,* from Late Latin *stannum,* tin, from Latin *stannum†,* an alloy of silver and lead.]

stannic chloride *n.* A colorless caustic liquid, $Na_2SnCl_6 \cdot H_2O$, made from tin treated with chlorine and used in the manufacture of textiles, sensitized papers, and perfumes.

stan·nif·er·ous (stə-nĭf′ər-əs) *adj.* Containing tin. [Late Latin *stannum,* tin + -FEROUS.]

stan·nite (stăn′īt′) *n.* A gray to black mineral, chiefly Cu_2FeSnS, having a metallic luster. Also called "tin pyrites." [German *Stannit* : Late Latin *stannum,* tin (see **stannic**) + -ITE.]

stan·nous (stăn′əs) *adj.* Of or containing tin, especially with valence 2. [Late Latin *stannum,* tin. See **stannic.**]

St. An·tho·ny's fire (sānt ăn′thə-nēz) *n. Pathology.* Erysipelas *(see).* [After *St. Anthony* (died c. A.D. 350).]

Stan·ton (stăn′tən), **Edwin McMasters** (1814-69). U.S. jurist and public official. Attorney general under James Buchanan (1860-61), he became secretary of war under Abraham Lincoln (1862) and served dutifully throughout the Civil War. During the Reconstruction period his disagreements with Andrew Johnson were the basis for Johnson's impeachment. When Johnson was found innocent, Stanton resigned his post (1868).

Stanton, Elizabeth Cady (1815-1902). U.S. feminist and social reformer. She helped organize the first women's rights convention, held in Seneca Falls, New York (1848), for which she composed a Declaration of Sentiments calling for the reform of discriminatory practices that perpetuated sexual inequality.

stan·za (stăn′zə) *n. Abbr.* **st.** One of the number of distinct and separate divisions of a poem, composed of two or more lines usually characterized by a common pattern of meter, rhyme, and number of lines. [Italian, "a stopping or standing," from Vulgar Latin *stantia* (unattested), from Latin *stāns,* present participle of *stāre,* to stand.] —**stan·za·ic** (stăn-zā′ĭk) *adj.*

sta·pe·lia (stə-pēl′yə, -lē-ə) *n.* Any plant of the African genus *Stapelia,* having fleshy stems, no leaves, and large, unpleasant-smelling

star

STAR LIFE, STAR DEATH
Each star has a unique life of its own

Stars form, change over time, and ultimately cease to shine. That much is accepted scientific fact. For each star, however, the timetable is different.

A widely accepted theory is that stars form from interstellar clouds—gigantic collections of hydrogen and dust that swirl among stars and galaxies. Eventually, as gravitational force builds up and begins to pull the hydrogen and dust together, the cloud becomes what some astronomers call a protostar. The process of contraction raises the temperature at the center of the protostar. When the temperature gets high enough, hydrogen atoms undergo fusion (typically into helium atoms), releasing incredible energy, and the star begins to shine.

At this stage, a star is said to have entered the main sequence, a classification in which it remains for as long as its nuclear fires continue to burn on hydrogen. For example, the sun (which astronomers call an ordinary star, or dwarf, in contrast to more massive giants and supergi-

ants) has been in its main-sequence period for about 5 billion years, and will probably remain there for as long in the future. When hydrogen atoms are depleted, stars of relatively low mass like the sun may expand into less-dense red giants. These may cool and shrink into dense white dwarfs, losing luminosity, and finally fade into balls of ash that are called black dwarfs.

Stars of relatively high mass may take a different course, with an accelerated tour (of just a few million years) through the main sequence. At one or more stages in their lifetimes, they may become variable stars, growing alternately hotter and colder and thus pulsating in brightness. Instead of becoming white dwarfs, some high-mass supergiants may explode into supernovae that eventually collapse into extremely dense neutron stars. The immense gravity of some of the biggest neutron stars causes them to swallow their own matter until they become black holes from which not even light can escape.

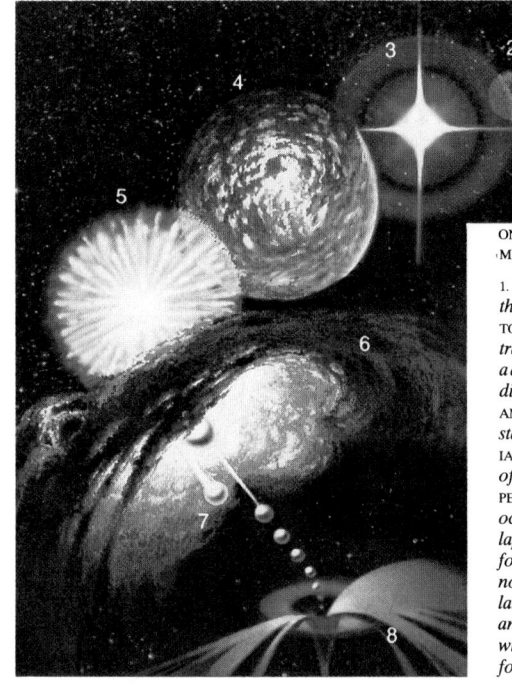

ONE STAR, MANY POSSIBLE STAGES

1. INTERSTELLAR CLOUD *is thought to spawn stars.* 2. PROTOSTAR *forms as cloud contracts.* 3. HIGH-MASS STAR *takes a different life path than an ordinary star.* 4. RED SUPERGIANT, *equivalent to "red giant" stage of ordinary stars.* 5. VARIABLE STAR, *a temporary stage of some massive stars.* 6. SUPERNOVA, *cosmic explosion occurs as red supergiant collapses.* 7. NEUTRON STAR, *forms in aftermath of supernova.* 8. BLACK HOLE, *speculated to exist, sucks in matter and energy—even light—with powerful attractive force.*

flowers. [New Latin, after J. B. van *Stapel* (died 1636), Dutch botanist.]

sta·pes (stā′pēz′) *n., pl.* **stapes** or **stapedes** (stā′pə-dēz′, stə-pē′-). A small sound-conducting bone of the inner ear, shaped somewhat like a stirrup. Also called "stirrup bone." Compare **anvil, malleus.** [New Latin, from Medieval Latin *stapēs,* perhaps variant of *staffa, stapha, stapeda,* stirrup : Latin *stāre,* to stand + *pēs* (stem ped-), foot.] —**sta·pe·di·al** (stə-pē′dē-əl) *adj.*

staphylo– *prefix.* Indicates: **1.** *Anatomy.* The uvula; for example, **staphylorrhaphy. 2.** *Microbiology.* Resembling a bunch of grapes; clustered; for example, **staphylococcus.** [New Latin, from Greek *staphulē,* bunch of grapes, grapevine, uvula.]

staph·y·lo·coc·cus (stăf′ə-lō-kŏk′əs) *n., pl.* **-cocci** (-kŏk′sī′). Any of various Gram-positive, spherical bacteria of the genus *Staphylococcus,* occurring in grapelike clusters. Also called "staph." [New Latin : STAPHYLO- + -COCCUS.] —**staph·y·lo·coc·cal** (stăf′ə-lō-kŏk′əl), **staph·y·lo·coc·cic** (stăf′ə-lō-kŏk′sĭk) *adj.*

staph·y·lo·plas·ty (stăf′ə-lō-plăs′tē) *n.* Corrective surgery of the uvula and the soft palate. [STAPHYLO- + -PLASTY.] —**staph·y·lo·plas·tic** (stăf′ə-lō-plăs′tĭk) *adj.*

staph·y·lor·rha·phy, staph·y·lor·a·phy (stăf′ə-lôr′ə-fē, -lôr′ə-fē) *n.* The correction of a cleft palate or divided uvula by plastic surgery. [STAPHYLO- + Greek *-rrhaphia,* sewing, suture, from *rhaptein,* to sew.]

sta·ple[1] (stā′pəl) *n.* **1.** A major commodity grown or produced in a region. **2.** A commodity in steady or constant demand, such as salt, flour, or coffee. **3.** A major part, element, or feature. **4.** Raw material. **5.** The graded fiber of cotton, wool, or flax. ~*adj.* **1.** In constant supply and demand. **2.** Important as an article of trade, production, or consumption in a particular region: *staple exports.* **3.** Principal; main: *a staple topic of conversation.* ~*tr.v.* **stapled, -pling, -ples.** To grade (fibers) according to length and fineness. [Middle English *staple,* market town, from Old French *estaple,* from Middle Dutch *stapel,* pillar, emporium.]

sta·ple[2] *n.* **1.** A U-shaped metal loop with pointed ends, driven into a surface to hold a bolt, hook, or hasp, or to hold wiring in place. **2.** A thin piece of wire having the shape of a square bracket, used, by being forced through and flattened, as a fastening for papers, cloth, and similar materials. ~*tr.v.* **stapled, -pling, -ples.** To fasten by means of a staple or staples. [Middle English *stapel, stapul,* Old English *stapol,* post, pillar, from Germanic.]

sta·pler[1] (stā′plər) *n.* One who deals in staple goods or fibers.

stapler[2] *n.* A machine or hand-operated device used to bind material together by means of staples.

star (stär) *n.* **1.** *Astronomy.* A light-emitting mass of gas in which the energy generated by nuclear reactions in the interior is balanced by the outflow of energy to the surface, and the inward-directed gravitational forces are balanced by the outward-directed gas and radiation pressures. **2.** Any of the celestial bodies visible at night from Earth as relatively stationary, usually twinkling points of light. **3.** Anything regarded as resembling such a body. **4. a.** A graphic design or emblem conventionally representing a star, having five or

more radiating points, and often used as a symbol, as of rank or excellence. **b.** Any of a number of such symbols used to indicate relative position on a recognized scale of quality: *a three-star restaurant.* **5.** An artistic performer or athlete whose superior talent or ability is acknowledged. **6.** An asterisk (*). **7.** A white spot on the forehead of a horse. **8. stars.** The constellations of the zodiac believed to influence a person's character or destiny. **9.** The future; fate or destiny. —**see stars.** To experience bright, flashing sensations, as from a blow on the head. —**thank one's (lucky) stars.** To be thankful for one's good fortune. ~*v.* **starred, starring, stars.** —*tr.* **1.** To ornament or set with stars. **2. a.** To award or mark with a star for excellence. **b.** To mark with an asterisk. **3.** To present or feature (a performer) in a leading role. —*intr.* **1.** To play the leading role in a film or theatrical production. **2.** To do an outstanding job; perform excellently. ~*adj.* **1.** Of or pertaining to a star: *star quality.* **2.** Pre-eminent; brilliant. [Middle English *ste(o)rre,* Old English *steorra.*]

star anise *n.* **1.** An aromatic tree, *Illicium verum,* of eastern Asia, having purple-red flowers and anise-scented fruit. **2.** The fruit of this tree, used in Oriental cooking. Also called "Chinese anise."

star apple *n.* **1.** A tropical American tree, *Chrysophyllum cainito,* bearing smooth-skinned greenish-purple fruit. **2.** The edible fruit of this tree, having a star-shaped core.

star·board (stär′bərd) *n.* The right-hand side of a ship or aircraft as one faces forward. Compare **port.** ~*adj.* On the right-hand side. ~*adv.* To or toward the right-hand side. ~*tr.v.* **starboarded, -boarding, -boards.** To turn or shift (a rudder or helm) to the right. [Middle English *sterbord,* Old English *stēorbord : stēor,* rudder + *bord,* side of a ship.]

starch (stärch) *n.* **1.** A naturally abundant nutrient carbohydrate consisting of linked units of D-glucose, found chiefly in the seeds, fruits, tubers, roots, and stem pith of plants, notably potatoes, wheat, and rice, varying widely in appearance according to source but commonly prepared as a white, amorphous, tasteless powder. **2.** Any of various substances, including natural starch, used to stiffen fabrics after washing them. **3.** Foods having a high content of starch. **4.** Stiffness or formality in manner or behavior. ~*tr.v.* **starched, starching, starches.** To stiffen with starch. [Middle English *sterche, starche,* from *sterchen,* to stiffen (with starch), Old English *stercan* (attested only by past participle *sterced-*).]

Star Chamber *n.* **1.** A former English court (abolished in 1641) consisting of judges who were appointed by the Crown and sat in closed session on cases involving the security of the state. **2. star chamber.** Any court or tribunal that resembles the Star Chamber, especially in the manner of its secrecy and the severity of its judgments. [So called because the ceiling of the original courtroom was decorated with gilded stars.]

starch·y (stär′chē) *adj.* **-ier, -iest. 1.** Of, of the nature of, or containing starch. **2.** Stiffened with starch. **3.** *Informal.* Stiff; formal. —**starch·i·ly** *adv.* —**starch·i·ness** *n.*

star connection *n. Electricity.* A connection of three or more phase

starfish *Rows of suctionlike tube feet enable the starfish to creep along the ocean floor. Its mouth is on the underside of the central part, and it devours small seabed creatures as it crawls over them. Many of the 1,800 different species can regenerate lost arms.*

starling *Adult starlings of both sexes have an iridescent summer plumage of black, purple, and green (above). In winter the bills darken and the plumage changes to black with white spots, which are more pronounced in the female.*

star-of-Bethlehem *Starlike flowers and the plant's abundance in the Holy Land have given* Ornithogalum umbellatum *its common name. The plant blooms in late spring, and the flowers close at night and do not open again until midmorning, which has given it another name—"nap-at-noon."*

supplies that joins one end of each branch at a common point. Compare **delta connection.**

star-crossed (stär′krôst′, -krŏst′) *adj.* Beset or dogged with bad luck: *star-crossed lovers.*

star·dom (stär′dəm) *n.* **1.** The status of an actor or other performer acknowledged as a star. **2.** Stars collectively, as of motion pictures.

star·dust (stär′dŭst′) *n.* **1.** Distant stars seen as a mass of tiny glittering lights. **2.** A dreamy, misty, romantic quality.

stare (stâr) *v.* **stared, staring, stares.** *—intr.* **1.** To look with a steady, often wide-eyed gaze, as from interest, astonishment, or hostility. **2.** *Chiefly British.* To stand out; be conspicuous or glaring. **3.** To stand on end or bristle, as animal hair or feathers. *—tr.* To affect by staring at: *He stared the boy into submission.* —See Synonyms at **gaze.** **—stare down.** To cause to waver or give in by or as if by staring.
∼n. The act of staring; an intent or fixed gaze. [Middle English *staren,* Old English *starian.*] **—star·er** *n.*

star facet *n.* Any of the eight small triangular facets in the crown of a brilliant-cut gem.

star·fish (stär′fĭsh′) *n., pl.* **starfishes** or collectively **starfish.** Any of various marine echinoderms of the class Asteroidea, characteristically having five arms extending from a central disk.

star·flow·er (stär′flou′ər) *n.* **1.** Any of several small North American plants of the genus *Trientalis,* having white, starlike flowers. **2.** Any of several other plants having starlike flowers.

star·gaze (stär′gāz′) *intr.v.* **-gazed, -gazing, -gazes.** **1.** To gaze at or study the stars. **2.** To daydream.

star·gaz·er (stär′gā′zər) *n.* **1. a.** One who stargazes. **b.** An astronomer or astrologer. Used humorously. **2.** Any of various marine bottom-dwelling fishes of the families Uranoscopidae and Dactyloscopidae, having eyes on the top of the head.

star grass *n.* Any of various plants of the genus *Hypoxis,* having grasslike leaves and star-shaped flowers.

stark (stärk) *adj.* **starker, starkest.** **1.** Without elaboration; bare; blunt: *stark truth.* **2.** Complete or utter; extreme: *stark poverty.* **3.** Harsh in appearance; bleak; grim: *stark cliffs.* **4.** Clearly defined; sharp: *in stark contrast.*
∼adv. Utterly; entirely; absolutely: *stark raving mad; stark naked.* [Middle English *stark(e), sterk(e),* Old English *stearc,* hard, stern, severe, cruel.] **—stark·ly** *adv.* **—stark·ness** *n.*

stark·ers (stär′kərz) *adj. British Slang.* Completely naked.

star·let (stär′lĭt) *n.* **1.** A small star. **2.** A young film actress publicized as a future star.

star·light (stär′līt′) *n.* The light given by the stars.
∼adj. Starlit.

star·ling[1] (stär′lĭng) *n.* Any of various Old World birds of the family Sturnidae, characteristically having dark, often iridescent plumage; especially, *Sturnus vulgaris.* [Middle English *sterling, starling,* Old English *stærlinc* : *stær,* starling + -LING.]

starling[2] *n.* A protective structure of pilings surrounding a pier of a bridge. [Probably alteration of Middle English *stadeline,* from *stadel, stathel,* foundation, Old English *stathol.*]

star·lit (stär′lĭt′) *adj.* Illuminated by starlight.

star-nosed mole (stär′nōzd′) *n.* A mole, *Condylura cristata,* of eastern North America, having 22 small fleshy tentacles encircling the end of its nose.

star-of-Beth·le·hem (stär′əv-bĕth′lə-hĕm′) *n.* **1.** A plant, *Ornithogalum umbellatum,* native to Europe, having narrow leaves and star-shaped white flowers. **2.** Any of several similar or related plants. [Probably from a fancied resemblance to the star that guided the Magi to the infant Jesus in Bethlehem (Matthew 2:2).]

Star of David *n.* A six-pointed star, or hexagram, formed by placing two triangles together, one upon the other or interlaced. It is a symbol of Judaism and appears on the Israeli flag. Also called "Magen David," "Shield of David."

Starr (stär), **Belle** (1848–89). U.S. outlaw. At the age of 18 she began her association with a succession of Texas and Oklahoma outlaws. Calling herself the bandit queen, she often donned an outfit of velvet or leather and participated in horse theft and petty thievery. She was fatally shot in the back by an unidentified gunman.

Starr, Ringo, born Richard Starkey (1940–). British rock musician. He was drummer with the rock group the Beatles (1962–70). When the group disbanded (1970), he pursued a separate career as a musician and actor.

star·ry (stär′ē) *adj.* **-rier, -riest.** **1.** Of or resembling a star, especially in shape or brilliance. **2.** Set or filled with or as if with stars or starlight: *a starry night; starry eyes.* **—star·ri·ness** *n.*

star·ry-eyed (stär′ē-īd′) *adj.* Naively enthusiastic or romantic.

Stars and Stripes *n.* The flag of the United States.

star sapphire *n.* A sapphire with a polished convex surface exhibiting a star-shaped figure.

star shell *n.* An artillery shell that explodes in midair with a shower of lights, used for illumination and signaling.

Star-Span·gled Banner (stär′spăng′gəld) *n.* **1.** The flag of the United States. **2.** The national anthem of the United States, written by Francis Scott Key in 1814.

start (stärt) *v.* **started, starting, starts.** *—intr.* **1. a.** To begin a journey or movement; move from a position of rest; set out: *started on her travels.* **b.** To begin a process, course of action, or undertaking: *Let's start at once. The show started with a dance routine.* **2. a.** To come into being or operation: *School starts at nine. The car won't start.* **b.** To have a beginning, origin, or lower limit: *Prices start at $100.* **3. a.** To move involuntarily: *started with fright.* **b.** To move suddenly; spring forth. **4.** To issue suddenly and forcefully; gush. **5.** To be in the line-up at the beginning of a race. **6.** To protrude or bulge: *eyes starting out of their sockets.* **7.** To become loosened or displaced, as from shrinkage. *—tr.* **1.** To set into motion, operation, or activity: *start the show.* Sometimes used with *off* or *up*: *Start up the engine. This started him off on one of his boring explanations.* **2. a.** To bring into being; initiate: *start a rumor; start a family.* **b.** To found; establish: *start a business.* **3. a.** To indicate the beginning of (a race). **b.** To enter in a race. **4.** To cause or enable to begin an activity or venture, often with encouragement or instruction: *started her on painting at an early age.* **5.** To rouse (game) from its hiding place or lair; flush. **6.** To cause to work loose. —See Synonyms at **begin.** **—start in.** To begin work or an activity. **—start out.** To set out on a journey, a course of action, or a career. **—start something.** To cause trouble. **—to start with.** First of all; as a first consideration.
∼n. **1.** A beginning; a commencement. **2.** A startled reaction or movement. **3. starts.** Quick, brief spurts of effort or activity. Used chiefly in the phrase *by fits and starts.* **4.** A part that has become displaced or loosened. **5. a.** A place of beginning; a starting line. **b.** A time of beginning; a starting point. **6.** A signal to begin a race. **7.** A position of advantage over others, as in a race or endeavor; a lead. **8.** An opportunity granted to pursue a career or course of action: *a good start in life.* **—for a start.** To start with. [Middle English *sterten,* Old English *styrtan* (attested only in the present participle *sturtende*), to leap up.]

START Strategic Arms Reduction Talks.

start·er (stär′tər) *n.* **1.** One that starts. **2.** An attachment for starting an internal-combustion engine without hand cranking. Also called "self-starter," "starter motor." **3.** One who signals the start of a race. **4.** A person or animal that starts in a race. **5.** *Chiefly British.* The first course of a meal. **6.** A chemical agent or bacterial culture used to start a reaction, as in the formation of acid in making yogurt, cheese, or vinegar. **—for starters.** *Informal.* To start with.

star thistle *n.* Any of several plants of the genus *Centaurea*; especially, *C. calcitrapa,* native to Eurasia, having spiny purplish flower heads.

starting block *n.* Either of a pair of fixed supports against which a runner pushes to gain initial momentum at the start of a race. Also called "block."

starting gate *n.* Any of a set of gates that are simultaneously raised to release the competitors in a horse or dog race.

starting grid *n.* An area where racing cars are staggered before the start of a race according to their relative practice times.

starting pistol *n.* A pistol that is fired to signal the start of a race.

starting price *n.* The last odds given by bookmakers before the start of a horse or dog race.

star·tle (stär′tl) *v.* **-tled, -tling, -tles.** *—tr.* **1.** To cause to make a quick involuntary movement or start; rouse suddenly. **2.** To alarm, frighten, or surprise. *—intr.* To become startled.
∼n. A sudden mild shock; a start. [Middle English *stertlen,* Old English *steartlian,* to kick, struggle, frequentative of *styrtan* (unattested), to leap up, START.] **—start·ling·ly** *adv.*

star tracker *n.* A telescopic instrument, used chiefly on rockets, that provides a guidance reference by remaining fixed on a celestial body.

star·va·tion (stär-vā′shən) *n.* **1.** The act or process of starving. **2.** The condition of being starved.

starve (stärv) *v.* **starved, starving, starves.** *—intr.* **1.** To suffer or die from extreme or prolonged lack of food. **2.** To suffer from deprivation; be in need. **3.** *Informal.* To be very hungry. **4.** *Archaic.* To suffer or die from cold. *—tr.* **1.** To cause to starve. **2.** To bring or force to a specified state by starving: *starved into surrender.* [Middle English *ste(o)rven,* Old English *steorfan,* to die.]

starve·ling (stärv′lĭng) *n.* One that is starving or ill-nourished.
∼adj. **1.** Hungry or ill-nourished. **2.** Poor in quality; inadequate.

Star Wars, star wars *n.* **1. STAR WARS.** A trademark for a space adventure film and for products associated with this film and its sequels. **2. Strategic Defense Initiative** (see).
∼adj. Of or pertaining to the Strategic Defense Initiative.

star·wort (stär′wûrt′, -wôrt′) *n.* **1.** Any of various plants having star-shaped flowers. **2.** Any of various aquatic plants of the genus *Callitriche,* having a rosette of floating leaves.

stash (stăsh) *tr.v.* **stashed, stashing, stashes.** To hide or store away in a secret place.
∼n. **1.** A secret store or cache, as of money, drugs, or valuables. **2.** Something hidden away. [18th century : origin obscure.]

sta·sis (stā′sĭs) *n., pl.* **-ses** (-sēz′). **1.** *Pathology.* Stagnation of a bodily fluid, especially of blood. **2.** A condition of balance among various forces. [New Latin, from Greek, a standing.]

-stasis *suffix.* Indicates: **1.** Slowing or stoppage; for example, **bacteriostasis.** **2.** A stable state or a balance; for example, **homeostasis.** [New Latin, from Greek *stasis,* a standing.]

Stas·sen (stăs′ən), **Harold Edward** (1907–). U.S. politician. He was elected to three terms as governor of Minnesota (1938–44) before serving in World War II. A delegate to the first United Nations conference (1945), he unsuccessfully sought the Republican presidential nomination in 1948, 1952, and 1964.

-stat *suffix.* Indicates stationary or making stationary; for example, **rheostat, thermostat.** [New Latin *-stata,* from Greek *-statēs,* one that causes to stand.]

stat. **1.** immediately. [Latin *statim*.] **2.** stationary. **3.** statistics. **4.** statuary. **5.** statute.

sta·tant (stā′tənt) *adj. Heraldry.* In profile and having all four feet on the ground: *a lion statant.* [Probably from Latin *stāre* (past participle *status*), to stand + -ANT.]

state (stāt) *n.* **1.** A condition or mode of being with regard to a set of circumstances; a position: *the state of play; a state of disrepair.* **2.** A condition of being in a stage or form, as of structure, growth, or development: *the fetal state.* **3.** A mental or emotional condition or disposition: *a state of shock.* **4.** *Informal.* A condition of excitement or distress: *got himself into a state.* **5.** *Physics.* The condition of a physical system as specified by a set of appropriate macroscopic or quantum variables: *the proton state of the nucleon.* **6.** A social position or rank: *lived in a way appropriate to her state.* **7.** Ceremony; pomp; formality: *robes of state.* **8.** *Sometimes* **State. a.** The supreme public power within a sovereign political entity. Often preceded by *the*: *has been taken over by the state.* **b.** The sphere of supreme civil power within a given polity, often contrasted with the religious authority of the church: *matters of state.* **9.** A mode of government marked by a specified characteristic: *a welfare state; a police state.* **10.** A body politic; specifically, one constituting a nation: *the member states of the European Economic Community.* **11. a.** Any of the more or less internally autonomous territorial and political units composing a federation under a sovereign government: *the United States of America.* **b.** **States.** The United States of America. —See Usage note at **nation.** —**lie in state.** To be placed in public view for honors prior to burial.

~*tr.v.* **stated, stating, states. 1.** To set forth in words; declare. **2.** To present in speech or writing in a formal and deliberate manner: *stated the argument with cool precision.* **3.** To fix or settle; specify: *stated their conditions; at the stated time.*

~*adj. Sometimes* **State. 1. a.** Of, pertaining to, or maintained by a national government: *a state school; state control.* **b.** Of, pertaining to, or maintained by the government of an internally autonomous state: *the State University of New York.* **2. a.** Of or involving pomp and ceremony. **b.** Reserved for, used for, or done on ceremonial occasions: *a state banquet.* [Middle English *stat(e),* from Old French *estat,* from Latin *status,* manner of standing, condition, position, attitude.]
  Synonyms: condition, situation, status.

state capitalism *n.* A form of capitalism in which state control of capital, as through ownership of industries, plays a major part in a country's economic direction.

state·craft (stāt′krăft′, -kräft′) *n.* The art of managing the affairs or business of a nation or state.

State Department *n.* The foreign affairs department of the U.S. government.

state·hood (stāt′hŏŏd′) *n.* The condition of being a state, especially one of the states of the U.S., rather than a territory or a dependency.

state house, State House *n.* A building in which a state legislature holds sessions.

state·less (stāt′lĭs) *adj.* Having no national status. —**state·less·ness** *n.*

state·ly (stāt′lē) *adj.* **-lier, -liest. 1.** Marked by a graceful, dignified formality: *the stately progress of the royal party.* **2.** Majestic; grand. —See Synonyms at **grand.**
  ~*adv.* In a grand, imposing manner. [Middle English *statly,* suitable to a person of rank, from *stat,* person of rank, STATE.] —**state·li·ness** *n.*

state·ment (stāt′mənt) *n.* **1.** The act of stating or declaring. **2.** Something stated; an assertion or formal declaration: *issued no statement.* **3.** An account showing an amount due, received, or paid, such as a bank sends regularly to one of its customers. **4.** The presentation of a phrase, tune, or theme in a musical composition. **5.** *Computer Science.* An elementary instruction in a computer's source language.

Stat·en Island (stăt′n). Island in New York Bay, in southeastern New York State, southwest of Manhattan Island. It forms the borough of Staten Island, one of the five boroughs of New York City, and is coextensive with Richmond County.

state of the art *n.* The level or stage of development reached in a particular area, as technology or industry, at a particular time.

state-of-the-art (stāt′əv-thē-ärt′) *adj.* Of, pertaining to, or using the most advanced technology.

state of war *n.* The condition of being at war; especially, this condition as recognized by a formal declaration of war and as officially acknowledged by the two parties in conflict.

state·room (stāt′rŏŏm′, -rŏŏm′) *n.* A private cabin or compartment on a ship or train.

state's attorney *n.* A prosecuting attorney for a state. Also called "state attorney."

state's evidence, State's evidence *n.* **1.** Evidence for the prosecution in U.S. state or federal trials. **2.** A person who gives evidence for the state in criminal proceedings.

States-Gen·er·al (stāts′jĕn′ər-əl) *n.* **1.** The legislative assembly in France before the Revolution. Also called "Estates-General." **2.** The two-chamber parliament of the Netherlands. [Translation of French *états généraux.*]

state·side, State·side (stāt′sīd′) *adj.* Of, pertaining to, or in the continental United States.
  ~*adv. Informal.* To, toward, or in the continental United States.

states·man (stāts′mən) *n., pl.* **-men** (-mĭn). One who takes a prominent part in national or international political affairs; especially, a political leader respected for his outstanding wisdom, ability, and integrity. —**states·man·like** (stāts′mən-līk′), **states·man·ly** (-lē) *adj.* —**states·man·ship** (-shĭp′) *n.*

state socialism *n.* A form of socialism in which the state has considerable control over key areas of finance and industry.

States' rights *pl.n.* **1.** All rights not delegated to the federal government by the Constitution nor denied by it to the states. **2.** A political stance advocating strict interpretation of the Constitution with regard to the limitation of federal powers. —**States' righter** *n.*

states·wom·an (stāts′wŏŏm′ən) *n., pl.* **-women** (-wĭm′ĭn). A woman who is a leader in the affairs of a nation.

stat·ic (stăt′ĭk) *adj.* Also **stat·i·cal** (-ĭ-kəl). **1.** *Physics.* **a.** Acting but causing no motion. Said of a force. **b.** Pertaining to or involving statics. **2.** *Electricity.* Of, pertaining to, or producing stationary charges; electrostatic. **3.** Of, pertaining to, or produced by random radio noise. **4.** Not changing or developing; fixed.
  ~*n.* **1.** Random noise in a receiver, as hissing or crackling in a radio or specks on a television screen. **2.** *Slang.* **a.** Back talk. **b.** Interference; obstruction. **c.** Angry criticism. [New Latin *staticus,* from Greek *statikos,* causing to stand, from *statos,* placed, standing.] —**stat·i·cal·ly** *adv.*

static electricity *n.* **1.** An accumulation of electric charge on an insulated body. **2.** Electric discharge resulting from this.

static line *n.* A line attached to a parachute and an aircraft to open the parachute when the wearer has jumped clear of the aircraft.

stat·ics (stăt′ĭks) *n. Used with a singular verb.* A branch of mechanics dealing with the study of the forces acting on systems of bodies in equilibrium. Compare **dynamics, kinetics.** [New Latin *statica,* from Greek *statikē (tekhnē),* (science) of weighing, from *statikos,* causing to stand, skilled in weighing. See **static.**]

sta·tion (stā′shən) *n.* **1.** The place or position where a person or thing stands or is assigned to stand; a post: *a sentry station.* **2.** The place, building, or establishment from which a service is provided or operations are directed: *a police station; a gas station.* **3. a.** A stopping place along a route, especially one on a railroad line where passengers and goods may be taken onto a train. **b.** The buildings of such a station. **4.** Social position; status; rank. **5.** An establishment equipped for observation and study: *a radar station.* **6.** An establishment equipped for radio or television transmission. **7. a.** The wavelength on which a particular television or radio program is broadcast. **b.** The organization broadcasting on this wavelength. **8.** In surveying, a point at which an observation may be taken. **9.** In Australia: **a.** A large farm for raising cattle or sheep. **b.** A sheep run or cattle run. **10.** A military post, especially one in which British officers and administrative officials formerly resided in India. **11.** Any of the stations of the cross.
  ~*tr.v.* **stationed, -tioning, -tions.** To assign to a position or station; post. [Middle English *stacioun,* a standing still, from Latin *statiō* (stem *statiōn-*), from *stāre,* to stand.]

sta·tion·ar·y (stā′shə-nĕr′ē) *adj. Abbr.* **sta., stat. 1. a.** Fixed in position; not moving. **b.** Not capable of being moved; not portable: *a stationary engine.* **2.** Remaining in a fixed state or at a fixed level: *Her temperature was stationary.* [Middle English *stationarye,* from Latin *stationārius,* from *statiō,* a standstill, STATION.]

stationary front *n.* A transition zone between two nearly stationary air masses of different density.

stationary orbit *n. Aerospace.* **Synchronous orbit** (see).

stationary point *n. Mathematics.* A point on a graph at which the tangent is either horizontal or vertical, indicating either a point of inflection or a maximum or minimum.

stationary satellite *n.* An artificial satellite in a synchronous orbit.

stationary wave *n.* A **standing wave** (see).

station break *n.* An intermission in a radio or television program for identification of the network or station.

sta·tion·er (stā′shə-nər) *n.* **1.** One who sells stationery. **2.** *Obsolete.* A publisher or bookseller. [Middle English *staciouner,* from Medieval Latin *stationārius,* shopkeeper, from *statiō,* shop, from Latin, STATION.]

sta·tion·er·y (stā′shə-nĕr′ē) *n.* **1.** Writing paper and envelopes. **2.** Writing materials such as paper, pens, and inks.

station house *n.* A building used as a station, especially a police station or a fire station.

sta·tion·mas·ter (stā′shən-măs′tər, -mä′stər) *n.* An official in charge of a railroad or bus station.

stations of the cross, Stations of the Cross *pl.n.* **1.** A series of usually 14 crosses, often accompanied by images, set up in a church or along a path commemorating 14 events in the Passion of Jesus. **2.** The devotional meditations performed before these crosses and images.

station wagon *n.* An automobile having an extended interior with a third seat or luggage platform and a tailgate.

stat·ism (stā′tĭz′əm) *n.* The act or policy of strengthening the economic and political power of a state, as by increasing its control over industries and the mass media. [STATE + -ISM.]

stat·ist (stā′tĭst) *n.* An advocate of statism. —**stat·ist** *adj.*

sta·tis·tic (stə-tĭs′tĭk) *n.* **1.** Any numerical datum. **2.** An estimate of a parameter, as of the population mean or variance, obtained from a sample. [Back-formation from STATISTICS.] —**sta·tis·ti·cal** (stə-tĭs′tĭ-kəl) *adj.* —**sta·tis·ti·cal·ly** *adv.*

statistical mechanics *n.* The study of the theory in which the properties of a physical system are predicted by the statistical behavior of their constituent particles.

steam *The Industrial Revolution was built on steam power, and by the 19th century engineers were using it to drive almost every mechanical device, including clocks such as this one in Vancouver, British Columbia.*

stat·is·ti·cian (stăt'ə-stĭsh'ən) *n.* **1.** A mathematician specializing in statistics. **2.** A compiler of statistical data.

sta·tis·tics (stə-tĭs'tĭks) *n. Abbr.* **stat. 1.** *Used with a singular verb.* The mathematics of the collection, organization, and interpretation of numerical data; especially, the analysis of population characteristics or social phenomena by inference from sampling. **2.** *Used with a plural verb.* A collection of numerical data. [German *Statistik,* originally "political science dealing with state affairs," from New Latin *statisticus,* of state affairs, from Latin *status,* state.]

sta·tive (stā'tĭv) *adj.* Belonging to or designating a class of verbs that express a state or condition; for example, *know, like,* and *doubt* are stative verbs.
~*n.* A verb of this class.

stato– *prefix.* Indicates: **1.** Position; for example, **statocyst. 2.** Resting, remaining, or surviving; for example, **statoblast.** [Greek *statos,* placed, standing.]

stat·o·blast (stăt'ə-blăst', -bläst') *n.* An asexually produced encapsulated bud of a freshwater bryozoan from which new individuals develop after the parent colony has disintegrated. [STATO- + -BLAST.]

stat·o·cyst (stăt'ə-sĭst') *n.* A small organ of balance in many invertebrates, consisting of a fluid-filled sac containing statoliths that help indicate position when the animal moves. Also called "otocyst." [STATO- + CYST.]

stat·o·lith (stăt'l-ĭth') *n.* **1.** A small, movable concretion of calcium carbonate, found in statocysts. **2.** Any of various starch grains found in some plant cells and thought to function in the plant's response to gravity. [STATO- + -LITH.]

sta·tor (stā'tər) *n.* The stationary part of a motor, dynamo, turbine, or other rotary machine. [New Latin, from Latin, one that stands, from *stāre* (past participle *status*), to stand.]

stat·o·scope (stăt'ə-skōp') *n.* A sensitive form of aneroid barometer used in aircraft to indicate small changes of height but not the absolute altitude. [Greek *statos,* stationary + -SCOPE.]

stat·u·ar·y (stăch'o͞o-ĕr'ē) *n., pl.* **-ies.** *Abbr.* **stat. 1.** Statues collectively. **2.** A sculptor. **3.** The art of making statues.
~*adj.* Of, pertaining to, or suitable for a statue or statues. [Latin *statuāria,* the art of making statues, and *statuārius,* sculptor, from *statuārius,* of a statue, from *statua,* STATUE.]

stat·ue (stăch'o͞o) *n.* A three-dimensional figure or image, as of a famous person, sculpted, modeled, carved, or cast in material such as stone, clay, wood, or bronze. [Middle English, from Old French, from Latin *statua,* from *statuere,* to set up, erect.]

Statue of Liberty. A colossal statue in New York Harbor representing liberty as a woman with a torch raised in one hand and a book in the other arm. The statue was a gift from France in 1876. Its centennial was the occasion of a gala celebration in July 1986.

stat·u·esque (stăch'o͞o-ĕsk') *adj.* Suggestive of a statue, as in proportion, grace, or dignity; stately. **—stat·u·esque·ly** *adv.*

stat·u·ette (stăch'o͞o-ĕt') *n.* A small statue.

stat·ure (stăch'ər) *n.* **1.** The natural height of a human or animal body in an upright position. **2. a.** A level, status, or degree, as of achievement or recognition; caliber. **b.** A high degree of worth or eminence. [Middle English *statur(e),* from Old French *(e)stature,* from Latin *statūra.*]

sta·tus (stā'təs, stăt'əs) *n.* **1.** The legal character or condition of a person or thing: *What is your marital status?* **2.** A relative position; especially, relative social or professional position. **3.** High standing; prestige. **4.** A state of affairs; situation. —See Synonyms at **state.** [Latin *status,* state.]

sta·tus quo (stā'təs kwō', stăt'əs) *n.* The existing condition or state of affairs. [Latin, "state in which."]

status symbol *n.* Something that is desirable because of the social prestige it confers upon its possessor: *He bought a sports car purely as a status symbol.*

stat·u·ta·ble (stăch'o͞o-tə-bəl) *adj.* Enacted, regulated, recognized, or authorized by statute; statutory.

stat·ute (stăch'o͞ot) *n. Abbr.* **st., St., stat. 1.** A law enacted by a legislative body and formally recorded in writing; often distinguished from **common law** *(see).* **2.** An established law or rule, as of a body or an institution: *club statutes.* [Middle English *statut(e),* from Old French *(e)statut,* from Late Latin *statūtum,* from the neuter of *statūtus,* past participle of *statuere,* to set up, decree.]

statute book *n.* A written record of enacted legislation: *put a law on the statute book.*

statute law *n.* A law or rule established by legislative enactment. Compare **common law.**

statute mile *n.* The standard **mile** (sense 1) *(see).*

statute of limitations *n. Law.* A statute setting a time limit on enforcement of a right in certain cases.

stat·u·to·ry (stăch'ə-tôr'ē, -tōr'ē) *adj.* **1.** Of or pertaining to a statute. **2.** Enacted, regulated, or authorized by statute. **3.** *Informal.* Designating an object, action, or behavior that has become typical through its frequency: *got up and had her statutory cup of coffee.* [STATUTE + -ORY.]

statutory offense *n.* A legal offense declared by statute; especially, statutory rape.

statutory rape *n.* Sexual intercourse with a female who is below the statutory age of consent.

St. Au·gus·tine (sānt ô'gə-stēn'). City of northeastern Florida, on a peninsula separated from the Atlantic Ocean by Anastasia Island. The oldest city in the United States, it was founded by the Spanish in 1565 and ceded to the United States in 1821. It has many old landmarks and today is a year-round resort center.

staunch (stônch, stŏnch) *adj.* **stauncher, staunchest.** Also **stanch** (stŏnch, stănch) **stancher, stanchest. 1.** Firm and steadfast; true. **2. a.** Strong or substantial in construction or constitution. **b.** Watertight. —See Synonyms at **faithful.**
~*tr.v.* Variant of **stanch.** [Middle English *staunche, stanch,* watertight, firm, strong, from Old French *estanche,* from *estanch(i)er,* to STANCH.] **—staunch·ly** *adv.* **—staunch·ness** *n.*

stau·ro·lite (stôr'ə-līt') *n.* A brownish-black mineral, $FeAl_4Si_2O_{10}(OH)_2$, often having crossed intergrown crystals and sometimes used as a gem. [French : Greek *stauros,* cross + -LITE.] **—stau·ro·lit·ic** (stôr'ə-lĭt'ĭk) *adj.*

stau·ro·scope (stôr'ə-skōp') *n.* An optical instrument used to study the crystal structure of minerals with polarized light. [Greek *stauros,* cross + -SCOPE.]

stave (stāv) *n.* **1.** A narrow strip of wood forming part of the sides of a barrel, tub, or the like. **2. a.** A rung of a ladder. **b.** A crosspiece on a chair. **3.** A long, thick stick, especially one used as a weapon. **4.** A musical **staff** *(see).* **5.** A set of verses; stanza.
~*v.* **staved** or **stove** (stōv), **staving, staves.** *—tr.* **1.** To break in or puncture the staves of. **2.** To break or smash a hole in: *staved in a boat.* **3.** To crush or smash inward. *—intr.* To be or become crushed or broken in. **—stave off.** To ward off; avert. [Back-formation from *staves,* plural of STAFF.]

Usage: The past tense and past participial form of this verb is usually *staved*: *I think we've staved off her visit. Stove* is restricted to nautical contexts: *The ship's side was stove in.*

staves. Alternate plural of **staff.**

staves·a·cre (stāvz'ā'kər) *n.* **1.** A larkspur, *Delphinium staphisagria,* of southern Europe, having deep blue flowers. **2.** The poisonous seeds of this plant, formerly used externally as a parasiticide. [Middle English *staphisagre, stafisagre,* from Latin *staphis agria,* from Greek, "wild raisin" : *staphis, astaphis*†, raisin + *agria,* feminine of *agrios,* wild, "of the field," from *agros,* field.]

stay[1] (stā) *v.* **stayed, staying, stays.** *—intr.* **1.** To remain or continue in a specified place or condition: *stayed behind; stayed in bed; stay out of trouble.* **2. a.** To remain or sojourn as a guest or lodger. **b.** *Scottish.* To reside permanently; live. **c.** To wait; pause. **3.** To hold on; endure. **4.** In poker, to meet a bet without raising it. **5. a.** To stop moving; cease. **b.** To keep up in a race or contest: *stayed with the rest of the runners till the last lap.* *—tr.* **1.** To stop or halt; check. **2.** To postpone; delay; especially, to delay or stop the effect or course of by intervening measures: *stayed legal proceedings.* **3.** To satisfy or appease (hunger, for example) temporarily. **4.** To remain for (a specified period of time): *She stayed the week.* **5.** To endure to the end; last out: *couldn't stay the course.* **6.** To wait for; await. **—stay put.** To remain in the place or position that one is occupying.
~*n.* **1.** The action of stopping or coming to a stop. **2.** A sojourn or visit. **3.** A suspension or postponement of a legal action or execution. [Middle English *steyen,* to halt, from Old French *ester* (present stem *estei-*), to stand, stop, from Latin *stāre.*] **—stay·er** *n.*

Synonyms: *abide, linger, remain, tarry, wait.*

stay[2] *tr.v.* **stayed, staying, stays. 1.** To brace, support, or prop up. Often used with *up.* **2.** To strengthen or sustain mentally or spiritually; comfort.
~*n.* **1.** A support or prop: *She was a stay during the crisis.* **2.** A strip of bone, plastic, or metal used to stiffen a garment or part such as a corset or shirt collar. **3. stays.** A corset stiffened with stays. [Old French *estayer,* to support, from *estaie,* support, from Germanic; see **stay** (rope).]

stay[3] *n.* **1.** A heavy rope or cable, usually of wire, used as a brace or support for a mast or spar. **2.** Any rope used for a similar purpose; a guy line. **—in stays.** In the process of coming about to the opposite tack. Said of a ship.
~*v.* **stayed, staying, stays.** *—tr.* **1.** To brace or support with a stay or stays. **2.** To put (a ship) on the opposite tack. *—intr.* To come about to the opposite tack. Used of a ship. [Middle English *stey, stay,* Old English *stæg,* from Germanic *staga-* (unattested).]

stay-at-home (stā'ət-hōm') *n.* One who habitually stays at home; especially, one who leads a sheltered, unadventurous life. **—stay-at-home** *adj.*

staying power *n.* The ability to endure or last.

stay·sail (stā'səl, -sāl') *n.* A triangular sail hoisted on a stay.

St. Ber·nard Pass (sānt' bər-närd'). Either of two Alpine passes. The Great St. Bernard Pass, height 2,472 meters (8,110 feet), links Piedmont, Italy, with Valais, Switzerland, and was the route by which Napoleon I crossed into Italy (1800). At its summit there is a hospice (11th century) founded by St. Bernard of Menthon, which formerly bred St. Bernard dogs to search for travelers trapped by snow. Beneath it is a road tunnel (1964). The Little St. Bernard Pass, height 2,187 meters (7,178 feet), which links Piedmont with Savoie, France, also has a hospice (11th century) founded by St. Bernard and was the route by which Hannibal is believed to have invaded Italy.

St. Chris·to·pher and Ne·vis (sānt krĭs'tə-fər; nē'vĭs, nĕv'ĭs). Also **St. Kitts-Ne·vis** (kĭts'nē'vĭs, -nĕv'ĭs). Formerly **St. Kitts-Ne·vis-An·guil·la** (-ăng-gwĭl'ə). Island state of the Caribbean. The two islands, five kilometers (three miles) apart, were the first Caribbean islands to be settled by the British (1623–28) but were also claimed by France until 1783. In 1967 the self-governing British Associated State of St. Kitts-Nevis-Anguilla was created. However, the Anguillans resented the link and finally became a separate United Kingdom dependency in 1980. St. Christopher and Nevis gained independence in 1983. Sugar is the mainstay of the economy; however, tourism is becoming a major source of income. Area, 262 square kilometers (101 square miles). Population, 44,400. Capital, Basseterre.

St. Croix (sānt kroi'). Island, 207 square kilometers (80 square miles), in the West Indies. It is the largest of the U.S. Virgin Islands.

STD sexually transmitted disease.

std. standard.

St. De·nis (săN də-nē'). Suburb of Paris, France, situated in the Seine-St. Denis department. Its abbey church (cathedral, 12th century) was the first in Gothic style. Several French monarchs are buried here.

St. Den·is (sānt dĕn'ĭs), **Ruth** (1878–1968). U.S. dancer and educator. Constantly exploring avenues as yet unknown to American dance, she studied the dance of foreign and ancient cultures and became interested in developing dance as a form of worship. She was married to the dancer Ted Shawn and worked often with him during her early career.

stead (stĕd) *n.* **1.** The place, position, or function properly or customarily occupied by another. **2.** Advantage; avail. Used chiefly in the phrase *stand someone in good stead.*
~tr.v. **steaded, steading, steads.** To be of advantage or service to; benefit; help. [Middle English, Old English *stede.*]

stead·fast, sted·fast (stĕd'făst', -fäst', -fəst) *adj.* **1.** Fixed or unchanging; steady: *a steadfast gaze.* **2.** Firmly loyal or constant; unswerving. —See Synonyms at **faithful.** [Middle English *stedefast,* Old English *stedefæst,* fixed in one place : *stede,* place, STEAD + *fæst,* fixed, FAST.] **—stead·fast·ly** *adv.* **—stead·fast·ness** *n.*

stead·y (stĕd'ē) *adj.* **-ier, -iest. 1.** Firm in position or place; fixed. **2.** Direct and unfaltering; sure: *a steady aim.* **3.** Regular, even, and continuous in action, movement, quality, or pace: *slow but steady progress.* **4.** Not easily excited or upset; controlled: *steady nerves.* **5. a.** Regular; habitual: *a steady boyfriend.* **b.** Reliable; dependable. **c.** Temperate; sober.
~v. **steadied, -ying, -ies.** *—tr.* To make steady; stabilize. *—intr.* To become steady.
~interj. **1.** Used to urge care and self-control. **2.** *Nautical.* Used to direct the helmsman to keep the ship's head in the same direction.
~n., pl. **steadies.** *Slang.* A regular boyfriend or girlfriend.
~adv. In a steady manner. **—go steady.** *Informal.* To go out socially on a regular basis with the same member of the opposite sex. [From STEAD, place (after Middle Low German *stēdig,* stable).] **—stead·i·er** *n.* **—stead·i·ly** *adv.* **—stead·i·ness** *n.*
Synonyms: *constant, equable, even, uniform.*

steady state *n.* A stable condition that does not change over time or in which change in one direction is continually balanced by change in another.

stead·y-state theory (stĕd'ē-stāt') *n.* A cosmological theory that assumes that the large-scale view of the universe is independent of the position of the observer in space and time and that the expansion of the universe, required on other grounds, is compensated for by the continuous creation of matter. Compare **big-bang theory.**

steak (stāk) *n.* **1.** A slice of meat, beef unless otherwise specified, typically cut thick and usually broiled or fried. **2.** A thick slice of a large fish cut across the body. **3.** A patty of ground meat broiled or fried: *hamburg steak.* [Middle English *ste(y)ke, styke,* from Old Norse *steik,* piece of meat roasted on a spit, from *steikja,* to roast on a spit.]

steak·house (stāk'hous') *n.* A restaurant that serves steaks as a specialty.

steak tar·tare (tär-tär', tär'tər) *n.* Raw ground beef mixed with onion, seasoning, and raw egg and eaten raw. Also called "tartare steak." [STEAK + French *tartare,* Tartar.]

steal (stēl) *v.* **stole** (stōl), **stolen** (stō'lən), **stealing, steals.** *—tr.* **1. a.** To take (an object) without right or permission, often in a surreptitious way. **b.** To take or appropriate (an idea, for example) without permission or acknowledging the source. **2.** To get, take, gain, or effect secretly or artfully: *steal a kiss; steal a glance.* **3.** To move, carry, or place surreptitiously. **4.** *Baseball.* To gain (a base) without the aid of a hit, error, or wild pitch. Used of a base runner. *—intr.* **1.** To commit theft. **2. a.** To move stealthily or unobtrusively: *stole away from the party.* **b.** To happen, pass, or elapse gently and imperceptibly: *The days stole past.* **3.** *Baseball.* To steal a base. —See Synonyms at **rob.**
~n. **1.** The act or an instance of stealing. **2.** *Informal.* A bargain. **3.** *Baseball.* The act of stealing a base. [Middle English *stelen,* Old English *stelan.*] **—steal·er** *n.*

stealth (stĕlth) *n.* **1.** The act of moving, proceeding, or acting in a covert way. **2.** Furtiveness; covertness. **3.** *Archaic.* The act of stealing. [Middle English *stalth, stelth,* probably from Old English *stǣlth* (unattested) : STEAL (to move stealthily) + -TH.]

stealth·y (stĕl'thē) *adj.* **-ier, -iest.** Characterized by stealth; cautiously unobtrusive and secretive. —See Synonyms at **secret.** **—stealth·i·ly** *adv.* **—stealth·i·ness** *n.*

steam (stēm) *n.* **1.** The hot gaseous phase of water formed when water boils. **2.** The white visible mist of water vapor containing small droplets of water, seen when hot water boils or evaporates. **3.** The use of steam as a source of power; especially, the use of steam-powered locomotives: *the age of steam.* Also used adjectivally: *a steam railroad.* **4. a.** The power generated by the use of steam: *get up steam.* **b.** *Informal.* Energy, driving force, or means of progress: *running out of steam; got here under my own steam.* **5.** Pent-up emotions or nervous energy: *letting off steam.*
~v. **steamed, steaming, steams.** *—intr.* **1.** To produce or emit steam. **2.** To become or rise up as steam. **3.** To become misted or covered with steam. Used with *up.* **4.** To move by means of steam power. **5.** *Informal.* To be extremely angry or emotional. **6.** *Informal.* To move energetically and rapidly. *—tr.* **1.** To cook (food) by exposing to steam. **2.** To expose or subject to steam: *steamed a stamp off an envelope.* **3.** *Informal.* To cause to become bad tempered or irritated. Often used in the passive with *up*: *no need to get all steamed up.* [Middle English *steme,* vapor, exhalation, Old English *stēam,* from West Germanic *stauma* (unattested).]

steam bath *n.* **1.** A bath in which bodily impurities are sweated out by the action and heat of steam. **2.** A place where one takes such a bath.

steam beer *n.* A highly effervescent western U.S. beer.

steam·boat (stēm'bōt') *n.* A **steamship** *(see).*

steam boiler *n.* A closed tank in which water is converted into steam under pressure.

steam chest *n.* A compartment in a steam engine that encloses the slide valve and through which steam is delivered from the boiler to a cylinder.

steam engine *n.* An engine that converts the heat energy of pressurized steam into mechanical energy, especially one in which steam drives a piston in a closed cylinder.

steam·er (stē'mər) *n. Abbr.* **str. 1.** A steamship. **2.** A container in which something, such as food, is steamed.

steamer trunk *n.* A small trunk originally designed to fit under the bunk of a steamship cabin.

steam·fit·ter (stēm'fĭt'ər) *n.* A person whose occupation is the installation and repair of heating, ventilating, refrigerating, and air-conditioning systems. **—steam·fit·ting** *n.*

steam heating *n.* A heating system by which steam is generated in a boiler and piped to radiators.

steam iron *n.* A pressing iron that holds and heats water to be emitted as steam on the cloth being pressed.

steam point *n.* The temperature at which the vapor phase of water is in equilibrium with the liquid phase. At standard pressure, the steam point is 100°C. Compare **ice point.**

steam radio *n. British Informal.* Radio broadcasting considered as being old-fashioned by comparison with television.

steam·roll·er (stēm'rō'lər) *n.* **1. a.** A steam-driven machine used chiefly for rolling road surfaces flat. **b.** Loosely, any heavy rolling machine similarly used. **2.** A ruthless or irresistible force or power.
~v. **steamrollered, -ering, -ers.** *—tr.* **1.** To work or roll (a surface) with a steamroller. **2. a.** To overwhelm or suppress ruthlessly; crush. **b.** To bring or impel by means of an irresistible force. *—intr.* To move or proceed with overwhelming or crushing force.

steam room *n.* A room filled with steam in which one can take a steam bath.

steam·ship (stēm'shĭp') *n. Abbr.* **SS, S.S.** A large vessel propelled by one or more steam-driven propellers. Also called "steamboat," "steamer."

steam shovel *n.* A steam-driven excavating machine.

steam table *n.* **1.** A table giving the properties of steam under different conditions of pressure. **2.** A table equipped to hold containers of cooked food kept warm by hot water or steam.

steam turbine *n.* A turbine operated by highly pressurized steam directed against or through vanes on a rotor.

steam·y (stē'mē) *adj.* **-ier, -iest. 1.** Filled with, covered with, or emitting steam. **2.** *Informal.* Full of sexual passion; erotic. **—steam·i·ly** *adv.* **—steam·i·ness** *n.*

ste·ap·sin (stē-ăp'sĭn) *n.* An enzyme of pancreatic juice that catalyzes the hydrolysis of fats to fatty acids and glycerol. [Greek *stear,* solid fat, suet, tallow (see **stearic**) + (PE)PSIN.]

ste·a·rate (stē'ə-rāt', stîr'āt') *n.* A salt or ester of stearic acid. [STEAR(IC) + -ATE.]

ste·ar·ic (stē-ăr'ĭk, stîr'ĭk) *adj.* Of, pertaining to, or similar to stearin or fat. [French *stéarique,* from Greek *stear,* solid fat, suet, tallow.]

stearic acid *n.* A colorless, odorless, waxlike fatty acid, $CH_3(CH_2)_{16}COOH$, occurring in natural animal and vegetable fats.

ste·a·rin (stē'ər-ĭn, stîr'ĭn) *n.* **1.** A colorless, odorless, tasteless ester of glycerol and stearic acid, $C_3H_5(C_{18}H_{35}O_2)_3$, used in the manufacture of soap and candles and for textile sizing. Also called "tristearin." **2.** Stearic acid, especially as used commercially. **3.** The solid form of fat. [French *stéarine* : Greek *stear,* solid fat, suet, tallow (see **stearic**) + -IN.]

ste·a·rop·tene (stē'ə-rŏp'tēn') *n.* The part of a natural essential oil that separates out as a white, crystalline solid on cooling or standing. [STEAR(IC) + Greek *ptēnos,* winged, "volatile."]

ste·a·tite (stē'ə-tīt') *n.* A massive, white-to-green talc used in paints, ceramics, and insulation. Also called "soapstone." [Latin *steatītis, steatītēs,* from Greek *steatitis, steatitēs,* "tallow stone" : STEAT(O)- + -ITE.] **—ste·a·tit·ic** (stē'ə-tĭt'ĭk) *adj.*

steato– *prefix.* Indicates fat; for example, **steatopygia.** [Greek, from *stear* (stem *steat-*), solid fat, tallow. See **stearic.**]

ste·a·tol·y·sis (stē'ə-tŏl'ə-sĭs) *n.* The digestive emulsification of fats prior to assimilation. [New Latin : STEATO- + -LYSIS.]

ste·at·o·pyg·i·a (stē-ăt'ə-pĭj'ē-ə, -pī'gē-ə) *n.* An excessive accumulation of fat on the buttocks. [STEATO- + Greek *pugē,* rump (see **pygidium**).] **—ste·at·o·pyg·ic** (stē-ăt'ə-pĭj'ĭk, -pī'jĭk), **ste·at·o·py·gous** (-pī'gəs) *adj.*

ste·at·or·rhe·a (stē-ăt'ə-rē'ə, stē'ə-tə-) *n.* **1.** Excessive discharge of

steam engine *An Italian steam locomotive. The first practical steam engines were stationary; they were used in 18th-century Britain to pump water from mines.*

steamroller *Road-building machines are no longer powered by steam, but the steamroller has entered the language as an image of unstoppable power. Steam-powered machines, like the one shown here, were first used in the 1860's.*

steinbok *Most antelopes instinctively bound away from danger. But the steinbok, which spends most of each year alone, may react by lying flat on the ground and relying on its natural camouflage. Steinboks make their homes in dry scrubland in southern and eastern Africa as far north as Kenya.*

PRONUNCIATION KEY

ă, pat; ā, pay; âr, care;
ä, father, are; b, **bib**;
ch, **church**; d, **deed**; ĕ, pet;
ē, be; f, **fife**; g, **gag**; h, **hat**;
hw, **which**; ĭ, pit; ī, pie;
îr, pier; j, **judge**; k, **kick**;
l, **lid**, **needle**; m, **mum**;
n, **no**, **sudden**; ng, **thing**;
ŏ, pot; ō, toe; ô, **paw**, for;
oi, noise; ou, **out**; ŏŏ, **book**;
ōō, **boot**; p, **pop**; r, **roar**;
s, **sauce**; sh, **ship**, **dish**;
t, **tight**; th, **thin**, **path**;
th, **this**, **bathe**; ŭ, cut; ûr, **fur**;
v, **valve**; w, **with**; y, **yes**;
z, **zebra**, **size**; zh, **vision**;
ə, **about**, **item**, **edible**,
gallop, **circus**, **peaceful**

IN FOREIGN WORDS:

à, *Fr.* ami; œ, *Fr.* **feu**, *Ger.* **schön**; ü, *Fr.* **tu**, *Ger.* **über**; KH, *Ger.* **ich**, *Scot.* **loch**; N, *Fr.* bon; y', *Fr.* Compiègne

STRESS MARKS:

Primary stress: ′
in·cite′ (ĭn-sīt′)
Secondary stress: ′
in′sight′ (ĭn′sīt′)

fat in the feces. **2.** Overaction of the sebaceous glands; seborrhea. [New Latin : STEATO- + -RRHEA.]

Stę·bark (stĕNm′bärk′). *German* **Tan·nen·berg** (tăn′ən-bûrg′, tä′nən-bĕrk′). Town in northeastern Poland, formerly in East Prussia. It was the site of a battle (1914) in which a German army commanded by Gen. Von Hindenburg defeated the Russians.

stedfast. Variant of **steadfast.**

steed (stēd) *n.* A horse, especially one that is spirited. [Middle English *stede,* Old English *stēda,* stallion.]

steel (stēl) *n.* **1.** Any of various generally hard, strong, durable, malleable alloys of iron and carbon, usually containing between 0.02 to 1.5 percent carbon, often with other constituents such as manganese, chromium, nickel, molybdenum, copper, tungsten, cobalt, or silicon, depending on the desired alloy properties, and widely used as a structural material. **2.** A quality suggestive of steel; especially, a hard, unflinching character. **3.** Something made of steel, especially: **a.** A weapon such as a sword, knife, or the like. **b.** A knife sharpener consisting of a handled steel rod. **c.** A slender strip or band of steel used for stiffening. **4.** *Finance.* **a.** The steel industry. **b. steels.** The market quotation for shares in the steel industry. **5. a.** A dark gray to purplish gray. Also called "steel gray." **b.** A dark grayish blue. Also called "steel blue."
~*adj.* **1.** Made of or with steel. **2. a.** Resembling the properties of steel. **b.** Of the color steel. **3.** Of or pertaining to the production of steel.
~*tr.v.* **steeled, steeling, steels. 1.** To cover, plate, edge, or point with steel. **2.** To make strong, resolute, or resistant; strengthen. [Middle English *stel(le), stiel,* Old English *stēli, stȳle.*]

steel band *n.* A musical band of a type originating in the West Indies, composed chiefly of percussion instruments fashioned from oil drums.

Steele (stēl), **Sir Richard** (1672–1729). Irish-born playwright and essayist. He founded *The Tatler* (1709) and was a leading contributor (1711–12) to the *Spectator,* for which he invented the character Sir Roger de Coverley, a jovial English squire.

steel engraving *n.* **1.** The art or process of engraving on a steel plate. **2.** An impression produced with an engraved steel plate.

steel·head (stēl′hĕd′) *n.* The rainbow trout of North America when occurring in marine waters or large inland lakes.

steel wool *n.* Fine fibers of steel woven or matted together to form an abrasive for cleansing, smoothing, or polishing.

steel·work (stēl′wûrk′) *n.* **1.** Something made of steel. **2. steelworks.** *Used with a singular or plural verb.* A plant where steel is made. **—steel·work·er** *n.*

steel·y (stē′lē) *adj.* **-ier, -iest. 1.** Made of steel. **2.** Like steel, as in coldness or hardness: *steely eyes.* **—steel·i·ness** *n.*

steel·yard (stēl′yärd′) *n.* A balance consisting of a scaled arm suspended off center, a hook at the shorter end on which to hang the object being weighed, and a counterbalance at the longer end. [STEEL + YARD (rod).]

Steen (stēn, stān), **Jan** (*c.* 1626–79). Dutch painter. He specialized in domestic and tavern scenes, among them *The Music Lesson, The Skittle Alley,* and *The Lute Player.*

steenbok. Variant of **steinbok.**

steep¹ (stēp) *adj.* **steeper, steepest. 1.** Having a sharp inclination; nearly perpendicular; precipitous. **2.** Rising or falling rapidly or precipitously. **3. a.** Excessive; exorbitant: *a steep price.* **b.** Difficult to believe, accept, or do.
~*n.* A precipitous slope; a steep place. [Middle English *stepe,* Old English *stēap,* lofty, deep, projecting.] **—steep·ly** *adv.* **—steep·ness** *n.*

steep² *v.* **steeped, steeping, steeps.** *—tr.* **1.** To soak in liquid in order to cleanse, soften, or extract some property. **2.** To infuse or subject thoroughly; immerse: *steeped in misery.* **3.** To make thoroughly wet. *—intr.* To undergo a soaking in liquid.
~*n.* **1. a.** The process of steeping. **b.** The state of being steeped. **2.** A liquid, bath, or solution in which something is steeped. [Middle English *stepen,* from Old English *stiepan* (unattested), from Germanic.] **—steep·er** *n.*

steep·en (stē′pən) *v.* **-ened, -ening, -ens.** *—tr.* To make steeper. *—intr.* To become steeper.

stee·ple (stē′pəl) *n.* **1.** A tall tower forming the superstructure of a building, especially a church, and usually surmounted by a spire. **2.** A spire. [Middle English *stepel, stepyl,* Old English *stīpel, stȳpel.*]

stee·ple·bush (stē′pəl-bŏŏsh′) *n.* A plant, the **hardhack** *(see).*

stee·ple·chase (stē′pəl-chās′) *n.* **1. a.** A horse race over a course provided with artificial obstacles. **b.** A horse race across open country. **2.** A long-distance running race over a course provided with hurdles and other obstacles.
~*intr.v.* **steeplechased, -chasing, -chases.** To take part in a steeplechase. [Church steeples were originally used as goals in such horse races.] **—stee·ple·chas·er** *n.*

stee·ple·jack (stē′pəl-jăk′) *n.* A worker on steeples or other very high structures. [STEEPLE + JACK (laborer).]

steer¹ (stîr) *v.* **steered, steering, steers.** *—tr.* **1.** To guide (a vessel or vehicle) by means of a device such as a rudder, paddle, or wheel. **2. a.** To direct the course of (a discussion or conversation, for example). **b.** To maneuver (a person) into a place or course of action. **3.** To set and follow (a particular course): *steered a course through the straits; tried to steer a middle course.* *—intr.* **1.** To guide a vessel or vehicle. **2.** To follow or move in a set course. **3.** To be capable of being steered or guided in a specified fashion: *a boat that steers easily.* **—steer clear of.** To avoid; keep away from.
~*n.* A piece of advice; hint or tip. [Middle English *steren,* Old English *stīeran.*] **—steer·a·ble** *adj.* **—steer·er** *n.*

steer² *n.* A young ox, especially one castrated and raised for beef. [Middle English *stere, steer,* Old English *stēor.*]

steer·age (stîr′ĭj) *n.* **1.** The action or practice of steering. **2.** The steering apparatus of a ship. **3.** The section of a passenger ship, originally near the rudder, providing the cheapest accommodation for passengers.

steer·age·way (stîr′ĭj-wā′) *n.* The minimum rate of motion required for the helm of a ship or boat to have effect.

steering committee *n.* A committee whose function it is to suggest issues to be considered and to arrange the order of business, as for a legislative body or other assembly.

steering gear *n.* The mechanism by which a vehicle, ship, or aircraft is steered.

steering wheel *n.* A wheel that is turned to control the steering gear, as on a motor vehicle or motorboat.

steers·man (stîrs′mən) *n., pl.* **-men** (-mĭn). A helmsman.

steeve¹ (stēv) *n.* A spar or derrick with a block at one end, used for stowing cargo.
~*tr.v.* **steeved, steeving, steeves.** To stow or pack (cargo) in the hold of a ship. [Middle English *steven,* to stow, from Spanish *estibar,* to cram, from Latin *stīpāre,* to stuff fully.]

steeve² *n. Nautical.* The angle formed by the bowsprit and the horizon or the keel.
~*v.* **steeved, steeving, steeves.** *Nautical.* *—tr.* To incline (a bowsprit) upward at an angle with the horizon or the keel. *—intr.* To have an upward inclination. Used of a bowsprit. [17th century : origin obscure.]

Stef·an-Boltz·mann law (stĕf′ən-bōlts′män′) *n.* A physical law stating that the total energy radiated from a blackbody is equal to the fourth power of its absolute temperature. [After Josef *Stefan* (1835–83), Austrian physicist, and Ludwig BOLTZMANN.]

Ste·fáns·son (stĕf′ən-sən), **Vilhjálmur** (1879–1962). Canadian explorer and ethnologist. In numerous expeditions to the Arctic, he explored much of the region and discovered that by following the Eskimos' diet and lifestyle it was possible for other people to be successful in living off the land in the far north.

Stef·fens (stĕf′ənz), **(Joseph) Lincoln** (1866–1936). U.S. journalist. As managing editor of *McClure's Magazine* (1901–06) he exposed corruption in city government, thereby beginning the era of muckraking journalism, though he eschewed the sensationalism employed by other muckrakers. Steffens later became interested in the revolutionary movements in Russia and Mexico and published a popular autobiography in 1931.

steg·o·don (stĕg′ə-dŏn′) *n.* Also **steg·o·dont** (-dŏnt′). Any of various extinct elephantlike mammals of the genus *Stegodon* and related genera, of the Pliocene to Pleistocene epoch. [New Latin *Stegodon,* "ridge-toothed" (from the distinctive ridges on its molars) : Greek *stegos,* roof, "ridge," from *stegein,* to cover + -ODONT.]

steg·o·saur (stĕg′ə-sôr′) *n.* Also **steg·o·sau·rus** (stĕg′ə-sôr′əs). Any of several herbivorous dinosaurs of the genus *Stegosaurus* and related genera, of the Triassic to the Cretaceous period, having a double row of upright bony plates along the back. [New Latin *Stegosaurus* : Greek *stegos,* roof, "ridge of plates" (see **stegodon**) + -SAUR.]

Stei·chen (stī′kən), **Edward Jean** (1879–1973). U.S. photographer, born in Luxembourg. After buying his first camera at the age of 16, he developed techniques to bring an impressionistic flavor to his work. While visiting Paris (1900–02) he became involved in the modern art movement. During both world wars he supervised aerial and combat photography.

Steiermark. See **Styria.**

stein (stīn) *n.* An earthenware mug, especially one for beer, usually holding about a pint. [German *Stein,* probably short for *Steingut,* stoneware, earthenware : *Stein,* stone + *Gut,* goods, ware.]

Stein (stīn), **Gertrude** (1874–1946). U.S. author and poet. Her unique style, which experimented with syntax, was influenced by her study of psychology. Her best-known work is *The Autobiography of Alice B. Toklas* (1933).

Stein·beck (stīn′bĕk′), **John Ernst** (1902–68). U.S. novelist. Many of his novels deal with social and economic conditions in California. His works include *The Grapes of Wrath* (1939) and *East of Eden* (1952). He won the Nobel Prize for literature in 1962.

Stein·berg (stīn′bûrg′, -bərg), **Saul** (1914–). U.S. graphic artist and cartoonist, born in Romania. He was already an established artist when he immigrated to the United States at the outbreak of World War II, and his water colors and murals earned him national recognition. His detailed and imaginative cartoons have adorned the pages of the *New Yorker* and other magazines for 30 years.

stein·bok (stīn′bŏk′) *n.* Also **steen·bok** (stēn′bŏk′, stān′-). **1.** An African antelope, *Raphicerus campestris neumanni,* having a brownish coat and short pointed horns in the male. **2.** An **ibex** *(see).* [Afrikaans, "stone buck."]

Stein·em (stī′nəm), **Gloria** (1935–). U.S. feminist and author. A vigorous campaigner for social reform, she became involved in the women's movement in 1968, helped organize the National Women's Political Caucus (1971), founded and edits *Ms.* magazine, and has become a highly respected advocate for sexual equality.

Stein·er (stī′nər, shtī′-), **Rudolf** (1861–1925). Austrian teacher and philosopher and the founder of anthroposophy.

Stein·metz (stīn′mĕts′), **Charles Proteus** (1865–1923). U.S. electrical engineer and inventor, born in Germany. A brilliant mathematician and physicist, he is best known for his theoretical studies of alternating current, which made possible advancements in electrical generators and motors.

ste·le (stē′lē) *n., pl.* **-les** or **-lae** (-lē). Also **ste·la** (stē′lə) *pl.* **-lae** (-lē) (for sense 1). **1.** An upright stone or slab with an inscribed or sculptured surface, used, especially in ancient times, to mark a grave, as a monument, or as a commemorative tablet. **2.** *Botany.* The central core of vascular tissue in a plant stem or root. [Latin *stēla,* from Greek *stēlē,* pillar.] **—ste·lar** (stē′lər) *adj.*

Stel·la (stĕl′ə), **Frank Philip** (1936–). U.S. painter. Noted for the emphasis of geometric shapes and color in his abstract works, he first achieved wide recognition with his series of black paintings that were exhibited in the Museum of Modern Art (1959–60).

stel·lar (stĕl′ər) *adj.* **1.** Of, relating to, or consisting of stars. **2.** Of, relating to, or worthy of a star performer. [Late Latin *stellāris,* from *stella,* star.]

stel·la·ra·tor (stĕl′ə-rā′tər) *n.* An apparatus used in thermonuclear research to contain a plasma in a toroidal vessel by means of a magnetic field. [STELLAR (the temperature used to heat the plasma approximates that in some stars) + -ATOR.]

stel·late (stĕl′āt′) *adj.* Also **stel·at·ed** (-ā′tĭd). *Biology.* Arranged or shaped like a star; radiating from a center. [Latin *stellātus,* from *stella,* star.] **—stel·late·ly** *adv.*

stel·li·form (stĕl′ə-fôrm′) *adj.* Star-shaped. [New Latin *stelliformis* : Latin *stella,* star (see **stellate**) + -FORM.]

stel·li·fy (stĕl′ə-fī′) *tr.v.* **-fied, -fying, -fies.** To transform into a star. [Middle English *stellifien,* from Old French *stellifier,* from Medieval Latin *stellificāre* : Latin *stella,* star + *facere,* to do, make.]

stel·lu·lar (stĕl′yə-lər) *adj.* **1.** Having the form of a small star or stars. **2.** Adorned with small stars. [Late Latin *stellula,* diminutive of Latin *stella,* star.]

St. El·mo's fire (sānt′ ĕl′mōz) *n.* A bluish electrical glow caused by corona discharge on masts and other high parts of a ship at sea before and during electrical storms. Also called "corposant." [After *St. Elmo,* patron saint of sailors.]

stem[1] (stĕm) *n.* **1. a.** The main ascending axis of a plant, which bears the leaves, flowers, and axillary buds. **b.** The corresponding part in nonflowering plants. **c.** A slender stalk supporting or connecting another plant part, such as a leaf or flower; a stalk. **2.** A banana stalk bearing several bunches of bananas. **3.** Something analogous to a plant stem, especially: **a.** The tube of a tobacco pipe. **b.** The slender upright support of a wine glass or goblet. **c.** The small projecting shaft bearing the knob with which a watch is wound. **d.** The rounded rod in the center of certain locks about which the key fits and is turned. **e.** The shaft of a feather or hair. **f.** The main line of descent of a family as distinguished from a branch. **g.** The upright stroke of a typeface or letter. **h.** The vertical line extending from the head of a musical note. **i.** The main part of a word to which inflectional affixes are added. **j.** The curved upright beam at the bow of a vessel into which the hull timbers are scarfed to form the prow. **k.** In an incandescent bulb or vacuum tube, the tubular glass structure mounting the filament or electrodes. **—from stem to stern.** From one end to the other; throughout.
~*v.* **stemmed, stemming, stems.** *—tr.* **1.** To remove the stem or stems of. **2.** To make headway against (a tide, current, or comparable force); breast. *—intr.* To have as a point of origin; derive or develop. Usually used with *from.* [Middle English *stem,* Old English *stemn, stefn,* stem, tree trunk, (timber used to build the) prow or stern of a ship.] **—stem·less** *adj.*

stem[2] *v.* **stemmed, stemming, stems.** *—tr.* **1.** To hold back (a flow, onrush, or movement) by or as if by damming. **2.** To plug or stop up (a blast hole, for example). **3.** To force the heel of (a ski or both skis) outward, as in performing a stem turn. *—intr.* To force the heel of one ski or both skis outward by shifting one's weight in order to slow down, stop, or make a turn.
~*n.* In skiing, a stem turn. [Middle English *stemmen,* from Old Norse *stemma.*]

stem cell *n.* An unspecialized cell that gives rise to a certain type of specialized cell, such as a blood cell.

stem·ma (stĕm′ə) *n., pl.* **stemmata** (stĕm′ə-tə) or **-mas. 1.** In ancient Rome, a scroll recording the genealogy of a family. **2.** Any family tree or pedigree. [Latin, garland, wreath, from Greek, from *stephein,* to encircle, crown, wreathe.]

stemmed (stĕmd) *adj.* **1.** Having the stem or stems removed. **2.** Provided with a stem or stems. Often used in combination: *thick-stemmed.*

stem·son (stĕm′sən) *n. Nautical.* A piece of supporting timber bolted to the stem and keelson at their junction near the bow of a wooden vessel. [STEM (prow) + (KEEL)SON.]

stem turn *n.* In skiing, a turn made by stemming the downhill ski and placing one's weight upon it while bringing the other ski into a parallel position. Also called "stem," "stem christie."

stem·ware (stĕm′wâr′) *n.* Glassware mounted on a stem.

stem-wind·er (stĕm′wīn′dər) *n.* A stem-winding watch.

stem-wind·ing (stĕm′wīn′dĭng) *adj.* Designating a watch that is wound by turning a knob mounted on the end of the stem.

sten. 1. stenographer. **2.** stenography.

stench (stĕnch) *n.* A strong and foul odor; a stink. —See Synonyms at **smell.** [Middle English *stench,* Old English *stenc,* from Germanic *stenkw-* (unattested); akin to *stinkwan* (unattested), to STINK.]

sten·cil (stĕn′səl) *n.* **1.** A sheet of celluloid, cardboard, or other material in which a desired lettering or design has been cut so that when ink or paint is passed over the sheet the pattern will be reproduced on the surface placed below. **2.** The lettering or design so produced. **3.** A sheet of thin waxed paper that can be typed or drawn on to produce a stencil suitable for use in a duplicator.
~*tr.v.* **stenciled** or **-cilled, -ciling** or **-cilling, -cils. 1.** To mark (a surface) with a stencil. **2.** To produce by stencil. [Middle English *stencel,* to adorn with brilliant colors, from Old French *estenceler,* "to cause to sparkle," from *estencele,* spark, from Latin *scintilla,* spark.] **—sten·cil·er, sten·cil·ler** *n.*

Sten·dhal (stĕn-däl′, stăN-), pen name of Henri Beyle (1783–1842). French writer. His work, which shows searching psychological insight, was an important influence on the development of the French novel. His novels include *Le Rouge et le Noir* (1830) and *La Chartreuse de Parme* (1839).

Sten·gel (stĕng′gəl), **Charles Dillon,** known as "Casey" (1891–1975). U.S. baseball player and manager. A player and manager on several different professional teams, he was hired to manage the New York Yankees (1948) and proceeded to lead that team to 10 American League pennants and 7 victorious World Series. He was elected to the Baseball Hall of Fame in 1966.

Sten gun (stĕn) *n.* A type of lightweight British submachine gun. [*St-* from the initials of the inventors' names, *S*hepherd and *T*urpin + *-en* as in BRENGUN.]

sten·o (stĕn′ō) *n., pl.* **-os.** *Informal.* **1.** A stenographer. **2.** Stenography.

steno– *prefix.* Indicates narrowness; for example, **stenophagous.** [Greek *stenos,* narrow.]

sten·o·graph (stĕn′ə-grăf′, -gräf′) *tr.v.* **-graphed, -graphing, -graphs.** To record in shorthand. [Back-formation from STENOGRAPHY.]

ste·nog·ra·pher (stə-nŏg′rə-fər) *n. Abbr.* **sten., steno.** A person skilled in shorthand; especially, one employed to take and transcribe dictation in an office or court.

ste·nog·ra·phy (stə-nŏg′rə-fē) *n. Abbr.* **sten., steno. 1.** The art or process of writing in shorthand. **2.** Material written down in shorthand. [STENO- + -GRAPHY.] **—sten·o·graph·ic** (stĕn′ə-grăf′ĭk) *adj.* **—sten·o·graph·i·cal·ly** *adv.*

sten·o·ha·line (stĕn′ə-hā′līn′, -hăl′īn′) *adj.* Able to live only within a narrow range of salt concentration. Said of certain aquatic organisms. Compare **euryhaline.** [STENO- + Greek *hals* (stem *hal-*), salt + -INE.]

ste·noph·a·gous (stə-nŏf′ə-gəs) *adj.* Feeding on a single kind or limited range of food. [STENO- + -PHAGOUS.]

ste·no·sis (stə-nō′sĭs) *n., pl.* **-ses** (-sēz′). *Pathology.* An abnormal narrowing of a passage or canal in the body. [New Latin, from Greek *stenōsis,* from *stenoun,* to constrict, from *stenos,* narrow.] **—ste·not·ic** (stə-nŏt′ĭk) *adj.*

sten·o·ther·mal (stĕn′ō-thûr′məl) *adj. Biology.* Of or designating organisms adapted to living only within a limited range of temperature. [German *stenotherm* : STENO- + *thermē,* heat, THERM.]

sten·o·trop·ic (stĕn′ō-trŏp′ĭk) *adj.* Also **sten·o·top·ic** (-tŏp′ĭk). *Biology.* Having narrow limits of adaptation to environmental conditions. [STENO- + -TROP(E) + -IC.]

sten·o·type (stĕn′ə-tīp′) *n.* **1.** A keyboard machine used to record dictation by a phonetic system. **2.** A symbol or combination of symbols representing a sound, word, or phrase, especially in shorthand. [STENO(GRAPHY) + TYPE.]

sten·o·ty·py (stĕn′ə-tī′pē) *n.* A form of shorthand using the letters of the alphabet to represent certain sounds or words. [STENOTYPE + -Y.] **—sten·o·ty·pist** *n.*

sten·tor (stĕn′tôr′) *n.* **1.** Any of several trumpet-shaped aquatic microorganisms of the genus *Stentor,* having cilia around the oral cavity. **2.** A person with an extremely loud voice. [New Latin *Stentor,* from Greek *Stentōr.* See **stentorian.**]

sten·to·ri·an (stĕn-tôr′ē-ən, stĕn-tōr′-) *adj.* Extremely loud. Said of the voice. [After *Stentōr,* a loud-voiced herald in the *Iliad,* from *stenein,* to groan, moan.]

step (stĕp) *n.* **1. a.** The single complete movement of raising one foot and putting it down in another spot in the act of walking, running, or dancing. **b.** A manner of walking; a gait. **c.** A fixed rhythm or pace, as in a march or dance: *break step; keep step.* **d.** The sound of a tread; a footstep. **e.** A footprint. **2. a.** The distance traversed by moving one foot ahead of the other. **b.** A very short distance: *just a step away.* **c. steps.** Course; path: *followed in his father's steps.* **3. a.** A rest for the foot in ascending or descending. **b. steps.** Stairs. **4. a.** Any of a series of actions or measures taken toward some end: *take steps to remedy the situation.* **b.** A stage in a process. **5.** A degree in progress or a grade or rank in a scale: *a step ahead of the others.* **6.** *Nautical.* The block in which the heel of a mast is fixed. **7.** A series of foot and body movements making up part of a dance: *hasn't learned the polka step.* **8.** A change in the level of a surface, as on a hillside or on the seabed, that resembles a step on a set of stairs. **9.** *Music.* **a.** A degree in a scale. **b.** The interval between two adjacent degrees in a scale. **—in step. 1.** Moving in rhythm or time. **2.** *Informal.* In conformity or harmony. **—out of step. 1.** Not in step. **2.** *Informal.* Not in conformity or harmony. **—step by step.** By degrees; gradually. **—watch one's step. 1.** To be careful and sensible. **2.** To behave as is demanded or required.
~*v.* **stepped, stepping, steps.** *—intr.* **1.** To put or press the foot; tread: *stepped on my toe.* **2.** To move or go, especially a short distance, by taking a step or steps: *step aside; step into my office.* **3.** To move using the feet in a particular manner: *step lively.* **4.** To move

stele *This stone stele depicts the storm god Baal holding his spear-pointed thunderbolt in his left hand. It was carved by Syrian craftsmen in about 1800* B.C.

into a new situation as if by taking a single step: *stepping into a life of ease.* —*tr.* **1.** To move by taking (a number of steps or paces): *step five paces.* **2.** To measure by pacing. Usually used with *off* or *out*: *step off ten yards.* **3.** To furnish with steps; make steps in. **4.** To set (the foot) down: *step foot on land.* **5.** *Nautical.* To place (a mast) in its step. —**step on.** To treat harshly or with arrogant indifference. —**step on it.** *Informal.* To hurry up; speed up. —**step out. 1.** To walk with brisk strides. **2.** To leave a place for a short time. **3.** *Informal.* To go out for a special evening of entertainment. [Middle English *step(pe),* Old English *stæpe.*]

step– *prefix.* Indicates relationship through the previous marriage of a spouse or through the remarriage of a parent rather than by blood; for example, **stepbrother.** [Middle English *step-, stip-,* Old English *stēop-.*]

step·broth·er (stĕp′brŭth′ər) *n.* The son of one's stepparent by a former marriage.

step·child (stĕp′chīld′) *n., pl.* **-children** (-chīl′drən). The child of one's spouse by a former marriage.

step·daugh·ter (stĕp′dô′tər) *n.* The daughter of one's spouse by a former marriage.

step down *intr.v.* **1.** To take a lesser position. **2.** To abdicate; resign. —*tr.v.* To reduce (power, for example) by stages.

step-down (stĕp′doun′) *adj.* Decreasing in stages. ~*n.* A reduction in amount or size.

step-down transformer *n.* A transformer that has a greater number of turns in the primary winding than in the secondary, used to transform high voltage to low voltage.

step·fa·ther (stĕp′fä′thər) *n.* The husband of one's mother by a later marriage.

step fault *n. Geology.* A series of parallel faults along which relative displacement downward has occurred on the same side.

steph·a·no·tis (stĕf′ə-nō′tĭs) *n.* Any climbing plant of the tropical genus *Stephanotis;* especially, *S. floribunda,* native to Madagascar and widely cultivated as a house plant for its white waxy flowers. [New Latin, from Greek (adjective), fit for a wreath, from *stephanos,* wreath, crown.]

Ste·phen (stē′vən) (c. 1097–1154). King of England. He was elected king (1135) on the death of Henry I, despite an oath of fealty to Henry's daughter Matilda. He was a weak king and most of his reign was marked by civil war. After the death of his son (1153) he acknowledged Matilda's son (Henry II) as his heir.

Stephen I, also called "Saint Stephen" (977–1038). First Hungarian king (1000–38). Crowned on Christmas Day, he is considered the founder of the Hungarian state. During his largely peaceful reign he maintained strong ties with the Roman Catholic Church, called for the building of churches and abbeys, and organized a standing army. He was canonized in 1083.

Stephen, Sir Leslie (1832–1904). English man of letters. He was the first editor of the *Dictionary of National Biography,* and his books include *Essays on Free Thinking and Plain Speaking* (1873).

Ste·phen·son (stē′vən-sən), **George** (1781–1848). British engineer. In 1815 he built the first successful steam locomotive, and in 1825 the world's first passenger railway. His engine, *The Rocket,* won (1829) a prize for maintaining an average speed of 29 miles per hour.

step in *intr.v.* To intervene or interfere, as to provide help or take charge of a situation.

step-in (stĕp′ĭn′) *adj.* Put on by being stepped into: *a step-in robe.* ~*n.* Often **step-ins.** A step-in garment, especially an undergarment.

step·lad·der (stĕp′lăd′ər) *n.* A portable ladder with a hinged supporting frame and usually topped with a small platform.

step·moth·er (stĕp′mŭth′ər) *n.* The wife of one's father by a later marriage.

step·par·ent (stĕp′pâr′ənt) *n.* A stepfather or a stepmother.

steppe (stĕp) *n.* A vast semiarid grass-covered plain, such as that found in southeastern Europe and Siberia. [Russian *step',* from Old Russian *step′†,* lowland.]

step·ping·stone (stĕp′ĭng-stōn′) *n.* **1.** A stone that provides a place to stand on, as in crossing a stream. **2.** An advantageous position for advancement toward some goal.

step pyramid *n.* A pyramid with outer faces made up of stone blocks rising in steps.

step rocket *n. Aerospace.* A **multistage rocket** (*see*).

step·sis·ter (stĕp′sĭs′tər) *n.* The daughter of one's stepparent by a former marriage.

step·son (stĕp′sŭn′) *n.* The son of one's spouse by a former marriage.

step up *tr.v.* To increase, especially by stages: *step up production.*

step-up (stĕp′ŭp′) *adj.* Increasing in steps or by stages. ~*n.* An increase in size, amount, or activity.

step-up transformer *n.* A transformer that has fewer turns in the primary winding than in the secondary, used to transform low voltage to high voltage.

step·wise (stĕp′wīz′) *adj.* **1.** Marked by a gradual progression as if step by step. **2.** *Music.* Moving from one musical tone to an adjacent one. —**step·wise** *adv.*

–ster *suffix.* Indicates: **1.** One who takes part in or is associated with; for example, **gangster, youngster. 2.** One who makes or is given to making; for example, **pollster, prankster.** [Middle English *-ster(e), -estere,* Old English *-estre, -ister,* from West Germanic *-strjōn* (unattested), agent-noun suffix (primarily feminine).]

ster. sterling.

stereoscope *A viewing device using pairs of pictures taken by a camera with two lenses, for a three-dimensional effect.*

ste·ra·di·an (stĭ-rā′dē-ən) *n. Abbr.* **sr** A unit of measure equal to the solid angle subtended at the center of a sphere by an area on the surface equal to the square of the radius: *The total solid angle of a sphere is 4π steradians.* [STE(REO)- + RADIAN.]

ster·co·ra·ceous (stûr′kə-rā′shəs) *adj.* Also **ster·co·rous** (stûr′kər-əs). Consisting of or pertaining to excrement. [Latin *stercus* (stem *stercor-*), dung + -ACEOUS.]

stere (stîr) *n. Abbr.* **s** A unit of volume equal to one cubic meter. [French *stère,* from Greek *stereos,* solid, hard.]

ster·e·o (stĕr′ē-ō′, stîr′-) *n., pl.* **-os. 1. a.** A stereophonic high-fidelity sound system. **b.** Stereophonic sound. **2.** *Printing.* A stereotype. **3.** A stereoscopic system or photograph. ~*adj.* **1.** Stereophonic. **2.** Stereoscopic.

stereo–, stere– *prefix.* Indicates solid, firm, or three-dimensional; for example, **stereophonic, stereoscope.** [Greek *stereos,* solid, hard.]

ster·e·o·bate (stĕr′ē-ō-bāt′, stîr′-) *n. Architecture.* **1.** A stylobate. **2.** The foundation of a stone building, its top course sometimes being a stylobate. [Latin *stereobata,* from Greek *sterebatēs,* "solid base" : *stereos,* solid, STEREO- + *-batēs,* "one that is based."]

ster·e·o·chem·is·try (stĕr′ē-ō-kĕm′ĭ-strē, stîr′-) *n.* The chemical study of spatial arrangements of atoms in molecules and of the effects of these arrangements on the molecule's properties.

ster·e·o·chro·my (stĕr′ē-ō-krō′mē, stîr′-) *n.* The art or process of painting murals using pigments mixed with water glass. [STEREO- + -CHROME + -Y.] —**ster·e·o·chrome** *n. & v.* —**ster·e·o·chro·mic** (stĕr′ē-ō-krō′mĭk, stîr′-) *adj.* —**ster·e·o·chro·mi·cal·ly** *adv.*

ster·e·o·gram (stĕr′ē-ō-grăm′, stîr′-) *n.* **1.** A picture or diagram designed to give the impression of solidity. **2.** A stereograph. [STEREO- + -GRAM.]

ster·e·o·graph (stĕr′ē-ō-grăf′, -gräf′, stîr′-) *n.* Two stereoscopic pictures, or one picture with two superposed stereoscopic images, designed to give a three-dimensional effect when viewed through a stereoscope or special glasses. ~*tr.v.* **stereographed, -graphing, -graphs.** To make (a stereographic picture) using stereoscopic images. [STEREO- + -GRAPH.]

stereographic projection *n.* An azimuthal map projection in which a point is projected onto the tangent plane from a point on the opposite end of the diameter. It is an orthomorphic projection.

ster·e·og·ra·phy (stĕr′ē-ŏg′rə-fē, stîr′-) *n.* The art or technique of depicting solid bodies on a plane surface. [STEREO- + -GRAPHY.] —**ster·e·o·graph·ic** (stĕr′ē-ə-grăf′ĭk, stîr′-), **ster·e·o·graph·i·cal** *adj.* —**ster·e·o·graph·i·cal·ly** *adv.*

ster·e·o·i·so·mer (stĕr′ē-ō-ī′sə-mər, stîr′-) *n. Chemistry.* Any of the structural molecular forms of a compound that exhibit stereoisomerism. See **isomer.**

ster·e·o·i·som·er·ism (stĕr′ē-ō-ī-sŏm′ə-rĭz′əm, stîr′-) *n.* Isomerism created by differences in the spatial arrangement of atoms in a molecule. —**ster·e·o·i·so·mer·ic** (stĕr′ē-ō-ī′sə-mĕr′ĭk, stîr′-) *adj.*

ster·e·om·e·try (stĕr′ē-ŏm′ə-trē, stîr′-) *n.* The science of measuring volume. [STEREO- + -METRY.] —**ster·e·o·met·ric** (stĕr′ē-ō-mĕt′rĭk, stîr′-), **ster·e·o·met·ri·cal** *adj.*

ster·e·o·mi·cro·scope (stĕr′ē-ō-mī′krə-skōp′, stîr′-) *n.* A microscope optically equipped for stereoscopic viewing.

ster·e·o·phon·ic (stĕr′ē-ō-fŏn′ĭk, stîr′-) *adj.* Of or pertaining to a high-fidelity sound system in which two channels are used to give an illusion of a more natural distribution of sources of sound. Compare **binaural, quadraphonic.** [STEREO- + PHONIC.] —**ster·e·o·phon·i·cal·ly** *adv.* —**ster·e·oph·o·ny** (stĕr′ē-ŏf′ə-nē, stîr′-) *n.*

ster·e·op·sis (stĕr′ē-ŏp′sĭs, stîr′-) *n.* Stereoscopic vision. [New Latin : STERE(O)- + -OPSIS.]

ster·e·op·ti·con (stĕr′ē-ŏp′tĭ-kŏn′, stîr′-) *n.* A **magic lantern** (*see*), especially one consisting of two separate units arranged so as to produce dissolving views. [New Latin : STEREO- + Greek *optikon,* neuter of *optikos,* OPTIC.]

ster·e·o·scope (stĕr′ē-ə-skōp′, stîr′-) *n.* An optical instrument used to impart a three-dimensional effect to two photographs of the same scene taken at slightly different angles and viewed through two eyepieces. [STEREO- + -SCOPE.]

ster·e·o·scop·ic (stĕr′ē-ə-skŏp′ĭk, stîr′-) *adj.* **1.** Of or pertaining to stereoscopy; especially, three-dimensional. **2.** Of or pertaining to a stereoscope. —**ster·e·o·scop·i·cal·ly** *adv.*

ster·e·os·co·py (stĕr′ē-ŏs′kə-pē, stîr′-) *n.* **1.** The viewing of objects as three-dimensional. **2.** The technique of making or using stereoscopes. [STEREO- + -SCOPY.] —**ster·e·os·co·pist** *n.*

ster·e·o·spe·cif·ic (stĕr′ē-ō-spĭ-sĭf′ĭk, stîr′-) *adj. Chemistry.* Pertaining to, involving, or producing a regular arrangement of atoms in a molecule. Said especially of polymers with a regular arrangement of atoms or of reactions or catalysts producing such compounds.

ster·e·o·tax·is (stĕr′ē-ō-tăk′sĭs, stîr′-) *n. Biology.* Thigmotaxis (*see*). —**ster·e·o·tac·tic** (stĕr′ē-ə-tăk′tĭk, stîr′-), **ster·e·o·tac·ti·cal** *adj.* —**ster·e·o·tac·ti·cal·ly** *adv.*

ster·e·o·type (stĕr′ē-ə-tīp′, stîr′-) *n.* **1.** A conventional, formulaic, and usually oversimplified conception, opinion, or belief. **2.** A person, group, event, or issue considered to typify or conform to an unvarying standard pattern or manner: *the stereotype of a banker.* Also used adjectivally: *a stereotype male chauvinist.* **3. a.** A metal printing plate cast from a mold made out of papier-mâché, plastic, or rubber and taken from a raised printing surface, such as type. **b.** The method or process of making such a plate. ~*tr.v.* **stereotyped, -typing, -types. 1.** To make a stereotype of. **2.** To print from a stereotype. **3.** To give a fixed, unvarying form to. [French *stéréotype* : STEREO- + TYPE.] —**ster·e·o·typ·er** *n.* —**ster·e·**

o·typ·ic (stĕr′ē-ə-tĭp′ĭk, stîr′-), **ster·e·o·typ·i·cal** *adj.*

ster·e·o·typed (stĕr′ē-ə-tīpt′, stîr′-) *adj.* **1.** Not individualized; unoriginal; conventional. **2.** Printed or reproduced from stereotype plates. —See Synonyms at **trite.**

ster·e·o·ty·py (stĕr′ē-ə-tī′pē, stîr′-) *n.* **1.** The process or art of making stereotype plates. **2.** Excessive repetition or lack of variation in movements, ideas, or patterns of speech.

ster·e·o·vi·sion (stĕr′ē-ō-vĭzh′ən, stîr′-) *n.* Visual perception of or exhibition in three dimensions.

ster·ic (stĕr′ĭk, stîr′-) *adj.* Of or pertaining to the spatial arrangement of atoms in a molecule. [STER(EO)- + -IC.] —**ster·i·cal·ly** *adv.*

ste·rig·ma (stə-rĭg′mə) *n., pl.* **-mata** (-mə-tə). A slender spore-bearing structure formed by certain fungi. [New Latin, from Greek *stērigma,* support, from *stērizein,* to support.]

ster·i·lant (stĕr′ə-lənt) *n.* A sterilizing agent.

ster·ile (stĕr′əl, -īl′) *adj.* **1. a.** Incapable of reproducing sexually; barren; infertile. **b.** Incapable of producing seed, fruit spores, or other reproductive structures. Said of plants or their parts. **2.** Capable of producing little or no vegetation: *sterile land.* **3.** Free from bacteria or other microorganisms. **4.** Lacking in imagination or vitality; not stimulating; dry. **5.** Failing to produce any useful result; fruitless: *a sterile discussion.* **6.** Containing no archaeological remains: *a sterile stratum.* [French *sterile,* from Latin *sterilis,* unfruitful.] —**ster·ile·ly** *adv.* —**ste·ril·i·ty** (stə-rĭl′ə-tē), **ster·ile·ness** *n.*
   Synonyms: barren, impotent, infertile, unfruitful.

ster·il·i·za·tion (stĕr′ə-lə-zā′shən) *n.* **1.** The procedure or act of sterilizing. **2.** The condition of being sterile or sterilized.

ster·il·ize (stĕr′ə-līz′) *tr.v.* **-ized, -izing, -izes.** To render sterile. —**ster·il·iz·er** *n.*

ster·let (stûr′lĭt) *n.* A sturgeon, *Acipenser ruthenus,* of the Caspian Sea and adjacent waters. [Russian *sterlyad′,* perhaps akin to Germanic *sturjōn* (unattested), STURGEON.]

ster·ling (stûr′lĭng) *n. Abbr.* **ster., stg. 1.** British money; especially, the pound as the basic monetary unit of the United Kingdom. **2.** British coinage of silver or gold, having as a standard of fineness 0.500 for silver and 0.91666 for gold. **3. a.** Sterling silver. **b.** Articles made of sterling silver, such as tableware.
   ~*adj. Abbr.* **ster., stg. 1.** Consisting of or relating to sterling or British money. **2.** Made of sterling silver. **3.** Of the highest quality; of genuine worth. [Middle English *sterling, starling,* "small star" (from the small star stamped on the silver pennies), probably from Old English *steorling* (unattested) : *steorra,* STAR + -LING.]

sterling silver *n.* **1.** An alloy of 92.5 percent silver with copper or another metal. **2.** Objects made of sterling silver.

stern[1] (stûrn) *adj.* **sterner, sternest. 1.** Not inclined to leniency; strict. **2.** Expressing disapproval or displeasure: *a stern rebuke.* **3.** Grave or severe in manner or appearance; grim; austere: *a silent, stern, rather forbidding manner.* **4.** Resolute; inflexible; unyielding: *a stern resolve to quit smoking.* **5.** Inexorable; relentless: *stern necessity.* —See Synonyms at **severe.** [Middle English *sterne, stierne,* Old English *styrne, stierne.*] —**stern·ly** *adv.* —**stern·ness** *n.*

stern[2] *n.* **1.** The rear part of a ship or boat. **2.** The rear part of anything. [Middle English *sterne,* probably from Old Norse *stjōrn,* steering, rudder, from *stȳra,* to STEER.]

Stern (stûrn), **Isaac** (1920-). U.S. violinist, born in Russia. Brought to the United States as an infant, he began studying the violin at the age of 8, and by the time of his first appearance at Carnegie Hall (1943) was considered among the world's greatest violinists. He has performed worldwide in as many as 90 concerts a year.

ster·nal (stûr′nəl) *adj. Anatomy.* Of, near, or pertaining to the sternum. [New Latin *sternalis,* from STERNUM.]

Stern·berg (shtĕrn′bĕrk′), **Josef von** (1894-1969). Austrian film director. He is best known for his series of films starring Marlene Dietrich, which include *The Blue Angel* (1930), *Blonde Venus* (1932), *Shanghai Express* (1932), and *The Scarlet Empress* (1934).

stern chaser *n.* A gun or cannon mounted on the stern of a ship for firing at a pursuing vessel.

Sterne (stûrn), **Laurence** (1713-68). English novelist and clergyman. He won fame with his witty, ribald novel *The Life and Opinions of Tristram Shandy, Gentleman* (1759-67). His other works include *A Sentimental Journey* (1768).

stern·fore·most (stûrn′fôr′mōst′, -fōr′mōst′, -məst) *adv. Nautical.* With the stern foremost; backward.

stern·most (stûrn′mōst′, -məst) *adj. Nautical.* Farthest astern.

stern·post (stûrn′pōst′) *n.* The principal upright post at the stern of a vessel, usually serving to support the rudder.

stern sheets *pl.n.* The stern area of an open boat.

stern·son (stûrn′sən) *n.* A bar of metal or wood set between the keelson and the sternpost to fortify the joint. Also called "stern knee." [STERN + (KEEL)SON.]

ster·num (stûr′nəm) *n., pl.* **-na** (-nə) or **-nums. 1.** A long flat bone articulating with the cartilages of and forming the midventral support of most of the ribs in tetrapod vertebrates, and also of the collarbone in humans and certain other vertebrates. Also called "breastbone." **2.** The chitinous plate that forms a protective covering on the ventral surface of the body segment of an arthropod. [New Latin, from Greek *sternon,* breast, breastbone.]

ster·nu·ta·tion (stûr′nyə-tā′shən) *n.* **1.** The act of sneezing. **2.** A sneeze. [Latin *sternūtātiō* (stem *sternūtātiōn-*), from *sternūtāre,* frequentative of *sternuere,* to sneeze.]

ster·nu·ta·tor (stûr′nyə-tā′tər) *n.* A substance that irritates the nasal and respiratory passages and causes sneezing.

ster·nu·ta·to·ry (stûr-nyōō′tə-tôr′ē, -tōr′ē) *adj.* Causing or tending to cause sneezing.
   ~*n., pl.* **sternutatories.** A sternutatory substance, such as pepper.

stern·ward (stûrn′wərd) *adv.* Also **stern·wards** (-wərdz). Toward the stern; astern.
   ~*adj.* In or at the stern.

stern·way (stûrn′wā′) *n.* The backward movement of a vessel.

stern·wheel·er (stûrn′hwē′lər) *n.* A steamboat propelled by a paddle wheel at the stern.

ster·oid (stĕr′oid′, stîr′-) *n.* Any of numerous naturally occurring, fat-soluble organic compounds having a 17-carbon-atom ring as a basis, and including the sterols and bile acids, many hormones, certain natural drugs such as digitalis compounds, and the precursors of certain vitamins. [STER(OL) + -OID.]

ste·roid·o·gen·e·sis (stĭ-roi′də-jĕn′ə-sĭs, stîr′oi-, stĕr′-) *n.* The production of steroids. —**ste·roid·o·gen·ic** *adj.*

ster·ol (stĕr′ôl′, -ōl′, stîr′-) *n.* Any of a group of predominantly unsaturated solid alcohols of the steroid group, as cholesterol and ergosterol, occurring in the fatty tissues of plants and animals. [Short for CHOLESTEROL.]

Ster·o·pe[1] (stĕr′ə-pē). Also **As·ter·o·pe** (ă-stĕr′ə-pē). *Greek Mythology.* One of the seven **Pleiades** *(see).* [Greek *(A)steropē,* from *(a)steropē, astrapē,* lightning, "twinkling."]

Sterope[2] *n.* One of the stars in the constellation **Pleiades** *(see).*

ster·tor (stûr′tər) *n.* A heavy snoring sound in deep sleep or a coma, caused by obstruction of the air passages. [New Latin, from Latin *stertere,* to snore.] —**ster·tor·ous** *adj.* —**ster·tor·ous·ly** *adv.*

stet (stĕt) *n. Abbr.* **st.** A printer's term directing that a letter, word, or other matter marked for omission or correction is to be retained.
   ~*tr.v.* **stetted, stetting, stets.** To cancel a correction or omission previously made in (printed matter) by underlining with a row of dots and marking the word *stet* in the margin. Compare **dele.** [Latin, 3rd person sing. of *stāre,* to stand.]

steth·o·scope (stĕth′ə-skōp′) *n.* An instrument consisting of a hollow disk connected by a tube to an earpiece used for listening to sounds produced within the body. [French *stéthoscope* : Greek *stēthos†,* chest, breast + -SCOPE.] —**steth·o·scop·ic** (stĕth′ə-skŏp′-ĭk) *adj.* —**steth·o·scop·i·cal·ly** *adv.* —**ste·thos·co·py** (stĕ-thŏs′kə-pē) *n.*

Stet·son (stĕt′sən) *n.* A trademark for a hat having a high crown and wide brim, popular in the western United States. [Designed by John *Stetson* (1830-1906), U.S. hatmaker.]

Stettin. See Szczecin.

Stet·tin·i·us (stĕ-tĭn′ē-əs, -tĭn′yəs), **Edward Reilly, Jr.** (1900-49). U.S. businessman and public official. An executive for General Motors (1926-34) and U.S. Steel (1934-39), he served in several war-related administrative positions, including chairman of the War Resource Board and secretary of state (1944-45). After World War II he helped organize the United Nations and was America's first delegate to the UN (1945-46).

Steu·ben (stōō′bən, styōō′-), **Baron Friedrich Wilhelm von** (1730-94). U.S. Revolutionary soldier, born in Prussia. After considerable European military action, he came to America to aid the rebelling colonists. His primary contribution involved training the previously undisciplined American troops.

Steu·ben·ville (stōō′bən-vĭl′, styōō′-). City of east-central Ohio, on the Ohio River. The city's major industry is the production of steel.

ste·ve·dore (stē′və-dôr′, -dōr′) *n.* A person employed in the loading or unloading of ships.
   ~*v.* **stevedored, -doring, -dores.** —*tr.* To load or unload the cargo of (a ship). —*intr.* To work as a stevedore. [Spanish *estibador,* from *estivar,* to pack, from Latin *stīpāre,* to stuff.]

stevedore's knot *n.* A knot used to prevent a line from coming out of a pulley.

Ste·ven·graph (stē′vən-grăf′, -gräf′) *n.* A colorful, usually small picture woven in silk. [After Thomas *Stevens,* 19th-century British weaver.]

Ste·vens (stē′vənz), **Wallace** (1879-1955). U.S. poet. His poetry is distinguished by its tight construction and its intellectual but lucid content, as in the collection *The Man with the Blue Guitar and Other Poems* (1937).

Ste·ven·son (stē′vən-sən), **Adlai Ewing** (1900-65). U.S. politician. He held various offices in Franklin Roosevelt's wartime administration and was governor (1949-53) of Illinois. Stevenson was a Democratic presidential candidate in 1952 and 1956 but was beaten both times by Dwight D. Eisenhower.

Stevenson, Robert Louis (1850-94). Scottish novelist, essayist, and poet. His works include *Travels with a Donkey in the Cévennes* (1879), *Virginibus Puerisque* (1881), *Treasure Island* (1883), and *The Strange Case of Dr. Jekyll and Mr. Hyde* (1886).

stew (stōō, styōō) *v.* **stewed, stewing, stews.** —*tr.* To cook (food) by simmering or boiling slowly. —*intr.* **1.** To undergo cooking by boiling slowly or simmering. **2.** *Informal.* To suffer with oppressive heat or stuffy confinement; swelter. **3.** *Informal.* To worry; fret. —*n.* **1.** A dish cooked by stewing; especially, a mixture of meat or fish and vegetables with stock. **2.** *Informal.* A state of mental agitation or difficulty: *in a stew over her lost keys.* **3.** *Often* **stews.** *Archaic.* A brothel. [Middle English *stewen,* originally to bathe in hot water or steam, from Old French *estuver,* from Vulgar Latin *extūfāre* (unattested) : probably *ex-,* out of + *tufus* (unattested), hot vapor, from Greek *tuphos,* smoke, vapor, from *tuphein,* to smoke.]

stew·ard (stōō′ərd, styōō′-) *n.* **1.** One who manages another's property, finances, or other affairs. **2.** One in charge of domestic ar-

rangements, as in an institution, club, or hotel. **3.** An officer on a ship in charge of provisions and dining arrangements. **4.** Any male member of the staff of a ship or airplane who waits on the passengers. **5.** An official who supervises or helps to manage an event. **6.** A **shop steward** *(see).*
~*v.* **stewarded, -arding, -ards.** *—tr.* To serve as steward of; manage; administer. *—intr.* To serve as a steward. [Middle English *stuarde, stywarde,* Old English *stigweard,* "keeper of the hall" : *stig,* hall (see **sty**) + *weard,* keeper, ward.]

stew·ard·ess (sto͞o′ər-dĭs, styo͞o′-) *n.* A woman who works as a steward, especially one who works as a flight attendant.

Stewart. See **Stuart.**

Stew·art (sto͞o′ərt, styo͞o′-), **James Maitland** (1908–). U.S. film actor. He is best known for his portrayals of incorruptible heroes in films such as *Destry Rides Again* (1939), *Mr. Smith Goes to Washington* (1939), and *The Philadelphia Story* (1940), for which he won an Academy Award as best actor.

stewed (sto͞od, styo͞od) *adj.* **1.** Cooked by stewing: *stewed prunes.* **2.** *Slang.* Drunk; intoxicated.

St. George's (sānt jôr′jĭz). Capital and port of Grenada, on the southwestern coast of the island. It was founded by the French (1705) and was the capital of the British Windward Isles (1885–1958).

St. Gott·hard Pass (sānt gŏt′ərd, gŏth′ərd). Alpine pass in southern Switzerland, in the St. Gotthard range of the Lepontine Alps. Rising to a height of 2,114 meters (6,935 feet), it has long been part of the main road and mail link between northern Europe and Italy. Beneath the pass there is a railway tunnel (1872–80) 15 kilometers (9.25 miles) long and a road tunnel (1970–80) 16 kilometers (10 miles) long.

Sth. South.

St. He·le·na (sānt′ hə-lē′nə). Volcanic island in the South Atlantic Ocean, 122 square kilometers (47 square miles) in area. Napoleon died here in exile (1812).

St. Hel·ens, Mount (sānt hĕl′ənz). Volcano in southwestern Washington State. It erupted in April, 1980, shearing *c.* 450 meters (1,500 feet) from its crest and covering a vast area with dust. Its height before the eruption was 2,948 meters (9,671 feet). Volcanic activity continues within the truncated cone.

St. Hel·ier (sānt hĕl′yər). Port on Jersey in the Channel Islands. It is a resort and market for cattle and early vegetables.

sthen·ic (sthĕn′ĭk) *adj.* Characterized by excessive energy; vigorous. [Greek *sthenos,* strength + -IC.]

Sthe·no (sthē′nō). *Greek Mythology.* One of the three Gorgons.

stib·ine (stĭb′ēn′) *n.* **1.** A colorless, flammable, poisonous gas, SbH_3, often used as a fumigant. **2.** A derivative of this formed by replacing one or more hydrogen atoms by hydrocarbon groups. [Latin *stibium,* variant of *stibi, stimmi,* antimony, from Greek, from Egyptian *stm* + -INE.]

stib·nite (stĭb′nīt′) *n.* A lead-gray mineral, Sb_2S_3, that is the chief source of antimony. Also called "antimony glance." [French *stibine,* stibnite, from Latin *stibium,* antimony (see **stibine**) + -ITE.]

stich (stĭk) *n.* A line of verse. [Greek *stikhos,* row, line, verse.]

sti·chom·e·try (stĭ-kŏm′ə-trē) *n.* The division of a prose piece into lines of fixed length or, occasionally, into lines whose lengths correspond to the natural divisions of sense, as in manuscripts written before the adoption of punctuation. [Greek *stikhos,* STICH + -METRY.] **—stich·o·met·ric** (stĭk′ə-mĕt′rĭk) *adj.*

stich·o·myth·i·a (stĭk′ə-mĭth′ē-ə) *n.* Also **sti·chom·y·thy** (stĭ-kŏm′ə-thē). An ancient Greek arrangement of dialogue in drama, poetry, and disputation in which single lines of verse are spoken by alternate speakers. [Greek *stikhomuthia,* from *stikhomuthein,* to speak in alternating lines : *stikhos,* STICH + *muthos,* speech, tale, MYTH.] **—stich·o·myth·ic** (stĭk′ə-mĭth′ĭk) *adj.*

-stichous *suffix.* Indicates rows; for example, **polystichous.** [Greek *-stikhos,* from *stikhos,* row, line, verse.]

stick[1] (stĭk) *n.* **1.** A long, slender piece of wood, especially: **a.** A branch or stem cut from a tree or shrub. **b.** A tree branch or other piece of wood used for fuel, cut for timber, or shaped for a specific purpose. **c.** A wand, staff, baton, or rod. **d.** Any of various stick-like implements used in games or sports: *a hockey stick.* **e.** A cane or walking stick. **2.** Something cut into or having the shape of a stick: *a stick of dynamite; a stick of rock.* **3.** *Aviation.* An airplane control that operates the elevators and ailerons. **4.** *Informal.* The lever or rod in a motor vehicle used for changing gear. **5.** *Nautical.* A mast or a part of a mast. **6.** *Printing.* **a.** A composing stick. **b.** The type contents of a composing stick. Also called "stickful." **7. a.** *Military.* A group of bombs released to fall across a target in a straight row. **b.** A group of paratroopers jumping in succession. **8.** A timber tree. **9.** *Informal.* An item of furniture. **10. sticks.** *Informal.* An area far from a city or town; backwoods: *They live way out in the sticks.* **11.** *Informal.* A person, especially one who is spiritless or boring: *a dry old stick.* **12.** A poke, thrust, or stab with a stick or similar object: *a stick in the ribs.* **13.** The state, condition, or power of adhering: *a glue with plenty of stick.*
~*tr.v.* **sticked, sticking, sticks.** **1.** To prop up (a vine or other plant) with sticks or brush on which to grow. **2.** *Printing.* To set (type) in a composing stick.
~*interj.* **sticks.** Used in hockey by the umpire to indicate that players have raised their sticks improperly above their shoulders. [Middle English, Old English *sticca,* from West Germanic *stikka* (unattested).]

stick[2] *v.* **stuck** (stŭk), **sticking, sticks.** *—tr.* **1.** To pierce, puncture, or penetrate with a pointed instrument, such as a knife or pin. **2.** To kill by piercing. **3.** To thrust or push (a knife, pin, or other pointed instrument) into or through another object. **4.** To fasten into place by forcing an end or point into something: *stick a hook into the wall.* **5.** To fasten or attach with or as if with pins, nails, or similar instruments. **6.** To fasten or attach with an adhesive material, glue, or tape: *stick a poster to the wall.* **7.** To cover or decorate with objects piercing the surface. **8.** To fix, impale, or transfix on a pointed object: *stick an olive on a toothpick.* **9.** To put, place, thrust, or poke into a specified place or position: *stick your hands up; stuck a cigarette in his mouth.* **10.** *Informal.* To detain or delay. Usually used in the passive: *was stuck at the dentist all morning.* **11.** *Chiefly British Slang.* To bear; abide: *can't stick his silly jokes.* **12.** To make incapable of movement or progress; bring to a standstill or impasse. Usually used in the passive: *can't shift it—it's completely stuck; stuck on question three.* **13.** *Informal.* To confuse, baffle, or puzzle. Usually used in the passive: *never stuck for an answer.* **14.** To burden or encumber with something unpleasant or unwanted; saddle: *stuck with paying the bill.* **15.** *Informal.* To write: *Stick your address at the top of the page.* *—intr.* **1.** To be or become fixed or embedded in place by having the point thrust in. **2.** To become or remain attached or in close association by or as if by adhesion; cling: *"I'm all for us English sticking together when we're abroad"* (Somerset Maugham). **3.** To remain firm, determined, or resolute: *stick to a resolution.* **4.** To persist, endure, or persevere. Used with *at, to,* or *with*: *must stick to it in order to succeed.* **5. a.** *Informal.* To remain in the vicinity; linger. Usually used with *about* or *around*: *Stick around until I get back.* **b.** To remain for a period of time: *Her face really stuck in my mind.* **6.** To scruple or hesitate. Used with *at* or *to*: *She sticks at nothing.* **7.** To be at or come to a standstill; become fixed, jammed, checked, or obstructed. **8.** To extend, project, or protrude. Used with *out, up, down,* or *through.* **—be stuck on.** *Informal.* To be infatuated by. **—stick by.** To remain loyal to. **—stick it out.** *Informal.* To persist or persevere to the end. **—stick out.** To be prominent. **—stick to the ribs.** *Informal.* To be substantial or filling. Used of food. **—stick up for.** To defend or support. [Middle English, Old English *stician.*]

stick·ball (stĭk′bôl′) *n.* A form of baseball played with a rubber ball and a stick or the handle of a broom for a bat.

stick·er (stĭk′ər) *n.* **1.** A person or thing that sticks. **2.** A gummed or adhesive label or patch. **3.** A tenacious, diligent, or persistent person. **4.** A thorn, prickle, or barb.

sticking plaster *n.* See **plaster** (sense 2).

stick insect *n.* A **walking stick** *(see).*

stick-in-the-mud (stĭk′ĭn-*thə*-mŭd′) *n. Informal.* A very staid person who lacks initiative, imagination, or enthusiasm.

stick·le (stĭk′əl) *intr.v.* **-led, -ling, -les.** **1.** To argue or contend stubbornly, especially about trivial or petty points. **2.** To have or raise objections; scruple. [Earlier *stightle,* to arbitrate, intervene, Middle English *stightlen,* Old English *stihtan, stihtian.*]

stick·le·back (stĭk′əl-băk′) *n.* Any of various small freshwater and marine fishes of the family Gasterosteidae, having erectile spines along the back. [Middle English *stykylbak,* "prickly back" : *stykyl-,* from Old English *sticel,* prick, sting + *bak,* BACK.]

stick·ler (stĭk′lər) *n.* **1.** A person who insists on something: *a stickler for neatness.* **2.** Anything puzzling or difficult.

stick·pin (stĭk′pĭn′) *n.* A decorative pin worn on a necktie.

stick·seed (stĭk′sēd′) *n.* Any of various plants of the genus *Lappula,* having small prickly fruits that cling to clothing or fur. Also called "beggar's-lice" and sometimes "burseed."

stick·tight (stĭk′tīt′) *n.* Any of various plants having barbed, clinging seeds or fruit, such as the **bur marigold** *(see).*

stick-to-it·ive·ness (stĭk-to͞o′ə-tĭv-nĭs) *n. Informal.* Unwavering pertinacity; perseverance.

stick up *tr.v. Slang.* To rob, especially at gunpoint.

stick·up (stĭk′ŭp′) *n. Slang.* A robbery, especially at gunpoint.

stick·weed (stĭk′wēd′) *n.* Broadly, any of various plants having clinging seeds or fruit, especially ragweed.

stick·y (stĭk′ē) *adj.* **-ier, -iest.** **1.** Having the property of adhering or sticking to a surface; adhesive. **2.** Covered with an adhesive agent: *a sticky floor.* **3.** Warm and humid; muggy. **4.** *Informal.* Painful or difficult: *a sticky problem.* **5.** *Economics.* Tending to remain the same despite changes in the economy. Said of prices or wages. **—stick·i·ly** *adv.* **—stick·i·ness** *n.*

sticky wicket *n. Informal.* A difficult or embarrassing problem or situation.

Stieg·litz (stēg′lĭts′), **Alfred** (1864–1946). American photographer, a pioneer of color photography and an early advocate of photography as an art form.

stiff (stĭf) *adj.* **stiffer, stiffest.** **1.** Difficult to bend or stretch; not flexible, pliant, or limp; rigid. **2. a.** Not moving or operating easily or freely; resistant: *a stiff hinge.* **b.** Aching and lacking ease of movement, as from exertion or old age: *a stiff neck; stiff all over.* **3.** Drawn tightly; taut. **4.** Rigidly or excessively formal, awkward, or constrained; without ease or grace. **5.** Not liquid, loose, or fluid; firm; thick: *stiff batter.* **6.** Firm in purpose or resistance; stubborn; unyielding. **7.** Having a strong, swift, steady force or movement: *a stiff breeze.* **8.** Potent or strong: *a stiff drink.* **9.** Difficult to perform or deal with; demanding; arduous: *a stiff hike; a stiff examination.* **10.** Difficult to accept; harsh or severe: *a stiff penalty.* **11.** Excessively high: *stiff prices.* **12.** *Nautical.* Not heeling over much in spite of great wind or the press of the sail. **13.** *Slang.* Well supplied; full: *The area was stiff with security men.*

PRONUNCIATION KEY

ă, pat; ā, pay; âr, care;
ä, father, are; b, bib;
ch, church; d, deed; ĕ, pet;
ē, be; f, fife; g, gag; h, hat;
hw, which; ĭ, pit; ī, pie;
îr, pier; j, judge; k, kick;
l, lid, needle; m, mum;
n, no, sudden; ng, thing;
ŏ, pot; ō, toe; ô, paw, for;
oi, noise; ou, out; o͝o, book;
o͞o, boot; p, pop; r, roar;
s, sauce; sh, ship, dish;
t, tight; th, thin, path;
th, this, bathe; ŭ, cut; ûr, fur;
v, valve; w, with; y, yes;
z, zebra, size; zh, vision;
ə, about, item, edible,
gallop, circus, peaceful

IN FOREIGN WORDS:

à, *Fr.* ami; œ, *Fr.* feu, *Ger.* schön; ü, *Fr.* tu, *Ger.* über; KH, *Ger.* ich, *Scot.* loch; N, *Fr.* bon; y', *Fr.* Compiègne

STRESS MARKS:

Primary stress: ′
in·cite′ (ĭn-sīt′)
Secondary stress: ′
in′sight′ (ĭn′sīt′)

~*adv.* **1.** To the point of being rigid: *frozen stiff.* **2.** Completely; totally: *bored stiff.*
~*n. Slang.* **1.** A corpse. **2.** An overformal, constrained, or priggish person: *a big stiff.* **3.** A drunk. **4.** A fellow; a man: *He's a lucky stiff.* **5.** A hobo; tramp. **6.** A person who tips poorly. [Middle English *stif(fe),* Old English *stīf.*] **—stiff·ly** *adv.* **—stiff·ness** *n.*

Synonyms: *stiff, rigid, inflexible, inelastic, tense, taut.* These adjectives are compared as they relate to physical stress and to human behavior and attitudes. Anything *stiff* cannot easily be bent. In reference to persons, *stiff* suggests firmness of position and either lack of ease in manner or cold formality. *Rigid* and *inflexible* apply to what cannot be bent physically, at least without damage or deformation; figuratively they describe unyielding positions or attitudes. *Inelastic* refers largely to what cannot be stretched, bent, or expanded without marked physical change. *Tense* describes the condition of being stretched tight; it is applied literally to muscles and other bodily structures and figuratively to persons under nervous strain. *Taut* is used both in the physical sense of being tightly drawn or stretched and in the related sense of nervous tension.

stiff·en (stĭf′ən) *v.* **-ened, -ening, -ens.** *—tr.* To make stiff or stiffer. *—intr.* **1.** To become stiff or stiffer. **2.** To become suddenly rigid or tense, as with indignation or fear. **—stiff·en·er** *n.*

stiff-necked (stĭf′nĕkt′) *adj.* Stubborn; unyielding. —See Synonyms at **obstinate.**

stiff upper lip *n.* Great restraint and composure; concealment of emotions or feelings, as of sadness or fear.

sti·fle¹ (stī′fəl) *v.* **-fled, -fling, -fles.** *—tr.* **1.** To kill by preventing respiration; smother or suffocate. **2.** To interrupt or cut off (the voice or breath). **3.** To keep or hold back; suppress; repress: *stifle his opinions.* *—intr.* **1.** To die of suffocation. **2.** To feel smothered or suffocated by or as if by close confinement in a stuffy room. —See Synonyms at **suppress.** [From Middle English *stufflen,* probably formed as a frequentative from Old French *estouffer,* to choke, smother.] **—sti·fler** *n.*

stifle² *n.* The joint of the hind leg corresponding to the human knee in certain quadrupeds, such as the horse. Also called "stifle joint." [Middle English *stiflet.*]

sti·fling (stī′flĭng) *adj.* Hot or stuffy almost to the point of being suffocating. **—sti·fling·ly** *adv.*

stig·ma (stĭg′mə) *n., pl.* **stigmata** (stĭg-mä′tə, stĭg′mə-tə) or **-mas** (especially for sense 6). **1.** A mark or token of shame, disgrace, or reproach: *a certain stigma attached to being divorced.* **2.** *Archaic.* A mark burned into the skin of a criminal or slave; a brand. **3.** A small mark; a scar or birthmark. **4.** *Medicine.* **a.** A mark or rash that occurs as a symptom of hysteria. **b.** A mark indicative of a history of a disease or abnormality. **5.** *Biology.* A small mark, spot, or pore, such as the respiratory spiracle of an insect or an eyespot in certain algae. **6.** *Botany.* The apex of the pistil of a flower upon which pollen is deposited at pollination. **7. stigmata.** Marks or sores corresponding to and resembling the crucifixion wounds of Jesus, sometimes appearing on the bodies of certain persons in a state of religious ecstasy or hysteria. [Latin *stigma* (plural *stigmata*), from Greek, tattoo mark, from *stizein,* to prick, tattoo.]

stig·mas·ter·ol (stĭg-măs′tə-rôl′, -rōl′, -rŏl′) *n.* A sterol, $C_{29}H_{48}O$, obtained from soybeans or Calabar beans. [New Latin *(Physo)stigma,* genus of the Calabar bean (see **physostigmine**) + STEROL.]

stig·mat·ic (stĭg-măt′ĭk) *adj.* **1.** Pertaining to, resembling, or having a stigma or stigmata. **2. Anastigmatic** *(see).*
~*n.* Also **stig·ma·tist** (stĭg′mə-tĭst). A person marked with religious stigmata.

stig·ma·tism (stĭg′mə-tĭz′əm) *n.* **1.** The state or condition of being affected by stigmata. **2.** *Optics.* The state of a refracting or reflecting system, especially the eye, that focuses light rays at a point from an off-axis point. **3.** Normal eyesight.

stig·ma·tize (stĭg′mə-tīz′) *tr.v.* **-tized, -tizing, -tizes.** **1.** To characterize or brand as disgraceful or ignominious. **2.** To brand or mark with a stigma or stigmata. **3.** To cause stigmata to appear on. [Medieval Latin *stigmatizāre,* to brand, from Greek *stigmatizein,* to mark, tattoo, from *stigma,* tattoo mark, STIGMA.] **—stig·ma·ti·za·tion** *n.* **—stig·ma·tiz·er** *n.*

Sti·kine (stĭ-kēn′). A river rising in northwestern British Columbia, Canada, and flowing 539 kilometers (335 miles) west and southwest through southern Alaska to the Pacific.

stil·bene (stĭl′bēn′) *n.* A colorless or yellowish crystalline compound, $C_{14}H_{12}$, used in the manufacture of dyes and optical bleaches and as a phosphor. [Greek *stilbos,* shining, shimmering, from *stilbein†,* to shimmer + -ENE.]

stil·bes·trol (stĭl-bĕs′trôl′, -trōl′) *n. Chemistry.* **Diethylstilbestrol** *(see).* [STILB(ENE) + ESTR(US) + -OL.]

stil·bite (stĭl′bīt′) *n.* A white or yellow lustrous zeolite mineral, essentially (Na, Ca_2) $Al_2Si_7O_{18}·7H_2O$. [French : Greek *stilbos,* shining, shimmering (see **stilbene**) + -ITE.]

stile¹ (stīl) *n.* **1.** A set or series of steps for getting over a fence or wall. **2.** A turnstile. [Middle English *stile,* Old English *stigel.*]

stile² *n.* A vertical member of a panel or frame, as in a door or window sash. [Probably from Dutch *stijl,* doorpost, from Middle Dutch, probably from Latin *stilus,* pole, post. See **style.**]

sti·let·to (stĭ-lĕt′ō) *n., pl.* **-tos** or **-toes.** **1.** A small dagger with a slender, tapering blade. **2.** A small, sharp-pointed instrument used for making eyelet holes in needlework. **3. a.** A high heel on a woman's shoe that tapers to a sharp point at the bottom. Also called "stiletto heel." **b. stilettos.** A pair of shoes with such heels. [Italian, diminutive of *stilo,* dagger, from Latin *stilus,* sharp-pointed post, pole, stake. See **style.**]

still¹ (stĭl) *adj.* **stiller, stillest.** **1.** Free from sound; silent; quiet. **2.** Low in sound; hushed; subdued. **3.** Without movement; at rest. **4.** Free from disturbance, commotion, or agitation; tranquil; serene. **5.** Free from noticeable current, as water might be. **6.** Not carbonated; lacking effervescence: *still wine.* **7.** *Photography.* Of, designating, or pertaining to a single or static photograph as opposed to a motion picture. —See Synonyms at **calm.**
~*n.* **1.** Silence; quiet; calm: *the still of the night.* **2.** A still photograph, especially one taken from a scene of a motion picture and used for promotional purposes.
~*adv.* **1.** Without movement; motionlessly: *stand still.* **2.** Up to or at the time specified; yet: *will still be here tomorrow; has still not finished.* **3.** In increasing amount or degree: *has become still worse.* **4.** Nevertheless; all the same: *I understand the difficulty, but I still think he should go.* **5.** Even: *worked still harder.* **6.** *Archaic & Regional.* Always; constantly.
~*conj.* But yet; nevertheless: *It was difficult; still, he tried.* —See Synonyms at **but.**
~*v.* **stilled, stilling, stills.** *—tr.* **1.** To make still, quiet, or tranquil. **2.** To make motionless. **3.** To allay; calm. *—intr.* To become still. [Middle English *still(e),* Old English *stille.*] **—still·ness** *n.*

Synonyms: *still, quiet, silent, noiseless, hushed, tranquil.* These adjectives refer to the relative absence of sound or movement. *Still* can apply to what is without sound or activity or both, as can *quiet. Still* is usually the more emphatic in all senses; *quiet* often implies merely the absence of noise, bustle, or customary activity. *Silent* refers only to what is without sound or noise. Like *noiseless* and *hushed,* it makes no clear indication with respect to movement or the absence thereof. *Noiseless* can mean without sound but usually implies freedom from excessive or disturbing sound. *Hushed* suggests a sudden condition of silence, especially one following noise or excitement. *Tranquil* primarily implies calm and lack of agitated movement.

still² *n.* **1.** An apparatus for distilling liquids, particularly alcohols, consisting of a vessel in which the substance is vaporized by heat and a cooling device in which the vapor is condensed. **2.** A distillery. [From *still,* to distill, Middle English *stillen,* short for *distillen,* to DISTILL.]

Still (stĭl), **Andrew Taylor** (1828–1917). U.S. pioneer osteopath. A largely self-taught medical practitioner, he surmised that disease was due to abnormalities in or near bodily joints that inhibit the body's natural healing processes. On this premise he founded osteopathy, a practice that has gained widespread acceptance.

stil·lage (stĭl′ĭj) *n.* A bench or frame, as in a factory, used to keep objects from touching the floor, as while they are draining or drying. [Probably from Dutch *stellagie,* frame, scaffold, from *stellen,* to stand.]

still alarm *n.* A fire alarm transmitted by means, as the telephone, other than sounding the regular signal apparatus.

still·birth (stĭl′bûrth′) *n.* **1.** The birth of a dead child, usually when gestation has continued for over 28 weeks. **2.** A child dead at birth.

still·born (stĭl′bôrn′) *adj.* **1.** Dead at birth. **2.** Failing right at the beginning; abortive.

still hunt *n.* The hunting of game by stalking or ambushing. **—still-hunt** (stĭl′hŭnt′) *v.*

stil·li·cide (stĭl′ə-sīd′) *n. Law.* A right or duty connected with the spilling of water from one person's roof onto another's land. [Latin *stillicidium : stilla,* drop (of water) + *-cidium,* from *cadere,* to fall.]

stil·li·form (stĭl′ə-fôrm′) *adj.* Shaped like a drop or globule. [Latin *stillis,* a drop (see **distill**) + -FORM.]

still life *n., pl.* **still lifes.** **1.** The representation of inanimate objects, such as flowers or fruit, in painting or photography. **2.** A picture of inanimate objects. **—still-life** (stĭl′līf′) *adj.*

still·man (stĭl′măn′) *n., pl.* **-men** (-mĕn′). **1.** A person who owns or manages a still or distillery. **2.** A person who operates a distillation apparatus, as in an oil refinery.

Still·son wrench (stĭl′sən) *n.* A trademark for a monkey wrench with serrated jaws, one of which has slight angular movement to facilitate gripping pipes and other round objects. Compare **pipe wrench.**

still·y (stĭl′ē) *adj.* **-ier, -iest.** Quiet; calm. **—stil·ly** *adv.*

stilt (stĭlt) *n., pl.* **stilts** or **stilt** (for sense 3). **1.** Either of a pair of long, slender poles, each equipped with a raised footrest enabling the wearer to walk elevated above the ground. **2.** Any of various tall posts or pillars used as support, as for a dock or building. **3. a.** A long-legged wading bird, *Himantopus mexicanus* (or *H. himantopus*), having black and white plumage and a long slender bill. **b.** A related bird, *Cladorhyncus leucocephala,* of Australia.
~*tr.v.* **stilted, stilting, stilts.** To place or raise on or as if on stilts. [Middle English *stilte,* stilt, crutch, perhaps of Low German origin, akin to Low German and Flemish *stilte.*]

stilt·ed (stĭl′tĭd) *adj.* **1.** Stiffly or artificially dignified or formal; stiff: *a very stilted manner.* **2.** *Architecture.* Having some vertical length between the impost and the beginning of the curve. Said of an arch. **—stilt·ed·ly** *adv.* **—stilt·ed·ness** *n.*

Stil·ton (stĭlt′n) *n.* A rich, blue-veined cheese made from whole milk with added cream and having a wrinkled rind. [After *Stilton,* Cambridgeshire, England.]

Stil·well (stĭl′wĕl′, -wəl), **Joseph Warren** (1883–1946). U.S. army officer. America's foremost political and military expert on China, he became chief of staff of Chinese and American forces (1941), a

stilt *The black-winged stilt (above) is one of nine species of this long-legged bird. Stilts live in temperate and tropical regions, on the shores of lakes, marshes, and pools where their long legs and bills enable them to probe deep for small animals.*

position he held through most of World War II. Late in the war he was active in the South Pacific and participated in the taking of Okinawa (1945).

Stim·son (stĭm′sən), **Henry Lewis** (1867–1950). U.S. public official. A successful New York lawyer, he served as secretary of war under William Howard Taft and later saw brief action in France during World War I. He served as governor-general of the Philippines (1927–29), as secretary of state under Herbert Hoover (1929–33), and as secretary of war and presidential adviser on atomic policy during World War II.

stim·u·lant (stĭm′yə-lənt) *n.* **1.** Anything that temporarily arouses or accelerates physiological activity, especially of a particular organ. **2.** A stimulus or incentive: *Social unrest often provides a stimulant to literature.* **3.** A drug, food, or drink that stimulates. ~*adj.* Serving as a stimulant. [Latin *stimulāns* (stem *stimulant-*), present participle of *stimulāre*, to STIMULATE.]

stim·u·late (stĭm′yə-lāt′) *v.* **-lated, -lating, -lates.** —*tr.* To rouse to activity or heightened action, as by spurring or goading; animate. —*intr.* To act or serve as a stimulant or stimulus. —See Synonyms at **provoke.** [Latin *stimulāre,* to goad on, from *stimulus,* STIMULUS.] —**stim·u·la·tor** *n.* —**stim·u·la·tion** *n.*

stim·u·la·tive (stĭm′yə-lā′tĭv) *adj.* Serving or tending to stimulate. —*n.* Anything that stimulates; a stimulus.

stim·u·lus (stĭm′yə-ləs) *n., pl.* **-li** (-lī′). **1.** Something causing or regarded as causing a response. **2.** An agent, action, or condition that elicits or accelerates a physiological or psychological activity. **3.** Something that incites or rouses to action: *a stimulus to the imagination.* [Latin *stimulus†,* a goad.]

sting (stĭng) *v.* **stung** (stŭng) *or obsolete* **stang** (stăng), **stung, sting·ing, stings.** —*tr.* **1.** To pierce or wound painfully with or as if with a sharp-pointed structure or organ, such as that of certain insects. **2.** To cause to feel a sharp, smarting pain: *stinging rain. Smoke stung our eyes.* **3.** To cause to suffer keenly in the mind or feelings: *Her words stung him bitterly.* **4.** To spur on by or as if by sharp irritation. **5.** *Slang.* To cheat or overcharge. —*intr.* **1.** To have, use, or wound with a sting. **2.** To feel a sharp, smarting pain. **3.** To cause a sharp, smarting pain or keen mental distress. ~*n.* **1.** The act of stinging. **2.** The wound or pain caused by or as if by stinging. **3.** A sharp, piercing organ or part, often ejecting a venomous secretion, such as the modified ovipositor of a bee or wasp or the spine of certain fishes. **4.** Stinging power, quality, or capacity: *"The sting of fear is anxiety"* (Paul Tillich). **5.** A keen stimulus or incitement; a goad or spur. **6.** *Informal.* A complicated confidence game, especially one undertaken by undercover agents to entrap criminals. [Sting, stung (or stang), stung; Middle English *stingen, stang* (past plural *stungen*), *stungen,* Old English *stingan, stang* (past plural *stungon*), *stungen.*] —**sting·ing·ly** *adv.*

sting·a·ree (stĭng′ə-rē′) *n.* A fish, the **stingray.** [Alteration of STINGRAY.]

sting·er (stĭng′ər) *n.* **1.** One that stings, as: **a.** A stinging organ or part. **b.** A sharp blow. **c.** Something that wounds mentally, such as an insult. **2.** A cocktail of crème de menthe and brandy.

stinging hair *n.* A glandular plant hair that if touched expels an irritant fluid to deter animal predators.

stinging nettle *n.* A nettle, especially *Urtica dioica,* with stinging hairs on the stem and leaves.

sting·ray (stĭng′rā′) *n.* Any of various rays of the family Dasyatidae, having a whiplike tail armed with a venomous spine capable of inflicting severe injury. Also called "stingaree."

stin·gy (stĭn′jē) *adj.* **-gier, -giest. 1.** Giving or spending reluctantly or unwillingly; penurious. **2.** Scanty or meager. [Obsolete *stingy,* stinging, from STING.] —**stin·gi·ly** *adv.* —**stin·gi·ness** *n.*

Synonyms: *stingy, close, close-fisted, niggardly, miserly, parsimonious, penny-pinching.* These adjectives, which are often interchangeable, suggest reluctance to spend one's money or part with one's possessions. *Stingy,* the most general, often implies, besides absence of generosity, an inclination toward meanness in dealings. *Close* and *close-fisted* describe one who is exceedingly and usually annoyingly cautious in money matters. *Niggardly* implies a tendency to be grudging, petty, and covetous. *Miserly* suggests greediness and hoarding of wealth for its own sake. *Parsimonious* emphasizes frugality carried to an extreme. *Penny-pinching* adds to *niggardly* the implication of foolish economy.

stink (stĭngk) *v.* **stank** (stăngk) *or* **stunk** (stŭngk), **stunk, stink·ing, stinks.** —*intr.* **1.** To emit a strong foul odor. **2. a.** To be highly offensive or abhorrent. **b.** To be in extremely bad repute. **3.** *Slang.* To have or embody something to an extreme or offensive degree. Usually used with *of* or *with: He stinks of success.* **4.** *Slang.* To be of extremely low or bad quality: *This film stinks.* —*tr.* **1.** To cause to stink. Usually used with *up: The smell of garlic stank the kitchen up.* **2.** To drive or force by a strong, foul, or suffocating smell. Used with *out.* ~*n.* **1.** A strong offensive odor; a stench. **2.** *Informal.* A great fuss or outcry: *raised a stink.* —See Synonyms at **smell.** [Stink, stank (or stunk), stunk; Middle English *stinken, stank* (past plural *stunken*), *stunken,* Old English *stincan, stanc* (past plural *stuncon*), *stuncen,* from Germanic *stinkwan* (unattested).]

stink ball *n.* See **stinkpot** (sense 1).

stink bomb *n.* A small bomb, often in the form of a capsule, that emits a foul odor on explosion.

stink·bug (stĭngk′bŭg′) *n.* Any of numerous insects of the family Pentatomidae, having a broad, flattened body and emitting a foul odor.

stink·er (stĭng′kər) *n.* **1.** One that stinks. **2.** *Slang.* A contemptible, disgusting, or irritating person. **3.** *Slang.* Something very difficult or very offensive: *The exam was a real stinker.*

stink·horn (stĭngk′hôrn′) *n.* Any of several foul-smelling fungi of the order Phallales, such as *Phallus impudicus,* having a thick, cylindrical stalk and a narrow cap.

stink·ing (stĭng′kĭng) *adj.* **1.** Having a foul smell; fetid; rank. **2.** *Slang.* Very unpleasant or repulsive. **3.** *Slang.* Very drunk. ~*adv. Slang.* To an offensive or extreme degree: *got stinking drunk; stinking rich.* —**stink·ing·ly** *adv.* —**stink·ing·ness** *n.*

stinking badger *n.* The **teledu** *(see).*

stinking chamomile *n.* A plant, the **mayweed** *(see).*

stinking iris *n.* A grayish-purple flowered iris, *Iris foetidissima,* the leaves of which emit a sickly sweet smell when crushed.

stink·pot (stĭngk′pŏt′) *n.* **1.** An earthenware jar containing combustibles emitting a suffocating smoke, formerly used in warfare. Also called "stink ball." **2.** *Slang.* A despised or mean person. **3.** A musk turtle, *Sternotherus odoratus,* of eastern North America.

stink·stone (stĭngk′stōn′) *n.* A variety of limestone that emits a disagreeable smell when struck or rubbed.

stink·weed (stĭngk′wēd′) *n.* **1.** A yellow-flowered plant, *Diplotaxis muralis,* that emits an unpleasant smell if bruised. Also called "wall mustard." **2.** Any of various other plants having flowers or foliage with an unpleasant smell.

stink·wood (stĭngk′wʊd′) *n.* **1. a.** A tree, *Ocotea bullata,* of southern Africa, having wood with an unpleasant smell. **b.** The hard, heavy wood of this tree, used in cabinetwork. **2.** Broadly, any of several other trees having wood with an unpleasant smell.

stint¹ (stĭnt) *v.* **stinted, stinting, stints.** —*tr.* **1. a.** To restrict or limit, as in amount or number; be sparing with: *stinting the rations to make them last.* **b.** To restrict or limit (oneself or another): *stinted himself in order to buy a car.* **2.** *Archaic.* To stop; desist. —*intr.* **1.** To be frugal or sparing. **2.** *Archaic.* To stop or desist. ~*n.* **1.** A fixed amount or share of work or duty to be performed within a given period of time. **2.** A limitation or restriction: *working without stint.* [Middle English *stinten,* to stop, cut short, Old English *styntan,* to blunt, dull.] —**stint·er** *n.*

stint² *n.* **1.** Any of several small sandpipers of the genus *Calidris,* of northern regions. **2.** *Archaic.* A **dunlin** *(see).* [Middle English *stynt†.*]

stipe (stīp) *n. Biology.* A stalk or stalklike structure, such as the stemlike support of the cap of a mushroom or the stalk of a seaweed frond. [French, from Latin *stīpes,* post, tree trunk.]

sti·pel (stī′pəl) *n. Botany.* A minute or secondary stipule at the base of a leaflet. [New Latin *stipella,* diminutive of *stipula,* STIPULE.] —**sti·pel·late** (stī-pĕl′ĭt, stī′pə-lĭt, -lāt′) *adj.*

sti·pend (stī′pĕnd′, -pənd) *n.* A fixed or regular payment, such as a salary for services rendered or an allowance; especially, the salary paid to a clergyman. [Middle English *stipendie,* from Old French, from Latin *stīpendium,* tax, tribute; akin to *stipulārī,* to STIPULATE.]

sti·pen·di·ar·y (stī-pĕn′dē-ĕr′ē) *adj.* **1.** Receiving a stipend. **2.** Compensated by stipend: *stipendiary services.* ~*n., pl.* **stipendiaries. 1.** A person, such as a clergyman, who receives a stipend. **2.** A stipendiary magistrate. [Latin *stīpendiārius,* from *stīpendium,* tribute, STIPEND.]

sti·pes (stī′pēz′) *n., pl.* **stipites** (stĭp′ə-tēz′). *Zoology.* **1.** A segment of the maxilla of an insect. **2.** Any stalklike support or structure. [New Latin, from Latin *stīpes,* post, tree trunk.] —**sti·pi·form** (stī′pə-fôrm′), **stip·i·ti·form** (stĭp′ə-tə-fôrm′) *adj.*

stip·i·tate (stĭp′ə-tāt′) *adj.* Having or supported on a stipe. [Latin *stīpes* (stem *stīpit-*), post, tree trunk. See **stipes.**]

stip·ple (stĭp′əl) *tr.v.* **-pled, -pling, -ples. 1.** To draw, engrave, or paint in dots or short strokes. **2.** To apply (paint, for example) in dots or short strokes. **3.** To dot, fleck, or speckle. ~*n.* **1.** The method of painting, drawing, or engraving by stippling. **2.** The effect produced by stippling or a work produced in this manner. [Dutch *stippelen,* frequentative of *stippen,* to speckle, dot, from *stip,* dot, point, from Middle Dutch.] —**stip·pler** *n.*

stip·u·lar (stĭp′yə-lər) *adj. Botany.* Of, pertaining to, or resembling a stipule or stipules.

stip·u·late¹ (stĭp′yə-lāt′) *v.* **-lated, -lating, -lates.** —*tr.* **1. a.** To lay down as a condition of an agreement; require by contract. **b.** To specify or arrange in an agreement: *stipulate the date and price.* **2.** To guarantee or promise in an agreement. —*intr.* **1.** To make an express demand or provision in an agreement. Used with *for.* **2.** To form an agreement. [Latin *stipulārī,* to bargain, demand.] —**stip·u·la·tor** *n.*

stip·u·late² (stĭp′yə-lĭt) *adj. Botany.* Having stipules.

stip·u·la·tion (stĭp′yə-lā′shən) *n.* **1.** The act of stipulating. **2.** Something stipulated; a term or condition in an agreement. —**stip·u·la·to·ry** (stĭp′yə-lə-tôr′ē, -tōr′ē) *adj.*

stip·ule (stĭp′yʊl) *n. Botany.* Any of the usually small, paired leaflike appendages at the base of a leaf or leafstalk in certain plants. [New Latin *stipula,* from Latin, stalk, stem; akin to *stipulārī,* to STIPULATE.]

stir¹ (stûr) *v.* **stirred, stirring, stirs.** —*tr.* **1. a.** To pass an implement through (a liquid, for example) in circular motions so as to mix or cool the contents. **b.** To introduce (an ingredient) into a liquid or mixture in this way: *stirred sugar into his tea.* **c.** To mix together the ingredients of (a cake, for example) prior to cooking or use. **2.** To cause a slight movement in or alter the placement of slightly. **3.** To move (oneself) briskly or vigorously; bestir. **4.** To rouse (a person), as from sleep or indifference. **5.** To incite, provoke, or instigate.

stinkbug *There are about 2,500 species of these sap-sucking insects, which are found all over the world and sometimes known as shieldbugs, from their shield-shaped bodies. When alarmed, stinkbugs give off an offensive smell as a defense mechanism.*

Often used with *up*: *stir up trouble; stir up old memories.* **6.** To excite the emotions of; move or affect strongly. *—intr.* **1.** To change position slightly: *stirred in her sleep.* **2. a.** To move about actively; bestir oneself. **b.** To move away from a customary place or position; venture: *The sentry did not stir from his post.* **3.** To take place; happen. **4.** To be capable of being stirred: *As the mixture started to set it stirred less easily.* —See Synonyms at **provoke.**
~n. **1.** An act of stirring; a mixing or poking movement. **2.** A very slight movement. **3.** A disturbance or commotion. **4.** An excited reaction; a ferment. [Middle English *stiren,* Old English *styrian,* to move, agitate, excite.] **—stir·rer** *n.*

stir[2] *n. Slang.* Prison. [19th century : origin obscure.]

stir crazy *adj. Slang.* Distraught or restless from long confinement in or as if in prison.

stirk (stûrk) *n.* A yearling heifer or bullock. [Middle English *stirk,* Old English *stirc.*]

Stir·ling's formula (stûr′lĭngz) *n. Mathematics.* A formula for the approximate value of the factorial of a large number: $\log n! = n\log n - n$. [After James *Stirling* (1692–1770), Scottish mathematician.]

Stir·ling·shire (stûr′lĭng-shîr′, -shər). Former county in central Scotland, south of the Forth River, now divided between the Central and Strathclyde regions.

stirps (stûrps) *n., pl.* **stirpes** (stûr′pēz′). **1. a.** A line of descendants of common ancestry; stock. **b.** *Law.* A person from whom a family is descended. **2. a.** A group of animals equivalent to a superfamily. **b.** A variety of plants with stable characteristics retained under cultivation. [Latin *stirps*†, stem, root, lineage.]

stir·ring (stûr′ĭng) *adj.* **1.** Rousing; thrilling: *a stirring call to arms.* **2.** Active; lively. —See Synonyms at **moving. —stir·ring·ly** *adv.*

stir·rup (stûr′əp, stĭr′-) *n.* **1.** A flat-based loop or ring hung from either side of a horse's saddle to support the rider's foot in mounting and riding. Also called "stirrup iron." **2.** Any of various parts or devices shaped like an inverted U, used to support, hold, or fix something. **3.** *Nautical.* A rope on a ship hanging from a yard and having an eye at the end through which a footrope is passed for support. [Middle English *stirope,* Old English *stigrāp.*]

stirrup bone *n. Anatomy.* The **stapes** *(see).*

stir·rup-cup (stûr′əp-kŭp′, stĭr′-) *n.* **1.** A farewell drink given to a rider who is mounted ready to depart. **2.** Any farewell drink.

stirrup leather *n.* The strap used to fasten a stirrup to a saddle. Also called "stirrup strap."

stirrup pump *n.* A type of small hand pump that is used for fighting fires or in gardening.

stish·ov·ite (stĭsh′ə-vīt′) *n.* A dense tetragonal form of silicon dioxide formed under great pressure. [After S. M. *Stishov,* 20th-century Russian mineralogist.]

stitch (stĭch) *n. Abbr.* **st. 1.** A single complete movement of a threaded needle in sewing or surgical suturing. **2.** A single loop of yarn around a knitting needle or similar implement. **3.** The link, loop, or knot made in this way. **4.** A particular method of arranging the threads in sewing, knitting, or crocheting: *a purl stitch.* **5.** A sudden sharp pain in the side. **6.** *Informal.* An article of clothing: *not a stitch on.* **7.** *Informal.* The least part; bit: *didn't do a stitch of work.* **—in stitches.** *Informal.* Laughing uncontrollably.
~v. **stitched, stitching, stitches.** *—tr.* **1. a.** To fasten or join with stitches. **b.** To mend or repair with stitches. Used with *up.* **2.** To decorate or ornament with stitches. **3.** To fasten together (sheets of a book, for example) with staples or thread. *—intr.* To make stitches; sew. [Middle English *stiche,* Old English *stice,* a sting, prick.] **—stitch·er** *n.* See feature, next page.

stitch·wort (stĭch′wûrt′, -wôrt′) *n.* Any of several low-growing plants of the genus *Stellaria,* having small, white flowers. [Middle English *stichewort,* Old English *sticwyrt,* agrimony : STITCH + WORT (from its alleged ability to cure sharp pains in the side).]

stith·y (stĭth′ē) *n., pl.* **-ies. 1.** An anvil. **2.** A forge or smithy. [Middle English *stethy,* from Old Norse *stedhi.*]

sti·ver (stī′vər) *n.* **1.** An obsolete Dutch coin worth $1/20$ of a guilder. **2.** Something of small value. [Dutch *stuiver,* from Middle Dutch *stuyver.*]

St. John (sānt jŏn′). Island, 52 square kilometers (20 square miles), in the U.S. Virgin Islands of the West Indies, located east of St. Thomas.

St. John River. A river rising in the northwestern part of the state of Maine and flowing 673 kilometers (450 miles), first northeast, then southeast through western New Brunswick, Canada, to the Bay of Fundy, forming part of the U.S.-Canadian border along its course.

St. Johns (sānt jŏnz′). A river of eastern Florida, flowing 459 kilometers (285 miles) north to the Atlantic east of Jacksonville.

St. John's[1] (sānt jŏnz′). Capital of Antigua and Barbuda, on Antigua Island in the British West Indies. It is a popular tourist center.

St. John's[2]. The capital of Newfoundland, eastern Canada. An Atlantic port, it is the most easterly city in North America.

St. John's bread *n.* The long blackish, sugary, edible pod of the **carob** *(see).* [After St. JOHN the Baptist, who lived on honey and locusts (probably locust beans, or carob) while preaching in the desert. Matthew 3:4.]

St. Johns·wort (sānt jŏnz′wûrt′, -wôrt′) *n.* Any of various plants or shrubs of the genus *Hypericum,* having yellow flowers with prominent stamens. [So called because it was gathered on *St. John's* Eve to ward off evil spirits.]

St. Joseph (sānt jō′zəf, -səf). A city of Missouri, in the northwest on the Missouri River.

St. Kitts-Nevis, Kitts-Nevis-Anguilla. See **St. Christopher and Nevis.**

St. Lau·rent (săN′ lô-räN′), **Louis Stephen** (1882–1973). Canadian prime minister from 1948 to 1957. The St. Lawrence Seaway (opened in 1959) was built during his premiership.

St. Law·rence (sānt lôr′əns, lŏr′əns). One of the principal rivers of North America. It issues from Lake Ontario and flows northeast to form part of the border between Canada and the United States, eventually entering the Gulf of St. Lawrence. Though partially icebound in winter, it remains a major artery for shipping between the Atlantic and the Great Lakes and was improved by the opening of the St. Lawrence Seaway. From Lake Ontario to Anticosti Island, the river is *c.* 1,200 kilometers (750 miles) long.

St. Lawrence, Gulf of. A gulf of the Atlantic Ocean, eastern Canada, into which the St. Lawrence River flows. It lies between Newfoundland and mainland Canada. Though closed to navigation by ice in the winter months, it has important fishing grounds.

St. Lawrence Island. An island of the state of Alaska 145 kilometers (90 miles) long and up to 35 kilometers (22 miles) wide, lying just south of Bering Strait.

St. Lawrence Seaway. A major waterway system connecting the Gulf of St. Lawrence and the Great Lakes. A joint U.S.-Canadian project, it was opened in 1959 and provides navigation channels between Montreal and Lake Ontario, and between Lake Ontario and Lake Erie. The seaway for the first time gave large oceangoing vessels access to the heart of North America.

St. Lou·is (sānt lo͞o′ĭs, lo͞o′ē). The largest city in Missouri, in the eastern part of the state. Founded in 1764 by the French, on the Mississippi just downstream from the confluence with the Missouri, it became an important center for fur traders and explorers opening up the West. It was ceded to the United States in 1804 and is now a communications, commercial, industrial, and cultural center.

St. Louis River. A river rising in northeastern Minnesota and flowing 354 kilometers (220 miles) in a wide southward bend to Lake Superior at Duluth.

St. Lu·cia (sānt lo͞o′shə). Volcanic island state in the Windward group of the West Indies. Discovered by Columbus (1502), it changed hands repeatedly between England and France before becoming an English colony in 1814. It won full independence in 1979. The economy is primarily agricultural, but tourism is increasingly important. Area, 616 square kilometers (238 square miles). Population, 115,700 (estimated). Capital, Castries. See map at **Latin America.**

St. Ma·lo (săN′ mä-lō′). A port and popular resort in Ille-et-Vilaine department, northwestern France. A tidal power station, one of the first in the world, was opened here in 1966.

St. Mar·tin (sānt märt′n). A Leeward Island of the West Indies constituting part of the Netherlands Antilles in the south and of French Guadeloupe in the north.

St. Mar·ys City (sānt mâr′ēz). Formerly **Saint Mar·ys.** A village in southern Maryland, the site of the first settlement in Maryland (1634) and of the state's first capital.

St. Marys River. 1. A river rising in Okefenokee Swamp, southeastern Georgia, and flowing 280 kilometers (175 miles) east to the Atlantic, forming part of the Georgia-Florida border. **2.** A river flowing 101 kilometers (63 miles) from Lake Superior to Lake Huron, forming the boundary between northeastern Michigan and Ontario, Canada.

St. Mau·rice (sānt mə-rēs′; *French* săN mô-rēs′). A river rising in central Quebec and flowing 325 miles southward to the St. Lawrence at Trois Rivières.

St. Mo·ritz (sānt′ mə-rĭts′, săN′ mô-rēts′). Alpine resort in Graubünden canton, southeastern Switzerland, in the upper Engadin (Inn valley). It is a famous winter-sports center.

sto·a (stō′ə) *n., pl.* **-as** or **stoae** (stō′ē′). An ancient Greek covered walk or colonnade, usually having columns on one side and a wall on the other. [Greek, porch.]

stoat (stōt) *n.* A small carnivorous mammal, *Mustela erminea,* similar to but larger than the weasel and having a black-tipped tail. In northern regions the brown coat turns white in winter and is called ermine. [Middle English *stote.*]

sto·chas·tic (stō-kăs′tĭk) *adj.* **1.** Of, designating, or characterized by conjecture; conjectural. **2.** *Statistics.* **a.** Random. **b.** Statistical. [Greek *stokhastikos,* capable of aiming, conjectural, from *stokhazesthai,* to aim at, guess at, from *stokhos,* target, aim.] **—sto·chas·ti·cal·ly** *adv.*

stochastic process *n. Statistics.* A process consisting of a number of steps having a random variable the successive values of which are not independent.

stochastic variable *n. Statistics.* A **random variable** *(see).*

stock (stŏk) *n. Abbr.* **stk. 1.** A supply accumulated for future use; a store or supply that may be drawn upon. **2.** The total merchandise kept on hand by a trader, commercial establishment, or manufacturer. **3.** All the animals kept or reared on a farm; livestock. **4.** *Finance.* **a.** The capital or fund that a company raises through the sale of shares entitling the holder to dividends and to other rights of ownership, such as voting rights. **b.** The number of shares that each stockholder possesses. **c.** The shares of a specified company or business enterprise. **d.** Formerly, the part of a tally or record of account given to a creditor. **e.** A debt symbolized by such a tally or tallies. **5.** The trunk or main stem of a tree or other plant as distinguished from the branches and roots. **6. a.** A plant or stem onto which a graft is made. **b.** A plant or tree from which cuttings and

stoa *A colonnaded promenade that the ancient Greeks used as a meeting place. This is the Stoa of Attalos in Athens.*

stoat Mustela erminea, *the stoat, normally has brown fur on its back and white fur on its undersides, as shown here. But in winter the coat turns completely white except for a black tip on the tail, and the animal is then known as an ermine.*

slips are taken. **7. a.** The original progenitor of a family line. **b.** The descendants of a common ancestor; a family line, especially one of a specified character: *comes from farming stock.* **c.** The type from which a group of animals or plants has descended. **d.** A race, family, or other related group of animals or plants. **e.** An ethnic group or other major division of mankind. **f.** A group of related languages. **g.** A group of related families of languages. **8.** The raw material out of which something is made. **9.** A broth in which meat, fish, bones, or vegetables have been simmered for a period of time, used as a base in preparing soup, gravy, or sauces. **10. a.** The chief upright part of something, particularly a supporting structure or block. **b. stocks.** The timber frame that supports a ship during construction. **c.** *Often* **stocks.** A frame in which a horse or other animal is held for shoeing or for veterinary treatment. **11. stocks.** Formerly, an instrument of punishment consisting of a heavy timber frame with holes for confining the ankles and, sometimes, the wrists. **12.** *Nautical.* The crosspiece at the end of an anchor's shank. **13.** The wooden block from which a bell is suspended. **14. a.** The rear wooden or metal handle or steadying support of a rifle, pistol, or automatic weapon, to which the barrel and mechanism are at-

---

stitch

THE ART OF DECORATIVE STITCHING

Embroidery goes back to the days of the ancient Egyptians

The art of decorative stitching, or embroidery, goes back to the ancient Egyptians, whose wall paintings show colorful examples of needlework. One of the earliest embroidered linen strips in existence is the 11th-century Bayeux Tapestry depicting the Norman conquest of England, which now hangs in the museum at Bayeux in Normandy.

Embroidery, as opposed to plain sewing, has been enjoyed by people from all walks of life. In 1502 Catherine of Aragon, the first wife of Henry VIII, brought with her from Spain samples of her own needlework in her trousseau. And in 1588 Elizabeth I, another keen needlewoman, refounded the ancient Company of Broderers (Embroiderers) in London.

During the late 18th century there was a vogue in Europe for "needlepainting" in which scenes and portraits were stitched with wool or silk on cloth to resemble oil paintings. Today there is a worldwide interest in needlework, ranging from canvaswork, or tapestry as it is often known, to blackwork—in which black silk threads are worked on a white or natural linen background. Six groups of stitches—blanket stitch, chain stitch, cross-stitch, featherstitch, running stitch, and weaving stitch—used in needlework are shown below.

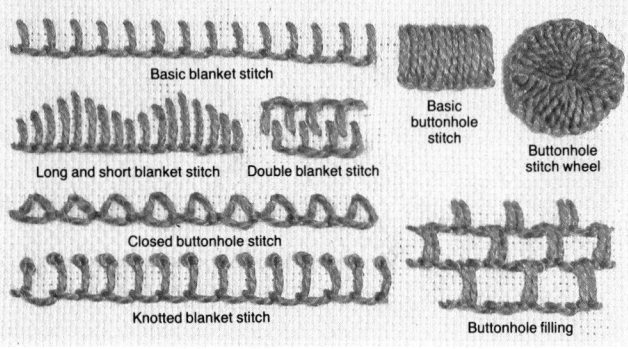

BLANKET STITCH *A broad stitch used for oversewing edges in plain needlework and also to embroider decorative outlines and borders.*

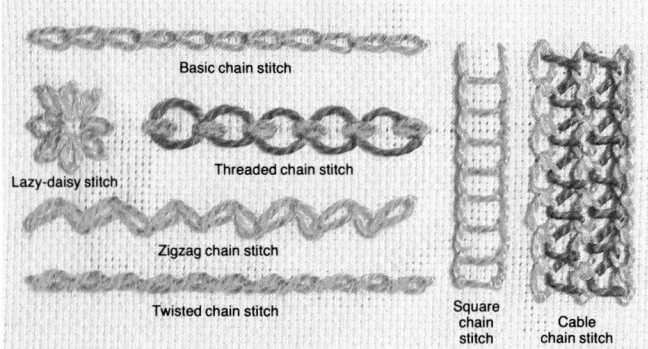

CHAIN STITCH *The basic chain stitch is a series of interlocking loops. When worked in close rows, it can be used to cover an area.*

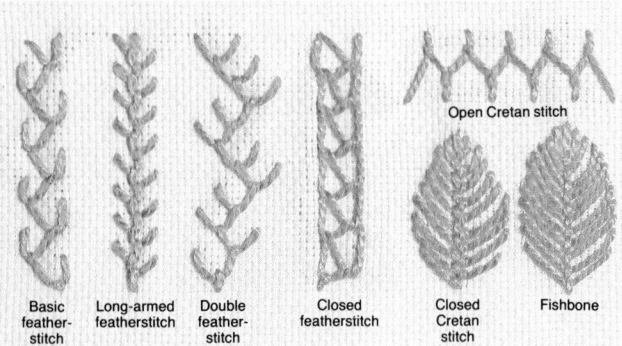

FEATHERSTITCH *The basic stitch and its variants are used mainly for borders. In 19th-century England they were used on smocks.*

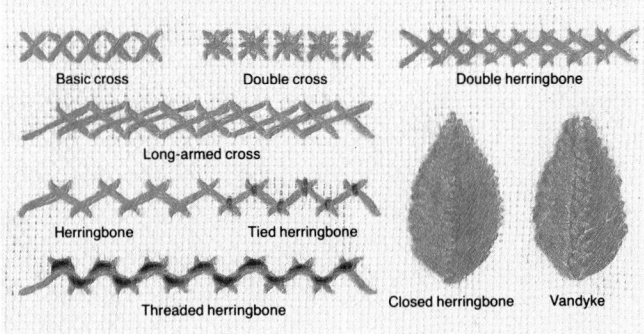

CROSS-STITCH *All types of cross-stitch are formed by two crossing arms. They can be used as outlines, borders, or to fill an area.*

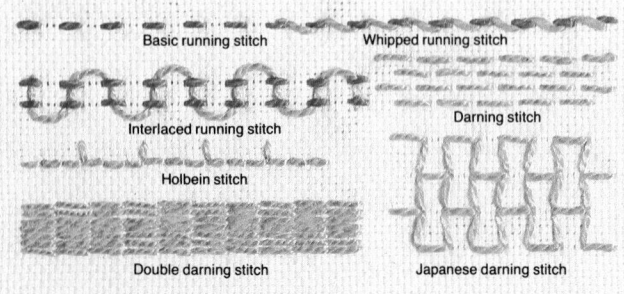

RUNNING STITCH *The basic running stitch is the main stitch in quilting. Variations are also used to decorate borders and bands.*

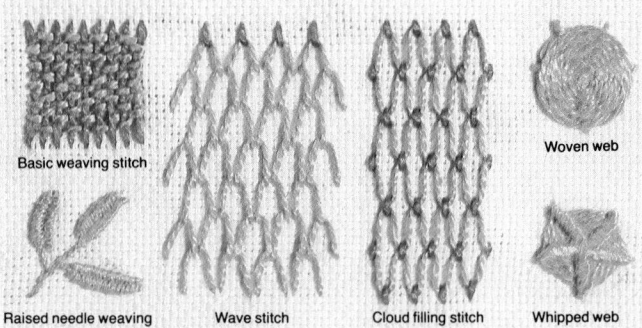

WEAVING STITCH *The basic weaving stitch, with its basketlike texture, is used to fill in an area with different colored threads.*

tached. Also called "gunstock." **b.** The long beam of field-gun carriages that trails along the ground to provide stability and support. **15.** Any handle, as of a whip, fishing rod, or various carpenter's tools. **16.** The frame of a plow, to which the share, handles, coulter, and other parts are fastened. **17.** *Theater.* **a.** A stock company. **b.** The repertoire of such a company. **c.** Any theater or theatrical activity, especially outside of a main theatrical center such as New York City: *a small role in summer stock.* **18.** Any of several plants of the genus *Matthiola,* native to the Old World; especially, *M. incana,* widely cultivated for its clusters of showy, fragrant, variously colored flowers, and *M. bicornis,* night-scented stock. **19.** That portion of a pack of cards or group of dominoes that is not dealt out but is drawn from during a game. **20.** *Geology.* An irregularly shaped intrusive body of igneous rock in the earth's crust, with an exposed surface of less than 100 square kilometers (40 square miles). **21. a.** Personal reputation or standing: *His stock with the students is falling.* **b.** Confidence or credence: *put no stock in his statement.* **22.** Unexposed film. **23. a.** A stiff, long neckcloth wound around the neck as a part of male dress in the 18th century. **b.** A long white cloth worn around the neck as a part of formal riding dress. **c.** A broad scarf worn around the neck. **24.** A brick of the kind most commonly used in building. **25. Rolling stock** *(see).* **26. Diestock** *(see).* **27.** *Archaic.* A stocking. **—in stock.** Available for sale or use. **—out of stock.** Not available for sale or use. **—take stock. 1.** To take an inventory. **2.** To make an estimate or reappraisal, as of resources, prospects, or a prevailing situation.
~v. **stocked, stocking, stocks.** *—tr.* **1.** To provide or furnish with a stock of something, especially: **a.** To supply (a shop) with merchandise. **b.** To supply (a farm) with livestock. **c.** To fill (a stream, for example) with fish. **2.** To keep in stock for future sale. **3.** To provide (a rifle, for example) with a stock. **4.** *Obsolete.* To put (someone) in the stocks as a punishment. *—intr.* **1.** To gather and lay in a supply of something. Used with *up* or *up on.* **2.** To put forth or sprout new shoots. Used of a plant.
~adj. **1.** Kept regularly in stock. **2.** Repeated regularly without any thought or originality; trite: *a stock answer.* **3. a.** Of or pertaining to the raising of livestock: *stock farming.* **b.** Used for breeding: *a stock mare.* **4.** Designating a conventional or traditional character of a particular dramatic genre, such as farce or pantomime. [Middle English *stok(ke),* Old English *stocc,* tree trunk.]

stock·ade (stŏ-kād′) *n.* **1.** A defensive barrier made of strong posts or timbers driven upright side by side into the ground. **2.** Any similarly fenced or enclosed area, especially one used for protection or imprisonment.
~tr.v. **stockaded, -ading, -ades.** To fortify, protect, or surround with a stockade. [Obsolete French *estocade,* from Spanish *estacada,* from *estaca,* stake, from Germanic.]

stock·breed·ing (stŏk′brē′dĭng) *n.* The raising of livestock. **—stock·breed·er** *n.*

stock·bro·ker (stŏk′brō′kər) *n.* A person who acts, for a commission, as an agent in the buying and selling of stocks or other securities. **—stock·bro·ker·age** *n.* **—stock·bro·king** *n.*

stock car *n.* **1.** An automobile of a standard make modified for racing. **2.** A railroad car for carrying livestock.

stock certificate *n.* A certificate establishing ownership of a certain number of shares in a corporation's stock.

stock company *n.* **1.** A company or corporation whose capital is divided into shares. **2.** *Theater.* A permanent company of actors and technicians attached to a single theater and performing in repertory.

stock dove *n.* A common Old World bird, *Columba oenas,* having grayish plumage. [Probably because it lives in hollow tree trunks.]

stock exchange *n.* **1.** A place where stocks and shares or other securities are bought and sold. **2.** An association of stockjobbers and stockbrokers who meet to buy and sell stocks and shares according to fixed regulations. Also called "stock market."

stock·fish (stŏk′fĭsh′) *n., pl.* **-fishes** or collectively **stockfish.** A fish, such as cod or haddock, cured by being split and air-dried without salt.

Stock·hau·sen (shtŏk′hou′zən), **Karlheinz** (1928–). German composer. He is one of the leading exponents of electronic music. His works include *Gruppen* (1955–57) and *Stimmung* (1968).

stock·hold·er (stŏk′hōl′dər) *n.* One who owns a share or shares of stock in a company. **—stock·hold·ing** *adj. & n.*

Stock·holm (stŏk′hōlm′, -hōm′). Capital of Sweden, occupying several peninsulas and islands on the Baltic Sea at the eastern tip of Lake Mälaren. It has been the capital since 1634 and is also an important port and shipbuilding center.

Stockholm syndrome *n.* The tendency of a hostage, under certain circumstances, to try to cooperate and occasionally even to aid his captors. [Referring to the cooperative behavior of hostages held in a bank robbery in STOCKHOLM (1973).]

stock·i·nette, stock·i·net (stŏk′ə-nĕt′) *n.* An elastic knitted fabric used especially in making undergarments, bandages, and babies' clothing. [Alteration of *stocking net.*]

stockinette stitch *n.* A knitting pattern consisting of alternate rows of plain and purl stitches. Also *chiefly British* "stocking stitch."

stock·ing (stŏk′ĭng) *n.* **1.** A close-fitting, usually knitted covering for the foot and leg. **2.** Something resembling such a covering. **—in one's stocking feet.** Wearing socks or stockings but no shoes. [Obsolete *stock,* to cover with hose, from obsolete *stock,* a stocking.]

stocking cap *n.* A close-fitting, knitted, conical hat, often having a long tapering tassel, that resembles a stocking.

stocking filler *n.* A small article, such as a toy or something to eat, for putting in a Christmas stocking.

stocking frame *n.* A knitting machine. Also called "stocking loom," "stocking machine."

stock in trade *n.* **1.** All the merchandise and equipment kept on hand and used in carrying on a business. **2.** The resources available to and habitually called upon by a person in a given situation: *A ready wit is her stock in trade.*

stock·ish (stŏk′ĭsh) *adj.* Slow-witted; stupid. [STOCK (trunk, stump) + -ISH.] **—stock·ish·ly** *adv.* **—stock·ish·ness** *n.*

stock·job·ber (stŏk′jŏb′ər) *n.* **1.** *British.* A person on the stock exchange who acts as an intermediary between brokers and does not deal with the public. **2.** A stockbroker. Often used derogatorily. **—stock·job·ber·y, stock·job·bing** *n.*

stock·man (stŏk′mən) *n., pl.* **-men** (-mĭn). **1.** A farmer who raises livestock. **2.** A worker employed to look after livestock. **3.** One employed in a stockroom or warehouse.

stock market *n.* **1.** A stock exchange. **2.** The business transacted at a stock exchange. **3.** The prices offered for stocks and bonds: *The stock market fell today.*

stock·pile (stŏk′pīl′) *n.* A supply of material stored for future use; especially, a carefully accrued reserve of essential or strategically important commodities.
~v. **stockpiled, -piling, -piles.** *—tr.* To accumulate a stockpile of. *—intr.* To accumulate a stockpile of a given material.

stock·pot (stŏk′pŏt′) *n.* **1.** A large pot used for simmering meat in order to make stock. **2.** A rich supply or resource.

stock·room (stŏk′ro͞om′, -ro͝om′) *n.* A room in which a store of goods or materials is kept.

stock saddle *n.* A large, heavy, often ornamented saddle with a raised, curved pommel used especially by stockmen.

stock-still (stŏk′stĭl′) *adv.* Completely motionless.

stock-tak·ing (stŏk′tā′kĭng) *n.* **1.** The process of taking an inventory of goods or stocks, as in a shop or factory. **2.** A reappraisal of a situation or of one's own position or prospects.

Stock·ton (stŏk′tən). **1.** A city and commercial center of California, in the center of the state on the San Joaquin River. **2.** Also **Stockton-on-Tees** (stŏk′tən-ŏn-tēz′, -ōn-tēz′). A city and shipbuilding center of England, in the north in Durham county.

stock whip *n. British.* A whip with a short handle and a long lash, used for herding cattle.

stock·y (stŏk′ē) *adj.* **-ier, -iest. 1.** Solidly built; sturdy. **2.** Chubby; plump. **—stock·i·ly** *adv.* **—stock·i·ness** *n.*

stock·yard (stŏk′yärd′) *n.* A large enclosed yard, usually with pens or stables, in which livestock is temporarily kept until slaughtered, sold, or shipped elsewhere.

stodg·y (stŏj′ē) *adj.* **-ier, -iest. 1. a.** Dull, unimaginative, and commonplace. **b.** Prim or pompous; stuffy. **2.** Heavy; indigestible and starchy. [From *stodge,* to cram.] **—stodg·i·ly** *adv.* **—stodg·i·ness** *n.*

sto·gy (stō′gē) *n., pl.* **-gies. 1.** A long, thin, inexpensive cigar. **2.** A roughly made heavy shoe or boot. [After *Conestoga,* town in Pennsylvania.]

sto·ic (stō′ĭk) *n.* **1.** A person seemingly indifferent to or unaffected by joy, grief, pleasure, or pain. **2. Stoic.** A member of a Greek school of philosophy, founded by Zeno about 308 B.C. and later forming an important feature of Roman culture, holding that one should be free from passion and calmly accept all occurrences in submission to divine will or the natural order.
~adj. Also **sto·i·cal** (-ĭ-kəl) (for sense 1). **1.** Indifferent to pleasure and steadfast in the endurance of pain or grief; impassive: *stoic resignation.* **2. Stoic.** Of or pertaining to the Stoics or their beliefs. [Latin *Stōicus,* a Stoic, from Greek *Stōikos,* from *stoa,* portico, the porch where Zeno taught.] **—sto·i·cal·ly** *adv.*

stoi·chi·o·met·ric (stoi′kē-ō-mĕt′rĭk) *adj.* **1.** Having exact proportions for chemical combination: *a stoichiometric reaction.* **2.** Of or pertaining to stoichiometry. [Greek *stoikheio(n),* element + -METRIC.] **—stoi·chi·o·met·ri·cal·ly** *adv.*

stoi·chi·om·e·try (stoi′kē-ŏm′ə-trē) *n.* The methodology and technology by which the quantities of reactants and products in chemical reactions are determined. [Greek *stoikheion,* element + -METRY.]

sto·i·cism (stō′ĭ-sĭz′əm) *n.* **1.** Indifference to pleasure or pain; impassivity; an attitude of endurance or bravery. **2. Stoicism.** The philosophy or doctrines of the Stoics.

stoke (stōk) *v.* **stoked, stoking, stokes.** *—tr.* **1.** To stir up and feed (a fire or furnace). Often used with *up.* **2.** To tend the fire of (a furnace). *—intr.* **1.** To feed or tend a furnace fire. **2.** *Informal.* To eat steadily and in large quantities. Used with *up.* [Back-formation from STOKER.]

stoke·hold (stōk′hōld′) *n.* The area or compartment into which a ship's furnaces or boilers open. Also called "stokehole."

stoke·hole (stōk′hōl′) *n.* **1. a.** The space about the opening in a furnace or boiler. **b.** The opening itself. **2.** A stokehold. [Translation of Dutch *stookgat.*]

Stoke-on-Trent (stōk′ŏn-trĕnt′). Also **Stoke-up·on-Trent** (-ə-pôn-trĕnt′). A city of west-central England, in Staffordshire; the center of the ceramics industry.

stok·er (stō′kər) *n.* **1.** One who is employed to feed fuel to and tend a furnace, as on a steamship or steam locomotive. **2.** A mechanical device for feeding coal to a furnace. [Dutch, from *stoken,* to poke, thrust, from Middle Dutch.]

stock dove Columba oenas, *the stock dove, is a bird of open woods, farmland, and parkland in Europe and Asia. It is smaller than its close relative, the wood pigeon, and lacks the pigeon's white neck and wing markings.*

PRONUNCIATION KEY

ă, pat; ā, pay; âr, care; ä, father, are; b, bib; ch, church; d, deed; ĕ, pet; ē, be; f, fife; g, gag; h, hat; hw, which; ĭ, pit; ī, pie; îr, pier; j, judge; k, kick; l, lid, needle; m, mum; n, no, sudden; ng, thing; ŏ, pot; ō, toe; ô, paw, for; oi, noise; ou, out; o͝o, book; o͞o, boot; p, pop; r, roar; s, sauce; sh, ship, dish; t, tight; th, thin, path; *th,* this, bathe; ŭ, cut; ûr, fur; v, valve; w, with; y, yes; z, zebra, size; zh, vision; ə, about, item, edible, gallop, circus, peaceful

IN FOREIGN WORDS:

à, *Fr.* ami; œ, *Fr.* feu, *Ger.* schön; ü, *Fr.* tu, *Ger.* über; KH, *Ger.* ich, *Scot.* loch; N, *Fr.* bon; y′, *Fr.* Compiègne

STRESS MARKS:

Primary stress: ′ **in·cite′** (ĭn-sīt′)
Secondary stress: ′ **in′sight′** (ĭn′sīt′)

stonechat *This small insect-eating moorland bird gets its name from its call—similar to the sound of two stones being clapped together. The male (above) is distinguished from the female by its white collar.*

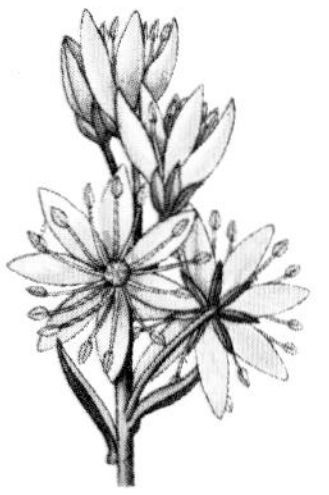

stonecrop *This creeping plant of rocks and walls stores water in its fleshy leaves. The leaves of* Sedum reflexum, *shown here, are sometimes eaten in soups and salads.*

stone marten *Found throughout Europe and western Asia, the stone marten is a member of the weasel family and feeds chiefly on squirrels and birds. It often nests in hollow trees.*

Sto·ker (stō′kər), **Bram,** original given name, Abraham (1819-1903). British writer, creator of *Dracula.*

stokes (stōks) *n. Symbol* **St** The centimeter-gram-second unit of kinematic viscosity equal to viscosity in poise divided by density in grams per cubic centimeter. [After Sir George *Stokes* (1819–1903), British physicist.]

Sto·kow·ski (stə-kôf′skē, -kou′skē), **Leopold** (1882–1977). British-born U.S. conductor. He was associated with many U.S. orchestras and was noted for his lavish orchestral arrangements.

STOL short takeoff and landing. Said of aircraft.

stole[1] (stōl) *n.* **1.** A woman's long scarflike garment of fur, feathers, or material, usually worn around the shoulders. **2.** A long scarf, usually of embroidered silk or linen, worn over the left shoulder by deacons and over both shoulders by priests and bishops while officiating. [Middle English *stole,* long robe, Old English *stol,* from Latin *stola,* from Greek *stolē,* garment, array, equipment.]

stole[2]. Past tense of **steal.**

sto·len. Past participle of **steal.**

stol·id (stŏl′ĭd) *adj.* Having or showing little emotion or sensibility; impassive: *stolid patience.* [Latin *stolidus.*] **—sto·lid·i·ty** (stə-lĭd′ə-tē), **stol·id·ness** *n.* **—stol·id·ly** *adv.*

stol·len (stō′lən) *n.* A rich yeast bread, originally from Germany, often containing raisins, citron, and chopped nuts. [German *Stollen,* loaf-shaped Christmas cake (symbolizing the Christ child in swaddling clothes), from Middle High German *stolle,* from Old High German *stollo,* post, support.]

sto·lon (stō′lŏn′, -lən) *n.* **1.** *Botany.* A stem growing along the ground and taking root at the nodes to form new plants. **2.** *Zoology.* A stemlike structure of certain colonial organisms from which new individuals develop by budding. [Latin *stolō* (stem *stolōn-*), branch, shoot.]

sto·lon·if·er·ous (stō′lə-nĭf′ər-əs) *adj.* Bearing or forming stolons. **—sto·lon·if·er·ous·ly** *adv.*

sto·ma (stō′mə) *n., pl.* **-mata** (-mə-tə) or **-mas. 1.** *Botany.* One of the minute pores in the epidermis of a leaf or stem through which gases and water vapor pass. **2.** *Anatomy.* **a.** An opening leading into the intestine or from one part of the intestine to another. **b.** A hypothetical opening in the surface of the peritoneum thought to be for the passage of fluid into the lymphatic vessels. **3.** *Zoology.* A mouthlike opening, such as the oral cavity of a nematode. [New Latin, from Greek, mouth.]

stom·ach (stŭm′ək) *n.* **1. a.** The enlarged, saclike portion of the alimentary canal, one of the principal organs of digestion, located in vertebrates between the esophagus and the small intestine. **b.** A similar digestive structure of many invertebrates. **2.** *Informal.* The abdomen or belly. **3.** An appetite for food. **4.** Any desire or inclination, especially for something difficult or unpleasant: *has no stomach for violence.* **5.** *Obsolete.* Courage or spirit. **6.** *Obsolete.* Pride or haughtiness.

~tr.v. **stomached, -aching, -achs. 1.** To bear; tolerate; endure. **2.** To take into or hold in the stomach; digest. [Middle English *stomak,* from Old French *stomaque,* from Latin *stomachus,* from Greek *stomakhos,* throat, mouth, gullet, from *stoma,* mouth.]

stom·ach·ache (stŭm′ək-āk′) *n.* Pain in the abdomen.

stom·ach·er (stŭm′ə-kər) *n.* A decorative, heavily embroidered or jeweled garment formerly worn, especially by women, over the chest and ending in a point over the stomach.

sto·mach·ic (stə-măk′ĭk) *adj.* Also **stom·ach·al** (stŭm′ə-kəl). **1.** Of or pertaining to the stomach; gastric. **2.** Beneficial to or stimulating digestion in the stomach.

~n. Any medicine or agent that strengthens or stimulates the stomach.

stomach pump *n.* A suction pump with a flexible tube inserted into the stomach through the mouth and esophagus to empty the stomach in an emergency, as in a case of poisoning.

stomach worm *n.* Any of various parasitic nematode worms that infest the stomachs of animals; especially, *Haemonchus contortus,* a parasite of sheep and other ruminants.

sto·ma·ta. Plural of **stoma.**

sto·ma·tal (stō′mə-təl) *adj.* Of or having a stoma or stomata.

sto·mat·ic (stō-măt′ĭk) *adj.* **1.** Of or relating to the mouth. **2.** Stomatal.

sto·ma·ti·tis (stō′mə-tī′tĭs) *n.* Inflammation of the mucous tissue of the mouth. [New Latin : STOMAT(O)- + -ITIS.]

stomato–, stomat– *prefix.* Indicates the mouth or a mouthlike part; for example, **stomatopod, stomatitis.** [Greek *stoma* (stem *stomat-*), mouth.]

sto·ma·tol·o·gy (stō′mə-tŏl′ə-jē) *n.* The medical study of the physiology and pathology of the mouth. [STOMATO- + -LOGY.]

sto·mat·o·pod (stō-măt′ə-pŏd′) *n.* Any of various marine crustaceans of the order Stomatopoda, which includes the squilla. [New Latin *stomatopoda* : STOMATO- + -POD.]

–stome *suffix.* Indicates the mouth or a mouthlike opening; for example, **cyclostome.** [Greek *stoma,* opening, mouth.]

sto·mo·de·um (stō′mə-dē′əm) *n., pl.* **-dea** (-dē′ə). *Embryology.* The primitive oral cavity of an embryo. [New Latin : Greek *stoma,* mouth (see **stoma**) + *hodaios,* on the way, from *hodos,* way.] **—sto·mo·de·al** *adj.*

stomp (stŏmp, stômp) *v.* **stomped, stomping, stomps.** *—tr.* To tread or trample heavily or violently on. See Usage note below. *—intr.* **1.** To tread or trample heavily or violently. **2.** To dance the stomp.

~n. **1.** A dance involving a rhythmical and heavy step. **2.** The jazz music for this dance. [Variant of STAMP (to pound).]

Usage: *Stomp* (verb) is established in the sense of trampling or violent treading: *trash stomped on by a stream of pedestrians; stomping wild horses. Stamp* would also be possible in these examples, and it is the form used in the related sense of eliminating: *stamp out a fire; stamp out poverty.* In the sense of striking the ground with the human foot, as in a fit of temper, *stamp* is the standard form: *She stamped her foot and began to cry.* Here *stomped* would be unacceptable, in writing, though it sometimes occurs in speech.

–stomy *suffix.* Indicates a surgical operation in which a usually permanent opening is made into a specified organ or part; for example, **colostomy.** [From Greek *stoma,* opening, mouth.]

stone (stōn) *n., pl.* **stones** or **stone** (for sense 9). *Abbr.* **st. 1.** Solid and compact earthy or mineral matter; rock. **2.** Such material of a particular type. Used in combination: *sandstone; soapstone.* **3.** A small piece of rock. **4.** Rock or a piece of rock shaped or finished for a particular purpose, especially: **a.** A stone used in construction work: *a coping stone; a paving stone.* **b.** A gravestone or tombstone. **c.** A grindstone, millstone, or whetstone. **d.** A milestone or boundary. **5.** A gem or precious stone. **6.** Something like a stone in shape or hardness, such as a hailstone. **7.** *Botany.* The hard covering enclosing the kernel in certain fruits, such as the cherry or plum. **8.** *Pathology.* A mineral concretion in a hollow organ, as in the kidney. See **calculus. 9.** A unit of weight in Britain and some other English-speaking countries, 14 pounds avoirdupois, used especially to express human body weight. **10.** *Printing.* A table with a smooth surface on which page forms are composed, originally made of stone. **11.** The oblate piece of stone or iron, with a gooseneck handle, used in the game of curling. **12. stones.** *Archaic.* The testicles. **13.** Dull light to dark gray. **—cast the first stone.** To be the first to criticize or accuse. [Biblical allusion to Jesus' saying, "He that is without sin among you, let him cast a stone at her . . ." (John 8:7).]

~adj. **1.** Pertaining to or made of stone: *a stone wall.* **2.** Made of stoneware or earthenware.

~adv. Utterly; completely: *stone cold.*

~tr.v. **stoned, stoning, stones. 1.** To hurl or throw stones at; pelt or kill with stones. **2.** To remove the stones from (fruit, for example). **3.** To furnish, fit, pave, or line with stones. **4.** To rub on or with a stone in order to polish or sharpen. **5.** *Obsolete.* To make hard like stone; make pitiless or indifferent. [Middle English *stane, stone,* Old English *stān.*] **—ston·er** *n.*

Stone (stōn), **Edward Durrell** (1902-78). U.S. architect. After studying at Harvard and MIT and in Europe, he moved to New York City and contributed to the designs for Rockefeller Center and Radio City Music Hall. Among his notable later designs are the Museum of Modern Art in New York, the U.S. embassy in New Delhi, India, and the Kennedy Center for the Performing Arts in Washington, D.C.

Stone, Harlan Fiske (1872-1946). Chief Justice of the U.S. Supreme Court (1941-46). After serving as dean of Columbia University Law School and U.S. attorney general, Stone was named to the Supreme Court (1925). During his long tenure he consistently maintained his liberal stance, most notably by upholding the reform legislation passed during the New Deal.

Stone, Lucy (1818-93). U.S. social reformer. Forced to earn her own living after the age of sixteen because her parents refused to believe a woman should attend college, she early became active in the fledgling women's rights movement. She helped organize the first national women's rights convention in 1850 and in 1869 founded the American Woman Suffrage Association to lobby state legislatures for the right to vote.

Stone Age *n.* The earliest known period of human culture, characterized by the use of stone tools.

stone ax *n.* An ax with two blunt edges used for hewing stone.

stone bass *n.* A large sea perch, *Polyprion americanus,* of Mediterranean and Atlantic waters. Also called "wreckfish."

stone-blind (stōn′blīnd′) *adj.* Completely blind.

stone boiling *n.* A primitive way of boiling water by putting heated stones into it.

stone bramble *n.* A bramble, *Rubus saxatilis,* with small white flowers and red fruit.

stone·chat (stōn′chăt′) *n.* A small Old World bird, *Saxicola torquata,* having dark plumage. [From the bird's cry, which resembles the sound of falling pebbles.]

stone·crop (stōn′krŏp′) *n.* **1.** Any of various plants of the genus *Sedum,* having fleshy leaves and variously colored flowers. **2.** Any of various related plants. [Middle English *stoncrop,* Old English *stāncropp* : *stān,* STONE + *cropp,* cluster, CROP.]

stone curlew *n.* A wading bird, *Burhinus oedicnemus,* with a large round head and staring yellow eyes. Also called "thick-knee," *South African* "dikkop."

stone·cut·ter (stōn′kŭt′ər) *n.* One that cuts or carves stone; especially, a machine that dresses stone. **—stone·cut·ting** *n.*

stoned (stōnd) *adj. Slang.* **1.** Intoxicated; drunk. **2.** Under the influence of a mind-altering drug.

stone-deaf (stōn′dĕf′) *adj.* Completely deaf.

stone·fish (stōn′fĭsh′) *n., pl.* **-fishes** or collectively **stonefish.** Any of several tropical marine fishes of the family Scorpaenidae, having spines that eject a deadly venom. [From the resemblance of the fish to encrusted stones.]

stone·fly (stōn′flī′) *n., pl.* **-flies.** Any of numerous winged insects of the order Plecoptera, occurring on banks of streams and used as fishing bait. [From their aquatic larvae, found under stones.]

stone fruit *n.* A drupe *(see)*.

Stone·henge (stōn′hĕnj′) *n.* A megalithic circle on Salisbury Plain, in southern England. Its surrounding bank and ditch date from *c.* 2800 B.C. The stone circle itself dates from *c.* 2200–1800 B.C. and was probably used as a religious center. The mathematical accuracy of the stones' positioning suggests that it was also an observatory, used as a calendar of the seasons and to predict eclipses.

stone lily *n.* A fossil crinoid.

stone marten *n.* **1.** A Eurasian mammal, *Martes foina,* having brown fur with lighter underfur. **2.** The fur of this animal. Also called "beech marten."

stone·ma·son (stōn′mā′sən) *n.* One who prepares and lays stones in building. **—stone·ma·son·ry** *n.*

stone mint *n.* A North American plant, *Cunila origanoides,* having clusters of small purplish or white flowers. Also called "dittany." [It grows in rocky places.]

stone parsley *n.* A hedgerow plant, *Sison amomum,* with small white flowers and a fetid smell.

stone pit *n. Chiefly British.* A quarry.

stone's throw *n.* A short distance.

stone·wall (stōn′wôl′) *v.* **-walled, -walling, -walls.** *—intr.* **1.** In cricket, to bat defensively rather than trying to score. **2.** *Informal.* **a.** To engage in delaying or obstructionist tactics. **b.** To refuse to answer or cooperate. *—tr. Informal.* To refuse to answer or cooperate with; resist or rebuff. **—stone·wall·er** *n.*

stone·ware (stōn′wâr′) *n.* A heavy, nonporous pottery fired at a high temperature and often glazed with salt.

stone·work (stōn′wûrk′) *n.* **1.** The technique or process of preparing, dressing, or working in stone. **2.** Work made of stone; stone masonry. **—stone·work·er** *n.*

stone·wort (stōn′wûrt′, -wôrt′) *n.* Any of various green algae of the family Characae that grow submerged in fresh or brackish water and are frequently encrusted with calcium carbonate deposits.

ston·y (stō′nē) *adj.* **-ier, -iest.** **1.** Covered with or full of stones. **2.** Hard as a stone. **3.** Hard and unfeeling. **4.** Impassive; showing no feeling or warmth: *a stony face.* **5.** Emotionally numbing or paralyzing: *a stony fear.* **—ston·i·ly** *adv.* **—ston·i·ness** *n.*

Stony Point. Village in southeastern New York, on the Hudson River. The Stony Point Battle Reservation nearby commemorates the storming of Stony Point by Anthony Wayne in the Revolution (1779).

stood. Past tense and past participle of **stand.**

stooge (stōōj) *n.* **1.** A person who acts as the butt or foil for a comedian's jokes, often by asking questions. **2.** Anyone who allows himself to be used for another's advantage. **3.** A planted spy. *—intr.v.* **stooged, stooging, stooges.** To be or behave as a stooge. [20th century : origin obscure.]

stook (stōōk, stŏŏk) *n.* A shock of sheaves of corn. *—tr.v.* **stooked, stooking, stooks.** To pile (sheaves of corn) into a shock. [Middle English *stouk,* probably from Middle Low German *stuke,* shock.]

stool (stōōl) *n.* **1.** A backless and armless single seat supported on legs or a pedestal. **2.** A low bench or support for the feet or knees in sitting or kneeling, such as a footrest or hassock. **3.** A seat enclosing a chamber pot; a commode. **4.** A piece of fecal matter. **5.** *Horticulture.* **a.** A stump or rootstock that produces shoots or suckers. **b.** A shoot or growth from such a stump or rootstock. **6.** In West Africa: **a.** The throne of a chief. **b.** The kingdom or sphere of sovereignty of a chief. *—intr.v.* **stooled, stooling, stools.** **1.** To send up shoots or suckers. **2.** To evacuate the bowels; defecate. **3.** *Slang.* To act as a stool pigeon. [Middle English *stol,* Old English *stōl.*]

stool·ie (stōō′lē) *n. Slang.* A stool pigeon for the police.

stool pigeon *n.* **1.** A pigeon used as a decoy. **2.** *Slang.* A person acting as a decoy or informer; especially, a spy for the police. [Decoy pigeons were originally tied to a stool.]

stoop¹ (stōōp) *v.* **stooped, stooping, stoops.** *—intr.* **1.** To bend forward and downward from the waist or middle of the back. **2.** To walk or stand, especially habitually, with the head and upper back bent forward. **3.** To bend or slope downward. **4.** To lower or debase oneself. Used with *to.* **5.** To descend from a superior position; condescend. Used with *to.* **6.** To swoop down. Used especially of a bird of prey. *—tr.* **1.** To bend (one's head or body) forward and downward. **2.** *Archaic.* To debase or subdue; humble. *—n.* **1.** The act of stooping. **2.** A forward bending of the head and upper back, especially when habitual. **3.** An act of self-abasement or condescension. **4.** A swooping down, as of a bird of prey. [Middle English *stupen,* Old English *stūpian.*]

stoop² *n.* A small porch, platform, or staircase leading to the entrance of a house or building. [Dutch *stoep,* front verandah, from Middle Dutch.]

stoop³. Variant of **stoup.**

stoop·ball (stōōp′bôl′) *n.* A game patterned on baseball in which a player throws a ball against a stoop or wall and then runs to base.

stop (stŏp) *v.* **stopped, stopping, stops.** *—tr.* **1.** To close (an opening) by covering, filling in, or plugging up. Often used with *up.* **2.** To stop the flow of something from; stanch: *stop a wound.* **3.** To constrict (an opening or orifice). **4.** To obstruct or block the passage of (traffic, for example). **5.** To prevent the flow or passage of: *tried to stop the blood.* **6. a.** To arrest the movement or progress of; cause to halt: *A man stopped me and asked the time.* **b.** To prevent from continuing an action; cause to cease or desist: *stopped their chatter by banging on the table.* **c.** To restrain or prevent from an

ANCIENT AND MODERN STONE AGE
The simultaneous evolution of man and his tools

The ability to make and use tools is one of the features that most clearly distinguishes man from ape. *Homo,* presumed to be the ancestor of Modern Man, emerged about 2 million years ago at the same time as the first stone tools and is believed to have used crudely split small rocks and rock flakes for butchering and other purposes, such as chopping and scraping.

The beginning of the Paleolithic period, or Old Stone Age, is dated from the appearance of early stone tools. It embraces the millennia during which *Homo* evolved into Modern Man, and the art of stone toolmaking advanced from the crude flaking of stones to the accurate shaping, by controlled hammer blows, of a core of flint into finely flaked spears, axheads, or scrapers.

Such tools may have been used for the killing and butchering of prehistoric animals.

As man evolved, his stoneworking became more refined and productive, so that by the Mesolithic period, or Middle Stone Age, which began about 9000 B.C., he had among his tools numerous small, sharp blades less than 2 millimeters ($^1/_{12}$ inch) thick. These could be set into shafts of wood or bone to be used as arrows or spears.

Agriculture began to spread outward from the Middle East in about 6000 B.C., initiating the Neolithic period, or New Stone Age. An astonishing variety of both chipped and ground tools, some of the latter perforated for hafting, were used for cultivation and butchering.

Flint handax of *c.* 300,000 B.C., about 200 millimeters (8 inches) long

Farmer's flint dagger of *c.* 2000 B.C., about 200 millimeters (8 inches) long

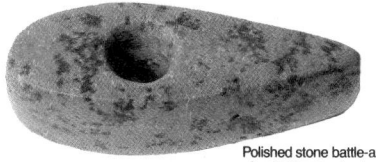

Polished stone battle-ax of *c.* 2000 B.C., about 200 millimeters (8 inches) long

Flint arrowhead of *c.* 1800 B.C., about 30 millimeters (1³/₁₆ inches) long

TECHNOLOGY IN STONE *Tools are valuable clues to prehistoric development. By the New Stone Age crudely flaked stones had been superseded by finely ground axes, farm tools, and weapons. They were significant aids in making permanent settlements.*

MODERN STONE AGE

A Nambicuara Indian (top) living near the Galera Caves in the Rondonia area of Brazil has little contact with the outside world. His people still use Stone Age tools that they find in the caves or that they make themselves from flints. These ancient stone axheads need only the addition of modern wooden handles in order to make them into useful tools once again (bottom).

intended action: *couldn't stop him from calling the police.* **7.** To desist from; cease doing. Often used with a gerund: *stop running.* **8.** To cause (a machine, for example) to cease operating, functioning, or moving; halt. **9.** To give instructions to one's banker to not honor (a check). **10.** To withhold; keep back: *stop his allowance.* **11.** In boxing, to defeat (an opponent) by rendering him unable to continue the fight. **12.** *Music.* **a.** To close (a hole on a wind instrument) with the finger in order to produce a desired pitch. **b.** To press down (a string on a stringed instrument) in order to produce a desired pitch. **c.** To put one's hand inside (the bell of a French horn) in order to alter the pitch or tone quality. **d.** To produce (a particular pitch) by any of these methods. **13.** To close (an organ pipe) at one end in order to make it sound an octave lower. **14.** In bridge, to hold a card or cards in (a particular suit) that will prevent one's opponents from winning all the tricks in that suit. *—intr.* **1.** To cease moving, progressing, acting, or operating; come to a halt or pause. **2.** To put an end to what one is doing; cease. **3.** To interrupt one's course or journey, as to make a quick visit or do an errand. Often used with *in* or *off: stop in at the supermarket.* **4.** *Informal.* To stay: *stopped at a friend's for a few nights.* **—stop at**

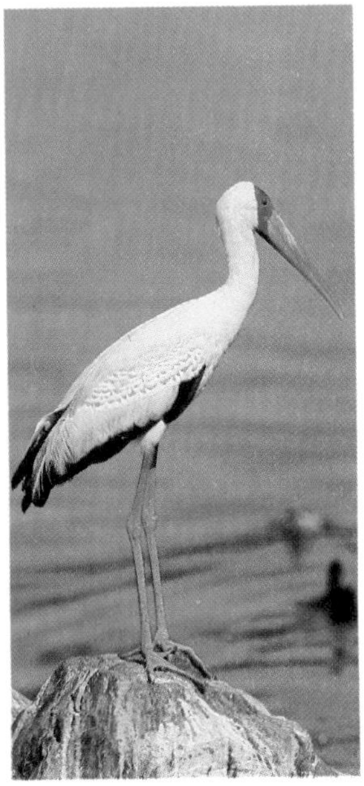

stork *The European white stork (above) is one of 17 species of the family Ciconiidae. Storks live near shores and marshes and feed on fish and small animals. They return to the same nest every year, rebuilding and enlarging it each time.*

PRONUNCIATION KEY

ă, pat; ā, pay; âr, care;
ä, father, are; b, bib;
ch, church; d, deed; ĕ, pet;
ē, be; f, fife; g, gag; h, hat;
hw, which; ĭ, pit; ī, pie;
îr, pier; j, judge; k, kick;
l, lid, needle; m, mum;
n, no, sudden; ng, thing;
ŏ, pot; ō, toe; ô, paw, for;
oi, noise; ou, out; o͝o, book;
o͞o, boot; p, pop; r, roar;
s, sauce; sh, ship, dish;
t, tight; th, thin, path;
th, this, bathe; ŭ, cut; ûr, fur;
v, valve; w, with; y, yes;
z, zebra, size; zh, vision;
ə, about, item, edible, gallop, circus, peaceful

IN FOREIGN WORDS:

à, *Fr.* ami; œ, *Fr.* feu, *Ger.* schön; ü, *Fr.* tu, *Ger.* über; KH, *Ger.* ich, *Scot.* loch; N, *Fr.* bon; y', *Fr.* Compiègne

STRESS MARKS:

Primary stress: ′
in·cite′ (ĭn-sīt′)
Secondary stress: ′
in′sight′ (ĭn′sīt′)

nothing. To act with absolute determination or lack of scruples. **—stop down.** To reduce the effective aperture of (a camera lens). **—stop out.** To cover (part of a printing plate, for example) in order to prevent it from being printed or etched.
~*n.* **1.** The act of stopping or the condition of being stopped; a cessation; a halt. **2.** A finish; an end. **3.** A stay or visit, as during a journey. **4. a.** An official stopping place: *a bus stop.* **b.** Any place stopped at. **5. a.** An act or instance of obstructing, blocking, or plugging up. **b.** A device or means that obstructs, blocks, or plugs up. **6. a.** A stop payment. **b.** A stop order. **7.** A part in a machine that stops or regulates movement. **8.** A perforated screen or diaphragm that limits the effective aperture of a lens, producing an image of improved definition but lowered intensity. **9.** A punctuation mark, especially a period. **10.** *Music.* **a.** The act of stopping a string or hole on a musical instrument. **b.** A device such as a key for closing the hole on a wind instrument. **11.** *Music.* **a.** A tuned set of pipes, as in an organ. **b.** A knob, key, or pull that regulates such a set of pipes. **12.** *Nautical.* A line used for securing something temporarily: *a sail stop.* **13.** *Phonetics.* A consonant articulated with a complete obstruction of the passage of breath; specifically, *p, b, t, d, k,* or *g* in English. Compare **continuant. 14.** The depression between the muzzle and top of the skull of a dog or cat. **15.** In bridge, a **stopper** *(see).* **16.** *Architecture.* A projecting stone, often carved, at the end of a molding. **—pull out all the stops.** To exert oneself to the utmost. [Middle English *stoppen,* Old English *stoppian,* from West Germanic *stoppōn* (unattested), to plug up, from Late Latin *stuppāre,* to stop up with a tow, from Latin *stuppa,* tow, from Greek *stuppē.*]

stop bath *n.* In photography, an acid solution used to check the developing process.

stop·cock (stŏp′kŏk′) *n.* A valve that regulates the flow of liquid through a pipe; a tap.

stope (stōp) *n.* A tunnel driven parallel to the strike of a vertical or near vertical vein so that ore can be excavated from the vein.
~*v.* **stoped, stoping, stopes.** —*tr.* To remove (ore) from a stope. —*intr.* To mine by means of a stope. [Perhaps from Low German *stope,* a step, from Middle Low German *stōpe.*]

Stopes (stōps), **Marie Charlotte Carmichael** (1880–1958). British scientist and pioneer advocate of birth control. With her husband she founded Britain's first birth-control clinic (1921). Her books include *Married Love* (1918) and *Enduring Passion* (1928).

stop·gap (stŏp′găp′) *n.* An improvised substitute for something lacking; a temporary expedient.

stop·ing (stō′pĭng) *n.* **1.** *Geology.* The breaking up of country rock by advancing intrusive magma. **2.** *Mining.* The mining of ore by means of stopes, often by a series of stopes.

stop·light (stŏp′līt′) *n.* **1.** A traffic light. **2.** A **brake light** *(see).*

stop order *n.* An order to a broker to buy or sell a stock when it reaches a stipulated level of decline or gain.

stop over *intr.v.* To make a stopover on a journey.

stop·o·ver (stŏp′ō′vər) *n.* **1.** An interruption in the course of a journey for stopping at or visiting a certain place; especially, a stop made in the course of a long-distance airline flight. **2.** A place visited briefly in the course of a journey.

stop·page (stŏp′ĭj) *n.* **1.** The act of stopping or the condition of being stopped; a halt. **2.** Something that stops, obstructs, or blocks. **3.** An amount withheld, as from a person's wages; a deduction. **4.** The act of stopping work, as during industrial action.

Stop·pard (stŏp′ärd′), **Tom** (1937–). Czech-born English playwright. He first achieved success with *Rosencrantz and Guildenstern Are Dead* (1967); later works include *Jumpers* (1972) and *The Real Thing* (1982). His plays are characterized by witty dialogue and often deal with philosophical or ethical themes.

stop payment *n.* An order to one's bank not to honor a check.

stop·per (stŏp′ər) *n.* **1.** Any device, such as a cork or plug, inserted to close an opening. **2.** One that causes something to stop. **3.** In bridge, a card or cards enabling one to prevent one's opponents from winning all the tricks. Also called "stop."
~*tr.v.* **stoppered, -pering, -pers.** To close with a stopper.

stop·ple (stŏp′əl) *n.* A stopper; a plug.
~*tr.v.* **stoppled, -pling, -ples.** To close with a stopple. [Middle English *stoppell,* from *stoppen,* to STOP.]

stop sign *n.* A traffic sign that orders traffic to come to a stop.

stop street *n.* A street intersection at which a vehicle must come to a complete stop before entering a through street.

stop·watch (stŏp′wŏch′) *n.* A timepiece that can be started and stopped by pushing a button to measure duration of time.

stor·age (stôr′ĭj, stōr′-) *n. Abbr.* **stge., stor. 1. a.** The act of storing goods, as in a warehouse. **b.** The state of being stored. **2.** Space for storing goods. **3.** The price charged for keeping goods stored. **4.** *Computer Science.* The process of storing information on a storage device. Also used adjectivally: *storage capacity.*

storage battery *n.* A group of reversible or rechargeable **secondary cells** *(see)* acting as a unit. Also called "secondary battery" or *chiefly British* "accumulator."

storage cell *n.* A **secondary cell** *(see).*

storage device *n. Computer Science.* A piece of equipment or medium on which information can be stored and from which it can be retrieved. Storage devices include magnetic tapes and tape cassettes, hard and floppy disks, and magnetic drums.

storage heater *n.* A type of electric heater that accumulates heat during off-peak electricity hours.

sto·rax (stôr′ăks′, stōr′-) *n.* **1.** Any of various trees of the genus *Styrax,* some of which yield an aromatic resin. **2.** An aromatic resin obtained from any of these trees. **3.** A brownish, aromatic resin used in perfume and medicine and obtained from any of several trees of the genus *Liquidambar,* especially from *L. orientalis,* of Asia Minor. In this sense, also called "styrax." [Middle English, from Latin, from Greek, variant of *sturax,* probably from Semitic; akin to Hebrew *tzŏrī.*]

store (stôr, stōr) *n.* **1.** A stock or supply reserved for future use. **2. stores.** Supplies, especially of food, clothing, or arms. **3.** A place where commodities are kept; a warehouse or storehouse. **4.** A great quantity or number; an abundance. **5.** *Chiefly British.* A computer **memory** *(see).* **6.** A place where merchandise is offered for sale; a shop. **—in store.** Set aside or reserved for the future; forthcoming. **—set** (or **lay** or **put**) **store by.** To regard as important or valuable.
~*tr.v.* **stored, storing, stores. 1.** To reserve or put away for future use. **2.** To fill, supply, or stock with something. **3.** To deposit or receive in a storehouse or warehouse for safekeeping. **4.** *Computer Science.* To place (data) in a storage device for retention. [Middle English *stor,* from Old French *estor,* from *estorer,* to build, restore, from Latin *instaurāre.*] **—stor·a·ble** *adj.*

store-bought (stôr′bôt′, stōr′-) *adj. Informal.* Manufactured and purchased at retail: *store-bought clothes.*

store·front (stôr′frŭnt′, stōr′-) *n.* **1.** The side of a shop facing a street. **2.** A room or set of rooms in a storefront. **—store·front** *adj.*

store·house (stôr′hous′, stōr′-) *n.* **1.** A place or building in which goods are stored; a warehouse. **2.** An abundant source or supply.

store·keep·er (stôr′kē′pər, stōr′-) *n.* **1.** A person in charge of receiving or distributing stores or supplies, especially military or naval supplies. **2.** A shopkeeper.

store·room (stôr′ro͞om′, -ro͝om′, stōr′-) *n.* A room in which things are stored.

storey. *Chiefly British.* Variant of **story** (level).

Sto·rey (stôr′ē, stōr′ē), **David** (1933–). British novelist and dramatist. His works include the novels *This Sporting Life* (1960) and *Saville* (1976) and the play *In Celebration* (1969).

sto·ried[1] (stôr′ēd, stōr′-) *adj.* **1.** Celebrated or famous in history or legend. **2.** Ornamented with designs representing scenes from history or legend: *storied tapestry.*

storied[2] *adj.* Having or consisting of a specified number of stories. Used in combination: *a three-storied house.*

stork (stôrk) *n.* Any of various large wading birds of the family Ciconiidae, having long red legs, a long, straight bill, and black and white plumage. [Middle English *stork,* Old English *storc.*]

stork's-bill (stôrks′bĭl′) *n.* Any of various plants of the genus *Erodium,* having fruit with a narrow, beaklike point.

storm (stôrm) *n.* **1.** An atmospheric disturbance manifested in strong winds accompanied by rain, snow, or other precipitation and often by thunder and lightning. **2.** *Meteorology.* A wind ranging from 64 to 72 miles per hour, force 11 on the Beaufort scale. **3.** A heavy shower of objects, such as bullets or missiles. **4.** A strong or violent outburst, as of emotion or protest. **5.** A violent disturbance or upheaval, as in political, social, or domestic affairs. **6.** *Military.* A violent, sudden attack on a fortified place. **—take by storm.** To have an overwhelming and captivating effect on (an audience, for example).
~*v.* **stormed, storming, storms.** —*intr.* **1.** To blow forcefully; rain, snow, hail, or otherwise precipitate violently. Used with *it*: *It stormed last night.* **2.** To be extremely angry; rant and rage. **3.** To move or rush tumultuously, violently, or angrily: *She stormed into the room.* —*tr. Military.* To capture or try to capture by a violent, sudden attack. —See Synonyms at **attack.** [Middle English, Old English *storm.*]

storm belt *n.* A tract of the earth's surface in which storms are frequent.

storm·bound (stôrm′bound′) *adj.* Delayed, confined, or cut off from communication by a storm.

storm cellar *n.* A cyclone cellar.

storm center *n.* **1.** *Meteorology.* The central area covered by a storm; especially, the point of lowest barometric pressure within a storm. **2.** A center or source of trouble, disturbance, or argument.

storm cloud *n.* **1.** A heavy, dark rain cloud that threatens stormy weather. **2.** Anything that presages violence, disturbance, or war.

storm collar *n.* A high coat collar, often one that buttons up.

storm cone *n. British.* A tarred cone hoisted to provide a warning of high winds.

storm door *n.* An outer or additional door added for protection against inclement weather.

storm glass *n.* A glass tube containing a liquid solution that forms crystals as an indication of bad weather.

storm in a teacup *n.* Great excitement or fuss over something trivial or unimportant.

storm petrel *n.* A small sea bird of the family Hydrobatidae; especially, *Hydrobates pelagicus,* of the North Atlantic and the Mediterranean. Also called "stormy petrel," "Mother Carey's chicken."

storm trooper *n.* **1.** A member of the Nazi militia noted for brutality and violence. **2.** A member of a force of shock troops.

storm warning *n.* A pattern of lights or flags displayed along a coastline or at a port to warn of an approaching storm.

storm window *n.* A secondary window attached over a window to protect against the wind and cold.

storm·y (stôr′mē) *adj.* **-ier, -iest. 1.** Subject to, characterized by, or affected by storms; tempestuous. **2.** Characterized by violent emotions, passions, speech, or actions: *a stormy argument.* —**storm·i·ly** *adv.* —**storm·i·ness** *n.*

stormy petrel *n.* **1.** A storm petrel. **2.** A person who brings discord or appears at the onset of trouble.

Stor·ting, Stor·thing (stôr′tĭng, stōr′-) *n.* The parliament of Norway. [Norwegian : *stor,* great + *thing,* assembly.]

sto·ry¹ (stôr′ē, stōr′ē) *n., pl.* **-ries. 1.** An account or recital of an event or series of events, either true or fictitious. **2.** A prose or verse narrative, usually fictional, intended to interest or amuse the hearer or reader; a tale. **3.** A type of fictional literary composition, a **short story** *(see).* **4.** An incident or experience that would be good material for a narrative. **5.** A plot, as of a novel or play. **6.** A report, statement, or allegation of facts. **7. a.** A news article. **b.** The event, situation, or other material for such an article. **8.** An anecdote. **9.** A lie. **10.** Romantic legend or tradition. —**the same old story.** The well-known or very familiar course of events.
~*tr.v.* **storied, -rying, -ries. 1.** To decorate with scenes representing historical or legendary events. **2.** *Archaic.* To tell as a story. [Middle English *storie,* from Norman French *estoire,* from Latin *historia,* HISTORY.]

story² *n., pl.* **-ries.** *Also chiefly British* **sto·rey,** *pl.* **-reys. 1.** A complete horizontal division of a building, comprising the area between two adjacent levels. **2.** The set of rooms on the same level of a building. [Middle English, from Medieval Latin *historia,* HISTORY (perhaps originally referring to a row of painted windows or of sculptures).]

sto·ry·book (stôr′ē-bŏŏk′, stōr′-) *n.* A book containing a collection of stories, usually for children.
~*adj.* Of the kind that occurs in a storybook; romantic; fairytale.

story line *n.* The plot of a book, film, or dramatic work.

sto·ry·tell·er (stôr′ē-tĕl′ər, stōr′-) *n.* **1.** A person who tells or writes stories. **2.** *Informal.* A person who tells lies; a fibber.

stoss (stŏs, stôs, shtōs) *adj.* Facing the direction from which a glacier or ice sheet moves. Said of a rock or slope in its path. [From German *stossen,* to push, thrust, from Old High German *stōzan.*]

sto·tin·ka (stō-tĭng′kə) *n., pl.* **-ki** (-kē). A monetary unit equal to ¹/₁₀₀ of the lev of Bulgaria. See feature at **currency.** [Bulgarian.]

Stough·ton (stōt′n), **William** (*c.* 1631-1701). Colonial official in Massachusetts. He served as lieutenant governor and acting governor of the colony, but is best known as the presiding judge at the Salem witchcraft trials (1692), where his overbearing manner and insistence on the admission of "spectral evidence" led to the hanging of 18 persons.

stound (stound, stōŏnd, stōōn) *n.* **1.** *Obsolete.* A short time; a while. **2.** *Chiefly Scottish.* A sudden tremor, as of pain or excitement. [Middle English *sto(u)nd,* Old English *stund.*]

stoup, stoop (stōōp) *n.* **1.** *Ecclesiastical.* A basin or font for holy water at the entrance of a church. **2.** *British Regional.* **a.** A bucket or pail. **b.** A cup, tankard, or other drinking vessel. [Middle English *stowp,* vessel, pail, from Old Norse *staup.*]

stour (stōŏr) *n.* *Chiefly Scottish.* **1.** Tumult; conflict. **2. a.** A driving storm. **b.** A sudden cloud of dust or spray. [Middle English, from Old French *estour,* armed combat, from Germanic; akin to Old High German *sturm,* STORM.]

stout (stout) *adj.* **stouter, stoutest. 1.** Determined, bold, or brave; resolute; staunch: *a stout heart.* **2.** Strong in body; sturdy. **3.** Strong in structure or substance; substantial; solid. **4.** Bulky in figure; thickset; inclined toward fatness. **5.** Powerful; forceful. —See Synonyms at **strong, fat.**
~*n.* A strong, very dark beer or ale brewed with malt or barley. [Middle English, from Old French *estout,* from Germanic.] —**stout·ly** *adv.* —**stout·ness** *n.*

stout·heart·ed (stout′här′tĭd) *adj.* Brave; courageous; dauntless. —**stout·heart·ed·ly** *adv.* —**stout·heart·ed·ness** *n.*

stove¹ (stōv) *n.* **1.** An apparatus in which electricity or a fuel is used to provide heat, as for cooking or comfort. **2.** A heated room or box used for a particular purpose, such as a kiln or hothouse.
~*tr.v.* **stoved, stoving, stoves.** To heat, treat, or keep in a stove. [Middle English, heated chamber, from Middle Low German or Middle Dutch.]

stove². Alternate past tense and past participle of **stave.**

stove enamel *n.* A type of heat-resistant enamel paint.

stove·pipe (stōv′pīp′) *n.* **1.** A pipe, usually iron, used to conduct smoke or fumes from a stove into a chimney flue. **2.** A man's tall silk hat. Also called "stovepipe hat."

sto·ver (stō′vər) *n.* Any of various kinds of animal feed made from clover, stubble, or the like. [Middle English, food, provisions, short for Norman French *estovers,* supplies, from Old French *estovier,* to be necessary, from Latin *est opus,* it is necessary : *est,* (it) is, from *esse,* to be + *opus,* need, necessity.]

stow (stō) *tr.v.* **stowed, stowing, stows. 1. a.** To place, arrange, or store away, especially in a neat, compact way. **b.** *Nautical.* To load or store (cargo, gear, or provisions) in the proper place. **2.** To fill by packing tightly. **3.** *Slang.* To cease; stop. Usually used in the imperative: *Stow it!* **4.** *Slang.* To consume (food) greedily. Often used with *away.* **5.** *Archaic.* To provide lodging for; quarter. [Middle English *stowen,* from *stowe,* a place, from Old English *stōw.*]

stow·age (stō′ĭj) *n.* **1. a.** The act, manner, or process of stowing. **b.** The state of being stowed. **2.** Space or room for storage. **3.** Goods in storage. **4.** A charge for storing goods.

stow away *intr.v.* To be a stowaway.

stow·a·way (stō′ə-wā′) *n.* One who hides aboard a ship or other form of transport in order to obtain free passage.

Stowe (stō), **Harriet Beecher** (1811–96). U.S. author. Her antislavery novel *Uncle Tom's Cabin* (1852) had great political influence and did much to advance the cause of abolition.

STP¹ (ĕs′tē-pē′) *n.* A synthetic hallucinogenic drug chemically related to amphetamine and mescaline. [Probably from the commercial name of the oil substitute *S.T.P.* (Scientifically Treated Petroleum).]

STP² 1. Professor of Sacred Theology [Latin *Sanctae Theologiae Professor*]. **2.** standard temperature and pressure.

St. Paul (sānt pôl′). Capital of Minnesota and an industrial and transportation center of the state on the Mississippi River. It is opposite the larger city of Minneapolis.

St. Peter Port (sānt pē′tər). The capital of Guernsey in the Channel Islands. It was the residence of Victor Hugo (1855-70).

St. Petersburg. See **Leningrad.**

St. Pierre (sānt pîr′). *French* **Saint-Pierre** (săN-pyâr′). **1.** A town in northwestern Martinique, destroyed by the eruption of Mount Pelée. **2.** An island of the St. Pierre and Miquelon group off Newfoundland, Canada. **3.** A fishing port on Réunion Island in the Indian Ocean.

St. Pi·erre and Mi·que·lon (sānt′ pē-âr′; mĭk′ə-lŏn′; săN pîr′; mē-klôN′). Two small island groups making up a French overseas department in the Atlantic Ocean south of Newfoundland. Frequently contested between England and France, the islands finally became French in 1814 and are the last French territory in North America.

str. 1. steamer. **2.** strait. **3.** stringed (instruments).

stra·bis·mus (strə-bĭz′məs) *n.* A visual defect in which one eye cannot focus with the other on an objective because of imbalance of the eye muscles. Also called "squint." See **walleye.** [New Latin, from Greek *strabismos,* from *strabizein,* to squint, from *strabos,* squinting.] —**stra·bis·mal, stra·bis·mic** *adj.*

Stra·bo (strā′bō) (*c.* 63 B.C.–*c.* A.D. 24). Greek geographer and historian. One of his great works, *Geography,* completed in A.D. 23, is the only extant text that describes the people and countries known to the Greeks and Romans during the reign of Augustus (27 B.C.–A.D. 14).

stra·bot·o·my (strə-bŏt′ə-mē) *n., pl.* **-mies.** The cutting of an ocular muscle or tendon to correct strabismus. [Greek *strabos,* squinting + -TOMY.]

Stra·chey (strā′chē), **(Giles) Lytton** (1880–1932). British biographer and historian. He is known chiefly for his revolutionary biographies, in which he debunked the grandeur of Victorian society. His works include *Eminent Victorians* (1918), *Queen Victoria* (1921), and *Elizabeth and Essex* (1928). He was a member of the Bloomsbury Group of writers and artists.

strad·dle (străd′l) *v.* **-dled, -dling, -dles.** —*tr.* **1.** To sit, stand, or be in a position astride of; bestride. **2.** To fire shots behind and in front of (a target) in order to determine the range. **3. a.** To fall on or take in parts of (two periods or areas, for example): *Her constituency straddles two counties.* **b.** To fall or lie on either side of (a dividing line). **4.** To vacillate between or seem to favor both sides of (an issue). —*intr.* **1.** To sit or stand with the legs apart. **2.** To be or be spread wide apart; sprawl. **3.** To favor or appear to favor both sides of an issue. —**straddle the fence.** To be in an indecisive or neutral position.
~*n.* **1.** The act or posture of sitting astride. **2.** The privileged option of either delivering or buying securities at a stated price within a stated period of time. Compare **call, put. 3.** An equivocal or noncommittal position. [From STRIDE.] —**strad·dler** *n.*

Usage: **Straddle** (verb), in the figurative sense of appearing to favor both sides of an issue, is not confined to expressly informal contexts despite its casual tone. Employed transitively, it is acceptable in the following, as an example in writing: *politicians, who straddle every controversial question.*

Strad·i·var·i (străd′ə-vär′ē, -vâr′ē, -vär′ē), **Antonio** (1644–1737). Italian violin maker. At his workshop in Cremona he brought violin making to its highest point of craftsmanship. He produced more than 1,000 instruments, some of which still survive.

Strad·i·var·i·us (străd′ə-vâr′ē-əs, -văr′ē-əs) *n., pl.* **-varii** (-vâr′ē-ī′, -văr′ē-ī′). Any of the famous violins made in the workshop of Antonio Stradivari. Also informally called "Strad."

strafe (strāf, străf) *tr.v.* **strafed, strafing, strafes.** To attack (ground troops, for example) with bombs or machine-gun fire from low-flying aircraft.
~*n.* An act of strafing. [From the German World War I slogan *(Gott) strafe (England),* "(God) punish (England)," from *strafen,* to punish, from Middle High German *strāfen†,* to rebuke.]

Straf·ford (străf′ərd), **Thomas Wentworth, 1st Earl of** (1593-1641). English statesman. After a volatile career in Parliament, he became chief adviser to King Charles I, advocating among other things the invasion of Scotland to stamp out Presbyterian insurgency. He was convicted of treason by Parliament and beheaded on Tower Hill.

strag·gle (străg′əl) *intr.v.* **-gled, -gling, -gles. 1.** To stray or fall behind. **2.** To grow, proceed, or spread out in a scattered or irregular manner or pattern. [Middle English *straglen,* perhaps frequentative of *straken,* to go, move, perhaps related to Old English *streccan,* to STRETCH.] —**strag·gler** *n.*

strag·gly (străg′lē) *adj.* **-glier, -gliest.** Spread out or proceeding irregularly.

straight (strāt) *adj.* **straighter, straightest. 1.** Extending continuously in the same direction. **2.** Free from curves, angles, or irregularities, as: **a.** Not wavy or curly: *straight hair.* **b.** Not bent or stooping: *a straight back.* **c.** Exactly vertical or horizontal; level or upright. **3.** Characterized by honesty and fairness; scrupulous. **4. a.** Logical; reasonable: *straight thinking.* **b.** Accurate; correct; in accordance with the truth: *set the record straight.* **5.** Direct and candid; not evasive: *a straight answer.* **6.** Uninterrupted; consecutive. **7.** Unmodified; unembellished: *gave us the straight facts.* **8.** Undiluted or unmixed: *straight whiskey.* **9.** Politically undeviating: *a straight party line.* **10.** Neatly arranged; orderly. **11.** Of, designating, or involved in serious drama as opposed to comedy, musicals, or the like: *a straight actor; a straight play.* **12.** *Slang.* Conventional; conforming to established norms, as in one's opinions, lifestyle, or sexual preferences, especially: **a.** Heterosexual. **b.** Not being a drug user. **13.** *Slang.* Not being under the influence of alcohol or drugs. **14.** Not deviating from the norm or strict form: *straight Freudian analysis.* **15.** Sold without discount regardless of the amount purchased. **16.** In poker, made up of five cards constituting a sequence: *a straight flush.* —*adv.* **1.** In a straight line. **2.** In an erect posture; upright. **3.** Directly; without detour or delay. **4.** Without circumlocution; candidly: *told her straight out that she was wrong.* **5.** Honestly or virtuously. **6.** Continuously. —**go straight.** *Informal.* To reform after having been a criminal. —*n.* **1.** A straight line, part, piece, or condition. **2.** A straight part on a racecourse, especially between the last turn and the winning post. **3.** A poker hand containing a numerical sequence of five cards of various suits. **4.** *Slang.* A normal or conventional person, especially: **a.** A heterosexual person. **b.** A person who is not a drug user. [Middle English *streit, streight,* from the past participle of *strecchen,* to STRETCH.] —**straight·ly** *adv.* —**straight·ness** *n.*

straight and narrow *n.* The path of honest, moral, and law-abiding behavior.

straight angle *n.* An angle of 180 degrees.

straight-arm (strāt′ärm′) *tr.v.* **-armed, -arming, -arms.** *Football.* To ward off (a tackler) by holding the arm out straight.

straight·a·way (strāt′ə-wā′) *adv.* At once; immediately. —*adj.* (strāt′ə-wā′). **1.** Extending or proceeding in a straight line or course. **2.** Unhesitating; immediate. —*n.* (strāt′ə-wā′). A straight course, stretch, or track.

straight chain *n. Chemistry.* An open linear molecular structure with no side chains. Compare **branched chain.**

straight·edge (strāt′ěj′) *n.* A rigid flat rectangular bar, as of wood or metal, with a straight edge for testing or drawing straight lines. —**straight·edged** *adj.*

straight·en (strāt′n) *v.* **-ened, -ening, -ens.** —*tr.* **1.** To make straight. **2.** To tidy. —*intr.* To become straight. —**straighten out.** **1.** To put to rights or restore order to; rectify. **2.** To reform or improve. —**straight·en·er** *n.*

straight face *n.* A face that betrays no sign of emotion, especially of amusement. —**straight-faced** (strāt′fāst′) *adj.*

straight flush *n.* In poker, a run of five consecutive cards of the same suit.

straight·for·ward (strāt-fôr′wərd) *adj.* **1.** Proceeding in a straight course; direct. **2.** Honest; frank; candid. **3.** Simple; uncomplicated. **4.** Unambiguous; cut-and-dried. —See Synonyms at **fair.** —*adv.* In a straightforward course. —**straight·for·ward·ly** *adv.* —**straight·for·ward·ness** *n.*

straightjacket. Variant of **straitjacket.**

straight-line (strāt′līn′) *adj.* **1.** Of, pertaining to, or designating a type of machinery whose linkage produces or copies motion in straight lines. **2.** Designating the most usual method of amortization of a loan or of providing for the depreciation of an asset, based on a series of equal payments or equal allowable amounts over a given period of time.

straight man *n.* One of two comedians who acts as a foil for his partner.

straight off *adv.* Without delay or hesitation; at once.

straight razor *n.* A razor consisting of a blade hinged to a handle into which it slips when not in use.

straight ticket *n.* A vote cast for all the candidates of one party. Compare **split ticket.**

straight·way (strāt′wā′, -wā′) *adv.* Immediately.

strain¹ (strān) *v.* **strained, straining, strains.** —*tr.* **1.** To pull, draw, or stretch tight. **2.** To exert or tax to the utmost. Often used reflexively. **3.** To injure or impair by overuse or overexertion; especially, to wrench: *strain a muscle.* **4. a.** To place too great a load on: *strained the lifting mechanism.* **b.** To stretch or force beyond the proper, reasonable, or legitimate limits: *strain a point.* **5.** To alter (the relations between the parts of a structure or shape) by applying an external force; deform. **6.** To pass (a substance) through a strainer or other filtering agent. **7.** To draw off or remove by filtration. **8.** To embrace or clasp tightly; hug. —*intr.* **1.** To make forceful and continuous efforts; exert oneself physically or mentally; strive hard. **2.** To be overexerted; especially, to be wrenched or twisted. **3.** To be subjected to great stress. **4.** To pull forcibly or violently: *straining at the leash.* **5.** To hesitate, as through scruple; balk. Used with *at.* **6.** To filter, trickle, or ooze. —*n.* **1. a.** The act of straining. **b.** The state of being strained. **2.** A great or extreme effort, exertion, or tension. **3.** Something that makes great or excessive demands on one's mental, emotional, or physical resources. **4.** A wrench or other injury resulting from excessive effort or use. **5.** *Physics.* A deformation produced by stress, measured by the change in dimension divided by the original di-

mension (length, area, or volume), or by the angular shear. —See Synonyms at **effort.** [Middle English *streynen,* from Old French *estreindre,* from Latin *stringere,* to draw tight, tie.]

strain² *n.* **1.** The collective descendants of a common ancestor; a race, stock, line, or breed. **2.** Any of the various lines of ancestry united in an individual or family; ancestry; lineage. **3.** *Biology.* A group of organisms of the same species, having distinctive characteristics but not usually considered a separate breed or variety. **4.** A kind; sort. **5. a.** An inborn or inherited tendency or character. **b.** A streak; a trace. **6.** The tone or tenor of a piece of speech or writing. **7.** *Often* **strains.** A passage of musical expression; an air; a tune. **8.** A passage of poetic expression. **9.** An outburst or flow of eloquent or impassioned language. [Middle English *stren(e),* Old English *strēon,* acquisition, generation, offspring.]

strained (strānd) *adj.* **1.** Forced; unnatural: *a strained smile.* **2.** Tense and uncomfortable, especially because of latent hostility: *a strained atmosphere.*

strain·er (strā′nər) *n.* One that strains, especially: **1.** A filter, sieve, or the like used to separate liquids from solids. **2.** An apparatus for tightening, stretching, or strengthening.

strain gauge *n.* A device for detecting or measuring strain using the change in electrical resistance of a distorted thin wire or a piezoelectric crystal.

strain hardening *n.* The process of hardening metal by straining it so as to increase the number of internal crystal dislocations.

straining beam *n. Architecture.* A horizontal tie beam connecting two queen posts in a roof truss. Also called "straining piece."

strait (strāt) *n. Abbr.* **St., str. 1.** *Often* **straits.** A narrow passage of water joining two larger bodies of water. **2.** *Usually* **straits.** A position of difficulty, perplexity, distress, or need: *in desperate straits.* —*adj. Archaic.* **1.** Narrow, constricting, or confined. **2.** Stringent or rigorous, as in moral conduct or religious observance. [Middle English *streit,* from Old French *estreit,* tight, narrow, from Latin *strictus,* from the past participle of *stringere,* to draw tight.]

strait·en (strāt′n) *tr.v.* **-ened, -ening, -ens. 1.** To make narrow; limit, contract, or restrict. **2.** To cause to experience difficulties or distress, particularly financial hardship. Used chiefly in the phrase *in straitened circumstances.*

strait·jack·et, straight·jack·et (strāt′jăk′ĭt) *n.* **1.** A long-sleeved jacketlike garment used to bind the arms tightly against the body as a means of restraining a violent patient or prisoner. **2.** Anything that restricts or restrains like a straitjacket, such as a rule or institution. —*tr.v.* **-jacketed, -eting, -ets.** To restrict or restrain by or as if by confining in a straitjacket.

strait-laced (strāt′lāst′) *adj.* Excessively strict in behavior, morality, or opinions; puritanical; prudish. [Originally referring to tightly laced dress, hence strict, exacting.]

Straits, The. 1. The waterway connecting the Black Sea and the Mediterranean, formed by the Bosporus and the Dardanelles. **2.** The former name for the **Strait of Gibraltar. 3.** See **Straits Settlements.**

Straits Settlements. Also **The Straits.** A former British crown colony, a division of British Malaya, that included Singapore, Penang, Malacca, Labuan, and a number of smaller islands.

strake (strāk) *n.* **1.** *Nautical.* A single continuous line of planking or metal plating extending on a vessel's hull from stem to stern. **2.** Any of the curved sections making up the metal rim of a wooden wheel. [Middle English *strake,* perhaps "thing stretched," related to Old English *streccan,* to STRETCH.]

stra·mo·ni·um (strə-mō′nē-əm) *n.* **1.** A plant, the **jimsonweed** (see). **2.** The dried poisonous leaves of the jimsonweed, used in the treatment of asthma. [New Latin, perhaps an alteration of Tatar *turman,* horse medicine.]

strand¹ (strănd) *n.* Land bordering a body of water; especially, the area between tide marks. —*v.* **stranded, stranding, strands.** —*tr.* **1.** To drive or force aground; beach. **2.** To bring into or leave in a difficult or helpless position: *The collapse of the airline left us stranded in New York.* —*intr.* To become stranded. [Middle English *strand,* Old English *strand,* shore, akin to Old Norse *strönd†.*]

strand² *n.* **1.** Any of the long stringlike pieces of material that are twisted together to form a rope, cable, or the like. **2.** Any single fiber, thread, or other filament: *a strand of hair.* **3. a.** A string of beads. **b.** The material on which they are strung. **4.** Anything that is plaited or twisted, such as a rope or a plait of hair. **5.** A single element forming part of an interwoven whole: *one of the strands in his complex narrative.* —*tr.v.* **stranded, stranding, strands. 1.** To make or form (a rope or cable, for example) by twisting strands together. **2.** To break one or more of the strands in (a rope, cable, or the like). [Middle English *strond†.*]

strand line *n.* A shore line, especially one marking an earlier and higher water level.

strange (strānj) *adj.* **stranger, strangest. 1.** Previously unknown; unfamiliar. **2.** Strikingly unusual; queer, unaccountable, or extraordinary. **3.** Not of one's own or a particular locality, environment, or kind; exotic. **4.** Inexperienced in or unacquainted with something: *still strange to the job.* **5.** Unwell or dizzy: *feeling strange.* **6.** *Archaic.* Alien or foreign. **7.** *Physics.* **a.** Designating a type of quark with unit quantum number strangeness. **b.** Of or designating an elementary particle that contains one or more charmed quarks and no charmed antiquarks.

~*adv.* In a strange manner: *acting strange.* [Middle English *straunge,* from Old French *estrange,* from Latin *extrāneus,* foreign, strange, from *extrā,* outside, beyond.] —**strange·ly** *adv.*

Synonyms: *strange, peculiar, odd, queer, quaint, outlandish, singular, eccentric.* These adjectives describe persons or things that are notably unusual. *Strange* refers especially to what is unfamiliar, unknown, or inexplicable. *Peculiar,* though often applied to anything unusual, is most applicable to what distinguishes a given person or thing from others. *Odd* suggests the quality of not fitting in, or lack of accord with associates, surroundings, or circumstances. *Queer* implies difference from the norm. *Quaint* often refers to peculiarity that seems old-fashioned but endearing. *Outlandish* suggests alien appearance or manner and often implies uncouthness. *Singular* describes what is unique, unparalleled, or unusual and thus arouses curiosity or wonder. *Eccentric* refers particularly to striking peculiarity of behavior.

strange·ness (strānj′nĭs) *n.* **1.** The quality of being strange. **2.** *Symbol* **S** *Physics.* A quantum number, a property of certain types of elementary particle, originally postulated to account for the long lifetime of kaons, sigma particles, and lambda particles. [Sense 2, from the original lack of understanding of the nature of the particles that it describes.]

strang·er (strān′jər) *n.* **1.** A person whom one does not know or does not know well. **2.** A foreigner, newcomer, or outsider. **3.** One who is unaccustomed to or unacquainted with something specified. Used with *to: no stranger to the bar.* **4.** A visitor or guest. **5.** *Law.* One who is neither privy nor party to an act, proceeding, or other form of business. [Middle English *straunger,* from Old French *estrangier,* from Vulgar Latin *extrāneārius* (unattested), from Latin *extrāneus,* STRANGE.]

stran·gle (străng′gəl) *v.* **-gled, -gling, -gles.** —*tr.* **1. a.** To kill by choking or suffocating; throttle. **b.** To kill by cutting off the oxygen supply of. **2.** To suppress, repress, or stifle. **3.** To inhibit the growth or action of; restrict: *strangled by convention.* —*intr.* To die or suffer from suffocation or strangulation; choke. [Middle English *stranglen,* from Old French *estrangler,* from Latin *strangulāre,* to STRANGULATE.] —**stran·gler** *n.*

stran·gle·hold (străng′gəl-hōld′) *n.* **1.** Powerful control that restricts or prevents freedom of thought or action. **2.** An illegal wrestling hold used to choke an opponent.

stran·gles (străng′gəlz) *n.* *Used with a singular verb.* An infectious disease of horses and related animals, caused by the bacterium *Streptococcus equi* and characterized by nasal inflammation and abscesses in the mouth. [From Middle English *strangle* (singular), strangulation, from *stranglen,* to STRANGLE.]

stran·gu·late (străng′gyə-lāt′) *v.* **-lated, -lating, -lates.** —*tr.* **1.** *Pathology.* To compress, constrict, or obstruct (a tube, duct, intestine, or other part) so as to cut off the flow of blood, air, or other fluid. **2.** To strangle. —*intr.* To be or become strangled or constricted. [Latin *strangulāre,* to strangle, from Greek *strangalan,* from *strangalē,* halter.]

stran·gu·la·tion (străng′gyə-lā′shən) *n.* **1.** The act of strangling. **2.** The state of being strangled.

stran·gu·ry (străng′gyə-rē) *n.* Slow, painful urination with spasms of the urethra and bladder. [Middle English, from Latin *strangūria,* from Greek *strangouria : stranx* (stem *strang-*), drop + -URIA.]

strap (străp) *n.* **1.** A flat, narrow strip of leather, canvas, or other material, usually fitted with a buckle or other adjustable fastener and used for binding, securing, or supporting objects. **2.** A flat, thin metal band used for fastening or clamping objects together or into position. **3.** A narrow band formed into a loop for grasping with the hand. **4.** A strip of leather used for beating, especially as a punishment in schools. —*tr.v.* **strapped, strapping, straps.** **1.** To fasten or secure with a strap. **2.** To beat with a strap. **3.** To bind (a wound or injured limb, for example) with bandages. Often used with *up.* [Alteration of STROP.]

strap·hang·er (străp′hăng′ər) *n.* A standing passenger, as on a bus or subway, who grips a hanging strap for support. —**strap·hang·ing** *n.*

strap·less (străp′lĭs) *adj.* Without a strap or straps. Said especially of a dress or undergarment designed to leave the shoulders bare. —*n.* A strapless garment.

strap·pa·do (strə-pā′dō, strə-pā′-) *n.,* *pl.* **-does.** **1.** A torture in which the victim's hands are tied behind his back and attached to a pulley by means of which he is pulled up off the ground and then dropped halfway down with a jerk. **2.** The apparatus so employed. [French *(e)strapade,* from Italian *strappata,* from *strappare,* to drag, from Old French *estraper,* variant of *estreper,* from Latin *extirpāre,* to pluck up by the stem : *ex-,* out + *stirps,* stem (see **stirps**).]

strapped (străpt) *adj.* *Informal.* Suffering from a shortage, especially of money: *strapped for cash.* [From STRAP.]

strap·per (străp′ər) *n.* A tall, sturdy person.

strap·ping (străp′ĭng) *adj.* *Informal.* Tall and sturdy.

Stras·berg (străs′bûrg′, -bərg, străs′-), **Lee** (1901–82). U.S. theatrical producer, director, and teacher, born in Austria. Trained in the tradition of Konstantin Stanislavsky, the originator of method acting, he became its premier American proponent, employing it in his own roles and teaching it to numerous students, including Marlon Brando, Anne Bancroft, and Robert De Niro.

Stras·bourg (străs′bŏŏrg′, -bûrg′, străz′-). City in northeastern France, lying close to the Franco-German border and formerly part of Germany (1871–1919). Its cathedral, built between the 11th and 15th centuries, is a notable example of Rhenish architecture.

strass (străs) *n.* A type of lead glass, **paste** (see). [German, after Josef *Strasser,* 18th-century German jeweler.]

stra·ta. Plural of **stratum.** See Usage note at **stratum.**

strat·a·gem (străt′ə-jəm) *n.* **1. a.** A military maneuver designed to deceive or surprise an enemy. **b.** Any trick or scheme used to gain an advantage. **2.** Deception; trickery. —See Synonyms at **artifice.** [French *stratagème,* from Latin *stratēgēma,* from Greek, "act of a general," from *stratēgein,* to be a general, from *stratēgos,* general : *stratos,* army + *agein,* to lead.]

stra·te·gic (strə-tē′jĭk) *adj.* Also **stra·te·gi·cal** (-jĭ-kəl). **1.** Of or pertaining to strategy. **2. a.** Dictated by or essential for the furtherance of a military or other strategy: *a strategic withdrawal.* **b.** Essential to the effective conduct of war. **c.** Designed to destroy at the source the military and economic potential of an enemy: *strategic nuclear weapons.* —**stra·te·gi·cal·ly** *adv.*

Strategic Defense Initiative, strategic defense initiative *n.* A planned system of defense that would include a network of satellites equipped for surveillance and destruction of ballistic missiles. Also called "SDI, S.D.I.," "Star Wars."

stra·te·gics (strə-tē′jĭks) *n.* *Used with a singular verb.* The art of strategy.

strat·e·gist (străt′ə-jĭst) *n.* One who is skilled in strategy.

strat·e·gy (străt′ə-jē) *n., pl.* **-gies.** **1.** The science or art of military command as applied to the overall planning and conduct of large-scale combat operations. Compare **tactics.** **2.** A plan of action resulting from the practice of this science. **3.** The use of skillful planning to secure one's own advantage, as in politics, business, or personal relations. **4.** A plan or design for achieving one's aims. [French *stratégie,* from Greek *stratēgia,* office of a general, from *stratēgos,* general. See **stratagem.**]

Strat·ford (străt′fərd) *n.* **1.** See **Stratford-upon-Avon.** **2.** A city of Connecticut, in the southeast on Long Island Sound; site of the American Shakespeare Festival. **3.** A city in southeastern Ontario, Canada; site of the Stratford Festival.

Strat·ford-up·on-A·von (străt′fərd-ə-pŏn-ā′vən, -ā′vŏn′). Town in Warwickshire, central England, famous for its associations with William Shakespeare, who was born and died here.

strath (străth) *n.* *Scottish.* A steep-sided, flat-floored valley wider than a glen. [Scottish Gaelic *srath,* (mountain) valley.]

Strath·clyde Region (străth′klīd′). An administrative region of western Scotland, formed in 1975 and comprising the former counties of Ayr, Bute, Dunbarton, Lanark, and Renfrew, with parts of Stirling and Argyll. Industries, including shipbuilding, mining, textiles, and distilling, are concentrated in the lower Clyde valley. Glasgow is the administrative center.

strath·spey (străth-spā′, străth′spā′) *n., pl.* **-speys.** A type of Scottish reel or the music that accompanies it. [After *Strathspey,* valley of the SPEY River.]

strati– *prefix.* Indicates stratum or strata; for example, **stratigraphy.** [From STRATUM.]

stra·tic·u·late (strə-tĭk′yə-lĭt) *adj.* Having thin strata. [From STRATUM.] —**stra·tic·u·la·tion** *n.*

strat·i·fi·ca·tion (străt′ə-fĭ-kā′shən) *n.* **1. a.** The act or process of stratifying. **b.** The state of being stratified. **2.** A stratified configuration. —**strat·i·fi·ca·tion·al** *adj.*

stratificational grammar *n. Linguistics.* A theory of grammar that conceives of language in terms of a hierarchical system of linked levels, ranging from the conceptual to the phonemic, each of which has its own rules.

strat·i·form (străt′ə-fôrm′) *adj.* Having the form of strata.

strat·i·fy (străt′ə-fī′) *v.* **-fied, -fying, -fies.** —*tr.* **1.** To form, arrange, or deposit in strata. **2.** To arrange or divide according to different levels of caste, class, or status: *a stratified society.* **3.** To preserve (seeds) by placing them between layers of moist sand or similar material. —*intr.* To become layered; develop physical or social strata. [French *stratifier,* from New Latin *stratificare :* STRATUM + Latin *facere,* to make, do.]

stra·tig·ra·phy (strə-tĭg′rə-fē) *n.* The study of rock strata, especially of their distribution, deposition, and chronological succession. [STRATI- + -GRAPHY.] —**strat·i·graph·ic** (străt′ə-grăf′ĭk), **strat·i·graph·i·cal** *adj.* —**strat·i·graph·i·cal·ly** *adv.*

stra·toc·ra·cy (strə-tŏk′rə-sē) *n., pl.* **-cies.** Government by the army. [Greek *stratos,* army + -CRACY.]

stra·to·cu·mu·lus (strā′tō-kyōōm′yə-ləs, străt′ō-) *n., pl.* **-li** (-lī′). A low-lying heavy cloud occurring at about 1,500 to 6,000 feet as rounded gray masses, often covering the sky but sometimes with small breaks. [STRAT(US) + CUMULUS.]

strat·o·pause (străt′ə-pôz′, strā′tə-) *n.* The boundary between the stratosphere and the mesosphere in the earth's atmosphere, at a height where the air becomes so thin that there are not enough oxygen molecules to form ozone. [STRATO(SPHERE) + PAUSE.]

strat·o·sphere (străt′ə-sfîr′) *n.* The part of the atmosphere between the troposphere and the mesosphere, extending from a height of about 9 to 30 miles and having a temperature that increases with height to a maximum of about 0°C. [French *stratosphère :* New Latin *stratum,* STRATUM + *sphère,* SPHERE.] —**strat·o·spher·ic** (străt′ə-sfîr′ĭk, -sfĕr′ĭk) *adj.*

stra·tum (strā′təm, străt′-, străt′əm) *n., pl.* **-ta** (-tə) or **-tums.** **1.** *Geology.* **a.** A bed or layer of rock having the same composition throughout. **b.** A number of beds or layers of rock of the same kind of material. **2.** A horizontal layer of any material, especially one of several parallel layers arranged one on top of the other, such as:

a. A layer of tissue or cells. **b.** Any of the layers making up the earth's atmosphere. **c.** A layer in which the archaeological remains of a particular stage or period are deposited. **3.** A class or category regarded as occupying a level in a hierarchy: *the middle strata of society.* [New Latin, from Latin *strātum,* neuter of *strātus,* stretched out. See **stratus.**] **—stra·tal** *adj.*

Usage: The standard singular form is *stratum.* The standard plural form is *strata* (or sometimes *stratums*) but not *stratas*: *All strata of society have been affected.*

stra·tus (strā'təs, străt'əs) *n., pl.* **strati** (strā'tī', străt'ī'). A low-altitude cloud usually occurring below 2,000 feet, and typically resembling a layer of fog. [Latin *strātus,* past participle of *sternere,* to stretch out, extend.]

Strauss, Johann[1] (strous, shtrous), known as "the Elder" (1804–49). Austrian violinist and composer. He composed many dances, especially waltzes, and is best known for his *Radetzky March.*

Strauss, Johann[2], known as "the Younger" (1825–99). Austrian composer and conductor. He is best known for his dance music, especially his waltzes, which include *The Blue Danube* (1867), and his operettas, such as *Die Fledermaus* (1874).

Strauss, Richard (1864–1949). German composer and conductor. He is known chiefly for his symphonic poems, which include *Till Eulenspiegel* (1895) and *Don Quixote* (1897), and his operas, among them *Salomé* (1905) and *Der Rosenkavalier* (1911).

Stra·vin·sky (strə-vĭn'skē), **Igor Feodorovich** (1882–1971). Russian composer. His early ballet, *The Rite of Spring* (1913), caused a scandal at its first performance but like many of his works has been recognized as one of the musical landmarks of the 20th century. His later pioneering works include the *Symphony of Psalms* (1930) and *The Rake's Progress* (1951).

straw (strô) *n.* **1. a.** Stalks of threshed grain used for thatching, as bedding or food for animals, and for weaving or braiding, as into hats or baskets. **b.** A single stalk of straw. **2.** A slender tube used for sucking up a liquid. **3.** Something of minimal value or importance. **4.** A usually worthless expedient resorted to in desperation: *clutching at straws.* **—straw in the wind.** A slight hint of something to come. **—the last straw.** The final blow to be withstood.

~tr.v. **strawed, strawing, straws. 1.** To cover (a surface, for example) with straw; strew. **2.** To provide with straw.

~adj. **1.** Made of straw: *a straw hat.* **2.** Of the color of straw; yellowish: *straw hair.* **3.** Of little or no value or substance. [Middle English *strawe,* Old English *strēaw.*]

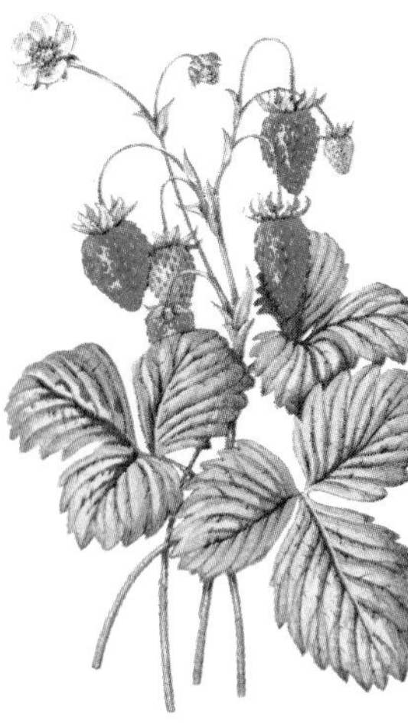

strawberry *The edible fruit of a ground-creeping plant of the genus* Fragaria. *Most cultivated varieties are said to have been developed from 18th-century hybrids between two American species.*

straw·ber·ry (strô'bĕr'ē) *n., pl.* **-ries. 1.** Any of various low-growing plants of the genus *Fragaria,* having white flowers and red, fleshy, edible fruit. **2.** The fruit of any of these plants. **3.** A related plant, the barren strawberry, *Potentilla sterilis,* having strawberrylike flowers but dry fruit. [Middle English *strawberry,* Old English *strēawberige* : STRAW (possibly from the strawlike slender runners trailing on the ground) + BERRY.]

strawberry blite *n.* A weedy plant, *Chenopodium capitatum,* of northern regions, having minute, petalless flowers and red, berrylike fruit.

straw·ber·ry-blond (strô'bĕr'ē-blŏnd') *adj.* Reddish-blond. Said of hair.

~n. A person with strawberry-blond hair.

strawberry bush *n.* A North American shrub, *Euonymus americanus,* having inconspicuous flowers and showy pinkish fruit.

strawberry mark *n.* A small, reddish birthmark.

strawberry roan *n.* A horse having reddish hair mixed with white.

strawberry shrub *n.* Any of several North American shrubs of the genus *Calycanthus,* having aromatic reddish-brown flowers.

strawberry tomato *n.* **1.** A North American plant, *Physalis pruinosa,* having yellow flowers and edible yellowish fruit enclosed in a husk. **2.** The fruit of the strawberry tomato.

strawberry tree *n.* A tree, *Arbutus unedo,* native to southern Europe, having evergreen leaves and strawberrylike fruit.

straw·board (strô'bôrd', -bōrd') *n.* A coarse yellow cardboard made of straw pulp.

straw boss *n. Informal.* A worker who acts as a boss or assistant foreman in addition to his regular duties.

straw·flow·er (strô'flou'ər) *n.* A plant, *Helichrysum bracteatum,* native to Australia, having flowers with showy, variously colored bracts that retain their color when dried.

straw-hat (strô'hăt') *adj.* Of or pertaining to a summer theater that operates in suburban and resort areas: *The show was a hit on the straw-hat circuit.* [So called because straw hats are worn in the summer.]

straw man *n.* **1.** A bundle of straw made into the likeness of a man and often used as a scarecrow. **2.** One who is set up as cover or front man for a questionable enterprise. **3.** One set up as an opponent to be easily defeated or refuted. Also called "man of straw."

straw vote *n.* An unofficial vote or poll indicating the trend of opinion on a candidate or issue.

straw wine *n.* A dessert wine made from grapes that have been dried on straw.

straw·worm (strô'wûrm') *n.* The destructive larva of a fly, *Hormolita grandis,* of western North America, that infests stalks of grain.

stray (strā) *intr.v.* **strayed, straying, strays. 1. a.** To wander from a given place or group or beyond established limits; roam. **b.** To become lost. **2.** To rove, wander about, or meander. **3.** To deviate from a course that is regarded as right or moral; go astray; err. **4.** To digress or wander from a given subject or line of thought. —See Synonyms at **wander.**

~n. One that has strayed; especially, a domestic animal at large or that has been lost.

~adj. **1.** Straying or having strayed; lost or at large. **2. a.** Scattered, random, or isolated: *a few stray cars.* **b.** Not in its proper place or context: *brushed back some stray hairs.* [Middle English *straien,* from Old French *estraier,* from Vulgar Latin *estragāre* (unattested) : Latin *extrā-,* outside of + *vagārī,* to wander, roam, from *vagus,* wandering, VAGUE.] **—stray·er** *n.*

streak (strēk) *n.* **1.** An irregular line, mark, or band differentiated by color or texture from its surroundings. **2.** A trace or element of a particular quality or characteristic; a strain: *a masochistic streak.* **3.** *Informal.* A brief stretch or run: *a losing streak.* **4.** *Geology & Chemistry.* The color of the powder of a mineral, used as a distinguishing characteristic. **5.** A single discharge of atmospheric lightning. Also used adjectivally: *streak lightning.* **6.** An act of streaking. **7.** *Biology.* A growth of microorganisms produced by streaking.

~v. **streaked, streaking, streaks.** *—tr.* To mark with a streak or streaks; stripe; striate. *—intr.* **1.** To form streaks or become streaked. **2.** To move at high speed; rush. **3.** To run naked or partly naked through or across a public place as a way of attracting attention or amusing the crowd. **4.** *Biology.* To inoculate a culture medium with microorganisms by drawing a contaminated wire along the surface. [Middle English *strick(e),* Old English *strica.*] **—streak·er** *n.*

streak·y (strē'kē) *adj.* **-ier, -iest. 1.** Marked with, characterized by, or occurring in streaks; streaked. **2.** Consisting of alternate streaks of meat and fat. Said of bacon. **3.** Variable or uneven in character or quality. **—streak·i·ly** *adv.* **—streak·i·ness** *n.*

stream (strēm) *n.* **1.** A body of running water; especially, such a body moving over the earth's surface in a channel or bed, as a brook or rivulet. **2.** A steady current in such a body of water. **3.** A steady current of any fluid. **4. a.** A steady flow or procession, as of people or traffic, moving in the same direction. **b.** An uninterrupted succession or outpouring: *a stream of invective.* **5.** A prevailing trend or general drift, as of opinion, thought, or history. **6.** *British.* In many schools, any of the sets into which children of a given age group are divided, usually according to ability. In this sense, compare **band. —on stream.** In or into production.

~v. **streamed, streaming, streams.** *—intr.* **1.** To flow in or as if in a stream: *"From the paddocks . . . there streamed the milky scent of ripe grass"* (Katherine Mansfield). **2.** To pour forth or give off a stream; flow. Often used with *with*: *eyes streaming with tears.* **3.** To move or proceed in large numbers: *"Hundreds of people were streaming by our house in wild panic"* (James Thurber). **4.** To extend, wave, or float outward in the air: *The banner streamed in the breeze.* **5.** To leave a continuous trail of light. *—tr.* **1.** To emit, discharge, or exude. **2.** *British.* To group (schoolchildren) into streams. [Middle English *streme,* Old English *strēam.*] **—stream·y** *adj.*

stream·er (strē'mər) *n.* **1.** A long, narrow flag, banner, or pennant. **2. a.** Any long, narrow pendant strip of ribbon, colored paper, or other material. **b.** Such a strip that is wound into a tight roll that unwinds when thrown, used for fun by children and as party decorations. **3.** A shaft or ray of light extending upward from the horizon. **4.** A newspaper headline that runs across a full page; a banner. **5.** A long, narrow, luminous electrical discharge, as in the aurora.

stream·line (strēm'līn') *n.* **1.** A line in a fluid such that the tangent at every point on the line is aligned with the fluid's local velocity. **2.** The path of any one particle in a flowing fluid. **3.** Any contour of a body constructed so as to offer minimum resistance to a fluid flow.

~tr.v. **streamlined, -lining, -lines.** To make streamlined.

stream·lined (strēm'līnd') *adj.* **1.** Designed, constructed, or shaped so as to offer the least resistance to fluid flow. **2.** Simplified, modernized, or reorganized so as to improve efficiency. **3.** Having simple, smooth, or elegant contours.

streamline flow *n.* A flow characterized by lack of turbulence or interruption. Compare **laminar flow, turbulent flow.**

stream of consciousness *n.* **1.** *Psychology.* The conscious experience of an individual regarded as a continuous rather than a discrete series of events. **2.** A literary technique in which the thoughts and feelings of a character in a novel are recorded as they develop by means of first-person narration. Compare **interior monologue.**

street (strēt) *n. Abbr.* **st., St. 1.** A public way or thoroughfare in a city, town, or village, usually including the pavements and the buildings lining either or both sides. **2.** Such a roadway for vehicles apart from the buildings and pavements. **3.** The people living, working, or habitually gathering in or along such a roadway: *The whole street knew about it.* **4. Street.** The financial area around the Stock Exchange in Wall Street, New York.

~adj. Pertaining to, taking place in, or found on a street or the streets of a town: *street life; a street party.* [Middle English *strete,* Old English *strǣt,* from West Germanic *strāta* (unattested), from Late Latin *strāta,* from Latin *strātus,* past participle of *sternere,* to extend, stretch out.]

street Arab *n.* A homeless child who lives on the streets of a city; an urchin.

street·car (strēt'cär') *n.* A public passenger car operated on rails along a regular route, usually through the streets of a city. Also called "trolley," "trolley car," *British* "tramcar," "tram."

street·light (strēt′līt′) *n.* Any of a series of lights that are attached to tall poles spaced at intervals along a public thoroughfare and are illuminated automatically from dusk to dawn.

street value *n.* The retail value of an illegal commodity, calculated on the basis of the price at which it is sold to the consumer (its *street price*): *cocaine with a street value of $300,000.*

street·walk·er (strēt′wô′kər) *n.* A prostitute who solicits in the streets. **—street·walk·ing** *n.*

street·wise (strēt′wīz′) *adj.* Experienced in the ways of rough urban areas; capable of surviving or being successful on the streets.

stre·ga (strā′gə) *n.* A sweet, orange-flavored Italian liqueur having a rich golden color. [From *Strega,* a trademark.]

Strei·sand (strī′sănd′, -zănd′), **Barbra** (1942–). American singer and actress. Her stage and film performances include *Funny Girl* (1968), *Hello Dolly* (1969), and *A Star Is Born* (1976).

stre·lit·zi·a (strə-lĭt′sē-ə) *n.* A plant of the South African genus *Strelitzia,* which includes the bird-of-paradise flower. [After Charlotte of Mecklenburg-*Strelitz* (1744–1818), queen of England.]

strength (strĕngkth, strĕngth) *n.* **1.** The state, quality, or property of being strong; physical power. **2. a.** The power of resisting force, attack, strain, or stress; durability, solidity, or impregnability. **b.** The ability to maintain a moral or intellectual position firmly, especially in the face of opposition or temptation: *strength of character.* **3.** Capacity or potential for effective action: *a show of strength.* **4.** Military capability in terms of manpower and material resources: *the strength of the fleet.* **5.** The number of personnel constituting the normal or ideal complement of an organization: *The police force is below strength.* **6.** Degree of intensity, force, effectiveness, or potency in terms of a particular property, as: **a.** Degree of concentration, distillation, or saturation. **b.** Operative effectiveness or potency. **c.** Intensity, as of sound or light. **d.** Degree of ardor or vehemence, as of feelings or language: *tried to gauge the strength of support for his idea.* **7. a.** A source of power or force. **b.** An attribute or quality of particular worth or utility; an asset. **8.** Effective or binding force; efficacy: *the strength of an argument.* **9.** Firmness of or a continuous rising tendency in prices, as on the stock market. **—go from strength to strength.** To become ever more powerful or successful. **—on the strength of.** Relying or depending on; based on: *hired her on the strength of your recommendation.* [Middle English *strengthe,* Old English *strengthu.*]

Synonyms: *strength, power, might, force, energy, potency.* These nouns are compared as they relate to the ability to act effectively. *Strength* is the capacity for thus acting, considered especially as the means of physical accomplishment. *Power* is also the source of effective action but has even wider application than *strength,* as in contexts where it implies authority or the ability to control work by superhuman or supernatural means. *Might* implies abundant or overmastering power. *Force* is the application of power or physical strength. *Energy* is power considered either as something expended or as a latent source of action. *Potency* is power considered as a means of achieving a desired result, and is often used to imply authority, influence, or chemical or medicinal value.

strength·en (strĕngk′thən, strĕng′-) *v.* **-ened, -ening, -ens.** *—tr.* To make strong or stronger. *—intr.* To become strong or stronger. **—strength·en·er** *n.*

stren·u·ous (strĕn′yo͞o-əs) *adj.* **1.** Requiring or characterized by great effort or exertion: *a strenuous task.* **2.** Vigorously active; energetic, persistent, or unremitting: *strenuous opposition.* [Latin *strēnuus*†, brisk, nimble, quick.] **—stren·u·os·i·ty** (strĕn′yo͞o-ŏs′ĭ-tē), **stren·u·ous·ness** *n.* **—stren·u·ous·ly** *adv.*

strep (strĕp) *n.* **1.** A sore throat caused by infection with bacteria of the genus *Streptococcus.* **2.** A streptococcus.
~adj. Streptococcal.

strepto– *prefix.* Indicates: **1.** A twisted chain; for example, **streptococcus. 2.** Streptococcus; for example, **streptokinase.** [Greek *streptos,* twisted, from *strephein,* to turn.]

strep·to·coc·cal (strĕp′tə-kŏk′əl) *adj.* Also **strep·to·coc·cic** (-kŏk′sĭk). Of, pertaining to, or caused by a streptococcus.

strep·to·coc·cus (strĕp′tə-kŏk′əs) *n., pl.* **-cocci** (-kŏk′sī′). Any of various round to ovoid, often pathogenic bacteria of the genus *Streptococcus,* occurring in pairs or chains. [New Latin : STREPTO- + -COCCUS.]

strep·to·kin·ase (strĕp′tə-kĭn′ās′, -āz′, -kī′nās′, -kī′nāz′) *n.* A proteolytic enzyme derived from hemolytic streptococci, capable of dissolving fibrin and used to dissolve blood clots. [STREPTO- + KINASE.]

strep·to·ly·sin (strĕp′tə-lī′sən) *n.* An antigenic hemolysin derived from strains of *Streptococcus pyogenes.* [STREPTO- + -LYS(IS) + -IN.]

strep·to·my·cin (strĕp′tə-mī′sən) *n.* An antibiotic, $C_{21}H_{39}N_7O_{12}$, produced from the bacterium *Streptomyces griseus* and used medicinally to combat various bacteria, especially tuberculosis. [New Latin *Streptomyces* : STREPTO- + Greek *mukēs,* fungus + -IN.]

strep·to·thri·cin (strĕp′tə-thrī′sən, -thrĭs′ən) *n.* An antibiotic, $C_{19}H_{34}N_8O_8$, isolated from the bacterium *Streptomyces lavendulae* (or *Actinomyces lavendulae*) and active against both Gram-positive and Gram-negative bacteria. [New Latin *Streptothrix,* a genus of bacteria : STREPTO- + Greek *thrix,* hair + -IN.]

Stre·se·mann (shtrā′zə-män′, strā′-), **Gustav** (1878–1929). German statesman. As minister of foreign affairs (1923–29), he negotiated the Locarno Pact (1925) of mutual security with France and Belgium and secured Germany's entry (1926) into the League of Nations. He shared the Nobel Peace Prize with Aristide Briand (1926).

stress (strĕs) *n.* **1.** Importance, significance, or emphasis placed upon something: *laid great stress on the need for economy.* **2. a.** The degree of force with which a sound or syllable is spoken. **b.** The emphasis placed upon the sound or syllable spoken loudest in a given word or phrase. **3. a.** The relative emphasis given a syllable or word in verse in accordance with a metrical pattern. **b.** A syllable receiving a strong relative emphasis. **4.** *Music.* An accent. **5.** *Physics.* An applied force or system of forces that tends to strain or deform a body, measured by the force acting per unit area. **6. a.** A mentally or emotionally disruptive or disquieting influence. **b.** A state of tension or distress caused by such an influence.
~tr.v. **stressed, stressing, stresses. 1.** To place phonetic emphasis on; accent. **2.** To attribute particular importance to; emphasize. **3.** To subject to mental, physical, or mechanical stress. [Middle English *stresse,* hardship, distress, from Old French *estresse,* narrowness, from Vulgar Latin *strictia* (unattested), from Latin *strictus,* STRICT.] **—stress·ful** *adj.*

-stress *suffix.* Indicates a feminine agent; for example, **seamstress.** [-ST(ER) + -ESS.]

stretch (strĕch) *v.* **stretched, stretching, stretches.** *—tr.* **1.** To lengthen, widen, or distend by pulling: *stretch a woolen sweater.* **2.** To cause to extend from one place to another or across a given space. **3.** To make taut; tighten. **4.** To reach or put forth; extend. Often used with *out*: *stretched out his hand.* **5.** To extend (oneself) at full length, usually in a prone position. Often used with *out.* **6.** To straighten (oneself) by extending the limbs or flexing the muscles. **7.** To make do with or eke out: *stretch the budget by careful spending.* **8.** To extend or enlarge (the scope of a law or meaning of a word, for example) beyond the usual or proper limits. **9. a.** To make the fullest possible use of or demands upon (one's intellectual or material resources): *felt that he wasn't being stretched in the job.* **b.** To subject to unreasonable or intolerable strain: *stretch one's patience.* **10.** To wrench or strain (a muscle or ligament, for example); sprain. **11.** To prolong: *stretch out an argument.* *—intr.* **1. a.** To become lengthened, widened, or distended. **b.** To admit of being stretched; be elastic. **2.** To extend or reach over a particular distance or area or in a particular direction: *Ahead of us stretched the plain.* **3.** To lie down at full length. Usually used with *out.* **4.** To straighten oneself by extending the limbs or flexing the muscles. **5.** To reach, usually with one's hand. Often used with *out.* **6.** To allow for or include something specified. Used with *to*: *My salary won't stretch to luxuries.* **7.** To extend over a given period of time: *This story stretches over two centuries.* **—stretch one's legs.** To stand up and stroll around after sitting for a long time.
~n. **1.** The act of stretching or the state of being stretched. **2.** The extent or scope to which something can be stretched; elasticity. **3.** A continuous or unbroken length, area, or expanse: *a stretch of highway.* **4.** A straight section of a racecourse or track, especially that section leading to the finishing line. **5. a.** A continuous period of time, especially considered as being occupied by a particular activity or marked by a particular state: *would work for three days at a stretch.* **b.** *Slang.* A term of imprisonment: *a two-year stretch.* **—by no stretch of the imagination.** By no means; not at all.
~adj. Capable of being stretched; elastic: *a stretch sock.* [Middle English *strecchen,* Old English *streccan,* to extend, from Germanic *strakkjan* (unattested).] **—stretch·a·ble** *adj.* **—stretch·y** *adj.*

stretch·er (strĕch′ər) *n.* **1.** A kind of portable bed, usually consisting of canvas stretched over a frame, used to transport the sick, wounded, or dead. **2.** Any of various devices used for stretching and shaping, such as the wooden framework upon which canvas is stretched for an oil painting. **3.** A usually horizontal tie beam or brace serving to support or extend a framework. **4.** A brick or stone laid parallel to the face of a wall. Compare **header.**

stretch·er-bear·er (strĕch′ər-bâr′ər) *n.* One who helps carry a stretcher or litter.

stretch mark *n.* A whitish line on the skin of the thighs, abdomen, or breasts, appearing especially as the result of stretching during pregnancy.

stretch-out (strĕch′out′) *n.* An increase in the work required of industrial workers without a commensurate pay increase.

stret·to (strĕt′ō) *n., pl.* **stretti** (strĕt′ē) or **-tos.** *Music.* **1.** A close succession or overlapping of voices in a fugue, especially in the final section. **2.** A final section, as of an oratorio, performed with an acceleration in tempo to produce a climax.
~adv. Music. More quickly. Used as a direction. [Italian, "tight," from Latin *strictus,* STRICT.]

streu·sel (stroi′zəl, stro͞o′-; *German* shtroi′səl) *n.* A crumblike topping for coffee cakes and rich breads, consisting of flour, sugar, butter, cinnamon, and sometimes chopped nutmeats. [German *Streusel,* "something strewn together," from Middle High German *ströusel,* from *ströuwen,* to sprinkle, strew, from Old High German *strouwen.*]

strew (stro͞o) *tr.v.* **strewn** (stro͞on) or **strewed, strewing, strews. 1.** To spread here and there; scatter; sprinkle. **2.** To cover (a surface) with things scattered or sprinkled. **3.** To be or become dispersed over (a surface). [Middle English *strewen,* Old English *strēowian.*]

strewth. Variant of **struth.**

stri·a (strī′ə) *n., pl.* **striae** (strī′ē′). **1.** A thin, narrow groove or channel. **2.** *Architecture.* A thin band between the grooves on a column. **3.** A thin line or band, especially any one of several that are parallel or close together and share a distinctive feature such as color or composition. [Latin, furrow, channel.]

PRONUNCIATION KEY

ă, pat; ā, pay; âr, care;
ä, father, are; b, bib;
ch, church; d, deed; ĕ, pet;
ē, be; f, fife; g, gag; h, hat;
hw, which; ĭ, pit; ī, pie;
îr, pier; j, judge; k, kick;
l, lid, needle; m, mum;
n, no, sudden; ng, thing;
ŏ, pot; ō, toe; ô, paw, for;
oi, noise; ou, out; o͝o, book;
o͞o, boot; p, pop; r, roar;
s, sauce; sh, ship, dish;
t, tight; th, thin, path;
th, this, bathe; ŭ, cut; ûr, fur;
v, valve; w, with; y, yes;
z, zebra, size; zh, vision;
ə, about, item, edible,
gallop, circus, peaceful

IN FOREIGN WORDS:

à, *Fr.* ami; œ, *Fr.* feu, *Ger.* schön; ü, *Fr.* tu, *Ger.* über; KH, *Ger.* ich, *Scot.* loch; N, *Fr.* bon; y′, *Fr.* Compiègne

STRESS MARKS:

Primary stress: ′
in·cite′ (ĭn-sīt′)
Secondary stress: ′
in′sight′ (ĭn′sīt′)

stri·ate (strī'āt') *adj.* Also **stri·at·ed** (-ā'tĭd). Marked with striae; striped, grooved, or ridged.
~*tr.v.* **striated, -ating, -ates.** To mark with striae. [Latin *striātus,* past participle of *striāre,* to make furrows, from *stria,* furrow, STRIA.]

striated muscle *n.* Muscle consisting of elongated, transversely striated fibers, often operating under voluntary control. Also called "skeletal muscle," "striped muscle."

stri·a·tion (strī-ā'shən) *n.* **1.** The state of being striated or having striae. **2.** An arrangement of striae. **3.** A stria.

strick·en (strĭk'ən) *adj.* **1.** Struck or wounded, as by a projectile. **2.** Afflicted with something overwhelming, such as strong emotion, disease, or trouble. Often used in combination: *conscience-stricken; grief-stricken.* **3.** Having the contents made even with the top of a measuring device or container; level. [Past participle of STRIKE.]

strick·le (strĭk'əl) *n.* **1.** An instrument used to level off grain or other material in a measure; a strike. **2.** A foundry tool used to shape a mold in sand or loam. **3.** A tool for sharpening scythes.
~*tr.v.* **strickled, -ling, -les.** To apply a strickle to (sand in a mold, for example). [Middle English *strikelle,* Old English *stricel.*]

strict (strĭkt) *adj.* **stricter, strictest. 1.** Precise; accurate; exact. **2.** Complete; absolute; maintained without exception or deviation: *strict hygiene.* **3.** Imposing an exacting discipline; allowing no indulgence or relaxation; not permissive: *strict standards.* **4.** Rigidly conforming to a particular code or norm: *a strict Muslim.* **5.** *Botany.* Stiff, narrow, and upright. —See Synonyms at **severe.** [Latin *strictus,* tight, narrow, from the past participle of *stringere,* to draw tight, tighten.] —**strict·ly** *adv.* —**strict·ness** *n.*

stric·ture (strĭk'chər) *n.* **1.** Something that restrains, limits, or restricts. **2.** An adverse remark or criticism; censure. **3.** *Pathology.* An abnormal narrowing of a duct or passage. [Middle English, from Latin *strictūra,* contraction, from *strictus,* STRICT.]

stride (strīd) *v.* **strode** (strōd) or *obsolete* **strid** (strĭd), **stridden** (strĭd'n) or *obsolete* **strid, striding, strides.** —*intr.* **1.** To walk with long steps, especially in a hasty or purposeful manner. **2.** To take a single long step, as in passing over an obstruction. —*tr.* **1.** To stride over, along, or through. **2.** To straddle; bestride.
~*n.* **1.** The act of striding. **2. a.** A single long step. **b.** The distance traveled in such a step. **3. a.** A single coordinated movement of the four legs of a horse or other animal, completed when the legs are returned to their initial relative position. **b.** The distance traveled in such a cycle of movements. **4.** A progressive development; an advance: *making great strides.* —**take in one's stride.** To cope with (an unfamiliar situation, for example) without effort or difficulty. [Stride, strode (or strid), stridden; Middle English *striden, strode* (or *stride*), *stridden,* Old English *strīdan, strād* (singular, only in *bestrād*), *stridon* (plural, unattested), *striden* (unattested), from Germanic *strīdan* (unattested).] —**strid·er** *n.*

stri·dent (strīd'dənt) *adj.* **1.** Loud, harsh, and grating; shrill. **2.** Having a disagreeably assertive or insistent quality. [Latin *strīdēns* (stem *strīdent-*), present participle of *strīdēre,* to make a harsh sound.] —**stri·dence, stri·den·cy** *n.* —**stri·dent·ly** *adv.*

stri·dor (strī'dər, -dôr') *n.* **1.** A strident sound. **2.** *Pathology.* A harsh, high-pitched sound in inhalation or exhalation. [Latin *strīdor,* from *strīdēre,* to make a harsh sound.]

strid·u·late (strĭj'ŏŏ-lāt') *intr.v.* **-lated, -lating, -lates.** To produce a shrill grating or creaking sound; chirp. Used especially of insects such as crickets. [Latin *strīdulus,* creaking, STRIDULOUS.] —**strid·u·la·tion** *n.* —**strid·u·la·to·ry** (strĭj'ə-lə-tôr'ē, -tōr'ē) *adj.*

strid·u·lous (strĭj'ŏŏ-ləs) *adj.* **1.** Making or characterized by a strident sound or chirp. **2.** Of or affected with stridor. [Latin *strīdulus,* creaking, from *strīdēre,* to make a harsh sound.]

strife (strīf) *n.* **1.** Heated, often violent dissension; a state of bitter conflict. **2.** A struggle between rivals; a dispute or conflict. **3.** Earnest endeavor or striving. —See Synonyms at **discord.** [Middle English *strif,* from Old French *estrif†.*]

strig·il (strĭj'əl) *n.* **1.** An instrument used in ancient Greece and Rome for scraping the skin after a bath. **2.** A structure on the first leg of certain insects, such as bees, used for cleaning the antennae. [Latin *strigilis,* from *stringere,* to draw tight.]

stri·gose (strī'gōs') *adj.* **1.** *Zoology.* Marked with fine, close-set grooves or streaks. **2.** *Botany.* Having stiff, closely pressed hairs or bristles. [New Latin *strigosus,* from Latin *striga,* swath, furrow.]

strike (strīk) *v.* **struck** (strŭk), **struck** or **stricken** (strĭk'ən), **striking, strikes.** —*tr.* **1. a.** To hit sharply or forcefully, as with the hand or fist or with a weapon or implement. **b.** To inflict: *struck a blow.* **2. a.** To collide with or crash into: *struck the rocks and quickly sank.* **b.** To cause to hit sharply or forcefully; dash: *fell and struck her head.* **3.** To bring into a specified condition by or as if by a blow: *struck him dead.* **4. a.** To launch a military attack upon; assault. **b.** *Archaic.* To do (battle). **5.** To afflict suddenly, as with disease or impairment: *stricken with a heart attack.* **6.** To wound with the fangs. Used of a snake. **7.** To hook (a fish) that has taken the bait. **8.** To produce or impress by stamping, printing, or punching: *strike a medallion.* **9.** To play or produce, as by hitting a key on a piano or typewriter: *strike a B flat.* **10.** To indicate (the time) by a percussive sound: *The clock struck nine.* **11. a.** To produce (a flame, light, or spark) by friction. **b.** To cause to ignite by friction: *strike a match.* **12.** To delete or cancel by or as if by the stroke of a pen: *Strike that remark from the record.* **13.** To come upon, usually as the result of a search; discover: *struck gold.* **14.** To reach; fall upon: *A bright light struck her face.* **15.** To come suddenly to the mind of; occur to: *It struck me that the whole thing was a hoax.* **16. a.** To make a particular impression upon; appear to: *How do the new arrangements strike you? His behavior struck me as odd.* **b.** To make a powerful impression upon: *We were struck by his obvious sincerity.* **17.** To cause (an emotion) to penetrate deeply: *struck terror into their hearts.* **18. a.** To make or conclude (a bargain or agreement). **b.** To achieve or produce, as by careful calculation or contrivance: *strike a balance.* **19.** To fall into or assume (a pose, for example). **20.** *Nautical.* **a.** To haul down (a mast or sail). **b.** To lower (a flag or sail) in salute or surrender. **c.** To lower (cargo) into a hold. **21.** To remove (theatrical properties or scenery, for example) from the stage or other playing area. **22.** To take down and pack up the tents of (a camp). **23.** To level or smooth (a measure, as of grain); strickle. **24.** To put forth or send down (roots). **25.** To undertake a strike against (an employer). —*intr.* **1. a.** To deal a blow or blows with or as if with the fist or a weapon; hit. **b.** To occur or appear with devastating effect, as if dealing a blow: *All was going well when tragedy struck.* **2.** To aim a stroke or blow. **3.** To make contact suddenly or violently; collide. **4.** To begin or deliver an attack: *struck at daybreak; strikes at the roots of our democratic institutions.* **5.** To pierce; penetrate. Used chiefly of wind, cold, or damp. **6.** To jerk the line in order to hook a fish that has taken the bait. **7. a.** To make a percussive sound. **b.** To be indicated by sounds: *The hour has struck.* **8.** To become ignited. **9.** To discover something suddenly or unexpectedly. Used with *on* or *upon.* **10.** To proceed, especially in a new direction; set out; head: *The hikers struck out at dawn.* **11.** To engage in a strike as a form of protest or to support a demand. —See Synonyms at **affect.** —**strike it rich.** To gain sudden wealth. —**strike off. 1.** To remove the name of, as from a list or record. **2.** To print: *struck off 50 copies.* —**strike up. 1.** To start to play or sound vigorously: *The band struck up a waltz.* **2.** To initiate (a friendship, for example).
~*n.* **1.** An act or gesture of striking; a hit or thrust. **2.** An attack; especially, a military air attack upon a single group of targets. **3. a.** A cessation of work by employees in support of demands made upon their employer, as for higher pay or improved conditions. **b.** Any cessation of normal activity undertaken as a form of protest: *a hunger strike.* **4. a.** A sudden discovery, as of a precious mineral. **b.** Any sudden or unexpected piece of good luck. **5.** A pull on a fishing line by which the fish is hooked. **6.** A quantity of coins or medals struck at the same time. **7.** In baseball, a pitched ball that is counted against the batter, swung at and missed, fouled off, or judged to have passed through the strike zone. **8.** In bowling, the knocking down of all the pins with the first bowl of a frame. **9.** *Geology.* The direction of a horizontal line in the plane of an inclined structural feature such as a rock bed or vein. **10.** A strickle. [Strike, struck (earlier stroke), stricken (or struck); Middle English *striken, strok* (or *strak*), *striken,* Old English *strīcan,* to stroke, rub, *strāc, stricen.*]

strike·bound (strīk'bound') *adj.* Closed, immobilized, or slowed down by a strike.

strike·break·er (strīk'brā'kər) *n.* One who works or provides an employer with workers during a strike. —**strike·break·ing** *n.*

strike fault *n. Geology.* A fault in the earth's crust parallel to the strike of the rock strata.

strike figure *n. Geology.* The pattern of cracks formed in a crystalline mineral when struck. Also called "percussion figure."

strike out *intr.v.* **1.** To begin a course of action or proceed with vigorous effort: *struck out on his own.* **2.** In baseball, to be retired after the recording of three strikes. —*tr.v.* In baseball, to retire (a batter) by the recording of three strikes.

strike·out (strīk'out') *n.* An act of striking out in baseball.

strik·er (strī'kər) *n.* **1.** One that strikes. **2.** An employee who is on strike against his or her employer. **3.** Any device for striking, such as the clapper in a bell or the firing pin in a gun. **4. a.** A harpoon. **b.** A harpooner. **5.** In the U.S. Navy, an enlisted man in training for a petty officer's rating.

strike-slip fault (strīk'slĭp') *n. Geology.* A fault in which the dominant movement on the fault plane is horizontal. Also called "transcurrent fault," "tear fault."

strike zone *n.* In baseball, the area over home plate through which a pitch must pass to be called a strike, defined as being between the batter's armpits and knees.

strik·ing (strī'kĭng) *adj.* Making an immediate or vivid impression because of remarkable or unusual qualities: *a striking beauty.* —**strik·ing·ly** *adv.* —**strik·ing·ness** *n.*

striking circle *n.* In field hockey, the semicircular area in front of the goal from which all scoring shots must be made. Also called "circle."

striking distance *n.* **1.** A distance over which it is possible to deliver an attack. **2.** A distance that is easily traversed: *within striking distance of the coast.*

Strind·berg (strĭnd'bûrg'), **(Johan) August** (1849–1912). Swedish dramatist and novelist. He was a leading exponent of psychological realism in drama. His plays include *The Father* (1887), *Miss Julie* (1888), and *The Dance of Death* (1901). His best-known novels are *The Red Room* (1879) and *The Ghost Sonata* (1907).

string (strĭng) *n.* **1.** A cord thicker than thread and usually made of twisted fibers, used for fastening, tying, or lacing. **2.** Anything shaped into a long, thin line. **3.** A tough plant fiber, such as one running along the side of a pod. **4.** A set of objects threaded together: *a string of beads.* **5.** A continuous series of related acts, events, or items: *a string of excuses.* **6. a.** A set of animals, especially racehorses, belonging to a single owner; a stable. **b.** A group of businesses belonging to a single owner. **7.** A group of players having a specified ranking according to ability: *He made the second string.* **8.** *Music.* **a.** A cord or wire stretched across the sounding board of an instrument that is struck, plucked, or bowed to produce a tone. **b. strings.** Instruments that have such strings; especially, the instruments of the violin family. **c. strings.** The members of an orchestra who play these instruments. **9.** Any of the cords arranged in a crisscross pattern in a sports racket. **10.** *Architecture.* **a.** A stringboard. **b.** A stringcourse. **11.** *Informal.* A limiting or hidden condition: *a gift with no strings attached.* —See Synonyms at **series.** **—on a string.** Totally under someone's control. **—pull strings.** To use one's influence or influential connections, often in secret, to gain an advantage.

~*adj.* Made of string or having a string or a mesh of strings: *a string bag.*

~*v.* **strung** (strŭng), **stringing, strings.** —*tr.* **1.** To fit or furnish with a string or strings: *string a guitar.* **2.** To thread on a string: *string beads.* **3.** To arrange or bring together so as to form a string: *managed to string together a few clichés.* **4.** To fasten, tie, or hang with a string or strings. **5.** To extend; stretch out: *string a wire across a room.* **6.** To remove the strings from (a vegetable). **7.** *Informal.* To hang (a person). Usually used with *up.* —*intr.* **1.** To form strings or become stringlike. **2.** To extend or progress in a string, line, or succession. **3.** In billiards and similar games, to determine the order of play by hitting the cue ball to the end cushion with the aim of bringing it back as close as possible to the head rail. **—string along. 1.** To follow another's lead; go along: *strung along with her friend's decision.* **2.** To keep (someone) waiting or dangling. **3.** To fool or deceive: *He strung them along with tales of buried treasure.* [Middle English *stringe,* Old English *streng.*]

string bass *n.* A **double bass** *(see).*

string bean *n.* **1.** A bushy or climbing plant, *Phaseolus vulgaris,* widely cultivated for its narrow, green, edible pods. **2.** The green pod of any bean prepared for cooking by breaking into sections that retain the beans. Also called "green bean," "snap bean." **3.** *Slang.* A tall, thin person. [From the stringy fibers on the pod.]

string·board (strĭng′bôrd', -bōrd') *n.* A board that runs along the side of a staircase to support or cover the ends of the steps. Also called "string," "stringer."

string·course (strĭng′kôrs', -kōrs') *n.* A distinctive horizontal band or molding set in the face of a building as a design element. Also called "cordon," "string," "table."

stringed instrument *n.* A musical instrument played by plucking, striking, or bowing taut strings. See feature, pages 1642-43.

strin·gen·do (strĭn-jĕn′dō) *adv. Music.* With an accelerating tempo. Used as a direction. [Italian, "tightening," from *stringere,* to press together, to tighten, from Latin.] **—strin·gen·do** *adj.*

strin·gent (strĭn′jənt) *adj.* **1.** Imposing rigorous and exacting standards or demands; severe. **2.** Constricted; tight: *"For the time grows stringent, frightfully pressing"* (Carlyle). **3.** Characterized by scarcity of money or by financial restrictions: *stringent market conditions.* [Latin *stringēns* (stem *stringent-*), present participle of *stringere,* to tighten.] **—strin·gen·cy** *n.* **—strin·gent·ly** *adv.*

string·er (strĭng′ər) *n.* **1.** A person or thing that strings. **2.** *Architecture.* **a.** A long, horizontal structural timber used for any of several connective or supportive purposes. **b.** A stringboard. **3.** A lengthwise timber used to support rails. **4.** A heavy longitudinal member serving to strengthen the hull of a ship or fuselage of a plane. **5.** A part-time or free-lance correspondent for a news publication. **6.** A person viewed as being at a particular level of proficiency or excellence: *a second-stringer.*

string·halt (strĭng′hôlt') *n.* Lameness accompanied by spasmodic movements in the hind legs of a horse. Also called "springhalt." [Perhaps STRING + HALT.]

string-pull·ing (strĭng′po͝ol'ĭng) *n.* The secret or unofficial use of influence to gain an advantage.

string quartet *n.* **1.** A quartet of musicians playing stringed instruments, traditionally a first and second violin, a viola, and a cello. **2.** A composition for such a quartet of performers.

string tie *n.* A very narrow necktie, usually tied in a bow.

string·y (strĭng′ē) *adj.* **-ier, -iest. 1.** Resembling, forming, or consisting of a string or strings. **2.** Slender and wiry. **3.** Fibrous or sinewy; tough: *stringy meat.* **—string·i·ly** *adv.* **—string·i·ness** *n.*

strip[1] (strĭp) *v.* **stripped** or *rare* **stript** (strĭpt), **stripping, strips.** —*tr.* **1. a.** To remove the clothing or other covering from. **b.** To remove (clothing or other covering). **2. a.** To remove the furnishings from. **b.** To remove (furnishings) from. **3. a.** To deprive of honors, rank, or the like; divest. **b.** To deprive of possessions; dispossess. **4.** To reduce to essentials; remove all excess detail or extraneous matter from. **5. a.** To remove the foliage or bark from. **b.** To remove the leaves from the stalks of (tobacco). **6. a.** To remove (paint, wallpaper, or varnish, for example), as from walls or furniture, either manually or by chemical or mechanical means. **b.** To remove paint or other coverings from (walls, for example) in this way. **7.** To dismantle (a mechanical apparatus) piece by piece. **8.** To damage or break the threads or teeth of (a nut, bolt, screw, or gear). **9.** To finish milking (a cow or other milk-giving creature). **10.** To rob; plunder; despoil. —*intr.* **1. a.** To undress completely. **b.** To perform a striptease. **2.** To fall away or be removed; peel. [Middle English *stripen,* Old English *(be)strīepan,* to plunder, from Germanic *straupjan* (unattested).]

Synonyms: *strip, divest, denude, bare.* These verbs refer to the act of removing coverings or possessions. *Strip* often suggests force or abrupt action and applies to removal of such diverse things as clothing, natural covering such as bark or foliage, components of machinery, and attributes such as honor, rank, or position. *Divest* more often specifies deprivation of authority or rank or of the physical things that symbolize them. *Denude* generally refers to making land barren by depriving it of natural covering, such as vegetation or topsoil. *Bare* usually implies uncovering, literally or figuratively, and exposing to view.

strip[2] *n.* **1.** A long, narrow piece or tract, usually of uniform width: *a strip of paper; a strip of land.* **2.** A heavily developed street or thoroughfare lined with stores, restaurants, and other business establishments. **3.** A **comic strip** *(see).* **4.** An **airstrip** *(see).*

~*tr.v.* **stripped, stripping, strips.** To cut or tear into strips. [Perhaps alteration of STRIPE (line).]

strip-crop·ping (strĭp′krŏp'ĭng) *n.* The growing of a cultivated crop, such as cotton, and a sod-forming crop, such as alfalfa, in alternating strips following the contour of the land, in order to minimize erosion.

stripe[1] (strīp) *n.* **1.** A long, narrow band distinguished, as by color or texture, from the surrounding material or surface. **2. a.** A fabric having such a band or bands. **b. stripes.** A garment of such fabric, especially a prisoner's uniform. **3.** A strip of cloth or braid worn on a uniform to indicate rank or length of service. **4.** Sort; kind: *men of a vicious stripe.*

~*tr.v.* **striped, striping, stripes.** To mark with a stripe or stripes. [Middle English *strype* (unattested), from Middle Dutch *strīpe,* akin to Middle High German *strīfe*†.]

stripe[2] *n.* A stroke or blow, as with a whip. [Middle English *strype,* perhaps from Middle Low German *strippe,* a lash, strap, from Germanic *strip-* (unattested).]

striped (strīpt, strī′pĭd) *adj.* Having a stripe or stripes.

striped bass *n.* A food and game fish, *Roccus saxatilis,* of North American coastal waters, having dark longitudinal stripes along its sides. Also called "rockfish," "striper."

striped muscle *n. Anatomy.* **Striated muscle** *(see).*

strip·er (strī′pər) *n.* **1.** *Slang.* A member of the armed forces who wears stripes designating rank or length of service. Usually used in combination: *a four-striper.* **2.** *Informal.* A striped bass.

strip light *n.* A long fluorescent light. **—strip lighting** *n.*

strip·ling (strĭp′lĭng) *n.* An adolescent youth. [Middle English.]

strip mine *n.* An open mine, especially a coal mine, whose seams or outcrops run close to ground level and are exposed by the removal of topsoil and overburden.

strip-mine (strĭp′mīn') *tr.v.* **-mined, -mining, -mines.** To mine (an ore) from a strip mine. **—strip-min·ing** *n.*

strip·per (strĭp′ər) *n.* **1.** One that strips; especially, a tool or chemical that strips wallpaper, paint, or some other coating. **2.** *Slang.* One who performs a striptease.

strip poker *n.* A poker game in which the losing players in each hand must remove an article of clothing.

strip·tease (strĭp′tēz') *n.* A form of entertainment featuring a performer, usually a woman, who slowly removes clothing to a musical accompaniment. **—strip·teas·er** *n.*

strip·y (strī′pē) *adj.* **-ier, -iest.** Suggestive of or marked with stripes.

strive (strīv) *intr.v.* **strove** (strōv) or *rare* **strived, striven** (strĭv′ən) or **strived, striving, strives. 1.** To exert much effort or energy: *"She strove to make him moral, religious"* (D.H. Lawrence). **2.** To struggle against another or one another; contend: *"Good nature now and passion strive/which of the two should be above"* (Suckling). [Middle English *striven,* from Old French *estriver,* perhaps from *estrif,* STRIFE. Strove, striven; Middle English *stroof, streven,* analogous formations, from *striven.*] **—striv·er** *n.*

strobe (strōb) *n.* **1.** A strobe light. **2.** A stroboscope.

strobe light *n.* An electric light that produces a series of repeated intense flashes, used in stroboscopes and in light displays. Also called "strobe." **—strobe lighting** *n.*

stro·bi·la (strō-bī′lə) *n., pl.* **-lae** (-lē'). **1.** The body of an adult tapeworm, consisting of a series of segments or proglottides. **2.** The segmented polyp stage of certain jellyfish. [New Latin, from Greek *strobilē,* plug of lint resembling a pine cone, from *strobilos,* pine cone, STROBILUS.]

stro·bi·la·ceous (strō'bə-lā′shəs) *adj. Botany.* Of or resembling a strobilus; conelike.

stro·bi·la·tion (strō'bə-lā′shən) *n.* Segmentation of the type found in tapeworms and certain jellyfish.

stro·bi·lus (strō-bī′ləs, strō′bə-ləs) *n., pl.* **-li** (-lī'). Also **stro·bile** (strō′bīl', -bəl). *Botany.* A fruiting structure characterized by rows of overlapping scales, such as a pine cone or the fruit of the hop. [New Latin *strobilus,* from Late Latin, a pine cone, from Greek *strobilos,* "round ball," from *strobos,* a whirling around, whirlwind.]

stro·bo·scope (strō′bə-skōp') *n.* Any of various instruments used to view, calibrate, balance, or otherwise adjust moving, rotating, or vibrating objects by making them appear stationary, using pulsed illumination or mechanical devices that intermittently interrupt observation. [Greek *strobos,* a whirling around + -SCOPE.] **—stro·bo·scop·ic** (strō'bə-skŏp′ĭk) *adj.* **—stro·bo·scop·i·cal·ly** *adv.*

strode. Past tense of **stride.**

stro·gan·off (strô′gə-nôf', strô-gä′nôf) *adj.* Sliced thin and cooked with onions, mushrooms, and seasonings, with a thick sour-cream sauce. [After Count *Stroganoff,* 19th-century Russian diplomat.]

Stro·heim (strō′hīm', shtrō′-), **Erich von** (1885–1957). Austrian-born U.S. film director and actor. As a director he was noted for uncompromising realistic detail, as in *Greed* (1923). As an actor

PRONUNCIATION KEY

ă, pat; ā, pay; âr, care; ä, father, are; b, bib; ch, church; d, deed; ĕ, pet; ē, be; f, fife; g, gag; h, hat; hw, which; ĭ, pit; ī, pie; îr, pier; j, judge; k, kick; l, lid, needle; m, mum; n, no, sudden; ng, thing; ŏ, pot; ō, toe; ô, paw, for; oi, noise; ou, out; o͝o, book; o͞o, boot; p, pop; r, roar; s, sauce; sh, ship, dish; t, tight; th, thin, path; *th*, this, bathe; ŭ, cut; ûr, fur; v, valve; w, with; y, yes; z, zebra, size; zh, vision; ə, about, item, edible, gallop, circus, peaceful

IN FOREIGN WORDS:

à, *Fr.* ami; œ, *Fr.* feu, *Ger.* schön; ü, *Fr.* tu, *Ger.* über; KH, *Ger.* ich, *Scot.* loch; N, *Fr.* bon; y', *Fr.* Compiègne

STRESS MARKS:

Primary stress: ′ in·cite′ (ĭn-sīt′) Secondary stress: ' in′sight' (ĭn′sīt')

he is remembered for his portrayal of Prussian officers, particularly in *La Grande Illusion* (1937).

stroke (strōk) *n.* **1. a.** The act or an action of striking; an impact; a blow. **b.** A blow, as from a cane or whip, imposed as a punishment: *sentenced to six strokes.* **2. a.** The striking of a bell, gong, or similar instrument. **b.** The sound so produced. **c.** The time so indicated: *the stroke of midnight.* **3.** An unexpected event having a powerful immediate effect for good or ill: *a stroke of luck.* **4. a.** A sudden severe attack, as of apoplexy or paralysis. **b. Apoplexy** (*see*). **5.** An inspired or effective idea or act: *a stroke of genius.* **6. a.** A single completed movement of the limbs and body, as in swimming or rowing. **b.** The rate or manner of executing such a movement. **7. a.** The member of a rowing crew who sits nearest the coxswain or the stern and sets the tempo of the other oarsmen. **b.** The position he occupies. **8. a.** A movement of the upper torso and arms for the purpose of striking a ball, as in tennis. **b.** The manner of executing such a movement. **9.** In golf, a single act of striking the ball, used as a unit of scoring. **10.** Any single act or movement: *has never done a stroke of work; cut interest rates at a stroke.* **11.** Any of a series of movements of a piston from one end of the limit of its motion to the other. **12.** A single mark made by a pen, brush, or other marking implement. **13.** A single deft touch, as in literary composition. **14.** A single flash of lightning. **15.** A light caressing movement, as of the hand. **16.** A positive gesture, expression, or action received from another person and causing a sense of well-being. *~tr.v.* **stroked, stroking, strokes. 1.** To give or apply a stroke to. **2.** To rub lightly, as with the hand or something held in the hand; caress. **3.** To set the pace for (a rowing crew). [Middle English *stroke,* Old English *strāc.*]

stroke play *n.* A method of scoring in golf, **medal play** (*see*).

stroll (strōl) *v.* **strolled, strolling, strolls.** *—intr.* **1.** To go for a leisurely walk. **2.** To travel from place to place giving performances: *strolling players.* *—tr.* To walk along or through at a leisurely pace: *stroll the beach.* *~n.* A leisurely walk. [Perhaps from German dialectal *strollen†.*]

stroll·er (strō′lər) *n.* **1.** One who strolls. **2.** A strolling player. **3.** A vagabond. **4.** A lightweight, collapsible baby carriage shaped like a chair in which a child rides in a sitting position.

---

stringed instruments

MUSIC PRODUCED BY THE VIBRATION OF STRINGS

One simple principle is used in a large family of musical instruments

Stringed instruments produce their sound by the vibrations of strings made of gut, wire, silk, or nylon. The strings may be vibrated by bowing (violin), plucking with the fingers (guitar), or striking with hammers (dulcimer). Pitch is most frequently altered by shortening the length of a vibrating string, which then produces a higher tone. Stringed instruments differ widely in size and methods of construction, and their range of sounds is therefore enormous. Modern instruments have been developed over several centuries, and many early types are no longer played.

In an orchestra the four main stringed instruments—the violin, the viola, the violoncello (generally called the cello), and the double bass—are all members of the violin family. Each consists of a soundbox to which is attached a projecting neck. Four strings of different thicknesses are stretched from a tailpiece, over a wooden bridge on the lower part of the soundbox, to the far end of the neck. The strings are stopped along the neck by the player's left hand to produce different tones. The strings are tuned by pegs at the end of the neck that tighten or slacken the tension and so raise or lower the pitch. A bow is drawn across the strings to produce vibrations that are transmitted by the bridge to the soundbox, where they are amplified to produce sound. The modern bow is a tapered stick with horsehair stretched across it.

The viol is not commonly played today, but the harp is often found in orchestras. The harp has the largest range of all orchestral instruments and is constructed with the soundbox forming one side of a triangle across which the strings are stretched. The strings are plucked with the fingers. The piano is a development of the harp, but is normally classed as a keyboard instrument. Because of their size, the harp, cello, and double bass are played resting on the ground.

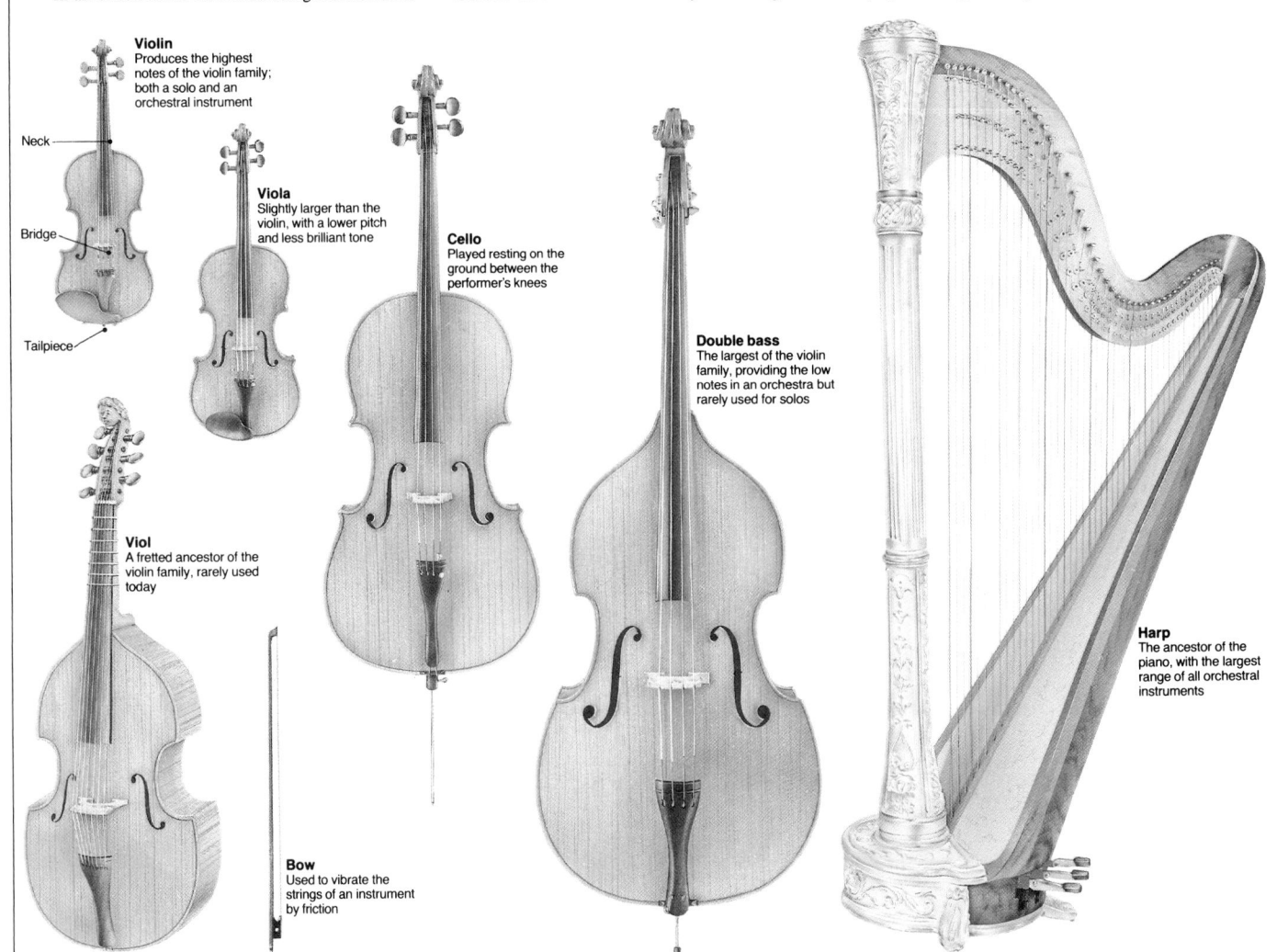

Violin
Produces the highest notes of the violin family; both a solo and an orchestral instrument

Neck

Bridge

Tailpiece

Viola
Slightly larger than the violin, with a lower pitch and less brilliant tone

Cello
Played resting on the ground between the performer's knees

Double bass
The largest of the violin family, providing the low notes in an orchestra but rarely used for solos

Viol
A fretted ancestor of the violin family, rarely used today

Bow
Used to vibrate the strings of an instrument by friction

Harp
The ancestor of the piano, with the largest range of all orchestral instruments

stro·ma (strō′mə) *n., pl.* **-mata** (-mə-tə). *Biology.* Tissue that serves as a framework, especially: **1.** The colorless dense material occurring around the grana in a chloroplast. **2.** A compact mass of fungal hyphae in which fruiting bodies are produced. **3.** The fibrous connective tissue forming the framework of the ovaries and testes. [New Latin, from Late Latin, from Greek *strōma*, bedspread, mattress.] **—stro·mat·ic** (strō-măt′ĭk) *adj.*

Strom·bo·li (strŏm′bə-lē). One of the volcanic Lipari islands in the Tyrrhenian Sea north of Sicily. Its crater contains molten lava and continuously emits gases; small-scale eruptions occur frequently. There were violent eruptions in 1930 and 1966.

strong (strông) *adj.* **stronger, strongest. 1.** Physically powerful; capable of exerting great physical force; muscular. **2. a.** In sound health; robust. **b.** Economically or financially sound or thriving: *a strong economy.* **3.** Having force of character, will, morality, or intellect. **4.** Having or showing impressive ability, talent, or resources in a specified field: *strong in chemistry; a strong batting line-up.* **5.** Capable of the effective exercise of authority: *a strong leader.* **6.** Capable of enduring; solid: *a strong building.* **7.** Capable of being defended: *a strong flank.* **8.** Having force of conviction or feeling; well-grounded: *a strong faith.* **9.** *Finance.* Showing firmness and a tendency to rise in price or value: *The dollar remained strong.* **10.** Not easily upset; resistant to harmful or unpleasant influences: *strong nerves; a strong stomach.* **11.** Having a specified number: *an army 15,000 strong.* **12.** Having force of motion or action: *a strong current.* **13. a.** Persuasive, effective, and cogent: *a strong argument.* **b.** Forceful and pointed; emphatic: *a strong statement.* **c.** Immoderate or profane: *strong language.* **14.** Extreme; drastic: *strong measures.* **15.** Intense in degree or quality: *a strong emotion.* **16.** Having an intense effect on the senses: *a strong smell.* **17.** Having a high concentration of an active or essential ingredient: *strong coffee.* **18.** Powerfully effective: *a strong painkiller.* **19.** Existing to a considerable or striking degree: *a strong resemblance; a strong possibility.* **20.** Characterized by a high degree of saturation. Said of a color. **21.** *Linguistics.* Of, pertaining to, or being a verb in a Germanic language that forms the past tense by a change in the root vowel rather than by means of a dental suffix such as *-ed*, as *drive, drove* or *sing, sang.* In this sense, compare **weak**.

The majority of nonorchestral stringed instruments also work on the principle of a strung neck attached to a soundbox. Unlike the violin family, these instruments are normally plucked and frequently have frets—narrow, slightly raised metal or wood bars across the width of the neck that facilitate the precise stopping of the strings usually with the left hand.

The lute was popular throughout Renaissance Europe and had a varying number of strings. It was gradually superseded by the guitar in the 17th century. The guitar was probably introduced into Spain by the Moors and grew in popularity throughout Europe from the 14th century. The classical guitar of today has six gut or nylon strings that are plucked and strummed and is a popular portable instrument. The folk guitar is generally larger than the classical guitar and has metal strings that give it greater volume. The electric guitar is unlike other stringed instruments in having no soundbox. The metal strings vibrate above a magnet wrapped in a metal coil. The vibrations alter the magnetic field and induce a small electrical charge in the coil that is then amplified and emitted through loudspeakers as sound. Electronic modification of the impulse makes the range of sounds almost limitless. The ukulele is a small four-string guitar that was developed in the 19th century in Hawaii and was popular with jazz bands until the mid-20th century. The banjo, which is also used in traditional jazz, was brought to the United States by African slaves and is a derivative of the lute. The mandolin is similar to the lute, played with a plectrum, and is most popular in Italy.

Throughout the world there is a great variety of stringed instruments. Other examples include the zither, which is popular in Austria and the Indian sitar, which has become more popular in the West since the 1960's.

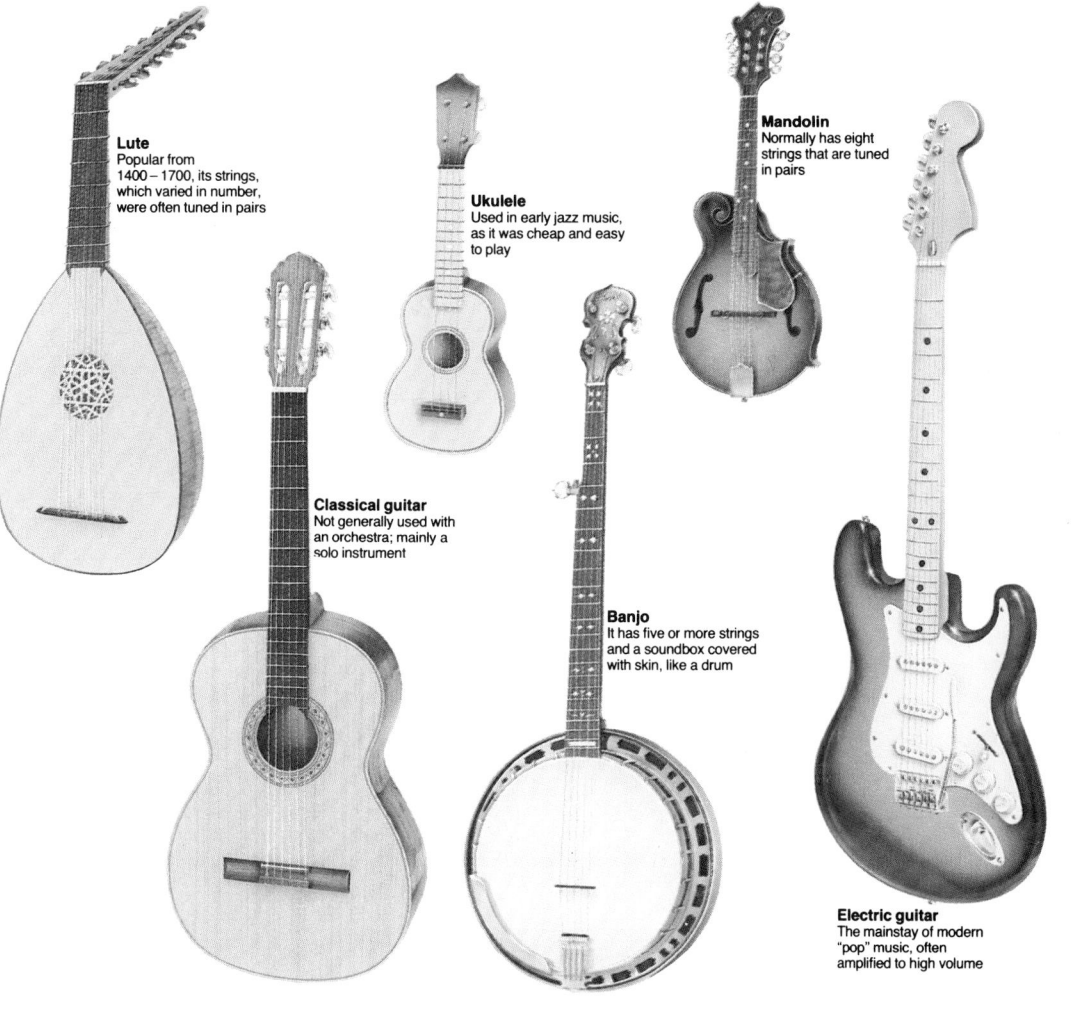

Lute
Popular from 1400 – 1700, its strings, which varied in number, were often tuned in pairs

Ukulele
Used in early jazz music, as it was cheap and easy to play

Mandolin
Normally has eight strings that are tuned in pairs

Classical guitar
Not generally used with an orchestra; mainly a solo instrument

Banjo
It has five or more strings and a soundbox covered with skin, like a drum

Electric guitar
The mainstay of modern "pop" music, often amplified to high volume

~adv. In a strong, powerful, or vigorous manner; forcibly; forcefully. **—going strong.** Still vigorous or effective. [Middle English *strong,* Old English *strang.*] **—strong·ly** *adv.*

Synonyms: strong, stout, sturdy, tough, stalwart, tenacious. These adjectives are compared as they relate to vigor, durability, or power of body or spirit. *Strong* is the most general. *Stout* stresses ability to endure by muscular strength, solid construction, or resoluteness. *Sturdy* is closely related to *stout* in its implications of rugged health, solidity, or firmness of spirit or purpose. *Tough* suggests strength of physique or moral fiber that resists opposition or hardship. *Stalwart* implies imposing strength, courage, or unwavering determination, dependability, or loyalty. *Tenacious* stresses ability to hold fast to positions, goals, or opinions.

strong-arm (strông′ärm′) *adj. Informal.* Using physical force or coercion: *strong-arm tactics.*

strong·box (strông′bŏks′) *n.* A stoutly made box or safe in which valuables are deposited.

strong breeze *n.* A wind having a speed of 25 to 30 miles per hour, force 6 on the Beaufort scale.

strong gale *n.* A wind having a speed of 47 to 54 miles per hour, force 9 on the Beaufort scale.

strong·hold (strông′hōld′) *n.* **1.** A fortress. **2.** A place of security; a refuge. **3.** An area of predominance: *a Republican stronghold.*

strong interaction *n.* A force that acts between certain elementary particles, hadrons, and is about 100 times stronger than the electromagnetic interaction but acts over only very short distances (10^{-15} meter). Compare **electromagnetic interaction, gravitational interaction, weak interaction.**

strong man *n.* **1.** One who performs feats of strength at a circus, fair, or other show. **2.** A leader, especially a military dictator, who retains power by the use or threat of force.

strong-mind·ed (strông′mīn′dĭd) *adj.* **1.** Having a determined will. **2.** Having a vigorous mentality. **—strong-mind·ed·ly** *adv.* **—strong-mind·ed·ness** *n.*

strong point *n.* A skill or quality in which one excels.

strong room *n.* A strongly built, secure, and fireproof room designed for the safekeeping of money or valuables.

strong suit *n.* A long suit *(see).*

stron·gyle, stron·gyl (strŏn′jĭl′, -jəl) *n.* Any of various nematode worms of the family Strongylidae, often parasitic in the gastrointestinal tract of mammals, especially horses. [New Latin *Strongylus* (genus), from Greek *strongulos†,* round, compactly formed.]

stron·gy·lo·sis (strŏn′jə-lō′sĭs) *n.* Infestation with strongyles.

stron·ti·a (strŏn′chē-ə, -tē-ə) *n.* **Strontium hydroxide** *(see).* [From *strontian,* variant of STRONTIUM.]

stron·ti·an·ite (strŏn′chē-ə-nīt′, -tē-ə-nīt′) *n.* A gray to yellowish-green strontium ore, essentially $SrCO_3$. [*Strontian,* variant of STRONTIUM + -ITE.]

stron·ti·um (strŏn′chē-əm, -tē-əm) *n. Symbol* **Sr** A soft, silvery, easily oxidized metallic element that ignites spontaneously in air when finely divided. It is used in pyrotechnic compounds and various alloys. Atomic number 38, atomic weight 87.62, melting point 769°C, boiling point 1,384°C, specific gravity 2.54, valence 2. [Earlier *strontian,* after *Strontian,* mining village in Argyllshire, Scotland, where it was discovered.] **—stron·tic** (strŏn′tĭk) *adj.*

strontium hydroxide *n.* A white deliquescent powder that normally occurs as the octahydrate, Sr (OH)₂·8 H₂O, and is used in sugar refining. Also called "strontia."

strontium 90 *n.* The strontium isotope with mass 90, having a half-life of 28 years, used for its high-energy beta emission in certain nuclear electric power sources and constituting a radiation hazard in fallout.

strontium unit *n. Abbr.* **SU** A measure of the concentration of strontium 90 in an organic medium, such as soil, milk, or bone, relative to the calcium concentration in the same medium; 10^{-12} curie of strontium 90 per gram of calcium.

strop (strŏp) *n.* A flexible strip of leather or canvas used for sharpening a razor.

~tr.v. **stropped, stropping, strops.** To sharpen (a razor) on a strop. [Middle English *stroppe,* band of leather, from Middle Low German or Middle Dutch *strop,* from West Germanic *strupa* (unattested), from Latin *struppus,* from Greek *strophos,* twisted cord, from *strephein,* to turn.]

stro·phan·thin (strō-făn′thĭn) *n.* A toxic glycoside or mixture of glycosides extracted from seeds of *Strophanthus Kombé* and used medicinally as a cardiac tonic. [New Latin *Strophanthus* (genus) : Greek *strophos,* twisted cord (see **strop**) + *anthos,* flower + -IN.]

stro·phe (strō′fē) *n.* **1. a.** A stanza, especially the first of a pair of stanzas of alternating form on which the structure of a given poem is based. **b.** A rhythmic system constituting a section of a poem, typically consisting of a series of asymmetric lines. **2.** The first division of the triad (strophe, antistrophe, and epode) constituting a section of a Pindaric ode. **3. a.** The movement of the chorus in classical Greek drama while turning from one side of the orchestra to the other. **b.** The part of a choral ode sung while this movement is executed. [Greek *strophē,* a turning, from *strephein,* to turn.] **—stro·phic** (strō′fĭk, strŏf′ĭk) *adj.*

stroph·u·lus (strŏf′yə-ləs) *n.* Formerly, any of various diseases causing a skin rash; especially, a disease of infants, sometimes associated with intestinal disturbances, characterized by a papular eruption of the skin. Also called "red gum." [New Latin, from Greek *strophos,* twisted cord, from *strephein,* to turn.]

strove. Past tense of **strive.**

struck (strŭk). Past tense and a past participle of **strike.**
~adj. Affected or shut down by a labor strike.

struck jury *n. Law.* A jury, particularly a special jury, selected from an original panel of 48 members from which each party strikes off names until the list is reduced to 12.

struck measure *n.* A dry measure having the contents leveled off and not heaped.

struc·tur·al (strŭk′chər-əl) *adj.* **1.** Of, pertaining to, having, or characterized by structure. **2.** Used in or necessary to construction. **3.** *Geology.* Of or pertaining to the structure of rocks and other aspects of the earth's crust. **4.** *Biology.* Of or pertaining to organic structure; morphological. **5.** Involved in or caused by the existing economic or political structure of a community or country: *structural unemployment.* **—struc·tur·al·ly** *adv.*

structural formula *n.* A chemical formula that represents the configuration of atoms and bonds in a molecule. Compare **empirical formula, molecular formula.**

structural gene *n.* A gene that forms part of an **operon** *(see)* and that determines a particular amino acid sequence in a protein.

struc·tur·al·ism (strŭk′chər-ə-lĭz′əm) *n.* **1.** An approach to linguistics characterized by the description of language in terms of irreducible structural features. **2.** An approach to the understanding of phenomena, as in the fields of anthropology, sociology, or literature, chiefly characterized by analysis or interpretation in terms of the underlying structures and principles that are felt to generate the phenomena in question. **—struc·tur·al·ist** *n.*

structural isomer. See **isomer.**

struc·tur·al·ize (strŭk′chər-ə-līz′) *tr.v.* **-ized, -izing, -izes.** To incorporate or arrange into a structure. **—struc·tur·al·i·za·tion** *n.*

structural steel *n.* Steel shaped for use in construction.

struc·ture (strŭk′chər) *n.* **1.** Something constructed by the bringing together of material parts, especially a building. **2.** Any complex entity made up of mutually connected elements. **3.** The manner in which something is constructed; the configuration or organization of constituent elements. **4.** Constitution; make-up. **5.** The interrelation of parts or the principle of organization in a complex entity.
~tr.v. **structured, -turing, -tures.** To provide with or form into a well-defined structure; give form or arrangement to. [Middle English, from Old French, from Latin *structūra,* from *struere* (past participle *structus*), to construct.]

stru·del (strōōd′l, shtrōōd′l) *n.* A kind of pastry made with fruit or cheese rolled up in a thin sheet of dough and baked. [German *Strudel,* from Middle High German *strudel,* whirlpool.]

strug·gle (strŭg′əl) *v.* **-gled, -gling, -gles.** *—intr.* **1.** To make violent or strenuous physical effort, as in opposing a material force or trying to escape confinement. **2.** To contend, compete, or fight. **3.** To be strenuously engaged with a problem, task, or anything presenting a difficulty; grapple. **4. a.** To make any strenuous effort; strive: *struggling to be polite.* **b.** To strive to achieve recognition: *a struggling writer.* **5.** To progress with difficulty. *—tr.* To move or place (something) with effort: *struggle a trunk into the car.*
~n. **1.** A strenuous physical effort. **2.** A determined effort to achieve a goal in spite of obstacles. **3.** Combat; strife. [Middle English *struglen†.*] **—strug·gler** *n.* **—strug·gling·ly** *adv.*

strum (strŭm) *v.* **strummed, strumming, strums.** *—tr.* To play (a stringed musical instrument) by running the fingers lightly over the strings. *—intr.* To play an instrument by strumming.
~n. The act or sound of strumming. [Perhaps blend of STRING and THRUM, to play (a stringed instrument) idly.] **—strum·mer** *n.*

stru·ma (strōō′mə) *n., pl.* **-mae** (-mē′) *or* **-mas.** **1.** *Pathology.* **a.** **Scrofula** *(see).* **b.** **Goiter** *(see).* **2.** *Botany.* A cushionlike swelling at the base of a moss capsule. [Latin *strūma†,* tumor.] **—stru·mat·ic** (strōō-măt′ĭk), **stru·mose** (strōō′mōs′), **stru·mous** (strōō′məs) *adj.*

Stru·ma (strōō′mə). *Greek* **Stry·mon** (strī′mən), **Stri·mon.** A river rising in southwestern Bulgaria near Sofia and flowing 348 kilometers (216 miles) generally southeast through Greece to the Aegean.

strum·pet (strŭm′pĭt) *n.* A prostitute. [Middle English *strompet†.*]

strung. Past tense and past participle of **string.**

strung out *adj. Slang.* **1.** Addicted to a drug. **2.** Stupefied from ingestion of a drug. **3.** Physically debilitated or emotionally distressed, as from long-term drug addiction.

strut (strŭt) *v.* **strutted, strutting, struts.** *—intr.* To walk with pompous bearing; swagger. *—tr.* To brace with a supporting bar or rod.
~n. **1.** A stiff, self-important gait. **2.** A bar or rod used to strengthen a framework by resisting longitudinal thrust. [Middle English *strouten,* to swell, stand out, protrude, Old English *strūtian,* to stand out stiffly.] **—strut·ter** *n.* **—strut·ting·ly** *adv.*

struth, strewth (strōōth) *interj.* Used to express surprise or annoyance. [From *God's truth.*]

stru·thi·ous (strōō′thē-əs, -thə-əs) *adj.* **1.** Of, pertaining to, or resembling a flightless bird, especially the ostrich. **2.** Deliberately ignoring the truth. [Latin *strūthiō,* ostrich, from Greek *strouthion,* from *strouthos†,* sparrow, ostrich.]

strych·nine (strĭk′nīn′, -nĭn, -nēn′) *n.* An extremely poisonous white crystalline alkaloid, $C_{21}H_{22}N_2O_2$, derived from nux vomica and related plants, used as a poison for rodents and formerly medicinally as a stimulant for the central nervous system. [French, from New Latin *Strychnos,* genus of plants including nux vomica, from Latin *strychnos,* nightshade, from Greek *strukhnos†.*]

strych·nin·ism (strĭk′nə-nĭz′əm) *n.* Poisoning from excessive or prolonged ingestion of strychnine, resulting in painful muscular spasms. [STRYCHNINE + -ISM.]

St. Thom·as (sānt tŏm′əs). Island, 83 square kilometers (32 square miles) in area, in the U.S. Virgin Islands of the West Indies. Tourism is central to its economy.

Stu·art, Stew·art (stōō′ərt, styōō′-). The family name of the royal family of Scotland (1371-1707), England (1603-1707), and Great Britain (1707-14).

Stuart, Charles Edward, known as "the Young Pretender" or "Bonnie Prince Charlie" (1720-88). Grandson of James II of England and son of James Edward Stuart. In 1745 he led the last Jacobite rising, claiming the British throne for his father. He was defeated at the battle of Culloden (1746) and escaped to France.

Stuart, Gilbert Charles (1755-1828). U.S. painter. Tutored by Benjamin West in London, he became a noted portrait artist in Great Britain. He returned to America (1793) and was commissioned to paint several prominent Americans. Perhaps his best-known work is the unfinished "Athenaeum Head" of George Washington (1796).

Stuart, James Ewell Brown, known as "Jeb" (1833-64). U.S. Confederate general. Noted for his brilliant commands during the battles of Bull Run (1861 and 1862), Antietam (1862), and Fredericksburg (1862), he was also present at Gettysburg (1863), where his decision to conduct a raid instead of delivering vital tactical information to Robert E. Lee contributed to the Confederate defeat. He was mortally wounded during the Wilderness Campaign (1864).

Stuart, James Francis Edward, known as "the Old Pretender" (1688-1766). Pretender to the British throne; son of James II. He made two unsuccessful attempts (1708 and 1715) to take the British throne. The Jacobite rising of 1745-46, led on James's behalf by his son Charles Edward Stuart, also failed.

stub (stŭb) n. **1.** The short blunt end remaining after something has been cut, broken off, or worn down, such as the stump of a tree, tooth, or pencil. **2.** A cigar or cigarette butt. **3.** Anything that has been shortened, blunted, or worn down. **4.** The part of a check or receipt retained as a record. **5.** The part of a ticket returned as a voucher of payment. ~tr.v. **stubbed, stubbing, stubs. 1.** To pull up by the roots. **2.** To clear (a field) of stubs. **3.** To strike (one's toe or foot) against something. **4.** To extinguish (a cigarette butt) by crushing. [Middle English stubbe, Old English stybb, stubb.]

stub axle n. A short axle that supports a front wheel of a motor vehicle.

stub·ble (stŭb′əl) n. **1.** The short, stiff stalks of a grain or hay crop remaining on a field after harvesting. **2.** Anything resembling stubble, especially the short, bristly hairs on a man's unshaven face. [Middle English stuble, from Old French, from Latin stup(u)la, variant of stipula, straw. See **stipule.**] —**stub·bly** adj.

stub·born (stŭb′ərn) adj. **1.** Doggedly and unreasonably asserting one's will or refusing to comply; refractory; obstinate. **2.** Characterized by perseverance; resolute or persistent: stubborn resistance. **3.** Difficult to treat or deal with; resistant to treatment or effort: stubborn stains. —See Synonyms at **contrary, obstinate.** [Middle English stoborne†.] —**stub·born·ly** adv. —**stub·born·ness** n.

Stubbs (stŭbz), **George** (1724-1806). English painter and engraver. He published Anatomy of the Horse (1766), a collection of engravings made from drawings of horses he had dissected.

stub·by (stŭb′ē) adj. **-bier, -biest. 1.** Resembling a stub; short and thick or thickset. **2.** Covered with or consisting of stubs; bristly. —**stub·bi·ly** adv. —**stub·bi·ness** n.

stub nail n. A short, thick nail.

stuc·co (stŭk′ō) n., pl. **-coes** or **-cos. 1.** A durable finish for exterior walls, applied wet and usually composed of cement, sand, and lime. **2.** A fine plaster for interior wall ornamentation, such as moldings. **3.** Ornamental work done using stucco. ~tr.v. **stuccoed, -coing, -coes** or **-cos.** To finish or decorate with stucco. [Italian, from Old High German stukki, fragment, crust.]

stuck. Past tense and past participle of **stick.**

stuck-up (stŭk′ŭp′) adj. Informal. Snobbish; conceited.

stud¹ (stŭd) n. **1. a.** A small knob, nail head, or rivet fixed in and slightly projecting from a surface, used chiefly for decorative purposes. **b.** An almost flat, usually square metal object projecting slightly from the surface of a road, usually used to mark off lanes. **c.** Any of several small metal cleats, as on a snow tire, designed to give extra grip. **2.** An upright post in the framework of a wall for supporting sheets of lath, wallboard, or similar material. **3.** A headless bolt threaded at both ends. **4.** A small ornamental button mounted on a short pin for insertion through an eyelet, as on a dress shirt. **5.** A small buttonlike earring. **6.** Any of various protruding pins or pegs in machinery. **7.** A metal crosspiece used as a brace in a link, as in a chain cable. ~tr.v. **studded, studding, studs. 1.** To provide with or construct with a stud or studs. **2.** To set or adorn with studs or other prominent objects. **3.** To be dotted about on, especially ornamentally: Daisies studded the meadow. [Middle English stode, post, prop, Old English studu, stuthu.]

stud² n. **1. a.** A group of animals, especially horses, kept for breeding. **b.** A stable or farm where they are kept. Also called "stud farm." **2.** A stallion or other male animal kept for breeding. **3.** The condition of being available for breeding purposes: at stud. **4.** Slang. A virile, sexually active man. **5.** Stud poker. [Middle English stod, Old English stōd, stable for breeding.]

stud·book (stŭd′bŏŏk′) n. A book registering the pedigrees of thoroughbred animals, especially of horses.

stud·ding (stŭd′ĭng) n. **1.** The wood framework of a wall or partition. **b.** Lumber cut for studs. **2.** Something with which a surface is studded.

stud·ding·sail (stŭd′ĭng-sāl′; Nautical stŭn′səl) n. Nautical. A narrow rectangular sail set from extensions of the yards of square-rigged ships. [Perhaps from Middle Low German and Middle Dutch stōting, a thrusting, from stōten, to force.]

stu·dent (stōō′dənt, styōō′-) n. **1.** A person following a course of study, especially one who attends a school, college, or university. Also used adjectivally: a student nurse. **2.** One who makes a study of something. **3.** An attentive observer: a student of world affairs. [Middle English, from Latin studēns (stem student-), present participle of studēre, to study, be diligent.]

student teacher n. A college student who practices teaching in an elementary or secondary school under supervision.

student union n. A building on a college campus with facilities for social and recreational student activities.

stud·fish (stŭd′fĭsh′) n., pl. **-fishes** or collectively **studfish.** Either of two small, brightly colored freshwater fishes, Fundulus catenatus or F. stellifer, of the southeastern United States. [Perhaps from STUD (post).]

stud·horse, stud horse (stŭd′hôrs′) n. A stallion.

stud·ied (stŭd′ēd) adj. **1. a.** Carefully prepared or considered; calculated: a studied effect. **b.** Lacking spontaneity; contrived: a studied smile. **2.** Learned; knowledgeable. —**stud·ied·ly** adv. —**stud·ied·ness** n.

stu·di·o (stōō′dē-ō′, styōō′-) n., pl. **-os. 1.** The workroom of an artist or photographer. **2.** An establishment where an art is taught or studied: a dance studio. **3.** A place where motion pictures are made. **4.** A room used for the recording or live transmission of television or radio productions. **5.** A place where music is recorded for commercial distribution; a recording studio. **6.** A studio apartment. [Italian, from Latin studium, STUDY.]

studio apartment n. A small apartment usually consisting of a single main room together with a kitchenette and bathroom.

studio couch n. A couch that can be made to serve as a double bed by sliding the frame of a cot from beneath it.

stu·di·ous (stōō′dē-əs, styōō′-) adj. **1.** Devoted to study. **2.** Earnest; diligent. **3.** Giving or suggestive of careful attention; heedful: studious of his appearance. **4.** Deliberate; studied. **5.** Conducive to study. [Middle English, from Latin studiōsus, from studium, STUDY.] —**stu·di·ous·ly** adv. —**stu·di·ous·ness** n.

stud poker n. Poker in which the first round of cards (and often the last) is dealt face down and the others face up. Also called "stud." [Shortened from stud horse poker, perhaps alluding to the cards being "at stud," that is, available to the player as long as he bets and stays in the game.]

stud·work (stŭd′wûrk′) n. **1.** Work ornamented or covered with studs. **2.** The supportive framework of a wall or partition.

stud·y (stŭd′ē) n., pl. **-ies. 1. a.** The act or process of studying; the pursuit of knowledge, as by reading, observation, or research. **b. studies.** The work of one engaged in this act or process. **2. a.** Attentive scrutiny or careful investigation. **b.** An inquiry or examination, especially of an academic or scientific nature. **3. a.** A subject to be investigated or studied: Human behavior proves a fascinating study. **b.** Often **studies.** A branch or department of learning; an academic or scientific subject: environmental studies. **4.** Something that deserves notice or requires careful attention: Her attitude was a study in polite condescension. **5.** Earnest aim or endeavor: made it my study to serve them. **6. a.** A work resulting from academic endeavor, such as a monograph or thesis. **b.** A literary work on a particular subject. **c.** A preliminary sketch, as for a work of art. **7.** A musical composition designed as a technical exercise; an étude. **8.** A state of mental absorption: She was in a deep study. **9.** A room intended for reading and private study. **10. a.** An actor who is memorizing a part. **b.** The memorizing of a part in a play. ~v. **studied, studying, studies.** —tr. **1. a.** To apply one's mind purposefully to the acquisition of knowledge or understanding of (any subject): study a language. **b.** To be engaged in the study of (a particular subject) as part of an educational course. **2.** To read or scrutinize with close attention: study a report; study a map. **3.** To memorize (a part in a play). **4.** To give careful thought to; contemplate: study the next move. **5.** To inquire into; investigate: study the mood of the country. —intr. **1.** To apply oneself to learning, especially by reading. **2.** To pursue a course of study. **3.** To ponder; reflect; meditate. [Middle English studie, from Old French estudie, from Latin studium, from studēre, to be eager, study.]

study hall n. **1.** A schoolroom reserved for study. **2.** A period set aside for study.

stuff (stŭf) n. **1.** The material out of which something is made or formed; substance. **2.** The basic substance or essential elements of anything; essence: the stuff heroes are made of. **3.** Any material not specifically identified: bought lots of stuff. **4.** Informal. Household or personal articles collectively; belongings. **5.** Worthless objects; refuse or junk. **6.** Foolish or empty words or ideas. Used chiefly in the interjection stuff and nonsense. **7.** British. Woven material; especially, woolen fabric. **8.** Informal. A person's field of knowledge or competence: knows her stuff. **9.** Slang. **a.** Money; cash. **b.** An illegal drug. **10.** Informal. Actions or remarks of a particular kind: That's kid stuff. —**do one's stuff.** Informal. To do what is expected of one; show one's particular skill. ~v. **stuffed, stuffing, stuffs.** —tr. **1. a.** To pack tightly; fill up; cram: stuff a Christmas stocking. **b.** To block (a passage or opening); plug: stuff a leak with plaster. **c.** To push roughly into a place:

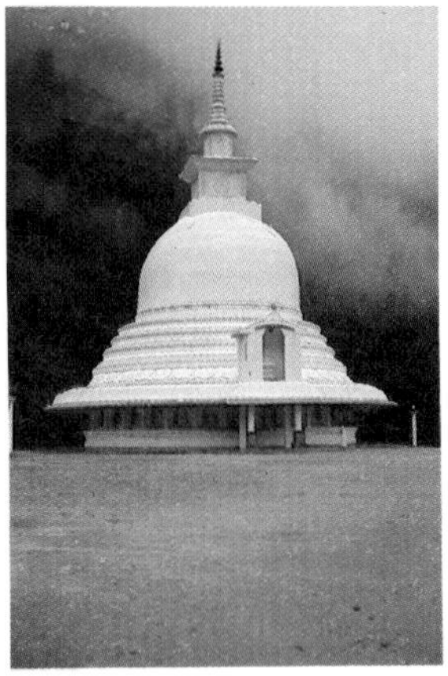

stupa *Buddhist shrines vary slightly in style in different countries, but almost all are built around a central dome—a shape derived from burial mounds that were common in India in pre-Buddhist times. Many—as on this Sri Lankan stupa—are topped by a stylized parasol, one of the traditional possessions of a Buddhist monk.*

stuffed the letter into my pocket. **2. a.** To fill with an appropriate stuffing: *stuff a pillow; stuff a turkey.* **b.** To fill the skin of (a dead animal) so as to restore its natural form for mounting. **3.** To fill to repletion with food. **4.** To fill (the mind): *He stuffs her head with silly ideas.* **5.** To put fraudulent votes into (a ballot box). **6.** To apply a preservative and softening agent to (leather). —*intr.* To overeat; gorge oneself. [Middle English *stuff(e),* from Old French *estoffe,* provisions, from *estoffer,* to cram, pad, from Germanic *stopfōn* (unattested), from Late Latin *stuppāre,* to plug up, from Latin *stuppa,* plug, cork, from Greek *stuppē.*] **—stuff·er** *n.*

stuffed derma *n.* **Derma** *(see).*

stuffed shirt *n. Informal.* A pompous, complacently self-important person.

stuff·ing (stŭf′ĭng) *n.* **1.** Material used to stuff or fill, especially: **a.** Padding put in cushions, pillows, and upholstered furniture. **b.** A seasoned mixture put in the cavity of meat or vegetables. **2.** *Informal.* Strength, vigor, or self-confidence: *His illness knocked the stuffing out of him.*

stuffing box *n.* An enclosure containing packing to prevent leakage around a moving machine part. Also called "packing box."

stuff·y (stŭf′ē) *adj.* **-ier, -iest. 1.** Lacking sufficient ventilation; airless; close. **2.** Having the respiratory passages blocked. **3.** *Informal.* Primly formal or boringly conventional; dull; stodgy: *a stuffy dinner party.* **—stuff·i·ly** *adv.* **—stuff·i·ness** *n.*

stull (stŭl) *n.* **1.** A timber or other prop supporting the roof of a mine opening. **2.** A platform braced against the sides of a working area in a mine. [Perhaps from German *Stollen,* a prop, from Old High German *stollo.*]

stul·ti·fy (stŭl′tə-fī′) *tr.v.* **-fied, -fying, -fies. 1.** To reduce to a state of uselessness, futility, or enfeeblement. **2.** To cause to appear stupid, illogical, or ridiculous. **3.** *Law.* To allege or prove (oneself or another) insane and hence not legally responsible. [Late Latin *stultificāre* : Latin *stultus,* foolish + *facere,* to make.] **—stul·ti·fi·ca·tion** *n.* **—stul·ti·fi·er** *n.*

stum (stŭm) *n.* **1.** Unfermented or partly fermented grape juice; must. **2.** Vapid wine renewed by an admixture of stum.
~*tr.v.* **stummed, stumming, stums. 1.** To revitalize (vapid wine) by adding stum so as to restart fermentation. **2.** To prevent further fermentation of (wine). [Dutch, from *stom,* unfermented, dumb, mute, translation of French *(vin) muet,* "mute (wine)."]

stum·ble (stŭm′bəl) *v.* **-bled, -bling, -bles.** —*intr.* **1. a.** To miss one's step in walking or running; trip and almost fall. **b.** To proceed unsteadily or falteringly; flounder. **c.** To act or speak falteringly or clumsily. **2.** To make a mistake; blunder. **3.** To fall into evil ways; err. **4.** To find accidentally or unexpectedly. Used with *on* or *upon*: *stumbled on the answer.* —*tr.* **1.** To cause to stumble. **2.** To puzzle or bewilder.
~*n.* The act or an instance of stumbling. [Middle English *stumblen,* perhaps from Old Norse *stumla* (unattested).] **—stum·bler** *n.* **—stum·bling·ly** *adv.*

stum·ble·bum (stŭm′bəl-bŭm′) *n. Slang.* **1.** A blundering or inept person. **2.** A punch-drunk or second-rate prizefighter. [STUMBLE + BUM (vagabond).]

stumbling block *n.* An obstacle or impediment.

stump (stŭmp) *n.* **1.** The part of a tree trunk left protruding from the ground after the tree has been felled. **2.** Any part, as of a branch, limb, or tooth, remaining after the main part has been cut away, broken off, or worn down. **3. stumps.** *Informal.* The legs. **4.** A short, thickset person. **5.** A heavy tread or footstep. **6.** A platform or other place used for making speeches in a political campaign. **7.** A short, thick roll of leather or paper or a wad of rubber for rubbing on a charcoal or pencil drawing to shade or soften it. **8.** In cricket, any one of the three upright sticks in a wicket. **—up a stump.** In a quandary.
~*v.* **stumped, stumping, stumps.** —*tr.* **1.** To reduce to a stump; lop; truncate. **2.** To clear stumps from: *stump a field.* **3.** To go through (a region) making political speeches: *The candidate stumped the state.* **4.** To shade (a drawing) with a stump. **5.** To baffle completely; confront with an insoluble problem. **6.** *Informal.* To challenge or dare (someone). **7.** *Regional.* To stub (a toe or foot). —*intr.* **1.** To walk clumsily or heavily. **2.** To travel around making political speeches. [Middle English *stumpe,* from Middle Low German *stump.*] **—stump·er** *n.* **—stump·i·ly** *adv.* **—stump·i·ness** *n.* **—stump·y** *adj.*

stump·age (stŭm′pĭj) *n.* **1.** Standing timber regarded as a commodity. **2.** The value of standing timber. **3.** The right to cut standing timber.

stun (stŭn) *tr.v.* **stunned, stunning, stuns. 1.** To daze or render senseless, as by a blow. **2.** To overwhelm or daze with a loud noise. **3.** To stupefy or overwhelm with shock or astonishment; astound.
~*n.* **1.** Something that stupefies. **2.** A state of stupefaction. [Middle English *stonen,* from Old French *estoner,* from Vulgar Latin *extonāre* (unattested) : Latin *ex-* (intensive) + *tonāre,* to thunder.]

stung. Past tense and past participle of **sting.**

stun grenade *n.* A grenade designed to detonate with a loud explosion and release smoke or disabling gas but without causing physical harm, used particularly in antiterrorist operations.

stunk. Past participle and alternate past tense of **stink.**

stun·ner (stŭn′ər) *n.* **1.** One that stuns. **2.** *Informal.* An exceptionally attractive person or thing.

stun·ning (stŭn′ĭng) *adj.* **1.** Causing or capable of causing loss of consciousness or emotional shock. **2.** *Informal.* **a.** Strikingly attractive: *a stunning necklace.* **b.** Extremely impressive: *a stunning performance.* **—stun·ning·ly** *adv.*

stunt[1] (stŭnt) *tr.v.* **stunted, stunting, stunts. 1.** To check the growth or development of. **2.** To check (growth or development).
~*n.* **1.** Retarded growth. **2.** One that is retarded in growth. **3.** A plant disease that causes dwarfing. [Probably from dialectal *stont,* short in duration, of Scandinavian origin.] **—stunt·ed·ness** *n.*

stunt[2] *n.* **1.** A feat displaying unusual strength, skill, or daring. **2.** Any unusual act or display intended to attract attention.
~*intr.v.* **stunted, stunting, stunts.** To perform a stunt or stunts. [19th century : origin obscure.]

stunt man *n.* A person who substitutes for a film actor in scenes requiring physical prowess or involving physical risk.

stu·pa (sto͞o′pə) *n.* A Buddhist shrine usually consisting of a large domed structure. Also called "tope." [Sanskrit *stūpa,* "tuft of hair," "crown of head."]

stupe (sto͞op, styo͞op) *n.* A hot compress, often treated with a counterirritant and applied to relieve pain. [Middle English, from Latin *stuppa,* tow, plug, from Greek *stuppē.*]

stu·pe·fa·cient (sto͞o′pə-fā′shənt, styo͞o′-) *adj.* Inducing stupor.
~*n.* A stupefacient drug, such as a narcotic. [Latin *stupefaciēns* (stem *stupefacient-*), present participle of *stupefacere,* to STUPEFY.]

stu·pe·fac·tion (sto͞o′pə-făk′shən, styo͞o′-) *n.* **1.** The act of stupefying or the state of being stupefied. **2.** Great astonishment or consternation.

stu·pe·fy (sto͞o′pə-fī′, styo͞o′-) *tr.v.* **-fied, -fying, -fies. 1.** To dull the senses of; put into a stupor. **2.** To stun with amazement; astonish. [French *stupéfier,* from Latin *stupefacere* : *stupēre,* to be stunned + *facere,* to make.] **—stu·pe·fi·er** *n.*

stu·pen·dous (sto͞o-pĕn′dəs, styo͞o-) *adj.* **1.** Of awesome size, degree, force, or quality; astounding; prodigious. **2.** *Informal.* Extremely impressive or enjoyable. —See Synonyms at **enormous.** [Latin *stupendus,* from *stupēre,* to be stunned.] **—stu·pen·dous·ly** *adv.* **—stu·pen·dous·ness** *n.*

stu·pid (sto͞o′pĭd, styo͞o′-) *adj.* **-pider, -pidest. 1.** In a stupor; stupefied. **2.** Slow to apprehend; dull; obtuse. **3.** Showing a lack of sense or intelligence. **4.** Boring or trivial: *a stupid job.* **5.** *Informal.* Infuriating or intractable: *The stupid car won't start.*
~*n. Informal.* A stupid person; dolt. [French *stupide,* from Latin *stupidus,* from *stupēre,* to be stunned.] **—stu·pid·ly** *adv.* **—stu·pid·ness** *n.*

Synonyms: *slow, dumb, stupid, dull, obtuse, dense, crass.* These adjectives mean lacking in mental acuity. *Slow* and the informal *dumb* imply chronic sluggishness of perception or understanding; *stupid* and *dull* occasionally suggest a mere temporary state. *Stupid* and *dumb* can also refer to individual actions that are extremely foolish. *Obtuse* implies insensitivity or unreceptiveness to instruction. *Dense* suggests a mind that is virtually impenetrable or incapable of grasping even elementary ideas. *Crass* refers especially to stupidity marked by coarseness or tastelessness.

stu·pid·i·ty (sto͞o-pĭd′ə-tē, styo͞o-) *n., pl.* **-ties. 1.** The quality or fact of being stupid: *"the elegant stupidity of private parties"* (Jane Austen). **2.** A stupid act, remark, or idea.

stu·por (sto͞o′pər, styo͞o′-) *n.* **1.** A state of near unconsciousness; lethargy; torpor. **2.** A state of mental confusion; a daze. [Middle English, from Latin, from *stupēre,* to be stunned. See **stupid.**] **—stu·por·ous** *adj.*

stur·dy[1] (stûr′dē) *adj.* **-dier, -diest. 1.** Substantially built; strong. **2.** Physically strong and healthy; robust. **3.** Vigorous; lusty: *"We admire Chaucer for his sturdy English wit"* (Thoreau). —See Synonyms at **strong.** [Middle English, giddy, rash, impetuous, from Old French *estourdi,* past participle of *estourir,* to stun, daze, from Vulgar Latin *exturdīre* (unattested), probably "to be stunned like a thrush drunk with grapes" : perhaps Latin *ex-,* completely + *turdus,* thrush.] **—stur·di·ly** *adv.* **—stur·di·ness** *n.*

sturdy[2] *n.* A disease of sheep, **gid** *(see).* [From STURDY (in earlier sense "giddy").] **—stur·died** *adj.*

stur·geon (stûr′jən) *n.* Any of various large, edible freshwater and marine fishes of the family Acipenseridae, of the Northern Hemisphere, valued as a source of caviar and isinglass. [Middle English, from Norman French, from Vulgar Latin *sturiō* (unattested), from Germanic *sturjōn* (unattested). See also **sterlet.**]

Sturluson, Snorri. See **Snorri Sturluson.**

Sturm·ab·teil·ung (shto͝orm′äp′tī′lo͝ongk) *n., pl.* **-teilungen** (-tī′lo͝ong-ən). *Abbr.* **S.A.** A Nazi militia organized about 1924 and notorious for its violent and terroristic methods. Also called "Brown Shirts," "storm troopers." [German, "storm division."]

Sturm und Drang (shto͝orm′ o͝ont drăng′) *n.* A German romantic literary movement of the late 18th century, the works of which typically depicted the impulsive man struggling against conventional society. [German, "storm and stress," originally the title of a romantic play (1776) by Friedrich Maximilian von Klinger (1752–1831), German poet and dramatist.]

stut·ter (stŭt′ər) *v.* **-tered, -tering, -ters.** —*intr.* To speak with a spasmodic hesitation, prolongation, or repetition of sounds. —*tr.* To say with or as if with a stutter.
~*n.* The act or habit of stuttering. [Frequentative of obsolete *stut,* from Middle English *stutten,* perhaps of Low German origin, akin to Middle Low German *stōtern,* to stutter.] **—stut·ter·er** *n.* **—stut·ter·ing·ly** *adv.*

Stutt·gart (stŭt′gärt′, shto͝ot′-). The capital of Baden-Württemberg, on the Neckar River in southwestern West Germany. It is a major industrial center producing electrical and photographic equipment, textiles, printed materials, and motor vehicles.

Stuy·ve·sant (stī'və-sənt), **Peter** or **Petrus** (*c.* 1592–1672). Dutch colonial administrator in America. An employee of the Dutch West India Company, he served as governor of several Caribbean islands and was later appointed director of New Netherland. While living in New Amsterdam, present-day New York City, he attempted to bring social and religious uniformity to the diverse populace, but was largely unsuccessful. He fought English attempts to subjugate the colony until 1664, when the colonists forced him to accept England's generous terms.

St. Vincent, Cape (sānt' vĭn'sənt). The southwestern extremity of Portugal and of continental Europe.

St. Vin·cent and the Gren·a·dines (sānt vĭn'sənt; grĕn'ə-dēnz', grĕn'ə-dēnz'). Island state of the Windward Islands, British West Indies. It comprises the island of St. Vincent and the northern islands of the Grenadines. The country became independent in 1979. Its major industries are food processing and tourism. Kingstown, on St. Vincent, is the capital. See map at **Latin America.**

St. Vi·tus' dance, St. Vi·tus's dance (sānt vī'tə-sĭz) *n. Pathology* A nervous disease, **chorea** *(see).* [After St. *Vitus,* a 3rd-century Christian child martyr.]

sty[1] (stī) *n., pl.* **sties. 1.** An enclosure or pen for swine. **2.** A filthy place: *Your room is a sty.*
~*v.* **stied, stying, sties.** —*tr.* To shut up in a sty. —*intr.* To live in a sty. [Middle English *sty,* Old English *stī, stig,* from Germanic *stijam* (unattested).]

sty[2], **stye** *n., pl.* **sties** or **styes.** Inflammation of one or more sebaceous glands at the edge of an eyelid. [Obsolete *styany* (taken as *sty-on-eye*), Middle English *styanye* : *styan* (unattested), sty, "swelling," from Old English *stīgend,* present participle of *stīgan,* to rise + EYE.]

styg·i·an, Styg·i·an (stĭj'ē-ən) *adj.* **1.** Of or pertaining to the river Styx. **2. a.** Gloomy and dark. **b.** Infernal; hellish. [Latin *Stygius,* from Greek *Stugios,* from *Stux,* STYX.]

sty·lar (stī'lər) *adj.* **1.** Of, pertaining to, or resembling a stylus. **2.** *Biology.* Of or pertaining to a style.

sty·late (stī'lāt') *adj. Biology.* Having a style or styles.

style (stīl) *n.* **1.** The way in which something is written, said, shown, or done as distinguished from its substance. **2.** The combination of distinctive features of literary or artistic expression, execution, or performance characterizing a particular person, people, school, or era. **3.** Sort; type: *a style of furniture.* **4.** A quality of imagination and individuality expressed in one's actions and tastes and personal appearance: *dresses with style. She's got style.* **5. a.** A comfortable and elegant way of living or behaving: *dined in style.* **b.** A particular mode of living: *the style of a gentleman.* **6. a.** The fashion of the moment, especially of dress; a vogue. Used chiefly in the phrases *out of style* and *in style.* **b.** A particular fashion. **7.** A particular set of conventions favored by a publisher or publication in presenting printed material, including matters of usage, punctuation, spelling, typography, and arrangement. **8.** A name or descriptive designation, especially a legal or official title. **9.** A slender, pointed instrument used to write on wax tablets in ancient times. **10.** An implement used for etching or engraving. **11.** The shadow-casting projection on a sundial; a gnomon. **12.** *Botany.* The usually slender part of a pistil, rising from the ovary and tipped by the stigma. **13.** *Zoology.* Any slender, tubular, or bristlelike process. **14.** *Obsolete.* A pen. **15.** A surgical probing instrument; a stylet. —See Synonyms at **fashion.** —**cramp someone's style.** *Informal.* To inhibit someone's freedom of action or expression.
~*tr.v.* **styled, styling, styles. 1.** To design; give style to: *style hair.* **2.** To make consistent with the rules of style. **3.** To call or name; designate: *"whatever is mine, you may style, and think, yours"* (Sterne). [Middle English, from Old French, from Latin *stilus*†, writing instrument, style.] —**styl·er** *n.*

-style *suffix.* Indicates being in or imitating a specified style: *a thirties-style dress.*

style book *n.* A book giving rules and examples of usage, spelling, punctuation, and typography, used in the preparation of copy for publication. Also called "style guide."

sty·let (stī'lĭt, stī-lĕt') *n.* **1.** A slender, pointed instrument or weapon, such as a stiletto. **2.** A surgical probe; a style. **3.** A wire inserted into a catheter to maintain its shape or remove an obstruction. **4.** *Zoology.* A small, stiff, needlelike process in some invertebrates, such as the mouth parts of an aphid. [French, from Italian *stiletto,* STILETTO.]

sty·li·form (stī'lə-fôrm') *adj. Zoology.* Having the shape of a style; bristlelike. [New Latin *styliformis* : Latin *stilus,* STYLE + *-formis,* -FORM.]

styl·ish (stī'lĭsh) *adj.* **1.** In step with current fashion. **2.** Showing or having natural elegance. —**styl·ish·ly** *adv.* —**styl·ish·ness** *n.*

styl·ist (stī'lĭst) *n.* **1.** A writer or performer who cultivates an approved or distinctive artistic style. **2.** A designer of or consultant on styles, as in interior decorating and clothing.

sty·lis·tic (stī-lĭs'tĭk) *adj.* Of or pertaining to style, especially to artistic or literary style. —**sty·lis·ti·cal·ly** *adv.*

sty·lis·tics (stī-lĭs'tĭks) *n. Used with a singular verb.* The study of the use of elements of language style, such as metaphor, in particular contexts.

sty·lite (stī'līt') *n.* Any early Christian ascetic who lived unsheltered on the tops of high pillars. [Late Greek *stulitēs* : Greek *stulos,* pillar + -ITE.] —**sty·lit·ic** (stī-lĭt'ĭk) *adj.* —**sty·lit·ism** (stī'lī-tĭz'əm) *n.*

styl·ize (stī'līz') *tr.v.* **-ized, -izing, -izes. 1.** To restrict or cause to conform to a particular style. **2.** To represent conventionally; conventionalize. —**styl·i·za·tion** *n.* —**styl·iz·er** *n.*

stylo–, styl– *prefix.* Indicates: **1.** *Biology.* A style; for example, **stylopodium. 2.** A point, pillar, or styloid process; for example, **stylograph.** [Latin *stilus,* stalk, STYLE.]

sty·lo·bate (stī'lə-bāt') *n. Architecture.* The immediate foundation of a row of classical columns. See **stereobate.** [Latin *stylobata,* from Greek *stulobatēs,* column base : *stulos,* column + *-bates,* "one that is based."]

sty·lo·graph (stī'lə-grăf', -gräf') *n.* A fountain pen having a tubular writing point instead of a nib. Also called "stylographic pen." [STYLO- + -GRAPH.]

sty·log·ra·phy (stī-lŏg'rə-fē) *n.* The art or a method of etching, engraving, or writing with a style. [STYLO- + -GRAPHY.] —**sty·lo·graph·ic** (stī'lə-grăf'ĭk), **sty·lo·graph·i·cal** *adj.*

sty·loid (stī'loid') *adj.* Slender and pointed. [New Latin *styloides,* resembling a style (after Greek *styloeidēs,* pillarlike) : STYL(O)- + -OID.]

sty·lo·lite (stī'lə-līt') *n.* A small columnar rock development in limestone and other calcareous rocks that is usually at right angles to the bedding planes and is of irregular cross section with striated sides. [STYLO- + -LITE.] —**sty·lo·lit·ic** (stī'lə-lĭt'ĭk) *adj.*

sty·lo·po·di·um (stī'lə-pō'dē-əm) *n., pl.* **-dia** (-dē-ə). *Botany.* An enlargement at the base of the style of certain flowers. [New Latin : STYLO- + -PODIUM.]

sty·lops (stī'lŏps') *n.* Any of various minute parasitic insects of the order Strepsiptera, which live inside other insects. [New Latin, from Greek : *stulos,* pillar, column + *ōps,* eye (referring to the stalked eye of the male).]

sty·lo·stix·is (stī'lə-stĭk'sĭs) *n.* **Acupuncture** *(see).* [New Latin, from Greek *stulos,* stylus, needle + *stixis,* spot, mark.]

sty·lus (stī'ləs) *n., pl.* **-luses** or **-li** (-lī'). **1.** A sharp, pointed instrument used for writing, marking, or engraving. **2.** A needle or jewel in the cartridge of a phonograph pickup that senses the undulations in the record grooves; a phonograph needle. **3.** The sharp, pointed tool used for cutting record grooves. [Latin *stilus,* STYLE.]

sty·mie, sty·my (stī'mē) *n.* **1.** A situation in golf in which one ball obstructs the line of play of another on the putting green. **2.** An impasse; a quandary.
~*tr.v.* **stymied, -mieing** or **-mying, -mies.** To block, thwart, or baffle. [19th century : origin obscure.]

styp·sis (stĭp'sĭs) *n.* The action or application of a styptic. [Late Latin *stypsis,* from Greek *stupsis,* contraction, astringency, from *stuphein,* to contract. See **styptic.**]

styp·tic (stĭp'tĭk) *adj.* Also **styp·ti·cal** (-tĭ-kəl). **1.** Tending to check bleeding; hemostatic. **2.** Contracting the tissues; astringent.
~*n.* A styptic drug or substance. [Middle English *stiptik,* from Late Latin *stypticus,* from Greek *stuptikos,* from *stuphein,* to contract.] —**styp·tic·i·ty** (stĭp-tĭs'ə-tē) *n.*

styptic pencil *n.* A small medicated stick, usually of alum, applied to shaving nicks and other small cuts to check bleeding.

sty·rax (stī'răks') *n.* **1.** A resin, **storax** *(see).* **2.** Any tree of the genus *Styrax.* —**sty·ra·ca·ceous** (stī'rə-kā'shəs) *adj.*

sty·rene (stī'rēn') *n.* A colorless oily liquid, C_8H_8, the monomer for **polystyrene** *(see).* [Latin *styrax, storax,* STORAX (from which styrene is obtained by distillation) + -ENE.]

Styr·i·a (stîr'ē-ə). *German* **Stei·er·mark** (shtī'ər-märk'). State and ancient province in southeastern Austria. It is mountainous and a mining area, with deposits of lignite, iron ore, and magnesite. Graz is the capital.

Sty·ro·foam (stī'rə-fōm') *n.* A trademark for a light, resilient polystyrene plastic.

Styx (stĭks) *n. Greek Mythology.* A river of Hades across which Charon ferried the souls of the dead. [Latin, from Greek *Stux.*]

SU strontium unit.

su·a·ble (so͞o'ə-bəl) *adj.* Legally subject to a court suit; liable to be sued. —**su·a·bil·i·ty** *n.*

sua·sion (swā'zhən) *n.* Persuasion. Used chiefly in the phrase *moral suasion.* [Middle English, from Latin *suāsiō* (stem *suāsiōn-*), from *suādēre* (past participle *suāsus*), to persuade.] —**sua·sive** (swā'sĭv, -zĭv) *adj.*

suave (swäv) *adj.* Smoothly gracious, as in social manner; urbane. [French, from Latin *suāvis,* delightful.] —**suav·i·ty** (swä'və-tē), **suave·ness** *n.* —**suave·ly** *adv.*

Synonyms: *suave, smooth, urbane, diplomatic, politic.* These adjectives refer to a controlled or refined manner. *Suave* suggests a polished exterior and outward sophistication. *Smooth* stresses conscious, sometimes excessive effort to avoid conflict with others. *Urbane* implies a high degree of refinement together with the assurance that comes from wide social experience. *Diplomatic* especially suggests tact in handling difficult situations, and *politic* adds to this the implication of artful management, sagacity, or shrewdness in gaining an end.

sub (sŭb) *n. Informal.* **1.** A submarine. **2.** A substitute. **3.** *British.* An advance payment of wages, especially as a subsistence allowance. **4.** A sandwich, the **hero** *(see).*
~*intr.v.* **subbed, subbing, subs.** *Informal.* To act as a substitute.

sub– *prefix.* Indicates: **1.** Under or beneath; for example, **submarine. 2.** Inferior or secondary in rank; for example, **sublieutenant. 3.** Somewhat short of or less than; for example, **subhuman, subtropical. 4.** Forming a subordinate or constituent part of a whole; for example, **subdivision, subset.** ***Note:*** Many compounds other than those entered here may be formed with *sub-.* In forming com-

PRONUNCIATION KEY

ă, pat; ā, pay; âr, care;
ä, father, are; b, bib;
ch, church; d, deed; ĕ, pet;
ē, be; f, fife; g, gag; h, hat;
hw, which; ĭ, pit; ī, pie;
îr, pier; j, judge; k, kick;
l, lid, needle; m, mum;
n, no, sudden; ng, thing;
ŏ, pot; ō, toe; ô, paw, for;
oi, noise; ou, out; o͝o, book;
o͞o, boot; p, pop; r, roar;
s, sauce; sh, ship, dish;
t, tight; th, thin, path;
th, this, bathe; ŭ, cut; ûr, fur;
v, valve; w, with; y, yes;
z, zebra, size; zh, vision;
ə, about, item, edible,
gallop, circus, peaceful

IN FOREIGN WORDS:

à, *Fr.* ami; œ, *Fr.* feu, *Ger.* schön; ü, *Fr.* tu, *Ger.* über;
KH, *Ger.* ich, *Scot.* loch;
N, *Fr.* bon; y', *Fr.* Compiègne

STRESS MARKS:

Primary stress: ′
in·cite′ (ĭn-sīt′)
Secondary stress: ′
in′sight′ (ĭn′sīt′)

pounds, *sub*- is normally joined with the following element without space or hyphen: *subbasement, subtitle.* [In borrowed Latin compounds, *sub*- indicates: 1. Under, as in **suppose.** 2. Below, beneath, as in **subaltern.** 3. Down, as in **supplicate.** 4. Up from under, from below, as in **supplant.** 5. Up, toward, as in **support.** 6. Subordinate, as in **subdeacon.** 7. Secretly, as in **suborn.** 8. In place of, as in **substitute.** Before *c, f, g, m, p,* and *r, sub*- becomes, respectively, *suc-, suf-, sug-, sum-, sup-,* and *sur-.* Sometimes it also becomes *sus-* before *c, p,* and *t.* Latin *sub-,* from *sub,* under, from below.]

sub. 1. *Logic.* subaltern. 2. *Music.* subito. 3. subscription. 4. substitute. 5. suburb; suburban.

sub·ac·id (sŭb′ăs′ĭd) *adj.* Moderately acid or tart. —**sub·a·cid·i·ty** (sŭb′ə-sĭd′ə-tē) *n.*

sub·a·cute (sŭb′ə-kyōōt′) *adj.* Between acute and chronic. Said of a disease. —**sub·a·cute·ly** *adv.*

sub·aer·i·al (sŭb′âr′ē-əl) *adj.* Located or occurring on or near the surface of the earth.

sub·al·pine (sŭb′ăl′pīn) *adj.* 1. Of or pertaining to regions at or near the foot of the Alps. 2. Of, designating, or growing or living in mountainous regions just below the timber line.

sub·al·tern (sŭb′ôl′tərn; *British* sŭb′əl-tûrn′) *adj.* 1. Lower in position or rank; secondary. 2. *Chiefly British.* Holding a military rank just below that of captain. 3. *Logic.* **a.** Designating a particular proposition in relation to a universal with the same subject, predicate, and quality. **b.** Designating such a relationship. —*n.* 1. A subordinate. 2. *Chiefly British.* A subaltern officer. 3. *Abbr.* **sub.** *Logic.* A subaltern proposition or relation. [Late Latin *subalternus* : Latin *sub-,* below + *alternus,* ALTERNATE.]

sub·al·ter·nate (sŭb′ôl′tər-nĭt) *adj.* 1. Subordinate. 2. Arranged alternately but tending to become opposite. Said of leaves. 3. Following in turn. —**sub·al·ter·na·tion** (sŭb-ôl′tər-nā′shən) *n.*

sub·ant·arc·tic (sŭb′ănt-ärk′tĭk, -är′tĭk) *adj.* Of or like regions just north of the Antarctic Circle.

sub·a·pi·cal (sŭb′ā′pĭ-kəl, -ăp′ĭ-kəl) *adj.* Located below or near an apex. —**sub·ap·i·cal·ly** *adv.*

sub·ap·o·stol·ic (sŭb′ăp′ə-stŏl′ĭk) *adj.* Of or pertaining to the era immediately following that of the Apostles.

sub·a·quat·ic (sŭb′ə-kwŏt′ĭk, -kwăt′ĭk) *adj.* 1. Living or growing partly on land and partly in water. 2. Underwater. [SUB- + Latin *aqua,* water.]

sub·a·que·ous (sŭb′ā′kwē-əs, -ăk′wē-əs) *adj.* 1. Formed or adapted for underwater use or operation. 2. Found or occurring under water.

sub·arc·tic (sŭb′ärk′tĭk, -är′tĭk) *adj.* Of or like regions just south of the Arctic Circle.

sub·ar·id (sŭb′ăr′ĭd) *adj.* Semiarid.

sub·a·tom·ic (sŭb′ə-tŏm′ĭk) *adj.* 1. Of or pertaining to the constituents of the atom. 2. Having dimensions or participating in reactions characteristic of these constituents.

sub·au·di·tion (sŭb′ô-dĭsh′ən) *n.* 1. The act of understanding and mentally supplying a word or thought that has been implied but not expressed. 2. A word or thought thus supplied. [Late Latin *subaudītiō,* from *subaudīre,* to supply an omitted word : *sub-,* secretly + *audīre,* to hear.]

sub·base (sŭb′bās′) *n. Architecture.* The lowermost front strip or molding of a pedestal or baseboard.

sub·base·ment (sŭb′bās′mənt) *n.* A story or floor beneath the main basement of a building.

sub·bass (sŭb′bās′) *n. Music.* A pedal stop on an organ that produces the lowest tones, having 16 or 32 feet.

sub·cal·i·ber (sŭb′kăl′ə-bər) *adj.* 1. Smaller in caliber than the barrel of the gun from which it is fired. Said of projectiles. 2. Of or pertaining to such projectiles.

sub·car·ti·lag·i·nous (sŭb′kär′tə-lăj′ə-nəs) *adj.* 1. Located beneath a cartilage. 2. Partly cartilaginous.

sub·cat·e·go·ry (sŭb′kăt′ĭ-gôr′ē, -gōr′ē) *n., pl.* **-ries.** A subdivision of a category.

sub·ce·les·tial (sŭb′sĭ-lĕs′chəl) *adj.* 1. Lower than celestial; terrestrial. 2. Mundane. —*n.* A subcelestial object.

sub·cep·tion (səb-sĕp′shən) *n. Psychology.* Subliminal perception. [*Subliminal* per*ception.*]

sub·chas·er (sŭb′chā′sər) *n.* A submarine chaser (see).

sub·class (sŭb′klăs′, -kläs′) *n.* 1. A subdivision of a class. 2. A taxonomic category ranking between a class and an order. 3. *Mathematics.* A subset. —*tr.v.* **subclassed, -classing, -classes.** To assign to a subclass.

sub·cla·vi·an (sŭb′klā′vē-ən) *adj. Anatomy.* 1. Situated beneath the clavicle. 2. Of or pertaining to a subclavian part. —*n.* A subclavian structure, such as a vein, nerve, or muscle. [New Latin *subclavius* : SUB- + Latin *clāvis,* key (see **clavicle**).]

subclavian artery *n.* A short part of a major artery originating under the clavicle and continuous with the axillary artery extending to the upper extremities or forelimbs.

subclavian vein *n.* A part of a major vein of the upper extremities or forelimbs that is continuous with the axillary vein and is situated beneath the clavicle.

sub·cli·max (sŭb′klī′măks′) *n.* 1. A stage in the ecological succession of a plant or animal community immediately preceding a climax, and often persisting because of the effects of fire, flood, or other conditions. 2. A plant or animal community at this stage. —**sub·cli·mac·tic** (sŭb′klī-măk′tĭk) *adj.*

sub·clin·i·cal (sŭb′klĭn′ĭ-kəl) *adj.* Of or pertaining to a disease or the stage of a disease in which signs and symptoms are not yet apparent. —**sub·clin·i·cal·ly** *adv.*

sub·com·mit·tee (sŭb′kə-mĭt′ē) *n.* A subordinate committee composed of members appointed from or by the main committee to deal with matters in more detail.

sub·con·scious (sŭb′kŏn′shəs) *adj.* 1. Not wholly conscious but capable of being made conscious. 2. Existing in the mind without being consciously recognized: *subconscious desires.* —*n.* The subconscious mind; the unperceived source of conscious emotions, fantasies, and dreams. —See Usage note at **conscious.** —**sub·con·scious·ly** *adv.* —**sub·con·scious·ness** *n.*

sub·con·ti·nent (sŭb′kŏn′tə-nənt) *n.* 1. A large land mass, as India, that is part of a continent but is independent of it in some geographic or political respect. 2. A large land mass, as Greenland, that is smaller than a continent. —**sub·con·ti·nen·tal** (sŭb′kŏn′tə-něn′təl) *adj.*

sub·con·tract (sŭb′kŏn′trăkt′) *n.* A contract that assigns some of the obligations of a prior contract to another party. —*v.* (sŭb′kŏn′trăkt′, sŭb-kən-trăkt′) **subcontracted, -tracting, -tracts.** —*tr.* To make a subcontract for. Used of the original contractor. —*intr.* To make a subcontract.

sub·con·trac·tor (sŭb′kən-trăk′tər, sŭb′kŏn′trăk′tər) *n.* A person or company that enters into a subcontract and assumes some of the obligations of the primary contractor; especially, one who undertakes a particular part of the work in the construction of a building.

sub·con·tra·oc·tave (sŭb′kŏn′trə-ŏk′tĭv) *n. Music.* The octave that begins on the fourth C below middle C.

sub·con·trar·y (sŭb′kŏn′trěr′ē) *adj. Logic.* Of, pertaining to, or being either or both of a pair of propositions related in such a way that they cannot both be false at once, although they may be true together. —*n., pl.* **subcontraries.** *Logic.* Either of two subcontrary propositions. —**sub·con·tra·ri·e·ty** (sŭb′kŏn′trə-rī′ə-tē) *n.*

sub·cor·tex (sŭb′kôr′těks) *n., pl.* **-tices** (-tə-sēz′). The portion of the brain immediately below the cerebral cortex. —**sub·cor·ti·cal** *adj.* —**sub·cor·ti·cal·ly** *adv.*

sub·crit·i·cal (sŭb′krĭt′ĭ-kəl) *adj.* Not having or involving a self-sustaining chain reaction. Said of nuclear reactions and reactors.

sub·cul·ture (sŭb′kŭl′chər) *n.* 1. One culture of microorganisms derived from another. 2. A cultural subgroup, especially of a nation, differentiated by ethnic background, religion, beliefs, lifestyle, or other factors that functionally unify the group and act collectively on each member. —*tr.v.* **subcultured, -turing, -tures.** To transfer (bacteria from a culture) on to a new culture medium. —**sub·cul·tur·al** (sŭb′kŭl′chər-əl) *adj.*

sub·cu·ta·ne·ous (sŭb′kyōō-tā′nē-əs) *adj.* Located or introduced just beneath the skin. —**sub·cu·ta·ne·ous·ly** *adv.*

sub·dea·con (sŭb′dē′kən) *n.* 1. **a.** Formerly in the Roman Catholic Church, a candidate ordained to the lowest of the major orders. **b.** In certain other churches, a clergyman with rank just below that of deacon. 2. A cleric who acts as assistant to the deacon at High Mass. [Middle English *subde(a)con,* from Late Latin *subdiaconus,* partial translation of Late Greek *hupodiakonos* : Greek *hupo-,* below, subordinate + *diakonos,* DEACON.]

sub·deb (sŭb′děb′) *n. Informal.* 1. A subdebutante. 2. A girl in her middle teens.

sub·deb·u·tante (sŭb′děb′yə-tänt′) *n.* 1. A teen-age girl approaching her debut. 2. A girl in her middle teens.

sub·di·ac·o·nate (sŭb′dī-ăk′ə-nĭt) *n.* The office, order, or rank of subdeacon. [Late Latin *subdiaconātus,* from *subdiaconus,* SUBDEACON.] —**sub·di·ac·o·nal** *adj.*

sub·di·vide (sŭb′dĭ-vīd′, sŭb′də-vīd′) *v.* **-vided, -viding, -vides.** —*tr.* 1. To divide (a part or parts resulting from earlier division) into smaller parts. 2. **a.** To divide into a number of parts. **b.** To divide (land) into lots for sale. —*intr.* To form into subdivisions. [Middle English *subdividen,* from Late Latin *subdīvidere* : Latin *sub-,* secondary, smaller + *dīvidere,* to DIVIDE.] —**sub·di·vid·er** *n.*

sub·di·vi·sion (sŭb′də-vĭzh′ən, sŭb′də-vĭzh′ən) *n.* 1. The act or process of subdividing. 2. Any of the subdivided parts. 3. *Botany.* A taxonomic category ranking between a division and a class. 4. An area composed of subdivided lots. —**sub·di·vi·sion·al** *adj.*

sub·dom·i·nant (sŭb′dŏm′ə-nənt) *n. Music.* 1. The fourth tone of a diatonic scale, next below the dominant. 2. A key or chord based on the subdominant. —*adj.* 1. Influential but not quite dominant. 2. *Music.* Of or pertaining to the subdominant.

sub·duc·tion (səb-dŭk′shən) *n.* A geological process in which one edge of crustal plate descends below another. [French, from Late Latin *subductiō,* act of taking away, from Latin *subdūcere,* to withdraw : *sub-,* under + *dūcere,* to lead.]

subduction zone *n.* A long narrow zone along which oceanic lithosphere moves down into and is assimilated by the earth's interior. Also called "Benioff zone."

sub·due (səb-dōō′, -dyōō′) *tr.v.* **-dued, -duing, -dues.** 1. To conquer and subjugate; put down; vanquish. 2. To quiet or bring under control by physical force or persuasion; make tractable. 3. To make less intense or prominent; suppress; tone down: *A vote of approval subdued his anger.* 4. To bring (land) under cultivation. —See Synonyms at **defeat.** [Middle English *subduen,* from Latin *subdūcere,* to lead away, withdraw (but influenced in meaning by Latin *subdere,* to put under, subdue) : *sub-,* from under, away + *dūcere,* to lead.] —**sub·du·a·ble** *adj.* —**sub·du·al** *n.* —**sub·du·er** *n.*

sub·dued (səb-do͞od′, -dyo͞od′) *adj.* **1.** Uncharacteristically quiet, as through tiredness or shyness. **2.** Gentle; of only moderate strength or intensity: *subdued lighting.* **3.** Expressed only in an inhibited way: *subdued laughter.*

sub·dur·al (səb-do͝or′əl, -dyo͝or′əl) *adj. Anatomy.* Situated or occurring below the dura mater. [SUB + *dural,* from DURA (MATER).] **—sub·dur·al·ly** *adv.*

sub·ed·it (sŭb′ĕd′ĭt) *tr.v.* **-ited, -iting, -its.** *British.* To re-edit and correct (written or printed material). **—sub·ed·i·tor** (sŭb′ĕd′ə-tər) *n.* **—sub·ed·i·to·ri·al** (sŭb′ĕd′ə-tôr′ē-əl, -tōr′ē-əl) *adj.*

sub·e·qua·to·ri·al (sŭb′ē′kwə-tôr′ē-əl, -tōr′ē-əl, sŭb′ĕk′wə-) *adj.* Belonging to a region adjacent to the equatorial area.

su·ber·ic acid (so͞o-bĕr′ĭk) *n.* **Octanedioic acid** *(see).* [French *subérique,* from Latin *sūber,* cork (from which the acid is obtained).]

su·ber·in (so͞o′bər-ĭn) *n.* A waxy waterproof substance present in the cell walls of cork tissue in plants. [French *subérine* : Latin *sūber,* cork (see **suberic acid**) + -IN.]

su·ber·ize (so͞o′bə-rīz′) *tr.v.* **-ized, -izing, -izes.** To cause (plant cell walls) to become impregnated with suberin during the formation of cork. [Latin *sūber,* cork. See **suberic acid.**] **—su·ber·i·za·tion** *n.*

su·ber·ose (so͞o′bə-rōs′) *adj.* Also **su·ber·ous** (so͞o′bər-əs). Of, pertaining to, or resembling cork or cork tissue; corky. [New Latin *suberosus,* from Latin *sūber,* cork. See **suberic acid.**]

sub·fam·i·ly (sŭb′făm′ə-lē) *n., pl.* **-lies. 1.** *Biology.* A taxonomic category ranking between a family and a genus. **2.** *Linguistics.* A division of languages below a family and above a branch.

sub·fix (sŭb′fĭks′) *n.* A subscript letter or sign.

sub·freez·ing (sŭb′frē′zĭng) *adj.* Below the freezing point.

sub·fusc (səb-fŭsk′, sŭb′fŭsk′) *adj.* Dull-colored; drab. [Latin *subfuscus,* dusky, from *fuscus,* dark brown.]

sub·ge·nus (sŭb′jē′nəs) *n., pl.* **-genera** (-jĕn′ər-ə). *Biology.* An occasionally used taxonomic category ranking below a genus and above a species. **—sub·ge·ner·ic** (sŭb′jə-nĕr′ĭk) *adj.*

sub·gla·cial (sŭb′glā′shəl) *adj.* Formed or deposited beneath a glacier. **—sub·gla·cial·ly** *adv.*

sub·group (sŭb′gro͞op′) *n.* **1.** A distinct group within a group. **2.** In algebra, a nonempty subset of a group. **3.** A subordinate group.

sub·head (sŭb′hĕd′) *n.* Also **sub·head·ing** (-hĕd′ĭng) (for sense 1). **1.** The heading or title of a subdivision of a printed subject. **2.** A subordinate heading or title.

sub·hu·man (sŭb′hyo͞o′mən) *adj.* **1.** Below the human race in evolutionary development. **2.** Not fully human.

Su·bic Bay (so͞o′bĭk). An inlet of the South China Sea, extending about 11 kilometers (7 miles) into west-central Luzon, Republic of the Philippines, north of Bataan.

sub·i·ma·go (sŭb′ĭ-mā′gō, -mä′gō) *n., pl.* **-goes** or **-gines** (-gə-nēz′). An insect, especially the mayfly, in a stage between the pupa and the imago. **—sub·i·ma·gi·nal** (sŭb′ĭ-mā′jə-nəl, -mä′jə-nəl) *adj.*

sub·in·dex (sŭb′ĭn′dĕks′) *n., pl.* **-dices** (-də-sēz′) or **-dexes. 1.** *Mathematics.* A distinguishing character or symbol directly beneath or next to and slightly below a number or letter; a subscript. **2.** An index to a section of a work.

sub·in·feu·date (sŭb′ĭn-fyo͞o′dāt′) *tr.v.* **-dated, -dating, -dates.** Also **sub·in·feud** (-ĭn-fyo͞od′) **-feuded, -feuding, -feuds.** To lease (lands) by subinfeudation.

sub·in·feu·da·tion (sŭb′ĭn′fyo͞o-dā′shən) *n.* **1.** The sublease of a portion of a feudal estate by a vassal to a subtenant who pays fealty to the vassal. **2.** The tenure established. **3.** The lands so leased.

sub·in·feu·da·to·ry (sŭb′ĭn-fyo͞o′də-tôr′ē, -tōr′ē) *adj.* Of or pertaining to subinfeudation.
~*n., pl.* **subinfeudatories.** A person who held his fief by subinfeudation.

sub·ir·ri·gate (sŭb′ĭr′ĭ-gāt′) *tr.v.* **-gated, -gating, -gates.** To irrigate from beneath, as by means of underground pipes. **—sub·ir·ri·ga·tion** *n.*

su·bi·to (so͞o′bē-tō′) *adv. Abbr.* **sub.** *Music.* Quickly; suddenly. Used as a direction. [Italian, from Latin *subitō,* suddenly, from *subire,* to come secretly, steal upon : *sub-,* secretly + *īre,* to go.]

subj. 1. subject. **2.** subjective. **3.** subjunctive.

sub·ja·cent (sŭb′jā′sənt) *adj.* **1.** Located beneath or below; underlying. **2.** Lying at a lower level but not directly beneath. [Latin *subjacēns* (stem *subjacent-*), present participle of *subjacēre,* to lie under : *sub-,* under + *jacēre,* to lie, from *jacere,* to throw.] **—sub·ja·cen·cy** *n.* **—sub·ja·cent·ly** *adv.*

sub·ject (sŭb′jĭkt, -jĕkt) *adj.* **1.** Under the power or authority of another; owing obedience or allegiance to another: *subject to the law.* **2.** Prone; disposed: *subject to colds.* **3.** Liable to incur or receive; exposed: *subject to misinterpretation.* **4.** Contingent, conditional, or dependent: *subject to approval.*
~*n. Abbr.* **subj. 1.** A person under the rule of another; especially, one who owes allegiance to a government or ruler: *a subject of the Crown.* **2. a.** A person or thing concerning which something is said or done; a topic. **b.** That which is treated or indicated in a work of art. **c.** *Music.* A melodic phrase that is subsequently developed, especially in a fugue; a theme. **3.** A course or area of study. **4.** A basis for action; a cause. Often used with *for*: *a subject for concern.* **5. a.** One that experiences or is subjected to something. **b.** One that is the object of clinical study, analysis, or treatment. **c.** A corpse intended for study and dissection. **6.** *Grammar.* A noun or noun phrase in a sentence that denotes the doer of the action, the receiver of the action in passive constructions, or that which is described or identified. **7.** *Logic.* The term of a proposition about which something is affirmed or denied. **8.** *Philosophy.* **a.** The essential nature or substance of something as distinguished from its attributes. **b.** The mind or thinking part as distinguished from the object of thought.
~*tr.v.* (səb-jĕkt′) **subjected, -jecting, -jects. 1.** To submit to some discipline or authority; bring under control. **2.** To render liable to something. Often used in the passive. **3.** To cause to experience or undergo. **4.** To bring under control; subjugate. **5.** To submit for consideration. [Middle English *su(b)get, subject,* from Old French *su(b)get,* from Latin *subicere* (past participle *subjectus*), to bring under : *sub-,* under + *jacere,* to throw.] **—sub·ject·a·ble** *adj.* **—sub·jec·tion** (səb-jĕk′shən) *n.*

Synonyms: *subject, matter, topic, theme.* These nouns relate to the principal idea of any discourse or creative work. *Subject* denotes the thing represented, discussed, or otherwise treated. *Matter* refers somewhat less specifically to the material involved in the work. *Topic* is either interchangeable with *subject* or else denotes a division of it. *Theme* is sometimes used in the sense of any of the foregoing terms but often refers specifically to a basic idea that underlies or unifies the material treated and either summarizes or interprets it.

sub·jec·ti·fy (səb-jĕk′tə-fī′) *tr.v.* **-fied, -fying, -fies.** To render subjective; interpret subjectively.

sub·jec·tive (səb-jĕk′tĭv) *adj. Abbr.* **subj. 1. a.** Proceeding from, pertaining to, or taking place within an individual's mind in a manner unrelated to external reality; unfounded: *subjective fears.* **b.** Affected by or arising from one's personality or experience rather than rational thought or observation: *a subjective view.* **c.** Particular to a given individual; personal. **2.** Pertaining to the real nature of something; essential. **3.** Moodily introspective. **4.** *Psychology.* Existing only within the mind and incapable of external verification. **5.** *Medicine.* Designating a symptom or condition perceived by the patient and not by the examiner. **6.** Expressing or bringing into prominence the individuality of the artist or author. **7.** *Grammar.* Designating or being in the nominative case. **—sub·jec·tive·ly** *adv.* **—sub·jec·tive·ness, sub·jec·tiv·i·ty** (sŭb′jĕk-tĭv′ə-tē) *n.*

subjective complement *n. Grammar.* A noun, noun phrase, or adjective serving as a complement to a verb and qualifying its subject. In *He made her a good husband, husband* is a subjective complement.

subjective genitive *n. Grammar.* **1.** The genitive case as indicating the subject of a specified action. In the phrase *my love for her,* meaning "the love I bear her," the subject *(I)* is transferred to the genitive case *(my).* Compare **objective genitive. 2.** A noun or pronoun in this case.

subjective idealism *n. Philosophy.* The theory that all experience is of ideas in the mind.

sub·jec·tiv·ism (səb-jĕk′tə-vĭz′əm) *n.* **1. a.** The doctrine that all knowledge is restricted to the conscious self and its sensory states. **b.** Any theory or doctrine, especially a theological one, that emphasizes the subjective elements in experience. **2.** The theory that individual conscience is the only valid standard of moral judgment. **3.** The quality of being subjective. **—sub·jec·tiv·ist** *n.* **—sub·jec·tiv·is·tic** (səb-jĕk′tə-vĭs′tĭk) *adj.*

subject matter *n.* The matter under consideration in a written work, speech, or discussion; the theme. [Translation of Latin *subjecta materia,* translation of Greek *hupokeimenē hulē,* "underlying matter."]

sub·join (səb-join′) *tr.v.* **-joined, -joining, -joins.** To add at the end; append; annex. [From obsolete French *subjoindre,* from Latin *subjungere* : *sub-,* in addition + *jungere,* to join.]

sub·join·der (səb-join′dər) *n.* Something subjoined.

sub ju·di·ce (sŭb jo͞o′də-sē′, yo͞o′dē-kā′) *adj. Law.* **1.** Under judicial deliberation; before a judge or court of law and thus outside the scope of public comment. **2.** Not yet decided; still subject to confidential discussion. [Latin, "under a judge."] **—sub ju·di·ce** *adv.*

sub·ju·gate (sŭb′jə-gāt′) *tr.v.* **-gated, -gating, -gates. 1.** To bring under dominion; conquer; subdue. **2.** To make subservient or submissive; enslave. —See Synonyms at **defeat.** [Middle English *subjugaten,* from Latin *subjugāre,* to place under a yoke : *sub-,* under + *jugum,* yoke.] **—sub·ju·ga·tion** *n.* **—sub·ju·ga·tor** *n.*

sub·junc·tion (səb-jŭngk′shən) *n.* **1.** The act of subjoining or the condition of being subjoined. **2.** Something that is subjoined. [Late Latin *subjunctiō* (stem *subjunctiōn-*), from *subjungere* (past participle *subjunctus*), to SUBJOIN.]

sub·junc·tive (səb-jŭngk′tĭv) *adj. Abbr.* **subj.** *Grammar.* Designating a verb form or set of forms used to express a contingent or hypothetical action or state, as one that is feared, desired, or doubted. Compare **indicative.**
~*n. Abbr.* **subj. 1.** The subjunctive mood. **2.** A subjunctive verb or construction. [Late Latin *(mōdus) subjunctīvus,* translation of Greek *hupotaktikē enklisis,* "mood of subordination" (originally regarded as proper to subordinate clauses), from Latin *subjungere,* to SUBJOIN.] **—sub·junc·tive·ly** *adv.*

sub·king·dom (sŭb′kĭng′dəm) *n. Biology.* A former taxonomic category constituting a major division of a kingdom.

sub·lap·sar·i·an·ism (sŭb′lăp-sâr′ē-ə-nĭz′əm) *n. Theology.* **Infralapsarianism** *(see).* [New Latin *sublapsarius* : SUB- + LAPSE.] **—sub·lap·sar·i·an** *adj. & n.*

sub·lease (sŭb′lēs′, -lēs′) *tr.v.* **-leased, -leasing, -leases. 1.** To sublet (property). **2.** To rent (property) under a sublease.
~*n.* A lease of property granted in turn by a lessee.

sub·les·see (sŭb′lĕ-sē′) *n.* One to whom a sublease is granted.

sub·les·sor (sŭb′lĕs′ôr′, sŭb′lĕ-sôr′) *n.* One granting a sublease.

sub·let (sŭb′lĕt′) *tr.v.* **-let, -letting, -lets. 1.** To rent (property one

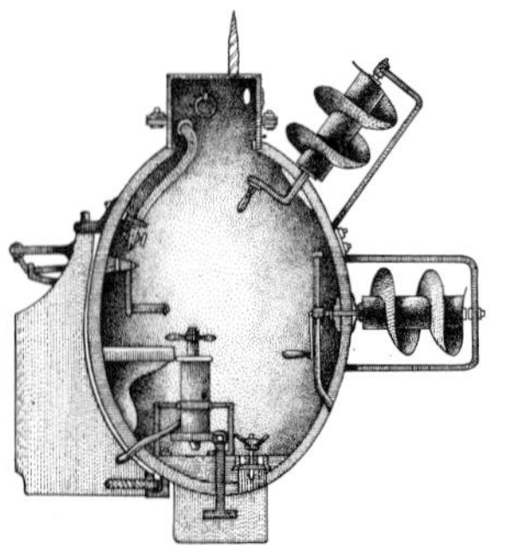

submarine *The earliest authenticated submarines, dating from the 1620's, were built of greased leather over a wooden frame and were propelled by oars. In use, however, they leaked badly under the pressure of water. The more reliable model shown here was a one-man craft known as the* Turtle. *Designed in 1776 by an American engineer, David Bushnell, it was the first to make use of buoyancy tanks—which could be flooded to submerge and pumped out to surface. The* Turtle *was moved underwater by cranking the propellers by hand.*

PRONUNCIATION KEY

ă, pat; **ā**, pay; **âr**, care;
ä, father, are; **b**, bib;
ch, church; **d**, deed; **ĕ**, pet;
ē, be; **f**, fife; **g**, gag; **h**, hat;
hw, which; **ĭ**, pit; **ī**, pie;
îr, pier; **j**, judge; **k**, kick;
l, lid, needle; **m**, mum;
n, no, sudden; **ng**, thing;
ŏ, pot; **ō**, toe; **ô**, paw, for;
oi, noise; **ou**, out; **o͝o**, book;
o͞o, boot; **p**, pop; **r**, roar;
s, sauce; **sh**, ship, dish;
t, tight; **th**, thin, path;
th, this, bathe; **ŭ**, cut; **ûr**, fur;
v, valve; **w**, with; **y**, yes;
z, zebra, size; **zh**, vision;
ə, about, item, edible, gallop, circus, peaceful

IN FOREIGN WORDS:

à, *Fr.* ami; **œ**, *Fr.* feu, *Ger.* schön; **ü**, *Fr.* tu, *Ger.* über; **KH**, *Ger.* ich, *Scot.* loch; **N**, *Fr.* bon; **y'**, *Fr.* Compiègne

STRESS MARKS:

Primary stress: **'**
in·cite' (ĭn-sīt')
Secondary stress: **'**
in'sight' (ĭn'sīt')

holds by lease) to another. **2.** To subcontract (work).
∼*n.* (-lĕt'). **1.** An instance of subletting. **2.** *Informal.* Property, especially an apartment, rented by a tenant to another party.

sub·lieu·ten·ant (sŭb'lo͞o-tĕn'ənt) *n. British.* A navy officer ranking next below a lieutenant. **—sub·lieu·ten·an·cy** *n.*

sub·li·mate (sŭb'lə-māt') *v.* **-mated, -mating, -mates.** *—tr.* **1.** *Psychology.* To transform (an instinctual impulse, especially a sexual urge) into a more socially acceptable form of expression or behavior. **2.** *Chemistry.* To cause (a solid or a gas) to change state without becoming a liquid. *—intr. Chemistry.* To change directly from the solid to the gaseous state or from the gaseous to the solid state without becoming a liquid.
∼*n. Chemistry.* The material formed by sublimating.
∼*adj.* Exalted or purified. [Latin *sublīmāre,* to raise, from *sublīmis,* uplifted, SUBLIME.]

sub·li·ma·tion (sŭb'lə-mā'shən) *n.* **1.** The act or process of sublimating. **2.** That which has been sublimated.

sub·lime (sə-blīm') *adj.* **1.** Characterized by nobility; grand; majestic. **2. a.** Of high spiritual, moral, or intellectual worth. **b.** Not to be excelled; supreme. Sometimes used ironically: *sublime ignorance.* **3.** Inspiring awe; impressive; moving. **4.** *Obsolete.* Of lofty appearance or bearing; proud. **5.** *Archaic.* Raised aloft; set high.
∼*n.* **1.** Something that is sublime. Preceded by *the.* **2.** The ultimate example of something. Preceded by *the.*
∼*v.* **sublimed, -liming, -limes.** *—tr.* **1.** To render sublime; elevate; ennoble. **2.** *Chemistry.* To cause to sublimate. *—intr. Chemistry.* To sublimate. [Latin *sublīmis.* See **limen.**] **—sub·lime·ly** *adv.* **—sub·lim·er** *n.* **—sub·lim·i·ty** (sə-blĭm'ə-tē), **sub·lime·ness** *n.*

sub·lim·i·nal (sŭb-lĭm'ə-nəl) *adj. Psychology.* **1.** Existing or acting below the threshold of conscious perception: *subliminal advertising.* **2.** Inadequate to produce conscious awareness. [SUB- + Latin *līmen* (stem *līmin-*), threshold (see **limen**).] **—sub·lim·i·nal·ly** *adv.*

sub·lin·gual (sŭb'lĭng'gwəl) *adj.* Situated beneath or on the underside of the tongue: *sublingual salivary glands.*

sub·lit·to·ral (sŭb'lĭt'ər-əl) *adj.* **1.** Near the seashore. **2.** Shallow and lying between the shoreline and the edge of the continental shelf or ranging in depth to about 50 fathoms.

sub·lu·na·ry (sŭb'lo͞o'nə-rē) *adj.* Also **sub·lu·nar** (-nər). **1.** Situated beneath the moon. **2.** Of this world; earthly; mundane: *"The princess thought, that of all sublunary things, knowledge was the best"* (Samuel Johnson). [Late Latin *sublūnāris* : Latin *sub-,* beneath + *lūna,* moon.]

sub·lux·a·tion (sŭb'lŭk-sā'shən) *n.* Incomplete dislocation of a bone in a joint.

sub·ma·chine gun (sŭb'mə-shēn') *n.* A lightweight automatic or semiautomatic gun fired from the shoulder or hip. Compare **machine gun.**

sub·man·dib·u·lar (sŭb'măn-dĭb'yə-lər) *adj.* Submaxillary.

sub·mar·gin·al (sŭb'mär'jə-nəl) *adj.* **1.** Beneath a margin. **2.** Below the minimum requirements. **3.** Of low productivity; infertile.

sub·ma·rine (sŭb'mə-rēn', sŭb'mə-rēn') *adj.* Located, occurring, or functioning beneath the surface of the water; undersea.
∼*n.* **1.** A vessel capable of operating submerged. **2.** A sandwich, the **hero** *(see).*

submarine chaser *n.* A small, fast patrol vessel designed to pursue and attack submarines. Also called "subchaser."

sub·mar·i·ner (sŭb'măr'ə-nər, -mə-rē'nər) *n.* A member of the crew of a submarine.

sub·max·il·lar·y (sŭb'măk'sə-lĕr'ē) *adj.* Of or relating to the lower jaw or the region adjacent to it; submandibular.
∼*n., pl.* **submaxillaries.** An anatomical part situated beneath the maxilla, such as the submaxillary salivary gland.

sub·me·di·ant (sŭb'mē'dē-ənt) *n. Music.* The sixth tone of a diatonic scale. Also called "superdominant."
∼*adj.* Of or pertaining to the submediant. [SUB- + MEDIANT.]

sub·merge (səb-mûrj') *v.* **-merged, -merging, -merges.** *—tr.* **1.** To place or plunge under water or other liquid. **2.** To cover with water; inundate. **3.** To hide from view; obscure. **4.** To overwhelm. *—intr.* To go under or as if under water. [Latin *submergere* : *sub-,* under + *mergere,* to immerse, plunge.] **—sub·mer·gence** *n.*

sub·merged (səb-mûrjd') *adj.* Also **sub·mersed** (-mûrst') (for sense 1). **1.** *Botany.* Growing or remaining under water: *submerged leaves.* **2.** Living in poverty and misery: *the submerged masses.* **3.** Hidden.

sub·merg·i·ble (səb-mûr'jə-bəl) *adj.* Submersible.

sub·merse (səb-mûrs') *tr.v.* **-mersed, -mersing, -merses.** To submerge. [Latin *submergere* (past participle *submersus*), to SUBMERGE.] **—sub·mer·sion** (səb-mûr'zhən, -shən) *n.*

sub·mers·i·ble (səb-mûr'sə-bəl) *adj.* Able to be plunged into or to remain under water.
∼*n.* A vessel capable of operating or remaining under water, as a bathysphere or submarine.

sub·mi·cro·scop·ic (sŭb'mī'krə-skŏp'ĭk) *adj.* Too small to be seen through an optical microscope. **—sub·mi·cro·scop·i·cal·ly** *adv.*

sub·min·i·a·ture (sŭb'mĭn'ē-ə-cho͝or', -chər) *adj.* Smaller than miniature; exceedingly small.

sub·min·i·a·tur·ize (sŭb'mĭn'ē-ə-chə-rīz') *tr.v.* **-ized, -izing, -izes.** To make subminiature; especially, to manufacture or design (electronic equipment) in subminiature size. **—sub·min·i·a·tur·i·za·tion** *n.*

sub·miss (səb-mĭs') *adj. Archaic.* **1.** Submissive. **2.** Soft in tone. [Latin *submissus,* past participle of *submittere,* to SUBMIT.]

sub·mis·sion (səb-mĭsh'ən) *n.* **1. a.** The act of submitting to the power of another. **b.** The state of having submitted. **2.** The state of being submissive or compliant; meekness. **3. a.** The act of submitting something, such as a document, for consideration. **b.** Something thus submitted. —See Synonyms at **surrender.**

sub·mis·sive (səb-mĭs'ĭv) *adj.* **1.** Disposed to submit; docile. **2.** Indicating or marked by submission. —See Synonyms at **obedient.** **—sub·mis·sive·ly** *adv.* **—sub·mis·sive·ness** *n.*

sub·mit (səb-mĭt') *v.* **-mitted, -mitting, -mits.** *—tr.* **1.** To yield or surrender (oneself) to the will or authority of another or others. **2.** To subject to some condition or process. **3.** To refer (something) to the consideration or judgment of another. **4.** To offer as a proposition or contention: *I submit that they lied.* *—intr.* **1.** To yield or give way, especially to one considered physically, intellectually, or morally superior. **2.** To allow oneself to be subjected to something: *submit to cross-examination.* —See Synonyms at **yield.** [Middle English *submitten,* from Latin *submittere,* to place under : *sub-,* under + *mittere,* to throw.] **—sub·mit·tal** *n.* **—sub·mit·ter** *n.*

sub·mon·tane (sŭb'mŏn'tān', sŭb'mŏn-tān') *adj.* Located under or at the base of a mountain or mountain range. [Late Latin *submontānus* : Latin *sub-,* under + *montānus,* mountainous, from *mōns,* mountain.] **—sub·mon·tane·ly** *adv.*

sub·mu·co·sa (sŭb'myo͞o-kō'sə, -zə) *n.* The layer of connective tissue that lies beneath a mucous membrane. **—sub·mu·co·sal** *adj.*

sub·mul·ti·ple (sŭb'mŭl'tə-pəl) *n.* A number that is an exact divisor of another number: *2 is a submultiple of 10.* **—sub·mul·ti·ple** *adj.*

sub·nor·mal (sŭb'nôr'məl) *adj.* **1.** Less than normal; below the average. **2.** Mentally deficient. See **mental deficiency.**
∼*n.* A person who is subnormal in some respect, as in intelligence or coordination. **—sub·nor·mal·ly** *adv.*

sub·nor·mal·i·ty (sŭb'nôr-măl'ə-tē) *n.* **1.** The state or condition of being subnormal. **2. Mental deficiency** *(see).*

sub·nu·cle·ar (sŭb'no͞o'klē-ər, -nyo͞o'klē-ər) *adj.* **1.** Of or pertaining to the constituents of the nucleus of an atom. **2.** Participating in reactions characteristic of subnuclear constituents.

sub·o·ce·an·ic (sŭb'ō'shē-ăn'ĭk) *adj.* Formed, situated, or occurring beneath the ocean or the ocean bed.

sub·or·der (sŭb'ôr'dər) *n.* **1.** *Biology.* A taxonomic category ranking after an order and before a family. **2.** A subdivision of any category termed an order. **—sub·or·di·nal** (sŭb'ôr'də-nəl) *adj.*

sub·or·di·nar·y (sŭb'ôr'də-nĕr'ē) *n., pl.* **-ies.** Any of various heraldic bearings that are less important that the ordinaries.

sub·or·di·nate (sə-bôr'də-nĭt) *adj.* **1.** Belonging to a lower or inferior class or rank; minor; secondary. **2.** Occupying a secondary position; of relatively little importance. **3.** Subject to the authority or control of another.
∼*n.* One that is subordinate.
∼*tr.v.* (sə-bôr'də-nāt') **subordinated, -nating, -nates. 1.** To put in a lower or inferior rank or class. **2.** To treat as having little or less importance. **3.** To make subservient; subdue. [Medieval Latin *subōrdinātus,* past participle of *subōrdināre,* to put in a lower rank : Latin *sub-,* below + *ōrdināre,* to arrange in order, from *ōrdō,* order.] **—sub·or·di·nate·ly** *adv.* **—sub·or·di·nate·ness, sub·or·di·na·tion** *n.* **—sub·or·di·na·tive** (sə-bôr'də-nā'tĭv) *adj.*

subordinate clause *n. Grammar.* A **dependent clause** *(see).*

subordinate conjunction *n. Grammar.* A conjunction that introduces a subordinate clause, such as *that, who, because,* or *if.* Compare **coordinate conjunction.**

sub·or·di·na·tion·ism (sə-bôr'də-nā'shə-nĭz'əm) *n. Theology.* The doctrine that the second and third persons of the Trinity are subordinate to the first person. **—sub·or·di·na·tion·ist** *n.*

sub·orn (sə-bôrn') *tr.v.* **-orned, -orning, -orns. 1. a.** To induce (a person) to commit a wrong or unlawful act. **b.** To induce (a person) to commit perjury. **2.** To procure (perjured testimony). [Latin *subōrnāre* : *sub-,* secretly + *ōrnāre,* to equip.] **—sub·or·na·tion** *n.* **—sub·orn·er** *n.*

sub·ox·ide (sŭb'ŏk'sīd') *n.* An oxide containing a lower proportion of oxygen than is present in the normal or most common oxide of the element.

sub·phy·lum (sŭb'fī'ləm) *n., pl.* **-la** (-lə). *Biology.* A taxonomic category ranking between a phylum and a class.

sub·plot (sŭb'plŏt') *n.* A plot, as in a novel or play, that is secondary and incidental to the main plot.

sub·poe·na (sə-pē'nə) *n.* A legal writ requiring appearance in court to give testimony.
∼*tr.v.* **subpoenaed, -naing, -nas.** To serve or summon with such a writ. [Latin *sub poenā,* under penalty (first words in the writ) : *sub-,* under + *poenā,* penalty, from Greek *poinē.*]

sub·po·lar (sŭb'pō'lər) *adj.* Near the polar regions.

sub·prin·ci·pal (sŭb'prĭn'sə-pəl) *n.* **1.** An assistant principal. **2.** An auxiliary or bracing rafter in a frame. **3.** *Music.* An open diapason subbass in an organ.

sub·re·gion (sŭb'rē'jən) *n.* A subdivision of a region, especially of an ecological region. **—sub·re·gion·al** *adj.*

sub·rep·tion (sŭb-rĕp'shən) *n.* **1.** A calculated misrepresentation through concealment of the facts. **2.** An inference drawn from such a misrepresentation. [Latin *subreptiō* (stem *subreptiōn-*), theft, from *subrepere* (past participle *subreptus*), to creep under, steal upon : *sub-,* under + *repere,* to creep.] **—sub·rep·ti·tious** (sŭb'rĕp-tĭsh'əs) *adj.*

sub·ro·gate (sŭb'rə-gāt') *tr.v.* **-gated, -gating, -gates. 1.** *Law.* To substitute (one person) for another. **2.** To substitute (one thing) for another. [Latin *subrogāre,* "to nominate an alternative candidate" : *sub-,* instead of + *rogāre,* to ask, propose.]

sub·ro·ga·tion (sŭb'rə-gā'shən) *n. Law.* The substitution of one person for another, especially of one creditor for another.

sub ro·sa (sŭb rō'zə) *adv.* In secret; privately; confidentially. [Latin, "under the rose," from the practice of hanging a rose over a meeting as a symbol of secrecy, from the legend that Cupid once gave Harpocrates, the god of silence, a rose to make him keep the secrets of Venus.] **—sub ro·sa** *adj.*

sub·rou·tine (sŭb'ro͞o-tēn') *n. Computer Science.* A self-contained section of a computer program that can be identified and used more than once during the running of the program.

subs. subscription.

sub·scap·u·lar (sŭb'skăp'yə-lər) *adj. Anatomy.* Situated below or on the underside of the scapula.
~*n.* A subscapular part, such as an artery or nerve.

sub·scribe (səb-skrīb') *v.* **-scribed, -scribing, -scribes.** *—tr.* **1.** To sign (one's name) at the end of a document. **2.** To sign one's name to in attestation, testimony, or consent: *subscribe a will.* **3.** To pledge or contribute (a sum of money). *—intr.* **1.** To contract to pay for regular receipt of a periodical or service: *subscribe to cable television.* **2.** To promise to pay or contribute money: *subscribe to charity.* **3.** To indicate agreement or approval; be in favor; assent. Used with *to*: *He does not subscribe to that view.* **4.** To sign one's name. **5.** To affix one's signature to a document as a witness or to show consent. **6.** To apply for shares in an offering of newly issued stocks or bonds. **7.** To undertake to purchase a book prior to publication. —See Synonyms at **assent.** [Middle English *subscriben,* from Latin *subscrībere* : *sub-,* under + *scrībere,* to write.] **—sub·scrib·er** *n.*

sub·script (sŭb'skrĭpt') *adj.* Written beneath.
~*n.* A distinguishing character or symbol written directly beneath or next to and slightly below a letter or number. Compare **superscript.** [Latin *subscriptus,* past participle of *subscrībere,* to SUBSCRIBE.]

sub·scrip·tion (səb-skrĭp'shən) *n. Abbr.* **sub., subs. 1.** An order for an advance purchase, as of the issues of a periodical over a certain period of time or of tickets for a series of concerts, plays, or other cultural events. **2.** *Chiefly British.* Dues paid in for membership in a society, association, or similar body. **3.** An application for newly issued stocks or bonds. **4.** The act of subscribing, especially: **a.** The act of setting one's signature on a document. **b.** The acceptance of a position or belief, especially an article of faith. **c.** The act of contributing money, as to a charitable cause or to finance a future publication. **5.** That which is subscribed, especially: **a.** An inscription. **b.** A charitable donation. **—sub·scrip·tive** *adj.* **—sub·scrip·tive·ly** *adv.*

sub·sec·tion (sŭb'sĕk'shən) *n.* A division of a section.

sub·se·quence (sŭb'sə-kwəns, -kwĕns') *n.* **1.** That which is subsequent; a sequel. **2.** The fact or quality of being subsequent.

sub·se·quent (sŭb'sə-kwənt, -kwĕnt') *adj.* **1.** Following in time or order; succeeding. **2.** Designating a river that is a tributary to a consequent river. In this sense, compare **obsequent.** —See Usage Note at **consequent. —subsequent to.** Following; coming after. [Middle English, from Old French, from Latin *subsequēns,* present participle of *subsequī,* to follow close after : *sub-,* close to, after + *sequī,* to follow.] **—sub·se·quent·ly** *adv.* **—sub·se·quent·ness** *n.*

Usage: *Subsequent, subsequent to* (used prepositionally), and *subsequently* are employed, in the sense of *later,* in the following typical constructions: *a subsequent discussion; a discussion held subsequent to the meeting; a discussion held subsequently.*

sub·serve (səb-sûrv') *tr.v.* **-served, -serving, -serves.** To serve to promote (some end); be useful to; further. [Latin *subservīre,* to serve, be subject to : *sub-,* under + *servīre,* to SERVE.]

sub·ser·vi·ent (səb-sûr'vē-ənt) *adj.* **1.** Subordinate in capacity or function. **2.** Excessively compliant or submissive; obsequious; servile. **3.** Useful only to further some other purpose; purely instrumental. [Latin *subserviēns* (stem *subservient-*), present participle of *subservīre,* to SUBSERVE.] **—sub·ser·vi·ence, sub·ser·vi·en·cy** *n.* **—sub·ser·vi·ent·ly** *adv.*

sub·set (sŭb'sĕt') *n.* A set, as in mathematics, contained within a set.

sub·shrub (sŭb'shrŭb') *n.* **1.** A herbaceous plant having a woody lower stem. **2.** A low shrub; an undershrub.

sub·side (səb-sīd') *intr.v.* **-sided, -siding, -sides. 1.** To sink to a lower or normal level. **2.** To sink or settle down, as into a sofa. **3.** To sink to the bottom; settle, as sediment. **4.** To become less agitated or active; abate. —See Synonyms at **decrease.** [Latin *subsīdere,* to sink down : *sub-,* down + *sīdere,* to settle.]

sub·si·dence (səb-sīd'ns, sŭb'sə-dəns) *n.* The act or process of subsiding; especially, the sinking or settling of ground or of buildings erected on it.

sub·sid·i·ar·y (səb-sĭd'ē-ĕr'ē) *adj.* **1.** Serving to assist or supplement; auxiliary. **2.** Secondary in importance; subordinate. **3.** Of, pertaining to, or of the nature of a subsidy.
~*n., pl.* **subsidiaries. 1.** One that is subsidiary. **2.** A subsidiary company. **3.** *Music.* A theme subordinate to a main theme or subject. [Latin *subsīdiārius,* in reserve, supporting, from *subsidium,* support, SUBSIDY.] **—sub·sid·i·ar·i·ly** (səb-sĭd'ē-âr'ə-lē) *adv.*

subsidiary company *n.* A company having more than half of its stock owned by another company. Also called "subsidiary."

sub·si·dize (sŭb'sə-dīz') *tr.v.* **-dized, -dizing, -dizes. 1.** To assist or support with a subsidy. **2.** To secure the assistance of by granting a subsidy. **—sub·si·di·za·tion** *n.* **—sub·si·diz·er** *n.*

sub·si·dy (sŭb'sə-dē) *n., pl.* **-dies. 1.** A sum of money provided to assist a person, enterprise, or nation, usually one unable to be self-financing; especially, government funds for such purposes as financing research, maintaining employment, encouraging development, or stabilizing price levels. **2.** Formerly, money granted to the British Crown by Parliament. —See Synonyms at **bonus.** [Middle English *subsidie,* aid, assistance, from Norman French, from Latin *subsidium,* reserve troops, hence support, help, from *subsidēre,* to sit down, remain, be placed in reserve : *sub-,* down + *sedēre,* to sit.]

sub·sist (səb-sĭst') *v.* **-sisted, -sisting, -sists.** *—intr.* **1.** To be sustained; manage to live. Used with *on* or *by*: *subsisting on a meager pension.* **2.** To reside in or consist of something specified: *The difference subsists in the quality of their work.* **3. a.** To exist; be. **b.** To remain or continue in existence. **4.** To be logically conceivable. *—tr.* To maintain or support with provisions. [Latin *subsistere,* to stand still, stand up, remain standing : *sub-,* from below, up + *sistere,* to cause to stand.] **—sub·sist·er** *n.*

sub·sis·tence (səb-sĭs'təns) *n.* **1.** The act or state of subsisting, especially in a very basic state. **2.** A means of subsisting; sustenance. **3.** That which has real or substantial existence. —See Synonyms at **livelihood.**
~*adj.* **1.** Of, pertaining to, or being an agricultural system in which farmers and their families consume what they produce, leaving little or nothing to sell. **2.** Of or being money paid to an employee as an advance or to cover incidental expenses. **3.** Of or designating a level of income that is barely sufficient to meet the necessities of life. **—sub·sis·tent** *adj.*

sub·soil (sŭb'soil') *n.* The partially decomposed layer of rock underlying the topsoil and overlying the solid rock beneath.
~*tr.v.* **subsoiled, -soiling, -soils.** To plow or turn up the subsoil of. **—sub·soil·er** *n.*

sub·so·lar (sŭb'sō'lər) *adj.* **1.** Situated directly beneath the sun. **2.** Located between the topics; equatorial.

sub·son·ic (sŭb'sŏn'ĭk) *adj.* **1.** Infrasonic. **2.** Having a speed less than that of sound in a designated medium.

sub·spe·cies (sŭb'spē'shēz, -sēz) *n., pl.* **subspecies.** *Abbr.* **ssp** *Biology.* A subdivision of a taxonomic species, usually based on geographic distribution. **—sub·spe·cif·ic** (sŭb'spə-sĭf'ĭk) *adj.*

subst. 1. substantive. **2.** substitute.

sub·stance (sŭb'stəns) *n.* **1.** *Philosophy.* The essential nature of anything, as considered apart from its form or attributes; the primary or basic element that receives modifications. **2.** Any kind of matter; a material of which something is composed. **3.** The essence of what is said or written; the gist. **4. a.** That which is solid or real; reality as opposed to appearance. **b.** A solid or substantial quality or character. **5.** Density; body: *Air has little substance.* **6.** Material possessions; wealth: *a man of substance.* [Middle English, essence, from Old French, from Latin *substantia,* from *substāns,* present participle of *substāre,* to be present : *sub-,* up + *stāre,* to stand.]

sub·stan·dard (sŭb'stăn'dərd) *adj.* **1.** Failing to meet a standard; below standard. **2.** Considered unacceptable usage by the educated members of a speech community.

sub·stan·tial (səb-stăn'shəl) *adj.* **1.** Of, pertaining to, or having substance; material. **2.** Not imaginary; true; real. **3.** Solidly built; strong. **4.** Ample; sustaining: *a substantial breakfast.* **5.** Considerable in importance, value, degree, amount, or extent: *won by a substantial margin.* **6.** Practical; virtual: *in substantial agreement.* **7.** Possessing wealth or property; well-to-do. **8.** *Informal.* Fat; stout. Used humorously: *"Running did not come easily to a middle-aged woman of her substantial proportions"* (Ivy St. David).
~*n.* **substantials. 1.** The essentials. **2.** Solid things. [Middle English *substancial,* from Late Latin *substantiālis,* from Latin *substantia,* SUBSTANCE.] **—sub·stan·ti·al·i·ty** (səb-stăn'shē-ăl'ə-tē), **sub·stan·tial·ness** *n.* **—sub·stan·tial·ly** *adv.*

sub·stan·ti·ate (səb-stăn'shē-āt') *tr.v.* **-ated, -ating, -ates. 1.** To support with proof or evidence; verify: *substantiate an accusation.* **2. a.** To give material form to; embody. **b.** To make firm or solid. **3.** To give substance to; make real or actual. —See Synonyms at **confirm.** [New Latin *substantiare,* from Latin *substantia,* SUBSTANCE.] **—sub·stan·ti·a·tion** *n.*

sub·stan·ti·val (sŭb'stən-tī'vəl) *adj. Grammar.* Of, pertaining to, or of the nature of a substantive. **—sub·stan·ti·val·ly** *adv.*

sub·stan·tive (sŭb'stən-tĭv) *adj. Abbr.* **s., sb., subst. 1.** Independent in existence or function; not subordinate. **2.** Not imaginary; genuine; real. **3.** Of or pertaining to the essence or substance of something; essential. **4.** Of substantial amount. **5.** Having a solid basis; firm. **6.** Effective and permanent. **7.** Expressing or denoting existence, as does the verb *to be.* **8.** Being or functioning as a noun or noun phrase. **9.** *Law.* Concerned with legal rights and duties rather than with procedure. Compare **adjective.**
~*n. Abbr.* **s., sb., subst.** A word or group of words acting as a noun. [Middle English *substantif,* from Old French, from Late Latin *substantīvus,* self-existent, from Latin *substantia,* "thing that exists," SUBSTANCE.] **—sub·stan·tive·ly** *adv.* **—sub·stan·tive·ness** *n.*

sub·sta·tion (sŭb'stā'shən) *n.* **1.** An electrical installation in which power from the generating station is converted or transformed for distribution. **2.** A subsidiary or branch station; especially, a branch post office.

sub·stit·u·ent (səb-stĭch'o͞o-ənt) *n. Chemistry.* An atom, radical, or group substituted for another in a compound as a result of a chemical reaction.
~*adj.* Of such an atom or group. [Latin *substituēns* (stem *substituent-*), present participle of *substituere,* to SUBSTITUTE.]

sub·sti·tute (sŭb'stə-to͞ot', -tyo͞ot') *n. Abbr.* **sub., subst. 1.** One that

takes the place or function of another; a replacement, as: **a.** A substance, especially an artificial or inferior one, used in place of another. **b.** In sports, a reserve player who may be called on to replace a member of a team, as for reasons of injury or tactics. **2.** *Grammar.* A word or construction used in place of another word, phrase, or clause.
~*v.* **substituted, -tuting, -tutes.** —*tr.* To put or use (a person or thing) in place of another: *substitute margarine for butter.* —*intr.* To take the place of another: *"Only art can substitute for nature"* (Leonard Bernstein). [Latin *substitūtus,* a replacement, from the past participle of *substituere,* to substitute : *sub-,* in place of + *statuere,* to cause to stand.] —**sub·sti·tut·a·bil·i·ty** *n.* —**sub·sti·tut·a·ble** *adj.* —**sub·sti·tute** *adj.*

sub·sti·tu·tion (sŭb'stə-tōō'shən, -tyōō'shən) *n.* **1. a.** The act of substituting. **b.** The state of being substituted. **2.** That which is substituted. —**sub·sti·tu·tion·al** *adj.* —**sub·sti·tu·tion·al·ly** *adv.*

sub·sti·tu·tive (sŭb'stə-tōō'tĭv, -tyōō'tĭv) *adj.* Serving or capable of serving as a substitute.

sub·strate (sŭb'strāt') *n.* **1.** A chemical substance that undergoes change as a result of being acted upon by an enzyme. **2.** *Biology.* The base on which a plant or animal lives. **3.** *Electronics.* The material upon which the elements of a semiconducting component or integrated circuit are deposited. **4.** A substratum. [From SUBSTRATUM.]

sub·stra·tum (sŭb'strā'təm, -străt'əm) *n., pl.* **-strata** (-strā'tə, -străt'ə) or **-stratums. 1.** An underlying layer. **2.** The foundation or groundwork for something. **3.** *Philosophy.* The characterless substance that supports attributes of reality. **4.** *Biology.* A substrate. **5.** A thin coating of hardened gelatin used to hold the emulsion on a photographic plate or film. **6.** *Linguistics.* An indigenous language that is replaced by the language of an incoming population but continues to exert an influence on the dominant language. In this sense, compare **superstratum.** [Medieval Latin *substrātum,* from Latin, neuter past participle of *substernere,* to lie under : *sub-,* under + *sternere,* to spread out flat.] —**sub·stra·tive** *adj.*

sub·struc·tion (səb-strŭk'shən) *n.* A foundation; substructure, as of a building. [Latin *substructiō* (stem *substructiōn-*), from *substruere* (past participle *substructus*), to build beneath : *sub-,* beneath + *struere,* to build.] —**sub·struc·tion·al** *adj.*

sub·struc·ture (sŭb'strŭk'chər) *n.* **1.** The supporting part of a structure; a foundation. **2.** The earth bank or bed supporting railroad tracks. —**sub·struc·tur·al** *adj.*

sub·sume (səb-sōōm') *tr.v.* **-sumed, -suming, -sumes.** To place or include in a more comprehensive category or under a general principle. [New Latin *subsumere* : Latin *sub-,* under + *sūmere,* to take up.] —**sub·sum·a·ble** *adj.*

sub·sump·tion (səb-sŭmp'shən) *n.* **1. a.** The act or an instance of subsuming. **b.** Something that is subsumed. **2.** *Logic.* The minor premise of a syllogism. [New Latin *subsumptio* (stem *subsumptiōn-*), from *subsumere,* to SUBSUME.] —**sub·sump·tive** *adj.*

sub·teen (sŭb'tēn') *n.* A child approaching the teenage years. —**sub·teen** *adj.*

sub·tem·per·ate (sŭb'tĕm'pər-ĭt, -tĕm'prĭt) *adj.* Of, pertaining to, or occurring within the colder regions of the Temperate Zones.

sub·ten·ant (sŭb'tĕn'ənt) *n.* One who rents land, a house, or other property from a tenant. —**sub·ten·an·cy** *n.*

sub·tend (səb-tĕnd') *tr.v.* **-tended, -tending, -tends. 1.** *Geometry.* To be opposite to and delimit: *The side of a triangle subtends the opposite angle.* **2.** To underlie so as to enclose or surround. [Latin *subtendere,* to extend beneath : *sub-,* beneath + *tendere,* to extend.]

sub·ter·fuge (sŭb'tər-fyōōj') *n.* An evasive or deceitful tactic used to avoid an unwanted situation or to gain one's ends. —See Synonyms at **artifice.** [French, from Late Latin *subterfugium,* from Latin *subterfugere,* to flee secretly : *subter,* secretly + *fugere,* to flee.]

sub·ter·mi·nal (sŭb'tûr'mə-nəl) *adj.* Coming nearly at the end.

sub·ter·ra·ne·an (sŭb'tə-rā'nē-ən) *adj.* **1.** Situated or operating beneath the earth's surface; underground. **2.** Existing or operating in secret; hidden. [Latin *subterrāneus* : *sub-,* under + *terra,* earth.] —**sub·ter·ra·ne·an·ly** *adv.*

sub·ter·res·tri·al (sŭb'tə-rĕs'trē-əl) *adj.* Subterranean.
~*n.* An animal that lives underground.

sub·text (sŭb'tĕkst') *n.* A message that is not made explicit but may be inferred from a statement or work of art or literature; an underlying meaning: *a political speech with a sinister subtext.*

sub·tile (sŭt'l, sŭb'təl) *adj.* Subtle. —**sub·tile·ly** *adv.* —**sub·tile·ness** *n.*

sub·til·ize (sŭt'l-īz', sŭb'tə-līz') *v.* **-ized, -izing, -izes.** —*tr.* To make subtle. —*intr.* To argue or discuss with subtlety; make fine distinctions. [Medieval Latin *subtīlizāre,* from Latin *subtīlis,* SUBTLE.] —**sub·til·i·za·tion** *n.*

sub·ti·tle (sŭb'tīt'l) *n.* **1.** A secondary and usually explanatory title, as of a literary work. **2. a.** A printed narration or portion of dialogue shown on the screen between the scenes of a silent film. **b.** A printed translation of the dialogue of a foreign-language film shown at the bottom of the screen during the scenes.

sub·tle (sŭt'l) *adj.* **-tler, -tlest. 1. a.** So slight as to be difficult to detect or analyze; elusive. **b.** Not immediately obvious; abstruse. **2.** Fine or delicate: *a subtle flavor.* **3.** Able to make fine distinctions; keen. **4. a.** Characterized by skill or ingenuity; clever. **b.** Marked by deftness or sensitivity: *the subtle approach.* **5. a.** Crafty or sly; devious. **b.** Operating in a hidden and usually injurious way; insidious. [Middle English *sutil, subtil,* thin, fine,

clever, ingenious, from Old French, from Latin *subtīlis,* thin, fine.] —**sub·tle·ness** *n.* —**sub·tly** *adv.*

sub·tle·ty (sŭt'l-tē) *n., pl.* **-ties. 1.** The quality or state of being subtle. **2.** Something subtle; especially, a nicety of thought or a fine distinction. —See Synonyms at **tact.**

sub·ton·ic (sŭb'tŏn'ĭk) *n. Music.* The seventh tone of a diatonic scale, immediately below the tonic.

sub·to·pi·a (sŭb'tō'pē-ə) *n. British.* A suburban area, especially one that has been developed in an unattractive way. Used derogatorily. [*Suburban* + *utopia.*] —**sub·to·pi·an** *adj.*

sub·tor·rid (sŭb'tôr'ĭd, -tŏr'ĭd) *adj.* Subtropical.

sub·to·tal (sŭb'tōt'l) *adj.* Less than total; incomplete.
~*n.* (sŭb'tōt'l). The total of part of a series of numbers.
~*tr.v.* (sŭb'tōt'l) **subtotaled** or **-talled, -taling** or **-talling, -tals.** To add up part of (a series of numbers).

sub·tract (səb-trăkt') *v.* **-tracted, -tracting, -tracts.** —*tr.* To take away; deduct. —*intr.* To perform the arithmetic operation of subtraction. [Latin *substrahere* (past participle *substractus*), to draw away : *sub-,* away + *trahere,* to draw.] —**sub·tract·er** *n.*

sub·trac·tion (səb-trăk'shən) *n.* **1.** The act or process of subtracting; deduction. **2.** The arithmetic process or operation of finding a number or quantity that when added to one of two quantities produces the other.

sub·trac·tive (səb-trăk'tĭv) *adj.* **1.** Producing or involving subtraction. **2.** Designating a color produced by light passing through more than one colorant, each of which inhibits certain wavelengths, as in mixtures of pigments. Compare **additive.** See **primary color. 3.** Designating a photographic process that produces a positive image by superposition or mixing of substances that selectively absorb colored light.

sub·tra·hend (sŭb'trə-hĕnd') *n.* A quantity or number to be subtracted from another. [Latin *subtrahendum,* gerundive of *subtrahere,* to SUBTRACT.]

sub·trop·i·cal (sŭb'trŏp'ĭ-kəl) *adj.* Of, relating to, or being the geographic areas adjacent to the tropics.

sub·trop·ics (sŭb'trŏp'ĭks) *pl.n.* Subtropical regions.

su·bu·late (sōō'byə-lĭt, -lāt', sŭb'yə-) *adj. Biology.* Awl-shaped; tapering to a point. [New Latin *subulatus,* from Latin *sūbula,* awl.]

sub·urb (sŭb'ûrb') *n. Abbr.* **sub. 1.** A usually residential area or community on the edge of a city or large town. **2. suburbs.** The perimeter of country around a major city; environs. [Middle English, from Old French *suburbe,* from Latin *suburbium* : *sub-,* near + *urbs,* city (see **urban**).]

sub·ur·ban (sə-bûr'bən) *adj. Abbr.* **sub. 1.** Of, pertaining to, or characteristic of a suburb or life in a suburb. **2.** Located or residing in a suburb. **3.** Typical of life in the suburbs.
~*n.* A suburbanite.

sub·ur·ban·ite (sə-bûr'bə-nīt') *n.* One who lives in a suburb.

sub·ur·bi·a (sə-bûr'bē-ə) *n.* **1.** Suburbs or suburbanites collectively. **2.** The typical values and lifestyle of suburbanites.

sub·ur·bi·car·i·an (sə-bûr'bĭ-kâr'ē-ən) *adj.* Designating any of the six dioceses surrounding Rome of which the pope is the metropolitan bishop. [Late Latin *suburbicārius,* situated near Rome : *sub-,* near + *urbicārius,* of the city (especially Rome), from Latin *urbicus,* from *urbs,* city (see **urban**).]

sub·ven·tion (səb-vĕn'shən) *n.* **1.** The provision of help, aid, or support. **2.** A grant of financial aid; an endowment or subsidy, as that given by a government to an institution for research. [Middle English *subvencioun,* from Old French *subvention,* from Late Latin *subventiō* (stem *subventiōn-*), from Latin *subvenīre* (past participle *subventus*), to come to help : *sub-,* from below, up + *venīre,* to come.] —**sub·ven·tion·ar·y** (səb-vĕn'shə-nĕr'ē) *adj.*

sub·ver·sion (səb-vûr'zhən, -shən) *n.* **1.** The act of subverting. **2.** The condition of being subverted. **3.** *Obsolete.* A cause of overthrow or ruin. [Middle English *subversioun,* from Old French *subversion,* from Late Latin *subversiō* (stem *subversiōn-*), from Latin *subvertere* (past participle *subversus*), to SUBVERT.] —**sub·ver·sion·ar·y** (səb-vûr'zhə-nĕr'ē, -shə-nĕr'ē) *adj.*

sub·ver·sive (səb-vûr'sĭv, -zĭv) *adj.* Intended or serving to subvert; especially, intended to overthrow or undermine an established government or other institution.
~*n.* One who advocates or is regarded as advocating subversive means or actions. —**sub·ver·sive·ly** *adv.* —**sub·ver·sive·ness** *n.*

sub·vert (səb-vûrt') *tr.v.* **-verted, -verting, -verts. 1.** To destroy completely; ruin: *"schemes to subvert the liberties of a great community"* (Alexander Hamilton). **2.** To undermine the character, morals, or allegiance of; corrupt. **3.** To overthrow completely: *subvert the democratic system.* [Middle English *subverten,* from Old French *subvertir,* from Latin *subvertere,* to turn upside down : *sub-,* from below, up + *vertere,* to turn.] —**sub·vert·er** *n.*

sub·way (sŭb'wā') *n.* **1. a.** An underground urban railroad, usually operated by electricity. **b.** A passage for such a railroad. **2.** An underground tunnel or passage, as for a water main.

sub·ze·ro (sŭb'zîr'ō) *adj.* **1.** Less than zero, especially on a temperature scale. **2.** Of, characterized by, or appropriate for use in temperatures below zero: *subzero nights.*

Su·car·yl (sōō'kə-rĭl) *n.* A trademark for either of two compounds used as low-calorie sweeteners.

suc·ce·da·ne·um (sŭk'sē-dā'nē-əm) *n., pl.* **-nea** (-nē-ə). A substitute. [New Latin, from Latin *succēdāneus,* substituted, "following," from *succēdere,* to SUCCEED.]

suc·ceed (sək-sēd') *v.* **-ceeded, -ceeding, -ceeds.** —*intr.* **1.** To come next in time, order, or sequence; follow after; especially, to replace another in an office or position. Often used with *to*: *succeed to the throne.* **2.** To accomplish something desired or intended: *succeeded in proving his case.* **3.** To turn out well; end favorably. *—tr.* **1.** To follow in time or order; come after. **2.** To replace; follow in office: *succeeded his father as chairman.* —See Synonyms at **follow.** [Middle English *succeden,* from Old French *succeder,* from Latin *succēdere,* to follow closely, go after : *sub-*, toward, next to + *cēdere,* to go.] **—suc·ce·dent** (sək-sēd'nt) *adj.* **—suc·ceed·er** *n.*

suc·cès de scan·dale (sük-sě' də skäɴ-däl') *n.* Acclaim or success accorded something, such as a work of art, purely on the basis of its shocking or scandalous nature. [French, "success of scandal."]

suc·cès d'es·time (sük-sě' dě-stēm') *n.* **1.** Success based on critical acclaim rather than popular appeal. **2.** A work that is admired without necessarily being read, seen, or heard. [French, "success of respect."]

suc·cès fou (sük-sě' fo͞o') *n.* An extraordinary success. [French, "mad success."]

suc·cess (sək-sěs') *n.* **1.** The achievement of something desired, planned, or attempted. **2. a.** The gaining of fame, prosperity, or status. **b.** The extent of such gain. **3.** One that is successful. **4.** *Obsolete.* Any result or outcome. [Latin *successus,* from the past participle of *succēdere,* to SUCCEED.]

suc·cess·ful (sək-sěs'fəl) *adj.* **1.** Having a favorable outcome. **2.** Having obtained something desired or intended. **3.** Having achieved fame, prosperity, or status. **—suc·cess·ful·ly** *adv.*

suc·ces·sion (sək-sěsh'ən) *n.* **1.** The act or process of following in order or sequence. **2.** A group of persons or things arranged or following in order; a sequence. **3. a.** The sequence in which one person after another succeeds to a title, throne, dignity, or estate. **b.** The right of a person or line of persons to so succeed. **c.** The person or line vested with such a right. **4. a.** The act or process of succeeding to the rights or duties of another. **b.** The act or process of becoming entitled as a legal beneficiary to the property of a deceased person. **5.** *Ecology.* The series of changes that take place in a community from its initial colonization of the habitat to formation of a stable **climax community** *(see).* —See Synonyms at **series.** **—in succession.** Following one after another, without interruption. **—suc·ces·sion·al** *adj.* **—suc·ces·sion·al·ly** *adv.*

suc·ces·sive (sək-sěs'ĭv) *adj.* **1.** Following in uninterrupted order or sequence. **2.** Of, characterized by, or involving succession. **—suc·ces·sive·ly** *adv.* **—suc·ces·sive·ness** *n.*

suc·ces·sor (sək-sěs'ər) *n.* One that succeeds another.

suc·ci·nate (sŭk'sə-nāt') *n.* A salt of succinic acid.

suc·cinct (sək-sĭngkt') *adj.* **1.** Clearly expressed in few words; concise. **2.** Characterized by brevity and clarity in speech or writing: *a succinct style.* **3.** *Archaic.* Encircled as if by a girdle; girded. —See Synonyms at **concise.** [Latin *succinctus,* girded, concise, from the past participle of *succingere,* to gird below : *sub-*, below + *cingere,* to gird.] **—suc·cinct·ly** *adv.* **—suc·cinct·ness** *n.*

suc·cin·ic (sək-sĭn'ĭk) *adj.* **1.** Of or relating to amber. **2.** Containing or derived from succinic acid. [French *succinique,* from Latin *succinum,* amber.]

succinic acid *n.* A colorless crystalline compound, $CO_2H(CH_2)_2CO_2H$, occurring naturally in amber and synthesized for use in pharmaceuticals and perfumes; 1, 4-butanedioic acid.

suc·cor (sŭk'ər) *n.* Also *chiefly British* **suc·cour. 1.** Assistance or help in time of distress; relief. **2.** One that affords assistance or relief.

~tr.v. **succored, -coring, -cors.** Also *chiefly British* **succoured, -couring, -cours.** To render assistance to in time of distress. —See Synonyms at **help.** [Middle English *sucurs* (taken as plural), from Old French, from Medieval Latin *succursus,* from Latin, past participle of *succurrere,* to turn to the aid of, run under : *sub-*, under + *currere,* to run.] **—suc·cor·a·ble** *adj.* **—suc·cor·er** *n.*

suc·co·ry (sŭk'ə-rē) *n., pl.* **-ries.** A plant, **chicory** *(see).* [Alteration of Middle English *cicoree,* CHICORY.]

suc·co·tash (sŭk'ə-tăsh') *n.* Kernels of corn and lima beans cooked together. [Narraganset *msíckquatash,* "boiled whole-grain corn (off the cob)" : Proto-Algonquian *mes-* (unattested), whole + *-īnkw-* (unattested), grain + *-etē-* (unattested), heated, cooked + *-wali* (unattested), inanimate plural suffix.]

Suc·coth, Suk·koth (so͝ok'ōt', -əs) *n.* A Jewish harvest festival celebrated for nine days beginning on the eve of the 15th of Tishri. [Hebrew *sukkōth,* "(feast of) booths," (commemorating the temporary shelter of the Jews in the wilderness), from *sukkāh,* booth.]

suc·cu·bus (sŭk'yə-bəs) *n., pl.* **-buses** or **-bi** (-bī'). Also **suc·cu·ba** (-bə), *pl.* **-bae** (-bē', -bī'). **1.** A female demon said to descend upon and have sexual intercourse with a man while he sleeps. Compare **incubus. 2.** Any evil spirit; a demon. [Medieval Latin, from Late Latin *succuba,* prostitute, from Latin *succubāre,* to lie under : *sub-*, under + *cubāre,* to lie.]

suc·cu·lent (sŭk'yə-lənt) *adj.* **1.** Full of juice or sap; juicy. **2.** *Botany.* Having thick, fleshy leaves or stems that conserve moisture. **3.** Desirable or attractive.

~n. A succulent plant, such as a sedum or a cactus. [Latin *succulentus,* from *succus,* juice.] **—suc·cu·lence, suc·cu·len·cy** *n.* **—suc·cu·lent·ly** *adv.*

suc·cumb (sə-kŭm') *intr.v.* **-cumbed, -cumbing, -cumbs. 1.** To yield to an overpowering force or overwhelming desire; give in or give up: *succumb to temptation.* **2.** To die: *succumbed to smallpox.* [Middle English *succomben,* from Old French *succomber,* from Latin *succumbere,* to lie down under : *sub-*, under + *cumbere,* to lie.]

suc·cus·sion (sə-kŭsh'ən) *n.* **1.** The act or process of shaking violently. **2.** The condition of being so shaken. **3.** *Medicine.* The shaking of a patient in order to detect a splashing sound, indicating the presence of fluid in a body cavity, especially the pleural cavity. [Latin *succussiō* (stem *succussiōn-*), from *succutere* (past participle *succussus*), to shake from beneath : *sub-*, beneath + *quatere,* to shake.] **—suc·cus·sa·to·ry** (sə-kŭs'ə-tôr'ē, -tōr'ē) *adj.*

such (sŭch) *adj.* **1.** Of this or that kind: *haven't had such fun in years.* **2.** Being the same as something implied but left undefined or unsaid: *Such people are never satisfied.* **3.** Being of the same quality or kind: *pins, needles, and other such sewing aids.* **4.** Of so extreme or great a degree or quality: *He's such a fool!* **—as such. 1.** As being the person or thing implied or previously mentioned: *A diplomat as such must negotiate.* **2.** In itself or by itself: *Money as such will seldom bring happiness.* **—such as. 1.** For example. **2.** Of the stated or implied kind or degree; like: *a statement such as this.*

~pron. **1.** Such a person or thing or persons or things: *enjoyed the compliment, if it was such.* **2.** Someone or something implied or indicated: *Such are the results of war.* **3.** The like: *papers and such.*

~adv. **1.** To such an extent or degree; so very: *such long hair.* **2.** Very: *has not been in such good health lately.* **3.** In such a manner or way. [Middle English *su(c)ch, swulc,* Old English *swylc, swelc.*]

such and such *adj.* Not named or specified: *They agreed to meet at such and such an hour.*

~pron. An unnamed or unspecified person or thing.

such·like (sŭch'līk') *adj.* Of a similar kind; like.

~pron. Persons or things of such a kind.

Su-chou. See **Suzhou.**

suck (sŭk) *v.* **sucked, sucking, sucks.** *—tr.* **1.** To draw (liquid) into the mouth by tensing muscles in the mouth and drawing in breath. **2. a.** To draw in by establishing a partial vacuum. **b.** To draw in by or as if by a current in a fluid. **c.** To absorb. Often used with *up* or *in.* **3.** To draw liquid or nourishment through or from. **4.** To hold, moisten, or maneuver (a piece of candy, for example) in the mouth, often by making sucking motions. *—intr.* **1.** To draw in by or as if by suction. **2.** To draw nourishment; suckle. **3.** To make a sucking sound or motion. **—suck in. 1.** *Slang.* To take advantage of; cheat; swindle. **2.** To contract and flatten (the abdomen). **—suck up to.** *Slang.* To flatter in order to gain favor.

~n. **1.** The act of sucking. **2.** Suction. **3.** Something drawn in by sucking. [Middle English *s(o)uken,* Old English *sūcan.*]

suck·er (sŭk'ər) *n.* **1.** One that sucks. **2.** *Informal.* One who is easily deceived; a gullible person. **3.** *Informal.* One unable to resist the appeal of something specified: *a sucker for kittens.* **4. a.** A piston or piston valve, as in a suction pump or syringe. **b.** A tube or pipe, such as a siphon, through which something is sucked. **5.** A flat or cup-shaped device, usually made of rubber, that can adhere to a surface by suction. **6.** A lollipop. **7.** Any of numerous chiefly North American freshwater fishes of the family Catostomidae, having a thick-lipped mouth adapted for feeding by suction. **8.** A structure or part adapted for sucking or clinging, as found in certain animals. **9.** *Botany.* A secondary shoot arising from the base of a tree trunk or from the lower part of some plants.

~v. **suckered, -ering, -ers.** *—tr.* **1.** To strip suckers or shoots from. **2.** *Slang.* To take advantage of the gullibility of; fool. *—intr.* To send out suckers or shoots.

suck·er·fish (sŭk'ər-fĭsh') *n., pl.* **-fishes** or collectively **suckerfish.** The **remora** *(see).*

suck·ing (sŭk'ĭng) *adj.* Too young to be weaned.

sucking louse *n.* Any insect of the order Anoplura. See **louse.**

suck·le (sŭk'əl) *v.* **-led, -ling, -les.** *—tr.* **1.** To cause or allow to take milk at the breast or udder; nurse. **2.** To take in as sustenance; have as nourishment. **3.** To bring up; rear; nourish; foster: *suckled in poverty.* *—intr.* To suck at the breast. [Probably back-formation from SUCKLING.] **—suck·ler** *n.*

suck·ling (sŭk'lĭng) *n.* A young mammal or child that has not been weaned. [Middle English : SUCK + -LING.]

Suck·ling (sŭk'lĭng), **Sir John** (1609–42). English poet, courtier, and wit. His works included *Aglaura* (1637), *Session of the Poets* (1637), and *Brennoralt, or The Discontented Colonel* (1640).

su·crase (so͞o'krās', -krāz') *n.* *Chemistry.* **Invertase** *(see).* [French *sucre,* SUGAR + -ASE.]

su·cre (so͞o'krā) *n.* **1.** The basic monetary unit of Ecuador, equal to 100 centavos. See feature at **currency. 2.** A coin worth one sucre. [Spanish, after Antonio José de *Sucre* (1795–1830), South American revolutionary.]

Su·cre (so͞o'krā). City in Bolivia, in a mountain valley on the eastern slope of the Andes at an altitude of 2,590 meters (8,500 feet). It is the legal capital of Bolivia, although the seat of government is La Paz. Sucre has oil refineries and is an agricultural center.

su·crose (so͞o'krōs', -krōz') *n.* A crystalline disaccharide carbohydrate, $C_{12}H_{22}O_{11}$, found in many plants, mainly sugar cane, sugar beet, and maple, and used widely as a sweetener, preservative, and in the manufacture of plastics and cellulose. Also called "sugar," "saccharose." [French *sucre,* SUGAR + -OSE.]

suc·tion (sŭk'shən) *n.* **1.** The act or process of sucking. **2.** The force that causes a fluid or solid to be drawn into an interior space or to adhere to a surface because of the difference between the external and internal pressures.

~adj. Creating or operating by suction. [Late Latin *sūctiō* (stem *sūctiōn-*), from Latin *sūgere* (past participle *sūctus*), to suck.]

suction pump *n.* A pump for drawing up a liquid by means of suction produced by a piston being drawn through a cylinder.

suction stop *n.* *Phonetics.* A **click** *(see).*

suc·to·ri·al (sŭk-tôr′ē-əl, -tōr′ē-əl) *adj. Biology.* **1.** Adapted for sucking or clinging by suction. **2.** Having suctorial organs or parts. [New Latin *sūctōrius,* from Latin *sūgere,* to suck. See **suction.**]

Su·dan¹ (sōō-dăn′, -dän′). Vast region of Africa lying between the Sahara and the tropical forest lands to the south. It stretches from the Atlantic to Ethiopia and Cameroon.

Sudan². The largest country in Africa, in the northeast of the continent. The north is desert or scrubland, and the south is mostly savannah, a vast area suitable only for livestock herding. About 77 percent of the labor force is in agriculture, mostly at subsistence level, and cotton, groundnuts, sesame seed, and hides and skins are the chief exports. Sudan is one of the world's poorest countries, with massive foreign debts. However, its rivers have great potential for irrigation. The country's mineral resources include extensive oil and gas reserves. The area was ruled jointly by Britain and Egypt from 1898 until independence, in 1956. A military coup (1969) brought Gen. Nemery to power, and the civil war (1955–72) between the predominantly Arab north and the black south was ended. Area, 2,503,813 square kilometers (967,500 square miles). Population, 18,700,000. Capital, Khartoum. —**Su·da·nese** (sōō′-n-ēz′, -ēs′) *adj. & n.*

Su·dan·ic (sōō-dăn′ĭk) *n.* The non-Bantu, non-Hamitic languages of the Sudan. —**Su·dan·ic** *adj.*

su·da·to·ri·um (sōō′də-tôr′ē-əm, -tōr′ē-əm) *n., pl.* **-toria** (-tôr′ē-ə, -tōr′ē-ə). A hot-air room used, especially in ancient Rome, for sweat baths. [Latin *sūdātōrium,* from *sūdāre,* to sweat.]

su·da·to·ry (sōō′də-tôr′ē, -tōr′ē) *adj.* Sudorific. —*n., pl.* **sudatories. 1.** A sudatorium. **2.** A sudorific.

sudd (sŭd) *n.* A floating mass of vegetation that often obstructs navigation on the White Nile. [Arabic, obstruction, from *sadda,* to obstruct.]

sud·den (sŭd′n) *adj.* **1.** Happening without warning; unforeseen. **2.** Characterized by hastiness; abrupt or rash. **3.** Characterized by rapidity; swift. —See Usage note at **impetuous.** —**all of a sudden.** Very quickly and unexpectedly; suddenly. [Middle English *sodan(e),* from Norman French *sodein, sudein,* from Late Latin *subitānus,* variant of Latin *subitāneus,* from *subitus,* sudden, past participle of *subīre,* to approach stealthily : *sub-,* secretly + *īre,* to go.] —**sud·den·ly** *adv.* —**sud·den·ness** *n.*

sudden death *n.* **1.** A death that is not preceded by any condition that would appear to be fatal. **2.** *Sports.* **a.** A game played to break a tie. **b.** Extra play added to a tied game and continuing only until one of the teams breaks the tie.

sudden infant death syndrome *n.* Unexplained death, usually during sleep, of an apparently healthy infant. Also called "crib death."

Su·de·ten·land (sōō-dāt′n-lănd′). Border region of northern Czechoslovakia, along the Sudeten Mts. (also called "the Sudetes"). It was transferred from Austria-Hungary to Czechoslovakia (1919) and had a significant proportion of German-speaking inhabitants. The area was granted to Nazi Germany by the Munich Agreement (1938) but together with similar areas of northwestern and south-western Czechoslovakia was returned to Czechoslovakia in 1945. The area's German-speaking populations were subsequently expelled.

Su·de·tes (sōō-dā′tēz). Also **Su·de·ten Mountains** (sōō-dāt′n). A mountain system extending *c.* 298 kilometers (185 miles) along the border between Czechoslovakia and East Germany and Czechoslovakia and Poland.

su·dor·if·er·ous (sōō′də-rĭf′ər-əs) *adj.* Producing or secreting sweat. [Late Latin *sūdōrifer* : Latin *sūdor,* sweat + -FEROUS.]

su·dor·if·ic (sōō′də-rĭf′ĭk) *adj.* Causing or increasing sweat. —*n.* A sudorific medicine. [New Latin *sūdōrificus* : Latin *sūdor,* sweat + -FIC.]

Su·dra (sōō′drə) *n.* **1.** The lowest of the major Hindu castes, originally composed of menials but later largely of artisans and laborers. **2.** A member of this caste. [Sanskrit *śūdra.*]

suds (sŭdz) *pl.n.* **1.** Soapy water containing soap bubbles. **2.** Foam; lather. **3.** *Slang.* Beer. [Possibly from Middle Dutch *sudse,* marsh.] —**suds·y** *adj.*

sue (sōō) *v.* **sued, suing, sues.** —*tr.* **1.** To make a petition to; appeal to; beseech. **2.** To institute legal proceedings against by bringing a civil action, usually for redress of grievances. **3.** *Archaic.* To court; woo. —*intr.* **1.** To institute legal proceedings. **2.** To make an appeal or entreaty. Usually used with *for: sue for mercy.* **3.** *Archaic.* To woo. [Middle English *sewen,* to pursue, prosecute, from Norman French *suer, suire,* from Vulgar Latin *sequere* (unattested), to follow, from Latin *sequī.*] —**su·er** *n.*

Sue (sōō, sü), **Eugène** (1804–57). French novelist. Known for his sensational novels that depicted the sordid side of city life, he was among the first writers to detail the problems associated with the French industrial revolution. Many of his novels, including *Arthur* (1838) and *Les Mystères de Paris* (1842–43), were published serially in newspapers.

suede, suède (swād) *n.* **1.** Leather with a soft napped surface, usually produced by rubbing the flesh side. **2.** Fabric made to resemble this leather. In this sense, also called "suede cloth." [From French *gants de suède,* Swedish gloves.]

su·et (sōō′ĭt) *n.* The hard fat around the kidneys of cattle and sheep, used in cooking and making tallow. [Middle English *sewet,* from Norman French *sewet* (unattested), diminutive of *sue, seu,* from Latin *sēbum,* tallow, suet. See **sebum.**]

Sue·to·ni·us (swĭ-tō′nē-əs), born Gaius Suetonius Tranquillus (c. A.D. 69–140). Roman historian and biographer. His *De Vita Caesarum,* lives of the first 12 Caesars from Julius Caesar to Domitian, survives almost complete.

Su·ez (sōō-ĕz′, sōō′ĕz′). Port in northeastern Egypt, at the northern end of the Gulf of Suez at the entrance to the Suez Canal.

Suez, Isthmus of. The strip of land in northeastern Egypt connecting Asia and Africa and traversed by the Suez Canal.

Suez Canal. A major shipping canal in northeastern Egypt, connecting the Mediterranean Sea with the Red Sea, via the Gulf of Suez. It is 165 kilometers (103 miles) long, and extends from Port Said in the north to Suez in the south. The canal was planned by the French engineer Ferdinand de Lesseps, who also supervised its construction (1859–69). Britain became the largest shareholder in the Suez Canal Company in 1875. In 1888 an international convention proclaimed the free right of transit to all shipping, to be guaranteed by Britain. An agreement of 1954 provided for British evacuation of the zone. In 1956 Gamal Nasser nationalized the canal company, provoking a crisis in which Britain, France, and Israel attacked Egypt but were quickly forced to withdraw due to hostile world opinion. The canal is now under Egyptian control.

suf. suffix.

suff. 1. sufficient. **2.** suffix.

Suff. 1. Suffolk. **2.** suffragan.

suf·fer (sŭf′ər) *v.* **-fered, -fering, -fers.** —*intr.* **1. a.** To feel pain or distress, as after sustaining loss, injury, or punishment. **b.** To be subject to a specified medical condition: *suffers from gout.* **2.** To endure evil, injury, harm, pain, or death. **3.** To appear at a disadvantage: *suffer by comparison.* —*tr.* **1.** To undergo or sustain (something painful, injurious, or unpleasant): *suffer a nasty wound.* **2.** To experience: *suffer a change of heart.* **3.** To endure or bear; stand: *He cannot suffer bores.* **4.** To permit; allow: *"Rulers must not be suffered thus to absolve themselves of their solemn responsibility"* (Macauley). —See Synonyms at **bear.** [Middle English *suff(e)ren,* to undergo, endure, allow, from Norman French *suffrir,* from Vulgar Latin *sufferīre* (unattested), from Latin *sufferre,* to sustain, "to bear up" : *sub-,* up from under + *ferre,* to bear.] —**suf·fer·er** *n.* —**suf·fer·ing·ly** *adv.*

suf·fer·a·ble (sŭf′ər-ə-bəl, sŭf′rə-bəl) *adj.* Capable of being suffered, endured, or permitted; tolerable. —**suf·fer·a·bly** *adv.*

suf·fer·ance (sŭf′ər-əns, sŭf′rəns) *n.* **1.** The capacity to tolerate pain or distress. **2.** Sanction or permission implied or given by failure to prohibit; tacit assent; tolerance. **3.** *Archaic.* Suffering; misery. **4.** *Archaic.* Patient endurance. —**on sufferance.** Out of a reluctant sense of tolerance. [Middle English *suffrance,* from Old French, from Late Latin *sufferentia,* from Latin *sufferre,* to SUFFER.]

suf·fer·ing (sŭf′ər-ĭng, sŭf′rĭng) *n.* **1.** The condition of one who suffers. **2.** The enduring of pain or distress.

suf·fice (sə-fīs′) *v.* **-ficed, -ficing, -fices.** —*intr.* **1.** To meet present needs or requirements; be sufficient: *These supplies will suffice until next week.* **2.** To be capable or competent; be equal to a specified task: *No words will suffice to convey his grief.* —*tr.* To be enough or sufficient for; satisfy the needs or requirements of. —**suffice it.** Let

Suffolk *The Suffolk, also known as Suffolk Punch, is a draft horse about 16 hands high and is always chestnut in color. Every horse of the breed can be traced back to a stallion foaled in 1768.*

SUDAN

EGYPT · Tropic of Cancer
LIBYA
L. Nasser · Wadi Halfa
Nubian Desert · 20°N
Red Sea
30°E
S A H A R A
Port Sudan
C H A D · Merowe · Atbara
Omdurman · Khartoum
KHARTOUM · North
S U D A N
Darfur 3071m · Kosti · Sennar
Nyala
Blue Nile
Nuba · White Nile · 10°N
CENTRAL AFRICAN REPUBLIC
S U D D · ETHIOPIA
Jonglei Canal
KENYA
ZAIRE · UGANDA
Km 0 · 400 · 800
Miles 0 · 200 · 400

it be enough; it is sufficient. Used chiefly in the phrase *suffice it to say.* [Middle English *suffisen,* from Old French *suffire* (present stem *suffis-*), from Latin *sufficere,* to put under, substitute, suffice : *sub-,* under + *facere,* to do, make.] **—suf·fic·er** *n.*

suf·fi·cien·cy (sə-fĭsh'ən-sē) *n.* **1.** The state or quality of being sufficient. **2.** Adequate supplies, ability, numbers, or resources; especially, an adequate but not luxurious standard of living.

suf·fi·cient (sə-fĭsh'ənt) *adj.* **1.** *Abbr.* **suff.** As much as is needed; enough; adequate: *sufficient food for survival.* **2.** *Archaic.* Capable; competent; efficient. [Middle English, from Old French, from Latin *sufficiēns* (stem *sufficient-*), present participle of *sufficere,* to SUFFICE.] **—suf·fi·cient·ly** *adv.*

Synonyms: *sufficient, enough, adequate.* These adjectives mean capable of fulfilling a need or requirement. *Sufficient* and *enough* refer to quantity and usually imply equality with the required amount or a slight excess. *Enough* can also be used ironically to indicate a quantity well in excess of what is desired. *Adequate* refers to both quantity and quality. With respect to quantity, it is approximately equivalent to *sufficient* and *enough* in their primary sense. With reference to quality, *adequate* implies capacity for meeting a modest standard and sometimes for barely meeting it.

sufficient condition *n. Logic.* A condition whose truth guarantees the truth of a proposition or state of affairs. For example, that it has just rained is a sufficient condition for the grass to be wet.

suf·fix (sŭf'ĭks') *n. Abbr.* **suf., suff.** An affix added to the end of a word or stem, serving to form a new word or to form an inflectional ending, as *-ness* in *gentleness, -ing* in *walking,* or *-s* in *sits.*
~tr.v (sŭf'ĭks', sə-fĭks') **suffixed, -fixing, -fixes. 1.** To fix or add at the end; append. **2.** To add as a suffix. [New Latin *suffixum,* from Latin *suffīxus,* neuter past participle of *suffīgere,* to affix, fasten beneath : *sub-,* beneath + *fīgere,* to fix.] **—suf·fix·al** (sŭf'ĭk'səl, sə-fĭk'səl) *adj.* **—suf·fix·ion** (sə-fĭk'shən) *n.*

suf·fo·cate (sŭf'ə-kāt') *v.* **-cated, -cating, -cates.** *—tr.* **1. a.** To kill (a person or animal) by preventing access of oxygen. **b.** To extinguish (a fire, for example) by cutting off a supply of oxygen. **2.** To impair the respiration of; cause a choking sensation in. **3.** To cause discomfort to by or as if by cutting off the supply of air. **4.** To suppress the development, imagination, or creativity of; stifle. *—intr.* **1.** To die through lack of oxygen. **2.** To be stifled; smother. [Latin *suffocāre* : *sub-,* under, down + *faucēs,* throat, FAUCES.] **—suf·fo·ca·tion** *n.* **—suf·fo·ca·tive** *adj.*

Suf·folk[1] (sŭf'ək). *Abbr.* **Suff.** County in East Anglia, England. With low and undulating terrain, it is primarily agricultural. Ipswich, the county town, is the chief industrial center.

Suffolk[2] *n.* **1.** Any of an English breed of hornless sheep producing high-quality mutton. **2.** Any of an English breed of thickset, chestnut-colored draft horses. [After SUFFOLK.]

suf·fra·gan (sŭf'rə-gən) *n. Abbr.* **Suff., Suffr. 1.** A bishop elected or appointed as an assistant to the bishop or ordinary of a diocese, having administrative and episcopal responsibilities but no jurisdictional functions. **2.** Any bishop regarded in his position as subordinate to his archbishop or metropolitan. Also called "suffragan bishop." [Middle English, from Old French, from Medieval Latin *suffrāgāneus,* from *suffrāgium,* SUFFRAGE.] **—suf·fra·gan** *adj.* **—suf·fra·gan·ship** *n.*

suf·frage (sŭf'rĭj) *n.* **1.** The right or privilege of voting; franchise. **2.** The exercise of such a right. **3.** A vote cast in deciding a disputed question or in electing a person to office. **4.** A short intercessory prayer. [Middle English, intercessory prayer, from Old French *suffrage, suffragies,* from Medieval Latin *suffrāgium,* vote, support, prayer, from Latin, ballot, right of voting.]

suf·fra·gette (sŭf'rə-jĕt') *n.* A female advocate of suffrage for women. **—suf·fra·get·tism** *n.*

suf·fra·gist (sŭf'rə-jĭst) *n.* An advocate of the extension of political voting rights, especially to women.

suf·fru·tes·cent (sŭf'ro͞o-tĕs'ənt) *adj.* Also **suf·fru·ti·cose** (sə-fro͞o'tĭ-kōs'). *Botany.* Having a woody stem or base and herbaceous branches; somewhat shrubby. [New Latin *suffrutescens* : SUB- + FRUTESCENT.]

suf·fuse (sə-fyo͞oz') *tr.v.* **-fused, -fusing, -fuses.** To spread through or over: *"The sky above the roof is suffused with deep colors"* (Eugene O'Neill). [Latin *suffundere* (past participle *suffūsus*), to pour underneath or into : *sub-,* underneath + *fundere,* to pour.] **—suf·fu·sion** (sə-fyo͞o'zhən) *n.* **—suf·fu·sive** (sə-fyo͞o'sĭv, -zĭv) *adj.*

Su·fi (so͞o'fē) *n.* A member of a Muslim mystic sect that dates from the 8th century A.D. and developed chiefly in Persia. [Arabic *ṣūfīy,* "(man) of wool," from *ṣūf,* wool (probably from their woolen garments).] **—Su·fic** (so͞o'fĭk), **Su·fis·tic** (so͞o-fĭs'tĭk) *adj.*

Su·fism (so͞o'fĭz'əm) *n.* The beliefs and practices of the Sufis.

sug·ar (sho͝og'ər) *n.* **1.** A sweet crystalline carbohydrate, **sucrose** *(see).* **2.** Any of a class of water-soluble crystalline carbohydrates, including sucrose and lactose, having a characteristically sweet taste. **3.** A particular amount of sugar, as a cube. **4.** Sweetheart; honey. Used as a term of endearment.
~v. **sugared, -aring, -ars.** *—tr.* **1.** To sprinkle or sweeten with sugar. **2.** To make less distasteful or more appealing. *—intr.* **1.** To form sugar; granulate. **2.** To make maple syrup or maple sugar. **—sugar off.** To complete the process of boiling maple sap to yield maple syrup and maple sugar. [Middle English *suker, sugre,* from Old French *sukere, zuchre,* from Italian *zucchero,* from Medieval Latin *zuccarum, succarum,* from Arabic *sukkar,* from Persian *shakar,* from Prakrit *sakkara,* from Sanskrit *śarkarā†,* pebble, gravel, sugar.] **—sug·ar·less** *adj.*

sugar apple *n.* A tree, the **sweetsop** *(see),* or its fruit.

sugar beet *n.* A form of the common beet, *Beta vulgaris,* having white roots from which sugar is obtained.

sug·ar·ber·ry (sho͝og'ər-bĕr'ē) *n., pl.* **-ries.** The **hackberry** *(see).*

sugar bush *n.* A grove of sugar maples used as a source of maple syrup or maple sugar.

sugar cane *n.* A tall grass, *Saccharum officinarum,* native to the East Indies, having thick, tough stems that are one of the chief commercial sources of sugar.

sug·ar-coat (sho͝og'ər-kōt') *tr.v.* **-coated, -coating, -coats. 1.** To coat with sugar. **2.** To cause to seem more appealing or pleasant.

sugar daddy *n. Slang.* A wealthy, usually older man who supports or gives expensive gifts to a young woman in return for sexual favors or companionship.

sug·ared (sho͝og'ərd) *adj.* **1.** Sweetened with sugar. **2.** Made more appealing or pleasant.

sugar gum *n.* An Australian eucalyptus tree, *Eucalyptus cladocalyx,* yielding heavy, yellow-brown timber.

sugaring off *n.* **1.** The process of boiling down maple sap to yield maple syrup and maple sugar. **2.** An informal social gathering in which the guests help make maple sugar.

sugar loaf *n.* **1.** A large conical mass of pure concentrated sugar. **2.** Something resembling a sugar loaf in shape. **—sug·ar-loaf** (sho͝og'ər-lōf') *adj.*

Sugar Loaf Mountain. Peak, 395 meters (1,296 feet) high, overlooking Guanabara Bay in Rio de Janeiro, Brazil. It is a famous symbol of the city.

sugar maple *n.* A maple tree, *Acer saccharum,* of eastern North America, having sap that is the source of maple syrup and maple sugar and yielding a hard wood used in cabinetmaking. Also called "hard maple."

sugar of lead *n.* **Lead acetate** *(see).*

sugar of milk *n.* **Lactose** *(see).*

sugar pea *n.* The **snow pea** *(see).*

sugar pine *n.* A tall evergreen timber tree, *Pinus lambertiana,* of the Pacific coast of North America.

sug·ar·plum (sho͝og'ər-plŭm') *n.* A small piece of sugary candy.

sug·ar·y (sho͝og'ə-rē) *adj.* **-ier, -iest. 1.** Composed of, tasting like, resembling, or containing sugar. **2.** Deceitfully or cloyingly sweet. **—sug·ar·i·ness** *n.*

sug·gest (səg-jĕst', sə-jĕst') *tr.v.* **-gested, -gesting, -gests. 1.** To offer for consideration or action; propose. **2.** To bring or call to mind by logic or association; evoke. **3.** To make evident indirectly; intimate; imply. **4.** To serve as or provide a motive for; prompt: *Such a crime suggests apt punishment.* [Latin *suggerere* (past participle *suggestus*), to carry or put underneath, furnish, suggest : *sub-,* underneath + *gerere,* to carry.] **—sug·gest·er** *n.*

Synonyms: *suggest, imply, hint, intimate, insinuate.* These verbs mean to impart thoughts or ideas by indirection. *Suggest,* in this context, usually refers to a process whereby something is called to mind by a listener or viewer as the result of an association of ideas or train of thought. *Imply* refers to conveying an unstated or indirectly stated thought as part of something otherwise more explicit. The implied, or secondary, part is deduced as a seemingly logical consequence of the whole. *Hint* refers to expression that is indirect but contains rather pointed clues. *Intimate* applies to veiled expression that may be the result of discretion or reserve. *Insinuate* refers to covert expression of something, usually unpleasant, in a manner that suggests underhandedness..

sug·gest·i·bil·i·ty (səg-jĕs'tə-bĭl'ə-tē, sə-jĕs'-) *n.* Responsiveness or susceptibility to suggestion.

sug·gest·i·ble (səg-jĕs'tə-bəl, sə-jĕs'-) *adj.* Readily influenced by suggestion.

sug·ges·tion (səg-jĕs'chən, sə-jĕs'-) *n.* **1.** The act of suggesting. **2.** Something suggested; an idea or proposal. **3.** A trace or slight indication. **4. a.** The psychological process by which an idea is induced in or adopted by an individual without argument, command, or coercion. **b.** Any idea or response so induced. **5.** The thought process by which one idea or concept leads to another.

sug·ges·tive (səg-jĕs'tĭv, sə-jĕs'-) *adj.* **1. a.** Tending to suggest thoughts or ideas. **b.** Conveying a hint or suggestion; indicative. **2.** Tending to suggest something sexually improper or indecent. **—sug·ges·tive·ly** *adv.* **—sug·ges·tive·ness** *n.*

Su·har·to (sə-här'tō, so͞o-) (1921–). Indonesian general and statesman. He assumed power (1967) after the downfall of Sukarno and was confirmed as president (1968). He adopted a peaceful policy toward Malaysia while suppressing all opposition.

Sui (swā). Chinese dynasty that ruled from 581–618.

su·i·cid·al (so͞o'ĭ-sīd'l) *adj.* **1. a.** Pertaining to, involving, or related to suicide. **b.** Showing a disposition to commit suicide. **2.** Dangerous to oneself or to one's interests; self-destructive; ruinous. **—su·i·cid·al·ly** *adv.*

su·i·cide (so͞o'ĭ-sīd') *n.* **1.** The act or an instance of intentionally killing oneself. **2.** The destruction or ruin of one's own interests. **3.** One who commits suicide.
~adj. Involving suicide or extreme danger: *a suicide mission.*
~v. **suicided, -ciding, -cides.** *—intr.* To commit suicide. *—tr.* To kill (oneself). [New Latin *suicida* (person), *suicidium* (act) : Latin *suī,* of oneself + -CIDE.]

su·i gen·er·is (so͞o'ī' jĕn'ər-ĭs, so͞o'ē) *adj.* Unique; individual. [Latin, "of its own kind."]

su·i ju·ris (so͞o'ī' jo͝or'ĭs, so͞o'ē) *adj. Law.* Capable of managing one's own affairs. [Latin, "of one's own right."]

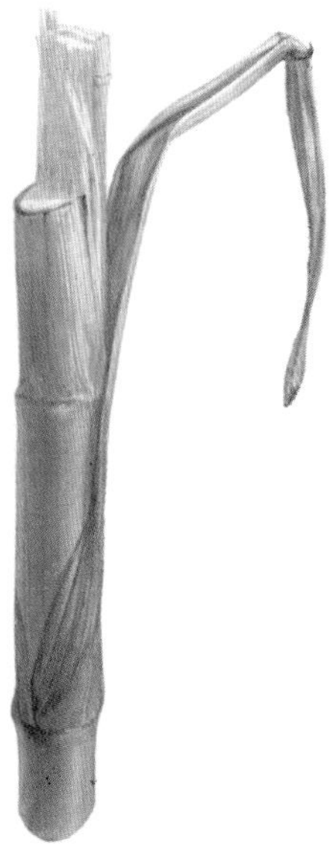

sugar cane *One of the bamboo family grown in tropical and subtropical regions around the world. Juice from the cane is boiled to remove the water and produce grains of sugar.*

su·int (sōō′ĭnt, swĭnt) *n.* A natural grease formed from dried perspiration found in the fleece of sheep, used as a source of potash. [French, from Old French *suer,* to sweat, from Latin *sūdāre.*]

Suisse. See **Switzerland.**

Sui·sun Bay (sə-sōōn′). The eastern arm of San Francisco Bay, in western California.

suit (sōōt) *n.* **1. a.** A set of outer garments consisting of a coat and trousers or skirt, and sometimes a vest, that match in color and fabric or that have been designed to be worn together. **b.** A garment or set of clothes designed to be worn for a specified purpose or as a fashionable outfit. Often used in combination: *a gym suit.* **2.** Any group of things united into a set or series by having a common form or function. **3.** Any of the four sets of 13 playing cards (spades, hearts, diamonds, and clubs), each with similar markings, that constitute a deck. **4. a.** *Law.* An act or instance of suing in court, usually to recover a right or claim; a lawsuit. **b.** An act of pleading; a request. **5.** The act or an instance of courting a woman. **—follow suit. 1.** To play a card of the same suit as the one led. **2.** To do as another has done; follow an example. ~*v.* **suited, suiting, suits.** —*tr.* **1.** To meet the requirements of; accommodate: *This candidate does not suit our needs.* **2. a.** To make appropriate or suitable; adapt: *We can suit the building to your specifications.* **b.** To be appropriate or suitable for; go well with: *Does the climate suit you?* **3.** To please; satisfy. **4.** *Archaic.* To dress. —*intr.* To be suitable or acceptable. **—suit oneself.** To do as one pleases in a given circumstance. [Middle English *su(i)te,* attendance at a sheriff's court, litigation, uniform, garb, from Old French *siute, suite,* from Vulgar Latin *sequita* (unattested), pursuit, from *sequere* (unattested), to follow. See **sue.**]

suit·a·ble (sōō′tə-bəl) *adj.* Appropriate to a given purpose or occasion; fitting. **—See Synonyms at fit. —suit·a·bil·i·ty, suit·a·ble·ness** *n.* **—suit·a·bly** *adv.*

suit·case (sōōt′kās′) *n.* A usually rectangular and flat piece of luggage having a handle and used for carrying personal belongings and clothing.

suite (swēt; *also* sōōt *for sense 3*) *n.* **1.** A succession of related things intended to be used together. **2.** A series of connected rooms used as a living unit. **3.** A set of matched furniture pieces. **4.** *Music.* **a.** A 17th- and 18th-century instrumental composition consisting of a number of movements in dance form. **b.** A modern instrumental composition consisting of a number of movements. **5.** A staff of attendants or a train of followers; a retinue. [French, from Old French *sieute,* following, retinue, from Vulgar Latin *sequita* (unattested). See **suit.**]

suit·ing (sōō′tĭng) *n.* Fabric from which suits are made.

suit·or (sōō′tər) *n.* **1.** A person who makes a petition or request. **2.** A person who sues in a court of law; a plaintiff; a petitioner. **3.** A man who is in the process of courting a woman. [Middle English *suitor,* from Norman French, follower, from Latin *secūtor,* from *sequī* (past participle *secūtus*), to follow.]

Su·kar·no (sōō-kär′nō), **Achmed** (1901–70). Indonesian statesman and first president of Indonesia (1945–67). He assumed dictatorial powers (1960) but was forced to relinquish power (1967) by the army.

Sukarno, Mount. See **Jaya Peak.**

su·ki·ya·ki (sōō′kē-yä′kē, skē-yä′kē) *n.* A Japanese dish consisting of sliced meat, vegetables, and bean curd seasoned with soy sauce and fried together. [Japanese.]

Sukkoth. Variant of **Succoth.**

Sulawesi. See **Celebes.**

sul·cate (sŭl′kāt′) *adj. Biology.* Having narrow longitudinal indentations; grooved. [Latin *sulcātus,* past participle of *sulcāre,* to furrow, from *sulcus,* furrow, SULCUS.]

sul·cus (sŭl′kəs) *n., pl.* **-ci** (-kī′, -sī′). **1.** A narrow, deep furrow or groove. **2.** *Anatomy.* Any of the narrow fissures separating adjacent cerebral convolutions. [Latin *sulcus,* furrow, groove.]

Su·lei·man I (sōō′lā-män′), known as "the Magnificent" (c. 1494–1566). Turkish sultan. He brought the Ottoman Empire to its peak, improved the administration of the country, and encouraged the arts and sciences.

sulf-, sulfo- *prefix.* Indicates sulfur; for example, **sulfide, sulfone.** *Note:* The spellings *sulph-* and *sulpho-* are no longer admitted by scientific publications. [From SULFUR.]

sul·fa·di·a·zine (sŭl′fə-dī′ə-zēn′) *n.* A sulfa drug, $C_{10}H_{10}N_4O_2S$, used in the treatment of various bacterial infections. [SULFA (DRUG) + DIAZINE.]

sul·fa drug (sŭl′fə) *n.* Any of a group of sulfonamide compounds, such as sulfathiazole and sulfadiazine, capable of inhibiting bacterial growth and activity and used to treat a wide variety of infections. [SULFA(NILAMIDE) + DRUG.]

sul·fa·nil·a·mide (sŭl′fə-nĭl′ə-mīd′) *n.* A white odorless crystalline sulfonamide, $H_2N.C_6H_4.SO_2NH_2$, used in the treatment of various bacterial infections. [SULF- + ANIL(INE) + AMIDE.]

sul·fate (sŭl′fāt′) *n.* A chemical compound containing the bivalent group SO_4. ~*v.* **sulfated, -fating, -fates.** —*tr.* **1.** To treat or react with sulfuric acid or a sulfate. **2.** *Electricity.* To cause lead sulfate to form on (the plates of a lead-acid storage battery). —*intr.* To become sulfated. [French : SULF- + -ATE.]

sul·fa·thi·a·zole (sŭl′fə-thī′ə-zōl′) *n.* A sulfa drug, $C_9H_9N_3O_2S_2$, used to treat a variety of bacterial infections.

sul·fide (sŭl′fīd′) *n.* A compound of bivalent sulfur with an electropositive element or group, usually a metal. [SULF- + -IDE.]

sul·fite (sŭl′fīt′) *n.* A salt or ester of sulfurous acid. [French, variant of SULFATE.] **—sul·fit·ic** (sŭl-fĭt′ĭk) *adj.*

sulfon– *prefix.* Indicates: **1.** Sulfonic; for example, **sulfonamide. 2.** Sulfonyl; for example, **sulfonmethane.** [From SULFONE.]

sul·fon·a·mide (sŭl-fŏn′ə-mīd′, -mĭd) *n.* Any of a group of organic sulfur compounds having the general formula RSO_2NH_2. The group includes the sulfa drugs.

sul·fo·nate (sŭl′fə-nāt′) *n.* A compound in which a hydrogen atom is replaced by the sulfonic acid group SO_2OH. ~*tr.v.* **sulfonated, -nating, -nates. 1.** To introduce one or more sulfonic-acid groups into (an organic compound), as by treating with concentrated sulfuric acid. **2.** To treat with sulfonic acid. [SULFON- + -ATE.] **—sul·fo·na·tion** *n.*

sul·fone (sŭl′fōn′) *n.* Any of various organic sulfur compounds having a sulfonyl group, -SO₂, attached to two carbon atoms, especially such a compound used to treat leprosy and tuberculosis. [SULF- + ONE.]

sul·fon·ic (sŭl-fŏn′ĭk) *adj.* Of or relating to the chemical group SO_3H.

sulfonic acid *n.* Any of several organic acids containing one or more sulfonic groups, -SO₂OH.

sul·fon·meth·ane (sŭl′fŏn-mĕth′ān′) *n.* A colorless crystalline or powdered compound, $C_7H_{16}S_2O_4$, used as a hypnotic.

sul·fo·nyl (sŭl′fə-nĭl′) *n.* The bivalent radical SO_2. Also called "sulfuryl." [SULFON- + -YL.]

sul·fur (sŭl′fər) *n.* Also **sul·phur.** *Symbol* **S** A pale-yellow nonmetallic element occurring widely in nature both free and combined in several allotropic forms. It is used in black gunpowder, rubber vulcanization, the manufacture of insecticides and pharmaceuticals, and in the preparation of important sulfur compounds, such as sulfuric acid. Atomic number 16, atomic weight 32.064, melting point (rhombic) 112.8°C, (monoclinic) 119.0°C, boiling point 444.6°C, specific gravity (rhombic) 2.07, (monoclinic) 1.957, valences 2, 4, 6. Also *obsolete* "brimstone." *Note:* The spelling *sulphur* is no longer admitted by scientific publications. However, it may occur in nonscientific contexts, especially when the reference is not directly to the element. See the entries beginning **sulphur.** [Middle English *sulphre,* from Latin *sulpur, sulfur†.*]

sul·fu·rate (sŭl′fə-rāt′, -fyə-rāt′) *tr.v.* **-rated, -rating, -rates.** To treat or combine with sulfur. [Late Latin *sulfurāre,* from Latin *sulpur, sulfur,* SULFUR.] **—sul·fu·ra·tion** *n.*

sulfur bacteria *pl.n.* Bacteria of the order Beggiatoales, which derive their energy from the oxidation of sulfides.

sulfur dioxide *n.* A colorless, extremely irritating gas or liquid, SO_2, used in many industrial processes, especially the manufacture of sulfuric acid. When dissolved in water it forms sulfurous acid.

sul·fu·re·ous (sŭl-fyōōr′ē-əs) *adj.* Sulfurous.

sul·fu·ret (sŭl′fə-rĕt′, -fyə-rĕt′) *tr.v.* **-reted** or **-retted, -reting** or **-retting, -rets.** To sulfurize. ~*n.* A sulfide. [New Latin *sulfuretum,* sulfide, from Latin *sulpur, sulfur,* SULFUR.]

sul·fu·ric (sŭl-fyōōr′ĭk) *adj.* Of, relating to, or containing sulfur, especially with valence 6.

sulfuric acid *n.* A highly corrosive, dense oily liquid, H_2SO_4, colorless to dark brown depending on purity, used to manufacture a variety of chemicals and materials including fertilizers, dyestuffs, paints, detergents, and explosives. Also called "oil of vitriol."

sul·fur·ize (sŭl′fə-rīz′, -fyə-rīz′) *tr.v.* **-ized, -izing, -izes. 1.** To treat or impregnate with sulfur; sulfuret. **2.** To bleach or fumigate with sulfur or sulfur dioxide. **—sul·fur·i·za·tion** *n.*

sul·fur·ous (sŭl′fər-əs, sŭl-fyōōr′əs) *adj.* **1.** Of, relating to, derived from, or containing sulfur, especially in its lower valence, 4. **2.** Characteristic of or emanating from burning sulfur. **3.** Fiery.

sulfurous acid *n.* A colorless solution of sulfur dioxide in water, H_2SO_3, characterized by a suffocating sulfurous odor, used as a bleaching agent, preservative, and disinfectant.

sulfur trioxide *n.* A corrosive compound, SO_3, having three solid forms that may coexist in a given sample, used in the sulfonation of organic compounds.

sul·fur·yl (sŭl′fə-rĭl′, -fyə-rĭl′) *n.* Sulfonyl (see).

sulfuryl chloride *n.* A colorless liquid, SO_2Cl_2, having a pungent odor, used as a chlorinating and dehydrating agent and solvent and in the manufacture of pharmaceuticals and dyestuffs.

sulk (sŭlk) *intr.v.* **sulked, sulking, sulks.** To be sullenly aloof or withdrawn, as in silent protest. ~*n.* A mood or display of sulking: *in a sulk; a case of the sulks.* [Back-formation from SULKY.]

sulk·y¹ (sŭl′kē) *adj.* **-ier, -iest. 1.** Sullenly aloof or withdrawn. **2.** Gloomy; dismal: *sulky weather.* [Perhaps from obsolete *sulke,* hard to sell.] **—sulk·i·ly** *adv.* **—sulk·i·ness** *n.*

sulky² *n., pl.* **-ies.** A light two-wheeled vehicle accommodating one person and drawn by one horse. [From SULKY (because it has only one seat for the driver).]

Sul·la (sŭl′ə), **Lucius Cornelius** (138–78 B.C.). Roman general. After a successful military career, he proclaimed himself dictator (82–79). He tried to reorganize Roman politics, but his influence did not long survive his retirement.

sul·lage (sŭl′ĭj) *n.* **1.** Silt deposited by a current of water. **2.** Sewage. [Probably from Old French *souiller,* to SOIL.]

sul·len (sŭl′ən) *adj.* **1.** Showing a brooding ill humor or a tendency to silent gloom and resentment; glumly bad-tempered; morose. **2.** Gloomy or somber in tone, color, or portent: *a sullen sky.* [Middle English *solein, solain,* from Norman French *solein* (unattested) alone, sullen, from Old French *seul, sol,* alone, single, from Latin *sōlus.*] **—sul·len·ly** *adv.* **—sul·len·ness** *n.*

Sul·li·van (sŭl′ə-vən), **Sir Arthur Seymour** (1842–1900). British composer. He is best known for his collaboration with W.S. Gilbert in light operas that include *H.M.S. Pinafore* (1878), *The Mikado* (1885), and *The Gondoliers* (1889).

Sullivan, John L(awrence) (1858–1918). U.S. boxer. He won (1882) the heavyweight championship by defeating Paddy Ryan in a bare-knuckles fight.

Sullivan, Louis Henri (1856–1924). U.S. architect. His experimental use of steel frames for the construction of skyscrapers earned him the title Father of Modernism. His famous dictum, "Form follows function," influenced many architects, notably his student Frank Lloyd Wright.

sul·ly (sŭl′ē) *tr.v.* **-lied, -lying, -lies.** 1. To mar the cleanness or luster of; soil; stain. 2. To defile; tarnish.
~*n., pl.* **sullies.** *Archaic.* Something that sullies; a stain or spot. [Probably from Old French *souiller,* to SOIL.]

Sul·ly (sŭl′ē, sü-lē′), **Maximilien de Béthune, Duc de** (1560–1641). French statesman. As finance minister (1598–1610) to Henry IV, he replenished the treasury and encouraged agriculture and industry.

Sul·ly (sŭl′ē), **Thomas** (1783-1871). British-born American painter of portraits and historical scenes such as *Washington's Passage of the Delaware.* He also wrote a treatise on painting, *Hints to Young Portrait Painters* (1873, reprinted 1965).

Sul·ly-Pru·dhomme (sü-lē′prü-dôm′), **René François Armand** (1839-1907). French poet. His early works are melancholic, while his later poems are concerned with scientific and philosophic theories. He won the Nobel Prize in literature (1901).

sulph-, sulpho-. See **sulf-.**

sulphur. Variant of **sulfur.** Not in scientific use.

sul·phur-bot·tom (sŭl′fər-bŏt′əm) *n.* The **blue whale** *(see).*

sulphur butterfly *n.* Any of various butterflies of the genus *Colias* and related genera, having yellow or orange wings marked with black.

sul·tan (sŭl′tən) *n.* The ruler of a Muslim country, especially of the former Ottoman Empire. [Middle French, from Medieval Latin *sultānus,* from Arabic *sulṭān,* ruler, from Aramaic *shulṭānā,* "power," from *shəlēṭ,* to have power.]

sul·tan·a (sŭl-tăn′ə, -tä′nə) *n.* 1. The wife, mother, sister, or daughter of a sultan. Also called "sultaness." 2. The mistress of a sultan, king, or prince. 3. A small, yellow, seedless raisin of a kind originally produced in Asia Minor. [Italian, feminine of *sultano,* sultan, from Arabic *sulṭān,* SULTAN.]

sul·tan·ate (sŭl′tə-nāt′) *n.* 1. The office, power, or reign of a sultan. 2. The domain of a sultan.

sul·try (sŭl′trē) *adj.* **-trier, -triest.** 1. Very hot and humid. 2. Sensual; voluptuous: *a sultry Spanish dance.* [From obsolete *sulter,* variant of SWELTER.] **—sul·tri·ly** *adv.* **—sul·tri·ness** *n.*

Su·lu (soo′loo) *n., pl.* **-lus** or collectively **Sulu.** 1. A Moro people inhabiting the Sulu Archipelago. 2. A member of this people. 3. The Austronesian language spoken by this people. [Sulu *sulug,* "current."] **—Su·lu·an** *adj. & n.*

Su·lu Archipelago (soo′loo). A group of islands, 2,813 square kilometers (1,086 square miles) in area, in the western Pacific Ocean, constituting the extreme southern province of the Republic of the Philippines.

Su·lu Sea (soo′loo). The section of the western Pacific Ocean between the central Philippines and Borneo.

sum (sŭm) *n.* 1. The amount obtained as a result of adding. 2. The whole amount, quantity, or number: *the sum of our knowledge.* 3. An amount of money: *paid a large sum.* 4. An arithmetic problem: *good at sums.* 5. A summary: gist.
~*v.* **summed, summing, sums.** *—tr.* 1. To restate briefly; summarize. 2. To find the total of by adding. *—intr.* To add up; amount.
—sum up. 1. To summarize; recapitulate briefly. 2. To form a judgment about and then outline succinctly: *summed up his character.* [Middle English *summe, somme,* from Old French, from Latin *summa,* from *summus,* highest.]

su·mac, su·mach (soo′măk′, shoo′-) *n.* 1. Any of various small trees, shrubs, or vines of the genus *Rhus.* Some species, such as **poison ivy** *(see),* cause an acute itching rash on contact. 2. The dried and powdered leaves of some *Rhus* species, especially *R. coraria,* used in tanning and dyeing. [Middle English, from Old French, from Arabic *summaq,* sumach tree, probably from Aramaic, "red."]

Su·ma·tra (soo-mä′trə). The westernmost and second-largest island of Indonesia. A volcanic range, which rises to 3,805 meters (12,483 feet), extends along the west coast, and the east is swampland, with dense rain forests in the interior. Sumatra has reserves of oil, natural gas, coal, and silver. Rubber, coffee, tea, and pepper are among the chief farm products. A Dutch colony from 1816, Sumatra was included in the new republic of Indonesia after World War II. **—Su·ma·tran** *adj. & n.*

Su·mer (soo′mər). The southern part of ancient Mesopotamia, the site of one of the world's oldest known civilizations, dating back to the 5th millenium B.C. The Sumerians, who spoke a non-Semitic language, are credited with the invention of the cuneiform system of writing, wheeled vehicles, and the plow. By the 3rd millennium a number of city-states had grown up on the alluvial plains of the lower Tigris and Euphrates, among them Kish, Uruk, and Ur. Sumer was overrun by Akkad (c. 2300 B.C.) and was briefly revived by the third dynasty at Ur (c. 2100 B.C.). The civilization declined after

Amorite invasions (c. 2000 B.C.) and was later absorbed into the empires of Babylon and Assyria.

Su·me·ri·an (soo-mîr′ē-ən, -mĕr′ē-ən) *adj.* Of or pertaining to ancient Sumer, its people, culture, or language.
~*n.* 1. A member of an ancient Babylonian people of Sumer. 2. The language of the Sumerians, of no known linguistic affiliation.

sum·ma cum lau·de (soom′ə koom lou′də, sŭm′ə kŭm lô′dē) *adv.* With the greatest praise. Used on university and college diplomas to designate the highest degree of academic distinction. Compare **cum laude, magna cum laude.** [Latin.]

sum·ma·rize (sŭm′ə-rīz′) *tr.v.* **-rized, -rizing, -rizes.** To make a summary of; abstract. **—sum·ma·rist** (sŭm′ər-ĭst), **sum·ma·riz·er** *n.* **—sum·ma·ri·za·tion** *n.*

sum·ma·ry (sŭm′ə-rē) *adj.* 1. Presenting the substance in a condensed form; concise. 2. Performed speedily and without ceremony: *summary justice.* 3. *Law.* Of or pertaining to the right of a court to try or judge a case without a jury: *summary jurisdiction.* **—See Synonyms at concise.**
~*n., pl.* **summaries.** A condensation of the substance of a larger work; an abstract or abridgment containing the main or important points. [Middle English, from Medieval Latin *summarius,* comprising the principal parts, from Latin *summa,* SUM.] **—sum·mar·i·ly** (sə-mâr′ə-lē) *adv.* **—sum·ma·ri·ness** *n.*

summary court-martial *n.* A court-martial consisting of one commissioned officer for trying relatively minor offenses.

sum·ma·tion (sə-mā′shən) *n.* 1. The act or process of adding or totaling; addition. 2. A sum or aggregate. 3. A concluding statement containing a summary of principal points, especially as made by the opposing attorneys in a trial. [Medieval Latin *summātiō* (stem *summātiōn-*), from *summāre,* to sum up, from Latin *summa,* SUM.]

sum·mer¹ (sŭm′ər) *n.* 1. The usually warmest season of the year, occurring between spring and autumn. In the Northern Hemisphere it extends from the summer solstice to the autumnal equinox and is popularly considered to comprise June, July, and August, while in the Southern Hemisphere it falls between the winter solstice and the vernal equinox or, popularly, December, January, and February. 2. Any period regarded as a time of warmth, fruition, fulfillment, happiness, or beauty.
~*adj.* Pertaining to, characteristic of, or occurring in summer.
~*v.* **summered, -mering, -mers.** *—tr.* To lodge or keep during the summer. *—intr.* To pass the summer. [Middle English *somer, sumer,* Old English *sumor.*] **—sum·mer·ly** *adj. & adv.*

summer² *n. Architecture.* 1. A heavy horizontal timber that serves as a supporting beam, especially for the floor above. 2. A lintel. 3. A large, heavy stone usually set on the top of a column or pilaster to support an arch or lintel. [Middle English *summer, somer,* from Norman French *sumer, somer,* "pack animal," from Vulgar Latin *saumārius* (unattested), variant of Late Latin *sagmārius,* from *sagma,* packsaddle, from Greek. See **sumpter.**]

summer cypress *n.* A plant, *Kochia scoparia,* native to Eurasia, having dense foliage that turns bright red in autumn. Also called "burning bush."

sum·mer·house (sŭm′ər-hous′) *n.* A small, roofed structure in a park or garden affording shade and rest; a gazebo.

summer lightning *n.* **Heat lightning** *(see).*

summersault, summerset. Variants of **somersault.**

summer savory *n.* A plant, **savory** *(see).*

summer school *n.* An academic session held during the summer.

summer solstice *n. Astronomy.* A **solstice** *(see).*

summer squash *n.* Any of several varieties of squash, such as the crookneck, that are eaten shortly after being picked rather than kept for storage.

summer stock *n.* The theatrical productions of stock companies presented during the summer.

sum·mer·time (sŭm′ər-tīm′) *n.* The summer season.

sum·mer·wood (sŭm′ər-wood′) *n.* Wood that develops during the latter part of the growing season and is harder and less porous than springwood. Compare **springwood.**

sum·mer·y (sŭm′ə-rē) *adj.* Pertaining to or suggesting summer.

sum·ming-up (sŭm′ĭng-ŭp′) *n.* The act or declaration of a person who sums up; especially, an attorney's summation in a trial.

sum·mit (sŭm′ĭt) *n.* 1. The highest point or part; the top, especially of a mountain. 2. The highest degree of achievement or status. 3. The highest level, especially of government. 4. A conference involving heads of government and sometimes leading government ministers. Also used adjectivally: *summit talks.* [Middle English *somette,* from Old French *sommette, sumet,* diminutive of *som, sum,* top, from Latin *summum,* neuter of *summus,* highest, topmost.]

Synonyms: *summit, peak, pinnacle, acme, apex, zenith, climax.* Each of these nouns is applicable to the highest point of a thing, physically or figuratively. *Summit* and *peak* refer literally to the top, as of a hill or mountain. Figuratively *summit* suggests the highest level attainable, and *peak* the highest point of achievement. *Pinnacle* refers to a tall, slender mass, such as a spire, that tapers to a point or figuratively, to a height reached by spectacular achievement. *Acme* is used figuratively, for the most part, to represent perfection. *Apex* is applied to the pointed tip or top of a figure, such as a cone, and figuratively to the focal point or culmination of any concerted effort. *Zenith* is that point in the heavens directly overhead or, by extension, the point of highest achievement, development, or power. *Climax* usually refers to the point of greatest development or intensity, marking the end of an ascending process.

sun

A THERMONUCLEAR FURNACE IN THE SKY

The closest star is our lifeline to the universe

Our sun is a vast globe of incandescent gas that provides the light and heat upon which all life on earth depends. In the universe, however, it is merely an average star and it seems so large and bright compared with other stars simply because it is so much closer.

Although the sun has a mass 330,000 times greater than that of the earth, it would have burned out millions of years ago if it blazed in the same way as wood or coal. In fact, the sun generates its power by the fusion process in which energy is created as the 15,000,000°C (27,000,000°F) heat at its core turns hydrogen gas into helium. It will continue radiating more energy per second than man has ever used for many eons to come.

THE STRUCTURE OF THE SUN

Radiation zone Heat travels outward from atom to atom, by radiation

The core A nuclear furnace converting hydrogen to helium at 15,000,000°C (27,000,000°F)

Photosphere Visible surface of the sun

Convection zone Heat rises in large gas masses, by convection

Sunspot A path of cooler gas on the surface

Chromosphere A layer of gas 1,600 – 4,800 kilometers (1,000 – 3,000 miles) thick

Solar prominence An arch of incandescent gas

Corona Outermost halo of light around the sun, extending millions of miles into space

Solar flare A violent eruption of energy

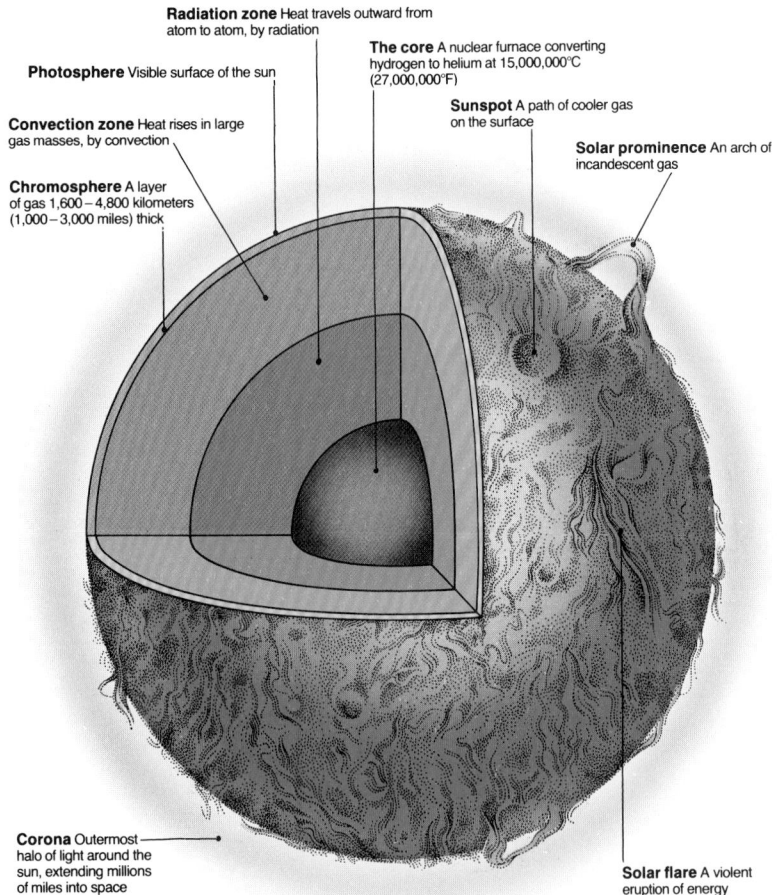

The sun is a nuclear reactor with a dense, intensely hot core that gives out most of its energy in the form of x-rays, which seep out to heat the surrounding material. By the time it reaches the surface the radiation has given way to convection. It takes about 30 million years for light generated in the core to reach the earth.

Escaping energy makes the outer region of the sun seethe and gyrate. Some of the gigantic flares that shoot out in this dramatic boiling-off process can dwarf the planet earth.

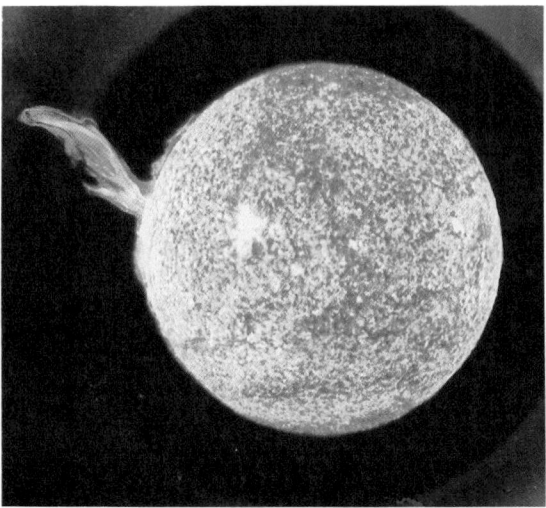

sum·mon (sŭm′ən) *tr.v.* **-moned, -moning, -mons.** **1.** To call together; convene. **2.** To send for; request to appear. **3.** To order (a person) to appear in court by the issue of a summons. **4.** To do a specified act: *summon the captain to surrender.* **5.** To call forth; rouse; muster. Often used with *up: He summoned up a smile.* [Middle English *somo(u)nen,* from Old French *somondre,* from Vulgar Latin *summonere* (unattested), from Latin *summonēre,* to remind secretly : *sub-,* secretly + *monēre,* to remind, warn.]

sum·mon·er (sŭm′ə-nər) *n.* **1.** A person who summons. **2.** Formerly, a court official who served summonses.

sum·mons (sŭm′ənz) *n., pl.* **-monses.** **1.** A call or order to appear or to do something. **2.** *Law.* An official order summoning a defendant or witness to report to a court. *~tr.v.* **summonsed, -monsing, -monses.** To serve a court summons to. [Middle English *somo(u)ns,* from Old French *som(o)unse,* from Gallo-Roman *summonsa* (unattested), from Latin *summonita,* from the feminine past participle of *summonēre,* to remind secretly, SUMMON.]

sum·mum bo·num (soŏm′əm bō′nəm) *n.* The greatest or supreme good. [Latin.]

Sum·ner (sŭm′nər), **Charles** (1811–74). U.S. politician. A Republican U.S. senator from Massachusetts (1851–74), he was an accomplished orator whose uncompromising stand against slavery and sustained efforts to bring about its abolition were a significant force in the political struggle for the emancipation of slaves.

su·mo (soŏ′mō) *n.* A Japanese form of wrestling in which the object is to make one's opponent touch the ground with his body or to force him out of the ring. [Japanese *sumō.*]

sump (sŭmp) *n.* **1.** The crankcase or oil reservoir of an internal-combustion engine. **2. a.** Any low area that receives drainage. **b.** A cesspool. **3.** A hole at the lowest point of a mine shaft into which water is drained to be pumped out. [Middle English *sompe,* a swamp, morass, from Middle Low German or Middle Dutch *sump.*]

sump·ter (sŭmp′tər) *n.* A pack animal. [Middle English *sumpter,* driver of a pack animal, from Old French *sometier,* from Vulgar Latin *saumatārius* (unattested), from Late Latin *sagma,* packsaddle, from Greek, from *sattein†,* to pack.]

sump·tu·ar·y (sŭmp′choŏ-ĕr′ē) *adj.* **1.** Pertaining to expenditure; especially, regulating or limiting expenses. **2.** Regulating personal behavior on moral or religious grounds: *sumptuary laws.* [Latin *sumptuārius,* from *sumptus,* expense, from the past participle of *sūmere,* to consume, spend, take.]

sump·tu·ous (sŭmp′choŏ-əs) *adj.* Of a size or splendor suggesting great expense; lavish. [Middle English, from Old French *sumptueux,* from Latin *sumptuōsus,* from *sumptus,* expense. See **sumptuary.**] —**sump·tu·ous·ly** *adv.* —**sump·tu·ous·ness** *n.*

Sum·ter (sŭm′tər), **Thomas** (1734–1832). U.S. Revolutionary general, politician, and diplomat. After the British conquest of South Carolina in 1780, he commanded a series of raids against the British and local loyalists. He was a member of the South Carolina convention that ratified the Constitution and later served as U.S. representative (1789–93 and 1797–1801) and senator (1801–10).

sun (sŭn) *n.* **1. a.** A star that is the basis of the Solar System and that sustains life on Earth, being the source of heat and light. It has a mean distance from Earth of about 93 million miles, a diameter of approximately 864,000 miles, and a mass about 330,000 times that of Earth. **b.** The sun in a particular aspect or at a particular time or place: *the midnight sun.* **2.** Any star that is the center of a planetary system. **3.** The radiant energy, especially heat and visible light, emitted by the sun; sunshine. **4.** *Archaic.* **a.** A day. **b.** A year. **—under the sun.** On earth; in the world. *~v.* **sunned, sunning, suns.** *—tr.* **1.** To expose to the sun's rays. **2.** To warm, dry, or tan in the sun. *—intr.* To bask in the sun. [Middle English *sonne, sunne,* Old English *sunne.*]

Sun. Sunday.

sun-baked (sŭn′bākt′) *adj.* Hardened by the heat of the sun.

sun bath *n.* Exposure of the body to the rays of the sun.

sun-bathe (sŭn′bāth′) *intr.v.* **-bathed, -bathing, -bathes.** To expose the body to the direct rays of the sun. —**sun·bath·er** *n.*

sun·beam (sŭn′bēm′) *n.* A ray of sunlight.

Sun·belt (sŭn′bĕlt′) *n.* The southern and southwestern states of the United States.

sun·bird (sŭn′bûrd′) *n.* Any of various small, tropical Old World birds of the family Nectariniidae, having a slender, downward-curving bill and often brightly colored plumage in the male.

sun bittern *n.* A cranelike tropical American bird, *Eurypyga helias,* having mottled brownish plumage.

sun·bon·net (sŭn′bŏn′ĭt) *n.* A wide-brimmed bonnet with a projecting flap at the back for protecting the neck from the sun.

sun·bow (sŭn′bō′) *n.* A rainbowlike display of colors resulting from the refraction of sunlight through a spray of water.

sun·burn (sŭn′bûrn′) *n.* Inflammation or blistering of the skin caused by overexposure to direct sunlight or a sunlamp. *~v.* **sunburned** or **-burnt** (-bûrnt′), **-burning, -burns.** *—tr.* To affect with sunburn. *—intr.* To be affected with sunburn.

sun·burst (sŭn′bûrst′) *n.* **1.** A sudden burst of sunlight, as through broken clouds. **2.** A pattern or design consisting of a central disk with radiating spires projecting in the manner of sunbeams. **3.** A jeweled brooch with such a design.

sun·dae (sŭn′dē, -dā′) *n.* A dish of ice cream with toppings such as syrup, fruits, nuts, and whipped cream. [19th century : origin obscure.]

Sun·da Islands (sŭn′də, soŏn′-). Group of islands lying between the Indian Ocean and South China Sea. The group comprises the Greater Sunda Islands, which include Java, Sumatra, Borneo, and Sulawesi, and the Lesser Sunda Islands, which include Bali, Sumbawa, Sumba, and Timor. The territory is Indonesian, with the exception of Brunei and the Malaysian states of Sabah and Sarawak.

sun dance *n.* A ritual dance performed by the North American Plains Indians at the summer solstice.

Sunda Strait. A channel between Sumatra and Java, connecting the Java Sea with the Indian Ocean.

Sun·day (sŭn′dē, -dā′) *n. Abbr.* **S., Sun.** The day of the week following Saturday; the Christian Sabbath. [Middle English *sone(n)day, sun(en)day,* Old English *sunnandæg,* "day of the sun."]

Sunday, William Ashley, known as "Billy" (1862–1935). U.S. evangelist. A professional baseball player as a young man, he underwent a religious conversion (1887) and was ordained a Presbyterian minister (1908). His flamboyant and popular sermons praised puritanical morality and denounced science and liberalism.

Sunday best *n. Informal.* One's best or smartest clothes.

Sunday driver *n. Informal.* A slow and exaggeratedly careful motorist, such as one who drives mainly for recreation.

Sunday school *n. Abbr.* **S.S. 1.** A school, generally affiliated with a church, that offers religious instruction for children on Sundays. **2.** The teachers and pupils of a Sunday school.

sun deck *n.* **1.** An exposed upper deck on a passenger ship. **2.** A roof, balcony, or terrace used for sunbathing.

sun·der (sŭn′dər) *v.* **-dered, -dering, -ders.** *—tr.* To break apart; divide; sever. *—intr.* To break into parts; become separated. —See Synonyms at **separate.**

∼n. A division or separation. [Middle English *sund(e)ren,* Old English *syndrian, sundrian.*] **—sun·der·ance** *n.*

Sun·der·land (sŭn′dər-lənd). Port and industrial town in Tyne and Wear, northeastern England, at the mouth of the Wear River. In Monkwearmouth, the area north of the river, there stands a 7th-century abbey, house of the Venerable Bede. Coal has been shipped from the port since 1396.

sun·dew (sŭn′do͞o′, -dyo͞o′) *n.* Any of several insectivorous plants of the genus *Drosera,* having leaves covered with sticky hairs that trap insects. [Translation of Latin *rōs sōlis.*]

sun·di·al (sŭn′dī′əl) *n.* An instrument that indicates local apparent solar time by measuring the hour angle of the sun with a style that casts a shadow on a calibrated dial.

sun disk *n.* A symbol in Egyptian art consisting of a disk set between outspread wings, representing the sun god.

sun·dog (sŭn′dôg′, -dŏg′) *n. Meteorology.* **1.** A **parhelion** *(see).* **2.** A small halo or rainbow near the horizon just off the parhelic circle.

sun·down (sŭn′doun′) *n.* Sunset.

sun·down·er (sŭn′dou′nər) *n. Informal.* **1.** In Australia, a tramp who looks for a place to sleep at sunset. **2.** *Chiefly British.* An alcoholic drink taken at sunset.

sun·dress (sŭn′drĕs′) *n.* A dress that exposes the back, shoulders, and arms to the sun.

sun·dries (sŭn′drēz) *pl.n.* Articles too small or numerous to be itemized; miscellaneous items. [From SUNDRY.]

sun·drops (sŭn′drŏps′) *n. Plural in form, used with a singular or plural verb.* Any of several New World plants of the genus *Oenothera,* having four-petaled yellow flowers. [So called because the flowers remain open during the hours of sunlight.]

sun·dry (sŭn′drē) *adj.* Various; several; miscellaneous. [Middle English *sundri, sondri,* Old English *syndrig,* apart, separate.]

sun·fish (sŭn′fĭsh′) *n., pl.* **-fishes** or collectively **sunfish. 1.** Any of various large marine fishes of the family Molidae; especially, the **ocean sunfish** *(see).* **2.** Any of various North American freshwater fishes of the family Centrarchidae, having a laterally flattened, often brightly colored body. [From its roundish body and bright colors.]

sun·flow·er (sŭn′flou′ər) *n.* **1.** Any of several plants of the genus *Helianthus*; especially, *H. annuus,* having tall, coarse stems and large yellow-rayed flowers that produce edible seeds rich in oil. **2.** Brilliant yellow to strong or vivid orange yellow.

sung. Past participle and alternate past tense of **sing.**

Sung. See **Song.**

Sun·ga·ri (so͝ong′gä′rē′). The major river of Manchuria, rising near the North Korean border and flowing 1,850 kilometers (1,150 miles) northwest, east, and finally northeast to the Amur at the Siberian border.

sun·glass (sŭn′glăs′, -gläs′) *n.* A **burning-glass** *(see).*

sun·glass·es (sŭn′glăs′ĭz, -glä′sĭz) *pl.n.* Eyeglasses with tinted or polarizing lenses to protect the eyes from the sun's glare.

sun·glow (sŭn′glō′) *n.* A rose or yellow glow in the sky preceding sunrise or following sunset.

sun god *n.* A god that personifies the sun.

sun·grebe (sŭn′grēb′) *n.* A bird, the **finfoot** *(see).*

sun·hat (sŭn′hăt′) *n.* A hat with a wide brim, worn to protect the head, face, and neck from the sun.

sunk. Past participle and alternate past tense of **sink.**

sunk·en (sŭng′kən). Alternate past participle of **sink.**

∼adj. **1.** Depressed, fallen in, or hollowed: *sunken cheeks.* **2.** Situated beneath the surface of the water or ground; submerged. **3.** Below the surrounding level: *a sunken meadow.*

sunk fence *n.* A **ha-ha** *(see).*

sun lamp *n.* **1.** A lamp that radiates over a wide range of the spectrum from ultraviolet to infrared and is used in therapeutic and cosmetic treatments. **2.** A high-intensity lamp with parabolic mirrors, used in photography.

sun·less (sŭn′lĭs) *adj.* **1.** Without sunlight; dark or overcast. **2.** Gloomy; cheerless. **—sun·less·ness** *n.*

sun·light (sŭn′līt′) *n.* The light of the sun; sunshine.

sun·lit (sŭn′lĭt′) *adj.* Illuminated by the sun.

sunn (sŭn) *n.* **1.** A plant, *Crotalaria juncea,* of tropical Asia and Australia, having clusters of yellow flowers. **2.** A tough fiber from the stems of this plant, used for cordage. Also called "Madras hemp," "sunn hemp." [Hindi *san,* from Sanskrit *śaṇaḥ,* hempen.]

Sun·na, Sun·nah (so͝on′ə) *n.* The body of traditional Muslim law, observed by the orthodox Muslims and based on the words and acts of Muhammad. [Arabic *sunnah,* form, course, rule.]

Sun·ni (so͝on′ē) *n.* The great branch of Islam following orthodox tradition and accepting the first four caliphs as rightful successors of Muhammad. Compare **Shiah.** [Arabic *sunnīy,* "adherent of the Sunna," from *sunnah,* SUNNA.]

Sun·nite (so͝on′īt′) *n.* A Muslim of the Sunni. [From SUNNI.]

sun·ny (sŭn′ē) *adj.* **-nier, -niest. 1.** Exposed to or filled with sunshine: *a sunny room.* **2.** Cheerful; light-hearted: *a sunny smile; a sunny soul.* **—sun·ni·ly** *adv.* **—sun·ni·ness** *n.*

sunny side *n.* **1.** The sunlit side, as of a street. **2.** The positive or encouraging aspect of a situation.

sun·ny-side up (sŭn′ē-sīd′ ŭp′) *adv.* Fried on one side only. Said of eggs. **—sunny-side up** *adj.*

sun·ray (sŭn′rā′) *n.* A sunbeam.

sun·rise (sŭn′rīz′) *n.* **1. a.** The event or time of the daily first appearance of the sun above the eastern horizon. **b.** The time when the center of the rising sun is on the horizon. **2.** The atmospheric effects of sunrise. **3.** An outset or emergence, as of civilization.

sun·roof (sŭn′ro͞of′, -ro͝of′) *n.* An automobile roof with a panel that can be slid back or lifted up.

sun·scald (sŭn′skôld′) *n.* An injury to woody plants characterized by localized death of plant tissues and caused by excessive sun in summer and by the combined effects of sun and low temperatures in winter.

sun·screen (sŭn′skrēn′) *n.* A substance or preparation that protects the skin by blocking harmful ultraviolet rays.

sun·seek·er (sŭn′sē′kər) *n.* **1.** A person who travels to sunny climates. **2.** A photoelectric device on a spacecraft that maintains a constant fix on the sun.

sun·set (sŭn′sĕt′) *n.* **1. a.** The event or time of the daily disappearance of the sun below the western horizon. **b.** The time when the center of the setting sun is on the horizon. **2.** The atmospheric effects of sunset. **3.** A decline or final phase, as of life.

sun·shade (sŭn′shād′) *n.* Anything used as a protection from the sun's rays, such as an awning or a parasol.

sun·shine (sŭn′shīn′) *n.* **1. a.** The light or warmth of the sun; the direct rays from the sun. **b.** An area lit up by the sun. **2. a.** Happiness or cheerfulness. **b.** A source of happiness or cheerfulness: *You are my sunshine.* **—sun·shin·y** *adj.*

sun·spot (sŭn′spŏt′) *n.* Any of the relatively dark spots that appear briefly in groups on the surface of the sun during an approximate 11-year cycle and are associated with strong magnetic fields.

sun·star (sŭn′stär′) *n.* Any starfish of the genus *Solaster,* having up to 13 arms.

sun·stone (sŭn′stōn′) *n.* A type of feldspar, **aventurine** *(see).*

sun·stroke (sŭn′strōk′) *n.* **Heat stroke** *(see)* caused by overexposure to the sun. Also called "insolation."

sun·tan (sŭn′tăn′) *n.* **1.** A tan skin color resulting from exposure to the ultraviolet rays of the sun or a sun lamp. **2. suntans.** A tan-colored summer military uniform. **—sun·tanned** *adj.*

sun·up (sŭn′ŭp′) *n.* The time of sunrise.

Sun Valley. A winter sports center in south-central Idaho.

sun·ward (sŭn′wərd) *adj.* Facing or directed toward the sun.

∼adv. Also **sun·wards** (-wərdz). Toward the sun.

sun·wise (sŭn′wīz′) *adv.* From left to right, like the sun's course as viewed in the Northern Hemisphere.

Sun Zhong-shan (so͝on′ jŏng′shăn′), also **Sun Yat-sen** (yät′sĕn′). (1866–1925). Chinese revolutionary politician. He united all the revolutionary parties under the Guomindang (1911) and was appointed provisional president of the republic after the fall of the Manchus. He resigned in 1912.

su·o ju·re (so͞o′ō jo͝or′ē) *adv. Law.* In one's own right. [Latin.]

su·o lo·co (so͞o′ō lō′kō) *adv. Law.* In a person or thing's rightful place. [Latin.]

Suomi. See **Finland.**

sup¹ (sŭp) *v.* **supped, supping, sups.** *—tr.* To take (a liquid) into the mouth by sips. *—intr.* To take liquid into the mouth in small amounts.

∼n. A mouthful or taste of liquid. [Middle English *s(o)upen,* Old English *sūpan.*]

sup² *intr.v.* **supped, supping, sups.** To eat the evening meal; have supper. [Middle English *soupen, suppen,* from Old French *s(o)uper,* from *soup,* piece of bread dipped in broth, soup, from Germanic.]

sup. 1. above [Latin *supra*]. **2.** superior. **3.** *Grammar.* superlative. **4.** supine (noun). **5.** supplement; supplementary. **6.** supply.

supe (so͞op) *n. Slang.* A supernumerary actor; an extra. [Short for SUPERNUMERARY.]

su·per (so͞o′pər) *n.* **1.** *Informal.* A superintendent in an apartment or office building. **2.** *Informal.* An extra person, especially a **supernumerary** *(see).* **3.** An article or product of a superior size, quality,

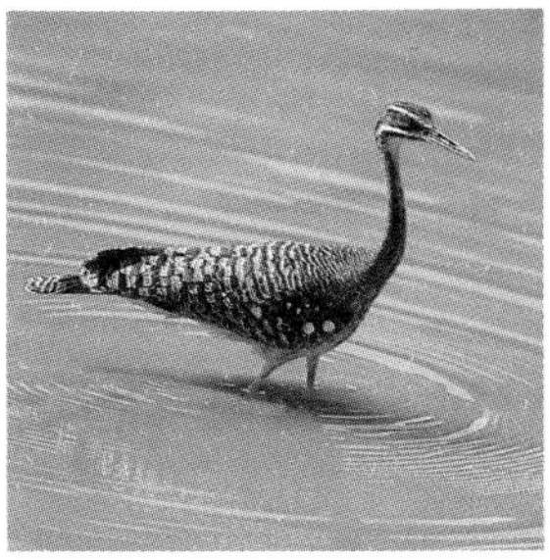

sun bittern *When startled, the sun bittern spreads its wings, displaying eye-shaped marks to deter its attacker. The birds live along the banks of forested rivers in South America and feed largely on insects.*

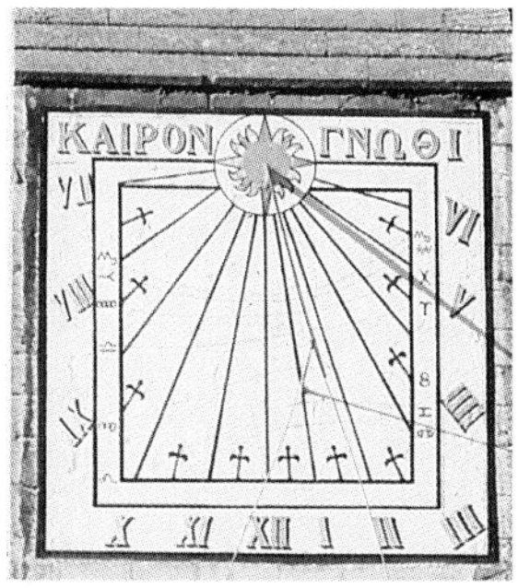

sundial *The shadow cast by the central gnomon on this 18th-century sundial gives the time at about 4:55* P.M.

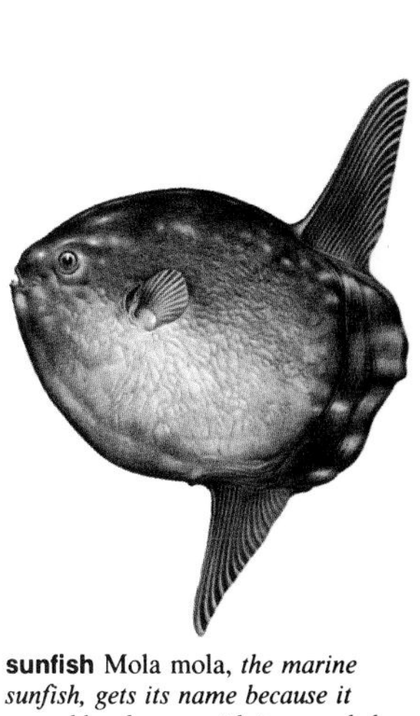

sunfish Mola mola, *the marine sunfish, gets its name because it resembles the sun with its rounded shape and radiating fins. Sunfish are the world's heaviest bony fish. One—captured off Sydney, Australia, in 1908—weighed 2.24 tons.*

or grade. **4.** A thin, starched cotton mesh used to reinforce books. —*adj. Slang.* Ideal; first-rate.

super– *prefix.* Indicates: **1.** Placement above, over, or outside; for example, **supercolumnar, superimpose. 2.** Superiority in size, quality, number, or degree; for example, **superfine, supermarket. 3. a.** A degree exceeding a specified level; for example, **supersonic. b.** An extraordinary degree; for example, **superhero. 4.** Addition; for example, **superadd. 5.** *Chemistry.* The presence of a specified ingredient in a high proportion; for example, **superphosphate.** *Note:* Many compounds other than those entered here may be formed with *super-.* In forming compounds, *super-* is normally joined with the following element without space or hyphen: *superrefined.* However, if the second element begins with a capital letter, it is separated with a hyphen: *super-American.* [Latin *super,* above, over.]

super. 1. superintendent. **2.** superior. **3.** supernumerary.

su·per·a·ble (so͞o′pər-ə-bəl) *adj.* Capable of being overcome or surmounted. [Latin *superābilis,* from *superāre,* to go over, overcome, from *super,* above, over.] —**su·per·a·bil·i·ty, su·per·a·ble·ness** *n.* —**su·per·a·bly** *adv.*

su·per·a·bound (so͞o′pər-ə-bound′) *intr.v.* **-bounded, -bounding, -bounds.** To be unusually or excessively abundant. [Middle English *superabounden,* from Late Latin *superabundāre* : Latin *super-,* excessively + *abundāre,* to ABOUND.]

su·per·a·bun·dant (so͞o′pər-ə-bŭn′dənt) *adj.* Abundant to excess; more than ample. [Middle English, from Late Latin *superabundāns* (stem *superabundant-*), present participle of *superabundāre,* to SUPERABOUND.] —**su·per·a·bun·dance** *n.* —**su·per·a·bun·dant·ly** *adv.*

su·per·add (so͞o′pər-ăd′) *tr.v.* **-added, -adding, -adds.** To add to something that has already been added to.

su·per·al·tern (so͞o′pər-ôl′tərn) *n. Logic.* A universal proposition that is a ground for the immediate inference of a corresponding subalternate. [SUPER- + *altern,* as in SUBALTERN.]

su·per·an·nu·ate (so͞o′pər-ăn′yo͞o-āt′) *tr.v.* **-ated, -ating, -ates. 1.** To allow to retire on a pension because of age or infirmity. **2.** To set aside or discard as old-fashioned or obsolete. [Back-formation from SUPERANNUATED.] —**su·per·an·nu·a·tion** *n.*

su·per·an·nu·at·ed (so͞o′pər-ăn′yo͞o-ā′tĭd) *adj.* **1.** Retired or discharged because of age or infirmity. **2.** Too old or out of date to be worth preserving. **3.** Obsolete. —See Synonyms at **old.** [Medieval Latin *superannuātus,* past participle of *superannuārī,* to be too old : Latin *super,* above + *annus,* year, time of life.]

su·perb (so͞o-pûrb′) *adj.* **1.** Of unusually high quality. **2.** Majestic; imposing. **3.** Rich; luxurious. [French *superbe,* from Latin *superbus,* superior, proud.] —**su·perb·ly** *adv.* —**su·perb·ness** *n.*

su·per·cal·en·der (so͞o′pər-kăl′ən-dər) *n.* A calender with a number of rollers for giving a high finish or gloss to paper.
—*tr.v.* **supercalendered, -dering, -ders.** To finish (paper) in a supercalendar.

su·per·car·go (so͞o′pər-kär′gō) *n., pl.* **-goes** or **-gos.** An officer on board a merchant ship who has charge of the cargo and its sale and purchase. [Variant of earlier *supracargo,* from Spanish *sobrecargo* : *sobre-,* over, from Latin *super-* + CARGO.]

su·per·charge (so͞o′pər-chärj′) *tr.v.* **-charged, -charging, -charges. 1.** To increase the power of (an engine) by fitting with a supercharger. **2.** To charge excessively, as with emotion or tension. **3.** To pressurize (a fluid).
—*n.* An excess or extra charge.

su·per·charg·er (so͞o′pər-chär′jər) *n.* A blower or compressor for supplying air under high pressure to the cylinders of an internal-combustion engine. Also called "booster."

su·per·cil·i·ar·y (so͞o′pər-sĭl′ē-ĕr′ē) *adj.* **1.** Of or pertaining to the eyebrow. **2.** Located over the eyebrow. [New Latin *superciliaris,* from Latin *supercilium,* eyebrow. See **supercilious.**]

su·per·cil·i·ous (so͞o′pər-sĭl′ē-əs) *adj.* Showing or characterized by haughty scorn or indifference; disdainful. —See Synonyms at **proud.** [Latin *superciliōsus,* from Latin *supercilium,* "upper eyelid," eyebrow, pride : *super-,* above + *cilium,* (lower) eyelid.] —**su·per·cil·i·ous·ly** *adv.* —**su·per·cil·i·ous·ness** *n.*

su·per·class (so͞o′pər-klăs′, -kläs′) *n. Biology.* A taxonomic category ranking below a phylum and above a class.

su·per·co·lum·nar (so͞o′pər-kə-lŭm′nər) *adj. Architecture.* **1.** Having one order of columns above another. **2.** Situated above a colonnade or column.

su·per·con·duc·tiv·i·ty (so͞o′pər-kŏn′dŭk-tĭv′ə-tē) *n.* A property of certain metals and alloys whereby they exhibit virtually no electrical resistance at temperatures close to absolute zero. —**su·per·con·duc·tive** (so͞o′pər-kən-dŭk′tĭv) *adj.* —**su·per·con·duc·tor** (so͞o′-pər-kən-dŭk′tər) *n.*

su·per·cool (so͞o′pər-ko͞ol′) *v.* **-cooled, -cooling, -cools.** —*tr.* To cool (a liquid) below a transition temperature without the transition occurring; especially, to cool below the freezing point without solidification. —*intr.* To become supercooled. Used of a liquid.

su·per·crit·i·cal (so͞o′pər-krĭt′ĭ-kəl) *adj. Physics.* Having or involving a chain reaction that is self-sustaining and uncontrolled. Said especially of nuclear reactions, reactors, and weapons.

su·per·dom·i·nant (so͞o′pər-dŏm′ə-nənt) *n.* The **submediant** (see).

su·per·du·per (so͞o′pər-do͞o′pər) *adj. Slang.* Great; marvelous. [Reduplication of SUPER.]

su·per·e·go (so͞o′pər-ē′gō, -ĕg′ō) *n., pl.* **-egos.** *Psychoanalysis.* The division of the psyche that develops by the incorporation of the perceived moral standards of the community as they are transferred from parent to child, is mainly unconscious, and includes the conscience. See **ego, id.**

su·per·el·e·va·tion (so͞o′pər-ĕl′ə-vā′shən) *n.* The difference in height between the outer and inner edges of a curve in a railway track or road.

su·per·em·i·nent (so͞o′pər-ĕm′ə-nənt) *adj.* Eminent beyond all others; pre-eminent. [Late Latin *superēminēns* (stem *superēminent-*), from Latin, present participle of *superēminēre,* to rise above : *super-,* above + *ēminēre,* to stand out (see **eminent**).] —**su·per·em·i·nence** *n.* —**su·per·em·i·nent·ly** *adv.*

su·per·er·o·gate (so͞o′pər-ĕr′ə-gāt′) *intr.v.* **-gated, -gating, -gates.** To do more than is required, ordered, or expected. [Late Latin *superērogāre,* to spend more : Latin *super-,* above + *ērogāre,* to spend : *ex-,* out of + *rogāre,* to ask.]

su·per·er·o·ga·tion (so͞o′pər-ĕr′ə-gā′shən) *n.* The performance of more than is required, ordered, or expected.

su·per·e·rog·a·to·ry (so͞o′pər-ə-rŏg′ə-tôr′ē, -tōr′ē) *adj.* Also **su·per·e·rog·a·tive** (-tĭv). **1.** Performed or observed beyond the degree required or expected. **2.** Superfluous; unnecessary: *"It was supererogatory for her to gloat"* (Mary McCarthy).

su·per·fam·i·ly (so͞o′pər-făm′ə-lē) *n., pl.* **-lies.** *Biology.* A taxonomic category ranking below an order or its subdivisions and above a family.

su·per·fat·ted (so͞o′pər-făt′ĭd) *adj.* Containing extra fat. Said of soap.

su·per·fe·cun·da·tion (so͞o′pər-fē′kən-dā′shən, -fĕk′ən-dā′shən) *n.* The fertilization of more than one ovum within a single menstrual cycle by separate acts of coitus, especially by different males.

su·per·fe·tate (so͞o′pər-fē′tāt′) *intr.v.* **-tated, -tating, -tates.** To conceive when a fetus is already present in the uterus. [Latin *superfē-tāre* : *super-,* over, in addition to + *fētāre,* to breed, impregnate, from *fētus,* young, fetus.]

su·per·fe·ta·tion (so͞o′pər-fē-tā′shən) *n.* The presence in the uterus of fetuses of different ages resulting from the fertilization of a second ovum some time after the start of pregnancy.

su·per·fi·cial (so͞o′pər-fĭsh′əl) *adj.* **1.** Of, affecting, or being on or near the surface: *a superficial wound.* **2. a.** Concerned with or comprehending only what is apparent, obvious, or insubstantial. **b.** Shallow; not thorough or searching. **3. a.** Apparent rather than actual or substantial: *a superficial likeness.* **b.** Trivial; insignificant. **4.** Involving only the surface area. Said of measurements. **5.** *Geology.* Lying on the surface; not derived from the rocks below. Said of a deposit. [Middle English, from Late Latin *superficiālis,* from Latin *superficiēs,* surface, SUPERFICIES.] —**su·per·fi·ci·al·i·ty** (so͞o′-pər-fĭsh′ē-ăl′ə-tē), **su·per·fi·cial·ness** *n.* —**su·per·fi·cial·ly** *adv.*

Synonyms: superficial, shallow, cursory, perfunctory. These adjectives mean lacking in depth or thoroughness. *Superficial* applies to thought and action concerned largely with the obvious, sometimes implying lack of genuine interest or sincerity. *Shallow* emphasizes lack of intellectual or emotional depth in persons or their works; more strongly than *superficial,* it implies lack of capacity for something better. *Cursory* and *perfunctory* principally describe action performed speedily and without thoroughness.

su·per·fi·cies (so͞o′pər-fĭsh′ĕz, -fĭsh′ē-ēz′) *n., pl.* **superficies. 1.** The surface of an area or body. **2.** The external appearance or aspect of a thing. [Latin *superficiēs,* surface : *super-,* above, over + *faciēs,* FACE.]

su·per·fine (so͞o′pər-fīn′) *adj.* **1.** Of exceptional quality or refinement. **2.** Of extra fine texture. **3.** Overdelicate or refined. —**su·per·fine·ness** *n.*

su·per·fix (so͞o′pər-fĭks′) *n. Linguistics.* A suprasegmental feature distinguishing the meaning or grammatical function of one word or phrase from that of another.

su·per·flu·id (so͞o′pər-flo͞o′ĭd) *n.* A fluid, such as a form of helium, exhibiting frictionless flow at temperatures close to absolute zero. —**su·per·flu·id·i·ty** (so͞o′pər-flo͞o-ĭd′ə-tē) *n.*

su·per·flu·i·ty (so͞o′pər-flo͞o′ə-tē) *n., pl.* **-ties. 1.** The quality or condition of being superfluous. **2.** Something that is superfluous. **3.** Overabundance; excess.

su·per·flu·ous (so͞o-pûr′flo͞o-əs) *adj.* **1.** Beyond what is required or sufficient; extra. **2.** Excessive; unnecessary or redundant. [Middle English, from Latin *superfluus,* overflowing, from *superfluere,* to overflow : *super-,* over + *fluere,* to flow.] —**su·per·flu·ous·ly** *adv.* —**su·per·flu·ous·ness** *n.*

su·per·gal·ax·y (so͞o′pər-găl′ək-sē) *n., pl.* **-ies.** A very large group of galaxies.

su·per·gene (so͞o′pər-jēn′) *n.* A group of genes closely linked on a chromosome so that they are rarely separated by crossing over and therefore tend to function as a single gene.

su·per·gi·ant (so͞o′pər-jī′ənt) *n.* Any of a class of bright low-density stars with diameters and luminosities thousands of times greater than that of the sun.

su·per·gla·cial (so͞o′pər-glā′shəl) *adj.* Formed or originating on the surface of a glacier.

su·per·graph·ics (so͞o′pər-grăf′ĭks) *n. Used with a singular or plural verb.* Brightly colored and simply designed graphic shapes of billboard proportions.

su·per·heat (so͞o′pər-hēt′) *tr.v.* **-heated, -heating, -heats. 1.** To heat excessively; overheat. **2.** To heat (steam or other vapor not in contact with its own liquid) beyond its saturation point at a given pressure. **3.** To heat (a liquid) above its boiling point at a given pressure without causing vaporization.
—*n.* (so͞o′pər-hēt′). **1.** The amount by which a vapor is superheated.

2. The heat imparted in the process of superheating. **—su·per·heat·er** *n.*
su·per·he·ro (so͞o′pər-hîr′ō) *n., pl.* **-heroes.** An imaginary or mythical personage, especially a cartoon character, endowed with superhuman strength or powers.
su·per·het·er·o·dyne (so͞o′pər-hĕt′ər-ə-dīn′) *adj.* Designating or pertaining to a form of radio reception in which the frequency of an incoming radio signal is converted to an intermediate frequency, by mixing with a locally generated signal, to facilitate amplification and the rejection of unwanted signals.
~n. A superheterodyne radio set. [SUPER(SONIC) + HETERODYNE.]
su·per·high frequency (so͞o′pər-hī′) *n. Abbr.* **shf, SHF** Any radio frequency between 3,000 and 30,000 megahertz.
su·per·high·way (so͞o′pər-hī′wā′) *n.* A broad highway for high-speed traffic, often with six or more lanes.
su·per·hu·man (so͞o′pər-hyo͞o′mən) *adj.* **1.** Above or beyond the human; divine. **2.** Beyond ordinary or normal human ability, power, or experience: *a superhuman effort.* **—su·per·hu·man·i·ty** (so͞o′pər-hyo͞o-măn′ə-tē) *n.* **—su·per·hu·man·ly** *adv.*
su·per·im·pose (so͞o′pər-ĭm-pōz′) *tr.v.* **-posed, -posing, -poses.** To lay or place upon or over something else. **—su·per·im·po·si·tion** (so͞o′pər-ĭm′pə-zĭsh′ən) *n.*
su·per·in·cum·bent (so͞o′pər-ĭn-kŭm′bənt) *adj.* Lying, resting, or suspended on or above something else. [Latin *superincumbēns* (stem *superincumbent-*), present participle of *superincumbere,* to lie down on or above : *super-,* above + *incumbere,* to lie down (see **incumbent**).] **—su·per·in·cum·bence, su·per·in·cum·ben·cy** *n.* **—su·per·in·cum·bent·ly** *adv.*
su·per·in·duce (so͞o′pər-ĭn-do͞os′, -dyo͞os′) *tr.v.* **-duced, -ducing, -duces.** To introduce as an addition. [Latin *superindūcere,* to bring upon : *super-,* on, over, in addition + *indūcere,* to lead in, INDUCE.] **—su·per·in·duce·ment, su·per·in·duc·tion** *n.*
su·per·in·fec·tion (so͞o′pər-ĭn-fĕk′shən) *n.* An infection that develops during the course of another infection, caused by microorganisms not susceptible to the drugs used to treat the first infection.
su·per·in·tend (so͞o′pər-ĭn-tĕnd′, so͞o′prĭn-) *tr.v.* **-tended, -tending, -tends.** To have charge of; exercise supervision over; manage. [Late Latin *superintendere,* to oversee : *super-,* over + *intendere,* to direct one's attention to, INTEND.] **—su·per·in·ten·dence** *n.*
su·per·in·ten·dent (so͞o′pər-ĭn-tĕn′dənt, so͞o′prĭn-) *n. Abbr.* **super., supt., Supt.** **1.** A person who supervises or directs some enterprise or institution. **2.** A caretaker in a building, especially an apartment house. **—su·per·in·ten·dent** *adj.* **—su·per·in·ten·den·cy** *n.*
su·pe·ri·or (so͞o-pîr′ē-ər) *adj. Abbr.* **sup., super.** **1.** Higher in rank, station, or authority: *a superior officer.* **2.** Of a higher nature or kind; far above average in comparison: *superior in tone to the modern instrument.* **3. a.** Of great value or excellence; extraordinary. **b.** Of high quality. **4.** Greater in number or amount: *defeated by superior numbers of troops.* **5.** Affecting an attitude of disdain or conceit. **6.** Above being affected or influenced; indifferent or immune: *superior to envy.* **7.** Located higher; upper. **8.** *Anatomy.* Designating a part or organ situated higher in the body in relation to another part. **9.** *Astronomy.* Having an orbit farther from the Sun than the orbit of the Earth. **10.** *Botany.* Located above and not in contact with the calyx and corolla. Said of an ovary. **11.** *Printing.* Set above the main line of type. **12.** *Logic.* Of wider or more comprehensive application; generic. Said of a term or proposition.
~n. Abbr. **sup., super.** **1.** One who surpasses another in rank, office, or quality. **2.** The head of a monastery, abbey, convent, or other ecclesiastical order or house. **3.** *Printing.* A superior character or letter. [Middle English, from Old French, from Latin, comparative of *superus,* situated above, upper, from *super,* above, over.] **—su·pe·ri·or·ly** *adv.*
Superior, Lake. The largest freshwater lake in the world and the largest of the Great Lakes of North America. The Canadian-United States border passes through it.
superior conjunction *n.* The position of a celestial body when it is on the opposite side of the sun from the earth.
superior court *n.* A court of general jurisdiction, above the inferior courts and below the higher courts of final appeal.
su·pe·ri·or·i·ty (so͞o-pîr′ē-ôr′ə-tē, -ŏr′ə-tē) *n.* The quality or state of being superior.
superiority complex *n.* **1.** An unfounded conviction that one is superior to others. **2.** A psychological defense mechanism in which feelings of superiority counter feelings of inferiority.
superior planet *n.* Any planet of this Solar System whose mean distance from the Sun is greater than that of the Earth.
su·per·ja·cent (so͞o′pər-jā′sənt) *adj.* Lying immediately above or upon something else. Used with *to.* [Latin *superjacēns* (stem *superjacent-*), present participle of *superjacēre,* to lie above or upon : *super-,* over + *jacēre,* to lie, from *jacere,* to throw, lay.]
su·per·la·tive (so͞o-pûr′lə-tĭv) *adj.* **1.** Of the highest order, quality, or degree; surpassing or superior to all others. **2.** Excessive or exaggerated. **3.** *Grammar. Abbr.* **sup., superl.** Expressing or involving the extreme degree of comparison of adjectives and adverbs. Compare **comparative, positive.**
~n. **1.** Something of the highest possible excellence. **2.** The highest degree; the acme. **3.** *Grammar. Abbr.* **sup., superl. a.** The superlative degree. **b.** An adjective or adverb expressing the superlative degree; for example, *brightest* is the superlative of *bright; most slowly* is the superlative of *slowly.* [Middle English *superlatyf,* from Old French *superlative,* from Late Latin *superlātīvus,* from *superlātus* (past participle of *superferre,* to carry over) : *super-,* over + *-lātus,* "carried."] **—su·per·la·tive·ly** *adv.*
su·per·lu·nar (so͞o′pər-lo͞o′nər) *adj.* Also **su·per·lu·na·ry** (-nə-rē). Situated beyond the Moon.
su·per·man (so͞o′pər-măn′) *n., pl.* **-men** (-mĕn′). **1.** A man with more than human powers. **2.** In the philosophy of Nietzsche, an ideal superior man who, through the exercise of creative power and his ability to forgo transient pleasure, would live at a level of experience beyond standards of good and evil and would represent the goal of human evolution. [Translation of German *Übermensch.*]
su·per·mar·ket (so͞o′pər-mär′kĭt) *n.* A large self-service retail market that sells food and household goods.
su·per·nal (so͞o-pûr′nəl) *adj.* **1.** Celestial; heavenly. **2.** Of, coming from, or being in the sky or high above. [Middle English, from Old French, from Latin *supernus.*] **—su·per·nal·ly** *adv.*
su·per·na·tant (so͞o′pər-nā′tənt) *adj.* Floating on the surface. [Latin *supernatāns* (stem *supernatant-*), present participle of *supernatāre,* to swim above, float : *super-,* above + *natāre,* to swim.] **—su·per·na·tant** *n.* **—su·per·na·ta·tion** (so͞o′pər-nə-tā′shən) *n.*
su·per·nate (so͞o′pər-nāt′) *n.* The clear supernatant fluid over a sediment or precipitate. [Short for SUPERNATANT.]
su·per·nat·u·ral (so͞o′pər-năch′ər-əl) *adj.* **1.** Of or pertaining to existence outside the natural world; especially, not attributable to natural forces. **2.** Attributed to the immediate exercise of divine power; miraculous. **3.** Of or pertaining to the miraculous.
~n. That which is supernatural. **—su·per·nat·u·ral·ly** *adv.* **—su·per·nat·u·ral·ness** *n.*
su·per·nat·u·ral·ism (so͞o′pər-năch′ər-ə-lĭz′əm) *n.* **1.** The quality of being supernatural. **2.** Belief in a supernatural agency that intervenes in the course of natural laws. **—su·per·nat·u·ral·ist** *adj. & n.* **—su·per·nat·u·ral·is·tic** (so͞o′pər-năch′ər-ə-lĭs′tĭk) *adj.*
su·per·nor·mal (so͞o′pər-nôr′məl) *adj.* Greatly exceeding the normal or average but still obeying natural laws. **—su·per·nor·mal·i·ty** (so͞o′pər-nôr-măl′ə-tē) *n.* **—su·per·nor·mal·ly** *adv.*
su·per·no·va (so͞o′pər-nō′və) *n., pl.* **-vae** (-vē) or **-vas.** A rare celestial phenomenon involving the explosion of most of the material in a star, resulting in an extremely bright, short-lived object that emits vast amounts of energy. Compare **nova.**
su·per·nu·mer·ar·y (so͞o′pər-no͞o′mə-rĕr′ē, -nyo͞o′-). *adj.* **1.** Exceeding a fixed, prescribed, or standard number; extra: *a supernumerary nipple.* **2.** Beyond the required or desired number.
~n., pl. **supernumeraries.** *Abbr.* **super.** **1.** Someone or something in excess of the regular, necessary, or usual number. **2.** An actor without a speaking part, as one who appears in a crowd scene. [Late Latin *supernumerārius,* (a soldier) added to a legion in excess of its fixed number, from Latin *super numerum,* over the number : *super,* over + *numerus,* number, division of an army.]
su·per·or·der (so͞o′pər-ôr′dər) *n. Biology.* A taxonomic category ranking above an order or one of its subdivisions and below a class.
su·per·or·di·nate (so͞o′pər-ôr′də-nĭt) *adj.* **1.** Of higher status or value. **2.** *Logic.* Bearing the relation of a universal proposition to a particular proposition in which the terms are the same. **—su·per·or·di·nate** *n.*
su·per·o·vu·la·tion (so͞o′pər-ō′vyə-lā′shən, -ŏv′yə-lā′shən) *n.* The production of a large number of ova at one time.
su·per·ox·ide (so͞o′pər-ŏk′sīd′) *n.* An oxide of an alkali or an alkaline-earth metal containing the ion O_2, such as NaO_2.
su·per·phos·phate (so͞o′pər-fŏs′fāt′) *n.* **1.** An acid phosphate. **2.** A fertilizer made by sulfuric acid acting on phosphate rock, consisting chiefly of tribasic calcium phosphate, to form a mixture of gypsum and monobasic calcium phosphate.
su·per·phys·i·cal (so͞o′pər-fĭz′ĭ-kəl) *adj.* **1.** Exceeding or beyond the purely physical. **2.** Not explained by known physical laws; supernatural.
su·per·pose (so͞o′pər-pōz′) *tr.v.* **-posed, -posing, -poses.** **1.** To place (one geometric figure) over another so that all like parts coincide. **2.** To set or place over or above; superimpose.
su·per·po·si·tion (so͞o′pər-pə-zĭsh′ən) *n.* **1.** The act of superposing or the state of being superposed. **2.** *Geology.* The principle that in a group of stratified sedimentary rocks the lowest were the earliest to be deposited.
su·per·pow·er (so͞o′pər-pou′ər) *n.* A powerful and influential nation; especially, a nuclear power that dominates its satellites and allies in an international power bloc.
su·per·sat·u·rate (so͞o′pər-săch′ə-rāt′) *tr.v.* **-rated, -rating, -rates.** **1.** To cause (a chemical solution) to be more highly concentrated than is normally possible under given conditions of temperature and pressure. **2.** To cause (a vapor) to exceed the normal saturation vapor pressure at a given temperature. **—su·per·sat·u·ra·tion** *n.*
su·per·scribe (so͞o′pər-skrīb′) *tr.v.* **-scribed, -scribing, -scribes.** **1.** To write on the outside or upper part of (a letter, for example). **2.** To write (a name or address, for example) on the top or outside. [Latin *superscrībere,* to write over : *super-,* over + *scrībere,* to write.]
su·per·script (so͞o′pər-skrĭpt′) *adj.* Written or printed above a character or line of print.
~n. A character that is set, printed, or written above and immediately to one side of another. For example, *2* is a superscript in x^2. Compare **subscript.** [Latin *superscriptus,* past participle of *superscrībere,* to SUPERSCRIBE.]
su·per·scrip·tion (so͞o′pər-skrĭp′shən) *n.* **1.** Something written above or outside something. **2.** The act of superscribing. **3.** The part of a prescription that bears the Latin word *recipe* represented by the symbol ℞ in a prescription.

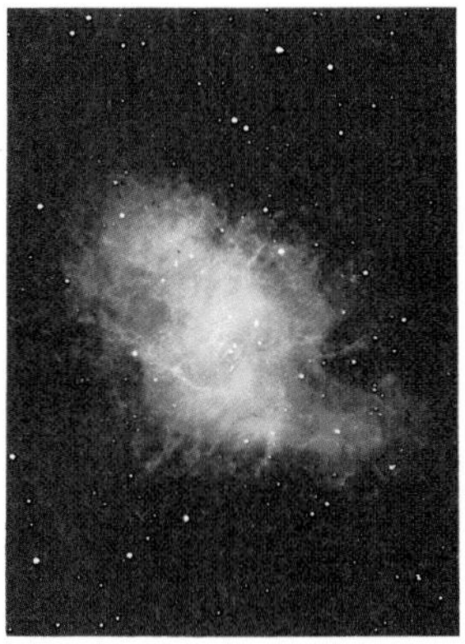

supernova *The Crab nebula (above)—which lies 6,000 light-years away in the constellation Taurus—is the glowing debris of a star that exploded into a supernova in about 5000 B.C. The glare of the explosion was seen on earth and recorded by Chinese astronomers in A.D. 1054. At the center of the nebula is a small faint star—all that survives of the original shattered star. In 1968 astronomers discovered that this remnant star was a pulsar, a tiny and extremely dense star, which was spinning 30 times a second. Pulsars are so called because they send out flashes, or "pulses," of radiation on each rotation like the beam of a lighthouse.*

PRONUNCIATION KEY

ă, pat; ā, pay; âr, care;
ä, father, are; b, bib;
ch, church; d, deed; ĕ, pet;
ē, be; f, fife; g, gag; h, hat;
hw, which; ĭ, pit; ī, pie;
îr, pier; j, judge; k, kick;
l, lid, needle; m, mum;
n, no, sudden; ng, thing;
ŏ, pot; ō, toe; ô, paw, for;
oi, noise; ou, out; o͝o, book;
o͞o, boot; p, pop; r, roar;
s, sauce; sh, ship, dish;
t, tight; th, thin, path;
th, this, bathe; ŭ, cut; ûr, fur;
v, valve; w, with; y, yes;
z, zebra, size; zh, vision;
ə, about, item, edible, gallop, circus, peaceful

IN FOREIGN WORDS:

à, *Fr.* ami; œ, *Fr.* feu, *Ger.* schön; ü, *Fr.* tu, *Ger.* über; KH, *Ger.* ich, *Scot.* loch; N, *Fr.* bon; y′, *Fr.* Compiègne

STRESS MARKS:

Primary stress: ′
in·cite′ (ĭn-sīt′)
Secondary stress: ′
in′sight′ (ĭn′sīt′)

su·per·sede (so͞o′pər-sēd′) *tr.v.* **-seded, -seding, -sedes. 1.** To replace or succeed. **2.** To cause (something outdated or inferior) to be set aside or displaced. —See Synonyms at **replace.** [Middle English *superceden,* to postpone, from Old French *superseder,* from Latin *supersedēre,* to sit above, desist from : *super-,* above + *sedēre,* to sit.] —**su·per·sed·ence** *n.* —**su·per·sed·er** *n.*

su·per·se·de·as (so͞o′pər-sē′dē-əs) *n. Law.* A writ containing a command to stay legal proceedings, as in the halting or delaying of the execution of a sentence. [Medieval Latin, from Latin, "you must desist," first word of the writ, from *supersedēre,* to SUPERSEDE.]

su·per·sen·si·ble (so͞o′pər-sĕn′sə-bəl) *adj.* Also **su·per·sen·so·ry** (-sĕn′sə-rē). Beyond or above perception by the senses. —**su·per·sen·si·bly** *adv.*

su·per·sen·si·tive (so͞o′pər-sĕn′sə-tĭv) *adj.* Hypersensitive.

su·per·ses·sion (so͞o′pər-sĕsh′ən) *n.* The act of superseding or the state of being superseded.

su·per·son·ic (so͞o′pər-sŏn′ĭk) *adj.* Having, caused by, or related to a speed greater than the speed of sound in a specific medium. —**su·per·son·ic** *n.* —**su·per·son·i·cal·ly** *adv.*

su·per·son·ics (so͞o′pər-sŏn′ĭks) *n. Used with a singular verb.* The study of phenomena produced by the motion of a body through a medium at velocities greater than that of sound.

supersonic transport *n. Abbr.* **SST** An aircraft capable of flight at speeds exceeding the speed of sound.

su·per·star (so͞o′pər-stär′) *n.* **1.** A widely acclaimed star, as in motion pictures or sports, who has great popular appeal. **2.** One that is a major attraction because of great popularity or prominence. —**su·per·star·dom** *n.*

su·per·sti·tion (so͞o′pər-stĭsh′ən) *n.* **1. a.** An unfounded belief that some action or circumstance completely unrelated to a course of events can influence its outcome. **b.** Fear of the mysterious or unknown. **2. a.** A belief, practice, or rite unreasoningly upheld by faith in magic, chance, or dogma. **b.** Fearful or abject dependence upon such beliefs, practices, or rites. [Middle English *supersticion,* from Old French *superstition,* from Latin *superstitiō* (stem *superstitiōn-*), from *superstāre,* to stand over : *super-,* over + *stāre,* to stand.]

su·per·sti·tious (so͞o′pər-stĭsh′əs) *adj.* **1.** Inclined to believe in superstitions. **2.** Of, characterized by, or proceeding from superstition. —**su·per·sti·tious·ly** *adv.* —**su·per·sti·tious·ness** *n.*

su·per·stra·tum (so͞o′pər-strā′təm, -străt′əm) *n., pl.* **-ta** (-tə). A layer superimposed upon another, especially: **1.** *Geology.* A layer or stratum overlying another. **2.** *Linguistics.* The language of an invading population imposed on the indigenous tongue. Compare **substratum.**

su·per·struc·ture (so͞o′pər-strŭk′chər) *n.* **1.** Any structure, whether physical or conceptual, that extends or develops from a basic form. **2.** That part of a building or other structure above the foundation. **3.** The parts of a ship's structure above the main deck. **4.** In Marxist theory, the institutions or ideology of a society as distinct from the basic relations of economy and material production. —**su·per·struc·tur·al** (so͞o′pər-strŭk′chər-əl) *adj.*

su·per·sub·stan·tial (so͞o′pər-səb-stăn′shəl) *adj.* Transcending material substance or all substance.

su·per·tank·er (so͞o′pər-tăng′kər) *n.* A large tanker, especially one that carries more than 75,000 tons of oil.

su·per·tax (so͞o′pər-tăks′) *n.* In Britain, income tax paid at higher rates on incomes above a certain level.

su·per·ton·ic (so͞o′pər-tŏn′ĭk) *n. Music.* The second tone of a diatonic scale.

su·per·vene (so͞o′pər-vēn′) *intr.v.* **-vened, -vening, -venes. 1.** To come or occur as something extraneous, additional, or unexpected. **2.** To follow immediately after; ensue. —See Synonyms at **follow, happen.** [Latin *supervenīre* : *super-,* in addition + *venīre,* to come.] —**su·per·ven·ience** (so͞o′pər-vēn′yəns) *n.* —**su·per·ven·ient** (so͞o′pər-vēn′yənt) *adj.* —**su·per·ven·tion** (so͞o′pər-vĕn′shən) *n.*

su·per·vise (so͞o′pər-vīz′) *tr.v.* **-vised, -vising, -vises. 1.** To direct and inspect the performance of (workers or work); oversee; superintend. **2.** To watch over (pupils in an examination, for example) to maintain order. —See Synonyms at **conduct.** [Medieval Latin *supervidēre* (past participle *supervīsus*), to look over : Latin *super-,* over + *vidēre,* to see.] —**su·per·vi·sion** (so͞o′pər-vĭzh′ən) *n.*

su·per·vi·sor (so͞o′pər-vī′zər) *n.* **1.** A person who supervises. **2.** An elected administrative officer in certain U.S. counties and townships. **3.** A person in charge of a particular department or unit, as in a governmental agency or a school system. —**su·per·vi·so·ry** (so͞o′pər-vī′zə-rē) *adj.*

su·pi·nate (so͞o′pə-nāt′) *v.* **-nated, -nating, -nates.** —*tr.* To turn or place (the hand and forearm) so that the palm is upward. —*intr.* To turn the palm and forearm upward. [Latin *supīnāre,* to bend backward, from *supīnus,* SUPINE.] —**su·pi·na·tion** *n.*

su·pi·na·tor (so͞o′pə-nā′tər) *n.* A muscle in the forearm that makes supination possible.

su·pine[1] (so͞o-pīn′, so͞o′pīn′) *adj.* **1.** Lying on the back or having the face upward. **2.** Having the palm upward. Said of the hand. **3.** Indisposed to act or object; lethargic; passive. **4.** Inclined; sloping. —See Usage note at **prone.** [Latin *supīnus.*] —**su·pine·ly** *adv.* —**su·pine·ness** *n.*

su·pine[2] (so͞o′pīn′) *n. Abbr.* **sup. 1.** A Latin verbal noun having an accusative in *-um* and an ablative in *-ū.* **2.** An English infinitive preceded by *to.* [Late Latin *supīnum,* from Latin *supīnus,* backward.]

supp. supplement; supplementary.

sup·per (sŭp′ər) *n.* **1.** An evening meal; especially, a light evening meal when dinner is taken at midday. **2.** A social gathering at which supper is served. **3.** A light meal eaten before going to bed. [Middle English *suppere,* from Old French *so(u)per,* from *so(u)per,* to SUP.]

suppl. supplement; supplementary.

sup·plant (sə-plănt′, -plänt′) *tr.v.* **-planted, -planting, -plants.** To take the place of, as by force; oust. —See Synonyms at **replace.** [Middle English *supplanten,* from Old French *supplanter,* from Latin *supplantāre,* to trip up one's heel : *sub-,* up from under + *planta,* sole of the foot.] —**sup·plan·ta·tion** (sŭp′lăn-tā′shən) *n.* —**sup·plant·er** *n.*

sup·ple (sŭp′əl) *adj.* **-pler, -plest. 1.** Readily bent; pliant. **2.** Moving and bending with agility; lithe. **3.** Mentally flexible. **4.** Yielding or changing readily; compliant. —See Synonyms at **flexible.** [Middle English *souple,* from Old French, from Latin *supplex,* beseeching, submissive.] —**sup·ple** *v.* —**sup·ple·ness** *n.* —**sup·ply** *adv.*

sup·ple·jack (sŭp′əl-jăk′) *n.* A walking stick made from a strong tropical American twining plant, *Paullinia curassavica.*

sup·ple·ment (sŭp′lə-mənt) *n. Abbr.* **sup., supp., suppl. 1.** Something added to complete a thing, make up for a deficiency, or extend or strengthen the whole. **2.** A section, sometimes published separately, added to a book or document to give further information or to correct errors. **3. a.** A separate section devoted to a special subject inserted into a newspaper or other periodical as an additional feature. **b.** A periodical devoted to a particular subject, associated with another publication but published separately. **4.** *Geometry.* **a.** An angle that with an adjacent angle forms an angle of 180°. **b.** An arc that with an adjacent arc forms a semicircle. **5.** A preparation, as of iron or calcium, taken to balance a diet or remedy a dietary deficiency.

~*tr.v.* (sŭp′lə-mĕnt′) **supplemented, -menting, -ments.** To provide or form a supplement to. [Middle English, from Latin *supplēmentum,* from *supplēre,* to complete, SUPPLY.] —**sup·ple·men·tal** (sŭp′lə-mĕn′təl) *adj & n.* —**sup·ple·men·ta·tion** (sŭp′lə-mĕn-tā′shən) *n.* —**sup·ple·ment·er** *n.*

Supplemental Security Income *n. Abbr.* **SSI** A program under the Social Security Administration that provides federal welfare payments for aged, blind, and disabled persons.

sup·ple·men·ta·ry (sŭp′lə-mĕn′tə-rē, -trē) *adj.* **1.** Provided or added as a supplement; additional. **2.** Of, pertaining to, or being an angle that is a supplement.

sup·ple·tion (sə-plē′shən) *n.* The occurrence of a phonetically unrelated form to complete an otherwise consistent paradigm, as *better* as the comparative of *good.* [Middle English, from Old French, from Medieval Latin *supplētiō* (stem *supplētiōn-*), a completing, from Latin *supplēre,* to fill up, SUPPLY.] —**sup·ple·tive** (sə-plē′tĭv, sŭp′lĭ-tĭv) *adj. & n.*

sup·pli·ant (sŭp′lē-ənt) *adj.* Asking humbly and earnestly.

~*n.* One who supplicates. [Middle English, from Old French, present participle of *supplier,* to entreat, from Latin *supplicāre,* to SUPPLICATE.] —**sup·pli·ance** *n.* —**sup·pli·ant·ly** *adv.*

sup·pli·cant (sŭp′lĭ-kənt) *n.* One who entreats or supplicates.

~*adj.* Supplicating.

sup·pli·cate (sŭp′lĭ-kāt′) *v.* **-cated, -cating, -cates.** —*tr.* **1.** To ask for humbly or earnestly. **2.** To make a humble entreaty to; beseech. —*intr.* To make a humble and earnest petition, especially to a deity. [Middle English *supplicaten,* from Latin *supplicāre,* to kneel down, beg humbly : *sub-,* down, underneath + *plicāre,* to fold up.] —**sup·pli·ca·tion** *n.* —**sup·pli·ca·to·ry** (sŭp′lĭ-kə-tôr′ē, -tōr′ē) *adj.*

sup·ply (sə-plī′) *v.* **-plied, -plying, -plies.** —*tr.* **1.** To make (something needed, desired, or lacking) available for use; provide: *supplied food for the needy.* **2.** To provide or equip (a person or place, for example) with what is needed or lacking: *supplies the city with water.* **3.** *Anatomy.* To provide (a body part) with nerve impulses or a vital fluid, such as blood. **4.** To fill sufficiently; satisfy: *supply a need.* **5.** To make up for (a deficiency, for example); compensate for. **6.** To serve temporarily as a substitute in (the position or office of another, especially in a church). —*intr.* To fill a position as a substitute.

~*n., pl.* **supplies.** *Abbr.* **sup. 1.** The act of supplying. **2.** Something that is or can be supplied, especially a basic facility such as water or electricity. **3.** An amount available or sufficient for a given use; a store; a stock. **4.** *Usually* **supplies.** Materials or provisions stored and dispensed when needed. **5.** *Economics.* The amount of a commodity available for meeting a demand or for purchase at a given price. **6.** One who substitutes for another; especially, a clergyman serving as a temporary pastor. [Middle English *suppl(y)en,* from Old French *so(u)pleer, soup(p)leier,* from Latin *supplēre,* to fill up, complete : *sub-,* from below + *plēre,* to fill.] —**sup·pli·er** *n.*

supply and demand *n.* The availability of and willingness of consumers to purchase goods or services, considered as the economic force governing prices in the absence of administrative control and through prices determining output and the distribution of income.

sup·ply-side (sə-plī′sīd′) *adj.* Designating or pertaining to an economic theory that advocates reductions in taxes as a means of encouraging investment and boosting productivity.

sup·port (sə-pôrt′, -pōrt′) *tr.v.* **-ported, -porting, -ports. 1.** To bear the whole or partial weight of, especially from below. **2.** To hold in position; prevent from falling, sinking, or slipping. **3.** To encourage or lend strength to, especially in difficulties. **4.** To provide for or maintain by supplying with money or other necessities. **5.** To furnish evidence for; corroborate or substantiate. **6. a.** To aid the

PRONUNCIATION KEY

ă, pat; ā, pay; âr, care; ä, father, are; b, bib; ch, church; d, deed; ĕ, pet; ē, be; f, fife; g, gag; h, hat; hw, which; ĭ, pit; ī, pie; îr, pier; j, judge; k, kick; l, lid, needle; m, mum; n, no, sudden; ng, thing; ŏ, pot; ō, toe; ô, paw, for; oi, noise; ou, out; o͝o, book; o͞o, boot; p, pop; r, roar; s, sauce; sh, ship, dish; t, tight; th, thin, path; *th,* this, bathe; ŭ, cut; ûr, fur; v, valve; w, with; y, yes; z, zebra, size; zh, vision; ə, about, item, edible, gallop, circus, peaceful

IN FOREIGN WORDS:

à, *Fr.* ami; œ, *Fr.* feu, *Ger.* schön; ü, *Fr.* tu, *Ger.* über; KH, *Ger.* ich, *Scot.* loch; N, *Fr.* bon; y′, *Fr.* Compiègne

STRESS MARKS:

Primary stress: ′ in·cite′ (ĭn-sīt′)
Secondary stress: ′ in′sight′ (ĭn′sīt′)

cause of by approving, favoring, or advocating. **b.** To be an adherent of; give one's loyalty to. **7.** To bear or endure; tolerate. **8. a.** To act in a secondary or subordinate role to (a leading actor). **b.** To accompany (the main act, showing, or performance). ~*n.* **1. a.** The act of supporting. **b.** The state of being supported. **2.** One that supports. **3.** Maintenance or subsistence. **4.** A medical appliance worn to support and ease an injured part. **5.** The solid material on which a painting is executed. [Middle English *supporten,* from Old French *supporter,* from Latin *supportāre,* to carry, convey : *sub-,* up, toward + *portāre,* to carry.]

Synonyms: *support, uphold, sustain, maintain, advocate, champion.* These verbs are compared in the sense of giving aid, encouragement, or the like to a person or cause. *Support* refers nonspecifically to any such aid. *Uphold* often implies aid to someone or something faced with strong opposition or a challenge. *Sustain* and *maintain* can refer to material or financial aid or support. In this comparison, however, *sustain* more often suggests keeping up a person's spirits in time of stress, whereas *maintain* applies to the defense of personal rights or a position or cause. *Advocate* implies verbal support, usually in the sense of pleading or arguing. *Champion* suggests aid in the form of defense of what is under attack or protection of what is unable to act in its own behalf.

sup·port·a·ble (sə-pôr′tə-bəl, -pōr′tə-bəl) *adj.* Bearable; endurable. —**sup·port·a·bil·i·ty** *n.* —**sup·port·a·bly** *adv.*

sup·port·er (sə-pôr′tər, -pōr′tər) *n.* **1.** A person or thing that supports. **2.** One who promotes or advocates; adherent. **3.** A sports fan loyal to a particular team or player. **4.** A support or binding for a part of the body; especially, a jockstrap. **5.** *Heraldry.* An animal or figure that supports a shield in a coat of arms.

sup·por·tive (sə-pôr′tĭv, -pōr′tĭv) *adj.* **1.** Furnishing support or assistance. **2.** Inclined to provide emotional or psychological support. —**sup·por·tive·ly** *adv.* —**sup·por·tive·ness** *n.*

support level *n.* A level at which the price of a security becomes attractive to investors.

support stockings *pl.n.* Elasticized stockings designed to reduce stress on the blood vessels in the legs, as for people with varicose veins. Also called "support hose."

support system *n.* A network of personal or professional contacts available to a person or organization to give practical or moral support when required.

sup·pose (sə-pōz′) *v.* **-posed, -posing, -poses.** —*tr.* **1.** To assume (something) to be true or real for the sake of an argument or explanation. **2.** To believe, especially on uncertain or tentative grounds; be inclined to think. **3.** To imply as an antecedent condition; presuppose. **4.** To consider as a suggestion. Often used to introduce a proposal: *Suppose we dine together.* **5.** To expect or require. Used in the passive: *I was not supposed to be home. You are supposed to obey the rules.* —*intr.* To make an assumption; conjecture. —See Synonyms at **presume.** [Middle English *supposen,* to believe, assume, from Old French *supposer,* from Latin *suppōnere* (past participle *suppositus*), to put under, substitute, forge : *sub-,* under + *pōnere,* to place.]

sup·posed (sə-pōzd′, -pō′zĭd) *adj.* Presumed to be true or genuine, especially on dubious grounds: *the supposed site of buried treasure; your supposed friends.* —**sup·pos·ed·ly** (sə-pō′zĭd-lē) *adv.*

sup·pos·ing (sə-pō′zĭng) *conj.* In the event that; assuming that: *Supposing you're right, what should we do?*

sup·po·si·tion (sŭp′ə-zĭsh′ən) *n.* **1.** The act of supposing. **2.** An unproven statement or assumption, especially one tentatively accepted. —**sup·po·si·tion·al** *adj.* —**sup·po·si·tion·al·ly** *adv.*

sup·po·si·tious (sŭp′ə-zĭsh′əs) *adj.* **1.** Hypothetical; supposed. **2.** Fraudulent; supposititious.

sup·pos·i·ti·tious (sə-pŏz′ə-tĭsh′əs) *adj.* **1.** Substituted with fraudulent intent; spurious; counterfeit. **2.** Hypothetical; supposed. [Latin *supposītīcius,* substituted, from *suppōnere* (past participle *suppositus*), to place under, substitute, SUPPOSE.] —**sup·pos·i·ti·tious·ly** *adv.* —**sup·pos·i·ti·tious·ness** *n.*

sup·pos·i·tive (sə-pŏz′ə-tĭv) *adj.* Of the nature of, including, or involving supposition. ~*n. Grammar.* A conjunction introducing a supposition, such as *if* or *providing.* —**sup·pos·i·tive·ly** *adv.*

sup·pos·i·to·ry (sə-pŏz′ə-tôr′ē, -tōr′ē) *n., pl.* **-ries.** A solid medication designed to melt within a body cavity other than the mouth, especially the rectum or vagina. [Medieval Latin *suppositōrium,* "something placed underneath," from Latin *suppositōrius,* "placed under," from Latin *suppōnere,* to place under, SUPPOSE.]

sup·press (sə-prĕs′) *tr.v.* **-pressed, -pressing, -presses. 1.** To put an end to forcibly; subdue; crush. **2.** To curtail or prohibit the activities of (a political party, for example). **3.** To keep from being revealed, published, or circulated; withhold from the public. **4.** To hold back (an impulse, for example); check: *suppress a smile.* **5.** To reduce the incidence or severity of (a hemorrhage, for example); arrest. **6.** To reduce or eliminate (noise or a specified frequency range) from an electronic signal or device. **7.** *Psychology.* To exclude (desires or thoughts) consciously from one's awareness. [Middle English *suppressen,* from Latin *supprimere* (past participle *suppressus*), to press down : *sub-,* down + *premere,* to press.] —**sup·pres·sant** *n.* —**sup·press·i·ble** *adj.* —**sup·pres·sive** *adj.*

Synonyms: *suppress, stifle.* These verbs refer to the exercise of power or control that either brings about extinction or severely limits force or function. *Suppress* implies crushing or restricting drastically in effectiveness. *Stifle* can refer to physical attack on a

person but more often applies to restraining or smothering, as emotions, coughs, or cries.

sup·pres·sion (sə-prĕsh′ən) *n.* **1.** The act of suppressing. **2.** The state of being suppressed. **3.** The act or process of suppressing an electronic frequency. **4.** *Psychology.* The conscious exclusion of painful desires or thoughts from awareness. **5.** *Botany.* The failure of an organ or part to develop.

sup·pres·sor, sup·press·er (sə-prĕs′ər) *n.* **1.** One that suppresses. **2.** A gene that reduces the phenotypic expression of a mutant gene. **3.** A device that reduces or eliminates electrical noise from the ignition system of an internal-combustion engine to prevent interference with an electronic device, such as a radio. **4.** An electrode placed between the screen grid and anode of an electronic vacuum tube to keep secondary electrons from the anode from reaching the screen. In this sense, also called "suppressor grid."

sup·pu·rate (sŭp′yə-rāt′) *intr.v.* **-rated, -rating, -rates.** To form or discharge pus; fester or maturate. [Latin *suppūrāre* : *sub-,* under + *pūs* (stem *pūr-*), pus.]

sup·pu·ra·tion (sŭp′yə-rā′shən) *n.* **1.** The formation or discharge of pus. Also called "maturation." **2.** Pus.

sup·pu·ra·tive (sŭp′yə-rā′tĭv) *adj.* **1.** Causing suppuration. **2.** Characterized by suppuration. —**sup·pu·ra·tive** *n.*

supr. supreme.

su·pra (soo′prə) *adv.* In the text that precedes; above. Compare **infra.** [Latin.]

supra– *prefix.* Indicates above, specifically: **1.** Higher than or over; for example, **suprarenal. 2.** Greater than; for example, **supramolecular. 3.** Preceding; for example, **supralapsarian.** [Latin, from *suprā,* above, beyond, earlier.]

su·pra·glot·tal (soo′prə-glŏt′l) *adj.* **1.** *Anatomy.* Above or anterior to the glottis. **2.** *Phonetics.* Produced by the speech organs anterior to the glottis.

su·pra·lap·sar·i·an (soo′prə-lăp-sâr′ē-ən) *n.* A Calvinist who believes that God's determination of the elect preceded the fall of man from grace and that the fall itself had been predestined. [SUPRA- + Latin *lapsus,* fall, from the past participle of *lābī,* to slide.] —**su·pra·lap·sar·i·an** *adj.* —**su·pra·lap·sar·i·an·ism** *n.*

su·pra·lim·i·nal (soo′prə-lĭm′ə-nəl) *adj.* Above the threshold of conscious perception. Said of stimuli.

su·pra·mo·lec·u·lar (soo′prə-mə-lĕk′yə-lər) *adj.* **1.** Consisting of more than one molecule. **2.** More complex than a molecule.

sup·ra·na·tion·al (soo′prə-năsh′ə-nəl) *adj.* Going beyond national boundaries or concerns.

su·pra·or·bi·tal (soo′prə-ôr′bĭ-təl) *adj.* Located above the orbit of the eye.

su·pra·re·nal (soo′prə-rē′nəl) *adj.* Located above or on the kidney. ~*n.* A suprarenal gland. [New Latin *suprarenalis* : SUPRA- + Latin *rēnēs,* the kidneys (see **renal**).]

suprarenal gland *n.* An adrenal gland (see).

su·pra·seg·men·tal (soo′prə-sĕg-mĕn′təl) *adj. Linguistics.* Designating those features, such as stress and juncture, that occur simultaneously with the individual segments of an utterance.

su·prem·a·cist (soo-prĕm′ə-sĭst) *n.* One who believes that a certain group is or should be supreme.

su·prem·a·cy (soo-prĕm′ə-sē) *n., pl.* **-cies. 1.** The condition or quality of being supreme. **2.** Supreme power.

su·prem·a·tism (soo-prĕm′ə-tĭz′əm) *n.* A school and theory of geometric abstract art that was originated by Russian artists such as Malevich in the early 20th century and that influenced constructivists. [From *suprematist,* an adherent of suprematism, from French *suprémacie,* SUPREMACY.] —**su·prem·a·tist** *n. & adj.*

su·preme (soo-prĕm′) *adj. Abbr.* **supr. 1.** Greatest in power, authority, or rank; paramount; dominant. **2.** Greatest in degree, significance, character, or achievement; utmost; extreme. **3.** Ultimate; final: *the supreme sacrifice.* [Latin *suprēmus,* superlative of *superus,* situated above, upper, from *super,* above.] —**su·preme·ly** *adv.* —**su·preme·ness** *n.*

su·prême (soo-prĕm′) *n.* A rich white sauce usually made with cream and egg yolks. [French, SUPREME.]

Supreme Court *n. Abbr.* **S.C. 1.** The highest federal court in the United States, consisting of nine justices and having jurisdiction over all other courts in the nation. **2.** *Sometimes* **supreme court.** The highest court in most states within the United States. Also called "high court."

Supreme Soviet *n.* The legislature of the Soviet Union, consisting of two equal houses, the *Soviet of the Union,* whose members are elected on the basis of population, and the *Soviet of the Nationalities,* whose members are elected by the various national groups.

su·pre·mo (soo-prē′mō) *n., pl.* **-mos.** *British Informal.* A chief or leader having overall authority. [Spanish, SUPREME.]

Supt., Supt. superintendent.

Su·qua·mish (sə-kwä′mĭsh) *n., pl.* **-mishes** or collectively **Suquamish. 1.** A member of a Salish-speaking people of North American Indians of the northwestern Pacific coast, west of Puget Sound. **2.** The Salish language of the Suquamish.

sur– *prefix.* Indicates: **1.** Over, above, or upon; for example, **surface, surprint. 2.** Additional; for example, **surtax.** [Middle English, from Old French *s(o)ur-,* from Latin *super-,* from *super,* above, over.]

sur. 1. surface. **2.** surplus.

su·ra (soor′ə) *n.* Any of the 114 chapters or sections of the Koran. [Arabic *sūrah,* "a step," from Hebrew *shūrāh,* row, line.]

Su·ra·ba·ya (soor′ə-bī′ə). Port in Indonesia, situated in northeastern Java at the mouth of the Mas River. It is the country's second-largest city and its major naval base.

su·rah (sŏŏr′ə) *n.* A soft twilled fabric of silk or of a blend of silk and rayon. [French *surat*, originally made at SURAT.]

su·ral (sŏŏr′əl) *adj.* Of or relating to the calf of the leg. [New Latin *suralis*, from Latin *sūra†*, calf of the leg.]

Su·rat (sŏŏr′ət, sə-răt′, -răt′). City in Gujarat state, India, on the Tapti River near its mouth on the Gulf of Khambat. It is an administrative and commercial center, a small port, and a railway junction. In the 17th century British and Dutch trading posts were established here.

sur·base (sûr′bās′) *n. Architecture.* A molding or border above the base of a structure such as a pedestal. [SUR- + BASE.]

sur·based (sûr′bāst′) *adj. Architecture.* **1.** Having a surbase. **2.** Pertaining to or designating an arch with a rise less than half its span. [French *surbaissé*, flattened (said of an arch), from the past participle of *surbaisser*, to depress, flatten : *sur-*, extremely + *baisser*, to lower, from *bas*, low, from Old French, low, BASE.]

sur·cease (sər-sēs′, sûr′sēs′) *v.* **-ceased, -ceasing, -ceases.** *Archaic.* —*tr.* To put an end to. —*intr.* To cease; stop.
—*n.* (sûr′sēs′, sər-sēs′). *Archaic.* A cessation; end. [Middle English *sursesen,* from Old French *surseoir* (past participle *sursis*), to refrain, delay, from Latin *supersedēre,* to desist from, SUPERSEDE.]

sur·charge (sûr′chärj′) *n.* **1.** An additional sum added to the usual amount or cost. **2.** An overcharge, especially when unlawful. **3.** An additional or excessive burden; an overload. **4. a.** A new value or denomination overprinted on a postage or revenue stamp. **b.** The stamp to which it has been applied. **5.** *Law.* The act of surcharging. —*tr.v.* **surcharged, -charging, -charges. 1.** To charge (a person) an additional sum. **2.** To overcharge (a person). **3. a.** To place an excessive burden upon; overload. **b.** To fill beyond usual capacity; overfill. **4.** To print a surcharge on (a postage or revenue stamp). **5.** *Law.* To show an omission of a credit in (an account). **6.** To require (a person) to reimburse funds spent without authorization. [Middle English *surchargen,* from Old French *surcharger : sur-,* excessively + *charg(i)er,* to CHARGE.]

sur·cin·gle (sûr′sing′gəl) *n.* **1.** A girth that binds a saddle, pack, or blanket to the body of a horse. **2.** *Archaic.* The fastening belt on a clerical cassock. [Middle English *surcengle,* from Old French *so(u)rcengle : sur-,* over + *cengle,* belt, from Latin *cingula,* from *cingere,* to gird.]

sur·coat (sûr′kōt′) *n.* **1.** A loose outer coat or cloak. **2.** A tunic worn in the Middle Ages by a knight over his armor. [Middle English *surcote,* "overcoat," from Old French : SUR- + COAT.]

sur·cu·lose (sûr′kyə-lōs′) *adj. Botany.* Producing suckers: *a surculose shrub.* [Latin *surculōsus,* woody, ligneous, from *surculus,* diminutive of *surus,* branch.]

surd (sûrd) *n.* **1.** A sum, such as $\sqrt{2} + \sqrt{3}$, containing one or more irrational roots of numbers. **2.** *Phonetics.* A voiceless sound.
—*adj. Phonetics.* Voiceless. [Latin *surdus,* deaf, mute (used in mathematics to translate Arabic *(jadhr) asạm,* deaf (root), translation of Greek *alogos,* speechless, irrational).]

sure (shŏŏr) *adj.* **surer, surest. 1.** Incapable of being doubted or disputed; completely true; certain: *sure proof of his innocence.* **2.** Not hesitating or wavering; stable; steady; firm: *sure convictions.* **3.** Confident of some established fact or future outcome; certain in one's knowledge or expectation. Used with a clause or *of: sure that I'm right; sure of victory.* **4. a.** Bound to come about or to happen; inevitable. **b.** Having one's course directed; destined; bound. **5.** Certain not to miss or err; steady. **6. a.** Worthy of being trusted or depended upon; reliable. **b.** Of which one may be confident; safe. **7.** *Obsolete.* Free from harm or danger; safe; secure. —**for sure.** Certainly; unquestionably: *We'll win for sure.* —**make sure. 1.** To establish something without doubt. **2.** To ensure something: *made sure you were told.* —**to be sure.** Indeed; of course.
—*adv. Informal.* Certainly; indeed; surely: *I sure hope so. It sure was easy.* —**sure enough.** As was to be expected.
—*interj.* Certainly; willingly. [Middle English *s(e)ure,* from Old French *sur,* from Latin *sēcūrus,* "free from care," safe : *sē,* without + *cūra,* care.] —**sure′ness** *n.*

Synonyms: *sure, certain, confident, assured.* These adjectives are compared as they apply to persons who do not doubt their own abilities. *Sure* and *certain* are frequently used interchangeably. *Sure,* however, is the more subjective term, whereas *certain* may imply belief based on experience or established evidence. *Confident* suggests belief founded on faith or reliance in oneself or in others. *Assured* suggests confidence or certainty based on knowledge that doubt has been removed.

sure-fire (shŏŏr′fīr′) *adj. Informal.* Bound to be successful or perform as expected: *a sure-fire plan.*

sure-foot·ed (shŏŏr′fŏŏt′ĭd) *adj.* Not liable to stumble or fall; agile. —**sure-foot·ed·ness** *n.*

sure·ly (shŏŏr′lē) *adv.* **1.** Firmly and with confidence; unhesitatingly. **2.** Undoubtedly; certainly. Often used: **a.** As an intensive: *You surely can't be serious.* **b.** In incredulous questions: *Surely it's not Monday already?* **3.** Without fail: *Slowly but surely spring returns.*
—*interj.* Of course; willingly.

sure thing *n. Informal.* A guaranteed success.
—*interj. Informal.* Certainly; of course.

sur·e·ty (shŏŏr′ə-tē) *n., pl.* **-ties. 1.** A person who has contracted to be responsible for another; especially, a person who assumes any responsibilities, debts, or obligations in the event of the default of another. **2.** A pledge or formal promise made to secure against loss, damage, or default; a guarantee or security. **3.** Something beyond doubt; a certainty. **4.** The condition of being sure, especially of oneself; self-assurance. —**sur·e·ty·ship** *n.*

surf (sûrf) *n.* **1.** The foaming white spray produced by waves as they break. **2.** The sound or effect of breaking waves.
—*intr.v.* **surfed, surfing, surfs.** To engage in surfing. [17th century : origin obscure.] —**surf′y** *adj.*

sur·face (sûr′fəs) *n. Abbr.* **sur. 1. a.** The outer or the topmost boundary or boundaries of an object. **b.** A material layer constituting such a boundary. **c.** Such a layer with regard to its texture. **2.** The uppermost level of the land or sea. **3.** *Geometry.* **a.** The boundary of any three-dimensional figure. **b.** The two-dimensional locus of points located in three-dimensional space. **4.** The superficial or outward appearance of anything as distinguished from inner substance or matter. **5.** *Aeronautics.* An airfoil. —**on the surface.** To all appearances. —**scratch the surface.** To make a slight beginning without achieving a deep effect.
—*adj.* **1.** Pertaining to, on, or at a surface: *surface algae in the water.* **2.** Superficial; apparent as opposed to real.
—*v.* **surfaced, -facing, -faces.** —*tr.* **1.** To form the surface of, as by smoothing or leveling; give a surface to. **2.** To provide with a particular surface. —*intr.* **1.** To rise to the surface. **2.** To emerge after concealment. **3.** To mine at or near the ground surface. [French : *sur-,* above + *face,* FACE.]

sur·face-ac·tive (sûr′fəs-ăk′tĭv) *adj.* Designating a substance capable of reducing the surface tension of a liquid in which it is dissolved. Said especially of detergents.

surface mail *n.* **1.** Mail transported over land and sea rather than by air. **2.** Transportation of surface mail.

surface noise *n.* Noise, largely of a high frequency, produced by a phonograph needle as it follows the groove of a rotating record.

surface of revolution *n. Geometry.* A surface generated by revolving a plane curve about an axis in its plane.

surface plate *n.* A **planometer** *(see).*

surface structure *n. Linguistics.* In the standard theory of transformational-generative grammar, the string of words and sounds as they occur in a sentence, or a diagrammatic representation of these, that can be analyzed according to transformational rules to reveal the underlying **deep structure** *(see).*

surface tension *n. Abbr.* **T 1.** A property of liquids arising from molecular cohesive forces at or near the surface, as a result of which the surface tends to contract to a minimum area and has properties resembling those of a stretched elastic membrane. **2.** A measure of this property.

sur·face-to-air missile (sûr′fəs-tōō-âr′) *n.* A missile launched from land or sea at an airborne target. Also called "SAM."

sur·face-to-sur·face missile (sûr′fəs-tōō-sûr′fəs) *n. Abbr.* **SSM** A missile launched from land or sea at a target that is also on the earth's surface.

sur·fac·tant (sər-făk′tənt) *n.* A surface-active agent, as a detergent. [SURF(ACE) + AC(TIVE) + -ANT.]

surf·bird (sûrf′bûrd′) *n.* A shore bird, *Aphriza virgata,* of the Pacific coast of North and South America, having dark, spotted plumage.

surf·board (sûrf′bôrd′, -bōrd′) *n.* A long, narrow, round-ended board used by surfers for riding waves to the shore.
—*intr.v.* **surfboarded, -boarding, boards.** To engage in surfing.

surf·boat (sûrf′bōt′) *n.* A strong seaworthy boat that can be launched or landed in heavy surf.

surf·cast·ing (sûrf′kăs′tĭng, -kä′stĭng) *n.* The sport of fishing from shore, casting one's line into the surf. —**surf·cast·er** *n.*

sur·feit (sûr′fĭt) *v.* **-feited, -feiting, -feits.** —*tr.* To feed or supply to fullness or excess; satiate. —*intr. Archaic.* To overindulge. —See Synonyms at **satiate.**
—*n.* **1.** The act or an instance of overindulging in food or drink. **2.** The result of such overindulgence; satiety; disgust. **3.** An excessive amount. [Middle English, from Old French, from Vulgar Latin *superfactum* (unattested), from the neuter past participle of *superficere* (unattested), to overdo : Latin *super-,* excessively + *facere,* to do.] —**sur·feit·er** *n.*

surf·er (sûr′fər) *n.* One who engages in surfing.

sur·fi·cial (sər-fĭsh′əl) *adj.* Of, pertaining to, or occurring on the earth's surface. [SURF(ACE) + (SUPERF)ICIAL.] —**sur·fi·cial·ly** *adv.*

surf·ing (sûr′fĭng) *n.* The sport of riding toward the shore on the crest or along the tunnel of a wave while standing or lying on a surfboard.

surf·perch (sûrf′pûrch′) *n., pl.* **-perches** or collectively **surfperch.** Any of various viviparous fishes of the family Embiotocidae, of North American Pacific coastal waters. Also called "sea perch."

surg. surgeon; surgery; surgical.

surge (sûrj) *v.* **surged, surging, surges.** —*intr.* **1.** To move in a billowing or swelling manner; rise and heave over violently, as waves. **2.** To roll or be tossed about on waves, as a boat. **3.** To move like advancing waves: *The fans surged forward to see her.* **4.** To well or rise up suddenly and strongly: *anger surging up within us.* **5.** To increase suddenly. Used of an electric current or voltage. **6.** To slip around a windlass. —*tr.* To loosen or slacken (a cable) gradually.
—*n.* **1.** A heavy, billowing, or swelling motion like that of great waves: *surge and flow.* **2. a.** A wave, ground swell, or billow. **b.** Such waves collectively. **c.** An undulating surface, such as one formed by hills. **3.** A sudden powerful onset, as of emotion. **4.** A sudden, transient increase in electric current. **5.** An instability in

the power output of an engine. **6.** *Astronomy.* A short-lived, violent disturbance occurring during the eruption of a solar flare. **7.** *Nautical.* **a.** A temporary release or slackening of a cable. **b.** The part of a windlass into which the cable surges. [Old French *sourgir,* from Old Spanish *surgir,* from Latin *surgere,* "to lead straight up," rise : *sub-,* up from below + *regere,* to lead, rule.]

sur·geon (sûr′jən) *n. Abbr.* **surg.** A physician who specializes in surgery. [Middle English *surg(i)en,* from Norman French, short for Old French *serurgien,* from *serurgie,* SURGERY.]

sur·geon·cy (sûr′jən-sē) *n., pl.* **-cies.** The position, office, or duties of a surgeon.

sur·geon·fish (sûr′jən-fĭsh′) *n., pl.* **-fishes** or collectively **surgeonfish.** Any of various bright-colored tropical marine fishes of the family Acanthuridae, having a sharp, erectile spine near the base of the tail. [From its lancetlike spines, which resemble surgeons' instruments.]

Surgeon General *n., pl.* **Surgeons General.** *Abbr.* **Surg. Gen. 1.** The chief general officer in the medical departments of the United States Army or Navy. **2.** The chief medical officer in the United States Public Health Service.

surgeon's knot *n.* Any of several knots used in surgery for tying ligatures or stitching incisions.

sur·ger·y (sûr′jə-rē) *n., pl.* **-ies.** *Abbr.* **surg. 1.** The branch of medicine concerned with the treatment of injury, deformity, and disease by manual and instrumental operations. **2.** The skill or work of a surgeon. **3.** An operating room or laboratory of a surgeon or of a hospital's surgical staff. **4.** An operation performed by a surgeon: *having surgery tomorrow.* **5.** *Chiefly British.* **a.** A place where general practitioners or dentists advise and treat patients. **b.** The period during which a doctor or other specialist is present in the surgery. [Middle English *surgerie,* from Old French, short for *serurgerie, cerurgerie,* from *serurgie, cerurgie,* from Latin *chirurgia,* from Greek *kheirurgia,* from *kheirurgos,* working by hand : *kheir,* hand + *ergon,* work.]

sur·gi·cal (sûr′jĭ-kəl) *adj. Abbr.* **surg. 1.** Pertaining to or characteristic of surgeons or surgery. **2.** Used in surgery. **3.** Resulting from or occurring after surgery. [From SURGEON.] **—sur·gi·cal·ly** *adv.*

su·ri·cate (so͝or′ĭ-kāt′) *n.* A small, grayish, gregarious burrowing mongoose, *Suricata suricatta,* of southern Africa, having a long tail. [French *suricate,* of African origin.]

Su·ri·nam (so͝or′ə-năm′). *Formerly* **Dutch Gui·a·na** (dŭch′ gē-ä′nə). *Dutch* **Su·ri·na·me** (so͝or′ə-nä′mə). A country in northeastern South America. It has a low-lying, marshy coastal strip, a belt of grassland, and the densely forested Guiana Highlands in the south. The major part of all cultivated land is used for rice growing. Other crops include sugar cane, bananas, citrus fruits, and coconuts. Surinam is one of the world's largest producers of bauxite and its products, which account for most of its foreign income. The population is mixed, with Creoles, Asian Indians, and Indonesians forming the largest groups. The first Europeans to reach the area were the Spanish (1499), but it was the British who established the first colony (1650). In 1667 the territory was ceded to the Dutch. Known as Dutch Guiana, it was renamed Surinam (1949) and became an internally autonomous part of the Netherlands (1954). It has been fully independent since 1975. Area, 163,265 square kilometers (63,037 square miles). Population, 350,000. Capital, Paramaribo. See map at **Guyana.**

Surinam toad *n.* A South American toad, the **pipa** *(see).*

sur·ly (sûr′lē) *adj.* **-lier, -liest.** Grumpy or habitually uncivil; gruff. [Variant of obsolete *sirly,* originally "lordly," masterful, imperious, from SIR.] **—sur·li·ly** *adv.* **—sur·li·ness** *n.*

sur·mise (sər-mīz′) *v.* **-mised, -mising, -mises.** *—tr.* To infer reasonably though without conclusive evidence. *—intr.* To make a guess or conjecture. —See Synonyms at **conjecture.**

∼n. An idea or opinion based upon insufficiently conclusive evidence; a guess; a conjecture. [Middle English *surmysen,* to charge on or against, accuse, from Old French *surmettre* (past participle *surmis*), from Medieval Latin *supermittere,* from Late Latin, to throw upon : Latin *super-,* upon + *mittere,* to send off, throw.]

sur·mount (sər-mount′) *tr.v.* **-mounted, -mounting, -mounts. 1.** To overcome (an obstacle, for example); conquer. **2.** To ascend to the top and cross to the other side of; get above and over. **3.** To place something above; top. **4.** To be above or on top of: *The church steeple surmounts the square.* **5.** *Obsolete.* **a.** To exceed in amount. **b.** To surpass. [Middle English *surmonten,* from Old French *surmonter* : *sur-,* above + *monter,* to MOUNT.] **—sur·mount·a·ble** *adj.* **—sur·mount·a·ble·ness** *n.* **—sur·mount·er** *n.*

sur·mul·let (sər-mŭl′ĭt, sûr′mŭl′ĭt) *n., pl.* **-lets** or collectively **surmullet.** The **goatfish** *(see).* [French *surmulet,* from Old French *sormulet* : probably *sor,* reddish brown, from Germanic + *mulet,* MULLET.]

sur·name (sûr′nām′) *n.* **1.** A family name as distinguished from a given name. **2.** A nickname or epithet added to a person's name.

∼tr.v. **surnamed, -naming, -names.** To give a surname to. [Middle English : SUR- + NAME.] **—sur·nom·i·nal** (sər-nŏm′ə-nəl) *adj.*

sur·pass (sər-păs′, -päs′) *tr.v.* **-passed, -passing, -passes. 1.** To go beyond the limit, powers, or extent of; transcend. **2.** To be or go beyond, as in quantity, degree, or amount; exceed. —See Synonyms at **excel.** [Old French *surpasser* : *sur-,* over + *passer,* to PASS.] **—sur·pass·a·ble** *adj.*

sur·pass·ing (sər-păs′ĭng, -pä′sĭng) *adj.* Exceptional; exceeding: *monuments of surpassing splendor.*

∼adv. Archaic. Extremely; exceedingly: *surpassing strange.* **—surpass·ing·ly** *adv.*

sur·plice (sûr′plĭs) *n.* A loose-fitting white gown reaching usually to the knees and having full flowing sleeves, worn over a cassock by certain clergymen and choristers. [Middle English *surplis,* from Old French *sourpeliz,* from Medieval Latin *superpellicium* : *super-,* over + *pellicium,* fur coat, from Latin *pellicius,* made of skin, from *pellis,* skin.] **—sur·pliced** *adj.*

sur·plus (sûr′plŭs′, -pləs) *adj. Abbr.* **sur.** Being more than or in excess of what is needed or required: *surplus grain.*

∼n. Abbr. **sur. 1.** An amount or quantity in excess of what is needed; something remaining or left over. **2.** The total of assets minus the sum of all liabilities. **3.** The excess of a company's net assets over the face value of its capital stock. **4.** The excess of receipts over expenditures. [Middle English, from Old French, from Medieval Latin *superplūs* : Latin *super-,* in addition + *plūs,* more.]

sur·plus·age (sûr′plŭs′ĭj, -plə-sĭj) *n.* **1.** A surplus. **2.** An excess of words. **3.** *Law.* Irrelevant matter in a pleading.

surplus value *n.* In the Marxian analysis of capitalism, the difference between the value of the product produced by labor and the actual price of labor as paid out in wages.

sur·print (sûr′prĭnt′) *tr.v.* **-printed, -printing, -prints. 1.** To overprint. **2.** To superimpose (a second negative) upon a previously printed image of the first negative.

∼n. Something that is surprinted.

sur·pris·al (sər-prī′zəl) *n.* The act of surprising or the condition of being surprised.

sur·prise, sur·prize (sər-prīz′) *tr.v.* **-prised, -prising, -prises** or **-prized, -prizing, -prizes. 1.** To cause to feel wonder or astonishment. **2.** To attack or capture suddenly and without warning. **3.** To take or catch (a person) unawares. **4. a.** To cause (a person) to do or say something unintended. **b.** To elicit or detect through surprise.

∼n. **1.** The act of surprising; an unexpected occurrence, encounter, or attack. **2.** The condition of being surprised; a feeling of amazement or wonder. **3.** Something that surprises, such as an unexpected encounter, event, or gift. [Middle English *surprysen,* to be seized with, from Old French *surprendre* (past participle *surpris*), "to overtake" : *sur-,* over + *prendre,* to take, from Latin *prehendere,* to seize.] **—sur·pris·ed·ly** (sər-prī′zĭd-lē) *adv.* **—sur·pris·er** *n.* **—sur·pris·ing·ly** *adv.*

Synonyms: *surprise, astonish, amaze, astound, dumbfound, flabbergast.* These verbs mean to fill a person with wonder or disbelief. All imply a reaction to what is unexpected. *Surprise* refers to the effect of what is unexpected or unusual. The remaining terms are considerably stronger. *Astonish* implies the condition of being momentarily overwhelmed and often dazed and speechless. *Amaze* suggests wonder and, often, bewilderment. *Astound* implies shock, as from something that seems incredible or has no precedent in one's experience. *Dumbfound* adds to *astound* the implication of speechlessness. *Flabbergast* is used informally, in the sense of *astound* or *dumbfound* and sometimes as the equivalent of *astonish* or *amaze.*

sur·ra (so͝or′ə) *n.* A dangerous infectious disease of horses and other domesticated animals. [Marathi.]

Sur·ratt (sə-răt′), **Mary Eugenia Jenkins** (*c.* 1820–65). U.S. alleged conspirator. Her son John conspired with John Wilkes Booth in the assassination of President Abraham Lincoln (1865). Implicated in the crime because the conspirators occasionally met at her boarding house, she was sentenced to hang and was executed, although it is possible that she had not known of the plot. Her son was never convicted.

sur·re·al (sə-rē′əl) *adj.* **1.** Having qualities attributed to surrealism. **2.** Dreamlike and distorted; surrealistic. [Back-formation from SURREALISM.] **—sur·re·al·ly** *adv.*

sur·re·al·ism (sə-rē′ə-lĭz′əm) *n.* A literary and artistic movement evolving from Dada and launched in 1924 by the French poet André Breton (1896–1966), proclaiming the radical transformation of social, scientific, and philosophical values through the total liberation of the unconscious. Its exponents include writers such as **Artaud** and **Beckett** and artists such as **Magritte** and **Dali** *(all of whom see),* whose work is characterized by fantastic imagery and incongruous juxtaposition of subject matter. [French *surréalisme* : *sur-,* beyond + *réalisme,* realism, from *réel,* real, from Old French, from Late Latin *reālis,* REAL.] **—sur·re·al·ist** *adj. & n.* **—sur·re·al·is·tic** *adj.* **—sur·re·al·is·ti·cal·ly** *adv.* See feature, next page.

sur·re·but·ter (sûr′rĭ-bŭt′ər) *n.* Also **sur·re·but·tal** (-bŭt′l). *Law.* The plaintiff's reply to the defendant's rebutter.

sur·re·join·der (sûr′rĭ-join′dər) *n. Law.* The plaintiff's reply to the defendant's rejoinder.

sur·ren·der (sə-rĕn′dər) *v.* **-dered, -dering, -ders.** *—tr.* **1.** To relinquish possession or control of to another because of demand or compulsion. **2.** To give up in favor of another. **3.** To give up or give back (that which has been granted): *surrender a contractual right.* **4.** To give up or abandon: *surrender all hope.* **5.** To give over or resign (oneself) to something, as to capture or to an influence or an emotion. **6.** *Law.* To restore (an estate, for example); especially, to give up (a lease) before expiration of the term. *—intr.* To give oneself up, as to an enemy. —See Synonyms at **relinquish.**

∼n. Abbr. **surr. 1.** The act of surrendering. **2.** *Law.* **a.** The delivery of a prisoner, fugitive from justice, or other principal in a suit into custody. **b.** The restoring of an estate. **c.** The act of surrendering or being surrendered to bail. [Middle English *sorendren,* from Old French *surrendre* : *sur-,* over + *rendre,* to deliver, RENDER.]

Synonyms: *capitulation, submission.*

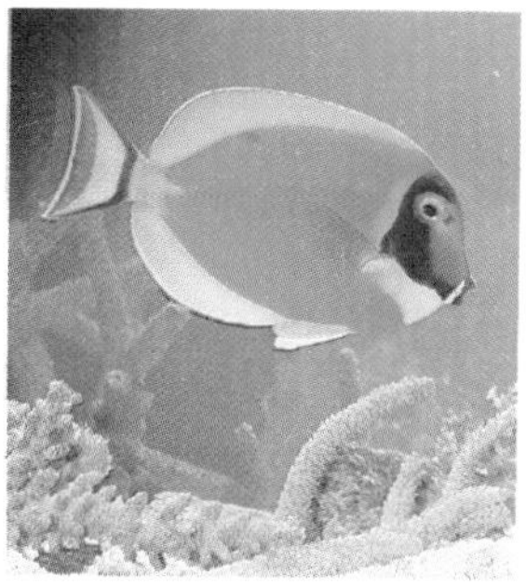

surgeonfish *Razor-sharp spines at the base of the tail give this fish its name. The species shown here is* Acanthurus leucosternon, *which is found in most warm seas, but particularly in the waters off Indonesia.*

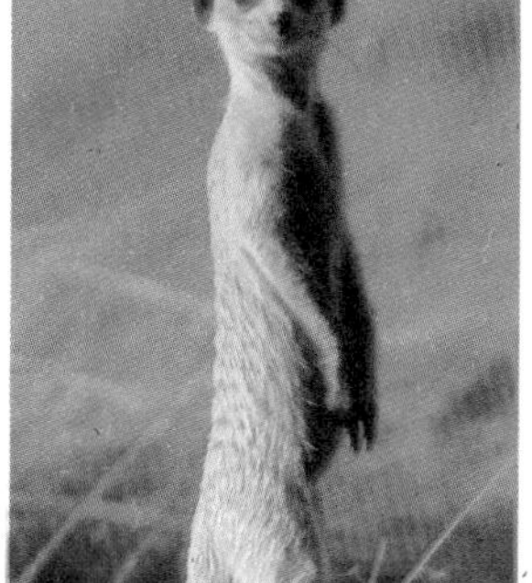

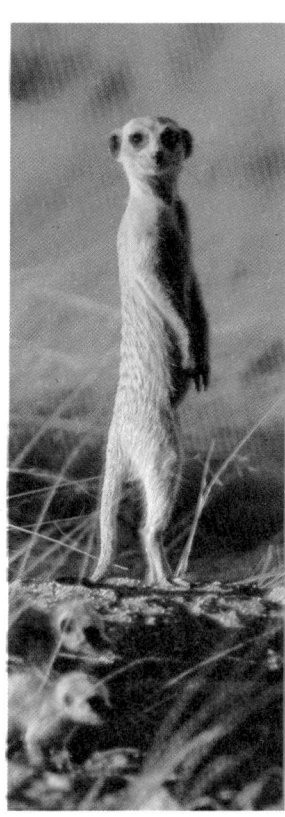

suricate *These small mongooses live in colonies of burrows in southern Africa. They are sometimes kept as pets and used to catch rats and mice.*

LIBERATING THE UNCONSCIOUS

A movement conceived by writers and realized by artists

The surrealist movement in literature and art asserted that the dream world of the unconscious has a reality superior to the world of the senses. The aim of the surrealist—according to the movement's leader, the French poet André Breton (1896–1966) in his *Surrealist Manifesto* of 1924—should be to integrate the two worlds into a superreality.

At first the surrealist movement was dominated by French writers, such as Louis Aragon (1897–1982) and Jean Cocteau (1889–1963), who, under Breton's severe guidance, sought to release the unconscious with illogical but startling associations of words and images. The founders' attempts to ally surrealism with the socialist movement foundered with the rise of Stalinism during the 1930's.

Surrealist painting had its roots in the Dada movement, whose adherents, deeply affected by World War I and influenced by Freud's emphasis on the significance of the unconscious mind, explored the value of absurdity and rejected conventional notions of art.

The first surrealist artist was a German, Max Ernst (1891–1976), whose collages of incongruous objects appealed directly to the unconscious. René Magritte (1898–1967), a Belgian artist, demonstrated that precise realism in technique accentuated the incongruity of oddly juxtaposed objects.

The Spanish artist Salvador Dali (1904–   ) attempted to portray the unconscious in disturbing, hallucinatory images. His distortions of objects, such as the human body or the limp watches in *The Persistence of Memory* (1931), have become surrealist clichés. The paintings of his compatriot Joan Miró (1893–1983) and the French artist André Masson (1896–   ) are still further removed from images of reality.

Surrealist art achieved lasting influence during the 1930's, partly owing to its adherents' wild and humorous exhibitions, far removed from the seriousness with which Breton propounded his original concept.

Surrealism was expressed in photography by the American painter Man Ray (1890–1976) and in film by Man Ray, by Cocteau, and by Dali and Luis Buñuel (1900–1983), his fellow countryman, who jointly directed *Un Chien Andalou* (1929) and *L'Age d'Or* (1930).

THE HUMAN CONDITION I (1933) *René Magritte's painting is an example of naturalistic surrealism, based on images of reality. A landscape painting resting on an easel in front of a window through which can be glimpsed the landscape in the painting temporarily confuses the viewer's perceptions. This picture within a picture seems to question our perception of the world and also the convention of admiring a painting as an artificial representation of a scene or object.*

surrender value *n.* The value of an insurance policy either to the owner or to the beneficiary upon its expiration.

sur·rep·ti·tious (sûr′əp-tĭsh′əs) *adj.* Performed, made, or acquired by secret or clandestine means or in a stealthy manner. —See Synonyms at **secret.** [Latin *surreptīcius,* from *surripere* (past participle *surreptus*), to seize or take away secretly : *sub-,* under, secretly + *rapere,* to seize.] —**sur·rep·ti·tious·ly** *adv.* —**sur·rep·ti·tious·ness** *n.*

sur·rey (sûr′ē) *n., pl.* **-reys.** A horse-drawn four-wheeled pleasure vehicle having two or four seats. [Short for *Surrey cart,* first built in SURREY.]

Sur·rey (sûr′ē). County in southeastern England. The North Downs cross it from east to west, their course broken by the valleys of the Wey and Mole rivers. The county has many bedroom suburbs from which workers commute into London (including Guildford, the county town).

Surrey, Henry Howard, Earl of (*c.* 1517–47). English poet. He and Sir Thomas Wyatt introduced Italian Renaissance verse forms, particularly the sonnet, into English literature. He also introduced blank verse with his translation of part of Virgil's *Aeneid.*

sur·ro·gate (sûr′ə-gĭt, -gāt′) *n.* **1.** A person or thing that is substituted for another; a substitute. **2.** A person or thing that functions as a substitute for another individual in the life of a person or animal, such as a substitute parent. Also used adjectivally: *a surrogate mother.* **3.** In New York and some other states, a judge having jurisdiction over the probate of wills and the settlement of estates. ~*tr.v.* (sûr′ə-gāt′) **surrogated, -gating, -gates. 1.** To put in the place of another, especially as a successor; replace. **2.** To appoint (another) as a replacement for oneself. [Latin *surrogāre, subrogāre,* to substitute, SUBROGATE.] —**sur·ro·gate·ship, sur·ro·ga·cy** (sûr′ə-gə-sē) *n.* —**sur·ro·ga·tion** *n.*

surrogate mother *n.* **1.** A woman who bears a child on behalf of an infertile woman by receiving her fertilized ova or the sperm of her male partner. **2.** One that acts as a mother substitute.

sur·round (sə-round′) *tr.v.* **-rounded, -rounding, -rounds. 1.** To extend on all sides of simultaneously; encircle; exist around. **2.** To enclose or confine on all sides so as to bar escape or outside communication. ~*n.* **1.** *Usually* **surrounds.** The grounds of a country mansion or estate. **2.** An area that surrounds; a border. [Middle English *sourrounden,* to submerge, overflow, from Old French *s(o)uronder,* from Late Latin *superundāre* : Latin *super-,* over + *undāre,* to rise in waves, from *unda,* wave.]

sur·round·ings (sə-roun′dĭngz) *n.* The external circumstances, conditions, and objects that affect the existence and development of something; an environment.

sur·round-sound (sə-round′sound′) *n.* High-fidelity sound reproduction that gives the impression of surrounding the listener.

sur·tax (sûr′tăks′) *n.* **1.** An additional tax. **2.** A graduated income tax added to the normal income tax, levied on the amount by which a person's net income exceeds a certain sum. —**sur·tax** *v.*

Sur·tees (sûr′tēz), **Robert Smith** (1803–64). British novelist. His humorous novels about Mr. Jorrocks, the hunting grocer, portray the spirit of Victorian sporting life and manners. His books include *Jorricks' Jaunts and Jollities* (1838) and *Mr. Sponge's Sporting Tour* (1853).

sur·tout (sŏŏr-tŏŏ′) *n.* A man's single-breasted frock coat with diagonal front pockets. [French, "over everything."]

sur·veil·lance (sər-vā′ləns) *n.* **1.** Close observation of a person or group, especially of one under suspicion. **2.** The act of observing or the condition of being observed. [French, from *surveiller,* to watch over. See **surveillant.**]

sur·veil·lant (sər-vā′lənt) *adj.* Exercising surveillance. ~*n.* One who keeps close watch. [French, present participle of *surveiller,* to watch over : *sur-,* over + *veiller,* to watch, from Latin *vigilāre,* from *vigil,* awake, watchful.]

sur·vey (sər-vā′, sûr′vā′) *v.* **-veyed, -veying, -veys.** —*tr.* **1.** To examine or look at in a comprehensive way. **2.** To inspect carefully; scrutinize: *"Two women were surveying the other people on the platform"* (Thomas Wolfe). **3.** To range one's gaze at leisure over: *From the hilltop she could survey the valley below.* **4.** To determine the boundaries, the area, or the elevations of (land or structures on the earth's surface) by means of measuring angles and distances on the ground or of aerial photography, and then using the techniques of geometry and trigonometry. **5.** *British.* To inspect and determine the structural condition of (a building). **6.** To conduct a statistical survey on. —*intr.* To make a survey. —See Synonyms at **see.** ~*n.* (sûr′vā′), *pl.* **surveys. 1.** A detailed inspection or investigation. **2.** A general or comprehensive view. **3. a.** The process of surveying. **b.** A report on or map of that which is surveyed. **c.** An area surveyed. **d.** A body of surveyors. **4. a.** A statistical inquiry, as into population characteristics or political trends, conducted through questionnaires, interviews, or general observation. **b.** A compilation of the results of such an inquiry. **c.** A random statistical sample. **5.** *British.* An inspection of a building to determine its structural condition. [Middle English *surveyen,* from Old French *survee(i)r,* from Medieval Latin *supervidēre,* to look over : Latin *super-,* over + *vidēre,* to look, see.]

survey course *n.* A course consisting of an overview of a broad topic or field of knowledge.

sur·vey·ing (sər-vā′ĭng) *n.* The measurement of dimensional relationships, as of horizontal distances, elevations, directions, and angles, on the earth's surface, especially for use in locating property boundaries, in construction layout, and in mapmaking.

sur·vey·or (sər-vā′ər) *n.* **1.** A person trained in the surveying and valuation of land or buildings. **2.** A person qualified to inspect something to assess its value or to confirm that it has the qualities attributed to it.

surveyor's level *n.* A level having a telescope and attached spirit level mounted on a tripod and rotating around a vertical axis.

surveyor's measure *n.* A system of measurement used by surveyors, based on the chain as a unit.

sur·viv·al (sər-vī′vəl) *n.* **1.** The act of surviving or the fact of having survived. **2.** Something that survives, such as an ancient custom.

survival kit *n.* A compact package of necessities designed to sustain a person in an emergency, such as a natural disaster.

survival of the fittest *n.* **Natural selection** *(see),* conceived of as a struggle in which only those organisms best adapted to existing conditions survive.

survival value *n.* Usefulness in a species' struggle for survival.

sur·vive (sər-vīv′) *v.* **-vived, -viving, -vives.** *—intr.* To remain alive or in existence. *—tr.* **1.** To live longer than; outlive: *She survived her husband by five years.* **2.** To live or persist through: *The plants survived the frost.* [Middle English *surviven,* from Old French *so(u)rvivre,* from Late Latin *supervīvere* : *super-,* over + *vīvere,* to live.] **—sur·viv·a·ble** (sər-vī′və-bəl) *adj.* **—sur·vi·vor** (sər-vī′vər) *n.*

sur·vi·vor·ship (sər-vī′vər-shĭp′) *n.* **1.** *Law.* The right of a person who survives a partner or joint owner to the entire ownership of that which was previously owned jointly. **2.** The condition of being a survivor.

survivor syndrome *n.* A range of symptoms any or all of which may be exhibited by the survivors of traumatic ordeals, such as earthquakes or concentration camps.

Su·san·na[1] (so͞o-zăn′ə). In the Apocrypha, a captive in Babylon falsely accused of adultery and saved from death by Daniel.

Susanna[2] *n.* The book of the Apocrypha containing the story of Susanna.

sus·cep·tance (sə-sĕp′təns) *n. Electricity.* The imaginary part of the complex representation of **admittance** *(see).* [*suscept*ibility + conduct*ance.*]

sus·cep·ti·bil·i·ty (sə-sĕp′tə-bĭl′ə-tē) *n., pl.* **-ties. 1.** The condition or quality of being susceptible. **2.** The capacity to be affected by deep emotions or strong feelings; sensitivity. **3. susceptibilities.** Sensibilities; sensitive feelings. **4. Magnetic susceptibility** *(see).*

sus·cep·ti·ble (sə-sĕp′tə-bəl) *adj.* **1.** Readily subject to an influence, agency, or force; unresistant; yielding. Usually used with *of* or *to.* **2.** Liable to be stricken with or by something: *susceptible to colds.* **3.** Capable or admitting of something. Used with *of*: *susceptible of misinterpretation.* **4.** Highly impressionable. [Late Latin *susceptibilis,* capable of receiving, from Latin *suscipere* (past participle *susceptus*), to take up, receive : *sub-,* up from under + *capere,* to take.] **—sus·cep·ti·ble·ness** *n.* **—sus·cep·ti·bly** *adv.*

sus·cep·tive (sə-sĕp′tĭv) *adj.* **1.** Receptive. **2.** Susceptible. **—sus·cep·tive·ness, sus·cep·tiv·i·ty** (sə-sĕp′tĭv′ə-tē) *n.*

su·shi (so͞o′shē) *n.* A type of cold food eaten in Japan, consisting of cakes of vinegared rice often wrapped in seaweed and enclosing or topped with pickled vegetables or raw fish. [Japanese.]

Su·si·an (so͞o′zē-ən) *n.* **Elamite** *(see).*

Susiana. See **Elam.**

sus·lik, sous·lik (so͞os′lĭk) *n.* A ground squirrel, *Citellus citellus,* of central Eurasia, with a yellowish-brown coat, large eyes, and small ears. [Russian.]

sus·pect (sə-spĕkt′) *v.* **-pected, -pecting, -pects.** *—tr.* **1.** To surmise to be true or probable; imagine: *I suspect she is quite disappointed.* **2.** To distrust; have doubts about: *suspected his motives.* **3.** To think (a person) guilty without proof: *suspect him of murder.* *—intr.* To have or feel suspicion.

∼n. (sŭs′pĕkt′). One who is suspected, especially of committing a crime.

∼adj. (sŭs′pĕkt′, sə-spĕkt′). Open to or viewed with suspicion. [Middle English, from Latin *suspectāre,* intensive of *suspicere* (past participle *suspectus*), to look up at, watch : *sub-,* up from under + *specere,* to look at.]

sus·pend (sə-spĕnd′) *v.* **-pended, -pending, -pends.** *—tr.* **1.** To bar for a period from a privilege, office, or position, usually as a punishment: *suspend a pupil from school.* **2.** To cause to stop for a period; interrupt: *suspended the trial.* **3. a.** To maintain in an undecided state; hold in abeyance: *suspend judgment; suspend sentencing.* **b.** To render temporarily ineffective or inoperative under certain conditions: *suspend parking regulations.* **4.** To hang so as to allow free movement: *suspend a mobile from the ceiling.* **5.** To support or keep from falling without apparent attachment, as by buoyancy. *—intr.* **1.** To cease for a period; delay. **2.** To fail to make payments or meet obligations. **3.** To hang; be held in suspension: *The door suspends from these hinges.* [Middle English *suspenden,* from Old French *suspendre,* from Latin *suspendēre,* to hang up : *sub-,* up from under + *pendere,* to hang.] **—sus·pend·i·ble** *adj.*

suspended animation *n.* A dormant condition resembling death, induced by suspension of the vital functions.

suspended sentence *n.* A prison sentence imposed on a convicted person but not to be served unless a further crime is committed.

sus·pend·er (sə-spĕn′dər) *n.* **1.** One that suspends. **2. suspenders.** A pair of straps, usually elasticized, worn over the shoulders to support trousers. **3.** *British.* An elasticized strap or garter used to hold up a sock or stocking.

suspender belt *n. British.* A **garter belt** *(see).*

sus·pense (sə-spĕns′) *n.* **1.** The state or quality of being undecided, uncertain, or doubtful. **2. a.** Anxiety or apprehension resulting from an uncertain, undecided, or mysterious situation. **b.** Excitement arising from uncertainty over an outcome. Also used adjectivally: *a suspense novel.* **3.** The condition of being suspended. [Middle English, from Old French, from the feminine of *suspens,* suspended, from Latin *suspensus,* past participle of *suspendēre,* SUSPEND.] **—sus·pense·ful** *adj.*

suspense account *n.* A temporary account in which entries of credits or charges are made until their correct place of entry is determined.

sus·pen·sion (sə-spĕn′shən) *n.* **1.** The act of suspending or the condition of being suspended, especially: **a.** A temporary abrogation or deferment. **b.** A debarment, as from office or privilege. **c.** A postponement of judgment, opinion, or decision. **2.** *Music.* **a.** The prolonging of one or more notes of a chord into a following chord to create a temporary dissonance. **b.** The note so prolonged. **3.** A device from which a part is suspended. **4.** The system of springs and other devices that insulates the body of a vehicle from shocks transmitted through the wheels. **5.** *Chemistry.* A relatively coarse, noncolloidal dispersion of solid particles in a liquid. See **colloid.** [French, or Latin *suspensio* (stem *suspensiōn-*). See **suspense.**]

suspension bridge *n.* A bridge having the roadway suspended from cables that are supported by two or more towers and are firmly anchored at both ends.

suspension points *pl.n.* A series of dots, usually three, used to indicate the omission of a word or words; an ellipsis.

sus·pen·sive (sə-spĕn′sĭv) *adj.* **1.** Serving or tending to suspend or temporarily stop something. **2.** Characterized by or causing suspense. **—sus·pen·sive·ly** *adv.* **—sus·pen·sive·ness** *n.*

sus·pen·soid (sə-spĕn′soid′) *n.* A suspension of solid particles in a liquid. Also called "suspensoid sol." [SUSPENS(ION) + -OID.]

sus·pen·sor (sə-spĕn′sər) *n.* **1.** *Botany.* A stalklike cellular structure that forms in the zygote in flowering plants and pushes the embryo into the endosperm. **2.** Variant of **suspensory.** [New Latin, from Medieval Latin, one that suspends, from Latin *suspendēre* (past participle *suspensus*), SUSPEND.]

sus·pen·so·ry (sə-spĕn′sə-rē) *adj.* **1.** Supporting or suspending: *a suspensory bandage.* **2.** Delaying the completion of something.

∼n., pl. **suspensories.** Also **sus·pen·sor** (-sər). **1.** A support or truss. **2.** A jockstrap.

suspensory ligament *n.* A ligament that supports an organ or bodily part, such as the structure that supports the lens of the eye.

sus·pi·cion (sə-spĭsh′ən) *n.* **1. a.** The act or an instance of suspecting the existence of something, especially of something wrong, without sufficient evidence or proof. **b.** The state of being suspected: *under suspicion.* **2.** A state of uncertainty; doubt. **3.** A minute amount; a hint; a trace: *a suspicion of lemon in the sauce.* [Middle English *suspicio(u)n,* from Old French *suspicion,* from Latin *suspīciō* (stem *suspīciōn-*), from Latin *suspicere* (past participle *suspectus*), to look at secretly, SUSPECT.] **—sus·pi·cion·al** *adj.*

sus·pi·cious (sə-spĭsh′əs) *adj.* **1.** Arousing or apt to arouse suspicion; questionable: *suspicious behavior.* **2.** Tending to suspect; distrustful: *a suspicious nature.* **3.** Expressing suspicion: *a suspicious look.* **—sus·pi·cious·ly** *adv.* **—sus·pi·cious·ness** *n.*

sus·pire (sə-spīr′) *intr.v.* **-pired, -piring, -pires.** *Poetic.* **1.** To breathe: *"And from that one intake of fire/All creatures still warmly suspire"* (Robert Frost). **2.** To sigh. [Middle English *suspiren,* from Latin *suspīrāre,* to draw a deep breath : *sub-,* up from below + *spīrāre,* to breathe.] **—sus·pi·ra·tion** *n.*

Sus·que·han·na (sŭs′kwə-hăn′ə). River in the eastern United States, 715 kilometers (444 miles) long. It rises in Otsego Lake, New York State, and flows chiefly south to Chesapeake Bay.

Sus·sex (sŭs′ĭks). Former English county. In 1974 it was divided into East Sussex and West Sussex.

Sussex spaniel *n.* A dog of a breed developed in Sussex, having long ears, short legs, and a silky golden-brown coat.

sus·tain (sə-stān′) *tr.v.* **-tained, -taining, -tains. 1.** To keep in existence; maintain; prolong: *"The historical process is sustained by man's desire to become other than what he is"* (Norman O. Brown). **2.** To supply with necessities or nourishment; provide for. **3.** To support from below; keep from falling or sinking; prop. **4.** To support the spirits, vitality, or resolution of; encourage: *"Pride of profession, scorn of competitors, devotion to his trade sustained him"* (Mark Van Doren). **5.** To keep up (a joke or an assumed role, for example) competently. **6.** To endure or withstand; bear up under: *sustain hardships.* **7.** To experience or suffer (loss or injury). **8.** To affirm the validity or justice of: *sustain an objection.* **9.** To prove or corroborate; confirm. —See Synonyms at **support.** [Middle English *suste(y)nen,* from Old French *sustenir,* from Latin *sustinēre,* to hold up : *sub-,* up from under + *tenēre,* to hold.] **—sus·tain·a·ble** *adj.* **—sus·tain·ment** *n.*

sus·tain·er (sə-stā′nər) *n.* **1.** One that sustains. **2.** A small rocket motor that sustains the velocity of a spacecraft after the booster has been jettisoned.

sustaining pedal *n.* The right pedal of a piano, which stops the action of the dampers, allowing the strings to vibrate freely. Also called "loud pedal," "reverberation pedal."

sustaining program *n.* A radio or television program that has no commercial announcements.

sus·te·nance (sŭs′tə-nəns) *n.* **1.** The act of sustaining or the condition of being sustained. **2.** The supporting of life or health; maintenance: *"to deliver in every morning six beeves, forty sheep, and other victuals for my sustenance"* (Jonathan Swift). **3.** Means of sustaining

PRONUNCIATION KEY

ă, pat; ā, pay; âr, care;
ä, father, are; b, bib;
ch, church; d, deed; ĕ, pet;
ē, be; f, fife; g, gag; h, hat;
hw, which; ĭ, pit; ī, pie;
îr, pier; j, judge; k, kick;
l, lid, needle; m, mum;
n, no, sudden; ng, thing;
ŏ, pot; ō, toe; ô, paw, for;
oi, noise; ou, out; o͝o, book;
o͞o, boot; p, pop; r, roar;
s, sauce; sh, ship, dish;
t, tight; th, thin, path;
th, this, bathe; ŭ, cut; ûr, fur;
v, valve; w, with; y, yes;
z, zebra, size; zh, vision;
ə, about, item, edible,
gallop, circus, peaceful

IN FOREIGN WORDS:

à, *Fr.* ami; œ, *Fr.* feu, *Ger.* schön; ü, *Fr.* tu, *Ger.* über; KH, *Ger.* ich, *Scot.* loch; N, *Fr.* bon; y′, *Fr.* Compiègne

STRESS MARKS:

Primary stress: ′
in·cite′ (ĭn-sīt′)
Secondary stress: ′
in′sight′ (ĭn′sīt′)

life or health; especially, food. **4.** Means of livelihood. [Middle English *sustena(u)nce,* from Old French *so(u)stenance,* from *so(u)stenir, sustenir,* SUSTAIN.]

sus·ten·tac·u·lar (sŭs'tən-tăk'yə-lər) *adj. Anatomy.* Supporting. Said of fibers, ligaments, and the like. [Latin *sustentāculum,* a support, from *sustentāre,* frequentative of *sustinēre,* SUSTAIN.]

sus·ten·ta·tion (sŭs'tən-tā'shən) *n. Rare.* Sustenance; food. [Middle English *sustentacion,* from Old French, from Latin *sustentātiō* (stem *sustentātiōn-*), from *sustentāre,* frequentative of *sustinēre,* SUSTAIN.] **—sus·ten·ta·tive** (sŭs'tən-tā'tĭv, sə-stĕn'tə-tĭv) *adj.*

Su·su (soo'soo) *n., pl.* **-sus** or collectively **Susu. 1.** A member of a West African people living in Guinea, the Sudan, and along the northern border of Sierra Leone. **2.** The Mande language spoken by the Susu.

su·sur·ra·tion (soo'sə-rā'shən) *n.* Also **su·sur·rus** (soo-sûr'əs). A soft, whispering, or rustling sound; a murmur; a whisper. [Middle English, from Late Latin *susurrātiō* (stem *susurrātiōn-*) from Latin *susurrāre,* to whisper, from *susurrus,* whisper.] **—su·sur·rant** (soo-sûr'ənt), **su·sur·rous** (soo-sûr'əs) *adj.* **—su·sur·rate** (soo'sə-rāt') *v.*

Suth·er·land (sŭth'ər-lənd). Former county of northern Scotland. In 1975 it was incorporated into Highland Region.

Sutherland, Graham Vivian (1903-80). British painter. He was an official war artist (1941-45) and is best known for his portraits and religious paintings. His works include *Somerset Maugham* (1949) and the tapestry *Christ in Majesty.*

Sutherland, Joan (1926-). Australian coloratura soprano. She has done much to revive the popularity of the bel canto operas of Bellini and Donizetti.

Sut·lej (sŭt'lĕj). One of the "Five Rivers" of Punjab. It flows *c.* 1,350 kilometers (850 miles) from southwest Tibet through the Himalayas.

sut·ler (sŭt'lər) *n.* A follower of an army camp who peddled provisions to the soldiers. [Middle Dutch *soeteler,* bad cook, camp cook, probably from Middle High German *sudelen,* to do sloppy work.]

su·tra (soo'trə) *n.* Also **sut·ta** (soo'tə). **1.** Any of various aphoristic doctrinal summaries produced generally between 500 and 200 B.C. and later incorporated into Hindu and Buddhist literature. **2.** *Buddhism.* Any scriptural narrative; especially, any text traditionally regarded as a discourse of the Buddha. [Sanskrit *sūtra,* thread, string, collection of aphorisms or rules.]

sut·tee (sŭ-tē', sŭt'ē') *n.* **1.** The act or practice, now forbidden by law, of a Hindu widow cremating herself on her husband's funeral pyre. **2.** A widow so cremated. [Sanskrit *satī,* good woman, faithful wife, from *sat,* "existing," virtuous.]

Sut·ter (sŭt'ər), **John Augustus** (1803-80). U.S. pioneer in California, raised in Switzerland. He made his way to present-day Sacramento, California, where he was granted a large tract of land (1839). He had established a successful ranch and trading post there when gold was discovered at a mill on his land, starting the Gold Rush of 1849. His hired hands left to seek gold, and his land was overrun by prospectors, leaving him in financial ruin.

Sut·ton Hoo (sŭt'n hoo'). An archaeological site in eastern England, situated near Woodbridge in Suffolk. In 1939 a Saxon ship measuring 27 meters (89 feet) long was excavated here with a hoard of richly ornamented weapons, jewelry, and utensils. The ship may have been buried as a memorial to King Redwald (died 624).

su·ture (soo'chər) *n.* **1. a.** The process of joining two surfaces or edges together along a line by or as if by sewing. **b.** The material used in this procedure, as thread, gut, or wire. **2.** The line so formed. **3.** *Anatomy.* The line of junction or an immovable joint between two bones, particularly of the skull. **4.** *Biology.* A seamlike joint or line of articulation, such as the line of dehiscence in a seed or fruit or the spiral seam marking the junction of whorls of a gastropod shell.
~tr.v. **sutured, -turing, -tures.** To join by means of sutures; sew up. [French, from Latin *sūtūra,* a sewing together, seam, suture, from *suere* (past participle *sūtus*), to sew.] **—su·tur·al** *adj.* **—su·tur·al·ly** *adv.*

Su·va (soo'və). The capital of Fiji, on the island of Viti Levu. It is a marketing center and port for sugar, cotton, and pineapples grown on the island. Tourism is also important.

Su·wan·nee (sə-wä'nē) or **Swa·nee** (swä'nē). River in the southern United States. It rises in the Okefenokee Swamp of southeast Georgia and flows south through Florida to the Gulf of Mexico. The river is *c.* 400 kilometers (250 miles) long.

su·ze·rain (soo'zə-rən, -rān') *n.* **1.** Formerly, a feudal lord to whom fealty was due. **2.** A nation that controls another nation in international affairs but allows it domestic sovereignty.
~adj. Characteristic of a suzerain; sovereign. [French *suzerain* : *sus,* up, above, from Latin *sūsum, sursum,* (turned) upward, up : *sub-,* up + *versum,* neuter past participle of *vertere,* to turn + *(souv)erain,* from Old French *so(u)verein,* SOVEREIGN.]

su·ze·rain·ty (soo'zə-rən-tē, -rān'tē) *n., pl.* **-ties.** The power or domain of a suzerain.

Su·zhou, Su·chou or **Soo·chow** (soo'jō'). Also **Wu·xian** or **Wu·hsien** (woo'syĕn'). City in Jiangsu province, eastern China, on the Grand Canal to the west of Shanghai. Founded in the 5th century B.C., it became a walled city and was noted for its pagodas and silk manufacture. Silk and cotton industries remain important.

Su·zu·ki method (soo-zoo'kē) *n.* A method of teaching the violin to very young children through imitation and repetition. [After the Japanese music teacher who devised it.]

s.v. sailing vessel.

Sval·bard (sväl'bärd). A Norwegian archipelago in the Arctic Ocean. It includes the Spitsbergen island group and is mountainous and mostly covered by ice fields and glaciers. The Treaty of Spitsbergen (1920), while recognizing Norwegian sovereignty, granted mineral and other rights to all 40 signatories, and both Norway and the U.S.S.R. maintain coal-mining settlements on the island. Svalbard commands the shipping lanes to Murmansk, the only major ice-free port in the U.S.S.R., and the two countries are in dispute over their common boundary across the Barents Sea, which has potentially valuable oil deposits.

svelte (svĕlt) *adj.* **svelter, sveltest.** Slender or graceful in figure or outline; slim and lithe. [French, from Italian *svelto,* "stretched," slender, from *svellere,* to pull out, stretch out, from Vulgar Latin *exvellere* (unattested), from Latin *evellere* : *ex-,* out + *vellere,* to pull.]

Sven·ga·li (svĕn-gä'lē) *n.* A person with an uncanny power to compel another to do his will. [After the villain in *Trilby* (1894), a novel by George DU MAURIER.]

Sverd·lovsk (svĕrd'lôfsk'). Formerly **E·kat·er·in·burg** (ĕ-kä'tər-ĭn-bûrg'). A city in the R.S.F.S.R., U.S.S.R., in the eastern foothills of the Ural Mts. It is an industrial and cultural center and a railway junction on the Trans-Siberian Railway.

Sverige. See **Sweden.**

Svizzera. See **Switzerland.**

sw short wave; short-wave.

SW southwest.

Sw. Sweden; Swedish.

S.W.A. South-West Africa.

swab, swob (swŏb) *n.* **1.** A small piece of cotton or other absorbent material, usually attached to the end of a small stick, and used for cleansing an area of the body or applying medication. **2.** A specimen of mucus or other material collected with such an instrument. **3. a.** A mop for cleaning decks, floors, or other large areas. **b.** A person who uses such a mop, especially on a ship. Also called "swabby." **4.** A lout. **5.** A sponge or patch of absorbent material used to clean the bore of a firearm.
~tr.v. **swabbed, swabbing, swabs.** To use a swab on; clean or treat with a swab. [Probably from Middle Dutch *swabbe,* mop.]

Swa·bi·a (swä'bē-ə). German **Schwa·ben** (shvä'bən). A medieval duchy in southwestern West Germany, which originally included parts of present-day France and Switzerland. The towns of Swabia formed a series of leagues starting in 1331, the most important being that of 1488-1534, a powerful association of cities, princes, churchmen, and knights, whose army became a bastion of Hapsburg authority under Maximilian I. In the reign of Charles V its members became divided over the Reformation, and the league collapsed. **—Swa·bi·an** *adj. & n.*

swad·dle (swŏd'l) *tr.v.* **-dled, -dling, -dles. 1.** To wrap or bind in bandages; swathe. **2.** To wrap (a baby) in swaddling clothes. **3.** To restrain or restrict; smother.
~n. A band or cloth used for swaddling. [Middle English *swadlen, swethelen,* from *swethel,* swaddling clothes, Old English *swæthel,* probably from *swathian,* to SWATHE.]

swaddling clothes *pl.n.* **1.** Formerly, strips of linen or other cloth wound about a newborn infant. **2.** Any restrictions imposed upon the immature. Also called "swaddling bands."

swag (swăg) *n.* **1. a.** Goods or property obtained by forcible or illicit means. **b.** Loosely, any goods or valuables, especially when improperly gained. **2. a.** A length of drapery, especially a curtain, bunched and secured at two points so that it hangs in a curve. **b.** An ornamental festoon of flowers or fruit. **c.** A carving or molding representing this. **3.** *Australian.* The pack of a swagman.
~intr.v. **swagged, swagging, swags. 1.** *Chiefly British.* To lurch or sway. **2.** *Australian.* To travel around with a pack or swag. [Probably from Scandinavian, akin to Norwegian *swagga,* to sway.]

swage (swāj) *n.* **1.** A tool used in bending or shaping cold metal. **2.** A stamp or die for marking or shaping metal with a hammer. **3.** A swage block.
~tr.v. **swaged, swaging, swages.** To bend or shape by using a swage. [19th century : from French *s(o)uage.*]

swage block *n.* A metal block having holes or grooves for shaping metal objects.

swag·ger (swăg'ər) *v.* **-gered, -gering, -gers. —intr. 1.** To walk or conduct oneself with an overconfident or insolent air; strut. **2.** To brag; bluster. **—tr.** To influence or affect by swaggering.
~n. **1.** A swaggering movement or gait. **2.** Boastful or conceited expression; braggadocio. **3.** A dashing, confident air. [Probably from SWAG.] **—swag·ger·er** *n.* **—swag·ger·ing·ly** *adv.*

swagger stick *n.* A short metal-tipped cane typically carried by military officers.

swag·man (swăg'măn') *n., pl.* **-men** (-mĕn'). *Australian.* A man who seeks casual work while traveling about carrying his pack or swag; an itinerant worker.

Swa·hi·li (swä-hē'lē) *n., pl.* **Swahili** or **-lis. 1.** A Bantu language of eastern and central Africa, widely used as a lingua franca. **2.** A member of a Bantu people of Zanzibar and the neighboring mainland who were original speakers of this language. [Swahili, "(people) belonging to the coasts" : Arabic *sawāhil,* plural of *sāhil,* coast + *-īy,* belonging to.] **—Swa·hi·li·an** *adj.*

swain (swān) *n.* **1.** *Archaic.* A country youth, especially a shepherd. **2.** A male lover. [Middle English *swein, swayne,* from Old Norse *sveinn,* a boy, herdsman.]

swale, swail (swāl) *n.* **1.** A low tract of land, especially moist or marshy ground. **2.** Shade. [Middle English, "a shade, shady place," perhaps from Scandinavian, akin to Old Norse *svalr,* cool.]

swal·low[1] (swŏl′ō) *v.* **-lowed, -lowing, -lows.** —*tr.* **1.** To cause (food, for example) to pass from the mouth via the throat and the esophagus into the stomach by muscular action; ingest. **2.** To consume or destroy as if by ingestion; devour. Often used with *up*: *swallow up smaller businesses.* **3.** To ingest (something unpleasant) reluctantly. Often used with *down.* **4. a.** To bear humbly; tolerate: *swallow an insult.* **b.** To refrain from expressing; suppress: *swallow one's feelings.* **c.** To take back; retract: *swallow one's words.* **5.** To believe without question. **6.** To utter (words) indistinctly. —*intr.* To perform the act of swallowing.
∼*n.* **1.** The act of swallowing; a gulp. **2.** The amount that is swallowed at any one time. **3.** *Nautical.* The channel through which a rope runs in a block or a mooring chock. [Middle English *swalowen, swolwen,* Old English *swelgan.*] **—swal·low·er** *n.*

swallow[2] *n.* **1.** Any of various birds of the family Hirundinidae; especially, *Hirundo rustica,* having long, pointed wings and a usually notched or forked tail. **2.** Broadly, any of various similar birds, such as a swift. [Middle English *swal(o)we, swalu,* Old English *sweal(e)we,* from Germanic *swalwi* (unattested).]

swallow dive *n. Chiefly British.* A **swan dive** *(see).*

swallow hole *n.* See **sinkhole** (sense 2).

swal·low·tail (swŏl′ō-tāl′) *n.* **1. a.** The deeply forked tail of a swallow. **b.** Anything resembling such a tail. **2.** *Informal.* A swallow-tailed coat. **3.** Any of various butterflies of the family Papilionidae having a taillike extension at the end of each hind wing.

swal·low-tailed (swŏl′ō-tāld′) *adj.* **1.** Having a deeply forked tail. Said of various birds. **2.** Resembling the tail of a swallow: *a swallow-tailed kite.*

swallow-tailed coat *n.* A **tailcoat** *(see).*

swal·low·wort (swŏl′ō-wûrt, -wôrt′) *n.* **1.** A plant, the **celandine** *(see).* **2.** Any of several vines of the genus *Cynanchum,* native to Europe; especially, *C. nigrum,* having clusters of small brownish-purple flowers. [Translation of Dutch *zwaluwenkruid* and German *Schwalbenwurz* (from the shape of its pod).]

swam. Past tense of **swim.**

swa·mi (swä′mē) *n., pl.* **-mis.** **1.** Lord; master. A Hindu title of respect. **2.** A Hindu religious teacher. **3.** Loosely, a mystic; a yogi. [Hindi *svāmī,* master, from Sanskrit *svāmin,* owner, prince, "one's own master."]

swamp (swŏmp, swômp) *n.* **1.** A lowland region permanently saturated with water. **2.** Loosely, a stretch of marsh ground.
∼*v.* **swamped, swamping, swamps.** —*tr.* **1.** To drench in or cover with water or other liquid. **2.** To inundate or burden; overwhelm: *swamped with work.* **3.** To fill with water or sink (a ship). —*intr.* To become swamped, as a ship. [Perhaps of Low German origin, akin to Low German *zwamp,* swamp.] **—swamp·y** *adj.*

swamp boat *n.* A flat-bottomed boat powered by an aircraft propeller projecting above the stern, used in swamps or shallow waters. Also called "airboat."

swamp·er (swŏm′pər, swôm′-) *n.* **1.** One who lives in or close to a swamp. **2.** One who clears a swamp or forest. **3. a.** A menial helper, as in a restaurant. **b.** A handyman; an assistant.

swamp fever *n.* **1.** A viral disease in horses, marked by progressive anemia, a staggering gait, and fever. **2.** Malaria.

swamp·land (swŏmp′lănd′, swômp′-) *n.* Land of swampy consistency; land having many swamps on it.

swan (swŏn) *n.* **1.** Any of various large aquatic birds, chiefly of the genus *Cygnus,* having webbed feet, a long slender neck, and usually white plumage. **2. Swan.** The constellation, **Cygnus** *(see).* Preceded by *the.* **3.** A poet; a bard. [Middle English *swan(ne), suan,* Old English *swan, suan.*]

Swan (swŏn), **Sir Joseph Wilson** (1828–1914). British physicist and inventor. He invented the photographic dry plate (1871) and bromide paper (1879). He also devised a carbon-filament electric lamp (1860), which he improved for commercial production (1881).

swan dive *n.* A dive performed with the legs together and straight, the back arched, and the arms at first stretched out from the sides and then brought together over the head as the diver enters the water.

Swanee. See **Suwannee.**

swank (swăngk) *intr.v.* **swanked, swanking, swanks.** To act in an ostentatious or pretentious way.
∼*n.* **1.** Ostentatious or pretentious behavior; swagger. **2.** Showy elegance; style. **3.** *Chiefly British.* A conceited or swaggering person.
∼*adj.* Variant of **swanky.** [Perhaps from Middle High German *swanken,* to swing.]

swank·y (swăng′kē) *adj.* **-ier, -iest.** **1.** Imposingly fashionable or elegant; grand. **2.** Ostentatious; showy. **—swank·i·ly** *adv.* **—swank·i·ness** *n.*

swan neck *n.* A bend in a handrail, tubing, or the like that is double-curved in the shape of a swan's neck.

swan·ner·y (swŏn′ə-rē) *n., pl.* **-ies.** A place where swans are bred and kept.

Swan River daisy *n.* An Australian plant, *Brachycome iberidifolia,* cultivated for its showy blue or white flower heads.

swan's-down, swans·down (swŏnz′doun′) *n.* **1.** The soft down of a swan. **2.** A fine, soft fabric made of wool or of cotton with a woolly nap on one side, used especially for baby clothes.

Swan·sea (swŏn′sē). Second-largest city in Wales, the administrative center of West Glamorgan. It is an industrial port on Swansea Bay at the mouth of the Tawe River, and coal and coke are major exports.

swan·skin (swŏn′skĭn′) *n.* **1.** The skin of a swan with the feathers attached. **2.** Any of several flannel or cotton fabrics with a soft nap.

Swan·son (swŏn′sən), **Gloria** (1899–1983). U.S. actress. A glamorous Hollywood star in the 1920's, she appeared in numerous movies, established a production company, and, in 1948, starred in her own television show. She made a heralded comeback in *Sunset Boulevard* (1950), in which she portrayed a fading movie queen.

swan song *n.* **1.** According to legend, the beautiful music uttered only once in a swan's life, just as it is dying. **2.** A farewell or final appearance, utterance, act, or work. [Translation of German *Schwanenlied.*]

swap, swop (swŏp) *v.* **swapped, swapping, swaps** or **swopped, swopping, swops.** *Informal.* —*intr.* To exchange one thing for another. —*tr.* To exchange.
∼*n. Informal.* An exchange of one thing for another. [Literally, "to strike hands in closing a bargain," Middle English *swappen,* to strike, hit, from Germanic (probably imitative); akin to German *schwappen,* to splash, whack.] **—swap·per** *n.*

SWAPO (swä′pō) *n.* South-West Africa People's Organization.

sward (swôrd) *n.* Land covered with grassy turf; a lawn or meadow. [Old English *sweard, swearth,* skin of the body, rind of bacon; akin to Old Norse *svörthr,* skin.] **—sward·ed** (swôr′dĭd) *adj.*

sware. *Archaic.* Past tense of **swear.**

swarf (swôrf) *n.* Fine metallic filings or shavings removed by a cutting tool. [Probably from Scandinavian, akin to Old Norse *svarf,* filings.]

swarm[1] (swôrm) *n.* **1.** A large number of insects or other small organisms, especially when in motion. **2.** A group of bees, led by a queen bee, in migration to establish a new colony. **3.** A dense throng of persons or animals, especially when moving in mass: *A swarm of reporters surrounded him.*
∼*v.* **swarmed, swarming, swarms.** —*intr.* **1. a.** To move or emerge in a swarm. **b.** To leave a hive as a swarm to start a new colony. Used of bees. **2.** To move as a large group or mass of creatures; congregate. **3.** To be overrun; teem: *a river bank swarming with insects.* —*tr.* To fill with a crowd; throng. [Old English *swearm.*] **—swarm·er** *n.*

swarm[2] *v.* **swarmed, swarming, swarms.** —*tr.* To climb quickly by gripping with the arms and legs. —*intr.* To climb something in this way. Usually used with *up.* [16th century : origin obscure.]

swart (swôrt) *adj. Archaic.* Swarthy. [Middle English *swarte, swe(o)rt,* Old English *sweart,* from Germanic *swartaz* (unattested).]

swarth·y (swôr′thē) *adj.* **-ier, -iest.** Having a dark or sunburned complexion. [Earlier *swarty,* from SWART.] **—swarth·i·ly** *adv.* **—swarth·i·ness** *n.*

swash (swŏsh, swôsh) *n.* **1.** The splashing of water or other liquid as it hits a solid surface: *the swash of the sea against the rocks.* **2.** The sound of such a splashing. **3.** A narrow channel through which tides flow. **4.** A bar over which waves wash freely. **5.** Swagger or bluster.
∼*v.* **swashed, swashing, swashes.** —*intr.* **1.** To strike, move, or wash with a splashing sound, as of water. **2.** To swagger. —*tr.* **1.** To splash (a liquid). **2.** To splash a liquid against. [16th century : imitative.]

swash·buck·ler (swŏsh′bŭk′lər, swôsh′-) *n.* **1.** A flamboyant swordsman or adventurer. **2.** Any sword-wielding bully or ruffian. Also called "swasher." [From the striking of bucklers in fighting.]

swash·buck·ling (swŏsh′bŭk′lĭng, swôsh′-) *adj.* Of or characteristic of a swashbuckler; flamboyant; full of bravado.

swash letter *n.* An ornamental italic letter formed with fancy flourishes and tails. [17th century : *swash*†, oblique, obliquely inclined.]

swas·ti·ka (swŏs′tĭ-kə) *n.* **1.** An ancient cosmic or religious symbol, formed by a Greek cross with the ends of the arms bent at right angles either clockwise or counterclockwise. **2.** The emblem of Nazi Germany, officially adopted in 1935 and still used as a symbol by fascist groups. [Sanskrit *svastika,* a sign of good luck, from *svasti,* well-being, good luck : *su-,* well + *asti,* "is," being.]

swat (swŏt) *tr.v.* **swatted, swatting, swats.** To deal a sharp blow to, usually with an instrument; slap: *swat flies.*
∼*n.* A quick, sharp, or violent blow. [Variant of SQUAT (obsolete sense to "lay flat with a blow").]

swatch (swŏch) *n.* **1.** A sample strip cut from a piece of cloth or other material. **2.** A characteristic sample or specimen. [17th century : origin obscure.]

swath (swŏth, swôth) *n.* Also **swathe** (swŏ*th*, swô*th*, swā*th*). **1.** The width of a scythe stroke or a mowing-machine blade. **2. a.** A path of this width made by mowing. **b.** The mown grass or grain lying on such a path. **3.** Something likened to a swath; a strip or belt. **4.** A devastating effect caused as if by a scythe: *cut a swath through her opponents.* **—cut a (wide) swath.** To create a great stir, impression, or display. [Middle English *swathe,* Old English *swæth, swathu,* track, trace, from Germanic *swath-* (unattested).]

swathe[1] (swŏ*th*, swô*th*, swā*th*) *tr.v.* **swathed, swathing, swathes.** **1.** To wrap or bind with bindings or bandages. **2.** To enfold or envelop: *swathed in furs.*
∼*n.* A wrapping, binding, or bandage. [Middle English *swathen,* Old English *swathian*†, to wrap up.] **—swath·er** *n.*

swathe[2]. Variant of **swath.**

swat·ter (swŏt′ər) *n.* **1.** One that swats. **2.** A small meshed or flexi-

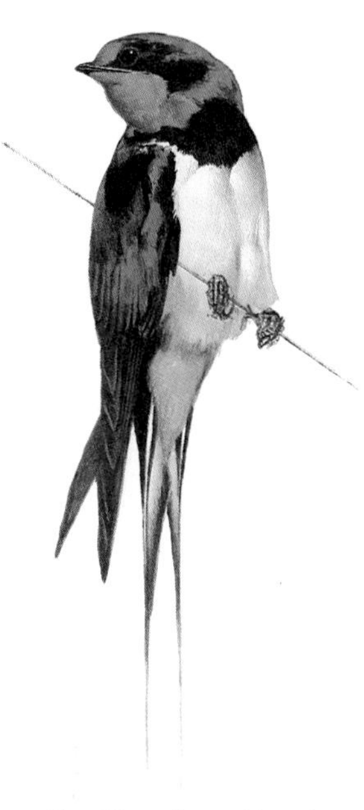

swallow *Flying fast and low, the swallow scoops up insects, such as gnats and midges, as they swarm on summer evenings. It is a close relative of the house martin and swift but has a longer forked tail and a distinctive red chin.*

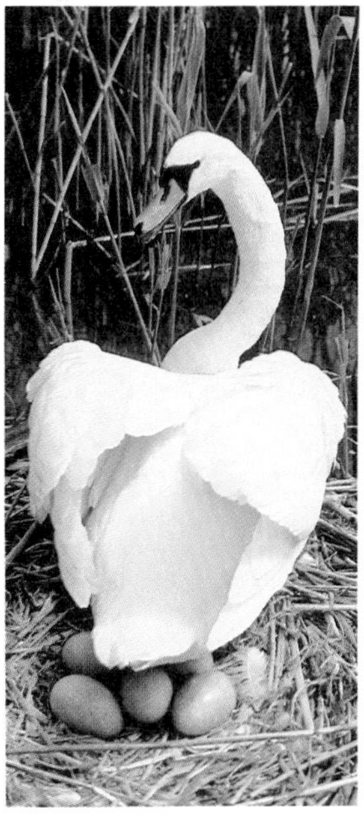

swan *The mute swan,* Cygnus olor *(above), is one of the heaviest flying birds, weighing up to about 23 kilograms (50 pounds).*

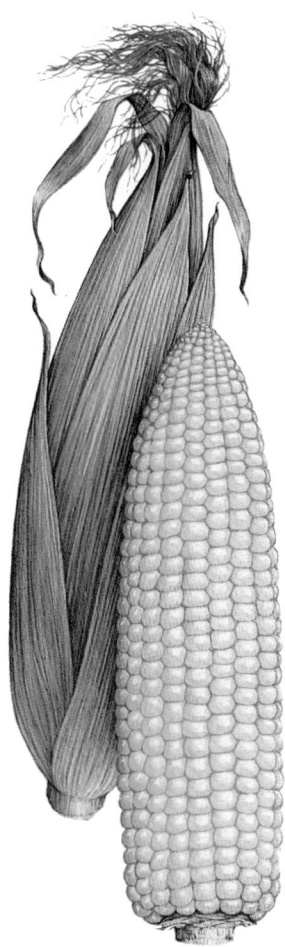

sweet corn *Corn, now grown around the world for the edible grains on its cob, is native to North and Central America. The grains are also ground into flour and crushed to extract cooking oil.*

sweet pea *There are many garden varieties of this scented annual,* Lathyrus odoratus, *which is native to southern Italy.*

ble flap attached to a handle, used for killing insects. Also called "fly swatter." **3.** *Baseball.* A hard-hitting batter.

sway (swā) *v.* **swayed, swaying, sways.** —*intr.* **1.** To move back and forth with a swinging motion; oscillate. **2.** To incline or bend to one side; veer. **3. a.** To incline toward change, as in opinion or feeling; vacillate. **b.** To fluctuate, as in outlook. —*tr.* **1.** To cause to swing from side to side. **2.** To cause to incline or bend toward one side. **3.** *Nautical.* To hoist (a mast or yard) into position. **4. a.** To deter or cause to swerve; dissuade. **b.** To exert influence on or control over: *His speech swayed the voters.* **5.** *Archaic.* **a.** To rule or govern. **b.** To wield, as a weapon or scepter. —See Synonyms at **swing.**
~*n.* **1.** The act of moving from side to side with a swinging motion. **2.** Power; influence. **3.** *Archaic.* Dominion or rule. [Middle English *sweyen, sweghen,* to move, go down, swing, probably from Old Norse *sveigja,* to bend, yield.] —**sway·ing·ly** *adv.*

sway·back (swā′băk′) *n.* An excessive inward or downward curvature of the spine, as in horses. —**sway·backed** *adj.*

Swa·zi (swä′zē) *n., pl.* **-zis** or collectively **Swazi. 1.** A member of the Bantu people of Swaziland. **2.** The language of this people, closely related to Zulu. —**Swa·zi** *adj.*

Swa·zi·land (swä′zē·lănd′). Small, landlocked African kingdom. In the 1970's foreign investment made it one of the most prosperous of the small African states, and forestry, mining, and manufacturing are expanding. Even so, *c.* 70 percent of workers are in farming, and many others work in South Africa. A British protectorate from 1903, Swaziland became independent in 1968. In 1973 Sobhuza II (reigned 1921–82) assumed supreme power and abolished the constitution. His son Makhosetive was installed as King Mswati III in 1986. Area, 17,363 square kilometers (6,704 square miles). Population, 550,000 in 1986. Capital, Mbabane. See map at **South Africa.**

SWbS southwest by south.
SWbW southwest by west.

swear (swâr) *v.* **swore** (swôr, swōr) or *archaic* **sware** (swâr), **sworn** (swôrn, swōrn), **swearing, swears.** —*intr.* **1.** To make a solemn declaration, invoking a deity or some person or thing held sacred, in confirmation of the honesty or truth of such a declaration: *I swear to God I spoke the truth.* **2.** To make a solemn promise; vow. **3.** To use swearwords; blaspheme or curse. **4.** *Law.* To give evidence or testimony under oath. —*tr.* **1.** To declare solemnly by invoking a sacred personage or thing. **2.** To promise or pledge with a solemn oath; vow. **3.** To utter or bind oneself to (an oath). **4.** To administer a legal oath to. **5.** To say or affirm earnestly and with great conviction. —**swear by. 1.** To name (a sacred personage or thing) as invocation in taking an oath. **2.** To have great reliance upon or confidence in. —**swear in.** To administer a legal or official oath to: *swear in the mayor.* —**swear off.** *Informal.* To pledge to renounce or give up. —**swear out.** To obtain (a warrant for arrest) by making a charge under oath. [Middle English *swer(i)en, swor, swor(n),* Old English *swerian, swōr* (past singular), *sworen.*] —**swear·er** *n.*

swear·word (swâr′wûrd′) *n.* A word used in an obscene, insulting, or blasphemous way.

sweat (swĕt) *v.* **sweated** or **sweat, sweating, sweats.** —*intr.* **1.** To excrete the secretion of the sweat glands through the pores in the skin; perspire. **2.** To exude in droplets, as moisture from certain cheeses or sap from a tree. **3.** To condense atmospheric moisture. **4. a.** To release moisture, as hay or plants left to dry out. **b.** To ferment, as tobacco during curing. **5.** *Informal.* To work long and hard. **6.** *Informal.* To suffer much, as for a misdeed. **7.** *Informal.* To fret or worry. —*tr.* **1.** To excrete (moisture) through a porous surface, such as the skin. **2.** To exude (moisture) in droplets on a surface. **3.** To cause to perspire, as by drugs, heat, or strenuous exercise. **4.** To make damp or wet with perspiration. **5.** To cause to work excessively; overwork. **6.** To overwork and underpay (employees). **7.** *Informal.* **a.** To interrogate (someone) under duress. **b.** To extract (information) from someone under duress. **8.** To heat (metal parts) in order to make a soldered joint. **9.** To steam (vegetables or other food). —**sweat blood.** *Slang.* **1.** To work strenuously. **2.** To worry intensely. —**sweat out.** *Slang.* **1.** To endure anxiously. **2.** To await (something) anxiously.
~*n.* **1.** The product of the sweat glands of the skin. **2.** Any condensation of moisture in the form of droplets on a surface. **3.** The process of sweating or condition of being sweated. **4.** Strenuous, exhausting labor; drudgery. **5.** An exercise run given to a horse before a race. **6.** *Informal.* An anxious or impatient condition: *in a sweat.* —**no sweat.** *Slang.* Easily done or handled. Often used as an interjection. [Middle English *sweten, swaten,* Old English *swǣtan.*] —**sweat·i·ly** *adv.* —**sweat·i·ness** *n.* —**sweat·y** *adj.*

sweat·band (swĕt′bănd′) *n.* **1.** A band of fabric or leather sewn inside the crown of a hat as protection against sweat. **2.** A cloth band worn around the forehead or wrist to absorb sweat.

sweat·box (swĕt′bŏks′) *n.* **1.** A box in which something, such as animal hides or fruit, is fermented by sweating. **2.** A confined place in which a person is made to sweat, especially as a punishment.

sweat·er (swĕt′ər) *n.* **1.** One that sweats, especially profusely. **2.** That which induces sweating; especially, a sudorific. **3.** A knitted or crocheted garment made of wool or synthetic yarns and worn on the upper part of the body.

sweat gland *n.* Any of the numerous small, tubular glands that in humans are found nearly everywhere in the skin and that secrete a watery fluid containing sodium chloride and urea externally through the pores.

sweat·ing sickness (swĕt′ĭng) *n.* **1.** An acute infectious disease that was epidemic in Europe during the 15th and 16th centuries, characterized by profuse sweating and fever. **2.** A disease of cattle that is transmitted by ticks and is widespread in southern Africa.

sweat·pants, sweat pants (swĕt′pănts′) *pl.n.* Cotton jersey pants having a drawstring or elasticized waist and close-fitting cuffs, worn especially for exercising.

sweat·shirt, sweat shirt (swĕt′shûrt′) *n.* A usually long-sleeved cotton jersey pullover worn especially as casual wear or for exercising.

sweat·shop (swĕt′shŏp′) *n.* A workplace or factory where employees work long hours for low wages under bad conditions.

sweat suit *n.* A two-piece outfit consisting of a sweatshirt and sweat pants.

Swed. Sweden; Swedish.

swede (swēd) *n.* A plant, the rutabaga *(see).* [So named because introduced into Scotland from Sweden in the 18th century.]

Swede (swēd) *n.* **1.** A native or inhabitant of Sweden. **2.** A person of Swedish descent.

Swe·den (swēd′n). *Abbr.* **Sw., Swed.** *Swedish* **Sve·ri·ge** (svär′yə). Kingdom of northern Europe, occupying the east of the mountainous Scandinavian Peninsula. It has one of the world's highest living standards, and also one of its most extensive welfare programs, taxes absorbing more than a third of the national income. Prosperity derives chiefly from manufacturing. The country has large forest and mineral resources, including iron, copper, lead, and uranium. It relies heavily on hydroelectric power and increasingly on nuclear power, having few fossil fuel deposits. Sweden emerged as a unified nation in the 11th century. It became a great power in the 17th century, but lost its empire early in the next century. Area, 449,964 square kilometers (173,732 square miles). Population, 8,300,000. Capital, Stockholm.

Swe·den·borg (swēd′n-bôrg′), **Emanuel** (1688–1772). Swedish scientist, philosopher, and religious writer. He began having visions (*c.* 1743) and afterward devoted himself to physical and spiritual research. Although he did not preach or found a religious sect, his

writings inspired his followers to set up the New Jerusalem Church.
Swe·den·bor·gi·an·ism (swēd'n-bôr'gē-ə-nĭz'əm, -bôr'jē-) *n.* Also *rare* **Swe·den·borg·ism** (-bôr'gĭz'əm). The theological philosophy of Emanuel Swedenborg that forms the basis for the New Jerusalem Church, claiming direct mystical communication between the world and the spiritual realm and affirming Christ as the true God. **—Swe·den·bor·gi·an** *n. & adj.*
Swed·ish (swē'dĭsh) *adj.* Of or pertaining to Sweden, the Swedes, or their culture or language.
~n. **1.** The North Germanic language of Sweden. **2.** *Used with a plural verb.* The people of Sweden. Preceded by *the.*
Swedish massage *n.* A European style of therapeutic massage and exercises for muscles and joints, developed in the 19th century.
Swedish turnip *n.* A vegetable, the **rutabaga** *(see).*
sweep (swēp) *v.* **swept** (swĕpt), **sweeping, sweeps.** *—tr.* **1.** To clean or clear the surface or interior of with or as if with a broom or brush: *sweep a chimney.* **2.** To clean or clear away (dust or dirt, for example) with or as if with a broom or brush: *sweep snow from the steps.* **3. a.** To clear (a space) with or as if with a broom. **b.** To clear (objects) away with or as if with a broom: *swept the papers off her desk.* **4.** To touch or brush lightly: *Willow branches swept the ground.* **5. a.** To move, remove, or convey with a flowing or driving motion: *The wind swept tiles from the roof.* **b.** To move or unbalance emotionally: *Love swept him off his feet.* **6.** To cause to depart; remove or destroy: *flood waters sweeping everything in their path.* **7.** To move across or along with speed or intensity; range throughout: *Plague swept Europe; fire sweeping the prairie.* **8.** To traverse, as when searching: *Her gaze swept the horizon.* **9.** To drag the bottom of (a body of water). **10.** To win all the stages of (a game or contest): *swept the World Series.* **11.** To win overwhelmingly in: *Their candidates swept the election.* *—intr.* **1.** To clear or clean a surface with or as if with a broom or brush. **2. a.** To move, surge, or flow with strong and steady force: *A cool wind swept over the plain.* **b.** To move swiftly or majestically: *She swept by in silence.* **3.** To trail, as a long garment: *Her veil swept to the floor.* **4.** To extend gracefully or majestically: *The hills sweep down to the sea.*
~n. **1.** The act of sweeping; removal with or as if with a broom or brush. **2.** The motion of sweeping: *a sweep of the arm.* **3.** The range or scope encompassed by sweeping: *the sweep of a machine gun.* **4. a.** A reach or extent: *a sweep of green lawn.* **b.** A curving driveway. **5.** Any curve or contour: *the sweep of her hair.* **6.** One who sweeps; especially, a chimney sweep. **7.** *Usually* **sweeps.** Sweepings. **8. a.** The winning of all stages of a game or contest. **b.** A total victory or success. **9.** A long oar used to propel a boat. **10.** A long pole attached to a pivot and with a bucket at one end, used to raise water from a well. **11.** *Informal.* A sweepstakes. **12.** *Electronics.* The steady motion of an electron beam across a cathode-ray tube. **—make a clean sweep.** To get rid of all unwanted objects, people, obligations, or other obstacles. [Middle English *swe(e)pen,* probably from Old English *swēop,* past singular of *swāpan,* to sweep.]
sweep·back (swēp'băk') *n. Aviation.* **1.** The backward slant of the leading edge of an airfoil. **2.** The degree of this slant.
sweep·er (swē'pər) *n.* **1.** A person who sweeps. **2.** A **carpet sweeper** *(see).*
sweep·ing (swē'pĭng) *adj.* **1.** Removing with or as if with a broom or brushing movement. **2.** Influencing or affecting a great area; wide-ranging: *sweeping changes.* **3.** Very general; without discrimination or reservation: *sweeping generalizations.* **4.** Overwhelming; complete: *a sweeping victory.* **5.** Curving in form or motion: *a sweeping gesture of the arm.*
~n. **1.** The action or occupation of one who sweeps. **2. sweepings.** That which is swept up; debris; litter. **—sweep·ing·ly** *adv.*
sweep-sec·ond hand (swēp'sĕk'ənd) *n.* A long hand on a clock or watch that measures seconds by moving the space of a minute for each second. Also called "sweep hand."
sweep·stakes (swēp'stāks') *n. Used with a singular or plural verb.* Also **sweep·stake** (-stāk'). **1.** A lottery in which the participants' contributions form a fund to be awarded as a prize to the winner or winners. **2.** Any event or contest, especially a horse race, the result of which determines the winner of such a lottery. **3.** The lottery prize won.
sweet (swēt) *adj.* **sweeter, sweetest. 1. a.** Having a sugary taste. **b.** Containing or derived from a sugar. **2.** Pleasing to the senses, feelings, or the mind; gratifying: *sweet music; Revenge is sweet.* **3.** Having a pleasing disposition; lovable: *a sweet child.* **4.** Kind; nice; pleasant and helpful: *It's sweet of you to give me a lift.* **5. a.** Not saline; fresh: *sweet water.* **b.** Unsalted: *sweet butter.* **6.** Not spoiled, sour, or decaying; fresh: *This milk is still sweet.* **7.** Free of acid. **8.** *Music.* **a.** Designating jazz characterized by adherence to a melodic line and to a time signature. **b.** Performing jazz in this way. **9.** Designating wine that retains some natural sugar; not dry. **—sweet on.** *Informal.* Fond of (a person); infatuated with.
~n. **1.** The quality of being sweet; sweetness. **2.** Something that is sweet or contains sugar. **3.** A candy, preserve, or confection. **4.** *Chiefly British.* Anything relatively sweet served as a dessert. **5.** A dear or beloved person. [Middle English *swe(e)te,* Old English *swēte.*] **—sweet·ish** *adj.* **—sweet·ly** *adv.* **—sweet·ness** *n.*
sweet alyssum *n.* A widely cultivated plant, *Lobularia maritima,* native to the Mediterranean region, having clusters of small, fragrant white or purplish flowers.
sweet-and-sour (swēt'n-sour') *adj.* Flavored with a sauce made of vinegar and sugar and often fruit, as in Chinese cooking: *sweet-and-sour pork.*
sweet basil *n.* A species of **basil** *(see).*
sweet bay *n.* A small tree, *Magnolia virginiana,* of the southeastern United States, having large, fragrant white flowers. Also called "bay."
sweet birch *n.* A tree, the **black birch** *(see).*
sweet·bread (swēt'brĕd') *n.* The pancreas or thymus gland of a calf or lamb, used for food. [SWEET + BREAD (euphemism).]
sweet·bri·ar, sweet·bri·er (swēt'brī'ər) *n.* A rose, *Rosa rubiginosa* (or *R. eglanteria*), native to Europe, having prickly stems, fragrant leaves, and pink flowers. Also called "eglantine."
sweet cherry *n.* **1.** A widely cultivated tree originating from the wild cherry *Prunus avium,* native to Eurasia, having white flowers and sweet, edible fruit. The sweet cherry group has two subdivisions, the **bigarreau** and the **gean** *(both of which see).* **2.** The fruit of this tree.
sweet chestnut *n.* See **chestnut** (sense 1).
sweet cicely *n.* **1.** Any of various North American plants of the genus *Osmorhiza,* having aromatic roots, compound leaves, and clusters of small white flowers. **2.** An aromatic European plant, *Myrrhis odorata,* having compound leaves and clusters of small white flowers. In this sense, also called "myrrh."
sweet cider *n.* Unfermented apple juice. Compare **hard cider.**
sweet clover *n.* A plant, the **melilot** *(see).*
sweet corn *n.* Any of several varieties of corn, especially *Zea mays saccharata,* having kernels that are sweet to eat when young.
sweet·en (swēt'n) *v.* **-ened, -ening, -ens.** *—tr.* **1.** To make sweet or sweeter by or as if by the addition of sugar. **2.** To make pleasurable or gratifying. **3.** To make bearable; alleviate; lighten. **4.** *Informal.* To increase the value of (collateral for a loan) by adding more securities. **5.** In poker, to increase the value of (an unwon pot) by adding stakes before reopening. *—intr.* To become sweet.
sweet·en·er (swēt'n-ər) *n.* **1.** That which is added to something to make it sweet; specifically, a sugar substitute such as saccharin. **2.** *Slang.* A bribe.
sweet·en·ing (swēt'n-ĭng) *n.* **1.** The act or process of making sweet. **2.** Something used to sweeten.
sweet fennel *n.* A variety of fennel, **finochio** *(see).*
sweet fern *n.* An aromatic shrub, *Comptonia peregrina,* of eastern North America, having shallowly lobed, fernlike, aromatic foliage.
sweet flag *n.* A plant, *Acorus calamus,* growing in moist places and having bladelike leaves, minute greenish flowers, and aromatic roots. Also called "calamus."
sweet gum *n.* **1.** A New World tree, *Liquidambar styraciflua,* having sharply lobed leaves, prickly, ball-like fruit clusters, and wood used to make furniture. Also called "bilsted." **2.** The wood or aromatic resin obtained from this tree.
sweet·heart (swēt'härt') *n.* **1.** One who loves and is loved by another. Often used as a term of affectionate address. **2.** A lovable, friendly, or generous person.
swee·tie (swē'tē) *n. Informal.* A sweetheart; a dear.
sweetie pie *n. Informal.* A sweetheart.
sweet·ing (swē'tĭng) *n.* **1.** A sweet apple. **2.** *Archaic.* A sweetheart.
sweet marjoram *n.* A species of **marjoram** *(see).*
sweet·meat (swēt'mēt') *n.* Any delicacy made with a sweetening agent, such as a piece of candy or crystallized fruit. [SWEET + MEAT (food).]
sweet myrtle *n.* A swamp shrub, *Myrica gale,* having aromatic, resinous leaves. Also called "bog myrtle," "gale."
sweet pea *n.* A climbing plant, *Lathyrus odoratus,* native to southern Italy, cultivated for its variously colored, fragrant flowers.
sweet pepper *n.* A plant, or its fruit, the **bell pepper** *(see).*
sweet potato *n.* **1.** A tropical American vine, *Ipomoea batatas,* cultivated for its thick, sweet, orange-colored, edible root. **2.** The root of this plant, eaten cooked as a vegetable. **3.** *Informal.* The ocarina.
sweet·shop (swēt'shŏp') *n. Chiefly British.* A small shop that sells candy and sometimes tobacco and other items.
sweet·sop (swēt'sŏp') *n.* **1.** A tropical American tree, *Annona squamosa,* having yellowish-green fruit with sweet, edible pulp. **2.** The fruit of this tree. Also called "sugar apple."
sweet talk *n.* Flattery.
sweet-talk (swēt'tôk') *v.* **-talked, -talking, -talks.** *—tr.* To coax or cajole with flattery. *—intr.* To use flattery.
sweet-tem·pered (swēt'tĕm'pərd) *adj.* Gentle and kind by nature. **—sweet-tem·pered·ly** *adv.*
sweet tooth *n.* A fondness for sugar or sweet things.
sweet William (wĭl'yəm) *n.* A widely cultivated plant, *Dianthus barbatus,* native to Eurasia, having flat, dense clusters of white, pink, red, or purple flowers.
swell (swĕl) *v.* **swelled, swelled** or **swollen** (swō'lən), **swelling, swells.** *—intr.* **1.** To increase in size or volume as a result of internal pressure; expand. **2. a.** To increase in force, size, number, or degree. **b.** To grow in loudness or intensity: *the sound swelled to a tremendous din.* **3.** To bulge out; protrude, as a sail. **4.** To rise in or like billows above the surrounding level, as waves or clouds. **5.** To rise up in level or overflow, as a river. **6.** To be or become filled or puffed up with an emotion, such as pride. *—tr.* To cause to swell: *swelled the chorus of protest.*
~n. **1. a.** The act or process of swelling. **b.** The condition of being swollen. **2.** A swollen part; a bulge or protuberance. **3.** A regular undulating movement of waves out in the open sea, with no breaking and considerable distance between successive crests. **4. a.** A rise

sweet William Dianthus barbatus, *a perennial flower that is a common garden plant, can grow to about 75 centimeters (2½ feet).*

PRONUNCIATION KEY

ă, pat; ā, pay; âr, care;
ä, father, are; b, bib;
ch, church; d, deed; ĕ, pet;
ē, be; f, fife; g, gag; h, hat;
hw, which; ĭ, pit; ī, pie;
îr, pier; j, judge; k, kick;
l, lid, needle; m, mum;
n, no, sudden; ng, thing;
ŏ, pot; ō, toe; ô, paw, for;
oi, noise; ou, out; o͝o, book;
o͞o, boot; p, pop; r, roar;
s, sauce; sh, ship, dish;
t, tight; th, thin, path;
th, this, bathe; ŭ, cut; ûr, fur;
v, valve; w, with; y, yes;
z, zebra, size; zh, vision;
ə, about, item, edible, gallop, circus, peaceful

IN FOREIGN WORDS:

à, *Fr.* ami; œ, *Fr.* feu, *Ger.* schön; ü, *Fr.* tu, *Ger.* über; KH, *Ger.* ich, *Scot.* loch; N, *Fr.* bon; y', *Fr.* Compiègne

STRESS MARKS:

Primary stress: '
in·cite' (ĭn-sīt')
Secondary stress: '
in'sight' (ĭn'sīt')

swift *Found almost everywhere except in polar regions, the swift spends most of its waking hours in flight. It can reach speeds of 110 kilometers (70 miles) per hour and catches insects on the wing with its wide-open mouth. This is the common swift,* Apus apus.

PRONUNCIATION KEY

ă, pat; ā, pay; âr, care;
ä, father, are; b, **bib**;
ch, **church**; d, **deed**; ĕ, pet;
ē, be; f, **fife**; g, **gag**; h, **hat**;
hw, **which**; ĭ, pit; ī, pie;
îr, pier; j, **judge**; k, **kick**;
l, lid, needle; m, **mum**;
n, no, sudden; ng, **thing**;
ŏ, pot; ō, toe; ô, paw, for;
oi, noise; ou, **out**; ŏŏ, **book**;
ōō, **boot**; p, **pop**; r, **roar**;
s, sauce; sh, **ship**, **dish**;
t, tight; th, **thin**, **path**;
th, **this**, **bathe**; ŭ, cut; ûr, **fur**;
v, valve; w, **with**; y, **yes**;
z, zebra, size; zh, **vision**;
ə, about, item, edible, gallop, circus, peaceful

IN FOREIGN WORDS:

à, *Fr.* ami; œ, *Fr.* **feu**, *Ger.* **schön**; ü, *Fr.* tu, *Ger.* **über**;
KH, *Ger.* **ich**, *Scot.* **loch**;
N, *Fr.* bon; y', *Fr.* Compiègne

STRESS MARKS:

Primary stress: ′
in·cite′ (ĭn-sīt′)
Secondary stress: ˌ
in′sight′ (ĭn′sīt′)

in the land; a rounded hill. **b.** A long, gently sloping elevation that rises from the sea bed but is far from the surface. **5.** *Informal.* One who is fashionably dressed or prominent in fashionable society. **6.** *Music.* **a.** A crescendo followed by a gradual diminuendo. **b.** The sign indicating this. **c.** A device on some instruments, such as an organ or harpsichord, for regulating volume.
~*adj.* **sweller, swellest.** *Informal.* **1.** Fashionably elegant; smart; stylish. **2.** Fine; excellent: *a swell guy.* [Middle English *swellen, swollen,* Old English *swellan, geswollen,* from Germanic *swellan* (unattested).]

swell box *n.* A chamber housing one or more sets of organ pipes and having shutters that can be opened or shut to regulate the volume of tone.

swelled head *n.* An unduly high opinion of oneself; conceit.

swell·fish (swĕl′fĭsh′) *n., pl.* **-fishes** or collectively **swellfish.** The **puffer** *(see).*

swell·head (swĕl′hĕd′) *n.* An arrogant, conceited person. **—swell·head·ed** *adj.* **—swell·head·ed·ness** *n.*

swell·ing (swĕl′ĭng) *n.* **1.** The act of expanding. **2.** The state of being swollen or expanded. **3.** Something that is swollen; especially, an abnormally swollen or protuberant area on the body.

swel·ter (swĕl′tər) *v.* **-tered, -tering, -ters.** *—intr.* To be affected by or sweat or feel faint from oppressive heat. *—tr.* **1.** To affect with oppressive heat. **2.** *Archaic.* To exude.
~*n.* Oppressive heat and humidity: *"All the swelter of that urban summer"* (Cyril Connolly). [Middle English *swelt(e)ren,* frequentative of *swelten,* to faint from heat, Old English *sweltan,* to die.]

swel·ter·ing (swĕl′tər-ĭng) *adj.* Also *rare* **swel·try** (swĕl′trē), **-trier, -triest.** **1.** Oppressively hot and humid. **2.** Suffering from oppressive heat. **—swel·ter·ing·ly** *adv.*

swept. Past tense and past participle of **sweep.**

swept·back (swĕpt′băk′) *adj.* Angled rearward from the points of attachment. Said especially of aircraft wings.

swept·wing (swĕpt′wĭng′) *adj.* Having sweptback wings.
~*n.* A sweptback wing.

swerve (swûrv) *v.* **swerved, swerving, swerves.** *—intr.* To turn aside suddenly and swiftly from a straight or planned course; veer. *—tr.* To cause to swerve; deflect; turn aside.
~*n.* A deflection or deviation; a swerving movement. [Middle English *swerven,* Old English *sweorfan,* to rub.]

S.W.G. Standard wire gauge.

swift (swĭft) *adj.* **swifter, swiftest.** **1.** Moving or able to move with great speed; fast; fleet. **2.** Coming, occurring, or accomplished quickly; instant: *a swift retort.* **3.** Ready in acting or reacting; prompt: *swift to take steps.* **—**See Synonyms at **fast.**
~*adv.* Quickly; swiftly. Often used in combination: *swift-running.*
~*n.* **1.** A cylinder on a carding machine. **2.** A reel used to hold yarn as it is being wound off. **3.** Any of various dark-colored, swallowlike birds of the family Apodidae, characteristically having long, narrow wings and a relatively short tail. **4.** Any of various small, fast-moving North American lizards of the genera *Sceloporus* and *Uta.* [Middle English *swift(e),* Old English *swift.*] **—swift·ly** *adv.* **—swift·ness** *n.*

Swift (swĭft), **Jonathan** (1667–1745). English satirist and poet, born in Ireland. His works include *A Tale of a Tub* (1704), which attacked religious extremism, and his masterpiece, *Gulliver's Travels* (1726), a satirical attack on the politics, philosophy, and science of his time.

swift·let (swĭft′lĭt) *n.* Any small cave-dwelling swift of the genus *Collocalia,* of southeast Asia and Australia, whose nests, constructed chiefly of solidified saliva, are used to make bird's-nest soup. [Diminutive of SWIFT. See **-let.**]

swift moth *n.* The **ghost moth** *(see).*

swig (swĭg) *n. Informal.* A large swallow, as of a liquid; a gulp.
~*v.* **swigged, swigging, swigs.** *—tr. Informal.* To drink eagerly and with great gulps. *—intr. Informal.* To take a large swallow; gulp. [16th century : origin obscure.]

swill (swĭl) *v.* **swilled, swilling, swills.** *—tr.* **1.** To drink eagerly, greedily, or to excess. **2.** To flood with water, as for cleaning or washing. **3.** To feed (animals) with slops. *—intr.* To drink greedily.
~*n.* **1.** The act or an instance of swilling. **2.** A mixture of liquid and solid food, such as table scraps, fed to animals, especially pigs; slops. **3.** Kitchen waste or garbage; refuse. [Middle English *swilen,* Old English *swilian,* to wash out.] **—swill·er** *n.*

swim (swĭm) *v.* **swam** (swăm), **swum** (swŭm), **swimming, swims.** *—intr.* **1.** To propel oneself through water by means of movements of the body. **2.** To move as though gliding through water. **3.** To float on water or other liquid. **4.** To be covered or flooded with a liquid; be immersed: *chicken swimming in gravy.* **5.** To experience a floating or dizzy sensation: *Her head swam from lack of food.* **6.** To appear to spin or reel lazily: *The room swam before her eyes.* *—tr.* **1.** To propel oneself through or across (a body of water) by swimming. **2.** To compete in (a race) by swimming. **3.** To perform (a particular stroke) in swimming. **4.** To cause to swim or float on a body of water.
~*n.* **1.** The act or movements of one that swims. **2.** A period or instance of swimming. **3.** A deep part in a river, containing many fish. **4.** A state of dizziness; a swoon. **—in the swim.** *Informal.* In the current trend of affairs; participating in what is fashionable. [Middle English *swimmen, swam(me), swummen,* Old English *swimman, swamm* (or *swom*), *swummen.*] **—swim·mer** *n.*

swim bladder *n.* An organ in fishes, the **air bladder** *(see).*

swim·mer·et (swĭm′ə-rĕt′) *n.* Any of the paired abdominal appendages of certain aquatic crustaceans, such as shrimps and lobsters, that function primarily as organs of respiration or locomotion. Also called "pleopod." [Diminutive of *swimmer,* from SWIM.]

swim·ming·ly (swĭm′ĭng-lē) *adv.* With great ease and a high degree of success: *The campaign is proceeding swimmingly.*

swimming pool *n.* A pool built for swimming. Also called "pool."

swim·suit (swĭm′sōōt′) *n.* A garment worn for swimming; bathing suit.

Swin·burne (swĭn′bərn), **Algernon Charles** (1837–1909). British poet and critic. He is best known for his magnificently musical, often erotic verse, in which he attacked the conventions of Victorian morality.

swin·dle (swĭn′dl) *v.* **-dled, -dling, -dles.** *—tr.* **1.** To cheat or defraud (a person or group) of money or property. **2.** To obtain (money or property, for example) by fraudulent means. *—intr.* To practice fraud as a habitual means of obtaining money.
~*n.* The act or an instance of swindling; a fraud. [Back-formation from *swindler,* from German *Schwindler,* dizzy person, from *schwindeln,* to be dizzy, from Old High German *swintilōn,* frequentative of *swintan,* to vanish, from Germanic *swindan* (unattested).] **—swin·dler** *n.*

swine (swīn) *n., pl.* **swine.** **1.** Any of the ungulate mammals of the family Suidae, which includes pigs, hogs, and boars. **2.** A contemptible, vicious, or coarse person. [Middle English *swin(e),* Old English *swīn.*]

swine·herd (swīn′hûrd′) *n.* A person who tends swine.

swine·pox (swīn′pŏks′) *n.* A disease of domesticated swine caused by a virus similar to that causing cowpox and smallpox and characterized by skin lesions.

swine vesicular disease *n.* A highly infectious viral disease of pigs, similar to foot-and-mouth disease, characterized by fever and painful blisters on the feet and snout.

swing (swĭng) *v.* **swung** (swŭng), **swung, swinging, swings.** *—intr.* **1. a.** To move rhythmically back and forth suspended or as if suspended from above; oscillate; sway: *a rope swinging from the mast.* **b.** To move back and forth, as a gate, while attached to a fixed point or support. **c.** To ride on or propel a swing. **2. a.** To walk or run with a free-swaying motion: *a team of horses swinging down the road.* **b.** To move from one fixed position or support to another with a free-swaying motion: *swinging from tree to tree.* **3. a.** To turn in place, as on a hinge or other pivot. **b.** To turn suddenly: *swung around.* **4.** To move in a curve; move from a straight path: *The car swung off the road. The ball swung in toward the plate.* **5.** To change one's attitudes, emotions, habits, or the like; vacillate. **6.** *Slang.* To be executed by hanging: *He'll swing for his crimes.* **7. a.** *Music.* To have a compulsive rhythm. **b.** To play with a compulsive rhythm. **8.** To hit or attempt to hit with a curving, swaying motion of the arm: *He swung at the ball.* **9.** *Slang.* **a.** To be spirited and up-to-date. **b.** To be sexually uninhibited. *—tr.* **1.** To cause to move back and forth. **2.** To move (a person on a swing) backward and forward by pulling or pushing. **3.** To cause to move back and forth with a sweeping motion: *Swing your arms while you walk.* **4.** To cause to move in a broad arc: *swing a bat; swung the car into the driveway.* **5.** To hang or suspend (something) so that it can sway or move freely. **6.** To cause to turn on hinges: *Swing the door shut.* **7.** To cause to change from one attitude, position, opinion, or emotion to another. **8.** *Slang.* To manipulate or manage successfully: *Can you swing this deal?* **9.** To arrange or perform (popular music) in the style of swing.
~*n.* **1.** The act or an instance of swinging, especially: **a.** A rhythmic back-and-forth movement. **b.** A single movement or series of movements in one particular direction. **c.** A punch or blow: *took a swing at him.* **d.** A movement from one attitude or opinion to another, such as a change of allegiance or voting: *a swing to conservatism.* **2.** The distance traversed while swinging: *The pendulum's swing is 12 inches.* **3.** The manner in which a person or thing swings something, such as a bat or golf club. **4.** Freedom and scope of movement or action. **5. a.** A swaying, graceful motion. **b.** A sweep or swoop: *the swing of a bird across the sky.* **6.** A seat suspended from above, on which one may ride back and forth in an arc for recreation. **7.** *Informal.* The normal rhythm or pace of life; the ordinary flow of activities: *back into the swing of things.* **8.** A steady, vigorous rhythm, as in poetry or music. **9. a.** An innovation in popular dance music developed about 1935, based on jazz but employing a larger band and simpler harmonic and rhythmic patterns. **b.** The rhythmic quality of this music. **—in full swing.** At full speed or intensity.
~*adj.* **1.** Pertaining to or performing swing: *a swing band.* **2.** Deciding an election: *the swing vote.* [Middle English *swingen, swang* (past singular), *swungen* (past plural), *swungen,* Old English *swingan,* to whip, strike, fling oneself, *swang, swungon, geswungen.*]

Synonyms: *swing, oscillate, sway, rock, vibrate, fluctuate, undulate, waver.* These verbs refer to movement marked in general by a back-and-forth or up-and-down pattern. *Swing* usually applies to arclike movement of something attached at one extremity and free at the other, or to rotating or pivoting movement around an axis. *Oscillate* more specifically refers to regular back-and-forth movement, such as that of a pendulum. *Sway* suggests the movement of something unsteady, light, or flexible. *Rock* can apply both to rhythmic and rather gentle movement and to violent tilting. *Vibrate,* in general usage, usually suggests rhythmic throbbing or pulsating;

thus it implies trembling or quivering motion rather than pronounced movement. *Fluctuate* usually applies to movement of nonphysical things, such as prices, and suggests fairly constant change that follows no set course. *Undulate* implies smooth, wavelike movement. *Waver* suggests unsteady and uncertain movement, such as tottering or faltering. In figurative usage it refers to indecisiveness.

swing bridge *n.* A river or canal bridge that can be pivoted on a vertical central axis to allow ships to pass. Also called "turn bridge."

swinge (swĭnj) *tr.v.* **swinged, swinges.** *Archaic.* To strike or beat. [Middle English *swengen*, to shake, dash, beat up, Old English *swengan*, to swing, shake.] —**swing·er** (swĭn'jər) *n.*

swing·er (swĭng'ər) *n.* **1.** One that swings. **2.** *Slang.* A person who actively seeks excitement and moves with the latest trends. **3.** *Slang.* A person who is sexually uninhibited.

swing·ing (swĭng'ĭng) *adj. Slang.* **1.** Spirited and up-to-date. **2.** Attracting a lively, trendy crowd: *a swinging nightclub.*

swinging door *n.* A door, often either of a pair, that is hung on double-sided hinges enabling it to be opened in either direction. Also **swing door.**

swin·gle·tree (swĭng'gəl-trē') *n.* A whiffletree (see). [From *swingle*, wooden instrument for beating hemp, Middle English *swingle*, from Middle Dutch *swinghel*.]

swing shift *n. Informal.* A factory work shift between the day and night shifts, as from about 4 P.M. to midnight.

swing-wing (swĭng'wĭng') *adj.* Being or pertaining to an aircraft with movable wings that can be swept back for fast flight and brought forward for lower speeds, as on takeoff and landing. ~*n.* **1.** A swing-wing aircraft. Also called "variable sweep." **2.** Either of the wings of such an aircraft.

swin·ish (swī'nĭsh) *adj.* Resembling or befitting swine; bestial; brutish. —**swin·ish·ly** *adv.* —**swin·ish·ness** *n.*

swipe (swīp) *n.* **1.** A heavy, sweeping blow. **2.** A critical remark. **3.** A lever, especially one that raises the bucket in a well. ~*v.* **swiped, swiping, swipes.** —*tr.* **1.** To hit with a sweeping blow. **2.** *Slang.* To steal; filch. —*intr.* To make a sweeping blow. [Perhaps alteration of SWEEP.]

swipes (swīps) *pl.n. British Informal.* Beer that is weak, inferior, or spoiled. [18th century : origin obscure.]

swirl (swûrl) *v.* **swirled, swirling, swirls.** —*intr.* **1.** To rotate or spin in or as if in a whirlpool or eddy. **2.** To be dizzy or faint; reel. —*tr.* To cause to move with a whirling motion. —See Synonyms at **turn.** ~*n.* **1.** The motion or act of whirling or spinning. **2.** Something that swirls; a whirlpool or eddy. **3.** Something that is or has been swirled, such as a twisting line or a curl of hair. **4.** Confusion; turbulence; disorder. [Middle English *swyrl*, eddy, probably of Low German origin.] —**swirl·y** *adj.*

swish (swĭsh) *v.* **swished, swishing, swishes.** —*intr.* **1.** To move with a sibilant whistle or hiss. **2.** To rustle, as certain fabrics. **3.** *Slang.* To move or act in an effeminate manner. —*tr.* **1.** To cause to make a swishing movement or sound. **2.** To cut off with a swishing sound. **3.** To whip with a rod. ~*n.* **1. a.** A sharp sibilant or rustling sound: *the swish of scythes.* **b.** A movement making such a sound. **2. a.** A rod used for whipping. **b.** A stroke made with such a rod. **3.** *Slang.* A highly effeminate male. ~*adj. Slang.* **1.** *Chiefly British.* Fashionable; posh; luxurious. **2.** Highly effeminate. [Imitative.]

swiss, Swiss (swĭs) *n.* A crisp, sheer cotton cloth used for curtains or light garments. [From SWISS (because it was first manufactured in Switzerland.)]

Swiss (swĭs) *adj.* Of, pertaining to, or characteristic of Switzerland, its inhabitants, or its culture. ~*n., pl.* **Swiss. 1.** A native or inhabitant of Switzerland. **2.** A person of Swiss descent. [Old French *Suisse*, from Middle High German *Swizer*, from *Swiz*, SWITZERLAND.]

Swiss chard *n.* A vegetable, **chard** (see).

Swiss cheese *n.* A firm whitish or pale yellow cheese with a nutlike flavor and many holes.

Swiss Guard *pl.n.* The group of bodyguards in the Vatican, made up of mercenaries from Switzerland.

swiss roll *n.* A cake made of a layer of sponge spread with a filling such as jam or cream and rolled into a cylindrical shape. [SWISS, from Switzerland, where it probably originated.]

Swiss steak *n.* A round or shoulder steak that is pounded with flour, braised, and usually served with a seasoned sauce.

switch (swĭch) *n. Abbr.* **sw. 1.** A slender flexible rod, stick, twig, or the like; especially, such a rod used for whipping. **2.** The bushy tip of the tail of certain animals: *a cow's switch.* **3.** A thick bunch of real or synthetic hair used by women as part of a hairstyle. **4.** A flailing or lashing, as with a slender rod. **5.** *Electricity.* A device used to break or open an electrical circuit or to divert current from one conductor to another. **6.** A device consisting of two sections of railway track and the accompanying apparatus, used to transfer rolling stock from one track to another. **7.** An exchange or swap, especially one done surreptitiously. **8.** Any sudden transference or shift, as of opinion or attention. ~*v.* **switched, switching, switches.** —*tr.* **1.** To whip with or as if with a switch. **2.** To jerk or swish abruptly or sharply. **3.** To shift, transfer, change, or divert: *switch the conversation.* **4.** To exchange: *switch sides.* **5.** To connect, disconnect, or divert (an electric current) by operating a switch. **6.** To cause (an electric current or appliance) to begin or cease operation: *switch on the lights; switch*

off the radio. **7.** To move (rolling stock) from one track to another; shunt. **8.** *Informal.* To provide or produce quickly and effortlessly: *switch on the charm.* —*intr.* **1.** To shift or change: *switch from coal to oil.* **2.** To be shifted or changed. —**switch off.** *Informal.* To lose interest; cease paying attention: *The lecturer's voice was so dull that I switched off after five minutes.* [Perhaps from Middle Dutch *swijch*, bough, twig.] —**switch·er** *n.*

switch·back (swĭch'băk') *n.* A road or trail that ascends a steep incline in a winding course.

switch·blade (swĭch'blād') *n.* A pocket knife having a spring-operated blade that unsheathes when a release on the handle is pressed. Also *British* "flick knife."

switch·board (swĭch'bôrd', -bōrd') *n.* **1.** An installation that controls the interconnection of telephone lines, as in a telephone exchange or office. **2.** A panel or set of panels with switches, indicators, and other apparatus for operating electric circuits.

switch hitter *n.* A baseball player who can bat either right-handed or left-handed.

switch·man (swĭch'mən) *n., pl.* **-men** (-mĭn). One who operates railroad switches.

switch·yard (swĭch'yärd') *n.* An area of a railroad yard where cars are switched and trains assembled.

Swith·in or **Swith·un** (swĭth'ən), **Saint** (died 862). English prelate. He was bishop of Winchester (852–62). According to tradition, if it rains on St. Swithin's Day (July 15), it will rain for 40 days following. On that day in 971 the saint's body was to be transferred from churchyard to cathedral, contrary to his wishes, and heavy rain delayed the proceedings.

Switz. Switzerland.

Swit·zer (swĭt'sər) *n.* **1.** A Swiss. **2.** A member of the Swiss Guard. [Middle High German *Swizer*, from *Swiz*, SWITZERLAND.]

Swit·zer·land (swĭt'sər-lənd). *Abbr.* **Switz.** French **Suisse** (swēs). German **Schweiz** (shvīts). Italian **Sviz·ze·ra** (svēt-sā'rä). Latin **Hel·ve·tia** (hĕl-vē'shə). Landlocked country in western Europe. It consists of three regions: the Alps in the south are divided from the Jura Mts. of the northwest by the Mittelland Plateau. The population includes German, French, and Italian speakers, with a small Romansch minority. Switzerland is a world center of finance and tourism. Its main exports are watches, jewelry, instruments, and textiles. It became part of the Holy Roman Empire (10th century), but by 1499 had achieved independence as a loose confederation of cantons. A federal constitution was adopted in 1848. Resolute neutrality kept Switzerland out of both world wars, and it is not a UN member. However, it has become the base of many international groups, including the Red Cross and the World Health Organization. Area, 41,288 square kilometers (15,937 square miles). Population, 6,400,000. Capital, Bern.

swiv·el (swĭv'əl) *n.* **1.** A link, pivot, or other fastening so designed that it permits free turning of attached parts. **2.** A pivoted support that allows an object, such as a chair or gun, to turn in a horizontal plane. **3.** A cannon that turns on a pivot. Also called "swivel gun." ~*v.* **swiveled** or **-elled, -eling** or **-elling, -els.** —*tr.* **1.** To turn or rotate on or as if on a swivel. **2.** To secure, fit, or support with a swivel. —*intr.* To turn on or as if on a swivel. —See Synonyms at **turn.** [Middle English *swyvel*.]

swivel chair *n.* A chair that swivels on its base.

swiv·el-hipped (swĭv'əl-hĭpt') *adj.* Characterized by or moving with an exaggerated swinging motion of the hips.

swiz·zle (swĭz'əl) *n.* Any of various tall mixed drinks, usually made with rum. [19th century : origin unknown.]

swizzle stick *n.* A rod for stirring mixed drinks.

swob. Variant of **swab.**

swol·len (swō'lən) Alternate past participle of **swell.** ~*adj.* Enlarged; distended.

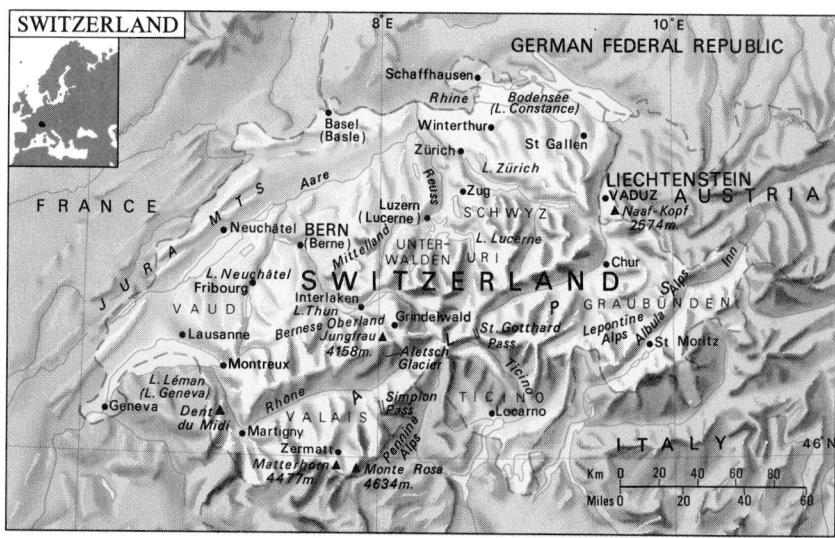

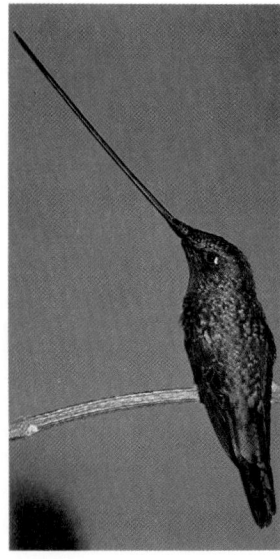

swordbill *One of about 320 species of hummingbird, found mostly in South America. All hummingbirds have long, slender bills, but the swordbill's is the longest—it is almost the length of the bird's body.*

swoon (swōōn) *intr.v.* **swooned, swooning, swoons. 1.** To faint. **2.** To become rapturous or ecstatic.
~*n.* A fainting spell. [Middle English *swounen,* probably from Old English *swōgan,* to suffocate.]

swoop (swōōp) *v.* **swooped, swooping, swoops. —***intr.* To make a sudden sweeping, pouncing movement, like a bird descending upon its prey. —*tr.* To take or snatch suddenly. Often used with *up.*
~*n.* A swift, sudden descent. —**at** (or **in**) **one fell swoop.** With one sudden action; all at once. [Perhaps alteration of Middle English *swopen,* to sweep along, Old English *swāpan,* to sweep.]

swoosh (swōōsh, swŏŏsh) *n.* A low, swishing, hissing sound.
~*v.* **swooshed, swooshing, swooshes. —***intr.* To make such a sound, especially by moving. —*tr.* To cause to make or move with such a sound. [Imitative.]

swop. Variant of **swap.**

sword (sôrd, sōrd) *n.* **1.** A weapon having a handle and a long blade for cutting or thrusting, often worn ceremonially as a symbol of power or authority. **2.** Any instrument of death, combat, or destruction. **3.** Something that resembles a sword. **4. a.** The use of force, as in war. **b.** Military power or jurisdiction. —**at swords' points.** Ready for combat; antagonistic. —**cross swords. 1.** To fight. **2.** To quarrel violently. —**put to the sword.** To kill, especially with a sword. [Middle English *sw(e)ord, swerd,* Old English *sw(e)ord.*]

sword arm *n.* **1.** The arm used to hold a sword. **2.** The right arm.

sword bayonet *n.* A long bayonet resembling and capable of functioning as a sword.

sword·bear·er (sôrd´bâr´ər, sōrd´-) *n.* A person who carries the sword of a monarch or dignitary on ceremonial occasions.

sword·bill (sôrd´bĭl´, sōrd´-) *n.* A hummingbird, *Ensifera ensifera,* of tropical South America, having a very long, slender bill.

sword cane *n.* A cane or light walking stick designed to conceal a sword in its hollow shaft.

sword dance *n.* A dance performed with swords, especially one performed around swords laid on the ground.

sword·fish (sôrd´fĭsh´, sōrd´-) *n., pl.* **-fishes** or collectively **swordfish.** A large marine game and food fish, *Xiphias gladius,* having a long, swordlike extension of the upper jaw. Also called "broadbill."

sword grass *n.* Any of various grasses or grasslike plants having bladelike, pointed leaves.

sword·knot (sôrd´nŏt´, sōrd´-) *n.* A decorative loop or tassel attached to the hilt of a sword.

sword lily *n.* A plant, the **gladiolus** *(see).* [Part translation of Latin *gladiolus,* small sword (referring to the sword-shaped leaves).]

Sword of Damocles *n.* An impending disaster or the constant threat of one. See **Damocles.**

sword·play (sôrd´plā´, sōrd´-) *n.* The action or art of using a sword; fencing. —**sword·play·er** *n.*

swords·man (sôrdz´mən, sōrdz´-) *n., pl.* **-men** (-mĭn). **1.** A person skilled in the use of the sword. **2.** A person armed with a sword. —**swords·man·ship** *n.*

sword·tail (sôrd´tāl´, sōrd´-) *n.* A small, brightly colored freshwater fish, *Xiphophorus helleri,* of Central America, popular in home aquariums, having a long, tapering extension of the tail fin in the male.

swore. Past tense of **swear.**

sworn. Past participle of **swear.**

swounds, swouns. Variants of **zounds.**

swum. Past participle of **swim.**

swung. Past tense and past participle of **swing.**

swung dash *n.* A curved dash (~) used, for example, to indicate the omission of a word or part of a word that has been previously spelled out, or, in symbolic logic, as the sign for negation. In this dictionary it is used to represent a headword before a second or subsequent part of speech label.

Syb·a·ris (sĭb´ə-rĭs´) Ancient Greek colony. It was near the site of the modern town of Terranova di Sibari in northern Calabria. In the 6th century Sybaris controlled trade with the Etruscans. Its wealth earned the Sybarites a reputation for pleasure-seeking luxury.

syb·a·rite, Syb·a·rite (sĭb´ə-rīt´) *n.* A person devoted to pleasure and luxury; a voluptuary: *"Dressed to a sybarite's most pampered wishes"* (Byron). [Latin *Sybarīta,* native of Sybaris, from Greek *Subarītēs,* from *Subaris,* SYBARIS.] —**syb·a·rit·ic** (sĭb´ə-rĭt´ĭk), **syb·a·rit·i·cal** *adj.* —**syb·a·rit·i·cal·ly** *adv.*

syc·a·mine (sĭk´ə-mīn´) *n.* A tree mentioned in the New Testament, thought to be a species of mulberry. Luke 17:6. [Latin *sȳcamīnus,* from Greek *sukaminos,* from Phoenician or Aramaic *shiqmīn* (plural), akin to Hebrew *shiqmīn,* plural of *shiqmāh,* mulberry tree. See also **sycamore.**]

syc·a·more (sĭk´ə-môr´, -mōr´) *n.* **1.** A Eurasian maple tree, *Acer pseudoplatanus,* having five-lobed leaves and winged fruits. **2.** A plane tree, *Platanus occidentalis,* of eastern North America, having lobed leaves, ball-like seed clusters, and bark that often flakes off in large patches. **3.** A tree, *Ficus sycomorus,* of northeastern Africa and adjacent Asia, related to the fig. This species is the sycamore of the Bible. [Middle English *sicamour,* from Old French *sicamor,* from Latin *sycomorus,* from Greek *sukamoros : suka-,* probably from Hebrew *shiqmāh,* mulberry tree (see **sycamine**) + *moron,* mulberry tree.]

syce, sice (sīs) *n.* A stableman or groom, especially formerly in India. [Hindi *sā'is,* from Arabic *sā'is,* from *sāsa,* to administer.]

sy·cee (sī-sē´) *n.* Lumps of pure silver bearing the stamp of a banker or assayer and formerly used in China as money. Also called "sycee silver." [Cantonese *sai si,* "fine silk" (so called because the pure silver can be spun into fine threads).]

sy·co·ni·um (sī-kō´nē-əm) *n., pl.* **-nia** (-nē-ə). Also **sy·co·nus** (sī-kō´nəs). The fleshy multiple fruit of the fig, consisting primarily of the enlarged floral receptacle. [New Latin, from Greek *sukon,* the fig, probably from the same Mediterranean source as Latin *fīcus,* FIG.]

syc·o·phan·cy (sĭk´ə-fən-sē) *n., pl.* **-cies.** The act, practice, or behavior of a sycophant; servile flattery.

syc·o·phant (sĭk´ə-fənt) *n.* One who attempts to win favor or advancement by flattering persons of influence; a servile self-seeker. [Latin *sycophanta,* from Greek *sukophantēs,* "fig-shower," "accuser" (from the use of the gesture of the fig in denouncing a criminal), hence an informer, flatterer : *sukon,* fig (see **syconium**) + *-phantēs,* shower, from *phainein,* to show.] —**syc·o·phan·tic** (sĭk´ə-făn´tĭk), **syc·o·phan·ti·cal** *adj.* —**syc·o·phan·ti·cal·ly** *adv.*
Synonyms: *flatterer, toady.*

sy·co·sis (sī-kō´sĭs) *n.* A chronic inflammation of the hair follicles, especially of the beard and scalp, caused by bacterial infection. [New Latin, from Greek *sukōsis,* eruption resembling a fig : *sukon,* fig (see **syconium**) + -OSIS.]

Syd·ney (sĭd´nē). The largest city in Australia and capital of New

---

sword

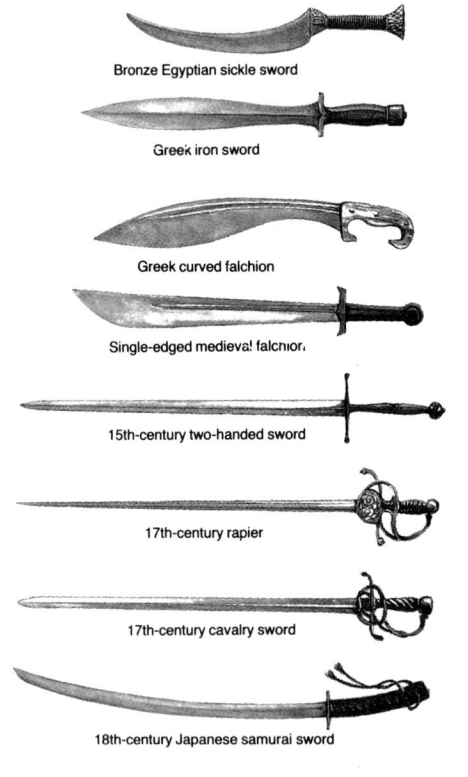

DEADLY CUT AND THRUST

Empires were built by the sword

The sword developed as a weapon from the spear, and for centuries it was the major instrument of warfare. It added a cutting action to the deadly thrust of the spear. From the Bronze Age (*c.* 3000 B.C.) onward, the skill of the metal-worker reached its peak in the making of sword blades, which had to be flexible, strong, and able to take an edge. Precise combinations of copper and tin repeatedly doubled over and hammered together could meet these requirements and so, later, could iron when heated then plunged into cold water to become an even harder metal—steel.

From its discovery in the Middle East about 1000 B.C. until the 19th century, steel was used almost exclusively for making swords or knives, and empires depended on it. Some swords, such as the curved Greek falchion and the sword used by the Japanese samurai, were purely slashing weapons of steel, strong enough to kill a man with one blow. The Roman Empire was built on the *gladius,* the short, double-edged cutting and thrusting weapon of the legions. Medieval Europe preferred a long, straight, double-edged weapon. From about the 16th century, as the use of armor declined, the lighter, pointed rapier, which was intended mainly for thrusting, was developed.

Bronze Egyptian sickle sword

Greek iron sword

Greek curved falchion

Single-edged medieval falchion

15th-century two-handed sword

17th-century rapier

17th-century cavalry sword

18th-century Japanese samurai sword

South Wales. It surrounds Port Jackson or Sydney Harbor, an inlet on the southeast coast. Sydney is the center of the nation's trade and finance. Its many beaches are popular tourist resorts. Other attractions include the Sydney Harbor Bridge (1932) and Sydney Opera House (1973). Sydney was developed by convict labor and rapidly expanded in the late 19th century. Today it is one of the leading cultural centers in the southern hemisphere.

Sydney, Philip. See Sir Philip **Sidney**.

sy·e·nite (sī′ə-nīt′) *n.* An igneous rock composed primarily of alkali feldspar together with other minerals, such as hornblende. [Latin *Syēnītēs (lapis),* "(stone) of Syene" (where it was first quarried), from *Syēnē,* Syene, from Greek *Suēnē.*] **—sy·e·nit·ic** (sī′ə-nĭt′ĭk) *adj.*

syl., syll. **1.** syllable. **2.** syllabus.

sy·li (sĭl′ī) *n., pl.* **-lis.** The basic monetary unit of Guinea, equal to 100 cauris. See feature at **currency.** [Native word in Guinea.]

syl·la·bar·y (sĭl′ə-bĕr′ē) *n., pl.* **-ies.** A list of syllables; especially, a list or set of written characters, each one representing a syllable. [New Latin *syllabārium,* from Latin *syllaba,* SYLLABLE.]

syl·lab·ic (sĭ-lăb′ĭk) *adj.* **1.** Of, pertaining to, or consisting of a syllable or syllables. **2.** Designating a consonant that forms a syllable without a vowel, as the *l* in *riddle* (rĭd′l). **3.** Pronouncing every syllable distinctly: *a syllabic reading of a line of poetry.* **4.** Designating a form of verse based on the number of syllables per line rather than on the arrangement of accents or quantities.
~n. A syllabic sound. [Medieval Latin *syllabicus,* from Greek *sullabikos,* from *sullabē,* SYLLABLE.] **—syl·lab·i·cal·ly** *adv.*

syl·lab·i·cate (sĭ-lăb′ə-kāt′) *tr.v.* **-cated, -cating, -cates.** Also **syl·lab·i·fy** (-fī′), **-fied, -fying, -fies.** To form or divide into syllables. **—syl·lab·i·ca·tion, syl·lab·i·fi·ca·tion** *n.*

syl·la·bism (sĭl′ə-bĭz′əm) *n.* **1.** The use of written characters that represent syllables. **2.** Division into syllables.

syl·la·bize (sĭl′ə-bīz′) *tr.v.* **-bized, -bizing, -bizes.** To syllabify. [Greek *sullabizein,* from *sullabē,* SYLLABLE.]

syl·la·ble (sĭl′ə-bəl) *n. Abbr.* **syl., syll.** **1.** A unit of spoken language consisting of a single uninterrupted sound formed by a vowel or diphthong alone, of a syllabic consonant alone, or of either with one or more consonants. *Of, spoken,* and *consisting* have, respectively, one, two, and three syllables. **2.** One or more letters or phonetic symbols written or printed to approximate a spoken syllable. **3.** The slightest bit or expression.
~tr.v. **syllabled, -bling, -bles.** To pronounce (a line of verse, for example) in syllables. [Middle English *sillable,* from Old French *sillabe,* from Latin *syllaba,* from Greek *sullabē,* "a gathering (of letters)," from *sullambanein,* to gather together, spell together : *sun-,* together + *lambanein,* to take, grasp.]

syl·la·bub, sil·la·bub (sĭl′ə-bŭb′) *n.* **1.** A cold dessert made with sweetened, thickened cream and wine, spirits, or fruit juice. **2.** A drink consisting of wine or spirits mixed with sweetened milk or cream. [16th century : origin obscure.]

syl·la·bus (sĭl′ə-bəs) *n., pl.* **-buses** or **-bi** (-bī′). *Abbr.* **syl., syll.** **1.** An outline or brief statement of the main points of a text, lecture, or course of study. **2.** *Law.* A short statement preceding a report on an adjudged case and containing the court rulings on the legal points involved. [Medieval Latin, list, from Greek *sullabus,* a misreading (in Cicero's *Letters to Atticus*) of *silluba,* earlier *sittuba*†, book title, label, table of contents.]

syl·lep·sis (sĭ-lĕp′sĭs) *n., pl.* **-ses** (-sēz′). *Grammar.* A construction in which one word seems to be in the same semantic relation to two or more other words but in fact is not; a zeugma. An example is: *She lost her coat and her temper.* [Late Latin, from Greek *sullēpsis,* "a taking together" : *sun-,* together + *lēpsis,* a taking, from *lambanein* (past participle *lēptos*), to take.] **—syl·lep·tic** *adj.*

syl·lo·gism (sĭl′ə-jĭz′əm) *n.* **1.** *Logic.* A form of deductive reasoning consisting of a major premise, a minor premise, and a conclusion; for example, *All men are foolish* (major premise); *Smith is a man* (minor premise); *therefore, Smith is foolish* (conclusion). **2.** Reasoning from the general to the specific; deduction. **3.** A subtle or specious piece of reasoning. [Middle English *silogisme,* from Old French, from Latin *syllogismus,* from Greek *sullogismos,* from *sullogizesthai,* to reckon together, infer : *sun-,* together + *logizesthai,* to reckon, reason, from *logos,* word, computation.]

syl·lo·gist (sĭl′ə-jĭst) *n.* A person who uses or is skilled in syllogistic reasoning.

syl·lo·gis·tic (sĭl′ə-jĭs′tĭk) *adj.* Also **syl·lo·gis·ti·cal** (-tĭ-kəl). Of, pertaining to, resembling, or consisting of a syllogism or syllogisms.
~n. Also **syl·lo·gis·tics.** *Used with a singular verb.* **1.** The branch of logic dealing with syllogisms. **2.** The art of reasoning by syllogism. **—syl·lo·gis·ti·cal·ly** *adv.*

syl·lo·gize (sĭl′ə-jīz′) *v.* **-gized, -gizing, -gizes.** *—intr.* To reason or argue by means of syllogisms. *—tr.* To deduce by syllogism. **—syl·lo·gi·za·tion** (sĭl′ə-jĭ-zā′shən) **—syl·lo·giz·er** *n.*

sylph (sĭlf) *n.* **1.** Any of a class of fairylike beings without souls that were believed to inhabit the air. **2.** A slim, graceful woman or girl. [New Latin *sylphus,* probably coined by Paracelsus by contracting Latin *sylvestris nympha,* nymph of the woods : *sylvestris,* from *sylva,* forest (see **sylvan**) + *nympha,* NYMPH.]

sylph·id (sĭl′fĭd) *n.* A young or diminutive sylph.
~adj. Pertaining to or resembling a sylph. [French *sylphide,* from *sylphe,* sylph, from New Latin *sylphus,* SYLPH.]

syl·va, sil·va (sĭl′və) *n.* **1.** The trees or forests of a region. **2.** A written work on such trees or forests. [Latin, forest. See **sylvan.**]

syl·van, sil·van (sĭl′vən) *adj.* **1.** Pertaining to or characteristic of woods or forest regions. **2.** Situated in or inhabiting a wood or forest. **3.** Abounding in trees; wooded. —See Synonyms at **rural.**
~n. One that lives in or frequents the woods. [Medieval Latin *silvānus,* from Latin *silva, sylva*†, forest.]

syl·van·ite (sĭl′və-nīt′) *n.* A pale brass-yellow to silver-white gold and silver ore, chiefly $(Au, Ag)Te_2$. [French; found in TRANSYLVANIA.]

syl·vat·ic (sĭl-văt′ĭk) *adj.* Growing or occurring in a wood. [Latin *silvaticus,* of the forest, wild, from *sylva,* forest (see **sylvan**).]

sylviculture. Variant of **silviculture.**

syl·vite (sĭl′vīt′) *n.* Also **syl·vin** (-vĭn), **syl·vine** (-vēn′, -vĭn), **syl·vin·ite** (-vĭn-īt′). A colorless vitreous potassium chloride mineral, a major source of potassium compounds. [French, from *sylvine,* from New Latin *(sal digestivus) Sylvii,* "(digestive salt) of Sylvius," probably after Franz de la Boë *Sylvius* (1614–72), Dutch physician.]

sym–. Variant of **syn-.**

sym. **1.** symbol. **2.** symphony.

sym·bi·ont (sĭm′bē-ŏnt′, -bī-ŏnt′) *n.* Also **sym·bi·ote** (-ōt′). Any of the organisms in a symbiotic relationship. [Greek *sumbiōn,* present participle of *sumbioun,* to live together. See **symbiosis.**]

sym·bi·o·sis (sĭm′bē-ō′sĭs, sĭm′bī-) *n. Biology.* Any relationship between two or more different organisms in close association, especially one that is of benefit to all the organisms involved. See **mutualism.** [New Latin, from Greek *sumbiōsis,* a living together, from *sumbioun,* to live together : *sun-,* together + *bios,* life.] **—sym·bi·ot·ic** (sĭm′bē-ŏt′ĭk, sĭm′bī-), **sym·bi·ot·i·cal** *adj.* **—sym·bi·ot·i·cal·ly** *adv.*

sym·bol (sĭm′bəl) *n. Abbr.* **sym.** **1.** Something that represents or stands for or is thought to typify something else by association, resemblance, or convention; especially, a material object used to represent something invisible such as an idea: *the dove is a symbol of peace.* **2.** A printed or written sign used to represent an operation, element, quantity, quality, or relation, as in mathematics or music: *"Au" is the symbol for gold. The symbol for addition is "+".*
~tr.v. **symboled, -boling, -bols.** To symbolize. [Latin *symbolum,* sign, token, from Greek *sumbolon,* token for identification (by comparing with its counterpart), from *sumballein,* to compare : *sun-,* together + *ballein,* to throw.]

sycamore A quick-growing Eurasian member of the maple family, Acer pseudoplatanus *is widely planted in the United States. Each sycamore seed is attached to a propellerlike vane (above), enabling it to whirl some distance from its parent tree before it falls to the ground.*

sym·bol·ic (sĭm-bŏl′ĭk) *adj.* Also **sym·bol·i·cal** (-ĭ-kəl). **1.** Of, pertaining to, or expressed by means of a symbol or symbols. **2.** Serving as a symbol. **3.** Characterized by the use of symbolism, as a work of art. **—sym·bol·i·cal·ly** *adv.* **—sym·bol·i·cal·ness** *n.*

symbolic logic *n.* A treatment of formal logic in which a calculus or rule-governed system of symbols is used to represent terms, propositions, and relationships. Also called "mathematical logic."

sym·bol·ism (sĭm′bə-lĭz′əm) *n.* **1.** The practice of representing things by means of symbols or of attributing symbolic meanings or significance to objects, events, or relationships. **2.** A system of symbols or representations. **3.** A symbolic meaning or representation. **4. Symbolism.** The theory or practice of the Symbolists.

sym·bol·ist (sĭm′bə-lĭst) *n.* **1.** A person who uses symbols or symbolism. **2. a.** One who interprets or represents conditions or truths by the use of symbolism. **b. Symbolist.** Any of a group of chiefly French artists and poets of the late 19th century who expressed their ideas and emotions indirectly through symbols. **—sym·bol·ist, sym·bol·is·tic** (sĭm′bə-lĭs′tĭc), **sym·bol·is·ti·cal** *adj.*

sym·bol·ize (sĭm′bə-līz′) *v.* **-ized, -izing, -izes.** *—tr.* **1.** To be or serve as a symbol of: *"His whole attitude was symbolized by his shrug and his flippantly red carnation"* (Willa Cather). **2.** To represent or identify by a symbol or symbols. *—intr.* To use symbols. **—sym·bol·i·za·tion** (sĭm′bə-lĭ-zā′shən) *n.*

sym·bol·o·gy (sĭm-bŏl′ə-jē) *n.* **1.** The study or interpretation of symbols or symbolism. **2.** The use of symbols. **—sym·bo·log·i·cal** (sĭm′bə-lŏj′ĭ-kəl) *adj.* **—sym·bol·o·gist** *n.*

sym·met·al·ism (sĭm-mĕt′l-ĭz′əm) *n.* A system of coinage in which a unit of currency consists of a combination of two or more metals in fixed proportions. [SYM- + METAL + -ISM.]

sym·met·ri·cal (sĭ-mĕt′rĭ-kəl) *adj.* Also **sym·met·ric** (-rĭk). **1.** Of, pertaining to, or showing symmetry. **2.** *Biology.* Actinomorphic. **3.** *Logic & Mathematics.* Of, pertaining to, or designating something, such as a function or proposition, that remains unchanged for all permutations of its constituent parts. **4.** *Chemistry.* Having repetitive, similar faces. Said of a crystal. **—sym·met·ri·cal·ly** *adv.* **—sym·met·ri·cal·ness** *n.*

sym·me·trize (sĭm′ə-trīz′) *tr.v.* **-trized, -trizing, -trizes.** To make symmetrical; impart perfect balance to. **—sym·me·tri·za·tion** (sĭm′ə-trĭ-zā′shən) *n.*

sym·me·try (sĭm′ə-trē) *n., pl.* **-tries.** **1.** A relationship of characteristic correspondence, equivalence, or identity among constituents of a system or between different systems: *symmetry in political and religious activism.* **2.** Exact correspondence of form and constituent configuration on opposite sides of a boundary, such as a line or plane or about a center or axis. **3.** Structural or functional independence of direction; isotropy. **4.** Beauty as a result of balance or harmonious arrangement. —See Synonyms at **proportion.** [Obsolete French *symmetrie,* from Latin *symmetria,* from Greek *summetria,* from *summetros,* "of like measure."]

sym·pa·thec·to·my (sĭm′pə-thĕk′tə-mē) *n., pl.* **-mies.** The removal of a part of a sympathetic nerve or a number of sympathetic ganglia. [SYMPATH(ETIC) + -ECTOMY.]

sym·pa·thet·ic (sĭm′pə-thĕt′ĭk) *adj.* **1.** Of, expressing, feeling, or resulting from sympathy. **2.** In agreement; favorable; inclined. Used with *to* or *toward: sympathetic to our proposal.* **3.** Agreeable; congenial: *sympathetic surroundings.* **4.** Pertaining to or acting on the sympathetic nervous system. **5.** Pertaining to or involving oscillation produced by a nearby oscillating system at the same frequency. Said, for example, of vibrations of strings in certain musical instruments. [New Latin *sympatheticus,* from Greek *sumpathētikos,* from *sumpatheia,* SYMPATHY.] **—sym·pa·thet·i·cal·ly** *adv.*

sympathetic ink *n.* **Invisible ink** *(see).*

sympathetic magic *n.* Magic that seeks to achieve an effect at a distance, as by means of an associated or symbolic object such as a doll intended to represent a person.

sympathetic nervous system *n.* The portion of the autonomic nervous system originating in the lumbar and thoracic parts of the spinal cord that stimulates the involuntary response to alarm, as by speeding the heart and raising blood pressure. Compare **parasympathetic nervous system.**

sym·pa·thin (sĭm'pə-thĭn) *n.* A substance, such as norepinephrine, released at sympathetic nerve endings and involved in the transmission of impulses. [SYMPATH(ETIC) + -IN.]

sym·pa·thize (sĭm'pə-thīz') *intr.v.* **-thized, -thizing, -thizes. 1.** To feel or express compassion; commiserate. Used with *with.* **2.** To share or understand another's feelings or ideas. Used with *with.* **3.** *Obsolete.* To agree in quality or disposition; correspond. **—sym·pa·thiz·er** *n.* **—sym·pa·thiz·ing·ly** *adv.*

sym·pa·tho·lyt·ic (sĭm'pə-thō-lĭt'ĭk) *adj.* Of or pertaining to an agent that opposes the activity of the sympathetic nervous system. *~n.* A sympatholytic agent. [SYMPATH(ETIC) + -LYTIC.]

sym·pa·tho·mi·met·ic (sĭm'pə-thō-mĭ-mĕt'ĭk, -mī-) *adj.* Of or pertaining to an agent that stimulates the sympathetic nervous system. *~n.* A sympathomimetic agent. [SYMPATH(ETIC) + MIMETIC.]

sym·pa·thy (sĭm'pə-thē) *n., pl.* **-thies. 1. a.** The act of or capacity for sharing or understanding the feelings of another person. **b.** A feeling or expression of pity or sorrow for the distress of another; commiseration. **2. a.** A relationship or affinity between persons or things in which whatever affects one correspondingly affects the other. **b.** Mutual understanding or affection arising from this. **3.** Favor; agreement; accord: *She is in sympathy with my beliefs.* **4.** A feeling of loyalty; allegiance. **5.** *Physiology.* The mutual influence of different parts of the body on each other. —See Synonyms at **pity.** [Latin *sympathīa,* from Greek *sumpatheia,* from *sumpathēs,* affected by like feelings : *sun-,* like + *pathos,* emotion, feelings.]

sympathy strike *n.* A strike by a body of workers for the purpose of supporting a cause or another group of strikers.

sym·pat·ric (sĭm-păt'rĭk) *adj. Ecology.* Occupying or occurring in the same or overlapping geographical areas. Said of populations of closely related species. Compare **allopatric.** [SYN- + Greek *patra, patrē,* fatherland, from *patēr,* father.] **—sym·pat·ri·cal·ly** *adv.*

sym·pet·al·ous (sĭm-pĕt'l-əs) *adj. Botany.* **Gamopetalous** *(see).*

sym·phon·ic (sĭm-fŏn'ĭk) *adj.* **1.** Pertaining to or having the character or form of a symphony. **2.** Harmonious in sound.

symphonic poem *n.* A musical composition for symphony orchestra, based on an extramusical theme such as a folk tale, usually consisting of a single, extended movement and typical chiefly of the late 19th century. Also called "tone poem."

sym·pho·ni·ous (sĭm-fō'nē-əs) *adj.* In accord; harmonious. **—sym·pho·ni·ous·ly** *adv.*

sym·pho·nist (sĭm'fə-nĭst) *n.* One who composes symphonies.

sym·pho·ny (sĭm'fə-nē) *n., pl.* **-nies. 1.** *Abbr.* **sym.** *Music.* A usually long sonata for orchestra, typically consisting of four related movements. **2. a.** An instrumental passage in a vocal or choral composition. **b.** An instrumental overture or interlude, as in early opera. **3.** Harmony, especially of sound or color. **4.** Anything characterized by a harmonious combination of elements. [Middle English *symphonie,* harmony of sound, from Old French, from Latin *symphōnia,* from Greek *sumphōnia,* from *sumphōnos,* harmonious : *sun-,* together + *phōnē,* voice, sound.]

symphony orchestra *n.* A large orchestra composed of string, woodwind, brass, and percussion sections, designed for playing symphonic works.

sym·phy·sis (sĭm'fə-sĭs) *n., pl.* **-ses** (-sēz'). **1.** *Anatomy.* **a.** A type of joint in which the bones are united by fibrocartilage, as between the vertebrae of the backbone. **b.** The line marking such a joint. **2.** The coalescence of similar parts or organs. [New Latin, from Greek *sumphusis,* a growing together (especially of bones), from *sumphuein,* to cause to unite : *sun-,* together + *phuein,* to make grow.] **—sym·phy·se·al** (sĭm'fə-sē'əl), **sym·phys·i·al** (sĭm-fĭz'ē-əl) *adj.*

sym·po·di·um (sĭm-pō'dē-əm) *n., pl.* **-dia** (-dē-ə). *Botany.* A primary axis that develops from a series of short lateral branches and has a zigzag or irregular form, as in a cymose inflorescence. Also called "pseudaxis." Compare **monopodium.** [New Latin : SYN- + Greek *podion,* small foot, base, from *pous* (stem *pod-*), foot.] **—sym·po·di·al** *adj.* **—sym·po·di·al·ly** *adv.*

sym·po·si·ac (sĭm-pō'zē-ăk') *adj.* Of, of the nature of, appropriate to, or occurring at a symposium. *~n. Archaic.* A meeting or conference; a symposium.

sym·po·si·arch (sĭm-pō'zē-ärk') *n.* **1.** The master or director of an ancient Greek symposium. **2.** A toastmaster. [Greek *sumposiarkhos, sumposiarkhēs* : *sumposion,* SYMPOSIUM + -ARCH.]

sym·po·si·um (sĭm-pō'zē-əm) *n., pl.* **-siums** or **-sia** (-zē-ə). **1.** A meeting or conference for discussion of some topic. **2.** A collection of writings on a particular topic, as in a magazine or other periodical. **3.** A convivial meeting among the ancient Greeks for drinking, music, and intellectual discussion. [Latin, from Greek *sumposion,* drinking party : *sun-,* together + *posis,* drink.]

PRONUNCIATION KEY

ă, pat; ā, pay; âr, care;
ä, father, are; b, bib;
ch, church; d, deed; ĕ, pet;
ē, be; f, fife; g, gag; h, hat;
hw, which; ĭ, pit; ī, pie;
îr, pier; j, judge; k, kick;
l, lid, needle; m, mum;
n, no, sudden; ng, thing;
ŏ, pot; ō, toe; ô, paw, for;
oi, noise; ou, out; ŏŏ, book;
ōō, boot; p, pop; r, roar;
s, sauce; sh, ship, dish;
t, tight; th, thin, path;
th, this, bathe; ŭ, cut; ûr, fur;
v, valve; w, with; y, yes;
z, zebra, size; zh, vision;
ə, about, item, edible, gallop, circus, peaceful

IN FOREIGN WORDS:

à, *Fr.* ami; œ, *Fr.* feu, *Ger.* schön; ü, *Fr.* tu, *Ger.* über; KH, *Ger.* ich, *Scot.* loch; N, *Fr.* bon; y', *Fr.* Compiègne

STRESS MARKS:

Primary stress: '
in·cite' (ĭn-sīt')
Secondary stress: '
in'sight' (ĭn'sīt')

symp·tom (sĭm'təm, sĭmp'-) *n.* **1.** Any circumstance or phenomenon regarded as an indication or characteristic of a condition or event. **2.** *Medicine.* Any phenomenon experienced by an individual as a departure from normal function, sensation, or appearance, generally indicating disorder or disease. —See Synonyms at **sign.** [Greek *sumptōma,* occurrence, phenomenon, from *sumpiptein,* to fall together, fall upon, happen : *sun-,* together + *piptein,* to fall.] **—symp·to·mat·ic** (sĭm'tə-măt'ĭk, sĭmp'-) *adj.* **—symp·to·mat·i·cal·ly** *adv.*

symp·tom·a·tol·o·gy (sĭm'tə-mə-tŏl'ə-jē, sĭmp'-) *n.* **1.** The medical science of disease symptoms. Also called "semiology." **2.** The complex of symptoms of a disease. [New Latin *symptomatologia* : Greek *sumptōma* (stem *sumptōmat-*), SYMPTOM + -LOGY.]

syn–, sym– *prefix.* Indicates: **1.** Together or with; for example, **syndactyl, symmetalism. 2.** Same, alike, similar, or at the same time; for example, **sympatric. 3.** Union or fusion; for example, **sympetalous, syncarp.** [Greek *sun-,* from *sun,* together, with.]

syn. synonym; synonymous; synonymy.

synaeresis. Variant of **syneresis.**

synaesthesia. Variant of **synesthesia.**

syn·a·gogue, syn·a·gog (sĭn'ə-gŏg') *n.* **1.** A building or place of meeting for Jewish worship and religious instruction. **2.** A congregation of Jews for worship or religious study. **3.** The Jewish religion as organized or typified in such local congregations. [Middle English *synagoge,* from Old French, from Latin *synagōga,* from Greek *sunagōgē,* assembly, from *sunagein,* to bring together : *sun-,* together + *agein,* to lead, drive.] **—syn·a·gog·al** (sĭn'ə-gŏg'əl), **syn·a·gog·i·cal** (sĭn'ə-gŏj'ĭ-kəl) *adj.*

syn·a·le·pha, syn·a·loe·pha (sĭn'ə-lē'fə) *n.* The blending of two adjacent syllables into one syllable, especially of two successive vowels of adjacent syllables; for example, *th' elite* for *the elite.* [New Latin, from Greek *sunaloiphē,* from *sunaleiphein,* to smear or melt together, unite two syllables : *sun-,* together + *aleiphein,* to anoint.]

syn·apse (sĭn'ăps', sĭ-năps') *n.* Also **syn·ap·sis** (sĭ-năp'sĭs), *pl.* **-ses** (-sēz'). The point at which a nerve impulse passes from an axon of one neuron to the dendrite of another. [New Latin *synapsis,* from Greek *sunapsis,* point of contact, from *sunaptein,* to join together : *sun-,* together + *haptein*†, to fasten, connect.]

syn·ap·sid (sĭ-năp'sĭd) *n.* A reptile of the subclass Synapsida, which existed during the Upper Carboniferous Permian and Triassic periods, having a single pair of lateral temporal openings in the skull. [New Latin *Synapsida.*]

syn·ap·sis (sĭ-năp'sĭs) *n., pl.* **-ses** (-sēz'). **1.** *Biology.* The fusion of homologous chromosome pairs during meiosis. **2.** Variant of **synapse.** [New Latin. See **synapse.**]

syn·ap·tic (sĭ-năp'tĭk) *adj.* Pertaining to a synapse or synapsis.

syn·ar·thro·sis (sĭn'är-thrō'sĭs) *n., pl.* **-ses** (-sēz'). Also **syn·ar·thro·di·a** (-dē-ə), *pl.* **-diae** (-dē-ē'). *Anatomy.* Any of several forms of bone articulation in which the bones are rigidly joined without an intervening cavity. [New Latin, from Greek *sunarthrōsis* : *sun-,* together + *arthrōsis,* articulation, from *arthron,* a joint.]

sync (sĭngk) *n. Informal.* Synchronization: *The sound is out of sync.* *~v.* **synced** (sĭngkt), **syncing** (sĭngk'ĭng), **syncs.** *Informal. —intr.* To synchronize. *—tr.* To synchronize (something) with another.

syn·carp (sĭn'kärp') *n. Botany.* A fleshy fruit composed of the fruits of several flowers or several carpels of a single flower. [SYN- + -CARP.]

syn·car·pous (sĭn-kär'pəs) *adj. Botany.* Having or consisting of united carpels. [SYN- + -CARPOUS.] **—syn·car·py** (sĭn'kär'pē) *n.*

syn·chon·dro·sis (sĭn'kŏn-drō'sĭs) *n.* A slightly movable joint in which the ends of the bones are separated by hyaline cartilage, such as occurs between the ribs and the breastbone in humans. [SYN- + Greek *khondros,* cartilage + -OSIS.]

syn·chro (sĭng'krō, sĭn'-) *n., pl.* **-chros.** *Machinery.* A **selsyn** *(see).* [Short for SYNCHRONOUS.]

synchro– *prefix.* Indicates synchronization; for example, **synchromesh.** [Shortened from SYNCHRONIZE.]

syn·chro·cy·clo·tron (sĭng'krō-sī'klə-trŏn', sĭn'-) *n.* A proton and positive ion accelerator, the chief components and configuration of which are similar to those of a **cyclotron** *(see)* and in which the phase of the accelerating potential is synchronized with the frequency of the accelerated particles by frequency modulation to compensate for relativistic increases in particle mass at high speeds.

syn·chro·flash (sĭng'krō-flăsh', sĭn'-) *n.* A device on a camera that synchronizes the peak of a flash created by a flash bulb with the widest opening of the shutter. **—syn·chro·flash** *adj.*

syn·chro·mesh (sĭng'krō-mĕsh', sĭn'-) *adj.* Designating a gearbox in a motor vehicle in which the gears are synchronized at the same speeds before engaging to effect a smooth change. *~n.* A system of gears using this principle.

syn·chron·ic (sĭng-krŏn'ĭk, sĭn-) *adj.* Also **syn·chron·i·cal** (-ĭ-kəl). **1.** Synchronous. **2. a.** Studying the events of a particular time or era without consideration of historical data. **b.** Pertaining to or designating the study of language and linguistic phenomena without reference to any historical perspective. Compare **diachronic. —syn·chron·i·cal·ly** *adv.*

syn·chro·nic·i·ty (sĭng'krə-nĭs'ə-tē, sĭn'-) *n.* Coincidence that is felt to be significant or meaningful; especially, in the philosophy of C.G. Jung, the simultaneous occurrence of two or more events that seem to be linked in a meaningful or significant way without apparently being causally related, as, for example, the sudden stopping of a clock at the moment of a person's death in the same vicinity.

syn·chro·nism (sĭng'krə-nĭz'əm, sĭn'-) *n.* **1.** The condition of being synchronized or synchronous. **2.** A chronological listing of historical personages or events so as to indicate parallel existence or occurrence. **3.** The representation in the same art work of two or more events that occurred at different times. **—syn·chro·nis·tic** (sĭng′krə-nĭs′tĭk, sĭn′-), **syn·chro·nis·ti·cal** (-tĭ-kəl) *adj.* **—syn·chro·nis·ti·cal·ly** *adv.*

syn·chro·nize (sĭng′krə-nīz′, sĭn′-) *v.* **-nized, -nizing, -nizes.** **—***intr.* **1.** To occur at the same time; be or become simultaneous. **2.** To operate in unison. **—***tr.* **1.** To cause to operate with exact coincidence in time or rate. **2.** To arrange (historical events) so as to indicate parallel existence or occurrence. **3. a.** To cause (sound effects or dialogue) to coincide with an action. **b.** To make sounds and actions coincide in (a film). [From SYNCHRONOUS.] **—syn·chro·ni·za·tion** (sĭng′krə-nĭ-zā′shən, sĭn′-) *n.*

synchronized swimming *n.* A rhythmic, dancelike form of swimming, synchronized to music.

syn·chro·nous (sĭng′krə-nəs, sĭn′-) *adj.* **1.** Occurring at the same time. **2.** Moving or operating at the same rate. **3. a.** Having identical periods. **b.** Having identical period and phase. **—**See Synonyms at **contemporary.** [Late Latin *synchronos,* from Greek *sunkhronos* : *sun-*, same + *khronos,* time (see **chronic**).] **—syn·chro·nous·ly** *adv.* **—syn·chro·nous·ness** *n.*

synchronous converter *n.* An electrical machine in which a double-wound armature is used to convert alternating current into direct current, or vice versa.

synchronous motor *n.* A motor having a speed directly proportional to the frequency of the electric current that operates it.

synchronous orbit *n.* An orbit having a period the same as the period of axial rotation of the earth and so oriented that any body in it maintains a position over one point on the earth's surface. Also called "stationary orbit."

synchronous rotation *n.* **Captured rotation** *(see).*

syn·chro·ny (sĭng′krə-nē, sĭn′-) *n., pl.* **-nies.** A synchronous occurrence, movement, or arrangement.

syn·chro·scope (sĭng′krə-skōp′, sĭn′-) *n.* Also **syn·chron·o·scope** (sĭng-krŏn′ə-skōp′, sĭn-). An instrument that indicates whether or not two periodic motions are synchronous. [SYNCHRO- + -SCOPE.]

syn·chro·tron (sĭng′krə-trŏn′, sĭn′-) *n.* An accelerator in which charged particles are accelerated around a fixed circular path by a radio-frequency potential and held to the path by a time-varying magnetic field. [SYNCHRO- + (ELEC)TRON.]

synchrotron radiation *n.* Electromagnetic radiation emitted by high-energy charged particles, such as electrons, spiraling along the lines of force produced by a strong magnetic field. The radiation is emitted at a tangent to the orbit of the particles and occurs in synchrotrons and in some astronomical systems, such as supernova remnants.

syn·cli·nal (sĭn-klī′nəl) *adj.* **1.** Sloping downward from opposite directions to meet in a common point or line. **2.** *Geology.* Pertaining to, formed by, or forming a syncline.
~ *n.* A syncline. [SYN- + Greek *klinein,* to lean.]

syn·cline (sĭn′klīn′) *n.* A low, troughlike area in bedrock, in which rocks incline together from opposite sides. [Back-formation from SYNCLINAL.]

syn·co·pate (sĭng′kə-pāt′, sĭn′-) *tr.v.* **-pated, -pating, -pates.** **1.** *Grammar.* **a.** To shorten (a word) by means of syncope. **b.** To drop (a letter or sound) from the spelling or pronunciation of a word. **2.** To modify (musical rhythm) by syncopation. [Medieval Latin *syncopāre,* from Late Latin *syncopē,* SYNCOPE.] **—syn·co·pa·tor** (sĭng′kə-pā′tər, sĭn′-) *n.*

syn·co·pa·tion (sĭng′kə-pā′shən, sĭn′-) *n.* **1.** The act of syncopating or the condition of being syncopated. **2.** Something syncopated. **3.** *Music.* The displacement of an accent or accents in a bar to parts that are not normally accented, as when a normally weak beat is stressed. **4.** *Grammar.* Syncope.

syn·co·pe (sĭng′kə-pē′, sĭn′-) *n.* **1.** *Grammar.* The shortening of a word by the omission of a sound, letter, or syllable from the middle of the word; for example, *bo's'n* for *boatswain.* **2.** *Pathology.* A brief loss of consciousness caused by a transient reduction of blood supply to the brain; a faint. [Late Latin, from Greek *sunkopē,* from *sunkoptein,* to chop up : *sun-*, together, thoroughly + *koptein,* to cut off.] **—syn·co·pal** (sĭng′kə-pəl, sĭn′-), **syn·cop·ic** (sĭn-kŏp′ĭk) *adj.*

syn·cre·tism (sĭng′krə-tĭz′əm, sĭn′-) *n.* **1.** The attempt or tendency to combine or reconcile differing beliefs, as in philosophy or religion. **2.** *Linguistics.* The diachronic fusion of two or more originally different inflectional forms into one. [New Latin *syncretismus,* from Greek *sunkrētismos,* union, from *sunkrētizein,* to unite (in the manner of the Cretan cities) against a common enemy : *sun-*, together + *Krēs* (stem *Krēt-*), CRETAN.] **—syn·cre·tist** *n.* **—syn·cret·ic** (sĭn-krĕt′ĭk, sĭng-), **syn·cre·tis·tic** (sĭng′krə-tĭs′tĭk, sĭn′-) *adj.*

syn·cre·tize (sĭng′krə-tīz′, sĭn′-) *v.* **-tized, -tizing, -tizes.** **—***tr.* To reconcile or attempt to reconcile (differing religious beliefs, for example). **—***intr.* To combine differing beliefs. [New Latin *syncretizare,* from Greek *sunkrētizein.* See **syncretism.**]

syn·cy·ti·um (sĭn-sĭsh′ē-əm) *n., pl.* **-cytia** (-sĭsh′ə, -ē-ə). *Biology.* A mass of protoplasm with many nuclei but no clear cell boundaries. [New Latin : SYN- + CYT(O)- + -IUM.] **—syn·cy·tial** *adj.*

synd. syndicate.

syn·dac·tyl, syn·dac·tyle (sĭn-dăk′təl) *adj.* Also **syn·dac·ty·lous** (-tə-ləs). *Biology.* Having two or more wholly or partially fused digits.
~ *n.* A syndactyl animal. [French *syndactyle* : SYN- + Greek *daktu-*

HOUSE OF ASSEMBLY, PRAYER, AND STUDY
The focal point of Jewish religious and cultural life

The first synagogues—the Jewish houses of assembly, prayer, and study—seem to have come into being as early as the 6th century B.C., during the exile of the Jews in Babylon, as substitutes for the Temple in Jerusalem. The word synagogue is from the Greek *sunagoge,* "assembly." The synagogue became the focal point of Jewish religious and cultural life and has remained so.

Although a synagogue is usually rectangular, with seats downstairs for men and a gallery for women (in Orthodox synagogues), it can be built on any plan. It normally contains a screened niche for the *aron hakodesh,* the Holy Ark that holds the scroll of Jewish law; the *ner tamid,* the light that is symbolic of the Eternal Light, is placed directly above the Ark. Most synagogues also have a *bema*—a raised platform or pulpit.

The religious life of a synagogue and its congregation is led by a lay rabbi (Hebrew for "my master"), who operates as a full-time minister. He is elected by a board of fellow laymen, his necessary qualification being his knowledge of Jewish law, faith, and practice. The synagogue is thus a democratic institution—and any group of Jews is free to establish one.

Three main synagogue associations now exist—the Orthodox, the Conservative, and the Reform.

ANCIENT SYMBOL *In the Book of Exodus, the Lord tells Moses to make a six-branched candlestick for the Tabernacle—the portable place of worship used on the journey to the Promised Land. Today there are such candlesticks in synagogues throughout the world.*

SET FOR A WEDDING *The red velvet canopy has been erected in this London synagogue for a wedding. Behind the canopy is the niche containing the Ark, with the Eternal Light hanging above it.*

los, finger, DACTYL.] **—syn·dac·tyl·ism** (sĭn-dăk′tə-lĭz′əm), **syn·dac·ty·ly** (sĭn-dăk′tə-lē) *n.*

syn·des·mo·sis (sĭn′dĕz-mō′sĭs, -dĕs-) *n.* The articulation of bones by ligaments. [New Latin, from Greek *sundesmos,* ligament, from *sundein,* to bind. See **syndetic.**] **—syn·des·mot·ic** (sĭn′dĕz-mŏt′ĭk, -dĕs-) *adj.*

syn·det·ic (sĭn-dĕt′ĭk) *adj.* Also **syn·det·i·cal** (-ĭ-kəl). **1.** Serving to connect, as a conjunction; copulative; conjunctive. **2.** Connected by a conjunction. [Greek *sundetikos,* from *sundetos,* bound together, from *sundein,* to bind together : *sun-*, together + *dein,* to bind.] **—syn·det·i·cal·ly** *adv.*

syn·dic (sĭn′dĭk) *n.* **1.** One appointed to represent a company, university, or other organization in business transactions; a business agent. **2.** In various European countries, a civil magistrate or similar government official. [French, from Late Latin *syndicus,* from Greek *sundikos,* assistant in a court of justice, public advocate : *sun-,* with + *dikē,* judgment.] —**syn·di·cal** *adj.*

syn·di·cal·ism (sĭn′dĭ-kəl-ĭz′əm) *n.* A radical political movement that advocates bringing industry and government under the control of trade unions, especially by the use of direct action such as general strikes and sabotage. [French *syndicalisme,* from *(chambre) syndicale,* trade union.] —**syn·di·cal·ist** *adj. & n.*

syn·di·cate (sĭn′dĭ-kĭt) *n. Abbr.* **synd.** **1. a.** An association of people or commercial firms organized to promote some common interest. **b.** An association of people formed to carry out a usually specified enterprise or activity: *a crime syndicate.* **2.** An agency that sells news articles and photographs for publication in a number of newspapers or periodicals simultaneously. **3.** The office, position, or jurisdiction of a syndic or body of syndics. ~*v.* (sĭn′dĭ-kāt′) **syndicated, -cating, -cates.** —*tr.* **1.** To organize into a syndicate. **2.** To sell (an article, for example) through a syndicate for publication. —*intr.* To organize a syndicate. [French *syndicat,* from *syndic,* SYNDIC.]

syn·di·o·tac·tic (sĭn′dē-ō-tăk′tĭk) *adj. Chemistry.* Designating a stereospecific polymer having alternating stereochemical configurations of the groups on successive carbon atoms in the chain. Compare **isotactic.** [Greek *sunduo,* two together + -TACTIC.]

syn·drome (sĭn′drōm′) *n.* **1.** A group of signs and symptoms that collectively indicate or characterize a disease, psychological disorder, or other abnormal condition. **2. a.** A set of signs or symptoms indicating the existence of an undesirable condition, problem, or quality. **b.** Such a condition, problem, or quality. [New Latin, from Greek *sundromē,* a running together, concurrence (of symptoms) : *sun-,* together + *dromos,* race, racecourse.] —**syn·drom·ic** (sĭn-drŏm′ĭk) *adj.*

syne (sīn) *adv. Scottish.* Since. —**syne** *conj. & prep.*

syn·ec·do·che (sĭ-nĕk′də-kē) *n.* A figure of speech by which a more inclusive term is used for a less inclusive term, or vice versa; for example, *head* for *cattle* or *the law* for *a policeman.* [Latin, from Greek *sunekdokhē,* from *sunekdekhesthai,* to take with : *sun-,* with + *ekdekhesthai,* to understand (*ek,* out of + *dekhesthai,* to take, receive).] —**syn·ec·doch·ic** (sĭn′ĕk-dŏk′ĭk) *adj.*

synecious. Variant of **synoecious.**

syn·e·col·o·gy (sĭn′ĭ-kŏl′ə-jē) *n.* The study of the environmental interrelationships among communities of organisms. Compare **autecology.** [SYN- + ECOLOGY.] —**syn·e·co·log·ic** (sĭn′ē-kə-lŏj′ĭk), **syn·e·co·log·i·cal** *adj.*

syn·er·e·sis, syn·aer·e·sis (sĭ-nĕr′ə-sĭs) *n., pl.* **-ses** (-sēz′). **1.** The drawing together into one syllable of two consecutive vowels ordinarily pronounced separately, as when *doest* (do̅o̅′ĭst) contracts to *dost* (dŭst). Compare **dieresis, synizesis. 2.** *Chemistry.* Exudation of the liquid component of a gel. [Late Latin *synaeresis,* from Greek *sunairesis,* from *sunairein,* to take or draw together, contract : *sun-,* together + *hairein,* to seize, take.]

syn·er·get·ic (sĭn′ər-jĕt′ĭk) *adj.* Also **syn·er·gic** (sĭ-nûr′jĭk). *Biology.* **1.** Of or pertaining to synergism. **2.** Working together.

syn·er·gid (sĭ-nûr′jĭd) *n.* Either of two haploid cells situated close to the egg cell in the embryo sac of flowering plants. [New Latin *synergida,* from Greek *sunergos,* working together. See **synergism.**]

syn·er·gism (sĭn′ər-jĭz′əm) *n.* Also **syn·er·gy** (-ər-jē) *pl.* **-gies** (for sense 1). **1.** *Biology.* The action of two or more substances, organs, or organisms to achieve an effect greater than the sum of their individual effects. **2.** *Theology.* The doctrine that individual salvation is achieved through a combination of human will and divine grace. [New Latin *synergismus,* from Greek *sunergos,* working together : *sun-,* together + *ergon,* work.]

syn·er·gist (sĭn′ər-jĭst) *n.* **1.** *Biology.* A synergetic organ, drug, or substance. **2.** *Theology.* An adherent of synergism. —**syn·er·gis·tic** (sĭn′ər-jĭs′tĭk), **syn·er·gis·ti·cal** *adj.*

syn·e·sis (sĭn′ə-sĭs) *n. Grammar.* A construction in which a form differs in number but agrees in meaning with the word governing it; for example, *If anyone arrives, tell them to wait.* [New Latin, from Greek *sunesis,* understanding, from *sunienai,* to understand : *sun-,* together + *hienai,* to send.]

syn·es·the·sia, syn·aes·the·sia (sĭn′əs-thē′zhə) *n.* **1.** The experiencing of a sensation in one part of the body resulting from the stimulation of a different part. **2.** The sensation of a sense other than the sense being stimulated, as when a sound invokes a sensation of color. [New Latin : SYN- + (AN)ESTHESIA.] —**syn·es·thet·ic** (sĭn′əs-thĕt′ĭk) *adj.*

syn·ga·my (sĭng′gə-mē) *n. Biology.* The fusion of two gametes; fertilization. [SYN- + -GAMY.] —**syn·gam·ic** (sĭn-găm′ĭk), **syn·ga·mous** (sĭng′gə-məs) *adj.*

Synge (sĭng), **John Millington** (1871–1909). Irish playwright. His plays, which draw on the speech and culture of Irish peasants and fishermen, include *Riders to the Sea* (1904) and *The Playboy of the Western World* (1907).

syn·gen·e·sis (sĭn-jĕn′ə-sĭs) *n. Biology.* Sexual reproduction. [New Latin : SYN- + -GENESIS.] —**syn·ge·net·ic** (sĭn′jə-nĕt′ĭk) *adj.*

syn·graft (sĭng′grăft′, -gräft′, sĭn′-) *n.* An **isograft** (see).

syn·i·ze·sis (sĭn′ĭ-zē′sĭs) *n., pl.* **-ses** (-sēz′). **1.** The contraction of two syllables into one by joining in pronunciation two adjacent vowels without forming a recognized diphthong, as when *tower* (tou′ər) is pronounced (tär). Compare **syneresis. 2.** *Biology.* The phase of

meiosis in which the chromatin contracts into a mass at one side of the nucleus. [Late Latin *synizēsis,* from Greek *sunizēsis,* "collapse," from *sunizein,* to collapse : *sun-,* together + *hizein,* to sit down.]

syn·kar·y·on (sĭn-kăr′ē-ŏn′, -ē-ən) *n.* The nucleus of a fertilized egg immediately after the male and female nuclei have fused. [New Latin : SYN- + Greek *karuon,* nut.] —**syn·kar·y·on·ic** *adj.*

syn·od (sĭn′əd) *n.* **1.** A council or assembly of churches or church officials; an ecclesiastical council. **2.** Any council or assembly. [Middle English, from Late Latin *synodus,* from Greek *sunodos,* meeting : *sun-,* together + *hodos,* road, way, journey.] —**syn·od·al** (sĭn′ə-dəl) *adj.*

sy·nod·i·cal (sĭ-nŏd′ĭ-kəl) *adj.* Also **sy·nod·ic** (-nŏd′ĭk). **1.** Pertaining to the conjunction of celestial bodies, especially the interval between two successive conjunctions of a planet or the moon with the sun: *a synodic month.* **2.** Of or pertaining to a synod. —**sy·nod·i·cal·ly** *adv.*

sy·noe·cious, sy·ne·cious (sĭ-nē′shəs) *adj. Botany.* Having male and female organs in the same flower or corresponding structure. [SYN- + (MON)OECIOUS.]

syn·o·nym (sĭn′ə-nĭm′) *n. Abbr.* **syn. 1.** A word having the same or nearly the same meaning as that of another word in the same language; for example, *mix, blend,* and *mingle* are synonyms. Compare **antonym. 2.** A word or expression accepted as a figurative or symbolic substitute for another word or expression; for example, *Her name has become a synonym for courage.* **3.** *Biology.* A taxonomic name of an organism that is equivalent to or has been superseded by another designation. [Middle English *sinonyme,* from Latin *synonymum,* from Greek *sunōnumon,* from *sunōnumos,* SYNONYMOUS.] —**syn·o·nym·ic** (sĭn′ə-nĭm′ĭk), **syn·o·nym·i·cal** *adj.* —**syn·o·nym·i·ty** (sĭn′ə-nĭm′ə-tē) *n.*

syn·on·y·mize (sĭ-nŏn′ə-mīz′) *tr.v.* **-mized, -mizing, -mizes.** To provide or analyze the synonyms of (a word). —**syn·on·y·mist** (sĭ-nŏn′ə-mĭst) *n.*

syn·on·y·mous (sĭ-nŏn′ə-məs) *adj. Abbr.* **syn. 1.** Expressing the same or a similar meaning; being a synonym or synonyms. **2.** Having a particular connotation through association with something specified: *Nazism is synonymous with evil.* [Medieval Latin *synonymus,* from Greek *sunōnumos : sun-,* same + *onoma, onuma,* name.] —**syn·on·y·mous·ly** *adv.*

syn·on·y·my (sĭ-nŏn′ə-mē) *n., pl.* **-mies.** *Abbr.* **syn. 1.** The quality of being synonymous; equivalence of meaning. **2.** The study and classification of synonyms. **3.** A list, book, or system of synonyms. **4.** The use of synonyms for rhetorical emphasis or effect. **5.** A chronological list or record of the scientific names that have been applied to a species and its subdivisions.

syn·op·sis (sĭ-nŏp′sĭs) *n., pl.* **-ses** (-sēz′). A brief statement or outline of a subject; a summary; an abstract. [Late Latin, from Greek *sunopsis,* a viewing all together : *sun-,* together + *opsis,* view.]

syn·op·size (sĭ-nŏp′sīz′) *tr.v.* **-sized, -sizing, -sizes.** To present or write a synopsis of. [Late Greek *sunopsizein,* from Greek *sunopsis,* SYNOPSIS.]

syn·op·tic (sĭ-nŏp′tĭk) *adj.* Also **syn·op·ti·cal** (-tĭ-kəl). **1.** Of or constituting a synopsis or summary. **2.** Presenting an account from the same point of view. **3.** *Often* **Synoptic.** Of or designating the first three Gospels of the New Testament (Matthew, Mark, and Luke), which correspond closely. **4.** Of or concerning the meteorological conditions at a given time: *a synoptic chart.* —**syn·op·ti·cal·ly** *adv.*

syn·os·to·sis (sĭn′ŏs-tō′sĭs) *n.* The fusion of two skeletal bones. [New Latin : SYN- + Greek *osteon,* bone + -OSIS.] —**syn·os·tot·ic** (sĭn′ŏs-tŏt′ĭk) *adj.*

syn·o·vi·a (sĭ-nō′vē-ə) *n.* A clear, viscid lubricating fluid secreted by the *synovial* membranes lining joint cavities, sheaths of tendons, and bursae. Also called "synovial fluid." [New Latin *synovia, sinovia* (coined by Paracelsus).] —**syn·o·vi·al** *adj.*

sy·no·vi·tis (sĭn′ə-vī′tĭs) *n.* Inflammation of the synovial membrane lining a joint cavity, resulting in pain and swelling. [SYNOV(IAL MEMBRANE) + -ITIS.]

syn·sep·al·ous (sĭn-sĕp′ə-ləs) *adj. Botany.* Gamosepalous.

syn·tac·tics (sĭn-tăk′tĭks) *n. Used with a singular or plural verb.* The branch of semiotics that deals with the formal properties of words and expressions, or, more generally, signs and symbols and their interrelations, without reference to their meaning. [From *syntactic,* of syntax, from New Latin *syntacticus,* from Greek *suntaktikos,* putting together, from *suntassein,* to put together. See **syntax.**]

syn·tax (sĭn′tăks′) *n.* **1. a.** The way in which words are put together grammatically to form phrases and sentences. **b.** The branch of grammar dealing with this. **c.** The rules for determining grammaticality. **2.** The system of rules governing the construction of well-formed formulas in a system of symbolic logic. **3.** The system of rules in operation in a computer program. [French *syntaxe,* from Late Latin *syntaxis,* from Greek *suntaxis,* from *suntassein,* to put together, arrange in order : *sun-,* together + *tassein,* to arrange.] —**syn·tac·tic** (sĭn-tăk′tĭk), **syn·tac·ti·cal** *adj.* —**syn·tac·ti·cal·ly** *adv.*

syn·the·sis (sĭn′thə-sĭs) *n., pl.* **-ses** (-sēz′). **1. a.** The combining of separate elements or substances to form a coherent whole. Compare **analysis. b.** The whole so formed. **2.** *Chemistry.* Formation of a compound from its constituents. **3.** *Philosophy.* **a.** Reasoning from the general to the particular; logical deduction. **b.** In the philosophy of Hegel, the combination of thesis and antithesis in the dialectical process. [Latin, from Greek, a putting together, from *suntithenai,* to put together.] —**syn·the·sist** *n.*

syn·the·size (sĭn′thə-sīz′) *v.* **-sized, -sizing, -sizes.** Also **syn·the·tize** (-tīz′). —*tr.* **1.** To combine so as to form a new, complex product.

2. To produce by combining separate elements. —*intr.* To form a synthesis.

syn·the·siz·er (sĭn'thə-sī'zər) *n.* **1.** One that synthesizes. **2.** A machine having a keyboard and using solid-state circuitry to produce a wide range of electronic musical sounds. See **Moog synthesizer.**

syn·thet·ic (sĭn-thĕt'ĭk), **syn·thet·i·cal** (-ĭ-kəl) *adj.* **1.** Pertaining to, involving, or of the nature of a synthesis. **2.** Produced by chemical synthesis; especially, not of natural origin; man-made. **3.** Not genuine; artificial; devised. **4.** *Linguistics.* Designating a language, such as Latin or Russian, that uses inflectional affixes to express syntactic relationships. In this sense, compare **analytic, polysynthetic. 5.** *Philosophy.* Designating a statement or proposition whose truth depends on some fact about the world, rather than depending entirely on the meanings of the words from which it is composed. In this sense, compare **analytic.** —See Synonyms at **artificial.**
~*n.* A synthetic chemical compound or material, as a plastic. [Greek *sunthetikos,* skilled in putting together, component, from *sunthetos,* put together, compounded, composite, from *suntithenai,* to put together. See **synthesis.**] —**syn·thet·i·cal·ly** *adv.*

synthetic philosophy *n.* **Spencerianism** (see).

sy·pher (sī'fər) *tr.v.* **-phered, -phering, -phers.** To overlap and even (chamfered or beveled plank edges) so that they form a flush surface. [Variant of CIPHER.]

syph·i·lis (sĭf'ə-lĭs) *n.* A chronic infectious venereal disease caused by a spirochete, *Treponema pallidum,* transmitted by direct contact, usually in sexual intercourse, or passed from the mother to the fetus, and progressing through three stages characterized respectively by (*primary syphilis*) local formation of chancres, (*secondary syphilis*) ulcerous skin eruptions, and (*tertiary syphilis*) systemic infection leading to **general paresis** (see). [New Latin, after the supposed first victim of the disease *Syphilus,* title character of a Latin poem *Syphilis, sive Morbus Gallicus* (1530) by Girolamo Fracastoro, Italian poet and physician.] —**syph·i·lit·ic** (sĭf'ə-lĭt'ĭk) *n. & adj.*

syph·i·loid (sĭf'ə-loid') *adj.* Characteristic of syphilis. [SYPHIL(IS) + -OID.]

syph·i·lol·o·gy (sĭf'ə-lŏl'ə-jē) *n.* The sum of knowledge concerning the origin, nature, course, complications, and treatment of syphilis. [SYPHIL(IS) + -LOGY.] —**syph·i·lol·o·gist** *n.*

syph·i·lo·ma (sĭf'ə-lō'mə) *n., pl.* **-mas** or **-mata** (-mə-tə). A lesion formed in an advanced stage of syphilis; a gumma. [New Latin : SYPHIL(IS) + -OMA.] —**syph·i·lom·a·tous** (sĭf'ə-lŏm'ə-təs) *adj.*

syphon. Variant of **siphon.**

Syr. Syria; Syriac; Syrian.

Syr·a·cuse (sĭr'ə-kyōōz'). *Italian* **Si·ra·cu·sa** (sĭr'ə-kōō'zə). Seaport on the east coast of Sicily, Italy. It was founded by colonists from Corinth in the 8th century B.C. and became a brilliant center of Greek culture. However, the city sided with Carthage in the Second Punic War and fell to the Romans in 212 B.C. Archimedes, a native, directed the city's defense and was killed during its subsequent sacking.

Syr Dar·ya (sĭr' där'yə). River in the southern U.S.S.R., *c.* 2,250 kilometers (1,400 miles) long. It rises in the Tian Shan range near the border with China and flows northwest to the Aral Sea.

Syr·i·a (sĭr'ē-ə). *Abbr.* **Syr.** Country in the Middle East. Much of it is mountain, steppe, or desert, with fertile lowlands along the coast and in the valleys of the Euphrates and Orontes. Most Syrians are of Arab descent, but there are substantial minorities of Kurds, Armenians, and Turkomans. Manufacturing and mining have replaced agriculture as the chief source of national income, though *c.* 30 percent of workers remain in farming. The main exports are crude oil, cotton, and cotton goods. Tourism is a major industry. Syria was a province of the Ottoman Empire (1516–1918). After 1920 it was a French League of Nations mandate. It became an independent republic (1946) and joined Egypt in the short-lived United Arab Republic (1958–61). The country took part in Arab-Israeli wars after 1948, being firmly aligned against Israel. Syrian troops intervened in the Lebanese civil war (1976) and remained in the country as a peace-keeping force. Area, 185,180 square kilometers (71,498 square miles). Population, 9,000,000. Capital, Damascus.

Syr·i·ac (sĭr'ē-ăk') *n. Abbr.* **Syr.** An ancient Aramaic language spoken in Syria (3rd–13th century A.D.), surviving as the liturgical language of certain eastern Christian churches. —**Syr·i·ac** *adj.*

Syr·i·an (sĭr'ē-ən) *adj. Abbr.* **Syr.** Of or pertaining to Syria, its culture, or inhabitants.
~*n.* **1.** A native or inhabitant of Syria. **2.** A member of a Christian church using the Syriac language.

sy·rin·ga (sə-rĭng'gə) *n.* Either of two shrubs, the **mock orange** or **lilac** (both of which see). [New Latin *syringa,* "pipe" (from the use of its hollow stems to make pipes), from Greek *surinx,* SYRINX.]

sy·ringe (sə-rĭnj', sĭr'ĭnj) *n.* **1.** A thin tube with a nozzle and a piston, rubber bulb, or other device that can draw in fluid by suction and expel it by force. **2.** A **hypodermic syringe** (see).
~*tr.v.* **syringed, -inging, -inges.** To clean, spray, or inject with a syringe. [Middle English *syring,* from Medieval Latin *syringa,* from Greek *surinx* (stem *suring-*), SYRINX.]

sy·rin·go·my·e·li·a (sə-rĭng'gō-mī-ē'lē-ə) *n.* A chronic disease of the spinal cord characterized by the presence of liquid-filled cavities and leading to spasticity and loss of awareness of pain and temperature. [New Latin : Greek *surinx,* spinal cavity (see **syrinx**) + *muelos,* marrow, from *mus,* muscle, mouse.]

SYRIA

syr·inx (sĭr'ĭngks) *n., pl.* **syringes** (sə-rĭn'jēz', -rĭng'gēz') or **syrinxes. 1. Panpipes** (see). **2.** *Zoology.* The vocal organ of a bird, consisting of thin, vibrating muscles at or close to the division of the trachea. [Latin, from Greek *surinx†,* shepherd's pipe, panpipe, pipe.] —**sy·rin·ge·al** (sə-rĭn'jē-əl) *adj.*

syr·phid (sûr'fĭd) *n.* Any fly of the family Syrphidae, many of which have a form or coloration mimicking that of bees or wasps. [New Latin *Syrphidae,* from Greek *surphos†,* gnat.] —**syr·phid** *adj.*

syr·up, sir·up (sĭr'əp, sûr'-) *n.* **1.** A thick, sweet, sticky liquid, consisting of a sugar base, natural or artificial flavoring, and water. **2.** A highly concentrated solution of sugar in water. **3.** The juice of a fruit or plant boiled with sugar until thick and sticky. **4.** A medicine in a sweet-tasting liquid. **5.** Cloying sentimentality. [Middle English *sirop,* from Old French, from Medieval Latin *siropus,* from Arabic *sharāb,* beverage.] —**syr·up·y** *adj.*

sys·sar·co·sis (sĭs'är-kō'sĭs) *n.* The union of bones, such as the hyoid bone and lower jaw, by muscle. [New Latin, from Greek *sussarkōsis,* a growing together with flesh, from *sussarkousthai,* to be grown together with flesh : *sun-,* together + *sarkousthai,* passive of *sarkoun,* to grow fleshy, from *sarx,* flesh.]

sys·tal·tic (sĭ-stôl'tĭk, -stăl'tĭk) *adj.* Alternately contracting and expanding, as the heart; pulsating. [Late Latin *systalticus,* from Greek *sustaltikos,* from *sustellein,* to draw together, contract : *sun-,* together + *stellein,* to send, bind, repress, make compact.]

sys·tem (sĭs'təm) *n.* **1.** A group of interacting, interrelated, or interdependent elements forming or regarded as forming a collective entity. **2.** A functionally related group of elements, as: **a.** The human body regarded as a functional physiological unit. **b.** A group of physiologically complementary organs or parts. **c.** A group of interacting mechanical or electrical components. **d.** A network of structures and channels, as for communications, travel, or distribution. **3.** A structurally or anatomically related group of elements or parts. **4.** A set of interrelated members, as of ideas, principles, rules, procedures, or laws: *metric system.* **5.** A social, economic, or political organizational form. **6.** A naturally occurring group of objects or phenomena. **7.** A set of objects or phenomena grouped together for classification or analysis, as in: **a.** A **crystal system** (see). **b.** *Geology.* The succession of rocks formed during a geological period. **c.** *Astronomy.* A group of associated stars, planets, or other bodies. **8.** An orderly way of doing something; a method. **9.** Orderliness: *bring some system into this chaos.* **10.** The established political, social, and economic order or power structure. —See Synonyms at **method.** —**get something out of one's system.** *Informal.* To purge oneself of a desire to do or say something by acting on it. [Late Latin *systēma,* from Greek *sustēma,* a composite whole, from *sunistanai,* to bring together, combine : *sun-,* together + *histanai,* to cause to stand.]

sys·tem·at·ic (sĭs'tə-măt'ĭk) *adj.* Also **sys·tem·at·i·cal** (-ĭ-kəl). **1.** Of, characterized by, based upon, or constituting a system. **2.** Carried on in a step-by-step procedure. **3.** Characterized by purposeful regularity; methodical. **4.** Of or pertaining to classification or taxonomy. —See Synonyms at **orderly.** —**sys·tem·at·i·cal·ly** *adv.*

systematic name *n. Chemistry.* A name given to a compound that describes the elements and groups that it contains using a set of formal rules. Compare **trivial name.**

sys·tem·at·ics (sĭs'tə-măt'ĭks) *n. Used with a singular verb. Biology.* The classification of organisms in an ordered system designed to indicate natural relationships.

sys·tem·a·tism (sĭs'tə-mə-tĭz'əm, sĭ-stĕm'ə-) *n.* **1.** The practice of classifying or systematizing. **2.** Adherence to a system.

sys·tem·a·tist (sĭs'tə-mə-tĭst, sĭ-stĕm'ə-) *n.* **1.** A person who adheres to or formulates a system. **2.** A taxonomist.

sys·tem·a·tize (sĭs'tə-mə-tīz') *tr.v.* **-tized, -tizing, -tizes.** Also **sys·tem·ize** (-tə-mīz'). To formulate or reduce to a system: *system-*

atizing research data. **—sys·tem·a·ti·za·tion** (sĭs′tə-mə-tĭ-zā′shən), **sys·tem·a·tiz·er** *n.*

Sys·tème in·ter·na·tio·nal d'u·ni·tés (sē-stĕm′ ăN-tĕr-nȧ-syô-nȧl′ dü-nē-tā′) *n. French.* International System of Units. See **SI unit.**

sys·tem·ic (sĭ-stĕm′ĭk) *adj.* **1.** Of or pertaining to a system or systems. **2.** Of, pertaining to, or affecting the entire body.
~*n.* A systemic poison or agent. **—sys·tem·i·cal·ly** *adv.*

systems analysis *n.* An analysis of an activity by mathematical means to determine its desired end and the most efficient means of obtaining this. **—systems analyst** *n.*

systems engineering *n.* The branch of engineering concerned with the design and organization of multi-component technological operations.

sys·to·le (sĭs′tə-lē) *n. Physiology.* The rhythmic contraction of the heart, especially of the ventricles, by which blood is driven through the aorta and pulmonary artery after each dilation or **diastole** *(see).* [Greek *sustolē,* contraction, from *sustellein,* to contract. See **systaltic.**] **—sys·tol·ic** (sĭs-tŏl′ĭk) *adj.*

syz·y·gy (sĭz′ə-jē) *n., pl.* **-gies. 1.** *Astronomy.* **a.** Either of two points in the orbit of a celestial body at which the body is in opposition to or in conjunction with the sun. **b.** Either of two points in the orbit of the moon at which the moon lies in a straight line with the sun and the earth. **c.** The configuration of the sun, the moon, and the earth lying in a straight line. **2.** In classical prosody, the combining of two feet into a single metrical unit. [Late Latin *syzygia,* from Greek *suzugia,* union, coupling, yoke, from *suzugos,* yoked, paired : *sun-,* together + *zugon,* a yoke.] **—sy·zyg·i·al** (sĭ-zĭj′ē-əl) *adj.*

Szcze·cin (shchĕ′tsĕn′). *German* **Stet·tin** (shtĕ′tĕn′). Port in northwestern Poland, at the mouth of the Oder River on the Baltic Sea. It is a major outlet for Polish coal and has important shipbuilding, chemical, textile, and engineering industries.

Szechwan. See **Sichuan.**

Szell (sĕl, zĕl), **George** (1897–1970). U.S. conductor, born in Hungary. A child prodigy and assistant to Richard Strauss, he was already widely experienced and respected when he immigrated to the United States (1939). In 1946, after several years as guest conductor for major American symphonies, he settled with the Cleveland Orchestra, which prospered under his direction.

Szi·lard (sē′lärd), **Leo** (1898–1964). Hungarian-born physicist. He immigrated to the United States in 1937 and during World War II worked on the construction of the atom bomb. He later regretted its construction and urged the abolition of all nuclear weapons.

t, T (tē) *n., pl.* **t's** or**T's. 1.** The 20th letter of the modern English alphabet. See feature at **alphabet. 2.** Any of the speech sounds represented by this letter. **3.** Something shaped like the letter T. **4.** The 20th in a series; 19th when *J* is omitted. **—to a T.** Perfectly; precisely: *She fits the role to a T.*

t, T, t., T. **Note:** As an abbreviation or symbol, *t* may be a small or a capital letter, with or without a period. Established forms or those generally preferred precede the definition. When no form is given, all four forms are in general use in that sense. **1. t.** in the time of [Latin *tempore*]. **2. T** *Physics.* surface tension. **3. T.** tablespoon; tablespoonful. **4. t.** *Commerce.* tare. **5. t.** teaspoon; teaspoonful. **6. T** temperature. **7. t.** tempo. **8. t., T.** *Music.* tenor. **9. t.** *Grammar.* tense. **10. T** *Physics.* tera-. **11. t., T.** territory. **12. T** tesla. **13. T.** Testament. **14. t., T.** time. **15. T** *Mathematics.* time reversal. **16. t** ton; tons. **17. t.** terminal. **18. t.** *Physics.* top. **19. t.** *Grammar.* transitive. **20. t** troy (weights). **21. T.** Tuesday (unofficial).

ta (tä) *interj.* British Informal. Used to express thanks.

Ta The symbol for the element tantalum.

T.A. transactional analysis.

Taal (täl) *n. South African.* **Afrikaans** (*see*). Preceded by *the.* [Dutch *taal*, language, speech, from Middle Dutch *tāle*.]

tab (tăb) *n.* **1.** A projection, flap, or short strip attached to an object to facilitate opening, handling, or identification. **2.** A small, usually decorative flap or tongue on a garment. **3.** A small auxiliary control surface attached to a larger one to stabilize an airplane. **4.** A bill, as for a meal in a restaurant. **5.** A tabulator, as on a typewriter. **6.** A metal ring that is pulled off the top of a can of drink in order to make an opening. Also called "pull-tab." **—keep tabs on.** To keep account of or watch carefully. **~***tr.v.* **tabbed, tabbing, tabs.** To supply with a tab or tabs. [17th century : origin obscure.]

TAB, T.A.B. typhoid-paratyphoid A and B (vaccine against).

tab. table.

ta·ba·nid (tə-bā′nĭd, -băn′ĭd) *n.* Any of various blood-sucking flies of the family Tabanidae, which includes the horseflies. [New Latin *Tabanidae*, from Latin *tabānus*†, horsefly.] **—ta·ba·nid** *adj.*

tab·ard (tăb′ərd) *n.* **1.** A short tunic or capelike garment worn by a knight over his armor and emblazoned with his coat of arms. **2.** A similar garment worn by a herald and bearing his lord's coat of arms. [Middle English, from Old French *tabart*†.]

tab·a·ret (tăb′ə-rĕt′) *n.* A strong upholstery fabric having alternating stripes of satin and moiré. [Probably from TABBY.]

Ta·bas·co (tə-băs′kō) *n.* A trademark for a hot, pungent sauce made from the fruit of a species of pepper plant.

tab·by (tăb′ē) *n., pl.* **-bies.** Also **tab·bis** (tăb′ĭs) (for sense 2). **1. a.** A striped or brindled domestic cat. **b.** A female domestic cat. **2.** A rich silk cloth with a watered or wavy pattern. **3.** A plain weave fabric. **4.** A prying woman; a gossip. **~***adj.* **1.** Striped or brindled. Said of domestic cats. **2.** Made of or resembling watered silk. [French *tabis*, from Old French *atabis*, from Arabic *'attābī*, after *Al-'attābīya*, a suburb of Baghdad, Iraq.]

tab·er·na·cle (tăb′ər-năk′əl) *n.* **1.** *Often* **Tabernacle. a.** The portable sanctuary in which the Jews carried the Ark of the Covenant through the desert. **b.** The Jewish temple. **c.** A temporary or portable dwelling, as used by the Jews during the Exodus. **2.** *Often* **Tabernacle.** A case or box on a church altar containing the consecrated host and wine of the Eucharist. **3.** A place of worship distinguished from a church; especially, one used by various denominations in Wales or by the Mormon Temple in the United States. **4.** A canopied niche used as a shrine. **5.** The body considered as the temporary residence of the soul. **6.** *Nautical.* A boxlike support in which the heel of a mast is stepped. **~***v.* **tabernacled, -cling, -cles.** **—***tr.* To enshrine. **—***intr.* To dwell temporarily. [Middle English, from Old French, from Latin *tabernaculum*, tent, diminutive of *taberna*, hut, perhaps from Etruscan. See also **tavern.**] **—tab·er·nac·u·lar** (tăb′ər-năk′yə-lər) *adj.*

ta·bes (tā′bēz′) *n., pl.* **tabes. 1.** Progressive bodily wasting or emaciation. **2.** Tabes dorsalis. [Latin *tābēs*, "a melting."] **—ta·bet·ic** (tə-bĕt′ĭk) *adj.*

tabes dor·sa·lis (dôr-sā′lĭs, -săl′ĭs, -sä′lĭs) *n.* A form of syphilis resulting in a hardening of the dorsal columns of the spinal cord and in shooting pains, unsteadiness, and loss of ability to coordinate voluntary movements. Also called "locomotor ataxia." [New Latin, "dorsal tabes."]

tab·la (tŭb′lə) *n.* A pair of small hand drums of India. [Hindi, from Arabic *ṭablə*, drum.]

tab·la·ture (tăb′lə-choŏr′, -chər) *n.* **1.** *Music.* An early system of notation, used especially for lute music, using letters and symbols to indicate playing directions. **2.** An engraved tablet or surface. [French, from Medieval Latin *tabulātūra*, from *tabulātus*, tablet, from Latin, boarded, floored, from *tabula*, board. See **table.**]

ta·ble (tā′bəl) *n. Abbr.* **tab. 1.** An article of furniture supported by one or more vertical legs and having a flat horizontal surface on which objects can be placed, especially: **a.** One at which meals are eaten: *a dinner table.* **b.** *Often* **tables.** One used in gambling games, as roulette or dice. **2.** The objects laid out for a meal upon a table: *lay the table.* **3.** The food and drink served at meals; fare: *kept an excellent table.* **4.** The company of people assembled around a table, as for a meal. **5.** The horizontal part of a machine tool where a piece is worked. **6.** Either of the leaves of a backgammon board. **7.** A plateau or tableland. **8. a.** A flat facet cut across the top of a gemstone. **b.** A stone cut in this fashion. **9.** *Music.* The front part of a stringed instrument, the **belly** (*see*). **10.** *Architecture.* **a.** A raised or sunken rectangular panel on a wall. **b.** A **stringcourse** (*see*). **11.** *Geology.* A horizontal rock stratum. **12.** In palmistry, a part of the palm framed by four lines. **13. a.** An orderly written, typed, or printed display of data, especially a rectangular array exhibiting one or more characteristics of designated entities or categories. **b. tables.** A set of such tables listing basic arithmetic calculations to be learned by heart. **14.** An abbreviated list, as of the contents of a book. **15.** A slab or tablet, as of stone, bearing an inscription or device. **16. tables.** A system of laws or decrees; a code: *the tables of Moses.* **—drink someone under the table.** *Slang.* To succeed in remaining relatively sober for longer than (someone with whom one is drinking). **—on the table. 1.** Submitted for consideration or acceptance. **2.** Postponed or put aside for consideration at a later date. **—turn the tables.** To reverse a situation and gain the upper hand. **—under the table.** *Informal.* In a secret, underhand, or stealthy manner: *paid him under the table to remain silent.* **~***tr.v.* **tabled, -bling, -bles. 1.** To put or place on a table. **2.** To submit (a proposal, for example) for consideration. **3.** To postpone consideration of (a piece of legislation, for example); shelve. **4.** To enter in a table; tabulate. [Middle English, *tablet*, board, table, from Old French, from Latin *tabula*†, board, list.]

tab·leau (tăb′lō′, tă-blō′) *n., pl.* **tableaux** or **-leaus** (tăb′lōz′, tă-blōz′). **1.** A vivid or graphic description. **2.** A striking incidental scene, as of a picturesque group of people. **3.** A moment during a scene of a play when all the actors on stage freeze in position and then resume action as before. **4.** A tableau vivant. [French, from Old French *tablel*, diminutive of *table*, TABLE.]

tab·leau vi·vant (tă-blō′ vē-väⁿ′) *n., pl.* **tableaux vivants** (*pronounced as singular*). A scene presented on stage by costumed actors who remain silent and motionless as if in a picture. [French, "living picture."]

ta·ble·cloth (tā′bəl-klôth′, -klŏth′) *n., pl.* **-cloths** (-klôths′, -klŏthz′, -klôths′, -klŏthz′). A cloth to cover a table, especially in preparation for a meal.

ta·ble-cut (tā′bəl-kŭt′) *adj.* Cut with a flat facet across the top. Said of a gemstone.

ta·ble d'hôte (tä′bəl dōt′) *n., pl.* **tables d'hôte** (*pronounced as singular*). **1.** A communal table for all guests at a hotel or restaurant. **2.** A meal consisting of several courses and offering a limited number of choices, served at a fixed price in a restaurant or hotel. In this sense, also called "prix fixe." Compare **à la carte.** [French, "table of (the) host."] **—ta·ble d'hôte** *adv.*

ta·ble-hop (tā′bəl-hŏp′) *intr.v.* **-hopped, -hopping, -hops.** To move around from table to table greeting friends, as in a restaurant or nightclub. —**ta·ble·hop·per** *n.*

ta·ble·land (tā'bəl-lănd') *n.* A flat, elevated region, especially one with steep sides; a plateau; a mesa.

table linen *n.* Tablecloths and napkins.

table money *n. British.* An allowance given, especially to senior officers in the armed services, for the official entertaining of visitors.

Table Mountain. The distinctive flat-topped mountain that rises steeply behind Cape Town, South Africa, to a height of 1,087 meters (3,567 feet).

table salt *n.* **1.** A refined mixture of salts, chiefly sodium chloride, used in cooking and as a seasoning. Also called "common salt." **2. Sodium chloride** *(see).*

ta·ble·spoon (tā'bəl-spoon') *n.* **1.** A large spoon used for serving food. **2.** *Abbr.* **T., tbs., tbsp.** A household cooking measure equivalent to three teaspoons or four liquid drams.

ta·ble·spoon·ful (tā'bəl-spoon'fool') *n., pl.* **-fuls.** *Abbr.* **T., tbs., tbsp.** The amount a tablespoon will hold.

table sugar *n.* Sucrose.

tab·let (tăb'lĭt) *n.* **1.** A small, flat pellet of compressed powdered medication to be taken orally. **2.** A slab or plaque, as of stone or ivory, with a surface intended for or bearing an inscription. **3.** A thin sheet or leaf, as of clay or ivory, used as a writing surface. **4.** A set of such leaves fastened together, as in a book. **5.** A pad of writing paper secured along one edge. **6.** A small, flat cake of a prepared substance, such as soap. [Middle English *tablette,* from Old French *tablete,* diminutive of *table,* TABLE.]

table talk *n.* Casual mealtime conversation; cultured chat.

table tennis *n.* A game that is like a scaled-down version of lawn tennis, played on a table with a net across it, using wooden paddles faced with rubber and a small celluloid ball. See **Ping-Pong.** —**ta·ble-ten·nis** (tā'bəl-tĕn'ĭs) *adj.*

ta·ble·top, table top (tā'bəl-tŏp') *n.* **1.** The upper surface of a table. **2.** The level top of a geological formation, as a mountain, hill, or rock. —**ta·ble·top** *adj.*

ta·ble·ware (tā'bəl-wâr') *n.* The dishes, glassware, and cutlery used in setting a table for a meal.

table wine *n.* A wine considered suitable to be served with a meal.

tab·loid (tăb'loid') *n.* A newspaper of small format giving the news in condensed form, usually with illustrated, often sensational material. [TABL(ET) + -OID.]

ta·boo, ta·bu (tə-boo', tă-) *n., pl.* **-boos** or **-bus. 1.** A ban or inhibition attached to something by social custom or emotional aversion. **2.** A prohibition, especially in Polynesia and other South Pacific islands, excluding something from use, approach, or mention because of its sacred and inviolable nature. **3.** An object, word, or act protected by such a prohibition.

~*adj.* Excluded or forbidden from use, approach, or mention.

~*tr.v.* **tabooed** or **tabued, -booing** or **-buing, -boos** or **-bus.** To exclude from use, approach, or mention; place under taboo. [Tongan *tabu,* perhaps "exceedingly marked," marked as sacred.]

Usage: When this word is used in a specialized discussion —for example, in anthropology—the spelling *tabu* is usual.

ta·bor, ta·bour (tā'bər) *n.* A small drum played by a fifer to accompany the fife. [Middle English *tabo(u)r,* from Old French, perhaps from Persian *ṭabīr,* drum. See also **tambour.**]

Ta·bor, Mount (tā'bər). Peak, 588 meters (1,929 feet) high, in Galilee, northern Israel, near Nazareth. Ruins of an ancient stronghold are on its summit.

tab·ou·ret, tab·o·ret (tăb'ə-rĕt', -rā') *n.* **1.** A low stool without a back or arms. **2.** A low stand or cabinet. **3.** An embroidery frame. [French *tabouret,* diminutive of Old French *tabour,* TABOR.]

Ta·briz (tă-brēz'). City in northwestern Iran close to the borders with Turkey and the U.S.S.R. It is a commercial, industrial, and communications center.

tab·u·lar (tăb'yə-lər) *adj.* **1.** Having a plane surface; flat. **2.** Organized or arranged in table form. **3.** Calculated by means of a table. [Latin *tabulāris,* from *tabula,* TABLE.] —**tab·u·lar·ly** *adv.*

tab·u·la ra·sa (tăb'yə-lə rä'sə, rä'zə) *n.* **1.** A need or opportunity to start from the beginning; a clean slate. **2.** The mind before it receives the impressions gained from experience; especially, in the philosophy of Locke, the unformed, featureless mind. [Latin, "erased tablet."]

tab·u·lar·ize (tăb'yə-lə-rīz') *tr.v.* **-ized, -izing, -izes.** To put into tabular form; tabulate. —**tab·u·lar·i·za·tion** *n.*

tab·u·late (tăb'yə-lāt') *tr.v.* **-lated, -lating, -lates. 1.** To arrange, set out, record, or write in tabular form; condense and list. **2.** To cut or form with a plane surface.

~*adj.* (-lĭt, -lāt'). Having a plane surface. [Latin *tabula,* TABLE.] —**tab·u·la·tion** *n.*

tab·u·la·tor (tăb'yə-lā'tər) *n.* **1.** A person who tabulates. **2.** A machine into which data can be fed for tabulation. **3.** A mechanism on a typewriter for setting automatic stops or margins for columns. Also called "tab." **4.** *Computer Science.* A device for reading data from punched cards and producing printed lists or totals of the result.

tac·a·ma·hac (tăk'ə-mə-hăk') *n.* **1.** Any of several aromatic resinous substances used in ointments and incenses. **2.** The **balsam poplar** *(see).* [Spanish *tacamahaca, tacamaca,* from Nahuatl *tecamaca.*]

tac·et (tās'ĭt, tā'sĭt, tä'kĕt). *Music.* Be silent. Used as a direction. [Latin, it is silent, from *tacēre,* to be silent.]

tache (tăch) *n. Archaic.* A clasp or buckle. [Middle English, from

Old French, nail, fastening, from Germanic.]

tach·i·na fly (tăk'ə-nə) *n.* Any of several bristly, usually grayish flies of the family Tachinidae, the larvae of which live as parasites within the bodies of other insects. [New Latin *Tachina,* type genus, from Greek *takhinos,* swift, from *takhos,* speed, akin to *takhus,* swift.]

tach·isme (tăsh'ĭz'əm) *n.* A French school of art, originating in the 1950's and very similar to the American school **action painting** *(see),* characterized by irregular dabs and splotches of color thrown haphazardly onto the canvas in a spontaneous fashion. [French, from *tache,* spot, stain.] —**tach·iste** *n. & adj.*

ta·chis·to·scope (tə-kĭs'tə-skōp') *n.* An apparatus that projects a series of images onto a screen at rapid speed, used in experiments, as those on visual perception or memory. [Greek *takhistos,* most swift, very swift, from *takhus,* swift + -SCOPE.]

tach·o·graph (tăk'ə-grăf', -gräf') *n.* A machine that records the measurements of a tachometer, especially one in a vehicle recording its speed and the times at which it was being driven. [Greek *takhos,* speed + -GRAPH.]

ta·chom·e·ter (tə-kŏm'ə-tər) *n.* An instrument used to determine speed, especially the rotational speed of a shaft. [Greek *takhos,* speed, akin to *takhus,* swift + -METER.] —**tach·o·met·ric** (tăk'-ə-mĕt'rĭk) *adj.* —**ta·chom·e·try** (tə-kŏm'ə-trē). *n.*

tachy- *prefix.* Indicates swift or accelerated; for example, **tachycardia, tachymeter.** [Greek *takhus†,* swift.]

tach·y·car·di·a (tăk'ĭ-kär'dē-ə) *n.* Excessively rapid heartbeat. [New Latin : TACHY- + Greek *kardia,* heart.]

ta·chyg·ra·phy (tə-kĭg'rə-fē) *n.* The art or practice of rapid writing or shorthand; especially, the stenography of the ancient Greeks and Romans. [Greek *takhugraphos,* "swift writer" : TACHY- + -GRAPH.] —**ta·chyg·ra·pher, ta·chyg·ra·phist** *n.* —**tach·y·graph·ic** (tăk'-ĭ-grăf'ĭk), **tach·y·graph·i·cal** *adj.* —**tach·y·graph·i·cal·ly** *adv.*

tach·y·lyte, tach·y·lite (tăk'ə-līt') *n.* A black, glassy basaltic rock. [German *Tachylyt,* "that which decomposes quickly (in acids)" : TACHY- + Greek *lutos,* soluble, from *luein,* to dissolve.] —**tach·y·lyt·ic** (tăk'ə-lĭt'ĭk) *adj.*

ta·chym·e·ter (tă-kĭm'ə-tər) *n.* A surveying instrument used for the rapid measurement of distances, elevations, and bearings. [TACHY- + -METER.] —**ta·chym·e·try** *n.*

tach·y·on (tăk'ē-ŏn') *n. Physics.* A hypothetical elementary particle that travels faster than the speed of light, mathematically equivalent to a normal particle moving backward in time. [TACHY- + -ON.]

tach·yp·ne·a (tăk'ĭp-nē'ə) *n.* Abnormally rapid breathing. [New Latin, from TACHY- + Greek *pnoea,* breathing.]

tac·it (tăs'ĭt) *adj.* **1.** Not spoken; implied or understood: *Her glare was a tacit accusation.* **2. a.** Implied by or inferred from actions or statements. **b.** *Law.* Arising by operation of the law rather than through direct expression. **3.** *Archaic.* Silent; not speaking. [Latin *tacitus,* silent, from the past participle of *tacēre,* to be silent.] —**tac·it·ly** *adv.* —**tac·it·ness** *n.*

tac·i·turn (tăs'ə-tûrn') *adj.* Habitually untalkative; laconic. [French *taciturne,* from Latin *taciturnus,* from *tacitus,* silent, TACIT.] —**tac·i·tur·ni·ty** (tăs'ə-tûr'nə-tē) *n.* —**tac·i·turn·ly** *adv.*

Tac·i·tus (tăs'ĭ-təs), **Publius Cornelius** (A.D. *c.* 55–*c.* 118). Roman historian and senator. Active during the reigns of Domitian and Trajan, he described the period between the deaths of Augustus (A.D. 14) and Domitian (A.D. 96) in his two major works, the *Annals* and the *Histories.*

tack¹ (tăk) *n.* **1.** A short, light nail with a sharp point and a flat head. **2.** *Nautical.* **a.** A rope for holding down the weather clew of a course. **b.** A rope for hauling the outer lower corner of a studdingsail to the boom. **c.** The part of a sail to which a tack is fastened, such as the weather clew of a course. **d.** The lower forward corner of a fore-and-aft sail. **3.** *Nautical.* **a.** The position of a vessel sailing to windward relative to the trim of its sails. **b.** The act of changing from one tack to another. **c.** The distance or leg sailed between changes of tack. **d.** A sailing course that involves continual changes of tack. **4. a.** A course of action meant to minimize opposition to the attainment of a goal. **b.** An approach, especially one of a series. **5.** A large, loose stitch made as a temporary binding or as a mark. **6.** Stickiness, as of a newly painted surface.

~*v.* **tacked, tacking, tacks.** —*tr.* **1.** To fasten or attach with or as if with a tack or tacks. **2.** To fasten or mark (cloth or a seam, for example) with a loose, temporary stitch. **3.** To put together loosely and arbitrarily: *tacked some stories together.* **4.** To append; add. Used with *on.* **5.** *Nautical.* To bring (a vessel) into the wind in order to change tack. —*intr.* **1.** *Nautical.* **a.** To change the tack of a vessel. **b.** To change tack. Used of a vessel. **2.** To change one's course of action. [Middle English *tak(ke),* from Old North French *taque,* variant of Old French *tache,* nail, fastening, from Germanic.]

tack² *n.* Food, especially inferior food. [Origin unknown.]

tack³ *n.* The harness for a horse, including the bridle and saddle. Also used adjectively: *tack room.* [Shortened from TACKLE.]

tack hammer *n.* A light hammer used to drive tacks.

tack·le (tăk'əl; *also* tā'kəl *for sense* 2) *n.* **1.** The equipment used in a sport or occupation, especially in fishing. **2. a.** A system of ropes and pulleys for raising and lowering weights. **b.** A rope and its pulley. **3.** *Sports.* **a.** Either of two line players in football positioned between the guard and the end. **b.** The position played by a tackle. **c.** The act of stopping another player by seizing and bringing him down.

~*v.* **tackled, -ling, -les.** —*tr.* **1.** To take on and wrestle with (an opponent or problem, for example) in order to overcome permanently; come to grips with. **2.** *Sports.* To seize and throw down (an opposing player in football). —*intr. Sports.* To tackle an opponent in football. [Middle English *takel,* probably from Middle Low German *takel,* from *taken,* to seize.] **—tack·ler** *n.*

tack·y[1] (tăk'ē) *adj.* **-ier, -iest.** Slightly adhesive or gummy to the touch; sticky. [From TACK (to attach).] **—tack·i·ness** *n.*

tacky[2] *adj.* **-ier, -iest.** *Informal.* **1.** Distasteful or offensive; tasteless. **2.** Shabby; shoddy. [19th century : origin obscure.] **—tack·i·ly** *adv.* **—tack·i·ness** *n.*

tac·node (tăk'nōd') *n. Geometry.* A point at which two branches of a curve touch and continue without crossing, so as to have a common tangent at this point. Also called "osculation." [Latin *tactus,* touch + NODE.]

ta·co (tä'kō) *n., pl.* **-cos.** A tortilla folded around a filling, as of ground meat or cheese. [Mexican Spanish, from Spanish, wad, roll, plug, probably from Germanic.]

Ta·co·ma (tə-kō'mə). City of western Washington State, on Puget Sound at the mouth of the Puyallup River. It is a major seaport and railroad terminus and has varied industries. Numerous recreational areas, including Mt. Rainier, are nearby.

tac·o·nite (tăk'ə-nīt') *n.* A type of chert containing magnetite and hematite, mined as a low-grade iron ore. [After the *Taconic* Mountains, New York and western New England.]

tact (tăkt) *n.* **1.** The ability to appreciate the delicacy of a situation and to do or say the kindest or most fitting thing; diplomacy. **2.** Skill or ability in dealing with others, especially skill in not giving offense. **3.** *Archaic.* The sense of touch. [French, from Latin *tactus,* sense of touch, from the past participle of *tangere,* to touch.]

***Synonyms:** tact, diplomacy, finesse, savoir-faire, subtlety.*

tact·ful (tăkt'fəl) *adj.* Possessing or showing tact; considerate; discreet. **—tact·ful·ly** *adv.* **—tact·ful·ness** *n.*

tac·tic (tăk'tĭk) *n.* An expedient for achieving a goal; a maneuver.

-tactic *suffix.* Indicates: **1.** Pattern, orientation, or position in space; for example, **isotactic, atactic. 2.** Movement; for example, **geotactic, phototactic.** [Greek *taktos,* arranged.]

tac·ti·cal (tăk'tĭ-kəl) *adj.* **1.** Of, pertaining to, or using tactics. **2.** Characterized by adroitness, ingenuity, or skill. **3.** *Military.* **a.** Of, pertaining to, used in, or involving operations that are smaller, closer to base, or of less long-term significance than strategic operations: *a tactical unit.* **b.** Carried out in support of military or naval operations: *tactical bombing.*

tactical voting *n.* The practice of voting for a candidate or party one does not positively favor so as to prevent the election of another.

tac·ti·cian (tăk-tĭsh'ən) *n.* **1.** A person skilled in the planning and execution of military tactics. **2.** A clever maneuverer.

tac·tics (tăk'tĭks) *n. Used with a singular or plural verb.* **1. a.** The technique or science of securing the objectives set by strategy; specifically, the art of deploying and directing troops, ships, and aircraft in efficient maneuvers against an enemy. **b.** The maneuvers so used. Compare **strategy. 2.** A procedure or set of maneuvers engaged in to achieve an end or aim. [New Latin *tactica,* from Greek *(ta) taktika,* "(the) matters of arrangement," from the neuter plural of *taktikos,* of order or arrangement, of tactics, from *taktos,* arranged, in order, from *tassein, tattein,* to arrange (in battle formation).]

tac·tile (tăk'təl, -tīl') *adj.* **1.** Perceptible to the sense of touch; tangible. **2.** Used for feeling: *a tactile organ.* **3.** Of, pertaining to, or proceeding from the sense of touch: *a tactile reflex.* [Latin *tactilis,* from *tactus,* sense of touch.] **—tac·til·i·ty** (tăk-tĭl'ə-tē) *n.*

tac·tion (tăk'shən) *n.* The act of touching; contact. [Latin *tactiō* (stem *tactiōn-*), from *tangere* (past participle *tactus*), to touch.]

tact·less (tăkt'lĭs) *adj.* Lacking in delicacy; bluntly inconsiderate or indiscreet. **—tact·less·ly** *adv.* **—tact·less·ness** *n.*

tac·tu·al (tăk'cho͞o-əl) *adj.* Of, producing, derived from, or pertaining to the sense of touch; tactile. [From Latin *tactus,* sense of touch.] **—tac·tu·al·ly** *adv.*

tad (tăd) *n. Informal.* **1.** A small boy. **2.** A small amount or degree; bit: *needed a tad more salt.* [Probably from English dialectal *tad,* toad, from Middle English *tadde, tode,* TOAD.]

Tadmor. See **Palmyra.**

tad·pole (tăd'pōl') *n.* The aquatic larval stage of a frog or toad, having a tail and external gills that disappear as the limbs develop and the adult stage is reached. [Middle English *taddepol,* "toad head" : *tadde, tode,* TOAD + *pol,* POLL (head).]

Ta·dzhik, Ta·jik (tä'jĭk, -jēk') *n., pl.* **Tadzhik** or **Tajik.** A member of a people of Iranian descent inhabiting the Tadzhik S.S.R. and regions of Afghanistan and China. **—Ta·dzhik** *adj.*

Tadzhik Soviet Socialist Republic. Also **Ta·dzhik·i·stan** (tä-jĭk'ĭ-stăn', -stän'). Constituent republic of the U.S.S.R. Predominantly mountainous, with parts of the Pamir systems, it contains Communism Peak, at 7,495 meters (24,590 feet) the highest mountain in the Soviet Union. The Amu Darya, Syr Darya, and Zeravshan are the principal rivers. Tadzhiks make up just over 50 percent of the population, which is primarily engaged in agriculture. Tadzhikistan became a constituent republic of the U.S.S.R. in 1929. Dushanbe is the capital.

tae·di·um vi·tae (tē'dē-əm vī'tē', tīd'ē-əm wē'tī') *n.* A feeling of great weariness and boredom with life. [Latin, weariness of life.]

Tae·gu (tī-go͞o'). City of South Korea, on the Kum River. It is a railroad junction and an industrial and commercial center. The city was the temporary capital of Korea in August, 1950.

Tae·jon (tī-jôn'). City of central South Korea. It is a railroad hub and agricultural center, with rice mills, silk and textile factories, and food-processing plants.

tael (tāl) *n.* **1.** Any of varying units of weight used in eastern Asia, the most common being equivalent to $1^1/_3$ ounces. **2.** A former Chinese monetary unit equivalent in value to a tael of standard silver. [Portuguese *tael,* from Malay *tahil, tail,* probably from Hindi *tolā,* a weight, from Sanskrit *tulā,* balance, weight.]

tae·ni·a, te·ni·a (tē'nē-ə) *n., pl.* **-niae** (-nē-ē'). **1.** A narrow band or ribbon for the hair worn in ancient Greece. **2.** *Architecture.* The band or fillet separating a Doric frieze from the architrave. **3.** A ribbonlike anatomical structure. **4.** A flatworm of the genus *Taenia,* which includes many tapeworms. [Latin, band, ribbon, from Greek *tainia.*]

taeniacide. Variant of **teniacide.**

taeniasis. Variant of **teniasis.**

taf·fe·ta (tăf'ə-tə) *n.* A glossy, stiff, plain-woven fabric of silk, rayon, or nylon, used especially for women's garments.

~adj. **1.** Made of or resembling taffeta. **2.** Reminiscent of shot taffeta in being changeable; inconsistent or fickle. [Middle English *taffeta,* from Old French *taffetas,* from Old Italian *taffettà,* from Turkish *tafta,* from Persian *tāftah,* "woven," from *tāftan,* to weave.]

taffeta weave *n.* **Plain weave** *(see).*

taff·rail (tăf'rəl, -rāl') *n. Nautical.* **1.** The rail around the stern of a vessel. **2.** The flat upper part of the stern of a vessel, made of wood and often richly carved. [Alteration of earlier *taff(e)rel,* "carved panel," from Dutch *taffereel,* variant of *tafeleel* (unattested), diminutive of *tafel,* panel, table, from Middle Dutch *tāvele,* from Latin *tabula,* TABLE.]

taf·fy (tăf'ē) *n., pl.* **-fies. 1.** A sweet, chewy candy of molasses or brown sugar boiled until very thick and then pulled with the hands or by machine until it is glossy and holds its shape. **2.** *Informal.* Wheedling flattery. [Perhaps from TOFFEE or TAFIA.]

Taf·fy (tăf'ē) *n., pl.* **-fies.** A Welshman. Also used as a term of address. Often considered offensive. [Alteration of *Dafydd,* the Welsh version of *David,* patron saint of Wales.]

taf·i·a, taf·fi·a (tăf'ē-ə) *n.* A cheap rum distilled from molasses and refuse sugar in the West Indies. [West Indian Creole, probably alteration of RATAFIA.]

Taft (tăft), **Robert Alphonso** (1889–1953). U.S. politician. He was a staunch Republican senator from Ohio (1938–53) who opposed many of Franklin D. Roosevelt's policies, supported isolationism, cosponsored the Taft-Hartley Act (1947), resisted American involvement in NATO, and endorsed Joseph McCarthy's investigations of Communist infiltration.

Taft, William Howard (1857–1930). 27th U.S. president (1909–13) and Supreme Court justice. An efficient lawyer and federal appeals judge, he presided over the Philippine Commission (1900–1904), served as Theodore Roosevelt's secretary of war (1904–08), and was elected president in 1908. His quietly efficient administration, marked by antitrust activity and the Payne-Aldrich Tariff Act (1909), did not attract wide public support. Defeated in his bid for re-election (1912), he was appointed chief justice of the Supreme Court (1921), a position he held until a month before his death.

tag[1] (tăg) *n.* **1.** A strip of leather, paper, metal, or plastic attached to something or hung from a wearer's neck for the purpose of identification, classification, or labeling: *a price tag.* **2. a.** The plastic or metal tip with which shoelaces and some kinds of string are finished for ease in passing them through eyelets and to prevent them from fraying. **b.** A loop or other attachment by which something may be gripped or hung up. **3.** The contrastingly colored tip of an animal's tail. **4.** A bright piece of feather, floss, or tinsel surrounding the shank of the hook on a fishing fly. **5. a.** A dirty, matted lock of wool. **b.** A loose lock of hair. **6.** A rag; a tatter. **7.** A small, loose fragment: *tags and snippets.* **8.** An ornamental flourish, as at the end of a signature. **9. a.** A brief quotation, as from the English or Latin classics or the Bible, inserted into a discourse to give it an air of erudition and authority: *Shakespearean tags.* **b.** A cliché, saw, or similar short, conventional idea used to embellish a discourse. **10. a.** The refrain or last lines of a song or poem. **b.** The closing lines of a speech in a play; a cue. **11.** A designation or epithet, especially when unwelcome. **12.** *Computer Science.* A label assigned to identify data in a computer memory.

~v. **tagged, tagging, tags.** —*tr.* **1.** To label, identify, or recognize with or as if with a tag: *tagged him as a loser.* **2.** To add as an appendage to: *tagged an extra paragraph on the letter.* **3.** To put a ticket on (an automobile) for a traffic or parking violation. **4.** To follow closely. **5.** To cut the tags from (a sheep). —*intr.* To follow along after; accompany: *tagged after his brother; insisted on tagging along.* [Middle English *tagge*†.]

tag[2] *n.* **1.** A children's game in which one player pursues the others until he is able to touch one of them, who then in turn becomes the pursuer. **2.** The act of touching one's partner in tag wrestling. **3.** The act of touching a runner to retire him in baseball, softball, or touch football.

~tr.v. **tagged, tagging, tags. 1.** To touch (another player) in the game of tag. **2. a.** To touch the hand of (one's partner) in tag wrestling. **b.** In baseball, to touch (a runner) with the ball or the glove holding the ball in order to retire him. **c.** In touch football, to touch (the runner) as a substitute for tackling him. [Variant of *tig,* perhaps from TICK (tapping sound, originally "a light touch").]

Ta·ga·log (tə-gä'lôg') *n., pl.* **-logs** or collectively **Tagalog. 1.** A member of a people native to the Philippines and inhabiting Manila and its adjacent provinces. **2.** The Austronesian language spoken

tahr *The tahr is a wild cousin of both the sheep and the goat—hence its scientific name,* Hemitragus *(semigoat)* jemlahicus. *It lives on wooded hillsides in the Himalayas, India, and Arabia.*

PRONUNCIATION KEY

ă, pat; ā, pay; âr, care; ä, father, are; b, bib; ch, church; d, deed; ĕ, pet; ē, be; f, fife; g, gag; h, hat; hw, which; ĭ, pit; ī, pie; îr, pier; j, judge; k, kick; l, lid, needle; m, mum; n, no, sudden; ng, thing; ŏ, pot; ō, toe; ô, paw, for; oi, noise; ou, out; o͝o, book; o͞o, boot; p, pop; r, roar; s, sauce; sh, ship, dish; t, tight; th, thin, path; *th*, this, bathe; ŭ, cut; ûr, fur; v, valve; w, with; y, yes; z, zebra, size; zh, vision; ə, about, item, edible, gallop, circus, peaceful

IN FOREIGN WORDS:

à, *Fr.* ami; œ, *Fr.* feu, *Ger.* schön; ü, *Fr.* tu, *Ger.* über; KH, *Ger.* ich, *Scot.* loch; N, *Fr.* bon; y', *Fr.* Compiègne

STRESS MARKS:

Primary stress: ′ in·cite′ (ĭn-sīt′)
Secondary stress: ′ in′sight′ (ĭn′sīt′)

by this people. [Tagalog, "(people) from the (Pasig) river" : *taga,* coming from + *ilog,* river.] —**Ta·ga·log** *adj.*

tag day *n.* A day on which collectors for a charitable fund solicit contributions, giving each contributor a tag.

tag·ger (tăg′ər) *n.* **1.** One that tags, especially the pursuer in the game of tag. **2. taggers.** A very thin sheet iron, usually plated with tin.

ta·glia·tel·le (täl′yä-tĕl′ē) *n.* A type of pasta cut in flat, narrow strips. [Italian, from *tagliare,* to cut.]

tag line *n.* **1.** An ending line, as in a play or joke, that serves to make a point. **2.** An often repeated phrase associated with an individual, organization, or commercial product.

Tagore (tə-gôr′, -gōr′), **Sir Rabindranath** (1861–1941). Indian author, poet, and philosopher. He won the Nobel Prize for literature in 1913 for his collection of poetry, *Gitanjali,* drawing on traditional Hindu themes.

tag question *n.* A question, such as *isn't it?* or *don't you think?,* appended to the end of a remark.

tag sale *n.* A **garage sale** *(see).*

Ta·gus (tā′gəs). *Portuguese* **Te·jo** (tā′zho͞o). *Spanish* **Ta·jo** (tä′hō). River of Spain and Portugal. It is 940 kilometers (585 miles) long and enters the Atlantic Ocean at Lisbon. Its estuary is one of Europe's finest harbors.

tag wrestling *n.* A wrestling contest between two teams of two wrestlers each, only one member of each team being allowed in the ring at any one time, the other being permitted to enter when he touches his partner on the hand.

ta·hi·ni (tə-hē′nē) *n.* A thick paste made from ground sesame seeds. [Arabic.]

Ta·hi·ti (tə-hē′tē). The largest of the Society Islands in French Polynesia. The first European to discover it (1767) was the English navigator Capt. Samuel Wallis (1728–95). The chief products are tropical fruits, copra, vanilla, and sugar cane. Papeete, the capital and chief port, is also the capital of French Polynesia.

Ta·hi·tian (tə-hē′shən) *n.* **1.** A native or inhabitant of Tahiti. **2.** The Polynesian language of Tahiti. —**Ta·hi·tian** *adj.*

Ta·hoe, Lake (tä′hō). Lake, 500 square kilometers (193 square miles), on the California-Nevada border. It is 1,900 meters (6,228 feet) above sea level in a basin in the Sierra Nevada and is *c.* 502 meters (1,645 feet) deep. The lake is a popular resort area.

tahr (tär) *n.* Any of several goatlike mammals of the genus *Hemitragus,* of mountainous regions of Asia. [Nepalese *thar.*]

tah·sil (tə-sēl′) *n.* An administrative subdivision of a district in India. [Hindi, from Arabic, "collection."]

tah·sil·dar, tah·seel·dar (tə-sēl′där′) *n.* An official in India in charge of revenues and taxation in a tahsil. [Urdu *taḥsīldār,* from Persian : Arabic *taḥsīl,* collection + Persian *-dār,* holder.]

Tai (tī) *n.* A family of languages spoken in Southeast Asia and southern China that includes Thai, Lao, and Shan. —**Tai** *adj.*

ta·i·a·ha (tä′ē-ə-hä′) *n.* A long, spearlike Maori weapon. [Maori.]

tai chi (tī′ chē′, jē′) *n.* Also **tai chi chuan** (chwän′, cho͞o-än′). A Chinese form of callisthenics consisting of a series of movements performed slowly and deliberately for training both the body and the mind in balance, control, and coordination. [Chinese *tài jí qúan,* great ultimate boxing.]

tai·ga (tī′gə) *n.* The subarctic coniferous forest of Siberia and of similar regions elsewhere in Eurasia and North America. [Russian *taĭga,* from Turkic *taiga,* rocky mountain.]

taiglach. Variant of **teiglach.**

tail¹ (tāl) *n.* **1.** The posterior part of an animal, especially when elongated and extending beyond the trunk or main part of the body. **2.** The bottom, rear, or hindmost part of anything: *the tail of a shirt.* **3.** The rear end of a wagon or other vehicle. **4.** *Aviation.* **a.** The rear portion of a fuselage. **b.** An assembly of stabilizing planes and control surfaces in this region. Also called "empennage." **5.** The vaned rear portion of any bomb or missile. **6.** Any appendage to the rear or bottom of a thing: *the tail of a kite.* **7.** The long, luminous stream of gas and dust forced from the head of a comet when it is close to the sun. **8.** Something that follows or takes the last place: *the tail of the journey.* **9.** A retinue or train of followers. **10.** The end of a line or series of persons or things. **11.** The short closing line of certain stanzas of verse. **12.** The refuse or dross remaining from such processes as distilling or milling. **13.** *Printing.* The bottom margin of a page. **14.** *Informal.* The trail of a person or animal in flight. **15.** *Informal.* A person assigned to watch and report on someone's movements and actions. **16.** *Slang.* The buttocks. **17. tails. a.** A formal evening costume worn by men. **b.** A swallow-tailed coat. **18. tails.** The reverse of a coin: *heads or tails.* —**turn tail.** To run away. —**with one's tail between one's legs.** In an utterly dejected or defeated state.
—*v.* **tailed, tailing, tails.** —*tr.* **1.** To provide with a tail: *tail a kite.* **2. a.** To deprive of a tail; dock. **b.** To cut the stalks off (fruit). **3.** To come toward the end of: *tailing the list.* **4.** To serve as the tail of: *The winning float tailed the parade.* **5.** To connect (objects often dissimilar or incongruous) by or as if by the tail or end: *tail two ideas together.* **6.** *Architecture.* To set one end of (a beam, board, or brick) into a wall. Used with *in* or *on.* **7.** *Informal.* To follow and keep under surveillance. —*intr.* **1.** *Architecture.* To be inserted at one end, as a floor timber or beam. **2.** *Informal.* To follow. Usually used with *after.* **3.** *Nautical.* **a.** To go aground with the stern foremost. **b.** To be pointed in some direction with the stern when riding at anchor or on a mooring. —**tail off** (or **away**). To dwindle.
—*adj.* **1.** Posterior; hindmost. **2.** Coming from behind: *a tail wind.* [Middle English *tayle,* Old English *tæg(e)l.*]

tail² *n. Law.* The limitation of the inheritance of an estate to a particular person or his direct descendants.
—*adj. Law.* In tail. Used after the noun and often in combination: *estate tail; fee-tail.* [Middle English *taille, tayle,* from Old French *taille,* cut, division, partition, from *taillier,* to cut, from Vulgar Latin *tāl(l)iāre* (unattested). See **tailor.**]

tail·back (tāl′băk′) *n. Football.* The back on the offensive team lining up farthest from the line of scrimmage.

tail beam *n. Architecture.* A **tailpiece** *(see).*

tail·board (tāl′bôrd′, -bōrd′) *n.* The tailgate of a vehicle.

tail·coat (tāl′cōt′) *n.* A man's black coat that is cut away at the front and has a tapering tail at the back that is split in two up to the waist, worn as part of very formal evening dress or as part of a morning suit. Also called "swallow-tailed coat," "tails."

tail end *n.* **1.** The rear or hindmost part of anything. **2.** The very end; the conclusion.

tail·gate (tāl′gāt′) *n.* **1.** Either of the pair of gates downstream in a canal lock. Compare **headgate. 2. a.** A hinged board forming the rear wall of a wagon or truck that can be removed or let down to serve as a ramp in loading or unloading. **b.** The sloping door that forms the back of a hatchback car.
—*v.* **tailgated, -gating, -gates.** —*tr.* To drive so closely behind (another vehicle) that one cannot stop or swerve in an emergency. —*intr.* To follow another vehicle too closely.

tail-heav·y (tāl′hĕv′ē) *adj.* Having too much weight at the rear either from overloading or from poor design and construction. Said especially of aircraft.

tail·ing (tā′lĭng) *n.* **1. tailings.** Refuse or dross remaining after such processes as milling, distilling, or mining. **2.** *Architecture.* The part of a tailed beam, brick, or board inside a wall.

taille (tä′yə, tāl) *n.* A form of direct royal taxation levied in France before 1789 on nonprivileged subjects and lands, and tending to weigh most heavily on the peasants. [French, a cut, division, from *tailler,* to cut, from Vulgar Latin *tāl(l)iāre* (unattested). See **tailor.**]

tail·light (tāl′līt′) *n.* A red light or one of a pair mounted on the rear end of a vehicle.

tai·lor (tā′lər) *n.* A person who makes, repairs, and alters garments such as suits, coats, and dresses.
—*v.* **tailored, -loring, -lors.** —*tr.* **1.** To make (a garment), especially to satisfy specific requirements or measurements. **2.** To fit or provide (a person) with clothes made to his measurements. **3.** To make, alter, or adapt for a particular end: *a speech tailored to a special audience.* —*intr.* To pursue the trade of a tailor. [Middle English *taillour,* from Norman French *taillour,* from Old French *tailler,* to cut, from Vulgar Latin *tāliāre, tālliāre,* to cut, from Latin *tālea*†, twig, cutting.]

tai·lor·bird (tā′lər-bûrd′) *n.* Any of several Old World tropical birds of the genus *Orthotomus,* characteristically using plant fibers to stitch leaves together in making its nest.

tai·lored (tā′lərd) *adj.* Simple, trim, or severe in line or design: *a tailored suit.*

tai·lor-made (tā′lər-mād′) *adj.* **1.** Made by a tailor. **2.** Perfectly fitted to a condition, preference, or purpose; made or as if made to order: *a job tailor-made for me.*
—*n.* **1.** A garment made by a tailor. **2.** *Informal.* A commercially manufactured cigarette as opposed to one rolled by hand.

tailor's chalk *n.* A thin piece of hard chalk used in tailoring for making temporary marks on clothing, as for seams or darts.

tail·piece (tāl′pēs′) *n.* **1.** Any piece forming an end to something; an appendage. **2.** *Printing.* An engraving or design placed as an ornament at the end of a chapter or at the bottom of a page. **3.** *Architecture.* A beam tailed into a wall. Also called "tail beam." **4.** *Music.* A triangular piece of ebony to which the lower ends of the strings of a stringed instrument are attached.

tail pipe *n.* The pipe through which exhaust gases from an engine are discharged; the final section of a vehicle's exhaust.

tail·plane (tāl′plān′) *n.* A horizontal airfoil fitted to the tail of an aircraft.

tail·race (tāl′rās′) *n.* **1.** The part of a millrace below the water wheel through which the spent water flows. Compare **headrace. 2.** A channel for floating away mine tailings and refuse.

tail rotor *n.* A small rotor fitted at the back of a helicopter to produce a sideways thrust, used to counteract the tendency of the body to rotate in the opposite direction to the main rotor.

tail·skid (tāl′skĭd′) *n.* A skid attached to the rear underside of certain aircraft to act as a runner.

tail·spin (tāl′spĭn′) *n.* **1.** The descent of an aircraft in a **spin** *(see),* characterized by the rapid spiral movement of the tail section. **2.** *Informal.* A state of emotional collapse; panic.

tail·stock (tāl′stŏk′) *n.* The adjustable stock of a lathe supporting the spindle containing the dead center.

tail wind *n.* A wind blowing in the same direction as that of the course of a vehicle.

tain (tān) *n.* **1.** A type of paper-thin tin plate. **2.** Tinfoil used as a backing for mirrors. [French, tinfoil, shortened from *étain,* tin, from Old French *estain,* from Latin *stagnum, stannum,* an alloy of silver and lead.]

Tai·no (tī′nō) *n., pl.* **-nos** or collectively **Taino. 1.** A member of an extinct aboriginal Arawakan Indian people of the West Indies. **2.** The language of this people. [Spanish, from a native name in the West Indies.] —**Tai·no** *adj.*

taint (tānt) *v.* **tainted, tainting, taints.** —*tr.* **1.** To stain or spoil (a

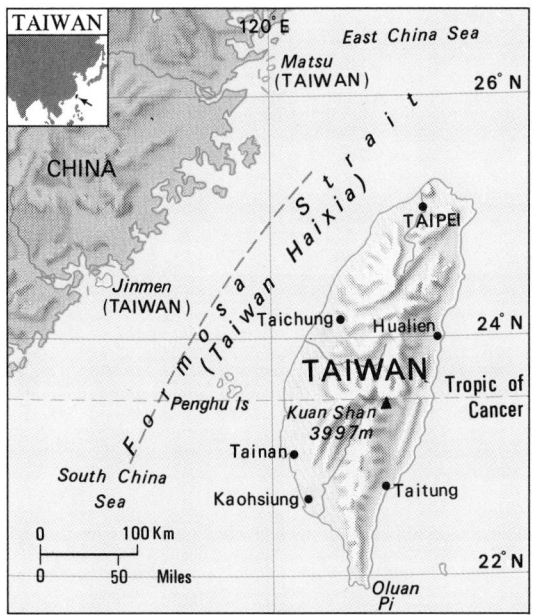

TAIWAN

East China Sea
Matsu (TAIWAN)   26° N
120° E

CHINA

TAIPEI

Jinmen (TAIWAN)

Taichung • • Hualien   24° N

TAIWAN   Tropic of Cancer

Penghu Is   Kuan Shan ▲ 3997m

Tainan •

South China Sea

Kaohsiung •   • Taitung

0   100 Km

0   50   Miles   22° N

Oluan Pi

person's honor or reputation). **2.** To make poisonous or rotten; infect or spoil. **3.** To affect with some unpleasant or harmful influence; corrupt. —*intr.* To become tainted or contaminated. ~*n.* **1.** A moral defect considered as a stain or spot. **2.** An infecting touch, influence, or tinge. [Middle English *taynten,* from Norman French *teinter,* from Old French *teint,* color, from Latin *tinctus,* past participle of *tingere,* to dip in liquid, dye.]

tai·pan (tī′păn′) *n.* A large venomous snake, *Oxyuranus scutellatus,* of Australia. [Native Australian name.]

Tai·pei (tī′pā′). Capital of Taiwan, at the northern end of the island. It is a major industrial center.

Tai·ping (tī′pĭng′) *n.* A Chinese insurrectionist who took part in an uprising (1850–64) against the Manchu dynasty. [Chinese, "great peace."] —**Tai·ping** *adj.*

Tai·wan (tī′wän′). Formerly **For·mo·sa** (fôr-mō′sə). Mountainous island off the southeastern coast of mainland China. The first Europeans to reach it were the Portuguese (1590). It became an important center for trade in the 19th century. China was forced to cede the island to Japan in 1895 but regained it after World War II, in 1945. Following defeats by the Communists, the Chinese Nationalists, led by Jiang Jieshi (Chiang Kai-shek), retreated to Taiwan and its neighboring islands (1949). Under U.S. sponsorship, rapid industrialization took place, and trade links between the two countries remain strong. Taiwan lost its United Nations seat to the People's Republic of China (1971), which regards Taiwan as one of its provinces. The United States broke off diplomatic relations with Taiwan and recognized the People's Republic in 1979. Electrical goods, clothing, and textiles are its main exports. Area, 35,989 square kilometers (13,895 square miles). Population, 16,610,000. Capital, Taipei. —**Tai·wan·ese** (tī′wə-nēz′, -nēs′) *adj. & n.*

taj (täzh, täj) *n.* A tall conical cap worn by certain Muslims as a headdress of distinction. [Arabic *tāj,* from Persian *tāj,* "crown."]

Tajik. Variant of **Tadzhik.**

Taj Ma·hal (täzh′ mə-häl′). A mausoleum in Agra, northern India. Built of white marble carved and inlaid with stones, it was constructed for the wife of Shah Jahan, who is also buried there.

Tajo. See **Tagus.**

ta·ka (tä′kə) *n.* The basic monetary unit of Bangladesh, equal to 100 paise. See feature at **currency.** [Bengali *tākā,* from Sanskrit *ṭaṅkaḥ,* coin.]

ta·ka·he (tə-kä′ē, tə-kī′) *n.* An almost extinct flightless bird, *Notornis mantelli,* of New Zealand, having a large bill and brightly colored plumage. [Maori *takahe* (imitative).]

take (tāk) *v.* **took** (tŏŏk), **taken** (tā′kən), **taking, takes.** —*tr.* **1.** To get into one's possession by force, skill, or artifice, especially: **a.** To capture physically; seize: *take an enemy fortress.* **b.** To kill, snare, or trap (fish or game, for example). **c.** To go away with; remove, often without proper permission: *Someone's taken my pen.* **d.** To capture in the course of a sport or game: *took my queen.* **e.** To obtain as a result of a victory; win: *took the seat at a by-election.* **f.** To seize authoritatively; confiscate. **2.** To grasp with the hands; grip: *take your partner's arm.* **3.** To carry along or cause to go with one to another place: *always takes his umbrella.* **4.** To encounter or catch in a particular situation; come upon; discover: *They'll never take me unawares.* **5.** To aim: *took a shot at the target.* **6.** To affect favorably; charm; captivate. Usually used in the passive: *completely taken by the puppy.* **7. a.** To put (food or drink, for example) into the body; eat, drink, inhale, or draw in: *take snuff.* **b.** To eat or drink habitually: *Do you take sugar?* **c.** To eat or drink as part of a course of medical treatment: *take tranquilizers.* **8.** To indulge or engage in (healthful or pleasurable treatment, for example): *take a*

vacation. **9. a.** To bring or receive into a particular relation, association, or other connection: *take a new partner into the firm.* **b.** To marry: *take a wife.* **10.** To have sexual intercourse with. Used of a man, as in romantic fiction. **11.** To accept and place under one's care or keeping: *take the children for the weekend.* **12. a.** To appropriate for one's own or another's use or benefit; obtain by purchase; buy. **b.** To buy regularly; especially, to subscribe to: *takes the Times.* **c.** To rent: *take a cottage for the summer.* **13. a.** To assume for or upon oneself: *take the blame.* **b.** To charge or oblige oneself with the fulfillment of (a task or duty, for example); deal with in the appropriate way: *The substitute took the sick teacher's class.* **c.** To pledge one's obedience to or adopt as a symbol of one's obedience; impose (a vow or promise) upon oneself: *take the veil.* **d.** To use (time) for a particular end. **e.** To accept or adopt for one's own: *took my side in the argument.* **f.** To require for a correct fitting: *takes size 14.* **g.** To require or have as a fitting or proper accompaniment: *Intransitive verbs take no direct object.* **14.** To obtain through competition: *took the prize.* **15.** To have or come to have: *took the form of a dialogue; taking shape.* **16. a.** To select; pick out; choose: *take any card.* **b.** To follow (a route or course of action): *took a wrong turn.* **c.** To use as a tool or instrument for doing something: *I'm going to take scissors to that hair of yours.* **d.** To use as a means of conveyance or transportation: *take a steamer to Europe.* **e.** To obtain or find: *take shelter.* **17.** To assume occupancy of: *take a seat.* **18.** To have as a requirement or necessity: *This job takes brains. It took three hours to get there.* **19.** To derive through conscious or unconscious influence: *She took her domineering tone from her mother.* **20. a.** To obtain or derive from a source or sources: *took the figures from an opinion poll.* **b.** To note or record: *took particulars of the case.* **21. a.** To put down in writing; write from dictation: *take a letter.* **b.** To put down an image, likeness, or representation of by or as if by drawing, painting, or photography: *take a photo.* **22. a.** To accept (something owed, offered, or given) either reluctantly or willingly: *took the bait.* **b.** To submit to (something inflicted); endure: *He can't take criticism.* **c.** To withstand or contain successfully: *The dam took the heavy flood waters.* **d.** To accept or believe (something put forth) as true or valid: *I'll take your word for it.* **e.** To follow (advice, a suggestion, or a lead, for example). **f.** To accept, handle, or deal with in a specified way: *takes things in his stride.* **g.** To consider in a particular relation or from a particular viewpoint: *Taken as a whole, it was a success.* **23. a.** To do, perform, or accomplish: *take a bath.* **b.** To perform or execute: *The horse took the jump.* **c.** To engage in or adopt, especially with an end in view: *taking precautions.* **24. a.** To allow to come in; admit; give access or admission to: *takes members only.* **b.** To provide room for; accommodate: *We can't take more than 300 guests.* **c.** To absorb or become saturated or impregnated with (dye, for example). **25. a.** To understand or interpret: *He took my criticism as an insult.* **b.** To consider; assume: *took her to be a policewoman.* Also used with *it: I take it you're coming.* **c.** To consider as a case in point: *Take children, for example.* **d.** To perceive or feel; experience: *took pride in her work. Don't take offense.* **26. a.** To convey or transport to a place: *This bus takes you to the station.* **b.** To conduct or lead: *That road takes us past the museum.* **c.** To cause to reach (a condition or state): *Her dedication took her to the top of her profession.* **27.** To go with, especially as a chaperone or as the person who pays: *take the children home; took him to the theater.* **28.** To remove; do away with: *takes all the joy out of life.* **29.** To cause to die; kill; destroy: *The war took both our sons.* **30.** To subtract: *take 15 from 30.* **31.** To commit oneself to the study of; enroll in: *take a course in physics.* **32.** *Slang.* To swindle; defraud; cheat: *taken for 40 dollars.* —*intr.* **1.** To acquire possession. **2.** To engage or mesh; catch, as gears or other mechanical parts do. **3.** To start growing; root; germinate: *Have the seeds taken?* **4.** To have the intended effect; operate; work: *Glue won't take on that surface.* **5.** To become. Used especially in the phrase *take ill.* —**take aback.** To bewilder; astonish; nonplus. —**take after. 1.** To follow as an example. **2.** To resemble in appearance, temperament, or character: *He takes after his father.* —**take amiss.** To be offended by through misunderstanding. —**take apart. 1.** To dissect or analyze (an object or theory, for example) into component parts; disassemble. **2.** *Informal.* To criticize or scold harshly or severely. **3.** *Slang.* **a.** To beat up; thrash. **b.** To defeat overwhelmingly, as in an argument; crush. —**take back. 1.** To retract something stated or written. **2.** To cause to recollect an earlier time: *takes you back.* —**take five** (or **ten**). *Informal.* To take a short rest or break, as of five to ten minutes. —**take for. 1.** To consider or suppose to be; regard as: *I take him for a fool.* **2.** To consider mistakenly: *We took you for dead.* —**take it.** *Informal.* To endure abuse, criticism, or other harsh treatment: *You've got to learn to take it in the army.* —**take it lying down.** *Informal.* To submit to unfair, harsh, or unjust treatment with no resistance. —**take it out on.** *Informal.* To abuse (another person or thing) in venting one's own anger or frustration. —**take on. 1.** To begin to employ; hire. **2.** To undertake or begin to handle (a task, for example). **3.** To oppose in competition. **4.** To begin to have or acquire: *take on a new image.* **5.** *Informal.* To display emotion; fuss: *Don't take on so!* —**take to. 1.** To have recourse to; go to, as for safety: *took to the woods.* **2.** To set out on: *take to the open road.* **3.** To develop as a habit or steady practice: *take to drink.* **4.** To become adept at: *took to it like a duck to water.* **5.** To become fond of or attached to: *They took to each other.* —**take up with.** To develop a friendship or association with. —See Usage note at **have.**

talapoin *The talapoin monkey lives in troops of up to 100 in the mangrove swamps and forests of central and western Africa.*

~*n.* **1.** The act or process of taking. **2.** The number of fish, game birds, or other animals killed or captured at one time. **3.** *Informal.* **a.** A quantity of anything collected at one time; especially, the amount of money stolen by a thief, profit or receipts taken by a business, or tickets sold by a theater. **b.** A share of money stolen or profits or receipts taken. **4. a.** The uninterrupted running of a motion-picture or television camera or set of recording equipment in making a film or television program or cutting a record. **b.** Any of a series of films or recordings of the same scene or sound, the best of which will be picked for final use. **5.** A scene filmed or televised without interrupting the run of the camera. **6. a.** Any physical reaction, such as a rash, indicating a successful vaccination. **b.** A successful skin graft. **7.** An amount of copy set in type at one time. **—on the take.** *Slang.* Receiving or appropriating money illegally. [Middle English *taken, took, taken,* Old English *tacan, tōc, tacen* (unattested), from Old Norse *taka, tōk, tekinn.*]

take down *tr.v.* **1.** To bring to a lower position from a higher one. **2.** To dismantle; take apart: *take down the scaffolding.* **3.** To lower the arrogance or self-esteem of (a person): *took him down a peg or two.* **4.** To put down in writing.

take•down (tāk′doun′) *adj.* Capable of being taken down or apart. Said chiefly of certain rifles.

take-home pay (tāk′hōm′) *n.* The amount of one's salary remaining after income tax has been paid and various other deductions have been made.

take in *tr.v.* **1.** To grant admittance to; receive as a guest or lodger. **2.** To reduce in size; make smaller or shorter: *take in a skirt.* **3.** To include or comprise. **4.** To understand; absorb mentally. **5.** *Informal.* To deceive; swindle. **6.** To look at thoroughly; survey: *take in the sights.* **7.** To accept work to be done in one's home for pay: *takes in sewing.*

take-in (tāk′ĭn′) *n. Informal.* An act or instance of taking in or being taken in, especially by deception.

take off *tr.v.* **1.** To remove (clothing, for example). **2.** To deduct as a discount: *took 20 percent off the bill.* **3.** To release: *took off the brake.* **4.** To discontinue: *took off the commuter special.* **5.** To leave off working for (a period of time): *take the afternoon off.* *—intr.v.* **1.** *Slang.* To go off; leave: *took off in a hurry.* **2.** *Slang.* To become widely used or popular. **3.** To rise up in flight. Used of an aircraft or rocket.

take•off (tāk′ôf′, -ŏf′) *n.* **1.** The act of rising in flight as an aircraft or rocket might do. **2.** *Informal.* An amusing or mocking imitation or caricature of another person. **—**See Synonyms at **caricature.**

take out *tr.v.* **1.** To extract; remove. **2.** To secure (a license, for example) by application to an authority. **3.** *Informal.* To escort, as on a date. **4.** In bridge, to cancel (a partner's bid) by bidding a different suit. **5.** *Slang.* **a.** To destroy or eliminate (enemy aircraft, for example). **b.** To kill. **6.** *Sports Informal.* To render (an opponent) ineffective, as by harsh tackling.

take•out (tāk′out′) *adj.* **1.** Selling food to be eaten off the premises: *a takeout Chinese restaurant.* **2.** Intended to be eaten off the premises: *a takeout lunch.*

~*n.* **1.** A store or restaurant selling takeout food. **2.** Takeout food.

take over *tr.v.* To assume the control or management of; especially, to buy the majority of the shares of (a company). *—intr.v.* **1.** To undertake something, such as a responsibility or task, especially by succeeding another person. **2.** To become prevalent: *Luxury apartments are taking over in the old neighborhoods.*

take•o•ver, take-o•ver (tāk′ō′vər) *n.* The act or an instance of assuming control over, management of, or responsibility for something, especially: **1.** The forcible seizure of power, as in a state or political organization. **2.** The acquisition of the majority of the shares of a company. **—take•o•ver** *adj.*

tak•er (tā′kər) *n.* A person who takes or takes up something, such as a wager or purchase.

take up *tr.v.* **1.** To raise up; lift. **2.** To reduce in size or length; shorten or tighten: *take up the slack.* **3.** To accept the offer, challenge, or bet of. Used with *on*: *I might take you up on that offer.* **4.** To accept (an offer, option, bet, challenge, or other proposal). **5.** To gather from a number of persons: *took up a collection.* **6.** To use up or occupy (space or time, for example). **7. a.** To develop an interest in or devotion to: *take up astronomy.* **b.** To enter into (a business or profession): *took up medicine.* **8.** To become the patron of: *a cause that was taken up by a well-known philanthropist.* **9.** To pursue or raise (a matter): *better take this up with the boss himself.* **10.** To begin to deal with: *takes up one question at a time.* **11.** To absorb (a liquid or gas). *—intr.v.* To begin again; resume: *take up where we left off.*

take-up (tāk′ŭp′) *n.* **1.** A device for reducing slack or taking up lost motion, as in a loom. **2.** The act of taking or tightening up.

ta•kin (tä′kēn′) *n.* A large buffalolike ruminant, *Budorcas taxicolor,* of the mountains of central Asia, having backward-pointing horns and a shaggy coat. [Of Tibeto-Burman origin.]

tak•ing (tā′kĭng) *adj.* **1.** Captivating; winning: *a taking smile.* **2.** *Informal.* Contagious; catching. Said of an infectious disease.

~*n.* **1.** The act of a person or thing that takes. **2.** Something that is taken, as a catch of fish. **3. takings.** Receipts, especially of money. **—tak•ing•ly** *adv.* **—tak•ing•ness** *n.*

ta•là (tä′lə) *n., pl.* **talà.** The basic monetary unit of Western Samoa, equal to 100 sene. [Samoan, from English DOLLAR.]

tal•a•poin (tăl′ə-poin′) *n.* A small African monkey, *Miopithecus talapoin* (or *Cercopithecus talapoin*), having a long tail and greenish fur. [French, "Buddhist monk" (from a fancied resemblance), from Portuguese *talapões,* plural of *talapão,* monk, from Mon *tala pōi,* "our lord" (polite address to a monk).]

talc (tălk) *n.* **1.** A fine-grained white, greenish, or gray mineral, essentially $Mg_3Si_4O_{10}(OH)_2$, having a soft, soapy texture and used in talcum and face powder, as a paper coating, and as a filler for paint and plastics. Also called "talcum." **2.** Talcum powder.

~*tr.v.* **talcked** or **talced, talcking** or **talcing, talcs.** To apply talc to (a photographic plate, for example). [French *talc,* from Medieval Latin *talcum,* from Arabic *ṭalq,* from Persian *talk*†.]

talc•ose (tăl′kōs′) *adj.* Also **talc•ous** (tăl′kəs), **talck•y** (tăl′kē). Made of, containing, or resembling talc.

tal•cum (tăl′kəm) *n.* **1.** Soapstone or talc. **2.** Talcum powder. [Medieval Latin, TALC.]

talcum powder *n.* A fine, often perfumed powder made from purified talc, for use on the skin.

tale (tāl) *n.* **1.** A report or revelation; a recital of facts or happenings: *told her tale of woe.* **2.** A malicious story, piece of gossip, or petty complaint. **3.** A deliberate lie; a falsehood. **4.** A diverting or edifying narrative of real or imaginary events; a story. **5.** *Usually* **tales.** Anything, whether true or false, told or revealed in breach of confidence, especially to one in authority: *tell tales.* **6.** *Archaic.* A reckoning; a total: *the earthquake's tale of thousands dead.* [Middle English *tale,* Old English *talu,* discourse, narrative.]

tale•bear•er (tāl′bâr′ər) *n.* One who spreads malicious stories or gossip; a telltale. **—tale•bear•ing** *adj.* & *n.*

tal•ent (tăl′ənt) *n.* **1.** Natural endowment or ability of a superior quality. **2.** A specific mental or physical aptitude; an innate ability to perform successfully in a particular field. **3.** Gifted people collectively: *local talent.* **4.** A variable unit of weight and money used in ancient Greece, Rome, and the Middle East. **—**See Synonyms at **ability.** [Middle English *talent(e),* from Old English *talente,* unit of weight or money, and Old French *talent,* aptitude, both from Latin *talentum,* unit of weight or money (in Medieval Latin, also "mental aptitude," extended sense from the parable of the talents in Matthew 25:14–30), from Greek *talanton.*]

talent scout *n.* An agent who goes in search of talented people for entertaining, sports, business, or the like.

ta•ler, tha•ler (tä′lər) *n.* Any of numerous silver coins serving as a unit of currency in certain Germanic countries from the 15th to 19th centuries. [German *Taler.* See **dollar.**]

ta•les (tā′lēz) *n., pl.* **tales.** *Law.* **1.** A group of persons summoned to fill vacancies on a jury that has become deficient in number. **2.** The writ allowing for such a summons of jurors. [Middle English, from the Medieval Latin phrase *tales de circumstantibus,* "such (persons) from those standing about" (used in the writ), from Latin *tālēs,* plural of *tālis,* such.]

tales•man (tālz′mən, tā′lēz-) *n., pl.* **-men** (-mĭn). *Law.* A person summoned under a writ of tales.

tale•tell•er (tāl′tĕl′ər) *n.* **1.** An oral narrator. **2.** A person who tells tales; a talebearer. **—tale•tell•ing** *adj.* & *n.*

ta•li. Plural of **talus.**

Ta-lien. See **Lü-da.**

tal•i•on (tăl′ē-ən) *n.* **1.** A punishment identical to the offense, such as the death penalty for murder. **2.** The principle of exacting compensation in this way. [Middle English *talioun,* from Old French *talion,* from Latin *tāliō* (stem *tāliōn-*), reciprocal punishment in kind.]

tal•i•ped (tăl′ə-pĕd′) *adj.* Afflicted with talipes; clubfooted.

~*n.* A person with a clubfoot.

tal•i•pes (tăl′ə-pēz′) *n.* A deformity of the human foot; especially, **clubfoot** *(see).* [New Latin *talipes* (stem *taliped-*), "walking on the ankles" : Latin *tālus,* ankle, TALUS + -PED.]

tal•i•pot (tăl′ə-pŏt′) *n.* A tall palm tree, *Corypha umbraculifera,* of tropical Asia. [Bengali *tālipōt,* palm leaf : Sanskrit *tālī,* fan palm, probably akin to *tāla* (see **toddy**) + *pattra,* feather, leaf.]

tal•is•man (tăl′ĭs-mən, tăl′ĭz-) *n., pl.* **-mans** (-mənz). **1.** A small object, such as a stone or amulet, usually marked with magical signs, that is believed to confer on its bearer supernatural powers or protection. **2.** Anything having apparently magical power. [French and Spanish *talisman,* from Arabic *ṭilsām* (plural *ṭilsamān*), from Late Greek *telesma,* completion, consecrated object, from *telein,* to fulfill, consecrate, from *telos,* aim, result.] **—tal•is•man•ic** (tăl′-ĭs-măn′ĭk, tăl′ĭz-) *adj.*

talk (tôk) *v.* **talked, talking, talks.** *—tr.* **1.** To articulate (something, such as thoughts and emotions) in words; express by means of speech: *talk treason.* **2.** To speak of or discuss (something): *talk music.* **3.** To speak or know how to speak in (an idiom or language). **4.** To gain, influence, or bring into a specified state by talking: *talked her into coming; talk his way out of trouble.* **5.** To spend (a period of time) by or as if by talking. Used with *away*: *talk the evening away.* *—intr.* **1. a.** To converse by means of spoken language. Often used with *to* or *with*: *talked to each other for hours.* **b.** To express thoughts, desires, hopes, or the like in words. Used with *about* or *of.* **2.** To articulate words: *The baby can talk.* **3.** To imitate the sounds of human speech: *The parrot talks.* **4.** To communicate one's thoughts in a way other than by spoken words: *talk with the hands.* **5.** To express one's thoughts in writing: *Voltaire talks about London in this text.* **6.** To parley or negotiate with someone: *Let's talk before fighting.* **7.** To gossip; spread rumors: *People will talk.* **8.** To allude to something: *What are you talking about?* **9.** To consult or confer with someone: *I'll have to talk to the others first.* **10.** To reveal information concerning oneself or others, especially under pressure: *Has the prisoner talked?* **11.** To be effica-

cious: *Nothing talks to them but money.* —See Synonyms at **speak.** **—talk about.** *Informal.* **1.** Used to express the opinion that the word or words immediately following are an understatement of the actual case: *Talk about stupid, he's a total idiot.* **2.** To imply as a result of what one is saying or doing: *If we decide to buy, we're talking about six years' savings gone.* **—talk at.** To address (someone) without regard to a response: *She talks at people, never to them.* **—talk big.** *Informal.* To brag. **—talk down. 1.** To address someone with insulting condescension: *talked down to his student.* **2.** To silence (a person), especially by speaking in a loud and domineering manner. **3.** To depreciate by talking: *talked down the importance of the move.* **—talk out. 1.** To discuss (a matter) exhaustively. **2.** To resolve or settle by discussion. **3.** *British.* To block (proposed legislation) by making prolonged speeches, introducing irrelevant material, or the like. **—talk over. 1.** To consider thoroughly in conversation; discuss: *Let's talk it over.* **2.** To win over by persuasion: *I talked her over to my position.* **—talk through.** To show (someone) how to do something by going through it giving step-by-step instructions or explanations. **—talk up. 1.** To speak in favor of; promote or advocate. **2.** To speak up in a frank or insolent manner.

~*n.* **1.** An exchange of ideas or opinions; a conversation. **2.** A speech or lecture. **3.** Any hearsay, rumor, or speculation concerning something: *talk of war.* **4.** Any subject of conversation: *the talk of the town.* **5.** A conference or negotiation: *peace talks.* **6. a.** A particular manner of speech: *baby talk.* **b.** Any jargon or slang: *street talk.* **7.** Any empty speech or unnecessary discussion: *too much talk and not enough action.* [Middle English *talkien, talken,* probably frequentative formation (with *k*) from Old English *talian,* to reckon, tell, relate.]

talk·a·tive (tô′kə-tĭv) *adj.* Having an inclination to talk; loquacious. **—talk·a·tive·ly** *adv.* **—talk·a·tive·ness** *n.*

Synonyms: *effusive, garrulous, loquacious, verbose, voluble, wordy.*

talk back *intr.v.* **1.** To make an impertinent reply: *His father slaps him when he talks back.* **2.** To make a belligerent response: *Our guns will talk back.*

talk·back (tôk′băk′) *n.* A system of communication links in a television or radio studio enabling directions to be given while a program is actually being produced.

talk·er (tô′kər) *n.* A person who talks, especially a loquacious or garrulous person.

talk·ie (tô′kē) *n.* *Informal.* A motion picture with a soundtrack.

talking book *n.* A tape recording or record of a reading of a book, designed for use by the blind.

talking head *n.* The image of a person on a television documentary or interview who talks at length directly to the camera and is usually seated, with only the head and upper part of the body visible.

talking picture *n.* A talkie. Used especially when such motion pictures were first introduced.

talk·ing-to (tô′kĭng-to͞o′) *n., pl.* **-tos.** *Informal.* A scolding, especially one given by a person in authority to a subordinate.

talk show *n.* A radio or television show in which usually noted individuals or celebrities participate in discussions or are interviewed. Also *British* "chat show."

tall (tôl) *adj.* **taller, tallest. 1. a.** Having greater than average height: *a tall woman.* **b.** Having considerable height, especially in relation to width; lofty: *tall trees.* **2.** Having a specified height: *three feet tall.* **3.** *Informal.* Fanciful or exaggerated: *tall tales.* **4.** *Informal.* Very difficult to fulfill or accomplish: *a tall order.* **5.** *Archaic.* **a.** Brave; courageous. **b.** Excellent; fine. —See Synonyms at **high.**

~*adv.* Straight; with proud bearing: *stand tall.* [Middle English *tall,* seemly, handsome, valiant, probably from Old English *getæl,* swift, ready.]

tal·lage (tăl′ĭj) *n.* **1.** An occasional tax levied by the Anglo-Norman kings on crown lands and royal towns. **2.** A tax levied by a feudal lord on his dependants.

~*tr.v.* **tallaged, -laging, -lages.** To levy a tax on. [Middle English *ta(i)llage,* from Old French *taillage,* "a cutting," from *taillier,* to cut, from Vulgar Latin *tāl(l)iāre* (unattested). See **tailor.**]

Tal·la·has·see (tăl′ə-hăs′ē). Capital of Florida, in the northwestern part of the state. The state government and two universities are the major sources of employment. An Indian settlement on the site was first visited by Hernando de Soto in 1539.

Tal·la·hatch·ie (tăl′ə-hăch′ē). River of Mississippi, rising in the northwest and flowing 370 kilometers (230 miles) south to the Yazoo River.

Tal·la·poo·sa (tăl′ə-po͞o′sə). River, 431 kilometers (268 miles) long, rising in northwestern Georgia and flowing generally southwest through eastern Alabama to join the Coosa River and form the Alabama River.

tall·boy (tôl′boi′) *n.* *British.* A tall chest of drawers, often constructed in separate sections that are mounted vertically together. Compare **highboy.**

Tal·ley·rand-Pé·ri·gord (tăl′ē-rănd′pĕr′ə-gôr′, tä′lĕ-räɴ′pā′rē-gôr′), **Charles Maurice de** (1754–1838). French statesman and diplomat. A politician whose diplomatic skills were matched by his keen sense of political survival, he was one of the few constants in the succession of five disparate French regimes between 1789 and 1849.

tall drink *n.* A drink served in a tall glass and consisting typically of a liquor base with any of various diluents and flavorings.

Tal·linn (tä′lĭn, tăl′ĭn). Baltic seaport in the U.S.S.R. Once a Hanseatic town, it is a naval and military base. It was the capital of the independent republic of Estonia (1918–40) and is now the capital of the Estonian S.S.R.

tal·lith (tä′lĭs, -lĭth) *n., pl.* **tallithim** (tä′lĭ-sēm′, -thēm′) or **talliths.** A fringed prayer shawl with bands of black or blue, worn especially by Orthodox Jewish men at prayer and on certain solemn occasions. [Hebrew (Mishnaic) *ṭallīth,* "cover," from Hebrew *tillēl,* he covered.]

tall oil (täl, tôl) *n.* An oily resinous liquid composed of a mixture of rosin acids and fatty acids obtained as a by-product in the treatment of pine pulp and used in soaps, emulsions, and lubricants. [Partial translation of German *Tallöl,* from Swedish *tallolja* : *tall,* pine, from Old Norse *thöll*†, young pine tree + *Öl,* oil.]

tal·low (tăl′ō) *n.* **1.** A mixture of the whitish, tasteless, solid or hard fat obtained from parts of the bodies of cattle, sheep, or horses, and used in foodstuffs or to make candles, leather dressing, soap, and lubricants. **2.** Any of various similar fats, as from plants.

~*tr.v.* **tallowed, -lowing, -lows.** To smear or cover with tallow. [Middle English *talg, talgh, talow,* from Middle Low German *talg, talch.*] **—tal·low·y** *adj.*

tal·low-drop (tăl′ō-drŏp′) *n.* A style of cutting a gemstone so that it is smooth and convex on one or both sides.

tal·low-wood (tăl′ō-wo͝od′) *n.* **1.** A large Australian eucalyptus tree, *Eucalyptus microcorys.* **2.** The hard, greasy wood of this tree.

tal·ly (tăl′ē) *n., pl.* **-lies. 1.** A stick on which notches are made, used, especially formerly, to keep a count or record, as of amounts paid or owing. **2. a.** The reckoning or score kept on such a stick. **b.** Any reckoning or score kept of a game, account, or the like. **3.** A mark or number of marks used in recording a number of acts or objects. **4.** A label, ticket, piece of metal, or the like used for identification or classification. **5.** Anything that is very similar or corresponds to something else; a double or counterpart. **6.** A metal plate attached to a ship's machinery and bearing instructions for its use.

~*v.* **tallied, -lying, -lies.** —*tr.* **1.** To record on a tally. **2.** To reckon or count. **3.** To label with a tally. **4.** To cause to correspond or agree. —*intr.* **1.** To be alike; agree; correspond. **2.** To keep the score or reckoning of a thing. [Middle English *taly, talye,* from Norman French *tallie,* from Medieval Latin *tal(l)ia,* from Latin *tālea,* twig, cutting, stick. See **tailor.**]

tal·ly·ho (tăl′ē-hō′) *interj.* Used to urge hounds in fox hunting.

~*v.* **tallyhoed, -hoing, -hos.** —*tr.* To urge on (hounds) or indicate the sighting of (a fox) by shouting "tallyho." —*intr.* To shout "tallyho."

~*n., pl.* **tallyhos. 1.** The cry of "tallyho." **2.** A kind of fast coach drawn by four horses. [Probably from French *taïaut,* from Old French *thialau, taho,* cry used to urge on hounds.]

tal·ly·man (tăl′ē-mən) *n., pl.* **-men** (-mĭn). **1.** A recorder or scorekeeper. **2.** *British.* A traveling salesman who sells goods on credit and collects weekly or monthly payments for them.

Tal·mi gold (tăl′mē) *n.* An alloy of gold and brass used in making jewelry. [German *Talmigold,* partial translation of French *Talmi-or,* contraction of *Tallois-demi-or,* "half gold (made by) Tallois (a Parisian)."]

Tal·mud (täl′mo͝od′, tăl′məd) *n.* The collection of ancient rabbinic writings consisting of the Mishnah and the Gemara, constituting the basis of religious authority for traditional Judaism. It exists in two versions, the *Palestinian Talmud* and the longer *Babylonian Talmud.* [Hebrew (Mishnaic) *talmūd,* learning, instruction, from *lāmadh,* he learned.] **—Tal·mu·dic** (täl-mo͞o′dĭk, -myo͞o′dĭk, tăl-), **Tal·mu·di·cal** *adj.* **—Tal·mud·ist** (täl′mo͝od′ĭst, tăl′mə-dĭst) *n.*

tal·on (tăl′ən) *n.* **1. a.** The claw of a bird of prey. **b.** The similar claw of a predatory animal. **2.** Anything similar to or suggestive of a claw. **3.** The part of a lock that the key presses in order to shoot the bolt. **4.** The part of the pack of cards in certain card games left on the table after the deal. **5.** *Architecture.* An ogee molding. [Middle English, originally "heel," "hinder claw," from Old French, heel, spur, from (unattested) Vulgar Latin *tālō* (stem *tālōn-*), variant of Latin *tālus,* ankle, TALUS.]

ta·luk (tä-lo͝ok′) *n.* In India: **1.** A subdivision of a tax district, consisting of several villages. **2.** Formerly, the hereditary estate of a family. [Urdu, estate, from Arabic.]

ta·lus[1] (tā′ləs) *n., pl.* **-li** (-lī′). **1.** A tarsal bone that articulates with the tibia and fibula to form the anklebone. Also called "anklebone," "astragalus." **2.** The ankle. [New Latin, from Latin *tālus,* ankle, probably from Celtic, akin to Irish *sal*†, talon.]

talus[2] *n., pl.* **-luses. 1. a.** A sloping mass of debris at the base of a cliff. **b.** A **scree** *(see).* **2.** A sloping side of a rampart, fortification, or the like. [Old French, sloping side of an earthwork.]

tam (tăm) *n.* **1.** A hat, the **tam-o'-shanter** *(see).* **2.** Variant of **tom** (a Rastafarian's hat).

ta·ma·le (tə-mä′lē) *n.* A Mexican dish made of fried chopped meat and crushed peppers, highly seasoned, rolled in cornmeal dough, wrapped in corn husks, and steamed. [Mexican Spanish *tamal,* from Nahuatl *tamalli.*]

ta·man·du·a (tə-măn′do͞o-ə, tə-măn′də-wä′) *n.* A chiefly arboreal anteater, *Tamandua tetradactyla,* of tropical America, having a dense, furry coat and a prehensile tail. [Portuguese *tamanduá,* from Tupi, "ant-catcher" : *tacy,* ant + *monduar,* to catch.]

tam·a·rack (tăm′ə-răk′) *n.* A North American larch tree, *Larix laricina,* having very small cones. Also called "hackmatack." [Algonquian.]

tam·a·rau, tam·a·rao (tăm′ə-rou′) *n.* A small, short-horned buffalo, *Anoa mindorensis,* of the island of Mindoro in the Philippines. [Tagalog *tamaráw, timaraw.*]

tamandua *Largely nocturnal, this South American anteater is a tree climber with a prehensile tail that it uses to grip branches. It has a long tongue and no teeth.*

PRONUNCIATION KEY

ă, pat; ā, pay; âr, care; ä, father, are; b, bib; ch, church; d, deed; ĕ, pet; ē, be; f, fife; g, gag; h, hat; hw, which; ĭ, pit; ī, pie; îr, pier; j, judge; k, kick; l, lid, needle; m, mum; n, no, sudden; ng, thing; ŏ, pot; ō, toe; ô, paw, for; oi, noise; ou, out; o͝o, book; o͞o, boot; p, pop; r, roar; s, sauce; sh, ship, dish; t, tight; th, thin, path; *th*, this, bathe; ŭ, cut; ûr, fur; v, valve; w, with; y, yes; z, zebra, size; zh, vision; ə, about, item, edible, gallop, circus, peaceful

IN FOREIGN WORDS:

à, *Fr.* ami; œ, *Fr.* feu, *Ger.* schön; ü, *Fr.* tu, *Ger.* über; KH, *Ger.* ich, *Scot.* loch; N, *Fr.* bon; y′, *Fr.* Compiègne

STRESS MARKS:

Primary stress: ′ in·cite′ (ĭn-sīt′)
Secondary stress: ′ in′sight′ (ĭn′sīt′)

tamarisk *A native of the Middle East, the tamarisk thrives in coastal areas, where it is often grown as a windbreak.*

tanager *There are over 200 species of tanager, all native to the Americas. They live chiefly in forests and feed on nectar, fruit, and insects. The blue-necked tanager (above) lives in the tropical forests of South America.*

PRONUNCIATION KEY

ă, pat; ā, pay; âr, care;
ä, father, are; b, **bib**;
ch, **church**; d, **deed**; ĕ, pet;
ē, be; f, **fife**; g, **gag**; h, **hat**;
hw, **which**; ĭ, pit; ī, pie;
îr, pier; j, **judge**; k, **kick**;
l, lid, needle; m, **mum**;
n, no, sudden; ng, **thing**;
ŏ, pot; ō, toe; ô, paw, for;
oi, noise; ou, **out**; o͝o, **book**;
o͞o, boot; p, **pop**; r, **roar**;
s, sauce; sh, **ship, dish**;
t, tight; th, **thin, path**;
th, **this, bathe**; ŭ, cut; ûr, fur;
v, valve; w, **with**; y, yes;
z, zebra, size; zh, vision;
ə, about, item, edible, gallop, circus, peaceful

IN FOREIGN WORDS:

à, *Fr.* ami; œ, *Fr.* **feu**, *Ger.* schön; ü, *Fr.* **tu**, *Ger.* über; KH, *Ger.* **ich**, *Scot.* loch; N, *Fr.* bon; y', *Fr.* Compiègne

STRESS MARKS:

Primary stress: ′
in·cite′ (ĭn-sīt′)
Secondary stress: ′
in′sight′ (ĭn′sīt′)

tam·a·rin (tăm′ər-ĭn, -ə-răn′) *n.* Any of various small, long-tailed monkeys of the family Callithricidae, of tropical South America. [French, from Galibi.]

tam·a·rind (tăm′ə-rĭnd′) *n.* **1.** A tropical Old World tree, *Tamarindus indica,* with compound leaves and red-striped yellow flowers. **2.** The fruit of this tree, consisting of a long pod with seeds embedded in an edible pulp. [Medieval Latin *tamarindus,* from Arabic *tamr hindī,* "date of India" : *tamr,* date + *hindī,* of India, from Persian *Hind,* India.] **—tam·a·rind** *adj.*

tam·a·risk (tăm′ə-rĭsk′) *n.* Any of numerous shrubs or small trees of the genus *Tamarix,* native to Eurasia, having small, scalelike leaves and spikelike clusters of flowers; especially, *T. tetrandra,* which is often grown as an ornamental for its feathery foliage. [Middle English *tamarisc, thamarike,* from Late Latin *tamariscus,* variant of Latin *tamarīx*†.]

tam·ba·la (täm-bä′lə) *n., pl.* **tambala** or **-las.** A monetary unit equal to 1/100 of the kwacha of Malawi. See feature at **currency.** [Bantu, "cockerel."]

tam·bour (tăm′bo͝or′, tăm-bo͝or′) *n.* **1.** A drum. **2. a.** A small wooden embroidery frame consisting of two concentric hoops over which the fabric is stretched. **b.** Embroidery made on such a frame. **3.** A rolling front or top for a desk, consisting of narrow strips of wood glued side by side onto canvas. **4.** *Architecture.* Any of various types of circular structure, especially: **a.** The wall of a circular building that is surrounded with columns. **b.** The vertical part of a cupola. **5.** The sloping buttress or projection on the side of a court designed for playing court tennis or fives.
~*v.* **tamboured, -bouring, -bours.** *—tr.* To do (embroidery) on a tambour. *—intr.* To use a tambour in doing embroidery. [Middle English, from Old French, from Arabic *ṭanbūr,* alteration (by confusion with *ṭanbūr,* lute, TAMBOURA) of Persian *ṭabīr,* drum, TABOR.]

tam·bou·ra, tam·bu·ra (tŭm-bo͝or′ə) *n.* An unfretted, four-stringed Indian musical instrument resembling a lute, used to provide a harmonic drone. [Hindi, from Persian *ṭanbūr,* from Arabic. See also **tambour.**]

tam·bou·rin (tăm′bo͝or′ĭn, täN′bo͞o-răN′) *n.* **1.** A long, narrow drum used in Provence. **2.** A Provençal dance in lively two-beat rhythm, accompanied by the tambourin. **3.** A piece of music composed for such a dance. [Provençal *tamborin,* diminutive of *tambor,* TAMBOUR.]

tam·bou·rine (tăm′bə-rēn′) *n.* A musical instrument consisting of a small drumhead with jingling disks fitted into the rim that is carried and shaken with one hand and struck with the other. [French *tambourin,* diminutive of TAMBOUR.]

tame (tām) *adj.* **tamer, tamest. 1.** Brought from natural wildness into a domesticated, tractable, or cultivated state. **2.** Naturally unafraid; not timid. Said of animals. **3.** Submissive; servile: *tame obedience.* **4.** Without spirit or excitement; insipid; flat: *a tame Christmas party.* **5.** Sluggish; languid; inactive: *a tame river.*
~*tr.v.* **tamed, taming, tames. 1.** To make tractable; domesticate. **2.** To subdue or curb. **3.** To soften; tone down. [Middle English *tame,* Old English *tam.*] **—tam·a·ble, tame·a·ble** *adj.* **—tame·ly** *adv.* **—tame·ness** *n.* **—tam·er** *n.*

Tam·er·lane (tăm′ər-lān′) (1336–1405). Also **Tam·bur·laine** (tăm′bər-lān′) or **Ti·mur** (tĭ-mo͝or′). Mongol conqueror. He led his nomadic hordes from his capital at Samarkand in central Asia to overrun vast areas of Persia, Turkey, Russia, and India.

Tam·il (tăm′əl, tŭm′-) *n., pl.* **-ils** or collectively **Tamil. 1.** A member of a Dravidian people of southern India and Sri Lanka. **2.** The Dravidian language of the Tamil. **—Tam·il** *adj.*

Tamil Na·du (nä′do͞o, nä-do͞o′). *Formerly* **Ma·dras** (mə-drăs′, -dräs′). State in southeastern India. After Indian independence the area of the Madras presidency was divided into new Indian states (1953–56). The Tamil-speaking area became Tamil Nadu, with its capital at Madras. It is one of the most highly urbanized and industrialized areas of India.

Tam·ma·ny (tăm′ə-nē) *n.* An organization of the Democratic Party in New York City, founded as a fraternal society in 1789 and notorious in the 19th century for its political corruption. Also called "Tammany Hall." [From *Tammany* Hall, its headquarters.] **—Tam·ma·ny·ism** *n.* **—Tam·ma·ny·ite** *n.*

Tam·muz, Tham·muz (tä′mo͞oz′) *n.* The tenth month in the Hebrew calendar. See feature at **calendar.** [Hebrew *Tammūz,* from Babylonian *Du'uzu, Duzu* (name of a god), contractions of *Dumu-zi,* "the son who rises."]

tam·my[1] (tăm′ē) *n.* A fine glazed woolen cloth formerly used for linings or undergarments. [17th century : origin obscure.]

tammy[2] *n., pl.* **-mies.** *Chiefly British.* A tam-o'-shanter.

tam-o'-shan·ter (tăm′ə-shăn′tər) *n.* A tight-fitting Scottish cap, usually woolen, often having a pompon, tassel, or feather in the center and usually pulled down to one side. Also called "tam," *chiefly British* "tammy." [After the hero of Robert Burns's poem *Tam o'Shanter.*]

tamp (tămp) *tr.v.* **tamped, tamping, tamps. 1.** To pack down tightly by a succession of blows. **2.** To pack clay, sand, or dirt into (a drill hole) above an explosive. [Back-formation from TAMPION.]

Tam·pa (tăm′pə). City of west-central Florida, a port of entry with a harbor on Tampa Bay, an inlet of the Gulf of Mexico. It is a resort and a processing and shipping center for phosphate, shrimp, citrus fruits, beer, and cigars.

Tam·pax (tăm′păks′) *n.* A trademark for a menstrual tampon having a cardboard applicator tube.

tam·per[1] (tăm′pər) *intr.v.* **-pered, -pering, -pers. 1.** To interfere in a harmful manner. Used with *with*: *tampering with a mechanism.* **2.** To meddle rashly or foolishly. Used with *with*: *tamper with her feelings.* **3.** To interfere or exert influence surreptitiously so as to bring about an improper state of affairs. Used with *with*: *tamper with a contract.* —See Synonyms at **interfere.** [Originally "to prepare (clay) by mixing," alteration of TEMPER.] **—tam·per·er** *n.*

tamp·er[2] (tăm′pər) *n.* **1.** One that tamps; especially, a small instrument for packing down tobacco into a pipe bowl. **2.** A neutron reflector in a nuclear bomb that also delays the expansion of the exploding material, making possible a longer-lasting, more energetic, and more destructive explosion.

Tam·pi·co (tăm-pē′kō). City of eastern Mexico, on the Pánuco River a few miles inland from the Gulf of Mexico. One of Mexico's most important ports, it has large fishing, processing, and petroleum industries.

tam·pi·on (tăm′pē-ən) *n.* Also **tom·pi·on** (tŏm′-). A plug or cover for the muzzle of a cannon or gun to keep out dust and moisture. [Middle English *tamp(y)on,* from Old French *tampon,* cotton plug, TAMPON.]

tam·pon (tăm′pŏn′) *n.* **1.** A plug of absorbent material inserted into the vagina to absorb menstrual blood. **2.** *Medicine.* An absorbent wad inserted into a bodily cavity or wound to check a flow of blood or absorb secretions.
~*tr.v.* **tamponed, -poning, -pons.** To plug or fill with a tampon. [French, from Old French, nasalized variant of *tapon,* from Frankish *tappo* (unattested), plug.]

tam-tam (tŭm′tŭm′, tăm′tăm′) *n.* Any of a set of musical instruments resembling the gong but made of thinner metal and having a shallower rim. [Hindi *ṭamṭam* (imitative).]

tan (tăn) *v.* **tanned, tanning, tans.** *—tr.* **1.** To convert (hide) into leather by treating it with a tanning agent, especially one containing tannin. **2.** To make brown by exposure to ultraviolet rays, especially those of the sun. **3.** *Informal.* To thrash; beat. *—intr.* To become brown from exposure to ultraviolet rays.
~*n.* **1.** Light or moderate yellowish brown to brownish orange. **2.** The brown color imparted to the skin by ultraviolet rays, especially those of the sun. **3. Tanbark** *(see).* **4. Tannin** *(see)* or a solution derived from it.
~*adj.* **1.** Of the color tan. **2.** Used in or pertaining to tanning. [Middle English *tannen,* from Old English *tannian* and Old French *tanner,* both from Medieval Latin *tannāre,* from *tannum,* oak bark (used in tanning), probably from Gaulish *tanno-,* oak, from Common Celtic *tann-* (unattested).]

tan tangent.

Ta·na (tä′nə). Also **Tsa·na** (tsä′nə). Lake in Ethiopia. It has a surface area of *c.* 3,100 square kilometers (1,197 square miles) and is 1,830 meters (6,000 feet) above sea level. It is the source of the Blue Nile.

tan·a·ger (tăn′ə-jər) *n.* Any of various small New World birds of the family Thraupidae, often having brightly colored plumage. [New Latin *tanagra,* from Portuguese *tangará,* from Tupi : *atá,* to walk + *carâ,* around.]

Ta·na·ka (tä-nä′kä), **Kakeui** (1918–). Japanese statesman. Secretary-general of the Liberal Democratic Party (1965–66 and 1968–71), he was appointed prime minister in 1972 but was forced to resign when he was implicated in a bribery scandal involving the Lockheed Corporation (1974). He remains one of Japan's most powerful politicians.

Tananarive. See **Antananarivo.**

tan·bark (tăn′bärk′) *n.* **1.** The bark of various trees, especially the oak and hemlock, used as a source of tannin. **2.** Shredded bark from which the tannin has been extracted, used to cover circus arenas, racetracks, and other surfaces. Also called "tan."

tan·dem (tăn′dəm) *n.* **1.** A two-wheeled carriage drawn by two horses harnessed one behind the other. **2.** A team of carriage horses harnessed in single file. **3.** A bicycle with two or more saddles for two or more riders seated one behind the other. **4.** An arrangement in which two or more persons or objects are placed one behind the other or in which they operate in conjunction: *working in tandem.*
~*adv.* One behind the other.
~*adj.* **1.** Positioned one behind the other. **2.** Working in conjunction with another or one another; cooperative. **3.** *British.* Designating, using, or pertaining to an intermediate automatic telephone exchange: *tandem dialing.* [Latin *tandem,* "exactly then," at length, finally (but taken to mean "lengthwise," "one after another") : *tam,* so, so much + *-dem,* demonstrative suffix.]

tan·doo·ri (tăn-do͝or′ē) *n.* A method that originated in India of cooking in a charcoal-fired clay oven. [Urdu *tandoor,* oven.] **—tan·doo·ri** *adj.*

tang[1] (tăng) *n.* **1.** A sharp, often acrid taste, as of lemon juice, flavor, as of onions, or smell, as of sea air. **2.** A distinctive quality that adds piquancy. **3.** A trace, hint, or suggestion of something. **4. a.** A sharp point, shank, tongue, or prong. **b.** A projection by which a tool, such as a chisel, sword blade, or knife, is attached to its handle or stock. In this sense, also called "shank."
~*tr.v.* **tanged, tanging, tangs. 1.** To furnish with a tang. **2.** To give a tang to. [Middle English *tange,* serpent's tongue, insect's sting, probably from Old Norse *tangi,* a sting, point.] **—tang·y** *adj.*

tang[2] *n.* A loud ringing or vibrating sound; a twang.
~*v.* **tanged, tanging, tangs.** *—tr.* To cause to twang or clang. *—intr.* To twang or clang. [Imitative.]

Tang (täng). **1.** Chinese dynasty (A.D. 618–907). A high cultural period, it is regarded as the golden age of Chinese poetry. Buddhism and its art forms flourished. Expansionist policies and increased trade made the capital Changan (now Xi'an) a famous cosmopolitan center. **2.** A second, minor dynasty that ruled China from 923 to 936. **—Tang** *adj. & n.*

Tan·gan·yi·ka[1] (tăn′gən-yē′kə, tăng′gən-). Lake in east-central Africa. It is in the Great Rift Valley, on the borders of Zaire, Burundi, Tanzania, and Zambia. Its surface area is *c.* 33,000 square kilometers (12,738 square miles).

Tanganyika[2]. See **Tanzania.**

tan·ge·lo (tăn′jə-lō′) *n., pl.* **-los. 1.** A hybrid citrus tree that is a cross between certain varieties of grapefruit and tangerine. **2.** The fruit of this tree, having an acid, orange pulp. [*Tange*rine + pome*lo.*]

tan·gen·cy (tăn′jən-sē) *n.* Also **tan·gence** (-jəns). The condition of being tangent.

tan·gent (tăn′jənt) *adj.* **1.** Making contact at a single point or along a line; touching but not intersecting. **2.** Diverging from the main point; irrelevant.
~*n.* **1.** A line, curve, or surface touching but not intersecting another line, curve, or surface. **2.** *Abbr.* **tan a.** The ratio of the ordinate to the abscissa of the endpoint of an arc of a unit circle centered at the origin of a Cartesian coordinate system, the arc being of length *x* and measured counterclockwise from the point (1, 0) if *x* is positive or clockwise if *x* is negative. **b.** The function of an acute angle in a right triangle that is the ratio of the length of the side opposite the angle to the length of the side adjacent to the angle. **3.** A sudden change of course, as in thought or speech; a digression: *went off on a tangent.* **4.** In a clavichord, a small upright brass pin at the back of a key that strikes the string when the key is depressed and produces the sound. [New Latin *linea tangēns,* "touching line," from Latin *tangēns* (stem *tangent-*), present participle of *tangere,* to touch.]

tangent galvanometer *n. Physics.* A simple galvanometer having a small magnetic needle free to rotate in a horizontal plane and mounted at the center on a flat vertical coil through which the current is passed.

tan·gen·tial (tăn-jĕn′shəl) *adj.* Also **tan·gen·tal** (-jĕnt′l). **1.** Of, pertaining to, or moving along or in the direction of a tangent. **2.** Only slightly connected; peripheral. **3.** Going off at a tangent; divergent. **—tan·gen·ti·al·i·ty** (tăn-jĕn′shē-ăl′ə-tē) *n.* **—tan·gen·tial·ly** *adv.*

tangent plane *n.* The plane containing all the lines tangent to a specified point on a surface.

tan·ger·ine (tăn′jə-rēn′) *n.* **1.** A widely cultivated citrus tree, *Citrus reticulata,* bearing edible fruit having an easily peeled deep-orange skin and sweet, juicy pulp. **2.** The fruit of the tangerine. **3.** A strong reddish orange to strong or vivid orange. [From French *Tanger,* TANGIERS.] **—tan·ger·ine** *adj.*

tan·gi·ble (tăn′jə-bəl) *adj.* **1. a.** Discernible by the touch; capable of being touched; palpable. **b.** Visible and capable of being valued; material; corporeal: *tangible property.* **2.** Capable of being clearly and exactly comprehended; having real substance; concrete: *tangible evidence.* **—**See Synonyms at **real.**
~*n.* **1.** Something palpable or concrete. **2. tangibles.** Material assets. [Old French *tangible,* from Late Latin *tangibilis,* from Latin *tangere,* to touch.] **—tan·gi·bil·i·ty, tan·gi·ble·ness** *n.* **—tan·gi·bly** *adv.*

Tan·gier (tăn-jîr′) Also **Tan·giers** (-jîrs′). *French* **Tan·ger** (täN-zhā′). Port on the Moroccan side of the Strait of Gibraltar. An ancient Phoenician city, it was held by the Portuguese (1471–1662) and British (1662–84). After 1923–24 it was administered as an international zone by Britain, France, and Spain, and after 1928 also by Italy. The city's international status was restored after World War II, but it was returned to Morocco in 1956.

tan·gle[1] (tăng′gəl) *v.* **-gled, -gling, -gles.** —*tr.* **1.** To mix together or intertwine in a confused mass; snarl. **2.** To involve in hampering or awkward complications; entangle. **3.** To trap; ensnare. —*intr.* **1.** To be or become entangled. **2.** To enter into argument, dispute, or conflict. Used with *with*: *tangled with the law.*
~*n.* **1.** A confused, intertwined mass. **2.** A jumbled or confused state or condition. **3.** A state of bewilderment. **4.** *Informal.* An argument; an altercation. [Middle English *tangilen,* nasalized variant of *tagilen,* probably from Scandinavian, akin to Swedish dialectal *taggla*†, to entangle.] **—tan·gly** *adj.*

tangle[2] *n.* **1.** A large brown seaweed, *Laminaria digitata,* found on the lower areas of a shore. **2.** Any large brown seaweed. [Scottish, probably from Old Norse *thöngull.*]

tan·gle·ber·ry (tăng′gəl-bĕr′ē) *n., pl.* **-ries.** A shrub, the **dangleberry** *(see).*

tan·gled (tăng′gəld) *adj.* Complicated in a random or confused way.

tan·go (tăng′gō) *n., pl.* **-gos. 1.** A Latin-American ballroom dance in 2/4 or 4/4 time, characterized by long gliding steps and sudden dramatic poses. **2.** The music for this dance.
~*intr.v.* **tangoed, -going, -gos.** To dance the tango. [American Spanish, originally an Afro-American drum dance, possibly of Niger-Congo origin.]

tan·gram (tăng′grəm) *n.* A Chinese puzzle consisting of a square cut into five triangles, a square, and a rhomboid, to be reassembled into different figures. [Possibly Chinese *táng,* TANG (Chinese dynasty, hence "the Chinese") + -GRAM.]

Tan·guy (täN-gē′), **Yves** (1900–55). U.S. painter, born in France. A self-taught artist, he was a leader of the French surrealist movement. Moving to America at the outbreak of World War II (1939), he continued to create his phantasmagoric landscapes, including *Indefinite Divisibility* (1942).

tanh hyperbolic tangent.

tan·ist (tăn′ĭst, thô′nĭst) *n.* Among the ancient Celts, the heir apparent to the chief, elected during the chief's lifetime. [Irish Gaelic *tānaiste,* "second person," from Old Irish *tānaise*†, second, next.]

tan·ist·ry (tăn′ĭ-strē, thô′nĭ-) *n.* The system of electing a tanist.

tank (tăngk) *n.* **1.** A large, often metallic container for liquids or gases. **2.** A large, usually man-made reservoir or cistern, as for drinking water or irrigation; especially, any of a kind common in India. **3.** *Military.* A powerful turreted heavily armored combat vehicle that is mounted with cannon and guns and has caterpillar treads to traverse rough terrain. **4.** *Slang.* A jail or jail cell.
~*tr.v.* **tanked, tanking, tanks.** To place, store, or process in a tank. **—tank up. 1.** *Informal.* To fill up a vehicle with gasoline. **2.** *Slang.* To drink to the point of drunkenness. [Portuguese *tanque,* pond, from Latin *stagnum.*]

tan·ka[1], thang·ka (täng′kä) *n.* A Tibetan religious painting, usually mounted on a piece of rich material in the form of a hanging scroll. [Tibetan *thaṅka.*]

tanka[2] *n.* A Japanese verse form in five lines, the first and third composed of five syllables and the rest of seven. [Japanese, "short poem," from Chinese : *duǎn,* short + *ge,* song, poem.]

Tan·ka (täng′kä) *n., pl.* **-kas** or collectively **Tanka.** A member of a people in southern China who live on small boats clustered in colonies. [Cantonese *tan ka* : *tan,* tribal name represented by the character *dan,* "egg" + *ka,* variant of Mandarin Chinese *jia,* family, people.]

tank·age (tăng′kĭj) *n.* **1.** The capacity or contents of a tank or tanks. **2.** The act or process of putting or storing in a tank. **3.** The fee for such storage. **4.** Animal residues left after rendering fat in a slaughterhouse and used for fertilizer or feed.

tank·ard (tăng′kərd) *n.* **1.** A large drinking cup having a single handle and often a hinged cover; especially, a tall pewter or silver mug. **2.** The amount of liquid contained in a tankard. [Middle English *tankard,* probably related to Middle Dutch *tanckaert*†.]

tankard *An ivory tankard mounted in silver gilt by the Swedish craftsman Didrik Hysing (1676–1702).*

tank destroyer *n.* A high-speed armored vehicle equipped with antitank guns.

tanked (tăngkt) *adj. Slang.* Drunk.

tank engine *n.* A steam locomotive in which the water is carried in tanks mounted on the boiler. Also called "tank locomotive."

tank·er (tăng′kər) *n.* A ship, plane, truck, railroad car, or other means of transport used to carry liquids, such as oil, in bulk.

tanker *Modern oil tankers are the largest ships ever built. This one, the* Haql Episkopi, *launched in Japan in 1968, is 345 meters (1,132 feet) long and has a carrying capacity of 326,585 deadweight tons (DWT).*

tank farming *n.* The cultivation of plants in tanks of water without soil.

tank top *n.* A sleeveless, tightfitting, usually knitted shirt with shoulder straps and no front opening.

tank town *n.* A small or unimportant town. [So called because trians would stop there only to replenish water.]

tan·nage (tăn′ĭj) *n.* **1.** The act, process, or skill of tanning. **2.** Something tanned.

Tannenberg. See **Stębark.**

tan·ner[1] (tăn′ər) *n.* A person who tans hides.

tanner[2] *n. British Slang.* A sixpenny piece (half a shilling). Not in current usage. [19th century : origin obscure.]

tan·ner·y (tăn′ə-rē) *n., pl.* **-ies.** A place where hides are tanned.

Tann·häu·ser (tăn′hoi′zər, tän′-). A minstrel knight of legend who after having spent a time of revelry with Venus, the goddess of love, sought absolution from the pope but was refused.

tan·nic (tăn′ĭk) *adj.* Pertaining to or obtained from tannin.

tannic acid *n.* A lustrous yellowish to light brown amorphous, powdered, flaked, or spongy mass having the approximate composition $C_{76}H_{52}O_{46}$, derived from the bark and fruit of many plants and used in tanning, as a mordant to fix dyes, to clarify wine and beer, and as an astringent and styptic. Also called "tannin."

tan·nin (tăn′ĭn) *n.* **1.** Tannic acid. **2.** Any of various chemically different substances capable of promoting tanning. Also called "tan." [French *tanin,* from *tanner,* to TAN.]

Ta·no·an (tä′nō-ən) *n.* A language family of several American Indian peoples of New Mexico and Arizona. **—Ta·no·an** *adj.*

tanrec. Variant of **tenrec.**

tan·sy (tăn′zē) *n., pl.* **-sies.** Any of several plants of the genus *Tanacetum*; especially, *T. vulgare,* native to the Old World, having clusters of buttonlike yellow flowers and pungent, aromatic juice sometimes used medicinally and as a flavoring. [Middle English, from Old French *tanesie,* perhaps from Late Latin *tanacitam.*]

tan·tal·ic (tăn-tăl′ĭk) *adj.* Of, pertaining to, or containing tantalum.

tan·ta·lite (tăn′tə-līt′) *n.* A black to red-brown mineral, essentially $(Fe,Mn)(Ta,Nb)_2O_6$, distinguished from columbite by the predominance of tantalum over niobium and used as an ore of both elements. [Swedish *tantalit,* from New Latin TANTALUM.]

tan·ta·lize (tăn′tə-līz′) *tr.v.* **-lized, -lizing, -lizes.** To tease or torment by or as if by exposing to view but keeping out of reach something that is much desired. [From TANTALUS.] **—tan·ta·li·za·tion** *n.* **—tan·ta·liz·er** *n.* **—tan·ta·liz·ing·ly** *adv.*

tan·ta·lous (tăn′tə-ləs) *adj. Chemistry.* Of or containing trivalent tantalum. [TANTAL(UM) + -OUS.]

tan·ta·lum (tăn′tə-ləm) *n. Symbol* **Ta** A very hard, heavy gray metallic element that is exceptionally resistant to chemical attack below 150°C. It is used to make light-bulb filaments, electrolytic capacitors, lightning conductors, nuclear reactor parts, and some surgical instruments. Atomic number 73, atomic weight 180.948, melting point 2,996°C, boiling point 5,425°C, specific gravity 16.6, valences 2, 3, 4, 5. [New Latin, after TANTALUS; when immersed in acid it is unaltered, like Tantalus standing in the water.]

tapestry *Detail from a Flemish tapestry,* The Hunt of the Unicorn, *made in about 1500.*

tan·ta·lus (tăn′tə-ləs) *n.* A stand in which decanters are displayed locked up. [After TANTALUS.]

Tan·ta·lus (tăn′tə-ləs). *Greek Mythology.* A king who for his crimes was condemned in Hades to stand in water that receded when he tried to drink it, and with fruit hanging above him that receded when he reached for it. [Greek *Tantalos,* "bearer," "sufferer."]

tan·ta·mount (tăn′tə-mount′) *adj.* Equivalent in effect or value. Used after the noun with *to.* [Originally a verb, "to be equal to," from Norman French *tant amunter,* to amount to so much : Old French *tant,* so much, from Latin *tantus,* from *tam,* so + *amo(u)nter,* to AMOUNT.]

tan·ta·ra (tăn-tăr′ə, -tär′ə) *n.* **1.** A fanfare of a trumpet or horn. **2.** A sound resembling such a fanfare. [Latin *taratantara* (imitative).]

tan·tiv·y (tăn-tĭv′ē) *adv.* At full gallop or at top speed.
~*n., pl.* **tantivies. 1.** A blast on a horn. **2.** A fast and furious gallop; top speed. [17th century : origin obscure.]

tant mieux (tän myœ′) *adv.* So much the better. [French.]

tan·to (tän′tō) *adv. Music.* So much. Used as part of a direction: *allegro non tanto.* [Italian.]

tant pis (tän pē′) *adv.* So much the worse. [French.]

tan·tra (tŭn′trə) *n.* Any of a comparatively recent class of Hindu or Buddhist religious writings, in Sanskrit, concerned with mysticism and magic. [Sanskrit, loom, warp, hence principle, doctrine, from *tanōti,* he stretches or weaves.]

tan·trum (tăn′trəm) *n.* A fit of bad temper, especially when childish or petulant. [18th century : origin obscure.]

tan·yard (tăn′yärd′) *n.* The part of a tannery where the tanning vats are located.

Tan·za·ni·a (tăn′zə-nē′ə, tăn-zā′nē-ə). Republic in East Africa formed by the union of Tanganyika and Zanzibar in 1964. The mainland formed part of German East Africa until World War I, after which it was administered by the British until its independence in 1961. The sultanate of Zanzibar gained its independence in 1963. Tanzania is mostly plateau, broken by the Great Rift Valley and mountain areas, including Mt. Kilimanjaro. More than 85 percent of the people are subsistence cultivators or herders of cattle. Cotton, coffee, cloves, sisal, and diamonds dominate the country's exports. Area, 945,087 square kilometers (364,804 square miles). Population, 17,500,000. Capital, Dodoma. —**Tan·za·ni·an** *adj. & n.*

tan·zan·ite (tăn′zə-nīt′) *n.* A hydrated calcium aluminum silicate mineral, exhibiting blue, violet, or greenish coloration, used as a gem. [TANZAN(IA) + -ITE.]

Tao, Dao (tou, dou) *n.* In the philosophy of Taoism: **1.** The universal force that produces harmony in nature. **2.** The way or course in all aspects of life that is the most effective and least conspicuous and is in harmony with the spirit of nature and the universe. [Chinese *dào,* way.]

Taoi·seach (thē′shəKH) *n.* The prime minister of the Republic of Ireland. [Irish, leader.]

Tao·ism, Dao·ism (tou′ĭz′əm, dou′-) *n.* **1.** A principal philosophy and system of religion of China founded upon the teachings of Lao-tse, thought to have lived in the 6th century B.C., and based upon the concept of Tao, seeking to achieve practical and spiritual harmony with the universe. **2.** A more recent, popular version of Taoism, incorporating the use of charms and magic. [TAO + -ISM.] —**Tao·ist** *adj. & n.* —**Tao·is·tic** (tou-ĭs′tĭk, dou-) *adj.*

Ta·or·mi·na (tä′ôr-mē′nə, tour′-). City of eastern Sicily, overlooking the Ionian Sea. At the foot of Mt. Etna, it is a popular winter resort.

Taos (tous, tä′ōs). Resort community in northern New Mexico, between the Rio Grande and the Sangre de Cristo Mts. It has long been known as a colony for artists and writers, including John Marin (1872–1953) and D.H. Lawrence (1885–1930).

tap¹ (tăp) *v.* **tapped, tapping, taps.** —*tr.* **1.** To strike gently but audibly and usually repeatedly. **2.** To give a light rap with: *tap a pencil.* **3.** To produce with a succession of light blows. **4.** To reinforce or repair (shoe heels or toes) by attaching metal taps or a layer of leather or rubber. —*intr.* **1.** To deliver a gentle, light blow or blows. **2.** To walk making light clicks.
~*n.* **1. a.** A gentle but audible blow. **b.** The sound made by it. **2. a.** A thin layer of leather or a leather substitute applied to a worn-down shoe heel or toe. **b.** A metal plate attached to the toe or heel of a shoe, as for tap-dancing. [Middle English, from Old French *taper,* from Germanic.]

tap² *n.* **1.** A device consisting of a valve and spout used to regulate delivery of a fluid at the end of a pipe. **2.** A plug for a bunghole, as in a cask; a spigot. **3. a.** Alcoholic drink drawn from a tap. **b.** Alcoholic drink of a particular brew, age, or quality. **4.** *Surgery.* The removal of bodily fluid: *a spinal tap.* **5.** A tool for cutting an internal screw thread. Compare **die. 6.** A connection made between two points of an electric circuit, as to provide an intermediate potential. **7.** A concealed listening or recording device fitted to a telephone line or other communications system. Also called "wiretap." **8.** *British.* A taproom (*see*). —**on tap. 1.** On draft; ready to be tapped from a cask or keg. Said especially of beer. **2.** *Informal.* Available for immediate use; ready.
~*tr.v.* **tapped, tapping, taps. 1.** To furnish (a cask, for example) with a spigot or tap. **2.** To pierce in order to draw off liquid: *tap a rubber tree.* **3. a.** To draw off (liquid) by tapping. **b.** To extract or exploit as if by tapping: *tapped every possible source of energy.* **4.** *Surgery.* To withdraw fluid from (a bodily cavity). **5.** To make a connection with or open outlets from: *tap a water main.* **6. a.** To fit an electronic tap to (a telephone line, for example). **b.** To listen to or record (a telephone conversation, for example) by means of a tap. **7.** To make a connection in (an electric circuit) so as to draw off an intermediate potential or current. **8.** To cut screw threads in (a collar, socket, or other fitting). **9.** *Slang.* To ask (a person) for money. [Middle English *tappe,* Old English *tæppa.*] —**tap·per** *n.*

ta·pa (tä′pə) *n.* **1.** The inner bark of the **paper mulberry** (*see*). **2.** A paperlike cloth made in the Pacific islands by pounding tapa or similar bark. [Marquesan and Tahitian.]

tap dance *n.* A dance in which the rhythm is tapped out by the heels and toes in rapid, often intricate steps, the sound emphasized by taps on the dancer's shoes. —**tap-dance** (tăp′dăns′, -däns′) *v.* —**tap dancer** *n.*

tape (tāp) *n.* **1.** A narrow strip of strong woven fabric, such as that used in sewing or bookbinding. **2.** Any continuous narrow, flexible strip of cloth, metal, paper, or plastic, such as adhesive tape, magnetic tape, or ticker tape. **3.** A string stretched across the finish line of a racetrack to be broken by the winner. **4.** A tape recording. **5.** A tape cartridge.
~*v.* **taped, taping, tapes.** —*tr.* **1. a.** To fasten, secure, strengthen, or wrap with tape. **b.** To bind together (the sections of a book) by applying strips of tape. **2.** To measure with a tape measure. **3.** To record (sounds or pictures) on magnetic tape. —*intr.* To make a recording on magnetic tape. [Middle English *tap(p)e,* Old English *tæppa, tæppe.*]

tape cartridge *n.* **1.** A cartridge containing an endless loop of magnetic tape and designed for automatic use on insertion into a compatible sound or video recorder or a computer system. Also called "tape." **2.** A similar but usually smaller cartridge containing unlooped tape. Also called "cassette," "tape."

tape deck *n.* **1.** A tape recorder and player having no built-in amplifiers or speakers, used as a component in a high-fidelity sound system. **2.** A system of spools, magnetic tape, and a read-write head, used as a computer storage system.

tape grass *n.* An aquatic plant, *Vallisneria spiralis,* having long, grasslike, submerged leaves. Also called "eelgrass."

tape-loop (tāp′lōōp′) *n.* A magnetic tape recording joined in an endless loop so that it constantly replays itself. Also called "loop."

tape machine *n. Chiefly British.* See **ticker** (sense 1).

tape measure *n.* A tape of cloth, paper, or steel marked off in a linear scale, as inches or centimeters, used for taking measurements.

tape player *n.* A self-contained machine for playing back recorded magnetic tapes.

ta·per (tā′pər) *n.* **1.** A small or very slender candle. **2.** A long waxcoated wick used to light candles or gas lamps. **3.** Something that gives off a feeble light. **4.** A gradual decrease in thickness or width of an elongated object.
~*v.* **tapered, -pering, -pers.** —*intr.* **1.** To become gradually narrower or thinner toward one end. **2.** To lessen gradually, as in intensity or significance; diminish; slacken and finally stop. Used with *off.* —*tr.* To cause to taper.
~*adj.* Gradually decreasing in size toward a point; tapering. [Middle English, from Old English *tapor, tapur,* probably altered from *papur* (unattested), from Latin *papȳrus,* papyrus, wick made of papyrus.] —**ta·per·ing·ly** *adv.*

tape-re·cord (tāp′rĭ-kôrd′) *tr.v.* **-corded, -cording, -cords.** To record on magnetic tape.

tape recorder *n.* An apparatus used to record sound on magnetic tape and, usually, to play back sound so recorded.

tape recording *n.* **1. a.** Magnetized tape on which sound has been recorded. **b.** The sound recorded on a magnetic tape. Also called "tape." **2.** The act of recording on magnetic tape.

tap·es·try (tăp′ĭ-strē) *n., pl.* **-tries. 1.** A heavy textile fabric having a varicolored, often pictorial design woven across the warp, used especially for wall hangings or furniture coverings. **2.** A textile imi-

TANZANIA

Taoism

TAOISM, PHILOSOPHY OF NATURE

Chinese sect believes in a natural path through life

There is a simple message in the Chinese philosophy of Taoism: follow the natural path of life. It declares that man can overcome all his difficulties by spontaneously following his nature—in much the same way that water effortlessly finds its own course. Taoism was founded in the 4th or 3rd century B.C. and was based on the teachings of the sage Lao-tse, who is reputed to have lived two centuries earlier. It takes its name from the book *Tao-te-Ching* ("The Way and Its Power") and was in sharp conflict with the earlier bureaucratic teaching of the philosopher Confucius. He urged a belief in loyalty, respect for authority, the justice of the state, and the right of talent to be recognized.

Taoists turned to a belief that there is a mystical harmony of man with his surroundings and that truth is to be found in a love of nature. Taoism became a formal religion in the 1st century B.C., with a pantheon of gods and a priesthood. It was practiced until recently, but it has declined since the People's Republic of China was formed in 1949.

MEETING OF MINDS *This painting by Wang Shu Ku shows a smiling encounter between Lao-tse (left) and Confucius, two philosophers whose beliefs were in sharp conflict.*

---

tating a tapestry. **3.** Something suggestive of tapestry, as in complexity, richness, or variety: *"the fair tapestry of human life"* (Thomas Carlyle). [Middle English *tapstery,* from Old French *tapisserie,* from *tapisser,* to cover with carpet, from *tapis, tapiz,* carpet, from Medieval Greek *tapition,* variant of Greek *tapētion,* diminutive of *tapēs,* carpet.]

ta·pe·tum (tə-pē′təm) *n., pl.* **-ta** (-tə). **1.** *Botany.* A layer of nutritive cells within the sporangium of ferns and related plants or within the anther of flowering plants. **2.** *Anatomy.* A membranous reflecting layer or region in the choroid coat of the eye of certain animals, notably nocturnal animals. **3.** A stratum of fibers of the corpus callosum. [New Latin, from Medieval Latin, carpet, from Latin *tapēte,* from Greek *tapēs.* See **tapestry.**] **—tap·e·tal** *adj.*

tape·worm (tāp′wûrm′) *n.* Any of various ribbonlike, often very long segmented flatworms of the class Cestoda that are parasitic in the intestines of vertebrates, including humans.

tap house *n.* A tavern or bar.

tap·i·o·ca (tăp′ē-ō′kə) *n.* A beady starch obtained from the root of the cassava, used for puddings and as a thickening agent in cooking. [Portuguese and Spanish, from Tupi *tipioca,* "residue."]

ta·pir (tā′pər, tə-pîr′) *n.* Any of several ungulate mammals of the genus *Tapirus,* of tropical America or southern Asia, having a heavy body, short legs, and a fleshy proboscis. [New Latin *Tapirus,* genus name, from Tupi *tapira,* tapir.]

tap·is (tăp′ē, tă-pē′) *n. Archaic.* A tapestry or similar cloth used as a wall hanging, table cover, or rug. **—on the tapis.** Being discussed or considered. [Middle English *tapistry,* a type of cloth, from Old French *tapiz,* from Vulgar Latin *tappetium* (unattested), from Late Latin, from Greek *tapētion,* diminutive of *tapēs* (stem *tapēt-*), tapestry.]

Tap·pan Zee (tăp′ən zē′). A widening of the Hudson River in southeastern New York State. In the nearby town of Tappan is the De Wint mansion, George Washington's headquarters in 1780 and 1783.

tap·pet (tăp′ĭt) *n.* A lever or projecting arm that moves or is moved by contact with another part, usually to communicate a certain motion, as between a driving mechanism and a valve. [From TAP (to strike lightly).]

tap·ping (tăp′ĭng) *n.* **1.** The act of one that taps. **2.** Something that is taken or drawn by tapping.

tap·pit-hen (tăp′ĭt-hĕn′) *n. Scottish.* **1.** A crested hen. **2.** A large mug with a knobbed lid. [Scottish *tappit,* tufted, crested, from *tap,* dialectal variant of TOP + HEN.]

tap·room (tăp′rōōm′, -rōōm′) *n.* A bar, as in a hotel or pub.

tap·root (tăp′rōōt′, -rōōt′) *n. Botany.* The main root of certain plants, usually stouter than the lateral roots and growing straight downward from the stem.

taps (tăps) *n. Used with a singular verb.* A military bugle call or a drum signal sounded at night as an order to put out lights, and also sounded at military funerals and memorial services. [From TAP (light blow, drumbeat).]

Ta·pu·ya (tä-pōō′yə) *n., pl.* **-yas** or collectively **Tapuya.** A Tapuyan-speaking Indian. [Tupi *Tapua.*] **—Ta·pu·ya** *adj.*

Ta·pu·yan (tä-pōō′yən) *n.* A South American Indian linguistic stock of Brazil.

~*adj.* Of or pertaining to this family of languages or its speakers.

tap water *n.* Water containing dissolved salts that is obtained from the normal domestic supply, distinguished from distilled or deionized water.

tar[1] (tär) *n.* **1.** A dark, oily, viscid mixture, consisting mainly of hydrocarbons, produced by the destructive distillation of organic substances such as wood, coal, or peat. **2. Coal tar** *(see).*

~*tr.v.* **tarred, tarring, tars.** To coat with tar. **—tar and feather.** To punish (a person) by covering first with tar and then with feathers. [Middle English *taar, terr,* Old English *te(o)ru.*] **—tar·ry** *adj.*

tar[2] *n. Informal.* A sailor. [Short for TARPAULIN.]

Tar·a (tär′ə). Village in County Meath, eastern Republic of Ireland. From ancient times until the 6th century the Hill of Tara was the seat of Irish kings.

Tar·a·ca·hi·tian (tär′ə-kə-hē′shən) *adj.* Of or pertaining to a language family of the Uto-Aztecan group. [From *Tarahumara* and *Cahita,* names of two peoples in Mexico.]

taradiddle. Variant of **tarradiddle.**

ta·ra·ma·sa·la·ta (tə-rä′mə-sə-lä′tə) *n.* A pale pink, creamy paste made from the dried, salted, and pressed roe of mullet or cod, seasoned with lemon juice, and served as a hors-d'oeuvre. [Modern Greek : *taramas,* cod's roe + *salata,* SALAD.]

tar·an·tel·la (tär′ən-tĕl′ə) *n.* **1.** A lively, whirling southern Italian dance once thought to be a remedy for tarantism. **2.** The music for this dance, in 6/8 time. [After *Taranto,* seaport in southern Italy, where tarantism was common.]

tar·an·tism (tär′ən-tĭz′əm) *n.* A malady characterized by an uncontrollable urge to dance, epidemic in southern Italy from the 15th to the 17th century and believed to result from the bite of the tarantula. [New Latin *tarantismus,* after *Taranto.* See **tarantella.**]

ta·ran·tu·la (tə-răn′chōō-lə) *n., pl.* **-las** or **-lae** (-lē′). **1.** Any of various large, hairy, chiefly tropical spiders of the family Theraphosidae, capable of inflicting a painful but not seriously poisonous bite. **2.** A wolf spider, *Lycosa tarentula,* of southern Europe, once thought to cause tarantism. [Medieval Latin *tarantula,* from Italian *tarantola,* from *Taranto* (see **tarantella**), where it is common.]

ta·rax·a·cum (tə-răk′sə-kəm) *n.* **1.** Any plant of the genus *Taraxacum,* which includes the common dandelion, *T. officinale.* **2.** The root of any of these plants, the latex of which is used as a tonic and mild laxative. [Medieval Latin, from Arabic *tarakhshaqūq,* from Persian *talkh,* bitter + *chaqūq,* purslane.]

tar·boosh, tar·bush (tär-bōōsh′) *n.* A brimless, usually red felt cap with a silk tassel, worn by Muslim men, either by itself or as the base of a turban. [Egyptian Arabic *ṭarbush,* "sweating cap" : Turkish *ter,* sweat + Persian *pūshidānt,* to cover.]

Tar·de·noi·sian (tär′də-noi′zhən) *adj.* Of, pertaining to, or designating a Mesolithic culture characterized by the use of small flint tools. [After *Tardenois,* France, where the tools were found.]

tar·di·grade (tär′də-grād′) *n.* Any of various minute, slow-moving arthropods of the class Tardigrada, having eight legs and living in water or damp moss. Also called "water bear."

~*adj.* **1.** Of or belonging to the Tardigrada. **2.** Slow in thought or action; sluggish. [New Latin *Tardigrada,* from Latin *tardigradus,* slow-moving : *tardus,* slow (see **tardy**) + -GRADE.]

tar·dy (tär′dē) *adj.* **-dier, -diest. 1. a.** Occurring or arriving later than

tapir *A hoofed mammal found in tropical forests near water in Central and South America and in Malaysia. Tapirs feed mostly on leaves.*

tarsier *This small nocturnal primate has large toe pads that enable it to grip even smooth-barked trees in the Southeast Asian forests where it lives.*

expected or scheduled; late. **b.** Acting more slowly than expected, as through reluctance; dilatory. **2.** Moving or progressing slowly; sluggish. [Middle English *tardif, tardive,* slow, from Old French, from Common Romance *tardīvus* (unattested), from Latin *tardus*†, slow.] **—tar·di·ly** *adv.* **—tar·di·ness** *n.*

Synonyms: *dilatory, lagging, late, overdue.*

tar·dy·on (tär′dē-ŏn′) *n.* An elementary particle that travels more slowly than the speed of light; a normal particle as opposed to a tachyon. [Latin *tardus,* slow + -ON, after TACHYON.]

tare[1] (târ) *n.* **1.** Any of various small vetches of the genus *Vicia,* such as *V. hirsuta.* **2.** Any of several other weedy plants that grow in cornfields. **3.** The seed of any of these weeds. **4. tares.** Noxious elements, likened to weeds growing among wheat. By allusion to Matthew 13:25: *"his enemy came and sowed tares among the wheat."* [Middle English *tare*†, seed of the vetch.]

tare[2] *n.* **1.** *Abbr.* **t.** The weight of a container or wrapper that is deducted from the gross weight to obtain net weight. **2.** A deduction from gross weight made to allow for the weight of a container. **3.** *Chemistry.* A counterbalance, especially an empty vessel used to counterbalance the weight of a similar container. **4.** The weight of a motor vehicle, especially a truck, without a load, passengers, or fuel.
~tr.v. **tared, taring, tares.** To determine, allow for, or indicate the tare of (a container). [Middle English, from Old French, waste, deficiency, from Medieval Latin *tara,* from Arabic *ṭarḥah,* thing thrown away, from *ṭaraḥa,* to reject, throw.]

targe (tärj) *n. Archaic.* A light shield or buckler. [Middle English, from Old French. See **target.**]

tar·get (tär′gĭt) *n.* **1.** An object with a marked surface that is shot at to test accuracy, as a padded disk with colored concentric circles for use in rifle or archery practice. Also used adjectivally: *target practice.* **2.** Something aimed or fired at. **3. a.** An object of criticism or attack. **b.** Something viewed as an object to be acted on with the aim of transforming it. **4.** A desired end; a goal: *Her target is to finish school.* Also used adjectivally: *a target figure.* **5.** A railroad signal that indicates the position of a switch by its color, position, and shape. **6.** The sliding sight on a surveyor's leveling rod. **7.** A small, round shield, especially one worn on the arm in medieval times. **8. a.** A structure in a camera tube with a storage surface that is scanned by an electron beam to generate a signal output current similar to the charge-density pattern stored on the surface. **b.** A usually metal part in an x-ray tube on which a beam of electrons is focused and from which x-rays are emitted.
~tr.v. **targeted, -geting, -gets. 1.** To have as a target. **2.** To make a target of. [Middle English, from Old French *targette,* diminutive of *targe,* light shield, from Frankish *targa* (unattested).]

target language *n.* The language into which something such as a text or document is to be translated. Also called "object language." Compare **source language.**

Tar·gum (tär′go͝om′, -go͞om′) *n., pl.* **-gums** or **Targumim** (tär′-go͞o-mēm′). Any of several Aramaic translations or paraphrasings of the Old Testament. [Mishnaic Hebrew *targūm,* translation, interpretation, from Hebrew *tirgēm,* he interpreted.] **—Tar·gum·ic** (tär-go͝om′ĭk, -go͞o′mĭk), **Tar·gum·i·cal** *adj.* **—Tar·gum·ist** *n.*

tar·iff (tăr′ĭf) *n.* **1.** A list or system of duties or taxes imposed by a government on imported, or sometimes exported, goods, levied in order to raise revenue and, often, to protect indigenous producers. **2.** A duty or tax in such a system. **3.** Any schedule of prices, fares, or fees, especially in a bar, hotel, or restaurant.
~tr.v. **tariffed, -iffing, -iffs. 1.** To fix a duty or price on, according to a tariff. **2.** To fix a tariff on or draw up a tariff for. [French *tarif,* from Italian *tariffa* and Spanish *tarifa,* from Turkish *ta'rifa,* from Arabic *ta'rīf,* "information," "notification," from *'arafa,* to notify.]

Tar·king·ton (tär′kĭng-tən), **(Newton) Booth** (1869–1946). U.S. author. A prolific and popular writer known for his tales of boyhood and life in the Midwest, he wrote 40 novels, including two Pulitzer Prize winners, *The Magnificent Ambersons* (1918) and *Alice Adams* (1921).

tar·la·tan (tär′lə-tən) *n.* A thin, stiffly starched open-weave muslin. [French *tarlatane,* perhaps from Portuguese *tarlatana,* irregular variant of *tiritana,* from French *tiretaine,* linsey-woolsey, TARTAN.]

tar·mac (tär′măk′) *n.* **1.** A bituminous substance used as a binder in paving. **2.** An area paved with tarmac; especially, the runway of an airport. **3.** A tarmacadam road or pavement. [Originally a trademark.] **—tar·mac** *adj.*

tar·mac·ad·am (tär′mə-kăd′əm) *n.* A hard flat surface, as for a road or pavement, consisting of layers of crushed stone with a tar binder that is rolled until smooth. [TAR + MACADAM.]

tarn (tärn) *n.* A small mountain lake, especially one in a cirque. [Middle English *terne, tarne,* from Old Norse *tjörn, tjarn*†.]

tar·na·tion (tär-nā′shən) *interj.* Damnation. Used euphemistically.

tar·nish (tär′nĭsh) *v.* **-nished, -nishing, -nishes.** *—tr.* **1.** To dull the luster of; discolor, especially by exposure to air or dirt. **2.** To detract from or spoil; taint. *—intr.* **1.** To lose luster; become dull or discolored. **2.** To become spoiled or tainted.
~n. **1.** The condition of being tarnished or tainted. **2.** Something that tarnishes; a stain or film that dulls or discolors. [French *ternir* (present stem *terniss-*), from Germanic *tarnjan* (unattested).] **—tar·nish·a·ble** *adj.*

ta·ro (tăr′ō, tär′ō) *n., pl.* **-ros. 1.** A widely cultivated tropical plant, *Colocasia esculenta,* having broad leaves and a large, starchy, edible rootstock. **2.** The rootstock of this plant. Also called "cocoyam," "dasheen," "eddoe." [Tahitian and Maori.]

tar·ok, tar·oc (tăr′ək) *n.* A card game developed in Italy in the 14th century, played with a 78-card pack consisting of four suits plus the 22 tarot cards as trumps. Also called "tarots." [Italian *tarocchi,* plural of *tarocco,* TAROT.]

tar·ot (tăr′ō) *n.* **1.** Any of a set of 22 playing cards consisting of a joker plus 21 cards depicting vices, virtues, and elemental forces, used in fortunetelling and as trumps in tarok games. **2. tarots.** Tarok. [French, from Italian *tarocco*†.]

tarp (tärp) *n.* A tarpaulin.

tar·pan (tär′păn′) *n.* An extinct wild horse, *Equus caballus,* once common in Europe. [Kirghiz.]

tar·pa·per (tär′pā′pər) *n.* Heavy paper impregnated or coated with tar, used as a waterproof protective material in building.

tar·pau·lin (tär-pô′lĭn, tär′pə-lĭn) *n.* **1.** Waterproof canvas used to cover and protect things from moisture. **2.** A sheet of this material. **3. a.** A sailor's hat made of this fabric. **b.** *Archaic.* A sailor. [Obsolete *tarpawling* : TAR + PALL (cover).]

tar·pon (tär′pən) *n., pl.* **tarpon** or **-pons.** Any of several fishes of the family Elopidae; especially, a large, silvery game fish, *Megalops atlantica,* of Atlantic coastal waters. [Dutch *tarpoen*†.]

tar·ra·did·dle, tar·a·did·dle (tăr′ə-dĭd′l, tăr′ə-dĭd′l) *n. Informal.* **1.** A petty falsehood; a fib. **2.** Absurd or pretentious twaddle; nonsense. [18th century: origin obscure.]

tar·ra·gon (tăr′ə-gŏn′, -gən) *n.* **1.** An aromatic herb, *Artemisia dracunculus,* native to Eurasia. **2.** The leaves of this plant, used as seasoning. [Medieval Latin *tragonia, tarchon,* from Medieval Greek *tarkhōn,* from Arabic *ṭarkhūn,* perhaps "dragon wort," from Greek *drakontion,* adderwort, from *drakōn,* DRAGON.]

tar·ri·ance (tăr′ē-əns) *n. Archaic.* The act or an instance of tarrying; a delay or sojourn.

tar·ry (tăr′ē) *v.* **-ried, -rying, -ries.** *—intr.* **1.** To delay or be late in going, coming, or acting. **2.** To wait; linger. **3.** To remain or stay temporarily; sojourn. *—tr. Archaic.* To await. **—See Synonyms at stay.**
~n., pl. **-ries.** A temporary stay; sojourn. [Middle English *tarien*†.] **—tar·ri·er** *n.*

tar·sal (tär′səl) *adj.* **1.** Of, pertaining to, or situated near the tarsus of the foot. **2.** Of or pertaining to the tarsus of the eyelid.
~n. Any of the seven small bones forming the posterior part of the skeleton of the foot. [New Latin *tarsālis,* from TARSUS.]

tarsal gland *n.* Any of the small sebaceous glands situated below the conjunctiva of the eyelids.

tar·si·er (tär′sē-ər, -sē-ā′) *n.* Any of several small nocturnal primates of the genus *Tarsius,* of the Philippines and Indonesia, having large, round eyes and a long tail. [French, from *tarse,* ankle (from its elongated ankles), from New Latin *tarsus,* TARSUS.]

tar·so·met·a·tar·sus (tär′sō-mĕt′ə-tär′səs) *n., pl.* **-si** (-sī′). A compound bone between the tibia and the toes of a bird's leg, formed by fusion of the tarsal and metatarsal bones. Also called "tarsus." [TARS(US) + METATARSUS.]

tar·sus (tär′səs) *n., pl.* **-si** (-sī′). **1. a.** The section of the vertebrate foot between the leg and the metatarsus. **b.** The seven bones making up this section. **2.** A fibrous plate that supports and shapes the edge of the eyelid. **3.** *Zoology.* **a.** The tarsometatarsus. **b.** The distal segmented structure on the leg of an insect or an arachnid. [New Latin, from Greek *tarsos,* frame of wickerwork, (hence) flat surface, sole of the foot, ankle.]

Tar·sus (tär′səs). City of southern Turkey, on the Tarsus River near the Mediterranean. Ancient Tarsus was one of the most important cities of Asia Minor and reached the height of its prosperity and cultural achievement under Roman rule. St. Paul was born here.

tart[1] (tärt) *adj.* **tarter, tartest. 1.** Having a sharp, pungent taste; sour. **2.** Sharp or bitter in tone or meaning; cutting. [Middle English *tart,* Old English *teart,* sharp, severe.] **—tart·ly** *adv.* **—tart·ness** *n.*

tart[2] *n.* **1.** A small pie with a sweet filling. **2.** *Chiefly British.* **a.** A pastry case with no top crust and a usually sweet filling, such as fruit, jam, or custard. **b.** A covered pastry case with a fruit filling; a fruit pie. **3.** A promiscuous woman, especially one dressed in a flashy, gaudy, or provocative manner; prostitute. **—tart up.** *Chiefly British.* **1.** To improve the appearance of, especially in a cheap, flashy, or gaudy manner; redecorate. **2.** To dress (oneself) up and put on make-up, especially so as to look sexy and provocative. [Middle English *tarte,* from Old French, variant (influenced by Medieval Latin *tartarum,* TARTAR) of *torte,* from Latin *torta,* round bread, "twisted," from *torquēre,* to turn, twist.]

tar·tan[1] (tärt′n) *n.* **1.** Any of numerous textile patterns consisting of stripes of varying widths and colors crossing at right angles against a solid background, each forming a distinctive design worn by the members of a particular Scottish clan. **2.** A twilled wool fabric or garment having such a pattern. **3.** Any fabric having a similar pattern; plaid. [Probably from Old French *tertaine, tiretaine,* linsey-woolsey, from Old Spanish *tiritaña,* a thin silk stuff, from *tiritar,* to rustle (imitative).] **—tar·tan** *adj.*

tartan[2] *n.* A small, single-masted Mediterranean ship with a large lateen sail. [French *tartane,* from Italian *tartana,* probably from Old Provençal *tartana*†, buzzard.]

tar·tar[1] (tär′tər) *n.* **1.** A reddish acid compound, chiefly potassium bitartrate, found in the juice of grapes and deposited on the sides of casks during wine-making. **2.** A hard, yellowish deposit on the teeth, consisting of organic secretions and food particles deposited in various salts, such as calcium carbonate. [Middle English *tartre, tartar,* from Old French *tartre,* from Medieval Latin *tartarum,* from Medieval Greek *tartaron*†.]

PRONUNCIATION KEY

ă, pat; ā, pay; âr, care;
ä, father, are; b, bib;
ch, church; d, deed; ĕ, pet;
ē, be; f, fife; g, gag; h, hat;
hw, which; ĭ, pit; ī, pie;
îr, pier; j, judge; k, kick;
l, lid, needle; m, mum;
n, no, sudden; ng, thing;
ŏ, pot; ō, toe; ô, paw, for;
oi, noise; ou, out; o͝o, book;
o͞o, boot; p, pop; r, roar;
s, sauce; sh, ship, dish;
t, tight; th, thin, path;
th, this, bathe; ŭ, cut; ûr, fur;
v, valve; w, with; y, yes;
z, zebra, size; zh, vision;
ə, about, item, edible,
gallop, circus, peaceful

IN FOREIGN WORDS:

à, *Fr.* ami; œ, *Fr.* feu, *Ger.* schön; ü, *Fr.* tu, *Ger.* über; KH, *Ger.* ich, *Scot.* loch; N, *Fr.* bon; y', *Fr.* Compiègne

STRESS MARKS:

Primary stress: ′
in·cite′ (ĭn-sīt′)
Secondary stress: ′
in′sight′ (ĭn′sīt′)

tarot

TRUMPS FOR TELLING THE FUTURE

Dual-purpose playing cards devised 800 years ago

No one knows where the tarot came from. An 18th-century French scholar, Comte de Gébelin, tried to trace the cards back to ancient Egypt, on the premise that the Egyptians had put all their wisdom and science into their hieroglyphic alphabet and that the tarot was related to this. Occult tradition has it that the town of Fez, in Morocco, became the world center of scholarship after the destruction of the Library at Alexandria in the 3rd century A.D., and that the tarot was invented there in about 1200 as a means of communication among the multilingual community. What is certain is that the 22 picture cards of the tarot were added to 56 number cards of oriental origin, probably in Italy in the 14th century.

Modern tarot games mostly use 54 cards: 32 suit cards and the 22 tarot cards, of which all but the fool are permanent trumps. The tarots are used for simple games and for fortunetelling, but the full pack is also used for more elaborate divination, when the tarot cards are called the major arcana; the suit cards are the minor arcana.

The identities of the trumps vary, but usually they are:

0.	The Fool	11.	Strength
1.	The Juggler	12.	The Hanged Man
2.	The Female Pope	13.	Death
3.	The Empress	14.	Temperance
4.	The Emperor	15.	The Devil
5.	The Pope	16.	The Tower (or Hospital)
6.	The Lovers	17.	The Star (or Stars)
7.	The Chariot	18.	The Moon
8.	Justice	19.	The Sun
9.	The Hermit	20.	The Day of Judgment
10.	The Wheel of Fortune	21.	The World

SIXTEENTH TRUMP *This hand-colored engraving of The Tower is from a 19th-century Italian tarot pack.*

tartar² *n. Often* **Tartar.** A ferocious, formidable, or violent-tempered person. [*Tartar,* variant of TATAR.]

Tartar. Variant of **Tatar.**

Tar·tar·e·an (tär-târ'ē-ən) *adj.* Of or pertaining to Tartarus.

tartar emetic *n.* A poisonous crystalline salt, potassium antimony tartrate, $K(SbO)C_4H_4O_6$, used in the medical treatment of amoebiasis and formerly as an emetic.

tar·tare steak (tär'tər) *n.* **Steak tartare** *(see).*

Tar·tar·i·an (tär-târ'ē-ən) *adj.* Of or pertaining to the Tatars or Tartary.

tar·tar·ic (tär-tär'ĭk) *adj.* Of, pertaining to, or derived from tartar or tartaric acid.

tartaric acid *n.* Any of four isomeric crystalline organic compounds, $C_4H_6O_6$, used to make cream of tartar, as a sequestrant, in tanning, and in effervescent drinks, baking powders, and photographic chemicals.

tar·tar·ize (tär'tə-rīz') *tr.v.* **-ized, -izing, -izes.** To treat, impregnate, or combine with tartar, tartar emetic, or cream of tartar. —**tar·tar·i·za·tion** *n.*

tar·tar·ous (tär'tər-əs) *adj.* Consisting of, derived from, or containing tartar.

tartar sauce, tartare sauce *n.* Mayonnaise mixed with chopped onion, olives, pickles, and capers and served as a sauce, especially with fish.

Tar·ta·rus (tär'tər-əs) *n.* **1.** *Greek Mythology.* **a.** The abysmal regions below Hades where the Titans were confined. **b.** A region of Hades reserved for the most wicked sinners. **2.** Any infernal or hellish region. [Latin, from Greek *Tartaros†.*]

Tar·ta·ry (tär'tə-rē) Also **Ta·ta·ry** (tä'-). A historical region comprising the areas of eastern Europe and Asia overrun by Tatars in the 13th and 14th centuries and extending as far east as the Pacific under Genghis Khan.

tart·let (tärt'lĭt) *n.* A small tart for an individual serving.

tar·trate (tär'trāt') *n.* A salt or ester of tartaric acid.

tar·trat·ed (tär'trā'tĭd) *adj.* Containing, combined with, or derived from tartaric acid.

Tar·tu (tär'tōō). *Swedish & German* **Dor·pat** (dôr'pät'). City in the western U.S.S.R., in Estonia, on the Ema River. It is an important industrial and commercial center.

tar·tuffe (tär-tōōf', -tōōf') *n.* A hypocrite, especially one who affects religious piety. [After *Tartuffe,* title character and hypocrite in Molière's comedy (1664).] —**tar·tuff·i·an** *adj.* —**tar·tuff·ism** *n.*

tart·y (tär'tē) *adj.* **-ier, -iest.** Sexually provocative in an obvious and vulgar way: *tarty behavior; tarty clothes.*

Tar·zan (tär'zən, -zăn') *n. Informal.* A man with a muscular physique who possesses great physical strength and virility. [After *Tarzan,* the hero of a number of stories by E.R. Burroughs.]

Tash·kent (tăsh-kĕnt'). City in the Central Asian U.S.S.R., in the foothills of the Tian Shan Mts. It is the capital of the Uzbek S.S.R. The city lies in a broad oasis along the Chirchik River that produces cotton and fruit and is one of the largest producers of finished textile goods in Asia.

ta·sim·e·ter (tə-sĭm'ə-tər) *n.* A device for measuring small temperature changes by the expansion or contraction of a solid. [Greek *tasis,* tension + -METER.]

task (tăsk, täsk) *n.* **1.** A specific piece of work assigned by a superior or done as part of one's duties. **2.** Something that has to be done, especially when difficult, tedious, or unpleasant. **3.** A function or duty to be performed: *My task is to assure fair play.* —**take to task.** To reprimand or censure.
~*tr.v.* **tasked, tasking, tasks. 1.** To assign a task to or impose a task upon. **2.** To overburden with labor; tax. [Middle English *taske, tasque,* tax, work imposed, task, from Norman French *tasque,* variant of Old French *tasche,* from Medieval Latin *tasca, taxa,* from *taxāre,* to TAX.]
   Synonyms: *assignment, chore, job.*

task force *n.* A temporary grouping of forces and resources, especially of military or police units, for the accomplishment of a specific objective.

task·mas·ter (tăsk'măs'tər, täsk'mä'stər) *n.* One who imposes work, especially heavy or exacting work.

Tas·ma·ni·a (tăz-mā'nē-ə, -mān'yə). Formerly **Van Die·man's Land** (văn dē'mənz). Island and state of Australia, lying off the southeastern coast of Australia and separated from the mainland by Bass Strait. The state also includes a number of small offshore islands. The capital is Hobart. The island was discovered by the Dutch explorer Abel Tasman in 1642. It was taken by Britain (1803), and its name changed to Tasmania (1853). In 1901 the island became a state of the Commonwealth of Australia. It is mountainous and much forested, and there are several large hydroelectric power projects. It exports iron, copper, zinc, tungsten, metal products, timber and wood products, textiles, and wool.

Tas·ma·ni·an devil (tăz-mā'nē-ən, -mān'yən) *n.* A burrowing carnivorous marsupial, *Sarcophilus harrisii,* of Tasmania, having a predominantly blackish coat, powerful jaws, and a long tail.

Tasmanian wolf *n.* A marsupial, the **thylacine** *(see).*

Tas·man Sea (tăz'mən). Arm of the South Pacific between Australia and New Zealand.

tass (tăs) *n. Chiefly Scottish.* **1.** A small cup or goblet. **2.** A small drink, especially of liquor. [Middle English, from Old French *tasse,* cup, from Arabic *tassah,* basin, from Persian *tast.*]

tasse (tăs) *n.* Also **tas·set** (tăs'ĭt). Any of a series of jointed overlapping metal plates hanging from the corselet, used as armor for the lower trunk and thighs. [Perhaps from Old French *tasse,* pouch, purse, from Middle High German *tasche,* from Old High German *tasca,* from Medieval Latin *tasca,* task, payment. See **task.**]

tas·sel (tăs′əl) *n.* **1.** An ornament consisting of a bunch of loose threads or cords bound at one end, hung from curtains, clothing, cushions, or the like. **2.** Something that resembles a tassel, as the pollen-bearing inflorescence of a corn plant. —*v.* **tasseled** or **-selled, -seling** or **-selling, -sels.** —*tr.* To fringe or decorate with tassels. —*intr.* To put forth a tassellike inflorescence. Used especially of corn. [Middle English, clasp, fibula, tassel, from Old French *tassel,* from Vulgar Latin *tascellus* (unattested), from Latin *taxillus,* small die.]

Tas·so (tăs′ō, tä′sō), **Torquato** (1544–95). Italian poet. Regarded as the greatest poet of the Italian High Renaissance, he wrote lyric love poems and discourses on the art of poetry and influenced Elizabethan literature with his masterpiece *Gerusalemme Liberata* (c. 1575), an epic account of the First Crusade.

taste (tāst) *v.* **tasted, tasting, tastes.** —*tr.* **1.** To distinguish, experience, or judge the flavor of by taking into the mouth. **2.** To eat or drink a small quantity of. **3.** To experience or partake of, especially for the first time: *tasted power.* **4.** *Archaic.* To like or appreciate. **5.** *Obsolete.* To test by touching. —*intr.* **1.** To distinguish, experience, or judge flavors in the mouth. **2.** To eat or drink a small amount. **3.** To have an experience; partake. Often used with *of.* **4.** To have a distinctive flavor: *The stew tastes salty. The salad tastes of garlic.* —*n.* **1. a.** The sense that distinguishes the sweet, sour, salty, and bitter qualities of dissolved substances in contact with the taste buds on the tongue. **b.** This sense in combination with the senses of smell and touch, which together receive a sensation of a substance in the mouth. **2. a.** The sensation of sweet, sour, salty, or bitter qualities produced by a substance in solution in the mouth. **b.** The sensation produced by any of these qualities together with a distinct smell and texture; flavor. **3.** A small quantity eaten or tasted. **4.** A brief spell of participating in or experiencing something, often for the first time; a sample: *a taste of fear.* **5.** A distinctive impression left by an event or experience. **6.** A personal preference or liking for something; an inclination. **7. a.** The faculty of discerning what is aesthetically excellent, pleasing, or appropriate; discrimination. **b.** A manner indicative of the quality of such discernment: *dressed with taste.* **8. a.** The sense of what is proper, seemly, or least likely to give offense in a given social situation; discretion. **b.** A manner indicative of the quality of this sense: *a remark in poor taste.* **9.** *Obsolete.* The act of testing; trial. —See Synonyms at **culture.** [Middle English *tasten,* to examine by touch, taste, from Old French *taster,* from Vulgar Latin *tastāre, taxitāre* (unattested), frequentative of Latin *taxāre,* to touch, frequentative of *tangere.*] —**tast·a·ble** *adj.*

taste bud *n.* Any of numerous spherical or ovoid nests of cells distributed over the tongue. The cells are embedded in the epithelium, consist of gustatory cells and supporting cells, and constitute the organs of taste.

taste·ful (tāst′fəl) *adj.* **1.** Exhibiting good taste. **2.** Tasty. —**taste·ful·ly** *adv.* —**taste·ful·ness** *n.*

taste·less (tāst′lĭs) *adj.* **1.** Lacking flavor; insipid. **2.** Exhibiting poor taste. —**taste·less·ly** *adv.* —**taste·less·ness** *n.*

tast·er (tā′stər) *n.* **1.** One who tastes, specifically: **a.** One who samples a food or drink for quality. **b.** One who samples food and drink prepared for another, as a king, as a precaution against poisoning. **2.** Any of several devices or implements used in tasting.

tast·y (tā′stē) *adj.* **-ier, -iest.** **1.** Having a pleasing flavor; savory. **2.** Very attractive or appealing. **3.** Having good taste; tasteful. —**tast·i·ly** *adv.* —**tast·i·ness** *n.*

tat (tăt) *v.* **tatted, tatting, tats.** —*intr.* To make tatting. —*tr.* To produce by tatting. [Probably back-formation from TATTING.] —**tat·ter** *n.*

ta·ta·mi (tä-tä′mē, tə-) *n.* Straw matting used as a floor covering, especially in Japan. [Japanese.]

Ta·tar (tä′tər) *n.* Also **Tar·tar** (tär′tər). **1.** A member of any of the Mongolian peoples of central Asia who overran western Asia and eastern Europe in the 13th century. **2.** A descendant of these Mongolian peoples, now living chiefly in parts of the Russian S.F.S.R. and Soviet Central Asia. **3.** Any of the Turkic languages of the Tatars. [Middle English *Tartre, Tatar,* from Old French *Tartare,* from Medieval Latin *Tartarus* (probably influenced by Latin *Tartarus,* TARTARUS), from Persian *Tātār,* from *Tata,* Turkic ethnic name.] —**Ta·tar, Tar·tar** *adj.*

Tatar Autonomous Soviet Socialist Republic. Constituent republic of the U.S.S.R. occupying the valleys of the middle Volga and lower Kama rivers. The capital is Kazan. It is a leading producer of natural gas and petroleum in the U.S.S.R.

Tatary. See **Tartary.**

Tate (tāt), **Allen** (1899–1979). U.S. poet, critic, editor, and biographer. Perhaps best known for his poetry, including "Ode to the Confederate Dead" (1926), he had a broad literary career, encompassing biographies, such as *Stonewall Jackson* (1928), works of criticism, including *Reason in Madness* (1941), and the editorship of the *Sewanee Review* (1944–46).

ta·ter (tā′tər) *n. Regional.* A potato. [Shortening and alteration of POTATO.]

Ta·tra Mountains (tä′trə). Highest chain of mountains in the Carpathian range of east-central Europe, lying in Poland and Czechoslovakia. The highest peak is Mt. Gerlachovka, which rises to 2,655 meters (8,710 feet).

tat·ter (tăt′ər) *n.* **1.** A torn and hanging piece of cloth; a shred. **2. tatters. a.** Torn and ragged clothing; rags. **b.** A condition of being reduced as if to shreds or rags: *left her nerves in tatters.* —*v.* **tattered, -tering, -ters.** —*tr.* To make ragged; reduce to shreds. —*intr.* To become ragged. [Middle English *tatter, tatar,* from Old Norse *taturr* (unattested), *töturr,* from Germanic *tath-* (unattested).]

tat·ter·de·mal·ion (tăt′ər-dĭ-māl′yən, -mä′lē-ən) *n.* A person wearing ragged or tattered clothing; a ragamuffin. —*adj.* Ragged; tattered. [TATTER + obscure second element.]

tat·tered (tăt′ərd) *adj.* **1.** Torn into shreds or tatters; ragged. **2.** Having ragged clothes; dressed in tatters.

tat·ter·sall, Tat·ter·sall (tăt′ər-sôl′, -səl) *n.* **1.** A pattern of variously colored lines forming squares on a plain, usually light background. **2.** Cloth woven with this pattern. Also used adjectivally: *tattersall check.* [Originally the pattern on blankets used at *Tattersall's* horse market in London, founded by Richard *Tattersall* (died 1795), English horseman.]

tat·ting (tăt′ĭng) *n.* **1.** Handmade lace fashioned by looping and knotting a single strand of strong thread on a small hand shuttle. **2.** The act or art of making tatting. [Perhaps related to Scottish *tate†,* tuft.]

tat·tle (tăt′l) *v.* **-tled, -tling, -tles.** —*intr.* **1.** To reveal the plans or activities of another by chattering; gossip. **2.** To chatter aimlessly; prate. —*tr.* To reveal through gossiping. —*n.* **1.** Aimless chatter; prattle. **2.** Gossip. [Middle Flemish *tatelen,* to babble (imitative).] —**tat·tling·ly** *adv.*

tat·tler (tăt′lər) *n.* **1.** A person who tattles. **2.** Any of several shore birds related to and resembling the sandpipers and characteristically having a loud call.

tat·tle·tale (tăt′l-tāl′) *n.* A person who tattles on others; talebearer. —*adj.* Revealing; telltale.

tat·too¹ (tă-tōō′) *n., pl.* **-toos. 1.** A signal sounded on a drum or bugle to summon soldiers or sailors to their quarters at night. **2.** A display of military exercises performed as entertainment, especially in the evening. **3.** A continuous even drumming or rapping. —*v.* **tattooed, -tooing, -toos.** —*intr.* To beat out an even rhythm, as with the fingers. —*tr.* To beat or tap rhythmically on. [Obsolete *taptoo,* from Dutch *taptoe,* "the shutting off of the taps" : *tap,* spigot, tap + *toe,* short for *doe toe,* "do to," shut.]

tattoo² *n., pl.* **-toos.** A permanent mark or design made on the skin by a process of pricking and ingraining an indelible pigment or by raising scars. —*tr.v.* **tattooed, -tooing, -toos. 1.** To mark (the skin) with a tattoo. **2.** To form (a mark or design) on the skin by tattooing. [Of Polynesian origin, akin to Tahitian *tatau,* Marquesan *ta-tu.*] —**tat·too·er,** **tat·too·ist** *n.*

tat·ty (tăt′ē) *adj.* **-tier, -tiest.** Shabby, untidy, or ragged, especially in dress or appearance. [16th century (Scottish) : ultimately akin to Old English *tættec,* TATTER.] —**tat·ti·ly** *adv.* —**tat·ti·ness** *n.*

Ta·tum (tā′təm), **Art** (1910–56). U.S. musician. A stylish improviser and soloist, he was an internationally admired jazz pianist in the 1930's, 1940's, and 1950's. His harmonic and rhythmic innovations influenced many other jazz musicians.

tau (tou, tô) *n.* The 19th letter of the Greek alphabet, written T, τ. Transliterated in English as *T, t.* See feature at **alphabet.** [Greek, from Semitic, akin to Hebrew *tāw,* TAV.]

tau cross *n.* A cross in the form of a T. Also called "Saint Anthony's cross."

taught. Past tense and past participle of **teach.**

taunt¹ (tônt) *tr.v.* **taunted, taunting, taunts. 1.** To deride or reproach with contempt; mock; jeer at. **2.** To provoke or incite by taunting: *taunted them into action.* —See Synonyms at **ridicule.** —*n.* A scornful remark or jibe; a jeer. [Perhaps from Old French *tanter, tenter,* to test, tempt, from Latin *temptāre,* to TEMPT.] —**taunt·er** *n.* —**taunt·ing·ly** *adv.*

taunt² *adj.* Unusually tall. Said of a mast. [Origin unknown.]

tau particle *n.* A short-lived elementary particle that together with its associated neutrino is a member of the lepton family.

taupe (tōp) *n.* A brownish gray to dark yellowish brown. [French, "mole," from Latin *talpa†.*] —**taupe** *adj.*

Tau·po (tou′pō). Largest lake in New Zealand, in the center of North Island in the district known as Hot Springs. Set among volcanic mountains, the lake is the hub of a popular resort area.

tau·rine¹ (tôr′īn′) *adj.* Of, pertaining to, or resembling a bull. [Latin *taurīnus,* from *taurus,* bull.]

tau·rine² (tôr′ēn′) *n.* A derivative of the amino acid cysteine, 2-aminoethane sulfonic acid, $C_2H_7NO_3S$, found in bile. [TAUR(O)- (so called because it was first obtained from ox bile) + -INE.]

tauro–, taur– *prefix.* Indicates bull or bovine; for example, **taurocholic, taurine.** [Latin *taurus* and Greek *tauros,* bull.]

tau·ro·cho·lic acid (tôr′ō-kō′lĭk, -kŏl′ĭk) *n.* A crystalline acid, $C_{26}H_{45}NO_7S$, occurring as a constituent of bile. [TAURO- (because it was first obtained from ox bile) + CHOLIC ACID.]

tau·rom·a·chy (tô-rŏm′ə-kē) *n., pl.* **-chies. 1.** Bullfighting. **2.** A bullfight. [Spanish *tauromaquia,* from Greek *tauromakhia* : TAURO- + *makhē,* battle, from *makhesthai,* to fight.]

Tau·rus (tôr′əs) *n.* **1.** A constellation in the Northern Hemisphere near Orion and Aries. **2. a.** The second sign of the **zodiac** (see). Also called "Bull." **b.** One born under this sign. [Middle English, from Latin, bull.] —**Tau·re·an** (tôr′ē-ən) *n. & adj.*

Taurus Mountains. Chain of peaks in southern Turkey, extending *c.* 565 kilometers (350 miles) roughly parallel to the Mediterranean coast of southern Asia Minor. The highest peak is Ala Dag, rising to 3,737 meters (12,251 feet).

taut (tôt) *adj.* **tauter, tautest. 1.** Pulled or drawn tight; not slack. **2.** Strained; tense: *Our nerves are taut.* **3.** Kept in good order and condition; neat and tidy: *a taut ship.* **4.** Strict in form; polished and well-organized: *a taut piece of writing.* —See Synonyms at **stiff.** [Earlier *taught, tought,* Middle English *toght, toht,* probably variant past participle of *togen, towen,* to pull, from Old English *togian.*] —**taut·ly** *adv.* —**taut·ness** *n.*

taut·en (tôt'n) *v.* **-ened, -ening, -ens.** —*tr.* To make taut; stretch tight. —*intr.* To become taut.

tauto-, taut- *prefix.* Indicates same or identical; for example, **tau·tomerism, tautonym.** [Greek *tautos,* identical, from *to auto,* the same (neuter) : *to,* the + *autos,* same.]

tau·tog, tau·taug (tô'tôg', -tŏg', tô-tôg', -tŏg') *n.* A dark-colored edible marine fish, *Tautoga onitis,* of the North American Atlantic coast. Also called "blackfish." [Narraganset *tautauog,* plural of *taut.*]

tau·tol·o·gize (tô-tŏl'ə-jīz') *intr.v.* **-gized, -gizing, -gizes.** To use tautology. —**tau·tol'o·gist** (tô-tŏl'ə-jĭst) *n.*

tau·tol·o·gy (tô-tŏl'ə-jē) *n., pl.* **-gies. 1. a.** Needless repetition of the same sense in different words, as in the statement *Pair off in twos.* **b.** An instance of such repetition. **2.** *Logic.* A statement composed of simpler statements in a fashion that makes it true whether the simpler statements are true or false; for example, *Either it will rain tomorrow or it will not rain tomorrow.* [Late Latin *tautologia,* from Greek, from *tautologos,* repeating the same ideas : TAUTO- + *logos,* saying, word (see -LOGY).] —**tau·to·log·i·cal** (tô'tə-lŏj'ĭ-kəl), **tau·tol·o·gous** (tô-tŏl'ə-gəs) *adj.* —**tau·to·log·i·cal·ly** *adv.*

tau·tom·er·ism (tô-tŏm'ə-rĭz'əm) *n.* Chemical isomerism characterized by relatively easy interconversion of isomeric forms in equilibrium. [TAUTO- + (ISO)MERISM.] —**tau·to·mer** (tô'tə-mər) *n.* —**tau·to·mer·ic** (tô'tə-mĕr'ĭk) *adj.*

tau·to·nym (tô'tə-nĭm') *n.* A taxonomic designation, such as *Gorilla gorilla,* in which the genus and species names are the same. Now used only in zoology. [TAUT(O)- + -ONYM.] —**tau·to·nym·ic** (tô'tə-nĭm'ĭk), **tau·ton·y·mous** (tô-tŏn'ə-məs) *adj.* —**tau·ton·y·my** *n.*

tav, taw (täf, tôf) *n.* The 23rd letter of the Hebrew alphabet, corresponding phonetically to *t* or *th* in English. See feature at **alphabet.** [Hebrew *tāw,* probably "mark," "cross."]

tav·ern (tăv'ərn) *n.* **1.** An establishment licensed to sell alcoholic drinks to be drunk on the premises. **2.** An inn for travelers. [Middle English *taverne,* from Old French, from Latin *taberna,* hut, inn, perhaps from Etruscan. See also **tabernacle.**]

taw[1] (tô) *tr.v.* **tawed, tawing, taws.** To convert (hide) into white leather by mineral tanning, as by soaking in alum and salt. [Middle English *tawen,* Old English *tawian.*] —**taw·er** *n.*

taw[2] *n.* **1.** A large, often fancy marble used for shooting. **2.** A game played with taws. **3.** The line from which a player shoots in marbles. [18th century : origin obscure.]

taw[3] Variant of **tav.**

taw·dry (tô'drē) *adj.* **-drier, -driest.** Gaudy and cheap-looking; vulgarly ornamental. [From *tawdry lace,* short for *Seynt Audries lace,* cheap and gaudy lace sold at fairs in honor of St. Audrey or Etheldrida (died A.D. 679), queen of Northumbria and patron saint of Ely, who died of a throat tumor regarded as punishment for her fondness for laces.] —**taw·dri·ly** *adv.* —**taw·dri·ness** *n.*

taw·ny (tô'nē) *n.* A light brown to brownish orange, like the color of a lion's body. [Middle English *taune, tawny,* from Norman French *taune,* variant of Old French *tane,* tanned, from *taner, tanner,* to TAN.] —**taw·ny** *adj.*

tawny owl *n.* A large common European owl, *Strix aluco,* ranging in color from tawny chestnut brown to grayish white.

tawse, taws (tôz) *n. Scottish.* A leather strap divided at one end into thin strips, used as an instrument of punishment in schools. [Probably originally the plural of obsolete *taw,* leather strip. See **taw** (to dress skins).]

tax (tăks) *n.* **1.** A contribution for the support of a government levied on the income, profits, or property of persons, groups, or businesses or on the cost of goods and services. **2.** A fee or due levied on the members of an organization to meet expenses. **3.** A burdensome or excessive demand; a strain: *a tax on his patience.* —*tr.v.* **taxed, taxing, taxes. 1.** To place a tax on (income, property, or goods). **2.** To exact a tax from (a person or organization). **3.** *Law.* To examine and assess (court costs, for example). **4.** To make exacting or excessive demands upon. **5.** To make a charge against; accuse: *He was taxed with hypocrisy.* [Middle English *taxen,* to assess, tax, from Old French *taxer,* from Medieval Latin *taxāre,* from Latin, frequentative of *tangere,* to touch.] —**tax·a·bil·i·ty, tax·a·ble·ness** *n.* —**tax·a·ble** *adj.* —**tax·er** *n.*

tax·a·tion (tăk-sā'shən) *n.* **1. a.** The act or practice of imposing taxes. **b.** The fact of being taxed. **2.** An amount of money levied by taxing.

tax avoidance *n.* The taking of legal measures to reduce one's tax liability.

tax-de·duct·i·ble (tăks'dĭ-dŭk'tə-bəl) *adj.* Exempt from inclusion in one's taxable income so that one's tax liability is reduced. Said especially of an expense incurred in the course of doing business.

tax·eme (tăk'sēm') *n.* A minimal linguistic feature of grammatical arrangement, such as the order or stress of words in a compound or phonemes in a word. [TAX(O)- + (PHON)EME.]

tax evasion *n.* The taking of illegal measures to reduce one's tax liability.

tax-ex·empt (tăks'ĭg-zĕmpt') *adj.* Not subject to taxation, as the capital or income of a philanthropic organization.

tax-free (tăks'frē') *adj.* Tax-exempt. —**tax-free** *adv.*

tax haven *n.* A place that is attractive to companies or individuals because of its relatively low rates of taxation.

tax·i (tăk'sē) *n., pl.* **-is** or **-ies.** A taxicab. ~*v.* **taxied, taxiing** or **taxying, taxies** or **taxis.** —*intr.* **1.** To be transported by taxi. **2.** To move slowly on the ground or on the surface of the water before takeoff or after landing. Used of an aircraft. —*tr.* **1.** To transport or convey in a taxi. **2.** To cause (an aircraft) to taxi. [Short for TAXICAB.]

tax·i·cab (tăk'sē-kăb') *n.* A car that carries passengers for a fare, usually calculated by a taximeter. [TAXI(METER) + CAB.]

taxi dancer *n.* A person, usually a woman, employed by a dance hall or nightclub to dance with the patrons for a fee.

tax·i·der·mist (tăk'sə-dûr'mĭst) *n.* One whose profession is taxidermy.

tax·i·der·my (tăk'sə-dûr'mē) *n.* The art or operation of preparing, stuffing, and mounting the skins of dead animals for exhibition in a lifelike state. [*Taxi-,* variant of TAXO- + -DERM + -Y.] —**tax·i·der·mal** (tăk'sə-dûr'məl), **tax·i·der·mic** (-mĭk) *adj.*

tax·i·me·ter (tăk'sē-mē'tər) *n.* An instrument installed in a taxicab to calculate and indicate the fare. [French *taximètre* : *taxe,* tax, charge, from Old French *taxer,* to TAX + -METER.]

tax·ing (tăk'sĭng) *adj.* Burdensome; wearing. —**tax·ing·ly** *adv.*

tax·i·plane (tăk'sē-plān') *n.* An airplane commercially available for hire.

taxi rank *n. British.* A taxi stand.

tax·is (tăk'sĭs) *n., pl.* **taxes** (tăk'sēz'). **1.** *Biology.* The responsive movement of an entire organism toward or away from an external stimulus. It is not a growth movement. **2.** The moving of an organ, as in a dislocation or hernia, into the normal position by manipulation. [Greek, arrangement, order, from *tattein,* to arrange.]

-taxis, -taxy *suffix.* Indicates: **1.** Order or arrangement; for example, **phyllotaxy. 2.** Movement toward or away from a specified stimulus; for example, **phototaxis.** [New Latin, from Greek *taxis,* arrangement, order.]

taxi stand *n.* An area reserved for taxis waiting for customers.

taxo-, tax-, taxi- *prefix.* Indicates arrangement or order; for example, **taxonomy.** [Greek *taxis,* arrangement, order. See **taxis.**]

tax·on (tăk'sŏn') *n., pl.* **taxa** (tăk'sə). *Biology.* A category or formal unit in taxonomic classification, as a phylum, order, family, genus, or species, characterized by common characteristics in varying degrees of distinction. [Back-formation from TAXONOMY.]

tax·on·o·my (tăk-sŏn'ə-mē) *n. Abbr.* **taxon. 1.** The science, laws, or principles of classification. **2.** *Biology.* The theory, principles, and process of classifying organisms in established categories according to observed similarities or supposed evolutionary relationships. [French *taxonomie* : TAXO- + -NOMY.] —**tax·o·nom·ic** (tăk'sə-nŏm'ĭk), **tax·o·nom·i·cal** (-ĭ-kəl) *adj.* —**tax·o·nom·i·cal·ly** *adv.* —**tax·on·o·mist** (tăk-sŏn'ə-mĭst) *n.* See feature, next page.

tax·pay·er (tăks'pā'ər) *n.* **1.** A person who pays or is legally liable to pay taxes. **2.** A building erected to bring in sufficient income to pay the taxes on the land it occupies.

tax shelter *n.* A financial operation, such as the acquisition of loss-making assets or the use of special depreciation allowances, used as a means to reduce taxes on current earnings.

Tay (tā). Longest river in Scotland, rising on Ben Lui in the Grampian Mts. and flowing for *c.* 190 kilometers (118 miles) through lochs Dochart and Tay and into the North Sea through the Firth of Tay.

Ta·yg·e·ta (tā-ĭj'ĭ-tə). *Greek Mythology.* One of the **Pleiades** (*see*).

Tay·lor (tā'lər), **Elizabeth** (1932–). U.S. actress, born in England. Coming to prominence as a child movie star in *National Velvet* (1944), she developed into a notable actress and received Academy Awards for her performances in *Butterfield 8* (1960) and *Who's Afraid of Virginia Woolf?* (1966). Her highly publicized personal life included two marriages to actor Richard Burton.

Taylor, Jeremy (1613–67). English bishop and theologian. Once the chaplain to Charles I, he produced two classic works of devotional writing, *Rule and Exercises of Holy Living* (1650) and *Rule and Exercises of Holy Dying* (1651), during his tenure as chaplain to the 2nd Earl of Carberry.

Taylor, Zachary (1784–1850). 12th U.S. president (1849–50) and army officer. Nicknamed Old Rough and Ready in recognition of his military actions in the Black Hawk War (1832) and the Battle of Lake Okeechobee against Seminole Indians (1837), he became a national hero in the Mexican War and, although apolitical for most of his life, was elected president in 1848. He died after less than two years in office.

Tay-Sachs disease (tā'săks') *n.* An inherited disorder in which excessive amounts of lipid accumulate in the brain, leading to mental retardation, blindness, convulsions, and early death. [After Warren *Tay* (1843–1927), British physician, and Bernard P. *Sachs* (1858–1944), U.S. neurologist.]

Tay·side (tā'sīd'). Region of eastern Scotland. It was formed in 1975 and includes the former counties of Angus, Perthshire, and Kinross. Dundee is the administrative center.

taz·za (tät'sə) *n.* A shallow vessel, such as a bowl or vase, shaped like a saucer and often mounted on a pedestal. [Italian, probably from Arabic *tassah,* basin. See **tass.**]

HOW ALL LIVING THINGS ARE CLASSIFIED

A system designed to cope with a myriad of different species

The system of classifying living things, called taxonomy, was developed by Carolus Linnaeus, Professor of Medicine at the University of Uppsala, Sweden, from 1741 until 1778. Linnaeus was working at a time when many species were being discovered all over the world by explorers. He divided all living creatures into two kingdoms—Animals and Plants—each with many subdivisions, including phylums, classes, orders, and families.

The name given to a species consists of two words. The first is the generic name: it always starts with a capital letter and is printed in italics (or underlined in handwriting). The second is the specific name, which is italicized but not capitalized. The two together are called the scientific name. The specific name may be an ad-

jective describing some characteristic of the species, such as the dark thrush, *Turdus obscurus.* Or it may be a place name or the name of a person, such as Naumann's thrush, *Turdus naumanni,* named after its discoverer. Common names will not suffice for classifying plants and animals, as an overwhelming number of species have no common names at all.

Since the time of Linnaeus, a great many creatures have been discovered that do not fit into either of the two kingdoms. A third kingdom of Protista is now used to classify viruses, protozoa (which have very small bodies), and other organisms not obviously plants or animals.

Below are examples of classifications for two species, animal and plant—the Siberian tiger and romaine lettuce.

SIBERIAN TIGER

ROMAINE

KINGDOM: Animalia

PHYLUM: Chordata
The chordates are complex, multicellular animals that at some stage in their development have a supporting skeletal rod, or notochord, and gills (human beings have gills in their embryonic stage). In most chordates, a backbone replaces the notochord as they grow.

CLASS: Mammalia
Mammals suckle their young, and all have some hair. Most are born fully developed, and some can walk within minutes of birth.

ORDER: Carnivora
Carnivores eat meat—although some also eat large amounts of vegetable matter—and have teeth adapted for tearing flesh and crushing bones. The collarbone is small, embedded in muscle, and not rigidly fixed, so will not break when the animal leaps on its prey.

FAMILY: Felidae
Cats of all sizes.

GENUS: *Panthera*
The big cats (lion, tiger, panther, jaguar). Linnaeus gave all the cats the same generic name, *Felis.* A refinement of his system has been the addition of more generic names as anatomical differences are better understood; *Panthera* is one of these.

SPECIES: *Panthera tigris*
The tiger. The best simple definition of "species" is that any male could mate with any female of the same species and produce fertile offspring.

SUBSPECIES: *Panthera tigris longipilis*
The Siberian tiger. It has longer hair *(longipilis)* because it lives in a cold climate.

KINGDOM: Plantae

DIVISION: Tracheophyta
Vascular plants, having clearly defined supporting and conductive tissues that carry water and sap. Includes ferns, which reproduce by means of spores, gymnosperms, and flowering plants.

CLASS: Angiospermae
Flowering plants that have seeds contained in an ovary or fruit, compared to Gymnospermae, such as conifers, which have their seeds more exposed.

SUBCLASS: Dicotyledonae
Having two embryonic seed leaves that function at germination. Monocotyledons have only one.

ORDER: Asteridae
Plants with complex flowers and usually fused petals. Includes bellflowers, foxgloves, mints, and composites.

FAMILY: Compositae
The composites have a head, or inflorescence, of flowers that looks like a single flower. This may contain flat-petaled ray flowers or small, tubular disk flowers, or both—as in the daisy. In all flowers the petals are fused into a tube.

GENUS: *Lactuca*
Having a flower head of ray flowers and milky juice in the stem.

SPECIES: *Lactuca sativa*
Cultivated lettuce.

VARIETY: *Lactuca sativa longifolia*
Cultivated lettuce with long leaves (romaine).

Tb The symbol for the element terbium.

TB, T.B. tuberculosis.

Tb. tubercle bacillus.

T-bar lift (tē'bär') *n.* A ski lift consisting of a bar suspended like an inverted T against which skiers lean while being towed uphill.

Tbi·li·si (tə-bē-lē'sē, tə-bĭl'ə-sē). Also **Tif·lis** (tĭf'lĭs). City in the southwestern U.S.S.R., the capital of the Georgian S.S.R., in the basin of the Kura River. It was a Muslim stronghold in the early Middle Ages and after the 13th century was ruled by Mongols, Iranians, and the Ottoman Turks until it passed under Russian control in 1800. It is now the most important commercial, administrative, and cultural center of Transcaucasia.

T-bone (tē'bōn') *n.* A tender steak taken from the small end of the loin and containing a T-shaped bone.

tbs., tbsp. tablespoon; tablespoonful.

Tc The symbol for the element technetium.

TCDD (tē'sē'dē'dē') *n.* **Dioxin** (see).

T cell *n.* A lymphocyte influenced by the thymus that functions in the defense against intracellular pathogens such as viruses and tubercle bacilli.

Tchad. See **Chad.**

Tchai·kov·sky (chī-kôf'skē, -kôv'skē), **Piotr Ilyich** (1840–93). Russian composer. His music, marked by romantic melodies and a freedom of form, includes many orchestral and stage works, such as the *Pathétique* symphony (1893) and the opera *Eugene Onegin* (1879).

td, TD, td. touchdown.

Te The symbol for the element tellurium.

tea (tē) *n.* **1.** A shrub, *Thea sinensis* or *Camellia sinensis,* of eastern Asia, having fragrant white flowers and evergreen leaves. **2.** The dried leaves of the tea plant, prepared by various processes and in various stages of growth. **3.** An aromatic, slightly bitter drink made by steeping tea leaves in boiling water. **4.** Any of various beverages made by steeping the leaves of certain plants or by extracting an infusion, especially of beef. **5.** Any of various plants having leaves used to make a tealike infusion. **6. a.** *Chiefly British.* An afternoon refreshment consisting usually of cookies, sandwiches, or light cakes served with tea. **b.** A social occasion, such as a tea party, at which tea is served. **7.** *Chiefly British.* An evening meal, **high tea** (see). **8.** *Slang.* Marijuana. [Earlier *tay, tee* (probably via Dutch *thee* and Malay *teh*), from Chinese (Amoy) *te,* equivalent of Mandarin *chá.*]

tea bag *n.* A small porous bag holding tea leaves that is dipped into a cup or pot of boiling water to make tea.

tea ball *n.* A small perforated metal ball used for immersing tea leaves in hot water.

tea·ber·ry (tē'bĕr'ē) *n., pl.* **-ries. 1.** A plant, the **wintergreen** (see). **2.** The fruit of the wintergreen.

tea biscuit *n.* Any of various plain cookies or biscuits often served with tea.

tea cake *n. British.* A light, flat, bunlike cake, often with currants, usually toasted and served with butter.

teach (tēch) *v.* **taught** (tôt), **teaching, teaches.** —*tr.* **1.** To impart knowledge or skill to; give instruction to: *taught foreign students on Saturdays.* **2.** To provide knowledge of or instruction in, as by giving formal lessons: *taught Latin at a local school.* **3. a.** To cause to learn by example or experience. **b.** To cause to appreciate the inadvisability of a particular course of action: *I'll teach him to go against my orders!* **4.** To advocate; preach: *a religion that teaches forgiveness.* —*intr.* To give instruction, especially as an occupation. [Teach, taught; Middle English *techen, tahte,* Old English *tǣcan, tǣhte* (past tense), *getǣht* (unattested past participle).]

　　Synonyms: *coach, discipline, drill, educate, instruct, school, train, tutor.*

Teach (tēch), **Edward,** known as "Blackbeard" (died 1718). English pirate. Among the world's most notorious pirates, he established a base on the North Carolina coast (1718), engaged in acts of piracy off the coast of the Colonies and in the Caribbean, and was killed during a battle with a British naval force.

teach·a·ble (tē'chə-bəl) *adj.* Capable of or receptive to being taught. —**teach·a·bil·i·ty, teach·a·ble·ness** *n.* —**teach·a·bly** *adv.*

teach·er (tē'chər) *n.* One who teaches; especially, a person who is employed to teach.

tea chest *n.* A large, lined box made of a light wood, used for transporting tea.

teach-in (tēch'ĭn') *n.* An extended critical discussion of an important topical issue, typically one held in a college or university with the participation of students, lecturers, and guest speakers.

teach·ing (tē'chĭng) *n.* **1.** The work or occupation of teachers. **2.** A precept or doctrine.

teaching aid *n.* Something, such as a film strip, tape recorder, or wall chart, that helps a teacher to convey information.

teaching fellow *n.* A postgraduate student who holds a fellowship that provides financial aid in exchange for some teaching duties. —**teaching fellowship** *n.*

teaching hospital *n.* A hospital associated with a medical school that provides medical students with practical experience.

teaching machine *n.* Any of various devices designed to teach by presenting the student with a planned sequence of statements and questions and providing an immediate response to the answers.

tea cozy *n.* A **cozy** (see).

tea·cup (tē'kŭp') *n.* A small cup for serving tea.

tea·cup·ful (tē'kŭp'fool') *n., pl.* **-fuls.** The amount that a teacup will hold.

tea dance *n.* A late-afternoon dance.

tea garden *n.* A garden open to the public where tea and light refreshments may be served to customers.
tea·house (tē′hous′) *n.* A public establishment, especially in the Far East, serving tea and other refreshments.
teak (tēk) *n.* **1. a.** A tall evergreen tree, *Tectona grandis,* of southeastern Asia, having hard, heavy, durable wood. **b.** The yellowish-brown hard wood of this tree, used for furniture and in shipbuilding. **2.** A yellowish brown or grayish to moderate brown. [Portuguese *teca,* from Malayalam *tēkka.*] **—teak** *adj.*
tea·ket·tle (tē′kĕt′l) *n.* A kettle, usually with a spout, used for boiling water for tea.
teal (tēl) *n., pl.* **teals** or collectively **teal. 1.** Any of several small, widely distributed river ducks of the genus *Anas,* many of which have brightly marked plumage; especially, *A. crecca,* the male of which has a chestnut-colored head with a distinctive green eye-stripe. **2.** A moderate or dark bluish green to greenish blue. In this sense, also called "teal blue." [Middle English *tele,* akin to Middle Dutch *talinc,* Middle Low German *telink*†.] **—teal** *adj.*
team (tēm) *n.* **1.** A group of players making up one of the sides in a game or contest. **2.** A group organized to work together: *a team of medical experts.* **3. a.** Two or more draft animals harnessed to a single vehicle or farm implement. **b.** The vehicle or implement along with the animal or animals harnessed to it. **4.** A group of animals exhibited or performing together, as horses at an equestrian show. **5.** A brood or flock. **6.** *Obsolete.* Offspring; lineage.
~v. **teamed, teaming, teams.** *—tr.* **1.** To harness or join together so as to form a team. **2.** To bring together with another so as to form a team: *The girls were teamed up with the boys in the spelling bee.* **3.** To transport or haul with a draft team. *—intr.* **1.** To form a team: *The two musicians teamed up as a duo.* **2.** To drive a team or truck. [Middle English *tem(e),* Old English *tēam,* offspring, brood, team of animals.]
team·mate (tēm′māt′) *n.* A fellow member of a team.
team play *n.* **1.** Collective play participated in by the members of a team. **2.** Mutual cooperative effort. **—team player** *n.*
team·ster (tēm′stər) *n.* **1.** A person who drives a team. **2.** A truck driver.
team·work (tēm′wûrk′) *n.* Cooperative effort by the members of a team to achieve a common goal.
tea party *n.* A social gathering, usually in the afternoon, at which tea is served.
tea·pot (tē′pŏt′) *n.* A covered pot with a spout in which tea is steeped and from which it is served.
tea·poy (tē′poi′) *n.* A small, usually three-legged table, especially one on which tea is served. [Alteration (influenced by TEA) of Hindi *tipāī* : Hindi *tīn,* three, from Sanskrit *tri* + Middle Persian *pāī,* foot.]
tear¹ (târ) *v.* **tore** (tôr, tōr), **torn** (tôrn, tōrn), **tearing, tears.** *—tr.* **1.** To pull apart or into pieces, especially so as to leave jagged or irregular edges; rend. **2.** To make (an opening) by ripping. **3.** To lacerate (one's skin, for example). **4.** To extract or separate forcefully; wrench: *tore the wrapping off the package.* **5.** To divide; disunite: *torn between conflicting choices.* *—intr.* **1.** To become torn. **2.** To move with heedless speed; rush headlong: *tore up the stairs to see what was wrong.* **—tear down. 1.** To demolish or destroy: *tear down slums.* **2.** To take apart; disassemble. **—tear into.** To attack with great violence or vigor: *tore into his arguments.* **—tear off.** To produce hurriedly and casually. **—tear up. 1.** To make an opening in: *tore up the tile floor to install a new drain.* **2.** To cancel or annul by or as if by tearing: *tore up their agreement.*
~n. **1.** An act of tearing. **2.** The result of tearing; a rip or rent. **3.** A great rush; a hurry. [Tear, tore, torn; Middle English *teren, tore* (earlier *taar*), *toren,* Old English *teran, tær, toren.*]
Synonyms: *cleave, rend, rip, sever, slash, slit, split.*
tear² (tîr) *n.* **1.** A drop of the clear saline liquid that is secreted by the lachrymal gland of the eye, often as a result of a strong emotion such as grief or joy, and that lubricates the surface between the eyeball and the eyelid. **2.** A drop of any liquid or hardened fluid. **3. tears.** The act of weeping: *We were bored to tears. The farewell party left her in tears.* **—without tears.** Presented so as to be easily absorbed or learned: *French without tears.*
~intr.v. **teared, tearing, tears.** To fill with tears: *My eyes always tear when I peel onions.* [Middle English *tere, tear,* Old English *tēar, tehher.*]
tear·a·way (târ′ə-wā′) *n. British.* A rash, impetuous youth.
~adj. British. Of or like a tearaway; rash and impetuous.
tear·drop (tîr′drŏp′) *n.* **1.** A single tear. **2.** Something in the shape of a tear.
tear duct (tîr) *n.* A **lachrymal duct** *(see).*
tear fault (târ) *n.* A **strike-slip fault** *(see).*
tear·ful (tîr′fəl) *adj.* **1.** Filled or accompanied by tears: *gave us a tearful account of her marriage.* **2.** So piteous as to cause tears; pathetic. **—tear·ful·ly** *adv.* **—tear·ful·ness** *n.*
tear gas (tîr) *n.* Any of various vapors that on dispersal, usually from grenades or projectiles, irritate the eyes and cause blinding tears. Also called "lachrymator."
tear·ing (târ′ĭng) *adj.* Reckless, rash, or impetuous: *left the house in a tearing hurry.*
tear-jerk·er (tîr′jûr′kər) *n. Slang.* A grossly pathetic story, drama, performance, or song that is liable to provoke sentimental tears. **—tear-jerk·ing** *adj.*
tea·room (tē′rōōm′, -rŏŏm′) *n.* A restaurant or shop serving tea and other refreshments. Also called "teashop."

tea rose *n.* **1.** Any of several cultivated roses derived from *Rosa odorata* and having fragrant, tea-scented yellowish or pink flowers. **2.** A pale to strong yellowish pink. **—tea-rose** (tē′rōz′) *adj.*
tear sheet (târ) *n.* A page, often perforated, that is designed to be detached easily from a newspaper or periodical.
Teas·dale (tēz′dāl′), **Sara** (1884–1933). U.S. poet. In her classically styled and straightforward works, she displayed consistent literary growth and deepening sensitivity toward her subject matter. Her collection entitled *Love Songs* (1918) won the Columbia University Poetry Society prize.
tea·shop (tē′shŏp′) *n.* A tearoom.
tease (tēz) *v.* **teased, teasing, teases.** *—tr.* **1.** To annoy by persistent pestering; bother. **2.** To make fun of; playfully mock. **3.** To arouse hope, curiosity, or desire in without affording satisfaction: *teased the dog by holding the bone just beyond his reach.* **4.** To cut (body tissue, for example) into pieces for microscopic examination. **5.** To disentangle and dress the fibers of (wool, for example). **6.** To raise the nap of (cloth) by dressing, as with a fuller's teasel. **7. a.** To coax; importune. **b.** To gain or achieve by persistent coaxing. **8.** To backcomb (the hair). *—intr.* To annoy or make fun of someone persistently.
~n. **1.** The act of teasing. **2.** One that teases, as: **a.** One given to playful mocking. **b.** A coquettish woman. **c.** A preliminary remark or action intended to whet the curiosity. [Middle English *tesen, teesen,* to card (wool), tear apart, Old English *tǣsan,* from West Germanic *taisjan* (unattested).] **—teas·ing·ly** *adv.*
tea·sel (tē′zəl) *n.* **1.** Any of several plants of the genus *Dipsacus,* native to the Old World, having thistlelike flowers surrounded by prickly bracts. **2. a.** The bristly flower head of *D. fullonum,* used to produce a napped surface on fabrics. **b.** A wire device used for the same purpose.
~tr.v. **teaseled** or **-selled, -seling** or **-selling, -sels.** To produce a napped surface on (a fabric). [Middle English *tesel, tasel,* Old English *tǣsel,* from West Germanic *taisilā* (unattested), from *taisjan* (unattested), to card, TEASE.] **—tea·sel·er** *n.*
teas·er (tē′zər) *n.* **1.** A person who teases. **2.** *Informal.* A problem or puzzle: *a brain teaser.*
tea service *n.* A set of articles, such as matching cups, saucers, and teapot, used in serving tea.
tea·spoon (tē′spōōn′) *n.* **1.** A small spoon used especially with tea, coffee, and desserts. **2.** *Abbr.* **t., tsp. a.** A household cooking measure equal to approximately 1/3 tablespoon or 13 milliliters. **b.** A teaspoonful.
tea·spoon·ful (tē′spōōn′fŏŏl′) *n., pl.* **-fuls.** *Abbr.* **t., tsp.** The amount that a teaspoon will hold.
teat (tēt, tĭt) *n.* **1.** A mammary gland or nipple. **2.** A rubber nipple on a nursing bottle. [Middle English *tet(t)e,* from Old French, from West Germanic *titta* (unattested), TIT.]
tea towel *n. British.* A dish towel.
tea tree *n.* Any of various Australian trees of the genus *Leptospermum,* the leaves of which were formerly used as a tea substitute.
tea trolley *n. British.* A tea wagon.
tea wagon *n.* A small table on wheels for serving tea or holding dishes.
Tebet, Tebeth. Variants of **Tevet.**
tech. **1.** technical. **2.** technology.
tech·ne·ti·um (tĕk-nē′shē-əm, -shəm) *n. Symbol* **Tc** A silvery-gray metal, the first synthetically produced element, having 14 isotopes with masses ranging from 92 to 105 and half-lives up to 2.6×10^6 years. It is used as a tracer and to eliminate corrosion in steel. Atomic number 43, melting point 2,200°C, specific gravity 11.50, valences 3, 4, 6, 7. [New Latin, from Greek *tekhnētos,* artificial, from *tekhnē,* art, skill. See **technical.**]
tech·nic (tĕk′nĭk) *n.* **1. techics.** The theory, principles, or study of an art or process, especially an industrial or mechanical one. **2. technics.** Technical details, rules, methods, or the like. **3.** Variant of **technique** (sense 2).
~adj. Technical.
tech·ni·cal (tĕk′nĭ-kəl) *adj. Abbr.* **tech. 1. a.** Of or pertaining to that aspect of an art or science requiring practical, applied, mechanical, or scientific skills or knowledge. **b.** Qualified or skilled in the practical, mechanical, or applied aspect of an art or science: *a technical expert.* **2.** Of, pertaining to, or characteristic of a specialized field or activity: *technical vocabulary.* **3.** Of, pertaining to, or providing knowledge of any of various subjects that involve practical, applied, mechanical, or industrial skills or knowledge: *a technical school.* **4.** Of, pertaining to, or derived from technique: *showed technical mastery but no feeling or imagination.* **5.** Characterized by or based on a rigorously strict interpretation of the rules: *a technical victory.* **6.** According to principle; especially, formal rather than practical: *had a technical advantage.* **7.** *Finance.* Of or designating a market condition in which prices are determined or affected by internal manipulation and speculation rather than by external factors. [Latin *technicus,* from Greek *tekhnikos,* of art or skill, from *tekhnē,* art, skill.] **—tech·ni·cal·ly** *adv.* **—tech·ni·cal·ness** *n.*
tech·ni·cal·i·ty (tĕk′nĭ-kăl′ə-tē) *n., pl.* **-ties. 1.** Something meaningful or relevant only to a specialist: *a legal technicality.* **2.** The condition or quality of being technical.
technical knockout *n. Abbr.* **TKO** In boxing, a victory, with immediate termination of the match, awarded by the referee when it appears that one fighter is in too bad a condition to continue.
tech·ni·cian (tĕk-nĭsh′ən) *n.* An expert in a particular skill or technique, as: **1.** A person whose occupation requires training in spe-

teal *Found throughout the Northern Hemisphere, the teal is a dabbling duck that lives in wetlands and marshes, rarely venturing into open water. It feeds on invertebrates and water plants.*

teasel *A tall plant with a prickly flower head. The spiky green bracts around the flower head are still used to tease, or raise, the nap of new woven cloth such as velour and cashmere.*

PRONUNCIATION KEY

ă, **pat**; ā, **pay**; âr, **care**;
ä, **father, are**; b, **bib**;
ch, **church**; d, **deed**; ĕ, **pet**;
ē, **be**; f, **fife**; g, **gag**; h, **hat**;
hw, **which**; ĭ, **pit**; ī, **pie**;
îr, **pier**; j, **judge**; k, **kick**;
l, **lid, needle**; m, **mum**;
n, **no, sudden**; ng, **thing**;
ŏ, **pot**; ō, **toe**; ô, **paw, for**;
oi, **noise**; ou, **out**; ŏŏ, **book**;
ōō, **boot**; p, **pop**; r, **roar**;
s, **sauce**; sh, **ship, dish**;
t, **tight**; th, **thin, path**;
th, **this, bathe**; ŭ, **cut**; ûr, **fur**;
v, **valve**; w, **with**; y, **yes**;
z, **zebra, size**; zh, **vision**;
ə, **about, item, edible, gallop, circus, peaceful**

IN FOREIGN WORDS:

à, *Fr.* **ami**; œ, *Fr.* **feu**, *Ger.* **schön**; ü, *Fr.* **tu**, *Ger.* **über**;
KH, *Ger.* **ich**, *Scot.* **loch**;
N, *Fr.* **bon**; y′, *Fr.* **Compiègne**

STRESS MARKS:

Primary stress: ′
in·cite′ (ĭn-sīt′)
Secondary stress: ′
in′sight′ (ĭn′sīt′)

cific technical skills and processes: *a lighting technician in a television studio.* **2.** One considered from the point of view of his technical skill as opposed to his originality or imagination: *a boring poet although a fine technician.* [TECHN(IC) + -ICIAN.]

Tech·ni·col·or (tĕk′nĭ-kŭl′ər) *n.* A trademark for a motion-picture color process.

tech·nique (tĕk-nēk′) *n.* Also **tech·nic** (tĕk′nĭk) (for sense 2). **1.** A systematic procedure by which a complex or specialized task is accomplished. **2.** The degree of skill or command of fundamentals exhibited in a performance, especially an artistic performance. [French, "technical," from Greek *tekhnikos.* See **technical.**]

tech·noc·ra·cy (tĕk-nŏk′rə-sē) *n., pl.* **-cies. 1.** A system of organization in which government and industry are controlled by scientific experts or technicians. **2.** A state or country under a technocracy. [Greek *tekhnē,* art, skill (see **technology**) + -CRACY.] —**tech·no·crat** (tĕk′nə-krăt′) *n.* —**tech·no·crat·ic** (tĕk′nə-krăt′ĭk) *adj.*

technol. technology.

tech·no·log·i·cal (tĕk′nə-lŏj′ĭ-kəl) *adj.* Also **tech·no·log·ic** (-lŏj′ĭk). **1.** Pertaining to or involving technology, especially scientific technology. **2.** Affected by or resulting from scientific and industrial progress. —**tech·no·log·i·cal·ly** *adv.*

tech·nol·o·gy (tĕk-nŏl′ə-jē) *n., pl.* **-gies.** *Abbr.* **tech., technol. 1. a.** The application of science, especially to industrial or commercial objectives. **b.** The entire body of methods and materials used to achieve such objectives. **2.** *Anthropology.* The body of knowledge available to a civilization that is of use in fashioning implements, practicing manual arts and skills, and extracting or collecting materials: *Iron Age technology.* [Greek *tekhnē,* skill, art + -LOGY.] —**tech·nol·o·gist** (tĕk-nŏl′ə-jĭst) *n.*

techy. Variant of **tetchy.**

tec·ton·ic (tĕk-tŏn′ĭk) *adj.* **1. a.** Pertaining to construction or building. **b.** Architectural. **2.** *Geology.* Pertaining to, causing, or resulting from structural deformation in the earth's crust. [Late Latin *tectonicus,* from Greek *tektonikos,* from *tektōn,* carpenter, builder.]

tec·ton·ics (tĕk-tŏn′ĭks) *n. Used with a singular verb.* **1.** The art or science of construction, especially of large buildings. **2.** The geology of the earth's structural deformation. See **plate tectonics.**

tec·to·ri·al membrane (tĕk-tôr′ē-əl, -tōr′ē-əl) *n.* The membrane covering the organ of Corti in the inner ear. [Latin *tectōrium,* plaster, from *tectōrius,* concerning the use of plaster, from *tectus* (past participle of *tegere,* to cover) + -tōrius.]

tec·trix (tĕk′trĭks) *n., pl.* **-trices** (-trə-sēz′). Any of the coverts of a bird's wing. [New Latin, feminine of Latin *tector,* coverer, from *tegere* (past participle *tectus*), to cover.]

tec·tum (tĕk′təm) *n., pl.* **-ta** (-tə). A rooflike bodily structure, especially the dorsal part of the midbrain. [New Latin, from Latin, roof, from the neuter past participle of *tegere,* to cover.]

Te·cum·seh (tə-kŭm′sə, -sĕ) or **Te·cum·tha** (-thə) (1768–1813). U.S. Shawnee Indian chief. He attempted to establish a pan-Indian confederation to unify Native Americans against white encroachment. Chief Tecumseh sided with the British in the War of 1812, was instrumental in the capture of Detroit (1812), and was killed in the Battle of the Thames (1813).

ted (tĕd) *tr.v.* **tedded, tedding, teds.** To strew or spread (newly mown grass, for example) for drying. [Middle English *tedden* (attested only in the gerund *teddyng*), from Old Norse *tedhja,* to spread dung, from *tadh,* spread dung.] —**ted·der** *n.*

ted·dy (tĕd′ē) *n., pl.* **-dies.** A woman's undergarment consisting of a camisole top and loose-fitting panties. [Origin unknown.]

teddy bear *n.* A child's toy bear, usually stuffed with soft material and covered with furlike material. [After President *Theodore* Roosevelt, once depicted in a cartoon as having spared the life of a bear cub on a hunting trip.]

Ted·dy boy (tĕd′ē) *n.* In Britain, especially during the 1950's, one of a group of tough youths affecting a modified style of Edwardian dress and often having swept-back hair and long sideburns. [From *Teddy,* nickname for Edward.]

Te De·um (tā dā′əm, tē dē′əm) *n.* **1.** A Latin hymn, probably written in the early 5th century A.D., beginning with the words *Te Deum laudamus,* "We praise Thee, O God," sung especially at matins or on special occasions, as a thanksgiving service. **2.** A musical setting of this text.

te·di·ous (tē′dē-əs) *adj.* Tiresome or uninteresting, especially by reason of extreme length or slowness; wearisome; boring; monotonous: *a tedious music lesson.* —See Synonyms at **boring.** [Middle English, from Old French *tedieus,* from Late Latin *taediōsus,* from Latin *taedium,* TEDIUM.] —**te·di·ous·ly** *adv.* —**te·di·ous·ness** *n.*

te·di·um (tē′dē-əm) *n.* **1.** The quality of being wearisome or monotonous; tediousness. **2.** The state of being bored; boredom; ennui. [Latin *taedium,* from *taedēre†,* to bore, weary.]

tee¹ (tē) *n.* **1.** The letter *t.* **2.** Something shaped like a capital T, as a T-shaped pipe connection.

tee² *n.* **1.** A small peg with a concave top on which a golf ball is placed for an initial drive. **2.** The area at the beginning of each hole from which a golfer makes his first stroke.

~*tr.v.* **teed, teeing, tees.** To place (a golf ball) on a tee. —**tee off. 1.** To drive a golf ball from the tee. **2.** *Slang.* To start; begin: *They teed off the fund-raising campaign with a toast.* **3.** *Slang.* To make or become angry: *What you just said really tees me off.* —**tee up.** To place or set up a golf ball for driving. [Earlier *teaz†.*]

tee³ *n.* A mark aimed at in certain games, such as curling or quoits. —**to a tee.** Perfectly; exactly. [Perhaps such marks were originally T-shaped.]

teehee. Variant of **tehee.**

teem¹ (tēm) *v.* **teemed, teeming, teems.** —*intr.* **1. a.** To be full and often in motion; abound or swarm: *A drop of water teems with microorganisms.* **b.** To exist in great quantity; be abundant: *Her mind teems with ideas.* **2.** *Obsolete.* To produce young. —*tr. Archaic.* To give birth to; bear; produce. [Middle English *temen, teamen,* to give birth to, breed, Old English *tīeman, tȳman.*] —**teem·er** *n.*

teem² *v.* **teemed, teeming, teems.** —*intr.* To flow or pour in great quantity. Used chiefly of rain. —*tr.* To pour out; empty: *teemed molten ore into a huge mold.* [Middle English *temen,* from Old Norse *tōma,* to empty, from Germanic *tōm-,* empty (unattested).]

teen¹ (tēn) *n.* A teenager.

~*adj.* Teenage.

teen² *n. Archaic.* Injury; grief. [Middle English *tene, teone,* Old English *tēona.*]

-teen *suffix.* Used in the names of the cardinal numbers **thirteen** to **nineteen.** [Middle English *-tene,* Old English *-tēne, -tȳne.*]

teen·age, teen-age (tēn′āj′) *adj.* Also **teen-aged** (-ājd′). Of, pertaining to, or designating a teenager or teenagers.

teen·ag·er, teen-ag·er (tēn′ā′jər) *n.* A person between the ages of 13 and 19 inclusive. —See Synonyms at **young.**

teens (tēnz) *pl.n.* **1.** The numbers that end in *-teen.* **2.** The years of one's age between 13 and 19 inclusive.

tee·ny (tē′nē) *adj.* **-nier, -niest.** Also **teen·sy** (tēn′sē), **-sier, -siest.** Tiny. [Alteration of TINY.]

teen·y·bop·per (tē′nē-bŏp′ər) *n. Informal.* A girl in early adolescence who is an avid follower of contemporary fashions and tastes, especially in matters of pop music and clothes. Also called "bopper." [TEEN(AGE) + BOP (music).]

teepee. Variant of **tepee.**

tee shirt. Variant of **T-shirt.**

Tees (tēz). River in northeastern England, rising in the northern Pennines and flowing for *c.* 110 kilometers (70 miles) into the North Sea.

tee·ter (tē′tər) *intr.v.* **-tered, -tering, -ters. 1.** To walk or move unsteadily or unsurely; totter. **2.** To be in a precarious position or condition: *teetering on the brink of disaster.* **3.** To waver; vacillate.

~*n.* A seesaw *(see).* [Earlier *titter,* from Middle English *titeren,* probably from Old Norse *titra,* to tremble.]

tee·ter-tot·ter (tē′tər-tŏt′ər) *n.* A seesaw *(see).*

teeth (tēth) *pl.n.* **1.** Plural of **tooth. 2.** Power; force: *The law lacks teeth.* —**cut one's teeth on.** To gain one's first experience with; begin with. —**get one's teeth into.** To become actively involved in or get a firm grasp of. —**in the teeth of. 1.** Directly and forcefully against. **2.** In defiance of. —**kick in the teeth.** To treat with utter disrespect and callousness. —**lie in one's teeth.** To lie directly to or as if to someone's face. —**set someone's teeth on edge.** To grate or jar against the sensibilities of; produce an acutely unpleasant sensation in. —**show one's teeth.** To show a readiness to fight. —**to the teeth.** To the fullest extent; completely: *armed to the teeth.*

teethe (tēth) *intr.v.* **teethed, teething, teethes.** To grow teeth; cut one's teeth in infancy. [Middle English *tethen,* from *tethe,* **tooth.**]

teething ring *n.* A ring of hard rubber or plastic upon which a baby can bite while teething.

tee·to·tal (tē′tōt′l) *adj.* **1.** Of, practicing, or advocating total abstinence from alcoholic liquors. **2.** Complete; entire. [TEE (first letter in TOTAL) + TOTAL.]

tee·to·tal·er, tee·to·tal·ler (tē′tōt′l-ər) *n.* A person who abstains completely from alcoholic liquors. [Probably from TEETOTAL (AB-STAIN)ER.]

tee·to·tum (tē′tō′təm) *n.* A top spun with the fingers that usually has four lettered sides and is used in games of chance. [Earlier *T-totum,* from the letter *T* inscribed on one of the four sides, standing for Latin *tōtum,* all, and signifying "take all."]

teff, tef, t'ef (tĕf) *n.* A cereal, *Eragrostis abyssinica,* widely grown in Ethiopia for grain and in certain other countries for fodder. [Amharic *tēf.*]

Tef·lon (tĕf′lŏn′) *n.* A trademark for a waxy, opaque material, polytetrafluoroethylene, used as a coating on cooking utensils and in industrial applications to prevent sticking.

teg (tĕg) *n. British.* A sheep in its second year. [Origin unknown.]

teg·men (tĕg′mən) *n., pl.* **-mina** (-mə-nə). *Biology.* A covering or integument, such as the tough, leathery forewing of certain insects or the inner coat of a seed. [New Latin, from Latin, covering, from *tegere,* to cover.]

te·gua (tā′gwə, tā′wə) *n.* An ankle-high moccasin worn by Mexicans and Indians. [Native word in Mexico.]

Te·gu·ci·gal·pa (tā-gōō′sē-gäl′pə). Capital and largest city of Honduras, in the south-central mountain region on the Choluteca River.

teg·u·lar (tĕg′yə-lər) *adj.* Also **teg·u·lat·ed** (-lā′tĭd). **1.** Pertaining to, arranged like, or resembling a tile. **2.** Overlapping; imbricate: *tegular scales.* [From Latin *tēgula,* tile, from *tegere,* to cover.] —**teg·u·lar·ly** *adv.*

teg·u·ment (tĕg′yə-mənt) *n.* An outer covering; an integument. [Middle English, from Latin *tegumentum,* from *tegere,* to cover.] —**teg·u·men·ta·ry** (tĕg′yə-mĕn′tə-rē), **teg·u·men·tal** (-mĕnt′l) *adj.*

te·hee, tee-hee (tē′hē′) *interj.* Used to express giggling, often mocking laughter.

~*intr.v.* **-heed, -heeing, -hees.** To laugh in a giggling, often mocking way; titter. [Middle English, imitative.]

Teh·ran (tā-rän′, -răn′). Also **Te·he·ran** (tā′ə-rän′, -răn′). Capital of

Iran, in the northern part of the country near Mt. Damavand. It is Iran's largest city and most important industrial and commercial center. It became the capital of Persia in 1788.

Te·huan·te·pec, Isthmus of (tə-wän'tə-pĕk'). The narrowest section of southern Mexico, *c.* 200 kilometers (125 miles) wide. It lies between the Gulf of Mexico and an arm of the Pacific Ocean.

Teil·hard de Char·din (tā-yär' də shär-dăN'), **Pierre** (1881–1955). French Jesuit theologian who maintained that the universe and mankind are in constant evolution toward a perfect state. He also made valuable contributions in the field of paleontology.

Tejo. See **Tagus.**

tek·tite (tĕk'tīt') *n.* A dark brown to green glassy mass, about 3/4 inch (20 millimeters) in diameter, that is composed largely of silica, is found in various parts of the world and on the moon, and is thought to have formed when a meteorite hit the ground. [Greek *tēktos,* molten (from *tēkein,* to melt) + -ITE.]

tel. 1. telegram; telegraph; telegraphic. **2.** telephone.

te·la (tē'lə) *n., pl.* **-lae** (-lē'). A weblike membrane that covers a portion of a bodily organ. [New Latin, from Latin *tēla,* web.]

telaesthesia. Variant of **telesthesia.**

tel·a·mon (tĕl'ə-mŏn') *n., pl.* **telamones** (tĕl'ə-mō'nēz). *Architecture.* A figure of a man used as a supporting pillar. Compare **caryatid.** [Latin, from Greek *telamōn,* bearer.]

tel·an·gi·ec·ta·sia (tĕl-ăn'jē-ĕk-tā'zhə) *n.* Also **tel·an·gi·ec·ta·sis** (-ĕk'tə-sĭs). A chronic dilation of groups of capillaries of the blood vascular system causing dark-red blotches on the skin. [New Latin : TEL(O)- (end) + Greek *angos,* vessel (see **angiology**) + *ectasis,* dilation, from Greek *ektasis,* expansion, stretching, from *ekteinein,* to stretch out : *ek-,* from *ex,* out + *teinein,* to stretch.] **—tel·an·gi·ec·tat·ic** (tĕl-ăn'jē-ĕk-tăt'ĭk) *adj.*

Tel A·viv–Jaf·fa (tĕl' ə-vēv'jăf'ə). Largest city in Israel, in the central part of the country on the Mediterranean coast. It is both a leading resort and the most important industrial and commercial city in the country. Jaffa is an ancient Phoenician city; Tel Aviv was founded in 1909 by Jews who wished to escape from Arab-dominated Jaffa. The two cities were merged in 1950.

tele–, tel– *prefix.* Indicates: **1.** Distance; for example, **telecommunication, telesthesia. 2.** Television; for example, **telecast.** [Greek *tēle,* at a distance, far off.]

tel·e·cast (tĕl'ə-kăst', -käst') *v.* **-cast** or **-casted, -casting, -casts.** *—intr.* To broadcast by television. *—tr.* To broadcast (a program) by television.
~n. A television broadcast. [TELE- (television) + (BROAD)CAST.] **—tel·e·cast·er** *n.*

tel·e·com·mu·ni·ca·tion (tĕl'ə-kə-myōō'nĭ-kā'shən) *n.* **1.** *Often* **telecommunications.** *Used with a singular verb.* The science and technology of communication by electronic transmission of impulses, as by telegraphy, cable, telephony, radio, or television. **2.** A message transmitted by telecommunication.

tel·e·du (tĕl'ə-dōō') *n.* A brownish-black carnivorous mammal, *Mydaus javanensis,* of southeastern Asia, that is capable of emitting an offensive odor. Also called "stinking badger." [Malay *tĕledu.*]

teleg. telegram; telegraph; telegraphic; telegraphy.

tel·e·gen·ic (tĕl'ə-jĕn'ĭk) *adj.* Presenting a pleasing appearance on television. [TELE- + (PHOTO)GENIC.]

te·leg·o·ny (tə-lĕg'ə-nē) *n.* The supposed influence of one sire on offspring sired by subsequent males on the same female. [TELE- (distance) + -GONY.] **—tel·e·gon·ic** (tĕl'ə-gŏn'ĭk), **te·leg·o·nous** (tə-lĕg'ə-nəs) *adj.*

tel·e·gram (tĕl'ə-grăm') *n. Abbr.* **tel., teleg.** A communication transmitted by telegraph. [TELE- + -GRAM.]

tel·e·graph (tĕl'ə-grăf', -gräf') *n. Abbr.* **tel., teleg. 1.** A communication system that transmits and receives simple unmodulated electric impulses, especially one in which the transmission and reception stations are directly connected by wires. **2.** A telegram.
~v. **telegraphed, -graphing, -graphs.** *—tr.* **1. a.** To transmit (a message) by telegraph. **b.** To send by means of a telegraphic message: *asked his bank to telegraph some money.* **2.** To send or convey a message to (a person) by telegraph. **3.** To make known in advance or unintentionally, as by a sign; especially, to make (an intended action, such as a pass) obvious to an opponent. *—intr.* To send or transmit a telegram. [TELE- + -GRAPH.] **—te·leg·ra·pher** (tə-lĕg'rə-fər), **te·leg·ra·phist** (-fĭst) *n.*

tel·e·graph·ese (tĕl'ə-gră-fēz', -ēs', -grä-fēz', -fēs') *n. Informal.* Language or speech that excludes all but the essential words to convey meaning.

tel·e·graph·ic (tĕl'ə-grăf'ĭk) *adj.* **1.** *Abbr.* **tel., teleg.** Pertaining to or transmitted by telegraph. **2.** Brief or concise, as the wording of a telegram typically is. **—tel·e·graph·i·cal·ly** *adv.*

telegraph plant *n.* A tropical Asian plant, *Desmodium gyrans,* having trifoliolate compound leaves, of which the lateral leaflets move or rotate.

te·leg·ra·phy (tə-lĕg'rə-fē) *n. Abbr.* **teleg.** The process of operating or act of using a telegraph system.

Telegu. Variant of **Telugu.**

tel·e·ki·ne·sis (tĕl'ə-kĭ-nē'sĭs, -kī-nē'sĭs) *n.* **1.** The movement of objects by scientifically unknown or inexplicable means, as by the exercise of mystical powers. **2.** The ability to produce telekinesis. [New Latin : TELE- + -KINESIS.] **—tel·e·ki·net·ic** (tĕl'ə-kĭ-nĕt'ĭk, -kī-nĕt'ĭk) *adj.*

Te·lem·a·chus (tə-lĕm'ə-kəs). In Homer, the son of Odysseus and Penelope who helped his father kill Penelope's suitors.

Te·le·mann (tā'lə-män'), **Georg Philipp** (1681–1767). German composer. Certainly one of the most prolific composers ever, he produced approximately 600 orchestral suites, 40 operas, and countless pieces of chamber music. His music occasionally lacks depth and had only minimal influence on other composers, but it has recently experienced renewed popularity.

tel·e·mark, Tel·e·mark (tĕl'ə-märk') *n.* A turn or stop in skiing executed by shifting the weight forward on the ski that will be on the outside of the turn and pulling its tip gradually inward. [Norwegian, after *Telemark,* region in southern Norway.]

te·lem·e·ter (tə-lĕm'ə-tər, tĕl'ə-mē'-) *n.* Any of various devices used in telemetry.
~tr.v. **telemetered, -tering, -ters.** To measure and transmit (data) automatically from a distant source, as from a spacecraft or electric power grid, to a receiving station for recording or display. [TELE- + -METER.]

te·lem·e·try (tə-lĕm'ə-trē) *n.* The science and technology of automatic measurement and transmission of data by wire, radio, or other means from remote sources, as from space vehicles, to a receiving station for recording and analysis. [TELE- + -METRY.] **—tel·e·met·ric** (tĕl'ə-mĕt'rĭk), **tel·e·met·ri·cal** (-rĭ-kəl) *adj.* **—tel·e·met·ri·cal·ly** *adv.*

tel·en·ceph·a·lon (tĕl'ĕn-sĕf'ə-lŏn', -lən) *n.* The anterior portion of the forebrain, including the cerebral cortex, olfactory lobes, and related parts. Also called "endbrain." [TEL(O)- + ENCEPHALON.] **—tel·en·ce·phal·ic** (tĕl'ĕn-sə-făl'ĭk) *adj.*

tel·e·ol·o·gy (tĕl'ē-ŏl'ə-jē, tē'lē-) *n., pl.* **-gies. 1.** The philosophical study of manifestations of design or purpose in natural processes or occurrences. **2. a.** Such overall purpose or design as is exhibited in natural phenomena. **b.** The doctrine that such overall purpose or design underlies and determines natural processes. [New Latin *teleologia* : Greek *teleos,* complete, from *telos,* completion, end + -LOGY.] **—tel·e·o·log·i·cal** (tĕl'ē-ə-lŏj'ĭ-kəl, tē'lē-), **tel·e·o·log·ic** *adj.* **—tel·e·o·log·i·cal·ly** *adv.* **—tel·e·ol·o·gist** (tĕl'ē-ŏl'ə-jĭst, tē'lē-) *n.*

tel·e·ost (tĕl'ē-ŏst', tē'lē-) *n.* Also **tel·e·os·te·an** (tĕl'ē-ŏs'tē-ən, tē'lē-). A member of the Teleostei (or Teleostomi), a group consisting of fishes having bony skeletons and including the majority of living species. [New Latin *Teleostei,* "ones having complete bony skeletons," and *Teleostomi,* "ones having complete mouths" : Greek *teleos,* complete (see **teleology**) + Greek *osteon,* bone, and *stoma,* mouth (see **stomach**).] **—tel·e·ost, tel·e·os·te·an** *adj.*

te·lep·a·thy (tə-lĕp'ə-thē) *n.* **1.** Transference of thoughts between people by scientifically unknown or inexplicable means. **2.** The ability to produce or engage in such communication. Also called "thought transference." [TELE- + -PATHY.] **—tel·e·path·ic** (tĕl'ə-păth'ĭk) *adj.* **—tel·e·path·i·cal·ly** *adv.* **—te·lep·a·thize** (tə-lĕp'ə-thīz') *v.* **—te·lep·a·thist** (tə-lĕp'ə-thĭst) *n.*

tel·e·phone (tĕl'ə-fōn') *n. Abbr.* **tel. 1.** An instrument that directly modulates carrier waves with voice or other acoustic source signals to be transmitted to distant locations and that directly reconverts received waves into audible signals; especially, such an instrument connected to others by wire. **2.** A system of such instruments together with connecting and supporting equipment.
~v. **telephoned, -phoning, -phones.** *—tr.* **1.** To call or communicate with (a person) by telephone. **2.** To transmit by telephone: *The reporter telephoned his article to the newspaper.* *—intr.* To communicate by telephone. [TELE- + -PHONE.] **—tel·e·phon·er** *n.* **—tel·e·phon·ic** (tĕl'ə-fŏn'ĭk) *adj.* **—tel·e·phon·i·cal·ly** *adv.*

telephone book *n.* A telephone directory.

telephone booth *n.* A small enclosure containing a public telephone.

telephone box *n. British.* A telephone booth.

telephone directory *n.* A book listing alphabetically all the telephone subscribers in a particular area, together with their addresses and telephone numbers. Also called "telephone book."

telephone exchange *n.* Any of numerous central systems of switches and other equipment that establish connections between individual telephones.

telephone number *n.* A set of digits used to identify and call individual subscribers to a telephone system.

telephone receiver *n.* The part of a telephone in which incoming electrical impulses are converted into sound.

te·leph·o·ny (tə-lĕf'ə-nē) *n.* The electrical transmission of sound between distant points, especially by radio or telephone.

tel·e·pho·to (tĕl'ə-fō'tō) *adj.* Of, pertaining to, or designating a photographic lens or lens system used to produce a large image of a distant object.

tel·e·pho·tog·ra·phy (tĕl'ə-fə-tŏg'rə-fē) *n.* **1.** The process or technique of photographing distant objects with a telephoto lens or telescope on a camera. **2.** The technique or process of transmitting charts, pictures, and photographs over a distance. **—tel·e·pho·to·graph·ic** (tĕl'ə-fō'tə-grăf'ĭk) *adj.*

tel·e·play (tĕl'ə-plā') *n.* A play written or adapted for television.

tel·e·print·er (tĕl'ə-prĭn'tər) *n.* A teletypewriter.

Tel·e·Promp·Ter (tĕl'ə-prŏmp'tər) *n.* A trademark for a device used in television to show an actor or speaker an enlarged line-by-line reproduction of a script, unseen by the audience.

tel·e·ran (tĕl'ə-răn') *n.* A system used in air-traffic control in which the image of a ground-based radar unit is televised to aircraft in the vicinity so that a pilot may see his position in relation to other aircraft. [Originally a trademark.]

tel·e·scope (tĕl'ə-skōp') *n.* An instrument for collecting and examining electromagnetic radiation, especially: **1.** An arrangement of lenses or mirrors or both that gathers visible light, permitting direct

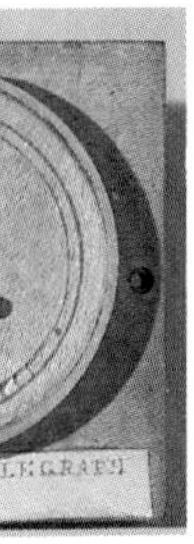

telegraph *The first electric telegraphic receiver (above) had a wooden disk that swung around to expose, letter by letter, the transmitted message. Invented by an Englishman, Francis Ronalds, the device was turned down by the British government in 1816. But the invention of faster equipment in 1837, and of the Morse code a year later, established the electric telegraph as a revolutionary means of communication.*

observation or photographic recording of distant objects. **2.** Any of various devices, such as a radio telescope, used to detect and observe distant objects by their emission, transmission, reflection, or other interaction with invisible radiation.

~*v.* **telescoped, -scoping, -scopes.** —*tr.* **1.** To cause to slide inward or outward in overlapping sections, as the cylindrical sections of a small hand telescope. **2.** To crush or compress inward or together, especially as the result of a collision. **3.** To make shorter or more precise; condense: *He telescoped his speech into a few dramatic phrases.* —*intr.* To slide inward or outward in or as if in overlapping cylindrical sections; become telescoped. [New Latin *telescopium* or Italian *telescopio,* from Greek *teleskopos,* farseeing : TELE- + *skopos,* watcher.]

tel·e·scop·ic (tĕl′ə-skŏp′ĭk) *adj.* **1.** Of or pertaining to a telescope. **2.** Seen through or obtained by means of a telescope. **3.** Visible only by means of a telescope. **4.** Incorporating a telescope: *a telescopic sight.* **5.** Able to discern distant objects; farseeing. **6.** Extensible or compressible by or as if by the successive sliding of overlapping concentric tubular sections: *a telescopic umbrella.* —**tel·e·scop·i·cal·ly** *adv.*

Tel·e·sco·pi·um (tĕl′ə-skō′pē-əm) *n.* A constellation in the Southern Hemisphere near Scorpius and Sagittarius. [New Latin, from *telescopium,* TELESCOPE.]

te·les·co·py (tə-lĕs′kə-pē) *n.* The art or study of making and operating telescopes. —**te·les·co·pist** *n.*

tel·e·spec·tro·scope (tĕl′ə-spĕk′trə-skōp′) *n.* A spectroscope used in conjunction with an astronomical telescope to enable a spectroscopic analysis to be made of radiation from distant stars or other celestial bodies. —**tel·e·spec·tro·scop·ic** (tĕl′ə-spĕk′trə-skŏp′ĭk) *adj.*

tel·e·ster·e·o·scope (tĕl′ə-stĕr′ē-ə-skōp′, -stîr′ē-ə-skōp′) *n.* A binocular telescope for stereoscopic viewing of distant objects.

tel·es·the·sia, tel·aes·the·sia (tĕl′ĭs-thē′zhə, -zhē-ə) *n.* Perception of or response to distant objects or stimuli by extrasensory means. [New Latin : TELE- + Greek *aisthēsis,* perception + -IA.] —**tel·es·thet·ic** (tĕl′ĭs-thĕt′ĭk) *adj.*

tel·e·tex (tĕl′ə-tĕks′) *n.* A system enabling typescript messages, especially those produced by word processors, to be electronically transmitted directly over the telephone system. [TELE- + TEX(T).]

tel·e·text (tĕl′ə-tĕkst′) *n.* **1.** An electronic communication system in which printed information is broadcast by television signal to sets equipped with a decoder. **2.** Information broadcast by teletext.

tel·e·ther·mo·scope (tĕl′ə-thûr′mə-skōp′) *n.* An apparatus for indicating or recording the temperatures of remote locations.

tel·e·thon (tĕl′ə-thŏn′) *n.* A long, continuous television program, usually to raise funds for charity. [TELE- + (MARA)THON.]

Tel·e·type (tĕl′ə-tīp′) *n.* A trademark for a teletypewriter.

tel·e·type·writ·er (tĕl′ə-tīp′rī′tər) *n.* An electromechanical typewriter that transmits and receives messages coded in electrical signals by telegraph or telephone wires. Also called "teleprinter."

te·leu·to·spore (tə-lōō′tə-spôr′, -spōr′) *n.* A teliospore. [Greek *teleutē,* end, from *telos,* end, completion + SPORE.] —**te·leu·to·spor·ic** (tə-lōō′tə-spôr′ĭk, -spōr′ĭk) *adj.*

tel·e·vise (tĕl′ə-vīz′) *v.* **-vised, -vising, -vises.** —*tr.* **1.** To broadcast (a program) by television. **2.** To film (an event) for a television broadcast. —*intr.* To broadcast by television. [Back-formation from TELEVISION.]

tel·e·vi·sion (tĕl′ə-vĭzh′ən) *n. Abbr.* **TV 1.** The transmission of visual images of moving and stationary objects, generally with accompanying sound, as electromagnetic waves and the reconversion of received waves into visual images. **2. a.** An electronic apparatus that receives electromagnetic waves and displays the reconverted images on a screen. **b.** The integrated audible and visible content of the electromagnetic waves received and converted by such an appara-

---

telescope

EXTENDING THE EYE'S VIEW OF THE UNIVERSE

Lenses, mirrors, and electronics focused on the stars

The first telescope about which there is any definite knowledge was made by the Dutch optician Hans Lippershey in 1608. The following year the Italian astronomer Galileo made his own telescope and used it to make a series of spectacular discoveries, including the four main satellites of Jupiter, the phases of Venus, and the numerous stars in the Milky Way.

Telescopes are of two main types: refractors and reflectors. With a refractor, the light is collected by a glass lens, or objective, and brought to focus. There are various drawbacks: to avoid the "false color" caused by the fact that light rays of different wavelengths are brought to different focal points, an objective has to be compound—made up of two parts made of different kinds of glass whose errors counteract each other. Moreover an objective has to be supported around its edge and if too large will distort under its own weight. The world's largest refractor telescope, at the Yerkes Observatory in Williams Bay, Wisconsin, has an objective 1 meter (40 inches) across.

With a reflector, the light is collected by a curved mirror, and

there is no false color problem. Various optical arrangements are in use, and very large mirrors have been made; the largest of all is the 6-meter (236-inch) reflector at Zelenchukskaya in the Caucasus. The largest reflector in full use is at Palomar in California and is 5 meters (200 inches) across. There is also the MMT, or Multi-Mirror Telescope, at Mount Hopkins in Arizona, where six 1.8-meter (72-inch) mirrors are used to bring light to a common focus.

Modern telescopes transfer the signals they receive to film or, in recent years, to electronic devices that are much more sensitive than film. They are also computer-controlled, and a modern observer need not be anywhere near the telescope, or even near the observatory, when carrying out an observational program. Yet the earth's atmosphere blurs images from space and limits the size of telescope that can be used efficiently. The next breakthrough will come with the Space Telescope, a 2.4-meter (94-inch) reflector due to be launched possibly in late 1987 from a space shuttle.

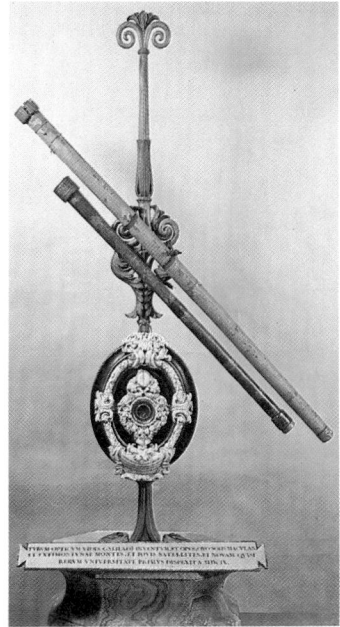

RADIO TELESCOPE *This radio telescope at Cambridge, England, collects the long wavelength electromagnetic radiations from space and records them in the form of a chart marked with an automatic pencil on moving paper.*

EARLY TELESCOPE *Two of Galileo's telescopes are now in the Science Museum in Florence. Small and imperfect though they were (magnifying only 30 times), they enabled Galileo to make observations supporting the theory that the earth moves around the sun. The Church was violently hostile to such a view; Galileo was condemned by the Inquisition and kept a virtual prisoner in his villa until his death in 1642.*

tus. **3.** The industry of broadcasting television programs. [French *télévision* : *télé-*, TELE- + *vision*, VISION.] —**tel·e·vi·sion·ar·y** (tĕl'-ə-vĭzh'ə-nĕr'ē) *adj.*

television tube *n.* A form of cathode-ray tube designed for use in a television receiver. Also called "picture tube."

tel·ex (tĕl'ĕks') *n.* **1.** A communication system consisting of teletypewriters connected to a telephonic network to send and receive signals. **2.** A message sent or received by telex. —*tr.v.* **telexed, -exing, -exes. 1.** To send (a message) by telex. **2.** To communicate with (a person) by telex. [TEL(ETYPEWRITER) + EX(CHANGE).]

telfer. Variant of **telpher.**

tel·ic (tĕl'ĭk, tē'lĭk) *adj.* Directed or tending toward a definite goal or purpose; purposeful. [Greek *telikos*, final, from *telos*, end.]

te·li·o·spore (tē'lē-ə-spôr', -spōr') *n.* A dark, thick-walled spore produced at the end of the summer by rust fungi. It remains dormant through the winter and germinates in the spring. Also called "teleutospore." [TELI(UM) + SPORE.]

te·li·um (tē'lē-əm) *n., pl.* **-lia** (-lē-ə). A dark, pustulelike structure formed on plant tissue infected by a rust fungus and giving rise to teliospores. [New Latin, from Greek *teleios*, complete (formed in the final stage of the cycle of rust fungi), from *telos*, end, completion.] —**te·li·al** *adj.*

tell[1] (tĕl) *v.* **told** (tōld), **telling, tells.** —*tr.* **1.** To give a detailed account of; narrate; recount: *tell a story.* **2.** To communicate by speech or writing; express with words: *tell a lie; told us the news.* **3.** To make something known to; notify; inform: *told the authorities.* **4.** To show, explain, or make clear: *His face told us he wasn't joking. Will you tell me how to work the copier?* **5.** To make known; reveal; disclose: *tell a secret.* **6. a.** To command; order: *Do what I tell you.* **b.** To warn; advise: *I told you that would happen.* **7.** *Informal.* To assure: *I tell you he's an honest man.* Often used for emphasis. **8.** To know or come to know, as through observation or experience; discern: *I can always tell when he's lying.* **9.** To distinguish or recognize; discriminate: *can't tell the difference between margarine and butter.* **10.** *Informal.* To make clear one's low or contemptuous opinion of (someone): *Well, that's certainly telling him!* —*intr.* **1.** To give an account, enumeration, or description. **2.** To give evidence or indication: *Silence told of their unease.* **3. a.** To have an effect or impact: *In this game every move tells.* **b.** To have an exhausting or detrimental effect: *Pressure began to tell on her.* **4.** To reveal the secrets of another: *Promise not to tell!* —**tell off. 1.** To count and set apart, especially aloud. **2.** *Informal.* To rebuke severely; scold. —**tell on.** *Informal.* To inform against; tattle on. —**tell someone where to get off.** *Slang.* To rebuff or correct in an aggressive manner. —**you're telling me.** I know that only too well. Used for emphasis. [Tell, told (past tense), told (past participle); Middle English *tellen, told* (or *tald*), *ytold* (or *ytald*), Old English *tellan, tealde, geteald.*] —**tell·a·ble** *adj.*

tell[2] *n.* A hillock, found especially in the Middle East, formed from the accumulation of debris, earth, or other material on the site of an ancient settlement. [Arabic *tall*, hillock.]

Tell (tĕl), **William.** Swiss hero. According to legend, he was sentenced to shoot an apple off his son's head with a crossbow for an act of disrespect to the Austrian bailiff Gessler. He did so, then shot Gessler. The events supposedly took place *c.* 1300.

tell·er (tĕl'ər) *n.* **1.** One who tells. **2.** A bank employee who deals directly with the public, receiving and paying out money. **3.** A person appointed to count votes, especially in a legislative assembly. —**tell·er·ship** *n.*

Tel·ler (tĕl'ər), **Edward** (1908–). U.S. physicist, born in Hungary. Immigrating to the United States in 1935, he joined the Manhattan Project, the unit of army engineers that produced the atomic bomb, and provided the theoretical groundwork for the hydrogen bomb, developed in 1952. In contrast to most of the scientific community, he advocated continued testing and refinement of nuclear weaponry.

tell·ing (tĕl'ĭng) *adj.* **1.** Having force or effect; striking. **2.** Full of underlying meaning; revealing: *a telling example of their selfishness.* —See Synonyms at **valid.** —**tell·ing·ly** *adv.*

tell·tale (tĕl'tāl') *n.* **1.** One who informs on another person; a tattler; a talebearer. **2.** Anything that provides evidence of something secret or hidden, as of a person's feelings or conduct; a revealing sign. Also used adjectivally: *a telltale blush; the telltale pile of empty wine bottles.* **3.** Any of various devices that indicate or register information, especially: **a.** A time clock for recording an employee's attendance. **b.** A device indicating the position of a ship's rudder. **c.** A compass used by the captain of a ship to check the course.

tel·lu·rate (tĕl'yə-rāt') *n.* A salt or ester of telluric acid.

tel·lu·ri·an (tĕ-lŏŏr'ē-ən) *adj.* Of, pertaining to, or inhabiting the earth. —*n.* **1.** An inhabitant of the earth; a terrestrial. **2.** Variant of **tellurion.** [Latin *tellūs* (stem *tellūr-*), earth.]

tel·lu·ric (tĕ-lŏŏr'ĭk) *adj.* **1.** Of or relating to the earth; earthly; terrestrial. **2.** Derived from or containing tellurium, especially with valence 6. [From Latin *tellūs* (stem *tellūr-*), earth.]

telluric acid *n.* A white, crystalline inorganic acid, H_6TeO_6, that is used as a chemical reagent.

tel·lu·ride (tĕl'yə-rīd') *n.* A binary compound of tellurium. [TELLUR(IUM) + -IDE.]

tel·lu·ri·on (tĕ-lŏŏr'ē-ŏn') *n.* Also **tel·lu·ri·an** (-ən). An instrument that shows how the movement of the earth on its axis and around

television

IMAGES THAT SPAN THE WORLD

Transmitting live pictures in a series of colored lines

Scientists dreamed of "seeing by telegraph" as early as the 1870's, but the first public demonstration of television was by John Logie Baird in London in 1926.

Since 1945 television has proved as significant an invention as printing. Within a generation it has linked every nation with instant worldwide news coverage. It has shown live pictures of moon landings, sports events, and presidential elections. With the rapid advance in satellite transmission and in video and computer technology, its role continues to grow.

Television works by scanning a scene in lines and transmitting them in sequence as radio signals. The lines flash on the receiving screen so fast that the eye sees them as one picture.

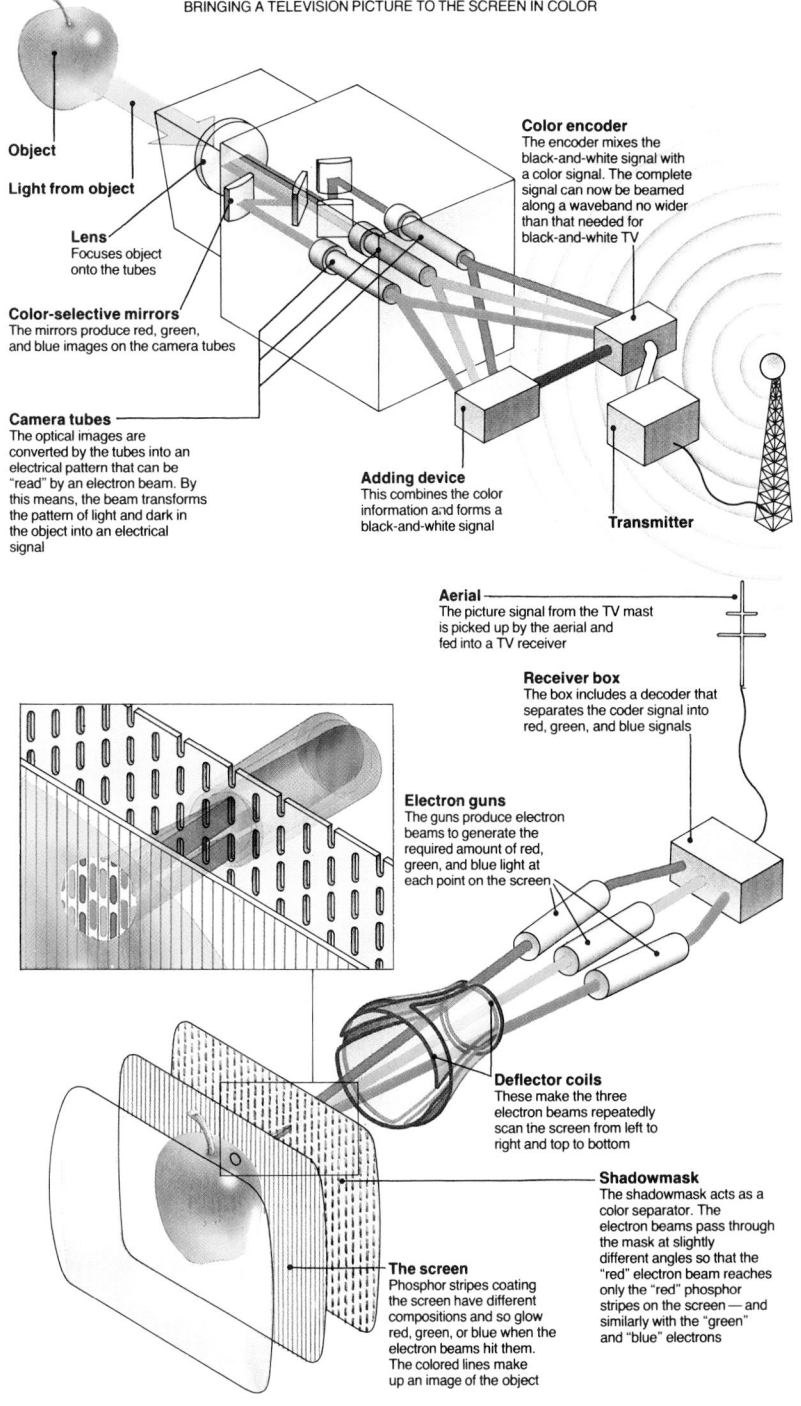

BRINGING A TELEVISION PICTURE TO THE SCREEN IN COLOR

Object

Light from object

Lens
Focuses object onto the tubes

Color-selective mirrors
The mirrors produce red, green, and blue images on the camera tubes

Camera tubes
The optical images are converted by the tubes into an electrical pattern that can be "read" by an electron beam. By this means, the beam transforms the pattern of light and dark in the object into an electrical signal

Adding device
This combines the color information and forms a black-and-white signal

Color encoder
The encoder mixes the black-and-white signal with a color signal. The complete signal can now be beamed along a waveband no wider than that needed for black-and-white TV.

Transmitter

Aerial
The picture signal from the TV mast is picked up by the aerial and fed into a TV receiver

Receiver box
The box includes a decoder that separates the coder signal into red, green, and blue signals

Electron guns
The guns produce electron beams to generate the required amount of red, green, and blue light at each point on the screen

Deflector coils
These make the three electron beams repeatedly scan the screen from left to right and top to bottom

Shadowmask
The shadowmask acts as a color separator. The electron beams pass through the mask at slightly different angles so that the "red" electron beam reaches only the "red" phosphor stripes on the screen — and similarly with the "green" and "blue" electrons

The screen
Phosphor stripes coating the screen have different compositions and so glow red, green, or blue when the electron beams hit them. The colored lines make up an image of the object

COLOR SIGNALS *Light from the scene is broken into its constituent wavelengths (colors), which are coded into radio signals. These are received and reconstituted as separate beams of color. They combine on the screen to reproduce the original scene in a series of lines and dots.*

temple *This Buddhist temple stands on the island of Penang in Malaysia.*

the sun causes day and night and the seasons. [Latin *tellūs* (stem *tellūr-*), earth + -ION.]

tel·lu·ri·um (tĕ-lo͝or'ē-əm) *n. Symbol* **Te** A brittle, silvery-white metallic element, occurring naturally combined with gold and other metals, produced commercially as a by-product of the electrolytic refining of copper, and used to alloy stainless steel and lead, in ceramics, and, in the form of bismuth telluride, in thermoelectric devices. Atomic number 52, atomic weight 127.60, melting point 449.8°C, boiling point 989.8°C, specific-gravity range 6.11–6.27, valences 2, 4, 6. [New Latin, from Latin *tellūs* (stem *tellūr-*), earth (by analogy with URANIUM, after the planet *Uranus*).]

tel·lu·rom·e·ter (tĕl'yə-rŏm'ĭ-tər) *n.* An electronic surveying device used to measure distances of up to 40 miles (64 kilometers) by the transmission of radio waves between two stations set up at the ends of the unknown distance and measurement of the time the waves take to travel between the stations. [Latin *tellūs* (stem *tellūr-*), earth + -METER.]

tel·lu·rous (tĕl'yər-əs, tĕ-lo͝or'əs) *adj.* Of, relating to, or derived from tellurium, especially with valence 4. [TELLUR(IUM) + -OUS.]

tel·ly (tĕl'ē) *n., pl.* **-lies.** *Chiefly British Informal.* Television.

telo–, tel– *prefix.* Indicates: **1.** Completion, perfection, or finality; for example, **telophase. 2.** End or situated at the end; for example, **telencephalon.** [From Greek *telos,* end, completion.]

te·lom·er·i·za·tion (tə-lŏm'ər-ĭ-zā'shən) *n.* The polymerization of a chemical substance in the presence of a chain transfer agent to give products of relatively low molecular weight. [TELO- + (POLY)MERIZATION.]

te·lo·phase (tē'lə-fāz', tĕl'ə-) *n.* The last phase of mitosis and meiosis, in which the daughter chromosomes are grouped either in two diploid daughter cells (mitosis) or four haploid gametes (meiosis). [TELO- + PHASE.]

tel·pher, tel·fer (tĕl'fər) *n.* Also **tel·pher·age** (-fər-ĭj) (for sense 2). **1.** A device for transporting loads consisting of a light car suspended from overhead wire cables and usually driven by electricity. **2.** A transport system using these cars.

~*tr.v.* **telphered, -phering, -phers.** To transport by telpher. [From TEL(E)- + Greek *pherein,* to carry.]

tel·son (tĕl'sən) *n.* A terminal structure of the posterior section of certain arthropods, as the sting of a scorpion or the middle lobe of the tail fin of a lobster or shrimp. [New Latin, from Greek, headland, limit, from *telos,* end.]

Tel·u·gu, Tel·e·gu (tĕl'ə-go͞o') *n., pl.* **-gus** or collectively **Telugu. 1.** A Dravidian language spoken chiefly in Andhra Pradesh, India. **2.** A member of a Dravidian people who speak this language. **—Tel·u·gu** *adj.*

tem·blor (tĕm'blər, -blôr') *n.* An earthquake. [Spanish, from *temblar,* to shake, from Vulgar Latin *tremulāre* (unattested), to TREMBLE.]

tem·er·ar·i·ous (tĕm'ə-râr'ē-əs) *adj.* Presumptuously or recklessly daring; rash. [Latin *temerārius,* rash, from *temere,* rashly. See **temerity.**] **—tem·e·rar·i·ous·ly** *adv.* **—tem·e·rar·i·ous·ness** *n.*

te·mer·i·ty (tə-mĕr'ə-tē) *n.* Foolhardy or heedless disregard of danger; foolish boldness; recklessness; rashness. [Middle English *temeryte,* from Latin *temeritās,* from *temere,* blindly, rashly.]

Synonyms: *audacity, cheek, effrontery, gall, impetuosity, nerve.*

temp (tĕmp) *n. Informal.* A person, such as a typist or secretary, who works on a temporary basis.

~*intr.v.* **temped, temping, temps.** *Informal.* To work as a temp.

temp. 1. in the time of [Latin *tempore*]. **2.** temperature.

Tem·pe, Vale of (tĕm'pē). Valley, *c.* 8 kilometers (5 miles) long, in east-central Greece, between Mt. Olympus and Mt. Ossa. The valley is famous for its rugged grandeur and in ancient times was considered sacred to Apollo.

tem·per (tĕm'pər) *v.* **-pered, -pering, -pers.** —*tr.* **1.** To modify by the addition of a moderating agent or quality; moderate: *tempered severity with kindness.* **2.** To bring to a suitable or desired consistency, texture, hardness, or other physical condition by or as if by blending, admixture, or kneading. **3.** To harden, strengthen, or toughen (a metal) by application of heat or by alternate heating and cooling. **4.** *Music.* To adjust (the pitch of a keyboard instrument) to a temperament. —*intr.* To be or become tempered.

~*n.* **1. a.** A person's habitual state of mind or emotions; disposition: *a sweet temper.* **b.** A temporary state of mind or emotions; mood: *in a foul temper.* **2.** Calmness of mind or emotions; composure: *lost my temper; keep one's temper.* **3. a.** A tendency to become easily angry or irritable: *Control your temper.* **b.** An outburst of rage: *a fit of temper.* **4. a.** The condition of being tempered. **b.** The degree of hardness and elasticity of a metal, chiefly steel, as a result of tempering. **5.** A substance or agent added to something to alter or modify it. **6.** *Archaic.* A middle course; a compromise between extremes. —See Synonyms at **mood.** [Middle English *temp(e)ren,* Old English *temprian,* to mingle, moderate, from Latin *temperāre,* "to mingle in due proportion," probably from *tempus* (stem *tempor-*), time, due season.] **—tem·per·a·bil·i·ty** *n.* **—tem·per·a·ble** *adj.* **—tem·per·er** *n.*

tem·per·a (tĕm'pər-ə) *n.* **1.** A painting medium in which pigment is mixed with water-soluble glutinous materials such as size or egg yolk. **2.** Painting done with tempera. [Italian, from *temperare,* to mingle, temper, from Latin *temperāre.* See **temper.**]

tem·per·a·ment (tĕm'prə-mənt, -pər-ə-mənt) *n.* **1. a.** The manner of thinking, behaving, or reacting characteristic of a particular individual: *a nervous temperament.* **b.** The distinguishing mental and physical characteristics that established the constitution of a person according to medieval physiology, caused by the dominance of one of the four humors. See **humor. 2.** A tendency to become irritable or to be too sensitive. **3.** *Music.* **Equal temperament** *(see).* —See Synonyms at **disposition.** [Middle English *temperament,* from Latin *temperāmentum,* "a mixing (of the humors)," from *temperāre,* to mingle, TEMPER.]

tem·per·a·men·tal (tĕm'prə-mĕnt'l, tĕm'pər-ə-) *adj.* **1.** Of, pertaining to, or arising from temperament or temper. **2.** Excessively sensitive or irritable; easily excited or angered; moody. **3.** Tending to behave or perform in an erratic or unpredictable manner: *a temperamental old car.* **—tem·per·a·men·tal·ly** *adv.*

tem·per·ance (tĕm'pər-əns, tĕm'prəns) *n.* **1.** The condition or quality of being temperate; moderation or self-restraint. **2. a.** Moderation in the consumption of alcoholic liquors. **b.** Total abstinence from alcoholic liquors. —See Synonyms at **abstinence.**

tem·per·ate (tĕm'pər-ĭt, tĕm'prĭt) *adj.* **1.** Exercising moderation and self-restraint, especially with regard to bodily and emotional indulgence: *a temperate drinker.* **2.** Moderate in degree or quality; tempered. **3. a.** Neither hot nor cold in climate; mild. **b.** Occurring in or characteristic of the temperate zone: *temperate vegetation.* [Middle English, from Latin *temperātus,* from the past participle of *temperāre,* to moderate, TEMPER.] **—tem·per·ate·ly** *adv.*

temperate zone *n. Often* **Temperate Zone.** Either of two middle latitude zones of the earth, the *North Temperate Zone* and the *South Temperate Zone,* lying between about 23°30' and 66°30' north and south.

tem·per·a·ture (tĕm'pər-ə-cho͝or', -chər, tĕm'prə-) *n. Abbr.* **temp.** *Symbol* **T 1. a.** The degree of hotness or coldness of a body or environment. **b.** A specific degree of hotness or coldness as indicated on or referred to a standard scale; a scalar quantity that is independent of the size of the system and that determines the direction of heat flow between any two systems in thermal contact. **2.** An abnormally high body temperature caused by illness; fever. [Originally "a tempering," moderate condition (of weather), from Latin *temperātūra,* from *temperāre,* to mix, TEMPER.]

temperature gradient *n.* The rate of change of temperature with displacement in a given direction from a given reference point.

tem·pered (tĕm'pərd) *adj.* **1.** Having a specified type of temper or disposition. Used in combination: *sweet-tempered.* **2.** *Music.* Tuned to temperament; specifically, tuned to equal temperament. Said of a scale, interval, semitone, or intonation. **3.** Having the requisite degree of hardness or elasticity. Said of a metal. **4.** Moderated by the admixture of another substance, quality, or factor.

tem·pest (tĕm'pĭst) *n.* **1.** A violent onrush or storm of wind, frequently accompanied by rain, snow, or hail. **2.** An agitated or tumultuous condition: *battered by the political tempest.*

~*tr.v.* **tempested, -pesting, -pests.** To disturb or agitate violently. [Middle English *tempeste,* from Old French, from Vulgar Latin *tempesta* (unattested), variant of Latin *tempestās,* storm, weather, season, from *tempus,* time, season. See **temporal.**]

tem·pes·tu·ous (tĕm-pĕs'cho͞o-əs) *adj.* **1.** Pertaining to, characterized by, or resembling a tempest: *tempestuous weather.* **2.** Tumultuous; turbulent: *a tempestuous marriage.* **—tem·pes·tu·ous·ly** *adv.* **—tem·pes·tu·ous·ness** *n.*

Tem·plar (tĕm'plər) *n.* **1.** A **Knight Templar** *(see).* **2. templar.** *British.* A barrister having chambers in the Middle or Lower Temple in London. [Middle English *templer,* from Norman French, variant of Old French *templier,* from Medieval Latin *(mīles) templāri(u)s,* "(soldier) of the temple," from Latin *templum,* TEMPLE.]

tem·plate, tem·plet (tĕm'plĭt) *n.* **1.** A pattern or gauge, such as a thin metal plate with a cut pattern, used as a guide in making something accurately, as in woodworking, or in replication of a standard object. **2.** A piece of stone or timber used to distribute weight or pressure, as over a door frame. **3.** A macromolecule, such as DNA, RNA, or messenger RNA, the structure of which serves as a guide for the assembly of nucleic acids and polypeptides. [Earlier *templet* (influenced by PLATE), from French, diminutive of Old French *temple,* TEMPLE (device in a loom).]

tem·ple¹ (tĕm'pəl) *n.* **1.** A building or place dedicated to religious worship or the presence of a deity. Used chiefly with reference to the sacred buildings of the ancient world and to those of eastern religions such as Hinduism, Buddhism, and Shintoism. **2. Temple.** Any of three successive buildings in ancient Jerusalem dedicated to the worship of God. **3.** A Christian church; especially, a Mormon or French Protestant church. **4.** Something considered to contain a divine presence: *The body is the temple of the soul.* **5.** A place or building serving as the focus of a special activity or of something especially valued: *a temple of learning.* **6. Temple.** Either of two Inns of Court in London, the **Inner Temple** and **Middle Temple** *(both of which see),* on the site formerly occupied by the Knights Templar. **7.** A synagogue. [Middle English *temple,* from Old English *tempel* and Old French *temple,* from Latin *templum,* sanctuary, space marked for observation by an augur.]

temple² *n.* The flat region on either side of the forehead above the cheekbone. [Middle English, from Old French, from Vulgar Latin *tempula* (unattested), variant of Latin *tempora,* plural of *tempus,* temple of the head.]

temple³ *n.* A device in a loom that keeps the cloth stretched to the correct width during weaving. [Middle English *tempylle,* from Old French *temple,* from Latin *templum,* small piece of wood.]

Tem·ple (tĕm'pəl), **Shirley** (1928–). U.S. actress and public official. An immensely popular child actress in the 1930's, she starred in several motion pictures, including *Bright Eyes* (1934), in which she sang "The Good Ship Lollypop." Retiring from acting in 1949, she married and as Shirley Temple Black served as a U.S. delegate to the United Nations (1968–70), ambassador to Ghana (1974–76), and as the State Department's chief of protocol (1976–77).

tem·po (tĕm'pō) *n., pl.* **-pos** or **-pi** (-pē). **1.** *Abbr.* **t.** *Music.* The relative speed at which a composition is to be played, as indicated by a descriptive or metronomic direction to the performer. **2.** A characteristic rate or rhythm of activity; pace: *the quick tempo of modern life.* [Italian, "time," from Latin *tempus.* See **temporal.**]

tem·po·ral[1] (tĕm'pər-əl, tĕm'prəl) *adj.* **1.** Pertaining to, concerned with, or limited by time. **2.** Pertaining to or concerned with earthly life or existence. **3.** Civil, secular, or lay as distinguished from ecclesiastical. **4.** *Grammar.* Expressing time: *a temporal conjunction.* [Middle English *temporal,* from Latin *temporālis,* from *tempus*† (stem *tempor-*), time.] **—tem·po·ral·ly** *adv.*

temporal[2] *adj.* Of, pertaining to, or near the temples of the skull. [Late Latin *temporālis,* from Latin *tempus* (stem *tempor-*), TEMPLE (of the head).]

temporal bone *n.* Either of two complex bones forming the sides and base of the skull and housing the middle and inner ear.

tem·po·ral·i·ty (tĕm'pə-răl'ə-tē) *n., pl.* **-ties. 1.** The condition of being temporal or temporary. **2. temporalities.** Temporal possessions, especially of the church or clergy.

temporal lobe *n.* The part of each cerebral hemisphere associated with the perception and interpretation of sound.

tem·po·rar·y (tĕm'pə-rĕr'ē) *adj.* Lasting, used, or enjoyed for a limited time; impermanent: *a temporary job; temporary relief.* —See Synonyms at **transient.**
~*n., pl.* **-ies.** One that is employed only for a limited time. [Latin *temporārius,* from *tempus* (stem *tempor-*), time. See **temporal.**] **—tem·po·rar·i·ly** (tĕm'pə-râr'ə-lē) *adv.* **—tem·po·rar·i·ness** *n.*

tem·po·rize (tĕm'pə-rīz') *intr.v.* **-rized, -rizing, -rizes. 1.** To compromise or act evasively in order to gain time, avoid argument, or postpone a decision: *preferred temporizing to taking an unpopular course of action.* **2. a.** To act or behave in a way appropriate to particular circumstances. **b.** To yield to what current conditions demand; compromise. [French *temporiser,* from Medieval Latin *temporizāre,* to wait one's time, from Latin *tempus* (stem *tempor-*), time. See **temporal.**] **—tem·po·ri·za·tion** *n.*

tempt (tĕmpt) *tr.v.* **tempted, tempting, tempts. 1.** To entice (a person) to commit a usually unwise or immoral act, especially by a promise of reward. **2.** To attract or invite: *I must say I'm tempted by the offer.* **3.** To provoke or to risk provoking: *It's wiser not to tempt fate.* **4.** To incline or dispose strongly: *I was tempted just to give the whole thing up.* **5.** *Archaic.* To put to the test: *God tempted Abraham.* —See Synonyms at **lure.** [Middle English *tempten,* from Old French *tempter,* from Latin *temptāre*†, to try, test, tempt.] **—tempt·a·ble** *adj.*

temp·ta·tion (tĕmp-tā'shən) *n.* **1.** The act of tempting or the condition of being tempted. **2.** Something that tempts or entices.

tempt·er (tĕmp'tər) *n.* One who tempts.

tempt·ing (tĕmp'tĭng) *adj.* Alluring, enticing, or seductive. **—tempt·ing·ly** *adv.* **—tempt·ing·ness** *n.*

temp·tress (tĕmp'trĭs) *n.* A woman who tempts.

tem·pu·ra (tĕm'po͝o-rə, tĕm-po͝or'ə) *n.* A Japanese dish of vegetables and seafood dipped in batter and fried in deep fat. [Japanese, "fried food."]

ten (tĕn) *n.* **1. a.** The cardinal number that is one more than nine. **b.** A symbol representing this, as 10, X, or x. **2.** A set made up of ten persons or things. **3. a.** The tenth in a series. **b.** A playing card marked with ten spots. **4.** Ten parts: *cut the pie in ten.* **5.** A size, as in clothing, designated as ten. **6.** A ten-dollar bill: *I'd like the money in tens.* **7.** Ten hours after midnight or midday: *We left at ten in the morning.* [Middle English *ten,* Old English *tīen, tēne, tȳn.*] **—ten** *adj. & pron.*

ten. 1. tenor. **2.** *Music.* tenuto.

ten·a·ble (tĕn'ə-bəl) *adj.* Capable of being defended or sustained, as against critical argument or military attack: *a tenable position.* [French *tenable,* from *tenir,* to hold, from Latin *tenēre.*] **—ten·a·bil·i·ty, ten·a·ble·ness** *n.* **—ten·a·bly** *adv.*

ten·ace (tĕn'ās', -ĭs, tĕ-nās') *n.* In card games such as bridge and whist, the combination or holding of a combination of two nonconsecutive high cards of a suit, as the king and the jack. [French, TENACIOUS.]

te·na·cious (tə-nā'shəs) *adj.* **1. a.** Holding or tending to hold or maintain firmly. **b.** Persistent, resolute, or stubborn. **2.** Holding together firmly; cohesive. **3.** Clinging to another object or surface; adhesive. **4.** Tending to retain; retentive: *a tenacious memory.* —See Synonyms at **strong.** [Latin *tenāx* (stem *tenāc-*), from *tenēre,* to hold.] **—te·na·cious·ly** *adv.* **—te·na·cious·ness** *n.*

te·nac·i·ty (tə-năs'ə-tē) *n.* The condition or quality of being tenacious. —See Synonyms at **courage, perseverance.**

te·nac·u·lum (tə-năk'yə-ləm) *n., pl.* **-la** (-lə). A long-handled, slender hooked instrument for lifting and holding parts, such as blood vessels, during surgery. [New Latin, from Late Latin, holder, from Latin *tenēre,* to hold.]

ten·an·cy (tĕn'ən-sē) *n., pl.* **-cies. 1.** The possession or occupancy of lands or buildings by title, under a lease, or on payment of rent. **2.** The period of a tenant's occupancy or possession. **3.** The occupation or period of occupation of an office or position; tenure.

ten·ant (tĕn'ənt) *n.* **1.** One who pays rent to use or occupy property, as land or a building, that is owned by another. **2.** *Law.* One who holds or possesses lands, tenements, and sometimes personal property by any kind of title. **3.** An occupant, inhabitant, or dweller.
~*v.* **tenanted, -anting, -ants.** —*tr.* To hold as a tenant. —*intr.* To be a tenant. [Middle English *tena(u)nt,* from Old French *tenant,* from the present participle of *tenir,* to hold, from Latin *tenēre,* to hold.]

tenant farmer *n.* One who farms land owned by another and pays rent in cash or as a proportion of his produce.

ten·ant·ry (tĕn'ən-trē) *n., pl.* **-ries. 1.** Tenants collectively, especially tenant farmers. **2.** The state or condition of being a tenant; tenancy.

tench (tĕnch) *n., pl.* **tenches** or collectively **tench.** An edible Eurasian freshwater fish, *Tinca tinca,* having small scales and two barbels near the mouth. [Middle English *tenche,* from Old French, from Late Latin *tinca,* perhaps from Gaulish.]

Ten Commandments *pl.n.* The ten injunctions given by God to Moses on Mount Sinai that constitute the basis of Mosaic Law. Exodus 20:1–17. Also called "Decalogue."

tend[1] (tĕnd) *intr.v.* **tended, tending, tends. 1.** To move or extend in a particular direction: *Our course tended toward the north.* **2.** To show a natural likelihood or inclination to act in a particular way or produce a particular effect; be apt: *War tends to defeat its purposes.* **3.** To be disposed or inclined: *He tends toward sarcasm.* [Middle English *tenden,* from Old French *tendre,* from Latin *tendere,* to stretch, direct one's course, be inclined.]

tend[2] *v.* **tended, tending, tends.** —*tr.* **1.** To minister to the needs of; look after: *tend a child.* **2.** To be in charge of; mind: *tend bar.* —*intr.* **1.** To serve or wait. Used with *on* or *upon.* **2.** *Informal.* To apply one's attention: *Tend to your own business.* [Middle English *tenden,* short for *attenden,* to ATTEND.]

Usage: *Tend* and *attend* are distinguished in formal English; one may *tend the sick people of the town* or *attend to the sick people of the town. To* is used with *tend* in the sense "apply one's attention" only in informal English.

ten·den·cy (tĕn'dən-sē) *n., pl.* **-cies.** A demonstrated inclination to think, act, develop, or behave in a certain way; a propensity: *a tendency to panic; a tendency to lie.* [Medieval Latin *tendentia,* from Latin *tendēns,* present participle of *tendere,* to stretch, TEND.]

Synonyms: *current, drift, inclination, trend.*

ten·den·tious, ten·den·cious (tĕn-dĕn'shəs) *adj.* Written or said with the aim of promoting a particular point of view; not impartial; biased. [From TENDENCY.] **—ten·den·tious·ly** *adv.* **—ten·den·tious·ness** *n.*

ten·der[1] (tĕn'dər) *adj.* **-derer, -derest. 1. a.** Easily damaged, bruised, or broken; delicate; fragile: *tender skin.* **b.** Easily chewed or cut: *tender beef.* **2.** Young and vulnerable: *of tender age.* **3.** Needing to be handled with tact and sensitivity: *a tender subject.* **4.** Sensitive to frost or severe cold; not hardy. Said of a plant. **5. a.** Easily hurt; sensitive: *a tender conscience.* **b.** Painful; sore. **6. a.** Gentle and solicitous: *a tender mother.* **b.** Expressing gentle emotions; loving: *a tender glance.* **c.** Given to sympathy or kindness; soft: *a tender heart.* **7.** Considerate and protective; careful to ward off harmful influences or prevent harmful action: *tender of her reputation.* **8.** *Nautical.* Apt to lean under sail; crank.
~*tr.v.* **tendered, -dering, -ders. 1.** To make tender. **2.** *Archaic.* To treat with tender regard. [Middle English *tender, tendre,* from Old French *tendre,* from Latin *tener,* tender, delicate.] **—ten·der·ly** *adv.* **—ten·der·ness** *n.*

tender[2] *n.* **1.** A formal offer, as: **a.** *Law.* An offer of money or goods in payment of an obligation. **b.** A written offer to supply goods or perform work at a stated cost or rate; a bid. **2.** Something that may be offered in payment, especially money: *legal tender.*
~*v.* **tendered, -dering, -ders.** —*tr.* **1.** To offer formally; present: *tendered my resignation.* **2.** To offer (money or goods) in payment: *tendered the correct fare.* —*intr.* To make a tender; bid: *tender for a contract.* —See Synonyms at **offer.** [From Old French *tendre,* to offer, stretch out; see **tend** (to move toward).] **—ten·der·er** *n.*

tender[3] *n.* **1.** One who tends something. **2.** *Nautical.* A vessel attendant on another vessel or vessels, especially one that ferries supplies between ship and shore. **3.** A railroad car attached to the rear of a steam locomotive and designed to carry fuel and water.

ten·der·foot (tĕn'dər-fo͝ot') *n., pl.* **-foots** or **-feet** (-fēt'). **1.** A newcomer not yet hardened to rough outdoor life; greenhorn. **2.** An inexperienced person; novice. **3.** A beginner in the ranks of the Boy Scouts.

ten·der·heart·ed (tĕn'dər-här'tĭd) *adj.* Easily moved by another's distress; compassionate. **—ten·der·heart·ed·ly** *adv.* **—ten·der·heart·ed·ness** *n.*

ten·der·ize (tĕn'də-rīz') *tr.v.* **-ized, -izing, -izes.** To make (meat) tender, as by marinating, pounding, or applying a tenderizer. **—ten·der·i·za·tion** *n.*

ten·der·iz·er (tĕn'də-rī'zər) *n.* A substance, as a plant enzyme, that tenderizes meat by breaking down the fibers.

ten·der·loin (tĕn'dər-loin') *n.* A cut of meat from under the short ribs that is the tenderest part of a loin, as of beef or pork.

ten·di·ni·tis (tĕn'də-nī'tĭs) *n.* Inflammation of a tendon and its muscle attachments. [New Latin *tendo* (stem *tendin-*), TENDON + -ITIS.]

ten·di·nous (tĕn'də-nəs) *adj.* **1.** Of, having, or resembling a tendon or tendons. **2.** Sinewy. [New Latin *tendinosus,* from *tendo* (stem *tendin-*), from Medieval Latin *tendō,* TENDON.]

ten·don (tĕn'dən) *n.* A band of tough, inelastic fibrous tissue that connects a muscle with its bony attachment; a sinew. [From Medieval Latin *tendō* (stem *tendin-*), from Latin *tendere,* to stretch.]

ten·dril (tĕn'drəl) *n.* **1.** A long, slender coiling extension, as of a

PRONUNCIATION KEY

ă, pat; ā, pay; âr, care;
ä, father, are; b, bib;
ch, church; d, deed; ĕ, pet;
ē, be; f, fife; g, gag; h, hat;
hw, which; ĭ, pit; ī, pie;
îr, pier; j, judge; k, kick;
l, lid, needle; m, mum;
n, no, sudden; ng, thing;
ŏ, pot; ō, toe; ô, paw, for;
oi, noise; ou, out; o͝o, book;
o͞o, boot; p, pop; r, roar;
s, sauce; sh, ship, dish;
t, tight; th, thin, path;
th, this, bathe; ŭ, cut; ûr, fur;
v, valve; w, with; y, yes;
z, zebra, size; zh, vision;
ə, about, item, edible, gallop, circus, peaceful

IN FOREIGN WORDS:

à, *Fr.* ami; œ, *Fr.* feu, *Ger.* schön; ü, *Fr.* tu, *Ger.* über; KH, *Ger.* ich, *Scot.* loch; N, *Fr.* bon; y', *Fr.* Compiègne

STRESS MARKS:

Primary stress: '
in·cite' (ĭn-sīt')
Secondary stress: '
in'sight' (ĭn'sīt')

stem, serving as an organ of attachment for certain climbing plants, such as the grape. **2.** Something resembling a tendril: *wispy tendrils of hair.* [Probably from obsolete French *tendrillon,* diminutive of Old French *tendron,* cartilage, young shoot, from Vulgar Latin *tenerūmen* (unattested), from Latin *tener,* tender, delicate.]

Ten·e·brae (tĕn′ə-brä′, -brē′) *n. Used with a singular or plural verb. Roman Catholic Church.* The office of matins and lauds sung on the last three days of Holy Week, with a ceremony of candles. [Medieval Latin, from Latin, darkness.]

ten·e·brif·ic (tĕn′ə-brĭf′ĭk) *adj.* Serving to obscure or darken. [Latin *tenebrae,* darkness (see **Tenebrae**) + -FIC.]

ten·e·brous (tĕn′ə-brəs) *adj.* Also **te·neb·ri·ous** (tə-nĕb′rē-əs). Dark and gloomy. [From Latin *tenebrae,* darkness. See **Tenebrae.**] **—ten·e·bros·i·ty** (tĕn′ə-brŏs′ə-tē) *n.*

ten·e·ment (tĕn′ə-mənt) *n.* **1.** A building to live in; residence. **2.** A large building divided into separate apartments for rent that typically meets only minimal standards of facilities and maintenance and is usually found in deprived urban areas. **3.** *Chiefly British.* A room or set of rooms leased to a tenant, especially one that is part of a large house or building. **4.** *Law.* Property of a permanent nature, as land, rents, or franchises, that may be held by one person for another; a holding. [Middle English *tenement,* from Old French, from Medieval Latin *tenementum,* feudal holding, house, from Latin *tenēre,* to hold.] **—ten·e·men·tal** (tĕn′ə-mĕnt′l), **ten·e·men·ta·ry** (-mĕn′tə-rē, -mĕn′trē) *adj.*

Ten·er·ife, Ten·er·iffe (tĕn′ə-rīf′, -rēf′). Largest and most populous of the Canary Islands and the site of the capital city of Santa Cruz. It is admired for its scenic beauty.

te·nes·mus (tə-nĕz′məs) *n.* **1.** A painful attempt to urinate or defecate. **2.** Pain associated with urination or defecation. [Medieval Latin, variant of Latin *tenesmos,* from Greek *teinesmos,* "a straining," from *teinein,* to stretch, strain.]

ten·et (tĕn′ĭt) *n.* A belief, doctrine, or principle held as being true by a person or especially by a group of people. [Latin, he holds, from *tenēre,* to hold.]

ten·fold (tĕn′fōld′) *adj.* **1.** Composed of ten parts or members. **2.** Being ten times as great or as many. **—ten·fold** *adv.*

ten·gal·lon hat (tĕn′găl′ən) *n.* A felt hat with an exceptionally tall crown and a wide brim.

Teng Hsaio-p'ing. See Deng Xiao-ping.

tenia. Variant of taenia.

te·ni·a·cide, tae·ni·a·cide (tē′nē-ə-sīd′) *n.* An agent that destroys tapeworms. [TENIA + -CIDE.]

te·ni·a·sis, tae·ni·a·sis (tē-nī′ə-sĭs) *n.* Infestation with tapeworms. [TEN(IA) + -IASIS.]

ten·ner (tĕn′ər) *n. Informal.* A ten-dollar bill.

Ten·nes·see¹ (tĕn′ə-sē′). State in the south-central United States, on the east bank of the Mississippi. It is an agricultural state and a leading producer of tobacco and cotton. Tennessee is the nation's leading producer of zinc, and its industries are expanding. The capital is Nashville; the largest city is Memphis.

Tennessee². River in the south-central United States, formed by the confluence of the Holston and French Broad rivers near Knoxville, Tennessee. It flows for *c.* 1,050 kilometers (650 miles) to the Ohio River at Paducah, Kentucky. The Tennessee Valley Authority (TVA), formed in 1933, implemented a development plan for the river basin by constructing dams, providing navigable waterways, flood and erosion control, and hydroelectric power.

Ten·niel (tĕn′yəl), **Sir John** (1820–1914). English cartoonist and artist. A popular staff cartoonist for *Punch* from 1850 to 1901, he also illustrated the first editions of *Alice's Adventures in Wonderland* (1865) and *Through the Looking-Glass* (1872).

ten·nis (tĕn′ĭs) *n.* **1.** A game played with rackets and a light ball by two players *(singles)* or two pairs of players *(doubles)* on a court divided by a net. Also used adjectivally: *a tennis shoe; a tennis ball.* **2. Lawn tennis** *(see).* **3. Court tennis** *(see).* [Middle English *tenetz, tennys,* probably from Old French *tenez,* imperative of *tenir,* to hold (probably from the call of the server to his opponent in the game), from Latin *tenēre,* to hold.]

tennis elbow *n.* A painful inflammation of the outer elbow resulting from excessive use of the muscles of the forearm.

Ten·no (tĕn′ō) *n., pl.* **Tenno** or **-nos.** *Sometimes* **tenno.** The emperor of Japan considered as a religious leader and a divine being. [Japanese *tennō,* "celestial emperor" : *ten,* from Chinese *tiān,* heaven + *no,* from Chinese *huang,* emperor.]

Ten·ny·son (tĕn′ə-sən), **Alfred, 1st Baron,** known as "Alfred, Lord Tennyson" (1809–92). British poet. His first publication, *Poems, Chiefly Lyrical,* appeared in 1830. In 1850 "In Memoriam," written after the death of a close friend, Arthur Henry Hallam, attracted the attention of Queen Victoria and the prime minister, W.E. Gladstone. In the same year Tennyson was made poet laureate. "Idylls of the King" (1859) and later poems were inspired by ancient and medieval mythology. Poems like "The Charge of the Light Brigade" (1854) are the best known, but his best work lies in poems such as "Ulysses" (1859). **—Ten·ny·so·ni·an** (tĕn′ə-sō′nē-ən) *adj. & n.*

teno- *prefix.* Indicates tendon; for example, **tenotomy.** [From Greek *tenōn,* tendon.]

Te·noch·ti·tlán (tā-nôch′tēt-län′). The ancient capital of the Aztec Empire, on the site now occupied by Mexico City.

ten·on (tĕn′ən) *n.* A projection on the end of a piece of wood shaped for insertion into a mortise.
—tr.v. **tenoned, -oning, -ons. 1.** To provide with a tenon. **2.** To join with a tenon. [Middle English, from Old French, from *tenir,* to hold, from Latin *tenēre.*]

ten·or (tĕn′ər) *n.* **1. a.** The general sense, meaning, or drift apparent in something written or spoken. **b.** A steady prevailing course or direction: *couldn't change the dramatic tenor of his life.* **2. a.** *Law.* The exact meaning or actual wording of a document as distinct from its effect. **b.** An exact copy or transcript of a document. **3.** *Abbr.* **t., T., ten.** *Music.* **a.** The highest natural adult male voice. **b.** A part for this voice. **c.** One who sings this part. **d.** The largest and lowest-pitched bell of a set.
~adj. Of, pertaining to, or having the range of a tenor: *a tenor saxophone.* [Middle English, general meaning, from Old French, from Latin *tenor,* uninterrupted course, from *tenēre,* to hold.]

ten·o·rite (tĕn′ə-rīt′) *n.* A black copper ore consisting predominantly of copper oxide, CuO, occurring in the oxidized zone of a weathered copper lode. [After G. *Tenore* (1780–1861), Italian botanist.]

te·nor·rha·phy (tə-nôr′ə-fē) *n., pl.* **-phies.** The surgical uniting of divided tendons with sutures. [TENO- + Greek *-rrhaphia,* from *rhaptein,* to sew.]

ten·o·syn·o·vi·tis (tĕn′ō-sĭn′ō-vī′tĭs) *n.* Inflammation of a tendon sheath. [TENO- + SYNOV(IA) + -ITIS.]

te·not·o·my (tə-nŏt′ə-mē) *n., pl.* **-mies.** The surgical cutting of a tendon for the relief of deformities caused by the shortening of a muscle. [TENO- + -TOMY.]

ten·pin (tĕn′pĭn′) *n.* **1. tenpins.** *Used with a singular verb.* The game of bowling. **2.** A bowling pin used in playing tenpins.

ten·rec (tĕn′rĕk′) *n.* Also **tan·rec** (tăn′-). Any of various insectivorous, often hedgehoglike mammals of the family Tenrecidae, of Madagascar and adjacent islands. [French, from Malagasy *tàndraka.*]

tense¹ (tĕns) *adj.* **tenser, tensest. 1.** Tightly stretched; taut and strained: *tense muscles.* **2.** In a state of mental or nervous tension. **3.** Nerve-racking; full of suspense: *a tense situation.* **4.** *Phonetics.* Enunciated with taut vocal muscles, as the consonant *t.* Compare **lax.** **—See Synonyms at stiff.**
~v. **tensed, tensing, tenses.** **—tr.** To make tense. **—intr.** To become tense. Often used with *up.* [Latin *tensus,* past participle of *tendere,* to stretch out.] **—tense·ly** *adv.* **—tense·ness** *n.*

tense² *n. Abbr.* **t. 1.** Any of the inflected forms in the conjugation of a verb that indicate the time (past, present, or future) as well as the continuance (imperfect) or completion (perfect) of the action or state. **2.** A set of such forms indicating a particular time: *the future tense.* [Middle English *tens,* tense, time, from Old French, from Latin *tempus,* time. See **temporal.**]

ten·sile (tĕn′səl, -sīl′) *adj.* **1.** Of or pertaining to tension. **2.** Capable of being stretched or extended; ductile. [New Latin *tensilis,* from Latin *tensus,* "stretched," TENSE.] **—ten·sil·i·ty** (tĕn-sīl′ə-tē) *n.*

tensile strength *n.* The resistance of a material to a force tending to tear it apart, expressed as the maximum longitudinal stress it can withstand.

ten·sim·e·ter (tĕn-sĭm′ə-tər) *n.* An apparatus used to measure differences in vapor pressure. [TENSI(ON) + -METER.]

ten·si·om·e·ter (tĕn′sē-ŏm′ə-tər) *n.* **1.** An instrument for measuring tensile strength. **2.** A torsion-balance apparatus used to measure the surface tension of a liquid. **3.** An instrument used to measure the moisture content of soil. [TENSIO(N) + -METER.]

ten·sion (tĕn′shən) *n.* **1. a.** The act or process of stretching. **b.** The condition of being stretched. **2. a.** A force tending to produce elongation or extension. **b.** The measure of such a force. **3. a.** Mental, emotional, or nervous strain. **b.** An uneasy and potentially explosive condition of latent hostility and mistrust between persons or groups: *tension in the Middle East.* **c.** An atmosphere of suspense or suppressed excitement: *Tension mounts as the big match approaches.* **4.** The density of knitted fabrics determined by the size of the needles and thickness of the yarn or the number of rows and stitches needed to complete a given sample of fabric; gauge. **5.** A device for regulating tautness; especially, a device regulating the tautness of thread on a sewing machine. **6.** *Electricity.* Voltage or potential; electromotive force.
~tr.v. **tensioned, -sioning, -sions.** To subject to tension; make taut. [Old French, from Latin *tensiō* (stem *tensiōn-*), from *tensus,* TENSE.] **—ten·sion·al** *adj.*

ten·si·ty (tĕn′sĭ-tē) *n.* The state of being tense.

ten·sive (tĕn′sĭv) *adj.* Of or causing tension.

ten·sor (tĕn′sər, -sôr′) *n.* **1.** *Anatomy.* Any muscle that tenses a part, making it firm. **2.** *Mathematics.* A set of components of a system in *n* dimensions, used to denote position determined within the context of more than one coordinate system, that may be linearly transformed between coordinate systems. **—ten·so·ri·al** (tĕn-sôr′ē-əl, -sōr′ē-əl) *adj.*

ten·strike (tĕn′strīk′) *n.* **1.** A strike in the game of bowling. **2.** *Informal.* A remarkably successful stroke or action.

tent¹ (tĕnt) *n.* **1.** A portable shelter of waterproof material, as canvas or plastic, stretched over a supporting framework of poles with ropes and pegs. **2.** Something resembling a tent in construction or outline; especially, a medical tent placed over a patient's head so that his air supply may be regulated.
~v. **tented, tenting, tents.** **—intr.** To encamp in a tent. **—tr. 1.** To form a tent over. **2.** To accommodate in tents. [Middle English *tente,* from Old French, from Vulgar Latin *tenta* (unattested), from the feminine past participle of *tendere,* to stretch.]

tent² *n.* A small roll or plug, usually of lint or gauze, for placing in a wound or orifice to keep it open or for probing. ~*tr.v.* **tented, tenting, tents.** To keep (a wound or cut) open with a tent. [Middle English, a probe, from Old French *tente,* from *tenter,* to probe, test, from Latin *tentāre,* variant of *temptāre,* to feel, try, TEMPT.]

tent³ *n. Scottish.* Attention; heed. Used chiefly in the phrase *take tent.* [Middle English *tenten,* from *tent,* attention, short for *attent,* from Old French *attente,* from Latin *attenta,* feminine past participle of *attendere,* to ATTEND.]

ten·ta·cle (těn′tə-kəl) *n.* **1.** *Zoology.* An elongated, flexible unsegmented protrusion, such as one of those surrounding the mouth or oral cavity of the hydra, sea anemone, or squid. **2.** *Botany.* One of the hairs on the leaves of insectivorous plants, such as the sundew. **3.** Something resembling a tentacle, especially in ability to grasp or hold. [New Latin *tentaculum,* from Latin *tentāre,* variant of *temptāre,* to touch, feel, TEMPT.] —**ten·tac·u·lar** (těn-tăk′yə-lər), **ten·tac·u·late** (-lĭt), **ten·ta·cled** *adj.*

tent·age (těn′tĭj) *n.* **1.** A supply of tents. **2.** Tent equipment.

ten·ta·tive (těn′tə-tĭv) *adj.* **1.** Of an experimental nature; provisional. **2.** Uncertain; hesitant: *a tentative smile.* [Medieval Latin *tentātīvus,* from Latin *tentātus,* past participle of *tentāre,* variant of *temptāre,* to feel, try, TEMPT.] —**ten·ta·tive** *n.* —**ten·ta·tive·ly** *adv.* —**ten·ta·tive·ness** *n.*

tent caterpillar *n.* Any of several widely distributed destructive caterpillars of the genus *Malacosoma* that live in colonies in tentlike webs constructed in deciduous trees.

tent dress *n.* A full dress that flares out toward the bottom and is not fitted at the waist.

tent·ed (těn′tĭd) *adj.* **1.** Covered with tents: *a tented shoreline.* **2.** Sheltered in tents. **3.** Resembling a tent in shape.

ten·ter (těn′tər) *n.* **1.** A framework upon which milled cloth is stretched for drying without shrinkage. **2.** *Archaic.* A tenterhook. [Middle English *teyntur,* from Norman French *tentur* (unattested), from Medieval Latin *tentōrium,* from Latin *tentus,* past participle of *tendere,* to stretch.]

ten·ter·hook (těn′tər-hŏŏk′) *n.* A hooked nail for securing cloth on a tenter. —**on tenterhooks.** In a state of uneasiness, suspense, or anxiety.

tenth (těnth) *n.* **1.** The ordinal number ten in a series. **2.** One of ten equal parts. [Middle English *tenthe,* variant of earlier *tethe,* Old English *tēotha, teogetha.*] —**tenth** *adj. & adv.*

tent stitch *n.* A short diagonal embroidery stitch that forms close, even parallel rows to fill in a pattern or a background.

ten·u·is (těn′yŏŏ-ĭs) *n., pl.* **-ues** (-yŏŏ-ēz′). *Phonetics.* A voiceless stop. [New Latin (translation of Greek *psilos,* plain), from Latin, TENUOUS.]

ten·u·ous (těn′yŏŏ-əs) *adj.* **1.** Lacking substance and strength; flimsy: *a tenuous argument.* **2.** Having a thin consistency; diluted. **3.** Having a thin or slender form. [Earlier *tenuious,* from Latin *tenuis,* thin, rare, fine.] —**ten·u·ous·ly** *adv.* —**ten·u·ous·ness** *n.*

ten·ure (těn′yər, -yŏŏr′) *n.* **1. a.** The fact or condition of holding something, as real estate or an office. **b.** The terms or conditions under which something is held. **c.** The period or duration during which something is held. **2.** Permanence of position, as that often granted to employees in certain fields after a fixed number of years. [Middle English, from Old French, from *tenir,* earlier *tenēure,* from Latin *tenēre,* to hold.] —**ten·u·ri·al** (těn-yŏŏr′ē-əl) *adj.* —**ten·u·ri·al·ly** *adv.*

ten·ured (těn′yərd, -yŏŏrd′) *adj.* Having academic tenure.

te·nu·to (tə-nŏŏ′tō) *adj. Abbr.* **ten.** *Music.* Held for the full time value; sustained. Said of a chord or tone. [Italian, past participle of *tenere,* to hold, from Latin *tenēre.*] —**te·nu·to** *adv.*

te·o·cal·li (tē′ə-kăl′ē) *n., pl.* **-lis.** Also **te·o·pan** (tē′ə-păn′). **1.** A temple of ancient Mexico and Central America, usually built upon a mound of a truncated pyramidal shape. **2.** The mound itself. [Nahuatl : *teotl,* god + *calli,* house.]

te·o·sin·te (tē′ə-sĭn′tē, tā′ō-) *n.* A tall Central American grass, *Euchlaena mexicana* (or *Zea mexicana*), closely related to corn and sometimes cultivated for fodder. [Mexican Spanish, from Nahuatl *teocentli* : *teotl,* god + *centli,* dried ear of corn.]

Te·o·ti·hua·cán (tā′ō-tē′wä-kän′). Ancient city of Mexico, one of the oldest urban settlements in ancient America.

te·pal (tē′pəl, těp′əl) *n. Botany.* A division of the perianth of a flower having petals and sepals that are indistinguishable. [French *tépale,* perhaps a blend of PETAL and SEPAL.]

te·pee, tee·pee, ti·pi (tē′pē) *n.* A cone-shaped tent of skins or bark, supported by poles, used by North American Indians. Compare **wigwam.** [Dakota *tipi,* dwelling.]

tep·id (těp′ĭd) *adj.* Moderately warm; lukewarm. [Latin *tepidus,* from *tepēre,* to be lukewarm.] —**te·pid·i·ty** (tě-pĭd′ə-tē), **tep·id·ness** *n.* —**tep·id·ly** *adv.*

te·qui·la (tə-kē′lə) *n.* An alcoholic liquor distilled from a Central American plant, *Agave tequilana.* [Mexican Spanish, from *Tequila,* district in Mexico.]

ter– *prefix.* Indicates three, third, or threefold; for example, **tercentenary.** [Latin *ter,* thrice.]

tera– *prefix. Symbol* **T** Indicates one trillion (10¹²); for example, **terahertz.** [Greek *teras,* monster. See **teratoid.**]

ter·a·hertz (těr′ə-hûrts′) *n. Abbr.* **THz** One trillion (10¹²) hertz.

ter·aph (těr′əf) *n., pl.* **-aphim** (-ə-fīm′). A small image or idol revered by ancient Semitic peoples. [Hebrew *tərāphīm,* a pejorative appellation of these idols, perhaps from *rəpha'im,* "shades."]

terato– *prefix.* Indicates: **1.** Abnormality; for example, **teratoma.** **2.** Something monstrous; for example, **teratoid.** [Greek *teras* (stem *terat-*), monster, marvel.]

te·rat·o·gen (tə-răt′ə-jən) *n.* An agent that induces abnormalities in a developing fetus. [TERATO- + -GEN.] —**ter·a·to·gen·ic** (těr′ə-tə-jěn′ĭk) *adj.* —**ter·a·tog·e·ny** (-tŏj′ə-nē) *n.*

ter·a·toid (těr′ə-toid′) *adj.* Like a monster; monstrous. [Greek *teras, terat-,* monster + -OID.]

ter·a·tol·o·gy (těr′ə-tŏl′ə-jē) *n.* The biological study of the development, anatomy, or abnormalities of monsters. [TERATO- + -LOGY.] —**ter·a·to·log·i·cal** (těr′ə-tə-lŏj′ĭ-kəl) *adj.*

ter·a·to·ma (těr′ə-tō′mə) *n., pl.* **-mas** or **-mata** (-mə-tə). A tumor consisting of different types of tissue. [TERATO- + -OMA.] —**ter·a·tom·a·tous** (těr′ə-tŏm′ə-təs, -tō′mə-təs) *adj.*

ter·bi·a (tûr′bē-ə) *n.* Terbium oxide.

ter·bi·um (tûr′bē-əm) *n. Symbol* **Tb** A soft, silvery-gray metallic rare-earth element, used as a solid-state dopant and as a laser material. Atomic number 65, atomic weight 158.924, melting point 1,356°C, boiling point 2,800°C, specific gravity 8.272, valences 3, 4. [Discovered in *Ytterby,* a village in Sweden.]

terbium metal *n.* Any of several rare-earth metals separable from other metals as a group and including europium, terbium, and gadolinium.

terbium oxide *n.* An insoluble dark brown powder, Tb₂O₃. Also called "terbia."

terce. Variant of **tierce.**

ter·cel (tûr′səl) *n.* Also **tier·cel** (tîr′-). A male hawk, especially one used in falconry. [Middle English, from Old French, from Vulgar Latin *tertiōlus* (unattested), from Latin *tertius,* third (from the belief that the third egg of a brood was a male).]

ter·cen·ten·a·ry (tûr′sěn-těn′ə-rē, tər-sěn′tə-něr′ē) *n., pl.* **-ries.** A 300th anniversary or its celebration.

tepee *Children at play outside a tepee, the traditional and movable home of many North American Indians.*

---

teocalli

HOUSES OF GOD IN THE LAND OF MONTEZUMA

The conquering Spaniards reported grisly doings in Mexican temples

At once fascinated and offended by the religious customs of the Aztecs, the conquistadors found no monuments more awesome than Mexico's looming stone- or brick-encased earthen mounds shaped into truncated pyramids and topped by ceremonial courtyards and temple-towers. These the Spaniards called teocallis (Spanish *teocali*) after the Nahuatl words *teotl,* "god," and *calli,* "house."

Bernal Diaz, chronicler of the Spanish conquest of Mexico (1519–21), tells of his leader Hernando Cortés bounding up the 114 steps of the great five-story teocalli at Tenochtitlán (Mexico City) to talk with the Aztec emperor Montezuma when the Spaniards first entered the city in 1519. Emerging from the stinking, blood-spattered chambers where eight freshly excised human hearts were on display, a righteous if impolitic Cortés lectured his royal host on the unholiness of human sacrifice.

Such tales have overshadowed the role of the teocalli as a center for tranquil worship and education. In and around cities were hundreds of teocallis, great and small, each the focus of a family clan's religious life. Only a few major teocallis have been restored.

DREAD *In his* History of the Conquest of Mexico *(1843), William H. Prescott describes how teocalli architecture must have magnified the authority of Aztec priests: "The top was a broad area, on which . . . long processions of priests and the dismal rites of sacrifice were all visible, impressing on the spectator's mind a superstitious veneration for the mysteries of his religion, and for the dread ministers by whom they were interpreted."*

termitarium *In tropical and subtropical countries, termites build mounds as high as 7 or 8 meters (about 25 feet), using mud that is brought from a similar depth. The mounds harden in the sun to a rocklike consistency.*

termite *Termites belong to a large family of social insects of the order Isoptera. This is a soldier termite from East Africa, a species that lives in giant colonies in large, pinnacled mounds.*

tern *The tern family holds the world record among birds for long-distance migration. Every year the arctic tern (above) flies nearly 39,000 kilometers (24,000 miles)—from the Arctic to the Antarctic and back.*

~*adj.* Of or pertaining to a span of 300 years or to a 300th anniversary. [TER- + CENTENARY.]

ter·cen·ten·ni·al (tûr′sĕn-tĕn′ē-əl) *adj.* Tercentenary. **—ter·cen·ten·ni·al** *n.*

ter·cet (tûr′sĭt) *n.* In prosody, a unit of three lines, often rhyming with each other or with other tercets. Also called "triplet." [Italian *terzetto,* diminutive of *terzo,* third, from Latin *tertius.*]

ter·e·bene (tĕr′ə-bēn′) *n.* A mixture of terpenes prepared from oil of turpentine, used as an expectorant and antiseptic. [French *térébène,* from *térébinthe,* from Old French *terebinte,* TEREBINTH.]

te·reb·ic acid (tə-rĕb′ĭk, -rē′bĭk) *n.* A white crystalline compound, $C_7H_{10}O_4$, resulting from the action of nitric acid on turpentine. [TEREB(INTH) + -IC.]

ter·e·binth (tĕr′ə-bĭnth′) *n.* A small tree, *Pistacia terebinthus,* of the Mediterranean region, that yields turpentine. [Middle English *therebinthe,* from Old French *t(h)erebinte,* from Latin *terebinthus,* from Greek *terebinthos, terminthos,* of Aegean origin.]

ter·e·bin·thine (tĕr′ə-bĭn′thĭn, -thīn′) *adj.* Also **ter·e·bin·thic** (-thĭk). **1.** Of or pertaining to the terebinth. **2.** Pertaining to, consisting of, or resembling turpentine.

te·re·do (tə-rē′dō, -rā′dō) *n., pl.* **-dos.** A marine mollusk of the genus *Teredo,* especially, the shipworm. [New Latin *Teredo,* from Latin *terēdō,* a kind of worm, from Greek *terēdōn.*]

Ter·ence (tĕr′əns) (*c.* 185–159 B.C.). Roman playwright. Taken to Rome as the young slave of a senator, he was educated and then freed by his master. His dramas, such as *Phormio* and *Adelphi,* are largely renditions of Greek comedies for the Roman stage that featured subtle humor and fine dialogue.

Te·re·sa (tə-rē′sə, -rā′zə), **Mother,** born Agnes Gonxha Bejaxhiu (1910–). Indian nun, born in Albania. Dedicated to relieving the suffering of India's desperately poor and dying people, she founded a Roman Catholic congregation of sisters, the Missionaries of Charity, in 1950. In 1979 she was awarded the Nobel Peace Prize.

Teresa, Saint. See **Theresa.**

Ter·esh·ko·va (tĕr′ĕsh-kô′və, -kō′və), **Valentina Vladimirovna** (1937–). Soviet cosmonaut. A textile factory worker recruited for the Soviet cosmonaut program, she orbited the earth 48 times aboard the *Vostok 6* in June, 1963, thereby becoming the first woman in space.

te·rete (tĕ-rēt′) *adj.* Cylindrical but usually slightly tapering at both ends, circular in cross section, and smooth-surfaced. [Latin *teres* (stem *teret-*), rounded.]

ter·giv·er·sate (tər-jĭv′ər-sāt′, tûr′jə-vûr′sāt′) *intr.v.* **-sated, -sating, -sates. 1.** To use evasions or ambiguities; equivocate. **2.** To change sides; apostatize. [Latin *tergiversārī,* "to turn the back," shift : *tergum,* back, TERGUM + *versus,* past participle of *vertere,* to turn.] **—ter·giv·er·sa·tion** *n.* **—ter·giv·er·sa·tor** *n.*

ter·gum (tûr′gəm) *n., pl.* **-ga** (-gə). *Zoology.* The upper or dorsal surface, especially of a body segment of an insect or other arthropod. [Latin *tergum*†, the back.] **—ter·gal** *adj.*

ter·i·ya·ki (tĕr′ē-yä′kē) *n.* A Japanese dish consisting of skewered and broiled slices of marinated meat or shellfish. [Japanese : *teri,* sunshine, flame + *yaki,* to broil.]

term (tûrm) *n.* **1.** A period of time, usually having clearly defined limits, for which something lasts or is intended to last, especially: **a.** A limited period of time that a person serves: *a term of office; a 15-year prison term.* **b.** A period when an educational institution or court of law is in session. **c.** An approximately specified period with regard to which plans or predictions are made: *in the short term.* **2.** A point of time beginning or ending a period, as: **a.** A fixed time by which a payment must be made. **b.** The end of a normal period of pregnancy. **3.** *Law.* **a.** A fixed period of time during which an estate may be held. **b.** The estate to be granted for a term. **c.** A period of time allowed a debtor to meet an obligation. **4. a.** A word or phrase that expresses a particular idea or has a particular function: *a term of abuse.* **b.** A word or expression that is part of the jargon of a particular group or activity: *a legal term.* **c. terms.** Language or manner of expression employed: *told us in no uncertain terms.* **5. terms. a.** Conditions or stipulations that define the nature and limits of an agreement: *peace terms.* **b.** Conditions of payment, as for a service or purchase: *easy credit terms.* **c.** The relation between two persons or groups; footing: *We're no longer on speaking terms.* **6.** *Mathematics.* **a.** Each of the quantities composing a ratio or a fraction or forming a series. **b.** Each of the quantities connected by addition or subtraction signs in an equation. **7.** *Logic.* **a.** The word or phrase constituting the subject or the predicate of a proposition. **b.** Any of the three parts of a syllogism. **8.** *Archaic.* A limit or boundary. **9.** A stone or post marking a boundary, especially a square and tapering pillar adorned with the figure of a human head or a human head and torso. **—bring to terms.** To force (a person) to submit or agree. **—come to terms.** To reach an agreement. **—come to terms with.** To face up to (a fact or condition); accept. **—in terms of.** With regard to; in relation to.

~*tr.v.* **termed, terming, terms.** To designate; call. [Middle English *terme,* from Old French, from Latin *terminus,* boundary line, boundary, limit.]

term. **1.** terminal. **2.** termination.

ter·ma·gant (tûr′mə-gənt) *n.* A quarrelsome, brawling, or scolding woman; a shrew.

~*adj.* Overbearing, abusive, or shrewish. [Middle English *Termagaunt, Tervagaunt,* vicious Muslim deity in medieval mystery plays, from Old French *Tervagan(t),* from Italian *Trivigante*†.]

term·er (tûr′mər) *n.* A person holding a position or confined to a place for a specified term. Usually used in combination: *These patients are long-termers.*

ter·mi·na·ble (tûr′mə-nə-bəl) *adj.* **1.** Capable of being terminated. **2.** Terminating after a designated date: *a terminable annuity.* **—ter·mi·na·bil·i·ty, ter·mi·na·ble·ness** *n.* **—ter·mi·na·bly** *adv.*

ter·mi·nal (tûr′mə-nəl) *adj. Abbr.* **term. 1.** Pertaining to, situated at, or forming the end or boundary of something: *a terminal post.* **2.** *Botany.* Growing or appearing at the end of a stem, branch, stalk, or similar part. **3.** Pertaining to or occurring at the end of a section or series; final. **4.** Pertaining to or occurring in or at the end of a term or each term: *terminal exams.* **5.** Ending in death; fatal. **6.** Very serious; especially, resulting in ruin or collapse: *terminal laziness.* —See Synonyms at **last.**

~*n. Abbr.* **term. 1.** A terminating point, limit, or part; extremity. **2.** An ornamental figure or object, as a finial of a lamp, situated at the end of another object. **3.** *Electricity.* **a.** A position in an electric circuit or device at which an electric connection is normally established or broken. **b.** A passive conductor at such a position used to facilitate the connection. **4. a.** Either end of a transportation line, as a railroad or bus line; terminus. **b.** A building at a terminal providing services for departing or incoming travelers; station. **5.** *Computer Science.* A device through which information can enter or leave a computer system, especially one that is remote from the computer itself. [Latin *terminālis,* from *terminus,* boundary, TERMINUS.] **—ter·mi·nal·ly** *adv.*

terminal velocity *n.* **1.** The maximum velocity attained by a body falling through a fluid in the earth's gravitational field. **2.** The maximum velocity attained by a projectile during its parabolic flight. **3.** The velocity of a projectile at the end of its flight. **4.** The maximum velocity that an aircraft can attain, as determined by its drag.

ter·mi·nate (tûr′mə-nāt′) *v.* **-nated, -nating, -nates.** —*tr.* **1.** To bring to an end or halt: *Terrorist action terminated the truce.* **2.** To occur at or form the end of; conclude. **3.** To discontinue the employment of: *terminated 300 workers when the contract was canceled.* —*intr.* **1.** To come to an end or halt: *Negotiations terminated yesterday.* **2.** To have as an end or result: *The war terminated in victory for the Allies.* **3.** To take form as a last part: *The headboard terminates in a scroll.* —See Synonyms at **complete.** [Latin *termināre,* to limit, to terminate, from *terminus,* TERMINUS.] **—ter·mi·na·tive** (tûr′mə-nā′tĭv) *adj.* **—ter·mi·na·tive·ly** *adv.*

ter·mi·na·tion (tûr′mə-nā′shən) *n. Abbr.* **term. 1.** The act of terminating or the condition of being terminated. **2. a.** The spatial end of something; a limit or boundary. **b.** The temporal end of something; conclusion or cessation. **3.** A result or outcome of something. **4.** The end of a word, as an inflectional ending, suffix, or final morpheme. **—ter·mi·na·tion·al** *adj.*

ter·mi·na·tor (tûr′mə-nā′tər) *n.* **1.** One that terminates. **2.** The dividing line between the bright and shaded regions of the disk of the moon or an inner planet.

ter·mi·nol·o·gy (tûr′mə-nŏl′ə-jē) *n., pl.* **-gies. 1.** The vocabulary of technical terms and usages appropriate to a particular field, subject, science, or art; nomenclature. **2.** The study of nomenclature. [Medieval Latin *terminus,* expression, from Latin, limit, TERMINUS + -LOGY.] **—ter·mi·no·log·i·cal** (tûr′mə-nə-lŏj′ĭ-kəl) *adj.* **—ter·mi·no·log·i·cal·ly** *adv.* **—ter·mi·nol·o·gist** *n.*

term insurance *n.* Insurance for a specifically stated period providing coverage for losses to the insured during that period but becoming void upon its expiration.

ter·mi·nus (tûr′mə-nəs) *n., pl.* **-nuses** or **-ni** (-nī′). **1.** The end of something; a final point, extremity, or goal. **2. a.** A terminal on a transportation line. **b.** The town in which such a terminal is located. **3. a.** A boundary or border. **b.** A stone or post marking such a border. [Latin, boundary line, boundary, limit.]

ter·mi·tar·i·um (tûr′mə-târ′ē-əm) *n., pl.* **-ia** (-ē-ə). The moundlike nest of a termite colony. [TERMIT(E) + -ARIUM.]

ter·mite (tûr′mīt′) *n.* Any of numerous superficially antlike social insects of the order Isoptera, many species of which feed on wood and are highly destructive to living trees and wooden structures. Also called "white ant." [Latin *termes* (stem *termit-*), variant of *tarmes*†, wood-eating worm.]

term·less (tûrm′lĭs) *adj.* **1.** Having no bounds or limits; unending. **2.** Unconditional.

term paper *n.* A lengthy report or essay required of a student on a topic drawn from the subject matter of a course of study.

tern[1] (tûrn) *n.* Any of various sea birds of the family Sterninae, related to and resembling the gulls but characteristically smaller and having black and white plumage and a forked tail. [Scandinavian, akin to Old Norse *therna*†.]

tern[2] *n.* **1.** A set of three; especially, a combination of three numbers that wins a lottery prize. **2.** A three-masted schooner. [Latin *ternī,* three each, from *ter,* thrice.]

ter·na·ry (tûr′nə-rē) *adj.* **1.** Composed of three or arranged in threes. **2.** *Mathematics.* **a.** Of, pertaining to, or being a number system that has three as its base. **b.** Involving three variables. **3.** *Chemistry.* Containing three different components or elements.

~*n., pl.* **ternaries.** A set or group of three. [Middle English, from Latin *ternārius,* from *ternī,* three each. See **tern** (set of three).]

ternary form *n.* A musical form in three parts of which the first and the third are the same.

ter·nate (tûr′nāt′, -nĭt) *adj.* Arranged in or consisting of groups or sets of three, as a compound leaf with three leaflets. [New Latin *ternatus,* from Medieval Latin *ternātus,* past participle of *ternāre,* to multiply by three, from *ternī,* three each, from *ter,* thrice.] **—ter·nate·ly** *adv.*

terne (tûrn) *n.* **1.** An alloy of three or four parts of lead to one part of tin, with a tiny percentage of antimony. **2.** Terneplate. [TERNE(PLATE).]

terne·plate (tûrn′plāt′) *n.* Sheet iron or steel plated with terne, used as a roofing material. Also called "terne." [Probably from French *terne,* dull, from Old French, from *ternir,* to tarnish + PLATE.]

ter·pene (tûr′pēn′) *n.* Any of various unsaturated hydrocarbons, $C_{10}H_{16}$, found in essential oils and oleoresins of plants such as conifers and used in organic syntheses. [Obsolete *terpentin,* TURPENTINE + -ENE.] **—ter·pe·nic** (tər-pē′nĭk), **ter·pe·noid** (tûr′pə-noid′, tər-pē′-) *adj.*

ter·pin·e·ol (tər-pĭn′ē-ôl′, -ōl′) *n.* Any of three isomeric alcohols, $C_{10}H_{17}OH$, occurring naturally in the essential oils of certain plants and used as a solvent and in perfumes, soaps, and medicine. [TERP(ENE) + -INE + -OL.]

Terp·sich·o·re (tûrp-sĭk′ə-rē). *Greek Mythology.* The Muse of dancing and choral singing. [Greek *Terpsikhorē* : *terpein,* to delight, cheer + *khoros,* dance.]

terp·sich·o·re·an (tûrp-sĭk′ə-rē′ən, tûrp′sĭ-kôr′ē-ən, -kōr′ē-ən) *adj.* Of or pertaining to dancing.

~n. A dancer. [From TERPSICHORE.]

terr. **1.** terrace. **2.** territorial; territory.

ter·ra al·ba (tĕr′ə ăl′bə, ôl′bə) *n.* **1.** Finely pulverized gypsum used in making paper, paints, and plastics. **2.** A clay, **kaolin** *(see).* [New Latin, "white earth."]

ter·race (tĕr′ĭs) *n. Abbr.* **terr.** **1. a.** An open, level, often paved area adjacent to a house, serving as an outdoor living area; a patio. **b.** The flat roof of a house serving a similar purpose, as in warmer climates. **c.** An open colonnaded platform, as a porch or promenade. **2.** A relatively narrow horizontal shelf of land on the side of a slope, typically one of a landscaped series, having vertical or sloping sides and used for cultivation. **3.** *Geology.* A horizontal or gently inclined shelf or bench, as along the side of a river valley. **4.** A row of buildings erected on raised ground or on a sloping site. **5. a.** A narrow strip of landscaped earth in the middle of a street. **b.** A street, especially one having such a terrace.

~tr.v. **terraced, -racing, -races.** To make into or supply with a terrace: *a terraced hillside.* [Old French *terrasse,* terrace, pile of earth, from Old Provençal *terrassa,* from *terra,* earth, from Latin.]

ter·ra cot·ta, ter·ra-cot·ta (tĕr′ə kŏt′ə) *n.* **1. a.** A hard, brownish red to yellow waterproof material composed of clay, fine sand, and sometimes pulverized pottery waste, usually unglazed, used in pottery and building construction. **b.** Ceramic wares made of this material. **2.** A brownish orange color. [Italian, "baked earth."] **—ter·ra-cot·ta** *adj.*

ter·ra fir·ma (tĕr′ə fûr′mə) *n.* Solid ground; dry land. [Latin.]

ter·rain (tə-rān′, tĕ-) *n.* **1.** A tract of land; ground. **2.** The physical character of land; topography. **3.** A particular geographic area; region. [French, from Latin *terrēnum,* from *terrēnus,* TERRENE.]

ter·ra in·cog·ni·ta (tĕr′ə ĭn′kŏg-nē′tə, ĭn-kŏg′nĭ-tə) *n.* Unknown or unmapped territory. [Latin.]

Ter·ra·my·cin (tĕr′ə-mī′sĭn) *n.* A trademark for oxytetracycline.

ter·ra·pin (tĕr′ə-pĭn) *n.* **1.** Any of various aquatic North American turtles of the genus *Malaclemys* and related genera. **2.** *British.* A partly terrestrial freshwater turtle. [Algonquian (Virginia), from Eastern Algonquian *toolepeiwa* (unattested).]

ter·ra·que·ous (tĕ-rā′kwē-əs, -răk′wē-əs) *adj.* Composed of both land and water. [Medieval Latin *terraqueus* : *terra,* earth, from Latin + *aqueus,* AQUEOUS.]

ter·rar·i·um (tə-râr′ē-əm) *n., pl.* **-ums** or **-ia** (-ē-ə). A small enclosure or closed container in which small plants are grown or small animals, such as turtles or lizards, are kept. [New Latin : Latin *terra,* earth + -ARIUM.]

ter·raz·zo (tə-rät′sō, -răz′ō) *n.* A flooring material of marble or other stone chips set in mortar and polished smooth when dry. [Italian, "terrace."]

Ter·re Haute (tĕr′ə hōt′, hŭt′). City of western Indiana, on the Wabash River. It is the commercial and trade center of a farming and coal-mining region and the seat of Indiana State University.

ter·rene (tĕ-rēn′, tĕr′ēn′) *adj.* Of or pertaining to the earth; earthly. [Middle English, from Latin *terrēnus,* from *terra,* earth.]

ter·re·plein (tĕr′ə-plān′) *n.* **1.** The level ground on an embankment. **2.** The platform behind a parapet where heavy guns are mounted. [French *terreplein,* from Italian *terrapieno,* from *terrapienare,* to fill with earth, terrace : *terra,* earth + *pieno,* full.]

ter·res·tri·al (tə-rĕs′trē-əl) *adj.* **1.** Of or pertaining to the Earth, especially as distinct from the Moon, the stars, and the planets. **2.** Having a worldly, mundane character or quality. **3.** Of, pertaining to, or composed of land as distinct from water or air. **4.** *Biology.* Living or growing on land; not aquatic. —See Usage note at **earthly.**

~n. An inhabitant of the earth, especially a human being. [Middle English, from Latin *terrestris,* from *terra,* earth.] **—ter·res·tri·al·ly** *adv.* **—ter·res·tri·al·ness** *n.*

terrestrial planet *n.* Any of the four planets nearest the Sun, resembling Earth in density and composition: Mercury, Venus, Earth, or Mars.

terrestrial space *n.* The region of space surrounding the Earth (up to about 2,500 kilometers (4,000 miles).

terrestrial telescope *n.* An optical telescope, usually containing a separate lens or prism to give an erect image, that is used to view objects on land or water rather than for making astronomical observations. Compare **astronomical telescope.**

ter·ret (tĕr′ĭt) *n.* **1.** Either of the metal rings on a horse's harness through which the reins pass. **2.** A similar ring on an animal's collar, used for attaching a leash. [Middle English *tyret, toret,* from Old French *to(u)ret,* diminutive of *tour,* "circular movement," from *tourner,* to TURN.]

terre-verte (târ′vârt′) *n.* An olive-green pigment used by artists and commonly made from **glauconite** *(see).* [French, "green earth."] **—terre-verte** *adj.*

ter·ri·ble (tĕr′ə-bəl) *adj.* **1.** Causing terror or fear; dreadful. **2.** Eliciting awe; formidable: *terrible responsibilities.* **3.** Extreme in extent or degree; intense: *a terrible storm.* **4.** Unpleasant; disagreeable: *had a terrible time at the party.* **5.** Extremely bad: *a terrible actor.* [Middle English, from Old French, from Latin *terribilis,* from *terrēre,* to frighten.] **—ter·ri·ble·ness** *n.*

ter·ri·bly (tĕr′ə-blē) *adv.* **1.** In a terrible manner: *terribly wounded.* **2.** To a great extent; very much: *Would you mind terribly if I opened the window?* **3.** Very. Used as an intensive: *terribly nice.*

ter·ric·o·lous (tĕ-rĭk′ə-ləs, tə-) *adj. Biology.* Living on or in the ground. [Latin *terricola,* land dweller : *terra,* earth + -COLOUS.]

ter·ri·er[1] (tĕr′ē-ər) *n.* Any of various usually small, active dogs originally bred for hunting animals that live in burrows. [French *(chien) terrier,* from *terrier,* burrow, from *terre,* earth, from Latin *terra.*]

terrier[2] *n. Law.* A document or book enumerating boundaries and acreage and the conditions of their tenure. [Old French *terrier,* from *terre,* land. See **terrier** (dog).]

ter·rif·ic (tə-rĭf′ĭk) *adj.* **1.** Very good or fine; splendid: *a terrific chef.* **2.** Awesome; astounding: *drove at a terrific rate of speed.* **3.** Causing terror or great fear; terrifying: *a terrific wail.* **4.** Very bad or unpleasant; frightful: *a terrific headache.* [Latin *terrificus* : *terrēre,* to frighten + -FIC.] **—ter·rif·i·cal·ly** *adv.*

ter·ri·fy (tĕr′ə-fī′) *tr.v.* **-fied, -fying, -fies.** **1.** To fill with terror; make deeply afraid. **2.** To force or drive by causing terror; scare; intimidate: *terrified him into signing the contract.* —See Synonyms at **frighten.** [Latin *terrificāre,* from *terrificus,* TERRIFIC.]

ter·rig·e·nous (tĕ-rĭj′ə-nəs, tə-) *adj.* Derived from the land, especially by erosive action. Said chiefly of sediments. [From Latin *terrigena,* born of the earth : *terra,* earth + -GENOUS.]

ter·rine (tə-rēn′, tĕ-) *n.* **1.** An earthenware dish with a tightly fitting lid that is used for cooking and serving foods, as pâtés. **2.** Food that is cooked in a terrine, especially a type of pâté. [French.]

ter·ri·to·ri·al (tĕr′ə-tôr′ē-əl, -tōr′ē-əl) *adj. Abbr.* **terr.** **1.** Of or pertaining to a territory or to its powers of jurisdiction. **2.** Pertaining or restricted to a particular territory; regional; local. **3.** Marked by or exhibiting a tendency to defend one's territory: *territorial instincts.* **4. Territorial.** Of, pertaining to, or designating a volunteer force maintained to provide a reserve: *the British Territorial Army.*

~n. **Territorial.** A member of a territorial army. **—ter·ri·to·ri·al·ly** *adv.*

ter·ri·to·ri·al·ism (tĕr′ə-tôr′ē-ə-lĭz′əm, tĕr′ə-tōr′-) *n.* **1.** A social system that gives authority and influence in a state to the landowners; landlordism. **2.** A system of church government based on the primacy of civil power. **—ter·ri·to·ri·al·ist** *n.*

ter·ri·to·ri·al·i·ty (tĕr′ə-tôr′ē-ăl′ə-tē, tĕr′ə-tōr′-) *n.* **1.** The status of a territory. **2. a.** The behavior of one who stays close to or jealously guards his territory. **b.** A behavior pattern in animals that consists of occupying and defending a territory.

ter·ri·to·ri·al·ize (tĕr′ə-tôr′ē-ə-līz′, tĕr′ə-tōr′-) *tr.v.* **-ized, -izing, -izes.** **1.** To make territorial, especially: **a.** To reduce to the status of a territory. **b.** To extend or restrict to a particular territory. **2.** To add to by the acquisition of territory. **3.** To distribute among particular territories. **—ter·ri·to·ri·al·i·za·tion** *n.*

territorial waters *pl.n.* Inland and coastal waters under the jurisdiction of a state; especially, the ocean waters within three miles of the shoreline.

ter·ri·to·ry (tĕr′ə-tôr′ē, -tōr′ē) *n., pl.* **-ries.** *Abbr.* **t., T., terr.** **1.** An area of land; region. **2.** The land and waters under the jurisdiction of a state, nation, or sovereign. **3. Territory. a.** A part of the United States that is not admitted as a state, that is administered by a governor, and that has its own legislature. **b.** A part of Canada or Australia not accorded statehood or provincial status. **c.** A semiautonomous geographic region, as a colonial possession, that is dependent on an external government. **4. a.** An area inhabited by an individual animal or a mating pair or group of animals and often vigorously defended against intruders. **b.** A comparable concrete or psychological area regarded by a person as his own inviolable domain. **5.** The area for which a person is responsible as representative or agent: *a salesman's territory.* **6.** The area of a sports field defended by a team. **7.** A sphere of action or interest; province. [Middle English, from Latin *territōrium,* from *terra,* land.]

ter·ror (tĕr′ər) *n.* **1. a.** Intense, overpowering fear. **b.** Something that instills such fear; a terrifying person, thing, or occurrence. **c.** The ability to instill such fear; terribleness: *the terror of the haunted house.* **2.** Systematic violence carried out against private citizens, public property, and political enemies with the aim of enforcing demands or maintaining supremacy: *a reign of terror.* **3.** *Informal.* An annoying or intolerable pest; a nuisance. —See Synonyms at **fear.** [Middle English *terrour,* from Old French, from Latin *terror,* from *terrēre,* to frighten.]

ter·ror·ism (tĕr′ə-rĭz′əm) *n.* The use of terror, violence, and intimi-

Terpsichore *According to Greek mythology, the Muses would sing, dance, and play music at the feasts of the gods. Terpsichore, the Muse of dance and choral singing, is shown playing a harp on this Greek vase made in about 440 B.C.*

terra cotta *In the 1880's French archaeologists discovered hundreds of terra-cotta figurines buried in tombs at Myrina, an ancient Greek settlement on the coast of modern-day Turkey. This fired-clay figure of Aphrodite—the Greek goddess of love and beauty—was made there in about A.D. 20.*

terrapin *Freshwater tortoises, or terrapins, are found throughout the tropics. This common species, the red-eared terrapin, is native to the Americas.*

dation to achieve an end, especially a political end. —**ter·ror·ist** *adj. & n.* —**ter·ror·is·tic** (tĕr′ə-rĭs′tĭk) *adj.*

ter·ror·ize (tĕr′ə-rīz′) *tr.v.* **-ized, -izing, -izes. 1.** To fill or overpower with terror; terrify. **2.** To coerce or maintain control over by intimidation or fear: *Vandals terrorized the neighborhood.* —See Synonyms at **frighten.** —**ter·ror·i·za·tion** *n.* —**ter·ror·iz·er** *n.*

ter·ror·strick·en (tĕr′ər-strĭk′ən) *adj.* Also **ter·ror·struck** (-strŭk′). Overcome by terror.

ter·ry (tĕr′ē) *n., pl.* **-ries. 1.** Any of the uncut loops that form the pile of a fabric. **2.** A pile fabric, usually woven of cotton, with uncut loops on both sides, used for such articles as bath towels and robes. In this sense, also called "terry cloth." [18th century : origin obscure.]

terse (tûrs) *adj.* **terser, tersest. 1.** Effectively concise; free of superfluity. **2.** Curt; brusque. —See Synonyms at **concise.** [Originally "polished," "refined," from Latin *tersus,* past participle of *tergēre,* to wipe off, polish. See **deterge.**] —**terse·ly** *adv.* —**terse·ness** *n.*

ter·tian fever (tûr′shən) *n.* A form of malaria that is caused by the invasion of *Plasmodium vivax* into new red blood cells and is characterized by a 48-hour life cycle in the human body with a recurrence of fever paroxysms at the end of each such period. Also called "tertian malaria." [*Tertian,* from Latin *tertiānus,* of the third, from *tertius,* third.]

ter·ti·ar·y (tûr′shē-ĕr′ē) *adj.* **1.** Third in place, order, degree, or rank. **2.** Of, designating, or providing education above the secondary level, as in a college or university: *an examination at the tertiary level.* **3.** *Chemistry.* **a.** Of or pertaining to salts of acids containing three replaceable hydrogen atoms. **b.** Of or pertaining to organic compounds in which a group, such as an alcohol or amine, is bound to three nonelementary radicals. **4.** Of or pertaining to the third order of a Roman Catholic monastic system. **5.** Of, pertaining to, or involving the provision of a service rather than the extraction or production of goods: *Transportation is a tertiary industry.* **6.** Of, pertaining to, or designating the short flight feathers nearest the body on the inner edge of a bird's wing.
∼*n., pl.* **tertiaries. 1.** A tertiary feather. **2.** A member of a Roman Catholic tertiary order. [Latin *tertiārius,* from *tertius,* third.]

Ter·ti·ar·y (tûr′shē-ĕr′ē) *adj.* Of, belonging to, or designating the geologic time, system of rocks, and sedimentary deposits of the first period of the Cenozoic era, extending from the Cretaceous period of the Mesozoic era to the Quarternary period of the Cenozoic era, characterized by the appearance of modern flora and of apes and other large mammals.
∼*n.* The Tertiary period or system of deposits.

tertiary stress *n. Linguistics.* A stress weaker than primary and secondary stress in phonetic systems recognizing three or more degrees of stress. Also called "tertiary accent." Compare **primary stress, secondary stress.**

tertiary color *n.* A color resulting from the mixture of two secondary colors.

ter·ti·um quid (tûr′shē-əm kwĭd′) *n.* Something that cannot be classified into either of two groups themselves considered to be exhaustive; an intermediate thing or factor. [Late Latin, "third something" (translation of Greek *triton ti*).]

Ter·tul·li·an (tər-tŭl′ē-ən, -tŭl′yən) (*c.* 160–230). Carthaginian theologian. Converted to Christianity (*c.* 193), he later broke with the church (207) and moved to Africa to join the Montanists soon after forming his own sect, the Tertullianists. His writings, such as *De Carne Christi,* greatly influenced Western thought and provide descriptions of early Christian belief and worship.

tervalent. Variant of **trivalent.**

Ter·y·lene (tĕr′ə-lēn′) *n.* A trademark for a synthetic polyester fiber that is used in making crease-resistant fabric.

ter·za ri·ma (tĕrt′sə rē′mə) *n., pl.* **terze rime** (tĕrt′sā rē′mā′). A verse form consisting of a series of tercets having 10- or 11-syllable lines of which the middle line of one tercet rhymes with the first and third lines of the following tercet. [Italian, "third rhyme."]

tes·la (tĕs′lə) *n. Abbr.* **T** The unit of magnetic flux density in the International System equal to one weber per square meter. [After Nikola TESLA.]

Tes·la (tĕs′lə), **Nikola** (1856–1943). Croatian-born U.S. electrical engineer and inventor. His many inventions include the first practical system for distributing alternating current.

tesla coil *n.* A transformer with an air-core primary and a capacitor-tuned secondary, used as a source of high-frequency high voltage, as for x-ray tubes.

tes·sel·late (tĕs′ə-lāt′) *tr.v.* **-lated, -lating, -lates.** To form into or inlay with a mosaic pattern, as by using small squares of stone or glass. [Latin *tessellātus,* from *tessella,* a small cube, diminutive of *tessera,* TESSERA.] —**tes·sel·la·tion** *n.*

tes·ser·a (tĕs′ər-ə) *n., pl.* **-serae** (-ə-rē′). One of the small squares of stone or glass used in making mosaic patterns. [Latin, "a square," from Greek *tesseres, tessares,* four.] —**tes·ser·al** *adj.*

tes·ser·act (tĕs′ə-răkt′) *n. Mathematics.* The four-dimensional extension of a cube. [Greek *tesseres,* four + *aktis,* ray.]

tes·si·tu·ra (tĕs′ə-to͝or′ə) *n. Music.* The range within which most notes of a voice part fall. [Italian, "texture."]

test[1] (tĕst) *n.* **1.** Any of various procedures by which a person or thing may be examined for certain properties or qualities, as: **a.** A series of questions or problems designed to assess knowledge, skill, or aptitude. **b.** A series of operations or functions designed to assess effectiveness or conformity to a standard: *nuclear weapons test.* **c.** A diagnostic medical examination: *a pregnancy test.* Also used adjectivally: *test conditions.* **2.** A criterion; standard. **3. a.** A physical or chemical reaction by which a substance may be detected or its properties ascertained. **b.** The reagent used in such determination. **c.** A positive result obtained. **4.** A cupel.
∼*v.* **tested, testing, tests.** —*tr.* **1.** To subject to a test; examine. **2. a.** To determine the presence or properties of (a substance). **b.** To assay (metal) in a cupel. **3.** To try; tax: *tested his patience.* —*intr.* **1.** To undergo a test. **2.** To achieve as a score or rating through testing. **3.** To exhibit certain properties under test conditions. **4.** To administer a test in order to analyze or diagnose: *test for acid content.* [Middle English, cupel for treating ores, from Old French, pot, from Latin *testum*†, earthen vessel.]

test[2] *n.* A hard external covering, such as that of certain insects and other invertebrates. [Latin *testa,* shell. See **testa.**]

tes·ta (tĕs′tə) *n., pl.* **-tae** (-tē′). The often thick or hard outer coat of a seed. [Latin *testa*†, clay, brick, tile, shell.]

tes·ta·ceous (tĕ-stā′shəs) *adj.* **1.** *Biology.* Of, pertaining to, or having a shell or shell-like outer covering. **2.** Having the characteristic reddish-brown or brownish-yellow color of bricks. [Latin *testāceus,* from *testa,* shell. See **test** (shell).]

tes·ta·cy (tĕs′tə-sē) *n. Law.* The condition of being testate.

tes·ta·ment (tĕs′tə-mənt) *n.* **1.** *Law.* A written document providing for the disposition of one's personal property after death; a will. Used chiefly in the phrase *last will and testament.* **2. a.** A tangible proof or tribute that testifies to or serves as evidence of something. **b.** A statement of belief or conviction; a credo. **3. a.** *Archaic.* A covenant between humanity and God. **b. Testament.** Either of the two main divisions of the Bible, the Old Testament and the New Testament. [Middle English, from Late Latin *testāmentum* (translation of Greek *diathēkē,* scripture), from Latin, will, from *testārī,* to be a witness, assert, make a will, from *testis,* witness.] —**tes·ta·men·ta·ry** (tĕs′tə-mĕn′tə-rē, -mĕn′trē) *adj.*

tes·tate (tĕs′tāt′) *adj.* Having made a legally valid will before death. [Middle English, from Latin *testātus,* past participle of *testārī,* to make a will. See **testament.**]

tes·ta·tor (tĕs′tā′tər, tĕs-tā′tər) *n.* A person who has made a legally valid will before death. [Middle English *testatour,* from Norman French, from Latin *testātor,* from *testārī,* to make a will. See **testament.**]

tes·ta·trix (tĕs-tā′trĭks, tĕs′tā′-) *n.* A female testator. [Latin *testātrix,* feminine of *testātor,* TESTATOR.]

test ban *n.* A mutual and voluntary agreement between nations to forgo atmospheric testing of nuclear weapons.

test case *n.* **1.** A legal action whose outcome is likely to set a precedent or test the constitutionality of a statute. **2.** An issue whose outcome is likely to be treated as a precedent.

test·cross (tĕst′krôs′, -krŏs′) *n. Genetics.* The crossing of a hybrid exhibiting the dominant phenotype of a particular gene back to a parent homozygous for the recessive allele of this gene in order to determine whether the hybrid is homozygous or heterozygous.

test-drive (tĕst′drīv′) *tr.v.* **-drove** (-drōv′), **-driven** (-drĭv′ən), **-driving, -drives.** To drive (an automobile, for example) to evaluate performance.

test·ed (tĕs′tĭd) *adj.* Having been subjected to a test or certified through testing. Used in combination: *tuberculin-tested; heat-tested; toxin-tested.*

tes·ter[1] (tĕs′tər) *n.* A canopy over a bed. [Middle English, from Medieval Latin *testerium,* headpiece, from Late Latin *testa,* skull, head, from Latin, shell. See **testa.**]

tes·ter[2] (tĕs′tər) *n.* A former English coin, the **teston** *(see).*

test·er[3] (tĕs′tər) *n.* One that tests.

tes·tes. Plural of **testis.**

tes·ti·cle (tĕs′tĭ-kəl) *n.* Either of the male reproductive organs, situated in an external scrotum behind the penis in humans and most mammals, that produce spermatozoa and secrete androgens. Also called "testis." [Middle English *testicule,* from Latin *testiculus,* diminutive of *testis,* TESTIS.]

tes·tic·u·late (tĕs-tĭk′yə-lĭt, -lāt′) *adj.* Also **tes·tic·u·lar** (-lər). **1.** Having the shape of a testicle; ovoid. **2.** Having testicles.

tes·ti·fy (tĕs′tə-fī′) *v.* **-fied, -fying, -fies.** —*intr.* **1.** To make a declaration of truth or fact under oath; submit testimony. **2.** To make a serious or solemn statement in support of an argument, position, or asserted fact; affirm. **3.** To serve as witness or evidence: *I can testify to their honesty.* **4.** To make an open profession of religious faith. —*tr.* **1.** To bear witness to; provide evidence for. **2.** To state or affirm under oath. **3.** To declare publicly; make known. [Middle English *testifien,* from Latin *testificārī* : *testis,* witness + *facere,* to make.] —**tes·ti·fi·ca·tion** *n.* —**tes·ti·fi·er** *n.*

tes·ti·mo·ni·al (tĕs′tə-mō′nē-əl) *n.* **1.** A written statement providing evidence of a person's character or ability; a letter of recommendation. **2.** Something given as a tribute for a person's service or achievement.
∼*adj.* Of, pertaining to, or being testimony or a testimonial. [Middle English, noun and adjective, from Old French, from Late Latin *testimōniālis,* from Latin *testimōnium,* TESTIMONY.]

tes·ti·mo·ny (tĕs′tə-mō′nē) *n., pl.* **-nies. 1.** A declaration or affirmation of fact or truth, such as that given before a court of law. **2.** Evidence in support of a fact or assertion; proof. **3.** The collective written and spoken testimony offered in a legal case. **4.** A public declaration regarding a religious experience. **5.** *Often* **Testimony. a.** The law of Moses, inscribed on the tablets of stone. Exodus 25:16. **b.** The ark containing these tablets. Exodus 16:34. [Middle English, from Latin *testimōnium,* from *testis,* witness.]

testing ground *n.* An area or environment where something is subjected to a critical test: *a nuclear testing ground.*

tes·tis (tĕs′tĭs) *n., pl.* **-tes** (-tēz′). A testicle. [Latin, "witness" (to masculinity).]

test match *n.* Any of a series of international sports matches, especially in cricket.

tes·ton (tĕs′tŏn′) *n.* Also **tes·toon** (tĕs-toon′). Any of various coins with the image of a head on one side, especially: **1.** A 16th-century silver coin of France. **2.** An English coin stamped with the head of Henry VIII, originally worth a shilling and later sixpence. In this sense, also called "tester." [Middle English, from Old French *teste* and Italian *testa,* head, both from Late Latin *testa,* skull, from Latin, shell. See **testa.**]

tes·tos·ter·one (tĕs-tŏs′tə-rōn′) *n.* A male sex hormone, $C_{19}H_{28}O_2$, produced in the testicles and functioning to control secondary sexual characteristics. [TEST(IS) + STER(OL) + -ONE.]

test paper *n.* **1.** A paper saturated with a reagent, such as litmus, used in making chemical tests. **2. a.** A paper or booklet bearing examination questions. **b.** A paper or booklet bearing a student's work for an examination.

test pilot *n.* A pilot who flies aircraft of new or experimental design to test them for conformity to planned standards.

test tube *n.* A clear cylindrical glass tube, usually open at one end and rounded at the other, used in laboratory experiments.

test-tube baby (tĕst′toob′, -tyoob′) *n.* A baby conceived by fertilization of an ovum outside the body and implanted in the womb at the blastocyst stage.

tes·tu·di·nal (tĕs-tood′n-əl, -tyood′n-əl) *adj.* Also **tes·tu·di·nar·y** (-tood′n-ĕr′ē, -tyood′n-ĕr′ē). **1.** Of, pertaining to, or resembling a tortoise or turtle. **2.** Of or pertaining to the shell of a tortoise or turtle.

tes·tu·do (tĕs-tood′dō, -tyood′dō) *n., pl.* **-dos.** An ancient Roman siege device consisting either of a movable arched screen or of shields held up to interlock over their bearers' heads, protecting the besiegers' approach to a wall. Also called "tortoise." [Latin *testūdo,* "tortoise," a covering, from *testa,* shell. See **testa.**]

tes·ty (tĕs′tē) *adj.* **-tier, -tiest. 1.** Irritable; touchy; peevish: *a testy old codger.* **2.** Characterized by irritability, impatience, or exasperation: *a testy remark.* [Middle English *testif,* headstrong, from Norman French, from Old French *teste,* head. See **teston.**] —**tes·ti·ly** *adv.* —**tes·ti·ness** *n.*

Tet (tĕt) *n.* The lunar New Year as celebrated during January or February in Southeast Asia. [Vietnamese *têt,* from Ancient Chinese *tsiet,* "festival" (Mandarin Chinese *jié*).]

te·tan·ic (tē-tăn′ĭk) *adj.* **1.** Of or pertaining to tetanus. **2.** Of or pertaining to tetany.
~*n.* A poison producing symptoms similar to those of tetanus. —**te·tan·i·cal·ly** *adv.*

tet·a·nize (tĕt′n-īz′) *tr.v.* **-nized, -nizing, -nizes.** To affect with tetanic convulsions; produce or induce tetanus in. —**tet·a·ni·za·tion** *n.* —**tet·a·niz·er** *n.*

tet·a·nus (tĕt′n-əs) *n.* **1.** An acute, often fatal infectious disease that is caused by a bacillus, *Clostridium tetani,* that generally enters the body through wounds, and is characterized by rigidity and spasmodic contraction of the voluntary muscles. Also called "lockjaw." **2.** A state of continuous muscular contraction caused by reaction to rapidly repeated stimuli, such as electric shocks. [Learned respelling of Middle English *tetane,* from Latin *tetanus,* from Greek *tetanos,* from adjective, "stretched," from *teinein,* to stretch.] —**tet·a·nal** (tĕt′n-əl), **tet·a·noid** (tĕt′n-oid′) *adj.*

tet·a·ny (tĕt′n-ē) *n.* An abnormal condition, occurring chiefly in young people, characterized by periodic painful muscular spasms caused by faulty calcium metabolism. [From TETANUS.]

tetch·y, tech·y (tĕch′ē) *adj.* **-ier, -iest.** Peevish; irritable. [Probably from obsolete *tecche, tache,* blemish, fault (of character), from Old French *tache, teche,* blemish, from Late Latin *tacca* (unattested), from Gothic *taikns,* sign.] —**tetch·i·ly** *adv.* —**tetch·i·ness** *n.*

tête-à-tête (tāt′ə-tāt′, tĕt′ə-tĕt′) *adv.* Together without the intrusion of others; in intimate privacy: *talk tête-à-tête.*
~*adj.* For or between two only; intimate and private.
~*n.* **1.** A private conversation between two people. **2.** A sofa for two, especially an S-shaped one allowing the occupants to face each other. [French, "head to head."]

tête-bêche (tāt′bāsh′, tĕt′bĕsh′) *adj.* Of, pertaining to, or designating a pair of postage stamps printed upside-down in relation to one another. [French : *tête,* head + *bechevet,* "double-headed" : *bes,* twice, from Latin *bis* (see **bi-**) + *chevet,* head (of a bed), from Latin *capitium,* head covering, from *caput,* head.]

teth (tĕt, tĕs) *n.* The ninth letter in the Hebrew alphabet. See feature at **alphabet.** [Hebrew *tēth.*]

teth·er (tĕth′ər) *n.* **1.** A rope, chain, or halter for an animal, tied fast at one end to allow only a limited range of movement. **2.** The range of one's resources; especially, the limits of one's endurance.
~*tr.v.* **tethered, -ering, -ers.** To restrict or bind with or as if with a tether. [Middle English *tethir,* from Old Norse *tjóthr.*]

Te·thys (tē′thĭs). *Greek Mythology.* A Titaness and sea goddess who was both sister and consort of Oceanus.

Te·ton (tē′tŏn). River, rising in several branches in the Rocky Mts. of northwestern Montana and flowing 230 kilometers (143 miles) eastward.

Teton Range. Part of the Rocky Mts. in northwestern Wyoming and southeastern Idaho, just south of Yellowstone National Park.

Grand Teton, the highest elevation (*c.* 5,000 meters; 13,770 feet), is included in Grand Teton National Park.

tet·ra (tĕt′rə) *n., pl.* **-ras** or collectively **tetra.** Any of various small, colorful tropical freshwater fishes of the family Characidae, popular in home aquariums. [Short for New Latin *Tetragonopterus* (former classification of tetras) : TETRAGON (from their squared-off dorsal fins) + -PTER.]

tetra-, tetr– *prefix.* Indicates four; for example, **tetrachloride, tetracid.** [Greek.]

tet·ra·ba·sic (tĕt′rə-bā′sĭk) *adj.* **1.** Containing four replaceable hydrogen atoms in a molecule. Said of an acid. **2.** Containing four univalent basic atoms or radicals. Said of a base or salt. —**tet·ra·ba·sic·i·ty** (tĕt′rə-bā-sĭs′ə-tē) *n.*

tet·ra·chlo·ride (tĕt′rə-klôr′īd′, -klōr′īd′) *n.* A chemical compound containing four chlorine atoms per molecule.

tet·ra·chord (tĕt′rə-kôrd′) *n. Music.* A series of four diatonic tones encompassing the interval of a perfect fourth. [Greek *tetrakhordon,* from *tetrakhordos* : TETRA- + *khordē,* string.]

te·trac·id (tē-trăs′ĭd) *adj.* **1.** Able to react with four molecules of a monobasic acid. Said of a base. **2.** Containing four replaceable hydrogen atoms. Said of an acid or acid salt.
~*n.* An acid containing four replaceable hydrogen atoms.

tet·ra·cy·cline (tĕt′rə-sī′klēn′) *n.* A yellow crystalline compound, $C_{22}H_{24}N_2O_8$, synthesized from chlortetracycline or derived from bacteria of the genus *Streptomyces* and used as an antibiotic. [TETRA- + CYCL(IC) + -INE.]

tet·rad (tĕt′răd′) *n.* **1.** A group or series of four. **2.** A tetravalent atom, radical, or element. **3. a.** A group of four chromatids formed during meiosis by the pairing of two homologous chromosomes that have each divided into two chromatids. **b.** A body formed of four cells, as pollen grains from one mother cell. [Greek *tetras* (stem *tetrad-*).] —**te·trad·ic** (tē-trăd′ĭk) *adj.*

tet·rad·y·mite (tē-trăd′ə-mīt′) *n.* A steel-gray bismuth ore, chiefly bismuth telluride. [Late Greek *tetradumos,* fourfold (since it occurs in compound twin crystals) : TETRA- + Greek *didumos,* double.]

tet·ra·dy·na·mous (tĕt′rə-dī′nə-məs) *adj. Botany.* Having six stamens of which two are shorter than the others. [TETRA- + Greek *dynamis,* power (see **dynamic**) + -OUS.]

tet·ra·eth·yl lead (tĕt′rə-ĕth′əl) *n.* A colorless, poisonous, oily liquid, $Pb(C_2H_5)_4$, used in gasoline for internal-combustion engines as an antiknock agent. Also called "lead tetraethyl."

tet·ra·gon (tĕt′rə-gŏn′) *n.* A four-sided polygon; quadrilateral. [Late Latin *tetragōnum,* from Greek *tetragōnon* : TETRA- + -GON.] —**te·trag·o·nal** (tē-trăg′ə-nəl) *adj.*

Tet·ra·gram·ma·ton (tĕt′rə-grăm′ə-tŏn′) *n.* The four Hebrew letters usually transliterated as YHWH or JHVH (Yahweh or Jehovah) and used as a symbol or substitute for the ineffable name of God. [Middle English *Tetragramaton,* from Greek *tetragrammaton,* four-letter word : TETRA- + *gramma* (stem *grammat-*), letter.]

tet·ra·he·dral (tĕt′rə-hē′drəl) *adj.* **1.** Having four plane faces. **2.** Of, pertaining to, or formed like a tetrahedron.

tet·ra·he·drite (tĕt′rə-hē′drīt′) *n.* A grayish-black copper ore, essentially $(CuFe)_{12}Sb_4S_{13}$, often containing other elements. [German *Tetraëdrit,* from Greek *tetraedros,* four-faced (it occurs in tetrahedral crystals). See **tetrahedron.**]

tet·ra·he·dron (tĕt′rə-hē′drən) *n., pl.* **-drons** or **-dra** (-drə). A polyhedron with four plane faces. [New Latin, from Late Greek *tetraedron,* from Greek *tetraedros* : TETRA- + *hedra,* face.]

tet·ra·hy·dro·can·nab·i·nol (tĕt′rə-hī′drə-kə-năb′ə-nôl′, -nōl′) *n.* A crystalline compound that is the primary intoxicant in marijuana.

te·tral·o·gy (tē-trăl′ə-jē, -trŏl′ə-jē) *n., pl.* **-gies. 1.** In ancient Athens, a series of four dramas, three tragic and one satiric, performed at the festivals dedicated to Dionysus. **2.** A series of four related theatrical or literary works. [Greek *tetralogia* : TETRA- + -LOGY.]

tetralogy of Fallot (fă-lō′) *n.* A congenital deformity involving four particular defects of the heart. [After E.-L.A. *Fallot* (1850–1911), French physician.]

te·tram·er·ous (tē-trăm′ər-əs) *adj.* **1.** Having or consisting of four similar parts. **2.** *Botany.* Having flower parts, such as sepals, petals, and stamens, in sets of four. [New Latin *tetramerus,* from Greek *tetramerēs* : TETRA- + -MEROUS.] —**te·tram·er·ism** *n.*

te·tram·e·ter (tē-trăm′ə-tər) *n.* A line of verse consisting of four metrical feet. [Late Latin *tetrametrus,* from Greek *tetrametros,* having four measures : TETRA- + -METER.] —**te·tram·e·ter** *adj.*

tet·ra·ploid (tĕt′rə-ploid′) *adj. Genetics.* Having four times the haploid number of chromosomes.
~*n. Genetics.* A tetraploid individual, cell, or nucleus. [TETRA- + -PLOID.]

tet·ra·pod (tĕt′rə-pŏd′) *adj.* Having four feet, legs, or leglike appendages. [Greek *tetrapous* (stem *tetrapod-*) : TETRA- + -POD.] —**tet·ra·pod** *n.*

tet·rap·ter·ous (tē-trăp′tər-əs) *adj.* Having four wings. Said of certain insects. [Greek *tetrapteros* : TETRA- + -PTEROUS.]

tet·rarch (tĕt′rärk′, tē′trärk′) *n.* **1.** A governor of one of any of the four divisions of a country or province, especially in the ancient Roman empire. **2.** One of four joint rulers. **3.** A subordinate ruler. **4.** The commander of a subdivision of a phalanx in ancient Greece. [Middle English, from Late Latin *tetrarcha,* from Latin *tetrarchēs,* from Greek *tetrarkhēs* : TETR(A)- + -ARCH.] —**tet·rarch·y** (tĕt′rär-kē, tē′trär-kē) *n.* —**te·trar·chic** (tĕ-trär′kĭk, tē-) *adj.*

tet·ra·spore (tĕt′rə-spôr′, -spōr′) *n. Botany.* Any of four spores produced in a group from a sporangium, as in certain algae. —**tet·ra·spor·ic** (tĕt′rə-spôr′ĭk, -spōr′ĭk), **tet·ra·spor·ous** (-əs) *adj.*

te·tras·ti·chous (tĕ-trăs'tĭ-kəs) *adj. Botany.* Arranged in four vertical rows. Said of leaves or flowers on a stalk. [Late Latin *tetrastichus,* having four lines, from Greek *tetrastikhos* : TETRA- + -STICHOUS.]

tet·ra·va·lent (tĕt'rə-vā'lənt) *adj.* Having valence 4.

tet·rode (tĕt'rōd') *n.* **1.** An electronic vacuum tube with four electrodes, a cathode, a control grid, a screen grid, and an anode. **2.** A transistor with two connections to the base or gate to improve high-frequency performance. [TETR(A)- + -ODE (path).]

te·trox·ide (tĕ-trŏk'sīd') *n.* A chemical compound containing four oxygen atoms per molecule. [TETR(A)- + OXIDE.]

tet·ryl (tĕt'rəl) *n.* A yellow crystalline explosive consisting of (NO₂)₃C₆H₂N(NO₂)CH₃, used chiefly as a primer or detonator. Also called "nitramine." [TETR(A)- + -YL.]

tet·ter (tĕt'ər) *n.* Any of various skin diseases, as psoriasis, herpes, and especially eczema, characterized by eruptions and itching. [Middle English *teter,* Old English *tet(e)r.*]

Tet·zel or **Te·zel** (tĕt'səl), **Johann** (*c.* 1465–1519). German monk. Appointed to sell indulgences to raise funds for the Catholic Church, he toured Germany, where his simplistic and unorthodox sermons were regarded as symptomatic of the abuses within the Church. Provoked by Tetzel's teachings, Martin Luther wrote his 95 theses (1517), which in turn sparked the Reformation.

Teu·to·burg Forest (tōō'tō-bûrg', tyōō'-). *German* **Teu·to·bur·ger Wald** (toi'tō-bŏŏr'gər vält'). Range of low, wooded hills in north-central West Germany. A monument commemorates the site (unknown) of a victory of the Germans over the Roman legions (A.D. 9) in which the Roman forces were nearly annihilated.

Teu·ton (tōōt'n, tyōōt'n) *n.* **1.** A member of an ancient people, probably of Germanic or Celtic origin, who lived in Jutland until the late 2nd century B.C., when they migrated southward. **2.** A member of a people speaking a Germanic language; especially, a German. [Latin *Teutonī.*]

Teu·ton·ic (tōō-tŏn'ĭk, tyōō-) *adj.* **1.** Of, relating to, or characteristic of the Germanic people or the Teutons. **2.** Of or relating to the Germanic languages.
~*n.* The subfamily of Germanic languages.

Teutonic Knights *pl.n.* German military religious order founded (1190–91) at Acre. In 1211 they moved from Palestine to eastern Europe and after 50 years of campaigning subdued Prussia and many of the eastern Baltic states. The order went into decline in the 15th century.

Teu·ton·ism (tōōt'n-ĭz'əm, tyōōt'n-) *n.* **1.** A German practice or idiom. **2.** German character or civilization.

Tevere. See Tiber.

Te·vet, Te·bet, Te·beth (tā-vāth', tā'vəs') *n.* The fourth month of the Hebrew year. See feature at **calendar.** [Hebrew *tēbhēth,* from Akkadian *ṭebētu,* perhaps "month of sinking in," "muddy month," from *ṭebū,* to sink in.]

Tewkes·bur·y (tōōks'bĕr'ē, -bə-rē, tyōōks'-). Borough in Gloucestershire, west-central England, on the Avon River near its junction with the Severn. At Bloody Meadow, south of the town, Edward IV defeated the Lancastrians in the Wars of the Roses (1471).

Tex·as (tĕk'səs). *Abbr.* **Tex.** State in the south-central United States, bordering on Mexico. It is the second largest state in the Union, after Alaska. Its chief agricultural products are cotton, rice, and cattle, and the chief industry is the manufacture of chemicals. However, the great wealth of Texas is its vast oil resources. Texas was owned by Spain until it gained independence in 1836. It was annexed to the United States in 1845 and admitted as a state of the Union. The capital is Austin; the largest cities are Houston, Dallas, and San Antonio. —**Tex·an** *adj. & n.*

Texas fever *n.* An infectious disease of cattle and related animals, caused by a parasitic microorganism, *Babesia bigemina,* and transmitted by ticks.

Texas tower *n.* A offshore radar tower. [After TEXAS.]

text (tĕkst) *n.* **1. a.** The wording or words of something written or printed. **b.** The words of something delivered orally, as a speech or song, appearing in print. **c.** The exact wording and word sequence of an author as opposed to translation, revision, or condensation. **2. a.** The body of a printed work as distinct from a preface, footnote, or appendix. **b.** The words in a book as distinct from pictures or illustrations. **3.** A scriptural passage to be read and expounded in a sermon. **4. a.** A reference used as the starting point of a discussion. **b.** The subject matter of a discourse. **5.** A textbook. [Middle English *texte,* from Old French, from Medieval Latin *textus,* (scriptural) text, from Latin, literary composition, "woven thing," from the past participle of *texere,* to weave.]

text·book (tĕkst'bŏŏk') *n.* A book used as a standard work for the formal study of a particular subject.
~*adj.* Conforming to a stereotype; typical: *a textbook example.*

tex·tile (tĕk'stīl', -stəl) *n.* **1.** Fabric, especially one that is woven or knitted; cloth. **2.** Fiber or yarn for weaving or making into fabric. Also used adjectively: *the textile industry.* [French, from Latin *textilis,* from *textus,* "woven thing." See text.]

tex·tu·al (tĕks'chōō-əl) *adj.* **1.** Of, pertaining to, or contained in a text. **2.** Based on or conforming to a text. [Middle English, from Old French *textuel.* See text, -al.] —**tex·tu·al·ly** *adv.*

textual criticism *n.* **1.** A study of a written work that seeks to establish the original text. **2.** See **criticism** (sense 5).

tex·tu·al·ism (tĕks'chōō-ə-lĭz'əm) *n.* **1.** Strict adherence to a text, especially of the Scriptures. **2.** Textual criticism, especially of the Scriptures. —**tex·tu·al·ist** *n.*

tex·tu·ar·y (tĕks'chōō-ĕr'ē) *adj.* Of, pertaining to, or contained in a text; textual.
~*n., pl.* **textuaries.** A specialist in the study of the Scriptures.

tex·ture (tĕks'chər) *n.* **1.** The appearance and feel of the surface of something: *the smooth texture of ivory.* **2. a.** The appearance of a fabric resulting from the woven arrangement of its yarns or fibers. **b.** A surface appearance suggesting the weave of a fabric. **c.** Consistency, as of a liquid. **3.** A grainy, fibrous, woven, or dimensional quality as opposed to a uniformly flat, smooth aspect; surface interest: *Brick walls give a room texture.* **4.** Distinctive or identifying qualities: *the texture of suburban life.* **5.** The representation of the structure of a surface as distinct from color or form. **6.** *Music.* A sound pattern created by melody, harmony, and rhythm.
~*tr.v.* **textured, -turing, -tures.** To give a distinctive texture to. [Originally, "weaving," from Latin *textūra,* from *textus,* woven thing. See text.] —**tex·tur·al** *adj.* —**tex·tur·al·ly** *adv.*

tex·tured (tĕks'chərd) *adj.* **1.** Having a specified kind of texture. Used in combination: *a rough-textured tweed.* **2.** Having marked texture: *a textured wall of stucco.*

tex·tus re·cep·tus (tĕk'stəs rĭ-sĕp'təs) *n.* Received text; specifically, the received text of the Greek New Testament. [Latin.]

Tezel, Johann. See Johann **Tetzel.**

tfr. transfer.

Th The symbol for the element thorium.

–th¹ *suffix.* Indicates: **1.** The act or result of the act expressed in the verb root; for example, **spilth. 2.** The quality suggested by the adjective root; for example, **width.** [Middle English *-th(e),* Old English *-thu, -tho,* from Common Germanic *-ithō* (unattested).]

–th², –eth *suffix.* Indicates ordinal numbers; for example, **millionth, fortieth.** [Middle English *-the, -te,* Old English *-(o)tha, -(o)the.*]

–th³. Variant of **-eth¹.**

Thack·er·ay (thăk'ə-rē, thăk'rē), **William Makepeace** (1811–63). English novelist and satirist, born in India. One of the most prominent Victorian novelists, he explored the ethical and social pretensions of what he felt was a largely amoral era. His greatest work, *Vanity Fair* (1847–48), is a satiric yet realistic portrayal of a self-interested young woman striving for social position.

Thai (tī) *n., pl.* **Thais** or collectively **Thai. 1. a.** A native or inhabitant of Thailand. **b.** A member of the predominant ethnic group of Thailand, a people with both Mongoloid and Indonesian characteristics. **2.** The official language of Thailand, a member of the Tai family. Also called "Siamese."
~*adj.* Of or pertaining to Thailand, its people, or its language. Also "Siamese."

Thai·land (tī'lănd'). Formerly **Si·am** (sī-ăm'). Kingdom in Southeast Asia. Its heartland is the great plain of the Chao Phraya, a major rice-growing area. Nearly 75 percent of the work force is in farming, but manufacturing is expanding rapidly, and fishing and tourism are also important. The present dynasty, founded in 1782, kept Thailand the only Southeast Asian country that was never occupied by a European power (except in war). Absolute monarchy was abandoned in 1932. Area, 514,000 square kilometers (198,250 square miles). Population, 46,500,000. Capital, Krung Thep (Bangkok).

thal·a·men·ceph·a·lon (thăl'ə-mĕn-sĕf'ə-lŏn') *n. Anatomy.* **1.** The hindmost part of the forebrain. **2.** The **diencephalon** (see). [THALA-

THAILAND

M(US) + ENCEPHALON.] —**thal·a·men·ce·phal·ic** (thăl'ə-měn'-sə-făl'ĭk) adj.

thal·a·mus (thăl'ə-məs) n., pl. **-mi** (-mī'). 1. Anatomy. Either of two large ovoid masses of gray matter that relay sensory stimuli to the cerebral cortex. 2. Botany. The receptacle of a flower. [New Latin, from Greek thalamos, inner chamber; perhaps akin to THOLOS.] —**tha·lam·ic** (thə-lăm'ĭk) adj. —**tha·lam·i·cal·ly** adv.

thal·as·se·mi·a (thăl'ə-sē'mē-ə) n. An inherited blood disease in which an abnormality in the protein portion of the hemoglobin molecule leads to severe anemia. Also called "Cooley's anemia." [Greek thalassa†, sea (that is, the Mediterranean) + -EMIA.] —**thal·as·se·mic** adj.

tha·las·sic (thə-lăs'ĭk) adj. 1. Of or pertaining to deep seas or oceans; pelagic. 2. Of, pertaining to, or situated about inland seas as distinguished from the oceans. [French thalassique, from Greek thalassa†, sea.]

thal·as·soc·ra·cy (thăl'ə-sŏk'rə-sē) n., pl. **-cies**. Supremacy on the seas. [From Greek thalassokratia : thalassa†, sea + -CRACY.] —**tha·las·so·crat** (thə-lăs'ə-krăt') n.

thaler. Variant of **taler**.

Tha·les (thā'lēz) (c. 640–546 B.C.). Greek philosopher. The first known Greek philosopher, he believed that the earth floated on water and that all things consisted of water. Because none of his writings survive, little about him is known for certain.

Tha·li·a (thə-lī'ə, thä'lē-ə). Greek Mythology. 1. The Muse of comedy and pastoral poetry. 2. One of the three **Graces** (see). [Greek Thaleia, "the blooming one," from thallein, to flourish.]

tha·lid·o·mide (thə-lĭd'ə-mīd') n. A sedative and hypnotic drug, $C_{13}H_{10}N_2O_4$, withdrawn from sale in 1961 following the discovery that its use during early pregnancy could lead to fetal abnormalities, most notably the malformation of limbs. [(PH)THAL(IC ACID) + (IM)ID(E) + (I)MIDE.]

thal·lic (thăl'ĭk) adj. Of, pertaining to, or containing thallium, especially with valence 3. [THALL(IUM) + -IC.]

thal·li·um (thăl'ē-əm) n. Symbol **TI** A soft, malleable, highly toxic metallic element that is used in rodent and ant poisons and in photocells, infrared detectors, and low-melting glass. Atomic number 81, atomic weight 204.37, melting point 303.5°C, boiling point 1,457°C, specific gravity 11.85, valences 1, 3. [New Latin : Latin thallus, green shoot, THALLUS (from its green spectral line) + -IUM.]

thal·loid (thăl'oid') adj. Also **thal·loi·dal** (thə-loid'l). Of, resembling, or constituting a thallus. [THALL(US) + -OID.]

thal·lo·phyte (thăl'ə-fīt') n. Any plant or plantlike organism of the now obsolete division Thallophyta, which included the algae, fungi, and bacteria. These are all now considered to be separate divisions. [New Latin Thallophyta : THALL(US) + -PHYTE.] —**thal·lo·phy·tic** (thăl'ə-fĭt'ĭk) adj.

thal·lous (thăl'əs) adj. Of, pertaining to, or containing thallium, especially with valence 1. [THALL(IUM) + -OUS.]

thal·lus (thăl'əs) n., pl. **thalli** (thăl'ī') or **-luses**. Botany. The undifferentiated stemless, rootless, leafless plant body characteristic of thallophytes. [New Latin, from Latin, young shoot, from Greek thallos, from thallein, to sprout.]

Thames (tĕmz). River in southeastern England. It rises in the Cotswolds, in Gloucestershire, and flows c. 340 kilometers (210 miles) generally eastward to the North Sea via a great estuary. In Oxford it is also known as the Isis. London lies at the head of navigation and is protected against storm surges by a gated flood barrier, completed in 1982.

than (thăn; unstressed thən) conj. 1. Used in comparative statements to introduce the second element or clause of a comparison of inequality: She's a better athlete than I am. 2. Used in statements of preference to introduce the less acceptable alternative: I would rather dance than eat. 3. Used in statements expressing difference, especially after else, other, and compounds in which they appear: elsewhere than in the country; turned out to be none other than my brother. 4. When. ~prep. 1. In comparison with: She is much cleverer than me. 2. Used with expressions of degree or quantity: more than twice the speed of sound; fewer than 100 people. —**other than**. Apart from; except for. [Middle English than(ne), Old English thanne, thænne.]

Usage: In sentences involving comparison, than is usually construed as a conjunction rather than as a preposition, especially in formal usage. Accordingly, the case of the word following than is felt to be governed by its function in the clause introduced by than: He speaks better than I do. This is true also of elliptical clauses in which the unexpressed words are clearly indicated: He is a better speaker than I (that is, than I am). The students disliked no one more than her (that is, than they disliked her). In the first example, I is construed as the subject of an unexpressed verb; in the second, her is construed as an object. In both examples, the words following than agree in case with their antecedents (the first members of the comparisons, he and no one). • Less formally, in some writing and especially in speech, than is construed as a preposition in such examples, and the word following than is in the objective case. Moreover, in some examples either a nominative or an objective pronoun can be justified when than is construed as a conjunction: We had no more faithful friend than her (her construed as in agreement with the object friend). • In the construction than whom the pronoun is always objective: Napoleon, than whom no more romantic soldier lived, is the subject of a new book. See also Usage notes at but and different.

than·age (thā'nĭj) n. 1. The rank, jurisdiction, or office of a thane;

thaneship. 2. The land held by a thane. [Middle English, from Norman French : THAN(E) + -AGE.]

Than·a·tos (thăn'ə-tŏs', -tōs') n. 1. Death as a personification or as a philosophical notion. 2. **thanatos.** Psychoanalysis. An alleged instinct to self-destruction; the death wish. [Greek, "death."] —**than·a·tot·ic** (thăn'ə-tŏt'ĭk) adj.

thane (thān) n. Also **thegn** (for sense 1). 1. In Anglo-Saxon England: **a.** A freeman granted land by the king in return for military service. **b.** A man ranking above an ordinary freeman and below a nobleman or ealdorman. 2. In medieval Scotland, a feudal lord holding land granted by the king and having the same rank as an earl's son. [Middle English thayn, theyn, Old English theg(e)n, from Germanic thegnaz (unattested); akin to Greek teknon, child.]

thane·ship (thān'shĭp') n. The position or office of a thane, especially in Scotland.

Than·et, Isle of (thăn'ĭt). Northeastern extremity of the county of Kent in southeastern England, formerly an island, now joined to the mainland by silting and the reclamation of land.

thangka. Variant of **tanka**.

thank (thăngk) tr.v. **thanked, thanking, thanks**. 1. To express gratitude to; give thanks to: thanked him for his help. Often used in interjections to express the speaker's thanks or relief: Thank goodness you're here. 2. To hold responsible; blame: I had only myself to thank for the mess I was in. [Middle English thanken, Old English thancian.]

thank·ful (thăngk'fəl) adj. 1. Grateful. 2. Expressive of thanks. —**thank·ful·ness** n.

thank·ful·ly (thăngk'fə-lē) adv. 1. In a thankful manner. 2. Informal. Fortunately: Thankfully, her injuries were only minor.

thank·less (thăngk'lĭs) adj. 1. Not feeling or showing gratitude; ungrateful. 2. Unappreciated; unlikely to be appreciated: a thankless task. —**thank·less·ly** adv. —**thank·less·ness** n.

thanks (thăngks) pl.n. 1. An acknowledgment of a favor, gift, or benefit; gratitude. 2. An expression of gratitude. —**no thanks to**. Without any help from; despite. —**thanks to**. On account of; because of. ~interj. Used to express thanks. [Plural of obsolete thank, Old English thanc, from Germanic thankaz (unattested).]

thanks·giv·ing (thăngks-gĭv'ĭng) n. 1. An act of giving thanks; an expression of gratitude, especially to God. 2. **Thanksgiving.** Thanksgiving Day.

Thanksgiving Day n. A national holiday set apart for giving thanks to God, celebrated in the United States on the fourth Thursday of November and in Canada on the second Monday of October. Also called "Thanksgiving."

thank·wor·thy (thăngk'wûr'the) adj. Worthy of thanks.

thank-you (thăngk'yōō') n. An act or expression of thanks. ~adj. Expressing thanks: a thank-you letter.

Thant (thänt, thănt), **U** (1909–74). Burmese statesman. Named Burma's permanent delegate to the UN (1957), he served as secretary-general from 1962 to 1971 and was involved in the settlements of the Cuban missile crisis (1963), the Congo crisis (1963), the civil war in Cyprus (1964), and the India-Pakistan War (1965).

Tha·sos (thā'sŏs'). Also **Thá·sos** (thä'sôs'). Greek island in the Aegean Sea off the northeastern coast of Greece. In ancient times the Phoenicians worked its gold mines, now exhausted; lead and zinc ores are still exploited.

that (thăt; unstressed thət) adj., pl. **those** (thōz). 1. Being the one indicated, mentioned, implied, or understood: that place; those books. 2. Being the one further removed or less obvious: That route is shorter than this one. ~pron., pl. **those**. 1. Used as a demonstrative pronoun with the sense of: **a.** The one indicated, mentioned, implied, or understood. **b.** The further or less immediate one. **c.** The one belonging to the kind or category specified: The best whiskey is that from Scotland. 2. Used as a demonstrative pronoun to indicate: **a.** The period, point in time, or incident already mentioned or implied: I felt for my key, and that was when I noticed it was missing. He tore up the contract and with that left the room. **b.** The place already mentioned or implied: spent years in the country, and that was where he learned to paint. **c.** The manner, means, or process indicated or already mentioned or implied: took a course in computer programming, and that's how she got her present job. You open it like that. Don't look at me like that! 3. Used as a relative pronoun: **a.** To introduce a restrictive clause: never got the letter that I sent him. **b.** To indicate at, in, to, or on which: the day that we met; every time that I tried; everywhere that we went. 4. **a.** Something: There is that about him which mystifies me. **b. those.** Some people: There are those who feel it is already too late. —**all that**. 1. All of the kind specified: good looks, intelligence, and all that. 2. **a.** More of the same type: a store selling nails, hammers, saws, and all that. **b.** To the degree indicated: It can't be as bad as all that. —**at that**. Furthermore; as well: scored a goal and a good one at that. —**like that**. Without effort or delay: solved the problem just like that. ~adv. 1. To such an extent or degree; to that extent; so: If it cost that much, it ought to be good. 2. To a great extent; very: I wasn't that worried. ~conj. 1. Used to introduce a subordinate clause stating a fact, wish, consequence, purpose, or reason: We supposed that you were lost. She wishes that you would come. He was so tired that he fell asleep in his chair. 2. Used to introduce an elliptical exclamation of desire: Oh, that I were rich! —See Usage note at **this**. [Middle English that, Old English thæt.]

thatch Thatching is one of the oldest and most effective methods of roofing a building and is still in use in many parts of the world. This English thatched cottage is near Wimborne Minster in Dorset.

that·a·way (*th*ăt′ə-wā′) *adv. Informal.* That way; in that direction.

thatch (thăch) *n.* **1. a.** Plant stalks or foliage, such as reeds or palm fronds, used for roofing. **b.** A roof made of this material. **2.** Something resembling the thatch on a roof, especially the hair of the head.
~*tr.v.* **thatched, thatching, thatches.** To cover with or as if with thatch. [Middle English *thacche,* from *thacchen,* to thatch, cover, Old English *theccan.*] **—thatch·er** *n.*

Thatch·er (thăch′ər), **Margaret Hilda** (1925–). British politician. She has been prime minister since 1979 and was the first woman chosen to lead the government of Great Britain.

that'll (*th*ăt′l). Contraction of *that will.*

that's (*th*ăts). Contraction of *that has* or *that is.*

thau·ma·trope (thô′mə-trōp′) *n.* A device, such as a card, with designs on each side that appear to merge when it is spun rapidly. [Greek *thauma,* wonder, marvel + *-tropos,* turning.]

thau·ma·turge (thô′mə-tûrj′) *n.* Also **thau·ma·tur·gist** (-tûr′jĭst). A performer of miracles or magic feats. [Medieval Latin *thaumaturgus,* from Greek *thaumatourgos* : *thauma* (stem *thaumat-*), wonder + *-ergos,* "working," from *ergon,* work.]

thau·ma·tur·gy (thô′mə-tûr′jē) *n.* The working of miracles or wonders. **—thau·ma·tur·gic** (thô′mə-tûr′jĭk), **thau·ma·tur·gi·cal** *adj.*

thaw (thô) *v.* **thawed, thawing, thaws.** *—intr.* **1.** To change from a frozen solid to a liquid by gradual warming. **2.** To lose stiffness, numbness, or impermeability by being warmed. **3.** To become warm enough for snow and ice to melt. **4.** To become less restrained or tense; relax. *—tr.* To melt or soften (a frozen solid) by gradual warming. —See Synonyms at **melt.**
~*n.* **1.** The process of thawing. **2.** A period of relatively warm weather during which ice and snow melt. **3.** A relaxation of reserve, restraints, hostilities, or tensions: *a thaw in East-West relations.* [Middle English *thawen,* from Old English *thāwian,* from Germanic *thawōjant* (unattested).]

the[1] (*th*ē *before a vowel; th*ə *before a consonant*). The definite article, functioning as an adjective. It is used: **1.** Before singular or plural nouns and noun phrases that denote particular or previously specified persons or things. **2.** Before a singular noun, making it generic: *the human arm; plays the violin.* **3. a.** Before a noun, and generally stressed, emphasizing its uniqueness or prominence: *That's the show to see this year.* **b.** Before a noun denoting one that is the best, most notable, or most desirable of its kind: *gave the performance of his life. This is the place to be!* **4. a.** Before a proper noun denoting something that is the only one of its kind: *the British Museum; the Bible.* **b.** Before a noun denoting any of various natural phenomena that are or are considered to be unique: *flew through the air; the wind and the rain; always snows in the winter.* **5. a.** Before a title of rank or office, designating its holder: *the queen; the prime minister.* **b.** Before a qualifying adjective or noun in certain epithets or titles: *Ivan the Terrible; Edward the Confessor.* **c.** Before the name of certain Scottish or Irish clans, designating the chieftain: *the O'Donoghue.* **6.** Before certain nouns referring to familiar features or adjuncts of daily life, typically indicating the most accessible individual example: *ought to see the doctor; listening to the radio; has gone to the library.* **7. a.** Instead of the possessive pronoun before nouns denoting parts of the body: *slapped him in the face.* **b.** Instead of the possessive pronoun before nouns denoting personal possessions or pets: *I put the car in the garage. We took the dog for a walk.* **8.** Before a noun, indicating the degree or amount of it required for a stated purpose or operation: *haven't the time to see her.* **9. a.** Before an adjective or participle, extending it to signify a class or group and giving it the function of a noun: *the British; a school for the blind; the sick, the wounded, and the dying.* **b.** Before certain passive past participles, indicating an individual in the specified condition: *The accused took the stand.* **c.** Before certain adjectives, indicating an abstract concept: *a taste for the bizarre.* **10.** Before an adjective used absolutely: *the finest we have to offer.* **11.** Before a present participle, signifying the action in the abstract: *the weaving of rugs.* **12.** Before a noun, with the force of *per*: *at a dollar the box.* [Middle English *the,* Old English *thē* (originally a demonstrative adjective, later superseding *sē,* masculine singular).]

the[2] (*thē before a vowel; thə before a consonant*) *adv.* To that extent; by that much: *the sooner the better.* [Middle English *the, thi,* Old English *thȳ, thē,* instrumental case of *thē,* THE, and *thæt,* THAT.]

the·an·thro·pism (thē-ăn′thrə-pĭz′əm) *n. Theology.* The doctrine of the union of human and divine natures in Christ. [Late Greek *theanthrōpos,* god-man (*theos,* god + *anthrōpos,* man) + -IC.] **—the·an·throp·ic** (thē′ən-thrŏp′ĭk) *adj.* **—the·an·thro·pist** (thē-ăn′thrə-pĭst) *n.*

the·ar·chy (thē′är′kē) *n., pl.* **-chies.** **1.** Government or rule by God or a god; theocracy. **2.** A hierarchy or order of gods. [Late Greek *thearkhia* : THE(O)- + -ARCHY.]

the·a·ter, the·a·tre (thē′ə-tər) *n.* **1.** A building, room, or outdoor structure, as an amphitheater, for the presentation of dramatic performances, as plays or motion pictures. **2.** A room with tiers of seats used for lectures or demonstrations, as of surgical procedures; auditorium. **3. a.** Dramatic literature or its performance considered as a branch of art; drama: *the theater of 16th-century England.* **b.** A school of dramatic theory. **c.** The milieu or world of actors and playwrights. **d.** The quality or effectiveness of a theatrical production: *This play is good theater.* **4.** The audience assembled for a dramatic performance. **5. a.** A place that is the setting for dramatic or remarkable events: *The legislature was the theater in which the hearing took place.* **b.** A large geographic area in which military operations are coordinated.
~*adj.* Of, pertaining to, or for the theater: *We bought theater tickets for the whole family.* [Middle English *theatre,* from Old French, from Latin *theātrum,* from Greek *theatron,* from *theasthai,* to watch, look at, from *thea*†, a viewing.]

the·a·ter·go·er (thē′ə-tər-gō′ər) *n.* A person who goes to the theater, especially habitually.

the·a·ter-in-the-round (thē′ə-tər-ĭn-*th*ə-round′) *n., pl.* **theaters-in-the-round.** A theater without a proscenium in which the stage is at the center of the auditorium. Also called "arena theater."

theater of the absurd *n.* A form of theater that rejects naturalism in order to present the absurdity of the human condition.

the·at·ric (thē-ăt′rĭk) *adj.* Theatrical.

the·at·ri·cal (thē-ăt′rĭ-kəl) *adj.* **1.** Of, relating to, or suitable for the theater or dramatic performance. **2.** Marked by exaggerated self-display or unnatural behavior; affectedly dramatic.
~*n.* **1.** *Often* **theatricals.** A dramatic performance, especially by amateurs. **2.** *British Informal.* An actor. **—the·at·ri·cal·ism** (thē-ăt′rĭ-kə-lĭz′əm), **the·at·ri·cal·i·ty** (thē-ăt′rĭ-kăl′ə-tē), **the·at·ri·cal·ness** *n.* **—the·at·ri·cal·ly** *adv.*

the·at·rics (thē-ăt′rĭks) *pl.n.* **1.** *Used with a singular verb.* The art of the theater. **2.** Theatrical effects or mannerisms; histrionics.

the·ba·ine (thē′bā-ēn′, thĭ-bā′ĭn) *n.* A poisonous alkaloid, $C_{19}H_{21}NO_3$, obtained from opium and having a slight narcotic action. [New Latin *thebaia,* (herb of) Thebes + -INE.]

the·be (thā′bā) *n., pl.* **thebe.** A monetary unit equal to $1/100$ of the pula of Botswana. See feature at **currency.** [Native word, "sword."]

Thebes[1] (thēbz). City of ancient Egypt, occupying the site now partially occupied by Al Uqsur and Karnak, on both sides of the Nile. It flourished from the mid-22nd to the 18th century B.C., both as a royal residence and as the center of the worship of the god Amen. Excavations have unearthed ruins of great archaeological and historical importance, among them the nearby Valley of the Tombs of the Kings and the temples of Karnak and Luxor.

Thebes[2]. City of ancient Greece, lying in eastern Boeotia northwest of Athens, on the site of present-day Thebes. Settlement of the site dates from the early Bronze Age and it is the scene of the legends of Oedipus and Antigone. Following the Peloponnesian War, Thebes gained military ascendancy in Greece by twice defeating Sparta (375 B.C. and 371 B.C.). Its heyday was short-lived. In 336 B.C. the city was almost completely destroyed by Alexander.

the·ca (thē′kə) *n., pl.* **-cae** (-sē′, -kē′). *Biology.* A case, covering, or sheath, such as the spore case of a moss capsule or the outer covering of the pupa of certain insects. [New Latin, from Latin *thēca,* a case, sheath, from Greek *thēkē.*] **—the·cal** *adj.*

the·cate (thē′kāt′) *adj.* Having a theca; encased or sheathed. [THEC(A) + -ATE.]

thé dan·sant (tā′ däN-säN′) *n., pl.* **thés dansants** (*pronounced as singular*). A tea dance. [French.]

thee (*th*ē) *pron. Archaic.* **1.** The objective case of the second person singular pronoun *thou,* used as the direct or indirect object of a verb, as the object of a preposition, or after *than* or *as* in comparisons in which the first term is in the objective case. **2.** Used in the nominative as well as the objective case in certain religious communities, especially by members of the Society of Friends in the 19th century.

thee·lin (thē′lĭn) *n.* A female sex hormone, **estrone** *(see).* [Irregularly from Greek *thēlus,* female + -IN.]

theft (thĕft) *n.* **1.** The act or an instance of stealing; the dishonest taking and removing of another's personal property; larceny. **2.** *Obsolete.* Something that is stolen. [Middle English *theft(he),* Old English *thēofth,* from Common Germanic *thiufith* (unattested), from *thiuf* (unattested), THIEF.]

thegn. Variant of **thane.**

the·ine (thē′ēn′, -ĭn) *n.* Caffeine. [New Latin *thea,* tea + -INE; originally believed to be peculiar to tea.]

their (*th*âr) *pron.* The possessive form of **they.** Used attributively to indicate possession or the agent or recipient of an action: *their house; doing their job; suffered their first defeat.* [Middle English, from Old Norse *their(r)a* (genitive plural).]

theirs (*th*ârz) *pron. Used with a singular or plural verb.* The one or ones belonging to them: *The blue boots are theirs. Mine is here, and theirs is the one on the stairs.* **—of theirs.** Belonging or pertaining to them: *a friend of theirs.* [Middle English, from THEIR.]

the·ism (thē′ĭz′əm) *n.* Belief in the existence of a god or gods; especially, belief in a personal God as creator and ruler of the world. Compare **deism, pantheism.** [THE(O)- + -ISM.] **—the·ist** *n.* **—the·is·tic** (thē-ĭs′tĭk), **the·is·ti·cal** (-tĭ-kəl) *adj.* **—the·is·ti·cal·ly** *adv.*

them (*th*ĕm; *unstressed th*əm) *pron.* The objective case of **they.** It is used: **1.** As the direct object of a verb: *She assisted them.* **2.** As the indirect object of a verb: *He offered them a new contract.* **3.** As the object of a preposition: *This letter is addressed to them.* **4.** After *than* or *as* in comparisons in which the first term is in the objective case: *The judges praised us more than them.* **5.** *Informal.* In place of the reflexive pronoun *themselves,* as the indirect object of a verb: *They went to buy them a car.* **6.** In various elliptical, absolute, or interjectional phrases in which it is neither subject nor object: *Them and their big ideas!* [Middle English *the(i)m,* partly from Old Norse *theim,* partly from Old English *thǣm.*]

the·mat·ic (thĭ-măt′ĭk) *adj.* **1.** Of, based on, constituting, or relating to a theme or themes. **2.** *Linguistics.* Constituting part of the theme or stem of a word.

~n. A thematic vowel or sound sequence. [Greek *thematikos,* from *thema* (stem *themat-*), proposition, THEME.] **—the·mat·i·cal·ly** *adv.*

theme (thēm) *n.* **1.** A topic of discourse, discussion, contemplation, or composition, often expressible as a phrase, proposition, or question. **2.** An idea, point of view, or perception embodied and expanded upon in a work of art; an underlying or essential subject of artistic representation; a motif: *the theme of the noble savage in literature.* **3.** A short composition assigned to a student as a writing exercise. **4.** *Music.* A melody forming the basis of development or variations in a composition. Also called "subject." **5.** *Linguistics.* **a.** A stem. **b.** A root. **—See Synonyms at subject.** [Middle English *t(h)eme,* theme (of a discussion), from Old French *teme,* from Latin *thema,* from Greek, "thing placed," proposition.]

theme song *n.* **1.** A melody or song recurring throughout a dramatic performance and often intended to convey a mood. **2.** A song that is identified with a performer or group or with a radio or television program.

The·mis (thē'mĭs). *Greek Mythology.* A daughter of Uranus and Gaea, and the goddess who personifies justice.

The·mis·to·cles (thə-mĭs'tə-klēz') (*c.* 527–460 B.C.). Athenian military and political leader. After persuading the people of Athens to build a navy (483), he led the new fleet to victory over Persia in the Battle of Salamis (480), thereby establishing Athens as the dominant power in the region.

them·selves (*th*ĕm-sĕlvz', *th*əm-) *pron.* A specialized form of the third person plural pronoun. It is used: **1.** As a reflexive pronoun forming the direct or indirect object of a verb or the object of a preposition: *hurt themselves; give themselves time; talk to themselves.* **2.** For emphasis after *they*: *They themselves weren't certain.* **3.** As an emphasizing substitute: *Themselves in debt, they couldn't help us.* Sometimes nonstandard: *The Smiths and themselves are in trouble.* **4.** As an indication of their real, normal, or healthy condition or identity: *They haven't been themselves lately.*

then (*th*ĕn) *adv.* **1.** At that time: *I was a lot younger then. If you're still in town then, come and visit us.* **2.** Next in time, space, or order; immediately afterward: *I watched the late movie and then went to bed.* **3.** In that case; accordingly: *If you want to do it, then tell him.* **4.** In consequence; with the result that: *If you leave by the back door, then nobody will notice.* **5.** In addition; moreover. **6. a.** As may be deduced from what has gone before: *I take it, then, that you're interested.* **b.** By way of summing up or concluding: *The allies, then, had suffered badly.* **7. a.** By way of qualifying what has just been stated: *didn't get the job, but then he never really wanted it.* **b.** In contrast; on the other hand: *Then again, we could go home.*
~pron. A particular time or moment: *Until then let's stay here.*
~adj. Being so at that time: *the then headmistress.* [Middle English *thenne, thann,* Old English *thanne, thænne.*]

the·nar (thē'när') *n.* **1.** The fleshy mound on the palm of the hand at the base of the thumb. **2.** The sole of the foot. [New Latin, from Greek *thenar,* palm of the hand.] **—the·nar** *adj.*

thence (*th*ĕns, thĕns) *adv.* **1.** From that place; from there. **2.** From that time; thenceforth. **3.** From that circumstance or source; therefrom. [Middle English *thannes,* from *thanne,* from there, Old English *thanon.*]

thence·forth (*th*ĕns-fôrth', -fōrth', thĕns-) *adv.* From that time forward; thereafter.

thence·for·ward (*th*ĕns-fôr'wərd, thĕns-) *adv.* Also **thence·for·wards** (-wərdz). From that time or place onward.

theo–, the– *prefix.* Indicates a god or gods; for example, **theism, theobromine.** [From Greek *theos,* god.]

the·o·bro·mine (thē'ō-brō'mēn', -mĭn) *n.* A bitter, colorless alkaloid, $C_7H_8N_4O_2$, derived principally from the cocoa bean and used as a diuretic and a cardiac stimulant. [New Latin *Theobroma,* "food of the gods," genus including the cacao tree : THEO- + Greek *brōma,* food + -INE.]

the·o·cen·tric (thē'ō-sĕn'trĭk) *adj.* Centering on God as the prime concern. [THEO- + CENTRIC.] **—the·o·cen·tric·i·ty** (thē'ō-sĕn-trĭs'ə-tē), **the·o·cen·trism** (-sĕn'trĭz'əm) *n.*

the·oc·ra·cy (thē-ŏk'rə-sē) *n., pl.* **-cies. 1.** A form of government in which a god is regarded as the supreme ruler and temporal power is in the hands of a priestly order claiming divine sanction. **2.** A state so governed. [Greek *theokratia* : THEO- + -CRACY.]

the·o·crat (thē'ə-krăt') *n.* **1.** One who rules in a theocracy. **2.** A believer in theocracy. [THEO- + -CRAT.] **—the·o·crat·ic** (thē'ə-krăt'ĭk), **the·o·crat·i·cal** (-ĭ-kəl) *adj.* **—the·o·crat·i·cal·ly** *adv.*

The·oc·ri·tus (thē-ŏk'rĭ-təs) (*fl.* 3rd century B.C.). Greek idyllic poet. His major work, the *Idylls,* a collection of 30 short poems on pastoral and mythical subjects, influenced Virgil's *Eclogues* and the genre of pastoral literature.

the·od·i·cy (thē-ŏd'ə-sē) *n., pl.* **-cies.** A vindication of divine justice in the face of the paradox that God is both omnipotent and benevolent and yet permits evil to exist among men. [French *Théodicée,* title of a work (1710) by Leibniz : THEO- + Greek *dikē,* judgment.]

the·od·o·lite (thē-ŏd'l-īt') *n.* A surveying instrument used to measure horizontal and vertical angles with a small telescope that can move in horizontal and vertical planes. [New Latin *theodelitus*†.]

The·o·do·ra (thē'ə-dôr'ə, -dōr'ə) (*c.* 508–48). Byzantine empress as wife of Justinian I. Allegedly an actress and harlot before her marriage to Justinian in 525, she exerted great influence on the emperor. Her encouragement during the Nika riot (532) persuaded him not to flee the capital and probably preserved his crown.

The·od·o·ric (thē-ŏd'ər-ĭk), known as "the Great" (A.D. *c.* 454–526). King of the Ostrogoths who established the Ostrogothic kingdom that dominated Italy from the late 5th to the 6th century.

the·og·o·ny (thē-ŏg'ə-nē) *n., pl.* **-nies.** The origin and genealogy of the gods, especially as recounted in ancient epic poetry. [Greek *theogonia* : THEO- + -GONY.] **—the·o·gon·ic** (thē'ə-gŏn'ĭk) *adj.* **—the·og·o·nist** (thē-ŏg'ə-nĭst) *n.*

the·o·lo·gian (thē'ə-lō'jən) *n.* One versed in or studying theology.

the·o·log·i·cal (thē'ə-lŏj'ĭ-kəl) *adj.* Also **the·o·log·ic** (-ĭk). Of or pertaining to theology. **—the·o·log·i·cal·ly** *adv.*

the·ol·o·gize (thē-ŏl'ə-jīz') *v.* **-gized, -gizing, -gizes.** *—tr.* To make theological in form or significance. *—intr.* To speculate about theology. **—the·ol·o·giz·er** *n.*

the·ol·o·gy (thē-ŏl'ə-jē) *n., pl.* **-gies. 1.** The study of the nature of God and religious truth; rational inquiry into religious questions, especially those posed by an organized religious community. **2.** An organized, often formalized body of opinions concerning divinity and humanity's relationship to God. **3.** A course of specialized religious study, usually at a college or seminary. [Middle English *theologie,* from Old French, from Latin *theologia,* from Greek : THEO- + -LOGY.]

the·o·ma·ni·a (thē'ō-mā'nē-ə, -măn'yə) *n.* Religious insanity; especially, a belief that one is God.

the·o·mor·phism (thē'ō-môr'fĭz'əm) *n.* The depiction or conception of man as having the form of a god or of God. [THEO- + MORPH(O)- + -ISM.] **—the·o·mor·phic** (thē'ō-môr'fĭk) *adj.*

the·oph·a·ny (thē-ŏf'ə-nē) *n., pl.* **-nies.** An appearance of God or of a god to a human being; a divine manifestation. [Medieval Latin *theophania,* from Late Greek *theophaneia* : THEO- + Greek *phainein,* to show.]

The·o·phras·tus (thē'ə-frăs'təs) (371–287 B.C.). Greek philosopher. Following in Aristotle's footsteps as leader of the Peripatetics, he developed and refined the empirical and scientific aspects of Aristotle's philosophy. Particularly influential in the field of botany, he is also known for his major extant works, *Doctrines of the Natural Philosophers* and *Characters.*

the·oph·yl·line (thē-ŏf'ə-lĭn, thē'ō-fĭl'ēn') *n.* A colorless crystalline alkaloid, $C_7H_8N_4O_2$, derived from tea leaves and also made synthetically. It is an isomer of and has effects similar to those of theobromine. [THEO(BROMINE) + PHYLL(O)- + -INE.]

the·or·bo (thē-ôr'bō) *n., pl.* **-bos.** A 17th-century lute having two necks and two sets of strings and pegs, one set above and somewhat to the side of the other. [Italian *tiorba*†.]

the·o·rem (thē'ər-əm, thîr'əm) *n.* **1.** *Mathematics & Logic.* A statement or proposition that can be or has been proved on the basis of reasoning from explicit assumptions. **2.** A rule or statement of relations, usually expressed as a formula or equation: *the binomial theorem.* [Late Latin *theōrēma,* from Greek, spectacle, intuition, theorem, from *theōrein,* to observe, look at, from *theōros,* spectator, from *thea,* a looking at.]

the·o·ret·i·cal (thē'ə-rĕt'ĭ-kəl) *adj.* Also **the·o·ret·ic** (-ĭk). **1.** Of, pertaining to, or based on theory. **2.** Restricted to theory, as: **a.** Lacking verification from experience or experiment. **b.** Lacking practical application. Compare **applied. 3.** Existing only in theory; hypothetical or speculative. [Late Latin *theōrēticus,* from Greek *theōrētikos,* able to perceive, from *theōrein,* to observe. See **theorem.**] **—the·o·ret·i·cal·ly** *adv.*

the·o·re·ti·cian (thē'ər-ə-tĭsh'ən) *n.* A person who formulates, studies, or is expert in the theory of a science or art.

the·o·ret·ics (thē'ə-rĕt'ĭks) *n. Used with a singular verb.* The theoretical part of a science or art; principles.

the·o·rize (thē'ə-rīz') *intr.v.* **-rized, -rizing, -rizes. 1.** To develop, analyze, or formulate theories. **2.** To think or analyze in terms of theory. **3.** To speculate. **—the·o·ri·za·tion** *n.* **—the·o·riz·er** *n.*

the·o·rist (thē'ər-ĭst) *n.* One skilled in the theoretical rather than the practical aspects of a subject.

the·o·ry (thē'ə-rē, thîr'ē) *n., pl.* **-ries. 1. a.** Systematically organized knowledge applicable in a relatively wide variety of circumstances; especially, a system of assumptions, accepted principles, and rules of procedure devised to analyze, predict, or otherwise explain the nature or behavior of a given set of phenomena: *the theory of evolution; Marxist economic theory.* **b.** Such knowledge or such a system distinguished from experiment or practice. **2. a.** The part of a subject dealing with its underlying rules and principles: *music theory.* **b.** The realm of abstract speculation or ideal circumstances: *In theory it should only take a week.* **3.** An assumption or guess based on limited information or knowledge; supposition or opinion. [Late Latin *theōria,* from Greek, contemplation, theory, from *theōros,* spectator, from *theasthai,* to observe, from *thea,* a viewing.]

theory of games *n. Mathematics.* **Game theory** *(see).*

the·os·o·phy (thē-ŏs'ə-fē) *n., pl.* **-phies. 1.** Any of various philosophical or religious systems concerned with a direct intuitive or mystical apprehension of God. **2.** *Often* **Theosophy.** The doctrines and beliefs of a modern religious sect, the Theosophical Society, incorporating aspects of Buddhism and Brahmanism. [Medieval Latin *theosophia,* from Late Greek *theosophia* : THEO- + -SOPHY.] **—the·o·soph·ic** (thē'ə-sŏf'ĭk), **the·o·soph·i·cal** (-ĭ-kəl) *adj.* **—the·o·soph·i·cal·ly** *adv.* **—the·os·o·phist** (thē-ŏs'ə-fĭst) *n.*

ther·a·peu·tic (thĕr'ə-pyōō'tĭk) *adj.* **1.** Having healing or curative powers. **2.** Performed or serving to maintain health. **3.** Of or pertaining to therapeutics. [Greek *therapeutikos,* from *therapeutēs,* one who administers, from *therapeuein,* to administer to (medically). See **therapy.**] **—ther·a·peu·ti·cal·ly** *adv.*

ther·a·peu·tics (thĕr'ə-pyōō'tĭks) *n. Used with a singular verb.* The medical treatment of disease. **—ther·a·peu·tist** *n.*

PRONUNCIATION KEY

ă, pat; ā, pay; âr, care; ä, father, are; b, bib; ch, church; d, deed; ĕ, pet; ē, be; f, fife; g, gag; h, hat; hw, which; ĭ, pit; ī, pie; îr, pier; j, judge; k, kick; l, lid, needle; m, mum; n, no, sudden; ng, thing; ŏ, pot; ō, toe; ô, paw, for; oi, noise; ou, out; ŏŏ, book; ōō, boot; p, pop; r, roar; s, sauce; sh, ship, dish; t, tight; th, thin, path; *th*, this, bathe; ŭ, cut; ûr, fur; v, valve; w, with; y, yes; z, zebra, size; zh, vision; ə, about, item, edible, gallop, circus, peaceful

IN FOREIGN WORDS:

à, *Fr.* ami; œ, *Fr.* feu, *Ger.* schön; ü, *Fr.* tu, *Ger.* über; KH, *Ger.* ich, *Scot.* loch; N, *Fr.* bon; y', *Fr.* Compiègne

STRESS MARKS:

Primary stress: ' in·cite' (ĭn-sīt')
Secondary stress: ' in'sight' (ĭn'sīt')

ther·a·pist (thĕr'ə-pĭst) *n.* A specialist in a form of therapy, such as physical therapy or psychotherapy.

the·rap·sid (thə-răp'sĭd) *n.* Any of the large, extinct reptiles of the order Therapsida that were widespread in Permian and Triassic times and are thought to be the ancestors of the mammals. [New Latin *Therapsida,* from Greek *theraps,* attendant.]

ther·a·py (thĕr'ə-pē) *n., pl.* **-pies. 1. a.** The remedial treatment of illness or disability: *speech therapy.* **b.** A course of such treatment. Often used in combination: *hydrotherapy.* **2. Psychotherapy** (see). [New Latin *therapīa,* from Greek *therapeia,* service, from *therapeuein,* to be an attendant, from *theraps,* attendant.]

Ther·a·va·da (thĕr'ə-vä'də) *n.* A branch of Buddhism, predominating in Sri Lanka and Southeast Asia, based on a somewhat literal interpretation of the Pali scripture and emphasizing monastic life. Also called "Hinayana." [Pali *theravāda,* "doctrine of the elders" : *thera,* old, elder, from Sanskrit *sthavira,* thick, stout, old + *vāda,* speech, doctrine, from Sanskrit *vad,* sound, statement.]

there (thâr) *adv.* **1.** At or in that place: *Sit over there.* **2.** To, into, or toward that place; thither: *wouldn't go there again.* **3.** At that point of action or time: *Hold it right there before you make a mistake.* **4.** In that matter or respect: *There we must agree to differ.*
~*pron.* **1.** Used, especially with the verb *be,* to introduce a sentence or clause whose real subject follows the verb: *There is someone at the door. There appears to be some disagreement.* **2.** Used in place of a name: *Hello there.*
~*adj.* **1.** Being in that place. Used for emphasis after a noun or demonstrative pronoun: *John there will help you. Take that one there.* **2.** Nonstandard. Used for emphasis between a demonstrative pronoun and a noun: *that there dog.*
~*n.* That place or point: *stopped and went on from there.*
~*interj.* Used to express emotion such as relief, satisfaction, or consolation: *There, now I can have some peace!* [Middle English *ther(e),* Old English *thǣr, thēr.*]
Usage: *There* frequently precedes a linking verb such as *be, seem,* or *appear* in beginning a sentence or clause: *There has been much trouble.* The number of the verb is governed by the subject, which in such constructions follows the verb: *There is a garage across the street. There seem to be many good candidates.* But a singular verb is also possible before a compound subject whose parts are joined by a conjunction or conjunctions, especially when the parts are singular: *There is much pain and toil involved. There appears to be a man and a wagon in the distance.* When the first element of such a subject is singular, a singular verb is also possible even though the other elements are plural: *There was (or were) a man and two children in the car.* But: *There were two children and a man.* *There* (adverb), meaning "in that place," comes after the noun, not before it, in constructions introduced by the demonstrative *that: That boy there* (not *that there boy) is to blame.*

there·a·bouts (thâr'ə-bouts') *adv.* Also **there·a·bout** (-bout'). **1.** Near that place or time. **2.** Near that number or degree: *She was 21 or thereabouts.*

there·af·ter (thâr-ăf'tər, -äf'tər) *adv.* From then on; after that: *an apprentice for three years, an assistant thereafter.*

there·at (thâr-ăt') *adv.* **1.** At that place or point. **2.** By reason of that; as a result of that.

there·by (thâr-bī') *adv.* **1.** By that means; as a result. **2.** In connection with that: *and thereby hangs a tale.*

there·for (thâr-fôr', -fōr') *adv. Archaic.* For that, this, or it.

there·fore (thâr'fôr', -fōr') *adv.* For that reason; consequently: *The rumor's false and your judgment therefore wrong.* Also used to indicate a logical connection with a preceding clause: *I lost my money; therefore I could not buy a ticket.*

there·from (thâr-frŏm', -frŭm') *adv.* From that time, place, circumstance, or thing.

there·in (thâr-ĭn') *adv.* **1.** In that place or context. **2.** In that matter or particular.

there·in·af·ter (thâr'ĭn-ăf'tər, -äf'tər) *adv.* In a later or subsequent portion, as of a statute or book.

there·of (thâr-ŏv', -ŭv') *adv.* **1.** Of or concerning this, that, or it. **2.** From that cause or origin; therefrom.

there·on (thâr-ŏn', -ŏn') *adv.* **1.** On or upon this, that, or it. **2.** Following that immediately; thereupon.

The·re·sa or **Te·re·sa** (tə-rē'sə, -rā'zə), **Saint,** known as "Theresa of Avila" (1515–82). Spanish nun and mystical author. Calling for a return by the Carmelites to a strict observance of austerity, she founded 17 reformed convents. Among her classic spiritual writings are *The Way of Perfection* (1583) and *The Interior Castle* (1588).

there·to (thâr-tōō') *adv.* **1.** To that, this, or it; thereunto: *affixed his seal thereto.* **2.** *Archaic.* In addition to that; furthermore.

there·to·fore (thâr'tə-fôr', -fōr') *adv.* Until or prior to that time; before that.

there·un·der (thâr-ŭn'dər) *adv.* Under this, that, or it.

there·up·on (thâr'ə-pŏn', -pôn') *adv.* **1.** Upon this, that, or it. **2.** Directly following that. **3.** In consequence of that; therefore.

there·with (thâr-wĭth', -wĭth') *adv.* **1.** With that, this, or it. **2.** Immediately thereafter.

the·ri·an·throp·ic (thĭr'ē-ăn-thrŏp'ĭk) *adj.* Partly human, partly animal. Said of such mythological creatures as the Minotaur. [Greek *thērion,* wild beast + ANTHROP(O)- + -IC.]

the·ri·o·mor·phic (thĭr'ē-ə-môr'fĭk) *adj.* Having the form of a beast: *theriomorphic gods.* [Greek *thērion,* wild beast + -MORPHIC.]

therm (thûrm) *n.* A unit of heat equal to: **a.** One hundred thousand British thermal units. **b.** One thousand large calories. **c.** The large

calorie. **d.** The small calorie. [From Greek *thermē,* heat, from *thermos,* hot.]

therm–. Variant of **thermo-.**

–therm *suffix.* Indicates heat; for example, **poikilotherm.** [From Greek *thermē,* heat. See **therm.**]

ther·mae (thûr'mē) *pl.n.* Public baths in the ancient Greek or Roman world. [Latin, from Greek *thermai,* from *thermē,* heat.]

ther·mal (thûr'məl) *adj.* Also **ther·mic** (-mĭk) (for sense 1). **1.** Of, pertaining to, using, producing, or caused by heat. **2.** Specially designed to minimize loss of body heat: *thermal underwear.*
~*n.* A rising current of warm air. [French, from Greek *thermē,* heat. See **therm.**] —**ther'mal·ly** *adv.*

thermal barrier *n.* A barrier to flight above a certain speed as a result of the heat produced by air friction. Also called "heat barrier."

thermal conductivity *n.* A measure of a substance's ability to transfer heat, expressed as the rate of conduction of heat between opposite faces of a hypothetical unit cube of the substance when there is unit temperature difference between the faces. It is measured in joules per second per meter per kelvin.

thermal equator *n.* An imaginary line around the earth that links the point on each meridian with the highest average temperatures.

thermal equilibrium *n.* A state of a system in which there is no net flow of heat among its components.

thermal spring *n.* A hot spring (see).

ther·mal·ize (thûr'mə-līz') *v.* **-ized, -izing, -izes.** —*tr.* To cause (neutrons) in a moderator to become thermal neutrons. —*intr.* To become thermal neutrons. —**ther·mal·i·za'tion** *n.*

thermal neutron *n.* A neutron in thermal equilibrium with the surrounding medium; especially, one produced by fission, slowed by a moderator, and having a mean velocity of about 2,200 meters per second. Also called "slow neutron."

thermal reactor *n.* A nuclear reactor in which most of the fissions are caused by thermal neutrons.

thermal shock *n.* Stress in a material caused by a sharp change of temperature.

therm·i·on (thûr'mī'ən, -ŏn') *n.* An electrically charged particle or ion emitted by a conducting material at high temperatures. [THERM(O)- + ION.] —**therm·i·on·ic** (thûr'mī-ŏn'ĭk) *adj.*

thermionic current *n.* A flow of thermions.

thermionic emission *n.* The emission of thermions from a conducting material at high temperatures.

therm·i·on·ics (thûr'mī-ŏn'ĭks) *n.* Used with a singular verb. The physics of thermionic phenomena; especially, the study and design of thermionic tubes.

thermionic tube *n.* An electronic vacuum tube in which the source of electrons is a heated electrode.

therm·is·tor (thûr'mĭs'tər) *n.* A resistor made of semiconductors having resistance that varies rapidly and predictably with temperature. [THERM(AL) + (RES)ISTOR.]

Ther·mit (thûr'mĭt, -mīt') *n.* A trademark for a welding and incendiary mixture of fine aluminum powder with a metallic oxide, as of iron, that when ignited produces an intense heat.

thermo–, therm– *prefix.* **1.** Indicates heat; for example, **thermogram. 2.** Indicates thermoelectricity; for example, **thermionics.** [From Greek *thermē,* heat, from *thermos,* hot.]

ther·mo·chem·is·try (thûr'mō-kĕm'ĭ-strē) *n.* The branch of chemistry concerned with the heat produced or absorbed during reactions and other heat-associated chemical phenomena. —**ther·mo·chem·i·cal** (thûr'mō-kĕm'ĭ-kəl) *adj.* —**ther·mo·chem·ist** *n.*

ther·mo·cline (thûr'mə-klīn') *n.* A temperature gradient in a body of water, such as a lake, in which there is a marked variation of temperature with depth. [THERMO- + -CLINE.]

ther·mo·cou·ple (thûr'mə-kŭp'əl) *n.* **1.** A pair of wires of different metals joined at one end, used to measure temperature by the voltage produced at the junction. **2.** A circuit formed by two different wires joined at both ends, with one junction kept at a constant low temperature and the other at the temperature to be measured. The temperature is proportional to the current in the circuit.

ther·mo·dy·nam·ics (thûr'mō-dī-năm'ĭks) *n.* Used with a singular verb. The physics of the relationships between heat and other forms of energy, especially when used to study the properties of matter. —**ther·mo·dy·nam·ic** *adj.*

thermodynamic scale *n.* A temperature scale based on thermodynamic properties such that zero on the scale is absolute zero.

thermodynamic temperature *n.* A physical quantity based on the average thermal energy of the random motion of the particles of a system in thermal equilibrium. The unit of thermodynamic temperature is the kelvin.

ther·mo·e·lec·tric·i·ty (thûr'mō-ĭ-lĕk'trĭs'ə-tē) *n.* **1.** Electricity generated by a flow of heat, as in a thermocouple. **2.** The branch of physics concerned with thermoelectricity and related phenomena. —**ther·mo·e·lec·tric** (thûr'mō-ĭ-lĕk'trĭk), **ther·mo·e·lec·tri·cal** (-trĭ-kəl) *adj.* —**ther·mo·e·lec·tri·cal·ly** *adv.*

ther·mo·e·lec·tron (thûr'mō-ĭ-lĕk'trŏn') *n.* An electron produced as a result of thermionic emission.

ther·mo·gen·e·sis (thûr'mō-jĕn'ə-sĭs) *n.* The production of heat by physiological processes in the body.

ther·mo·gram (thûr'mə-grăm') *n.* A record made by a thermograph. [THERMO- + -GRAM.]

ther·mo·graph (thûr'mə-grăf', -gräf') *n.* A thermometer that records temperatures automatically. [THERMO- + -GRAPH.]

ther·mog·ra·phy (thər-mŏg'rə-fē) *n.* A printing or writing process involving heat; especially, a letterpress technique that produces a raised effect, as on calling cards, by heating printed matter that has been dusted with powder. [THERMO- + -GRAPHY.]

ther·mo·junc·tion (thûr′mō-jŭngk′shən) *n.* A point of contact between two dissimilar metals at which a thermoelectric current is produced.

ther·mo·la·bile (thûr′mō-lā′bīl, -bəl) *adj.* Subject to destruction, decomposition, or great change by moderate heating. Said especially of certain biochemical compounds. Compare **thermostable.** [THERMO- + LABILE.]

ther·mo·lu·mi·nes·cence (thûr′mō-lōō′mə-nĕs′əns) *n.* Phosphorescence produced by gentle heating of some minerals that have previously absorbed radiation. —**ther·mo·lu·mi·nes·cent** *adj.*

ther·mol·y·sis (thər-mŏl′ə-sĭs) *n.* **1.** *Physiology.* The loss of heat from the body. **2.** *Chemistry.* The dissociation or decomposition of compounds by heat. [THERMO- + -LYSIS.] —**ther·mo·lyt·ic** (thûr′mə-lĭt′ĭk) *adj.*

ther·mo·mag·net·ic (thûr′mō-măg-nĕt′ĭk) *adj.* Of or pertaining to a change in the temperature of a body as a result of magnetization or demagnetization.

ther·mom·e·ter (thər-mŏm′ə-tər) *n.* An instrument for measuring temperature; especially, one consisting of a graduated sealed glass tube with a bulb containing a liquid, typically mercury, that expands and rises in the tube as the temperature increases. [French *thermomètre* : THERMO- + -METER.]

ther·mom·e·try (thər-mŏm′ə-trē) *n.* **1.** The measurement of temperature. **2.** The science and technology of temperature measurement. [THERMO- + -METRY.] —**ther·mo·met·ric** (thûr′mə-mĕt′rĭk) *adj.*

ther·mo·mo·tor (thûr′mō-mō′tər) *n.* An engine operated by heat, especially by the expansion of heated air.

ther·mo·nu·cle·ar (thûr′mō-nōō′klē-ər, -nyōō′klē-ər) *adj.* **1.** Of, pertaining to, or derived from the fusion of atomic nuclei at high temperatures. **2.** Of or pertaining to nuclear weapons based on fusion, especially as distinguished from those based on fission.

ther·mo·pe·ri·od·ism (thûr′mō-pîr′ē-ə-dĭz′əm) *n.* Also **ther·mo·pe·ri·o·dic·i·ty** (-pîr′ē-ə-dĭs′ə-tē). The response of organisms, as certain plants, to the alternation of low and high temperatures over a period, as of days and nights or of successive seasons.

ther·mo·phil·ic (thûr′mə-fĭl′ĭk) *adj. Biology.* Requiring high temperatures for normal development, as certain bacteria do. Compare **mesophilic, psychrophilic.** [THERMO- + -PHIL(E) + -IC.] —**ther·mo·phile** (thûr′mə-fīl′), **ther·mo·phil** (-fĭl) *n.*

ther·mo·pile (thûr′mə-pīl′) *n.* A device to measure temperature or generate current that consists of a number of thermocouples connected in series. [THERMO- + PILE (a heap, "series").]

ther·mo·plas·tic (thûr′mə-plăs′tĭk, -plä′stĭk) *adj.* Becoming soft when heated and hard when cooled.
~*n.* A thermoplastic resin, such as polystyrene.

Ther·mop·y·lae (thər-mŏp′ə-lē) *n.* A locality in eastern Greece, south of Lamia. A pass between the sea and Mt. Oeta to the south, it is the site of a heroic but unsuccessful defense by the Spartans against the Persians (480 B.C.).

Ther·mos bottle (thûr′məs) *n.* A trademark for a vacuum flask. Also called "Thermos."

ther·mo·set·ting (thûr′mō-sĕt′ĭng) *adj.* Permanently hardening or solidifying on being heated. Said of certain synthetic resins.

ther·mo·si·phon (thûr′mə-sī′fən) *n.* A cooling system in which the circulation of the coolant relies on differences in density between hot and cold parts of the fluid.

ther·mo·sphere (thûr′mə-sfîr′) *n.* The outermost shell of the atmosphere, between the mesosphere and outer space, within which temperatures increase steadily with altitude.

ther·mo·sta·ble (thûr′mō-stā′bəl) *adj.* Unaffected by relatively high temperatures. Said especially of biochemical compounds. Compare **thermolabile.** —**ther·mo·sta·bil·i·ty** (thûr′mō-stə-bĭl′ə-tē) *n.*

ther·mo·stat (thûr′mə-stăt′) *n.* A device that automatically responds to temperature changes to maintain a fixed temperature or activate control switches, as in refrigerators and air conditioners. [THERMO- + -STAT.] —**ther·mo·stat·ic** (thûr′mə-stăt′ĭk) *adj.*

ther·mo·tax·is (thûr′mə-tăk′sĭs) *n.* **1.** The directional movement of an entire cell or organism in response to heat. **2.** The normal regulation or adjustment of body temperature. [New Latin : THERMO- + -TAXIS.] —**ther·mo·tac·tic** (thûr′mə-tăk′tĭk) *adj.*

ther·mo·ther·a·py (thûr′mō-thĕr′ə-pē) *n.* Therapy by application of heat.

ther·mot·ro·pism (thər-mŏt′rə-pĭz′əm) *n. Biology.* Directional growth of plants in response to heat. [THERMO- + -TROPISM.] —**ther·mo·trop·ic** (thûr′mə-trŏp′ĭk) *adj.*

-thermy *suffix.* Indicates heat; for example, **diathermy.** [New Latin -*thermia,* from Greek *thermē,* heat, from *thermos,* hot.]

the·ro·phyte (thĭr′ə-fīt′) *n.* A plant that overwinters as a seed; an annual. [Greek *theros,* summer + -PHYTE.]

the·ro·pod (thĭr′ə-pŏd′) *n.* Any of various bipedal carnivorous dinosaurs of the suborder Theropoda, of the Jurassic and Cretaceous periods, characteristically having small, grasping forelimbs. [New Latin *Theropoda* : Greek *thēr,* beast + -POD.] —**the·rop·o·dan** (thī-rŏp′ə-dən) *adj. & n.*

Ther·si·tes (thər-sī′tēz). An ugly, abusive Greek soldier slain by Achilles in the Trojan War.

the·sau·rus (thĭ-sôr′əs) *n., pl.* **-sauri** (-sôr′ī) or **-ruses. 1.** A book of selected words or concepts, as a specialized vocabulary of a particular field, as music or medicine. **2.** A book of systematically classified words with their synonyms and often their antonyms. [Latin *thēsaurus,* TREASURE.]

these. Plural of **this.**

The·se·us (thē′sē-əs, -syōōs′). *Greek Mythology.* A hero of Athens who united Attica, slew the Minotaur, and married Phaedra.

the·sis (thē′sĭs) *n., pl.* **-ses** (-sēz′). **1.** A dissertation advancing an original point of view as a result of research, especially as a requirement for an academic degree. **2.** A proposition or theory that is maintained by argument. **3.** A hypothetical proposition, especially one put forth for the sake of argument; a premise. **4.** The first stage of dialectic. **5. a.** The unstressed part of a foot in verse. **b.** The accented section of a musical measure. Compare **arsis.** [Late Latin, from Greek, a placing, a laying down, position, affirmation, from *tithenai,* to put, place.]

thes·pi·an (thĕs′pē-ən) *adj.* **1.** *Thespian.* Of or pertaining to Thespis. **2.** Of or pertaining to drama; dramatic.
~*n.* An actor or actress.

Thes·pis (thĕs′pĭs). Greek poet of the 6th century B.C.; reputed inventor of tragic drama.

Thes·sa·lo·ni·ans (thĕs′ə-lō′nē-ənz) *pl.n. Used with a singular verb. Abbr.* **Thess.** Either of two books of the New Testament consisting of Epistles from the Apostle Paul to the Christians of Thessalonica.

Thes·sa·lo·ni·ki (thĕs′ə-lə-nē′kē). *Ancient name* **Thes·sa·lo·ni·ca** (thĕs′ə-lō′nĭ-kə, -lŏn′ĭ-kə). *English* **Sa·lon·i·ka** (sə-lŏn′ĭ-kə, săl′ə-nē′kə). Port and second-largest city of Greece, in the northeast of the country. It was founded *c.* 315 B.C. and later became the capital of the ancient Roman province of Macedonia.

Thes·sa·ly (thĕs′ə-lē). *Greek* **Thes·sa·lí·a** (thä′sə-lē′ə). Region of central Greece, consisting of a flat, fertile plain between upland Epirus and the Aegean Sea.

the·ta (thā′tə, thē′-) *n.* The eighth letter in the Greek alphabet, written Θ, θ. Transliterated in English as *th.* See feature at **alphabet.** [Greek *thēta,* from a Phoenician cognate of Hebrew *tēth,* TETH.]

The·tis (thē′tĭs). *Greek Mythology.* One of the Nereids, the wife of Peleus and mother of Achilles.

the·ur·gy (thē′ûr-jē) *n., pl.* **-gies. 1.** Divine or supernatural intervention in human affairs. **2.** Magic performed supposedly with the aid of beneficent spirits, as practiced by Neo-Platonists. [Late Latin *theurgia,* from Greek *theourgia,* sacramental rite, "mystery" : THEO- + -URGY.] —**the·ur·gic** (thē-ûr′jĭk), **the·ur·gi·cal** (-jĭ-kəl) *adj.* —**the·ur·gist** (thē′ûr-jĭst) *n.*

thew (thyōō) *n.* **1.** A well-developed sinew or muscle. **2. a.** *thews.* Muscular power or strength. **b.** Vigor. [Middle English, habit, characteristic, good physical quality, Old English *thēaw,* usage, custom, characteristic.] —**thew·y** *adj.*

they (thā) *pron.* The third person plural pronoun in the nominative case. **1.** Used to represent the persons or things last mentioned or implied: *I have three blouses and they all fit perfectly.* **2. a.** Used to represent unspecified persons or people in general: *They say he's having an affair. He's as tough as they come.* **b.** Used to represent those in positions of power; the authorities: *They've changed the regulations to prevent cheating.* **3.** Used of persons as a demonstrative pronoun in the sense of *those:* "*Blessed are they which are persecuted*" (Matthew 5:10). **4.** *Informal.* Used in referring to an indefinite singular antecedent; he or she: *If anyone wants a drink, they can get it themselves.* —See Usage note at **me.** [Middle English *thei,* partly from Old Norse *their,* partly from Old English *thā.*]

they'd (thād). Contraction of *they had* or *they would.*

they'll (thāl). Contraction of *they will* or *they shall.*

they're (thâr). Contraction of *they are.*

they've (thāv). Contraction of *they have.*

thi–. Variant of **thio-.**

thi·a·mine (thī′ə-mĭn, -mēn′) *n.* Also **thi·a·min** (-mĭn). A B-complex vitamin, $C_{12}H_{17}ClN_4OS$, produced synthetically and occurring naturally in the bran coat of grains, in yeast, and in meat, that is necessary for carbohydrate metabolism, maintenance of normal neural activity, and the prevention of beriberi. Also called "vitamin B_1." [THI(O)- + (VIT)AMIN.]

thi·a·zine (thī′ə-zēn′) *n.* Any of a class of organic chemical compounds containing a ring composed of one sulfur atom, one nitrogen atom, and four carbon atoms. [THI(O)- + AZINE.]

thi·a·zole (thī′ə-zōl′) *n.* **1.** A colorless or pale-yellow liquid, C_3H_3NS, containing a five-member ring composed of a nitrogen atom, a sulfur atom, and three carbon atoms, used in making dyes and fungicides. **2.** Any of various derivatives of thiazole. [THI(O)- + AZOLE.]

thick (thĭk) *adj.* **thicker, thickest. 1. a.** Relatively great in depth or in extent from one surface to the opposite; not thin: *a thick board.* **b.** Relatively great in diameter or cross section: *I used thick yarn because I wanted the sweater to be good and warm.* **2.** Measuring in thickness: *The book is two inches thick.* **3.** Having constituent parts in a close, compact arrangement; dense: *a thick forest.* **4.** Having a viscous consistency; not thin, watery, or fluid: *a thick tomato sauce.* **5. a.** Existing in great numbers; numerous: *In that garden the flowers were thick.* **b.** Densely crowded or closely packed; swarming: *The area was thick with security men.* **6.** Impenetrable by the eyes; deep: *a thick, gloomy night.* **7.** Not easy to hear or understand; indistinctly articulated: *the thick slurrings of a drunkard.* **8.** Very noticeable; pronounced: *a thick foreign accent.* **9.** Foggy, misty, or hazy: *thick weather.* **10.** *Informal.* Lacking mental agility; stupid: *Get that through your thick head.* **11.** *Informal.* Very friendly; intimate: *quite thick with his business partners.* **12.** *Informal.* Going be-

thimble *This seamstress's finger cap—of white and yellow gold inlaid with turquoise—is thought to have been made in England in the early 19th century.*

yond what is tolerable; excessive: *thought it a bit thick to be scolded by a child.*
~*adv.* So as to be thick; thickly: *Slice it thick.* **—lay it on thick.** *Informal.* **1.** To overstate or give an exaggerated account of something. **2.** To flatter someone excessively. **—thick and fast.** In rapid succession and great profusion.
~*n.* **1.** The thickest part of something. **2.** The most active, intense, or dense part: *in the thick of the fighting.* **—through thick and thin.** In both good and bad times. [Middle English *thikke,* Old English *thicce.*] **—thick·ish** *adj.* **—thick·ly** *adv.*

thick·en (thĭk'ən) *v.* **-ened, -ening, -ens.** *—tr.* To make thick or thicker. *—intr.* **1.** To become thickened. **2.** To become more intense, intricate, or complex: *The plot thickens.* **—thick·en·er** *n.*

thick·en·ing (thĭk'ə-nĭng) *n.* **1.** Any material used to thicken a liquid. **2.** A thickened part of something.

thick·et (thĭk'ĭt) *n.* **1.** A dense growth of shrubs or underbrush; a copse. **2.** Something suggestive of a thicket in impenetrability or thickness: *a thicket of unreality.* [Middle English *thikket* (unattested), Old English *thiccet,* from *thicce,* THICK.]

thick·head (thĭk'hĕd') *n.* A stupid person; a blockhead; a numbskull. **—thick·head·ed** (thĭk'hĕd'ĭd) *adj.*

thick-knee (thĭk'nē') *n.* A **stone curlew** *(see).*

thick·ness (thĭk'nĭs) *n.* **1.** The state or condition of being thick. **2.** The dimension between two of an object's surfaces, usually taken to be the dimension of least measure. **3.** A layer, sheet, stratum, or ply. **4.** The thick part or main body of something.

thick·set (thĭk'sĕt') *adj.* **1.** Heavily or stockily built; stout and compact. **2.** Positioned or placed closely together: *thickset rose bushes.*

thick-skinned (thĭk'skĭnd') *adj.* **1.** Having a thick skin. **2. a.** Insensitive. **b.** Not easily offended.

thick-wit·ted (thĭk'wĭt'ĭd) *adj.* Stupid; dull.

thief (thēf) *n., pl.* **thieves** (thēvz). One who commits theft; especially, a person who steals using surreptitious rather than violent means. [Middle English *thefe,* Old English *thīof, thēof,* from Germanic *theubhaz* (unattested).]

Thiers (tē-âr'), **Louis Adolphe** (1797–1877). French statesman and historian. A member of the French assembly under Napoleon III, he was a founder and the first president of the new Third Republic upon the emperor's fall after the Franco-Prussian War. Also a noted historian, he wrote *History of the French Revolution* (1823–27) and *History of the Consulate and the Empire* (1845–62).

Thieu (tyōō), **Nguyen Van** (1923–). Vietnamese military and political leader; president of South Vietnam (1967–75). After fighting with the French against the Viet Minh (1946–54) and helping lead the coup against Ngo Dinh Diem (1963), he became military chief of state of South Vietnam (1965) and served as president from 1967 to 1975, when the country fell to North Vietnamese forces.

thieve (thēv) *v.* **thieved, thieving, thieves.** *—tr.* To take by theft; steal. *—intr.* To act as or be a thief; commit theft. —See Synonyms at **rob.** [Old English *thēofian,* from *thēof,* THIEF.]

thiev·er·y (thē'və-rē) *n., pl.* **-ies.** The act or an instance of thieving.

thiev·ish (thē'vĭsh) *adj.* **1.** Given to thieving or stealing. **2.** Of, similar to, or characteristic of a thief; stealthy; furtive. **—thiev·ish·ly** *adv.* **—thiev·ish·ness** *n.*

thigh (thī) *n.* **1.** The portion of the human leg between the hip and the knee. **2.** A corresponding structure in other animals. [Middle English *thih,* Old English *thēoh.*]

thigh·bone (thī'bōn') *n.* The **femur** *(see).*

thig·mo·tax·is (thĭg'mə-tăk'sĭs) *n.* Movement of an entire cell or organism in response to a direct tactile stimulus. Also called "stereotaxis." [New Latin : Greek *thigma,* touch, from *thinganein,* to touch + -TAXIS.] **—thig·mo·tac·tic** (thĭg'mə-tăk'tĭk) *adj.* **—thig·mo·tac·ti·cal·ly** *adv.*

thig·mot·ro·pism (thĭg-mŏt'rə-pĭz'əm) *n.* Directional growth of plants in response to contact with a surface or object. Also called "haptotropism." [Greek *thigma,* touch (see **thigmotaxis**) + -TROPISM.] **—thig·mo·trop·ic** (thĭg'mə-trŏp'ĭk) *adj.*

thill (thĭl) *n.* Either of the two long shafts between which an animal is fastened when pulling a wagon. [Middle English *thille*†.]

thim·ble (thĭm'bəl) *n.* **1. a.** A small metal, ceramic, or plastic cup worn to protect the finger that pushes the needle in sewing. **b.** A thimbleful. **2.** Any of various tubular sockets or sleeves in machinery. **3.** *Nautical.* **a.** A metal ring fitted in an eye of a sail to prevent chafing. **b.** A metal ring around which a rope splice is passed. [Middle English *thymbyl,* Old English *thȳmel,* from *thūma,* THUMB.]

thim·ble·ful (thĭm'bəl-fōōl') *n., pl.* **-fuls.** A very small quantity.

thim·ble·rig (thĭm'bəl-rĭg') *n.* **1.** A gambling game, usually a swindle, in which the operator shuffles three inverted thimble-shaped cups under one of which he has placed a marker, as a pea, and spectators bet on the location of the marker. **2.** A person who operates a thimblerig.
~*tr.v.* **thimblerigged, -rigging, -rigs.** To swindle with or as if with a thimblerig. **—thim·ble·rig·ger** *n.*

Thim·phu (thĭm'pōō'). Also **Thim·bu** (-bōō'). Capital of Bhutan, high in the Chinchu valley in the west of the country.

thin (thĭn) *adj.* **thinner, thinnest. 1. a.** Relatively small in depth or in extent from one surface to the opposite; not thick. **b.** Not great in diameter or cross section; narrow in relation to length: *a thin strand.* **2.** Lean or slender of figure. **3. a.** Having constituent parts widely separated; sparse: *a thin rain. The crowd grew thinner.* **b.** More rarefied than normal: *thin air.* **4.** Lacking force, substance, or body: *a thin brew.* **5.** Unconvincing, feeble, or flimsy: *That excuse is wearing a bit thin.* **6.** Difficult, uncomfortable, or disappointing: *having rather a thin time.* **7.** Lacking resonance or fullness; tinny. Said of sound or tone. **8.** Lacking radiance or intensity. Said of light or color. **9.** *Photography.* Not having enough contrast to make satisfactory prints. Said of a negative.
~*adv.* So as to be thin; thinly.
~*v.* **thinned, thinning, thins.** *—intr.* **1.** To become thin or thinner. **2.** To become less dense. Often used with *out: The crowd began to thin out.* *—tr.* **1.** To make thin or thinner. **2. a.** To make less dense or crowded: *Plague thinned the enemy's ranks.* **b.** To remove so as to make less dense: *thin out seedlings.* [Middle English *thinne,* Old English *thynne.*] **—thin·ly** *adv.* **—thin·ness** *n.*

thin air *n.* A state of being invisible: *vanished into thin air.*

thine (*th*īn) *pron. Archaic.* Absolute form of *thy.* **1.** Belonging to thee. **2.** The one or ones belonging to thee: *Thine is the kingdom.* **3.** Used instead of *thy* before an initial vowel or *h*: *thine enemy.* [Middle English *thin,* Old English *thīn.*]

thing (thĭng) *n.* **1.** Something perceived, known, or thought to have a separate existence; an entity. **2.** The real or concrete substance of an entity as distinguished from its appearances or from the name, word, or symbol denoting it. **3.** An entity actually existing in space or time in contrast to one merely postulated; an object or fact. **4.** An inanimate object as distinct from a living being: *seems more interested in things than in people.* **5.** A living being. Used to emphasize an attitude of pity, affection, contempt, or reproach: *the poor thing.* **6. a.** *Law.* That which can be possessed or owned as distinguished from a person. **b. things.** Possessions; belongings. **7.** An article of clothing; garment. **8. things.** The equipment needed for an activity or purpose: *Where are my sewing things?* **9.** An object or entity that cannot or need not be named specifically: *What's this thing for?* **10. a.** An act, deed, or achievement: *expects great things of us. I hope I've done the right thing.* **b.** A product of work: *likes making things with his hands.* **11.** A thought, notion, or statement: *What a funny thing to say!* **12.** A piece of information. **13.** An example or representative of a class: *the latest thing in home computers.* **14. a.** A matter to be dealt with; a concern: *a lot of things on her mind.* **b.** A point, factor, or reason: *and for another thing, it's far too expensive.* **15. things. a.** The general state of affairs; conditions: *How are things?* **b.** A particular or prevailing situation: *helped me to see things differently.* **16.** A characteristic; a particular feature: *one of the things I like about her.* **17.** A turn of events; a circumstance: *the nicest thing that's happened all day.* **18. a.** An illogical feeling or preoccupation; an obsession: *has a thing about cats.* **b.** Something to which undue importance is given: *no need to make such a thing of it.* **19.** *Slang.* An activity uniquely suitable and satisfying to one: *doing his thing.* **—first thing.** Before anything else; right away. **—know a thing or two.** To have considerable knowledge or skill, especially as a result of long experience. **—see** (or **hear**) **things.** To have hallucinations. **—the thing. 1.** What is conventionally regarded as proper or correct: *His behavior wasn't quite the thing.* **2.** What is most important or most necessary: *The great thing is to keep on trying.* **3.** What is most fashionable; the rage: *Streaked hair was the thing last year.* **4.** The point at issue: *The thing is, do you think he'll believe it?* [Middle English *thing,* Old English *thing,* creature, thing, deed, assembly, from Germanic *thingam* (unattested).]

thing·a·ma·bob, thing·u·ma·bob (thĭng'ə-mə-bŏb') *n. Informal.* A thingamajig. [From THING.]

thing·a·ma·jig, thing·u·ma·jig (thĭng'ə-mə-jĭg') *n. Informal.* Something for which the exact name has been forgotten or is not known. [From THING.]

thing-in-it·self (thĭng'ĭn-ĭt-sĕlf') *n., pl.* **things-in-them·selves** (thĭngz'ĭn-thəm-sĕlvz'). An ultimate metaphysical reality conceived by Kant as beyond the perception of human senses and thought; a noumenon. [Translation of German *Ding an sich.*]

think (thĭngk) *v.* **thought** (thôt), **thinking, thinks.** *—tr.* **1.** To have as a thought; formulate in the mind: *think great thoughts.* **2. a.** To reason about or reflect on; ponder: *Think how complex language is.* Often used with *through* or *over: Think the matter through.* **b.** To consider carefully: *Think what you need to bring.* Often used with *out: thought the problem out.* **3.** To judge or regard; look upon: *I think it only fair.* **4.** To believe; suppose: *I think it is true.* **5. a.** To have in mind; plan or intend: *I think I'll go to bed. We thought we'd arrive early but didn't.* **b.** To expect; anticipate: *I don't think you'll have any trouble.* **6.** To remember; call to mind: *I can't think now what his name was.* **7. a.** To visualize; imagine: *Think what a difference it would make.* **b.** To fathom; understand: *can't think why he did it.* **8.** To bring into a specified condition by mental activity: *She thought herself into a terror of going.* **9.** To be sufficiently thoughtful or attentive: *didn't think to say good-by.* **10.** To center one's thoughts on; think largely or exclusively in terms of. *—intr.* **1. a.** To exercise the power of reason; conceive of ideas, draw inferences, and use judgment. **b.** To turn over ideas; ponder; reflect. **2.** To weigh the idea; consider the matter: *Think before you answer.* Often used with *about* or *of: They are thinking of moving.* **3.** To recall a thought or image to mind: *can't think of his name; think back to last summer.* **4.** To believe; suppose: *Do you think so?* **5.** To dispose the mind in a specified way: *Think rich.* **—think aloud.** To say what one is thinking. **—think better of.** To decide against after reconsidering. **—think nothing of.** To regard as routine or usual. **—think of. 1.** To regard in the specified way; have as one's opinion of: *always thought of him as reasonable. What do you think of the latest offer?* **2.** To value or approve to the specified extent: *don't think much of that idea.* **3.** To have care or consideration for; be mindful of: *Think of your future.* **4.** To hit on the idea of: *never*

thought of phoning the police. —**think twice.** To weigh something carefully. —**think up.** To devise or invent.
~*n.* An act of thinking. [Think, thought, thought; Middle English *thenken, thoughte, thought,* Old English *thencan, thōhte, gethōht.*]

think·a·ble (thǐng′kə-bəl) *adj.* Capable of being or fit to be considered; conceivable. —**think·a·bly** *adv.*

think·er (thǐng′kər) *n.* **1.** A person who devotes his time to thinking or has a special ability to think. **2.** A person who thinks or reasons in a specified way: *a careful thinker.*

think·ing (thǐng′kǐng) *n.* **1.** Mental activity; thought. **2.** A way of reasoning; judgment: *not to my thinking a good idea.*
~*adj.* Characterized by thoughtfulness; rational: *Man is a thinking animal.*

think tank *n.* An institution or group of people organized, as by a government or business, to undertake detailed study of particular issues or problems.

thin·ner (thǐn′ər) *n.* A liquid, such as turpentine, mixed with paint to reduce viscosity for ease in application.

thin-skinned (thǐn′skǐnd′) *adj.* **1.** Having a thin rind or skin. **2.** Oversensitive, especially to reproach or insult.

thio-, thi- *prefix. Chemistry.* Indicates a compound containing a divalent sulfur atom, especially one in which sulfur has replaced oxygen; for example, **thiophene, thiol.** [From Greek *theion,* sulfur.]

thi·o·car·bam·ide (thī′ō-kär′bə-mīd′) *n.* Thiourea *(see).*

thi·o·cy·an·ic acid (thī′ō-sī-ǎn′ĭk) *n.* An unstable weak acid, HSCN, existing as a colorless gas or white solid.

thi·o·e·ther (thī′ō-ē′thər) *n.* Any of various organic compounds containing sulfur and having the general formula RSR′, where R and R′ are organic groups. [THIO- + ETHER.]

Thi·o·kol (thī′ə-kôl′, -kōl′) *n.* A trademark for any of various polysulfide polymers in the form of liquids, water dispersions, and rubbers used in seals and sealants.

thi·ol (thī′ôl′, -ōl′) *n.* Any of various organic compounds containing sulfur and having the general formula RSH, where R is an organic group. Also called "mercaptan." [THI(O)- + -OL.]

thion- *prefix.* Indicates sulfur; for example, **thionine.** [From Greek *theion,* sulfur.]

thi·o·nine (thī′ə-nēn′, -nǐn) *n.* A crystalline thiazene derivative used as a violet dye in microscopy. [THION- + -INE.]

thi·o·nyl (thī′ə-nǐl′) *adj.* Of, pertaining to, or containing the divalent group SO. [THION- + -YL.]

thi·o·pen·tal sodium (thī′ō-pěn′tǎl′, -tôl′) *n.* Also **thi·o·pen·tone sodium** (-tōn′). A hygroscopic powder, $C_{11}H_{17}N_2O_2SNa$, injected intravenously as a general anesthetic. Also called "sodium pentothal." [THIO- + PENT(OBARBIT)AL.]

thi·o·phene (thī′ə-fēn′) *n.* A colorless liquid, C_4H_4S, used as a solvent. [THIO- + PH(ENO)- + -ENE.]

thi·o·sul·fate (thī′ō-sŭl′fāt′) *n.* A salt of thiosulfuric acid.

thi·o·sul·fu·ric acid (thī′ō-sŭl-fyŏŏr′ĭk) *n.* An acid, $H_2S_2O_3$, formed by the replacement of an oxygen atom by a sulfur atom in sulfuric acid, known only in solution or by its salts and esters.

thi·o·u·ra·cil (thī′ō-yŏŏr′ə-sǐl′) *n.* A white crystalline substance, $C_4H_4N_2OS$, used in the treatment of hyperthyroidism. [THIO- + URACIL.]

thi·o·u·re·a (thī′ō-yŏŏ-rē′ə) *n.* A white, lustrous crystalline compound, $(NH_2)_2CS$, used in photography, photocopying paper, and various organic syntheses. Also called "thiocarbamide." [THIO- + UREA.]

Thi·ra (thîr′ə). Also **San·to·rin** (săn′tə-rēn′). Southernmost of the Cyclades Islands in the Aegean Sea. It is the remains of an ancient volcano. Excavations in the 1960's revealed remains of a rich Minoan settlement.

third (thûrd) *n.* **1.** The ordinal number three in a series. Also written 3rd. **2.** One of three equal parts. **3.** *Music.* **a.** An interval of three degrees in a diatonic scale. **b.** A tone separated by three degrees from a given tone; especially, the third tone of a scale. **c.** The harmonic combination of two tones separated by a third. **4.** The gear immediately above second in a motor vehicle transmission. **5.** *Baseball.* Third base.
~*adv.* Also **third·ly** (thûrd′lē). In the third place, rank, or order. [Middle English *thride, thirde,* Old English *third(d)a, thridda.*] —**third** *adj.*

third base *n. Baseball.* **1.** The third base to be reached by a runner, up the left-field foul line from home base. **2.** The position played by the third baseman.

third baseman *n. Baseball.* The infielder stationed near third base.

third class *n.* **1.** The group or class that is next below the second in quality, value, or the like. **2.** The class of accommodation on a train or other means of transport ranking next below second class and usually of the lowest level of luxury and price. **3.** A class of mail in the United States comprising unsealed printed matter, other than newspapers and magazines, that weighs less than 16 ounces. —**third-class** (thûrd′klǎs′, -kläs′) *adj. & adv.*

third degree *n.* Rough treatment or torture of a prisoner to obtain information or a confession.

third-de·gree burn (thûrd′dǐ-grē′) *n.* A severe burn in which the epidermis and dermis are destroyed, the tissues below are damaged, and sensitive nerve endings are exposed.

third dimension *n.* **1.** The dimension of depth or thickness. **2.** The quality of seeming real or lifelike. —**third-di·men·sion·al** (thûrd′-dǐ-měn′shə-nəl) *adj.*

Third Estate *n. Sometimes* **third estate.** The third-highest social

order in a country; specifically, the commons in contrast to the nobility and clergy.

third·hand (thûrd′hǎnd′) *adj.* **1.** Acquired from or through two intermediate sources. **2.** Previously used by two other owners.

Third International *n.* See International.

Third Order *n.* A confraternity of laymen associated with any of various religious orders of the Roman Catholic Church.

third party *n.* **1.** *Law.* A person or party other than the principals in a transaction, agreement, or case. **2.** A political party organized as opposition to the existing parties in a two-party system.

third-par·ty (thûrd′pär′tē) *adj.* Providing insurance cover against liability arising from accident to other persons or their property.

third person *n. Grammar.* The form of a pronoun or verb used in referring to a person or thing other than the speaker or the one spoken to.

third rail *n.* The rail through which the current runs to power the train on an electric railway.

third-rate (thûrd′rāt′) *adj.* Of third quality or value; especially, distinctly inferior.

third reading *n.* The final reading of a legislative bill before a vote is taken.

Third World *n.* Underdeveloped or developing countries, especially those not allied with the Communist or non-Communist blocs.

thirst (thûrst) *n.* **1. a.** A sensation of dryness in the mouth related to a need or desire to drink. **b.** A need or desire to drink. **c.** Dehydration produced by a lack of water. **2.** An insistent desire; craving.
~*intr.v.* **thirsted, thirsting, thirsts.** **1.** To feel a need to drink. **2.** To have a strong craving; yearn. Used with *for.* —See Synonyms at **yearn.** [Middle English *thurst, thirst,* Old English *thurst.*]

thirst·y (thûr′stē) *adj.* **-ier, -iest.** **1.** Desiring or needing to drink. **2.** Arid; parched. **3.** Feeling a strong desire; eager: *thirsty for news.* —**thirst·i·ly** *adv.* —**thirst·i·ness** *n.*

thir·teen (thûr-tēn′) *n.* **1. a.** The cardinal number that is one more than twelve. **b.** A symbol representing this, as 13 or XIII. **2.** A set made up of thirteen persons or things. **3.** The thirteenth in a series. [Middle English *thrittene,* Old English *thrēotīne* : THREE + -TEEN.] —**thir·teen** *adj. & pron.*

thir·teenth (thûr-tēnth′) *n.* **1.** The ordinal number 13 in a series. Also written 13th. **2.** One of 13 equal parts. —**thir·teenth** *adj. & adv.*

thir·ti·eth (thûr′tē-ĭth) *n.* **1.** The ordinal number 30 in a series. Also written 30th. **2.** One of 30 equal parts. —**thir·ti·eth** *adj. & adv.*

thir·ty (thûr′tē) *n., pl.* **-ties.** **1. a.** The cardinal number that is 10 more than 20. **b.** A symbol representing this, as 30 or XXX. **2. thirties. a.** The range of numbers from 30 to 39, considered as a range, as of age, price, or temperature. **b.** The years 30 to 39 in a century. Also used adjectively: *a thirties film.* [Middle English *thritty,* Old English *thrītig* : THREE + -TY.] —**thir·ty** *adj. & pron.*

thir·ty-sec·ond note (thûr′tē-sĕk′ənd) *n.* A musical note with a time value equivalent to 1/32 of a whole note. Also *chiefly British* "demisemiquaver."

thir·ty-two-mo (thûr′tē-tōō′mō) *n., pl.* **-mos.** **1.** The page size (3½ by 5½ inches) that results when a printers' sheet is folded into 32 equal sections. **2.** A book composed of pages of thirty-twomos.

Thirty Years' War. A series of wars fought mainly in central and western Europe (1618–48).

this (thĭs) *adj., pl.* **these** (thēz). **1.** Being just mentioned or present in space, time, or thought. **2.** Being nearer than another or compared with another. **3.** Being about to be stated or described: *began with this word.*
~*pron., pl.* **these. 1.** The person or thing present, nearby, or just mentioned or understood. **2.** What is about to be stated. **3.** The one that is nearer than another or the one compared with the other: *This is mine.* **4.** The present occasion or time: *said he'd be back before this.*
~*adv.* To this extent; so: *a book about this thick.* [This, these; Middle English *this, thes,* Old English *thes* or *thēs, thēos, this* (masculine, feminine, neuter singular).] —**this·ness** *n.*

Usage: This and *that* are both used as demonstrative pronouns to refer to a thought expressed earlier: *The letter was unopened; that* (or *this) in itself casts doubt on the inspector's theory. That* is sometimes prescribed as the better choice in referring to what has gone before (as in the preceding example). When the referent is yet to be mentioned, only *this* is used: *This* (not *that) is what bothers me: we have no time to consider late applications.* This use of *this* appears as an emphatic variant of the indefinite article *a*: *This friend of mine came to visit me last night. I have this terrible headache.* This usage should be avoided in writing.

this·tle (thĭs′əl) *n.* **1.** Any of numerous weedy plants, chiefly of the genera *Cirsium, Carduus,* or *Onopordum,* having prickly leaves and usually purplish flowers surrounded by prickly bracts. **2.** Any of various similar or related plants. [Middle English *thistel,* Old English *thistel,* from Germanic *thistilaz* (unattested).]

this·tle·down (thĭs′əl-doun′) *n.* The silky down attached to the seeds of a thistle.

thith·er (thĭth′ər, thĭth′-) *adv.* To or toward that place; in that direction; there: *hither and thither.*
~*adj.* Located or being on the more distant side; farther: *the thither side of the pond.* [Middle English *thither, thider,* Old English *thider, thæder.*]

thith·er·ward (thĭth′ər-wərd, thĭth′-) *adv.* In that direction; thither.

thix·ot·ro·py (thĭk-sŏt′rə-pē) *n.* The property exhibited by certain gels, such as emulsion paints, of liquefying when stirred or shaken

thistle *A prickly weed that seems to flourish in any habitat. The spear thistle, shown here, grows up to 1.8 meters (6 feet) tall.*

and returning to the semisolid state upon standing. [Greek *thixis,* "touching," from *thinganein,* to touch + -TROPY.] —**thix·o·trop·ic** (thĭk′sə-trŏp′ĭk) *adj.*

tho, tho' (thō) *conj. & adv. Informal.* Though.

thole[1] (thōl) *tr.v.* **tholed, tholing, tholes.** *Regional.* To endure; bear. [Middle English *tholen,* Old English *tholian,* to endure.]

thole[2] *n.* Also **thole·pin** (thōl′pĭn′). Either of a pair of wooden pegs set in the gunwale of a boat to serve as an oarlock. [Middle English *tholle,* Old English *thol(l).*]

tho·los (thō′lŏs′) *n., pl.* **tholoi** (thō′loi′). A dome-shaped tomb of the type associated with the Mycenaean culture of ancient Greece. [Greek *tholos†.*]

Thom·as (tŏm′əs), **Saint,** known as "Didymus." One of the Twelve Apostles. According to the New Testament, he refused to believe that Jesus had risen from the dead until he had seen the wounds on the hands and side of the resurrected Christ.

Thomas, Dylan Marlais (1914–53). Welsh poet. Known for his bardic voice and successful experiments with syllabic verse, he wrote highly personal poems, such as "Fern Hill" (1946), as well as essays, short fiction, and pieces for the radio, including *A Child's Christmas in Wales* (1954) and *Under Milk Wood* (1954).

Thomas, Norman Mattoon (1884–1968). U.S. socialist leader. As a Presbyterian minister (1911–31) in East Harlem, he saw the problems of poverty and the ineffectual social policies of the government. He joined the Socialist Party in 1918, helped found the American Civil Liberties Union (1920), and ran for president six times between 1928 and 1948.

Thomas à Becket. See Saint Thomas **Becket.**

Thomas à Kem·pis (ə kĕm′pĭs, ä) (1380–1471). German ecclesiastic and writer. After entering an Augustinian monastery (1407) and being ordained (1413), he spent most of his life there writing devotional literature. *The Imitation of Christ,* a classic religious work attributed to him, delineates a life of religious devotion.

Tho·mism (tō′mĭz′əm) *n.* The theological and philosophical system of St. Thomas Aquinas, which became the basis of scholasticism. —**Tho·mist** (tō′mĭst) *n.* —**Tho·mis·tic** (tō-mĭs′tĭk) *adj.*

Thomp·son (tŏmp′sən, tŏm′sən), **Benjamin,** known as "Count Rumford" (1753–1814). U.S. physicist, philanthropist, and loyalist. He is primarily known for the 11 years (1784–95) he spent in Bavaria, where he made significant improvements in military and welfare conditions, and for his scientific studies of heat and friction. He is credited with many inventions related to his experiments, including the drip coffee-maker.

Thompson submachine gun *n.* A type of .45-caliber submachine gun. Also informally called "Tommy gun." [After its co-inventor, John *Thompson* (1860–1940), U.S. army officer.]

thong (thông, thŏng) *n.* **1.** A narrow strip of leather or other material used for binding or lashing. **2.** A sandal held on the foot by a thong that fits between the toes. Also called "flip-flop." [Middle English *thong,* Old English *thwong, thwang.*]

Thor (thôr). *Norse Mythology.* The god of thunder. [Old Norse *thōrr,* thunder.]

tho·rac·ic (thə-răs′ĭk) *adj.* Of, relating to, or situated in or near the thorax.

thoracic duct *n.* The main duct of the lymphatic system, ascending along the spinal cord and discharging into veins in the neck.

tho·ra·cot·o·my (thôr′ə-kŏt′ə-mē, thōr′-) *n., pl.* **-mies.** Surgical incision of the chest wall. [Latin *thōrāx* (stem *thōrāc-*), THORAX + -TOMY.]

tho·rax (thôr′ăks′) *n., pl.* **-raxes** or **thoraces** (thôr′ə-sēz′, thōr′-). **1.** *Anatomy.* **a.** The part of the human body between the neck and the diaphragm, partially encased by the ribs; the chest. **b.** A corresponding part in other animals. **2.** The second or middle region of the body of an arthropod, in insects bearing the true legs and wings. [Latin *thōrāx,* from Greek *thōrax†* (stem *thōrak-*), breastplate, coat of mail, chest covering.]

Tho·reau (thə-rō′, thô-, thôr′ō), **Henry David** (1817–62). U.S. essayist and poet. One of the premier figures in American intellectual history, he lived in Concord, Massachusetts, for much of his life. There he became associated with the Transcendentalists and for two years lived in solitude on the shore of Walden Pond. Among his classic works are "Civil Disobedience" (1849) and *Walden, or Life in the Woods* (1854).

Thor·finn Karl·sef·ni (thôr′fĭn kärl′sĕv′nē, thōr′-) (born *c.* 980). Icelandic explorer and colonist. Following the explorations of present-day Newfoundland by Leif Ericson, he led a colonizing expedition to the region (*c.* 1010). After a severe winter the colony migrated south, possibly to present-day Massachusetts, before becoming discouraged and returning to their homeland.

tho·rite (thôr′īt, thōr′-) *n.* A vitreous brownish-yellow or black thorium ore, essentially ThSiO₄. [THOR(IUM) + -ITE.]

tho·ri·um (thôr′ē-əm, thōr′-) *n. Symbol* **Th** A silvery-white metallic element with 13 radioactive isotopes, only one of which, thorium 232, occurs naturally. It is used in magnesium alloys and isotope 232 is a potential source of nuclear energy. Atomic number 90, atomic weight 232.038, approximate melting point 1,700°C, approximate boiling point 4,000°C, approximate specific gravity 11.66, valence 4. [New Latin, after THOR.]

thorium dioxide *n.* A heavy white powder, ThO₂, used mainly in ceramics, gas mantles, and nuclear fuels.

thorn (thôrn) *n.* **1.** *Botany.* A modified branch in the form of a sharp, woody structure. **2.** Any of various shrubs, trees, or woody plants, as the hawthorn, bearing thorns. **3.** Any of various sharp,

spiny protuberances; a prickle or spine. **4.** A source of continual annoyance or distress: *a thorn in one's flesh.* **5.** The runic letter originally representing the sounds (th), as in *thin,* and (th), as in *the,* adapted into the Roman alphabet and used in Old English and Middle English manuscripts. It now survives only in Icelandic representing the sound (th) in *thin.* [Middle English *thorn,* Old English *thorn,* thorn, thornbush.]

thorn apple *n.* Any of various plants of the genus *Datura,* especially the **jimsonweed** (*see*).

thorn·back (thôrn′băk′) *n.* Either of two rays, *Raja clavata,* of European waters, or *Platyrhinoidis triseriata,* of Pacific waters, having spines along the back.

thorn·y (thôr′nē) *adj.* **-ier, -iest. 1.** Full of or covered with thorns or thorny plants. **2.** Thornlike; spiny. **3.** Painfully controversial or difficult to resolve; vexatious: *a thorny problem.* —**thorn·i·ness** *n.*

tho·ron (thôr′ŏn′, thōr′-) *n.* A radioactive isotope of radon having a half-life of 54.5 seconds and produced by the disintegration of thorium. [THOR(IUM) + -ON.]

thor·ough (thûr′ō) *adj.* **1.** Complete in every respect or detail; exhaustive: *a thorough search.* **2.** Being completely as described; utter: *a thorough rogue.* **3.** Painstakingly accurate or careful: *a thorough worker.* [Middle English *thorow,* from *thurgh* (adverb), through, Old English *thuruh,* from *thurh,* THROUGH.] —**thor·ough·ly** *adv.* —**thor·ough·ness** *n.*

thor·ough·bred (thûr′ō-brĕd′, thûr′ə-) *adj.* **1.** Bred of pure stock; purebred. **2.** Thoroughbred. Pertaining or belonging to the Thoroughbred breed of horses. **3.** Thoroughly trained, accomplished, or educated; well-bred. **4.** Marked by characteristics associated with a thoroughbred: *a thoroughbred sports car.* ~*n.* **1.** A purebred or pedigreed animal. **2.** Thoroughbred. A horse of a breed originating from a cross of Arab stallions with English mares and used widely in horseracing. **3.** A well-bred person.

thor·ough·fare (thûr′ō-fâr′, thûr′ə-) *n.* **1.** A main road or public highway. **2. a.** A place of passage from one location to another. **b.** Right to such passage: *no thoroughfare.* **3.** A heavily traveled passage, as a waterway, strait, or channel. [Middle English *thurghfare : thurgh,* THROUGH + FARE (passage).]

thor·ough·go·ing (thûr′ō-gō′ĭng, thûr′ə-) *adj.* **1.** Very thorough; complete. **2.** Unmitigated; unqualified; out-and-out.

thor·ough·paced (thûr′ō-pāst′, thûr′ə-) *adj.* **1. a.** Trained in all paces or gaits. Said of a horse. **b.** Thoroughly trained. **2.** Thoroughgoing.

thor·ough·pin (thûr′ō-pĭn′, thûr′ə-) *n.* An abnormal swelling on either side of the hock joint of horses and related animals. [From THOROUGH (passing through); it appears as if a pin were piercing the joint.]

thor·ough·wort (thûr′ō-wûrt′, -wôrt′, thûr′ə-) *n.* A plant, the **bone·set** (*see*).

thorp (thôrp) *n. Obsolete.* A hamlet or village. [Middle English *thorp,* Old English *throp, thorp.*]

Thorpe (thôrp), **James Francis,** called "Jim" (1888–1953). U.S. Indian athlete. He first distinguished himself as a two-time all-American football player (1911–12) and later played football and baseball professionally. Perhaps his greatest athletic achievement was winning the decathlon and pentathlon in the 1912 Olympic Games.

Thors·havn (tôrs′houn′). Capital and chief town of the Faeroes, situated on the island of Stremoy.

those. Plural of **that.**

Thoth (thōth, tōt). *Egyptian Mythology.* The god of the moon and of wisdom and learning, whose sacred bird was the ibis. He is represented with the head and neck of an ibis or as a baboon.

thou[1] (thou) *pron. Archaic.* The second person singular pronoun in the nominative case. **1.** Used to represent the person or personal being who is spoken to: *"Thou wilt never get thee a husband"* (Shakespeare). **2.** Used in apposition before a noun to indicate address: *"Thou drone, thou snail, thou slug, thou sot!"* (Shakespeare). [Thou, thee, thy or thine; Middle English *thu, the(e), thi* (before a consonant) and *thin* (before a vowel), Old English *thu* (or *thū*), *the* (or *thē*), *thīn.*]

thou[2] (thou) *n. Slang.* A thousand.

though (thō) *conj.* **1.** Despite the fact that; while; although: *Though I failed, I'm glad I tried.* **2.** Conceding or supposing that; even if: *Though I may fail, I will still try.* ~*adv.* However; nevertheless: *She can be unpleasant. I still like her, though.* —**as though.** As if. [Middle English *thoh, though,* from Old Norse *thō.*]

Usage: The use of *though* as an adverb at the end of a sentence or clause is very common: *He said he wouldn't come; he did, though.* The construction is most appropriate to informal contexts. See also Usage note at **although.**

thought (thôt). Past tense and past participle of **think.** ~*n.* **1. a.** The act or process of thinking; cogitation. **b.** The faculty or power of reasoning. **2. a.** An object of thinking; what one is thinking about: *lofty thoughts.* **b.** A product of thinking; an idea, opinion, or judgment. **3.** The intellectual activity or output of a particular time, place, or group. **4.** Serious consideration: *give the matter some thought.* **5.** Heed; regard: *with no thought for his life.* **6.** Intention; purpose. **7.** Expectation; hope; anticipation. **8.** A trifle; a bit: *a thought more considerate.* —See Synonyms at **idea.** [Middle English *thought,* a thought, Old English *(ge)thōht.*]

thought·ful (thôt′fəl) *adj.* **1.** Given to or occupied with thought; contemplative. **2.** Well thought-out: *a thoughtful essay.* **3.** Careful;

Thoth *In ancient Egypt, Thoth was the scribe of the gods, the inventor of numbers and measurer of time, from which he became the god of wisdom and magic. He was also the moon god and was usually, as here, represented with the head of an ibis.*

heedful. **4.** Showing regard for others; considerate. —**thought·ful·ly** *adv.* —**thought·ful·ness** *n.*
 Synonyms: *considerate, indulgent, solicitous.*
thought·less (thôt′lĭs) *adj.* **1.** Showing lack of thought, as: **a.** Careless; unthinking. **b.** Reckless; rash. **c.** Inconsiderate; inattentive. **2.** Unable to think. —See Synonyms at **careless.** —**thought·less·ly** *adv.* —**thought·less·ness** *n.*
thought-out (thôt′out′) *adj.* Produced or developed through the application of thought: *a well thought-out plan.*
thought-pro·vok·ing (thôt′prə-vō′kĭng) *adj.* Stimulating serious or deep thinking: *a thought-provoking lecture.*
thought reading *n.* **Mind reading** *(see).*
thought transference *n.* **Telepathy** *(see).*
thou·sand (thou′zənd) *n.* **1.** The cardinal number written 1,000, 1000, 10³, or in Roman numerals M. **2.** *Often* **thousands.** An indefinitely large number: *thousands of people.* [Middle English *thousande,* Old English *thūsend.*] —**thou·sand** *adj. & pron.*
Thousand and One Nights *pl.n.* The **Arabian Nights** *(see).*
Thousand Island dressing *n.* A salad dressing made of mayonnaise with chili sauce or ketchup and various seasonings. [Probably after the THOUSAND ISLANDS.]
Thousand Islands. A group of more than 1,800 islands and 3,000 shoals in the St. Lawrence River, stretching for *c.* 80 kilometers (50 miles) east of Lake Ontario. The largest is Wolfe Island.
thou·sandth (thou′zəndth, -zənth) *n.* **1.** The ordinal number thousand in a series. Also written 1,000th. **2.** One of a thousand equal parts. —**thou·sandth** *adj. & adv.*
thp thrust horsepower.
Thrace (thrās). Region of southeastern Europe, now mostly in northeastern Greece but also occupying parts of southern Bulgaria and European Turkey. It was colonized by Greeks in the 7th century B.C. and later passed successively to the Roman, Byzantine, and Ottoman empires.
Thra·cian (thrā′shən) *n.* **1.** A native or inhabitant of Thrace. **2.** The Indo-European language spoken by the ancient inhabitants of Thrace. —**Thra·cian** *adj.*
Thrale, Mrs. See Hester Lynch **Piozzi.**
thrall (thrôl) *n.* **1.** A person, as a slave or serf, who is held in bondage or servitude. **2.** One who is a slave to a powerful influence, as an addiction. **3.** Servitude; bondage. **4.** A state of being enthralled or transfixed.
~*tr.v.* **thralled, thralling, thralls.** *Archaic.* To make a thrall of; enslave. [Middle English *thral(l),* Old English *thrǣl,* from Old Norse *thrǣll,* from Germanic *thrah-* (unattested), to run.] —**thrall·dom, thral·dom** *n.*
thrash (thrăsh) *v.* **thrashed, thrashing, thrashes.** —*tr.* **1.** To beat or flog with or as if with a whip. **2.** To swing or strike wildly in a manner suggestive of the action of a flail: *thrashing her arms about.* **3.** To defeat utterly; vanquish. **4.** To thresh. **5.** *Nautical.* To sail (a boat) against opposing winds or tides. —*intr.* **1.** To move the body or a bodily part wildly or violently. **2.** To strike or flail. **3.** To thresh. **4.** *Nautical.* To make one's way against opposing tides or winds. —**thrash out. 1.** To discuss fully and bring to a conclusion. **2.** To produce (a plan or agreement, for example) by thorough discussion.
~*n.* **1.** The act of thrashing. **2.** A swimming kick in the backstroke and crawl. [Alteration of THRESH.] —**thrash·er** *n.*
thrash·er¹ (thrăsh′ər) *n.* Any of various New World thrushlike songbirds of the genus *Toxostoma,* having a long tail, a long, curved beak, and, in several species, a spotted breast. [Perhaps alteration of dialectal *thrusher,* from THRUSH (songbird).]
thrasher². Variant of **thresher** (sense 3).
thrash·ing (thrăsh′ĭng) *n.* A severe beating; a whipping.
thra·son·i·cal (thrā-sŏn′ĭ-kəl, thrə-) *adj.* Boastful. [Latin *Thrasō* (stem *Thrasōn-*), a bragging character in Terence's comedy *Eunuchus,* from Greek *Thrasōn,* from *thrasus,* bold, brave.] —**thra·son·i·cal·ly** *adv.*
thread (thrĕd) *n.* **1. a.** A fine cord of a fibrous material, such as cotton or flax, made of two or more filaments twisted together and used in needlework and the weaving of cloth. **b.** A piece of this material. **2.** A strand, fiber, or filament of natural or manufactured material. **3.** Something suggestive of the fineness or thinness of thread. **4.** Something suggestive of the continuousness and sequence of thread: *I've lost the thread of my argument.* **5.** A helical or spiral ridge on a screw, nut, or bolt. **6. threads.** *Slang.* Clothes.
~*v.* **threaded, threading, threads.** —*tr.* **1.** To pass one end of a thread through the eye of (a needle or similar device). **2.** To string (beads or similar objects) onto a thread. **3. a.** To pass or feed (thread or tape, for example) through or into something. **b.** To pass or feed tape, film, or similar material through or into (a machine or camera, for example). **4. a.** To pass cautiously through. **b.** To make (one's way) cautiously, as through a crowded or narrow place. **5.** To occur throughout; pervade. **6.** To machine a thread on (a screw, nut, or bolt). —*intr.* **1.** To wind cautiously through obstacles or along a narrow path. **2.** To proceed by a winding course. **3.** To form a thread when dropped from a spoon, as boiling sugar syrup. [Middle English *thre(e)d,* Old English *thrǣd.*] —**thread·er** *n.* —**thread·like** *adj.*
thread·bare (thrĕd′bâr′) *adj.* **1.** Having the nap worn down so that the filling or warp threads show through; frayed or shabby. Said of cloth. **2.** Wearing old, shabby clothing. **3.** Hackneyed; stale. —See Synonyms at **trite.** —**thread·bare·ness** *n.*
thread·fin (thrĕd′fĭn′) *n.* Any of various chiefly tropical marine

fishes of the subfamily Polynemidae, having threadlike rays extending from the lower part of the pectoral fin.
thread mark *n.* A marking made in paper currency by a threading of colored silk fibers to make counterfeiting difficult.
thread·worm (thrĕd′wûrm′) *n.* Any of various threadlike nematode worms, especially the **pinworm** *(see).*
thread·y (thrĕd′ē) *adj.* **-ier, -iest. 1.** Consisting of or resembling thread; fibrous. **2.** Tending to form threads, as a syrupy liquid does; viscid. **3.** *Medicine.* Weak and shallow. Said especially of a pulse. **4.** Lacking fullness of tone; thin; weak. —**thread·i·ness** *n.*
threat (thrĕt) *n.* **1.** An expression of an intention to inflict pain, injury, evil, or punishment on a person or thing. **2.** An indication of the impending arrival or occurrence of something harmful or undesirable: *the threat of rain.* **3.** A person, thing, or idea regarded as a possible danger; a menace.
~*tr.v.* **threated, threating, threats.** *Archaic.* To threaten. [Middle English *thret,* Old English *thrēat,* oppression, use of force, threat.]
threat·en (thrĕt′n) *v.* **-ened, -ening, -ens.** —*tr.* **1.** To express a threat against: *threatened him with dismissal.* **2.** To serve as a threat to; endanger; menace. **3.** To give signs or warning of; portend. **4.** To express as a threat. —*intr.* **1.** To express or use threats. **2.** To indicate danger or other harm. [Middle English, Old English *thrēatnian.*] —**threat·en·er** *n.* —**threat·en·ing·ly** *adv.*
 Synonyms: *intimidate, menace.*
three (thrē) *n.* **1. a.** The cardinal number that is one more than two. **b.** A symbol representing this, as 3, III, or iii. **2.** A set made up of three persons or things. **3.** The third in a series: *the three of diamonds.* **4.** Three parts: *cut the apple in three.* **5.** A size, as in clothing, designated as three. **6.** Three hours after midnight or midday; three o'clock. [Middle English *three,* Old English *thrī(e), thrēo.*] —**three** *adj & pron.*
three-bag·ger (thrē′băg′ər) *n. Baseball.* A three-base hit.
three-base hit (thrē′bās′) *n. Baseball.* A base hit that allows the batter to reach third base without being put out.
three-card mon·te (thrē′kärd mŏn′tē) *n.* A gambling game in which each participant bets that he can identify a particular card of three lying face downward.
three-col·or (thrē′kŭl′ər) *adj.* Designating a color printing or photographic process in which three primary colors are transferred by three different plates or filters to a surface, reproducing all the colors of the subject matter.
three-cor·nered (thrē′kôr′nərd) *adj.* **1.** Having three corners; triangular: *a three-cornered hat.* **2.** Involving three contestants or parties: *a three-cornered fight.*
three-D, 3-D (thrē′dē′) *adj.* Three-dimensional.
~*n.* A three-dimensional medium, display, or performance, especially a cinematic or graphic display in three dimensions.
three-day event (thrē′dā′) *n.* An equestrian competition that lasts three days during which riders do a dressage test, ride over a cross-country course, and do a round of showjumping.
three-day measles *n. Informal.* German measles.
three-deck·er (thrē′dĕk′ər) *n.* **1.** A ship having three decks; especially, one of a class of sail-powered warships with guns on three decks. **2.** Anything with three layers; especially, a sandwich having three slices of bread.
three-di·men·sion·al (thrē′dĭ-mĕn′shə-nəl, thrē′dī-) *adj.* **1.** Of, pertaining to, having, or existing in three dimensions. **2.** Having or appearing to have extension in depth; three-D.
three·fold (thrē′fōld′) *adj.* **1.** Having or consisting of three parts. **2.** Being three times as many or as much; treble.
~*adv.* Three times as much or as great; trebly.
three-gait·ed (thrē′gā′tĭd) *adj.* Trained in the walk, the trot, and the canter. Said of a horse.
Three Graces *pl.n.* The **Graces** *(see).*
three-leaved (thrē′lēvd′) *adj.* Also **three-leafed** (-lēft′). *Botany.* Divided into three leaflets: *a three-leaved clover.*
three-leg·ged race (thrē′lĕg′ĭd, -lĕgd′) *n.* A race in which pairs of people run side by side with their adjacent legs tied together.
three-line whip (thrē′līn′) *n.* In the British Parliament, the strongest form of notice issued by the leaders of a political party, requiring its members to vote on a forthcoming issue. [From the three underlinings on the written notice, indicating the greatest urgency.]
three-mast·er (thrē′măs′tər, -mä′stər) *n.* A ship, usually a schooner, with three masts.
three-mile limit (thrē′mīl′) *n. International Law.* The outer limit of the area extending three miles out to sea from the coast of a country that constitutes that country's territorial waters.
three·pence (thrĕp′əns, thrĭp′-, thrŭp′-; thrē′pĕns′ *for sense 2) n., pl.* **threepence** *or* **-pences. 1.** A former British coin worth three pennies. **2.** The sum of three pennies.
three·pen·ny (thrĕp′ə-nē, thrĭp′-, thrŭp′-) *adj. British.* **1.** Worth or priced at threepence. **2.** Of little worth; trifling.
three-phase (thrē′fāz′) *adj. Electricity.* Designating or pertaining to an electrical supply with three different equal voltages that have the same frequency and differ in phase by 120°.
three-piece (thrē′pēs′) *adj.* Made in or consisting of three parts or pieces: *a three-piece suit.*
three-ply (thrē′plī′) *adj.* **1.** Consisting of three layers. **2.** Having three strands. Said especially of knitting yarn.
three-point landing (thrē′point′) *n.* An airplane landing in which the tailskid or tail wheel and the two forward wheels all touch the ground simultaneously; a perfect landing.
three-point turn *n.* A way of turning a vehicle in a confined space

by moving it first forward, then backward, and then forward again so that it ends up facing in the opposite direction.

three-quar·ter (thrē′kwôr′tər) *adj.* Pertaining to, consisting of, showing, or extending to three quarters of the full or normal length of something.

three-quarter binding *n.* A type of bookbinding in which the leather or fabric covering the spine extends onto the covers for one third of their width.

three-ring circus (thrē′rĭng′) *n.* **1.** A circus having simultaneous performances in three separate rings. **2.** A situation characterized by bewildering, engrossing, or amusing activity.

three R's *pl.n.* Reading, writing, and arithmetic, considered as the fundamentals of elementary education. [From the facetious spelling *reading, 'riting, and 'rithmetic.*]

three·score (thrē′skôr′, -skōr′) *adj.* Sixty; three times twenty. **—three·score** *n.*

three·some (thrē′səm) *adj.* Consisting of or performed by three. ~*n.* **1.** A group of three persons. **2.** Any activity involving three persons; especially, a golf match in which one player competes against two others who alternate their play.

three-square (thrē′skwâr′) *adj.* Having an equilateral triangular cross section: *a three-square file.*

three-wheel·er (thrē′hwē′lər) *n.* A vehicle, such as a motorcycle or a tricycle, with three wheels.

threm·ma·tol·o·gy (thrĕm′ə-tŏl′ə-jē) *n.* The scientific breeding of domestic plants and animals. [Greek *thremma* (stem *thremmat*-), creature, nursling + -LOGY.]

thren·o·dy (thrĕn′ə-dē) *n., pl.* **-dies.** A song of mourning or lamentation. [Greek *thrēnōidia* : *thrēnos,* dirge, lament + *ōidē,* song, ODE.] **—thre·no·di·al** (thrə-nō′dē-əl), **thre·nod·ic** (-nŏd′ĭk) *adj.* **—thren·o·dist** (thrĕn′ə-dĭst) *n.*

thresh (thrĕsh) *v.* **threshed, threshing, threshes.** —*tr.* **1. a.** To beat the stems and husks of (grain or cereal plants) with a machine or flail to separate the grain or seeds from the straw. **b.** To separate (grain or seed) in this manner. **2.** To go over (an issue, for example) repeatedly. **3.** To beat severely; thrash. —*intr.* **1.** To thresh grain. **2.** To thrash about; toss. [Middle English *thresshen,* Old English *therscan.*]

thresh·er (thrĕsh′ər) *n.* Also **thrash·er** (thrăsh′-) (for sense 3). **1.** One who threshes. **2.** A threshing machine. **3.** Any of various large sharks of the genus *Alopias,* especially *A. vulpinus,* having a tail with a long, whiplike upper lobe.

threshing machine *n.* A farm machine used in threshing grain or seed plants. Also called "thresher."

thresh·old (thrĕsh′ōld′, thrĕsh′hōld′) *n.* **1.** The piece of wood or stone placed beneath a door; a doorsill. **2.** An entrance or doorway. **3.** The place or point of beginning; outset or verge: *on the threshold of his career.* **4.** A point or level above which a specified phenomenon occurs and below which it does not: *a tax threshold.* **5.** The intensity below which a mental or physical stimulus cannot be perceived and can produce no response: *a low threshold of pain.* **6.** The value or intensity of a physical quantity that produces a specific effect in a system or device and below which no effect occurs. ~*adj.* Of, pertaining to, resembling, or being a threshold: *a threshold voltage.* [Middle English *threshhold,* Old English *therscold, threscold.*]

threw. Past tense of **throw.**

thrice (thrīs) *adv.* **1.** Three times. **2.** In a threefold quantity or degree. **3.** *Archaic.* Extremely; greatly. [Middle English *thries,* adverbial genitive of *thrie,* Old English *thriga, thriwa.*]

thrift (thrĭft) *n.* **1.** Wise economy in the management of money and other resources; frugality. **2.** Vigorous growth of living things such as plants. **3.** Any of several densely tufted, chiefly European plants of the genus *Armeria;* especially, *A. maritima,* having rounded clusters of pink flowers. In this sense, also called "sea pink." [Middle English, prosperity, a flourishing, savings, from Old Norse, prosperity, from *thrifask,* to THRIVE.]

thrift·less (thrĭft′lĭs) *adj.* **1.** Lacking value or usefulness. **2.** Careless in handling money; wasteful.

thrift shop *n.* A shop that sells used articles and especially clothing, often to benefit a charitable organization.

thrift·y (thrĭf′tē) *adj.* **-ier, -iest. 1.** Practicing thrift; economical and frugal. **2.** Industrious and thriving; prosperous. **3.** Growing vigorously, as a plant might; thriving. —See Synonyms at **sparing.** **—thrift·i·ly** *adv.* **—thrift·i·ness** *n.*

thrill (thrĭl) *v.* **thrilled, thrilling, thrills.** —*tr.* **1.** To cause to feel a sudden intense sensation; excite greatly. **2.** To give great pleasure to; delight. **3.** To cause to quiver or vibrate. —*intr.* **1.** To feel a sudden tingle of emotion. **2.** To quiver, tremble, or vibrate. ~*n.* **1.** A sensation of great excitement. **2.** A tingling or trembling passing through the body as a result of sudden emotion. **3.** An exciting quality or situation. **4.** *Pathology.* A slight vibration that accompanies a heart or vascular murmur, felt when the hand is placed on the chest wall. [Middle English *thrillen,* variant of *thirlen,* to pierce, Old English *thyrlian,* from *thyr(e)l,* hole.]

thrill·er (thrĭl′ər) *n.* One that thrills. **2.** A book, motion picture, or play that is full of mystery and suspense.

thrill·ing (thrĭl′ĭng) *adj.* **1.** Extremely exciting. **2.** Vibrating or pulsating.

thrips (thrĭps) *n., pl.* **thrips.** Any of various small, often wingless insects of the order Thysanoptera, many of which are destructive to plants. [Latin, woodworm, from Greek *thrips†.*]

thrive (thrīv) *intr.v.* **throve** (thrōv) or **thrived, thrived** or **thriven**

(thrĭv′ən), **thriving, thrives. 1.** To grow vigorously; flourish. **2.** To improve steadily, as in wealth or position; prosper. [Thrive, throve, thriven; Middle English *thriven, throfe, thriven,* to increase, flourish, from Old Norse *thrīfask,* "to grasp for oneself," reflexive of *thrīfa†,* to seize.] **—thriv·er** *n.* **—thriv·ing·ly** *adv.*

throat (thrōt) *n.* **1.** *Anatomy.* **a.** The part of the digestive tract that lies between the rear of the mouth and the esophagus and includes the pharynx. **b.** The front part of the neck. **2.** *Botany.* The outer, expanded part of a tubular corolla. **3.** Any narrow passage or part shaped like the human throat: *the throat of a tennis racket.* **—jump down someone's throat.** To speak sharply and critically to. **—stick in one's throat.** *Informal.* To be difficult to express or accept. [Middle English *throte,* Old English *throte, throtu,* from Germanic *thrut-* (unattested).]

throat·latch (thrōt′lăch′) *n.* A strap passing under the neck of a horse or other animal for holding a bridle or halter in place.

throat microphone *n.* A small microphone that when held or fastened next to the throat is activated by vibrations of the larynx.

throat·y (thrō′tē) *adj.* **-ier, -iest.** Uttered or sounding as if uttered deep in the throat; guttural, hoarse, or husky. **—throat·i·ly** *adv.* **—throat·i·ness** *n.*

throb (thrŏb) *intr.v.* **throbbed, throbbing, throbs. 1.** To beat rapidly or violently; pound. **2.** To vibrate, pulsate, or sound with a steady, pronounced rhythm. —See Synonyms at **pulsate.** ~*n.* The act of throbbing; a beat, palpitation, or vibration. [Middle English *throbben* (attested only in the present participle); imitative.] **—throb·bing·ly** *adv.*

throe (thrō) *n.* **1.** A severe pang or spasm of pain, as in childbirth. **2. throes.** A condition of agonizing struggle or effort: *a country in the throes of economic collapse.* [Middle English *throwe,* Old English *thrawe†,* paroxysm.]

throm·bin (thrŏm′bĭn) *n.* An enzyme in blood that facilitates clotting by reacting with fibrinogen to form fibrin. [THROMB(O)- + -IN.]

thrombo-, thromb– *prefix.* Indicates a blood clot; for example, thromboplastin, thrombin. [From Greek *thrombos,* THROMBUS.]

throm·bo·cyte (thrŏm′bə-sīt′) *n.* A blood platelet.

throm·bo·cy·to·pe·ni·a (thrŏm′bə-sī′tə-pē′nē-ə) *n.* A decrease in the number of platelets in the blood, resulting in reduced ability of the blood to clot. [THROMBOCYTE + Greek *penia,* poverty, want.]

throm·bo·em·bo·lism (thrŏm′bō-ĕm′bə-lĭz′əm) *n.* The blocking of a blood vessel by a thrombus dislodged from a vein.

throm·bo·phle·bi·tis (thrŏm′bō-flĭ-bī′tĭs) *n.* Inflammation of a vein associated with the formation of a blood clot in it.

throm·bo·plas·tic (thrŏm′bō-plăs′tĭk, -plă′stĭk) *adj.* **1.** Causing or promoting blood clotting. **2.** Of or pertaining to thromboplastin.

throm·bo·plas·tin (thrŏm′bō-plăs′tĭn, -plă′stĭn) *n.* A protein complex essential for thrombin formation and blood clotting. [THROMB(O)- + -PLAST + -IN.]

throm·bose (thrŏm′bōz′, -bōs′) *v.* **-bosed, -bosing, -boses.** —*tr.* To affect with thrombosis. —*intr.* To become affected with thrombosis. [Back-formation from THROMBOSIS.]

throm·bo·sis (thrŏm-bō′sĭs) *n., pl.* **-ses** (-sēz′). The formation, presence, or development of a thrombus. [New Latin, from Greek *thrombōsis,* a clotting, from *thrombousthai,* to clot, from *thrombos,* THROMBUS.] **—throm·bot·ic** (thrŏm-bŏt′ĭk) *adj.*

throm·bus (thrŏm′bəs) *n., pl.* **-bi** (-bī′). A blood clot that forms in and blocks a blood vessel or that is formed in a heart cavity. [New Latin, from Greek *thrombos†,* lump, clot.]

throne (thrōn) *n.* **1.** The chair occupied by a sovereign, bishop, or other exalted personage on state or ceremonial occasions. **2.** The power, dignity, or rank of one who occupies a throne; sovereignty. **3. thrones.** *Theology.* The third of the nine orders of angels. See **angel. 4.** *Slang.* A toilet. ~*v.* **throned, throning, thrones.** —*tr.* To enthrone. —*intr.* To occupy a throne; reign. [Middle English, learned respelling of earlier *trone,* from Old French, from Latin *thronus,* from Greek *thronos.*]

throng (thrông, thrŏng) *n.* **1.** A large group of people gathered or crowded closely together. **2.** Any large group of things; a host. ~*v.* **thronged, thronging, throngs. 1.** To crowd into; fill completely. **2.** To press to upon; surround in large numbers. —*intr.* To gather, press, or move in a throng. [Middle English *throng, thrang,* Old English *thrang,* probably from Germanic *thring-* (unattested), to press, crowd.]

thros·tle (thrŏs′əl) *n.* **1.** Any of various Old World thrushes; especially, the **song thrush** (see). **2.** A machine formerly used for spinning fibers such as cotton or wool. [Middle English *throstle,* Old English *throstle.*]

throt·tle (thrŏt′l) *n.* **1. a.** A valve in an internal-combustion engine that regulates the amount of vaporized fuel entering the cylinders. **b.** A similar valve in a steam engine regulating the amount of steam. **c.** A lever or pedal controlling either of these valves. **2. a.** The throat. **b.** The windpipe. ~*tr.v.* **throttled, -tling, -tles. 1. a.** To regulate the flow of (fuel) in an engine. **b.** To regulate the speed of (an engine) with a throttle. **2.** To strangle; choke. **3.** To suppress. [Noun sense 1, perhaps diminutive of THROAT; verb senses 2 and 3, Middle English *throtelen,* to throttle, perhaps from *throte,* THROAT.] **—throt·tler** *n.*

through (thrōō) *prep.* **1.** In at one side and out at the opposite or another side of: *pushed the needle through the fabric.* **2.** Among or between; in the midst of: *a walk through the flowers.* **3.** By way of: *went out through the door.* **4.** By the means or agency of: *got the job*

through his father. **5.** Here and there in; around: *a tour through France.* **6. a.** From the beginning to the end of: *stayed up through the night.* **b.** Up to and including: *Monday through Friday.* **7.** At or to the end of; done or finished with, especially successfully: *We are through the initial testing period.* **8.** Without stopping for: *drove through a red light.* **9.** Because of: *succeeded through hard work.*
~adv. **1.** From one end or side to another or opposite end or side. **2.** From beginning to end: *slept the whole night through.* **3.** Completely; thoroughly: *soaked through; tried to think the problem through.* **4.** To a conclusion or accomplishment: *see the matter through.* **5.** Out into the open: *The sun broke through.* **—through and through. 1.** In every part; throughout. **2.** In every respect; completely: *I am disgusted through and through.*
~adj. **1.** Passing or extending from one end, side, or surface to another: *a through beam.* **2.** Allowing continuous passage; unobstructed: *a through road.* **3.** Conveying passengers directly to a destination with few or no stops and no transfers: *a through bus.* **4.** Having arrived at completion; finished: *We're finally through with the project.* **5.** At the end of one's effectiveness or resources: *He's through financially.* **6.** No longer involved in an emotional relationship. [Middle English *thru(g)h, thurh,* Old English *thurh.*]

through·ly (thro͞o'lē) *adv. Archaic.* Thoroughly.

through·out (thro͞o-out') *prep.* In, to, through, or during every part of; all through.
~adv. **1.** In or through all parts; everywhere. **2.** During the entire time or extent.

through·put (thro͞o'po͝ot') *n.* Output or production, as of a computer program, over a period of time.

throughway. Variant of **thruway.**

throve. Past tense of **thrive.**

throw (thrō) *v.* **threw** (thro͞o), **thrown** (thrōn), **throwing, throws.** *—tr.* **1.** To propel through the air with a swift motion of the arm; hurl. **2.** To discharge into the air by any means. **3.** To hurl with great force, suddenness, or carelessness: *She threw her clothes into the closet. He threw himself at his opponent.* **4.** To apply (oneself, for example) with energy: *threw herself into her new job.* **5.** To surrender (oneself) to something: *threw himself on the mercy of the court.* **6. a.** To put on or off hastily or carelessly: *throw on a cape.* **b.** To put quickly into use or place: *throw in extra troops.* **7.** To put abruptly or forcibly into a specified condition or place: *threw him into total confusion; threw the prisoner into jail.* **8.** To form on a potter's wheel: *throw a vase.* **9.** To twist (fibers) into thread. **10. a.** To roll (dice). **b.** To roll (a particular combination) with dice. **11.** To discard or play (a card). **12. a.** To cast (a shadow). **b.** To direct; send: *threw an anxious glance at him.* **13.** To bear (young), as cows or horses. **14.** To deliver (a blow or punch). **15.** To move (a controlling lever or switch). **16.** To send (an opponent in wrestling) to the ground. **17.** To cause (a rider) to leave the saddle and fall to the ground. Used of a horse. **18. a.** To project (the voice). **b.** To cause (one's voice) to appear to be coming from elsewhere than one's mouth. **19.** To give way to (an emotional outburst): *throw a fit.* **20.** To disconcert; nonplus: *The news really threw her.* **21.** *Slang.* To arrange or give (a party, for example). **22.** *Informal.* To lose (a contest) intentionally. *—intr.* To cast, fling, or hurl something. **—throw in. 1.** To add (something extra) at no additional charge. **2.** To add or contribute (a remark) to a conversation. **—throw in the towel** (or **sponge**). To give up in a contest or undertaking; admit defeat: *finally threw in the towel after 15 years of teaching.* [Originally in boxing, a contestant acknowledged defeat by throwing his towel or sponge into the ring.] **—throw off. 1.** To cast out; reject. **2.** To give off; emit. **3.** To rid oneself of: *can't seem to throw off this cold.* **4.** To escape; evade: *managed to throw off his pursuers.* **—throw one's weight around.** To exert power or authority, especially in an excessive or heavy-handed way. **—throw out. 1.** To give off; emit. **2.** To reject or discard. **3.** To dismiss or expel. **4.** To offer (a suggestion or plan, for example). **5.** To eject, especially in an abrupt or unexpected manner. —See Synonyms at **eject. —throw over. 1.** To overturn. **2.** To abandon (a lover, for example). **—throw up. 1.** To abandon; relinquish: *throw up a job.* **2.** To construct hurriedly. **3.** To vomit. **4.** To refer to repeatedly and often reproachfully: *threw up his past to him whenever they argued.*
~n. **1.** An act of throwing; hurl. **2.** The distance, height, or direction of something thrown: *a low throw.* **3. a.** A roll or cast of dice. **b.** The numbers obtained by rolling or casting dice. **4.** A chance or attempt. **5.** The technique used to throw an opponent in wrestling. **6. a.** A light coverlet such as an afghan. **b.** A scarf or shawl. **7.** *Machinery.* **a.** The length of the radius of a circle described by a crank, cam, or similar part. **b.** The maximum displacement of a part moved by a crank, cam, or the like. **8.** *Geology.* The vertical distance between a rock on one side of a fault and its continuation on the other side. **9.** *Physics.* A single movement of the indicator of a measuring instrument, as in a ballistic galvanometer. [Middle English *throwen, thrawen,* to turn, twist, hence to hurl, cast, Old English *thrāwan,* to turn, twist.] **—throw·er** *n.*
Synonyms: *cast, fling, heave, hurl, sling, toss.*

throw away *tr.v.* **1.** To discard as useless. **2.** To fail to use (an opportunity, for example). **3.** To use in a foolish manner; waste.

throw·a·way (thrō'ə-wā') *adj.* **1.** Designed or intended to be discarded after use. **2.** Written or delivered in a low-key or offhand manner: *throwaway lines.*
~n. **1.** Something designed to be discarded after use. **2.** A free handbill distributed on the street.

throw back *intr.v.* To revert to an earlier type or stage in one's past. *—tr.v.* To cause or compel to be dependent: *Her husband's death threw her back on her own resources.*

throw·back (thrō'băk') *n.* **1.** A reversion to a former type or ancestral characteristic. **2.** An atavism. **3.** Something that refers back to or results from a previous incident, period, or the like: *Her tidiness is a throwback to her days at boarding school.*

thrown. Past participle of **throw.**

throw pillow *n.* A small pillow used especially for decoration, as in a living room.

throw rug *n.* A **scatter rug** *(see).*

thru (thro͞o) *prep., adv., & adj. Informal.* Through.

thrum[1] (thrŭm) *v.* **thrummed, thrumming, thrums.** *—tr.* **1.** To play (a stringed instrument) idly or monotonously. **2.** To repeat or recite in a monotonous tone of voice. *—intr.* To strum idly on a stringed instrument.
~n. A thrumming sound. [Imitative.] **—thrum·mer** *n.*

thrum[2] *n.* **1. a.** The fringe of warp threads left on a loom after the cloth has been cut off. **b.** Any of these threads. **2.** Any loose end, fringe, or tuft of thread. **3. thrums.** *Nautical.* Short bits of rope yarn inserted into canvas to roughen the surface so that it can be used to prevent chafing.
~tr.v. **thrummed, thrumming, thrums. 1.** To cover or trim with thrums; fringe. **2.** *Nautical.* To sew thrums into (canvas). [Middle English *thrum,* Old English *thrum.*]

thrush[1] (thrŭsh) *n.* **1.** Any of various songbirds of the family Turdidae, characteristically having brownish upper plumage and a spotted breast. **2.** Any of various similar or related birds. [Middle English *thrusch(e),* Old English *thrysce.*]

thrush *Common across Eurasia but found worldwide, thrushes are songbirds that live in woods and gardens. They feed chiefly on snails, often smashing open the shells on stones, but they also eat insects and fruit. This is a European species—the mistle, or missel, thrush.*

thrush[2] *n.* **1.** An oral infection with a fungus, *Candida albicans,* characterized by white eruptions. **2.** A suppurative infection of a horse's foot caused by standing in a wet, unhygienic stall. [Probably of Scandinavian origin.]

thrust (thrŭst) *v.* **thrust, thrusting, thrusts.** *—tr.* **1. a.** To push or drive quickly and forcibly. **b.** To cause to pierce or stab. **2.** To force (oneself or another) into a specified condition or situation. *—intr.* **1.** To shove against something; push. **2.** To pierce or stab at something with or as if with a pointed weapon. **3.** To force one's way. **4.** To push or project upward.
~n. **1.** A forceful shove or push; a lunge. **2. a.** A driving force or pressure. **b.** The forward-directed force developed in a jet or rocket engine as a reaction to the backward ejection of fuel gases at high velocities. **3.** A stab. **4.** The general direction or tendency: *the thrust of an argument.* **5.** *Architecture.* Outward or lateral stress in a structure, such as an arch. **6.** *Geology.* A force of compression in the earth's crust producing folding. [Middle English *thrusten,* from Old Norse *thrȳsta,* to thrust, compress.]

thrust bearing *n. Machinery.* A type of bearing designed to transmit a force along a shaft as well as at right angles to it.

thrust·er (thrŭs'tər) *n.* A small rocket motor used to control a spacecraft.

thrust fault *n. Geology.* A reverse fault with a dip so low that the upthrow has moved far forward over the downthrow.

thru·way, through·way (thrū'wā') *n.* An expressway.

Thu·cyd·i·des (tho͞o-sĭd'ə-dēz'). Greek historian of the 5th century B.C., author of *History of the Peloponnesian War.*

thud (thŭd) *n.* **1.** A dull sound, as that of a heavy object striking a solid surface. **2.** A blow or fall causing a thud.
~intr.v. **thudded, thudding, thuds.** To make a thud. [Middle English *thudden,* Old English *thyddan* (imitative).] **—thud** *adv.*

thug (thŭg) *n.* **1.** A violent and criminally disposed man; hoodlum. **2.** One of a band of professional assassins formerly active in northern India. [Hindi *ṭhag,* cheat, thief, from Sanskrit *sthaga,* robber, from *sthagati,* to cover, hide.] **—thug·ger·y** *n.* **—thug·gish** *adj.*

thug·gee (thŭg'ē) *n.* The practices or methods of the thugs of India. [Hindi *ṭhagī,* robbery, from *ṭhag,* THUG.]

Thu·le[1] (tho͞o'lē, thyo͞o'-). The most northerly region of the ancient habitable world, conceived as an island north of Britain by ancient geographers.

Thu·le[2] (to͞o'lē). Town in northwestern Greenland. It is the site of a strategically important U.S. air base begun during World War II and completed in 1953.

thu·li·um (tho͞o'lē-əm, thyo͞o'-) *n. Symbol* **Tm** A bright silvery rare-earth element having 18 known isotopes with mass numbers ranging from 153 to 176. The x-ray emitting isotope Tm 170 is used in small portable medical x-ray units. Atomic number 69, atomic weight 168.934, melting point 1,545°C, boiling point 1,727°C, specific gravity 9.332, valence 3. [From THULE (island).]

thumb (thŭm) *n.* **1.** The short first digit of the human hand, opposable to each of the other four digits. **2.** A corresponding digit in other animals, especially primates. **3.** The part of a glove or mitten that covers the thumb. **4.** *Architecture.* An **ovolo** *(see).* **—all thumbs.** Clumsy; awkward. **—under someone's thumb.** Under someone's influence, authority, or power.
~v. **thumbed, thumbing, thumbs.** *—tr.* **1.** To handle, wear, or soil by careless or frequent handling with the thumb. **2.** *Informal.* To solicit (a ride) from a passing vehicle by signaling with the thumb, especially by pointing it in the direction in which one is traveling. *—intr.* To hitchhike. **—thumb one's nose.** To express scorn or derision by or as if by placing the thumb on the nose and wiggling the fingers. **—thumb through.** To browse rapidly through the

pages of (a book or magazine). [Middle English *thom(b)e*, Old English *thūma*.]

thumb·hole (thŭm′hōl′) *n.* The hole on a wind instrument that is opened or closed with the thumb.

thumb index *n.* A series of rounded indentations cut into the front edge of a book, each labeled, as with a letter, to indicate a section of the book.

thumb·in·dex (thŭm′ĭn′dĕks) *tr.v.* **-dexed, -dexing, -dexes.** To furnish with a thumb index.

thumb·nail (thŭm′nāl′) *n.* The nail of the thumb. ～*adj.* **1.** Of the size of a thumbnail. **2.** Brief: *a thumbnail sketch.*

thumb piano *n.* Any of various small African musical instruments played with the thumbs.

thumb·print (thŭm′prĭnt′) *n.* An impression of the ball of the thumb, especially when used as a means of identification.

thumb·screw (thŭm′skrōō′) *n.* **1.** A screw so designed that it can be turned with the thumb and fingers. **2.** An instrument of torture formerly used to compress the thumb. In this sense, also called "screws."

thumbs down *n.* A gesture or indication of rejection, disapproval, or prohibition.

thumb·stall (thŭm′stôl′) *n.* A sheath or cap worn on the thumb to protect it or to aid in such tasks as counting money.

thumbs up *n.* A gesture or indication of approval, acceptance, or encouragement.

thumb·tack (thŭm′tăk′) *n.* A tack with a smooth, rounded head that can be pressed into place with the thumb. ～*tr.v.* **thumbtacked, -tacking, -tacks.** To affix with a thumbtack.

Thummim. See Urim and Thummim.

thump (thŭmp) *n.* **1.** A blow with or as if with a blunt instrument. **2. a.** The muffled sound produced by a thump; thud. **b.** A muted noise similar to a thump; thud. ～*v.* **thumped, thumping, thumps.** —*tr.* **1.** To beat with or as if with a blunt or dull instrument so as to produce a muffled sound or thud. **2.** *Informal.* To thrash soundly or thoroughly; drub. —*intr.* **1.** To hit or fall in such a way as to produce a thump. **2.** To walk with heavy steps; stomp. **3.** To throb audibly; pound. [16th century : imitative.] —**thump** *adv.* —**thump·er** *n.*

thump·ing (thŭm′pĭng) *adj. Informal.* **1.** Large; enormous. **2.** Thoroughly enjoyable. —**thump·ing·ly** *adv.*

thun·ber·gia (thŭn-bûr′jə, -jē-ə) *n.* Any climbing plant of the genus *Thunbergia*, native to Old World tropical regions. See **black-eyed Susan.** [After Carl *Thunberg* (1734–1828), Swedish botanist.]

thun·der (thŭn′dər) *n.* **1.** The rumbling or crashing sound emitted by rapidly expanding gases along the path of the electrical discharge of lightning. **2.** A sound similar to thunder. —**steal someone's thunder. 1.** To anticipate or adopt someone's idea or practice and get the credit oneself. **2.** To divert attention, praise, or recognition from another to oneself. ～*v.* **thundered, -dering, -ders.** —*intr.* **1.** To produce thunder. **2.** To produce sounds like thunder. **3.** To utter loud, vociferous remarks or threats; roar. —*tr.* To express violently, commandingly, or angrily; roar. [Middle English *thunder, thon(d)re,* Old English *thunor.*]

thun·der·bird (thŭn′dər-bûrd′) *n.* In the mythology of some North American Indians, thunder, lightning, and rain personified as a huge bird.

thun·der·bolt (thŭn′dər-bōlt′) *n.* **1.** The discharge of lightning that accompanies thunder. **2.** A flash of lightning imagined as a bolt or dart hurled from the heavens. **3.** Someone or something resembling a thunderbolt, as in suddenness or destructive effect.

thun·der·box (thŭn′dər-bŏks′) *n. British Slang.* A toilet, especially a portable one.

thun·der·clap (thŭn′dər-klăp′) *n.* **1.** A single sharp crash of thunder. **2.** Something, such as a startling or shocking piece of news, that is similar to a thunderclap in violence or suddenness.

thun·der·cloud (thŭn′dər-kloud′) *n.* **1.** A large, dark cloud charged with electricity and producing lightning and thunder; a cumulonimbus cloud. **2.** Something dreadful or menacing: *thunderclouds of impending war.*

thun·der·head (thŭn′dər-hĕd′) *n.* The swollen upper portion of a thundercloud, often associated with the coming of a thunderstorm.

thun·der·ing (thŭn′dər-ĭng) *adj. British Informal.* Used as an intensive: *a thundering bore.* ～*adv. British Informal.* Used as an intensive: *a thundering good show.*

thun·der·ous (thŭn′dər-əs) *adj.* **1.** Of or pertaining to thunder or to a similar sound. **2.** Loud and unrestrained: *thunderous applause.* —**thun·der·ous·ly** *adv.*

thun·der·show·er (thŭn′dər-shou′ər) *n.* A brief rainstorm accompanied by thunder and lightning.

thun·der·stick (thŭn′dər-stĭk′) *n.* A bullroarer *(see).*

thun·der·stone (thŭn′dər-stōn′) *n.* **1.** Any of various mineral concretions formerly supposed to be thunderbolts; especially, a **belemnite** *(see).* **2.** *Archaic.* A flash of lightning conceived as a stone.

thun·der·storm (thŭn′dər-stôrm′) *n.* A storm in which intense heating induces air to rise rapidly and form vast cumulonimbus clouds, with heavy rain, lightning, thunder, and sometimes hail.

thun·der·struck (thŭn′dər-strŭk′) *adj.* Also **thun·der·strick·en** (-strĭk′ən). Struck with sudden astonishment or amazement: *We were thunderstruck at the news.*

thun·der·y (thŭn′də-rē) *adj.* **1.** Indicating or characterized by thunder: *thundery weather.* **2.** Resembling thunder.

Thur., Thurs. Thursday.

Thur·ber (thûr′bər), **James Grover** (1894–1961). U.S. humorist and cartoonist. His drawings and writings are collected in *My Life and Hard Times* (1933) and *The Thurber Carnival* (1945).

thu·ri·ble (thōōr′ə-bəl) *n.* An incense vessel, a **censer** *(see).* [Middle English *thoryble,* from Old French *thurible,* from Latin *t(h)ūribulum,* from *t(h)ūs* (stem *t(h)ūr-*), incense, from Greek *thuos,* (sacrificial) incense, (burnt) offering.]

thu·ri·fer (thōōr′ə-fər) *n.* A person, as an acolyte, who carries a thurible. [New Latin, from Latin *thūrifer,* "incense bearing" : *thūs* (stem *thūr-*), incense (see **thurible**) + -FER.]

Thu·rin·gi·a (thōō-rĭn′jē-ə, -jə). Former state of Germany, south of the Harz Mts. It was created in 1920 from a number of former duchies and principalities. After World War II it passed into the control of Soviet-occupied East Germany and was abolished as an administrative unit in 1952. —**Thu·rin·gi·an** *adj. & n.*

Thurs·day (thûrz′dē, -dā′) *n. Abbr.* **Thur., Thurs.** The day following Wednesday; the fourth day of the working week. [Middle English *thur(e)sday,* Old English *thūr(e)s dæg* (influenced by Old Norse *thōrsdagr,* "Thor's day"), from earlier *thunresdæg,* "Thor's day" (translation of Late Latin *Jovis diēs,* "Jupiter's day") : *thunres,* genitive of *thunor,* THUNDER + *dæg,* DAY.]

thus (thŭs) *adv.* Also *nonstandard* **thus·ly** (thŭs′lē) (for sense 1). **1.** In a manner previously stated or to be stated; in this manner. **2.** To a stated degree or extent; so: *thus far.* **3.** Therefore; consequently. [Middle English, Old English *thus.*]

thwack (thwăk) *tr.v.* **thwacked, thwacking, thwacks.** To strike or hit with something flat; whack. ～*n.* A hard blow with something flat; a whack. [Imitative.] —**thwack** *adv.* —**thwack·er** *n.*

thwart (thwôrt) *tr.v.* **thwarted, thwarting, thwarts. 1.** To prevent from taking place or being realized; frustrate. **2.** To challenge, oppose, or offend. —See Synonyms at **frustrate.** ～*n.* A seat across a boat on which the oarsman sits. ～*adj.* **1.** Extending, lying, or passing across something; transverse. **2.** Perverse; stubborn. **3.** Adverse; unfavorable. Said of winds and currents. ～*adv. Archaic.* Athwart; across. ～*prep. Archaic.* Athwart; across. [Middle English *thwert,* athwart, across, perverse, from Old Norse *thvert,* neuter of *thverr,* transverse.] —**thwart·ed·ly** *adv.* —**thwart·er** *n.*

thy (thī). *Archaic & Poetic.* The possessive form of the pronoun *thou.* Used attributively to indicate possession, agency, or reception of an action by the one addressed by the speaker: *"He sees his brood about thy knee"* (Tennyson). [Middle English *thy, thin,* Old English *thīn,* thine.]

thy·la·cine (thī′lə-sīn′) *n.* A wolflike marsupial, *Thylacinus cynocephalus,* of forest areas of Tasmania, having dark transverse bands across its back. Also called "Tasmanian wolf." [New Latin *thylacinus,* from Greek *thulakos†,* a sack.]

thyme (tīm) *n.* **1.** Any of several aromatic herbs or low shrubs of the genus *Thymus;* especially, *T. vulgaris,* of southern Europe, having small purplish flowers. **2.** The leaves of the thyme, used as seasoning. [Middle English *t(h)yme,* from Old French *thym,* from Latin *thymum,* from Greek *thumon.*]

–thymia *suffix.* Indicates state of mind or temperament; for example, **schizothymia.** [New Latin, from Greek *thumos,* soul, spirit, mind, temper.]

thy·mic (thī′mĭk) *adj.* Of or pertaining to the thymus.

thy·mi·dine (thī′mə-dēn′) *n. Biochemistry.* A nucleoside consisting of thymine and the sugar ribose. [THYM(INE) + -ID(E) + -INE.]

thy·mine (thī′mēn′) *n. Biochemistry.* A pyrimidine base, $C_5H_6N_2O_2$, occurring in DNA. [THYM(IC) + -INE.]

thy·mol (thī′môl′, -mōl′) *n.* A white, crystalline, aromatic compound, $(CH_3)_2CHC_6H_3(CH_3)OH$, derived from thyme oil and other oils and used as an antiseptic, in perfumery, and as a preservative. [THYM(E) + -OL.]

thy·mus (thī′məs) *n.* **1.** A ductless glandlike structure, situated just behind the top of the breastbone, that during early childhood plays some part in building resistance to disease by producing lymphocytes but in adults is usually vestigial. **2.** A structure corresponding to the thymus in nonhuman vertebrates. [New Latin, from Greek *thumos†.*]

thy·ra·tron (thī′rə-trŏn′) *n. Electronics.* A gas-filled tube having three electrodes such that an electrical discharge and consequent current flow between the anode and cathode is initiated but not controlled by a potential applied to a grid. The device is used as a relay and particle counter. [Originally a trademark, from Greek *thura,* door, valve + -TRON.]

thy·ris·tor (thī-rĭs′tər) *n. Electronics.* A semiconductor rectifier, such as a silicon-controlled rectifier, in which passage of current is initiated by a voltage applied to a third electrode. It is the solid-state equivalent of a thyratron. [THYR(ATRON) + (TRANS)ISTOR.]

thy·ro·cal·ci·to·nin (thī′rō-kăl′sĭ-tō′nĭn) *n.* A hormone, **calcitonin** *(see).* [THYRO(ID) + CALCITONIN.]

thy·roid (thī′roid) *adj.* Of or relating to the thyroid gland or the thyroid cartilage. ～*n.* **1.** The thyroid gland. **2.** The thyroid cartilage. **3.** A dried and powdered preparation of the thyroid gland of certain domestic animals, used in the treatment of hypothyroid conditions, such as cretinism. [Obsolete French *thyroide,* from Greek *thuroidēs, thureoeidēs,* shaped like a door or oblong shield, from *thureos,* door-shaped : *thura,* door + -OID.]

---

thyroid cartilage *n.* The largest cartilage of the larynx, having two broad processes that join in front to form the Adam's apple. Also called "thyroid."

thyroid colloid *n. Physiology.* **Colloid** *(see).*

thy·roid·ec·to·my (thī′roi-dĕk′tə-mē) *n., pl.* **-mies.** The surgical removal of all or part of the thyroid gland.

thyroid gland *n.* A two-lobed endocrine gland found in all vertebrates, located in front of and on either side of the trachea in humans, and producing the hormone thyroxin. Also called "thyroid."

thy·roid·i·tis (thī′roi-dī′tĭs) *n.* Inflammation of the thyroid gland.

thyroid stimulating hormone *n. Abbr.* **TSH** **Thyrotropin** *(see).*

thy·ro·tox·i·co·sis (thī′rō-tŏk′sĭ-kō′sĭs) *n.* The condition resulting from excessive production of thyroid hormone, characterized by weight loss, increased appetite, tremor, palpitations, anxiety, and intolerance of heat. [New Latin : THYRO(ID) + TOXICOSIS.]

thy·ro·tro·pin (thī′rə-trō′pĭn) *n.* Also **thy·ro·tro·phin** (-fĭn). A hormone secreted by the anterior pituitary that stimulates and regulates the development and secretion of the thyroid gland hormone. Also called "thyroid stimulating hormone." [THYRO(ID) + -TROP(E) + -IN.]

thy·rox·in (thī-rŏk′sĭn) *n.* Also **thy·rox·ine** (-sēn′, -sĭn). An iodine-containing hormone, $C_{15}H_{11}I_4NO_4$, produced by the thyroid gland to regulate metabolism and made synthetically for treatment of underactivity of the thyroid gland. [THYR(OID) + OX(Y)- + -IN.]

thyrse (thûrs) *n. Botany.* A branched flower cluster, as of the lilac, whose main axis does not terminate in a flower. [New Latin *thyrsus,* THYRSUS.] **—thyr·soid** (thûr′soid′) *adj.*

thyr·sus (thûr′səs) *n., pl.* **-si** (-sī′) A staff tipped with a pine cone and twined with ivy, represented as carried by Dionysus and his devotees. [New Latin, from Latin, from Greek *thursos†.*]

thy·self (thī-sĕlf′) *pron. Archaic & Poetic.* Yourself. Used as the reflexive or emphatic form of *thee* or *thou.*

THz terahertz.

ti¹ (tē) *n. Music.* A syllable representing the seventh tone of the diatonic scale in solmization. [Alteration of SI, short for Latin *Sancte iohannes,* "Saint John," from a stanza sung in a hymn to St. John the Baptist. See **gamut.**]

ti² *n.* Any of several trees or shrubs of the genus *Cordyline,* of tropical Asia and adjacent Pacific regions; especially, *C. australis,* of New Zealand, having a terminal tuft of long, narrow palmlike leaves. [Tahitian and Maori.]

Ti The symbol for the element titanium.

Ti·a·hua·na·co (tē′ə-wə-nä′kō). Ruins near the southeastern end of Lake Titicaca, western Bolivia. The Tiahuanaco culture preceded that of the Incas, flourishing from *c.* A.D. 1000 to 1300, and spread through Bolivia, northern Chile, and Peru.

Tian·jin (tyän′jĭn′). Formerly **Tien·tsin** (tĭn′tsĭn′). Port in Hebei province, northeastern China, lying at the confluence of the Hai River and the Grand Canal. It is an important industrial center.

Tian Shan, Tien Shan (tyän′ shän′). Mountain chain of central Asia, extending from the Pamirs in Tadzhik S.S.R., U.S.S.R., through northwestern China to the China-Mongolia border.

ti·ar·a (tē-ăr′ə, -âr′ə, -ä′rə) *n.* **1.** An ornamental semicircular headpiece, made of precious metal and often decorated with jewels, worn by women on formal occasions. **2.** The triple crown worn by the pope. [Latin *tiāra,* from Greek *tiara(s)†.*]

Ti·ber (tī′bər). Italian **Te·ve·re** (tā′vā-rā′). River of central Italy. It rises in the Tuscan Apennines and flows *c.* 406 kilometers (252 miles) through Rome to the Tyrrhenian Sea at Ostia.

Tiberias, Sea of. See **Galilee, Sea of.**

Ti·be·ri·us (tī-bîr′ē-əs) (42 B.C.–A.D. 37). Roman emperor (A.D. 14–37). An accomplished general, he was made heir to the throne by Augustus in A.D. 4 and was proclaimed emperor upon the death of Augustus in A.D. 14. His reign was marked by suspicion and the execution of several aides, senators, and relatives.

Ti·bet (tĭ-bĕt′). Chinese **Xi·zang** (shĕd′zäng′). Autonomous region of China, occupying a high plateau in the southwestern extremity of the country to the north and west of the Himalayas. Apart from the fertile valley of the Tsangpo, in southern Tibet, most of the land is suitable only for grazing. Tibet has rich reserves of salt, gold, radioactive ores, and copper. It rose to prominence as an independent kingdom in the 7th century. From the 13th to the 18th century it was under the sway of the Mongols. In 1720 the Manchu dynasty of China took control of the region, and thereafter China exercised more or less effective suzerainty over it until 1951, when Tibet was formally made an autonomous region of China. It is a center of Lamaist Buddhism, but the Dalai Lama and thousands of followers fled the country in 1954. Its capital is Lhasa.

Ti·bet·an (tĭ-bĕt′n) *adj.* Of or pertaining to Tibet, its people, or their language or culture.
~*n.* **1.** A member of the Mongoloid people of Tibet. **2.** The Tibeto-Burman language of Tibet.

Ti·bet·o-Bur·man (tĭ-bĕt′ō-bûr′mən) *n.* Also **Ti·bet·o-Bur·mese** (-bər-mēz′, -mēs′). A branch of the Sino-Tibetan language family that principally includes Tibetan, Burmese, Lolo, and Balti. **—Ti·bet·o-Bur·man, Ti·bet·o-Bur·mese** *adj.*

tib·i·a (tĭb′ē-ə) *n., pl.* **-iae** (-ē-ē′) or **-ias.** **1. a.** The inner and larger of the two bones of the lower human leg from the knee to the ankle. Also called "shin," "shinbone." **b.** A homologous bone in animals. **2.** The fourth division of an insect's leg, between the femur and the tarsi. **3.** A kind of ancient flute originally made from an animal's leg bone. [Latin *tĭbia†,* shinbone, pipe.] **—tib·i·al** *adj.*

Ti·bul·lus (tə-bŭl′əs), **Albius** (*c.* 54–18 B.C.). Roman elegiac poet. Primarily concerned with his poetry and rural living, he remained distant from the political complexities that involved his contemporaries Horace and Ovid. In the two volumes attributed to him, he laments the passing of two mistresses and a young friend, Marathus.

tic (tĭk) *n.* **1.** A habitual spasmodic muscular contraction, usually of the face or extremities. **2.** Tic douloureux. [French, originally a veterinary term (perhaps imitative).]

tic dou·lou·reux (dōō′lə-rōō′, -rœ′) *n.* **Trigeminal neuralgia** *(see).* [French, "painful tic."]

tick¹ (tĭk) *n.* **1.** The recurring sharp, clicking sound made by a machine, especially by a clock. **2.** *British Informal.* A moment. **3.** A mark used to call attention to an item or indicate that it has been approved, dealt with, or noted.
~*v.* **ticked, ticking, ticks.** *—intr.* **1.** To emit recurring clicking sounds, as a clock does. **2.** To function in a characteristic way, as if by means of a motivating mechanism: *What makes him tick?* *—tr.* **1.** To count or record by means of ticks: *The meter ticked off the fare. The clock was ticking away the hours.* **2.** To mark (a sum, for example) with a tick. **—tick off. 1.** *Slang.* To make angry; annoy. **2.** *Chiefly British Informal.* To scold or rebuke. [Middle English *tek* (noun; perhaps imitative); verb, 16th century, of Germanic origin.]

tick² *n.* **1.** Any of numerous bloodsucking parasitic arachnids of the families Ixodidae and Argasidae within the order Acarina, many of which transmit infectious diseases. **2.** Any of various usually wingless, louselike insects of the family Hippoboscidae, which are parasitic on sheep, goats, and other animals. [Middle English *tyke, teke,* Old English *ticca* (unattested).]

tick³ *n.* **1.** The cloth case of a mattress or pillow. **2.** Ticking. [Middle English *tikke,* perhaps from Middle Dutch *tēke,* from West Germanic *tēka* (unattested), from Latin *thēca,* cover, case, from Greek *thēkē.*]

tick⁴ *n. British Informal.* Credit; trust: *on tick.* [Short for TICKET.]

tick bird *n.* The oxpecker *(see).*

tick-borne (tĭk′bôrn′, -bōrn′) *adj.* Transmitted by ticks. Said of diseases such as typhus.

tick·er (tĭk′ər) *n.* **1. a.** A telegraphic instrument that receives and records stock-market quotations on a paper tape. **b.** Any of various devices that record similar information by electronic means. **2.** *Slang.* A watch. **3.** *Slang.* The heart.

ticker tape *n.* The paper strip on which a telegraphic ticker prints.

tick·er-tape parade (tĭk′ər-tāp′) *n.* A traditional hero's welcome, especially in New York City, in which ticker tape and shredded paper are thrown from buildings as the celebrity parades by.

tick·et (tĭk′ĭt) *n.* **1.** A paper slip or card indicating that its holder has paid for or is entitled to a service, right, or consideration, such as: **a.** One entitling its holder to use public transportation: *a bus ticket.* **b.** One entitling its holder to admission, as to a place of entertainment or a lecture: *a theater ticket.* **2.** A card or piece of paper enabling property, especially articles of clothing, to be identified and reclaimed by the owner: *a dry-cleaning ticket; a checkroom ticket.* **3.** A certifying document; especially, a captain's or pilot's license. **4.** An identifying or descriptive tag attached to an item to give information such as price; label. **5.** A list of candidates proposed or endorsed by a political party. **6.** A **parking ticket** *(see).* **7.** *Informal.* The proper thing: *A change of scene would be just the ticket for her.* **8.** A way of obtaining something sought or desired: *Study and practice are the ticket to a successful concert career.*
~*tr.v.* **ticketed, -eting, -ets. 1.** To provide with a ticket for admission or passage. **2.** To attach a tag to; label. **3.** To designate for a specified use or end; destine. **4. a.** To serve (a violator) with a parking ticket. **b.** To place a parking ticket on (a motor vehicle). [Obsolete French *etiquet,* ticket, label, from Old French *estiquet(te),* from *estiquier,* to stick, from Middle Dutch *steken.*]

ticket agency *n.* An agency that sells tickets for theatrical and other performances and for transportation. **—ticket agent** *n.*

ticket office *n.* An office, as in a theater or railroad station, where reservations can be made and tickets can be bought.

ticket scalper *n.* A profiteer who buys up desirable admission tickets for popular events and resells them at inflated prices.

tick fever *n.* A febrile infectious disease transmitted by ticks.

tick·ing (tĭk′ĭng) *n.* A strong, tightly woven fabric of cotton or linen used especially to make mattress or pillow coverings. Also called "tick."

tick·ing-off (tĭk′ĭng-ôf′, -ŏf′) *n. Chiefly British Informal.* A rebuke; a scolding.

tick·le (tĭk′əl) *v.* **-led, -ling, -les.** *—tr.* **1.** To touch (the body) lightly so as to provoke a tingling sensation causing laughter or twitching movements. **2. a.** To tease or excite pleasurably; titillate. **b.** To fill with mirth or pleasure; delight. *—intr.* To feel or cause a tingling sensation. **—tickle pink.** *Informal.* To please; delight. Usually used in the passive: *She was tickled pink by the gift.*
~*n.* **1.** The act of tickling. **2.** A tickling sensation. [Middle English *tikelen,* probably from *tiken, ticken†,* to touch lightly.]

tick·ler (tĭk′lər) *n.* **1.** One that tickles. **2.** A memorandum book or file to aid the memory. **3.** *Chiefly British Informal.* A difficult problem.

tick·lish (tĭk′lĭsh) *adj.* **1.** Sensitive to tickling. **2.** Requiring skillful or tactful handling; delicate. **3.** Easily offended or upset; touchy. **—tick·lish·ly** *adv.* **—tick·lish·ness** *n.*

Tick·nor (tĭk′nər, -nôr′), **George** (1791–1871). U.S. language instructor and author. As the first Smith Professor of French and Spanish at Harvard (1819–35), he effectively reorganized the language department and helped legitimize the study of modern foreign languages.

tick·seed (tĭk'sēd') *n.* A plant, the **coreopsis** (see). [So called from its shape.]

tick·tack, tic-tac (tĭk'tăk') *n.* **1.** A steady ticking sound, as of a clock. **2.** A prankster's device for tapping on a door or window from a distance. **3.** *British.* A system of sign language by which bookmakers communicate odds to each other at a series of races. [Imitative.]

tick·tack·toe, tic-tack-toe (tĭk'tăk'tō') *n.* A game played by two persons, each trying to make a line of three X's or three O's in a boxlike figure with nine spaces. Also called "crisscross," *chiefly British* "noughts and crosses." [Probably TICKTACK (from the

sounds made on slates on which an earlier form of the game was played) + TOE.]

tick·tock (tĭk'tŏk') *n.* The ticking sound made by a clock, especially a pendulum clock. [Imitative.] **—tick·tock** *v.*

tick trefoil *n.* Any of various plants of the genus *Desmodium,* having compound leaves with three leaflets, clusters of small purplish or white flowers, and jointed seed pods with easily separable sticky segments. Also called "beggar-ticks." [Its sticky seed pods adhere like ticks to animals.]

tick·y-tack·y (tĭk'ē-tăk'ē) *n.* Cheap, shoddy material. [Reduplication of TACKY (cheap).]

Ti·con·der·o·ga (tī-kŏn'də-rō'gə). Resort village in northeastern New York State, on a neck of land between lakes George and Champlain. Fort Ticonderoga, now a museum, was captured from the British by troops led by Benedict Arnold and Ethan Allen (1775).

t.i.d. *Medicine.* three times a day [Latin *ter in die.*]

tid·al (tīd'l) *adj.* **1.** Pertaining to, affected by, or having tides: *a tidal river.* **2.** Dependent upon or scheduled by the state or times of the tide: *a tidal ship.* [TID(E) + -AL.] **—tid·al·ly** *adv.*

tidal wave *n.* **1.** An unusual rise or incursion of water along the seashore, as from a storm or a combination of wind and spring tide. **2.** A tsunami. **3.** An overwhelming manifestation of sentiment, desire, or opinion.

tid·bit (tĭd'bĭt') *n.* Also **tit·bit** (tĭt'-). A choice morsel, as of food or gossip. [Perhaps dialectal *tid,* tender + BIT.]

tid·dly (tĭd'lē) *adj. Chiefly British Slang.* Drunk. [19th century (meaning "a drink") : origin obscure.]

tid·dly·winks (tĭd'lē-wĭngks') *n.* Also **tid·dle·dy·winks** (tĭd'l-dē-). *Used with a singular verb.* A game in which players try to snap small disks into a cup by pressing them on the edge with a larger disk. [Perhaps dialectal *tiddly,* little + WINK.]

tide[1] (tīd) *n.* **1. a.** The twice-daily rise and fall in the surface level of the oceans, seas, and lower courses of rivers caused by the gravitational attraction of the moon and, to a lesser extent, the sun. **b.** A specific occurrence of such a variation. **c.** The waters in such a variation. See **ebb tide, flood tide, neap tide, spring tide.** **2.** Stress exerted on a body or part of a body by the gravitational attraction of another: *atmospheric tide; solar tide.* **3.** A tendency or movement regarded as alternating and inexorable: *The tide of public opinion has turned.* **4.** A time or season. Usually used in combination: *springtide; Christmastide.* **5.** *Archaic.* A favorable occasion; an opportunity. **—swim with** (or **against**) **the tide.** To submit to (or oppose) majority views or trends. **—v. tided, tiding, tides.** **—intr. 1.** To rise and fall like the tide. **2.** To drift or ride with the tide. **—tr.** To carry along with or as if with the tide. **—tide over.** To support through a difficult period: *The five dollars tided him over until payday.* [Middle English *tid(e),* season, time, tide, Old English *tīd,* season, time.] **—tide·less** *adj.*

tide[2] *intr.v.* **tided, tiding, tides.** *Archaic.* To betide; befall. [Middle English *tiden,* Old English *tīdan,* "to fall as one's lot."]

tide-mark (tīd'märk') *n.* **1.** A line or artificial indicator marking the high-water or low-water limit of the tides. **2.** *Chiefly British.* A mark showing the level a liquid has reached, as that left when a bathtub has been emptied. **3.** *Chiefly British Informal.* A dirty mark on the skin showing an area that has been left unwashed.

tide-wait·er (tīd'wā'tər) *n.* A customs officer who boards incoming ships at a harbor.

tide-wa·ter (tīd'wô'tər, -wŏt'ər) *n.* **1.** Water that inundates land at high tide. **2.** Water affected by the tides; especially, tidal streams. **3.** Low coastal land drained by tidal streams.

tide-way (tīd'wā') *n.* **1.** A channel in which a tidal current runs. **2.** The current that runs through a tideway.

tid·ings (tī'dĭngz) *pl.n.* Information; news: *tidings of great joy.* [Plural of *tiding,* an event, Middle English *tiding,* Old English *tīdung,* perhaps from Old Norse *tidhendi,* events, from *tidhr,* occurring.]

ti·dy (tī'dē) *adj.* **-dier, -diest. 1.** Orderly and neat in appearance or procedure. **2.** Orderly in habits; methodical. **3.** Substantial; considerable: *a tidy nest egg.* **4.** Adequate; satisfactory.

—v. tidied, -dying, -dies. —tr. To make tidy; put in order. **—intr.** To put things in order. Often used with *up.*

—n., pl. tidies. 1. A fancy protective covering for the arms or headrest of a chair. **2.** *British.* A small container for miscellaneous objects: *a desk tidy.* [Middle English, timely, seasonable, fair, excellent, from *tid,* season, TIDE.] **—ti·di·ly** *adv.* **—ti·di·ness** *n.*

tie (tī) *v.* **tied, tying, ties. —tr. 1.** To fasten or secure with a cord, rope, or strap: *tied the dog to a tree.* **2.** To fasten by drawing together the parts or sides of and knotting with strings or laces: *tie one's shoes.* **3. a.** To make (a knot or bow). **b.** To put a knot or bow in: *tie a ribbon.* **4.** To confine or restrict as if with cord: *tied down to his job.* **5.** To bring together closely; unite: *tied by bonds of affection.* **6. a.** To end (a match or contest) with an equal score. **b.** To equal (an opponent) in a match or contest. **7.** To restrict the freedom of action or choice of: *Responsibilities tied him to his impoverished lifestyle.* **8.** *Music.* To join (notes) by a tie. **—intr. 1.** To be fastened with strings. **2.** To achieve equal scores in a match or contest. **—tie one on.** *Slang.* To get drunk. **—tie the knot. 1.** To get married. **2.** To perform a marriage ceremony.

—n. 1. A cord, string, or other means by which something is tied. **2. a.** Something that unites; a bond: *marital ties.* **b.** Something that restricts one's freedom of action or choice: *He wanted to avoid the ties of a wife and children.* **3.** A necktie. **4.** A beam or rod that joins parts and gives support. **5.** One of the timbers laid across a railroad

THE OCEAN'S EBB AND FLOW

The earth's waters are subject to remote gravitational forces

The twice-daily rise and fall of the oceans is caused by the gravitational effect on the earth of the moon and, less importantly, the sun. Tidal ranges vary dramatically: the greatest is in the Bay of Fundy, Canada, where high and low water may differ by 15 meters (49 feet).

At any given time there are two high tides on the earth, the direct tide on the side facing the moon and the indirect tide on the opposite side.

The direct tide is a bulge produced by the moon pulling the earth's water toward it more powerfully than it can pull the earth itself.

The indirect tide occurs because the moon's

pull on the center of the earth is greater than on the water on the side of the earth farthest from the moon, causing the earth to be drawn away from the water most distant from the moon, producing a second bulge.

As the moon is in motion, circling the earth once a month, the tides do not exactly coincide with the earth's 24-hour cycle, but occur 50 minutes later each successive day. The sun has less effect than the moon—just under half—because of its distance. Its influence is mostly masked by the moon's, except at spring and neap tides, which occur every two weeks.

SPRING TIDES

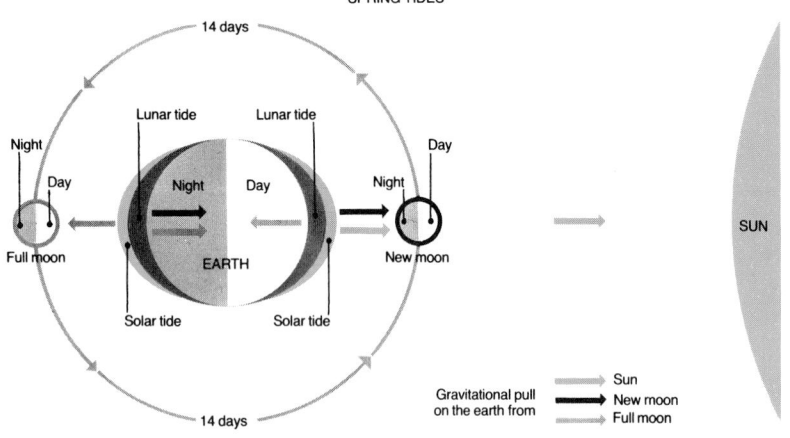

SPRING TIDE *When the moon, the earth, and the sun are in alignment, their gravitational pulls complement one another and produce an exceptionally* *high tide called a spring tide. Spring tides occur every 14 days, at the time the moon is full and also when it is new.*

NEAP TIDES

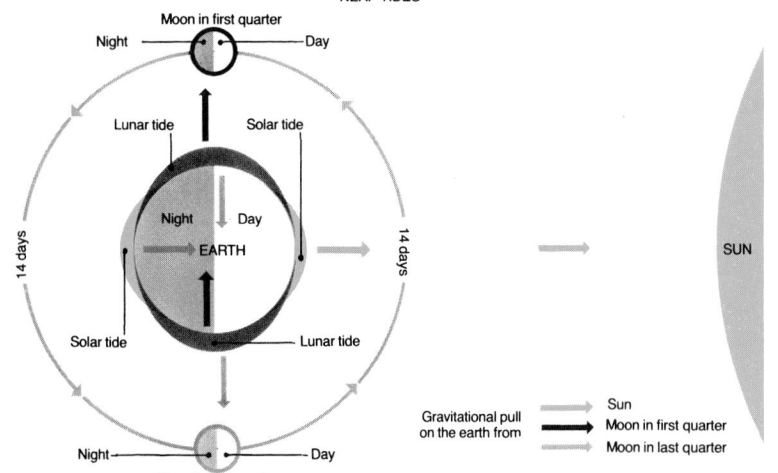

NEAP TIDE *When the moon, the earth, and the sun are at right angles, the sun's pull partly neutralizes the moon's, so that high-water and low-water lev-* *els are less pronounced than at other times. These neap tides occur when the moon is in its first quarter and its last quarter.*

bed to support the tracks. **6. a.** A state of equality of scores, votes, or performance in a contest. **b.** A contest resulting in a tie; a draw. **7.** *Music.* A curved line put either above or below two notes of the same pitch, indicating that the tone is to be sustained for their combined duration. [Middle English *t(e)yen,* Old English *tīgan.*]

tie·back (tī′băk′) *n.* **1.** A decorative loop of fabric, cord, or metal for parting and draping curtains to the sides. **2. tiebacks.** A pair of curtains meant to be tied back at about midlength.

tie beam *n.* A horizontal beam that connects the rafters in a roof.

tie·break·er (tī′brā′kər) *n.* A match to decide the winner of a contest when the competitors are tied.

tie clasp *n.* An ornamental device that holds the ends of a necktie to the shirt front.

tied house *n. British.* A pub that is owned by a brewery and sells only the beers made by the brewery. Compare **free house.**

tie-dye (tī′dī′) *tr.v.* **-dyed, -dyeing, -dyes.** To dye (fabric) after tying parts of the fabric so that they will not absorb the dye, giving the fabric a streaked or mottled look.

tie in *tr.v.* **1.** To bring into conformity; coordinate. **2.** To use as a tie-in. —*intr.v.* To be in conformity; correspond or fit in.

tie-in (tī′ĭn′) *n.* **1.** A connection or relation. **2.** An item such as a book, record, or souvenir designed to be sold after a demand has been created, as by a film or television series. **3. a.** The sale of two or more products or services so that a minor item is expected to be purchased with the major one. **b.** One of the products or services so offered, usually the minor one.

Tien Shan. See **Tian Shan.**

Tientsin. See **Tianjin.**

tie·pin (tī′pĭn′) *n. Chiefly British.* A **stickpin** *(see).*

Ti·e·po·lo (tē-ā′pə-lō′, -ĕp′ə-lō′), **Giambattista** (1696–1770). Italian painter. With his unrivaled command of perspective, light, color, and composition, he produced a large body of secular and ecclesiastical works, including *The Banquet of Cleopatra* (*c.* 1745–50) and the *Martyrdom of Saint Agatha* (1750).

tier[1] (tîr) *n.* **1.** Any of a series of rows placed one above another, as in a theater balcony. **2.** A level; a stratum: *tiers of local government.* ~*v.* **tiered, tiering, tiers.** —*tr.* To arrange in tiers. —*intr.* To rise in tiers. [Earlier *tire,* from French, sequence, rank, from *tirer,* to draw out, from Vulgar Latin *tīrāre*† (unattested).]

ti·er[2] (tī′ər) *n.* One that ties.

tierce (tîrs) *n.* **1. a.** The third of seven canonical hours. **b.** The time of day set aside for this prayer, usually the third hour after sunrise. **2.** A former measure of liquid capacity equal to a third of a pipe, or 42 gallons. **3.** In card games, a sequence of three cards of the same suit. **4.** The third position in fencing from which a parry or thrust can be made. **5.** *Music.* An interval of a third. [Middle English, one third, the third canonical hour, from Old French, from Latin *tertia* (noun), from Latin *tertius,* third.]

tiercel. Variant of **tercel.**

Ti·er·ra del Fu·e·go (tē-ĕr′ə dĕl fo͞o-ā′gō, fyo͞o-). Archipelago of islands off the extreme southeastern tip of South America, separated from the mainland by the Strait of Magellan. The eastern half belongs to Argentina, the western to Chile.

tie tack *n.* A short pin with a decorative head used to attach a tie to a shirt front by means of a snap or chain.

tie up *tr.v.* **1. a.** To invest (money) in such a way that it is not available to be withdrawn and used: *Her money is all tied up in real estate.* **b.** To subject (assets, for example) to such restrictions that they cannot be realized. **2.** To hinder, delay, or stop: *The strike tied up traffic for hours.* **3.** To connect; associate: *The police tied up the murder with the robbery.* **4.** *Informal.* To bring to a successful completion: *tie up a contract.* **5.** *Informal.* **a.** To keep busy or very occupied: *I'm tied up tonight.* **b.** To monopolize or pre-empt the use of: *He ties up the phone for hours.* —*intr.v.* To moor. Used of a ship.

tie-up (tī′ŭp′) *n.* **1. a.** A link or connection. **b.** An association or partnership. **2.** A temporary condition of immobilization such as a traffic jam, work stoppage, or mechanical breakdown.

tiff (tĭf) *n.* **1.** A petty quarrel. **2.** A fit of irritation. ~*intr.v.* **tiffed, tiffing, tiffs.** To quarrel. [18th century : origin obscure.]

tif·fa·ny (tĭf′ə-nē) *n., pl.* **-nies.** A thin, transparent gauze of silk or cotton muslin. [Originally, dress for wearing on Twelfth Night (Epiphany), from Old French *tifanie,* Epiphany, from Medieval Latin *theophania,* THEOPHANY.]

Tif·fa·ny glass (tĭf′ə-nē) *n.* Stained or iridescent glass of a kind popular in the early 1900's for decorative objects or lamps. Also called "favrile glass." [After Louis *Tiffany* (1848–1933), U.S. artist.]

tif·fin (tĭf′ĭn) *n. Chiefly British.* A light lunch or snack. ~*intr.v.* **tiffined, -fining, -fins.** *Chiefly British.* To eat tiffin. [Short for obsolete *tiffing,* gerund of *tiff*†, to sip.]

Tiflis. See **Tbilisi.**

ti·ger (tī′gər) *n.* **1. a.** A large carnivorous feline mammal, *Panthera tigris,* of Asia, having a tawny coat with transverse black stripes. **b.** Any of various other similar felines. **2.** A fierce, aggressive, or audacious person. [Middle English *tigre,* from Old French, from Latin *tigris,* from Greek.] —**ti·ger·ish** *adj.* See feature, next page.

tiger beetle *n.* Any of numerous active, long-legged predatory beetles of the family Cicindelidae, chiefly of warm, sandy regions.

tiger cat *n.* Any of various small felines resembling the tiger in appearance or behavior.

ti·ger-eye (tī′gər-ī′) *n.* Also **ti·ger's-eye** (tī′gərz-). A yellow-brown semiprecious gemstone of quartz colored by iron oxide. [From a fancied resemblance to the eye of a tiger.]

tiger lily *n.* A plant, *Lilium tigrinum,* native to Asia, having large, black-spotted reddish-orange flowers.

tiger moth *n.* Any of numerous moths of the family Arctiidae, characteristically having wings marked with spots or lines.

tiger shark *n.* A large, chiefly tropical shark, *Galeocerdo cuvieri,* having a grayish-brown body marked with darker stripes.

tiger snake *n.* A venomous snake of the genus *Notechis,* of Australia and Tasmania, marked with brown and yellow stripes.

tight (tīt) *adj.* **tighter, tightest. 1.** Of such close construction, texture, or organization as to be impermeable, especially by water or air. Often used in combination: *airtight.* **2.** Fastened, held, or closed securely. **3. a.** Compressed, leaving few or no intervening spaces; compact. **b.** Very full; leaving no spare time or room: *a tight schedule.* **4.** Drawn out to the fullest extent; taut. **5.** Cramped; constrained. **6.** Snug, often uncomfortably so: *a tight fit.* **7.** Constricted: *a tight feeling in the chest.* **8.** Close-fisted; stingy. **9. a.** Difficult to obtain: *Money is tight.* **b.** Affected by scarcity: *a tight market.* **10.** Difficult to deal with or get out of: *a tight spot.* **11. a.** Strict in discipline or control. **b.** Characterized by strict discipline or control: *runs a tight ship.* **12.** Closely contested: *a tight match.* **13.** *Regional.* Neat and trim. **14.** *Slang.* Drunk. **15.** *Slang.* Very friendly; intimate. ~*adv.* **1.** Firmly; securely. **2.** Soundly: *sleep tight.* [Middle English, probably variant of *thyght,* thickset, dense, from Old Norse *thēttr,* watertight, dense.] —**tight·ly** *adv.* —**tight·ness** *n.*

tight·en (tīt′n) *v.* **-ened, -ening, -ens.** —*tr.* To make tight or tighter. —*intr.* To become tight or tighter. —**tight·en·er** *n.*

tight·fist·ed (tīt′fĭs′tĭd) *adj.* Giving or spending reluctantly. —See Synonyms at **stingy.**

tight-knit (tīt′nĭt′) *adj.* **1.** Closely connected or integrated: *a tight-knit community.* **2.** Carefully and closely organized.

tight·lipped (tīt′lĭpt′) *adj.* **1.** Having the lips pressed together, as when tense or angry. **2.** Reticent.

tight·rope (tīt′rōp′) *n.* **1.** A tightly stretched rope, usually of wire, on which acrobats perform high above the ground. **2.** A difficult or dangerous situation.

tights (tīts) *pl.n.* **1.** A close-fitting, stretchable garment covering the body from the waist or neck down and worn especially by dancers and gymnasts. **2.** *British.* Pantyhose.

tight·wad (tīt′wŏd′) *n. Slang.* One who hates to spend money; a miser. [TIGHT + WAD (money).]

tig·lic acid (tĭg′lĭk) *n.* A thick, syrupy poisonous liquid, $CH_3CH{:}C(CH_3)CO_2H$, derived from croton oil, having a spicy odor and used in making perfumes and flavoring agents. [From New Latin *(Croton) tiglium,* a seed of the (Croton) species, perhaps from Greek *tilos*†, liquid feces (from the use of the seeds as a purgative).]

ti·glon (tī′glən) *n.* Also **ti·gon** (tī′gən). The hybrid offspring of a male tiger and a female lion. [Blend of TIGER and LION.]

Ti·gré (tē-grā′) *n.* A Semitic language of northern Ethiopia.

ti·gress (tī′grĭs) *n.* **1.** A female tiger. **2.** A fierce, aggressive, or audacious woman.

Ti·gri·nya (tə-grēn′yə) *n.* A Semitic language of northern Ethiopia.

Ti·gris (tī′grĭs). River in southwestern Asia, rising in the Taurus Mts. of eastern Turkey and flowing *c.* 1,850 kilometers (1,150 miles) through Iraq to join the Euphrates and form the Shatt al Arab waterway, which passes through a delta and into the northern end of the Persian Gulf. Its flood banks, along with those of the Euphrates, supported the agriculture on which the ancient civilization of Mesopotamia was based.

Ti·jua·na (tē-wä′nə, -hwä′nə, tē′ə-). City in northwestern Mexico, just south of the U.S. border of California. It is noted for its racetracks and bullfighting rings.

Ti·kal (tē-käl′). Ruined Mayan city in northern Guatemala. The largest and possibly the oldest of the Mayan cities, it has nine groups of courts and plazas built on hilly land surrounding swamps and interconnected by bridges and causeways.

tik·chung (tĭk′chŭng′) *n.* A monetary unit of Bhutan equal to 1/100 of a ngultrum. See feature at **currency.** [Native word in Bhutan.]

tike. Variant of **tyke.**

ti·ki (tē′kē) *n.* **1. Tiki.** A male figure in Polynesian mythology, sometimes identified as the first man. **2.** A wood or stone image of a Polynesian god. **3.** A Maori figurine representing an ancestor, often intricately carved from greenstone and worn about the neck as a talisman. [Maori.]

til (tĭl) *n.* The sesame plant, especially as used in India as a source of food and oil. [Hindi *til,* from Sanskrit *tila*†.]

ti·la·pi·a (tĭ-lä′pē-ə, -lā′pē-ə) *n.* An African cichlid fish of the genus *Tilapia,* which hatches eggs and young in the mouth and is used as a food fish. [New Latin, probably from an African name.]

til·bur·y (tĭl′bĕr′ē, -bə-rē) *n., pl.* **-ies.** A light open gig seating two persons, popular in the early 19th century. [After *Tilbury,* a 19th-century London coach builder.]

Til·bur·y (tĭl′bĕr′ē, -bə-rē). Dockyard district in Essex on the north bank of the Thames River, southeastern England. Tilbury serves as the chief container port of London.

til·de (tĭl′də) *n.* The diacritical mark (˜) placed over the letter *n* in Spanish to indicate the palatal nasal sound (ny), as in *cañon,* or over a vowel in Portuguese to indicate nasalization, as in *lã, pão.* [Spanish, from Latin *titulus,* superscription, TITLE.]

Til·den (tĭl′dən), **William Tatem, Jr.,** known as "Big Bill" (1893–1953). U.S. tennis player. The dominant tennis player of the

tiger moth *This medium-size moth, having a wingspan of up to 6 1/2 centimeters (2 1/2 inches), is found in marshes and woodlands throughout most of the United States.*

tiki *New Zealand Maoris wore carved figurines like this jade tiki around their necks as good luck charms. Each tiki was believed to house the spirit of an ancestor.*

PRONUNCIATION KEY

ă, pat; ā, pay; âr, care; ä, father, are; b, bib; ch, church; d, deed; ĕ, pet; ē, be; f, fife; g, gag; h, hat; hw, which; ĭ, pit; ī, pie; îr, pier; j, judge; k, kick; l, lid, needle; m, mum; n, no, sudden; ng, thing; ŏ, pot; ō, toe; ô, paw, for; oi, noise; ou, out; o͝o, book; o͞o, boot; p, pop; r, roar; s, sauce; sh, ship, dish; t, tight; th, thin, path; *th,* this, bathe; ŭ, cut; ûr, fur; v, valve; w, with; y, yes; z, zebra, size; zh, vision; ə, about, item, edible, gallop, circus, peaceful

IN FOREIGN WORDS:

à, *Fr.* ami; œ, *Fr.* feu, *Ger.* schön; ü, *Fr.* tu, *Ger.* über; KH, *Ger.* ich, *Scot.* loch; N, *Fr.* bon; y′, *Fr.* Compiègne

STRESS MARKS:

Primary stress: ′ **in·cite′** (ĭn-sīt′)
Secondary stress: ′ **in′sight′** (ĭn′sīt′)

tiger

STRIPED FELINE OF INDIA AND EASTERN ASIA

"Did he who made the Lamb make thee?"

Tyger! Tyger! burning bright
In the forests of the night,
What immortal hand or eye
Could frame thy fearful symmetry?

—William Blake

The tiger's "fearful symmetry" has long inspired awe throughout its native range from Siberia to Sumatra. In India it is linked with the worship of Shiva and Kali, deities of nature's destructive and procreative energies. In China the white tiger is the emblem of the western sky and autumn. To this day, tiger-bone wine is sold as a tonic among the Chinese. Throughout eastern Asia, folklore of tigers changing into people and vice versa parallels that of the werewolf in Europe. Europeans saw their first tiger when one was sent to Athens in the aftermath of Alexander the Great's expedition to India.

The world's largest cats, tigers can weigh up to 250 kilograms (550 pounds) and reach a length of 4 meters (13 feet). Males are bigger than females. These massive animals hunt at night, stalking deer and other hooved animals; they also prey on fish, frogs, and even insects.

Because tigers require large hunting territories, they have become endangered throughout their range. One subspecies that is native to the island of **Bali** is now extinct.

A tiger's stripes help it blend into the background. It also moves with a minimum of noise, so it can creep up on prey undetected.

Tigers are much less social than lions. In the wild they generally hunt alone, though sometimes they are seen sharing food. A mated pair or a group of siblings may also stay together for some time.

Not all tigers have tawny fur: occasional individuals—the so-called white tigers—are ivory-colored. Their coloration is an inherited trait.

1920's, he won the U.S. men's singles championship seven times (1920–25, 1930), was a three-time singles champion at Wimbledon (1920–21, 1930), and was also successful in doubles competition.

tile (tīl) *n.* **1.** A thin, flat, or convex slab of baked clay, plastic, concrete, cork, or other material, laid in rows to cover walls, floors, and roofs. **2.** A short length of pipe made of clay or concrete, used in sewers and drains. **3.** A hollow fired clay or concrete block used for building walls. **4.** Tiles collectively. **5.** Any of the marked playing pieces in games such as mahjong.
~*tr.v.* **tiled, tiling, tiles.** To cover or provide with tiles. [Middle English *til(e), teyele,* Old English *tigele,* from West Germanic *tegala* (unattested), from Latin *tēgula,* from *tegere,* to cover.] —**til·er** *n.*
til·ing (tī′lĭng) *n.* **1.** The laying of tiles. **2.** Tiles collectively. **3.** A tiled surface.

till¹ (tĭl) *tr.v.* **tilled, tilling, tills.** To prepare (land) for the growing of crops by plowing, harrowing, and fertilizing. [Middle English *tilien, til(l)en,* Old English *tilian,* to work at, labor, cultivate, from Germanic *tilōjan* (unattested), from *tilam* (unattested), aim, fixed point.] —**till·a·ble** *adj.*
till² *prep.* Until.
~*conj.* Until. [Middle English *till,* Old English *til,* probably from Germanic *tilam* (unattested), fixed point. See **till** (to cultivate).]
till³ *n.* A drawer, small box, or compartment for money, especially in a store. [Middle English *tylle†.*]
till⁴ *n. Geology.* **Boulder clay** (*see*). [Origin unknown.]
till·age (tĭl′ĭj) *n.* **1.** The cultivation of land. **2.** The state of being tilled. **3.** Land that is or has been tilled for crops.
til·land·si·a (tĭ-lănd′zē-ə) *n.* Any of various usually epiphytic plants of the genus *Tillandsia,* such as Spanish moss, of tropical and sub-tropical America. [New Latin, after Elias *Tillands* (died 1693), Swedish botanist.]
till·er¹ (tĭl′ər) *n.* One that tills land.
tiller² *n.* A lever used to turn a rudder and steer a boat. [Middle English *tiler, telor,* beam of a crossbow, from Norman French *telier,* weaver's beam, from Medieval Latin *tēlārium,* from Latin *tēla,* web, warp of a fabric, weaver's beam.]
tiller³ *n.* **1.** A shoot, especially one that sprouts from the base of a grass. **2.** A sapling.
~*intr.v.* **tillered, -lering, -lers.** To send forth tillers. [Middle English *tiller* (unattested), Old English *telgor, telgra.*]
Til·lich (tĭl′ĭk), **Paul Johannes** (1886–1965). U.S. theologian and philosopher, born in Germany. Considered one of the most creative and influential intellectuals of the 20th century, he wrote and spoke widely on religion and culture, formulating a philosophy that inextricably united the two.
til·sit (tĭl′sĭt) *n.* A type of pale, firm, slightly pungent cheese with holes in it. [From *Tilsit* (now Sovetsk, U.S.S.R.).]
tilt¹ (tĭlt) *v.* **tilted, tilting, tilts.** —*tr.* **1.** To cause to slope, as by raising one end; incline; tip. **2. a.** To aim or thrust (a lance) in a joust. **b.** To charge (an opponent). **3.** To forge with a tilt hammer. —*intr.* **1.** To slope; incline. **2.** To joust. Used with *at.* **3.** To quarrel. Used with *at.* **4.** To incline toward a specified view or position.
~*n.* **1. a.** An inclination from the horizontal or vertical; a slant. **b.** A sloping surface, as of the ground. **2.** The act of tilting. **3. a.** A medieval sport in which two mounted knights with lances charged together and attempted to unhorse each other. **b.** A thrust or blow with a lance. **4.** A dispute or other encounter between opponents. **5.** A tilt hammer. **6.** An inclination or bias toward a particular view

or position. **—at full tilt.** At full speed. [Middle English *tylten, tilten,* perhaps from Old English *tyltan* (unattested; akin to *tealt,* unsteady), from Germanic.]

tilt[2] *n.* A canopy or awning for a boat, cart, or wagon.
~tr.v. **tilted, tilting, tilts.** To cover with a tilt. [Middle English *tild, teld,* Old English *teld,* a tent.]

tilth (tĭlth) *n.* **1.** The cultivation of land; tillage. **2.** The condition of land or soil with respect to encouraging plant growth. **3.** Tilled earth. [Middle English *tilth,* Old English *tilth,* from *tilian,* to TILL (cultivate).]

tilt hammer *n.* A heavy forge hammer having a pivoted lever by which it is tilted up and then allowed to drop.

tilt·yard (tĭlt′yärd′) *n.* An enclosed area for tilting contests.

Tim. Timothy (New Testament).

tim·bal, tym·bal (tĭm′bəl) *n.* **1.** A kettledrum. **2.** A small cylindrical drum similar to a bongo that is used in Latin-American music. [French *timbale,* variant (influenced by *cymbale,* cymbal) of obsolete *tamballe,* variant (influenced by *tambour,* tambour) of Spanish *atabal,* a kettledrum, from Arabic *aṭ-ṭabl,* the drum.]

tim·bale (tĭm′bəl, tĭm-bäl′, tăm-) *n.* **1.** A custardlike dish, usually of meat, fish, or vegetables, baked in a drum-shaped mold of pastry, rice, or pasta. **2.** A mold in which a timbale is baked. [French, "kettledrum," TIMBAL.]

tim·ber (tĭm′bər) *n.* **1.** Trees or wooded land considered as a source of wood. **2. a.** Wood as a building material. **b.** A prepared piece of wood; especially, a beam in a structure. **c.** A rib in a ship's frame. **3.** Suitable or potential material: *He's executive timber.*
~tr.v. **timbered, -bering, -bers.** To support or shore up with timbers.
~interj. Used to warn of a falling tree. [Middle English *timber,* building, building material, Old English *timber.*]

tim·bered (tĭm′bərd) *adj.* **1. a.** Constructed of or covered with timber. **b.** Built with exposed timbers. **2.** Wooded.

tim·ber·head (tĭm′bər-hĕd′) *n. Nautical.* A timber end that projects above a ship's deck and is used as a bollard.

timber hitch *n. Nautical.* A knot used for fastening a rope around a spar or log to be hoisted or towed.

tim·ber·ing (tĭm′bər-ĭng) *n.* Timber or work made of it.

tim·ber·land (tĭm′bər-lănd′) *n.* Forested land, especially land with timber that can be sold commercially.

tim·ber·line, timber line (tĭm′bər-līn′) *n.* The limit of altitude in mountainous regions beyond which trees do not grow. Also called "tree line."

timber wolf *n.* A grayish wolf, *Canis lupus,* of forested northern regions, especially of North America. Also called "gray wolf."

tim·ber·work (tĭm′bər-wûrk′) *n.* The part of a structure made with timbers, as the framework of a boat or house.

tim·bre (tăm′bər, tĭm′-) *n.* The quality of a sound that distinguishes it from other sounds of the same pitch and volume; especially, the distinctive tone of a musical instrument, a voice, or a voiced speech sound. [French, from Old French, a bell struck with a hammer, timbrel, timbre, from Vulgar Latin *timbano* (unattested), a drum, from Medieval Greek *timbanon,* from Greek *tumpanon.* See **tympanum.**] **—tim·bral** (tăm′brəl, tĭm′-) *adj.*

tim·brel (tĭm′brəl) *n.* An ancient percussion instrument similar to a tambourine. [Diminutive of Middle English *timbre,* from Old French, a drum, TIMBRE.]

Tim·buk·tu (tĭm′bŭk-to͞o′). City in central Mali, near the Niger River, to which it is connected by a series of canals. It was founded in the 11th century and rose to become one of the great trading centers (especially for gold) and a leading intellectual center of Islam. It was sacked by Moroccans in 1593 and never regained its economic or cultural status.

time (tīm) *n.* **1. a.** A nonspatial continuum in which events occur in apparently irreversible succession from the past through the present to the future. **b.** A point or period on this continuum, as a day, month, or year. **2.** A quantity measuring duration by comparison with a periodic process, such as the earth's rotation or the vibration of electromagnetic radiation, regarded in relativity theory as a fourth coordinate required to specify an event completely. See **space-time.** **3.** An indefinite but finite period on this continuum: *Time will tell. You'll recover in time.* **4.** A specific point on the continuum reckoned in hours and minutes: *Can you tell me the time?* **5.** A system by which such intervals are measured or such numbers are reckoned: *Greenwich mean time.* **6. a.** *Often* **times.** An interval marked by similar events, conditions, or phenomena; especially, a span of years; an era: *Edwardian times; a time of troubles.* **b. times.** The present with respect to prevailing conditions and trends: *move with the times.* **7. a.** One's lifetime. **b.** One's heyday. **8.** A suitable or opportune moment or season. **9. a.** A moment or period designated, as by custom, for a specified activity: *harvest time; bedtime.* **b.** A moment or period designated for something to happen: *got to work on time.* **c.** A period allotted or given over to a specific activity: *Your time is up. I need time to think.* **d.** A period at one's disposal: *free time. Have you time for a chat?* **10.** An appointed or fated moment, especially of death or giving birth: *died before his time. Her time is near.* **11. a.** One of several instances: *We called on you twice, but both times you were out.* **b. times.** Used to indicate the number of instances by which a quantity is or is to be multiplied: *It's at least three times as big.* **12.** An occasion or experience of a specified kind: *had a marvelous time; showed us a good time.* **13.** *Informal.* A prison sentence: *do time.* **14. a.** The customary period of work: *work full time.* **b.** The period spent working. **c.** A period of apprenticeship: *serve one's time.* **d.** The hourly pay rate: *earned double time on Sundays.* **15.** The rate of speed of a measured activity: *marching in double time.* **16.** The characteristic beat of musical rhythm: *three-quarter time.* **17.** *British.* The hour at which a bar in a pub closes; closing time: *Time, gentlemen, please!* **—against time.** With a quickly approaching time limit. **—at one time. 1.** Simultaneously. **2.** At a period or moment in the past. **—at the same time.** However; nonetheless. **—at times.** On occasion; sometimes. **—behind the times.** Out-of-date; old-fashioned. **—bide one's time.** To wait for an opportune moment. **—for the time being.** Temporarily. **—from time to time.** Once in a while; at intervals. **—gain time.** To run too fast. Said of a timepiece. **—have no time for.** To be intolerant of; dislike: *I have no time for slackers.* **—high time.** Past the appropriate or required time; long overdue. **—in good time. 1.** In a reasonable length of time. **2.** At or before the proper time. **3.** Quickly. **—in no time.** Almost instantly; immediately. **—in time. 1.** Before the expiration of a time limit. **2.** Within an indefinite amount of passing time. **3.** In proper tempo or rhythm. **—keep time. 1.** To indicate the correct time. **2.** To maintain the tempo or rhythm. **—kill time.** To occupy oneself in a desultory way while waiting for time to pass. **—lose time. 1.** To operate too slowly. Said of a timepiece. **2.** To delay advancement. **—make up time.** To compensate for lost time. **—mark time. 1.** To move the feet as though marching but without moving forward. **2.** To act or function in an unproductive or purposeless fashion. **3.** To stop doing something temporarily, usually with a view to restarting when conditions permit. **—once upon a time.** Long ago; once. Used especially to introduce fairy tales. **—on time. 1.** According to schedule; promptly. **2.** By paying in installments. **—pass the time of day.** To chat about general topics such as the weather. **—play for time.** To use delaying tactics in order to gain extra time. **—take one's time.** To do something in a careful or leisurely fashion. **—time after time.** Repeatedly. **—time and (time) again.** Often; frequently. **—time of one's life.** A highly pleasurable experience. **—time out of mind.** Time immemorial.
~adj. **1.** Of or relating to time. **2.** Constructed so as to operate at or indicate a particular moment: *a time charge.* **3.** Payable on a future date or dates: *a time loan.*
~tr.v. **timed, timing, times. 1.** To set the time for (an event or occasion). **2.** To adjust to keep accurate time. **3.** To regulate for the most appopriate sequence of movements or events. **4.** To record the speed or duration of. **5.** To set or maintain the tempo, speed, or duration of. [Middle English *time,* Old English *tīma.*]

time and a half *n.* A rate of pay that is one and a half times the regular rate, as for overtime work.

time and motion study *n.* An analysis of the working methods involved in an industrial operation with a view to improving efficiency. Also called "motion study," "time study."

time base *n. Electronics.* An electronic circuit that repeatedly produces a voltage increasing to a given value and falling abruptly to zero or a minimum value, used to deflect the electron beam horizontally in an oscilloscope or television.

time bill *n.* A bill of exchange payable at an indicated future time.

time bomb *n.* **1.** A bomb with a detonating mechanism that can be set for a particular time. **2.** Something, such as a situation or a personality characteristic, with potentially disastrous repercussions.

time capsule *n.* A sealed container preserving articles and records of contemporary culture for study in the distant future.

time·card (tīm′kärd′) *n.* A card, either maintained by an employee or stamped by a time clock, recording the employee's arrival and departure time each day.

time clock *n.* A clock that records the arrival and departure times of employees, usually by punching timecards.

time constant *n. Physics.* A measure of the amount of damping in an oscillating system, such as a vibrating structure or a circuit carrying an alternating signal, measured by the time taken for the amplitude to fall to a value $1/e$ (about 0.368) of its initial value or to increase to $(1 - 1/e)$ (0.632) of its final steady value.

time-con·sum·ing (tīm′kən-so͞o′mĭng) *adj.* Taking up a great deal of time.

time deposit *n.* A bank deposit that cannot be withdrawn before a date specified at the time of deposit.

time dilatation *n.* Also **time dilation.** The relativistic slowing of a clock that moves with respect to a stationary observer.

time exposure *n.* **1.** A photographic exposure made for a relatively long period of time. **2.** An image made by time exposure.

time fuse *n.* A fuse designed to set off an explosive charge after a preset period of time.

time-hon·ored (tīm′ŏn′ərd) *adj.* Honored because of age or age-old observance.

time immemorial *n.* Time long past, beyond memory or record.

time·keep·er (tīm′kē′pər) *n.* **1.** A timepiece. **2.** A person who keeps track of time, as in a sports event or in a place of employment. **—time·keep·ing** *n.*

time lag *n.* The interval of time between two events, the second of which is usually a result of the first.

time-lapse (tīm′lăps′) *adj.* Of or using a motion-picture technique for filming a naturally slow process, such as the unfolding of a leaf, by photographing it at intervals so that the continuous projection of the frames gives an accelerated view of it.

time·less (tīm′lĭs) *adj.* **1.** Independent of time; unending; eternal. **2.** Unaffected by time; ageless. **—time·less·ly** *adv.* **—time·less·ness** *n.*

PRONUNCIATION KEY

ă, pat; ā, pay; âr, care;
ä, father, are; b, bib;
ch, church; d, deed; ĕ, pet;
ē, be; f, fife; g, gag; h, hat;
hw, which; ĭ, pit; ī, pie;
îr, pier; j, judge; k, kick;
l, lid, needle; m, mum;
n, no, sudden; ng, thing;
ŏ, pot; ō, toe; ô, paw, for;
oi, noise; ou, out; o͝o, book;
o͞o, boot; p, pop; r, roar;
s, sauce; sh, ship, dish;
t, tight; th, thin, path;
th, this, bathe; ŭ, cut; ûr, fur;
v, valve; w, with; y, yes;
z, zebra, size; zh, vision;
ə, about, item, edible,
gallop, circus, peaceful

IN FOREIGN WORDS:

à, *Fr.* ami; œ, *Fr.* feu, *Ger.* schön; ü, *Fr.* tu, *Ger.* über;
KH, *Ger.* ich, *Scot.* loch;
N, *Fr.* bon; y′, *Fr.* Compiègne

STRESS MARKS:

Primary stress: ′
in·cite′ (ĭn-sīt′)
Secondary stress: ′
in′sight′ (ĭn′sīt′)

timothy Phleum pratense *was regarded as a weed until the middle of the 18th century when an American agriculturalist, Timothy Hanson, discovered its value as fodder. Now it is grown in most temperate countries.*

tinamou *The largely solitary tinamou of Central and South America spends most of its time on the ground and is a poor flier. This is the crested tinamou.*

time loan *n.* A loan to be paid within or by a specified time.
time lock *n.* A lock set to open at a specific time.
time•ly (tīm′lē) *adj.* **-lier, -liest. 1.** Occurring at a suitable or opportune time; well-timed. **2.** *Archaic.* Early; premature.
∼*adv.* **1.** Opportunely; in time. **2.** *Archaic.* Early; soon. [Middle English : TIME + -LY.] **—time•li•ness** *n.*
time machine *n.* A machine or device that in theory permits travel backward and forward in time.
time money *n.* A time loan.
time note *n.* An instrument such as a promissory note that specifies a date or dates of payment.
time off *n.* A period of absence or rest from work or study.
time•ous (tī′məs) *adj. Scottish.* Timely. [TIME + -OUS.] **—time•ous•ly** *adv.*
time-out, time out (tīm′out′) *n.* **1.** A brief cessation of play at the request of a sports team for rest or consultation. **2.** Any short break from work or play.
time•piece (tīm′pēs′) *n.* An instrument, such as a clock or chronometer, that measures, registers, or records time.
tim•er (tī′mər) *n.* **1.** A switch or regulator that controls or activates another mechanism at preset intervals. **2.** A timepiece, especially one used for measuring intervals of time. **3.** A person who keeps track of time; a timekeeper.
time reversal *n. Symbol* **T** A mathematical operation representing a transformation from a given physical system undergoing a given sequence of events (states) to a system in which the exact reverse sequence of states is undergone.
times (tīmz) *prep.* Multiplied by: *Five times two is ten.*
time's arrow *n. Physics.* The existence of a single direction for the passage of time such that time reversal does not occur in physical systems, as indicated by such phenomena as spontaneous increase in entropy, the spreading of waves from a source, or the expansion of the universe.
time•sav•ing (tīm′sā′vĭng) *adj.* Saving time through an efficient method or a shorter route. **—time•sav•er** *n.*
time scale *n.* A sequence of events used as a measure of duration or the passing of time.
time•serv•er (tīm′sûr′vər) *n.* A person who conforms to the prevailing ways and opinions of his time or condition for personal advantage; an opportunist. **—time•serv•ing** *adj.* & *n.*
time-shar•ing (tīm′shâr′ĭng) *n.* **1.** *Computer Science.* A system in which two or more users communicate with a computer at the same time, data being processed successively for short periods in a way controlled by the computer so that each terminal appears to have sole use of the machine. Compare **batch processing. 2.** The joint ownership or lease of vacation property through which the principals occupy the property individually for set periods of time. **—time-share** *v.*
time sheet *n.* A sheet that records the number of hours worked by employees during a pay period.
time signal *n.* An announcement, usually on the radio, of the correct time.
time signature *n. Music.* A symbol in the form of a numerical fraction placed on a staff at the beginning of a piece of music to indicate the meter. The numerator indicates the number of notes to the bar, and the denominator indicates the time value of each note. Thus 3/4 means that there are three quarter notes to the measure. Also called "signature."
time study *n.* Time and motion study.
time•switch (tīm′swĭch′) *n.* A switch whereby a mechanism can be preset to start or finish operating automatically.
time•ta•ble (tīm′tā′bəl) *n.* **1.** A list of the times at which certain events, such as arrivals and departures at an airport or railroad station, are expected to take place. **2.** A plan giving the times when classes or lectures will take place, as in a school or college. **3.** A schedule for a planned sequence of events.
time-test•ed (tīm′tĕs′tĭd) *adj.* Having been proved effective by prolonged testing.
time trial *n.* A competitive event, as in sports, that must be completed within a given time.
time value *n.* The length of a musical tone, note, or rest in relation to others in the score or in relation to the tempo.
time warp *n.* An imaginary distortion or interruption in the flow of time from past to future, featured typically in science fiction.
time•work (tīm′wûrk′) *n.* Work paid for in specific time units, as by the hour. **—time•work•er** *n.*
time•worn (tīm′wôrn′, -wōrn′) *adj.* **1.** Showing the effects of long use or wear. **2.** Used too often; trite.
time zone *n.* Any of the 24 equal longitudinal divisions of the earth's surface in which a standard time, the mean time of a meridian near the center, is kept, the primary division being that bisected by the Greenwich meridian. Each zone is 15 degrees of longitude in width, with local variations, and observes a clock time one hour earlier than the zone immediately to the east. Also called "international time zone."
tim•id (tĭm′ĭd) *adj.* **-ider, -idest. 1.** Shrinking from dangerous or difficult circumstances; hesitant or fearful. **2.** Shrinking from public attention; shy. **3.** Characterized by hesitancy or lack of courage. —See Synonyms at **shy.** [Latin *timidus,* from *timēre*†, to fear.] **—ti•mid•i•ty** (tĭ-mĭd′ə-tē), **tim•id•ness** *n.* **—tim•id•ly** *adv.*
tim•ing (tī′mĭng) *n.* **1.** The art or operation of regulating occurrence, pace, or coordination to achieve the most desirable effects, as in music, the theater, or athletics. **2.** The way in which the distribution of electricity to the plugs of an internal-combustion engine is synchronized with the speed of the engine.
ti•moc•ra•cy (tī-mŏk′rə-sē) *n., pl.* **-cies. 1.** A state described by Plato in which love of honor is the guiding principle. **2.** An Aristotelian state in which political power is proportional to the property one owns. [Old French *tymocracie,* from Medieval Latin *tīmocratia,* from Greek *timokratia* : *timē,* honor, worth + -CRACY.] **—ti•mo•crat•ic** (tī′mə-krăt′ĭk) *adj.*
Ti•mor (tē′môr′, tē-môr′). Mountainous Indonesian island, the largest and easternmost of the Lesser Sunda Islands. The western half of the island, formerly Netherlands Timor, became part of Indonesia in 1949. The eastern half was formerly Portuguese Timor, an overseas province of Portugal from 1914 until 1975.
tim•or•ous (tĭm′ər-əs) *adj.* Full of apprehensiveness; timid. [Middle English, from Old French *timoureus,* from Medieval Latin *timorōsus,* from Latin *timor,* fear, from *timēre*†, to fear.] **—tim•or•ous•ly** *adv.* **—tim•or•ous•ness** *n.*
tim•o•thy (tĭm′ə-thē) *n.* A grass, *Phleum pratense,* native to Eurasia, that has narrow, cylindrical flower spikes and is widely cultivated for hay. [After *Timothy* Hanson, American farmer who introduced it in the Carolinas about 1720.]
Tim•o•thy (tĭm′ə-thē) *n. Abbr.* **Tim.** Either of two books of the New Testament, each an epistle to St. Timothy attributed to St. Paul.
Timothy, Saint. Christian leader of the 1st century A.D. He was a convert and companion of St. Paul and a legendary martyr.
tim•pa•ni, tym•pa•ni (tĭm′pə-nē) *pl.n.* A set of kettledrums. [Italian, plural of *timpano,* kettledrum, from Latin *tympanum,* TYMPANUM.] **—tim•pa•nist** *n.*
timpanum. Variant of **tympanum.**
Timur. See **Tamerlane.**
tin (tĭn) *n.* **1.** *Symbol* **Sn** A malleable, silvery metallic element obtained chiefly from cassiterite. It is used to coat other metals to prevent corrosion, and forms part of numerous alloys, such as soft solder, pewter, type metal, and bronze. Atomic number 50, atomic weight 118.69, melting point 231.89°C, boiling point 2,507°C, specific gravity 7.31, valences 2, 4. **2.** Tin plate. **3.** A tin container or box. **4.** *British.* **a.** A container for preserved foodstuffs; can. **b.** The contents of such a container. **5.** *British.* A loaf of bread baked in a long rectangular tin. **6.** *British Slang.* Money.
∼*tr.v.* **tinned, tinning, tins. 1.** To plate or coat with tin. **2.** *Chiefly British.* To preserve by sealing in airtight tins; can. [Middle English *tin,* Old English *tin,* from Germanic *tinam* (unattested).]
tin•a•mou (tĭn′ə-mo͞o′) *n.* Any of various chickenlike or quaillike birds of the family Tinamidae, of Central and South America. [French, from Galibi *tinamu.*]
tin•cal (tĭng′kəl) *n.* Crude borax. [Malay *tingkal,* from Sanskrit *ṭankaṇa*†.]
tin can *n.* **1.** A container of tin-plated metal used especially for preserving food. **2.** *Slang.* A naval destroyer.
tinct (tĭngkt) *n. Archaic.* A color or tint.
∼*adj. Archaic.* Colored or tinted. [Latin *tinctus,* past participle of *tingere,* to TINGE.]
tinct. tincture.
tinc•to•ri•al (tĭngk-tôr′ē-əl, -tōr′ē-əl) *adj.* Pertaining to the processes of dyeing or coloring. [Latin *tinctōrius,* from *tinctus,* past participle of *tingere,* to TINGE.]
tinc•ture (tĭngk′chər) *n. Abbr.* **tinct. 1.** A dyeing substance; pigment. **2.** An imparted color; a tinge; a tint. **3.** A trace or hint. **4.** *Pharmacology.* An alcohol solution of a nonvolatile medicine: *tincture of iodine.* **5.** A heraldic metal, color, or fur. **6.** A component of a substance extracted by means of a solvent.
∼*tr.v.* **tinctured, -turing, -tures. 1.** To stain or tint with a color. **2.** To infuse, as with a quality; impregnate. [Middle English, from Latin *tinctūra,* a dyeing, from *tinctus,* past participle of *tingere,* to TINGE.]
Tindal or **Tindale, William.** See William **Tyndale.**
tin•der (tĭn′dər) *n.* Readily combustible material, such as dry twigs, used to kindle fires. [Middle English *tinder,* Old English *tynder,* from Germanic *tund-* (unattested), past participial form of *tend-* (unattested), to burn, kindle.]
tin•der•box (tĭn′dər-bŏks′) *n.* **1.** A metal box for holding tinder and usually flint and steel. **2.** A potentially explosive place, person, or situation.
tine (tīn) *n.* **1.** A branch of a deer's antlers. **2.** A prong on a fork, pitchfork, or similar implement. [Middle English *tind, tene,* Old English *tind,* from Germanic *tind-* (unattested), point.]
tin•e•a (tĭn′ē-ə) *n.* Any of several fungous skin diseases, especially ringworm. [Latin *tinea*†, a gnawing worm, moth.]
tinea cap•i•tis (kăp′ə-tĭs) *n.* A fungous infection of the scalp. [New Latin, "worm of the head."]
tin ear *n. Informal.* An inability to reproduce accurately or distinguish between different sounds, especially different musical tones.
tin•foil (tĭn′foil′) *n.* **1.** A thin, pliable sheet of tin or of tin-lead alloy, used as a protective wrapping. **2.** A thin metal foil, such as aluminum foil.
ting (tĭng) *n.* A single high-pitched metallic sound, as of a small bell.
∼*intr.v.* **tinged** (tĭngd), **tinging, tings.** To give forth a ting. [Middle English *tyngen* (imitative).]
ting•a•ling (tĭng′ə-lĭng′, tĭng′ə-lĭng′) *n.* The high-pitched sound made by a small bell. [Imitative.] **—ting•a•ling** *adv.*
tinge (tĭnj) *tr.v.* **tinged** (tĭnjd), **tingeing** or **tinging, tinges. 1.** To impart a trace of color to; tint. **2.** To modify, as by the admixture of a contrasting quality: *comedy tinged with tragedy.*

~*n.* **1.** A faint trace of a color incorporated or added. **2.** A slight admixture of a modifying quality or property. [Middle English *tyn-gen,* from Latin *tingere,* to moisten, plunge, dye.]

tin·gle (tĭng′gəl) *v.* **-gled, -gling, -gles.** —*intr.* **1.** To have a prickling, stinging sensation, as from the cold or excitement: *tingle all over with joy.* **2.** To cause a prickling, stinging sensation: *The slap tingled on his cheek.* —*tr.* To cause to tingle.
~*n.* A tingling sensation. [Middle English *tinglen,* originally, to be affected with a ringing sound in the ears, perhaps variant of TIN-KLE.] —**tin·gler** *n.* —**tin·gly** *adj.*

tin god *n.* **1.** A person who is unjustifiably or mistakenly revered. **2.** A self-important person in a position of some authority.

tin hat *n.* A protective steel helmet.

tin·horn (tĭn′hôrn′) *n. Slang.* A petty braggart, especially a gambler, who pretends to be wealthier than he is.

tin·ker (tĭng′kər) *n.* **1.** A traveling mender of metal household utensils. **2.** A person who enjoys repairing and experimenting with machine parts. **3.** One who is clumsy at his work; bungler.
~*v.* **tinkered, -kering, -kers.** —*intr.* **1.** To work as a tinker. **2.** To work at or fiddle with something, often clumsily or ineffectually, with the aim of effecting repairs or improvements. —*tr.* To mend, patch up, or experiment with. —See Synonyms at **interfere.** [Middle English *tyn(e)kere,* perhaps from *tynken,* to TINKLE (perhaps from the sounds made by a tinker at work).]

tinker's damn, tinker's dam *n. Slang.* Something of the smallest value: *not worth a tinker's damn.* [From the tinker's reputed habit of cursing.]

Tin·ker·toy (tĭng′kər-toi′) *n.* A trademark for a construction toy consisting of pieces that fit together.

tin·kle (tĭng′kəl) *v.* **-kled, -kling, -kles.** —*intr.* To make a series of light metallic sounds, such as those of a small bell. —*tr.* To cause to tinkle.

~*n.* **1.** A light, clear metallic sound or series of sounds. **2.** *British Informal.* A telephone call; a ring. **3.** *British Informal.* An act of urinating. [Middle English *tynclen,* frequentative of *tynken* (imitative).] —**tin·kly** *adj.*

tin liz·zie (lĭz′ē) *n. Slang.* **1.** An automobile, the **Model T** *(see).* **2.** A dilapidated or cheap car. [From *Lizzie,* a nickname for *Elizabeth.*]

tin·ner (tĭn′ər) *n.* **1.** A tin miner. **2.** A person who makes or deals in wares made of tin; tinsmith.

tin·ni·tus (tĭn′ə-təs) *n.* A sound in the ears, such as buzzing, ringing, or whistling, caused by disease of the inner ear, certain drugs, or a defect in the auditory nerve. [Latin *tinnītus,* from the past participle of *tinnīre,* to ring, tinkle (imitative).]

tin·ny (tĭn′ē) *adj.* **-nier, -niest. 1.** Of, containing, or yielding tin. **2.** Shiny and attractive but cheaply and badly made. **3.** Having a thin metallic sound. **4.** Tasting or smelling of tin, as food from a tin can.
~*n., pl.* **tinnies.** *Australian Slang.* A can of beer. —**tin·ni·ly** *adv.* —**tin·ni·ness** *n.*

Tin Pan Alley *n.* **1.** A district associated with players, composers, and publishers of popular music. **2.** The publishers, players, and composers of popular music considered as a group; the world of commercial popular music. [From the use of *tin pans* for drums.]

tin plate *n.* Thin sheet iron or steel coated with tin.

tin-plate (tĭn′plāt′) *tr.v.* **-plated, -plating, -plates.** To coat with tin. —**tin-plat·er** *n.*

tin·pot (tĭn′pŏt′) *adj.* Worthless; contemptible: *a tinpot dictator.*

tin pyrites *n.* A mineral, **stannite** *(see).*

tin·sel (tĭn′səl) *n.* **1.** A very thin sheet, strip, or thread of a glittering material used as a decoration. **2.** Something superficially fine or attractive but basically valueless.
~*adj.* **1.** Made of, decorated with, or covered with tinsel. **2.** Gaudy and showy but basically valueless.

---

time zone

MAKING THE CLOCK CHASE THE SUN

What time it is depends on where you are

Midday is the time when the sun is at its highest in the sky but, because the world rotates once every 24 hours, this occurs at different hours around the globe. Using the sun's position as the arbiter of the clock, actual time varies minutely with every mile to the east or west, and it differs very significantly over more substantial distances. Noon in New York, for example, would be 8 P.M. (20:00) in Moscow.

With the beginning of rapid travel by railroad this variation began to pose timetable difficulties. In 1884 the International Meridian Conference adopted a plan for rationalizing times proposed by Canadian railroad planner Sir Sandford Fleming. The 360 degrees of longitude were divided by 24 to give a 15-degree section, or time zone, for each hour of the day. As the line 0° longitude ran through the Royal Observatory at Greenwich, England, the time there became known as Greenwich Mean Time.

On the other side of the globe at 180° longitude, where time is always 12 hours different from Greenwich, the longitude line became the International Date Line. Those crossing it from east to west add 24 hours and lose a day. Those going the other way subtract 24 hours and repeat a day. Like all the dividing lines of the time zones, the IDL generally follows its longitude line but deviates to avoid land areas or island groups under one government.

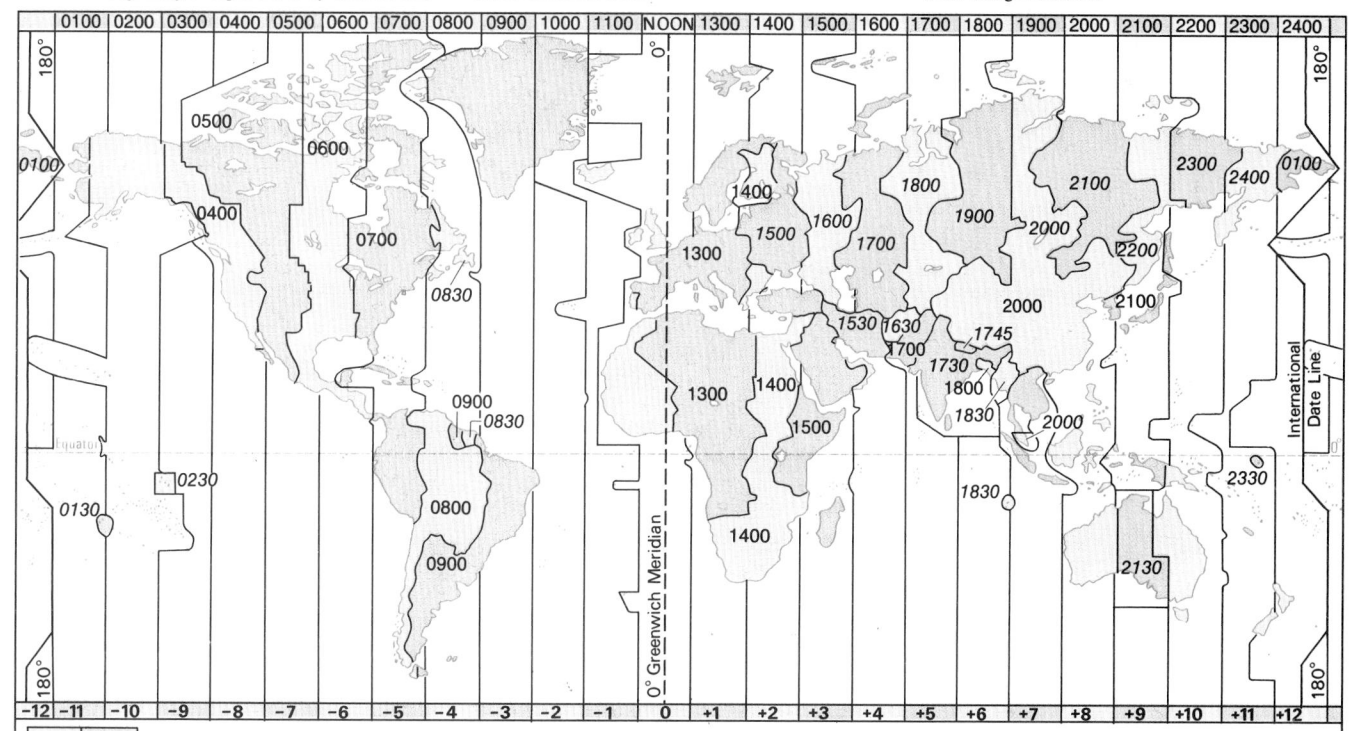

CHANGES FROM STANDARD TIME *Daylight-saving time is adopted by some countries for part of the year. During daylight-saving time, these countries are one hour ahead of the time shown on the map. The United States uses daylight-saving time from April to October. Time zones in the U.S.S.R. are 1 hour ahead of standard time.*

Standard Time Zones
Upright figures = Standard Time (e.g. 1700)
Italic figures = variations from standard time (e.g. *1530*)
Figures with minus = hours behind GMT (e.g. -4)
Figures with plus = hours ahead of GMT (e.g. +4)

~tr.v. **tinseled** or **-selled, -seling** or **-selling, -sels. 1.** To decorate with or as if with tinsel. **2.** To give a superficially fine or showy appearance to. [Earlier *tinselle,* adorned with metallic threads, probably from Old French *estincelle,* a spark, from Vulgar Latin *stincilla* (unattested), variant of Latin *scintilla,* spark.] **—tin·sel·ly** *adj.*

tin·smith (tĭn'smĭth') *n.* One who makes and repairs things made of light metal, such as tin.

tin·snips (tĭn'snĭps') *pl.n.* **Snips** *(see).*

tin·stone (tĭn'stōn') *n.* A mineral, **cassiterite** *(see).*

tint (tĭnt) *n.* **1.** A shade of a color, especially a pale or delicate variation; a tinge. **2.** A gradation of a color made by adding white to it to lessen its saturation. **3.** A slight coloration; a hue. **4.** A barely detectable modifying quality; a trace. **5.** In engraving, a shaded effect produced by a series of fine parallel lines. **6.** *Printing.* A panel of usually pale color on which matter in another color, as an illustration, may be printed. **7.** A dye for the hair. *~tr.v.* **tinted, tinting, tints.** To imbue with a tint; color. [Variant (probably influenced by Italian *tinto,* tint) of earlier *tinct,* from Latin *tinctus,* a dipping or dyeing, from the past participle of *tingere,* to wet, dip.]

tin·tack (tĭn'tăk') *n. Chiefly British.* A small, tin-covered nail, usually made of iron, with a broad flat head.

Tin·tag·el (tĭn-tăj'əl). Village on the northern coast of Cornwall, in southwestern England. It is the site of a ruined 12th-century castle reputed to have been the birthplace of King Arthur.

tin·tin·nab·u·la·tion (tĭn'tĭ-năb'yə-lā'shən) *n.* The ringing or tinkling of bells. [From TINTINNABULUM.]

tin·tin·nab·u·lum (tĭn'tĭ-năb'yə-ləm) *n., pl.* **-la** (-lə). A small, tinkling bell or set of bells. [Latin, from *tintinnāre, tintinnīre,* to jingle, reduplication of *tinnīre,* to ring. See **tinnitus.**] **—tin·tin·nab·u·lar** (tĭn'tĭ-năb'yə-lər), **tin·tin·nab·u·lar·y** (-lĕr'ē) *adj.*

tin·tom·e·ter (tĭn-tŏm'ə-tər) *n.* A colorimeter for measuring concentration. [TINT + -METER.]

Tin·to·ret·to (tĭn'tə-rĕt'ō) (1518–94). Venetian painter. Called Il Tintoretto because his father was a dyer, he was a versatile painter, handling religious, mythological, and historical subjects as well as portraits. Among his many surviving works are *St. George and the Dragon* (c. 1550) and a series of paintings illustrating the life of Christ and the Virgin (1576–88).

tin·type (tĭn'tīp') *n.* A **ferrotype** *(see).*

tin whistle *n.* A **penny whistle** *(see).*

tin·works (tĭn'wûrks') *pl.n. Used with a singular or plural verb.* A place where tin is smelted and rolled.

ti·ny (tī'nē) *adj.* **-nier, -niest.** Extremely small; minute. **—See Synonyms at small.** [From Middle English *tinet* (adjective and noun, "a little") + -Y.]

–tion *suffix.* Indicates action, process, condition, or result; for example, *adsorption.* [Middle English *-cioun,* from Old French *-tion,* from Latin *-tiō* (stem *-tiōn-*) : *-t-,* of the past participial stem + *-iōn-,* -ION.]

tip¹ (tĭp) *n.* **1.** The end or extremity of something, especially of something pointed or tapering. **2.** A piece or attachment, such as a ferrule, the end of a billiard cue, or the filter on a cigarette, fitted to the end of something. **3.** The bud of a leaf on a tea plant. **—the tip of the iceberg.** A small perceptible part of something, such as a problem or task, that hides its true dimensions. *~tr.v.* **tipped, tipping, tips. 1.** To furnish with a tip. **2.** To cover, decorate, or remove the tip of. **3.** To attach (an insert) in a book by gluing along the binding edge. Often used with *in.* **4.** To dye strands or ends of (hair or fur) in order to blend or improve appearance. [Middle English *tip(pe),* probably from Old Norse *typpi* (noun), *typpa* (verb), from Germanic *tupp-* (unattested), TOP.]

tip² *v.* **tipped, tipping, tips.** *—tr.* **1.** To knock over or upset. Usually used with *over.* **2.** To bring to a slanting position; tilt. **3.** To touch or raise (one's hat) in greeting. **4.** *British.* **a.** To empty (the contents of a container) or by as if by tilting. **b.** To dump (rubbish). *—intr.* **1.** To topple; overturn. Usually used with *over.* **2.** To become tilted; slant. *~n.* **1.** An act of tipping. **2.** A tilt or slant; incline. **3.** *British.* **a.** A place for dumping rubbish. **b.** *Informal.* A very dirty or untidy place. [Middle English *typen, tipent.*]

tip³ *tr.v.* **tipped, tipping, tips. 1.** To strike gently; tap. **2.** To hit (a baseball) with the side of the bat so that it glances off. *~n.* A light blow; tap. [Middle English *tippen,* perhaps from Low German.]

tip⁴ *n.* **1.** A small sum of money given as an acknowledgment of services rendered; a gratuity. **2. a.** A piece of advance or inside information given as a guide, as to speculation on the stock market or betting on a race. **b.** A piece of useful or helpful information. *~v.* **tipped, tipping, tips.** *—tr.* **1.** To give a tip or gratuity to. **2.** To give advance or inside information to. **3.** To mention or regard as a profitable investment or likely winner. *—intr.* To give a tip or tips. **—tip one's hand.** To reveal one's sources or intentions. [From slang *tip,* to give.] **—tip·per** *n.*

tip-cart (tĭp'kärt') *n.* A cart with a body that can be tilted to facilitate unloading.

tipi. Variant of **tepee.**

tip off *tr.v.* To provide with a tip-off; warn.

tip-off (tĭp'ôf', -ŏf') *n. Informal.* An item of advance or inside information; a hint or warning.

Tip·pe·ca·noe (tĭp'ē-kə-nōō'). River, c. 275 kilometers (170 miles) long, rising in northeastern Indiana and flowing southwest to the Wabash River. On the site of present-day Battle Ground, Indiana, Gen. William Henry Harrison was victorious over the Shawnee Indians (1811), a victory that inspired the slogan "Tippecanoe and Tyler Too" for Harrison's successful presidential campaign of 1840.

Tip·per·ar·y (tĭp'ə-râr'ē). County in south-central Republic of Ireland. It includes the Golden Vale, one of Ireland's most fertile agricultural regions. The county town, also called Tipperary, has the ruins of a 13th-century Augustinian abbey.

tip·pet (tĭp'ĭt) *n.* **1.** A covering for the shoulders, as of fur, with long ends that hang in front. **2.** A long stole worn by clergymen of the Anglican Church. **3.** A long, hanging part, as of a sleeve, hood, or cape. [Middle English *tipet,* probably a diminutive of TIP (end).]

tip·ple (tĭp'əl) *v.* **-pled, -pling, -ples.** *—intr.* To drink alcoholic liquor, especially habitually. *—tr.* To drink (alcoholic liquor), especially habitually. *~n.* An alcoholic drink, especially one taken habitually. [Back-formation from obsolete *tippler,* drunkard, from Middle English *tipeler†,* bartender.] **—tip·pler** *n.*

tip·staff (tĭp'stăf', -stäf') *n., pl.* **-staves** (-stāvz', -stăvz', -stävz') or **-staffs. 1.** A staff with a metal tip that is carried as a sign of office. **2.** An official, as a bailiff or constable, who carries a tipstaff. [Alteration of *tipped staff.*]

tip·ster (tĭp'stər) *n. Informal.* A person who gives or sells tips, especially to bettors or speculators.

tip·sy (tĭp'sē) *adj.* **-sier, -siest. 1.** Slightly drunk. **2.** Likely to tip over; unsteady; crooked. [From TIP (to tilt, be unsteady).] **—tip·si·ly** *adv.* **—tip·si·ness** *n.*

tipsy cake *n. British.* A cake soaked with wine or sherry, decorated with almonds, and served with custard.

tip·toe (tĭp'tō') *intr.v.* **-toed, -toeing, -toes. 1.** To walk or move with the heels raised and only the toes and the ball of the foot touching the ground. **2.** To walk stealthily or quietly. *~n.* The tip of a toe. **—on tiptoe. 1.** Full of anticipation; eager. **2.** Silently; stealthily. *~adj.* **1.** Standing or walking on or as if on tiptoe. **2.** Stealthy; wary. *~adv.* On or as if on tiptoe.

tip·top (tĭp'tŏp', -tŏp') *n.* The highest point or degree. *~adj.* Excellent; first-rate. *~adv.* At the highest point of excellence.

tip-up (tĭp'ŭp') *adj.* Having a horizontal part that may be tilted into an upright position, as a seat in a theater.

ti·rade (tī'rād, tī-rād') *n.* A long vehement or blustering speech, especially of denunciation or censure; a diatribe. [French, "a stretching" (as in *tout d'une tirade,* all at once stretch), from Italian *tirata,* a volley, act of drawing, from *tirare,* to draw, from Vulgar Latin *tīrāre* (unattested). See **tier** (layer).]

Ti·ra·na, Ti·ra·në (tĭ-rä'nə). Capital of Albania, on the Ishm River in Albania's central plain. It is the largest and industrially most important city in the country.

tire¹ (tīr) *v.* **tired, tiring, tires.** *—intr.* **1.** To become weak or fatigued as a result of exertion. **2.** To lose interest or grow impatient; weary. Often used with *of: He tired of reading. —tr.* **1.** To diminish the strength or energy of; weary; fatigue. Often used with *out.* **2.** To exhaust the interest or patience of; bore. [Middle English *tyren,* to stop, tire, Old English *tēorian†.*]

tire² *n. Also British* **tyre. 1.** A solid or air-filled covering for a wheel, typically made of rubber reinforced with cords of material such as nylon or fiber glass, fitted around the wheel's rim to absorb shock and provide traction. **2.** A hoop of metal or rubber fitted around a wheel. [Middle English *tyre,* curved metal plates for wheels, probably from *tyr,* attire.]

tire³ *tr.v.* **tired, tiring, tires.** *Archaic.* To adorn or attire. *~n. Archaic.* **1.** Attire. **2.** A covering or ornament for the head or hair. [Middle English *tiren,* short for *attiren,* to ATTIRE.]

tire chain *n.* A **snow chain** *(see).*

tired (tīrd) *adj.* **1. a.** Worn-out; fatigued. **b.** Impatient, fed up, or no longer interested. **2.** Overused; hackneyed. **—tired·ness** *n.*
   Synonyms: *exhausted, fatigued, jaded, weary.*

tire·less (tīr'lĭs) *adj.* Untiring; indefatigable. **—tire·less·ly** *adv.* **—tire·less·ness** *n.*

Ti·re·si·as (tī-rē'sē-əs, -zē-əs). A blind prophet of Thebes prominent in many Greek myths and tragedies.

tire·some (tīr'səm) *adj.* Causing boredom or annoyance; tedious or irritating. **—See Synonyms at boring. —tire·some·ly** *adv.* **—tire·some·ness** *n.*

tire·wom·an (tīr'wŏom'ən) *n., pl.* **-women** (-wĭm'ĭn). *Archaic.* A lady's maid. [From TIRE (attire).]

tiro. Variant of **tyro.**

Tirol. See **Tyrol.**

Ti·ryns (tī'rĭnz, tîr'ĭnz). Ancient city of Greece, in the northeastern Peloponnese, near Argos. Excavations of the site have revealed extensive pre-Homeric palaces of the Mycenaean period and other prehistoric remains.

'tis (tĭz). *Archaic & Poetic.* Contraction of *it is.*

ti·sane, pti·san (tĭ-zăn', -zän') *n.* A preparation such as an herbal infusion drunk as a beverage or for its mildly medicinal effect. [French, from Latin *ptisana,* barley, PTISAN.]

Tish·ri (tĭsh'rē) *n.* The first month of the civil year in the Hebrew calendar. See feature at **calendar.** [Hebrew *Tishrī,* from Akkadian *Tashrītu,* from *shurrū,* to begin.]

Ti·siph·o·ne (tĭ-sĭf'ə-nē). One of the three **Furies** *(see).*

tis·sue (tĭsh'ōō) *n.* **1.** *Biology.* **a.** An aggregation of cells that are

tit *The Paridae family of small Eurasian birds. The great tit (above) is the largest member of the family, growing to a length of about 14 centimeters (5½ inches). Tits are readily attracted to nuts hung in gardens, but in the wild they feed largely on caterpillars and other insects; it has been estimated that a pair of adult great tits will catch more than 2,000 insects a week to feed themselves and their nestlings.*

specialized to perform a certain function: *nervous tissue.* **b.** Cellular matter regarded as a collective entity. **2.** A soft, very absorbent piece of paper, generally made up of two thin layers, and used as a disposable handkerchief or towel. **3.** Unsized thin, translucent paper used for packing, wrapping, or protecting delicate articles. Also called "tissue paper." **4.** A woven fabric, usually of a fine, delicate texture. **5.** An interwoven or interrelated series; web; network: *His evidence was nothing but a tissue of lies.* [Middle English *tissu,* a rich cloth, fine gauze, from Old French, from the past participle of *tistre,* to weave, from Latin *texere.*]

tissue culture *n.* **1.** The growth in a suitable medium of specimens of tissue removed from a living organism. **2.** The tissue so grown.

tit[1] (tĭt) *n.* **1.** Any of various small Old World birds of the family Paridae, such as the **blue tit** *(see),* typically feeding on insects and seeds. Sometimes called "titmouse." **2.** Any of various similar or related birds. [Probably from Scandinavian, from a word referring to small objects; compare Icelandic *titlingr,* sparrow.]

tit[2] *n.* A teat or nipple. [Middle English *titte,* Old English *titt,* from West Germanic *titta* (unattested).]

Tit. Titus (New Testament).

ti·tan (tīt′n) *n.* A person of colossal size, strength, ability, or achievement. [From TITAN.]

Ti·tan[1] (tīt′n). *Greek Mythology.* One of a family of primordial gods, the children of Uranus and Gaea, overthrown and succeeded by the Olympian gods. [Middle English, from Latin, from Greek *Titan,* from *titō†,* day, sun.]

Titan[2] *n. Astronomy.* The largest satellite of Saturn and probably the largest in the solar system. [After TITAN.]

ti·tan·ate (tīt′n-āt′) *n.* A salt of titanic acid. [TITAN(IUM) + -ATE (salt).]

Ti·tan·ess (tīt′n-ĭs) *Greek Mythology.* A female Titan.

Ti·ta·ni·a[1] (tĭ-tā′nē-ə, tī-). In medieval folklore, the queen of the fairies, wife of Oberon.

Titania[2] *n.* One of the satellites of the planet Uranus.

ti·tan·ic[1] (tī-tăn′ĭk) *adj.* **1. a.** Having great stature or enormous strength; huge; colossal. **b.** Of enormous scope, power, or influence. **2. Titanic.** Of or pertaining to the Titans. [After TITAN.] —**ti·tan·i·cal·ly** *adv.*

ti·tan·ic[2] (tī-tăn′ĭk, -tā′nĭk, tī-) *adj.* Pertaining to or containing titanium. Said especially of compounds containing titanium with a valence of 4. [TITAN(IUM) + -IC.]

titanic acid *n.* **1.** A white, powdered inorganic acid, H_2TiO_3, derived from an acid solution of titanates and used as a mordant. **2.** Titanium dioxide.

ti·tan·if·er·ous (tīt′n-ĭf′ər-əs) *adj.* Containing or yielding titanium. [TITANI(UM) + -FEROUS.]

Ti·tan·ism (tīt′n-ĭz′əm) *n.* The spirit of rebellion; defiance of and revolt against authority, convention, or the established order. [After TITAN.]

ti·tan·ite (tīt′n-īt′) *n.* A mineral, **sphene** *(see).* [German *Titanit* : TITAN(IUM) + -ITE.]

ti·ta·ni·um (tī-tā′nē-əm, tī-) *n. Symbol* **Ti** A strong, low-density, highly corrosion-resistant, lustrous white metallic element that occurs widely in igneous rocks and is used to alloy aircraft metals for low weight, strength, and high-temperature stability. Atomic number 22, atomic weight 47.90, melting point 1,677°C, boiling point 3,277°C, specific gravity 4.54, valences 2, 3, 4. [New Latin, from Greek *Titan,* TITAN.]

titanium dioxide *n.* A white powder, TiO_2, used as an opaque white pigment. Also called "titanic acid."

titanium white *n.* Titanium dioxide used as a paint pigment with great covering power and durability.

ti·tan·o·there (tī-tăn′ə-thîr′) *n.* Any of various extinct herbivorous mammals of the genus *Brontotherium* and related genera, of the Eocene and Oligocene epochs, resembling the rhinoceros. [New Latin *Titanotherium,* "gigantic beast" : TITAN + -THERE.]

ti·tan·ous (tī-tăn′əs, -tā′nəs, tī-) *adj.* Pertaining to or containing titanium. Said especially of compounds containing titanium with a valence of 3. [TITAN(IUM) + -OUS.]

titbit. Variant of **tidbit.**

ti·ter, ti·tre (tī′tər) *n.* **1.** The concentration of a substance in solution or the strength of such a substance determined by titration. **2.** The minimum volume needed to cause a particular result in titration. **3.** A measure of the amount of antibody present in blood serums. [French *titre,* a title, designation of rank, qualification, fineness of gold or silver in an alloy, from Old French *title,* TITLE.]

tit for tat *n.* Repayment in kind, as for an injury; retaliation. [Alteration of *tip for tap.*]

tithe (tīth) *n.* **1.** A tenth part of one's annual income or produce, either in kind or money, contributed voluntarily for charitable purposes or due as a tax for the support of the clergy or church. **2.** Any tax or levy of one tenth. **3. a.** The tenth part of something. **b.** A very small part; a fraction. ~*v.* **tithed, tithing, tithes.** —*tr.* **1.** To contribute or pay a tenth part of (one's annual income). **2.** To levy a tithe upon. —*intr.* To pay a tithe. [Middle English *tithe,* Old English *tēotha, teogetha,* TENTH.] —**tith·a·ble** (tī′thə-bəl) *adj.* —**tith·er** (tī′thər) *n.*

tith·ing (tī′thĭng) *n.* **1.** The act of levying or paying tithes. **2.** A tithe. **3.** In English history: **a.** A unit consisting of ten householders in the system of **frankpledge** *(see).* **b.** A rural administrative division originally corresponding to the area occupied by such a unit.

ti·ti (tĭ′tĭ′, tē′tē′) *n.* Any of various small, long-tailed South American

monkeys of the genus *Callicebus,* having long, soft, often brightly colored fur. [Spanish, perhaps of Tupian origin.]

ti·tian (tĭsh′ən) *n.* A golden red or auburn. [After TITIAN, from his frequent use of the color in his paintings.] —**ti·tian** *adj.*

Ti·tian (tĭsh′ən), born Tiziano Vecellio *(c.* 1488–1576). Venetian painter. His greatest works include the altarpiece *The Assumption of the Virgin* (1518), the *Pesaro Madonna (c.* 1520), and *Paul III and His Grandsons* (1546). Titian's brilliant use of color and his use of backgrounds, landscapes, and sunsets as part of the composition made him one of the greatest Renaissance artists.

Ti·ti·ca·ca (tē′tē-kä′kə). Lake of South America, lying high in the Andes on the Peru-Bolivia border. It covers *c.* 9,065 square kilometers (3,500 square miles) and is the largest freshwater lake in South

---

Titian

VIGOR AND VIBRANCY IN AN ITALIAN MASTER
The 16th-century painter whose free style anticipated Impressionism

Although Titian (Tiziano Vecellio, *c.* 1488–1576) trained under Gentile and Giovanni Bellini, he was greatly influenced by Giorgione. After the deaths of these masters, Titian was the most important painter of the Venetian school and brought to it a vigor and color it had not previously known. With his vibrant colors, especially reds and blues, he painted religious and mythological subjects and portraits.

In 1516 he succeeded Giovanni Bellini as official painter of Venice and in the same year began the large, dramatic *Assumption of the Virgin* (finished in 1518) for the Frari church, which established his reputation. He painted other studies of the Madonna, including *The Madonna of the Cherries (c.* 1515) and *The Madonna with a Rabbit* (1530).

He also delighted in painting beautiful women

with richly colored auburn hair; among them were *Flora (c.* 1521), *Venus Anadyomene (c.* 1525), *La Bella (c.* 1536), *St. Mary Magdalen (c.* 1533), and *Venus of Urbino* (1538).

Titian was much sought after by Italian and European rulers, and in 1532 the emperor Charles V became his patron. In 1548 he painted his famous equestrian portrait, *Charles V at the Battle of Muhlberg.* Earlier works, for the Duke of Ferrara, included *The Bacchanal of the Andrians, The Worship of Venus,* and *Bacchus and Ariadne.*

In his later years, Titian developed a very free style that almost anticipated Impressionism, and is said to have applied paint with his fingers almost as much as with a brush so as to achieve the correct tonal effects. Among the works of his old age is a self-portrait.

A LANDMARK IN FORM *Titian achieved a remarkably lifelike quality in his* Young Englishman (c.*1540*), *the eyes gazing directly from warm flesh tones offset by the deeper-toned background.*

America. It is plied by steamboats and at a height of 3,810 meters (12,500 feet) above sea level is the world's highest large lake.

tit·il·late (tĭt'l-āt') *tr.v.* **-lated, -lating, -lates.** **1.** To stimulate by tickling or touching lightly. **2.** To arouse or excite agreeably. [From Latin *tītillāre* (past participle *tītillātus*), to tickle, of imitative origin.] **—tit·il·lat·ing·ly** *adv.* **—tit·il·la·tion** *n.* **—tit·il·la·tive** *adj.*

tit·i·vate, tit·ti·vate (tĭt'ə-vāt') *tr.v.* **-vated, -vating, -vates.** To enhance the appearance of by means of decorative additions; smarten up. [Perhaps TIDY + (CULTI)VATE.] **—tit·i·va·tion** *n.*

tit·lark (tĭt'lärk') *n.* A bird, the **pipit** *(see).* [TIT(MOUSE) + LARK.]

ti·tle (tīt'l) *n.* **1.** An identifying name given to a book, play, film, musical composition, work of art, or the like. **2. a.** All the material that appears on the title page of a book. **b.** A general or descriptive heading, as of a book chapter. **c.** A particular book or other publication, rather than any one copy of it: *They publish mainly historical titles.* **3. a. titles.** Written matter included in a motion picture or television program to give credits. **b.** A subtitle in a motion picture. **4. a.** The heading that names a legal document or statute. **b.** The heading given to any legal action or proceeding, showing the name of the court, the name of the parties involved, and other relevant information. **5.** A division of a law book, declaration, or statute, generally larger than a section or article. **6.** *Law.* **a.** The sum of all the factors or events that constitute or justify a person's legal right to control and dispose of property or a claim. **b.** The legal instrument, such as a title deed, that provides evidence of such a right. **7. a.** Anything that provides ground for or justifies a claim. **b.** An acknowledged or alleged right. **8. a.** A formal appellation, such as *Mrs., Dr., Sir,* or *Professor,* prefixed to or substituted for a person's name, and used as a respectful term of address indicating office, rank, or attainment. **b.** Such an appellation as an indication of nobility. **9.** A descriptive appellation; an epithet. **10.** *Sports.* A championship. **11.** Proof that one has a source of income or area of work, as a prerequisite for ordination in the Church of England. **12.** *Roman Catholic Church.* A titular church. —See Synonyms at **right.**
~*tr.v.* **titled, -tling, -tles.** To give a title to; confer a name upon. [Middle English, from Old French, from Latin *titulus,* superscription, label, title.]

ti·tled (tīt'əld) *adj.* Having a title, especially of nobility.

title deed *n.* A deed that shows or provides evidence for a person's title to real property.

ti·tle·hold·er (tīt'l-hōl'dər) *n.* The unbeaten champion in a particular sports competition.

title page *n. Abbr.* **t.p.** A page at the front of a book giving the complete title, the names of the author and publisher, and the place of publication.

title role *n.* The part of the character after whom a play or film is named.

tit·mouse (tĭt'mous') *n., pl.* **-mice** (-mīs'). A bird, the **tit** *(see).* [Middle English *titmose* : TIT (bird) + Old English *māse,* titmouse, from West Germanic *maisō* (unattested); assimilated to MOUSE.]

Ti·to (tē'tō), **Marshal,** born Josip Broz (1892–1980). Communist leader of Yugoslavia. He led the Yugoslav resistance to Nazi occupation from 1941 to 1945. After the war the Yugoslav monarchy was abolished, and Tito became prime minister (1945) and president (1953). In 1948 he broke with the U.S.S.R. and developed Yugoslavia's own brand of national communism, preserving a neutral position in foreign affairs and accepting aid from East and West.

Ti·to·grad (tē'tō-grăd'). Capital of Montenegro, southern Yugoslavia, known as Podgorica until 1946. It was almost completely rebuilt after being severely damaged in World War II.

Ti·to·ism (tē'tō-ĭz'əm) *n.* The Communist policies and practices associated with Marshal Tito of Yugoslavia; especially, the assertion by a Communist state of its national interests independently of and often in opposition to Soviet policy. **—Ti·to·ist** *n. & adj.*

ti·trant (tī'trənt) *n. Chemistry.* The solution added in regulated amounts in a titration.

ti·trate (tī'trāt') *v.* **-trated, -trating, -trates.** —*tr.* To determine the concentration of (a solution) by titration. —*intr.* To perform the operation of titration. [From French *titrer,* from *titre,* TITER.]

ti·tra·tion (tī-trā'shən) *n.* **1.** The process or method of determining the concentration of a substance in solution by adding to it a standard reagent of known concentration in carefully measured amounts until a reaction of definite and known proportion is completed, as shown by a color change or by electrical measurement. **2.** An analogous technique applied to mixtures of gases.

titre. Variant of **titer.**

tit·ter (tĭt'ər) *intr.v.* **-tered, -tering, -ters.** To utter a nervous, stifled giggle, as in ridicule or childish amusement. [Imitative.] **—tit·ter** *n.* **—tit·ter·er** *n.* **—tit·ter·ing·ly** *adv.*

tittivate. Variant of **titivate.**

tit·tle (tĭt'l) *n.* **1.** A small diacritical mark, such as an accent, vowel point, or dot over an *i.* **2.** The tiniest bit; an iota. [Middle English *titel,* a diacritical mark, from Medieval Latin *titulus,* from Latin, TITLE.]

tit·tle-tat·tle (tĭt'l-tăt'l) *n.* Petty gossip; trivial talk.
~*intr.v.* **tittle-tattled, -tling, -tles.** To engage in idle talk or gossip; prattle. [Reduplication of TATTLE.]

tit·tup (tĭt'əp) *intr.v.* **-tuped** or **-tupped, -tuping** or **-tupping, -tups.** To move in an affected, lively manner; prance.
~*n.* A lively, affected manner of moving or walking; a prance or caper. [Imitative of the sounds of a horse's hoofs.]

tit·u·ba·tion (tĭch'ŏŏ-bā'shən) *n.* A staggering or stumbling gait associated with a nodding movement of the head, characteristic of certain nervous disorders. [Latin *titubātiō* (stem *titubātiōn-*), from *titubātus,* past participle of *titubāre*†, to reel, stagger.]

tit·u·lar (tĭch'ŏŏ-lər) *adj.* **1.** Pertaining to, having the nature of, or constituting a title. **2.** Existing as such in name only; nominal: *the titular head of the company.* **3.** Bearing a title. **4.** Of or designating one of the ancient churches in or near Rome from which a cardinal takes his title.
~*n.* Also **tit·u·lar·y** (tĭch'ŏŏ-lĕr'ē) *pl.* **-ies.** A person who holds a title. [From Latin *titulus,* TITLE.] **—tit·u·lar·ly** *adv.*

titular bishop *n. Roman Catholic Church.* A bishop who normally acts as an auxiliary bishop in a diocese and who is nominally appointed to a diocese in a remote part of the world.

Ti·tus (tī'təs) *n. Abbr.* **Tit.** An epistle in the New Testament attributed to Saint Paul and addressed to Titus, his disciple.

Ti·u (tē'ŏŏ). *Germanic Mythology.* The god of war and the sky, identified with the Norse god Tyr. [Old English *Tīw,* from Germanic *Tīwaz* (unattested), akin to Latin *deus,* god. See **Tuesday.**]

Tiv·o·li (tĭv'ə-lē). City in central Italy. It is the site of the Villa d'Este, with its famous Renaissance gardens, built in 1550, and it also has several Roman ruins, including the villa of Emperor Hadrian.

tiz·zy (tĭz'ē) *n., pl.* **-zies.** *Slang.* A state of nervous confusion; a dither. [20th century : origin obscure.]

T-junc·tion (tē'jŭngk'shən) *n.* A right-angled junction, as of two roads or pipes, forming a shape like the letter T.

TKO technical knockout.

Tl The symbol for the element thallium.

Tlax·ca·la (tlä-skä'lä). State in east-central Mexico, formerly the territory of the Tlaxcaltec Indians. The state capital, also called Tlaxcala, is the site of the oldest Christian church in the New World, founded by Cortés in 1521.

TLC (tē'ĕl-sē') *n. Informal.* Tender loving care.

Tlin·git (tlĭng'gĭt) *n., pl.* **-gits** or collectively **Tlingit. 1.** A member of any of a group of North American Indian seafaring peoples inhabiting the coastal areas of southern Alaska and northern British Columbia. **2.** A linguistic family of the Na-Dene phylum consisting only of the language of the Tlingit.

T lymphocyte *n.* A **T cell** *(see).*

Tm The symbol for the element thulium.

TM transcendental meditation.

tme·sis (tmē'sĭs, mē'-) *n.* The separation of the parts of a compound word by one or more intervening words, as *where I go ever* instead of *wherever I go.* [Late Latin *tmēsis,* "a cutting," from Greek, from *temnein,* to cut.]

TMV tobacco mosaic virus.

TN Tennessee (used with a Zip Code).

TNT (tē'ĕn-tē') *n.* An explosive compound, **trinitrotoluene** *(see).*

to (tŏŏ; *unstressed* tə) *prep.* **1.** In a direction toward; so as to approach or come near: *the road to Paris; bear to the right.* **2.** So as to reach or terminate in: *a trip to Scotland.* **3.** Altogether and including: *drunk to the last man.* **4.** Through an intervening space or time; right up until: *a nine-to-five job; rotten to the core.* **5.** Through a standard intervening series or arrangement and terminating in: *from A to Z; strong to gale force winds.* **6.** To the extent of: *starved to death.* **7.** In contact with: *dancing cheek to cheek; apply polish to the shoes.* **8.** In front of: *face to face.* **9.** For the attention, benefit, or possession of: *Tell it to me.* **10.** For the purpose of; for: *She worked to that end.* **11.** For, of, or associated with: *the belt to this dress; secretary to the director.* **12.** Concerning or regarding; in response to: *deaf to her pleas.* **13.** In relation with: *parallel to the road.* **14.** Together with or as an accompaniment or addition for: *Sing to the music.* **15.** With regard to: *the way to his heart.* **16.** Composing or constituting; in: *two pints to the quart.* **17.** In correspondence or accordance with: *not to my liking; add sugar to taste.* **18.** So as to reach a specified total or result: *The bill came to $25. It all adds up to a remarkable victory.* **19.** Before: *ten to five; only three weeks to Christmas.* **20.** In honor of: *a toast to his success.* **21.** Used in expressions of comparison or contrast: *bears no resemblance to the original plan; odds of 20 to 1.* **22.** Used to indicate: **a.** A progression toward a specified condition: *her rise to power.* **b.** An action resulting in a specified condition: *The flag was torn to shreds. To my amazement he agreed.* **c.** A process of change resulting in a specified condition: *Their laughter soon turned to tears.*
~*adv.* **1.** Into a position or condition, especially shut or closed: *He slammed the door to.* **2.** Into consciousness: *He came to.* **3.** Into a state of application to the matter, action, or work at hand: *We sat down for lunch and fell to.* **4.** In proximity: *have never seen him close to.* **5.** *Nautical.* Turned into the wind. Used of a sailing vessel. [Middle English *to,* Old English *tō, te.*] —See Usage note at **try.**

toad (tōd) *n.* **1.** Any of numerous tailless amphibians chiefly of the family Bufonidae, related to and resembling the frogs but characteristically more terrestrial and having rougher, drier skin. **2.** A lizard, the **horned toad** *(see).* **3.** A repulsive person. [Middle English *tadde, tode,* Old English *tādi(g)e*†.]

toad·eat·er (tōd'ē'tər) *n.* A toady.

toad·fish (tōd'fĭsh') *n., pl.* **-fishes** or collectively **toadfish.** Any of various bottom-dwelling, chiefly marine fishes of the family Batrachoididae, having a broad, flattened head and a wide mouth.

toad·flax (tōd'flăks') *n.* Any of various plants of the genus *Linaria,* having narrow leaves and spurred, two-lipped flowers; especially,

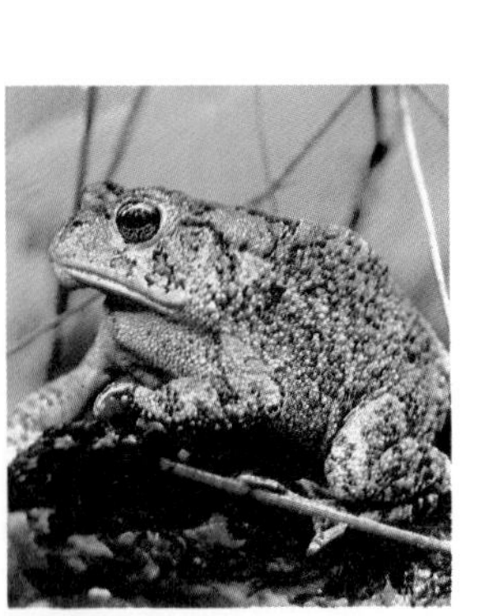

toad *Worldwide, there are about 250 species of toad, all members of the scientific family Bufonidae. The large glands behind their eyes contain a poison that makes them distasteful to predators.*

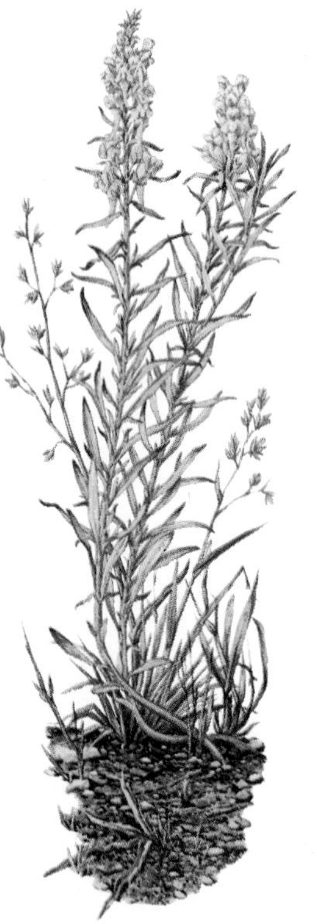

toadflax *Creeping roots spread this plant over uncultivated land.*

the common wildflower, **butter-and-eggs** *(see).* [TOAD + FLAX (from the flaxlike appearance of its foliage).]
toad-in-the-hole (tōd′ĭn-*thə*-hōl′) *n. British.* A dish consisting of sausages baked in a batter.
toad spit *n.* An insect secretion, **cuckoo spit** *(see).*
toad·stone (tōd′stōn′) *n.* A dark-colored basaltic or glassy volcanic rock. It is often associated with mineral veins but contains no ore. [Probably from German *Tödestein,* dead or worthless stone.]
toad·stool (tōd′sto͞ol′) *n.* An inedible fungus with an umbrella-shaped fruiting body, as distinguished from an edible mushroom.
toad·y (tō′dē) *n., pl.* **-ies.** A servile flatterer; a sycophant. —See Synonyms at **sycophant.**
~*v.* **toadied, -ying, -ies.** *—tr.* To be a toady to. *—intr.* To be a toady; fawn. [From TOADEATER.]
to and fro *adv.* In one direction and then the opposite; back and forth. **—to-and-fro** (to͞o′ən-frō′) *adj.*
toast¹ (tōst) *v.* **toasted, toasting, toasts.** *—tr.* **1.** To heat and brown (bread, for example) by placing close to a fire, under a grill, or in a toaster. **2.** To warm thoroughly, as before a fire: *toast one's feet. —intr.* To become toasted.
~*n.* Sliced bread heated and browned. [Middle English *tosten,* from Old French *toster,* from Vulgar Latin *tostāre* (unattested), from Latin *torrēre* (past participle *tostus*), to dry, parch.]
toast² *n.* **1.** A person, institution, sentiment, or the like to whose health or in whose honor a group of people drink. **2.** The act of proposing the health or honor of a person or thing as a toast. **3.** One receiving much acclaim. **4.** *Archaic.* A lady to whose beauty or charms toasts are frequently proposed.
~*v.* **toasted, toasting, toasts.** *—tr.* To drink to the health or honor of. *—intr.* To propose or drink a toast. [From TOAST (from the use of spiced toast to flavor drinks).]
toast·er (tō′stər) *n.* A device used to toast bread by exposure to electrically heated wire coils.
toast·mas·ter (tōst′măs′tər, -mäs′tər) *n.* One who proposes the toasts and introduces the guests or speakers at a banquet.
toast·mis·tress (tōst′mĭs′trĭs) *n.* A woman who serves as a toastmaster.
to·bac·co (tə-băk′ō) *n., pl.* **-cos** or **-coes.** **1.** Any of various plants of the genus *Nicotiana;* especially, *N. tabacum,* native to tropical America, widely cultivated for its leaves, which are used primarily for smoking. **2.** The leaves of cultivated tobacco, dried and processed chiefly for use in cigarettes, snuff, or cigars, or for smoking in pipes. **3.** Products made from tobacco. **4.** The habit of using tobacco: *gave up tobacco for good.* **5.** A crop of tobacco. [Earlier *tabac(c)o,* from Spanish *tabaco,* perhaps from a Taino word referring to leaves rolled for smoking (taken by the Spanish as referring to the plant itself).]
tobacco mosaic virus *n. Abbr.* **TMV** The virus that causes mosaic disease in tobacco plants and the first virus to be discovered (1892).
to·bac·co·nist (tə-băk′ə-nĭst) *n.* **1.** *Chiefly British.* A shopkeeper who sells tobacco, cigarettes, pipes, matches, and other equipment used by smokers. **2.** A dealer in tobacco. [Irregularly from TOBACCO + -IST.]
Tobago Island. See **Trinidad and Tobago.**
to-be (to͞o-bē′, tə-bē′) *adj.* That is to be; future. Usually used in combination: *bride-to-be.*
To·bit (tō′bĭt) *n.* A book of the Old Testament Apocrypha, named after its hero, a Hebrew captive in Nineveh. Also called "Tobias."
to·bog·gan (tə-bŏg′ən) *n.* **1.** A long, light, runnerless vehicle made of thin boards curved upward at the front, originally used by Canadian Indians for transporting goods over snow and ice. **2.** A similar vehicle, often equipped with runners, used for coasting down slopes.
~*intr.v.* **tobogganed, -ganing, -gans.** **1.** To coast, ride, or travel on a toboggan. **2.** To decline or fall rapidly: *His good fortune tobogganed.* [Canadian French *tobagan,* from Algonquian; compare Micmac *tobākan.*] **—to·bog·gan·er, to·bog·gan·ist** *n.*
to·by, To·by (tō′bē) *n., pl.* **-bies.** A drinking mug usually in the shape of a stout man wearing a large three-cornered hat. Also called "Toby jug." [After *Toby,* a nickname for *Tobias.*]
toc·ca·ta (tə-kä′tə) *n.* A composition for organ or other keyboard instrument in a free style intended to show off the technical virtuosity of the performer. [Italian, "a touching" (originally a piece intended to show touch technique), from the feminine past participle of *toccare,* to touch, from Vulgar Latin *toccāre* (unattested), to strike, TOUCH.]
To·char·i·an, To·khar·i·an (tō-kâr′ē-ən, -kär′ē-ən) *n.* **1.** A member of a people of possible European origin living in Asia until about the 10th century A.D. **2.** An Indo-European language with eastern and western dialects, *Tocharian A* and *Tocharian B,* respectively, attested in documents of the 7th century. [French *Tocharien,* from Latin *Tochari,* from Greek *Tokharoi*†.]
to·col·o·gy, to·kol·o·gy (tō-kŏl′ə-jē) *n.* Obstetrics. [Greek *tokos,* childbirth, from *tiktein,* to beget + -LOGY.]
to·coph·er·ol (tō-kŏf′ə-rôl′, -rōl′) *n.* Any of a group of four chemically related compounds, differing slightly in structure, that together constitute **vitamin E** *(see).* Deficiency leads to sterility in rodents, and the vitamin is thought to be necessary for fertility in other vertebrates. [Greek *tokos,* childbirth (see **tocology**) + Greek *pherein,* to carry, bear + -OL.]
Tocque·ville (tŏk′vĭl′, tōk′-, tôk-vēl′), **Alexis-Charles-Henri Clérel de** (1805–59). French statesman, traveler, and historian. After touring the United States (1831–32), he wrote his classic study, *Democracy in America* (1832), which helped establish the view of the United States as a land of equality and opportunity.
toc·sin (tŏk′sĭn) *n.* **1.** An alarm sounded on a bell, or the bell on which it is sounded. **2.** Any warning sign; an omen. [French, from Old French *toquesain,* from Old Provençal *tocasenh* : *tocar,* to strike (a bell), touch, from Vulgar Latin *toccāre* (unattested), to ring a bell, TOUCH + *senh,* bell, from Latin *signum,* token, SIGN.]
tod¹ (tŏd) *n.* **1.** *Chiefly British.* A unit of weight used in the wool trade, usually equivalent to 28 pounds. **2.** *British.* A bushy clump, especially of ivy. [Middle English *todd(e),* a unit of weight, probably from Low Dutch; akin to Middle Low German *toddelen,* to fall apart into bunches, and Old High German *zot(t)a,* a tuft, from Germanic *toddōn* (unattested).]
tod² *n. Chiefly Scottish.* A fox. [Middle English : origin obscure.]
to·day (tə-dā′) *adv.* **1.** During or on this present day. **2.** During or at the present time.
~*n.* The present day, time, or age. [Middle English *to day,* Old English *tōdæg(e),* on this day : TO + *dæge,* dative of *dæg,* DAY.]
tod·dle (tŏd′l) *intr.v.* **-dled, -dling, -dles.** **1.** To walk with short, unsteady steps, as a young child does. **2.** *Informal.* **a.** To saunter; stroll: *toddle down to the pub.* **b.** To depart: *must toddle off.* [16th century : origin obscure.] **—tod·dle** *n.*
tod·dler (tŏd′lər) *n.* **1.** A young child who has learned to walk but not yet perfectly. **2.** A size of clothing for children between the ages of about one and three years.
tod·dy (tŏd′ē) *n., pl.* **-dies.** **1.** A drink consisting of whiskey or other liquor combined with hot water, sugar, spices, and lemon. Also called "hot toddy." **2. a.** The sweet sap of several tropical Asian palm trees, especially *Caryota urens,* used as a drink and as a leavening agent. **b.** An alcoholic drink fermented from this sap. [Hindi *tārī,* sap of a palm, from *tār,* palm yielding toddy, from Sanskrit *tāla.*]
to-do (tə-do͞o′) *n., pl.* **-dos** (-do͞oz′). *Informal.* A commotion or fuss.
to·dy (tō′dē) *n., pl.* **-dies.** Any of various small, colorful birds of the family Todidae, of the West Indies. [French *todier,* from Latin *todus*†, name of a small bird.]
toe (tō) *n.* **1. a.** One of the digits of the human foot. **b.** The corresponding digit in other vertebrate animals. **2.** The part of a shoe, sock, or the like that covers the toes. **3. a.** The base or lower tip of something, such as the end of the head on a golf club. **b.** Anything suggestive of a toe in form, function, or location. **—on one's toes.** Alert; ready to act. **—step** (or **tread**) **on someone's toes.** To offend or annoy someone, especially by interfering in his sphere of action or responsibility. **—toe the mark** (or **line**). **1.** To touch a mark or line with the toes or hands in readiness for the start of a race or competition. **2.** To obey rules conscientiously.
~*v.* **toed, toeing, toes.** *—tr.* **1.** To touch, kick, or trace with the toe. **2.** To drive (a golf ball) with the toe of the club. **3. a.** To drive (a nail or spike, for example) obliquely. **b.** To secure (beams, for example) with nails driven obliquely. *—intr.* To walk or move with the toes pointed in a specified direction: *He toes out.* [Middle English *ta, to,* Old English *tā.*]
toe·a (toi′ə) *n., pl.* **toea.** A monetary unit equal to 1/100 of the kina of Papua New Guinea. See feature at **currency.** [Probably Pidgin English, from English DOLLAR.]
toe·cap (tō′kăp′) *n.* A reinforced covering of leather or metal for the toe of a shoe or boot.
toe clip *n.* An attachment to a bicycle pedal that fits over the foot to prevent it from slipping.
toed (tōd) *adj.* Having a toe or toes, especially of a specified kind or number. Usually used in combination: *a two-toed sloth.*
toe dance *n.* A dance performed on the toes by means of specially reinforced ballet slippers. **—toe dancer** *n.*
toe·hold (tō′hōld′) *n.* **1.** A small indentation or ledge on which the toe can find support in climbing; a small foothold. **2.** Any slight or initial advantage or means of access providing a basis for future progress: *Family connections gave him a toehold in politics.* **3.** A wrestling hold in which one competitor wrenches the other's foot.
toe-in (tō′ĭn′) *n.* The adjustment of the front wheels of a motor vehicle so that they turn slightly inward.
toe·nail (tō′nāl′) *n.* **1.** The nail on a toe. **2.** A nail driven obliquely, as to join vertical and horizontal beams.
~*tr.v.* **toenailed, -nailing, -nails.** To secure (beams) with obliquely driven nails.
toff (tŏf) *n. British Slang.* **1.** A dandy. **2.** Any member of the upper classes. [Probably variant of TUFT, a titled undergraduate (from the gold tassel formerly worn on caps by titled students).]
tof·fee (tŏf′ē, tô′fē) *n.* **1.** A hard or chewy candy made of brown sugar and butter boiled together. **2.** A small piece of toffee. [Alteration of TAFFY.]
tof·fee-nosed (tŏf′ē-nōzd′, tô′fē-) *adj. Chiefly British Slang.* Snobbish; stuck-up.
toft (tôft, tŏft) *n. British Archaic.* **1.** A homestead. **2.** A hillock. [Middle English *toft,* Old English *toft,* site of a building, homestead, from Old Norse *topt.*]
to·fu (tō′fo͞o) *n.* **Bean curd** *(see).* [Japanese, from Chinese.]
tog (tŏg, tôg) *n. Informal.* **1.** A coat or cloak. **2. togs.** Clothes.
~*tr.v.* **togged, togging, togs.** *Informal.* To dress or clothe. Often used with *up* or *out.* [Short for 16th-century cant *togeman(s), togman* : probably obsolete *toge,* cloak, from Middle English, from Old French *tog(u)e,* from Latin *toga,* TOGA + *-mans*†, a cant noun suffix.]
to·ga (tō′gə) *n., pl.* **-gas.** **1.** A draped one-piece outer garment worn

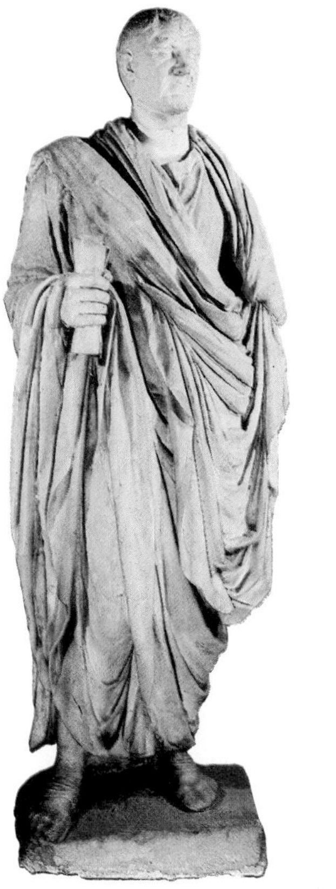

toga *This heavy outer garment made from fine white wool was difficult to drape—it was about 6 meters (20 feet) long and up to about 2 meters (7 feet) wide—hard to keep in place, and cumbersome to wear. Nevertheless, all men who were citizens of ancient Rome were required to wear it on public occasions.*

PRONUNCIATION KEY

ă, pat; ā, pay; âr, care;
ä, father, are; b, bib;
ch, church; d, deed; ĕ, pet;
ē, be; f, fife; g, gag; h, hat;
hw, which; ĭ, pit; ī, pie;
îr, pier; j, judge; k, kick;
l, lid, needle; m, mum;
n, no, sudden; ng, thing;
ŏ, pot; ō, toe; ô, paw, for;
oi, noise; ou, out; o͝o, book;
o͞o, boot; p, pop; r, roar;
s, sauce; sh, ship, dish;
t, tight; th, thin, path;
th, this, bathe; ŭ, cut; ûr, fur;
v, valve; w, with; y, yes;
z, zebra, size; zh, vision;
ə, about, item, edible,
gallop, circus, peaceful

IN FOREIGN WORDS:

à, *Fr.* ami; œ, *Fr.* feu, *Ger.* schön; ü, *Fr.* tu, *Ger.* über; KH, *Ger.* ich, *Scot.* loch; N, *Fr.* bon; y′, *Fr.* Compiègne

STRESS MARKS:

Primary stress: ′
in·cite′ (ĭn-sīt′)
Secondary stress: ′
in′sight′ (ĭn′sīt′)

in public by citizens of ancient Rome. **2.** Any robe or gown characteristic of a particular office or profession. [Latin, from *tegere,* to cover.] **—to·gaed** (tō′gəd) *adj.*

toga vi·ri·lis (və-rē′lĭs, -rĭl′ĭs) *n.* A white toga symbolizing manhood that boys of ancient Rome were allowed to wear at age 15. [Latin, toga of a man.]

to·geth·er (tə-gĕth′ər) *adv.* **1.** In or into a single group, body, mass, or place: *We gather together. I stuck it together with glue.* **2.** Against or in contact with one another: *He rubbed his hands together.* **3.** One with another; mutually or reciprocally: *The shirt and tie go well together.* **4.** Regarded collectively; in total: *She is worth more than all of us together.* **5.** Simultaneously: *All the bells rang out together.* **6.** In uninterrupted succession; at a stretch: *delirious for days together.* **7.** In harmony or accord: *We stand together on this issue.* **8.** *Informal.* **a.** In or into a coherent, compact, well-ordered aggregation: *Try to get your ideas together. I got all my bits and pieces together.* **b.** In or into a state of self-possession or effective operation: *Pull yourself together. We got a show together on short notice.* **—get it together.** *Informal.* To manage to act effectively. **—together with.** As well as; and in addition.
∼*adj. Slang.* **1.** Stable and well-organized; self-possessed. **2.** Unified and performing effectively. [Middle English *togeder(e),* Old English *tōgædere* : TO + *gad-* (unattested), as in *gæd,* fellowship; akin to GATHER.]

Usage: When *together with* is used following the subject of a sentence, it does not alter the agreement in number between the subject and the verb. Thus in the sentence *The king, together with the two princes, is expected to arrive tonight,* the verb remains in the singular, agreeing with *king,* despite the plural noun following. A similar rule applies to such other phrases as *in addition to, as well as, along with,* and *like*: *Common sense as well as training is a requisite for a good job.*

to·geth·er·ness (tə-gĕth′ər-nĭs) *n.* The quality of being in close relationship or harmony; comradeship or intimacy.

tog·ger·y (tŏg′ə-rē, tô′gə-) *n., pl.* **-ies.** *Informal.* Clothing; togs.

tog·gle (tŏg′əl) *n.* **1.** A device used to secure or hold something, especially: **a.** A pin inserted in a nautical knot to keep it from slipping. **b.** A bar-shaped crosspiece or button, as on sports clothes, attached to the end of or inserted in a loop in a rope, chain, or strap to prevent slipping, to tighten, or to fasten. **2.** An apparatus having a toggle joint.
∼*tr.v.* **toggled, -gling, -gles.** To furnish or fasten with a toggle or toggles. [18th century (nautical use) : origin obscure.]

toggle bolt *n.* A fastener consisting of a threaded bolt and a mated toggle.

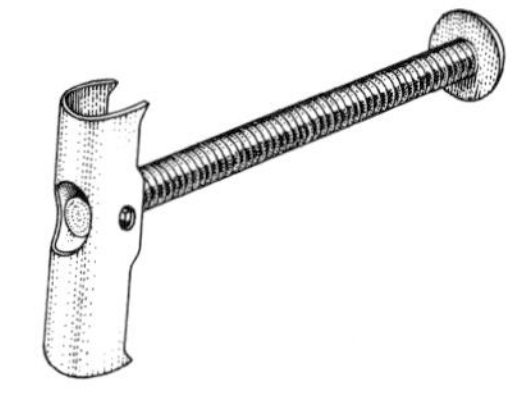

toggle bolt *A bolt with a threaded swivel fitting that swings down at right angles to the bolt after it is pushed through a drilled hole. The bolt is then tightened, and the swivel grips the surface behind the hole.*

toggle joint *n.* An elbowlike joint composed of two arms pivoted so that a force applied to their hinge to straighten them produces an outward force at the ends.

toggle switch *n.* A switch in which a projecting lever employing a toggle joint with a spring is used to open or close an electric circuit.

To·go (tō′gō). Republic of West Africa on the Gulf of Guinea. Coffee and cocoa are exported, but the economy is dominated by minerals, with phosphates accounting for 40 percent of exports. From 1894 to 1914 the area was the German protectorate of Togoland but was subsequently divided between Britain and France. In 1956 the west voted to join Ghana on its independence (1957). French Togo became independent as the Republic of Togo in 1960. Area, 56,785 square kilometers (21,919 square miles). Population, 2,500,000. Capital, Lomé. See map at **West African States. —To·go·lese** (tō′gə-lēz′, -lēs′) *n. & adj.*

Togo, Heihachiro (1847–1934). Japanese admiral. While leading the Japanese fleet to victory during the Russo-Japanese War he developed a naval tactic, later called "crossing the enemy's T," that brings the broadsides of a fleet to bear on an advancing column of enemy vessels. His strategic brilliance forced Western countries to view Japan as a naval force.

Togo, Shigenori (1882–1950). Japanese diplomat and politician. After serving as ambassador to Germany (1937) and to the U.S.S.R. (1938–40), he became the Japanese foreign minister, a position he held throughout World War II. He was later tried as a war criminal and received a 20-year prison sentence.

togue (tōg) *n.* The **lake trout** *(see).* [Canadian French.]

to·he·ro·a (tō′ə-rō′ə) *n., pl.* **-roas** or collectively **toheroa. 1.** A New Zealand bivalve mollusk, *Amphidesma ventricosum.* **2.** A soup made of toheroa. [Maori.]

toil[1] (toil) *intr.v.* **toiled, toiling, toils. 1.** To labor continuously and untiringly; work strenuously. **2.** To proceed or make one's way with difficulty, pain, or strenuous effort: *toiling over the mountains.*
∼*n.* **1.** Exhausting labor or effort. **2.** *Archaic.* Strife; contention. —See Synonyms at **work.** [Middle English *toilen,* to struggle, to battle, from Norman French *toiler,* to strive, from Old French *toillier,* to stir, agitate, from Latin *tudiculāre,* to stir about, from *tudicula,* a mill for crushing olives, diminutive of *tudes,* a hammer.]

toil[2] *n.* **1.** A long net or a series of nets for trapping game. **2.** *Usually* **toils.** Anything in which one is trapped or caught up. [Old French *toile,* a net, from Latin *tēla;* akin to *texere,* to weave.]

toile (twäl) *n.* **1.** A sheer linen fabric. **2.** Fine cretonne printed in a single color. **3.** A copy of a garment made in inexpensive material so that alterations can be made to the design. [French, cloth, net. See **toil** (net).]

toi·let (toi′lĭt) *n.* Also **toi·lette** (twä-lĕt′) (for sense 2). **1. a.** A disposal apparatus consisting of a porcelain bowl that is fitted with a hinged seat and a flushing device, used for urination and defecation. **b.** A room or booth containing a toilet. **2.** The act or process of grooming and dressing oneself. **3.** *Archaic.* A dressing table. **4.** The cleansing of a bodily part, as in preparation for a surgical procedure. [French *toilette,* lavatory, dressing table, from Old French, cloth cover for a dressing table, a dressing table, diminutive of TOILE.]

toilet paper *n.* Thin, absorbent paper, usually in rolls, used for cleansing oneself after defecation or urination. Also called "toilet tissue."

toi·let·ry (toi′lĭ-trē) *n., pl.* **-ries.** Any article or cosmetic used in dressing or grooming oneself.

toi·lette (twä-lĕt′) *n.* **1.** Toilet (sense 2). **2.** A person's dress or style of dress. **3.** A costume; outfit. [French. See TOILET.]

toilet training *n.* The process of training a child to control bladder and bowel movements and to use the toilet. **—toi·let-train** (toi′lĭt-trān′) *v.*

toilet water *n.* Cologne or mild perfume.

toil·some (toil′səm) *adj.* Characterized by or requiring toil; done with difficulty. **—toil·some·ly** *adv.* **—toil·some·ness** *n.*

to-ing and fro-ing (tōō′ĭng-ən-frō′ĭng) *n., pl.* **to-ings and fro-ings.** Busy movement back and forth.

To·jo (tō′jō), **Hideki** (1885–1948). Japanese army officer and prime minister (1941–44). A leading advocate of Japanese military aggression during World War II, he became prime minister and soon after approved the attack on Pearl Harbor (1941). He was executed as a war criminal after the fall of Japan.

to·ka·mak (tō′kə-măk′, tŏk′ə-) *n.* A small doughnut-shaped nuclear reactor in which a plasma is heated and confined by electric and magnetic fields. [Russian.]

to·kay (tō′kā′) *n.* A tropical Asian lizard, *Gekko gecko.* See **gecko.** [From Malay *toke* (imitative of its cry).]

To·kay (tō-kā′) *n.* **1.** A variety of grape originally grown near Tokay, Hungary. **2.** A sweet wine made from these grapes.

toke (tōk) *n. Slang.* A puff on a cigarette or, especially, a marijuana cigarette. [20th century : origin obscure.]

to·ken (tō′kən) *n.* **1.** Something that serves as an indication or representation, as of some fact, event, or emotion; a sign; symbol. **2.** Something that tangibly signifies something, such as authority, validity, or identity: *The scepter is a token of kingship.* **3.** A keepsake or souvenir. **4.** A piece of stamped metal or plastic used as a substitute for a coin, as in a public telephone, slot machine, or the like. **5.** A voucher exchangeable for a specified commodity of a stated value: *a record token.* —See Synonyms at **sign. —by the same token.** In the same manner; likewise.
∼*tr.v.* **tokened, -kening, -kens.** To signify, betoken, or symbolize.
∼*adj.* **1.** Done, made, or undertaken as a token, as of good faith or strength of feeling: *a token payment; a token strike.* **2. a.** Purely for the sake of form; nominal; perfunctory: *token resistance.* **b.** Indicative of minimal effort to comply with a statutory requirement or fulfill a moral obligation: *a token woman on the board.* [Middle English *taken, token,* Old English *tāc(e)n.*]

to·ken·ism (tō′kə-nĭz′əm) *n.* The practice or policy of making only a superficial effort or symbolic gesture toward the accomplishment of a goal, such as racial integration.

Tokharian. Variant of **Tocharian.**

To·klas (tō′kləs), **Alice Babette** (1877–1967). U.S. author. As Gertrude Stein's secretary and companion for nearly 40 years, she became so inextricably entwined in Stein's life and work that Stein entitled her own memoirs *The Autobiography of Alice B. Toklas* (1931). After Stein's death in 1946 Toklas wrote cookbooks and a volume of memoirs, *What Is Remembered* (1963).

tokology. Variant of **tocology.**

To·ky·o (tō′kē-ō′). Formerly **Ed·o** (ĕd′ō). Capital of Japan, and one of the world's largest cities, in east-central Honshu at the head of Tokyo Bay. It has extensive industrial complexes and is the financial, administrative, educational, and cultural center of Japan. Founded on the 12th-century village of Edo, it has been extensively rebuilt since World War II. Its seaport is Yokohama.

to·la (tō′lə, tō-lä′) *n.* A unit of weight used in India, equal to the weight of one silver rupee, or 180 troy grains. [Hindi *tolā,* from Sanskrit *tulā,* balance, weight.]

tol·booth, toll·booth (tōl′bōōth′) *n. Scottish.* **1.** A town hall. **2.** A prison. [Middle English *tolbothe,* toll station, tax-collection booth, town hall (beneath which there were prison cells) : TOLL + BOOTH.]

tol·bu·ta·mide (tŏl-byōō′tə-mīd′) *n.* A white powder, $C_{12}H_{18}N_2O_3S$, administered by mouth in the treatment of diabetes. [TOL(U) + BUT(YRIC ACID) + AMIDE.]

told. Past tense and past participle of **tell.**

tole, tôle (tōl) *n.* Lacquered or enameled metalware, usually gilded, popular in the 18th century. [French *tôle,* sheet metal, sheet iron, from French dialect, a slab, table, variant of *table,* from Latin *tabula,* a board. See **table.**]

To·le·do[1] (tə-lē′dō). Capital of Toledo province, central Spain, on the Tagus River. It was an important Roman city, the capital of the Visigoth kingdom (534–712), and a Moorish provincial capital (712–1031), when it became famous as a center of Arab and Hebrew learning. It was reconquered by El Cid and Alfonso VI of León and Castile (1085).

Toledo[2]. City of northwestern Ohio, with a fine natural harbor on Lake Erie. It is a shipping and manufacturing center.

tol·er·a·ble (tŏl′ər-ə-bəl) *adj.* **1.** Able to be tolerated; endurable. **2.** Fair or adequate; passable. —See Synonyms at **average.** [Mid-

PRONUNCIATION KEY

ă, pat; ā, pay; âr, care;
ä, father, are; b, bib;
ch, church; d, deed; ĕ, pet;
ē, be; f, fife; g, gag; h, hat;
hw, which; ĭ, pit; ī, pie;
îr, pier; j, judge; k, kick;
l, lid, needle; m, mum;
n, no, sudden; ng, thing;
ŏ, pot; ō, toe; ô, paw, for;
oi, noise; ou, out; ŏŏ, book;
ōō, boot; p, pop; r, roar;
s, sauce; sh, ship, dish;
t, tight; th, thin, path;
th, this, bathe; ŭ, cut; ûr, fur;
v, valve; w, with; y, yes;
z, zebra, size; zh, vision;
ə, about, item, edible,
gallop, circus, peaceful

IN FOREIGN WORDS:

à, *Fr.* ami; œ, *Fr.* feu, *Ger.* schön; ü, *Fr.* tu, *Ger.* über; KH, *Ger.* ich, *Scot.* loch; N, *Fr.* bon; y′, *Fr.* Compiègne

STRESS MARKS:

Primary stress: ′
in·cite′ (ĭn-sīt′)
Secondary stress: ′
in′sight′ (ĭn′sīt′)

dle English, from Old French, from Latin *tolerābilis.* See **tolerate.**]
—**tol·er·a·bil·i·ty, tol·er·a·ble·ness** *n.* —**tol·er·a·bly** *adv.*

tol·er·ance (tŏl′ər-əns) *n.* **1.** A disposition toward or capacity for allowing or respecting the beliefs or behavior of others when these differ from one's own. **2. a.** Leeway for variation from a standard. **b.** The permissible deviation from a specified value of a structural dimension. **3.** The capacity to endure hardship or pain; endurance. **4. a.** Physiological resistance to poison. **b.** The capacity to absorb a drug continuously or in large doses without experiencing its pharmacological effects. [Middle English, from Old French, from Latin *tolerantia.* See **tolerate.**]

tol·er·ant (tŏl′ər-ənt) *adj.* **1.** Inclined to tolerate the beliefs or behavior of others; forbearing. **2.** Able to withstand or endure an adverse environmental condition. [From French *tolérant,* present participle of *tolérer,* to TOLERATE.] —**tol·er·ant·ly** *adv.*

tol·er·ate (tŏl′ə-rāt′) *tr.v.* **-ated, -ating, -ates. 1.** To show tolerance toward; especially, to allow (beliefs or practices that differ from one's own) to exist without interference or prohibition. **2.** To put up with; endure or countenance: *would not tolerate laziness.* **3.** *Medicine.* To have tolerance for (a drug or poison). —See Synonyms at **bear.** [From Latin *tolerāre,* to bear, tolerate.] —**tol·er·a·tive** *adj.* —**tol·er·a·tor** *n.*

tol·er·a·tion (tŏl′ə-rā′shən) *n.* **1.** The act of tolerating or inclination to tolerate. **2.** Official recognition of the rights of individuals and groups to hold dissenting opinions, especially on religion. [From French, from Latin *tolerātio* (stem *tolerātiōn-*). See **tolerate.**]

tol·i·dine (tŏl′ə-dēn′) *n.* Any of several isomeric bases, (H₂NC₆H₃CH₃)₂, derived from toluene, used in the manufacture of dyes and synthetic resins. [TOL(UENE) + -ID(E) + -INE.]

toll¹ (tōl) *n.* **1.** A fixed charge or tax for an access or privilege, especially for passage across a bridge or along a road. **2.** An amount or loss, as of lives, property, or health, incurred as a result of war, disaster, or other adverse condition: *took a heavy toll in lives.* **3.** A charge for a long-distance telephone call.
~*tr.v.* **tolled, tolling, tolls.** To exact as a toll. [Middle English *tol(le),* Old English *toll,* from Late Latin *tolonium, telōnium,* a tollbooth, from Greek *telōnion,* from *telos,* tax.]

toll² *v.* **tolled, tolling, tolls.** —*tr.* **1.** To sound (a large bell) slowly at regular intervals. **2.** To announce or summon by tolling. —*intr.* To ring with slow and regular strokes. Used of a bell.
~*n.* **1.** The act of tolling. **2.** The sound of a tolling bell. [Middle English *tollen,* probably special use of *tollen, tullen,* to entice, lure, perhaps Old English *tollian* (unattested), perhaps from Germanic *tull* (unattested).]

toll·booth (tōl′bōōth′) *n.* **1.** A booth at a tollgate, where a toll is collected. Also called "tollhouse." **2.** Variant of **tolbooth.**

toll·bridge (tōl′brĭj′) *n.* A bridge at which a toll is charged for crossing.

toll call *n.* A telephone call for which a higher rate is charged than that standard for a local call.

toll·gate (tōl′gāt′) *n.* A gate barring passage to a road, tunnel, or bridge until a toll is collected.

toll·house (tōl′hous′) *n.* A house or booth where tolls are collected.

Tol·stoy, Tol·stoi (tōl′stoi′, tôl′-), **Count Lev** or **Leo Nikolayevich** (1828-1910). Russian author and philosopher. In his great novels, *War and Peace* (1862-69) and *Anna Karenina* (1873-76), he displayed the richness of detail and psychological acumen that pervaded all his work. After he developed his doctrine of nonresistance and nonparticipation, his literary efforts became more didactic.

Tol·tec (tōl′tĕk′, tôl′-) *n., pl.* **-tecs** or collectively **Toltec.** A member of an ancient Nahuatl people of central and southern Mexico whose culture flourished in about A.D. 1000. —**Tol·tec, Tol·tec·an** (tōl-tĕk′ən, tôl-) *adj.*

to·lu (tə-lōō′) *n.* An aromatic resin obtained from the tree *Myroxylon balsamum,* of South America. [Spanish *tolú,* from Santiago de *Tolú,* Colombia, its place of origin.]

tol·u·ene (tŏl′yōō-ēn′) *n.* A colorless flammable liquid, CH₃C₆H₅, obtained from coal tar or petroleum and used in aviation and other high-octane fuels, in dyestuffs, in explosives, and as a solvent for gums and lacquers. Also called "toluol." [TOLU (from which it was originally obtained) + -ENE.]

tol·u·i·dine (tə-lōō′ə-dēn′) *n.* Any of three isomeric compounds, H₂NC₆H₄CH₃, used to make dyes. [TOLU(ENE) + -ID(E) + -INE.]

tol·u·ol (tŏl′yōō-ôl′, -ōl′) *n.* Toluene. [TOLU + -OL.]

tol·yl (tŏl′əl) *n.* The univalent organic radical CH₃C₆H₄. [TOL(U) + -YL.]

tom (tŏm) *n.* **1.** The male of various animals; especially, a male cat that has not been neutered. **2. Tom.** See **Uncle Tom** (sense 2).
~*adj.* Male. [From *Tom,* nickname for *Thomas.*]

tom·a·hawk (tŏm′ə-hôk′) *n.* **1.** A light ax used as a tool or weapon by North American Indians. **2.** Any similar implement or weapon. **3.** *Australian.* A hatchet.
~*tr.v.* **tomahawked, -hawking, -hawks. 1.** To attack or kill with or as if with a tomahawk. **2.** *Australian.* To shear (a sheep) roughly, as if using a hatchet. [Virginia Algonquian *tamahaac, tomahake* : Proto-Algonquian *temah-* (unattested), to cut off by tool + *-aakan* (unattested), noun suffix.]

to·mal·ley (tə-mǎl′ē, tŏm′ăl′ē) *n., pl.* **-leys.** The liver of a lobster, esteemed as a culinary delicacy. [Of Cariban origin, akin to Carib *tumali,* sauce of lobster or crab liver.]

Tom and Jer·ry (tŏm′ ən jĕr′ē) *n.* A hot drink consisting of rum, a beaten egg, milk or water, sugar, and spices. [After Corinthian *Tom*

and *Jerry* Hawthorn, characters in the novel *Life in London* (1821), by Pierce Egan (1772-1849).]

to·ma·to (tə-mā′tō, -mä′tō) *n., pl.* **-toes. 1.** A plant, *Lycopersicon esculentum,* native to South America, widely cultivated for its edible, fleshy, usually red fruit. **2.** The fruit of this plant. [Variant of earlier *tomate,* from Spanish, from Nahuatl *tomatl.*]

tomb (tōōm) *n.* **1.** A vault or chamber serving as a repository for a dead body. **2.** Any grave or place of burial. **3.** A monument commemorating the dead. [Middle English *t(o)umbe,* from Norman French *tumbe,* from Old French *tombe,* from Late Latin *tumba,* sepulchral mound, from Greek *tumbos.*]

tom·bac (tŏm′băk′) *n.* Any one of several alloys of copper and zinc, used in making inexpensive jewelry. [French, from Dutch *tombak,* from Malay *tambāga,* copper.]

tom·bo·la (tŏm-bō′lə) *n. Chiefly British.* **1.** A lottery game in which winning tickets are drawn out of a revolving container. **2.** A simple form of the game of **bingo** (see). [Probably from Italian, from *tombolare,* to tumble.]

tom·boy (tŏm′boi′) *n.* A high-spirited girl who prefers boys' games to those conventionally played by girls. [TOM (male) + BOY.] —**tom·boy·ish** *adj.*

tomb·stone (tōōm′stōn′) *n.* A stone or monument, usually inscribed, marking a grave; gravestone.

Tomb·stone (tōōm′stōn′). Resort city in southeastern Arizona. Between 1877 and *c.* 1890 it established a reputation for rich silver mines and lawlessness. Among its picturesque attractions are Boot Hill Graveyard and the O.K. Corral, site of a famous gun battle between the Clanton gang and Wyatt Earp, his brother Virgil, and "Doc" Holliday.

tom·cat (tŏm′kăt′) *n.* A male cat, especially one that has not been neutered. [After *Tom,* hero of the anonymous work *The Life and Adventures of a Cat* (1760).]

Tom Col·lins (kŏl′ĭnz) *n.* A cocktail of gin, lemon or lime juice, soda water, and sugar. [Said to be the name of the bartender who invented it.]

Tom, Dick, and Har·ry (tŏm′ dĭk′ ən hăr′ē) *n.* Anyone at all; everyone: *Every Tom, Dick, and Harry came to the party.*

tome (tōm) *n.* **1.** A book; especially, a weighty or scholarly book. Often used humorously. **2.** One of the books in a work of several volumes. [French, from Latin *tomus,* cut, tome, roll of paper, from Greek *tomos,* from *temnein,* to cut, slice.]

-tome *suffix.* Indicates a cutting instrument; for example, **microtome.** [From New Latin *-tomus,* from Greek *-tomos,* a cutting, from *temnein,* to cut.]

to·men·tose (tō-mĕn′tōs′, tō′mən-tōs′) *adj. Biology.* Covered with dense, short, matted hairs. [New Latin *tomentosus,* from Latin *tōmentum,* cushion stuffing, TOMENTUM.]

to·men·tum (tō-mĕn′təm) *n., pl.* **-ta** (-tə). **1.** *Anatomy.* A network of extremely small blood vessels in the brain passing between the pia mater and cerebral cortex. **2.** *Biology.* A covering of closely matted woolly hairs. [New Latin, from Latin *tōmentum†,* cushion stuffing.]

tom·fool (tŏm′fōōl′) *n.* A stupid or foolish person; blockhead.
~*adj.* Extremely foolish. [Middle English *Tom* (name) + FOOL.]

tom·fool·er·y (tŏm-fōō′lə-rē) *n., pl.* **-ies. 1.** Foolish behavior. **2.** Something trivial or foolish; nonsense.

tom·my (tŏm′ē) *n., pl.* **-mies.** *British Informal.* **1.** Often **Tommy.** A British soldier, especially a private; a Tommy Atkins. **2.** *Archaic.* A workman's provisions. [From *Tommy,* nickname for *Thomas.*]

Tommy At·kins (ăt′kĭnz) *n.* A private of the regular British army. Also called "tommy." [Originally a name used in sample forms for privates in the British army.]

tommy bar *n.* A short metal bar used as a lever, as to turn a capstan screw.

Tommy gun *n.* A Thompson submachine gun (see).

tom·my·rot (tŏm′ē-rŏt′) *n. Informal.* Utter foolishness; nonsense. [Dialectal *tommy,* fool + ROT.]

to·mog·ra·phy (tō-mŏg′rə-fē) *n.* Any of several techniques for making x-ray pictures of a predetermined plane section of a solid object by blurring out the images of other planes. [Greek *tomos,* a cut, section (see **tome**) + -GRAPHY.]

to·mor·row (tə-môr′ō, -mŏr′ō) *n.* **1.** The day following today. **2.** The future, especially the near future.
~*adv.* On the day following today. [Middle English *to morge, to mor(o)we,* Old English *tō morgen(ne)* : TO (at, on) + *morgenne,* dative of *morgen,* MORROW.]

tompion. Variant of **tampion.**

Tom Thumb (tŏm′ thŭm′) *n.* **1.** A diminutive hero of English folklore. **2.** A tiny person; a midget.

tom·tit (tŏm′tĭt′) *n. British.* A tit or other small bird, especially a blue tit. [*Tom* (name) + TIT(MOUSE).]

tom-tom (tŏm′tŏm′) *n.* **1.** A small-headed, usually long and narrow drum that is beaten with the hands. **2.** A monotonous rhythmical drumbeat or similar sound. [Hindi *ṭamṭam* See **tam-tam.**]

-tomy *suffix.* Indicates a cutting of a specified part or tissue; for example, **craniotomy.** [From New Latin *-tomia,* from Greek *-tomos,* cut, -TOME.]

ton¹ (tŭn) *n.* **1.** Abbr. **t. a.** An avoirdupois unit of weight in the U.S. Customary System equal to 2,240 pounds (1016.05 kilograms). Also called "long ton." **b.** An avoirdupois unit of weight in the U.S. Customary System equal to 2,000 pounds (907.18 kilograms). Also called "short ton," "net ton." **2.** Any of various units of weight or capacity used in shipping, as: **a.** A unit of weight or volume used for measuring freight and varying according to the material being

tomb *In many ancient cultures tombs were furnished with goods for the use of the spirits of the dead. The Tomb of the Rilievi (above), at Cerveteri, Italy, dates from the second century B.C.; it contains household goods, and there are beds in the alcoves.*

shipped. Its most usual value is a weight of 1000 kilograms or a volume of either 40 cubic feet or 1 cubic meter. Also called "freight ton." **b.** A unit of volume for freight equal to 40 cubic feet. Also called "freight ton," "shipping ton," "measurement ton." **c.** A unit of capacity of ships equal to 100 cubic feet. Also called "register ton." **d.** A unit of displacement of ships equal to a displacement of 35 cubic feet of sea water. Also called "displacement ton." **3.** A **metric ton** (*see*). **4.** Often **tons.** *Informal.* A very large quantity. [Middle English *toun, tunne,* a measure of weight. See TUN.]

ton² (tŏN) *n.* Fashionable distinction; elegant style. [French, TONE.]
to·nal (tō′nəl) *adj.* Of or pertaining to a tone, tones, or tonality. [Medieval Latin *tonālis,* from *tonus,* TONE.] —**to·nal·ly** *adv.*
to·nal·i·ty (tō-năl′ə-tē) *n., pl.* **-ties. 1.** *Music.* **a.** A system or arrangement of seven tones built upon a tonic key. **b.** The arrangement of all the tones and chords of a musical composition in relation to a tonic. **2.** The scheme or interrelation of the tones in a painting.
ton·do (tŏn′dō) *n., pl.* **-di** (-dē) or **-dos.** A circular painting or sculpted relief. [Italian, from *rotondo,* from Latin *rotundus,* round.]
tone (tōn) *n.* **1. a.** A sound of distinct volume, pitch, duration, and quality; musical note. **b.** Quality or character of sound: *the sweet, clear tones of the lute.* **2.** *Music.* The interval of a major second; a whole tone as distinguished from a semitone. **3.** Vocal or instrumental quality or timbre: *discussed the problem in low tones.* **4.** The pitch of a word used to determine its meaning or to distinguish differences in meaning, as in Chinese. **5.** The particular or relative pitch of a word, phrase, or sentence. **6.** Manner of expression in speech or writing: *an angry tone of voice.* **7.** A general or prevailing character or atmosphere: *The tone of the debate was antagonistic.* **8. a.** A color or shade of color. **b.** The general effect produced, as in a picture, by light and color. **9.** *Physiology.* **a.** The tension in resting muscles. Also called "tonus." **b.** Normal firmness of tissue. **10.** *Informal.* High quality; distinction: *A duke added tone to the occasion.*
~*v.* **toned, toning, tones.** —*tr.* **1.** To give a particular tone or inflection to. **2.** To soften or change the color of (a photographic negative, for example). **3.** To sound monotonously; intone. —*intr.* **1.** To assume a particular color quality. **2.** To harmonize in color. —**tone down. 1.** To lessen or soften in tone. **2.** To make or become less pronounced or emphatic; moderate. —**tone up. 1.** To increase the tone of. **2.** To improve the tone of; strengthen. [Middle English *ton,* from Old French, from Latin *tonus,* a stretching, tone, sound, from Greek *tonos.*]
tone arm *n.* The pivoted arm of a record player that holds the cartridge and stylus.
tone color *n.* The timbre of a singing voice or instrument. [Translation of German *Klangfarbe.*]
tone-deaf (tōn′dĕf′) *adj.* Incapable of perceiving subtle distinctions of musical pitch.
tone language *n.* A language that distinguishes meanings among words of similar form by variations in pitch and tone.
tone·less (tōn′lĭs) *adj.* **1.** Lacking tone. **2.** Lacking vitality; listless. —**tone·less·ly** *adv.* —**tone·less·ness** *n.*
to·neme (tō′nēm) *n. Linguistics.* A feature of pitch that in a tone language distinguishes two otherwise identical words or forms. [TON(E) + -EME.]
tone poem *n.* A symphonic poem (*see*).
tone row *n.* A fixed sequence of tones, typically consisting of the 12 tones of the chromatic scale, used as a basis for musical composition.
tong (tông, tŏng) *n.* **1.** A Chinese association, clan, or fraternity. **2.** A secret society of Chinese in the United States, at one time believed to control criminal activity among Chinese Americans. [Cantonese *tong,* a hall, auditorium, assembly hall, from Mandarin Chinese *táng.*]
ton·ga (tŏng′gə) *n.* A light two-wheeled horse-drawn cart or carriage used in India. [Hindi *tāṅgā.*]
Tong·a (tŏng′gə) *n.* Also **Friend·ly Islands** (frĕnd′lē). Kingdom in the South Pacific comprising some 169 tropical islands, 38 of which are inhabited. Most of the people live by fishing and growing fruit and vegetables. Coconut products and bananas are the chief exports, and tourism is important. Offshore oil has been discovered. A British-protected state after 1900, Tonga became an independent member of the Commonwealth in 1970. Area, 699 square kilometers (270 square miles). Population 90,000. Capital, Nukualofa on Tongatabu Island. See map at **Pacific Ocean.**
Ton·gan (tŏng′gən) *n.* **1.** A Polynesian language spoken in Tonga. **2.** A native or inhabitant of Tonga.
Tongking. See **Tonkin.**
tongs (tôngz, tŏngz) *pl.n.* A grasping device consisting of two arms joined at one end by a pivot or hinge. [Middle English *tang(e)s,* Old English *tangan,* plural of *tang(e).*]
tongue (tŭng) *n.* **1.** The fleshy muscular organ, attached in most vertebrates to the floor of the mouth, that is the principal organ of taste, an important organ of speech in humans, and moves to aid chewing and swallowing. **2.** A homologous invertebrate structure, as in insects or certain mollusks. **3.** The tongue of an animal, such as a cow, used as food. **4. a.** The faculty of speech. **b.** A particular spoken language or dialect. **5.** Style of utterance or manner of expression: *has a sharp tongue.* **6.** Anything resembling a tongue in shape, especially in being long, often tapering, and attached at one end, such as: **a.** The flap of material under the laces or buckles of a shoe. **b.** A narrow spit of land; a promontory. **c.** A jet of flame. **d.** A bell clapper. **e.** The harnessing pole attached to the front axle

of a horse-drawn vehicle. **7.** A protruding strip along the edge of a board that fits into a matching groove on the edge of another board. —**give tongue. 1.** To bay, as hounds do when pursuing their quarry. **2.** To voice; utter. —**hold one's tongue.** To keep silent. —**on the tip of one's tongue.** On the verge of being remembered or expressed.
~*v.* **tongued, tonguing, tongues.** —*tr.* **1.** To articulate (musical notes on a wind instrument) by the technique of tonguing. **2.** To touch or lick with the tongue. **3. a.** To provide (a board) with a tongue. **b.** To join (boards) by means of a tongue and groove. **4.** *Archaic.* To scold. —*intr.* **1.** To articulate notes on a wind instrument by the technique of tonguing. **2.** To project, as a promontory. [Middle English *t(o)unge,* Old English *tunge.*]
tongue and groove *n.* A joint made by fitting a tongue on the edge of a board into a matching groove on another board.
tongue·fish (tŭng′fĭsh′) *n., pl.* **-fishes** or collectively **tonguefish.** Any of various marine flatfishes of the family Cynoglossidae, having the posterior part of the body tapering to a point. [From its tongue-shaped body.]
tongue-in-cheek (tŭng′ĭn-chēk′) *adj.* Meant or expressed ironically or facetiously. —**tongue in cheek** *adv.*
tongue-lash·ing (tŭng′lăsh′ĭng) *n. Informal.* A severe scolding.
tongue-tie (tŭng′tī′) *n.* Restricted mobility of the tongue resulting from abnormal shortness of the fold of tissue connecting the tongue to the floor of the mouth.
~*tr.v.* **tongue-tied, -tying, -ties.** To make tongue-tied.
tongue-tied (tŭng′tīd′) *adj.* **1.** Speechless or confused in expression, as from shyness, embarrassment, or astonishment. **2.** Affected with tongue-tie.
tongue twister *n.* **1.** A word or phrase difficult to articulate rapidly, usually because of a succession of similar consonant sounds, as *Shall she sell seashells?* **2.** Something difficult to pronounce.
tongu·ing (tŭng′ĭng) *n. Music.* Interruption of the wind stream through an instrument by movement of the tongue.
-tonia *suffix.* Indicates tonicity; for example, **myotonia.** [New Latin, from TONUS.]
ton·ic (tŏn′ĭk) *n.* **1.** Anything that invigorates, refreshes, or restores. **2.** A medicine or other agent that restores or increases bodily well-being. **3.** *Music.* The first note of a diatonic scale; a keynote. **4.** *Linguistics.* **a.** A tonic accent. **b.** *Obsolete.* A voiced sound. **5. a.** Quinine water. **b.** *Regional.* A flavored carbonated beverage. —*adj.* **1.** Producing or stimulating physical, mental, or emotional vigor. **2.** *Music.* Pertaining to or based on the tonic. **3.** *Linguistics.* Carrying the principal stress; accented. Said of a syllable. **4.** *Physiology.* **a.** Of or pertaining to normal muscular tension. **b.** Characterized by continuous muscular contraction: *a tonic spasm.* [From New Latin *tonicus,* of tension or tone, from Greek *tonikos,* from *tonos,* a stretching, TONE.]
tonic accent *n.* A stress produced by rising pitch as distinguished from increased volume. Also called "pitch accent," "tonic."
to·nic·i·ty (tō-nĭs′ə-tē) *n.* **1.** The property of having mental or physical tone, or of being tonic. **2.** Tonus (*see*).
to·night (tə-nīt′) *adv.* In or during the present or coming night. ~*n.* This night or the night of this day. [Middle English *to night,* Old English *tōniht:* TO (at, on) + *niht,* NIGHT.]
ton·ka bean (tŏng′kə) *n.* **1.** Any of several South American trees of the genus *Dipteryx,* having seeds that yield coumarin. **2.** The seed of any of these trees. [Perhaps from Galibi *tonka.*]
Ton·kin (tŏn′kĭn′, tŏng′-). Also **Tong·king** (tŏng′kĭng′). Region of northern Vietnam on the Gulf of Tonkin. It was part of French Indochina (1887–1946), and after the expulsion of the French it formed the nucleus of North Vietnam (1954–75). Its chief city, Hanoi, is now the capital of the Socialist Republic of Vietnam.
Tonkin, Gulf of. Arm of the South China Sea, between Vietnam and southern China, bounded in the east by the island of Hainan. The Gulf of Tonkin Resolution, prompted by a reported North Vietnamese attack on U.S. destroyers, led to increased U.S. involvement in the Vietnamese War.
ton·nage (tŭn′ĭj) *n. Abbr.* **tonn. 1.** The number of tons of water a ship displaces afloat. See **displacement ton. 2.** The capacity of a merchant ship in units of 100 cubic feet. **3.** A duty or charge per ton on cargo, as at a port or canal. **4.** The total shipping of a country or port, expressed in tons, with reference to carrying capacity. **5.** Weight measured in tons. [TON + -AGE.]
tonne (tŭn) *n. Abbr.* **t** A metric ton (*see*). [French, from *tonne,* a tun, from Old French. See tunnel.]
ton·neau (tə-nō′, tŏn′ō) *n., pl.* **-neaus** or **tonneaux** (tə-nōz′, tŏn′ōz′). **1.** The rear seating compartment of an early type of automobile. **2.** A detachable waterproof cover used to protect the passenger seats of an open car. In this sense, also called "tonneau cover." [French, "barrel," "cask," from Old French *tonnel.* See tunnel.]
to·nom·e·ter (tō-nŏm′ĭ-tər) *n.* **1.** Any of various instruments for measuring fluid or vapor pressure; especially, one for measuring fluid pressure within the eye. **2.** *Music.* An instrument or device, such as a graduated set of tuning forks, used to determine the pitch of a sound. [Greek *tonos,* tension, TONE + -METER.] —**to·no·met·ric** (tō′nə-mĕt′rĭk) *adj.* —**to·nom·e·try** *n.*
to·no·plast (tō′nə-plăst′, -plăst′) *n.* The membrane surrounding the large central vacuole in plant cells. [From Greek *tonos,* a stretching, tension (referring to its regulation of the pressure exerted by cell sap) + -PLAST.]
ton·sil (tŏn′səl) *n.* A mass of lymphoid tissue; especially, either of two such masses embedded in the lateral walls of the aperture be-

tween the mouth and the pharynx. See **adenoids.** [Latin *tonsillae* (plural), probably from *tōlēs†,* goiter.] —**ton·sil·lar** *adj.*

ton·sil·lec·to·my (tŏn′sə-lĕk′tə-mē) *n., pl.* **-mies.** The surgical removal of a tonsil. [Latin *tonsillae,* TONSIL(S) + -ECTOMY.]

ton·sil·li·tis (tŏn′sə-lī′tĭs) *n.* Inflammation of the tonsils. [New Latin : Latin *tonsillae,* TONSIL(S) + -ITIS.]

ton·sil·lot·o·my (tŏn′sə-lŏt′ə-mē) *n., pl.* **-mies.** 1. The surgical incision of a tonsil. 2. The surgical removal of part of a tonsil. [Latin *tonsillae,* TONSIL(S) + -OTOMY.]

ton·so·ri·al (tŏn-sôr′ē-əl, -sōr′ē-əl) *adj.* Of or pertaining to a barber or to barbering. [From Latin *tonsōrius,* from *tonsor,* a barber, from *tonsus,* past participle of *tondēre,* to shear.]

ton·sure (tŏn′shər) *n.* 1. The act of shaving the head or the top or crown of the head, especially as a preliminary to becoming a priest or a member of a monastic order. 2. The part of a monk's or priest's head so shaven.

~*tr.v.* **tonsured, -suring, -sures.** To shave the head of. [Middle English, from Old French, from Medieval Latin *tonsūra,* from Latin, a shearing, from *tonsus,* past participle of *tondēre,* to shear, shave.]

ton·tine (tŏn′tēn′, tŏn-tēn′) *n.* 1. An insurance plan whereby a group of participants share an annuity, each participant's share becoming larger as one of the others dies, the final survivor receiving the whole. 2. Each member's share of a tontine. 3. The total subscriptions to a tontine. 4. The subscribers to a tontine collectively. [French, after Lorenzo *Tonti,* Neapolitan banker who introduced this scheme in France in about 1653.]

Ton·ton Ma·coute (tŏn′tŏn mä-kōōt′) *n.* A member of a notorious personal police force set up by the Haitian dictator François Duvalier. [Haitian Creole, bogeyman.]

to·nus (tō′nəs) *n.* The normal condition of slight tension that occurs in a muscle even when at rest. Also called "tone," "tonicity." [New Latin, from Latin, tension, TONE.]

ton·y (tō′nē) *adj.* **-ier, -iest.** Marked by an elegant or exclusive manner or quality: *a tony country club.*

To·ny (tō′nē) *n., pl.* **-nies.** Any of several annual awards presented for outstanding achievement in the theater. [After *Tony* (Antoinette) Perry, American actress (died 1946).]

too (tōō) *adv.* 1. In addition; also; as well: *He's coming too.* 2. To a greater degree than is necessary or desirable; excessively: *working too hard.* 3. Very; extremely; immensely: *only too willing to be of service.* 4. *Informal.* Indeed; so. Used for emphasis: *said she'd leave him, and she did too.* —See Synonyms at **also.** [Emphatic form of Middle English *to,* in addition to, TO.]

too·dle·oo (tōōd′l-ōō′) *interj. British Informal.* Good-by. [Imitative, perhaps of a car horn.]

took. Past tense of **take.**

tool (tōōl) *n.* 1. An instrument, such as a hammer or rake, used by hand to accomplish work. 2. **a.** A machine, such as a lathe, used to cut and shape machinery parts; a machine tool. **b.** The cutting part of such a machine. 3. Anything used in the performance of an operation; an instrument: *the economic and intellectual tools to restore prosperity.* 4. Anything regarded as necessary to the carrying out of one's occupation or profession: *Words are the tools of his trade.* 5. A person used to carry out the designs of another; a dupe. 6. **a.** A bookbinder's hand stamp. **b.** A design impressed on a book cover by this means.

~*v.* **tooled, tooling, tools.** —*tr.* 1. To form, work, or decorate with a tool or tools. 2. To provide (a factory, industry, or shop) with the necessary tools, machinery, or equipment. Often used with *up.* 3. To ornament (a book cover) with a bookbinder's tool. —*intr.* 1. To work with a tool or tools. 2. *Informal.* To travel in a vehicle. Often used with *along: tooling along the road.* —**tool up.** To prepare an industry or a factory for production by providing machinery and tools suitable for a particular job. [Middle English *to(o)l,* Old English *tōl.*] —**tool·er** *n.*

Synonyms: *appliance, gadget, implement, instrument, utensil.*

tool·box (tōōl′bŏks′) *n.* A case for carrying or storing hand tools.

tool·ing (tōō′lĭng) *n.* Work or ornamentation done with tools; especially, stamped or gilded designs on books or leather.

tool·mak·er (tōōl′mā′kər) *n.* A master machinist skilled in making tools and parts. —**tool·mak·ing** *n.*

tool·shed (tōōl′shĕd′) *n.* A small building in which tools are kept; especially, a shed containing gardening tools.

toon (tōōn) *n.* 1. A tall tree, *Cedrela toona* (or *Toona ciliata*), of tropical Asia and Australia, closely related to the mahoganies and having reddish, aromatic wood. 2. The wood of this tree. [Hindi *tūn,* from Sanskrit *tunna†.*]

toot (tōōt) *v.* **tooted, tooting, toots.** —*intr.* 1. To sound a horn or whistle in short blasts. 2. To make this sound or a sound resembling this. —*tr.* To blow or sound (a horn or whistle).

~*n.* 1. The act or sound of tooting. 2. *Slang.* A lively time; a spree, especially a drinking spree. Used chiefly in the phrase *go on a toot.* [Probably from Middle Low German *tūten* (imitative).] —**toot·er** *n.*

tooth (tōōth) *n., pl.* **teeth** (tēth). 1. In most vertebrates, any of a set of hard, bonelike structures rooted in sockets in the jaws, typically composed of a core of soft pulp surrounded by a layer of hard dentine that is coated with cement or enamel at the crown, and used to seize, hold, or masticate. 2. A similar structure in invertebrates, such as any of the pointed denticles or ridges on the exoskeleton of an arthropod or the shell of a mollusk. 3. Any usually small projection resembling a tooth in shape or function, as on a comb, gear, or saw. 4. A small, notched projection along a margin, especially of a

leaf. See also **teeth.** —**long in the tooth.** Old or elderly. —**tooth and nail.** With great ferocity; as hard as possible.

~*v.* (tōōth, tōōth) **toothed, toothing, tooths.** —*tr.* 1. To furnish (a tool, for example) with teeth. 2. To make a jagged edge on. —*intr.* To mesh; become interlocked. [Tooth, teeth; Middle English *to(o)th, te(e)th,* Old English *tōth, tēth.*]

tooth·ache (tōōth′āk′) *n.* An aching pain in or near a tooth.

tooth·brush (tōōth′brŭsh′) *n.* A small, long-handled brush used for cleaning teeth.

toothed (tōōtht, tōōthd) *adj.* 1. Having teeth. 2. Having a specified number or type of teeth. Used in combination: *saw-toothed.*

toothed whale *n.* Any whale of the suborder Odontoceti, characterized by having rudimentary teeth. Compare **whalebone whale.**

tooth·less (tōōth′lĭs) *adj.* 1. Lacking teeth. 2. Lacking force; ineffectual. —**tooth·less·ly** *adv.* —**tooth·less·ness** *n.*

tooth·paste (tōōth′pāst′) *n.* A paste used for cleaning the teeth, usually applied with a toothbrush.

tooth·pick (tōōth′pĭk′) *n.* A small piece of wood or other material for removing food particles from between the teeth.

tooth·pow·der (tōōth′pou′dər) *n.* A powder used for cleaning the teeth; a powdered dentifrice.

tooth shell *n.* Any of various burrowing marine mollusks of the class Scaphopoda, having a long, tapering, slightly curved tubular shell. Also called "scaphopod," "tusk shell."

tooth·some (tōōth′səm) *adj.* 1. Delicious; savory: *a toothsome morsel of pie.* 2. Pleasant; attractive; tempting: *a toothsome offer.* —**tooth·some·ly** *adv.* —**tooth·some·ness** *n.*

tooth·wort (tōōth′wûrt′, -wôrt′) *n.* Any of various parasitic European plants of the genus *Lathraea;* especially *L. squamaria,* having pinkish flowers and a scaly rhizome.

tooth·y (tōō′thē) *adj.* **-ier, -iest.** Having or showing prominent teeth. —**tooth·i·ly** *adv.*

too·tle (tōōt′l) *v.* **-tled, -tling, -tles.** —*tr.* To toot softly on (a flute, for example). —*intr.* 1. To toot softly and repeatedly, as on a flute. 2. To move or travel gently or pleasurably. Often used with *along.* [Frequentative of TOOT.] —**too·tle** *n.* —**too·tler** *n.*

tooth

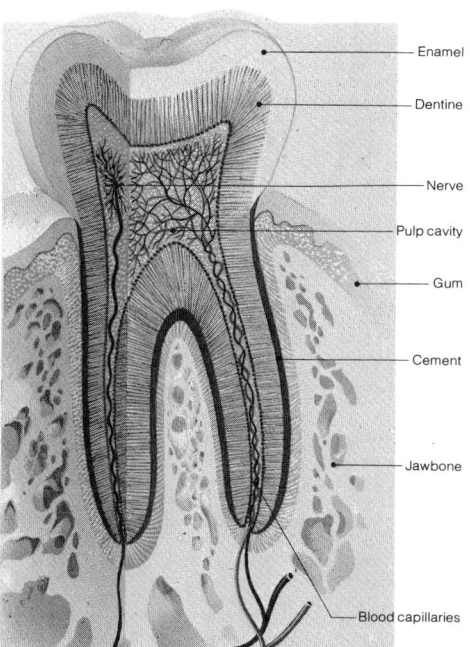

BITING, CUTTING, TEARING, AND GRINDING

Different types of teeth for different functions

Adult humans, who eat many varieties of food, have 32 teeth consisting of four types: 8 chisel-shaped incisors for biting, 4 canines for tearing, 8 premolars to cut food, and 12 molars (including the wisdom teeth) to grind food. Each tooth has a hard enamel surface covering a layer of dentine that is almost as hard. The part of the tooth in the jaw is covered with cement, which anchors it in place. The only soft part of the tooth is its pulpy core of blood vessels and nerves.

HUMAN TOOTH *The enamel is the hardest part but it is the most vulnerable because it cannot repair itself when it decays. Dentine is made up of cells that the body replaces.*

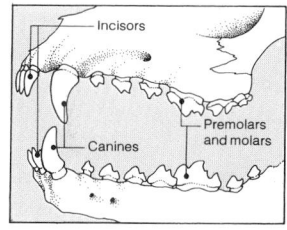

CARNIVORE *A wolf has large canines for tearing flesh. Premolars and molars cut and grind the food.*

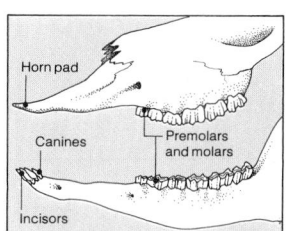

HERBIVORE *A cow has a horn pad in the upper jaw for incisors in the lower jaw to bite against.*

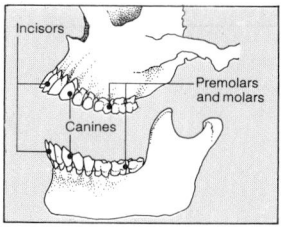

OMNIVORE *Man finds all four types of teeth necessary to deal efficiently with a meat and plant diet.*

toots (to͝ots) *n.* Also **toot·sy, toot·sie** (to͝ot′sē). *Slang.* Dear; sweetheart. Used affectionately or humorously. [Probably from **tootsy.**]

toot·sy, toot·sie (to͝ot′sē) *n., pl.* **-sies. 1.** A person's foot. **2.** *Usually* **tootsie.** Toots. [Alteration of *footsy,* from FOOT.]

top[1] (tŏp) *n.* **1.** The uppermost part, point, surface, or end of anything. **2.** The crown of the head. **3.** The part of a plant, such as a carrot, turnip, or beet, that is above the ground. **4.** Something that covers or forms the uppermost part of something, such as a lid or cap. **5.** *Nautical.* **a.** A platform enclosing the head of each mast of a sailing ship, to which the topmast rigging is attached. **b.** A similar platform, used as a gunsight or for observation, in a warship. **6. a.** In various sports and games, a stroke that lands above the center of the ball, giving it topspin. **b. Topspin** *(see).* **7.** The highest degree, pitch, or point; a peak; acme; zenith. **8. a.** The highest, most important, or most successful position or rank. **b.** A person in this position. **9.** In various card games, the highest card or cards in a suit or a hand. **10.** The best part; the pick; the cream. **11.** A garment, such as a blouse or T-shirt, that covers the upper part of the body. **12.** The upper part of something, especially when differentiated in some way, as by being of a different material, color, or consistency. **13.** The earliest part or beginning: *the top of the first inning.* **14.** *Chemistry.* The most volatile component of a distilled mixture; the component that distills first. **15.** *Abbr.* **t.** A quantum number, a property of certain postulated elementary particles. Also called "truth." **—blow one's top.** *Slang.* To lose one's temper. **—off the top of one's head.** Extemporaneously; impromptu. **—on top.** In a dominant, controlling, or successful position. **—on top of. 1.** *Informal.* **a.** In control of. **b.** Fully informed about. **2.** Besides; in addition to. **3.** In close proximity to. **4.** Following closely upon; coming immediately after. **—on top of the world.** In a position of great happiness or success. **—over the top. 1.** Over the front of a fortification, as an attack in trench warfare. **2.** Surpassing a goal or quota. **—up top.** In terms of mental ability: *He hasn't got much up top.*
~*adj.* **1.** Of, pertaining to, situated on, or forming the top; uppermost. **2.** Utmost; highest. Often used in combination: *top-priority; top-quality; top-rank.* **3.** *Physics.* **a.** Designating a quark flavor required in certain models of elementary particle theory to complement bottom. **b.** *Abbr.* **t.** Designating a particle that contains the top quark.
~*v.* **topped, topping, tops.** *—tr.* **1. a.** To remove the top from. **b.** To prune the upper branches from. **2. a.** To furnish with a top. **b.** To form or serve as the top of. **3.** To reach the top of. **4.** To go over the top of. **5.** To exceed or surpass. **6.** To be at the head or top of; lead: *He topped the list of this season's goal scorers.* **7.** In various sports and games, to strike the upper part of (a ball), giving it forward spin. **8.** *Chemistry.* To remove (the most volatile component) by distillation. *—intr.* To top a ball. **—top off.** To finish, usually in a satisfying way; complete. **—top out. 1.** To put the framework for the top story on (a building). **2. a.** To lay the last or highest brick or stone of a building. **b.** To celebrate this event in a ceremony. [Middle English *top(pe),* Old English *topp,* from Germanic *toppaz* (unattested).]

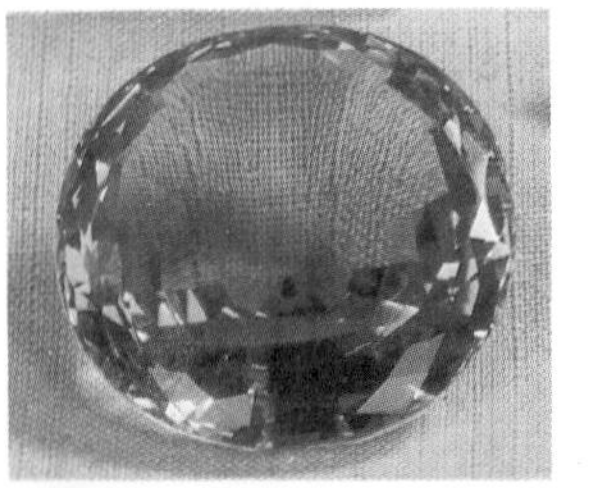

topaz *An aluminum- and silicon-based mineral that is valued as a gemstone. This prized sherry brown variety is found only in Brazil.*

top[2] *n.* A toy consisting of a symmetrical rigid body spun on a pointed end about the axis of symmetry. [Middle English *to(o)p,* Old English *topp*†.]

top–. Variant of **topo-.**

to·paz (tō′păz′) *n.* **1.** A colorless, blue, yellow, brown, or pink aluminum silicate mineral, often found in association with granitic rocks and valued as a gemstone, especially in the brown and pink varieties. **2.** Any of various yellow gemstones, especially a yellow variety of sapphire. **3.** A light-yellow variety of quartz. **4.** Either of two colorful South American hummingbirds, *Topaza pyra* or *T. pella.* [Middle English *topace,* from Old French *topace, topaze,* from Latin *topazus,* from Greek *topazos*†.]

top banana *n. Informal.* **1.** The main comedian in a burlesque show. **2.** The head person, as of a group or project. [So called from the presentation of a banana to the comedian who has the punch line in a three-man burlesque routine.]

top boot *n.* A high boot usually having its upper part trimmed with a contrasting color or texture of leather.

top brass *n.* The most important people, as in a business or army.

top·coat (tŏp′kōt′) *n.* **1.** A lightweight overcoat. **2.** A final covering of paint.

top dog *n. Informal.* A person or group considered to have the highest status or authority, especially as a result of victory in some struggle or competition. **—top-dog** (tŏp′dôg′, -dŏg′) *adj.*

top-drawer (tŏp′drôr′) *adj. Informal.* Of the highest importance, privilege, merit, or rank.

top-dress (tŏp′drĕs′) *tr.v.* **-dressed, -dressing, -dresses.** To cover (land or a road surface) with loose material that is not worked in; especially, to cover (land that is to be cultivated) with fertilizer.

top dressing *n.* **1.** A covering of fertilizer spread on soil without being plowed under. **2.** A covering of loose gravel on a road.

tope[1] (tōp) *v.* **toped, toping, topes.** *—tr.* To drink (alcoholic liquors) habitually and excessively. *—intr.* To drink to excess habitually. [Probably from obsolete *tope,* an interjection used in proposing a toast.]

tope[2] *n.* Any of several small sharks, especially *Galeorhinus galeus.* [17th century : perhaps from Cornish.]

tope[3] *n.* A Buddhist shrine, a **stupa** *(see).* [Hindi *tōp,* probably from Prakrit *thūpo,* from Sanskrit *stūpa,* tuft of hair, crown.]

topee. Variant of **topi.**

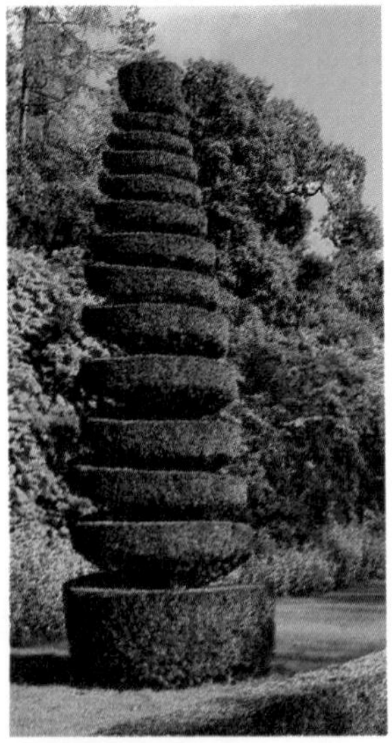

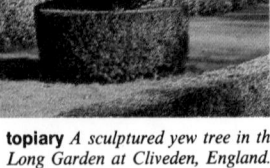

topiary *A sculptured yew tree in the Long Garden at Cliveden, England.*

To·pe·ka (tə-pē′kə). Capital of Kansas, in the northeastern part of the state. It is a major commercial center for the state's livestock, wheat, and other farm products.

top·er (tō′pər) *n.* A chronic drinker; drunkard. [From TOPE (to drink).]

top·flight (tŏp′flīt′) *adj.* First-rate; superior.

top·full (tŏp′fo͝ol′) *adj.* Full to the brim.

top·gal·lant (tə-găl′ənt, tŏp-) *adj. Nautical.* Designating the mast above the topmast, its sails, or its rigging. [Alluding to its superior position and to its making a gallant show.]

top-ham·per, top hamper (tŏp′hăm′pər) *n.* **1.** *Nautical.* Any rigging, cables, spars, or other materials or weight not immediately necessary and stored either aloft or on the upper decks. **2.** Cumbersome and unnecessary or meaningless matter.

top hat *n.* A man's hat having a narrow brim and a tall cylindrical crown, usually made of silk and worn only on formal occasions.

top-heav·y (tŏp′hĕv′ē) *adj.* **-ier, -iest. 1.** Too heavy on top for the lower part. **2.** Having too many executives in senior positions and not enough actual workers. Said of a business enterprise. **3.** *Finance.* Overcapitalized. **—top-heav·i·ness** *n.*

To·phet (tō′fĕt′, -fĭt) *n.* **1.** A place near Gehenna where human sacrifices were made. Jeremiah 19:4. **2.** Hell or a hellish place. [Middle English *Tophet(h),* from Hebrew *tōpheth,* probably "altar," place where children were burned, from the root *t-ph-th,* to burn.]

top-hole (tŏp′hōl′) *adj. British Informal.* Very good; excellent.

to·phus (tō′fəs) *n., pl.* **-phi** (-fī′). *Physiology.* A urate deposit found in tissue, such as cartilage, around the joints of people suffering from gout. Also called "chalkstone." [Latin *tōphus,* TUFA.] **—to·pha·ceous** (tō-fā′shəs) *adj.*

to·pi, to·pee (tō-pē′, tō′pē) *n., pl.* **-pis** or **-pees.** A pith helmet worn for protection against sun and heat. [Hindi *topī*†, hat.]

to·pi·ar·y (tō′pē-ĕr′ē) *adj.* Of, designating, or characterized by the clipping or trimming of shrubs or trees into decorative shapes, such as those of animals, birds, or geometric forms.
~*n., pl.* **topiaries. 1.** Topiary work or art. **2.** A topiary garden. [French *topiaire,* from Latin *topiārius,* of gardening, from *topia,* landscape gardening, from Greek *topia,* plural of *topion,* a field, small place, diminutive of *topos,* a place. See **topic.**] **—to·pi·a·rist** (tō′pē-ər-ĭst) *n.*

top·ic (tŏp′ĭk) *n.* **1.** A subject treated in a speech, essay, thesis, or portion of a discourse; a theme. **2.** A subject of discussion or conversation. **3.** A subdivision of a theme, thesis, or outline. **—**See Synonyms at **subject.** [Originally from Aristotle's *Topics,* which contains commonplace arguments, from Latin *Topica,* from Greek *(Ta) Topika,* from *topikos,* of a place, commonplace, from *topos*†, a place.]

top·i·cal (tŏp′ĭ-kəl) *adj.* **1.** Pertaining or belonging to a particular location or place; local. **2.** *Medicine.* Of, pertaining to, or applied to an isolated part of the body. **3.** Contemporary in reference or allusion; of current interest. **4.** Of or pertaining to a particular topic or topics. [Greek *topikos,* of a place. See **topic.**] **—top·i·cal·i·ty** (tŏp′ĭ-kăl′ə-tē) *n.* **—top·i·cal·ly** *adv.*

topic sentence *n.* The sentence within a paragraph that states the main thought, usually placed at the beginning.

top kick *n. Slang.* A first sergeant.

top·knot (tŏp′nŏt′) *n.* **1.** A crest or knot of hair or feathers on the crown of the head. **2.** Any decorative ribbon, bow, or the like, worn as a headdress. **3.** Any of various spiny-scaled flatfish of the genera *Zeugopterus* and *Phrynorhombus*; especially, *Z. punctatus.*

top·less (tŏp′lĭs) *adj.* **1. a.** Having no top. **b.** Having no part covering the breasts: *a topless bathing suit.* **c.** Not wearing a top: *a topless waitress.* **2.** So high as to appear to extend out of sight: *the topless Alps.* **—top·less** *adv.*

top-lev·el (tŏp′lĕv′əl) *adj.* Occurring at the highest level of authority, management, diplomacy, or the like: *top-level negotiations.*

top·loft·y (tŏp′lôf′tē, -lŏf′tē) *adj.* **-ier, -iest.** *Informal.* Haughty; pretentious. [Probably originally from TOP (highest part) + LOFTY, or from *top loft,* topmost story or gallery.] **—top·loft·i·ness** *n.*

top·mast (tŏp′məst, -măst′, -mäst′) *n. Nautical.* The mast that is below the topgallant mast in a square-rigged ship and just above the lower mast in a fore-and-aft-rigged ship.

top·most (tŏp′mōst′) *adj.* Highest; uppermost.

top·notch (tŏp′nŏch′) *adj. Informal.* First-rate; excellent.

topo–, top– *prefix.* Indicates place or region; for example, **topology, toponymy.** [Greek *topos,* a place.]

to·pog·ra·pher (tə-pŏg′rə-fər) *n.* **1.** A person skilled in topography. **2.** A person who describes and maps the surface features of geographic regions.

to·pog·ra·phy (tə-pŏg′rə-fē) *n., pl.* **-phies.** *Abbr.* **topog. 1.** The detailed and accurate description of a place or region. **2.** The art of graphically representing on a map the exact physical configuration of a place or region. **3.** The features of a place or region. **4.** The surveying of the features of a place or region. [Middle English *topographie,* from Late Latin *topographia,* from Greek, from *topographein,* to describe a place : TOPO- + *graphein,* to write (see **-graphy**).] **—top·o·graph·ic** (tŏp′ə-grăf′ĭk), **top·o·graph·i·cal** *adj.* **—top·o·graph·i·cal·ly** *adv.*

to·pol·o·gy (tə-pŏl′ə-jē) *n.* **1.** The topographical study of a given place in relation to its history. **2.** The anatomy of specific areas of the body. **3.** *Mathematics.* The study, by means of continuous mappings, of the properties of geometric configurations that are invariant under transformation; the study of those properties of a figure or solid that are unaffected by continuous distortion, as stretching

or twisting. In this sense, also formerly called "analysis situs." [TOPO- + -LOGY.] —**top·o·log·i·cal** (tŏp'ə-lŏj'ĭ-kəl), **top·o·log·ic** *adj.* —**to·pol·o·gist** (tə-pŏl'ə-jĭst) *n.*
top·o·nym (tŏp'ə-nĭm') *n.* **1.** Any name derived from a place or region. **2.** The name of a place. [Back-formation from TOPONYMY.] —**top·o·nym·ic** (tŏp'ə-nĭm'ĭk), **top·o·nym·i·cal** *adj.*
to·pon·y·my (tə-pŏn'ə-mē, tō-) *n., pl.* **-mies. 1.** The study of place names. **2.** *Anatomy.* Nomenclature with respect to a region of the body rather than to organs or structures. Not in current technical usage. [TOP(O)- + -ONYMY.]
to·pos (tō'pŏs', tŏp'ŏs') *n., pl.* **topoi** (tō'poi', tŏp'oi'). A basic or stereotypical theme, idea, or the like, especially in literature. [Greek, stock topic, commonplace.]
top·o·type (tŏp'ə-tīp') *n. Biology.* A specimen of an organism taken from the area typical for that species. [TOPO- + -TYPE.]
top·per (tŏp'ər) *n.* **1.** One that takes off tops: *a carrot topper.* **2.** *Informal.* A top hat. **3.** A short, lightweight topcoat for a girl or woman. **4.** *Informal.* Something that outdoes or caps what has gone before, especially a bantering remark.
top·ping (tŏp'ĭng) *n.* A sauce, icing, or garnish for food.
~*adj. Chiefly British Informal.* First-rate; excellent.
top·ple (tŏp'əl) *v.* **-pled, -pling, -ples.** —*tr.* **1.** To push over; overturn. **2.** To overthrow, as from an elevated or powerful position. —*intr.* **1.** To totter and fall. **2.** To lean over as if about to fall. [Frequentative of TOP (to remove the top of).]
top round *n.* A cut of meat, as steak or a roast, taken from the inner section of a round of beef.
tops (tŏps) *adj. Informal.* First-rate; excellent. —**the tops.** *Informal.* A first-rate or excellent person or thing.
top·sail (tŏp'səl, -sāl') *n.* **1.** A square sail set above the lowest sail on the mast of a square-rigged ship. **2.** A triangular or square sail set above the gaff of a lower sail on a fore-and-aft-rigged ship.
top-se·cret (tŏp'sē'krĭt) *adj.* Designating materials or information of the highest level of security classification.
top sergeant *n. Informal.* A first sergeant.
top shell *n.* Any primitive, winklelike, marine mollusk of the family Trochidae.
top·side (tŏp'sīd') *n. Often* **topsides.** The upper parts of a ship that are above the main deck.
~*adv.* On or to the upper parts of a ship; on deck.
Top-Sid·er (tŏp'sī'dər) *n.* A trademark for a soft leather or canvas shoe with a rubber sole.
top·soil (tŏp'soil') *n.* The surface layer of soil.
~*tr.v.* **topsoiled, -soiling, -soils. 1.** To remove the topsoil from (land). **2.** To cover or spread with topsoil.
top·spin (tŏp'spĭn') *n. Sports.* A forward spin given to a ball by hitting it with a sharp, slightly forward-curved stroke.
top·stitch (tŏp'stĭch') *tr.v.* **-stitched, -stitching, -stitches.** To sew a line of decorative stitching close to the seam or edge of (a garment) on the right side of the fabric.
top·sy-tur·vy (tŏp'sē-tûr'vē) *adv.* **1.** Upside-down. **2.** In a state of utter confusion or disorder.
~*adj.* In a confused or disordered condition.
~*n.* Confusion; chaos. [Earlier *topsy-tervy, topsy-tirvy* : probably TOP + obsolete *tervy,* to overturn, Middle English *turven,* to wallow, probably from Old English *tierfan* (unattested), to roll.] —**top·sy-tur·vi·ly** *adv.* —**top·sy-tur·vi·ness** *n.*
toque (tōk) *n.* **1.** A small brimless, close-fitting woman's hat. **2.** A plumed velvet cap with a full crown and small rolled brim, especially as worn by men and women in 16th-century France. [French, from Spanish *toca*†.]
tor (tôr) *n.* **1.** A high rock or pile of rocks on the top of a hill. **2.** A rocky peak or hill. [Middle English *torre,* Old English *torr,* probably from Old Welsh *twrr,* bulge.]
to·rah (tôr'ə, tōr'ə) *n.* **1.** The body of Jewish literature and oral tradition as a whole, containing the laws and teachings of the religion. **2. Torah. a.** The Pentateuch. **b.** The scroll of parchment or leather on which the Pentateuch is written, used in a synagogue during services. [Hebrew *tōrāh,* a law, instruction, from *yārāh,* to teach, instruct.]
tor·bern·ite (tôr'bər-nīt') *n.* A green hydrous crystalline phosphate of uranium and copper. [German *Torbernit,* after *Torbern* O. Bergman (1735–84), Swedish chemist.]
torch (tôrch) *n.* **1.** A portable light produced by the flame of an inflammable material wound about the end of a stick of wood and ignited; a flambeau. **2.** A portable apparatus that produces a very hot flame by the combustion of gases, used in welding and brazing. **3.** Anything that serves to illuminate, enlighten, or guide. **4.** *British.* A flashlight. —**carry a** (or **the**) **torch for.** To love (someone) unrequitedly.
~*tr.v.* **torched, torching, torches.** *Slang.* To set on fire with or as if with a torch. [Middle English *torche,* from Old French, a torch originally made of twisted straw dipped in wax, from Vulgar Latin *torca* (unattested), from *torquēre,* to twist.]
torch·bear·er (tôrch'bâr'ər) *n.* **1.** A person who carries a torch. **2.** A person who imparts knowledge, truth, or inspiration to others, as a leader of a movement.
tor·chère (tôr-shâr') *n.* A tall narrow table or stand, especially for supporting candlesticks. [French, from *torche,* TORCH.]
tor·chon lace (tôr'shŏn') *n.* A lace made of coarse linen or cotton thread twisted in simple geometric patterns. [French *torchon,* duster, dishcloth, from Old French, twisted straw, from *torche,* TORCH.]
torch song *n.* A sentimental, often highly emotional popular song. [From the phrase *to carry a torch for.*] —**torch singer** *n.*
torch·wood (tôrch'wo͝od') *n.* **1.** Any of several tropical American trees of the genus *Amyris*; especially, *A. balsamifera,* having resinous wood that burns with a torchlike flame. **2.** The wood of such a tree.
tore[1]. Past tense of **tear** (to pull apart).
tore[2] (tôr, tōr) *n. Mathematics & Architecture.* A **torus** *(see).* [French, from Latin TORUS.]
tor·e·a·dor (tôr'ē-ə-dôr') *n.* A bullfighter, especially one mounted on a horse. [Spanish, from *torear* (past participle *toreado*), to fight bulls, from *toro,* a bull, from Latin *taurus.*]
to·re·ro (tə-râr'ō) *n., pl.* **-ros.** A matador or one of his team. [Spanish, from Late Latin *taurārius,* from Latin *taurus,* a bull.]
to·reu·tics (tə-ro͞o'tĭks) *n. Used with a singular verb.* The art of working metal or other materials by the use of embossing and chasing to form minute detailed reliefs. [From *toreutic,* from Greek *toreutikos,* from *toreutos,* worked in relief, from *toreuein,* to bore through, from *toreus,* a boring tool.] —**to·reu·tic** *adj.*
to·ri. Plural of **torus.**
tor·ic (tôr'ĭk, tŏr'-) *adj.* Of, pertaining to, or shaped like a torus or a part of a torus.
toric lens *n.* A spectacle lens used to correct astigmatism that has one torus-shaped surface with different focal lengths in different directions.
to·ri·i (tôr'ē-ē', tōr'-) *n., pl.* **torii.** The gateway of a Shinto temple, consisting of two uprights with a straight crosspiece at the top and a concave lintel above the crosspiece. [Japanese, "bird residence" : *tori,* bird + *i-,* from *iru,* to dwell.]
Torino. See **Turin.**
tor·ment (tôr'mĕnt') *n.* **1.** Great physical pain or mental anguish. **2.** A source of harassment, annoyance, or pain.
~*tr.v.* (tôr-mĕnt', tôr'mĕnt') **tormented, -menting, -ments. 1.** To cause to undergo great physical pain or mental anguish. **2.** To agitate or upset greatly. **3.** To annoy, pester, or harass. —See Synonyms at **harass.** [Middle English, instrument of torture, torment, from Old French, from Latin *tormentum, torquementum* (unattested), a twisted rope, (instrument of) torture, from *torquēre,* to twist.] —**tor·ment·ing·ly** *adv.*
tor·men·til (tôr'mən-tĭl') *n.* A Eurasian plant, *Potentilla erecta* (or *P. tormentilla*), having yellow flowers and leaves divided into five leaflets. [Middle English *tormentille,* from Medieval Latin *tormentilla*†.]
tor·men·tor, tor·ment·er (tôr-mĕn'tər, tôr'mĕn'tər) *n.* **1.** One that torments. **2.** A hanging used at each side of the stage in a theater directly behind the proscenium to block the wing area and sidelights from the audience. **3.** A sound-absorbent screen used on a motion-picture set to prevent echo.
torn. Past participle of **tear** (to pull apart).
tor·na·do (tôr-nā'dō) *n., pl.* **-does** or **-dos. 1.** A rotating column of air usually accompanied by a funnel-shaped downward extension of a cumulonimbus cloud and having a vortex several hundred yards in diameter whirling destructively at speeds of up to 480 kilometers (300 miles) per hour. Also called "cyclone." Compare **waterspout. 2.** A violent thunderstorm in West Africa and nearby Atlantic waters. **3.** Any whirlwind or hurricane. **4.** Anything resembling a tornado in vigor or destructiveness. —See Synonyms at **wind.** [Variant (influenced by Spanish *tornado,* turned) of Spanish *tronada,* thunderstorm, from the past participle of *tronar,* to thunder, from Latin *tonāre.*] —**tor·na·dic** (tôr-nā'dĭk, -năd'ĭk) *adj.*
to·roid (tôr'oid', tōr'-) *n.* **1.** In geometry: **a.** A surface generated by a closed curve rotating about, but not intersecting or containing, an axis in its own plane. **b.** A solid having such a surface. **2.** An object having the shape of such a figure. [TOR(US) + -OID.] —**to·roi·dal** (tô-roid'l) *adj.*
To·ron·to (tə-rŏn'tō). Capital of Ontario, eastern Canada, on Lake Ontario. It is the cultural center of English-speaking Canada, a major port, a financial and industrial center, and an important transportation hub. It was founded *c.* 1787, and, as York, it became the capital of Upper Canada (1793), but was incorporated as the city of Toronto in 1834.
to·rose (tôr'ōs', tōr'-) *adj. Biology.* Cylindrical and having ridges or swellings. [Latin *torōsus,* from *torus,* TORUS.]
tor·pe·do (tôr-pē'dō) *n., pl.* **-does. 1.** A cigar-shaped, self-propelled underwater projectile launched from an aircraft, ship, or submarine, and designed to detonate on contact with or in the vicinity of a target. **2.** Any of various submarine explosive devices, especially a submarine mine. **3.** An explosive fired in an oil or gas well to begin or increase the flow. **4.** Any of several cartilaginous fishes of the genus *Torpedo,* related to the skates and rays. See **electric ray. 5.** See **hero** (sense 5).
~*tr.v.* **torpedoed, -doing, -does. 1.** To attack, explode, or destroy with or as if with a torpedo or torpedoes. **2.** To immobilize or render ineffective (a scheme, policy, or the like). [New Latin *Torpedo,* genus of fish that give electric shocks, from Latin *torpēdō,* stiffness, numbness, the torpedo (fish), from *torpēre,* to be stiff.]
torpedo boat *n.* A fast, thinly plated boat equipped with heavy machine guns and torpedoes.
tor·pe·do-boat destroyer (tôr-pē'dō-bōt') *n.* A fast vessel, larger and more heavily armed than a torpedo boat, designed to destroy the latter, but often serving the same purpose.
tor·pe·fy (tôr'pə-fī') *tr.v.* **-fied, -fying, -fies.** To make torpid. [Latin *torpefacere* : *torpēre,* to be sluggish + *-facere,* -FY.]
tor·pid (tôr'pĭd) *adj.* **1.** Deprived of the power of motion or feeling;

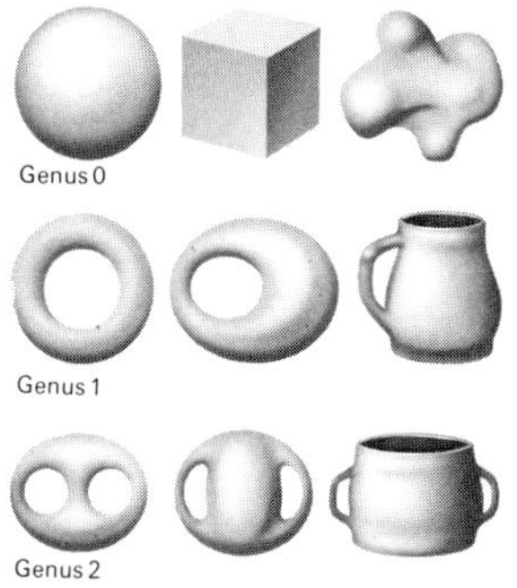

topology *In topological mathematics, the genus of an object is defined by the number of holes through it. If the shapes above were made of infinitely malleable Plasticine, those in each row could be changed into one another with no cutting, piercing, or joining. But they could not, under the same restrictions, be changed into the shapes of any other row.*

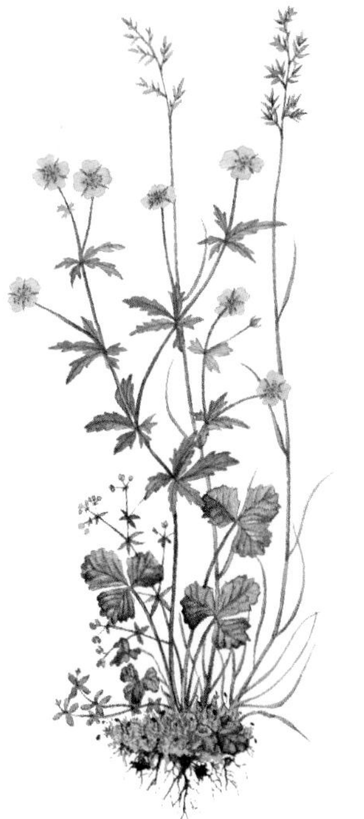
tormentil *A plant of heaths, fens, and bogs. Its roots were once used to produce a red dye and were also thought to cure the torment of stomachache—hence its name.*

benumbed. **2.** Dormant; hibernating. **3.** Lethargic; apathetic. —See Synonyms at **inactive.** [Latin *torpidus,* from *torpēre,* to be stiff. See **torpedo.**] —**tor·pid·i·ty** (tôr-pĭd′ə-tē), **tor·pid·ness** *n.* —**tor·pid·ly** *adv.*

tor·por (tôr′pər) *n.* **1.** A condition of mental or physical inactivity or insensibility. **2.** Lethargy; apathy. —See Synonyms at **lethargy.** [Latin, from *torpēre,* to be stiff. See **torpedo.**]

torque[1] (tôrk) *n.* **1.** The moment of a force, a measure of its tendency to produce torsion and rotation about an axis, equal to the vector product of the radius vector from the axis of rotation to the point of application of the force by the force applied. **2.** Broadly, a turning or twisting force. [Latin *torquēre,* to twist.]

torque[2] *n.* A collar, necklace, or armband made of a strip of twisted metal, worn by the ancient Gauls, Germans, and Britons. [French, from Latin *torquēs,* twisted necklace, from *torquēre,* to twist.]

torque converter *n.* A mechanical or hydraulic device for changing the ratio of torque to speed between the input and output shafts of a mechanism.

Tor·que·ma·da (tôr′kə-mä′də), **Tomás de** (1420–98). Spanish grand inquisitor. The organizer of the Spanish Inquisition, he was appointed grand inquisitor by Pope Innocent VIII (1487). Under his authorization, thousands of Jews, suspected witches, and other so-called offenders were killed or tortured.

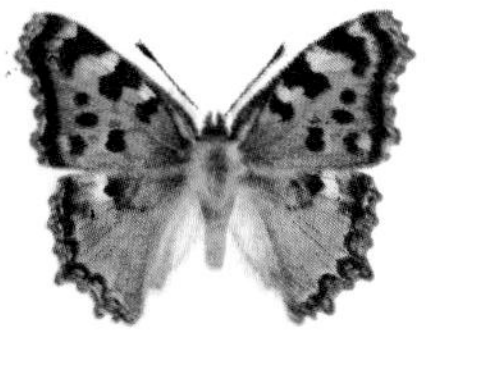

tortoiseshell *The large tortoiseshell butterfly,* Nymphalis polychloros, *has a wingspan of about 60 millimeters (2½ inches).*

tor·ques (tôr′kwēz′) *n. Zoology.* A distinctive band of feathers, hair, skin, or coloration around the neck. [Latin *torquēs,* TORQUE (collar).]

torque wrench *n.* A wrench with a torque gauge built into it to enable nuts and bolts to be tightened to a given torque.

torr (tôr) *n., pl.* **torr.** A unit of pressure equal to one millimeter of mercury (133.32 pascals). [After Evangelista TORRICELLI; see **Torricellian vacuum.**]

tor·re·fy, tor·ri·fy (tôr′ə-fī′, tŏr′-) *tr.v.* **-fied, -fying, -fies.** To scorch, roast, or dry (metallic ores or drugs, for example) by exposing to intense heat. [French *torréfier,* from Latin *torrefacere* : *torrēre,* to parch + *-facere,* -FY.] —**tor·re·fac·tion, tor·ri·fac·tion** (tôr′ə-făk′shən, tŏr′-) *n.*

tor·rent (tôr′ənt, tŏr′-) *n.* **1.** A turbulent, swift-flowing stream. **2.** A raging flood; a deluge. **3.** Any turbulent or overwhelming flow: *a torrent of abuse.* [French, from Italian *torrente,* from Latin *torrēns* (stem *torrent-*), a burning, a torrent, from the present participle of *torrēre,* to dry, burn.]

tor·ren·tial (tô-rĕn′shəl, tə-) *adj.* **1.** Of, pertaining to, or having the character of a torrent. **2.** Resembling a torrent; turbulent or unrestrained: *torrential applause.* **3.** Resulting from the action of a torrent or torrents: *torrential erosion.* —**tor·ren·tial·ly** *adv.*

Tor·res Strait (tôr′əs). Channel between New Guinea and Cape York, Australia, linking the Arafura and Coral seas. It is notorious for its reefs and shoals.

Tor·ri·cel·li (tôr′ə-chĕl′ē), **Evangelista** (1608–47). Italian mathematician and physicist. He proposed the experiment that led to the development of the barometer and formulated Torricelli's theorem, after showing that the flow of a liquid through an opening is proportional to the square root of the height of the liquid.

Tor·ri·cel·li·an vacuum (tôr′ə-chĕl′ē-ən) *n.* The vacuum formed at the top of a vertical glass tube with one sealed end that has been evacuated, partly filled with mercury, and inverted into a mercury reservoir so that its open end is submerged beneath the mercury. It functions as an indicator of atmospheric pressure. [After Evangelista TORRICELLI.]

tor·rid (tôr′ĭd, tŏr′-) *adj.* **1.** Parched with the heat of the sun. **2.** Intensely hot; scorching; burning. **3.** Passionate; ardent. [Latin *torridus,* from *torrēre,* to dry, parch.] —**tor·rid·i·ty** (tô-rĭd′ə-tē), **tor·rid·ness** *n.* —**tor·rid·ly** *adv.*

Torrid Zone *n.* The region of the earth's surface between the tropics of Cancer and Capricorn.

tor·sade (tôr-säd′, -săd′) *n.* A decorative trimming for hats, consisting of twisted ribbon or cord. [French, from (obsolete) *tors,* twisted, from Late Latin *torsus,* from the past participle of Latin *torquēre,* to twist.]

tor·sion (tôr′shən) *n.* **1. a.** The act of twisting or turning. **b.** The condition of being twisted or turned. **2.** The stress caused when one end of an object is twisted in one direction and the other end is held motionless or twisted in the opposite direction. [Middle English, from Old French, from Late Latin *torsiō* (stem *torsiōn-*), from *torsus,* "twisted." See **torsade.**] —**tor·sion·al** *adj.* —**tor·sion·al·ly** *adv.*

torsion balance *n.* An instrument with which small forces, such as those of gravity, electricity, or magnetism, are measured by means of the torsion they produce in a wire or slender rod.

torsion bar *n.* A part of a motor vehicle's suspension consisting of a bar that twists to maintain stability.

torsk (tôrsk) *n., pl.* **torsks** or collectively **torsk.** A marine fish, *Brosme brosme,* of the family Gadidae, found mainly in the north Atlantic. Also called "tusk." [Of Scandinavian origin; compare Norwegian *torsk.*]

tor·so (tôr′sō) *n., pl.* **-sos** or **-si** (-sē′). **1.** The trunk of the human body. **2.** A statue of the trunk of the human body, especially with the head and limbs missing or truncated. **3.** Any truncated or unfinished thing. [Italian, a stalk, trunk (of a statue), from Latin *thyrsus,* THYRSUS.]

tort (tôrt) *n. Law.* Any wrongful act, damage, or injury done willfully, negligently, or in circumstances involving strict liability, but not involving breach of contract, for which a civil lawsuit for damages can be brought. [Middle English, from Old French, from Medieval Latin *tortum,* from Latin, twisted, distorted, from the neuter past participle of *torquēre,* to twist.] —**tor·tious** (tôr′shəs) *adj.* —**tor·tious·ly** *adv.*

torte (tôrt, tôr′tə) *n., pl.* **tortes** or **torten** (tôrt′n). A rich layer cake made with many eggs and little flour and usually containing chopped nuts, cream, fruit, or jam. [German *Torte,* perhaps from Italian *torta,* from Late Latin *tōrta*†, a kind of bread.]

tor·tel·li·ni (tôrt′l-ē′nē) *pl.n.* Small, round pieces of pasta folded over a filling. [Italian, diminutive of *tortelli,* another type of pasta, ultimately from Late Latin *torta.* See **tart** (pie).]

tort·fea·sor (tôrt′fē′zər) *n. Law.* One who is guilty of tort. [French *tortfaiseur* : TORT + *faiseur,* doer, from *faire,* to do.]

tor·ti·col·lis (tôr′tĭ-kŏl′ĭs) *n.* A contracted state of the neck muscles producing an unnatural position of the head. Also called "wryneck." [New Latin : Latin *tortus,* past participle of *torquēre,* to twist (see **tort**) + *collum,* the neck.] —**tor·ti·col·lar** (tôr′tĭ-kŏl′ər) *adj.*

tor·til·la (tôr-tē′yə) *n.* A thin unleavened pancake made of corn meal, characteristic of Mexican cookery, usually served hot with various fillings. [American Spanish, diminutive of Spanish *torta,* a round cake, from Late Latin *torta,* TORTE.]

tor·toise (tôr′təs) *n.* **1. a.** Any of various terrestrial reptiles of the order Chelonia, characteristically having thick, scaly limbs and a high, rounded shell. **b.** *Chiefly British.* A pond or water tortoise; a **terrapin** *(see).* **2.** One that moves slowly. **3.** A **testudo** *(see).* [Middle English *tortuce, tortu,* from Old French *tortue,* probably from Medieval Latin *tortūca*†.]

tor·toise·shell (tôr′təs-shĕl′) *n.* **1.** The mottled, translucent brownish covering of the carapace of certain of the sea turtles, especially the hawksbill, used to make combs, jewelry, and other articles. **2.** Any of various synthetic substances similar to tortoiseshell. **3.** A domestic cat having fur with brown, black, and yellowish markings. **4.** Any of several butterflies, chiefly of the family Nymphalidae, especially *Nymphalis polychloros,* the large tortoiseshell, and *Aglais urticae,* the small tortoiseshell, having wings with orange, black, and brown markings. **5.** A mottled yellowish-brown. —**tor·toise·shell** *adj.*

Tor·to·la (tôr-tō′lə). Largest (54 square kilometers; 21 square miles) of the British Virgin Islands in the West Indies.

Tor·tu·ga (tôr-too͞′gə). Island, *c.* 180 square kilometers (70 square miles) in area, off the northern coast of Haiti. It was a notorious rendezvous of pirates in the 17th century.

tor·tu·os·i·ty (tôr′cho͞o-ŏs′ə-tē) *n., pl.* **-ties. 1.** The state of being tortuous; twistedness; crookedness. **2.** A bent or twisted part, passage, or thing; a twist; turn; winding.

tor·tu·ous (tôr′cho͞o-əs) *adj.* **1.** Having or marked by repeated turns or bends; winding; twisting. **2.** Not straightforward; deceitful; devious. **3.** Highly involved; circuitous; complex. [Middle English, from Old French, from Latin *tortuōsus,* from *tortus,* a twist, from the past participle of *torquēre,* to twist.] —**tor·tu·ous·ly** *adv.* —**tor·tu·ous·ness** *n.*

tor·ture (tôr′chər) *n.* **1.** The infliction of severe physical pain, especially as a means of punishment or coercion. **2.** The undergoing of such pain. **3.** Mental anguish. **4.** A cause of such pain or anguish. ~*tr.v.* **tortured, -turing, -tures. 1.** To subject (a person or animal) to torture. **2.** To afflict with great physical or mental pain. **3.** To twist or turn abnormally; distort. [French, from Late Latin *tortūra,* a twisting, torment, from Latin *tortus,* "twisted." See **tortuous.**] —**tor·tur·er** *n.*

tor·tur·ous (tôr′chər-əs) *adj.* **1.** Of or pertaining to torture. **2.** Causing or inflicting torture. **3.** Excruciatingly painful.

to·rus (tôr′əs, tōr′-) *n., pl.* **tori** (tôr′ī′, tōr′ī′). **1.** *Architecture.* A large molding of convex semicircular cross section, usually found just above the plinth of the base of a classical column. Also called "tore." **2.** *Anatomy.* A bulging or rounded projection or swelling. **3.** *Biology.* A moundlike or rounded structure, such as the receptacle of a flower. **4.** In geometry, a toroid generated by a circle; a surface having the shape of a doughnut. In this sense, also called "anchor ring," "tore." [New Latin, from Latin *torus*†, a protuberance, round swelling.]

To·ry (tôr′ē, tōr′ē) *n., pl.* **-ries. 1. a.** One who supported James II of England and opposed the Glorious Revolution of 1689. **b.** A member of a British political party, founded in 1689, that was the opposition party to the Whigs, became identified with conservative interests, and has been known as the Conservative Party since about 1832. **2.** An American who during the American Revolution favored the English side. **3.** *Sometimes* **tory. a.** A member or supporter of a Conservative Party, as in Canada. **b.** A conservative or right-wing person. [Irish Gaelic *tōraidhe,* robber, from Old Irish *tōir,* pursuit.] —**To·ry** *adj.* —**To·ry·ism** *n.*

Tos·ca·ni·ni (tŏs′kə-nē′nē), **Arturo** (1867–1957). Italian conductor. He is remembered especially for his interpretations of Beethoven, Wagner, and Verdi.

tosh (tŏsh) *n. Informal.* Nonsense; rubbish. [19th century : origin obscure.]

toss (tôs, tŏs) *v.* **tossed, tossing, tosses.** —*tr.* **1.** To throw casually or lightly. Often used with *out, aside, down,* or other adverbs. **2.** To throw, fling, or heave continuously about; pitch to and fro. **3. a.** To throw lightly with or as if with the hand or hands; pitch gently or with a sudden slight jerk. **b.** To throw upward. **4.** *Informal.* To discuss informally; bandy about. **5.** To move or lift (the head) with rapidity: *"'Idiot!' said the Queen, tossing her head impatiently"* (Lewis Carroll). **6.** To disturb or agitate; upset. **7. a.** To throw (a rider) to the ground. Used of a horse. **b.** To throw (a matador, for

example) into the air, using the head or horns. Used of a bull. **8. a.** To throw (a coin) up in order to make a decision according to the side facing upward when it lands. **b.** To throw a coin in this way with (someone) in order to decide something. **9.** To mix (a salad) lightly so as to cover with dressing, oil, or the like. **10.** To throw (a pancake) up in the air and catch it again in the pan with the reverse side upward. *—intr.* **1.** To be thrown here and there; be flung to and fro: *The boat tossed in the turbulent water.* **2.** To move oneself about vigorously; throw oneself from side to side: *toss in one's sleep.* **3.** To throw a coin to decide something. —See Synonyms at **throw.** **—toss down.** To drink in one draft by suddenly tilting: *tossed down one beer after another.* **—toss off. 1.** To drink up in one swallow. **2.** To do, finish, accomplish, or perform in a casual, easy manner: *toss off a few jokes.*
~n. **1.** The act of tossing or the condition of being tossed. **2.** The distance something can be tossed. **3.** A rapid movement or lift, as of the head. **4.** A fall from or the experience of being thrown from a horse. [Possibly of Scandinavian origin.] **—toss·er** *n.*

toss·pot (tôs'pŏt', tŏs'-) *n.* A drunkard.

toss up *intr.v.* To toss a coin to settle an issue.

toss·up (tôs'ŭp', tŏs'-) *n. Informal.* **1.** The tossing of a coin to settle an issue. **2.** An even chance or choice.

tot[1] (tŏt) *n.* **1.** A small child. **2.** A small amount of something. **3.** A small measure of liquor. [18th century : origin obscure.]

tot[2] *tr.v.* **totted, totting, tots.** *Informal.* To total or add. Usually used with *up.* [Shortening of TOTAL.]

to·tal (tōt'l) *n.* **1.** The amount or quantity obtained by addition; a sum. **2.** A whole quantity; an entirety.
~adj. **1.** Constituting or pertaining to the whole; entire. **2.** Complete; utter; absolute.
~v. **totaled** or **-talled, -taling** or **-talling, -tals.** *—tr.* **1.** To determine the sum or total of. **2.** To equal a total of; amount to. **3.** *Slang.* To demolish (a vehicle) completely in a road accident. *—intr.* To add up; amount. Often used with *to*: *It totals to three dollars.* [Middle English, of the whole, from Old French, from Medieval Latin *tōtālis,* from Latin *tōtus,* whole.]

total eclipse *n.* An eclipse in which the eclipsed body as seen from the earth is totally hidden. Compare **partial eclipse.**

to·tal·i·tar·i·an (tō-tăl'ə-târ'ē-ən) *adj.* Of or designating a government or political regime whose main characteristic is considered to be the imposition of monolithic unity in every sphere of the life of its subjects, upheld by authoritarian means. [TOTAL + (AUTHOR)ITARIAN.] **—to·tal·i·tar·i·an·ism** *n.*

to·tal·i·ty (tō-tăl'ə-tē) *n., pl.* **-ties. 1.** The state or condition of being total. **2.** The whole amount. **3.** The aggregate amount; a sum. **4. a.** The state of an eclipse when it is total. **b.** The length of time during which an eclipse is total.

to·tal·i·za·tor (tōt'l-ə-zā'tər) *n.* See **pari-mutuel** (sense 2).

to·tal·ize (tōt'l-īz') *tr.v.* **-ized, -izing, -izes.** To make or combine into a total. **—to·tal·i·za·tion** *n.*

to·tal·iz·er (tōt'l-ī'zər) *n.* **1.** A pari-mutuel machine. **2.** An adding machine.

to·tal·ly (tōt'l-ē) *adv.* Entirely; wholly; completely.

to·ta·quine (tō'tə-kwīn', -kwēn', -kwĭn) *n.* A powdered yellowish, bitter mixture of quinine and alkaloids from cinchona bark, formerly used as an antimalarial. [New Latin *totaquina* : TOTA(L) + Spanish *quina,* cinchona bark (see **quinine**).]

to·ta·ra (tō'tər-ə) *n.* A conifer, *Podocarpus totara,* of New Zealand, having hard reddish wood used in building and in making furniture. [Maori.]

tote[1] (tōt) *tr.v.* **toted, toting, totes.** *Informal.* **1.** To haul; lug. **2.** To have on one's person; pack: *toting guns.*
~n. Informal. **1.** A load; a burden. **2.** A tote bag. [17th century (U.S.) : origin obscure.] **—tot·er** *n.*

tote[2] *n. Informal.* A pari-mutuel machine. [Short for TOTALIZATOR.]

tote bag *n. Informal.* A very large handbag or shopping bag. Also called "tote."

to·tem (tō'təm) *n.* **1.** An animal, plant, or natural object serving among certain primitive peoples as the emblem of a clan or family by virtue of an asserted ancestral relationship. **2.** A representation of this being. **3.** A social group having a common totemic affiliation. **4.** Any venerated emblem or symbol. [Algonquian; compare Ojibwa *nintōtēm,* "my family mark," from a stem *ōtē-* (unattested), "to be from a local group."]

to·tem·ic (tō-tĕm'ĭk) *adj.* **1.** Of, pertaining to, characteristic of, or like a totem or totemism. **2.** Practicing or founded on totemism.

to·tem·ism (tō'tə-mĭz'əm) *n.* **1.** The belief in kinship through common totemic affiliation or the identification of an individual or group with a totem. **2.** The primitive kinship system of which this is a reflection. **—to·tem·ist** *n.* **—to·tem·is·tic** (tō'tə-mĭs'tĭk) *adj.*

totem pole *n.* **1.** A post carved and painted with a series of totemic symbols and erected before a dwelling, as by certain Indian peoples of the northwestern coast of North America. **2.** *Slang.* A hierarchy: *low man on the totem pole.*

toth·er, t'oth·er (tŭth'ər) *pron. Archaic & Regional.* The other. [Middle English *the tother,* mistaken division of *thet other* : *thet,* the, Old English *thæt,* THAT + OTHER.]

to·ti·pal·mate (tō'tĭ-păl'māt') *adj.* Having webbing that connects each of the four toes, as water birds such as pelicans and gannets have. [Latin *tōtus,* whole (see **total**) + PALMATE.]

to·tip·o·ten·cy (tō-tĭp'ə-tən-sē, tō'tĭ-pōt'n-sē) *n.* Also **to·tip·o·tence** (tō-tĭp'ə-təns, tō'tĭ-pōt'ns). **1.** The capacity of a blastomere to develop into a fully formed embryo. **2.** The ability of meristematic cells to specialize in response to hormones from growth centers. [Latin *tōtus,* whole (see **total**) + POTENCY.] **—to·tip·o·tent** *adj.*

tot·ter (tŏt'ər) *intr.v.* **-tered, -tering, -ters. 1. a.** To sway as if about to fall. **b.** To appear about to collapse: *a tottering empire.* **2.** To walk unsteadily or feebly. **3.** To waver; vacillate.
~n. The act or condition of tottering. [Middle English *tot(e)ren,* from Middle Dutch *touteren,* to stagger, from Old Saxon *taltron* (unattested).] **—tot·ter·er** *n.* **—tot·ter·y** *adj.*

tou·can (to͞o'kăn', -kän') *n.* Any of various tropical American birds of the family Ramphastidae, having an extremely large, brightly colored bill and variously colored plumage. [French, from Portuguese *tucano,* from Tupi *tucana.*]

touch (tŭch) *v.* **touched, touching, touches.** *—tr.* **1. a.** To cause or permit a part of the body to come into contact with. **b.** To cause or permit a part of the body, especially the hand, to come into contact with so as to feel. **2.** To bring something into contact with: *touched the water with my toes.* **3.** To bring (something) into contact with something else: *touch the match to the paper.* **4.** To tap or nudge very lightly. **5.** To strike or lay hands on in violence. Usually used in the negative: *Don't you dare touch her!* **6.** To use or partake of. Usually used in the negative: *She didn't touch her food.* **7.** To disturb or move by handling. **8. a.** To meet; adjoin; border. **b.** In geometry, to be tangent to. **9.** To come up to; equal in quality: *His work couldn't touch his master's.* **10. a.** To handle or be involved in. Usually used in the negative: *I wouldn't touch that business.* **b.** To treat of; deal with as a subject. **11.** To be pertinent to; concern. **12.** To have an effect upon; act on; change. **13.** To injure or spoil slightly. **14.** To color slightly; tinge. **15.** To affect the emotions of; move to tender response. **16.** To draw, mark, or shade with light strokes. Often used with *in.* **17.** *Archaic.* To strike or pluck the keys or strings of (a musical instrument). **18.** *Archaic.* To play or sing (a musical piece). **19.** *Archaic.* To set fire to or kindle. **20.** *Archaic.* To stamp (tested metal). **21.** *Informal.* To borrow from; beg a loan from. Usually used with *for*: *He touched me for $50.* *—intr.* **1.** To touch someone or something. **2.** To be or come into contact. —See Synonyms at **affect.** **—touch at.** To stop briefly at (a port, for example). **—touch off. 1.** To cause to explode; fire. **2.** To initiate (a chain of events, for example); trigger. **—touch on** (or **upon**). **1.** To deal with (a topic) in passing. **2.** To pertain to; concern. **3.** To approach being; verge on.
~n. **1.** The act or an instance of touching. **2.** The physiological sense by which external objects or forces are perceived through contact with the body. **3.** A sensation experienced in touching something with a characteristic texture. **4.** A mild tap or shove. **5.** A discernible mark or effect left by contact with something. **6.** A subtle effect wrought by a small change or addition. **7.** A suggestion; a hint; a tinge. **8.** A mild attack: *a touch of flu.* **9.** A small amount; a trace; a dash: *a touch of paprika.* **10. a.** A manner or technique of striking the keys of a keyboard instrument, such as a piano or typewriter. **b.** The resistance to being struck by the fingers characteristic of a keyboard. **11. a.** A person's characteristic manner or style of doing something. **b.** A characteristic manner in one's personal relationships. **12.** A facility; a knack: *lose one's touch.* **13.** The state of being in contact or communication: *kept in touch; afraid she's getting out of touch with reality.* **14.** A test or trial, as to establish quality. Used chiefly in the phrase *put to the touch.* **15.** The official stamp indicating the quality of a metal product; hallmark. **16.** *Slang.* **a.** The act of approaching someone to borrow or beg a loan. **b.** A sum of money borrowed. **c.** A person liable to be the victim of an approach for a loan. Often used in the phrases *soft touch* and *easy touch.* **17. a.** In soccer, the area just outside the sidelines. **b.** In Rugby football, the area outside and including the sidelines. **18.** In fencing, a scoring hit. [Middle English *to(u)chen,* from Old French *tochier,* from Vulgar Latin *toccāre* (unattested), to strike, ring a bell, touch (probably imitative).] **—touch·a·ble** *adj.* **—touch·a·ble·ness** *n.* **—touch·er** *n.*

touch-and-go, touch and go (tŭch'ən-gō') *adj.* Of unclear outcome; critical; risky.

touch·back (tŭch'băk') *n. Football.* The act of touching the ball to the ground behind one's own goal line, the ball having been impelled over the line by an opponent.

touch down *intr.v.* To land, especially briefly, as for repairs. Used of aircraft or spacecraft.

touch·down (tŭch'doun') *n. Abbr.* **TD, td., td 1.** The contact, or moment of contact, of a landing aircraft or spacecraft with the landing surface. **2.** *Football.* A play worth six points, accomplished by being in possession of the ball when it is declared dead on or behind the opponent's goal line.

tou·ché (to͞o-shā') *interj.* **1.** Used in fencing to acknowledge that one has been touched by one's opponent's foil. **2.** Used to express concession to an opponent for a point well made, as in an argument. [French, "touched."]

touched (tŭcht) *adj.* **1.** Emotionally affected or moved. **2.** Slightly demented or mentally unbalanced.

touch football *n.* A variety of football for playing on an improvised field and without protective equipment, involving the substitution of touching for tackling.

touch·hole (tŭch'hōl') *n.* The opening in early firearms and cannons through which the powder was ignited.

touch·ing (tŭch'ĭng) *adj.* Eliciting a tender reaction; moving. —See Synonyms at **moving.**
~prep. Concerning; about. **—touch·ing·ly** *adv.*

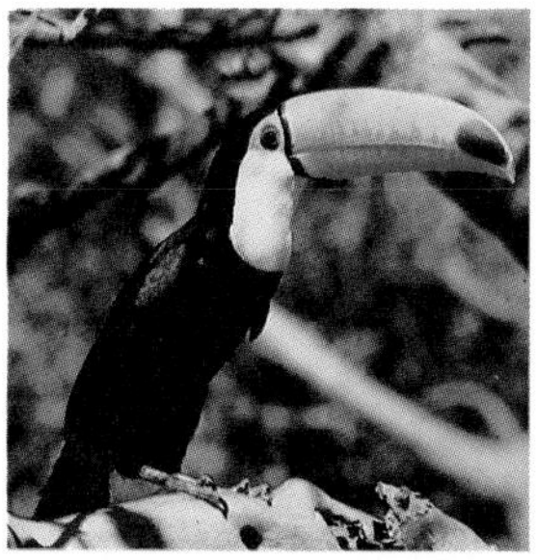

toucan *With its huge beak, which has a light honeycombed structure, the toucan is able to reach and pick fruit from trees. The birds are native to the tropical forests of the Americas.*

PRONUNCIATION KEY

ă, pat; ā, pay; âr, care;
ä, father, are; b, bib;
ch, church; d, deed; ĕ, pet;
ē, be; f, fife; g, gag; h, hat;
hw, which; ĭ, pit; ī, pie;
îr, pier; j, judge; k, kick;
l, lid, needle; m, mum;
n, no, sudden; ng, thing;
ŏ, pot; ō, toe; ô, paw, for;
oi, noise; ou, out; o͝o, book;
o͞o, boot; p, pop; r, roar;
s, sauce; sh, ship, dish;
t, tight; th, thin, path;
th, this, bathe; ŭ, cut; ûr, fur;
v, valve; w, with; y, yes;
z, zebra, size; zh, vision;
ə, about, item, edible, gallop, circus, peaceful

IN FOREIGN WORDS:

à, *Fr.* ami; œ, *Fr.* feu, *Ger.* schön; ü, *Fr.* tu, *Ger.* über; KH, *Ger.* ich, *Scot.* loch; N, *Fr.* bon; y', *Fr.* Compiègne

STRESS MARKS:

Primary stress: '
in·cite' (ĭn-sīt')
Secondary stress: '
in'sight' (ĭn'sīt')

touch·line (tŭch'līn') *n.* In various field sports such as soccer and Rugby football, either of the sidelines bordering the playing field.

touch-me-not (tŭch'mē-nŏt') *n.* Any of several plants of the genus *Impatiens* whose seed pods burst open at the slightest touch when ripe. See **jewelweed.**

touch paper *n.* A type of paper impregnated with saltpeter so that it burns slowly and without a flame. [From TOUCH (archaic sense "to kindle").]

touch·stone (tŭch'stōn') *n.* **1.** A hard black stone, such as jasper or basalt, formerly used to test the quality of gold or silver by comparing the streak left on the stone by one of these metals with that of a standard alloy. **2.** A criterion; a standard.

touch-type (tŭch'tīp') *intr.v.* **-typed, -typing, -types.** To type without having to look at the keyboard, the fingers being trained to locate the keys by position. —**touch-typ·ist** *n.*

touch up *tr.v.* To make minor changes, additions, or improvements in (a work, photograph, or the like).

touch-up (tŭch'ŭp') *n.* The act or process of finishing or improving by small alterations and additions.

touch·wood (tŭch'wŏŏd') *n.* Decayed wood or similar material used as tinder; punk. [From TOUCH (archaic sense "to kindle").]

touch·y (tŭch'ē) *adj.* **-ier, -iest. 1.** Apt to take offense with very slight cause; oversensitive. **2.** Requiring tact or skill; precarious; risky: *a touchy situation.* **3.** Sensitive to touch. Said of a bodily part. **4.** Easily ignited; flammable. —**touch·i·ly** *adv.* —**touch·i·ness** *n.*

tough (tŭf) *adj.* **tougher, toughest. 1.** Strong and resilient; able to withstand great strain without tearing or breaking. **2.** Hard to cut or chew. **3.** Physically hardy; rugged. **4.** Severe; harsh. **5.** Aggressive; pugnacious. **6.** Demanding or troubling; difficult. **7.** Strong-minded; resolute. **8.** Vicious; rough. **9.** *Informal.* Unfortunate; too bad. —See Synonyms at **strong.**
~*n.* A hoodlum; thug.
~*tr.v.* **toughed, toughing, toughs.** To remain unyielding in adverse circumstances. Used chiefly in the phrase *tough it out.* [Middle English *togh,* Old English *tōh.*] —**tough·ly** *adv.* —**tough·ness** *n.*

tough·en (tŭf'ən) *v.* **-ened, -ening, -ens.** —*tr.* To make tough or tougher. —*intr.* To become tough or tougher. —**tough·en·er** *n.*

toughened glass *n.* See **safety glass.**

tough·ie (tŭf'ē) *n. Informal.* **1.** A tough person or thing. **2.** A tough or tricky problem.

tough-mind·ed (tŭf'mīn'dĭd) *adj.* Not sentimental or timorous. —**tough-mind·ed·ly** *adv.* —**tough-mind·ed·ness** *n.*

Tou·lon (tŏŏ-lôn'). City in Var department, southeastern France. It has been a major naval base since the 17th century.

Tou·louse (tŏŏ-lŏŏz'). Capital of Haute-Garonne department, southern France. A major market, cultural center, and canal port, it is also the center of the French aviation industry.

Tou·louse-Lau·trec (tŏŏ-lŏŏz'lō-trĕk'), **Henri Marie Raymond de** (1864-1901). French artist. He settled in Paris in 1881 and painted an unconventional side of life among the music halls and cafés of Montmartre.

tou·pee (tŏŏ-pā') *n.* **1.** A partial wig or hairpiece worn, usually by men, to cover a bald spot. **2.** A curl or lock of hair worn during the 18th century as a topknot on a periwig. [French *toupet,* a tuft of hair, forelock, diminutive of Old French *toup,* tuft; see **top** (summit).]

tour (tŏŏr) *n.* **1.** A comprehensive trip or journey, usually taken for pleasure or education, with visits to places of interest. **2.** A group organized for such a trip or for a shorter sightseeing excursion. **3.** A brief trip to or through a place for the purpose of seeing it: *a tour of the house.* **4.** A journey to fulfill a round of engagements in several places: *a concert tour.* **5.** A period of duty at a single place or job. —**on tour.** Giving a series of engagements, as theatrical or concert performances, on a tour.
~*v.* **toured, touring, tours.** —*intr.* To go on a tour. —*tr.* **1.** To make a tour of: **2.** To present (a theatrical performance) on a tour. [Middle English, one's turn, a turning, from Old French *tour, to(u)rn,* turn, circuit, from Latin *tornus,* lathe. See **turn.**]

tou·ra·co, tu·ra·co (tŏŏr'ə-kō') *n., pl.* **-cos.** Any of various African birds of the family Musophagidae, many of which have brightly colored plumage. [French, from a West African name.]

Tou·raine (tŏŏ-rĕn', -rān'). Former province of west-central France. A rich agricultural area famous for its grain, fruit, and wines, it is sometimes called the garden of France. It is also a major tourist area noted for its chateaus. Tours is the chief city.

Tourane. See **Da Nang.**

tour·bil·lion (tŏŏr-bĭl'yən) *n.* **1.** A whirlwind. **2.** A firework sky-rocket that has a spiral flight. [French *tourbillon,* ultimately from Latin *turbō* (stem *turbin-*), whirlwind. See **turbine.**]

tour de force (tŏŏr' də fôrs', fōrs') *n., pl.* **tours de force** (pronounced as singular). A feat of strength or virtuosity. [French.]

touring car *n.* A large open automobile for five or more persons, popular in the 1920's.

tour·ism (tŏŏr'ĭz'əm) *n.* Also **tour·is·try** (tŏŏr'ĭ-strē) (for sense 1). **1.** The practice of traveling for pleasure. **2.** The business of providing tours and services for tourists.

tour·ist (tŏŏr'ĭst) *n.* A person who is traveling for pleasure.
~*adj.* Also **tour·is·tic** (tŏŏ-rĭs'tĭk). Of or for tourists.

tourist class *n.* A grade of travel accommodations for passengers that is less luxurious than first class or cabin class.

tourist trap *n. Informal.* A place or event to which large numbers of tourists are attracted, and at which visitors are often exploited, as by overcharging.

tour·ist·y (tŏŏr'ĭ-stē) *adj. Informal.* Like, suitable for, full of, or spoiled by tourists. Used derogatorily.

tour·ma·line (tŏŏr'mə-lĭn, -lēn') *n.* A complex crystalline silicate containing aluminum, boron, and other elements, used in electronic instrumentation and as a gemstone. [French, from Sinhalese *toramalli,* cornelian.]

tour·na·ment (tŏŏr'nə-mənt, tûr'-) *n.* **1.** A contest involving a number of contestants who compete in a series of elimination games or trials. **2. a.** A medieval sport in which mounted contestants endeavored to unseat one another with lances or swords; a jousting match. **b.** A meeting or festivity at which such matches and other chivalric displays took place. [Middle English *tornement,* from Old French *torneiement,* from *torneier,* to TOURNEY.]

tour·ne·dos (tŏŏr'nə-dō') *n., pl.* **-dos** (-dō', -dōz'). A small fillet of beef cut from the tenderloin, often bound in bacon or suet for cooking. [French : *tourner,* to TURN + *dos,* back.]

tour·ney (tŏŏr'nē, tûr'-) *intr.v.* **-neyed, -neying, -neys.** To compete in a medieval tournament.
~*n., pl.* **tourneys.** A medieval tournament. [Middle English *torneyen,* from Old French *torneier,* "to turn around" (from the combatants' turning around for each attack), from Vulgar Latin *tornidiāre* (unattested), to wheel, turn, from Latin *tornus,* a lathe, TURN.]

tour·ni·quet (tŏŏr'nĭ-kĭt, tûr'-) *n.* Any device used to stop temporarily the flow of blood through a large artery in a limb; especially, a cloth band tightened around a limb, often over a pad placed to focus pressure on the artery. [French, "a turning instrument," swivel.]

Tours (tŏŏr). Capital of Indre-et-Loire department, west-central France. It is a tourist center for the Loire valley and a market and manufacturing center.

tou·sle (tou'zəl) *tr.v.* **-sled, -sling, -sles. 1.** To disarrange or rumple; dishevel: *tousled the child's hair.* **2.** To handle roughly; mistreat.
~*n.* **1.** A disheveled mass, as of hair. **2.** A disheveled state. [Middle English *touselen,* frequentative of *tousen,* to pull roughly (in Middle English only in compounds).]

tous-les-mois (tŏŏ'lā-mwä') *n.* **1.** A West Indian plant, *Canna edulis,* with red flowers and purple stems, widely cultivated for its edible starchy rhizomes. **2.** The rhizome or starch obtained from this plant. [French, "every month," probably a phonetic approximation of West Indian *tolomane* (native name).]

Tous·saint L'Ou·ver·ture (tŏŏ-săn' lŏŏ'vĕr-tür'), **Pierre Dominique** (*c.* 1743-1803). Haitian revolutionary. With the help of the French he led a force that expelled the British and Spanish (1798). The French later seized him (1802), and he died in a French prison.

tout (tout) *v.* **touted, touting, touts.** *Informal.* —*intr.* **1.** To solicit customers, votes, or patronage, especially in a brazen way. **2.** *Chiefly British.* **a.** To obtain horseracing information for use in betting, as by spying on the training of racehorses. **b.** To deal in such information. —*tr.* **1.** To solicit or importune. **2.** *Chiefly British.* To obtain or sell information on (a racing horse or stable) for the guidance of bettors. **3.** To publicize as being of great worth; praise excessively: *highly touted by the press.*
~*n. Informal.* **1.** A person who obtains information on racehorses and their prospects and sells it to bettors. **2.** A person who solicits customers persistently or brazenly. [Middle English *tuten,* to peep, watch, Old English *tūtian* (unattested), from Germanic *tūt-* (unattested), to stick out, protrude.] —**tout·er** *n.*

to·va·risch, to·va·rish, to·va·rich (tə-vär'ĭsh, -ĭch) *n.* A comrade. Used as a term of address. [Russian.]

tow[1] (tō) *tr.v.* **towed, towing, tows.** To draw, drag, or pull along, usually by a chain or rope.
~*n.* **1.** An act of towing. **2.** The condition of being towed. Used chiefly in the phrases *on tow* or *in tow.* **3.** Something being towed, such as a barge or car. **4.** Something that tows, such as a tugboat. **5.** A rope or cable used in towing. —**in tow. 1.** Following or accompanying. **2.** Under one's sway or control; in one's charge. [Middle English *togen, towen,* Old English *togian.*]

tow[2] *n.* **1.** Coarse broken flax or hemp fiber, either prepared for spinning or to be discarded. **2.** A bunch of synthetic fibers. [Middle English *towe,* probably Old English *tow-,* "spinning."]

tow·age (tō'ĭj) *n.* **1.** The act or service of towing. **2.** A charge for towing.

to·ward (tôrd, tōrd, tə-wôrd') *prep.* Also **to·wards** (tôrdz, tōrdz, tə-wôrdz'). **1.** In the direction of. **2.** In a position facing: *The back of the chair was toward me.* **3.** Just before in time; approaching: *It began to rain toward morning.* **4.** With regard to; in relation to: *I can't understand his attitude toward us.* **5. a.** In furtherance of or partial fulfillment of: *$100 a month toward a new car.* **b.** By way of achieving; with a view to: *efforts toward peace.*
~*adj.* (tôrd, tōrd). **1.** Favorable. **2.** In progress or imminent. **3.** Tractable; docile. [Middle English *toward,* Old English *tōweard,* coming, favorable, future : TO + -WARD.]

to·ward·ly (tôrd'lē, tōrd'-) *adj. Archaic.* **1.** Promising. **2.** Advantageous; favorable. —**to·ward·li·ness** *n.*

tow·bar (tō'bär') *n.* A rigid metal bar that can be attached to a vehicle for towing something, such as another vehicle or a boat.

tow·boat (tō'bōt') *n.* A tugboat (see).

tow·el (tou'əl) *n.* A piece of absorbent cloth or paper used for wiping or drying.
~*v.* **toweled** or **-elled, -eling** or **-elling, -els.** —*tr.* To wipe or rub dry with a towel. —*intr.* To dry oneself with a towel. [Middle English *towelle,* from Old French *toail(l)e,* from Frankish *thwahljō* (unattested), from Germanic *thwahan* (unattested), to bathe.]

tow·el·ette (tou′ə-lĕt′) *n.* A small, usually moist piece of material used for cleansing, as of the hands and face.

tow·el·ing (tou′ə-lĭng) *n.* Any of various absorbent fabrics, usually of cotton or linen and having a nap, used for making towels.

tow·er (tou′ər) *n.* **1. a.** An exceptionally tall, usually equilateral, square, or circular building. **b.** An exceptionally tall part of a building, usually having a particular function: *a church tower.* **2.** A tall framework or structure, the elevation of which is functional, as for observation, signaling, or pumping. **3.** A fortress or prison, often consisting of or incorporating a tower. **4.** A tall mobile wooden framework used in medieval warfare to help soldiers scale the walls of an enemy castle. —*intr.v.* **towered, -ering, -ers. 1.** To rise to a conspicuous height; loom: *towering above our heads.* **2.** To be pre-eminent: *He towers above all others.* **3.** To soar or to fly directly upward before swooping or falling. Used of certain birds. [Middle English *to(u)r,* from Old English *torr* and Old French *tor, tur,* both from Latin *turris,* from Greek, probably of Mediterranean origin.] —**tow·ered** *adj.*

tower crane *n.* A crane consisting of a cantilever beam pivoted so that it can rotate at the top of a framework tower.

tow·er·ing (tou′ər-ĭng) *adj.* **1.** Of imposing height. **2.** Outstanding; pre-eminent. **3.** Awesomely intense; furious: *a towering rage.* —See Synonyms at **high.**

tower of strength *n.* An extremely supportive or dependable person. [From Shakespeare's *Richard III* (1594): " . . . the King's name is a tower of strength" (Act V, scene 3).]

tow·head (tō′hĕd′) *n.* **1.** A head of white-blond hair. **2.** One having such hair. [From ⲧⲟⲱ (hemp).] —**tow·head·ed** *adj.*

tow·hee (tō′hē, tō-hē′) *n.* Any of several North American birds of the genera *Pipilo* or *Chlorura;* especially, *P. erythrophthalmus,* having black, white, and rust-colored plumage in the male. [Imitative of the song of some of these birds.]

tow·line (tō′lĭn′) *n.* A towrope *(see).*

town (toun) *n.* **1.** A large group of buildings and roads within a fixed boundary, where people live and work, larger than a village and, typically, smaller than most cities. **2.** The commercial district or center of a town. **3.** The nearest town: *drove to town.* **4.** Towns in general or urban life: *I prefer the country to the town.* **5.** The residents of a town. **6.** The ordinary, permanent inhabitants of a university town, as opposed to the academic community. Compare **gown. 7.** The dominant city or town of an area. —**go to town.** *Informal.* To do something energetically with no inhibitions or restrictions; go all out. —**on the town.** *Informal.* On a spree. —**paint the town red.** *Informal.* To go on an elaborate or wild spree. [Middle English *t(o)un, town,* Old English *tūn,* an enclosed place, homestead, village.]

town clerk *n.* **1.** A public official in charge of keeping the records of a town. **2.** Until 1974, the chief administrative officer, secretary, and legal adviser of a British town.

town crier *n.* A person formerly employed by a town to walk the streets proclaiming announcements. Also called "bellman."

town hall *n.* The building where many of the local government officials of a town are based, where municipal business is conducted, and where public meetings may be held.

town house *n.* **1.** A person's house or other residence in the city as distinguished from one in the country. **2.** One of a row of houses connected by common side walls.

town·ie, town·y (tou′nē) *n., pl.* **-ies.** *Informal.* **1.** A town-dweller as opposed to a country-dweller. **2.** A resident of a university town as opposed to a student.

town meeting *n.* A legislative assembly of townspeople.

town planning *n.* The designing of a town or urban area such that houses, roads, and public amenities are planned as an integrated whole. —**town planner** *n.*

towns·folk (tounz′fōk′) *pl.n.* **Townspeople** *(see).*

town·ship (toun′shĭp′) *n.* **1.** A subdivision of a county in most northeastern and midwestern states, having the status of a unit of local government with varying governmental powers. **2.** A public land surveying unit of 36 sections or 36 square miles. **3.** Formerly in England, a unit of local government such as a parish, part of a town, or a small town. **4.** The residents of a township.

towns·man (tounz′mən) *n., pl.* **-men** (-mĭn). **1.** A resident of a town. **2.** A fellow resident of one's town.

towns·peo·ple (tounz′pē′pəl) *pl.n.* The inhabitants or citizens of a town or city. Also called "townsfolk."

towns·wom·an (tounz′wŏŏm′ən) *n., pl.* **-women** (-wĭm′ĭn). **1.** A woman resident of a town. **2.** A woman residing in the same town as oneself.

tow·path (tō′păth′, -päth′) *n., pl.* **-paths** (-păthz′, -päthz′). A path along a canal or river used by animals towing boats.

tow·rope (tō′rōp′) *n.* A strong rope or cord used in towing a vehicle, especially a car. Also called "towline."

tox-, toxo-, toxico- *prefix.* Indicates poison; for example, **toxemia.** [From Latin *toxicum,* poison. See **toxic.**]

tox·al·bu·min (tŏk′săl-byōō′mĭn) *n.* Any of various toxic albumin proteins.

tox·e·mi·a (tŏk-sē′mē-ə) *n.* **1.** A condition in which bacterial toxins produced at a local source of infection are contained in the blood. Also called "blood poisoning." **2.** The condition of pre-eclampsia or eclampsia in the later stages of pregnancy. [New Latin : TOX- + -EMIA.] —**tox·e·mic** *adj.*

tox·ic (tŏk′sĭk) *adj.* **1.** Of or pertaining to a toxin. **2.** Harmful, destructive, or deadly; poisonous. [Late Latin *toxicus,* from·Latin

toxicum, poison for arrows, from Greek *toxikon,* from *toxikos,* of or for a bow, from *toxon,* a bow.] —**tox·i·cal·ly** *adv.*

tox·i·cant (tŏk′sĭ-kənt) *n.* A poison or poisonous agent. —*adj.* Poisonous; toxic. [Medieval Latin *toxicāns* (stem *toxicant-*), present participle of *toxicāre,* to poison, from Latin *toxicum,* poison. See **toxic.**]

tox·ic·i·ty (tŏk-sĭs′ĭ-tē) *n., pl.* **-ties. 1.** The quality or condition of being toxic. **2.** The degree to which a poison is toxic.

tox·i·co·gen·ic (tŏk′sĭ-kō-jĕn′ĭk) *adj.* **1.** Producing poison or toxic substances. **2.** Derived from toxic matter.

tox·i·col·o·gy (tŏk′sĭ-kŏl′ə-jē) *n.* The study of the nature, effects, and detection of poisons and the treatment of poisoning. [TOXIC + -LOGY.] —**tox·i·co·log·i·cal** (tŏk′sĭ-kə-lŏj′ĭ-kəl) *adj.* —**tox·i·co·log·i·cal·ly** *adv.* —**tox·i·col·o·gist** *n.*

tox·i·co·sis (tŏk′sĭ-kō′sĭs) *n., pl.* **-ses** (-sēz′). Any pathological condition resulting from poisoning. [New Latin : TOXIC + -OSIS.]

toxic shock syndrome *n.* A rare infection that is characterized by vomiting, fever, a rash, and a sharp drop in blood pressure. Most known cases have occurred in women using vaginal tampons.

tox·in (tŏk′sĭn) *n.* Also **tox·ine** (-sēn′). A poisonous substance secreted by certain organisms and capable of causing toxicosis when introduced into the body tissues but also capable of inducing a counteragent or an antitoxin. [TOX- + -IN.]

tox·in-an·ti·tox·in (tŏk′sĭn-ăn′tĭ-tŏk′sĭn) *n.* A mixture of a toxin, as from diphtheria, and its antitoxin with a slight excess of toxin, formerly used as an active (live) vaccine.

tox·oid (tŏk′soid′) *n.* A toxin that has lost toxicity but has retained the capacity to stimulate the production of or combine with antitoxins, used in immunization. [TOX- + -OID.]

tox·oph·i·lite (tŏk-sŏf′ə-līt′) *n.* A lover of archery. —*adj.* Also **tox·o·phil·ic** (tŏk′sə-fĭl′ĭk). Of, pertaining to, or loving archery. [From *Toxophilus* (1545), a book by Roger ASCHAM, from Greek *toxon,* bow + -*philos,* -PHILE + -ITE.]

tox·o·plas·mo·sis (tŏk′sō-plăz-mō′sĭs) *n.* A disease caused by infection with a microorganism, *Toxoplasma gondii,* usually producing only mild symptoms except if contracted by a pregnant woman, when it can cause blindness and mental retardation in the fetus. [New Latin *toxoplasma,* from Latin : *toxicum,* poison (see **toxic**) + PLASMA + -OSIS.] —**tox·o·plas·mic** (tŏk′sō-plăz′mĭk) *adj.*

toy (toi) *n.* **1.** An object designed to be played with, especially by children. Also used adjectivally: *toy soldiers.* **2.** Something of little importance; a trifle. **3.** A small ornament; bauble; trinket. **4.** A diminutive thing or person. **5.** A dog of a very small breed or one much smaller than is characteristic of its breed, usually kept as a pet. Also used adjectivally: *a toy poodle.* —*intr.v.* **toyed, toying, toys.** To amuse oneself idly; trifle. Used with *with.* [Middle English *toye†,* dallying, amorous sport.]

Toyn·bee (toin′bē), **Arnold Joseph** (1889-1975). English historian and educator. His search for patterns in the development and decay of civilizations resulted in his best-known work, *Study of History* (1934-61), in which he explains the nontraditional philosophy of history that made him a controversial yet influential historian.

toy·on (toi′ŏn′) *n.* An evergreen shrub, *Heteromeles arbutifolia* (or *Photinia arbutifolia*), of the Pacific coast of southern North America, having clusters of fragrant white flowers and red berrylike fruit. Also called "Christmas berry." [American Spanish *tollon,* probably of Mexican Indian origin.]

t.p. title page.

tpk. turnpike.

tr. 1. *Grammar.* transitive. **2.** translated; translation; translator. **3.** transpose; transposition. **4.** treasurer. **5.** *Law.* trust; trustee.

tra·be·at·ed (trā′bē-ā′tĭd) *adj.* Also **tra·be·ate** (-bē-ĭt, -āt′). *Architecture.* Having horizontal beams or lintels rather than arches. [From Latin *trabs,* a beam, timber.] —**tra·be·a·tion** *n.*

tra·bec·u·la (trə-bĕk′yə-lə) *n., pl.* **-lae** (-lē′). **1.** A small supporting beam or bar. **2.** *Anatomy.* Any of the supporting strands of connective tissue projecting into an organ and constituting part of the framework of that organ. **3.** *Botany.* A transverse rodlike or platelike structure, often extending across a cavity. [New Latin, from Latin, diminutive of *trabs,* a beam.] —**tra·bec·u·lar** *adj.*

Trab·zon (trăb-zŏn′). Also **Treb·i·zond** (trĕb′ĭ-zŏnd′). City of northeastern Turkey, a port on the Black Sea. A commercial center, it exports food products and tobacco. The city was founded in the 8th century B.C. by Greek colonists.

trace¹ (trās) *n.* **1.** A visible mark or sign of the former presence or passage of some person, thing, or event. **2.** A barely perceptible indication of something; a touch. **3. a.** A minute quantity. **b.** A quantity of rainfall or other precipitation too small to be measured. **c.** A constituent, such as a chemical compound or element, present in quantities less than a standard limit. **4. a.** A footprint or track left by an animal or person. **b.** A path or trail through a wilderness that has been beaten out by the passage of animals or people. **5.** *Archaic.* A way or route followed. **6.** A line drawn by a recording instrument, such as a cardiograph. —*v.* **traced, tracing, traces.** —*tr.* **1.** To follow the course or trail of. **2.** To ascertain the successive stages in the development or progress of. **3. a.** To search back or in time to find the origin of. Often used with *back.* **b.** To locate or discover (a cause, for example) by searching or researching evidence. **4. a.** To delineate or sketch (a figure). **b.** To give an outline or rough idea of (a plan). Often used with *out.* **5.** To imprint (a design) on something. **6.** To form (letters) with special concentration or care. **7.** To copy by following lines seen through a sheet of transparent paper. **8.** To make a design or series of markings on (a surface). **9.** To cover or decorate with tracery. **10.** To record (a variable), as on a graph. —*intr.* **1.** To make one's way; follow a path. Used with *along* or *through.* **2.** To have origins; be traceable. Used with *back.* [Middle English, a path, a course, from Old French, from *tracier,* to make one's way, from Vulgar Latin *tractiāre* (unattested), to drag, from Latin *tractus,* a dragging. See **tract** (expanse).] —**trace·a·bil·i·ty, trace·a·ble·ness** *n.* —**trace·a·ble** *adj.* —**trace·a·bly** *adv.* —**trace·less** *adj.* —**trace·less·ly** *adv.*

Synonyms: spoor, track, trail, vestige.

trace² *n.* **1.** Either of two side straps or chains connecting a harnessed draft animal to the vehicle it is pulling. **2.** In fishing, a short connecting piece of line between the hook and the main line. **3.** A bar or rod, hinged at either end to another part, that transfers movement from one part of a machine to another. —**kick over the traces.** To free oneself from constraints; become unruly. [Middle English *trais,* a pair of traces, from Old French, plural of *trait,* a pulling, a strap, from Latin *tractus,* a dragging. See **tract** (expanse).]

trace element *n.* An element required in minute amounts by an organism to maintain certain essential physiological processes.

trac·er (trā'sər) *n.* **1.** One that traces. **2.** A person employed to locate missing goods or persons. **3.** An investigation or inquiry organized to trace missing goods or persons. **4.** Any of several instruments used in making tracings or other drawings. **5.** A tracer bullet. **6.** An identifiable substance, such as a dye or radioactive isotope, that can be followed through the course of a mechanical or biological process, providing information on the process or on the redistribution of the parts or elements involved.

tracer bullet *n.* A bullet that leaves a luminous or smoky trail and whose path can therefore be observed. Also called "tracer."

trac·er·y (trā'sə-rē) *n., pl.* **-ies.** Ornamental work or a pattern of interlaced and ramified lines; specifically, the lacy openwork in a Gothic window. [From TRACE (to draw).] —**trac·er·ied** *adj.*

tra·che·a (trā'kē-ə) *n., pl.* **-cheae** (-kē-ē') or **-as. 1.** *Anatomy.* A thin-walled tube of cartilaginous and membranous tissue descending from the larynx to the bronchi and carrying air to the lungs. Also called "windpipe." **2.** *Zoology.* Any of the internal respiratory tubes of insects and some other terrestrial arthropods. **3.** *Botany.* A vessel (sense 5) *(see).* [Middle English *trache,* from Medieval Latin *trāchēa,* from Late Latin *trāchīa,* from Greek *(artēria) trakheia,* "rough (artery)," from the feminine of *trakhus,* rough.] —**tra·che·al** (trā'kē-əl), **tra·che·ate** (-āt', -ĭt) *adj.*

tra·che·id (trā'kē-ĭd) *n.* Any of the elongated, tapering, supporting and conductive cells in woody tissue. [TRACHE(O)- + -ID.]

tra·che·i·tis (trā'kē-ī'tĭs) *n.* Inflammation of the trachea. [New Latin : TRACHE(O)- + -ITIS.]

tracheo-, trache- *prefix.* Indicates the trachea; for example, **tracheotomy, tracheitis.** [New Latin, from Medieval Latin *trāchēa,* TRACHEA.]

tra·che·o·phyte (trā'kē-ə-fīt') *n.* Any plant with xylem- and phloem-conducting tissues; a vascular plant.

tra·che·ot·o·my (trā'kē-ŏt'ə-mē) *n., pl.* **-mies.** The act or procedure of cutting into the trachea through the neck, usually to facilitate breathing when the upper air passage is obstructed. Also called "tracheostomy." [TRACHEO- + -TOMY.]

tra·cho·ma (trə-kō'mə) *n.* A contagious viral disease of the conjunctiva of the eye characterized by inflammation and scarring of the cornea. [New Latin, from Greek *trakhōma* : *trakhus,* rough + -OMA.] —**tra·cho·ma·tous** (trə-kō'mə-təs) *adj.*

tra·chyte (trā'kīt', trăk'īt') *n.* A light-colored, fine-grained, igneous rock consisting essentially of alkali feldspar. [French, "rough stone" : Greek *trakhus,* rough (see **trachea**) + -ITE.] —**tra·chyt·ic** (trə-kĭt'ĭk), **tra·chy·toid** (trā'kĭ-toid') *adj.*

trac·ing (trā'sĭng) *n.* **1.** A reproduction made by placing a transparent sheet on top of the original and copying the lines seen through it. **2.** A graphic record made by a recording instrument, such as a cardiograph.

track (trăk) *n.* **1. a.** A mark, such as a footprint, left by the passage of a person, animal, or thing; a trace. **b.** The path, route, or course indicated by such marks; a trail. **2.** A path or course traveled, such as a line of flight. **3.** A course of action; a method of inquiry or proceeding: *on the right track.* **4.** A rough path or road. **5. a.** A specially prepared road or course laid out for racing or running events. **b.** Athletic competition on such a course; track events. **c.** **Track and field** *(see).* **6.** A rail or set of parallel rails, such as those on which a train runs. **7.** An endless segmented band of metal plates driven by the wheels of certain tractors and tanks to enable them to move across rough ground. **8.** The distance between each of a pair of wheels, such as the front wheels of a motor vehicle or the paired wheels of an aircraft undercarriage. **9.** The path of a particle as observed in a cloud chamber, bubble chamber, or photographic emulsion. **10.** A separate path on a magnetic recording tape: *nine-track tape.* **11.** A separate section of a phonograph record on which a particular composition, song, or movement is recorded. —See Synonyms at **trace.** —**cover one's tracks.** To keep what one has done secret or hidden. —**in one's tracks.** Exactly where one is at a given moment. —**keep track of.** To follow the course or progress of. —**lose track of.** To fail to follow the course or progress of. —**make tracks.** *Informal.* To move or go hurriedly. —**on the track of. 1.** Following in pursuit. **2.** Coming near to an understanding of the character or intentions of. —*v.* **tracked, tracking, tracks.** —*tr.* **1.** To follow the footprints or traces of; trail. **2.** To pursue successfully; seek and find. Often used

with *down: tracked down the culprit.* **3.** To move over or along; traverse. **4.** To observe or monitor the course of (aircraft, for example), as by radar. **5.** To focus on and film (a moving person or object) by swiveling or changing position. Used of a camera or camera operator. —*intr.* **1.** To keep a constant distance apart. Used of a pair of wheels. **2.** To be in alignment. **3.** To pursue a track; trail. **4.** To move around, often in a set path, while focusing on and filming an object. Used of a camera. **5.** To move in the groove of a phonograph record. Used of a stylus or pickup. [Middle English *trak,* trace, trail, from Old French *trac,* perhaps from Middle Dutch *trek,* a drawing, from *trekken,* to draw, pull. See **trek.**] —**track·a·ble** *adj.* —**track·er** *n.*

track·age (trăk'ĭj) *n.* **1.** Railway tracks. **2. a.** The right of one railroad company to use the track system of another. **b.** The charge for this.

track and field *n. Sports.* Athletic events performed on a running track and the field associated with it. Also called "track." —**track-and-field** (trăk'ən-fēld') *adj.*

track events *pl.n.* The running and racing events at a track meet as distinguished from the field events.

tracking station *n.* An observing station for maintaining radar or radio contact with an object in the atmosphere or in space.

track-lay·ing vehicle (trăk'lā'ĭng) *n.* A motor vehicle, such as a tank and certain tractors and excavators, in which the wheels drive an endless track to enable it to move across rough ground.

track·less (trăk'lĭs) *adj.* **1.** Not running on tracks or rails. **2.** Unmarked by trails or paths.

track·man (trăk'mən) *n., pl.* **-men** (-mĭn). A workman employed to maintain or inspect railroad traks.

track meet *n.* A competition of track-and-field events.

track record *n.* A record of performance or accomplishment: *an executive's excellent track record.*

track rod *n.* A rod joining the front wheels of a motor vehicle to ensure that they can be steered together.

track shoe *n.* Either of a pair of light shoes worn by runners, often having steel spikes attached to the soles to give them a firm grip.

track suit *n.* A warm jacket and trousers that are tight-fitting around the ankles, wrists, and waist and loose elsewhere, worn to keep warm, as during training or exercise.

tract¹ (trăkt) *n.* **1.** An expanse of land; a region. **2.** *Anatomy.* **a.** A system of organs and tissues that together perform one specialized function: *the digestive tract.* **b.** A bundle of nerve fibers having a common origin, termination, and function. **3.** *Archaic.* A stretch or lapse of time. [Latin *tractus,* "a drawing," course, tract, region, from *trahere* (past participle *tractus*), to draw.]

tract² *n.* A distributed paper or pamphlet containing a declaration or appeal, especially one put out by a religious or political group. [Middle English *tracte,* shortened from Latin *tractātus,* a discussion, treatise, from the past participle of *tractāre,* to pull violently, discuss. See **tractable.**]

tract³ *n.* The verses from Scripture sung during Lent or on Ember days after the gradual in the Roman Catholic Mass. [Middle English *tracte,* from Medieval Latin *tractus,* from Latin, "a drawing out" (the verses are sung without a break by one voice). See **tract** (area).]

trac·ta·ble (trăk'tə-bəl) *adj.* **1.** Easily managed or controlled; governable. **2.** Easily handled or worked; malleable. —See Synonyms at **obedient.** [Latin *tractābilis,* from *tractāre,* to pull violently, to take in hand, manage, frequentative of *trahere* (past participle *tractus*), to draw, pull.] —**trac·ta·bil·i·ty, trac·ta·ble·ness** *n.* —**trac·ta·bly** *adv.*

Trac·tar·i·an·ism (trăk-târ'ē-ə-nĭz'əm) *n.* The religious opinions and principles of the founders of the Oxford movement, put forth in a series of 90 pamphlets entitled *Tracts for the Times,* published in Oxford (1833–41). —**Trac·tar·i·an** *adj.* & *n.*

trac·tate (trăk'tāt') *n.* A treatise; an essay. [Latin *tractātus,* TRACT.]

trac·tile (trăk'tĭl, -tīl') *adj.* Capable of being drawn out in length, as certain metals; ductile. [Late Latin *tractilis,* from Latin *trahere,* to draw.] —**trac·til·i·ty** (trăk-tĭl'ə-tē) *n.*

trac·tion (trăk'shən) *n.* **1.** The act of drawing or pulling something, as a load, especially by motive power. **2.** The condition of being drawn or pulled. **3.** Adhesive friction, as of a wheel on a road surface or rail. **4.** The pulling power of a locomotive. **5.** *Medicine.* The use of weights, straps, and the like to exert a continuous pull on a part of the body to assist the healing of injuries. [Medieval Latin *tractiō* (stem *tractiōn-*), from Latin *tractus,* past participle of *trahere,* to draw, pull.] —**trac·tion·al, trac·tive** (trăk'tĭv) *adj.*

traction engine *n.* A steam-powered vehicle formerly used on roads or over rough ground to pull heavy loads.

trac·tor (trăk'tər) *n.* **1.** A small vehicle, powered by an internal-combustion engine, having large, heavily treaded tires, or sometimes tracks, and used in farming for pulling machinery. **2.** A short, powerful motor vehicle having a cab and no body, used for pulling large vehicles such as vans or trailers. **3.** An aircraft having a propeller mounted in front of the supporting surfaces. In this sense, also called "tractor aircraft." [New Latin, from Latin *tractus.* See **traction.**]

trade (trād) *n.* **1.** An occupation, especially one requiring skilled labor; a craft. **2.** The business of buying and selling; commerce. **3. a.** A particular business, industry, or market. **b.** The persons working in or associated with a specific business or industry. **4. a.** The customers collectively of a specific business or industry. **b.** The amount of custom of a business or industry at a particular

time or place: *the holiday trade.* **5.** An instance of buying or selling; a transaction. **6.** An exchange of one thing for another. **7. trades.** The trade winds. —See Usage note at **business.**
~*v.* **traded, trading, trades.** —*intr.* **1. a.** To engage in buying and selling for profit. **b.** To have business relations. Often used with *with: prepared to trade with Cuba.* **2.** To make an exchange of one thing for another. **3.** To shop or buy regularly at a given store. —*tr.* **1.** To give in exchange for something else. **2.** To buy and sell (shares, for example). **3.** To pass back and forth: *We traded anecdotes.* —**trade on.** To put to advantage; exploit: *He traded on his war wounds for sympathy.* [Middle English *tra(i)d,* trade, a course, way, track, from Middle Low German *trade,* a track, path.]

trade acceptance *n.* A bill of exchange for the amount of a purchase drawn by the seller on the purchaser, bearing the purchaser's signature and specifying time and place of payment.

trade book *n.* A book published for distribution to the general public through booksellers, as distinguished from a textbook or a limited edition.

trade cycle *n.* A regular fluctuation in the trade or economic conditions of most capitalist countries consisting of a movement from a state of high activity (prosperity or boom) to a state of low activity (depression) and back again.

trade discount *n.* A discount on the list price granted by a manufacturer or wholesaler to buyers in the same trade.

trade gap *n. Economics.* **1.** An excess of a country's visible imports over its visible exports. **2.** The amount of this excess.

trade in *tr.v.* To give (an old item) to a dealer as partial payment for a new purchase.

trade-in (trăd'ĭn') *n.* **1.** A piece of merchandise accepted as partial payment for a new purchase. **2.** A transaction involving such an item. **3.** The amount allowed for such an item. Also used adjectivally: *trade-in value.*

trade·mark (trăd'märk') *n.* **1.** A name, symbol, or other device identifying a product, officially registered and legally restricted to the use of the owner or manufacturer. **2.** A distinctive sign by which a person or thing comes to be known.
~*tr.v.* **trademarked, -marking, -marks. 1.** To label (a product) with a trademark. **2.** To register as a trademark.

trade name *n.* **1.** The name by which a commodity, service, process, or the like is known to the trade. **2.** A trademark consisting solely of a name. **3.** The name under which a business enterprise operates.

trade-off, trade-off (trăd'ôf', -ŏf') *n.* An exchange of one thing in return for another; especially, a giving up of something desirable for something else regarded as more desirable. —**trade-off** *adj.*

trade paper *n.* A newspaper or periodical published regularly by or for a particular business or industry to give pertinent news and developments. Also called "trade journal," "trade magazine."

trade price *n.* The price charged by a wholesaler to a retailer.

trad·er (trā'dər) *n.* **1.** A person who trades; a dealer. **2.** A member of a stock exchange who trades for himself and not as a broker for customers. **3.** A ship employed in foreign trade.

trade rat *n.* The pack rat *(see).*

trade route *n.* A sea lane used by trading ships.

trad·es·can·tia (trăd'ə-skăn'chə, -chē-ə) *n.* Any plant of the genus *Tradescantia,* characteristically having a jointed succulent stem and three-petaled flowers, such as the house plant **wandering Jew** *(see).* [New Latin, after John *Tradescant* (1608–62), English botanist.]

trade secret *n.* **1.** A secret formula, method, or device that gives a manufacturer an advantage over competitors. **2.** Something, such as a scheme or trick, to which a person attributes his success and which he keeps secret.

trades·man (trādz'mən) *n., pl.* **-men** (-mĭn). **1.** A person engaged in the retail trade, especially a shopkeeper; dealer. **2.** A skilled worker; a craftsman.

trades·peo·ple (trādz'pē'pəl) *pl.n.* People engaged in the retail trade, especially shopkeepers.

trades·wom·an (trādz'wŏom'ən) *n., pl.* **-women** (-wĭm'ĭn). A woman engaged in trade.

trade union *n.* Also *chiefly British* **trades union.** *Abbr.* **T.U.** A labor union, especially one limited in membership to people in the same trade as distinguished from people in the same company or industry. —**trade unionism** *n.* —**trade unionist** *n.*

trade wind *n.* An extremely consistent system of winds occupying most of the tropics, constituting the major component of the general circulation of the atmosphere, blowing northeasterly in the Northern Hemisphere and southeasterly in the Southern Hemisphere. [From the phrase *to blow trade,* to blow in a regular course, from TRADE (in the obsolete sense of a course).]

trading cards *pl.n.* Picture cards or playing cards with designs on the backs, collected and traded by children.

trading post *n.* A station or general store in a sparsely settled area established by traders to barter supplies for local products.

trading stamp *n.* A stamp given by a retailer to a buyer for each purchase of a specified amount and able to be redeemed in quantity, by the buyer, for merchandise.

tra·di·tion (trə-dĭsh'ən) *n.* **1.** The passing down of elements of a culture from generation to generation, especially by oral communication. **2. a.** A mode of thought or behavior followed by a people continuously from generation to generation; a cultural custom or usage. **b.** A set of such customs and usages viewed as a coherent body of precedents influencing the present. **c.** A set of such customs followed in a particular art. **3.** A body of unwritten religious

precepts. **4.** Any time-honored practice or a set of such practices. **5.** *Law.* The transfer of property to another. [Middle English *tradicion,* a handing down, a surrender, from Old French, from Latin *trāditiō* (stem *trāditiōn-*), from *trādere,* to hand over : *trāns-,* over + *dare,* to give.]

tra·di·tion·al (trə-dĭsh'ə-nəl) *adj.* Also **tra·di·tion·ar·y** (trə-dĭsh'-ə-nĕr'ē). Pertaining to or in accord with tradition. —**tra·di·tion·al·ize** (trə-dĭsh'ə-nə-līz') *v.* —**tra·di·tion·al·ly** *adv.*

tra·di·tion·al·ism (trə-dĭsh'ə-nə-lĭz'əm) *n.* **1.** Adherence to tradition; especially, excessive reverence for religious tradition. **2.** A religious doctrine holding that all knowledge is derived from original divine revelation and is transmitted by tradition. —**tra·di·tion·al·ist** *n. & adj.* —**tra·di·tion·al·is·tic** (trə-dĭsh'ə-nə-lĭs'tĭk) *adj.*

tra·di·tion·di·rect·ed (trə-dĭsh'ən-də-rĕk'tĭd) *adj.* Guided by tradition and the values of one's forebears rather than by independent personal principles: *a tradition-directed personality.* Compare **inner-directed, other-directed.**

trad·i·tor (trăd'ə-tər) *n., pl.* **traditores** (trăd'ə-tôr'ēz', -tōr'ēz'). Any of the early Christians who surrendered sacred objects or betrayed fellow Christians during the Roman persecutions. [Middle English *traditour,* from Latin *trāditor,* traitor, from *trādere,* to hand over, betray. See **tradition.**]

tra·duce (trə-dōōs', -dyōōs') *tr.v.* **-duced, -ducing, -duces.** To speak falsely or maliciously of; slander; defame. —See Synonyms at **malign.** [Latin *trādūcere,* to lead across, make public, expose to ridicule : *trāns-,* across + *dūcere,* to lead.] —**tra·duce·ment** *n.* —**tra·duc·er** *n.* —**tra·duc·i·ble** *adj.* —**tra·duc·ing·ly** *adv.*

tra·du·cian·ism (trə-dōō'shə-nĭz'əm, trə-dyōō'-) *n. Theology.* The belief that the soul is inherited from the parents along with the body. Compare **creationism.** [Medieval Latin *trāduciānus,* believer in this doctrine, from *trādux,* inheritance, from Latin *trādūcere,* to lead across, TRADUCE.] —**tra·du·cian·ist** *n.* —**tra·du·cian·is·tic** (trə-dōō'shə-nĭs'tĭk, -dyōō'-) *adj.*

Tra·fal·gar, Cape (trə-fǎl'gər). Headland of southwestern Spain, between the Strait of Gibraltar and the Gulf of Cadiz. It gave its name to a naval battle of 1805 in which the British, under Adm. Nelson, destroyed Napoleon's fleet.

traf·fic (trăf'ĭk) *n.* **1. a.** The commercial exchange of goods; trade. **b.** Illicit or improper trade: *traffic in drugs.* **2. a.** The business of moving passengers and cargo by means of a system of transportation. **b.** The amount of cargo or number of passengers conveyed. **3. a.** The passage of persons, vehicles, or messages through routes of transportation or communication. **b.** The vehicles using a particular road or route: *heavy traffic.* **c.** The volume of messages passing through a system of communication. **4.** Connections; dealings. —See Usage note at **business.**
~*intr.v.* **trafficked, -ficking, -fics. 1.** To carry on trade, especially illegal trade. **2.** To have dealings. Usually used with *with.* [French *traffique,* from Old Italian *traffico,* from *trafficare†,* to trade.] —**traf·fick·er** *n.*

traf·fi·ca·tor (trăf'ĭ-kā'tər) *n. British.* An illuminated arm on motor vehicles that can be raised to indicate a left or right turn. Compare **indicator.** [Blend of TRAFFIC and INDICATOR.]

traffic circle *n.* A circular one-way road at a junction of thoroughfares, facilitating uninterrupted traffic. Also called "rotary."

traffic island *n.* A raised area over which cars may not pass, placed at a junction of thoroughfares or between opposing traffic lanes. Also called "island."

traffic jam *n.* A situation in which a large number of motor vehicles on the road are brought to a standstill or can move only very slowly, as caused by heavy traffic or an accident.

traffic light *n.* A road signal that beams a red or green light or an amber warning light to direct traffic to stop, proceed, or proceed with caution. Also called "traffic signal."

trag·a·canth (trăg'ə-kănth', trăj'-) *n.* **1.** Any of various thorny shrubs of the genus *Astragalus,* of northern temperate regions, yielding a gum used in pharmacy, adhesives, and textile printing. **2.** The gum of such a shrub. [French, from Latin *tragacantha,* from Greek *tragakantha,* "goat's thorn" : *tragos,* goat (see **tragedy**) + *akantha,* thorn.]

tra·ge·di·an (trə-jē'dē-ən) *n.* **1.** A writer of tragedies. **2.** An actor of tragic roles. [Middle English *tragedien,* from Old French, from *tragedie,* TRAGEDY.]

tra·ge·di·enne (trə-jē'dē-ĕn') *n.* A woman who plays tragic roles in the theater. [French *tragédienne.*]

trag·e·dy (trăj'ə-dē) *n., pl.* **-dies. 1.** A dramatic or literary work in which the principal character engages in a morally significant struggle ending in ruin or profound disappointment, specifically: **a.** A classical verse drama in which a noble principal character is brought to ruin essentially as a consequence of some extreme quality that is both his greatness and his downfall. **b.** A Renaissance or modern drama resembling the classical model in representing terrible struggle and calamity but freer in style and choice of principal character. **c.** A serious play or narrative that deals with sad or calamitous events and has an unhappy and usually morally significant ending. **2.** The branch of drama dealing with such plays. **2.** A dramatic, disastrous event, especially one of some moral significance. **3.** The tragic aspect or element of something. [Middle English *tragedie,* from Old French, from Latin *tragoedia,* from Greek *tragōidia,* "goat-song" (probably the name of a form of choric ceremony associated with goat-satyr plays) : *tragos†,* goat + *ōidē,* song from *aeidein,* to sing.]

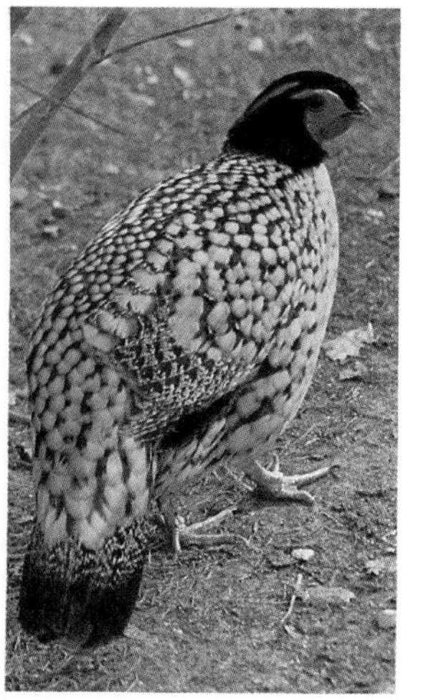

***tragopan** The tragopan is a pheasant that lives in the high mountain forests of Asia. Unlike other pheasants, it nests in trees and the male is able to puff out two brightly colored fleshy horns from its head during courtship. The species shown here is the Cabot's tragopan.*

PRONUNCIATION KEY

ă, pat; ā, pay; âr, care; ä, father, are; b, bib; ch, church; d, deed; ĕ, pet; ē, be; f, fife; g, gag; h, hat; hw, which; ĭ, pit; ī, pie; îr, pier; j, judge; k, kick; l, lid, needle; m, mum; n, no, sudden; ng, thing; ŏ, pot; ō, toe; ô, paw, for; oi, noise; ou, out; o͝o, book; o͞o, boot; p, pop; r, roar; s, sauce; sh, ship, dish; t, tight; th, thin, path; *th*, this, bathe; ŭ, cut; ûr, fur; v, valve; w, with; y, yes; z, zebra, size; zh, vision; ə, about, item, edible, gallop, circus, peaceful

IN FOREIGN WORDS:

à, *Fr.* ami; œ, *Fr.* feu, *Ger.* schön; ü, *Fr.* tu, *Ger.* über; KH, *Ger.* ich, *Scot.* loch; N, *Fr.* bon; y', *Fr.* Compiègne

STRESS MARKS:

Primary stress: ′
in·cite′ (ĭn-sīt′)
Secondary stress: ′
in′sight′ (ĭn′sīt′)

trag·ic (trăj′ĭk) *adj.* Also **trag·i·cal** (trăj′ĭ-kəl). **1.** Pertaining to, in the style of, or having the character of tragedy. **2.** Writing or performing in tragedy: *a tragic poet.* **3.** Having the elements of tragedy; involving death, grief, or destruction: *a tragic accident.* **4.** Mournful or grave: *Don't look so tragic!* [French *tragique,* from Latin *tragicus,* from Greek *tragikos,* from *tragos,* goat. See **tragedy**.] **—trag·i·cal·ly** *adv.* **—trag·i·cal·ness** *n.*

tragic flaw *n.* A flaw in the character of the protagonist of a tragedy that brings about his or her ruin.

trag·i·com·e·dy (trăj′ĭ-kŏm′ə-dē) *n., pl.* **-dies. 1.** A drama that combines elements of both tragedy and comedy. **2.** The branch of drama dealing with such plays. **3.** An incident or situation having both comic and tragic elements. [French *tragicomédie,* from Late Latin *tragicōmoedia,* from Latin *tragicocōmoedia* : TRAGIC + COMEDY.] **—trag·i·com·ic** *adj.* **—trag·i·com·i·cal·ly** *adv.*

trag·o·pan (trăg′ə-păn′) *n.* Any of several Asian pheasants of the genus *Tragopan,* of which the male has brightly colored plumage and two hornlike appendages on the head. [Latin *tragopān,* fabulous bird in Ethiopia, from Greek *tragopan,* "goat of Pan" : *tragos,* goat (see **tragedy**) + *Pan,* PAN.]

tra·gus (trā′gəs) *n., pl.* **-gi** (-gī′, -jī′). **1.** The projection of skin-covered cartilage in front of the opening of the external ear. **2.** Any of the hairs growing at the entrance of the external ear. [New Latin, from Greek *tragos,* goat (the hair resembles a goat's beard).]

trail (trāl) *v.* **trailed, trailing, trails.** *—tr.* **1.** To allow to drag or stream behind, as along the ground. **2.** To drag, pull, or tow. **3. a.** To form (a course, path, or track). **b.** To make a path or track through. **4.** To follow the traces or scent of, as in hunting; track. **5. a.** To follow slowly or wearily. **b.** To lag behind (an opponent). *—intr.* **1.** To drag or be dragged along, brushing the ground. **2.** To extend, grow, or droop along the ground or over a surface, as a vine or plant might. **3.** To drift in a tenuous stream, as smoke from a cigarette. **4.** To become gradually fainter. Usually used with *away* or *off*: *Her voice trailed off sadly.* **5. a.** To walk slowly or wearily. **b.** To walk with dragging steps; trudge. **6.** To fall behind in competition; lag.
~n. **1.** Something that hangs down loosely or drags along the ground: *trails of ribbon.* **2.** Something that is drawn along or follows behind; a train. **3.** The part of a gun carriage that rests or slides on the ground. **4. a.** A mark, trace, course, or path left by a moving body. **b.** The scent of a person or animal. **c.** A blazed path or beaten track, as through woods or wilderness. **d.** A chain of consequences: *a trail of bitter recriminations.* **5.** The act or an instance of trailing. **—**See Synonyms at **trace, way.** [Middle English *trailen,* probably from Old French *trailler* and Middle Low German *treilen,* to tow, both from Vulgar Latin *tragulāre* (unattested), to drag, from Latin *trāgula,* dragnet, from *trahere,* to pull.]

trail bike *n.* A light, strong motorcycle with special suspension and ridged tires, used for riding over rough ground.

trail·blaz·er (trāl′blā′zər) *n.* **1.** One who blazes a trail. **2.** A leader in any field; a pioneer. **—trail·blaz·ing** *n.* & *adj.*

trail boss *n.* The man in charge of a cattle drive in the West.

trail·er (trā′lər) *n.* **1.** One that trails. **2.** A large transport vehicle designed to be hauled by a truck or tractor. **3.** A two- or four-wheeled road vehicle used to carry a boat or other load to be towed behind a car. **4.** A short filmed advertisement for a motion-picture or television program. **5.** A furnished van drawn by a truck or automobile and used as a dwelling or office when parked.

trailing arbutus *n.* A low-growing plant, *Epigaea repens,* of eastern North America, having evergreen leaves and clusters of fragrant pink or white flowers. Also called "mayflower."

trailing edge *n.* The rearmost edge of a structure, especially of an airfoil.

train (trān) *n.* **1.** Something that follows or is drawn along behind, such as part of a dress or robe that trails behind the wearer. **2.** A body of persons following behind in attendance; a retinue: *a train of admirers.* **3.** A service unit of men, vehicles, and equipment following and attending an army. **4.** A long line of moving persons, animals, or vehicles. **5.** A string of connected railroad cars. **6.** An orderly succession of related events or thoughts; a sequence. **7.** A set of linked mechanical parts: *a train of gears.* **8.** A string of gunpowder that acts as a fuse for exploding a charge. **—**See Synonyms at **series.**
~v. **trained, training, trains.** *—tr.* **1.** To coach in or accustom to some mode of behavior or performance. **2.** To make proficient with specialized instruction and practice. **3.** To prepare physically, as with exercise or a regimen; make fit: *train a long-distance runner.* **4.** To cause (a plant, for example) to take a desired course or shape, as by manipulating. **5.** To focus or direct; aim. Usually used with *on* or *upon*: *Train your sights on the hilltop.* **6.** To draw, drag, or trail. *—intr.* To give or undergo a course of instruction, coaching, or exercises. **—**See Synonyms at **teach.** [Middle English *trayne,* from Old French *train,* from *tra(h)iner,* to drag, from Vulgar Latin *trāgināre* (unattested), from *tragere* (unattested), variant of Latin *trahere.*] **—train·a·ble** *adj.*

train·band (trān′bănd′) *n.* A militia trained as a supplement to the army in England from the 16th to the 18th century. [Originally *trained band.*]

train·bear·er (trān′bâr′ər) *n.* An attendant who holds up the train of a robe or dress, as in a procession.

train·ee (trā-nē′) *n.* A person who is being trained. **—train·ee·ship** (trā-nē′shĭp′) *n.*

train·er (trā′nər) *n.* **1.** One who trains, especially one who coaches athletes, racehorses, or show animals. **2.** A contrivance or apparatus used in training. **3.** The member of a naval gun crew who trains the cannon horizontally.

train·ing (trā′nĭng) *n.* **1.** The act, process, or routine of one who trains. **2.** The state of being trained.

training school *n.* **1.** A school that gives practical vocational and technical instruction. **2.** A detention house for juvenile delinquents that offers vocational training.

train·load (trān′lōd′) *n.* The full capacity of a freight or passenger train.

train·man (trān′mən) *n., pl.* **-men** (-mĭn). A member of the operating crew on a railroad train, especially the brakeman.

train oil *n.* Oil obtained from the blubber of a whale or other marine animal. [Middle English *trane,* train oil, from Middle Low German *trān.*]

traipse (trāps) *intr.v.* **traipsed, traipsing, traipses.** *Informal.* **1.** To walk about casually. **2.** To walk wearily or slowly; trudge.
~n. Informal. A tiring walk. [Origin unknown.]

trait (trāt) *n.* **1.** A distinguishing feature, as of a person's character. **2.** A trace; a touch. **—**See Synonyms at **quality.** [French, from Old French, pencil mark, stroke, from Latin *tractus,* a pulling, a drawing, from the past participle of *trahere,* to pull, drag.]

trai·tor (trā′tər) *n.* A person who betrays his country, a cause, or a trust; especially, one who has committed treason. [Middle English *traitour,* from Old French, from Latin *trāditor.* See **traditor.**]

trai·tor·ous (trā′tər-əs) *adj.* **1.** Having the character of a traitor; disloyal. **2.** Constituting treason: *a traitorous act.* **—**See Synonyms at **faithless. —trai·tor·ous·ly** *adv.* **—trai·tor·ous·ness** *n.*

trai·tress (trā′trĭs) *n.* A woman who is a traitor.

Tra·jan (trā′jən) (A.D. *c.* 52–117). Roman emperor (98–117). With the support of the military he came to power upon the death of the emperor Nerva. His reign was marked by aggressive expansion, an extensive building program, and compassionate treatment of the poor.

tra·ject (trə-jĕkt′) *tr.v.* **-jected, -jecting, -jects.** To transmit (light, for example). [Latin *trājicere* (past participle *trājectus*), to throw across : *trāns-,* across + *jacere,* to throw.] **—tra·jec·tion** *n.*

tra·jec·to·ry (trə-jĕk′tə-rē) *n., pl.* **-ries. 1.** The path of a moving particle or body, especially such a path in three dimensions. **2.** In geometry, a curve that cuts all of a given family of curves or surfaces at the same angle. [Originally an adjective, from Medieval Latin *trājectōrius,* from Latin *trājectus.* See **traject.**]

Tra·lee (trə-lē′). County seat of Kerry, in the southwestern Republic of Ireland. It is a seaport, and boots, shoes, knitwear, and plastics are produced.

tram[1] (trăm) *n.* **1.** *Chiefly British.* **a.** A **streetcar** *(see).* **b.** A **tramway** *(see).* **2.** A four-wheeled, open box-shaped wagon or iron car run on tracks in a mine. In both senses, also called "tramcar." [Originally "shaft or frame of a truck," from Middle Low German *trame,* beam.]

tram[2] *n.* **1.** A machine gauge, a **trammel** *(see).* **2.** Accurate mechanical adjustment: *The device is in tram.*
~tr.v. **trammed, tramming, trams.** To adjust or align (mechanical parts) with a trammel. [Shortened from TRAMMEL.]

tram[3] *n.* A heavy silk thread used for the weft, or cross threads, in fine velvet or silk. [French *trame,* from Old French *traime,* woof, from Latin *trāma*†.]

tram·car (trăm′kär′) *n.* **1.** *Chiefly British.* A **streetcar** *(see).* **2.** A coal car in a mine, a **tram** *(see).*

tram·lines (trăm′līnz′) *pl.n. British.* The rails on which a tram runs. Also called "tramway."

tram·mel (trăm′əl) *n.* **1.** *Often* **trammels.** Something that restricts activity or free movement; a hindrance. **2.** A shackle used to teach a horse to amble. **3.** A vertically set fishing net of three layers, consisting of a finely meshed net between two nets of coarse mesh. Also called "trammel net." **4. a.** An instrument for describing ellipses. **b.** A **beam compass** *(see).* **c.** The pivoted beam of a beam compass. **5.** An instrument for gauging and adjusting parts of a machine. Also called "tram." **6.** An arrangement of links and a hook in a fireplace for raising or lowering a kettle.
~tr.v. **trammeled** or **-melled, -meling** or **-melling, -mels. 1.** To confine or hinder. **2.** To entrap. Sometimes used with *up.* **3.** To adjust (a machine) by means of a trammel. [Middle English *tramale,* trammel net, from Old French *tramail,* from Late Latin *tremaculum* : *trēs,* three + *macula,* mesh, spot.] **—tram·mel·er** *n.*

tra·mon·ta·na (trä′mən-tä′nə) *n.* A cold north wind sweeping down from the mountains, especially in Italy. [Italian, feminine form of *tramontano* (see **tramontane**).]

tra·mon·tane (trə-mŏn′tān′, trăm′ən-) *adj.* **1. a.** Dwelling beyond or coming from the far side of the mountains, especially the Alps as viewed from Italy. **b.** Foreign. **c.** Barbarous. **2.** Sweeping down from the mountains. Said of a wind.
~n. **1.** A person who lives beyond the mountains; an outsider; foreigner. **2.** In Italy, a north or cold wind. [Middle English, from Italian *tramontano,* from Latin *trānsmontānus* : *trāns-,* beyond + *montānus,* mountainous (see **mountain**).]

tramp (trămp) *v.* **tramped, tramping, tramps.** *—intr.* **1.** To walk with a firm, heavy step; trudge. **2. a.** To go on foot; hike. **b.** To wander about aimlessly. *—tr.* **1.** To traverse on foot: *tramp the fields.* **2.** To tread down; trample: *tramp the snow down.*
~n. **1. a.** A heavy footfall. **b.** A heavy rhythmic tread, as of a marching army. **c.** The sound produced by heavy walking or

marching. **2. a.** A walking trip; a hike. **b.** An arduous walk. **3.** A person who travels aimlessly about on foot, doing odd jobs or begging for a living; a vagrant. **4.** *Slang.* **a.** A prostitute. **b.** A promiscuous girl or woman. **5.** A cargo vessel that has no regular schedule but takes on freight wherever it may be found and discharges it wherever required. Also called "tramp steamer." **6. a.** A metal plate attached to the sole of a shoe for protection, as when using a spade to dig ground. **b.** The part of the spade on which the foot rests. [Middle English *trampen,* probably from Middle Low German.] **—tramp·er** *n.*

tram·ple (trăm′pəl) *v.* **-pled, -pling, -ples.** *—tr.* **1.** To beat down with the feet so as to crush, bruise, violate, or destroy; stamp upon. **2.** To treat harshly or ruthlessly, as if stepping or stamping upon. *—intr.* **1.** To tread heavily. **2.** To treat contemptuously or insensitively. Used with *on: He trampled on her feelings whenever he could.* *~n.* The action or sound of treading underfoot. [Middle English *tramp(e)len,* frequentative of *trampen,* to TRAMP.] **—tram·pler** *n.*

tram·po·line (trăm′pə-lēn′, -lĭn) *n.* A sheet of strong, taut canvas attached with springs to a metal frame and used for jumping on and performing acrobatic feats on, either as a competitive sport or for pleasure and exercise. *~intr.v.* **trampolined, -lining, -lines.** To compete, perform, or exercise on a trampoline. [From Italian *trampolino,* "performance on stilts," from *trampoli,* stilts, from Germanic.] **—tram·po·lin·er, tram·po·lin·ist** *n.*

tram·way (trăm′wā′) *n. British.* **1. a.** A street track or railway for trams. **b.** A streetcar line. **2.** A cable or system of cables for a cable car.

trance (trăns, träns) *n.* **1.** A hypnotic, cataleptic, or ecstatic state. **2.** A state of detachment from one's physical surroundings, as in contemplation or daydreaming. **3.** A dazed state, as between sleeping and waking; a stupor. *~tr.v.* **tranced, trancing, trances.** To put into a trance. [Middle English *traunce,* from Old French *transe,* from *transir,* "to pass (from life to death)," depart, from Latin *transīre,* to go across. See **transit.**]

tran·quil (trăng′kwəl, trăn′kwəl) *adj.* **1.** Free from agitation or other disturbance; calm; unruffled; serene: *a tranquil rural life.* **2.** Steady; even: *a tranquil flame.* —See Synonyms at **calm, still.** [Latin *tranquillus.*] **—tran·quil·li·ty, tran·quil·i·ty** (trăng-kwĭl′ə-tē, trăn′-) *n.* **—tran·quil·ly** *adv.* **—tran·quil·ness** *n.*

tran·quil·ize (trăng′kwə-līz′, trăn′kwə-) *v.* **-ized, -izing, -izes.** Also **tran·quil·lize, -lized, -lizing, -lizes.** *—tr.* To make tranquil; quiet. *—intr.* To become tranquil. **—tran·quil·i·za·tion** *n.*

tran·quil·iz·er (trăng′kwə-lī′zər, trăn′kwə-) *n.* **1.** Something that tranquilizes, such as music. **2.** Any of various drugs used to calm or pacify.

trans– *prefix.* Indicates: **1.** Across or over; for example, **transpolar. 2.** Beyond or above; for example, **transcend, transpontine. 3.** From one place to another; for example, **translocate. 4.** Moving, transferring, or transporting; for example, **transship. 5.** Changing; for example, **transliterate. 6.** Having a greater atomic number; for example, **transuranic. 7.** A chemical compound in which two identical atoms or groups are on opposite sides of the plane of a double bond. Compare **cis–. Note:** Many compounds other than those entered here may be formed with *trans-.* In forming compounds, *trans-* is normally joined with the following element without space or hyphen: *transculturation.* If the second element begins with a capital letter, it is usually separated with a hyphen: *trans-Canadian.* Note, however, that certain compounds have become one word: *transatlantic, Transcaucasia.* [Latin *trāns,* across, over, beyond, through, through and through.]

trans. 1. transaction. **2.** *Grammar.* transitive. **3.** translated; translation; translator. **4.** transportation. **5.** transpose; transposition. **6.** transverse.

trans·act (trăn-săkt′, -zăkt′) *v.* **-acted, -acting, -acts.** *—tr.* To do, carry out, perform, manage, or conduct (business or affairs, for example). *—intr.* To do business; negotiate. [Latin *transigere* (past participle *transactus*), to drive or carry through, complete : *trāns-,* through + *agere,* to drive.] **—trans·ac·tor** *n.*

trans·ac·ti·nide (trăn-săk′tə-nīd′, trăn-zăk′-) *n.* Any of the artificially produced chemical elements with an atomic number in excess of 103. [TRANS- + ACTINIDE.]

trans·ac·tion (trăn-săk′shən, -zăk′shən) *n. Abbr.* **trans. 1.** The act of transacting or the fact of being transacted. **2.** Something transacted; especially, a piece of business. **3. transactions.** Published papers, discussions, or other proceedings, as of a conference, academic meeting, or the like. **—trans·ac·tion·al** *adj.*

transactional analysis *n.* A method of psychotherapy concentrating on an individual's social exchanges or transactions in his relationships with others. Such exchanges are analyzed in terms of roles (child, parent, or adult), goals, games, and the like.

trans·al·pine (trăns-ăl′pīn′, trănz-) *adj.* Pertaining to, living on, or coming from the other side of the Alps, especially as seen from Italy. *~n.* One who lives beyond the Alps.

Transalpine Gaul (gôl). The section of Gaul northwest of the Alps.

trans·at·lan·tic (trăns′ət-lăn′tĭk, trăn′zət-) *adj.* **1.** On or from the other side of the Atlantic. **2.** Spanning or crossing the Atlantic.

Trans·cau·ca·sia (trăns′kô-kā′zhə, trănz′-). Region of the southwest-central U.S.S.R., between the Black and Caspian seas. After the Russian Revolution, this oil-rich region was a short-lived

train

THE VEHICLE THAT REPLACED THE HORSE
Development of the train over two centuries

The railroad age began in 1804 when a steam locomotive, built by the Cornish engineer Richard Trevithick, ran between two nearby points in Wales. Trevithick's engine could pull far more freight than a horse but the weight soon damaged the rails and the scheme was abandoned.

In 1830 the world's first passenger railroad was opened between Manchester and Liverpool, England, by George Stephenson and his son Robert. Electric traction was pioneered in Germany in 1879; in the 1930's diesels came into use. In the early 1980's the fastest train was the French high-speed train, whose gas-turbine engine drives it at speeds up to 260 kilometers (160 miles) an hour. More recent trains, developed in the late 1980's in Europe and Japan, hover over a single rail, making speeds up to 800 kilometers (500 miles) an hour.

WINNING DESIGN *George and Robert Stephenson's* Rocket *won trials held by the Liverpool and Manchester Railway Company in 1829.* Rocket *pulled a 14-ton train at 46 kilometers (29 miles) an hour—twice as fast as its rivals.*

1850 EXPRESS TRAIN *U.S. rail mileage exceeded 9,000 miles in 1850. Henry David Thoreau commented in* Walden *(1854): "If railroads are not built, how shall we get to heaven in season?"*

1864 EXPRESS TRAIN *Identifying railroads with political as well as economic progress, Ralph Waldo Emerson wrote in his* Journals *in 1866: "Whenever I see a railroad I look for a republic."*

TRAINS AT HORNELLSVILLE, N.Y. *The English critic John Ruskin observed, "Your railroad, when you come to understand it, is only a device for making the world smaller."*

Soviet republic (1917–23). It is now divided between Georgia, Armenia, and Azerbaijan.

trans·ceiv·er (trăn-sē′vər) *n.* A device consisting of a radio receiver and transmitter. [TRANS(MITTER) + (RE)CEIVER.]

tran·scend (trăn-sĕnd′) *v.* **-scended, -scending, -scends.** —*tr.* **1. a.** To pass beyond (a limit that humans can grasp): *an emotion that transcends understanding.* **b.** To exist above and independently of (material experience or the universe): *God transcends the world of phenomena.* **2.** To rise above or across; surpass; exceed: *Try to transcend your selfish desires.* —*intr.* To be outstanding; excel. —See Synonyms at **excel.** [Middle English *transcenden,* from Old French *transcendre,* from Latin *transcendere,* "to climb over" : *trāns-,* over + *scandere,* to climb.]

tran·scen·dent (trăn-sĕn′dənt) *adj.* **1.** Surpassing others of the same kind; pre-eminent. **2. a.** *Philosophy.* Transcending the Aristotelian categories. **b.** Especially in Kant's theory of knowledge, designating knowledge that is beyond the limits of experience. **3.** Above and independent of the material universe. Said of God. In this sense, compare **immanent.** —**tran·scen·dence, tran·scen·den·cy, tran·scen·dent·ness** *n.* —**tran·scen·dent·ly** *adv.*

tran·scen·den·tal (trăn′sĕn-dĕnt′l) *adj.* **1.** *Philosophy.* **a.** Concerned with the a priori or intuitive basis of knowledge. **b.** Asserting a fundamental irrationality or supernatural element in experience. **2.** Rising above common thought or ideas; exalted; mystical. **3.** *Mathematics.* **a.** Not capable of being determined by any combination of a finite number of equations with rational number coefficients. **b.** Not expressible as an integer or quotient of integers. Said of numbers, especially nonrepeating infinite decimals. —**tran·scen·den·tal·ly** *adv.*

tran·scen·den·tal·ism (trăn′sən-dĕnt′l-ĭz′əm) *n.* **1.** *Philosophy.* **a.** The belief that knowledge of reality is dependent on a priori or intuitive knowledge rather than on objective experience. **b.** Any doctrine based on this belief, such as the philosophies of Kant and Emerson. **2.** The quality or condition of being transcendental. **3. a.** Any unrigorous philosophizing or casual speculation. **b.** Exalted or irrational language. —**tran·scen·den·tal·ist** *n.*

transcendental meditation *n. Abbr.* **T.M.** A simple form of meditation derived from Hindu traditions, but practiced mainly in Western countries, in which mental relaxation is promoted by the repeated silent utterance of a mantra.

trans·con·ti·nen·tal (trăns′kŏn′tə-nĕn′təl, trănz′-) *adj.* Spanning or crossing a continent.

tran·scribe (trăn-skrīb′) *tr.v.* **-scribed, -scribing, -scribes.** **1.** To write or type a copy of; write out fully, as from shorthand notes: *transcribe a letter.* **2.** *Computer Science.* To transfer (information) from one recording and storing system to another. **3.** To adapt or arrange (a musical composition) for a voice or instrument other than the original. **4.** To record, usually on tape, for broadcasting at a later date. **5.** To represent (speech sounds) by phonetic symbols. **6.** To represent in a different alphabet; transliterate. **7.** *Genetics.* To cause transcription of (DNA). [Latin *transcrībere,* to copy, "write over" : *trāns-,* from one place to another, across + *scrībere,* to write.] —**tran·scrib·a·ble** *adj.* —**tran·scrib·er** *n.*

tran·script (trăn′skrĭpt′) *n.* Something transcribed; especially, a written, typed, or printed copy, as of a legal record or a student's academic record. [Middle English *transcri(p)t,* from Old French *transcrit,* from Latin *transcriptum,* from the past participle of *transcrībere,* to TRANSCRIBE.]

tran·scrip·tion (trăn-skrĭp′shən) *n.* **1. a.** The act or process or an instance of transcribing. **b.** The state of being transcribed. **2.** Something that has been transcribed, especially: **a.** A representation of speech sounds in phonetic symbols. **b.** An adaptation of a musical composition. **c.** A recorded radio or television program. **3.** *Genetics.* The transfer of genetic information in DNA to RNA, usually by the synthesis of messenger RNA in which DNA acts as a template. —**tran·scrip·tion·al, tran·scrip·tive** *adj.* —**tran·scrip·tion·al·ly, tran·scrip·tive·ly** *adv.*

trans·cul·tu·ra·tion (trăns′kŭl′chə-rā′shən, trănz′-) *n.* Cultural change induced by the introduction of elements of a foreign culture. [TRANS- + CULTUR(E) + -ATION.]

trans·cur·rent (trăns-kûr′ənt, trănz-) *adj.* Extending, passing, or running transversely.

transcurrent fault *n.* A **strike-slip fault** *(see).*

trans·duc·er (trăns-dōō′sər, -dyōō′sər, trănz-) *n. Physics.* Any of various substances or devices, such as a piezoelectric crystal or a photoelectric cell, that convert input energy of one form into output energy of another. [Latin *transdūcere,* to lead across, transfer : *trāns-,* across + *dūcere,* to lead.] —**trans·duce** *v.*

trans·duc·tion (trăns-dŭk′shən, trănz-) *n.* **1.** The transfer of genetic material from one bacterial cell to another by a bacteriophage. **2.** *Physics.* The process of converting energy from one form into another. [Latin *transductiō* (stem *transductiōn-*), a transfer, from *transdūcere,* to transfer. See **transducer.**]

tran·sect (trăn-sĕkt′) *tr.v.* **-sected, -secting, -sects.** To divide by cutting transversely. [TRANS- + Latin *secāre* (past participle *sectus*), to cut.] —**tran·sec·tion** *n.*

tran·sept (trăn′sĕpt′) *n. Architecture.* **1.** The shorter portion of a cross-shaped church, consisting of two arms that run across and at right angles to the main body of the church. **2.** Either of the two arms. [New Latin *transeptum* : TRANS- + SEPTUM (partition).]

trans·e·unt (trăn′sē-ənt) *adj. Philosophy.* Productive of effects outside of the mind. Compare **immanent.** [Latin *transiēns* (oblique stem *transeunt-*), going over, TRANSIENT.]

trans·fec·tion (trăns-fĕk′shən) *n.* The infection of a cell with purified viral nucleic acid with subsequent replication of the virus in the cell. [TRANS- + (IN)FECTION.] —**trans·fect** *v.*

trans·fer (trăns-fûr′, trăns′fər) *v.* **-ferred, -ferring, -fers.** —*tr.* **1.** To convey or shift from one person, thing, or place to another: *was transferred to a new job.* **2.** To change or shift (the meaning of a word, phrase, or the like), especially by figurative use. **3.** To make over the possession or legal title of to another. **4.** To convey (a drawing, pattern, mural, or design) from one surface to another. **5.** To sell or move (a professional sportsman) from one club to another. —*intr.* **1.** To move oneself, as from one location, job, or school to another. **2.** To change from one train, airplane, or the like to another. —See Synonyms at **convey.**

∼*n.* (trăns′fər). Also **trans·fer·al, trans·fer·ral** (trăns-fûr′əl) (for senses 1, 2). *Abbr.* **tfr., transf.** **1. a.** The act or process of transferring. **b.** The state of being transferred. **2. a.** Any person or object that has or has been transferred. **b.** A design conveyed or to be conveyed from one surface, usually paper, to another. **3. a.** A ticket entitling a passenger to change from one train, bus, or the like to another. **b.** A place where such changes are permitted or required. **4.** *Law.* **a.** The conveyance of title, property, or shares from one owner to another. **b.** The document effecting such conveyance. [Middle English *transferren,* from Old French *transferer,* from Latin *trānsferre,* to bear across : *trāns-,* across + *ferre,* to bear.] —**trans·fer·a·bil·i·ty** *n.* —**trans·fer·a·ble** *adj.* —**trans·fer·rer** *n.*

trans·fer·ase (trăns′fər-ās′, -āz′) *n.* Any of various enzymes that catalyze the transfer of radicals from one molecule to another.

trans·fer·ee (trăns′fə-rē′) *n.* **1.** *Law.* One to whom a transfer of title or property is made. **2.** One who is transferred.

trans·fer·ence (trăns-fûr′əns, trăns′fər-əns) *n.* **1. a.** An act, the process, or an instance of transferring. **b.** The condition of being transferred. **2.** The process in and by which an individual's feelings, thoughts, and wishes shift from one person to another; especially, this process in psychoanalysis, where the analyst is made the object of the shift. —**trans·fer·en·tial** (trăns′fə-rĕn′shəl) *adj.*

transfer income *n.* Income regarded as a simple transfer of funds from one part of the community to another, rather than as a return for goods and services. It includes government subsidies, unemployment benefits, pensions, and the like, and is not calculated as part of the national income. Also called "transfer payment."

trans·fer·or (trăns-fûr′ər) *n. Law.* A person who makes a transfer of title or property.

transfer paper *n.* Any of various types of specially coated paper used for transferring designs from one surface to another.

trans·fer·rin (trăns-fĕr′ĭn) *n.* A blood globulin that can combine reversibly with and transport iron ions in the body. [TRANS- + FERR(O)- + -IN.]

transfer RNA *n.* Any of various small RNA molecules, each specific for a particular amino acid, that during synthesis carry amino acids to the ribosomes and arrange them along the messenger RNA molecule, where they are joined by peptide bonds to form a protein. Also called "s RNA," "soluble RNA," "t RNA."

trans·fig·u·ra·tion (trăns-fĭg′yə-rā′shən) *n.* **1.** A radical transformation of figure or appearance; metamorphosis. **2. Transfiguration. a.** The sudden emanation of radiance from Jesus' person that occurred on the mountain. Matthew 17:2; Mark 9:2. **b.** The Christian commemoration of this, observed on August 6. **3.** The act or an instance of transfiguring, or the state of being transfigured.

trans·fig·ure (trăns-fĭg′yər) *tr.v.* **-ured, -uring, -ures.** **1.** To transform the figure or appearance of; alter radically, especially so as to improve. **2.** To exalt; glorify. [Middle English, from Latin *trānsfigūrāre* : *trāns-,* change + *figūra,* FIGURE.] —**trans·fig·ure·ment** *n.*

trans·fi·nite (trăns-fī′nīt′) *adj.* Beyond the finite.

transfinite number *n.* Any cardinal or ordinal number representing the size of a set of numbers too large to be counted.

trans·fix (trăns-fĭks′) *tr.v.* **-fixed, -fixing, -fixes.** **1.** To pierce through with or as if with a pointed weapon. **2.** To fix fast; impale. **3.** To render motionless, as with terror, amazement, or awe. [Latin *transfīgere* (past participle *transfīxus*) : *trans-,* through + *fīgere,* to pierce, fix.] —**trans·fix·ion** (trăns-fĭk′shən) *n.*

trans·form (trăns-fôrm′) *v.* **-formed, -forming, -forms.** —*tr.* **1.** To change markedly the form, character, or appearance of, especially for the better: *His new wife has transformed him!* **2.** To change the nature, function, or condition of; convert. **3.** *Mathematics.* To subject to a mathematical transformation. **4.** *Electricity.* To subject to the action of a transformer. —*intr.* To undergo a transformation. —See Synonyms at **change.**

∼*n.* (trăns′fôrm′). The result, especially a mathematical quantity or linguistic construction, of a transformation. [Middle English, from Old French, from Latin *transformāre* : TRANS- + FORM.] —**trans·form·a·ble** *adj.*

trans·for·ma·tion (trăns′fər-mā′shən) *n.* **1. a.** The act of transforming. **b.** The state or an instance of being transformed. **c.** Something that has been transformed. **2.** Any extreme or radical change, especially for the better. **3.** *Mathematics.* **a.** The replacement of the variables in an algebraic expression by their values in terms of another set of variables. **b.** A mapping of one space onto another or onto itself. **4.** *Physics.* A change of one nuclide into another as a result of an alpha decay or a beta decay. **5.** *Linguistics.* **a.** The process of converting a syntactic construction into a semantically equivalent construction according to the rules shown to generate the syntax of the language. **b.** A construction derived by such transformation. [Middle English, from Late Latin *transformātio* (stem *transformātiōn-*). See **transform.**] **—trans·for·ma·tive** (trăns-fôr′mə-tĭv) *adj.*

trans·for·ma·tion·al grammar (trăns′fər-mā′shə-nəl, trăns′fôr-) *n. Linguistics.* A grammar that accounts for the constructions of a language by linguistic transformations and phrase structures, on the assumption that languages have a **deep structure** and a **surface structure** *(both of which see).* Also called "transformational-generative grammar."

trans·form·er (trăns-fôr′mər) *n.* **1.** One that transforms. **2.** A device used to transfer electric energy, usually that of an alternating current, from one circuit to another; especially, a pair of multiply wound, inductively coupled wire coils that effect such a transfer with a change in voltage, current, phase, or other electric characteristic. See **step-down transformer, step-up transformer.**

trans·fuse (trăns-fyo͞oz′) *tr.v.* **-fused, -fusing, -fuses. 1.** To transfer (liquid) by pouring from one vessel into another. **2.** To permeate; infuse. **3.** *Medicine.* To administer a transfusion of or to. [Middle English *transfusen,* from Latin *trānsfundere* (past participle *trānsfūsus*) : *trāns-,* from one place to another + *fundere,* to pour.] **—trans·fus·er** *n.* **—trans·fus·i·ble** *adj.* **—trans·fu·sive** (trăns-fyo͞o′sĭv, -zĭv) *adj.*

trans·fu·sion (trăns-fyo͞o′zhən) *n.* **1.** The act or process or an instance of transfusing. **2.** *Medicine.* The injection of whole blood, plasma, or another solution into the bloodstream.

trans·gress (trăns-grĕs′, trănz-) *v.* **-gressed, -gressing, -gresses.** *—tr.* **1.** To go beyond or over (a limit or boundary). **2.** To act in violation of (the law, for example). *—intr.* To trespass; sin. [Latin *trānsgredī* (past participle *trānsgressus*), to step across : *trāns-,* across + *gradī,* to step.] **—trans·gress·i·ble** *adj.* **—trans·gres·sive** *adj.* **—trans·gres·sive·ly** *adv.* **—trans·gres·sor** *n.*

trans·gres·sion (trăns-grĕsh′ən, trănz-) *n.* **1.** The violation of a law, command, or duty; a crime or sin. **2.** The exceeding or overstepping of due bounds or limits. —See Synonyms at **breach.**

tranship. Variant of **transship.**

trans·hu·mance (trăns-hyo͞o′məns, trănz-) *n.* The movement of livestock and herders to different grazing grounds with the changing of the seasons. [French, from *transhumer,* to make seasonal movement of livestock, from Spanish *transhumar* : Latin *trāns-,* from one place to another + *humus,* earth, ground.] **—trans·hu·mant** *adj. & n.*

tran·sient (trăn′shənt, -zhənt, -zē-ənt) *adj.* **1.** Passing away with time; transitory; fleeting. **2.** Passing through from one place to another; stopping only briefly: *transient laborers.* **3.** *Physics.* Decaying with time, especially as a simple exponential function of time. **4.** *Music.* Used only in passing from one key to a different key in a modulation: *a transient chord.*
~n. **1.** One that is transient. **2.** *Physics.* A transient phenomenon or property, especially a transient electric current. [Latin *transiēns* (stem *transient-*), present participle of *transīre,* to go over : *trāns-,* over, across + *īre,* to go.] **—tran·sience** (trăn′shəns, -zhəns, -zē-əns), **tran·sien·cy** (trăn′shən-sē, -zhən-sē, -zē-ən-sē), **tran·sient·ness** *n.* **—tran·sient·ly** *adv.*
Synonyms: *ephemeral, evanescent, fleeting, fugitive, momentary, provisional, temporary, transitory.*

trans·il·lu·mi·nate (trăns′ĭ-lo͞o′mə-nāt′, trănz′-) *tr.v.* **-nated, -nating, -nates.** *Medicine.* To examine (a bodily part or organ) by passing a light through its walls. **—trans·il·lu·mi·na·tion** *n.* **—trans·il·lu·mi·na·tor** *n.*

tran·sis·tor (trăn-zĭs′tər, trăn-sĭs′-) *n.* **1.** A semiconductor device used for amplification, switching, and detection, typically containing two rectifying junctions and usually having three terminals, and characteristically operating so that the current between one pair of terminals controls the current between the other pair, one terminal being common to input and output. **2.** A radio equipped with transistors. In this sense, also called "transistor radio." [TRANS(FER) + (RES)ISTOR.]

tran·sis·tor·ize (trăn-zĭs′tə-rīz′, trăn-sĭs′-) *tr.v.* **-ized, -izing, -izes. 1.** To equip (an electronic circuit or device) with transistors. **2.** To design or refit (a machine, factory, or the like) to use transistors.

tran·sit (trăn′sĭt, -zĭt) *n.* **1. a.** The act of passing over, across, or through; passage. **b.** The movement or conveyance of goods or persons from one place to another, especially on a local public transportation system. **2.** A transition or change, especially from one life to another at death. **3.** *Astronomy.* **a.** The apparent passage of a celestial body across the observer's meridian. **b.** The passage of a smaller celestial body across the disk of a larger celestial body. **4.** A surveying instrument similar to a theodolite that measures horizontal and vertical angles. **5.** A way, passage, or route.. **—in transit. 1.** While being moved or conveyed. **2.** Only stopping temporarily; continuing one's journey. Said especially of airline passengers.
~v. **transited, -siting, -sits.** *—tr.* **1.** To pass over, across, or through. **2.** To revolve (the telescope of a surveying transit) about its horizontal transverse axis in order to reverse its direction. *—intr. Astronomy.* To make a transit. [Latin *transitus,* from the past participle of *transīre,* to go across. See **transient.**]

transit instrument *n.* A telescope mounted on a horizontal east-west axis used to observe the passage of stars across the meridian.

tran·si·tion (trăn-zĭsh′ən, -sĭsh′ən) *n.* **1. a.** The act or process or an instance of changing from one form, state, activity, or place to another. **b.** The length of time involved in such a change. **2.** Passage from one subject to another, as in discourse. **3.** *Music.* **a.** A modulation, especially a brief one. **b.** A passage connecting two themes. **4.** *Physics.* **a.** In quantum mechanics, the change of a system from one energy state to another. **b.** A change in a nuclide involving either a transformation to another nuclide or a change in energy level as a result of gamma-ray emission. **5.** In various arts, a change from one tradition or style to another or a combination of elements of an older style and a newer style, as in transitional architecture. **—tran·si·tion·al, tran·si·tion·ar·y** (trăn-zĭsh′ə-nĕr′ē) *adj.* **—tran·si·tion·al·ly** *adv.*

transitional architecture *n.* Architecture of the period, around the year 1100, of transition from the Romanesque to the Gothic. In Britain it is marked by a combination of the Norman and early English styles.

transition element *n.* **1.** Any of the elements that serve as transitional links between the most and the least electropositive in a series of elements and that are characterized by high melting points, densities, magnetic moments, multiple valences, and the ability to form stable complex ions. **2.** Any of the elements in which an inner electron shell rather than an outer shell is only partially filled, generally taken to include elements 21–30, 39–48, and 57–80. Also called "transition metal."

transition temperature *n.* The temperature at which there is a sudden change in a particular physical property of a substance, such as its crystalline structure, conductivity, or magnetism. Also called "transition point."

tran·si·tive (trăn′sə-tĭv, trăn′zə-) *adj.* **1.** *Abbr.* **t., tr., trans.** *Grammar.* **a.** Expressing an action that is carried from the subject to the object. **b.** Designating a verb or verb construction that requires a direct object to complete its meaning. **2.** Characterized by or effecting transition. **3.** *Mathematics & Logic.* Designating a relationship such that if A and B have a particular relation and B and C have the same relation, then so do A and C. For example, if A is a number that has a value less than that of B and the value of B is less than that of C, then A is less than C; therefore "is less than" is a transitive relationship.
~n. Abbr. **t., tr., trans.** *Grammar.* A transitive verb. Compare **intransitive.** [Late Latin *transitīvus,* passing over (as from the subject to the object), from Latin *transitus,* TRANSIT.] **—tran·si·tive·ly** *adv.* **—tran·si·tive·ness, tran·si·tiv·i·ty** (trăn′sə-tĭv′ə-tē) *n.*

tran·si·to·ry (trăn′sə-tôr′ē, -tōr′ē, trăn′zə-) *adj.* Existing or occurring only briefly; short-lived; passing. —See Synonyms at **transient.** [Middle English *transitorie,* from Norman French, from Late Latin *transitōrius,* from Latin, having a passageway, from *transitus,* TRANSIT.] **—tran·si·to·ri·ly** (trăn′sə-tôr′ə-lē, -tōr′ə-lē, trăn′zə-) *adv.* **—tran·si·to·ri·ness** *n.*

transitory action *n.* A legal action or case that may be brought in any country and not merely in the one in which it originated.

Transjordan. See **Jordan.**

Trans·kei (trăns-kī′). An autonomous region of South Africa. Consisting of the homelands of the Xhosa tribe, it was established by the South African government in 1963 to implement its policy of apartheid. No other nation has recognized Transkei's sovereignty. Area, 43,077 square kilometers (16,632 square miles). Population, 2,000,000. Capital, Umtata. **—Trans·kei·an** *n. & adj.*

transl. translated; translation.

trans·late (trăns-lāt′, trănz-, trăns′lāt′, trănz′-) *v.* **-lated, -lating, -lates.** *—tr.* **1.** To express in another language, systematically retaining the original sense. **2. a.** To put in simpler terms; explain. **b.** To see the significance of; infer; interpret. **3.** To convey from one form or style to another; convert. **4.** To transfer (a bishop) to another see. **5.** To move or transfer. **6.** *Theology.* To convey to heaven without natural death. **7.** *Physics.* To subject (a body) to translation. **8.** *Genetics.* To cause translation of (messenger RNA). **9.** *Archaic.* To transport; enrapture. *—intr.* **1. a.** To make a translation. **b.** To work as a translator. **2.** To admit of or be capable of translation. **3.** *Aerospace.* To move from one place to another in space by means of reaction power. [Middle English *translaten,* to transport, to translate, from Latin *translātus* (past participle of *transferre,* to carry across, transfer, translate) : *trāns-,* across + *-lātus,* "carried."] **—trans·lat·a·bil·i·ty, trans·lat·a·ble·ness** *n.* **—trans·lat·a·ble** *adj.*

trans·la·tion (trăns-lā′shən, trănz-) *n. Abbr.* **transl., trans., tr. 1. a.** The act or process or an instance of translating, especially from one language to another. **b.** The condition of being translated. **2.** A translated version of a text. **3.** *Physics.* Motion of a body in which every point of the body moves parallel to, and the same distance as, every other point of the body; nonrotational displacement. **4.** *Biochemistry.* The decoding of the genetic information in a messenger RNA molecule so that it may be used to synthesize protein molecules. **—trans·la·tion·al** *adj.*

trans·la·tor (trăns-lā′tər, trănz-, trăns′lā′tər, trănz′-) *n. Abbr.* **tr., trans. 1.** One who translates; especially, one professionally employed to translate written works. **2.** An interpreter. **—trans·la·to·ri·al** (trăns′lə-tôr′ē-əl, -tōr′ē-əl, trănz′-) *adj.*

trans·lit·er·ate (trăns-lĭt′ə-rāt′, trănz-) *tr.v.* **-ated, -ating, -ates.** To represent (letters or words) in the corresponding characters of another alphabet. [TRANS- + Latin *littera,* LETTER + -ATE.] **—trans·lit·er·a·tion** *n.*

trans·lo·cate (trăns′lō-kāt′, trănz′-) *tr.v.* **-cated, -cating, -cates.** To cause to change from one position to another; displace; move.

trans·lo·ca·tion (trăns′lō-kā′shən, trănz′-) *n.* **1.** A change in location. **2.** *Genetics.* A chromosomal aberration in which sections from different chromosomes are interchanged. **3.** The movement of mineral nutrients, food materials, and the like in plants.

PRONUNCIATION KEY

ă, pat; ā, pay; âr, care;
ä, father, are; b, bib;
ch, church; d, deed; ĕ, pet;
ē, be; f, fife; g, gag; h, hat;
hw, which; ĭ, pit; ī, pie;
îr, pier; j, judge; k, kick;
l, lid, needle; m, mum;
n, no, sudden; ng, thing;
ŏ, pot; ō, toe; ô, paw, for;
oi, noise; ou, out; o͝o, book;
o͞o, boot; p, pop; r, roar;
s, sauce; sh, ship, dish;
t, tight; th, thin, path;
th, this, bathe; ŭ, cut; ûr, fur;
v, valve; w, with; y, yes;
z, zebra, size; zh, vision;
ə, about, item, edible,
gallop, circus, peaceful

IN FOREIGN WORDS:

à, *Fr.* ami; œ, *Fr.* feu, *Ger.* schön; ü, *Fr.* tu, *Ger.* über;
KH, *Ger.* ich, *Scot.* loch;
N, *Fr.* bon; y′, *Fr.* Compiègne

STRESS MARKS:

Primary stress: ′
in·cite′ (ĭn-sīt′)
Secondary stress: ′
in′sight′ (ĭn′sīt′)

trans·lu·cent (trăns-lo͞o′sənt, trănz-) *adj.* Transmitting light but causing sufficient diffusion to eliminate perception of distinct images. Compare **transparent, opaque.** [Latin *translūcēns* (stem *translūcent-*), present participle of *translūcēre,* to shine through : *trāns-,* through + *lūcēre,* to shine.] —**trans·lu·cence, trans·lu·cen·cy** *n.* —**trans·lu·cent·ly** *adv.*

trans·lun·ar (trăns-lo͞o′nər, trănz-) *adj.* Lying beyond the moon. Compare **cislunar.**

trans·lu·na·ry (trăns-lo͞o′nə-rē, trănz-) *adj.* **1.** Translunar. **2.** Unearthly; visionary. [TRANS- + Latin *lūna,* moon + -ARY.]

trans·ma·rine (trăns′mə-rēn′, trănz′-) *adj.* **1.** Crossing the sea. **2.** Being beyond or coming from across the sea. [Latin *transmarīnus* : *trāns-,* across, beyond + *mare,* sea.]

trans·mi·grant (trăns-mī′grənt, trănz-) *n.* **1.** One who transmigrates; an immigrant. **2.** An immigrant in transit through a country on his way to the country in which he intends to settle.

trans·mi·grate (trăns-mī′grāt′, trănz-) *intr.v.* **-grated, -grating, -grates. 1.** To migrate. **2.** To pass into another body after death. Used of the soul. —**trans·mi·gra·tor** *n.* —**trans·mi·gra·to·ry** (trăns-mī′grə-tôr′ē, -tōr′ē, trănz-) *adj.*

trans·mi·gra·tion (trăns′mī-grā′shən, trănz′-) *n.* **1.** The act or process of transmigrating. **2.** The passing of a soul into another body after death; metempsychosis. Also called "transmigration of souls." —**trans·mi·gra·tion·ism** *n.*

trans·mis·si·ble (trăns-mĭs′ə-bəl, trănz-) *adj.* Capable of being transmitted. —**trans·mis·si·bil·i·ty** *n.*

trans·mis·sion (trăns-mĭsh′ən, trănz-) *n.* **1. a.** The act or process of transmitting. **b.** The state of being transmitted. **2.** Something transmitted, such as a message. **3. a.** An assembly of gears and associated parts by which power is transmitted from the engine of a motor vehicle to a driving axle. **b.** A system of gears. **4.** The sending of modulated carrier waves from a transmitter; a broadcast. [Latin *transmissiō* (stem *transmissiōn-*), from *transmissus,* past participle of *transmittere,* to TRANSMIT.] —**trans·mis·sive** (trăns-mĭs′ĭv) *adj.*

transmission line *n.* A coaxial cable, waveguide, or other system of conductors used to transfer information from one place to another.

trans·mis·siv·i·ty (trăns′mĭ-sĭv′ə-tē, trănz′-) *n. Physics.* A measure of the ability of a medium to transmit radiation given by the internal transmittance of unit length of a material.

trans·mis·som·e·ter (trăns′mĭ-sŏm′ĭ-tər, trănz′-) *n.* A device used to measure the transmission of light through a medium. [TRANSMIS-S(ION) + -METER.] —**trans·mis·som·e·try** *n.*

trans·mit (trăns-mĭt′, trănz-) *v.* **-mitted, -mitting, -mits.** —*tr.* **1.** To send from one person, thing, or place to another; convey. **2.** To cause to spread; pass on: *transmit an infection.* **3.** To impart or convey to others by heredity; hand down. **4.** *Electronics.* **a.** To send (a signal), as by wire or radio. **b.** To broadcast (a television or radio program). **5.** *Physics.* To cause (a disturbance) to propagate through a medium. **6.** To convey (force or energy) from one part of a mechanism to another. —*intr.* To send out a signal. —See Synonyms at **convey.** [Middle English *transmitten,* from Latin *transmittere,* to send across : *trāns-,* across + *mittere,* to send.] —**trans·mit·ta·ble** *adj.* —**trans·mit·tal** (trăns-mĭt′l, trănz-) *n.*

trans·mit·tance (trăns-mĭt′ns, trănz-) *n.* **1.** The act or process of transmitting; a transmission. **2.** *Physics.* The ratio of the radiant energy transmitted to the total radiant energy incident on a given body. Compare **absorptance, reflectance.**

trans·mit·tan·cy (trăns-mĭt′n-sē, trănz-) *n. Physics.* The transmittance of a solution divided by the transmittance of a pure solvent of identical dimensions.

trans·mit·ter (trăns-mĭt′ər, trănz-) *n.* **1.** One that transmits. **2.** A telegraphic sending instrument. **3.** The portion of a telephone that converts the incident sounds into electrical impulses that are conveyed to a remote receiver. **4.** Electronic equipment that generates and amplifies a carrier wave, modulates it with a signal derived from speech or other sources, and radiates the resulting signal from an aerial. **5.** In physiology, a **neurotransmitter** *(see).*

trans·mog·ri·fy (trăns-mŏg′rə-fī′, trănz-) *tr.v.* **-fied, -fying, -fies.** To change into a different shape or form, especially one that is fantastic or bizarre. [17th century : origin obscure.] —**trans·mog·ri·fi·ca·tion** *n.*

trans·mon·tane (trăns-mŏn′tān′, trănz-, trăns′mŏn-tān′, trănz′-) *adj.* Located beyond a mountain or mountain range; tramontane. [Latin *trānsmontānus,* TRAMONTANE.]

trans·mu·ta·tion (trăns′myo͞o-tā′shən, trănz′-) *n.* **1.** The act of transmuting. **2.** The state of being transmuted. **3.** In alchemy, the alleged conversion of base metals into gold or silver. **4.** *Physics.* The transformation of one element into another by one or a series of nuclear reactions. [Middle English, from Old French, from Late Latin *transmūtātiō* (stem *transmūtātiōn-*). See **transmute.**] —**trans·mu·ta·tion·al, trans·mu·ta·tive** (trăns-myo͞o′tə-tĭv, trănz-) *adj.*

trans·mute (trăns-myo͞ot′, trănz-) *tr.v.* **-muted, -muting, -mutes.** To change from one form, nature, substance, or state into another; transform. —See Synonyms at **change.** [Middle English *transmuten,* from Latin *transmūtāre* : *trāns-,* from one to another + *mūtāre,* to change.] —**trans·mut·a·bil·i·ty, trans·mut·a·ble·ness** *n.* —**trans·mut·a·ble** *adj.* —**trans·mut·a·bly** *adv.* —**trans·mut·er** *n.*

trans·na·tion·al (trăns-năsh′ə-nəl, trănz-) *adj.* Not confined to a single nation; extending across national frontiers.

trans·o·ce·an·ic (trăns′ō′shē-ăn′ĭk, trănz′-) *adj.* **1.** Situated beyond or on the other side of the ocean. **2.** Spanning or crossing the ocean.

tran·som (trăn′səm) *n.* **1.** A horizontal bar that is situated between a door and a window above it. **2.** A horizontal dividing bar of wood or stone in a window. **3.** A window that has been divided with a transom. **4.** A rectangular window over a door, often serving to admit light to a passage or hall. Also *British* "fanlight." **5.** *Nautical.* Any of several transverse beams affixed to the sternpost of a wooden ship and forming part of the stern. **6.** The horizontal beam on a cross or gallows, or the top piece of a trilith. [Middle English *traunson,* crossbeam, lintel, perhaps from Latin *transtrum* : *trāns-,* across + *-trum,* suffix denoting an instrument.] —**tran·somed** *adj.*

tran·son·ic (trăn-sŏn′ĭk) *adj.* Of or pertaining to aerodynamic flow or flight conditions at speeds close to the speed of sound. [TRANS- + (SUPER)SONIC.]

transp. transportation.

trans·pa·cif·ic (trăns′pə-sĭf′ĭk) *adj.* **1.** Crossing the Pacific Ocean. **2.** Situated across or beyond the Pacific Ocean.

trans·par·en·cy (trăns-pâr′ən-sē, -păr′ən-sē) *n., pl.* **-cies.** Also **trans·par·ence** (-pâr′əns, -păr′əns) (for sense 1). **1.** The quality or state of being transparent. **2.** A transparent object; especially, a photographic slide whose image is made visible by light shining through from behind.

trans·par·ent (trăns-pâr′ənt, -păr′ənt) *adj.* **1.** Capable of transmitting light so that objects or images can be seen clearly. Compare **translucent, opaque. 2.** Permeable to electromagnetic radiation of specified frequencies, as to visible light or radio waves. **3.** Of such fine or open texture that objects may be easily seen on the other side; diaphanous; sheer. **4.** Easily understood or detected; flimsy or obvious: *transparent lies.* **5.** Guileless; candid; open. [Middle English, from Old French, from Medieval Latin *trānspārēns* (stem *transpārent-*), present participle of *trānspārēre,* to be seen through : Latin *trāns-,* through + *pārēre,* to show (see **appear**).] —**trans·par·ent·ly** *adv.* —**trans·par·ent·ness** *n.*

tran·spi·ra·tion (trăn′spə-rā′shən) *n.* The act or process of transpiring, especially through the stomata of plant tissue or the pores of the skin.

tran·spire (trăn-spīr′) *v.* **-spired, -spiring, -spires.** —*tr.* **1.** To secrete (water containing waste products) through the pores of the skin; perspire. **2.** To lose (water vapor) from the surface of a plant, mainly through open stomata. **3.** To become known; come to light. Used impersonally with a clause. **4.** *Informal.* **a.** To happen; occur. **b.** To come to pass; turn out. Used impersonally with a clause. —*intr.* **1.** To secrete water containing waste products through animal pores. **2.** To lose water vapor from a plant surface. **3.** To become known; come to light. **4.** *Informal.* **a.** To happen; occur. **b.** To come to pass; turn out. [French *transpirer,* from Old French : Latin *trāns-,* out + *spīrāre,* to breathe.]

Usage: *Transpire* has long been used in the sense "to become known": *It soon transpired that he had known all along.* The meaning "to happen" or "to take place" has come into use more recently: *He wondered what would transpire next.* This use, though widespread, has attracted criticism from purists.

trans·plant (trăns-plănt′, -plänt′) *v.* **-planted, -planting, -plants.** —*tr.* **1.** To uproot and replant (a growing plant). **2.** To transfer from one place or residence to another; resettle; relocate. **3.** In surgery, to transfer (tissue or an organ) from one body or body part to another. —*intr.* **1.** To admit or be capable of being transplanted. **2.** To survive transplanting.
~*n.* (trăns′plănt′, -plänt′). **1.** Something transplanted. **2.** The act or process of transplanting: *a heart transplant.* [Middle English *transplaunten,* from Late Latin *transplantāre* : Latin *trans-,* across + *plantāre,* to plant (see **plant**).] —**trans·plan·ta·tion** (trăns′plăn-tā′shən, trăns′plän-) *n.* —**trans·plant·er** *n.*

trans·po·lar (trăns-pō′lər) *adj.* Extending across or crossing over either of the geographic polar regions.

tran·spond·er (trăn-spŏn′dər) *n.* A radio or radar receiver-transmitter activated for transmission by reception of a predetermined signal. [TRAN(SMITTER) + (RE)SPONDER.]

trans·pon·tine (trăns-pŏn′tīn′) *adj.* **1.** Situated across or beyond a bridge. **2.** Of or pertaining to the melodramatic plays once performed in the part of London on the south side of the Thames. [TRANS- + Latin *pōns* (stem *pont-*), bridge + -INE.]

trans·port (trăns-pôrt′, -pōrt′) *tr.v.* **-ported, -porting, -ports. 1.** To carry from one place to another; convey. **2.** To move to strong emotion; enrapture; carry away: *transported by the scene.* **3.** Especially formerly, to send abroad to a penal colony; deport. —See Synonyms at **banish, convey.**
~*n.* (trăns′pôrt′, -pōrt′). **1.** The act of transporting; conveyance. **2.** The state or condition of being transported by emotion; rapture. **3.** A ship used to transport troops or military equipment. **4.** A vehicle, such as an aircraft, used to transport passengers, mail, or freight. **5. a.** The system of transporting passengers or goods in a particular country or area. **b.** The vehicles, such as buses and trains, used in such a system. **6.** Especially formerly, a deported convict. —See Synonyms at **ecstasy.** [Middle English *transporten,* from Old French *transporter,* from Latin *trānsportāre* : *trāns-,* from one place to another + *portāre,* to carry.] —**trans·port·a·bil·i·ty** *n.* —**trans·port·a·ble** *adj.* —**trans·port·er** *n.* —**trans·port·ive** *adj.*

trans·por·ta·tion (trăns′pər-tā′shən) *n. Abbr.* **trans., transp. 1.** The act of transporting. **2.** The state of being transported. **3. a.** A means of transport; a conveyance. **b.** The business of transporting passengers, goods, materials, or the like. **4.** A charge for transporting; a fare.

PRONUNCIATION KEY

ă, pat; ā, pay; âr, care;
ä, father, are; b, bib;
ch, church; d, deed; ĕ, pet;
ē, be; f, fife; g, gag; h, hat;
hw, which; ĭ, pit; ī, pie;
îr, pier; j, judge; k, kick;
l, lid, needle; m, mum;
n, no, sudden; ng, thing;
ŏ, pot; ō, toe; ô, paw, for;
oi, noise; ou, out; o͝o, book;
o͞o, boot; p, pop; r, roar;
s, sauce; sh, ship, dish;
t, tight; th, thin, path;
th, this, bathe; ŭ, cut; ûr, fur;
v, valve; w, with; y, yes;
z, zebra, size; zh, vision;
ə, about, item, edible, gallop, circus, peaceful

IN FOREIGN WORDS:

à, *Fr.* ami; œ, *Fr.* feu, *Ger.* schön; ü, *Fr.* tu, *Ger.* über; KH, *Ger.* ich, *Scot.* loch; N, *Fr.* bon; y′, *Fr.* Compiègne

STRESS MARKS:

Primary stress: ′
in·cite′ (ĭn-sīt′)
Secondary stress: ′
in′sight′ (ĭn′sīt′)

trans·pose (trăns-pōz′) *v.* **-posed, -posing, -poses.** —*tr.* **1.** To reverse or transfer the order or place of; interchange. **2.** To put into a different place or order: *transpose the words of a sentence.* **3.** *Mathematics.* To move (a term) from one side of an algebraic equation to the other side, reversing its sign to maintain equality. **4.** *Music.* To write or perform (a composition) in a key other than the original or given key. **5.** *Obsolete.* To transform. —*intr.* **1.** *Music.* To write or perform music in a key other than the original or given key. **2.** To admit of being transposed.
~*n.* (trăns′pōz′). *Mathematics.* A matrix that is generated by interchanging the rows and columns of the original matrix. [Middle English *transposen,* from Old French *transposer* : Latin *trāns-,* from one place to another + French *poser,* to place, POSE.] **—trans·pos·a·ble** *adj.* **—trans·pos·er** *n.*
trans·po·si·tion (trăns′pə-zĭsh′ən) *n.* Also **trans·pos·al** (trăns-pō′zəl). *Abbr.* **tr. 1.** The act of transposing. **2.** The state of being transposed. **3.** Something that has been transposed. [French. See **trans-, position.**] **—trans·po·si·tion·al** *adj.*
trans·ra·cial (trăns-rā′shəl, trănz-) *adj.* Involving two or more races.
trans·sex·u·al (trăns-sĕk′sho͞o-əl) *n.* **1.** A person with an overwhelming desire to become a member of the opposite sex. **2.** A person who has undergone a sex change, usually through surgery and hormone therapy. **—trans·sex·u·al** *adj.* **—trans·sex·u·al·ism, trans·sex·u·al·i·ty** *n.*
trans·ship (trăns-shĭp′) *v.* **-shipped, -shipping, -ships.** Also **tran·ship** (trăn-shĭp′, trăns-). —*tr.* To transfer from one vessel or vehicle to another for reshipment. —*intr.* To transfer cargo from one vessel or vehicle to another. **—trans·ship·ment** *n.*
trans·tho·rac·ic (trăns′thə-răs′ĭk) *adj.* Across the thoracic cavity. **—trans·tho·rac·i·cal·ly** *adv.*
tran·sub·stan·ti·ate (trăn′səb-stăn′shē-āt′) *tr.v.* **-ated, -ating, -ates. 1.** To change (one substance) into another; transmute; transform. **2.** *Theology.* To change the substance of (the Eucharistic bread and wine) into the body and blood of Christ. [Medieval Latin *transubstantiāre* : Latin *trāns-,* change + *substantia,* SUBSTANCE.]
tran·sub·stan·ti·a·tion (trăn′səb-stăn′shē-ā′shən) *n.* **1.** *Theology.* The doctrine that the bread and wine of the Eucharist are transformed into the body and blood of Christ, although their appearance remains the same. Compare **consubstantiation. 2.** The conversion of one substance into another; a transformation. **—tran·sub·stan·ti·a·tion·al·ist** *n.*
tran·su·date (trăn-so͞o′dāt′, -syo͞o′dāt′, trăn′so͞o-dāt′, -syo͞o-dāt′) *n.* A substance that has undergone transudation.
tran·su·da·tion (trăn′so͞o-dā′shən, trăn′syo͞o-) *n.* The passage of a fluid with some of its dissolved salts through a membrane or skin.
tran·sude (trăn-so͞od′, -syo͞od′) *intr.v.* **-suded, -suding, -sudes.** To exude or pass through a membrane or skin, in the manner of perspiration. [New Latin *transudare* : Latin *trāns-,* through + *sūdāre,* to sweat.] **—tran·su·da·to·ry** (trăn-so͞o′də-tôr′ē, -tōr′ē, trăn-syo͞o′-) *adj.*
trans·u·ran·ic (trăns′yo͞o-răn′ĭk, trănz′-) *adj.* Also **trans·u·ra·ni·an** (-rā′nē-ən), **trans·u·ra·ni·um** (-nē-əm). Having an atomic number greater than 92. [TRANS- + URAN(IUM) + -IC.]
Trans·vaal (trăns-väl′, trănz-). Province of northeastern South Africa, between the Vaal and Limpopo rivers. It is South Africa's richest province, having enormous mineral wealth, especially gold and diamonds, and fertile veldt for crops and grazing. Pretoria is the capital and Johannesburg the largest city. Boer settlers set up the South African Republic (1857), which was annexed by Britain (1877). After enormous gold finds on the Witwatersrand (1886) settlers, particularly Britons, flocked in. Tensions led to war between Britain and the Boers (1899), and as a result Transvaal was made a crown colony (1902). It joined the Union of South Africa in 1910.
trans·val·ue (trăns-văl′yo͞o, trănz-) *tr.v.* **-ued, -uing, -ues.** To evaluate by a new standard or principle, especially one that varies from conventional standards. **—trans·val·u·a·tion** *n.*
trans·ver·sal (trăns-vûr′səl, trănz-) *adj.* Transverse.
~*n.* In geometry, a line that intersects a system of lines. Also called "traverse."
trans·verse (trăns-vûrs′, trănz-, trăns′vûrs′, trănz′-) *adj. Abbr.* **trans.** Situated or lying across; crosswise.
~*n.* (trăns′vûrs′, trănz′-). *Abbr.* **trans.** Something, as a part or beam, that is transverse. [Latin *trānsversus,* from the past participle of *trānsvertere,* to turn or direct across : *trāns-,* across + *vertere,* to turn.] **—trans·verse·ly** *adv.* **—trans·verse·ness** *n.*
transverse colon *n.* The part of the colon that lies across the upper part of the abdominal cavity.
transverse flute *n.* A flute that is held horizontally, having its embouchure on the side of the cylinder. Said of the modern flute as distinguished from the recorder.
transverse process *n.* A lateral projection from a vertebra.
transverse wave *n.* A wave in which the displacement of the transmitting field or medium is at right angles to the direction of propagation. Compare **longitudinal wave.**
trans·vest·ism (trăns-vĕs′tĭz′əm, trănz-) *n.* Also **trans·ves·tit·ism** (-vĕs′tĭ-tĭz′əm). The practice or condition of being a transvestite. Also called "eonism."
trans·ves·tite (trăns-vĕs′tīt′, trănz-) *n.* A person who for sexual stimulation wears clothes normally worn by the opposite sex. [From German *transvestit* : Latin *trāns-,* across + *vestīre (*past participle *vestītus*), to dress.] **—trans·ves·tite** *adj.*
Tran·syl·va·ni·a (trăn′sĭl-vā′nē-ə, -vān′yə). Plateau region of central Romania, between the Carpathians and the Transylvanian Alps. Transylvania is rich in mineral, agricultural, and forest resources, and it has large iron and steel, chemical, and textile industries. **—Tran·syl·va·ni·an** *adj. & n.*
Transylvanian Alps (ălps). Mountain range of central Romania. It extends 360 kilometers (225 miles) eastward from the Iron Gate gorge on the Danube. Mt. Moldoveanu is its highest peak (2,543 meters; 8,343 feet).
trap¹ (trăp) *n.* **1.** A device for catching and holding animals, such as a net, a concealed pit, or a sensitive clamplike apparatus that springs shut suddenly. **2. a.** Any stratagem or device for betraying, tricking, or exposing an unwary or unsuspecting person. **b.** Anything that serves to catch or ensnare an unwary or unsuspecting person: *fell into the trap of underestimating amateur opposition.* **c.** Anything that attracts, catches, and holds. Also used in combination: *Our garden is a real suntrap.* **3.** A device for sealing a passage against the escape of gases; especially, a U-shaped or S-shaped bend in a drainpipe that prevents the return flow of gases by holding a quantity of water as a barrier. **4.** A device that hurls clay pigeons or disks into the air to be shot at. **5.** In golf, a **bunker** *(see).* **6.** A light two-wheeled vehicle with springs. **7.** A trap door. **8.** Any of the stall-like compartments in which a greyhound is held and which springs open to release the dog at the start of a race. **9.** *Usually* **traps.** *Informal.* In jazz, percussion instruments, such as snare drums, cymbals, or bells. **10.** *Slang.* The mouth.
~*v.* **trapped, trapping, traps.** —*tr.* **1.** To catch in or as if in a trap; ensnare. **2.** To seal off (gases) by a trap. **3.** To furnish or provide with a trap or traps. **4.** To place in a confining or embarrassing position. —*intr.* **1.** To set traps for game. **2.** To trap fur-bearing animals, especially as an occupation. [Middle English *trappe,* Old English *træppe*†.]
trap² *n. Often* **traps.** Personal belongings or household goods.
~*tr.v.* **trapped, trapping, traps.** To furnish with trappings. Often used with *out.* [Middle English *trappe,* probably from Old French *drap,* cloth, from Late Latin *drappus,* from Celtic.]
trap³ *n.* **1.** A fine-grained igneous rock with a characteristically steplike configuration. Also called "traprock." **2.** A structure of rock strata in which oil or gas may collect. [Swedish *trapp,* from *trappa,* step, stair, from Middle Low German *trappe.*] **—trap·pe·an** (trăp′ē-ən), **trap·pous** (trăp′əs) *adj.*
trapan. Variant of **trepan** (to trick).
trap cut *n.* A method of cutting a gem so that it has a flat crown and an intricately shaped pavilion. [Probably from Dutch *trap,* stairs, flight of steps; akin to TRAP (steplike configuration).]
trap door *n.* **1.** A hinged or sliding door in a floor, roof, or ceiling. **2.** The opening covered by a trap door.
trap-door spider (trăp′dôr′, -dōr′) *n.* Any of various spiders of the family Ctenizidae that construct a silk-lined burrow concealed by a hinged lid.

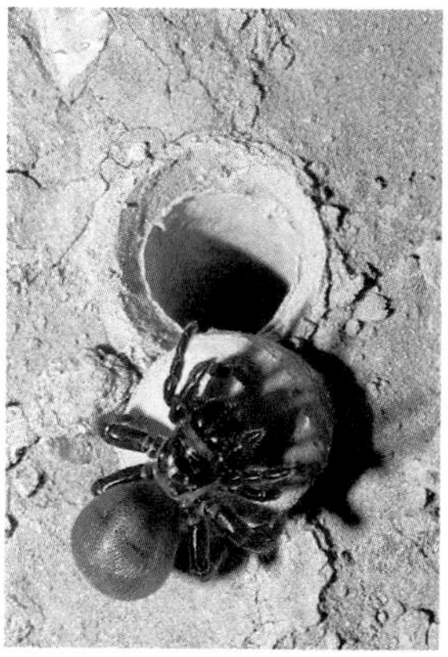

trap-door spider *The burrow of the trap-door spider is concealed by a mud lid hinged with silk. The spider, which is found in tropical and subtropical regions around the world, lies in wait in the burrow, then flips open the door to pounce on passing prey.*

tra·peze (tră-pēz′, trə-) *n.* A short horizontal bar suspended from the ends of two parallel ropes, used for exercises or for acrobatic stunts. [French *trapèze,* from Late Latin *trapezium,* TRAPEZIUM.]
tra·pe·zi·form (trə-pē′zə-fôrm′) *adj.* Formed in the shape of a trapezium. [TRAPEZI(UM) + -FORM.]
tra·pe·zi·um (trə-pē′zē-əm) *n., pl.* **-ums** or **-zia** (-zē-ə). **1. a.** A quadrilateral having no parallel sides. Also *British* "trapezoid." **b.** *British.* See **trapezoid** (sense 1a). **2.** A bone in the wrist at the base of the thumb. [Late Latin, from Greek *trapezion,* small table, diminutive of *trapeza,* table, "four-footed" : *tra-,* four + *peza,* foot.]
tra·pe·zi·us (trə-pē′zē-əs) *n., pl.* **-uses.** Either of two large, flat, triangular muscles running from the base of the back of the head to the middle of the back and across to the shoulder blade. They support and make it possible to raise the head and shoulders. [New Latin *(musculus) trapezius,* "trapezium-shaped (muscle)."]
tra·pe·zo·he·dron (trə-pē′zō-hē′drən, trăp′ə-zō-) *n., pl.* **-drons** or **-dra** (-drə). Any of several forms of crystal with trapeziums as faces. Also called "trisoctahedron." [TRAPEZ(IUM) + -HEDRON.]
trap·e·zoid (trăp′ə-zoid′) *n.* **1. a.** A quadrilateral having two parallel sides. Also *British* "trapezium." **b.** *British.* See **trapezium** (sense 1a). **2.** A small bone in the wrist. [New Latin *trapezoides,* from Greek *trapezoeidēs,* trapezium-shaped : *trapeza,* table (see **trapezium**) + -OID.] **—trap·e·zoid, trap·e·zoi·dal** (trăp′ə-zoid′l) *adj.*
trap·per (trăp′ər) *n.* One whose occupation is trapping animals for their furs.
trap·pings (trăp′ĭngz) *pl.n.* **1.** An ornamental covering or harness for a horse; a caparison. **2.** Articles of dress or adornment, especially those that are characteristic of or symbolize something, such as a particular position or office: *the trappings of a judge.* **3.** Objects, marks, or appearances that are characteristic of or symbolize something: *the trappings of power.*
Trap·pist (trăp′ĭst) *n.* A member of a branch of the Cistercian order of monks, known for austerity and absolute silence, established in 1664 in La Trappe, Normandy. **—Trap·pist** *adj.*
trap·rock (trăp′rŏk′) *n.* An igneous rock, **trap** *(see).*
trap·shoot·ing (trăp′sho͞o′tĭng) *n.* The sport of shooting at clay pigeons or other objects hurled into the air from spring traps. **—trap·shoot·er** *n.*
tra·pun·to (trə-po͝on′tō) *n., pl.* **-tos.** Quilting having a raised effect made by outlining the design with running stitches and then filling it with padding such as cotton. [Italian, from the past participle of *trapungere,* to embroider : Latin *trans-,* through + *pungere,* to prick, pierce.]
trash (trăsh) *n.* **1.** Worthless or discarded material or objects; refuse. **2. a.** Cheap or empty language, talk, or ideas. **b.** Worthless literary or artistic material. **3.** Something broken off or removed to

be discarded; especially, plant trimmings. **4.** The bits of sugar cane that remain after the extraction of its juice. **5.** A person or group of persons held in disdain.
~*tr.v.* **trashed, trashing, trashes. 1.** To cut off leaves or branches from; especially, to lop off the outer leaves from (growing sugar cane). **2.** *Slang.* **a.** To disprove or discredit (an argument). **b.** To beat (someone) up. **c.** To virtually destroy; reduce to trash. [16th century : origin obscure.] **—trash·i·ly** *adv.* **—trash·i·ness** *n.* **—trash·y** *adj.*

trash can *n.* A large, often cylindrical container for household trash or garbage.

trass (trăs) *n.* A volcanic earth used in hydraulic cement. [Dutch *terras,* from French *terrasse,* pile of earth, from Old French *terrasse, terrace,* TERRACE.]

trat·to·ri·a (trăt'ə-rē'ə) *n.* An Italian restaurant. [Italian, from *trattore,* innkeeper, restaurateur, from French *traiteur,* from *traiter,* to entertain, TREAT.]

Trau·bel (trou'bəl), **Helen** (1903–72). U.S. operatic soprano. After making her debut with the St. Louis Symphony in 1925, she joined the Metropolitan Opera Company in New York and was particularly noted for her Wagnerian roles.

trau·ma (trou'mə, trô'-) *n., pl.* **-mas** or **-mata** (-mə-tə). **1.** *Pathology.* A wound, especially one produced by sudden physical injury. **2.** *Psychiatry.* An emotional shock that creates substantial and lasting damage to the psychological development of the individual, generally leading to neurosis. [Greek, wound, hurt.]

trau·mat·ic (trou-măt'ĭk, trô-) *adj.* **1.** Of or causing a trauma: *a traumatic shock.* **2.** *Informal.* Awful; unpleasant. [Late Latin *traumăticus,* from Greek, from TRAUMA.] **—trau·mat·i·cal·ly** *adv.*

trau·ma·tism (trou'mə-tĭz'əm, trô'-) *n.* **1.** A trauma. **2.** Any condition arising from a trauma.

trau·ma·tize (trou'mə-tīz', trô'-) *tr.v.* **-tized, -tizing, -tizes. 1.** To wound or injure. **2.** To cause (someone) to undergo a psychological trauma. **—trau·ma·ti·za·tion** *n.*

tra·vail (trə-vāl', trăv'āl') *n.* **1. a.** Strenuous mental or physical exertion; labor; toil. **b.** Tribulation or agony; anguish. **2.** The labor of childbirth.
~*intr.v.* **travailed, -vailing, -vails. 1.** To labor strenuously; toil. **2.** To be in the labor of childbirth. [Middle English, from Old French, from *travailler,* to work hard, from Vulgar Latin *tripāliāre* (unattested), to torture, from *tripālium* (unattested), torture instrument (made of three stakes), from Latin *tripālis,* having three stakes : *tri-,* three + *pālus,* stake.]

trave (trāv) *n.* **1.** A wooden frame for confining a lively horse so that it can be shod. **2.** *Architecture.* **a.** A crossbeam. **b.** A section, as of a ceiling, formed by crossbeams. [Middle English, from Old French, stake, beam, from Latin *trabs.*]

trav·el (trăv'əl) *v.* **-eled** or **-elled, -eling** or **-elling, -els.** —*intr.* **1.** To go from one place to another; journey: *traveled all over Europe.* **2.** To be transmitted; move, as sound or light moves. **3.** To move, advance, or proceed, especially in a specified way: *traveling faster than the speed of sound.* **4.** To be a traveling salesman: *He travels for a record company.* **5.** To admit of being transported without damage or loss of quality: *Some wines travel poorly.* **6.** *Informal.* To move swiftly. —*tr.* To pass or journey over or through; traverse.
~*n.* **1.** The act or process of traveling. **2.** The distance moved by a mechanical part. **3. travels. a.** A series of journeys. **b.** A written account of these. [Middle English *travailen,* to toil, make a toilsome journey, from Old French *travailler,* to TRAVAIL.]

travel agency *n.* A business that makes travel arrangements for customers, as by booking tickets for flights and other journeys, booking accommodations, arranging tours, or the like. **—travel agent** *n.*

trav·eled, trav·elled (trăv'əld) *adj.* **1.** Having traveled widely; experienced in travel. **2.** Much frequented by travelers. Usually used in combination: *a well-traveled route.*

trav·el·er, trav·el·ler (trăv'ə-lər, trăv'lər) *n.* **1. a.** A person who is traveling. **b.** One who has traveled or who customarily travels. **2.** *Chiefly British.* A traveling salesman. **3.** *Nautical.* **a.** A metal ring that moves freely back and forth on a rope, rod, or spar. **b.** The rope, rod, or spar on which such a ring moves. **4.** A part of a mechanism that can move only in a fixed direction.

traveler's check *n.* An internationally redeemable draft purchasable in various denominations from a bank, express company, or travel agency and valid only with the holder's own endorsement against his original signature.

trav·el·er's-joy (trăv'ə-lərz-joi', trăv'lərz-) *n.* Any of several climbing vines of the genus *Clematis;* especially, *C. vitalba,* of the Old World, having clusters of greenish flowers and pale gray feathery fruit in dense clusters.

traveling salesman *n.* A salesman who solicits business orders or sells merchandise through personal dealings with potential customers met by traveling within a given territory. Also *British* "commercial traveler," *chiefly British* "traveler."

traveling wave *n.* A wave in which the peaks and troughs move continuously away from the source.

trav·e·logue, trav·e·log (trăv'ə-lôg', -lŏg') *n.* **1.** A lecture illustrated by travel slides or films. **2.** A narrated film about travels. [TRAVEL + -LOGUE.]

travel sickness *n.* **Motion sickness** *(see).*

tra·verse (trə-vûrs', trăv'ərs) *v.* **-versed, -versing, -verses.** —*tr.* **1.** To travel across, over, or through. **2.** To move to and fro over; cross and recross. **3. a.** To go up or down (a slope) diagonally, as when climbing or skiing. **b.** To go across rather than down (a slope), as when skiing. **4.** To move (a gun, for example) laterally; cause to swivel. **5.** To extend across; cross. **6.** To look over carefully; examine. **7.** To go counter to; thwart. **8.** *Law.* To deny formally (an allegation of fact by the opposition) in a suit. **9.** *Nautical.* To brace (a yard) fore and aft. —*intr.* **1.** To move or go along, across, or back and forth. **2.** To turn laterally; swivel. **3.** To traverse a slope. **4.** In fencing, to slide one's blade down toward the hilt of an opponent's weapon while exerting pressure against his blade.
~*n.* **trav·erse** (trăv'ərs, trə-vûrs'). **1. a.** The act of traversing; a passing across, over, or through. **b.** A route or path, as across a slope. **2.** Something lying across something else, especially: **a.** An intersecting line, a **transversal** *(see).* **b.** *Architecture.* A structural crosspiece; a transom. **c.** *Architecture.* A gallery, deck, or loft crossing from one side of a building, such as a church, to the other. **d.** A railing, curtain, screen, or other barrier. **e.** A defensive barrier across a rampart or trench, as a bank of earth thrown up for protection from enfilade fire. **3.** Something that obstructs and thwarts; an obstacle. **4. a.** *Nautical.* The zigzag route of a vessel forced by contrary winds to sail on different courses. **b.** A diagonal or horizontal course made by a skier across a slope. **5.** The horizontal swivel of a mounted gun. **6. a.** A lateral movement, as of a lathe tool across a piece of work. **b.** A part of a mechanism that moves in this manner. **7.** In surveying, a line established by sighting in the measurement of a tract of land. **8.** *Law.* The formal denial of an allegation of fact in a suit.
~*adj.* **trav·erse** (trăv'ərs, trə-vûrs'). Lying or extending across; transverse. [Middle English *traversen,* from Old French *traverser,* from Late Latin *trā(ns)versāre,* from Latin *transversus,* TRANSVERSE.] **—tra·vers·a·ble** *adj.* **—tra·vers·al** (trə-vûr'səl) *n.* **—tra·vers·er** *n.*

trav·er·tine (trăv'ər-tēn', -tĭn) *n.* **1.** A light-colored, porous calcite, $CaCO_3$, deposited from solution in ground or surface waters. **2.** A compact type of calcium carbonate, used as a facing material in construction. [Italian *travertino,* earlier *tivertino,* from Latin *(lapis) Tīburtīnus,* "(stone) of Tibur."]

trav·es·ty (trăv'ĭ-stē) *n., pl.* **-ties. 1.** An exaggerated or grotesque imitation intended to ridicule; especially, a farcical and grotesque parody of a serious literary work or theme. **2.** Broadly, any event or situation that has become or been turned into a parody of itself: *The debate became a travesty.*
~*tr.v.* **travestied, -tying, -ties.** To make a travesty of; ridicule. [French *travesti,* past participle of *travestir,* to ridicule, from Italian *travestire,* "to disguise" : *tra-,* across, TRANS- + *vestire,* to dress, from Latin *vestīre,* from *vestis,* garment.]

tra·vois (trə-voi', trăv'oi') *n., pl.* **travois** (trə-voiz', trăv'oiz') or **travoises** (trə-voi'zĭz, trăv'oi'zĭz). A primitive sledge formerly used by the Plains Indians of North America, consisting of a platform or netting supported by two long trailing poles, the forward ends of which are fastened to a dog or horse. [Canadian French, alteration of French *travail.*]

trawl (trôl) *n.* **1.** A large, tapered fishing net of flattened conical shape, towed along the sea bottom. Also called "trawl net." **2.** A multiple fishing line, a **setline** *(see).* Also called "trawl line."
~*v.* **trawled, trawling, trawls.** —*tr.* To catch (fish) by means of a trawl. —*intr.* **1.** To fish with a trawl net or line. **2.** To troll. [Perhaps from Dutch *tragel,* dragnet, from Middle Dutch *traghel,* from Latin *trāgula,* from *trahere,* to pull, draw.]

trawl·er (trô'lər) *n.* **1.** A vessel used for trawling. **2.** One who trawls.

tray (trā) *n.* **1.** A flat, shallow receptacle, as of wood or metal, with a raised edge or rim, used for carrying, holding, or displaying articles. **2.** A tray with food on it: *brought her up a tray.* **3.** A shallow, open, boxlike receptacle often made of wire and used to hold items such as papers or letters. [Middle English *tray,* Old English *trīg, trēg,* from Germanic *traujam* (unattested); akin to TREE.]

treach·er·ous (trĕch'ər-əs) *adj.* **1.** Betraying a trust; traitorous; disloyal. **2. a.** Not to be relied upon; not dependable. **b.** Not to be trusted; deceptive; dangerous: *treacherous waters.* **—treach·er·ous·ly** *adv.* **—treach·er·ous·ness** *n.*

treach·er·y (trĕch'ə-rē) *n., pl.* **-ies. 1.** Willful betrayal of fidelity, confidence, or trust; perfidy; treason. **2.** An act or instance of this. [Middle English *trecherie, tricherie,* from Old French, from *trichier,* to TRICK.]

trea·cle (trē'kəl) *n.* **1. a.** *British.* **Molasses** *(see).* **b.** A kind of syrup. **2.** A medicinal compound formerly used as an antidote for poison. **3.** Cloying speech or sentiment. [Middle English *triacle,* antidote for poison, from Old French, from Latin *thēriaca,* from Greek *(antidotos) thēriakē,* from *thērion,* poisonous beast, diminutive of *thēr,* beast.] **—trea·cly** (trē'klē) *adj.*

tread (trĕd) *v.* **trod** (trŏd) or *archaic* **trode** (trōd), **trodden** (trŏd'n) or **trod, treading, treads.** —*tr.* **1.** To walk on, over, or along. **2.** To press down on with the foot; trample: *treading grapes.* **3.** To treat harshly or cruelly. **4.** To make (a path, for example) by walking or trampling. **5.** To perform or execute by walking or dancing. Used chiefly in the phrase *tread a measure.* **6.** To copulate with. Used of male birds. —*intr.* **1.** To go on foot; walk; step. **2. a.** To tread so as to press, crush, or injure someone or something. Used with *on* or *upon.* **b.** To subdue or hurt. Used with *on* or *upon*: *trod on her feelings.* **—tread lightly.** To act or proceed tactfully and sensitively. **—tread water.** To keep one's head above water while in an upright position by moving the feet up and down as if walking.
~*n.* **1. a.** The act, manner, or sound of treading. **b.** An instance of treading; a step. **2.** The horizontal part of a step in a staircase. Also

PRONUNCIATION KEY

ă, pat; ā, pay; âr, care;
ä, father, are; b, bib;
ch, church; d, deed; ĕ, pet;
ē, be; f, fife; g, gag; h, hat;
hw, which; ĭ, pit; ī, pie;
îr, pier; j, judge; k, kick;
l, lid, needle; m, mum;
n, no, sudden; ng, thing;
ŏ, pot; ō, toe; ô, paw, for;
oi, noise; ou, out; ŏŏ, book;
ōō, boot; p, pop; r, roar;
s, sauce; sh, ship, dish;
t, tight; th, thin, path;
th, this, bathe; ŭ, cut; ûr, fur;
v, valve; w, with; y, yes;
z, zebra, size; zh, vision;
ə, about, item, edible, gallop, circus, peaceful

IN FOREIGN WORDS:

à, *Fr.* ami; œ, *Fr.* feu, *Ger.* schön; ü, *Fr.* tu, *Ger.* über; KH, *Ger.* ich, *Scot.* loch; N, *Fr.* bon; y', *Fr.* Compiègne

STRESS MARKS:

Primary stress: '
in·cite' (ĭn-sīt')
Secondary stress: '
in'sight' (ĭn'sīt')

called "treadboard." **3.** The part of a wheel that makes contact with the ground or rails. **4. a.** The grooved face of a motor-vehicle tire. **b.** The thickness of the grooves and ridges on a tire: *not much tread left.* **5.** The part of the sole of a shoe that touches the ground. [Tread, trod (or trode), trodden; Middle English *treden, trode, troden,* Old English *tredan, træd* (plural *trædon*), *treden.*] —**tread·er** *n.*

tread·le (trĕd′l) *n.* A pedal or lever operated by the foot for circular drive, as in a potter's wheel or sewing machine.
~*intr.v.* **treadled, -ling, -les.** To work a treadle. [Middle English *tredel,* Old English *tredel,* step of a stair, from *tredan,* to TREAD.] —**tread·ler** *n.*

tread·mill (trĕd′mĭl′) *n.* **1.** A mechanism used to produce rotary motion that is operated by one or more persons or animals walking on moving steps inside a wheel or treading an endless sloping belt. **2.** A monotonous task or routine.

treas. treasurer; treasury.

trea·son (trē′zən) *n.* **1.** Violation of allegiance toward one's sovereign or country; especially, the betrayal of one's own country by waging war against it or by consciously and purposely acting to aid its enemies. **2.** Any betrayal of trust or confidence; treachery. [Middle English *treison,* from Norman French *tre(i)soun,* from Medieval Latin *trāditiō* (stem *trāditiōn-*), from Latin, a handing over. See **tradition.**] —**trea·son·ous** *adj.* —**trea·son·ous·ly** *adv.*

trea·son·a·ble (trē′zə-nə-bəl) *adj.* Pertaining to or involving treason. —**trea·son·a·ble·ness** *n.* —**trea·son·a·bly** *adv.*

treas·ure (trĕzh′ər) *n.* **1.** Accumulated, stored, or cached wealth in the form of valuables such as money or jewels. **2.** A person or thing considered especially precious or valuable.
~*tr.v.* **treasured, -uring, -ures. 1.** To accumulate and save for future use; hoard. **2.** To value or prize highly: *treasured fond memories.* —See Synonyms at **appreciate.** [Middle English *tresor,* from Old French, from Vulgar Latin *tresaurus* (unattested), from Latin *thēsaurus,* from Greek *thēsauros†*.] —**treas·ur·a·ble** *adj.*

treasure house *n.* Any place that contains treasure or something considered to be treasure: *a treasure house of humor.*

treasure hunt *n.* A game in which players seek to be the first to find a hidden prize using a series of clues.

treas·ur·er (trĕzh′ər-ər) *n. Abbr.* **tr., treas. 1.** A person having charge of funds or revenues for a corporation, club, society, or the like. **2.** A financial officer or recorder of public funds for a government. [Middle English *tresourer,* from Old French *tresorier,* from *tresor,* TREASURE.] —**treas·ur·er·ship** *n.*

treasure trove (trōv) *n.* **1.** *Law.* Any treasure found hidden or buried and whose owner is unknown. In English law, treasure trove is money, bullion, or objects made of precious metal, and it belongs to the Crown. **2.** Any discovery of great value. [Norman French *tresor trove,* "discovered treasure" : Old French *tresor,* TREASURE + *trove,* past participle of *trover,* to find, compose (see **trouvère**).]

treas·ur·y (trĕzh′ə-rē) *n., pl.* **-ies.** *Abbr.* **treas. 1.** A place where treasure is kept or stored. **2.** A place where private or public funds are received, kept, managed, and disbursed. **3.** Such funds or revenues. **4. a.** Any collection of valuables or things considered to be valuable. **b.** A source of something valuable, such as wisdom. **5. Treasury.** The executive department of a government in charge of the collection, management, and expenditure of the public revenue. [Middle English *tresorie,* from Old French, from *tresor,* TREASURE.]

treasury note *n.* A note or bill issued by the U.S. Treasury as legal tender for all debts.

treat (trēt) *v.* **treated, treating, treats.** —*tr.* **1.** To act or behave in a specified manner toward: *treated her horse well.* **2.** To regard or consider in a certain way. Usually used with *as: treated the affair as a joke.* **3. a.** To consider and deal with in a specified manner: *You haven't treated his case fairly.* **b.** To deal with in writing or speech, usually in a specified manner or style: *The book treats certain philosophical questions in detail.* **4.** To deal with or represent in a specified manner or style, as in art or literature: *treat a subject poetically.* **5. a.** To entertain or provide with a gift at one's own expense: *treated her to dinner and dancing.* **b.** To give (someone or oneself) something as a treat: *treated myself to chocolates.* **6.** To subject to some process, action, or change, especially: **a.** To give medical aid to. **b.** To subject to a chemical or physical process or application. —*intr.* **1.** To deal with a subject or topic in writing, speaking, or thought. Usually used with *of: The essay treats of courtly love.* **2.** To pay for another's entertainment, food, or the like. **3.** To negotiate; bargain. Used with *with.*
~*n.* **1.** Something, such as food or entertainment, paid for by someone other than the person invited to enjoy it. **2.** The act of treating. **3.** Something considered to be a special delight or pleasure. [Middle English *treten,* from Old French *traitier,* from Latin *tractāre,* to drag, handle, treat, frequentative of *trahere* (past participle *tractus*), to draw, drag.] —**treat·a·ble** *adj.* —**treat·er** *n.*

trea·tise (trē′tĭs) *n.* A formal account in writing treating systematically of some subject. [Middle English *tretis,* from Norman French, from Old French *traitier,* to TREAT.]

treat·ment (trēt′mənt) *n.* **1.** The act or manner of treating something, such as a person or a literary subject: *sensitive treatment of characters.* **2. a.** The application of remedies with the object of effecting a cure; therapy. **b.** The substance or remedy applied. **3.** *Slang.* Aggressive, rough, or bad handling. Used with *the: gave the opposing team the treatment.*

trea·ty (trē′tē) *n., pl.* **-ties. 1. a.** A formal agreement between two or more states containing terms of trade, peace, alliance, or the like; a pact. **b.** A document embodying this. **2.** Any contract or agreement; especially, one between two persons concerning the buying of property. **3.** Negotiation for the purpose of reaching an agreement. [Middle English *tretee,* from Old French *traite,* from Medieval Latin *tractātus,* from Latin, past participle of *tractāre,* to TREAT.]

treaty port *n.* A port kept open for trade according to the terms of a treaty; especially, formerly in the Far East, any of several such ports open to foreign commerce.

Trebizond. See **Trabzon.**

tre·ble (trĕb′əl) *adj.* **1.** Triple; threefold. **2.** *Music.* Of, having, or performing the highest part, voice, or range. **3.** High-pitched; shrill. ~*n.* **1.** *Music.* **a.** The highest part, voice, instrument, or range; soprano. **b.** A player who performs the highest instrumental part. **c.** A singer who performs the highest voice part, especially a boy singer as opposed to a female soprano. **2.** A high, shrill sound or voice. **3.** A number or amount three times as much or as many as another. **4. a.** In darts, the narrow ring between the double and the bull's eye. **b.** A score obtained by hitting this ring. ~*v.* **trebled, -ling, -les.** —*tr.* To make triple. —*intr.* To become triple. [Middle English, from Old French, from Latin *triplus,* TRIPLE.] —**treb·le·ness** *n.* —**treb·ly** (trĕb′lē) *adv.*

treble clef *n. Music.* A symbol, 𝄞, centered on the second line of the staff to indicate the position of G above middle C. Also called "G clef."

treb·u·chet (trĕb′ə-shĕt′, trĕb′yə-) *n.* Also **treb·uc·ket** (trĕb′ə-kĕt′). A medieval catapult for hurling heavy stones. [Middle English, from Old French, pitfall, from *trebucher,* to stumble.]

tre·cen·to (trā-chĕn′tō) *n.* The 14th century, with reference especially to Italian art and literature. [Italian, "three hundred," short for *(mil) trecento,* (one thousand) three hundred : *tre,* three, from Latin *trēs* + *cento,* hundred, from Latin *centum.*]

tree (trē) *n.* **1.** A usually tall woody plant, distinguished from a shrub by having comparatively greater height and, characteristically, a single trunk with branches arising at an appreciable dis-

tree

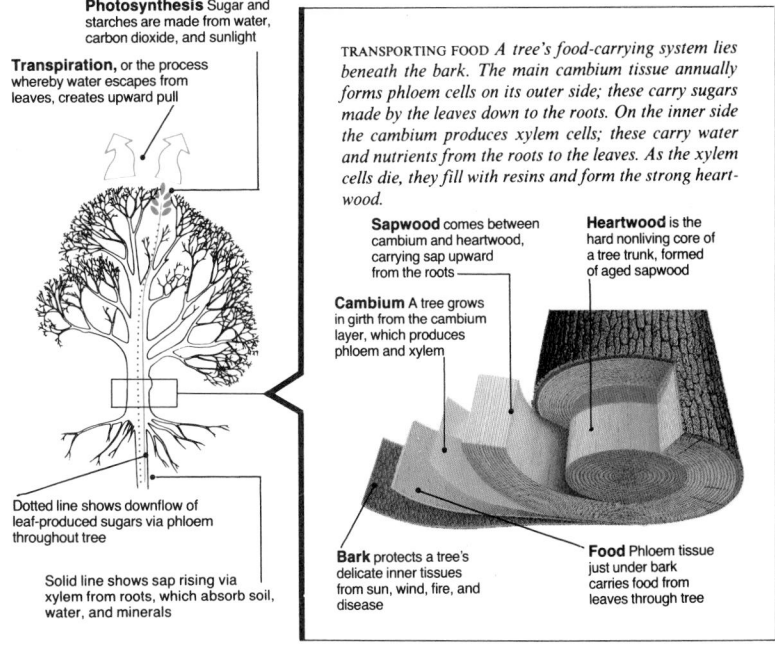

THE LONG GROWING LIFE OF TREES
Annual renewal of tissue keeps trees functioning efficiently

Some trees grow for hundreds of years; new tissues formed each year by the cambium layers and by the tips of shoots and roots regularly renew a tree's ability to function efficiently.

Two layers of cambium tissue lying beneath the bark are responsible for the increase in girth of a tree's branches, trunk, and roots. The main cambium produces food-carrying cells and the outer cambium produces corky bark.

The main cambium manufactures microscopic cells that give rigid support, carry watery sap from the roots to the crown, store food, and carry food in solution both up and down the tree. Every spring this layer manufactures cells with thin walls and large spaces for carrying all the water and nutrients needed for growth; every summer it produces denser wood composed of cells with thicker walls.

The spring and summer cells together form one annual growth ring. Often this is so clearly visible that the number of growth rings in a log can give a reliable indication of its age.

Below ground the cambium cells in the roots increase the diameter of the roots each year and so help to anchor the tree in the ground. In the tree's crown the cambium cells in the shoots increase the diameter of the twigs and branches.

Different cells are responsible for the onward extension of shoots and roots. The cells located in the tip of each twig and root divide frequently and enable the tree to grow upward, outward, and downward.

Photosynthesis Sugar and starches are made from water, carbon dioxide, and sunlight

Transpiration, or the process whereby water escapes from leaves, creates upward pull

Dotted line shows downflow of leaf-produced sugars via phloem throughout tree

Solid line shows sap rising via xylem from roots, which absorb soil, water, and minerals

TRANSPORTING FOOD *A tree's food-carrying system lies beneath the bark. The main cambium tissue annually forms phloem cells on its outer side; these carry sugars made by the leaves down to the roots. On the inner side the cambium produces xylem cells; these carry water and nutrients from the roots to the leaves. As the xylem cells die, they fill with resins and form the strong heartwood.*

Sapwood comes between cambium and heartwood, carrying sap upward from the roots

Cambium A tree grows in girth from the cambium layer, which produces phloem and xylem

Heartwood is the hard nonliving core of a tree trunk, formed of aged sapwood

Bark protects a tree's delicate inner tissues from sun, wind, fire, and disease

Food Phloem tissue just under bark carries food from leaves through tree

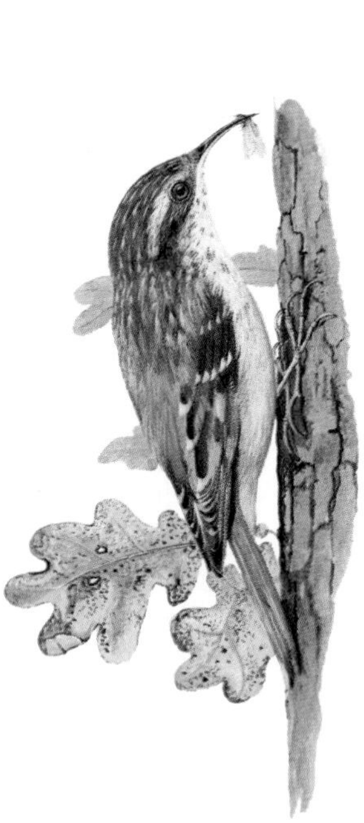

tree creeper *The tree creeper gets its name from its habit of walking on the trunks of trees in search of beetles, earwigs, and wood lice beneath the bark. It lives chiefly in coniferous forests and is found in North America, Europe, and Asia.*

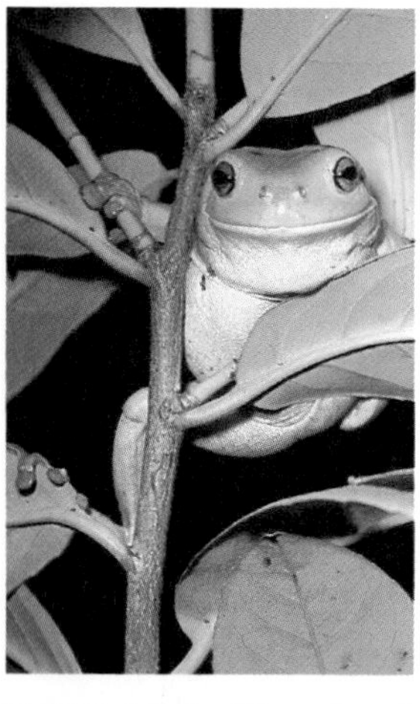

tree frog *Adhesive disks on the ends of the tree frog's toes help it to grip branches as it climbs through trees hunting for the insects on which it chiefly feeds. This is White's tree frog,* Litoria caerulea, *a species native to the tropical forests of New Guinea and parts of Australia.*

tance from the ground, rather than several stems. **2.** Broadly, a plant or shrub resembling a tree but without a woody trunk, such as a palm. **3.** A wooden beam, post, stake, or bar used as a part of a framework or structure. **4.** *Archaic.* A gallows; a gibbet. **5.** *Often* **Tree.** *Archaic.* The cross on which Jesus was crucified. **6.** A **saddletree** *(see).* **7.** Something suggestive of a tree: *a clothes tree.* **8.** A diagram showing a family lineage; a family tree. **9.** A **Christmas tree** *(see).* **—bark up the wrong tree.** *Informal.* To expend one's energies uselessly through a misapprehension. **—grow on trees.** To be in abundant free supply: *Money doesn't grow on trees.* **—up a tree.** *Informal.* In a situation of hopeless confusion or embarrassment.

~tr.v. **treed, treeing, trees. 1.** To force to climb a tree in evasion of pursuit. **2.** *Informal.* To force into a difficult position; corner. **3.** To stretch (shoes) on a shoetree. [Middle English *tree,* Old English *treo(w).*]

tree creeper *n.* A small, brown-speckled bird, *Certhia familiaris,* having a downward-curved beak and habitually found creeping around tree trunks in search of food.

tree diagram *n.* A branching diagram especially suited to represent the analysis of a structure, such as a sentence, by subdividing it into component parts.

tree farm *n.* An area of forest land on which trees are grown for commercial use.

tree fern *n.* Any of various treelike tropical ferns, especially of the family Cyatheaceae, having a woody, trunklike stem and a terminal crown of large, divided fronds.

tree frog *n.* Any of various small, arboreal frogs of the family Polypedatidae, having long toes terminating in adhesive disks. Also called "tree toad."

tree heath *n.* See **briar** (sense 1).

tree-hop·per (trē'hŏp'pər) *n.* Any insect of the family Membracidae that damages trees by sucking sap.

tree house *n.* A structure built by or for children among the limbs of a tree.

tree line *n.* **1.** The limit of northern or southern latitude beyond which trees do not grow except as stunted forms. **2.** The **timberline** *(see).*

tree mallow *n.* A tall biennial mallow plant, *Lavatera arborea,* of coastal regions, having purple-veined, dark pink flowers.

tree·nail, tre·nail (trē'nāl', trĕn'əl, trŭn'əl) *n.* Also **trun·nel** (trŭn'əl). A wooden peg that swells when wet and that is used to fasten timbers, especially in shipbuilding.

tree of heaven *n.* A tree, the **ailanthus** *(see).*

tree of knowledge *n.* The tree in the Garden of Eden whose forbidden fruit was eaten by Adam and Eve, causing loss of innocence. Genesis 2:9, 17; 3:6. Also called "tree of knowledge of good and evil."

tree of life *n.* **1.** A tree, the **arborvitae** *(see).* **2.** A tree in the Garden of Eden whose fruit, if eaten, gave man immortality. Genesis 3:22. **3.** The tree in the new Jerusalem whose leaves were for the healing of the nations. Revelation 22:2.

tree-run·ner (trē'rŭn'ər) *n.* Any of various Australian birds. See **sittella.**

tree-shrew (trē'shrōō') *n.* A squirrellike primate, the **banxring** *(see).*

tree sparrow *n.* A European woodland bird, *Passer montanus,* similar to the house sparrow but having a chestnut crown and white head markings.

tree surgery *n.* The treatment of diseased or damaged trees by filling cavities, pruning, and bracing branches. **—tree surgeon** *n.*

tree toad *n.* A **tree frog** *(see).*

tree·top (trē'tŏp') *n.* The uppermost part of a tree.

tref (trāf) *adj.* Unclean and unfit for consumption according to Jewish dietary law, as pork, lobster, or horse meat are. Compare **kosher.** [Yiddish *treyf,* from Hebrew *terēphāh,* "torn," flesh of an animal torn by wild beasts, from *tāraf,* to tear.]

tre·foil (trē'foil', trĕf'oil') *n.* **1.** Any of various plants of the genera *Trifolium* and *Lotus,* having compound leaves with three leaflets. See **bird's-foot trefoil. 2.** Any ornament, symbol, or architectural form having the appearance of a trifoliate leaf. [Middle English, from Norman French *trifoil,* from Latin *trifolium,* three-leaved grass : *tri-,* three + *folium,* leaf.] **—tre·foiled** *adj.*

tre·ha·la (trĭ-hä'lə) *n.* A sugarlike, edible substance obtained from the pupal case of an Old World beetle, *Larinus maculatus.* [New Latin, from Turkish *tīgāla,* from Persian *tīghāl*†.]

tre·ha·lose (trĭ-hä'lōs', -lōz') *n.* A sweet-tasting, crystalline disaccharide, $C_{12}H_{22}O_{11} \cdot 2H_2O$, found in trehala and in many fungi that store it instead of starch. [TREHAL(A) + -OSE.]

treil·lage (trē-yäzh', trā'lĭj) *n.* Latticework; especially, a trellis for vines. [French, from Old French, from *treille,* arbor, from Latin *trichila*†, bower, arbor.]

trek (trĕk) *intr.v.* **trekked, trekking, treks. 1.** To make a slow or arduous journey. **2.** *South African.* **a.** To draw or pull a wagon. Used of an ox. **b.** To travel by ox wagon.

~n. **1.** A journey or a part of a journey, especially when slow or difficult. **2.** A migration; especially, one involving a slow journey with wagons, such as the migration of the Boers from 1835 to 1837. [Afrikaans, from Middle Dutch *trekken,* to pull, draw, travel, akin to Old High German *trechan*†.] **—trek·ker** *n.*

trel·lis (trĕl'ĭs) *n.* **1.** A structure of open latticework; especially, one used for supporting vines and other creeping plants. **2.** An arbor or arch made with such a structure.

~tr.v. **trellised, -lising, -lises. 1.** To provide with a trellis; especially, to support (a creeping plant) on a trellis. **2.** To make into or in the form of a trellis. [Middle English *trelis,* from Old French *treliz,* a coarse fabric, later (influenced by *treillage,* TREILLAGE) trellis, from Vulgar Latin *trilīcius* (unattested), from Latin *trilīx,* triple-twilled : *tri-,* three + *līcium*†, thread.]

trel·lis·work (trĕl'ĭs-wûrk') *n.* Latticework.

trem·a·tode (trĕm'ə-tōd') *n.* Any of numerous parasitic flatworms of the class Trematoda, having a thick outer cuticle and one or more suckers for attaching to host tissue. Also called "fluke."

~adj. Of or belonging to the Trematoda. [New Latin *Trematoda,* from Greek *trēmatōdēs,* having a vent to the intestinal canal (taken to mean "having holes," perhaps from the cavity of the suckers) : *trēma,* perforation + -ODE (-like).]

trem·ble (trĕm'bəl) *intr.v.* **-bled, -bling, -bles. 1.** To shake involuntarily, as from fear, cold, or sickness; quake or shiver; shake. **2.** To feel or express fear or anxiety: *I tremble at the thought.* **3.** To vibrate; quiver: *leaves trembling in the wind.* —See Synonyms at **shake.**

~n. **1.** The act or state of trembling. **2.** *Sometimes* **trembles.** A convulsive fit of trembling, especially as a result of a disease. [Middle English *trem(b)len,* from Old French *trembler,* from Vulgar Latin *tremulāre* (unattested), from Latin *tremulus,* TREMULOUS.] **—trem·bler** *n.* **—trem·bling·ly** *adv.* **—trem·bly** *adj.*

trem·bles (trĕm'bəlz) *n. Used with a singular verb.* In veterinary medicine, **louping ill** *(see).*

tre·men·dous (trĭ-mĕn'dəs) *adj.* **1.** Capable of making one tremble; terrible: *the tremendous tragedy of war.* **2. a.** Extremely large in amount, extent, or degree; enormous: *a tremendous task.* **b.** *Informal.* Marvelous; wonderful; excellent: *We had a tremendous time.* [Latin *tremendus,* gerundive of *tremere,* to tremble.] **—tre·men·dous·ly** *adv.* **—tre·men·dous·ness** *n.*

trem·o·lite (trĕm'ə-līt') *n.* A white to dark-gray calcium magnesium amphibole, $Ca_2Mg_5Si_8O_{22}(OH)_2$, usually occurring in aggregates, used as a substitute for asbestos. [French *trémolite,* first found in *Tremola,* valley in southern Switzerland.]

trem·o·lo (trĕm'ə-lō') *n., pl.* **-los.** *Music.* **1. a.** A tremulous effect produced by the rapid repetition of a single tone, especially on a stringed instrument played with a bow. **b.** A similar effect produced by the rapid alternation of two tones, often separated by an interval of a third. Compare **trill. 2.** A device on an organ for producing a tremolo. Also called "tremolant," "tremulant." **3.** A vibrato in singing, used for emotional effect or resulting from poor vocal control. Compare **vibrato.** [Italian, "tremulous."]

trem·or (trĕm'ər) *n.* **1.** A shaking or vibrating movement or short series of movements of the earth; a small earthquake: *an earth tremor.* **2. a.** An involuntary trembling motion of the body, as from a state of nervous agitation or illness. **b.** A mental or emotional state characterized by such trembling. **3.** A nervous quiver or shiver. **4.** Any trembling, shaking, or vibrating movement: *a tremor of aspen leaves.* **5.** A tremulous sound; a quaver. [Middle English *tremour,* from Old French, from Latin *tremor,* from *tremere,* to tremble.]

trem·u·lous (trĕm'yə-ləs) *adj.* Also **trem·u·lant** (-lənt). **1. a.** Vibrating or quivering; trembling. **b.** Produced by or suggestive of someone with a tremor: *tremulous handwriting.* **2.** Timid; fearful; timorous. [Latin *tremulus,* from *tremere,* to tremble.] **—trem·u·lous·ly** *adv.* **—trem·u·lous·ness** *n.*

trenail. Variant of **treenail.**

trench (trĕnch) *n.* **1.** A deep furrow. **2.** A ditch. **3. a.** A long, narrow ditch embanked with its own soil and used for concealment and protection in warfare. **b. trenches.** A system of such ditches, used especially as a defensive position. **4.** A long, deep, narrow depression in the seabed.

~v. **trenched, trenching, trenches.** *—tr.* **1.** To cut or dig a trench or trenches in. **2.** To fortify with a trench or trenches. **3.** To carve or make a cut in. *—intr.* **1.** To dig a trench or ditch. **2.** To verge or encroach. Used with *on* or *upon.* [Middle English *trenche,* long narrow ditch, path cut through, from Old French, from *trenchier,* to cut, dig, probably from Vulgar Latin *trincāre* (unattested), from Latin *truncāre,* to mutilate, from *truncus,* torso.]

trench·ant (trĕn'chənt) *adj.* **1.** Keen; incisive; penetrating: *trenchant comments.* **2.** Forceful; effective; vigorous: *a trenchant argument.* **3.** Distinct; sharply defined; clear-cut. **4.** *Archaic & Poetic.* Sharp-edged. Said of a sword. —See Synonyms at **incisive.** [Middle English, cutting, from Old French, present participle of *trenchier,* to cut. See **trench.**] **—trench·an·cy** *n.* **—trench·ant·ly** *adv.*

trench coat *n.* A loose-fitting, belted raincoat having many pockets and flaps, suggesting a military style.

trench·er[1] (trĕn'chər) *n.* **1.** A wooden board or plate on which food is cut or served. **2.** *Obsolete.* One who carves meat. [Middle English *trenchour,* cutting board, from Norman French, from Old French *trenchier,* to cut. See **trench.**]

trencher[2] *n.* One that digs trenches.

trench·er·man (trĕn'chər-mən) *n., pl.* **-men** (-mĭn). **1.** A hearty eater. **2.** *Archaic.* A sponger; a parasite; hanger-on.

trench fever *n.* An acute infectious relapsing fever caused by a microorganism, *Rickettsia quintana,* and transmitted by a louse, *Pediculus humanus.*

trench foot *n.* A form of frostbite of the feet, often afflicting soldiers obliged to stand in cold water for long periods of time.

trench knife *n.* A knife used in warfare, having a long, double-edged blade.

trench mortar *n.* *Military.* See **mortar** (sense 3).

trench mouth *n.* A form of gingivitis characterized by pain, foul odor, and the formation of a gray film over the diseased area. Also called "Vincent's disease."

trench warfare *n.* Warfare conducted between two armies who are facing each other in trenches.

trend (trĕnd) *n.* **1.** A direction of movement; a course; flow: *a trend of thought.* **2.** A general inclination or tendency: *a trend away from smoking.* **3.** A fashion; a style. —See Synonyms at **tendency.** ~*intr.v.* **trended, trending, trends.** **1.** To extend, bend, turn, or move in a specified direction: *The prevailing wind trends east-northeast.* **2.** To have a general tendency; tend: *a mood trending toward gloom.* [Middle English *trenden,* to turn, roll, revolve, Old English *trendan,* from Germanic *trand-* (unattested).]

trend·set·ter (trĕnd'sĕt'ər) *n.* One who initiates or popularizes a fashion or trend. —**trend·set·ting** *adj.*

trend·y (trĕn'dē) *adj.* **-ier, -iest.** *Informal.* **1.** Of, in accordance with, or consciously following the latest fad or fashion. **2.** Of or involving trendy people: *a trendy party.* ~*n., pl.* **trendies.** *Informal.* A trendy person. —**trend·i·ly** *adv.* —**trend·i·ness** *n.*

Trent (trĕnt). River of central England. Rising on Staffordshire's Biddulph Moor, it flows 270 kilometers (170 miles) to join the Ouse, forming the Humber estuary.

Trent, Council of *n.* A council of the Roman Catholic Church held periodically in Trento, Italy, between 1545 and 1563, that attempted to find a political solution to the Reformation, clarified Catholic doctrine, and initiated reform within the church.

trente et qua·rante (tränt' ā' kä-ränt') *n.* **Rouge et noir** (*see*).

Tren·ti·no-Al·to A·di·ge (trĕn-tē'nō-äl'tō ä'dē-jā'). Autonomous alpine region of northeastern Italy. Agriculture, forestry, and tourism are the principal industries. Trento is the capital.

Tren·ton (trĕn'tən). Capital of New Jersey, in the western part of the state at the head of navigation on the Delaware River. Settled in 1679, it was the site of an important American victory during the Revolution (December, 1776). Today it is a leading transportation hub and industrial center.

tre·pan¹ (trī-păn') *n.* **1.** A rock-boring tool used in mining for sinking shafts. **2.** An early type of trephine used in surgery. **3.** A tool for making large circular holes or grooves. ~*tr.v.* **trepanned, -panning, -pans.** **1.** To bore (a shaft) with a trepan. **2.** To cut a disk from with a trepan. **3.** In surgery, to trephine. [Middle English *trepane,* from Medieval Latin *trepanum,* from Greek *trupanon,* auger, borer, from *trupan,* to pierce, from *trupē,* hole.] —**trep·a·na·tion** (trĕp'ə-nā'shən) *n.*

trepan² *tr.v.* **-panned, -panning, -pans.** Also **tra·pan.** *Archaic.* To trap; ensnare; trick. ~*n. Archaic.* **1.** A prankster; a trickster. **2.** A trick; a stratagem. [17th century: originally *trapan,* probably thieves' slang for TRAP.]

tre·pang (trī-păng') *n.* **1.** Any of several sea cucumbers of the genus *Holothuria,* of the southern Pacific and Indian oceans. **2.** The eviscerated and dried or smoked body of any of these animals, used as food in China and the East Indies. Also called "bêche-de-mer." [Malay *těripang.*]

tre·phine (trī-fīn', -fēn') *n.* A surgical instrument having circular, sawlike edges, used to cut out disks of tissue, usually bone from the skull. ~*tr.v.* **trephined, -phining, -phines.** In surgery, to operate on with a trephine; trepan. [Earlier *trafine,* from Latin *trēs fīnes,* three ends.] —**treph·i·na·tion** (trĕf'ə-nā'shən) *n.*

trep·i·da·tion (trĕp'ə-dā'shən) *n.* **1.** A state of alarm or dread; nervous apprehension. **2.** A quivering or trembling movement, especially as caused by disease or illness. —See Synonyms at **fear.** [Latin *trepidātiō* (stem *trepidātiōn-*), from *trepidāre,* to hurry with alarm, tremble at, from *trepidus,* alarmed.]

trep·o·neme (trĕp'ə-nēm') *n.* Also **trep·o·ne·ma** (trĕp'ə-nē'mə). Any of a group of spirochetes of the genus *Treponema,* including those that cause syphilis and yaws. [New Latin *Treponema,* "twisted thread" (from its shape) : Greek *trepein,* to turn + *nēma,* thread.]

tres·pass (trĕs'pəs, -păs', -päs') *intr.v.* **-passed, -passing, -passes.** **1.** To commit an offense or sin; err; transgress. **2.** To infringe upon the privacy, time, or attention of another. Used with *on* or *upon:* *"I must . . . not trespass too far on the patience of a good-natured critic"* (Henry Fielding). **3.** *Law.* To invade the property, rights, or person of another without his consent and with the intention, actual or implied, of committing violence; especially, to commit the tort of entering onto another's land without permission and causing damage. ~*n.* **1.** The transgression of a moral or social law, code, or duty. **2.** An intrusion or infringement upon another. **3.** *Law.* **a.** The tort of trespassing. **b.** A legal suit brought for this. —See Synonyms at **breach.** [Middle English *trespassen,* from Old French *trespasser,* from Medieval Latin *transpassāre* : Latin *trāns-,* across + Medieval Latin *passāre* to PASS.] —**tres·pass·er** *n.*

tress (trĕs) *n.* **1.** A lock, plait, or braid of hair, especially of a woman's hair. **2. tresses.** The long flowing hair of a woman. [Middle English *tresse,* from Old French *tresse, trece†.*]

tres·tle (trĕs'əl) *n.* **1.** A horizontal beam or bar held up by two pairs of divergent legs and used as a support. **2.** A framework consisting of vertical, slanted supports and horizontal crosspieces supporting a bridge. [Middle English *trestel,* from Old French, from Vulgar Latin *transtellum* (unattested), diminutive of Latin *transtrum,* crossbeam. See **transom.**]

trestle table *n.* A table consisting of a board or boards supported by a trestle.

tres·tle·tree (trĕs'əl-trē') *n. Nautical.* Either of two horizontal beams set into a masthead to support the crosstrees.

tres·tle·work (trĕs'əl-wûrk') *n.* A trestle or system of trestles, such as that supporting a bridge.

tret (trĕt) *n.* Formerly, an allowance made to purchasers of goods sold by weight so as to account for waste occurring during transport. [Middle English, from Norman French, from Old French, a drawing, draft, variant of TRAIT.]

tre·val·ly (trə-văl'ē) *n.* Any Australian food fish of the genus *Caranx.* [Probably alteration of CAVALLY.]

trews (trōōz) *pl.n.* Close-fitting, usually tartan trousers. [Scottish Gaelic *triubhas.*]

trey (trā) *n.* A card, die, or domino with three pips. [Middle English *treis, treye,* from Old French *treis,* from Latin *trēs,* three.]

tri- *prefix.* Indicates: **1.** Three, as in number of parts or elements; for example, **trioxide.** **2. a.** Appearance or occurrence in intervals of three; for example, **tricentennial.** **b.** Appearance or occurrence three times during; for example, **triweekly.** [Latin and Greek, three.]

tri·a·ble (trī'ə-bəl) *adj.* **1.** Capable of being tried. **2.** *Law.* Subject to judicial examination. —**tri·a·ble·ness** *n.*

tri·ac·id (trī-ăs'ĭd) Also **tri·a·cid·ic** (trī'ə-sĭd'ĭk). **1.** Able to react with three molecules of a monobasic acid. Said of a base. **2.** Containing three replaceable hydrogen atoms. Said of an acid or an acid salt. ~*n.* An acid containing three replaceable hydrogen atoms.

tri·ad (trī'ăd, -əd) *n.* **1.** A group of three persons or things; a trinity. **2.** *Music.* A chord of three tones; especially one built on a given root plus a major or minor third and a perfect fifth. **3.** A literary form used in medieval Welsh and Irish literature, consisting of aphorisms grouped in threes. [Late Latin *trias* (stem *triad-*), the number three, from Greek.] —**tri·ad·ic** (trī-ăd'ĭk) *adj.*

tri·age (trē-äzh', trē'äzh') *n.* **1.** The act of sorting according to quality. **2.** The act or process of assigning or allocating limited resources so as to achieve the greatest possible benefit; especially, the allocating of limited treatment facilities for battlefield casualties so as to maximize the number of survivors. [French, sorting : *trier,* to pick out, sift (see **try**) + -AGE.]

tri·al (trī'əl, trīl) *n.* **1.** *Law.* The examination of evidence and applicable law by a competent tribunal, such as a judge and jury, to decide on a charge or claim: *a murder trial.* **2. a.** The act or process of testing, trying, or putting to the proof by actual or simulated use and experience: *a trial of one's faith.* **b.** A single complete instance of such testing, especially as part of a series of tests or experiments: *The new aircraft crashed during its third trial.* **3.** An effort or attempt: *He succeeded on his fourth trial.* **4.** A trouble, problem, or difficulty: *Life is full of little trials.* **5.** A test of patience or endurance: *She was a trial to her parents.* **6.** Usually **trials.** A series of competitions or tests designed to establish the individual ability and skill of the participants: *horse trials; held trials to pick the team.* —**on trial. 1.** In the state or process of being tried, as before a court of law. **2.** In the state or process of being tested or tried out. ~*adj.* **1.** Of or pertaining to a trial or trials. **2.** Made, done, used, or performed during the course of a trial or trials: *gave his car a trial run.* [Norman French *trial, triel,* from Old French *trier,* to TRY.]

trial and error *n.* **1.** An empirical method of attempting to solve a problem or achieve a certain result, consisting of repeating experiments until error is eliminated or the desired result is achieved. **2.** A method of learning or acquiring a skill by trying out various actions or processes until success is achieved. —**tri·al-and-er·ror** (trī'əl-ən-ĕr'ər, trīl'-) *adj.*

trial balance *n. Abbr.* **t.b.** In bookkeeping, a statement of all the open debit and credit items in a double-entry ledger made to make sure they are equal.

trial balloon *n.* A preliminary statement or campaign tried out on a small scale to test public reaction. [Originally applied to a balloon for testing weather conditions.]

trial court *n. Law.* The court in which a case is first heard and where issues of fact are decided.

trial jury *n.* A petit jury (*see*).

trial marriage *n.* A period during which a couple lives together in order to ascertain their compatibility with regard to marriage.

tri·am·cin·o·lone (trī'ăm-sĭn'ə-lōn') *n.* A synthetic corticosteroid hormone applied as a cream or lotion to reduce inflammation. [*Tri-* + *amy*l + *cin*ene (a terpine) + prednis*olone.*]

tri·an·gle (trī'ăng'gəl) *n.* **1.** The plane figure formed by connecting three points not in a straight line by straight-line segments; a three-sided polygon. **2.** Something having the shape of this figure, such as the wooden frame in which billiard balls are placed at the start of a game. **3.** Any of various flat, three-sided drawing and drafting guides, used especially to draw straight lines at specific angles. **4.** *Music.* A percussion instrument consisting of a piece of metal in the shape of a triangle, open at one angle. **5.** An **eternal triangle** (*see*). [Middle English, from Old French, from Latin *triangulum,* from *triangulus,* three-angled : *tri-,* three + *angulus,* ANGLE.]

triangle of vectors *n. Mathematics.* A triangle formed by three lines representing the magnitudes and directions of three vectors, such as forces or velocities that are in equilibrium.

tri·an·gu·lar (trī-ăng'gyə-lər) *adj.* **1.** Of, pertaining to, or shaped like a triangle; three-cornered; three-sided. **2.** Having a triangle for a base: *a triangular pyramid.* **3.** Pertaining to, involving, or consisting of three interrelated entities, such as three persons, objects, or ideas. **—tri·an·gu·lar·i·ty** (trī-ăng'gyə-lăr'ə-tē) *n.* **—tri·an·gu·lar·ly** *adv.*

tri·an·gu·late (trī-ăng'gyə-lāt') *tr.v.* **-lated, -lating, -lates. 1.** To divide into triangles. **2.** To survey by triangulation. **3.** To make triangular. **4.** To measure by using trigonometry.
∼*adj.* (trī-ăng'gyə-lĭt). **1.** Of or pertaining to triangles; triangular. **2.** Made up of or marked with triangles.

tri·an·gu·la·tion (trī-ăng'gyə-lā'shən) *n.* **1.** A surveying technique in which a region is divided into a series of triangular elements based on a line of known length so that accurate measurements of distances and directions may be made by the application of trigonometry. **2.** The network of triangles so laid out. **3.** The location of an unknown point, as in navigation, by forming a triangle having the unknown point and two known points as the vertices.

Tri·an·gu·lum (trī-ăng'gyə-ləm) *n.* A constellation in the northern sky near Aries and Andromeda. [Latin, TRIANGLE.]

Triangulum Aus·tra·le (ô-strā'lē) *n.* A constellation in the southern sky near Apus and Norma. [Latin, "southern triangle."]

tri·ar·chy (trī'är'kē) *n., pl.* **-chies. 1.** Government by three persons; a triumvirate. **2.** A country governed by three rulers. [Greek *triarkhia* : *tri-,* three + -ARCHY.]

Tri·as·sic (trī-ăs'ĭk) *adj.* Of, belonging to, or designating the geologic period, system of rocks, and sedimentary deposits of the first period of the Mesozoic era, after the Permian period of the Paleozoic era and before the Jurassic period of the Mesozoic era.
∼*n. Geology.* The Triassic period or system of deposits. Preceded by *the.* [Late Latin *trias,* TRIAD (from the subdivision of the strata of this period into three groups in Germany).]

tri·a·tom·ic (trī'ə-tŏm'ĭk) *adj. Chemistry.* Containing three atoms per molecule.

tri·ax·i·al (trī-ăk'sē-əl) *adj.* Having three axes.

tri·a·zine (trī'ə-zēn', trī-ăz'ēn') *n.* **1.** Any of three isomeric compounds, $C_3H_3N_3$, each having three carbon and three nitrogen atoms in a six-membered ring. **2.** Any compound derived from these isomers.

tri·a·zole (trī'ə-zōl', trī-ăz'ōl') *n.* **1.** Any of several compounds with composition $C_2H_3N_3$, having a five-membered ring of two carbon atoms and three nitrogen atoms. **2.** Any compound derived from one of these isomers.

trib·ade (trĭb'əd, trə-băd', -băd') *n.* A lesbian. [French, from Latin *tribas,* from Greek, "she who rubs," from *tribein,* to rub.] **—trib·a·dism** (trĭb'ə-dĭz'əm) *n.*

trib·al (trī'bəl) *adj.* Pertaining to or of the nature of a tribe or tribes. **—trib·al·ly** *adv.*

trib·al·ism (trī'bə-lĭz'əm) *n.* **1.** The condition of being made up of or organized into tribes. **2.** The organization, culture, or beliefs of a tribe. **3.** The sense of belonging to a tribe; tribal loyalty. **—trib·al·ist** *n.* **—trib·al·is·tic** (trī'bə-lĭs'tĭk) *adj.*

tri·ba·sic (trī-bā'sĭk) *adj.* **1.** Containing three replaceable hydrogen atoms per molecule. Said of an acid. **2.** Containing three univalent basic atoms or radicals per molecule. Said of a base or salt.

tribe (trīb) *n.* **1.** A unit of social organization, especially among primitive peoples but also surviving in some modern societies, consisting of a group of people claiming a common ancestry, usually sharing a common culture, and originally living together under a chief or headman. **2.** A political, ethnic, or ancestral division of ancient states and cultures, especially: **a.** Any of the three divisions of the ancient Romans, namely, the Latin, Sabine, and Etruscan. **b.** Any of the 12 divisions of ancient Israel. **c.** A phyle of ancient Greece. **3. a.** A group of persons with a common occupation, interest, or habit: *a tribe of schoolchildren.* **b.** *Informal.* A large family. **4.** *Biology.* A taxonomic category sometimes placed between a family and a genus. [Middle English *tribu, tribe,* from Old French *tribu,* from Latin *tribus,* division of the Roman people, perhaps from *tri-* (unattested), three (referring to Latin, Sabine, and Etruscan).]

tribes·man (trībz'mən) *n., pl.* **-men** (-mĭn). A member of a tribe.

tribes·wom·an (trībz'wo͝om'ən) *n., pl.* **-women** (-wĭm'ĭn). A woman who is a member of a tribe.

tribo– *prefix.* Indicates friction; for example, **triboelectricity, triboluminescence.** [From Greek *tribos,* rubbing.]

tri·bo·e·lec·tric·i·ty (trī'bō-ĭ-lĕk'trĭs'ĭ-tē, -ē'lĕk-trĭs'ə-tē, trĭb'ō-) *n. Physics.* Electricity that is produced by friction. **—tri·bo·e·lec·tric** (trī'bō-ĭ-lĕk'trĭk, trĭb'ō-) *adj.*

tri·bol·o·gy (trī-bŏl'ə-jē, trĭ-bŏl'-) *n.* The study of friction and lubrication.

tri·bo·lu·mi·nes·cence (trī'bō-lo͞o'mə-nĕs'əns, trĭb'ō-) *n. Physics.* Luminescence produced by certain crystals as a result of friction or crushing. **—tri·bo·lu·mi·nes·cent** *adj.*

tri·brach (trī'brăk') *n.* A metrical foot of three short or unstressed syllables. [Latin *tribrachys,* from Greek *tribrakhus* : *tri-,* three + *brakhus,* short.] **—tri·brach·ic** (trī-brăk'ĭk) *adj.*

tri·bro·mo·eth·a·nol (trī-brō'mō-ĕth'ə-nôl', -nōl') *n.* A white crystalline compound, CBr_3CH_2OH, having a slight aromatic odor and taste and used to produce complete unconsciousness.

trib·u·la·tion (trĭb'yə-lā'shən) *n.* **1.** *Often* **tribulations.** Great affliction, trial, or distress; suffering: *the tribulations of the persecuted.* **2.** An experience or condition that causes such distress. [Middle English *tribulacioun,* from Old French *tribulation,* from Late Latin *trībulātiō* (stem *trībulātiōn-*), from *trībulāre,* to oppress, from Latin, to press, from *trībulum,* threshing sledge.]

tri·bu·nal (trī-byo͞o'nəl, trĭ-) *n.* **1.** A seat or court of justice. **2.** The platform or seat upon which a judge or other presiding officer sits in court. **3.** A committee or board set up to adjudicate or investigate a particular matter or dispute: *a rent tribunal.* **4.** Anything having the power of determining or judging: *the tribunal of public opinion.* [Latin *tribūnāl(e),* court of the tribunes, tribunal, from *tribūnālis,* of a tribune, from *tribūnus,* TRIBUNE (official).]

trib·u·nate (trĭb'yə-nāt', trĭ-byo͞o'nĭt) *n.* The rank, office, dignity, or authority of a tribune.

trib·une[1] (trĭb'yo͞on', trĭ-byo͞on') *n.* **1.** In ancient Rome, an official chosen by the plebs to protect their rights against the patricians. **2.** Any protector or champion of the common people. [Middle English, from Latin *tribūnus,* "head of the tribe," tribune, from *tribus,* TRIBE.] **—trib·u·nar·y** (trĭb'yə-nĕr'ē) *adj.* **—trib·une·ship** *n.*

tribune[2] *n.* **1.** A raised platform or dais from which a speaker addresses an assembly. **2. a.** An apse. **b.** A bishop's throne within an apse. **c.** A raised area or gallery in a church. [French, from Italian *tribuna,* from Medieval Latin *tribūna,* variant of Latin *tribūnāl(e),* TRIBUNAL.]

trib·u·tar·y (trĭb'yə-tĕr'ē) *adj.* **1.** Making additions or offering supplies; contributory; subsidiary. **2.** Having the nature of a tribute: *a tributary payment.* **3.** Paying or required to pay tribute. **4.** Flowing into a larger body of water. Said of a river or stream.
∼*n., pl.* **tributaries. 1.** One that pays tribute. **2.** *Abbr.* **trib.** A stream or river flowing into a larger stream or river. In this sense, compare **distributary.** **—trib·u·tar·i·ly** (trĭb'yə-târ'ə-lē) *adv.*

trib·ute (trĭb'yo͞ot) *n.* **1. a.** A gift, payment, declaration, or other acknowledgment of gratitude, respect, or admiration: *"To love and grief tribute of verse belongs"* (John Donne). **b.** That which is a worthy or creditable reflection of the person or thing mentioned: *The new church was a tribute to their faith.* **2. a.** A sum of money or other valuables paid by one ruler or nation to another as acknowledgment of submission or as the price for protection by that nation. **b.** Any payment made for protection. **3. a.** In feudal times, any payment or tax given by a vassal to his overlord. **b.** The obligation to make such a payment. [Middle English *tribut,* from Latin *tribūtum,* from the neuter past participle of *tribuere,* to give, distribute (as among the Roman tribes), from *tribus,* TRIBE.]

tri·car·box·yl·ic acid cycle (trī-kär'bŏk-sĭl'ĭk) *n.* The **Krebs cycle** *(see).*

trice (trīs) *tr.v.* **triced, tricing, trices.** To hoist and secure (a sail, for example); lash. Usually used with *up.*
∼*n.* A very short period of time; moment; instant. Used chiefly in the phrase *in a trice.* —See Synonyms at **moment.** [Middle English *trisen,* from Middle Dutch, akin to Middle Dutch *trise*†, pulley; noun sense, Middle English *at a tryse,* "at a pull."]

tri·cen·ten·ni·al (trī'sĕn-tĕn'ē-əl) *adj.* Tercentenary.
∼*n.* A tercentenary event or celebration.

tri·ceps (trī'sĕps') *n., pl.* **triceps** or **-cepses** (-sĕp'sĭz). Any three-headed muscle, especially the large muscle running along the back of the upper arm and serving to extend the forearm. [Latin, three-headed : *tri-,* three + *caput,* head.]

tri·cer·a·tops (trī-sĕr'ə-tŏps') *n.* A three-horned herbivorous dinosaur of the genus *Triceratops,* of the Cretaceous period, having a bony plate covering the neck. [New Latin *Triceratops* : TRI- + Greek *keras* (stem *kerat-*), horn + *ōps,* eye, face.]

trich–. Variant of **tricho–.**

tri·chi·a·sis (trĭ-kī'ə-sĭs) *n.* **1.** A condition of ingrowing hairs about an orifice, especially of ingrowing eyelashes. **2.** The presence of hairlike bodies in the urine. [Late Latin, from Greek *trikhiasis* : TRICH(O)- + -IASIS.]

tri·chi·na (trĭ-kī'nə) *n., pl.* **-nae** (-nē) or **-nas.** A parasitic nematode worm, *Trichinella spiralis,* infesting the intestines of various mammals and having larvae that move through the blood vessels and become encysted in the muscles. [New Latin, from Greek *trikhinos,* hairy, from *thrix,* hair.]

trich·i·nize (trĭk'ə-nīz') *tr.v.* **-nized, -nizing, -nizes.** To infect with trichinae. **—trich·i·ni·za·tion** *n.*

trich·i·no·sis (trĭk'ə-nō'sĭs) *n.* Also **trich·i·ni·a·sis** (-nī'ə-sĭs). A disease caused by eating inadequately cooked meat containing trichinae and characterized by intestinal disorders, fever, muscular swelling, pain, and delirium. [New Latin : TRICHIN(A) + -OSIS.]

tri·chi·nous (trĭ-kī'nəs, trĭk'ə-nəs) *adj.* **1.** Containing trichinae: *trichinous pork.* **2.** Of or relating to trichinae or trichinosis.

trich·ite (trĭk'īt') *n.* A small needle-shaped filament or crystal. [German *Trichit* : TRICH(O)- + -ITE.] **—tri·chit·ic** (trĭ-kĭt'ĭk) *adj.*

tri·chlor·fon (trī-klôr'fŏn', -klōr'fŏn') *n.* A colorless crystalline compound, $C_4H_8Cl_3O_4P$, used as an agricultural insecticide. [TRI- + CHLOR(O)- + *-fon* (from PHOSPHONATE).]

tri·chlo·ride (trī-klôr'īd', -klōr'īd') *n.* A compound containing three chlorine atoms per molecule.

tri·chlo·ro·a·ce·tic acid (trī-klôr'ō-ə-sē'tĭk, trī-klōr'ō-) *n.* A colorless, deliquescent, corrosive, crystalline compound, CCl_3COOH, used as a herbicide and applied locally as an astringent and antiseptic.

tri·chlo·ro·eth·yl·ene (trī-klôr'ō-ĕth'ə-lēn', trī-klōr'ō-) *n.* Also **tri·chlor·eth·yl·ene** (trī'klôr-ĕth'ə-lēn', trī'klōr-). A colorless, toxic liquid, $CHCl{:}CCl_2$, that is used to degrease metals, as an extraction solvent for oils and waxes, as a refrigerant, in dry cleaning, and as a fumigant.

tri·chlo·ro·phe·nox·y·a·ce·tic acid (trī-klôr'ō-fə-nŏk'sē-ə-sē'tĭk, trī-klōr'ō-) *n.* A synthetic auxin, 2,4,5-trichlorophenoxyacetic acid, $C_8H_5Cl_3O_3$, that is used as a herbicide. Also called "2, 4, 5-T."

tricho–, trich– *prefix.* Indicates hair or hairlike part; for example, **trichopteran, trichogyne.** [Greek *trikho-,* from *thrix* (stem *trikh-*), hair.]

PRONUNCIATION KEY

ă, pat; ā, pay; âr, care;
ä, father, are; b, bib;
ch, church; d, deed; ĕ, pet;
ē, be; f, fife; g, gag; h, hat;
hw, which; ĭ, pit; ī, pie;
îr, pier; j, judge; k, kick;
l, lid, needle; m, mum;
n, no, sudden; ng, thing;
ŏ, pot; ō, toe; ô, paw, for;
oi, noise; ou, out; o͝o, book;
o͞o, boot; p, pop; r, roar;
s, sauce; sh, ship, dish;
t, tight; th, thin, path;
th, this, bathe; ŭ, cut; ûr, fur;
v, valve; w, with; y, yes;
z, zebra, size; zh, vision;
ə, about, item, edible,
gallop, circus, peaceful

IN FOREIGN WORDS:

à, *Fr.* ami; œ, *Fr.* feu, *Ger.* schön; ü, *Fr.* tu, *Ger.* über;
KH, *Ger.* ich, *Scot.* loch;
N, *Fr.* bon; y', *Fr.* Compiègne

STRESS MARKS:

Primary stress: '
in·cite' (ĭn-sīt')
Secondary stress: '
in'sight' (ĭn'sīt')

trich•o•cyst (trĭk'ə-sĭst') *n.* One of the minute capsulelike bodies in the outer cytoplasm of certain protozoans, capable of ejecting a threadlike or bristlelike extension. [TRICHO- + -CYST.] —**trich•o•cys•tic** (trĭk'ə-sĭs'tĭk) *adj.*

trich•o•gyne (trĭk'ə-jīn', -gīn') *n.* A receptive filament of the female reproductive structure of certain fungi or algae.

trich•oid (trĭk'oid', trī'koid') *adj.* Resembling hair; hairlike. [Greek *trikhoeidēs* : TRICH(O)- + -OID.]

tri•chol•o•gy (trĭ-kŏl'ə-jē) *n.* The study of hair and its diseases.

trich•ome (trĭk'ōm', trī'kōm') *n.* A hairlike or bristlelike outgrowth, as from the epidermis of a plant. [German *Trichom,* from Greek *trikhōma,* hair growth, from *trikhoun,* to furnish with hair, from *thrix* (stem *trikh-*), hair.] —**tri•chom•ic** (trĭ-kŏm'ĭk, -kō'mĭk, trī-) *adj.*

trich•o•mo•nad (trĭk'ə-mō'năd') *n.* Any of various flagellate protozoans of the genus *Trichomonas,* occurring in the digestive and urogenital tracts of vertebrates. [New Latin *Trichomonas* (stem *Trichomonad-*) : TRICHO- + MONAD.]

trich•o•mo•ni•a•sis (trĭk'ə-mə-nī'ə-sĭs) *n.* **1.** A vaginal infection caused by a protozoan, *Trichomonas vaginalis,* and resulting in inflammation and discomfort. **2.** Any infection caused by trichomonads. [New Latin : *Trichomonas,* TRICHOMON(AD) + -IASIS.]

tri•chop•ter•an (trĭ-kŏp'tər-ən) *n.* Any insect of the order Trichoptera, which comprises the caddis flies. [New Latin *Trichoptera,* "hairy winged" : TRICHO- + -PTER.]

tri•cho•sis (trĭ-kō'sĭs) *n.* Disease of the hair. [New Latin, from Greek *trikhōsis,* growth of hair, from *trikhoun,* to furnish with hair. See **trichome.**]

tri•chot•o•my (trī-kŏt'ə-mē) *n., pl.* **-mies.** A dividing into three parts. [Greek *trikha,* in three parts + -TOMY.] —**trich•o•tom•ic** (trĭk'ə-tŏm'ĭk), **tri•chot•o•mous** (trī-kŏt'ə-məs) *adj.*

-trichous *suffix.* Indicates specified kinds of hair; for example, **amphitrichous.** [Greek *-trikhos,* from *thrix* (stem *trikh-*), hair.]

tri•chro•ism (trī'krō-ĭz'əm) *n.* The property possessed by certain minerals of exhibiting three different colors when illuminated by white light and viewed from three different directions. [Greek *trikhroos,* "tricolored" : TRI- + -CHRO(OUS) + -ISM.] —**tri•chro•ic** (trī-krō'ĭk) *adj.*

tri•chro•mat•ic (trī'krō-măt'ĭk) *adj.* Also **tri•chrome** (trī'krōm'), **tri•chro•mic** (trī-krō'mĭk). **1.** Of, relating to, or having three colors, as in photography or printing. **2.** Having visual perception of the three primary colors, as in normal vision. —**tri•chro•ma•tism** (trī-krō'mə-tĭz'əm) *n.*

trick (trĭk) *n.* **1.** A device or action designed to achieve an end by deceptive or fraudulent means; stratagem; ruse. **2.** A mischievous action; practical joke; prank. **3.** A deceptive or delusive appearance; an illusion: *a trick of the sunlight.* **4.** A peculiar trait or characteristic, such as a mannerism: *had the trick of blinking as she spoke.* **5.** The best quality or method needed to accomplish something; knack: *Patience is the trick here.* **6.** A feat of magic or legerdemain. **7.** A difficult, dexterous, or clever act designed to amuse or entertain. **8.** In card games: **a.** All the cards played in a single round, one from each player. **b.** One such round. **9.** A period or turn of duty, as at the helm of a ship. **10.** *Slang.* **a.** A prostitute's client. **b.** A session with any one client, as carried out by a prostitute. —See Synonyms at **artifice.** —**do the trick.** *Informal.* To bring about the desired result. —**how's tricks.** *Informal.* Used to inquire how a person is or how things are going.
~*v.* **tricked, tricking, tricks.** —*tr.* **1.** To swindle or cheat; deceive; delude. **2.** To ornament, dress, or adorn. Used with *up* or *out.* —*intr.* To practice deception or trickery.
~*adj.* **1.** Of, pertaining to, or involving tricks. **2.** Capable of doing tricks: *a trick dog.* **3.** Designed or made for doing a trick or tricks: *trick dice.* **4.** Weak, defective, or liable to fail: *a trick knee.* [Middle English *trik,* from Old North French *trique,* from Old French *triche,* from *trichier,* to deceive, perhaps from Vulgar Latin *triccāre* (unattested), from Latin *trīcarī,* to start difficulties, play tricks, from *trīcae*†, trifles, tricks. See also **intricate, extricate.**] —**trick•er** *n.*

trick•er•y (trĭk'ə-rē) *n., pl.* **-ies.** The practice or use of tricks; deception by stratagem; artifice.

trick•ish (trĭk'ĭsh) *adj.* Characterized by or tending to use tricks or trickery. —**trick•ish•ly** *adv.* —**trick•ish•ness** *n.*

trick•le (trĭk'əl) *v.* **-led, -ling, -les.** —*intr.* **1.** To flow or fall in drops or in a thin, intermittent stream; drip gently but steadily. **2.** To move or proceed slowly or bit by bit: *The audience trickled in.* —*tr.* To cause to trickle: *trickle oil onto the salad.*
~*n.* **1.** The act or condition of trickling. **2.** Any slow, small, or irregular quantity of something that moves, proceeds, or occurs intermittently. [Middle English *triklen* (perhaps imitative).]

trick or treat *n.* The custom practiced by children on Halloween of going from door to door dressed in costume and saying "trick or treat" as a demand for a treat, as candy.

trick•ster (trĭk'stər) *n.* One who plays tricks or deceives.

trick•sy (trĭk'sē) *adj.* **-sier, -siest. 1.** Prankish; mischievous. **2.** *Archaic.* Crafty or sly. **3.** *Archaic.* Smart; dapper.

trick•y (trĭk'ē) *adj.* **-ier, -iest. 1.** Given to or characterized by deception or trickery; crafty; sly; wily: *a tricky politician.* **2.** Requiring caution or skill; difficult: *a tricky question; a tricky situation.* —See Synonyms at **dishonest, sly.** —**trick•i•ly** *adv.* —**trick•i•ness** *n.*

tri•clin•ic (trī-klĭn'ĭk) *adj.* Having three unequal axes intersecting at oblique angles. Said of certain crystals. [TRI- + -CLINIC.]

tri•clin•i•um (trī-klĭn'ē-əm) *n., pl.* **-ia** (-ē-ə). **1.** A couch or set of couches surrounding three sides of a table, used by the ancient Romans for reclining at meals. **2.** A room containing such a couch or couches. [Latin *triclīnium,* from Greek *triklinion,* diminutive of *triklinos,* room with three couches : *tri-,* three + *klinē,* couch.]

tri•col•or (trī'kŭl'ər) *adj.* Also **tri•col•ored** (-ərd). Having three colors.
~*n.* **1.** A tricolor flag. **2. Tricolor.** The French flag.

tri•corn, tri•corne (trī'kôrn') *n.* A hat having the brim turned up on three sides.
~*adj.* Having three projections, horns, or corners. [French *tricorne,* from Latin *tricornis,* three-horned : *tri-,* three + *cornū,* horn.]

tri•cor•nered (trī'kôr'nərd) *adj.* Having three corners.

tri•cos•tate (trī-kŏs'tāt') *adj.* Having three costae or riblike ridges.

tri•cot (trē'kō) *n.* **1.** A plain, warp-knitted cloth of any of various yarns. **2.** A soft ribbed cloth of wool or a wool blend, usually used for dresses. [French, from *tricoter*†, to knit.]

tric•o•tine (trĭk'ə-tēn', trē'kə-) *n.* A sturdy worsted fabric with a double twill, used for dresses and suits. [French, from TRICOT.]

tri•crot•ic (trī-krŏt'ĭk) *adj. Medicine.* Having three waves or elevations to one beat of the pulse. [From Greek *trikrotos,* having a triple beat : *tri-,* three + *krotein,* to beat.] —**tri•cro•tism** (trī'krə-tĭz'əm) *n.*

tri•cus•pid (trī-kŭs'pĭd) *adj.* Also **tri•cus•pi•dal** (-pə-dəl), **tri•cus•pi•date** (-pə-dāt'). **1.** Having three points or cusps, as a molar tooth. **2.** *Anatomy.* Pertaining to the tricuspid valve of the heart.
~*n. Anatomy.* A tricuspid organ or part, especially a tooth. [Latin *tricuspis* (stem *tricuspid-*) : *tri-,* three + *cuspis,* point, CUSP.]

tricuspid valve *n.* The three-segmented valve of the heart that keeps the blood from flowing back from the right ventricle into the right atrium.

tri•cy•cle (trī'sĭk'əl, -sĭ-kəl) *n.* A vehicle, used especially by small children, that has three wheels, two at the back and one at the front and is usually propelled by pedals. Also informally called "trike."
—**tri•cy•cle** *v.*

tri•cy•clic (trī-sī'klĭk, -sĭk'lĭk) *adj. Chemistry.* Having or pertaining to a molecular structure with three rings.

tri•dac•tyl (trī-dăk'təl) *adj.* Also **tri•dac•ty•lous** (-tə-ləs). Having three toes, claws, or similar parts on each limb. [Greek *tridaktulos,* three-fingered : *tri-,* three + *daktulos,* finger (see **dactyl**).]

tri•dent (trīd'ənt) *n.* A long, three-pronged fork or weapon as used by one hunting fish or formerly by gladiators; especially, the three-pronged spear carried by Neptune or Poseidon.
~*adj.* Also **tri•den•tate** (trī-dĕn'tāt'). Having three teeth, prongs, or similar protrusions. [Latin *tridēns* (stem *trident-*), three-toothed : *tri-,* three + *dēns,* tooth.]

Tri•den•tine (trī-dĕn'tīn', -tēn') *adj.* Of or relating to the Council of Trent or to the results or decrees of that Council.
~*n.* A Roman Catholic who conforms rigorously to the Tridentine Creed formulated at the Council of Trent. [Medieval Latin *Tridentīnus,* from *Tridentum,* TRENT.]

Tridentine Mass *n.* The Mass in the rite laid down by Pius V in 1570 following the reforms of the Council of Trent, used throughout the Roman Catholic Church until replaced by the various revisions that followed the Second Vatican Council.

triecious. Variant of **trioecious.**

tried. Past tense and past participle of **try.**

tri•en•ni•al (trī-ĕn'ē-əl) *adj.* **1.** Occurring every third year. **2.** Lasting three years.
~*n.* **1.** A third anniversary. **2.** A triennial thing, event, or celebration. [From TRIENNIUM.] —**tri•en•ni•al•ly** *adv.*

tri•en•ni•um (trī-ĕn'ē-əm) *n., pl.* **-ums** or **-ennia** (-ĕn'ē-ə). A period of three years. [Latin *triennium* : *tri-,* three + Latin *annus,* year.]

tri•er (trī'ər) *n.* One that tries; especially, a person who continues to make repeated attempts at something despite failure.

tri•er•arch (trī'ə-rärk') *n.* In ancient Greece: **1.** The captain of a trireme. **2.** An Athenian who had the responsibility of outfitting and maintaining a trireme as a part of his civic duties. [Latin *triērarchus,* from Greek *triērarkhos* : *triērēs,* trireme + -ARCH.]

tri•er•ar•chy (trī'ə-rär'kē) *n., pl.* **-chies.** In ancient Greece: **1.** The authority or office of the commander of a trierarch. **2.** The ancient Athenian system whereby individual citizens furnished and maintained triremes as a part of their public duty.

Tri•este (trē-ĕst'). Seaport and capital of Friuli-Venezia Giulia region, northeastern Italy. It is an important industrial and tourist center. It was held by Austria from 1382 until 1919 and was the subject of a dispute with Yugoslavia after World War II.

tri•fa•cial (trī-fā'shəl) *adj. Anatomy.* Trigeminal.

tri•fid (trī'fĭd) *adj.* Divided or cleft into three narrow parts or lobes. [Latin *trifidus* : *tri-,* three + -FID.]

tri•fle (trī'fəl) *n.* **1.** Something of slight importance or very little value. **2.** A small amount; a little: *The book only cost a trifle.* **3.** A dessert typically consisting of a layer of sponge cake covered with jam or fruit, soaked in wine, sprinkled with almonds, and topped with custard and whipped cream. **4. a.** A moderately hard variety of pewter. **b. trifles.** Utensils made from this.
~*v.* **trifled, -fling, -fles.** —*intr.* **1.** To deal with something as if it were of little significance or value. Usually used with *with*: *not a person to be trifled with.* **2.** To act, perform, or speak with little seriousness or purpose; jest. **3.** To play or toy with something; handle things idly. —*tr.* To waste (time or money, for example). Often used with *away.* —**a trifle.** Slightly; somewhat: *a trifle stingy.* [Middle English *trifle, truf(f)le,* from Old French *truf(f)le,* variant of *tru(f)fe*†, trickery, deceit.] —**tri•fler** *n.*

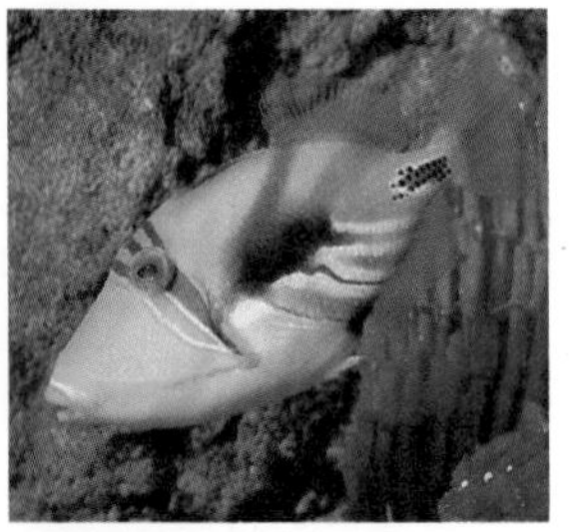

triggerfish *The Hawaiian triggerfish,* Rhineacanthus aculeatus *(above), is one of a family that derives its name from a triggering mechanism in the spines of the dorsal fin. The first spine can be locked erect and once in this position can be released only by the second spine. The mechanism enables the fish to hold its position in protective crevices.*

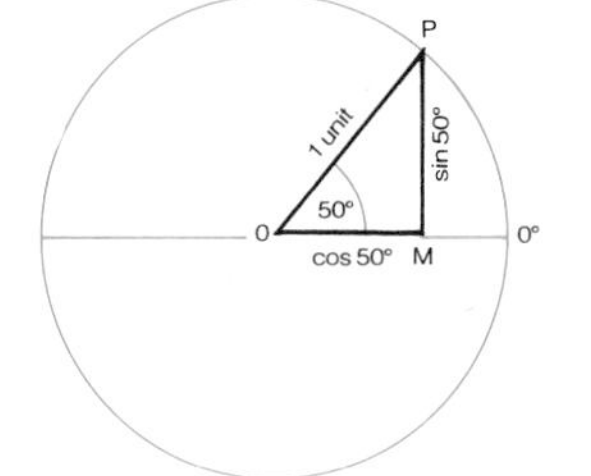

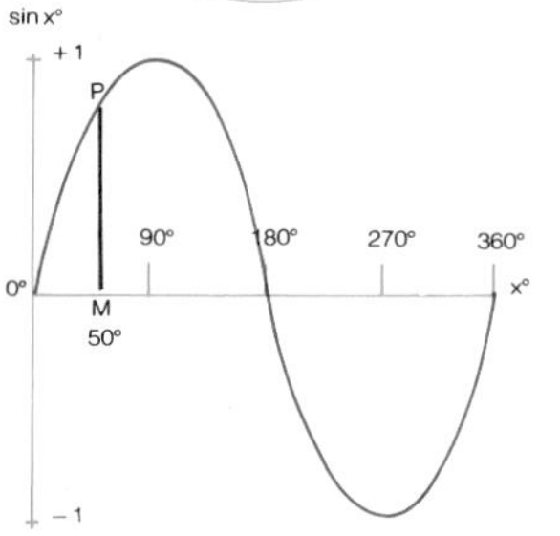

trigonometry *A knowledge of the relationships between the angles and sides of a right-angled triangle—the study called trigonometry—is useful in navigation, surveying, and other disciplines where distances have to be calculated from the measurement of angles. Three main ratios are used: sine, cosine, and tangent. In the triangle above (upper illustration), the sine of the 50° angle is the ratio of the height, PM, to the length of the longest side, or hypotenuse, OP. The cosine is the ratio of OM to OP. And the tangent is the ratio of PM to OM. If the hypotenuse is 1 unit long, the lengths of the other two sides are equal to the sine and cosine. If OP were 2 units long, PM would equal twice the sine, and so on. The graph (lower illustration) shows how the sine ratio changes as the angle increases from 0° to 360°. The graph of the cosine has a similar wavelike pattern.*

tri·fling (trīʹflĭng) *adj.* **1.** Of slight importance; insignificant. **2.** Characterized by frivolity or idleness. —See Synonyms at **trivial.** —**tri·fling·ly** *adv.*

tri·fo·cal (trī-fōʹkəl) *adj.* Having three focal lengths.
∼*n.* **trifocals.** Glasses having trifocal lenses.

tri·fold (trīʹfōldʹ) *adj.* Triple; having three parts. [TRI- + -FOLD.]

tri·fo·li·ate (trī-fōʹlē-ĭt) *adj.* Also **tri·fo·li·at·ed** (-fōʹlē-āʹtĭd). Having three leaves, leaflets, or leaflike parts: *a trifoliate compound leaf.*

tri·fo·li·o·late (trī-fōʹlē-ə-lātʹ) *adj.* Having three leaflets.

tri·fo·ri·um (trī-fôrʹē-əm, -fōrʹē-əm) *n., pl.* **-foria** (-fôrʹē-ə, -fōrʹē-ə). *Architecture.* A gallery of arches set in the wall above the arches of the nave choir, and sometimes the transept, of a church. [Medieval Latin *triforium*†, special name (in Gervase of Canterbury, *c.* 1185) applied to the gallery in Canterbury Cathedral, but subsequently taken to mean "structure with three openings" (Latin *tri-,* three + *fores,* doors) and thus applied to the elevated gallery characteristic of Gothic architecture, sometimes having three arches or openings.]

tri·form (trīʹfôrmʹ) *adj.* Having three different forms or parts.

tri·fur·cate (trī-fûrʹkĭt, -kātʹ, trīʹfər-kātʹ) *adj.* Also **tri·fur·cat·ed** (trīʹ-fər-kāʹtĭd). Having three forks or branches. —**tri·fur·ca·tion** *n.*

trig[1] (trĭg) *adj.* **1.** Trim; neat. **2.** In good condition.
∼*tr.v.* **trigged, trigging, trigs.** To make trim or neat, especially in dress. Often used with *up* or *out.* [Middle English, true, active, from Old Norse *tryggr,* akin to TRUE.] —**trig·ly** *adv.* —**trig·ness** *n.*

trig[2] *tr.v.* **trigged, trigging, trigs. 1.** To stop (a wheel) from rolling, as with a trig. **2.** To prop up; support.
∼*n.* A wedge or other braking device. [Perhaps from Scandinavian, akin to Old Norse *tryggr,* true, firm.]

trig. trigonometric; trigonometry.

tri·gem·i·nal (trī-jĕmʹə-nəl) *adj. Anatomy.* Pertaining to the trigeminal nerve; trifacial.

trigeminal nerve *n.* Either of the fifth pair of cranial nerves that divides into the ophthalmic, maxillary, and mandibular nerves. [New Latin, from Latin, three born at a birth, threefold (probably from its three branches) : *tri-,* three + *geminus,* twin-born, twin.]

trigeminal neuralgia *n.* Intensely painful paroxysms of the facial area around the trigeminal nerve. Also called "tic douloureux."

trig·ger (trĭgʹər) *n.* **1.** The lever pressed by the finger to discharge a firearm. **2.** Any similar device used to release or activate a mechanism. **3.** Anything that activates or sets off an action or series of events: *Murder was the trigger for the uprising.* **4.** *Electronics.* A pulse or a circuit that initiates the action of another component.
∼*tr.v.* **triggered, -gering, -gers. 1.** To initiate; activate; set off: *The tax rise triggered a public outcry.* **2.** To fire or explode (a weapon). [Earlier *tricker,* from Dutch *trekker,* something pulled, from Middle Dutch *trecker,* from *trecken,* to pull, travel. See **trek.**]

trig·ger·fish (trĭgʹər-fĭshʹ) *n., pl.* **-fishes** or collectively **triggerfish.** Any of various brightly colored fishes of the family Balistidae, of warm coastal seas, characteristically having sharp, erectile dorsal spines.

trigger flower *n.* Any of numerous plants of the genus *Stylidium,* confined mainly to Australia, that have a column of fused stamens that dusts the backs of insects with pollen.

trig·ger-hap·py (trĭgʹər-hăpʹē) *adj. Informal.* Inclined to react in a violent, rash manner at the slightest provocation.

tri·glyc·er·ide (trī-glĭsʹə-rīdʹ) *n.* A natural fat or oil formed by the combination of one molecule of glycerol with three molecules of fatty acids.

tri·glyph (trīʹglĭfʹ) *adj. Architecture.* An ornament in a Doric frieze consisting of a projecting block having three parallel vertical channels on its face. [Latin *trīglyphus,* from Greek *trigluphos* : *tri-,* three + *gluphē,* carving, GLYPH.] —**tri·glyph·ic** (trī-glĭfʹĭk) *adj.*

tri·gon (trīʹgŏnʹ) *n.* **1.** A triangular lyre or harp of Roman and Greek antiquity. **2.** In astrology, a **triplicity** *(see).* **3.** *Archaic.* A triangle. [Latin *trigonum,* triangle, from Greek *trigōnon,* from *trigōnos,* triangular : *tri-,* three + -GON.]

trig·o·nal (trĭgʹə-nəl) *adj.* **1.** Triangular. **2.** In crystallography, pertaining to or belonging to the crystal system with three unequal axes that are equally inclined to each other at an angle other than 90°.

trigonometric function *n.* **1.** A function of an angle expressed as the ratio of two of the sides of a right triangle that contains the angle, named sine, cosine, tangent, or the like. In general, for any angle formed in a coordinate plane by the intersection of the abscissal axis with the radius vector from the origin to a point in the plane, the ratio of any two of the values abscissa, ordinate, and radius vector of that point. Also called "circular function." **2.** A function composed of a combination of trigonometric functions.

trig·o·nom·e·try (trĭgʹə-nŏmʹə-trē) *n. Abbr.* **trig.** The study of the properties and applications of trigonometric functions. [New Latin *trigonometria* : Greek *trigōnon,* triangle, TRIGON + -METRY.] —**trig·o·no·met·ric** (trĭgʹə-nə-mĕtʹrĭk), **trig·o·no·met·ri·cal** *adj.* —**trig·o·no·met·ri·cal·ly** *adv.*

trig·o·nous (trĭgʹə-nəs) *adj.* Three-sided, especially in cross section: *a trigonous stem.* Compare **triquetrous.** [From Greek *trigōnos,* three-cornered. See **tri-, -gon.**]

tri·graph (trīʹgrăfʹ, -gräfʹ) *n.* A conjunction of three letters representing a single speech sound; for example, the letters *e, a,* and *u* in the word *beau* form a trigraph. Also called "triphthong." [TRI- + -GRAPH.]

tri·he·dral (trī-hēʹdrəl) *adj.* Formed by the plane surfaces of a trihedron.
∼*n.* A trihedron.

tri·he·dron (trī-hēʹdrən) *n., pl.* **-drons** or **-dra** (-drə). A figure formed by the intersection of three noncoplanar lines. Also called "trihedral." [New Latin : TRI- + -HEDRON.]

tri·hy·drate (trī-hīʹdrātʹ) *n.* A compound containing three molecules of water of crystallization per molecule in the compound.

tri·hy·dric (trī-hīʹdrĭk) *adj.* Also **tri·hy·drox·y** (trīʹhī-drŏkʹsē). Containing three hydroxide groups per molecule. Said especially of alcohols.

trike (trīk) *n. Informal.* A **tricycle** *(see).*

tri·lat·er·al (trī-lătʹər-əl) *adj.* Having three sides. [Latin *trilaterus* : *tri-,* three + *latus* (stem *later-*), side (see **lateral**).] —**tri·lat·er·al·ly** *adv.*

tri·lat·er·al·ism (trī-lătʹər-ə-lĭzʹəm) *n.* The political policy of encouraging friendly relations among three nations or regions, especially among North America, Japan, and Western Europe. —**tri·lat·er·al·ist** *n.* —**tri·lat·er·al·is·tic** *n.*

tril·by (trĭlʹbē) *n., pl.* **-bies.** *British.* A soft felt hat with a deeply creased crown and a narrow brim. [19th century : after the heroine of *Trilby,* a novel by George du Maurier. The hat was popularized in the stage version.]

tri·lin·e·ar (trī-lĭnʹē-ər) *adj.* Pertaining to, having, or bounded by three lines.

tri·lin·gual (trī-lĭngʹgwəl) *adj.* Having or expressed in three languages.

tri·lit·er·al (trī-lĭtʹər-əl) *adj.* Consisting of three letters. Used chiefly of consonantal roots in Semitic languages.
∼*n.* A three-letter word or word element.

tri·lith (trīʹlĭthʹ) *n.* A group of three large stones, usually with two standing upright and supporting a third, often found in prehistoric henge monuments. [Greek *trilithon* : TRI- + -LITH.]

trill (trĭl) *n.* **1.** A fluttering or tremulous sound, such as that made by certain birds; a warble. **2.** *Music.* The rapid alternation of two tones either a whole tone or a half tone apart. **3.** *Phonetics.* **a.** A rapid vibration of one speech organ against another, as of the tongue against the alveolar ridge in Spanish *rr.* **b.** A speech sound pronounced with such a vibration.
∼*v.* **trilled, trilling, trills.** —*tr.* **1.** To sound, sing, or play with a trill. **2.** *Phonetics.* To articulate with a trill. —*intr.* To produce or give forth a trill. [Italian *trillo,* from *trillare*†, to trill.]

tril·lion (trĭlʹyən) *n.* **1.** The cardinal number represented by 1 followed by 12 zeros, usually written 10^{12}. **2.** *Chiefly British.* The cardinal number represented by 1 followed by 18 zeros, usually written 10^{18}. **3. trillions.** An indefinitely large number; a great many. [French : *tri-,* third power + *(m)illion,* million.] —**tril·lion** *adj.*

tril·lionth (trĭlʹyənth) *n.* **1.** The ordinal number one trillion in a series. **2.** One of a trillion equal parts. —**tril·lionth** *adj. & adv.*

tril·li·um (trĭlʹē-əm) *n.* Any of various plants of the genus *Trillium,* of North America and eastern Asia, usually having a single whorl of three leaves, and a variously colored, three-petaled flower. [New Latin *Trillium,* genus name, from Swedish *trilling,* triplet (from its three leaves).]

tri·lo·bate (trī-lōʹbātʹ) *adj.* Also **tri·lo·bal** (-lōʹbəl), **tri·lo·bat·ed** (-lōʹ-bāʹtĭd), **tri·lobed** (trīʹlōbdʹ). Having three lobes, as certain leaves do.

tri·lo·bite (trīʹlə-bītʹ) *n.* Any of numerous extinct marine arthropods of the class Trilobita, of the Paleozoic era, having a segmented exoskeleton divided by furrows into three longitudinal lobes. [New Latin *Trilobites* (division), from Greek *trilobos,* "three-lobed" : *tri-,* three + *lobos,* LOBE.] —**tri·lo·bit·ic** (trīʹlō-bĭtʹĭk) *adj.*

tri·loc·u·lar (trī-lŏkʹyə-lər) *adj.* Having three chamberlike divisions or cavities. Said especially of plant reproductive structures.

tril·o·gy (trĭlʹə-jē) *n., pl.* **-gies.** A group of three dramatic or literary works by the same author that are related in subject or theme, such as three ancient Greek tragedies written to be performed in immediate succession. [Greek *trilogia* : TRI- + -LOGY.]

trim (trĭm) *v.* **trimmed, trimming, trims.** —*tr.* **1.** To make neat or tidy by clipping, smoothing, or pruning: *trimmed his beard.* **2. a.** To remove the excess from by or as if by cutting: *trimmed the budget.* **b.** To remove by or as if by cutting: *trim off the rotten bark.* **3.** To ornament; decorate: *trim the dress with a band of lace.* **4.** *Informal.* **a.** To thrash. **b.** To defeat soundly. **c.** To cheat. **d.** To rebuke or scold. **5.** *Nautical.* **a.** To adjust (the sails and yards of a ship) so that they receive the wind properly. **b.** To balance (a ship) by shifting its cargo or contents. **6.** To balance (an aircraft in flight) by regulating the control surfaces and tabs. —*intr.* **1.** *Nautical.* **a.** To be in or retain equilibrium. Used of a ship. **b.** To make the sails and yards of a ship ready for sailing. **2. a.** To affect or maintain cautious neutrality between conflicting interests. **b.** To fashion one's views for momentary popularity or advantage.
∼*n.* **1. a.** Order, arrangement, or appearance; condition: *in good trim.* **b.** A condition of good health, fitness, or order: *got himself in trim.* **2. a.** Moldings, framework, or other exterior ornamentation. **b.** Adornment or decoration, as for clothing. **3.** Dress or equipment. **4.** Excised or rejected material, such as film that has been cut in editing. **5.** A clipping or trimming to make neat: *The hedge needs a trim. My hair needs a trim.* **6.** A commercial window display. **7.** *Nautical.* **a.** The readiness of a vessel for sailing with regard to ballast, sails, and yards. **b.** The balance of a ship. **c.** The difference between the draft at the bow and at the stern. **8.** The position of an aircraft relative to its horizontal axis.
∼*adj.* **trimmer, trimmest. 1. a.** In good or neat order. **b.** In good condition; especially, slim. **2.** Having lines, edges, or forms of neat and pleasing simplicity.

~*adv.* In a trim manner. [Perhaps from Middle English *trimmen* (unattested), from Old English *trymman, trymian,* to strengthen, arrange.] —**trim·ly** *adv.* —**trim·ness** *n.*

tri·ma·ran (trī′mə-răn′) *n.* A sailing vessel with three hulls set side by side. [TRI- + (CATA)MARAN.]

tri·mer (trī′mər) *n. Chemistry.* A polymeric compound consisting of three identical monomeric molecules or groups. [TRI- + -MER.] —**tri·mer·ic** (trī-mĕr′ĭk) *adj.*

trim·er·ous (trĭm′ər-əs) *adj.* **1.** Having three similar segments or parts. **2.** *Botany.* Having flower parts, such as petals, sepals, and stamens, in sets of three. Also written *3-merous.* [New Latin *trimerus,* from Greek *trimerēs :* TRI- + -MEROUS.] —**trim·er·ism** *n.*

tri·mes·ter (trī-mĕs′tər, trī′mĕs′tər) *n.* **1.** A period or term of three months. **2.** In some universities, any of three equal academic terms into which the year is divided. Compare **semester.**
~*adj.* Also **tri·mes·tral** (-trəl), **tri·mes·tri·al** (-trē-əl). Of or pertaining to periods of three months. [French *trimestre,* from Latin *trimestris,* "of three months" : *tri-,* three + *mēnsis,* month.]

trim·e·ter (trĭm′ə-tər) *n.* A line of verse consisting of three metrical feet. [Latin *trimetrus,* from Greek *trimetros :* TRI- + METER.] —**tri·met·ric** (trī-mĕt′rĭk), **tri·met·ri·cal** *adj.*

tri·meth·a·di·one (trī-mĕth′ə-dī′ōn′) *n.* A granular, crystalline substance, $C_6H_9NO_3$, used in treating petit mal epilepsy. Also called "troxidone."

trimetric projection *n.* A method of projection, used especially for mechanical drawings, in which the representation involves three axes with arbitrary angles and scales.

tri·met·ro·gon (trī-mĕt′rə-gŏn′) *n.* A system of aerial photography in which one vertical and two oblique photographs are simultaneously taken for use in topographic mapping. [TRI- + Greek *metron,* measure, METER + -GON.]

trim·mer (trĭm′ər) *n.* **1.** A person or machine that trims; especially, any of various devices used for trimming, as a hedge trimmer. **2.** A person who changes his opinions to suit the needs of the moment; a timeserver. **3.** *Electronics.* A variable component used to make fine adjustments to capacity, resistance, or the like. **4.** *Architecture.* A beam across an opening, such as a hearth, into which the ends of joists can be fitted.

trim·ming (trĭm′ĭng) *n.* **1.** That which is added as decoration; especially, a band of lace, embroidery, or the like used to decorate clothing. **2. trimmings.** Accessories; extras: *roast turkey with all the trimmings.* **3. trimmings.** That which is removed when something is trimmed; excess. **4.** *Informal.* A sound defeat, beating, or punishment.

tri·mo·lec·u·lar (trī′mə-lĕk′yə-lər) *adj.* Pertaining to or formed from three molecules.

tri·month·ly (trī-mŭnth′lē) *adj.* Done, occurring, or appearing every three months. —**tri·month·ly** *adv.*

tri·morph (trī′môrf′) *n.* **1.** A substance that occurs in three distinct forms. **2.** One of the forms in which such a substance occurs. [Back-formation from TRIMORPHIC.]

tri·mor·phic (trī-môr′fĭk) *adj.* Also **tri·mor·phous** (-fəs). **1.** *Biology.* Having or occurring in three differing forms. **2.** *Chemistry.* Crystallizing in three distinct forms. [TRI- + -MORPH(OUS) + -IC.] —**tri·mor·phi·cal·ly** *adv.* —**tri·mor·phism** *n.*

Tri·mur·ti (trĭ-mŏŏr′tē) *n. Hindu Mythology.* The Vedaic triad of Brahma, Vishnu, and Shiva. [Sanskrit *trimūrti : tri,* three + *mūrti†,* form.]

tri·nal (trī′nəl) *adj.* Having three parts; threefold; triple. [Latin *trīnālis,* from Latin *trīnus,* TRINE.]

tri·na·ry (trī′nə-rē) *adj.* Consisting of three parts or proceeding by threes; ternary. [From Late Latin *trīnārius,* from Latin *trīnus,* TRINE.]

trine (trīn) *adj.* **1.** Threefold; triple. **2.** In astrology, of or designating the trine aspect of two planets.
~*n.* **1.** A group of three. **2.** In astrology, the aspect of two planets when 120 degrees apart. [Middle English, from Old French, from Latin *trīnus,* from *trīnī,* three each.]

Trin·i·dad and To·ba·go (trĭn′ĭ-dăd′; tə-bā′gō). An island republic of the southeastern Caribbean. Both islands are woody and hilly; oil and asphalt have replaced sugar as the chief product. Population, 1,100,000. The capital is Port of Spain.

Tri·nil man (trē′nĭl) *n. Pithecanthropus (see).* [After *Trinil,* village in Java where remains were found.]

Trin·i·tar·i·an (trĭn′ə-târ′ē-ən) *adj.* **1.** Describing or relating to the Trinity. **2.** Believing or professing belief in the Trinity or the doctrine of the Trinity. Compare **Unitarian.** **3.** Pertaining to the Order of the Holy Trinity.
~*n.* **1.** A person who believes in the doctrine of the Trinity. **2.** A member of the Order of the Holy Trinity, founded in 1198 for the ransoming of Christian captives from the Muslims. —**Trin·i·tar·i·an·ism** *n.*

tri·ni·tro·ben·zene (trī′nī′trō-bĕn′zēn′, -bĕn-zēn′) *n.* A yellow crystalline compound, $C_6H_3(NO_2)_3$, derived from trinitrotoluene and used as an explosive.

tri·ni·tro·cre·sol (trī′nī′trō-krē′sôl′, -sōl′) *n.* A yellow crystalline compound, $CH_3C_6H_2(NO_2)_3OH$, used in high explosives.

tri·ni·tro·glyc·er·in (trī′nī′trō-glĭs′ər-ĭn) *n. Chemistry.* **Nitroglycerin** (*see*).

tri·ni·tro·phe·nol (trī′nī′trō-fē′nôl′, -nōl′) *n.* **Picric acid** (*see*).

tri·ni·tro·tol·u·ene (trī′nī′trō-tŏl′yŏŏ-ēn′) *n.* A yellow crystalline compound, $CH_3C_6H_2(NO_2)_3$, used mainly as a high explosive. Also called "TNT," "trinitrotoluol."

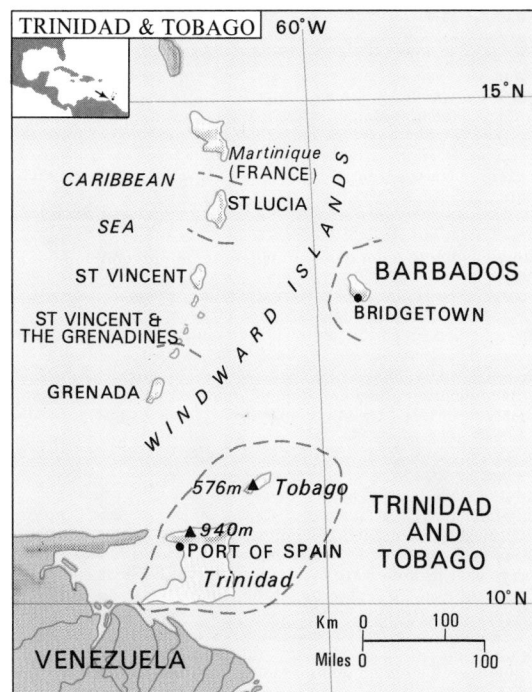

trillium *There are 30 species of trillium, all distinguished by having their leaves, sepals, and petals in groups of three. This is Trillium grandiflorum, a native of eastern North America.*

trin·i·ty (trĭn′ə-tē) *n., pl.* **-ties. 1.** The state or condition of being three. **2.** A group of three; a triad. Also called "triunity." **3.** Trinity. **a.** *Theology.* The union of three divine figures, the Father, Son, and Holy Ghost, in one Godhead. **b.** Trinity Sunday. [Middle English *trinite,* from Old French, from Latin *trīnitās,* from *trīnus,* TRINE.]

Trinity Brethren *pl.n.* The members of Trinity House.

Trinity House *n.* A British association that takes measures to safeguard shipping around the coastline, as by providing and maintaining lighthouses and buoys.

Trinity Sunday *n.* The first Sunday after Pentecost, or Whitsunday, dedicated to the Trinity. Also called "Trinity."

Trinity term *n.* In some British universities and colleges, the summer term. [After TRINITY SUNDAY.]

trin·ket (trĭng′kĭt) *n.* **1.** Any small ornament, such as a piece of jewelry. **2.** A trivial thing; a trifle. [16th century : origin obscure.]

tri·noc·u·lar (trī-nŏk′yə-lər) *adj.* Pertaining to or having a binocular eyepiece with an additional lens system for photographic recording. Said especially of microscopes. [TRI- + (BI)NOCULAR.]

tri·no·mi·al (trī-nō′mē-əl) *adj.* **1.** Consisting of three names or terms, as a taxonomic designation may. **2.** *Mathematics.* Having three algebraic terms connected by plus or minus signs.
~*n.* **1.** A three-part taxonomic designation indicating genus, species, and subspecies or variety, such as *Brassica oleracea botrytis,* the cauliflower. **2.** *Mathematics.* A trinomial algebraic expression. [TRI- + (BI)NOMIAL.]

tri·o (trē′ō) *n., pl.* **-os. 1.** A group of three people or things joined or associated. **2.** *Music.* **a.** A composition for three performers. **b.** The group of people performing a trio. **c.** The middle section of a minuet or scherzo, of a march, or of various dance forms. [French, composition for three voices, from Italian, from *tre,* three, from Latin *trēs.*]

tri·ode (trī′ōd′) *n.* A type of thermionic valve containing an anode, a cathode, and a control grid. [TRI- + -ODE (path).]

tri·oe·cious, tri·e·cious (trī-ē′shəs) *adj. Botany.* Having male, female, and hermaphroditic flowers borne on separate plants. [New Latin *Trioecia,* former order of such plants : TRI- + Greek *oikia,* dwelling, from *oikos,* house.] —**tri·oe·cious·ly** *adv.*

tri·ol (trī′ôl′, -ŏl′) *n. Chemistry.* Trihydric alcohol. [TRI- + -OL.]

tri·o·le·in (trī-ō′lē-ĭn) *n. Chemistry.* **Olein** (*see*).

tri·o·let (trē′ə-lā′, trē′ə-lĭt, trī′-) *n.* A poem or stanza of eight lines constructed on two rhymes, the scheme being *abaaabab.* [French, diminutive of *trio,* TRIO.]

tri·ox·ide (trī-ŏk′sīd′) *n.* Also **tri·ox·id** (-ŏk′sĭd). A chemical compound containing three oxygen atoms per molecule.

trip (trĭp) *n.* **1. a.** A going from one place to another, especially by ship or airplane; a journey: *a trip to England.* **b.** Any excursion or journey: *a trip to the mall.* **2.** *Slang.* **a.** The mental state or experience induced by a hallucinogen, such as LSD: *an acid trip.* **b.** Any experience or state of mind that is considered similar to the effects of a hallucinogenic drug in being stimulating, exciting, or extremely subjective: *a power trip.* **3.** A light or nimble tread or step. **4.** A stumble or fall. **5.** A way of causing a stumble or fall, as by catching the foot of someone walking. **6.** A mistake, slip, or blunder. **7. a.** A catch for tripping a mechanism. **b.** The action of such a catch.
~*v.* **tripped, tripping, trips.** —*intr.* **1.** To stumble. **2.** To move nimbly with or as if with light, rapid steps: *trip along.* **3.** To make a

trilobite *Some of the oldest fossils on earth show that these marine shellfish, now extinct, flourished for 350 million years and were in existence at least 600 million years ago. Trilobites had compound eyes similar to those of a modern insect, and some deep-sea species developed a special double lens to help them see in the low light. The horseshoe crab is their only living relative.*

mistake; go wrong: *tripped up on the last question.* **4.** To be released, as a tooth on an escapement wheel in a watch. **5.** To take a trip. **6.** *Slang.* To experience a hallucinogenic drug. —*tr.* **1.** To cause to stumble or fall. Often used with *up.* **2.** To trap or catch in an error or inconsistency. **3.** *Archaic.* To perform (a dance) nimbly. **4.** To release a catch, trigger, or switch that sets (a mechanism, for example) in operation. **5.** *Nautical.* **a.** To raise (an anchor) from the bottom. **b.** To tip or turn (a yardarm) into a position for lowering. **c.** To lift (an upper mast) in order to remove the pin or fid before lowering. [Middle English, short journey, light movement, from *trippen,* to move nimbly, cause to stumble, from Old French *trip(p)er,* from Middle Dutch *trippen,* to hop.]

tripod *The device used by surveyors and cameramen is a very ancient invention. On this Greek vase, painted in the fifth century B.C., Hercules is shown holding a sacred tripod he has stolen from the Delphi oracle. On the right, the oracle's patron god, Apollo, pleads with him to return it.*

tri·pal·mi·tin (trī-păl'mə-tĭn) *n. Chemistry.* **Palmitin** *(see).*

tri·par·tite (trī-pär'tīt') *adj.* **1.** Composed of or divided into three parts. **2.** Pertaining to or executed by three parties. **3.** *Botany.* Divided into three parts. Said especially of leaves.

tri·par·ti·tion (trī'pär-tĭsh'ən) *n.* Division into three parts or among three parties: *the tripartition of a defeated nation.*

tripe (trīp) *n.* **1.** The pale, rubbery lining of the stomach of cattle or other ruminants, used as food. **2.** *Informal.* Anything with no meaning or value; rubbish or nonsense. [Middle English, from Old French *tripe*†.]

tri·ped·al (trī-pĕd'l) *adj.* Having three feet or legs; tripodal. [Latin *tripedālis* : *tri-,* three + *pēs* (stem *ped-*), foot.]

tri·pet·al·ous (trī-pĕt'l-əs) *adj. Botany.* Having three petals.

trip·ham·mer, trip hammer (trĭp'hăm'ər) *n.* A heavy power-operated hammer that is lifted by a cam or lever and then dropped.

tri·phen·yl·meth·ane (trī'fĕn'əl-mĕth'ān', trī'fē'nəl-) *n.* A colorless crystalline hydrocarbon, $(C_6H_5)_3CH$, from which a large number of synthetic dyes are derived by substitution.

tri·phib·i·ous (trī-fĭb'ē-əs) *adj.* Taking place on land, at sea, and in the air. Said of military operations. [TRI- + (AM)PHIBIOUS.]

triph·thong (trĭf'thông', -thŏng', trĭp'-) *n.* **1.** A compound vowel sound resulting from the combination of three simple ones and functioning as a unit. **2.** A **trigraph** *(see).* [TRI- + (DI)PHTHONG.] —**triph·thon·gal** (trĭf-thông'əl, -thŏng'əl, trĭp-) *adj.*

triph·y·lite (trĭf'ə-līt') *n.* Also **triph·y·line** (-lēn'). A vitreous bluish-gray mineral, $LiFePO_4$. [TRI- + Greek *phulon,* tribe (see **phyletic**) + -ITE (from its three bases).]

tri·pin·nate (trī-pĭn'āt') *adj. Botany.* Divided into leaflets that are subdivided into smaller, further subdivided leaflets or lobes, as are the fronds of some ferns. —**tri·pin·nate·ly** *adv.*

tri·plane (trī'plān') *n.* An airplane with wings placed above each other in three levels.

tri·ple (trĭp'əl) *adj.* **1.** Consisting of three parts; threefold. **2.** Three times as many or as much.
~*n.* **1.** A number or quantity three times as great as another. **2.** A group or set of three; a triad. **3.** *Baseball.* A three-base hit.
~*v.* **tripled, -pling, -ples.** —*tr.* To make three times as great in number or amount. —*intr.* **1.** To be or become three times as great in number or amount. **2.** *Baseball.* To make a three-base hit. [Middle English, from Old French, from Latin *triplus* : *tri-,* three + *-plus,* "-fold."] —**tri·ply** *adv.*

triptych *A triptych altarpiece, now in the Museum of Folklore in Basel, Switzerland.*

Triple Alliance *n.* An alliance among three countries, especially: **1.** The alliance of England, Sweden, and the Netherlands against France in 1668. **2.** The alliance of England, France, and the Netherlands against Spain in 1717, called the Quadruple Alliance when joined by Austria in 1718. **3.** The Dreibund formed by Germany, Austria, and Italy in 1882.

Triple Entente *n.* The military alliance formed by Great Britain, France, and Russia prior to World War I as a means of counterbalancing the Dreibund.

triple play *n. Baseball.* A rare defensive play in which three putouts, as two base runners and the batter, are executed during one turn at bat, thereby ending suddenly the offensive threat and the inning.

triple point *n. Physics.* The point at which the solid, liquid, and gas phases of a given substance are all in equilibrium with each other.

trip·let (trĭp'lĭt) *n.* **1.** A group or set of three of one kind. **2.** Any of three children born at one birth. **3.** In prosody, a **tercet** *(see).* **4.** A group of three musical notes having the time value of two notes of the same kind. **5.** *Physics.* A **multiplet** *(see)* with three components. [*Triple* + *doublet.*]

tri·ple·tail (trĭp'əl-tāl') *n.* Any of several chiefly marine fishes of the genus *Labotes*; especially, *L. surinamensis,* of North America, having prominent dorsal and anal fins that resemble extra tails.

triple time *n.* A musical time or rhythm having three beats in each bar, with the accent on the first beat. Also called "triple measure." —**tri·ple-time** (trĭp'əl-tīm') *adj.*

tri·ple-tongu·ing (trĭp'əl-tŭng'ĭng) *n.* The articulation of triplets in a fast tempo on a wind instrument by touching the tongue to the upper teeth or alveolar ridge as if to pronounce *t, k,* and *t* in succession. Compare **double-tonguing** and **single-tonguing.** —**tri·ple-tongue** *v.*

tri·plex (trĭp'lĕks', trī'plĕks') *adj.* Composed of three parts; threefold; triple. [Latin, threefold, triple.] —**tri·plex** *n.*

trip·li·cate (trĭp'lĭ-kĭt) *adj.* Threefold; especially, made with three identical copies.
~*n.* **1.** Any of a set of three identical objects or copies. **2.** The state of being in three copies: *The contract was in triplicate.*
~*tr.v.* (trĭp'lĭ-kāt') **triplicated, -cating, -cates.** **1.** To increase threefold; triple. **2.** To make three identical copies of. [Latin *triplicātus,* past participle of *triplicāre,* to triple, from *triplex* (stem *triplic-*), TRIPLEX.] —**trip·li·cate·ly** *adv.* —**trip·li·ca·tion** *n.*

tri·plic·i·ty (trī-plĭs'ə-tē, trī-) *n., pl.* **-ties.** **1.** The condition or quality of being triple. **2.** A group or set of three. **3.** In astrology, any of four groups of the zodiac, each consisting of three signs. In this sense, also called "trigon." [Middle English *triplicite,* a trigon, from Late Latin *triplicitās,* quality of being triple, from TRIPLEX.]

trip·lo·blas·tic (trĭp'lō-blăs'tĭk) *adj.* Having a body made up of three embryonic germ layers. Said of all animals except protozoans, sponges, and coelenterates. Compare **diploblastic.** [*Triplo-,* threefold, from Greek *triploos* + -BLAST + -IC.]

trip·loid (trĭp'loid') *adj.* Having three times the haploid number of chromosomes in each nucleus.
~*n.* An organism having such sets of chromosomes. [Greek *triploos,* triple + (HAPL)OID.]

tri·pod (trī'pŏd') *n.* **1.** A three-legged stool, table, or the like. **2.** An adjustable three-legged stand, as for supporting a camera. [Latin *tripūs* (stem *tripod-*), from Greek *tripous,* three-footed : *tri-,* three + *-pous,* -POD.] —**trip·o·dal** (trĭp'ə-dəl, trī'pŏd'l) *adj.*

trip·o·li (trĭp'ə-lē) *n.* A porous, lightweight, siliceous rock of various colors, used as an abrasive. [After TRIPOLI, Libya.]

Trip·o·li (trĭp'ə-lē). Capital and chief port of Libya. Founded by the Phoenicians, probably in the 7th century B.C., it was held in turn by the Romans, Vandals, Byzantines, and Arabs. It fell to the Ottoman Turks (1551) and was a stronghold of Barbary pirates (16th–19th centuries). The city was taken by the Italians (1910) and British (1943).

tri·pos (trī'pŏs') *n., pl.* **-poses.** At Cambridge University, England, any of the courses or examinations for the B.A. degree with honors. [Alteration of Latin *tripūs,* TRIPOD, from the stool on which an appointed bachelor of arts formerly sat at a graduation ceremony to deliver a humorous address.]

trip·per (trĭp'ər) *n.* **1.** *Chiefly British Informal.* One who takes a short pleasure trip. **2.** A tripping device on a mechanism.

trip·pet (trĭp'ĭt) *n.* A cam or projection in a mechanism designed to strike another part at regular intervals. [Middle English *tripet,* piece of wood used in a game, from *trippen,* to TRIP.]

trip·ping (trĭp'ĭng) *adj.* Moving or stepping lightly and briskly; easy; nimble. —**trip·ping·ly** *adv.*

trip·tane (trĭp'tān') *n.* A liquid hydrocarbon, C_7H_{16}, used as an antiknock additive in aviation fuels. [Short for *trimethylbutane.*]

trip·tych (trĭp'tĭk) *n.* **1.** A work of art consisting of three hinged or folding panels, especially one bearing a religious theme, used as an altarpiece. **2.** A hinged writing tablet consisting of three leaves, used in ancient times. [Greek *triptukhos,* threefold : *tri-,* three + *ptukhē,* fold (see **diptych**).]

trip·tyque (trĭp-tēk') *n.* A customs permit for the passage of a motor vehicle. [French, TRIPTYCH (referring to its three sections).]

trip·wire (trĭp'wīr') *n.* A wire that activates an alarm, trap, or the like when brushed in passing.

tri·que·trous (trī-kwē'trəs) *adj.* Triangular and acutely angled, especially in cross section: *a triquetrous stem.* Compare **trigonous.** [Latin *triquetrus,* three-cornered.]

tri·reme (trī'rēm') *n.* An ancient Greek or Roman galley or warship having three tiers of oars on each side. [Latin *trirēmis,* having three tiers of oars : *tri-,* three + *rēmus,* oar.]

tri·sac·cha·ride (trī-săk'ə-rīd', -rĭd) *n. Chemistry.* A carbohydrate that upon hydrolysis yields three monosaccharides.

tri·sect (trī'sĕkt', trī-sĕkt') *tr.v.* **-sected, -secting, -sects.** To divide into three usually equal parts. [TRI- + -SECT.] —**tri·sec·tion** *n.* —**tri·sec·tor** *n.*

tri·sep·al·ous (trī-sĕp'ə-ləs) *adj.* Having three sepals.

tri·skel·i·on (trī-skĕl'ē-ən, trĭs-kĕl'-) *n., pl.* **-ia** (-ē-ə). Also **tri·skele, tri·scele** (trī'skēl', trĭs'kēl'). A figure consisting of three curved lines or branches, or three stylized human arms or legs, radiating from a common center. [New Latin, from Greek *triskelēs,* three-legged : *tri-,* three + *skelos,* leg.]

tris·mus (trĭz'məs) *n. Pathology.* See **lockjaw** (sense 2). [Greek *trismos, trigmos,* a scream, a grating (of the teeth).] —**tris·mic** *adj.*

tris·oc·ta·he·dron (trĭs'ŏk'tə-hē'drən) *n., pl.* **-drons** or **-dra** (-drə). **1.** In geometry, a solid figure having 24 congruent triangular faces and an octahedron as a base. **2.** In crystallography, a **trapezohedron** *(see).* [Greek *tris,* thrice + OCTAHEDRON.] —**tris·oc·ta·he·dral** *adj.*

tri·so·di·um (trī-sō'dē-əm) *adj.* Containing three sodium atoms.

tri·so·mic (trī-sō'mĭk) *adj. Genetics.* Having one chromosome represented three times in an otherwise diploid set. [TRI- + (CHROMO)SOM(E) + -IC.] —**tri·some** (trī'sōm') *n.*

Tris·tan (trĭs'tən, -tăn', -tän'). Also **Tris·tram** (trĭs'trəm). A hero of medieval legend who fell in love with Iseult, the bride of King Mark of Cornwall, after they accidentally drank a love potion.

Tris·tan da Cu·nha (trĭs'tən də ko͞o'nə). Group of volcanic islands in the South Atlantic. Only one of the four, Tristan, is inhabited, by fewer than 300 people, descendants of a British garrison posted here in 1816 when Napoleon was exiled to St. Helena, of which the group is a dependency. Edinburgh is the capital.

tri·ste·a·rin (trī-stē'ər-ĭn) *n. Chemistry.* See **stearin** (sense 1).

trist·ful (trĭst'fəl) *adj.* Also **triste** (trĭst, trēst). *Archaic.* Sorrowful; gloomy. [Middle English *trist,* from Old French *triste,* from Latin *trīstis*†, gloomy.] —**trist·ful·ly** *adv.* —**trist·ful·ness** *n.*

tris·tich (trĭs'tĭk) *n.* A stanza or strophic unit of three lines. [TRI- + (DI)STICH.] —**tri·stich·ic** (trĭ-stĭk'ĭk) *adj.*

tri·stim·u·lus (trī-stĭm'yə-ləs) *adj.* Of or pertaining to the values of the three primary colors that when combined additively produce a color to match the color of an unknown sample.

tri·sul·fide, tri·sul·phide (trī-sŭl′fīd′) *n.* Also **tri·sul·fid, tri·sul·phid** (-fĭd). A sulfide containing three sulfur atoms per molecule.

tri·syl·la·ble (trī′sĭl′ə-bəl, trī-sĭl′ə-bəl) *n.* A word consisting of three syllables. —**tri·syl·lab·ic** (trī′sĭ-lăb′ĭk) *adj.*

tri·ta·no·pi·a (trī′tə-nō′pē-ə) *n.* A rare visual defect involving an inability to distinguish the color blue. [New Latin, "ability to see only one third" : Greek *tritos,* a third + *anopia,* blindness : AN- (not) + -OPIA.] —**tri·ta·nop·ic** (trī′tə-nŏp′ĭk) *adj.*

trite (trīt) *adj.* **triter, tritest.** **1.** Overused and commonplace; lacking interest or originality. **2.** *Archaic.* Frayed or worn by use. [Latin *trītus,* past participle of *terere,* to rub (away), wear out.] —**trite·ly** *adv.* —**trite·ness** *n.*

Synonyms: *banal, commonplace, hackneyed, shopworn, stale, stereotyped, threadbare.*

tri·the·ism (trī′thē-ĭz′əm) *n.* A belief in three gods; specifically, the belief that the Father, Son, and Holy Ghost are three separate and distinct gods. —**tri·the·ist** *n.* —**tri·the·is·tic** (trī′thē-ĭs′tĭk) *adj.*

trit·i·ate (trĭt′ē-āt′, trĭsh′ē-) *tr.v.* **-ated, -ating, -ates.** To treat with tritium; especially, to replace the hydrogen atoms in (a molecule) by tritium atoms for labeling. [TRITI(UM) + -ATE.] —**trit·i·a·tion** *n.*

trit·i·ca·le (trĭt′ĭ-kä′lē) *n.* A fertile, hybrid cereal obtained by crossing wheat and rye. [Latin *triticum,* wheat + *secale,* rye.]

trit·i·um (trĭt′ē-əm, trĭsh′ē-əm) *n.* A rare radioactive hydrogen isotope with atomic mass 3 and half-life 12.5 years, prepared artificially for use as a tracer and as a constituent of hydrogen bombs. [New Latin, from Greek *tritos,* third.]

tri·ton¹ (trīt′n) *n.* Any of various chiefly tropical marine gastropod mollusks of the genus *Cymatium* and related genera, having a pointed, spirally twisted, often colorfully marked shell. [After TRITON, whose trumpet is a shell.]

tri·ton² (trī′tŏn′) *n.* The nucleus of a tritium atom consisting of two neutrons and one proton. [TRIT(IUM) + -ON.]

Tri·ton (trīt′n). *n.* **1.** *Greek Mythology.* **a.** A god of the sea, son of Poseidon and Amphitrite, portrayed as having the head and trunk of a man and the tail of a fish. **b.** Any of a race of lesser sea deities. **2.** The larger satellite of the planet Neptune. [Latin, from Greek *Tritōn.*]

tri·tone (trī′tōn′) *n. Music.* An interval composed of three whole tones. [Greek *tritonos,* having three tones : TRI- + TONE.]

trit·u·rate (trĭch′ə-rāt′) *tr.v.* **-rated, -rating, -rates.** To crush, grind, or pound into fine particles or a powder; pulverize. ~*n.* (trĭch′ər-ĭt). A triturated substance, especially a powdered drug. Also called "trituration." [Late Latin *trītūrāre,* to pulverize corn, from Latin *trītūra,* a rubbing or chafing, from *trītus,* past participle of *terere,* to rub.] —**trit·u·ra·ble** (trĭch′ər-ə-bəl) *adj.*

trit·u·ra·tion (trĭch′ə-rā′shən) *n.* **1.** The act or process of triturating something. **2.** A triturate. **3.** The composing of a dental amalgam by mortar and pestle.

tri·umph (trī′əmf) *intr.v.* **-umphed, -umphing, -umphs.** **1.** To be victorious or successful; win; prevail. **2.** To rejoice over a success or victory; exult. **3.** In ancient Rome, to receive honors upon return from a victory. ~*n.* **1.** The instance or fact of being victorious; success. **2.** A remarkable achievement or feat. **3.** Exultation or merriment derived from victory or success. **4.** A public celebration in ancient Rome to welcome a returning victorious commander and his army. [Middle English, from Old French *triumphe(r),* from Latin *triumphāre,* from *triumphus,* a triumph, variant of Old Latin *triumpus,* probably from Greek *thriambos,* hymn to Bacchus.] —**tri·umph·er** *n.*

tri·um·phal (trī-ŭm′fəl) *adj.* **1.** Pertaining to or having the nature of a triumph. **2.** Celebrating or commemorating a victory: *a triumphal procession; a triumphal arch.* —See Usage note at **triumphant.**

tri·um·phant (trī-ŭm′fənt) *adj.* **1.** Exulting in success or victory. **2.** Victorious; conquering; successful. —**tri·um·phant·ly** *adv.*

Usage: *Triumphant* and *triumphal* are not usually interchangeable. *Triumphant* now generally means exulting in success or victory: *The football team returned home triumphant. Triumphal* is a more specific term, describing the formal celebration of a triumph: *There was a triumphal procession to mark the navy's return.*

tri·um·vir (trī-ŭm′vər) *n., pl.* **-virs** or **-vir·i** (-və-rī′). Any of three men sharing public administration or civil authority, as in ancient Rome. [Latin, singular of *triumvirī,* from *trium virōrum,* "(one) of three men," genitive of *trēs virī,* three men.] —**tri·um·vi·ral** *adj.*

tri·um·vi·rate (trī-ŭm′vər-ĭt) *n.* **1.** A group of three men jointly governing a realm. **2. a.** The office or term of a triumvir. **b.** Government by triumvirs. **3.** Any association or group of three. [Latin *triumvirātus,* from *triumvir,* TRIUMVIR.]

tri·une (trī′yōōn′) *adj.* Being three in one. Said especially of the single Godhead of the Trinity. ~*n.* **1.** A trinity. **2. Triune.** The holy Trinity. [TRI- + Latin *ūnus,* one.]

tri·u·ni·ty (trī-yōō′nə-tē) *n., pl.* **-ties.** See **trinity** (sense 2).

tri·va·lent (trī-vā′lənt) *adj.* Also **ter·va·lent** (tər-vā′lənt, tûr′vā′lənt). *Chemistry.* **1.** Having a valence of 3. **2.** Having three valences. —**tri·va·lence, tri·va·len·cy** *n.*

tri·valve (trī′vălv′) *adj.* Having three valves.

triv·et (trĭv′ĭt) *n.* **1.** A three-legged stand made of iron or a similar metal, used for supporting cooking vessels in a fireplace. **2.** A metal stand with short feet, used under a hot dish on a table. [Middle English *trevet,* probably Old English *trefet,* from Latin *tripēs,* "three-footed" : *tri-,* three + *pēs,* foot.]

triv·i·a¹ (trĭv′ē-ə) *pl.n.* Insignificant or inessential matters; trifles. [New Latin, *trivia,* "that which comes from the street," from Latin,

plural of *trivium,* place where three roads meet, public square. See **trivium.**]

triv·i·a². Plural of **trivium.**

triv·i·al (trĭv′ē-əl) *adj.* **1.** Of little importance or significance; trifling. **2.** Ordinary; commonplace. **3.** Concerned with or involving trivia. **4.** *Mathematics.* Having or pertaining to solutions with zero values. **5.** Of or pertaining to the trivium. [Latin *triviālis,* pertaining to the TRIVIUM (hence, commonplace, of little account; sense development perhaps influenced by later scorn for medieval learning).] —**triv·i·al·ly** *adv.*

Synonyms: *paltry, petty, trifling.*

triv·i·al·i·ty (trĭv′ē-ăl′ə-tē) *n., pl.* **-ties.** **1.** The condition or quality of being trivial. **2.** A trivial matter, idea, or occurrence.

triv·i·al·ize (trĭv′ē-ə-līz′) *tr.v.* **-ized, -izing, -izes.** To make trivial; devalue. —**triv·i·al·i·za·tion** *n.*

trivial name *n.* **1.** In taxonomic nomenclature, the term following the genus name and designating the species, as *troglodytes* in *Pan troglodytes,* the chimpanzee. **2.** A vernacular name as distinguished from a taxonomic designation. **3.** *Chemistry.* A name for a compound that is not systematic and gives no indication of the compound's molecular structure, such as *toluene* for *methylbenzene.*

triv·i·um (trĭv′ē-əm) *n., pl.* **-ia** (-ē-ə). The first division of the seven liberal arts in medieval schools, consisting of grammar, logic, and rhetoric. Compare **quadrivium.** [Medieval Latin, from Latin, place where three roads meet : *tri-,* three + *via,* road, way.]

tri·week·ly (trī-wēk′lē) *adj.* Happening, done, or appearing: **1.** Three times a week. **2.** Every three weeks. ~*adv.* **1.** Three times a week. **2.** Every three weeks. ~*n., pl.* **triweeklies.** A periodical published triweekly.

-trix *suffix.* Indicates: **1.** Feminine agency, corresponding to masculine or common nouns in *-tor;* for example, **testatrix. 2.** A geometric line, point, or surface; for example, **directrix.** [Latin *-trix* (stem *-tric-*).]

t RNA *n.* **Transfer RNA** (see).

Tro·as (trō′ăs′). Also **Tro·ad** (-ăd′). Region around ancient Troy, on the northwestern coast of Asia Minor, in present-day northwestern Turkey, scene of the events in the *Iliad.*

Tro·bri·and Islands (trō′brē-änd′). Archipelago lying off Papua New Guinea, by which the islands are administered. The chief island is Kirwana (or Trobriand).

tro·car (trō′kär′) *n.* A sharp-pointed surgical instrument within a cannula, used to puncture a body cavity and remove fluid. [French *trocart,* "three-sided instrument" (referring to its triangular shape) : *trois,* three + *carre,* side.]

tro·cha·ic (trō-kā′ĭk) *adj.* Of, pertaining to, or consisting of trochees. ~*n.* A trochaic metrical foot, line of verse, or poem. [French *trochaïque,* from Latin *trochaicus,* from Greek *trokhaikos,* from *trokhaios.* See **trochee.**]

tro·chal (trō′kəl) *adj.* Shaped like a wheel: *the trochal disk of a rotifer.* [Greek *trokhos,* wheel, from *trekhein,* to run.]

tro·chan·ter (trō-kăn′tər) *n.* **1.** Any of several bony processes on the upper part of the femur of many vertebrates. **2.** The second proximal segment of the leg of an insect. [Greek *trokhantēr,* from *trekhein,* to run. See **trochal.**]

tro·che (trō′kē) *n.* A small circular medicinal lozenge; a pastille. [Earlier *trochies* (plural), from Middle English *trociske* (singular), from Late Latin *trochiscus,* from Greek *trokhiskos,* diminutive of *trokhos,* wheel. See **trochal.**]

tro·chee (trō′kē) *n.* A metrical foot consisting of one long or stressed syllable followed by one short or unstressed syllable. There are four trochees in the following line: *Peter, Peter, pumpkin eater.* Also called "trochaic." Compare **iamb.** [Latin, from Greek *trokhaios (pous),* running (foot), from *trekhein,* to run.]

troch·le·a (trŏk′lē-ə) *n., pl.* **-leae** (-lē-ē′). An anatomical structure that resembles a pulley, such as the part of the distal end of the humerus that articulates with the ulna. [Latin, system of pulleys, from Greek *trokhileia.*]

troch·le·ar (trŏk′lē-ər) *adj.* **1.** Of, resembling, or situated near a trochlea. **2.** Of or pertaining to the trochlear nerve. **3.** *Botany.* Shaped like a pulley. ~*n.* The trochlear nerve.

trochlear nerve *n.* Either of the fourth pair of cranial nerves that supplies the superior oblique muscle of the eyeball. Also called "trochlear."

tro·choid (trō′koid′, trŏk′oid′) *adj.* Also **tro·choi·dal** (trō-koid′l, trŏk-oid′l). **1.** Capable of or exhibiting rotation about a central axis. **2.** Permitting rotation, as does a pulley or pivot. ~*n. Geometry.* A plane curve formed by the locus of a point on the radius or on an extension of the radius of a circle as the circle rolls along a fixed straight line. [Greek *trokhoeidēs,* resembling a wheel, wheellike, circular : *trokhos,* wheel (see **troche**) + -OID.] —**tro·choi·dal·ly** *adv.*

troch·o·phore (trŏk′ə-fôr′, -fōr′) *n.* The small aquatic larva of various invertebrates, including certain mollusks and annelids. [Greek *trokhos,* wheel (see **troche**) + -PHORE (from its spheroidal body and ring of cilia).]

trod. Past tense and alternate past participle of **tread.**

trod·den. Past participle of **tread.**

trode. *Archaic.* Past tense of **tread.**

trof·fer (trŏf′ər, trô′fər) *n.* An inverted, usually metal trough suspended from a ceiling as a fixture for fluorescent lighting tubes. [Alteration of TROUGH.]

trogon *There are more than 30 species of trogon, an insect-eating bird mostly native to the tropical forests of the Americas, Africa, and Asia. The copper-tailed trogon (above) is the only species found in the United States.*

trompe l'oeil *A section of Peruzzi's painting* View of Rome *illustrates the artistic device called* trompe l'oeil, *a French phrase meaning literally "deceives the eye."*

trog (trôg, trŏg) *intr.v.* **trogged, trogging, trogs.** *British Informal.* To trudge; plod wearily. [TRUDGE + SLOG.]

trog·lo·dyte (trŏg'lə-dīt') *n.* **1.** A prehistoric cave dweller. **2.** A person likened to a caveman, as in reclusiveness or brutishness. **3.** An anthropoid ape, such as the gorilla. [Latin *Trōglodyta,* from Greek *Trōglodutēs,* singular of *Trōglodutai,* variant (influenced by *trōglos,* cave, and *-dutai,* those who enter) of *Trōgodutai*†, name of an Ethiopian people.] **—trog·lo·dyt·ic** (trŏg'lə-dĭt'ĭk), **trog·lo·dyt·i·cal** *adj.*

tro·gon (trō'gŏn') *n.* Any of various colorful tropical birds of the family Trogonidae, which includes the quetzal. [New Latin, "gnawer," from Greek *trōgōn,* present participle of *trōgein,* to gnaw.]

troi·ka (troi'kə) *n.* **1. a.** A kind of small Russian carriage drawn by a team of three horses abreast. **b.** A team of three horses abreast. **2.** A triumvirate. [Russian *troyka,* from *troye,* three (collectively).]

Troi·lus (troi'ləs, trō'ə-ləs). *Greek Mythology.* A son of Priam of Troy, killed by Achilles. He is depicted as Cressida's lover in medieval romance.

Tro·jan (trō'jən) *n.* **1.** A native or inhabitant of ancient Troy. **2.** A person of courageous determination or energy.
~adj. Of or pertaining to ancient Troy or its residents. [Middle English, from Latin *Trōjānus,* from *Trōjā,* TROY.]

Trojan horse *n.* **1.** *Greek Mythology.* The hollow wooden horse in which the Greeks hid and gained entrance to Troy, later opening the gates to their army. In this sense, also called "Wooden Horse." **2.** Any subversive group or device insinuated within enemy ranks.

Trojan War *n.* *Greek Mythology.* The prehistoric ten-year war waged against Troy by the confederated Greeks, ending in the burning of Troy. It is known chiefly through Homeric legend, which gives the cause as the abduction of the Spartan queen, Helen, by Paris, a Trojan prince.

troll[1] (trōl) *v.* **trolled, trolling, trolls.** *—tr.* **1.** To fish for by trailing a baited line from behind a slowly moving boat. **2.** To trail (a baited line) in fishing. **3.** To sing in succession the parts of (a round, for example). **4.** To sing heartily: *troll a carol.* **5.** To roll or revolve. *—intr.* **1.** To fish by trailing a line, as from a moving boat. **2.** To sing heartily or gaily. **3.** To be sung or uttered in a rolling, hearty manner: *The tune trolled on.* **4.** To roll or spin around. **5.** To wander about; stroll. Often used with *along.*
~n. **1.** The act of trolling for fish. **2.** A lure used for trolling, such as a spoon or spinner. [Middle English *trollen*†, to ramble, roll.]

troll[2] *n.* A supernatural creature of Scandinavian folklore variously portrayed as a friendly or mischievous dwarf, or sometimes a dangerous giant, that lives in caves, in the hills, or under bridges. [Old Norse *troll*†, monster, demon.]

trol·ley (trŏl'ē) *n., pl.* **-leys. 1.** A **streetcar** *(see).* **2.** A wheeled carriage, cage, or basket that is suspended from and travels on an overhead track. **3.** A device that collects electric current from an underground conductor, an overhead wire, or a third rail, and transmits it to the motor of an electric vehicle. **4.** A small truck or car operating on a track and used in a mine, quarry, or factory for conveying materials. **5.** *Chiefly British.* A cart.
~v. **trolleyed, -leying, -leys.** *—tr.* To convey by trolley. *—intr.* To travel by trolley. [Probably from TROLL (to move about).]

trolley bus *n.* An electric bus that does not run on tracks and is powered by electricity from an overhead wire.

trolley car *n.* A streetcar *(see).*

trol·lop (trŏl'əp) *n.* **1.** A slovenly, untidy woman. **2.** A loose woman; a strumpet. [17th century : perhaps from TRULL.]

Trol·lope (trŏl'əp), **Anthony** (1815–82). British novelist. His ecclesiastical novels set in the imaginary county of Barsetshire include *The Warden* (1885), *Barchester Towers* (1857), and *The Last Chronicle of Barset* (1867). Among his novels dealing with political life are *Phineas Finn* (1869) and *The Eustace Diamonds* (1873).

trom·bic·u·li·a·sis (trŏm-bĭk'yə-lī'ə-sĭs) *n.* Also **trom·bic·u·lo·sis** (-lō'sĭs), **trom·bi·di·a·sis** (trŏm'bə-dī'ə-sĭs). *Pathology.* Infestation with mites of the genus *Trombicula,* which if untreated results in severe dermatitis. [New Latin : *Trombicula,* genus of mites, diminutive of *Trombidium*† + -IASIS.]

trom·bone (trŏm-bōn', trəm-, trŏm'bōn') *n.* **1.** A brass musical instrument consisting of a long cylindrical tube bent upon itself twice, ending in a bell-shaped mouth, and having a movable U-shaped slide for producing different pitches. **2.** A member of an orchestra who plays the trombone. [French, from Italian, augmentative of *tromba,* trumpet, from Old High German *trumpa,* TRUMP.] **—trom·bon·ist** *n.*

trom·mel (trŏm'əl) *n.* A revolving cylindrical sieve used for sizing rock and ore. [German *Trommel,* barrel, drum, from Middle High German *trummel,* from *trumme,* drum, akin to Middle Dutch *tromme,* DRUM.]

tromp (trŏmp) *v.* **tromped, tromping, tromps.** *Informal.* *—intr.* To walk heavily and noisily; tramp. *—tr.* **1.** To trample underfoot. **2.** To defeat soundly; trounce. **—tromp on.** *Informal.* To abuse verbally. [Alteration of TRAMP.]

trompe (trŏmp) *n.* An apparatus in which water falling through a perforated pipe entrains air into and down the pipe to produce an air blast for a furnace or forge. [French, "trumpet," from Old French. See **trump** (trumpet).]

trompe l'oeil (trômp loi') *n.* **1.** A technique of depicting objects so realistically that the viewer is tricked into believing they really exist in three dimensions. **2.** A trick painting in this style, such as a window frame on a sheer brick wall. [French, "deceive the eye."]

tron (trŏn) *n.* Also **trone** (trōn). *Scottish.* A bulk weighing machine for merchandise. [Middle English, from Old French *trone,* from Latin *trutina,* from Greek *trutanē,* balance, pair of scales.]

-tron *suffix.* Indicates: **1.** A vacuum tube; for example, **dynatron. 2.** A device for manipulating subatomic particles; for example, **cyclotron.** [Greek, suffix denoting instrument.]

tro·na (trō'nə) *n.* A natural vitreous gray or white mineral, $Na_2CO_3 \cdot NaHCO_3 \cdot 2H_2O$, used as a source of sodium compounds. [Swedish, probably from Arabic *trōn,* short for *naṭrūn,* natron.]

Trond·heim (trŏn'hām'). Formerly **Ni·da·ros** (nē'dä-rōs'). Seaport of central Norway. Founded (997) on the south side of Trondheim Fjord, it is an important fishing center.

troop (tro͞op) *n. Abbr.* **trp. 1.** A group or company of people, animals, or things. **2.** *Military.* **a.** A division of a cavalry unit, commanded by a captain. **b.** A group of soldiers. **3. troops.** Military units; soldiers. **4.** A unit of at least five Boy Scouts or Girl Scouts under the guidance of an adult leader. **5.** *Informal.* A great many; a lot.
~intr.v. **trooped, trooping, troops. 1.** To move or go as a throng. **2.** To proceed; move along: *children trooping home.* **3.** To consort; associate. Used with *with.* [French *troupe,* back-formation from *troupeau,* herd, from Medieval Latin *troppus*†.]

troop carrier *n.* A vehicle, aircraft, or ship built to carry troops.

troop·er (tro͞o'pər) *n.* **1. a.** A cavalryman. **b.** A cavalry horse. **2.** A mounted police officer. **3.** A state police officer.

troop·ship (tro͞op'shĭp') *n.* A ship, often one that has been modified or converted, for carrying troops.

troost·ite (tro͞o'stīt') *n.* A reddish mineral, a variety of **willemite** *(see),* in which the zinc is partly replaced by manganese. [After Gerald *Troost* (1776–1850), U.S. geologist.]

trop. tropic; tropical.

tro·pae·o·lum (trō-pē'ə-ləm) *n., pl.* **-lums** or **-la** (-lə). Any trailing or climbing succulent plant of the South American genus *Tropaeolum;* especially, the garden nasturtium, *T. majus,* which has orange, yellow, or red spurred flowers and smooth leaves. [New Latin, from Latin *tropaeum,* TROPHY (referring to the leaves and flowers, which resemble shields and helmets).]

trope (trōp) *n.* **1.** The figurative use of a word or expression; a figure of speech. **2.** A word or phrase interpolated as an embellishment in the sung parts of certain medieval liturgies. [Latin *tropus,* from Greek *tropos,* a turn, way, manner, from *trepein,* to turn.]

-trope *suffix.* Indicates: **1.** Orientation or development toward; for example, **heliotrope. 2.** A version; for example, **allotrope.** [Greek *tropos,* turn, turning, from *trepein,* to turn.]

troph·al·lax·is (trŏf'ə-lăk'sĭs, trō'fə-) *n.* The mutual exchange of food between adults and larvae that occurs among certain social insects such as ants and wasps. [New Latin, from TROPHO- + Greek *allaxis,* exchange, from *allassein,* to change.]

tro·phic (trō'fĭk, trŏf'ĭk) *adj.* Of or pertaining to nutrition or to the nutritive processes. [Greek *trophikos,* nursing, from *trophē,* food, from *trephein,* to nourish.] **—tro·phi·cal·ly** *adv.*

trophic level *n. Ecology.* A group of organisms that occupy the same position in a food chain in that they obtain their food, ultimately from plants, by the same number of steps.

tropho- *prefix.* Indicates nutrition; for example, **trophoblast.** [Greek *trophē,* food, from *trephein,* to nourish.]

tro·pho·blast (trō'fə-blăst', -bläst') *n.* The outermost layer of cells of the morula that attaches the fertilized ovum to the wall of the mammalian uterus and acts as a nutritive pathway. Also called "trophoderm." [TROPHO- + -BLAST.] **—tro·pho·blas·tic** (trō'fə-blăs'tĭk-) *adj.*

tro·pho·zo·ite (trō'fə-zō'īt') *n.* A protozoan of the class Sporozoa in the active feeding stage. [TROPHO- + ZO(O)- + -ITE.]

tro·phy (trō'fē) *n., pl.* **-phies. 1.** A prize or memento, such as a cup or plaque, received as a symbol of victory, especially in sports. **2.** An accumulation of captured arms or other spoils kept as a memorial of victory. **3.** A specimen or part, such as a lion's head, preserved as a token of a successful hunt. **4.** In ancient Greece and Rome, the captured arms and spoils of a defeated enemy set up as a memorial, often on the field of battle. **5.** *Architecture.* A marble carving or bronze casting depicting a group of weapons or armor placed upon a four-sided or circular base as an ornament. **6.** A memento, as of one's personal achievements. [Old French *trophee,* from Latin *trophaeum,* from Greek *tropaion,* "monument of the enemy's defeat," from *tropaios,* of turning, of defeat, from *tropē,* a turn, repulse of the enemy. See **trope.**]

-trophy *suffix.* Indicates a specified type of nutrition or growth; for example, **hypertrophy.** [New Latin *-trophia,* from Greek, from *trophē,* food. See **tropho-.**]

trop·ic (trŏp'ĭk) *n. Abbr.* **trop. 1.** *Astronomy.* Either of two circles on the celestial sphere parallel to and at an angular distance of 23° 27' from the equator and forming the limits of the apparent northern and southern passages of the sun. **2.** *Geography.* Either of the two corresponding parallels of latitude on the earth that constitute the boundaries of the Torrid Zone. See **tropic of Cancer, tropic of Capricorn. 3. tropics.** The region of the earth's surface lying between these latitudes; the Torrid Zone.
~adj. Of or pertaining to the tropics; tropical. [Middle English *tropik,* solstice point at which the sun "turns" back and moves toward the earth, from Late Latin *tropicus,* from Greek *tropikos,* of turning, from *tropē,* a turn. See **trope.**]

-tropic *suffix.* Indicates turning in response to a specified stimulus; for example, **phototropic.** [Greek *tropos,* a turn, TROPE.]

trop·i·cal¹ (trŏp′ĭ-kəl) *adj.* *Abbr.* **trop.** **1.** Of, indigenous to, or characteristic of the tropics. **2.** Hot and humid; sultry; torrid. **—trop·i·cal·ly** *adv.*

tro·pi·cal² (trō′pĭ-kəl, trŏp′ĭ-) *adj.* Of or pertaining to a rhetorical trope.

tropical cyclone *n.* A very low pressure area 80 to 160 kilometers (50 to 100 miles) in radius that originates in tropical regions and is frequently marked by winds of hurricane strength circulating around the calm eye in the center of the region.

tropical fish *n.* Any of various small, brightly colored fishes native to tropical waters and often kept in home aquariums.

trop·i·cal·ize (trŏp′ĭ-kə-līz′) *tr.v.* **-ized, -izing, -izes. 1.** To make tropical. **2.** To make suitable for a tropical climate, as by adapting to tropical temperatures.

tropical storm *n.* A tropical cyclone having winds ranging from 48 kilometers (30 miles) to 160 kilometers (75 miles) per hour.

tropical year *n.* The time interval between two successive passages of the sun through the vernal equinox; the calendar year, or 365.2422 mean solar days. Also called "solar year." See **year.**

trop·ic·bird (trŏp′ĭk-bûrd′) *n.* Any of several predominantly white sea birds of the genus *Phaëthon,* of warm regions, having a pair of long, slender, projecting tail feathers.

tropic of Cancer *n.* The parallel of latitude 23° 30′ north of the equator, the northern boundary of the Torrid Zone, and the most northerly latitude at which the sun reaches an altitude of 90°.

tropic of Capricorn *n.* The parallel of latitude 23° 30′ south of the equator, the southern boundary of the Torrid Zone, and the most southerly latitude at which the sun reaches an altitude of 90°.

tro·pine (trō′pēn′, -pĭn) *n.* Also **tro·pin** (-pĭn). A white, crystalline, poisonous alkaloid, $C_8H_{15}NO$, having an odor like that of tobacco and used to treat spasms. [Short for ATROPINE.]

tro·pism (trō′pĭz′əm) *n.* *Biology.* The directional growth movement of a plant part in response to an external stimulus. Also called "tropic movement." [Greek *tropos,* turn (see **-trope**) + -ISM.] **—tro·pis·mat·ic** (trō′pĭz-măt′ĭk), **tro·pis·tic** (trō-pĭs′tĭk) *adj.*

-tropism *suffix.* Indicates the growth of a plant part in response to a specified stimulus; for example, **phototropism.** [Greek *tropos,* turn. See **tropo-.**]

tropo- *prefix.* Indicates turning or change, especially change of temperature or condition; for example, **troposphere.** [Greek *tropos,* a turn, change.]

tro·pol·o·gy (trō-pŏl′ə-jē) *n., pl.* **-gies. 1.** The use of tropes in speech or writing. **2.** A mode of Biblical scholarship insisting on the morally edifying interpretation of tropes in Scripture. [Late Latin *tropologia,* from Late Greek : Greek *tropos,* TROPE + -LOGY.] **—tro·po·log·ic** (trŏ′pə-lŏj′ĭk, trŏp′ə-), **tro·po·log·i·cal** *adj.* **—tro·po·log·i·cal·ly** *adv.*

tro·po·pause (trō′pə-pôz′, trŏp′ə-) *n.* The boundary between the upper troposphere and the lower stratosphere that varies in altitude from 8 kilometers (5 miles) at the poles to 16 kilometers (10 miles) at the equator.

tro·po·phyte (trō′pə-fīt′, trŏp′ə-) *n.* A plant adapted to changeable climatic conditions. **—tro·po·phyt·ic** (trō′pə-fĭt′ĭk, trŏp′ə-) *adj.*

tro·po·sphere (trō′pə-sfîr′, trŏp′ə-) *n.* The lowest region of the atmosphere between the earth's surface and the tropopause, characterized by decreasing temperature with increasing altitude. **—tro·po·spher·ic** (trō′pə-sfîr′ĭk, -sfĕr′ĭk, trŏp′ə-) *adj.*

-tropous *suffix.* Indicates a turning away; for example, **amphitropous, anatropous.** [Greek *-tropos,* of turning, from *trepein,* to turn.]

trop·po (trŏ′pō) *adv.* *Music.* Too much. Usually used with the negative in the cautionary phrase *ma non troppo,* as a direction: *allegro ma non troppo.* [Italian.]

-tropy *suffix.* Indicates the condition of turning; for example, **allotropy, thixotropy.** [Greek *-tropia,* from *-tropos,* -TROPOUS.]

trot (trŏt) *n.* **1.** The gait of a horse or other four-footed animal, between a walk and a canter in speed, in which diagonal pairs of legs move forward together. **2.** A ride on a horse at this pace. **3.** A human gait faster than a walk; a jog. **4.** A race for trotters. **5.** *Archaic.* An old woman; crone. **6.** *Informal.* A literal translation used by a student. **7. trots.** *Slang.* Diarrhea. Used with *the.*
~v. **trotted, trotting, trots.** *—intr.* **1.** To go or move at a trot. **2. a.** To proceed rapidly; hurry. **b.** To go; move. Often used with *along.* **3.** To fish in a fast-moving current using a weighted line. *—tr.* To cause to move at a trot. **—trot out.** *Informal.* To bring out and show for or as if for inspection or admiration. [Middle English, from Old French, from *troter,* to trot, from Vulgar Latin *trottāre* (unattested), from Frankish *trottōn* (unattested).]

troth (trôth, trŏth, trōth) *n.* **1.** Good faith; fidelity. **2.** One's pledged fidelity; especially, a betrothal: *plight one's troth.*
~tr.v. **trothed, trothing, troths.** *Archaic.* To pledge or betroth. [Middle English *trouth(e),* Old English *trēowth,* TRUTH.]

troth·plight (trôth′plīt′, trŏth′-, trōth′-) *n.* *Archaic.* A betrothal.
~tr.v. **trothplighted, -plighting, -plights.** *Archaic.* To betroth. [Middle English *trouth plight* : TROTH + PLIGHT (pledge).]

trot·line (trŏt′līn′) *n.* A fishing line, a **setline** *(see).* [Perhaps TROT (to run) + LINE.]

Trot·sky (trŏt′skē), **Leon,** born Lev Davidovich Bronstein (1879–1940). Russian revolutionary. He was one of the leaders of the Bolshevik Revolution (1917). His policy for permanent revolution led to dismissal from the Politburo by Stalin (1926) and eventual exile from Russia (1929). He moved to Mexico (1937), where he was assassinated three years later.

Trot·sky·ism (trŏt′skē-ĭz′əm) *n.* The theories of Communism advocated by Leon Trotsky and his followers, who argued for the permanent worldwide revolution of the proletariat and bitterly opposed the leadership of Stalin. **—Trot·sky·ist, Trot·sky·ite** *adj.* & *n.*

trot·ter (trŏt′ər) *n.* **1.** A horse that trots; especially, one trained for harness racing. **2.** *Informal.* A foot; especially, the foot of a pig prepared as food.

trotter *A trotter is a horse that has been trained to race competitively without breaking into a canter or a gallop while drawing a sulky. The sport of harness racing is especially popular in the United States.*

trou·ba·dour (trōō′bə-dôr′, -dōr′, -dŏŏr′) *n.* **1.** Any of a class of lyric poets of the 12th and 13th centuries attached to the courts of Provence and northern Italy, who composed songs in complex metrical forms. Compare **trouvère. 2.** A strolling minstrel. [French, from Old Provençal *trobador,* from *trobar,* to invent, compose poetry, variant of Old French *trover.* See **trouvère.**]

troub·le (trŭb′əl) *n.* **1.** A state of distress, affliction, danger, or need. **2.** Something that contributes to such a state; a difficulty or problem: *One trouble after another delayed the job.* **3.** Exertion; effort; pains: *went to a lot of trouble.* **4.** A condition of pain, disease, or malfunction: *heart trouble.* **—in trouble.** *Informal.* **1.** At a disadvantage. **2.** Due to be admonished or punished: *in big trouble with the boss.* **3.** Pregnant out of wedlock.
~v. **troubled, -ling, -les.** *—tr.* **1.** To agitate; stir up: *troubled waters.* **2.** To afflict with pain or discomfort. **3.** To cause distress or confusion in; vex; perturb. **4.** To inconvenience; bother: *Please don't trouble yourself. May I trouble you to close the window?* *—intr.* To take pains: *They trouble over every detail.* [Middle English, from Old French, from *troubler,* to trouble, from Vulgar Latin *turbulāre,* from *turbulus,* confused, from Latin *turbidus,* TURBID.] **—troub·ler** *n.* **—troub·ling·ly** *adv.*

troub·le·mak·er (trŭb′əl-mā′kər) *n.* A person who habitually stirs up trouble or strife. **—troub·le·mak·ing** *adj.* & *n.*

troub·le·shoot·er (trub′əl-shōō′tər) *n.* A person who locates and eliminates sources of trouble, as in mechanical operations or diplomatic affairs. **—troub·le·shoot·ing** *n.* & *adj.*

troub·le·some (trŭb′əl-səm) *adj.* **1.** Causing trouble, especially repeatedly; worrisome. **2.** Difficult; trying. —See Synonyms at **hard. —troub·le·some·ly** *adv.* **—troub·le·some·ness** *n.*

trouble spot *n.* A place of recurring trouble or unrest, especially political unrest.

troub·lous (trŭb′ləs) *adj.* Attended with trouble; uneasy; troubled. **—troub·lous·ly** *adv.* **—troub·lous·ness** *n.*

trou-de-loup (trōō′də-lōō′) *n., pl.* **trous-de-loup** *(pronounced as singular). Military.* Any of a series of conical pits having pointed stakes set upright in their centers, formerly used to provide an obstacle to enemy cavalry. [French, "wolf's pit."]

trough (trôf, trŏf) *n.* **1.** A long, narrow, generally shallow receptacle, especially one for holding water or feed for animals. **2.** A gutter under the eaves of a roof. **3.** A long, narrow depression, as between waves or ridges. **4.** A low point in a business cycle or on a statistical graph. **5.** *Meteorology.* An elongated region of low atmospheric pressure, often associated with a front. **6.** *Physics.* A minimum point in a wave or alternating signal. [Middle English *trough,* Old English *trog.*]

trounce (trouns) *tr.v.* **trounced, trouncing, trounces. 1.** To thrash; beat. **2.** To defeat decisively. [16th century (meaning "to harass, afflict") : origin obscure.]

troupe (trōōp) *n.* A company or group, especially of touring actors, singers, or dancers.
~intr.v. **trouped, trouping, troupes.** To tour with a theatrical company. [French, TROOP.]

troup·er (trōō′pər) *n.* **1.** A member of a theatrical company. **2.** A veteran actor or performer. **3.** *Informal.* A plucky and staunch colleague or worker.

trou·pi·al (trōō′pē-əl) *n.* Any of several tropical American birds of the genus *Icterus,* related to the orioles and New World blackbirds; especially, *I. icterus,* having orange and black plumage. [French *troupiale,* from *troupe,* flock, TROOP (from its living in flocks).]

trou·ser (trou′zər) *adj.* Of, for, or being a part of trousers: *a trouser pocket.* [Back-formation from TROUSERS.]

trou·sers (trou′zərz) *pl.n.* An outer garment for covering the body from the waist to the ankles, divided into two tubelike sections to fit each leg separately. [From obsolete *trouse,* from Scottish Gaelic *triubhas* (singular), TREWS.]

trou·ser-suit (trou′zər-sōōt′) *n.* *Chiefly British.* A woman's **pantsuit** *(see).*

trous·seau (trōō′sō, trōō-sō′) *n., pl.* **-seaux** (trōō′sōz, trōō-sōz′) or **-seaus.** The possessions, such as clothing and linen, assembled by a bride before her wedding. [French, from Old French, diminutive of *trusse,* a bundle. See **truss.**]

trout (trout) *n., pl.* **trouts** (for all senses) or **trout** (for senses 1, 2). **1.** Any of various freshwater or anadromous food and game fishes of the genera *Salmo* and *Salvelinus,* usually having a speckled body. **2.** Broadly, any of various similar fishes. **3.** *British Slang.* A silly old person. [Old English *trūht,* from Late Latin *tructa*†.]

trout lily *n.* The **dogtooth violet** *(see).* [From the spots on the leaves resembling the speckles on a trout.]

trou·vère (trōō-vâr′) *n.* Also **trou·veur** (-vûr′). Any of a school of poets flourishing in northern France from the 11th to the 13th centuries who chiefly wrote narrative works, such as the chansons de geste. Compare **troubadour.** [French, from Old French *trovere,* from *trover,* to invent, find, compose poetry, from Vulgar Latin *tropāre* (unattested), to use tropes, from Latin *tropus,* TROPE.]

trove (trōv) *n.* Something of value discovered or found; a find. [Short for TREASURE TROVE.]

PRONUNCIATION KEY

ă, pat; ā, pay; âr, care;
ä, father, are; b, bib;
ch, church; d, deed; ĕ, pet;
ē, be; f, fife; g, gag; h, hat;
hw, which; ĭ, pit; ī, pie;
îr, pier; j, judge; k, kick;
l, lid, needle; m, mum;
n, no, sudden; ng, thing;
ŏ, pot; ō, toe; ô, paw, for;
oi, noise; ou, out; ŏŏ, book;
ōō, boot; p, pop; r, roar;
s, sauce; sh, ship, dish;
t, tight; th, thin, path;
th, this, bathe; ŭ, cut; ûr, fur;
v, valve; w, with; y, yes;
z, zebra, size; zh, vision;
ə, about, item, edible,
gallop, circus, peaceful

IN FOREIGN WORDS:

à, *Fr.* ami; œ, *Fr.* feu, *Ger.* schön; ü, *Fr.* tu, *Ger.* über; KH, *Ger.* ich, *Scot.* loch; N, *Fr.* bon; y′, *Fr.* Compiègne

STRESS MARKS:

Primary stress: ′
in·cite′ (ĭn-sīt′)
Secondary stress: ′
in′sight′ (ĭn′sīt′)

tro·ver (trō'vər) *n. Law.* A common-law action to recover damages for personal property illegally withheld or wrongfully converted to use by another. [Norman French, from Old French. See **trouvère.**]

trow (trō) *intr.v.* **trowed, trowing, trows.** *Archaic.* To think; suppose; trust. [Middle English *trowen, trewen,* Old English *trēowian.*]

trow·el (trou'əl) *n.* **1.** A flat-bladed hand tool for leveling, spreading, or shaping substances such as cement or mortar. **2.** A small implement with a pointed, scoop-shaped blade used in gardening for digging or lifting plants.
~*tr.v.* **troweled** or **-elled, -eling** or **-elling, -els.** To spread, smooth, dig, or scoop with or as if with a trowel. [Middle English *trowell,* from Old French *truelle,* from Late Latin *truella,* variant of Latin *trulla,* diminutive of *trua†,* stirring spoon, ladle.]

trox·i·done (trŏk'sĭ-dōn') *n.* **Trimethadione** *(see).*

troy (troi) *adj. Abbr.* **t** Of or expressed in troy weight. [Middle English *troye,* from Norman French, probably first used at a fair in *Troyes,* France.]

Troy (troi). *Latin* **Il·i·um** (ĭl'ē-əm). Ancient city in northwestern Asia Minor near the Dardanelles. Its remains were first excavated (1870–90) by Heinrich Schliemann. The site revealed 10 major periods of occupation since the Early Bronze Age. The Troy of Homer's *Iliad* and *Odyssey* was probably a city destroyed by fire in the middle of the 13th century B.C. after a long siege.

troy weight *n. Abbr.* **t** A system of units used in weighing precious metals and gems in which the grain is the same as in the avoirdupois system and the pound contains 12 ounces, 240 pennyweights, or 5,760 grains. [See **troy.**]

trp. troop.

trs. transpose.

tru·an·cy (trōō'ən-sē) *n., pl.* **-cies.** Also **tru·ant·ry** (-ən-trē), *pl.* **-ries. 1.** An act or instance of playing truant. **2.** The condition of being truant.

tru·ant (trōō'ənt) *n.* **1.** One who is absent without permission, especially from school. **2.** A person who shirks work or duty.
~*adj.* **1.** Absent without permission, especially from school. **2.** Idle, lazy, or neglectful. —**play truant.** To absent oneself from school, especially habitually, without authorization.
~*intr.v.* **truanted, -anting, -ants.** To be truant. [Middle English, beggar, idle rogue, from Old French, of Celtic origin.]

truce (trōōs) *n.* A temporary cessation or suspension of hostilities by agreement of the contending forces; an armistice. [Middle English *trewes,* plural of *trewe,* truce, peace, Old English *trēow,* faith, pledge.]

Trucial States. See **United Arab Emirates.**

truck[1] (trŭk) *n.* **1.** Any of various heavy automotive vehicles designed for transporting loads. **2.** A two-wheeled barrow for moving heavy objects by hand. **3.** A wheeled platform, sometimes equipped with a motor, for conveying loads in a warehouse or freight yard. **4.** *British.* A railroad freight car without a top. **5.** One of the swiveling frames of wheels under each end of a railroad car, trolley car, or the like. **6.** The swiveling frame of wheels under a skateboard. **7.** *Nautical.* A disk-shaped block at the head of a mast with holes used for hoisting or lowering flags or sails.
~*v.* **trucked, trucking, trucks.** —*tr.* To transport by truck. —*intr.* **1.** To carry goods by truck. **2.** To drive a truck. **3.** *Slang.* To move along, especially in a carefree way. [Perhaps short for TRUCKLE ("pulley").]

truck[2] *v.* **trucked, trucking, trucks.** —*tr.* **1.** To exchange; barter. **2.** To peddle. —*intr.* To have dealings or commerce; traffic.
~*n.* **1.** Trade goods; articles of commerce. **2.** Barter; exchange. **3.** The payment of wages in goods or kind rather than in money. **4.** Garden produce grown for the market. **5.** *Informal.* Dealings; business: *I'll have no truck with them.* **6.** *Informal.* Worthless articles; rubbish. [Middle English *trukken,* from Norman French, akin to Medieval Latin *trocāre,* to exchange, barter.]

truck·age (trŭk'ĭj) *n.* **1.** The transportation of goods by truck. **2.** A charge for this.

truck·er (trŭk'ər) *n.* **1.** A truck driver. **2.** A person or company engaged in trucking goods.

truck farm *n.* A farm producing vegetables for the market. Also called "truck garden," *chiefly British* "market garden." —**truck farmer** *n.* —**truck farming** *n.*

truck·le (trŭk'əl) *n.* A small wheel or roller; a caster.
~*intr.v.* **truckled, -ling, -les.** To be servile or submissive; yield weakly. Used with *to.* [Middle English *trocle,* pulley, from Norman French, from Latin *trochlea,* system of pulleys. See **trochlea.**]

truckle bed *n. British.* A **trundle bed** *(see).*

truck·load (trŭk'lōd') *n.* The quantity or weight that a truck carries.

truck·man (trŭk'mən) *n., pl.* **-men** (-mĭn). **1.** A truck driver. **2.** A person engaged in the trucking business; a trucker. **3.** A member of the crew of a hook-and-ladder fire truck.

truck system *n.* The system of paying wages in goods instead of money, especially as practiced during the Industrial Revolution.

truc·u·lence (trŭk'yə-ləns) *n.* Also **truc·u·len·cy** (-lən-sē). **1.** Pugnacity; belligerence. **2.** Savagery.

truc·u·lent (trŭk'yə-lənt) *adj.* **1.** Disposed to fight; pugnacious. **2.** Savage and cruel; fierce. **3.** Vitriolic; scathing. [Latin *truculentus,* from *trux* (stem *truc-*), fierce.] —**truc·u·lent·ly** *adv.*

Tru·deau (trōō'dō, trōō-dō'), **Pierre Elliott** (1919–). Canadian statesman. As prime minister (1968–79) he opposed French separatism and introduced (1970) a brief spell of martial law to counteract agitation in Quebec. He was also prime minister from 1980 to 1984, when he retired.

trudge (trŭj) *intr.v.* **trudged, trudging, trudges.** To walk in a laborious or weary way; plod.
~*n.* A long, tedious walk. [16th century : origin obscure.]

trudg·en, trudg·eon (trŭj'ən) *n.* A swimming stroke in which a double overarm movement is combined with a scissors kick. Also called "trudgen stroke." [Introduced from Argentina by John *Trudgen,* 19th-century British swimmer.]

true (trōō) *adj.* **truer, truest. 1.** Consistent with fact or reality; not false or erroneous. **2. a.** Exactly conforming to a rule, standard, or pattern: *true to form.* **b.** Proper: *a true soufflé.* **3.** Reliable; accurate: *a true prophecy.* **4.** Real; genuine: *true suede.* **5.** Faithful, as to a friend, vow, or cause; steadfast; loyal: *a true socialist.* **6.** *Archaic.* Honorable; upright. **7.** Sincerely felt or expressed; unfeigned: *true sorrow.* **8.** Fundamental; essential: *her true motives.* **9.** Rightful; legitimate: *the true heir.* **10.** Accurately shaped or fitted. **11.** Accurately placed, delivered, or thrown. **12.** Determined with reference to the earth's axis, not the magnetic poles: *true north.* **13.** Conforming to the definitive criteria of a natural group: *The horseshoe crab is not a true crab.* **14.** Flat and horizontal: *a true level.* **15.** *Physics.* Not apparent or relative. Said of a physical property. —See Synonyms at **real, faithful.** —**come true.** To become fact; conform to expectation or prediction. —**too true.** *Chiefly British.* Correct; right. Often used as a rueful interjection.
~*adv.* **1.** Rightly; truthfully. **2.** Unswervingly; exactly: *aimed true.* **3.** So as to conform to the ancestral type or stock: *breed true.*
~*tr.v.* **trued, truing** or **trueing, trues.** To adjust or fit so as to conform with a standard. Often used with *up.*
~*n.* **1.** Truth. **2.** Proper alignment or adjustment: *in or out of true.* [Middle English *trewe,* Old English *trēowe,* loyal, trustworthy.] —**true·ness** *n.*

true bearing *n.* The angular distance clockwise from a meridian of longitude.

true bill *n. Law.* A bill of indictment endorsed by a grand jury.

true-blue, true blue (trōō'blōō') *n.* A person of unswerving loyalty. [Originally a 17th-century Scottish Presbyterian or Covenanter, from the color blue adopted in opposition to the Royalists' red.] —**true-blue** *adj.*

true-born (trōō'bôrn') *adj.* Being authentically or genuinely as specified by birth.

true-life (trōō'līf') *adj.* Based on fact; having happened in reality. Said of reports, stories, and works of literature.

true-love (trōō'lŭv') *n.* **1.** One's beloved; a sweetheart. **2.** A plant, **herb Paris** *(see).*

true lovers' knot *n.* A stylized knot, usually a form of bowknot, used as an emblem of love. Also called "love knot," "truelove knot."

true-pen·ny (trōō'pĕn'ē) *n., pl.* **-nies.** An honest fellow; a trusty person. [By association with a genuine coin.]

true rhyme *n.* **Perfect rhyme** *(see).*

true rib *n.* Any of the ribs, in humans any of the upper seven, that are attached to the sternum by a costal cartilage.

Truf·faut (trōō-fō', trü-), **François** (1932–84). French film director. His films include *Les Quatre-cents Coups* (a prize winner at the Cannes Film Festival in 1959), *Jules et Jim* (1961), and *Le Dernier Métro* (1980).

truf·fle (trŭf'əl, trōō'fəl) *n.* **1.** Any of various fleshy subterranean fungi, chiefly of the genus *Tuber,* often valued as food. **2.** A small, round, rich candy made from chocolate, egg, and butter, and usually flavored with a liqueur. [Old French *truffe,* from Old Provençal *trufa,* from Vulgar Latin *tūfera* (unattested), from Latin *tūber,* tuber, truffle.]

trug (trŭg) *n. British.* A shallow, usually oval basket made from strips of wood and used for carrying flowers, vegetables, or fruit. [16th century : dialectal variant of TROUGH.]

tru·ism (trōō'ĭz'əm) *n.* A statement of an obvious or self-evident truth. —See Synonyms at **cliché.** —**tru·is·tic** (trōō-ĭs'tĭk) *adj.*

Tru·jil·lo Mo·li·na (trōō-hē'ō mō-lē'nə), **Rafael Leonidas** (1891–1961). Dominican dictator, president (1930–38 and 1942–52) of the Dominican Republic. His policies brought some social and economic progress, but his tyranny led to his assassination.

Truk (trŭk, trōōk). Island group, *c.* 100 square kilometers (39 square miles) in area, in the western Pacific Ocean, in the Caroline Islands. The volcanic islands are surrounded by an atoll reef and many islets. It was the site of a Japanese naval base in World War II.

trull (trŭl) *n. Archaic.* A strumpet; a harlot. [Perhaps from German *Trulle,* from Middle High German *trolle,* clumsy person, akin to Old Norse *troll,* creature, TROLL.]

tru·ly (trōō'lē) *adv.* **1.** Sincerely; genuinely. **2.** Truthfully; accurately. **3.** Indeed; really: *truly ugly.*

Tru·man (trōō'mən), **Harry S.** (1884–1972). U.S. statesman. He was the 33rd president of the United States (1945–53), succeeding to office on the death of F.D. Roosevelt. As president he authorized (1945) the use of the nuclear bomb against Japan, which ended World War II. He also initiated (1949) the establishment of NATO.

tru·meau (trōō-mō') *n., pl.* **-meaux** (-mōz'). *Architecture.* A divider, as a wall or pillar, between two openings, as a pair of windows or a twin archway. [French, panel between two windows, from Old French *trumel,* from Frankish *thrum* (unattested), piece, bit.]

trump[1] (trŭmp) *n.* **1.** In card games: **a.** *Often* **trumps.** A suit whose cards are declared to outrank all other cards for the duration of a hand or game. **b.** Any card of such a suit. **2.** A key resource to be used at the opportune moment. **3.** *Informal.* A reliable or admira-

ble person. **—come up trumps. 1.** To turn out well; end satisfactorily. **2.** To be successful.
~v. **trumped, trumping, trumps.** *—tr.* **1.** To take (a card or trick) with a trump. **2.** To outdo (an opponent) with or as if with a trump. *—intr.* To play a trump card. **—trump up.** To devise fraudulently; concoct; counterfeit. [Alteration of TRIUMPH.]

trump[2] *n. Archaic.* A trumpet or trumpet call: *the last trump.* [Middle English *trompe,* from Old French, from Old High German *trumpa,* akin to Old Norse *trumba*†.]

trump card *n.* **1.** A playing card cut or turned up to determine which suit shall be trumps. **2.** Any card of the agreed trump suit. **3.** A powerful resource or gambit used when all else has failed.

trumped-up (trŭmpt′ŭp′) *adj.* Devised in order to deceive; concocted: *trumped-up charges.*

trump•er•y (trŭm′pə-rē) *n., pl.* **-ies. 1.** Showy but worthless finery; bric-a-brac. **2.** Nonsense; rubbish. **3.** Deception; trickery.
~adj. Showy but valueless. [Middle English *trompery,* from Old French *tromperie,* from *tromper*†, to cheat.]

trum•pet (trŭm′pĭt) *n.* **1. a.** A soprano brass wind instrument consisting of a long metal tube looped once and ending in a flared bell, the modern type being equipped with three valves for producing variations in pitch. **b.** A member of an orchestra who plays the trumpet. **2.** Something shaped like or sounding like a trumpet. **3.** An organ stop that produces a tone like that of the trumpet. **4. a.** Music produced by a trumpet. **b.** A resounding call, such as that of the elephant. **5.** An ear trumpet.
~v. **trumpeted, -peting, -pets.** *—intr.* **1.** To play a trumpet. **2.** To give forth a resounding call. Used especially of an elephant. *—tr.* To sound or proclaim loudly. [Middle English *trompette,* from Old French, diminutive of *trompe,* TRUMP (trumpet).]

trum•pet•er (trŭm′pĭ-tər) *n.* **1.** A trumpet player, especially one in a cavalry regiment. **2.** A person who announces something, as on a trumpet; a herald. **3.** Any of several large birds of the genus *Psophia,* of tropical South America, having a loud, resonant call. **4.** The trumpeter swan. **5.** Any of several large Australian and New Zealand food fishes; especially, the species *Latris lineata,* which is silvery with yellow stripes. **6.** A breed of domestic pigeon.

trumpeter swan *n.* A large white swan, *Cygnus buccinator,* of western North America, having a black bill and a loud, buglelike call. Also called "trumpeter."

trum•pet-ma•jor (trŭm′pĭt-mā′jər) *n.* Formerly, the head trumpeter of a cavalry regiment.

trun•cal (trŭng′kəl) *adj.* Of or pertaining to a trunk, as of a body or tree. [Alteration of TRUNK + -AL.]

trun•cate (trŭng′kāt′) *tr.v.* **-cated, -cating, -cates. 1. a.** To shorten by or as if by cutting off the end or top; lop. **b.** To cut short; abbreviate (a quoted passage, for example). **2.** To replace (the edge of a crystal) with a plane face.
~adj. **1.** Appearing to terminate abruptly, as a leaf or a coiled gastropod shell that lacks a spire. **2.** Truncated. [Latin *truncāre,* to maim, from *truncus,* torso, TRUNK.] **—trun•cate•ly** *adv.* **—trun•ca•tion** *n.*

trun•cat•ed (trŭng′kā′tĭd) *adj.* **1.** Having the apex cut off and replaced by a plane, especially one parallel to the base. Said of a solid geometric figure such as a cone or pyramid. **2.** Cut short or abbreviated, as a quoted passage may be. **3.** Truncate.

trun•cheon (trŭn′chən) *n.* **1.** A short cudgel carried by policemen. **2.** A staff carried as a symbol of office or authority; a baton. **3.** A thick cutting from a plant, as for grafting.
~tr.v. **truncheoned, -cheoning, -cheons.** *Archaic.* To beat with a truncheon; bludgeon. [Middle English *tronchon,* fragment, club, from Old French, from Vulgar Latin *trunciō,* from Latin *truncus,* torso, TRUNK.]

trun•dle (trŭnd′l) *n.* **1.** The motion or noise of rolling. **2.** A small wheel or roller. **3.** A trundle bed. **4.** A low-wheeled cart; dolly.
~v. **trundled, -dling, -dles.** *—tr.* **1.** To push or propel on wheels or rollers. **2.** To spin; twirl. *—intr.* To move along in a slow and cumbersome manner by or as if by rolling. [Variant of dialectal *trendle,* wheel, from Middle English *trendil,* Old English *trendel,* circle, from Germanic *trand-*; akin to TREND.] **—trun•dler** *n.*

trundle bed *n.* A low bed on casters that can be rolled under another bed when not in use. Also *British* "truckle bed."

trunk (trŭngk) *n.* **1.** The main woody axis of a tree. **2. a.** The human body excluding the head and limbs; the torso. **b.** An analogous part of other organisms, such as the thorax of an insect. **3.** A main body, apart from tributaries or appendages. **4.** *Architecture.* The shaft of a column. **5.** A proboscis; specifically, the long, prehensile proboscis of an elephant. **6.** A trunk line. **7.** A large packing case or box that is fastened with clasps, used as luggage or for storage. **8.** A covered compartment for luggage and storage, generally at the rear of an automobile. **9.** A chute or conduit. **10.** *Nautical.* **a.** A shaft connecting two or more decks. **b.** The housing for the centerboard of a vessel. **c.** A structure projecting above part of a main deck, such as a covering over a ship's hatches or a cabin. **11. trunks.** Men's shorts worn for swimming or athletics.
~adj. Of or designating the main body or line of a system: *a trunk road.* [Middle English *trunke,* from Old French *tronc,* a tree trunk, from Latin *truncus.*]

trunk•fish (trŭngk′fĭsh′) *n., pl.* **-fishes** or collectively **trunkfish.** Any of various tropical marine fishes of the family Ostraciidae, having boxlike armor enclosing the body. Also called "boxfish."

trunk hose *pl.n.* Short, ballooning breeches, extending from the waist to midthigh, worn by men in the 16th and 17th centuries. Also called "trunk breeches." [Probably from obsolete *trunk,* to cut short, from Latin *truncāre,* to TRUNCATE.]

trunk line *n.* **1.** A direct line between two distant telephone switchboards. **2.** The main line of a transport system, such as a railroad or canal system.

trunnel. Variant of **treenail.**

trun•nion (trŭn′yən) *n.* A pin or gudgeon; especially, either of two small cylindrical projections on a cannon or movable container forming an axis on which it pivots. [French *trognon,* core of fruit, tree trunk, from Old French, perhaps from *estrongner,* to cut off the branches, variant of *estronchier* : *es-,* from Latin *ex-,* off + *tronchier,* to cut, from Latin *truncāre,* to TRUNCATE.] **—trun•nioned** *adj.*

Tru•ro (tro͝or′ō). Administrative center of Cornwall, southwestern England. Lying at the confluence of the Kenwyn and Allen rivers, it is a small port and tourist center.

truss (trŭs) *n.* **1.** *Medicine.* A supportive device or belt worn to prevent the protrusion of a hernia. **2.** *Engineering.* A framework of wooden beams or metal bars, often arranged in triangles, to support a roof, bridge, or similar structure. **3.** *Architecture.* A bracket; a corbel. **4.** Something gathered into a bundle; a pack. **5.** *British.* A bundle of a set weight of straw or hay, generally 60 pounds (27 kilograms) of new hay, 56 pounds (25 kilograms) of old hay, or 36 pounds (16 kilograms) of straw. **6.** *Nautical.* An iron fitting by which a lower yard is secured to a mast. **7.** A compact cluster of flowers or fruit at the end of a stalk.
~tr.v. **trussed, trussing, trusses. 1.** To tie up or bind. Often used with *up.* **2.** To bind or skewer the wings or legs of (a fowl) before cooking. **3.** To enclose or confine (the body) in tight-fitting clothes. Often used with *up.* **4.** To support or brace with a truss. [Middle English *trusse,* a bundle, from Old French *tr(o)usse,* from *tr(o)usser,* to tie in a bundle, perhaps from Vulgar Latin *torsāre* (unattested), from *torsus* (unattested), past participle of Latin *torquēre,* to twist.]

truss bridge *n.* A bridge supported by trusses.

truss•ing (trŭs′ĭng) *n.* **1.** The parts forming a truss. **2.** A system of trusses supporting a structure.

trust (trŭst) *n.* **1.** Firm reliance on the integrity, ability, or character of a person or thing; confident belief; faith. **2.** The person or thing in which confidence is placed. **3.** Custody; care. **4.** Something committed into the care of another; a charge. **5.** The condition and resulting obligation of having confidence placed in one: *a position of public trust.* **6.** Reliance on something in the future; hope. **7.** Reliance on the intention and ability of a purchaser to pay in the future; credit. **8.** *Abbr.* **tr.** *Law.* **a.** A legal title to property held by one party (the trustee) for the benefit of another (the beneficiary). **b.** The confidence reposed in a trustee when giving him legal title to property to administer for another, and his obligation with respect to the property and the beneficiary. **c.** The property so held. **d.** The right of the beneficiary to the property. **9.** A group of companies organized for the purpose of reducing competition and controlling prices throughout a business or industry. **10.** A **trust territory** *(see).* **—in trust.** In the charge of a trustee.
~v. **trusted, trusting, trusts.** *—intr.* **1.** To rely; depend. Used with *in* or *to.* **2.** To be confident; hope. **3.** To sell on credit. *—tr.* **1.** To have confidence in; feel sure of. **2.** To expect with assurance; assume. **3.** To believe. **4.** To place in the care of another; entrust. **5.** To grant discretion to confidently: *Shall I trust her with the boat?* **6.** To extend credit to. —See Synonyms at **rely.**
~adj. Maintained in trust. [Middle English *truste,* probably from Old Norse *traust,* confidence, firmness.] **—trust•a•bil•i•ty** *n.* **—trust•a•ble** *adj.* **—trust•er** *n.*
Synonyms: *confidence, dependence, faith, reliance.*

trust account *n.* **1.** A savings account deposited in the name of a trustee, after whose death the balance is payable to a specified beneficiary. Also called "trustee account." **2.** Property under trustee control.

trust•bust•er (trŭst′bŭs′tər) *n. Informal.* One, as a government official, who seeks to prosecute or dissolve business trusts.

trust company *n.* A commercial bank or other company that manages trusts.

trus•tee (trŭ-stē′) *n. Abbr.* **tr. 1.** A person or agent, such as a bank, holding legal title to property in order to administer it for a beneficiary. **2.** A member of a board elected or appointed to direct the funds and policy of an institution. **3.** A garnishee.
~tr.v. **trusteed, -teeing, -tees. 1.** To place (property) in the care of a trustee. **2.** To garnishee (property).

trustee process *n.* See **garnishment** (sense 2b).

trus•tee•ship (trŭ-stē′shĭp′) *n.* **1.** The position or function of a trustee. **2. a.** The administration of a territory by a country or countries, supervised by the United Nations. **b.** *Often* **Trusteeship.** A region so administered; a trust territory. Compare **mandate.**

trust•ful (trŭst′fəl) *adj.* Trusting. **—trust•ful•ly** *adv.*

trust fund *n.* An estate, especially money and securities, held or settled in trust.

trust•ing (trŭs′tĭng) *adj.* Inclined to believe or confide readily; full of trust. **—trust•ing•ly** *adv.* **—trust•ing•ness** *n.*

trust territory *n.* A colony or territory placed under the administration of a country or countries by commission of the United Nations. Also called "trust." Compare **mandate.**

trust•wor•thy (trŭst′wûr′*thē*) *adj.* Warranting trust; dependable; reliable. **—trust•wor•thi•ly** *adv.* **—trust•wor•thi•ness** *n.*

trust•y (trŭs′tē) *adj.* **-ier, -iest.** Dependable; faithful; reliable.
~n., pl. **trusties.** A trusted person; specifically, a convict granted privileges for good behavior. **—trust•i•ly** *adv.* **—trust•i•ness** *n.*

trumpeter swan *The trumpeter of North America is the largest of the swan family. Fully grown, it can be 1.5 meters (5 feet) long and have a wingspan of nearly 2.5 meters (more than 8 feet). Once hunted to near extinction for its meat and feathers, it is now a protected species and the population has increased to about 5,000 birds, mostly in Alaska.*

truth (trōōth) *n., pl.* **truths** (trōō*th*z, trōōths). **1.** Conformity to knowledge, fact, or logic. **2.** Fidelity to an original or standard. **3. a.** Reality; actuality. **b.** *Often* **Truth.** That which is considered to be the supreme reality and to have the ultimate meaning and value of existence. **c. Truth.** *Christian Science.* God. **4.** A statement proven to be or accepted as true; the opposite of a falsehood. **5.** Sincerity; integrity; honesty. **6.** *Physics.* See **top** (sense 15). —**truth to tell.** To tell the truth; speaking frankly. [Middle English *trewthe, treothe,* Old English *trēowth, trīewth.*]

Synonyms: veracity, verisimilitude, verity.

truth·ful (trōōth'fəl) *adj.* **1.** Consistently telling the truth; honest. **2.** Corresponding to reality; true. —**truth·ful·ly** *adv.* —**truth·ful·ness** *n.*

truth-func·tion (trōōth'fŭngk'shən) *n.* A compound proposition in logic, such as a conjunction or negation, the truth-value of which is always determined by the truth-values of the components.

truth serum *n. Informal.* Any drug that reduces inhibitions and promotes relaxation, as used by certain authorities during interrogation. Also called "truth drug."

truth set *n. Mathematics & Logic.* A set of values that satisfy a given equation or statement. Also called "solution set."

truth table *n. Logic.* A table listing the truth-values of a proposition that result from all the possible combinations of the truth-values of its components.

truth-val·ue (trōōth'văl'yōō) *n. Logic.* The truth or the falsity of a proposition.

try (trī) *v.* **tried, trying, tries.** —*tr.* **1.** To taste, sample, or otherwise test in order to determine strength, effect, worth, or desirability. Often used with *out.* **2. a.** To examine or hear (evidence or a case) by judicial process. **b.** To put (an accused person) on trial. **3.** To subject to strain or hardship; tax: *The last steep ascent tried her every muscle.* **4.** To melt (lard, for example) in order to separate out impurities; render down. Often used with *out.* **5.** To make an effort to do or accomplish (something); attempt: *tried to ski.* **6.** To smooth, fit, or align accurately. —*intr.* To make an effort; strive. —**try one's hand.** To attempt to do something for the first time. —*n., pl.* **tries. 1.** An attempt; effort. **2.** A test; trial. **3. a.** In Rugby football, the act of touching the ball down behind the opposing team's goal line, giving the team the right to kick for a goal. **b.** The score so gained. [Middle English *trien,* to separate, pick out, sift, from Old French *trier†.*]

Usage: Try and is commonly used in speech for *try to,* especially in such established phrases as *try and stop me* and *try and get some rest.* In most contexts, however, it is usually not interchangeable with *try to* unless the level of usage is clearly informal.

try·ing (trī'ĭng) *adj.* Causing annoyance, strain, or distress. —**try·ing·ly** *adv.* —**try·ing·ness** *n.*

trying plane *n.* A long plane used to produce level surfaces on planks.

try·ma (trī'mə) *n., pl.* **-mata** (-mə-tə). A drupe, such as a walnut, having a tough epicarp that separates from the shell of the fruit. [New Latin, from Greek *truma, trumē,* a hole (from the hollow drupe).]

try on *tr.v.* To put on (an article of clothing) to see whether it fits or suits one.

try-on (trī'ŏn', -ôn') *n.* The act of trying on.

try out *intr.v.* To undergo a competitive qualifying test, as for an athletic team or a theatrical role: *tried out for the debating team.*

try·out (trī'out') *n. Informal.* **1.** An experimental test or trial. **2.** A test to ascertain the qualifications of applicants.

try·pan·o·some (trĭ-păn'ə-sōm', trĭp'ə-nə-) *n.* Any of various parasitic protozoans of the genus *Trypanosoma,* transmitted to the vertebrate bloodstream by certain insects, and often causing diseases such as sleeping sickness. [New Latin *Trypanosoma,* "augerbodied" (from its shape) : Greek *trupanon,* an auger, borer, from *trupan,* to bore, from *trupa, trupē,* a hole + -SOME (body).] —**try·pan·o·so·mic** (trĭ-păn'ə-sō'mĭk, trĭp'ə-nə-) *adj.*

try·pan·o·so·mi·a·sis (trĭ-păn'ə-sō-mī'ə-sĭs, trĭp'ə-nō-sō-sĭs) *n., pl.* **-ses** (-sēz'). A disease caused by a trypanosome. [New Latin : TRYPANOSOM(E) + -IASIS.]

try·pars·am·ide (trĭ-pär'sə-mīd') *n.* A white crystalline powder, $C_8H_{10}AsN_2O_4Na·½H_2O$, used in the treatment of spirochetal and trypanosomic diseases. [Originally a trade name : *trypan*osome + *arsenic* + *amide.*]

tryp·sin (trĭp'sĭn) *n.* One of the proteolytic enzymes of the pancreatic juice, important in the digestive processes. [Greek *tripsis,* a rubbing (first obtained by rubbing the pancreas with glycerin), from *tribein,* to rub + -IN.] —**tryp·tic** (trĭp'tĭk) *adj.*

tryp·sin·o·gen (trĭp-sĭn'ə-jən) *n.* The substance produced by the pancreas that is converted into trypsin when acted upon by certain enzymes. [From TRYPSIN + -GEN.]

tryp·to·phan (trĭp'tə-făn') *n.* Also **tryp·to·phane** (-fān'). An amino acid, $C_{11}H_{12}N_2O_2$, found in a variety of proteins, that is produced in the digestive process and is an essential element in human nutrition. [TRYP(SIN) + (PEP)T(IC) + -PHAN(E).]

try·sail (trī'sāl, -səl) *n. Nautical.* A small fore-and-aft sail hoisted abaft the foremast and mainmast in a storm to keep a ship's bow to the wind. Also called "spencer." [TRY, "to lie to in a storm" + SAIL.]

try square *n.* A carpenter's tool consisting of a ruled metal straightedge set at right angles to a wooden straight piece, used for measuring and marking square work. Also called "square."

tryst (trĭst) *n.* **1.** An agreement, as between lovers, to meet at a certain time and place. **2.** A meeting or meeting place that has been agreed upon. —*intr.v.* **trysted, trysting, trysts.** To arrange or keep a tryst. [Middle English, from Old French *triste,* an appointed station in hunting, perhaps from Scandinavian, akin to Old Norse *treysta,* to trust, make firm.] —**tryst·er** *n.*

T.S. *Physics.* tensile strength.

tsade. Variant of **sade.**

Tsana. See **Tana, Lake.**

tsar. Variant of **czar.**

tset·se disease (tsĕt'sĕ, tsĕt'sē) *n.* **Nagana** *(see).*

tset·se fly, tzet·ze fly (tsĕt'sĕ, tsĕt'sē) *n.* Any of several bloodsucking African flies of the genus *Glossina,* often carrying and transmitting pathogenic trypanosomes to human beings and livestock. [Afrikaans, from Tswana.]

TSH thyroid stimulating hormone.

Tshi. Variant of **Twi.**

Tshi·lu·ba (chĭ-lōō'bə) *n.* The language of the Luba people, used as a trade language in Zaire. See **Luba.** —**Tshi·lu·ba** *adj.*

T-shirt, tee shirt (tē'shûrt') *n.* A short-sleeved, collarless casual shirt worn by both sexes. [So called from its shape.]

Tshom·be (chŏm'bā'), **Moise Kapenda** (1919–69). Congolese statesman. He was president (1960–63) of the breakaway province of Katanga and prime minister of the Congo (1964–65) until dismissed and condemned to death in absentia in 1967.

tsim·mes, tzim·mes (tsĭm'ĭs) *n.* **1.** A stew of vegetables or fruits cooked slowly over very low heat. **2.** *Informal.* A state of confusion. [Yiddish, "vegetable or fruit stew."]

Tsinan. See **Jinan.**

Tsinghai. See **Qinghai.**

tsp. teaspoon; teaspoonful.

T-square (tē'skwär') *n.* A T-shaped ruler with a short, sometimes sliding perpendicular crosspiece at one end, used by draftsmen for establishing and drawing parallel lines.

tsu·na·mi (tsōō-nä'mē) *n.* A very large ocean wave caused by an underwater earthquake or volcanic eruption; tidal wave. [Japanese : *tsu,* port + *nami,* wave.] —**tsu·na·mic** (tsōō-nä'mĭk) *adj.*

tsu·ris, tzu·ris (tsōōr'ĭs, tsôr'-) *n. Informal.* Trouble; aggravation. [Yiddish *tsores.*]

tsu·tsu·ga·mu·shi disease (tsōō'tsə-gə-mōō'shē) *n.* **Scrub typhus** *(see).* [Japanese : *tsutsuga,* illness + *mushi,* an insect.]

Tswa·na (tswä'nə, sä'-) *n.* **1.** A member of a Bantu people of southern Africa, living mainly in Botswana. **2.** The Sotho language of the Tswana people. Also called "Bechuana." —**Tswa·na** *adj.*

T.T. **1.** teetotal; teetotaler. **2.** tuberculin-tested.

TTL **1.** through the lens; used to designate a type of camera light meter. **2.** transistor–transistor logic.

T.U. trade union.

Tuan (twän) *n.* A Malayan form of respectful address equivalent to the English *Sir* or *Mr.* [Malay, master, lord.]

Tua·reg (twä'rĕg) *n., pl.* **-regs** or collectively **Tuareg.** A member of one of the tall, nomadic, Hamitic-speaking peoples who occupy the western and central Sahara and an area along the Niger and have adopted the Muslim religion. [Arabic *Tawāriq.*] —**Tua·reg** *adj.*

tu·a·ta·ra (tōō'ə-tär'ə) *n.* A lizardlike reptile, *Sphenodon punctatum,* of New Zealand, the only surviving representative of the order Rhynchocephalia that flourished during the Mesozoic era. [Maori.]

tub (tŭb) *n.* **1. a.** A round, open, flat-bottomed vessel, usually wider than it is tall, originally made of wooden staves held together with hoops, and used for packing, storing, or washing. **b.** A small container resembling such a vessel in shape and used for packaging foods, as butter or margarine. **c.** The contents of a tub. **d.** The amount that a tub will hold. Also called "tubful." **2. a.** A **bathtub** *(see).* **b.** A bath taken in a bathtub. **3.** *Informal.* **a.** A wide, clumsy, slow-moving boat. **b.** A strong broad boat used for rowing practice. **4. a.** A bucket used for conveying ore or coal up a mine shaft. **b.** A coal wagon used in a mine.
—*v.* **tubbed, tubbing, tubs.** —*tr.* **1.** To pack or store in a tub. **2.** To wash or bathe in a tub. —*intr.* To take a bath. [Middle English *tubbe, tobbe,* from Middle Dutch and Middle Low German *tubbe†.*] —**tub·ba·ble** *adj.* —**tub·ber** *n.*

tu·ba (tōō'bə, tyōō'-) *n., pl.* **-bas** or **-bae** (-bē) (for sense 3). **1.** A large, valved, brass musical wind instrument with a bass pitch. **2.** A reed stop in an organ, having eight-foot pitch. **3.** An ancient Roman war trumpet. [Italian, from Latin, a trumpet, akin to Latin *tubus,* TUBE.]

tu·bal (tōō'bəl, tyōō'-) *adj.* Of, pertaining to, or occurring in a tube, especially the Fallopian tube.

tu·bate (tōō'bāt', tyōō'-) *adj.* Forming or having a tube.

tub·by (tŭb'ē) *adj.* **-bier, -biest. 1.** *Informal.* Short and fat. **2.** Having a dull sound; lacking resonance. —**tub·bi·ness** *n.*

tube (tōōb, tyōōb) *n.* **1. a.** A hollow cylinder that conveys a fluid or functions as a passage. **b.** An organic structure so shaped or so functioning; a duct. **2.** A small, flexible cylindrical container sealed at one end and having a cap at the other, for pigments, toothpaste, or other pastelike substances. **3.** The cylindrical part of a wind instrument. **4. a.** A **vacuum tube** *(see).* **b.** An **electron tube** *(see).* **5.** *Botany.* The lower, joined part of a gamopetalous corolla or a gamosepalous calyx. **6.** *British.* **a.** An underground railroad. **b.** An underground railroad system, especially the one in London. **7.** *Informal.* **a.** Television. **b.** A television set. **8. tubes.** *Informal.*

tsetse fly *The tsetse fly is exclusive to Africa, where it transmits sleeping sickness to humans and a similar disease, nagana, to cattle.*

The Fallopian tubes. —**down the tubes** (or **tube**). *Slang.* Into a state of failure or ruin: *saw all her dreams go down the tubes.*
~*tr.v.* **tubed, tubing, tubes. 1.** To provide with a tube or tubes; insert a tube in: *tube a tire.* **2.** To place in or enclose in a tube. [French, from Latin *tubus†.* See also **tuba.**]

tube foot *n.* Any of the numerous external, fluid-filled muscular tubes of echinoderms, such as the starfish, serving primarily as organs of locomotion.

tube·less tire (tōōb′lĭs, tyōōb′-) *n.* A pneumatic vehicular tire in which the air is held in the assembly of casing and rim without an inner tube.

tu·ber (tōō′bər, tyōō′-) *n.* **1.** *Botany.* A swollen, usually underground stem or root, such as the potato or dahlia, bearing buds from which new plant shoots arise. **2.** *Anatomy.* A swelling; a tubercle. [Latin *tūber,* a lump, swelling, tumor.]

tu·ber·cle (tōō′bər-kəl, tyōō′-) *n.* **1.** A small, rounded prominence or growth, such as a wartlike excrescence on the roots of some leguminous plants or a knoblike projection in the skin or on a bone. **2.** *Pathology.* **a.** A nodule or swelling. **b.** The characteristic lesion of tuberculosis. [Latin *tūberculum,* diminutive of *tūber,* TUBER.]

tubercle bacillus *n.* A rod-shaped bacterium, *Mycobacterium tuberculosis,* that causes tuberculosis.

tu·ber·cu·lar (tōō-bûr′kyə-lər, tyōō-) *adj.* **1.** Of, pertaining to, or covered with tubercles; tuberculate. **2.** Of, pertaining to, or suffering from tuberculosis. **3.** Possessing or characterized by the presence of tubercles.
~*n.* A person suffering from tuberculosis.

tu·ber·cu·late (tōō-bûr′kyə-lĭt, tyōō-) *adj.* Also **tu·ber·cu·lat·ed** (-lā′tĭd). **1.** Having tubercles. **2.** Tubercular. —**tu·ber·cu·late·ly** *adv.* —**tu·ber·cu·la·tion** *n.*

tu·ber·cu·lin (tōō-bûr′kyə-lĭn, tyōō-) *n.* A sterile liquid derived from cultures of tubercle bacilli, used in the diagnosis and treatment of tuberculosis. [Latin *tūberculum,* TUBERCLE + -IN.]

tuberculin test *n.* The **Mantoux test** *(see).* —**tu·ber·cu·lin-test·ed** (tōō-bûr′kyə-lĭn-tĕs′tĭd, tyōō-) *adj.*

tu·ber·cu·loid (tōō-bûr′kyə-loid′, tyōō-) *adj.* **1.** Resembling tuberculosis. **2.** Resembling a tubercle.

tu·ber·cu·lo·sis (tōō-bûr′kyə-lō′sĭs, tyōō-) *n. Abbr.* **TB, T.B. 1.** An infectious disease of humans and animals caused by a microorganism, *Mycobacterium tuberculosis,* and manifesting itself in lesions of the lung, bone, and other parts of the body. **2.** Tuberculosis of the lungs. In this sense, also called "consumption," "phthisis." [New Latin : Latin *tūberculum,* TUBERCLE + -OSIS.]

tu·ber·cu·lous (tōō-bûr′kyə-ləs, tyōō-) *adj.* **1.** Of, pertaining to, or having tuberculosis. **2.** Of, affected with, or caused by tubercles. [New Latin *tuberculosus,* from Latin *tūberculum,* TUBERCLE.]

tube·rose (tōōb′rōz′, tyōōb′-, tōō′bə-rōz′, -rōs′, tyōō′-) *n.* A tuberous plant, *Polianthes tuberosa,* native to Mexico, cultivated for its fragrant white flowers, which yield an expensive perfume, *tuberose obsolete.* [New Latin *(Polianthes) tuberosa,* from the feminine of Latin *tūberōsus,* TUBEROUS.]

tu·ber·os·i·ty (tōō′bə-rŏs′ə-tē, tyōō′-) *n., pl.* **-ties.** A projection or protuberance, especially one at the end of a bone for the attachment of a muscle or tendon.

tu·ber·ous (tōō′bər-əs, tyōō′-) *adj.* Also **tu·ber·ose** (-bə-rōs′, -rōz′). **1.** *Botany.* **a.** Producing or bearing tubers. **b.** Resembling a tuber: *a tuberous root.* **2.** Covered with small, rounded projections; knobby. [Latin *tūberōsus,* full of lumps, from *tūber,* TUBER.]

tube worm *n.* Any sedentary, tube-dwelling bristle worm, such as the lugworm or the ragworm.

tub·ful (tŭb′fōōl′) *n.* The amount held by a tub.

tu·bi·fex (tōō′bə-fĕks′, tyōō′-) *n., pl.* **-fexes** or collectively **tubifex.** Any of various small, slender, reddish freshwater worms of the genus *Tubifex,* often used as food for tropical aquarium fish. [New Latin *Tubifex* : Latin *tubus,* TUBE (each one is partially enclosed in a tube) + *-fex,* "maker."]

tub·ing (tōō′bĭng, tyōō′-) *n.* **1.** A length of tube or material in the form of a tube. **2.** Tubes collectively. **3.** A system of tubes.

Tub·man (tŭb′mən), **Harriet** (1820–1913). U.S. abolitionist. Born a slave on a Maryland plantation, she escaped to the North in 1849 and became the most renowned conductor on the Underground Railroad, making 19 trips into the South and leading more than 300 slaves to freedom.

tub thumper *n. Informal.* A soapbox orator; a vehement public speaker. —**tub-thump·ing** (tŭb′thŭm′pĭng) *n. & adj.*

tu·bu·lar (tōō′byə-lər, tyōō′-) *adj.* **1.** Having the form of a tube. **2.** Made or consisting of a tube or tubes. —**tu·bu·lar·i·ty** (tōō′byə-lâr′ə-tē, tyōō′-) *n.*

tubular bells *pl.n.* A musical instrument consisting of a set of long metal tubes that are tuned to the musical scale and struck with a mallet to simulate the sound of bells.

tu·bu·late (tōō′byə-lĭt, -lāt′, tyōō′-) *adj.* Also **tu·bu·lat·ed** (-lā′tĭd). **1.** Formed into or resembling a tube; tubular. **2.** Provided with a tube.
~*tr.v.* (tōō′byə-lāt′, tyōō′-) **tubulated, -lating, -lates.** To provide with or form into a tube. [Latin *tubulātus,* from *tubulus,* diminutive of *tubus,* TUBE.] —**tu·bu·la·tion** *n.* —**tu·bu·la·tor** *n.*

tu·bule (tōō′byōōl, tyōō′-) *n.* A very small tube or tubular structure. [Latin *tubulus,* diminutive of *tubus,* TUBE.]

tu·bu·lif·er·ous (tōō′byə-lĭf′ər-əs, tyōō′-) *adj.* Having or consisting of tubules. [TUBULE + -FEROUS.]

tu·bu·li·flo·rous (tōō′byə-lə-flôr′əs, tyōō′-) *adj.* Having

THE KILLER WAVES
Monstrous ripples that follow an earthquake under the sea

Essentially, tsunamis are no more than ripples. But they come on a monstrous scale.

Just as circular ripples spread from a pebble tossed into a pond, so tsunamis surge across the sea from an underwater earthquake or volcanic eruption. In deep water, the swells are so long and so slight that ships hardly notice them. But as tsunamis reach shallow water, they pile up into crests that can be as much as 60 meters (200 feet) high. Their speed is astonishing, too: many travel faster than 600 kilometers (375 miles) an hour; one, in April 1946, is known to have raced across 3,620 kilometers (2,250 miles) of the Pacific to Hawaii in 4 hours and 34 minutes, an average speed of more than 790 kilometers (nearly 495 miles) an hour.

Almost all tsunamis are confined to the Pacific, the ocean whose basin is surrounded by a ring of volcanoes. The word itself comes from Japan; it was adopted by scientists of other countries to replace the misleading phrase "tidal wave" because tsunamis are triggered by geological, not tidal, movements.

Usually, just before a tsunami strikes a coast, the sea itself is sucked back, leaving ships in harbors beached. Then the vast wave smashes onto the land, often causing enormous destruction. In 1883, for example, 30,000 people died on Java in a tsunami triggered by the eruption of Krakatoa. In 1896, a tsunami killed more than 20,000 people and flattened 10,000 homes in Sanriku, a town on Tokyo Bay.

A MOUNTAIN OF WATER *A tsunami reaches out for the land in a print by the 19th-century Japanese artist Hokusai. On a miniature scale in the background appears the volcanic cone of Mount Fuji. The Japanese have long known the connection between the gigantic killer waves and movements of the earth's crust. Ancient monuments along the coast of Japan carry inscriptions that give the warning: "When you feel an earthquake, expect a tsunami."*

---

flowers or florets with tubular corollas. [From TUBUL(E) + -FLOROUS.]

tu·bu·lous (tōō′byə-ləs, tyōō′-) *adj.* **1.** Tubular. **2.** Composed of tubes or having tubular parts. [New Latin *tubulosus,* from Latin *tubulus,* TUBULE.] —**tu·bu·lous·ly** *adv.*

Tu·ca·na (tōō-kā′nə, -kä′nə, tyōō-) *n.* A constellation in the polar region of the Southern Hemisphere near Indus and Hydrus, containing the smaller **Magellanic cloud** *(see).* [Tupi *tucana,* TOUCAN.]

Tuch·man (tŭk′mən), **Barbara Wertheim** (1912–). U.S. historian and author. Concerned with accurately recounting historic events in a highly readable literary style, she has written numerous popular and critically acclaimed works, including *The Guns of August* (1962), *Stillwell and the American Experience in China, 1911–1945* (1971), and *The March of Folly: From Troy to Vietnam* (1984).

tu·chun (dōō′jōōn′, -jün′) *n., pl.* **-chuns** or **tuchun.** A Chinese military governor of a province. [Chinese *dū jūn* : *dū,* to supervise + *jūn,* army.] —**tu·chun·ate** *n.* —**tu·chun·ism** *n.*

tuck¹ (tŭk) *v.* **tucked, tucking, tucks.** —*tr.* **1.** To make one or more folds in. **2.** To gather up the ends of (a garment, for example) and thrust into a space between two surfaces so as to secure or confine: *tuck one's shirt into one's trousers.* **3. a.** To put (something) into a place or space where it will be concealed, confined, or snug: *tuck the letter into your bag; a cabin tucked away in the woods.* **b.** To store in a safe spot; save. Used with *away: He has millions tucked away.* **4.** To cover (a child, for example) snugly in bed. Used with *in.* **5.** To draw in; contract. —*intr.* To make tucks. —**tuck in** (or **away**). *Informal.* To consume (food) heartily or greedily.
~*n.* **1.** A flattened pleat or fold in a garment, especially a very narrow one stitched in place. **2.** An act of tucking something in. **3.** *Nautical.* The part of a ship's hull under the stern where the ends of the bottom planks come together. **4. a.** A bodily position, as in diving, in which the knees are bent, the thighs are drawn close to

tuatara *The lizardlike tuatara is the sole survivor of a group of reptiles that flourished 150 million years ago. It grows to about 70 centimeters (28 inches) long and is found only on a few islands off the coast of New Zealand.*

the chest, and the hands are clasped around the shins. **b.** A position in skiing in which the skier squats while holding the poles parallel to the ground and under the arms. **5.** *British Informal.* Food, especially candy and pastry. [Middle English *tukken, tucken,* from Old English *tūcian,* to torment.]

tuck[2] *n. Scottish.* A beat or tap, especially on a drum. [From obsolete *t(o)uk,* to beat the drum, sound the trumpet, from Middle English *tukken,* from Old North French *toquer,* to strike, touch, from Vulgar Latin *toccāre* (unattested), to TOUCH.]

tuck[3] *n. Archaic.* A slender sword; a rapier. [Earlier *to(c)ke,* from French (Normandy dialect) *étoc,* from Old French *estoc,* "a tree trunk," sword, sword point, from Frankish *stok* (unattested).]

tuck•er[1] (tŭk′ər) *n.* **1.** One that tucks. **2.** A piece of linen or frill of lace formerly worn by women around the neck and shoulders. [TUCK (fold, food) + -ER.]

tucker[2] *tr.v.* **-ered, -ering, -ers.** *Informal.* To weary; exhaust. Usually used in the passive and with *out*: *I'm all tuckered out.* [Frequentative of TUCK (to pull under).]

Tuck•er (tŭk′ər), **Sophie** (1884–1966). U.S. entertainer, born in Russia. In a show-business career that spanned 60 years and encompassed vaudeville, burlesque, nightclub, and television performances, she roused audiences with her renditions of blues and jazz standards.

tuck•et (tŭk′ĭt) *n.* A trumpet fanfare. [From obsolete *t(o)uk,* to sound the trumpet. See **tuck** (drumbeat).]

tuck-shop (tŭk′shŏp′) *n. British.* A shop that sells candy and pastry, especially one in a school. [From TUCK (food).]

Tuc•son (to͞o′sŏn′). City in southeastern Arizona, in a desert valley surrounded by mountains. It is an important transportation and tourist center whose dry, sunny climate attracts many vacationers and sun-seeking winter visitors.

-tude *suffix.* Indicates a condition or state of being; for example, **exactitude.** [Old French, from Latin *-tūdō.*]

Tu•dor (to͞o′dər, tyo͞o′-) *n.* **1.** The family name of the English royal family from Henry VII (1485) to Elizabeth I (1603). **2.** A member of the Tudor family, especially when a monarch: *the Tudors and Stuarts.*

~adj. **1.** Of or pertaining to the Tudors. **2. a.** Of, pertaining to, or characteristic of the period of the Tudors (1485–1603). **b.** Of, designating, or characteristic of the architectural style of the Tudor period, with exposed beams as a typical feature.

Tues•day (to͞oz′dē, -dā′, tyo͞oz′-) *n. Abbr.* **Tues.** The third day of the week, following Monday and preceding Wednesday. [Middle English *tiwesday, tuesdai,* Old English *tīwesdæg,* "day of Tiu" : *Tīw,* TIU + *dæg,* DAY.]

tufted duck *Found in Europe and parts of Asia, and a seasonal visitor to North American shores, the tufted duck lives on lakes and ponds. It feeds mainly on freshwater mussels, fish, frogs, and insects and will dive down more than 3 meters (about 10 feet) to find food.*

tu•fa (to͞o′fə, tyo͞o′-) *n.* **1.** The porous, spongy calcium carbonate deposited around a spring. **2. Tuff** *(see).* [Obsolete Italian *tufa, tufo,* from Latin *tōphus, tōfus*†.] **—tu•fa•ceous** (to͞o-fā′shəs, tyo͞o-) *adj.*

tuff (tŭf) *n.* A rock composed of cemented or fused fragments less than 2 millimeters (1/12 inch) in diameter that have been ejected from a volcano. Also called "tufa." [French *tuf, tuffe,* from obsolete Italian *tufo,* TUFA.] **—tuff•a•ceous** (tŭ-fā′shəs) *adj.*

tuf•fet (tŭf′ĭt) *n.* **1.** A clump or tuft of grass. **2.** A small mound or hillock. **3.** A stool or low seat. [Alteration of TUFT.]

tuft (tŭft) *n.* **1.** A short cluster of hair, feathers, grass, or the like, attached at the base or growing close together. **2.** A dense clump of trees or bushes.

~v. **tufted, tufting, tufts.** *—tr.* **1.** To provide or ornament with a tuft or tufts. **2.** To pass threads through the layers of (a quilt, mattress, or upholstery), securing the thread ends with a knot or button in the depressions thus created. *—intr.* To separate or form into tufts; grow in a tuft. [Middle English *tuft, toft,* from Old French *tof(f)e,* from Germanic.] **—tuft•er** *n.* **—tuft•y** *adj.*

tufted duck *n.* A diving duck, *Aythya fuligula,* with a drooping purple-black crest in the male.

tug (tŭg) *v.* **tugged, tugging, tugs.** *—tr.* **1.** To pull at vigorously; strain at. **2.** To move by pulling with great effort or exertion; haul; drag: *tugged her out of bed.* **3.** To tow by tugboat. *—intr.* **1.** To pull hard: *She tugged at my boots.* **2.** To toil or struggle; strain. **3.** To vie; contend.

~n. **1.** A strong pull or pulling force: *the tug of the sea.* **2.** A hard struggle between opposing forces or parties: *a tug between duty and desire.* **3.** A tugboat. **4.** A rope, chain, or strap used in hauling; especially, a harness trace. [Middle English *tuggen, toggen,* intensive form akin to Old English *tēon,* to draw, pull, tow.] **—tug•ger** *n.*

tug•boat (tŭg′bōt′) *n.* A powerful small boat designed for towing larger vessels. Also called "towboat," "tug."

tug of war *n.* **1.** A contest of strength and skill in which two teams tug on opposite ends of a rope, each trying to pull the other across a line marked out between them. **2.** A struggle for supremacy.

tug•rik (to͞o′grĭk) *n.* The basic monetary unit of the Mongolian People's Republic, equal to 100 mongo. See feature at **currency.** [Mongolian *dughurik,* "round object," wheel.]

tu•i (to͞o′ē) *n.* A New Zealand honeyeater, *Prosthemadera novaeseelandiae,* having greenish-brown plumage and two patches of curly white feathers at the throat. Also called "parson bird." [Maori.]

tu•i•tion (to͞o-ĭsh′ən, tyo͞o-) *n.* **1.** Teaching or instruction, especially of individuals or small groups. **2.** A fee for instruction, especially at a formal institution of learning. **3.** *Archaic.* Guardianship. [Middle English, protection, tutelage, from Old French, from Latin *tuitiō* (stem *tuitiōn-*), protection, a watching, from *tuērī,* to look at, watch, protect.] **—tu•i•tion•al, tu•i•tion•ar•y** (to͞o-ĭsh′ə-nĕr′ē, tyo͞o-) *adj.*

tu•la•re•mi•a (to͞o′lə-rē′mē-ə, tyo͞o′-) *n.* An infectious disease caused by the bacterium *Pasteurella tularensis,* transmitted from infected rodents to humans by insect vectors or by handling infected animals, and characterized by fever and swelling of the lymph nodes. Also called "rabbit fever." [New Latin : *Tulare,* a county in California where it was discovered + -EMIA.]

tu•lip (to͞o′lĭp, tyo͞o′-) *n.* **1.** Any of several bulbous plants of the genus *Tulipa,* native to Asia, widely cultivated for their showy, bell-shaped, variously colored flowers. **2.** The flower or bulb of this plant. [New Latin *Tulipa,* from Turkish *tül(i)bend,* TURBAN (from its turban-shaped flower).]

tulip tree *n.* Either of two trees of the genus *Liriodendron, L. tulipifera,* of North America, or *L. chinensis,* of China, both having tulip-shaped yellow flowers and soft, easily worked wood. Also called "tulip poplar," "yellow poplar."

tu•lip•wood (to͞o′lĭp-wo͝od′, tyo͞o′-) *n.* **1.** The wood of the tulip tree. **2.** The irregularly striped, ornamental wood of any of several other trees. **—tu•lip•wood** *adj.*

tulle (to͞ol) *n.* A fine, often starched net of silk, rayon, or nylon, used especially for veils, tutus, or evening dresses. [French, originally produced in *Tulle,* southwestern France.]

tum (tŭm) *n. British Informal.* The stomach. [Back-formation from TUMMY.]

Tu•ma•ca•co•ri National Monument (to͞o′mə-kä′kə-rē). Site, 4 hectares (10 acres) in area, in southern Arizona, south of Tucson, containing the ruins of a 17th-century Spanish mission.

tum•ble (tŭm′bəl) *v.* **-bled, -bling, -bles.** *—intr.* **1. a.** To fall or roll end over end: *kittens tumbling over each other.* **b.** To fall helplessly or precipitately; pitch headlong. **c.** To move in confusion or disorder; proceed haphazardly: *Children tumbled out of the bus.* **2.** To perform acrobatic feats, such as somersaults or twists. **3. a.** To fall or be toppled, as from a position of power or eminence. **b.** To collapse: *and the walls came tumbling down.* **c.** To drop suddenly and rapidly: *Prices tumbled.* **4.** To come upon accidentally; happen upon. **5.** *Informal.* To come to a sudden understanding; catch on: *tumbled to what she was saying.* *—tr.* **1.** To cause to fall suddenly or violently; overturn or overthrow. **2.** To spill, throw, or mix together haphazardly. **3.** To disturb the order of; disarrange; rumple. **4.** To toss or whirl in a drum or tumbler, especially: **a.** To treat in a tumbling box. **b.** To dry in a tumble dryer.

~n. **1.** An act of tumbling; a fall. **2.** A condition of confusion or disorder. **3.** A disorderly heap or mass. [Middle English *tumblen,* from Middle Low German *tummelen,* Old High German *tumalōn,* frequentative of *tūmōn*; akin to Old English *tumbian,* to dance, and French *tomber,* to fall.]

tum•ble•bug (tŭm′bəl-bŭg′) *n.* Any of various beetles of the family Scarabaeidae that roll up balls of dung to protect their eggs and serve as food for the newly hatched larvae.

tum•ble-down (tŭm′bəl-doun′) *adj.* Dilapidated; rickety.

tumble dryer *n.* A machine that dries clothes by tumbling them in a heated rotating drum.

tum•ble-home (tŭm′bəl-hōm′) *n.* The inward curve of a ship's or boat's topsides above the point of greatest breadth. [From *tumble,* to slope inward (obsolete).]

tum•bler (tŭm′blər) *n.* **1.** One that tumbles; specifically, an acrobat or gymnast. **2. a.** A drinking glass, originally with a rounded bottom. **b.** A flat-bottomed glass having no handle or stem. **c.** The contents of or the amount held by a drinking glass; a tumblerful. **3.** A toy made with a weighted, rounded base so that it can rock over and then right itself. **4.** Any of a breed of domestic pigeons characteristically tumbling or somersaulting in flight. **5.** A piece in a gunlock that forces the hammer forward by action of the mainspring. **6.** The part in a lock that releases the bolt when moved by a key. **7. a.** The drum of a tumble dryer. **b.** A tumbling box. **8. a.** A projecting piece on a revolving or rocking part in a mechanism that transmits motion to the part it engages. **b.** The rocking frame that moves a gear into place in a selective transmission, as in a motor vehicle.

tumbler gear *n. Machinery.* A set of gears operated by a tumbler.

tum•ble•weed (tŭm′bəl-wēd′) *n.* Any of various densely branched New World plants, chiefly of the genus *Amaranthus,* that when withered break off and are rolled about by the wind.

tumbling box *n.* A revolving drum in which objects, such as gemstones, are reduced in size, polished, or cleaned by tumbling with abrasives. Also called "rumble," "tumbler," "tumbling barrel."

tum•brel, tum•bril (tŭm′brəl) *n.* **1.** A two-wheeled covered cart formerly used to transport tools and ammunition. **2.** A farm cart that can be tilted to dump a load, as of dung. **3.** A crude cart used to carry condemned prisoners, as to the stake or to the guillotine during the French Revolution. [Middle English *tumberell,* from Old French *tomberel,* from *tomber,* to let fall, from Frankish *tūmon,* perhaps from Germanic *tumōjan-* (unattested), to leap. See **tumble.**]

tu•me•fa•cient (to͞o′mə-fā′shənt, tyo͞o′-) *adj.* Producing or tending to produce swelling or tumefaction. [Latin *tumefaciēns* (stem *tumefacient-*), present participle of *tumefacere,* to cause to swell : *tumēre,* to swell + *facere,* to make.]

tu•me•fac•tion (to͞o′mə-făk′shən, tyo͞o′-) *n.* **1. a.** The action or process of puffing or swelling. **b.** A swollen condition. **2.** A swollen part. [French, from Latin *tumefactus,* past participle of *tumefacere,* to cause to swell. See **tumefacient.**] **—tu•me•fac•tive** *adj.*

tu•me•fy (to͞o′mə-fī′, tyo͞o′-) *v.* **-fied, -fying, -fies.** *—tr.* To cause to swell. *—intr.* To swell; become tumid. [Old French *tumefier* : Latin *tumēre,* to swell + -FY.]

tu·mes·cent (tōō-mĕs′ənt, tyōō-) adj. Swelling; somewhat tumid. [Latin tumēscēns (stem tumescent-), present participle of tumēscere, to begin to swell, from tumēre, to swell.] —**tu·mes·cence** n.

tu·mid (tōō′mĭd, tyōō′-) adj. 1. Swollen; distended. Said of a bodily part or organ. 2. Of a bulging shape; protuberant. 3. Overblown; bombastic: tumid prose. [Latin tumidus, from tumēre, to swell.] —**tu·mid·i·ty** (tōō-mĭd′ə-tē, tyōō-), **tu·mid·ness** n. —**tu·mid·ly** adv.

tum·my (tŭm′ē) n., pl. -**mies**. Informal. The stomach. [Alteration of STOMACH.]

tu·mor (tōō′mər, tyōō′-) n. 1. A noninflammatory abnormal growth arising from existing tissue but growing independently of the normal rate or structural development of such tissue and serving no physiological function. 2. Any swollen part. [Latin tumor, from tumēre, to swell.]

tu·mor·i·gen·ic (tōō′mər-ə-jĕn′ĭk, tyōō′-) adj. Causing the formation of tumors. —**tu·mor·i·ge·nic·i·ty** (tōō′mər-ə-jə-nĭs′ə-tē) n.

tu·mult (tōō′mŭlt, tyōō′-) n. 1. The din and commotion of a great crowd: the tumult of the marketplace. 2. A disorderly commotion or disturbance; especially, a riot or insurrection. 3. Agitation of the mind or emotions. [Middle English tumulte, from Old French, from Latin tumultus.]

tu·mul·tu·ar·y (tōō-mŭl′chōō-ĕr′ē, tyōō-) adj. Marked by haste, disorder, or confusion. [Latin tumultuārius, from tumultus, TUMULT.]

tu·mul·tu·ous (tōō-mŭl′chōō-əs, tyōō-) adj. 1. Full of tumult and commotion; noisy; clamorous: tumultuous applause. 2. Making a tumult; turbulent; riotous: a tumultuous crowd. 3. Confusedly or violently agitated: a tumultuous heart. —**tu·mul·tu·ous·ly** adv. —**tu·mul·tu·ous·ness** n.

tu·mu·lus (tōō′myə-ləs, tyōō′-) n., pl. -**li** (-lī′). An ancient artificial mound; especially, a burial mound or barrow. [Latin, a raised heap of earth, hillock, tumulus.] —**tu·mu·lar** adj.

tun (tŭn) n. 1. A large cask for liquids, especially beer or wine. 2. A measure of liquid capacity, especially one equivalent to 252 gallons. [Middle English tunne, tonne, a measure of wine, Old English tunne, cask, vat.]

tu·na¹ (tōō′nə, tyōō′-) n., pl. -**nas** or collectively **tuna**. 1. a. Any of various often large marine food fishes of the genus Thunnus and related genera, many of which, including T. thynnus and the albacore, are commercially important sources of canned fish. Also called "tunny." b. Any of several related fishes, such as the bonito. 2. The canned or commercially processed flesh of any of these fishes. In this sense, also called "tuna fish." [American Spanish, ultimately from Latin thunnus. See tunny.]

tuna² n. 1. Any of several tropical American cacti of the genus Opuntia, which includes the prickly pears; especially, O. tuna, bearing edible red fruit. 2. The fruit of such a plant. [Spanish, from Taino.]

tun·a·ble, tune·a·ble (tōō′nə-bəl, tyōō′-) adj. 1. Archaic. Tuneful or melodious. 2. Able to be tuned. —**tun·a·ble·ness** n.

tun·dra (tŭn′drə) n. An area between the perpetual snow and ice of arctic regions and the tree line, having a permanently frozen subsoil and supporting low-growing vegetation such as lichens, mosses, dwarf shrubs, and stunted trees. [Russian, from Lapp tundar; akin to Finnish tunturi, an arctic hill, a bare hill.]

tune (tōōn, tyōōn) n. 1. A succession of musical tones forming a melody, especially one of simple and easily remembered character. 2. a. Correct musical pitch. b. The state of being properly adjusted for pitch: a piano out of tune. 3. a. Agreement in pitch: play in tune with the piano. b. Concord or agreement; harmony: in tune with the times. c. Archaic. Frame of mind; disposition. 4. Electronics. The adjustment of a receiver or circuit for maximum response to a given signal or frequency. 5. Archaic. A musical sound or tone. —**call the tune.** To be in a position to control events. —**change one's tune.** To change one's approach or attitude. —**to the tune of.** To the sum or amount of. ~v. **tuned, tuning, tunes.** —tr. 1. To put (a musical instrument) in the desired pitch with mechanical adjustments. 2. To adjust so as to bring into harmony or accord; adapt; attune: tune oneself to life in the tropics. 3. To adjust (an engine) for maximum performance. 4. To adjust (a radio or television receiver) to receive signals at a particular frequency. 5. Archaic. To utter musically; sing. —intr. To become attuned. —**tune in.** 1. To tune a radio or television to receive a particular program. 2. Slang. To make or become aware or responsive. —**tune out.** 1. To tune a radio or television not to receive a particular program. 2. Slang. To dissociate oneself from one's environment. 3. Slang. To become unresponsive to; ignore. [Middle English, variant of TONE.]

tune·ful (tōōn′fəl, tyōōn′-) adj. 1. Full of tune; melodious; musical. 2. Producing musical sounds. —**tune·ful·ly** adv. —**tune·ful·ness** n.

tune·less (tōōn′lĭs, tyōōn′-) adj. 1. Not melodious or tuneful; unmusical. 2. Giving no music; silent. —**tune·less·ly** adv. —**tune·less·ness** n.

tun·er (tōō′nər, tyōō′-) n. 1. One that tunes: a piano tuner. 2. A device used for tuning; especially, an electronic circuit or device used to select signals at a specific radio frequency for amplification and conversion to sound.

tune up tr.v. 1. To bring (a musical instrument) into proper pitch. 2. To adjust (a motor or engine) to efficient working order. —intr.v. To bring an instrument or group of instruments, as in an orchestra, into proper pitch before a performance or rehearsal.

tune-up (tōōn′ŭp′, tyōōn′-) n. An adjustment of a motor or engine to put it in the most efficient working order.

tung oil (tŭng) n. A yellow oil extracted from the seeds of the tung tree and used as a drying agent in varnishes and paints and for waterproofing. Also called "Chinese wood oil."

tung·state (tŭng′stāt′) n. A chemical compound derived from tungstic acid and containing tungsten with a valence of 6. [TUNGST(EN) + -ATE.]

tung·sten (tŭng′stən) n. Symbol **W** A hard, brittle, corrosion-resistant, gray to white metallic element extracted from wolframite, scheelite, and other minerals, having the highest melting point and lowest vapor pressure of any metal. Tungsten and its alloys are used in high-temperature structural materials, electrical elements, notably lamp filaments, and instruments requiring thermally compatible glass-to-metal seals. Atomic number 74, atomic weight 183.85, melting point 3,410°C, boiling point 5,927°C, specific gravity 19.3 (20°C), valences 2, 3, 4, 5, 6. Also rare "wolfram." [Swedish, "heavy stone" : tung, heavy, from Old Norse thungr + sten, from Old Norse steinn.] —**tung·sten·ic** (tŭng-stĕn′ĭk) adj.

tungsten carbide n. An extremely hard, fine gray powder with composition WC, used in tools, wear-resistant machine parts, and abrasives.

tungsten lamp n. An incandescent electric lamp with a tungsten filament.

tungsten steel n. A hard, heat-resistant steel containing tungsten.

tung·stic (tŭng′stĭk) adj. Of, pertaining to, or containing tungsten, especially with a valence of 6. [From TUNGSTEN.]

tungstic acid n. Any of various acids containing tungstites; especially, a powder, H_2WO_4, used in making textiles and plastics.

tung·stite (tŭng′stīt′) n. A yellow or yellowish-green mineral, essentially WO_3, resulting from the alteration of tungsten ores. [TUNGST(EN) + -ITE.]

tung tree n. Any of several Asian trees of the genus Aleurites; especially, A. cordata, cultivated for its seeds that yield a commercially valuable drying oil. Also called "tung-oil tree." [Mandarin Chinese tóng, tung tree + TREE.]

Tun·gus (tōōng-gōōz′) n., pl. -**guses** or collectively **Tungus**. 1. A member of a Mongoloid people inhabiting eastern Siberia. 2. The Tungusic language of this people. [Russian Tunguz, a Tungus, from Yakut tungus, from Turkic tungus, pig (probably because many Tungus were pig breeders).] —**Tun·gus** adj.

Tun·gus·ic (tōōng-gōō′zĭk) n. A subfamily of the Altaic family of languages, including the Tungus and Manchu languages, spoken in eastern Siberia and northern Manchuria. ~adj. Of or pertaining to the Tungus people or to Tungusic.

tu·nic (tōō′nĭk, tyōō′-) n. 1. a. A loose-fitting garment, sleeved or sleeveless, extending to the knees and worn by women and men especially in ancient Greece and Rome. b. A medieval surcoat. 2. a. A long plain close-fitting jacket, usually with a high stiff collar, forming part of a military or police uniform. b. A long plain sleeved or sleeveless blouse worn over a skirt by women. 3. Anatomy. A coat or layer enveloping an organ or part. 4. Botany. A membranous outer covering, as of a seed. 5. A tunicle. [Latin tunica, a sheath, tunic, from a Phoenician source, from Aramaic kittūnā, akin to Hebrew kəthōnet. See also chiton.]

tu·ni·ca (tōō′nĭ-kə, tyōō′-) n., pl. -**cae** (-kē′, -kī′, -sē′). Anatomy. An enclosing membrane or layer of tissue; integument. [New Latin, from Latin, TUNIC.]

tu·ni·cate (tōō′nĭ-kĭt, -nĭ-kāt′, tyōō′-) n. Any of various chordate marine animals of the subphylum Urochordata (or Tunicata), having a cylindrical or globular body enclosed in a tough outer covering, or tunic, and including the sea squirts and salps. ~adj. 1. Of or pertaining to the tunicates. 2. Anatomy. Having a tunic or tunica. 3. Botany. Having concentric layers, as does the bulb of an onion. [Latin tunicātus, past participle of tunicāre, to clothe with a tunic, from tunica, TUNIC.]

tu·ni·cle (tōō′nĭ-kəl, tyōō′-) n. A short vestment worn over the alb by a subdeacon or with the dalmatic by a bishop or cardinal. Also called "tunic." [Middle English, from Latin tunicula, diminutive of tunica, TUNIC.]

tuning fork n. A small two-pronged metal device that when struck produces a sound of fixed pitch.

Tu·nis (tōō′nĭs, tyōō′-). Capital of Tunisia. In the northeast of the country on a lagoon inland from the Gulf of Tunis, it is southwest of the site of Carthage.

Tu·ni·sia (tōō-nē′zhə, -zhē-ə, -nĭzh′ə, -nĭzh′ē-ə, tyōō′-). Largely desert country of North Africa. The economy is dominated by oil, which accounts for more than a third of the country's exports. Despite little farmland, 40 percent of workers are in agriculture, and olive oil is a major export. A French protectorate from 1881, Tunisia became independent in 1956. Area, 163,610 square kilometers (63,170 square miles). Population, 6,400,000. Capital, Tunis. —**Tu·ni·sian** n. & adj. See map, next page.

tun·nel (tŭn′əl) n. 1. A passage excavated underground, through a hill or mountain, or under a river or sea, especially one for a road or railway. 2. An underground gallery in a mine. 3. An animal's burrow. 4. Archaic. The flue of a chimney. ~v. **tunneled** or -**nelled, -neling** or -**nelling, -nels.** —tr. 1. To make a tunnel under or through. 2. To make by or as if by excavating: tunnel a passage; tunnel one's way out. —intr. 1. To make a tunnel. 2. Physics. To pass through a barrier by the tunnel effect. Used of a particle. [Middle English tonel, a pipelike net for catching birds, from Old French ton(n)el, a cask, from tonne, a tun, from Medieval Latin tunna, tonna, TUN.] —**tun·nel·er, tun·nel·ler** n.

tunnel diode n. Electronics. A semiconductor diode with a very

turkey *The wild turkey (above), native to the woodlands of North America, was introduced into Europe in the 16th century. It is the ancestor of modern farmyard breeds reared for their meat, such as the turkey below.*

narrow, heavily doped p-n junction across which electrons travel by the tunnel effect. Also called "Esaki diode."

tunnel disease *n. Medicine.* **Decompression sickness** *(see).*

tunnel effect *n. Physics.* An effect, explained by quantum mechanics, by which a particle can pass through a barrier even though it does not have enough energy to overcome the barrier according to classical mechanics.

tunnel vision *n.* **1.** A defect or restriction of lateral vision. **2.** *Informal.* An inability to take a broad or long-term view of a situation because of obsessive concentration on a single one of its problems or aspects.

Tun·ney (tŭn′ē), **James Joseph,** known as "Gene" (1898–1978). U.S. prizefighter. A lightweight champion in 1922 and 1923, he began fighting as a heavyweight in 1924 and defeated Jack Dempsey in their 1926 championship bout. After two title defenses he retired as undefeated world heavyweight champion (1928).

tun·ny (tŭn′ē) *n., pl.* **-nies** or collectively **tunny.** See **tuna** (sense 1a). [Old Italian *tonnos,* from Old Provençal *ton,* from Latin *thynnus,* from Greek *thunnos,* akin to Hebrew *tannīn,* "great sea monster."]

tup (tŭp) *n.* **1.** *Chiefly British.* A male sheep; a ram. **2.** A heavy metal body; especially, the head of a power hammer.
~*tr.v.* **tupped, tupping, tups.** To copulate with (a ewe). Used of a ram. [Middle English *toupe, tup(pe)†,* a ram.]

Tu·pa·ma·ro (tŏŏ′pə-mär′ō) *n., pl.* **-ros.** A member of an extreme left-wing urban guerrilla organization in Uruguay. [After *Tupac Amaru,* 18th-century Peruvian Indian leader of a rebellion against the Spanish.] —**Tu·pa·ma·ro** *adj.*

tu·pe·lo (tŏŏ′pə-lō′, tyŏŏ′-) *n., pl.* **-los.** **1.** Any of several trees of the genus *Nyssa;* especially, *N. aquatica,* of the southeastern United States, having soft, light wood. **2.** The wood of any of these trees. [Creek *ito opilwa,* "swamp tree" : *ito,* tree + *opilwa,* swamp.]

Tu·pi (tŏŏ′pē, tŏŏ-pē′) *n., pl.* **-pis** or collectively **Tupi.** **1.** A member of a group of South American Indian peoples living along the coast of Brazil, in the Amazon valley, and in Paraguay. **2.** The language of these peoples, a branch of Tupi-Guarani. —**Tu·pi, Tu·pi·an** (tŏŏ′pē-ən, tŏŏ-pē′ən) *adj.*

Tu·pi-Gua·ra·ni (tŏŏ-pē′gwär′ə-nē′, tŏŏ′pē-) *n.* A family of languages spoken throughout large areas of coastal Brazil, the Amazon valley, and northeastern South America. —**Tu·pi-Gua·ra·ni, Tu·pi-Gua·ra·ni·an** *adj.*

tuppence. *British Informal.* Variant of **twopence.**

tuppenny. *Chiefly British Informal.* Variant of **twopenny.**

Tup·per·ware (tŭp′ər-wâr′) *n.* A trademark for a range of polyethylene containers used especially in the home for storing food.

tu quo·que (tŏŏ kwō′kwē, kō′kwē, tyŏŏ) *n.* A retort accusing an accuser of a similar fault or offense. [Latin, "you also."]

turaco. Variant of **touraco.**

Tu·ra·ni·an (tŏŏ-rā′nē-ən, tyŏŏ-) *n.* **1.** A language group, **Ural-Altaic** *(see).* **2.** A member of any of the peoples who speak languages of this group. [Persian *Tūrān,* region north of the Oxus River.] —**Tu·ra·ni·an** *adj.*

tur·ban (tûr′bən) *n.* **1.** A man's headdress of Muslim origin but also worn by Sikhs and some Hindus that consists of a long scarf of linen, cotton, or silk wound around the head or a cap. **2.** Any hat or headdress resembling a turban; especially, a type of brimless hat worn by women. [French *turbant, tolliban,* from Italian *turbante, tolipante,* from Turkish *tül(i)bend,* Persian *dulband†.*] —**tur·baned** *adj.*

tur·ba·ry (tûr′bə-rē) *n., pl.* **-ries. 1.** A place where peat can be dug; a peat bog. **2.** *Law.* In England, the right to dig peat or turf on common land or someone else's ground. [Middle English *turbary(e),* turf land, peat bog, from Norman French, from Old French *t(o)ur-*

berie, Medieval Latin *turbaria,* from *turba,* turf, from Germanic.]

tur·bel·lar·i·an (tûr′bə-lâr′ē-ən) *n.* Any of various chiefly aquatic ciliate flatworms of the class Turbellaria. [New Latin *Turbellaria,* from Latin *turbellae* (plural), bustle, stir (their cilia vibrate and produce little whirls in the water), from *turba,* turmoil, uproar. See **turbid.**] —**tur·bel·lar·i·an** *adj.*

tur·bid (tûr′bĭd) *adj.* **1.** Containing sediment or foreign particles stirred up or suspended; muddy; cloudy: *turbid water.* **2.** Heavy, dark, or dense, as smoke or fog. **3.** In turmoil; muddled: *turbid feelings.* [Latin *turbidus,* wild, confused, muddy, from *turba,* turmoil, uproar, probably from Greek *turbē,* disorder.] —**tur·bid·i·ty** (tûr-bĭd′ə-tē), **tur·bid·ness** *n.* —**tur·bid·ly** *adv.*

tur·bi·nal (tûr′bə-nəl) *adj.* **1.** Having the shape of a cone resting on its apex. **2.** Having the shape of a scroll.
~*n. Anatomy.* A turbinate bone. [Latin *turbō* (stem *turbin-*), a spinning thing, top. See **turbine.**]

tur·bi·nate (tûr′bə-nĭt, -nāt′) *adj.* Also **tur·bi·nat·ed** (-nā′tĭd). **1.** *Zoology.* Spiral and decreasing sharply in diameter from base to apex. Said of a shell. **2.** *Anatomy.* Designating a small scroll-like bone that extends horizontally along the lateral wall of the nasal passage. **3.** Shaped like a top. **4.** Spinning like a top. [Latin *turbinātus,* from *turbō* (stem *turbin-*), a top. See **turbine.**]

tur·bine (tûr′bĭn, -bīn′) *n.* Any of various machines in which the kinetic energy of a moving fluid is converted to rotational energy by the impulse or reaction of the fluid with a series of buckets or blades arrayed about the circumference of a wheel or cylinder. See **gas turbine, impulse turbine, reaction turbine.** [French, from Latin *turbō* (stem *turbin-*), a spinning thing, top, whirlwind, perhaps from Greek *turbē,* disorder.]

tur·bit (tûr′bĭt) *n.* Any of a breed of domestic pigeons having a small crested head and a ruffled breast. [Perhaps from Latin *turbō,* top (see **turbine**), referring to its shape.]

tur·bo (tûr′bō′) *n., pl.* **-bos.** A car or other vehicle with an engine fitted with a turbocharger [Probably shortened from TURBO-CHARGER or TURBOSUPERCHARGER.]

turbo– *prefix.* Indicates: **1.** Turbine; for example, **turbocharger.** **2.** Pertaining to or driven by a turbine; for example, **turbojet.** [From TURBINE.]

tur·bo·charg·er (tûr′bō-chär′jər) *n.* A device that uses the exhaust gas of an internal-combustion engine to drive a turbine that in turn drives a supercharger attached to the engine.

tur·bo·elec·tric (tûr′bō-ĭ-lĕk′trĭk) *adj.* Designating, pertaining to, or using electricity produced by a turbine.

tur·bo·fan (tûr′bō-făn′) *n.* **1.** A turbojet engine in which a fan supplements the total thrust by forcing air diverted from the main engine directly into the hot turbine exhaust. **2.** An aircraft in which such an engine is used.

tur·bo·gen·er·a·tor (tûr′bō-jĕn′ə-rā′tər) *n.* A large electric generator in a power station that is driven by a turbine.

tur·bo·jet (tûr′bō-jĕt′) *n.* **1.** A jet engine having a turbine-driven compressor and developing thrust from the exhaust of hot gases. **2.** An aircraft in which such an engine is used.

tur·bo·prop (tûr′bō-prŏp′) *n.* **1.** A turbojet engine used to drive an external propeller. Also called "prop-jet." **2.** An aircraft in which such an engine is used. [Short for *turbopropeller.*]

tur·bo·ram·jet (tûr′bō-răm′jĕt′) *n.* **1.** A turbojet engine that at high speeds compresses air taken in as a ramjet and increases exhaust velocities with an afterburner. **2.** An aircraft in which such an engine is used.

tur·bo·su·per·charg·er (tûr′bō-sŏŏ′pər-chär′jər) *n.* A supercharger that uses an exhaust-driven turbine to maintain air-intake pressure in high-altitude aircraft.

tur·bot (tûr′bət) *n., pl.* **-bots** or collectively **turbot. 1.** A European flatfish, *Scophthalmus maximus,* prized as food. **2.** Any of various similar or related flatfishes. [Middle English, from Old French *torbaut,* probably from Old Swedish *törnbut,* turbot, "thorn-flatfish" : *törn,* thorn + *but,* flatfish.]

tur·bu·la·tor (tûr′byə-lā′tər) *n.* Any device designed to cause turbulence in fluids. [From TURBULENT.]

tur·bu·lence (tûr′byə-ləns) *n.* **1.** The state or quality of being agitated, violently disturbed, or in commotion. **2.** Turbulent flow. **3.** Disturbances in the atmosphere, such as air pockets and currents.

tur·bu·lent (tûr′byə-lənt) *adj.* **1.** Violently agitated or disturbed: *turbulent rapids.* **2.** Having a restless, uncertain, or chaotic character; stormy: *a turbulent period of history.* **3.** Inclined to unrest or disorder; unruly; tumultuous. [Latin *turbulentus,* from *turba,* confusion. See **turbid.**] —**tur·bu·lent·ly** *adv.*

turbulent flow *n.* The motion of a fluid having local velocities and pressures that fluctuate randomly. Also called "turbulence." Compare **laminar flow, streamline flow.**

Turcoman. Variant of **Turkoman.**

tu·reen (tŏŏ-rēn′, tyŏŏ-) *n.* A broad, deep, often oval dish with a lid, used for serving soups, stews, or the like. [Earlier *ter(r)ene,* from French *terrine,* "earthen vessel," from Old French, feminine of *terrin,* from Vulgar Latin *terrīnus,* from Latin *terra,* earth.]

turf (tûrf) *n., pl.* **turfs** or archaic **turves** (tûrvz). **1.** A surface layer of earth containing a dense growth of grass and its matted roots; sod. **2.** A piece cut from such a layer of earth or sod. **3.** A piece of peat that is burned for use as fuel. **4.** *Slang.* **a.** The area claimed by a juvenile gang as its personal territory. **b.** An indefinite geographic area; territory. **5. a.** A racetrack. **b.** The sport or business of racing horses; the world of racing. [Middle English *turf,* Old English *turf.*] —**turf·y** *adj.*

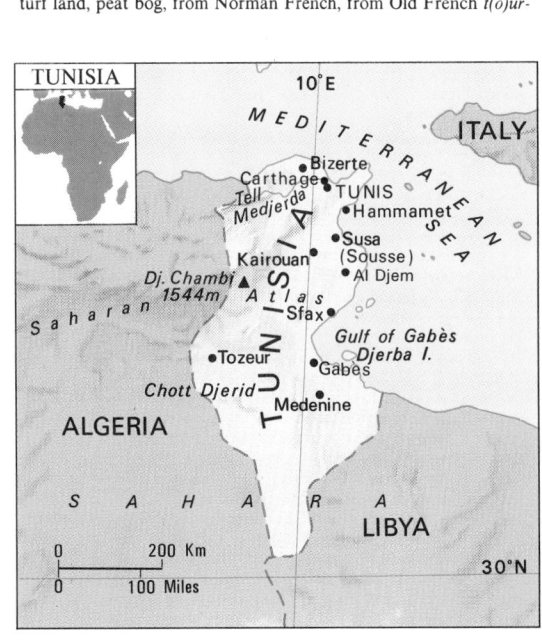

turf accountant *n. British.* A bookmaker *(see).*

Tur·ge·nev (tōōr-gān′yəf), **Ivan Sergeyevich** (1818–83). Russian writer. His collection of stories, *A Sportsman's Sketches* (1852), contributed toward the emancipation of the serfs. His novels, such as *Fathers and Children* (1862), are eloquent portrayals of the ineffectual Russian gentry.

tur·ges·cence (tûr-jĕs′əns) *n.* **1.** The process of swelling up, or the condition of being swollen. **2.** Pomposity; self-importance. [Latin *turgēscens* (stem *turgēscent-*), present participle of *turgēscere*, inceptive of *turgēre*, to be swollen. See **turgid.**] —**tur·ges·cent** *adj.*

tur·gid (tûr′jĭd) *adj.* **1.** Distended; swollen; bloated. **2.** Excessively ornate in style or language; grandiloquent. **3.** Fully expanded from water intake. Said of plants. [Latin *turgidus,* from *turgēre†*, to be swollen, swell.] —**tur·gid·i·ty** (tûr-jĭd′ə-tē), **tur·gid·ness** *n.* —**tur·gid·ly** *adv.*

tur·gor (tûr′gər, -gôr) *n. Biology.* The normal fullness or tension produced by the fluid content of blood vessels, capillaries, and plant or animal cells. The maintenance of turgor is the primary method of support in herbaceous plants. [Late Latin, from Latin *turgēre,* to be swollen. See **turgid.**]

Tu·rin (tōōr′ĭn, tyōōr′-). *Italian* **To·ri·no** (tô-rē′nō). City of northwestern Italy. The capital of Piedmont and of Turin province, it was founded by the Romans at the confluence of the Po and Dora Riparia rivers. It is the former capital of the kingdom of Sardinia (1720) and of Italy (1861–65). The 15th-century cathedral has a chapel containing the Shroud of Turin, considered by some to be the cloth in which the body of Christ was wrapped after the Crucifixion.

tu·ri·on (tōōr′ē-ən) *n.* A bud produced by many aquatic plants that is shed from the parent plant and remains dormant until the spring. [French, from Latin *turiō* (stem *turiōn-*), shoot.]

Turk (tûrk) *n.* **1.** A native or inhabitant of Turkey. **2.** A person speaking a Turkic language. **3.** *Informal.* A brutal or tyrannical person. [Middle English, from Old French *Turc,* from Medieval Latin *Turcus,* from Turkish *Türk.*]

Turk. Turkey; Turkish.

Turkestan. Variant of **Turkistan.**

Turkestan, Chinese. See **Xinjiang Uigur Zizhiqu.**

tur·key (tûr′kē) *n., pl.* **-keys** or collectively **turkey. 1. a.** A large North American bird, *Meleagris gallopavo,* that has brownish plumage and a bare, wattled head and neck and is widely domesticated for food. **b.** A related bird, *Agriocharis ocellata,* of Mexico and Central America. **2.** *Slang.* A film, play, or other production that fails; a flop. **3.** *Slang.* A person regarded as inept or undesirable. —**talk turkey.** *Informal.* To discuss in a straightforward and direct manner. [After **TURKEY,** from a confusion with the guinea fowl imported from Turkish territory.]

Tur·key (tûr′kē). *Abbr.* **Turk.** Republic of southeastern Europe and western Asia, mostly covering the Anatolian plateau (Asia Minor). Farming is the main occupation, with cotton, tobacco, and textile yarns and fabrics making up 66 percent of the exports. Turkey has reserves of coal, lignite, oil, and iron, and chrome is exported. Tourism is an important source of foreign exchange. The country was the center of the Ottoman Empire for almost 700 years, but became a republic in 1923. There have been several military governments since 1946, and Turkey pursues a course between East and West, joining NATO (1952) and signing a nonaggression and trade pact with the U.S.S.R. (1978). Relations with Greece are uneasy because of Cyprus and the disputed border. Istanbul is the largest city and chief port. Area, 780,756 square kilometers (301,382 square miles). Population, 45,200,000. Capital, Ankara. See map, next page.

turkey buzzard *n.* A New World vulture, *Cathartes aura,* having dark plumage and a bare red head and neck similar to that of the turkey. Also called **"turkey vulture."**

turkey cock *n.* **1.** A male turkey. **2.** *Informal.* A strutting, conceited man.

Turkey red *n.* A brilliant red. [The color was often used in cotton cloth manufactured in Turkey.]

turkey trot *n.* A ragtime dance of the early 20th century, characterized by a springy walk with the feet well apart and a swinging up-and-down movement of the shoulders.

Tur·ki (tûr′kē) *adj.* **1.** Of or pertaining to Turkic. **2.** Of or pertaining to the Turkic-speaking peoples, especially those speaking an Eastern Turkic language.
~*n.* Any Turkic language or Turkic speaker.

Tur·kic (tûr′kĭk) *n.* A subdivision of the Altaic family of languages, including Turkish, Turkoman, Azerbaidzhani, Tatar, Uzbek, Uigur, Kirgiz, Karakalpak, Chuvash, Chagatai, and Yakut.
~*adj.* **1.** Of or pertaining to the language or people of Turkey. **2.** Of or pertaining to Turkic.

Turk·ish (tûr′kĭsh) *adj. Abbr.* **Turk. 1.** Of or pertaining to Turkey or the Turks. **2.** Of or pertaining to the Turkic language of Turkey.
~*n. Abbr.* **Turk.** The Turkic language of Turkey. When written in the Arabic script, as it was until 1930, it is generally referred to as Ottoman Turkish or Osmanli.

Turkish bath *n.* **1.** A steam bath inducing heavy perspiration, usually followed by a shower and often a massage. **2.** *Often* **Turkish baths.** An establishment where such bathing facilities are available.

Turkish coffee *n.* Strong, sweet black coffee made from very finely ground beans and served in tiny cups.

Turkish delight *n.* A gelatinous candy of Turkish origin, cut into cubes and dredged in powdered sugar.

Turkish Empire. See **Ottoman Empire.**

---

turbine

THE ENGINE WITH CONTINUOUS ROTARY MOTION
The turbine principle is found in powerhouses and jet aircraft

A turbine, which moves with a spinning motion, is more efficient than a reciprocating engine, which has a to-and-fro movement. In the latter the constant change of direction wastes energy, but the smooth, continuous motion of the turbine allows it to attain very high speeds.

Running water was mankind's earliest power source and a Frenchman, Benoît Fourneyron, is generally credited with building the first practical water-driven turbine in 1827. Now, about a quarter of the world's electricity is generated by water turbines. However, water sources suitable for driving hydroelectric generators are not available everywhere, and steam-driven turbines

were developed for other locations. The first working device was produced in 1883 by a Swiss, Carl Gustaf de Laval, but the British engineer Charles A. Parsons built a more practical model in 1884. Steam-turbine generators are now in worldwide use. Some produce enough power for a city of a million people.

Work on gas turbines started in this century. They are useful standby generators at powerhouses and have dramatically affected the field of aviation as jet engines—first built in the 1930's by two engineers working independently of each other, Hans Pabst von Ohain of Germany and Frank Whittle of Great Britain.

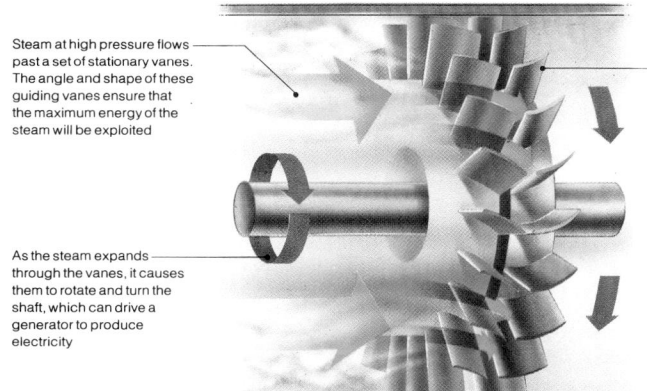

Steam at high pressure flows past a set of stationary vanes. The angle and shape of these guiding vanes ensure that the maximum energy of the steam will be exploited.

The steam hits the next set of vanes, attached to a rotating shaft. In an actual turbine the steam would pass on through many more sets of stationary and rotating vanes

As the steam expands through the vanes, it causes them to rotate and turn the shaft, which can drive a generator to produce electricity

STEAM TURBINE *Modern turbines follow essentially the same pattern as that used by Parsons in 1884. Only two sets of vanes are shown above, but a typical turbine would have many sets, alternately guiding and rotating, to extract maximum energy from the steam.*

Turkish Federated State of Cyprus. The northern part of Cyprus, occupied by Turkey in 1974 and proclaimed a federated state the following year.

Turkish towel *n.* A thick rough terry towel.

Tur·ki·stan, Tur·ke·stan (tûr′kĭ-stăn′, -stän′). Region of central Asia. A crossroads for trade and conquest, it has historically been the subject of dispute and is now divided between China, Afghanistan, and the U.S.S.R. Soviet Turkistan is divided into the Kazakh, Kirgiz, Tadzhik, Turkmen, and Uzbek Soviet Socialist Republics.

Turk·men Soviet Socialist Republic (tûrk′mən). Also **Turk·men·i·stan** (tûrk-mĕn′ĭ-stăn′, -stän′), **Turk·me·ni·a** (tûrk-mē′nē-ə, -mĕn′yə). Constituent republic of the U.S.S.R., east of the Caspian Sea, established as a republic in 1925. Largely consisting of the desert of the Kara Kum, it has a population concentrated around oases, where subsistence farming is the chief occupation. Ashkhabad is the capital. —**Turk·me·ni·an** *adj.*

Tur·ko·man, Tur·co·man (tûr′kə-mən) *n., pl.* **-mans. 1.** Any of a formerly nomadic people inhabiting the Turkmen, Uzbek, Kazakh, and Kara-Kalpak republics of the U.S.S.R. **2.** The Turkic language of this people. —**Tur·ko·man, Tur·co·man** *adj.*

Turks and Cai·cos Islands (tûrks; kī′kəs). Two groups of islands in the Bahamas, western Atlantic Ocean, forming a self-governing British colony. Grand Turk is the seat of government.

Turk's-cap lily (tûrks′kăp′) *n.* Any of various cultivated lilies having colorful, turban-shaped flowers, such as the **martagon** *(see).*

Turk's-head (tûrks′hĕd′) *n. Nautical.* A turban-shaped knot made by winding a smaller rope around a larger one.

Turkut. See **Old Turkic.**

tur·mer·ic (tûr′mər-ĭk) *n.* **1.** A plant, *Curcuma longa,* of India, having yellow flowers and an aromatic rootstock. **2.** The powdered rootstock of this plant, used to flavor or color food and as a yellow dye. **3.** Any of several other plants having similar roots. [Earlier *tarmaret,* from Old French *terre mérite,* from Medieval Latin *terra merita,* "meritorious earth," alteration of a native name.]

turmeric paper *n.* Paper saturated with turmeric and used as an indicator for the presence of alkalis, which turn the paper brown, or for boric acid, which turns it red-brown.

tur·moil (tûr′moil′) *n.* A state of violent agitation or utter confusion; tumult. [16th century : origin obscure.]

turn (tûrn) *v.* **turned, turning, turns.** —*tr.* **1.** To cause to move around a central point; cause to rotate or revolve: *The wind turns the sails of the windmill.* **2.** To cause to move around in order to achieve a desired result: *turn the handle to open.* **3.** To alter or

PRONUNCIATION KEY

ă, pat; ā, pay; âr, care; ä, father, art; b, bib; ch, church; d, deed; ĕ, pet; ē, be; f, fife; g, gag; h, hat; hw, which; ĭ, pit; ī, pie; îr, pier; j, judge; k, kick; l, lid, needle; m, mum; n, no, sudden; ng, thing; ŏ, pot; ō, toe; ô, paw, for; oi, noise; ou, out; ŏŏ, book; ōō, boot; p, pop; r, roar; s, sauce; sh, ship, dish; t, tight; th, thin, path; *th,* this, bathe; ŭ, cut; ûr, fur; v, valve; w, with; y, yes; z, zebra, size; zh, vision; ə, about, item, edible, gallop, circus, peaceful

IN FOREIGN WORDS:

à, *Fr.* ami; œ, *Fr.* feu, *Ger.* schön; ü, *Fr.* tu, *Ger.* über; KH, *Ger.* ich, *Scot.* loch; N, *Fr.* bon; y′, *Fr.* Compiègne

STRESS MARKS:

Primary stress: ′
  in·cite′ (ĭn-sīt′)
Secondary stress: ′
  in′sight′ (ĭn′sīt′)

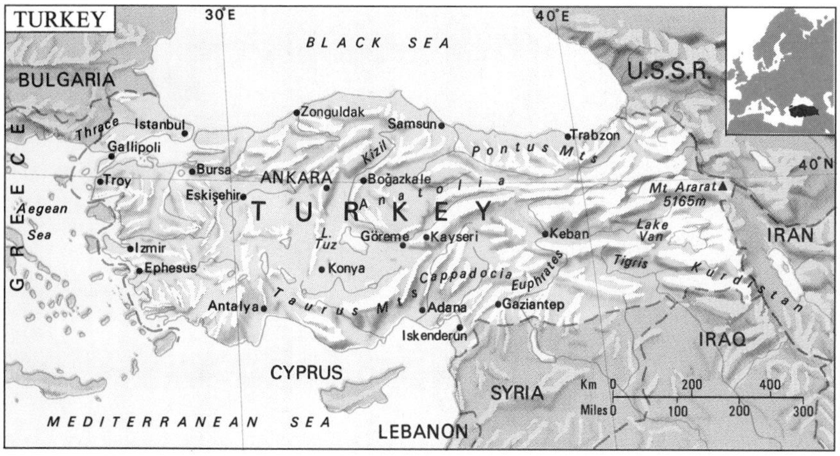
TURKEY
30°E
40°E
BLACK SEA
BULGARIA
U.S.S.R.
Zonguldak
Samsun
Trabzon
Thrace
Istanbul
Gallipoli
Kizil
Pontus Mts
Bursa
ANKARA
Boğazkale
Anatolia
40°N
Troy
Eskişehir
Mt Ararat
5165m
GREECE
Aegean Sea
TURKEY
L. Tuz
Göreme
Kayseri
Keban
Lake Van
IRAN
Izmir
Ephesus
Konya
Cappadocia
Euphrates
Tigris
Kurdistan
Antalya
Taurus Mts
Adana
Gaziantep
Iskenderun
IRAQ
CYPRUS
SYRIA
Km 0 200 400
Miles 0 100 200 300
MEDITERRANEAN SEA
LEBANON

control the functioning of (a mechanical device, for example), especially by means of a rotating or similar movement: *turn the radio down.* **4.** To perform or accomplish by rotating or revolving: *turn a somersault.* **5. a.** To change the position of so that the underside becomes the upperside: *turn the steak.* **b.** To dig or plow (soil) to bring the undersoil to the surface. **c.** To reverse the material of (a collar or cuff, for example) so that the inner side becomes the outer. **d.** To reverse or fundamentally disturb the order, disposition, or character of: *turned the room upside down in her search; turned the argument completely around.* **6. a.** To produce a rounded shape in (wood or metal, for example) by applying a cutting tool while rotating on a lathe. **b.** To produce a rounded form in by any means: *turn a heel in knitting a sock.* **c.** To give shape or form to by rotating: *turn a vase on a potter's wheel.* **d.** To give distinctive, artistic, or elegant form to: *turn a phrase.* **7.** To weigh in the mind; think over; ponder. Often used with *over*: *turn an idea over.* **8. a.** To change the position of by moving through an arc of a circle: *turned her chair to face me.* **b.** To change the position of by folding, twisting, or bending: *turn the blankets down.* **c.** To change the position of so as to show another side: *turn the page.* **d.** To injure by twisting: *turn an ankle.* **e.** To upset or make nauseated: *That turns my stomach.* **9. a.** To change the direction or course of: *turn the car around.* **b.** To cause (a cricket ball) to change direction on pitching; spin. **10.** To divert or deflect: *turn aside a blow.* **11.** To reverse the course of; cause to retreat: *turn the enemy.* **12.** To make a course around or about: *turn the corner.* **13.** To change, affect, or influence the character or tendency of: *a speech that turned the election.* **14.** To disturb the emotional or mental balance of; unsettle: *"Sudden prosperity had turned Garrick's head"* (Lord Macaulay). **15.** To set or point in a specified way or direction: *turned her back on them.* **16.** To set going in a specified direction; direct: *turned our steps toward home.* **17.** To aim or focus; train: *turn a spotlight on the intruders.* **18.** To direct (the attention, interest, or mind, for example) toward or away from something: *turn a deaf ear.* **19.** To devote or apply (oneself or one's efforts, for example) to something: *turned my hand to a bit of decorating.* **20.** To reach or surpass (a specified age, time, or amount): *just turned thirty.* **21.** To cause to act or go against; make antagonistic. **22.** To send, drive, or let go: *threatened to turn us out; turn the dog loose.* **23.** To pour, let fall, or otherwise release (contents) from a receptacle: *turn the dough onto a floured board.* **24.** To make sour; curdle: *Lemon juice turns milk.* **25.** To affect or change the color of: *Autumn turns the leaves.* **26.** To change or convert; transform. Often used with *into*: *turned the rundown house into a showplace.* **27.** To cause to take on a specified character, nature, or appearance: *Worry turned her hair gray.* **28. a.** To make a bend or curve in: *turn a bar of steel.* **b.** To blunt or dull (the edge of a cutting instrument). **29.** To earn: *turn an honest penny.* —*intr.* **1.** To move around an axis or center; rotate; revolve. **2.** To appear to revolve or whirl, as in dizziness or giddiness: *My head keeps turning.* **3.** To roll from side to side or back and forth: *tossed and turned all night.* **4.** To operate a lathe. **5.** To change one's position so as to face in a different or opposite direction: *turned away at the sight. Everyone turned around as I entered.* **6. a.** To move so as to follow a different or opposite course; take a new direction: *turned and ran; turned into a side street.* **b.** To change direction on pitching. Used of a cricket ball. **7.** To change in behavior or attitude so as to become hostile or antagonistic: *turned against her former colleagues.* **8.** To attack suddenly and violently with no apparent motive: *The dog turned on me.* **9.** To direct one's attention, interest, or thought toward or away from something. **10.** To adopt a new religion; become converted. **11.** To switch one's loyalty from one side or party to another. **12.** To have recourse for help, support, or information: *didn't know whom to turn to; turned to drugs.* **13.** To devote or apply oneself to something, as to a field of study. **14. a.** To depend for an outcome; rely: *Success turns on the effectiveness of our advertising.* **b.** To have a particular focal point or central feature; hinge: *The debate turned on the issue of subsidies.* **15. a.** To undergo a change: *Our luck finally turned.* **b.** To change by passing from one state into another; become transformed: *Our surprise turned to horror.* **c.** To change so as to assume the specified nature, role, or characteristics; become: *turned traitor. It suddenly turned cold.* **16.** To become sour; curdle or ferment. **17.** To change color. **18.** To become dull or blunt after bending back. Used of the edge of a cutting instrument. **—turn down. 1.** To reduce the speed, volume, intensity, or flow of. **2.** *Informal.* To reject or refuse (an offer or proposal, for example). **—turn in. 1. a.** To deliver over, as to the police: *turned herself in.* **b.** To hand in; give in: *turn in an income-tax return.* **2.** To register or produce: *turned in a creditable performance.* **3.** *Informal.* To go to bed. **—turn tail.** To run away; flee. **—turn to.** To begin work; apply oneself to a task.

∼*n.* **1.** An act of turning or being turned around an axis or center; a rotation or revolution. **2.** The act or an action of turning to face or move in a different or opposite direction: *a right turn.* **3.** A point at which something turns or turns off; a bend or junction; a turning: *take the first turn on the left.* **4.** A point of change in time: *the turn of the century.* **5.** A deviation from an existing course or trend; a new departure or development: *took a turn for the worse.* **6.** A right, duty, or opportunity to do something allotted to an individual according to some roster or implicitly agreed order of succession: *my turn to do the dishes.* **7.** A period of participation in something: *a turn at creative writing.* **8.** A characteristic mood, style, or habit; a natural inclination: *a speculative turn of mind.* **9.** A propensity or adeptness: *a turn for carpentry.* **10.** A deed or action having a specified effect on another: *One good turn deserves another.* **11.** Advantage or purpose: *It served her turn.* **12.** A short walk or excursion: *a turn in the park.* **13.** A twist or other distortion in shape. **14.** The condition of being twisted or wound. **15. a.** A winding of one thing about another. **b.** A single wind or convolution, as of wire upon a spool. **16.** *Music.* A figure or ornament consisting of four notes in rapid succession, the second and fourth of which are identical, with the first a degree above, and the third a degree below. **17.** A distinctive form of style or expression: *a nice turn of phrase.* **18.** An attack of illness or severe nervousness; a fit; a spell. **19.** *Informal.* A momentary shock or scare: *I had quite a turn when I heard the news.* **20. a.** A brief performance, as in the theater or circus; an act: *the turns of a vaudeville show.* **b.** A performer in such an act. **21. a.** A transaction on the stock market involving both a sale and a purchase. **b.** A similar commercial transaction. **—at every turn.** At every point or moment; continually. **—by turns.** Alternately; one after another. **—in turn.** In the proper order or sequence. **—out of turn. 1.** Not in the proper order or sequence. **2.** At an inappropriate time or in an inappropriate manner. **—take turns.** To take part or do something in order, one after another. **—to a turn.** To a precise degree; perfectly: *The roast was done to a turn.* [Middle English *turnen, tornen,* from Old English *tyrnan, turnian* and Old French *to(u)rner,* both from Latin *tornāre,* to turn in a lathe, round off, from *tornus,* a lathe, from Greek *tornos,* tool for drawing a circle, circle, lathe.]

Synonyms: *circle, eddy, gyrate, revolve, roll, rotate, spin, swirl, swivel, whirl.*

turn·a·bout (tûrn′ə-bout′) *n.* **1.** The act of turning around and facing or moving in the opposite direction. **2.** A shift or reversal in opinion, policy, or allegiance.

turn·a·round (tûrn′ə-round′) *n.* **1.** A space, as in a driveway, permitting the turning around of a vehicle. **2.** The time needed to load, unload, and service a ship, airplane, or the like. **3.** A turnabout.

turn bridge *n.* A **swing bridge** *(see).*

turn·buck·le (tûrn′bŭk′əl) *n.* A metal coupling device consisting of an oblong piece internally threaded at both ends, into each end of which a threaded rod is screwed. It is used for tightening a rod or wire rope.

turn·coat (tûrn′kōt′) *n.* One who traitorously switches allegiance.

turn·er (tûr′nər) *n.* One who or that which turns; specifically, a person who works a lathe.

Tur·ner (tûr′nər), **Joseph Mallord William** (1775–1851). British painter. Perhaps the most original of English painters, his abstract treatment of light, color, and space influenced the French impressionists. His works include *The Fighting Téméraire* (1839) and *Rain, Steam, and Speed* (1844).

Turner, Nat (1800–31). U.S. slave leader. Believing himself to be the divinely appointed emancipator of slaves, he led a violent mob on a two-day trek to Jerusalem, Virginia (1831), during which they killed more than 50 people before being stopped by the Virginia militia. The massacre led to stricter slave codes in most Southern states. Turner was tried and hanged for his role in the killings.

turn·er·y (tûr′nə-rē) *n., pl.* **-ies. 1.** The work or workshop of a lathe operator. **2.** Objects made on a lathe.

turn·ing (tûr′nĭng) *n.* **1. a.** A deviation or change of course. **b.** A point at which a road or path turns off from another: *missed our turning and got lost.* **2.** The shaping of metal or wood on a lathe.

turning circle *n.* The circle with the smallest circumference within which a motor vehicle can turn.

turning point *n.* **1.** A point at which significant changes occur or a crucial decision must be made; a decisive moment. **2.** *Mathematics.* A maximum or minimum point on a curve.

tur·nip (tûr′nĭp) *n.* **1.** A widely cultivated plant, *Brassica rapa,* native to the Old World, having a large, edible yellow or white root. **2.** The root of this plant, eaten as a vegetable. **3.** Any of several similar or related plants, such as the **rutabaga** *(see).* [Earlier *turnepe* : *tur-* (origin and meaning unknown) + *nepe,* turnip, from Middle English *nepe,* Old English *nǣp,* from Latin *nāpus* (see **napiform**).]

turnip cabbage *n.* A vegetable, **kohlrabi** *(see).*

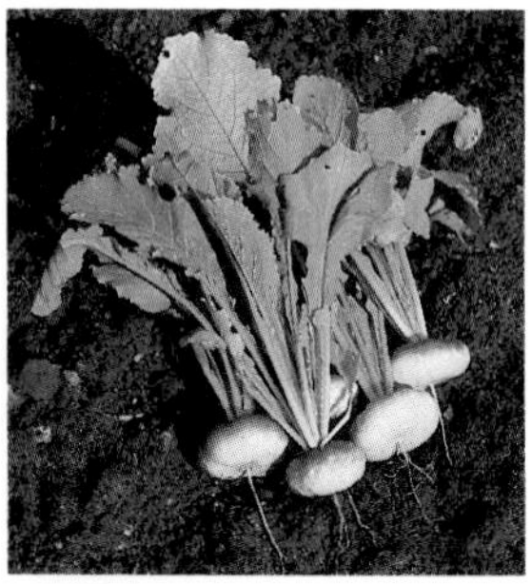

turnip *A root crop of Asiatic origin related to cabbages, cauliflowers, and broccoli. It is grown as a vegetable and as winter feed for sheep.*

Turner

"HE SEEMS TO PAINT WITH TINTED STEAM"
The artist who pursued the mystery of light and space

From his humble beginnings as a barber's son in London, Joseph Mallord William Turner rose to fame and fortune faster than any other English landscape painter. He first had a water color accepted by the Royal Academy in 1790, when he was 15. By the time he was 24 he had more commissions for water colors and drawings than he could handle; at 27 he was elected a member of the Royal Academy.

To discover subjects for his work, Turner spent his summers touring. In Britain he visited Yorkshire, the Lake District, Scotland, and Wales. In 1802 in Paris, Turner saw the Italian paintings Napoleon had seized and made many copies. In 1819 he made the first of several visits to Italy, which led to a great development in his treatment of light and color.

No artist has excelled Turner's originality in the use of color, treatment of light, and creation of mood. He painted a wide range of subjects and strove to treat significant themes. His early works include historical landscapes featuring human events, such as the Roman legend of Dido and Aeneas. His later works include magnificent studies of nature's power, especially in sea and sky. In his quest to unravel the mysteries of light, Turner pushed beyond the understanding of his contemporaries. But Constable understood him: "He seems to paint with tinted steam, so evanescent, so airy." Although he was always harshly criticized for his lack of finish, Turner enjoyed success and recognition until he was 40, when he decided to paint only what suited him and to experiment with his ideas of light and space. His work fell out of favor and was not rediscovered until modern times.

Most of the 19,500 oils, water colors, and drawings he left to Great Britain are in the Tate Gallery and the British Museum.

RADIANT SKY AND SEA Keelmen Heaving in Coals by Night *(1835) displays Turner's unsurpassed skill in giving a luminous quality and a mood of drama to a scene. His original and imaginative approach to landscape presaged the impressionist style.*

---

turn·key (tûrn′kē′) *n., pl.* **-keys.** The keeper of the keys in a prison; a jailer. *—adj.* Installed, supplied, or constructed so as to be fully operational: *a turnkey apartment.*

turn off *tr.v.* **1.** To stop the operation, activity, or flow of; shut off or switch off. **2.** *British.* To discharge (an employee). **3.** *Slang.* **a.** To fail to interest, especially sexually. **b.** To annoy, bore, or repel: *This continuous chatter turns me off.* *—intr.v.* To leave a path or road at a particular point and take another: *turn off at exit 14.*

turn-off (tûrn′ôf′, -ŏf′) *n.* **1.** The point where a road or path branches off from the main thoroughfare. **2.** *Slang.* Something that is irritating or repellent, especially sexually.

turn on *tr.v.* **1. a.** To cause to operate or flow by turning a switch or control: *turn on the television.* **b.** *Informal.* To produce as if by turning a switch: *turn on the charm.* **2.** *Slang.* **a.** To excite sexually. **b.** To produce a pleasurable response in; delight or stimulate. *—intr.v. Slang.* To take a hallucinogenic or narcotic drug.

turn-on (tûrn′ŏn′, -ôn′) *n. Slang.* Someone or something that excites, stimulates, or interests, especially sexually.

turn out *tr.v.* **1.** To switch off (a light, for example). **2.** To produce or manufacture. **3.** To empty the contents of: *turn out the attic.* **4.** To dress or equip. **5.** To put (a horse) out to pasture for rest or retirement. *—intr.v.* **1.** To come out or assemble, as for a public event or entertainment. **2. a.** To be found or proved, as after experience or trial: *It turned out that she had been lying all along.* **b.** To come to be in the end; end up: *turned out to be a fine day.* **3.** *Informal.* To get out of bed.

turn-out (tûrn′out′) *n.* **1.** The number of people at a gathering; attendance. **2.** The proportion of registered voters actually voting in a given election. **3.** The amount of goods produced; output. **4.** The way in which a person or group is dressed or equipped. **5.** An outfit of a carriage with its horse or horses; an equipage. **6.** A space next to a highway where vehicles may pull in to park temporarily or to allow other vehicles to pass.

turn over *tr.v.* **1.** To transfer or hand over, especially to the police. **2.** To cause (an internal-combustion engine) to go through at least one cycle. **3. a.** To buy and resell (stock) or invest and get back (capital) in the course of trade. **b.** To do business to the extent or amount of: *turn over millions every year.* *—intr.v.* To go through at least one cycle. Used of an internal-combustion engine.

turn·o·ver (tûrn′ō′vər) *n.* **1.** The act of turning over; an upset or overthrow. **2.** A small pastry made by covering one half of a circular piece of dough with fruit, preserves, or other filling and sealing the other half over on top. **3. a.** The number of times a particular stock of goods is sold and restocked during a given period of time. **b.** The rate at which a stock of goods is turned over. **4. a.** The total amount or value of business transacted during a given period of time. **b.** The ratio of this amount to the value of a company's issued shares, showing the number of times the company's share-capital has been turned over in the given period. **5. a.** The number of

---

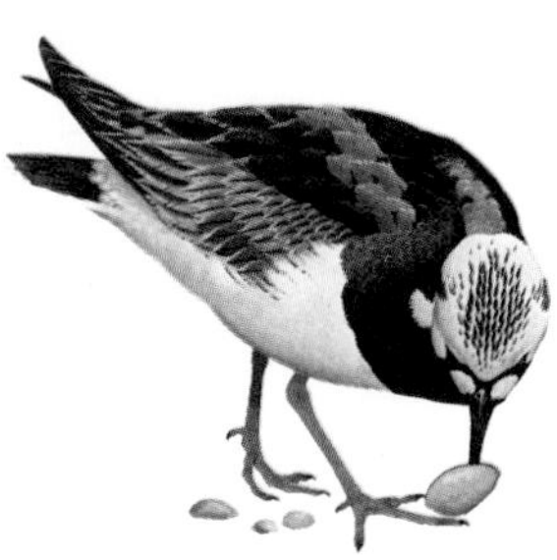

turnstone *At low tide this wader walks along sands and rocks, lifting not only stones but wood, shells, seaweed, and anything else that may hide the sandhoppers and mud dwellers it eats. The turnstone breeds on the most northerly coasts of Europe, Asia, and North America, but it flies south in the winter, sometimes as far as South America and Australia.*

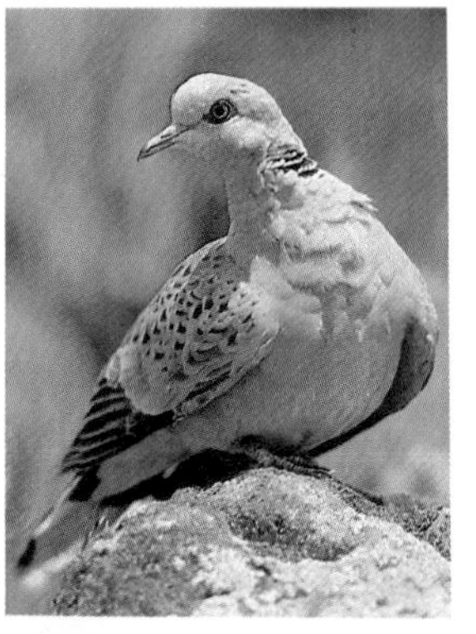

turtledove *The European turtledove,* Streptopelia turtur *(above), is noted for its soft cooing call in summer. Turtledoves are referred to in the Bible's Song of Solomon as symbols of summer, when "The flowers appear on the earth, the time of the singing of birds is come, and the voice of the turtle is heard in our land."*

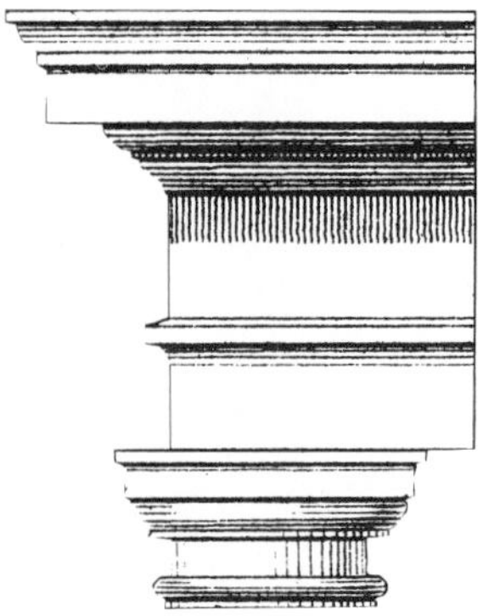

Tuscan order *A simplification of the Doric order of architecture, developed by the Etruscans in ancient Italy.*

workers taken on by an employer to replace those who have left. **b.** The ratio of this number to the number of employed workers. ~*adj.* Capable of being folded down or over: *a turnover collar.*

turn·pike (tûrn′pīk′) *n. Abbr.* **tpk. 1.** A road; especially, a wide, modern highway with toll gates. **2.** A tollgate. [Middle English *turnepike,* a revolving barrier furnished with spikes used to block a road : *turnen,* to TURN + PIKE.]

turn·sole (tûrn′sōl′) *n.* Any plant, such as the heliotrope, that moves or is believed to move in response to the sun. [Middle English *turnesole,* from Old French *tournesol,* Italian *tornasole* : *tornare,* from Latin *tornāre,* to TURN + *sole,* the sun, from Latin *sōl.*]

turn·spit (tûrn′spĭt′) *n.* One that turns a roasting spit; especially, a small dog formerly used in a treadmill to turn a roasting spit.

turn·stile (tûrn′stīl′) *n.* **1.** A mechanical device used to control passage from one public area to another, typically consisting of several horizontal arms supported by and radially projecting from a central vertical post. **2.** A similar structure that permits the passage of persons but not of horses or cattle.

turn·stone (tûrn′stōn′) *n.* A wading bird, *Arenaria interpres,* having plumage that is tortoiseshell colored in summer and dull brown in winter. [From its habit of turning over stones in search of food.]

turn·ta·ble (tûrn′tā′bəl) *n.* **1.** A circular horizontal rotating platform equipped with a railway track, used for turning locomotives. **2.** A similar device for turning road vehicles. **3. a.** The circular horizontal rotating platform of a record player on which the record is placed. **b.** The mechanical path of a record player excluding the amplifying circuitry and speakers. **4.** Any similar rotating platform or disk, as on a microscope.

turntable ladder *n.* A ladder, usually mounted on a fire engine, that can be mechanically rotated and extended.

turn up *tr.v.* To find; unearth. *—intr.v.* **1.** To be found; come to light: *The missing book turned up at last.* **2.** To make an appearance; arrive. **3.** *Informal.* To happen, especially unexpectedly. **—turn up one's nose.** To regard with scorn.

turn·up (tûrn′ŭp′) *n. British.* **1.** Something that is turned up or turns up; specifically, the turned-up fold at the bottom of a trouser leg. **2.** *Informal.* An unexpected occurrence or turn of events. Often used in the phrase *a turnup for the books.*
~*adj.* Turned up or capable of being turned up.

tur·pen·tine (tûr′pən-tīn′) *n. Abbr.* **turp. 1.** A thin volatile essential oil, consisting of a mixture of terpenes, obtained by steam distillation or other means from the wood or the exudate of certain pine trees and used as a paint thinner and solvent and medicinally as a liniment. Also called "oil of turpentine," "spirits of turpentine," "turps." **2.** The sticky mixture of resin and volatile oil from which this oil is distilled. **3.** A similar resinous liquid obtained from the terebinth. **4.** Any of several similar liquids obtained from petroleum and used as thinners for paints and varnishes. Also called "turpentine substitute," "white spirit."
~*tr.v.* **turpentined, -tining, -tines. 1.** To apply turpentine to or mix turpentine with. **2.** To extract turpentine from (a tree). [Middle English *turpentyne,* resin of the terebinth, from Old French *ter(e)bentine,* from Latin *terebinthina,* from *terebinthus,* TEREBINTH.]

tur·peth (tûr′pĭth) *n.* **1.** A vine of the genus *Ipomoea,* of tropical Asia and Australia, having roots that yield a resinous substance used medicinally as a purgative. **2.** The root of this plant. [Middle English *turbit,* from Old French, from Medieval Latin *turbit(h)um, turpetum,* from Arabic *turbiḍ, turbeḍ.*]

tur·pi·tude (tûr′pə-to͞od′, -tyo͞od′) *n.* **1.** Baseness; depravity. **2.** A base, immoral act. [Latin *turpitūdō,* from *turpis*†, ugly, vile.]

turps (tûrps) *n. Used with a singular verb. Informal.* Turpentine. [Shortening and alteration of TURPENTINE.]

tur·quoise (tûr′kwoiz′, -koiz′) *n.* **1.** A blue to blue-green mineral, a basic hydrous phosphate of aluminum and copper, mainly $CuAl_6(PO_4)_4(OH)_8 \cdot 4H_2O$. It is prized as a gemstone in its polished blue form. **2.** Light to brilliant bluish green. [Middle English *turkeis,* from Old French *(pierre) turqueise,* "Turkish (stone)," from *turqueis,* Turkish (it was first found in Turkistan), from *Turc,* TURK.] **—tur·quoise** *adj.*

tur·ret (tûr′ĭt) *n.* **1.** A small ornamented tower or tower-shaped projection on a building. **2.** *Military.* A low, heavily armored structure, usually rotating horizontally, containing mounted guns and their crew, as on a warship or tank. **3.** A domelike gunner's enclosure projecting from the fuselage of a military aircraft. **4.** A tall wooden structure mounted on wheels, used in ancient warfare by besiegers to scale the walls of a fortress. **5.** An attachment for a lathe consisting of a rotating, cylindrical block holding various cutting tools. [Middle English *t(o)uret,* from Old French *t(o)urete,* diminutive of *t(o)ur,* a TOWER.]

tur·ret·ed (tûr′ĭ-tĭd) *adj.* **1.** Furnished with a turret or turrets. **2.** Having the shape or form of a turret, as do certain long-spired gastropod shells.

tur·tle[1] (tûrt′l) *n.* **1.** Any of various marine reptiles of the order Chelonia, having horny, toothless jaws and the body enclosed in a bony or leathery shell into which the head, limbs, and tail can be withdrawn in most species. **2.** *Chiefly British.* A marine chelonian. **—turn turtle.** To turn upside-down; capsize.
~*intr.v.* **turtled, -tling, -tles.** To hunt for turtles, especially as an occupation. [Perhaps from French *tortue,* TORTOISE.]

turtle[2] *n. Archaic.* A turtledove: *"the voice of the turtle is heard in our land"* (Song of Solomon 2:12). [Middle English *turtle,* Old English *turtla, turtle,* from Latin *turtur*†.]

tur·tle·back (tûrt′l-băk′) *n.* A projection built so as to arch over the deck of a ship at the bow and sometimes also at the stern as a protection against high seas.

tur·tle·dove (tûrt′l-dŭv′) *n.* A slender European dove, *Streptopelia turtur,* having a white-edged tail and a soft, cooing voice. [TURTLE (dove) + DOVE.]

turtle grass *n.* A grasslike aquatic plant, *Thalassia testudinum,* of warm Atlantic waters, often forming extensive submerged beds.

tur·tle·head (tûrt′l-hĕd′) *n.* Any of several plants of the genus *Chelone*; especially, *C. glabra,* of eastern North America, having white or pink flowers. Also called "snakehead." [From the shape of its flower.]

tur·tle·neck (tûrt′l-nĕk′) *n.* **1.** A relatively high, turned-down collar that fits closely about the neck. **2.** A sweater or other garment having such a collar.

turves. *Archaic.* Plural of **turf.**

Tus·ca·loo·sa (tŭs′kə-lo͞o′sə). City in west-central Alabama, on the Black Warrior River. It is the seat of the University of Alabama and a transportation, manufacturing, and medical center. It was the state capital from 1826 to 1846.

Tus·can (tŭs′kən) *adj.* **1.** Of or pertaining to Tuscany, its people, or their dialect of Italian. **2.** Of or pertaining to the Tuscan order.
~*n.* **1.** A native or inhabitant of Tuscany. **2.** Any of the Italian dialects spoken in Tuscany, especially the dialect of Florence. [Latin *Tuscānus,* from *Tuscus,* Etruscan.]

Tuscan order *n. Architecture.* A classical order similar to Roman Doric, but having an unfluted shaft with a simplified base, capital, and entablature.

Tus·ca·ny (tŭs′kə-nē). Region of west-central Italy. It was inhabited in pre-Roman times by the Etruscans and became, with the rise of the Medicis of Florence, a grand duchy (1569–1860). Its dialect was selected as the model of standard Italian at the time of Italy's unification. The chief cities are Florence (the capital), Livorno, and Pisa.

Tus·ca·ro·ra (tŭs′kə-rôr′ə, -rōr′ə) *n., pl.* **-ras** or collectively **Tuscarora. 1.** A tribe of Iroquoian-speaking North American Indians formerly inhabiting North Carolina, and now living in New York and Ontario, Canada. **2.** A member of this tribe. **3.** The language of this tribe. [From Tuscarora *Skărū̆reⁿ,* "hemp gatherers."]

tu·sche (to͝osh′ə) *n.* A substance used for drawing in lithography and as a resist in etching and silk-screen printing. [German *Tusche,* from *tuschen,* to ink up, from French *toucher,* to TOUCH.]

tush[1] (tŭsh) *interj.* Used to express mild reproof, disapproval, or admonition: *Tush, tush, my dear, it's nothing to fuss about.* [Middle English *tussch.*]

tush[2] *n.* A tusk. [Middle English *tusche,* Old English *tūsc.*]

tush[3] (to͝osh) *n. Slang.* The buttocks. [Yiddish *toches.*]

tusk[1] (tŭsk) *n.* **1.** An elongated, pointed tooth, usually one of a pair, extending outside the mouth in certain animals, such as the walrus, elephant, or wild boar. **2.** Any long, projecting tooth or toothlike part.
~*tr.v.* **tusked, tusking, tusks.** To dig or gore with the tusks or a tusk. [Middle English *tux, tuske,* Old English *tūx, tūsc.*]

tusk[2] *n.* A fish, the **torsk** *(see).* [Of Scandinavian origin; see TORSK.]

tusk·er (tŭs′kər) *n.* An animal bearing tusks, such as a wild boar.

tusk shell *n.* A **tooth shell** *(see).*

tus·sah (tŭs′ə, tŭs′ô′) *n.* Also **tus·sore** (tŭs′ôr′, -ōr′). **1.** An Asian silkworm, *Antheraea paphia,* that produces a coarse brownish or yellowish silk. **2.** The silk itself, or a fabric woven from it. [Hindi *tasar,* from Sanskrit *tasara,* a shuttle (probably from the shape of the tussah's cocoon).]

Tus·saud (to͞o-sō′), **Madame,** born Marie Gresholtz or Grosholtz (1760–1850). French-born wax modeler. She was imprisoned during the French Revolution and modeled heads of the guillotined victims. In 1802 she moved to England and eventually opened a museum that is still a tourist attraction in London.

tus·sis (tŭs′ĭs) *n. Medicine.* A cough. [Latin.] **—tus·sal, tus·sive** *adj.*

tus·sle (tŭs′əl) *intr.v.* **-sled, -sling, -sles.** To fight or struggle roughly.
~*n.* **1.** A rough-and-tumble struggle; a scuffle. **2.** Any disorderly struggle or conflict: *a tussle for power.* [Middle English *tussillen,* frequentative of *tousen,* to pull roughly.]

tus·sock (tŭs′ək) *n.* **1.** A clump or tuft of growing grass or a similar plant. **2.** A tuft, as of hair or feathers. [Probably variant of dialectal *tusk*†, a tuft of hair, rushes.] **—tus·sock·y** *adj.*

tussock grass *n.* Any of various grasses or sedges that typically grow in tussocks; especially, species of the genus *Poa.*

tussock moth *n.* Any of various moths of the family Lymantriidae, having hairy caterpillars that are often destructive to trees.

tut (tŭt) *interj.* Also **tut-tut** (tŭt′tŭt′). Used to express annoyance, impatience, or mild reproof.

Tut·ankh·a·men, Tut·ankh·a·mon (to͞o′tăng-kä′mən). (*c.* 1358–1340 B.C.). Egyptian pharaoh of the 18th dynasty. His tomb with its magnificent contents was discovered almost intact (1922) by the British archaeologists Howard Carter and the Earl of Carnarvon.

tu·te·lage (to͞ot′l-ĭj, tyo͞ot′-) *n.* **1.** The function or capacity of a guardian; guardianship. **2.** The act or capacity of a tutor; instruction; teaching. **3.** The state of being under a guardian or tutor. [Latin *tūtēla,* a watching, from *tūtor,* TUTOR.]

tu·te·lar·y (to͞ot′l-ĕr′ē, tyo͞ot′-) *adj.* Also **tu·te·lar** (-ər). **1.** Of or pertaining to a guardian or guardianship. **2.** Acting as a guardian or

protector, especially over a particular place or person; protective.
~n. A tutelary saint, deity, or spirit. [Late Latin *tūtēlāris,* from Latin *tūtēla,* TUTELAGE.]

tu·tor (to͞o′tər, tyo͞o′-) *n.* **1. a.** A private teacher, often employed by a household. **b.** One who gives additional, special, or remedial instruction. **2.** In some universities and colleges, a teacher or teaching assistant with a rank lower than that of an instructor. **3.** In most British universities and colleges, a member of the staff who is responsible for the welfare of a number of students and usually for supervising their studies. **4.** In Roman and Scottish law, the guardian of a minor and of the minor's property.
~v. **tutored, -toring, -tors.** *—tr.* **1.** To act as a tutor to; especially, to instruct or teach privately. **2.** To discipline or treat sternly, as a tutor might. **3.** To act as the guardian to; have the care of. *—intr.* To function as a tutor or private instructor. **—See Synonyms at teach.** [Middle English *tutour,* from Old French, from Latin *tūtor,* a guardian, from *tūtus,* past participle of *tuērī,* to watch, protect.]

tu·to·ri·al (to͞o-tôr′ē-əl, -tōr′ē-əl, tyo͞o-) *n.* A period of intensive tuition given, especially in a university, to an individual student or a small number of students.
~adj. Of or pertaining to a tutor. [Latin *tūtōrius.* See **tutor, -al.**]

tutorial system *n.* An instructional system in which college or university tutors are responsible for the special supervision of students individually or in small groups.

tu·tor·ship (to͞o′tər-shĭp′, tyo͞o′-) *n.* **1.** The office or functions of a tutor. **2.** Tutelage.

tut·san (tŭt′sən) *n.* **1.** A yellow-flowered evergreen undershrub, *Hypericum androsaemum,* having berries that turn purplish black when ripe. **2.** Either of two related plants, *H. hircinum* or *H. inodorum.* [Middle English, from Norman French *tutsaine,* from French *toute-saine,* "all healthy" (the plants were believed to have various healing properties).]

tut·ti (to͞o′tē) *adv. Music.* All. Used as a direction to indicate that all performers are to take part.
~n., pl. **tuttis. 1.** A passage of ensemble music intended to be executed by all the performers simultaneously. **2.** The effect produced by a passage played tutti. [Italian, plural of *tutto,* all, from Latin *tōtus.*] **—tut·ti** *adj.*

tut·ti-frut·ti (to͞o′tē-fro͞o′tē) *n.* **1.** A confection, especially ice cream, containing a variety of chopped candied fruits. **2.** A flavoring simulating the flavor of many fruits. **3.** A preserve of chopped, mixed fruits.
~adj. Having a combination of fruit flavors. [Italian : *tutti,* all + *frutti,* fruits.]

tut-tut (tŭt′tŭt′) *interj.* Tut.

tut·ty (tŭt′ē) *n.* An impure zinc oxide obtained as a sublimate from the flues of zinc-smelting furnaces and used as a polishing powder. [Middle English *tutie,* from Old French, from Arabic *tūtiyā.*]

tu·tu (to͞o′to͞o) *n.* A skirt worn for classical ballet consisting of many layers of gathered sheer fabric, which is either brief and encircles the waist or extends to below the knee. [French.]

Tu·tu (to͞o′to͞o), **Desmond Mpilo, Archbishop** (1931–). Prominent South African theologian and campaigner for black rights. He won the Nobel Peace Prize in 1984.

Tu·tu·o·la (to͞o′to͞o-ō′lə), **Amos** (1920–). Nigerian writer. A native speaker of Yoruba who received little formal education, he wrote his first novel, *The Palm-Wine Drinkard* (1952), in English, using the rich West African dialect in a story inspired by regional folklore. He has written several other novels, all in English, and is considered the first African writer to achieve international fame.

Tu·va Autonomous Soviet Socialist Republic (to͞o′və). Administrative division of extreme southern Siberian U.S.S.R., on the Mongolian border. Cattle, grain, lumber, and furs are important to its economy. The capital is Kyzyl.

Tu·va·lu (to͞o-vä′lo͞o, -vä′ro͞o). *Formerly* **El·lice Islands** Country of the southwestern Pacific, consisting of nine islands. Established as a British protectorate in 1892, it became part of the Gilbert and Ellice Islands Colony in 1915, from which it broke away in 1975. Independence was granted in 1978. Area, 26 square kilometers (10 square miles). Population, 7,500. Capital, Fongafela on Funafuti. See map at **Pacific Ocean.**

tux·e·do (tŭk-sē′dō) *n., pl.* **-dos** or **-does. 1.** A man's usually dark jacket with satin or grosgrain lapels worn for formal or semiformal occasions. Also called "dinner jacket." **2.** A complete outfit including a tuxedo jacket, black trousers with a stripe down the side, and a black bow tie. [From the name of a club in *Tuxedo* Park, New York, where it became popular.]

tu·yère (twē-yâr′) *n.* The pipe, nozzle, or other opening through which air is forced into a blast furnace or forge to facilitate combustion. [French, from Old French *tuyere,* from *tuyau,* a pipe, probably from Frankish *thūta* (unattested), imitative.]

Tu·zi·goot National Monument (to͞o′zĭ-go͝ot′). Area, 17 hectares (43 acres), in central Arizona, set aside to preserve the ruins of a prehistoric Indian village.

TV (tē′vē′) *n. Informal.* Television. **—TV** *adj.*

TV Dinner *n.* A trademark for a packaged ready-to-serve meal, usually frozen in an aluminum tray, that can be heated in an oven.

Twad·dell scale (twŏ-dĕl′) *n.* A scale for measuring specific gravity, especially of acids. [After William *Twaddell* (died *c.* 1840), Scottish inventor.]

twad·dle (twŏd′l) *intr.v.* **-dled, -dling, -dles.** To talk foolishly.
~n. **1.** Foolish, trivial, or idle talk or chatter. **2.** Silly pretentious speech or writing. [From earlier *twattle,* alteration of TATTLE.] **—twad·dler** *n.*

twain (twān) *adj. Archaic.* Two.
~n. Poetic. A set of two: *"Oh, East is East, and West is West, and never the twain shall meet"* (Rudyard Kipling). [Middle English *tweien, tweyen,* Old English *twēgen* (nominative and accusative masculine), two.]

Twain, Mark. See Samuel Langhorne **Clemens.**

twang (twăng) *v.* **twanged, twanging, twangs.** *—intr.* **1.** To emit a sharp, vibrating sound, as the string of a musical instrument sounds when plucked. **2.** To be released or to resound with a sharp, vibrating sound. Used especially of an arrow. *—tr.* **1.** To cause to make a sharp, vibrating sound. **2.** To utter with a twang.
~n. **1.** A sharp, vibrating sound, such as that made by a plucked string. **2.** A notably nasal tone of voice, especially as a peculiarity of certain regional accents. **3.** Any sound resembling either of these. [Imitative.] **—twang·y** *adj.*

'twas (twəz, twŏz). *Regional and Poetic.* Contraction of *it was.*

tway·blade (twā′blād′) *n.* **1.** Any of various small terrestrial orchids of the genus *Listera,* having two basal, unstalked leaves and a terminal cluster of greenish or reddish flowers. **2.** Any other orchid with only two leaves. [Translation of Medieval Latin *bifolium,* "two-leaved" : obsolete English *tway,* two, Middle English *twei,* Old English *twēge,* short for *twēgen,* TWAIN + BLADE.]

tweak (twēk) *tr.v.* **tweaked, tweaking, tweaks.** To pinch, pluck, or twist sharply.
~n. A sharp, twisting pinch. [Probably variant of dialectal *twick,* from Middle English *twikken,* from Old English *twiccian.*]

twee (twē) *adj. British Informal.* **1.** Excessively or affectedly pretty, sentimental, or quaint. **2.** Sweet; cute. [From *tweet,* childish or affected pronunciation of SWEET.]

tweed (twēd) *n.* **1.** A coarse, rugged, often nubby woolen cloth made in any of various twill weaves and used chiefly for suits and coats. Also used adjectivally: *a tweed suit.* **2. tweeds.** Clothing made of this cloth. [Originally a trademark, misspelling (influenced by the river TWEED) of *tweel, tweeled,* Scottish variants of TWILL.]

Tweed (twēd). River of northern Great Britain. Rising in the Tweedsmuir Hills in the Borders Region of Scotland, it flows *c.* 156 kilometers (97 miles) to the North Sea at Berwick.

Tweed, William Marcy, called "Boss Tweed" (1823–78). U.S. politician. The leader of the Tweed Ring, New York City's most notoriously corrupt political administration, he oversaw the graft of millions of dollars of city funds between 1860 and 1871. Editorial campaigns by *Harper's Weekly* and the *New York Times* helped bring Tweed to justice. He died in prison.

twee·dle·dum and twee·dle·dee (twēd′l-dŭm′; twēd′l-dē′) *n.* Two persons or groups resembling each other so closely that they are practically indistinguishable. [After *Tweedledum and Tweedledee,* proverbial rival violinists supposedly representative of Handel and G.B. Bononcini, who had a musical rivalry.]

tweed·y (twē′dē) *adj.* **tweedier, tweediest. 1.** Of or resembling tweed: *tweedy wallpaper.* **2.** *Chiefly British Informal.* Given to or fond of the healthy, outdoor country life, especially that led by members of the British gentry: *the tweedy set.* **3. a.** Wearing tweeds. **b.** *Informal.* Suggestive of casual, informal taste, habits, and lifestyle: *a tweedy look.* **—tweed·i·ness** *n.*

'tween (twēn). *Poetic.* Contraction of *between.*

tween-decks (twēn′dĕks′) *n.* The space between two decks of a ship. **—tween-deck** *adj.*

tweet (twēt) *intr.v.* **tweeted, tweeting, tweets.** To utter a weak, chirping sound, as a young or small bird does.
~n. A weak, chirping sound.
~interj. Also **tweet tweet.** Used to imitate the sound of a bird. [Imitative.]

tweet·er (twē′tər) *n.* A loudspeaker designed to reproduce high-pitched sounds in a high-fidelity audiofrequency system. Compare **woofer.** [From TWEET.]

tweeze (twēz) *tr.v.* **tweezed, tweezing, tweezes.** To handle or extract with tweezers. [Back-formation from TWEEZERS.]

tweez·ers (twē′zərz) *pl.n.* A small, usually metal pincerlike tool used for plucking or handling small objects. [Originally "a set or case of small instruments," from obsolete *tweezes,* plural of *tweeze, etweese,* from the plural of *etwee,* from French *étui,* ÉTUI.]

twelfth (twĕlfth) *n.* **1.** The ordinal number 12 in a series. **2.** Any of 12 equal parts. **3.** *Music.* **a.** A 12-degree interval in a diatonic scale; an octave plus a fifth. **b.** A tone 12 degrees below or above a given tone. [Middle English *twelfthe,* Old English *twelfta.*] **—twelfth** *adj. & adv.*

Twelfth-day (twĕlfth′dā′) *n.* The day of Epiphany, January 6, which comes 12 days after Christmas and traditionally marks the end of the Christmas season.

Twelfth-night (twĕlfth′nīt′) *n.* The evening of January 5, before Twelfth-day, formerly celebrated with various festivities. **—Twelfth-night** *adj.*

Twelfth·tide (twĕlfth′tīd′) *n.* The season of Epiphany.

twelve (twĕlv) *n.* **1. a.** The cardinal number that is one more than 11; a dozen. **b.** A symbol representing this, such as 12 or XII. **2.** A set made up of twelve persons or things. **3.** The twelfth in a series. **4.** A size, as in clothing, designated as 12. **5.** Midnight or midday. Also called "twelve o'clock." [Middle English *twelfe, twelve,* Old English *twelf.*] **—twelve** *adj. & pron.*

Twelve Apostles *pl.n.* The 12 disciples chosen by Jesus.

twelve·mo (twĕlv′mō′) *n., pl.* **-mos. Duodecimo** *(see).*

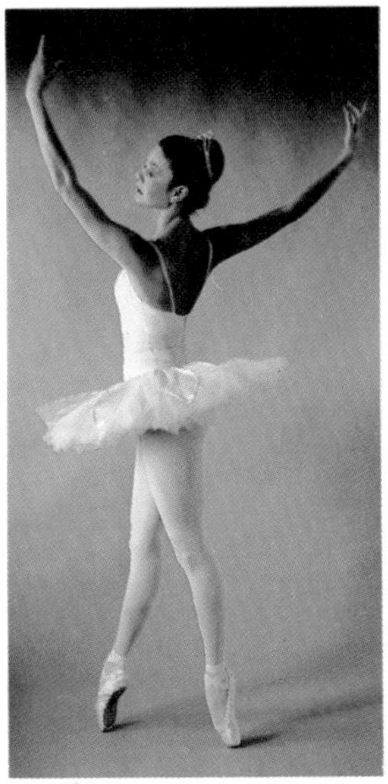

tutu *The tutu is the standard ballet dancer's skirt. There are two kinds, the brief tutu seen here and the romantic tutu, which extends below the knees to about 30 centimeters (12 inches) from the floor.*

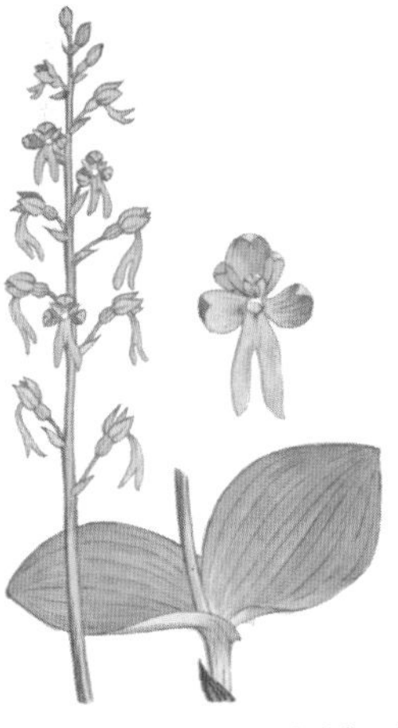

twayblade *A common orchid found in damp woods and meadows. It gets its name from its two, or "tway," leaves growing at the base of the stem.*

twelve·month (twĕlv′mŭnth′) *n.* A year or period of twelve months.
Twelve Tables *n.* The earliest code of Roman laws, written down 451–450 B.C. Preceded by *the.* [Translation of Latin *Duodecim Tabulae,* referring to the 12 original compilations (5th century B.C.) that when complete were incised on bronze plates and hung in the Forum.]
twelve·tone (twĕlv′tōn′) *adj. Music.* Pertaining to, consisting of, or based on an atonal arrangement of the traditional 12 chromatic tones.
twen·ti·eth (twĕn′tē-ĭth) *n.* **1.** The ordinal number 20 in a series. Also written 20th. **2.** Any of 20 equal parts. **—twen·ti·eth** *adj. & adv.*
twen·ty (twĕn′tē) *n., pl.* **-ties. 1. a.** The cardinal number that is 10 more than 10. **b.** A symbol representing this, such as 20 or XX. **2.** A set made up of 20 persons or things. **3.** The twentieth in a series. **4.** A size, as in clothing, designated as 20. **5.** A twenty-dollar bill. **6. twenties.** The range of numbers from 20 to 29, considered as a range, as of age, price, or temperature: *The thermometer dropped into the twenties.* **b.** The years numbered 20 to 29 in a century. Also used adjectively: *a twenties hairstyle.* [Middle English, Old English *twēntig.*] **—twen·ty** *adj. & pron.*
twen·ty-one (twĕn′tē-wŭn′) *n.* A card game, **blackjack** *(see).*
twen·ty-twen·ty (twĕn′tē-twĕn′tē) *adj.* Having normal visual acuity. Usually written *20/20.* [From a method of testing vision by reading charts at a distance of 20 feet.]
'twere (twûr). *Poetic.* Contraction of *it were.*
twerp, twirp (twûrp) *n. Slang.* A silly, stupid, or contemptible person; a fool. [20th century : origin obscure.]
Twi, Tshi (chwē, chē) *n.* A language spoken in western Africa, especially by the Ashanti. **—Twi, Tshi** *adj.*
twi·bil, twi·bill (twī′bĭl′) *n.* **1.** A battle-ax with two cutting edges. **2.** A mattock with one arm like an ax and the other like an adz. [Middle English, Old English *twibil(l)* : *twi-,* two + BILL (instrument).]
twice (twīs) *adv.* **1.** In two cases or on two occasions; two times. **2.** In doubled degree or amount: *twice as many.* [Middle English *twice, twiges,* Old English *twiges,* from *twige, twiga,* twice.]
twice-laid (twīs′lād′) *adj.* Made from strands of old or used rope.
twid·dle (twĭd′l) *v.* **-dled, -dling, -dles.** *—tr.* To turn over or around, especially idly or lightly; fiddle with: *twiddle the knobs on the radio.* *—intr.* **1.** To turn something over or around idly or lightly; fiddle. Used with *with.* **2.** To twirl or rotate aimlessly. **—twiddle one's thumbs. 1.** To twirl one's thumbs idly around each other. **2.** To do little or nothing; be idle. *—n.* The act of twiddling; an idle, twirling motion. [Probably a blend of TWIRL and FIDDLE.] **—twid·dler** *n.*
twig¹ (twĭg) *n.* A small branch or slender shoot, as of a tree or shrub. [Middle English *twig(ge),* Old English *twigge.*]
twig² *v.* **twigged, twigging, twigs.** *British Informal.* *—intr.* To suddenly comprehend a situation; catch on. *—tr.* **1.** To understand. **2.** To observe or watch; to notice. [Irish Gaelic *tuigim,* "I understand."]
twig·gy (twĭg′ē) *adj.* **-gier, -giest. 1.** Resembling a twig or twigs; slender; fragile. **2.** Abounding in twigs.
twi·light (twī′līt′) *n.* **1.** The time interval during which the sun's center is below the horizon at an angle less than 6° *(civil twilight),* 12° *(nautical twilight),* or 18° *(astronomical twilight).* **2.** The state of illumination of the atmosphere during this interval, especially after a sunset. **3.** Any dim or faint illumination. **4.** Any period or condition of decline, as after growth, glory, or success; a waning: *in the twilight of her life.* *—adj.* Pertaining to or characteristic of twilight. [Middle English *twilight,* "light between (night and day)," half-light : *twi-,* half, two, Old English *twi-* + LIGHT.]
Twilight of the Gods *n.* **Götterdämmerung** *(see).*
twilight sleep *n.* An analgesic and amnesic condition induced by an injection of morphine and scopolamine, characterized by the absence of sensibility to pain without loss of consciousness, and administered during labor in childbirth.
twilight zone *n.* An area or state that is not clearly defined or limited.
twill (twĭl) *n.* **1.** A cloth with diagonal parallel ribs produced by passing the weft yarn alternately over one warp yarn and then under two or more. **2.** The weave used to produce such cloth. *—tr.v.* **twilled, twilling, twills.** To weave (cloth) so as to produce the pattern of twill. [Middle English *twyl(l), twyle,* Old English *twilic,* "two-threaded" : *twi-,* two (see twilight) + Latin *(bi)līx,* "two-threaded" : BI- + *līcium,* a thread (see trellis).] **—twill** *adj.*
'twill (twĭl). *Regional and Poetic.* Contraction of *it will.*
twilled (twĭld) *adj.* Woven so as to have diagonal parallel ribs.
twin (twĭn) *n.* **1.** Either of two offspring born at the same birth. **2.** Either of two identical or similar persons, animals, or things; a counterpart. **3. Twins.** The constellation and sign of the zodiac **Gemini** *(see).* Preceded by *the.* **4.** A crystal composed of two parts that are oriented differently but are joined together so that a crystallographic direction or plane is common to both. In this sense, also called "macle." *—adj.* **1.** Being two or either of two offspring born at the same birth. **2.** Being either of two identical or similar persons, animals, or things. **3.** Consisting of two identical or similar related or connected parts. *—v.* **twinned, twinning, twins.** *—intr.* **1.** To give birth to twins. **2.** *Archaic.* To be either of twin offspring. **3.** To be paired or cou-

pled. *—tr.* **1.** To link together; couple. **2.** To provide a match or counterpart to; pair. [Middle English *twin, twyn* (adjective and noun), Old English *twinn* (adjective only), *getwinn.*]
twin·ber·ry (twĭn′bĕr′ē) *n., pl.* **-ries.** The **partridgeberry** *(see).* [From the single berry formed from a pair of flowers.]
Twin Cities. Minneapolis and St. Paul, Minnesota, lying opposite each other on the Mississippi River. St. Paul is the capital.
twine (twīn) *v.* **twined, twining, twines.** *—tr.* **1.** To twist (threads, for example) together; intertwine. **2.** To form by twisting, intertwining, or interlacing. **3.** To encircle or coil about: *A vine twined the fence.* **4.** To wind, coil, or wrap around (something): *twined a rope around the post.* *—intr.* **1.** To become twisted, interlaced, or interwoven. **2.** To wind or coil. Usually used with *around.* **3.** To go in a winding course; twist about: *a stream twining through the forest.* *—n.* **1.** A strong string or cord formed from two or more threads of hemp, cotton, or the like twisted together. **2.** Any thing or part formed by twining: *a twine of dough.* **3.** A tangle; a knot. **4.** The act or process of twining. [Middle English *twinen,* from *twin,* a rope of two strands, Old English *twīn,* from *twī-,* two.] **—twin·er** *n.*
twin-flow·er (twĭn′flou′ər) *n.* A creeping evergreen plant, *Linnaea borealis,* of northern regions, having roundish leaves and paired, bell-shaped, pinkish flowers.
twinge (twĭnj) *n.* **1.** A sharp, sudden physical pain. **2.** A mental or emotional pang: *a twinge of conscience.* *—v.* **twinged, twinging** or **twingeing, twinges.** *—tr.* **1.** To cause to feel a sharp pain. **2.** *Obsolete.* To tweak; pinch. *—intr.* To feel a twinge or twinges. [Middle English *twengen, twynchen,* to pinch, wring, Old English *twengan.*]
twi-night (twī′nīt′) *adj. Baseball.* Designating a double-header in which the first game begins in late afternoon. [TWI(LIGHT) + NIGHT.]
twin·kle (twĭng′kəl) *v.* **-kled, -kling, -kles.** *—intr.* **1.** To shine with slight, intermittent gleams, as distant lights or stars do; flicker or glimmer. **2.** To be bright or sparkling, as with delight. Used of the eyes. **3.** *Archaic.* To blink or wink. *—tr.* To cause to twinkle. —See Usage note at **flash.** *—n.* **1.** A slight, intermittent gleam of light; a glimmer; sparkle. **2.** A sparkle of merriment or delight in the eye. **3.** A brief interval; a twinkling. [Middle English *twynklen,* Old English *twinclian,* frequentative of *twincan* (unattested), to wink, from West Germanic *twink-* (unattested).] **—twin·kler** *n.*
twin·kling (twĭng′klĭng) *n.* The time it takes to blink once; an instant. Also called "twinkling of an eye."
twin-leaf (twĭn′lēf′) *n., pl.* **-leaves** (-lēvz′). A woodland plant, *Jeffersonia diplylla,* of eastern North America, having leaves deeply cleft into two lobes, and a solitary white flower.
twinned (twĭnd) *adj.* **1.** Born at a single birth. **2.** Paired or coupled with something identical or similar. **3.** Formed from crystals by the process of twinning.
twin·ning (twĭn′ĭng) *n.* **1.** The bearing of twins. **2.** A pairing or union of two similar or identical things. **3.** The formation of twin crystals.
twin-screw (twĭn′skrōō′) *adj.* Having two propellers, one on either side of the keel, that usually revolve in opposite directions. Said of a ship.
twin-size (twĭn′sīz′) *adj.* Relating to or being a bed that is 39 inches by 75 inches in dimension.
twirl (twûrl) *v.* **twirled, twirling, twirls.** *—tr.* **1.** To rotate or revolve briskly; swing in a circle; spin. **2.** To twist or swing around: *twirl thread on a spindle.* *—intr.* **1.** To move or spin around rapidly, suddenly, or repeatedly. **2.** To whirl or turn suddenly; make an about-face. Usually used with *about* or *around.* *—n.* **1.** A twirling or being twirled; a quick spinning or twisting. **2.** Something twirled; a curl or twist. [Perhaps alteration (influenced by WHIRL) of obsolete *tirl,* TRILL.]
twirp. Variant of **twerp.**
twist (twĭst) *v.* **twisted, twisting, twists.** *—tr.* **1. a.** To entwine (two or more threads) so as to produce a single strand. **b.** To form in this manner: *twist a length of rope.* **2.** To wind or coil (vines or rope, for example) around something. **3.** To interweave: *twist flowers in one's hair.* **4. a.** To impart a coiling or spiral shape to. **b.** To turn repeatedly while holding one end firm. **5. a.** To turn or open by turning. **b.** To pull, break, or snap by turning. Used with *off: twist off a dead branch.* **6.** To wrench or sprain: *twist one's wrist.* **7.** To alter the normal aspect of; contort: *twist one's mouth into a wry smile.* **8.** To alter or distort the intended meaning of. *—intr.* **1.** To be or become twisted. **2.** To move or progress in a winding course; meander. **3.** To squirm; writhe: *twist with pain.* **4. a.** To turn around, especially in an uneasy way. **b.** To rotate or revolve. **5.** To dance the twist. —See Usage note at **distort.** *—n.* **1.** Something twisted or formed by winding, especially: **a.** A length of yarn, cord, or thread, especially a strong silk thread used mainly to bind the edges of buttonholes. **b.** Tobacco leaves processed into the form of a rope or roll. **c.** *British.* A simple packet made by rolling a piece of paper around something and twisting the ends. **d.** Bread or other bakery products for which the dough was twisted before baking. **e.** A sliver of citrus peel twisted over or dropped into a drink to impart flavor. **2. a.** The act of twisting or the condition of being twisted; a spin or twirl; rotation. **b.** A sharp bend or turn. **3.** A vigorous wrench or turn. **4. a.** The state of being twisted into a spiral; torsional stress or strain. **b.** The degree or angle of such stress. **5.** A sprain or wrench, as of a muscle. **6. a.** A sudden or unexpected change in a course of events or a surprising

revelation, as in a novel, play, or the like: *Saki's stories always have a twist at the end.* **b.** A sudden change or departure from a pattern, usually for the worse: *a twist of fate.* **7.** A contortion or distortion, as of the face. **8.** A personal inclination or eccentricity; a penchant or flaw: *a twist in her character.* **9.** A dance, popular especially in the 1960's, characterized by vigorous twisting of the waist and hips from side to side with the knees bent. Preceded by *the.* **10.** *British Informal.* A trick or swindle. [Middle English *twysten,* from Old English *-twist,* a rope.] **—twist·a·bil·i·ty** *n.* **—twist·a·ble** *adj.* **—twist·ing·ly** *adv.*

twist drill *n.* A drill having deep helical grooves along the shank from the point.

twist·ed (twĭs′tĭd) *adj.* Perverted; weird and evil: *a twisted mind.*

twist·er (twĭs′tər) *n.* **1.** One that twists; specifically, a mechanical device for spinning or twisting yarn or rope. **2.** A ball thrown or batted with a twist. **3.** *Informal.* A cyclone or a tornado.

twist grip *n.* A ratchet-controlled, rotating device attached to the ends of some handlebars. On some bicycles and motorcycles it is used as a gear-changing control and on most motorcycles it is used as an accelerator.

twit (twĭt) *tr.v.* **twitted, twitting, twits.** To taunt, ridicule, or tease, especially for embarrassing mistakes or faults. —See Synonyms at **ridicule.**
~n. **1.** The act of twitting. **2.** A reproach, gibe, or taunt. **3.** A silly or stupid person. [Earlier *(a)twite,* Middle English *atwiten,* Old English *ætwitan,* to reproach with : *æt-* (indicating opposition), from *æt,* from, AT + *witan,* to reproach, ascribe to.]

twitch (twĭch) *v.* **twitched, twitching, twitches.** *—tr.* To draw, pull, or move suddenly and sharply; jerk: *The fisherman twitched his line.* *—intr.* **1.** To move jerkily or spasmodically. **2.** To ache sharply from time to time; twinge.
~n. **1.** A sudden involuntary or spasmodic muscular movement: *a nervous twitch.* **2.** A sudden pulling; a jerk or tug. **3.** A looped cord used to restrain a horse by tightening it around the animal's upper lip. **—in a twitch.** *Informal.* In a state of nervousness or agitation. [Middle English *twicchen,* perhaps of Low German origin, akin to Low German *twikken.*] **—twitch·ing·ly** *adv.*

twitch grass *n.* **Couch grass** *(see).*

twitch·y (twĭch′ē) *adj.* **-ier, -iest.** *Informal.* Agitated or nervous.

twite (twīt) *n.* A Eurasian finch, *Acanthis flavirostris,* resembling the linnet, but having no red plumage on the crown, and found in moorland regions. [Imitative of its call.]

twit·ter (twĭt′ər) *v.* **-tered, -tering, -ters.** *—intr.* **1.** To utter a succession of light chirping or tremulous sounds, as a bird does; chirrup. **2.** To titter; giggle. **3.** To tremble or talk nervously, as with excitement. *—tr.* To utter or say with a twitter: *twittered his greeting.*
~n. **1.** The light chirping sounds made by certain birds. **2.** Light, tremulous speech or laughter. **3.** A state of agitation or excitement; a flutter. Used especially in the phrase *in a twitter.* [Middle English *twiteren,* akin to Old High German *zwizzirōn,* from West Germanic *twittwīrōjan* (imitative; unattested).] **—twit·ter·er** *n.* **—twit·ter·ing·ly** *adv.* **—twit·ter·y** *adj.*

twixt, 'twixt (twĭkst) *prep. Archaic & Poetic.* Betwixt.

two (to͞o) *n.* **1. a.** The cardinal number that is one more than one. **b.** A symbol representing this, such as 2, II, or ii. **2.** A set made up of two persons or things. **3. a.** The second in a series. **b.** A playing card marked with two pips. **4.** A size, as in clothing, designated as two. **5.** Two hours after midnight or midday. **—in two. 1.** So as to be in two separate units: *split in two.* **2.** So as to have two thicknesses or layers: *fold in two.* **—put two and two together.** To reach a correct, usually obvious conclusion after considering a given set of circumstances. **—that makes two of us.** That is true of or applies to myself as well as to another. [Middle English *two,* Old English *twā, tū.*] **—two** *adj. & pron.*

two-base hit (to͞o′bās′) *n. Baseball.* A hit enabling the batter to reach second base; a double. Also called "two-bagger."

two-bit (to͞o′bĭt′) *adj. Slang.* **1.** Worth very little; insignificant. **2.** Cheap; shoddy.

two bits *pl.n. Informal.* **1.** Twenty-five cents. **2.** A petty sum.

two-by-four (to͞o′bī-fôr′, -fōr′, to͞o′bə-) *adj.* **1.** Measuring two by four inches, or in the same ratio in other units. **2.** *Informal.* Small in size; cramped: *a two-by-four apartment.*
~n. Any length of timber measuring about 2 by 4 inches or trimmed to 1 5/8 inches in thickness and 3 3/8 inches in width.

two-di·men·sion·al (to͞o′dĭ-mĕn′shə-nəl) *adj.* **1.** Having only two dimensions, usually length and width; planar; flat. **2.** *Informal.* Lacking dimension or completion; limited in range or depth: *two-dimensional characters in a novel.*

two-edged (to͞o′ĕjd′) *adj.* **1.** Having a cutting edge on both sides. Said especially of a knife, razor, or sword blade. **2.** Having two contrasting effects, meanings, or interpretations.

two-faced (to͞o′fāst′) *adj.* **1.** *Informal.* Hypocritical or double-dealing; deceitful. **2.** Having two faces or surfaces. **—two-fac·ed·ly** (to͞o′fā′sĭd-lē, -fāst′lē) *adv.* **—two-fac·ed·ness** *n.*

two-fist·ed (to͞o′fĭs′tĭd) *adj. Informal.* Aggressively vigorous: *a two-fisted drinker.*

two·fold (to͞o′fōld′, -fōld′) *adj.* **1.** Having two components. **2.** Having twice as much or twice as many; double.
~adv. (to͞o′fōld′). Two times as much or as many; doubly.

2,4,5-T (to͞o′fôr′fīv′tē′) *n.* **Trichlorophenoxyacetic acid** *(see).*

two-hand·ed (to͞o′hăn′dĭd) *adj.* **1.** Requiring the use of two hands at once: *a two-handed sledgehammer.* **2.** Made to be operated or engaged in by two people. **3.** Able to use both hands with equal facility; ambidextrous. **4.** Having two hands.

two-mast·er (to͞o′măs′tər, -mä′stər) *n.* A sailing vessel rigged with two masts.

two-name (to͞o′nām′) *adj. Finance.* Pertaining to or designating a commercial paper bearing the signatures of two persons liable to the obligation.

two-par·ty system (to͞o′pär′tē) *n.* A political system, such as currently prevails in the United States and traditionally in Great Britain, in which two major political parties dominate.

two·pence (tŭp′əns) *n.* Also *Informal* **tup·pence.** *British.* **1.** Two pennies regarded as a monetary unit. **2.** A silver coin worth two pennies, since 1662 minted only for distribution on Maundy Thursday. **3.** A copper coin of this value minted during the reign of George III. **4.** A very small amount; a whit: *didn't care twopence about politics.*

two·pen·ny (tŭp′ə-nē, to͞o′pĕn′ē) *adj.* Also *British Informal* **tup·pen·ny.** **1.** Worth or costing twopence. **2.** Cheap; worthless.

two-phase (to͞o′fāz′) *adj.* Pertaining to two alternating electrical currents with phases at 90°; quarter-phase.

two-piece (to͞o′pēs′) *adj.* Made in or consisting of two parts or pieces: *a two-piece suit.*
~n. A two-piece suit or swimsuit.

two-ply (to͞o′plī′) *adj.* **1.** Made of two interwoven layers. **2.** Consisting of two thicknesses or strands: *two-ply knitting yarn.*
~n., pl. **-plies.** Any two-ply material, such as wool or yarn.

two-seat·er (to͞o′sē′tər) *n.* A motor vehicle, especially a sports car, or an airplane that has seating for two people.

Two Sic·i·lies, the (sĭs′ə-lēz). The former kingdoms of Sicily and Naples, first ruled jointly (1443–58; 1504–1713; 1759–1815) and then united (1815–60).

two-sid·ed (to͞o′sī′dĭd) *adj.* Having two sides or involving two positions: *a two-sided dispute.*

two·some (to͞o′səm) *n.* **1.** Two people together; a pair or couple; a duo. **2.** A game played by two people, as a round of golf.

two-step (to͞o′stĕp′) *n.* **1.** A ballroom dance in 2/4 time that is characterized by long, sliding steps. **2.** The music composed for a two-step. **—two-step** *adj.*

two-stroke (to͞o′strōk′) *adj.* Designating an internal-combustion engine in which the piston or pistons make two strokes for each explosion. Compare **four-stroke.**

two-time (to͞o′tīm′) *tr.v.* **-timed, -timing, -times.** *Slang.* **1.** To deceive or betray. **2.** To be unfaithful to (a spouse or lover). **—two-tim·er** *n.* **—two-tim·ing** *adj.*

two-tone (to͞o′tōn′) *adj.* Of two shades or colors: *two-tone shoes.*

'twould (two͝od). *Regional and Poetic.* Contraction of *it would.*

two-way (to͞o′wā′) *adj.* **1.** Affording passage to vehicular traffic in two directions: *a two-way street.* **2.** Permitting communication in two directions: *two-way radio.* **3. a.** Expressive of or involving mutual action or responsibility. **b.** Involving two participants on a reciprocal basis. **4.** Permitting the flow in either of two directions: *a two-way valve.* **5.** Controlling an electric current at two places.

twp. township.

TX Texas (used with a Zip Code).

-ty[1] *suffix.* Indicates a condition or quality; for example, **royalty.** [Middle English *-te(e), -tie,* from Old French *-te, -tet,* from Latin *-tās* (stem *-tāt-*), akin to Greek *-tēs,* Sanskrit *-tat, -tati.*]

-ty[2] *suffix.* Indicates a multiple of ten; for example, **forty, fifty, sixty.** [Middle English *-ty, -ti,* Old English *-tig.*]

ty·coon (tī-ko͞on′) *n.* **1.** *Informal.* A wealthy and powerful businessman or industrialist; a magnate. **2.** A title formerly applied to the Japanese shogun. [Japanese *taikun,* title of a shogun, from Ancient Chinese *t'ai kiuən,* emperor : *tài,* great (Mandarin *dà*) + *kiuən,* prince, sovereign (Mandarin *jūn*).]

tyke, tike (tīk) *n.* **1.** *Informal.* A small child, especially a mischievous one. **2.** A mongrel or cur. **3.** *Chiefly Scottish.* A mean or uncouth fellow; a boor. [Middle English mongrel, from Old Norse *tīk,* a bitch.]

Ty·ler (tī′lər), **John** (1790–1862). 10th U.S. president (1841–44). A Democratic U.S. congressman (1816–21) and senator (1827–36) from Virginia, he initiated the Compromise Tariff of 1833 and soon after joined the newly formed Whig party. He was elected vice president under William H. Harrison and assumed the presidency upon Harrison's death within a month of inauguration. Tyler's administration was highlighted by the the annexation of Texas (1845).

Tyler, Wat (died 1381). English rebel. He led the Peasants' Revolt (1381) against Richard II's poll tax. He was killed by the lord mayor of London, Sir William Walworth, after making fresh demands of the king, who had already made concessions.

ty·lo·sin (tī′lə-sĭn) *n.* An antibiotic, $C_{45}H_{77}NO_{17}$, obtained from the actinomycete *Streptomyces fradiae* and used as an antibacterial drug in veterinary medicine. [Origin unknown.]

ty·lo·sis (tī-lō′sĭs) *n., pl.* **-ses** (-sēz′). Also **ty·lose** (tī′lōz′, -lōs′). *Botany.* An ingrowth from an adjoining cell into a water-conducting vessel, often found in old, damaged, or diseased wood, that may wholly block the vessel. [Greek *tulōsis* : *tulē,* callus + -OSIS.]

tymbal. Variant of **timbal.**

tym·pan (tĭm′pən) *n.* **1.** *Printing.* A padding of paper or cloth placed over the platen of a printing press to provide support for the sheet being printed. **2.** *Architecture.* A tympanum. **3.** A tightly stretched sheet or membrane, as on the head of a drum. [Middle English *tympan, timpan,* a drum, Old English *timpana,* from Latin *tympanum.* See **tympanum.**]

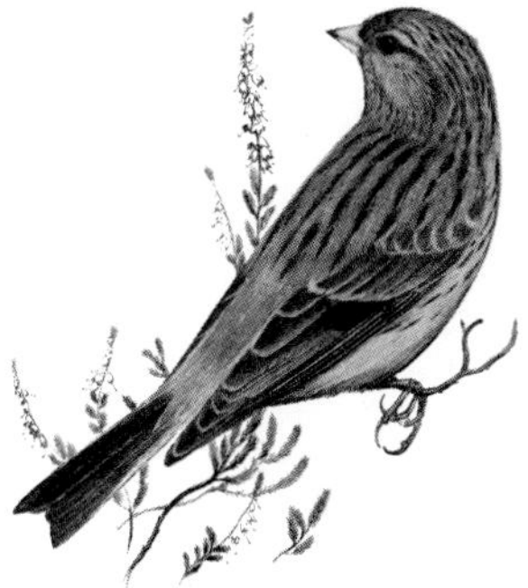

twite *Found throughout Europe and Asia, twites live in colonies on hill slopes and moorlands, often moving to coastal marshes in winter. They feed chiefly on plants and get their name from their nasal call, which sounds like "twa-it."*

PRONUNCIATION KEY

ă, pat; ā, pay; âr, care;
ä, father, are; b, bib;
ch, church; d, deed; ĕ, pet;
ē, be; f, fife; g, gag; h, hat;
hw, which; ĭ, pit; ī, pie;
îr, pier; j, judge; k, kick;
l, lid, needle; m, mum;
n, no, sudden; ng, thing;
ŏ, pot; ō, toe; ô, paw, for;
oi, noise; ou, out; o͝o, book;
o͞o, boot; p, pop; r, roar;
s, sauce; sh, ship, dish;
t, tight; th, thin, path;
th, this, bathe; ŭ, cut; ûr, fur;
v, valve; w, with; y, yes;
z, zebra, size; zh, vision;
ə, about, item, edible, gallop, circus, peaceful

IN FOREIGN WORDS:

à, *Fr.* ami; œ, *Fr.* feu, *Ger.* schön; ü, *Fr.* tu, *Ger.* über; KH, *Ger.* ich, *Scot.* loch; N, *Fr.* bon; y', *Fr.* Compiègne

STRESS MARKS:

Primary stress: ′
in·cite′ (ĭn-sīt′)
Secondary stress: ′
in′sight′ (ĭn′sīt′)

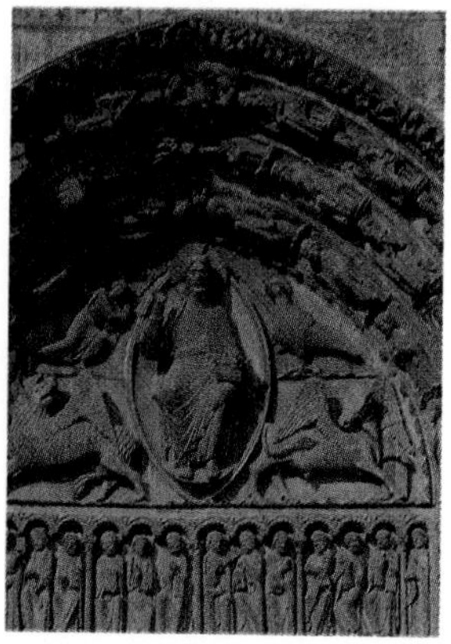

tympanum *Above an entrance to the 12th-century cathedral of Chartres in France, this tympanum is decorated with the figure of Christ triumphant, surrounded by symbols of the evangelists.*

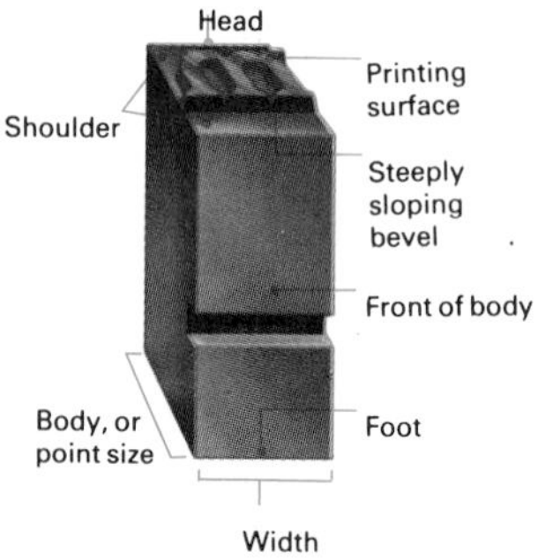
Head
Printing surface
Shoulder
Steeply sloping bevel
Front of body
Body, or point size
Foot
Width

type *The use of movable type for printing, invented in Europe in the 15th century, is no different in principle from the woodblock printing of illustrations, practiced for centuries before in China. A piece of metal type, such as the lower-case letter "m" (above), is cast in a mold of a chosen size and style. Modern printing is increasingly done on film, rendering the "hot metal" tradition obsolete.*

tympani. Variant of **timpani.**

tym·pan·ic (tĭm-păn′ĭk) *adj.* Also **tym·pa·nal** (tĭm′pə-nəl) (for sense 2). **1.** Pertaining to or resembling a drum. **2.** *Anatomy.* Of or pertaining to the tympanum. [From TYMPANUM.]

tympanic bone *n.* The part of the temporal bone of the skull that partially encloses the auditory canal and supports the tympanic membrane.

tympanic cavity *n.* The **middle ear** *(see).*

tympanic membrane *n.* The thin, semitransparent, oval-shaped membrane separating the middle ear from the external ear. Also called "eardrum," "tympanum."

tym·pa·nist (tĭm′pə-nĭst) *n.* A member of an orchestra who plays the kettledrums and other percussion instruments. [Latin *tympanista,* from Greek *tumpanistēs,* from *tumpanizein,* to beat a drum, from *tumpanon,* a drum. See **tympanum.**]

tym·pa·ni·tes (tĭm′pə-nī′tēz) *n.* A distension of the abdomen resulting from the accumulation of gas or air in the abdomen. [Middle English, from Late Latin *tympanītēs,* from Greek *tumpanitēs,* from *tumpanon,* a drum. See **tympanum.**]

tym·pa·ni·tis (tĭm′pə-nī′tĭs) *n.* Inflammation of the middle ear. [TYMPAN(UM) + -ITIS.]

tym·pa·num, tim·pa·num (tĭm′pə-nəm) *n., pl.* **-na** (-nə) or **-nums.** **1. a.** The **middle ear** *(see).* **b.** The tympanic membrane; the eardrum. **c.** The middle ear and the tympanic membrane combined. **2.** *Zoology.* A membranous external auditory structure, as in certain insects. **3.** *Architecture.* **a.** The recessed, ornamental space or panel enclosed by the cornices of a triangular pediment. **b.** A similar space between an arch and the lintel of a portal. Also called "tympan." **4.** The diaphragm of a telephone. **5.** The tympan on a drum; a drumhead. [Medieval Latin, the eardrum, from Latin, a drum, from Greek *tumpanon.*]

tym·pa·ny (tĭm′pə-nē) *n., pl.* **-nies.** **1.** Tympanites. **2.** *Archaic.* An inflated manner or style; bombast. **3.** A low-pitched resonance obtained by percussion. [Medieval Latin *tympanias,* "a drumlike swelling," from Greek *tumpanias,* from *tumpanon,* a drum.]

Tyn·dale, Tin·dal, Tin·dale (tĭn′dəl), **William** (*c.* 1494–1536). English Protestant reformer and biblical translator. His highly literary translation of the New Testament (begun at Cologne in 1525) became the basis of the Authorized, or King James, Version of the Bible. He was strangled at the stake as a heretic, and his body was afterward burned.

Tyn·dall effect (tĭn′dəl) *n.* The Rayleigh scattering of light by very small particles. [After John *Tyndall* (1820–93), Irish physicist.]

Tyne (tīn). River of northeastern England. Formed by the confluence of the North and South Tynes at Hexham, it flows 48 kilometers (30 miles) east to the North Sea.

Tyne and Wear (wâr). Metropolitan county of northeastern England. Established in 1974, it includes areas formerly in Northumberland and Durham. Newcastle upon Tyne is the administrative center.

Tyn·wald (tĭn′wəld) *n.* The parliament of the Isle of Man. [From Old Norse *thingwall-,* unattested stem of *thingvǫllr* (thing, assembly (see **thing**) + *vǫllr,* field, plain).]

typ·al (tī′pəl) *adj.* Pertaining to or serving as a type; typical.

type (tīp) *n.* **1. a.** A group of persons or things sharing common traits or characteristics that distinguish them as an identifiable group or class; a kind; category. **b.** A subdivision of a kind or category: *three main types of error.* **2.** A person or thing having the features of a group or class; a standard example: *a type of the red-haired Celt.* **3.** An example or model; an embodiment: *"He was the perfect type of a military dandy"* (Joyce Cary). **4.** *Informal.* **a.** A person regarded as being typical of a specified class, such as a profession, rank, or social group: *a restaurant full of executive types.* **b.** One embodying the features or characteristics associated with a specified group or class: *She's not the ballet type.* **5.** A figure, representation, or symbol of something to come, such as an event in the Old Testament that foreshadows another in the New Testament. **6. a.** A taxonomic designation, such as the name of a species or genus, used as the basis of ascription to or characterization of the next highest taxonomic category. **b.** A specimen or sample used as the basis of description of a species; a holotype. **7.** *Printing.* **a.** A small block of metal or wood bearing a raised letter or character on the upper end that when inked and pressed upon paper leaves a printed impression. **b.** Such pieces collectively. **c.** Letters or characters photographically exposed onto light-sensitive material, such as film or bromide paper, subsequently used to prepare a printing image in photocomposition. **d.** A typeface: *in heavy type.* **e.** Letters and characters produced by traditional printing methods or by photocomposition; printed matter. **8.** A pattern, design, or image impressed or stamped upon the face of a coin. **—true to type.** Appearing or behaving in a characteristic way.
~*adj.* **1.** Standard; typical: *type examples.* **2.** Of or pertaining to printing or typesetting: *type size.*
~*v.* **typed, typing, types.** —*tr.* **1.** To write (something) with a typewriter; typewrite. **2.** To determine the type of (a blood sample or tissue). **3.** To classify according to a particular type: *typed her a heroine.* **4.** To represent or typify. **5.** To prefigure; foreshadow. —*intr.* To work at a typewriter; typewrite. [Middle English, from Late Latin *typus,* a form, type, from Latin, figure, image, from Greek *tupos,* a blow, impression, from *tuptein,* to strike.]
Synonyms: *character, ilk, kind, nature, sort.*
Usage: In standard English, *type* is followed by *of* in constructions such as *that type of leather,* though the *of* is sometimes omitted in regional speech. Many people prefer to restrict their use of *type* to those contexts where a specific, clearly definable category is involved and to use *kind* or *sort* where the reference is more general *(that sort of thing; the kind of person I would trust).*

-type *suffix.* Indicates: **1.** Type or representative form; for example, **monotype.** **2.** Stamping or printing type or photographic process; for example, **collotype.** **3. a.** Belonging to a specified type or class: *reference-type works.* **b.** Resembling or related to something specified: *a Chablis-type wine.* [French, from Latin *-typus,* from Greek *-tupos,* from *tupos,* TYPE; senses 3a. and 3b. from TYPE.]

type-bar (tīp′bär′) *n.* Any of the movable bars in a typewriter carrying letters or characters.

type·case (tīp′kās′) *n.* A case divided into compartments for holding printing type.

type·cast (tīp′kăst′, -käst′) *tr.v.* **-cast, -casting, -casts.** **1.** To cast in an acting role akin or suited to one's own personality, background, or physical appearance. **2.** To assign repeatedly to the same kind of part or role.

type·face (tīp′fās′) *n.* *Printing.* **1.** The surface of a body of type that makes the impression. **2.** The impression itself. **3.** The size, design, or style of the letter or character on the type. **4.** The full range of type of the same design. Also called "face."

type foundry *n.* A factory where metal printing type is cast. **—type founder** *n.* **—type founding** *n.*

type genus *n.* The name of a taxonomic genus that is designated as representative of the family to which it belongs; for example, the genus *Canis,* which includes dogs and wolves, is the type genus of the family Canidae.

type-high (tīp′hī′) *adj.* *Printing.* As high as the standard height of type, 0.9186 of an inch.

type metal *n.* *Printing.* An alloy used for making metal types, consisting mainly of tin, lead, and antimony.

type·script (tīp′skrĭpt′) *n.* **1.** A typewritten copy, as of a book or document. **2.** Typewritten matter.

type·set (tīp′sĕt′) *tr.v.* **-set, -setting, -sets.** To set (type) for printing.

type·set·ter (tīp′sĕt′ər) *n.* **1.** A person who sets type; a compositor. **2.** A machine used for setting type.

type species *n.* The name of a taxonomic species designated as representative of the genus to which it belongs; for example, *Panthera pardus,* the leopard, is the type species of the genus *Panthera.*

type specimen *n.* A **holotype** *(see).*

type·write (tīp′rīt′) *v.* **-wrote** (-rōt′), **-written** (-rĭt′n), **-writing, -writes.** —*tr.* To write (a letter, for example) with a typewriter; type. —*intr.* To write with a typewriter; type. [Back-formation from TYPEWRITER.]

type·writ·er (tīp′rī′tər) *n.* *Abbr.* **typw.** **1.** A keyboard machine that prints characters and numerals, traditionally by means of a set of metal hammers bearing raised type that strike the paper through an inked ribbon or carbon tape, or using various other devices, such as a **daisywheel** or **golfball** *(both of which see),* when actuated by pressed keys. **2.** *Archaic.* A typist. **3.** *Printing.* A style of type that resembles typewritten copy.

type·writ·ing (tīp′rī′tĭng) *n.* **1.** The act, process, or skill of using a typewriter. **2.** Copy produced by typewriting; typescript.

typh·li·tis (tĭf-lī′tĭs) *n.* Inflammation of the cecum. [New Latin, from Greek *tuphlon,* cecum (from *tuphlos,* blind) + -ITIS.] **—typh·lit·ic** (tĭf-lĭt′ĭk) *adj.*

ty·phoid (tī′foid′) *n.* Typhoid fever.
~*adj.* Also **ty·phoid·al** (tī-foid′l). Of, relating to, or resembling typhoid fever. [TYPH(US) + -OID.]

typhoid fever *n.* An acute, highly infectious disease caused by the typhoid bacillus, *Salmonella typhosa,* transmitted by contaminated food or water and characterized by red rashes, high fever, and, in severe cases, intestinal hemorrhaging. Also called "enteric fever."

Typhoid Mary *n.* A person from whom something undesirable or deadly spreads to those around him or her. [After *Mary* MALLON, a typhoid carrier.]

Ty·phon (tī′fŏn′). *Greek Mythology.* A monster called by Hesiod the son of Typhoeus; father of the Winds.

ty·phoon (tī-fo͞on′) *n.* A small, intense tropical cyclone occurring in the western Pacific or the China Sea. —See Synonyms at **wind.** [Cantonese *daai fung,* "great wind," corresponding to Chinese (Mandarin) *dàfēng¹* : *dà,* great + *fēng,* wind (but in form influenced by Greek *Tuphōn,* TYPHON).] **—ty·phon·ic** (tī-fŏn′ĭk) *adj.*

ty·phus (tī′fəs) *n.* Any of several forms of an infectious disease caused by microorganisms of the genus *Rickettsia,* especially when flea-borne as in *endemic typhus,* louse-borne as in *epidemic typhus,* or mite-borne as in *scrub typhus,* and characterized generally by severe headache, sustained high fever, depression, delirium, and widespread rashes. Also called "ship fever," "typhus fever." [New Latin, from Greek *tuphos,* (fever-causing) delusion, from *tuphein,* to make smoke.] **—ty·phous** *adj.*

typ·i·cal (tĭp′ĭ-kəl) *adj.* Also **typ·ic** (-ĭk). **1.** Exhibiting the traits or characteristics peculiar to a kind, class, group, or the like; representative of a whole group: *a typical suburban community.* **2. a.** Of or pertaining to a representative specimen; characteristic; distinctive. **b.** Characteristic of a particular individual: *That sort of behavior is typical of her.* **3. a.** Conforming to a type. **b.** *Biology.* Having the characteristics of a particular taxonomic category. **4.** Of the nature of, constituting, or serving as a type; emblematic. —See Synonyms at **characteristic, usual.** [Late Latin *typicālis,* from *typicus,* typical, from Greek *tupikos,* impressionable, from *tupos,* impression, TYPE.] **—typ·i·cal·i·ty** (tĭp′ĭ-kăl′ə-tē), **typ·i·cal·ness** *n.*

typ·i·cal·ly (tĭp'ĭ-klē', -kə-lē) *adv.* **1.** In the respects usually associated with the specified category: *typically American.* **2.** In normal or typical circumstances; usually: *Roads are typically used by cars.*
typ·i·fy (tĭp'ə-fī') *tr.v.* **-fied, -fying, -fies. 1.** To serve as a typical example of; embody the essential characteristics of. **2.** To represent by an image, form, or model; symbolize. [TYP(E) + -FY.] —**typ·i·fi·ca·tion** *n.* —**typ·i·fi·er** *n.*
typ·ist (tī'pĭst) *n.* One who operates a typewriter, especially as a form of employment.
ty·po (tī'pō) *n., pl.* **-pos.** *Informal.* A typographical error.
ty·pog·ra·pher (tī-pŏg'rə-fər) *n.* **1.** A printer or compositor. **2.** One skilled in the design or layout of printed matter.
typographical error *n.* A mistake in printing, typing, or writing.
ty·pog·ra·phy (tī-pŏg'rə-fē) *n., pl.* **-phies. 1. a.** The process of printing material from movable type. **b.** The art and technique of this. **2.** The arrangement or appearance of printed matter. [Medieval Latin *typographia* : Greek *tupos,* impression, TYPE + -GRAPHY.] —**ty·po·graph·ic** (tī'pə-grăf'ĭk), —**ty·po·graph·i·cal** *adj.* —**ty·po·graph·i·cal·ly** *adv.*
ty·pol·o·gy (tī-pŏl'ə-jē) *n., pl.* **-gies. 1.** The study of types, especially according to a systematic classification. **2.** A theory or doctrine of types, as in scriptural studies. [Greek *tupos,* impression, TYPE + -LOGY.] —**ty·po·log·i·cal** (tī'pə-lŏj'ĭ-kəl) *adj.* —**ty·po·log·i·cal·ly** *adv.* —**ty·pol·o·gist** *n.*
typw. typewriter; typewritten.
Tyr, Tyrr (tîr). *Norse Mythology.* A god of war, son of Odin. [Old Norse *Týr.*]
ty·ra·mine (tī'rə-mēn') *n.* A colorless, crystalline amine, $C_8H_{11}NO$, found in mistletoe, putrefied animal tissue, certain cheeses, and ergot, and also produced synthetically, used in medicine. [TYR(OSINE) + AMINE.]
ty·ran·ni·cal (tĭ-răn'ĭ-kəl, tī-) *adj.* Also **ty·ran·nic** (-răn'ĭk). **1.** Of, pertaining to, or characteristic of a tyrant. **2.** Despotic; arbitrary; oppressive. —**ty·ran·ni·cal·ly** *adv.* —**ty·ran·ni·cal·ness** *n.*
ty·ran·ni·cide (tĭ-răn'ə-sīd', tī-) *n.* **1.** The killing of a tyrant. **2.** One who kills a tyrant. —**ty·ran·ni·cid·al** (tĭ-răn'ə-sīd'l, tī-) *adj.*
tyr·an·nize (tîr'ə-nīz') *v.* **-nized, -nizing, -nizes.** —*intr.* **1.** To exercise absolute power, especially arbitrarily. **2.** To rule as a tyrant. —*tr.* To treat tyrannically; crush; oppress. [French *tyranniser,* from Late Latin *tyrannizāre,* from Latin *tyrannus,* TYRANT.] —**tyr·an·niz·er** *n.* —**tyr·an·niz·ing·ly** *adv.*
ty·ran·no·saur (tĭ-răn'ə-sôr', tī-) *n.* Also **ty·ran·no·saur·us** (tĭ-răn'ə-sôr'əs, tī-). Any large carnivorous dinosaur of the genus *Tyrannosaurus,* of the Cretaceous period; especially, *T. rex,* which had small forelimbs and a large head. [New Latin : Greek *turannos,* TYRANT + -SAUR.]
tyr·an·nous (tîr'ə-nəs) *adj.* Characterized by tyranny; despotic; tyrannical. —**tyr·an·nous·ly** *adv.*
tyr·an·ny (tîr'ə-nē) *n., pl.* **-nies. 1.** A government in which a single ruler exercises absolute power, especially in an unjust, cruel, or arbitrary manner. **2.** The office, authority, or jurisdiction of such a ruler. **3.** Absolute power, especially when exercised unjustly or cruelly. **4.** The arbitrary use of such power; a tyrannical act. **5.** Excessively rigorous control: *the tyranny of etiquette.* [Middle English *tyrannye,* from Old French *tyrannie,* from Late Latin *tyrannia,* from Greek *turannia,* from *turannos,* TYRANT.]

ty·rant (tī'rənt) *n.* **1.** An absolute ruler who governs arbitrarily without constitutional or other restrictions, especially one in ancient Greece. **2.** A ruler who exercises power in a harsh, cruel manner; an oppressor. **3.** Any tyrannical or despotic person. [Middle English *tyra(u)nt,* from Old French *tyran(t),* from Latin *tyrannus,* from Greek *turannos,* probably from a source in Asia Minor.]
tyrant flycatcher *n.* A bird of the family Tyrannidae, the **flycatcher** *(see).* [Referring to its habit of repelling all birds from the territory surrounding its nest.]
tyre. *British.* Variant of **tire** (wheel covering).
Tyre (tīr). Ancient port of northwestern Lebanon. Founded by the Phoenicians, it became one of the great trade centers of the ancient world. Taken by the Crusaders in 1124, it was destroyed by Muslims in 1291 and was never completely rebuilt.
Tyr·i·an purple (tîr'ē-ən) *n.* A reddish dyestuff obtained from the bodies of certain mollusks of the genus *Murex* and highly prized in ancient times. [After *Tyre,* source of the dye.]
ty·ro, ti·ro (tī'rō) *n., pl.* **-ros.** An inexperienced person; a beginner; a neophyte. [Medieval Latin *tyrō,* from Latin *tīrō†,* a young soldier, recruit.]
Tyr·ol, Ti·rol (tĭ-rōl', tī'rōl'). Province in western Austria. The province is almost entirely occupied by the Tyrolean Alps and is a famous skiing center. Its capital is Innsbruck. —**Ty·ro·le·an** (tĭ-rō'lē-ən, tī-) *n. & adj.*
Tyr·o·lese (tîr'ə-lēz', -lēs', tī'rə-) *n., pl.* **Tyrolese.** A native or inhabitant of Tyrol.
~*adj.* Of or pertaining to Tyrol or the Tyrolese.
ty·ro·li·enne (tĭ-rō'lē-ĕn', tī-) *n.* **1.** A Tyrolean peasant dance in ³/₄ time. **2.** A song composed for this dance, featuring the yodel. [French *(danse) tyrolienne,* Tyrolean (dance).]
Ty·rone (tĭ-rōn'). County of western Northern Ireland. It is a hilly, predominantly agricultural county, and its traditional flax and brewing industries have declined. Omagh is the county town.
ty·ros·i·nase (tī-rŏs'ə-nās', -nāz') *n.* A copper-containing enzyme of plant and animal tissues that catalyzes the production of melanin from tyrosine. [TYROSIN(E) + -ASE.]
ty·ro·sine (tī'rə-sēn') *n.* A white crystalline nonessential amino acid, $C_9H_{11}NO_3$, derived from the hydrolysis of protein, that is a precursor of adrenaline, thyroxin, and melanin. [Greek *turos,* cheese + -INE.]
ty·ro·thri·cin (tī'rō-thrī'sĭn) *n.* A grayish to brown mixture of antibiotics obtained from cultures of the soil bacterium *Bacillus brevis* and applied locally for the treatment of infections caused by Grampositive bacteria. [New Latin *Tyrothrix* (stem *Tyrothric-*), generic name for certain spore-forming bacteria, "cheese-haired" : Greek *turos,* cheese + *thrix,* hair + -IN.]
Tyrr. Variant of **Tyr.**
Tyr·rhe·ni·an Sea (tĭ-rē'nē-ən). Section of the Mediterranean Sea lying between Italy and the islands of Corsica, Sardinia, and Sicily. The Strait of Messina connects it with the Ionian Sea.
tzar. Variant of **czar.**
tzetze fly. Variant of **tsetse fly.**
Tzi·gane (tsē-gän') *n.* A Gypsy, especially a Hungarian Gypsy.
~*adj.* Of or pertaining to Tziganes or their music. [French, from Hungarian *czigány.*]
tzimmes. Variant of **tsimmes.**
tzuris. Variant of **tsuris.**

PRONUNCIATION KEY

ă, pat; ā, pay; âr, care;
ä, father, are; b, bib;
ch, church; d, deed; ĕ, pet;
ē, be; f, fife; g, gag; h, hat;
hw, which; ĭ, pit; ī, pie;
îr, pier; j, judge; k, kick;
l, lid, needle; m, mum;
n, no, sudden; ng, thing;
ŏ, pot; ō, toe; ô, paw, for;
oi, noise; ou, out; ŏŏ, book;
ōō, boot; p, pop; r, roar;
s, sauce; sh, ship, dish;
t, tight; th, thin, path;
th, this, bathe; ŭ, cut; ûr, fur;
v, valve; w, with; y, yes;
z, zebra, size; zh, vision;
ə, about, item, edible,
gallop, circus, peaceful

IN FOREIGN WORDS:

à, *Fr.* ami; œ, *Fr.* feu, *Ger.*
schön; ü, *Fr.* tu, *Ger.* über;
KH, *Ger.* ich, *Scot.* loch;
N, *Fr.* bon; y', *Fr.* Compiègne

STRESS MARKS:

Primary stress: '
in·cite' (ĭn-sīt')
Secondary stress: '
in'sight' (ĭn'sīt')

U

u, U (yōō) *n., pl.* **u's** or **U's. 1.** The 21st letter of the modern English alphabet. See feature at **alphabet. 2.** Any of the speech sounds represented by this letter. **3.** Anything shaped like the letter U. Often used in combination: *a U-turn.* **4.** The 21st in a series; 20th when *J* is omitted.

u, U, u., U. *Note:* As an abbreviation or symbol, *u* may be a capital or a small letter, with or without a period. Established forms or those generally preferred precede the definition. When no form is given, all four forms are in general use in that sense. **1. u., U.** uncle. **2. U** *Mathematics.* union. **3. u.** unit. **4. U.** university. **5. u., U.** upper. **6. U** The symbol for the element uranium.

U¹ (yōō) *adj. British Informal.* Considered to be typical of or appropriate to the upper class, especially in language usage. Compare **non-U.** [Abbreviation of *upper class.*]

U² (ōō) *n.* A Burmese title of respect used before the name of a man.

U.A.E. United Arab Emirates.

UAM underwater-to-air missile.

UAR, U.A.R. United Arab Republic.

UART *n.* Universal asynchronous receiver transmitter; a type of radio set.

U.A.W. 1. United Automobile, Aerospace, and Agricultural Implement Workers. **2.** United Automobile Workers.

Ubangi-Shari. See **Central African Republic.**

Ü·ber·mensch (ü′bĕr-mĕnsh′) *n., pl.* **-menschen** (-mĕn′shən). *German.* A superman, as in the philosophy of Nietzsche. [German, "over-man."]

u·bi·e·ty (yōō-bī′ə-tē) *n.* The condition of being located in a particular place. [Medieval Latin *ubietās,* from *ubi,* where.]

u·biq·ui·tous (yōō-bĭk′wə-təs) *adj.* Being or seeming to be everywhere at the same time; omnipresent: *their ubiquitous influence.* [From UBIQUITY.] —**u·biq·ui·tous·ly** *adv.* —**u·biq·ui·tous·ness** *n.*

u·biq·ui·ty (yōō-bĭk′wə-tē) *n.* Existence everywhere at the same time; omnipresence. [New Latin *ubiquitas,* from Latin *ubīque,* everywhere : *ubī,* where + *-que,* generalizing particle.]

u·bi su·pra (ōō′bē sōō′prä). *Abbr.* **u.s.** *Latin.* Where (mentioned) above.

U-boat (yōō′bōt′) *n.* A German submarine. [German *U-boot,* short for *Unterseeboot,* "undersea boat."]

U-bolt (yōō′bōlt′) *n.* A bolt shaped like the letter U, fitted with a thread and nut at each end.

UBV photometry (yōō′bē-vē′) *n.* A system of photometry used to obtain stellar magnitudes by comparing observed magnitudes to a standard sequence of stars. [U(LTRAVIOLET) + B(LUE) + V(ISUAL).]

u.c. *Printing.* upper case.

Uc·cel·lo (ōō-chĕl′ō), **Paolo,** born Paolo di Dono (1397–1475). Florentine painter and craftsman, best known for his experiments with perspective and foreshortening. Among his works are three paintings of *The Battle of San Romano* (1456–60).

UCMJ Uniform Code of Military Justice.

UCS universal character set.

U.D.A., UDA Ulster Defense Association (in Northern Ireland).

u·dal (yōō′dəl) *n.* A system of freehold possession of land that preceded the feudal system and is still used in the Orkney and Shetland islands. [Orkney and Shetland dialect, from Old Norse *ōthal,* corresponding to Old English *ēthel, ōthel,* from Germanic *ōth-* (unattested); akin to ATHELING.] —**u·dal** *adj.*

U·dall (yōō′dôl), **Nicholas** (*c.* 1505–56). English playwright, translator, and schoolmaster. He is primarily remembered as the writer of the first known English comedy, *Ralph Roister Doister* (*c.* 1553). Although it is based on the works of Plautus and Terence, its characters, incidents, and idiomatic dialogue are English.

UDC Universal Decimal Classification.

ud·der (ŭd′ər) *n.* The baglike mammary organ characteristic of cows, sheep, and goats, having two or more teats. [Middle English *udder,* Old English *ūder.*]

UDI Unilateral Declaration of Independence.

u·do (ōō′dō) *n.* A Japanese plant, *Aralia cordata,* of which the young shoots are cooked and eaten as a vegetable. [Japanese.]

u·dom·e·ter (yōō-dŏm′ə-tər) *n.* A **rain gauge** *(see).* [French *udomè-*

tre, from Latin *ūdus,* damp + -METER.]

UFO, U.F.O. (yōō′ĕf′ō′, yōō′fō′) *n., pl.* **UFOs, U.F.O.'s** An **unidentified flying object** *(see).*

u·fol·o·gy (yōō-fŏl′ə-jē) *n.* The study of unidentified flying objects or the practice of trying to spot them. [UFO + -LOGY.] —**u·fo·log·i·cal** (yōō′fə-lŏj′ĭ-kəl) *adj.* —**u·fol·o·gist** (yōō-fŏl′ə-jĭst) *n.*

U·gan·da (yōō-gän′də, -găn′-). Landlocked republic in east-central Africa. Most of the country lies on a high plateau, more than 1,070 meters (3,500 feet) above sea level. Some 90 percent of Ugandans live by subsistence farming, and coffee accounts for over 75 percent of exports. There are reserves of copper and tin, and the Owen Falls hydroelectric scheme satisfies most energy needs. A British protectorate from 1894, Uganda became independent in 1962, with the kabaka (king) of Buganda as president. He was succeeded by Milton Obote (1966), who returned to power in 1980, following the overthrow of the dictatorship of Idi Amin (1971–78). Area, 236,036 square kilometers (91,134 square miles). Population, 12,600,000. Capital, Kampala. —**U·gan·dan** *n. & adj.*

U·ga·rit (ōō′gə-rēt′). Ancient city and city-state in western Syria. The city was probably occupied from Neolithic times. By the 4th millennium it had reached a high stage of development and enjoyed its greatest prosperity in the 15th and 14th centuries B.C. Cuneiform tablets dating from the 14th century B.C. record the poetic works and myths of the ancient Canaanites.

U·ga·rit·ic (ōō′gə-rĭt′ĭk) *n.* The Semitic language of the ancient city-state of Ugarit (on the site of Ras Shamra in present-day Syria). —**U·ga·rit·ic** *adj.*

ugh (ŭкн, ōōкн, ŭg) *interj.* Used to express horror, disgust, or repugnance.

ug·li (ŭg′lē) *n., pl.* **-lis** or **-lies.** A citrus fruit indigenous to Jamaica, produced by crossing a grapefruit and a tangerine and having a loose, wrinkled yellow rind. Also called "ugli fruit." [Perhaps from UGLY (from its ugly wrinkled rind).]

ug·li·fy (ŭg′lə-fī′) *tr.v.* **-fied, -fying, -fies.** To make ugly; disfigure. [UGLY + -FY.] —**ug·li·fi·ca·tion** *n.*

ug·ly (ŭg′lē) *adj.* **-lier, -liest. 1.** Displeasing to the eye; unsightly. **2.** Repulsive or offensive in any way; objectionable. **3.** Morally reprehensible. **4.** Threatening; ominous: *ugly weather.* **5.** Marked by or inclined toward anger or bad feelings: *An ugly scene developed.* [Middle English *ugli(c),* frightful, repulsive, from Old Norse *uggligr,* from *uggr†,* fear.] —**ug·li·ly** *adv.* —**ug·li·ness** *n.*

ugly duckling *n.* One considered ugly or unpromising at first but having the potential of becoming beautiful or admirable in maturity. [After the cygnet in the story by Hans Christian Andersen.]

U·gri·an (ōō'grē-ən, yōō'-) *n.* **1.** A member of a group of Finno-Ugric peoples of western Siberia and Hungary, including the Magyars. **2.** Ugric. [Old Russian *Ugrin'* (plural *Ugre*), from Common Slavic *Og'rin'* (unattested), from Turkic *Onogouroi.* See also **Hungary**.] —**U·gri·an** *adj.*

U·gric (ōō'grĭk, yōō'-) *n.* A branch of the Finno-Ugric subfamily of languages consisting of Magyar (Hungarian), Ostyak, and Vogul. —**U·gric** *adj.*

ug·some (ŭg'səm) *adj. Archaic.* Disgusting; loathsome. [Middle English *ugsom* : *uggen,* to inspire dread or disgust, from Old Norse *ugga,* to fear, UGLY + -SOME.]

UGT urgent (telegram).

uhf, UHF ultrahigh frequency.

uh-huh (ə-hŭ') *interj. Informal.* Yes.

uh·lan, u·lan (ōō'län', yōō'lən) *n.* A member of a body of cavalry armed with lances that formed part of the former Polish army, and later, the former German army. [German *u(h)lan,* from Polish *ulan,* from Turkish *oğlan,* "youth," from *oğul,* son.]

UHT *n.* Milk that has been heated rapidly and then cooled in a process that enables it to stay usable longer in an unopened container. [*U*ltra *H*igh *T*emperature.]

uh-uh (ŭ'ə) *interj. Informal.* No.

u·hu·ru (ōō-hōō'rōō, ōō-hōōr'ōō) *n. East African.* Liberty; freedom. Used chiefly as a slogan by African independence movements. [Swahili.]

Ui·gur, Ui·ghur (wē'gōōr) *n.* **1.** A member of a Turkic people dominant in Mongolia and eastern Turkestan from the 8th to the 12th centuries, now inhabiting northwestern China. **2.** The East Turkic language of this people. —**Ui·gu·ri·an** (wē-gōōr'ē-ən), **Ui·gu·ric** (wē-gōōr'ĭk) *adj.*

u·in·ta·ite (yōō-ĭn'tə-īt') *n.* A bitumen, **gilsonite** *(see).* [After the *Uinta* basin (Utah and Wyoming), where it was discovered.]

u·in·ta·there (yōō-ĭn'tə-thîr') *n.* Any of a number of extinct mammals resembling the rhinoceros, fossils of which have been found in North America. [After the *Uinta* Mountains, Utah, where fossil remains were discovered + *-there,* from Greek *thērion,* wild beast.]

uit·land·er (oit'län'dər, īt'-) *n. South African.* **1.** A foreigner. **2. Uitlander.** A native of Great Britain who resided in either of the former republics of the Orange Free State and Transvaal. [Afrikaans, from Dutch.]

u·ja·maa (ōō'jə-mä') *n.* **1.** A plan for developing cooperation and communal ideals amongst different peoples in Tanzania. Also used adjectivally: *an ujamaa village.* **2.** A village practicing this. [Swahili, family, brother : *u-,* prefix indicating state or condition + *jamaa,* family, from Arabic *jamā'a,* community.]

U.K., UK United Kingdom.

u·kase (yōō-kās', -kāz', yōō'kās, -kāz') *n.* **1.** A proclamation of the czar having the force of law in imperial Russia. **2.** Any authoritative order or decree; an edict. [French, from Russian *ukaz,* decree, from *ukazat',* to order, direct : *u-,* intensive prefix, "away" + *-kazat',* to show.]

uke (yōōk) *n. Informal.* A ukulele.

u·ki·yo·e (ōō-kē'yō-ā') *n.* A Japanese style of art in painting and printmaking, characterized by the simple depiction of scenes or objects from ordinary life. [Japanese : *ukiyo,* life + *e,* picture.]

U·krain·i·an (yōō-krā'nē-ən) *n.* **1.** An inhabitant or native of the Ukraine. **2.** A Slavic language, similar to but distinct from Russian, that is spoken by most natives of the Ukraine. Also formerly called "Little Russian." [Ukrainian *Ukrayina,* from Old Russian *Ukraina,* "borderland" : *u-,* away from, at + *kraĭ,* edge, brink, end.] —**U·krain·i·an** *adj.*

Ukrainian Soviet Socialist Republic. Also **Ukraine** (yōō-krān'). Constituent republic of the U.S.S.R., in the southwestern part of the country. The capital is Kiev. After the Russian Federative S.S.R. the Ukraine is the most heavily populated and economically important of the Soviet republics. Its steppe lands are one of the great wheat-producing regions of Europe, and the republic as a whole provides nearly a quarter of the U.S.S.R.'s food supply. It is also a major producer of coal and iron ore.

u·ku·le·le (yōō'kə-lā'lē, ōō'kə-) *n.* A small four-stringed guitar originally from Hawaii. [Hawaiian *'ukulele,* "jumping little flea" (said to be nickname of Edward Purvis, 19th-century British officer, who popularized the instrument) : *'uku,* flea + *lele,* jumping.]

ulan. Variant of **uhlan.**

U·lan Ba·tor (ōō'län' bä'tôr'). Capital of the Mongolian People's Republic, on the Tola River. It is the chief commercial and industrial city of the country and, lying on the Trans-Siberian Railway, is also the main transport junction.

U·la·no·va (ōō-lä'nə-və), **Galina Sergeyevna** (1910–). Russian prima ballerina. She is noted for her roles in *Swan Lake* and *Giselle.* Since 1962 she has been ballet mistress of the Bolshoi.

–ular *suffix.* Indicates a relationship or resemblance; for example, **tubular.** [Latin *-ulāris,* from *-ulus,* -ULE.]

Ul·bricht (ōōl'brĭkt), **Walter** (1893–1973). East German statesman. He was general secretary of the Socialist Unity Party after 1950 and became chairman (1960) of the newly established council of state. He erected the Berlin Wall (1961).

ul·cer (ŭl'sər) *n.* **1. a.** An inflammatory, often suppurating lesion on the skin or an internal mucous surface of the body, resulting in necrosis of the tissue and taking a long time to heal. **b.** A necrotic

lesion of the stomach or duodenum. **2.** Any corrupting condition or influence. [Middle English, from Old French *ulcere,* from Latin *ulcus* (stem *ulcer-*), a sore, ulcer.]

ul·cer·ate (ŭl'sə-rāt') *v.* **-ated, -ating, -ates.** —*intr.* To become affected with or as if with an ulcer. —*tr.* To affect with ulcers. —**ul·cer·a·tive** (ŭl'sə-rā'tĭv, ŭl'sər-ə-tĭv) *adj.*

ul·cer·a·tion (ŭl'sə-rā'shən) *n.* **1.** The development of an ulcer. **2.** An ulcer or ulcerous condition.

ul·cer·ous (ŭl'sər-əs) *adj.* **1.** Pertaining to or exhibiting ulcers. **2.** Corrupting; having a bad influence. —**ul·cer·ous·ly** *adv.*

–ule *suffix.* Indicates smallness; for example, **valvule, granule, valvule.** [French *-ule,* from Latin *-ulus* (masculine), *-ula* (feminine), *-ulum* (neuter), diminutive suffixes.]

u·le·ma, u·la·ma (ōō'lə-mä') *n., pl.* **-mas** or **-ma. 1.** The body of scholars or priests trained in traditional Muslim religion and law. **2.** A Muslim scholar or religious leader. [Turkish *'ulemā,* from Arabic *'ulamā,* "wise men," plural of *'ālim,* wise, learned, from *'alima,* to know.]

–ulent *suffix.* Indicates abundance or fullness; for example, **flatulent.** [Old French, from Latin *-ulentus.*]

u·lex·ite (yōō'lĕk-sīt', yōō-lĕk'sīt') *n.* A mineral, NaCaB$_5$O$_9$·8H$_2$O, that is white and forms round masses of very fine acicular crystals. [After George *Ulex* (died 1883), German chemist + -ITE.]

ul·lage (ŭl'ĭj) *n.* **1.** The amount of liquid, grain, or the like within a container that is lost during shipment or storage, as through leakage. **2.** The amount by which a container, such as a cask or bottle, falls short of being full. [Middle English, from Norman French *ulliage,* Old French *ouillage,* from *ouiller,* to fill up a cask to the bunghole, from *oeil,* eye, bunghole, from Latin *oculus.*]

Ulm (ōōlm). Industrial city in southern West Germany, on the Danube River. Mentioned in records as early as the mid-9th century, it was a leading commercial center during the Middle Ages.

ul·na (ŭl'nə) *n., pl.* **-nas** or **-nae** (-nē'). *Anatomy.* **1.** The bone extending from the elbow to the wrist on the side opposite to the thumb. **2.** The corresponding bone in the forelimb of other vertebrates. [New Latin, from Latin, elbow, arm.] —**ul·nar** (ŭl'nər) *adj.*

u·lot·ri·chous (yōō-lŏt'rĭ-kəs) *adj.* Having wiry or woolly hair. Said especially of Negroid peoples. [New Latin, "woolly-haired," from Greek *oulothrix* (stem *oulotrikh-*) : *oulos,* woolly, curly + *thrix,* hair.] —**u·lot·ri·chy** (yōō-lŏt'rĭ-kē) *n.*

ul·ster (ŭl'stər) *n.* A loose, long overcoat made of a heavy cloth and often belted. [After ULSTER (the coat was first made in Belfast).]

Ul·ster (ŭl'stər). Northernmost of the four ancient provinces of Ireland, no longer of political or administrative meaning. It consisted of nine counties, six of which (Antrim, Armagh, Down, Fermanagh, Londonderry, and Tyrone) now constitute Northern Ireland, itself still popularly known as Ulster. The three other counties (Cavan, Donegal, and Monaghan) are in the Republic of Ireland.

Ul·ster·man (ŭl'stər-mən, -män') *n., pl.* **-men** (-mĭn, -mĕn'). A native or inhabitant of Ulster.

Ul·ster·wom·an (ŭl'stər-wōōm'ən) *n., pl.* **-women** (-wĭm'ĭn). A woman who is a native or inhabitant of Ulster.

ult. 1. ultimate; ultimately. **2.** ultimo.

ul·te·ri·or (ŭl-tîr'ē-ər) *adj.* **1.** Lying beyond what is evident, revealed, or avowed; especially, concealed intentionally so as to deceive: *an ulterior motive.* **2.** Lying beyond or outside the area of immediate interest. **3.** Occurring later; subsequent. [Latin, farther, comparative of *ulter* (unattested), on the other side.]

ul·ti·ma (ŭl'tə-mə) *n.* The last syllable of a word. [Latin, feminine of *ultimus,* farthest, last. See **ultimate**.]

ul·ti·mate (ŭl'tə-mĭt) *adj. Abbr.* **ult. 1.** Completing a series or process; final; conclusive. **2.** Representing the farthest possible extent of analysis or division into parts: *ultimate constituent.* **3.** Fundamental; elemental. **4.** Of the greatest possible size or significance; maximum. **5.** Farthest; most remote. **6.** Representing the greatest possible sophistication or development of something: *the ultimate bicycle.* —See Synonyms at **last.** —*n.* **1.** The basic or fundamental element or principle. **2.** The final point; the conclusive result. **3.** The maximum; the greatest extreme. [Medieval Latin *ultimātus,* past participle of *ultimāre,* to come to an end, from Latin *ultimus,* farthest, last, superlative degree of *ulter* (unattested), on the other side.] —**ul·ti·mate·ness** *n.*

ul·ti·mate·ly (ŭl'tə-mĭt-lē) *adv.* At last; in the end; eventually.

ultima Thu·le (thōō'lē, thyōō'-) *n.* **1.** The northernmost region of the habitable world as thought of by ancient geographers. **2.** Any distant territory or destination. **3.** A remote goal or ideal. [Latin, "farthest Thule."]

ul·ti·ma·tum (ŭl'tə-mā'təm, -mä'təm) *n., pl.* **-tums** or **-ta** (-tə). **1.** A final statement of terms made by one party to another. **2.** A statement that expresses or implies the threat of serious penalties if the terms are not accepted. [New Latin, from Medieval Latin, neuter of *ultimātus,* last, ULTIMATE.]

ul·ti·mo (ŭl'tə-mō') *adv. Abbr.* **ult.** In or of the month before the present one. Compare **instant, proximo.** [Latin *ultimo (mense),* in last (month), from *ultimus,* last, ULTIMATE.]

ul·ti·mo·gen·i·ture (ŭl'tə-mō-jĕn'ə-chər) *n. Law.* A principle by which the youngest child inherits the estate of one or both parents. Compare **primogeniture.** [Latin *ultimus* + *-geniture,* as in PRIMOGENITURE.]

ul·tra (ŭl'trə) *adj.* Immoderately adhering to a belief, fashion, or course of action; extreme. —*n.* An extremist. [Originally shortened from French *ultra-royaliste.* See **ultra-**.]

ul·tra– *prefix.* Indicates: **1.** Surpassing or beyond a specified limit, range, or scope; for example, **ultramicroscopic, ultrasonic. 2.** Exceeding what is usual, moderate, or proper to an extreme degree; for example, **ultraconservative. Note:** Many compounds other than those entered here may be formed with *ultra-.* In forming compounds, *ultra-* is normally joined with the following element without a space or hyphen: *ultramodern; ultrafashionable.* However, if the second element begins with a capital letter or with the letter *a,* it is separated with a hyphen: *ultra-British, ultra-atomic.* [Latin, from *ultrā,* beyond, from *ulter* (unattested), on the other side.]

ul·tra·cen·tri·fuge (ŭl′trə-sĕn′trə-fyōōj′) *n.* A convection-free high-velocity centrifuge used in the separation of colloidal or submicroscopic particles. —**ul·tra·cen·trif·u·gal** (ŭl′trə-sĕn-trĭf′yə-gəl, -ə-gəl) *adj.* —**ul·tra·cen·trif·u·ga·tion** (ŭl′trə-sĕn-trĭf′yə-gā′shən, -ə-gā′-shən) *n.*

ul·tra·con·ser·va·tive (ŭl′trə-kən-sûr′və-tĭv) *adj.* Conservative to an extreme, especially in political beliefs; reactionary.
—*n.* One who is extremely conservative.

ul·tra·crep·i·dar·i·an (ŭl′trə-krĕp′ə-dâr′ē-ən) *adj.* Acting or speaking outside one's experience, knowledge, or ability.
—*n.* One who acts or speaks beyond the sphere of his experience or knowledge; especially, an ignorant critic. [Latin *ultrā crepidam,* "beyond the sole," alluding to a story about the Greek painter Apelles and a cobbler, who pointed out to Apelles that he had painted a slipper with the wrong number of ties. Having made this successful criticism, the cobbler criticized on the following day the leg of the figure in the painting, to which Apelles replied that he should confine himself to remarks about slippers and not judge "beyond the sole."]

ul·tra·fiche (ŭl′trə-fēsh′) *n.* A microfiche in which the reduction factor is 100 or more. [ULTRA- + (MICRO)FICHE.]

ul·tra·fil·tra·tion (ŭl′trə-fĭl-trā′shən) *n.* Filtration of colloidal solution through a semipermeable membrane. —**ul·tra·fil·ter** (ŭl′trə-fĭl′tər) *n.*

ul·tra·high frequency (ŭl′trə-hī′) *n. Abbr.* **uhf, UHF** A band of radio frequencies from 300 to 3,000 megahertz.

ul·tra·ism (ŭl′trə-ĭz′əm) *n.* Extremism, especially in politics; radicalism. [ULTRA + -ISM.] —**ul·tra·ist** *adj.* & *n.* —**ul·tra·is·tic** (ŭl′trə-ĭs′tĭk) *adj.*

ul·tra·ma·rine (ŭl′trə-mə-rēn′) *n.* **1.** A blue pigment made from powdered lapis lazuli. **2.** Any similar pigment made synthetically by heating clay, sodium carbonate, and sulfur together. **3.** Vivid or strong blue to purplish blue.
—*adj.* **1.** Having a deep to purplish blue color. **2.** Of or from some place beyond the sea. [Medieval Latin *ultrāmarīnus,* "(coming from) beyond the sea" (because lapis lazuli was imported from Asia by sea) : Latin *ultrā-,* beyond + *mare,* sea.]

ul·tra·mi·crom·e·ter (ŭl′trə-mī-krŏm′ə-tər) *n.* An extremely accurate micrometer.

ul·tra·mi·cro·scope (ŭl′trə-mī′krə-skōp′) *n.* A microscope with high-intensity illumination used to study very minute objects by means of their diffraction system, which appears as a bright spot against a black background. Also called "dark-field microscope." —**ul·tra·mi·cros·co·py** (ŭl′trə-mī-krŏs′kə-pē) *n.*

ul·tra·mi·cro·scop·ic (ŭl′trə-mī′krə-skŏp′ĭk) *adj.* **1.** Too small to be seen with an ordinary microscope. **2.** Of or relating to an ultramicroscope.

ul·tra·mod·ern (ŭl′trə-mŏd′ərn) *adj.* Extremely modern; absolutely up-to-date. —**ul·tra·mod·ern·ism** *n.* —**ul·tra·mod·ern·ist** *n.* —**ul·tra·mod·ern·is·tic** (ŭl′trə-mŏd′ər-nĭs′tĭk) *adj.*

ul·tra·mon·tane (ŭl′trə-mŏn′tān′, -mŏn-tān′) *adj.* **1.** Of or designating peoples or regions lying on the other side of the mountains; especially, south of the Alps. **2.** Strongly supporting the authority of the papal court over national or diocesan authority in the Roman Catholic Church.
—*n.* **1.** A person living beyond the mountains; especially, one from south of the Alps. **2. Ultramontane.** A Roman Catholic who advocates support of papal policy in ecclesiastical and political matters. [Medieval Latin *ultrāmontānus,* beyond the mountain (applied by the French to the papal court at Rome) : Latin *ultrā-,* beyond + *mōns* (stem *mont-*), mountain.]

Ul·tra·mon·ta·nism (ŭl′trə-mŏn′tə-nĭz′əm) *n.* The policy that absolute authority in the Roman Catholic Church should be vested in the pope. Compare **Gallicanism.** —**Ul·tra·mon·ta·nist** *n.*

ul·tra·mun·dane (ŭl′trə-mŭn′dān′, -mŭn-dān′) *adj.* Extending or being beyond the world or the limits of the universe. [Latin *ultrāmundānus* : *ultrā-,* beyond + *mundus,* the world.]

ul·tra·na·tion·al·ism (ŭl′trə-nāsh′ən-əl-ĭz′əm) *n.* Extreme nationalism, especially when opposed to international cooperation. —**ul·tra·na·tion·al** *adj.* —**ul·tra·na·tion·al·ist** *n.* & *adj.* —**ul·tra·na·tion·al·is·tic** (ŭl′trə-nāsh′ən-ə-lĭs′tĭk) *adj.*

ul·tra·short (ŭl′trə-shôrt′) *adj.* Designating or pertaining to radio waves with a wavelength less than 10 meters.

ul·tra·son·ic (ŭl′trə-sŏn′ĭk) *adj.* Pertaining to or designating acoustic frequencies above the range audible to the human ear, or above approximately 20 kilohertz.

ul·tra·son·ics (ŭl′trə-sŏn′ĭks) *n. Used with a singular verb.* **1.** The acoustics of ultrasonic sound. **2.** A technology using ultrasonic sound, as for medical therapy.

ul·tra·sound (ŭl′trə-sound′) *n.* Ultrasonic sound.

ul·tra·struc·ture (ŭl′trə-strŭk′chər) *n.* The detailed structure of a cell, tissue, or organ that can be seen by electron microscopy but

not by light microscopy. Also called "fine structure." —**ul·tra·struc·tur·al** (ŭl′trə-strŭk′chər-əl) *adj.*

ul·tra·vi·o·let (ŭl′trə-vī′ə-lĭt) *adj. Abbr.* **UV, U.V. 1.** Of, belonging to, or designating the range of radiation wavelengths from about 4,000 angstroms, just beyond the violet in the visible spectrum, to about 40 angstroms, on the border of the x-ray region. **2.** Generating, using, or sensitive to such radiation.
—*n.* Ultraviolet radiation or the ultraviolet region of the electromagnetic spectrum.

ultraviolet lamp *n.* A mercury-vapor lamp that produces ultraviolet light.

ul·tra vi·res (ŭl′trə vī′rēz′, ōōl′trə vĕr′āz′) *adv. Law.* Beyond one's legal authority or rights. [Latin.] —**ul·tra vi·res** *adj.*

ul·tra·vi·rus (ŭl′trə-vī′rəs) *n.* A virus small enough to pass through the finest filter.

ul·u·late (ŭl′yə-lāt′, yōōl′-) *intr.v.* **-lated, -lating, -lates.** To howl, hoot, wail, or lament loudly. [Latin *ululāre,* to howl (imitative).] —**ul·u·la·tion** (ŭl′yə-lā′shən, yōōl′-) *n.*

Ulysses. The Latin name for **Odysseus.**

um (ŭm, əm) *interj.* Used when hesitating in speech, or to express doubt or uncertainty.

u·man·gite (yōō-măng′gīt′) *n.* A rare ore of selenium, Cu₃Se₂. [German *Umangit,* after Sierra de *Umango,* province in northwestern Argentina + -ITE.]

U·may·yad (ōō-mī′yăd′). Also **Om·mi·ad** (ə-mī′ăd′). A dynasty of rulers of the Muslim Empire (A.D. 661–750) and Muslim Spain (A.D. 756–1031). [After *Ummayah,* its founder.]

um·bel (ŭm′bəl) *n. Botany.* A flat-topped or rounded flower cluster in which the individual flower stalks arise from about the same point, as in the carrot and related plants. [New Latin *umbella,* from Latin, an umbrella, diminutive of *umbra,* shadow.]

um·bel·late (ŭm′bə-lāt′, ŭm′bĕl′ĭt) *adj.* Having, forming, or of the nature of an umbel.

um·bel·lif·er (ŭm-bĕl′ə-fər) *n.* Any umbelliferous plant.

um·bel·lif·er·ous (ŭm′bə-lĭf′ər-əs) *adj. Botany.* **1.** Bearing umbels. **2.** Belonging to the plant family Umbelliferae. [New Latin *umbellifer* : *umbella,* UMBEL + -FEROUS.]

um·bel·lule (ŭm′bəl-yōōl′, ŭm-bĕl′yōōl′) *n.* Also **um·bel·let** (ŭm′bə-lĭt). *Botany.* Any of the smaller secondary umbels forming a compound umbel. [New Latin *umbellula,* diminutive of *umbella,* UMBEL.]

um·ber (ŭm′bər) *n.* **1.** A natural brown earth composed of ferric oxide, silica, alumina, lime, and manganese oxides and used as pigment. **2.** Any of the shades of brown produced by umber in its various states.
—*tr.v.* **umbered, -bering, -bers.** To coat or color with or as if with umber. [Old French *umbre,* short for *terre d'Umbre,* "earth of Umbria."] —**um·ber** *adj.*

Um·ber·to I (ŭm-bĕr′tō) (1844–1900). King of Italy. He succeeded his father, Victor Emmanuel II, in 1878 and led Italy into the Triple Alliance with Austria and Germany (1882). He was assassinated by an anarchist at Monza.

Umberto II (1904–83). Last King of Italy. He became king (May 1946) on the abdication of his father, Victor Emmanuel III, but was forced to abdicate a month later when a national referendum voted for a republic.

um·bil·i·cal (ŭm-bĭl′ĭ-kəl) *adj.* **1.** Of, pertaining to, or resembling an umbilicus. **2.** Pertaining to or located near the central area of the abdomen.
—*n. Aerospace.* See **umbilical cord** (sense 2b).

umbilical cord *n.* **1.** *Anatomy.* The flexible, cordlike structure connecting the fetus at the navel with the placenta and containing two umbilical arteries and one vein that nourish the fetus and remove its wastes. **2.** *Aerospace.* **a.** Any of various external electrical lines or fluid tubes supplying a rocket before launch. **b.** The line that supplies an astronaut with oxygen and in some cases with communications while he is outside the spacecraft. In this sense, also called "umbilical."

um·bil·i·cate (ŭm-bĭl′ĭ-kĭt, -kāt′) *adj.* Also **um·bil·i·cat·ed** (-kā′tĭd). **1.** Having a central mark or depression resembling a navel. **2.** Having an umbilicus. —**um·bil·i·ca·tion** (ŭm-bĭl′ĭ-kā′shən) *n.*

um·bil·i·cus (ŭm-bĭl′ĭ-kəs, ŭm′bə-lī′kəs) *n., pl.* **-ci** (-sī′). **1.** The navel. **2.** *Biology.* Any similar small opening or depression, such as the hollow at the base of the shell of some gastropod mollusks or an opening in the shaft of a feather. [Latin *umbilicus;* akin to Greek *omphalos,* navel, and UMBO.]

um·bles (ŭm′bəlz) *pl.n. Archaic.* Entrails, **numbles** (see).

um·bo (ŭm′bō) *n., pl.* **umbones** (ŭm-bō′nēz). **1.** A boss or knob at the center of a shield. **2.** *Biology.* A similar knoblike protuberance, such as the central hump on a mushroom cap. **3.** *Anatomy.* A small projection at the center of the outer surface of the tympanic membrane of the ear. [Latin *umbō* (stem *umbōn-*); akin to NAVEL.]

um·bo·nate (ŭm′bə-nāt′, -nĭt) *adj.* Also **um·bo·nal** (ŭm′bə-nəl), **um·bon·ic** (ŭm-bŏn′ĭk). Having or resembling a knob or knoblike protuberance. [Latin *umbō* (stem *umbōn-*), knob + -ATE.]

um·bra (ŭm′brə) *n., pl.* **-bras** or **-brae** (-brē). **1.** A dark area; specifically, the blackest part of a shadow from which all light is cut off. **2.** *Astronomy.* **a.** The shadow region over an area of the earth where a solar eclipse is total. **b.** The darkest region of a sunspot. [Latin *umbra,* shadow.]

um·brage (ŭm′brĭj) *n.* **1.** Offense; resentment: *took umbrage at their rudeness.* **2.** *Archaic.* **a.** Something that affords shade. **b.** Shadow or shade. **3.** *Obsolete.* A shadowy or indistinct indication; a hint.

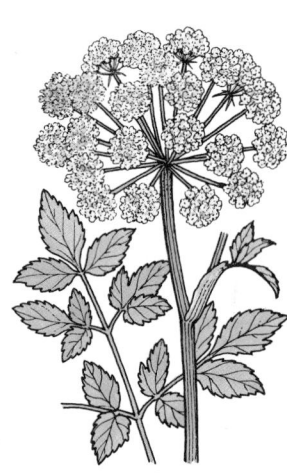

umbel *The flower heads of wild angelica,* Angelica sylvestris, *are arranged on spokes that spread from the central stem. The parsley family, of which angelica is a member, is known to botanists as the* Umbelliferae, *or "umbel bearers," because of this umbrellalike arrangement.*

[Middle English, shade, from Old French, from Vulgar Latin *umbrāticum* (unattested), neuter of Latin *umbrāticus*, of a shadow, from *umbra*, shadow, UMBRA.]

um·bra·geous (ŭm-brā'jəs) *adj.* **1.** Affording or forming shade; shady or shading. **2.** Inclined to take umbrage; touchy. —**um·bra·geous·ly** *adv.* —**um·bra·geous·ness** *n.*

um·brel·la (ŭm-brĕl'ə) *n.* **1.** A device for protection from the weather consisting of a collapsible canopy mounted on a central rod. **2.** Anything that covers or protects. **3.** *Military.* An air cover. **4.** An all-encompassing category, organization, or authority by means of which many different things or groups are linked. **5.** *Zoology.* The contractile gelatinous, rounded mass constituting the major part of the body of most jellyfishes. ~*adj.* Covering or encompassing a wide variety of things: *an umbrella term.* [Italian *ombrella,* diminutive of *ombra,* shade, from Latin *umbra.*]

umbrella bird *n.* Any of several tropical American birds of the genus *Cephalopterus;* especially, *C. ornatus,* having a retractile black crest and a long, feathered wattle.

umbrella tree *n.* **1.** Any of several trees of the genus *Magnolia,* of the southeastern United States; especially, *M. tripetala,* having large leaves clustered in an umbrellalike form at the ends of the branches. **2.** Any of several other trees having leaves growing in an umbrella-like cluster.

Um·bri·a (ŭm'brē-ə). Largely mountainous region of central Italy, comprising the provinces of Perugia and Terni. The principal town is Perugia. It gets its name from the tribe called the Umbri, who settled in the region in the 7th century B.C.

Um·bri·an (ŭm'brē-ən) *adj.* **1.** Of or pertaining to Umbria or its people, culture, dialect, or ancient language. **2.** Designating a Renaissance school of painting which included Perugino and Raphael. ~*n.* **1.** An inhabitant or native of ancient or modern Umbria. **2.** The extinct Italic language of ancient Umbria.

u·mi·ak, oo·mi·ak (ōō'mē-ăk') *n.* A large open Eskimo boat made of skins stretched on a wooden frame, usually propelled by paddles. Compare **kayak.** [Eskimo.]

um·laut (ōōm'lout') *n. Linguistics.* **1.** A change in a vowel sound caused by partial assimilation to a vowel or semivowel, originally occurring in the following syllable, now usually lost. An example is English *bed,* produced by umlaut from the earlier Germanic form in Gothic *badi.* Also called "vowel mutation." Compare **ablaut. 2.** A vowel sound changed in this manner, such as the German *ä, ö,* or *ü.* **3.** The diacritical mark (¨) placed over a vowel to indicate an umlaut, especially in German. See **dieresis.** ~*tr.v.* **umlauted, -lauting, -lauts. 1.** To modify (a vowel sound) by umlaut. **2.** To write or print (a vowel) with an umlaut. [German *Umlaut* : *um-,* prefix indicating alteration, "around," from Middle High German *um(b)-,* from *umbe,* from Old High German *umbi* + *Laut,* sound, from Middle High German *lūt,* from Old High German *hlūt.*]

um·pir·age (ŭm'pī'rĭj, -pə-rĭj) *n.* **1.** The position, function, or authority of an umpire. **2.** A ruling or decision of an umpire.

um·pire (ŭm'pīr') *n.* **1.** A person appointed to make rulings and control the progress of the game in various sports, especially baseball. Compare **referee. 2.** A person selected or empowered to settle a dispute between other persons or groups. **3.** A judge; an arbiter. —See Synonyms at **judge.** ~*v.* **umpired, -piring, -pires.** —*tr.* To act as umpire in or of; referee; arbitrate. —*intr.* To be or act as an umpire. [Middle English *(an) oumpere,* originally *(a) noumpere,* (an) umpire, from Old French *nomper, nonper,* "non-peer" (that is, not a contestant but a third person called in to arbitrate) : *non-,* not + *per,* match, equal, PEER.] —**um·pire·ship** (ŭm'pīr-shĭp') *n.*

ump·teen (ŭmp'tēn', ŭm'-) *adj. Informal.* Large but indefinite in number: *umpteen reasons; umpteen guests.* [Slang *umpty,* dash in Morse code + *-teen,* as in *thirteen.*] —**ump·teen** *pron.* —**ump·teenth** *adj.*

UMW United Mine Workers.

un-¹ *prefix.* Indicates not or contrary to; for example, **unhappy. Note:** Many compounds other than those entered here may be formed with *un-.* In forming compounds, *un-* is normally joined with the following element without space or a hyphen: *unnamed.* However, if the second element begins with a capital letter, it is separated with a hyphen: *un-American.* [Middle English *un-,* Old English *un-.*]

un-² *prefix.* Indicates: **1.** Reversal of an action; for example, **unlock, unmake. 2.** Deprivation; for example, **unman, unsex, unfrock. 3.** Release or removal from; for example, **unearth, unyoke, unhorse. 4.** Intensified action; for example, **unloose.** [Middle English *un-,* Old English *un-,* variant of *ond-, and-,* against.]

Usage: Un-, used in combination to indicate negation, is distinguished from *in-* (and its assimilated forms *il-, im-, ir-*) in the following general sense: *un-* is frequently confined to stressing mere lack and is consequently rather neutral and literal; *in-* and its variants more often give the original term a more strongly negative sense or one contrary to the meaning of the original. Thus *unhuman* and *unartistic* primarily apply to what is outside the realm of the human and artistic. *Inhuman* and *inartistic* imply the contrary of what is human and artistic, such as cruelty and lack of taste or talent. This applies, however, only where the *un-* and *in-* forms of words are both in current usage. See Usage note at **non-.**

'un, un (ən) *pron. Informal & Regional.* One; a person, animal, or thing of a specified kind: *She's a good 'un.* [Weak form of **one.**]

UN, U.N. United Nations.

UNA United Nations Association.

un·a·bashed (ŭn'ə-băsht') *adj.* Not disconcerted or embarrassed; poised. —**un·a·bash·ed·ly** (ŭn'ə-băsh'ĭd-lē) *adv.*

un·a·bat·ed (ŭn'ə-bā'tĭd) *adj.* With no loss of force or intensity: *They fought with unabated violence.* —**un·a·bat·ed·ly** *adv.*

un·a·ble (ŭn-ā'bəl) *adj.* **1.** Lacking the necessary power, authority, or means; not able. **2.** Lacking mental or physical capability or efficiency: *unable to walk.*

un·a·bridged (ŭn'ə-brĭjd') *adj.* Having the original content; not condensed or shortened. Said of books, documents, or the like.

un·ac·cent·ed (ŭn-ăk'sĕn-tĭd) *adj.* **1.** Having no diacritical mark. Said of a word, syllable, or letter. **2.** Having weak stress or no stress, or lacking some other specific phonological feature. Said of a speech segment or syllable.

un·ac·com·pa·nied (ŭn'ə-kŭm'pə-nēd) *adj.* **1.** Not accompanied: *unaccompanied luggage.* **2.** *Music.* Solo; without accompaniment.

un·ac·com·plished (ŭn'ə-kŏm'plĭsht) *adj.* **1.** Not completed or done; unfinished. **2.** Lacking accomplishments.

un·ac·count·a·ble (ŭn'ə-koun'tə-bəl) *adj.* **1.** Not able to be accounted for; inexplicable. **2.** Not liable to be held to account; not accountable. —**un·ac·count·a·bil·i·ty** (ŭn'ə-koun'tə-bĭl'ə-tē), **un·ac·count·a·ble·ness** *n.* —**un·ac·count·a·bly** *adv.*

un·ac·count·ed-for (ŭn'ə-koun'tĭd-fôr') *adj.* **1.** Not explained, understood, or taken into account. **2.** Missing or absent without explanation, as from a roll call or after a military operation.

un·ac·cus·tomed (ŭn'ə-kŭs'təmd) *adj.* **1.** Not used to; not accustomed. Used with *to.* **2.** Unfamiliar: *unaccustomed surroundings.*

u·na cor·da (ōō'nə kôr'də) *adv. Music.* With the soft pedal depressed. Used as a direction to a pianist. [Italian, "one string" (the action of the pedal causes one piano string to be struck instead of three.)]

un·a·dorned (ŭn'ə-dôrnd') *adj.* Without embellishment or artificiality; simple; natural.

un·a·dul·ter·at·ed (ŭn'ə-dŭl'tə-rā'tĭd) *adj.* **1.** Not mingled or diluted with extraneous matter; pure. **2.** Out-and-out; utter.

un·ad·vised (ŭn'əd-vīzd') *adj.* **1.** Having received no advice; not informed. **2.** Ill-advised; rash; imprudent. —**un·ad·vis·ed·ly** (ŭn'-əd-vī'zĭd-lē) *adv.* —**un·ad·vis·ed·ness** *n.*

un·af·fect·ed¹ (ŭn'ə-fĕk'tĭd) *adj.* Not changed, modified, or affected.

unaffected² *adj.* Without affectation; genuine. —See Synonyms at **naive, sincere.** —**un·af·fect·ed·ly** *adv.* —**un·af·fect·ed·ness** *n.*

un·al·loyed (ŭn'ə-loid') *adj.* **1.** Not in mixture with other metals; pure. **2.** Complete; unqualified: *an unalloyed success.*

un·a·neled (ŭn'ə-nēld') *adj. Archaic.* Not having received extreme unction.

u·nan·i·mous (yōō-năn'ə-məs) *adj.* **1.** Sharing the same opinions or views; in complete accord. **2.** Based on or characterized by the assent or agreement of all. [Latin *ūnanimus,* "of one mind" : *ūnus,* one + *animus,* soul, mind.] —**u·na·nim·i·ty** (yōō'nə-nĭm'ə-tē), **u·nan·i·mous·ness** *n.* —**u·nan·i·mous·ly** *adv.*

un·an·swer·a·ble (ŭn-ăn'sər-ə-bəl, ŭn-ăn'-) *adj.* **1.** Impossible to answer. Said of a question. **2.** Irrefutable; incontrovertible.

un·ap·peal·a·ble (ŭn'ə-pē'lə-bəl) *adj. Law.* Not subject to appeal.

un·ap·proach·a·ble (ŭn'ə-prō'chə-bəl) *adj.* **1.** Not friendly; aloof; distant. **2.** Not accessible; inapproachable. —**un·ap·proach·a·bil·i·ty** (ŭn'ə-prō'chə-bĭl'ə-tē), **un·ap·proach·a·ble·ness** *n.* —**un·ap·proach·a·bly** *adv.*

un·apt (ŭn-ăpt') *adj.* **1.** Not suitable or appropriate; inapt. Often used with *for.* **2.** Not likely; not liable. Used with *to.* **3.** Slow-witted; stupid. —**un·apt·ly** *adv.* —**un·apt·ness** *n.*

un·arm (ŭn-ärm') *tr.v.* **-armed, -arming, -arms.** *Archaic.* To divest of armor or arms; especially, to assist in taking off armor.

un·armed (ŭn-ärmd') *adj.* **1.** Lacking weapons or armor; defenseless. **2.** *Biology.* Having no thorns or spines. **3.** Not fitted with a detonator. Said of a bomb, missile, or other explosive device.

un·a·shamed (ŭn'ə-shāmd') *adj.* **1.** Open and without restraint or embarrassment: *unashamed luxury.* **2.** Not feeling or revealing any remorse, shame, or need for apology. —**un·a·sham·ed·ly** (ŭn'-ə-shā'mĭd-lē) *adv.* —**un·a·sham·ed·ness** *n.*

un·asked (ŭn-ăskt', -äskt') *adj.* **1.** Uninvited. **2.** Not requested or demanded.

un·as·sail·a·ble (ŭn'ə-sā'lə-bəl) *adj.* **1.** Not capable of being disputed or disproven; undeniable; unquestionable. **2.** Not capable of being attacked or seized successfully; impregnable. —**un·as·sail·a·bil·i·ty** (ŭn'ə-sā'lə-bĭl'ə-tē), **un·as·sail·a·ble·ness** *n.* —**un·as·sail·a·bly** *adv.*

un·as·sum·ing (ŭn'ə-sōō'mĭng) *adj.* Not pretentious, boastful, or ostentatious; modest. —**un·as·sum·ing·ly** *adv.* —**un·as·sum·ing·ness** *n.*

un·at·tached (ŭn'ə-tăcht') *adj.* **1.** Not attached or joined, especially to surrounding tissue. **2. a.** Not committed to or dependent upon a person, group, or organization. **b.** Not engaged, married, or involved in a serious sexual or romantic relationship. **3.** *Law.* Not possessed or seized as security.

un·at·tend·ed (ŭn'ə-tĕn'dĭd) *adj.* **1.** Not being attended to, looked after, or watched. **2.** Without attendants; not in company; alone. **3.** Not being paid attention to or listened to.

un·at·test·ed (ŭn'ə-tĕs'tĭd) *adj.* Not attested. Used in linguistic descriptions, as in the etymologies of this dictionary, to designate a form whose existence is not established by documentary evidence but is reliably inferred from comparative evidence.

u·nau (yōō′nou, ōō′-, -nô) *n.* A two-toed **sloth** *(see).*

un·a·vail·ing (ŭn′ə-vā′lĭng) *adj.* Having no effect; achieving nothing; futile. —**un·a·vail·ing·ly** *adv.*

u·na vo·ce (yōō′nə vō′sē) *adv. Latin.* With one voice; unanimously.

un·a·void·a·ble (ŭn′ə-voi′də-bəl) *adj.* **1.** Not able to be avoided; inevitable. **2.** *Law.* Not able to be voided or nullified. —**un·a·void·a·bil·i·ty, un·a·void·a·ble·ness** *n.* —**un·a·void·a·bly** *adv.*

un·a·ware (ŭn′ə-wâr′) *adj.* Not aware or cognizant.
~*adv.* Unawares.

un·a·wares (ŭn′ə-wârz′) *adv.* **1.** By surprise; unexpectedly: *"Sorrow comes to all, and to the young it comes with bittered agony because it takes them unawares"* (Abraham Lincoln). **2.** Without knowledge or plan: *We came upon it unawares.* [Middle English *unwares,* variant of *unware* (adverb), Old English *unwær :* UN- + AWARE + -S (adverbial suffix).]

un·backed (ŭn-băkt′) *adj.* **1.** Lacking backing or support. **2.** Not having a back, as a bench. **3.** Never ridden. Said of a horse.

un·bal·ance (ŭn-băl′əns) *tr.v.* **-anced, -ancing, -ances. 1.** To upset the balance, stability, or equilibrium of. **2.** To derange.
~*n.* The condition of being unbalanced; lack of balance.

un·bal·anced (ŭn-băl′ənst) *adj.* **1.** Not balanced. **2. a.** Mentally deranged. **b.** Not of sound judgment; erratic; irrational. **3.** Not satisfactorily adjusted, so that debit and credit do not correspond. Said of an account.

un·bar (ŭn-bär′) *tr.v.* **-barred, -barring, -bars.** To remove the bar or bars from; unlock; open.

un·bat·ed (ŭn-bā′tĭd) *adj.* **1.** Unabated. **2.** *Archaic.* Not blunted by a guard on the tip. Said of a fencing foil, sword, or the like.

un·bear·a·ble (ŭn-bâr′ə-bəl) *adj.* Not able to be endured; intolerable. —**un·bear·a·bly** *adv.*

un·beat·a·ble (ŭn-bē′tə-bəl) *adj.* **1.** Unable to be surpassed or defeated. **2.** First-rate; excellent. —**un·beat·a·bly** *adv.*

un·beat·en (ŭn-bēt′n) *adj.* **1. a.** Undefeated. **b.** Not surpassed. **2.** Untrodden.

un·be·com·ing (ŭn′bĭ-kŭm′ĭng) *adj.* **1.** Not appropriate, attractive, or flattering: *an unbecoming dress.* **2.** Not seemly; indecorous; improper: *an unbecoming remark.* —See Usage note at **improper.** —**un·be·com·ing·ly** *adv.* —**un·be·com·ing·ness** *n.*

un·be·got·ten (ŭn′bĭ-gŏt′n) *adj.* **1.** Not yet begotten; as yet unborn. **2.** Self-existent; eternal.

un·be·known (ŭn′bĭ-nōn′) *adv.* Also **un·be·knownst** (-nōnst′). Without the knowledge of. Usually used with *to.*
~*adj.* Also **un·be·knownst.** Not known. Usually used with *to.* [UN- + obsolete *beknown,* known, Middle English *beknowen,* past participle of *beknowen,* to get to know, Old English *becnāwan :* BE- + *cnāwan,* KNOW.]

un·be·lief (ŭn′bĭ-lēf′) *n.* Lack of belief or faith, especially in religious matters.

un·be·liev·a·ble (ŭn′bĭ-lē′və-bəl) *adj.* Incapable of being believed; incredible. —**un·be·liev·a·bil·i·ty, un·be·liev·a·ble·ness** *n.* —**un·be·liev·a·bly** *adv.*

un·be·liev·er (ŭn′bĭ-lē′vər) *n.* One who lacks belief or faith, especially in a particular religion.

un·be·liev·ing (ŭn′bĭ-lē′vĭng) *adj.* Lacking belief; skeptical, especially in religious matters. —**un·be·liev·ing·ly** *adv.*

un·bend (ŭn-bĕnd′) *v.* **-bent** (-bĕnt′), **-bending, -bends.** —*tr.* **1.** To relax; release from mental tension, strain, or formality. **2.** To release (a bow, for example) from flexure or tension. **3.** *Nautical.* To untie or loosen (a rope or sail). **4.** To straighten (something crooked or bent). —*intr.* **1.** To become less tense; relax. **2.** To become less strict or less formal. **3.** To become straight.

un·bend·ing (ŭn-bĕn′dĭng) *adj.* **1.** Unyielding or uncompromising. **2.** Stern or severe. —**un·bend·ing·ly** *adv.* —**un·bend·ing·ness** *n.*

un·bi·ased (ŭn-bī′əst) *adj.* Without bias or prejudice; impartial. —See Synonyms at **fair.** —**un·bi·ased·ly** *adv.* —**un·bi·ased·ness** *n.*

un·bid·den (ŭn-bĭd′n) *adj.* **1.** Not commanded; voluntary. **2.** Not invited; unasked: *unbidden company.*

un·bind (ŭn-bīnd′) *tr.v.* **-bound** (-bound′), **-binding, -binds. 1.** To untie or unfasten (wrappings or bindings, for example). **2.** To release from restraints or bonds; free.

un·blessed (ŭn-blĕst′) *adj.* **1.** Deprived of a blessing. **2.** Unholy; evil. —**un·bless·ed·ness** (ŭn-blĕs′ĭd-nĭs) *n.*

un·blink·ing (ŭn-blĭng′kĭng) *adj.* **1.** Without blinking. **2.** Without visible emotion. **3.** Fearless in facing reality: *her unblinking self-criticism.* —**un·blink·ing·ly** *adv.*

un·blown (ŭn-blōn′) *adj.* Unopened. Said of a flower.

un·blush·ing (ŭn-blŭsh′ĭng) *adj.* **1.** Without shame or embarrassment. **2.** Not blushing. —See Synonyms at **shameless.** —**un·blush·ing·ly** *adv.*

un·bolt (ŭn-bōlt′) *tr.v.* **-bolted, -bolting, -bolts.** To release the bolts of (a door or gate); unlock.

un·bolt·ed (ŭn-bōl′tĭd) *adj.* Not sifted: *unbolted flour.*

un·born (ŭn-bôrn′) *adj.* Not yet in existence; not yet born.

un·bos·om (ŭn-bŏŏz′əm -bōō′zəm) *v.* **-omed, -oming, -oms.** —*tr.* **1.** To confide (one's thoughts or feelings). **2.** To relieve (oneself) of troublesome thoughts or feelings by revealing them. —*intr.* To reveal one's thoughts or feelings.

un·bound (ŭn-bound′). Past tense and past participle of **unbind.**
~*adj.* **1.** Not bound. Said of a book. **2.** Free from bonds or shackles; unconfined. **3.** *Linguistics.* Designating a morpheme that is or can be a full and independent word when standing alone.

un·bound·ed (ŭn-boun′dĭd) *adj.* **1.** Having no boundaries or limits.

2. Not kept within bounds; unrestrained: *unbounded enthusiasm.* —**un·bound·ed·ly** *adv.* —**un·bound·ed·ness** *n.*

un·bowed (ŭn-boud′) *adj.* **1.** Not bowed; not bent. **2.** Not subdued; unyielding: *The warriors returned bloody but unbowed.*

un·brace (ŭn-brās′) *tr.v.* **-braced, -bracing, -braces. 1.** To set free by removing bands or braces. **2.** To release from tension; relax. **3.** To weaken; make slack.

un·bred (ŭn-brĕd′) *adj.* **1.** Not taught or instructed; untaught. **2.** *Archaic.* Ill-bred; impolite.

un·bri·dle (ŭn-brī′dəl) *tr.v.* **-dled, -dling, -dles. 1.** To take the bridle off (a horse). **2.** To remove restraints from; free.

un·bri·dled (ŭn-brī′dəld) *adj.* **1.** Not wearing or fitted with a bridle. **2.** Unrestrained; uncontrolled. —**un·bri·dled·ly** *adv.*

un·bro·ken (ŭn-brō′kən) *adj.* **1.** Not broken or tampered with; intact. **2.** Not violated or breached. **3.** Uninterrupted; continuous; even. **4.** Not tamed; not trained to accept a harness. Said of a horse. **5.** Not disordered or disturbed. **6.** Not surpassed. Said of a record, as in sports. —**un·bro·ken·ly** *adv.* —**un·bro·ken·ness** *n.*

un·buck·le (ŭn-bŭk′əl) *tr.v.* **-led, -ling, -les. 1.** To loosen or undo the buckle or buckles of. **2.** To remove by unbuckling.

un·bur·den (ŭn-bûrd′n) *tr.v.* **-dened, -dening, -dens.** To free from or relieve of a burden or trouble: *unburden one's mind.*

un·but·ton (ŭn-bŭt′n) *v.* **-toned, -toning, -tons.** —*tr.* **1.** To unfasten the button or buttons of. **2.** To free or remove (a button) from a buttonhole. **3.** To make informal or relaxed. —*intr.* **1.** To undo a button or buttons. **2.** To relax.

un·called-for (ŭn-kôld′fôr′) *adj.* **1.** Unwarranted; impertinent; unnecessary. **2.** Not required or requested.

un·can·ny (ŭn-kăn′ē) *adj.* **-nier, -niest. 1.** So beyond the normal or expected as to suggest the supernatural: *a fortune-teller's uncanny accuracy.* **2.** Exciting wonder and fear; strange: *an uncanny laugh.* —See Synonyms at **weird.** —**un·can·ni·ly** *adv.* —**un·can·ni·ness** *n.*

un·cap (ŭn-kăp′) *v.* **-capped, -capping, -caps.** —*tr.* To remove the cap or covering of (a container). —*intr.* To remove one's head covering as a sign of deference.

un·cared-for (ŭn-kârd′fôr′) *adj.* Not looked after; neglected.

un·car·ing (ŭn-kâr′ĭng) *adj.* Devoid of concern or sympathy.

Un·cas (ŭng′kəs) (c. 1588–1683). U.S. Indian leader. As chief of the Mohegans, the western division of the Pequot tribe, he led a rebellion against the tribe's leadership. After successfully deposing the sachem, he assumed leadership, reunited the tribe, and in a series of battles with other New England tribes, emerged as the leader of the most powerful Indians in the region.

un·ceas·ing (ŭn-sē′sĭng) *adj.* Not ceasing or letting up; continuous. —**un·ceas·ing·ly** *adv.* —**un·ceas·ing·ness** *n.*

un·cer·e·mo·ni·ous (ŭn-sĕr′ə-mō′nē-əs) *adj.* **1.** Without the due formalities; abrupt; rude. **2.** Not ceremonious; informal. —**un·cer·e·mo·ni·ous·ly** *adv.* —**un·cer·e·mo·ni·ous·ness** *n.*

un·cer·tain (ŭn-sûrt′n) *adj.* **1.** Not known or established; questionable; doubtful: *an uncertain outcome.* **2.** Not determined; vague; undecided: *uncertain plans.* **3.** Not having sure knowledge. **4.** Subject to change; variable: *uncertain weather.* **5.** Unsteady; fitful: *uncertain light.* —**un·cer·tain·ly** *adv.*

un·cer·tain·ty (ŭn-sûrt′n-tē) *n., pl.* **-ties.** Also **un·cer·tain·ness** (-nĭs) (for sense 1). **1.** The condition of being in doubt; lack of certainty. **2.** Something that is uncertain.
Synonyms: doubt, dubiety, mistrust, skepticism.

uncertainty principle *n.* The principle in quantum mechanics that the product of the uncertainties in the values of certain related variables, as of the position and momentum of a particle, is greater than or equal to Planck's constant divided by 4π. Also called "Heisenberg uncertainty principle."

un·chain (ŭn-chān′) *tr.v.* **-chained, -chaining, -chains.** To release from or as if from a chain or bond; set free.

un·chan·cy (ŭn-chăn′sē) *adj. Scottish.* **1.** Unlucky; ill-fated. **2.** Threatening; dangerous. [UN- (not) + CHANCY (in obsolete sense, "lucky").]

un·charged (ŭn-chärjd′) *adj.* **1.** Not loaded. Said of a weapon. **2.** *Law.* **a.** Not subject to a charge. Said of land. **b.** Not formally accused. **3.** Lacking electric charge.

un·char·i·ta·ble (ŭn-chăr′ə-tə-bəl) *adj.* Not charitable or generous; unkind; judging harshly. —**un·char·i·ta·ble·ness** *n.* —**un·char·i·ta·bly** *adv.*

un·chart·ed (ŭn-chär′tĭd) *adj.* Not charted or recorded on or as if on a map or plan; unexplored; unknown.

un·chaste (ŭn-chāst′) *adj.* Not chaste or modest. —**un·chaste·ly** *adv.* —**un·chaste·ness, un·chas·ti·ty** (ŭn-chăs′tə-tē) *n.*

un·chris·tian (ŭn-krĭs′chən) *adj.* **1.** Not in accordance with the spirit or principles of Christianity. **2.** Not Christian; heathen. **3.** Uncivilized; barbarous.

un·church (ŭn-chûrch′) *tr.v.* **-churched, -churching, -churches. 1.** To expel from a church or from church membership; excommunicate. **2.** To deprive (a congregation, sect, or building) of the status of a church.

un·cial (ŭn′shəl, -shē-əl, -sē-əl) *adj. Sometimes* **Uncial.** Of, pertaining to, or designating a style of writing characterized by somewhat rounded shapes and found especially in Greek and Latin manuscripts of the 4th to the 9th century A.D. It provided the model from which most of the capital letters in the modern Roman alphabet are derived.
~*n. Sometimes* **Uncial. 1.** The uncial style or hand. **2.** An uncial letter or manuscript. [Late Latin *unciāles (litterae),* "letters of an inch long" (applied loosely by St. Jerome to uncial letters), plural of

Latin *unciālis*, of an inch, from *uncia*, a twelfth part, ounce, inch, from *ūnus*, one.]

un·ci·form (ŭn′sə-fôrm′) *adj.* Hook-shaped. [New Latin *unciformis* : Latin *uncus*, hook + -FORM.]

unciform bone *n.* The hamate bone *(see)*.

un·ci·nate (ŭn′sə-nāt′, -nĭt) *adj.* 1. Hooked at the tip. 2. Of or possessing uncini. [Latin *uncīnātus*, from *uncīnus*, hook, UNCINUS.]

un·ci·nus (ŭn-sī′nəs) *n., pl.* **-ni** (-nī′). A small hooklike structure, such as any of the setae of certain annelid worms. [New Latin, from Latin, hook, barb, from *uncus*, hook.]

un·cir·cum·cised (ŭn-sûr′kəm-sīzd′) *adj.* 1. Not circumcised. 2. Not Jewish; Gentile. 3. Heathen. 4. Spiritually impure. —**un·cir·cum·ci·sion** (ŭn-sûr′kəm-sĭzh′ən) *n.*

un·civ·il (ŭn-sĭv′əl) *adj.* 1. Impolite; discourteous; rude. 2. *Archaic.* Uncivilized; barbarous. —**un·civ·il·ly** *adv.*

un·civ·i·lized (ŭn-sĭv′ə-līzd′) *adj.* 1. Not civilized; barbarous. 2. Lacking education, manners, culture, or sophistication.

un·clad (ŭn-klăd′) *adj.* Not wearing clothes; naked.

un·clasp (ŭn-klăsp′, -kläsp′) *v.* **-clasped, -clasping, -clasps.** —*tr.* 1. To release or loosen the clasp of. 2. To release or loosen from a grasp or embrace. —*intr.* To release or relax a clasp or grasp.

un·clas·si·fied (ŭn-klăs′ə-fīd′) *adj.* 1. Not placed or included in order or in a class or category. 2. Not classified for security purposes. Said of information.

un·cle (ŭng′kəl) *n.* 1. *Abbr.* **u., U. a.** The brother of one's mother or father. **b.** The husband of one's aunt. 2. A form of respectful address to an older man, used especially by children. 3. A kindly counselor. 4. *Slang.* A pawnbroker. ~*interj. Informal.* Used to express surrender: *They beat him until he cried uncle.* [Middle English *uncle*, from Old French *oncle*, from Late Latin *aunculus*, variant of Latin *avunculus*, maternal uncle, diminutive of *avus*, grandfather.]

un·clean (ŭn-klēn′) *adj.* **-cleaner, -cleanest.** 1. Not clean; foul or dirty. 2. Morally defiled; unchaste. 3. Ceremonially impure. —**un·clean·ness** *n.*

un·clean·ly (ŭn-klĕn′lē) *adj.* **-lier, -liest.** Unclean; dirty. ~*adv.* (ŭn-klēn′lē). In an unclean manner. —**un·clean·li·ness** (ŭn-klĕn′lē-nĭs) *n.*

un·clear (ŭn-klîr′) *adj.* **-clearer, -clearest.** Not clearly defined; confused or ambiguous.

un·clench (ŭn-klĕnch′) *v.* **-clenched, -clenching, -clenches.** —*tr.* To loosen from a clenched position; relax; open: *unclench one's fists.* —*intr.* To become unclenched.

Uncle Sam *n. Abbr.* **U.S.** A personification of the U.S. Government, represented as a tall, thin man with a white beard and wearing a blue swallow-tailed coat, red-and-white striped trousers, and a tall hat with a band of stars. [Extension from *U.S.* (for *U*nited *S*tates); said to be a jocular interpretation of this abbreviation (stamped on U.S. Army supply packages during the War of 1812).]

Uncle Tom *n.* 1. A black person who is held to be humiliatingly subservient or deferential to whites. 2. Any person regarded as a traitor to his own group by excessive tolerance of or cooperation with the oppressors of that group. [After the black slave in *Uncle Tom's Cabin* (1851–52), novel by Harriet Beecher Stowe.]

un·clog (un-klŏg′) *tr.v.* **-clogged, -clogging, -clogs.** To clear a blockage from (a drain, for example).

un·close (ŭn-klōz′) *v.* **-closed, -closing, -closes.** —*tr.* 1. To open. 2. To disclose. —*intr.* To become opened.

un·clothe (ŭn-klōth′) *tr.v.* **-clothed** or **-clad** (-klăd′), **-clothing, -clothes.** To remove the clothing or cover from; strip.

un·co (ŭng′kō) *adj. Scottish.* 1. Unusual; odd; striking. 2. Mysterious; uncanny. ~*n., pl.* **uncos.** *Scottish.* 1. An unusual or amazing person. 2. A stranger. 3. **uncos.** News. ~*adv. Scottish.* To an excessive degree; remarkably. [Middle English (Scottish) *unkow*, variant of UNCOUTH.]

un·coil (ŭn-koil′) *v.* **-coiled, -coiling, -coils.** —*tr.* To unwind; untwist. —*intr.* To become unwound or untwisted.

un·com·fort·a·ble (ŭn-kŭmf′tə-bəl, -kŭm′fər-tə-bəl) *adj.* 1. Experiencing physical discomfort. 2. Uneasy; ill-at-ease. 3. Causing anxiety; disquieting. —**un·com·fort·a·ble·ness** *n.* —**un·com·fort·a·bly** *adv.*

un·com·mer·cial (ŭn′kə-mûr′shəl) *adj.* 1. Not engaged in or involving trade or commerce. 2. Not in accordance with the spirit or methods of commerce; not businesslike. 3. Uneconomical.

un·com·mit·ted (ŭn′kə-mĭt′ĭd) *adj.* Not pledged to a specific cause or course of action.

un·com·mon (ŭn-kŏm′ən) *adj.* **-moner, -monest.** 1. Not common; unusual; rare. 2. Wonderful; remarkable. 3. Unusually large or intense. —**un·com·mon·ly** *adv.* —**un·com·mon·ness** *n.*

un·com·mu·ni·ca·tive (ŭn′kə-myōō′nĭ-kā′tĭv, -nĭ-kə-tĭv) *adj.* Not disposed to be communicative; taciturn; reserved. —**un·com·mu·ni·ca·tive·ly** *adv.* —**un·com·mu·ni·ca·tive·ness** *n.*

un·com·pro·mis·ing (ŭn-kŏm′prə-mī′zĭng) *adj.* Not making concessions; inflexible; rigid. —**un·com·pro·mis·ing·ly** *adv.*

un·con·cern (ŭn′kən-sûrn′) *n.* 1. Lack of interest; indifference; apathy. 2. Lack of concern or apprehensiveness.

un·con·cerned (ŭn′kən-sûrnd′) *adj.* 1. Not interested; indifferent. 2. Not anxious or apprehensive; unworried. —See Synonyms at **indifferent.** —**un·con·cern·ed·ly** (ŭn′kən-sûr′nĭd-lē) *adv.* —**un·con·cern·ed·ness** *n.*

un·con·di·tion·al (ŭn′kən-dĭsh′ən-əl) *adj.* Without conditions or limitations; absolute. —**un·con·di·tion·al·ly** *adv.*

un·con·di·tioned (ŭn′kən-dĭsh′ənd) *adj.* 1. Unconditional; absolute; unrestricted. 2. *Psychology.* Not resulting from conditioning or learning; reflex or instinctive.

unconditioned response *n.* A response evoked by a stimulus independently of any learning or conditioning process. Formerly called "unconditioned reflex."

unconditioned stimulus *n.* A stimulus that evokes a certain response before the initiation of a conditioning process.

un·con·form·a·ble (ŭn′kən-fôr′mə-bəl) *adj.* 1. Not conforming or capable of conforming. 2. *Geology.* Showing unconformity. —**un·con·form·a·bil·i·ty** (ŭn′kən-fôr′mə-bĭl′ə-tē), **un·con·form·a·ble·ness** *n.* —**un·con·form·a·bly** *adv.*

un·con·for·mi·ty (ŭn′kən-fôr′mə-tē) *n., pl.* **-ties.** 1. Lack of conformity; nonconformity. 2. *Geology.* An eroded space, or space caused by lack of deposit, that separates younger strata from older rocks. Compare **disconformity.**

un·con·nect·ed (ŭn′kə-nĕk′tĭd) *adj.* 1. Not joined or connected. 2. Not coherent; disconnected. —**un·con·nect·ed·ly** *adv.* —**un·con·nect·ed·ness** *n.*

un·con·quer·a·ble (ŭn-kŏng′kər-ə-bəl) *adj.* Incapable of being overcome or defeated.

un·con·scion·a·ble (ŭn-kŏn′shən-ə-bəl) *adj.* 1. Not restrained by conscience; unscrupulous. 2. Beyond prudence or reason; immoderate; excessive. —**un·con·scion·a·ble·ness** *n.* —**un·con·scion·a·bly** *adv.*

un·con·scious (ŭn-kŏn′shəs) *adj.* 1. Completely lacking in awareness, as in a coma or deep sleep. 2. Without conscious awareness. 3. Pertaining to or originating in the unconscious; unavailable for direct conscious scrutiny: *unconscious resentment.* 4. Not consciously intended; involuntary. ~*n.* The division of the psyche not subject to direct conscious observation but inferred from its effects on conscious processes and behavior. Preceded by *the.* —See Usage note at **conscious.** —**un·con·scious·ly** *adv.* —**un·con·scious·ness** *n.*

un·con·sid·ered (ŭn′kən-sĭd′ərd) *adj.* 1. Not reasoned or considered; rash: *an unconsidered remark.* 2. Not taken into account; disregarded.

un·con·sti·tu·tion·al (ŭn′kŏn-stə-tōō′shən-əl, -tyōō′shən-əl) *adj.* Not in accord with or not permitted by the principles set forth in a constitution. —**un·con·sti·tu·tion·al·i·ty** (ŭn′kŏn-stə-tōō′shə-năl′ə-tē) *n.* —**un·con·sti·tu·tion·al·ly** *adv.*

un·con·trol·la·ble (ŭn′kən-trō′lə-bəl) *adj.* Not able to be controlled or governed. —**un·con·trol·la·bil·i·ty, un·con·trol·la·ble·ness** *n.* —**un·con·trol·la·bly** *adv.*

un·con·ven·tion·al (ŭn′kən-vĕn′shən-əl) *adj.* Not adhering to or in accord with conventional standards, manners, or styles. —**un·con·ven·tion·al·i·ty** (ŭn′kən-vĕn′shə-năl′ə-tē) *n.* —**un·con·ven·tion·al·ly** *adv.*

un·co·or·di·nat·ed (ŭn′kō-ôr′də-nā′tĭd) *adj.* 1. Lacking planning, method, or organization. 2. Lacking physical or mental coordination. —**un·co·or·di·nat·ed·ly** *adv.*

un·cork (ŭn-kôrk′) *tr.v.* **-corked, -corking, -corks.** 1. To draw the cork from. 2. To free from a sealed or constrained state: *uncork feelings of anger.*

un·count·a·ble (ŭn-koun′tə-bəl) *adj.* Countless; innumerable.

un·count·ed (ŭn-koun′tĭd) *adj.* 1. Not counted. 2. Unable to be counted; innumerable: *uncounted hosts of angels.*

un·cou·ple (ŭn-kŭp′əl) *tr.v.* **-pled, -pling, -ples.** 1. To disconnect (something coupled). 2. To release; unleash.

un·couth (ŭn-kōōth′) *adj.* 1. Crude; unrefined; rude. 2. Awkward or clumsy; ungraceful: *an uncouth gait.* 3. *Archaic.* Foreign; unfamiliar. [Middle English *unc(o)uth*, unknown, strange, Old English *uncūth* : *un-*, not + *cūth*, known, past participle of *cunnan*.] —**un·couth·ly** *adv.* —**un·couth·ness** *n.*

un·cov·e·nant·ed (ŭn-kŭv′ə-nən-tĭd) *adj.* 1. Not bound by a covenant. 2. Not promised or guaranteed by a covenant. 3. Not approved or permitted by a covenant.

un·cov·er (ŭn-kŭv′ər) *v.* **-ered, -ering, -ers.** —*tr.* 1. To remove the cover from; unveil or uncap. 2. To bring to light or disclose; reveal. 3. To remove the hat from (one's head) in respect or reverence. —*intr.* 1. To remove a cover. 2. To bare the head in respect or reverence.

un·cov·ered (ŭn-kŭv′ərd) *adj.* 1. Having no cover or protection. 2. Lacking the protection of insurance or collateral security. 3. Bareheaded.

un·cross (ŭn-krôs′, -krŏs′) *tr.v.* **-crossed, -crossing, -crosses.** To move (one's legs, for example) from a crossed position.

un·crowned (ŭn-kround′) *adj.* 1. Not having yet been crowned. 2. Having the power or influence of a monarch or other prominent figure but not the title.

unc·tion (ŭngk′shən) *n.* 1. The act of anointing as part of a religious, ceremonial, or healing ritual. See **extreme unction.** 2. An ointment or oil; a salve. 3. Something that serves to soothe or restore; a balm. 4. Affected, insincere, or exaggerated charm or earnestness; unctuousness. [Middle English, from Latin *unctiō* (stem *unctiōn-*), from *unguere* (past participle *unctus*), to anoint.]

unc·tu·ous (ŭngk′chōō-əs) *adj.* 1. Having the quality or characteristics of oil or ointment; greasy; slippery. 2. Containing or composed of oil or fat. 3. Characterized by affected, exaggerated, or insincere charm or earnestness. 4. Abundant in organic materials; soft and rich: *unctuous soil.* [Middle English, from Medieval Latin *unctuōsus*, from Latin *unctum*, ointment, from *unctus*, past participle of *unguere,* to anoint.] **—unc·tu·os·i·ty** (ŭngk'cho͞o-ŏs'ə-tē), **unc·tu·ous·ness** *n.* **—unc·tu·ous·ly** *adv.*

un·cus (ŭng'kəs) *n., pl.* **unci** (ŭn'sī'). *Biology.* A hook-shaped part or process; especially, the projection from the lower surface of the cerebrum. [New Latin, from Latin, hook.]

un·cut (ŭn-kŭt') *adj.* **1.** Not cut. **2.** Having the page edge not slit or trimmed. Said of a book. **3.** Not ground to a specific shape. Said of a gemstone. **4.** Not condensed, abridged, or shortened, as by an editor or censor.

un·damped (ŭn-dămpt') *adj.* **1.** *Physics.* Not tending toward a state of rest; not damped. Said of oscillations. **2.** Not stifled or discouraged; unchecked: *His ardor was undamped.*

un·daunt·ed (ŭn-dôn'tĭd, -dän'tĭd) *adj.* Not discouraged or disheartened; resolute; fearless. —See Synonyms at **brave.** **—un·daunt·ed·ly** *adv.* **—un·daunt·ed·ness** *n.*

un·dec·a·gon (ŭn-dĕk'ə-gŏn') *n.* A polygon having eleven angles and eleven sides. [Latin *undecim,* eleven, after *decagon.*]

un·de·ceive (ŭn'dĭ-sēv') *tr.v.* **-ceived, -ceiving, -ceives.** To free from illusion or deception. **—un·de·ceiv·er** *n.*

un·de·cid·ed (ŭn'dĭ-sī'dĭd) *adj.* **1.** Not yet determined or settled; open. **2.** Not having reached a decision; uncommitted. **—un·de·cid·ed·ly** *adv.* **—un·de·cid·ed·ness** *n.*

un·de·fend·ed (ŭn'dĭ-fĕn'dĭd) *adj.* **1.** Not defended. **2.** Without having a defense entered. Said of a lawsuit.

un·de·mon·stra·tive (ŭn'dĭ-mŏn'strə-tĭv) *adj.* Not disposed to expressions of feeling; reserved. **—un·de·mon·stra·tive·ly** *adv.* **—un·de·mon·stra·tive·ness** *n.*

un·de·ni·a·ble (ŭn'dĭ-nī'ə-bəl) *adj.* **1.** Not able to be denied; irrefutable; certain. **2.** Unquestionably good; outstanding; excellent. **—un·de·ni·a·bly** *adv.*

un·de·pend·a·ble (ŭn'dĭ-pĕn'də-bəl) *adj.* Not capable of being relied upon; untrustworthy. —See Synonyms at **faithless.**

un·der (ŭn'dər) *prep.* **1.** In or to a lower position or place than: *a caption under a picture.* **2.** Beneath the surface of: *under the ground.* **3.** Beneath the assumed surface or guise of: *under a false name.* **4.** Less than; smaller than. **5.** Less than the required amount or degree of; less than the standard of: *under voting age.* **6.** Inferior to in quality, status, or rank. **7. a.** Subject to the authority, rule, instruction, or influence of: *under a dictatorship; under the impression that it was already finished.* **b.** During the reign, regime, or government of: *Under Stalin there was little free discussion.* **8.** During the time conventionally assigned to (a specified sign of the zodiac): *born under Virgo.* **9.** Undergoing or receiving the effects of: *under intensive care.* **10.** Subject to the restraint or obligation of: *under contract.* **11.** Within the group or classification of: *listed under biology; under the heading of.* **12.** In the process of: *under discussion.* **13.** In view of; because of: *under these conditions.* **14.** With the authorization of; attested by; by virtue of: *under the king's seal.* **15.** Sowed or planted with: *an acre under oats.* **16.** Powered or propelled by: *under steam.* —See Usage Note at **below.**
~*adv.* **1.** In or into a place below or beneath something. **2.** In or into a subordinate or inferior condition or position. **3.** So as to be submerged or enveloped by something. **4.** *Informal.* In or into a state of unconsciousness. **5.** So as to be less than the required amount or degree. **—go under. 1.** To sink or drown. **2.** To yield or surrender, as to sleep or unconsciousness. **3.** To fail or fall through. Used of a business.
~*adj.* **1.** Located or moving beneath or on the lower surface. **2.** Lower in rank, power, or authority; subordinate; inferior. **3.** Less than is required or customary; substandard. **4.** Lower in amount or degree. [Middle English *under,* Old English *under.*]

under– *prefix.* Indicates: **1.** Location below or under; for example, **underground, underclothes. 2.** Inferiority in rank or importance; for example, **undersecretary. 3.** Degree, rate, or quantity that is lower or less than normal, proper, or sufficient; for example, **underestimate, undernourished. 4.** Secrecy or treachery; for example, **undermine, underhand.** ***Note:*** Many compounds other than those entered here may be formed with *under-*. In forming compounds, *under-* is joined with the following element without space or a hyphen: *underrate; undergrow.* [Middle English *under-,* Old English *under-,* from UNDER.]

un·der·a·chieve (ŭn'dər-ə-chēv') *intr.v.* **-chieved, -chieving, -chieves.** To perform below an expected level, especially in schoolwork. **—un·der·a·chiev·er** *n.*

un·der·act (ŭn'dər-ăkt') *v.* **-acted, -acting, -acts.** —*tr.* **1.** To perform (a dramatic role) weakly or with insufficient expressiveness. **2.** To understate (a dramatic role) intentionally. —*intr.* To perform a dramatic role weakly or with intentional restraint.

un·der·age (ŭn'dər-āj') *adj.* Below the customary or required age; especially, below the legal age, as for drinking or voting.

un·der·arm[1] (ŭn'dər-ärm') *adj.* **1.** Located, placed, or used under the arm. **2.** In or of the armpit.
~*n.* The armpit.

underarm[2] *adj. Sports.* Executed with the hand kept below the level of the shoulder: *an underarm toss; a pitcher's underarm delivery.*
~*adv.* With an underarm motion or delivery.

un·der·bel·ly (ŭn'dər-bĕl'ē) *n., pl.* **-lies. 1.** The lowest part of an animal's body. **2.** Any vulnerable or weak part or aspect: *"the soft underbelly of Europe"* (Winston Churchill).

un·der·bid (ŭn'dər-bĭd') *v.* **-bid, -bidding, -bids.** —*tr.* **1.** To bid lower than (a competitor). **2.** *Bridge.* To bid less than the full value of (one's hand). —*intr.* To make an unnecessarily low bid. **—un·der·bid·der** *n.*

undercroft *The tomb of the Duc de Berry (1340–1416) lies in the undercroft beneath Bourges Cathedral in France.*

un·der·bod·y (ŭn'dər-bŏd'ē) *n.* The underside or lower part, as of an animal's body or a vehicle.

un·der·bred (ŭn'dər-brĕd') *adj.* **1.** Not of pure stock; of mixed breeding. Said of an animal. **2.** Ill-bred; vulgar. Said of a person.

un·der·brush (ŭn'dər-brŭsh') *n.* Small trees, shrubs, or similar plants growing beneath the taller trees in a forest.

un·der·buy (ŭn'dər-bī') *tr.v.* **-bought** (-bôt'), **-buying, -buys. 1.** To buy something at a lower price than (someone else). **2.** To buy for less than the actual value. **3.** To buy an insufficient quantity of.

un·der·cap·i·tal·ize (ŭn'dər-kăp'ə-tə-līz') *tr.v.* **-ized, -izing, -izes.** To provide (a commercial enterprise or other venture) with insufficient capital for efficiency or viability.

un·der·car·riage (ŭn'dər-kăr'ĭj') *n.* **1.** The landing gear of an aircraft. **2.** The supporting framework of a carriage or other vehicle.

un·der·charge (ŭn'dər-chärj') *v.* **-charged, -charging, -charges.** —*tr.* **1.** To charge (someone) less than is customary or required. **2.** To load (a firearm) with an insufficient charge. —*intr.* To make or levy charges lower than is customary or required.
~*n.* (ŭn'dər-chärj'). An insufficient or improper charge.

un·der·class (ŭn'dər-klăs', -kläs') *n.* A lower social class, especially an oppressed or disadvantaged one.

un·der·class·man (ŭn'dər-klăs'mən, -kläs'mən) *n., pl.* **-men** (-mĭn). A student in the freshman or sophomore class at a secondary school or college. Also called "lowerclassman."

un·der·clothes (ŭn'dər-klōz', -klō*th*z') *pl.n.* Also **un·der·cloth·ing** (-klō'*th*ĭng). **Underwear** *(see).*

un·der·coat (ŭn'dər-kōt') *n.* Also **un·der·coat·ing** (-kō'tĭng) (for senses 3, 4). **1.** A coat worn beneath another coat. **2.** A covering of short hairs or fur concealed by the longer outer hairs of an animal's coat. **3. a.** A coat of paint or sealing material applied to a surface before the topcoat is applied. **b.** The paint or sealing material used for this. **4.** A tarlike substance sprayed on the underside of an automobile to prevent rusting.
~*tr.v.* **undercoated, -coating, -coats.** To apply an undercoat to.

un·der·cool (ŭn'dər-ko͞ol') *tr.v.* **-cooled, -cooling, -cools.** To **supercool** *(see).*

un·der·cov·er (ŭn'dər-kŭv'ər) *adj.* Performed or acting in secret; especially, concerned with or engaged in espionage or secret inquiries: *an undercover investigation.*

un·der·croft (ŭn'dər-krôft', -krŏft') *n.* An underground chamber or vault; especially, a crypt. [Middle English *under croft* : UNDER + *croft(e),* vault, from Medieval Latin *crupta,* variant of Latin *crypta,* CRYPT.]

un·der·cur·rent (ŭn'dər-kûr'ənt) *n.* **1.** A current, as of air or water, below another current or beneath a surface. **2.** An underlying feeling, tendency, force, or influence often contrary to what is superficially evident: *spoke quietly but with an undercurrent of passion.*

un·der·cut (ŭn'dər-kŭt') *v.* **-cut, -cutting, -cuts.** —*tr.* **1.** To make a cut under or below. **2.** To cut material away from, as in carving, in order to create an overhang. **3.** To charge less than (a competitor) for goods or services. **4.** To undermine or outmaneuver (a rival), as by swift or unexpected action. **5.** To strike (a ball) with backspin by hitting downward as well as forward, as in golf and tennis. —*intr.* To undercut someone or something.
~*n.* (ŭn'dər-kŭt'). **1.** A cut made in the under part to remove material. **2.** A part so removed. **3.** *Chiefly British.* The tender under part of a sirloin of beef. **4.** *Sports.* **a.** A spin given to a ball opposite to its direction of movement; backspin. **b.** A cut or slice imparting such a spin. **5.** A notch cut in a tree to direct its fall and ensure a clean break.

un·der·de·vel·oped (ŭn'dər-dĭ-vĕl'əpt) *adj.* **1.** Not adequately or normally developed; immature; deficient: *an underdeveloped mind; underdeveloped fruit.* **2.** In photography, processed in too weak a developing solution, or for too short a time, or at too low a temperature to produce a normal degree of contrast. **3.** Poor and economically primitive, usually because of insufficient capital and an inadequate social infrastructure. **—un·der·de·vel·op·ment** *n.*

un·der·dog (ŭn'dər-dôg', -dŏg') *n.* **1.** One who loses or is expected to lose a contest or struggle, as in sports or politics. **2.** One who is at a disadvantage or is being oppressed.

un·der·done (ŭn'dər-dŭn') *adj.* Cooked lightly or insufficiently.

un·der·draw·ers (un'dər-drôrz') *pl.n.* Shorts or briefs worn as undergarments; underpants.

un·der·dressed (ŭn'dər-drĕst') *adj.* Dressed too informally for a given situation.

un·der·drive (ŭn'dər-drīv') *n.* A gearing device causing the output drive shaft to rotate at a slower rate than the engine input shaft.

un·der·em·ployed (ŭn'dər-ĕm-ploid') *adj.* Not adequately or fully employed.

un·der·es·ti·mate (ŭn'dər-ĕs'tə-māt') *v.* **-mated, -mating, -mates.** —*tr.* **1.** To estimate at too low a quantity, degree, or size. **2.** To have too low a regard for the worth, strength, or character of. —*intr.* To make too low an estimate of a quantity, degree, or size.
~*n.* (ŭn'dər-ĕs'tə-mĭt). An estimate that is too low. **—un·der·es·ti·ma·tion** (ŭn'dər-ĕs'tə-mā'shən) *n.*

un·der·ex·pose (ŭn'dər-ĭk-spōz') *tr.v.* **-posed, -posing, -poses.** To expose insufficiently; especially, to expose (film, for example) to light for too short a time or to insufficient light or radiation to produce normal image contrast. **—un·der·ex·po·sure** (ŭn'dər-ĭk-spō'zhər) *n.*

un·der·feed (ŭn'dər-fēd') *tr.v.* **-fed** (-fĕd'), **-feeding, -feeds. 1.** To feed insufficiently. **2.** To supply with fuel from below.

un·der·floor (ŭn′dər-flôr′) *adj.* Located beneath the floor: *underfloor heating.*

un·der·foot (ŭn′dər-fŏŏt′) *adv.* **1.** Under the foot or feet, and often on the ground: *trampled the flowers underfoot.* **2.** Below one's feet; directly below. **3.** In the way: *The cat's always underfoot.*

un·der·fur (ŭn′dər-fûr′) *n.* The dense, soft, fine fur beneath the coarse outer hairs of certain mammals.

un·der·gar·ment (ŭn′dər-gär′mənt) *n.* A garment that is worn under outer garments; especially, one worn next to the skin.

un·der·gird (ŭn′dər-gûrd′) *tr.v.* **-girded** or **-girt** (-gûrt′), **-girding, -girds.** To gird, support, or strengthen from beneath.

un·der·glaze (ŭn′dər-glāz′) *adj.* Applied to pottery before it is glazed. Said of a pigment or decoration.
~*n.* (ŭn′dər-glāz′). A pigment or decoration so applied.

un·der·go (ŭn′dər-gō′) *tr.v.* **-went** (-wĕnt′), **-gone** (-gôn′, -gŏn′), **-going, -goes** (-gōz′). **1.** To experience; be subjected to. **2.** To endure; suffer; sustain. [Middle English *undergon*, to submit to, go through : *under,* UNDER + *gon,* to GO.]

un·der·grad·u·ate (ŭn′dər-grăj′ŏŏ-ĭt) *n.* A university student who has not yet received a first degree. Also informally called "undergrad." —**un·der·grad·u·ate** *adj.*

un·der·ground (ŭn′dər-ground′) *adj.* **1.** Occurring, operating, or situated below the surface of the earth. **2.** Hidden or concealed; clandestine. **3.** Of, pertaining to, or designating an organization involved in secret or illegal activity, such as the subversion of an established political or social order. **4.** Of, pertaining to, or describing an avant-garde movement or its music, publications, and art, usually privately produced and often concerned with social or artistic experiment.
~*n.* **1.** A clandestine, often nationalist, organization engaged in or encouraging the usually violent overthrow of a government in power, such as an occupying military government. **2.** *Chiefly British.* A subway system. Usually preceded by *the.*
~*adv.* (ŭn′dər-ground′, ŭn′dər-ground′). **1.** Below the surface of the earth. **2.** In or into secrecy or hiding: *They went underground.*

underground railroad *n.* **1.** A tunneled railroad system below the surface of the earth; subway. Also called "underground railway." **2. Underground Railroad.** A secret network of cooperation in the ante-bellum United States, by which fugitive slaves were helped to reach the free states or Canada.

un·der·grown (ŭn′dər-grōn′) *adj.* Not fully grown; puny.

un·der·growth (ŭn′dər-grōth′; ŭn′dər-grŏth′ *for sense 3*) *n.* **1.** Low-growing plants, saplings, and shrubs beneath taller trees. **2.** Something resembling this, as a growth of short, fine hairs beneath longer ones. **3.** The condition of being undergrown.

un·der·hand (ŭn′dər-hănd′) *adj.* **1.** Secret and deceitful; treacherous; sneaky; underhanded. **2.** *Sports.* Underarm. —See Synonyms at **dishonest, secret.**
~*adv.* **1.** With an underhand movement. **2.** Slyly and secretly.

un·der·hand·ed (ŭn′dər-hăn′dĭd) *adj.* **1.** Secret and deceitful. **2.** Lacking the required number of workers or players; shorthanded. —**un·der·hand·ed·ly** *adv.* —**un·der·hand·ed·ness** *n.*

un·der·hung (ŭn′dər-hŭng′) *adj.* **1. a.** Protruding beyond the upper jaw. Said of a lower jaw. **b.** Having such a lower jaw. **2.** Resting on or mounted along a supporting track. Said of a sliding door.

un·der·in·sure (ŭn′dər-ĭn-shŏŏr′) *tr.v.* **-sured, -suring, -sures.** **1.** To insure (possessions) below their full value. **2.** To fail to protect (oneself) with adequate insurance.

un·der·laid (ŭn′dər-lād′) *adj.* **1.** Placed or laid underneath. **2.** Supported or raised by something from beneath; having an underlay.

un·der·lay (ŭn′dər-lā′) *tr.v.* **-laid, -laying, -lays.** **1.** To put (one thing) under another. **2.** To provide with a base or sublining. **3.** *Printing.* To raise or support by underlays.
~*n.* (ŭn′dər-lā′). **1.** Something laid underneath; especially, felt or foam rubber placed under a carpet for added insulation and resilience. **2.** *Printing.* A piece of paper or other material used under type to raise the level of a printing bed.

un·der·let (ŭn′dər-lĕt′) *tr.v.* **-let, -letting, -lets.** **1.** To let (property) at less than the proper value. **2.** To sublet.

un·der·lie (ŭn′dər-lī′) *tr.v.* **-lay** (-lā′), **-lain** (-lān′), **-lying, -lies.** **1.** To lie or be located under or below. **2.** To be the support or basis of; account for: *Many facts underlie my decision.* **3.** *Finance.* To take precedence over (another claim, security, liability, or the like).

un·der·line (ŭn′dər-līn′, ŭn′dər-līn′) *tr.v.* **-lined, -lining, -lines.** **1.** To draw a line under, especially to distinguish or emphasize (a written word or passage). **2.** To emphasize or stress.
~*n.* (ŭn′dər-līn′). A line drawn under writing to indicate emphasis or italic type.

un·der·ling (ŭn′dər-lĭng) *n.* A subordinate or lackey.

un·der·lip (ŭn′dər-lĭp′) *n.* The lower lip.

un·der·ly·ing (ŭn′dər-lī′ĭng, ŭn′dər-lī′ĭng) *adj.* **1.** Basic; fundamental. **2.** Implicit; hidden: *an underlying meaning.* **3.** *Finance.* Taking precedence; prior: *an underlying claim.*

un·der·manned (ŭn′dər-mănd′) *adj.* Without sufficient workers or troops; short-handed.

un·der·mine (ŭn′dər-mīn′) *tr.v.* **-mined, -mining, -mines.** **1.** To dig a mine or tunnel beneath. **2.** To weaken by wearing away a base or foundation: *Water undermined the foundations.* **3.** To weaken or impair by degrees or imperceptibly; sap: *Late hours undermine one's health; The ridicule undermined the chairman's authority.*

un·der·most (ŭn′dər-mōst′) *adj.* Lowest in position, rank, or place.
~*adv.* In or to the lowest place.

un·der·neath (ŭn′dər-nēth′) *adv.* In or to a place beneath; below.

~*prep.* Under; below; beneath. —See Usage note at **below.**
~*adj.* Lower; under.
~*n.* The lower part or side. [Middle English *undernethe,* from Old English *underneothan* : UNDER + *neothan,* below.]

un·der·nour·ish (ŭn′dər-nûr′ĭsh) *tr.v.* **-ished, -ishing, -ishes.** To provide with insufficient quantity or quality of nourishment to sustain proper health and growth. —**un·der·nour·ish·ment** *n.*

un·der·paint·ing (ŭn′dər-pān′tĭng) *n.* A sketch of a painting, indicating the design, shading, and often coloring, over which the final painting is executed.

un·der·pants (ŭn′dər-pănts′) *pl.n.* An undergarment worn over the lower abdomen, buttocks, hips, and sometimes thighs.

un·der·part (ŭn′dər-pärt′) *n.* **1.** A part on the lower surface, especially of an animal or plant. **2.** A subordinate role, as in a play.

un·der·pass (ŭn′dər-păs′, -päs′) *n.* **1.** A passage underneath something; especially, a section of road that passes under another road or a railroad. **2.** An intersection formed in this way.

un·der·pay (ŭn′dər-pā′) *tr.v.* **-paid** (-pād′), **-paying, -pays.** To pay insufficiently or less than deserved. —**un·der·pay·ment** *n.*

un·der·pin (ŭn′dər-pĭn′) *tr.v.* **-pinned, -pinning, -pins.** **1.** To support from below, as with props, girders, masonry, or the like. **2.** To corroborate or substantiate.

un·der·play (ŭn′dər-plā′, ŭn′dər-plā′) *v.* **-played, -playing, -plays.** —*tr.* **1.** To act (a role) subtly or with restraint. **2.** To present or deal with subtly or with restraint; play down. —*intr.* **1.** To underplay a role. **2.** In card games, to play a low card while holding a higher card of the same suit.

un·der·plot (ŭn′dər-plŏt′) *n.* A subsidiary plot, as in a play or novel.

un·der·price (ŭn′dər-prīs′) *tr.v.* **-priced, -pricing, -prices.** To price below normal or appropriate value.

un·der·priv·i·leged (ŭn′dər-prĭv′ə-lĭjd) *adj.* Lacking the rights, opportunities, and economic or educational advantages enjoyed by other members of one's community; deprived.

un·der·pro·duc·tion (ŭn′dər-prə-dŭk′shən) *n.* Production below full capacity or below demand.

un·der·proof (ŭn′dər-prŏŏf′) *adj.* Having a smaller proportion of alcohol than **proof spirit** (see).

un·der·prop (ŭn′dər-prŏp′) *tr.v.* **-propped, -propping, -props.** **1.** To prop (something) from below. **2.** To support or sustain.

un·der·quote (ŭn′dər-kwōt′) *tr.v.* **-quoted, -quoting, -quotes.** **1.** To offer (goods or services) for sale at a price lower than the official list or market price; undersell. **2.** To quote a lower price than that quoted by (another).

un·der·rate (ŭn′dər-rāt′) *tr.v.* **-rated, -rating, -rates.** To regard (someone's abilities, for example) as having less value or quality than is due; undervalue; underestimate.

un·der·run (ŭn′dər-run′) *tr.v.* **-ran** (-răn′), **-run, -running, -runs.** **1.** To run or pass beneath. **2.** *Nautical.* To haul (a line or cable) onto a boat for inspection or repair.

un·der·score (ŭn′dər-skôr′, -skōr′) *tr.v.* **-scored, -scoring, -scores.** **1.** To draw a line under. **2.** To emphasize or stress.
~*n.* A line drawn under writing to indicate emphasis or italic type.

un·der·sea (ŭn′dər-sē′) *adj.* Pertaining to, existing, occurring, or designed for use beneath the surface of the sea.
~*adv.* (ŭn′dər-sē′). Beneath the surface of the sea.

un·der·seal (ŭn′dər-sēl′) *tr.v.* **-sealed, -sealing, -seals.** To place a protective coating on the underside of.

un·der·sec·re·tar·y (ŭn′dər-sĕk′rə-tĕr′ē) *n., pl.* **-ies.** An official directly subordinate to a Cabinet member.

un·der·sell (ŭn′dər-sĕl′) *tr.v.* **-sold** (-sōld′), **-selling, -sells.** **1.** To sell goods at a lower price than (another seller). **2.** To sell (goods) for less than the full or normal price. **3.** To advertise or publicize moderately or inadequately. **4.** To present or regard (oneself) as having less ability or worth than one actually has. —**un·der·sell·er** *n.*

un·der·set (ŭn′dər-sĕt′) *n.* An ocean undercurrent.

un·der·sexed (ŭn′dər-sĕkst′) *adj.* Having less sexual potency or desire than normal.

un·der·shirt (ŭn′dər-shûrt′) *n.* An upper undergarment, with or without sleeves, worn next to the skin under a shirt.

un·der·shoot (ŭn′dər-shŏŏt′) *v.* **-shot** (-shŏt′), **-shooting, -shoots.** —*tr.* **1.** To shoot a projectile below or short of (a target). **2.** *Aeronautics.* **a.** To start one's final approach to (a landing area) too low or too soon. **b.** To land an aircraft short of (a landing area). —*intr.* **1.** To shoot short of a target. **2.** To land short of a landing area.

un·der·shot (ŭn′dər-shŏt′) *adj.* **1.** Driven by water passing from below. Said of a waterwheel. **2.** Projecting beyond the upper jaw. Said of a lower jaw.

un·der·shrub (ŭn′dər-shrŭb′) *n.* A low-growing shrub.

un·der·side (ŭn′dər-sīd′) *n.* The side or surface that is underneath; the bottom side.

un·der·sign (ŭn′dər-sīn′) *tr.v.* **-signed, -signing, -signs.** To sign one's name at the bottom of (a letter or document).

un·der·signed (ŭn′dər-sīnd′) *adj.* **1.** Having placed one's signature at the bottom of a document. **2.** Having a signature at the bottom or the end. Said of documents. **3.** Signed at the bottom of a document: *the undersigned names.*
~*n., pl.* **undersigned.** The person who has signed at the bottom of a document. Preceded by *the.*

un·der·sized (ŭn′dər-sīzd′) *adj.* Also **un·der·size** (-sīz′). Being of less than normal or sufficient size.

un·der·skirt (ŭn′dər-skûrt′) *n.* **1.** A skirt worn under another; a petticoat. **2.** One skirt of a layered dress or gown over which outer skirts are draped.

un·der·sleeve (ŭn′dər-slēv′) n. A sleeve worn under an outer sleeve; especially, an ornamental sleeve designed to extend below or show through slashes in the outer sleeve.

un·der·slung (ŭn′dər-slŭng′) adj. 1. Having springs attached to the axles from below. Said of a vehicle. 2. Supported from above. 3. Having a low center of gravity.

un·der·soil (ŭn′dər-soil′) n. Soil below the ground surface.

un·der·staffed (ŭn′dər-stăft′) adj. Having too small a staff; having insufficient personnel: an understaffed hospital.

un·der·stand (ŭn′dər-stănd′) v. **-stood** (-stood′), **-standing, -stands.** —tr. **1.** To perceive and comprehend the nature and significance of: "I don't pretend to understand the Universe—it's a great deal bigger than I am" (Thomas Carlyle). **2.** To know thoroughly by close contact with or long experience of: understood the customs of the Far East. **3. a.** To grasp or comprehend the meaning intended or expressed by (another): "for thank God I can read and perhaps understand Shakespeare to his depths" (Keats). **b.** To comprehend the meaning, language, sounds, form, or symbols of: Do you understand French? **4.** To know and be tolerant or sympathetic toward (the needs, feelings, or views of): My wife doesn't understand me. **5.** To learn indirectly, as by hearsay; gather; assume. **6.** To take something as meaning; conclude; infer: Am I to understand that you are staying the night? **7.** To accept as an agreed fact or condition; regard as definite: It is understood that the fee will be five dollars. **8.** To supply or add (a meaning or words, for example) mentally. —intr. **1.** To have understanding, knowledge, sympathy, or comprehension: "Hear and understand" (Matthew 15:10). **2.** To learn indirectly or at secondhand; gather: They were just married, or so I understand. **3.** To draw an inference. **—give someone to understand.** To cause (someone) to believe or think. —See Synonyms at **apprehend.** [Middle English understanden, Old English understandan : UNDER- + STAND.] **—un·der·stand·a·ble** adj. **—un·der·stand·a·bly** adv.

un·der·stand·ing (ŭn′dər-stăn′dĭng) n. **1.** The quality or condition of one who understands; comprehension. **2.** The faculty by which one understands; intelligence. **3.** Individual or specified judgment or outlook in a matter; opinion; interpretation. **4.** An agreement between two or more persons or groups, especially when informal and implicit. **5.** A reconciliation of differences; an agreement: The two factions finally reached an understanding. **—on the understanding that.** On condition that. —See Synonyms at **reason.** ~adj. **1.** Having or characterized by comprehension, good sense, or discernment. **2.** Intelligently sympathetic and compassionate. **—un·der·stand·ing·ly** adv.

un·der·state (ŭn′dər-stāt′) v. **-stated, -stating, -states.** —tr. **1.** To express with undue restraint and cause to seem less important than is the case. **2.** To express with restraint or lack of emphasis, especially ironically or for dramatic impact. **3.** To state (a number, quantity, or the like) lower than is correct: understate one's age. —intr. To understate something.

un·der·state·ment (ŭn′dər-stāt′mənt) n. **1.** A statement or disclosure that is less than complete. **2.** Intentional lack of emphasis, as for dramatic effect; restrained expression.

un·der·steer (ŭn′dər-stîr′) intr.v. **-steered, -steering, -steers.** To turn or tend to turn less sharply than the driver intends. Used of a motor vehicle. ~n. (ŭn′dər-stîr′). A tendency toward understeering.

un·der·stood (ŭn′dər-stood′) adj. **1.** Agreed upon; assumed. **2.** Not expressed; implied.

un·der·strap·per (ŭn′dər-străp′ər) n. A subordinate; an underling.

un·der·stra·tum (ŭn′dər-strā′təm, -străt′əm) n., pl. **-strata** (-strā′tə, -străt′ə) or **-tums.** A substratum.

un·der·stud·y (ŭn′dər-stŭd′ē) v. **-ied, -ying, -ies.** —tr. **1.** To study or know (a role) so as to be able to replace the regular actor or actress when required. **2.** To act as an understudy to. —intr. To act as an understudy. ~n., pl. **understudies. 1.** An actor or actress who studies a role so as to be able to replace the regular actor or actress when required. **2.** Any person trained to do the work of another.

un·der·sur·face (ŭn′dər-sûr′fəs) n. An underside.

un·der·take (ŭn′dər-tāk′) v. **-took** (-took′), **-taken, -taking, -takes.** —tr. **1. a.** To decide or agree to do: undertake a task. **b.** To set about; begin. **2.** To take upon oneself; commit oneself to: He undertook to pay all the costs. **3.** To promise; guarantee. —intr. Archaic. To make oneself responsible. Used with for. [Middle English undertaken, to accept, take in hand : UNDER- + TAKE.]

un·der·tak·er (ŭn′dər-tā′kər for sense 1; ŭn′dər-tā′kər for sense 2) n. **1.** One who undertakes a task or job; especially, an entrepreneur. **2.** One whose business it is to arrange for the burial or cremation of the dead and to assist at funeral rites; a mortician.

un·der·tak·ing (ŭn′dər-tā′kĭng) n. **1. a.** A task or assignment undertaken. **b.** An enterprise or venture. **2.** A guaranty, engagement, or promise. **3.** The profession or duties of an undertaker.

un·der-the-count·er (ŭn′dər-thə-koun′tər) adj. Transacted or sold illicitly. Compare **over-the-counter.**

un·der-the-ta·ble (ŭn′dər-thə-tā′bəl) adj. Not straightforward; secret or underhand.

un·der·things (ŭn′dər-thĭngz′) pl.n. Underwear.

un·der·thrust (ŭn′dər-thrŭst′) n. Geology. A reverse geological fault in which the rocks on the undersurface of a fault plane move below the static rocks on the upper surface.

un·der·tint (ŭn′dər-tĭnt′) n. A slight or subtle tint.

un·der·tone (ŭn′dər-tōn′) n. **1.** A tone of low pitch or volume, especially of spoken sound. **2. a.** A pale or subdued color. **b.** A color applied under or seen through another color. **3.** An underlying or implied tendency or meaning; an undercurrent.

un·der·tow (ŭn′dər-tō′) n. **1.** The seaward pull of waves receding after they have broken on a shore. **2.** Any strong undercurrent moving in a direction other than that of the surface current.

un·der·trick (ŭn′dər-trĭk′) n. A trick, especially in bridge, the loss of which prevents a declarer from making his contract.

un·der·trump (ŭn′dər-trŭmp′) intr.v. **-trumped, -trumping, -trumps.** In card games, to play a trump lower than one already played when a trump has not been led.

un·der·val·ue (ŭn′dər-văl′yōō) tr.v. **-ued, -uing, -ues. 1.** To assign too low a value to; underestimate. **2.** To have too little regard or esteem for. **—un·der·val·u·a·tion** (ŭn′dər-văl′yōō-ā′shən) n.

un·der·vest (ŭn′dər-vĕst′) n. Chiefly British. An undershirt.

un·der·wa·ter (ŭn′dər-wô′tər, -wŏt′ər) adj. Being, occurring, used, or performed beneath the surface of the water. **—un·der·wa·ter** adv.

under way adv. **1.** In motion or operation; started: The game got under way at noon. **2.** Already commenced or initiated; in progress; afoot. **3.** Nautical. Not anchored and not moored to a fixed object.

un·der·wear (ŭn′dər-wâr′) n. Clothing worn under the outer clothes and next to the skin. Also called "underclothes," "underclothing."

un·der·weight (ŭn′dər-wāt′) adj. Weighing less than is normal, healthy, or required. ~n. Insufficiency of weight.

underwent. Past tense of **undergo.**

un·der·whelm (ŭn′dər-hwĕlm′, -wĕlm′) tr.v. **-whelmed, -whelming, -whelms.** Informal. To fail to excite or make enthusiastic. Often used humorously. [UNDER- + -whelm, as in OVERWHELM.]

un·der·wing (ŭn′dər-wĭng′) n. **1.** Either of a pair of hind wings partially or wholly covered by the forewings, as in certain moths. **2.** Any of various moths of the genus Calocala, having brightly colored underwings.

un·der·wood (ŭn′dər-wood′) n. Shrubs and small trees growing beneath taller trees; underbrush; undergrowth.

un·der·world (ŭn′dər-wûrld′) n. **1.** Any region, realm, or dwelling place conceived to be below the surface of the earth; especially, the world of the dead in classical mythology; Hades. **2.** The part of society habitually engaged in crime or vice; the milieu of criminals. **3.** The opposite side of the earth; the antipodes. **4.** Archaic. The world beneath the heavens; the earth.

un·der·write (ŭn′dər-rīt′) v. **-wrote** (-rōt′), **-written** (-rĭt′n), **-writing, -writes.** —tr. **1. a.** To write (one's signature, for example) at the bottom; subscribe. **b.** To sign or endorse (a document). **2.** To assume financial responsibility for; guarantee (an enterprise) against failure: underwrite a theatrical production. **3. a.** To sign (an insurance policy), thus assuming liability in case of certain losses. **b.** To insure. **c.** To insure against losses totaling (a given amount). **4.** Finance. To guarantee the purchase of (a full issue of shares or bonds); specifically, to agree to buy the unsold part of (a share issue) at a fixed time and price. **5.** To support or agree to (a decision, for example). —intr. To act as an underwriter; especially, to issue an insurance policy. [Middle English, translation of Latin subscrībere.]

un·der·writ·er (ŭn′dər-rī′tər) n. Abbr. **UW 1.** A person or firm engaged in an insurance business; specifically, an insurance agent who assesses the risk of enrolling an applicant for coverage or a policy. **2.** A person or company that guarantees the purchase of a full issue of shares or bonds.

un·de·scend·ed testicle (ŭn′dĭ-sĕn′dĭd) n. A testicle that has remained within the inguinal canal and has not descended to the scrotum.

un·de·served (ŭn′dĭ-zûrvd′) adj. Not merited; unjustifiable; unfair. **—un·de·serv·ed·ly** (ŭn′dĭ-zûr′vĭd-lē) adv.

un·de·sir·a·ble (ŭn′dĭ-zīr′ə-bəl) adj. **1.** Not desirable; unwanted. **2.** Unpleasant; objectionable. ~n. An undesirable person. **—un·de·sir·a·bil·i·ty** (ŭn′dĭ-zīr′ə-bĭl′ə-tē) n. **—un·de·sir·a·bly** adv.

un·de·vel·oped (ŭn′dĭ-vĕl′əpt) adj. **1.** Not developed or fully grown; immature. **2.** Not put to full use or not having reached full potential: undeveloped talent. **3.** Not yet economically exploited.

un·dies (ŭn′dēz) pl.n. Informal. Underwear.

un·dine (ŭn-dēn′, ŭn′dēn′) n. A female water spirit who, according to Paracelsus, could earn a soul by marrying a mortal and bearing his child. [New Latin Undina, from Latin unda, wave.]

un·di·rect·ed (ŭn′dĭ-rĕk′tĭd, -dī-rĕk′tĭd) adj. **1.** Without object or purpose. **2.** Having no prescribed destination. Said of mail.

un·dis·charged (ŭn′dĭs-chärjd′) adj. **1.** Not unloaded. Said of a ship's cargo. **2. a.** Not fulfilled: an undischarged obligation. **b.** Not paid: an undischarged debt.

un·dis·tin·guished (ŭn′dĭs-tĭng′gwĭsht) adj. **1.** Not set apart; without any distinction: His appearance was undistinguished. **2.** Having no particularly good features; mediocre.

un·dis·trib·u·ted (ŭn′dĭs-trĭb′yə-tĭd) adj. Logic. Not referring or applying to all members of a class. Said of a term or proposition.

un·do (ŭn-dōō′) v. **-did** (-dĭd′), **-done** (-dŭn′), **-doing, -does** (-dŭz′). —tr. **1.** To reverse or erase; cancel; annul. **2.** To untie, disassemble, or loosen: undo a shoelace. **3.** To open (a parcel, for example); unwrap. **4. a.** To ruin the reputation or prospects of. **b.** To throw into confusion; unsettle. —intr. To come open or undone. [Middle English undon, from Old English undōn, to unfasten, untie, annul, destroy : UN- + dōn, to DO.] **—un·do·er** n.

un·do·ing (ŭn-dōō'ĭng) *n.* **1.** The act of reversing or annulling something accomplished; cancellation. **2.** The act of unfastening or loosening. **3. a.** Ruin; destruction. **b.** The act of bringing to ruin. **c.** The cause of ruin; downfall.

un·doubt·ed (ŭn-dou'tĭd) *adj.* Accepted as beyond question.

un·doubt·ed·ly (ŭn-dou'tĭd-lē) *adv.* **1.** Without doubt. **2.** It is not to be doubted that. —See Usage note at **doubtless.**

un·dreamt-of (ŭn-drĕmpt'ŭv') *adj.* Also **un·dreamed-of** (ŭn-drĕmd'ŭv'). Barely or not entertained even in wishful fantasy: *undreamt-of success.*

un·dress (ŭn-drĕs') *v.* **-dressed, -dressing, -dresses.** —*tr.* **1.** To remove the clothing of; strip. **2.** To remove the bandages from (a wound or burn, for example). —*intr.* To take off one's clothing; strip. ~*n.* **1.** Informal as distinguished from formal dress or uniform. **2.** Nakedness or near nakedness.

un·dressed (ŭn-drĕst') *adj.* **1. a.** Naked. **b.** Not fully dressed. **2.** Not specially prepared or processed: *undressed leather.* **3. a.** Not prepared for cooking or eating. Said of certain meats. **b.** Without dressing or sauce. Said of a salad. **4.** Not treated or bandaged: *an undressed wound.*

un·due (ŭn-dōō', -dyōō') *adj.* **1.** Exceeding what is appropriate or normal; excessive: *"I was grateful, without showing undue excitement"* (Katherine Mansfield). **2.** Not just, proper, or legal: *undue use of power.* **3.** Not yet payable or due.

un·du·lant (ŭn'jōō-lənt, ŭn'dyə-, ŭn'də-) *adj.* Resembling waves in occurrence, appearance, or motion. [UNDUL(ATE) + -ANT.]

undulant fever *n.* **Brucellosis** *(see).*

un·du·late (ŭn'jōō-lāt', ŭn'dyə-, ŭn'də-) *v.* **-lated, -lating, -lates.** —*tr.* **1.** To cause to move in a smooth wavelike motion. **2.** To give a wavelike appearance or form to. —*intr.* **1.** To move in waves or in a smooth wavelike motion; ripple. **2.** To have a wavelike appearance or form. —See Synonyms at **swing.** ~*adj.* (ŭn'jōō-lĭt, -lāt', ŭn'dyə-, ŭn'də-). Also **un·du·la·ted** (-lā'tĭd). Having a wavy outline or appearance: *leaves with undulate margins.* [Late Latin *undulāre,* from *undula,* diminutive of Latin *unda,* wave.]

un·du·la·tion (ŭn'jōō-lā'shən, ŭn'dyə-, ŭn'də-) *n.* **1.** A regular rising and falling or movement to alternating sides; a movement in waves. **2.** A wavelike form, outline, or appearance. **3.** Any of a series of waves or wavelike segments; a pulsation.

un·du·la·to·ry (ŭn'jōō-lə-tôr'ē, ŭn'dyə-, -tōr'ē) *adj.* Of, pertaining to, or caused by undulation; undulating.

un·du·ly (ŭn-dōō'lē, -dyōō'lē) *adv.* **1.** Excessively; immoderately. **2.** In disregard of a legal or moral precept.

un·du·ti·ful (ŭn-dōō'tĭ-fəl, ŭn-dyōō'-) *adj.* **1.** Lacking a sense of duty. **2.** Unreliable or disobedient.

un·dy·ing (ŭn-dī'ĭng) *adj.* Endless; everlasting; immortal.

un·earned (ŭn-ûrnd') *adj.* **1.** Not gained by work or service. **2.** Not deserved. **3.** Not yet earned: *unearned interest.*

unearned income *n.* An income coming from property, interests, or other investments as opposed to wages and salaries.

unearned increment *n.* An increase in the value of a property resulting from factors independent of the owner's efforts, such as a general rise in demand for land.

un·earth (ŭn-ûrth') *tr.v.* **-earthed, -earthing, -earths.** **1.** To bring up out of the earth; dig up; uproot. **2.** To bring to light; discover.

un·earth·ly (ŭn-ûrth'lē) *adj.* **-lier, -liest.** **1.** Not of the earth; spiritual or supernatural. **2.** Ghostly; weird and unaccountable; unnatural: *"a shriek so loud, piercing and unearthly . . . that the blood seemed to freeze in my veins"* (W.H. Hudson). **3.** Ridiculously unreasonable or uncustomary; absurd: *out of bed at an unearthly hour.* —See Synonyms at **weird.** —**un·earth'li·ness** *n.*

un·ease (ŭn-ēz') *n.* A sense of discomfort or apprehension.

un·eas·y (ŭn-ē'zē) *adj.* **-ier, -iest.** **1.** Lacking a sense of security; anxious or apprehensive: *The farmers were uneasy until the crop was in.* **2.** Causing constraint or awkwardness: *an uneasy silence.* **3.** Awkward or unsure in manner; constrained: *uneasy with strangers.* **4.** Not conducive to or causing rest: *an uneasy sleep.* —**un·eas'i·ly** *adv.* —**un·eas'i·ness** *n.*

un·ed·u·cat·ed (ŭn-ĕj'ōō-kā'tĭd) *adj.* Not educated; especially, lacking in literacy. —See Synonyms at **ignorant.**

un·em·ploy·a·ble (ŭn'ĭm-ploi'ə-bəl) *adj.* Not able to find or keep a job. ~*n.* One who cannot be employed.

un·em·ployed (ŭn'ĭm-ploid') *adj.* **1.** Out of work; jobless. **2.** Not being used; idle.

un·em·ploy·ment (ŭn'ĭm-ploi'mənt) *n.* **1.** The state of being out of work. **2.** The number or percentage of people in a community who are out of work.

unemployment benefit *n.* A regular payment made by a government agency to an unemployed person, especially one who has been laid off. Also called "unemployment compensation."

un·en·light·ened (ŭn'ĭn-līt'nd) *adj.* **1.** Not educated; ignorant. **2.** Not informed of something. **3.** Prejudiced, superstitious, and unreasoning.

un·e·qual (ŭn-ē'kwəl) *adj.* **1.** Not the same in extent, quantity, rank, or social position. **2.** Consisting of or having ill-matched opponents: *an unequal running race.* **3.** Having unbalanced sides or parts; asymmetric. **4.** Not even or consistent; variable; irregular. **5.** Not having the required abilities; inadequate. Used with *to: "It was maddening to be unequal to many enterprises"* (D.H. Lawrence). ~*n.* One that is unequal. —**un·e·qual·ly** *adv.*

un·e·qualed, un·e·qualled (ŭn-ē'kwəld) *adj.* Not matched or paralleled by others of its kind; unrivaled.

un·e·quiv·o·cal (ŭn'ĭ-kwĭv'ə-kəl) *adj.* Admitting of no doubt or misunderstanding; unambiguous; clear. —**un·e·quiv·o·cal·ly** *adv.*

un·err·ing (ŭn'ûr'ĭng, -ĕr'ĭng) *adj.* Committing no mistakes; consistent, accurate. —**un·err·ing·ly** *adv.*

UNESCO (yōō-nĕs'kō). United Nations Educational, Scientific, and Cultural Organization.

un·es·sen·tial (ŭn'ə-sĕn'shəl) *adj.* Not necessary; not of importance. ~*n.* A nonessential.

un·e·ven (ŭn-ē'vən) *adj.* **-vener, -venest.** **1. a.** Not equal, as in size, length, or quality. **b.** Having ill-matched opponents. **2. a.** Not consistent or uniform: *an uneven color.* **b.** Not consistent in quality: *an uneven performance.* **3.** Not smooth or level: *uneven surface of a cobblestone road.* **4.** Not straight or parallel: *uneven margins.* **5.** Archaic. Not fair or equitable. **6.** Designating an odd number. —See Synonyms at **rough.** —**un·e·ven·ly** *adv.* —**un·e·ven·ness** *n.*

un·e·vent·ful (ŭn'ĭ-vĕnt'fəl) *adj.* Lacking in significant or disrupting incidents. —**un·e·vent·ful·ly** *adv.* —**un·e·vent·ful·ness** *n.*

un·ex·am·pled (ŭn'ĭg-zăm'pəld, -zäm'pəld) *adj.* Without precedent; unparalleled: *"Witchcraft blazed forth with unexampled virulence"* (Montague Summers).

un·ex·cep·tion·a·ble (ŭn'ĭk-sĕp'shən-ə-bəl) *adj.* Beyond any reasonable objection; quite satisfactory. —See Usage note at **unexceptional.** —**un·ex·cep·tion·a·ble·ness** *n.* —**un·ex·cep·tion·a·bly** *adv.*

un·ex·cep·tion·al (ŭn'ĭk-sĕp'shən-əl) *adj.* **1.** Not varying from the normal; usual; ordinary. **2.** Not subject to exceptions; absolute. —**un·ex·cep·tion·al·ly** *adv.*

Usage: Unexceptional and *unexceptionable* are not interchangeable. *Unexceptional* means "usual; ordinary"; *unexceptionable* means "not open to objection," "to which one cannot take exception." Compare: *Her argument was unexceptional* (it was familiar), *Her argument was unexceptionable* (it was quite acceptable).

un·ex·pect·ed (ŭn'ĭk-spĕk'tĭd) *adj.* Coming without warning; unforeseen. —**un·ex·pect·ed·ly** *adv.* —**un·ex·pect·ed·ness** *n.*

un·fail·ing (ŭn-fā'lĭng) *adj.* **1.** Constant; unflagging: *unfailing patience.* **2.** Inexhaustible; endless: *an unfailing supply.* **3.** Incapable of error; infallible. —**un·fail·ing·ly** *adv.*

un·fair (ŭn-fâr') *adj.* **-fairer, -fairest.** **1.** Not just or even-handed; biased: *an unfair decision.* **2.** Contrary to laws or conventions; unethical: *unfair trading.* —**un·fair·ly** *adv.* —**un·fair·ness** *n.*

un·faith·ful (ŭn-fāth'fəl) *adj.* **1.** Not adhering to a pledge or contract; disloyal. **2.** Having sexual relations with someone who is not one's spouse or long-term sexual partner; specifically, guilty of adultery. **3.** Not justly representing or reflecting the original; inaccurate: *an unfaithful translation.* **4.** Obsolete. Without or deficient in religious faith; unbelieving. —See Synonyms at **faithless.** —**un·faith·ful·ly** *adv.* —**un·faith·ful·ness** *n.*

un·fa·mil·iar (ŭn'fə-mĭl'yər) *adj.* **1.** Not within one's knowledge; strange: *unfamiliar faces.* **2.** Not being acquainted; not conversant: *unfamiliar with flying.* —**un·fa·mil·i·ar·i·ty** (ŭn'fə-mĭl-yăr'ə-tē, -mĭl'ē-ăr'ə-tē) *n.* —**un·fa·mil·iar·ly** *adv.*

un·fas·ten (ŭn-făs'ən, -fä'sən) *v.* **-tened, -tening, -tens.** —*tr.* To separate the connecting parts of; unloosen or open. —*intr.* To become loosened or separated.

un·fa·thered (ŭn-fä'thərd) *adj.* **1. a.** Having no father; fatherless. **b.** Having no known father; illegitimate; bastard. **2.** Of uncertain or unknown origin or authenticity: *unfathered rumors.*

un·fath·om·a·ble (ŭn-făth'əm-ə-bəl) *adj.* **1.** Too deep to be measured. **2.** Incomprehensible; inscrutable. —**un·fath·om·a·ble·ness** *n.* —**un·fath·om·a·bly** *adv.*

un·fa·vor·a·ble (ŭn-fā'vər-ə-bəl, -fā'vrə-bəl) *adj.* **1.** Unpromising; not propitious. **2.** Adverse; opposed. **3.** Harmful. **4.** Unpleasing. —**un·fa·vor·a·ble·ness** *n.* —**un·fa·vor·a·bly** *adv.*

un·feed (ŭn-fēd') *adj.* Not paid a fee.

un·feel·ing (ŭn-fē'lĭng) *adj.* **1.** Not sensitive to others' feelings; unsympathetic; callous. **2.** Having no physical feeling or sensation; insentient. —**un·feel·ing·ly** *adv.* —**un·feel·ing·ness** *n.*

un·feigned (ŭn-fānd') *adj.* Not simulated; genuine. —See Synonyms at **sincere.** —**un·feign·ed·ly** (ŭn-fā'nĭd-lē) *adv.*

un·fet·tered (ŭn-fĕt'ərd) *adj.* Unrestrained; free.

un·fin·ished (ŭn-fĭn'ĭsht) *adj.* **1.** Not brought to an end; incomplete: *unfinished business.* **2.** Not having received special processing; natural: *unfinished wood.*

un·fit (ŭn-fĭt') *adj.* **1.** Not meant or adapted for some usually specified purpose; inappropriate. Usually used with *for.* **2.** Below the required standard; unqualified. Usually used with *for.* **3.** Not in good health; in bad physical condition. ~*tr.v.* **unfitted, -fitting, -fits.** To cause to be unsuited or unqualified; disqualify. —**un·fit·ly** *adv.* —**un·fit·ness** *n.*

un·fix (ŭn-fĭks') *tr.v.* **-fixed, -fixing, -fixes.** To unfasten.

un·flag·ging (ŭn-flăg'ĭng) *adj.* Not weakening or stopping; untiring.

un·flap·pa·ble (ŭn-flăp'ə-bəl) *adj.* Informal. Not easily upset or excited, even in a crisis; calm. —**un·flap·pa·bil·i·ty** *n.*

un·fledged (ŭn-flĕjd') *adj.* **1.** Not yet sufficiently developed to fly. Said of a young bird lacking flight feathers. **2.** Inexperienced; immature, or untried.

un·flinch·ing (ŭn-flĭn'chĭng) *adj.* Without fear or indecision; unshrinking; resolute. —**un·flinch·ing·ly** *adv.*

un·fold (ŭn-fōld') *v.* **-folded, -folding, -folds.** —*tr.* **1.** To open and spread out; extend (something folded). **2.** To remove the coverings from; disclose to view. **3.** To reveal gradually by written or spoken explanation; make known. —*intr.* **1.** To become spread out; open out. **2.** To be revealed gradually to the understanding. **3.** To develop.

un·for·get·ta·ble (ŭn′fər-gĕt′ə-bəl) *adj.* Earning a permanent place in the memory; memorable. —**un·for·get′ta·bly** *adv.*

un·formed (ŭn-fôrmd′) *adj.* **1.** Having no definite shape or structure; shapeless and unorganized. **2.** Not yet developed to maturity. **3.** Not yet given a physical existence; uncreated.

un·for·tu·nate (ŭn-fôr′chə-nĭt) *adj.* **1.** Characterized by undeserved lack of good fortune; unlucky. **2.** Causing misfortune; disastrous. **3.** Regrettable; deplorable: *an unfortunate lack of good manners.* ~*n.* A victim of bad luck, disaster, poverty, or other misfortune. —**un·for′tu·nate·ly** *adv.* —**un·for′tu·nate·ness** *n.*

un·found·ed (ŭn-foun′dĭd) *adj.* **1.** Not yet established. **2.** Not based on fact or sound evidence; groundless: *unfounded accusations.* —**un·found′ed·ly** *adv.* —**un·found′ed·ness** *n.*

un·freeze (ŭn-frēz′) *v.* **-froze** (-frōz′), **-frozen** (-frō′zən), **-freezing, -freezes.** —*tr.* **1.** To thaw out. **2.** To ease or eliminate restrictions on (wages, prices, credit, or manufactured goods). —*intr.* To thaw.

un·fre·quent·ed (ŭn′frĭ-kwĕn′tĭd, ŭn-frē′kwən-tĭd) *adj.* Receiving few or no visitors.

un·friend·ly (ŭn-frĕnd′lē) *adj.* **-lier, -liest. 1.** Not disposed to friendship; hostile; disagreeable. **2.** Indicating a bad prospect; unfavorable. —**un·friend′li·ness** *n.*

un·frock (ŭn-frŏk′) *tr.v.* **-frocked, -frocking, -frocks.** To strip of priestly privileges and functions.

un·fruit·ful (ŭn-frōōt′fəl) *adj.* **1.** Not bearing fruit or offspring; barren. **2.** Unprofitable or unsuccessful. —See Synonyms at **sterile.** —**un·fruit′ful·ly** *adv.* —**un·fruit′ful·ness** *n.*

un·furl (ŭn-fûrl′) *v.* **-furled, -furling, -furls.** —*tr.* To spread or open out; unroll. —*intr.* To become spread or opened out.

un·gain·ly (ŭn-gān′lē) *adj.* **-lier, -liest. 1.** Without grace or ease of movement; clumsy. **2.** Difficult to move or use; unwieldy. —See Synonyms at **awkward.** ~*adv.* In a clumsy manner. —**un·gain′li·ness** *n.*

un·gen·er·ous (ŭn-jĕn′ər-əs) *adj.* **1.** Not generous; stingy. **2.** Harsh in judgment; unkind. —**un·gen′er·ous·ly** *adv.*

un·get-at-a·ble (ŭn′gĕt-ăt′ə-bəl) *adj. Informal.* Inaccessible.

un·girt (ŭn-gûrt′) *adj. Archaic.* **1.** Having the belt, girdle, or other restraining or supporting garment removed or loosened. **2.** Loose or free; slack.

un·glued (ŭn-glōōd′) *adj.* Loosened or separated; unfastened. —**come unglued.** *Slang.* To lose one's composure; fall apart emotionally.

un·god·ly (ŭn-gŏd′lē) *adj.* **-lier, -liest. 1.** Not revering God; impious. **2.** Sinful; wicked. **3.** *Informal.* **a.** Outrageous; unreasonable: *He called at an ungodly hour.* **b.** Very unpleasant or annoying: *an ungodly din.* —**un·god′li·ness** *n.*

un·gov·ern·a·ble (ŭn-gŭv′ər-nə-bəl) *adj.* Not able to be controlled: *an ungovernable temper.* —See Synonyms at **unruly.** —**un·gov′ern·a·ble·ness** *n.* —**un·gov′ern·a·bly** *adv.*

un·gra·cious (ŭn-grā′shəs) *adj.* **1.** Lacking social manners; rude. **2.** Not welcome or acceptable; unattractive: *an ungracious task.* —**un·gra′cious·ly** *adv.* —**un·gra′cious·ness** *n.*

un·gram·mat·i·cal (ŭn′grə-măt′ĭ-kəl) *adj.* **1.** Not in accord with the rules of a prescriptive grammar. **2.** Not in accord with a language as used by a native speaker.

un·grate·ful (ŭn-grāt′fəl) *adj.* **1.** Without due feeling or expression of gratitude, thanks, or appreciation. **2.** Not agreeable or pleasant; repellent: *"I will not perform the ungrateful task of comparing cases of failure"* (Abraham Lincoln). —**un·grate′ful·ly** *adv.* —**un·grate′ful·ness** *n.*

un·grudg·ing (ŭn-grŭj′ĭng) *adj.* Generous; willing or freely given: *ungrudging praise.* —**un·grudg′ing·ly** *adv.*

un·gual (ŭng′gwəl) *adj.* **1.** Of or pertaining to the fingernails or toenails. **2.** Of, resembling, or bearing a hoof, nail, or claw. [Latin *unguis,* UNGUIS.]

un·guard·ed (ŭn-gär′dĭd) *adj.* **1.** Without guard or protection; vulnerable. **2.** Unprepared or imprudent; incautious: *caught in an unguarded moment.* **3.** Free from guile; open. —**un·guard′ed·ly** *adv.* —**un·guard′ed·ness** *n.*

un·guent (ŭng′gwənt) *n.* A soothing salve; an ointment. [Middle English, from Latin *unguentum,* from *unguere,* to anoint.]

un·guic·u·late (ŭng-gwĭk′yə-lĭt, -lāt′) *adj.* **1.** *Zoology.* Having nails or claws. Said of a mammal. **2.** *Botany.* Having a claw-shaped base: *unguiculate petals.* ~*n.* A mammal having nails or claws. [New Latin *unguiculatus,* from Latin *unguiculus,* fingernail, diminutive of *unguis,* UNGUIS.]

un·guis (ŭng′gwĭs) *n., pl.* **-gues** (-gwēz′). **1.** A nail, claw, hoof, or clawlike structure. **2.** The clawlike base of some petals. [Latin *unguis,* claw, nail.]

un·gu·la (ŭng′gyə-lə) *n., pl.* **-lae** (-lē). *Mathematics.* **1.** A cone or cylinder truncated by a plane not parallel to its base. **2.** *Rare.* A hoof. [Latin, "hoof" (from its shape), diminutive of UNGUIS.] —**un·gu·lar** (ŭng′gyə-lər) *adj.*

un·gu·late (ŭng′gyə-lĭt, -lāt′) *adj.* **1. a.** Having hoofs. **b.** Hooflike. **2.** Of or belonging to the former order Ungulata, now divided into the orders Perissodactyla and Artiodactyla, and including hoofed mammals such as horses, cattle, deer, and pigs. ~*n.* An ungulate mammal. [Late Latin *ungulātus,* from Latin *ungula,* diminutive of *unguis,* UNGUIS.]

un·gu·li·grade (ŭng′gyə-lə-grād′) *adj.* Walking on hoofs. Said of

horses and similar animals. [Latin *ungula,* hoof (see **ungula**) + -GRADE.]

Unh The symbol for the element unnilhexium.

un·hal·low (ŭn-hăl′ō) *tr.v.* **-lowed, -lowing, -lows.** *Archaic.* To profane; desecrate.

un·hal·lowed (ŭn-hăl′ōd) *adj.* **1.** Not hallowed or consecrated. **2.** Immoral; wicked.

un·hand (ŭn-hănd′) *tr.v.* **-handed, -handing, -hands.** To remove one's hand or hands from; let go: *"Unhand me, you villain."*

un·hand·y (ŭn-hăn′dē) *adj.* **-ier, -iest. 1.** Difficult to handle or manage; unwieldy; cumbersome: *an unhandy desk.* **2.** Lacking manual skill or dexterity. —**un·hand′i·ly** *adv.* —**un·hand′i·ness** *n.*

un·hap·py (ŭn-hăp′ē) *adj.* **-pier, -piest. 1.** Not happy or joyful; sad. **2.** Not bringing or enjoying good fortune; unlucky. **3.** Not suitable or tactful; inappropriate. —**un·hap·pi·ly** (ŭn-hăp′ə-lē) *adv.* —**un·hap·pi·ness** *n.*

un·har·ness (ŭn-här′nĭs) *tr.v.* **-nessed, -nessing, -nesses. 1.** To remove the harness from. **2.** To release or liberate (energy or emotions, for example). **3.** To take armor off (someone).

un·health·y (ŭn-hĕl′thē) *adj.* **-ier, -iest. 1.** In a state of ill health; sick. **2.** Characterizing or symptomatic of ill health: *an unhealthy pallor.* **3.** Causing or conducive to poor health; unwholesome. **4. a.** Harmful to character or moral health; corrupting. **b.** Indicating a morbid or disturbed mental state: *an unhealthy interest in violence.* **5.** *Informal.* Of a risky nature; dangerous. —**un·health′i·ly** (ŭn-hĕl′thə-lē) *adv.* —**un·health′i·ness** *n.*

un·heard (ŭn-hûrd′) *adj.* **1.** Not sensed by the ear. **2.** Not given a hearing; not listened to. **3.** *Archaic.* Obscure; unknown.

un·heard-of (ŭn-hûrd′ŭv′, -ŏv′) *adj.* **1.** Not previously known; unknown. **2.** Without precedent. **3.** Highly offensive or outrageous.

un·hes·i·tat·ing (ŭn-hĕz′ə-tā′tĭng) *adj.* **1.** Prompt; ready. **2.** Unfaltering; steadfast. —**un·hes′i·tat·ing·ly** *adv.*

un·hinge (ŭn-hĭnj′) *tr.v.* **-hinged, -hinging, -hinges. 1.** To remove (a door) from the hinges. **2.** To confuse; disrupt. **3.** To derange; unbalance: *He was unhinged by a traumatic shock.*

un·hitch (ŭn-hĭch′) *tr.v.* **-hitched, -hitching, -hitches.** To release from or as if from a hitch; unfasten.

un·ho·ly (ŭn-hō′lē) *adj.* **-lier, -liest. 1.** Not hallowed or consecrated. **2.** Wicked; immoral. **3.** *Informal.* Outrageous; unreasonable. —**un·ho·li·ly** *adv.* —**un·ho·li·ness** *n.*

un·hook (ŭn-hōōk′) *tr.v.* **-hooked, -hooking, -hooks. 1.** To release or remove from a hook. **2.** To unfasten the hooks of.

un·hoped-for (ŭn-hōpt′fôr′) *adj.* Not expected but pleasant; beyond what was anticipated.

un·horse (ŭn-hôrs′) *tr.v.* **-horsed, -horsing, -horses. 1.** To cause to fall from a horse. Usually used in the passive. **2.** To overthrow or dislodge; upset.

un·hou·seled (ŭn-hou′zəld) *adj. Obsolete.* Not having received the Eucharist. Said of a dying or dead person. [UN- (not) + HOUSEL.]

uni- *prefix.* Indicates the state of being single or of having or consisting of only one; for example, **unicameral, unicostate.** [Latin, from *ūnus,* one.]

U·ni·at (yōō′nē-ăt′) *n.* Also **U·ni·ate** (yōō′nē-ĭt, -āt′). A member of a Uniat Church. ~*adj.* Of or pertaining to a Uniat Church or its members, practices, or doctrines. [Russian *uniyat,* from Polish *uniat,* from *unja,* "church-union" (of the Greek and the Roman Catholic Churches), from Late Latin *ūniō,* UNION.]

Uniat Church *n.* Also **Uniate Church.** Any Eastern Orthodox Church that acknowledges the supremacy of the pope but retains its own distinctive liturgy.

u·ni·ax·i·al (yōō′nē-ăk′sē-əl) *adj.* **1.** Having only one axis; monaxial. Said especially of plants having a single main stem. **2.** Having one direction along which double refraction of light does not take place. Said of a crystal.

u·ni·cam·er·al (yōō′nĭ-kăm′ər-əl) *adj.* Having or consisting of a single legislative chamber. [UNI- + CAMERA (chamber).]

UNICEF (yōō′nĭ-sĕf′) United Nations International Children's Emergency Fund.

u·ni·cel·lu·lar (yōō′nĭ-sĕl′yə-lər) *adj. Biology.* Consisting of one cell; one-celled: *unicellular organisms.*

u·ni·col·or (yōō′nĭ-kŭl′ər) *adj.* Of a single color; monochromatic.

u·ni·corn (yōō′nə-kôrn′) *n.* **1.** An imaginary creature usually represented as a white horse with a spiraled horn projecting from its forehead. **2.** A two-horned animal, possibly the wild ox or rhinoceros, mentioned in the Old Testament. [Middle English, from Old French, from Latin *ūnicornis* : UNI- + *cornū,* horn.]

u·ni·cos·tate (yōō′nĭ-kŏs′tāt′) *adj.* Having a single main costa, rib, or riblike part: *a unicostate leaf.* [UNI- + COSTA.]

u·ni·cy·cle (yōō′nĭ-sī′kəl) *n.* A vehicle consisting of a frame mounted over a single wheel and usually propelled by pedals. Also called "monocycle." —**u·ni·cy·clist** (yōō′nĭ-sī′klĭst) *n.*

un·i·den·ti·fied flying object (ŭn′ī-dĕn′tĭ-fīd′) *n.* **1.** *Abbr.* **UFO, U.F.O.** A flying or apparently flying object of an unknown nature. **2.** A flying saucer (*see*).

u·ni·di·men·sion·al (yōō′nĭ-dī-mĕn′shən-əl) *adj.* **1.** Existing in one dimension only. **2.** Lacking depth; superficial.

u·ni·di·rec·tion·al (yōō′nĭ-dĭ-rĕk′shən-əl) *adj.* Having, operating, or moving in one direction only.

Unification Church *n.* A contemporary religious sect that combines elements of Christian fundamentalism and Buddhism. It was founded by Sun Myung Moon, a Korean evangelist.

unified field theory *n.* A physical theory that combines the treatment of two or more types of fields in order to deduce previously unrecognized interrelationships; especially, such a theory, as yet unidentified, unifying the theories of nuclear, electromagnetic, and gravitational forces.

u·ni·fi·lar (yōō′nĭ-fī′lər) *adj.* Having or utilizing only one thread, wire, fiber, or the like.

u·ni·fo·li·ate (yōō′nĭ-fō′lē-ĭt, -āt′) *adj.* Having a single leaf.

u·ni·fo·li·o·late (yōō′nĭ-fō′lē-ə-lāt′) *adj.* Compound in structure, but having a single leaflet.

u·ni·form (yōō′nə-fôrm′) *adj.* **1. a.** Always the same; unchanging; unvarying: *a uniform gait.* **b.** Without fluctuation or variation; consistent; regular: *a uniform flow.* **2.** Being the same as another or others; identical; consonant: *a uniform size.* **3.** Consistent in appearance; having an unvaried texture, color, or design. —See Synonyms at **steady.** ~*n.* **1.** Distinctive dress intended to identify those who wear it as members of a specific group: *soldiers in uniform.* **2.** A single outfit of such dress. ~*tr.v.* **uniformed, -forming, -forms. 1.** To make uniform. **2.** To provide with or dress in a uniform. [Old French *uniforme,* from Latin *ūniformis,* of one form : UNI- + -FORM.] —**u·ni·for·mi·ty** (yōō′nə-fôr′mə-tē), **u·ni·form·ness** *n.* —**u·ni·form·ly** *adv.*

u·ni·for·mi·tar·i·an·ism (yōō′nə-fôr′mə-târ′ē-ə-nĭz′əm) *n. Geology.* The theory that all geological phenomena can be explained as the result of existing forces having operated in the past. —**u·ni·for·mi·tar·i·an** *adj. & n.*

u·ni·fy (yōō′nə-fī′) *v.* **-fied, -fying, -fies.** —*tr.* **1.** To make into a unit; consolidate. **2.** To make uniform. —*intr.* To be made into a unit. [French *unifier,* from Late Latin *ūnificāre* : UNI- + Latin *facere,* to make.] —**u·ni·fi·ca·tion** (yōō′nə-fĭ-kā′shən) *n.* —**u·ni·fi·er** *n.*

u·ni·lat·er·al (yōō′nĭ-lăt′ər-əl) *adj.* **1. a.** Of, on, pertaining to, having, or affecting only one side. **b.** Performed or undertaken by only one side: *unilateral disarmament.* **2.** Obligating only one of two or more parties, nations, or persons: *a unilateral contract.* **3.** Emphasizing or recognizing only one side of a subject. **4.** Tracing the lineage of one parent only: *a unilateral genealogy.* Compare **bilateral. 5.** *Botany.* Having leaves or other parts on one side of an axis only. —**u·ni·lat·er·al·ly** *adv.*

u·ni·lat·er·al·ist (yōō′nĭ-lăt′ər-ə-lĭst) *n.* One who favors unilateral action, especially unilateral disarmament. Compare **multilateralist.** —**u·ni·lat·er·al·ism** *n.* —**u·ni·lat·er·al·ist** *adj.*

u·ni·loc·u·lar (yōō′nĭ-lŏk′yə-lər) *adj. Botany.* Having a single compartment or chamber: *a unilocular ovary.* [UNI- + LOCULUS.]

un·i·mag·in·a·ble (ŭn′ĭ-măj′ĭ-nə-bəl) *adj.* Beyond one's comprehension; inconceivable. —**un·i·mag·in·a·bly** *adv.*

un·im·peach·a·ble (ŭn′ĭm-pē′chə-bəl) *adj.* **1.** Beyond doubt; unquestionable. **2.** Blameless; beyond reproach. —**un·im·peach·a·bil·i·ty** (ŭn′ĭm-pē′chə-bĭl′ə-tē) *n.* —**un·im·peach·a·bly** *adv.*

un·im·proved (ŭn′ĭm-prōōvd′) *adj.* **1.** Not improved; not bettered. **2.** Not made use of or put to advantage. **3.** Not built upon or cultivated so as to increase in value. Said of land.

un·in·hab·it·a·ble (ŭn′ĭn-hăb′ĭ-tə-bəl) *adj.* Not fit for habitation.

un·in·hib·it·ed (ŭn′ĭn-hĭb′ə-tĭd) *adj.* **1.** Not inhibited; open: *uninhibited laughter.* **2.** Free from external social or moral constraints. —**un·in·hib·it·ed·ly** *adv.* —**un·in·hib·it·ed·ness** *n.*

un·in·spired (ŭn′ĭn-spīrd′) *adj.* Not stimulating to the mind or imagination; mediocre; dull.

un·in·tel·li·gent (ŭn′ĭn-tĕl′ə-jənt) *adj.* **1.** Not intelligent; stupid. **2.** Not endowed with intelligence. Said of nonsentient beings. —**un·in·tel·li·gence** *n.* —**un·in·tel·li·gent·ly** *adv.*

un·in·ten·tion·al (ŭn′ĭn-tĕn′shən-əl) *adj.* Not deliberate or intended. —**un·in·ten·tion·al·ly** *adv.*

un·in·ter·est (ŭn-ĭn′trĭst, -tər-ĭst) *n.* Lack of interest.

un·in·ter·est·ed (ŭn-ĭn′trĭs-tĭd, -ĭn′tə-rĕs′tĭd) *adj.* **1.** Not interested; indifferent. **2.** Not having an interest, especially a financial interest. —See Usage note at **disinterested.** —**un·in·ter·est·ed·ly** *adv.* —**un·in·ter·est·ed·ness** *n.*

un·in·ter·rup·ted (ŭn′ĭn-tə-rŭp′tĭd) *adj.* Without interruption; continuous. —**un·in·ter·rup·ted·ly** *adv.*

u·ni·nu·cle·ate (yōō′nĭ-nōō′klē-ĭt, -āt′, yōō′nĭ-nyōō′-) *adj.* Having a single nucleus. Said of a cell.

un·ion (yōōn′yən) *n.* **1.** The act of uniting or the state of being united. **2.** A combination so formed; especially, an alliance or confederation of persons, parties, or political entities for mutual interest or benefit. **3.** *Symbol* **U** *Mathematics.* A set consisting of all members of two or more given sets. Compare **intersection. 4.** Agreement, especially resulting from an alliance; concord; harmony. **5. a.** The state of matrimony. **b.** A marriage. **c.** Sexual intercourse. **6.** Formerly in Britain: **a.** A combination of parishes for joint administration of relief for the poor. **b.** A workhouse maintained by such a union. **7.** A **labor union** (*see*). **8.** A coupling device for connecting parts, as pipes or rods. **9.** A device on a flag or ensign, occupying the upper inner corner or the entire field, that signifies the union of two or more sovereignties. **10. Union. a.** An organization or society at a college or university that deals with student administration and provides facilities for recreation. **b.** A building housing such facilities. **11.** A piece of fabric made from two different kinds of yarn. —**the Union. 1.** The United States of America, especially during the Civil War. **2. a.** The union of the English and Scottish thrones (1603–1707) or parliaments (from 1707). **b.** The union of Great Britain and Ireland (1801–1920) or of Great Britain and Northern Ireland (since 1920).

A MYTHICAL SYMBOL OF PURITY
A beast that looks as if it should exist

The unicorn has a long pedigree. It was portrayed on Assyrian reliefs, was firmly accepted by the Greeks and Romans, and was familiar in art and legend in medieval Europe, the Middle East, and China. Supposedly, it lived in India, and the myth may have originated in garbled descriptions of the one-horned Indian rhinoceros. In European art the unicorn hunt was a favorite subject and the animal remains a common heraldic beast. Its true significance, however, is allegorical. The unicorn was portrayed as pure white—a symbol of purity, often of Christ himself. The horn was believed to have magical properties and "unicorn horn"—often from a rhinoceros or narwhal (a single-horned whale)—was much valued as a talisman.

MEDIEVAL MYTH *The unicorn in this Gothic tapestry shows in its body the attributes of a horse and in its beard and cloven hooves those of a goat. The common medieval motif of a lady with a unicorn recalls the myth that the animal could be caught only by a virgin.*

~*adj.* Of or pertaining to a labor union. [Middle English, from Late Latin *ūniō* (stem *ūniōn-*), unity, from Latin *ūnus,* one.]

union card *n.* A membership card in a labor union.

union catalogue *n.* A library catalogue combining the contents of a number of catalogues or the contents of more than one library.

un·ion·ism (yōōn′yə-nĭz′əm) *n.* **1.** The principle or theory of forming a union. **2.** The principles, theory, or system of unions, especially labor unions. **3.** Loyalty to a union, especially to a labor union. **4. Unionism.** Loyalty to the Federal government during the Civil War. **5. Unionism.** Loyalty to the Union of Great Britain and Ireland or Northern Ireland. —**un·ion·ist** *n.*

Unionist Party *n.* Formerly, the dominant political party of Northern Ireland, identified with the Union with Britain.

un·ion·ize (yōōn′yə-nīz′) *v.* **-ized, -izing, -izes.** —*tr.* **1.** To organize (a group of workers) into a labor union. **2.** To recruit into a labor union. —*intr.* **1.** To organize or form a labor union. **2.** To join a labor union. —**un·ion·i·za·tion** *n.*

Union Jack *n.* **1.** The flag of the United Kingdom. Also officially called the "Union Flag." **2. union jack.** Any flag consisting entirely of a union. [UNION (device on a flag, specifically the combined

UNION OF SOVIET SOCIALIST REPUBLICS

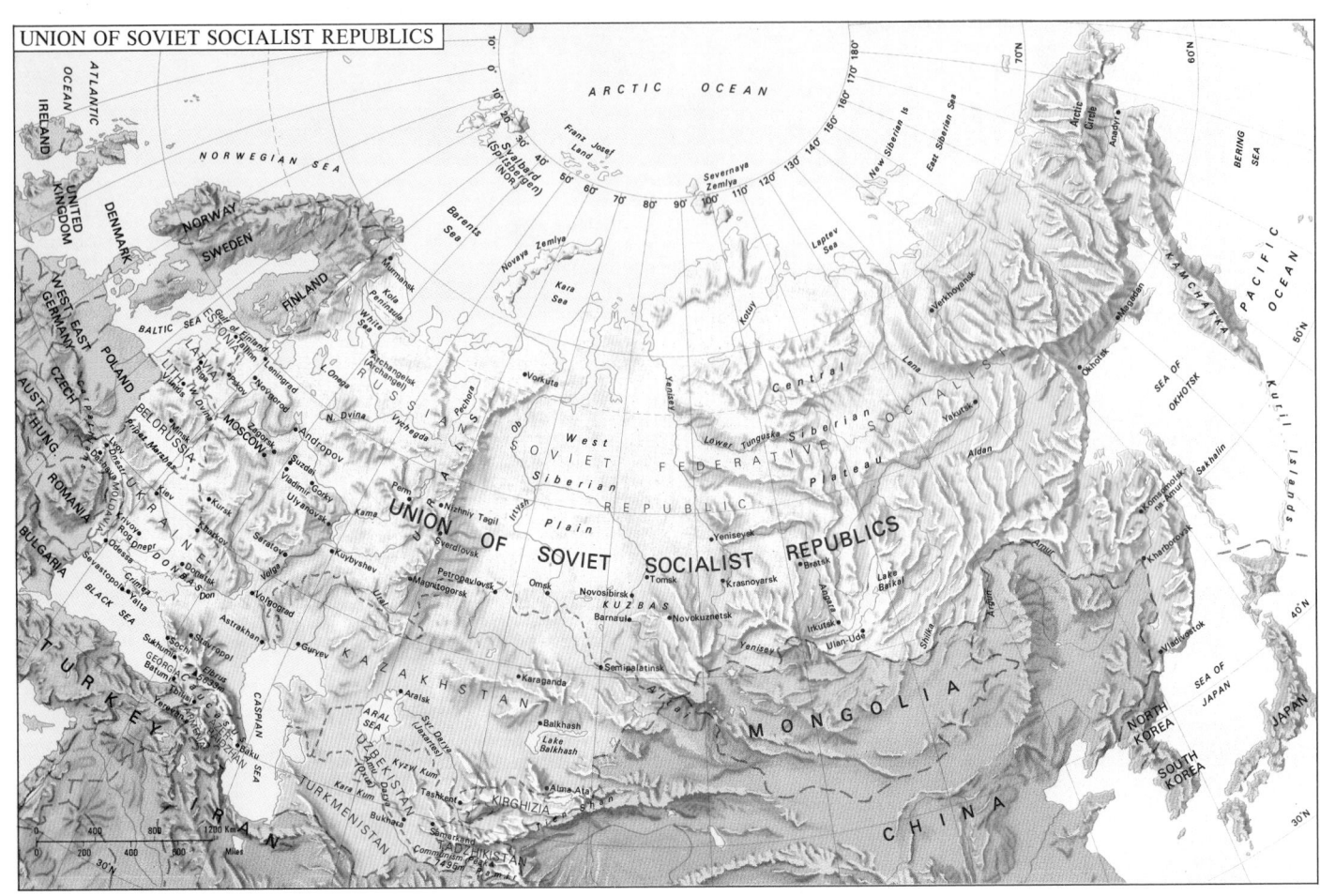

crosses of St. George, St. Andrew, and St. Patrick) + JACK (flag).]

Union of Soviet Socialist Republics. *Abbr.* **USSR, U.S.S.R.** Also **Soviet Union.** Formerly **Rus·sia** (rŭsh'ə). Federation of 15 national republics lying in eastern Europe and northern Asia, in extent the largest, and in population the third-largest, country in the world. The population is concentrated west of the Urals, in the Volga-Baikal belt, and in central Asia; Moscow, Leningrad, and Kiev are the biggest cities. The largely industrial economy is centrally planned. The country is self-sufficient in most minerals and in energy, and its chief exports are machinery, crude oil, natural gas, iron and steel, timber, and coal, mostly to other Comecon countries. Cereals, potatoes, sugar beet, livestock, and cotton are the main farm products. A unified Russian state emerged when several principalities united under Moscow (15th century) and gradually expanded into Asia. The Russian empire became a great power in the 18th century, and by 1914 its boundaries were roughly those of today. The Revolution (1917) brought Lenin and the Communists to power, and the U.S.S.R. was set up (1922). Area, 22,402,200 square kilometers (8,649,539 square miles). Population, 262,500,-000. Capital, Moscow.

union shop *n.* A business or other place of employment whose employees are required to join an often named labor union within a stated period after being hired. Compare **closed shop, open shop.**

union suit *n.* An undershirt and underdrawers combined in a single garment.

u·nip·a·rous (yo͞o-nĭp'ər-əs) *adj.* **1.** Producing only one offspring at a time. **2.** Having produced only one offspring. Said of a woman. **3.** *Botany.* Forming a single axis at each branching. Said of some flower clusters. [UNI- + -PAROUS.]

u·ni·per·son·al (yo͞o'nĭ-pûr'sən-əl) *adj.* **1.** Being manifested as or existing in the form of only one person: *a unipersonal spirit.* **2.** *Grammar.* Used only in one person; specifically, used only in the third person singular. Said of certain verbs, for example *snows.*

u·ni·pla·nar (yo͞o'nĭ-plā'nər, -när') *adj.* Situated or occurring in one plane.

u·ni·po·lar (yo͞o'nĭ-pō'lər) *adj.* **1.** *Physics.* Having, acting by means of, or produced by a single pole. **2.** *Anatomy.* Of or designating a nerve cell having a single process extending from the cell body.

u·nique (yo͞o-nēk') *adj.* **1.** Being the only one of its kind; solitary; sole. **2.** Being without an equal or equivalent; unparalleled. **3.** *Informal.* Outstanding; remarkable. **4.** *Mathematics.* Giving, having, or designating a single solution: *a unique solution to an equation.* —See Synonyms at **single.** [French, from Latin *ūnicus,* only, sole.] —**u·nique·ly** *adv.* —**u·nique·ness** *n.*

> **Usage:** The absolute sense of the word *unique* precludes its use

in any comparative way. In traditional usage, intensifying adverbs (such as *more, most, rather, very,* or *somewhat*) are avoided. Appropriate substitutes for *unique* can usually be found among *unusual, remarkable, rare, exceptional,* or the like, which are weaker and can be qualified freely. Like other absolute words such as *chief* and *unanimous,* however, *unique* can be modified by words like *almost* and *nearly.* Phrases such as *the most unique,* in the sense of "most unusual," are often encountered in casual speech, and suggest that a less absolute sense has emerged in modern English, although this readily attracts criticism.

u·ni·sex (yo͞o'nĭ-sĕks') *adj.* **1.** Designed to be worn or used by people of either sex: *a unisex sauna.* **2.** Selling or using unisex goods.

u·ni·sex·u·al (yo͞o'nĭ-sĕk'sho͞o-əl) *adj.* **1.** Of only one sex. **2.** *Biology.* Having either male or female sexual organs but not both. —**u·ni·sex·u·al·i·ty** (yo͞o'nĭ-sĕk'sho͞o-ăl'ə-tē) *n.* —**u·ni·sex·u·al·ly** *adv.*

u·ni·son (yo͞o'nə-sən, -zən) *n.* **1. a.** Identity of musical pitch; the interval of a perfect prime. **b.** The agreement or coincidence in pitch of musical parts. **c.** The performance or combination of musical parts at the same pitch or in octaves. **2.** A speaking of the same words simultaneously by two or more speakers. **3.** An instance of agreement; concord; harmony. —**in unison. 1.** In harmony or agreement. **2.** Simultaneously. [Old French, from Late Latin *ūnisonus,* of the same sound : UNI- + Latin *sonus,* sound.]

u·nis·o·nous (yo͞o-nĭs'ə-nəs) *adj.* Also **u·nis·o·nal** (-nəl), **u·nis·o·nant** (-nənt). Sounding or composed to sound in unison.

u·nit (yo͞o'nĭt) *n. Abbr.* **u. 1. a.** A single individual or entity. **b.** An individual, group, structure, or other entity regarded as an elementary structural or functional constituent of a whole. **2.** A group regarded as a distinct entity within a larger group. **3. a.** A mechanical part or module. **b.** An entire apparatus or the equipment that performs a specific function. **c.** A group of people performing a usually specified function: *an editorial unit.* **4.** A precise quantity in terms of which the magnitudes of other quantities of the same kind can be stated. **5. a.** The number immediately to the left of the decimal point in the Arabic numeral system. **b.** The smallest positive integer; one. **6.** A single share in a unit trust. **7.** A place in a building or complex set aside for a specified activity: *an intensive care unit.* **8.** A piece of furniture to be fitted and used with complementary pieces: *a kitchen unit.* **9.** *Military.* **a.** An organized tactical or administrative group that is a subdivision of a larger group. **b.** A large piece of equipment, such as a tank or ship. **10.** An amount of a drug required to produce a specific result.

~*adj.* Designating or having a value of one in some unitary system: *a line of unit length.* [16th century : from Latin *ūnus,* one, probably by analogy with *digit* (used to replace *unity* as a translation of Greek *monas*, MONAD, in Euclid).]

Unit. Unitarian; Unitarianism.

U·ni·tar·i·an (yōō'nə-târ'ē-ən) *n.* **1.** A monotheist who rejects the doctrine of the Trinity. Compare **Trinitarian.** **2.** *Abbr.* **Unit.** A member of a Christian denomination that rejects the doctrine of the Trinity and emphasizes freedom and tolerance in religious belief and the autonomy of each congregation. See **Universalist.** —*adj. Abbr.* **Unit.** Of, pertaining to, or supporting the Unitarians or their beliefs. [New Latin *unitarius*, from Latin *ūnitās*, UNITY.] —**U·ni·tar·i·an·ism** *n.*

u·ni·tar·y (yōō'nə-tĕr'ē) *adj.* **1.** Of, pertaining to, or characteristic of a unit. **2.** Having the nature of a unit; whole. **3.** Based on or characterized by unity. **4.** Serving or used as a unit, especially of measurement. **5.** Pertaining to or designating a political system in which all governing power rests with a central government.

unit cell *n.* The smallest group of atoms, ions, or molecules having a spatial configuration characteristic of a particular crystal lattice.

unit character *n. Genetics.* A character inherited as a single unit and determined by a single gene.

u·nite (yōō-nīt') *v.* **united, uniting, unites.** —*tr.* **1.** To bring together into a whole. **2.** To bring together or combine (people) in interest, purpose, or action, as in an association. **3.** To join (a couple) in marriage. **4.** To cause to adhere; bond. **5.** To have or demonstrate in combination: *He unites common sense with vision.* —*intr.* **1.** To become or seem to become joined, formed, or combined into a unit. **2.** To join and act together in a common purpose or endeavor. **3.** To be or become bound together by adhesion. —See Synonyms at **join.** [Middle English *uniten,* from Late Latin *ūnīre* (past participle *ūnītus*), from Latin *ūnus*, one.]

u·nit·ed (yōō-nī'tĭd) *adj.* **1.** Joined; combined. **2.** Produced by two or more people acting jointly. **3.** Being in agreement. —**u·nit·ed·ly** *adv.*

United Ar·ab E·mir·ates (ăr'əb ĭ-mîr'ĭts, -āts'). Formerly **Tru·cial States** (trōō'shəl). Federation of seven emirates (Abu Dhabi, Ajman, Dubai, Fujairah, Ras al Khaimah, Sharjah, and Umm al Qaiwain) on the southern coast of the Persian Gulf. Most of the land is flat, sandy desert. The mainstay of the economy is petroleum production. The seven emirates, known as the "Pirate Coast," concluded a treaty with Britain (1853), and after 1892 Britain looked after their foreign affairs and defense. The present federation (formed 1971) has a friendship treaty with Britain. A single council of ministers replaced the emirate ministries in 1974. Area, 83,600 square kilometers (32,278 square miles). Population, 1,000,000. Capital, Abu Dhabi. See map at **Gulf States.**

United Arab Republic. *Abbr.* **UAR, U.A.R.** The union of the Arab Republic of Egypt and the Syrian Arab Republic (1958–61).

United Church of Christ *n.* A Protestant denomination founded in 1957 by a merger of the Congregational Christian Church and the Evangelical and Reformed Church.

United Kingdom. *Abbr.* **UK, U.K.** Official name **United Kingdom of Great Britain and Northern Ireland.** Constitutional monarchy of northwest Europe, comprising England, Wales, Scotland, and Northern Ireland. Manufacturing is the largest sector of its economy, employing some 30 percent of the work force, and the main exports are machinery, chemicals, crude oil (extracted from the North Sea since the mid-1970's), and motor vehicles. The country is self-sufficient in energy, fossil fuels providing 95 percent of its needs. Agriculture employs only 2 percent of workers, yet provides 50 percent of the nation's food. Some 30 percent of workers are in the public sector. The country joined the European Economic Community in 1973. London, Birmingham, and Glasgow are the major cities. Wales became an English principality in 1284. Scotland and England were officially joined as Great Britain in 1707. The United Kingdom was formed by the union of Great Britain and Ireland in 1801, but southern Ireland broke away in 1921. Area, 244,046 square kilometers (94,201 square miles). Population, 55,700,000. Capital, London.

United Methodist Church *n.* A Protestant church formed in 1968 by the union of the Methodist Church and the Evangelical United Brethren.

United Nations *n. Abbr.* **UN, U.N.** An international organization of independent countries, with headquarters in New York City, formed in 1945 to promote international security and cooperation. See feature, next page.

United Nations Trust Territory *n.* A trust territory *(see).*

United Provinces. 1. The Dutch republic that existed from the revolt of the Netherlands against Spain to its conquest by France (1579–1795). **2.** See **Uttar Pradesh.**

United Reformed Church *n.* A Protestant church formed by the merger of the Presbyterian Church of England and some Congregational Churches in England and Wales in 1972.

United States of A·mer·i·ca (ə-mĕr'ə-kə). *Abbr.* **USA, U.S.A.** Federal republic of 50 constituent states and the District of Columbia, smaller than Canada in extent, but in population the fourth-largest country in the world. It is both the world's leading industrial nation and one of the world's major food suppliers. It is the world's leading producer of coal, natural gas, beef, corn, cheese, soy beans, copper, aluminum, and synthetic rubber. The country is largely self-sufficient, enjoying one of the world's highest living standards. However, crude oil accounts for nearly 25 percent of its imports. Machinery, chemicals, motor vehicles, and cereals (corn and wheat) are the chief exports. The industrial centers of New York, Chicago,

Los Angeles, Philadelphia, Houston, and Detroit are the largest cities. The union was formed in 1787, the original 13 states being the Thirteen Colonies along the Atlantic seaboard. The last two states to be admitted to the Union were Alaska and Hawaii. Area, 9,363,123 square kilometers (3,614,165 square miles). Population, 226,500,000. Capital, Washington, D.C. See map, page 1795.

unit factor *n.* A gene that determines a unit character.

u·ni·tive (yōō'nə-tĭv, yōō-nī'-) *adj.* Tending to promote unity.

unit magnetic pole *n.* The strength of a magnetic pole that will repel a similar magnetic pole with a force of one dyne when the poles are one centimeter apart.

unit of account *n.* **1.** A money of account *(see).* **2.** The standard currency unit of a country. **3.** An artificial currency unit used, for example, by the European Community for fixing farm prices.

unit price *n.* A price of goods calculated for each unit of measure, such as a pound or quart. —**unit pricing** *n.*

unit process *n.* Any of several standard chemical engineering processes, such as distillation, used in industry.

unit rule *n.* A rule of procedure at a national political convention,

WORKING TOWARD WORLD PEACE

The dream that inspired the founding of the United Nations

The United Nations came formally into being on October 24, 1945, succeeding the League of Nations. It was formed at the initiative of the countries that had fought Hitler's Germany.

Under the UN charter, member states bound themselves to "settle their international disputes by peaceful means" and to "refrain . . . from the threat or use of force against . . . any state." Although these promises have not always been realized, the organization has created an international forum that embraces the vast majority of the world's nations.

From an original membership of 51 in 1945, the total has risen to 159. There are still some states that are not members, such as Tonga and Monaco.

The central body of the UN—its parliament—is the General Assembly, based in New York, but its subsidiary agencies are located throughout the world. The International Court of Justice, for instance, is in The Hague; the World Health Organization in Geneva; the Food and Agriculture Organization in Rome; and the International Monetary Fund in Washington.

The most powerful arm of the UN is the Security Council, which, in theory, has the authority to impose decisions on member states. (The General Assembly has the right only to make recommendations to governments.) The council has 15 members: 10 of them are elected by the General Assembly for two years each, and five are permanent members. The five are the world's leading nuclear powers—the Soviet Union, the United States, China, Britain, and France; each has the right to veto any Security Council resolution.

The UN, through the Security Council, helps to keep the peace throughout the world and has sent observers and troops to such trouble spots as Lebanon, Cyprus, Korea, Kashmir, and the Congo (now Zaire). Through its Economic and Social Council it also coordinates worldwide campaigns against poverty and disease. The UN civil service, the Secretariat, is headed by a Secretary-General who is elected by the General Assembly. It is funded by contributions from member states; the largest single contributor, the United States, has long provided roughly a quarter of the UN budget.

GENERAL ASSEMBLY

SECURITY COUNCIL

SECRETARIAT

INTERNATIONAL COURT OF JUSTICE

MILITARY OBSERVERS AND PEACEKEEPING FORCES

ECONOMIC AND SOCIAL COUNCIL

SPECIALIST AGENCIES, INCLUDING:

International Atomic Energy Agency

U.N. Conference on Trade and Development

U.N. Children's Fund

U.N. High Commission for Refugees

U.N. Development Program

SPECIALIST AGENCIES, INCLUDING:

International Telecommunication Union	International Monetary Fund
World Meteorological Organization	International Bank for Reconstruction and Development (World Bank)
U.N. Educational, Scientific, and Cultural Organization	International Civil Aviation Organization
World Health Organization	Food and Agriculture Organization
International Labor Organization	General Agreement on Tariffs and Trade

UNITED STATES OF AMERICA

under which a state's entire vote must be cast for the candidate preferred by a majority of the state's delegates.

unit trust *n.* **1.** An investment company that purchases long-term bonds and issues equal units of each series of purchased bonds for public sale. **2.** *British.* A mutual fund *(see).*

u·ni·ty (yōō′nə-tē) *n., pl.* **-ties. 1.** The state of being one; singleness. **2.** The quality or condition of harmony or agreement; concord. **3.** The state of being combined into a whole; unification. **4.** A combination or union of parts into a whole. **5. a.** An ordering of all elements in a work of art or literature so that each contributes to a unified aesthetic effect. **b.** The effect thus produced. **6.** Singleness or constancy of purpose or action; continuity. **7.** *Mathematics.* **a.** The number l. **b.** An element *I* in a groupoid satisfying $x \cdot I = x = I \cdot x$ for each x in the groupoid. **8.** Any of three principles of dramatic composition derived from Aristotle's *Poetics*, the unities of action, time, and place. They require that a drama should have only one plot, the action of which should be contained within one day and confined to one locality. [Middle English *unite*, from Old French, from Latin *ūnitās* (stem *ūnitāt-*), from *ūnus*, one.]

univ. 1. universal. **2.** university.

Univ. 1. Universalist. **2.** University.

u·ni·va·lent (yōō′nĭ-vā′lənt) *adj. Chemistry.* Monovalent.

—*n. Genetics.* A chromosome that is not paired with its homologue during meiosis.

u·ni·valve (yōō′nĭ-vălv′) *n.* **1.** A mollusk, especially a gastropod, having a shell consisting of a single piece. **2.** The shell of such a mollusk.

—*adj.* Pertaining to or having such a shell.

u·ni·ver·sal (yōō′nə-vûr′səl) *adj. Abbr.* **univ. 1.** Of, pertaining to, extending to, or affecting the entire world or all within the world; worldwide. **2.** Including, pertaining to, or affecting all members of the class or group under consideration: *the universal admiration of the critics.* **3.** Applicable or common to all purposes, conditions, or situations. **4.** Of or pertaining to the universe or cosmos; cosmic. **5.** Comprising all or many subjects; comprehensively broad: *universal interests.* **6.** *Mechanics.* Adapted or adjustable to many sizes or uses. **7.** *Logic.* Predicable of all the members of a class or genus denoted by the subject. Said of a proposition. Compare **particular.**

—*n.* **1.** *Philosophy.* **a.** A universal logical proposition. **b.** A general or abstract concept or term considered absolute or axiomatic, such as a Platonic idea. **2.** Any general or widely held principle, concept, or notion. **3.** A trait or pattern of behavior characteristic of all the members of a particular culture or of all human beings. **4.** *Linguistics.* **a.** A feature posited as an obligatory characteristic of all languages. **b.** A formal rule posited as essential for the analysis of any language. —**u·ni·ver·sal·ly** *adv.* —**u·ni·ver·sal·ness** *n.*

universal constant *n.* A fundamental constant *(see).*

universal donor *n.* A person of blood type O, which is compatible with most other blood types and can therefore be safely used for most transfusions.

universal gas constant *n. Physics.* The gas constant *(see).*

u·ni·ver·sal·ism (yōō′nə-vûr′sə-lĭz′əm) *n.* **1. Universalism.** *Theology.* The doctrine of universal salvation. Also called "apocatastasis." **2.** Universality. —**u·ni·ver·sal·is·tic** (yōō′nə-vûr′sə-lĭs′tĭk) *adj.*

U·ni·ver·sal·ist (yōō′nə-vûr′sə-lĭst) *n. Abbr.* **Univ.** One who believes that salvation is extended to all humankind; especially, a member of a Christian denomination that adheres to this doctrine. In 1961, the Universalists merged with the Unitarians, forming the Unitarian Universalist Association.

—*adj.* Of or pertaining to Universalism or Universalists.

u·ni·ver·sal·i·ty (yōō′nə-vər-sǎl′ə-tē) *n., pl.* **-ties. 1.** The quality, fact, or condition of being universal. **2.** Intellectual versatility.

u·ni·ver·sal·ize (yōō′nə-vûr′sə-līz′) *tr.v.* **-ized, -izing, -izes.** To make universal; generalize. —**u·ni·ver·sal·i·za·tion** (yōō′nə-vûr′sə-lĭ-zā′shən) *n.*

universal joint *n.* A joint or coupling that allows parts of a machine not collinear with each other limited freedom of movement in any direction while transmitting rotary motion. Also called "universal coupling."

universal language *n.* An artificial language, such as Esperanto, designed for use by all nationalities.

universal motor *n.* An electric motor capable of running on either a direct-current or an alternating-current supply.

universal set *n.* A mathematical set containing all elements of the variety under consideration.

Universal Soul *n.* The Hindu concept of Brahman as the sacred syllable Om. Also called "Universal Spirit."

universal suffrage *n.* National suffrage extended to all adults above a certain age regardless of sex or race unless they are judged criminal or insane.

universal time *n. Abbr.* **U.T.** Greenwich mean time *(see).*

u·ni·verse (yōō′nə-vûrs′) *n.* **1.** All existing things, including the earth, the heavens, the galaxies, and all therein, regarded as a whole; the cosmos. **2. a.** The earth together with all its inhabitants and created things. **b.** All humankind. **3.** In science fiction: **a.** Another system of time, space, and matter coexisting with or corresponding to our own. **b.** A vast and undiscovered star system or galaxy spatially distant from our own. **4.** The sphere or realm in which something exists or takes place. **5.** *Logic.* A universe of discourse *(see).* **6.** *Statistics.* A population *(see).* [Middle English, from Old French *univers*, from Latin *ūniversum*, the whole world (translation of Greek *to holon*, "the whole"), neuter of *ūniversus*,

universe

THE MIRACLE OF THE CREATION IS ALL AROUND US

The visible universe is as astonishing as any science fiction

The study of the universe—its origins and its history—is called cosmology. The prevailing scientific belief is that all the matter in the universe came into existence when a "primeval atom" (or "cosmic egg") exploded at a definite moment more than 15 billion years ago.

There is much evidence for this theory (generally known as the big bang theory): wherever radio astronomers point their instruments, they pick up background radiation—the aftermath of the "big bang." The change in the wavelength of the light from distant galaxies (it shifts toward the red end of the spectrum) indicates that they are moving away at immense speed.

The oscillating universe theory predicts that the galaxies will eventually slow down, stop, and draw together again for a new big bang, so beginning a new cycle.

THE BIG BANG THEORY

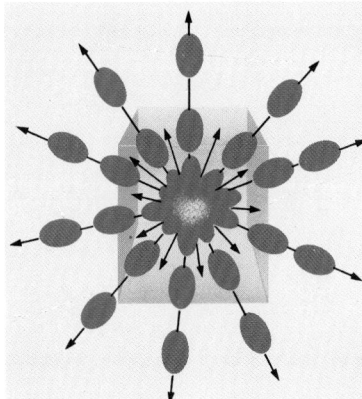

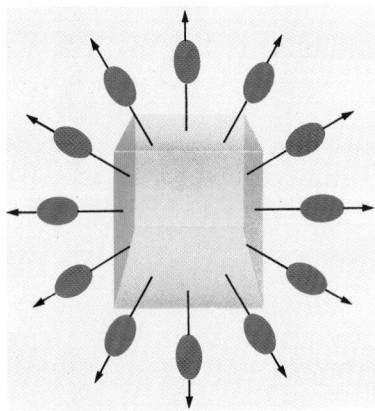

According to this theory, the universe had its origin in an enormous explosion. The gas and dust flung out from the explosion condensed into galaxies that are still moving outward. Present knowledge fits this theory back to the instant of the big bang, about which nothing is known.

THE OSCILLATING UNIVERSE THEORY

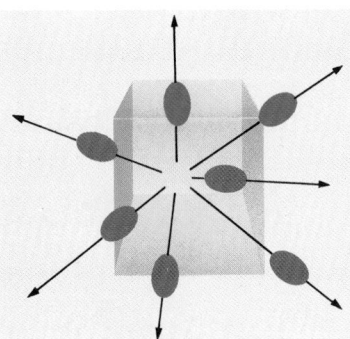

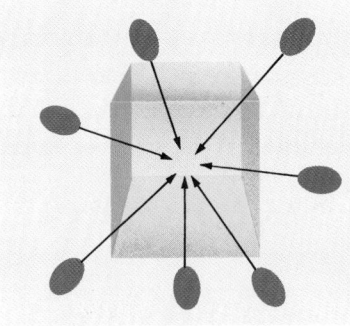

Every particle of matter exerts an attractive force on every other particle. Some scientists believe that the universe expands and contracts in endless cycles; the laws of physics may differ in each cycle. Some estimates of the critical amount of matter in the universe suggest this cannot be so.

THE STEADY-STATE THEORY

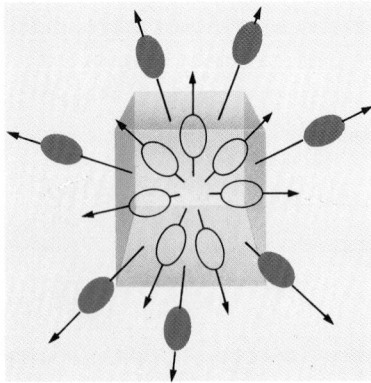

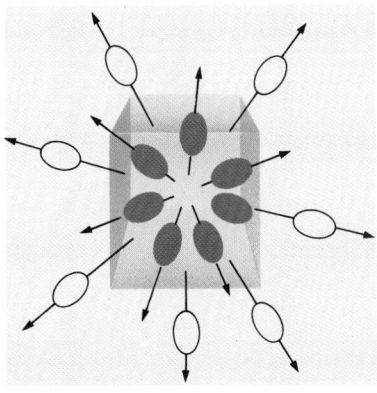

An alternative to the big bang theory was proposed in the 1940's. The steady-state theory (now generally abandoned) holds that the universe was not created at any given time, nor will it ever die. Its appearance remains constant because, as it expands, new matter is created to fill the space.

---

whole, entire, "turned into one" : UNI- + *versus,* past participle of *vertere,* to turn.]

universe of discourse *n. Logic.* A field containing all the entities referred to in a discourse or argument. Also called "universe."

u·ni·ver·si·ty (yōō'nə-vûr'sə-tē) *n., pl.* **-ties.** *Abbr.* **U., uni., univ., Univ. 1.** An institution for higher learning with teaching and research facilities that awards undergraduate and postgraduate degrees. **2.** The buildings and grounds of a university. **3.** The students, teaching staff, and governing body of a university, regarded collectively. [Middle English *universite,* from Old French, from Medieval Latin *ūniversitās (magistrorum et scholarium),* "society (of masters and students)," from Late Latin *ūniversitās* (stem *ūniversitāt-),* a society, guild, from Latin, the whole, from *ūniversus,* whole. See **universe.**]

u·niv·o·cal (yōō-nĭv'ə-kəl) *adj.* Having only one meaning. ~*n.* A word or term having only one meaning. [Late Latin *ūnivōcus* : UNI- + Latin *vōx* (stem *vōc-*), voice.] —**u·niv·o·cal·ly** *adv.*

un·just (ŭn-jŭst') *adj.* **1.** Violating principles of justice; unfair. **2.** *Archaic.* Faithless; dishonest. —**un·just·ly** *adv.* —**un·just·ness** *n.*

un·kempt (ŭn-kĕmpt') *adj.* **1. a.** Uncombed; disheveled: *unkempt hair.* **b.** Lacking a neat or cared-for appearance; untidy: *an unkempt lawn.* **2.** *Archaic.* Unpolished; rude; rough. —See Synonyms at **sloppy.** [UN- (not) + *kempt,* past participle of archaic *kemb,* to comb, Middle English *kemben,* Old English *cemban.*] —**un·kempt·ly** *adv.* —**un·kempt·ness** *n.*

un·ken·nel (ŭn-kĕn'əl) *tr.v.* **-neled** or **-nelled, -neling** or **-nelling, -nels. 1. a.** To drive from a lair or den. **b.** To loose from a kennel. **2.** To uncover; disclose.

un·kind (ŭn-kīnd') *adj.* **-kinder, -kindest. 1.** Lacking kindness; cruel. **2.** Causing pain; harsh: *an unkind wind.* —**un·kind·ness** *n.*

un·kind·ly (ŭn-kīnd'lē) *adv.* In an unkind manner. ~*adj.* **-lier, -liest.** Unkind. —**un·kind·li·ness** *n.*

un·knit (ŭn-nĭt') *v.* **-knit** or **-knitted, -knitting, -knits.** —*tr.* **1.** To unravel or undo (something knitted or tied). **2.** To smooth out (something wrinkled, especially the brow). —*intr.* To become unknit or undone.

un·know·a·ble (ŭn-nō'ə-bəl) *adj.* Impossible to know or comprehend; beyond the range of human experience or understanding. ~*n.* Something that cannot be known. —**the Unknowable.** The ultimate reality underlying all phenomena that is beyond human comprehension. —**un·know·a·ble·ness** *n.* —**un·know·a·bly** *adv.*

un·know·ing (ŭn-nō'ĭng) *adj.* Not knowing; uninformed; unaware. —**un·know·ing·ly** *adv.*

un·known (ŭn-nōn') *adj.* **1.** Not known; unfamiliar; strange. **2. a.** Not identified, discovered, or ascertained: *an unknown factor.* **b.** Not established or verified. **3.** Not famous: *an unknown actor.* —**unknown to.** Without the knowledge of. ~*n.* **1.** One that is unknown. **2.** The world postulated as existing beyond sensory perception; the supernatural. Preceded by *the.* **3.** *Mathematics.* **a.** A quantity of unknown numerical value. **b.** The symbol for this quantity. —**un·known·ness** *n.*

unknown quantity *n.* A person, thing, or event whose outcome, behavior, or effects cannot be predicted.

Unknown Soldier *n.* An anonymous soldier whose tomb is set up in public as a memorial to all the unidentified casualties of a national war. Preceded by *the.*

un·lace (ŭn-lās') *tr.v.* **-laced, -lacing, -laces. 1. a.** To loosen or undo the lace or laces of. **b.** To remove or loosen the clothing of. **2.** *Obsolete.* To disgrace.

un·lade (ŭn-lād') *v.* **-laded, -lading, -lades.** —*tr.* **1.** To unload (a cargo). **2.** To unload (a ship). —*intr.* To discharge a cargo.

un·lash (ŭn-lăsh') *tr.v.* **-lashed, -lashing, -lashes.** To untie the lashing of; loosen.

un·latch (ŭn-lăch') *v.* **-latched, -latching, -latches.** —*tr.* To unfasten or open by releasing the latch. —*intr.* To become or admit of being unfastened or opened.

un·law·ful (ŭn-lô'fəl) *adj.* **1.** Not lawful; in violation of law; illicit. **2.** *Archaic.* Illegitimate. Said of offspring. —**un·law·ful·ly** *adv.* —**un·law·ful·ness** *n.*

unlawful assembly *n.* An assembly of three or more people collaborating for any unlawful purpose.

un·lay (ŭn-lā') *v.* **-laid** (-lād'), **-laying, -lays.** *Nautical.* —*tr.* To untwist the strands of (a cable or rope). —*intr.* To untwist.

un·lead·ed (ŭn-lĕd'ĭd) *adj.* **1.** Not surfaced or weighted with lead. **2.** Not mixed with lead. Said of fuels. **3.** *Printing.* Not spaced or separated with lead; set solid. Said of typeset matter.

un·learn (ŭn-lûrn') *tr.v.* **-learned** or **-learnt** (-lûrnt'), **-learning, -learns.** To put (something learned) out of the mind; forget.

un·learn·ed (ŭn-lûr'nĭd *for senses 1, 2;* ŭn-lûrnd' *for sense 3) adj.* **1.** Not educated; ignorant or illiterate. **2.** Not skilled or versed in a specified discipline. **3.** Not acquired by training or studying: *an unlearned response.* —See Synonyms at **ignorant.** —**un·learn·ed·ly** (ŭn-lûr'nĭd-lē) *adv.*

un·leash (ŭn-lēsh') *tr.v.* **-leashed, -leashing, -leashes.** To release or loose from or as if from a leash: *unleash one's fury.*

un·leav·ened (ŭn-lĕv'ənd) *adj.* **1.** Made without leavening. Said especially of the bread of the Passover. **2.** Not lightened or alleviated: *a week of drudgery unleavened by amusement.*

un·less (ŭn-lĕs') *conj.* Except on the condition that; except under the circumstances that. ~*prep. Rare.* Except; except for. [Middle English *unlesse,* alteration of *onlesse (than* or *that),* originally *(up)on less than,* "on a less condition than," hence "except, if . . . not" : ON + LESS.]

Usage: The expressions *unless and until* and *unless or until* are sometimes heard in emphatic speech and writing, but they attract criticism because the senses of the two words overlap. Either *unless* or *until,* used singly and chosen in accordance with the desired sense, is usually sufficient: *Unless* (or *until*) *this sum is paid, no further credit can be extended.*

un·let·tered (ŭn-lĕt′ərd) *adj.* **1. a.** Not educated. **b.** Illiterate. **2.** Without lettering. —See Synonyms at **ignorant.**

un·li·censed (ŭn-lī′sənst) *adj.* **1.** Having no license. **2.** Unauthorized. **3.** Unrestrained.

un·licked (ŭn-lĭkt′) *adj.* **1.** Not licked clean. Said of the newborn young of some animals. **2.** Unpolished; crude.

un·like (ŭn-līk′) *adj.* **1.** Not alike; different; dissimilar. **2.** Not equal.

~*prep.* **1.** Different from; not like. **2.** Not typical of: *It's unlike Emily to lose her cool that way.*

un·like·li·hood (ŭn-līk′lē-hŏŏd′) *n.* The state of being unlikely or improbable; improbability.

un·like·ly (ŭn-līk′lē) *adj.* **-lier, -liest. 1.** Not likely; improbable. **2.** Likely to fail: *a most unlikely candidate.* —**un·like′li·ness** *n.*

un·like·ness (ŭn-līk′nĭs) *n.* The condition or quality of being unlike. —See Usage note at **difference.**

un·lim·ber (ŭn-lĭm′bər) *v.* **-bered, -bering, -bers.** —*tr.* **1.** To detach (a gun or caisson) from its limber. **2.** To make ready for action. —*intr.* To prepare for action.

un·lim·it·ed (ŭn-lĭm′ĭ-tĭd) *adj.* **1.** Having no limits, bounds, or qualifications. **2.** *British Finance.* Unlimited in liability should business fail. —**un·lim·it·ed·ly** *adv.* —**un·lim·it·ed·ness** *n.*

un·lined (ŭn-līnd′) *adj.* **1.** Not marked with lines. **2.** Not wrinkled: *an unlined brow.* **3.** Not backed with a lining: *an unlined coat.*

un·link (ŭn-lĭngk′) *tr.v.* **-linked, -linking, -links.** To disconnect the links of; unfasten.

un·list·ed (ŭn-lĭs′tĭd) *adj.* **1.** Not appearing on a list; especially, not listed in a telephone directory: *an unlisted number.* **2.** Designating stock or securities not listed on a stock exchange.

un·live (ŭn-lĭv′) *tr.v.* **-lived, -living, -lives.** To live in such a manner as to undo or annul (earlier years or their consequences); reverse.

un·load (ŭn-lōd′) *v.* **-loaded, -loading, -loads.** —*tr.* **1. a.** To take the load or cargo from. **b.** To discharge (a cargo or load). **2. a.** To relieve (oneself) of something oppressive; unburden. **b.** To relieve oneself of (a duty, for example) by giving it to another. **c.** To pour forth (one's troubles). **3.** To remove the charge from (a firearm). **4.** To dispose of, especially by selling in great quantity; dump. —*intr.* To discharge a cargo or other burden. —**un·load′er** *n.*

un·lock (ŭn-lŏk′) *v.* **-locked, -locking, -locks.** —*tr.* **1. a.** To undo (a lock) by turning a key or a corresponding part. **b.** To undo the lock of. **2. a.** To cause to open; unfasten. **b.** To give access to: *unlocked her heart.* **3.** To set free; release. **4.** To provide a solution to: *unlock a mystery.* —*intr.* To become unlocked.

un·looked-for (ŭn-lŏŏkt′fôr′) *adj.* Not looked for or expected; unforeseen.

un·loose (ŭn-lōōs′) *tr.v.* **-loosed, -loosing, -looses. 1.** To let loose or unfasten; release; set free. **2.** To relax; ease, as a hold upon something. [Middle English *unlo(o)sen*: UN- (intensive) + *lo(o)sen,* to loosen, from *lo(o)s,* LOOSE.]

un·loos·en (ŭn-lōō′sən) *tr.v.* **-ened, -ening, -ens.** To make less tight or firmly secured; unloose.

un·love·ly (ŭn-lŭv′lē) *adj.* **-lier, -liest.** Not beautiful or pleasant; disagreeable; repugnant. —**un·love′li·ness** *n.*

un·luck·y (ŭn-lŭk′ē) *adj.* **-ier, -iest. 1.** Subjected to or marked by misfortune. **2.** Forecasting bad luck; inauspicious. **3.** Not producing the desired outcome; disappointing; regrettable. —**un·luck′i·ly** *adv.* —**un·luck′i·ness** *n.*

un·made (ŭn′mād′, ŭn′-) *adj.* Not made up tidily for sleeping in. Said of a bed.

un·make (ŭn-māk′) *tr.v.* **-made** (-mād′) **-making, -makes. 1.** To deprive of position, rank, or authority; depose. **2.** To ruin; destroy. **3.** To alter the characteristics of. —**un·mak′er** *n.*

un·man (ŭn-măn′) *tr.v.* **-manned, -manning, -mans. 1.** To cause to lose courage: *"The idea of the grisly occupant unmanned him"* (R. L. Stevenson). **2.** To deprive of virility; emasculate. **3.** To remove the men from.

un·man·age·a·ble (ŭn-măn′ĭ-jə-bəl) *adj.* Difficult to control.

un·man·ly (ŭn-măn′lē) *adj.* **-lier, -liest. 1.** Not showing or marked by qualities conventionally associated with men, such as strength or self-control. Said typically of a man. **2. a.** Dishonorable; degrading. **b.** Cowardly; repugnant. —**un·man′li·ness** *n.*

un·manned (ŭn-mănd′) *adj.* **1.** Without a crew: *an unmanned ship.* **2.** *Obsolete.* Untrained. Said of a hawk.

un·man·nered (ŭn-măn′ərd) *adj.* **1.** Without manners; rude. **2.** Without mannerisms.

un·man·ner·ly (ŭn-măn′ər-lē) *adj.* Rude; ill-mannered. —**un·man′ner·li·ness** *n.*

un·marked (ŭn-märkt′) *adj.* **1.** Not bearing a mark. **2.** Not observed or noticed. **3.** Not marked with corrections, a price, or the like. **4.** *Linguistics.* Of or pertaining to that one of a connected pair of words or linguistic units which is the more general or neutral; for example, in the pairs *dog* and *dogs* and *dog* and *bitch, dog* is the unmarked form.

un·mask (ŭn-măsk′, -mäsk′) *v.* **-masked, -masking, -masks.** —*tr.* **1.** To remove a mask from. **2.** To disclose the true character of; expose. **3.** *Military.* To expose the presence of (weapons), as by removing camouflage. —*intr.* To remove one's mask.

un·mean·ing (ŭn-mē′nĭng) *adj.* **1.** Meaningless. **2.** Expressionless; vacant. —**un·mean′ing·ly** *adv.* —**un·mean′ing·ness** *n.*

un·meas·ured (ŭn-mĕzh′ərd) *adj.* **1.** Not yet measured. **2.** Measureless. **3.** *Music.* Without a fixed beat or bars.

un·men·tion·a·ble (ŭn-mĕn′shən-ə-bəl) *adj.* **1.** Not fit to be mentioned. **2.** Unspeakable. —**un·men·tion·a·ble·ness** *n.* —**un·men·tion·a·bly** *adv.*

un·men·tion·a·bles (ŭn-mĕn′shən-ə-bəlz) *pl.n.* Underwear.

un·mer·ci·ful (ŭn-mûr′sĭ-fəl) *adj.* **1.** Having no mercy; merciless. **2.** Unrelenting: *unmerciful heat.* —**un·mer·ci·ful·ly** *adv.* —**un·mer·ci·ful·ness** *n.*

un·mind·ful (ŭn-mīnd′fəl) *adj.* Careless; forgetful; oblivious. Used with *of: unmindful of the time.* —See Synonyms at **forgetful.** —**un·mind·ful·ly** *adv.* —**un·mind·ful·ness** *n.*

un·mis·tak·a·ble (ŭn′mĭ-stā′kə-bəl) *adj.* Obvious; evident; easily identifiable. —**un·mis·tak·a·ble·ness** *n.* —**un·mis·tak·a·bly** *adv.*

un·mit·i·gat·ed (ŭn-mĭt′ə-gā′tĭd) *adj.* **1.** Not diminished or moderated in intensity or severity; unrelieved. **2.** Absolute; unqualified: *an unmitigated lie.* —**un·mit·i·gat·ed·ly** *adv.*

un·moor (ŭn-mŏŏr′) *v.* **-moored, -mooring, -moors.** —*tr.* **1.** To release from or as if from moorings. **2.** To release (a ship) from all but one anchor. —*intr.* To cast off moorings.

un·mor·al (ŭn-môr′əl, -mŏr′əl) *adj.* Having no moral quality or sense; amoral. —**un·mo·ral·i·ty** (ŭn′mə-răl′ə-tē) *n.* —**un·mor·al·ly** *adv.*

un·muz·zle (ŭn-mŭz′əl) *tr.v.* **-zled, -zling, -zles. 1.** To remove the muzzle from. **2.** To free from censorship; allow to speak or write freely.

un·my·e·lin·a·ted (ŭn-mī′ə-lĭ-nā′tĭd) *adj.* Lacking a myelin sheath. Said of certain nerve fibers.

un·named (ŭn-nāmd′) *adj.* **1.** Having no name. **2.** Not referred to by name.

un·nat·u·ral (ŭn-năch′ər-əl) *adj.* **1.** Violating natural law. **2.** Inconsistent with an individual pattern or custom. **3.** Deemed to deviate from a behavioral, ethical, or social norm: *unnatural practices.* **4.** Contrived or constrained; artificial: *an unnatural manner.* **5.** Outrageously violating natural or proper feelings; inhuman. —**un·nat·u·ral·ly** *adv.* —**un·nat·u·ral·ness** *n.*

un·nec·es·sar·y (ŭn-nĕs′ə-sĕr′ē) *adj.* Not necessary; needless or superfluous. —**un·nec·es·sar·i·ly** (ŭn-nĕs′ə-sâr′ə-lē) *adv.* —**un·nec·es·sar·i·ness** *n.*

un·nerve (ŭn-nûrv′) *tr.v.* **-nerved, -nerving, -nerves.** To deprive of composure, confidence, or firmness of resolve.

unnil- *prefix.* Indicates a chemical element with an atomic number between 101 and 109. [From Latin *ūnus,* one + *nil,* zero.]

un·nil·bi·um (yōō-nĭl′bē-əm) *n.* The chemical element **nobelium** (see).

un·nil·hex·i·um (yōō′nəl-hĕk′sē-əm) *n.* *Symbol* **Unh** A synthetic radioactive chemical element with an atomic number of 106.

un·nil·pent·i·um (yōō′nəl-pĕn′tē-əm) *n.* *Symbol* **Unp** A synthetic radioactive chemical element with an atomic number of 105.

un·nil·quad·i·um (yōō′nəl-kwŏd′ē-əm) *n.* *Symbol* **Unq** A synthetic radioactive chemical element with an atomic number of 104. Formerly called "rutherfordium."

un·nil·sept·i·um (yōō′nəl-sĕp′tē-əm) *n.* *Symbol* **Uns** A synthetic radioactive chemical element with an atomic number of 107.

un·nil·tri·um (yōō′nəl-trī′əm) *n.* The chemical element **lawrencium** (see).

un·nil·un·i·um (yōō′nəl-yōō′nē-əm) *n.* The chemical element **mendelevium** (see).

un·num·bered (ŭn-nŭm′bərd) *adj.* **1.** Not numbered; countless. **2.** Not marked with an identifying number.

U.N.O. United Nations Organization.

un·ob·tru·sive (ŭn′əb-trōō′sĭv) *adj.* **1.** Not readily noticeable. **2.** Discreet. —**un·ob·tru·sive·ly** *adv.* —**un·ob·tru·sive·ness** *n.*

un·oc·cu·pied (ŭn-ŏk′yə-pīd′) *adj.* **1.** Not inhabited; vacant. **2.** Not occupied by foreign troops. **3.** Unemployed; idle.

un·of·fi·cial (ŭn′ə-fĭsh′əl) *adj.* **1.** Not official. **2.** Not acting officially. **3.** Not ratified by official labor union representatives: *unofficial strike action.* —**un·of·fi·cial·ly** *adv.*

un·or·gan·ized (ŭn-ôr′gə-nīzd′) *adj.* **1.** Lacking order, system, or unity. **2.** Having no organic properties. **3.** Not unionized.

un·or·tho·dox (ŭn-ôr′thə-dŏks′) *adj.* Not orthodox. —**un·or·tho·dox·ly** *adv.* —**un·or·tho·dox·y** (ŭn-ôr′thə-dŏk′sē) *n.*

Unp The symbol for the element unnilpentium.

un·pack (ŭn-păk′) *v.* **-packed, -packing, -packs.** —*tr.* **1.** To remove the contents of (a suitcase, for example). **2.** To remove from a container or from packaging. **3. a.** To remove a pack from (a pack animal). **b.** To unload the contents of (a motor vehicle). —*intr.* To unpack goods, a trunk, or the like. —**un·pack′er** *n.*

un·paid (ŭn-pād′) *adj.* **1.** Not yet paid: *an unpaid bill.* **2.** Serving without pay; unsalaried. **3.** Awaiting wages due.

un·pal·at·a·ble (ŭn-păl′ə-tə-bəl) *adj.* **1.** Unpleasant to the taste. **2.** Disagreeable; unpleasant: *unpalatable truths.*

un·par·al·leled (ŭn-păr′ə-lĕld′) *adj.* Without parallel; unmatched; unequaled.

un·par·lia·men·ta·ry (ŭn′pär-lə-mĕn′tə-rē, -mĕn′trē) *adj.* Not in accordance with parliamentary procedure.

un·peg (ŭn-pĕg′) *tr.v.* **-pegged, -pegging, -pegs. 1.** To remove the peg or pegs from. **2.** To allow (wages, prices, and the like) to fluctuate without restriction.

un·peo·ple (ŭn-pē′pəl) *tr.v.* **-pled, -pling, -ples.** To depopulate.

un·per·fo·rat·ed (ŭn-pûr′fə-rā′tĭd) *adj.* **1.** Lacking perforations. **2.** *Philately.* Imperforate.

un·per·son (ŭn′pûr′sən) *n., pl.* **unpersons. 1.** A person whose existence is denied or ignored by the authorities, especially in a totalitarian state. **2.** An insipid or unimpressive person. In both senses, also called "nonperson."

un·pick (ŭn-pĭk′) *tr.v.* **-picked, -picking, -picks.** To undo (sewing) by removing stitches: *unpick a seam.*

un·pin (ŭn-pĭn′) *tr.v.* **-pinned, -pinning, -pins. 1.** To remove a pin or pins from. **2. a.** To open or unfasten by removing pins. **b.** To free. **3.** *Chess.* To free (a piece) from a pin.

un·pleas·ant (ŭn-plĕz′ənt) *adj.* **-anter, -antest.** Not pleasing; offensive; disagreeable. **—un·pleas·ant·ly** *adv.*

un·pleas·ant·ness (ŭn-plĕz′ənt-nĭs) *n.* **1.** The condition or quality of being unpleasant. **2. a.** An unpleasant experience or situation. **b.** An argument or quarrel.

un·plug (ŭn-plŭg′) *tr.v.* **-plugged, -plugging, -plugs. 1.** To remove a plug, stopper, or obstruction from. **2. a.** To remove (an electric plug) from a socket. **b.** To disconnect (an electric appliance) by removing its plug from a socket.

un·plumbed (ŭn-plŭmd′) *adj.* Not explored as to depth or meaning; not fathomed: *unplumbed waters; an unplumbed theory.*

un·pop·u·lar (ŭn-pŏp′yə-lər) *adj.* **1.** Lacking public approval or acceptance. **2.** Not approved of; out of favor: *You're unpopular with her these days.* **—un·pop·u·lar·i·ty** (ŭn-pŏp′yə-lăr′ə-tē) *n.*

un·prec·e·dent·ed (ŭn-prĕs′ə-dĕn′tĭd) *adj.* Without precedent; unheard-of. **—un·prec·e·dent·ed·ly** *adv.*

un·pre·dict·a·ble (ŭn′prĭ-dĭk′tə-bəl) *adj.* Not predictable. **—un·pre·dict·a·bil·i·ty** (ŭn′prĭ-dĭk′tə-bĭl′ə-tē), **un·pre·dict·a·ble·ness** *n.* **—un·pre·dict·a·bly** *adv.*

un·prej·u·diced (ŭn-prĕj′ə-dĭst) *adj.* Free from prejudice; impartial. —See Synonyms at **fair.**

un·pre·med·i·tat·ed (ŭn′prĭ-mĕd′ə-tā′tĭd) *adj.* Spontaneous; not planned: *an unpremeditated crime.* —See Synonyms at **extemporaneous.**

un·pre·pared (ŭn′prĭ-pârd′) *adj.* **1.** Having made few or no preparations. **2.** Not equipped to meet a contingency: *The rain caught us unprepared.* **3.** Not steeled, as to face a shock. **4.** Impromptu: *an unprepared speech.* **—un·pre·par·ed·ly** (ŭn′prĭ-pâr′ĭd-lē, -pârd′lē) *adv.* **—un·pre·par·ed·ness** *n.*

un·pre·pos·sess·ing (ŭn′prē-pə-zĕs′ĭng) *adj.* Failing to impress favorably; unattractive; nondescript: *his unprepossessing appearance.* **—un·pre·pos·sess·ing·ly** *adv.*

un·pre·ten·tious (ŭn′prĭ-tĕn′shəs) *adj.* Lacking affectation or pretention; unostentatious; modest. **—un·pre·ten·tious·ness** *n.*

un·priced (ŭn-prīst′) *adj.* Having no fixed or attached price.

un·prin·ci·pled (ŭn-prĭn′sə-pəld) *adj.* Lacking principles or moral scruples; unscrupulous: *unprincipled behavior.*

un·print·a·ble (ŭn-prĭn′tə-bəl) *adj.* Not fit for publication, especially on grounds of infringing public taste or morality, libel laws, or the like.

un·pro·duc·tive (ŭn′prə-dŭk′tĭv) *adj.* **1.** Producing or yielding little or nothing. **2.** *Economics.* Adding nothing to exchangeable value. **—un·pro·duc·tive·ly** *adv.* **—un·pro·duc·tive·ness** *n.*

un·pro·fes·sion·al (ŭn′prə-fĕsh′ən-əl) *adj.* **1.** Not conforming to the standards of a profession. **2.** Amateurish. **3. a.** Not in a profession. **b.** Not a qualified member of a professional group. **—un·pro·fes·sion·al·ly** *adv.*

un·prof·it·a·ble (ŭn-prŏf′ĭ-tə-bəl) *adj.* **1.** Not making a profit. **2.** Not profitable; serving no purpose; useless. **—un·prof·it·a·bil·i·ty** (ŭn-prŏf′ĭ-tə-bĭl′ə-tē) *n.* **—un·prof·it·a·bly** *adv.*

un·prompt·ed (ŭn-prŏmp′tĭd) *adj.* Spontaneous; not asked for or suggested.

un·pro·nounce·a·ble (ŭn′prə-noun′sə-bəl) *adj.* **1.** Difficult to pronounce correctly. **2.** Not fit to be mentioned.

un·pro·vid·ed (ŭn′prə-vī′dĭd) *adj.* Not supplied, furnished, or equipped. Used with *with.* **—unprovided for.** Not provided with an adequate means of support: *He left his children unprovided for.*

Unq The symbol for the element unnilquadium.

un·qual·i·fied (ŭn-kwŏl′ə-fīd′) *adj.* **1.** Lacking the required qualifications: *If you are under 18, you are unqualified to vote.* **2.** Without reservations; unconditional: *unqualified admiration.* Often used as an intensive: *an unqualified disaster.*

un·ques·tion·a·ble (ŭn-kwĕs′chən-ə-bəl) *adj.* Beyond question or doubt; indisputable; certain. **—un·ques·tion·a·bil·i·ty, un·ques·tion·a·ble·ness** *n.* **—un·ques·tion·a·bly** *adv.*

un·ques·tioned (ŭn-kwĕs′chənd) *adj.* **1.** Not subjected to questioning. **2. a.** Unquestionable. **b.** Not called into question or examination; not doubted.

un·ques·tion·ing (ŭn-kwĕs′chən-ĭng) *adj.* Asking no questions; not doubting or hesitating. **—un·ques·tion·ing·ly** *adv.*

un·qui·et (ŭn-kwī′ĭt) *adj.* **-eter, -etest. 1.** Emotionally or mentally uneasy; agitated; disturbed. **2.** Characterized by unrest or uncertainty; turbulent: *unquiet times.* **—un·qui·et·ly** *adv.* **—un·qui·et·ness** *n.*

un·quote (ŭn′kwōt′) *interj.* Used in speaking to indicate the end of a quotation.

un·rav·el (ŭn-răv′əl) *v.* **-eled, -eling, -els** or *chiefly British* **-elled, -elling, -els. —tr. 1. a.** To undo or unpick the knitted or woven fabric of. **b.** To separate (entangled threads). **2.** To separate and clarify the elements of (something mysterious or baffling); solve. **—intr.** To become unraveled.

un·read (ŭn-rĕd′) *adj.* **1.** Not read, studied, or perused. **2.** Having read little; ignorant: *unread in the classics.*

un·read·a·ble (ŭn-rē′də-bəl) *adj.* **1.** Illegible. **2.** Not interesting to read; dull. **3.** Incomprehensible; obscure. **—un·read·a·bil·i·ty, un·read·a·ble·ness** *n.* **—un·read·a·bly** *adv.*

un·read·y (ŭn-rĕd′ē) *adj.* **-ier, -iest. 1.** Not ready or prepared. **2.** Slow in grasp or response; not prompt. **—un·read·i·ly** *adv.* **—un·read·i·ness** *n.*

un·re·al (ŭn-rē′əl, -rēl′) *adj.* **1.** Not real or substantial; imaginary; artificial. **2.** *Slang.* Amazing; astonishing. **—un·re·al·i·ty** (ŭn′rē-ăl′ə-tē) *n.*

un·re·al·is·tic (ŭn′rē-ə-lĭs′tĭk) *adj.* **1.** Lacking verisimilitude. **2.** Unlikely. **3. a.** Deluded; irrational. **b.** Not feasible or practicable. **—un·re·al·is·ti·cal·ly** *adv.*

un·rea·son (ŭn-rē′zən) *n.* **1.** Absence or lack of reason; irrationality. **2.** Nonsense; absurdity.

un·rea·son·a·ble (ŭn-rē′zə-nə-bəl) *adj.* **1.** Not governed by or based upon reason. **2.** Exceeding reasonable limits; exorbitant; immoderate. —See Synonyms at **excessive. —un·rea·son·a·ble·ness** *n.* **—un·rea·son·a·bly** *adv.*

unreasonable behavior *n. Law.* Misconduct by a spouse given as grounds for divorce, especially when this demonstrates emotional or sexual incompatibility.

un·rea·son·ing (ŭn-rē′zə-nĭng) *adj.* Not governed by reason; irrational. **—un·rea·son·ing·ly** *adv.*

un·reck·on·a·ble (ŭn-rĕk′ə-nə-bəl) *adj.* Incalculable.

un·re·con·struct·ed (ŭn′rē-kən-strŭk′tĭd) *adj.* **1.** Left unrepaired: *unreconstructed ruins.* **2.** Unreconciled to social and economic change: *an unreconstructed male chauvinist.*

un·reeve (ŭn-rēv′) *v.* **-reeved** or **-rove** (-rōv′), **-reeved** or **-roven** (-rō′vən), **-reeving, -reeves.** *Nautical.* **—tr.** To withdraw (a rope, cable, or line) from a block, thimble, or other opening. **—intr. 1.** To become unreeved. **2.** To unreeve a rope.

UNREF United Nations Refugee Emergency Fund.

un·re·fined (ŭn′rĭ-fīnd′) *adj.* **1.** Not processed. Said of natural products such as oil or sugar. **2.** Coarse or brutish.

un·re·gen·er·ate (ŭn′rĭ-jĕn′ər-ĭt) *adj.* **1.** Not reformed or repentant. **2.** Obstinately prejudiced. **—un·re·gen·er·a·cy** (ŭn′rĭ-jĕn′ər-ə-sē) *n.* **—un·re·gen·er·ate·ly** *adv.*

un·re·hearsed (ŭn′rĭ-hûrst′) *adj.* Not rehearsed. —See Synonyms at **extemporaneous.**

un·re·lent·ing (ŭn′rĭ-lĕn′tĭng) *adj.* **1.** Inexorable; merciless: *unrelenting fate.* **2.** Not diminishing in intensity, speed, or effort. **—un·re·lent·ing·ly** *adv.* **—un·re·lent·ing·ness** *n.*

un·re·li·a·ble (ŭn′rĭ-lī′ə-bəl) *adj.* Not reliable. **—un·re·li·a·bil·i·ty, un·re·li·a·ble·ness** *n.* **—un·re·li·a·bly** *adv.*

un·re·lieved (ŭn′rĭ-lēvd′) *adj.* Not varied in any way; uniform: *unrelieved boredom.* **—un·re·liev·ed·ly** (ŭn′rĭ-lē′vĭd-lē) *adv.*

un·re·li·gious (ŭn′rĭ-lĭj′əs) *adj.* **1.** Irreligious. **2.** Having no connection with religion. **—un·re·li·gious·ly** *adv.*

un·re·mit·ting (ŭn′rĭ-mĭt′ĭng) *adj.* Never slackening; incessant; persistent. **—un·re·mit·ting·ly** *adv.* **—un·re·mit·ting·ness** *n.*

un·re·quit·ed (ŭn′rĭ-kwī′tĭd) *adj.* Not reciprocated. Said of feelings: *He pined away from unrequited love.*

un·re·served (ŭn′rĭ-zûrvd′) *adj.* **1.** Not reserved for a particular use or person: *an unreserved seat.* **2.** Given without reservation; unqualified: *unreserved praise.* **3.** Not reserved in manner; frank. **—un·re·serv·ed·ly** (ŭn′rĭ-zûr′vĭd-lē) *adv.* **—un·re·serv·ed·ness** *n.*

un·re·spon·sive (ŭn′rĭ-spŏn′sĭv) *adj.* Not responsive. **—un·re·spon·sive·ly** *adv.* **—un·re·spon·sive·ness** *n.*

un·rest (ŭn-rĕst′) *n.* **1.** Uneasiness; disquiet. **2.** Agitation; rebellion: *social unrest.*

un·re·strained (ŭn′rĭ-strānd′) *adj.* **1. a.** Unchecked. **b.** Not given to restraint. **2.** Not constrained; natural. **—un·re·strain·ed·ly** (ŭn′rĭ-strā′nĭd-lē) *adv.*

un·rid·dle (ŭn-rĭd′l) *tr.v.* **-dled, -dling, -dles.** To solve or explain (a riddle or mystery).

un·ri·fled (ŭn-rī′fəld) *adj.* Having a smooth bore. Said of a gun.

un·rig (ŭn-rĭg′) *tr.v.* **-rigged, -rigging, -rigs.** *Nautical.* To strip (a vessel) of rigging.

un·right·eous (ŭn-rī′chəs) *adj.* **1.** Not righteous; wicked: *an unrighteous man.* **2.** Not right or fair; unjust: *unrighteous laws.* **—un·right·eous·ly** *adv.* **—un·right·eous·ness** *n.*

un·rip (ŭn-rĭp′) *tr.v.* **-ripped, -ripping, -rips.** To open, separate, or detach by ripping. [UN- (intensive) + RIP.]

un·ripe (ŭn-rīp′) *adj.* **-riper, -ripest.** Also **un·rip·ened** (-rī′pənd). **1.** Not matured or ripe. **2.** Not fully developed; immature. **3.** Not ready or prepared. **—un·ripe·ness** *n.*

un·ri·valed (ŭn-rī′vəld) *adj.* Unequaled; supreme.

un·roll (ŭn-rōl′) *v.* **-rolled, -rolling, -rolls. —tr. 1.** To unwind and open out (something rolled up). **2.** To unfold; reveal. **—intr.** To become unrolled.

un·root (ŭn-rōōt′, -rŏŏt′) *tr.v.* **-rooted, -rooting, -roots.** To uproot.

un·round (ŭn-round′) *tr.v.* **-rounded, -rounding, -rounds.** *Phonetics.* To pronounce (a vowel sound) with the lips in a flattened or neutral position.

UNRRA (ŭn′rə.) United Nations Relief and Rehabilitation Administration.

un·ruf·fled (ŭn-rŭf′əld) *adj.* Not ruffled or agitated; calm. —See Synonyms at **cool.**

un·ru·ly (ŭn-rōō′lē) *adj.* **-lier, -liest.** Difficult or impossible to govern; not amenable to control or discipline: *unruly locks of hair; the* *unruly mob.* [Middle English *unruly* : UN- + *ruly,* easy to govern, from *rule,* RULE.] —**un·ru·li·ness** *n.*

Synonyms: *headstrong, intractable, recalcitrant, refractory, ungovernable, wayward, willful.*

UNRWA United Nations Relief and Works Agency.

Uns The symbol for the element unnilseptium.

un·sad·dle (ŭn-săd′l) *v.* **-dled, -dling, -dles.** —*tr.* **1.** To remove the saddle from. **2.** To throw from the saddle; unhorse. —*intr.* To remove the saddle from a horse.

un·said (ŭn-sĕd′) *adj.* Not mentioned: *best left unsaid.*

un·sat·u·rate (ŭn-săch′ə-rĭt) *n.* An unsaturated chemical compound.

un·sat·u·rat·ed (ŭn-săch′ə-rā′tĭd) *adj.* **1.** Of or designating a compound, especially of carbon, containing atoms that share more than one valence bond. **2.** Capable of dissolving more of a solute at a given temperature. —**un·sat·u·ra·tion** (ŭn-săch′ə-rā′shən) *n.*

un·sa·vor·y (ŭn-sā′və-rē) *adj.* **1.** Distasteful or disagreeable. **2.** Morally offensive: *an unsavory scandal.* —**un·sa·vor·i·ly** *adv.* —**un·sa·vor·i·ness** *n.*

un·say (ŭn-sā′) *tr.v.* **-said** (-sĕd′), **-saying, -says** (-sĕz′). To retract (something said).

un·scathed (ŭn-skā*th*d′) *adj.* Unharmed; uninjured.

un·schooled (ŭn-skōōld′) *adj.* **1.** Not schooled; uninstructed. **2.** Not the result of training; natural.

un·sci·en·tif·ic (ŭn′sī-ən-tĭf′ĭk) *adj.* **1.** Not in accordance with the principles of science; especially, lacking in objectivity or proper methodology: *an unscientific opinion poll.* **2.** Not familiar with science. —**un·sci·en·tif·i·cal·ly** *adv.*

un·scram·ble (ŭn-skrăm′bəl) *tr.v.* **-bled, -bling, -bles. 1.** To disentangle; straighten out; resolve. **2.** To restore (a scrambled message) to intelligible form. —**un·scram·bler** *n.*

un·screw (ŭn-skrōō′) *v.* **-screwed, -screwing, -screws.** —*tr.* **1.** To take out the screw or screws from: *unscrewed the cover and lifted it off.* **2.** To loosen, adjust, or detach by rotating. —*intr.* To become or admit of being unscrewed.

un·scru·pu·lous (ŭn-skrōō′pyə-ləs) *adj.* Without scruples; contemptuous of what is right or honorable. —**un·scru·pu·lous·ly** *adv.* —**un·scru·pu·lous·ness** *n.*

un·seam (ŭn-sēm′) *tr.v.* **-seamed, -seaming, -seams.** To undo the seam or seams of.

un·search·a·ble (ŭn-sûr′chə-bəl) *adj.* Beyond research; inscrutable; imponderable.

un·sea·son·a·ble (ŭn-sē′zə-nə-bəl) *adj.* **1.** Not suitable to or appropriate for the season. **2.** Not characteristic of the time of year. **3.** Poorly timed; inopportune. —**un·sea·son·a·ble·ness** *n.* —**un·sea·son·a·bly** *adv.*

un·sea·soned (ŭn-sē′zənd) *adj.* **1.** Not made savory with seasoning. **2.** Inadequately aged or seasoned; not ripe or mature: *unseasoned wood.* **3.** Inexperienced. —**un·sea·soned·ness** *n.*

un·seat (ŭn-sēt′) *tr.v.* **-seated, -seating, -seats. 1.** To remove from a seat, especially from a saddle. **2.** To dislodge from a position or office.

un·seem·ly (ŭn-sēm′lē) *adj.* **-lier, -liest.** Not in good taste; indecorous; unbecoming. —See Usage note at **improper.** *~adv.* In an unseemly manner. —**un·seem·li·ness** *n.*

un·seen (ŭn-sēn′) *adj.* **1.** Not directly evident; invisible. **2.** Not previously read or studied: *an unseen translation.*

un·sel·fish (ŭn-sĕl′fĭsh) *adj.* Not selfish; generous. —**un·sel·fish·ly** *adv.* —**un·sel·fish·ness** *n.*

un·set (ŭn-sĕt′) *adj.* **1.** Not yet firm, stiff, or solidified, as jelly or concrete. **2.** Unmounted. Said especially of a precious stone. **3.** *Printing.* Not yet typeset.

un·set·tle (ŭn-sĕt′l) *v.* **-tled, -tling, -tles.** —*tr.* **1.** To displace from a settled condition; disrupt. **2.** To agitate mentally; make uneasy; disturb. —*intr.* To become unsettled.

un·set·tled (ŭn-sĕt′əld) *adj.* **1. a.** Disordered; disturbed: *unsettled times.* **b.** Worried; restless. **2.** Variable; uncertain: *unsettled weather.* **3.** Not determined or resolved: *an unsettled issue.* **4.** Not paid or adjusted: *an unsettled bill.* **5.** Not disposed of according to law: *an unsettled estate.* **6.** Unpopulated. **7.** Not fixed or established, as in a residence or routine. —**un·set·tled·ness** *n.*

un·sex (ŭn-sĕks′) *tr.v.* **-sexed, -sexing, -sexes.** To deprive of sexual capacity or sexual attributes.

un·shack·le (ŭn-shăk′əl) *tr.v.* **-led, -ling, -les.** To release from or as if from confinement or shackles; set free.

un·shak·a·ble, un·shake·a·ble (ŭn-shā′kə-bəl) *adj.* Incapable of being shaken or weakened; rigid; entrenched: *unshakable convictions.* —**un·shak·a·bly** *adv.*

un·shap·en (ŭn-shā′pən) *adj.* Also **un·shaped** (-shāpt′) (for sense 1). **1.** Not shaped or formed. **2.** Misshapen.

un·sheathe (ŭn-shē*th*′) *tr.v.* **-sheathed, -sheathing, -sheathes.** To draw from or as if from a sheath or scabbard.

un·shell (ŭn-shĕl′) *tr.v.* **-shelled, -shelling, -shells.** To remove from a shell.

un·ship (ŭn-shĭp′) *v.* **-shipped, -shipping, -ships.** —*tr.* **1.** To unload from a ship; discharge. **2.** To remove (a tiller or other piece of nautical gear) from its proper place. —*intr.* To be removable or detachable.

un·sight·ed (ŭn-sī′tĭd) *adj.* **1.** Not sighted or examined. **2.** Not equipped with or assisted by a sight for aiming. **3.** Blind. **4.** Not having a clear view. —**un·sight·ed·ly** *adv.*

un·sight·ly (ŭn-sīt′lē) *adj.* **-lier, -liest.** Unpleasant or offensive to look at; unattractive. —**un·sight·li·ness** *n.*

un·sized (ŭn-sīzd′) *adj.* Not coated or treated with size.

un·skilled (ŭn-skĭld′) *adj.* **1.** Lacking skill or technical training. **2.** Requiring no training or skill. **3.** Showing no skill; crude.

un·skill·ful (ŭn-skĭl′fəl) *adj.* Without skill or proficiency; not adroit; clumsy. —**un·skill·ful·ly** *adv.* —**un·skill·ful·ness** *n.*

un·slaked lime (ŭn-slākt′) *n.* Calcium oxide *(see).*

un·sling (ŭn-slĭng′) *tr.v.* **-slung** (-slŭng′), **-slinging, -slings. 1.** To remove from a sling or a slung position. **2.** *Nautical.* To remove the slings of (a yard, for example).

un·snap (ŭn-snăp′) *tr.v.* **-snapped, -snapping, -snaps.** To undo the snaps of; unfasten.

un·snarl (ŭn-snärl′) *tr.v.* **-snarled, -snarling, -snarls.** To free of snarls; disentangle.

un·so·cia·ble (ŭn-sō′shə-bəl) *adj.* **1.** Not disposed to seek the company of others; not companionable; reserved. **2.** Not conducive to social exchange: *an unsociable atmosphere.* **3.** Not congenial; incompatible. —**un·so·cia·bil·i·ty** (ŭn-sō′shə-bĭl′ə-tē), **un·so·cia·ble·ness** *n.* —**un·so·cia·bly** *adv.*

un·so·cial (ŭn-sō′shəl) *adj.* Not companionable; unsociable. —**un·so·cial·ly** *adv.*

un·so·lic·it·ed (ŭn-sə-lĭs′ə-tĭd) *adj.* Not solicited or asked for.

un·so·phis·ti·cat·ed (ŭn′sə-fĭs′tĭ-kā′tĭd) *adj.* Not sophisticated. —See Synonyms at **naive.** —**un·so·phis·ti·cat·ed·ly** *adv.*

un·sound (ŭn-sound′) *adj.* **-sounder, -soundest. 1.** Not in strong or healthy condition; not sound or stable. **2.** Not soundly based in logic or fact; fallacious. **3.** Not based on sound commercial or economic principles; not viable. **4.** Failing to conform to a given set of principles or dogmas: *an ideologically unsound policy.* —**un·sound·ly** *adv.* —**un·sound·ness** *n.*

un·spar·ing (ŭn-spâr′ĭng) *adj.* **1.** Not frugal. **2.** Unmerciful; severe. —**un·spar·ing·ly** *adv.* —**un·spar·ing·ness** *n.*

un·speak·a·ble (ŭn-spē′kə-bəl) *adj.* **1.** Beyond description; inexpressible: *unspeakable happiness.* **2.** Inexpressibly bad or objectionable. —**un·speak·a·ble·ness** *n.* —**un·speak·a·bly** *adv.*

un·spe·cial·ized (ŭn-spĕsh′ə-līzd′) *adj.* Having no special function; without specialty or specialization.

un·sphere (ŭn-sfîr′) *tr.v.* **-sphered, -sphering, -spheres.** *Rare.* To remove from a sphere or place in the heavens.

un·spoiled (ŭn-spoild′) *adj.* Also **un·spoilt** (-spoilt′). Not marred in beauty or character by modernization, industrialization, or the like: *an unspoiled fishing village.*

un·spo·ken (ŭn-spō′kən) *adj.* **1.** Not uttered or expressed: *She bristled with unspoken resentment.* **2.** Understood without the need for words: *an unspoken pact between them.* —**un·spo·ken·ly** *adv.*

un·spot·ted (ŭn-spŏt′ĭd) *adj.* **1.** Unnoticed; unseen. **2.** Not spotted or stained. **3.** Morally unblemished. —**un·spot·ted·ness** *n.*

un·sta·ble (ŭn-stā′bəl) *adj.* **-bler, -blest. 1. a.** Tending strongly to change. **b.** Not constant; fluctuating. **2. a.** Of fickle temperament; irresponsible. **b.** Psychologically maladjusted. **3.** Not firmly placed; unsteady. **4.** *Chemistry.* **a.** Decomposing readily. **b.** Highly or violently reactive. **5.** *Physics.* **a.** Decaying with relatively short lifetime. Said of subatomic particles. **b.** Radioactive. —**un·sta·ble·ness** *n.* —**un·sta·bly** *adv.*

un·stead·y (ŭn-stĕd′ē) *adj.* **-ier, -iest. 1.** Not securely in place; unstable. **2.** Fluctuating; inconstant. **3.** Wavering; uneven: *an unsteady voice.* **4.** Unsure; precarious: *unsteady legs.* *~tr.v.* **unsteadied, -ying, -ies.** To cause to become unsteady. —**un·stead·i·ly** *adv.* —**un·stead·i·ness** *n.*

un·step (ŭn-stĕp′) *tr.v.* **-stepped, -stepping, -steps.** *Nautical.* To remove (a mast) from a step.

un·stick (ŭn-stĭk′) *tr.v.* **-stuck** (-stŭk′), **-sticking, -sticks.** To free from being stuck.

un·stop (ŭn-stŏp′) *tr.v.* **-stopped, -stopping, -stops. 1.** To remove a stopper or stop from. **2.** To remove an obstruction from; open.

un·stopped (ŭn-stŏpt′) *adj.* **1.** Not stopped. **2.** *Phonetics.* Capable of being prolonged. Said of vowels, nasals, and fricative or liquid consonants. Not in current technical usage. **3.** Subject to enjambment. Said of a line of poetry.

un·strat·i·fied (ŭn-străt′ə-fīd′) *adj.* Lacking definite layers. Said of rocks.

un·stressed (ŭn-strĕst′) *adj.* **1.** Not stressed or having the weakest stress. Said of a segment of speech. **2.** Not emphasized.

un·stri·at·ed (ŭn-strī′ā′tĭd) *adj.* **1.** Lacking striations; smooth-textured. **2.** Composed of spindle-shaped cells that lack striations; unstriped. Said of involuntary muscle.

un·string (ŭn-strĭng′) *tr.v.* **-strung** (-strŭng′), **-stringing, -strings. 1.** To remove from a string. **2.** To unfasten the strings of. **3.** To weaken the nerves or resolve of; unnerve.

un·striped (ŭn-strīpt′) *adj.* **1.** Not striped. **2.** Unstriated. Said of involuntary muscle.

un·struc·tured (ŭn-strŭk′chərd) *adj.* **1.** Lacking a clear or formal structure or organization. **2.** *Psychology.* **a.** Having no intrinsic or objective meaning; meaningful by subjective interpretation only. Said of items, such as inkblots or incomplete sentences, on projective tests. **b.** Not regulated or regimented: *an unstructured setting.*

un·strung (ŭn-strŭng′) *adj.* **1.** Having a string or strings loosened or removed. **2.** Emotionally upset; unnerved.

un·stuck (ŭn-stŭk′) *adj.* **1.** Freed from being stuck. **2.** Mentally unhinged. —**come unstuck.** *Informal.* To fail to achieve an intended result; go wrong: *All her plans came unstuck.*

un·stud·ied (ŭn-stŭd′ēd) *adj.* **1.** Not contrived for effect; natural. **2.** Not having been instructed; unversed. Used with *in.*

un·sub·stan·tial (ŭn-səb-stăn′shəl) *adj.* **1.** Lacking material sub-

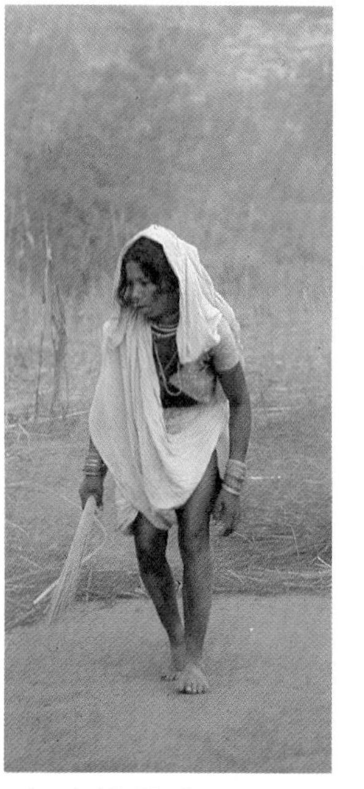

untouchable *The harijans, or "untouchables," form the lowest level in the Indian caste system. Traditionally, they were allowed only limited contact with other Hindu castes and were restricted to menial occupations. Officially, the Indian government has outlawed untouchability and given special privileges to former untouchables; but in practice discrimination lingers on.*

stance; insubstantial. **2.** Lacking firmness or strength; flimsy. **3.** Lacking basis in fact; insubstantial. **—un•sub•stan•ti•al•i•ty** (ŭn′səb-stăn′shē-ăl′ə-tē) *n.* **—un•sub•stan•tial•ly** *adv.*

un•suc•cess•ful (ŭn′sək-sĕs′fəl) *adj.* Not succeeding; without success. **—un•suc•cess•ful•ly** *adv.* **—un•suc•cess•ful•ness** *n.*

un•suit•a•ble (ŭn-so͞o′tə-bəl) *adj.* Not suitable; inappropriate. **—un•suit•a•bil•i•ty, un•suit•a•ble•ness** *n.* **—un•suit•a•bly** *adv.*

un•sung (ŭn-sŭng′) *adj.* **1.** Not sung. **2.** Not honored or praised in song; uncelebrated: *unsung heroes.*

un•sure (ŭn-sho͝or′) *adj.* **1.** Lacking confidence. **2.** Uncertain of the facts. **3.** Precarious; unstable; unreliable. **—un•sure•ly** *adv.* **—un•sure•ness** *n.*

un•sus•pect•ed (ŭn′sə-spĕk′tĭd) *adj.* **1.** Not under suspicion. **2.** Not known to exist. **—un•sus•pect•ed•ly** *adv.*

un•sus•pect•ing (ŭn′sə-spĕk′tĭng) *adj.* Not suspicious; trusting. **—un•sus•pect•ing•ly** *adv.*

un•swathe (ŭn-swŏ*th*′, -swô*th*′, -swā*th*′) *tr.v.* **-swathed, -swathing, -swathes.** To remove the swathings from; unbind.

un•swear (ŭn-swâr′) *v.* **-swore** (-swôr′, -swōr′), **-sworn** (-swôrn′, -swōrn′), **-swearing, -swears.** *—tr.* To retract (an oath). *—intr.* To recant or retract something sworn.

un•swerv•ing (ŭn-swûr′vĭng) *adj.* Unwavering; constant: *unswerving loyalty.* **—un•swerv•ing•ly** *adv.*

un•tan•gle (ŭn-tăng′gəl) *tr.v.* **-gled, -gling, -gles. 1.** To free from a tangle; disentangle. **2.** To clarify; resolve.

un•tapped (ŭn-tăpt′) *adj.* **1.** Not having been tapped: *an untapped cask of wine.* **2.** Not utilized: *untapped resources.*

un•taught (ŭn-tôt′) *adj.* **1.** Not instructed; ignorant. **2.** Not acquired by instruction; natural; untutored. —See Synonyms at **ignorant.**

un•teach (ŭn-tēch′) *tr.v.* **-taught** (-tôt′), **-teaching, -teaches. 1.** To cause to forget or unlearn something. **2.** To negate (what has been taught) with contradictory information.

un•ten•a•ble (ŭn-tĕn′ə-bəl) *adj.* **1.** Incapable of being maintained, defended, or vindicated: *an untenable proposition.* **2.** Not suitable for occupation. **—un•ten•a•bil•i•ty** *n.*

Un•ter den Lin•den (o͝on′tər dĕn lĭn′dən). The main street of East Berlin, extending from the Brandenburg Gate to the center of the city.

Un•ter•mey•er (ŭn′tər-mī′ər), **Louis** (1885–1977). U.S. author and editor. With each new edition of his two best-known anthologies, *Modern American Poetry* (1919) and *Modern British Poetry* (1920), he collected an eclectic body of contemporary works that indicated the changing reputation and popularity of established literary figures and provided a medium for emerging poets.

un•think (ŭn-thĭngk′) *tr.v.* **-thought** (-thôt′), **-thinking, -thinks.** To dismiss from the mind; disregard.

un•think•a•ble (ŭn-thĭng′kə-bəl) *adj.* **1.** Not thinkable; inconceivable. **2.** Not to be thought of or considered; out of the question. **3.** Contrary to what is reasonable or probable. **—un•think•a•ble•ness** *n.* **—un•think•a•bly** *adv.*

un•think•ing (ŭn-thĭng′kĭng) *adj.* **1.** Not thinking or mindful; inattentive; heedless. **2.** Not deliberate; inadvertent. **—un•think•ing•ly** *adv.* **—un•think•ing•ness** *n.*

un•thought-of (ŭn-thôt′ŭv′) *adj.* Inconceivable; not imagined or considered.

un•thread (ŭn-thrĕd′) *tr.v.* **-threaded, -threading, -threads. 1.** To draw out the thread from (a needle, for example). **2.** To unravel. **3.** To find one's way out of (a labyrinth, for example).

un•ti•dy (ŭn-tī′dē) *adj.* **-dier, -diest. 1.** Not neat and tidy; slovenly. **2.** Lacking orderliness or organization: *untidy thinking.* —See Synonyms at **sloppy.**
~*tr.v.* **untidied, -dying, -dies.** To make untidy. **—un•ti•di•ly** *adv.* **—un•ti•di•ness** *n.*

un•tie (ŭn-tī′) *v.* **-tied, -tying, -ties.** *—tr.* **1.** To undo or loosen (a knot or something knotted). **2.** To free from something that binds or restrains. **3.** To straighten out (difficulties or perplexities). *—intr.* To become untied.

un•til (ŭn-tĭl′) *prep.* **1. a.** Up to the time of: *We danced until dawn.* **b.** As far as: *Keep going straight until the third set of traffic lights.* **2.** Before a specific time. Used with a negative: *not until Friday.* **3.** *Chiefly Scottish.* To; unto.
~*conj.* **1.** Up to the time that. **2.** Before. Used with a negative: *You can't have your dessert until you eat your salad.* **3.** To the point or extent that. [Middle English *until(l),* to, toward, up to, till : *un-,* from Old Norse *und,* unto + *til,* TILL.]

un•time•ly (ŭn-tīm′lē) *adj.* **-lier, -liest. 1.** Occurring or done at an inappropriate time; inopportune. **2.** Occurring too soon; premature: *untimely death.*
~*adv.* **1.** Inopportunely. **2.** Prematurely. **—un•time•li•ness** *n.*

un•tir•ing (ŭn-tīr′ĭng) *adj.* **1.** Not tiring. **2.** Not ceasing despite fatigue or difficulties; persistent. **—un•tir•ing•ly** *adv.*

un•ti•tled (ŭn-tī′təld) *adj.* **1.** Having no right or claim. **2.** Having no title: *an untitled novel; untitled nobility.*

un•to (ŭn′to͞o) *prep. Poetic & Archaic.* To: *Unto us a child is born.* [Middle English *un-,* to (see **until**) + TO.]

un•told (ŭn-tōld′) *adj.* **1.** Not told or revealed: *untold secrets.* **2.** Beyond description or enumeration: *untold suffering.*

un•touch•a•ble (ŭn-tŭch′ə-bəl) *adj.* **1.** Not to be touched. **2.** Out of reach; unobtainable. **3.** Beyond the reach of criticism, impeachment, or attack. **4.** Loathsome, unpleasant, or defiling to the touch.
~*n.* *Often* **Untouchable.** A member of the lowest Hindu caste, who was considered unclean and with whom physical contact was considered defiling by Hindus of higher castes. Also called "harijan." **—un•touch•a•bil•i•ty** *n.*

un•touched (ŭn-tŭcht′) *adj.* **1.** Not used or touched: *untouched by human hand.* **2.** Not discussed or referred to. **3.** Not moved emotionally. **4.** Not harmed or damaged: *emerged from the wreck untouched.* **5.** Not modified or changed: *untouched photographs.*

un•to•ward (ŭn-tôrd′, -tōrd′) *adj.* **1.** Unfavorable; unpropitious. **2.** Characterized by disaster or misfortune. **3.** Inappropriate; offensive: *untoward advances.* **4.** *Archaic.* Hard to control; refractory. **—un•to•ward•ly** *adv.* **—un•to•ward•ness** *n.*

un•tram•meled (ŭn-trăm′əld) *adj.* Unrestrained; not confined to rigid boundaries.

un•trav•eled (ŭn-trăv′əld) *adj.* **1.** Not traversed, as a road. **2.** Not having traveled widely or far.

un•tread (ŭn-trĕd′) *tr.v.* **-trod** (-trŏd′), **-trodden** (-trŏd′n) or **-trod, -treading, -treads.** To retrace (one's course).

un•tried (ŭn-trīd′) *adj.* **1.** Not attempted, tested, or proved. **2.** Not tried in court.

un•true (ŭn-tro͞o′) *adj.* **-truer, -truest. 1.** Contrary to fact; false. **2.** Deviating from a standard; not straight, even, or exact. **3.** Disloyal; unfaithful. **—un•tru•ly** *adv.*

un•truss (ŭn-trŭs′) *v.* **-trussed, -trussing, -trusses.** *—tr.* **1.** To unfasten; undo. **2.** *Archaic.* To undress. *—intr. Archaic.* To remove one's clothes, especially one's breeches.

un•truth (ŭn-tro͞oth′) *n.* **1.** A lie. **2.** The state or quality of being untrue; falsity.

un•truth•ful (ŭn-tro͞oth′fəl) *adj.* **1.** Given to falsehood; mendacious. **2.** Contrary to truth. —See Synonyms at **dishonest. —un•truth•ful•ly** *adv.* **—un•truth•ful•ness** *n.*

un•tuck (ŭn-tŭk′) *tr.v.* **-tucked, -tucking, -tucks.** To cause to hang out or not be tucked in: *Your shirt has become untucked.*

un•tu•tored (ŭn-to͞o′tərd, -tyo͞o′tərd) *adj.* **1.** Having had no formal education or instruction: *an untutored genius.* **2.** Unsophisticated; unrefined: *an untutored palate.* —See Synonyms at **ignorant.**

un•twine (ŭn-twīn′) *v.* **-twined, -twining, -twines.** *—tr.* **1.** To loosen or separate (strands of twisted fiber, for example). **2.** To disentangle. *—intr.* To become untwined.

un•twist (ŭn-twĭst′) *v.* **-twisted, -twisting, -twists.** *—tr.* To loosen or separate (that which is twisted together) by turning in the opposite direction; unwind. *—intr.* To become untwisted.

un•used (ŭn-yo͞ozd′ *for senses 1, 2;* ŭn-yo͞ost′ *for sense 3*) *adj.* **1.** Not in use or put to use. **2.** Never having been used. **3.** Not accustomed. Used with *to*: *unused to city traffic.*

un•u•su•al (ŭn-yo͞o′zho͞o-əl) *adj.* Not usual or common. **—un•u•su•al•ly** *adv.* **—un•u•su•al•ness** *n.*

un•ut•ter•a•ble (ŭn-ŭt′ər-ə-bəl) *adj.* **1.** Not capable of being uttered or expressed; too profound to be expressed in words. **2.** Not capable of being pronounced. **3.** Utter; complete: *an unutterable idiot.* **—un•ut•ter•a•ble•ness** *n.* **—un•ut•ter•a•bly** *adv.*

un•var•nished (ŭn-vär′nĭsht) *adj.* **1.** Not varnished. **2.** Not softened or disguised; straightforward: *the unvarnished truth.*

un•veil (ŭn-vāl′) *v.* **-veiled, -veiling, -veils.** *—tr.* **1.** To remove a veil or other covering from. **2.** To disclose; reveal. *—intr.* To take off one's veil; reveal oneself.

un•veil•ing (ŭn-vā′lĭng) *n.* A ceremony at which a portrait, monument, or other work of art is disclosed for the first time to public view.

un•voice (ŭn-vois′) *tr.v.* **-voiced, -voicing, -voices.** *Phonetics.* To utter without vibrating the vocal cords; devoice.

un•voiced (ŭn-voist′) *adj.* **1.** Not expressed or uttered. **2.** *Phonetics.* Voiceless.

un•war•rant•a•ble (ŭn-wôr′ən-tə-bəl, ŭn-wŏr′-) *adj.* Not justifiable; inexcusable. **—un•war•rant•a•bly** *adv.*

un•war•rant•ed (ŭn-wôr′ən-tĭd, ŭn-wŏr′-) *adj.* Having no justification; groundless.

un•war•y (ŭn-wâr′ē) *adj.* **-ier, -iest.** Not alert to danger or deception; unguarded. **—un•war•i•ly** *adv.* **—un•war•i•ness** *n.*

un•washed (ŭn-wŏsht′, -wôsht′) *adj.* Not washed; unclean.
~*n.* The lower classes or the masses. Used derogatorily in the phrase *the great unwashed.*

un•wa•ver•ing (ŭn-wā′vər-ĭng) *adv.* Not wavering; constant: *unwavering accuracy; unwavering honesty.* **—un•wa•ver•ing•ly** *adv.*

un•wea•ried (ŭn-wîr′ēd) *adj.* **1.** Not tired; fresh. **2.** Never wearying; tireless. **—un•wea•ried•ly** *adv.*

un•well (ŭn-wĕl′) *adj.* **1.** Not well; ailing; ill. **2.** Menstruating. —See Synonyms at **sick.**

un•wept (ŭn-wĕpt′) *adj.* **1.** Not mourned or wept for: *the unwept dead.* **2.** Not shed. Said of tears.

un•whole•some (ŭn-hōl′səm) *adj.* **1.** Injurious to physical, mental, or moral health. **2.** Suggestive of disease or degeneracy. **3.** Offensive or loathsome. **—un•whole•some•ly** *adv.* **—un•whole•some•ness** *n.*

un•wield•y (ŭn-wēl′dē) *adj.* **-ier, -iest. 1.** Difficult to carry or manage because of bulk or shape. **2.** Cumbersomely large or unmanageable: *an unwieldy bureaucracy.* **3.** Clumsy; ungainly. —See Synonyms at **heavy. —un•wield•i•ly** *adv.* **—un•wield•i•ness** *n.*

un•willed (ŭn-wĭld′) *adj.* Involuntary; spontaneous.

un•will•ing (ŭn-wĭl′ĭng) *adj.* **1.** Hesitant; loath. **2.** Done, given, or said reluctantly: *unwilling consent.* **—un•will•ing•ly** *adv.* **—un•will•ing•ness** *n.*

un•wind (ŭn-wīnd′) *v.* **-wound** (-wound′), **-winding, -winds.** *—tr.* **1.** To reverse the winding or twisting direction of; unroll; uncoil. **2.** To separate the tangled parts of; disentangle. **3.** To free from tension. —*intr.* **1.** To become unwound. **2.** *Informal.* To become less tense; relax. —**un·wind·a·ble** *adj.*

un·wink·ing (ŭn-wĭng′kĭng) *adj.* Vigilant; careful. —**un·wink·ing·ly** *adv.* —**un·wink·ing·ness** *n.*

un·wis·dom (ŭn-wĭz′dəm) *n.* Lack of wisdom; foolishness.

un·wise (ŭn-wīz′) *adj.* **-wiser, -wisest.** Lacking wisdom; foolish or imprudent. —**un·wise·ly** *adv.* —**un·wise·ness** *n.*

un·wish (ŭn-wĭsh′) *tr.v.* **-wished, -wishing, -wishes. 1.** To cease to wish for. **2.** To wish out of existence.

un·wished-for (ŭn-wĭsht′fôr′) *adj.* Not wished for or desired: *unwished-for criticism.*

un·wit·ting (ŭn-wĭt′ĭng) *adj.* **1.** Not knowing; unaware: *an unwitting victim of fraud.* **2.** Not intended; unintentional. [Middle English *un-,* not + *witting,* present participle of *wit(t)en,* to know, Old English *witan.*] —**un·wit·ting·ly** *adv.* —**un·wit·ting·ness** *n.*

un·wont·ed (ŭn-wôn′tĭd, -wōn′tĭd, -wŭn′tĭd) *adj.* Not habitual; unusual: *"Her unwonted breach of delicacy . . . perplexed him"* (George Meredith). —**un·wont·ed·ly** *adv.* —**un·wont·ed·ness** *n.*

un·world·ly (ŭn-wûrld′lē) *adj.* **-lier, -liest. 1.** Not of this world; extraterrestrial. **2.** Concerned with matters of the spirit or soul. **3.** Not worldly-wise; naive. —**un·world·li·ness** *n.*

un·wor·thy (ŭn-wûr′thē) *adj.* **-thier, -thiest. 1.** Insufficient in worth; undeserving. Usually used with *of: a bad plan unworthy of consideration.* **2.** Not suiting or befitting. Usually used with *of: "The acquaintances she had already formed were unworthy of her"* (Jane Austen). **3.** Lacking value or merit; worthless. **4.** Vile; despicable. —**un·wor·thi·ly** *adv.* —**un·wor·thi·ness** *n.*

un·wrap (ŭn-răp′) *v.* **-wrapped, -wrapping, -wraps.** —*tr.* To remove the wrappings from; open. —*intr.* To become or admit of being unwrapped.

un·writ·ten (ŭn-rĭt′n) *adj.* **1.** Not written or recorded. **2.** Forceful or effective through custom or tradition; not codified: *an unwritten rule.*

unwritten law *n.* A code, rule, or law of morality, conduct, or procedure whose authority comes from custom, tradition, or general usage rather than formal legislation or regulation.

un·yield·ing (ŭn-yēl′dĭng) *adj.* Inflexible; unwilling to move from a given position. —See Synonyms at **inflexible.**

un·yoke (ŭn-yōk′) *v.* **-yoked, -yoking, -yokes.** —*tr.* **1.** To release (a draft animal) from a yoke. **2.** To separate or disjoin. **3.** To liberate. —*intr.* **1.** To remove a yoke. **2.** *Archaic.* To stop working.

un·zip (ŭn-zĭp′) *v.* **-zipped, -zipping, -zips.** —*tr.* To open or unfasten (a zipper or something held by a zipper). —*intr.* To become unzipped.

up (ŭp) *adv.* **1.** From a lower to a higher position. **2.** In or toward a higher position. **3. a.** From a reclining to an upright position: *setting up the deck chairs.* **b.** Out of bed: *It's time you got up.* **4. a.** Above a surface: *coming up for air.* **b.** From or off a surface: *pick it up.* **c.** Above the horizon: *The sun came up.* **5. a.** Into view or consideration: *brought up the problem of unemployment.* **b.** Into existence or operation: *set up a committee.* **6. a.** In or toward a position conventionally regarded as higher, as on a scale, chart, or map. **b.** *British.* In or toward a capital city or university, especially Oxford or Cambridge: *I'm going up to London. She's going up to Oxford.* **7.** Toward the speaker or the place or person referred to: *She went right up to the policeman.* **8.** In or toward a better position: *going up in the world.* **9.** To or at a higher price. **10.** So as to advance, increase, or improve: *Sales have gone up again.* **11. a.** With or to a greater volume: *turn the music up.* **b.** To a higher pitch. **12.** Into a state of excitement or turbulence: *He's quite wound up.* **13.** So as to detach or unearth: *pull up weeds.* **14.** To a stop: *She drew up at the curb.* **15.** *Nautical.* To windward. **16.** Used as an intensive to suggest thoroughness or conclusiveness of an action: *cleaning up; typing up a list; finishing up my work.* **17.** Each; apiece: *The score was eight up.* **18.** Completely; entirely. —**up** or **up with** Used interjectionally as a cry of support: *Up the Irish!* —*adj.* **1.** High or relatively high. **2. a.** Standing; erect. **b.** Out of bed. **3.** Moving or directed upward: *an up escalator.* **4.** Actively functioning; healthy: *up and around; up and doing.* **5.** Rising toward the flood level. **6. a.** Marked by agitation or acceleration: *The winds are up.* **b.** Prepared to fight: *up in arms.* **7.** *Informal.* Taking place; going on: *What's up?* **8.** Being considered; under study: *a contract up for renewal.* **9.** Charged; on trial: *up for manslaughter.* **10.** Running as a candidate: *up for re-election.* **11.** Finished; over: *His time was up.* **12.** Failed or lost hopelessly: *It's all up with me.* **13.** *Informal.* Well-informed: *not up on sports.* **14.** Being ahead of an opponent: *up two holes in a golf match.* **15.** *Baseball.* At bat. **16.** In tennis and similar games, not having bounced twice. Said of the ball. **17.** In the saddle. Said of a jockey. **18.** *Nautical.* Bound for a specified place. **19.** As a bet; at stake. —**up against.** Confronted with; facing: *up against great odds.* —**up to. 1.** Occupied with; especially, devising or scheming: *idlers up to no good.* **2.** Primed or prepared for: *Are you up to the challenge?* **3.** Dependent upon: *It's up to us.* **4.** As many as and including: *up to five of them.* —*prep.* **1.** From a lower to or toward a higher point on. **2.** Toward or at a point farther along: *up the road.* **3.** In a direction toward the source of: *up river.* **4.** Against: *up the wind.* —*n.* **1.** An upward slope; a rise or ascent, as of a projectile. **2.** An upward movement or trend. —**on the up and up.** *Slang.* **1.** Open and honest. **2.** *British.* Rising rapidly in status, achievement, or mood. —*v.* **upped, upping, ups.** —*tr.* **1.** To increase or improve. **2.** To raise. —*intr.* **1.** To get up; rise. **2.** *Informal.* To act suddenly or

unexpectedly. Usually used with *and* followed by a verb: *"She upped and perjured her immortal soul"* (Margery Allingham). —See Usage note at **down** (direction). [Middle English *up,* upward, and *uppe,* on high, Old English *ŭp* and *uppe.*]

up– *prefix.* Indicates: **1.** Up; for example, **uplift. 2.** Upper or better; for example, **upmost. 3.** Upward; for example, **upsweep. 4.** Upside-down; for example, **upend, upturn. 5.** Resulting; for example, **upshot. Note:** Many compounds other than those entered here may be formed with **up–.** In this dictionary in forming compounds, **up–** is normally joined with the following element without space or hyphen: **upend.** However, the separate word **up** appears in a few phrases that are hyphenated. Among those entered here are: **up-and-coming, up-and-down, up-bow,** and **up-to-the-minute.** [Middle English *up-,* Old English *ŭp-, upp-,* upward, on high.]

up-and-com·ing (ŭp′ən-kŭm′ĭng) *adj.* Likely to achieve success or improved status; promising or enterprising: *an up-and-coming young actress; an up-and-coming suburb.* —**up-and-com·er** *n.*

up and down *adv.* Backward and forward or in all directions: *pacing up and down.*

up-and-down (ŭp′ən-doun′) *adj.* **1.** Characterized by alternating upward and downward movement. **2.** Vertical; perpendicular.

up-and-o·ver (ŭp′ən-ō′vər) *adj.* Opened by being raised and slipped over into a horizontal position: *an up-and-over door.*

U·pan·i·shad (ōō-păn′ə-shäd′) *n.* Any of a group of philosophical treatises contributing to the theology of Hinduism, elaborating upon the earlier Vedas. [Sanskrit *upaniṣad,* "a sitting down near to" : *úpa,* near to + *ni,* down + *ṣad-,* to sit.] —**U·pan·i·shad·ic** (ōō-păn′ə-shăd′ĭk) *adj.*

u·pas (yōō′pəs) *n.* **1.** A tree, *Antiaris toxicaria,* of tropical Asia, once thought to be fatal to anyone who came near to or touched it, that yields a juice used as an arrow poison. Also called "upas-tree." **2.** The poison obtained from this tree or similar trees or plants. [Javanese, poison, dart poison.]

up·beat (ŭp′bēt′) *n.* **1.** *Music.* An unaccented beat, upon which the conductor's hand is raised; especially, the last beat of a bar. Compare **downbeat. 2.** An upward trend, as in one's fortunes or career. Used chiefly in the phrase *on the upbeat.* —*adj. Informal.* Optimistic; happy; cheerful.

up·bow (ŭp′bō′) *n.* A stroke executed from the tip toward the heel of the bow on a violin or similar stringed instrument. Compare **down-bow.**

up·braid (ŭp′brād′) *tr.v.* **-braided, -braiding, -braids.** To reprove sharply; scold or chide vehemently; censure. —See Synonyms at **scold.** [Middle English *upbreyden,* Old English *ŭpbrēdan,* "to throw up against," reproach : *ŭp-,* up + *bregdan,* to move quickly, throw, weave.] —**up·braid·er** *n.* —**up·braid·ing·ly** *adv.*

up·bring·ing (ŭp′brĭng′ĭng) *n.* The rearing and training received during childhood.

up·build (ŭp′bĭld′) *tr.v.* **-built** (-bĭlt′)**, -building, -builds.** To build up; enlarge or enhance. —**up·build·er** *n.*

up·cast (ŭp′kăst′, -käst′) *adj.* Directed or thrown upward. —*n.* **1.** Something cast upward. **2.** A ventilating shaft, as in a mine.

up·com·ing (ŭp′kŭm′ĭng) *adj.* Anticipated; forthcoming.

up·coun·try (ŭp′kŭn′trē) *n.* The inland or interior region of a country. —*adj.* (ŭp′kŭn′trē). **1.** Located in, originating from, or characteristic of the upcountry. **2.** Countrified; unsophisticated. —*adv.* (ŭp′kŭn′trē). In, to, or toward the upcountry.

up·date (ŭp′dāt′) *tr.v.* **-dated, -dating, -dates. 1.** To bring up to date: *update a textbook.* **2.** *Computer Science.* To amend (data or programs, for example) so as to produce a new version, with a new address number. —*n.* (ŭp′dāt′). **1.** Current or updated information. **2.** The act or an instance of updating something.

Up·dike (ŭp′dīk′)**, John Hoyer** (1932–). U.S. author. A regular contributor and one-time reporter for the *New Yorker* magazine, he is best known for his tragicomic novels about the troubles of middle-class American life, including *Rabbit, Run* (1960), *Rabbit Redux* (1971), and his Pulitzer Prize winner *Rabbit is Rich* (1981).

up·draft (ŭp′drăft′, -dräft′) *n.* An upward current of air. —*adj.* Designating a carburetor in which the mixture is drawn upward against gravity.

up·end (ŭp′ĕnd′) *v.* **-ended, -ending, -ends.** —*tr.* **1.** To stand, set, or turn on one end. **2.** To overturn or overthrow; upset. —*intr.* To be upended.

up-front, up front (ŭp′frŭnt′) *adj.* **1.** Frank; direct; forthright: *up-front about his own shortcomings.* **2.** Required or paid in advance: *up-front cash.* —**up-front** *adv.*

up·grade (ŭp′grād′) *tr.v.* **-graded, -grading, -grades. 1.** To raise to a higher grade, standard, or position. **2.** To improve the quality of (a manufactured product, for example). —*n.* An incline leading uphill. —*adj.* Uphill. —*adv.* Uphill.

up·growth (ŭp′grōth′) *n.* **1.** Upward growth or development. **2.** Something that has grown up.

up·heav·al (ŭp′hē′vəl) *n.* **1.** A sudden and violent disruption or upset. **2.** *Geology.* A lifting up of the earth's crust by the movement of stratified or other rocks. [UP- + HEAVE + -AL.]

up·hill (ŭp′hĭl′) *adj.* **1.** Going up a hill or slope. **2.** Prolonged and laborious. —*n.* (ŭp′hĭl′). An upward slope or incline.

~*adv.* (ŭp'hīl'). **1.** To or toward higher ground; upward. **2.** Against adversity; with difficulty.

up·hold (ŭp-hōld') *tr.v.* **-held** (-hĕld'), **-holding, -holds. 1. a.** To maintain or affirm in the face of a challenge: *"The Declaration of Right upheld the principle of hereditary monarchy"* (Edmund Burke). **b.** To support or stand by (a person or cause, for example). **2.** To prevent from falling or sinking; support. **3.** To hold aloft; raise. —See Synonyms at **support.** [Middle English *upholden* : UP- + HOLD.] —**up·hold·er** *n.*

up·hol·ster (ŭp-hōl'stər) *tr.v.* **-stered, -stering, -sters. 1.** To provide (chairs, sofas, or similar soft furniture) with stuffing, springs, cushions, and covering fabric. **2.** To furnish (rooms) with curtains, carpets, and similar accessories. [Back-formation from UPHOLSTERER.]

up·hol·ster·er (ŭp-hōl'stər-ər) *n.* A person who upholsters furniture as an occupation. [Obsolete *upholster,* a dealer in or repairer of small wares, Middle English *upholdester,* one who upholds or repairs, from *upholden,* to UPHOLD.]

up·hol·ster·y (ŭp-hōl'stər-ē, -strē) *n., pl.* **-ies. 1.** The fabrics and other materials used in upholstering. **2.** The act, craft, or business of upholstering.

UPI, U.P.I. United Press International.

up·keep (ŭp'kēp') *n.* **1.** The act or process of maintaining something in good condition and repair. **2.** The cost of such maintenance.

up·land (ŭp'lənd, -lănd') *n.* Often **uplands.** The higher parts of a region, country, or tract of land. —**up·land** *adj.*

upland cotton *n.* **1.** A cotton plant, *Gossypium hirsutum,* native to tropical America and widely cultivated for its fiber. **2.** The fiber of this plant.

up·lift (ŭp-lĭft') *tr.v.* **-lifted, -lifting, -lifts. 1.** To lift up or raise aloft. **2.** To raise to a higher spiritual, intellectual, or social level; exalt; elevate.
~*adj.* (ŭp'lĭft'). Uplifting: *an uplift bra.*
~*n.* (ŭp'lĭft'). **1.** The act, process, or result of raising or lifting up. **2.** Any agent or influence causing upward movement or lifting. **3.** A movement to improve social, moral, or intellectual standards. **4.** *Geology.* An upheaval.

up·load (ŭp'lōd') *tr.v.* **-loaded, -loading, -loads.** *Computer Science.* To transfer (data or programs) from a small computer to a main computer. Compare **download.** [*upline* + *load.*]

upmost. Variant of **uppermost.**

up·on (ə-pŏn', ə-pôn') *prep.* On. [Middle English (formed after Old Norse *upp ā*) : UP + ON.]
Usage: **Upon** is frequently interchangeable with *on,* although it is slightly more formal. It is always used, however, in such fixed phrases as: *Once upon a time; upon my word; (winter) is almost upon us; (row) upon (row) of (seats).* —See Usage note at **on.**

up·per (ŭp'ər) *adj. Abbr.* **up., u., U. 1.** Higher in place, power, position, or rank: *the upper bunk.* **2. a.** Situated on higher ground. **b.** Lying farther inland. **c.** *Northern: Michigan's upper peninsula.* **3. Upper.** *Geology & Archaeology.* Being a later division of the period named: *artifacts of the Upper Paleolithic.* **4.** *Mathematics.* Designating or pertaining to the highest value in a set.
~*n.* **1.** That part of a shoe or boot above the sole. **2.** *Informal.* An upper berth. **3. uppers.** *Informal.* The upper teeth or a set of upper dentures. **4.** *Slang.* A drug, often an amphetamine, used as a stimulant. Compare **downer.** —**on one's uppers.** *Informal.* **1.** Wearing shoes with worn-out soles. **2.** Impoverished; destitute.

upper atmosphere *n.* That part of the atmosphere above 18 miles high and inaccessible to direct observation by balloon.

Upper Avon. See **Avon** (Northamptonshire).

upper bound *n. Mathematics.* A number that is not exceeded by any number in a given set.

upper case *n. Abbr.* **u.c. 1.** Capital letters. **2.** The case of printing type containing the capital letters and special characters.

up·per-case (ŭp'ər-kās') *adj. Abbr.* **u.c.** *Printing.* Pertaining to or designating capital letters; capital.
~*tr.v.* **upper-cased, -casing, -cases.** To print in upper-case letters.

upper class *n.* **1.** Often **upper classes.** The usually small class in a society considered to rank highest, socially or economically; especially, the aristocracy. **2.** The junior or senior class in a secondary school or college. —**up·per-class** (ŭp'ər-klăs', -kläs') *adj.*

up·per·class·man (ŭp'ər-klăs'mən) *n., pl.* **-men** (-mĭn). A student in the junior or senior class of a secondary school or college.

upper crust *n. Informal.* The upper class.

up·per·cut (ŭp'ər-kŭt') *n. Boxing.* A short swinging blow directed upward, as to the opponent's chin. —**up·per·cut** *v.*

upper hand *n.* A position of control or advantage. Preceded by *the.*

Upper House *n.* Often **upper house.** The branch of a bicameral legislature that is smaller and less broadly representative of the population, such as the U.S. Senate. Also called "Upper Chamber." Compare **Lower House.**

up·per·most (ŭp'ər-mōst') *adj.* Also **up·most** (ŭp'mōst'). Highest in position, place, rank, or influence; topmost; foremost.
~*adv.* In the highest or most prominent rank, position, or place; first: *whatever concern is uppermost in your mind.*

Upper Vol·ta (vōl'tə). Also **Bur·ki·na Fa·so** (bûr-kē'nə fä'sō). Landlocked state in the Sahel region of West Africa. It is one of the world's poorest countries, depending on aid, mostly from France. Over 90 percent of its people are farmers, most at subsistence level. Some cattle and cotton are exported. A French colony from 1896, Upper Volta became independent in 1960. Area, 274,200 square kilometers (105,869 square miles). Population, 6,900,000. Capital, Ouagadougou. See map at **West African States.**

up·pish (ŭp'ĭsh) *adj. British Informal.* Tending to be snobbish or arrogant. [UP + -ISH.] —**up·pish·ly** *adv.* —**up·pish·ness** *n.*

up·pi·ty (ŭp'ə-tē) *adj. Informal.* Snobbish; haughty. [From UP.]

Upp·sa·la or **Up·sa·la** (ŭp'sə-lä'). City in eastern Sweden, on the Fyrisån River, just northwest of Stockholm. Its 13th-century cathedral has traditionally been used for the coronation of Swedish monarchs.

up·raise (ŭp-rāz') *tr.v.* **-raised, -raising, -raises.** To raise or lift up; elevate.

up·rear (ŭp-rîr') *v.* **-reared, -rearing, -rears.** —*tr.* To raise or lift up. —*intr.* To be raised up; rise.

up·right (ŭp'rīt') *adj.* **1. a.** In a vertical position, direction, or stance. **b.** Erect in posture or carriage. **2.** Morally respectable; honorable; righteous. —See Synonyms at **vertical.**
~*adv.* In a vertical or erect position: *walk upright.*
~*n.* **1.** A perpendicular position; verticality. **2.** Something standing upright, such as a beam. **3.** An upright piano. [Middle English *upright,* Old English *ūpriht* : UP- + RIGHT.] —**up·right·ly** *adv.* —**up·right·ness** *n.*

upright piano *n.* A piano having the strings mounted vertically in a rectangular case with the keyboard at a right angle to the case. Also called "upright." Compare **grand piano.**

up·rise (ŭp-rīz') *intr.v.* **-rose** (-rōz'), **-risen** (-rĭz'ən), **-rising, -rises. 1.** To get up or stand up; rise. **2.** To go, move, or incline upward; ascend. **3.** To rise into view, especially from below the horizon.
~*n.* (ŭp'rīz'). **1.** The act or process of rising up. **2.** Something that rises or slopes up.

up·ris·ing (ŭp'rī'zĭng) *n.* **1.** A revolt; an insurrection. **2.** An upward slope. **3.** An act of rising or rising up. —See Synonyms at **rebellion.**

up·riv·er (ŭp'rĭv'ər) *adv.* Toward or near the source of a river; in the direction opposite to that of the flow of water.
~*n.* A region lying upriver. —**up·riv·er** *adj.*

up·roar (ŭp'rôr', -rōr') *n.* **1.** A condition of noisy excitement and confusion; a tumult. **2.** A heated controversy. —See Synonyms at **noise.** [Alteration (influenced by ROAR) of Dutch *oproer,* from Middle Dutch : *op,* up + *roer,* confusion.]

up·roar·i·ous (ŭp-rôr'ē-əs, ŭp-rōr'-, ŭp'-) *adj.* **1.** Causing or accompanied by an uproar. **2.** Loud and full, as laughter; boisterous. **3.** Causing hearty laughter; hilarious. [UPROAR + -IOUS.] —**up·roar·i·ous·ly** *adv.* —**up·roar·i·ous·ness** *n.*

up·root (ŭp-rōōt', -rŏŏt') *tr.v.* **-rooted, -rooting, -roots. 1.** To tear or remove (a plant and its roots) from the ground. **2.** To destroy or remove completely; eradicate. **3.** To force to leave an accustomed or native location. —**up·root·ed·ness** *n.* —**up·root·er** *n.*

up·rush (ŭp'rŭsh') *n.* An upward rush, as of blood to the face or an emotion from the subconscious.

Upsala. See **Uppsala.**

ups and downs *pl.n.* Alternating periods of good and bad fortune or high and low spirits.

up·scale (ŭp'skāl') *adj.* Of, being, or intended for consumers belonging to the higher socioeconomic classes: *gourmet food with an upscale appeal; an upscale neighborhood.*

up·set (ŭp-sĕt') *v.* **-set, -setting, -sets.** —*tr.* **1.** To overturn or capsize; tip over. **2.** To disturb in usual or normal functioning, order, or course. **3.** To distress or perturb mentally or emotionally. **4.** To defeat unexpectedly. **5.** To cause illness or indigestion in (the stomach). **6.** To make shorter and thicker by hammering on the end; swage. —*intr.* **1.** To become overturned; tip over; capsize. **2.** To beccme disturbed.
~*n.* (ŭp'sĕt'). **1. a.** An act of upsetting. **b.** The condition of being upset. **2.** A disturbance, disorder, or agitation. **3.** A bodily disorder: *a stomach upset.* **4.** A game or contest in which the side expected to win is defeated. **5. a.** A tool used for upsetting; a swage. **b.** An upset part or piece.
~*adj.* (ŭp-sĕt', ŭp'sĕt'). **1.** Overturned; capsized. **2.** Disordered; disturbed. **3.** Suffering from indigestion, nausea, or a similar condition: *an upset stomach.* **4.** Agitated; distraught. **5.** Overthrown; defeated. [Originally "to set up," "erect," later "to overset," Middle English *upsetten* : UP- + *setten,* to SET.] —**up·set·ter** *n.*

upset price *n.* The lowest price at which merchandise or property will be auctioned or sold at public sale.

up·shot (ŭp'shŏt') *n.* The final result; the outcome. —See Synonyms at **effect.** [Originally the last shot at an archery contest, hence an outcome or decision.]

up·side-down (ŭp'sīd'doun') *adj.* **1.** Overturned completely so that the upper side is down. **2.** In great disorder or confusion; topsy-turvy.
~*adv.* Also **upside down. 1.** With the upper side down. **2.** Topsy-turvy. —**turn upside-down.** To ransack. [Alteration (influenced by obsolete *upside*) of earlier *upsedown,* Middle English *up so doun,* "up as if down" : UP + SO + DOWN.] —**up·side-down·ness** *n.*

upside-down cake *n.* A single-layer cake baked with sliced fruit at the bottom, then served with the fruit side up.

up·si·lon (ŭp'sə-lŏn') *n.* The 20th letter in the Greek alphabet, written Υ, υ. Transliterated in English as *U, u,* or *y,* and as *v* or *f* when it follows a vowel in Modern Greek. See feature at **alphabet.** [Medieval Greek *u psilon,* "simple upsilon" (name adopted for graphic *u* as distinguished from graphic *oi,* both of which were pronounced identically in Late Greek) : Greek *u,* upsilon + *psilon,* neuter of *psilos,* bare, simple, mere.]

up·spring (ŭp'sprĭng') *intr.v.* **-sprang** (-sprăng') or **-sprung**

(-sprŭng'), -sprung, -springing, -springs. 1. To spring up, as from the soil. 2. To come into being; arise.
~n. (ŭp'sprĭng'). A leap or spring upward.

up·stage (ŭp'stāj') *adj.* 1. At, pertaining to, or involving the rear of a stage. 2. *Informal.* Haughty; aloof.
~*adv.* Toward, to, on, or at the back part of the stage.
~*tr.v.* **upstaged, -staging, -stages.** 1. To distract the audience's attention from (another actor), as by moving behind him and thus forcing him to face upstage. 2. *Informal.* To steal the show from; force out of the spotlight. 3. *Informal.* To treat haughtily.

up·stairs (ŭp'stârz') *adv.* 1. In, on, or to an upper floor or story; up the stairs. 2. *Informal.* In or to a higher rank. 3. *Informal.* Mentally: *not all there upstairs.* —**kick upstairs.** *Informal.* To dispose of by promoting to an ineffectual position.
~*adj.* Of or on an upper floor or floors: *an upstairs bathroom.*
~*n.* Used with a singular or plural verb. A floor or the floors above ground level or a given level.

up·stand·ing (ŭp'stăn'dĭng, ŭp'-) *adj.* 1. Standing erect or upright. 2. Morally upright; honest. —**up·stand·ing·ness** *n.*

up·start (ŭp'stärt') *n.* 1. One that springs up suddenly; specifically, a person of humble origin who attains sudden wealth or consequence; a parvenu. 2. A person having an exaggerated sense of his own importance or ability: *cocky little upstart.*
~*adj.* 1. Suddenly raised to a position of consequence. 2. Characteristic of an upstart; self-important; presumptuous.
~*intr.v.* (ŭp'stärt') **upstarted, -starting, -starts.** To spring or start up suddenly.

up·state (ŭp'stāt') *adj.* Pertaining to or designating that part of a state lying inland or farther north of a large city.
~*n.* The upstate region. —**up·state** *adv.* —**up·stat·er** *n.*

up·stream (ŭp'strēm') *adv.* In, at, or toward the source of a stream or current.
~*adj.* 1. In a direction opposite to that of a stream's current. 2. *Finance.* Closer to the point of production or manufacture than to the point of sale. Compare **downstream.**

up·stroke (ŭp'strōk') *n.* 1. An upward stroke, as of a brush. 2. The upward movement of a piston in a reciprocating engine or pump in which the cylinder is cleared of fluid.

up·surge (ŭp'sûrj') *n.* A rapid upward swell or rise.

up·sweep (ŭp'swēp') *n.* 1. A curve or sweep upward. 2. A hairstyle that is smoothed upward at the back and piled on top of the head.
~*tr.v.* **upswept** (-swĕpt'), **-sweeping, -sweeps.** To brush, curve, or sweep upward.

up·swing (ŭp'swĭng') *n.* An upward swing or trend; an increase, as in movement or activity: *an upswing on the stock market.*

up·sy-dai·sy (ŭp'sē-dā'zē) *interj.* Used when lifting or swinging a child. [From earlier *up-a-daisy;* irregularly from UP; compare LACKADAISICAL.]

up·take (ŭp'tāk') *n.* 1. Understanding; comprehension: *very quick on the uptake.* 2. A passage for drawing up smoke or air; a flue or ventilating shaft. 3. An act of taking in or absorbing, especially into a living organism.

up·throw (ŭp'thrō') *n.* 1. A throwing upward. 2. *Geology.* An upward displacement of rock on one side of a fault.

up·thrust (ŭp'thrŭst') *n.* 1. A thrusting or pushing upward. 2. *Geology.* An upheaval of the earth's surface.

up·tight (ŭp'tīt') *adj. Slang.* 1. Tense; nervous; repressed. 2. Angry. —**up·tight·ness** *n.*

up·time (ŭp'tīm') *n.* The time during which a computer or other device is functioning or available for use.

up-to-date, up to date (ŭp'tə-dāt') *adj.* Informed of or reflecting the latest improvements, facts, or style; modern. —**up-to-date·ly** *adv.* —**up-to-date·ness** *n.*

up-to-the-min·ute, up to the minute (ŭp'tə-thə-mĭn'ĭt) *adj.* Being or having the most recent information, style, or fashion. —**up-to-the-min·ute·ness** *n.*

up·town (ŭp'toun') *adv.* In or toward the upper part of a town or city.
~*n.* The upper part of a town or city. Compare **downtown.** —**up·town** (ŭp'toun') *adj.*

up·turn (ŭp'tûrn', ŭp'tûrn') *v.* **-turned, -turning, -turns.** —*tr.* 1. To turn (soil, for example) up or over. 2. To upset; overturn. 3. To direct upward. —*intr.* To turn over or up.
~*n.* (ŭp'tûrn', ŭp'tûrn'). An upward movement, curve, or trend.

UPU Universal Postal Union.

up·ward (ŭp'wərd) *adv.* Also **upwards** (-wərdz). 1. In, to, or toward a higher place, level, or position. 2. To or toward the source, origin, or interior. 3. Toward the head or upper parts. 4. Toward a higher amount, degree, or rank: *Prices soared upward.* 5. Toward a later time or greater age. 6. Toward something greater or better. —**upward (or upwards) of.** More than; in excess of: *"The onslaught of upwards of seventy divisions"* (Winston Churchill). [Middle English *upward,* from Old English *ūpweard:* UP- + -WARD.] —**up·ward** *adj.* —**up·ward·ly** *adv.* —**up·ward·ness** *n.*

up·wind (ŭp'wĭnd') *adv.* In or toward the direction from which the wind blows.
~*adj.* 1. Going against the wind. 2. On the windward side.

Ur (ŭr, oŏr). Ancient city of Sumer, southern Mesopotamia, whose site was discovered in the 19th century. The great ziggurat of Ur, which still stands in crumbling condition, was built by King Ur-Nammu, who established the third dynasty of Ur in *c.* 2060 B.C.

ur-¹. 1. Variant of **uro-¹.** 2. Variant of **uro-².**

ur-² *prefix. Sometimes* **Ur-.** Indicates: 1. Primitive, basic; for exam-

ple, *ur-legend.* 2. The original version of; for example, **Urtext.** [German.]

u·ra·cil (yoŏr'ə-sĭl') *n.* A pyrimidine, $C_4H_4N_2O_2$, a constituent of RNA. [UR(O)- + AC(ETIC) + -IL(E).]

uraemia. Variant of **uremia.**

u·rae·us (yoŏ-rē'əs) *n., pl.* **uraei** (yoŏ-rē'ī) or **uraeuses.** The figure of the sacred serpent, depicted on the headdress of ancient Egyptian rulers and deities as an emblem of sovereignty. [New Latin, from Late Greek *ouraios,* from Egyptian for "cobra."]

U·ral (yoŏr'əl). River in the U.S.S.R., rising in the south Ural Mts. and flowing south and west for *c.* 2,540 kilometers (1,580 miles) until it empties into the Caspian Sea at Gurjev.

U·ral-Al·ta·ic (yoŏr'əl-ăl-tā'ĭk) *n.* A hypothetical group of languages including the Uralic and Altaic families, characterized by agglutination and vowel harmony. Also called "Turanian." —**U·ral-Al·ta·ic** *adj.*

U·ral·ic (yoŏ-răl'ĭk) *n.* Also **U·ra·li·an** (yoŏ-rā'lē-ən). A family of languages including the Finno-Ugric and Samoyed subfamilies.
~*adj.* Of or designating this language family.

u·ral·ite (yoŏr'ə-līt') *n.* An amphibole mineral that replaces pyroxene in some igneous and metamorphic rocks. [German *Uralit,* after the URAL MOUNTAINS + -ITE.]

Ural Mountains. Also **Urals.** Mountain range of the U.S.S.R., extending for *c.* 2,400 kilometers (1,500 miles) southward from the Arctic coast. It is generally considered to form, with the river Ural, the boundary between the European and the Asian U.S.S.R.

uran-. Variant of **urano-.**

u·ra·ni·a (yoŏ-rā'nē-ə) *n.* **Uranium dioxide** (see). [New Latin : URANIUM + -a (oxide).]

U·ra·ni·a (yoŏ-rā'nē-ə, -rān'yə). *Greek Mythology.* The Muse of astronomy. [Latin, from Greek *Ourania,* "the heavenly one", from *ouranos,* heaven. See **Uranus.**]

U·ra·ni·an (yoŏ-rā'nē-ən, -rān'yən) *adj.* 1. Of or pertaining to the planet Uranus. 2. Celestial. 3. Of or pertaining to astronomy or to the Muse Urania. 4. *Rare.* Of or pertaining to homosexuality.
~*n.* 1. A fictional inhabitant of the planet Uranus. 2. *Rare.* A homosexual.

u·ran·ic (yoŏ-răn'ĭk, -rā'nĭk) *adj.* 1. *Archaic.* Of or relating to the heavens; celestial. 2. *Chemistry.* Of, pertaining to, or derived from uranium, especially with a valence higher than in comparable uranous compounds. [Sense 1, from Latin *ūranus,* heaven, from Greek *ouranos.* See **Uranus.** Sense 2, from URANIUM.]

u·ran·ide (yoŏr'ə-nīd') *n.* Any element having an atomic number in excess of 91. [URAN(IUM) + -IDE.]

u·ra·ni·nite (yoŏ-rā'nə-nīt') *n.* A complex brownish-black mineral, chiefly UO_2 partially oxidized to U_3O_8, and containing variable amounts of radium, lead, thorium, rare-earth metals, helium, argon, and nitrogen. [German *Uranin,* uraninite : URAN(IUM) + -ITE.]

u·ran·ism (yoŏr'ə-nĭz'əm) *n. Rare.* Homosexuality, especially of males. [19th century : from German *Uranismus,* from *Urania,* name for Aphrodite, Greek goddess of love (from Greek *ouranios,* heavenly, from *ouranos†,* sky, heaven).]

u·ran·ite (yoŏr'ə-nīt') *n.* Either of two uranium-bearing minerals, **torbernite** (copper uranite) or **autunite** (lime uranite). [URAN(IUM) + -ITE.]

u·ra·ni·um (yoŏ-rā'nē-əm) *n. Symbol* **U** A heavy silvery-white metallic element, radioactive, easily oxidized, and having 14 known isotopes of which uranium 238 is the most abundant in nature. The element occurs in several minerals, including uraninite and carnotite, from which it is extracted and processed for use in research, nuclear fuels, and nuclear weapons. Atomic number 92, atomic weight 238.03, melting point 1,132°C, boiling point 3,818°C, specific gravity 18.95, valences 3, 4, 5, 6. [New Latin, after the planet URANUS (to contrast with the recently named TELLURIUM).]

uranium 235 *n.* The uranium isotope with mass number 235 and half-life 7.13 × 10⁸ years, fissionable with slow neutrons and capable in a critical mass of sustaining a chain reaction that can proceed explosively with appropriate mechanical arrangements.

uranium 238 *n.* The most common isotope of uranium, having mass number 238 and half-life 4.51 × 10⁹ years, nonfissionable but when irradiated with neutrons producing fissionable plutonium 239.

uranium dioxide *n.* A black toxic crystalline powder, UO_2, formerly used in ceramic glazes, now used to pack nuclear fuel rods. Also called "urania."

uranium series *n.* A radioactive series of elements that starts with uranium 238 and ends with the stable element lead 206.

uranium trioxide *n.* A radioactive orange powder, UO_3, used in uranium refining and as a coloring agent in ceramics.

urano-, uran- *prefix.* Indicates: 1. The heavens; for example, **uranography.** 2. Uranium; for example, **uranyl.** [Greek *ouranos†,* sky, heaven.]

u·ra·nog·ra·phy (yoŏr'ə-nŏg'rə-fē) *n.* The branch of astronomy concerned with mapping the stars, galaxies, or other heavenly bodies. [URANO- + -GRAPHY.] —**u·ra·nog·ra·pher** (yoŏr'ə-nŏg'rə-fər), **u·ra·nog·ra·phist** *n.* —**u·ra·no·graph·ic** (yoŏr'ə-nə-grăf'ĭk), **u·ra·no·graph·i·cal** *adj.*

u·ra·nous (yoŏ-rā'nəs, yoŏr'ə-nəs) *adj. Chemistry.* Of or pertaining to uranium, especially with a valence lower than in comparable uranic compounds.

U·ra·nus¹ (yoŏr'ə-nəs, yoŏ-rā'nəs). *Greek Mythology.* The earliest supreme god, a personification of the sky, who was the son and consort of Gaea and the father of the Cyclopes and Titans. [Latin *Ūranus,* from Greek *Ouranos,* personification of *ouranos†,* heaven.]

uraeus *The serpent emblem—the ancient Egyptian symbol of protection, sovereignty, and power—was put on the headdresses of gods and kings, at whose enemies it was expected to spit venom. Here it is worn by a prince, a son of the pharaoh Rameses III.*

Uranus² *n.* The seventh planet from the sun, revolving about it every 84.02 years at a distance of approximately 1,790,000,000 miles (2,880,110,000 kilometers). It has an equatorial diameter of 32,200 miles (51,810 kilometers), a mass 14.6 times that of Earth, and 15 known satellites. [After the god URANUS.]

u·ra·nyl (yŏŏr′ə-nĭl′, yŏŏ-rā′nəl) *n.* The divalent radical UO₂. [URAN(IUM) + -YL.]

urase. Variant of **urease.**

u·rate (yŏŏr′āt′) *n.* A salt or ester of uric acid. [UR(IC ACID) + -ATE.] **—u·rat·ic** (yŏŏ-rắt′ĭk) *adj.*

ur·ban (ûr′bən) *adj.* **1.** Pertaining to, located in, living in, or constituting a town or city. **2.** Characteristic of the geography, life, or functions of a town or city. Compare **rural.** [Latin *urbānus,* from *urbs†,* city.]

ur·bane (ûr-bān′) *adj.* Having or showing the refined manners of polite society; elegant. —See Synonyms at **suave.** [French *urbain, urbaine,* from Latin *urbānus,* characteristic of city life, URBAN.] **—ur·bane·ly** *adv.* **—ur·bane·ness** *n.*

ur·ban·ism (ûr′bə-nĭz′əm) *n.* **1.** The culture or lifestyle of city dwellers. **2.** Urbanization.

ur·ban·ite (ûr′bə-nīt′) *n.* A city dweller.

ur·ban·i·ty (ûr-băn′ə-tē) *n., pl.* **-ties. 1.** Refinement and elegance of manner; polished courtesy. **2. urbanities.** Courtesies; civilities.

ur·ban·ize (ûr′bə-nīz′) *tr.v.* **-ized, -izing, -izes. 1.** To make urban in nature or character. **2.** To cause or increase the migration of (country people) into cities. **—ur·ban·i·za·tion** *n.*

ur·ban·ol·o·gist (ûr′bə-nŏl′ə-jĭst) *n.* A specialist in the problems and sociology of cities. **—ur·ban·ol·o·gy** *n.*

urban renewal *n.* The government-sponsored destruction of slum areas with a view to the construction of new housing.

urban sprawl *n.* The spread of urban areas into the countryside.

ur·bi et or·bi (ûr′bē ĕt ôr′bē) *Latin.* To the city (of Rome) and to the world. Said of a solemn blessing by the pope.

U.R.C. United Reformed Church.

ur·ce·o·late (ûr′sē′ə-lĭt, ûr′sē-ə-lāt′) *adj.* Urn-shaped: *an urceolate corolla.* [New Latin *urceolatus,* from Latin *urceolus,* diminutive of *urceus,* jug, akin to *urna,* URN.]

ur·chin (ûr′chĭn) *n.* **1.** A poor, dirty, ragged child; a ragamuffin. **2.** A small, mischievous child; a scamp. **3.** A **sea urchin** (*see*). **4.** *Archaic.* A hedgehog. [Middle English variant of *(h)irchon,* hedgehog, from Norman French *herichon,* from Latin *(h)ērīcius,* from *(h)ēr,* hedgehog.]

ur·dé, ur·dee (ûr′dē, -dā′) *adj. Heraldry.* Having points; pointed. [16th century : probably a misreading of French *videé* in *crois aiquisseé et videé,* cross sharply pointed and reduced.]

Ur·du (ŏŏr′dŏŏ, ûr′-) *n.* A Hindustani language spoken in Pakistan, where it is the principal language, in Afghanistan, and by Muslims in India. [Hindi *urdū,* short for *zabān-i-urdū,* "language of the camp" : Persian *zabān,* language + *urdū,* army, camp, from Turkish *ordū,* HORDE.]

–ure *suffix.* Indicates: **1.** An act or process; for example, **erasure. 2.** A resulting condition; for example, **composure. 3.** A function or office or a body performing a function; for example, **legislature.** [Middle English, from Old French, from Latin *-ūra.*]

u·re·a (yŏŏ-rē′ə) *n.* A white crystalline or powdery compound, CO(NH₂)₂, found as an excretion product of protein metabolism in mammalian urine and other body fluids. A synthesized form is used as fertilizer, in animal feed, and in resins. [New Latin, from French *urée,* formed from *urine,* URINE.] **—u·re·al** (yŏŏ-rē′əl), **u·re·ic** (yŏŏ-rē′ĭk) *adj.*

u·re·a-for·mal·de·hyde resin (yŏŏ-rē′ə-fôr-măl′də-hīd′) *n.* Any of various thermosetting resins made by combining urea and formaldehyde and widely used to make molded household and mechanical objects and in cavity wall insulation.

u·re·ase (yŏŏr′ē-ās′, -āz′) *n.* Also **u·rase** (yŏŏr′ās′, -āz′). An enzyme occurring in urine, various plants, and as a secretion of certain microorganisms that catalyzes the hydrolysis of urea to ammonia and carbon dioxide and is used to determine the urea content of blood and urine. [URE(A) + -ASE.]

u·re·di·um (yŏŏ-rē′dē-əm) *n., pl.* **-dia** (-dē-ə). Also **u·re·din·i·um** (yŏŏr′ə-dĭn′ē-əm), *pl.* **-ia** (-ē-ə). A reddish, pustulelike structure formed on the tissue of a plant infected by a rust fungus, having hyphae that produce uredospores. Also called "uredosorus." [New Latin, from Latin *ūrēdo* (stem *ūrēdin-*), blight, burning itch, UREDO.] **—u·re·di·al** *adj.*

u·re·do (yŏŏ-rē′dō) *n., pl.* **uredines** (yŏŏ-rē′də-nēz′). *Pathology.* **Urticaria** (*see*). [Latin *ūrēdo,* blight, burning itch, from *ūrere,* to burn.]

u·re·do·spore (yŏŏ-rē′də-spôr′, -spōr′) *n.* A reddish spore that is produced in the uredium of a rust fungus and that spreads to and infects other plants.

u·re·ide (yŏŏr′ē-īd′) *n. Chemistry.* Any of various derivatives of urea. [URE(A) + -IDE.]

u·re·mi·a, u·rae·mi·a (yŏŏ-rē′mē-ə) *n.* The presence of excess urea and other waste products in the blood, a condition that often occurs in kidney disease and is characterized by headache, nausea, vomiting, and lethargy. Also called "azotemia." [New Latin : UR(O)- + -EMIA.] **—u·re·mic** (yŏŏ-rē′mĭk) *adj.*

u·re·o·tel·ic (yŏŏr′ē-ō-tĕl′ĭk, -tē′lĭk) *adj.* Excreting most excess nitrogen in the form of urea. Said of such animals as amphibians and mammals. [UREA + Greek *telos,* end + -IC (referring to urea as the end-product).]

u·re·ter (yŏŏr′ə-tər, yŏŏ-rē′tər) *n.* The long, narrow duct that conveys urine from the kidney to the urinary bladder. [New Latin,

from Greek *ourētēr,* from *ourein,* to urinate, from *ouron,* urine.] **—u·re·ter·al** (yŏŏ-rē′tə-rəl), **u·re·ter·ic** (yŏŏr′ə-tĕr′ĭk) *adj.*

u·re·thane (yŏŏr′ə-thān′) *n.* **1.** A colorless crystalline or white granular compound, C₃H₇NO₂, used as a treatment for leukemia and as a solvent. Also called "ethyl carbamate." **2.** Any of several esters, other than the ethyl ester, of carbamic acid. **3.** Polyurethane (*see*). [French *uréthane* : UR(O)- (urine) + ETH(YL) + -AN(E).]

u·re·thra (yŏŏ-rē′thrə) *n., pl.* **-thras** or **-thrae** (-thrē). The canal through which urine is discharged in most mammals and which serves as the male genital duct. [Late Latin *ūrēthra,* from Greek *ourēthra,* from *ourein,* to urinate, from *ouron,* urine.] **—u·re·thral** (yŏŏ-rē′thrəl) *adj.*

u·re·thri·tis (yŏŏr′ə-thrī′tĭs) *n.* Inflammation of the urethra. [New Latin : URETHR(A) + -ITIS.] **—u·re·thrit·ic** (yŏŏr′ə-thrĭt′ĭk) *adj.*

u·re·thro·scope (yŏŏ-rē′thrə-skōp′) *n.* An instrument for examining the interior of the urethra. [URETHR(A) + -SCOPE.] **—u·re·thros·co·py** (yŏŏr′ə-thrŏs′kə-pē) *n.*

u·ret·ic (yŏŏ-rĕt′ĭk) *adj.* Of or relating to urine; urinary. [Late Latin *ūrēticus,* from Greek *ourētikos,* from *ourein,* to urinate, from *ouron,* urine.]

U·rey (yŏŏr′ē), **Harold Clayton** (1893–1981). U.S. physicist. He is known chiefly for his discovery (1931) of deuterium and his work on the separation of isotopes and the structure of atoms and molecules. He won the Nobel Prize for chemistry (1934).

urge (ûrj) *v.* **urged, urging, urges.** *—tr.* **1.** To drive forward or onward forcefully; impel; spur. **2.** To entreat earnestly and repeatedly; plead with; exhort: *Urge your senators to vote for the bill.* **3.** To advocate persistently; recommend emphatically: *urge caution in driving at night.* **4.** To persuade, force, or otherwise move to some course of action. **5.** To stimulate; excite: *"It urged him to an intensity like madness"* (D.H. Lawrence). *—intr.* **1.** To present a forceful argument, claim, or case. **2.** To exert an impelling force; push vigorously.
~ *n.* **1.** The act of urging. **2.** An irresistible or impelling force, influence, or instinct. [Latin *urgēre,* to push, press.]
Synonyms: *coax, encourage, exhort, press.*

ur·gen·cy (ûr′jən-sē) *n., pl.* **-cies. 1.** The quality or condition of being urgent; imperativeness; pressing importance: *the urgency of their appeal.* **2.** A pressing necessity.

ur·gent (ûr′jənt) *adj.* **1.** Compelling immediate action; imperative; pressing: *She's away on urgent business.* **2.** Insistent or importunate; earnest: *urgent pleas.* **3.** Conveying or relating a sense of urgency: *an urgent tone.* [Middle English, from Old French, from Latin *urgēns* (stem *urgent-*), present participle of *urgēre,* to push, press, URGE.] **—ur·gent·ly** *adv.*
Synonyms: *imperative, pressing.*

–urgy *suffix.* Indicates a technique or technology; for example, **metallurgy, theurgy.** [New Latin *-urgia,* from Greek *-ourgos,* "worker," from *ergon,* work.]

–uria *suffix. Pathology.* Indicates: **1.** A diseased condition of the urine or urination; for example, **dysuria, pyuria. 2.** A substance in the urine; for example, **albuminuria.** [New Latin, from Greek *-ouria,* from *ouron,* urine.]

U·ri·ah (yŏŏ-rī′ə). A Hittite officer in the Israelite army and the husband of Bathsheba, whose death was contrived by David in order that he might marry Bathsheba. II Samuel 11:3–27. [Hebrew *ūriyāh,* probably "Yahweh is my light."]

u·ric (yŏŏr′ĭk) *adj.* Pertaining to, contained in, or obtained from urine. [UR(O)- + -IC.]

uric acid *n.* A white crystalline compound, C₅H₄N₄O₃, the end product of purine metabolism in man and other primates, birds, terrestrial reptiles, and most insects.

u·ri·co·su·ric (yŏŏr′ĭ-kō-sŏŏr′ĭk, -shŏŏr′ĭk) *adj.* Promoting the excretion of uric acid in the urine. Said of certain drugs used to treat gout. [*Urico-,* combining form of URIC ACID + -s- (connective) + URIC.]

u·ri·co·te·lic (yŏŏr′ĭ-kō-tĕl′ĭk) *adj.* Excreting most excess nitrogen in the form of uric acid. Said of birds. [*Urico-,* combining form of URIC ACID + Greek *telos,* end + -IC (referring to uric acid as the end-product).]

ur·i·dine (yŏŏr′ĭ-dēn′) *n.* A white, odorless powder, C₉H₁₂N₂O₆, that is the nucleoside of uracil, important in carbohydrate metabolism and used in biochemical experiments. [UR(O)- + -ID(E) + -INE.]

U·ri·el (yŏŏr′ē-əl). One of the four archangels in Hebrew tradition. [Hebrew *ūrī'ēl,* probably "God is my light."]

U·rim and Thum·mim (yŏŏr′ĭm; thŭm′ĭm) *pl.n.* Objects carried by the chief priests of ancient Israel and probably used to divine the will of God. Exodus 28:30; Leviticus 8:8.

urin-. Variant of **urino-.**

u·ri·nal (yŏŏr′ə-nəl) *n.* **1. a.** An upright wall fixture used by men for urinating. **b.** A room or other place containing such a fixture or fixtures. **2.** A receptacle for urine, such as one used by a bedridden patient. Also called "urinary." [Middle English, chamber pot, from Old French *urinal,* from Late Latin *ūrīnal,* from *ūrīna,* URINE.]

u·ri·nal·y·sis (yŏŏr′ə-năl′ə-sĭs) *n., pl.* **-ses** (-sēz′). The chemical analysis of urine. [New Latin : URIN(O)- + (AN)ALYSIS.]

u·ri·nant (yŏŏr′ə-nənt) *adj. Heraldry.* With the head downward. [Latin *ūrīnāns* (stem *ūrīnant-*), diving, present participle of *ūrīnāri,* to dive.]

u·ri·nar·y (yŏŏr′ə-nĕr′ē) *adj.* Of or relating to urine, its production, function, or excretion.
~ *n., pl.* **urinaries.** A urinal.

urinary bladder *n.* A muscular membrane-lined sac situated in the anterior part of the pelvic cavity and used as a urine reservoir prior to excretion.

urinary calculus *n.* A solid concretion of mineral and organic substances in the urinary system. Also called "urolith."

u·ri·nate (yōōr′ə-nāt′) *intr.v.* **-nated, -nating, -nates.** To excrete urine. [Medieval Latin *ūrīnāre*, from Latin *ūrīna*, URINE.] —**u·ri·na·tion** (yōōr′ə-nā′shən) *n.* —**u·ri·na·tive** (yōōr′ə-nā′tĭv, -nə-tĭv) *adj.*

u·rine (yōōr′ĭn) *n.* The fluid and dissolved substances, including urea, secreted by the kidneys, stored in the bladder, and excreted from the body through the urethra. [Middle English, from Old French, from Latin *ūrīna.*]

u·ri·nif·er·ous (yōōr′ə-nĭf′ər-əs) *adj.* Conveying urine.

urino–, urin– *prefix.* Indicates urine; for example, **urinalysis**, **urinogenital.** [Latin *ūrīna*, URINE.]

urinogenital. Variant of **urogenital.**

u·ri·nous (yōōr′ə-nəs) *adj.* Also **u·ri·nose** (-nōs′). Of, resembling, or containing urine.

urn (ûrn) *n.* **1.** A vase of varying size and shape, usually large with a pedestal, and used especially as a receptacle for the ashes of the cremated dead. **2.** A large vaselike vessel, often made of stone and planted with flowers, used as a garden ornament. **3.** A large closed metal vessel with a tap used for warming or serving tea or coffee; a samovar. **4.** *Botany.* The spore-bearing part of a moss capsule. [Middle English *urne*, a vessel containing the ashes of the dead, burial urn, from Latin *urna.*]

uro–¹, ur– *prefix.* Indicates urine or the urinary tract; for example, **urogenital, uridine.** [New Latin, from Greek *ouro-*, from *ouron*, urine.]

uro–², ur– *prefix.* Indicates a tail; for example, **uropod.** [New Latin, from Greek *oura*, tail.]

u·ro·chord (yōōr′ə-kôrd′) *n.* *Zoology.* A notochord limited to the caudal region, as in larval tunicates. [URO- (tail) + CHORD.] —**u·ro·chor·dal** (yōōr′ə-kôr′dəl) *adj.*

u·ro·chrome (yōōr′ə-krōm′) *n.* The pigment responsible for the normal yellow color of urine. [URO- + -CHROME.]

u·ro·dele (yōōr′ə-dēl′) *n.* Any amphibian of the order Urodela, characterized by a long body and tail and including the newts and salamanders. [French *urodèle* : URO- (tail) + Greek *dēlos*, evident.] —**u·ro·dele** *adj.*

u·ro·gen·i·tal (yōōr′ō-jĕn′ə-təl) *adj.* Also **u·ri·no·gen·i·tal** (yōōr′ə-nō-). Of, pertaining to, or involving both the urinary and genital functions.

u·ro·lith (yōōr′ə-lĭth′) *n.* *Pathology.* A **urinary calculus** (see). [URO- + -LITH.] —**u·ro·lith·ic** (yōōr′ə-lĭth′ĭk) *adj.*

u·rol·o·gy (yōō-rŏl′ə-jē) *n.* The medical study of the physiology and pathology of the urogenital tract. [URO- + -LOGY.] —**u·ro·log·i·cal** (yōōr′ə-lŏj′ĭ-kəl) *adj.* —**u·rol·o·gist** (yōō-rŏl′ə-jĭst) *n.*

–uronic *suffix.* Indicates a connection with urine; for example, **hyaluronic.** [Greek *ouron*, urine.]

u·ro·pod (yōōr′ə-pŏd′) *n.* Either of a pair of posterior abdominal appendages of certain crustaceans, such as the lobster or shrimp. [URO- (tail) + -POD.] —**u·rop·o·dal** (yōō-rŏp′ə-dəl), **u·rop·o·dous** (yōō-rŏp′ə-dəs) *adj.*

u·ro·py·gi·al gland (yōōr′ə-pĭj′ē-əl, -pĭj′ē-əl) *n.* An oil-secreting gland at the base of a bird's tail. Also called "oil gland."

u·ro·pyg·i·um (yōōr′ə-pĭj′ē-əm) *n.* The posterior part of a bird's body, from which the tail feathers grow; the rump. [New Latin, from Greek *ouropugion* : URO- (tail) + *pugē*, rump.] —**u·ro·pyg·i·al** *adj.*

u·ros·co·py (yōō-rŏs′kə-pē) *n., pl.* **-pies.** *Medicine.* The examination of urine with a microscope. [URO- + -SCOPY.]

u·ro·style (yōōr′ə-stīl′) *n.* A rod-shaped bone forming the terminal section of the backbone in frogs and toads. [URO- (tail) + Greek *stulos*, column.]

–urous *suffix.* Indicates a tail or type of tail; for example, **anurous.** [New Latin *-urus*, from Greek *-ouros*, from *oura*, tail.]

Ur·sa Major (ûr′sə) *n.* A constellation in the region of the north celestial pole, near Draco and Leo, containing the seven stars that form the Big Dipper. Also called the "Great Bear." [Latin *ursa*, feminine of *ursus*, bear. See **ursine.**]

Ursa Minor *n.* A constellation having the shape of a ladle with **Polaris** (see) at the tip of its handle. Also "Little Bear," "Little Dipper."

ur·sine (ûr′sīn′) *adj.* Of or characteristic of a bear. [Latin *ursīnus*, from *ursus*, bear.]

Ur·spra·che (ōōr′shprä′кнə) *n.* A reconstructed language set up as the parent of groups of related languages, as, for example, Indo-European, the hypothetical ancestor of Latin, Greek, Slavic, Celtic, and Germanic. Compare **protolanguage.** [German, "protolanguage."]

Ur·su·line (ûr′sə-lĭn, -līn′, -lēn′, ûr′syə-) *n.* A member of an order of nuns of the Roman Catholic Church, founded in about 1537 and devoted to the education of girls. [After Saint *Ursula*, legendary Christian British princess supposedly martyred at Cologne in the 5th century A.D.] —**Ur·su·line** *adj.*

Ur·text (ōōr′tĕkst′) *n.* **1.** A reconstructed proto-text set up as the basis of variants in extant later texts. **2. urtext.** The original text of a work of art, especially a musical composition. [German, "proto-text."]

ur·ti·cant (ûr′tĭ-kənt) *adj.* Causing itching or stinging.
~*n.* A substance that causes itching or stinging.

ur·ti·car·i·a (ûr′tĭ-kâr′ē-ə) *n.* A skin condition characterized by in-

tensely itching red, raised patches and usually caused by allergic reactions to internal or external agents. Also called "hives," "nettle rash," "uredo." [New Latin, from Latin *urtīca*, nettle. See **urticate.**]

ur·ti·cate (ûr′tĭ-kāt′) *v.* **-cated, -cating, -cates.** —*intr.* To produce urticaria or a stinging sensation. —*tr.* To practice urtication on. [Medieval Latin *urtīcāre*, from Latin *urtīca*, nettle.]

ur·ti·ca·tion (ûr′tĭ-kā′shən) *n.* **1.** The sensation of having been stung by nettles. **2.** *Medicine.* Formerly, a lashing with nettles as treatment of a paralyzed part of the body. **3.** Urticaria.

U·ru·guay¹ (yōōr′ə-gwī′, -gwā′). Republic on the east coast of South America. Its economy depends principally on cattle and sheep, with meat, hides, and wool accounting for 70 percent of its exports. Disputed by Spain and Portugal from the 17th century and by Brazil and Argentina in the 19th century, Uruguay emerged as an independent nation in 1828. Area, 176,215 square kilometers (68,019 square miles). Population, 2,900,000. Capital, Montevideo. —**U·ru·guay·an** *n. & adj.*

Uruguay². River in South America. It flows for *c.* 1,610 kilometers (1,000 miles) from southern Brazil into the Río de la Plata.

U·rum·qi or **U·rum·ch'i** (ōō-rōōm′chē). Capital of Xinjiang Uigur Zizhiqu, northwest China. It is a major agricultural and industrial center.

u·rus (yōōr′əs) *n.* An extinct bovine mammal, the **aurochs** *(see).* [Latin *ūrus*, from Germanic.]

u·ru·shi·ol (ə-rōō′shē-ôl′, -ōl′) *n.* A toxic substance present in the resin of plants of the genus *Rhus*, which includes poison ivy and the lacquer tree, *R. verniciflua*, from which a black Japanese lacquer is obtained. [Japanese *urushi*, lacquer + -OL.]

us (ŭs) *pron.* The objective case of the first person plural pronoun *we.* It is used: **1.** As the direct object of a verb: *He assisted us.* **2.** As the indirect object of a verb: *They offered us a ride.* **3.** As the object of a preposition: *They came to us first.* **4.** After *than* or *as* in comparisons in which the first term is in the objective case: *They gave you more than us.* **5.** *Informal.* In place of the reflexive pronoun *ourselves*, as the indirect object of a verb: *We'll get us some dinner.* **6.** In various elliptical, absolute, or interjectional phrases: *Who, us? Lucky us!* —See Usage notes at **me, we.** [Middle English *us*, Old English *ūs.*]

u.s. 1. ubi supra. **2.** ut supra.

U.S., US 1. United States. **2.** unserviceable. **3.** useless.

U.S.A., USA 1. United States of America. **2.** United States Army. **3.** Union of South Africa.

us·a·ble, use·a·ble (yōō′zə-bəl) *adj.* **1.** Capable of being used. **2.** In a fit condition for use; intact or operative. —**us·a·bil·i·ty** (yōō′zə-bĭl′ə-tē), **us·a·ble·ness** *n.* —**us·a·bly** *adv.*

USAF, U.S.A.F. United States Air Force.

us·age (yōō′sĭj, -zĭj) *n.* **1. a.** The act or manner of using or treating; use or employment. **b.** The act of using. **2.** Customary practice; habitual use. **3.** The actual or expressed way in which a language or its elements are used, interrelated, or pronounced in expression: *contemporary English usage.* **4.** An instance of this; a particular expression in speech or writing: *a nonce usage.* —See Synonyms at **habit.** [Middle English, from Old French, from *user*, to USE.]

Usage: Usage is a more specialized term than *use. Use* is preferred when the sense relates broadly to employment or usefulness: *Those materials are in wide use today. Usage* is preferred when the sense relates to "customary use," as in the "Usage notes" throughout this dictionary.

us·ance (yōō′zəns) *n.* **1.** *Commerce.* The length of time, established by custom and varying between countries, that is allowed for payment of a foreign bill of exchange. **2.** *Archaic.* Interest accruing on a loan. [Middle English *usaunce*, custom, usage, from Old French *usance*, from Vulgar Latin *ūsantia* (unattested), from *ūsāre* (unattested), to USE.]

USAR United States Army Reserve.

U.S.C. United States Code.

USCG, U.S.C.G. United States Coast Guard.

USDA United States Department of Agriculture.

use (yōōz) *v.* **used** (yōōzd; yōōst *for intr. sense*), **using, uses.** —*tr.* **1.** To bring or put into service; employ, as for some purpose: *use*

soap for washing; use our telephone. **2. a.** To make a practice or a habit of employing: *uses margarine in her sandwiches; doesn't use his wits.* **b.** To employ or utter (words or phrases): *uses clichés all the time.* **3.** To conduct oneself toward in a specified manner: *"the peace-offering of a man who once used you unkindly"* (Laurence Sterne). **4.** To consume or expend the whole of; deplete or exhaust. Often used with *up.* **5.** *Informal.* To exploit for one's own advantage or gain: *He gave nothing to his friends; he merely used them.* **6.** To take or partake of, as tobacco, alcohol, or drugs. —*intr.* To do or be habitually. Now used only in the past tense to show a former habitual action or state: *This museum used to be a house. I used to play football every Saturday.* —See Usage note at **utilize.** ~*n.* (yōōs). **1. a.** The act of using; the application or employment of something, as for some purpose: *the use of a pencil for writing.* **b.** The condition or fact of being used or occupied: *This toilet is no longer in use.* **c.** The fact of having been used: *This car has had a lot of use.* **2.** The manner of using; usage: *the proper use of power tools.* **3. a.** The permission, privilege, or benefit of using something: *have use of the car.* **b.** The power or ability to use something: *lose the use of one arm.* **4.** The need or occasion to use or employ: *Do you still have any use for this book?* **5.** The quality of being suitable or adaptable to an end; usefulness: *There's no use in discussing it.* **6.** The goal, object, or purpose for which something is used. **7.** Accustomed or usual procedure; habitual practice; custom. **8.** *Law.* **a.** The enjoyment of property, as by occupying or exercising it. **b.** The benefit or profit of lands and tenements of which the legal title and possession are vested in another who holds them in trust for the beneficiary. **c.** The arrangement establishing the equitable right to such benefits and profits. **9.** The special or distinctive form of ritual, ceremony, or public worship practiced in a particular church, ecclesiastical district, or community. —See Synonyms at **habit.** —**have no use for.** To have no tolerance for or patience with; dislike. —**make use of. 1.** To find occasion to use. **2.** To exploit. [Middle English *usen,* from Old French *user,* from Vulgar Latin *ūsāre* (unattested), frequentative of Latin *ūtī*† (past participle *ūsus*), to use.]

Usage: The following examples illustrate *use* as an auxiliary verb in positive, negative, and interrogative constructions: *They used to go there. They used not to go* (or *did not use to go*). *Did* (or *didn't*) *they use to go?*

used (yōōzd) *adj.* Not new; secondhand: *a used car.* —**used to** (yōōst). Accustomed to or familiar with: *I'm not used to all this rich food.*

use·ful (yōōs′fəl) *adj.* **1.** Capable of being used advantageously or beneficially; serviceable. **2.** Commendably productive: *doing some useful work at school.* —**use·ful·ly** *adv.* —**use·ful·ness** *n.*

use·less (yōōs′lĭs) *adj.* **1.** Having no beneficial purpose or use; of little or no worth; meaningless. **2.** Futile; pointless; to no avail. —**use·less·ly** *adv.* —**use·less·ness** *n.*

us·er (yōō′zər) *n.* **1.** One that uses. **2.** *Law.* The exercise or enjoyment of any right or property. **3.** *Slang.* A drug addict.

us·er-friend·ly (yōō′zər-frĕnd′lē) *adj.* Easy to use. [Possibly a translation of German *benutzerfreundlich: Benutzer,* user + *freundlich,* friendly.] —**us·er-friend·li·ness** *n.*

ush·er (ŭsh′ər) *n.* **1.** One who serves as official doorkeeper and usually keeps order, as in a court-room or legislative chamber. **2.** A person employed to escort people to their seats, as in a theater, church, or stadium. **3.** A male attendant at a wedding. **4.** An official who precedes persons of rank in a procession. ~*tr.v.* **ushered, -ering, -ers. 1.** To serve as an usher to; escort. **2.** To lead or conduct; cause to enter. Used with *through* or *into*: *ushered her through the door.* **3.** To precede and introduce; serve as the beginning of. Usually used with *in.* [Middle English, from Norman French *usser,* variant of Old French *ussier,* from Medieval Latin *ūstiārius,* variant of Latin *ōstiārius,* doorkeeper, from *ōstium,* entrance, river mouth, from *ōs,* mouth, orifice.]

ush·er·ette (ŭsh′ə-rĕt′) *n.* A woman who shows people to their seats, as in a theater.

USIA United States Information Agency.

U.S.M. United States Mail.

USMC, U.S.M.C. United States Marine Corps.

USN, U.S.N. United States Navy.

USO, U.S.O. United Service Organizations.

U.S.P.O., USPO United States Post Office.

us·que·baugh (ŭs′kwĭ-bô′, -bä′) *n. Irish & Scottish.* Whiskey. [Irish and Scots Gaelic *uisge beatha,* "water of life."]

U.S.S. 1. United States Senate. **2.** United States Ship.

U.S.S.R., USSR Union of Soviet Socialist Republics.

Us·ti·nov (yōō′stə-nôf′, -nôv′), **Peter Alexander** (1921–). British actor, director, and playwright. His films include *Spartacus* (1960), for which he got an Academy Award, and *Murder on the Nile* (1978).

u·su·al (yōō′zhōō-əl) *adj. Abbr.* **usu. 1.** Such as is commonly or frequently encountered, experienced, observed, or used; ordinary; normal. **2.** Habitual or customary; particular. [Middle English, from Old French, from Late Latin *ūsuālis,* ordinary, from Latin *ūsus,* use, custom, from the past participle of *ūtī,* to USE.] —**u·su·al·ly** *adv.* —**u·su·al·ness** *n.*

Synonyms: *accustomed, customary, habitual, typical.*

u·su·fruct (yōō′zə-frŭkt′, yōō′zyōō-) *n. Law.* The right to make use of and enjoy the profits and advantages of something belonging to another so long as the property is not damaged or altered in any way. [Latin *ūsusfrūctus,* "use (and) enjoyment" : *ūsus,* use (see

usual) + *frūctus,* enjoyment, FRUIT.]

u·su·fruc·tu·ar·y (yōō′zə-frŭk′chōō-ĕr′ē, yōō′zyōō-) *n., pl.* **-ies.** A person who holds property by usufruct. ~*adj.* Of or of the nature of a usufruct.

u·su·rer (yōō′zhər-ər) *n.* **1.** A person who lends money at an exorbitant or unlawful rate of interest. **2.** *Obsolete.* A moneylender. [Middle English, from Norman French, from Medieval Latin *ūsūrārius,* from Latin *ūsūra,* interest, USURY.]

u·su·ri·ous (yōō-zhŏor′ē-əs) *adj.* **1.** Practicing usury. **2.** Of, pertaining to, or constituting usury: *a usurious rate of interest.* —**u·su·ri·ous·ly** *adv.* —**u·su·ri·ous·ness** *n.*

u·surp (yōō-sûrp′, -zûrp′) *v.* **-surped, -surping, -surps.** —*tr.* **1.** To seize and hold (the power, position, or rights of another) by force and without legal right or authority. **2.** To take over or occupy physically and wrongfully (territory or possessions, for example); to appropriate. —*intr.* To commit such illegal seizure; encroach. [Middle English *usurpen,* from Old French *usurper,* from Latin *ūsūrpāre,* to take forcibly into use.] —**u·sur·pa·tion** (yōō′sər-pā′shən, yōō′zər-) *n.* —**u·surp·er** *n.*

u·su·ry (yōō′zhə-rē) *n., pl.* **-ries. 1.** The act or practice of lending money at an exorbitant or illegal rate of interest. **2.** Such an excessive rate of interest. **3.** *Archaic.* The act or practice of lending money at any rate of interest. [Middle English, from Norman French *usurie* (unattested), from Medieval Latin *ūsūria,* from Latin *ūsūra,* use of money lent, interest, from *ūsus,* use. See **usual.**]

ut (ŭt, ōōt) *n. Music.* A syllable representing the note *C,* otherwise represented by *do,* in the French system of solmization. See **gamut.** [Latin *ut,* that (first word of a hymn to St. John the Baptist).]

UT Utah (used with a Zip Code).

U.T. universal time.

U·tah (yōō′tô′). State in the western United States, one of the Rocky Mt. states. It is an important mining state, and has valuable deposits of petroleum. The region was first settled permanently in 1847 by Mormons seeking refuge from persecution, and the state has ever since been the home of the U.S. Mormons. The capital and largest city is Salt Lake City.

Ute (yōōt) *n., pl.* **Ute** or **Utes. 1.** A member of a Uto-Aztecan-speaking North American Indian people formerly inhabiting Utah, Colorado, and New Mexico and now living on reservations in Utah and Colorado. **2.** The language of this people.

u·ten·sil (yōō-tĕn′səl) *n.* **1.** An instrument or container, especially one used domestically, as in a kitchen. **2.** Any instrument or tool; an implement. —See Synonyms at **tool.** [Middle English *utensele,* from Old French *utensile,* from Latin *ūtēnsilia,* "things for use," from the neuter plural of *ūtēnsilis,* fit for use, from *ūtī,* to USE.]

u·ter·ine (yōō′tər-īn, -tə-rīn′) *adj.* **1.** Of or pertaining to the uterus. **2.** Having the same mother but different fathers. [Late Latin *uterīnus,* from *uterus,* UTERUS.]

u·ter·us (yōō′tər-əs) *n.* **1.** A pear-shaped muscular organ located in the pelvic cavity of female mammals that receives and holds the fertilized ovum during the development of the fetus and is the principal agent in its expulsion at birth. Also called "womb." **2.** A similar part of the female reproductive tract in many invertebrates, serving as a repository for the storage or development of eggs or embryos. [Latin *uterus.*]

Ut·gard (ōōt′gärd′). *Norse Mythology.* The home of Utgard-Loki. Also called "Jotunheim."

Ut·gard-Lo·ki (ōōt′gärd′lō′kē). *Norse Mythology.* An invincible giant.

U·ther Pen·drag·on (yōō′thər pĕn-drăg′ən). A legendary king of Britain and father of King Arthur.

u·tile (yōō′tĭl, -tīl′) *adj. Rare.* Useful. [Middle English *utyle,* from Old French *utile,* from Latin *ūtilis.* See **utility.**]

u·til·i·tar·i·an (yōō-tĭl′ə-târ′ē-ən) *adj.* **1.** Of or pertaining to utilitarianism. **2.** Useful and practical rather than decorative. ~*n.* An advocate of utilitarianism. [UTILIT(Y) + -ARIAN.]

u·til·i·tar·i·an·ism (yōō-tĭl′ə-târ′ē-ə-nĭz′əm) *n.* **1.** The ethical theory, originally proposed by Jeremy Bentham and John Stuart Mill, that all moral, social, or political action should be directed toward achieving the greatest good for the greatest number of people. **2.** The belief that what is useful is good.

u·til·i·ty (yōō-tĭl′ə-tē) *n., pl.* **-ties. 1.** The condition or quality of being useful; usefulness. **2.** A useful article or device. **3.** A public service, such as gas, electricity, water, or transportation. **4.** In utilitarianism, the principle that the greatest good is the greatest happiness for the greatest number. ~*adj.* **1.** Useful or practical for various purposes: *a utility knife.* **2.** For the storage of tools and appliances: *a utility closet.* **3.** Capable of serving as a substitute player in various positions: *a utility infielder.* **4.** Of the lowest U.S. Government grade of meat. [Middle English *utilite,* usefulness, from Old French, from Latin *ūtilitās* (stem *ūtilitāt-*), from *ūtilis,* useful, from *ūtī,* to USE.]

u·til·ize (yōō′tə-līz′) *tr.v.* **-ized, -izing, -izes.** To put to use for a certain purpose. [French *utiliser,* from Italian *utilizzare,* from *utile,* useful, from Latin *ūtilis.* See **utility.**] —**u·til·iz·a·ble** *adj.* —**u·til·i·za·tion** *n.* —**u·til·iz·er** *n.*

Usage: The tendency for *utilize* to replace *use* in business and official English is open to criticism as an example of needless jargon. Careful usage maintains a distinction between these verbs, *use* having a general sense of "put into service" (*The machinery should be used as little as possible*) and *utilize* having a narrower sense of "make useful or productive for a particular end" (*We shall utilize the spare parts to save money*).

ut in·fra (ŭt ĭn′frə, ōot ĭn′frä). *Abbr.* **ut inf.** *Latin.* As below.

u·ti pos·si·de·tis (yōō′tī pŏs′ə-dē′tĭs) *n.* A principle of international law providing that a belligerent state is entitled to absolute possession and control of the territory occupied by it at the end of a war. [Latin, as you possess.]

ut·most (ŭt′mōst′) *adj.* **1.** Being or situated at the farthest limit or point; most extreme. **2.** Of the highest or greatest degree, amount, intensity, or the like: *a matter of the utmost secrecy.*
~*n.* The greatest possible amount, degree, or extent; the maximum. [Middle English *utmost, ut(te)mast,* Old English *ūt(e)mest, outermost : ūt(e),* out + *-mest,* -MOST.]

U·to-Az·tec·an (yōō′tō-ăz′tĕk′ən) *n.* **1.** A large language family of North and Central American Indians, including Ute, Pima, Hopi, Nahuatl, and other languages. **2.** A member of a people speaking a Uto-Aztecan language. [UTE + AZTEC.] —**U·to-Az·tec·an** *adj.*

u·to·pi·a (yōō-tō′pē-ə) *n. Sometimes* **Utopia. 1.** A condition, place, or situation of social or political perfection. **2.** Any idealistic goal or concept for social and political reform. Compare **dystopia.** [After *Utopia,* an imaginary island and ideal commonwealth, the subject of Sir Thomas More's book of this title (1516) : New Latin, "no-place" : Greek *ou†,* not, no + *topos,* place (see **topic**).]

u·to·pi·an (yōō-tō′pē-ən) *adj.* Excellent or ideal but existing only in visionary or impractical thought or theory.
~*n.* A zealous but impractical reformer of human society.

u·to·pi·an·ism (yōō-tō′pē-ə-nĭz′əm) *n.* The ideals or principles of a utopian; idealistic and impractical social theory.

U·trecht (yōō′trĕkt′). City in the central Netherlands, on a branch of the lower Rhine. It was a leading commercial town in the Middle Ages and is now an industrial and financial center. The Peace of Utrecht brought the War of the Spanish Succession to an end in 1713–14.

u·tri·cle (yōō′trī-kəl) *n.* Also **u·tric·u·lus** (yōō-trĭk′yə-ləs), *pl.* **-li** (-lī′). **1.** A small, delicate membranous sac connecting with the semicircular canals of the inner ear and functioning in the maintenance of bodily equilibrium and coordination. **2.** *Botany.* A small, bladderlike one-seeded fruit. [French *utricule,* from Latin *ūtriculus,* diminutive of *ūter,* leather bag or bottle, perhaps from Greek *hudria,* water pot, pitcher, from *hudōr,* water.] —**u·tric·u·lar** (yōō-trĭk′yə-lər) *adj.*

U·tril·lo (yōō-trĭl′ō, ü-trē-ō′), **Maurice** (1883–1955). French painter, best known for his paintings of Paris street scenes.

ut su·pra (ŭt sōō′prə, ōot sōō′prä). *Abbr.* **u.s., ut sup.** *Latin.* As above.

Ut·tar Pra·desh (ōōt′ər prə-dāsh′). Formerly **United Provinces.** State in north-central India. With more than 88 million people, it is the country's most populous state. The capital is Lucknow. Agriculture and food processing are the chief economic activities.

ut·ter¹ (ŭt′ər) *tr.v.* **-tered, -tering, -ters. 1.** To express audibly; emit (a sound): *uttered a sigh of relief.* **2.** To express in words; say or write: *uttered his name; uttered the truth.* **3.** To put (counterfeit money, for example) into circulation. —See Synonyms at **vent.** [Middle English *utt(e)ren, outren,* from Middle Dutch *ūteren,* to drive away, announce, speak.] —**ut·ter·a·ble** *adj.* —**ut·ter·er** *n.*

utter² *adj.* Complete; absolute; entire. [Middle English *utter,* Old English *ūtera, ūttra,* outer, external, comparative of *ūt,* OUT.]

ut·ter·ance¹ (ŭt′ər-əns) *n.* **1. a.** The act of uttering or expressing vocally. **b.** The power of speaking. **2.** Something uttered.

utterance² *n. Obsolete.* The uttermost extremity; bitter end: *fight to the utterance.* [Middle English *utt(e)raunce,* from Old French *outrance,* from *outrer,* to go beyond limits, from Vulgar Latin *ultrāre* (unattested), from Latin *ultrā,* beyond, from *uls,* beyond.]

ut·ter·ly (ŭt′ər-lē) *adv.* Completely; absolutely; entirely.

ut·ter·most (ŭt′ər-mōst′) *adj.* **1.** Utmost. **2.** Farthest.
~*n.* Utmost. [Middle English *uttermost, uttermest : UTTER (outer, complete) + -MOST.]

U-turn (yōō′tûrn′) *n.* **1.** A turn, as by a vehicle, completely reversing the direction of travel. **2.** Any complete reversal, as of mind or policy: *Will the government make a U-turn on amnesty?*

UV, U.V. Ultraviolet.

u·va·rov·ite (yōō-vär′ə-vīt′, ōō-) *n.* An emerald-green garnet, Ca₃Cr₂(SiO₄)₃, found in chromium deposits. [German *Uvarovit;* discovered by Count Sergei *Uvarov* (1785–1855), Russian statesman.]

u·ve·a (yōō′vē-ə) *n.* The pigmented vascular layer of the eye including the iris, ciliary body, and choroid. [Medieval Latin *ūvea,* from Latin *ūva,* grape (from its round shape).] —**u·ve·al** (yōō′vē-əl) *adj.*

u·ve·i·tis (yōō′vē-ī′tĭs) *n.* Inflammation of the uvea. [New Latin : UVE(A) + -ITIS.]

u·vu·la (yōō′vyə-lə) *n.* The small, conical, fleshy mass of tissue suspended from the center of the soft palate above the back of the tongue. [Middle English, from Late Latin, "small grape" (from the shape of the uvula), diminutive of Latin *ūva,* a grape.]

u·vu·lar (yōō′vyə-lər) *adj.* **1.** Pertaining to or associated with the uvula. **2.** *Phonetics.* Articulated by vibration of the uvula or with the back of the tongue near or touching the uvula.

u·vu·li·tis (yōō′vyə-lī′tĭs) *n.* Inflammation of the uvula. [New Latin : UVUL(A) + -ITIS.]

UW underwriter.

ux·o·ri·al (ŭk-sôr′ē-əl, ŭk-sōr′-, ŭg-zôr′-, ŭg-zōr′-) *adj.* Pertaining to, characteristic of, or befitting a wife. [From Latin *uxōrius,* of a wife, UXORIOUS.]

ux·o·ri·cide (ŭk-sôr′ə-sīd′, ŭk-sōr′-, ŭg-zôr′-, ŭg-zōr′-) *n.* **1.** The killing of a wife by her husband. **2.** A man who kills his wife. [Medieval Latin *uxōricīdium,* the murder of one's wife : Latin *uxor,* wife + -CIDE.] —**ux·o·ri·cid·al** (ŭk-sôr′ə-sīd′l) *adj.*

ux·o·ri·ous (ŭk-sôr′ē-əs, ŭk-sōr′-, ŭg-zôr′-, ŭg-zōr′-) *adj.* **1.** Excessively or irrationally devoted to one's wife. **2.** Indicative of or revealing such devotion. [Latin *uxōrius,* from *uxor,* wife.] —**ux·o·ri·ous·ly** *adv.* —**ux·o·ri·ous·ness** *n.*

Uz·bek (ōōz′bĕk, ŭz′-) *n.* Also **Uz·beg** (-bĕg). **1.** A member of a group of Turkic people inhabiting the Uzbek S.S.R. **2.** The Turkic language spoken by the Uzbeks.

Uzbek Soviet Socialist Republic. Also **Uz·bek·i·stan** (ōōz-bĕk′ĭ-stän′, -stän′, ŭz-). Constituent republic of the U.S.S.R., in central Asia. The capital and largest city is Tashkent. It is the chief supplier of cotton and rice to the U.S.S.R. and has also valuable reserves of petroleum and natural gas.

v, V (vē) *n., pl.* **v's** or **V's.** **1.** The 22nd letter of the modern English alphabet. **2.** Any of the speech sounds represented by this letter. **3.** Anything shaped like the letter V. **4.** The Roman numeral for five. **5.** The 22nd in a series; 21st when *J* is omitted.

v, V, v., V. *Note:* As an abbreviation or symbol, *v* may be a small or a capital letter, with or without a period. Established forms or those generally preferred precede the definition. When no form is given, all four forms are in general use in that sense. **1. V** The symbol for the element vanadium. **2. V** *Physics.* velocity. **3. V.** venerable (in titles). **4. v.** verb. **5. v.** verse. **6. v.** version. **7. v.** verso. **8. v.** versus. **9. v., V.** very. **10. v., V.** vice (in titles). **11. V** victory (used by the Allies in World War II). **12. v.** vide [Latin, "See."] **13. v., V.** village. **14. v.** violin. **15. V.** viscount; viscountess. **16. v.** vocative. **17. v.** voice. **18. V** *Electricity.* volt. **19. V** volume. **20. v.** volume (book). **21. v.** vowel.

V-1 (vē'wǔn') *n.* A robot bomb (*see*). [German *Vergeltungswaffe eins,* "retaliation weapon (number) one."]

V-2 (vē'tōō') *n.* A long-range liquid-fueled rocket used by the Germans as a ballistic missile in World War II. [German *Vergeltungswaffe zwei,* "retaliation weapon (number) two."]

VA **1.** Veterans' Administration. **2.** Virginia (used with a Zip Code).

Va. Virginia.

V.A. **1.** Veterans' Administration. **2.** vicar apostolic. **3.** vice admiral.

Vaal (väl). River in northeastern South Africa, rising in the southeastern Transvaal and flowing southwest for *c.* 1,200 kilometers (750 miles) into the Orange River.

vac. vacuum.

va·can·cy (vā'kən-sē) *n., pl.* **-cies.** **1.** The state or condition of being vacant or unoccupied; emptiness. **2.** An empty or unoccupied space; a gap. **3.** A position, office, or place of accommodation that is unfilled or unoccupied. **4.** Emptiness of mind; inanity. **5.** A crystal defect caused by the absence of an atom, ion, or molecule in a crystal lattice. **6.** *Archaic.* A period of leisure; idleness.

va·cant (vā'kənt) *adj.* **1.** Containing nothing; empty; unfilled. **2.** Without an incumbent or occupant: *a vacant professorship.* **3.** Not occupied or put to use: *a vacant lot.* **4.** *Law.* Not claimed, as by an heir: *a vacant estate.* **5. a.** Lacking intelligence or knowledge: *a vacant mind.* **b.** Expressionless; blank; unresponsive: *a vacant stare.* **6.** Unfilled by any activity: *vacant hours.* —See Synonyms at **empty.** [Middle English *vaca(u)nt,* from Old French *vacant,* from Latin *vacāns* (stem *vacānt-*), present participle of *vacāre,* to be empty.] —**va·cant·ly** *adv.* —**va·cant·ness** *n.*

vacant possession *n. Law.* Ownership of an unoccupied house or dwelling, and hence the right of immediate occupation.

va·cate (vā'kāt') *v.* **-cated, -cating, -cates.** —*tr.* **1. a.** To cease to occupy or hold; give up; leave. **b.** To empty of occupants or incumbents. **2.** *Law.* To make void; countermand; annul. —*intr.* To leave a job, office, lodging, or the like. [Latin *vacāre,* to be empty.]

va·ca·tion (vā-kā'shən) *n.* **1.** A period of time devoted to pleasure, rest, or relaxation, especially one with pay granted to an employee. **2. a.** A holiday. **b.** A fixed period of holidays; especially, one during which the law courts and universities suspend activities. **3.** *Archaic.* An act or instance of vacating. —*intr.v.* **vacationed, -tioning, -tions.** To take or spend a vacation. [Middle English *vacacioun,* from Old French *vacation,* from Latin *vacātiō* (stem *vacātiōn-*), freedom, release from occupation, from *vacāre,* to be empty, be free. See **vacate.**] —**va·ca·tion·er** *n.*

va·ca·tion·ist (vā-kā'shən-ĭst) *n.* A person on vacation.

vac·ci·nal (văk'sə-nəl) *adj.* Caused by or pertaining to vaccine or vaccination.

vac·ci·nate (văk'sə-nāt') *v.* **-nated, -nating, -nates.** *Medicine.* —*tr.* To inoculate with a vaccine in order to produce immunity against smallpox, diphtheria, typhoid fever, poliomyelitis, cholera, typhus, and other infectious diseases. —*intr.* To perform a vaccination. [From VACCINE.] —**vac·ci·na·tor** *n.*

vac·ci·na·tion (văk'sə-nā'shən) *n.* **1.** Inoculation with a vaccine in order to protect against a given disease. **2.** A scar left on the skin by such an inoculation.

vac·cine (văk-sēn') *n.* **1.** A suspension of attenuated or killed disease-causing microorganisms, as of viruses or bacteria, incapable of inducing severe infection but capable, when inoculated, of stimulating the production of antibodies (and therefore conferring immunity) against the virulent microorganisms. **2.** Such a suspension prepared from the cowpox virus and inoculated against smallpox. ~*adj.* **1.** Of or derived from cows, especially from cows infected with cowpox. **2.** Of or pertaining to cowpox. **3.** Of or pertaining to vaccination. [French *(virus) vaccine,* (virus) of cowpox, from Latin *vaccīnus,* pertaining to cows, from *vacca,* cow.]

vac·cin·i·a (văk-sĭn'ē-ə) *n.* **Cowpox** (*see*). [New Latin, from Latin *vaccīnus,* of cows. See **vaccine.**]

vac·il·late (văs'ə-lāt') *intr.v.* **-lated, -lating, -lates.** **1.** To swing indecisively from one course of action or opinion to another; be irresolute; waver. **2.** To sway from one side to the other; fluctuate; oscillate. —See Synonyms at **hesitate.** [Latin *vacillāre†,* to waver.] —**vac·il·la·tion** *n.* —**vac·il·la·tor** *n.*

vac·il·lat·ing (văs'ə-lā'tĭng) *adj.* Also *rare* **vac·il·lant** (văs'ə-lənt). **vac·il·la·to·ry** (-lə-tôr'ē, -tōr'ē). Inclined to waver; irresolute. —**va·cil·lat·ing·ly** *adv.*

va·cu·i·ty (vă-kyōō'ə-tē) *n., pl.* **-ties.** **1.** Total absence of matter; emptiness. **2.** An empty space; a vacuum. **3.** Lack of thought or intelligence; emptiness of mind. **4.** Absence of meaningful occupation; idleness: *"the crew, being patient people, much given to slumber and vacuity"* (Washington Irving). **5.** The quality or fact of being devoid of something specified: *a vacuity of taste.* **6.** Something, especially a remark, utterly without substance or point; an inanity. [Old French *vacuite,* from Latin *vacuitās* (stem *vacuitāt-*), from *vacuus,* empty. See **vacuum.**]

vac·u·o·lat·ed (văk'yōō-ə-lā'tĭd) *adj.* Also **vac·u·o·late** (văk'yōō-ə-lāt', -lĭt). Containing a vacuole or vacuoles.

vac·u·ole (văk'yōō-ōl') *n.* Any small cavity in the cytoplasm of a cell, plant, or animal, that contains air, water, sap, partially digested food or other materials. [French, "little vacuum," from Latin *vacuum,* VACUUM.] —**vac·u·o·lar** *adj.* —**vac·u·o·la·tion** *n.*

vac·u·ous (văk'yōō-əs) *adj.* **1.** Devoid of matter; empty. **2. a.** Stupid; dull. **b.** Expressionless. **3.** Devoid of substance or meaning; inane. **4.** Purposeless; unoccupied; idle. —See Synonyms at **empty.** [Latin *vacuus,* empty. See **vacuum.**] —**vac·u·ous·ly** *adv.* —**vac·u·ous·ness** *n.*

vac·u·um (văk'yōō-əm, -yōōm) *n., pl.* **-ums** or **vacua** (văk'yōō-ə) (except for sense 4). *Abbr.* **vac.** **1. a.** The absence of matter. **b.** A space empty of matter. **c.** A space in which the pressure is significantly lower than atmospheric pressure. **d.** A space relatively empty of matter. **2.** A state or feeling of emptiness; a void. **3.** A state of being sealed off from external or environmental influences; isolation. **4.** A vacuum cleaner. ~*adj.* **1.** Pertaining to or used to create a vacuum. **2.** Containing air or other gas at a reduced pressure. **3.** Working by means of suction or by maintaining of a partial vacuum. ~*v.* **vacuumed, -uming, -ums.** —*tr.* To clean with a vacuum cleaner. —*intr.* To use a vacuum cleaner. [Latin, neuter of *vacuus,* empty, from *vacāre,* to be empty.]

vacuum aspiration *n. Medicine.* A therapeutic method of abortion carried out under anesthetic, before the twelfth week of pregnancy.

vacuum bottle *n.* A bottle or flask having a vacuum between its inner and outer walls, designed to maintain the desired temperature of the contents.

vacuum casting *n.* The casting of metals under a vacuum.

vacuum cleaner *n.* An electrical appliance that draws light dirt from surfaces by suction. —**vacuum-clean** *v.*

vacuum coffee maker *n.* A coffee maker consisting of two bowls, the upper one having a tubular part that fits into the lower one. As the water in the lower chamber boils, it rises, blends with the ground coffee in the upper chamber, and then is drawn back down by suction.

vacuum distillation *n.* A form of distillation in which the liquid to be distilled is maintained at a reduced pressure in order to lower its boiling point.

vacuum extractor *n. Medicine.* A suction cap that can be attached to the head of a fetus in order to aid delivery.

vacuum gauge *n.* A device for determining the pressure in a partial vacuum.

vac·u·um-packed (văk′yōō-əm-păkt′, văk′yōōm-păkt′) *adj.* 1. Packed in an airtight container with little or no air. 2. Sealed under low pressure or a partial vacuum.

vacuum pump *n.* 1. A pump used to evacuate an enclosure. 2. A **pulsometer** (*see*).

vacuum tube *n.* An electron tube having an internal vacuum sufficiently high to permit electrons to move with low interactions with any remaining gas molecules.

va·de me·cum (vä′dē mē′kəm) *n., pl.* **vade mecums.** 1. A useful thing that a person constantly carries with him. 2. A guidebook or other ready reference book. [Latin, "go with me."]

V. Adm. vice admiral.

va·dose (vä′dōs′) *adj.* Of, pertaining to, or designating water that occurs below the earth's surface and above the water table. [Latin *vadōsus,* full of shallows, from *vadum,* ford.]

Va·duz (vä-dōōts′). Capital of Liechtenstein. It is a tourist center and the site of a castle, built in 16th-century style.

vag·a·bond (văg′ə-bŏnd′) *n.* 1. A person without a fixed home who moves from place to place and has no apparent means of support. 2. A vagrant; a tramp. 3. A wandering rogue; a rascal. ~*adj.* 1. Of, pertaining to, or characteristic of a wanderer; nomadic. 2. Aimless; drifting; straying. 3. Irregular in course or behavior; unpredictable. ~*intr.v.* **vagabonded, -bonding, -bonds.** To lead a vagabond's life; roam about. [Middle English *vagabound,* from Old French *vagabond,* from Latin *vagābundus,* wandering, from *vagārī,* to wander, from *vagus,* wandering, undecided, VAGUE.] —**vag·a·bond·age** *n.* —**vag·a·bond·ism** *n.*

va·gal (vä′gəl) *adj.* Of or pertaining to the vagus nerve.

va·gar·y (vä′gə-rē, və-gâr′ē) *n., pl.* **-ies.** An extravagant or erratic notion or action; a flight of fancy. —See Synonyms at **caprice.** [Originally "a roaming tour," ramble, from Latin *vagārī,* to wander, from *vagus,* wandering, undecided, VAGUE.]

va·gil·i·ty (və-jĭl′ĭ-tē, vă-) *n.* The capacity or tendency of an organism to become widely dispersed. [From obsolete *vagile,* free to move about, from Latin *vagus,* wandering.]

va·gi·na (və-jī′nə) *n., pl.* **-nas** or **-nae** (-nē) 1. *Anatomy.* **a.** The passage leading from the external genital orifice to the uterus in female mammals. **b.** A similar structure in some invertebrates. 2. *Biology.* A sheathlike structure or part, such as that formed by the base of a leaf enclosing a stem. [Latin *vāgīna,* sheath.] —**vag·i·nal** (văj′ə-nəl) *adj.*

vag·i·nate (văj′ə-nĭt, -nāt′) *adj.* Also **vag·i·nat·ed** (-nā′tĭd). Forming or enclosed in a sheath.

vag·i·nec·to·my (văj′ə-nĕk′tə-mē) *n., pl.* **-mies.** 1. Surgical excision of all or part of the vagina. 2. Surgical excision of the serous membrane covering the testis and epididymis. [VAGIN(O)- + -ECTOMY.]

vag·i·nis·mus (văj′ə-nĭz′məs, -nĭs′məs) *n.* Sudden and painful contraction of the muscles surrounding the vagina. [New Latin : VAGIN(O)- + -ISM.]

vag·i·ni·tis (văj′ə-nī′tĭs) *n.* Inflammation of the vagina. Also called "colpitis." [New Latin : VAGIN(O)- + -ITIS.]

vagino-, vagin– *prefix.* Indicates the vagina; for example, **vaginectomy.** [From Latin *vāgīna.*]

va·got·o·my (vā-gŏt′ə-mē) *n., pl.* **-mies.** Surgical cutting of any of the branches of the vagus nerve, used to diminish the secretion of acid and pepsin by the stomach and to control a peptic ulcer. [VAG(US) + -TOMY.]

va·go·to·ni·a (vā′gə-tō′nē-ə) *n.* Pathological overactivity of the vagus nerve. [New Latin : VAG(US) + -TONIA.]

va·go·trop·ic (vā′gə-trŏp′ĭk) *adj.* Affecting or acting on the vagus nerve. Said chiefly of drugs. [VAG(US) + -TROPIC.]

va·gran·cy (vā′grən-sē) *n., pl.* **-cies.** 1. The state of being a vagrant. 2. The conduct or mode of existence of a vagrant. 3. A wandering in mind or thought.

va·grant (vā′grənt) *n.* 1. A person who wanders from place to place without a fixed home or livelihood and ekes out a living by begging or stealing; a tramp; a vagabond. 2. A wanderer; a rover. 3. One who lives on the streets and constitutes a public nuisance. ~*adj.* 1. Wandering from place to place; homeless and without work; roving. 2. Wayward; unrestrained. 3. Moving in a random fashion; not fixed in place. [Middle English *vag(a)raunt,* from Norman French, probably from Latin *vagārī,* to wander, from *vagus,* wandering, undecided, VAGUE.] —**va·grant·ly** *adv.*

vague (vāg) *adj.* **vaguer, vaguest.** 1. Not clearly expressed or outlined; inexplicit; indefinite: *vague instructions.* 2. **a.** Uncertain or indefinite in thought or expression: *She was vague about her future.* **b.** Mildly confused or muddled, as in one's thinking. 3. Lacking definite shape, form, or character; not clearly defined: *vague plans.* 4. Ambiguous in meaning or application: *"Right" and "wrong" seem vague to too many people.* 5. Indistinctly felt, perceived, understood, or recalled; hazy: *a vague uneasiness.* [Old French, from Latin *vagus†,* wandering, undecided, vague. See also **extravagant.**] —**vague·ly** *adv.* —**vague·ness** *n.*

va·gus (vā′gəs) *n., pl.* **-gi** (-gī′). Either of the tenth and longest pair of cranial nerves, passing through the neck and thorax into the abdomen and supplying sensation to part of the ear, the larynx, and the pharynx, motor impulses to the vocal-cord muscles, and motor and secretory impulses to the abdominal and thoracic viscera. Also called "vagus nerve," "pneumogastric nerve." [New Latin *vagus (nervus),* "wandering (nerve)," from Latin *vagus,* wandering, VAGUE.]

vahine. Variant of **wahine.**

vail (vāl) *v.* **vailed, vailing, vails.** *Archaic.* —*tr.* 1. To lower (a banner, for example). 2. To doff (a hat or headpiece) as a token of respect or submission. —*intr.* 1. To descend; to lower. 2. To doff one's hat. [Middle English *valen,* short for *avalen,* to let fall, from Old French *avaler,* to lower, from Vulgar Latin *advallāre* (unattested), from Latin *ad vallem,* "to the valley" : *ad,* to + *vallis, vallēs,* valley.]

vain (vān) *adj.* **vainer, vainest.** 1. Not yielding the desired outcome; unsuccessful; futile; fruitless: *a vain attempt.* 2. Lacking substance or worth; hollow; idle: *vain talk.* 3. Showing undue preoccupation with or pride in one's appearance or accomplishments; conceited: *He wasn't just immodest, he was shamelessly vain.* 4. *Archaic.* Foolish. —**in vain.** 1. Without effect or avail; to no use or purpose: *Our labor was in vain.* 2. Without due respect or piety; profanely. Used chiefly in the phrase *take the name of God in vain.* [Middle English, from Old French, from Latin *vānus,* empty.] —**vain·ly** *adv.* —**vain·ness** *n.*

vain·glo·ri·ous (vān-glôr′ē-əs, -glōr′ē-əs) *adj.* 1. Showing excessive vanity; boastful. 2. Characterized by or proceeding from vainglory. —**vain·glo·ri·ous·ly** *adv.* —**vain·glo·ri·ous·ness** *n.*

vain·glo·ry (vān′glôr′ē, -glōr′ē) *n., pl.* **-ries.** 1. Boastful and unwarranted pride in one's accomplishments or qualities. 2. Vain and ostentatious display. [Middle English *vein glory, waynglori,* from Old French *vaine glorie,* from Latin *vānus glōria,* empty pride : *vānus,* VAIN + *glōria,* pride, GLORY.]

vair (vâr) *n.* 1. A fur, probably squirrel, much used in medieval times to line and trim robes. 2. *Heraldry.* A heraldic representation of squirrel fur. [Middle English *veir, vaire,* variegated fur, from Old French *vair,* from Latin *varius,* variegated, VARIOUS.]

Vaish·na·va (vīsh′nə-və) *n.* A Hindu sect that worships Vishnu. [Sanskrit *viṣṇava,* of Vishnu, from *Viṣṇu,* VISHNU.] —**Vaish·na·vism** *n.*

Vais·ya (vīs′yə, vī′shə) *n.* 1. The Hindu merchant and business caste, originally composed of farmers and herders. 2. A member of this caste. See **caste.** [Sanskrit *vaisya,* "settler."]

val. valuation; value.

val·ance (văl′əns) *n.* 1. A short ornamental curtain or piece of drapery hung across the top of a window or along a shelf, canopy, or the like, or from the frame or mattress of a bed to the floor, often to conceal structural detail. 2. A decorative board or metal strip similar to this. ~*tr.v.* **valanced, -ancing, -ances.** To supply with a valance. [Middle English *valaunce,* perhaps from Norman French *valance* (unattested), equivalent to Old French *avaler,* to lower (see **vail**) + -ANCE.]

vale¹ (vāl) *n. Archaic & Poetic.* 1. A valley; a dale. 2. The world as a scene of sorrow: *this vale of dross and tears.* [Middle English *vale, vaal,* from Old French *val,* from Latin *vallēs, vallis.*]

va·le² (vā′lē, wä′lā) *interj. Archaic.* Used to express leave-taking or farewell. ~*n. Archaic.* A farewell. [Latin *vale,* imperative of *valēre,* to be strong or well.]

val·e·dic·tion (văl′ə-dĭk′shən) *n.* 1. An act or instance of saying goodbye; a farewell; a leave-taking. 2. A speech or statement made at a time of leaving. [From Latin *valedīcere,* to take farewell : *vale,* VALE (farewell) + *dīcere,* to say (by analogy with *benediction*).]

val·e·dic·to·ri·an (văl′ə-dĭk-tôr′ē-ən, -tōr′ē-ən) *n.* A student, usually ranking highest in the graduating class, who delivers the farewell address at commencement.

val·e·dic·to·ry (văl′ə-dĭk′tə-rē) *adj.* Pertaining to or by way of a farewell. ~*n., pl.* **valedictories.** A farewell address.

va·lence (vā′ləns) *n., pl.* **-cies.** Also **va·len·cy** (vā′lən-sē). 1. *Chemistry.* **a.** The capacity of an atom or group of atoms to combine in specific proportions with other atoms or groups of atoms. **b.** An integer, often one of several for any given element, used to represent this capacity in terms of an arbitrary assignment of 1 to an atom or group capable of forming a single bond with chlorine and of –1 to an atom or group capable of forming a single bond with hydrogen. 2. Broadly, the capacity of something to unite, react, or interact with something else. [Late Latin *valentia,* strength, capacity, from Latin *valēns* (stem *valent-*), present participle of *valēre,* to be strong.]

valence bond *n.* A covalent bond between atoms.

valence electron *n.* An electron in an outer or next to the outer shell of an atom that can participate in forming chemical bonds with other atoms.

valence shell *n.* A shell of an atom that contains the valence electrons.

Va·len·cia¹ (və-lĕn′chē-ə, -shē-ə). Region of eastern Spain, lying on the Mediterranean coast and comprising the provinces of Alicante, Castellón de la Plana, and Valencia. Its fertile coastal plain has won it the name of the garden of Spain.

Valencia². City in eastern Spain on the Turia River, with a port on the Mediterranean. It is the capital of the province of the same name and the third-largest city in Spain. It dates from at least the

2nd century B.C. and was the headquarters of the Loyalist government (1936–37) during the Spanish Civil War.

Va·len·ci·ennes (və-lĕn′sē-ĕn′, -ĕnz′, văl′ən-sĕ-). *n.* A fine type of lace with a floral pattern originally manufactured at Valenciennes, France. Also called "Valenciennes lace."

val·en·tine (văl′ən-tīn′) *n.* **1. a.** A greeting card of a sentimental or humorous nature sent, usually, to one of the opposite sex on Saint Valentine's Day (February 14). **b.** A card or gift sent as a token of love to one's sweetheart on Saint Valentine's Day. **2.** A person singled out as one's sweetheart on Saint Valentine's Day.

Val·en·tine (văl′īn-tīn′), **Saint** (*fl.* late 3rd century A.D.). Christian martyr, killed during the reign of Emperor Claudius. His feast day is February 14, and though he has long been considered the patron saint of lovers, the custom of sending valentines on his festival is not connected to the saint.

Valentine's Day, Valentines Day *n.* **Saint Valentine's Day** *(see).*

Val·en·ti·no (văl′īn-tē′nō), **Rudolf**, born Rodolpho Gugliemi di Valentina d'Antonguolla (1895–1926). Italian-born U.S. film actor. His roles in *The Sheik* (1921), *Blood and Sand* (1922), and other romantic motion pictures of the silent cinema made him the leading idol of the 1920's.

Valera, Eamon De. See Eamon **De** Valera.

va·le·ri·an (və-lîr′ē-ən) *n.* **1.** Any of various plants of the genera *Valeriana* or *Centranthus*, having dense clusters of small white or pinkish flowers; especially, *V. officinalis*, native to Eurasia and widely cultivated. This species is also called "garden heliotrope." **2.** The dried roots of *V. officinalis*, used medicinally as a sedative. [Middle English, from Old French *valeriane*, from Medieval Latin *valeriāna (herba)*, apparently from Latin *Valeriānus*, of Valeria, Roman province, from *Valerius*, name of a Roman gens.]

Va·le·ri·an (və-lîr′ē-ən) (died *c.* 269 A.D.). Roman emperor. He was chosen emperor by the Roman military in 253 and ruled until 260. During his reign the empire was in great turmoil, and Valerian was powerless against the increasing attacks of the Goths, Persians, Alemanni, and other barbarians. He was captured during a battle with the Persians (260) and later put to death.

va·le·ric acid (və-lĕr′ĭk, -lîr′ĭk) *n.* Pentanoic acid *(see).* [Obtained from the root of VALERIAN.]

Va·lé·ry (và-lā-rē′), **Paul Ambroise** (1871–1945). French poet, essayist, and critic. He is best remembered for his philosophical poems, *La Jeune Parque* (1917) and *Charmes* (1922).

val·et (văl′ĭt, -lā′) *n.* **1.** A man's male servant, who looks after his clothes and performs other personal services. **2.** An employee in a hotel or on a ship, for example, who performs personal services for guests or passengers.
~*v.* **valeted, -eting, -ets.** —*tr.* To act as a personal servant to; attend. —*intr.* To work as a valet. [French, from Old French *vaslet,* originally "young nobleman," "squire," from Medieval Latin *vassellitus* (unattested), diminutive of *vassus* (unattested), VASSAL.]

va·let de cham·bre (vă-lā′ də shäN′br′) *n., pl.* **valets de chambre** (*pronounced as singular*). *French.* A man's valet.

Valetta. See **Valletta.**

val·e·tu·di·nar·i·an (văl′ə-tōōd′n-âr′ē-ən, văl′ə-tyōōd′-) *n.* A chronic invalid; especially, one who is constantly and morbidly concerned with his or her health.
~*adj.* **1.** Chronically ailing; sickly; infirm. **2.** Endeavoring to recover health. **3.** Constantly and morbidly concerned with one's health. [Latin *valetūdinārius,* in poor health, from *valetūdō* (stem *valetūdin-*), state of health, from *valēre,* to be strong.] —**val·e·tu·di·nar·i·an·ism** *n.*

val·e·tu·di·nar·y (văl′ə-tōō′də-năr′ē, -tyōō′-) *adj.* Valetudinarian.
~*n.* A valetudinarian.

val·gus (văl′gəs) *adj. Pathology.* Displaced outward from the central line of the body.
~*n., pl.* **valguses. 1.** A deformity of the foot causing the sufferer to walk on the outer side of the foot. **2.** Any of various other deformities involving a turning or twisting from the midline of the body. [Latin *valgus†,* bowlegged.]

Val·hal·la (văl-hăl′ə) *n.* Also **Wal·hal·la** (văl-, wŏl-). *Norse Mythology.* The great hall of immortality in which the souls of warriors slain heroically were received by Odin and enshrined. [Old Norse *Valhöll : valr,* those slain in battle + *höll,* hall.]

val·iant (văl′yənt) *adj.* Possessing, acting with, or showing valor; brave; courageous. —See Synonyms at **brave.** [Middle English *valiaunt,* from Norman French, from Vulgar Latin *valiente* (unattested), from Latin *valēns,* present participle of *valēre,* to be strong.] —**val·ian·cy, val·iance, val·iant·ness** *n.* —**val·iant·ly** *adv.*

val·id (văl′ĭd) *adj.* **1.** Well-grounded; sound; supportable: *a valid objection.* **2.** Producing the desired results; efficacious: *valid methods.* **3. a.** Legally sound and effective; incontestable; binding: *a valid title.* **b.** Current; in effect: *valid till the end of the month.* **4.** *Logic.* **a.** Containing premises from which the conclusion may logically be derived: *a valid argument.* **b.** Correctly inferred or deduced from a premise: *a valid conclusion.* **5.** *Archaic.* Of sound health; robust. [French *valide,* from Old French, from Latin *validus,* strong, effective, from *valēre,* to be strong.] —**val·id·i·ty** (və-lĭd′ə-tē), **va·lid·ness** *n.* —**val·id·ly** *adv.*
Synonyms: conclusive, convincing, sound, telling.

val·i·date (văl′ə-dāt′) *tr.v.* **-dated, -dating, -dates. 1.** To declare or make legally valid. **2.** To substantiate; verify. —See Synonyms at **confirm.** —**val·i·da·tion** *n.*

val·ine (văl′ēn, vā′lēn) *n.* A crystalline amino acid, $C_5H_{11}NO_2$, essential for normal growth and health. [VAL(ERIC ACID) + -INE.]

va·lise (və-lēs′) *n.* A piece of hand luggage such as a small suitcase or bag. [French, from Italian *valigia,* akin to Medieval Latin *valisia†.*]

Val·i·um (văl′ē-əm) *n.* A trademark for a tranquilizer or sedative used to relieve tension and anxiety. Also called "diazepam."

Val·ky·rie (văl-kîr′ē, -kī′rē) *n.* Also **Wal·ky·rie** (văl-, wŏl-). *Norse Mythology.* Any of Odin's handmaidens who hover over battlefields, choosing warriors to be victorious and conducting the souls of slain heroes to Valhalla. [Old Norse *valkyrja,* "chooser of the slain."]

Val·la·do·lid (văl′ə-də-lĭd′). City in northern Spain, the capital of the province of the same name, lying at the confluence of the Pisuerga and Esgueva rivers.

val·la·tion (vă-lā′shən) *n. Archaic.* An earthwork wall used for military defense; a rampart. [Late Latin *vallātiō* (stem *vallātiōn-*), from Latin *vallāre,* to surround with a rampart, from *vallum,* palisade, rampart, from *vallus,* stake.] —**val·la·to·ry** *adj.*

val·lec·u·la (vă-lĕk′yə-lə) *n., pl.* **-lae** (-lē′). *Biology.* A shallow groove, depression, or furrow. [Late Latin, variant of Latin *vallicula,* diminutive of *vallēs,* VALLEY.] —**val·lec·u·lar** (vă-lĕk′yə-lər), **val·lec·u·late** (vă-lĕk′yə-lĭt, -lāt′) *adj.*

Val·le d'A·os·ta (vä′lā dä-ōs′tə). Region of northwestern Italy, occupying the upper basin of the Dora Baltea River. It has a distinct French linguistic and cultural heritage and was made an autonomous region in 1945. Aosta is the capital.

Val·lee (văl′ē), **Rudy** (1901–86). U.S. singer. Considered the first great crooner of the 20th century, he became famous for his soft-voiced renditions of "I'm Just a Vagabond Lover" and "My Time is Your Time." During the 1920's and 1930's, his singing voice, amplified by an ever-present megaphone, and his trademark greeting, "Heigh-ho, everybody!" helped make him the idol of millions.

Val·let·ta or **Va·let·ta** (və-lĕt′ə). Capital of Malta, on a high promontory between two deep harbors on the northeastern coast. It contains numerous relics of the Knights of Malta as well as a 16th-century cathedral and the governor's palace.

val·ley (văl′ē) *n., pl.* **-leys. 1.** An elongated lowland between ranges of mountains or hills, or other uplands, often having a river or stream running along the bottom. **2.** An extensive land area drained or irrigated by a river system: *the Indus Valley.* **3.** Any depression or hollow resembling or suggesting a valley, as where two slopes of a roof meet. [Middle English *valey,* from Norman French, from Vulgar Latin *vallāta* (unattested), from Latin *vallis, vallēs.*]

Valley Forge. Site of the Schuylkill River, in northeastern Pennsylvania northwest of Philadelphia. George Washington established his main camp here during the brutal winter of 1777–78.

Valley of Ten Thousand Smokes. Valley in the Katmai National Monument, a national park in southern Alaska. Since the massive volcanic eruption of Mt. Katmai in 1912, the valley has emitted hot gases through its countless cracks.

Valley of the Kings. Long, narrow valley in Egypt, the site of ancient Thebes and now occupied by Luxor and Karnak. It is the site of at least 60 tombs of Egyptian pharaohs of the 18th, 19th, and 20th dynasties, including the tomb of Tutankhamen.

val·lum (văl′əm) *n.* A large rampart erected as a means of defense, especially one built by the ancient Romans. [Latin, collective noun from *vallus,* stake.]

Va·lois[1] (văl-wä′). French royal dynasty, ruling from 1328 to 1589. They succeeded the Capetian line when Philip, Count of Valois, was called to the throne as Philip VI (1328–50). They were succeeded by the Bourbons.

Valois[2]. A historic region and former duchy of northern France.

va·lo·ni·a (və-lō′nē-ə, -lōn′yə). An extract from the dried acorn cups of an oak tree, *Quercus aegilops,* of eastern Europe and Asia Minor, used chiefly in tanning and dyeing. [Italian *vallonia,* from Modern Greek *balania,* plural of *balani,* acorn, from Greek *balanos.*]

val·or (văl′ər) *n.* Also *chiefly British* **val·our.** Courage and boldness, especially as shown in battle; bravery in the face of great danger. —See Synonyms at **courage.** [Middle English *valour,* value, worth, from Old French, from Latin *valor,* from *valēre,* to be strong, be of value.]

val·or·ize (văl′ə-rīz′) *tr.v.* **-ized, -izing, -izes.** To establish and maintain the price of (a commodity) artificially, especially by government action. [Portuguese *valorizar,* from *valor,* value, price, from Latin. See valor.] —**val·or·i·za·tion** *n.*

val·or·ous (văl′ər-əs) *adj.* Having or showing great personal bravery; valiant. —See Synonyms at **brave.** —**val·or·ous·ly** *adv.* —**val·or·ous·ness** *n.*

Val·pa·rai·so (văl′pə-rī′zō). City in central Chile, on the Pacific coast just to the northwest of Santiago. It is Chile's chief port and second-largest city. The city is built on a natural amphitheater, and funicular railways connect the industrial lowlands with the higher residential districts.

valse (väls, văls) *n.* A waltz. Used especially in titles of pieces of music. [French.]

val·u·a·ble (văl′yōō-ə-bəl, văl′yə-) *adj.* **1.** Having considerable monetary or material value for use or exchange. **2.** Highly useful or serviceable for a particular purpose: *valuable advice.* **3.** Having admirable or esteemed qualities or characteristics. —See Synonyms at **costly.**
~*n.* **valuables.** Valuable personal possessions, such as jewelry. —**val·u·a·ble·ness** *n.* —**val·u·a·bly** *adv.*

val·u·ate (văl′yo͞o-āt′) *tr.v.* **-ated, -ating, -ates.** To set a value for; appraise. [Back-formation from VALUATION.]

val·u·a·tion (văl′yo͞o-ā′shən) *n. Abbr.* **val. 1.** The act or process of assessing the value or price of something; an appraisal. **2.** The assessed value or price of something. **3.** An estimation or appreciation of the worth, merit, or character of something: *set a high valuation on friendship.* **—val·u·a·tion·al** *adj.*

val·u·a·tor (văl′yo͞o-ā′tər) *n.* One who makes valuations; an appraiser.

val·ue (văl′yo͞o) *n. Abbr.* **val. 1.** An amount, as of goods, services, or money, considered to be a fair and suitable equivalent for something else; a fair price or return. **2. a.** The amount of money for which something can be exchanged on the open market; monetary or material worth. **b.** Power to buy or exchange: *The value of the dollar has fallen.* **3. a.** Relative worth in terms of utility, quality, desirability, or importance: *the value of a good education; a novel of little value.* **b.** The usefulness of something in producing a particular effect or furthering a particular end: *The gesture cost them nothing, but had great propaganda value.* **4. values.** Those qualities regarded by a person or group as important and desirable; a set of standards and principles: *rejected the materialistic values of western society.* **5.** Precise meaning or import, as of a carefully considered word. **6.** *Mathematics.* An assigned or calculated numerical quantity. **7.** *Music.* The relative duration of a note or rest. **8.** The relative darkness or lightness of a color in a picture. **9.** *Phonetics.* The sound quality of a letter or diphthong.
~*tr.v.* **valued, -uing, -ues. 1.** To determine or estimate the worth or value of; appraise. **2.** To regard highly; prize; esteem. **3.** To rate according to relative estimate of worth or desirability; evaluate. **4.** To assign a value to (a unit of currency, for example). —See Synonyms at **appreciate.** [Middle English, from Old French, from the feminine past participle of *valoir,* to be worth, from Latin *valēre,* to be strong, be of value.] **—val·u·er** *n.*

val·ue-ad·ded tax (văl′yo͞o-ăd′ĭd) *n. Abbr.* **VAT, V.A.T.** A tax on the estimated market value added to any product or service at each stage of its manufacture or distribution, ultimately passed on to the consumer.

val·ued (văl′yo͞od) *adj.* Highly regarded; much esteemed.

valued policy *n.* An **agreed-value policy** *(see).*

value judgment *n.* A judgment based upon or reflecting one's personal moral and aesthetic values; a subjective evaluation.

val·ue·less (văl′yo͞o-lĭs) *adj.* Having no value; worthless.

val·vate (văl′vāt′) *adj.* **1.** Having valvelike parts. **2.** *Botany.* Meeting at the edges without overlapping, as petals may.

valve (vălv) *n.* **1. a.** Any of various devices that regulate the flow of gases, liquids, or loose materials through structures, such as piping, or through apertures by opening, closing, or obstructing ports or passageways. **b.** The movable control element of such a device. **c.** *Music.* A device in a brass wind instrument that permits change in pitch by allowing a rapid varying of the air column in a tube. **2.** *Anatomy.* A membranous structure in a hollow organ or passage, as in an artery or vein, that retards or prevents the return flow of a bodily fluid. **3.** *Biology.* **a.** Any of the paired, hinged shells of many mollusks and of brachiopods. **b.** A similar paired part, as of the cell wall of a diatom. **4.** *Botany.* **a.** Any of the sections into which a seed pod or other dehiscent fruit splits. **b.** A lidlike covering of an anther. **5.** *Chiefly British.* An **electron tube** *(see).* **6.** *Archaic.* Any of the leaves of a double or folding door.
~*tr.v.* **valved, valving, valves. 1.** To provide with a valve or valves. **2.** To control by means of a valve or valves. [Middle English, leaf of a door, from Latin *valva.*]

valve-in-head engine *n.* An internal-combustion engine having the inlet and exhaust valves in the cylinder head instead of in the engine block, as in some automobiles.

val·vu·lar (văl′vyə-lər) *adj.* Pertaining to, having, or operating by means of valves or valvelike parts.

val·vule (văl′vyo͞ol′) *n.* Also **val·vu·la** (văl′vyə-lə) *pl.* **-lae** (-lē′). A small valve or valvelike structure. [New Latin *valvula,* diminutive of Latin *valva,* leaf of a door, VALVE.]

val·vu·li·tis (văl′vyə-lī′tĭs) *n.* Inflammation of a valve, especially of a cardiac valve. [New Latin : *valvula,* VALVUL(E) + -ITIS.]

vam·brace (văm′brās′) *n.* Armor used to protect the forearm. [Middle English *va(u)mbras,* from Norman French *vauntbras,* short for Old French *avauntbras,* "forearm" : *avant,* before (see **vanguard**) + *bras,* arm, from Latin *bracchium.*] **—vam·braced** *adj.*

va·moose (vă-mo͞os′, və-) *intr.v.* **-moosed, -moosing, -mooses.** *Slang.* To leave hurriedly. [Spanish *vamos,* "let's go," from Latin *vādāmus,* from *vādere,* to go.]

vamp¹ (vămp) *n.* **1.** The upper part of a boot or shoe covering the instep and extending over the toe. **2. a.** Something patched up or refurbished. **b.** Something rehashed, such as a book based on old material. **3.** An improvised musical accompaniment.
~*v.* **vamped, vamping, vamps.** —*tr.* **1.** To provide (a shoe) with a new vamp. **2.** To patch up; refurbish. **3.** To put together; fabricate or improvise. Usually used with *up.* **4.** *Music.* To improvise (a simple accompaniment or tune). —*intr.* To improvise simple accompaniments, variations of tunes, or the like. [Middle English *vampe,* from Norman French *vaumpé* (unattested), Old French *avantpie* : *avant,* before + *pie(d),* foot, from Latin *pēs.*] **—vamp·er** *n.*

vamp² *n. Informal.* An unscrupulously seductive woman who uses her sex appeal to entrap and exploit men.
~*v.* **vamped, vamping, vamps.** *Informal.* —*tr.* To seduce or exploit (a man) in the manner of a vamp. —*intr.* To play the part of a vamp. [Shortening of VAMPIRE.]

vam·pire (văm′pīr′) *n.* **1.** In folklore, a reanimated corpse that rises from the grave at night to bite and then suck the blood of sleeping persons. **2.** One who preys upon others, as an extortionist or a vamp. **3. a.** Any of various tropical American bats of the family Desmodontidae, that feed on the blood of living mammals. **b.** Any of various other bats, such as those of the family Megadermatidae, erroneously believed to feed on blood. In senses 3a and 3b, also called "vampire bat." [French, from German *Vampir,* from Magyar *vampir,* probably from Russian *upyr',* from Kazan Tatar *ubyr,* witch.] **—vam·pir·ic** (văm-pîr′ĭk) *adj.*

vam·pir·ism (văm′pīr-ĭz′əm) *n.* **1.** Belief in the vampires of folklore. **2.** The practice of a vampire; bloodsucking.

van¹ (văn) *n.* **1. a.** A large covered truck or wagon for transporting goods or livestock. **b.** An enclosed, boxlike motor vehicle having rear or side doors and side panels, used especially for transporting people. **2.** *Chiefly British.* A closed railroad car for carrying baggage or freight. [Short for CARAVAN.]

van² *n.* The vanguard; the forefront. [Short for VANGUARD.]

van³ *n.* **1.** *Archaic.* Any winnowing device, such as a fan. **2.** *Poetic.* A wing. [Middle English *van(ne),* fan, Old English *fann* and Old French *van,* both from Latin *vannus.*]

van·a·date (văn′ə-dāt′) *n.* Any of three anions, VO_3, VO_4, or V_2O_7. [From VANADIUM.]

va·nad·ic (və-năd′ĭk) *adj.* Of or containing trivalent or pentavalent vanadium. [VANAD(IUM) + -IC.]

vanadic acid *n.* **1.** An acid containing a vanadate group, especially HVO_3, H_3VO_4, or $H_4V_2O_7$, not existing in a pure state. **2.** Vanadium pentoxide. [VANADATE + -IC.]

va·nad·i·nite (və-năd′n-īt′) *n.* A deep ruby-red or yellow to brown mineral of vanadium and lead sometimes with impurities of arsenic and phosphorus, essentially $(PbCl)Pb_4(VO_4)_3$. [VANAD(IUM) + -IN + -ITE.]

va·na·di·um (və-nā′dē-əm) *n. Symbol* **V** A bright-white soft ductile metallic element found in several minerals, notably vanadinite and carnotite, having good structural strength and used in rust-resistant high-speed tools, as a carbon stabilizer in some steels, as a titanium-steel bonding agent, and as a catalyst. Atomic number 23, atomic weight 50.942, melting point 1,917°C, boiling point 3,000°C, specific gravity 6.11, valences 2, 3, 4, 5. [New Latin, after Old Norse *Vanadīs,* name of the goddess Freya : *vana-,* akin to *Vanr,* fertility god + *dīs*†, woman, goddess.]

vanadium pentoxide *n.* A yellow to red crystalline powder, V_2O_5, used as a catalyst in various organic reactions and as a starting material for other vanadium salts. Also called "vanadic acid."

vanadium steel *n.* Steel alloyed with vanadium for added strength, hardness, and high-temperature stability.

van·ad·ous (və-năd′əs, văn′əd-) *adj.* Of or containing divalent vanadium. [VANAD(IUM) + -OUS.]

Van Allen belt *n.* Either of two zones of electrically charged particles, trapped by the earth's magnetic field, which form two belts above the atmosphere over the equatorial regions. They lie at about 3,200 kilometers (2,000 miles) and 17,700 kilometers (11,000 miles) from the earth. [After James A. *Van Allen* (1914–), U.S. physicist.]

va·nas·pa·ti (və-nŭs′pə-tē, və-näs′-) *n.* A hydrogenated vegetable fat used in India as a cooking oil in place of ghee. [Hindi, from Sanskrit, name of a plant : *vana,* forest + *pati,* lord.]

Van·brugh (văn′brə, văn-bro͞o′), **Sir John** (1664–1726). English architect and playwright. He designed Castle Howard and Blenheim Palace. His plays include *The Provok'd Wife* (1697) and *The Relapse* (1696).

Van Bur·en (văn byo͝or′ən), **Martin** (1782–1862). 8th U.S. president (1837–41). A powerful New York politician, he served in the U.S. Senate (1822–28), as secretary of state (1828–31), and as vice president under Andrew Jackson (1832–37), before being elected president in 1836. He unsuccessfully sought re-election in 1840, 1844, and 1848.

Vance (văns), **Cyrus** (1917–). U.S. statesman. He represented President Lyndon Johnson in Korea (1968) and was U.S. negotiator at the Paris peace talks on Vietnam (1968–69). He was secretary of state (1977–80).

van·co·my·cin (văng′kə-mī′sĭn, văn′kə-) *n.* An antibiotic produced by the bacterium *Streptomyces orientalis,* effective against staphylococci and spirochetes. [*vanco-* (of unknown origin) + -MYCIN.]

Van·cou·ver (văn-ko͞o′vər). City in southwestern British Columbia, Canada, lying across the Strait of Georgia from Vancouver Island. It is Canada's chief Pacific port and third-largest city.

Vancouver, George (1757–98). British navigator. After sailing with Capt. James Cook on two voyages, Vancouver commanded his own expedition to the Pacific, exploring the coasts of Australia, New Zealand, and the Hawaiian Islands (1791–92) and the Pacific coast of North America (1792–95), circumnavigating the island that was named for him.

Vancouver Island. Island off British Columbia, Canada. It is the largest offshore island on the west coast of North America, occupying 32,137 square kilometers (12,408 square miles).

van·dal (văn′dl) *n.* **1.** A person who willfully or maliciously defaces or destroys public or private property. **2.** One who spoils or destroys artistic or cultural achievement. [From VANDAL.]

Van·dal (văn′dl) *n.* A member of a Germanic people that overran Gaul, Spain, and northern Africa in the 4th and 5th centuries A.D.

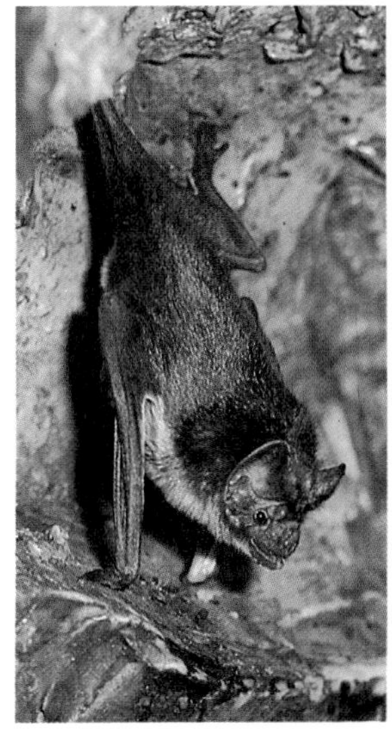

vampire Desmodus rotundus, *the common vampire bat, which is native to Central and South America, is one of several species known as vampire bats. All are small—between 60 and 90 millimeters (2½–3½ inches) long and weighing up to only 50 grams (1¾ ounces)—and all feed on the blood of living mammals, occasionally including humans. The bats feed at night, biting their resting victims so lightly that the prey often remain undisturbed. The bites are not serious in themselves, but they can transmit rabies and other diseases.*

and sacked Rome in A.D. 455. [Latin *Vandalus,* "wanderer" from Germanic.] **—Van·dal·ic** (văn-dăl′ĭk) *adj.*

van·dal·ism (vănd′l-ĭz′əm) *n.* The willful or malicious destruction of public or private property, especially of anything beautiful or artistic.

van·dal·ize (vănd′l-īz′) *tr.v.* **-ized, -izing, -izes.** To commit an act of vandalism on. [From VANDAL.]

Van de Graaff generator (văn′ də grăf′) *n.* An electrostatic generator in which electric charge is either removed from or transferred to a large hollow spherical electrode by a rapidly moving belt, in some configurations producing potentials over a million volts, and used with an acceleration tube as an electron or ion accelerator. [After Robert *Van de Graaff* (1901–67), U.S. physicist.]

Van-den·berg (văn′dĭn-bûrg′), **Arthur Hendrick** (1884–1951). U.S. diplomat and politician. A Republican senator from Michigan, he was an ardent isolationist and recommended a neutral stance in World War II until the attack on Pearl Harbor (1941), after which he became a central figure in the bipartisan support of the war effort.

Van·der·bilt (văn′dər-bĭlt′), **Cornelius,** known as "Commodore Vanderbilt" (1794–1877). U.S. businessman. He was founder of the family fortune, which he accumulated through railway and shipping interests. His heirs included his son **William Henry** (1821–85), financier and philanthropist, and his grandsons **Cornelius** (1843–99), railroad director; **William Kissam** (1849–1920), railroad executive, yachtsman, and philanthropist; **Frederick William** (1856–1938), expert in railroad management and noted yachtsman; and **George Washington** (1862–1914), stockbreeder and pioneer in scientific forestry. The Commodore's numerous grandchildren included **Harold Stirling** (1884–1970), who won the America's Cup three times (1930, 1934, and 1937); **Alfred Gwynne** (1877–1915), sportsman who died in the sinking of the *Titanic;* and **Reginald Claypoole** (1880–1925), sportsman and father of **Gloria** (1924–), designer and merchandiser.

Van der Post (văn′ dər pōst′), **Sir Laurens Jan** (1906–). South African author. Among his best-known works are *The Lost World of the Kalahari* (1958) and *A Story like the Wind* (1972).

van der Rohe, Ludwig Mies. See *Ludwig Mies van der Rohe.*

van der Waals force (văn′ dər wôlz′) *n.* A weak interatomic or intermolecular attraction arising from the interaction of dipoles induced in neighboring atoms or molecules. [After Johannes D. *van der Waals* (1837–1923), Dutch physicist.]

Van Diemen's Land. See **Tasmania.**

van Dong·en (văn dŏng′ən), **Kees** (1877–1968). Dutch-born painter. He moved to Paris in 1897 and became a naturalized French citizen in 1929. Van Dongen is best known for his fauvist-style paintings of elegant Parisian Women.

Van Dor·en (văn dôr′ən), **Carl Clinton** (1885–1950). U.S. critic, biographer, and historian. His biography of Benjamin Franklin (published 1938) won a Pulitzer Prize. He and his brother Mark were noted for the high quality of their literary criticism.

Van Dor·en (văn dôr′ən, dôr′-), **Mark Albert** (1894–1972). U.S. poet and critic. Literary editor (1924–28) and movie critic (1935–38) of the *Nation,* he wrote several works of fiction and literary criticism but perhaps is best known as a poet. His many volumes of verse include his Pulitzer Prize winner *Collected Poems* (1939).

Van·dyke (văn-dīk′) *n.* **1.** A painting by Sir Anthony Vandyke. **2.** A Vandyke beard or collar. **3.** A V-shaped point that is part of a decorative border or edging, or a border made up of such points. ~*tr.v.* **vandyked, -dyking, -dykes.** To cut or shape (cloth) with deeply indented or scalloped edges, as on a Vandyke collar.

Vandyke or **Van Dyck** (văn dīk′), **Sir Anthony** (1599–1641). Flemish painter. He was painter to Charles I and is famous for his portraits of the English court. His style greatly influenced the development of British portraiture. His works include *Charles I on Horseback* and *Thomas Killigrew and Lord Croft.*

Vandyke beard *n.* A short, pointed beard. Also called "Vandyke." [A style worn by subjects in many Vandyke portraits.]

Vandyke brown *n.* Moderate to dark brown. [From its frequent use by VANDYKE.] **—Van-dyke-brown** *adj.*

Vandyke collar *n.* A large collar of linen or lace having a deeply indented or scalloped edge. Also called "Vandyke." [A type of collar depicted in many Vandyke portraits.]

vane (vān) *n.* **1.** A thin plate of wood or metal, often having the shape of a rooster or an arrow, that pivots on an elevated vertical spindle to indicate the direction of the wind; a weather vane; a weathercock. **2.** Any of several usually relatively thin, rigid, flat, or sometimes curved surfaces radially mounted along an axis, that is turned by or used to turn a fluid, such as a blade in a turbine or a sail on a windmill. **3.** The flattened part of a feather, consisting of a series of barbs on either side of the shaft. **4. a.** The movable target on a leveling rod. **b.** A sight on a quadrant or compass. **5.** Any of the metal guidance or stabilizing fins attached to the tail of a bomb or other missile. [Middle English *vane, fane,* Old English *fana,* banner, from Germanic *fanon* (unattested).]

Vane (vān), **Sir Henry** or **Harry** (1613–62). English colonial administrator and statesman. A Puritan convert, he was the colonial governor of Massachusetts (1636–37) before returning to England to serve in the Short and the Long parliaments. Although he opposed some of Oliver Cromwell's policies, he was a leading parliamentarian during the English Civil War. Upon the restoration of the monarchy, he was tried and executed for high treason.

va·nes·sa (və-nĕs′ə) *n.* Any butterfly of the genus *Vanessa,* such as

the painted lady and red admiral. Also called "vanessid butterfly." [New Latin (reason for name obscure).]

van Eyck (văn īk′), **Jan** (*c.* 1390–1441). Flemish painter. He is noted for his realistic paintings, brilliant coloring, and minute detail. His works include *The Arnolfini Marriage, Man in a Red Turban,* and *The Adoration of the Lamb,* begun by his brother Hubert (*c.* 1366–1426).

vang (văng) *n.* *Nautical.* A guy rope running from the peak of a gaff or derrick to the deck. [Earlier *fang,* a device for gripping, Old English, from Old Norse *fang,* catch, grasp; akin to Dutch *vang,* from *vangen,* to catch, seize.]

van Gogh (văn gō′, gôkн′), **Vincent** (1853–90). Dutch painter. His early work portrayed Dutch peasant life in somber, dark colors; his later work in Provence (1888) was painted in bold, brilliant colors. His life was filled with suffering and despair, culminating in insanity and his suicide.

van·guard (văn′gärd′) *n.* **1. a.** The foremost position in an army or fleet advancing into battle. **b.** The foremost or leading position, as in an artistic or intellectual trend or movement. **2.** Those occupying any such position. Also called "van." [Middle English *vantgard,* short for *avaunt garde,* from Old French *avant-garde : avant,* before, from Latin *abante : ab-,* from + *ante,* before, in front of + *garde,* guard, from *garder,* to GUARD.]

va·nil·la (və-nĭl′ə) *n.* **1.** Any of various tropical American orchids of

van Gogh

AN ARTIST OF UNFILTERED IDEALS
Van Gogh's evangelism, a key to his powerful painting

The eldest son of a Protestant clergyman, Vincent Willem van Gogh (1853–90) was born at Groot-Zundert, the Netherlands. From childhood he seems to have had trouble tempering his ideals—whether of love, friendship, religious sincerity, social justice, or his own artistic vision—with any touch of compromise. His life was marked by depressions alternating with bursts of happiness and creative surges. Later came bouts of self-destructive madness that led him to cut off part of his right ear and, a year and a half later at the age of 37, to end his life by shooting himself.

Van Gogh set out to become a minister like his father, bringing comfort to the poor and sick; but that dream ended when his antiestablishment evangelism alienated church officials. Deeply dispirited, he turned to painting in 1880. Over the final 10 years of his life he poured out more than 1,500 paintings and drawings. Dark canvases of peasants typified his early work; then in a rush he discovered Japanese prints, the impasto technique, and the masters of impressionism. Edgar Degas, Paul Gauguin, Georges Seurat, and others became his friends in Paris, 1886–88. Then, at Arles in Provence, he did his greatest work; but there, too, his depressions reached the breaking point, as mental illness eroded his ability to paint and, finally, his will to live.

SELF-DESTRUCTION *A terrible honesty must have compelled van Gogh to paint himself showing a bandage covering the ear he had mutilated after a quarrel with Paul Gauguin at Arles in December 1888. Van Gogh killed himself in July 1890.*

the genus *Vanilla;* especially, *V. planifolia,* cultivated for its long, narrow seed pods from which a flavoring agent is obtained. **2.** The aromatic seed pod of this plant. Also called "vanilla bean." **3.** A flavoring extract prepared from these seed pods or produced synthetically. Also used adjectivally: *vanilla ice cream.* [Spanish *vainilla,* "little sheath" (from its elongated fruit), from *vaina,* sheath, pod, from Latin *vāgīna.*]

va·nil·lic (və-nĭl′ĭk) *adj.* Of, pertaining to, or derived from vanilla or vanillin.

va·nil·lin (və-nĭl′ĭn, văn′əl-ĭn) *n.* A white or yellowish crystalline compound, $C_8H_8O_3$, found in vanilla beans and certain balsams and resins and used in perfumes, flavorings, and pharmaceuticals.

Va·nir (vä′nîr) *pl.n. Norse Mythology.* An early race of gods who dwelt with the Aesir in Asgard. [Old Norse *Vanr,* fertility god.]

van·ish (văn′ĭsh) *v.* **-ished, -ishing, -ishes.** —*intr.* **1.** To disappear or become invisible, especially quickly or in an unexplained or magical manner. **2.** To fade or decay to nothing; pass out of perceived existence: *The choir's last notes vanished.* **3.** *Mathematics.* To become zero. Used of a function or variable. —*tr.* To cause to disappear. [Middle English *vanisshen,* from Old French *esvanir* (present stem *esvaniss-*), from Vulgar Latin *exvānīre* (unattested), variant of Latin *ēvānēscere* : *ex-,* away from + *vānēscere,* to disappear, "become empty," from *vānus,* empty.] —**van·ish·er** *n.*

vanishing cream *n.* A cosmetic face cream containing less oil than cold cream, which becomes colorless when applied and is used as a powder base or skin cleanser.

vanishing point *n.* **1.** A point in a drawing at which parallel lines drawn in perspective converge or seem to converge. **2.** A point at which a thing disappears or ceases to exist.

van·i·ty (văn′ĭ-tē) *n., pl.* **-ties. 1.** The quality or condition of being vain; preoccupation with or excessive pride in one's appearance or accomplishments; conceit. **2.** Lack of usefulness, worth, or effect; hollowness; futility; worthlessness. **3. a.** Something that is vain, futile, or worthless. **b.** Something about which one is vain or conceited. **4.** A dressing table. [Middle English *vanite,* from Old French, from Latin *vānitās* stem *vānitāt-*), from *vānus,* empty, vain.]

vanity case *n.* A small handbag or case used by women for carrying cosmetics or toiletries.

Vanity Fair *n. Sometimes* **vanity fair.** Any place or scene of empty, idle amusement and ostentation, especially the social world. [From the fair in Bunyan's *Pilgrim's Progress.*]

vanity plate *n.* An automobile license plate bearing a combination of letters or numbers selected by the purchaser. Also *British* "cherished number plate."

vanity press *n.* A publisher that publishes a book at the author's expense. Also called "vanity publisher."

van·quish (văng′kwĭsh, văn′-) *tr.v.* **-quished, -quishing, -quishes. 1. a.** To defeat or conquer in battle; subjugate. **b.** To defeat in any contest, conflict, or competition. **2.** To overcome or subdue (an emotion, for example); suppress: *His success vanquished his fears.* —See Synonyms at **defeat.** [Middle English *vencusen, vaynquysshen,* from Old French *vainquir* (present stem *vanquiss-*), variant of *vaintre,* from Latin *vincere.*] —**van·quish·a·ble** *adj.* —**van·quish·er** *n.* —**van·quish·ment** *n.*

Van Rens·se·laer (văn rĕn′sə-lîr′, rĕn′sə-lər), **Killian** or **Killiaen** (1595–1644). Dutch merchant. A founder of the Dutch West India Company (1621), he acquired an expansive estate in present-day New York from the Indians. On it he founded Rensselaerswyck (1635), the only successful privately held colony in America.

Van Rensselaer, Stephen (1764–1839). U.S. political leader. A descendant of Killian Van Rensselaer, he inherited the family estate in New York, saw limited military action in the War of 1812, and was a major figure in state politics. An early advocate of the Erie Canal, he oversaw the Canal Commission from 1825 to 1839.

Van Rie·beeck (văn rē′bĕk), **Jan Anthonisz** (1619–77). Dutch commander of the first settlement at the Cape of Good Hope, established in 1652. He is now considered the founding father of white South Africa.

van·tage (văn′tĭj) *n.* **1. a.** An advantage in a competition or conflict; superiority. **b.** A position, condition, or opportunity likely to provide superiority or advantage. Often used in the phrase *vantage ground.* **2.** A position that affords a broad overall view or perspective as of a place or situation. Often used in the phrase *vantage point.* **3.** In tennis, an **advantage** *(see).* [Middle English, from Norman French, short for Old French *avantage,* ADVANTAGE.]

van't Hoff (vänt hôf′), **Jacobus Henricus** (1852–1911). Dutch chemist, a pioneer in the field of stereochemistry. In 1901 he was awarded the first Nobel Prize for chemistry.

van·ward (văn′wərd) *adj.* Located in the van or front; advanced. ~*adv.* Toward or to the van or front; forward.

Va·nu·a·tu (vä′no͞o-ä′to͞o). Formerly **New Heb·ri·des** (hĕb′rĭ-dēz′). Group of 12 small islands and numerous islets in the southwest Pacific Ocean. The largest island is Espiritu Santo. The islands are largely volcanic and forested. The chief exports are copra, fish, and beef. After 1897 the islands were administered by France and Great Britain until 1980, when they became independent. Area, 14,763 square kilometers (5,699 square miles). Population, 112,500. Capital, Vila, on Efate.

Van·zet·ti (văn-zĕt′ē), **Bartolomeo** (1888–1927). U.S. anarchist, born in Italy. He was convicted of murder and executed along with Nicola **Sacco** *(see).*

vap·id (văp′ĭd, vā′pĭd) *adj.* **1.** Lacking life, spirit, or animation; dull; insipid: *vapid conversation.* **2.** Lacking taste, zest, or flavor; flat; stale: *vapid beer.* [Latin *vapidus.*] —**va·pid·i·ty** (vă-pĭd′ĭ-tē, vă-, və-), **vap·id·ness** *n.* —**vap·id·ly** *adv.*

va·por (vā′pər) *n.* Also *chiefly British* **va·pour. 1.** Any barely visible or cloudy diffused matter, such as mist, fumes, or smoke, suspended in the air. **2. a.** The state of a substance that exists below its critical temperature and that may be liquefied by application of sufficient pressure. **b.** Broadly, the gaseous state of any substance that is liquid or solid under ordinary conditions. **3. a.** The vaporized form of a substance for use in industrial, military, or medical processes. **b.** A mixture of a vapor and air, such as the explosive gasoline-air mixture burned in an internal-combustion engine. **4.** *Archaic.* **a.** Something unsubstantial, worthless, or fleeting. **b.** A fantastic or foolish idea. **5. vapors.** *Archaic.* **a.** Exhalations within a body organ, especially the stomach, supposed to affect the mental or physical condition. **b.** A nervous disorder such as depression or hysteria. Preceded by *the.*

~*v.* **vapored, -poring, -pors.** —*tr.* To vaporize. —*intr.* **1.** To be emitted or dispersed as vapor. **2.** To engage in idle, boastful talk. **3.** *Archaic.* To rise as vapor. [Middle English *vapour,* from Old French *vapeur, vapour,* from Latin *vapor,* steam.]

vapor bath *n.* **1.** A closed compartment or bath with an apparatus for applying steam to the body. **2.** A bath taken in such a place.

vapor density *n.* The density of a gas or vapor divided by the density of hydrogen both at standard temperature and pressure.

va·por·er moth (vā′pər-ər) *n.* A common moth, *Orgyia antiqua,* the tufted caterpillars of which are a serious pest of trees. [From VAPOR (verb, in archaic sense, "to rise as vapor"), referring to the rapid flight of the male.]

va·por·es·cence (vā′pə-rĕs′əns) *n.* The formation of vapor.

va·po·ret·to (vä′pə-rĕt′ō) *n., pl.* **-ti** (-tē) or **tos.** A steamboat carrying passengers along a regular route, especially one that operates like a bus along the canals of Venice. [Italian, diminutive of *vapore,* steamboat, ultimately from Latin *vapor,* steam.]

va·por·if·ic (vā′pə-rĭf′ĭk) *adj.* **1.** Producing or turning to vapor. **2.** Having the nature of vapor; vaporous. [VAPOR + -FIC.]

va·por·ing (vā′pə-rĭng) *adj.* Foolishly bombastic; boastful. ~*n.* Boastful or bombastic talk or behavior. —**va·por·ing·ly** *adv.*

va·por·ish (vā′pə-rĭsh) *adj.* **1.** Suggestive of or like vapor. **2.** *Archaic.* Affected by the vapors; inclined toward low spirits.

va·por·ize (vā′pə-rīz′) *v.* **-ized, -izing, -izes.** —*tr.* To convert (a solid or liquid) to vapor, especially by heating. —*intr.* To be converted into vapor. —**va·por·iz·a·ble** *adj.* —**va·por·i·za·tion** *n.*

va·por·iz·er (vā′pə-rī′zər) *n.* One that vaporizes; especially, a device used to vaporize medicine for inhalation.

vapor lock *n.* A pocket of vaporized gasoline in the fuel line of an internal-combustion engine that obstructs normal flow of fuel.

va·por·ous (vā′pə-rəs) *adj.* **1.** Pertaining to or resembling vapor. **2. a.** Producing vapors; volatile. **b.** Giving off or full of vapors. **3.** Insubstantial, vague, or ethereal: *"the imponderable mysterious and vaporous illusions of twilight"* (John Cowper Powys). **4.** Extravagantly fanciful; high-flown: *vaporous conjecture.* —**va·por·os·i·ty** (vā′pə-rŏs′ə-tē), **va·por·ous·ness** *n.* —**va·por·ous·ly** *adv.*

vapor pressure *n.* The pressure exerted by a vapor in equilibrium with its solid or liquid phase.

vapor trail *n.* A visible condensation trail in the sky caused by a high-flying aircraft passing through a region of supercooled air. Also called "condensation trail," "contrail."

va·que·ro (vä-kâr′ō) *n., pl.* **-ros.** *Southwestern U.S.* A cowboy; a herdsman. [Spanish, from *vaca,* cow, from Latin *vacca.*]

var. 1. variable. **2.** variant. **3.** variation. **4.** variety. **5.** various.

va·ra (vä′rä) *n.* A Spanish, Portuguese, and Latin American unit of linear measure, varying from 80 to 110 centimeters (32 to 43 inches). [Spanish and Portuguese, "rod," "yardstick," from Latin *vāra,* forked pole, from *vārus,* bent inward.]

va·rac·tor (və-răk′tər, vă-) *n.* A semiconductor device in which the capacitance is sensitive to the applied voltage at the boundary of the semiconductor material and an insulator. [*Var*ying re*actor.*]

Va·ra·na·si (və-rä′nə-sē′). Formerly **Be·na·res** (bə-när′əs, -ēz). City in the state of Uttar Pradesh, in north-central India, on the Ganges River. It is the holiest Hindu city, called Kasi by Hindus, and has more than 1,500 temples, shrines, and palaces.

Va·ran·gi·an (və-răn′jē-ən) *n.* Any of a group of Scandinavian seafarers who established a dynasty in Russia in the 9th century, and from whom Byzantine emperors in the 10th and 11th centuries recruited their bodyguards (the *Varangian Guard*). [Medieval Latin *Varangus,* from Medieval Greek *Barangos,* from Old Norse *Væringi,* probably "confederate," from *vār,* agreement, pledge.]

var·ec (văr′ĕk) *n.* The ash of **kelp** *(see).* [French, from Old Norse *wrek* (unattested), something driven ashore, WRECK.]

va·ri·a (vâr′ē-ə) *n.* A miscellany, especially of literary works. [Latin, neuter plural of *varius,* VARIOUS.]

va·ri·a·ble (vâr′ē-ə-bəl) *adj. Abbr.* **var. 1. a.** Liable, likely, or able to change or vary; subject to variation; changeable. **b.** Inconstant; fickle. **c.** Of uneven quality. **2.** *Mathematics.* Having no fixed quantitative value. **3.** Changing, as in direction or intensity: *variable winds.* **4.** Designating an electrical component, the value of which can be varied: *a variable resistor.*

~*n. Abbr.* **var. 1.** Anything that varies or is liable to variation. **2.** A variable star. **3.** *Mathematics.* **a.** A quantity capable of assuming any of a set of values. **b.** A symbol representing such a quantity. **4.** *Logic.* **a.** A symbol, often *p, q,* or *r,* representing a proposition. **b.** A symbol, often *x, y,* or *z,* representing a class of objects or the name of an individual object in a function or a sentence. —**va·ri·a·bil·i·ty, va·ri·a·ble·ness** *n.* —**va·ri·a·bly** *adv.*

variable cost *n.* Cost that fluctuates directly with output changes.

variable star *n.* A star whose brightness varies because of internal changes or periodic eclipsing of component stars.

va·ri·ance (vâr′ē-əns) *n.* **1. a.** The act of varying; alteration or modification. **b.** The state or quality of being variant or variable; variation; difference. **c.** A difference between what is expected and what actually occurs. **2.** A difference of opinion; dissension; a dispute. **3.** *Law.* **a.** A discrepancy between two statements or documents in a legal proceeding. **b.** A license to engage in an act contrary to a usual rule. **4.** *Statistics.* The dispersion of a set of data as measured by taking the mean of the squares of the variations from the mean of the frequency distribution. **5.** *Chemistry.* The number of thermodynamic variables required to specify a state of equilibrium of a system, given by the phase rule. —See Synonyms at **discord.** —**at variance. 1.** In a state of discrepancy; differing; conflicting. Said of things: *The facts are at variance.* **2.** In a state of dispute or dissension; quarreling: *The factions are at variance.*

va·ri·ant (vâr′ē-ənt) *adj.* **1.** Having or exhibiting variation; differing. **2.** Tending or liable to vary; variable; changeable. **3. a.** Deviating from a standard or norm. **b.** Exhibiting slight difference.
~*n. Abbr.* **var.** Something that differs, usually only slightly, from another in form, such as a different spelling or pronunciation of the same word. [Middle English, from Old French, from Latin *variāns* (stem *variānt-*), present participle of *variāre,* VARY.]

va·ri·ate (vâr′ē-ĭt, -āt′) *n.* **1.** *Statistics.* A random variable with a numerical value that is defined on a given sample space. **2.** *Rare.* Something that varies; a variable. [Latin *variāre,* VARY.]

va·ri·a·tion (vâr′ē-ā′shən) *n. Abbr.* **var. 1. a.** The act, process, or result of varying; change or deviation. **b.** The state or fact of being varied. **2.** The extent or degree of such varying or deviation: *a variation of ten pounds in weight.* **3.** A natural compass error, **magnetic declination** *(see).* **4.** Something that is slightly different from another of the same type. **5.** *Biology.* **a.** Marked difference or deviation from characteristic form, function, or structure. **b.** An organism or plant exhibiting such difference or deviation. **6.** *Mathematics.* A function that relates the values of one variable to those of other variables. **7. a.** A musical form that is an altered version of some given theme, diverging from it by melodic ornamentation and by changes in harmony, rhythm, or key. **b.** Any of a series of such forms based on a single theme. **8.** In classical ballet, a solo dance. —See Usage note at **difference.** [Middle English, from Old French, from Latin *variātiō* (stem *variātiōn-*), from *variāre,* VARY.] —**var·i·a·tion·al** *adj.*

var·i·cel·la (văr′ə-sĕl′ə) *n.* **Chickenpox** *(see).* [New Latin, irregular diminutive of VARIOLA.] —**var·i·cel·loid** *adj.*

var·i·ces. Plural of **varix.**

varico-, varic- *prefix.* Indicates varix or varicose veins; for example, **varicocele, varicosis.** [Latin *varix* (stem *varic-*), VARIX.]

var·i·co·cele (văr′ə-kō-sēl′) *n.* **1.** A varicose condition of the veins of the testicle, producing a swelling of the scrotum. **2.** Any of various other varicose conditions. [VARICO- + -CELE (tumor).]

va·ri·col·ored (vâr′ĭ-kŭl′ərd) *adj.* Having a variety of colors; variegated; motley.

var·i·cose (văr′ĭ-kōs′) *adj.* **1.** Designating blood or lymph vessels that are abnormally dilated, knotted, and tortuous, as in the legs or less commonly in the rectum or testes. **2.** Causing unusual swelling. [Latin *varicōsus,* from VARIX.]

var·i·co·sis (văr′ə-kō′sĭs) *n.* The state of being varicose. [VARIC(O)- + -OSIS.]

var·i·cos·i·ty (văr′ə-kŏs′ə-tē) *n., pl.* **-ties. 1.** Varicosis. **2. a.** A varicose distension or swelling. **b.** The state of having varicose veins.

var·i·cot·o·my (văr′ə-kŏt′ə-mē) *n., pl.* **-mies.** Subcutaneous incision to remove varicose veins. [VARICO- + -TOMY.]

va·ried (vâr′ēd) *adj.* **1.** Having various kinds or forms; marked by variety. **2.** Modified or altered. **3.** Varicolored; variegated. —See Synonyms at **miscellaneous.** —**var·ied·ly** *adv.*

va·rie·gate (vâr′ə-gāt′) *tr.v.* **-gated, -gating, -gates. 1.** To change the appearance of, especially by marking with different colors; streak. **2.** To give variety to; make varied. [Late Latin *variēgāre,* from Latin *varius,* VARIOUS.]

va·rie·gat·ed (vâr′ē-ə-gā′tĭd) *adj.* **1.** Having streaks, marks, or patches of a different color or colors. **2.** Having lighter or white areas due to mutation or infection, for example. Said of leaves and petals. **3.** Distinguished or characterized by variety; diversified.

va·rie·ga·tion (vâr′ē-ə-gā′shən) *n.* The state of being variegated; diversified coloration.

va·ri·e·tal (və-rī′ə-təl) *adj.* Of, indicating, or named after a biological variety. [From VARIETY.] —**va·ri·e·tal·ly** *adv.*

va·ri·e·ty (və-rī′ə-tē) *n., pl.* **-ties.** *Abbr.* **var. 1. a.** The condition or quality of being various or varied; diversity. **b.** A lack of monotony or sameness that keeps something interesting. **2.** A number or collection of varied things, especially of a particular group; an assortment: *a great variety of food at the buffet.* **3. a.** A different kind, sort, or form of something of the same general classification. **b.** Something belonging to such a kind, form, or sort. **4.** *Biology.* **a.** A taxonomic group below the species. Used by specialists in different fields as a substitute for various taxonomic categories such as race, stock, strain, and breed. **b.** An organism, especially a plant, belonging to such a group. **5.** The type of theatrical entertainment or branch of the theater consisting of variety shows. Also used adjectivally: a *variety act.* [French *variete,* from Latin *varietās* (stem *varietāt-*), from *varius,* VARIOUS.]

variety meat *n.* Meat taken from a part other than skeletal muscles, as liver or sweetbreads, or processed, as sausage.

variety show *n.* A theatrical entertainment consisting of successive diverse acts, such as songs, dances, and comedy sketches.

variety store *n.* A retail store carrying a large variety of usually inexpensive merchandise. Also called "variety shop."

va·ri·form (vâr′ə-fôrm′) *adj.* Having a variety of forms; diversiform. [VARI(O)- + -FORM.]

vario-, vari- *prefix.* Indicates variety or difference; for example, **variometer, variform.** [Latin *varius,* VARIOUS.]

va·ri·o·la (və-rī′ə-lə) *n.* **Smallpox** *(see).* [New Latin, from Medieval Latin, pustule, from Latin *varius,* speckled, VARIOUS.]

va·ri·o·late (vâr′ē-ə-lāt′, -lĭt) *adj.* Having pustules or scars like those of smallpox.
~*tr.v.* **variolated, -lating, -lates.** To inoculate with smallpox. —**va·ri·o·la·tion** *n.*

va·ri·o·lite (vâr′ē-ə-līt′) *n.* A basic rock, originally glassy, that has developed a variolitic texture. [Medieval Latin *variola,* smallpox, VARIOL(A) + -ITE.]

var·i·o·lit·ic (vâr′ē-ə-lĭt′ĭk) *adj.* Of or designating a structure or texture consisting of spherules of minute radiating fibers, generally of plagioclase, and having a pock-marked appearance.

va·ri·o·loid (vâr′ē-ə-loid′) *n.* A mild form of smallpox in persons who have previously been vaccinated or who have previously had the disease.
~*adj.* Resembling smallpox. [VARIOL(A) + -OID.]

va·ri·o·lous (vâr′ē-ə-ləs) *adj.* Pertaining to, characteristic of, or resembling smallpox. [VARIOL(A) + -OUS.]

va·ri·om·e·ter (vâr′ē-ŏm′ə-tər) *n.* **1.** A variable inductor used to measure variations in terrestrial magnetism. **2.** A form of variable inductor. **3.** An indicator in a glider or other aircraft showing the rate of climb or descent. [VARIO- + -METER.]

va·ri·o·rum (vâr′ē-ôr′əm, -ōr′əm) *n.* **1.** An edition particularly of the complete works of a classical author, with notes by scholars or editors. **2.** An edition containing various versions of a text.
~*adj.* Designating or pertaining to a variorum. [Short for Latin *editiō cum notīs variōrum,* edition with the notes of various (commentators), from *variōrum,* genitive plural of *varius,* VARIOUS.]

va·ri·ous (vâr′ē-əs, văr′-) *adj. Abbr.* **var. 1. a.** Of diverse kinds. **b.** Unlike; different. **2.** More than one; numerous; several. **3.** Many-sided; varying; versatile. **4.** Having a variegated nature or appearance. **5.** Being one of a class or group but individual and separate: *The various reports all agreed.* **6.** *Archaic.* Changeable; variable.
~*pron. Nonstandard.* Some; a certain amount: *spoke to various of the demonstrators.* [Latin *varius,* speckled, variegated, changeable.] —**var·i·ous·ly** *adv.* —**var·i·ous·ness** *n.*

Var·is·can (və-rĭs′kən) *adj.* Hercynian.

var·is·cite (văr′ə-sīt′) *n.* A green mineral, a hydrated phosphate of aluminum, essentially $AlPO_4.2H_2O$, that occurs as modular masses. [German *Variscit,* from Medieval Latin *Variscia,* ancient name of the Vogtland district of Saxony + -ITE.]

var·i·sized (vâr′ĭ-sīzd′, văr′-) *adj.* Of different sizes.

va·ris·tor (vă-rĭs′tər) *n.* A semiconductor device with a variable, voltage-dependent resistance; especially, one with a negative voltage characteristic. [From *var*ying tran*sistor.*]

va·ri·type (vâr′ĭ-tīp′) *v.* **-typed, -typing, -typing.** —*tr.* To prepare and set (copy) on a Varityper. —*intr.* To use a Varityper. —**var·i·typ·ist** *n.*

Va·ri·Typ·er (vâr′ĭ-tī′pər) *n.* A trademark for a typewriter that can be used to prepare copy in a variety of typefaces.

va·rix (văr′ĭks) *n., pl.* **-ices** (văr′ĭ-sēz′). **1.** A vein that is abnormally dilated and twisted. **2.** Any of the longitudinal ridges marking a resting stage in the development of the lip of a gastropod shell. [Latin, swollen vein.]

var·let (vär′lĭt) *n. Archaic.* **1.** An attendant or servant. **2.** A knight's page. **3.** A rascal; knave. [Middle English, from Old French, variant of *vaslet, valet,* VALET.]

var·let·ry (vär′lĭ-trē) *n. Archaic.* **1.** A crowd of attendants or menials. **2.** A disorderly crowd; a rabble.

var·mint (vär′mənt) *n. Regional.* A person or animal considered undesirable, obnoxious, or troublesome. [Variant of VERMIN.]

var·nish (vär′nĭsh) *n.* **1. a.** An oil-based preparation containing a solvent and an oxidizing or an evaporating binder, used to coat a surface with a hard, glossy, thin film. Also called "oil varnish." **b.** A similar preparation consisting of shellac or a synthetic resin, which is dissolved in a solvent, such as alcohol. The solvent evaporates leaving a hard glossy film. Also called "spirit varnish." **c.** A naturally produced substance, such as the sap of certain trees, that dries forming a hard glossy surface. Also called "natural varnish." **2. a.** The smooth coating or gloss resulting from the application of varnish. **b.** Something resembling or likened to varnish. **3.** Any deceptively attractive external appearance; an outward show.
~*tr.v.* **varnished, -nishing, -nishes. 1.** To cover with varnish. **2.** To give a smooth and glossy finish to. **3.** To give a deceptively nice appearance to; gloss over. **4.** *Chiefly British.* To cover (nails) with nail polish. [Middle English *vernisch,* from Old French *vernis,* from Medieval Latin *veronix,* sandarac, from Medieval Greek *berenikē,* perhaps from Greek *Berenikē,* Berenice, city in Cyrenaica, Libya, where varnishes were first used.] —**var·nish·er** *n.*

varnish tree *n.* Any of several trees having milky juice used to make varnish; especially, the **lacquer tree** *(see).*

Var·ro (vărʹō), **Marcus Terentius** (116–27 B.C.). Roman encyclopedist. The first universal scholar of Roman civilization, he reputedly produced over 600 volumes, although only about 50 of them are presently known. His highly influential and diversified works include *On Agriculture, The Latin Language,* and *History of Human and Divine Concerns.*

var·si·ty (värʹsə-tē) *n., pl.* **-ties. 1.** The principal team representing a university, college, or school in sports or other competitions. **2.** *Chiefly British Informal.* A university. [Shortened and altered from UNIVERSITY.] —**var·si·ty** *adj.*

Var·u·na (värʹŏŏ-nə, vûrʹ-) *n. Hinduism.* The Vedic god of the skies and seas. [Sanskrit *Varuṇa.*]

va·rus (vârʹəs) *n. pl.* **-uses. 1.** A deformity of the legs causing them to bend inward; knock-knee. **2.** A deformity of the foot causing the person to walk on the inner edge of the sole. [Latin, crooked.]

varve (värv) *n. Geology.* **1.** A layer of sediment deposited in one year. **2.** A pair of distinct layers of sediment, indicating seasonal deposits. [Swedish *varv,* layer, turn, from *varva,* to bend, turn, from Old Norse *hverfa.*]

va·ry (vârʹē) *v.* **-ied, -ying, -ies.** —*tr.* **1.** To make or cause changes in the characteristics or attributes of; modify or alter. **2.** To make diverse; give variety to: *vary one's diet.* **3.** To introduce under new aspects; express in a different manner. —*intr.* **1. a.** To undergo or show change: *a varying society.* **b.** To vary in direct relation to a specified variable. Used with *with: Her temper varies with the number of children at home.* **2.** To be different; deviate or depart. Used with *from.* **3.** To undergo successive or alternate changes in attributes or qualities. —See Synonyms at **change.** [Middle English *varien,* from Old French *varier,* from Latin *variāre,* from *varius,* speckled, changeable.] —**var·i·er** *n.*

varying hare *n.* A **snowshoe rabbit** *(see).*

vas (văs) *n., pl.* **vasa** (vāʹsə). An organic vessel or duct. [Latin *vās†,* vessel.]

Va·sa·re·ly (vä-zä-rĕ-lēʹ), **Victor** (1908–). Hungarian-born painter. He moved to Paris (1930), where his abstract works showed the influence of constructivism. By the 1960's he was regarded as one of the leading exponents of op art.

Va·sa·ri (və-zärʹē, -särʹē), **Giorgio** (1511–74). Italian painter, architect, and art historian. His *Lives of the Most Eminent Italian Architects, Painters, and Sculptors* traces the history of Renaissance art from Giotto to Michelangelo.

vas·cu·lar (văsʹkyə-lər) *adj. Biology.* Of, characterized by, or containing vessels for the transmission or circulation of plant or animal fluids such as blood, lymph, or sap. [Latin *vāsculum,* diminutive of *vās,* vessel, VAS.]

vascular bundle *n.* A strand of supportive and conductive plant tissue consisting essentially of xylem and phloem.

vas·cu·lar·i·za·tion (văsʹkyə-lə-rə-zāʹshən) *n.* The development of vessels, especially new blood capillaries, in an organ or part.

vascular plant *n.* Any plant of the division Tracheophyta, which includes the ferns and seed-bearing plants characterized by a system of specialized conductive and supportive tissue.

vascular tissue *n.* Plant tissue consisting of vascular bundles.

vas·cu·la·ture (văsʹkyə-lə-chŏŏr, -chər) *n.* The arrangement of blood vessels in the body or in an organ or part of the body.

vas·cu·lum (văsʹkyə-ləm) *n., pl.* **-la** (-lə). A small box or case used for carrying newly collected plant specimens. [Latin *vāsculum,* small vessel. See **vascular.**]

vas def·er·ens (văsʹ dĕfʹər-ənz, -ə-rĕnzʹ) *n., pl.* **va·sa def·er·en·ti·a.** Either of a pair of vertebrate ducts that carry sperm from the epididymal duct to the ejaculatory duct. [New Latin, "carrying-off vessel."]

vase (văs, vāz, väz) *n.* An open vessel, usually tall and often shaped like a cylinder, made of glass, crystal, earthenware, or the like, and used chiefly for holding flowers or as an ornament. [French, from Latin *vās,* vessel, VAS.]

va·sec·to·my (vă-sĕkʹtə-mē) *n., pl.* **-mies.** Surgical cutting of the vas deferens, used, when both are cut, as a means of male sterilization. [VAS (DEFERENS) + -ECTOMY.]

Vas·e·line (văsʹə-lēn) *n.* A trademark for a petroleum jelly used primarily as a vehicle for external applications of medicinal agents, as a soothing or lubricating covering for the skin, and as a protective coating for metal surfaces.

vaso-, vas– *prefix.* Indicates a blood vessel; for example, **vasomotor.** [Latin *vās,* vessel, VAS.]

va·so·ac·tive (vāʹzō-ăkʹtĭv) *adj.* Causing dilation or constriction of the blood vessels, especially the arteries. —**va·so·ac·tiv·i·ty** (vāʹzō-ăk-tĭvʹĭ-tē) *n.*

va·so·con·stric·tion (vāʹzō-kən-strĭkʹshən) *n.* Constriction of a blood vessel.

va·so·con·stric·tor (vāʹzō-kən-strĭkʹtər) *n.* An agent, such as a nerve or a drug, that causes vasoconstriction. —**va·so·con·stric·tive** *adj.*

va·so·dil·a·ta·tion (vāʹzō-dĭlʹə-tāʹshən, -dīʹlə-) *n.* Also **va·so·dil·a·tion** (-dī-lāʹshən, -dī-). Dilation of a blood vessel.

va·so·di·la·tor (vāʹzō-dī-lāʹtər, -dī-) *n.* An agent, such as a nerve or drug, that causes vasodilatation. —**va·so·di·la·tive** *adj.*

va·so·mo·tor (vāʹzō-mōʹtər) *adj.* Causing or regulating vasoconstriction or vasodilatation.

va·so·pres·sin (vāʹzō-prĕsʹĭn) *n.* A hormone secreted by the pituitary gland that increases the reabsorption of water by the kidneys and constricts the blood vessels. Also called "antidiuretic hormone." [Originally a trademark.]

vas·sal (văsʹəl) *n.* **1.** A person who held land from a feudal lord and received protection in return for homage and allegiance. **2.** One that is subject or subservient to another; a subordinate or dependent. Also used adjectively: *a vassal state.* **3.** Loosely, a minion or slave. [Middle English, from Old French, from Medieval Latin *vassallus,* from Vulgar Latin *vassus* (unattested), servant, valet, from Celtic *wasso-* (unattested), young man, squire.]

vas·sal·age (văsʹə-lĭj) *n.* **1.** The condition of being a vassal. **2.** The service, homage, and fealty required of a vassal. **3.** *Literary.* A position of subordination or subjection; servitude. **4.** The land held by a vassal; a fief. **5.** Vassals collectively or the vassals of a particular lord.

vast (văst, väst) *adj.* **vaster, vastest. 1.** Very great in size, number, amount, or quantity. **2.** Very great in area or extent; immense. **3.** Very great in degree or intensity: *made a vast difference.* —See Synonyms at **enormous.** ~*n.* **1.** *Archaic & Poetic.* An immense space. **2.** *Regional.* A great number, amount, or quality. [Latin *vastus,* immense, vast.] —**vast·ly** *adv.* —**vast·ness** *n.*

vas·ti·tude (văsʹtĭ-tōōdʹ, -tyōōdʹ) *n.* Also **vas·ti·ty** (-tē). Immensity; vastness. [Latin *vastitās,* from *vastus,* VAST.]

vast·y (văsʹtē) *adj.* **-ier, -iest.** *Archaic.* Vast.

vat (văt) *n.* A large vessel, such as a tub, cistern, or barrel, used to store or hold liquids. ~*tr.v.* **vatted, vatting, vats.** To place into or treat in a vat. [Middle English *vat, fat,* Old English *fæt,* from Germanic *fatam* (unattested), vessel.]

VAT, V.A.T. (often văt). Value-added tax.

vat dye *n.* Any of a series of dyes that produce a fast color by impregnating the fiber with a reduced soluble form that is then oxidized to an insoluble form.

vat·ic (vătʹĭk) *adj.* Also **vat·i·cal** (-ĭ-kəl). Of or characteristic of a prophet; oracular. [Latin *vātēs,* prophet.]

Vat·i·can (vătʹĭ-kən) *n.* *Abbr.* **Vat. 1.** The official residence of the pope in Vatican City, within the city of Rome, Italy. Preceded by *the.* **2.** The papal government; the papacy. Also used adjectively: *a Vatican decree.* [French, from Latin *Vāticānus (mōns),* the Vatican (Hill), of Etruscan origin.]

Vatican City. Italian **Cit·tà del Vat·i·ca·no** (chē-täʹ dĕl vä-tē-käʹnō). Independent state, the smallest in the world, lying within Rome, in central Italy. Its independence was established by the Lateran Treaty (1929) between Pius XI and King Victor Emmanuel III. The state is ruled by the pope and administered by a lay governor and council appointed by him. It is the supreme government of the Roman Catholic Church, which with tourism and sale of its postage stamps provides the state's income. St. Peter's Basilica lies within the Vatican City, sometimes known as the Holy See. Area, 44 hectares (0.17 square miles). Population, 700.

Vatican Council *n.* Either of two Roman Catholic ecumenical councils: **1.** *First Vatican Council* (1869–70), which accepted the definition of papal infallibility. **2.** *Second Vatican Council* (1962–65), which was convened to discuss the position of the Church in the modern world and which led to wide-ranging reforms, in particular the replacement of Latin by vernacular languages in public worship.

Vat·i·can·ism (vătʹĭ-kə-nĭzʹəm) *n.* The policies and authority of the Vatican, especially with regard to papal infallibility.

va·tic·i·nal (və-tĭsʹə-nəl) *adj.* Prophetic.

va·tic·i·nate (və-tĭsʹə-nātʹ) *v.* **-nated, -nating, -nates.** —*tr.* To prophesy; foretell. —*intr.* To be a prophet. [Latin *vāticinārī,* from *vātēs,* prophet. See **vatic.**] —**va·tic·i·na·tor** *n.*

va·tic·i·na·tion (və-tĭsʹə-nāʹshən) *n.* **1.** The act of prophesying. **2.** A prediction or prophecy.

va·tu (väʹtōō) *n.* The basic monetary unit of Vanuatu, equal to 100 cents.

vau. Variant of **vav.**

vau·de·ville (vôdʹvĭlʹ, vōdʹ-, vôʹdə-vĭlʹ) *n.* **1. a.** Stage entertainment offering a variety of short acts such as slapstick turns, song-and-dance routines, and juggling performances. **b.** A theatrical performance of this kind; variety show. Also *chiefly British* "music hall." **2.** A light comic play that often includes songs, pantomime, and dances. **3.** A popular, often satirical, song. [French, from Old French *vaudevire,* short for *chanson du Vau de Vire,* type of satirical song, especially those of Olivier Basselin, 15th-century poet born in *Vau de Vire,* in the Valley of Vire, a region in Normandy, from *vau, val,* VALE.]

vau·de·vil·li·an (vôd-vĭlʹyən, vōd-, vô'də-vĭlʹ-) *n.* One who works in vaudeville, especially a performer. ~*adj.* Of or pertaining to vaudeville.

Vau·dois (vō-dwäʹ) *pl.n.* The **Waldenses** *(see).*

Vaughn (vôn), **Sarah** (1924–). U.S. singer. One of the foremost jazz vocalists, she is known for her complex bebop phrasing and her scat-singing virtuosity.

Vaughan Wil·liams (wĭlʹyəmz), **Ralph** (1872–1958). British composer. He was greatly influenced by folk tunes and Tudor music, as is evident in his *Fantasia on a Theme by Thomas Tallis* (1910). His works include nine symphonies, the ballet *Job* (1931), and the opera *The Pilgrim's Progress* (1948–49).

vault¹ (vôlt) *n.* **1. a.** An arch, usually of stone, brick, or concrete, forming the supporting structure of a ceiling or roof. **b.** Any arched overhead covering resembling or thought to resemble a vault, such

vase *The Portland vase (above) is one of the finest surviving examples of Roman art. It is made of dark blue glass decorated with white figures and is thought to date from about the first century A.D. It was named after the Duke of Portland, who acquired it in the 18th century. It is now in the British Museum, London.*

as the sky. **2.** A room or space with arched walls and ceiling, especially when underground, such as a cellar or storeroom. **3.** A room or compartment, often built of steel, for the safekeeping of valuables: *a bank vault.* **4.** A burial chamber, especially when underground. **5.** *Anatomy.* An arched cavity.

~tr.v. **vaulted, vaulting, vaults. 1.** To construct or supply with an arched ceiling; cover with a vault. **2.** To build or make in the shape of a vault; arch. [Middle English *vaute, voute,* from Old French, from Vulgar Latin *vol(vi)ta* (unattested), a turn, vault, variant of Latin *volūta,* feminine past participle of *volvere,* to turn.]

vault² *v.* **vaulted, vaulting, vaults.** *—tr.* To jump or leap over, especially with the aid of a support, such as the hands or a pole. *—intr.* **1.** To jump or leap, especially with the use of the hands or a pole. **2.** To achieve or surmount something, as if by bounding vigorously: *vaulted into a position of wealth.*

~n. The act of vaulting; a jump. [Old French *volter,* from Italian *voltare,* to turn (a horse), leap, gambol, from Vulgar Latin *volvitāre* (unattested), frequentative of Latin *volvere,* to turn.] **—vault·er** *n.*

vault·ing¹ (vôl′tĭng) *n.* **1.** The practice or craft of building vaults. **2.** Vaults collectively. **3.** A vault or vaulted construction.

vaulting² *adj.* **1.** Leaping upward or over. **2.** Reaching too far; exaggerated: *vaulting ambition.* **3.** Used for leaping over: *a vaulting pole.*

vaunt (vônt, vŏnt) *v.* **vaunted, vaunting, vaunts.** *—tr.* To describe in boastful terms; brag about. *—intr.* To boast; brag. —See Synonyms at **boast.**

~n. A boastful remark or speech of extravagant self-praise. [Middle English *va(u)nten,* from Old French *vanter,* from Late Latin *vānitāre* (attested only in the present participle *vānitāns*), to be vain, from Latin *vānus,* empty, vain.] **—vaunt·er** *n.* **—vaunt·ing·ly** *adv.*

vaunt-cour·i·er (vônt′kŏŏr′ē-ər, -kûr′-, -kŭr′-, vŏnt′-) *n. Archaic.* One sent in advance, especially a herald. [Old French *avant-cour(r)ier : avant,* in front of + COURIER.]

Vaux (vôks), **Calvert** (1824–95). English-born U.S. landscape architect. He worked on the landscaping for the grounds of the U.S. Capitol (1850–52) and with Frederick Law Olmsted on the designs for several parks in Chicago and New York, including Central Park. His design for Brooklyn's Prospect Park was accepted in 1865.

vav (väv, vôv) *n.* Also **vau, waw.** The sixth letter of the Hebrew alphabet. See feature at **alphabet.** [Hebrew.]

vav·a·sour, vav·a·sor, vav·as·sor (văv′ə-sôr′, -sōr′) *n.* In the feudal system, a vassal who ranked directly below a baron or peer, with other vassals under him. [Middle English *vavasour,* from Old French, from Medieval Latin *vavassor,* perhaps contraction of *vassus vassōrum,* "vassal of vassals." See **vassal.**]

vb. verb; verbal.

V.C. 1. vice chairman. **2.** vice chancellor. **3.** vice consul. **4.** Victoria Cross. **5.** Vietcong.

VCR video cassette recorder.

VD, V.D. venereal disease.

v.d. 1. vapor density. **2.** various dates.

VDT video display terminal.

VDU *n., pl.* **VDUs.** a **visual display unit** *(see).*

Ve·a·dar, Ve·a·dar (vā′ä-där′) *n.* An extra month of the Hebrew year, having 29 days, added in leap years after the regular month of Adar. Also called "Adar Sheni." See feature at **calendar.** [Hebrew *va'adhar,* "and Adar."]

veal (vēl) *n.* The meat of a calf. [Middle English *veel,* from Old French, from Latin *vitellus,* diminutive of *vitulus,* calf, "yearling."]

veal·y (vē′lē) *adj.* **-ier, -iest. 1.** Of or like veal. **2.** Not fully developed; immature.

Veb·len (vĕb′lən), **Thorstein Bunde** (1857–1929). U.S. economist. Best known for his books *The Theory of the Leisure Class* (1899) and *The Theory of Business Enterprise* (1904), he introduced the idea of "conspicuous consumption" and argued that there is a fundamental conflict between the providing of goods and the making of money.

vec·tor (vĕk′tər) *n.* **1.** *Mathematics.* A quantity completely specified by a magnitude and a direction. Compare **scalar. 2.** *Pathology.* An organism that carries pathogens from one host to another. **3.** Broadly, any force or influence.

~tr.v. **vectored, -toring, -tors.** To guide (a pilot, aircraft, or the like) by means of radio communication, according to vectors. [Latin *vector,* carrier, from *vehere* (past participle *vectus*), to carry.] **—vec·to·ri·al** (vĕk-tôr′ē-əl, -tōr′ē-əl) *adj.*

vector field *n.* A region of space in which a vector quantity exerts a field, at any point of which the field strength can be represented by a vector.

vector product *n.* A vector, *C,* that has magnitude equal to the product of the magnitudes of two vectors, *A* and *B,* and the sine of the angle between *A* and *B,* and having a direction perpendicular to the plane containing *A* and *B* and in a right-handed coordinate system directed so that a right-handed rotation about *C* carries *A* into *B* through an angle not greater than 180 degrees. It is usually written *A* × *B.* Also called "cross product." Compare **scalar product.**

vector sum *n.* A vector that is the resultant of two other vectors, as determined by the parallelogram rule.

Ve·da (vā′də, vē′-) *n.* Any of the oldest sacred writings of Hinduism, including the psalms, incantations, hymns, and formulas of worship incorporated in four collections called the Rig-Veda, the Yajur-Veda, the Sama-Veda, and the Atharva-Veda. [Sanskrit *veda,* "knowledge."]

ve·da·li·a (vĭ-dāl′yə) *n.* An Australian beetle, *Rodolia cardinalis,* that

is used in many citrus-growing regions to control the scale insect *Icerya purchasi.* [New Latin : origin obscure.]

Ve·dan·ta (vĭ-dän′tə, -dăn′tə) *n.* The system of Hindu philosophy that further develops the implications in the Upanishads that all reality is a single principle, Brahman, and teaches that the believer's goal is to transcend the limitations of individual consciousness and realize his unity with Brahman. [Sanskrit *vedanta,* "complete knowledge of the Veda" : *veda,* VEDA + *anta,* end.] **—Ve·dan·tic** *adj.* **—Ve·dan·tism** *n.* **—Ve·dan·tist** *n.*

V-E Day (vē′ē′) *n.* The day of victory for the Allied forces in Europe during World War II; officially, May 8, 1945. [Short for *Victory in Europe Day.*]

Ved·da, Ved·dah (vĕd′ə) *n.* Any of a small, dark-skinned, wavy-haired aboriginal people of Sri Lanka. [Singhalese, "hunter," from Dravidian, akin to Tamil *vēṭṭam,* hunting.]

ve·dette, vi·dette (vĭ-dĕt′) *n.* **1.** A mounted sentry stationed in advance of an outpost. **2.** A small scouting boat used to observe and report on an opposing naval force. In this sense, also called "vedette boat." [French, from Italian *vedetta,* variant (influenced by *vedere,* to see) of *veletta,* from Spanish *vela,* a watch, from *velar,* to watch, from Latin *vigilāre,* from *vigil,* awake.]

Ve·dic (vā′dĭk, vē′-) *adj.* Of or pertaining to the Veda or Vedas or to the Hindu culture that produced them.

~n. The early Sanskrit in which the Vedas are written.

veep (vēp) *n. Slang.* **1.** A vice president. **2.** Veep. The Vice President of the United States. [From the abbreviation *V.P.*]

veer¹ (vîr) *v.* **veered, veering, veers.** *—intr.* **1.** To turn aside from a course, direction, or purpose; swerve; shift. **2.** To shift in direction by a clockwise motion. Used of the wind. Compare **back. 3.** *Nautical.* To change the direction of a ship by turning the head away from the direction of the wind; wear ship. *—tr.* **1.** To alter the direction of; turn. **2.** *Nautical.* To change the course of (a ship) by turning away from the direction of the wind.

~n. A change in direction; a swerve. [French *virer,* from Vulgar Latin *vīrāre* (unattested), perhaps variant (influenced by Latin *vibrāre,* VIBRATE) of Latin *gȳrāre,* GYRATE.]

veer² *tr.v.* **veered, veering, veers.** *Nautical.* To let out or release (an anchor chain or line, for example). [Middle English *veren,* from Middle Dutch *vieren.*]

veg (vĕj) *n., pl.* **veg.** *British Informal.* A vegetable: *meat and two veg.*

Ve·ga (vē′gə, vā′-) *n.* The brightest star in the constellation Lyra. [Medieval Latin, from Arabic *(al nasr) al wāqi',* the constellation Lyra, "the falling (vulture)."]

Ve·ga (vā′gə), **Lope Felix de** (1562–1635). Spanish poet and his country's first great dramatist. Most of his themes were drawn from history, and 500 of his almost 2,000 plays survive.

veg·an (vĕj′ən, -ăn, vē′gən) *n.* A strict vegetarian; one who consumes or uses no animal products at all. [Shortened from VEGETARIAN.] **—veg·an** *adj.* **—veg·an·ism** (vĕj′ə-nĭz′əm, vē′gə-) *n.*

veg·e·ta·ble (vĕj′tə-bəl, vĕj′ĭ-tə-) *n.* **1. a.** A plant cultivated for an edible part or parts, such as its roots, stems, leaves, or flowers. **b.** The edible part of such a plant. **2.** An organism classified as a plant; a member of the plant kingdom. **3.** A person who leads a monotonous, passive, or merely physical existence.

~adj. **1.** Of, pertaining to, or derived from a plant or plants. **2.** Suggesting or like a vegetable, as in passivity or dullness of existence; monotonous; inactive. [Middle English, living, growing, from Old French, from Medieval Latin *vegetābilis,* from Late Latin, enlivening, from Latin *vegetāre,* to enliven, from *vegetus,* lively, from *vegēre,* to be lively.]

vegetable ivory *n.* A hard, ivorylike material obtained from the **ivory nut** *(see)* and used in making small objects such as buttons.

vegetable marrow *n. Chiefly British.* An edible squash having very large, elongated greenish fruit. Also called "marrow squash."

vegetable oil *n.* Any of various oils obtained from plants, used in food products and industrially.

vegetable oyster *n.* A plant, **salsify** *(see).*

vegetable silk *n.* Any of several silky fibers from the seed pods of certain plants.

vegetable sponge *n.* See **loofa** (sense 1).

vegetable tallow *n.* Any of various waxy fats obtained from certain plants used in making soap and candles.

vegetable wax *n.* A waxy substance of plant origin, usually secreted in thin flakes by the epidermal cells.

veg·e·tal (vĕj′ə-təl) *adj.* **1.** Of, pertaining to, or characteristic of a plant or plants. **2.** Pertaining to growth rather than to sexual reproduction; vegetative. [French, from Old French *vegeter,* to grow, from Late Latin *vegetāre,* from Latin, to enliven. See **vegetable.**]

veg·e·tar·i·an (vĕj′ə-târ′ē-ən) *n.* **1.** One who eats no meat or fish. **2.** One who practices or advocates vegetarianism.

~adj. **1.** Eating no meat or fish. **2.** Pertaining to, practicing, or advocating vegetarianism. **3.** Consisting of vegetables or nonflesh foods: *a vegetarian diet.* **4.** Serving, presenting, or advocating no meat or fish: *a vegetarian cookbook; a vegetarian restaurant.* [From VEGETABLE (coined in 1847 by the Vegetarian Society at Ramsgate, England).]

veg·e·tar·i·an·ism (vĕj′ə-târ′ē-ə-nĭz′əm) *n.* The practice of or belief in avoiding eating meat or fish or, more strictly, eating only vegetables and plant products, usually for health or moral reasons.

veg·e·tate (vĕj′ĭ-tāt′) *intr.v.* **-tated, -tating, -tates. 1.** To grow or sprout as a plant does. **2.** *Pathology.* To grow or spread abnormally. **3.** To lead an existence that is monotonous, passive, or lacks mental stimulation. [Late Latin *vegetāre,* to grow, from Latin, to enliven. See **vegetable.**]

veg·e·ta·tion (vĕj′ə-tā′shən) *n.* **1.** The plants of an area or region; plant life collectively. **2.** The act or process of vegetating. **3.** *Pathology.* Any abnormal growth on the body.

veg·e·ta·tive (vĕj′ə-tā′tĭv) *adj.* Also **veg·e·tive** (vĕj′ə-tĭv). **1.** Of, pertaining to, or characteristic of plants or plant growth. **2.** *Biology.* **a.** Of, pertaining to, or capable of growth. **b.** Of, pertaining to, or functioning in processes such as growth or nutrition, rather than sexual reproduction. **c.** Of or pertaining to asexual reproduction, such as fission or budding. **3.** Monotonous, passive, or lacking mental stimulation.

ve·he·ment (vē′ə-mənt) *adj.* **1.** Characterized by forcefulness of expression or intensity of emotion, passion, or conviction; ardent; emphatic: *vehement denial.* **2.** Marked by or full of vigor or energy; strong; violent. [Old French, from Latin *vehemēns*† (stem *vehement-*).] **—ve·he·mence, ve·he·men·cy** *n.* **—ve·he·ment·ly** *adv.*

ve·hi·cle (vē′ĭ-kəl) *n.* **1.** Any conveyance for carrying passengers, goods, or equipment, moving along the ground or in the air or space, often one moving on wheels, such as a car. **2.** Anything through or by which something, such as thought, power, or information is conveyed, transmitted, expressed, or achieved: *The play was a vehicle for her political views.* **3.** A play, role, or piece of music used to display the special talents of one performer or company. **4.** *Pharmacology.* A substance of no therapeutic value used as the medium in which active medicines are administered. **5.** A substance, such as oil, in which paint pigments are mixed for application. [French *véhicule,* from Latin *vehiculum,* from *vehere,* to carry.] **—ve·hic·u·lar** (vē-hĭk′yə-lər) *adj.*

veil (vāl) *n.* **1.** A piece of cloth, often wide-meshed and semitransparent, worn by women over the head, shoulders, and often part of the face for concealment, protection, or as a token of modesty. **2.** A length of netting attached to a woman's hat or headdress for decoration, hanging before all or part of the face. **3.** The part of a nun's headdress that frames the face and falls over the shoulders. **4.** A piece of light fabric hung to separate or conceal what is behind it; a curtain. **5.** Anything that conceals, separates, or screens like a curtain: *a veil of secrecy.* **6.** *Biology.* A membranous covering, such as that partially or completely enveloping the developing fruiting body of certain mushrooms; a velum. **—beyond the veil.** In the afterlife; after death. **—draw a veil over.** To refrain from discussing or describing. **—take the veil.** To become a nun.
∼*v.* **veiled, veiling, veils.** *—tr.* **1.** To cover with a veil. **2.** To conceal, mask, or disguise with or as if with a veil: *veiling kindness under apparent severity.* *—intr.* To wear a veil. [Middle English *veile,* from Norman French, from Latin *vēla,* neuter plural of *vēlum,* covering, veil.]

veiled (vāld) *adj.* **1.** Covered with a veil. **2.** Partially concealed, masked, or disguised: *veiled threats; veiled promises.*

veil·ing (vā′lĭng) *n.* **1.** A veil. **2.** Gauzy material used for veils.

vein (vān) *n.* **1.** *Anatomy.* A vessel that transports blood toward the heart. **2.** Loosely, any blood vessel. **3.** *Botany.* Any of the vascular bundles that form the branching framework and support of a leaf. **4.** *Zoology.* Any of the chitinous, usually longitudinal ribs that stiffen and support the wing of an insect. **5.** *Geology.* A sheet of rock or mineral that infills a fissure or crevice in a pre-existing rock and is an economic source of ore; a lode. Compare **bed, mass. 6.** A long, wavy strip with a color different from its surrounding material, as in wood or marble, or as mold in cheese. **7.** Any fissure, crack, or cleft. **8.** A distinctive character, quality, or tendency; a strain or streak: *a vein of pessimism.* **9.** A transient or temporary attitude or mood; turn of mind: *a talk in a serious vein.*
∼*tr.v.* **veined, veining, veins. 1.** To supply or fill in streaked patterns with or as if with veins. **2.** To mark or decorate with veins. [Middle English *veine,* from Old French, from Latin *vēna*†, vein.] **—vein·al, vein·y** *adj.*

veined (vānd) *adj.* Exhibiting veins; having veinlike features or markings.

vein·let (vān′lĭt) *n.* A small or secondary vein, as of an insect's wing.

vein·stone (vān′stōn′) *n.* Mineral matter in a vein exclusive of the ore; gangue.

Ve·la (vē′lə) *n.* A constellation of the Southern Hemisphere in the Milky Way, near Antlia and Carina. [Latin *vēla,* sail, VEIL (from the saillike shape of the constellation).]

ve·la·men (vĭ-lā′mən) *n., pl.* **velamina** (və-lăm′ə-nə). **1.** *Anatomy.* Any membranous covering or integument; a velum. **2.** *Botany.* The spongy outer covering of the aerial roots of epiphytic orchids and certain other plants, capable of absorbing atmospheric moisture. [Latin *vēlamen,* covering, from *vēlāre,* to cover, from *vēlum,* covering. See **velum.**] **—vel·a·men·tous** (vĕl′ə-mĕn′təs) *adj.*

ve·lar (vē′lər) *adj.* **1. a.** Of or pertaining to a velum. **b.** Concerning or using the soft palate. **2.** *Phonetics.* Formed with the back of the tongue on or near the soft palate, as (g) in *good* and (k) in *cup.*
∼*n.* A velar sound. Also called "guttural." [New Latin *velaris,* from Latin *vēlum,* VELUM.]

ve·lar·ize (vē′lə-rīz′) *tr.v.* **-ized, -izing, izes.** *Phonetics.* To articulate (a sound) by retracting the back of the tongue toward the soft palate. **—ve·lar·iz·a·tion** *n.*

ve·late (vē′lĭt, -lāt′) *adj. Biology.* Having or covered by a velum or veil. [Latin *vēlātus,* past participle of *vēlāre,* to cover, from *vēlum,* veil, covering. See **velum.**]

Ve·láz·quez or **Ve·lás·quez** (və-lăs′kəs, -läs′-), **Diego Rodriguez de Silva y** (1599–1660). Spanish painter. He was appointed (1623) court painter to Philip IV and worked on many portraits of the royal family. Among his other works are *Pope Innocent X* and the *Rokeby Venus.*

Vel·cro (vĕl′krō′) *n.* A trademark for a material used as a fastener, usually consisting of a backing with a surface of minute nylon hooks and loops that fasten tightly with another piece of Velcro when pressed together. The two surfaces can be separated with a strong tug or abrupt pulling action.

veld, veldt (fĕlt, vĕlt) *n.* **1. a.** The open grassland area of South Africa; open country. **b.** Grazing or farming land. **2.** A particular tract of such land. [Afrikaans *veld,* from Middle Dutch *velt, veld,* field, open country.]

vel·i·ger (vē′lə-jər, vĕl′ə-) *n.* The free-swimming larva of certain marine gastropods. [New Latin : *vel(um),* sail + Latin *gerere,* to bear.]

vel·le·i·ty (vĕ-lē′ə-tē) *n., pl.* **-ties.** *Rare.* **1.** The lowest level of volition. **2.** A mere wish not accompanied by action or effort to obtain it. [Medieval Latin *velleitās,* from Latin *velle,* to wish.]

vel·lum (vĕl′əm) *n.* **1.** A fine parchment made from the skins of calf, lamb, or kid and used for the pages and binding of fine books. **2.** A work written or printed on vellum. **3.** A heavy off-white fine-quality paper resembling vellum. [Middle English *velim,* from Old French *velin,* from *veel,* calf, VEAL.] **—vel·lum** *adj.*

ve·lo·ce (vā-lō′chā) *adv. Music.* Rapidly. Used as a direction. [Italian, from Latin *vēlōx* (stem *vēlōc-*), fast. See **velocity.**]

vel·o·cim·e·ter (vē′lō-sĭm′ĭ-tər, vĕl′ō-) *n.* A device for measuring velocity or speed. [Latin *vēlōx* (stem *vēlōc-*) + -METER.]

ve·loc·i·pede (və-lŏs′ə-pēd′) *n.* **1.** An early bicycle propelled by pushing the feet along the ground while straddling the vehicle. **2.** Any of several early bicycles having pedals attached to the front wheel. [French *vélocipède,* "swift-footed" : Latin *vēlōx,* fast (see **velocity**) + -PED.]

ve·loc·i·ty (və-lŏs′ə-tē) *n., pl.* **-ties. 1.** Broadly, rapidity or speed. **2.** *Abbr.* **v** *Physics.* A vector quantity, the rate of change of position in a given direction. **3.** Distance traveled in a given amount of time. [French *vélocité,* from Latin *vēlōcitās* (stem *vēlōcitāt-*), from *vēlōx* (stem *vēlōc-*), fast.]

velocity modulation *n.* The modulation of an electron beam by alternately accelerating and decelerating them by means of a radio-frequency field in a cavity resonator.

ve·lo·drome (vĕl′ə-drōm′, vē′-) *n.* A sports arena specially built with a banked track for cycle and, often, motorcycle racing. [French *vélodrome,* from Latin *vēlōx,* swift + -DROME.]

ve·lours, ve·lour (və-lo͝or′) *n., pl.* **-lours** (-lo͝orz′). **1.** Any of various closely napped, velvetlike fabrics, used chiefly for clothing and upholstery. **2.** A felt resembling velvet, used in making hats. [French, from Old French *velo(u)s,* from Latin *villōsus,* hairy, from *villus,* shaggy hair, wool.]

ve·lou·té (və-lo͞o-tā′) *n.* A white sauce made with flour, butter, and a chicken or veal stock. [French, "velvety."]

vel·skoen (fĕl′sko͞on′, vĕl′-) *n. South African.* A shoe or ankle boot of rough suede. Also called "veldskoen." [Afrikaans, "hide shoe."]

ve·lum (vē′ləm) *n., pl.* **-la** (-lə) **1.** *Biology.* A covering or partition of thin membranous tissue, such as the veil of a mushroom. **2.** *Anatomy.* Any of various veillike structures, such as the soft palate. [New Latin, from Latin *vēlum,* veil, covering, sail.]

ve·lure (və-lo͝or′) *n.* **1.** *Obsolete.* Velvet or a velvetlike fabric. **2.** A soft pad used for smoothing silk hats. [Variant of French *velours,* VELOURS.]

ve·lu·ti·nous (və-lo͞ot′n-əs) *adj.* Covered with dense, soft, silky hairs; velvety. [New Latin *velutinus,* from Medieval Latin *velūtum,* velvet, from *villūtus,* velvety, shaggy. See **velvet.**]

vel·vet (vĕl′vĭt) *n.* **1. a.** A fabric made usually of silk or a synthetic fiber such as rayon or nylon, and having a smooth, dense pile and a plain back. **b.** Anything likened to the surface of this fabric. **2.** Smoothness; softness. **3.** The soft covering on the newly developing antlers of deer and related animals. **—on velvet.** A position of prosperity or advantage.
∼*adj.* **1.** Made of or covered with velvet. **2.** Resembling velvet. **3.** Soft and rich: *velvet tones.* [Middle English *veluet,* from Old French *veluotte,* from *velu,* shaggy, from Medieval Latin *villūtus,* from Latin *villus,* shaggy hair, wool.] **—vel·vet·y** *adj.*

velvet ant *n.* Any of various wasps of the family *Mutillidae,* having a dense, hairy, often brightly colored covering.

vel·vet·een (vĕl′və-tēn′) *n.* A velvetlike fabric made of cotton.

velvet plant *n.* A species of mullein *(see).*

Ven. venerable.

ve·na (vē′nə, vā′-) *n., pl.* **venae** (vē′nē′, vā′nī′). *Anatomy.* A vein. [Latin *vēna,* VEIN.]

ve·na ca·va (vē′nə kā′və, vā′nə kä′və) *pl.* **venae cavae** (vē′nē′ kā′vē′, vā′nī′ kä′vī′). Either of the two large veins in air-breathing vertebrates that enter and return blood to the right atrium of the heart. [Latin, "hollow vein."]

ve·nal (vē′nəl) *adj.* **1. a.** Open or susceptible to bribery. **b.** Capable of betraying one's honor, duty, or scruples for a price; corruptible. **2.** Marked by corrupt or morally reprehensible dealings: *a venal era.* **3.** Obtainable by purchase or bribery rather than by merit. [Latin *vēnālis,* for sale, from *vēnum,* sale.] **—ve·nal·ly** *adv.*

ve·nal·i·ty (vē-năl′ə-tē, vĭ-) *n., pl.* **-ties. 1.** The quality of being open to bribery or corruption. **2.** The use of a position of trust for dishonest gain.

ve·nat·ic (vē-năt′ĭk) *adj.* Also **ve·nat·i·cal** (-ĭ-kəl). **1.** Pertaining to or used in hunting. **2.** Devoted to or engaged in hunting for sport or livelihood. [Latin *vēnāticus,* from *vēnārī,* to hunt.]

ve·na·tion (vē-nā′shən, vā-) *n.* The distribution or arrangement of veins in a leaf or insect's wing. [From VENA.] **—ve·na·tion·al** *adj.*

vend (vĕnd) *v.* **vended, vending, vends.** —*tr.* **1.** *Law.* To sell. **2.** To sell small goods, especially in the street; peddle. **3.** To offer (an idea, for example) for public consideration. —*intr.* **1.** To sell goods; be a vendor. **2.** To have a market. [French *vendre*, from Latin *vēndere* : *vēnum*, sale + *dare*, to give.]

Ven·da¹ (vĕn′də) *n., pl.* **-das** or collectively **Venda. 1.** A member of a black South African people living chiefly in Venda and northern Transvaal. **2.** The Bantu language of this people. **—Ven·da** *adj.*

Venda². One of the segregated Bantu homelands in South Africa, lying in eastern Transvaal. It officially became a republic in 1979, but only South Africa recognizes its independence. Its capital is Thohoyandou.

ven·dace (vĕn′dās′) *n., pl.* **-daces** or collectively **vendace.** A small whitefish, *Coregonus albula*, found in certain lakes in northern Europe. [New Latin *vandesius*, from Old French *vendese, vendoise*, from Gaulish *vindesia* (unattested); akin to Gaulish *vindos* (unattested); white.]

vend·ee (vĕn-dē′) *n.* A buyer.

Ven·dée (vän-dā′). Department in western France, on the Bay of Biscay. It is largely an agricultural region, with some forest land and fishing ports. The administrative center is La Roche-sur-Yon. The Vendée Wars were a series of peasant revolts (1793–96).

vend·er, vend·or (vĕn′dər; *for sense 2 also* vĕn′dôr′) *n.* **1.** A person who sells or vends; a peddler or salesman. **2.** *Law.* The party to a contract who sells something, especially a piece of property. **3.** A vending machine.

ven·det·ta (vĕn-dĕt′ə) *n.* **1.** A hereditary blood feud between two families, perpetuated by retaliatory acts of revenge. **2.** A hostile and malicious campaign. **3.** Any act or attitude motivated by vengeance. [Italian, revenge, from Latin *vindicta*, from the feminine past participle of *vindicāre*, to revenge, VINDICATE.]

vend·i·ble (vĕn′də-bəl) *adj.* Capable of being sold; suitable for sale. —*n.* Something that can be sold.

vending machine *n.* A machine that dispenses goods such as cigarettes or confectionery when money is inserted. Also called "vendor."

ven·due (vĕn-dōō′, -dyōō′) *n.* A public sale; an auction. [Dutch *vendu*, from Old French *vendue*, from *vendre*, VEND.]

ve·neer (və-nîr′) *n.* **1.** A thin finishing or surface layer, as of fine wood or laminated plastic, bonded to an inferior substratum, such as an inexpensive wood. **2.** Any of the thin layers glued together in making plywood. **3.** An outward show that enhances but misrepresents what lies beneath; a superficially impressive appearance: *a veneer of politeness.* —*tr.v.* **veneered, -neering, -neers. 1.** To overlay (a surface) with a decorative or fine material. **2.** To glue together (layers of wood) in making plywood. **3.** To conceal (something common or crude) with an attractive but superficial appearance; gloss over. [Earlier *fineer*, from German *Furnier*, from *furnieren*, to furnish, veneer, from French *fournir*, to FURNISH.] **—ve·neer·er** *n.*

ve·neer·ing (və-nîr′ĭng) *n.* **1.** Material used as a veneer. **2.** A surface of veneer.

venepuncture. Variant of **venipuncture.**

ven·er·a·ble (vĕn′ər-ə-bəl) *adj.* **1.** Worthy of reverence or respect by virtue of dignity, character, position, or age. **2.** Commanding respect or reverence by association: *venerable relics.* **3.** *Abbr.* **V., Ven.** Honored above others. Used as: **a.** A title of respect for an Anglican archdeacon. **b.** A title given to a Roman Catholic who has attained the first degree of sanctity. —See Synonyms at **old.** [Middle English, from Old French, from Latin *venerābilis*, from *venerārī*, VENERATE.] **—ven·er·a·ble·ness, ven·er·a·bil·i·ty** *n.* **—ven·er·a·bly** *adv.*

ven·er·ate (vĕn′ə-rāt′) *tr.v.* **-ated, -ating, -ates.** To regard with respect, reverence, or heartfelt deference. —See Synonyms at **revere.** [Latin *venerārī*, from *venus* (stem *vener-*), love.] **—ven·er·a·tor** *n.*

ven·er·a·tion (vĕn′ə-rā′shən) *n.* **1.** The act of venerating. **2.** Profound respect or reverence. **3.** The condition or status of one who is venerated. —See Synonyms at **honor.**

ve·ne·re·al (və-nîr′ē-əl) *adj.* **1.** Of or pertaining to sexual intercourse. **2. a.** Transmitted by sexual intercourse. **b.** Of or pertaining to venereal disease. **3.** Of or pertaining to the genitals. [Middle English *venerealle*, from Latin *venereus*, from *venus* (stem *vener-*), love, lust.]

venereal disease *n. Abbr.* **V.D., VD** Any of several contagious diseases, such as syphilis and gonorrhea, contracted through sexual intercourse.

ve·ne·re·ol·o·gy (və-nîr′ē-ŏl′ə-jē) *n.* The medical study of venereal disease. [VENERE(AL) + -LOGY.] **—ve·ne·re·ol·o·gist** *n.*

ven·er·y¹ (vĕn′ər-ē) *n. Archaic.* Indulgence in or the pursuit of sexual activity. [Middle English *venerie*, from Medieval Latin *veneria*, from Latin *venus* (stem *vener-*), love.]

venery² *n. Archaic.* The act, art, or sport of hunting; the chase. [Middle English *venerie*, from Old French, from *vener*, to hunt, from Latin *vēnārī*.]

ven·e·sec·tion (vĕn′ə-sĕk′shən) *n. Surgery.* **Phlebotomy** *(see).* [Medieval Latin *vēnae sectiō*, cutting of a vein : Latin *vēnae*, genitive of *vēna*, vein, VENA + *sectiō*, SECTION.]

Ve·ne·tia (və-nē′shə). Region of northeastern Italy, on the Adriatic Sea. Venice is the capital.

Ve·ne·tian (və-nē′shən) *adj.* Of or pertaining to Venice, its culture, or its inhabitants. —*n.* **1.** A native or inhabitant of Venice. **2.** *Usually* **venetian.** A venetian blind. [Middle English *Venecien*, from Old French, from Medieval Latin *Venetiānus*, from Latin *Venetia*, VENICE.]

venetian blind *n. Often* **venetian blinds.** A window screen consisting of a number of thin horizontal slats that may be raised and lowered by means of one cord and all set at a desired angle by means of another cord, thus regulating the amount of light admitted. Also called "Venetian."

venetian blue *n.* Strong blue to greenish blue.

Venetian glass *n.* Fine, delicate glassware originally made near Venice.

venetian red *n.* **1.** Deep to strong reddish brown. **2.** A pigment of this color made from ferric oxide.

Venetian school *n.* A school of painting originating in Venice in the 15th century and flourishing in the 16th century, notable for its mastery of color and perspective.

Venezia. See Venice.

Ven·e·zue·la (vĕn′ə-zwā′lə). Country on the northern coast of South America. It is a major oil producer and one of Latin America's richest countries. Oil and oil products account for 90 percent of its exports, iron ore another 5 percent. The economy is being restructured and new industries developed. Ruled by Spain after 1500, Venezuela was liberated by Simón Bolívar (1821), forming part of Gran Colombia until 1830. A series of dictators ended with the overthrow of Pérez Jimenéz (1958). Venezuela claims the Essequibo territory, some 73 percent of neighboring Guyana. Area, 912,050 square kilometers (352,145 square miles). Population, 14,000,000. Capital, Caracas. **—Ven·e·zue·lan** *n. & adj.*

venge (vĕnj) *tr.v.* **venged, venging, venges.** *Archaic.* To avenge. [Middle English *vengen*, from Old French *venger*. See **vengeance.**]

venge·ance (vĕn′jəns) *n.* The act or motive of punishing another in payment for a wrong or injury committed; retribution: *He had been betrayed and now wanted vengeance.* **—with a vengeance. 1.** With great violence or fury. **2.** To a greater extent; excessively. Used as an intensive: *The weather has turned cold with a vengeance.* [Middle English, from Old French, from *venger*, to revenge, from Latin *vindicāre*, to revenge, VINDICATE.]

venge·ful (vĕnj′fəl) *adj.* **1.** Desiring vengeance; vindictive. **2.** Indicating or proceeding from a desire for revenge: *a vengeful frown.* **3.** Inflicting or serving to inflict vengeance: *a vengeful blow.* —See Synonyms at **vindictive.**

ve·ni·al (vē′nē-əl, vēn′yəl) *adj.* Easily excused or forgiven; pardonable: *a venial offense.* [Middle English, from Old French, from Late Latin *veniālis*, from *venia*, forgiveness.] **—ve·ni·al·i·ty** (vē′nē-ăl′ə-tē, vēn·yăl′-), **ve·ni·al·ness** *n.* **—ve·ni·al·ly** *adv.*

venial sin *n. Theology.* A sin which, though evil, does not totally estrange the soul from God's grace. Compare **mortal sin.**

Ven·ice (vĕn′ĭs). *Italian.* **Ve·ne·zia** (vā-nā′tsyä). Port in northeastern Italy. The capital of Venetia and of Venezia province, it lies in a lagoon on 118 alluvial islands, mostly separated by narrow canals crossed by some 400 bridges. A road and rail causeway links it to the mainland. Founded in the 5th century A.D., Venice built a wealthy maritime empire around the northeastern Mediterranean by the 13th century. As the Venetian Republic it gained extensive lands in northern Italy (15th century); however, after 1600 its eastern territories were lost to the Turks, and the republic fell to Austria (1797) and was ceded to Italy (1866). Venice is world famous for its art and architecture, including the Byzantine cathedral of St. Mark (begun in 830). Tourism, textiles, and glass are its main industries. The city is sinking, but since severe flooding in 1966 its art treasures are being preserved following international appeals.

ven·i·punc·ture, ve·ne·punc·ture (vĕn′ə-pŭngk′chər) *n.* Puncture of a vein, as for drawing blood, intravenous feeding, or administration of medicine. [VENA + PUNCTURE.]

ve·ni·re (vĭ-nī′rē) *n. Law.* **1.** A writ issued by a judge to a sheriff, ordering him to summon prospective jurors. Also called "venire facias." **2.** The panel of prospective jurors from which a jury is selected. [Medieval Latin *venīre (facias)*, "(you are to cause) to come" (words used in the writ), from Latin *venīre*, to come.]

VENEZUELA

ve·ni·re·man (və-nī'rē-mən) *n., pl.* **-men** (-mĭn). A person summoned to jury duty under a venire.

ven·i·son (vĕn'ĭ-sən, -zən) *n.* **1.** The flesh of a deer, used for food. **2.** *Archaic.* The flesh of any game animal thus used. [Middle English *veneso(u)n,* from Old French, from Latin *vēnātiō* (stem *vēnātiōn-*), hunting, game, from *vēnārī,* to hunt.]

Venn diagram (vĕn) *n.* A diagram in which mathematical sets or the terms of a logical argument or syllogism are represented by circles, the position and overlap of which indicate the way in which the different sets or terms are related. [After John *Venn* (1834–1923), British logician.]

ven·o·gram (vē'nə-grăm') *n.* An x-ray picture of a vein or veins. [Latin *vēna,* VEIN + -GRAM.]

ve·no·graph·y (vĭ-nŏg'rə-fē) *n.* The study using x-rays of a vein or veins following the injection of a radio-opaque substance. [Latin *vēna,* VEIN + -GRAPHY.]

ven·om (vĕn'əm) *n.* **1.** A poisonous secretion of some animals, such as certain snakes, spiders, scorpions, or insects, usually transmitted by a bite or sting. **2.** *Rare.* Any poison. **3.** Malice; evil; spite. [Middle English *venim,* from Old French, from Vulgar Latin *venīmen* (unattested), variant of Latin *venēnum,* poison.]

ven·om·ous (vĕn'ə-məs) *adj.* **1.** Secreting and transmitting venom: *a venomous snake.* **2.** Full of or containing venom. **3.** Malicious; malignant; spiteful: *a venomous utterance.* **—ven·om·ous·ly** *adv.* **—ven·om·ous·ness** *n.*

ve·nose (vē'nōs') *adj.* **1.** Having noticeable veins or veinlike markings. **2.** Venous. [Latin *vēnōsus,* VENOUS.]

ve·nos·i·ty (vĭ-nŏs'ə-tē) *n.* **1.** The condition or quality of being venous or venose. **2.** An accumulation of blood in the venous system.

ve·nous (vē'nəs) *adj.* **1.** Of or pertaining to a vein or veins. **2.** Designating or pertaining to blood carried in the veins. [Latin *vēnōsus,* from *vēna,* vein.] **—ve·nous·ly** *adv.* **—ve·nous·ness** *n.*

vent¹ (vĕnt) *n.* **1.** An opening permitting the passage or escape of liquids, gases, fumes, steam, or the like: *a vent above the kitchen stove.* **2.** A means of escaping or leaving a confined space; an exit. **3.** The small hole at the breech of an ancient gun through which the charge is ignited. **4.** *Geology.* A volcano shaft or an aperture in the earth's crust through which lava and gases can escape. **5.** *Zoology.* The cloacal or anal excretory opening in animals such as birds, reptiles, amphibians, and fish. **—give vent to.** To give utterance to; express or release: *gave vent to their indignation.*

~*v.* **vented, venting, vents.** *—tr.* **1.** To give utterance to; express: *venting his sorrows.* **2.** To relieve through the expression of emotion. **3.** To discharge through a vent. **4.** To provide with a vent. *—intr.* To come to the surface to breathe. Used of an otter or beaver. [Middle English *venten,* to provide with an outlet, Old French *esventer,* to let out air, from Vulgar Latin *exventāre* (unattested) : Latin *ex-,* out + *ventus,* wind.] **—vent·less** *adj.*

Synonyms: *vent, express, utter, voice, air, broach.* These verbs mean to give an outlet to thought or emotion. *Vent* is applied to speech, writing, or other action by which a person unburdens himself of a strong, hitherto pent-up emotion such as anger or grief. *Express,* a more comprehensive word, can refer to communication by any means, including the nonverbal. *Utter* involves vocal expression, either words or inarticulate sounds; with reference to speech it often implies forthright or even bold public statement. *Voice* generally refers to the public expression, in speech or writing, of ideas, opinions, or beliefs. *Air* especially suggests public discussion of such ideas or opinions. *Broach* refers to introducing a subject usually after careful thought, as a topic of discussion or written discourse.

vent² *n.* A narrow opening, often forming a flap, at the side or back of a garment such as a jacket. [Middle English *vent, fent,* from Old French *fente,* slip, from Vulgar Latin *findita* (unattested), from past participle of Latin *findere,* to cleave.]

vent·age (vĕn'tĭj) *n.* **1.** A small opening; a vent. **2.** Any of the small finger holes in the tube of a wind instrument such as a recorder.

ven·tail (vĕn'tāl') *n.* The lower front part of a medieval helmet, fitting over the neck. [Middle English, from Old French *vantail,* leaf of a window, from *vent,* wind, air, from Latin *ventus.*]

vent·er¹ (vĕn'tər) *n.* One that vents.

ven·ter² (vĕn'tər) *n.* **1. a.** *Biology.* The abdomen or belly. **b.** The wide swelling portion of a muscle. **2.** *Botany.* The swollen base of an archegonium containing the developing egg cell. **3.** *Law.* The womb as the source of offspring. [Norman French, from Latin, belly, womb.]

ven·ti·late (vĕnt'l-āt') *tr.v.* **-lated, -lating, -lates.** **1.** To admit fresh air into in order to replace stale air. **2.** To circulate within (a room or mine, for example) in order to freshen. Used of air. **3.** To provide with a vent or a similar means of airing. **4.** To expose (a substance) to the circulation of fresh air, as for the purpose of retarding spoilage. **5.** To expose to public discussion or examination: *The workers ventilated their grievances.* **6.** To aerate or oxygenate (blood). [Middle English *ventilaten,* to blow away, from Latin *ventilāre,* to fan, from *ventus,* wind.] **—ven·ti·la·tion** *n.*

ven·ti·la·tor (vĕnt'l-ā'tər) *n.* **1.** One that ventilates; especially, a device, such as an exhaust fan, that expels stale air and circulates fresh air. **2.** *Medicine.* A device used to ensure the passage of air into and out of the lungs in patients who cannot breathe normally. **—ven·ti·la·to·ry** (vĕnt'l-ə-tôr'ē, -tōr'ē) *adj.*

ven·tral (vĕn'trəl) *adj.* **1.** *Anatomy.* **a.** Pertaining to or situated on or close to the belly; abdominal. **b.** Pertaining to the anterior aspect or front of the human body or the lower surface of the body of an animal. **2.** *Botany.* Of or on the upper or inner surface of an organ such as a leaf facing the main axis; adaxial. [French, from Latin *ventrālis,* from *venter,* VENTER.] **—ven·tral·ly** *adv.*

ventral fin *n. Zoology.* A **pelvic fin** *(see).*

ven·tri·cle (vĕn'trĭ-kəl) *n.* A small anatomical cavity or chamber, as of the brain or heart, especially: **1.** The chamber on the left side of the heart that receives arterial blood from the left atrium and contracts to drive it into the aorta. **2.** The chamber on the right side of the heart that receives venous blood from the vena cava and drives it via the right atrium into the pulmonary artery. **3.** Any of the four fluid-filled cavities of the brain. Also called "ventriculus." [Middle English, from Old French, from Latin *ventriculus,* diminutive of *venter,* VENTER.] **—ven·tric·u·lar** (vĕn-trĭk'yə-lər) *adj.*

ven·tri·cose (vĕn'trĭ-kōs') *adj.* Also **ven·tri·cous** (-kəs). *Biology.* Inflated or swollen, especially on one side. [New Latin *ventricosus,* from Latin *venter,* VENTER (abdomen).] **—ven·tri·cos·i·ty** *n.*

ven·tric·u·lus (vĕn-trĭk'yə-ləs) *n., pl.* **-li** (-lī'). **1.** A hollow digestive organ; especially, the stomach of an insect or the gizzard of a bird. **2.** A ventricle. [Latin, VENTRICLE.]

ven·tril·o·quism (vĕn-trĭl'ə-kwĭz'əm) *n.* Also **ven·tril·o·quy** (-kwē). A method of producing vocal sounds so that they seem to originate in a source other than the speaker, as from a mechanical dummy. [Late Latin *ventriloquus,* "speaking from the belly" : Latin *venter,* VENTER + *loquī,* to speak.] **—ven·tri·lo·qui·al** (vĕn'trə-lō'kwē-əl) *adj.* **—ven·tri·lo·qui·al·ly** *adv.* **—ven·tril·o·quist** (vĕn-trĭl'ə-kwĭst) *n.* **—ven·tril·o·quis·tic** *adj.*

ven·tril·o·quize (vĕn-trĭl'ə-kwīz') *intr.v.* **-quized, -quizing, -quizes.** To engage in ventriloquism.

Ven·tris (vĕn'trĭs), **Michael George Francis** (1922–56). British architect and scholar. He deciphered Linear B, a hieroglyphic script of late Minoan Crete.

ven·ture (vĕn'chər) *n.* **1.** An undertaking that is dangerous, daring, or of doubtful outcome. **2.** Something at hazard in such an undertaking; a stake. **—at a venture.** By mere chance or fortune; at hazard; at random.

~*v.* **ventured, -turing, -tures.** *—tr.* **1.** To expose to danger or risk; stake: *ventured her entire fortune on the enterprise.* **2.** To brave the dangers of: *ventured the high seas in a light boat.* **3.** To express at the risk of denial, criticism, or censure; dare: *ventured a mild protest.* *—intr.* **1.** To take a risk or dare; make a venture. **2.** To go somewhere by or as if by taking a risk: *ventured into the forest.* [Middle English *venturen, venteren,* short for *aventuren,* from *aventure,* ADVENTURE.] **—ven·tur·er** *n.*

ven·ture·some (vĕn'chər-səm) *adj.* **1.** Disposed to venture or to take risks; daring; bold. **2.** Involving risk or danger; hazardous. **—ven·ture·some·ly** *adv.* **—ven·ture·some·ness** *n.*

ven·tu·ri (vĕn-tŏŏr'ē) *n.* **1.** A short tube with a constricted throat that is used to determine fluid pressures and velocities by measurement of differential pressures generated at the throat as a fluid traverses the tube. Also called "venturi tube." **2.** A constricted throat in the air passage of a carburetor, causing a reduction in pressure by means of which fuel vapor is drawn out of the carburetor bowl. [After G.B. *Venturi* (1746–1822), Italian physicist, whose study inspired its invention.]

ven·tur·ous (vĕn'chər-əs) *adj.* **1.** Courageous and daring; adventurous; bold. **2.** Hazardous, dangerous, or risky. **—ven·tur·ous·ly** *adv.* **—ven·tur·ous·ness** *n.*

ven·ue (vĕn'yōō) *n.* **1.** A location designated for an event, such as a meeting, concert, or sports match. **2.** *Law.* **a.** The locality where a crime is committed or a cause of action occurs. **b.** Formerly, the locality or political division from which a jury must be called and in which a trial must be held. **c.** Formerly, the clause within a declaration naming the locality in which the trial is occurring or will occur. **3.** Formerly, the clause in an affidavit naming the locality where it was made and sworn to. [Middle English, arrival, assault, from Old French, from the feminine past participle of *venir,* to come, from Latin *venīre.*]

ven·ule (vĕn'yōōl) *n.* A minute vein, such as one joining with a capillary or branching from a vein in an insect's wing. [Latin *vēnula,* diminutive of *vēna,* VEIN.] **—ven·u·lar** (vĕn'yə-lər) *adj.*

Ve·nus¹ (vē'nəs). *Roman Mythology.* The goddess of love and beauty, identified with the Greek Aphrodite. [Middle English *Venus,* Old English *Venus,* from Latin, personification of *venus,* love.]

Venus² *n.* The second planet from the sun, having an average radius of 6,100 kilometers (3,800 miles), a mass 0.815 times that of Earth, and a sidereal period of revolution about the sun of 224.7 days at a mean distance of approximately 108 million kilometers (67.2 million miles). [After the goddess VENUS.] See feature, next page.

Ve·nu·sian (vĭ-nōō'zhən, -nyōō'zhən) *adj.* Pertaining to or characteristic of the planet Venus.

~*n.* A hypothetical inhabitant of the planet Venus.

Venus's flower basket *n.* A sponge of the genus *Euplectella,* of deep marine waters, having a delicate, white, latticelike, cylindrical skeleton.

Ve·nus's-fly·trap (vē'nəs-flī'trăp', vē'nə-sĭz-) *n.* Also **Venus flytrap.** An insectivorous plant, *Dionaea muscipula,* of boggy areas of the southeastern United States, having hinged leaf blades that close and entrap insects.

Venus's girdle *n.* A ribbon-shaped marine animal, *Cestum veneris,* having a jellylike iridescent body up to 1.5 meters (5 feet) in length.

Ve·nus's-hair (vē'nə-sĭz-hâr') *n.* A maidenhair fern, *Adiantum capillus-veneris,* of subtropical and temperate areas.

Ve·nus's-look·ing-glass (vē'nə-sĭz-lŏŏk'ĭng-glăs', -gläs') *n.* Any of

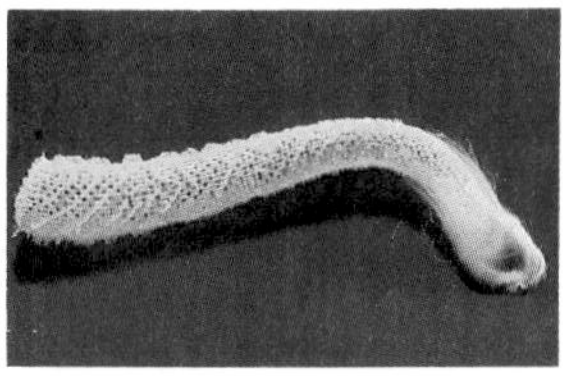

Venus's flower basket *The glassy, latticed skeleton of the Venus's flower basket sponge is traditionally given to newlyweds in Japan as a symbol of fidelity. The sponge often becomes the permanent home of pairs of small crustaceans that enter through the holes in its walls to feed in safety and grow too large to escape.*

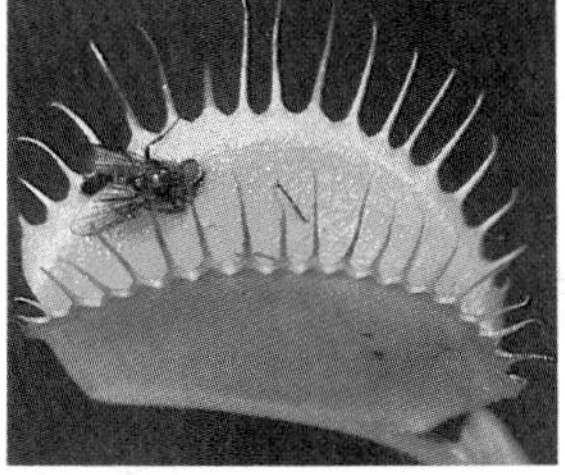

Venus's-flytrap *An insect-eating plant of the southeastern United States. Any insect landing on the trap touches trigger hairs that cause the trap—a modified leaf—to close tight. The insect is then dissolved by a digestive secretion.*

various annual weedy plants of the genus *Legousia* (or *Specularia*); especially *L. hybrida,* which has purple flowers.

ver. **1.** verse. **2.** version.

ve·ra·cious (və-rā′shəs) *adj.* **1.** Honest; truthful. **2.** Accurate; precise. [Latin *vērāx* (stem *vērāc-*), truth.] **—ve·ra·cious·ly** *adv.* **—ve·ra·cious·ness** *n.*

ve·rac·i·ty (və-răs′ə-tē) *n., pl.* **-ties.** **1.** Habitual adherence to the truth. **2.** Conformity to truth or fact; accuracy; precision. **3.** Something that is true. —See Synonyms at **honesty, truth.** [Medieval Latin *vērācitās,* from Latin *vērāx,* truth. See **veracious.**]

Ve·ra·cruz (vĕr′ə-krōōz′). City and port in Veracruz state, Mexico, lying on the Gulf of Mexico. It is the industrial center of one of Mexico's richest oil-producing regions.

ve·ran·dah, ve·ran·da (və-răn′də) *n.* A porch or balcony, usually

Venus

roofed and often partly enclosed, extending along the outside of a building. [Hindi, from Portuguese, from *varare* (unattested), to surround with poles, from *vara,* pole, from Latin *vāra,* forked pole, from *vārus,* bent inward.] **—ver·ran·dahed** *adj.*

ve·rat·ri·dine (və-răt′rə-dēn′, -dĭn) *n.* A yellowish-white, amorphous powdered alkaloid, C₃₆H₅₁NO₁₁, obtained from sabadilla seeds. [VERATR(INE) + -ID + -INE.]

ver·a·trine (vĕr′ə-trēn′, -trĭn) *n.* A poisonous mixture of colorless crystalline alkaloids extracted from sabadilla seeds and formerly used medicinally as a counterirritant. [French *vératrine,* from New Latin *Veratrum,* genus name of a hellebore, from Latin *vērātrum,* hellebore, perhaps from *veru,* spit.]

verb (vûrb) *n. Abbr.* **v., vb.** **1.** In most languages, that part of speech that expresses existence, action, or occurrence. **2.** Any of the words exemplifying this part of speech; for example, *be, run,* or *conceive.* **3.** Any phrase or other construction used as a verb.
~*adj. Grammar.* Verbal: *a verb phrase.* [Middle English *verbe,* from Old French, from Latin *verbum,* word.]

ver·bal (vûr′bəl) *adj. Abbr.* **vb.** **1.** Of, pertaining to, or associated with words: *a verbal symbol.* **2.** Concerned with words rather than with the facts or ideas they represent: *a merely verbal ceasefire.* **3.** Expressed or transmitted in speech; unwritten: *a verbal contract.* **4.** Literal; word for word: *a verbal translation.* **5.** *Grammar.* **a.** Pertaining to, having the nature or function of, or derived from a verb. **b.** Used to form verbs: *a verbal suffix.*
~*n. Grammar.* **1.** A verbal noun, adjective, or other word based on a verb and preserving some of the verb's characteristics. **2.** *Slang.* A spoken, as opposed to written, confession made by a suspect during police questioning and introduced as evidence at his trial. [Old French, from Late Latin *verbālis,* from Latin *verbum,* word, VERB.] **—ver·bal·ly** *adv.*

Usage: *Verbal* is used as well as *oral* to express the notion of "by word of mouth," but it can also refer to what is written (*He sent me a verbal account of what was said at the meeting*). *Oral* can refer only to what is spoken, and is thus often preferred when there is a possibility of ambiguity (in such phrases as *verbal agreement*).

ver·bal·ism (vûr′bə-lĭz′əm) *n.* **1.** An expression in words; a word or phrase. **2.** A meaningless or clichéd phrase or sentence, especially one resulting from an emphasis on words over content or idea. **3.** A disposition toward or the habitual use of such merely declamatory, ornate, or empty constructions.

ver·bal·ist (vûr′bə-lĭst) *n.* **1.** One skilled at using words. **2.** One who favors words over ideas or facts. **—ver·bal·is·tic** *adj.*

ver·bal·ize (vûr′bə-līz′) *v.* **-ized, -izing, -izes.** *—tr.* **1.** To express in words: *He couldn't verbalize what he was feeling.* **2.** To convert (a noun, for example) to verbal use. *—intr.* **1.** To express oneself in words. **2.** To be verbose. **—ver·bal·i·za·tion** *n.* **—ver·bal·i·zer** *n.*

verbal noun *n.* A noun that is derived from a verb and that in some uses preserves the verb's characteristics and sense.

ver·ba·tim (vûr-bā′tĭm) *adj.* Using exactly the same words; word for word. [Middle English, from Medieval Latin, from Latin *verbum,* word, VERB.] **—ver·ba·tim** *adv.*

ver·be·na (vər-bē′nə) *n.* **1.** Any of various chiefly New World plants of the genus *Verbena;* especially, any of several species cultivated for their showy, variously colored flowers. See **vervain.** **2.** Any of several similar or related plants, such as the **lemon verbena** (see). [New Latin *Verbena,* from Latin *verbēna,* usually in plural *verbēnae,* sacred boughs of olive or myrtle. See **vervain.**]

ver·bi·age (vûr′bē-ĭj) *n.* Words in excess of those needed for clarity or precision; wordiness. **2.** The favoring or use of such an excess of words. **3.** The manner in which one expresses oneself in words; diction. [French, from Latin *verbum,* word, VERB.]

verb·i·fy (vûr′bə-fī′) *v.* **-fied, -fying, -fies.** *—tr.* To use (a noun, for example) as a verb; form into a verb. *—intr.* To be verbose.

ver·bose (vər-bōs′) *adj.* Using or containing an excessive number of words; wordy; prolix. —See Synonyms at **talkative.** [Latin *verbōsus,* from *verbum,* word, VERB.] **—ver·bose·ly** *adv.* **—ver·bose·ness, ver·bos·i·ty** (vər-bŏs′ə-tē) *n.*

ver·bo·ten (fər-bōt′n, vər-) *adj. Informal.* Rigorously forbidden. [German, from Old High German *farboten,* past participle of *farbiotan,* to forbid.]

verb. sap. (vûrb′ săp′) *Latin.* Used to conclude a remark or clinch an argument by suggesting that no further explanation is needed. [Abbreviation of Latin phrase *verbum sapienti (sat est),* a word to the wise (suffices).]

ver·dant (vûr′dənt) *adj.* **1.** Green with vegetation; covered with a green growth: *verdant, fertile land.* **2.** Green in color. **3.** Inexperienced or unsophisticated. [Perhaps from Old French *verdeant,* present participle of *verdoier, verdier,* to become green, from *verd, vert,* green, from Latin *viridis,* from *virēre,* to be green.] **—ver·dan·cy** *n.* **—ver·dant·ly** *adv.*

verd antique, verde antique (vûrd) *n.* **1.** A dull-green mottled or veined serpentine marble used in interior decoration. **2.** Verdigris on ancient bronze, copper, and brass. **3.** A green porphyry. [French, "ancient green."]

Verde, Cape (vûrd). Peninsula of Senegal, jutting into the Atlantic ocean. Its tip, Cape Almadies, is the westernmost extremity of the African continent.

ver·der·er (vûr′dər-ər) *n.* Formerly, the official in charge of the royal forests of England. [Norman French, from Old French *verdier,* from *verde, verte,* green, "forest." See **verdant.**]

Ver·di (vâr′dē), **Giuseppe** (1813-1901). Italian composer. Among his works are the operas *Rigoletto* (1851), *Il Trovatore* (1853), *La*

OUR NEAREST NEIGHBOR IN THE SKY

The atmosphere of the planet Venus is hot and poisonous

Venus is almost a twin of the earth in size and mass, and, as it is closer to us than any other planet, it shines brightly in the night sky. Spacecraft from the United States and the U.S.S.R. have shown that the atmosphere is very dense, giving a pressure 90 times the pressure of the air on Earth. It is made up mainly of carbon dioxide, and the clouds that surround the planet contain large amounts of sulfuric acid. The surface of Venus has volcanoes that are probably active, a huge rolling plain, and two high areas of land. The temperature exceeds 475°C (887°F).

No life can exist on Venus now, but in the early days of the Solar System, when the Sun was less luminous, Venus may have had oceans and life may have appeared. As the Sun grew brighter, the oceans boiled and evaporated, and Venus became a furnacelike world.

THE CLOUDS OF VENUS *Unmanned spacecraft have sent back photographs of Venus from space and from the surface. Photographs from space (above) show that the planet is covered by permanent cloud. Pictures from the surface show a gloomy, rock-strewn landscape. Winds are sluggish (a few miles per hour), but in the very dense atmosphere they have tremendous force.*

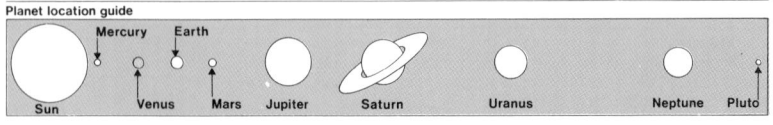

Planet location guide

Traviata (1853), and *Aida* (1871). His work introduced the new status of music drama to Italian opera.

ver·dict (vûr′dĭkt) *n.* **1.** The decision reached by a jury at the conclusion of a legal proceeding: *a verdict of not guilty.* **2.** An expressed conclusion; a judgment: *the verdict of history.* [Middle English *verdit,* from Norman French, variant of Old French *veirdit, voirdit,* "true saying" : *veir,* true, from Latin *vērus* + *dit,* saying, from Latin *dictum,* from the neuter past participle of *dīcere,* to speak, say.]

ver·di·gris (vûr′də-grēs, -grĭs) *n.* **1.** A blue or green basic copper acetate, used as a paint pigment, fungicide, and insecticide. **2.** A green patina or crust of copper carbonate formed on copper, brass, and bronze exposed to air or sea water for long periods of time. In this sense, also called "aerugo," "verd antique." Compare **patina.** [Middle English *vertegres,* from Old French *vertegrez, vert-de-Grice,* "green of Greece."]

ver·din (vûr′dĭn) *n.* A small grayish bird, *Auriparus flaviceps,* of the southwestern United States and adjacent Mexico, having a yellowish head and throat. [French *verdin*†, yellowhammer.]

ver·di·ter (vûr′də-tər) *n.* Either of two basic carbonates of copper, azirite and malachite, used as a blue or green pigment. [Old French *verd de terre,* "green of earth."]

Ver·dun (vər-dŭn′). Town in northeastern France, on the Meuse River. In 1916 the Battle of Verdun, lasting from February to December, was one of the longest and fiercest battles of World War I.

ver·dure (vûr′jər) *n.* **1.** The fresh, vibrant greenness of flourishing vegetation. **2.** Such vegetation itself: *lush verdure.* **3.** Any fresh or flourishing condition: *the verdure of childhood.* [Middle English, from Old French, from *verd,* green. See **verdant.**] **—ver·dur·ous** *adj.* **—ver·dur·ous·ness** *n.*

verge[1] (vûrj) *n.* **1.** The extreme edge, rim, or margin of something; the brink: *the verge of a stream.* **2. a.** An enclosing boundary. **b.** The space enclosed by such a boundary. **3.** *British.* The stretch of grass bordering a road. **4.** The point beyond which an action, state, or condition is likely to begin or occur: *the verge of a nervous breakdown.* **5.** *Architecture.* **a.** The edge of the tiling that projects over a roof gable. **b.** The body of a classical column; a pillar. **6.** A rod, wand, or staff carried as an emblem of authority or office. **7.** In feudal times, the rod held by a tenant swearing fealty to his lord. **8.** Formerly, the area of jurisdiction of the Lord High Steward, especially the surroundings of the royal court. **9.** The spindle of a balance wheel in an early clock or watch; especially, such a spindle in a clock with vertical escapement. **10.** The male reproductive organ of an invertebrate. —See Synonyms at **border.**
~*intr.v.* **verged, verging, verges. 1.** To approach the verge or limit; come near. Usually used with *on* or *upon: Her idea verged on genius.* **2.** To constitute a verge or limit; be a border. Used with *on* or *upon: a housing development verging on the slum area.* [Middle English, margin, from Old French, from Latin *virga*†, rod, strip.]

verge[2] *intr.v.* **verged, verging, verges.** To slope or incline. Used with *to* or *toward.* [Latin *vergere,* to tend toward.]

verg·er (vûr′jər) *n.* **1.** A person who takes care of the interior of a church and acts as an attendant during ceremonies. **2.** A person who carries the verge before a scholastic, legal, or religious dignitary in a procession.

Vergil. See **Virgil.**

ver·glas (vâr′glä′) *n.* A thin coating of ice or sleet, as on a rock. [French, from Old French *verre-glaz,* "glass-ice" : *verre,* from Latin *vitrum,* glass + *glaz,* ultimately from Latin *glaciēs,* ice.]

ve·rid·i·cal (və-rĭd′ĭ-kəl) *adj.* Also **ve·rid·ic** (və-rĭd′ĭk). **1.** Expressing the truth; accurate; veracious. **2.** *Psychology.* Designating dreams, visions, hallucinations, or the like that coincide accurately with future events or apparently unknowable present realities. [Latin *vēridicus* : *vērus,* true + *dīcere,* to say.] **—ve·rid·i·cal·i·ty** (və-rĭd′ĭ-kăl′ĭ-tē) *n.* **—ve·rid·i·cal·ly** *adv.*

ver·i·est (vĕr′ē-ĭst) *adj. Archaic.* Used as an intensive: *the veriest fop and fool.* [Superlative of VERY.]

ver·i·fi·ca·tion (vĕr′ə-fĭ-kā′shən) *n.* **1.** The act of verifying or condition of being verified. **2. a.** A confirmation of the truth of a theory or fact. **b.** The evidence for such a confirmation. **c.** A formal statement of such a confirmation. **3.** *Law.* **a.** Formerly, a short formulaic oath concluding a pleading and affirming that the pleader is ready to prove his allegations. **b.** The evidence used in trying to prove such allegations. **—ver·i·fi·ca·tive** (vĕr′ə-fĭ-kā′tĭv) *adj.*

ver·i·fy (vĕr′ə-fī′) *tr.v.* **-fied, -fying, -fies. 1.** To prove the truth of by the presentation of evidence or testimony; substantiate. **2.** To determine or test the truth or accuracy of, as by comparison, investigation, or reference: *Scientific claims are not accepted until verified.* **3.** *Law.* **a.** To affirm formally or under oath. **b.** To append a verification to (a pleading); conclude with a verification. —See Synonyms at **confirm.** [Middle English *verifien,* from Old French *verifier,* from Medieval Latin *vērificāre* : Latin *vērus,* true + *facere,* to make.] **—ver·i·fi·a·ble** *adj.* **—ver·i·fi·er** *n.*

ver·i·ly (vĕr′ə-lē) *adv. Archaic.* **1.** In truth; in fact; of a certainty. **2.** With confidence; assuredly. [Middle English *verraily,* from *verray,* true, VERY.]

ver·i·sim·i·lar (vĕr′ə-sĭm′ə-lər) *adj.* Appearing to be true or real; probable; likely. [Latin *vērisimilis* : *vērī,* of truth, from *vērum,* truth, from *vērus,* true + *similis,* SIMILAR.] **—ver·i·sim·i·lar·ly** *adv.*

ver·i·si·mil·i·tude (vĕr′ə-sĭm-ĭl′ə-to͞od′, -tyo͞od′) *n.* **1.** The quality of appearing to be true or real; likelihood. **2.** Something that has the appearance of being true or real. —See Synonyms at **truth.** [Latin *vērisimilitūdō,* from *vērisimilis,* VERISIMILAR.]

ver·ism (vĕr′ĭz′əm) *n.* Realistic portrayal in art and literature. [Italian *verismo,* from *vero,* true, from Latin *vērus.*] **—ver·ist** *n.* & *adj.* **—ve·ris·tic** (və-rĭs′tĭk) *adj.*

ve·ris·mo (vā-rēz′mō) *n.* A late 19th-century artistic movement, originating in Italy and influential particularly in opera, which concentrated on realistic, everyday themes, and tended to treat them in a melodramatic way. [Italian, from *vero,* true.]

ver·i·ta·ble (vĕr′ə-tə-bəl) *adj.* **1.** Unquestionably true; actual: *The house was a veritable pigpen.* **2.** Having the qualities of. Used as an intensive: *He's a veritable workaholic.* —See Synonyms at **real.** [Middle English, from Old French, from *verite,* VERITY.] **—ver·i·ta·ble·ness** *n.* **—ver·i·ta·bly** *adv.*

ver·i·ty (vĕr′ə-tē) *n., pl.* **-ties. 1.** The condition or quality of being real, accurate, or correct. **2.** A statement, principle, or belief considered to be of established and permanent truth. —See Synonyms at **truth.** [Middle English *verite,* from Old French, from Latin *vēritās* (stem *vēritāt-*), from *vērus,* true.]

ver·juice (vûr′jo͞os′) *n.* **1.** The acidic juice of sour or unripe fruit, such as grapes or crab apples. **2.** Bitterness or sourness, as of temper. [Middle English *verjus,* from Old French *vertjus* : *vert,* green (see **verdant**) + *jus,* JUICE.]

ver·kramp·te (fər-krămp′tə, -krŭmp′-) *n.* **1.** In South Africa, a person of very conservative political views who opposes liberalization of government policy, especially in respect to the race laws. **2.** *South African.* Any extremely conservative, bigoted, or narrow-minded person. Compare **verligte.** [Afrikaans, "restricted."] **—ver·kramp, ver·kramp·te** *adj.*

Ver·laine (vĕr-lān′, -lĕn′), **Paul** (1844–96). French poet. After associating with the Parnassian poets, whose influence is evident in his early poetry, he became a leader of the symbolists. His works include *Les Poètes Maudits* (1884) and *Sagesse* (1881).

ver·lig·te (fər-lĭ*KH*′tə) *n.* **1.** In South Africa, any of the more progressive National Party supporters who favor a slight liberalization of government and party policy, especially in respect of the race laws. **2.** *South African.* Any relatively progressive and broad-minded person. Compare **verkrampte.** [Afrikaans, "enlightened."] **—ver·lig, ver·lig·te** *adj.*

Ver·meer (vər-mîr′, -mâr′), **Jan** (1632–75). Dutch painter. He painted mostly interior scenes, where he used to great effect his mastery of highlighting and color. About 40 of his paintings are known, including *The Lady Standing at the Virginals.*

ver·meil (vûr′mĭl, -māl′) *n.* **1.** *Poetic.* Vermilion or bright-red. **2.** Gilded metal, such as silver, bronze, or copper.
~*adj.* Bright red in color. [Middle English *vermayl,* from Old French *vermeil,* from Late Latin *vermiculus,* from Latin, small worm, cochineal (which yields a red dye), from *vermis,* worm.]

vermi- *prefix.* Indicates a worm or worms; for example, **vermicide.** [Latin *vermis,* worm.]

ver·mi·cel·li (vûr′mə-chĕl′ē, -sĕl′ē) *n.* A food consisting of wheat flour paste made into long threads, thinner than spaghetti. [Italian, plural of *vermicello,* diminutive of *verme,* worm, from Latin *vermis.*]

ver·mi·cide (vûr′mə-sīd′) *n.* A substance used to kill worms. [VERMI- + -CIDE.] **—ver·mi·cid·al** (vûr′mə-sīd′l) *adj.*

ver·mic·u·lar (vər-mĭk′yə-lər) *adj.* **1.** Having the shape or motion of a worm. **2.** Having wormlike markings; vermiculate. **3.** Caused by or pertaining to worms. [Medieval Latin *vermiculāris,* from Latin *vermiculus,* diminutive of *vermis,* worm.] **—ver·mic·u·lar·ly** *adv.*

ver·mic·u·late (vər-mĭk′yə-lāt′) *tr.v.* **-lated, -lating, -lates.** To adorn or decorate with wavy or winding lines: *vermiculate a jar.*
~*adj.* (vər-mĭk′yə-lĭt, -lāt′). **1.** Bearing wormlike wavy lines. **2.** Having a wormlike motion; twisting or wriggling. **3.** Sinuous; tortuous; devious. **4.** Infested with worms; worm-eaten. [Latin *vermiculārī,* to be full of worms, from *vermiculus,* small worm. See **vermeil.**]

ver·mic·u·la·tion (vər-mĭk′yə-lā′shən) *n.* **1.** Motion resembling that of a worm; especially, the wavelike contractions of the intestine; peristalsis. **2.** Wormlike marks or carvings, as in a mosaic or masonry. **3.** The condition of being worm-eaten.

ver·mic·u·lite (vər-mĭk′yə-līt′) *n.* Any of a group of micaceous hydrated silicates of varying composition, related to the chlorites and used as heat insulation and as a planting medium for starting plant seeds and cuttings. [Latin *vermiculus,* small worm (see **vermeil**) + -ITE (from the wormlike projections it forms when subjected to the blowpipe).]

ver·mi·form (vûr′mə-fôrm′) *adj.* Resembling or having the shape of a worm. [New Latin *vermiformis* : VERMI- + -FORM.]

vermiform appendix *n.* The wormlike, closed projection of the cecum found in certain mammals including humans, in whom it is vestigial. Also called "appendix," "vermiform process."

ver·mi·fuge (vûr′mə-fyo͞oj′) *n.* Any agent that expels or destroys intestinal worms. Also called "anthelminthic." [VERMI- + -FUGE.] **—ver·mi·fug·al** *adj.*

ver·mil·ion, ver·mil·lion (vər-mĭl′yən) *n.* **1.** A bright-red **mercuric sulfide** *(see),* used as a pigment. **2.** Vivid red to reddish orange. Also called "Chinese red."
~*adj.* Also **ver·mil·lion.** Vivid red to reddish orange in color.
~*tr.v.* **vermilioned, -ioning, -ions.** Also **ver·mil·lion, -lioned, -lioning, -lions.** To color or dye vermilion. [Middle English *vermelyon,* from Old French *vermeillon,* from *vermeil,* VERMEIL.]

ver·min (vûr′mĭn) *n., pl.* **vermin. 1.** Collectively, various small animals or insects that are destructive, annoying, or injurious to health, such as cockroaches or rats. **2.** Collectively, various animals that prey on game, such as foxes or weasels. **3. a.** *Rare.* A vile, destructive, or worthless person. **b.** Such persons collectively: *"the most*

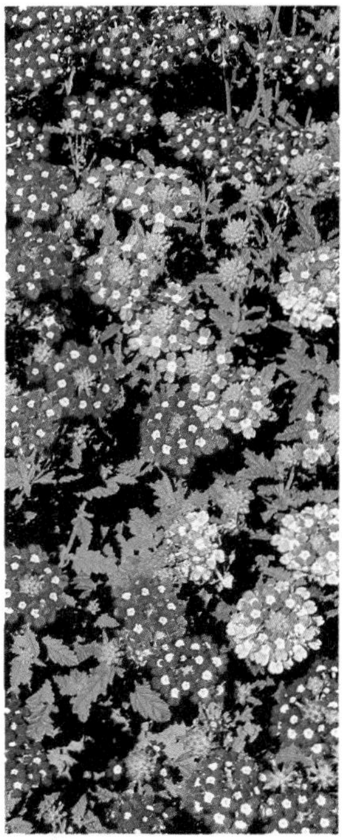

verbena *Most of the 250 species of verbena are native to the tropics, but cultivated varieties, such as those shown here, are now grown worldwide as garden plants. One species of verbena—*Verbena officinalis, *or vervain—was once used in medicine and is still used in teas as a cold remedy.*

PRONUNCIATION KEY

ă, **pat;** ā, **pay;** âr, **care;**
ä, **father, are;** b, **bib;**
ch, **church;** d, **deed;** ĕ, **pet;**
ē, **be;** f, **fife;** g, **gag;** h, **hat;**
hw, **which;** ĭ, **pit;** ī, **pie;**
îr, **pier;** j, **judge;** k, **kick;**
l, **lid, needle;** m, **mum;**
n, **no, sudden;** ng, **thing;**
ŏ, **pot;** ō, **toe;** ô, **paw, for;**
oi, **noise;** ou, **out;** o͝o, **book;**
o͞o, **boot;** p, **pop;** r, **roar;**
s, **sauce;** sh, **ship, dish;**
t, **tight;** th, **thin, path;**
th, **this, bathe;** ŭ, **cut;** ûr, **fur;**
v, **valve;** w, **with;** y, **yes;**
z, **zebra, size;** zh, **vision;**
ə, **about, item, edible, gallop, circus, peaceful**

IN FOREIGN WORDS:

à, *Fr.* **ami;** œ, *Fr.* **feu,** *Ger.* **schön;** ü, *Fr.* **tu,** *Ger.* **über;**
KH, *Ger.* **ich,** *Scot.* **loch;**
N, *Fr.* **bon;** y', *Fr.* **Compiègne**

STRESS MARKS:

Primary stress: ′
in·cite′ (ĭn-sīt′)
Secondary stress: ′
in′sight′ (ĭn′sīt′)

pernicious race of little odious vermin that nature ever suffered to crawl upon the surface of the earth" (Jonathan Swift). [Middle English, from Old French, from Vulgar Latin *vermīnum* (unattested), from Latin *vermis* (stem *vermin-*), worm.]

ver·mi·na·tion (vûr′mə-nā′shən) *n.* **1.** Infestation with vermin or worms. **2.** The breeding of worms, larvae, or vermin.

ver·min·ous (vûr′mə-nəs) *adj.* **1.** Of, pertaining to, or infested with vermin. **2.** Of the nature of vermin; repulsive; noxious. **—ver·mi·nous·ly** *adv.*

ver·miv·o·rous (vər-mĭv′ər-əs) *adj.* Feeding on worms. [VERMI- + -VOROUS.]

Ver·mont (vər-mŏnt′). State in the northeastern United States, one of the New England states, to the east of upper New York State with a northern boundary with Canada. The capital is Montpelier; the largest city is Burlington.

ver·mouth (vər-mōōth′) *n.* Any of several white wines, either sweet or dry, flavored with aromatic herbs and spices, and often used chiefly as an ingredient in cocktails. [French *vermout,* from German *Wermut,* WORMWOOD.]

ver·nac·u·lar (vər-năk′yə-lər) *n.* **1.** The standard native language of a country or locality. **2.** The informal everyday speech of a country or locality. **3.** The idiom of a particular trade or profession: *in the legal vernacular.* **4.** An idiomatic word, phrase, or expression. **5.** The commonly used name of a plant or animal as distinguished from the taxonomic designation.

~*adj.* **1.** Native to or commonly spoken by the members of a particular country or locality. Said of a language or dialect. **2.** Using the native language of a locality as distinct from literary language. Said of a writer. **3.** Pertaining to, spoken in, or written in the native language or dialect. **4.** Pertaining to the style of architecture and decoration peculiar to a specific culture or period. **5.** *Rare.* Occurring or existing in a particular locality; endemic: *a vernacular disease.* **6.** Designating or pertaining to the commonly used nonscientific name of a plant or animal. [Latin *vernāculus,* domestic, from *verna,* native slave, probably from Etruscan.] **—ver·nac·u·lar·ly** *adv.*

ver·nac·u·lar·ism (vər-năk′yə-lə-rĭz′əm) *n.* **1.** The use of or the doctrine favoring the use of the vernacular. **2.** A vernacular word, phrase, or expression.

ver·nal (vûr′nəl) *adj.* **1.** Of, pertaining to, or occurring in the spring. **2.** Characteristic of or resembling spring. **3.** Fresh and young; youthful. [Latin *vernālis,* from *vernus,* of spring, from *vēr,* spring.] **—ver·nal·ly** *adv.*

vernal equinox *n.* **1.** *Astronomy.* The point in Aries at which the ecliptic intersects the celestial equator, the sun having a northerly motion. **2.** The time when the sun passes through this point, about March 21, when day and night are approximately equal all over the earth. Compare **autumnal equinox.**

vernal grass *n.* Any of various Eurasian grasses of the genus *Anthoxanthum,* such as the sweet-scented *A. odoratum.*

ver·nal·i·za·tion (vûr′nə-lə-zā′shən) *n.* The exposure of certain plants or their seeds to a period of low temperature that is necessary for them to flower or flower earlier than usual. Used especially of winter varieties of cereals.

ver·na·tion (vər-nā′shən) *n. Botany.* The arrangement of the folded leaves in a bud. [New Latin *vernatio,* from Latin *vernāre,* to flourish, from *vernus,* VERNAL.]

Verne (vûrn), **Jules** (1828–1905). French writer. The founder of modern science fiction, he foresaw submarines and space travel. The best known of his adventure stories are *Journey to the Center of the Earth* (1864) and *Around the World in 80 Days* (1873).

Ver·ner's Law (vûr′nərz, vĕr′-) *n. Linguistics.* A law stating essentially that Proto-Germanic noninitial voiceless fricatives in voiced environments became voiced when the previous syllable was unstressed in Proto-Indo-European. [After Karl Adolf *Verner* (1846–96), Danish philologist.]

ver·ni·er (vûr′nē-ər) *n.* **1.** A small, movable auxiliary graduated scale attached parallel to a main graduated scale, calibrated to indicate fractional parts of the subdivisions of the larger scale, and used on certain precision instruments to increase accuracy in measurement. **2.** Any auxiliary device designed to facilitate fine adjustments or measurements on precision instruments. Also called "vernier scale."

~*adj.* Of or pertaining to a vernier. [After Pierre *Vernier* (1580–1637), French mathematician.]

vernier caliper *n.* A measuring instrument consisting of an L-shaped frame with a linear scale along its longer arm and an L-shaped sliding attachment with a vernier scale, used to read directly the dimension of an object represented by the separation between the inner or outer edges of the two shorter arms.

vernier rocket *n.* A small rocket engine used primarily to make fine adjustments in velocity and trajectory. Also called "thruster," "vernier engine."

Ve·ro·na (və-rō′nə). City in northeastern Italy, on the Adige River in the Venetia region. A strategic pre-Roman city, it is now a major industrial and agricultural center.

ver·o·nal (vĕr′ə-nôl′, -nəl) *n.* A type of **barbital** (see). [Originally a trademark.]

Ve·ro·ne·se (vĕr′ə-nā′sĕ, -zĕ), **Paolo,** born Paolo Caliari. (1528–1588). Italian painter of the Venetian school. He is known particularly as a decorative artist. His works include *Marriage at Cana* and the *Feast in the House of Levi.*

ve·ron·i·ca¹ (və-rŏn′ĭ-kə) *n.* Any of various plants of the genus *Ve-*

ronica, which includes the speedwells. [Perhaps from the name *Veronica.*]

veronica² *n.* **1.** The representation or image of the face of Jesus, which, according to legend, was impressed upon the handkerchief offered to him by Saint Veronica on the road to Calvary. **2.** The handkerchief itself. **3.** Any similar representation of Jesus' face on a textile fabric. [Medieval Latin, from Late Latin *Veraiconica,* (Saint) Veronica : *vēra, vērus,* true + *iconica, iconicus,* pertaining to an image, from *icon,* image, ICON.]

veronica³ *n.* In bullfighting, a maneuver in which the matador stands immobile and passes the cape slowly before the charging bull. [Spanish, from the name *Veronica.*]

Ver·ra·za·no or **Ver·raz·za·no** (vĕr′-ə-zä′nō), **Giovanni da** (*c.* 1485–1528). Italian explorer. Commissioned by the French king, Francis I, to find a western sea passage to China, he explored much of the Atlantic coast of North America, erroneously identifying either the Delaware River or Chesapeake Bay as a route to the Pacific Ocean (1524).

Ver·roc·chio (və-rō′kē-ō), **Andrea del,** born Andrea di Michele de Francesco di Cioni. (1435–88). Florentine sculptor, painter, and craftsman. He is best known for his magnificent equestrian statue of General Bartolommeo Colleoni at Venice.

ver·ru·ca (və-rōō′kə) *n., pl.* **-cas** or **-cae** (-sē). **1.** *Medicine.* A wart, especially on the sole of the foot. **2.** *Biology.* A wartlike projection, as on some leaves. [Latin *verrūca.*]

ver·ru·cose (və-rōō′kōs′, vĕr′ə-kōs′) *adj.* Also **ver·ru·cous** (-kəs). Covered with warts or wartlike projections. [Latin *verrucōsus,* from *verrūca,* VERRUCA.]

vers versed sine.

Ver·sailles (vər-sī′, vĕr-). City in north-central France, on the southwestern outskirts of Paris. It was a village until Louis XIV built his palace and transferred his court to it (1682). Both the German Empire and the Third French Republic were proclaimed at Versailles (1871), and the negotiations that ended World War I by the Treaty of Versailles (1919) were conducted here.

Versailles, Treaty of *n.* **1.** The treaty (1919) imposed on Germany after the end of World War I. **2.** The treaty (1783) ending the American Revolution. See **Paris, Treaty of.**

ver·sant (vûr′sənt) *n.* **1.** The slope of a side of a mountain or mountain range. **2.** The general slope of any region. [French, from Latin *versāns* (stem *versānt-*), present participle of *versārī,* to turn frequently. See **versatile.**]

ver·sa·tile (vûr′sə-təl, -tīl′) *adj.* **1.** Capable of turning competently from one task, subject, or occupation to another; having a generalized aptitude. **2.** Having varied uses or serving many functions: *The potato is a most versatile vegetable.* **3.** Inconstant or variable; changeable. **4.** *Biology.* Capable of moving freely in all directions, as the antenna of an insect or the loosely attached anther of a flower. [French, from Latin *versātilis,* from *versārī,* frequentative of *vertere,* to turn.] **—ver·sa·tile·ly** *adv.* **—ver·sa·til·i·ty** (vûr′sə-tĭl′ĭ-tē), **ver·sa·tile·ness** *n.*

verse (vûrs) *n. Abbr.* **v., ver. 1. a.** A line of words arranged in accordance with the principles of prosody; one line of poetry. **b.** A subdivision of any metrical composition, such as a stanza of a hymn or of a long poem. **2.** Metrical or rhymed composition; poetry as distinct from prose. **3.** Light metrical composition as distinct from serious poetry. **4.** An instance of such composition; a light poem. **5.** A specified type of metrical composition, such as blank verse or free verse. **6.** A specified type of metrical structure: *iambic verse.* **7.** Any of the numbered subdivisions of a chapter in the Bible.

~*v.* **versed, versing, verses.** *Rare.* —*tr.* To versify (prose, for example). —*intr.* To versify; write poetry. [Middle English *vers,* from Old English *fers* and Old French *vers,* from Latin *versus,* "a turning of the plow," furrow, line, verse, from the past participle of *vertere,* to turn.]

versed (vûrst) *adj.* Knowledgeable, skilled, or trained. Used with *in: versed in canon law.* [French *versé* or Latin *versātus,* past participle of *versārī,* to be engaged in, frequentative of *vertere,* to turn.]

versed cosine *n. Abbr.* **covers** *Mathematics.* A trigonometric function of an angle equal to one minus the sine of that angle. Also called "coversine."

versed sine *n. Abbr.* **vers** *Mathematics.* A trigonometric function of an angle equal to one minus the cosine of that angle. Also called "versine." [New Latin *sinus versus,* "inverse-order sine," from Latin *versus,* turned. See **verse** (poetry).]

ver·si·cle (vûr′sĭ-kəl) *n.* **1.** A short verse. **2.** A short sentence spoken or chanted by a priest and followed by a response from the congregation. [Middle English, from Old French *versicule,* from Latin *versiculus,* diminutive of *versus,* VERSE.] **—ver·si·cu·lar** (vûr-sĭk′yə-lər) *adj.*

ver·si·col·or (vûr′sĭ-kŭl′ər) *adj.* Also **ver·si·col·ored** (-kŭl′ərd). **1.** Having a variety of colors; variegated. **2.** Changing in color; iridescent. [Latin : *versus,* turned, changed (see **verse**) + COLOR.]

ver·si·fi·er (vûr′sə-fī′ər) *n.* One who versifies. **—See Synonyms at poet.**

ver·si·fy (vûr′sə-fī′) *v.* **-fied, -fying, -fies.** —*tr.* **1.** To change from prose into metrical form. **2.** To treat or tell in verse; write a poem about: *versify Bible stories.* —*intr.* To write verses; especially, to write light or worthless poetry. [Middle English *versifien,* from Old French *versifier,* from Latin *versificāre* : *versus,* VERSE + -FY.] **—ver·si·fi·ca·tion** *n.*

ver·sine (vûr′sīn′) *n. Mathematics.* A versed sine.

ver·sion (vûr′zhən, -shən) *n. Abbr.* **v., ver. 1.** A description, narration, or account related from the specific or subjective viewpoint of the narrator: *Her version of the accident differed from his.* **2. a.** A translation. **b.** *Usually* **Version.** A translation of the entire Bible or of a part of it: *the King James Version.* **3.** A variation of any prototype; a variant: *"At home we played soccer . . . and sometimes a version of hurling"* (Brendan Behan). **4.** An adaptation of a work of art or literature into another medium or style: *Lamb's version of Shakespeare; the film version of the novel.* **5.** *Medicine.* **a.** Manipulation of a fetus in the uterus to bring it into a favorable position for delivery. **b.** A deflection of an organ, such as the uterus, from its normal position. [From Medieval Latin *versiō* (stem *versiōn-*), conversion, translation, from Latin *vertere,* to turn, change.] **—ver·sion·al** *adj.*

vers li·bre (vĕr lē'br') *n. French.* **Free verse** *(see).*

ver·so (vûr'sō) *n., pl.* **-sos.** *Abbr.* **v., vo.** **1.** *Printing.* The left-hand page of a book or the reverse side of a sheet of paper as opposed to the **recto** *(see).* **2.** The back of a coin or medal. Compare **obverse.** [Latin *versō (folio),* "(the page) being turned," the page one sees when the leaf is turned over, ablative of *versus,* turned. See **versus.**]

verst (vûrst) *n.* A Russian measure of linear distance, equivalent to just over a kilometer (about two-thirds of a mile). [French *verste,* from Russian *versta,* "line."]

ver·sus (vûr'səs) *prep. Abbr.* **v., vs.** **1.** Against. Used in law and in sports: *the plaintiff versus the defendant; Yale versus Harvard.* **2.** As an alternative to; in contrast with: *death versus dishonor.* [Medieval Latin, from Latin, turned toward, from the past participle of *vertere,* to turn.]

vert (vûrt) *n.* **1.** In former English forest law: **a.** Any green vegetation that can serve as cover for deer. **b.** The right to cut such vegetation. **2.** *Heraldry.* The color green. [Middle English *verte,* from Old French *vert,* green. See **verdant.**]

vert. vertical.

ver·te·bra (vûr'tə-brə) *n., pl.* **-brae** (-brē) or **-bras.** Any of the bones or cartilaginous segments forming the spinal column. [Latin, joint, vertebra, "something to turn on," from *vertere,* to turn.]

ver·te·bral (vûr'tə-brəl) *adj.* **1.** Relating to or of the nature of a vertebra. **2.** Having or consisting of vertebrae.

vertebral canal *n. Anatomy.* The **spinal canal** *(see).*

vertebral column *n. Anatomy.* The **spinal column** *(see).*

ver·te·brate (vûr'tə-brāt', -brĭt) *n.* Any member of the subphylum Vertebrata, a primary division of the phylum Chordata that includes the fishes, amphibians, reptiles, birds, and mammals, all of which are characterized by a segmented bony or cartilaginous spinal column.

~adj. **1.** Having a backbone or spinal column. **2.** Of or characteristic of a vertebrate or vertebrates. [Latin *vertebrātus,* from *vertebra,* VERTEBRA.]

ver·te·bra·tion (vûr'tə-brā'shən) *n.* The process or result of division into vertebrae or similar segments.

ver·tex (vûr'tĕks') *n., pl.* **-texes** or **-tices** (-tə-sēz'). **1.** The highest point of anything; apex; summit. **2.** *Anatomy.* **a.** The highest point of the skull. **b.** The top of the head. **3.** *Astronomy.* The highest point reached in the apparent motion of a celestial body. **4.** *Geometry.* **a.** The point at which two or more lines or edges intersect. **b.** The fixed point that is one of the three generating characteristics of a conic section. [Latin, whirl, crown of the head, highest point, from *vertere,* to turn.]

ver·ti·cal (vûr'tĭ-kəl) *adj. Abbr.* **vert.** **1.** At right angles to the horizon; extending perpendicularly from a plane; upright. Compare **horizontal.** **2.** Pertaining to or situated at the vertex or highest point; directly overhead. **3.** *Anatomy.* Of or pertaining to the vertex of the head. **4.** *Economics.* Pertaining to, composed of, or controlling all the grades, stages, or levels in the manufacture and sale of a product. **5.** Moving straight up or down or up and down.

~n. Abbr. **vert.** **1.** A vertical line, plane, circle, or the like. **2.** A vertical position. **3.** A vertical pillar, pole, or the like. [French, from Late Latin *verticālis,* from Latin *vertex* (stem *vertic-*), VERTEX.] **—ver·ti·cal·i·ty** (vûr'tĭ-kăl'ĭ-tē), **ver·ti·cal·ness** *n.* **—ver·ti·cal·ly** *adv.*

Synonyms: *perpendicular, plumb, upright.*

vertical circle *n. Astronomy.* Any great circle on the celestial sphere, passing through the zenith and the nadir, and thus perpendicular to the horizon.

vertical file *n.* A collection of articles such as pamphlets, sheets of paper, and mounted photographs that have been collected and arranged for ready reference, as in a library.

vertically opposite angles *pl.n.* Either pair of the two pairs of equal angles formed opposite each other by two intersecting lines.

vertical take-off *n.* The take-off of an aircraft in a perpendicularly upward direction.

vertical union *n.* A labor union in which workers are organized according to the industry for which they work instead of by their particular craft or skill.

ver·ti·ces. Alternate plural of **vertex.**

ver·ti·cil (vûr'tə-səl) *n. Biology.* A circular arrangement, as of flowers or leaves, about a point on an axis; a whorl. [Latin *verticillus,* the whirl of a spindle, diminutive of *vertex,* whirl, VERTEX.]

ver·ti·cil·las·ter (vûr'tə-sə-lăs'tər) *n. Botany.* An inflorescence, such as that of the white dead nettle, resembling a whorl but actually arising in axils of opposite leaves. [VERTICIL + -ASTER.] **—ver·ti·cil·las·trate** (vûr'tə-sə-lăs'trāt') *adj.*

ver·ti·cil·late (vûr'tə-sĭl'ĭt, -āt') *adj.* Also **ver·ti·cil·lat·ed** (-sĭl'ā'tĭd). Arranged in or forming a whorl or whorls. **—ver·ti·cil·late·ly** *adv.* **—ver·ti·cil·la·tion** *n.*

ver·tig·i·nous (vər-tĭj'ə-nəs) *adj.* **1.** Revolving; whirling; rotary. **2.** Affected by vertigo; dizzy. **3.** Tending to produce vertigo: *vertiginous speed.* **4.** Liable to quick change; unstable; inconstant. [Latin *vertīginōsus,* from *vertīgō* (stem *vertīgin-*), VERTIGO.] **—ver·tig·i·nous·ly** *adv.* **—ver·tig·i·nous·ness** *n.*

ver·ti·go (vûr'tĭ-gō') *n., pl.* **-goes** or **vertigines** (vər-tĭj'ə-nēz') **1.** The sensation of dizziness and the feeling that oneself or one's environment is whirling about. **2.** A confused, disoriented state of mind. [Latin *vertīgō,* "a whirling," from *vertere,* to turn.]

vertu. Variant of **virtu.**

ver·vain (vûr'vān') *n.* A perennial plant, *Verbena officinalis,* native to Europe having clusters of tiny, purplish-blue flowers. [Middle English *verveine,* from Old French, from Latin *verbēna,* often in plural *verbēnae,* sacred leaves or twigs of olive, myrtle, or laurel.]

verve (vûrv) *n.* **1.** Energy and enthusiasm in the expression of ideas and especially in artistic endeavor: *The play lacks verve.* **2.** Vitality; liveliness; vigor. [French, from Old French, fancy, fanciful expression, from Latin *verba,* plural of *verbum,* word.]

ver·vet (vûr'vĭt) *n.* A small, long-tailed African monkey, *Cercopithecus aethiops,* having a yellowish-brown or greenish coat. [French, short for *vert grivet* : *vert,* green (see **verdant**) + GRIVET.]

Ver·woerd (fər-vŏŏrt'), **Hendrik Frensch** (1901–66). South African statesman. While prime minister (1958–66), he pursued a policy of apartheid and took South Africa out of the Commonwealth (1961). He was assassinated in Cape Town.

ver·y (vĕr'ē) *adv. Abbr.* **v., V.** **1.** In a high degree; extremely; exceedingly: *very happy.* **2.** Truly. Used as an intensive with superlatives: *the very best way to proceed.* **3.** Precisely: *the very same one.* **—not very. 1.** Not at all: *not very satisfied with the service.* **2.** Only a little: *He's not very hungry.*

~adj. **verier, -iest. 1.** Complete; absolute; utter: *at the very end of his career.* **2.** Identical; selfsame: *There goes the very man I met.* **3.** Used as an intensive to emphasize the importance of the thing described: *The very mountains crumbled.* **4.** Particular; precise: *the very center of town.* **5.** Mere: *The very mention of the name was frightening.* **6.** Actual: *caught in the very act.* **7.** As if actual. Used to reinforce a metaphor: *His fists are very rocks.* **8.** *Archaic.* Genuine; real; true: *"Like very sanctity she did approach"* (Shakespeare). [Middle English *verray,* from Old French *ver(r)ai,* true, real, from Vulgar Latin *vērāius* (unattested), from Latin *vērus,* true.]

Usage: *Very* may be used to modify a past participle, as in *She was very tired; She seems very interested,* where the past participle clearly has an adjectival function. However, in such sentences as *she was delayed/disliked/inconvenienced,* where the participle still seems partly verbal in function, more formal usage prefers *much, very much,* or *greatly,* and *very* has often been criticized in this kind of context.

very high frequency *n. Abbr.* **VHF, vhf** A band of radio frequencies falling between 30 and 300 megahertz.

Ve·ry light (vĕr'ē) *n.* A colored flare fired from a pistol (a *Very pistol*) as a signal or for temporary illumination. [After Edward W. *Very* (1847–1910), U.S. naval officer.]

very low frequency *n. Abbr.* **VLF, vlf** A band of radio frequencies falling between 3 and 30 kilohertz.

Ve·sa·li·us (vĭ-sā'lē-əs, -zā'-), **Andreas** (1514–64). Flemish anatomist. Often called the father of modern anatomy, he based his major work, *On the Structure of the Human Body* (1543), on his meticulous dissection of human cadavers, his careful illustration and description of human anatomy, and his skeptical view of many ancient anatomical works.

Ve·sey (vē'zē), **Denmark** (*c.* 1767–1822). U.S. slave insurrectionist. A freedman in Charleston, South Carolina, he was a successful carpenter and noted preacher who was implicated in a suspected slave conspiracy (1822). Although few details about the alleged plot were ever uncovered, he was hanged with five other men. The event caused heightened hysteria among slave owners and resulted in more severe slave codes in many Southern states.

ve·si·ca (və-sī'kə, -sē'kə) *n., pl.* **-cae** (-sē). **1.** A bladder; especially, the urinary bladder or the gallbladder. **2.** A **vesica piscis** *(see).* [Latin *vēsīca,* bladder, blister.] **—ves·i·cal** (vĕs'ĭ-kəl) *adj.*

vesica pis·cis (və-sī'kə pĭs'ĭs) *n.* A pointed oval shape formed by or as if by the intersection of two circles and used in medieval art, often as an aureole, to surround a sacred figure. Also called "vesica." [Latin, "fish's bladder."]

ves·i·cant (vĕs'ĭ-kənt) *n.* A blistering agent; especially, such an agent, as mustard gas, used in chemical warfare. **—ves·i·cant** *adj.*

ves·i·cate (vĕs'ĭ-kāt') *v.* **-cated, -cating, -cates.** *—tr.* To blister. *—intr.* To be or become blistered. [Late Latin *vēsīcāre,* from Latin *vēsīca,* bladder, blister, VESICA.] **—ves·i·ca·tion** *n.*

ves·i·ca·to·ry (vĕs'ĭ-kə-tôr'ē, -tōr'ē) *adj.* Vesicant.

~n., pl. **vesicatories.** A vesicant.

ves·i·cle (vĕs'ĭ-kəl) *n.* **1.** A small bladderlike vacuole, cell, or cavity. **2.** *Anatomy.* A small bladder or sac, especially one containing fluid. **3.** *Pathology.* A serum-filled blister formed in or beneath the skin. **4.** An air-filled cavity found in certain aquatic plants. **5.** A small cavity formed in volcanic rock during solidification. [French *vésicule,* from Latin *vēsīcula,* diminutive of *vēsīca,* VESICA.]

ve·sic·u·lar (və-sĭk'yə-lər) *adj.* **1.** Of or pertaining to vesicles. **2.** Composed of or containing vesicles. **3.** Having the form of a vesicle. **—ve·sic·u·lar·ly** *adv.*

ve·sic·u·late (və-sĭk'yə-lāt') *v.* **-lated, -lating, -lates.** *—tr.* To make vesicular; blister. *—intr.* To become blistered or vesicular.

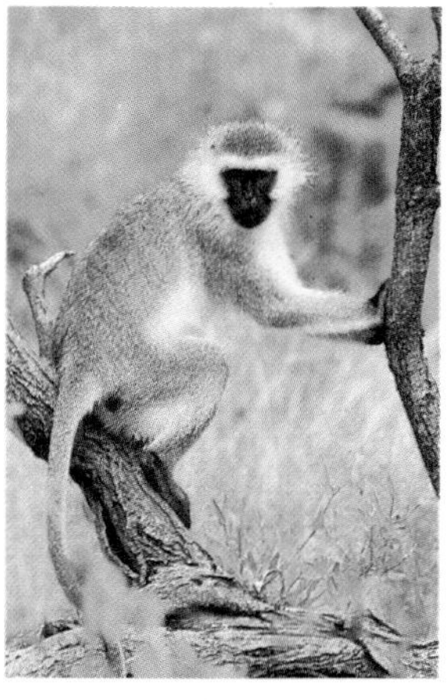

vervet *One of the commonest monkeys in East Africa, the vervet,* Cercopithecus aethiops, *is recognizable by its black face and often greenish fur.*

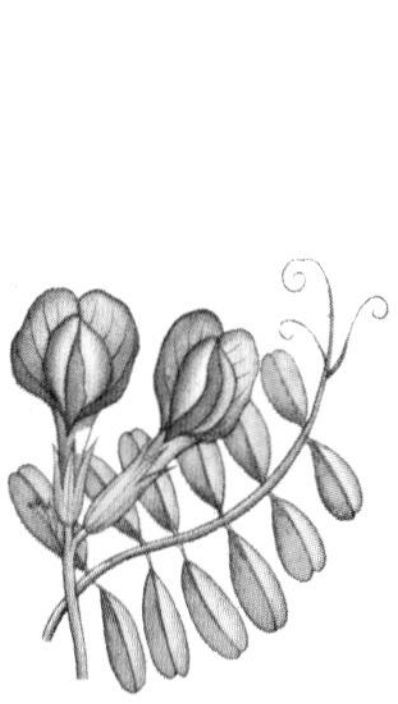

vetch *A clinging wild plant that winds its way through bushes. Its flowers, similar to the pea, are purple or white.*

PRONUNCIATION KEY

ă, pat; ā, pay; âr, care;
ä, father, are; b, bib;
ch, church; d, deed; ĕ, pet;
ē, be; f, fife; g, gag; h, hat;
hw, which; ĭ, pit; ī, pie;
îr, pier; j, judge; k, kick;
l, lid, needle; m, mum;
n, no, sudden; ng, thing;
ŏ, pot; ō, toe; ô, paw, for;
oi, noise; ou, out; o͝o, book;
o͞o, boot; p, pop; r, roar;
s, sauce; sh, ship, dish;
t, tight; th, thin, path;
th, this, bathe; ŭ, cut; ûr, fur;
v, valve; w, with; y, yes;
z, zebra, size; zh, vision;
ə, about, item, edible, gallop, circus, peaceful

IN FOREIGN WORDS:

à, *Fr.* ami; œ, *Fr.* feu, *Ger.* schön; ü, *Fr.* tu, *Ger.* über; KH, *Ger.* ich, *Scot.* loch; N, *Fr.* bon; y', *Fr.* Compiègne

STRESS MARKS:

Primary stress: ′
in·cite′ (ĭn-sīt′)
Secondary stress: ′
in′sight′ (ĭn′sīt′)

~*adj.* (və-sĭk′yə-lĭt, -lāt′) **1.** Of, pertaining to, or resembling vesicles. **2.** Full of or bearing vesicles; vesicular. **—ve·sic·u·la·tion** *n.*

Ves·pa·sian (vĕs-pā′zhən), Latin name Titus Flavius Vespasianus (A.D. 9–79). Roman emperor (69–79). He restored the empire's finances, reformed the army, patronized the arts, and began the building of the Colosseum.

ves·per (vĕs′pər) *n.* **1.** A bell used to summon persons to vespers. Also called "vesper bell." **2.** *Archaic.* Evening.
~*adj.* **1.** Of or pertaining to vespers. **2.** Pertaining to, appearing in, or appropriate for evening: *a vesper serenade.* [From VESPER.]

Ves·per (vĕs′pər) *n.* Formerly, the **evening star** *(see).* [Middle English, from Latin, evening, the evening star.]

ves·per·al (vĕs′pər-əl) *n.* **1.** A book containing the words and hymns to be used at vespers. **2.** A covering used to protect the altar cloth between services.

ves·pers (vĕs′pərz) *pl.n. often* **Vespers. 1. a.** The sixth of the seven **canonical hours** *(see).* **b.** The time of day set aside for this prayer, in the late afternoon or evening. **2.** Any service of worship held in the late afternoon or evening. **3.** *Roman Catholic Church.* A service held on Sundays or holy days which includes the office of vespers.

ves·per·tine (vĕs′pər-tĭn, -tīn′) *adj.* Also **ves·per·ti·nal** (vĕs′pər-tī′nəl) **1.** Pertaining to or appearing in the evening. **2.** *Botany.* Opening or blooming in the evening. **3.** *Zoology.* Becoming active in the evening; crepuscular. **4.** *Astronomy.* Moving toward the horizon in the evening. [Latin *vespertīnus,* from *vesper,* evening, VESPER.]

ves·pi·ar·y (vĕs′pē-ĕr′ē) *n., pl.* **-ies.** A nest or colony of wasps or hornets. [Latin *vespa,* wasp + (AP)IARY.]

ves·pid (vĕs′pĭd) *n.* Any of various insects of the family Vespidae, which includes the common wasp and hornet. [New Latin *Vespidae,* from Latin *vespa,* wasp. See **vespiary.**] **—ves·pid** *adj.*

ves·pine (vĕs′pīn′, -pĭn) *adj.* Of, pertaining to, or resembling a wasp or wasps. [From Latin *vespa,* wasp. See **vespiary.**]

Ves·puc·ci (vĕs-po͞o′chē), **Amerigo** (1454–1512). Italian navigator. He made several voyages to the New World and discovered (1499) the mouths of the Amazon and (1501) the mouth of the Río de la Plata. America is named after him.

ves·sel (vĕs′əl) *n.* **1.** A hollow utensil used as a container, especially for liquids. **2.** A boat, ship, barge, or the like designed to transport passengers or freight on water. **3.** An airship. **4.** *Anatomy.* A duct, canal, or other tube for containing or circulating a bodily fluid: *a blood vessel.* **5.** *Botany.* Any of the tubular conductive structures of plant vascular tissue, consisting of cylindrical cells that are attached end to end. **6.** A person considered as a receptacle or agent of some specified quality: *a vessel of mercy.* [Middle English, from Old French *vaissel, vessel,* from Late Latin *vascellum,* diminutive of Latin *vās,* vessel, VAS.]

vest (vĕst) *n.* **1. a.** A short, close-fitting sleeveless collarless garment, often buttoning down the front, worn over a shirt or blouse and often under a suit coat or jacket. Also *chiefly British* "waistcoat." **b.** A warm, lightweight, usually water-repellent sleeveless jacket: *a down vest.* **2.** *Rare.* A fabric trimming or decoration worn by women to cover the bosom. **3.** *Chiefly British.* An undershirt. **4.** *Archaic.* Clothing; dress. **5.** *Obsolete.* An ecclesiastical vestment.
~*v.* **vested, vesting, vests.** *—tr.* **1.** To clothe or dress, as with ecclesiastical vestments. **2.** To place (authority, property, or rights, for example) in the control of someone. Used with *in: He vested his estate in his son.* **3.** To place authority, power, or the like, in the control of. Used with *with: The council was vested with enormous power.* *—intr.* **1.** To dress oneself, especially in ecclesiastical vestments. **2.** To be or become legally vested in a person or persons; come into the possession of someone. [French *veste,* from Italian, from Latin *vestis,* garment.]

ves·ta (vĕs′tə) *n.* A short friction match made of wax or wood. [After the goddess VESTA.]

Ves·ta¹ (vĕs′tə). *Roman Mythology.* The goddess of the hearth, identified with the Greek goddess Hestia and worshiped in a temple containing the sacred fire tended by the vestal virgins. [Latin.]

Vesta² *n.* The third-largest asteroid in the solar system, having a diameter of approximately 380 kilometers (240 miles). [After the goddess VESTA.]

ves·tal (vĕs′təl) *adj.* **1.** Pertaining to or sacred to Vesta. **2.** Pertaining to or characteristic of the vestal virgins; chaste; pure.
~*n.* **1.** A vestal virgin. **2.** A virgin woman. **3.** *Rare.* A nun.

vestal virgin *n.* Any of the four or six virgin priestesses who tended the sacred fire in the temple of Vesta in ancient Rome.

vest·ed (vĕs′tĭd) *adj.* **1.** *Law.* **a.** Settled, complete, or absolute; without contingency. Said of property or a right. **b.** Having unqualified present or future possession of a property or right. Said of a person, persons, or an organization. **2.** Dressed or clothed, especially in ecclesiastical vestments.

vested interest *n.* **1.** *Law.* A right or title to ownership of property that can be conveyed to another. **2.** A strong concern for something, such as a state of affairs or an institution, from which one expects private benefit. **3.** *Usually* **vested interests.** A group that has a vested interest.

ves·ti·ar·y (vĕs′tē-ĕr′ē) *adj.* Of or pertaining to clothes.
~*n., pl.* **vestiaries.** A dressing room, cloakroom, or vestry. [Middle English *vestiarie,* from Old French, from Medieval Latin *vestiārium,* from Latin, wardrobe, from *vestiārius,* of clothes, from *vestis,* garment.]

vestibular nerve *n.* A division of the **acoustic nerve** *(see).*

ves·ti·bule (vĕs′tə-byo͞ol′) *n.* **1.** A small entrance hall or antechamber between two doors of a house or building. **2.** An enclosed area at the end of a passenger car on a railroad train. **3.** *Anatomy.* Any cavity, chamber, or channel that serves as an approach or entrance to another cavity or canal. [French, from Latin *vestibulum*†.] **—ves·tib·u·lar** (vĕ-stĭb′yə-lər) *adj.*

ves·tib·u·lo·coch·le·ar nerve (vĕ-stĭb′yo͞o-lō-kŏk′lē-ər) *n.* The **acoustic nerve** *(see).*

ves·tige (vĕs′tĭj) *n.* **1.** A visible trace, evidence, or sign of something that has once existed but now no longer exists or appears. **2.** A very small quantity; a hint: *a vestige of garlic; not a vestige of truth in his claim.* **3.** *Biology.* A small, degenerate, or rudimentary organ or part existing in an organism as a usually nonfunctioning remnant of an organ or part fully developed and functional in a preceding generation or earlier developmental stage. —See Synonyms at **trace.** [French, from Latin *vestīgium*†, footprint, trace.]

ves·tig·i·al (vĕ-stĭj′ē-əl) *adj.* **1.** Of, pertaining to, or constituting a vestige. **2.** *Biology.* Occurring or persisting as a rudimentary or degenerate structure. **—ves·tig·i·al·ly** *adv.*

vest·ment (vĕst′mənt) *n.* **1.** A garment; especially, a robe or gown worn as an indication of office or state. **2.** *Ecclesiastical.* Any of the ritual robes worn by clergymen, altar boys, or other assistants at services or rites; especially, a garment worn at the celebration of the Eucharist. [Middle English *vestiment,* from Old French, from Latin *vestimentum,* from *vestīre,* to dress, from *vestis,* garment. See **vest.**] **—vest·ment·al** *adj.*

vest-pock·et (vĕst′pŏk′ĭt) *adj.* **1.** Designed to fit into a vest pocket. **2.** Relatively small; diminutive.

ves·try (vĕs′trē) *n., pl.* **-tries. 1.** A room in or adjoining a church where the clergy put on their vestments and where these robes and other sacred objects are stored; a sacristy. **2.** A meeting room in a church. **3.** In the Anglican and Episcopal churches, a committee of members of the parish or congregation that administers the affairs of the parish or congregation. **4.** *Anglican Church.* A meeting of this group or of the entire congregation or the place in which it is held. [Middle English *vestrie,* variant of *vestiarie,* VESTIARY.]

ves·try·man (vĕs′trē-mən) *n., pl.* **-men** (-mĭn). A member of a vestry.

ves·ture (vĕs′chər) *n. Archaic.* **1.** Clothing; apparel. **2.** Anything that covers or cloaks: *hills in a vesture of mist.*
~*tr.v.* **vestured, -turing, -tures.** *Archaic.* To cover with vesture; clothe. [Middle English, clothes, from Old French, from Late Latin *vestītūra,* from Latin *vestīre,* to clothe. See **vestment.**]

ve·su·vi·an (və-so͞o′vē-ən) *n.* A match formerly used for lighting cigars; a fusee. [From VESUVIUS.]

ve·su·vi·an·ite (və-so͞o′vē-ə-nīt′) *n.* A mineral, **idocrase** *(see).* [*Vesuvian,* of VESUVIUS (because first found in the lava of the volcano) + -ITE.]

Ve·su·vi·us (və-so͞o′-vē-əs). Active volcano in southern Italy. Rising some 1,280 meters (4,200 feet) from the Bay of Naples, it has a seismological station on its west slope. In A.D. 79 the first recorded eruption destroyed Pompeii, Stabiae, and Herculaneum.

vet¹ (vĕt) *n. Informal.* A veterinarian.
~*tr.v.* **vetted, vetting, vets. 1.** *Informal.* To practice veterinary medicine upon. **2.** To examine or investigate and appraise for acceptability: *vet a manuscript.* [Shortening of VETERINARY.]

vet² *n. Informal.* A military veteran.

vet. 1. veteran. **2.** veterinarian; veterinary.

vetch (vĕch) *n.* **1.** Any of various climbing or twining plants of the genus *Vicia,* having pinnate leaves and small, usually purplish flowers. **2.** Any of various similar related plants such as the milk vetches and the kidney vetch. [Middle English *fecche,* from Old North French *veche,* from Latin *vicia.*]

vetch·ling (vĕch′lĭng) *n.* Any of several plants of the genus *Lathyrus,* having pinnate leaves, slender tendrils, winged or angled stems, and variously colored pealike flowers. [VETCH + -LING.]

veter. veterinary.

vet·er·an (vĕt′ər-ən, vĕt′rən) *n. Abbr.* **vet. 1.** One who has a long record of service in a given activity or capacity or long experience. **2.** One who has been a member of the armed forces.
~*adj.* **1.** Experienced because of long service: *a veteran politician.* **2.** Pertaining to or suggestive of a veteran or veterans. [French *vétéran,* from Latin *veterānus,* from *vetus* (stem *veter-*), old.]

veteran car *n. British.* A motor car made before 1919. Compare **vintage car.**

Veterans' Administration *n. Abbr.* **VA, V.A.** A Federal agency concerned with the welfare of veterans of the armed forces.

Veterans Day *n.* November 11, a national holiday celebrated in memory of the armistice ending World War I (1918) and in honor of veterans of the armed services. Formerly called "Armistice Day."

vet·er·i·na·ri·an (vĕt′ər-ə-nâr′ē-ən, vĕt′rə-) *n.* A person trained and authorized to treat animals medically.

vet·er·i·nar·y (vĕt′ər-ə-nĕr′ē, vĕt′rə-) *adj. Abbr.* **vet., veter.** Of, pertaining to, or designating the science of the diagnosis and treatment of diseases and injuries of animals, especially domestic animals.
~*n., pl.* **veterinaries.** A veterinarian. [Latin *veterīnārius,* from *veterīnae,* cattle.]

veterinary medicine *n.* The medical science of the prevention, diagnosis, and treatment of animal diseases and injuries. Also called "veterinary science."

veterinary surgeon *n. Abbr.* **V.S.** A veterinarian.

vet·i·ver (vĕt′ə-vər) *n.* **1.** A grass, *Vetiveria zizanioides,* of tropical Asia, cultivated for its aromatic roots that yield an oil used in perfumery. **2.** The root of this plant. [French *vetiver, vetyver,* from Tamil *veṭṭivēru* : *veṭṭi,* worthlessness + *vēru,* useless.]

ve·to (vē′tō) *n., pl.* **-toes. 1.** The vested power or constitutional right

of a sovereign or a branch or department of government, especially the right of a chief executive or an upper legislative body, to reject a bill passed by a (lower) legislative body and thus prevent or delay its enactment into law. **2.** The exercise of this right. **3.** The official document communicating the rejection and the reasons for it. Also called "veto message." **4.** The right of any full or permanent member of various other policy-making bodies, such as the United Nations Security Council, to prevent the passage of a resolution. **5.** Any authoritative prohibition or rejection of a proposed or intended act.
~*tr.v.* **vetoed, -toing, -toes. 1.** To prevent (a legislative bill) from becoming law by exercising the power of veto. **2.** To forbid or prevent authoritatively; prohibit. [Latin *vetō,* I forbid, from *vetāre*†, to forbid.] **—ve·to·er** *n.*

vex (vĕks) *tr.v.* **vexed, vexing, vexes. 1.** To irritate or annoy, as with petty matters; bother; pester. **2.** To cause serious suffering to; plague or afflict. **3.** To confuse; baffle; puzzle. **4.** *Formal.* To debate (a problem) at length; bring up repeatedly for discussion. **5.** *Archaic.* To toss about or stir up; agitate. —See Synonyms at **annoy.** [Middle English *vexen,* from Old French *vexer,* from Latin *vexāre,* to shake, annoy.] **—vex·er** *n.* **—vex·ing·ly** *adv.*

vex·a·tion (vĕk-sā'shən) *n.* **1.** The act of vexing. **2.** The state or condition of being vexed; annoyance. **3.** One that vexes; a source of irritation or annoyance.

vex·a·tious (vĕk-sā'shəs) *adj.* **1.** Causing or creating vexation; annoying; irksome. **2.** Full of vexation; disturbed; annoyed. **3.** *Law.* Instituted without sufficient grounds, to serve solely as an annoyance to a defendant. Said of legal actions. **—vex·a·tious·ly** *adv.* **—vex·a·tious·ness** *n.*

vexed (vĕkst) *adj.* **1.** Irritated; annoyed; troubled. **2.** Much debated; subject to controversy. Used chiefly in the phrase *a vexed question.* **—vex·ed·ly** (vĕk'sĭd-lē) *adv.* **—vex·ed·ness** *n.*

vex·il·lar·y (vĕk'sə-lĕr'ē) *n., pl.* **-ies. 1.** A member of the oldest class of army veterans who served under a special standard in ancient Rome. **2.** A standard-bearer.
~*adj.* Also **vex·il·lar** (vĕk'sə-lər). Of or pertaining to a banner or standard. [Latin *vexillārius,* from *vexillum,* flag. See **vexillum.**]

vex·il·late (vĕk'sə-lāt', vĕk-sĭl'ĭt) *adj.* Having a vexillum.

vex·il·lol·o·gy (vĕk'sĭ-lŏl'ə-jē) *n.* The study of flags. [Latin *vexillum,* flag + -LOGY.] **—vex·il·lol·o·gist** *n.*

vex·il·lum (vĕk-sĭl'əm) *n., pl.* **vexilla** (vĕk-sĭl'ə) **1.** *Botany.* A usually enlarged upper petal of certain flowers; a standard. **2.** *Zoology.* The weblike part of a feather; a vane. **3.** In ancient Rome, a military flag or standard. **4.** The small division of troops serving under such a standard. **5.** A ceremonial flag of a bishop, used especially in processions. [Latin, flag, diminutive of *vēlum,* cloth, veil, sail.]

V.F. 1. vicar forane. **2.** video frequency. **3.** visual field.

V format *n. Computer Science.* A method of presenting data-processor output in such a way as to begin each record with an indication of its length.

v.g. very good.

V.G. vicar general.

vhf, VHF very high frequency.

v.i. vide infra.

V.I. 1. Virgin Islands. **2.** volume indicator.

vi·a (vī'ə, vē'ə) *prep.* **1.** By way of; through. **2.** By means of. [Latin *viā,* ablative of *via,* road, way.]

vi·a·ble (vī'ə-bəl) *adj.* **1.** Capable of living. Said of a newborn infant, or a fetus that has reached the stage of development that will permit it to survive and develop under normal conditions. **2.** Capable of living, developing, or germinating under favorable conditions. Said of seeds, spores, or eggs. **3.** Capable of actualization, as a project might be; practicable: *a viable method of reducing costs.* —See Synonyms at **possible.** [French, from Old French, from *vie,* life, from Latin *vīta.*] **—vi·a·bil·i·ty** *n.*

Vi·a Do·lo·ro·sa (vī'ə dŏl'ə-rō'sə, vē'ə dō'lə-rō'sə) *n.* **1.** Jesus' route from Pilate's judgment hall to Calvary. **2.** A difficult or painful course or experience. [Latin, road of sorrow.]

vi·a·duct (vī'ə-dŭkt') *n.* A series of spans or arches used to carry a road or railroad over a wide valley or over other roads or railroads. [Latin *via,* road, way (see **via**) + (AQUA)DUCT.]

vi·al (vī'əl) *n.* A small container, usually glass, for liquids. Also called "phial."
~*tr.v.* **vialed** or **vialled, -aling** or **-alling, -als.** To put or keep in or as if in a vial. [Middle English *viole,* variant of *fiole,* PHIAL.]

vi·a me·di·a (vī'ə mē'dē-ə, vē'ə mā'dē-ə) *n.* A middle route, policy, or course avoiding extremes. [Latin.]

vi·and (vī'ənd) *n.* **1.** An article of food. **2. viands.** Provisions; victuals. [Middle English *viaunde,* from Old French *viande,* from Vulgar Latin *vī(v)anda* (unattested), variant of Latin *vīvenda,* gerundive of *vīvere,* to live.]

Viangchan. See **Vientiane.**

vi·at·ic (vī-ăt'ĭk) *adj.* Also **vi·at·i·cal** (-ĭ-kəl). Of or pertaining to traveling, a road, or a way. [Latin *viāticus.* See **viaticum.**]

vi·at·i·cum (vī-ăt'ĭ-kəm, vē-) *n., pl.* **-ca** (-kə) or **-cums. 1.** Holy communion as given to a dying person or one in danger of death. **2.** Supplies for a journey. [Latin *viāticum,* traveling provisions, from *viāticus,* of a road or journey, from *via,* way, road. See **via.**]

vibes (vībz) *pl.n.* **1.** *Slang.* An unspoken and often unconscious message given by one person or group to another, or the resulting emotional reaction; vibrations: *good vibes.* **2.** *Informal.* A vibraphone. [Shortened from VIBRATIONS.]

vi·brac·u·lum (vī-brăk'yə-ləm) *n., pl.* **-la** (-lə). *Zoology.* Any of the long, whiplike filaments on the surface of certain bryozoan colonies. [New Latin, diminutive formation from Latin *vibrāre,* to shake, brandish, VIBRATE.] **—vi·brac·u·lar** *adj.* **—vi·brac·u·loid** *adj.*

vi·bra·harp (vī'brə-härp') *n.* A **vibraphone** *(see).*

vi·brant (vī'brənt) *adj.* **1.** Exhibiting, characterized by, or resulting from vibration; vibrating. **2.** Pulsing or throbbing with energy or activity: *vibrant verse.* [Latin *vibrāre* (see **vibrate**) + -ANT.] **—vi·bran·cy** *n.* **—vi·brant·ly** *adv.*

vi·bra·phone (vī'brə-fōn') *n.* An electronic percussion instrument similar to a marimba but having metal bars and rotating disks in the resonators to produce a vibrato. Also called "vibraharp," informally "vibes." [VIBRA(TE) + -PHONE.] **—vi·bra·phon·ist** *n.*

vi·brate (vī'brāt') *v.* **-brated, -brating, -brates.** —*intr.* **1.** To move back and forth rapidly; oscillate. **2.** To produce a sound; resonate. **3.** To be moved emotionally; thrill: *vibrate with excitement.* **4.** To fluctuate or waver in making choices; vacillate. —*tr.* **1.** To cause to tremble or quiver. **2.** To cause to move back and forth rapidly. **3.** To produce (sound) by vibration. —See Synonyms at **swing.** [Latin *vibrāre.*]

vi·bra·tile (vī'brə-tĭl, -tīl') *adj.* **1.** Characterized by vibration. **2.** Capable of or adapted to vibratory motion. [French, from Latin *vibrāre,* VIBRATE.] **—vi·bra·til·i·ty** (vī'brə-tĭl'ə-tē) *n.*

vi·bra·tion (vī-brā'shən) *n.* **1.** The act or an instance of vibrating. **2.** The condition of being vibrated. **3.** *Physics.* **a.** A rapid linear motion of a particle or of an elastic solid about an equilibrium position. **b.** Any periodic process. **4.** A single complete vibrating motion; quiver; tremor. **5.** *Usually* **vibrations.** Also **vibes.** *Slang.* **a.** A distinctive emotional reaction by a person to another person or thing, capable of being instinctively sensed or experienced. **b.** The atmosphere or subtle message producing such a reaction. **—vi·bra·tion·al** *adj.*

vi·bra·to (vĭ-brä'tō, vē-) *n., pl.* **-tos.** *Music.* A tremulous or pulsating effect produced in an instrumental or vocal tone by barely perceptible minute and rapid variations in pitch. Compare **tremolo.** [Italian, from Latin *vibrātus,* past participle of *vibrāre,* VIBRATE.]

vi·bra·tor (vī'brā'tər) *n.* **1.** Something that vibrates. **2.** An electrically or battery operated device used for massage. **3.** A dildo with a vibrating tip, used for sexual stimulation. **4.** An electrical device consisting basically of a vibrating conductor interrupting a current.

vi·bra·to·ry (vī'brə-tôr'ē, -tōr'ē) *adj.* Also **vi·bra·tive** (vī'brā'tĭv, vī'brə-). **1.** Of, characterized by, or consisting of vibration. **2.** Causing vibration. **3.** Vibrating or capable of vibration.

vib·ri·o (vĭb'rē-ō') *n., pl.* **-os.** Any of various S-shaped or comma-shaped microorganisms of the genus *Vibrio,* especially *V. cholerae,* which causes cholera. [New Latin, arbitrarily from Latin *vibrāre,* VIBRATE (from their vibratory motion).] **—vib·ri·oid** (vĭb'rē-oid') *adj.*

vi·bris·sa (vī-brĭs'ə, vĭ-) *n., pl.* **-brissae** (-brĭs'ē). A stiff hair or hairlike projection, such as a nostril hair, any of the whiskers of a cat, or any of the modified feathers near the beak of an insectivorous bird. [Latin *vibrissae* (plural), from *vibrāre,* VIBRATE.]

vi·bur·num (vī-bûr'nəm) *n.* **1.** Any of various shrubs or trees of the genus *Viburnum,* characteristically having clusters of small white flowers and berrylike red or black fruit. **2.** The bark of certain of these trees containing substances used medicinally. [New Latin *Viburnum,* from Latin *vīburnum*†, wayfaring tree.]

vic. 1. vicar. **2.** vicinity.

vic·ar (vĭk'ər) *n. Abbr.* **vic. 1.** In the Church of England, the appointed priest of a parish. **2.** In the Episcopal Church of the United States, a clergyman in charge of a chapel. **3.** In the Anglican Communion generally, a clergyman acting in the place of a rector or bishop. **4.** *Roman Catholic Church.* A deputy or representative for an ecclesiastic. See **Vicar of Christ. 5.** One who fulfills the duties of another; substitute; deputy. [Middle English, from Old French *vicaire,* from Latin *vicārius,* a substitute, from *vicārius,* substituting, acting for, from *vicis,* change, turn, office.]

vic·ar·age (vĭk'ər-ĭj) *n.* **1.** The residence of a vicar. **2.** *Rare.* The benefice of a vicar. **3.** The duties or office of a vicar.

vicar apostolic *n., pl.* **vicars apostolic.** *Abbr.* **V.A.** *Roman Catholic Church.* **1. a.** A titular bishop who, as a representative of the Holy See, administers a region that is not yet a diocese. **b.** A titular bishop appointed to administer a vacant see in which the succession of bishops has been interrupted. **2.** Formerly, a bishop delegated by the pope to act in his stead in a particular region.

vicar fo·rane (vĭk'ər fô-rān', fō-) *n., pl.* **vicars forane.** *Abbr.* **V.F.** *Roman Catholic Church.* A priest who by a bishop's appointment exercises limited jurisdiction over the clergy in a distant district of a diocese. [From Late Latin *forānus,* FOREIGN.]

vicar general *n., pl.* **vicars general.** *Abbr.* **V.G. 1.** *Roman Catholic Church.* A priest acting as deputy to a bishop to assist him in the administration of his diocese. **2.** An ecclesiastical official, usually a layman, who assists an Anglican archbishop or bishop in administrative and judicial duties.

vi·car·i·al (vī-kâr'ē-əl, vĭ-) *adj.* **1.** Of or pertaining to a vicar or vicars. **2.** Acting as or having the position of a vicar. **3.** Vicarious or delegated, as powers of an ecclesiastical office might be.

vi·car·i·ate (vī-kâr'ē-ĭt, -āt', vĭ-) *n.* Also **vic·ar·ate** (vĭk'ər-ĭt). **1.** The office rank, or authority of a vicar. **2.** The district under a vicar's jurisdiction. [Medieval Latin *vicāriātus,* from Late Latin *vicārius,* vicar, VICARIOUS.]

vi·car·i·ous (vī-kâr'ē-əs, vĭ-) *adj.* **1.** Performed or endured by one person substituting for another; fulfilled by the substitution of the actual offender with some other person or thing: *vicarious punish-*

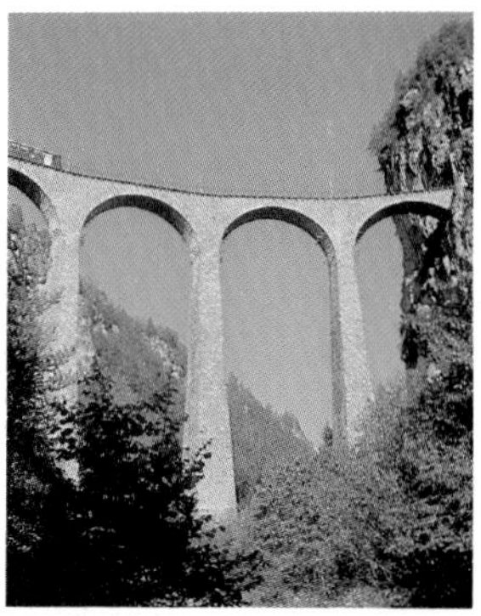

viaduct *A railroad viaduct crosses a sheer-sided valley near Filisur, in Switzerland.*

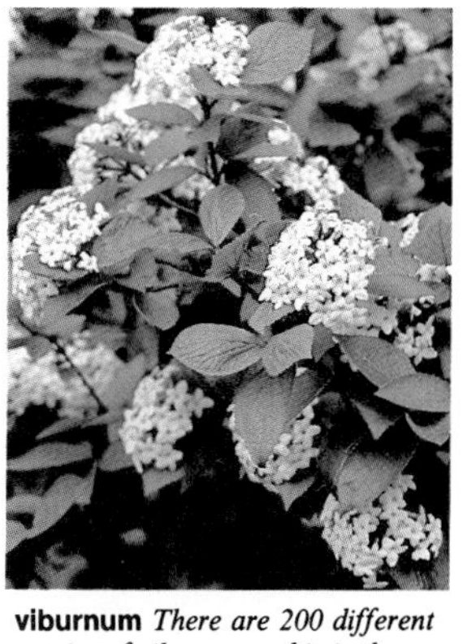

viburnum *There are 200 different species of viburnum—this is the hybrid shrub* Viburnum juddii. *The genus, which is common in temperate regions around the world, also includes the guelder rose and the wayfaring tree.*

ment. **2.** Acting in place of someone or something else; delegated; substituted: *a vicarious power of authority.* **3.** Experienced or enjoyed through sympathetic or imaginative participation in the experiences of another: *a vicarious thrill.* **4.** *Physiology.* Occurring in or performed by a part of the body not normally associated with a certain function. [Latin *vicārius,* substituting, from *vicis,* change, turn, office.] —**vi·car·i·ous·ly** *adv.* —**vi·car·i·ous·ness** *n.*

Vicar of Christ *n. Roman Catholic Church.* The pope considered as the earthly deputy of Christ.

vic·ar·ship (vĭk′ər-shĭp′) *n.* The office or tenure of a vicar.

vice¹ (vīs) *n.* **1.** An evil, degrading, or immoral practice or habit; a serious moral failing. **2.** Wicked or evil conduct or habits; indulgence in degrading practices; depravity; corruption. **3. a.** Sexual immorality; especially, prostitution. **b.** Sexual perversion. **4.** A slight personal failing; a foible: *His only vice is a partiality for practical jokes.* **5.** A flaw or imperfection; defect; fault: *the vices in his theory.* **6.** *Archaic.* A physical defect or weakness. **7.** An item of abnormal or perverse behavior in a domestic animal, such as a tendency in a horse to bite. **8. Vice.** A character representing a particular or generalized vice, often represented in English morality plays as a jester or buffoon. —See Synonyms at **fault.** [Middle English, from Old French, from Latin *vitium,* blemish, offense, vice.]

vice² Variant of **vise.**

vice³ *n. Abbr.* **v., V.** Someone who acts in the place of another; a deputy.

~*prep.* **vi·ce** (vī′sē). In place of; replacing. [Latin *vice,* ablative of *vicis,* change.]

vice– *prefix.* Indicates one representing or substituting or able to act or deputize for another; for example, **vice-chairman,** **vice-chamberlain, viceregal.** [Middle English *vis–,* from Old French, from Late Latin *vice–,* from Latin *vice,* in place of, VICE.]

vice admiral *n. Abbr.* **V.A., V. Adm.** An officer in the Navy or Coast Guard ranking next below an admiral.

vice-ad·mi·ral·ty (vīs-ăd′mər-əl-tē) *n., pl.* **-ties.** The office, rank, or command of a vice admiral.

vice-chan·cel·lor (vīs-chăn′sə-lər, -chăns′lər) *n. Abbr.* **V.C. 1.** *Law.* A judge in equity courts ranking below a chancellor. **2.** A deputy or assistant chancellor in a university. **3.** A deputy or substitute for a head of state or official bearing the title chancellor. —**vice-chan·cel·lor·ship** *n.*

vice-con·sul (vīs-kŏn′səl) *n. Abbr.* **V.C.** A consular officer who is subordinate to and a deputy of a consul or consul general. —**vice-con·su·lar** *adj.* —**vice-con·su·late** *n.* —**vice-con·sul·ship** *n.*

vice-ge·ren·cy (vīs-jîr′ən-sē) *n., pl.* **-cies. 1.** The position, function, or authority of a vicegerent. **2.** A district under a vicegerent's jurisdiction.

vice-ge·rent (vīs-jîr′ənt) *n.* **1.** A person appointed by a ruler or head of state to act as an administrative deputy. **2.** *Roman Catholic Church.* **a.** The pope. **b.** Any other bishop or priest considered as the earthly deputy of God or Christ. [Medieval Latin *vicegerēns* : VICE- + GERENT.] —**vice-ge·ral, vice-ge·rent** *adj.*

vi·cen·nar·y (vīs′ə-nĕr′ē) *adj.* **1.** Consisting of or pertaining to 20. **2.** Designating a notation system based on 20. [Latin *vīcēnārius,* from *vīcēnī,* 20 each, from *vīgintī,* 20.]

vi·cen·ni·al (vī-sĕn′ē-əl) *adj.* **1.** Happening once every 20 years. **2.** Existing or lasting for 20 years. [Late Latin *vīcennium,* period of 20 years : Latin *vīciēs,* 20 times, from *vīgintī,* 20 + *annus,* year.]

Vi·cen·za (vē-chĕn′zä). City in Venetia, northeastern Italy. The capital of Vicenza province, it is an industrial center. A powerful medieval city, it has a Gothic cathedral and some fine examples of Palladian architecture.

vice president *Abbr.* **V.P., V. Pres. 1.** An officer ranking immediately below a president, usually empowered to assume the president's duties under such conditions as absence, illness, or death. **2.** A deputy of a president, especially in a large business enterprise, in charge of a separate department or location: *vice president in charge of marketing.* —**vice-pres·i·den·cy** (vīs-prĕz′ĭ-dən-sē, -dĕn′-) *n.* —**vice-pres·i·den·tial** (vīs′prĕz′ĭ-dĕn′shəl) *adj.*

vice-re·gal (vīs-rē′gəl) *adj.* **1.** Of or pertaining to a viceroy. **2.** *Chiefly Australian.* Of or pertaining to a governor-general. [VICE- + REGAL.] —**vice-re·gal·ly** *adv.*

vice regent (vīs-rē′jənt) *n.* One who acts as a regent's deputy. —**vice-re·gen·cy** (vīs-rē′jən-sē) *n.* —**vice-re·gent** *adj.*

vice-reine (vīs′rān′) *n.* **1.** The wife of a viceroy. **2.** *Rare.* A woman who functions as a viceroy. [French : VICE- + *reine,* queen, from Latin *rēgīna,* feminine of *rēx,* king.]

vice·roy (vīs′roi′) *n., pl.* **-roys. 1.** A governor of a country, province, or colony, ruling as the representative of a sovereign or king. **2.** An orange and black North American butterfly, *Limenitis archippus,* resembling but somewhat smaller than the monarch. [French : *vice-* + *roi,* king, from Latin *rēx.*]

vice·roy·al·ty (vīs′roi′əl-tē, vīs-roi′-) *n., pl.* **-ties. 1.** The office, rank, or authority of a viceroy. **2.** The term of service of a viceroy. **3.** A district or province governed by a viceroy. Also called "viceroyship."

vice squad *n.* A police division charged with the control of vice, especially prostitution and gambling.

vi·ce ver·sa (vī′sə vûr′sə, vīs′-) *Abbr.* **v.v.** The order or meaning being reversed; with principal items transposed; conversely. Said of a preceding statement: *He betrayed her, or vice versa.* [Latin, "the position being changed" : *vice,* ablative singular of *vicis,* change,

office, position + *versā,* ablative feminine singular of *versus,* past participle of *vertere,* to turn, change.]

Vi·chy (vĭsh′ē, vē-shē′). A health resort of central France. Situated on the Allier River in the Allier department, it is world famous for its mineral springs. During World War II it was the seat of the Pétain government.

vi·chy·ssoise (vĭsh′ē-swäz′, vē′shē-) *n.* A thick, creamy leek and potato soup, usually served cold. [French, "of Vichy."]

Vichy water *n.* **1.** A naturally effervescent mineral water from the springs at Vichy, France, reputed to have medicinal benefits. **2.** Any sparkling mineral water resembling this. Also called "Vichy," "vichy."

vic·i·nage (vĭs′ə-nĭj) *n.* **1. a.** A limited region around a particular area; neighborhood; vicinity. **b.** A number of places collectively that are situated near one another. **2.** The residents of a particular neighborhood. **3.** The state of living in a neighborhood; proximity; nearness. [Middle English *vesinage,* from Old French *visenage,* from Vulgar Latin *vīcīnāticum* (unattested), from *vīcīnus,* neighbor. See **vicinity.**]

vic·i·nal (vĭs′ə-nəl) *adj.* **1.** Of, belonging to, or restricted to a limited area or neighborhood; nearby; adjacent. **2.** Designating a local road as opposed to a main road or highway. **3.** *Crystallography.* Approximating, resembling, or taking the place of a fundamental crystal form or face. Compare **gem. 4.** *Chemistry.* Designating or pertaining to the consecutive positions of substituted elements or radicals on a benzene ring. [Latin *vīcīnālis,* from *vīcīnus,* neighbor. See **vicinity.**]

vi·cin·i·ty (vĭ-sĭn′ə-tē) *n., pl.* **-ties.** *Abbr.* **vic. 1.** The state of being near in space or relationship; proximity; propinquity: *two restaurants in close vicinity.* **2.** A nearby, surrounding, or adjoining region; neighborhood; locality. [Latin *vīcīnitās* (stem *vīcīnitāt-*), from *vīcīnus,* neighbor, from *vīcus,* village.]

vi·cious (vĭsh′əs) *adj.* **1.** Having the nature of vice, evil, or immorality; depraved; debased. **2.** Addicted to vice, immorality, or depravity; malicious; reprobate; evil. **3.** Characterized by spite or malice: *vicious gossip.* **4.** Failing to meet a standard or criterion; having a fault, flaw, or defect: *a vicious syllogism.* **5.** *Archaic.* Impure; foul; diseased. **6.** Disposed to or characterized by violence or destructive behavior. **7.** Behaving in an unruly or potentially dangerous manner: *a vicious animal.* **8.** Being of an extreme or intense degree: *a vicious hurricane.* —See Synonyms at **cruel.** [Middle English, from Old French, from Latin *vitiōsus,* from *vitium,* VICE.] —**vi·cious·ly** *adv.* —**vi·cious·ness** *n.*

vicious circle *n.* **1.** A situation in which the solution of one problem in a chain of circumstances creates a new problem that leads back to the original problem and increases the difficulty of solving it. **2.** A condition in which a disorder or disease gives rise to another which subsequently affects the first. **3.** *Logic.* See **circle** (sense 10).

vi·cis·si·tude (vĭ-sĭs′ə-tōod′, -tyōod′) *n.* **1.** *Usually* **vicissitudes.** Any change or variation in something; mutability. **2.** Natural change or variation; alterations manifested in nature and human affairs. **3.** An alteration or variation in fortune. **4.** An alternating change; a succession. [From French, from Latin *vicissitūdō,* from *vicissim,* in turn, from *vicis,* change, turn.]

vi·cis·si·tu·di·nar·y (vĭ-sĭs′ə-tōod′n-ĕr′ē, -tyōod′-) *adj.* Also **vi·cis·si·tu·di·nous** (-əs). Characterized by or subject to vicissitudes.

Vick·ers (vĭk′ərz), **Jon** (1926–). Canadian tenor. He is acclaimed for his performances in operas by Wagner and Verdi.

Vicks·burg (vĭks′bûrg′). City of western Mississippi, on the Mississippi River at its confluence with the Yazoo River. It was the site of a siege in the Civil War that culminated in the surrender of the Confederate forces (1863).

Vi·co (vē′kō), **Giambattista** or **Giovanni Battista** (1668–1744). Italian historical philosopher. He was the first philosopher to see history in terms of the rise and fall of human societies and to make use of myths and legends as historical evidence.

vic·tim (vĭk′tĭm) *n.* **1.** Someone who is put to death or subjected to torture or suffering by another. **2.** A living creature slain and offered as a sacrifice to a deity or as part of a religious rite. **3.** One who is harmed or made to suffer from an act, circumstance, agency, or condition: *victims of war.* **4.** A person who suffers injury, loss, or death as a result of a voluntary undertaking: *a victim of his own scheming.* **5.** A person who is tricked, swindled, or taken advantage of; a dupe. [Latin *victima.*]

vic·tim·ize (vĭk′tə-mīz′) *tr.v.* **-ized, -izing, -izes. 1.** To single out unfairly for punishment or abuse; discriminate against and bully. **2.** To subject to a swindle or fraud. **3.** To make a victim of by or as if by slaying. —**vic·tim·i·za·tion** *n.* —**vic·tim·iz·er** *n.*

vic·tim·less (vĭk′tĭm-lĭs) *adj.* Designating a legal offense, such as possession of drugs, in which there is no victim involved, except perhaps the offender himself.

vic·tor (vĭk′tər) *n.* **1.** One who defeats or vanquishes an adversary; the winner in a fight, battle, or war. **2.** A winner of a contest or struggle. [Middle English, from Latin, from *vincere* (past participle *victus*), to conquer.]

Vic·tor Em·man·u·el II (vĭk′tər ĭ-măn′yōo-əl) (1820–78). The last king of Sardinia and first king of Italy. He became king of Sardinia (1849–61) on the abdication of his father, Charles Albert. After becoming king of Italy (1861), he completed its unification by acquiring Venice (1866) and Rome (which he made his capital in 1871).

vic·to·ri·a (vĭk-tôr′ē-ə, -tōr′ē-ə) *n.* **1.** A low, light, four-wheeled carriage for two with a folding top and an elevated driver's seat in front. **2.** A touring car with a folding top usually covering only the rear seat. **3.** A victoria plum *(see).* **4.** Any of various water lilies of the South American genus *Victoria,* having large, round, floating leaves. [After Queen VICTORIA.]

Vic·to·ri·a¹ (vĭk-tôr′ē-ə, -tōr′-). State of southeastern Australia. The second smallest and most densely populated of the Australian states, it is, with irrigation, a leading farming region, producing cereals, fruits and vegetables, dairy produce, wine, meat, and wool. It supplies some 70 percent of Australia's petroleum, its other minerals including natural gas, brown coal, and gold. Victoria's industries, concentrated around the capital, Melbourne, include metals and machinery, textiles, clothing, footwear, and vehicles.

Victoria². The capital of British Columbia, Canada. Situated on the southeastern tip of Vancouver Island, it was founded (1843) by the Hudson Bay Company.

Victoria³. Capital of Hong Kong. Lying on the northeastern shore of Hong Kong Island, it is the colony's biggest city and chief port. It is also known as Hong Kong.

Victoria⁴. Capital and only urban center and port of the Seychelles. It is located on Mahé Island.

Victoria, Lake. Also **Victoria Ny·an·za** (nī-ăn′zə). Africa's largest lake and the world's second-largest freshwater body. It covers 69,452 square kilometers (26,815 square miles) and lies in a shallow depression between the two arms of the Great Rift Valley. The Victoria Nile is its only outlet. The lake was originally named Lake Ukerewe.

Victoria, Queen (1819–1901). Queen of Great Britain and Empress of India. She was the daughter of George III's fourth son, Edward, Duke of Kent, and became queen (1837) on the death of her uncle, William IV. In 1876 she was proclaimed empress of India by Disraeli. Her great sense of duty and strict moral code set the pattern for 19th-century Britain. During her reign constitutional government was fully developed and the crown's prestige restored.

Victoria Cross *n. Abbr.* **V.C.** An award in the shape of a bronze Maltese cross, the highest military decoration in the British and Commonwealth armed forces for conspicuous valor.

Victoria Falls. Falls on the Zambezi River, on the border between Zambia and Zimbabwe. There are three main sections: the Eastern Cataract, the Rainbow Falls, and the Main Falls. Forming the world's third-largest falls, their total width can span over a kilometer (just over half a mile). They were discovered (1855) by David Livingstone and named in honor of Queen Victoria.

Victoria Land. Section of eastern Antarctica, south of new Zealand. Bounded on the east by Ross Sea and on the west by Wilkes Land, it consists of ranges of the Transantarctic Mts., with a high plateau in the interior.

Vic·to·ri·an (vĭk-tôr′ē-ən, -tōr′ē-ən) *adj.* **1.** Of or pertaining to Queen Victoria or the period of her reign: *a Victorian novel.* **2.** Exhibiting qualities usually associated with the time of Queen Victoria, such as moral severity or hypocrisy, middle-class stuffiness, and pompous conservatism. **3.** Pertaining to, designating, or constructed in the highly ornamented, massive style of architecture, decor, and furnishings popular in 19th-century England. **4.** Of or pertaining to any of the various geographical units named Victoria. ~*n.* A person belonging to or exhibiting characteristics typical of the period of Queen Victoria.

Vic·to·ri·a·na (vĭk-tôr′ē-ăn′ə, -ä′nə, -tōr′-) *n. Used with a singular verb.* Assorted objects such as photographs and ornaments of the Victorian period. [VICTORIA + -ANA.] See feature, next page.

Vic·to·ri·an·ism (vĭk-tôr′ē-ə-nĭz′əm, vĭk-tōr′-) *n.* **1.** The state of having Victorian characteristics, as in attitude, style, or taste. **2.** Something exhibiting Victorian characteristics.

victoria plum *n.* A plum of a variety having large, red, sweet fruits. Also called "victoria." [After Queen VICTORIA.]

vic·to·ri·ous (vĭk-tôr′ē-əs, -tōr′ē-əs) *adj.* **1.** Having overcome an opponent or enemy; triumphant; conquering. **2.** Characteristic of or expressing a sense of victory or fulfillment: *a victorious smile.* [Middle English, from Latin *victōriōsus,* from *victōria,* VICTORY.] —**vic·to·ri·ous·ly** *adv.* —**vic·to·ri·ous·ness** *n.*

vic·to·ry (vĭk′tə-rē) *n., pl.* **-ries.** *Abbr.* **V 1.** Final and complete defeat of the enemy in a military engagement. **2.** Any successful struggle against an opponent or obstacle. **3.** The state of having triumphed. [Middle English, from Old French *victorie,* from Latin *victōria,* from *victor,* VICTOR.]

Usage: victory, conquest, triumph. These nouns refer to the fact of winning, as in war or in a competition. *Victory,* the general term, is broadly interchangeable with the others but lacks their overtones. *Conquest* connotes physically subjugating or harnessing something, such as an enemy nation or a rampaging river, or it can refer to surmounting (a mountain peak) or overcoming barriers to knowledge, understanding, and control: *conquest of yellow fever. Triumph* refers to a victory or success that is especially noteworthy because it is decisive, significant, or spectacular.

vic·tress (vĭk′trĭs) *n.* A woman who is a victor.

vict·ual (vĭt′l) *n.* Also *nonstandard* **vit·tle.** *Usually* **victuals. 1.** Food fit for human consumption. **2.** Provisions; food supplies. ~*v.* **victualed** or **-ualled, -ualing** or **-ualling, -uals.** Also *nonstandard* **vit·tle, -tled, -tling, -tles.** —*tr.* To provide with food. —*intr.* **1.** To lay in food supplies. **2.** *Rare.* To eat. [Middle English *vitaille,* from Old French, from Late Latin *victuālia,* plural of *victuālis,* pro-

vision, from Latin *victus,* sustenance, from the past participle of *vīvere,* to live.]

vict·ual·er (vĭt′lər) *n.* Also **vict·ual·ler. 1.** A supplier of victuals; a sutler. **2.** A supply ship. **3.** *Chiefly British.* One who is allowed to sell alcohol, such as an innkeeper or publican.

vi·cu·ña (vĭ-kōōn′yə, -kōō′nə, -kyōō′nə, vī-) *n.* Also **vi·cu·na. 1.** A llamalike ruminant mammal, *Vicugna vicugna,* of the central Andes, having fine, silky fleece. **2. a.** The fleece of this animal. **b.** Fabric made from this fleece. [Spanish, from Quechua *wikúña.*]

Vi·dal (vĭ-däl′), **Gore** (1925–). U.S. novelist and essayist. His works include *Burr* (1974), a historical study, and *Myra Breckinridge* (1968), a satirical novel.

vi·de (vī′dē, vē′dā′) *Latin. Abbr.* **v., vid.** See. Used to direct a reader's attention: *vide page 64.* [Imperative of *vidēre,* to see.]

vide an·te (ăn′tē) *Latin.* See before.

vide in·fra (ĭn′frə) *Abbr.* **v.i.** *Latin.* See below.

vi·de·li·cet (vĭ-dĕl′ə-sĭt) *adv. Abbr.* **viz.** That is; namely. Used to introduce examples, lists, or items. See note at **viz.** [Latin *vidēlicet,* it is easy (literally, permissible) to see, plainly, namely : *vidēre,* to see (see **vide**) + *licet,* it is permitted, from *licēre,* to be permitted. See **leisure.**]

vid·e·o (vĭd′ē-ō′) *adj.* Of or pertaining to television, especially to systems for recording and playing back television sound and images. ~*n., pl.* **videos. 1.** A video cassette recorder or video player. **2.** A recording made for playing back on a television set. **3.** A short video film made as promotional material or especially to accompany the playing of a pop music record. **4.** The visual portion of a televised broadcast, as distinguished from **audio** *(see).* **5.** Television: *a star of stage, screen, and video.* [From Latin *vidēre,* to see. See **vide.**]

video camera *n.* A small hand-held camera similar to a motion-picture camera but recording on video cassettes for subsequent playback through a television set.

video cassette *n.* A videotape contained in a cassette.

video cassette recorder *n. Abbr.* **VCR** A device for receiving broadcast television signals and for recording and playing back television pictures and sound by means of magnetic tape cassettes. Also called "video."

vid·e·o·disc (vĭd′ē-ō-dĭsk′) *n.* Also **vid·e·o·disk.** A flat disc on which moving pictures and sound are recorded for playing through a television set. A laser beam is used to sense variations in height on the surface of the disc, and convert them into electronic pulses for playback.

video display terminal *n. Abbr.* **VDT** A visual display unit *(see).*

video frequency *n.* A frequency suitable for use in producing television images, lying in the range 50 hertz to 5 megahertz.

video game *n.* Any of various games, played either between two persons or between one person and the machine, in which electronic controls are manipulated to maneuver small images on a display screen such as a television screen.

vid·e·o·gen·ic (vĭd′ē-ō-jĕn′ĭk) *adj.* Appearing to advantage on television; telegenic. [VIDEO + (PHOTO)GENIC.]

Vid·e·o·phone (vĭd′ē-ō-fōn′) *n.* A trademark for a communication device that incorporates both telephone and television, allowing two people to talk to each other and see each other at the same time. [VIDEO + (TELE)PHONE.]

video player *n.* A device for playing video discs or tapes through a television set. Also called "video."

video recorder *n.* A device for recording and playing back television signals using magnetic tape, cassettes, or other media. Also called "videotape recorder."

Vid·e·o·scan (vĭd′ē-ō-skăn′) *n.* A trademark for a technique of machine character recognition in which a video camera records the shapes of the characters and matches the signals with data held in machine storage.

vid·e·o·tape (vĭd′ē-ō-tāp′) *n.* A relatively wide **magnetic tape** *(see)* used to record television images, usually together with the associated sound, for subsequent playback or broadcasting. —**vid·e·o·tape** *v.*

videotape recorder *n.* A device used for making a videotape recording.

video terminal *n.* A visual display unit *(see).*

vid·e·o·tex (vĭd′ē-ō-tĕks′) *n.* Any system for transmitting a wide variety of computer-stored information in teletext or viewdata form.

vide post (pōst) *Latin.* See below; see after.

vide su·pra (sōō′prə) *Abbr.* **v.s.** *Latin.* See above.

vi·dette. Variant of **vedette.**

vid·i·con (vĭd′ə-kŏn′) *n.* A small television camera tube that forms a charge-density image on a photoconductive surface for subsequent electron-beam scanning, used especially for hand-held cameras and closed-circuit television. [VID(EO) + ICON(OSCOPE).]

vie (vī) *v.* **vied, vying, vies.** —*intr.* To strive for victory or superiority; contend; compete, as in an athletic contest. Used with *for* or *with.* —*tr. Archaic.* **1.** To offer or display for the sake of competition; match. **2.** To wager; bet. —See Synonyms at **rival.** [Shortened from Middle English *envien,* from Old French *envier,* to challenge, bid, from Latin *invītāre,* INVITE.]

Vi·en·na (vē-ĕn′ə). *German* **Wien** (vēn). The capital of Austria, on the Danube River. In 1918, with the collapse of the Austro-Hungarian empire, Vienna was reduced from being the capital of one of the world's largest empires to the capital of a small country. Hitler's

Victoriana

POPULAR ART OF THE VICTORIAN AGE

Increased wealth created a new demand for household ornaments

The reign of Queen Victoria (1837–1901) in Britain was a period of industrial expansion when new techniques of mass production made household goods cheaper and more widely available. Increased prosperity also created a fresh demand for decorative art, but because the new middle class had no tradition of art appreciation, its taste was largely for bright, gaudy, ornate goods. Victoriana—the everyday art of the Victorian period—varies greatly in style and quality of construction. Although much of it lacks sophistication by today's standards, there is some which modern taste finds highly desirable.

Throughout the period there was a demand for papier-mâché goods such as firescreens, trays, and small tables, which were varnished and sometimes inlaid with mother-of-pearl. Increased wealth and travel by the newly developed railroads led to a demand for souvenirs from places people visited. Fairings—china figures with captions on the bases—were popular souvenirs at fairs, and potteries produced miniatures of Bronze Age vases, Roman ewers, and Celtic drinking cups. Colored glass bowls,

vases, and candlestick holders were popular, as was painted tinware. In the 1860's the advent of electroplating led to the demise of the Sheffield-plate industry, and surviving examples of the silverplated products are much sought after today. Other examples of Victoriana include statues made of brass or gunmetal, ornate clocks, and embroideries for wall hanging.

The movement to greater ornament and richness was exemplified by the Great Exhibition of 1851 at the Crystal Palace in London, at which many exhibits were grotesquely overelaborate. In contrast, however, many copies of Sheraton and Hepplewhite furniture designs were being made by the 1870's. In late Victorian times the designer and craftsman William Morris helped lead a move to greater simplicity of design and better workmanship; and Japanese art was discovered in the 1890's. In modern times Victoriana has become much sought after since it exists in sufficient quantities to be within the range of most collectors. Even where it lacks sophistication it often has an innocent charm.

A VICTORIAN DRAWING ROOM *This drawing room shows the Victorian love of decoration, with every available space filled with ornaments. On the high wall shelf there are vases and dishes and beneath them are drawings, paintings, and early photographs. Other ornaments include a bronze nymph, copies of Etruscan vases, and gilt Venetian mirrors.*

march into Vienna (1938) temporarily united Austria and Germany, but at the end of World War II the Allies divided the city into occupied sectors; it was not until 1955 that it was again a free city. An important cultural center, Vienna was the home of Haydn, Mozart, Beethoven, Schubert, Brahms, Mahler, and Strauss. **—Vi·en·nese** *n. & adj.*

Vienna sausage *n.* A small sausage resembling a frankfurter, often served as an hors d'oeuvre.

Vien·tiane (vyĕn-tyän′). Also **Viang·chan** (vyäng-chän′). Capital and largest city of Laos. It is on the north bank of the Mekong (the border with Thailand) and has many canals. It is the country's main trade outlet via Bangkok and has been its capital since 1899. Nearby is the ruined capital of a Lao kingdom (1707–1827).

Vi·et·cong (vĕ′ĕt-kŏng′, vyĕt′-) *n., pl.* **Vietcong.** Also **Vi·et Cong.** *Abbr.* **V.C. 1.** In the Vietnam war, the National Liberation Front of South Vietnam, a communist revolutionary movement. **2.** The guerrilla and armed forces of this movement. **3.** A member of this movement or these forces. [Short for Vietnamese *Viet Nam Cong Sam,* Vietnamese Communist.] **—Vi·et·cong** *adj.*

Vi·et·minh (vĕ′ĕt-mĭn′, vyĕt′-) *n., pl.* **Vietminh.** Also **Vi·et Minh. 1.** The Vietnamese league for national independence formed by an alliance of patriotic and revolutionary forces under the leadership of Ho Chi Minh that defeated the Japanese and the French between 1941 and 1954. **2.** A member of this front, especially of its armed forces. [Vietnamese, short for *Viet Nam Doc Lap Dong Minh Hoi,* Vietnam Federation of Independence.] **—Vi·et·minh** *adj.*

Vi·et·nam or **Vi·et Nam** (vĕ-ĕt′näm′, -näm′, vyĕt′-). State of Southeast Asia. It has two fertile rice-growing areas, the Mekong and Red-Black river deltas, separated by the Annamese range. The Kinh (Han Chinese people) founded the province of Tonkin in North Vietnam (c. 100 B.C.). Independent by 939, it expanded to control all Vietnam by 1802 but was incorporated into French Indochina in the late 19th century. Liberation movements arose, and the Vietminh, active during the Japanese occupation of World War II, defeated the French at Dien Bien Phu (1954). The country was then divided at the 17th parallel into North Vietnam, a Soviet puppet state led by Ho Chi Minh, and South Vietnam. The French withdrew from the south (1956), and after 1960 the north attempted to destabilize it. This brought U.S. intervention to aid the south, which ended in 1973. The south fell to the communists (1975), and the present state was set up (1976). Ethnic Chinese began fleeing the country (1978), and Vietnamese "boat people" became an international refugee problem. Vietnam occupied Kampuchea in late 1978. Some 70 percent of Vietnamese are farmers, and since 1976 there have been government development schemes, and reallocation of land. The north's considerable mineral resources, including coal, lignite, iron ore, chrome, bauxite, oil and gas, have been used in rapid industrialization. Vietnam is a member of Comecon. Area, 329,556 square kilometers (127,209 square miles). Population, 52,700,000. Capital, Hanoi.

Vi·et·nam·ese (vē′ĕt-nə-mēz′, -mēs′, vyĕt′-) n., pl. **Vietnamese.** **1.** A native or inhabitant of Vietnam. **2.** The language of Vietnam, commonly considered as belonging to the Mon-Khmer subfamily of Austro-Asiatic languages. Formerly called "Annamese." —**Vi·et·nam·ese** adj.

view (vyōō) n. **1.** An examination or inspection. **2.** A systematic survey; coverage: *a wide-ranging view of trends in philosophy.* **3.** *Often* **views.** A specific perception, observation, or interpretation; a thought: *her views on the situation.* **4.** *Often* **views.** A personal opinion. **5.** The field of vision: *The ship came into view.* **6. a.** A prospect or vista: *From here you get a fine view of the town.* **b.** Visual access or vantage: *a room with a view.* **c.** A picture of a landscape. **d.** An aspect, as of something seen from a given vantage point. **7.** Consideration: *have a plan in view.* **8.** Expectation; chance: *has no view of success.* **9.** In hunting, especially fox-hunting, a sighting of the quarry. **10.** *Law.* A formal inspection by a judge or jury of a corpse, a disputed property, or the scene of an alleged crime. —See Synonyms at **opinion.** —**in view of.** Taking into account; in consideration of. —**on view.** Being exhibited; placed so as to be seen. —**take a dim** (or **poor**) **view of.** To regard disapprovingly or unfavorably. —**with a view to.** With the intention or hope of. ~tr.v. **viewed, viewing, views. 1.** To see; behold; be present at a showing of: *view the exhibition.* **2.** To examine; inspect: *view the totals.* **3.** To survey or study mentally; consider: *We view the recent developments with alarm.* **4.** In hunting, especially fox-hunting, to sight (the quarry). **5.** To watch (television). **6.** To visit and inspect (a house, for example) when considering a purchase. **7.** *Law.* To inspect formally (a corpse, a disputed property, or the scene of an alleged crime). —See Synonyms at **see.** [Middle English *vewe,* from Old French *veue,* from the feminine past participle of *veoir,* to see, from Latin *vidēre.*]

VIETNAM

view·da·ta (vyōō′dāt′ə, -dăt′ə) n. **1.** A two-way system for transmitting information to subscribers by telephone or cable television to an adapted television set or computer terminal. **2.** Information transmitted by this method.

view·er (vyōō′ər) n. **1.** One who views; especially, one who views television. **2.** Any of various optical devices used to facilitate the viewing of photographic transparencies by illuminating or magnifying them.

view·find·er (vyōō′fīn′dər) n. A system of lenses in a camera enabling the operator to see the scene that is to be photographed. Also called "finder."

view hal·loo, view hal·loa (vyōō′hə-lōō′) n. **1.** A strident call given during a fox hunt by a servant or a follower to inform the huntsman that a fox has been sighted. **2.** A loud cry or clarion call announcing a sudden appearance or advent. ~interj. Used in fox-hunting to announce the sighting of a fox.

view·ing (vyōō′ĭng) n. **1.** The act or habit of watching television. **2.** Television programs collectively: *prime-time viewing.*

view·less (vyōō′lĭs) adj. **1.** Lacking a view. **2.** *Poetic.* Invisible.

view·point (vyōō′point′) n. A point of view.

vi·ges·i·mal (vī-jĕs′ə-məl) adj. **1.** Twentieth. **2.** Proceeding or occurring in intervals of 20. **3.** Based on or pertaining to 20. [From Latin *vīgēsimus, vīcēsimus,* twentieth, from *vīcēnī,* twenty each, from *vīgintī,* twenty.]

vig·il (vĭj′əl) n. **1. a.** A watch kept during normal sleeping hours. **b.** The duration of such a watch. **2.** The eve of a religious festival as observed by devotional watching. **3.** *Usually* **vigils.** Ritual devotions observed on the eve of a holy day. [Middle English *vigile,* from Old French, from Latin *vigilia,* from *vigil,* alert.]

vig·i·lance (vĭj′ə-ləns) n. **1.** The state or quality of being vigilant; watchfulness. **2.** A chronic inability to sleep.

vigilance committee n. A volunteer group of citizens that without authority takes on itself powers such as pursuing and punishing those suspected of being criminals or offenders.

vig·i·lant (vĭj′ə-lənt) adj. On the alert; watchful. [Middle English, from Old French, from Latin *vigilāns* (stem *vigilant-*), present participle of *vigilāre,* to be alert, from *vigil,* alert.] —**vig·i·lant·ly** adv.

vig·i·lan·te (vĭj′ə-lăn′tē) n. One belonging to a vigilance committee. [Spanish, from Latin *vigilāns,* VIGILANT.]

vigil light n. **1.** A small candle kept burning in the chancel of some Christian churches to symbolize the presence of the Blessed Sacrament; an altar light. **2.** A candle lit by a worshiper for a special devotional purpose.

vi·gnette (vĭn-yĕt′) n. **1. a.** An unenclosed decorative design placed at the beginning or end of a book or a chapter of a book. **b.** Decorative tracery along the border of a page. **2.** An unbordered portrait that shades off into the surrounding color at the edges. **3.** A literary, dramatic, or cinematic sketch having the intimate charm and subtlety attributed to vignette portraits: *The film was just a series of vignettes of medieval life.* ~tr.v. **vignetted, -gnetting, -gnettes. 1.** To soften the edges of (a picture) in the style of a vignette. **2.** To illustrate or embellish with vignettes. **3.** To portray in a vignette. [French, from Old French, "young vine," diminutive of *vigne,* VINE.]

vi·gnet·ter (vĭn-yĕt′ər) n. Also **vi·gnet·tist** (-ĭst) (for sense 2). **1.** A device used to print borderless illustrations and photographs. **2.** A person who makes or specializes in vignettes.

Vi·gny (vēn-yē′), **Alfred Victor, Comte de** (1797–1863). French poet, novelist, and dramatist. He was one of the leaders of the French romantic movement. His works include the play *Chatterton* (1835), *Cinq Mars* (1826), a historical novel, and *Les Destinées* (1864), a collection of poems that reveal his stoical pessimism.

vig·or (vĭg′ər) n. Also *chiefly British* **vig·our. 1.** Active physical or mental strength. **2.** The capacity for natural growth and survival, as of plants or animals. **3.** Expressive power or forcefulness, as of language. **4.** The most flourishing or active stage; the prime; the high point: *in the vigor of manhood.* **5.** Legal effectiveness or validity. **6.** Energetic and rigorous exercise of power: *effected with vigor and resolution.* [Middle English *vigour,* from Old French, from Latin *vigor,* from *vigēre,* to be lively or vigorous.]

vi·go·ro·so (vē′gô-rô′sō) adv. *Music.* Vigorous; with emphasis and spirit. Used as a direction. [Italian, from Medieval Latin *vigōrōsus,* from Latin *vigor,* VIGOR.] —**vi·go·ro·so** adj.

vig·or·ous (vĭg′ər-əs) adj. **1.** Strong and healthy; robust; hardy. **2.** Energetic; lively. —See Synonyms at **active, healthy.** —**vig·or·ous·ly** adv. —**vig·or·ous·ness** n.

Vi·king (vī′kĭng) n. *Sometimes* **viking.** Any of the Scandinavian mariners whose pirate bands attacked and pillaged coastal settlements of northern and western Europe from the 8th to the 11th centuries. [Old Norse *vīkingr†.*] See feature, next page.

vil. village.

vi·la·yet (vē′lä-yĕt′) n. An administrative division of Turkey. [Turkish *vilâyet,* from Arabic *wilāyah,* province, from *wāli,* governor.]

vile (vīl) adj. **viler, vilest. 1.** Loathsome to the mind or senses; disgusting: *vile language; a vile smell.* **2.** Unpleasant or objectionable: *a vile play.* **3.** Miserably poor; wretched: *a vile existence.* **4.** Depraved; ignoble. **5.** Degrading; menial. [Middle English *vyle,* from Old French *vil,* from Latin *vīlis†.*] —**vile·ly** adv. —**vile·ness** n.

vil·i·fy (vĭl′ə-fī′) tr.v. **-fied, -fying, -fies.** To defame; denigrate. —See Synonyms at **malign.** [Middle English *vilifien,* from Late Latin *vīlificāre* : Latin *vīlis,* VILE + *facere,* to make.] —**vil·i·fi·ca·tion** n. —**vil·i·fi·er** n.

Viking

SEA WARRIORS FROM SCANDINAVIA

Viking colonies ranged from North America to Russia

"From the fury of the Northmen deliver us, O Lord!" For more than two centuries this prayer was uttered by Christians throughout Europe and the British Isles as the Vikings—the fierce, Scandinavian sea warriors—sailed out in their longships in search of new domains. The pagan Norsemen—from Norway, Sweden, and Denmark—sought new territories because of overpopulation at home. Their incursions were also encouraged by the comparative weakness of the European nations.

The Viking expansion began between 786 and 800, when they raided the coasts of Saxon England, sacking the Northumbrian monasteries of Lindisfarne (Holy Island) in 793 and Jarrow in 794. In the 850's their tactics changed from raids to sustained invasion. This Danish Viking influx was checked by Alfred the Great of Wessex and his successors. A second wave of raids in the late 960's culminated 50 years later in the English acceptance of Canute—a former raider and the son of a Danish king—as sole ruler (1015-34).

The Vikings used their longboats to navigate rivers as well as oceans, and in the 9th and 10th centuries they settled in Iceland, Ireland, Spain, Italy, and Normandy (Norman is a variant of Northman). Eventually, their colonies extended from central Russia to North America—where, in the 980's, they landed at a place that they named "Vinland" after the wild grapes growing there. It may have been the Canadian island of Newfoundland, where the remains of a Viking settlement were discovered in 1963.

In the wake of the warriors came the Viking farmers and craftsmen. Trade routes were forged from the Baltic Sea to Byzantium, and Viking merchants brought to Europe furs and amber from the Far North and silks and spices from the East. The Viking colonies had a system of law and social order, and the Vikings introduced their rich literary culture, including the stirring Norse sagas and legends.

By the end of the 11th century the Viking Age had ended. In the autumn of 1066 (shortly before the successful Norman invasion) King Harold of England defeated a force of Viking raiders at Stamford Bridge, near York. It was the Vikings' last major attack abroad and within a few decades most of the once all-conquering warriors had returned to their homes in Scandinavia. They lacked the wealth, manpower, political expertise, and endurance to stay where they were not wanted. Those who did remain eventually became part of the societies they had once overrun and ruled.

SHIP OF WAR *An armed crew of sixty-four crammed into this Viking warship, which was excavated at a funeral mount at Gokstad in Norway in 1880. The oak-built vessel dates from about 850 and is 23 meters (75½ feet) long and 5.25 meters (17 feet) wide. Although it was mainly a sailing ship, it could also be rowed, and there are holes for 16 pairs of slender spruce oars. It was later used as the "tomb" of an unknown Viking king, who was placed in a wooden burial chamber in the ship with his weapons, animals, and personal possessions. The vessel is now in the Viking Ship Hall in Oslo.*

vil·i·pend (vĭl'ə-pĕnd') *tr.v.* **-pended, -pending, -pends.** **1.** To view or treat with contempt; despise. **2.** To disparage or abuse. [Middle English *vilipenden*, from Old French *vilipender*, from Latin *vīlipendere* : *vīlis*, VILE + *pendere*, to weigh, consider.]

vil·la (vĭl'ə) *n.* **1.** A large, luxurious country residence. **2.** In ancient Rome, a country estate with a substantial house. **3.** *Chiefly Scottish.* A detached or semidetached middle-class house in the suburbs. **4.** *Chiefly British.* A vacation home, as at a seaside resort. [Italian, from Latin *villa*, country house.]

Vil·la (vē'ə), **Francisco,** known as "Pancho," born Doroteo Arango (1877–1923). Mexican bandit and revolutionary. He was active in successive revolts against Mexican governments (1910-15). After coming to terms with the Mexican government (1920), he disbanded his army. He was assassinated.

vil·lage (vĭl'ĭj) *n. Abbr.* **v., V., vil.** **1.** A small group of dwellings in a rural area, usually ranking in size between a hamlet and a town. **2.** In some U.S. states, an incorporated community smaller in population than a town. **3.** An old and distinctive urban district having its own particular character, usually quainter and better preserved than its surroundings, and in some cases actually being a former rural village now absorbed into a metropolitan or suburban area. **4.** The inhabitants of a village; villagers.
—*adj.* **1.** Of or pertaining to a village. **2.** Characteristic of villages; rustic. [Middle English, from Old French, from *ville*, village, farm, from Latin *villa*, VILLA.]

vil·lag·er (vĭl'ĭ-jər) *n.* An inhabitant of a village.

vil·lain (vĭl'ən) *n.* **1.** A depraved, base-minded person; a scoundrel. **2.** A dramatic or fictional character who is typically at odds with the hero. **3.** *British Slang.* A criminal. **4.** *Obsolete.* A vile, brutish peasant. **5.** Variant of **villein.** [Middle English *vilain*, from Old French, originally "feudal serf," from Medieval Latin *vīllānus*, from Latin *villa*, country house.]

vil·lain·ess (vĭl'ə-nĭs) *n.* A woman who is a villain.

vil·lain·ous (vĭl'ə-nəs) *adj.* **1.** Viciously wicked or criminal. **2.** Extremely unpleasant; obnoxious. —**vil·lain·ous·ly** *adv.* —**vil·lain·ous·ness** *n.*

vil·lain·y (vĭl'ə-nē) *n., pl.* **-ies.** **1.** Viciousness of conduct or action. **2.** Baseness of mind or character. **3.** A treacherous or vicious act.

Vil·la-Lo·bos (vē'lə-lō'bŏs), **Heitor** (1887–1959). Brazilian composer. He was mainly self-taught, and his many works are influenced by Brazilian folk songs.

vil·la·nelle (vĭl'ə-nĕl') *n.* A 19-line poem of fixed form consisting of five tercets and a final quatrain based on two rhymes, with the first and third lines of the first tercet repeated alternately as a refrain closing the succeeding stanzas and joined as the final couplet of the quatrain. [French, from Italian *villanella*, an old rustic Italian song, from *villanello*, rustic, from *villano*, peasant, from Medieval Latin *vīllānus*. See **villain.**]

vil·lat·ic (vĭ-lăt'ĭk) *adj.* Rustic; rural. [Latin *vīllāticus*, from *villa*, VILLA.]

-ville *suffix.* Indicates a place or condition of a specified kind; for example, *dullsville; thrillsville.* [Abstracted from common U.S. town names (for example, *Charlottesville*), from French *ville*, town, ultimately from Latin *villa*.]

vil·lein (vĭl'ən) *n.* Also **vil·lain.** In feudal times, a member of a class of serfs who held the legal status of freemen in their dealings with all persons except their lord, to whom they owed certain services or rents in return for their land. [Middle English *villein*, variant of *vilain*, VILLAIN.]

vil·lein·age (vĭl'ə-nĭj) *n.* **1.** The legal status or condition of a villein. **2.** The legal tenure by which a villein held his land. Also called "bondage."

Vil·lel·la (və-lĕl'ə), **Edward** (1936–). U.S. ballet dancer. Beginning his long association with the New York City Ballet in 1957, he appeared in numerous productions, including *Harlequinade* (1965) and *Watermill* (1972). His dynamic and popular performances helped make dancing an acceptable career for men.

vil·li·form (vĭl'ə-fôrm') *adj.* Having the form of a villus or the appearance of villi.

Vil·lon (vē-ôN'), **François** (c. 1431–1463). French poet. He led a life of vagrancy after studying at the University of Paris. A sentence to hang was commuted to banishment in 1463, and nothing is known of him after that date. His only surviving works are the satirical *Testament* (c. 1461) and a few other poems.

vil·los·i·ty (vĭ-lŏs'ə-tē) *n., pl.* **-ties.** **1.** The condition of being villous. **2.** A villous surface or coating. **3.** A villus or set of villi.

vil·lous (vĭl'əs) *adj.* Also **vil·lose** (-ōs'). **1.** Of, pertaining to, resembling, or covered with villi. **2.** *Botany.* Covered with fine, unmatted hairs. [Middle English, from Latin *villōsus*, from *villus*, shaggy hair, VILLUS.] —**vil·lous·ly** *adv.*

vil·lus (vĭl'əs) *n., pl.* **villi** (vĭl'ī'). **1.** *Biology.* Any minute projection arising from a mucous membrane. **2.** *Botany.* A fine, hairlike epidermal outgrowth. [Latin, shaggy hair.]

Vil·ni·us (vĭl'nē-əs). Capital of the Lithuanian S.S.R. Founded in the 10th century on the Neris River, it became the capital of the grand duchy of Lithuania in 1323. In 1569 it was severely damaged in the wars following the union between Poland and Lithuania and became part of Russia on the partition of Poland (1795). Between 1920 and 1939 it again reverted to Poland.

vim (vĭm) *n. Informal.* Ebullient vitality and energy. [Latin *vim,* accusative of *vīs,* power.]

Vim·i·nal (vĭm'ə-nəl). One of the seven hills of Rome. [Latin *Vīmi-*

nālis (collis), "(hill) of osiers" (from the willow copse on the hill), from *vīmen,* osier.]

vi·min·e·ous (vĭ-mĭn′ē-əs) *adj. Botany.* Having or pertaining to long, flexible shoots. [Latin *vīmineus,* from *vīmen,* osier.]

vin-. Variant of **vini-.**

vi·na (vē′nä) *n.* A stringed musical instrument of India that has a long, fretted fingerboard with resonating gourds at each end. [Hindi *vīṇā,* from Sanskrit *vīṇāh†*.]

vi·na·ceous (vī-nā′shəs) *adj.* Having the color of red wine; wine-red. [Latin *vīnāceus,* of wine, from *vīnum,* wine.]

vin·ai·grette (vĭn′ə-grĕt′) *n.* **1.** A small decorative bottle or container with a perforated top, used for holding an aromatic restorative, such as smelling salts. **2.** Vinaigrette sauce.
~*adj.* Served or prepared with vinaigrette sauce. [French, from Old French *vinaigre,* VINEGAR.]

vinaigrette sauce *n.* A cold sauce or dressing made of vinegar and oil flavored with herbs and other seasonings.

vi·nasse (vī-năs′) *n.* The residue left in a still after the process of distillation. [French, from Latin *vīnācea,* feminine of *vīnāceus,* of wine, VINACEOUS.]

vin·blas·tine (vĭn-blăs′tēn) *n.* An alkaloid obtained from a periwinkle plant, *Vinca rosea,* that is used to treat cancer of the lymphatic system. [Shortened from *vincaleucoblastine* : New Latin *vinca,* periwinkle + *leucoblast* (LEUCO- + -BLAST) + -INE.]

vin·ca (vĭng′kə) *n.* Any plant of the genus *Vinca,* especially, a **periwinkle** *(see).* [New Latin, from Latin *(per)vinca,* PERIWINKLE.]

Vin·cennes (văn-sĕn′). Town in Val-de-Marne department, north-central France. A royal residence since the 12th century, it was particularly favored by Louis IX. Other French kings who lived here included Charles V, Charles IX, and Francis I. Vincennes today is an industrial and residential suburb of Paris.

Vin·cent de Paul (vĭn′sənt də pôl), Saint (1581–1660). French priest. Known for his benevolence and his skill in organizing practical charities, he founded the Congregation of the Priests of the Mission (1625), the Sisters of Charity (1634), and many foundling hospitals in Paris.

Vin·cent's disease (vĭn′sənts) *n. Pathology.* **Trench mouth** *(see).* Also called "Vincent's angina." [After Hyacinthe *Vincent* (1862–1950), French physician.]

Vinci, Leonardo da. See **Leonardo da Vinci.**

vin·ci·ble (vĭn′sə-bəl) *adj.* Capable of being overcome or defeated; surmountable. [Latin *vincibilis,* from *vincere,* to conquer.] —**vin·ci·bil·i·ty** *n.*

vin·cu·lum (vĭng′kyə-ləm) *n.,* pl. **-la** (-lə). **1.** *Mathematics.* A bar drawn over two or more algebraic terms to indicate that they are to be treated as a single term. **2.** *Anatomy.* **a.** A ligament. **b.** Any connecting band or fold, such as the umbilical cord or the membranes below the tongue. **3.** A bond or tie. [Latin, band, cord, from *vincīre†*, to tie.]

Vin·da·loo (vĭn′də-lōō′) *adj.* Served with a hot, sour curry sauce: *chicken Vindaloo.* [Hindi.]

vin·di·ca·ble (vĭn′dĭ-kə-bəl) *adj.* Justifiable. [VINDIC(ATE) + -ABLE.]

vin·di·cate (vĭn′dĭ-kāt′) *tr.v.* **-cated, -cating, -cates. 1.** To clear of accusation, blame, suspicion, or doubt with supporting arguments or proof. **2.** To justify or support: *vindicate one's claim.* **3.** To justify or prove the worth of, especially in the light of later developments. [Latin *vindicāre,* to claim, defend, revenge, from *vindex,* claimant, defender, avenger.] —**vin·di·ca·tor** *n.*

vin·di·ca·tion (vĭn′dĭ-kā′shən) *n.* **1.** The act of vindicating or condition of being vindicated. **2.** The evidence, argument, event, or the like, that serves to justify a claim or deed.

vin·dic·a·to·ry (vĭn′dĭ-kə-tôr′ē, -tôr′ē) *adj.* **1.** Vindicating; justifying. **2.** Exacting retribution; punitive.

vin·dic·tive (vĭn-dĭk′tĭv) *adj.* **1.** Disposed to seek revenge; revengeful. **2.** Unforgiving; bitter; spiteful. **3.** *Law.* Designating damages awarded in excess of simple compensation in order to punish the defendant. [From Latin *vindicta,* vengeance, from *vindicāre,* to revenge, VINDICATE.] —**vin·dic·tive·ly** *adv.* —**vin·dic·tive·ness** *n.*
Synonyms: *revengeful, spiteful, vengeful.*

vine (vīn) *n.* **1.** Any plant having a flexible stem supported by climbing, twining, or creeping along a surface. **2.** The stem of such a plant. **3. a.** A grapevine. **b.** Grapevines collectively: *products of the vine.* [Middle English, from Old French *vine, vigne,* from Latin *vīnea,* from the feminine of *vīneus,* of wine, from *vīnum,* wine.] —**vin·y** *adj.*

vine-dress·er (vīn′drĕs′ər) *n.* A person who cultivates and tends grapevines.

vin·e·gar (vĭn′ĭ-gər) *n.* **1.** A sour, impure dilute solution of acetic acid obtained by fermentation beyond the alcohol stage and used as a condiment and preservative. **2.** *Informal.* Sourness; ill temper. [Middle English *vinegre,* from Old French *vinaigre, vyn egre* : *vin,* wine, from Latin *vīnum* + *aigre,* sour, from Latin *acer,* sharp.]

vinegar eel *n.* A small nematode worm, *Turbatrix aceti,* that feeds on the organisms that cause fermentation in vinegar. Also called "eelworm," "vinegar worm."

vinegar fly *n.* Any of various flies of the genus *Drosophila* that often become pests by breeding in poorly sealed preserves and pickles.

vin·e·gar·roon (vĭn′ĭ-gə-rōōn′) *n.* Also **vin·e·ga·rone** (-rōn′). A large, nonvenomous scorpionlike arachnid, *Mastigoproctus giganteus,* of the southern United States and Mexico, that emits a strong odor of vinegar when disturbed. [Mexican Spanish *vinagrón,* from Spanish *vinagre,* vinegar, from Old French *vinaigre.* See **vinegar.**]

vin·e·gar·y (vĭn′ĭ-gə-rē) *adj.* Also **vin·e·gar·ish** (-gər-ĭsh). **1.** Having the nature of vinegar; sour; acid: *a vinegary taste.* **2.** Sour in disposition or speech; ill-tempered.

Vineland. See **Vinland.**

vine maple *n.* A maple, *Acer circinatum,* of western North America, having red fruits and white and purple flowers.

vin·er·y (vī′nə-rē) *n.,* pl. **-ies.** An area or greenhouse for growing vines.

vine·yard (vĭn′yərd) *n.* **1.** A plot of ground planted with cultivated grapevines. **2.** *Informal.* A sphere of spiritual, mental, or physical endeavor.

vingt-et-un (văn′tā′ən′) *n.* A card game, **blackjack** *(see).* [French, twenty-one (the maximum score of a hand).]

vini-, vino-, vin- *prefix.* Indicates wine, for example, **viniculture, vinometer.** [From Latin *vīnum,* wine.]

vi·nic (vī′nĭk) *adj.* Of, contained in, or derived from wine. [From Latin *vīnum,* wine. See **vine.**]

vin·i·cul·ture (vĭn′ĭ-kŭl′chər, vī′nĭ-) *n.* The cultivation of grapes and making of wine; viticulture. —**vin·i·cul·tur·al** *adj.* —**vin·i·cul·tur·al·ly** *adv.* —**vin·i·cul·tur·ist** *n.*

Vin·land (vĭn′lənd). Also **Vine·land** (vīn′-). An area of Newfoundland. Situated around the Hudson Straits and the Gulf of St. Lawrence according to the Vinland Map (1440), the area was supposedly explored by Leif Ericson in the 11th century.

vi·no (vē′nō) *n.,* pl. **-nos.** *Informal.* Wine. [Italian and Spanish, from Latin *vīnum,* wine. See **vine.**]

vi·nom·e·ter (vī-nŏm′ə-tər, vĭ-) *n.* A hydrometer used to determine the percentage of alcohol in a wine.

vin or·di·naire (văn ôr-dē-nâr′) *n.,* pl. **vins ordinaires** *(pronounced as singular).* *French.* An ordinary inexpensive wine; a table wine.

vi·nous (vī′nəs) *adj.* **1.** Of or pertaining to wine or its consumption: *a vinous party.* **2.** Affected or caused by the consumption of wine: *a vinous nose; vinous laughter.* **3.** Having the color of wine. [Latin *vinōsus,* from *vīnum,* wine. See **vine.**] —**vi·nos·i·ty** *n.*

Vin·son Massif (vĭn′sən). A mountain peak of Antarctica. One of the Ellsworth Mts., it rises to 5,139 meters (16,860 feet), the continent's highest point.

vin·tage (vĭn′tĭj) *n.* **1.** The yield of wine or grapes from a particular vineyard or district during one season. **2.** Wine, usually of high quality, identified as to year and vineyard or district of origin. Also called "vintage wine." **3.** The year in which or place where a particular wine was bottled. **4.** The harvesting of a grape crop or the initial stages of winemaking. **5.** The season for such harvesting or winemaking. **6.** *Informal.* Any group or collection of persons or things sharing certain characteristics. **7.** *Informal.* A year or period of origin: *a dress of 1942 vintage.*
~*adj.* **1.** Designating wine of an outstandingly good year. **2.** Characterized by excellence, maturity, and enduring appeal; venerable; classic. **3.** Typical of the best work of a specified author or other artist: *vintage O'Neill.* **4.** Old or outmoded. [Middle English *vyntage,* variant (influenced by *vineter,* VINTNER) of *vendage,* from Old French, from Latin *vindēmia,* grape gathering : *vīnum,* wine (see **vine**) + *dēmere,* to take off : *dē-,* off + *emere,* to take.]

vintage car *n. British.* A motor car made between 1919 and 1930. Compare **veteran car.**

vin·tag·er (vĭn′tĭ-jər) *n.* A harvester of wine grapes.

vintage year *n.* **1.** The year in which a vintage wine is produced. **2.** Any year of outstanding achievement or success.

vint·ner (vĭnt′nər) *n.* A wine merchant. [Middle English *vineter,* from Old French *vinetier,* from Medieval Latin *vīnātārius,* from Latin *vīnētum,* vineyard, from *vīnum,* wine. See **vine.**]

vi·nyl (vī′nəl) *n.* **1.** The univalent chemical radical CH_2:CH-, derived from ethene. **2.** Any of various compounds containing this group, typically highly reactive, easily polymerized, and used as basic materials for plastics. **3.** Any of various synthetic resins, typically tough, flexible, and shiny, used, for example, in coverings, clothing, and paints. [VIN(I)- + -YL.] —**vi·nyl** *adj.*

vinyl chloride *n.* A flammable gas, CH_2:CHCl, used as a monomer for polyvinyl chloride (PVC). Also called "chloroethene."

vi·ol (vī′əl) *n.* **1.** Any of a family of stringed instruments, chiefly of the 16th and 17th centuries, having a fretted fingerboard, usually six strings, a flat back, and played with a curved bow. **2.** A viola da gamba. [Old French *viole,* from Old Provençal *viola,* VIOLA (instrument).]

vi·o·la[1] (vē-ō′lə, vī-) *n.* **1.** A four-stringed musical instrument of the violin family, slightly larger than a violin, tuned a fifth lower, and having a deeper, more sonorous tone; the alto or tenor violin. **2.** An organ stop usually of eight-foot or four-foot pitch yielding stringlike tones. [Italian, from Old Provençal *viola, viula,* perhaps from *violar,* to play the viola (imitative).]

vi·o·la[2] (vī-ō′lə, vē-, vī′ə-lə) *n.* Any plant of the genus *Viola,* which includes the violets and pansies. [New Latin *Viola,* from Latin *viola,* VIOLET.]

vi·o·la·ble (vī′ə-lə-bəl) *adj.* Capable of being violated or easily broken. —**vi·o·la·bil·i·ty, vi·o·la·ble·ness** *n.* —**vi·o·la·bly** *adv.*

vi·o·la·ceous (vī′ə-lā′shəs) *adj.* **1.** Of or belonging to the family Violaceae, of the violets and pansies. **2.** Having a violet color. [Latin *violāceus* : *viola,* VIOLET + -ACEOUS.]

vi·o·la da brac·cio (vē-ō′lə də brä′chō) *n.* A stringed instrument of the viol family with approximately the range of the viola. [Italian, "viola of the arm."]

vi·o·la da gam·ba (vē-ō′lə də găm′bə). **1.** A stringed instrument, the bass of the viol family, with approximately the range of the cello.

vineyard *Part of the vineyard at Schloss Staufenberg, near Durbach in West Germany.*

Also called "viol," "bass viol," "gamba." **2.** An organ stop of eight-foot pitch yielding tones similar to those of the viola da gamba. [Italian, "viola of the leg."]

vi·o·la d'a·mo·re (vē-ō'lə dä-môr'ā) *n.* A stringed instrument, the tenor of the viol family, having 7 stopped strings and 7 or 14 sympathetic strings that produce a characteristic silvery tone. [Italian, "viola of love."]

vi·o·late (vī'ə-lāt') *tr.v.* **-lated, -lating, -lates. 1.** To break (a law or regulation, for example) intentionally or unintentionally; fail to keep; transgress; disregard: *violate a promise.* **2.** To injure the person or property of; especially, to rape. **3.** To do harm to (property or qualities considered sacred); profane; desecrate. **4.** To disturb rudely or improperly; break in upon without right: *violate the peace.* [Middle English *violaten,* from Latin *violāre,* from *vīs,* force.] **—vi·o·la·tive** *adj.* **—vi·o·la·tor** *n.*

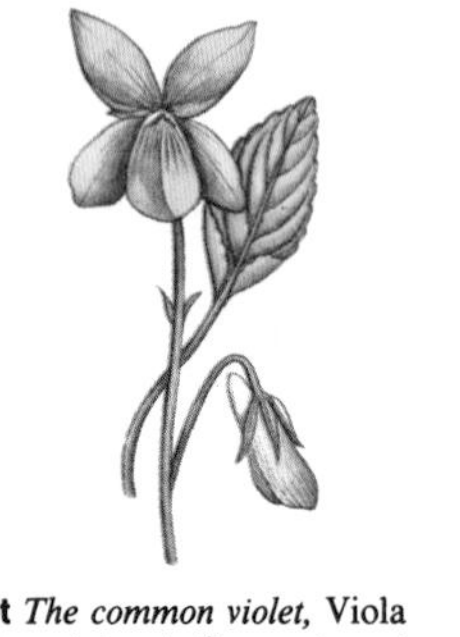

violet *The common violet,* Viola riviniana *(above), flowers in spring in woodlands and meadows throughout temperate regions.*

vi·o·la·tion (vī'ə-lā'shən) *n.* **1.** The act of violating or the condition of being violated. **2.** An instance of violation; a transgression: *violations of the ceasefire.* —See Synonyms at **breach.**

vi·o·lence (vī'ə-ləns) *n.* **1.** Physical force exerted for the purpose of violating, damaging, or abusing: *"The essence of war is violence"* (T.B. Macaulay). **2.** An act or instance of violent action or behavior. **3.** Intensity or severity, as in natural phenomena; untamed force: *the violence of a hurricane.* **4.** The abusive or unjust exercise of power; an outrage; a wrong. **5.** Abuse or injury to meaning, content, or intent: *do violence to a text.* **6.** Vehemence of feeling or expression; fervor.

vi·o·lent (vī'ə-lənt) *adj.* **1.** Displaying or proceeding from extreme or uncontrolled physical force or rough action. **2.** Exhibiting intense force or effect; extreme: *violent contrast.* **3.** Caused by or displaying undue mental or emotional force: *a violent antipathy.* **4.** Characterized by the immoderate use of force; severe; harsh. **5.** Caused by unexpected force or injury rather than by natural causes: *a violent death.* [Middle English, from Old French, from Latin *violentus.*] **—vi·o·lent·ly** *adv.*

violent storm *n.* A wind whose speed is 28.5 to 32.6 meters per second (56 to 63 knots), force 11 on the Beaufort scale.

vi·o·let (vī'ə-lĭt) *n.* **1.** Any of various low-growing plants of the genus *Viola,* having spurred, irregular flowers that are characteristically purplish-blue but sometimes yellow or white. **2.** Any of several similar but unrelated plants, such as the **African violet** *(see).* **3.** Any of a group of colors, reddish blue in hue, that may vary in lightness and saturation; the hue of that portion of the spectrum that may be evoked in the normal observer by radiant energy of wavelengths approximately 420 nanometers. **4.** A dye or pigment of this color. **5. a.** Any object of this color. **b.** Clothing of this color. [Middle English, from Old French *violete,* diminutive of *viole,* from Latin *viola,* from the same Mediterranean origin as Greek *ion,* violet. See **iodine.**] **—vi·o·let** *adj.*

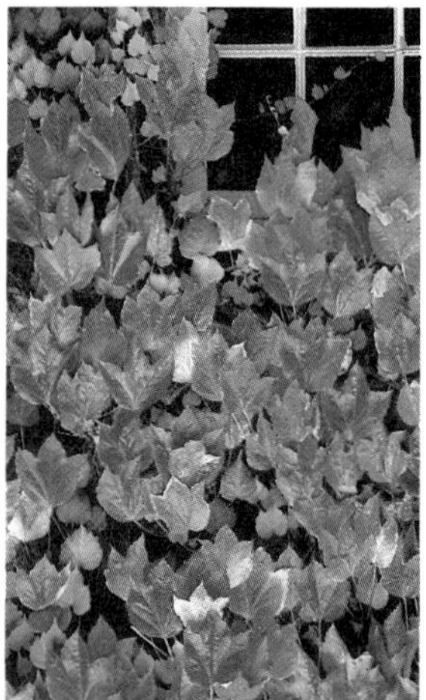

Virginia creeper Parthenocissus tricuspidata veitchii, *the small-leafed Virginia creeper (above), is a native of China and Japan. It has tendrils with adhesive tips that allow it to climb walls and fences.*

vi·o·lin (vī'ə-lĭn') *n. Abbr.* **v. 1.** A stringed instrument played with a bow, having four strings tuned at intervals of a fifth, an unfretted fingerboard, and a shallower body than the viol, and capable of great flexibility in range, tone, and dynamics. Also informally called "fiddle." **2.** A violinist. [Italian *violino,* diminutive of *viola,* VIOLA (instrument).]

vi·o·lin·ist (vī'ə-lĭn'ĭst) *n.* A person who plays the violin.

vi·o·list (vē-ō'lĭst) *n.* **1.** A person who plays the viola. **2.** A person who plays a viol.

Viol·let-le-Duc (vē'ə-lā'lə-do͝ok'), **Eugène Emmanuel.** (1814–79). French architect and author. He was a leader of the Gothic revival in France and designed the restoration of the city of Carcassonne and many medieval buildings, including Notre Dame in Paris.

vi·o·lon·cel·list (vē'ə-lən-chĕl'ĭst) *n.* A person who plays the cello; a cellist.

vi·o·lon·cel·lo (vē'ə-lən-chĕl'ō) *n., pl.* **-los.** A **cello** *(see).* [Italian, diminutive of *violone,* VIOLONE.]

vi·o·lone (vyō-lō'nā) *n.* **1.** A stringed instrument, the double bass of the viol family, with approximately the range of a modern double bass. **2.** A 16-foot organ stop yielding stringlike tones similar to a cello. [Italian, augmentative of *viola,* VIOLA (instrument).]

vi·o·my·cin (vī'ə-mī'sĭn) *n.* An antibiotic obtained from various species of the bacterium *Streptomyces,* used to treat tuberculosis. [VIO(LET) (referring to the color of the soil mold) + -MYCIN.]

vi·os·ter·ol (vī-ŏs'tə-rōl) *n.* Ultraviolet irradiated ergosterol, **vitamin** $\mathbf{D_2}$ *(see).*

VIP (vē'ī'pē') *n., pl.* **VIPs.** *Informal.* A person regarded as being very important, and therefore accorded special, courteous, or luxurious treatment; a dignitary or celebrity. [*V*ery *I*mportant *P*erson.]

vi·per (vī'pər) *n.* **1.** Any of various venomous Old World snakes of the family Viperidae; especially, a common Eurasian species, *Vipera berus,* which is also called "adder." **2.** A **pit viper** *(see).* **3.** Broadly, any venomous or supposedly venomous snake. **4.** A treacherous or malicious person. [Old French *vipere,* from Latin *vīpera,* snake, contracted from *vivipara* (unattested), "that which produces living young" (from the ancient belief that vipers were viviparous) : *vīvus,* alive + *parere,* to produce.]

vi·per·ine (vī'pər-īn, -pə-rīn') *adj.* Of, resembling, or characteristic of a viper.

vi·per·ous (vī'pər-əs) *adj.* Also **vi·per·ish** (-ĭsh). **1.** Suggestive of a viper or venomous snake. **2.** Venomous; spiteful; malicious.

viper's bugloss *n.* A bristly plant, *Echium vulgare,* native to Eurasia, having bright-blue flowers. Also called "blueweed."

vir·a·gin·i·ty (vîr'ə-jĭn'ə-tē) *n.* Masculine mentality and psychology in a woman. [From Latin *virāgō* (stem *virāgin-*), manlike woman, VIRAGO.] **—vir·a·gin·ous** (vĭ-răj'ə-nəs) *adj.*

vi·ra·go (vĭ-rä'gō, -rā'gō, vī-) *n., pl.* **-goes** or **-gos. 1.** A noisy, domineering woman; a scold. **2.** *Archaic.* A large, strong, or courageous woman; an Amazon. [Latin *virāgō,* from *vir,* man.]

vi·ral (vī'rəl) *adj.* Of, pertaining to, or caused by a virus. [From VIRUS.]

vir·e·lay (vîr'ə-lā') *n.* Also *French* **vi·re·lai** (vēr-lĕ'). Any of several medieval French verse and song forms, especially one in which each stanza has two rhymes, the end rhyme recurring as the first rhyme of the following stanza. [Middle English *virelai,* from Old French, variant (influenced by *lai,* LAY) of *vireli,* perhaps originally a meaningless refrain.]

vir·e·o (vîr'ē-ō') *n., pl.* **-os.** Any of various small New World birds of the genus *Vireo,* having grayish or greenish plumage. [Latin *vireo,* greenfinch, from *virēre,* to be green.]

vi·res·cence (vĭ-rĕs'əns) *n.* The state or process of becoming green; specifically, the abnormal development of green coloration in plant parts normally not green.

vi·res·cent (vĭ-rĕs'ənt) *adj.* Becoming green; greenish. [Latin *virēscēns* (stem *virēscent-*), present participle of *virēscere,* to become green, from *virēre,* to be green.]

vir·ga (vûr'gə) *n.* Wisps of precipitation streaming from a cloud but evaporating before reaching the earth. [Latin, twig, stripe.]

vir·gate[1] (vûr'gĭt, -gāt') *adj.* Shaped like a wand or rod; straight, long, and slender. [Latin *virgātus,* made of twigs, from *virga,* twig. See **virga.**]

virgate[2] *n.* An early English measure of land area of varying extent but most often equivalent to about 30 acres. [Medieval Latin *virgāta,* from *virga,* a measure, yard, from Latin, twig. See **virga.**]

Vir·gil or **Ver·gil** (vûr'jəl), born Publius Vergilius Maro (70–19 B.C.). Roman poet. His greatest work is his epic poem *Aeneid,* which tells of the wanderings of Aeneas after the sack of Troy, the founding of Rome, and the Julian dynasty. Among his other works are his *Eclogues* and the *Georgics.*

vir·gin (vûr'jĭn) *n.* **1.** A person who has not experienced sexual intercourse. **2.** A chaste or unmarried woman; a maiden. **3.** An unmarried woman who has taken religious vows of chastity. **4. Virgin.** Mary, the mother of Jesus. Preceded by *the.* Also called "Blessed Virgin." **5.** Any female animal that has not mated. **6. Virgin.** The constellation and the sign of the zodiac, **Virgo** *(see).*
~*adj.* **1.** Characteristic of or appropriate to a virgin; chaste. **2.** In a pure or natural state; untouched; unsullied: *virgin snow.* **3.** Unused, uncultivated, or unexplored: *the virgin West of 19th-century America.* **4.** Existing in native or raw form; not processed or refined. **5.** Happening for the first time; initial: *"guiding my virgin steps on the hard road of letters"* (Somerset Maugham). **6.** Obtained directly from the first pressing. Said of vegetable oils. **7.** Unprocessed. Said of wool. **8.** Obtained by smelting ore, rather than recycling scrap. Said of metals. **9.** *Physics.* Not having experienced any collisions. Said of neutrons. [Middle English, from Old French *virgine,* from Latin *virgō*† (stem *virgin-*).]

vir·gin·al[1] (vûr'jə-nəl) *adj.* **1.** Pertaining to, characteristic of, or befitting a virgin; chaste; pure. **2.** Remaining in a state of virginity. **3.** Untouched or unsullied; fresh.

virginal[2] *n. Often* **virginals.** A small, legless rectangular harpsichord popular in the 16th and 17th centuries. [From VIRGIN (because it was played by young girls).]

virgin birth *n. Sometimes* **Virgin Birth.** *Theology.* The doctrine that Jesus was miraculously begotten by God and born of Mary, who was a virgin.

Vir·gin·ia[1] (vûr-jĭn'yə). State of the United States. Bordering the Mid-Atlantic, it has land borders with Maryland, West Virginia, Kentucky, Tennessee, and North Carolina. First settled by the English (1607), it was named after Queen Elizabeth, "the Virgin Queen." One of the original 13 states, it was readmitted to the Union in 1870, following the Civil War, during which it was part of the Confederacy. Richmond is the capital.

Virginia[2] *n.* Cured tobacco of a kind originally grown in Virginia.

Virginia City. Village of western Nevada, southeast of Reno, at an altitude of 1,983 meters (6,500 feet). It was founded in 1859 when rich deposits of gold and silver, including the Comstock Lode, were discovered nearby. During the 1870's it was the mining metropolis of the West, with a population of some 35,000. It began to decline in the late 1880's and is now a tourist center as a ghost town.

Virginia cowslip *n.* A plant, *Mertensia virginica,* of eastern North America, having clusters of nodding blue flowers.

Virginia creeper *n.* **1.** A North American climbing vine, *Parthenocissus quinquefolia,* having compound leaves with five leaflets and bluish-black, berrylike fruit. Also called "woodbine." **2.** A similar vine from China and Japan, *P. tricuspidata* (or *Ampelopsis veitchii*).

Virginia deer *n.* The **white-tailed deer** *(see).*

Virginia fence *n.* A **worm fence** *(see).* Also called "Virginia rail fence."

Virginia reel *n.* **1.** A country dance in which couples, initially facing each other from two parallel lines, perform various figures to the instructions of a caller. **2.** A piece of music for this dance.

virginia stock *n. Sometimes* **Virginia.** An annual plant, *Malcolmia maritima,* from southern Europe, having four-petaled lilac, red, or white flowers and often grown in gardens. [After *Virginia,* where it was cultivated.]

Virgin Islands. An archipelago in the Caribbean. A group of *c.* 100 islands east of Puerto Rico in the West Indies. About one third of

the islands are owned by Britain; the remaining two thirds are the property of the United States.

Virgin Islands of the United States. Group of islands administered by the U.S. Department of the Interior. The main islands include St. Croix, St. John, and St. Thomas. The Virgin Islanders first elected their own governor in 1970 and also have a nonvoting representative in the U.S. Congress. The capital is Charlotte Amalie on St. Thomas.

vir·gin·i·ty (vər-jĭn′ə-tē) *n., pl.* **-ties. 1.** The condition of being a virgin; virginal chastity. **2.** The state of being pure, unsullied, or untouched.

Virgin Mary *n.* The mother of Jesus, **Mary** *(see).* Usually preceded by *the.*

Virgin Queen *n.* See **Elizabeth I.** Usually preceded by *the.*

vir·gin's-bow·er (vûr′jĭnz-bou′ər) *n.* Any of several plants of the genus *Clematis,* especially *C. virginiana,* of eastern North America, having clusters of white flowers and plumed seeds.

Vir·go (vûr′gō) *n.* **1.** A constellation in the region of the celestial equator near Leo and Libra. **2. a.** The sixth sign of the **zodiac. b.** One born under this sign. Also called the "Virgin." [Latin *virgō,* VIRGIN.]

vir·gu·late (vûr′gyə-lĭt, -lāt′) *adj.* Shaped like a small rod. [From Latin *virgula,* small rod. See **virgule.**]

vir·gule (vûr′gyo͞ol) *n.* A diagonal mark (/) used especially to separate alternatives, as in *and/or,* to represent the word *per,* as in *miles/hour,* and to indicate the ends of verse lines printed continuously, as in *Candy/Is dandy.* Also called "oblique," "slash," "shilling," "solidus." [French, comma, from Latin *virgula,* small rod, from *virga,* rod, twig.]

vir·id (vîr′ĭd) *adj.* Green with or as if with vegetation; verdant. [Latin *viridis,* green, from *virēre,* to be green.] **—vi·rid·i·ty** (və-rĭd′ə-tē) *n.*

vir·i·des·cent (vîr′ə-dĕs′ənt) *adj.* **1.** Green or slightly green. **2.** Turning green. [Latin *viridis,* green, VIRID + -ESCENT.] **—vir·i·des·cence** *n.*

vi·rid·i·an (və-rĭd′ē-ən) *n.* A durable bluish-green pigment. [From Latin *viridis,* green, VIRID.]

vir·ile (vîr′əl, -īl′) *adj.* **1.** Of or having the characteristics of an adult male. **2.** Having qualities traditionally associated with men, such as strength, vigor, or force. **3.** Of or pertaining to male sexual functions. [Middle English, from Old French *viril,* from Latin *virīlis,* from *vir,* man.]

vir·i·lism (vîr′ə-lĭz′əm) *n.* The development of male secondary sexual characteristics in a woman. [VIRILE + -ISM.]

vi·ril·i·ty (və-rĭl′ə-tē) *n., pl.* **-ties. 1. a.** Masculine vigor; potency. **b.** Manhood. **2.** Qualities of strength or forcefulness traditionally ascribed to men.

vi·ri·on (vī′rē-ŏn′, vîr′ē-) *n.* The complete inert form of a virus as found outside a host cell, consisting of a protein coat surrounding a strand or strands of nucleic acid. [From *viri-,* combining form of VIRUS + -ON (particle).]

vi·rol·o·gy (vī-rŏl′ə-jē) *n.* The study of viruses and viral diseases. [VIR(US) + -LOGY.] **—vi·ro·log·i·cal** (vī′rə-lŏj′ĭ-kəl) **—vi·rolo·gist** *n.*

vir·tu, ver·tu (vər-to͞o′, vûr′to͞o) *n.* **1.** A knowledge of or taste for the fine arts. **2.** The quality of being beautiful, rare, or otherwise interesting to a collector. Used in the phrases *articles of virtu* and *objects of virtu.* **3.** Such articles or objects collectively. [Italian *virtu,* taste, virtue, from Latin *virtūs,* VIRTUE.]

vir·tu·al (vûr′cho͞o-əl) *adj.* Being as specified in essence or effect though not in actual fact, form, or name: *He resigned from his job, but it was a virtual dismissal.* [Middle English *virtuall,* effective, powerful, from Medieval Latin *virtuālis,* from Latin *virtūs,* capacity, VIRTUE.] **—vir·tu·al·i·ty** (vûr′cho͞o-ăl′ə-tē) *n.*

virtual focus *n.* The point from which divergent rays of reflected or refracted light seem to have emanated, as from the image of a point in a plane mirror.

virtual image *n.* An image from which rays of reflected or refracted light appear to diverge, as from an image seen in a plane mirror.

vir·tu·al·ly (vûr′cho͞o-ə-lē) *adv.* In essence or in effect though not in actual fact; for all practical purposes; essentially.

virtual particle *n. Physics.* A particle that is not detected but is considered to exist for a very brief period of time, during which it is emitted by one real particle and absorbed by another, thereby transmitting a force between the two. Electromagnetic interaction, for example, is considered to result from exchange of *virtual photons* between charged particles.

virtual storage *n. Computer Science.* Memory in which the effective capacity is increased by the linking of the main memory to an external memory, such as a magnetic disk, so that they function together.

vir·tue (vûr′cho͞o) *n.* **1.** The quality of moral excellence, righteousness, and responsibility; probity; goodness. **2.** Conformity to standard morality or mores, as by abstention from vices; rectitude. **3. a.** A specific type of moral excellence or other exemplary quality considered meritorious; a worthy practice or ideal: *the virtue of integrity.* **b.** Any of the particular moral excellences considered exemplary in philosophy and theology. See **cardinal virtues. 4.** Chastity or virginity, especially that of a woman. **5. a.** A particular efficacious or beneficial quality. **b.** A preferable quality; an advantage: *The plane has the virtue of speed.* **6.** Effective force or power; efficacy. **7. virtues.** *Theology.* One of the orders of angels. See **angel. —by** (or **in**) **virtue of.** On the grounds or basis of; by reason of. **—make a virtue of necessity.** To appear to do freely or by inclination what one is forced to do anyway. [Middle English *vertu,* from Old French, from Latin *virtūs,* manliness, strength, capacity, from *vir,* man.]

vir·tu·o·sa (vûr′cho͞o-ō′sə, -zə) *n.* A woman who is a virtuoso. [Italian, feminine of *virtuoso,* virtuoso.]

vir·tu·os·i·ty (vûr′cho͞o-ŏs′ə-tē) *n., pl.* **-ties.** The technical skill, fluency, or style exhibited by a virtuoso.

vir·tu·o·so (vûr′cho͞o-ō′sō) *n., pl.* **-sos** or **-si** (-sē). **1.** A musician with masterly ability, technique, or personal style; a brilliant performer. **2.** One with masterly skill or technique in any field, especially in the arts. **3.** A connoisseur or dilettante.

~adj. Showing or requiring virtuosity: *a virtuoso performance.* [Italian, from Late Latin *virtuōsus,* virtuous, skillful, from Latin *virtūs,* VIRTUE.] **—vir·tu·os·ic** (vûr′cho͞o-ŏs′ĭk) *adj.*

vir·tu·ous (vûr′cho͞o-əs) *adj.* **1.** Exhibiting virtue; righteous: *virtuous conduct.* **2.** Possessing or characterized by chastity; pure: *a virtuous woman.* —See Synonyms at **moral. —vir·tu·ous·ly** *adv.* **—vir·tu·ous·ness** *n.*

vir·u·lent (vîr′yə-lənt, vîr′ə-) *adj.* **1.** Extremely harmful or pathogenic and taking rapid effect. Said of a disease, toxin, or microorganism. **2.** Bitterly hostile or antagonistic; venomously spiteful; full of hate. **3.** Intensely irritating, obnoxious, or harsh: *virulent prejudice.* [Middle English, from Latin *vīrulentus,* from *vīrus,* VIRUS.] **—vir·u·lence** (vîr′yə-ləns) *n.* **—vir·u·lent·ly** *adv.*

vi·rus (vī′rəs) *n., pl.* **-ruses. 1.** Any of various submicroscopic pathogens consisting essentially of a core of a single nucleic acid surrounded by a protein coat, having the ability to replicate only inside a living cell. **2.** Any disease believed to be caused by a virus. **3.** Any malevolent and corrupting force: *the virus of racism.* —See Usage note at **germ.** [Latin *vīrus,* poison, slime.]

vis. 1. visibility. **2.** visual.

vi·sa (vē′zə) *n.* **1.** An official authorization appended to a passport or similar document, permitting entry into and travel within a particular country or region. **2.** Any authorization or mark of authorization.

~tr.v. **visaed, -saing, -sas. 1.** To make a visa in (a passport). **2.** To give a visa to. [French, from Latin *vīsa,* "things seen," neuter plural of *vīsus,* past participle of *vidēre,* to see.]

vis·age (vĭz′ĭj) *n.* **1.** The face or facial expression of a person; a countenance. **2.** Appearance; aspect: *the visage of winter.* [Middle English, from Old French, from *vis,* face, from Latin *vīsus,* from the past participle of *vidēre,* to see.]

vis·aged (vĭz′ĭjd) *adj.* Having a specified kind of visage. Used in combination: *square-visaged.*

visard. Variant of **vizard.**

vis-à-vis (vē′zə-vē′) *n., pl.* **vis-à-vis** (-vēz′, -vē′). **1.** Either of two persons or things opposite each other, such as partners in various dances. **2.** Either of two persons corresponding to each other in status, ability, or position; a counterpart.

~adv. Face to face.

~prep. **1.** Compared with; in relation to. **2.** Opposite to; face to face with. [French, "face to face."] **—vis-à-vis** *adj.*

Vi·sa·yan (vē-sä′yən) *n., pl.* **-yans** or collectively **Visayan.** Also **Bi·sa·yan** (bē-). **1.** A member of the largest group of native people of the Philippines, found in the Visayan Islands. **2.** The Austronesian language spoken by these people. **—Vi·sa·yan** *adj.*

Visayan Islands. An island group of the Republic of the Philippines, 62,160 square kilometers (24,000 square miles) in area, lying between Luzon and Mindanao.

Visc. viscount; viscountess.

vis·ca·cha, viz·ca·cha (vĭs-kä′chə) *n.* Any of several gregarious, burrowing South American rodents of the genera *Lagostomus* and *Lagidium,* related to and resembling the chinchilla. [Spanish, from Quechua *wiscacha.*]

vis·cer·a (vĭs′ər-ə) *pl.n. Singular* **viscus** (vĭs′kəs). **1.** The internal organs of the body, especially those contained within the abdominal and thoracic cavities. **2.** Loosely, the intestines. [Latin *vīscera,* plural of *vīscus*†, body organ.]

vis·cer·al (vĭs′ər-əl) *adj.* **1.** Pertaining to, situated in, or affecting the viscera. **2.** Pertaining to or derived from emotions and intuition rather than the intellect: *"The scientific approach to life is not really appropriate to states of visceral anguish"* (Anthony Burgess).

vis·cer·o·mo·tor (vĭs′ə-rō-mō′tər) *adj. Physiology.* Producing or related to movements of the viscera. [VISCER(A) + MOTOR.]

vis·cid (vĭs′ĭd) *adj.* **1.** Thick and adhesive. Said of a fluid. **2.** Covered with a sticky or clammy coating, as certain leaves are. [Late Latin *viscidus,* from Latin *viscum,* mistletoe, birdlime. See **viscous.**] **—vis·cid·i·ty** (vĭ-sĭd′ĭ-tē), **vis·cid·ness** *n.* **—vis·cid·ly** *adv.*

vis·com·e·ter (vĭs-kŏm′ə-tər) *n.* Any of various instruments or pieces of apparatus used to measure viscosity. Also called "viscosimeter." [VISCO(SITY) + -METER.] **—vis·co·met·ric** (vĭs′kō-mĕt′rĭk) *adj.*

Vis·con·ti (vĭs-kŏn′tē), **Gian Galeazzo** (1351–1402). Duke of Milan (1378–1402). By conquest, intrigue, and purchase, he united Milan with neighboring cities into one powerful state.

Visconti, Luchino, born Luchino Visconti de Modrone (1906–76). Italian film director. His films, which are noted for their visual composition, include *The Leopard* (1963), *The Damned* (1969), and *Death in Venice* (1971).

vis·cose (vĭs′kōs′) *n.* **1.** A thick, golden-brown viscous solution of cellulose xanthate, used in the manufacture of rayon and cellophane. **2.** Viscose rayon.

~adj. **1.** Viscous. **2.** Of, relating to, or made from viscose. [Middle

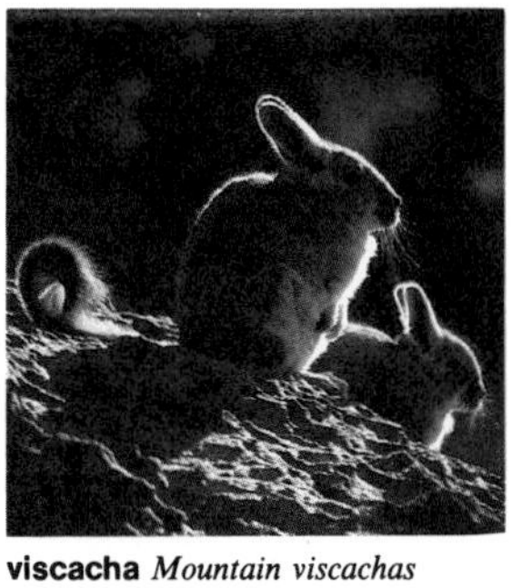

viscacha *Mountain viscachas (above) shelter in rock crevices and burrows at night, emerging to feed on plants by day. They live in the mountains of South America at altitudes of up to 5,000 meters (nearly 16,500 feet).*

PRONUNCIATION KEY

ă, pat; ā, pay; âr, care; ä, father, are; b, bib; ch, church; d, deed; ĕ, pet; ē, be; f, fife; g, gag; h, hat; hw, which; ĭ, pit; ī, pie; îr, pier; j, judge; k, kick; l, lid, needle; m, mum; n, no, sudden; ng, thing; ŏ, pot; ō, toe; ô, paw, for; oi, noise; ou, out; o͝o, book; o͞o, boot; p, pop; r, roar; s, sauce; sh, ship, dish; t, tight; th, thin, path; *th,* this, bathe; ŭ, cut; ûr, fur; v, valve; w, with; y, yes; z, zebra, size; zh, vision; ə, about, item, edible, gallop, circus, peaceful

IN FOREIGN WORDS:

à, *Fr.* ami; œ, *Fr.* feu, *Ger.* schön; ü, *Fr.* tu, *Ger.* über; KH, *Ger.* ich, *Scot.* loch; N, *Fr.* bon; y′, *Fr.* Compiègne

STRESS MARKS:

Primary stress: ′ **in·cite′** (ĭn-sīt′)
Secondary stress: ′ **in′sight′** (ĭn′sīt′)

English, sticky, viscid, from Late Latin *viscōsus*, VISCOUS.]

viscose rayon *n.* A rayon made by reconverting cellulose from a soluble xanthate form to tough fibers by washing in acid.

vis·co·sim·e·ter (vĭs′kə-sĭm′ə-tər) *n.* A viscometer.

vis·cos·i·ty (vĭs-kŏs′ə-tē) *n., pl.* **-ties. 1.** The condition or property of being viscous. **2.** *Physics. Symbol* η. The degree to which a fluid resists flow under an applied force, measured by the tangential stress on the fluid divided by the resulting velocity gradient under conditions of streamline flow. [Middle English, from Medieval Latin *viscōsitās* (stem *viscōsitāt-*), from *viscōsus*, VISCOUS.]

vis·count (vī′kount′) *n. Abbr.* **V., Visc., Visct.** A peer ranking below an earl and above a baron. [Middle English, from Old French *visconte*, from Medieval Latin *vicecomes* : VICE (substitute) + *comes*, COUNT.] **—vis·count·cy** (vī′kount′sē), **vis·count·y** *n.*

vis·count·ess (vī′koun′tĭs) *n. Abbr.* **V., Visc., Visct. 1.** The wife or widow of a viscount. **2.** A woman who holds the rank of viscount.

vis·cous (vĭs′kəs) *adj.* **1.** Having relatively high resistance to flow. **2.** Viscid; sticky. [Middle English *viscouse*, from Norman French *viscous*, from Late Latin *viscōsus*, from Latin *viscum*, mistletoe, birdlime (made from mistletoe berries).] **—vis·cous·ly** *adv.* **—vis·cous·ness** *n.*

Visct. viscount; viscountess.

vis·cus. Singular of **viscera.**

vise (vīs) *n.* Also **vice.** A clamping device of metal or wood, usually consisting of two jaws closed or opened by a screw or lever, used in carpentry or metalworking to hold a piece in position.

~tr.v. **vised, vising, vises.** Also **vice, viced, vicing, vices.** To hold in or as in a vise. [Middle English *vis*, winding staircase, screw, from Latin *vitis*, (winding) vine.]

Vi·shin·ski (vĭ-shĭn′skē), **Andrei Yanuarievich** (1883–1954). Soviet jurist and diplomat. As the chief Soviet prosecutor from 1935 to 1939 and the conductor of the Great Purge trials in Moscow, he was a principal figure in the Stalin terror. He later served as a Soviet delegate to the United Nations (1946–54) and as foreign minister (1949–53).

Vish·nu (vĭsh′no͞o) *n.* The Hindu deity worshiped as the preserver and second member of the trinity with Brahma and Shiva, and as the chief deity by the Vaishnava. [Sanskrit *Viṣṇuḥ*.]

vis·i·bil·i·ty (vĭz′ə-bĭl′ə-tē) *n., pl.* **-ties. 1.** The fact, state, or degree of being visible. **2.** *Abbr.* **vis.** The greatest distance under given weather conditions to which it is possible to see without the aid of instruments. [French *visibilité*, from Latin *vīsibilis*, VISIBLE.]

vis·i·ble (vĭz′ə-bəl) *adj.* **1.** Capable of being seen; perceptible to the eye: *a visible object.* **2.** Obvious to the eye: *a visible change of expression.* **3.** Manifest; apparent: *no visible solution.* **4.** Available; on hand: *the visible supply.* **5.** Publicly conspicuous; in the public eye: *a highly visible politician.* **6.** Prepared to receive visitors. **7.** Constructed or designed to keep important parts in easily accessible view: *a visible file.* **8.** Represented visually, as by symbols. **9.** *Economics.* Designating items of international trade consisting of goods rather than services. Compare **invisible.**

~n. **visibles.** *Economics.* Imports and exports of goods as opposed to those of services. Compare **invisible.** [Middle English, from Old French, from Latin *vīsibilis*, from *vīsus*, sight, VISION.] **—vis·i·ble·ness** *n.* **—vis·i·bly** *adv.*

visible horizon *n.* See **horizon** (sense 1).

visible radiation *n.* Electromagnetic radiation that can be detected by the normal human eye; light.

visible speech *n.* A system of phonetic notation used as an aid for teaching speech to the deaf and consisting of diagrams of the organs of speech in the positions required to articulate sounds.

Vis·i·goth (vĭz′ə-gŏth′) *n.* A member of the western group of Goths that invaded the Roman Empire in the 4th century A.D. and settled in France and Spain, establishing a monarchy that lasted until the early 8th century A.D. Compare **Ostrogoth.** [From Late Latin *Visigothi* (plural), probably "West Goths."] **—Vis·i·goth·ic** *adj.*

vi·sion (vĭzh′ən) *n.* **1. a.** The faculty of sight: *poor vision.* **b.** That which can be, is, or has been seen. **2.** Unusual competence in discernment or perception; intelligent foresight: *a woman of vision.* **3.** The manner in which one sees or conceives of something. **4.** A mental image produced by the imagination: *He has visions of himself as a hero.* **5. a.** The mystical experience of seeing as if with the eyes the supernatural or a supernatural being. **b.** That which is thus experienced or seen. **6.** A person or thing of extraordinary beauty. **7.** The image on a television screen.

~tr.v. **visioned, -sioning, -sions.** To see in or as if in a vision. [Middle English, from Old French, from Latin *vīsiō* (stem *vīsiōn-*), from *vīsus*, sight, from the past participle of *vidēre*, to see.] **—vi·sion·al** *adj.* **—vi·sion·al·ly** *adv.*

vi·sion·ar·y (vĭzh′ə-nĕr′ē) *adj.* **1.** Characterized by vision or foresight: *a visionary statesman.* **2.** Having the nature of or seen in fantasies or dreams. **3.** Characterized by or given to mystical visions, prophecies, or revelations. **4.** Characterized by or given to impractical ideas; unrealistic: *a visionary fool* **5.** Not practicable at present; idealistic; utopian: *a visionary scheme.*

~n., pl. **visionaries. 1.** One who has visions; a seer; prophet. **2.** One who is given to impractical or speculative ideas; a dreamer. **3.** One with great imagination or foresight.

vis·it (vĭz′ĭt) *v.* **-ited, -iting, -its.** *—tr.* **1.** To go or come to see (a person), as by way of friendship or duty; call on: *visiting his sister.* **2.** To go or come to see (a place), as on a tour: *visit a museum.* **3.** To stay with as a guest. **4. a.** To go or come to see in a professional capacity: *The priest visited the condemned man.* **b.** To go or come to (an institution, for example) in an official capacity, as to inspect or examine. **5.** To go or come to for a particular purpose: *I visit the bank on Fridays.* **6.** To go or come to for medical or other treatment: *visit the dentist.* **7.** To afflict; assail: *A plague visited the village.* **8. a.** To inflict punishment upon or for: *"I shall visit their sin upon them."* (Exodus 32:34). **b.** To inflict (anger or retribution, for example) upon someone or something. **9.** *Archaic.* To come to in order to comfort or bless. Said of the Deity. *—intr.* **1.** To pay a call or calls. **2.** To inflict punishment; take revenge. **3.** *Informal.* To converse or chat: *Stay and visit with me for a while.*

~n. **1.** An act or instance of visiting a person, place, or thing. **2.** A stay or sojourn as a guest. **3. a.** An act of visiting in a professional capacity: *The doctor's visit was very brief.* **b.** An act of visiting in an official capacity, as for an inspection or examination. **4.** *Law.* The boarding of a foreign ship during wartime to establish its nationality, purpose, and cargo. Used especially in the phrase *right of visit and search.* [Middle English *visiten*, from Old French *visiter*, from Latin *visitāre*, to go to see, from *vīsāre*, to view, from *vīsus*, sight, VISION.]

vis·it·a·ble (vĭz′ə-tə-bəl) *adj.* **1.** Capable of being visited socially. **2.** Subject to or allowing official visit, as for inspection.

vis·i·tant (vĭz′ə-tənt) *n.* **1.** A supernatural being; a ghost or specter. **2.** A visitor; especially, a pilgrim or tourist. **3.** A migratory animal or bird that stops in a particular place for a limited period of time.

~adj. Archaic. Visiting. [Latin *visitāns* (stem *visitānt-*), present participle of *visitāre*, to VISIT.]

vis·i·ta·tion (vĭz′ə-tā′shən) *n.* **1.** A visit for the purpose of making an official inspection or examination, such as one made by a bishop to a church in his diocese. **2. a.** A visit or social call. **b.** A visit or social call that is unwelcome or unduly long. Used humorously. **3.** A divorced or separated parent's right of access to the children of the marriage. **4. a.** A visit of punishment or affliction or of comfort and blessing, regarded as being ordained by God. **b.** A calamitous event or experience; a grave misfortune. **5.** The appearance or arrival of a supernatural being. **6. Visitation. a.** The visit of the Virgin Mary to her cousin Elizabeth. Luke 1:39–56. **b.** The Church festival held on July 2 in commemoration of this visit. **—vis·i·ta·tion·al** *adj.*

vis·i·ta·to·ri·al (vĭz′ə-tə-tôr′ē-əl, -tōr′ē-əl) *adj.* Also **vis·i·to·ri·al** (vĭz′ə-tôr′ē-əl, -tōr′ē-əl). **1.** Of or pertaining to an official visitor or visit. **2.** Having the right or power of visitation.

visiting card *n. British.* A **calling card** *(see).*

visiting fireman *n. Informal.* **1.** An influential visitor who is entertained impressively. **2.** A visitor to a city who is welcomed because he is thought to be a free spender.

visiting nurse *n.* A registered nurse employed by a public health agency or hospital to promote community health and especially to visit sick persons in their homes.

visiting professor *n.* A person, especially a lecturer or professor on sabbatical leave, holding a professorship at the invitation of a university or other institution, often in another country for an academic year.

visiting teacher *n.* **1.** A school social worker who works individually with students having special problems in adjusting to school or in functioning well in school. **2.** In some states, a teacher who visits and instructs sick or physically impaired students who are unable to attend school.

vis·i·tor (vĭz′ə-tər) *n.* **1.** One who pays a visit; a guest; caller. **2.** A sightseer or tourist. **3.** A migratory animal, especially a bird, pausing in transit at a place; a visitant. **4.** An official, especially at a college, holding nominal powers of inspection or supervision.

vis ma·jor (vĭs mā′jər) *n., pl.* **vires majores** (vī′rēz′ mə-jôr′ēz′, -jōr′ēz′). *Law.* An overwhelming force of circumstance or nature having unavoidable consequences that can exempt one from the obligations of a contract. [Latin, "greater force."]

vi·sor, vi·zor (vī′zər) *n.* **1.** A fixed or movable shield fitted at the top of a car windshield to protect against glare. **2.** A protective shield held or worn in front of the face, used when welding or doing other dangerous tasks. **3.** A peak on a cap. **4.** The front piece of the helmet of a suit of armor, capable of being raised and lowered and designed to protect the eyes, nose, and forehead. **5.** *Archaic.* Any means of concealment or disguise; a mask.

~tr.v. **visored, -soring, -sors.** Also **vi·zor, -zored, -zoring, -zors.** To mask or protect with a visor. [Middle English *viser*, from Norman French, from Old French *vis*, face, from Latin *vīsus*, sight, VISION.]

vis·ta (vĭs′tə) *n.* **1.** A distant view seen through a passage, as between buildings or rows of trees; scene; prospect. **2.** The passage framing the approach to such a scene; an avenue. **3.** A comprehensive awareness of a series of remembered, present, or anticipated events: *"He opened a vista into a mean life."* (Rebecca West). [Italian, from *visto*, past participle of *vedere*, to see, from Latin *vidēre*.]

Vis·tu·la (vĭs′cho͞o-lə). *Polish* **Wis·la** (vēs′lä). River in Poland. Rising in the Beskid Mts., it flows 1,094 kilometers (680 miles) north and northwest to enter the Baltic Sea at Gdańsk.

vis·u·al (vĭzh′o͞o-əl) *adj. Abbr.* **vis. 1.** Serving, resulting from, or pertaining to the sense of sight. **2.** Capable of being seen by the eye; visible. **3.** *Physics.* Optical. **4.** Done, maintained, or executed by the sight only: *visual navigation.* **5.** Having the nature of or producing an image in the mind. **6.** Involving sight: *visual instruction; visual humor.*

~n. Usually **visuals.** Any form of graphic material, such as a film, display, or photograph, used for educational or publicity purposes.

PRONUNCIATION KEY

ă, pat; ā, pay; âr, care;
ä, father, are; b, bib;
ch, church; d, deed; ĕ, pet;
ē, be; f, fife; g, gag; h, hat;
hw, which; ĭ, pit; ī, pie;
îr, pier; j, judge; k, kick;
l, lid, needle; m, mum;
n, no, sudden; ng, thing;
ŏ, pot; ō, toe; ô, paw, for;
oi, noise; ou, out; o͝o, book;
o͞o, boot; p, pop; r, roar;
s, sauce; sh, ship, dish;
t, tight; th, thin, path;
th, this, bathe; ŭ, cut; ûr, fur;
v, valve; w, with; y, yes;
z, zebra, size; zh, vision;
ə, about, item, edible,
gallop, circus, peaceful

IN FOREIGN WORDS:

à, *Fr.* ami; œ, *Fr.* feu, *Ger.* schön; ü, *Fr.* tu, *Ger.* über; KH, *Ger.* ich, *Scot.* loch; N, *Fr.* bon; y′, *Fr.* Compiègne

STRESS MARKS:

Primary stress: ′
in·cite′ (ĭn-sīt′)
Secondary stress: ′
in′sight′ (ĭn′sīt′)

[Middle English, from Late Latin *vīsuālis*, from Latin *vīsus*, VISION.] —**vis·u·al·ly** *adv.*

visual aids *pl.n.* Graphic material and the device's for presenting it, such as posters and display boards, used in education to impart instruction by visual means.

visual arts *pl.n.* Arts such as painting and sculpture whose works exist in permanent and static form rather than requiring performance, as ballet does, and whose aesthetic appeal is primarily to the visual sense, as opposed to such arts as music and poetry.

visual display unit *n.* An electronic device for displaying computer-prompted words and diagrams on a cathode-ray screen. Also called "VDU," "video terminal," "video display terminal."

visual field *n. Abbr.* **V.F.** The entire area visible to the immobile eye or eyes at a given moment; the field of vision.

vis·u·al·ize (vĭzh′ŏo-ə-līz′) *v.* **-ized, -izing, -izes.** —*tr.* To form a mental image or vision of; envisage. —*intr.* To form a mental image or images. —**vis·u·al·i·za·tion** *n.* —**vis·u·al·iz·er** *n.*

visual purple *n.* A red-light-sensitive pigment of the retina, **rhodopsin** *(see).*

vi·tal (vīt′əl, vīt′l) *adj.* **1.** Of, affecting, or characteristic of life: *vital processes.* **2.** Necessary to the continuation of life; life-sustaining: *vital functions.* **3.** Full of life; energetic; vigorous; animated: *Her dancing is vital yet controlled.* **4.** *Poetic.* Imparting life or animation; invigorating. **5. a.** Having immediate importance; essential; indispensable: *vital to our success.* **b.** Crucial; decisive: *a vital inning.* **6.** Concerned with or recording data pertinent to lives. **7.** *Archaic.* Destructive to life; fatal; deadly: *a vital wound.* —See Synonyms at **necessary.** [Middle English, from Old French, from Latin *vītālis*, from *vīta*, life.] —**vi·tal·ly** *adv.* —**vi·tal·ness** *n.*

vital capacity *n. Physiology.* The maximum amount of air that can be expelled from the lungs after breathing in as deeply as possible.

vital force *n.* A hypothetical living force suggested by early biologists as the driving force behind the evolution and development of organisms. [Translation of French *élan vital.*]

vi·tal·ism (vīt′l-ĭz′əm) *n.* The philosophical doctrine that life processes possess a unique character radically different from physiochemical phenomena and therefore cannot be explained in empirical terms. —**vi·tal·ist** *n.* —**vi·tal·is·tic** *adj.*

vi·tal·i·ty (vī-tăl′ə-tē) *n., pl.* **-ties. 1.** Vigor; energy; exuberance. **2.** The power to survive or evolve: *impaired the firm's vitality.* **3.** That which distinguishes the living from the nonliving; an energy, force, or principle characteristic of life; vital force. **4.** The capacity to live, grow, or develop.

vi·tal·ize (vīt′l-īz′) *tr.v.* **-ized, -izing, -izes. 1.** To endow with life. **2.** To invigorate or animate. —**vi·tal·i·za·tion** *n.* —**vi·tal·iz·er** *n.*

vi·tals (vīt′əlz) *pl.n.* **1.** Any bodily parts or organs regarded as the center or source of life: *sensed disaster in his vitals.* **2.** Those bodily organs whose continued functioning is essential for life. **3.** The reproductive organs, especially those of the male. **4.** Those elements essential to continued functioning, as in a system.

vital stain *n.* Any biological stain that can be used to color living material, as for examination under a microscope.

vital statistics *pl.n.* **1.** Data that record significant events and dates in human life, as the rate of births, deaths, and marriages. **2.** *Informal.* The measurements of a woman's bust, waist, and hips.

vi·ta·min (vīt′ə-mĭn) *n.* Also *rare* **vi·ta·mine** (-mēn, -mĭn). Any of various relatively complex organic substances occurring naturally in plant and some animal tissue, and essential in small amounts for the control of metabolic processes. [German *Vitamine* : Latin *vīta*, life + AMINE (so called because it was once thought to contain an amino acid).] —**vi·ta·min·ic** *adj.*

vitamin A *n.* Vitamin A_1 or a mixture of vitamins A_1 and A_2, occurring principally in fish-liver oils and some yellow and dark-green vegetables, functioning in normal cell growth and development. A deficiency causes hardening and roughening of the skin, night blindness, and degeneration of mucous membranes. Also called "retinol."

vitamin A_1 *n.* A yellow crystalline compound, $C_{20}H_{30}O$, extracted from fish-liver oils. See **vitamin A.**

vitamin A_2 *n.* A golden-yellow oil, $C_{20}H_{28}O$, occurring in pike-liver oils and having approximately 40 percent of the biological activity of vitamin A_1. See **vitamin A.**

vitamin B *n.* **1.** Vitamin B complex. **2.** A member of the vitamin B complex, especially thiamine.

vitamin B_c *n.* **Folic acid** *(see).*
vitamin B_1 *n.* **Thiamine** *(see).*
vitamin B_2 *n.* **Riboflavin** *(see).*
vitamin B_6 *n.* **Pyridoxine** *(see).*

vitamin B_{12} *n.* A complex, cobalt-containing coordination compound produced in the normal growth of certain microorganisms, found in liver, and widely used to treat pernicious anemia. Also called "cyanocobalamin."

vitamin B complex *n.* A group of vitamins originally thought to be a single substance, generally regarded as including thiamine, riboflavin, niacin, pantothenic acid, biotin, pyridoxine, folic acid, lipoic acid, inositol, and vitamin B_{12}, and occurring chiefly in yeast, liver, eggs, and some meats.

vitamin C *n.* **Ascorbic acid** *(see).*

vitamin D *n., pl.* **D vitamins.** Any of several chemically similar compounds, especially vitamin D_2 and vitamin D_3, produced in general by ultraviolet irradiation of sterols, obtained from milk, fish, and eggs, required for normal bone growth, and used to treat rickets in children and osteomalacia in adults.

vitamin D_2 *n.* A white crystalline compound, $C_{28}H_{44}O$, produced by ultraviolet irradiation of ergosterol. Also called "calciferol," "ergocalciferol," "viosterol." See **vitamin D.**

vitamin D_3 *n.* A colorless crystalline compound, $C_{27}H_{44}O$, with essentially the same biological activity as vitamin D_2 but significantly more potent in poultry. See **vitamin D.**

vitamin E *n.* Any of several chemically related viscous oils, especially $C_{29}H_{50}O_2$, found chiefly in grains and vegetable oils. A deficiency causes sterility in certain mammals, but the effects in humans are uncertain. Also called "tocopherol."

vitamin G *n.* **Riboflavin** *(see).*
vitamin H *n.* **Biotin** *(see).*

vitamin K *n., pl.* **K vitamins.** Any of several natural and synthetic substances essential for the promotion of blood clotting and prevention of hemorrhage; especially menaquinone *(vitamin K_2)* and phylloquinone *(vitamin K_1).*

vitamin P *n.* **Bioflavonoid** *(see).*

vi·tel·lin (vī-tĕl′ĭn, vĭ-) *n.* A protein found in egg yolk. [VITELL(US) + -IN.]

vi·tel·line (vī-tĕl′ĭn, vĭ-) *adj.* **1.** Pertaining to or associated with the yolk of an egg: *the vitelline membrane.* **2.** Having the yellow color of an egg yolk; dull yellow. [VITELL(US) + -INE.]

vitelline membrane *n. Zoology.* A membrane that forms around a fertilized egg to prevent other sperm from entering.

vi·tel·lus (vī-tĕl′əs, vĭ-) *n., pl.* **-luses** or **-li** (-lī). *Rare.* The yolk of an egg. [Latin.]

vi·ti·ate (vīsh′ē-āt′) *tr.v.* **-ated, -ating, -ates. 1.** To impair the value or quality of; make faulty or impure; spoil. **2.** To corrupt morally; pervert. **3.** To invalidate or render (a contract, for example) legally ineffective. [Latin *vitiāre*, from *vitium*, defect, fault.] —**vi·ti·a·ble** (vĭsh′ē-ə-bəl) *adj.* —**vi·ti·a·tion** *n.* —**vi·ti·a·tor** *n.*

vit·i·cul·ture (vĭt′ĭ-kŭl′chər, vī′tĭ-) *n.* The cultivation of grapes, especially for winemaking. [Latin *vītis*, vine + CULTURE.] —**vit·i·cul·tur·al** *adj.* —**vit·i·cul·tur·ist** *n.*

Vi·ti Le·vu (vē′tē lā′vōō). The principal island of the Fiji Islands, 10,386 square kilometers (4,010 square miles); the site of Suva, the capital of the republic.

vit·i·li·go (vĭt′l-ī′gō) *n.* A skin disease, **leucoderma** *(see).* [Latin *vitilīgō*, cutaneous eruption.]

vit·re·ous (vĭt′rē-əs) *adj.* **1.** Pertaining to, resembling, or having the nature of glass; glassy. **2.** Obtained or made from glass. **3.** Of or pertaining to the vitreous humor. [Latin *vitreus*, from *vitrum†*, glass.] —**vit·re·os·i·ty** (vĭt′rē-ŏs′ə-tē), **vit·re·ous·ness** *n.*

vitreous body *n.* A gelatinous body of matter composed mainly of vitreous humor that fills the part of the eyeball between the retina and the lens.

vitreous enamel *n.* Porcelain enamel *(see).*

vitreous humor *n.* A watery fluid that is a major component of the vitreous body.

vitreous silica *n.* Silica that has been fused to form a hard transparent heat-resistant glass, used especially for making scientific apparatus.

vi·tres·cence (vī-trĕs′əns) *n.* **1.** Transformation into glass. **2.** The state of becoming vitreous or like glass.

vi·tres·cent (vī-trĕs′ənt) *adj.* **1.** Tending to become glass or like glass. **2.** Capable of being turned into glass. [Latin *vitrum*, glass (see **vitreous**) + -ESCENT.]

vit·ri·fi·ca·tion (vĭt′rə-fə-kā′shən) *n.* **1.** The act or process of vitrifying or the state of being vitrified. **2.** Something vitrified.

vit·ri·form (vĭt′rə-fôrm′) *adj.* Resembling glass in form or appearance. [Latin *vitrum*, glass + -FORM.]

vit·ri·fy (vĭt′rə-fī′) *v.* **-fied, -fying, -fies.** —*tr.* To change or make into glass or a similar substance, especially through melting. —*intr.* To become vitreous. [French *vitrifier*, from Old French : Latin *vitrum*, glass (see **vitreous**) + -FY.] —**vit·ri·fi·a·bil·i·ty** *n.* —**vit·ri·fi·a·ble** *adj.*

vit·ri·ol (vĭt′rē-ōl′) *n.* **1.** *Chemistry.* **a.** Sulfuric acid. **b.** Any of various sulfates of metals, such as ferrous sulfate (green vitriol), zinc sulfate (white vitriol), or copper sulfate (blue vitriol). **2.** Vituperative statements or feelings.

~*tr.v.* **vitrioled** or **-olled, -oling** or **-olling, -ols. 1.** To expose or subject to vitriol. **2.** To attack or injure with vitriol. [Middle English, from Old French, from Medieval Latin *vitriolum*, from Latin *vitrum*, glass (from the appearance of its sulfates). See **vitreous.**]

vit·ri·ol·ic (vĭt′rē-ōl′ĭk) *adj.* **1.** Of, similar to, or derived from a vitriol. **2.** Bitterly scathing; caustic: *a vitriolic review.*

vit·ri·ol·ize (vĭt′rē-ə-līz′) *tr.v.* **-ized, -izing, -izes. 1.** To expose or subject to vitriol. **2.** To convert into vitriol. **3.** To attack or injure with vitriol. —**vit·ri·ol·i·za·tion** *n.*

Vi·tru·vi·us (vī-trōō′vē-əs), (late 1st century B.C. and early 1st century A.D.). Roman architect and engineer. His treatise *De Architectura*, the only complete Roman architectural work that has survived, influenced architects of the classical revival, such as Palladio and Alberti.

vit·ta (vĭt′ə) *n., pl.* **vittae** (vĭt′ē). **1.** *Biology.* A streak or band of color. **2.** *Botany.* An oil tube in the fruit of certain plants, such as the carrot or parsley. [Latin, headband.] —**vit·tate** (vĭt′āt′) *adj.*

vittle. *Nonstandard.* Variant of **victual.**

vi·tu·per·ate (vī-tōō′pə-rāt′, vĭ-tyōō′-, vī-) *tr.v.* **-ated, -ating, -ates.** To rail against severely or abusively; revile; berate. —See Synonyms at **malign.** [Latin *vituperāre.*] —**vi·tu·per·a·tor** *n.*

vi·tu·per·a·tion (vī-tōō′pə-rā′shən, vĭ-tyōō′-, vī-) *n.* **1.** Abusive censure or blame. **2.** Invective; railing. **3.** The act of vituperating.

vi·tu·per·a·tive (vī-tōō′pər-ə-tĭv, vĭ-tyōō′-, vī-) *adj.* Harshly abusive;

acrimonious: *a vituperative note.* —**vi·tu·per·a·tive·ly** *adv.*

vi·va¹ (vē′vä) *interj.* Used to express acclamation, salute, or applause. —*n.* A shout of "viva." [Italian, from *vivere,* to live, from Latin *vīvere.*]

vi·va² (vī′və) *n.* *British.* An examination consisting of an interview rather than of written papers; a viva voce examination. [Shortened from VIVA VOCE.]

vi·va·ce (vē-vä′chā) *adv. Music.* Lively; vivaciously; briskly. Used as a direction. [Italian, from Latin *vīvāx,* VIVACIOUS.]

vi·va·cious (vĭ-vā′shəs, vī-) *adj.* Animated; sprightly; spirited. [Latin *vīvāx* (stem *vīvāci-*), lively, from *vīvere,* to live.] —**vi·va·cious·ly** *adv.* —**vi·va·cious·ness** *n.*

vi·vac·i·ty (vĭ-văs′ə-tē, vī-) *n.* The condition or quality of being vivacious; liveliness.

Vi·val·di (vĭ-väl′dē), **Antonio** (1675–1741). Italian composer and violinist. He is chiefly remembered for his concertos, particularly *The Four Seasons,* a set of four violin concertos.

vi·van·dière (vē-vänd-dyâr′) *n.* Formerly, especially in France, a woman who accompanied troops to sell them extra food, supplies, and drink. [French, feminine of *vivandier,* provisioner, from Old French, from *viande,* VIAND.]

vi·var·i·um (vī-vâr′ē-əm) *n., pl.* **-ums** or **-ia** (-ē-ə). A place or enclosure for keeping and breeding living animals for observation or research. [Latin : *vīvus,* alive (see vivify) + -ARIUM.]

vi·va vo·ce (vī′və vō′sē) *adj.* By word of mouth; spoken; oral. —*n.* A viva voce examination. [Middle Latin, "with the living voice."] —**vi·va vo·ce** *adv.*

vive (vēv) *interj. French.* Used to acclaim, salute, or applaud a person or personification specified: *Vive la France!*

vi·ver·rine (vī-vĕr′īn, -ĭn′, vī-) *n.* A member of the family Viverridae, which includes carnivorous mammals such as the civets and mongooses. [From Latin *viverra,* ferret.] —**vi·ver·rine** *adj.*

viv·id (vĭv′ĭd) *adj.* **1.** Perceived as bright and distinct; brilliant: *the vivid evening star.* **2. a.** Having intensely bright colors: *a vivid tapestry.* **b.** Very bright or strong. Said of color. **3.** Full of the vigor and freshness of immediate experience: *vivid emotions.* **4. a.** Evoking lifelike images within the mind; heard, seen, or felt as if real: *a vivid description.* **b.** Active in forming or retaining lifelike images: *a vivid imagination.* [Latin *vīvidus,* full of life, lifelike, from *vīvere,* to live.] —**viv·id·ly** *adv.* —**viv·id·ness** *n.*

viv·i·fy (vĭv′ə-fī′) *tr.v.* **-fied, -fy·ing, -fies. 1.** To give or bring life to; animate. **2.** To make more lively, intense, or striking; enliven. [French *vivifier,* from Late Latin *vīvificāre* : Latin *vīvus,* alive + *facere,* to do.] —**viv·i·fi·ca·tion** *n.* —**viv·i·fi·er** *n.*

vi·vip·a·rous (vī-vĭp′ər-əs) *adj.* **1.** *Zoology.* Giving birth to living offspring that develop within the mother's body. Said of most mammals. Compare **oviparous, ovoviviparous. 2.** *Botany.* **a.** Germinating or producing seeds that germinate before becoming detached from the parent plant. **b.** Producing bulbils or new plants rather than seed. [Latin *vīviparus* : *vīvus,* alive (see vivify) + -PAROUS.] —**viv·i·par·i·ty** (vĭv′ə-păr′ə-tē) *n.* —**vi·vip·a·rous·ly** *adv.*

viv·i·sect (vĭv′ə-sĕkt′) *v.* **-sected, -secting, -sects.** —*tr.* To perform vivisection on (a live animal). —*intr.* To carry out vivisection. [Back-formation from VIVISECTION.] —**viv·i·sec·tor** *n.*

viv·i·sec·tion (vĭv′ə-sĕk′shən) *n.* **1.** The act of cutting into or dissecting the body of a living animal, especially for scientific research. **2.** Extremely detailed and often destructive criticism or analysis, as of a motion picture or book. [Latin *vīvus,* alive (see vivify) + -SECTION.] —**viv·i·sec·tion·al** *adj.*

viv·i·sec·tion·ist (vĭv′ə-sĕk′shə-nĭst) *n.* **1.** A person who performs a vivisection. **2.** A person who favors the continued use of vivisection for scientific research and opposes the movement to abolish it.

vix·en (vĭk′sən) *n.* **1.** A female fox. **2.** A quarrelsome, shrewish, or malicious woman. [Middle English *fixene,* Old English *fyxe,* she-fox.] —**vix·en·ish** *adj.* —**vix·en·ly** *adj. & adv.*

Vi·yel·la (vī-ĕl′ə) *n.* A trademark for a soft fabric made of a mixture of wool and cotton, used especially for clothing. —**Vi·yel·la** *adj.*

viz. videlicet. *Note: Viz.* is never pronounced (vĭz) when formally reading something aloud: it is replaced by its gloss, "namely." In informal speech, however, it is often pronounced (vĭz). Though *viz* is an abbreviation of *videlicet,* it is rarely read out as "videlicet"—except in humorous or highly formal contexts.

viz·ard, vis·ard (vĭz′ərd) *n. Archaic.* **1.** A visor on a helmet. **2.** A mask. [Earlier *vizar, viser,* variants of VISOR.]

vizcacha. Variant of **viscacha.**

vi·zier (vĭ-zîr′, vĭz′yər) *n.* Also **vi·zir** (vĭ-zîr′). A high officer, such as a provincial governor or chief adviser, in various Muslim governments, especially in the Ottoman Empire. [French *vizir,* from Turkish *vezîr,* from Arabic *wazīr,* porter, from *wazara,* to bear, carry.] —**vi·zier·i·al** *adj.*

vi·zier·ate (vĭ-zîr′ĭt, -āt′, vĭz′yər-ĭt, -yə-rāt′) *n.* The office, authority, or term of office of a vizier. Also called "vizieralty," "viziership."

vizor. Variant of **visor.**

vizs·la (vĭzh′lô′) *n.* A hunting dog of a Hungarian breed, having a smooth golden-red coat. [After *Vizsla,* Hungary, where the breed originated.]

V-J Day (vē′jā′) *n.* The day of victory for the Allied forces over Japan in World War II; in Britain, August 15, 1945, and in the United States, September 2, 1945. [Short for *Victory in Japan Day.*]

Vlach (vläKH) *n.* A member of a widely scattered people, speaking a Romanian dialect, living in southeastern Europe in early medieval times.

~*adj.* Of, pertaining to, or designating this people, their culture, or their Romanian dialect.

Vla·di·mir I (vlăd′ə-mîr′), **Saint ,** also known as Vladimir the Great (c. 965–1015). The first Christian ruler of Russia. He extended Russia's dominions from the Ukraine to the Baltic Sea, making Kiev his capital.

Vla·di·vos·tok (vlăd′ə-vŏs-tŏk′, -vŏs′tŏk). A Pacific seaport of the U.S.S.R., between Amur Bay and the Golden Horn. It is a major Russian naval base.

Vla·minck (vlə-măŊK′), **Maurice de** (1876–1958). French painter. With Derain and Matisse he was one of the leading exponents of fauvism. He is noted for his stormy, aggressive landscapes.

vlf, VLF very low frequency.

V.M.D. Doctor of Veterinary Medicine [Latin *Veterinariae Medicinae Doctor.*]

V neck (vē′nĕk′) *n.* **1.** A neck or collar of a garment that has a V-shaped front, tapering to a point rather than being rounded. **2.** A garment, especially a sweater, having such a neck. —**V-neck, V-necked** *adj.*

vo. verso.

voc. vocative.

vocab. vocabulary.

vo·ca·ble (vō′kə-bəl) *n.* **1.** A word considered only as a sequence of sounds or letters rather than as a unit of meaning. **2.** A sound that can be voiced; a vowel. ~*adj.* Capable of being voiced or spoken. [French, from Old French, from Latin *vocābulum,* an appellation, from *vocāre,* to call.]

vo·cab·u·lar·y (vō-kăb′yə-lĕr′ē) *n., pl.* **-ies.** *Abbr.* **vocab. 1.** A list of words and often phrases, usually arranged alphabetically and defined or translated; a lexicon or glossary. **2.** All the words of a language. **3.** The sum of words used by, understood by, or at the command of a particular person or group. **4.** A command or reserve of expressive techniques; repertoire: *a dancer's vocabulary of movement.* [Medieval Latin *vocābulārium,* from *vocābulārius,* of words, from Latin *vocābulum,* an appellation, name. See vocable.]

vo·cal (vō′kəl) *adj.* **1. a.** Of or pertaining to the voice. **b.** For or rendered by the voice rather than an instrument: *a vocal line.* **2.** Uttered or produced by the voice: *a vocal prayer.* **3.** Having a voice; capable of emitting sound or speech. **4.** Full of voices; resounding with speech: *a vocal gathering.* **5.** Quick to speak or criticize; outspoken: *vocal dissidents.* **6.** *Phonetics.* **a.** Vocalic. **b.** Voiced. ~*n.* **1.** *Phonetics.* A vocal sound. **2. vocals.** The music sung by a vocalist, rather than the instrumental accompaniment. [Middle English, from Latin *vōcālis,* speaking, talking, from *vōx,* voice.] —**vo·cal·ly** *adv.* —**vo·cal·ness** *n.*

vocal cords *pl.n.* The lower of two pairs of bands or folds in the larynx that vibrate when pulled together and when air passes over them from the lungs, thereby producing vocal sounds. Also called "vocal folds."

vo·cal·ic (vō-kăl′ĭk) *adj.* **1.** Containing many vowel sounds. **2.** Pertaining to or having the nature of a vowel or vowels.

vo·cal·ise (vō-kă-lēz′) *n.* A wordless musical composition, especially for the voice. [French.]

vo·cal·ism (vō′kə-lĭz′əm) *n.* **1.** The use of the voice in speaking or singing. **2.** The act, technique, or art of singing. **3.** A vowel or vocalic sound. **4.** A system of vowels, as within a specific language.

vo·cal·ist (vō′kə-lĭst) *n.* A singer, especially in a jazz or pop group.

vo·cal·ize (vō′kə-līz′) *v.* **-ized, -izing, -izes.** —*tr.* **1.** To make vocal; produce with the voice. **2.** To give voice to; articulate. **3.** To mark (a vowelless Hebrew text, for example) with diacritical vowel points. **4.** *Phonetics.* **a.** To change (a consonant) into a vowel. **b.** To voice. —*intr.* **1.** To use the voice; especially, to sing. **2.** *Phonetics.* To be changed into a vowel. —**vo·cal·i·za·tion** *n.* —**vo·cal·iz·er** *n.*

vocal score *n.* A musical score transcribing the voice parts in full and the orchestral parts reduced to a piano accompaniment.

vo·ca·tion (vō-kā′shən) *n.* **1.** A regular occupation or profession; especially, one for which one is specially suited or qualified. **2.** An urge or predisposition to undertake a certain kind of work, especially a religious career; a calling. [Middle English *vocacioun,* divine call to a religious life, from Old French *vocation,* from Latin *vōcātiō* (stem *vōcātiōn-*), a calling, summoning, from *vōcāre,* to call.]

vo·ca·tion·al (vō-kā′shən-əl) *adj.* **1.** Of or pertaining to vocations or one's vocation. **2.** Pertaining to, providing, or undergoing training in a special skill to be pursued as a trade or profession. —**vo·ca·tion·al·ly** *adv.*

voc·a·tive (vŏk′ə-tĭv) *adj.* **1.** Pertaining to, characteristic of, or used in calling. **2.** *Abbr.* **v., voc.** Designating, pertaining to, or inflected in the grammatical case used in certain languages, such as Latin or Polish, to denote the person or thing being addressed. ~*n.* *Abbr.* **v., voc. 1.** The vocative case. **2.** A form or construction in this case. [Middle English *vocatif,* from Old French, from Latin *vocātīvus,* from *vocāre,* to call. See vocation.] —**voc·a·tive·ly** *adv.*

vo·cif·er·ate (vō-sĭf′ə-rāt′) *v.* **-ated, -ating, -ates.** —*intr.* To cry out vehemently, especially in protest; exclaim. —*tr.* To utter (a protest, for example) loudly and insistently. [Latin *vōciferārī* : *vōx* (stem *vōci-*), voice (see vocal) + *ferre,* to bear] —**vo·cif·er·a·tion** *n.*

vo·cif·er·ous (vō-sĭf′ər-əs) *adj.* **1.** Making an outcry, as in protest. **2.** Characterized by loudness and vehemence. [From VOCIFERATE.] —**vo·cif·er·ous·ly** *adv.* —**vo·cif·er·ous·ness** *n.*

Synonyms: vociferous, blatant, boisterous, strident, clamorous. These adjectives describe what is conspicuously loud, usually offensively so. *Vociferous* suggests the noise of an outcry, as of vehement demanding or protesting. *Blatant* suggests noise associated with coarseness, vulgarity, or obtrusive behavior. *Boisterous* is even stronger in implying a combination of noise and rowdy behavior, caused usually by unruliness or high spirits. *Strident* describes noise that is offensively harsh, shrill, or discordant. *Clamorous* adds to *vociferous* the idea of long duration; or the term can refer to any combination of loud, distracting sounds.

vo·coid (vō'koid') *n.* A speech sound articulated with air from the lungs flowing through the mouth over the center of the tongue without friction; a vowel or semivowel. [Latin *vōx* (stem *vōc-*), voice (see **vowel**) + -OID.] **—vo·coid** *adj.*

vod·ka (vŏd'kə) *n.* An alcoholic drink of Russian origin, formerly distilled from fermented wheat mash, now also made from a mash of rye, wheat, or potatoes. [Russian, diminutive of *voda,* water.]

voet·stoots (fo͝ot'sto͝orts') *adj. South African Law.* Designating a sale of an item, especially a house, in which its condition, good or bad, is accepted by the buyer who cannot then claim redress if it proves unsatisfactory. [Afrikaans, from Dutch, from phrase *met de voet te stoten,* "to push (aside) with the foot," hence figuratively, (to sell) without assuming responsibility.] **—voet·stoots** *adv.*

vogue (vōg) *n.* **1.** The prevailing fashion, practice, or style: *in vogue.* **2.** Popular acceptance or favor; popularity. —See Synonyms at **fashion.**

~*adj.* Fashionable; in widespread current use; popular: *vogue words.* [French, fashion, "rowing," from *voguer,* to row, go along smoothly, from Old French, from Old Low German *wogon* (unattested).] **—vogu·ish** *adj.*

Vo·gul (vō'go͝ol) *n.* **1.** A member of a people living in western Siberia. **2.** The language of this people, of the Finno-Ugric family of languages. [Russian, from Ostyak *Uogal', Uogat'.*]

voice (vois) *n. Abbr.* **v. 1. a.** The sound or sounds produced by the vocal organs of a vertebrate, especially by those of a human being. **b.** The natural and characteristic manner of speaking or sound of the speech of a specified person: *recognized your voice.* **2.** The ability to produce such sounds: *lost her voice.* **3.** Any sound resembling or reminiscent of vocal utterance: *the voice of the bugles.* **4.** The specified quality, condition, or timbre of vocal sound: *a hoarse voice.* **5. a.** Oral or verbal expression: *give voice to one's anger.* **b.** Any means of making something known: *the voice of the nation; the voice of experience.* **c.** The right or opportunity to express a choice or opinion: *had no voice in their own future.* **6.** *Obsolete.* **a.** Rumor or report. **b.** Reputation or fame. **7.** *Grammar.* A verb form indicating the relation between the subject and the action expressed by the verb. See **active, passive. 8.** *Phonetics.* The expiration of air through vibrating vocal cords, used in the production of the vowels and voiced consonants. Compare **breath. 9. a.** Musical tone produced by the vibration of vocal cords and resonated within the throat and head cavities. **b.** The quality or condition of a person's singing: *a bass voice; in excellent voice.* **c.** A singer: *a choir of fine voices.* **10.** Any of the melodic parts for a musical composition. In this sense, also called "voice part." **—throw one's voice.** To make one's voice seem to come from elsewhere, as a ventriloquist does. **—with one voice.** In unison; unanimously.

~*tr.v.* **voiced, voicing, voices. 1.** To express or utter; give voice to: *voice an objection.* **2.** *Phonetics.* To utter with voice. **3.** *Music.* To regulate the tone of (the pipes of an organ, for example). —See Synonyms at **vent.** [Middle English, from Old French *vois, voix,* from Latin *vōx.*]

voice box *n.* The larynx.

voiced (voist) *adj.* **1.** Having a voice or having a specified kind of voice. Often used in combination: *harsh-voiced.* **2.** *Phonetics.* Uttered with vibration of the vocal cords, as the consonants *d* and *b* in English. Compare **voiceless.**

voice·ful (vois'fəl) *adj. Poetic.* Having a voice; especially, having a loud voice; resounding. **—voice·ful·ness** *n.*

voice·less (vois'lĭs) *adj.* **1. a.** Having no voice; mute; silent. **b.** Not expressed by means of the voice. **2.** *Phonetics.* Uttered without vibration of the vocal cords, as the consonants *t* and *p* are in English. Compare **voiced. 3.** Unable to sing. **4.** Not having the right to speak or vote. —See Synonyms at **dumb. —voice·less·ly** *adv.* **—voice·less·ness** *n.*

voice-o·ver (vois'ō'vər) *n.* **1.** In motion pictures and television, the voice of a narrator or commentator who does not appear on camera. **2.** The script read by such a narrator.

voice part *n. Music.* See **voice** (sense 10).

voice·print (vois'prĭnt') *n.* An electronically recorded graphic representation of voice, typically with time plotted on the horizontal axis, frequency on the vertical, and amplitude exhibited in a series of contour lines.

voic·er (voi'sər) *n.* One that voices organ pipes.

voice vote *n.* A parliamentary vote that is decided on the relative volume of noise of those shouting "aye" and "no."

void (void) *adj.* **1.** Containing no matter; empty. **2.** Unoccupied; unfilled. Said of an office or position. **3.** Devoid; lacking. Used with *of: void of understanding.* **4.** Ineffective; useless. **5.** Having no legal force or validity; null. **6.** Having no cards in a suit: *The hand was void in diamonds.* —See Synonyms at **empty.**

~*n.* **1.** Something that is void; an empty space; a vacuum. **2.** An open space or break in continuity; a gap. **3.** A feeling or state of emptiness, loneliness, or loss. **4.** In card games, the state of not having any cards in a particular suit. **5.** An empty space or gap, as in a wall for a window.

~*v.* **voided, voiding, voids.** —*tr.* **1.** To make void or of no effect; invalidate. **2. a.** To empty or take out (the contents of something). **b.** To evacuate (body wastes). **3.** *Archaic.* To leave; vacate. —*intr.* To evacuate body wastes. —See Synonyms at **nullify.** [Middle English, from Old French *voide, vuide,* from Vulgar Latin *vocitus* (unattested), from *vocāre,* to be empty.] **—void·er** *n.*

void·a·ble (voi'də-bəl) *adj.* Capable of being voided; especially, capable of being annulled. **—void·a·ble·ness** *n.*

void·ance (voi'dəns) *n.* **1. a.** The act of voiding, emptying, or evacuating. **b.** The act of making legally void; annulment. **2.** The condition of being vacant; emptiness.

void·ed (voi'dĭd) *adj. Heraldry.* Having the central area cut out or left vacant, leaving a narrow border or outline.

voile (voil) *n.* A light sheer fabric of cotton, rayon, silk, or wool used in dressmaking or for furnishings. [French, from Latin *vēla,* neuter of *vēlum,* cloth, veil.]

voir dire (vwär dîr') *n. Law.* **1.** A preliminary examination concerning the competence of a prospective witness or juror. **2.** The oath administered in such an examination. [Old French, "to speak the truth" : *voir,* truth, from Latin *vērus* + *dire,* to say, from Latin *dīcere.*]

voix cé·leste (vwä' sā-lĕst') *n.* An organ stop that produces a gentle tremolo effect. Also called "vox angelica." [French, "celestial voice."]

vol. **1.** volcano. **2.** volume. **3.** volunteer.

Vo·lans (vō'lănz') *n.* A constellation in the polar region of the Southern Hemisphere near Carina and Dorado. [Latin *volans,* present participle of *volare,* to fly.]

vo·lant (vō'lənt) *adj.* **1.** Flying or capable of flying. **2.** *Poetic.* Moving quickly or nimbly; agile. **3.** *Heraldry.* Depicted with the wings extended as in flying. [Latin *volāns* (stem *volānt-*), present participle of *volāre,* to fly.]

Vo·la·pük (vō'lə-pük') *n.* An international language invented in 1879, based mainly on English, Latin, and German, and other European languages. [*Vol,* from English WORLD + *pük,* from English SPEECH: coined by its inventor Johann Schleyer (1831–1912), German linguist.] **—Vo·la·pük·ist** *n.*

vo·lar (vō'lər) *adj.* Of or pertaining to the sole of the foot or the palm of the hand. [From Latin *vola,* palm, sole.]

vol·a·tile (vŏl'ə-tĭl; *chiefly British* -tīl') *adj.* **1.** Evaporating readily at normal temperatures and pressures. **2.** Capable of being readily vaporized. **3.** Changeable, as: **a.** Inconstant; fickle. **b.** Tending to violence; explosive. **c.** Lighthearted; flighty. **d.** Unstable; unpredictable. **e.** Ephemeral; fleeting. **4.** Designating a computer memory that loses stored information when power is cut off. **5.** *Obsolete.* Flying or capable of flying; volant.

~*n.* A volatile substance. [Middle English *volatil,* flying, fleeting, from Old French, from Latin *volātilis,* from *volāre,* to fly.]

volatile oil *n.* A rapidly evaporating oil, especially an essential oil, that does not leave a stain.

vol·a·til·i·ty (vŏl'ə-tĭl'ə-tē) *n.* The quality or state of being volatile.

vol·a·til·ize (vŏl'ə-tə-līz') *v.* **-ized, -izing, -izes.** —*intr.* **1.** To become volatile. **2.** To pass off in vapor; evaporate. —*tr.* **1.** To make volatile. **2.** To cause to evaporate. **—vol·a·til·iz·a·ble** *adj.* **—vol·a·til·i·za·tion** *n.* **—vol·a·til·iz·er** *n.*

vol-au-vent (vô'lō-väN') *n.* A light pastry shell filled with a ragout of meat or fish. [French, "flight in the wind."]

vol·can·ic (vŏl-kăn'ĭk) *adj.* **1.** Of or resembling an erupting volcano. **2.** Produced by or discharged from a volcano. **3.** Powerfully explosive: *a volcanic temper.*

volcanic glass *n.* A volcanic igneous rock of vitreous or glassy texture, such as obsidian or pitchstone.

vol·can·ism (vŏl'kə-nĭz'əm) *n.* Also **vul·can·ism** (vŭl'-). Volcanic force or activity. [VOLCANO + -ISM.]

vol·can·ize (vŏl'kə-nīz') *tr.v.* **-ized, -izing, -izes.** To subject to or change by the effects of volcanic heat. **—vol·can·i·za·tion** *n.*

vol·ca·no (vŏl-kā'nō) *n., pl.* **-noes** or **-nos.** *Abbr.* **vol. 1.** A vent in the earth's crust through which molten lava and gases are ejected. **2.** A mountain formed by the materials so ejected. [Italian, from Latin *Volcānus,* VULCAN.] See feature, next page.

Volcano Islands. Three small islands 30 square kilometers (11 square miles) in the western Pacific, among them Iwo Jima, administered by the United States from 1945 to 1968, when they were restored to Japan.

vol·can·ol·o·gy (vŏl'kə-nŏl'ə-jē) *n.* Also **vul·can·ol·o·gy** (vŭl'-). The branch of earth science concerned with volcanic phenomena. **—vol·can·o·log·i·cal** (vŏl'kə-nə-lŏj'ĭ-kəl) *adj.* **—vol·can·ol·o·gist** *n.*

vole[1] (vōl) *n.* Any of various rodents of the genus *Microtus* and related genera, resembling rats or mice but having a relatively short tail. [Earlier *volemouse,* "field mouse," from Norwegian *voll,* field, from Old Norse *vǫllr.*]

vole[2] *n.* The winning of all the tricks in a card game; a grand slam. [French, from *voler,* to fly, from Old French, from Latin *volāre.*]

Vol·ga (vŏl'gə). River of European U.S.S.R. Europe's longest river and the U.S.S.R's most important, it rises in the Valdai Hills and flows 3,690 kilometers (2,293 miles) east into the Caspian Sea at Astrakhan. Almost entirely navigable, it provides hydroelectric power and irrigation.

Vol·go·grad (vŏl'gə-grăd'). Formerly **Sta·lin·grad** (stä'lĭn-grăd'). City in the U.S.S.R. on the Volga River. It is an important river port and trading center. The Battle of Stalingrad (1942–43), in which the city was almost destroyed, was a turning point in World War II.

vol·i·tant (vŏl'ə-tənt) *adj.* **1.** Flying or capable of flying. **2.** Moving

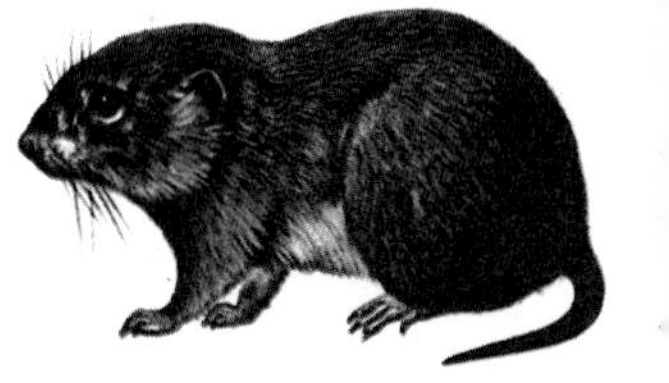

vole *The common field vole (above) builds its nest in meadowland and lives on grass, roots, and seeds. Voles, which are related to field mice, are native to North and Central America, Europe, and Asia.*

PRONUNCIATION KEY

ă, pat; ā, pay; âr, care;
ä, father, are; b, bib;
ch, church; d, deed; ĕ, pet;
ē, be; f, fife; g, gag; h, hat;
hw, which; ĭ, pit; ī, pie;
îr, pier; j, judge; k, kick;
l, lid, needle; m, mum;
n, no, sudden; ng, thing;
ŏ, pot; ō, toe; ô, paw, for;
oi, noise; ou, out; o͝o, book;
o͞o, boot; p, pop; r, roar;
s, sauce; sh, ship, dish;
t, tight; th, thin, path;
th, this, bathe; ŭ, cut; ûr, fur;
v, valve; w, with; y, yes;
z, zebra, size; zh, vision;
ə, about, item, edible, gallop, circus, peaceful

IN FOREIGN WORDS:

à, *Fr.* ami; œ, *Fr.* feu, *Ger.* schön; ü, *Fr.* tu, *Ger.* über;
KH, *Ger.* ich, *Scot.* loch;
N, *Fr.* bon; y', *Fr.* Compiègne

STRESS MARKS:

Primary stress: '
in·cite' (ĭn-sīt')
Secondary stress: '
in'sight' (ĭn'sīt')

volcano

THE FIRE BENEATH THE CRUST OF THE EARTH
Molten rock from deep underground is still altering the land surface

Volcanoes exist because molten rock in the earth's interior is held under pressure, like air in a car's tire. A volcano grows where this molten rock, or magma, erupts through a crack in the earth's outer skin of solid rock.

The eruption can be slow and relatively steady, so that cooling magma builds up into a cone around the crack, or vent. It was this sort of eruption that gave birth in 1963 to the new Icelandic island of Surtsey. Or the outburst can

be devastatingly explosive. The eruption in 1980 of Mount St. Helens in Washington State, for instance, blew off the top 400 meters (about 1,300 feet) of the peak with a force equivalent to 500 Hiroshima bombs.

There are more than 500 active volcanoes around the world. Most are on the Ring of Fire that circles the Pacific, and almost all lie along the edges of the shifting continent-size "plates" that make up the earth's crust.

NEW VOLCANO *The steaming cone of a volcano that appeared on Heimaey Island, Iceland, in 1973.*

HOW A VOLCANO GETS ITS SHAPE

Hot molten lava issues from the central cone and from lateral intrusions that cut through the rock strata

Ash and gas cloud from the central cone contains water vapor and carbon dioxide

Crater

Central cone

Lateral intrusion

Lava flow

Pyroclastic layers

Secondary cone will begin to form around the outlet of a lateral intrusion

Conduit

Lava solidified in fissures forms riblike dikes that strengthen the cone

Rock strata in the earth's outer crust

Magma chamber contains molten rock

The classic cone shape of a volcano grows from the debris of its own eruptions. Each time fragments of rock, or lava, are hurled from the central conduit, some fall back around the crater to harden into a solid skin. Rocks in these layers are known as pyroclastic, from Greek words meaning "broken by fire."

about rapidly. [Latin *volitāns* (stem *volitānt-*), present participle of *volitāre*, frequentative of *volāre*, to fly.]

vol·i·ta·tion (vŏl′ə-tā′shən) *n.* The act of flying or the ability to fly; flight. **—vol·i·ta·tion·al** *adj.*

vo·li·tion (və-lĭsh′ən) *n.* **1.** An act of willing, choosing, or deciding. **2.** A conscious choice; a decision. **3.** The power or capability of choosing; the will. [French, from Medieval Latin *volitiō* (stem *voli-tiōn-*), from Latin *velle* (present stem *vol-*), to wish.] **—vo·li·tion·al** *adj.* **—vo·li·tion·al·ly** *adv.*

vol·i·tive (vŏl′ə-tĭv) *adj.* **1.** Pertaining to or originating in the will. **2.** Expressing a wish or permission.

volk (fôlk) *n. Often* **Volk.** *South African.* The Afrikaner people. Preceded by *the.* [Afrikaans, from Dutch, people.]

volks·lied (fôk′slēt′, fôlk′-) *n., pl.* **volkslieder** (-slē′dər) A folk song. [German : *Volk,* people + *Lied,* song.]

vol·ley (vŏl′ē) *n., pl.* **-leys. 1. a.** The simultaneous discharge of a number of missiles. **b.** The missiles thus discharged. **2.** A bursting forth of a number of things simultaneously: *a volley of oaths.* **3.** *Sports.* A shot, stroke, hit, or kick made at a moving ball before it touches the ground.
~v. **volleyed, -leying, -leys.** *—tr.* **1.** To discharge (missiles or abuse, for example) in or as if in a volley. **2.** *Sports.* To strike, hit, or kick (a moving ball) before it touches the ground. *—intr.* **1.** To be discharged in or as if in a volley. **2.** To sound loudly and continuously, as guns may. **3.** *Sports.* To make a volley. [French *volée,* from Vulgar Latin *volāta* (unattested), flight, from Latin *volātus,* past participle of *volāre,* to fly.] **—vol·ley·er** *n.*

vol·ley·ball (vŏl′ē-bôl′) *n.* **1.** A court game in which two teams volley a ball by hand over a high net, each team attempting to ground it on the opposing team's side. **2.** The ball used in this game.

vo·lost (vŏl′ôst′, vōl′-) *n.* **1.** In the Soviet Union, a local unit of the government; a rural soviet. **2.** In czarist Russia, an administrative division consisting of several villages. [Russian.]

vol·plane (vŏl′plān′) *intr.v.* **-planed, -planing, -planes.** To glide toward the ground with the engine cut off. Used of an aircraft or winged missile.
~n. The glide of an aircraft. [French *vol plané* : *vol,* flight, from *voler,* to fly, from Latin *volāre* (see **volant**) + *plané,* past participle of *planer,* to PLANE (to soar).]

Vol·sci (vŏl′sē) *pl.n.* A people of ancient Latium in southwestern Italy whose territory was conquered by the Romans in the 4th century B.C.

Vol·scian (vŏl′shən) *n.* **1.** The Italic language of the Volsci, related to Umbrian. **2.** A member of the Volsci. **—Vol·scian** *adj.*

Volstead (vŏl′stĕd′, vôl′-, vōl′-), **Andrew John** (1860–1947). U.S. legislator. A U.S. congressman from Minnesota (1903–23), he introduced the Volstead Act, passed in 1919, that provided the means to investigate and punish violators of Prohibition. When Prohibition was repealed in 1933, the Volstead Act expired.

Vol·sun·ga Saga (vŏl′sŏŏng′gə) *n.* An Icelandic saga, recorded in the 13th century, dealing with the exploits of a family of warriors, in particular Sigurd, descended from the great heroic king Volsung. The saga is related to the German **Nibelungenlied** *(see).* [Old Norse, "Saga of the Volsungs."]

volt[1] (vōlt) *n. Abbr.* **V** The SI unit of electric potential and electromotive force, equal to the difference of electric potential between two points on a conducting wire carrying a constant current of one ampere when the power dissipated between the points is one watt. [After Count **VOLTA**.]

volt[2], **volte** (vōlt) *n.* **1.** A circular movement executed by a horse in dressage. **2.** In fencing, a sudden movement made in order to avoid a thrust. [French *volte,* a turn, from Italian *volta,* from Vulgar Latin *volvita* (unattested), from *volvitāre* (unattested), frequentative of Latin *volvere,* to turn.]

vol·ta (vōl′tə) *n., pl.* **-te** (-tā′). **1.** A brisk dance, in triple time, that was popular in the 16th century. **2.** A piece of music for such a dance. **3.** *Music.* A time, turn, or occasion of a specified ordinal number. Used as a direction: *prima volta.* [Italian, turn, from feminine past participle of *volgere,* to turn, from Latin *volvere,* to roll.]

Vol·ta (vōl′tə). River of Ghana. West Africa's chief river, it is formed by the union of the Black Volta and the White Volta. Its course carries it 1,125 kilometers (700 miles) southeast and south to the Gulf of Guinea. It has been dammed to produce hydro-electricity.

Vol·ta (vōl′tə, vôl′-), **Alessandro Giuseppe Antonio Anastasio, Count** (1745–1827). Italian physicist. A pioneer in the sphere of electricity, he invented the *electrophorus* (1775), a device to accumulate electricity, and the voltaic pile (1800).

volt·age (vōl′tĭj) *n.* Electromotive force or potential difference, usually expressed in volts.

voltage divider *n.* A resistor or series of resistors provided with taps at certain points to make available a fixed or variable fraction of the applied voltage.

vol·ta·ic (vŏl-tā′ĭk) *adj.* **1.** Pertaining to or designating electricity or electric current produced by chemical action; galvanic. **2.** Producing electricity by chemical action. [After Count **VOLTA**.]

voltaic battery *n.* An electric battery composed of a primary cell or cells.

voltaic cell *n. Electricity.* A **primary cell** *(see).*

voltaic couple *n.* A pair of dissimilar conductors in contact or in the same electrolytic solution, resulting in a difference of potential between them. Also called "galvanic couple."

voltaic pile *n.* A source of direct current consisting of a number of alternating disks of two different metals separated by acid-moistened pads, forming primary cells connected in series. Also called "galvanic pile," "pile."

Vol·taire (vōl′târ, vŏl′-), pen name of François-Marie Arouet (1694–1778). French philosopher and writer. His writings epitomize the Age of Enlightenment, often attacking injustice and intolerance. His best-known works include *Candide* (1759) and the *Dictionnaire Philosophique* (1764).

vol·ta·ism (vŏl′tə-ĭz′əm) *n. Electricity.* **Galvanism** *(see).* [VOLTA(IC) + -ISM.]

vol·tam·e·ter (vōl-tăm′ət-ər, vŏl′tə-mē′tər) *n.* An instrument for determining the quantity of electricity passed through a medium by the amount of electrolysis generated. Also called "coulombmeter," "coulometer."

volt·am·me·ter (vōlt′ăm′mē′tər) *n.* An instrument designed to measure current or potential. [VOLT-AM(PERE) + -METER.]

volt-am·pere (vōlt′ăm′pîr′) *n.* A unit of electric power equal to the product of one volt and one ampere, equivalent to one watt.

volte. Variant of **volt** (movement).

volte-face (vôlt-fäs′, vôl′tə-) *n., pl.* **-faces** *(pronounced as singular)* or **volte-face.** *French.* An about-face; a reversal, as in policy.

volt·me·ter (vōlt′mē′tər) *n.* An instrument, such as a galvanometer, for measuring potential differences in volts.

vol·u·ble (vŏl′yə-bəl) *adj.* **1.** Characterized by a ready flow of words in speaking; fluent; loquacious. **2.** *Archaic.* Turning easily on an axis; rotating. **3.** Twining or twisting, as a plant. —See Synonyms at **talkative.** [French, from Latin *volūbilis,* from *volvere* (past participle *volūtus*), to turn.] —**vol·u·bil·i·ty** (vŏl′yə-bĭl′ə-tē), **vol·u·ble·ness** *n.* —**vol·u·bly** *adv.*

vol·ume (vŏl′yo͞om, -yəm) *n.* **1.** *Abbr.* **v., vol.** A collection of written or printed sheets bound together; a book. **2.** *Abbr.* **v., vol.** A book that forms part of a series or set of books. Also used adjectivally and in combination: *a two-volume edition.* **3.** Any written material that has been assembled as an individual unit, such as a set of issues of a magazine in a library. **4.** A roll of parchment; a scroll. **5.** *Abbr.* **V a.** The size or extent of a three-dimensional object or region of space. **b.** Broadly, the capacity of such a region or of a specified container. **6.** *Often* **volumes.** A large amount: *volumes of praise.* **7. a.** The amplitude or loudness of a sound. **b.** A control, as on a radio, for adjusting loudness. **8.** A quantity or total: *The volume of sales has increased.* —**speak volumes.** To be informative or deeply significant. [Middle English, roll of parchment, from Old French, from Latin *volūmen,* from *volvere,* to roll, turn.]

vol·umed (vŏl′yo͞omd) *adj. Poetic.* Forming a rounded or dense mass: *volumed smoke.*

vo·lu·me·ter (və-lo͞o′mə-tər) *n.* Any of several instruments for measuring the volume of liquids, solids, and gases.

vol·u·met·ric (vŏl′yə-mĕt′rĭk) *adj.* Of or pertaining to measurement of volume. Compare **gravimetric.** —**vol·u·met·ri·cal·ly** *adv.*

volumetric analysis *n.* **1.** Quantitative analysis using accurately measured, especially titrated, volumes of standard chemical solutions. **2.** The analysis of a gas by volume.

vo·lu·mi·nous (və-lo͞o′mə-nəs) *adj.* **1.** Having great volume, fullness, size, or number. **2. a.** Filling or capable of filling volumes. Said of writing. **b.** Prolific in speech or writing. **3.** *Archaic.* Having many coils; winding: *the voluminous labyrinth.* [Late Latin *volūminōsus,* having many folds, from Latin *volūmen,* roll of writing, VOLUME.] —**vo·lu·mi·nos·i·ty** (və-lo͞o′mə-nŏs′ə-tē), **vo·lu·mi·nous·ness** *n.* —**vo·lu·mi·nous·ly** *adv.*

vol·un·ta·rism (vŏl′ən-tə-rĭz′əm) *n.* **1.** *Philosophy.* The doctrine that the will is primary or dominant over the intellect. **2.** The view that a project or course of action should be based on voluntary participation. **3.** The principle or practice of reliance on voluntary action or volunteers. Also called "voluntaryism." —**vol·un·ta·rist** *n.* —**vol·un·ta·ris·tic** *adj.*

vol·un·tar·y (vŏl′ən-tĕr′ē) *adj.* **1.** Arising from one's own free will; acting on one's own initiative: *"Ignorance, when it is voluntary, is criminal"* (Samuel Johnson). **2.** Acting or serving in a specified capacity willingly and without constraint or guarantee of reward. **3.** Controlled by, consisting of, supported by, or done with the aid of contributions or volunteers: *voluntary organizations.* **4.** Capable of exercising will; volitional. **5.** Proceeding from impulse; spontaneous. **6.** *Law.* **a.** Acting or performed without external persuasion or compulsion. **b.** Without legal obligation. **c.** Without payment: *a voluntary conveyance.* **7.** Normally controlled by or subject to individual volition: *voluntary responses.*

~*n., pl.* **voluntaries. 1.** Any act or work not imposed or demanded by another. **2.** The section of a competitor's performance whose contents are chosen by the competitor himself, as in a music or skating competition. **3.** *Music.* **a.** A piece of solo organ music, occasionally improvised, that is played usually before and sometimes during or after a church service. **b.** A composition based on or intended for such a performance. **4.** A volunteer. [Middle English, from Latin *voluntārius,* from *voluntās,* will, free will, from *velle* (present stem *vol-*), to wish.] —**vol·un·tar·i·ly** *adv.* —**vol·un·tar·i·ness** *n.*

Synonyms: *voluntary, intentional, deliberate, willful, willing, spontaneous.* These adjectives mean unforced. *Voluntary* is applied in several related senses to what is done by choice, to physical movement subject to regulation by the will, and less often to action that is not only of one's choice but premeditated. The last-named sense is more basic to *intentional* and *deliberate;* in addition, *deliberate* stresses the idea of action taken with full awareness of the consequences. *Willful* can mean merely in accordance with one's will but often implies headstrong persistence in a self-determined course of action. *Willing* suggests acceding to a course proposed by another, without reluctance or even eagerly. *Spontaneous* refers to behavior that seems wholly unpremeditated, a natural response and a true reflection of one's feelings.

vol·un·tar·y·ism (vŏl′ən-tĕr′ē-ĭz′əm) *n.* Voluntarism (sense 3). —**vol·un·tar·y·ist** *n.*

voluntary muscle *n.* Muscle normally controlled by individual volition. See **striated muscle.**

vol·un·teer (vŏl′ən-tîr′) *n. Abbr.* **vol. 1.** A person who performs or gives his services of his own free will. **2.** *Law.* **a.** A person who renders aid, performs a service, or assumes an obligation voluntarily. **b.** A person who holds property under a deed made without requiring anything in return, such as the heir in a will. **3.** A person who voluntarily does military service, especially when temporary. **4.** A cultivated plant growing from self-sown or accidentally dropped seed.

~*adj.* **1.** Pertaining to or consisting of volunteers: *a volunteer militia.* **2.** Enlisted or serving as a volunteer. **3.** Growing from self-sown or accidentally dropped seed. Said of a plant or crop.

~*v.* **volunteered, -teering, -teers.** —*tr.* To give or offer to give on one's own initiative. —*intr.* To enter into or offer to enter into any undertaking of one's own free will. [French *volontaire,* from Latin *voluntārius,* VOLUNTARY.]

vol·un·teer·ism (vŏl′ən-tîr′ĭz′əm) *n.* The theory, act, or practice of being a volunteer or of using volunteers in community service work. Also called "voluntarism," "voluntaryism."

vo·lup·tu·ar·y (və-lŭp′cho͞o-ĕr′ē) *n., pl.* **-ies.** A person whose life is given over to luxury and sensual pleasures; a sensualist. [Latin *voluptuārius,* from *voluptārius,* from *voluptās,* pleasure. See **voluptuous.**] —**vo·lup·tu·ar·y** *adj.*

vo·lup·tu·ous (və-lŭp′cho͞o-əs) *adj.* **1.** Consisting of or characterized by strong visual and tactile delights: *voluptuous sculpture.* **2.** Devoted to or frequently indulging in sensual gratifications. **3. a.** Full and appealing in form, especially in a sexually appealing way: *a voluptuous mouth.* **b.** Directed toward or anticipating sensuous gratification: *voluptuous thoughts.* **c.** Arising from the satisfying of luxurious or sensual desires. [Middle English, from Old French *voluptueux,* from Latin *voluptuōsus,* from *voluptās,* pleasure.] —**vo·lup·tu·ous·ly** *adv.* —**vo·lup·tu·ous·ness** *n.*

vo·lute (və-lo͞ot′) *n.* **1.** A spiral, scroll-like ornament such as that used on an Ionic capital. **2.** A twisted or spiral formation, such as any of the whorls of a gastropod shell. **3.** Any of various marine gastropod mollusks of the family Volutidae, having a spiral, often colorfully marked shell.

~*adj.* Also **vo·lut·ed** (və-lo͞o′tĭd). Having a spiral form; spirally twisted or rolled. [French, from Latin *volūta,* scroll, from the feminine past participle of *volvere,* to turn.]

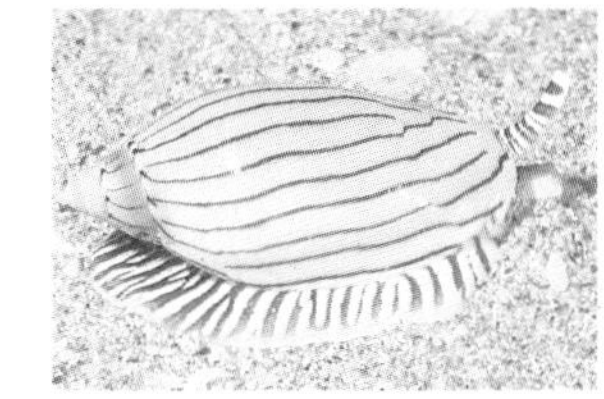

volute *A marine snail, the volute generally has a large, colorful shell and is most commonly found in warm, shallow waters. This is a Jamrack's volute, found off the west coast of Australia.*

vo·lu·tion (və-lo͞o′shən) *n.* **1.** A turn or twist about a center; a spiral. **2.** *Zoology.* Any of the whorls of a spiral shell. [From Latin *volvere* (past participle *volūtus*), to turn. See **volute.**]

vol·va (vŏl′və) *n., pl.* **-vae** (-vē). A cuplike structure around the base of the stalk of certain fungi, a remnant of the **veil** *(see).* [Latin *volva, vulva,* covering.] —**vol·vate** (vŏl′vāt′) *adj.*

vol·vox (vŏl′vŏks′) *n.* Any of various flagellate green algae of the genus *Volvox,* that form hollow, spherical multicellular colonies. [New Latin, from Latin *volvere,* to turn, roll. See **volute.**]

vol·vu·lus (vŏl′vyə-ləs) *n., pl.* **-luses.** A partial or complete obstruction of the intestine caused by abnormal twisting. [New Latin, from Latin *volvere,* to turn. See **volute.**]

vo·mer (vō′mər) *n.* A flat thin bone that forms part of the nasal septum. [Latin *vōmer,* plowshare.] —**vo·mer·ine** (vō′mər-ĭn, vŏm′-ər-ĭn) *adj.*

vom·i·ca (vŏm′ĭ-kə) *n., pl.* **-cae** (-sē). **1.** The profuse expectoration of putrid matter. **2. a.** An abnormal pus-containing cavity in a lung, caused by the deterioration of tissue. **b.** The purulent matter contained in such a cavity. [Latin, boil, ulcer, from *vomere,* to VOMIT.]

vom·it (vŏm′ĭt) *v.* **-ited, -iting, -its.** —*intr.* **1.** To eject part or all of the contents of the stomach through the mouth, usually in a series of involuntary spasmodic movements. **2.** To be discharged forcefully and abundantly; spew forth. —*tr.* **1.** To eject from the stomach through the mouth. **2.** To eject or discharge in a gush.

~*n.* **1.** The act of ejecting matter from the stomach. **2.** Matter ejected from the stomach. **3.** An emetic. [Middle English *vomiten,* from Latin *vomere* (past participle *vomitus*).] —**vom·it·er** *n.*

vomiting gas *n. Chemistry.* **Chloropicrin** *(see).*

vom·i·tive (vŏm′ĭ-tĭv) *adj.* Pertaining to or causing vomiting.

~*n.* An emetic.

vom·i·to·ry (vŏm′ə-tôr′ē, -tōr′ē) *adj.* Inducing vomiting; vomitive.

~*n., pl.* **vomitories. 1.** Something that induces vomiting. **2.** An aperture through which matter is discharged. **3.** Any of the passageways of a Roman amphitheater leading from the outside wall to the foot of the banked seats.

vom·i·tu·ri·tion (vŏm′ə-cho͞o-rĭsh′ən) *n.* Forceful but ineffectual attempts at vomiting; retching. [VOMIT + (MICT)URITION.]

vom·i·tus (vŏm′ə-təs) *n.* **1.** Vomited matter. **2.** Vomiting. [Latin, past participle of *vomere,* to VOMIT.]

Von·ne·gut (vŏn′ĭ-gət), **Kurt, Jr.** (1922–). U.S. author. First attracting a large readership in the 1960's and 1970's, he has written science-fiction novels, such as *The Sirens of Titan* (1959), and stories about underdogs coping with an overbearing world, including *Slaughterhouse Five* (1963), *Jailbird* (1979), and *Galápagos* (1985).

PRONUNCIATION KEY

ă, pat; ā, pay; âr, care;
ä, father, are; b, bib;
ch, church; d, deed; ĕ, pet;
ē, be; f, fife; g, gag; h, hat;
hw, which; ĭ, pit; ī, pie;
îr, pier; j, judge; k, kick;
l, lid, needle; m, mum;
n, no, sudden; ng, thing;
ŏ, pot; ō, toe; ô, paw, for;
oi, noise; ou, out; o͝o, book;
o͞o, boot; p, pop; r, roar;
s, sauce; sh, ship, dish;
t, tight; th, thin, path;
th, this, bathe; ŭ, cut; ûr, fur;
v, valve; w, with; y, yes;
z, zebra, size; zh, vision;
ə, about, item, edible, gallop, circus, peaceful

IN FOREIGN WORDS:

à, *Fr.* ami; œ, *Fr.* feu, *Ger.* schön; ü, *Fr.* tu, *Ger.* über; KH, *Ger.* ich, *Scot.* loch; N, *Fr.* bon; y′, *Fr.* Compiègne

STRESS MARKS:

Primary stress: ′
in·cite′ (ĭn-sīt′)
Secondary stress: ′
in′sight′ (ĭn′sīt′)

voo·doo (vo͞o′do͞o) *n., pl.* **-doos. 1.** A religious cult of African origin practiced in the Western Hemisphere mainly in Haiti and characterized by a belief in sorcery and fetishes and by rituals in which participants communicate by trance with ancestors, saints, or animistic deities. **2.** A charm, fetish, spell, or curse believed by adherents of this cult to hold magic power. **3.** A person who practices voodoo. **—**See Synonyms at **magic.**
~tr.v. **voodooed, -dooing, -doos.** To place under the influence of a voodoo spell. [Dahomey *vodu.*] **—voo·doo** *adj.*

voo·doo·ism (vo͞o′do͞o-ĭz′əm) *n.* **1.** The view of life and death embodied in the voodoo cult. **2.** The practice of voodoo. **—voo·doo·ist** *n.* **—voo·doo·is·tic** *adj.*

vo·ra·cious (vô-rā′shəs, vō-, və-) *adj.* **1.** Consuming or eager to consume great amounts of food; ravenous. **2.** Having an insatiable appetite for some activity or pursuit: *a voracious reader.* [Latin *vorax* (stem *vorāci-*), from *vorāre,* to devour.] **—vo·ra·cious·ly** *adv.* **—vo·rac·i·ty** (vô-răs′ə-tē, vō-, və-), **vo·ra·cious·ness** *n.*

vor·la·ge (fôr′lä′gə, fōr′-) *n.* A posture assumed in skiing in which the skier leans forward from the ankles, usually without lifting the heels. [German *Vorlage* : *vor,* before, from Old High German *fora* + *Lage,* stance, from Old High German *lāga.*]

Vo·ro·shi·lov (vô-rŏ-shē′lôf, -ləf, -lôf), **Kliment Efremovich** (1881–1969). Soviet military and political leader. A veteran of the civil war following the Russian Revolution in 1917, he held several high-ranking military positions under Joseph Stalin. He was later involved in the effort to remove Nikita Khrushchev in 1957.

-vorous *suffix.* Indicates eating or feeding on; for example, **herbivorous.** [Latin *-vorus,* from *vorāre,* to devour.]

Vor·ster (fôr′stər), **Balthazar Johannes** (1915–83). South African politician, prime minister (1966–78), and subsequently president of South Africa (1978–79). He was a leading advocate of apartheid.

vor·tex (vôr′tĕks) *n., pl.* **-texes** or **-tices** (-tə-sēz′). **1.** Fluid flow involving rotation about an axis; a whirlwind; whirlpool. **2.** Any activity or situation that is regarded as drawing into its center and engulfing all that surrounds it: *"As happened with so many theater actors, he was swept up in the vortex of Hollywood"* (New York Times). [Latin *vortex, vertex,* from *vertere,* to turn.]

vor·ti·cal (vôr′tĭ-kəl) *adj.* Also **vor·ti·cose** (-kōs′). Pertaining to or resembling a vortex; whirling. [From Latin *vortex* (stem *vortic-*), VORTEX.] **—vor·ti·cal·ly** *adv.*

vor·ti·cel·la (vôr′tə-sĕl′ə) *n., pl.* **-lae** (-lē). Any of various bell-shaped, ciliated, stalked protozoans of the genus *Vorticella.* [New Latin *Vorticella,* from Latin *vortex* (stem *vortic-*), VORTEX.]

vor·ti·cism (vôrt′ə-sĭz′əm) *n.* A short-lived English art movement that arose in 1914 as a result of the impact of futurist ideas on a small group of artists and writers led by Wyndham Lewis. **—vor·ti·cist** *n.*

vor·tig·i·nous (vôr-tĭj′ə-nəs) *adj.* Whirling; vortical. [From Latin *vortīgō* (stem *vortīgin-*), variant of *vertīgō,* a whirling, from *vertere,* to turn. See **vortex.**]

Vosges Mountains (vōzh). Mountain range of eastern France. Extending 240 kilometers (150 miles) south-southwest to north-northeast, it is separated from Germany's Black Forest by the rift valley of the Rhine River. Before World War I the mountains formed the border between Germany and France.

vo·tar·ess (vō′tə-rəs). *n.* Also **vo·tress** (vō′trəs). A woman who is a votary.

vo·ta·ry (vō′tə-rē) *n., pl.* **-ries.** Also **vo·ta·rist** (vō′tə-rĭst). **1.** A person bound by vows to live the religious life; a monk or nun. **2.** Any person fervently devoted, as to a religion, leader, or ideal.
~adj. Archaic. **1.** Consecrated by a vow. **2.** Resembling or pertaining to a vow. [From Latin *vōtus,* past participle of *vovēre,* to vow.]
Usage: *votary, devotee, habitué, fan.* These nouns mean an adherent of a person, cause, or activity. *Votary* and *devotee* imply strong personal commitment to the service of a person or thing, usually in a favorable sense. Both can refer to religious dedication or, by extension, to attachment to a branch of learning, a hobby, or a cultural pursuit. *Habitué* refers to one in regular attendance at a place offering a certain kind of activity. *Fan* is an informal term for an ardent enthusiast or admirer.

vote (vōt) *n.* **1.** A formal expression of preference, opinion, or will, as in favor of a candidate for office or a proposed resolution of an issue. **2.** Something by which such a preference is made known, such as a raised hand or a ballot. **3.** The number of votes cast in an election or to resolve an issue: *a heavy vote in his favor.* **4.** A group of voters: *the labor vote.* **5.** The result of an election, referendum, or the like. **6. a.** The right to participate as a voter; suffrage. **b.** A person who has such a right. **7.** Something that is to be or has been decided, expressed, or granted by voting. **—cast one's vote.** To make known, deposit, or give in one's vote.
~v. **voted, voting, votes.** *—intr.* **1.** To express one's preference, will, or opinion by a vote; cast one's vote. **2.** To cast one's vote in a specified manner: *vote Democrat.* *—tr.* **1.** To express one's preference for; endorse by a vote. **2.** To bring into existence or make available by vote: *vote new funds for a program.* **3.** To bring to a specified condition by voting: *voted her out; voted the Republicans into office.* **4.** To declare or pronounce by general consent: *voted the play a success.* **5.** *Informal.* To suggest; advocate: *I vote that we forget all about it.* **—vote down.** To defeat by casting a negative vote. [Latin *vōtum,* vow, from *vōtus,* past participle of *vovēre,* to vow.] **—vot·a·ble, vote·a·ble** *adj.* **—vot·er** *n.*

vote getter *n.* **1.** A candidate with abilities and qualities that attract votes in his or her favor. **2.** A means of drawing votes.

PRONUNCIATION KEY

ă, pat; ā, pay; âr, care;
ä, father, are; b, bib;
ch, church; d, deed; ĕ, pet;
ē, be; f, fife; g, gag; h, hat;
hw, which; ĭ, pit; ī, pie;
îr, pier; j, judge; k, kick;
l, lid, needle; m, mum;
n, no, sudden; ng, thing;
ŏ, pot; ō, toe; ô, paw, for;
oi, noise; ou, out; o͝o, book;
o͞o, boot; p, pop; r, roar;
s, sauce; sh, ship, dish;
t, tight; th, thin, path;
th, this, bathe; ŭ, cut; ûr, fur;
v, valve; w, with; y, yes;
z, zebra, size; zh, vision;
ə, about, item, edible,
gallop, circus, peaceful

IN FOREIGN WORDS:

à, *Fr.* ami; œ, *Fr.* feu, *Ger.* schön; ü, *Fr.* tu, *Ger.* über; KH, *Ger.* ich, *Scot.* loch; N, *Fr.* bon; y′, *Fr.* Compiègne

STRESS MARKS:

Primary stress: ′
in·cite′ (ĭn-sīt′)
Secondary stress: ′
in′sight′ (ĭn′sīt′)

vote·less (vōt′lĭs) *adj.* Having no vote, especially denied a political vote.

voting machine *n.* An apparatus for use at polling places that mechanically records and counts votes.

vo·tive (vō′tĭv) *adj.* **1.** Given or dedicated in fulfillment of a vow or pledge: *a votive offering.* **2.** Expressing a wish, desire, or vow: *a votive prayer.* [Latin *vōtīvus,* from *vōtum,* vow, VOTE.]

votive mass *n. Roman Catholic Church.* A mass that may be celebrated at the priest's discretion, as for a special intention or in honor of a given saint, instead of the mass appointed for the day.

vouch (vouch) *v.* **vouched, vouching, vouches.** *—tr.* **1.** To substantiate by supplying evidence; verify. **2.** *Law.* Formerly, to summon (a landowner) as a witness to give proof of ownership. **3.** *Archaic.* To cite (an authority, doctrine, or principle, for example) as supporting evidence for one's statements, opinions, or actions. **4.** *Obsolete.* To assert; declare. *—intr.* **1.** To furnish a guarantee; give personal assurance. Used with *for.* **2.** To function or serve as a guarantee; furnish supporting evidence. Used with *for: a feat that vouched for his courage.*
~n. Obsolete. A declaration of opinion; an assertion. [Middle English *vouchen,* to summon (as a witness), from Old French *voucher,* from Latin *vōcāre,* to call.]

vouch·er (vou′chər) *n.* **1.** A person who vouches; a supporter, sponsor, or witness. **2.** A signed or stamped document that serves as proof that the terms of a transaction have been met. **3.** *Chiefly British.* A document or card that can be exchanged for goods or services: *a gift voucher.*

vouch·safe (vouch-sāf′) *tr.v.* **-safed, -safing, -safes.** To condescend to grant or bestow (a reply, favor, or privilege, for example); deign: *vouchsafed us no explanation.* [Middle English *vouchen sauf,* "to warrant as safe" : VOUCH (obsolete sense "to warrant") + SAFE.] **—vouch·safe·ment** *n.*

vous·soir (vo͞o-swär′) *n.* Any of the wedge-shaped stones that form the curved parts of an arch or vaulted ceiling. [French, from Old French *vossoir,* from Vulgar Latin *volsōrium* (unattested), from *volsus* (unattested), variant of Latin *volutus.* See **volution.**]

vow (vou) *n.* **1.** An earnest promise or pledge that binds one to perform a specified act or behave in a certain manner; especially, a solemn promise to live and act in accordance with the prescriptions of a religious body: *a nun's vows.* **2.** A formal declaration or assertion. **—take vows.** To enter a religious order.
~v. **vowed, vowing, vows.** *—tr.* **1.** To promise or pledge solemnly. **2.** To make a pledge or threat to undertake: *vowing revenge on their persecutors.* **3.** To declare or assert emphatically or formally: *"Well, I vow it is as fine a boy as ever was seen!"* (Henry Fielding). *—intr.* To express a promise or pledge; make a vow. [Middle English *vowe,* from Old French, from Latin *vōtum.* See **vote.**] **—vow·er** *n.*

vow·el (vou′əl) *n. Abbr.* **v. 1.** *Phonetics.* A speech sound created by the relatively free passage of breath through the larynx and oral cavity, usually forming the most prominent and central sound of a syllable. Compare **consonant. 2.** A letter that represents such a sound, as, in the English alphabet, *a, e, i, o, u,* and sometimes *y.*
~adj. Of or constituting a vowel or vowels. [Middle English *vowelle,* from Old French *vouel,* from Latin *(littera) vōcālis,* "sounding (letter)," from *vōx* (stem *vōc-*), voice.] **—vowel·less** *adj.*

vowel fracture *n. Linguistics.* **Breaking** *(see).*

vowel gradation *n. Linguistics.* **Ablaut** *(see).*

vow·el·ize (vou′ə-līz′) *tr.v.* **-ized, -izing, -izes.** To provide with vowel points. **—vow·el·i·za·tion** *n.*

vowel mutation *n. Linguistics.* **Umlaut** *(see).*

vowel point *n.* Any of a number of diacritical marks written above or below consonants to indicate a preceding or following vowel, as in languages such as Hebrew and Arabic that are usually written without vowel letters.

vox an·gel·i·ca (vŏks′ ăn-jĕl′ĭ-kə) *n.* An organ stop, the **voix céleste** *(see).* [Latin, "angelic voice."]

vox hu·ma·na (vŏks′ hyo͞o-mā′nə, -mä′nə) *n.* An organ reed stop that produces tones supposedly imitative of the human voice. [Latin, "human voice."]

vox po·pu·li (vŏks′ pŏp′yə-lī′, -lē) *n.* Popular opinion or sentiment. [Latin, "voice of the people."]

voy·age (voi′ĭj) *n.* **1.** A long journey, usually to a foreign or distant land; especially, a journey across an open sea or ocean. **2.** A record or account of a journey of exploration or discovery. **3.** *Obsolete.* An ambitious project or undertaking.
~v. **voyaged, -aging, -ages.** *—intr.* To make a voyage. *—tr.* To travel or sail over in a journey. [Middle English, from Old French *veiyage,* from Latin *viāticum.* See **viaticum.**] **—voy·ag·er** *n.*

vo·ya·geur (vwä-yä-zhœr′) *n., pl.* **-geurs** *(pronounced as singular).* A woodsman, boatman, or guide, especially one employed by fur companies to transport furs and supplies between remote stations in the U.S. and Canadian northwest. [French, "voyager."]

voy·eur (voi-yûr′) *n.* One who derives sexual pleasure from watching other people undress or engage in sexual activity, especially from a secret vantage point. [French, "watcher," from *voir,* to see.] **—voy·eur·ism** *n.* **—voy·eur·is·tic** *adj.* **—voy·eur·is·ti·cal·ly** *adv.*

Voz·ne·sen·ski (vŏz-nə-sĕn′skē), **Andrei** (1933–). Soviet poet. One of the most prominent poets to emerge in the post-Stalin era, he strove to free the Russian literary language from the stilted, rhetorical style associated with Stalin. Despite his outspoken opposition to the Soviet government, his poems, such as "Goyya" (1960), are apolitical sketches of personal suffering.

V.P. vice president.

V-par·ti·cle (vē′pär′tĭ-kəl) *n.* Any of several neutral elementary particles with half-lives in the range of 10^{10} to 10^6 second. [From the V-shaped tracks left by their decay products in a cloud chamber.]

V. Pres. vice president.

V.R. **1.** Queen Victoria [Latin *Victoria Regina*]. **2.** variant reading. **3.** Volunteer Reserve.

vrai·sem·blance (vrä′səm-bläns′) *n.* The outward appearance of being true or true to life, especially in literature; verisimilitude. [French : *vrai*, true + SEMBLANCE.]

V. Rev. Very Reverend.

V.R.I. Victoria, Queen and Empress [Latin *Victoria Regina et Imperatrix*].

Vriesland. See **Friesland.**

vroom (vrōōm) *interj.* Used to imitate the sound of a fast-moving motor vehicle.

vrouw, vrow (frou, frō) *n.* A Dutch woman. [Dutch, woman, from Middle Dutch *vrouwe*.]

vs. versus.

v.s. vide supra.

V.S. veterinary surgeon.

V-shaped (vē′shāpt′) *adj.* Having the shape of the letter *V:* geese flying in a V-shaped formation.

V sign *n.* **1.** A symbol of victory formed by holding the raised index and middle fingers in the shape of a V, with the palm facing outward. **2.** The same sign but with the palm facing inward, used as an indication of hate, contempt, or defiance.

V.S.O. **1.** very special old (applied to cognac, Armagnac, or port). **2.** Voluntary Service Overseas; a British organization that arranges for young people to do voluntary work and teaching in developing countries.

V.S.O.P. very superior old pale (usually applied to cognac or Armagnac that is at least four years old).

VT Vermont (used with a Zip Code).

Vt. Vermont.

VT fuze *n. Military.* A **proximity fuze** (see). [V(ARIABLE) T(IME) FUZE.]

VTOL vertical takeoff and landing.

VTR videotape recorder.

vug, vugh (vŭg) *n. Geology.* A small cavity in a rock or vein, especially one lined with crystals. [Cornish *vooga*, cave.]

Vuil·lard (vwē′yär′), **(Jean) Édouard** (1868–1940). French painter. A postimpressionist and principal figure of the Nabis, a band of painters devoted to an antinaturalistic theory of painting, he is known for his intimate interior scenes, such as *Actress in her Dressing-room* (1892) and *Woman in a Blue Bodice* (c. 1910–13).

Vul. Vulgate.

Vul·can (vŭl′kən). *Roman Mythology.* The god of fire and craftsmanship, especially metalworking, identified with the Greek god Hephaestus. [Latin *Vulcānus, Volcānus*, perhaps obscurely related to Cretan *Welkhanoc*, from Hittite *Valhannasses†*.]

vul·ca·ni·an (vŭl-kā′nē-ən) *adj.* Also **Vul·ca·ni·an, Vul·can·ic** (-kăn′ĭk) (for sense 2).) **1.** *Geology.* Pertaining to or coming from a volcano or volcanic eruption. **2. a.** Pertaining to the god Vulcan. **b.** Pertaining to craftsmanship or metalworking.

vulcanism. Variant of **volcanism.**

vul·can·ite (vŭl′kə-nīt′) *n.* A hard material made by heavy vulcanization of rubber, used for insulators and containers. [VULCAN + -ITE.]

vul·can·ize (vŭl′kə-nīz′) *tr.v.* **-ized, -izing, -izes.** **1.** To improve the strength, resiliency, and freedom from stickiness and odor of (rubber) by combining with sulfur or other additives in the presence of heat and pressure. **2.** To treat (other substances) similarly. [From VULCAN.] **—vul·can·iz·a·ble** *adj.* **—vul·can·i·za·tion** *n.* **—vul·can·iz·er** *n.*

vulcanology. Variant of **volcanology.**

vulg. vulgar.

Vulg. Vulgate.

vul·gar (vŭl′gər) *adj.* **1. a.** Deficient in taste, delicacy, or refinement. **b.** Ill-bred; boorish; crude. **c.** Tasteless in appearance or quality; garish: *a vulgar display of wealth.* **2.** Obscene or indecent; offensive; coarse or bawdy: *a vulgar joke.* **3.** Of or associated with the masses as distinguished from the educated or cultivated classes; common. **4.** *Abbr.* **vulg.** Spoken by or expressed in a form of a language spoken by the common people; vernacular: *the vulgar tongue.* —See Synonyms at **coarse.**

~*n.* **1.** *Archaic.* The common people; especially, the ignorant and uncultivated: *"The vulgar thus through imitation err"* (Alexander Pope). **2.** *Obsolete.* The vernacular. [Middle English, from Latin *vulgāris*, from *vulgus†*, the common people.] **—vul·gar·ly** *adv.* **—vul·gar·ness** *n.*

vul·gar·i·an (vŭl-gâr′ē-ən) *n.* A vulgar person; especially, one who makes a conspicuous display of his money.

vul·gar·ism (vŭl′gə-rĭz′əm) *n.* **1.** Vulgarity. **2.** A word, phrase, or manner of expression common in ordinary speech but considered incorrect. **3.** An obscene, indecent, or crude word or phrase.

vul·gar·i·ty (vŭl-găr′ə-tē) *n., pl.* **-ties. 1.** The condition or quality of being vulgar; tastelessness; coarseness. **2.** Something, as an act or expression, that offends good taste or propriety.

vul·gar·ize (vŭl′gə-rīz′) *tr.v.* **-ized, -izing, -izes. 1.** To render vulgar; debase; cheapen. **2.** To popularize. **—vul·gar·i·za·tion** *n.* **—vul·gar·iz·er** *n.*

Vulgar Latin *n.* The common speech of ancient Rome, differing from the literary or standard Latin used by the educated classes and forming the basis for the development of the Romance languages. Compare **Classical Latin.**

vul·gate (vŭl′gāt′, -gĭt) *n.* **1.** The common speech of a people; the vernacular. **2.** A widely accepted text or version of a work.

~*adj.* Widely distributed and accepted; popular. [From Latin *vulgātus*, common, popular. See **Vulgate.**]

Vulgate *n. Abbr.* **Vul., Vulg.** The Latin translation of the Bible made by Saint Jerome at the end of the 4th century A.D., now used in a revised form as the Roman Catholic authorized version. See **Bible.** [Late Latin *vulgāta (ēditiō)*, "the popular (edition)," from Latin *vulgātus*, common, popular, from *vulgāre*, to make commonly known, from *vulgus*, common people. See **vulgar.**] **—Vul·gate** *adj.*

vul·ner·a·ble (vŭl′nər-ə-bəl) *adj.* **1.** Susceptible to injury, either physical or emotional; unprotected from danger. **2.** Susceptible to physical attack; insufficiently defended. **3. a.** Liable to censure or criticism; assailable. **b.** Suffering from emotional or psychological insecurity. **c.** Liable to succumb to persuasion or temptation. **4.** *Bridge.* In a position to receive greater penalties or bonuses. Said of the team that has won one game of a rubber. [Late Latin *vulnerābilis*, from Latin *vulnerāre*, to wound, from *vulnus* (stem *vulner-*), wound.] **—vul·ner·a·bil·i·ty** (vŭl′nər-ə-bĭl′ə-tē), **—vul·ner·a·ble·ness** *n.* **—vul·ner·a·bly** *adv.*

vul·ner·ar·y (vŭl′nə-rĕr′ē) *adj. Rare.* Used in the healing or treating of wounds.

~*n. Rare.* A remedy so used. [Latin *vulnerārius*, from *vulnus* (stem *vulner-*), wound. See **vulnerable.**]

Vul·pec·u·la (vŭl-pĕk′yə-lə) *n.* A constellation in the Northern Hemisphere near Cygnus and Sagitta. [Latin *vulpēcula*, diminutive of *vulpēs*, fox. See **vulpine.**]

vul·pine (vŭl′pīn, -pĭn′) *adj.* **1.** Of, resembling, or characteristic of a fox. **2.** Clever; devious; cunning. [Latin *vulpīnus*, from *vulpēs*, fox.]

vul·ture (vŭl′chər) *n.* **1.** Any of various large birds of the family Accipitridae, of the Old World, or the family Cathartidae, of the New World, characteristically having dark plumage, a naked head and neck, and feeding on carrion. **2.** A person of a rapacious or predatory nature. [Middle English, from Old French *voltour*, from Latin *vultur*.]

vul·tur·ine (vŭl′chə-rīn′, -chər-ĭn) *adj.* Also **vul·tur·ous** (-chər-əs). **1.** Pertaining to or characteristic of a vulture. **2.** Suggestive of a vulture; rapacious; predatory.

vul·va (vŭl′və) *n., pl.* **-vae** (-vē). The external female genitalia including the labia majora, labia minora, clitoris, and vestibule of the vagina. [Latin *vulva, volva*, womb, covering.] **—vul·val, vul·var, vul·vate** (vŭl′vāt′, -vĭt) *adj.* **—vul·vi·form** (vŭl′və-fôrm′) *adj.*

vul·vi·tis (vŭl-vī′tĭs) *n. Pathology.* Inflammation of the vulva. [New Latin : VULV(A) + -ITIS.]

vul·vo·vag·i·ni·tis (vŭl′vō-văj′ə-nī′tĭs) *n. Pathology.* Inflammation of the vulva and vagina. [*Vulvo-*, combining form of VULVA + VA-GIN(A) + -ITIS.]

vv. verses.

v.v. vice versa.

vy·ing (vī′ĭng) *adj.* Competing; contending. **—vy·ing·ly** *adv.*

vulture *Adapted for feeding on dead animals, vultures have feeble claws but powerful beaks. Some species can tear the toughest hides. The largest have wingspans of more than 2.5 meters (nearly 9 feet).*

w, W (dŭb′əl-yōō, -yōō) n., pl. **w's** or **W's. 1.** The 23rd letter of the modern English alphabet. See feature at **alphabet. 2.** Any of the speech sounds represented by this letter. **3.** Something shaped like the letter W. **4.** The 23rd in a series; 22nd when *J* is omitted.

w, W, w., W. *Note:* As an abbreviation or symbol, *w* may be a small or a capital letter, with or without a period. Established forms or those generally preferred precede the definition. When no form is given, all four forms are in general use in that sense. **1. W** The symbol for the element tungsten [German *Wolfram*]. **2. W** *Electricity.* watt. **3. W.** Wednesday. **4. w.** week. **5. w.** weight. **6. W.** Welsh. **7.** west; western. **8. w.** width. **9. w.** wife. **10. w.** with. **11. w, W** *Physics.* work.

WA Washington (used with a Zip Code).

W.A. Western Australia.

WAAC Women's Army Auxiliary Corps.

WAAF Women's Auxiliary Air Force.

Wa·bash (wô′băsh). River, *c.* 765 kilometers (475 miles) long, rising in western Ohio and flowing through Indiana, then along the Indiana-Illinois border to join the Ohio River. It is the largest northern tributary of the Ohio.

wabble. Variant of **wobble.**

Wac (wăk) n. A member of the Women's Army Corps of the United States Army, organized during World War II. [Abbreviation of *Women's Army Corps.*]

WAC, W.A.C. Women's Army Corps.

wack (wăk) n. Also **whack** (hwăk). *Slang.* A wacky person; nut. [Probably from **WACKY.**]

wack·y (wăk′ē) adj. **-ier, -iest.** Also **whack·y** (hwăk′ē). **1.** Highly irrational or erratic: *a wacky person.* **2.** Crazy or silly: *a wacky outfit.* [Probably variant of dialectal *whacky,* a fool, from *whackhead,* "one stunned by a heavy blow on the head," from **WHACK.**]

Wa·co (wā′kō). City in east-central Texas, *c.* 129 kilometers (80 miles) south of Fort Worth. Located on the Brazos River, it is a trading, shipping, and industrial center. It is also the seat of Baylor University.

wad (wŏd) n. **1.** A small mass of soft material, often folded or rolled, used especially for padding, stuffing, packing, or stopping holes. **2.** A compressed ball, roll, or lump of something, as tobacco. **3. a.** A plug, as of cloth or paper, used to hold in a powder charge in a muzzleloading gun or cannon. **b.** A disk, as of felt or paper, to keep the powder and shot in place in a shotgun cartridge. **4.** *Informal.* A large bundle of something rolled up tightly; especially, a bundle of paper money. **5.** *Informal.* A large amount, especially of money. **6.** *Geology.* Hydrated manganese oxides, usually in a soft, black, earthy form, probably resulting from the decomposition of other manganese minerals.

~v. **wadded, wadding, wads.** —*tr.* **1.** To compress into a wad. **2.** To pad, pack, line, or plug with wadding. **3. a.** To hold (shot or powder) in place with a wad. **b.** To insert a wad in (a gun). —*intr.* To form into a wad. [Perhaps akin to Dutch *watten,* padding.]

wad·ding (wŏd′ĭng) n. **1. a.** A wad. **b.** Wads collectively. **2.** A soft or fibrous substance, especially layers of carded cotton or wool used for padding or stuffing. **3.** Material for gun wads.

wad·dle (wŏd′l) intr.v. **-dled, -dling, -dles. 1.** To walk with short steps that tilt the body from side to side, as a duck does. **2.** To walk heavily and clumsily with a pronounced sway.

~n. A waddling gait. [Probably frequentative of **WADE.**]

wad·dy¹ (wŏd′ē) n., pl. **-dies.** A heavy straight stick used as a club or thrown as a missile by Australian aborigines.

~tr.v. **waddied, -dying, -dies.** To strike with a waddy. [An Australian native name, perhaps from English **WOOD.**]

waddy² n., pl. **-dies.** Also **wad·die.** *Western U.S.* **1.** A cowboy. **2.** Formerly, a cattle rustler. [Origin unknown.]

wade (wād) v. **waded, wading, wades.** —*intr.* **1.** To walk in or through water or something that similarly impedes normal movement. **2.** To make one's way arduously. Often used with *through: wade through a boring report.* **3.** To make a vigorous and determined start or attack. Used with *in* or *into.* —*tr.* To cross or pass through by wading.

~n. The act of wading. [Middle English *waden,* to go, walk through (water), Old English *wadan,* to go, wade.]

Wade (wād), **(Sarah) Virginia** (1945-). British tennis player. She won the Wimbledon women's singles championship (1977). She also won the United States (1968), Italian (1971), and Australian (1972) titles.

wad·er (wā′dər) n. **1.** One that wades. **2.** Any of numerous long-legged birds of the order Charadriiformes, such as cranes, that frequent shallow water. **3. waders.** Waterproof hip boots or a waterproof garment that covers the legs and extends as far as the waist, worn especially by fishermen and hunters.

wadge, wodge (wŏj) n. *British Informal.* A thick bundle; a wad. [Alteration of **WEDGE** (probably influenced by **WAD**).]

wa·di (wŏd′ē) n., pl. **-dis.** Also **wa·dy,** pl. **-dies.** In northern Africa and southwestern Asia, a valley, gully, or riverbed that remains dry except during the rainy season. [Arabic *wādī.*]

wad·mal (wŏd′məl) n. A rough, thick, woolen cloth formerly used for outer garments by country people in northern Europe. [Middle English, from Old Norse *vathmal* : *vath,* cloth + *mal,* measure.]

wad·set (wŏd′sĕt′) n. An obsolete Scottish form of mortgage. [Middle English : *wad,* Scottish variant of obsolete *wed* ("covenant," "pledge") + **SET**; probably from the Old English phrase *tō wedde settan* (unattested), to put to pledge.]

WAF, W.A.F. Women in the Air Force.

wa·fer (wā′fər) n. **1.** A small, thin, crisp cake, biscuit, or candy. **2.** *Ecclesiastical.* A small, thin disk of unleavened bread used in the Eucharist. **3.** *Pharmacology.* A flat tablet of rice paper or dried flour paste encasing a powdered drug. **4.** A small disk of adhesive material used as a seal for papers. **5.** *Electronics.* A small, thin, flat circular disk of a semiconducting material, such as pure silicon, that is masked, oxide-coated, doped, and otherwise processed for ultimate separation into numerous individual electronic devices or for packaging as an integrated circuit.

~tr.v. **wafered, -fering, -fers. 1.** To seal or fasten together with a wafer. **2.** *Electronics.* To divide into wafers. [Middle English *wafre,* from Norman French, from Old North French *waufre,* from Middle Low German *wāfel.* Compare **waffle.**]

waff (wăf, wŏf) v. **waffed, waffing, waffs.** *British Regional.* —*intr.* To wave; flutter. —*tr.* To cause to wave or flutter.

~n. *British Regional.* **1.** A waving motion. **2.** A gust of air; waft. **3.** A glimpse. [Middle English (northern) *waffen,* variant of *waven,* to **WAVE.**]

waf·fle¹ (wŏf′əl) n. A light, crisp batter cake baked in a waffle iron. [Dutch *wafel,* from earlier *waefel,* from Middle Low German *wāfel.* Compare **wafer.**]

waffle² intr.v. **-fled, -fling, -fles.** *Informal.* To speak or write evasively; willfully mislead.

~n. *Informal.* Evasive, vague, or misleading speech or writing. [Probably frequentative of *waff,* to yelp.]

waffle iron n. An appliance having hinged, indented metal plates that impress a grid pattern into waffle batter as it bakes.

waft (wŏft, wăft) v. **wafted, wafting, wafts.** —*tr.* To carry, cause to go, or send floating gently through the air or over water: *a breeze wafting the odor of roses.* —*intr.* To float easily and gently through or as if through the air; drift.

~n. **1.** Something, such as a scent, carried through the air. **2.** A light breeze; a rush of air. **3.** The act of wafting or waving. **4.** *Nautical.* **a.** A flag used for signaling or indicating wind direction. **b.** A signal with such a flag. [Originally "to convoy (ships)," from obsolete *wafter,* a convoy, Middle English *waughter,* from Middle Dutch *wachter,* a guard, from *wachten,* to watch, guard.]

waft·age (wŏf′tĭj, wăf′-) n. Conveyance over water or passage through the air.

waf·ture (wŏf′chər, wăf′-) n. **1.** The act or action of waving. **2.** The action of wafting.

wag¹ (wăg) v. **wagged, wagging, wags.** —*intr.* **1.** To move briskly and repeatedly from side to side, to and fro, or up and down. **2.** To move rapidly in talking, especially in gossiping. Used of the tongue. **3.** To walk with a clumsy sway; waddle. —*tr.* To wag (a part of the

body), as in playfulness, agreement, admonition, or chatter: *wagged his tail.*
~*n.* An act or motion of wagging. [Middle English *waggen,* ultimately from Old English *wagian,* to totter.] **—wag·ger** *n.*
wag² *n.* A humorous, mischievous, or facetious person. [Perhaps from obsolete *waghalter,* someone likely to be hanged : WAG (verb) + HALTER (hangman's noose).]
wage (wāj) *n.* **1.** Payment to a worker for labor or services; especially, remuneration on an hourly, daily, or weekly basis or by the piece. Also used adjectivally: *wage package.* Compare **salary.** **2. wages.** *Economics.* The portion of the national product that represents the aggregate paid for all contributing labor and services as distinguished from the portion retained by management or reinvested in capital goods. **3. wages.** *Used with a singular or plural verb.* A fitting return; recompense: *the wages of sin.*
~*tr.v.* **waged, waging, wages.** To engage in or carry on (something aggressive and sustained, such as a war or campaign). [Middle English, a pledge, wage, soldier's pay, from Old North French, from Germanic *wadhjam* (unattested).]
wage earner *n.* **1.** A person who works for wages. **2.** One whose earnings support a household.
wa·ger (wā'jər) *n.* **1.** An agreement under which each better pledges a certain amount to the other depending upon the outcome of an unsettled matter. **2.** A matter bet on; gamble. **3.** Something staked on an uncertain outcome; a bet.
~*v.* **wagered, -gering, -gers.** —*tr.* To risk or stake (an amount or possession) on an uncertain outcome; bet. —*intr.* To make a wager; bet. [Middle English, a pledge, prize at a contest, from Norman French *wageure,* from Old North French *wagier,* to pledge, from *wage,* a pledge, WAGE.] **—wa·ger·er** *n.*
wage scale *n.* The scale of wages paid to employees for the various jobs within an industry or organization.
wage·work·er (wāj'wûr'kər) *n.* A wage earner.
Wag·ga Wag·ga (wŏg'ə wŏg'ə). Town of New South Wales, southeastern Australia. On the Murrumbidgee River, it is a trade and service center for the Riverina and Western Slopes regions.
wag·ger·y (wăg'ə-rē) *n., pl.* **-ies.** **1.** Waggish behavior or spirit; drollery. **2.** A droll remark or act. [From WAG (joker).]
wag·gish (wăg'ĭsh) *adj.* Characteristic of a wag; playfully humorous. —See Synonyms at **playful.** **—wag·gish·ly** *adv.* **—wag·gish·ness** *n.*
wag·gle (wăg'əl) *v.* **-gled, -gling, -gles.** —*tr.* To move (an attached part) with short, quick motions: *She waggled her foot impatiently.* —*intr.* To move shakily; wobble.
~*n.* A waggling motion. [Frequentative of WAG.] **—wag·gly** *adj.*
Wag·ner (väg'nər), **(Wilhelm) Richard** (1813–83). German composer. He developed the use of leitmotifs to pioneer opera as music drama. His most famous work is his operatic cycle, *Der Ring des Nibelungen,* an epic treatment of German mythology.
Wag·ne·ri·an (väg-nîr'ē-ən) *adj.* Of, pertaining to, or characteristic of Richard Wagner, his music, or his theories.
~*n.* Also **Wag·ner·ite** (väg'nə-rīt'). An admirer or disciple of Richard Wagner.
wag·on (wăg'ən) *n.* Also *chiefly British* **wag·gon.** **1.** A four-wheeled, usually horse-drawn vehicle with a large rectangular body for transporting loads. **2. a.** A light automotive transport or delivery vehicle. **b.** A **station wagon** *(see).* **c.** A police patrol wagon. **3.** A child's low four-wheeled cart hauled by a handle that governs the direction of the front wheels. **4.** A cart on wheels serving drinks or food. **5.** *British.* An open railroad freight car. **6. Wagon.** The **Big Dipper** *(see).* **—off the wagon.** *Slang.* No longer abstaining from alcoholic drinks. **—on the wagon.** *Slang.* Abstaining from alcoholic drinks.
~*tr.v.* **wagoned, -oning, -ons.** Also *chiefly British* **wag·gon, -goned, -goning, -gons.** To transport by wagon. [Dutch *wagen,* from Middle Dutch; akin to Old English *wægn,* WAIN.]
wag·on·age (wăg'ə-nĭj) *n. Archaic.* **1.** Conveyance by wagon. **2.** The cost of such conveyance.
wag·on·er (wăg'ə-nər) *n.* A wagon driver.
wag·on·ette (wăg'ə-nĕt') *n.* A light horse-drawn wagon with two seats facing lengthwise, placed behind the driver's seat.
wa·gon-lit (vä'gôN-lē') *n., pl.* **wagons-lits** or **wagon-lits** *(pronounced as singular).* A sleeping car on a European railroad train. [French : *wagon,* railroad car + *lit,* bed.]
wag·on·load (wăg'ən-lōd') *n.* The load held by one wagon.
wagon train *n.* A line or train of wagons traveling cross-country.
Wa·gram (vä'gräm). Village of northeastern Austria, near Vienna. It was the site (July 5–6, 1809) of one of Napoleon's most brilliant victories over the Austrian forces.
wag·tail (wăg'tāl') *n.* Any of various birds of the genus *Motacilla* and related genera, having a long, wagging tail.
Wah·ha·bi, Wa·ha·bi (wä-hä'bē) *n.* Also **Wah·ha·bite** (-bīt). A member of a Muslim sect founded by Abdul Wahhab in the 18th century, known for its strict observance of the Koran and flourishing mainly in Saudi Arabia. **—Wah·ha·bism, Wa·ha·bism** (wä-hä'bĭz'əm) *n.*
wa·hi·ne (wä-hē'nē, -nā') *n.* Also **va·hi·ne** (vä-). A woman or wife, especially a Polynesian or Maori woman. [Hawaiian and Maori.]
wa·hoo¹ (wä-ho͞o', wä'ho͞o) *n., pl.* **-hoos.** A shrub or small tree, *Euonymus atropurpureus,* of eastern North America, having small purplish flowers and red fruit. [Dakota *wāhu.*]
wa·hoo² (wä-ho͞o', wä'ho͞o) *n., pl.* **-hoos.** **1.** An elm, *Ulmus alata,* of the southeastern United States, having twigs with winged, corky edges. **2.** Any of several similar trees. [Creek *ûhawhu.*]
wa·hoo³ (wä-ho͞o', wä'ho͞o) *n., pl.* **-hoos** or collectively **wahoo.** A tropical marine game fish, *Acanthocybium solanderi.* [Origin unknown.]
wa·hoo⁴ (wä'ho͞o') *interj. Chiefly Western U.S.* Used to express exuberance.
wah-wah, wa-wa (wä'wä') *n.* **1.** A wavering sound produced by alternately covering and uncovering the bell of a trumpet or trombone with a mute. **2.** A sound similar to a wah-wah produced, as on an electric guitar, by means of an electronic attachment operated by a foot pedal. [Imitative.]
waif¹ (wāf) *n.* **1. a.** A stray homeless person, especially a forsaken or orphaned child. **b.** An abandoned young animal. **2.** Something found and unclaimed, as an object cast up by the sea. [Middle English *waife, wayf,* ownerless property, from Norman French *waif, weif,* variant of Old North French *gaif,* from Scandinavian.]
waif² *n.* A small flag for signaling; a waft. [Probably from Scandinavian, akin to Old Norse *veif,* a waving thing.]
Wai·ka·to (wī'kä'tō). Longest river of New Zealand. Rising in Lake Taupo on North Island, it flows 425 kilometers (260 miles) through dairylands to the Tasman Sea south of Auckland.
Wai·ki·ki (wī'kē-kē', wī'kē-kē'). A famous beach and resort center southeast of Honolulu, Hawaii, on the southern shore of Oahu. Surfboard riding is the major sport at Waikiki, which is noted for its huge waves.
wail (wāl) *v.* **wailed, wailing, wails.** —*intr.* **1.** To grieve or protest loudly and bitterly; lament. **2.** To make a prolonged, high-pitched sound suggestive of a cry: *wailing winds.* —*tr.* **1.** *Archaic.* To lament over; bewail. **2.** To express plaintively. —See Synonyms at **cry.**
~*n.* **1.** A long, loud, high-pitched cry, as of grief or pain. **2.** Any similar sound. [Middle English *wailen, weilen,* probably from Old Norse *veila* (unattested), to moan, lament; akin to *vei,* WOE.] **—wail·er** *n.* **—wail·ing·ly** *adv.*
wail·ful (wāl'fəl) *adj.* **1.** Resembling a wail; mournful; plaintive. **2.** Issuing a sound like a wail.
Wail·ing Wall (wā'lĭng) *n.* A wall in the old city of Jerusalem believed to be a remnant of the Temple of Solomon and revered by Jews as a place of pilgrimage, lamentation, and prayer. Also called "Western Wall."
wain (wān) *n.* **1.** A large, open farm wagon. **2.** The **Big Dipper** *(see).* [Middle English, Old English *wæg(e)n, wǣn.*]
wain·scot (wān'skət, -skŏt', -skōt') *n.* **1.** A facing or paneling, usually of wood, applied to the walls of a room. **2.** The lower part of an interior wall when finished in a material different from that of the upper part.
~*tr.v.* **wainscoted** or **-scotted, -scoting** or **-scotting, -scots.** To line or panel (a room or wall) with wainscot. [Middle English *waynscot(te), weynshet,* from Middle Low German *wagenschot,* perhaps "timber for wagons" : *wagen,* WAGON + *schot,* planking.]
wain·scot·ing, wain·scot·ting (wān'skə-tĭng, -skŏt'ĭng, -skō'tĭng) *n.* **1.** A wainscoted surface of a wall; paneling. **2.** Wood or other material for wainscoting.
wain·wright (wān'rīt') *n.* A builder and repairer of wagons.
waist (wāst) *n.* **1.** The part of the human trunk between the bottom of the rib cage and the pelvis. **2. a.** The part of a garment that encircles the waist of the body. **b.** The upper part of a garment extending from the shoulders to the waistline; especially, the bodice of a woman's dress. **c.** A blouse. **d.** A child's undershirt. **3.** The middle section or part of an object, especially when narrower than the rest, as on a violin or hourglass. **4.** *Nautical.* The middle part of the deck of a ship between the forecastle and the quarter-deck. **5.** The center portion of the fuselage of an airplane. [Middle English *wa(a)st,* Old English *wæst* (unattested), growth, size of body; akin to WAX (to grow).]
waist·band (wāst'bănd') *n.* A band of material encircling and fitting the waist, as on a pair of trousers or a skirt.
waist·cloth (wāst'klôth', -klŏth') *n., pl.* **-cloths** (-klôths', -klôthz', -klŏths', -klŏthz'). A loincloth.
waist·coat (wĕs'kĭt, wāst'kōt') *n.* **1.** *Chiefly British.* A man's vest. **2.** A garment formerly worn by men under a doublet.
waist·ed (wā'stĭd) *adj.* **1.** Having a waist or a part like a waist. **2.** Having a waist of a specified kind. Used in combination: *short-waisted.*
waist·line (wāst'līn') *n.* **1. a.** The natural indentation of the body at the waist; the place at which the circumference of the waist is smallest. **b.** The measurement of this circumference. **2.** The point or line at which the skirt and bodice of a dress join.
wait (wāt) *v.* **waited, waiting, waits.** —*intr.* **1. a.** To remain inactive, defer action, or stay in one spot until something anticipated occurs or until a specified time: *I had to wait for the doctor to arrive.* **b.** To tarry until another catches up: *Wait for me.* **2.** To be in a state of readiness or expectancy: *waiting for the results of the test.* **3.** To be temporarily neglected, unattended to, or postponed: *The trip had to wait.* **4.** To work as a waiter or waitress. —*tr.* **1.** To remain or stay in expectation of; await: *wait one's turn.* **2.** *Informal.* To delay (a meal or event); postpone: *They waited lunch.* **3.** To be a waiter or waitress at: *wait table.* —See Synonyms at **stay.** **—wait on** (or **upon).** **1. a.** To serve the needs of; be in attendance upon. **b.** To take orders from and serve food and drink to (customers in a restaurant). **c.** To be the waiter in attendance on (a table in a restaurant). **2.** To make a formal call upon; visit. **3.** To follow as a result. **4.** To wait for. **—wait out.** To wait until the termination of: *wait out a war.* **—wait up.** **1.** To postpone going to bed in anticipation

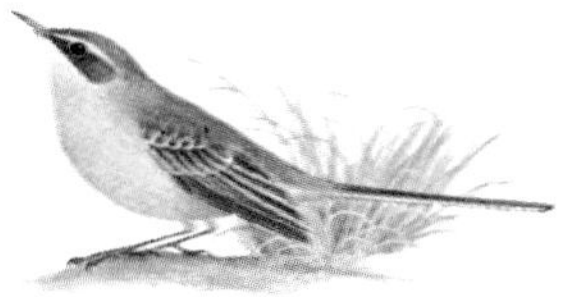

wagtail *Like other wagtails, the yellow wagtail (above) likes water and is found in marshes and river meadows. It nests on the ground among grasses.*

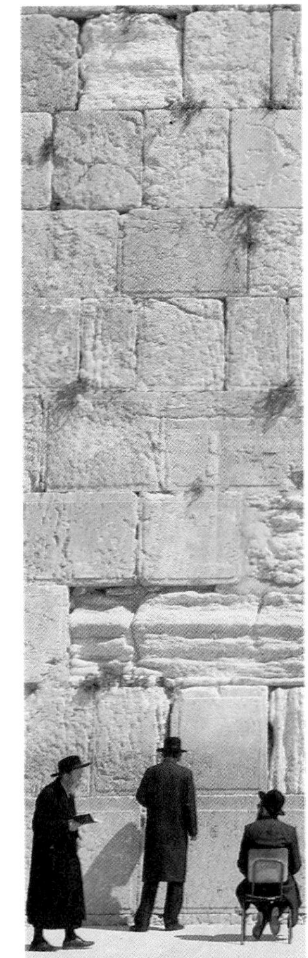

Wailing Wall *The Wailing, or Western, Wall is a place of prayer and pilgrimage sacred to the Jews. Part of it, dating from the second century B.C., is all that remains of the Second Temple of Jerusalem, destroyed by the Romans in A.D. 70. Fifty meters (160 feet) high, it is now part of a larger wall around a mosque.*

of something or someone. **2.** *Informal.* To stop or pause so that another can catch up.
~*n.* **1.** The act of waiting or the time spent waiting. **2.** *British.* **a.** One of a group of musicians employed, usually by a town or city, to play in parades or public ceremonies. **b.** One of a group of musicians who perform carols in the streets at Christmastime. —**lie in wait.** To be on the watch; especially, to wait in ambush. [Middle English *waiten, wayten,* to watch, lie in wait, wait, from Old North French *waitier,* from Germanic *wahtan* (unattested) to watch.]
   Usage: Wait is generally used intransitively (*I'll wait*); *await* is generally transitive (*A car awaits her at the station*). When used with reference to persons and physical objects, *wait for* is normal (*We were waiting for a train*), *await* being formal (*We were awaiting the train*). When used with reference to intangible things or abstract notions, *await* is much less restricted (*We're awaiting the announcement*) and is only a little more formal than *wait for.*
wait-a-bit (wā′tə-bĭt′) *n.* Any of several plants having sharp, often hooked thorns. [Translation of Afrikaans *wacht-en-bitje* (because the thorns catch hold of passers-by).]
wait-er (wā′tər) *n.* **1.** A man who serves at a table, as in a restaurant. **2.** A tray or salver.
wait-ing (wā′tĭng) *n.* **1.** The act of remaining stationary or inactive. **2.** A period of time spent in waiting. —**in waiting.** In attendance, especially at a royal court.
waiting game *n.* The stratagem of deferring action and allowing time to pass in order to gain an advantage.
waiting list *n.* A list of persons waiting, as for an appointment or for filling a vacancy.
waiting room *n.* A room, as at a railroad station or doctor's office, for the use of persons waiting.
wait-ress (wā′trĭs) *n.* A woman or girl who serves at a table, as in a restaurant.
waive (wāv) *tr.v.* **waived, waiving, waives. 1.** To relinquish or give up (a claim or right) voluntarily. **2.** To refrain from insisting upon or enforcing (a rule or penalty, for example); dispense with. **3.** To put aside temporarily; defer. —See Synonyms at **relinquish.** [Middle English *weiven,* to outlaw, abandon, relinquish, from Norman French *weyver,* variant of Old North French *gaiver,* from *gaif,* ownerless property. See **wait.**]
waiv-er (wā′vər) *n.* **1.** The intentional relinquishment of a right, claim, or privilege. **2.** A document that evidences a waiver. [Norman French *weyver,* from Old North French *weyver,* to WAIVE.]
Wa-kash-an (wô-kăsh′ən, wô′kăsh′-) *n.* A family of North American Indian laguages spoken by tribes in the state of Washington and in British Columbia. [From Wakashan *waukash,* good.]
wake¹ (wāk) *v.* **woke** (wōk) or *rare* **waked, waked** or **woken** (wō′kən) or *chiefly British & Regional* **woke, waking, wakes.** —*intr.* **1. a.** To cease to sleep; become awake: *overslept and woke up late.* **b.** To be brought into a state of awareness, attention, or alertness: *suddenly woke to the danger we were in; wake up and listen.* **2.** To keep watch or guard, especially over a corpse. **3.** To be or remain awake: *worked at his research during all his waking hours.* —*tr.* **1.** To rouse from sleep; awaken. Often used with *up.* **2.** To stir, as from a dormant or inactive condition; rouse: *wake old animosities.* **3.** To make aware; alert: *It woke him to the facts.* **4. a.** To keep a vigil over. **b.** To hold a wake over.
~*n.* **1. a.** A watch; vigil. **b.** A watch over the body of a deceased person before burial, sometimes accompanied by festivity. **2.** *British.* **a.** A parish festival held annually, often in honor of the patron saint. **b.** *Usually* **wakes.** Used with a singular or plural verb. An annual holiday in northern England during which many factories close for a week or more. **3.** The condition of being awake: *between wake and sleep.* [Middle English *wakien* and *waken,* Old English *wacian,* to be awake, and *wacan* (unattested), to rouse.]
   Usage: The verbs *wake, waken, awake,* and *awaken* each have transitive and intransitive uses. *Awake* is largely used intransitively (*I awoke at six*), and *waken* transitively (*I wakened her at six*). In passive constructions, the verbs *awaken* and *waken* are more widely used than the verbs *awake* or *wake* (*I was awakened/wakened by the phone*). *Wake* is especially common with *up,* is the most frequently used of all these verbs, and may be transitive or intransitive. *Awake* and *awaken* are the more prevalent verbs in figurative usage: *She awoke to the danger. Her suspicions were awakened.*
wake² *n.* **1.** The visible track of turbulence left by something moving through water: *the wake of a ship.* **2.** The track or course left behind anything that has passed: *The war left nothing but destruction in its wake.* —**in the wake of. 1.** Following directly upon. **2.** In the aftermath of; as a consequence of. [Probably Middle Low German *wake,* from Old Norse *vök,* a hole or crack in ice.]
Wake Island (wāk). Atoll in the central Pacific, between Hawaii and Guam. Discovered by the Spanish in 1568 and visited and named by the British in 1796, it was annexed by the United States in 1898. It is now a commercial and military base and has no indigenous population.
wake-ful (wāk′fəl) *adj.* **1. a.** Not sleeping or not able to sleep. **b.** Without sleep; sleepless. **2.** Watchful; alert; vigilant. —**wake-ful-ly** *adv.* —**wake-ful-ness** *n.*
wake-less (wāk′lĭs) *adj.* Unbroken. Said of sleep.
wak-en (wā′kən) *v.* **-ened, -ening, -ens. 1.** To rouse from sleep; awake. **2.** To rouse from a quiescent or inactive state; stir. —*intr.* To become awake; wake up. —See Usage note at **wake** (rouse). [Middle English *wak(e)nen,* Old English *wæcn(i)an.*] —**wak-en-er** *n.*

wake-rife (wāk′rīf′) *adj. Chiefly Scottish.* Wakeful; alert; vigilant. [Middle English : WAKE (noun) + RIFE.]
wake-rob-in (wāk′rŏb′ĭn) *n.* Any of various plants of the family Araceae, especially the cuckoopint. [WAKE (to rouse) + *Robin* (man's name).]
Waks-man (wăks′mən), **Selman Abraham** (1888–1973). Russian-born U.S. biologist. He discovered the antibiotics actinomycin (1940) and streptomycin (1943). He won the Nobel Prize for physiology and medicine (1952).
Wa-la-chi-a (wō-lā′kē-ə). Region of south Romania, southeastern Europe. Situated between the Transylvanian Alps and the Danube River, it was founded as a principality (1290) and was ruled by Turkey from 1387 until united with Moldavia (1859) to form Romania. Its chief town is Bucharest.
Wal-den Pond (wôl′dən). Pond in northeastern Massachusetts near Concord. Henry David Thoreau lived in a cabin on the lake from July 4, 1845, to September 6, 1847, and wrote about his life in his most famous book, *Walden* (1854).
Wal-den-ses (wôl-dĕn′sēz) *pl.n.* A Christian sect of dissenters originating in southern France in the late 12th century under the leadership of Peter Waldo, a Lyons merchant. Also called "Vaudois." —**Wal-den-sian** (wôl-dĕn′shən, -sē-ən) *adj & n.*
wald-grave (wôld′grāv′) *n.* **1.** Formerly, a king's officer in charge of a royal forest. **2.** A former German title of nobility. [German *Waldgraf* : *Wald,* forest, from Old High German + *Graf,* count, ruler, from Middle High German *grāve,* from Old High German *grāvo.*]
Wald-heim (wôld′hīm, vält′-), **Kurt** (1918–). Austrian diplomat and politician. Secretary-general of the United Nations (1972–81), he was elected president of Austria in 1986 despite worldwide controversy over his alleged Nazi affiliations in World War II.
Wal-dorf salad (wôl′dôrf′) *n.* A salad of diced raw apples, celery, and walnuts mixed with mayonnaise. [Originally served in the *Waldorf*-Astoria Hotel, New York City.]
wale¹ (wāl) *n.* **1.** A mark raised on the flesh, as by a whip; a weal. **2. a.** Any of the parallel ribs or ridges in the surface of a fabric such as corduroy. **b.** The texture or weave of such a fabric: *a wide wale.* **3.** A ridge woven around a basket to strengthen it. **4.** *Nautical.* **a.** The gunwale. **b.** Any of the heavy planks or strakes extending along the sides of a wooden ship.
~*tr.v.* **waled, waling, wales.** To mark (the skin) with wales. [Middle English *wale,* a ridge, gunwale, Old English *walu,* a ridge of earth or stone, weal.]
wale² *n. British Regional.* **1.** A choice. **2.** Something that is chosen or picked out as the best.
~*tr.v.* **waled, waling, wales.** *British Regional.* To choose; select. [Middle English, from Old Norse *val,* choice.]
Wal-er (wā′lər) *n.* A horse exported from Australia, especially from New South Wales. [(New South) Wal(es) + -ER.]
Wales (wālz). Welsh **Cym-ru** (kĭm′rōō). Principality of Great Britain. Bounded by the Irish Channel to the north and west, the Bristol Channel to the south, and England to the east, it forms the western peninsula of Great Britain. It is crossed by many mountains, including the Cambrians, which rise to 1,085 meters (3,560 feet) at Mt. Snowdon, and is drained by the Usk, Severn, Dee, and Wye rivers. The north is an agricultural region where livestock are bred and cereals and vegetables are grown, while the extensive coalfield of the south has fueled many industries including iron and steel, tinplate, and copper manufacture. Decreased demand during the 1970's and 1980's, however, has led to the closure of many plants and diversification into light industry. Incorporated with England since the Act of Union (1536), it has a distinctive culture and a language still widely spoken. Its capital is Cardiff.
Wa-le-sa (wä-lĕn′sə), **Lech** (1943–). Polish trade union leader. He was an electrician at the Lenin shipyard in Gdańsk between 1966 and 1976 and after 1980. He became the chairman of the Strike Committee in 1980 and was chairman of Solidarity, an independent trade union banned in 1981. He won the Nobel Peace Prize (1983).
Walhalla. Variant of **Valhalla.**
walk (wôk) *v.* **walked, walking, walks.** —*intr.* **1.** To move over a surface by taking steps with the feet at a pace slower than a run. **2.** To roam about in a visible form, as a ghost; appear: *The specter walks at midnight.* **3.** To travel or go on foot, especially for pleasure or exercise. **4.** To conduct oneself or behave in a particular manner; live. **5.** *Baseball.* To go to first base after the pitcher has thrown four balls. **6.** *Basketball.* To move illegally while holding the ball; travel. **7.** To move in a manner suggestive of walking: *The malfunctioning washing machine walked across the floor.* —*tr.* **1.** To go or pass over, on, or through by walking: *walk the streets.* **2.** To bring to a specified condition or state by walking: *walk someone to exhaustion.* **3.** To cause to walk or proceed at a walk: *walk a horse uphill.* **4.** To accompany in walking; escort on foot: *walk her home.* **5.** To assist or force to walk. **6.** To traverse on foot in order to survey or measure; pace off. **7.** To move (a heavy or cumbersome object) in a manner suggestive of walking. **8.** *Baseball.* To allow (a batter) to go to first base by pitching four balls. —**walk (all) over.** To treat contemptuously or inconsiderately. —**walk away from. 1.** To outdo, outrun, or defeat with little difficulty. **2.** To survive (an accident) with very little injury. —**walk away with.** To win very easily. —**walk into.** To encounter or be caught by (a trap, for example) inadvertently or through carelessness. —**walk off.** To purge or rid oneself of by walking: *walked off his anger.* —**walk off with. 1.** To walk away with. **2.** To steal. —**walk out on.** *Informal.*

To desert; abandon. **—walk the plank.** To be executed at sea by walking the length of a plank and falling into the water.
∼*n.* **1. a.** The gait of a human being or other biped in which the feet are lifted alternately with one part of a foot always on the ground. **b.** The gait of a quadruped, slower than a trot, in which at least two feet are always touching the ground. **c.** The gait of a horse in which the feet touch the ground in the four-beat sequence of near hind foot, near forefoot, off hind foot, off forefoot. **d.** The self-controlled movement in space of an astronaut. **2.** The act or an instance of walking; especially, a stroll for pleasure or exercise. **3. a.** The rate at which one walks; a walking pace. **b.** The characteristic way in which one walks. **4.** The distance covered or to be covered by walking. **5.** A place, as a sidewalk or promenade, on which one may walk. **6.** A route or circuit particularly suitable for walking: *one of the prettiest walks in the area.* **7.** A track event in which contestants compete in walking a specified distance. **8.** An enclosed area for the exercise or pasture of livestock. **9. a.** An arrangement of trees or shrubs planted in widely spaced rows. **b.** The space between such rows. **10. a.** *Baseball.* The act or an instance of taking first base after four balls have been pitched. **b.** *Basketball.* The act or an instance of traveling with the ball. [Middle English *walken* and *walkien,* respectively from Old English *wealcan,* to roll, toss, and *wealcian,* to roll up, muffle up.]
walk·a·bout (wô′kə-bout′) *n.* **1.** A period spent by an Aborigine wandering in the bush as a respite from regular work. **2. a.** A walking trip. **b.** *British.* A stroll made by an important person, as a monarch, among a crowd.
walk·a·way (wô′kə-wā′) *n.* A contest or victory easily won.
walk·er (wô′kər) *n.* **1.** One that walks. **2.** A framework used to support a baby learning to walk or a disabled or convalescent person.
Walk·er (wô′kər), **David** (1785–1830). U.S. abolitionist. A regular contributor to *Freeman's Journal,* he wrote and published three editions of *Walker's Appeal* (1829–30), an antislavery pamphlet that urged violent slave insurrections and began the militant abolitionist movement.
Walker, James John, known as "Jimmy" (1881–1946). U.S. politician. A liberal New York state senator (1914–25), he was elected mayor of New York City in 1925 and became widely known for his fondness of nightlife. In 1932, amid numerous charges of impropriety, he resigned from office but remained highly popular with the public.
Walker, Joseph Reddeford (1798–1876). U.S. frontiersman and guide. A fur trapper familiar with the geography, travel routes, and Indian tribes of the vast American West, he led several explorations and groups of settlers to the frontier.
Walker, William (1824–60). U.S. adventurer and South American revolutionary. After establishing a short-lived colony in Mexico (1853–54), he traveled to Nicaragua, where he founded a new government and was elected president (1856). After becoming entangled with American business interests in the regions, he returned to the United States. In 1860 he attempted to return to Central America but was captured by British naval forces, turned over to Honduran officials, court-martialed, and executed.
walk·ie-talk·ie, walk·y-talk·y (wô′kē-tô′kē) *n. pl.* **-ies.** A battery-powered, portable sending and receiving radio set.
walk-in (wôk′ĭn′) *adj.* **1.** Large enough to admit entrance: *a walk-in closet.* **2.** Located so as to be entered directly from the street: *a walk-in apartment.*
∼*n.* **1.** A room, especially a storage room, large enough to admit entrance. **2.** An easily won victory, especially in an election. **3.** A person who walks in without an appointment.
walk·ing (wô′kĭng) *adj.* Regarded as having the capabilities or qualities of a specified inanimate object: *He is a walking dictionary.*
walking bass (bās) *n.* A repetitive bass figure composed of nonsyncopated eighth notes, used in jazz.
walking delegate *n.* A trade-union official appointed to inspect and confer with local unions or to serve as a representative of the union in dealings with an employer.
walking fern *n.* A North American fern, *Camptosorus rhizophyllus,* having leaflike fronds with slender tips that often take root.
walking papers *pl.n. Informal.* Notice of discharge or dismissal.
walking stick *n.* **1.** A cane or staff used as an aid in walking. **2.** Any of various insects of the family Phasmidae, having the appearance of twigs or sticks. Also called "stick insect."
walk of life *n.* An occupation, profession, or social class: *People from all walks of life supported the cause.*
walk-on (wôk′ŏn′, -ôn′) *n.* **1.** A minor role, usually nonspeaking, in a theatrical production. **2.** An actor playing a walk-on.
walk out (wôk′out′) *intr.v.* **1.** To go on strike. **2.** To leave or resign abruptly, especially as a sign of disagreement or anger.
walk-out (wôk′out′) *n.* **1.** A labor strike. **2.** The act of leaving a meeting, company, or organization as a sign of protest.
walk over *tr.v.* **1.** *Informal.* To treat inconsiderately or contemptuously. **2.** To gain an easy or uncontested victory over.
walk·o·ver (wôk′ō′vər) *n.* **1.** A horse race in which only one horse is entered. **2.** A walkaway.
walk through *tr.v.* To perform (a play, for example) in a perfunctory fashion, as at a first rehearsal.
walk-through (wôk′thro͞o′) *n.* A rehearsal at which the performers walk through their parts.
walk·up, walk-up (wôk′ŭp′) *n.* **1.** An apartment house or office building with no elevator. **2.** An apartment or office in a walkup. **—walk·up** *adj.*
walk·way (wôk′wā′) *n.* A passage or path for walking.
Walkyrie. Variant of **Valkyrie.**
wall (wôl) *n.* **1.** An upright structure of building material such as masonry, wood, or plaster that serves to enclose, divide, or protect an area; specifically, a vertical construction forming an inner partition or exterior side of a building. **2.** *Often* **walls.** A continuous structure of material such as masonry forming a rampart and built for defensive purposes. **3.** A structure, as of stonework or cement, built to retain a flow of water; a dam, levee, or dyke. **4.** Something resembling a wall in appearance, function, or construction, as the exterior surface of a bodily organ: *the abdominal wall.* **5.** In surfing, the vertical surface of an ocean wave. **6.** Something resembling a wall in impenetrability or strength: *a wall of silence.* **7.** An extreme or desperate condition or position, as defeat or ruin: *driven to the wall by poverty.* **—up the wall.** *Informal.* Into a state of extreme frustration, anger, or distress: *Your complaints are driving me up the wall.*
∼*tr.v.* **walled, walling, walls. 1.** To enclose, surround, or fortify with or as if with a wall. **2.** To divide or separate with or as if with a wall: *wall off half a room.* **3.** To enclose within a wall; immure. **4.** To block or close (an opening or passage, for example) with or as if with a wall. [Middle English *wal(le),* Old English *weall,* from Latin *vallum,* palisade, wall, from *vallus,* stake.]
wal·la·by (wŏl′ə-bē) *n., pl.* **-bies** or collectively **wallaby.** Any of various marsupials of the genus *Wallabia* and related genera, of Australia and adjacent islands, related to and resembling the kangaroos but smaller. [Australian native name *wolabā.*]
wallaby grass *n.* Any of various tussock grasses of the genus *Danthonia,* abundant in Australasia and used as winter fodder.
Wal·lace (wŏl′ĭs), **Alfred Russel** (1823–1913). English naturalist. After his expeditions to the Amazon and the Malay Archipelago, he developed a theory of evolution that paralleled the work of Charles Darwin. The two naturalists presented their theories jointly in 1858.
Wallace, De Witt (1889–1981) and **Lila Bell Acheson** (1899–1984). U.S. publishers. Married in New York City in 1921, they published the first issue of *Reader's Digest* in 1922 and continued to manage the monthly magazine throughout their lives. In its first 50 years the magazine's circulation increased from 1,500 to over 20 million.
Wallace, Henry Agard (1888–1965). U.S. politician and agriculturalist. The editor of *Wallace's Farmer,* a distinguished farming journal, he served as U.S. secretary of agriculture (1933–40) and as Franklin D. Roosevelt's vice president (1941–45). He later was secretary of commerce (1945–46) and ran for president in 1948 on the Progressive Party ticket.
Wallace, Irving (1916–). U.S. author. Originally known for his best-selling novels, such as *The Chapman Report* (1960) and *The Prize* (1962), he has also written biographies, including one on P.T. Barnum (1959), and has collaborated on several collections of interesting little-known facts, such as *The People's Almanac* (1975).
Wallace, Lewis, known as "Lew" (1827–1905). U.S. soldier, diplomat, and author. Wallace served in the Union Army throughout the Civil War and later was governor of the New Mexico Territory (1878–81) and minister to Turkey (1881–85). His real love was writing, and he is best known for his sprawling historical novel *Ben Hur* (1880), one of the most popular books ever published in the United States.
Wallace, Sir William (*c.* 1270–1305). Scottish patriot. He led the resistance to Edward I and captured Stirling Castle (1297). He was proclaimed warden of Scotland, but was later routed at Falkirk (1298) and eventually captured and hanged.
Wal·lace's line (wŏl′ə-sĭz) *n.* The hypothetical dividing line between the Oriental and Australasian zoogeographic regions, running between the Indonesian islands Bali and Lombok. [After Alfred Russel WALLACE.]
wal·lah, wal·la (wŏl′ə) *n.* **1.** *Anglo-Indian.* One employed in a specified occupation or activity. Used in combination: *a kitchen wallah.* **2.** *British Informal.* A man; chap. [Hindi *-wālā,* adjectival suffix, mistaken by Europeans for a suffix indicating a man.]
wal·la·roo (wŏl′ə-ro͞o′) *n., pl.* **-roos.** A kangaroo, *Macropus robustus* or *Osphranter robustus,* of hilly regions of Australia. Also called "euro." [Australian native name *wolárū.*]
Wal·la Wal·la (wŏl′ə wŏl′ə). City in southeastern Washington, on the Walla Walla River near the Oregon border. It is a trade, processing, and distributing center for a rich farm area.
wall·board (wôl′bôrd′, -bōrd′) *n.* Any of several structural boards or sheets of various materials, such as gypsum plaster encased in paper or compressed wood fibers and chips, used in construction as a substitute for plaster or wood panels.
wall creeper *n.* A long-billed crimson and grayish bird, *Tichodroma muraria,* of alpine regions of the Old World, characteristically seeking food on rocky cliffs or walls.
walled plain *n.* A very large, flat-bottomed craterlike feature on the moon's surface.
Wal·ler (wôl′ər), **Edmund** (1606–87). British poet. He is known chiefly for his harmonious love lyrics, which include *On a Girdle* and *Go, Lovely Rose* (from his *Poems* of 1645).
Waller, Thomas Wright, known as "Fats" (1904–43). U.S. jazz musician and songwriter. His many compositions include *Honeysuckle Rose* and *Ain't Misbehavin'.*
wal·let (wŏl′ĭt) *n.* **1.** A small, flat folding case, often made of leather or vinyl material, for holding articles such as paper money, cards, or photographs. **2.** A small bag for carrying personal necessities on a

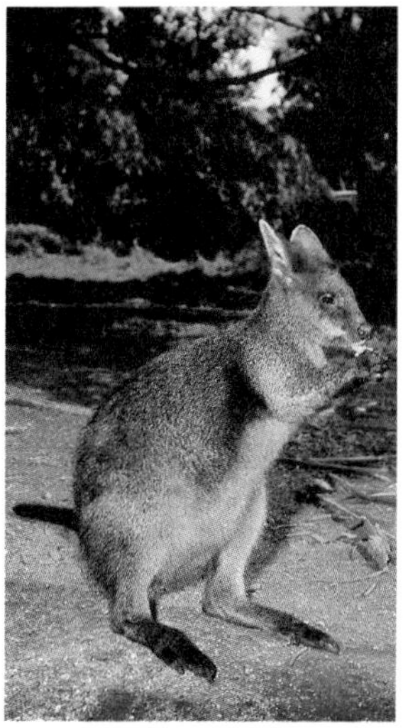

wallaby *Native to Australasia, wallabies resemble their larger cousins, the kangaroos.*

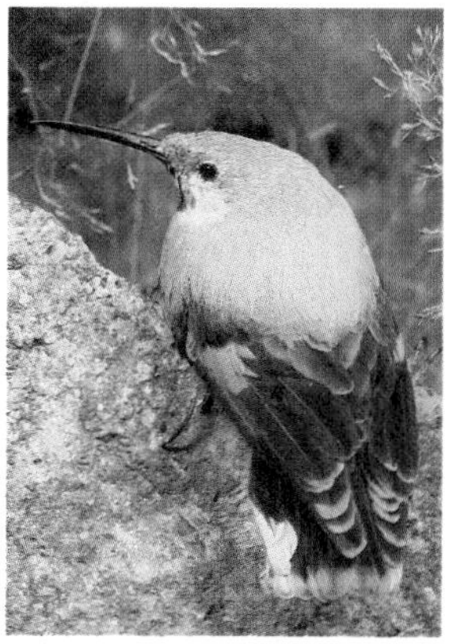

wall creeper *The ability of* Tichodroma muraria, *the wall creeper (above), to half-climb, half-flutter on rock faces looking for food has earned it the name butterfly bird among mountaineers. It inhabits alpine areas from southern Europe to the Chinese Himalayas.*

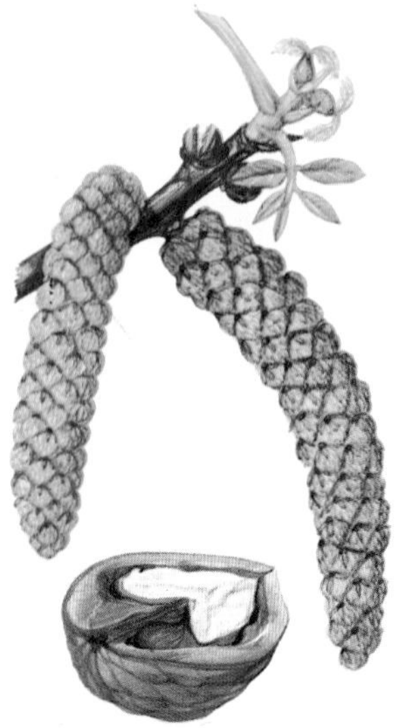

walnut *The edible fruit of the walnut tree; the male flowers are carried in slender catkins.*

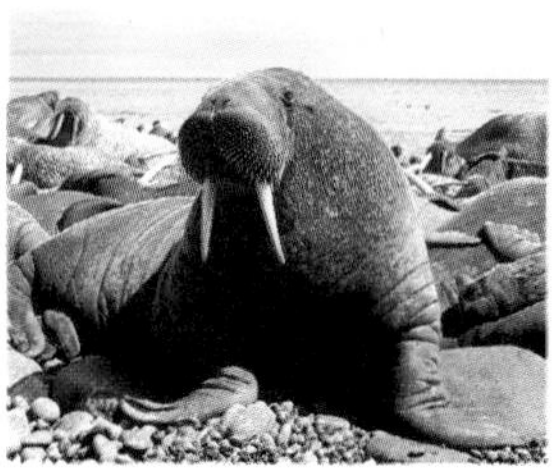

walrus *These arctic mammals feed largely on shellfish raked up by their tusks, which can grow up to a meter (3.3 feet) long.*

PRONUNCIATION KEY

ă, pat; ā, pay; âr, care;
ä, father, are; b, **bib**;
ch, **church**; d, **deed**; ĕ, pet;
ē, be; f, **fife**; g, **gag**; h, **hat**;
hw, **which**; ĭ, pit; ī, pie;
îr, **pier**; j, **judge**; k, **kick**;
l, lid, needle; m, **mum**;
n, no, sudden; ng, **thing**;
ŏ, pot; ō, toe; ô, paw, for;
oi, noise; ou, **out**; o͝o, **book**;
o͞o, **boot**; p, **pop**; r, **roar**;
s, sauce; sh, **ship**, **dish**;
t, **tight**; th, **thin**, **path**;
th, **this**, **bathe**; ŭ, cut; ûr, **fur**;
v, valve; w, **with**; y, **yes**;
z, zebra, size; zh, vision;
ə, about, item, edible, gallop, circus, peaceful

IN FOREIGN WORDS:

à, *Fr.* **ami**; œ, *Fr.* **feu**, *Ger.* **schön**; ü, *Fr.* **tu**, *Ger.* **über**; KH, *Ger.* **ich**, *Scot.* **loch**; N, *Fr.* **bon**; y', *Fr.* **Compiègne**

STRESS MARKS:

Primary stress: ′
in·cite′ (ĭn-sīt′)
Secondary stress: ′
in′sight′ (ĭn′sīt′)

journey, especially one formerly used by a pilgrim. [Middle English *walet,* a pilgrim's knapsack or provisions bag, probably from Norman French *walet* (unattested), from Germanic.]

wall·eye (wôl′ī′) *n.* **1. a.** An eye in which the cornea is white or opaque. **b.** Leukoma of the cornea. **c.** An eye in which the iris is white, partly colored, or of a different color from the other eye. **d.** A divergent strabismus. **2.** A freshwater food and game fish, *Stizostedium vitreum,* of North America, having large, conspicuous eyes. Also called "dory," "walleyed pike," or "pike perch." [Back-formation from WALLEYED.]

wall·eyed (wôl′īd′) *adj.* **1.** Having or affected with walleye. **2.** Having large bulging or staring eyes, as some fish do. [Variant (influenced by WALL) of Middle English *wawil-eghed,* from Old Norse *vagleygr* : *vagl* (unattested), perhaps film over the eye + *-eygr,* -eyed, from *auga,* an eye.]

wall fern *n.* A fern, the common **polypody** *(see).*

wall·flow·er (wôl′flou′ər) *n.* **1. a.** A widely cultivated plant, *Cheiranthus cheiri,* native to Europe, having fragrant, variously colored flowers. **b.** Any of various similar, related plants. **2.** *Informal.* A person who does not participate in the activity at a social event, especially a dance, because of shyness or unpopularity.

wall knot *n. Nautical.* A knot made at the end of a rope by undoing the strands and weaving them together to prevent unraveling. [18th century: probably from Scandinavian and akin to Norwegian and Swedish *valknut,* Danish *valknude,* double knot, secure knot.]

wall mustard *n.* A plant, **stinkweed** *(see).*

Wal·loon (wŏ-lo͞on′) *n.* **1.** A member of a French-speaking people of Celtic descent inhabiting southern and southeastern Belgium and adjacent regions of France. Compare **Fleming. 2.** The dialect of French spoken by the Walloons. [Old French *Wallon,* from Medieval Latin *Wallō* (stem *Wallōn-*), a foreigner, Welshman, from Germanic.] **—Wal·loon** *adj.*

wal·lop (wŏl′əp) *v.* **-loped, -loping, -lops.** *Informal. —tr.* **1.** To beat soundly; thrash. **2.** To defeat thoroughly. *—intr.* **1.** To move in a rolling, clumsy manner; lumber. **2.** To boil noisily and vigorously. Said of a liquid.

~n. Informal. **1.** A hard or severe blow. **2. a.** The capacity to strike a wallop: *a punch that packs a wallop.* **b.** The capacity to create a forceful effect; impact. **3.** *British Slang.* Beer. [Earlier "to make violent, heavy motions," from Middle English *walopen,* to gallop, from Old North French *waloper,* from Frankish *walahlaupan* (unattested), "to jump well" : *wala* (unattested), well + *hlaupan* (unattested), to jump, run.]

wal·lop·er (wŏl′ə-pər) *n.* **1.** *Informal.* One that wallops. **2.** *Australian Slang.* A policeman.

wal·lop·ing (wŏl′ə-pĭng) *adj. Informal.* **1.** Very large; huge: *a walloping fish.* **2.** Very fine; impressive.

~adv. Informal. Used as an intensifier: *a walloping huge lie.*

~n. Informal. A sound thrashing or defeat.

wal·low (wŏl′ō) *intr.v.* **-lowed, -lowing, -lows. 1.** To roll the body about indolently or clumsily in or as if in water, snow, or mud. **2.** To indulge oneself; luxuriate: *wallow in self-pity.* **3.** To be plentifully supplied: *wallowing in money.* **4.** To move with difficulty in a clumsy or rolling manner; flounder. **5.** To swell or surge forth; billow.

~n. **1.** An act of wallowing. **2.** A pool of water or mud where animals go to wallow. **3.** The depression, pool, or pit produced by wallowing animals. [Middle English *walowen,* Old English *wealwian.*] **—wal·low·er** *n.*

wall·pa·per (wôl′pā′pər) *n.* Paper, usually colored and printed with designs, pasted to the wall as a decorative covering.

~v. **wallpapered, -pering, -pers.** *—tr.* To cover with wallpaper. *—intr.* To decorate a wall or room with wallpaper.

wall plate *n.* **1.** A horizontal timber situated along the top of a wall at eaves level for bearing the ends of joists or rafters. **2.** A plate used to attach a bracket or similar device to a wall.

wall plug *n.* An electric socket, usually located in a wall, that is connected to and used as a source of electric power.

wall rock *n.* The rock that forms the walls of a vein or lode.

wall rocket *n.* Any of various yellow-flowered plants of the genus *Diplotaxis,* found growing on lime rocks and walls.

wall rue *n.* A small, delicate fern, *Asplenium ruta-mararia,* growing on rocks or in rocky crevices.

Wall Street *n.* The controlling financial interests of the United States. [From the name of the main street of the financial district of New York City.]

wall-to-wall (wôl′tə-wôl′) *adj.* **1.** Covering a floor completely: *wall-to-wall carpeting.* **2.** Present throughout an entire area; pervasive: *wall-to-wall people at the convention.*

wal·ly (wŏl′ē) *adj. Scottish.* **1.** Made of china. Said of an ornament. **2.** Fine; excellent.

~n., pl. **-lies.** *Scottish.* An ornament. [16th century (adjective, "excellent"), 18th century (noun, "toy, trinket") : origin obscure.]

wal·nut (wôl′nŭt′, -nət) *n.* **1.** Any of several trees of the genus *Juglans,* having round fruit enclosing an edible nut. **2.** The ridged or corrugated two-lobed nut of such a tree. **3.** The hard, dark-brown wood of such a tree, used for gunstocks and in cabinetwork. **4.** A moderate yellowish brown.

~adj. **1.** Made of the wood of the walnut. **2.** Of the color walnut. [Middle English *walnot,* Old English *walhhnutu* (translation of Latin *nux gallia,* "Gaulish or foreign nut").]

Walnut Canyon National Monument. Area, 656 hectares (1,641 acres), in north-central Arizona, set aside to preserve 12th-century Indian cliff dwellings.

Wal·pole (wôl′pōl, wŏl′-), **Horace, 4th Earl of Orford** (1717–97). British writer and wit. His novel *The Castle of Otranto* (1765) set the fashion for Gothic literature.

Walpole, Sir Robert, 1st Earl of Orford (1676–1745). British statesman. As first lord of the Treasury and Chancellor of the Exchequer (1715–17, 1721–42) he led the Whig administration and was regarded as Britain's first prime minister (although the office was not officially recognized until 1905).

Wal·pur·gis Night (väl-po͝or′gĭs). **1.** The eve of May Day which according to German legend was the occasion of a witches' Sabbath. **2.** An episode or situation having the quality of nightmarish wildness associated with Walpurgis Night. [Partial translation of German *Walpurgisnacht* : *Walpurgis,* St. Walburga, 7th-century English nun and missionary, whose feast day falls on May Day + NIGHT.]

wal·rus (wôl′rəs, wŏl′-) *n., pl.* **-ruses** or collectively **walrus.** A large marine mammal, *Odobenus rosmarus,* of Arctic regions, having tough, wrinkled skin and large tusks. [Probably from Dutch, perhaps a metathetic formation influenced by *walvisch,* "whale fish," from a Germanic source akin to Old English *horschwæl,* Old Norse *hrosshvalr,* "horse-whale."]

walrus mustache *n.* A bushy, drooping mustache. [From the resemblance to the tusks of a walrus.]

Wal·ter (väl′tər), **Bruno,** born B.W. Schlesinger (1876–1962). German conductor. His repertory was wide, but he is remembered especially for his interpretations of Mozart and Mahler.

Wal·ter Mit·ty (wôl′tər mĭt′ē) *n.* An ordinary, often inadequate person who indulges in fantastic daydreams about his own triumphs. [After the hero of *The Secret Life of Walter Mitty,* a story by James Thurber.]

Wal·ton (wôl′tən), **Ernest Thomas Sinton** (1903–). Irish physicist. With Sir John Cockcroft he was the first to succeed (1931) in splitting the atom. He and Cockcroft shared the Nobel Prize (1951) for their work in nuclear physics.

Walton, Izaak (1593–1683). English author. He wrote biographies of John Donne and other churchmen, but is best known for the fishing classic *The Compleat Angler* (1653, enlarged frequently).

Walton, Sir William Turner (1902–83). British composer. He established his reputation (1923) with *Façade,* an extravaganza accompanying poems by Edith Sitwell, but his later work, such as the oratorio *Belshazzar's Feast* (1931), *Symphony No. 1* (1935), and his film music, is neoromantic in style.

waltz (wôlts) *n.* **1.** A smooth, flowing ballroom dance in triple time with a strong accent on the first beat. **2. a.** A piece of music for the waltz. **b.** An instrumental or vocal composition in triple time.

~v. **waltzed, waltzing, waltzes.** *—intr.* **1.** To dance the waltz. **2.** To move effortlessly, confidently, or casually: *waltzed up and said hello.* **3.** To accomplish a task, chore, or assignment with little effort. Often used with *through*: *waltzed through her exams. —tr.* **1.** To dance the waltz with. **2.** To lead or force to move briskly and purposefully; march: *waltzed him into the headmaster's office.* [German *Walzer,* from Middle High German *walzen,* to roll, turn, dance, from Old High German *walzan,* to roll.] **—waltz·er** *n.*

wam·ble (wŏm′bəl, wăm′-) *intr.v.* **-bled, -bling, -bles. 1.** To move in a weaving, wobbling, or rolling manner. **2.** To turn or roll. Used of the stomach.

~n. **1.** A wobble or roll. **2.** A feeling of nausea. [Middle English *wam(e)len,* to feel nausea, probably from Scandinavian; akin to Old Norse *vamla.*] **—wam·bling·ly** *adv.* **—wam·bly** *adj.*

Wam·pa·no·ag (wăm′pə-nō′ăg′) *n., pl.* **-ags** or collectively **Wampanoag. 1.** A member of an Algonquian-speaking North American Indian people formerly inhabiting eastern Rhode Island and adjacent parts of Massachusetts. **2.** The language of this people. [Natick *Wampan-okhe,* "(people of the) eastern land."] **—Wam·pa·no·ag** *adj.*

wam·pum (wŏm′pəm) *n.* **1.** Small cylindrical beads made from polished shells that were formerly used by North American Indians as currency and as jewelry. Also called "peag." **2.** *Informal.* Money. [Short for WAMPUMPEAG.]

wam·pum·peag (wŏm′pəm-pēg′) *n.* Wampum made from white shell beads. [From Algonquian (southeastern New England) *wampumpeage,* "white strings."]

wan (wŏn) *adj.* **wanner, wannest. 1.** Unnaturally pale, as from physical or emotional distress. **2.** Suggestive of or indicating weariness, illness, or unhappiness; melancholy: *a wan expression.*

~intr.v. **wanned, wanning, wans.** To become pale. [Middle English *wan,* gloomy, wan, Old English *wann†,* dusky, dark, livid.] **—wan·ly** *adv.* **—wan·ness** *n.*

wand (wŏnd) *n.* **1.** A thin, supple rod, twig, or stick. **2.** A stick or baton used by a magician, conjurer, or diviner. **3.** A slender rod carried as a symbol of office in a procession. **4.** A conductor's baton. [Middle English *wand(e), wend(e),* from Old Norse *vöndr.*]

wan·der (wŏn′dər) *v.* **-dered, -dering, -ders.** *—intr.* **1.** To move about with no destination or purpose; roam aimlessly. **2.** To make one's way by an indirect route or in a leisurely fashion; amble: *wander toward town.* **3.** To proceed in an irregular course; meander: *This path wanders over hill and dale.* **4.** To go astray: *wander from the path of righteousness.* **5.** To think or express oneself unclearly or incoherently: *His mind is beginning to wander.* **6.** To stray from a subject or issue; digress: *wandering off the point. —tr.* To wander across or through: *wander the forests.*

~n. The act or an instance of wandering; a stroll; an amble. [Mid-

dle English *wand(e)ren,* Old English *wandrian.*] —**wan·der·er** *n.* —**wan·der·ing·ly** *adv.*

Synonyms: *meander, ramble, range, roam, rove, stray.*

wandering albatross *n.* The largest of the albatrosses, *Diomedea exulans,* having a wingspan of over ten feet.

wandering Jew *n.* Either of two trailing plants, *Tradescantia fluminensis* or *Zebrina pendula,* native to tropical America, having usually striped variegated foliage and popular as house plants. [Fancifully named after the WANDERING JEW.]

Wandering Jew *n.* A Jew of medieval legend who was condemned to wander until the Day of Judgment for having mocked Christ on the day of Crucifixion.

wan·der·lust (wŏn′dər-lŭst′) *n.* A strong or irresistible impulse to travel. [German *Wanderlust : wandern,* to wander + *Lust,* desire, delight.]

wan·der·oo (wŏn′də-rōō′) *n.* A monkey, *Macaca silenus,* of south-central Asia, having a glossy black coat and a ruff of gray hair about the face. [Singhalese *vanduru,* plural of *vandurā,* "forest-dweller," monkey, from Sanskrit *vānara,* from *vana,* a forest.]

wan·doo (wŏn-dōō′) *n.* A white-barked eucalyptus tree, *Eucalyptus wandoo* (or *E. redunca*), having durable, reddish-brown wood. [From a native Australian language.]

wane (wān) *intr.v.* **waned, wan·ing, wanes. 1.** To decrease gradually in extent, intensity, or degree; dwindle; decline: *Their influence was waning.* **2.** To show a decreasing illuminated area from full moon to new moon. Used of the moon. Compare **wax. 3.** To approach an end. —*n.* **1.** The act or process of waning; a gradual decline or diminution. **2.** A period or phase of waning; specifically, the period of the decrease of the moon's visible surface. **3.** A defective edge of a plank where it has been imperfectly sawed. —**on the wane.** In a period of decline; waning. [Middle English *wan(i)en,* Old English *wanian,* to lessen. In the sense "defective edge of a log," from Middle English *wane,* defect, shortage, Old English *wana.*]

wan·gle (wăng′gəl) *v.* **-gled, -gling, -gles.** *Informal.* —*tr.* **1.** To make, achieve, or get by contrivance: *tried to wangle his way into the top job.* **2.** To manipulate or juggle (accounts, for example), especially fraudulently. **3.** To extricate (oneself) from difficulty. —*intr.* **1.** To use indirect, devious, or fraudulent methods. **2.** To extricate oneself by subtle or indirect means, as from difficulty. —*n.* *Informal.* An act of wangling. [Originally a printer's term, "to manipulate or devise a substitute for," perhaps a blend of WAGGLE and dialectal *wankle,* unsteady, wavering, Middle English *wankel,* Old English *wancol.*] —**wan·gler** *n.*

wan·i·gan, wan·ni·gan (wŏn′ə-gən) *n.* **1.** A supply chest used in a logging camp. **2.** A shelter in a logging camp that is mounted on wheels or on a platform on a raft or boat. [Ojibwa *wanikkan,* "man-made hole."]

Wan·kel engine (väng′kəl, wäng′-) *n.* A rotary internal-combustion engine in which a triangular rotor turning in a specially shaped housing performs the functions allotted to the pistons of a conventional engine, thereby allowing great savings in weight and moving parts. [After Felix *Wankel* (1902–), German engineer.]

want (wŏnt, wônt) *v.* **wanted, wanting, wants. 1.** To wish for; desire: *He wants to leave. The child always wants the biggest piece of cake.* **2.** To need or require: " 'Your hair wants cutting,' said the Hatter." (Lewis Carroll). **3. a.** To desire the presence or assistance of: *You're wanted by the boss.* **b.** To seek with intent to capture: *The fugitive is wanted by the police.* **4. a.** To fall short of (something, especially a desirable quality); lack: *She wants tact.* **b.** To fall short by (a specified amount): *"Wants a few minutes of five o'clock"* (Charles Dickens). **5.** To have an inclination toward; like: *You can say what you want; I say he's incompetent.* **6.** *Informal.* To be obliged; should or ought. Used with the infinitive: *You want to get your head examined.* —*intr.* **1.** To have need; be lacking. Used with *for: wants for nothing.* **2.** To be destitute or needy. **3.** To be disposed; like; wish: *Call her if you want. Informal.* **1.** To wish to enter (or leave): *The dog wants out.* **2.** To wish to join (or leave) a project, business, or other undertaking.

—*n.* **1.** The condition or quality of lacking something usual or necessary; lack or absence: *stayed at home for want of anything better to do.* **2.** Pressing need; destitution: *live in want.* **3.** Something needed or desired: *moderate wants.* [Middle English *wanten,* from Old Norse *vanta,* to be lacking.]

Usage: When *want* is followed immediately by an infinitive construction, it does not take *for: I want you to go* (not *want for you*). When *want* and the infinitive are separated in the sentence, however, *for* is used: *What I want is for you to go. I want very much for you to go.*

want ad *n.* *Informal.* A classified advertisement.

want·ing (wŏn′tĭng, wôn′-) *adj.* **1.** Absent, lacking, or deficient. **2.** Not up to standards or expectations. —*prep.* **1.** Without. **2.** Minus; less: *an hour wanting fifteen minutes.*

wan·ton (wŏn′tən, wôn′-) *adj.* **1.** Immoral or unchaste; lewd. **2. a.** Gratuitously cruel; malicious. **b.** Marked by unprovoked, gratuitous maliciousness; capricious and unjust: *wanton destruction.* **3.** Unrestrainedly excessive: *wanton extravagance.* **4.** Luxuriant; overabundant: *wanton tresses.* **5.** Frolicsome; playful. **6.** *Obsolete.* Rebellious; refractory. —*v.* **wantoned, -toning, -tons.** —*intr.* To act, grow, or move in a wanton manner; be wanton. —*tr.* To waste or squander wantonly. —*n.* An immoral, lewd, or licentious person, especially a woman. [Middle English *wantowen,* lacking discipline, lewd : *wan-, un-,* lack-

---

Wankel engine

THE SEARCH FOR EFFICIENCY: FELIX WANKEL'S SOLUTION

A masterpiece of ingenuity and design—but not yet practical enough

In all conventional gasoline and diesel engines the rotary motion needed to turn a crankshaft is produced indirectly by reciprocating parts—pistons and connecting rods that move back and forth thousands of times a minute. Engineers have long looked for engines that dispense with reciprocating parts and rotate a shaft directly. The most successful of these is the jet engine, but the most successful on a smaller scale is the Wankel engine, designed by a German, Felix Wankel, and first brought into production in 1956.

In the Wankel engine a triangular rotor geared to a drive shaft is driven around inside a cylinder. As it rotates, the rotor draws in fuel, compresses it so that a spark ignites it, and finally expels the burned gases as in a conventional four-stroke cycle. The result is a simple, smooth-running, and powerful engine that has been used in several production-model cars. It has fewer moving parts and runs well at high speeds. But problems of high fuel consumption, wear at the rotor tips, and high exhaust emissions have so far limited its application.

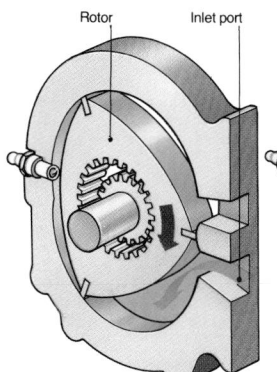 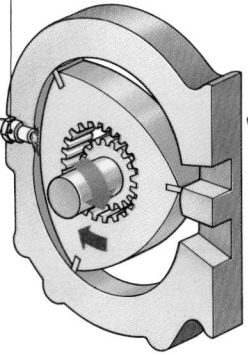 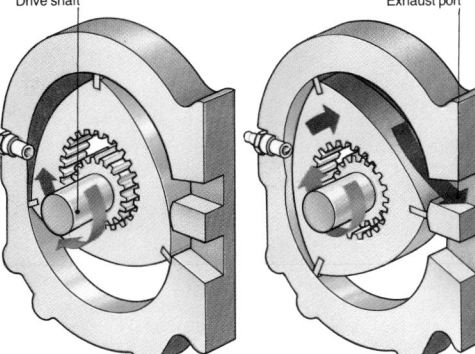

1. Rotation of rotor draws mixture through inlet port into space between rotor and cylinder wall

2. Mixture is compressed into a smaller space by the turning rotor; spark plug sparks

3. Mixture, ignited by spark from spark plug, explodes and drives rotor around

4. As rotor turns, exhaust outlet is exposed and burned gases are expelled

WANKEL ENGINE *The central rotor is a triangle with bulging sides that rotates inside a cylinder. There are holes in the side of the cylinder for fuel intake and exhaust outlet. The spaces between the* rotor and the cylinder alter in size as the rotor turns. Where the spark occurs, the space is small, compressing the fuel. The spark explodes it, turning the rotor and with it the shaft.

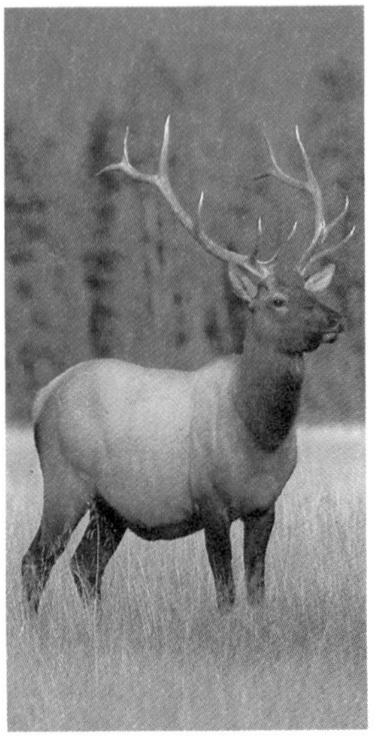

wapiti *Also called the American elk, the wapiti is the largest living deer after the moose, standing over 1.5 meters (5 feet) high at the shoulder and with antlers up to 1.2 meters (4 feet) long. It was once common throughout North America but is now confined to mountainous regions.*

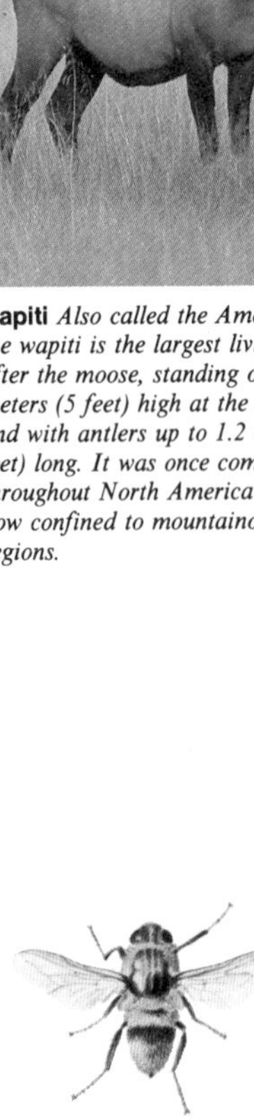

warble fly *A parasitic fly whose larvae burrow under the skin of cattle, ending up along the animals' backs where they raise lumps, or warbles. The larvae make holes in the skin, through which they breathe, ruining the hide's value as leather.*

ing, Old English *wan-* + *towen,* Old English *togen,* past participle of *tēon,* to draw, bring up.] **—wan·ton·ly** *adv.* **—wan·ton·ness** *n.*

wap·en·take (wŏp′ən-tāk′, wăp′-) *n.* A historical division of some northern counties in England, corresponding roughly to the hundred in other shires. [Middle English *wapentake,* subdivision, court of each division, Old English *wǣpengetæc,* from Old Norse *vāpnatak,* "taking of weapons" (vote by an assembly by brandishing of weapons, hence assembly) : *vāpna,* genitive plural of *vāpn,* a weapon + *tak,* a taking, from *taka,* to take.]

wap·i·ti (wŏp′ə-tē) *n., pl.* **-tis** or collectively **wapiti.** A large North American deer, *Cervus canadensis.* Also called "American elk," "elk." [Shawnee *wapiti,* "white rump" : Proto-Algonquian *wap-* (unattested), white + *-itwiy-* (unattested), rump.]

wap·pen·shaw, wap·pen·schaw (wŏp′ən-shô′, wăp′-) *n.* Also **wap·pen·shaw·ing** (-shô′ĭng). A former periodic muster or inspection of the fighting men of a district of Scotland. [16th century (later revived by Sir Walter Scott) : northern and Scottish dialectal *wapen,* from Old Norse *vapn,* WEAPON + *s(c)haw,* SHOW.]

war (wôr) *n.* **1. a.** A state of open, armed, often prolonged conflict carried on between nations, states, or parties. **b.** The period of such conflict. **2. a.** A condition of active antagonism or contention: *an advertising war.* **b.** A concerted effort or campaign to combat or put an end to something: *the continuing war against disease.* **3.** The techniques or procedures of war; military science or strategy. **—at war.** In an active state of conflict or contention: *"Life and death are at war within us"* (Thomas Merton). **—declare war on. 1.** To state formally the intention to carry on hostilites against. **2.** To state one's intent to suppress or eradicate: *declared war on the sale of pornographic magazines.*
~intr.v. **warred, warring, wars. 1.** To wage or carry on warfare. **2.** To be in a state of antagonism or rivalry; contend.
~adj. Of, resulting from, or used in war: *a war wound; a war cry.* [Middle English *werre, warre,* from Old North French *werre;* akin to Old High German *werra,* confusion, strife.]

war. warrant.

war·a·tah (wôr′ə-tô′, -tä′) *n.* A shrub of the genus *Telopea,* of Australia; especially *T. speciosissima,* which has bright red flowers borne in terminal clusters. [From a native Australian language.]

war baby *n.* A child born during wartime, especially during World War I or World War II.

War Between the States *n.* The **Civil War** *(see)* in the United States.

war·ble[1] (wôr′bəl) *v.* **-bled, -bling, -bles.** *—tr.* To sing with trills, runs, or other melodic embellishments. *—intr.* **1.** To sing with trills, runs, or quavers. **2.** To produce a warbling sound.
~n. The act or an instance of warbling. [Middle English, from Old North French *werbler,* from *werble,* a warbling, melody, from Frankish *hwirbilōn* (unattested), to whirl, trill.]

warble[2] *n.* **1.** An abscessed swelling under the hide of the back of cattle or other animals caused by the larva of a warble fly. **2.** The warble fly, especially in its larval stage. **3.** A hard lump of tissue on a horse's back caused by rubbing of the saddle. [16th century : perhaps from a Scandinavian compound corresponding to obsolete Swedish *varbulde.*] **—war·bled** *adj.*

warble fly *n.* Any of several flies of the family Oestridae, especially of the genus *Hypoderma,* whose larvae form warbles within the bodies of cattle and other animals.

war·bler (wôr′blər) *n.* **1.** Any of various small brownish or grayish Old World birds of the subfamily Sylviinae. **2.** Any of various small New World birds of the family Parulidae, many of which have yellowish plumage or markings. **3.** One that warbles.

war bonnet *n.* A ceremonial headdress used by some North American Plains Indians consisting of a cap or band and a trailing extension decorated with erect feathers.

war bride *n.* A woman who marries a serviceman during wartime, especially when she and her husband are of different nationalities.

war chest *n.* **1.** An accumulation of funds that is used to finance a war effort. **2.** A fund that is reserved for a particular purpose, as a political campaign.

war club *n.* A weapon consisting of a weight of iron or stone fixed to a handle, formerly used by American Indians.

war correspondent *n.* A journalist, reporter, or commentator assigned to report directly from a war or combat area.

war crime *n.* Any of various crimes, such as mistreatment of prisoners of war or genocide, committed during a war and considered to be in violation of the conventions of warfare. **—war criminal** *n.*

war cry *n.* **1.** A cry uttered by combatants as they attack; a battle cry. **2.** A phrase or slogan used to rally people to a cause.

ward (wôrd) *n.* **1.** A division of a city or town for administrative and representative purposes; especially, an electoral district. **2.** A historical division of some northern English and Scottish counties corresponding roughly to the hundred or wapentake. **3.** A large room in a hospital, especially one set aside for the care of a particular group of patients: *a maternity ward.* **4.** One of the divisions of a penal institution, as a prison. **5.** An open court or area of a castle or fortification enclosed by walls. **6. a.** *Law.* A minor or an incompetent person placed under the care or protection of a guardian or court. Also called "ward of court." **b.** A person under the protection or care of another. **7.** The state of being under guard; custody. **8.** The act of guarding or protecting; especially, guardianship of a minor or incompetent. **9.** A means of protection; a defense. **10.** A defensive movement or attitude, especially in fencing; a guard. **11. a.** The projecting ridge of a lock or keyhole that prevents the turning of any key other than the proper one. **b.** The notch cut into a key that corresponds to such a ridge.
~tr.v. **warded, warding, wards. 1. a.** To turn aside; parry: *ward off an opponent's blows.* **b.** To try to prevent or avert: *took vitamins to ward off colds.* **2.** To watch over; guard or protect. [Middle English *ward(e),* a guarding, place for guarding, person or thing in one's care, Old English *weard,* a watching over.]

-ward, -wards *suffix.* Indicates direction toward; for example, **skyward, westwards.** [Middle English *-ward,* Old English *-weard.*]
Usage: The suffixes *-ward* and *-wards* are both used to express direction of movement: *backward(s), eastward(s), homeward(s).* As adverbs, the forms without *-s* are predominant in American English, while those with *-s* prevail in British English. Only the forms without *-s* are regularly used as adjectives: *a backward glance.*

Ward (wôrd), **Artemas** (1727–1800). U.S. Revolutionary general. A French and Indian War veteran, he was commander of the Massachusetts troops during the American Revolution until George Washington relieved him of his command and drove the British from Boston on March 17, 1776. Later Ward served in the Continental Congress and in the U.S. House of Representatives (1791–95).

Ward, Artemus. Pen name of Charles Farrar **Browne.**

Ward, Barbara, Baroness Jackson (1914–81). British economist and conservationist. Her books on ecology and political economy include *Spaceship Earth* (1966) and *Only One Earth* (1972).

war dance *n.* A tribal dance performed before a battle or as a celebration after a victory.

ward·ed (wôr′dĭd) *adj.* Having notches or wards. Said of a key or lock.

war·den (wôrd′n) *n.* **1.** A person who is in charge of or takes care of someone or something. **2.** An official charged with the enforcement of certain laws and regulations: *an air raid warden; a fire warden.* **3.** *British.* The principal or governor of certain colleges, universities, schools, or hospitals. **4.** *British.* **a.** The chief executive official in charge of a port or market. **b.** Any of various crown officers having administrative duties. **5.** A churchwarden. **6.** The chief administrative official of a prison. [Middle English *wardein,* from Old North French, variant of Old French *guarden,* GUARDIAN.]

war·den·ry (wôrd′n-rē) *n., pl.* **-ries.** Also **war·den·ship** (-shĭp′). The office, duties, or jurisdiction of a warden.

ward·er[1] (wôr′dər) *n.* **1.** A guard, porter, or watchman of a gate or tower. **2.** A prison guard. [Middle English, from Norman French *wardere,* from Old North French *warder,* variant of Old French *garder,* to keep, GUARD.] **—war·der·ship** *n.*

warder[2] *n.* A baton formerly used by a ruler or commander as a symbol of authority and to signal orders. [Short for Middle English *warderer,* perhaps a jocular use of obsolete *warderere,* "look out behind" : Norman French *ware,* beware, from Germanic + *derere,* behind, from Vulgar Latin *dē retrō* (unattested) : Latin *dē,* from + *retrō,* behind.]

ward heel·er (hē′lər) *n. Slang.* A worker for the ward organization of a political machine.

ward·i·an case (wôr′dē-ən) *n.* A case with glass sides, used for growing or transporting living plants such as delicate ferns. [After N.B. *Ward* (died 1868), British botanist.]

ward·mote (wôrd′mōt′) *n.* A meeting of the citizens of a ward; especially, a meeting of the liverymen and the alderman of a ward in the City of London. [Middle English. See **ward, moot.**]

ward·ress (wôr′drĭs) *n.* A prison matron.

ward·robe (wôr′drōb′) *n.* **1.** A tall cabinet, small room, or closet in which clothes are kept. **2.** Garments collectively; especially, all the articles of clothing belonging to one person. **3. a.** The costumes belonging to a theater or theatrical company. **b.** The place in which theatrical costumes are kept. **4.** The department in charge of wearing apparel, jewelry, and accessories in a royal or noble household. [Middle English *warderobe,* from Old North French : *warder,* to guard, keep, from Germanic + *robe,* ROBE.]

wardrobe trunk *n.* A large trunk that stands on end and has drawers and a pole on which clothes may be hung.

ward·room (wôrd′ro͞om′, -ro͝om′) *n.* **1.** The living area and dining room for the commissioned officers, excepting the captain, on a warship. **2.** The commissioned officers on a warship.

-wards. Variant of **-ward.**

ward·ship (wôrd′shĭp′) *n.* **1.** The state of being a ward or in the charge of a guardian. **2.** Guardianship; custody.

ware[1] (wâr) *n.* **1.** Manufactured articles of the same general kind. Often used in combination to indicate: **a.** Articles made of a specified material: *glassware.* **b.** Articles of a specified type: *ovenware; computer software.* **c.** Pottery or ceramics of a specified type or make: *earthenware.* **2. wares. a.** Articles of commerce; goods. **b.** An immaterial asset or benefit, such as a service or personal accomplishment, that is regarded as an article of commerce. [Middle English *ware,* Old English *waru.*]

ware[2] *tr.v.* **wared, waring, wares.** *Archaic.* To beware of. Used chiefly in the imperative: *Ware hounds!*
~adj. Obsolete. **1.** Watchful; wary. **2.** Aware. [Middle English *waren,* Old English *warian.*]

ware[3] *tr.v.* **wared, waring, wares.** *Chiefly Scottish.* To spend, waste, or squander (money, goods, or time, for example). [Middle English, from Old Norse *verja,* to invest, spend money, literally, to clothe; akin to Old English *werian,* to clothe, WEAR.]

ware·house (wâr′hous′) *n.* **1.** A place in which goods or merchan-

dise are stored; a storehouse. **2.** *British.* A large shop, usually one that sells goods wholesale.
~*tr.v.* (-houz′, -hous′) **warehoused, -housing, -houses.** To place or store in a warehouse, especially in a bonded or government warehouse.
ware·house·man (wâr′hous′mən) *n., pl.* **-men** (-mĭn). A person who owns, manages, or works in a warehouse.
ware·room (wâr′ro͞om′, -ro͝om′) *n.* A room used for the storage or display of goods or wares.
war·fare (wôr′fâr′) *n.* **1. a.** The waging of war against an enemy; armed conflict. **b.** Military operations marked by a specified characteristic: *guerrilla warfare; chemical warfare.* **2.** A state of disharmony or conflict; strife: *constant stress and warfare in the household.* **3.** Acts engaged in to destroy or undermine the strength of another: *psychological warfare.* [Middle English *werrefare,* a going to war : *warre, werre,* WAR + *fare,* a journey, Old English *faru* and *fær.*]
war·fa·rin (wôr′fər-ĭn) *n.* A colorless crystalline compound, $C_{19}H_{16}O_4$, used to kill rodents and medicinally as an anticoagulant. [After *W*isconsin *A*lumni *R*esearch *F*oundation + (COUM)ARIN.]
war game *n.* **1.** A simulated battle in military training maneuvers. **2.** A board game that tests tactical knowledge using models or blocks to represent troops and weapons.
war hawk *n.* **1.** A member of the Twelfth U.S. Congress (1811–13) who advocated war with Great Britain. **2.** A person who advocates war.
war·head (wôr′hĕd′) *n.* A part of the armament system in the forward part of a projectile, such as a guided missile, torpedo, or bomb, containing the explosive charge.
War·hol (wôr′hôl′), **Andy,** born Andrew von Warhol (1931–87). American pop artist and film producer. He became known in the 1960's with outsize paintings of everyday objects such as soup cans and silk-screen portraits of film stars. His films, which are usually erotic and controversial, include *The Chelsea Girls* (1966).
war·horse (wôr′hôrs′) *n.* **1.** A horse used in combat; a charger. **2.** *Informal.* A person who has been through many battles, struggles, or fights; an old campaigner. **3.** *Informal.* A musical or dramatic work that has become hackneyed.
war·i·son (wăr′ə-sən) *n.* A bugle call giving the command to attack; a war cry. [Middle English, wealth, reward, from Old North French, variant of Old French *garison,* provision, store, defense, GARRISON; sense derives from misuse by Sir Walter Scott.]
war·like (wôr′līk′) *adj.* **1.** Belligerent; hostile. **2.** Of or pertaining to war; martial. **3.** Threatening or indicative of war.
war·lock (wôr′lŏk′) *n.* A male witch, sorcerer, or wizard. [Middle English *warloghe,* Old English *wǣrloga,* "oath-breaker" : *wǣr,* faith, pledge + *-loga,* liar, from *lēogan,* to lie.]
war·lord (wôr′lôrd′) *n.* A military commander exercising civil power in a given region, whether in nominal allegiance to the national government or in defiance of it.
warm (wôrm) *adj.* **warmer, warmest. 1.** Somewhat hotter than temperate; having or producing a comfortable and agreeable degree of heat; moderately hot: *a warm climate.* **2.** Having the natural heat of living beings. **3.** Preserving or imparting heat: *a warm overcoat.* **4.** Having or causing a sensation of unusually high bodily heat, as from exercise or hard work. **5.** Marked by enthusiasm; fervent; ardent: *warm support.* **6.** Characterized by liveliness, excitement, or disagreement; heated; animated: *a warm debate.* **7.** Marked by or revealing friendliness or sincerity; sympathetic; cordial: *a warm reception.* **8.** Loving; passionate; amorous: *a warm embrace.* **9.** Excitable, impetuous, or quick to be aroused: *a warm temper.* **10.** Predominantly red or yellow in tone; suggesting heat: *a warm sunset.* **11.** Recently made; fresh: *a warm trail.* **12.** Close to discovering, guessing, or finding something, as in certain games. **13.** *Informal.* Uncomfortable because of danger or annoyance.
~*v.* **warmed, warming, warms.** —*tr.* **1.** To make warm or warmer. Often used with *up.* **2.** To make zealous or ardent; inspire with life, zest, or color; enliven. **3.** To fill with pleasant emotions: *warmed by the thought of her return.* —*intr.* **1.** To become warm or warmer. Often used with *up.* **2.** To become ardent, enthusiastic, or animated. Usually used with *to*: *began to warm to his subject.* **3.** To become kindly disposed or friendly. Usually used with *to* or *toward*: *felt the audience warming to her.*
~*n. Informal.* A warming or heating. [Middle English *warm,* Old English *wearm.*] **—warm·er** *n.* **—warm·ish** *adj.* **—warm·ly** *adv.* **—warm·ness** *n.*
warm-blood·ed (wôrm′blŭd′ĭd) *adj.* **1.** *Zoology.* Maintaining a relatively constant and warm body temperature independent of environmental temperature; homoiothermic. **2.** Ardent; passionate. **—warm-blood·ed·ness** *n.*
warmed-o·ver (wôrmd′ō′vər) *adj. Informal.* **1.** Reheated; warmed up. Said of food. **2.** Not new, fresh, or spontaneous; stale.
warm front *n.* A front along which an advancing mass of warm air rises over a mass of cold air.
warm-heart·ed (wôrm′här′tĭd) *adj.* Kind; friendly; sympathetic. **—warm-heart·ed·ly** *adv.* **—warm-heart·ed·ness** *n.*
warming pan *n.* A metal pan with a cover and a long handle, designed to hold hot liquids or coals and used to warm a bed. Sometimes called "bedpan."
war·mon·ger (wôr′mŭng′gər, -mŏng′gər) *n.* One who advocates or attempts to stir up war. **—war·mon·ger·ing** *adj.* & *n.*
warmth (wôrmth) *n.* **1.** The state, sensation, or quality of producing or having a moderate degree of heat. **2.** Excitement or intensity, as of love or passion; ardor. **3.** Friendliness, sincerity, or affection. **4.** The glowing effect produced by using predominantly red or yellow colors. [Middle English *warmth,* Old English *wiermthu* (unattested).]
warm up *intr.v.* **1.** To exercise or practice, as in preparation for an athletic event. **2.** To become ready for operation. Used of an engine, for example. **3.** To become more enthusiastic, exciting, or animated. —*tr.v.* **1.** To reheat (food). **2.** To make (a car, for example) ready for operation by raising to efficient working temperature. **3.** To exercise (a horse, for example) immediately prior to a competition. **4.** To make more enthusiastic, exciting, or animated: *warm up the conversation with some juicy gossip.*
warm-up (wôrm′ŭp′) *n.* An act, process, or period of warming up.
warn (wôrn) *v.* **warned, warning, warns.** —*tr.* **1.** To make aware of potential or probable harm, danger, or evil; caution. **2.** To admonish as to action or behavior. **3.** To notify (a person) to go or stay away. Usually used with *off* or *away.* **4.** To notify or apprise in advance: *He warned us that he might be late.* —*intr.* To give a warning. [Middle English *warnen,* Old English *w(e)arnian,* to take heed, warn.] **—warn·er** *n.*
Synonyms: *admonish, caution, forewarn.*
War·ner (wôr′nər). U.S. family of filmmakers, including **Harry Morris** (1881–1958) and his brothers **Albert** (1884–1967), **Samuel Louis** (1887–1927), and **Jack** (1892–1978), who founded Warner Brothers Pictures in Hollywood (1918). Their company produced the first talkie, *The Jazz Singer* (1927) and numerous classic films such as *Casablanca* (1942) and was the first Hollywood studio to produce television programs.
warn·ing (wôr′nĭng) *n.* **1.** An intimation, threat, or sign of impending danger or evil. **2. a.** Advice to beware, as of a person or thing. **b.** Counsel to desist from an undesirable course of action. **3.** A cautionary or deterrent example.
~*adj.* Acting or serving as a warning. **—warn·ing·ly** *adv.*
warning coloration *n.* The conspicuous markings by which an animal can be recognized by potential predators. Also called "aposematic coloration."
War of American Independence *n. British.* The **American Revolution** *(see).*
War of 1812 *n.* A war between the United States and Great Britain (1812–14), fought over the rights of neutrals on the high seas and issues related to American westward expansion.
war of nerves *n.* A conflict in which attempts are made to wear down or destroy the morale of one's opponent by psychological means, such as progaganda, delaying tactics, and intimidation.
War of Secession *n.* The **Civil War** *(see)* in the United States.
War of the Spanish Succession *n.* A war fought by Great Britain, the Netherlands, and the Holy Roman Empire against France and Spain (1701–14) over the succession in Spain after the death of Charles II. The Treaty of Utrecht placed Louis XIV's grandson Philip V on the Spanish throne.
warp (wôrp) *v.* **warped, warping, warps.** —*tr.* **1.** To turn or twist out of shape. **2.** To turn from a correct, healthy, or true course; pervert. **3.** In weaving, to arrange (strands of yarn or thread) so that they can run lengthwise. **4.** *Nautical.* To move (a vessel) by hauling on a line that is fastened to or around a piling, anchor, or pier. —*intr.* **1.** To become bent or twisted out of shape, as wood. **2.** To turn aside from a correct, healthy, or true course; go astray. **3.** *Nautical.* To warp a vessel. —See Usage Note at **distort.**
~*n.* **1.** The state of being bent or twisted out of shape. **2.** A distortion or twist, especially in a piece of wood. **3.** A mental or moral aberration or deviation. **4.** The threads that run lengthwise in a fabric, crossed at right angles by the weft. **5.** *Nautical.* A towline used in warping a vessel. [Middle English *werpen,* to warp, throw, Old English *weorpan,* to throw (away).] **—warp·er** *n.*
war paint *n.* **1.** Pigments applied to the face or body by certain tribes, such as the Indians of North America, preparatory to going to war. **2.** *Informal.* Cosmetics such as lipstick, rouge, or mascara. **3.** *Informal.* Official dress; regalia.
warp and woof *n.* The underlying structure upon which something is built; a foundation; base.
war·path (wôr′păth′, -päth′) *n., pl.* **-paths** (-păthz′, -päthz′, -păths′, -päths′). **1.** The route taken by a party of North American Indians on the attack. **2.** A hostile course or mood. Used in the phrase *on the warpath.*
war·plane (wôr′plān′) *n.* A combat aircraft.
war·ra·gal, war·ri·gal (wôr′ə-gəl, wŏr′-) *n. Australian.* A dingo. [From a native Australian language.]
war·rant (wôr′ənt, wŏr′-) *n. Abbr.* **war., wrnt. 1.** Authorization or certification; sanction. **2.** Justification, as for an action or belief; grounds. **3.** Something that provides assurance or confirmation. **4.** An order, as a writ, that serves as authorization for something, specifically: **a.** A voucher authorizing payment or receipt of money. **b.** *Law.* A judicial writ authorizing an officer to make a search, seizure, or arrest or to carry out a judicial sentence. **c.** *Military.* A warrant officer's certificate of appointment.
~*tr.v.* **warranted, -ranting, -rants. 1. a.** To guarantee the truth of (a statement). **b.** To assure (a person) of a fact. **2.** To attest to or make oneself answerable for the quality or authenticity of; especially, to guarantee (a product) to be as represented. **3.** To guarantee the immunity or security of. **4.** To provide adequate grounds for; justify. **5.** To grant authorization or sanction to; authorize or empower. **6.** *Law.* To guarantee clear title to (real property, for example). [Middle English *war(r)ant,* protector, protection, authorization, from Old North French *warant,* probably from Medieval

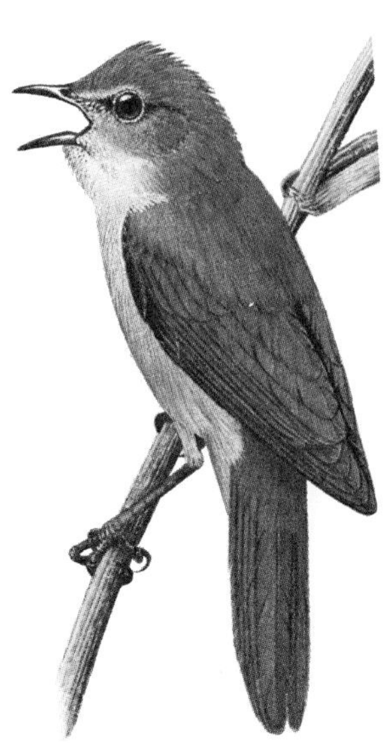

warbler *The reed warbler (above) lives on reed beds and is a favorite target of the cuckoo, which often lays its eggs in the reed warbler's nest. Warblers, which are found throughout Europe, Africa, and Asia, live on wood lice, insects, and berries.*

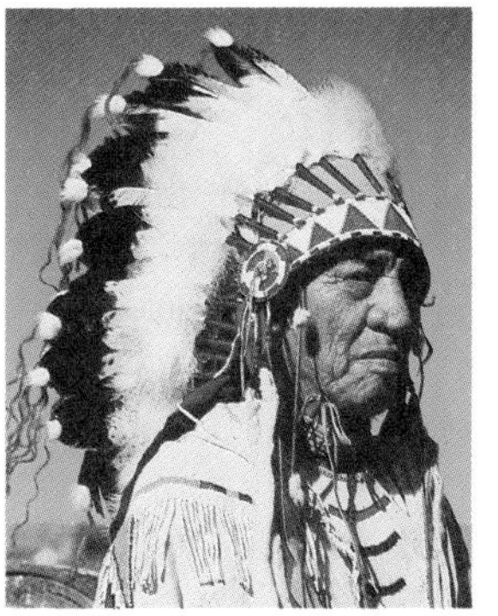

war bonnet *A tribal chieftain of the North American plains displays the ceremonial headdress, with its eagle feathers, which his ancestors wore into battle.*

Latin *warantus,* from Old High German *werenti,* "the one protecting," present participle of *werren,* to protect, guarantee.] —**warrant·a·ble** *adj.* —**war·rant·a·ble·ness** *n.* —**war·rant·a·bly** *adv.*

war·ran·tee (wôr'ən-tē', wôr'-) *n. Law.* A person to whom a warranty is made.

warrant officer *n. Abbr.* **WO, W.O.** *Military.* An officer who is intermediate in rank between a noncommissioned officer and a commissioned officer and has authority by virtue of a warrant.

war·ran·tor (wôr'ən-tər, -tôr', wôr'-) *n. Law.* A person who makes a warrant or gives a warranty to another.

war·ran·ty (wôr'ən-tē, wôr'-) *n., pl.* -ties. 1. Official authorization, sanction, or warrant. 2. Justification or valid grounds for an act or course of action. 3. *Law.* **a.** An assurance by the seller of goods or property that the goods or property are as represented or will be as promised. **b.** A guarantee by a party being insured that the facts are as stated in reference to an insurance risk or that conditions will be fulfilled to keep the contract effective. **c.** A covenant by which the seller of land binds himself and his heirs to defend the security of the estate conveyed. **d.** A judicial writ; a warrant. [Middle English *warantie,* from Old North French, from the feminine past participle of *warantir,* to guarantee, from *warant,* protection, WARRANT.]

war·ren (wôr'ən, wôr'-) *n.* 1. **a.** An area where rabbits live in burrows. **b.** A colony of rabbits. 2. An enclosure for small game animals. 3. **a.** An overcrowded living area. **b.** A mazelike place in which one may easily get lost. [Middle English *warenne,* from Old North French, from Germanic.]

War·ren (wôr'ən, wôr'ən), **Earl** (1891-1974). U.S. jurist, chief justice of the Supreme Court (1953-69). After serving two terms as governor of California (1943-53), he was appointed chief justice in 1953 and was involved in several historic decisions, such as *Brown vs. Board of Education* (1954) and *Miranda vs. Arizona* (1966), both of which displayed his devotion to civil liberties.

Warren, Robert Penn (1905-). U.S. author. A multitalented writer, he was associated with the Fugitives, a group of young Southern writers; taught literature at various universities, including Yale (1950-56 and 1961-73); and is widely respected as a poet, novelist, and critic. Both his novel *All the King's Men* (1946) and his volume of poetry *Promises* (1957) won Pulitzer Prizes.

war·ren·er (wôr'ə-nər, wôr'-) *n.* One who keeps a warren.

warrigal. Variant of **warragal.**

war·ri·or (wôr'ē-ər, wôr'-) *n.* One engaged or experienced in battle. Also used adjectivally: *a warrior race.* [Middle English *werreour,* from Old North French *werreieor,* from *werreier,* to make war, from *werre,* WAR.]

war·saw (wôr'sô) *n.* A large grouper, *Epinephelus nigritus,* of warm Atlantic waters. Also called "warsaw grouper." [Variant (influenced by WARSAW) of Spanish *guasa,* probably from a native name in the West Indies.]

War·saw (wôr'sô). *Polish* **War·sza·wa** (vär-shä'vä). Capital of Poland on the Vistula River. It was founded in the 13th century, first became the capital in 1596, and was ruled by Russia as an independent kingdom (1815-1917), becoming the capital again in 1918. It was badly damaged during the German occupation, and its Jewish ghetto was destroyed. Some 400,000 of the Jewish population were moved to concentration camps, and the remaining 60,000 or so were massacred after an attempted uprising (1943). Rebuilt according to its previous plan, it is a major cultural, commercial, industrial, and educational center.

Warsaw Pact *n.* A treaty of mutual military alliance signed in Warsaw in 1955 by Albania, Bulgaria, Czechoslovakia, East Germany, Hungary, Poland, Romania, and the U.S.S.R. Also called "Eastern European Mutual Assistance Treaty."

war·ship (wôr'shĭp') *n.* Any ship constructed or equipped for use in battle.

Wars of the Roses. See **Roses, Wars of the.**

wart (wôrt) *n.* 1. A small, usually hard elevation on the skin that is caused by a virus, covered with a keratinous layer, and occurs typically on the hands or feet. 2. A protuberance similar to a wart. —**warts and all.** Including faults and defects. [Middle English *werte, wart,* Old English *wearte.*]

wart hog *n.* A wild African pig, *Phacochoerus aethiopicus,* having tusks and wartlike protuberances on the face.

war·time (wôr'tīm') *n.* A period during which a war is in progress. Often used adjectivally: *wartime austerities.*

wart·y (wôr'tē) *adj.* -ier, -iest. 1. Having or covered with warts or wartlike protuberances. 2. Of or resembling a wart or warts.

war whoop *n.* A war cry, especially of North American Indians.

War·wick (wôr'ĭk, wôr'-), **Richard Neville, Earl of** (1428-71). English statesman, known as "the Kingmaker." During the Wars of the Roses he fought for the Yorkists and secured the throne (1461) for Edward IV. He then changed sides and restored (1470) the Lancastrian Henry VI. He was killed at the Battle of Barnet, which regained the throne for Edward.

War·wick·shire (wôr'ĭk-shîr', -shər, wôr'-) County of central England. Having lost its industrial region around Coventry and Birmingham to the newly created metropolitan county of West Midlands (1974), its economy is now mainly agricultural, including market gardening, wheat growing, and dairy farming.

war·y (wâr'ē) *adj.* -ier, -iest. 1. On one's guard; alert to possible danger or deception; watchful. 2. Characterized by caution: *a wary glance.* [From obsolete *ware,* wary, from Middle English *ware,* Old English *wær.*] —**war·i·ly** *adv.* —**war·i·ness** *n.*

wart hog *Unlike other members of the pig family, the wart hog—* Phacochoerus aethiopicus—*goes down on bent forelimbs to dig for food. It inhabits much of Africa south of the Sahara.*

was (wŏz, wŭz; *unstressed* wəz). First and third person singular past indicative mood of **be.**

wash (wŏsh, wôsh) *v.* **washed, washing, washes.** —*tr.* 1. To cleanse, using water or other liquid, and usually a cleaning agent such as soap or bleach, by immersing, flushing, rubbing, or scrubbing: *washed the clothes; wash windows.* 2. To remove by or as if by washing: *wash a stain from one's hands.* Often used with *off, out,* or *away: wash away one's guilt; wash out a dirty mark.* 3. To clean (the fur) by licking. Used of an animal. 4. To make moist or wet; dampen; drench: *Tears washed her cheeks.* 5. To flow over, against, or past: *shores washed by ocean tides.* 6. To carry along or sweep away through the action of flowing or moving water. Often used with *off, out,* or *away: His body was washed out to sea.* 7. To erode, remove, damage, or destroy by moving water. Used with *out* or *away: The roads were washed out.* 8. To serve as an effective cleaning agent for: *This soap washes wool.* 9. To cover or coat with a watery layer of paint or other coloring substance. 10. *Chemistry.* **a.** To purify (a gas) by passing through or over a liquid, as to remove soluble matter. **b.** To pass a solvent, such as distilled water, through (a precipitate). 11. *Mining.* To remove particulate constituents from (an ore) by immersion in or agitation with water. 12. To cause to undergo a swirling action: *washed the tea around in the cup.* —*intr.* 1. To wash oneself: *wash for dinner.* 2. To wash something, as clothes or dishes, in or by means of water or other liquid. 3. To undergo washing without fading, shrinkage, or other damage: *This fabric washes poorly.* 4. *Informal.* To hold up under examination; be convincing: *Your excuse won't wash.* 5. To be carried away, removed, or drawn along by the action of flowing or moving water: *Bits of wreckage washed up on the shore.* Often used with *out* or *away: Some of the topsoil washed away in the storm.* 6. To flow, sweep, or beat with a characteristic lapping sound: *The waves washed over the pilings.* —**wash down.** 1. To clean (a car, for example) by washing with water from top to bottom. 2. To follow the ingestion of (food, for example) with a drink: *washed the doughnut down with coffee.* —**wash one's hands of.** 1. To refuse to accept responsibility for. 2. To abandon or renounce. —**wash up.** 1. To wash one's face and hands. 2. *Chiefly British.* To wash the dishes after a meal.

~*n.* 1. The act or process of washing or being washed. 2. A quantity of articles, especially clothing, washed or intended for washing. 3. Kitchen refuse fed to pigs; swill. 4. A substance such as malt undergoing fermentation prior to distillation. 5. A preparation or product used in washing or coating, especially: **a.** A cosmetic or medicinal liquid, such as a mouthwash. **b.** A thin water-based paint or distemper. 6. **a.** A thin layer of water color or India ink spread on a drawing. **b.** A light tint or hue: *a wash of red sunset.* 7. **a.** The rush or surge of water or waves. **b.** The sound of this. 8. **a.** The removal or erosion of soil, subsoil, or the like by the action of moving water. **b.** A deposit of recently eroded debris. 9. **a.** An area of low or marshy ground washed by tidal waters. **b.** A stretch of shallow water. 10. A turbulence in air or water caused by the motion or action of an oar, propeller, jet, or airfoil. 11. *Western U.S.* The dry bed of a stream. —**come out in the wash.** 1. To turn out well in the end. 2. To come inevitably to light. Used especially of scandal.

~*adj.* 1. Used for washing. 2. Capable of being washed; washable. [Middle English *waschen, wasshen,* Old English *wæscan, wacsan,* from Germanic *wa(t)skan* (unattested).]

Wash. Washington (state).

wash·a·ble (wŏsh'ə-bəl, wô'shə-) *adj.* Capable of being washed without fading or other damage.

wash-and-wear (wŏsh'ən-wâr', wô'shən-) *adj.* Treated so as to be easily or quickly washed or rinsed clean and to require little or no ironing: *a wash-and-wear shirt.*

wash·ba·sin (wŏsh'bā'sĭn, wôsh'-) *n.* A washbowl.

wash·board (wŏsh'bôrd', -bōrd', wôsh'-) *n.* 1. **a.** A board having a corrugated surface, as of metal, upon which clothes can be rubbed in the process of laundering. **b.** A similar board used as a percussion instrument. 2. A baseboard. 3. *Nautical.* A thin plank fastened to the side of a boat or to the sill of a port to keep out the sea.

wash·bowl (wŏsh'bōl', wôsh'-) *n.* A basin that can be filled with water for washing oneself.

wash·cloth (wŏsh'klôth', -klŏth', wôsh'-) *n., pl.* -cloths (-klôthz', -klŏthz', -klôths', -klŏths'). A small cloth of absorbent material used for washing the face or body.

wash·day (wŏsh'dā', wôsh'-) *n.* A day, often the same day of every week, set aside for doing the household washing.

wash drawing *n.* A drawing or painting in which washes of color are used.

washed-out (wŏsht'out', wôsht'-) *adj.* 1. Lacking color or intensity; faded. 2. Exhausted; tired-looking.

washed-up (wŏsht'ŭp', wôsht'-) *adj.* 1. No longer successful or needed; finished. 2. Ready to give up in disgust.

wash·er (wŏsh'ər, wôsh'ər) *n.* 1. One that washes. 2. A small perforated disk, as of metal, rubber, leather, or plastic, placed beneath a nut or at an axle bearing or joint to relieve friction, prevent leakage, or distribute pressure. 3. A machine or apparatus for washing, especially, one for washing clothes or dishes. 4. *Australian.* A washcloth.

wash·er·wom·an (wŏsh'ər-wŏom'ən, wô'shər-) *n., pl.* -women (-wĭm'ĭn). A woman who washes clothes for a living; a laundress.

wash·ing (wŏsh'ĭng, wô'shĭng) *n.* 1. The act or process of one that washes. 2. Articles washed or intended to be washed at one time:

the week's washing. **3.** The residue after an ore or other material has been washed. **4.** A thin coat of liquid, as paint.
washing machine *n.* A usually automatic machine for washing clothes and linen.
washing soda *n.* A hydrated sodium carbonate used as a general cleanser.
Wash·ing·ton[1] (wŏsh′ĭng-tən, wôsh′-). *Abbr.* **Wash.** Coastal state of the northwestern United States. Bordering Canada and the Pacific Ocean, which indents the state at Puget Sound, it is chiefly mountainous except for the basin of the Columbia River in the east. It is crossed by the Cascade and Coast mountain ranges. The capital is Olympia. **—Wash·ing·to·ni·an** *adj. & n.*
Washington[2]**.** Capital of the United States. In the east of the country on the Potomac River, it is coterminous with the District of Columbia and was designed as a planned city by a Frenchman, Pierre L'Enfant, and built in 1790–1800. The federal capital since 1800, it was burned by the British (1814). Its many famous buildings include the White House, the Capitol, and the Lincoln Memorial.
Washington, Booker Taliaferro (1856–1915). U.S. educator and author. Born a slave, he acquired an education after emancipation and became the nationally prominent principal of Tuskegee Institute, which flourished under his tutelage. He also wrote several books, including *Up From Slavery* (1901).
Washington, George (1732–1799). American statesman and general. He commanded the American forces during the Revolution (1775–83) and became (1789) the first president of the United States. He served two terms in office (1789–97).
Washington, Lake. Lake, *c.* 32 kilometers (20 miles) long and 6 kilometers (4 miles) wide, in west-central Washington, east of Seattle. Around the lake are many parks and recreational facilities.
Washington, Martha Dandridge Custis (1731–1802). U.S. first lady. After the death of her first husband (1757), she married Gen. George Washington (1759) and acted as his hostess during his two terms as president (1789–97).
Washington, Mount. The highest (1,918 meters; 6,288 feet) of the Presidential Range of the White Mts. in northern New Hampshire.
wash leather *n.* **1.** Soft leather such as chamois or split sheepskin. **2.** *British.* A piece of wash leather, typically used for cleaning cars and windows or polishing metal.
wash out *tr.v.* **1.** To cause to fade by or as if by laundering: *Bleach washed the colors out.* **2.** To cause the postponement or abandonment of (an outdoor event) by rain: *The match was washed out by a freak storm.* **3.** To deplete of vitality or energy: *felt washed out by evening.* **4.** To eliminate as unsatisfactory: *was washed out of officers' training school.* *—intr.v.* **1.** to fade by or as if by laundering. **2.** To become depleted of vitality or energy. **3.** To be eliminated as unsatisfactory.
wash·out (wŏsh′out′, wôsh′-) *n.* **1. a.** The erosion of a relatively soft surface, as a roadbed, by a transient stream of water. **b.** A channel produced by washout. **2. a.** A total failure or disappointment. **b.** One who fails to measure up to a standard, especially one who fails a course of training or study.
wash·room (wŏsh′ro͝om′, -ro͞om′, wôsh′-) *n.* A bathroom, rest room, or lavatory.
wash sale *n.* The illegal buying of stock by a seller's agents to give the impression of an active market.
wash·stand (wŏsh′stănd′, wôsh′-) *n.* A stand designed to hold a basin and pitcher of water for washing.
wash·tub (wŏsh′tŭb′, wôsh′-) *n.* A tub for washing clothes.
wash·y (wŏsh′ē, wô′shē) *adj.* **-ier, -iest. 1.** Watery; diluted: *washy tea.* **2.** Lacking intensity or strength. **—wash·i·ness** *n.*
was·n't (wŏz′ənt, wŭz′-). Contraction of *was not.*
wasp (wŏsp, wôsp) *n.* Any of numerous social or solitary insects, chiefly of the superfamilies Vespoidea and Sphecoidea, commonly having a slender body with a constricted abdomen, membranous wings, and in the females an ovipositor often modified as a sting. [Middle English *waspe,* Old English *wæsp, wæps.*]
Wasp, WASP (wŏsp, wôsp) *n.* A person of Caucasoid, northern European, largely Protestant stock whose members are held by some to constitute the most privileged and influential group in American society. [*W*hite *A*nglo-*S*axon *P*rotestant.] **—Wasp·ish, Wasp·y** *adj.*
wasp·ish (wŏs′pĭsh, wô′spĭsh) *adj.* **1.** Pertaining to or suggestive of a wasp. **2.** Easily irritated or annoyed; irascible; snappish. **—wasp·ish·ly** *adv.* **—wasp·ish·ness** *n.*
wasp waist *n.* A very slender or tightly corseted waist. **—wasp-waist·ed** (wŏsp′wā′stĭd, wôsp′-) *adj.*
wasp·y (wŏs′pē, wô′spē) *adj.* **-ier, -iest.** Characteristic of a wasp; wasplike.
was·sail (wŏs′əl, wŏ-sāl′) *n.* **1. a.** A salutation or toast formerly given in drinking someone's health or as an expression of good will at a festivity. **b.** The drink used in such toasting, commonly ale or wine spiced with roasted apples and sugar. **2.** A festivity characterized by much drinking.
∼intr.v. **wassailed, -sailing, -sails.** To engage in or drink a wassail. [Middle English *wassayl,* contraction of *wæs hæil,* from Old Norse *ves heill,* be in good health : *ves,* imperative singular of *vesa, vera,* to be + *heill,* hale, healthy.] **—was·sail·er** *n.*
Was·ser·mann test (wä′sər-mən, vä′-) *n.* A diagnostic test for syphilis involving the fixation or inactivation of a complement by an antibody in a blood serum sample. [After August von *Wassermann* (1866–1925), German bacteriologist.]
wast·age (wā′stĭj) *n.* **1.** Loss by deterioration, wear, or destruction. **2.** The process of wasting. **3.** An amount that is wasted.
waste (wāst) *v.* **wasted, wasting, wastes.** *—tr.* **1.** To use, consume, or expend thoughtlessly or carelessly; squander. **2.** To cause to lose energy, strength, or vigor; weaken or enfeeble. **3.** To fail to take advantage or make profitable use of; lose: *waste an opportunity.* **4. a.** To destroy completely. **b.** *Slang.* To kill. *—intr.* **1.** To lose energy, strength, weight, or vigor; become weak or enfeebled: *wasting away from an illness.* **2.** To pass without being put to use: *Time is wasting.* **—waste one's breath.** To speak without accomplishing anything.
∼n. **1.** The act of wasting or the condition of being wasted: *a waste of talent; gone to waste.* **2.** A place, region, or land that is uninhabited or uncultivated; a desert or wilderness. **3. a.** A useless or worthless by-product, as of a manufacturing process. **b.** Something, as steam, that escapes without being used. **4.** Garbage; trash. **5.** The undigested residue of food eliminated from the body.
∼adj. **1.** Regarded or discarded as worthless or useless: *waste paper.* **2.** Used as a conveyance or container for refuse: *a waste bin.* **3.** Excreted from the body as useless. [Middle English *wasten,* from Old North French *waster,* from Vulgar Latin *wāstāre* (unattested), from Latin *vāstāre,* to make empty, from *vāstus,* empty.]
waste·bas·ket (wāst′băs′kĭt, -bä′skĭt) *n.* An open-topped container for rubbish.
wast·ed (wā′stĭd) *adj.* **1.** Needless or superfluous: *wasted words.* **2.** Physically haggard, as from disease or dissipation. **3.** Not profitably used or maintained: *wasted money.* —See Synonyms at **haggard.**
waste·ful (wāst′fəl) *adj.* Characterized by or given to waste; extravagant. **—waste·ful·ly** *adv.* **—waste·ful·ness** *n.*
waste·land (wāst′lănd′) *n.* **1.** An uncultivated or desolate area; a barren or ravaged land. **2.** A place, era, or aspect of life considered as lacking in spiritual, aesthetic, or other humanizing qualities; a vacuum: *a cultural wasteland.*
waste·pa·per (wāst′pā′pər) *n.* Discarded paper.
waste pipe *n.* A pipe carrying off liquid waste.
waste product *n.* **1.** Useless or worthless debris produced during or as a result of a manufacturing or other process. **2.** Organic waste matter such as urine, feces, or dead cells.
wast·er (wā′stər) *n.* **1. a.** One that wastes: *a procedure that is a time waster.* **b.** A spendthrift; wastrel. **2.** One that lays waste; destroyer.
wast·ing (wā′stĭng) *adj.* **1.** Gradually deteriorating; declining. **2.** Sapping the strength, energy, or substance of the body; emaciating: *a wasting disease.*
wasting asset *n.* A fixed asset, such as a mine or an oil well, that diminishes in value over the years.
wast·rel (wā′strəl) *n.* A profligate or loafer; a good-for-nothing. [WASTE + *-rel,* diminutive suffix (often derogatory), from Old French *-erel(le).*]
wa·tap (wä-täp′, wä-) *n.* Also **wa·ta·pe** (-tä′pē). A stringy thread made from the roots of various conifers and used by American Indians in sewing and weaving. [Cree *watapiy.*]
watch (wŏch) *v.* **watched, watching, watches.** *—intr.* **1.** To look or observe attentively or carefully. **2.** To look and wait expectantly or in anticipation: *watch for your chance.* **3.** To act as a spectator; look on. **4.** To stay awake at night while serving as a guard, sentinel, or watchman. **5.** To stay alert as a religious exercise; keep vigil. *—tr.* **1.** To look at steadily; observe carefully or continuously: *watched the parade.* **2.** To keep a watchful eye on; guard. **3.** To observe the course of mentally; keep informed about: *watching the opinion polls.* **4.** To tend (a flock, for example). **—watch it.** *Informal.* To be careful. Usually used in the imperative. **—watch one's step.** To act or proceed with caution. **—watch out.** To be careful or on the alert; take care. **—watch over.** To be in charge of; superintend.
∼n. **1.** The act or process of keeping awake or mentally alert, especially for the purpose of guarding. **2.** Any of the periods into which the night is divided; a part of the night. **3.** A period of close observation, often in order to discover something. **4.** A person or group of persons serving, especially at night, to guard or protect. **5.** The post or period of duty of a guard, sentinel, or watchman. **6.** A small, portable timepiece, especially one worn on the wrist or carried in the pocket. **7. a.** A period of wakefulness, especially one observed as a religious vigil. **b.** A wake. **8.** *Nautical.* **a.** Any of the periods of time into which the day aboard ship is divided and during which a part of the crew is assigned to duty. **b.** The members of a ship's crew on duty during a specific watch. **c.** A chronometer on a ship. **—on the watch.** On the lookout; waiting expectantly. [Middle English *wa(c)chen, wecchen,* Old English *wæccan,* to be or stay awake, keep vigil.]
watch cap *n.* A knitted cap in dark blue worn in cold weather, especially by enlisted naval personnel.
watch·case (wŏch′kās′) *n.* The casing for the mechanism of a watch.
watch·dog (wŏch′dôg′, -dŏg′) *n.* **1.** A dog trained to guard property. **2.** A person who serves as a guardian or protector against waste, loss, or illegal practices. Often used adjectivally: *a watchdog committee.*
watch·er (wŏch′ər) *n.* **1.** One that watches or observes. **2.** One who observes the progress or development of something. Used in combination: *a China watcher.* **3.** A person keeping vigil, as at a sick person's bedside.
watch·ful (wŏch′fəl) *adj.* **1.** Closely observant or alert; vigilant.

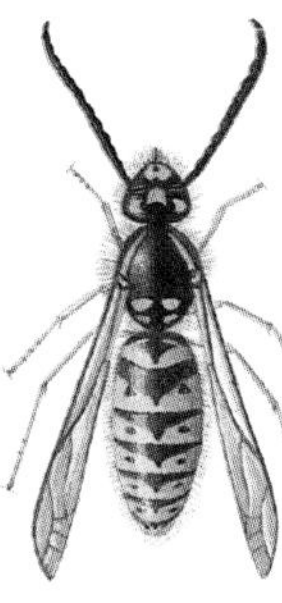

wasp *Rows of wasp pupae—insects in the dormant stage between larva and adult—fill the cells of a comb (below); the white grubs on the edge of the comb are wasp larvae. Most species of social wasp—including the common wasp (shown above 1½ times life size)—build a new colony each year. The queen builds the first cells out of wasp "paper," made by chewing dry wood into a pulp. Later, new worker wasps enlarge the nest until, by late summer, the colony may contain 2,000 insects.*

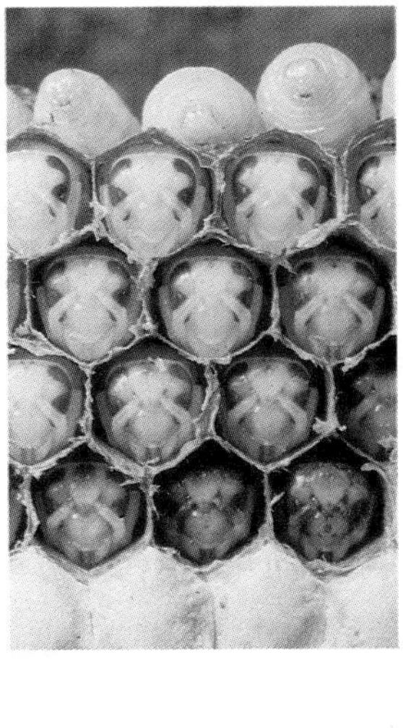

PRONUNCIATION KEY
ă, pat; ā, pay; âr, care;
ä, father, are; b, bib;
ch, church; d, deed; ĕ, pet;
ē, be; f, fife; g, gag; h, hat;
hw, which; ĭ, pit; ī, pie;
îr, pier; j, judge; k, kick;
l, lid, needle; m, mum;
n, no, sudden; ng, thing;
ŏ, pot; ō, toe; ô, paw, for;
oi, noise; ou, out; o͝o, book;
o͞o, boot; p, pop; r, roar;
s, sauce; sh, ship, dish;
t, tight; th, thin, path;
th, this, bathe; ŭ, cut; ûr, fur;
v, valve; w, with; y, yes;
z, zebra, size; zh, vision;
ə, about, item, edible,
gallop, circus, peaceful

IN FOREIGN WORDS:
à, *Fr.* ami; œ, *Fr.* feu, *Ger.* schön; ü, *Fr.* tu, *Ger.* über; KH, *Ger.* ich, *Scot.* loch; N, *Fr.* bon; y′, *Fr.* Compiègne

STRESS MARKS:
Primary stress: ′
in·cite′ (ĭn-sīt′)
Secondary stress: ′
in′sight′ (ĭn′sīt′)

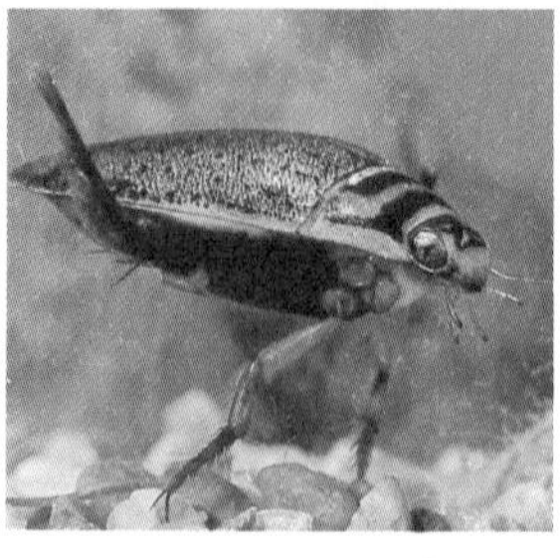

water beetle *A predator of rivers, lakes, and streams. The water beetle and its larvae will sometimes attack and eat small fish, such as sticklebacks. The beetle lays its eggs in the stems of water plants.*

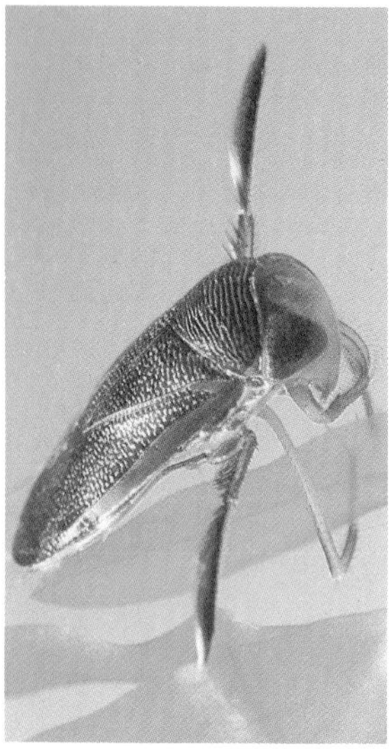

water boatman *This pond-dwelling insect propels itself underwater by using its powerful back legs as oars. Water boatmen feed on algae and diatoms that they draw from the ooze of the pond bed.*

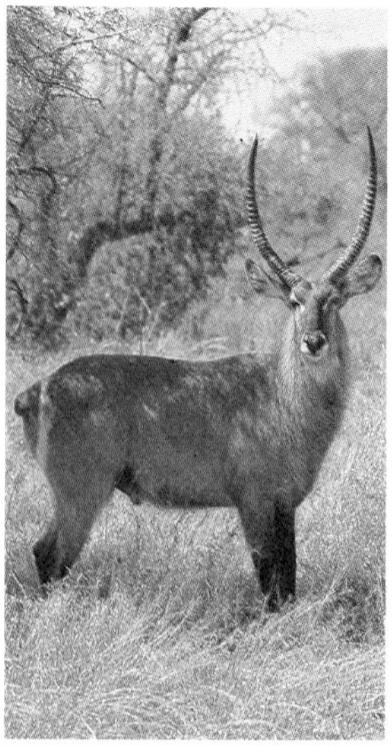

waterbuck *Despite its name, this large coarse-haired antelope from East Africa is found on plains and in woodlands as well as beside lakes and rivers. It does, however, always graze within range of water.*

2. *Archaic.* Not sleeping; awake. —See Synonyms at **aware.** **—watch•ful•ly** *adv.* **—watch•ful•ness** *n.*

watch glass *n.* **1.** A concavo-convex glass disk used to cover the face of a watch. **2.** A shallow glass dish used as a beaker cover or evaporating surface.

watch•mak•er (wŏch'mā'kər) *n.* One whose occupation is making or repairing watches. **—watch•mak•ing** *n.*

watch•man (wŏch'mən) *n., pl.* **-men** (-mĭn). A man employed to stand guard or keep watch.

watch night *n.* **1.** New Year's Eve. **2.** A religious service held on New Year's Eve.

watch pocket *n.* A small pocket in a vest, originally intended for holding a pocket watch.

watch•tow•er (wŏch'tou'ər) *n.* An observation tower upon which a guard or lookout is stationed to keep watch, as for enemies or forest fires or over prisoners.

watch•word (wŏch'wûrd') *n.* **1.** A prearranged reply to a challenge, as from a guard or sentry; a password. **2.** A slogan embodying the essential principles of a group; rallying cry.

wa•ter (wô'tər, wŏt'ər) *n.* **1.** A clear, colorless, nearly odorless and tasteless liquid, H_2O, essential for most plant and animal life and the most widely used of all solvents. Melting point 0°C (32°F), boiling point 100°C (212°F), specific gravity (4°C) 1.0000; weight per gallon (15°C) 8.337 pounds. **2. a.** Any of various forms of water: *salt water.* **b.** *Often* **waters.** Naturally occurring mineral water, as at a spa: *went to a resort to take the waters.* **3. a.** A body of water, such as a sea, lake, river, or stream. **b. waters.** A particular stretch of sea or ocean; especially, the territorial waters of a state: *escorted out of British waters.* **4.** Water as supplied to consumers; the water supply: *turning off the water for repairs.* **5. a.** Depth of water considered in terms of its suitability for navigation. **b.** The level of the tide: *high water.* **6.** Any of the liquids passed out of the body, as urine, perspiration, or tears. **7.** The fluid surrounding the fetus in the uterus; amniotic fluid. **8.** An aqueous solution of a substance, especially a gas: *ammonia water.* **9.** A wavy finish or sheen, as of a fabric. **10. a.** The valuation of the assets of a business firm beyond their real value. **b.** Stock issued in excess of paid-in capital. **11. a.** The transparency and luster of a gem. **b.** Level of excellence: *a musician of the first water.* **12.** In ancient thought, one of the four **elements** *(see).* **—above water.** Out of trouble. **—by water.** By boat. **—hold water.** To be logical or consistent: *His story doesn't hold water.* **—in deep water.** In great difficulty. **—make** (or **pass**) **water.** To urinate. **—throw** (or **pour**) **cold water on.** *Informal.* To speak scornfully about (a plan, for example) as being without merit, unjustified, or ill-advised; discourage. **—water under the bridge.** An occurrence, especially an unfortunate one, that cannot be undone.
~*v.* **watered, -tering, -ters.** *—tr.* **1.** To pour or sprinkle water upon; make wet: *watered the flowers.* **2. a.** To give drinking water to. **b.** To lead (an animal) to drinking water. **3.** To dilute or weaken by adding water: *a bar that served watered whiskey.* **4.** To give a sheen to the surface of (silk, linen, or metal). **5.** To increase (the share capital of a company) without any corresponding increase in the true value of the company's assets. **6.** To irrigate (land). *—intr.* **1.** To produce or discharge fluid: *eyes watering from the smoke.* **2.** To produce saliva in anticipation of food: *My mouth watered at the aroma of the freshly baked cookies.* **3.** To take on a supply of water. Used of a ship. **4.** To drink water. Used of an animal. **—make one's mouth water.** To cause to anticipate with relish. [Middle English *water,* Old English *wæter.*] **—wa•ter** *adj.* **—wa•ter•er** *n.* **—wa•ter•ish** *adj.*

wa•ter•age (wô'tər-ĭj, wŏt'ər-) *n. British.* **1.** The movement of goods or merchandise by water. **2.** The fee paid for this.

water bailiff *n. British.* An official responsible for enforcing laws on fishing or shipping.

water ballet *n.* **1.** The art of dancelike movement in water; synchronized swimming. **2.** A performance of water ballet.

water bear *n.* A **tardigrade** *(see).*

Water Bearer *n.* The constellation and sign of the zodiac **Aquarius** *(see).* [Translation of Latin *aquarius.*]

wa•ter•bed (wô'tər-bĕd', wŏt'ər-) *n.* An inflatable mattress designed to be filled with water and used as a bed.

water beetle *n.* Any of various aquatic beetles, especially of the family Dytiscidae, characteristically having a smooth, oval body and flattened hind legs especially adapted for swimming.

water bird *n.* Any swimming or wading bird.

water biscuit *n.* A biscuit made of flour and water.

water blister *n.* A blister having a nonpurulent watery content.

water bloom *n.* A growth of algae at or near the surface of a body of water, as a pond.

water boatman *n.* Any of various aquatic insects of the families Corixidae and Notonectidae, having long, oarlike hind legs adapted for swimming.

wa•ter•borne (wô'tər-bôrn', -bōrn', wŏt'ər-) *adj.* **1.** Floating on or supported by water; afloat. **2.** Transported by water, as freight may be. **3.** Transmitted in water, as a disease germ may be.

wa•ter•brain (wô'tər-brān', wŏt'ər-) A disease of sheep, **gid** *(see).*

water brash *n.* Regurgitation of watery acid from the stomach.

wa•ter•buck (wô'tər-bŭk', wŏt'ər-) *n.* Any of several African antelopes of the genus *Kobus,* having curved, ridged horns and frequenting swamps or bodies of water.

water buffalo *n.* A large buffalo, *Bubalus bubalis,* of southern Eurasia, having spreading backward-curving horns and often domesticated, especially as a draft animal. Also called "carabao."

water bug *n.* Any of various insects of wet places; especially, a large aquatic insect of the family Belostomatidae.

wa•ter•bus (wô'tər-bŭs', wŏt'ər-) A large motorboat used for carrying passengers on rivers or canals, as in Venice.

water cannon *n.* An apparatus capable of firing water at high pressure, used especially to disperse crowds or control riots.

water chestnut *n.* **1. a.** A Chinese sedge, *Eleocharis tuberosa,* having an edible corm. **b.** The succulent corm of this plant, used in Oriental cooking. **2.** A floating aquatic plant, *Trapa natans,* native to Asia, bearing nutlike fruit.

water chin•qua•pin (chĭng'kə-pĭn') *n.* A North American aquatic plant, *Nelumbo lutea,* related to the lotus and the water lilies, having large, cup-shaped leaves, large pale-yellow flowers, and edible, nutlike seeds.

water clock *n.* Any of various time-keeping or time-measuring devices, such as a **clepsydra** *(see),* based on the motion of running water. Also called "water glass."

water closet *n. Abbr.* **w.c.** A room or booth containing a toilet and often a washbowl.

water color, wa•ter•col•or, wa•ter•col•or (wô'tər-kŭl'ər, wŏt'ər-) *n.* **1.** A paint composed of a water-soluble pigment. **2.** A work done in water colors. **3.** The art of using water colors. **—wa•ter•col•or, wa•ter•col•or** *adj.* **—water colorist** *n.*

wa•ter-cool (wô'tər-kōōl', wŏt'ər-) *tr.v.* **-cooled, -cooling, -cools.** To cool (an engine) with water, especially with circulating water.

water cooler *n.* A vessel, device, or apparatus for cooling, storing, and dispensing drinking water.

wa•ter•course (wô'tər-kôrs', -kōrs', wŏt'ər-) *n.* **1.** A **waterway** *(see).* **2.** The bed or channel of a waterway.

wa•ter•cress (wô'tər-krĕs', wŏt'ər-) *n.* **1.** A plant, *Nasturtium officinale,* native to Eurasia, growing in freshwater ponds and streams and having pungent leaves used in salads, soups, and as a garnish. **2.** Any of several similar, related plants.

water cure *n. Medicine.* Hydropathy or hydrotherapy.

water cycle *n.* The cycle of evaporation and condensation that controls the distribution of the earth's water as it evaporates from the seas, rivers, and lakes into the atmosphere, condenses into a precipitated form, as rain, sleet, or snow, and flows back into the sea by way of rivers. Also called "hydrologic cycle."

water dog *n.* **1.** A dog accustomed to water, especially one trained to retrieve waterfowl. **2.** One who is at home in or on the water.

water down *tr.v.* To reduce or dilute the strength, effectiveness, or impact of.

wa•tered-down (wô'tərd-doun', wŏt'ərd-) *adj.* Reduced in strength, effectiveness, or impact.

wa•ter•fall (wô'tər-fôl', wŏt'ər-) *n.* A steep descent of water from a height; a cascade.

water flea *n.* Any of various small aquatic crustaceans of the order Cladocera, as the **daphnia** *(see),* which characteristically swim with jerking, flealike motions.

Wa•ter•ford (wô'tər-fərd, wŏt'ər-). County of Munster province, south Republic of Ireland. Bordering the Atlantic Ocean, it includes the Comeragh and Monavullagh mountain ranges and is crossed by the Suir and Blackwater rivers. Its chief industries are the raising of cattle, fishing, brewing, distilling, and glassmaking. Waterford is the county town.

wa•ter•fowl (wô'tər-foul', wŏt'ər-) *n., pl.* **-fowls** or collectively **waterfowl. 1.** A swimming bird, such as a duck or goose. **2.** Swimming game birds collectively.

wa•ter•front (wô'tər-frŭnt', wŏt'ər-) *n.* An area of land, especially built-up land in a town or city, abutting on a body of water, such as a lake or harbor. Also used adjectivally: *a waterfront café.*

water gap *n.* A transverse cleft in a mountain ridge through which a stream flows.

water gas *n.* A fuel gas containing about 40 percent carbon monoxide, 50 percent hydrogen, and small amounts of carbon dioxide and nitrogen, made by passing steam and air over heated coke.

water gate *n.* **1.** A **floodgate** *(see).* **2.** A gate that provides access to a body of water.

Wa•ter•gate (wô'tər-gāt', wŏt'ər-) *n. Informal.* A scandal that involves official violation of public trust through abuses of power, bribery, skullduggery, and a cover-up. [After *Watergate,* a building complex in Washington, D.C., the site of illegal activities that gave rise to such a scandal.]

water gauge *n.* An instrument indicating the level of water, as in a boiler, tank, reservoir, or stream.

water glass *n.* **1.** A drinking glass or goblet. **2.** A tube or similar structure having a glass bottom for making observations below the surface of the water. **3. Sodium silicate** *(see).* **4.** A water gauge made of glass. **5.** A **water clock** *(see).*

water hammer *n.* **1.** A banging noise heard in a water pipe following an abrupt alteration of the flow with resulting pressure surges. **2.** A similar noise in steam pipes, caused by steam bubbles entering a cold pipe partially filled with water.

water hemlock *n.* Any of several poisonous plants of the genus *Cicuta;* especially, *C. maculata,* of marshy areas, having clusters of small white flowers. Also called "cowbane."

water hen *n.* Any of various birds of the family Rallidae, especially the gallinule.

water hole *n.* A small natural depression in which water collects; especially, a pool used by animals as a watering place.

water hyacinth *n.* A floating aquatic plant, *Eichhornia crassipes*, native to tropical America, having bluish-purple flowers and often forming dense masses in ponds and streams.

water ice *n.* A dessert made from sweetened, flavored finely crushed ice.

watering can *n.* A watering pot.

watering hole *n. Informal.* A place serving alcoholic drinks to the public.

watering place *n.* 1. A place where animals find water. 2. A health resort with mineral springs; a spa. 3. A watering hole.

watering pot *n.* A vessel with a long spout and sometimes a perforated nozzle that is used to water plants.

water jacket *n.* A casing containing water circulated by a pump, used around a part to be cooled, especially in water-cooled internal-combustion engines.

water jump *n.* An obstacle consisting of a pond or ditch, usually preceded by a fence, over which riders or athletes must jump in a steeplechase or show jumping competition.

wa·ter·leaf (wô′tər-lēf′, wŏt′ər-) *n., pl.* **-leafs** or collectively **water-leaf.** Any of various North American plants of the genus *Hydro-phyllum*, having clusters of white or purplish flowers.

wa·ter·less (wô′tər-lĭs, wŏt′ər-) *adj.* 1. Without water; dry. 2. Not requiring water. Said especially of a cooling system.

water level *n.* 1. The height of the surface of a body of water. 2. *Geology.* A water table (*see*). 3. The water line of a ship.

water lily *n., pl.* **water lilies.** 1. Any of various aquatic plants of the genus *Nymphaea*, having floating leaves and showy, variously colored flowers; especially, the common white water lily, *N. alba.* 2. Any of various similar or related plants.

water line *n.* 1. *Nautical.* **a.** The line on the hull of a ship to which the water surface rises. **b.** Any of several lines parallel to this marked on the hull of a ship, indicating the depth to which the ship sinks under various loads. 2. A line or stain, as that left on a sea wall, indicating the height to which water has risen or may rise.

wa·ter·log (wô′tər-lôg′, -lŏg′, wŏt′ər-) *tr.v.* **-logged, -logging, -logs.** To soak or saturate with water; cause to lose buoyancy.

wa·ter·logged (wô′tər-lôgd′, wŏt′ər-lŏgd′) *adj.* 1. Heavy and sluggish in the water because of flooding in the hold. Said of a ship. 2. Soaked or saturated with water: *water-logged fields.* [WATER + *-logged,* probably "made (unmanageable) like a log in water," from LOG.]

wa·ter·loo (wô′tər-lōō′, wŏt′ər-) *n., pl.* **-loos.** A disastrous or crushing defeat. Usually used in the phrase *meet one's waterloo.* [After *Waterloo,* the town in Belgium where Napoleon met his final defeat (1815).]

water main *n.* A principal pipe in a system of pipes for conveying water, especially one installed underground.

wa·ter·man (wô′tər-mən, wŏt′ər-) *n., pl.* **-men** (-mĭn). A boatman.

wa·ter·mark (wô′tər-märk′, wŏt′ər-) *n.* 1. A mark showing the height to which water has risen; especially, a line indicating the levels of high and low tide. 2. **a.** A translucent design impressed on paper during manufacture and visible when the finished paper is held to the light. **b.** The metal pattern that produces this design. ~*tr.v.* **watermarked, -marking, -marks.** 1. To mark (paper) with a watermark. 2. To impress (a pattern or design) as a watermark.

water meadow *n.* A meadow irrigated and fertilized by the periodic flooding of a nearby stream, as a river.

wa·ter·mel·on (wô′tər-mĕl′ən, wŏt′ər-) *n.* 1. A vine, *Citrullus vulgaris,* native to Africa, cultivated for its large, edible fruit. 2. The fruit of this plant, having a hard green rind and sweet, watery pink or reddish flesh.

water meter *n.* An instrument that records the quantity of water passing through a pipe.

water milfoil *n.* Any of various aquatic plants of the genus *Myriophyllum,* having feathery, finely dissected leaves. Also called "milfoil."

water mill *n.* A mill with water-driven machinery.

water moccasin *n.* A venomous snake, *Agkistrodon piscivorus,* of the southern United States. Also called "cottonmouth."

water mole *n. Australian.* The duck-billed platypus (*see*).

water nymph *n.* A nymph, as the naiad, living in or near water.

water of crystallization *n.* Water in chemical combination with a crystal and necessary for the maintenance of crystalline properties but capable of being removed by sufficient heat.

water of hydration *n.* Water chemically combined with a substance so that it can be removed, as by heating, without substantially changing the chemical composition of the substance.

water on the brain *n.* Hydrocephalus (*see*).

water ouzel *n.* A bird, the dipper (*see*).

water pepper *n.* 1. A marsh plant, *Polygonum hydropiper,* having reddish stems, greenish flowers, and acrid-tasting leaves. 2. Any of various similar or related plants. Also called "smartweed."

water pimpernel *n.* A plant, the **brookweed** (*see*).

water pipe *n.* 1. A pipe that carries water. 2. A hookah (*see*).

water pistol *n.* A toy gun that squirts water.

water plantain *n.* Any of various aquatic plants of the genus *Alisma,* having branching clusters of small white or pinkish flowers.

water polo *n.* A water sport with two teams of swimmers, each of which tries to pass a ball into the other's goal.

wa·ter·pow·er (wô′tər-pou′ər, wŏt′ər-) *n.* 1. **a.** The power of running or falling water as used for driving machinery, especially for generating electricity. **b.** A source of such power, as a waterfall. 2. A water right owned by a mill.

water mill

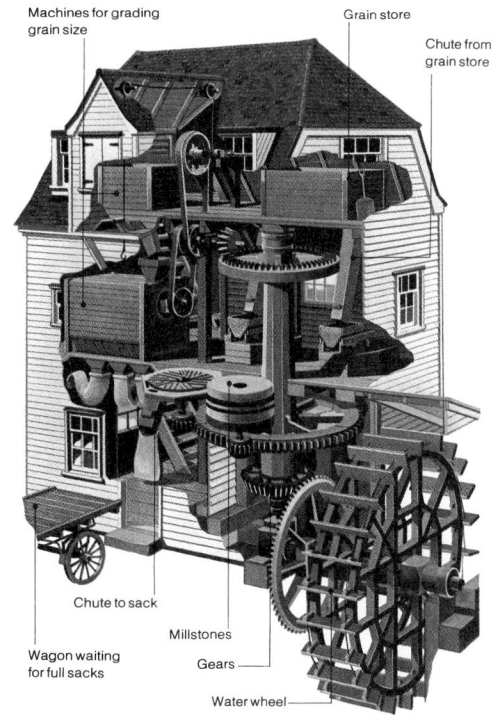

POWER FROM WATER WHEELS
The principal source of energy for 1,500 years

Simple water mills—half-horsepower water wheels set horizontally on an axle—were known to the ancient Greeks. The Romans devised vertical wheels that could generate about 3 horsepower. These remained the principal source of energy for 1,500 years. By the 18th century Europe had some 500,000 water mills, the best of which generated 5–10 horsepower. Their uses included grinding corn, crushing ore, pounding iron, drilling gun barrels, and fulling cloth. Water mills began to become obsolete as the steam engine spread in the early 19th century.

Machines for grading grain size

Grain store

Chute from grain store

Chute to sack

Millstones

Wagon waiting for full sacks

Gears

Water wheel

HOW A WATER MILL WORKS *A grain mill—shown with some sections cut away—used a vertical water wheel. The wheel's motion was accelerated and transferred to the horizontal millstones by gear wheels. Early medieval wheels were set directly in a stream and so were subject to little control.*

Later it was discovered that they could be controlled more easily by setting the wheel in a channel from the river; the water flow in the channel could be regulated with sluice gates. The grain to be ground into flour was stored on the top floor of the mill and dropped down a chute to the millstones, where another chute guided the ground meal into sacks, to be removed by wagons.

waterfall *Yosemite Falls in Yosemite National Park, California, have a total drop of 740 meters (2,400 feet).*

water lily *These long-stemmed plants grow in ponds and slow-flowing streams. The stems of the white water lily,* Nymphaea alba *(above), are sometimes eaten as a delicacy in parts of Europe.*

wa·ter·proof (wô′tər-prōōf′, wŏt′ər-) *adj.* 1. Impenetrable to or unaffected by water. 2. Made of or treated with rubber, plastic, or a sealing agent to resist water penetration. ~*n.* 1. A waterproof material. 2. *Chiefly British.* A raincoat. ~*tr.v.* **waterproofed, -proofing, -proofs.** To make waterproof. [WATER + -PROOF.]

water purslane *n.* 1. An aquatic plant, *Didiplis diandra,* having small greenish flowers. 2. A marsh plant, *Ludwigia palustris,* having reddish stems and small reddish flowers.

water rail *n.* A shy, marsh-dwelling bird of northern Europe, *Rallus aquaticus,* having a long, red bill.

water rat *n.* 1. Any of various semiaquatic rodents, as one of the genus *Hydromis,* of Australia and adjacent islands, or *Neofiber alleni,* of Florida and southern Georgia, resembling the muskrat. 2. *Slang.* One who frequents a waterfront area, especially a loafer or petty thief.

wa·ter·re·pel·lent (wô′tər-rĭ-pĕl′ənt, wŏt′ər-) *adj.* Resisting penetration by but not entirely impervious to water.

wa·ter·re·sis·tant (wô′tər-rĭ-zĭs′tənt, wŏt′ər-) *adj.* Resistant to wetting but not waterproof.

water right *n.* 1. The right to draw water from a particular source, such as a lake, irrigation canal, or stream. 2. The right to navigate on particular waters.

Wa·ters (wô'tərz, wŏt'ərz), **Ethel** (1896–1977). U.S. singer and actress. Born in extreme poverty in Philadelphia, she began singing on the stage at age 17. She worked in vaudeville and small clubs, then the Plantation Club in Harlem (1925), which led to offers to appear on Broadway and later in motion pictures. Her greatest dramatic success was in Carson McCullers's *The Member of the Wedding* (1950, on stage, and in the 1952 film version).

water sapphire *n.* A deep-blue cordierite from Sri Lanka often used as a gemstone.

wa·ter·scape (wô'tər-skāp', wŏt'ər-) *n.* A seascape.

water scorpion *n.* Any of various aquatic insects of the family Nepidae, having a respiratory tube that resembles a scorpion's tail.

wa·ter·shed (wô'tər-shĕd', wŏt'ər-) *n.* **1.** A ridge of high land dividing two areas that are drained by different river systems. **2.** The region draining into a river, river system, or body of water. **3.** A crucially important time or event; a turning point. [Probably translation of German *Wasserscheide.*]

wa·ter·side (wô'tər-sīd', wŏt'ər-) *n.* Land bordering a body of water; a bank or shore. —**wa·ter·side** *adj.*

wa·ter·ski (wô'tər-skē', wŏt'ər-) *intr.v.* **-skied, -skiing, -skis.** To ski on water while being towed by a speedboat.

~*n.* A broad ski used in water-skiing. —**wa·ter·ski·er** *n.*

water snake *n.* Any of various aquatic or semiaquatic snakes, especially of the genus *Natrix.*

water softener *n.* A substance used to reduce the hardness of water.

water soldier *n.* A perennial aquatic plant, *Stratiotes aloides,* that remains submerged except at flowering time, when rosettes of long, narrow serrated leaves surrounding three-petaled white flowers break the surface.

water spaniel *n.* A spaniel of a breed characterized by a curly, water-resistant coat, often used for retrieving waterfowl.

water spider *n.* A spider, *Argyroneta aquatica,* that constructs and lives in an underwater chamber, which it fills with air bubbles trapped in the hairs of its body.

wa·ter·spout (wô'tər-spout', wŏt'ər-) *n.* **1.** A funnel-shaped tornado or lesser whirlwind occurring over water and resulting in a whirling column of spray and mist. Compare **tornado.** **2.** A hole or pipe from which water is discharged.

water sprite *n.* A sprite or nymph living in or near the water.

water strider *n.* Any of various insects of the family Gerridae, having long, slender legs with which they support themselves on the surface of water. Also called "skater," "pond skater."

water supply *n.* **1.** The water available for a community or region. **2.** The sources and delivery system of such water.

water system *n.* **1.** A river and all its tributaries. **2.** A water supply.

water table *n.* **1.** The level under the ground in permeable or porous rock below which the ground is completely saturated with water. Also called "water level." **2.** A projecting ledge, molding, or stringcourse on a building, designed to throw off rainwater.

water thrush *n.* Either of two brownish New World birds, *Seiurus noveboracensis* or *S. motacilla,* characteristically walking along the edges of streams or ponds.

water tiger *n.* The predacious larva of a **diving beetle** *(see).*

wa·ter·tight (wô'tər-tīt', wŏt'ər-) *adj.* **1.** So assembled or constructed that water cannot enter or escape; waterproof. **2.** Having no flaws or loopholes; incapable of being faulted or misconstrued: *a watertight argument; a watertight contract.*

water tower *n.* A standpipe or tank mounted on a tower used as a reservoir or for maintaining equal pressure in a water system.

water turkey *n.* A blackish New World bird, *Anhinga anhinga,* of swampy regions, having a long, slender, flexible neck. Also called "anhinga," "darter," "snakebird."

water vapor *n.* Water diffused as a vapor in the atmosphere, especially at a temperature below the boiling point.

water vole *n.* A large aquatic vole, *Arvicola terrestris.*

water wagtail *n.* The **pied wagtail** *(see).*

wa·ter·way (wô'tər-wā', wŏt'ər-) *n.* **1.** A river, channel, canal, or other navigable body of water used for travel or transport. Also called "watercourse." **2.** A channel at the edge of a ship's deck to drain away water.

wa·ter·weed (wô'tər-wēd', wŏt'ər-) *n.* Any of various aquatic plants, such as the pondweed.

water wheel *n.* **1.** A wheel propelled by falling or running water that is used as a source of power. **2.** A wheel with buckets attached to its rim used for raising water.

water wings *pl.n.* A device consisting of a pair of joined inflatable waterproof bags placed under the arms of a person, especially a child, learning to swim.

wa·ter·works (wô'tər-wûrks', wŏt'ər-) *pl.n. Used with a singular or plural verb.* **1. a.** The apparatus, as reservoirs, tanks, buildings, pumps, and pipes, that constitute a public water-supply system. **b.** A single unit, such as a pumping station, within such a system. **2.** An exhibition of moving water, as artificial fountains or waterfalls. **3.** *Informal.* **a.** Tears: *turned on the waterworks.* **b.** The urinary system.

wa·ter·y (wô'tə-rē, wŏt'ə-) *adj.* **-ier, -iest. 1.** Filled with, consisting of, or containing water; moist; wet: *watery soil.* **2.** Resembling or suggestive of water; liquid. **3. a.** Containing too much water; diluted: *watery soup.* **b.** Sodden, as from overcooking in water. **4.** Without force; insipid: *watery prose.* **5.** Secreting or discharging water or watery fluid, especially as a symptom of disease. —**wa·ter·i·ness** *n.*

Watling Island. See **San Salvador Island.**

Wat·son (wŏt'sən), **James Dewey** (1928–). American biologist. With Francis Crick he worked out the detailed structure of DNA (deoxyribonucleic acid), which led to the unraveling of the genetic code. He shared the Nobel Prize for medicine (1962).

Wat·son-Crick model (wŏt'sən-krĭk') *n.* The molecular model constructed by J.D. Watson and F.H.C. Crick to show the structure of DNA. See **double helix.**

watt (wŏt) *n. Abbr.* **W** An SI unit of power equal to one joule per second. [After James WATT.]

Watt (wŏt), **James** (1736–1819). British engineer. He made fundamental improvements to the Newcomen steam engine, which resulted in the modern high-pressure steam engine (patented 1769).

wat·tage (wŏt'ĭj) *n.* **1.** An amount of power, especially electric power, expressed in watts. **2.** The electric power required by an appliance or device.

Wat·teau (wä-tō', vä-), **Jean Antoine** (1684–1721). French painter, the originator of the *fêtes galantes* (scenes of gallantry). Among his masterpieces is *The Embarkation for Cythera* (1717).

watt-hour (wŏt'our') *n. Abbr.* **W-hr, whr.** A unit of energy, especially electrical energy, equal to the energy of one watt acting for one hour and equivalent to 3,600 joules.

wat·tle (wŏt'l) *n.* **1. a.** Poles intertwined with twigs, reeds, or branches for use in construction, as of walls or fences. **b.** Materials thus used. **2.** A fleshy, often brightly colored fold of skin hanging from the neck or throat, characteristic of certain birds and some lizards. **3.** Any of various Australian trees or shrubs of the genus *Acacia.* ~*tr.v.* **wattled, -tling, -tles. 1.** To construct from wattle. **2.** To weave into wattle. **3.** To bind together by intertwining twigs or other material. [Middle English *wattel,* Old English *watel, watul†.*] —**wat·tled** *adj.*

wattle and daub *n.* Wattle plastered with clay or mud and used as a building material. —**wattle-and-daub** *adj.*

wat·tle·bird (wŏt'l-bûrd') *n.* **1.** Any of several birds of the genus *Anthochaera,* of Australia and adjacent regions, having wattles on each side of the head. **2.** Any of various New Zealand birds of the family Callaeidae, having wattles on either side of the bill.

watt·me·ter (wŏt'mē'tər) *n.* An instrument for measuring in watts the power flowing in a circuit.

Wa·tu·si (wŏ-tōō'sē, -zē) *n., pl.* **-sis** or collectively **Watusi.** A member of a pastoral people of Rwanda and Burundi in central equatorial Africa, distinguished by their tall stature.

Waugh (wô), **Alec** (1898–1981). British author of novels and travel books. Among his best-known works are *The Loom of Youth* (1918), *Island in the Sun* (1956), and *The Fatal Gift* (1973). He also wrote several autobiographical volumes, including *My Brother Evelyn and Other Profiles* (1967).

Waugh, Evelyn Arthur St. John (1903–66). British novelist. His satirical novels, such as *Decline and Fall* (1928) and *Vile Bodies* (1930), lampooned fashionable society. His later works, notably *Brideshead Revisited* (1945), revealed his interest in Roman Catholicism, to which he was converted (1930).

wave (wāv) *v.* **waved, waving, waves.** —*intr.* **1.** To be moved back and forth or up and down by or as if by a current of air; shake, sway, flutter, or undulate: *branches waving in the wind.* **2.** To make a signal with an up-and-down or back-and-forth movement with the hand or with an object in the hand: *waved at us from across the street.* **3.** To have an undulating, wavelike form or appearance; curve or curl: *Her hair waves naturally.* —*tr.* **1.** To move or sweep back and forth or up and down through the air, either once or repeatedly: *waved her fan; waved his magic wand.* **2. a.** To signal or express by waving the hand or something held in the hand: *He waved good-by.* **b.** To signal to (a person) to move in a specified direction: *waved us on; waved him aside.* **3.** To arrange into curves, curls, or undulations: *wave one's hair.*

~*n.* **1. a.** A ridge or swell moving along the surface of a large body of water and generated by the action of gravity or the wind. **b.** A small ridge or swell moving across the interface of two fluids and dependent on the surface tension. **2.** *Often* **waves.** The sea or the surface of the sea: *vanished beneath the waves.* **3.** Something resembling a wave or waves, as: **a.** A moving curve or a succession of curves in or upon a surface; an undulation: *waves of wheat in the wind.* **b.** A curve or succession of curves, as in the hair. **c.** A curved shape, outline, or pattern. **4.** A movement up and down or back and forth: *a wave of the hand.* **5.** A sudden rise, as of an emotion or pattern of behavior, sweeping irresistibly over an individual or through a group; a surge: *a wave of indignation; a wave of panic selling.* **6.** A widespread, persistent meteorological condition, especially of temperature: *a cold wave.* **7.** A group of people, animals, or events that act, move, or exist together, especially one of a series or succession: *came with the first wave of settlers.* **8.** *Physics.* **a.** A disturbance or oscillation propagated from point to point in a medium or in space and described, in general, by mathematical specification of its amplitude, velocity, frequency, and phase. **b.** A graphic representation of the variation of such a disturbance with time. **c.** A single cycle of such a disturbance. —**make waves.** To cause a disturbance or upset. [As a verb, Middle English *waven,* Old English *wafian,* to move back and forth (especially with the hands). As a noun, perhaps variant (influenced by the verb WAVE) of Middle English *wawe, waghe,* probably Old English *wǣg,* motion, wave.] —**wave·like** *adj.* —**wav·er** *n.*

wave·band (wāv'bănd') *n.* A range of frequencies, especially any of those assigned to radio transmissions.

wave equation *n.* **1.** A partial differential equation in one, two, or three dimensions, the solution of which represents the propagation of a wave with constant velocity. **2.** The fundamental equation of wave mechanics, the **Schrödinger wave equation** *(see).*

wave·form (wāv′fôrm′) *n.* The mathematical representation of a wave, especially a graph of amplitude at a fixed point against time.

wave front *n.* A surface of a propagating wave that is the locus of all points having identical phase, the surface being usually, but not always, perpendicular to the direction of propagation.

wave function *n.* A mathematical function used in wave mechanics to describe a given state of a quantum system, the square of the amplitude of the function at a given point being representative of the probability of the system in that state being found at that point.

wave·guide (wāv′gīd′) *n. Electronics.* A system of material boundaries in the form of a solid dielectric rod or dielectric-filled tubular conductor, usually of rectangular cross section, capable of guiding high-frequency electromagnetic waves.

wave·length (wāv′lĕngth′) *n.* **1.** *Physics.* In a periodic wave, the distance between two points of corresponding phase in consecutive cycles. **2.** *Informal.* A person's characteristic way of thinking and feeling: *We're not on the same wavelength.*

wave·let (wāv′lĭt) *n.* A small wave or ripple.

wa·vell·ite (wā′və-līt′) *n.* A white, yellowish, or brownish hydrated aluminum phosphate, $Al_6(PO_4)_4(OH)_6 \cdot 9H_2O$, that occurs usually as small spheres with radiating internal structure. [After William *Wavell* (died 1829), British physician.]

wave mechanics *n.* The formulation of quantum mechanics based on the wave equation of Schrödinger.

wave·me·ter (wāv′mē′tər) *n.* A device for determining the wavelength or frequency of radio waves.

wave number *n.* The frequency of a wave divided by its velocity of propagation; the reciprocal of the wavelength.

wave-par·ti·cle duality (wāv′pär′tĭ-kəl) *n. Physics.* The exhibition of both wavelike and particlelike properties by a single entity, such as a photon or an electron. See **quantum theory.**

wave power *n.* Energy obtained by using the momentum of waves to generate electricity. See feature, next page.

wa·ver (wā′vər) *intr.v.* **-vered, -vering, -vers. 1.** To swing or move back and forth; sway. **2.** To show irresolution or indecision; vacillate. **3.** To become uncertain or unsure; falter: *Her confidence never wavered.* **4.** To tremble, quaver, or shake. Used of a sound, such as a voice or a musical note. **5.** To flicker, flash, or glimmer. Used of light. —See Synonyms at **hesitate, swing.**
∼*n.* An act of wavering. [Middle English *waveren,* to wander, stray, fluctuate, from Old Norse *vafra,* to move unsteadily, hover.] **—wa·ver·er** *n.* **—wa·ver·ing·ly** *adv.*

wave theory *n.* A theory put forward by Christian Huygens (1629–95) that light is transmitted in the form of waves. Compare **corpuscular theory.**

wave train *n. Physics.* A succession of similar wave pulses.

wave trap *n.* An electronic filtering device designed to exclude unwanted signals or interference from a receiver.

wa·vy (wā′vē) *adj.* **-ier, -iest. 1.** Moving or proceeding in a wavelike form or motion; sinuous. **2.** Having curls, curves, or undulations: *wavy hair.* **3.** Characteristic of, resembling, or suggestive of waves. **4.** Abounding in, having, or rising in waves: *a wavy sea.* **—wav·i·ly** *adv.* **—wav·i·ness** *n.*

waw. Variant of **vav.**

wa-wa. Variant of **wah-wah.**

wax[1] (wăks) *n.* **1. a.** Any of various natural or synthetic viscous or solid heat-sensitive substances consisting essentially of high molecular weight hydrocarbons or esters of fatty acids, characteristically insoluble in water but soluble in most organic solvents. **b.** A substance secreted by bees; beeswax. **c.** A waxy substance found in the ears; cerumen. **2.** A solid plastic or pliable liquid substance of mineral origin, primarily petroleum, such as ozocerite or paraffin, used in paper coating, as insulation, in crayons, and often in medicinal preparations. **3.** A resinous mixture used by shoemakers to wax their thread. **4.** Something resembling or suggestive of wax in being readily molded or impressionable. **5.** A preparation containing wax used for polishing surfaces, as of floors.
∼*tr.v.* **waxed, waxing, waxes.** To coat or treat with wax.
∼*adj.* Made of or resembling wax. [Middle English *wax, wexe,* Old English *weax, wæx,* beeswax.]

wax[2] *intr.v.* **waxed, waxing, waxes. 1.** To increase gradually in size, number, strength, or intensity. **2.** To show a progressively larger light surface, as the moon does in passing from new to full. Compare **wane. 3.** To grow or become as specified: *wax angry.* [Middle English *wexen,* Old English *weaxan.*]

wax[3] *n.* A fit of anger; rage. [Perhaps from WAX (to increase).]

wax bean *n.* A variety of string bean with yellow pods. Also called "butter bean."

wax·ber·ry (wăks′bĕr′ē) *n., pl.* **-ries.** The waxy fruit of the wax myrtle or the snowberry.

wax·bill (wăks′bĭl′) *n.* Any of various tropical Old World birds of the genus *Estrilda* and related genera, having a short, often brightly colored waxy beak.

wax·en (wăk′sən) *adj.* **1.** Consisting of or covered with wax. **2.** Suggestive of wax, as: **a.** Pale. **b.** Smooth and shiny. **c.** Pliable or impressionable.

wax insect *n.* Any of various insects of the family Coccidae that secrete a waxy substance.

wax moth *n.* A **bee moth** *(see).*

wax myrtle *n.* A shrub, *Myrica cerifera,* of the southeastern United States, having evergreen leaves and small, berrylike fruit with a waxy coating. Also called "candleberry."

wax palm *n.* Any of several palm trees that yield wax, as *Copernica cerifera,* the source of carnauba wax, or *Ceroxylon andicola,* of South America.

wax paper *n.* Also **waxed paper.** Paper that has been made moistureproof by treatment with wax.

wax·plant (wăks′plănt′, -plänt′) *n.* A tropical Old World vine, *Hoya carnosa,* having waxy white or pinkish flowers.

wax·wing (wăks′wĭng′) *n.* Any of several birds of the genus *Bombycilla,* having crested heads, predominantly brown plumage, and waxy red tips on the secondary wing feathers.

wax·work (wăks′wûrk′) *n.* **1.** The art of modeling in wax. **2.** A figure or ornament made of wax; especially, a life-size wax representation of a famous person. **3. waxworks.** *Used with a singular or plural verb.* An exhibition of waxwork in a museum. **—wax·work·er** *n.*

wax·y (wăk′sē) *adj.* **-ier, -iest. 1.** Resembling wax in color or consistency, especially: **a.** Pale, smooth, and lustrous. **b.** Pliable or impressionable. **2.** Consisting of, abounding in, or covered with wax. **—wax·i·ness** *n.*

way (wā) *n.* Also *regional* **ways** (wāz) (for sense 9). **1. a.** A road, path, or track providing a route from one place to another. **b.** An opening affording passage: *This door is the only way into the attic.* **c.** A right of way in law. **2. a.** Room or space free of obstacles and allowing forward movement: *clear the way for a parade; get out of my way.* **b.** An absence of factors impeding progress or action; opportunity for advance or activity: *an agreement that has opened the way for a lasting peace.* **3.** A course that is or may be used in going from one place to another: *Show me the way to go home.* **4. a.** Progress or travel along a particular route, in a particular direction, or toward a particular end: *on my way to work; leading the way in the fight against cancer.* **b.** Forward movement or progress toward a desired end, effected as specified: *elbowed his way to the front; fought her way to the top in a competitive business.* **c.** Forward motion or rate of progress of a vessel through water: *The ship gathered way.* **5.** A path or course of experience, life, or conduct: *went our separate ways after the war.* **6. a.** A method or manner of performing an action or achieving an end: *There must be some way of mending it. Should I do it this way?* **b.** A means or expedient that may be employed to effect a result: *had no way of contacting you.* **7. a.** A characteristic or habitual mode of living, behaving, or happening: *the American way of life; mend one's ways. These little debts have a way of mounting up.* **b.** A particularly effective or persuasive manner: *a way with words; has a way with children.* **8.** Freedom or scope to do as one wishes: *if I had my way; always gets her own way.* **9.** Distance in general, whether spatial, temporal, or conceptual: *a good way off; have come some way toward an agreement.* **10. a.** Direction of motion or aspect: *come this way; glanced my way.* **b.** A district or region considered as lying in a specified direction: *Drop in if you're ever over our way.* **11.** An aspect, particular, or feature: *I agree with you in some ways. The situation is in no way comparable.* **12.** The range or scope of one's observation or experience: *Wealth never came his way.* **13.** *Informal.* A state or condition, especially with regard to health or prosperity: *in a bad way financially.* **14.** Type, category, or description: *not much in the way of a plot.* **15. ways.** A set of parallel longitudinal strips on a surface that serves to guide a moving part in a machine. **16. ways.** *Nautical.* The timbered structure from which a ship slides when launched. —See Synonyms at **method. —by the way.** Incidentally; in passing. **—by way of. 1.** Through; by route of. **2.** As a means of; in order to serve as: *He made no comment by way of apology.* **—give way. 1.** To yield, submit, or agree. **2.** To fall or break down under pressure. **—go out of one's** (or **the) way.** To inconvenience oneself in doing something beyond what is required. **—have** (or **want) it both ways.** To have (or want) the benefit or enjoyment of two states of affairs that are mutually incompatible. **—in a way.** To some extent. **—put someone in the way of.** To provide (someone) with an opportunity of gaining an advantage. **—see one's way (clear) to.** To be willing or find it possible to do something.
∼*adv. Informal.* **1.** At a great distance; far: *way off yonder.* **2.** By a great distance or to a great degree: *way over budget.* [Middle English *wey(e), wei(e), way,* Old English *weg,* a road, path. Adverbial use, from AWAY.]
Synonyms: *course, pass, passage, path, route, trail.*

way·bill (wā′bĭl′) *n.* A document containing a list of goods and shipping instructions relative to a shipment.

way·far·er (wā′fâr′ər) *n.* One who travels; especially, one who travels on foot. [Middle English *weyfarere* : *wey,* WAY + *fare,* a journey, traveling, Old English *faru.*] **—way·far·ing** *adj.*

wayfaring tree *n.* A shrub, *Viburnum lantana,* having clusters of white flowers and berries that turn from red to black. [It frequently grows along roadsides.]

way·lay (wā′lā′) *tr.v.* **-laid** (-lād′), **-laying, -lays. 1.** To lie in wait for and ambush. **2.** To stop and accost unexpectedly. **—way·lay·er** *n.*

way·leave (wā′lēv′) *n.* A right of way over or through land, as for the transport of goods or the running of a pipeline, that differs from an ordinary right of way in being granted to an applicant for a specific purpose. [WAY + LEAVE (permission).]

Wayne (wān), **Anthony,** known as "Mad Anthony" (1745–96). U.S. Revolutionary general. One of the colonies' boldest military leaders, he was involved in numerous campaigns, including the battles of Brandywine (1777) and Monmouth (1778). His seizure of Stony

waxbill *The small seed-eating waxbill is an African relative of the sparrow. Its nest is a frequent target of the whydah bird that lays its eggs there and leaves the waxbill to raise its young.*

waxwing *Berries are the favorite food of the waxwing, which breeds in the far north of Europe, Asia, and North America, but can move as far south as Mediterranean latitudes during the winter. The bird gets its name from the red blobs at the ends of some of its wing feathers; the blobs look like red sealing wax.*

wave power

MAKING USE OF THE OCEANS' PERPETUAL MOTION

Wave power may be a reliable source of "free" energy

As the world's oil and fossil fuel resources are depleted, nations are searching for cheap energy from renewable supplies. In certain maritime countries wave power seems to hold out real hope in an uncertain future.

In some parts of the oceans waves generate power more continuously than in others. The size of the waves depends on the wind—not only on its strength but also on the distance of open sea over which it is blowing. Where winds blow frequently in the same direction—as they do across the North Atlantic toward the coasts of Britain—their energy is stored and concentrated in powerful waves. In equatorial regions there is too little wind and in the polar regions there is too much ice for waves to build up. Only the areas between the latitudes 35° and 60° north and south can expect to benefit from wave power if it becomes a practical source of energy.

Wave power, where available, has some advantages over competing forms of renewable energy. The seas are rougher in winter, so more power is available when it is most needed, which is not the case with solar power. Wave power would also be more reliable than wind power, because the surface of the ocean is rarely motionless (less than one percent of the time), but the air does have long periods of calm. Although wave power promises much and does not require complex technology, there are still difficulties to be faced before it is applied.

One of the most promising devices being investigated is the Salter Duck, which is efficient enough to use 35 percent of the waves' energy; but it is estimated that a 2,000-megawatt-producing power unit of ducks (which would supply about one-twelfth of Britain's present annual need) would stretch for 30 kilometers (19 miles). The cost of building such huge machines and the difficulties of keeping them securely anchored and working reliably in greatly varying seas have meant that the capital cost of installing wave power makes it uneconomic.

THE BRISTOL OSCILLATING CYLINDER

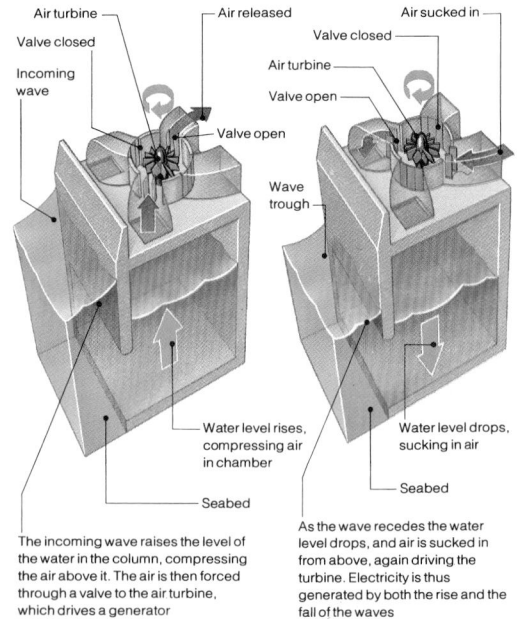

The Bristol Oscillating Cylinder bobs up and down on the waves; this motion is used by pumps on the seabed to suck in water and pump it at high pressure to a water turbine.

THE SALTER DUCK

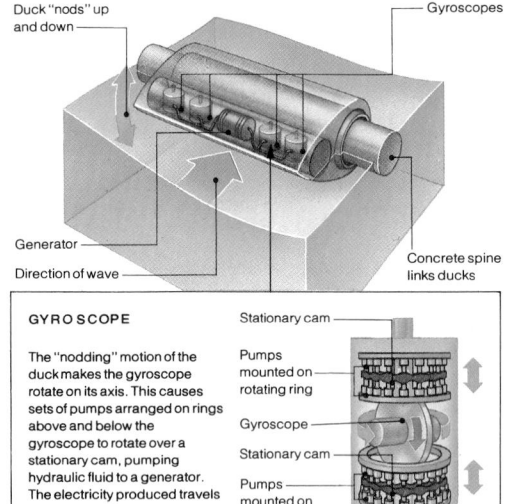

GYROSCOPE

The "nodding" motion of the duck makes the gyroscope rotate on its axis. This causes sets of pumps arranged on rings above and below the gyroscope to rotate over a stationary cam, pumping hydraulic fluid to a generator. The electricity produced travels through a cable to land

The nodding motion of the Salter Duck absorbs power from the waves more efficiently than most competitors, but it transfers that power through gyroscopes and pumps in a complex system whose reliability is so far unproved.

THE OSCILLATING WATER COLUMN

The incoming wave raises the level of the water in the column, compressing the air above it. The air is then forced through a valve to the air turbine, which drives a generator

As the wave recedes the water level drops, and air is sucked in from above, again driving the turbine. Electricity is thus generated by both the rise and the fall of the waves

The principle of the Oscillating Water Column was applied by the Japanese in the 1960's to illuminate small navigational buoys. Larger devices are now producing electricity and aiding research in both Japan and Britain.

Point, a British defense post (1779), displayed the tactical brilliance and audacity that gave rise to his nickname.

Wayne, John, born Marion Michael Morrison (1907–79). U.S. film actor. He was noted for his tough hero roles in classic westerns such as *Stagecoach* (1939), *Red River* (1948), and *True Grit* (1969), for which he won an Academy Award.

way·out (wā'out') *adj. Slang.* Strange or unconventional.

–ways *suffix.* Indicates way, manner, direction, or position; for example, **sideways.** [Middle English *-ways, -weys,* from *way(e)s, wey(e)s,* in (such) a way, Old English *weges,* adverbial genitive of *weg,* WAY.]

ways and means *pl.n.* **1.** Methods or resources that may be used to achieve a particular end. **2.** The methods of raising the revenue

needed to meet the expenditures of a country or state.

way·side (wā'sīd') *n.* The side or edge of a road. —**fall by the wayside.** To fail to continue; give up.
~*adj.* Near or at the edge of a road: *a wayside inn.*

way·ward (wā'wərd) *adj.* **1.** Wanting one's own way in spite of the advice or wishes of another; willful and headstrong. **2.** Swayed by caprice; unpredictable. —See Synonyms at **contrary, unruly.** [Middle English, short for *awayward,* turned away : AWAY + -WARD.] —**way·ward·ly** *adv.* —**way·ward·ness** *n.*

way·worn (wā'wôrn', -wōrn') *adj.* Wearied from traveling.

Wb *Physics.* weber.

WbN west by north.

WbS west by south.

w.c. **1.** water closet. **2.** without charge.
W/Cdr. Wing Commander.
we (wē) *pron.* The first person plural pronoun in the nominative case. **1.** Used to represent the speaker or writer and one or more others that share in the action of a verb. **2.** Sometimes used instead of *I* by a monarch or by an editor who purports to speak for a publication. **3.** *Informal.* Used in place of *you* in playful intimacy, especially with children, or in a patronizing manner: *Are we going to eat our cereal?* **4.** Often used to represent people in general: *We cannot see beyond the grave.* [Middle English *we,* Old English *wē.*]
Usage: The choice between *we* (nominative) and *us* (objective) is determined by the function served by these pronouns, and this is equally true when the terms are followed by nouns: *We students are entitled to a hearing. For us teachers, the choice is not easy. Let us visitors show respect for their customs.* See also Usage note at **me.**
weak (wēk) *adj.* **weaker, weakest. 1.** Lacking physical strength, energy, or vigor; feeble: *He was weak after his illness.* **2.** Liable to fail under pressure, stress, or strain; lacking resistance: *a weak link in a chain.* **3.** Lacking firmness of character, strength of will, or force of conviction. **4. a.** Lacking effectiveness or force; inadequate: *a weak defense.* **b.** Not easily defended or sustained: *in a weak bargaining position.* **5. a.** Lacking strength or intensity: *a weak voice.* **b.** Having a low concentration of an active or essential ingredient: *weak tea; a weak gin and tonic.* **6.** Lacking the capacity to function well or in a normal manner; unsound or easily upset: *a weak stomach; a weak heart.* **7.** Having or showing less than average ability, talent, or resources in a specified field: *a weak student; a weak batting line-up.* **8.** Based on or showing faulty logic, lack of coherence, or poor presentation; not persuasive or convincing: *a weak argument; a weak plot.* **9.** Incapable of the effective exercise of authority; lacking the power or political will to rule: *a weak government; weak leadership.* **10.** Lacking or deficient in a specified thing, as a quality or component. **11.** *Linguistics.* Of or designating those verbs in English and other Germanic languages that form a past tense by means of a dental suffix; for example, *start, started; have, had; bring, brought.* Compare **strong. 12.** *Phonetics.* Unstressed or unaccented. **13.** *Prosody.* Designating a verse ending having a final unstressed syllable. **14.** *Finance.* Marked by or showing lack of firmness and a falling tendency in prices or value: *a weak dollar.* [Middle English *waike, we(i)ke,* from Old Norse *veikr,* pliant, flexible.] **—weak·ly** *adv.*
Synonyms: *debilitated, decrepit, feeble, frail, infirm.*
weak·en (wē′kən) *v.* **-ened, -ening, -ens.** *—tr.* To make weak or weaker. *—intr.* To become weak or weaker. **—weak·en·er** *n.*
weak·fish (wēk′fĭsh′) *n., pl.* **-fishes** or collectively **weakfish.** Any of several marine food and game fishes of the genus *Cynoscion;* especially, *C. regalis,* of North American Atlantic waters. [Obsolete Dutch *weekvische, weekvis* : *week,* soft, WEAK (probably from its soft, fleshy mouth, which pulls very weakly on a line when caught) + Middle Dutch *visch, vis,* FISH.]
weak interaction *n.* A fundamental interaction between elementary particles that is some 10^{12} times weaker than the electromagnetic interaction and is responsible for some particle decay, for nuclear beta decay, and for neutrino emission and absorption. Compare **electromagnetic interaction, gravitational interaction, strong interaction.**
weak-kneed (wēk′nēd′) *adj.* Irresolute; timid.
weak·ling (wēk′lĭng) *n.* A person of weak constitution or character.
weak·ly (wēk′lē) *adj.* **-lier, -liest.** Delicate in health; sickly.
~adv. **1.** With little strength or force. **2.** With little strength of character.
weak-mind·ed (wēk′mīn′dĭd) *adj.* **1.** Irresolute; indecisive. **2.** Feeble-minded; foolish. **—weak-mind·ed·ness** *n.*
weak·ness (wēk′nĭs) *n.* **1. a.** The state or quality of being weak. **b.** An instance or display of this. **2.** A personal defect or failing. **3. a.** A special fondness or liking: *a weakness for chocolates.* **b.** Something for which one has an irresistible desire. —See Synonyms at **fault.**
weak sister *n. Slang.* A member of a group who is considered a weakling or an incompetent.
weal[1] (wēl) *n.* **1.** Prosperity; happiness: *in weal and woe.* **2.** The welfare of the community; the general good: *the public weal.* [Middle English *we(o)le,* Old English *we(o)la,* wealth, well-being.]
weal[2] *n.* A ridge on the flesh raised by a blow; a welt. [Variant (influenced by WHEAL) of WALE (ridge).]
weald (wēld) *n. British.* **1.** A woodland. **2.** An area of open rolling upland. [Middle English *weld(e), weeld,* Old English *weald,* variant of *wald,* WOLD.]
wealth (wĕlth) *n.* **1.** A great quantity of valuable material possessions or resources; riches. **2.** The state of being rich; affluence. **3.** A profusion or abundance: *a wealth of advice.* **4.** *Economics.* All goods and resources having economic value. [Middle English *welthe,* well-being, riches, from *wele,* WEAL (welfare).]
wealth·y (wĕl′thē) *adj.* **-ier, -iest. 1.** Prosperous; affluent. **2.** Marked by abundance. **—wealth·i·ly** *adv.* **—wealth·i·ness** *n.*
wean[1] (wēn) *tr.v.* **weaned, weaning, weans. 1.** To accustom (the young of a mammal) to solid food after a diet of mother's milk. **2.** To cause (a person) to give up something to which he is accustomed or devoted. [Middle English *wenen, wa(i)nen,* Old English *wenian,* to accustom, train, wean.]
wean[2] (wēn, wān) *British Regional. n.* A child. [Contraction of Scottish *wee ane,* wee one.]
wean·ling (wēn′lĭng) *n.* A recently weaned child or animal.
~adj. Recently weaned.
weap·on (wĕp′ən) *n.* **1.** An instrument or bodily part used as a means of attack or defense in combat. **2.** A means employed to disarm, persuade, or get the better of another.
~tr.v. **weaponed, -oning, -ons.** To supply with a weapon; arm. [Middle English *wepen, wepne,* Old English *wǣp(e)n,* from Germanic *wæpnam*† (unattested).]
weap·on·eer (wĕp′ə-nîr′) *n.* **1.** An individual who arms and otherwise prepares a nuclear weapon for release onto a target. **2.** An individual who designs or devises weapons, especially nuclear weapons. **—weap·on·eer·ing** *n.*
weap·on·ry (wĕp′ən-rē) *n.* **1.** Weapons collectively. **2.** The design and manufacture of weapons.
wear[1] (wâr) *v.* **wore** (wôr, wōr), **worn** (wôrn, wōrn), **wearing, wears.** *—tr.* **1.** To be dressed in or have on or about the body, as for clothing, adornment, or protection: *wearing a hat; must wear your seat belt; wore a delightful perfume.* **2.** To have or carry habitually on one's person: *wears glasses.* **3.** To affect or exhibit: *wear a smile.* **4.** To bear, carry, or maintain in a specified manner: *wears her hair long.* **5.** To fly or display (colors), as a ship, jockey, or knight does. **6.** To impair, consume, waste, efface, or erode by or as if by long or hard use, friction, or exposure to the elements. Often used with *away, down,* or *off: shoes worn down at the heels.* **7. a.** To produce by constant use, rubbing, or exposure: *They eventually wore hollows in the steps.* **b.** To bring to a specified condition through attrition or prolonged use: *pebbles worn smooth.* **8. a.** To fatigue; weary: *worn by the effort.* **b.** To diminish; exhaust: *His incessant criticism wore her patience.* *—intr.* **1. a.** To withstand the effects of use or activity: *fabric that wears well.* **b.** To withstand the effects of time and experience: *Those friendships wear best that are based on mutual understanding.* **2.** To be brought to a specified condition through attrition or prolonged use: *The gold ring has worn through; His excuses wore thinner over the years.* **3.** To pass gradually or tediously: *The hours wore on endlessly.* **—wear down.** To break down the resistance of by relentless pressure. **—wear off. 1.** To diminish gradually and vanish: *The pain wore off.* **2.** To become effaced; rub off: *The gilt soon wore off.* **—wear out. 1.** To make or become unusable through heavy use. **2.** To use up; consume: *She is wearing out her welcome.* **3.** To tire completely; exhaust.
~n. **1.** The act of wearing or state of being worn; use: *The coat has had heavy wear.* **2.** Clothing, especially of a specified kind or for a specified use: *men's wear; evening wear.* Often used in combination: *footwear; rainwear.* **3.** Gradual impairment, waste, or diminution from use or attrition: *signs of wear.* **4.** The capacity to withstand use; durability: *The engine has plenty of wear left.* [Middle English *wer(i)en,* Old English *werian,* wear, carry.] **—wear·a·bil·i·ty** *n.* **—wear·a·ble** *adj.* **—wear·er** *n.*
wear[2] (wâr) *v.* **wore** (wôr, wōr), **worn** (wôrn, wōrn), **wearing, wears.** *Nautical. —tr.* To make (a sailing ship) come about with the wind aft: *wear ship. —intr.* To come about with the stern to windward. [Earlier *weare*†.]
wear and tear *n.* Loss, damage, or depreciation resulting from ordinary use or exposure.
wea·ri·ful (wîr′ē-fəl) *adj.* **1.** Wearisome; tedious. **2.** Full of weariness. **—wea·ri·ful·ly** *adv.* **—wea·ri·ful·ness** *n.*
wea·ri·less (wîr′ē-lĭs) *adj.* Tireless. **—wea·ri·less·ly** *adv.* **—wea·ri·less·ness** *n.*
wear·ing (wâr′ĭng) *adj.* **1.** Intended to be worn: *wearing apparel.* **2.** Causing fatigue or wear; tiring: *a wearing day.* **—wear·ing·ly** *adv.*
wea·ri·some (wîr′ē-səm) *adj.* Causing exasperation or fatigue; tedious. **—wea·ri·some·ly** *adv.* **—wea·ri·some·ness** *n.*
wea·ry (wîr′ē) *adj.* **-rier, -riest. 1.** Exhausted, especially from prolonged exertion; fatigued. **2.** Expressive of or prompted by fatigue or resignation: *a weary smile.* **3.** Exhausted in patience, tolerance, spirit, or interest: *weary of his jibes.* **4. a.** Causing fatigue; exhausting. **b.** Irksome; tedious; wearisome. —See Synonyms at **tired.**
~v. **wearied, -rying, -ries.** *—tr.* To make weary; fatigue. *—intr.* To become weary; grow tired or exasperated. [Middle English *wery, weri(e),* Old English *wērig,* from Germanic *wōriga* (unattested).] **—wea·ri·ly** *adv.* **—wea·ri·ness** *n.*
wea·sand (wē′zənd) *n.* The gullet or throat. [Middle English *wesa(u)nt, wesand, wosen,* Old English *wāsend, wǣsend* (unattested), gullet, from West Germanic *wāsand-* (unattested).]
wea·sel (wē′zəl) *n.* **1.** Any of various small carnivorous mammals of the genus *Mustela,* having a slender body, a long tail, short legs, and brownish fur that in many species turns white in winter. **2.** A treacherous or sneaky person.
~intr.v. **weaseled, -seling, -sels.** To be evasive; equivocate. **—weasel out.** *Informal.* To back out of a situation or commitment in a sneaky or cowardly manner. [Middle English *wesele, wesill,* Old English *we(o)sule, wesle,* from West Germanic *wisulōn*† (unattested).] **—wea·sel·y** *adj.*
weasel word *n.* A word of an equivocal nature used to deprive a statement of its force or to evade a direct commitment. [Alluding to the weasel's supposed ability to suck up the contents of an egg without doing obvious damage to the shell.]
weath·er (wĕth′ər) *n.* **1.** The state of the atmosphere at a given time and place, described by specification of variables such as temperature, moisture, wind velocity, and pressure. **2. a.** The unpleasant or destructive effects of atmospheric conditions: *We must protect the house from the weather.* **b.** Violent conditions, such as high winds and heavy rain, at sea and in the air: *We flew into weather over the*

weasel *A slim, short-legged mammal that uses its acute hearing to hunt its prey of mice, frogs, and sometimes rabbits. Weasels, which are native to Eurasia and the Americas, are closely related to stoats. This is a European species,* Mustela nivalis.

PRONUNCIATION KEY

ă, pat; ā, pay; âr, care;
ä, father, are; b, bib;
ch, church; d, deed; ĕ, pet;
ē, be; f, fife; g, gag; h, hat;
hw, which; ĭ, pit; ī, pie;
îr, pier; j, judge; k, kick;
l, lid, needle; m, mum;
n, no, sudden; ng, thing;
ŏ, pot; ō, toe; ô, paw, for;
oi, noise; ou, out; o͝o, book;
o͞o, boot; p, pop; r, roar;
s, sauce; sh, ship, dish;
t, tight; th, thin, path;
th, this, bathe; ŭ, cut; ûr, fur;
v, valve; w, with; y, yes;
z, zebra, size; zh, vision;
ə, about, item, edible, gallop, circus, peaceful

IN FOREIGN WORDS:

à, *Fr.* ami; œ, *Fr.* feu, *Ger.* schön; ü, *Fr.* tu, *Ger.* über; KH, *Ger.* ich, *Scot.* loch; N, *Fr.* bon; y′, *Fr.* Compiègne

STRESS MARKS:

Primary stress: ′
in·cite′ (ĭn-sīt′)
Secondary stress: ′
in′sight′ (ĭn′sīt′)

weather

UNDERSTANDING A METEOROLOGICAL PHOTOGRAPH

Satellite pictures help to predict the weather

Weather prediction, or meteorology, has become more precise in the past decade with the development of satellite photography and computer techniques. Weather conditions can now be seen on photographs taken at high level and on which meteorological symbols have been superimposed.

Isobars are lines drawn between points of equal atmospheric pressure, in the way that contour lines on a map show areas of equal height. At the center of a high-pressure region, the weather is commonly warm and dry. At the center of a low-pressure region it is generally cool and rainy.

In the Northern Hemisphere, winds in a high-pressure area circulate in a clockwise direction. Winds in a low-pressure area circulate in a counterclockwise direction. The reverse applies in the Southern Hemisphere. Wind direction is marked on a weather map by arrows. The closer the isobars are together, the stronger will be the winds around the centers of pressure.

Boundaries between warm and cool air are called fronts. A warm front is where warm air is replacing cold air on the earth's surface; it is represented on a map by shaded semicircles along a line pointing in the direction in which the front is moving. A cold front is where cold air is replacing warm air and is represented by triangles on a line pointing in the direction of movement. A warm front brings a period of fairly steady rain; a cold front generally brings sharp showers with sunny intervals.

An occluded front is represented by alternating triangles and semicircles; it occurs where the temperature is fairly even at ground level but varies considerably at higher altitudes. This gives rise to cloud and frequently to rain.

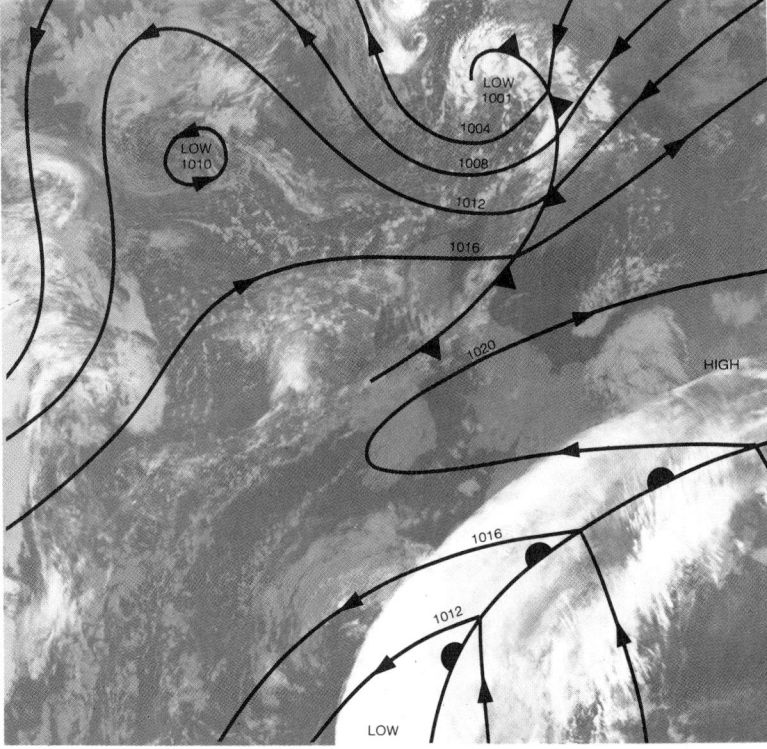

WEATHER SYMBOLS

〰️●〰️● Warm front   ▲▲▲▲ Cold front   ●▲●▲● Occluded front   ——→ Isobar
(arrow indicates direction of wind)

A COLD OCTOBER MORNING *This photograph was taken by a satellite at 9:09 A.M. (GMT) on October 16, 1981. The infrared process was used, so that the lighter images indicate lower temperatures. Thus the higher (therefore colder) clouds appear whiter than lower and warmer clouds. The ground temperature of the British Isles was close to freezing, the sea about 12°C (54°F), so the land appears paler than the sea.*

The brilliant white cloud mass in the bottom right of the picture is associated with a depression that had passed over southern Britain, causing *rain. The sharp edge of this cloud mass indicates a jet stream, or very strong winds, at about 9,000 meters (30,000 feet), while the winds at ground level were very light. The spirals of cloud north of Shetland (top center) and south of Iceland (top left) are small low-pressure centers.*

The band of cloud stretching from Norway to Northern Ireland is the remains of a decaying cold front. The cloud on the left edge of the picture is another depression, which brought gales and rain to northern Britain two days later. The numbers represent millibars of atmospheric pressure.

safely; survive: *weather a crisis.* **4.** To cause (a roof, for example) to slope so as to shed water. **5.** *Nautical.* To pass to windward of despite bad weather. —*intr.* **1.** To become discolored, disintegrate, or otherwise show the effects of exposure to the weather: *The cottage walls had weathered and mellowed.* **2.** To resist or withstand the effects of weather or adverse conditions. —*adj.* **1.** Of, pertaining to, or designating the side of a ship toward the wind; windward. **2.** Of, pertaining to, or used in weather forecasting. [Middle English *weder, wethyr,* Old English *weder.*]

weather balloon *n.* A balloon used to carry instruments aloft to gather meteorological data in the atmosphere.

weath·er·beat·en (wĕth′ər-bēt′n) *adj.* **1.** Worn by exposure to the weather. **2.** Tanned or coarsened from being outdoors.

weath·er·board (wĕth′ər-bôrd′, -bōrd′) *n.* **Clapboard** (see).

weath·er·board·ing (wĕth′ər-bôr′dĭng, -bōr′dĭng) *n.* Weatherboards collectively.

weath·er·bound (wĕth′ər-bound′) *adj.* Delayed, halted, or kept indoors by bad weather.

Weather Bureau *n.* A bureau of the U.S. Department of Commerce responsible for the gathering of meteorological data for weather forecasts and weather study.

weath·er·cast (wĕth′ər-kăst′, -käst′) *n.* A broadcast of weather conditions. —**weath·er·cast·er** *n.*

weath·er·cock (wĕth′ər-kŏk′) *n.* **1.** A weather vane in the form of a rooster. **2.** One that is fickle. —*intr.v.* **weathercocked, -cocking, -cocks.** To have a tendency to veer in the direction of the wind. Used of an aircraft or a missile.

weather deck *n.* The deck of a ship that is open to the sky.

weath·ered (wĕth′ərd) *adj.* **1.** Worn, stained, or warped by or as if by exposure to weather: *weathered shingles.* **2.** *Architecture.* Sloped to allow water to run off: *a weathered masonry joint.* —**weathered in.** Unable to fly because of adverse weather conditions.

weather eye *n.* An eye trained to recognize indications of weather changes. —**keep one's weather eye open.** To stay alert; keep on the lookout.

weather forecast *n.* A description of prevailing and expected weather conditions, as in a newspaper or a television broadcast. —**weather forecaster** *n.*

weath·er·glass (wĕth′ər-glăs′, -gläs′) *n.* A barometer or similar instrument used to indicate atmospheric conditions.

weath·er·ing (wĕth′ər-ĭng) *n.* Any of the chemical or mechanical processes by which rocks exposed to the weather decay to soil.

weath·er·ize (wĕth′ə-rīz′) *tr.v.* **-ized, -izing, -izes.** To protect (a building, for example) against cold weather, as by insulating.

weath·er·ly (wĕth′ər-lē) *adj. Nautical.* Capable of sailing close to the wind with little drift to leeward. —**weath·er·li·ness** *n.*

weath·er·man (wĕth′ər-măn′) *n., pl.* **-men** (-mĕn′). A person who makes weather forecasts, especially on radio or television.

weather map *n.* A map or chart depicting the meteorological conditions over a specific geographic area at a specific time.

weath·er·proof (wĕth′ər-pro͞of′) *adj.* Able to withstand exposure to weather without damage. —*tr.v.* **weatherproofed, -proofing, -proofs.** To make weatherproof.

weather ship *n.* An oceangoing vessel equipped to make meteorological observations.

weather station *n.* A station at which meteorological observations are gathered, recorded, and released.

weath·er·strip (wĕth′ər-strĭp′) *tr.v.* **-stripped, -stripping, -strips.** To fit or equip with weather stripping.

weather stripping *n.* **1.** A narrow piece of material, such as rubber, felt, or metal, installed around doors and windows to protect an interior from external extremes of temperature. **2.** Weather stripping collectively.

weather vane *n.* A vane for indicating wind direction.

weath·er·wise (wĕth′ər-wīz′) *adj.* Skilled in predicting shifts, as in the weather or public opinion.

weath·er·worn (wĕth′ər-wôrn′, -wōrn′) *adj.* Weather-beaten.

weave (wēv) *v.* **wove** (wōv) or **weaved, woven** (wō′vən) or *rare* **wove, weaving, weaves.** —*tr.* **1. a.** To make (cloth) by interlacing the threads of the weft and the warp on a loom. **b.** To interlace (threads) into cloth. **2.** To construct by interlacing or interweaving strips or strands of material: *weave a basket.* **3. a.** To interweave or combine (elements) into a whole: *He wove the incidents into a story.* **b.** To fashion or contrive (something complex or elaborate) in this way. **4.** To introduce (something new or contrasting) into a material or composition: *wove folk tunes into the symphony.* **5.** To spin (a web or cocoon, for example). Used of a spider or insect. **6.** To make (a path or way) by winding in and out or from side to side: *weave one's way through traffic.* —*intr.* **1. a.** To engage in weaving an article. **b.** To work at a loom. **2.** To move in and out or from side to side: *The dancers wove in and out of the trees. He was so drunk that he wove from side to side.* —*n.* The pattern, method of weaving, or construction of a fabric: *a twill weave; a loose weave.* [Weave, wove, woven; Middle English *weven, wo(o)f, woven* or *weven,* Old English *wefan, wæf, wefen.*]

weav·er (wē′vər) *n.* **1.** One who weaves, especially as an occupation. **2.** A weaverbird.

weav·er·bird (wē′vər-bûrd′) *n.* Any of various chiefly tropical Old World birds of the family Ploceidae, many of which build complex communal nests of intricately woven vegetation. Also called "weaver."

weaver's hitch *n. Nautical.* A knot, the **sheet bend** (see). Also called "weaver's knot."

Azores. —**make heavy weather of.** To exaggerate the difficulty of something to be done. —**under the weather.** *Informal.* **1.** Slightly indisposed; unwell. **2. a.** Drunk. **b.** Suffering from a hangover. —*v.* **weathered, -ering, -ers.** —*tr.* **1.** To expose to the action of the weather, as for drying, seasoning, or coloring. **2.** To discolor, disintegrate, wear, or otherwise affect by exposure. **3.** To pass through

web (wĕb) *n.* **1. a.** A textile fabric, especially one being woven on a loom or in the process of being removed from it. **b.** The structural part of cloth as distinguished from its pile or pattern. **2.** A latticed or woven structure; an interlacing of materials. **3.** A structure of threadlike filaments characteristically spun by spiders or certain insect larvae. **4.** Something intricately constructed; a complex or elaborate network, especially one designed to ensnare or deceive: *a web of lies.* **5.** A fold of skin or membranous tissue; especially, the membrane connecting the toes of certain water birds and mammals. **6.** The vane of a feather. **7.** *Architecture.* The surface between the ribs of a ribbed vault. **8.** A metal sheet or plate connecting the heavier sections, ribs, or flanges of a structural element. **9.** A thin metal plate or strip, as the bit of a key or the blade of a saw. **10.** A continuous roll of paper, such as newsprint, especially of the kind used in web presses.
∼*tr.v.* **webbed, webbing, webs. 1.** To provide with a web. **2.** To cover or envelop with a web. **3.** To ensnare in a web. [Middle English *web(be),* Old English *web(b).*] **—webbed** *adj.* **—web·by** *adj.*

Webb (wĕb), **Beatrice,** born Beatrice Potter (1858–1943). British socialist. In 1892 she married Sidney Webb, and together they helped found the *New Statesman* (1913), wrote many books, and worked for the advancement of socialism.

Webb, Sidney James, 1st Baron Passfield (1859–1947), British economist and socialist. He was one of the founders of the London School of Economics (1895). He and his wife, Beatrice Webb, helped found the Fabian Society (1884). Together they wrote *History of Trade Unionism* (1894) and *English Local Government* (1906–29).

web·bing (wĕb′ĭng) *n.* **1.** Sturdy cotton or nylon fabric woven in widths generally of from one to six inches, for use where strength is required, as for seat belts, brake lining, or upholstering. **2.** Something forming a web.

web·er (wĕb′ər) *n. Abbr.* **Wb** The SI System unit of magnetic flux equal to the magnetic flux that in linking a circuit of one turn produces in it an electromotive force of one volt as it is uniformly reduced to zero within one second. [After Wilhelm E. *Weber* (1804–91), German physicist.]

Web·er (vā′bər), **Carl Maria von** (1786–1826). German composer. He is best known for his opera *Der Freischütz* (1821), which was the first in the German romantic tradition.

Weber[1], **Max** (1864–1920). German social scientist. He was one of the founders of the modern analytical method of sociology. His works include *The Protestant Ethic and the Spirit of Capitalism* (1904) and *Methodology of the Social Sciences* (1904).

Weber[2], **Max** (1881–1961). U.S. artist, born in Russia. During a three-year visit to Europe (1905–08), he became acquainted with and influenced by the leading modernist painters. Upon his return to America, his work went unappreciated until late in his career, when his diverse paintings were recognized as pioneer works in American modern art.

Webern (vā′bərn), **Anton von** (1883–1945). Austrian composer. His works, which are characterized by brevity and tonal dissonance, include 2 symphonies and a concerto for nine instruments (1934).

web-foot·ed (wĕb′fo͝ot′ĭd) *adj.* Having feet with webbed toes.

web member *n.* Any of the structural elements connecting the top and bottom flanges of a lattice girder or the outside members of a truss.

web offset *n.* An offset method of printing using a web press.

web press *n.* A rotary printing press that prints on a continuous roll of paper.

web·ster (wĕb′stər) *n. Obsolete.* A weaver. [Middle English *web(e)ster,* Old English *webbestre,* feminine of *webba,* a weaver, from *webb,* a WEB.]

Web·ster (wĕb′stər), **Daniel** (1782–1852). U.S. politician. A U.S. congressman from New Hampshire (1813–17), he later moved to Massachusetts, which he represented as a congressman (1823–27) and senator (1827–41 and 1845–50). A noted orator who espoused preservation of the Union, he twice served as secretary of state (1841–43 and 1850–52), and sought the presidency in 1836 and 1852.

Webster, John (*c.* 1580–1634). English dramatist. His works include *The White Devil* (1612) and *The Duchess of Malfi* (*c.* 1613).

Webster, Noah (1758–1843). U.S. lexicographer and author. He is best known for his *American Dictionary of the English Language* (1828), which did much to standardize American spelling.

web·wheel (wĕb′hwēl′) *n.* **1.** A wheel in which the rim, spokes, and hub are cast or formed from one piece of metal. **2.** A spokeless wheel.

wed (wĕd) *v.* **wedded, wed** or **wedded, wedding, weds.** *—tr.* **1.** To take as husband or wife; marry. **2.** To perform the marriage ceremony for; join in matrimony. **3. a.** To join, unite, or associate. **b.** To cause to be indissolubly attached or devoted. Used chiefly in the passive: *wedded to socialism.* *—intr.* To take a husband or wife; marry. [Middle English *wedden,* Old English *weddian,* to engage (to do something), marry.]

we'd (wēd). Contraction of *we had, we should,* or *we would.*

Wed. Wednesday.

Wed·dell Sea (wĕd′l). Inlet of the South Atlantic, in western Antarctica, between Coats Land and the Antarctic Peninsula. The vast Ronne and Filchner ice shelves are at the head of the sea. It is named for James Weddell, a British navigator who claimed to have discovered the sea in 1823.

wed·ding (wĕd′ĭng) *n.* **1. a.** The act of marrying. **b.** The ceremony or celebration of a marriage. Also used adjectivally: *wedding guests.* **2.** The anniversary of a marriage: *a silver wedding.* **3.** A close association or union. —See Synonyms at **marriage.**

wedding cake *n.* A large decorated cake, often arranged in tiers, pieces of which are given to wedding guests and kept for absent friends and relations.

wedding ring *n.* A ring, often a plain gold band, given by one spouse to the other during the wedding ceremony.

wedge (wĕj) *n.* **1.** A piece of material such as metal or wood tapered in a solid V shape for insertion in a narrow crevice and used for splitting, tightening, securing, or levering. **2.** Something in the shape of a wedge: *a wedge of cheese.* **3.** A wedge-shaped formation, as in football or ground warfare. **4.** A tactic, event, policy, or idea that tends to divide or split associations of people. **5.** *Meteorology.* A region of relatively high atmospheric pressure in which the isobars are V-shaped. **6.** *Golf.* An iron with a very slanted face used to lift the ball, as from sand. **7.** Any of the triangular characters of cuneiform writing.
∼*v.* **wedged, wedging, wedges.** *—tr.* **1.** To split or force apart with or as if with a wedge. **2.** To tighten or fix in place with a wedge. **3.** To crowd, push, or force into a limited space. *—intr.* To become lodged or jammed like a wedge. [Middle English *wegge,* Old English *wecg,* a wedge, ingot of metal.]

wedg·ie (wĕj′ē) *n.* A shoe with a wedge-shaped heel joined to a half-sole so as to form a continuous undersurface. [Originally a trademark.]

Wedg·wood (wĕj′wo͝od′) *n.* A trademark for a type of pottery or china made by Josiah Wedgwood (1730–95) and his successors.

Wedgwood blue *n.* A clear pale or grayish blue, characteristically found as an unglazed background on Wedgwood pottery.

wed·lock (wĕd′lŏk′) *n.* The state of being married; matrimony. —See Synonyms at **marriage. —out of wedlock.** Of, to, or by parents not married to each other: *born out of wedlock.* [Middle English *wedlo(c)ke,* Old English *wedlāc,* "pledge-giving," marriage vow : *wedd,* a pledge + *-lāc,* suffix denoting activity.]

Wednes·day (wĕnz′dē, -dā′) *n. Abbr.* **W., Wed.** The day of the week following Tuesday; the third day of the working week. [Middle English *Wodnesday,* Old English *Wōdnesdæg,* "Woden's day" (translation of Latin *Mercurii diēs,* "day of Mercury").]

wee (wē) *adj.* **weer, weest. 1.** Very small; tiny. **2.** Very early: *in the wee hours of the night.*
∼*n. Scottish.* A short time; a little bit: *bide a wee.* [Middle English *we,* from *we(i),* a little, a small amount, Old English *wǣge,* a weight.]

weed[1] (wēd) *n.* **1. a.** A plant considered undesirable, unattractive, or troublesome; especially, one growing where it is not wanted in cultivated ground. **b.** A rank growth of weeds. **2.** Any of various usually common or abundantly growing plants. Usually used in combination: *chickweed.* **3.** A water plant, especially seaweed. **4.** The leaves or stems of a plant as distinguished from the seeds: *dill weed.* **5. a.** *Informal.* Tobacco. **b.** *Informal.* A cigarette. **c.** *Slang.* Marijuana. **6.** Something useless, detrimental, or worthless; especially, an animal unfit for breeding.
∼*v.* **weeded, weeding, weeds.** *—tr.* **1.** To remove weeds from; clear of weeds: *weed a flowerbed.* **2. a.** To remove (weeds). Usually used with *out: weed out dandelions.* **b.** To eliminate as unsuitable or unwanted. Usually used with *out: weed out unqualified applicants.* *—intr.* To remove weeds from a plot. [Middle English *weed,* Old English *wēod*†.] **—weed·er** *n.*

weed[2] *n.* **1.** A token of mourning, as a black band worn usually on the sleeve. **2. weeds.** A widow's mourning clothes. **3.** *Often* **weeds.** An article of clothing; garment. [Middle English *wede,* a garment, Old English *wǣd* and *wǣde,* a garment, from Germanic *wǣdhiz* (unattested).]

weed·kill·er (wēd′kĭl′ər) *n.* Any substance, such as a synthetic plant hormone, used to kill weeds.

weed·y (wē′dē) *adj.* **-ier, -iest. 1.** Full of or consisting of weeds. **2.** Resembling or characteristic of a weed. **3.** Of a thin, slight build; scrawny, spindly, or gawky. **—weed·i·ly** *adv.* **—weed·i·ness** *n.*

week (wēk) *n. Abbr.* **w., wk. 1. a.** A period of seven days: *a week of rain.* **b.** A seven-day calendar period, especially one starting with Sunday and continuing to the next Saturday: *this week.* **2. a.** A week designated by an event or holiday occurring within it: *Christmas week.* **b.** A week set aside for the honoring of a cause or institution: *Home Safety Week.* **3.** The part of a calendar week devoted to work, school, or business: *working a three-day week.* **4. a.** One week from a specified day: *I'll see you Friday week.* **b.** One week ago from a specified day: *It was Friday week that we last met.* [Middle English *wike, weke,* Old English *wice, wicu.*]

week·day (wēk′dā′) *n.* Any day of the week except Sunday and sometimes Saturday.

week·end (wēk′ĕnd′) *n.* The end of the week; Saturday and Sunday and often the period from Friday evening to the end of Sunday evening.
∼*adj.* **1.** Occurring or done on the weekend: *a weekend job.* **2.** For use on weekends: *a weekend cottage.*
∼*intr.v.* **weekended, -ending, -ends.** To spend the weekend.

week·end·er (wēk′ĕn′dər) *n.* **1.** A person who vacations or visits, especially habitually, on weekends. **2.** A small suitcase or bag for carrying clothing and toiletries for a weekend. **3.** *Australian.* A weekend or vacation cottage.

week·ly (wēk′lē) *adv.* **1.** Once a week. **2.** Every week. **3.** By the week.

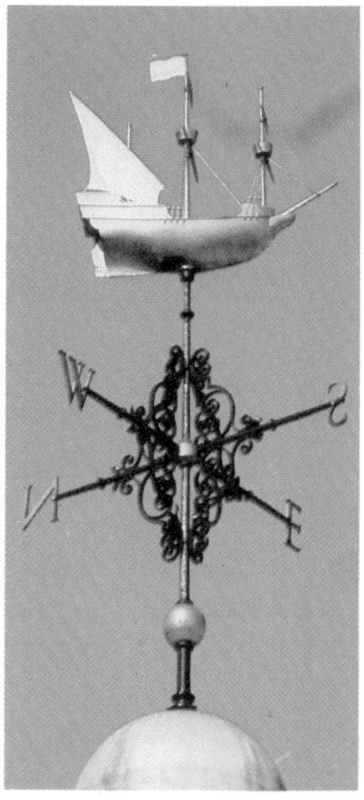

weather vane *A ship replaces the more usual rooster on this weather vane on top of London's Trinity House.*

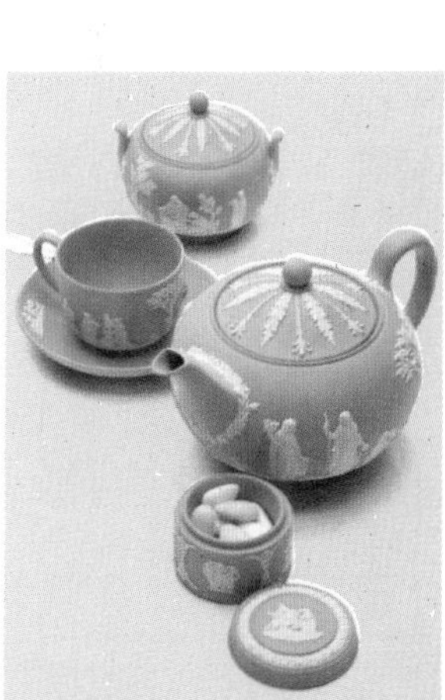

Wedgwood *Stoneware decorated with white classical figures is properly called Jasperware. It was developed in about 1774 by the British potter Josiah Wedgwood, and all genuine Jasperware carries the name Wedgwood. Jasperware is made in blue, green, lavender, yellow, and black, but it is the blue stoneware that is best known and has given rise to the term "Wedgwood blue."*

~*adj.* **1.** Occurring or done once a week or each week. **2.** Computed by the week.
~*n., pl.* **weeklies.** A publication issued once a week.
week·night (wēk′nīt′) *n.* The night or evening of a weekday.
Weems (wēmz), **Mason Locke,** known as "Parson Weems" (1759–1825). Clergyman, bookseller, and author. He is best known for a laudatory, fictionalized biography of George Washington, first published in 1800. In the fifth edition (1808) appeared the famous story about Washington chopping down the cherry tree with his hatchet. The book was a popular success and went through 29 editions before Weems's death.
ween (wēn) *tr.v.* **weened, weening, weens.** *Archaic.* To think; suppose. [Middle English *wenen,* Old English *wēnan,* from Germanic *wǣniz* (unattested), opinion.]
wee·ny (wē′nē) *adj.* **-nier, -niest.** *Informal.* Very small; tiny; wee. [Blend of WEE and TINY or TEENY.]
weep (wēp) *v.* **wept** (wĕpt), **weeping, weeps.** *—tr.* **1.** To mourn; lament, or bewail. **2.** To shed (tears). **3.** To bring to a specified condition by weeping: *She wept herself into a state of exhaustion.* **4.** To ooze, exude, or let fall (liquid or drops of liquid), as a wound or sore might. *—intr.* **1.** To express intense, usually painful emotion by shedding tears; shed tears. **2.** To mourn or grieve: *wept for the bereaved family.* **3.** To emit or run with drops of moisture. —See Synonyms at **cry.**
~*n. Often* **weeps.** A period or fit of weeping. [Middle English *we(o)pen,* Old English *wēpan.*]
weep·er (wē′pər) *n.* **1.** One that weeps. **2.** A hired mourner. **3.** A token of mourning, such as a black hatband or veil.
weep·ing (wē′pĭng) *adj.* Having slender, drooping branches: *a weeping fig.*
weeping willow *n.* A widely cultivated tree, *Salix babylonica,* native to China, having long, drooping branches and narrow leaves.
weep·y (wē′pē) *adj.* **-ier, -iest.** Prone to crying; tearful.
~*n., pl.* **weepies.** *British Informal.* A sentimental work of fiction, especially a film.
wee·ver (wē′vər) *n.* Any of several marine fishes of the family Trachinidae, having venomous spines. [Perhaps from Old French *wivre,* a serpent, viper, from Latin *vīpera,* VIPER.]
wee·vil (wē′vəl) *n. Zoology.* Any of numerous beetles, chiefly of the family Curculionidae, characteristically having a downward-curving snout, that are destructive to plants and stored plant products. Also called "snout beetle." [Middle English *wevel,* Old English *wifel,* a beetle.] **—wee·vil·y, wee·vil·ly** *adj.*

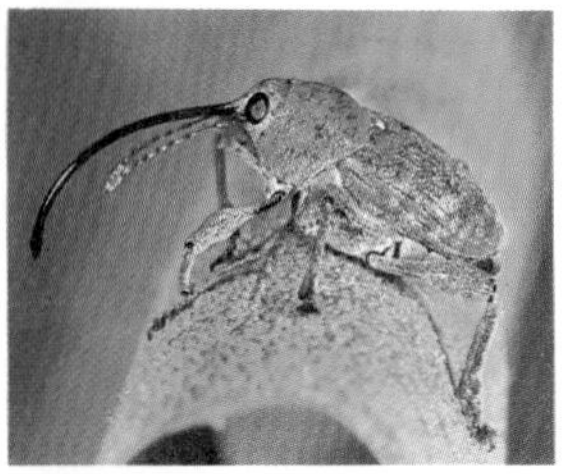

weevil *The 60,000 species of weevil make up the most widespread and numerous family of beetles. Many weevils feed on a single species or genus of plant, and most of their larvae feed on the internal tissues of roots, stems, or seeds, often causing considerable damage to crops.*

weft (wĕft) *n.* **1. a.** The horizontal threads interlaced through the warp in a woven fabric; filling; woof. **b.** Yarn to be used for the weft. **2.** Woven fabric. [Middle English *wefte, weft,* Old English *wefta, weft,* from Germanic *weft-* (unattested), from *webh-* (unattested), WEAVE.]
Wei (wā). Name of several Chinese dynasties (A.D. 220–65, 386–534, and 535–56).
wei·ge·la (wī-jē′lə, -gē′lə) *n.* Any of various shrubs of the genus *Weigela;* especially, *W. florida,* widely cultivated for its pink, white, or red flowers. [New Latin, after Christian E. *Weigel* (1748–1831), German physician.]
weigh[1] (wā) *v.* **weighed, weighing, weighs.** *—tr.* **1.** To determine the weight of by or as if by using a scale or balance: *weighs herself every morning.* **2.** To measure off, especially by using scales, an amount equal in weight to. Usually used with *out: weigh out a pound of cheese.* **3. a.** To balance in one's mind to determine the worth of; evaluate, consider, or compare: *weighed the alternatives and decided to take his friend's advice.* **b.** To choose carefully; deliberate over: *weigh one's words.* **4.** To cause to sag by the addition of weights or burdens; bend down: *apple trees weighed down with fruit.* **5.** *Nautical.* To raise (anchor). *—intr.* **1.** To have or be of a specific weight. **2.** To carry weight; be considered important or have influence; especially, to have a specific degree of importance or influence: *a fact that weighed heavily in his favor.* **3.** To be a burden; oppress. Used with *on* or *upon: His troubles weighed heavily on him.* **4.** *Nautical.* **a.** To raise anchor. **b.** To sail out of port. [Middle English *weghen, weien,* Old English *wegan,* to carry, balance in the scale, weigh.] **—weigh·a·ble** *adj.* **—weigh·er** *n.*
weigh[2] *n. Nautical.* Way. Used only in the phrase *under weigh.* [Variant (erroneously from the phrase *to weigh anchor*) of WAY.]
weigh·bridge (wā′brĭj′) *n.* A weighing machine that is flush with a road, has a metal platform, and is used for weighing heavy loads such as vehicles.
weigh in *intr.v.* **1.** To be weighed before or after a sports contest. **2.** To have a specified weight measured at a weigh-in: *weighed in at 100 pounds.* **3.** To have one's luggage weighed and checked, as before boarding an airplane. **4.** *Informal.* To enter as a participant, especially in order to contribute a telling point: *She weighed in with a few pertinent facts.*
weigh-in (wā′ĭn′) *n.* An act or instance of weighing in as a sports contestant, as a boxer before a fight or a jockey after a race.
weight (wāt) *n. Abbr.* **w., wt. 1.** A measure of the heaviness or mass of an object. **2.** The gravitational force exerted by the earth or another celestial body on an object, equal to the product of the object's mass and the local value of the acceleration of free fall. **3. a.** A unit measure of gravitational force: *a table of weights and measures.* **b.** A system of such measures: *avoirdupois weight; troy weight.* **4.** The measured heaviness of a specific object: *put a two-pound weight on the scale.* **5.** An object used principally to exert a force by virtue of its gravitational attraction to the earth, especially: **a.** A metallic solid used as a standard of comparison in weighing. **b.** An object used to hold something down. **c.** A counterbalance in a machine. **d.** A heavy object, as a dumbbell or a solid metal disk balanced on a crossbar, lifted for exercise or in athletic competition. **6.** *Mathematics.* One of a set of numbers assigned as multipliers to quantities to be averaged to indicate the relative importance of each quantity's contribution to the average. **7. a.** Something heavy; a load. **b.** Burden; oppressiveness; pressure: *the weight of responsibilities.* **8.** The greatest part or stress; preponderance: *the weight of evidence.* **9. a.** Influence, importance, or authority: *His opinions carried little weight with her.* **b.** Ponderous quality; significance: *the weight of his words.* **10.** A classification according to comparative lightness or heaviness. Usually used in combination: *a heavyweight boxer; a lightweight suit.* —See Synonyms at **importance. —by weight.** According to weight rather than volume or other measure. **—pull one's weight.** To do one's fair share. **—throw one's weight around (**or **about).** To make an aggressive show of one's importance.
~*tr.v.* **weighted, weighting, weights. 1.** To add heaviness to by or as if by attaching a weight; make heavy or heavier. **2.** To load down; burden. **3.** To treat (fabric) with chemical substances in order to give it body or extra weight. **4.** *Mathematics.* To assign a weight or weights to. **5.** To cause to have a particular bias or confer a particular advantage: *The entry procedure tends to be weighted in favor of university graduates.* **6.** To assign to (a horse) the weight it must carry as a handicap in a race. [Middle English *wighte, weit(e),* Old English *wiht, gewiht.*]
weight·less (wāt′lĭs) *adj.* **1.** Having little or no weight. **2.** Experiencing little or no gravitational force. **—weight·less·ly** *adv.* **—weight·less·ness** *n.*
weight·lift·ing (wāt′lĭf′tĭng) *n.* The lifting of heavy weights in a prescribed manner as an exercise or in athletic competition. **—weight·lift·er** *n.*
weight·y (wā′tē) *adj.* **-ier, -iest. 1.** Heavy; ponderous. **2.** Burdensome; oppressive. **3.** Of great consequence; momentous: *weighty decisions.* **4.** Carrying weight, as: **a.** Forceful; efficacious: *a weighty argument.* **b.** Authoritative; influential. —See Synonyms at **heavy. —weight·i·ly** *adv.* **—weight·i·ness** *n.*
Wei Ho (wā′ hō′). River of China, rising in western Gansu province and flowing *c.* 725 kilometers (450 miles) generally east to the Huang He (Yellow River). Its wide, alluvial valley was the site of some of the earliest centers of Chinese civilization.
Weill (wīl, vīl), **Kurt** (1900–50). German composer. He collaborated with Bertolt Brecht on *The Threepenny Opera* (1928) and *The Rise and Fall of the City of Mahagonny* (1927).
Wei·mar (vī′mär′). City of Erfurt district, southwestern East Germany, on the Ilm River. It was a cultural center during the 18th and 19th centuries. Weimar was the capital of Saxe-Weimar-Eisenach (1815–1918) and was where the constitution of the Weimar Republic (1918–33), the name of the German Republic, was drawn up. The republic was overthrown by Hitler.
Wei·mar·an·er (vī′mə-rä′nər, wī′-) *n.* A large dog of a breed originating in Germany, having a smooth grayish coat. [German, from WEIMAR.]
weir (wîr) *n.* **1.** A dam placed across a river or canal to raise or divert the water, as for a millrace, or to regulate the flow. **2.** A fence or wattle placed in a stream to catch or retain fish. [Middle English *wer(r)e,* Old English *wer.*]
weird (wîrd) *adj.* **weirder, weirdest. 1.** Suggestive of or concerned with the supernatural; unearthly; eerie; uncanny. **2.** Of an odd and inexplicable character; unusual; bizarre; fantastic. **3.** *Archaic.* Of or pertaining to fate or the Fates.
~*n. Scottish & Archaic.* **1.** Fate; destiny. **2.** One's assigned lot or fortune; kismet. [Middle English *werde, wirde,* having power to control fate, from *wird, werd,* fate, destiny, Old English *wyrd.*] **—weird·ly** *adv.* **—weird·ness** *n.*
Synonyms: *eerie, uncanny, unearthly.*
weird·o (wîr′dō) *n., pl.* **-oes.** Also **weird·ie** (-dē). *Slang.* An unusually strange or eccentric person.
Weiss (vīs), **Peter** (1916–82). Swedish author, born in Germany. His works include *The Persecution and Assassination of Marat* (1964) and *The Investigation* (1965).
Weiss·mul·ler (wīs′mŭl′ər), **Johnny** (1903–84). U.S. swimmer and actor. During a remarkable competitive swimming career, he amassed 52 national championships, 3 Olympic gold medals, and set 67 world records. After retiring from athletics, he played Tarzan in 19 jungle adventure films.
Weiz·mann (vīts′mən), **Chaim Azriel** (1874–1952). Israeli statesman and chemist, born in Russia. He was the first president of Israel (1949–52).
wek·a (wĕk′ə) *n.* A flightless bird, *Gallirallus australis,* of New Zealand, having brown, mottled plumage. [Maori.]
welch. Variant of **welsh.**
Welch. *Archaic.* Variant of **Welsh.**
wel·come (wĕl′kəm) *adj.* **1.** Received with pleasure and hospitality into one's company or home: *a welcome guest.* **2.** Agreeable or gratifying: *a welcome respite.* **3.** Cordially permitted or invited, as to do or enjoy: *You're welcome to join us.* **4.** Freely granted one's courtesy. Used to acknowledge an expression of gratitude, usually in the exchange "Thank you!" "You're welcome!"
~*n.* **1.** A cordial greeting to or reception of an arriving person. **2.** The state of being welcome: *Don't outstay your welcome.* **3.** A greeting or reception of a particular kind: *an unfriendly welcome.*

~*tr.v.* **welcomed, -coming, -comes. 1.** To greet, receive, or entertain cordially or hospitably. **2.** To receive or accept gladly: *welcome a little privacy.*
~*interj.* Used to express a cordial welcome to a visitor or recent arrival. [Middle English *welcume,* alteration (by influence of WELL and of Old French *bien venu*) of Old English *wilcuma,* a welcome guest, and *wilcume,* the greeting of welcome : *wil-,* pleasure + *cuma,* comer.] **—wel·come·ly** *adv.* **—wel·come·ness** *n.* **—wel·com·er** *n.*

weld¹ (wĕld) *v.* **welded, welding, welds.** *—tr.* **1. a.** To join (metals) by applying heat, sometimes with pressure and sometimes with an intermediate or filler metal having a high melting point. **b.** To produce by welding. **2.** To bring into close association; bring together as a unit. *—intr.* To be capable of being welded.
~*n.* **1.** The union of two metal parts by welding. **2.** The joint so formed. [Variant (influenced by past tense and past participle *welled*) of WELL (to pour forth, in the obsolete sense "to weld").] **—weld·a·ble** *adj.* **—weld·a·bil·i·ty —weld·er** *n.*

weld² *n.* **1.** A plant, the **dyer's rocket** *(see).* **2.** The yellow dye obtained from this plant. [Middle English *welde, wold,* Old English *wealde, walde* (unattested).]

wel·fare (wĕl′fâr′) *n.* **1. a.** Health, happiness, and general well-being. **b.** Prosperity. **2.** Welfare work. **3.** The provision of economic or social benefits, especially by the government or by a private agency, to people, as the needy or disabled, in need of assistance; relief. [Middle English *welfare,* well-being, from the phrase *wel faren,* to fare well, Old English *wel faran* : *wel,* WELL + *faran,* to go, FARE.]

welfare state *n.* **1.** A social system whereby a state assumes primary responsibility for the welfare of its citizens, as by means of government-run health and social-security plans. **2.** A nation characterized by its adoption of the welfare system.

welfare work *n.* Organized efforts, especially on the part of a government or a charitable agency, to improve the social and economic conditions of the poor and other disadvantaged members of society.

wel·far·ism (wĕl′fâr′ĭz′əm) *n.* The set of policies, practices, and social attitudes associated with a welfare state.

Welk (wĕlk), **Lawrence** (1903–). U.S. musician and bandleader. He formed his own band in 1927 and steadily gained popularity in the Big Band Era of the late 1930's to early 1950's. Welk appeared on network television and later syndicated television for some 30 years after 1955. He was widely known for his accordion playing, his Champagne Music, and his exuberant manner, including his high-stepping polkas.

wel·kin (wĕl′kĭn) *n. Archaic.* **1.** The vault of heaven; the sky: *make the welkin ring.* **2.** The upper air. [Middle English *w(e)olcne, welken,* a cloud, the sky, firmament, Old English *wolc(e)n.*]

well¹ (wĕl) *n.* **1.** A deep hole or shaft dug or drilled to obtain water, oil, gas, or brine. **2.** A cavity or space resembling a well in shape or function, as an inkwell. **3.** An open space extending vertically through the floors of a building, as for stairs or ventilation. **4.** An enclosure in a ship's hold for the pumps. **5.** A cistern with a perforated bottom in the hold of a fishing vessel for keeping fish alive. **6.** *British.* The central space in a law court, directly in front of the judge's bench, where the counsel or solicitor sits. **7. a.** A spring or fountain. **b.** A mineral spring. **c. wells.** A watering place; a spa. **8.** A source to be drawn upon: *a well of information.*
~*v.* **welled, welling, wells.** *—intr.* **1.** To rise to the surface, ready to flow: *Tears welled in her eyes.* **2.** To rise or surge from an inner source: *She felt anger welling up in her.* *—tr.* To pour forth. [Middle English *well(e), walle,* Old English *wælla, well, wiella.*]

well² *adv.* **better** (bĕt′ər), **best** (bĕst). **1.** In an adequate manner; satisfactorily: *The interview went quite well.* **2. a.** In a good or proper manner; with skill: *sing well.* **b.** With care or attention: *Listen well to what I tell you.* **3.** In a comfortable or affluent manner: *live well.* **4.** In a manner affording benefit or gain; advantageously: *married well.* **5. a.** With reason or propriety; reasonably: *I can't very well say no.* **b.** In all likelihood; indeed: *You may well need your umbrella.* **6.** In a sensible manner; prudently: *You would do well to say nothing.* **7.** Closely or familiarly; intimately: *I know him well.* **8.** In a kindly or approving manner; favorably: *speak well of him.* **9.** Thoroughly; completely: *well cooked.* **10.** Entirely; fully: *well worth seeing.* **11.** To a considerable or suitable extent or degree: *I'm well pleased.* **12.** To a considerable degree; far: *I was ready well in advance of the deadline.* ***Note:*** The adverb *well* combines with many adjectives, usually derived from the participles of verbs, to form attributive modifiers before nouns: *a well-regulated life; a well-read woman.* In such use the elements are joined with a hyphen. However, when *well* modifies an adjective used predicatively, the two words are usually written separately: *His life was well regulated. The woman is well read.* **—as well. 1.** In addition; also. **2.** With equal or better effect: *I might as well go.* **—as well as.** In addition to; moreover. **—in well with.** In a position to influence or be favored by: *in well with the management.* **—pretty well.** Nearly; almost: *We had pretty well finished dinner.* **—well and truly.** Completely; absolutely.
~*adj.* **1.** In a satisfactory state or circumstances; right or proper: *We were worried, but all is well now.* **2. a.** In good health; not ailing or diseased: *She's not a well woman.* **b.** Cured or healed, as a wound: *His broken arm is well again.* **3. a.** Advisable; prudent: *It would be well not to ask.* **b.** Being a ground for gratitude; fortunate: *It is well that you stayed.* —See Synonyms at **healthy. —leave well enough alone.** To refrain from meddling with what is satisfactory.
~*interj.* **1.** Used to express surprise. **2.** Used to introduce a remark, resume a narrative, or simply to gain time to collect one's thoughts. [Middle English *wel(e), well,* Old English *wel.*]
Usage: *As well as,* in the sense "in addition to," does not have the force of *and,* and therefore a singular noun preceding *as well as* continues to govern a singular verb: *The parent firm as well as its subsidiary was named in the indictment.* A plural verb is sometimes casually used but is not generally acceptable.

well-ad·vised (wĕl′əd-vīzd′) *adj.* **1.** Acting or proceeding in a sensible manner; prudent. **2.** Showing careful thought; considered: *a well-advised decision.*

Wel·land Ship Canal (wĕl′ənd). An artificial waterway, 44 kilometers (28 miles) long, connecting Lake Ontario with Lake Erie and by-passing Niagara Falls. Built between 1914 and 1932, it can accommodate the largest lake ships. It is part of the St. Lawrence Seaway system.

well-ap·point·ed (wĕl′ə-poin′tĭd) *adj.* Properly furnished and equipped: *a well-appointed apartment.*

we'll (wēl). Contraction of *we will* and *we shall.*

well·a·way (wĕl′ə-wā′) *interj.* Also **well·a·day** (-dā′). *Archaic.* Alas! Woe is me!
~*n., pl.* **wellaways.** Also **well·a·day.** *Archaic.* A lamentation. [Middle English *weilawey, wellaway,* Old English *wei lā wei,* variant (influenced by Old Norse *vei,* woe) of *wā lā wā* : *wā,* woe + *lā,* LO + *wā,* woe.]

well-bal·anced (wĕl′băl′ənst) *adj.* **1.** Evenly proportioned, balanced, or regulated. **2.** Mentally stable; sensible; sane.

well-be·ing (wĕl′bē′ĭng) *n.* The state of being healthy, happy, or prosperous; welfare.

well-born (wĕl′bôrn′) *adj.* Coming of good stock; especially, born of a noble family.

well-bred (wĕl′brĕd′) *adj.* **1.** Of good upbringing; well-mannered; refined. **2.** Of good breed or pedigree. Said of an animal.

well-built (wĕl′bĭlt′) *adj.* Soundly built; especially, shapely and muscular.

well-cho·sen (wĕl′chō′zən) *adj.* Carefully chosen for a deliberate effect: *well-chosen words.*

well-con·nect·ed (wĕl′kə-nĕk′tĭd) *adj.* Connected with and especially related to influential people.

well-dis·posed (wĕl′dĭ-spōzd′) *adj.* Disposed to be kindly, friendly, or sympathetic.

well-done (wĕl′dŭn′) *adj.* **1.** Cooked all the way through: *a well-done steak.* **2.** Satisfactorily or properly accomplished.

well-earned (wĕl′ûrnd′) *adj.* Fully deserved.

Welles (wĕlz), **(George) Orson** (1915–85). American actor and film director. He starred in and directed *Citizen Kane* (1940). His other films include *The Magnificent Ambersons* (1942), *The Third Man* (1949), *The Trial* (1962), and *Catch-22* (1970).

well-fa·vored (wĕl′fā′vərd) *adj.* Attractive; comely; handsome.

well-fixed (wĕl′fĭkst′) *adj. Informal.* Financially secure; well-to-do.

well-formed (wĕl′fôrmd′) *adj.* **1.** Having a good shape or attractive form. **2.** Properly constituted according to a set of logical or grammatical rules: *a well-formed sentence.*

well-found (wĕl′found′) *adj.* Properly furnished or equipped.

well-found·ed (wĕl′foun′dĭd) *adj.* Based on sound judgment, reasoning, or evidence; substantiated well.

well-groomed (wĕl′gro͞omd′, -gro͝omd′) *adj.* **1.** Attentive to personal appearance; neat. **2.** Carefully tended or curried: *a well-groomed horse.* **3.** Trim and tidy: *well-groomed hair.*

well-ground·ed (wĕl′groun′dĭd) *adj.* **1.** Adequately versed in a subject; having a sound basic knowledge. **2.** Having a sound basis; well-founded.

well-han·dled (wĕl′hăn′dld) *adj.* **1.** Managed well. **2.** Showing signs of much handling.

well·head (wĕl′hĕd′) *n.* **1.** The source of a well or stream. **2.** The top of a structure built over a well, especially an oil well. **3.** A principal source or fountainhead.

well-heeled (wĕl′hēld′) *adj. Slang.* Having plenty of money.

well-in·formed (wĕl′ĭn-fôrmd′) *adj.* **1.** Informed on a wide variety of subjects, especially on current news and events. **2.** Very well versed on a particular subject.

Wel·ling·ton (wĕl′ĭng-tən). Capital of New Zealand, on Cook Strait on the southern coast of North Island. It was founded in 1840 and has been the seat of government since 1865. Surrounded by mountains, it is a port exporting dairy produce, wool, and meat and has engineering, textiles, soap, and brick industries.

Wellington, Arthur Wellesley, 1st Duke of, known as "the Iron Duke" (1769–1852). British soldier and statesman. He commanded the British army during the Peninsular War, defeating the Napoleonic forces in Spain in 1813 and invading France in 1814. He defeated Napoleon at the Battle of Waterloo (1815), which finally ended the Napoleonic Wars. As prime minister (1828–30) he passed the Catholic Relief Bill (1829) but opposed the Reform Bill (1831–32).

Wellington boot *n.* **1.** A calf- or knee-length waterproof, rubber, or rubberized boot. Also called "gumboot." **2.** A leather boot extending to the top of the knee in front but cut lower at the back. [After the 1st Duke of WELLINGTON.]

wel·ling·ton·i·a (wĕl′ĭng-tō′nē-ə) *n.* A redwood tree, the **giant sequoia** *(see).* [After the 1st Duke of WELLINGTON.]

well-in·ten·tioned (wĕl′ĭn-tĕn′shənd) *adj.* **1.** Well-meant. **2.** Well-meaning.

well-knit (wĕl′nĭt′) *adj.* Strongly knit, especially strongly and firmly constructed: *a well-knit story.*

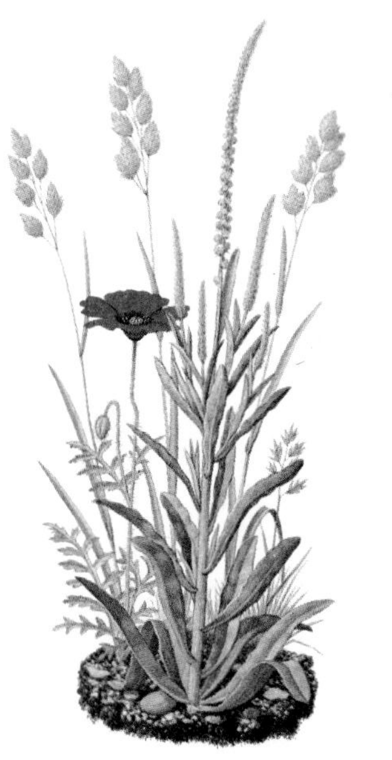

weld *This wildflower, more commonly called dyer's rocket, was once cultivated for a deep butter-colored dye that was squeezed from its flowers and used in the woolen industry. It is shown here growing in front of a poppy and several grasses.*

PRONUNCIATION KEY

ă, pat; ā, pay; âr, care;
ä, father, are; b, bib;
ch, church; d, deed; ĕ, pet;
ē, be; f, fife; g, gag; h, hat;
hw, which; ĭ, pit; ī, pie;
îr, pier; j, judge; k, kick;
l, lid, needle; m, mum;
n, no, sudden; ng, thing;
ŏ, pot; ō, toe; ô, paw, for;
oi, noise; ou, out; o͝o, book;
o͞o, boot; p, pop; r, roar;
s, sauce; sh, ship, dish;
t, tight; th, thin, path;
th, this, bathe; ŭ, cut; ûr, fur;
v, valve; w, with; y, yes;
z, zebra, size; zh, vision;
ə, about, item, edible,
gallop, circus, peaceful

IN FOREIGN WORDS:

à, *Fr.* ami; œ, *Fr.* feu, *Ger.* schön; ü, *Fr.* tu, *Ger.* über;
KH, *Ger.* ich, *Scot.* loch;
N, *Fr.* bon; y′, *Fr.* Compiègne

STRESS MARKS:

Primary stress: ′
in·cite′ (ĭn-sīt′)
Secondary stress: ′
in′sight′ (ĭn′sīt′)

well-known (wĕl′nōn′) *adj.* **1.** Widely known; familiar or famous. **2.** Fully known.

well-man·nered (wĕl′măn′ərd) *adj.* Polite; courteous.

well-mean·ing (wĕl′mē′nĭng) *adj.* Having or prompted by good intentions, though often with unhappy consequences: *a well-meaning but incompetent effort to help.*

well-meant (wĕl′mĕnt′) *adj.* Kindly or honestly intended.

well-nigh (wĕl′nī′) *adv.* Nearly; almost.

well-off (wĕl′ôf′, -ŏf′) *adj.* **1.** In fortunate circumstances. **2.** Wealthy; prosperous. **3.** Adequately provided.

well-oiled (wĕl′oild′) *adj. British Informal.* Drunk.

well-pre·served (wĕl′prĭ-zûrvd′) *adj.* Not seeming or looking old: *had a well-preserved face without wrinkles.*

well-read (wĕl′rĕd′) *adj.* Knowledgeable through having read extensively.

well-round·ed (wĕl′roun′dĭd) *adj.* **1.** Apt and complete: *a well-rounded speech.* **2.** Plump and pleasantly curving; shapely: *a well-rounded figure.* **3. a.** Marked by breadth, fullness, and variety: *a well-rounded education.* **b.** Having a broad, full, and varied background and education.

Wells (wĕlz). City of Somerset, southwest England, at the foot of the Mendips. It is known for its cathedral (12th–13th century) with its carved west front and for its medieval city walls.

Wells, Herbert George, known as "H.G. Wells" (1866–1946). British novelist. He won success with science-fiction works such as *The Time Machine* (1895). His concern for social and political issues was expressed in comic novels such as *The History of Mr. Polly* (1910) and in later theoretical works such as *The Outline of History* (1920).

well-spo·ken (wĕl′spō′kən) *adj.* **1.** Having an educated, socially acceptable way of speaking. **2.** Chosen or expressed with aptness or propriety.

well·spring (wĕl′sprĭng′) *n.* **1.** The source of a stream or spring; a fountainhead. **2.** An abundant source or supply: *a wellspring of ideas.*

well-tem·pered (wĕl′tĕm′pərd) *adj. Music.* Adjusted to or conforming to the system of equal temperament. Said of a musical instrument.

well-thought-of (wĕl′thôt′ŭv′, -ŏv′) *adj.* Respected; esteemed.

well-thought-out (wĕl′thôt-out′) *adj.* Carefully considered or devised.

well-thumbed (wĕl′thŭmd′) *adj.* Showing signs of frequent use. Said of a book.

well-tim·bered (wĕl′tĭm′bərd) *adj.* Covered with a good amount of growing timber: *well-timbered land.*

well-timed (wĕl′tīmd′) *adj.* Occurring or done at an opportune time: *a well-timed arrival.*

well-to-do (wĕl′tə-dōō′) *adj.* Prosperous; affluent; well-off. —*n.* Used with a plural verb. Persons who are well-to-do: *Only the well-to-do can afford such a house.* [From the phrase *to do well.*]

well-tried (wĕl′trīd′) *adj.* Thoroughly tested; of proven value.

well-turned (wĕl′tûrnd′) *adj.* **1.** Shapely: *a well-turned ankle.* **2.** Concisely or aptly expressed: *a well-turned phrase.*

well-wish·er (wĕl′wĭsh′ər) *n.* A person who wishes another well; one who extends good wishes. —**well-wish·ing** *adj. & n.*

well-worn (wĕl′wôrn′, -wōrn′) *adj.* **1.** Showing signs of much wear or use: *a well-worn sweater.* **2.** Repeated too often; trite; hackneyed: *a well-worn joke.*

Weis·bach burner (wĕlz′băk′, -bäk′) *n.* A trademark for a gauze mantle impregnated with cerium and thorium compounds and used with a gas burner that becomes incandescent when heated, producing light. [After Baron Carl Auer von Welsbach (1858–1929), Austrian chemist.]

welsh (wĕlsh, wĕlch) *intr.v.* **welshed, welshing, welshes.** Also **welch** (wĕlch) **welched, welching, welches.** *Slang.* **1.** To swindle a person by not paying a debt or wager. **2.** To fail to fulfill an obligation: *welsh on a promise.* [19th century : origin obscure.] —**welsh·er** *n.*

Welsh (wĕlsh) *adj.* Also *archaic* **Welch.** *Abbr.* **W.** Of or pertaining to Wales, its people, its language, or its culture. —*n.* **1.** Used with a plural verb. The people of Wales. **2.** The Celtic language of Wales. [Middle English *Wal(i)sche,* Old English *Wǣlisc, Wel(i)sc,* from *W(e)alh,* a Welshman, from Germanic *walhaz* (unattested), foreign, from Latin *Volcae,* name of a Celtic people.]

Welsh corgi *n.* A corgi *(see).*

Welsh dresser *n.* A dresser consisting of a set of open shelves on top of a sideboard or set of cupboards. [Originally made and used in Wales.]

Welsh·man (wĕlsh′mən) *n., pl.* **-men** (-mĭn). A native of Wales.

Welsh onion *n.* A perennial plant, *Allium fistulosum,* originally from Siberia, bearing globose clusters of yellowish-white flowers on a swollen hollow stem.

Welsh poppy *n.* A poppy, *Meconopsis cambrica,* with large yellow flowers.

Welsh rabbit *n.* A dish made of melted cheese, milk or cream, seasonings, and sometimes ale, served over toast or crackers. [A fanciful culinary term.]

Welsh rare·bit (râr′bĭt) *n.* Welsh rabbit.

Welsh springer spaniel *n.* See **springer spaniel.**

Welsh terrier *n.* A terrier of a breed originating in Wales, having a wiry black-and-tan coat and resembling a small Airedale.

welt (wĕlt) *n.* **1.** A strip of leather or other material stitched into a shoe between the sole and the upper. **2.** A strip of material, such as tape or covered cord, sewn into a seam as reinforcement or trim-

Wensleydale *The rams of this prolific English breed of sheep are often crossed with other breeds. Wensleydales grow into large animals with a heavy fleece of long, curly wool.*

ming; welting. **3. a.** A ridge or bump raised on the skin by a lash or blow or sometimes by an allergic disorder; a weal. **b.** A lash or blow producing such a mark. —*tr.v.* **welted, welting, welts. 1.** To reinforce or trim with a welt or welting. **2.** To beat severely; flog. **3.** To raise a welt or welts on. [Middle English *welte, walt,* perhaps Old English *wealt†, waelt* (both unattested).]

Welt·an·schau·ung (vĕlt′än′shou′ŏŏng) *n., pl.* **-ungs** or **-ungen** (-ŏŏng-ən). *German.* A comprehensive world view or philosophy of life, especially from a particular standpoint. [German, literally "world view."]

wel·ter (wĕl′tər) *intr.v.* **-tered, -tering, -ters. 1.** To writhe, roll, or wallow, as in mud or high seas. **2.** To lie soaked in a liquid, as blood. **3.** To be deeply immersed or involved in something. **4.** To roll and surge, as the sea does. —*n.* **1.** Turbulence; tossing: *"bright welter of wave-cords"* (Ezra Pound). **2. a.** A state of upheaval or turmoil. **b.** A confused mass; a jumble: *a welter of papers and magazines.* [Middle English *welteren,* perhaps from Middle Dutch.]

wel·ter·weight (wĕl′tər-wāt′) *n.* **1. a.** An amateur boxer weighing between 135 and 145 pounds (63.5 and 66 kilograms). **b.** A professional boxer weighing between 135 and 147 pounds (63.5 and 66.5 kilograms). **2.** A wrestler weighing between 150 and 163 pounds (68 and 74 kilograms). [19th century *welter†,* heavyweight horseman or boxer + WEIGHT.]

welt·ing (wĕl′tĭng) *n.* Material, such as a cord or strip, used to welt a seam.

Welt·schmerz (vĕlt′shmĕrts′) *n.* Sadness over the evils of the world, especially as an expression of romantic pessimism. [German, "world pain."]

Wel·ty (wĕl′tē), **Eudora** (1909–). U.S. author. Renowned for her revealing stories of rural Southern life, she wrote several short novels, including *Delta Wedding* (1946), but her reputation rests primarily on her numerous short stories, published in collections such as *The Golden Apples* (1949) and *The Optimist's Daughter* (1972).

wel·witsch·i·a (wĕl-wĭch′ē-ə) *n.* A gymnosperm plant, *Welwitschia mirabilis,* of desert regions of southwestern Africa, having a short, upright, mainly underground stem, two straplike leaves, and flowers in conelike arrangements. [After F.M.J. *Welwitsch* (1807–72), Austrian-born Portuguese botanist.]

wen¹ (wĕn) *n.* A cyst containing sebaceous matter, especially one on the scalp. [Middle English *wenne, wen,* Old English *wen(n), wæn(n).*]

wen² *n.* An Old English runic letter represented by Modern English *w.* [Old English *wen,* variant of *wyn(n),* pleasure, joy (a word beginning with the letter chosen to represent the letter).]

wench (wĕnch) *n.* **1.** A young woman or girl; especially, a peasant girl. Now used familiarly or humorously. **2.** A female servant. **3.** A wanton woman; a prostitute. —*intr.v.* **wenched, wenching, wenches. 1.** To be promiscuous. **2.** To consort with prostitutes. [Middle English *wenche,* short for *wenchel,* a girl, maid, Old English *wencel,* a child of either sex; maid.] —**wench·er** *n.*

wend (wĕnd) *v.* **wended** or *archaic* **went** (wĕnt), **wending, wends.** —*tr.* To proceed on or along (one's way); go. —*intr. Archaic.* To go one's way; proceed. [Middle English *wenden,* Old English *wendan,* to turn around or away, direct, happen.]

Wend (wĕnd) *n.* A member of a Slavic people inhabiting Saxony and Brandenburg. Also called "Sorb," "Sorbian." [German *Wende,* from Old High German *Winida.*]

Wend·ish (wĕn′dĭsh) *adj.* Of or pertaining to the Wends or their language. —*n.* The West Slavic language of the Wends. Also called "Lusatian," "Sorbian."

Wens·ley·dale (wĕnz′lē-dāl′) *n.* **1.** A long-haired breed of sheep. **2.** A type of white or sometimes blue cheese with a crumbly texture. [After *Wensleydale,* North Yorkshire, England.]

went. 1. Past tense of **go.** **2.** *Archaic.* Past tense and past participle of **wend.**

wen·tle·trap (wĕnt′l-trăp′) *n.* Any of various marine snails of the family Epitoniidae, having a tapering spiral shell with raised longitudinal ridges. [Dutch *wenteltrap,* from Middle Dutch *wendeltrappe,* "winding stair," spiral shell : *wendel,* winding, from *wenden,* to wind + *trappe,* a step, stairs.]

wept. Past tense and past participle of **weep.**

were (wûr). **1.** Plural and second person singular of the past indicative of **be.** **2.** Past subjunctive of **be.**

Usage: In clauses expressing clearly hypothetical conditions, *were* is the standard form of the verb *be: I would go if I were you. She spoke as if she were ill. Was* is often heard in such sentences but generally only in informal speech. When the clause expresses a condition that is not purely hypothetical or contrary to fact, *was* is standard: *I looked to see if/whether the way was clear.* This is also the case in indirect speech: *She asked whether I was happy with the car.* There are, however, several occasions when the hypothetical status of the expression is unclear, and in such cases usage is mixed (*She spoke as though everything were/was settled*); here *were* continues to predominate in formal contexts, especially in American English. In formal conditional sentences *were* may be inverted: *Were she to study, she would learn.*

we're (wîr). Contraction of *we are.*

were·n't (wûrnt, wûr′ənt). Contraction of *were not.*

were·wolf (wîr′wŏŏlf′, wûr′-, wâr′-) *n., pl.* **-wolves** (-wŏŏlvz′). In legend and folklore, a person transformed into a wolf or capable of assuming the form of a wolf; a lycanthrope. [Middle English *wer(e)wolf,* Old English *wer(e)wulf* : probably *wer,* man + *wulf,* WOLF.]

wer·geld (wûr′gĕld′) *n.* Also **wer·gild** (-gĭld′). In Anglo-Saxon and Germanic law, a price set upon a man's life on the basis of his rank and paid as compensation by the family of a slayer to the kindred or lord of a slain man to free the culprit of further punishment or obligation. [Middle English (Scottish) *weregehelde,* Old English *wergeld,* "man-payment" : *wer,* a man + *geld,* payment.]

wer·ner·ite (wûr′nə-rīt′) *n. Mineralogy.* **Scapolite** *(see).* [French, after A.G. *Werner* (1750–1817), German mineralogist.]

wert (wûrt). *Archaic.* Second person singular past indicative and past subjunctive of **be.**

We·ser (vā′zər). River, *c.* 480 kilometers (300 miles), in east-central West Germany, flowing generally northward to the North Sea through a long estuary.

wes·kit (wĕs′kĭt) *n.* A waistcoat; vest. [Variant of WAISTCOAT.]

Wes·ley (wĕs′lē, wĕz′-), **John** (1703–91). English religious leader and founder of Methodism. He and his brother **Charles** (1707–88), a writer of hymns, were ordained into the Church of England, but came under the influence of the more austere evangelical Christianity of the Moravians. Wesley traveled throughout the country preaching at open-air meetings, often to large working-class audiences. Although Methodism encountered the opposition of the Anglican Church, it was only formally founded after Wesley's death. **—Wes·ley·an** (wĕs′lē-ən, wĕz′-) *adj.* Of or pertaining to John or Charles Wesley or to Methodism. **~***n.* A Methodist, especially one belonging to the Wesleyan Methodist denomination based on the teachings of John and Charles Wesley. **—Wes·ley·an·ism** *n.*

Wes·sex (wĕs′ĭks). Former kingdom of the West Saxons, England. With varying boundaries it extended from the English Channel to the Thames and beyond and from Devon to Sussex.

west (wĕst) *n. Abbr.* **w, W, w., W. 1. a.** The direction opposite that of the earth's axial rotation; the general direction of the sunset. **b.** The cardinal point on the mariner's compass 270° clockwise from north and directly opposite east. **2.** *Often* **West.** Any area or region lying in the west. **3.** *Often* **West.** The part of the earth west of Asia and Asia Minor, especially Europe and North America; the Occident. **b.** The Western Hemisphere. **c.** The western part of a country or region. **d.** The western part of the United States; especially, the region west of the Mississippi River or, formerly, the region west of the Allegheny Mountains. **e.** The developed countries of the non-Communist world, especially Europe and North America. **4. a.** The one of four positions arranged like the four compass points that faces the west. **b.** In card games such as bridge, a player considered to occupy this position. **~***adj.* **1.** To, toward, of, facing, or in the west. **2.** Coming from or originating in the west, as the wind. **3.** **West.** Officially or conventionally designating the western part of a country, continent, or other geographic area: *West Germany.* **~***adv.* In, from, or towards the west. **—go west.** *Informal.* **1.** To die. **2.** To move to the western part of the United States or Canada. [Middle English *west,* Old English *west.*]

West (wĕst), **Benjamin** (1738–1820). U.S. painter. The first American to study art in Italy (1760–63), he settled in England where he quickly became a prominent artist. He was appointed painter to the king and served as president of the Royal Academy of Arts (1792–1801). *The Death of General Wolfe* (1770) is one of his many important works.

West, Mae (1892–1980). U.S. actress. She is remembered as a sex symbol of the 1930's in comedies such as *I'm No Angel* (1933) and *My Little Chickadee* (1939).

West, Dame Rebecca, born Cicely Isabel Fairfield (1892–1983). British novelist, journalist, and critic. Among her books are *The Thinking Reed* (1936) and *The Birds Fall Down* (1966).

West African States. Region of Africa between the Sahara and the Gulf of Guinea. With the exception of Liberia, all eleven states are former colonies of European countries that gained their independence after World War II.

West Atlantic *n.* A branch of the Niger-Congo language family that includes Fulani and Wolof.

West Bank. Territory on the west bank of the Jordan River. It was part of Palestine before passing to Jordan in 1949 and was captured by the Israelis (1967). Including part of Jerusalem, Nablus, Hebron, and the hills of Judaea and Samaria, it is considered to be strategically important by the Israelis and to be the natural homeland for the Palestinians by the Palestine Liberation Organization.

West Bengal. State of northeast India. Situated on the Bay of Bengal and bordered by Bangladesh in the east, it was part of the former province of Bengal partitioned in 1947 between India and Pakistan. It includes a portion of the Ganges delta and extends to the Himalayas in the far north. Its capital is Calcutta.

West Berlin. See **Berlin.**

west·bound (wĕst′bound′) *adj.* Going toward the west.

west by north *n. Abbr.* **WbN** The direction or point on the mariner's compass halfway between due west and west-northwest; 78° 45′ west of due north.

west by south *n. Abbr.* **WbS** The direction or point on the mariner's compass halfway between due west and west-southwest; 101° 15′ west of due north.

West End. The western part of central London, well known for its

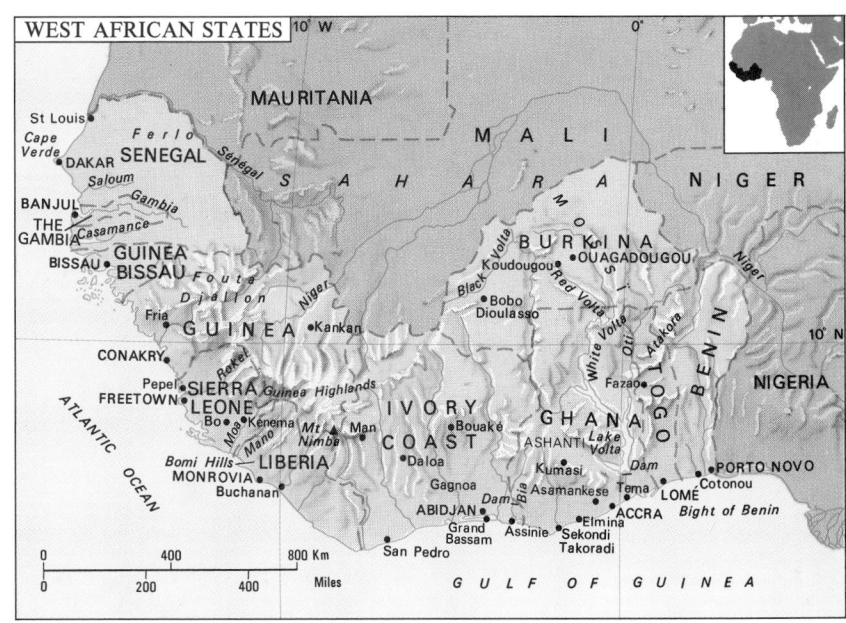

WEST AFRICAN STATES

fashionable shops and places of entertainment and including Mayfair, Piccadilly Circus, Oxford Street, and Hyde Park.

west·er (wĕs′tər) *intr.v.* **-ered, -ering, -ers. 1.** To move westward. Used of the sun, the moon, or a star. **2.** To shift to the west. Used of the wind. **~***n.* A westerly. [Middle English *west(e)ren,* from WEST.]

west·er·ly (wĕs′tər-lē) *adj.* **1.** Situated in or toward the west. **2.** Coming from the west. Said of the wind. **~***n., pl.* **westerlies.** A storm or wind from the west. [From obsolete *wester,* western, from Middle English *wester,* Old English *westra.*] **—west·er·ly** *adv.*

west·ern (wĕs′tərn) *adj. Abbr.* **w, W, w., W. 1.** Situated toward, in, or facing the west. **2.** Coming from the west. Said of the wind. **3.** Growing in the west. **4.** *Often* **Western.** Of, pertaining to, or characteristic of western regions or the West. **5. Western.** Of, pertaining to, or characteristic of Europe and the Western Hemisphere; Occidental: *Western technology.* **6.** *Often* **Western.** Of, pertaining to, or characteristic of the American West. **7. Western.** Of or pertaining to the Western Church. **~***n. Often* **Western.** A novel, motion picture, or radio or television program dealing with cowboys or frontier life in the American West. [Middle English *west(e)ren,* Old English *westerne.*]

Western Aus·tra·lia (ô-strāl′yə). *Abbr.* **W.A.** Largest state of Australia. Covering approximately a third of the country, it is bounded by the Indian Ocean on the north, west, and south and is mainly desert in the interior. Its mineral reserves include gold, iron, coal, oil, and bauxite. Its population is densest in the fertile southeast where wheat and fruit are grown and livestock are raised, while industries, chiefly situated around the capital, Perth, include oil refining and iron and steel.

Western Bug. See **Bug** (Poland-Ukraine).

Western Church *n.* **1.** The church of the Western Roman Empire, acknowledging the primacy of the see of Rome. **2.** Any of the churches that have developed from the Western Church, especially the Roman Catholic Church.

Western Dvina. See **Dvina, Western.**

west·ern·er (wĕs′tər-nər) *n.* **1.** A native or inhabitant of the west. **2.** *Often* **Westerner.** A native or inhabitant of the western United States.

Western Eu·rope (yoor′əp). Political region of Europe. Most of the 24 independent states of Western Europe look to the United States for military alliance, while the countries of Eastern Europe fall into the Soviet sphere of influence. Switzerland and Austria maintain strict neutrality. See map, next page.

Western Ghats. See **Ghats.**

Western Hemisphere. The half of the earth that includes all of North and South America, the surrounding waters, and all neighboring islands.

western hemlock *n.* A sprucelike tree, *Tsuga heterophylla,* of the Pacific Northwest, characteristically having drooping leaf shoots and branches in irregular whorls.

west·ern·ize (wĕs′tər-nīz′) *v.* **-ized, -izing, -izes. —***tr.* To cause to adopt customs and styles of living characteristic of the industrially developed countries of the West. **—***intr.* To become westernized. **—west·ern·i·za·tion** *n.*

Western Isles. See **Hebrides.**

west·ern·most (wĕs′tərn-mōst′) *adj.* Farthest west.

western omelet *n.* An omelet cooked with diced ham, chopped green pepper, and onion.

western roll *n.* A technique of performing the high jump in which the body is flung upward and rolls over the bar in a position paral-

WESTERN EUROPE

lel to it. [Apparently so called to contrast this technique with the *eastern roll*.]

Western Roman Empire. The western part of the Roman Empire, especially after the division established by the emperor Theodosius in A.D. 395 and lasting until A.D. 475. See **Byzantine Empire.**

Western Sa·har·a (sə-hâr′ə, -hä′rə). Formerly **Spanish Sahara.** Territory of northwestern Africa. Bordering the Atlantic Ocean, it is extremely arid and has reserves of phosphates. It was divided (1976) between Morocco and Mauritania, although Mauritania later withdrew (1979). The Polisario Front, a guerrilla movement resisting Moroccan rule, proclaimed (1976) the Saharan Arab Democratic Republic and was supported by Algeria and Libya.

Western Sa·mo·a (sə-mō′ə). Independent state, part of the archipelago of Samoa. It was controlled by Germany (1900–19) and then by New Zealand until 1962, when it became the first independent Polynesian state. The largest island is Savaii. The second largest, Upolu, has about two thirds of the population. Exports include copra, taro, and timber, and tourism is increasingly important. Area, 2,842 square kilometers (1,097 square miles). Population, 152,000. Capital, Apia, on Upolu. See map at **Pacific Ocean.**

western sandwich *n.* A sandwich having a western omelet as a filling.

Western Wall. See **Wailing Wall.**

West Frisians. See **Frisian Islands.**

West Germanic *n.* A subdivision of the Germanic languages that includes High German, Low German, Dutch, Afrikaans, Flemish, Frisian, English, and Yiddish.

West Ger·ma·ny (jûr′mə-nē). Official name **Federal Republic of Germany.** Republic of central Europe, on the North and Baltic seas and bordering on the Netherlands, Belgium, Luxembourg, France, Austria, Czechoslovakia, and East Germany. It was established in 1949 from the states occupied by the United States, Great Britain, and France after World War II. Northern West Germany is mainly agricultural, producing milk, eggs, potatoes, sugar beets, wheat, barley, rye, oats, cattle, hogs, and poultry. The central section includes West Germany's chief mining and industrial region, including the Ruhr and Saar basins. The primary minerals produced are coal, lignite, potash, petroleum, and iron ore. The country's industrial products include iron and steel, chemicals, motor vehicles, electric and electronic equipment, precision instruments, textiles, refined petroleum, and food products. Area, 247,973 square kilometers (95,742 square miles). Population, 61,700,000. Capital, Bonn. —**West Ger·man** adj. & n. See map at **Germany**.

West Gla·mor·gan (glə-môr′gən). County of southern Wales. It comprises the Tawe and Neath valleys, Swansea Bay, and the Gower peninsula and borders the Bristol channel. It was formed (1974) from the former county of Glamorganshire and the county borough of Swansea, which is the administrative center.

West Greek n. A principal dialectal division of Ancient Greek comprising Doric and Northwest Greek.

West Highland terrier n. A small dog of a breed of terrier that originated in Scotland and has short legs and tail and a white coat. Also called "West Highland white terrier."

West In·dies (ĭn′dēz). Abbr. **W.I.** Archipelago of Central America. Extending between Florida and Venezuela, it separates the Atlantic Ocean from the Caribbean Sea and the Gulf of Mexico. It includes the Greater Antilles (Cuba, Hispaniola, Jamaica, and Puerto Rico), the Lesser Antilles (Barbados, Trinidad, Tobago, and the Leeward and Windward Isles) and independent Bahama Islands, Cuba, Dominican Republic, Haiti, and the Virgin Islands.

west·ing (wĕs′tĭng) n. **1.** Nautical. **a.** The distance sailed by a ship on a westerly course. **b.** The longitudinal distance from a given meridian on a westward course. **2.** A westward direction or movement. [From WEST.]

West·ing·house (wĕs′tĭng-hous′), **George** (1846–1914). U.S. engineer and manufacturer. The recipient of more than 400 patents, he invented the air brake (1869) and an automatic signaling system (1882), both of which made railroading considerably safer. His research of alternating current yielded a practical electrical power distribution system that was further refined by the Westinghouse Electric Company, which he founded in 1886.

West I·ri·an (ĭr′ē-än). Indonesian **I·ri·an Ja·ya** (jī′ə). Province of Indonesia, Southeast Asia, the western half of New Guinea. Before its transfer to Indonesia (1963), it was known as Netherlands New Guinea. It is largely swampland.

West Lo·thi·an (lō′thē-ən). Former county of east-central Scotland, bordering the Firth of Forth. It was absorbed (1975) into Lothian Region, of which it is now a district.

West·meath (wĕst′mēth′). Inland county of Leinster province, north-central Republic of Ireland. It has many lakes, including loughs Ree and Ennell.

West Mid·lands (mĭd′ləndz). Metropolitan county of west-central England. Covering most of the Black Country, and with Birmingham at its center, it was created (1974) from northeastern Worcestershire, southeastern Staffordshire, and northwest Warwickshire.

West·min·ster, City of (wĕst′mĭn′stər). Borough of Greater London, southeastern England. Situated on the north bank of the Thames River, it contains many famous buildings, including the Houses of Parliament, Westminster Abbey, and Buckingham Palace, as well as Hyde Park.

West·more·land (wĕst′môr′lənd, -mōr′-), **William Childs** (1914–). U.S. general. A veteran of World War II and the Korean War, he served as the senior U.S. military commander in Vietnam (1964–68). His optimistic reports from the field were a major factor in the escalation of the war.

West·mor·land (wĕst′môr′lənd, -mōr′-). Former county of northwestern England. Incorporated into Cumbria (1974), it included much of the Lake District. The county town was Appleby.

west-north·west (wĕst′nôrth-wĕst′; Nautical -nôr-wĕst′) n. Abbr. **WNW** The direction or point on the mariner's compass halfway between west and northwest; 67° 30′ west of due north. —adj. Situated toward, facing, or in this direction. —adv. In, from, or toward this direction.

West Pakistan. See **Pakistan**.

West·phal·i·a (wĕst-fāl′yə). Former province of Prussia, part of North Rhine-Westphalia, western West Germany, since 1946. It was created as a duchy (12th century), passing to Prussia through the Congress of Vienna (1815). Chiefly low-lying, it includes the industrial Ruhr valley in the west.

West Saxon n. **1.** The dialect of Old English that was spoken in Wessex, the chief literary dialect of England before the Norman Conquest. **2.** A member of a Saxon people inhabiting Wessex during the centuries before the Norman Conquest.

West Slavic n. The western division of the Slavic languages, consisting of Czech, Polish, and Slovak.

west-south·west (wĕst′south-wĕst′; Nautical -sou-wĕst′) n. Abbr. **WSW** The direction or point on the mariner's compass halfway between west and southwest; 112° 30′ west of due north. —adj. Situated toward, facing, or in this direction. —adv. In, from, or toward this direction.

West Sus·sex (sŭs′ĭks). County of southern England. Extending northward from the English Channel across the South Downs to the west end of the Weald, it is mainly agricultural, producing dairy goods, barley, and vegetables. The administrative center is Chichester.

West Vir·gin·ia (vər-jĭn′yə). Mountain state of east-central United States. Divided by the Allegheny Mts., 80 percent of the state lies to the west on the hilly Appalachian plateau, while to the east lies the Great Appalachian Valley. The capital is Charleston.

West York·shire (yôrk′shĭr′, -shər). County of north-central England. Created (1974) from part of the former West Riding of Yorkshire and the industrial county boroughs of Bradford, Dewsbury,

Halifax, Huddersfield, Leeds, and Wakefield. It has textile industries and coal fields. Wakefield is the administrative center.

west·ward (wĕst′wərd) adj. At, toward, facing, or in the west. ~n. A westward direction, point, or region. ~adv. Toward the west: drove westward. —**west·ward·ly** adj. & adv. —**west·wards** adv.

wet (wĕt) adj. **wetter, wettest. 1.** Consisting of, covered with, or saturated with a liquid, especially water; damp: got his shoes wet; hands wet with perspiration. **2.** Not yet dry or firm: wet paint; wet plaster. **3.** Stored or preserved in liquid. **4.** Using or prepared by means of a liquid, especially water. **5. a.** Rainy, humid, or foggy: wet weather. **b.** Characterized by frequent or heavy rainfall or snowfall: a wet climate. **6.** Of, pertaining to, or being a process, system, or device in which liquids play a prominent part: a wet photocopier. **7.** Informal. **a.** Allowing the sale of alcoholic beverages: a wet state. **b.** British. Allowing the sale of alcoholic drinks on Sundays: a wet county. **8.** British Informal. Marked by weakness of character; faint-hearted. **9.** British Informal. Of, pertaining to, characteristic of, or composed of the liberal members of a group, especially of the liberal wing of the British Conservative party: a wet rebellion in the Cabinet. —**all wet**. Slang. Completely mistaken. —**wet behind the ears**. Lacking experience; green. ~n. **1.** Something that wets; moisture. **2.** Rainy or snowy weather: go out into the wet. **3.** Informal. One who supports the legality of the production and sale of alcoholic beverages. **4.** British. **a.** Informal. A feeble, timid, or stupid person. **b.** Informal. A liberal member of a group; especially, a member of the British Conservative party, typically opposing hard-line economic policies: political wets. **c.** Slang. A drink. ~v. **wetted** or **wet, wetting, wets.** —tr. **1.** To make wet; moisten or dampen: wet a sponge. **2.** To make (a bed, one's clothes, or oneself) wet by urinating. —intr. To become wet. —**wet one's whistle**. To take a drink. [Middle English wet, Old English wǣt, wēt.]

Synonyms: damp, dank, humid, moist.

wet-and-dry-bulb thermometer (wĕt′n-drī′bŭlb′) n. A **psychrometer** (see).

wet·back (wĕt′băk′) n. A Mexican immigrant who crosses the U.S. border illegally, as by swimming or wading across the Rio Grande. Compare **bracero**.

wet blanket n. Informal. One that discourages or dampens enjoyment or enthusiasm. [Originally a soaked blanket was used in putting out fires.]

wet cell n. A primary cell having an electrolyte in the form of a liquid bath. Compare **dry cell**.

wet dream n. An erotic dream accompanied by sexual climax and in a man or boy by the emission of semen.

wet fly n. An artificial fishing fly designed to be used under water. Compare **dry fly**.

weth·er (wĕth′ər) n. A gelded male sheep. [Middle English wether, wether, a ram, Old English wether.]

wet·land (wĕt′lənd, -lănd′) pl.n. Often **wetlands**. A lowland area, such as a marsh or swamp, that is saturated with moisture, especially when thought of as the natural habitat of wildlife.

wet look n. A very shiny finish given to the surface of fabrics used to make clothes, shoes, and accessories. Also used adjectivally: a wet-look handbag.

wet monsoon n. Meteorology. A monsoon (see).

wet nurse n. A woman who breast-feeds another woman's child.

wet-nurse (wĕt′nûrs′) tr.v. **-nursed, -nursing, -nurses. 1.** To serve as a wet nurse for. **2.** To treat with excessive care or solicitude.

wet pack n. A therapeutic pack made of a material, as gauze, that has been moistened in hot or cold water and then wrung out.

wet rot n. **1.** A disease of timber caused by various fungi of the genus Coniophora. **2.** Any fungus causing wet rot.

wet suit n. A tight-fitting permeable suit worn, as by skin divers, in order to retain body heat.

wetting agent n. Any compound that causes a liquid to spread more easily across or penetrate into the surface of a solid by reducing the surface tension of the liquid.

we've (wēv). Contraction of we have.

Wex·ford (wĕks′fərd). County of Leinster province, southeastern Republic of Ireland. Bordering on the Irish Sea, it was the first county colonized by the English (1169). The county town is also named Wexford.

Wey·den (wīd′n, vīd′n), **Rogier van der**, also known as "Roger de la Pasture" (c. 1400–64). Flemish painter. He is best known for his altarpiece The Deposition (c. 1435).

wf Printing. wrong font.

WFTU World Federation of Trade Unions.

w.g. wire gauge.

wh. white.

whack¹ (hwăk, wăk) v. **whacked, whacking, whacks.** —tr. **1. a.** To strike with a sharp blow; slap. **b.** To cut by or as if by whacking: whacked off the chicken wings and added them to the soup. **2.** British. To score or get by hitting. Usually used with up: whacked up a huge number of runs. —intr. To deal a sharp, resounding blow. ~n. **1. a.** A sharp, swift blow. **b.** The sound made by such a blow. **2.** Informal. A fair share: Give me my whack. **3.** Informal. An attempt or opportunity; a try: Give me a whack at driving the new car. —**out of whack**. Informal. Improperly ordered or balanced; not functioning correctly. [Perhaps variant of THWACK.]

whack². Variant of **wack**.

whacked (hwăkt) adj. British Informal. Tired out; exhausted.

***wheatear** A migratory bird, the wheatear spends the winter in Africa and Asia and the spring and summer in Europe. It also appears in Alaska, Greenland, and northern Canada and sometimes strays as far south as the United States. It lives chiefly on uplands and moorlands and feeds on insects and spiders.*

PRONUNCIATION KEY

ă, pat; ā, pay; âr, care;
ä, father, are; b, bib;
ch, church; d, deed; ĕ, pet;
ē, be; f, fife; g, gag; h, hat;
hw, which; ĭ, pit; ī, pie;
îr, pier; j, judge; k, kick;
l, lid, needle; m, mum;
n, no, sudden; ng, thing;
ŏ, pot; ō, toe; ô, paw, for;
oi, noise; ou, out; o͝o, book;
o͞o, boot; p, pop; r, roar;
s, sauce; sh, ship, dish;
t, tight; th, thin, path;
th, this, bathe; ŭ, cut; ûr, fur;
v, valve; w, with; y, yes;
z, zebra, size; zh, vision;
ə, about, item, edible, gallop, circus, peaceful

IN FOREIGN WORDS:

à, *Fr.* ami; œ, *Fr.* feu, *Ger.* schön; ü, *Fr.* tu, *Ger.* über; KH, *Ger.* ich, *Scot.* loch; N, *Fr.* bon; y', *Fr.* Compiègne

STRESS MARKS:

Primary stress: ′
in·cite′ (ĭn-sīt′)
Secondary stress: ′
in′sight′ (ĭn′sīt′)

whacked-out (hwăkt′out′, wăkt′-) *adj. Slang.* **1.** Extremely tired; exhausted. **2.** Crazy; wacky.

whack·ing (hwăk′ĭng) *adj. Chiefly British Informal.* Superlative; very great.
~adv. Chiefly British Informal. Used as an intensive: *whacking great tusks.*

whacky. Variant of **wacky.**

whale[1] (hwāl, wāl) *n., pl.* **whales** or collectively **whale. 1.** Any of various marine mammals of the order Cetacea, having a generally fishlike form with forelimbs modified to form flippers and a tail with horizontal flukes; especially, one of the very large species as distinguished from the smaller dolphins, porpoises, and others. **2.** *Informal.* A superlative example of something specified: *We had a whale of a good time.*
~intr.v. **whaled, whaling, whales.** To engage in the hunting of whales. [Middle English *whale,* Old English *hwæl.*]

whale[2] *v.* **whaled, whaling, whales.** *—tr.* **1.** To strike repeatedly and forcefully, as with a whip or stick; flog. **2.** To defeat thoroughly; whip. *—intr.* To attack vehemently: *The poet whaled away at his critics.* [Variant of WALE.]

whale·back (hwāl′băk′, wāl′-) *n.* A steamship with the bow and upper deck rounded so as to shed water.

whale·boat (hwāl′bōt′, wāl′-) *n.* **1.** A long rowboat, pointed at both ends and designed to move and turn swiftly, formerly used in the pursuit and harpooning of whales. **2.** Any boat of similar size and shape. Also called "whaler."

whale·bone (hwāl′bōn′, wāl′-) *n.* **1.** The durable, elastic, hornlike material forming plates or strips in the upper jaw of whalebone whales. Also called "baleen." **2.** An object made of this material, such as a corset stay.

whalebone whale *n.* Any of various whales of the suborder Mysticeti, lacking teeth and characteristically filtering plankton through plates of whalebone. Also called "mysticete." Compare **toothed whale.**

whale oil *n.* A yellowish oil obtained from whale blubber, used in making soap and candles and as a lubricating oil.

whal·er (hwā′lər, wā′-) *n.* **1.** One who hunts or processes whales. **2.** A whaling ship. **3.** A whaleboat.

whale shark *n.* A large shark, *Rhincodon typus,* of warm marine waters, having a spotted body and feeding chiefly on plankton.

whal·ing (hwā′lĭng, wā′-) *n.* The business or practice of hunting, killing, and processing whales.

wham (hwăm, wăm) *n.* **1.** A forceful, resounding crash or blow. **2.** The sound of such a crash or blow; a thud.
~v. **whammed, whamming, whams.** *—tr.* To strike or smash into with great force and resounding impact. *—intr.* To smash with great force and resounding impact. [Imitative.]

whang[1] (hwăng, wăng) *n. Informal.* **1.** A thong or whip made of hide or leather. **2. a.** A lashing blow, as by a whip. **b.** The sound of such a blow.
~tr.v. **whanged, whanging, whangs.** *Informal.* **1.** To beat or whip with a thong. **2.** To beat with a sharp blow or blows. [Variant of Middle English *thwang,* THONG.]

whang[2] *v.* **whanged, whanging, whangs.** *Informal. —tr.* To strike so as to produce a loud, reverberant noise. *—intr.* To produce a loud, reverberant noise.
~n. Informal. A loud, reverberant noise. [Imitative.]

whang·ee (hwăng-gē′, wăng-) *n.* **1.** Any of several bamboolike Asian grasses of the genus *Phyllostachys.* **2.** A walking stick made from the woody stem of such a plant. [Chinese *huáng,* a type of bamboo, probably *Phyllostachys aurea.*]

wharf (hwôrf, wôrf) *n., pl.* **wharves** (hwôrvz, wôrvz) or **wharfs. 1.** A landing place, such as a concrete platform, at which vessels may tie up and load or unload passengers or cargo. **2.** *Obsolete.* A shore or river bank.
~v. **wharfed, wharfing, wharfs.** *—tr.* **1.** To moor (a vessel) at a wharf. **2.** To take to or store (cargo) on a wharf. **3.** To furnish, equip, or protect with a wharf or wharves. *—intr.* To berth at a wharf. [Middle English *wharfe, wherf,* Old English *hwearf.*]

wharf·age (hwôr′fĭj, wôr′-) *n.* **1.** The use of a wharf or wharves. **2.** The charges for this. **3.** Wharves collectively.

wharf·in·ger (hwôr′fĭn-jər, wôr′-) *n.* The owner or manager of a wharf. [WHARF + *-inger,* as in words like HARBINGER.]

Whar·ton (hwôrt′n, wôrt′n), **Edith Newbold Jones** (1862–1937). U.S. novelist. Her novels include *The House of Mirth* (1905) and *The Age of Innocence* (1920).

what (hwŏt, hwŭt, wŏt, wŭt; *unstressed* hwət, wət) *pron.* **1.** Used as an interrogative pronoun in various types of questions: **a.** Used in questions asking for a specification or identification: *What is your name? What does she do for a living? What are these papers on my desk?* **b.** Used in requests for repetition, clarification, or explanation: *He said what? What are these papers doing on my desk? What do you think she meant by that? What did you do that for?* **c.** Used when questioning the value or significance of a person or thing: *What are possessions to a dying man?* **d.** Used in rhetorical questions as the equivalent of a negative statement: *What's the point in arguing?* **2.** That or those which. Used as a relative pronoun: **a.** The thing or things that: *What I like about him is his honesty. Listen to what I tell you.* **b.** Anything or everything that; whichever thing that: *come what may; did what they could to save him.* **3. a.** *Nonstandard.* Which, who, or that: *It's the poor what gets the blame.* **b.** *Informal.* Something: *I'll tell you what.* **—and what not.** And other less prominent or unspecified things; and so on: *bought nails, bolts, screws, and what not.* **—what about. 1.** What information is there on. **2.** What do you think about; have you considered. **—what for.** A strong reprimand; scolding: *The student who was late for class got what for from the teacher.* **—what have you.** What remains and need not be mentioned; all the rest: *sell it, give it away, throw it out, or what have you.* **—what if. 1.** What would occur if: *What if you knew he was lying?* **2.** What difference does it make if: *I don't mind, but anyhow, what if I did?* **—what of it.** How is it important; what does it matter: *So you disagree—what of it?* **—what's what.** *Informal.* The fundamentals and details of a situation or process; the true state or condition. **—what with.** Taking into consideration; in view of: *What with the heat and humidity, we really suffered.*
~adj. **1.** Which particular one or ones of many: *What university are you attending? What sort of car is that? You should know what musical that song is from.* **2.** Of what kind or nature: *What news have you heard about the election returns?* **3.** Whatever; all that; as much or as many as: *They soon repaired what damage had been done.* **4.** How astonishing or exceptional in good or bad qualities: *What weather! What a bore! I'd forgotten what a fool he was.* **5.** *Archaic.* How much; which degree of: *What love do you bear for her?*
~adv. **1.** How; how much; in what respect: *What does it matter?* **2.** To what an astonishing or exceptional degree: *What lovely weather!*
~interj. **1.** Used to express surprise, incredulity, or other strong and sudden excitement. **2.** *British Informal.* Used to request agreement: *A fine evening, what?* Now chiefly used humorously. [Middle English *what,* Old English *hwæt.*]

what·ev·er (hwŏt-ĕv′ər, hwŭt-, wŏt-, wŭt-) *pron.* Also *poetic* **what·e'er** (-âr′). **1.** Everything or anything that: *Do whatever you please.* **2.** What amount that; the whole of what: *Whatever is left over is yours.* **3.** No matter what; regardless of what: *Whatever happens, we'll meet here tonight.* **4.** *Informal.* What. Used as an intensive: *Whatever does he mean?* **5.** An unspecified but similar thing: *write with pencils, pens, or whatever.*
~adj. **1.** Of any number or kind; any: *Whatever requests you make will be granted.* **2.** All of; the whole of: *He applied whatever strength he had left to the task.* **3.** No matter what: *Help from whatever source will be most welcome.* **4.** Of any kind at all. Used for emphasis following the noun modified: *No campers whatever are allowed.*

what·not (hwŏt′nŏt′, hwŭt′-, wŏt′-, wŭt′-) *n.* **1.** A minor or unspecified object or article; a trivial item. **2.** A set of light, open shelves for small objects, especially ornaments.

what's (hwŏts, hwŭts, wŏts, wŭts). **1.** Contraction of *what is.* **2.** Contraction of *what has.*

what·so·ev·er (hwŏt′sō-ĕv′ər, hwŭt′-, wŏt′-, wŭt′-) *pron.* Also *poetic* **what·so·e'er** (-âr′). Whatever.
~adj. Whatever. Used for emphasis: *no power whatsoever.*

wheal (hwēl, wēl) *n.* A small acute swelling on the skin. [Variant (influenced by obsolete *wheal,* to suppurate) of WALE (ridge).]

wheat (hwēt, wēt) *n.* **1.** Any of various cereal grasses of the genus *Triticum;* especially, *T. aestivum,* widely cultivated in many varieties for its edible grain. **2.** The grain of a wheat plant, ground to produce flour used in cooking, especially for bread and cakes, and pasta products such as spaghetti and macaroni. [Middle English *whet(e),* Old English *hwǣte.*]

wheat·ear (hwēt′îr′, wēt′-) *n.* A brown, black, and white bird, *Oenanthe oenanthe,* of northern regions. [Back-formation from *wheatears* (taken as plural), "white-rumped (bird)" : probably WHITE + Middle English *ers,* ARSE.]

wheat·en (hwēt′n, wēt′n) *adj.* Of, pertaining to, or derived from wheat.

wheat germ *n.* The vitamin-rich embryo of the wheat kernel that is separated before milling for use as a cereal or food supplement.

wheat·meal (hwēt′mēl′) *n. British.* Brown wheat flour.
~adj. British. Of, pertaining to, or being flour or bread made from such flour, from which a proportion of the wheat kernel has been extracted.

wheat rust *n.* **1.** A destructive disease of wheat. **2.** A fungus, such as *Puccinia gyraminis,* that causes wheat rust.

Wheat·stone bridge (hwēt′stōn′, wēt′-) *n.* An instrument or circuit consisting of four resistors, or their equivalent, connected in a loop, with a galvanometer linking the junction between one pair and the other, used to determine the value of an unknown resistance when the other three resistances are known. [After Sir Charles *Wheatstone* (1802–75), British physicist.]

wheat·worm (hwēt′wûrm′, wēt′-) *n.* A nematode worm, *Anguina tritici,* that is parasitic on and destructive to wheat.

whee (hwē, wē) *interj.* Used to express enthusiasm or delight.

whee·dle (hwēd′l, wēd′l) *v.* **-dled, -dling, -dles.** *—tr.* **1.** To persuade or attempt to persuade by flattery or guile; cajole: *wheedled us into agreeing.* **2.** To obtain through the use of flattery or guile: *wheedled permission from their parents.* *—intr.* To use flattery or cajolery to achieve one's ends: *Children who wheedle can be annoying.* [Perhaps from German *wedeln,* "to wag the tail," fawn, from Middle High German *wadelen,* from Old High German *wadal,* tail.] **—whee·dler** *n.* **—whee·dling·ly** *adv.*

wheel (hwēl, wēl) *n.* **1.** A solid disk or a rigid circular ring connected by spokes to a hub, that is designed to turn around an axle passed through the center. **2.** Something that resembles a wheel in appearance or movement or that has a wheel as its principal part or characteristic, as: **a.** In the Middle Ages, an instrument to which a victim was bound for torture. **b.** A type of firework that rotates while burning. **c.** A device for directing the course of a ship. **d.** The steering device on a vehicle. **e.** *Informal.* A bicycle. **f.** A spinning wheel. **g.** A water wheel. **h.** A potter's wheel. **i.** A device used in roulette and other games of chance. **3. wheels.** The forces, procedures, and processes that provide energy, movement, or direction: *the wheels of commerce.* **4. a.** The act or process of turning; a revolution or rotation. **b.** Circular motion. **5.** *Military.* A maneuver to change the direction of movement of a formation, as of troops or ships, in which the formation is maintained while the outer unit describes an arc and the inner unit remains stationary as a pivot. **6. wheels.** *Slang.* **a.** A motor vehicle. **b.** Access to a motor vehicle. **7.** *Slang.* A person with a great deal of power or influence. Usually used in the phrase *a big wheel.* **—at (or behind) the wheel. 1.** Operating the steering mechanism of a vehicle; driving. **2.** In charge; directing or controlling. **—oil the wheels.** To make things go smoothly. **—wheels within wheels.** A complex series of actions and interactions.

~*v.* **wheeled, wheeling, wheels.** —*tr.* **1.** To roll, move, or transport on a wheel or wheels, especially: **a.** To push (a container or vehicle equipped with wheels). **b.** To transport (a person or object) in or on a container or vehicle equipped with wheels. **c.** To propel (oneself) in a wheelchair. **2.** To cause to turn around or as if around a central axis; revolve or rotate. **3.** To provide with a wheel or wheels. —*intr.* **1.** To turn around or as if around a central axis; revolve or rotate. **2.** To roll or move on or as if on a wheel or wheels. **3.** To fly or move in a curving or circular course: *A flock of gulls wheeled over the beach.* **4.** To turn or whirl around in the opposite direction; pivot: *The actor wheeled around and walked off-stage.* **5.** To reverse one's opinion, practice, or course of action. **—wheel and deal.** *Informal.* To engage in the advancement of one's own interests, especially in a complex, scheming way. [Middle English *wheel(e),* Old English *hwēol, hweogol.*]

wheel and axle *n.* A mechanical device, analogous to the lever, consisting of two coaxial wheels of different diameter conjoined so that the effort applied by a cord to the larger wheel in the form of a torque is transmitted as an action by a cord around the circumference of the smaller, yielding a mechanical advantage equal to the ratio of the diameters of the wheels.

wheel animalcule *n.* A microorganism, a **rotifer** *(see).*

wheel·back chair (hwēl'băk', wēl'-) *n.* An upright wooden chair with a back designed to resemble a wheel.

wheel balancing *n.* The process of checking that the wheels of a motor vehicle are perfectly balanced in order to prevent unwanted vibrations at high speed.

wheel·bar·row (hwēl'băr'ō, wēl'-) *n.* A one- or two-wheeled vehicle with handles, used to convey small, heavy, or unwieldy loads by hand, as in a garden or on a building site.

wheel·base (hwēl'bās', wēl'-) *n.* The distance from front to rear axle in a motor vehicle.

wheel bug *n.* A large predatory insect, *Arilus cristatus,* with a notched wheellike projection on the thorax.

wheel·chair (hwēl'châr', wēl'-) *n.* A chair mounted on large wheels for the use of the sick or disabled.

wheeled (hwēld, wēld) *adj.* Having a wheel or wheels. Often used in combination: *four-wheeled.*

wheel·er (hwē'lər, wē'lər) *n.* **1.** One that wheels. **2.** A thing that moves on or is equipped with a wheel or wheels. Often used in combination: *a three-wheeler.* **3.** A wheel horse.

Whee·ler (hwē'lər, wē'-), **Joseph** (1836–1906). U.S. Confederate general and politician. One of the South's most popular and aggressive Civil War commanders, he provided the only substantial opposition to Sherman's March to the Sea (1865). He later saw further military action in the Spanish-American War and in the Philippines (1899).

wheel·er-deal·er (hwē'lər-dē'lər, wē'-) *n. Informal.* A person who wheels and deals; a sharp operator.

wheel horse *n.* **1.** The horse in a team of horses that follows the leader and is harnessed nearest to the front wheels. **2.** A diligent, dependable worker, especially in a political organization.

wheel·house (hwēl'hous', wēl'-) *n.* A **pilothouse** *(see).*

wheel·ie (hwē'lē, wē'lē) *n. Informal.* An act of riding a vehicle such as a bicycle or motorcycle with the front wheel or wheels momentarily lifted off the ground. [Diminutive of WHEEL.]

wheel lock *n.* A firing mechanism in certain obsolete small arms in which a small wheel produces sparks by revolving against a flint.

wheel·man (hwēl'mən, wēl'-) *n., pl.* **-men** (-mĭn). Also **wheels·man** (hwēlz'mən, wēlz'-) (for sense 2). **1.** A bicyclist. **2.** One who steers a ship; a helmsman.

Whee·lock (hwē'lŏk', wē'-), **Eleazar** (1711–79). U.S. clergyman and educator. A Congregationalist minister dedicated to educating Native Americans, he established a school in Connecticut (1754). After its failure he moved to New Hampshire, where he founded Dartmouth College (1769) and acted as its first president (1769–79).

wheel·work (hwēl'wûrk', wēl'-) *n.* An arrangement of gears or wheels in a mechanical device.

wheel·wright (hwēl'rīt', wēl'-) *n.* One whose trade is the building and repairing of wheels.

wheen (hwēn) *n. Scottish.* A small number; a few: *a wheen of bairns.* [Middle English, Old English *hwēne,* instrumental of *hwōn,* (a) few.]

wheeze (hwēz, wēz) *v.* **wheezed, wheezing, wheezes.** —*intr.* **1.** To breathe with difficulty, producing a hoarse whistling sound. **2.** To make a sound suggestive of laborious breathing. —*tr.* To produce or utter with a hoarse whistling sound.

~*n.* **1.** A wheezing sound. **2.** *Informal.* An old joke. [Middle English *whesen,* probably from Old Norse *hvæsa,* to hiss.] **—wheez·er** *n.* **—wheez·ing·ly** *adv.*

wheez·y (hwē'zē, wē'-) *adj.* **-ier, -iest. 1.** Given to wheezing. **2.** Making a wheezing sound. **—wheez·i·ly** *adv.* **—wheez·i·ness** *n.*

whelk[1] (hwĕlk, wĕlk) *n.* **1.** Any of various large, sometimes edible marine snails of the family Buccinidae, having pointed, turreted shells. **2.** The flesh of an edible whelk, eaten as food. [Middle English *w(h)elke,* Old English *weoloc, wioloc†.*]

whelk[2] *n. Pathology.* A swelling, protuberance, or pustule. [Middle English *whelke,* Old English *hwylca†.*] **—whelk·y** *adj.*

whelm (hwĕlm, wĕlm) *tr.v.* **whelmed, whelming, whelms. 1.** To overwhelm. **2.** To cover with water; submerge. [Middle English *whelmen,* to turn over, Old English *hwelman* (unattested).]

whelp (hwĕlp, wĕlp) *n.* **1.** A young offspring of a mammal such as a dog or wolf. **2. a.** A mere child; young girl or boy. **b.** An impudent boy or young man. **3.** Any of the ridges on the barrel of a windlass or capstan.

~*v.* **whelped, whelping, whelps.** —*intr.* To give birth to a whelp or whelps. —*tr.* To give birth to (a whelp or whelps). [Middle English *w(h)elpe,* Old English *hwelp,* from Germanic.]

when (hwĕn, wĕn) *adv.* **1.** At what time: *When does the show start? I'll tell you when you can leave.* **2.** During which time: *When was he away?* **3.** At, on, or during which. Used with expressions of time: *on the day when war was declared; one of those weeks when everything goes wrong.*

~*conj.* **1.** At the time that: *in the spring, when the snow melts.* **2.** At the moment at which; as soon as: *Switch off the pump when the pressure reaches 30 pounds.* **3.** At the times at which; whenever: *When the wind blows, the doors rattle.* **4.** During the time at which; while: *when I was younger.* **5.** Despite the fact that: *continued talking when he knew we were bored.* **6.** Considering that; since; if: *Why bother when you know he'll refuse?* **7.** Whereupon; and then: *We were in a strong position when suddenly it began to rain.*

~*pron.* What or which time: *Since when has this been going on?*

~*n.* The time or date: *Have they decided the where and when?* [Middle English *when, wane,* Old English *hwanne, hwenne.*]

Usage: In informal style *when* is often used to mean "a situation or event in which," as in *A dilemma is when you don't know which way to turn.* This usage is best avoided in formal writing.

when·as (hwĕn-ăz', wĕn-) *conj. Archaic.* **1.** When. **2.** Whereas.

whence (hwĕns, wĕns) *adv.* **1.** From where; from what place, source, or cause: *whence came this man?* **2.** From or out of which: *returned to the land whence he came.*

~*conj.* **1.** From or out of which: *The path led to a sundial, whence it continued to the end of the garden.* **2.** By reason of which; and from this: *He was not dead, whence we derived some comfort.* [Middle English *whennes,* from *whenne,* whence, Old English *hwanon.*]

whence·so·ev·er (hwĕns'sō-ĕv'ər, wĕns'-) *adv.* From whatever place or source.

~*conj.* From any place or source that.

when·ev·er (hwĕn-ĕv'ər, wĕn-) *adv.* Also **when ever** (for sense 2), *poetic* **when·e'er** (-âr'). **1.** At whatever time: *Whenever you feel like leaving, just let me know.* **2.** When. Used as an intensive: *Whenever did you hear that?* **3.** *Informal.* At any unspecified time: *next Tuesday, Wednesday, or whenever.*

~*conj.* Also *poetic* **when·e'er. 1.** At any time that: *Come whenever it suits you.* **2.** Every time that: *He smiles whenever he sees her.*

when·so·ev·er (hwĕn'sō-ĕv'ər, wĕn'-) *adv.* At whatever time at all; whenever.

~*conj.* Whenever.

where (hwâr, wâr) *adv.* **1.** At or in what place: *Where is the telephone?* **2.** In what situation or position: *Where would we be without your help?* **3.** From what place or source: *Where did you get this idea?* **4.** To what place or toward what end: *Where is this argument leading?* **5.** At or in which. Used with expressions of place: *the house where I live; the point where his argument is least convincing.*

~*conj.* **1.** In the place in which: *Where she works, they have a staff cafeteria.* **2.** In or to a place in which: *Her health is bad, so she has to live where the weather is warm.* **3.** In or to any place in which; wherever: *has to go where the work is.* **4.** In a situation in which: *Where anyone else would have been furious, she just laughed.* **5.** In which place; and there: *walked outside, where I was waiting.*

~*n.* **1.** The place or occasion: *We know the when but not the where of it.* **2.** What place, source, or cause: *Where did they come from?* [Middle English *wher(e),* Old English *hwǣr.*]

where·a·bouts (hwâr'ə-bouts', wâr'-) *adv.* About where; in, at, or near what place: *Whereabouts do you live?*

~*n. Used with a singular or plural verb.* The approximate location of someone or something.

where·as (hwâr-ăz', wâr-) *conj.* **1.** It being the fact that; inasmuch as. Often used to introduce a formal document. **2. a.** While on the one hand. **b.** While on the contrary; by contrast with that.

where·at (hwâr-ăt', wâr-) *conj. Archaic.* **1.** At which place. **2.** At which point or event; whereupon.

where·by (hwâr-bī', wâr-) *conj.* In accordance with or by means of which: *a new law, whereby some players may be banned.*

~*adv. Archaic.* By what means; how.

where·fore (hwâr'fôr', -fōr', wâr'-) *adv. Archaic.* **1.** For what purpose or reason; why: *Wherefore did he come?* **2.** On account of which.

~*n.* A purpose or cause. Now used chiefly in the phrase *whys and wherefores.* [Middle English *wherfor* : WHERE + FOR.]

whelk *A marine snail that lives on the fringes of the sea and can grow up to 15 centimeters (6 inches) long. It feeds on other small marine animals or carrion, hunting by scent. Some species are edible.*

where·from (hwâr′frŏm′, -frŭm′, wâr′-) *adv. Archaic.* From what or where; whence.

where·in (hwâr-ĭn′, wâr-) *adv.* In what way; how: *Wherein did I sin?* ~*conj.* **1.** In which location; where: *the bed wherein I lay.* **2.** In which way; how: *showed them wherein they were wrong.*

where·in·to (hwâr-ĭn′tōō, wâr-) *adv. Archaic.* Into what or which.

where·of (hwâr-ŏv′, -ŭv′, wâr-) *conj.* **1.** Of what or which: *I know whereof I speak.* **2.** Of whom.

where·on (hwâr-ŏn′, -ôn′, wâr-) *adv. Archaic.* On which or what.

where·so·ev·er (hwâr′sō-ĕv′ər, wâr′-) *conj.* Also *poetic* **where·so·e'er** (-âr′). In, to, or from whatever place at all; wherever.

where·through (hwâr-thrōō′, wâr-) *adv.* Through, because of, or during which.

where·to (hwâr′tōō′, wâr′-) *adv.* To what place; toward what end. ~*conj.* To which.

where·up·on (hwâr′ə-pŏn′, -pôn′, wâr′-) *conj.* **1.** On which. **2.** In close consequence of which: *The president entered the room, whereupon the reporters rose.*

wher·ev·er (hwâr-ĕv′ər, wâr-) *adv.* Also **where ever** (for sense 2), *poetic* **wher·e'er** (-âr′). **1.** In, at, or to whatever place: *Wherever is she going?* **2.** Where. Used as an intensive: *Wherever did you hear that?* **3.** *Informal.* In, at, or to an unspecified place; anywhere: *can be used in the home, the office, or wherever.* ~*conj.* Also *poetic* **where·e'er.** **1.** In, at, or to whichever place or situation that: *sit wherever you like.* **2.** In, at, or to every place or situation that: *followed wherever she went.* [Middle English *wherever* : WHERE + EVER.]

where·with (hwâr′wĭth′, -wĭth′, wâr′-) *adv.* With what or which. ~*conj.* By means of which: *the pen wherewith I write.* ~*pron. Archaic.* The thing or things with which: *"Make ready wherewith I may sup"* (Luke 17:8).

where·with·al (hwâr′wĭth-ôl′, -wĭth-ôl′, wâr′-) *adv. Archaic.* Wherewith. ~*pron. Archaic.* Wherewith. ~*n.* The necessary means, especially financial means: *didn't have the wherewithal to live without working.*

wher·ry (hwĕr′ē, wĕr′ē) *n., pl.* **-ries. 1.** A light, swift rowboat built for one person and often used in racing. **2.** A kind of sailing barge used in East Anglia. [Middle English *wheryt*.]

whet (hwĕt, wĕt) *tr.v.* **whet·ted, whet·ting, whets. 1.** To sharpen (a knife or other tool); hone. **2.** To make more keen; stimulate or heighten: *The noise whetted his curiosity.* ~*n.* **1.** Something that whets. **2.** *Informal.* **a.** An appetizer. **b.** An apéritif. [Middle English *whetten,* Old English *hwettan.*]

wheth·er (hwĕth′ər, wĕth′-) *conj.* **1.** If it is so that; if the case is that. Used in indirect questions to introduce one alternative: *Ask whether the museum is open.* **2.** If it happens that; in case. Used to introduce the first of a set of possibilities and sometimes one or more other possibilities: *Whether he wins or (whether he) loses, this is his last fight. I'm seeing her, whether in Rome, London, or Paris.* —See Usage note at **if.** ~*pron. Obsolete.* Which of the two. Used in direct or indirect questions. —**whether or no** (or **not**). Regardless of circumstances. [Middle English *whether,* Old English *hwæther, hwether.*]

whet·stone (hwĕt′stōn′, wĕt′-) *n.* A stone for honing tools.

whew (hwōō, hwyōō) *interj.* Used to express relief or amazement. Usually partially unvoiced in imitation of a whistle. [Middle English *whewe* (imitative).]

whey (hwā, wā) *n.* The watery part of milk that separates from the curds, as in the process of making cheese. Also called "serum." [Middle English *whey,* Old English *hwæg,* from Germanic *khwuja-* (unattested).] —**whey′ey** *adj.*

whey-face (hwā′fās′, wā′-) *n.* A person with a pallid face. —**whey′faced** (hwā′fāst′, wā′-) *adj.*

which (hwĭch, wĭch) *pron.* **1.** What particular one or ones: *Which of these is yours? One of these is yours, but I'm not sure which.* **2.** The thing, animal, group of people, or event previously designated or implied, specifically: **a.** Used as a relative pronoun in a clause that provides additional information about the antecedent: *my house, which is small and old.* **b.** Used as a relative pronoun preceded by *that* or *those* or by a preposition in a clause that defines or restricts the antecedent: *the subject on which he spoke; took those which belonged to him.* **c.** Used instead of *that* as a relative pronoun in a clause that defines or restricts the antecedent: *The movie which was shown later was better.* **3.** *Archaic.* The person designated or implied. Used as a relative pronoun: *Our Father, which art in Heaven.* **4.** Any of the things, events, or persons designated or implied; whichever: *Choose which you like best.* **5.** A thing or circumstance that: *He left early, which was wise.* ~*adj.* **1.** What particular one or ones of a number of things or persons: *Which part of town? He asked me which color I preferred.* **2.** Any one or any number of; whichever: *Use which door you please.* **3.** Being the one or ones previously designated: *It started to rain, at which point we ran.* [Middle English *which, wilke,* Old English *hwilc, hwelc.*]

which·ev·er (hwĭch-ĕv′ər, wĭch-) *pron.* Whatever one or ones; no matter which. ~*adj.* Being any one or any number of a group of things or persons; no matter which: *Read whichever books you please. It's a long trip whichever road you take.*

which·so·ev·er (hwĭch′sō-ĕv′ər, wĭch′-) *pron.* Whichever. ~*adj.* Whichever. Used for emphasis.

whimbrel *A shorter curved bill and a striped forehead distinguish the whimbrel from its close relative, the curlew. Its call—a series of high-pitched whistles, often in groups of seven cries—has given it the colloquial name of seven whistler.*

whick·er (hwĭk′ər, wĭk′-) *intr.v.* **-ered, -ering, -ers.** To whinny. ~*n.* A whinny. [Imitative.]

whi·dah. Variant of **whydah.**

whiff (hwĭf, wĭf) *n.* **1.** A slight, gentle gust or breath of air; a waft: *a whiff of cool air.* **2.** A brief, passing odor carried in the air; a momentary smell: *"a whiff of lilac drifted across the room"* (Elizabeth Bowen). **3.** A slight trace or suggestion: *a whiff of scandal.* **4.** An inhalation, as of air, perfume, or tobacco smoke: *Take a whiff of this pipe.* **5.** *British.* A small cigar. ~*v.* **whiffed, whiffing, whiffs.** —*intr.* **1.** To be carried in brief gusts; waft. **2.** To draw in or breathe out a vapor, as air or smoke. **3.** *British Informal.* To emit an unpleasant smell. —*tr.* **1.** To blow or convey in whiffs. **2.** To inhale through the nose; smell; sniff. **3.** To draw in or breathe out (air or tobacco smoke, for example). [Imitative.] —**whiff′er** *n.*

whif·fle (hwĭf′əl, wĭf′-) *v.* **-fled, -fling, -fles.** —*intr.* **1.** To move or think erratically; vacillate. **2.** To blow in fitful gusts; puff. Used of the wind. **3.** To produce a light whistling sound. **4.** To move as if blown by wind; flutter. —*tr.* To blow, displace, or scatter with gusts of air. [From WHIFF (to blow).]

whif·fle·tree (hwĭf′əl-trē, wĭf′-) *n.* The pivoted horizontal crossbar to which the harness traces of a draft animal are attached and which is in turn attached to a vehicle or an implement. Also called "singletree," "swingletree," "whippletree."

Whig (hwĭg, wĭg) *n.* **1.** In the 17th century, a supporter of the Presbyterian cause in Scotland. **2.** From the late 17th to the mid-19th century, a member or supporter of one of the two major British political parties, opposed to the Tories and eventually succeeded by the Liberals. Early Whigs chiefly represented the aristocracy and sought the limitation of the power of the monarchy, while in the late 18th and early 19th centuries the Whigs came increasingly to represent the new industrial interests and to become a party of reform. **3.** A person who identifies strongly with the Whig political tradition. **4.** A supporter of the war against England during the American Revolution. **5.** A 19th-century American political party formed to oppose the Democratic Party, succeeded by the Republican Party, and favoring high tariffs and a loose interpretation of the Constitution. [Probably short for *Whiggamore,* one of a body of 17th-century Scottish insurgents : perhaps *whigt,* to drive + Middle English *mere,* horse, MARE.] —**Whig, Whig·gish** *adj.*

Whig·ger·y (hwĭg′ə-rē, wĭg′-) *n., pl.* **-ies.** Also **Whig·gism** (-ĭz′əm). The principles or practices of Whigs.

while (hwīl, wīl) *n.* **1.** A period of time: *stay for a while; sang all the while.* **2.** The time, effort, or trouble taken in doing something: *It is not worth my while to go yet.* —**once in a while.** Now and then; very occasionally. ~*conj.* **1.** As long as; during the time that: *It was lovely while it lasted.* **2.** At the same time that; although: *While I respect your opinion, I can't agree with you.* **3.** When on the contrary; whereas: *The soles are leather, while the uppers are canvas.* ~*prep. British Regional.* Until. ~*tr.v.* **whiled, whiling, whiles.** To spend (time) idly or pleasantly: *whiled the hours away playing solitaire.* [Middle English *while, qwile,* Old English *hwīl.*]

   Usage: The use of *while* in sentences like *Jean is French, John is English, while Jan is Polish* tends to attract criticism from purists, who find it inelegant. Indeed, all senses of *while* other than the strictly temporal have received criticism, usually on the grounds of a potential ambiguity: *She spent her youth in Wales, while her mother grew up in England.*

whiles (hwīlz, wīlz) *conj. Archaic.* While. [Middle English, adverbial genitive of WHILE.]

whi·lom (hwī′ləm, wī′-) *adj.* Having once been; former. ~*adv. Archaic.* Formerly. [Middle English *whilom,* Old English *hwīlum,* dative plural of *hwīl,* WHILE.]

whilst (hwīlst, wīlst) *conj. Chiefly British.* While. [Middle English *whylst,* from WHILES.]

whim (hwĭm, wĭm) *n.* **1.** A sudden or capricious idea; a passing fancy. **2.** Arbitrary thought or impulse; caprice: *governed by whim.* **3.** *Mining.* A vertical horse-powered drum used as a hoist. —See Synonyms at **caprice.** [Short for earlier *whim-whamt*.]

whim·brel (hwĭm′brəl, wĭm′-) *n.* A grayish-brown wading bird, *Numenius phaeopus,* having long legs and a long, downward-curving bill. [Origin unknown.]

whim·per (hwĭm′pər, wĭm′-) *v.* **-pered, -pering, -pers.** —*intr.* **1.** To cry or sob with soft intermittent sounds. **2.** To complain. —*tr.* To utter in a whimper. —See Synonyms at **cry.** ~*n.* A low, broken, sobbing sound. [Dialectal *whimp* (imitative).] —**whim·per·er** *n.* —**whim·per·ing·ly** *adv.*

whim·si·cal (hwĭm′zĭ-kəl, wĭm′-) *adj.* **1.** Capricious, playful, or fanciful. **2.** Unusual, fantastic, or odd. [From WHIMSY.] —**whim·si·cal·i·ty** (hwĭm′zĭ-kăl′ə-tē, wĭm′-) *n.* —**whim·si·cal·ly** *adv.*

whim·sy, whim·sey (hwĭm′zē, wĭm′-) *n., pl.* **-sies, -seys. 1.** A tendency to have or show a fanciful, often humorous approach to life; whimsicality: *loved whimsy and nonsense verse.* **2.** An odd or capricious idea; an idle fancy. **3.** Something quaint, fanciful, or odd. [Probably from WHIM.]

whin[1] (hwĭn, wĭn) *n.* A spiny shrub, **gorse** *(see).* [Middle English *whynnet*.]

whin[2] *n.* Whinstone. [Middle English *quint*.]

whin·chat (hwĭn′chăt′, wĭn′-) *n.* A brownish Old World bird, *Saxicola rubetra,* frequenting open country. [From WHIN (gorse) (the bird is often found around gorse bushes).]

whine (hwīn, wīn) *v.* **whined, whining, whines.** —*intr.* **1.** To utter a plaintive, high-pitched, protracted sound, as in pain, fear, supplication, or complaint. **2.** To complain or protest in a childish, annoying fashion. **3.** To produce a sustained noise of relatively high pitch: *jet engines whining.* —*tr.* To utter with a whine.
∼*n.* **1.** A whining sound. **2.** A complaint uttered in a plaintive tone. [Middle English *whinen,* Old English *hwīnan.*] **—whin·er** *n.* **—whin·ing·ly** *adv.* **—whin·y** *adj.*

whinge (hwĭnj, wĭnj) *intr.v.* **whinged, whinging, whinges.** *British Informal.* To whine or complain.
∼*n. British Informal.* A whine or complaint. [Northern English dialect, from Late Old English *hwinsian* (imitative); akin to German *winseln,* to WHINE.]

whin·ny (hwĭn′ē, wĭn′-) *v.* **-nied, -nying, -nies.** —*intr.* To neigh, especially in a gentle tone. Used chiefly of a horse. —*tr.* To express in a whinny.
∼*n., pl.* **whinnies.** The sound made in whinnying; a neigh. [Probably WHINE (imitative).]

whin·stone (hwĭn′stōn′, wĭn′-) *n.* Any of various hard, dark-colored rocks, especially basalt and chert. Also called "whin."

whip (hwĭp, wĭp) *v.* **whipped** or **whipt** (hwĭpt, wĭpt), **whipping, whips.** —*tr.* **1.** To strike with repeated strokes, as of a lash, strap, or rod; beat. **2. a.** To punish or chastise by whipping; flog or thrash. **b.** To afflict, castigate, or reprove severely. **3.** To drive, urge, force, or bring by or as if by whipping: *whipped his horse on; tried to whip the team into shape.* **4.** To strike or affect in a manner similar to whipping or lashing: *Icy winds whipped his face.* **5.** To beat (cream or eggs, for example) into a froth or foam. **6.** To move (something) with a sudden rapid motion; take, put, or remove quickly: *whipped out a revolver; whipped off his cap.* **7.** To sew with a loose overcast or overhand stitch; whipstitch. **8.** To wrap or bind (a rope, for example) with twine to prevent unraveling or fraying. **9.** *Nautical.* To hoist by means of a rope passing through an overhead pulley. **10.** To fish (a stream or pool) by casting the line onto the water with a whipping motion. **11.** *Informal.* To defeat; outdo: *well and truly whipped by a superior team.* —*intr.* **1.** To move or proceed briskly: *just going to whip down to the shops; whipped through the report in 10 minutes.* **2.** To move in a manner similar to whipping; thrash or snap about: *Branches whipped against the windows.*
∼*n.* **1.** An instrument, either a flexible rod or a flexible thong or lash attached to a handle, used for driving animals or administering corporal punishment. **2.** A whipping or lashing motion or stroke. **3.** A blow, wound, or cut made by or as if by whipping. **4.** Something, such as an automobile radio antenna, that is similar to a whip in form or flexibility. **5.** Flexibility, as in the shaft of a golf club. **6.** A legislative whipper-in. **7. a.** A member of a legislative body, as the U.S. Congress or the British Parliament, charged by his party with enforcing party discipline and especially with ensuring attendance. **b.** A notice requiring party members in a legislative body to attend a particular session and vote according to the party line. **8.** A dessert made of sugar and stiffly beaten egg whites or cream, often with fruit or fruit flavoring: *prune whip.* **9.** A kitchen utensil used for whipping foods. **10.** A windmill arm. **11.** *Nautical.* A hoist consisting of a single rope passing through an overhead pulley. **12.** A ride in an amusement park consisting of small cars that move in a rapid, whipping motion. **—whip in.** To keep (a pack of hounds) together by using a whip; act as a whipper-in. **—whip up. 1.** To arouse; excite: *whip up a crowd; whip up enthusiasm.* **2.** *Informal.* To prepare (a meal, for example) quickly. [Middle English *wippen,* perhaps from Middle Low German or Middle Dutch, to vacillate, swing.] **—whip·per** *n.*

whip bird *n.* Any of various Australian birds such as *Psophodes olivaceus,* having a cry resembling the crack of a whip.

whip·cord (hwĭp′kôrd′, wĭp′-) *n.* **1.** A worsted fabric with a distinct diagonal rib. **2.** A strong twisted or braided cord sometimes used in making whiplashes.

whip graft *n.* A horticultural graft in which a tongue cut on the sloping base of the scion is inserted into a slit made on the sloping top of the stock.

whip hand *n.* **1.** The hand in which a driver holds the whip. **2.** A dominating position; upper hand.

whip·lash (hwĭp′lăsh′, wĭp′-) *n.* **1.** The lash of a whip. **2.** An injury to the spine in the neck region caused by an abrupt jerking motion of the head, either backward or forward. In this sense, also called "whiplash injury." **—whip·lash** *adj.*

whip·per-in (hwĭp′ər-ĭn′, wĭp′-) *n., pl.* **whippers-in. 1.** In foxhunting, one who assists the huntsman in handling a pack of hounds. Also called "whip." **2.** A legislative whip.

whip·per·snap·per (hwĭp′ər-snăp′ər, wĭp′-) *n.* An impertinent but insignificant person. [Perhaps from *whipsnapper,* suggesting noisy but insignificant activity.]

whip·pet (hwĭp′ĭt, wĭp′-) *n.* A short-haired, swift-running dog of a breed developed in England, resembling the greyhound but smaller. [Perhaps from obsolete *whippet,* to move quickly, from *whip it.*]

whip·ping (hwĭp′ĭng, wĭp′-) *n.* **1.** A thrashing administered especially as punishment. **2.** Material, such as cord or thread, used to lash or bind parts.

whipping boy *n.* **1.** One who gets the blame for the faults of others, especially of his superiors; a scapegoat. **2.** A boy formerly educated with a prince or other young nobleman and whipped for the latter's misdeeds.

whip·ple·tree (hwĭp′əl-trē′, wĭp′-) *n.* A **whiffletree** *(see).* [Alteration of WHIP + TREE.]

whip·poor·will (hwĭp′ər-wĭl′, wĭp′-, hwĭp′ər-wĭl′, wĭp′-) *n.* A brownish nocturnal North American bird, *Caprimulgus vociferus,* having a distinctive call of which its name is imitative.

whip·saw (hwĭp′sô′, wĭp′-) *n.* A narrow two-man crosscut saw.
∼*tr.v.* **whipsawed** or **-sawn** (-sôn′), **-sawing, -saws. 1.** To cut with a whipsaw. **2.** To defeat or get the better of in two ways at once or by the joint action of two parties.

whip scorpion *n.* Any of various nonvenomous scorpionlike arachnids of the order Pedipalpi, as the vinegarroon.

whip snake *n.* Any of various slender nonvenomous snakes, such as *Coluber gemonensis,* of Eurasia, or one of the genus *Masticophis,* of the New World.

whip·stall (hwĭp′stôl′, wĭp′-) *n.* A usually intentional stall in which an aircraft enters a vertical climb, pauses, slips backward momentarily, and then drops nose downward.

whip·stitch (hwĭp′stĭch′, wĭp′-) *tr.v.* **-stitched, -stitching, -stitches.** To sew with overcast stitches, as in finishing a fabric edge or binding two pieces of fabric together.
∼*n.* A stitch or stitches made in this manner.

whip·stock (hwĭp′stŏk′, wĭp′-) *n.* The handle of a whip.

whipt. Alternate past tense and past participle of *whip.*

whip·tail (hwĭp′tāl′, wĭp′-) *n.* Any of various New World lizards of the genus *Cnemidophorus,* having a long, slender tail.

whip·worm (hwĭp′wûrm′, wĭp′-) *n.* A slender, parasitic roundworm, *Trichuris trichiura,* that infests the large intestine in humans.

whir, whirr (hwûr, wûr) *intr.v.* **whirred, whirring, whirs** or **whirrs.** To move so as to produce a continuous vibrating or buzzing sound, as some machines or the wings of certain birds do.
∼*n.* A sound of buzzing or vibration. [Middle English *whirren,* from Scandinavian, akin to Danish *hvirre.*]

whirl (hwûrl, wûrl) *v.* **whirled, whirling, whirls.** —*intr.* **1.** To revolve rapidly about a center or axis. **2.** To rotate or spin rapidly. **3.** To turn aside or away rapidly; wheel. **4.** To have the sensation of spinning; reel. **5.** To move along rapidly in or as if in a wheeled vehicle. —*tr.* **1.** To cause to rotate or turn rapidly. **2.** To drive or carry along at great speed in a circular or curving course. **3.** *Obsolete.* To hurl. —See Synonyms at **turn.**
∼*n.* **1.** The act of rotating or revolving rapidly. **2.** Something that whirls or is whirled, as a cloud of dust. **3.** A state of confusion; a tumult; a turmoil. **4.** A hurried succession or round of events: *the social whirl.* **5.** A state of mental confusion or giddiness; dizziness: *My head is in a whirl.* **6.** *Informal.* A short trip; a spin. **7.** *Informal.* A brief try: *Let's give it a whirl.* [Middle English *whirlen,* from Old Norse *hvirfla.*] **—whirl·er** *n.*

whirl·i·gig (hwûr′lĭ-gĭg′, wûr′-) *n.* **1.** Any of various spinning toys. **2.** A carousel or merry-go-round. **3.** Something that is continuously whirling or in a state of constant movement or change. **4.** The whirligig beetle. [Middle English *whirlegigge* : *whirlen,* to WHIRL + *gigg(e),* spinning top.]

whirligig beetle *n.* Any of various beetles of the family Gyrinidae that circle about rapidly on the surface of quiet water.

whirl·pool (hwûrl′po͞ol′, wûrl′-) *n.* **1.** Water in rapid rotating movement, as from the converging of two tides, tending to draw any floating object into its center and down; an eddy or vortex. **2.** Something suggesting the rapid turbulence of whirling water. **3.** A gripping force into which one may be inextricably drawn.

whirl·wind (hwûrl′wĭnd′, wûrl′-) *n.* **1. a.** A column of air centered on an area of low atmospheric pressure, rotating violently around a more or less vertical axis and moving forward; a tornado. **b.** A small, momentary current of such whirling air over dusty flat land; a dust devil. **2.** Something rushing or whirling impetuously, confusedly, or destructively. —See Synonyms at **wind.**
∼*adj.* Very rapid or impetuous: *a whirlwind courtship.*

whirl·y·bird (hwûr′lē-bûrd′, wûr′-) *n. Slang.* A helicopter. [From WHIRL + BIRD.]

whisht (hwĭsht) *interj. Scottish & Irish.* Hush. [Middle English (imitative).]
∼*tr.v.* **whishted, whishting, whishts.** *Scottish & Irish.* To hush; silence. [Middle English (imitative).]

whisk (hwĭsk, wĭsk) *v.* **whisked, whisking, whisks.** —*tr.* **1.** To move or remove with quick light sweeping motions: *whisked the crumbs off the table.* **2.** To carry or convey quickly and unobtrusively: *was whisked off to the theater in a limousine.* **3.** To whip (eggs or cream). —*intr.* To move lightly, nimbly, and rapidly.
∼*n.* **1.** A quick light sweeping motion. **2.** A small bundle, as of twigs or feathers, especially one used for brushing away dust or flies. **3.** A kitchen utensil, typically made of looped wire, for beating or whipping foodstuffs. [Middle English (Scottish) *quhisken,* from Scandinavian, akin to Swedish *viska†.*]

whisk·broom (hwĭsk′bro͞om′, -bro͝om′, wĭsk′-) *n.* A small short-handled broom used especially to brush clothes.

whisk·er (hwĭs′kər, wĭs′-) *n.* **1. a. whiskers.** The unshaven hair on a man's face, especially that part of it growing on the chin and the sides of the face; beard. **b.** A single hair of the beard or mustache. **2.** Any of the long stiff bristles or hairs growing near the mouth of certain animals. **3.** *Informal.* A narrow margin; hairsbreadth: *He lost by a whisker.* **4.** *Nautical.* One of two spars or booms projecting from the side of a bowsprit for spreading the jib or flying-jib guys. Also called "whisker boom." **5.** *Chemistry.* Any of the extremely fine filamentary crystals that can be grown from supersaturated solutions of certain minerals and metals and that possess extraor-

PRONUNCIATION KEY

ă, pat; ā, pay; âr, care;
ä, father, are; b, bib;
ch, church; d, deed; ĕ, pet;
ē, be; f, fife; g, gag; h, hat;
hw, which; ĭ, pit; ī, pie;
îr, pier; j, judge; k, kick;
l, lid, needle; m, mum;
n, no, sudden; ng, thing;
ŏ, pot; ō, toe; ô, paw, for;
oi, noise; ou, out; o͝o, book;
o͞o, boot; p, pop; r, roar;
s, sauce; sh, ship, dish;
t, tight; th, thin, path;
th, this, bathe; ŭ, cut; ûr, fur;
v, valve; w, with; y, yes;
z, zebra, size; zh, vision;
ə, about, item, edible,
gallop, circus, peaceful

IN FOREIGN WORDS:

à, *Fr.* ami; œ, *Fr.* feu, *Ger.* schön; ü, *Fr.* tu, *Ger.* über;
KH, *Ger.* ich, *Scot.* loch;
N, *Fr.* bon; y′, *Fr.* Compiègne

STRESS MARKS:

Primary stress: ′
in·cite′ (ĭn-sīt′)
Secondary stress: ′
in′sight′ (ĭn′sīt′)

white clover *A plant important to beekeepers because of the abundant nectar its flowers contain. Its leaves usually grow in groups of three; the rarer four-leaf clover is said to bring good luck to the finder.*

dinary shear strength and unusual electrical or surface properties. [From WHISK.] **—whisk·ered, whisk·er·y** *adj.*

whis·key (hwĭs′kē, wĭs′-) *n., pl.* **-keys.** Also **whis·ky** *pl.* **-kies. 1.** An alcoholic liquor distilled from fermented grain, typically from malted barley in Scotland and Ireland and from corn or rye in the United States and Canada, and containing approximately 40 to 50 percent ethyl alcohol by volume. **2.** A drink of whiskey. [Shortened from obsolete *whiskybae,* alteration of USQUEBAUGH.]

Usage: *Whiskey* is the usual American spelling, and it is also used of Irish whiskey. *Whisky* is the spelling for liquor made in Scotland or Canada.

whiskey sour *n.* A cocktail made with whiskey, lemon juice, and sugar.

whis·per (hwĭs′pər, wĭs′-) *n.* **1.** Soft speech produced without vibration of the vocal cords. **2.** Something uttered very softly. **3.** A secretly or surreptitiously expressed belief, rumor, or hint. **4.** A low rustling sound.

∼v. **whispered, -pering, -pers.** *—intr.* **1.** To speak softly, without the resonance produced by vibration of the vocal cords. **2.** To speak quietly or secretively, as by way of gossip, slander, or intrigue. **3.** To make a soft rustling sound, as surf or leaves do. *—tr.* **1.** To utter very softly. **2.** To say or suggest secretly or confidentially. [Middle English *whisperen,* Old English *hwisprian* (imitative).] **—whis·per·er** *n.*

whispering campaign *n.* A concerted effort to discredit a person or group by disseminating unfavorable allegations and rumors by word of mouth.

whist (hwĭst, wĭst) *n.* A card game for two pairs of players in which each pair tries to win as many as possible of the 13 available tricks. [Origin unknown.]

whis·tle (hwĭs′əl, wĭs′-) *v.* **-tled, -tling, -tles.** *—intr.* **1.** To produce a clear musical sound or series of sounds by forcing air through an aperture formed by pursing the lips. **2.** To produce a clear, shrill, sharp musical sound or series of sounds by blowing on or through a device. **3.** To produce a high-pitched sound when moving swiftly through the air: *The book whistled past his head.* **4.** To emit a sharp, high-pitched, often shrill note or cry, as some birds and animals do. **5.** To summon or signal by whistling: *whistled to his dog to follow him.* **6.** *Informal.* To request or expect something with no chance of success: *wants his money back, but he can whistle for it.* *—tr.* **1.** To produce by whistling: *whistle a tune.* **2.** To summon, signal, or direct by whistling.

∼n. **1. a.** A small wind instrument for making whistling sounds by means of the breath. **b.** A device for making whistling sounds by means of forced air or steam: *a factory whistle.* **2.** A sound produced by a whistle or by whistling through the lips. **3.** A whistling sound, as of an animal, a projectile, or the wind. **4.** The act of whistling. **5.** A whistling sound used to summon or command or to give a signal. **—blow the whistle on.** *Informal.* **1.** To expose and put a stop to (shady or undesirable activity). **2.** To give incriminating information about; inform on. [Middle English *whist(e)len,* Old English *hwistlian* (imitative).]

whis·tler (hwĭs′lər, wĭs′-) *n.* **1.** One that whistles. **2.** Any of various birds that produce a whistling sound, as certain Australian flycatchers and the goldeneye duck. **3.** A marmot, *Marmota caligata,* of the mountains of northwestern North America, having a grayish coat and a shrill, whistling cry. **4.** *Physics.* An electromagnetic wave of audio frequency produced by atmospheric disturbances such as lightning and having a characteristically decreasing frequency responsible for a whistling sound of descending pitch in detection equipment. **5.** A horse having a respiratory disease characterized by wheezing.

Whis·tler (hwĭs′lər, wĭs′-), **James Abbott McNeill** (1834–1903). U.S. painter. His works concentrate more on tone and color than on draughtsmanship. They include a portrait of his mother *Arrangement in Grey and Black* (1872) and *Old Battersea Bridge.*

whistle stop *n.* **1.** A small town at which a train stops only if signaled. **2.** One of a series of brief visits or appearances, especially by a candidate in an election.

whis·tle-stop (hwĭs′əl-stŏp′, wĭs′-) *intr.v.* **-stopped, -stopping, -stops.** To conduct a political campaign by making brief appearances or speeches in a series of small towns.

whistling swan *n.* A North American swan, *Olor columbianus,* having a black beak marked with yellow at the base.

whit (hwĭt, wĭt) *n.* The least bit; iota: *not a whit afraid.* [Variant of Middle English *wi(g)ht,* creature, WIGHT.]

white (hwīt, wīt) *n. Abbr.* **wh. 1.** An achromatic color of maximum lightness, the complement of black, the other extreme of the neutral gray series. Although typically a response to maximum stimulation, white appears always to depend upon contrast. **2.** The white or nearly white part of something, as: **a.** The albumen of an egg. **b.** The white part of an eyeball. **c.** A blank area on a printed surface. **3.** Something white or nearly white, as: **a.** White clothes: *dressed all in white.* **b. whites.** A white or cream outfit or item of clothing, as worn for some sports: *tennis whites.* **c.** A white wine. **d.** A white pigment: *titanium white.* **e.** A white breed of animal. **f.** Often **whites.** Products of a white color, as flour, salt, and sugar. **4. a.** The white or light-colored pieces in checkers or chess. **b.** The player using these pieces. **5. a.** The outermost ring of a target. **b.** A hit in the outermost ring of a target. **6.** A Caucasoid. **7.** Any of various butterflies of the family Pieridae, having white wings with some black markings, as the **cabbage white** *(see).* **8. whites.** *Medicine.* Leukorrhea. **9.** A member of any of several reactionary or counterrevolutionary political groups active in Europe from the 18th to the early 20th centuries.

∼adj. **whiter, whitest. 1.** Being of the color white; devoid of hue, as new snow is. **2.** Approaching the color white, as: **a.** Translucent and almost colorless: *white wine.* **b.** Pale green. Said of certain grapes. **c.** Pale gray; silvery and lustrous, as silver or tin or objects made of silver or tin. **d.** Silvery or light gray with age: *white hair.* **e.** Bloodless, as from illness or fear; blanched. **3.** Light or whitish in color or having light or whitish parts. Used with animal and plant names: *the white whale; white clover.* **4. a.** Having the comparatively pale complexion typical of Caucasoids. **b.** Of, pertaining to, characteristic of, or dominated by Caucasians. **5.** Not written or printed upon; blank. **6. a.** Pure; untainted; innocent. **b.** *Informal.* Fair; decent; honorable. **7. a.** Wearing a white habit: *white nuns.* **b.** Marked by the wearing of white by the bride: *a white wedding.* **8.** Accompanied by or mantled with snow: *a white Christmas.* **9. a.** Incandescent: *white heat.* **b.** Intensely heated; impassioned: *white with fury.* **10.** Reactionary or counterrevolutionary. **11.** Whitish in color as a result of processing. Said of some foodstuffs: *white bread; white rice.* Compare **brown. 12.** *Chiefly British.* With milk or cream added. Used of tea or coffee.

∼tr.v. **whited, whiting, whites. 1.** *Printing.* To create or leave blank spaces in (printed or illustrated matter). **2.** To efface with correction fluid: *made an error in typing and had to white out the line.* **3.** *Archaic.* **a.** To whiten; whitewash. **b.** To blanch. [Middle English *white,* Old English *hwīt,* white, white of an egg.] **—whit·ish** *adj.*

White (hwīt, wīt), **Elwyn Brooks,** known as "E. B." (1899–1985). U.S. author, humorist, and editor. He spent most of his career writing for *The New Yorker,* contributing essays, editorials, and parodies in prose and verse. He also wrote children's books, including *Charlotte's Web* (1952), edited anthologies of short stories and American humor, and revised William Strunk, Jr.'s 1918 manual, *The Elements of Style.*

White, John (died *c.* 1593). English painter and cartographer. During the first expedition to Roanoke Island (1585–86) he executed paintings of the flora and fauna of the region and produced several maps of the coastline. Appointed governor of the second Roanoke Island colony (1587), he was on a mission to England when all the colonists, including his granddaughter Virginia Dare, mysteriously disappeared.

White, Stanford (1853–1906). U.S. architect. A member of the influential architectural firm McKim, Mead & White, he worked in a large number of styles, occasionally combining complementary styles in a single building. Among his famous works are several buildings at the University of Virginia and the first Madison Square Garden (1889).

White, Terence Hanbury, known as "T. H." (1906–64). British author. He is best known for his novels about the Arthurian legend, including *The Sword in the Stone* (1937). The four books about Arthur were published collectively as *The Once and Future King* (1958). He also wrote *Mistress Masham's Repose* (1946).

White, Theodore Harold, known as "T.H." (1915–86). U.S. author. A longtime reporter on the political scene, White is best known for his series of books entitled *The Making of the President,* the first of which covered in a wealth of detail the presidential campaign of 1960.

White, William Allen (1868–1944). U.S. editor and author. In 1923 he won a Pulitzer Prize for his politically influential and widely reprinted editorials. Although primarily a newspaperman, he also wrote several books, including his autobiography, published posthumously in 1946, which earned him another Pulitzer Prize.

white admiral *n.* A Eurasian butterfly, *Limenitis camilla,* having brown wings marked with white.

white alkali *n.* **1.** Any of several mineral salts, such as sodium sulfate or sodium chloride, that appear as a white deposit on certain alkaline soils. **2.** Refined sodium carbonate.

white ant *n.* A **termite** *(see).*

white asbestos *n.* A variety of asbestos, **chrysotile** *(see).*

white·bait (hwīt′bāt′, wīt′-) *n.* **1.** The young of various fishes, such as the herring, considered a delicacy when fried. **2.** Any of various other small edible fishes.

white·beam (hwīt′bēm′, wīt′-) *n.* A European tree, *Sorbus aria,* the leaves of which have a whitish down on the undersurface. [Probably WHITE + BEAM.]

white birch *n.* Any of several birch trees having white bark, such as *Betula pendula,* of Europe, or the **paper birch** *(see).*

white blood cell *n.* A **leucocyte** *(see).*

white bryony *n.* A climbing European vine, *Bryonia dioica,* having lobed leaves, greenish-white flowers, and scarlet berries.

white·cap (hwīt′kăp′, wīt′-) *n.* A wave with a crest of foam.

white cedar *n.* **1.** Any of several North American coniferous trees, chiefly of the genus *Chamaecyparis,* having light-colored wood. **2.** The wood of any of these trees.

white cell *n.* A **leucocyte** *(see).*

white cloud *n.* A small, brightly colored freshwater fish, *Tanichthys albonubes,* native to China and popular in home aquariums.

white clover *n.* A common clover, *Trifolium repens,* native to Eurasia, having rounded white flower heads. Also called "Dutch clover."

white coal *n.* Water regarded as a source of power.

white-col·lar (hwīt′kŏl′ər, wīt′-) *adj.* Of, pertaining to, or designating those workers, usually salaried, whose work usually does not involve manual labor and who may be expected to dress with some degree of formality. Compare **blue-collar.**

white corpuscle *n.* A **leucocyte** *(see).*

white crappie *n.* See **crappie.**

white currant *n.* **1.** A shrub, *Ribes sativum,* cultivated for its edible berries. **2.** The small, round, white berry of this shrub.

white daisy *n.* See **daisy.**

white damp *n.* A poisonous gas consisting primarily of carbon monoxide that occurs in coal mines.

whited sepulcher *n.* An evil person who pretends to be holy or good; a hypocrite. Matthew 23:27.

white dwarf *n.* A faint highly dense star believed to represent the final stage in the evolution of a star of about the mass of the sun.

white elephant *n.* **1.** A rare whitish or light-gray form of the Asian elephant, often regarded with special veneration in regions of south-eastern Asia. **2.** Something that is large, costly, and perhaps impressive, but expensive to maintain, unproductive, and conse-quently unwanted. **3.** An expensive project or venture which comes to nothing or turns out to be a failure. **4.** Any possession no longer wanted by its owner. [Referring to a custom of the kings of Siam, who would express displeasure with a courtier by the gift of a white elephant, the upkeep of which was ruinously expensive.]

white-eye (hwīt′ī′, wīt′-) *n.* Any of various small greenish birds of the genus *Zosterops,* of Africa, southern Asia, and the Pacific is-lands, having a narrow ring of white feathers around each eye. Also *Australian* "silver-eye."

white-face (hwīt′fās′, wīt′-) *n.* Completely white make-up, as worn by clowns.

white-faced (hwīt′fāst′, wīt′-) *adj.* **1.** Pale; pallid. **2.** Having a white patch extending from the muzzle to the forehead.

white feather *n.* A sign of cowardice. [A gamecock with a white feather is regarded as a poor fighter.]

white-fish (hwīt′fĭsh′, wīt′-) *n., pl.* **-fishes** or collectively **whitefish.** **1.** Any of various freshwater food fishes of the genus *Coregonus,* occurring in the Northern Hemisphere and having a generally sil-very color. **2.** Any of various similar or related fishes.

white flag *n.* A white cloth or flag signaling surrender or truce.

white-fly (hwīt′flī′, wīt′-) *n., pl.* **-flies.** Any of various small whitish insects of the family Aleyrodidae, often injurious to plants.

white-foot-ed mouse (hwīt′foot′ĭd, wīt′-) *n.* The **deer mouse** *(see).*

white fox *n.* The **arctic fox** *(see)* in its winter color phase.

White Friar *n.* A **Carmelite** (sense 1) *(see).* [After the color of his habit.]

white frost *n.* **Hoarfrost** *(see).*

white gold *n.* An alloy of gold and nickel or palladium, and some-times containing small amounts of silver, copper, or zinc, having the color of platinum.

white goods *pl.n.* **1.** Household linens, such as sheets and towels, originally or typically white. **2.** Electrical household appliances such as refrigerators and washing machines, typically having a white exterior.

White-hall (hwīt′hôl′, wīt′-) *n.* The British government; especially, the government departments as distinguished from Parliament. [From *Whitehall,* a street in London where many departments of the government are located.]

White-head (hwīt′hĕd′, wīt′-), **Alfred North** (1861-1974). British philosopher and mathematician. One of the founders of mathemat-ical logic, his *Principia Mathematica* (1910-13) was written in col-laboration with Bertrand Russell.

white-head-ed (hwīt′hĕd′ĭd, wīt′-) *adj.* **1.** Having white hair or plumage on the head. Said of a bird or animal. **2. a.** White-haired, as from old age. **b.** Fair-haired. **3.** Favorite; darling: *the white-headed boy.*

white heat *n.* **1. a.** The temperature of a white-hot substance. **b.** The physical condition of a white-hot substance. **2.** A state of intense emotion or excitement.

white hole *n.* A hypothetical astrophysical object formed by the emergence of matter and energy from a space-time singularity through the event horizon.

white hope *n.* See **great white hope.**

white horehound *n.* A plant, the **horehound** (sense 1) *(see).*

white horse *n.* A wave capped with foam; whitecap.

White-horse (hwīt′hôrs′, wīt′-). Capital of the Yukon Territory, Canada, in the southern part of the territory on the Yukon River. It is the center of a copper-mining, hunting, and fur-trapping region and attracts many tourists.

white-hot (hwīt′hŏt′, wīt′-) *adj.* So hot as to glow with a bright white light; broadly, hotter than red-hot.

White House *n.* **1.** The official residence of the president of the United States in Washington, D.C. **2.** The supreme executive au-thority of the U.S. government.

white iron pyrites *n.* A mineral, **marcasite** *(see).*

white lead *n.* **1.** A heavy white poisonous compound of basic lead carbonate, lead silicate, or lead sulfate, used in paint pigments. Also called "ceruse." **2.** A form of putty consisting of white lead in boiled linseed oil.

white leather, whit-leath-er (hwīt′lĕth′ər, wīt′-) *n.* Leather that has been specially treated so as to make it white.

white leg *n.* A disease, **milk leg** *(see).*

white lie *n.* A diplomatic or well-intentioned untruth.

white light *n.* Light, such as sunlight, that contains the whole spec-trum of visible radiation in approximately equal proportions.

white line *n.* A solid or broken line of white paint marked on a road surface to indicate traffic lanes.

white magic *n.* Magic used for good purposes or against evil.

white man's burden *n.* The gratuitously assumed duty of the white peoples to govern and bring white civilization to the nonwhite peo-ples of the world. [From "The White Man's Burden" (1899), a poem by Rudyard Kipling.]

white matter *n.* White brain and spinal-cord tissue, consisting mostly of myelinated nerve fibers. Compare **gray matter.**

white meat *n.* Light-colored meat, especially of poultry. Compare **red meat.**

white metal *n.* Any of various whitish alloys, as pewter, having relatively low melting points and containing high percentages of tin, lead or antimony.

white mica *n.* A mineral, **muscovite** *(see).*

White Mountains. Part of the Appalachians in northern New Hampshire and southwestern Maine, rising in two main groups, the Presidential Range and the Franconia Mts., separated by Crawford Notch. Mt. Washington, in the Presidential Range, is the highest peak.

white mulberry *n.* A tree, *Morus alba,* native to China, having whit-ish or purplish fruit. Its leaves provide food for silkworms.

white mustard *n.* A Eurasian plant, *Brassica hirta* (or *Sinapis alba*), from whose seeds the condiment mustard is prepared.

whit-en (hwīt′n, wīt′n) *v.* **-ened, -ening, -ens.** —*tr.* To make white, as by bleaching or the application of whitewash. —*intr.* To become white. —**whit-en-er** *n.*

white-ness (hwīt′nĭs, wīt′-) *n.* **1.** The condition or quality of being white. **2.** Paleness or pallor. **3.** Moral purity; innocence. **4.** A white substance or area.

White Nile (nīl). River, 970 kilometers (600 miles) long, flowing northward from Lake No, in Sudan, to Khartoum, where it joins the Blue Nile to form the Nile proper.

white noise *n.* Acoustical or electrical noise in which the intensity is the same at all frequencies within a given band.

white oak *n.* A large oak, *Quercus alba,* of eastern North America, having heavy, hard, light-colored wood.

white-out (hwīt′out′, wīt′-) *n.* A polar weather condition caused by a heavy cloud cover over the snow, in which the light coming from above is approximately equal to the light reflected from below, and which is characterized by the absence of shadow, the invisibility of the horizon, and the discernibility of only very dark objects.

white paper *n.* Often **White Paper.** An official statement or report published by a government, providing information on a particular issue and presenting the government's own policy.

white pepper *n.* See **pepper.**

white perch *n.* A small food fish, *Roccus americanus,* of the Atlantic coast and freshwater ponds of North America.

white pine *n.* **1.** A timber tree, *Pinus strobus,* of eastern North America, having needles in clusters of five and durable, easily worked wood. **2.** The wood of the white pine.

white pointer *n.* A **white shark** *(see).*

white poplar *n.* A tree, *Populus alba,* native to Eurasia, having leaves with whitish undersides. Also called "abele."

white-print (hwīt′prĭnt′, wīt′-) *n.* A photomechanical copy, usually of line drawings, in which black or colored lines appear on a white background.

white rat *n.* A white variety of rat used as a laboratory animal in scientific research.

White Russia. See **Belorussian S.S.R.**

White Russian *n.* Belorussian *(see).*

White Sands. Uninhabited desert area in south-central New Mex-ico. It includes the White Sands Proving Grounds, a missile-testing range and the site of the first explosion of an atomic bomb (July 16, 1945). White Sands National Monument, 567 square kilometers (219 square miles), has been set aside to protect wind-drifted gyp-sum sands. There is also a wildlife refuge here.

white sapphire *n.* A pure form of corundum, used as a gem.

white sauce *n.* A sauce made with butter, flour, and milk, cream, or stock, sometimes used as a basis for other sauces.

White Sea. *Russian* **Be-lo-ye Mo-re** (bə-lô′yə môr′ə). Gulf of the Barents Sea, northwestern U.S.S.R. Part of the Arctic Ocean, it lies between the Kola and Kanin peninsulas and has the port of Arch-angel on its shore. It is linked by canal with the Baltic Sea.

white shark *n.* A large, whitish, man-eating shark, *Carcharodon carcharias.* Also called "great white shark," "white pointer."

white slave *n.* A woman held unwillingly for purposes of prostitu-tion. —**white-slave** *adj.* —**white slavery** *n.*

white slaver *n.* A procurer of white slaves.

white snakeroot *n.* A poisonous North American plant, *Eupato-rium rugosum,* having heart-shaped leaves and flat-topped clusters of small white flowers.

white squall *n.* A sudden squall occurring in tropical or subtropical waters, characterized by the absence of a dark cloud and the pres-ence of white-capped waves or broken water.

white supremacy *n.* The theory that the white race is inherently superior to and therefore entitled to rule over all other races. —**white supremacist** *n.*

white-tailed deer (hwīt′tāld′, wīt′-) *n.* A North American deer, *Odocoileus Virginianus,* having a grayish coat that turns red-dish-brown in summer and a tail that is white on the underside.

white-throat (hwīt′thrōt′, wīt′-) *n.* Either of two Old World song-

white-eye *There are about 80 species of this warblerlike bird, living in Africa, Asia, and the Pacific regions. This is an oriental white-eye,* Zosterops palpebrosa, *which ranges from Afghanistan to the islands of Southeast Asia.*

birds, *Sylvia communis* or *S. curruca,* having brownish plumage and a white throat.

white-throat-ed sparrow (hwīt'thrō'tĭd, wīt'-) *n.* A North American sparrow, *Zonotrichia albicollis,* having a white throat and a distinctive song.

white tie *n.* **1.** A white bow tie worn as a part of men's formal evening dress. **2.** The most formal type of men's evening dress, which includes a tailcoat. Compare **black tie.**

white trash *n. Offensive Slang.* A poor white or poor whites as a class.

white vitriol *n. Chemistry.* **Zinc sulfate** *(see).*

white-wall tire (hwīt'wôl', wīt'-) *n.* A tire on a motor vehicle having a white band on the visible side. Also called "whitewall."

white-wash (hwīt'wŏsh', -wôsh', wīt'-) *n.* **1.** A mixture of lime and water, often with whiting, size, or glue added, that is used to whiten walls, concrete, or the like. **2.** An attempt to conceal or gloss over mistakes or failures, especially so as to free those responsible from possible blame. **3.** *Informal.* A defeat in a game in which the loser scores no points. ~*tr.v.* **whitewashed, -washing, -washes. 1.** To paint or coat with or as if with whitewash. **2.** To gloss over (a mistake, for example). **3.** *Informal.* To prevent (an opponent) from scoring any points in a game. —**white-wash-er** *n.*

white water *n.* Turbulent or frothy water, as in rapids.

white whale *n.* A small whale, *Delphinapterus leucas,* white when full-grown, chiefly of northern waters. Also called "beluga."

white-wood (hwīt'wŏŏd', wīt'-) *n.* The soft, light-colored wood of any of various trees such as the tulip tree, basswood, or cottonwood. —**white-wood** *adj.*

whitey (hwī'tē, wī'-) *n. pl.* **-eys. 1.** *Slang.* A blond man or boy. **2.** *Offensive slang.* A white person.

whith-er (hwĭth'ər, wĭth'-) *adv.* **1.** To what place, result, or condition: *Whither are we wandering?* **2.** To which specified place or position: *the shores whither the storm tossed them.* **3.** To whatever place, result, or condition: *"Whither thou goest, I will go"* (Ruth 1:16). [Middle English *whider, whither,* Old English *hwider.*]

whith-er-so-ev-er (hwĭth'ər-sō-ĕv'ər, wĭth'-) *adv.* To whatever place; to any place whatsoever.

whit-ing[1] (hwī'tĭng, wī'-) *n.* A pure white grade of chalk that has been ground and washed for use in paints, ink, and putty. [Middle English *whityng,* from *whiten,* to white, from WHITE.]

whiting[2] *n.* **1.** A food fish, *Gadus merlangus,* of European Atlantic waters, related to the cod. **2.** Any of various Australian marine food fishes of the genus *Sillago.* **3.** Any of several marine fishes of the genera *Menticirrhus* and *Merluccius,* of North American coastal waters. [Middle English *whitynge,* from Middle Dutch *wijting* : apparently WHIT(E) + -ING (one having the quality of).]

whit-ish (hwī'tĭsh, wī'-) *adj.* Somewhat or almost white.

whitleather. Variant of **white leather.**

whit-low (hwĭt'lō, wĭt'-) *n.* An abscess of the area of a finger or toe around the nail. [Middle English *whitflawe, whit(f)lowe* : WHITE + *flawe,* fissure, FLAW.]

Whit-man (hwĭt'mən, wĭt'-), **Marcus** (1802–47) and **Narcissa Prentice** (1808–47). U.S. frontier missionaries. Married in 1836, they established a missionary post near present-day Walla Walla, Washington, where they introduced Christianity, schooling, and medical advances to the Native Americans. After an outbreak of smallpox, the Indians distrusted the couple and in a sudden raid killed them along with several settlers. Narcissa Whitman was the first white woman to settle west of the Rockies.

Whitman, Walter, known as "Walt" (1819–92). U.S. poet. His *Leaves of Grass* (1855), which he later expanded, was written without regard to conventional meter and rhyme and examines ideas that include freedom and comradeship.

Whit-mon-day, Whit-Mon-day (hwĭt'mŭn'dē, -dā', wĭt'-) *n.* Also **Whit-sun-Mon-day** (hwĭt'sən-, wĭt'-). The Monday following Whitsunday, observed as a legal holiday in England.

Whit-ney (hwĭt'nē, wĭt'-), **Asa** (1791–1874). U.S. inventor and manufacturer. The superintendent of the Mohawk & Hudson Railroad from 1833 to 1839, he invented an improved cast-iron railroad car wheel and founded a highly successful company to manufacture it (1849). He later was the president of the Philadelphia & Reading Railroad (1860–61).

Whitney, Eli (1765–1825). U.S. inventor and manufacturer. Primarily remembered for his invention of the cotton gin, which revolutionized the cotton industry (1793), he also established the first factory to assemble muskets with interchangeable parts. This development was the first instance of modern mass production.

Whitney, Mount. Peak, 4,420 meters (14,494 feet) high, in eastern California, in the Sierra Nevada. It is the second-highest mountain in the United States.

Whit-sun (hwĭt'sən, wĭt'-) *adj.* Of, pertaining to, or observed on Whitsunday or at Whitsuntide. ~*n.* Whitsuntide. [Middle English *whitsone,* short for *whitsonday,* WHITSUNDAY.]

Whit-sun-day (hwĭt'sən-dē, -dā', wĭt'-) *n.* **Pentecost** *(see).* [Middle English *whitsonday,* Old English *hwīta sunnandæg,* "white Sunday" (from a tradition of clothing the newly baptized in white robes on Whitsunday).]

Whit-sun-tide (hwĭt'sən-tīd', wĭt'-) *n.* The week beginning with Pentecost, especially the first three days of this week.

Whit-ti-er (hwĭt'ē-ər, wĭt'-), **John Greenleaf** (1807–92). U.S. poet. One of the foremost American poets of his time, he published several

eral volumes of poetry, including *Voices of Freedom* (1846), a collection of works that displayed his abolitionist views, and *Snow-Bound* (1866), his most popular book. He was a founder of the *Atlantic Monthly* (1857).

Whit-ting-ton (hwĭt'ĭng-tən, wĭt'-), **Richard,** known as "Dick" (c. 1358–1423). English merchant and mayor of London. A fabulously wealthy storekeeper, he served three terms as lord mayor of London (1397–99, 1406–07, and 1419–20) and loaned large sums of money to Henry IV and Henry V. His rise to prominence is a subject of English folklore.

whit-tle (hwĭt'l, wĭt'l) *v.* **-tled, -tling, -tles.** —*tr.* **1.** To cut small bits or pare shavings from (a piece of wood). **2.** To fashion or shape in this way. **3.** To reduce, wear down, or destroy gradually as if by whittling with a knife. Usually used with *down, away,* or *off: He whittled down his expenses by 60 dollars.* —*intr.* To whittle wood with a knife. [Middle English *whyttel,* knife, alteration of *thwitel,* from *thwiten,* to whittle down, Old English *thwītan.*] —**whit-tler** *n.*

whit-tlings (hwĭt'lĭngz, wĭt'-) *pl.n.* The chips and shavings from a piece of wood being whittled.

whiz, whizz' (hwĭz, wĭz) *v.* **whizzed, whizzing, whizzes.** —*intr.* **1.** To make a whirring, buzzing, or hissing sound, as of something rushing through the air. **2.** To rush past. —*tr.* To cause to whiz: *The pitcher whizzed the ball to first.* ~*n., pl.* **whizzes. 1.** A whizzing sound or a swift movement producing such a sound. **2.** A quick trip. **3.** *Slang.* One who has remarkable skill in a specified field: *a whiz at tennis.* [Imitative.]

whiz kid *n.* A person who achieves great success, especially in business, at a relatively early age, usually as a result of exceptional talent or acumen.

whizz-bang (hwĭz'băng', wĭz'-) *n.* A small-caliber high-speed shell used during World War I. It was fired in a flat trajectory and so was heard only an instant before landing and exploding.

who (hŏŏ) *pron.* **1.** What or which person or persons: *Who left?* **2.** That. Used as a relative pronoun to introduce a clause when the antecedent is a human or is understood to be a human: *The boy who came yesterday; informed sources who denied the story.* **3.** The person or persons that; whoever. [Who, whose, whom; Middle English *who* or *qwa, whoos, whom(e),* Old English *hwā, hwæs, hwǣm.*]

Usage: The traditional rules that determine the use of *who* and *whom* are relatively simple: *who* is used for a grammatical subject, where a nominative pronoun like *I* or *he* would be appropriate, and *whom* is used elsewhere. Thus, we write *the actor who played Hamlet was there,* since *who* stands for the subject of *played Hamlet;* and *who do you think is the best candidate,* where *who* stands for the subject of *is the best candidate.* But we write *to whom did you give the letter,* since *whom* is the object of the preposition *to;* and *the man whom the papers criticized did not show up,* since *whom* is the object of the verb *criticized.* It requires considerable effort and attention to apply the rules correctly in complicated sentences, however. To produce correctly a sentence like *I met the man whom the government had tried to get France to extradite,* we must anticipate when we write *whom* that it will function as the object of the verb *extradite,* several clauses distant from it. In consequence, few writers and speakers succeed in getting *who* and *whom* right all of the time, and a slavish adherence to the rules, especially in informal contexts, may be taken as a sign of pedantry. When the relative stands for the object of a preposition left at the end of a sentence. *whom* is technically the correct form. The strict grammarian will insist on *Whom* (not *who) did you give it to?* But grammarians since Noah Webster have argued that the excessive formality of *whom* in these cases is at odds with the relative informality associated with the practice of stranding the preposition and that the use of *who* in these cases should be regarded as entirely acceptable. The grammatical rules governing the use of *who* and *whom* apply equally to *whoever* and *whomever.* The relative pronoun *who* may be used both in restrictive relative clauses, in which case it is not preceded by a comma, or in nonrestrictive relative clauses, in which case a comma is required. Thus, we may say either the *scientist who discovers a cure for cancer will be immortalized,* where the clause *who discovers a cure for cancer* indicates which scientist will be immortalized; or the *mathematician over there, who solved the four-color theorem, is widely known,* where the clause *who solved the four-color theorem* adds information about a person already identified by the phrase *the mathematician over there.* Some grammarians have argued that only *who,* and not *that,* should be used to introduce a restrictive relative clause that identifies a person. But this restriction has no basis either in logic or in the usage of the best writers; it is entirely acceptable to write either *the man that wanted to talk to you* or *the man who wanted to talk to you.*

WHO World Health Organization.

whoa (hwō, wō) *interj.* Used in commanding a horse to stop. [Middle English *whoo,* variant of HO (halt).]

who'd (hŏŏd). Contraction of *who would* or *who had.*

who-dun-it, who-dun-nit (hŏŏ-dŭn'ĭt) *n. Informal.* A mystery story, typically one based on a search for the perpetrator of a crime, usually a murder. [WHO + DONE + IT.]

who-ev-er (hŏŏ-ĕv'ər) *pron.* **1.** Anyone that; any person who. **2.** No matter who; regardless of which person or persons: *The culprit will be punished, whoever he is.* **3.** What person ever; who. Used as an intensive: *Whoever told you that?*

whole (hōl) *adj.* **1.** Containing all the appropriate component parts; complete: *The archaeologists found a whole 12th-century chess set.* **2.** Not divided or disjoined; in one unit: *bake the apples whole.*

3. a. Sound; healthy or intact: *a whole organism.* **b.** Restored; healed: *a whole man again.* **4.** Constituting the full amount, extent, or duration; entire: *He cried the whole trip home.* **5.** Having the same parents: *a whole sister.* **6.** *Mathematics.* Integral; not fractional.
~*adv.* Completely; wholly: *gave us a whole new perspective.*
~*n.* **1.** All of the component parts or elements of a thing. **2.** A complete entity or system. **—as a whole.** Altogether; all things considered. **—on the whole.** Considering everything; in general. [Middle English *hool, (w)holle,* sound, unharmed, Old English *hāl.*]
whole blood *n.* Blood drawn from a living human being for use in transfusion, from which no constituent has been removed.
whole gale *n.* A wind of 24.5 to 28.4 meters per second (55 to 63 miles per hour); force 10 on the Beaufort Wind Scale.
whole-heart-ed (hōl'här'tĭd) *adj.* Marked by or undertaken with sincerity, enthusiasm, or complete commitment. **—See Synonyms at sincere. —whole-heart-ed-ly** *adv.* **—whole-heart-ed-ness** *n.*
whole hog *n. Slang.* The whole way or the fullest extent. Used chiefly in the phrase *go the whole hog.*
whole life insurance *n.* A type of life insurance policy whereby the insured pays premiums throughout his lifetime, and the sum insured is payable on his death, whenever it may be.
whole-meal (hōl'mēl') *adj.* Whole-wheat.
whole milk *n.* Milk from which no constituent has been removed.
whole-ness (hōl'nĭs) *n.* The state or quality of being whole.
whole note *n. Music.* A note having, in common time, the value of four beats. Also called *chiefly British* "semibreve."
whole number *n.* **1.** An integer. **2.** A natural number.
whole-sale (hōl'sāl') *n. Abbr.* **whsle.** The sale of goods in large quantities, as for resale by a retailer.
~*adj.* **1.** Pertaining to or engaged in the sale of goods in this way. **2.** Sold in large bulk or quantity, usually at a lower cost. **3.** Made or accomplished extensively and indiscriminately; blanket: *the wholesale elimination of life by nuclear weapons.*
~*adv.* **1.** In large bulk or quantity; on wholesale terms. **2.** Extensively and indiscriminately.
~*v.* **wholesaled, -saling, -sales.** *—tr.* To sell wholesale. *—intr.* **1.** To engage in wholesale selling. **2.** To be sold wholesale. [From the phrase *by (the) whole sale.*] **—whole-sal-er** *n.*
whole-some (hōl'səm) *adj.* **1.** Conducive to sound health or well-being; salutary. **2.** Conducive to moral or social well-being; salubrious. **3.** Physically, mentally, or morally sound; healthy. **—See Synonyms at healthy.** [Middle English *holsom,* Old English *hālsum* (unattested).] **—whole-some-ly** *adv.* **—whole-some-ness** *n.*
whole step *n.* A musical interval equal to two half steps. Also called "whole tone."
whole-wheat (hōl'wēt') *adj.* **1.** Made from the entire grain of wheat, including the bran: *whole-wheat flour.* **2.** Made with whole-wheat flour, as bread.
who'll (hōol). Contraction of *who will* or *who shall.*
whol-ly (hō'lē, hōl'lē) *adv.* **1.** Entirely; totally: *wholly irrelevant.* **2.** Exclusively; without reservation or exception: *a life wholly devoted to the cause.*
whom (hōom) *pron.* The objective case of **who.** See Usage note at **who.**
whom-ev-er (hōom-ĕv'ər) *pron.* The objective case of **whoever.**
whom-so-ev-er (hōom'sō-ĕv'ər) *pron.* The objective case of **whosoever.**
whoop (hōop, hwōop, wōop) *n.* **1.** A cry of exultation or excitement. **2.** A hooting cry, as of a bird. **3.** The paroxysmal gasp characteristic of whooping cough.
~*v.* **whooped, whooping, whoops.** *—intr.* **1.** To utter a loud shout or cry expressing exultation or excitement. **2.** To utter a hooting cry. **3.** To make the paroxysmal gasp characteristic of whooping cough. *—tr.* **1.** To utter with a whoop. **2.** To chase, call, urge on, or drive with a whoop or whoops: *whooping the horses on down the road.* **—whoop it up.** *Slang.* **1.** To have a wild, noisy celebration. **2.** To arouse interest or enthusiasm. [Middle English (imitative).]
whoop-ee (hwōo'pē, wōo'-, hwōo'-, wōo'-) *interj. Slang.* Used to express excitement and exuberance. **—make whoopee. 1.** To celebrate riotously. **2.** To make love. [From WHOOP.]
whoop-er (hōo'pər, hwōo'-, wōo'-) *n.* **1.** One that whoops. **2.** An Old World swan, *Cygnus cygnus* (or *Olor cygnus*), having a loud cry. Also called "whooper swan."
whoop-ing cough (hōo'pĭng, hōop'ĭng) *n.* An infectious disease caused by the bacterium *Haemophilus pertussis,* involving catarrh of the respiratory passages and characterized by spasms of coughing interspersed with deep, noisy inspiration. Also called "pertussis."
whooping crane *n.* A large, long-legged North American bird, *Grus americana,* now very rare, having black and white plumage and a shrill, trumpeting cry.
whoops (hwōops, wōops, hwōops, wōops) *interj.* Used to express mild surprise or apology, as in reaction to a fall or mistake. [Probably alteration of OOPS.]
whoosh (hwōosh, wōosh, hwōosh, wōosh) *intr.v.* **whooshed, whooshing, whooshes.** To hurtle or gush with a low hissing sound suggestive of great speed.
~*n.* A whooshing sound. [Imitative.]
whop (hwŏp, wŏp) *tr.v.* **whopped, whopping, whops. 1.** To beat; thrash. **2.** To defeat utterly.
~*n.* A heavy blow or thud. [Middle English *whappen,* variant of dialect *wappen†.]*

whop-per (hwŏp'ər, wŏp'-) *n.* **1.** Something exceptionally big or remarkable. **2.** A gross untruth. [WHOP + -ER.]
whop-ping (hwŏp'ĭng, wŏp'-) *adj.* Exceptionally big or remarkable. ~*adv.* Thoroughly; resoundingly: *a whopping great lie.*
whore (hôr, hōr) *n.* **1.** A prostitute. **2.** A promiscuous woman. Used derogatorily.
~*intr.v.* **whored, whoring, whores. 1.** To have sexual intercourse or consort with whores. **2.** To be or act as a whore. [Middle English *ho(o)re,* Old English *hōre.*]
whore-dom (hôr'dəm, hōr'-) *n.* **1.** Fornication or prostitution. **2.** In Biblical use, idolatry. [Middle English *hordom,* from Old Norse *hōrdōmr.*]
whore-house (hôr'hous', hōr'-) *n.* A brothel.
whore-mas-ter (hôr'măs'tər, hōr'-) *n.* One who consorts with whores; a fornicator.
whore-mong-er (hôr'mŭng'gər, -mŏng'gər, hōr'-) *n.* A whoremaster.
whore-son (hôr'sən, hōr'-). *n.* To A bastard. Used derogatorily, sometimes in direct address.
~*adj.* Abominable; bastardly.
whor-ish (hôr'ĭsh, hōr'-) *adj.* Characteristic of a whore; lewd. **—whor-ish-ly** *adv.* **—whor-ish-ness** *n.*
whorl (hwôrl, wôrl, hwûrl, wûrl) *n.* **1.** A small flywheel that regulates the speed of a spinning wheel. **2.** *Botany.* An arrangement of three or more parts, such as leaves or petals, radiating from a single organ or node. **3.** *Zoology.* A single turn or volution of a spiral shell. **4.** One of the three basic patterns by which fingerprints are classified, characterized by ridges forming complete circles. Compare **arch, loop. 5.** *Architecture.* An ornamental device consisting of stylized vine leaves and tendrils. **6.** A coil, curl, or convolution: *whorls of golden hair.* [Middle English *whorle,* perhaps alteration of *whirle,* a whirl, from *whirlen,* to WHIRL.]
whorled (hwôrld, wôrld, hwûrld, wûrld) *adj.* Having, forming, or arranged in a whorl or whorls.
whor-tle-ber-ry (hwûrt'l-bĕr'ē, wûrt'-) *n., pl.* **-ries.** *Botany.* **1.** A small European shrub, *Vaccinium myrtillus,* having edible blackish berries. **2.** The fruit of this shrub. Also called "bilberry," "huckleberry." [Dialectal alteration of earlier *hurtleberry,* from Middle English *hurtilberi : hurtil,* akin to Old English *hortan,* whortleberries + *beri,* BERRY.]
whose (hōoz) *pron.* **1.** The possessive form of *who. Whose is that bike?* **2.** The possessive form of *which: The legislature has recently passed a law whose provisions are not yet clear.* [Middle English *whos, whas, hwas,* Old English *hwæs.*]
who-so (hōo'sō) *pron.* Who; whoever; whatever person.
who-so-ev-er (hōo'sō-ĕv'ər) *pron.* Whoever.
W-hr, whr. *Electricity.* watt-hour.
whsle. wholesale.
why (hwī, wī) *adv.* For what purpose, reason, or cause; with what intention, justification, or motive: *Why were you absent?*
~*conj.* **1.** The reason, cause, or purpose for which: *I know why you left.* **2.** On account of which; for which: *the reason why he was so annoyed.*
~*n., pl.* **whys. 1.** The cause or intention underlying a given action or situation: *the whys and wherefores.* **2.** A difficult problem or question; a mystery.
~*interj.* Used to express indignation, surprise, or impatience. [Middle English *why,* Old English *hwȳ.*]
Usage: In the construction *the reason why,* the repetition of the notion of "reason," which is part of the sense of *why,* often leads to criticism. Critics would prefer using *why* or *reason* alone.
whyd-ah, whid-ah (hwĭd'ə, wĭd'ə) *n.* Any of several African weaverbirds of the genus *Vidua,* the breeding plumage of the male being predominantly black with long tail feathers. Also called "widow bird." [Alteration of WIDOW (BIRD), altered by association with *Whidah* (Ouidah), Dahomey.]
WI Wisconsin (used with Zip Code).
w.i. when issued (financial stock).
W.I. West Indian; West Indies.
Wich-i-ta¹ (wĭch'ə-tô) *n., pl.* **-tas** or collectively **Wichita. 1.** A member of a confederacy of Caddoan-speaking North American Indians, formerly living between the Arkansas river and central Texas. **2.** The language of these people.
Wichita². City in south-central Kansas, southwest of Kansas City. It is the chief commercial and industrial center of southern Kansas and has a huge aircraft industry. McConnell Air Force Base is nearby.
wick¹ (wĭk) *n.* **1.** A cord or strand of loosely woven, twisted fibers, as on a candle or oil lamp, that draws up fuel to the flame by capillary action. **2.** Any similar device that conveys liquid by capillary action. [Middle English *wike,* Old English *wēoce,* akin to Middle Low German *wēke* and Old High German *wiohha†.]*
wick² *n. Obsolete.* A village or town. Now surviving only in place names such as *Warwick.* [Middle English *wik(e),* Old English *wīc,* from West Germanic *wīka* (unattested), from Latin *vīcus.*]
wick-ed (wĭk'ĭd) *adj.* **-eder, -edest. 1. a.** Evil; depraved; bad; sinful: *wicked habits.* **b.** Vicious; savage: *a wicked murder.* **2.** Mischievous or playfully malicious: *a wicked joke.* **3.** Harmful; pernicious: *a wicked cough.* **4.** Obnoxious; offensive: *a wicked stench.* **5.** *Informal.* Formidable; excellent: *had a wicked, spinning tennis serve.* [Middle English, from *wicke,* wicked, Old English *wicca,* wizard.] **—wick-ed-ly** *adv.* **—wick-ed-ness** *n.*

whortleberry *Native to Europe and northern Asia,* Vaccinium myrtillus *(above) produces blue-black berries in autumn, which are relished by songbirds and game birds. The plant is also known as bilberry.*

whydah *Like the cuckoo, some species of whydah use foster parents to rear their young. The female lays her eggs in the nest of the waxbill—then leaves the waxbill to hatch and feed the nestlings. Whydahs are native to the grasslands of Africa and feed on seeds and insects.*

wick·er (wĭk′ər) *n.* **1.** A flexible shoot, as of a willow, used in weaving baskets or certain articles of furniture. **2.** Wickerwork. *~adj.* Constructed, consisting of, or covered with wicker. [Middle English *wiker*, from Scandinavian, akin to Swedish *viker*.]

wick·er·work (wĭk′ər-wûrk′) *n.* **1.** Woven wicker. **2.** Objects or articles made of this.

wick·et (wĭk′ĭt) *n.* **1.** A small door or gate, especially one built into or near a larger one. **2.** A sluice gate for regulating the amount of water in a millrace or a canal or for emptying a lock. **3.** A small window or opening, often fitted with glass or a grating. **4.** In cricket: **a.** Either of the two sets of three stumps, topped by bails, that forms the target of the bowler and is defended by the batsman. **b.** The area between these two sets of stumps, the **pitch** (*see*). **c.** The turn of a batsman or the termination of his innings. **d.** The period during which two batsmen are in together. **5.** In croquet, any of the small arches, usually made of wire, through which one tries to direct the ball. [Middle English, from Old North French *wiket*, from Germanic.]

wick·et·keep·er (wĭk′ĭt-kē′pər) *n.* In cricket, the player positioned immediately behind the wicket guarded by the batsman who is facing the bowling.

wick·i·up, wik·i·up (wĭk′ē-ŭp′) *n.* A frame hut covered with matting, bark, brush, or similar materials, used by the nomadic Indians of North America. [Fox *wikiyapi*, "house," from Proto-Algonquian *wikiwahmi* (unattested), WIGWAM.]

Wick·low (wĭk′lō), Coastal county of Leinster province, Republic of Ireland. Bordering on the Irish Sea, it is largely pastureland with the Wicklow Mts. at its center, rising to 926 meters (3,039 feet) at Lugnaquilla. The county town and port is Wicklow.

wic·o·py (wĭk′ə-pē) *n.*, *pl.* **-pies.** Any of several North American trees, shrubs, or plants, especially the **leatherwood** (see). [Cree *wikopiy*, willow bark.]

Wi·dal reaction (vē-däl′) *n.* A test for typhoid fever in which the presence or absence of antibodies against the causative bacteria is determined by agglutination techniques. [After Fernand *Widal* (1862–1929), French physician.]

widdershins. Variant of **withershins.**

wide (wīd) *adj.* **wider, widest. 1.** Extending over a relatively large area from side to side; broad. **2.** Having a specified extent from side to side; in width: *a ribbon two inches wide.* **3. a.** Having great range or scope: *a wide selection; wide reading.* **b.** Including or extending to many different things: *a wide observation.* **4.** Full or ample, as clothing might be. **5.** Fully open or extended: *look with wide eyes.* **6.** Landing or located away from or missing a given goal or point: *wide of the target.* **7.** Failing to realize or deal with a relevant point or issue: *wide of the mark.* **8.** Phonetics. Lax. *~adv.* **1.** Over a large area; extensively: *journey far and wide.* **2.** To the full extent; completely: *the door was open wide.* **3.** So as to miss the target; astray. *~n.* A ball bowled outside of the batsman's reach in cricket, counting as a run for the batting team. [Middle English *wide*, Old English *wīd*.] —**wide·ly** *adv.* —**wide·ness** *n.*

-wide *suffix.* **1.** Extending over a specified area or region: *citywide.* **2.** Throughout a specified area or region: *statewide.* [From WIDE.]

wide-an·gle lens (wīd′ăng′gəl) *n.* A lens that has a relatively short focal length and permits an angle of view wider than about 70°.

wide-a·wake (wīd′ə-wāk′) *adj.* **1.** Completely awake. **2.** Alert; watchful. *~n.* A soft felt hat with a wide brim.

wide-bodied (wīd′bŏd′ēd) *adj.* Also **wide-body** (-bŏd′ē). Designating a jet aircraft having a wide fuselage to accomodate a large number of passengers.

wide-eyed (wīd′īd′) *adj.* **1.** With the eyes completely opened, as in wonder. **2.** Innocent; credulous.

wid·en (wīd′n) *v.* **-ened, -ening, -ens.** *—tr.* To make wider. *—intr.* To be or become wide or wider. —**wid·en·er** *n.*

wide-o·pen (wīd′ō′pən) *adj.* **1.** Opened completely: *a wide-open door.* **2.** Vulnerable, as to attack: *left himself wide-open.* **3.** With the outcome uncertain: *a wide-open match.* **4.** Without laws or law enforcement: *a wide-open town.*

wide receiver *n.* Football. A receiver who usually lines up several yards to the side of an offensive formation.

wide-screen (wīd′skrēn′) *adj.* Pertaining to or involving a screen that is wide in proportion to its height.

wide-spread (wīd′sprĕd′) *adj.* **1.** Spread or scattered over a considerable extent. **2.** Occurring or accepted widely.

widgeon. Variant of **wigeon.**

wid·ow (wĭd′ō) *n.* **1.** A woman whose husband has died and who has not remarried. **2.** In card games, an additional hand dealt to the table. **3.** Printing. **a.** An incomplete line of type, especially one ending a paragraph, carried over to the top of the next page or column. **b.** A short line at the bottom of a page or column. *~tr.v.* **widowed, -owing, -ows.** To make a widow of. Used chiefly in the past participle: *She was widowed during the war.* [Middle English *wid(e)we*, Old English *widuwe*.] —**wid·ow·hood** *n.*

widow bird *n.* The **whydah** (*see*). [From its black plumage.]

wid·ow·er (wĭd′ō-ər) *n.* A man whose wife has died and who has not remarried. [Middle English *widewer*, from *widewe*, WIDOW.]

widow's cruse *n.* An unfailing or inexhaustible supply. [Biblical allusion (I Kings 17:10–16).]

widow's mite *n.* A small but relatively generous contribution made by one who has little. [Biblical allusion (Mark 12:42).]

widow's peak *n.* A hairline having a V-shaped point at the middle

wigeon *Flocks of wigeons make their homes along estuaries and mud flats in North America and Europe. They are sometimes mistaken for geese because they graze on grass.*

of the forehead. Also called "peak." [From the superstition that it is a sign of early widowhood.]

widow's walk *n.* A railed, rooftop gallery on a dwelling, designed to observe vessels at sea.

width (wĭdth, wĭth) *n.* Abbr. **w. 1.** The state, quality, or fact of being wide. **2.** The measurement of the extent of something from side to side; the size of something in terms of its wideness. **3.** Something that has a particular width; especially, in sewing, a piece of fabric measured from selvage to selvage: *a skirt having four widths.* **4.** The distance extending parallel with the shortest sides of a rectangular swimming pool. [From WIDE.]

width·wise (wĭdth′wīz′, wĭth′-) *adv.* Also **width·ways** (-wāz). From side to side; in terms of width.

wield (wēld) *tr.v.* **wielded, wielding, wields. 1.** To handle (a weapon or tool, for example). **2.** To exercise or exert (power or influence). —See Usage note at **handle.** [Middle English *welden*, Old English *wealdan* and *wieldan*.] —**wield·a·ble** *adj.* —**wield·er** *n.*

wield·y (wēl′dē) *adj.* **-ier, -iest.** Easily wielded or managed.

Wien. See **Vienna.**

wie·ner (wē′nər) *n.* A wienerwurst. [German, short for WIENERWURST.]

Wie·ner (wē′nər), **Norbert** (1894–1964). U.S. mathematician. Having earned a doctorate in mathematics at the age of 19, he dedicated himself to the study of information processing and control by machines, a field he named cybernetics.

Wie·ner schnit·zel (vē′nər shnĭt′səl) *n.* A breaded veal cutlet. [German, "Vienna cutlet."]

Wie·ner·wald (vē′nər-vält). Mountain range in northeastern Austria, just west of Vienna. An outlying part of the Eastern Alps, it rises to 894 meters (2,930 feet) in the Schöpfl. It is a favorite excursion and resort area for the Viennese.

wie·ner·wurst (wē′nər-wûrst′, -wŏŏrst′) *n.* A type of smoked pork or beef sausage, similar to a frankfurter. Also called "wiener." [German, "Vienna sausage."]

Wies·ba·den (vēs′bä′dən). City of central West Germany, on the Rhine River. The city is an industrial center and a market for Rhine wines. Wiesbaden was founded as a Celtic settlement in the 3rd century B.C. and is one of the most famous spas in Europe.

wife (wīf) *n.*, *pl.* **wives** (wīvz). Abbr. **w. 1.** A woman married to a man. **2.** Archaic. A woman. Now used chiefly in certain phrases: *old wives' tales.* —**take to wife.** To marry. [Middle English *wif(e)*, Old English *wīf*, from Germanic *wīf* (unattested), woman.] —**wife·hood, wife·dom** *n.* —**wife·less** *adj.* —**wife·ly** *adj.*

wig (wĭg) *n.* A headpiece of artificial or human hair worn as personal adornment, part of a costume, or to conceal baldness. *~tr.v.* **wigged, wigging, wigs.** To scold or censure. [Shortened from PERIWIG.] —**wigged** *adj.* —**wig·less** *adj.*

wig·an (wĭg′ən) *n.* A stiff fabric used for stiffening. [First made in *Wigan*, northwest England.]

wig·eon, wid·geon (wĭj′ən) *n.*, *pl.* **-eons** or **-geons** or collectively **wigeon** or **widgeon.** Either of two ducks, *Mareca americana*, of North America, or *M. penelope*, of Europe, having brownish plumage. [Origin unknown.]

wig·ger·y (wĭg′ə-rē) *n.*, *pl.* **-ies. 1.** A wig or wigs collectively. **2.** The practice of wearing wigs.

wig·ging (wĭg′ĭng) *n.* A telling off or scolding. [19th century : slang or informal use of WIG (false hair).]

wig·gle (wĭg′əl) *v.* **-gled, -gling, -gles.** *—intr.* To move, twist, or proceed with short irregular movements from side to side or up and down. *—tr.* To cause to move in such a fashion: *wiggle one's toes.* *~n.* The act of wiggling; a wiggling movement or course. —**get a wiggle on.** Slang. To hurry or hurry up. [Middle English *wiglen*, from Middle Dutch or Middle Low German *wiggelen*.] —**wig·gly** *adj.*

wig·gler (wĭg′lər) *n.* **1.** One that wiggles. **2.** The larva or pupa of a mosquito.

wight¹ (wīt) *n.* A human being; a person. [Middle English *wight*, Old English *wiht*.]

wight² *adj.* Archaic. Courageous; brave. [Middle English *wiht*, from Old Norse *vīgt*, neuter of *vīgr*, able to fight.]

Wight, Isle of (wīt). County and island off the south of England. Separated from the mainland by the Solent and Spithead channels, it is a chiefly agricultural area.

Wig·town (wĭg′tən, -toun). Former county of southwest Scotland. It was merged in 1975 with Dumfries and Galloway.

wig·wag (wĭg′wăg′) *v.* **-wagged, -wagging, -wags.** *—tr.* **1.** To move (a flag, for example) back and forth, especially as a means of signaling. **2.** To signal (a message) by such motions. *—intr.* **1.** To move back and forth; to wag. **2.** To signal by waving the hand or a device, such as a flag. *~n.* **1.** The act or practice of giving signals by wigwagging. **2.** A message so relayed. [Dialectal *wig*, to move + WAG.] —**wig·wag·ger** *n.*

wig·wam (wĭg′wŏm′) *n.* **1.** A North American Indian dwelling, commonly having an arched or domed framework overlaid with bark, hides, or mats. Compare **tepee. 2.** Loosely, any tent used by North American Indians. [Eastern Abnaki *wikəwam*, from Proto-Algonquian *wikiwahmi* (unattested), perhaps from root *wik-* (unattested), to dwell.]

wikiup. Variant of **wickiup.**

Wil·ber·force (wĭl′bər-fôrs′, -fōrs′), **William** (1759–1833). British politician and social reformer. He served as an M.P. (1780–1825) and campaigned for the abolition of the slave trade, achieved in 1807, and for the abolition of slavery, achieved in 1833.

wil·co (wĭl′kō) *interj.* Used, especially in radio communications, to indicate that one will carry out an instruction. [Abbreviation of *I will comply.*]

wild (wīld) *adj.* **wilder, wildest. 1.** Occurring, growing, or living in a natural state; not domesticated, cultivated, or tamed: *wild strawberries.* **2.** Not inhabited; desolate: *wild country.* **3.** Uncivilized or barbarous; savage: *wild natives.* **4. a.** Lacking discipline, restraint, or control; unruly. **b.** Excessive in noise and behavior; lively and loud: *a wild party; the conference became wild.* **5.** Disorderly; disarranged: *Her hair was wild.* **6.** Boisterous; ungoverned; frenzied: *wild laughter.* **7. a.** Full of intense, irrepressible emotion: *wild with jealousy.* **b.** Attracted or excited: *wild about her new byfriend; not wild about rice pudding.* **8. a.** Eccentric; notoriously odd or amusing: *a wild character.* **b.** Extravagant; fantastic: *a wild idea.* **9.** Furiously disturbed or turbulent; tempestuous: *a wild night at sea.* **10.** Reckless; risky: *a wild gamble.* **11.** Random or spontaneous; whimsical: *make a wild guess.* **12.** Deviating widely; erratic: *a wild shot.* **13.** In card games, having an arbitrary equivalence or value determined by the holder's needs or choice: *playing poker with jokers wild.*
~*adv.* In a wild manner. **—run wild.** To live, behave, or grow in an unrestrained manner.
~*n.* **1.** An uninhabited or uncultivated region: *the wilds of Greenland.* **2.** A natural, unrestrained life or state; nature. [Middle English *wilde,* Old English *wilde.*] **—wild·ly** *adv.* **—wild·ness** *n.*

wild basil *n.* See **basil** (sense 2).

wild bergamot *n.* An aromatic plant, *Monarda fistulosa,* of eastern North America, having clusters of lilac-purple flowers.

wild boar *n.* A wild pig, *Sus scrofa,* of Eurasia and northern Africa, having a gray or black coat and prominent tusks. Also called "boar."

wild carrot *n.* A plant, **Queen Anne's lace** *(see).*

wild·cat (wīld′kăt) *n.* **1.** A Eurasian wild cat, *Felis sylvestris,* with a thick coat and a bushy tail. **2.** Any of various wild felines of small to medium size; especially, one of the genus *Lynx.* **3.** A quick-tempered or fierce person, especially a woman. **4.** An oil well drilled in an area not known to yield oil.
~*adj.* **1.** Risky or unsound, especially financially. **2.** Accomplished or operating without official sanction or authority.
~*v.* **wildcatted, -catting, -cats.** *—tr.* To prospect for (oil, for example) in an area not known to be productive. *—intr.* To wildcat in an area not known to be productive. **—wild·cat·ter** *n.*

wildcat strike *n.* A strike not authorized by the appropriate union.

wild celery *n.* An aromatic plant, *Apium graveolens,* that is the ancestor of cultivated celery.

wild cherry *n.* A Eurasian cherry tree, *Prunus avium,* having white flowers and red round fruits. It is the ancestor of the cultivated sweet cherry. Also called "gean."

wild dog *n.* The **dingo** *(see).*

Wilde (wīld), **Oscar Fingal O'Flahertie Wills** (1854–1900). Irish-born dramatist, poet, and humorist. Renowned as a wit in London literary circles, he achieved recognition with the novel *The Picture of Dorian Grey* (1891); other works include *Poems* (1881) and the plays *Lady Windermere's Fan* (1892) and *The Importance of Being Earnest* (1895). Convicted and sentenced (1895) to two years' imprisonment for a homosexual relationship with Lord Alfred Douglas (1870–1945), on his release he went into exile in France, where he wrote his most famous poem, *The Ballad of Reading Gaol* (1898).

wil·de·beest (wĭl′də-bēst′, vĭl′-) *n., pl.* **-beests** or collectively **wildebeest.** A mammal, the **gnu** *(see).* [Obsolete Afrikaans : Dutch *wild,* wild, from Middle Dutch *wilt, wilde* + *beest,* beast, from Middle Dutch *beeste,* from Old French *beste,* BEAST.]

wil·der (wĭl′dər) *v.* **-dered, -dering, -ders.** *Archaic. —tr.* **1.** To lead astray; mislead. **2.** To bewilder; confuse; perplex. *—intr.* **1.** To lose one's way. **2.** To become bewildered. [Perhaps from WILDERNESS.] **—wil·der·ment** *n.*

Wil·der (wĭl′dər), **Billy Samuel** (1906–). Austrian-born U.S. film director. His films include *Double Indemnity* (1944), *Some Like It Hot* (1959), and *Fedora* (1978).

Wilder, Thornton Niven (1897–1975). U.S. playwright and novelist. His work includes the novel the *Bridge of San Luis Rey* (1927) and the plays *Our Town* (1938) and *The Skin of Our Teeth* (1942).

wil·der·ness (wĭl′dər-nĭs) *n.* **1.** Any unsettled, uncultivated region left in its natural condition, especially: **a.** A large wild tract of land covered with dense vegetation or forests. **b.** An extensive area that is barren or empty, such as a desert or ocean; a waste. **c.** A piece of land set aside to grow wild. **2.** Something likened to a wild region in bewildering vastness, confusion, or unchecked profusion: *a wilderness of industrial parks.* **3.** A period of being removed from a usually specified activity: *has come out of the political wilderness.* [Middle English *wildernesse,* Old English *wildēornes,* from *wildēor,* wild beast.]

Wilderness, the. Region in north-central Virginia, the site of a major Civil War battle (May 1864) between forces led by generals Ulysses S. Grant and Robert E. Lee.

wild-eyed (wīld′īd′) *adj.* Glaring in or as if in anger, terror, stupor, or madness.

wild·fire (wīld′fīr′) *n.* **1.** A highly flammable material formerly used in warfare. **2.** A raging fire that travels and spreads rapidly. **3.** Lightning occurring without thunder being heard. **4.** A luminosity that appears at night hovering over marshland; ignis fatuus.

wild·flow·er, wild flow·er (wīld′flou′ər) *n.* **1.** A flowering plant that grows in a natural, uncultivated state. **2.** The flower of such a plant.

wild·fowl (wīld′foul′) *n., pl.* **-fowls** or collectively **wildfowl.** A wild bird, such as a duck, goose, or quail, hunted as game.
~*intr.v.* **wildfowled, -fowling, -fowls.** To hunt wildfowl. **—wild·fowl·er** *n.*

wild geranium *n.* A North American woodland plant, *Geranium maculatum,* having rose-purple flowers.

wild ginger *n.* A North American plant, *Asarum canadense,* having broad leaves, a single brownish flower, and an aromatic root.

wild-goose chase (wīld′go͞os′) *n.* A hopeless or foolish pursuit of an unattainable or imaginary object. [Originally a race similar to the flight of geese, where the object was to follow accurately and at a definite interval.]

wild hyacinth *n.* A plant, *Camassia scilloides,* of the central United States, having narrow leaves and a cluster of pale-blue or white flowers.

wild·ing (wīl′dĭng) *n.* **1.** A plant that grows wild or has escaped from cultivation; especially, a wild apple tree or its fruit. **2.** A wild animal. [From WILD.]

wild·life (wīld′līf′) *n.* Wild animals and vegetation; especially, animals living in a natural, undomesticated state.

wild·ling (wīld′lĭng) *n.* A wild plant or animal; especially, a wild plant transplanted to a cultivated spot.

wild marjoram *n.* See **marjoram** (sense 2).

wild mustard *n.* **Charlock** *(see).*

wild oat *n.* **1.** *Often* **wild oats.** A grass, *Avena fatua,* native to Eurasia, related to the cultivated oat. **2. wild oats.** The indiscretions of youth, especially sexually promiscuous behavior. Used in the phrase *sow one's wild oats.*

wild olive *n.* Any of various trees resembling the olive; especially, the **oleaster** *(see).*

wild pansy *n.* Any of several pansylike plants of the genus *Viola.*

wild pink *n.* Any of several North American plants of the genus *Silene*; especially, *S. caroliniana,* having pink or white flowers.

wild pitch *n. Baseball.* An erratic pitch that the catcher cannot be expected to catch and that enables a runner to advance.

wild rice *n.* **1.** A tall aquatic grass, *Zizania aquatica,* of northern North America, bearing edible grain. **2.** The grain of this plant.

wild rose *n.* Any of various uncultivated roses having a single whorl of petals.

wild rye *n.* Any of various grasses of the genus *Elymus,* resembling cultivated rye in having bristly spikes.

wild type *n.* The typical form of an organism as it occurs in nature, as distinguished from mutant specimens that may result from selective breeding.

wild vanilla *n.* A plant, *Trilisa odoratissima,* of the southeastern United States, having vanilla-scented leaves.

Wild West. The western United States during the period of its settlement, especially with reference to its lawlessness.

wild·wood (wīld′wo͝od′) *n.* A forest or wooded area in its natural state.

wile (wīl) *n.* **1.** *Usually* **wiles. a.** A deceitful stratagem or trick. **b.** A disarming or seductive manner, device, or procedure. **2.** Trickery; cunning; deceit. —See Synonyms at **artifice.**
~*tr.v.* **wiled, wiling, wiles.** To influence or lead by means of wiles; entice; lure. [Middle English *wil,* perhaps from Old Norse *wihl-* (unattested).]

wilful. Variant of **willful.**

Wil·hel·mi·na (wĭl′ə-mē′nə), in full **Wilhelmina Helena Pauline Maria of Orange-Nassau** (1880–1962). Queen of the Netherlands (1890–1948), under the regency of her mother from 1890–98. She sought refuge in England during World War II but continued to encourage the Dutch resistance to the Germans. In 1948 she abdicated in favor of her daughter Juliana.

Wilkes Land (wĭlks). A section of Antarctica bordering on the Indian Ocean, south of Australia.

Wil·kins (wĭl′kĭnz), **Maurice Hugh Frederick** (1916–). British biophysicist. Born in New Zealand, he worked during World War II on the atomic bomb in California. He shared the Nobel Prize with Crick and Watson (1962) for work on the structure of DNA.

Wilkins, Roy (1901–81). U.S. civil-rights leader. Long associated with the NAACP, he edited its official publication, *The Crisis* (1934–49), and became executive director in 1965. He was opposed to violent demonstrations, believing that racial equality should be achieved through the American democratic process.

Wil·kin·son (wĭl′kĭn-sən), **Jemima** (1752–1819). U.S. religious leader. A resident of colonial Rhode Island, she declared that she was possessed by a prophetic spirit (1775) and, calling herself the "Universal Publik friend," attracted a considerable following. In 1789 she founded "Jerusalem," a religious colony in New York.

will[1] (wĭl) *n.* **1.** The mental faculty by which one deliberately chooses or decides upon a course of action. **2.** A disposition to exercise this faculty; determination: *a will to win.* **3.** That which is desired or decided upon, especially by a person in authority. **4.** Deliberate intention or wish: *against his will.* **5.** Free discretion; pleasure; inclination: *wandered about at will.* **6.** Bearing or attitude toward others; disposition: *full of good will.* **7.** The power to exert control over conflicting mental and emotional tendencies and arrive at one's own decision: *He's got enough will to resist temptation.* **8. a.** A legal declaration of how a person wishes his possessions to be disposed of after his death. **b.** The document containing this

wild boar *The ancestor of the domestic pig, the wild boar was hunted in England in medieval times, but it is now found only in mainland Europe, northern Africa, and southern Asia. It can run at speeds of up to 50 kilometers (30 miles) per hour and is ferocious if cornered.*

PRONUNCIATION KEY

ă, pat; ā, pay; âr, care; ä, father, are; b, bib; ch, church; d, deed; ĕ, pet; ē, be; f, fife; g, gag; h, hat; hw, which; ĭ, pit; ī, pie; îr, pier; j, judge; k, kick; l, lid, needle; m, mum; n, no, sudden; ng, thing; ŏ, pot; ō, toe; ô, paw, for; oi, noise; ou, out; o͝o, book; o͞o, boot; p, pop; r, roar; s, sauce; sh, ship, dish; t, tight; th, thin, path; *th*, this, bathe; ŭ, cut; ûr, fur; v, valve; w, with; y, yes; z, zebra, size; zh, vision; ə, about, item, edible, gallop, circus, peaceful

IN FOREIGN WORDS:

à, *Fr.* ami; œ, *Fr.* feu, *Ger.* schön; ü, *Fr.* tu, *Ger.* über; KH, *Ger.* ich, *Scot.* loch; N, *Fr.* bon; y′, *Fr.* Compiègne

STRESS MARKS:

Primary stress: ′
in·cite′ (ĭn-sīt′)
Secondary stress: ′
in′sight′ (ĭn′sīt′)

declaration. **—at will.** Just as one wishes. **—with a will.** With eagerness and energy.

~v. willed, will·ing, wills. *—tr.* **1.** To decide upon; choose: *Tell me what you have willed.* **2.** To desire; yearn for: *will one's own death.* **3.** To decree; dictate; order: *The queen willed that he should be exiled.* **4.** To resolve with a forceful will; determine: *as God wills.* **5.** To influence or induce by sheer force of will or by supernatural power: *We tried to will the sun to come out.* **6.** To bequeath; grant in a legal will. *—intr.* **1.** To exercise the will; use the power of the will. **2.** To decree or make a firm choice. [Middle English *will(e)*, Old English *will, willa.*] **—will·a·ble** *adj.*

will² (wĭl) *v.* past **would** (wŏŏd) also *archaic* **wouldest** (wŏŏd′ĭst) or **wouldst** (wŏŏdst) for second person singular, present **will** (also *archaic* **wilt** (wĭlt) for second person singular. Used as an auxiliary followed by an infinitive without *to* or, in reply to a question or suggestion, with the infinitive understood. It can indicate: **1.** Simple futurity: *They will appear later.* **2. a.** Likelihood or certainty: *You will regret this.* **b.** Inevitability: *Everyone will make mistakes.* **3.** Willingness: *Will you help me with this package?* **4.** Requirement or command: *You will report to me afterward.* **5.** Customary or habitual action: *She would spend hours in the library.* **6.** Capacity or ability: *This metal will not crack under heavy pressure.* **7.** *Informal.* Probability or expectation: *That will be the postman ringing.* **8.** Intention: *I will too if I feel like it.* —See Usage note at **shall.** *—intr.* To have a desire: *Sit here, if you will.* *—tr.* To desire; wish: *Do what you will.* [Will, would, wouldest; Middle English *willen, wolde, woldest,* Old English *wyllan, wolde, woldest.*]

willed (wĭld) *adj.* Having a will of a specified kind. Usually used in combination: *weak-willed.*

wil·lem·ite (wĭl′ə-mīt′) *n.* A vitreous to resinous silicate of zinc, Zn_2SiO_4, a minor ore of zinc. [Dutch *willemit,* from *Willem,* William, after *William* I (1772–1843), king of the Netherlands.]

Wil·lem·stad (vĭl′əm-stät′). Capital of the Netherlands Antilles, on the southern coast of Curaçao. It is the commercial and industrial center of the Netherlands Antilles as well as a free port and tourist center. It has a distinctive Dutch character.

wil·let (wĭl′ĭt) *n.* A long-billed New World shore bird, *Catoptrophorus semipalmatus.* [Imitative of its cry.]

will·ful (wĭl′fəl) *adj.* Also **wil·ful.** **1.** Said or done in accordance with one's will; deliberate. **2.** Inclined to impose one's will; unreasoningly obstinate. —See Synonyms at **contrary, unruly, voluntary.** **—will·ful·ly** *adv.* **—will·ful·ness** *n.*

Wil·liam I¹ (wĭl′yəm), known as "William the Conqueror" (c. 1027–87). The first Norman king of England (1066–87) and Duke of Normandy (1035–87). He invaded England (1066) on the grounds that succession to the English throne had been promised to him by his cousin Edward the Confessor. He defeated Harold at Hastings and as king adopted a feudal constitution.

William I², known as "William the Silent" (1533–84). Prince of Orange. Inheriting the principality in 1544, he was made governor of Holland, Zeeland, and Utrecht (1559) by Philip II of Spain, whom he opposed for his persecution of Protestants. He led the revolt against Spanish rule (1568) but succeeded only briefly in unifying the Protestant north with the Catholic south.

William II¹ (1859–1941). German emperor (1888–1918). The grandson of Queen Victoria, he pursued aggressive policies, supporting the Afrikaners in South Africa and Austria's demands on Serbia (1914), although when war became probable, he strove for peace. He was forced to abdicate after Germany's defeat in World War I.

William II², known as "William Rufus" (c. 1056–1100). King of England (1087–1100). He was the second son of William the Conqueror, on whose death he succeeded to the throne.

William III, known as "William of Orange" (1650–1702). King of England (1689–1702). Married to Mary, daughter of James II (1677), he was asked by the opposition to James to invade England (1688). He was proclaimed joint monarch with Mary (1689) after James fled.

William IV (1765–1837). King of Great Britain and Ireland (1830–37). The third son of George III and brother of George IV, he was known as the Sailor King because of his naval career, rising to the office of lord high admiral (1827–28). He left no surviving legitimate children and was succeeded by his niece Victoria.

Wil·liams, Tennessee, born Thomas Lanier Williams (1911–83). U.S. playwright. His works examine family tensions and feelings of frustration, particularly in women. Frequently set in the South, his plays include *The Glass Menagerie* (1944), *A Streetcar Named Desire* (1947), and *Cat on a Hot Tin Roof* (1955).

Williams, William Carlos (1883–1963). U.S. imagist poet. It was not until the 1940's that he established his reputation with a work in five volumes, *Paterson* (1946–58). His poetry is noted for its clarity, naturalism, and concern with American themes.

Wil·liams·burg (wĭl′yəmz-bûrg′). Historic city of southeastern Virginia, on a peninsula between the James and York rivers. It was settled in 1632 and as the capital of Virginia was the scene of important conventions during the movement for American independence. Williamsburg declined after the capital was moved to Richmond in 1779, but in 1926, with the financial support of John

D. Rockefeller, Jr., a large-scale restoration was begun. It is now a popular tourist attraction.

William Tell. See **Tell, William.**

William the Lion (1143–1214). King of Scotland (1165–1214). The brother of Malcolm IV and grandson of David I, he invaded Northumberland and was captured and taken to France. He was forced to perform homage for his kingdom as the price of freedom, but in 1189 Richard I of England abandoned all claims on payment of 10,000 marks.

wil·lies (wĭl′ēz) *pl.n. Slang.* Feelings of uneasiness: *This place gives me the willies.* [19th century : origin obscure.]

will·ing (wĭl′ĭng) *adj.* **1.** Disposed to accept or tolerate; prepared: *willing to overlook your mistakes.* **2.** Acting or ready to act gladly; eagerly compliant: *very willing to help; willing helpers.* **3.** Done, given, accepted, or offered freely and heartily. —See Synonyms at **voluntary.** **—will·ing·ly** *adv.* **—will·ing·ness** *n.*

wil·li·waw (wĭl′ē-wô′) *n.* **1.** A violent gust of cold wind blowing seaward from a mountainous coast. **2.** A sudden gust of wind; squall. [19th century : origin obscure.]

Will·kie (wĭl′kē), **Wendell Lewis** (1892–1944). U.S. politician. The 1940 Republican presidential nominee, he opposed the incumbent Franklin D. Roosevelt's economic policies but endorsed many of his social programs. He was soundly defeated. During World War II, he advocated an international organization to promote peace.

will-o'-the-wisp (wĭl′ə-thə-wĭsp′) *n.* **1. Ignis fatuus** (*see*). **2.** One that is alluring, delusive, or misleading. [Originally *Will with the wisp,* from *Will,* pet form of *William* + WISP, in obsolete sense handful of hay (used as torch).]

wil·low (wĭl′ō) *n.* **1.** Any of various deciduous trees or shrubs of the genus *Salix,* having usually narrow leaves, flowers borne in catkins, and strong, lightweight wood. **2.** The wood of any of these trees. **3.** Something made from willow, especially a cricket bat. **4.** A textile machine consisting of a spiked drum revolving inside a chamber fitted internally with spikes, used to open and clean unprocessed cotton or wool.
~tr.v. **willowed, -low·ing, -lows.** To open and clean (textile fibers) with a willow. [Middle English *wilowe,* Old English *welig.*]

Wil·low (wĭl′ō). City near Anchorage in Alaska, that is scheduled to be the new state capital, replacing Juneau.

willow herb *n.* Any of various plants of the genus *Epilobium,* such as *E. angustifolium,* rosebay willow herb, having narrow leaves and terminal clusters of pink, purplish, or white flowers. Also called "fireweed."

willow oak *n.* A timber tree, *Quercus phellos,* of the southern and central United States, having narrow, willowlike leaves.

willow pattern *n.* A traditional, Chinese-style, blue-on-white design typically consisting of a willow tree, bridge, river, and figures, used on household china.

willow warbler *n.* A Eurasian warbler, *Phylloscopus trochilus,* having a yellowish-brown plumage with pale underparts.

wil·low·ware (wĭl′ō-wâr′) *n.* Household china decorated with the willow pattern.

wil·low·y (wĭl′ō-ē) *adj.* **-i·er, -i·est. 1.** Planted with or abounding in willows. **2.** Resembling or suggestive of a willow tree, especially: **a.** Flexible; pliant. **b.** Slender and graceful.

will·pow·er (wĭl′pou′ər) *n.* The ability to exercise control over one's actions and bring them into line with one's decisions or wishes; strength of mind and purpose.

wil·ly-nil·ly (wĭl′ē-nĭl′ē) *adv.* Whether desired or not.
~adj. Being or occurring whether desired or not. [Variant of *will I nill I,* "be I willing, be I unwilling."]

Wil·ming·ton (wĭl′mĭng-tən). City of northern Delaware, on the Delaware River. It was founded by Swedes in 1638 and is an important port with extensive shipyards.

Wil·son (wĭl′sən), **Alexander** (1766–1813). U.S. ornithologist, born in Scotland. In 1808, after conducting extensive field studies throughout the eastern United States, he published the first volume of his remarkably inclusive work, *American Ornithology.*

Wilson, Charles Thomson Rees (1869–1959). British physicist. He invented the Wilson cloud chamber, which permitted the observation and photography of the movement of charged particles (1911). He won the Nobel Prize in physics (1927).

Wilson, Edmund (1895–1972). U.S. author and critic. His works include *Axel's Castle* (1931), a study of the symbolist movement in art and literature, *To The Finland Station* (1940), *The Scrolls from the Dead Sea* (1955), and *The American Earthquake* (1958).

Wilson, (James) Harold, Baron Wilson of Rievaulx (1916–). British Labour prime minister (1964–70 and 1974–76). He succeeded Hugh Gaitskell as party leader (1963), became prime minister with the Labour victory of 1964, and faced many problems, including those of Rhodesia and Northern Ireland and resistance among his supporters to the introduction of a prices and incomes policy. He resigned in 1976.

Wilson, (Thomas) Woodrow (1856–1924). 28th president of the United States (1913–21). During his presidency prohibition was introduced. Wilson resisted U.S. involvement in World War I, but he reversed himself after the German U-boat campaign (1917). He laid the basis for a peace settlement and at the Paris Peace Conference achieved the acceptance of the League of Nations in the Treaty of Versailles (1919). He was awarded the Nobel Peace Prize (1919), but the treaty was rejected by the U.S. Senate.

Wilson's disease (wĭl′sənz) *n.* A hereditary disorder of copper metabolism in which excess copper is deposited in tissues and organs, such as the liver (causing jaundice and cirrhosis) and brain (causing mental deterioration). [After Samuel *Wilson* (1877–1937), U.S.-born British neurologist.]

wilt¹ (wĭlt) *v.* **wilted, wilting, wilts.** —*intr.* **1.** To become limp or flaccid; droop: *Plants wilted in the heat.* **2.** To become less active, energetic, or spirited; weaken. —*tr.* To cause to wilt. ~*n.* **1.** The act of wilting or the state of being wilted. **2.** Any of various plant diseases characterized by slow or rapid collapse of terminal shoots, branches, or entire plants. [Variant of dialectal *wilk, welk,* from Middle English *welken,* from Middle Dutch.]

wilt² *Archaic.* Second person singular present tense of **will.**

Wil·ton (wĭl′tən) *n.* A kind of carpet having a velvety surface formed by the cut loops of a pile. [From *Wilton,* Wiltshire, England.]

Wilt·shire¹ (wĭlt′shîr, -shər). County of south-central England. With the Marlborough Downs in the north and Salisbury Plain in the south, it is chiefly agricultural. Inhabited since ancient times, the area has prehistoric remains at Stonehenge, Avebury, and Silbury Hill. The county town is Salisbury.

Wiltshire² *n.* A sheep of a horned breed with very short fleece, reared for meat.

wi·ly (wī′lē) *adj.* **-lier, -liest.** Full of wiles; guileful; calculating. —See Synonyms at **sly.** [WILE + -LY.] —**wil·i·ly** *adv.* —**wil·i·ness** *n.*

wim·ble (wĭm′bəl) *n.* Any of numerous hand tools for the boring of holes, as a brace and bit or a gimlet. ~*tr.v.* **wimbled, -bling, -bles.** To bore with or as if with a wimble. [Middle English, from Anglo-French, perhaps from Middle Dutch *wimmel.*]

Wim·ble·don (wĭm′bəl-dən). District in the Greater London borough of Merton. It is the location of the All-England Lawn Tennis Club, where international championships have been held since 1877.

wimp (wĭmp) *n.* One who lacks strength of character or resolution; an insipidly ineffectual person. [Perhaps back-formation from W(H)IMPER.]

wim·ple (wĭm′pəl) *n.* **1.** A cloth wound around the head, framing the face, and drawn into folds beneath the chin, worn by women in medieval times and as part of the habit of certain orders of nuns. **2. a.** A fold or pleat in cloth. **b.** A ripple, as on the surface of water. **c.** A curve or bend. **d.** *Scottish.* A cunning twist. ~*v.* **wimpled, -pling, -ples.** —*tr.* **1.** To cover or furnish with a wimple. **2. a.** To cause to form ripples. **b.** To cause to form or lie in folds. —*intr.* **1.** To form or lie in folds. **2. a.** To ripple. **b.** To meander. [Middle English *wimpel,* Old English *wimpel.*]

Wim·py (wĭm′pē) *n. Chiefly British.* A trademark for a type of hamburger.

Wims·hurst machine (wĭmz′hûrst′) *n.* An electrostatic generator having mica or glass disks rotating in opposite directions with metal carriers on which charges are produced by induction, used chiefly as a demonstration apparatus. [After J. *Wimshurst,* (1832–1903), British engineer.]

win (wĭn) *v.* **won** (wŭn), **winning, wins.** —*intr.* **1.** To achieve victory over others in any kind of contest. **2.** To achieve success in an effort or venture. **3.** To struggle through to a desired place or condition: *We won through. They won free and escaped.* **4.** To finish first in a race: *won by a length.* —*tr.* **1.** To achieve victory in: *win a race; win an argument.* **2.** To be the successful party in predicting or guessing (an outcome, such as the result of a bet). **3.** To receive or gain through victory in a contest: *won the World Cup.* **4.** To receive as a reward for performance: *won a medal for heroism.* **5.** To achieve through effort or merit: *win an advantage; won recognition.* **6.** To take in battle; capture. **7.** To succeed in gaining the favor or support of; prevail upon. Often used with *over: His eloquence won us over.* **8. a.** To gain the affection or loyalty of: *won a friend for life.* **b.** To appeal successfully to (someone's loyalty, sympathy, or other emotion). **c.** To persuade (a person) to marry one. **9.** *Mining.* **a.** To discover and open (a vein or deposit); render fit for mining. **b.** To extract from a mine. **10.** To reach with effort or difficulty: *The ship won a safe port.* —**win out.** *Informal.* To succeed, prevail, or be victorious. ~*n.* **1.** A victory or success, especially in a competition. **2.** An amount won or earned: *a lottery win.* [Win, won, won; Middle English *winnen,* to win, strive, Old English *winnan,* to strive.]

wince¹ (wĭns) *intr.v.* **winced, wincing, winces.** To shrink or start involuntarily, as in pain or distress; flinch. ~*n.* A wincing movement or gesture. [Middle English *wincen,* to kick, wince, from Norman French *wencir* (unattested), from Germanic.] —**winc·er** *n.*

wince² *n.* A roller on which cloth may be moved and lowered into a vat of dye. [Variant of WINCH.]

winch (wĭnch) *n.* **1.** A stationary motor-driven or hand-powered hoisting machine having a drum around which a rope or chain winds as the load is lifted. **2.** The crank used to give motion to a grindstone or similar device. ~*tr.v.* **winched, winching, winches.** To hoist or move with or as if with a winch. [Middle English *winche,* a pulley, Old English *wince.*] —**winch·er** *n.*

Win·chell (wĭn′chəl), **Walter** (1897–1972). U.S. journalist. In his celebrity column "On Broadway," he reported events in entertainment and politics in a highly original and often idiomatic style (1924–63). In 1932 he began his popular radio newscasts that always began with "Good evening, Mr. and Mrs. America, from border to border and coast to coast and all the ships at sea."

Win·ches·ter¹ (wĭn′chĕs′tər, -chə-stər). County town of Hampshire, southern England, on the Itchen River. It was once the capital of Wessex, and after the Norman Conquest and the rise of London, it remained England's chief seat of learning. Its Norman cathedral, built on the foundation of a Saxon church, is the longest in Britain and the burial place of many Saxon monarchs.

Win·ches·ter² (wĭn′chĕs′tər) *n.* A trademark for a breechloading repeating rifle with lever action and a magazine attached horizontally under the barrel. [After Oliver WINCHESTER.]

Winchester, Oliver Fisher (1810–80). U.S. firearms manufacturer. The owner of a successful shirt business, he bought a firearms company and began producing reliable repeating rifles and pistols that were popular with state militias in the Civil War.

Winck·el·mann (vĭng′kəl-män′), **Johann Joachim** (1717–68). German archaeologist and antiquary. Considered the father of archaeology, he was the first to study ancient art as history. His most influential work, *History of the Art of Antiquity,* was published in 1764.

wind¹ (wĭnd) *n.* **1.** A current of air moving at any speed; especially, a natural and perceptible movement of air parallel to or along the ground. **2. a.** A movement or current of air blowing from one of the four cardinal points of the compass: *the four winds.* **b.** The direction from which a strong or prevailing current of air comes: *The wind is northeast.* **3.** Moving air carrying an odor, scent, or sound. **4.** A current or stream of air generated by a fan, bellows, or other artificial means. **5. a.** A wind instrument, such as a flute or clarinet. **b.** The section of an orchestra or band that plays these instruments. **6.** Gas produced in the body during digestion; flatulence. **7.** Respiration; breath; especially, normal or adequate breathing. **8.** A pervasive or irresistible force or influence: *a wind of change.* **9.** Utterance empty of meaning; verbiage. —**before the wind.** Moving forward with the wind behind. —**break wind.** To eject intestinal gas from the anus. —**close to the wind.** As close as possible to the main force of the wind. —**get wind of.** To receive a hint or intimation of. —**have the wind of. 1.** To be to windward of. **2.** To hold an advantage over. —**how the wind blows (or lies).** What developments arise or what the current trends are. —**in the wind.** Likely to occur; in the offing. —**near the wind. 1.** Close to the wind. **2.** Close to danger. —**sail close to the wind. 1.** To sail or travel as directly against the wind as possible. **2.** To live or manage frugally and economically. **3.** To approach near to the limits of what is acceptable; verge on impropriety, dishonesty, or danger. —**take the wind out of someone's sails.** To rob of an advantage; deflate. —**under the wind. 1.** To leeward. **2.** In a location protected from the wind. ~*tr.v.* **winded, winding, winds. 1.** To expose to the free movement of air; ventilate or dry. **2. a.** To catch a scent or trace of. **b.** To pursue by following a scent. **3.** To cause to be out of or short of breath, especially by a blow to the stomach. **4.** To afford a recovery of breath: *winded their horses after a gallop.* [Middle English *wind,* Old English *wind.*] See feature, next page.

   Synonyms: blast, breeze, gale, gust, hurricane, tornado, typhoon, whirlwind, zephyr.

wind² (wīnd) *v.* **wound** (wound), **winding, winds.** —*tr.* **1.** To wrap (something) around an object or center once or repeatedly: *wound thread around a reel; wound a scarf around his neck.* **2.** To wrap or encircle in a series of coils; entwine. **3.** To unwind or remove by unwinding. Used with *off.* **4.** To proceed on (one's way) with a curving or twisting course. **5.** To present or introduce in a disguised or devious manner: *He wound a plea for money into his letter.* **6.** To turn (a crank or handle, for example) in a series of circular motions. **7.** To coil the spring of (a clock or other mechanism) by turning a stem, cord, or the like. Often used with *up.* **8.** To lift or haul by means of a windlass or winch. —*intr.* **1.** To move in or as if in a bending or coiling course: *The road winds around up to the monastery.* **2. a.** To move in or have a spiral or circular course. **b.** To be or become coiled or spiraled about something. **3.** To be twisted or warped. Used of a board, for example. **4.** To proceed misleadingly or insidiously in speech or conduct. **5.** To become wound. —**wind down.** To decrease or diminish in activity, energy, intensity, or scope, especially so as to stop gradually: *winds down after work. We are currently winding down our South African company operations.* ~*n.* **1.** The act of winding. **2.** A single turn, twist, or curve. [Wind, wound, wound; Middle English *winden, wond, wonden,* Old English *windan, wond, wunden.*]

wind³ (wĭnd) *tr.v.* **winded** (wĭn′dĭd, wīn′-) or **wound** (wound), **winding, winds. 1.** To blow (a wind instrument). **2.** To sound by blowing. [From WIND (air).] —**wind·er** *n.*

wind·age (wĭn′dĭj) *n.* **1. a.** The effect of wind on the course of a projectile. **b.** The point or degree at which the wind gauge or sight of a rifle or gun must be set to compensate for the effect of the wind. **2.** In ballistics, the difference, in a given firearm, between the diameter of the projectile fired and the diameter of the bore of the firearm. **3.** The disturbance of air caused by the passage of a fast-moving object, such as a railroad train or missile. **4.** *Nautical.* The part of the surface of a ship that is left exposed to the wind.

wind·bag (wĭnd′băg′) *n. Informal.* A talkative person who communicates nothing of substance or interest.

wind·blast (wĭnd′blăst′) *n.* **1.** A very strong gust of wind. **2.** Injury caused by air friction to the pilot of a high-speed aircraft who has used his ejection seat.

wind·blown (wĭnd′blōn′) *adj.* **1.** Blown or dispersed by the wind.

2. Growing or shaped in a manner governed by the prevailing winds. **3.** Cut short and curled or combed toward the front of the head: *a wind-blown hair style.*

wind·borne (wĭnd′bôrn′, -bōrn′) *adj.* Carried by the wind. Said especially of plant seeds and pollen.

wind·bound (wĭnd′bound′) *adj.* Unable to sail because of high or contrary winds. Said of a sailing ship.

wind·break (wĭnd′brāk′) *n.* A hedge, row of trees, or fence serving to lessen or break the force of the wind.

Wind·break·er (wĭnd′brā′kər) *n.* A trademark for a warm outer jacket having close-fitting, often elastic, cuffs and waistband.

wind·bro·ken (wĭnd′brō′kən) *adj.* Suffering from the heaves or some other impairment of respiration. Used of horses.

wind·burn (wĭnd′bûrn′) *n.* Reddening and irritation of the skin caused by prolonged exposure to strong winds. **—wind·burned** *adj.*

wind·cheat·er (wĭnd′chē′tər) *n. Chiefly British.* A windbreaker.

WHY THE WIND BLOWS

Air temperature differences cause winds and breezes

The world's winds are caused by unequal air temperatures in different parts of the globe. Air heated by the sun at the equator expands and rises, moving outward at high levels. As it cools, most of it subsides around 30°N and 30°S—just beyond the tropics. Its weight creates regions of high pressure, which send winds blowing at low levels into the low-pressure areas near the equator. These north-south winds are deflected by the rotation of the earth, so they blow from the northeast in the Northern Hemisphere and the southeast in the Southern Hemisphere; they are known as the trade winds because they were used by merchant sailing ships. Over the polar regions the cold ground causes the air to sink, and winds blow outward.

Between the tropical and polar air movements in each hemisphere there is a variable zone where cold polar air meets warm tropical air. This creates cyclonic depressions ("lows"), but the general air movement is deflected eastward as westerly winds.

If the earth were a smooth ball covered entirely by either sea or flat land, these air movements would be uniform. It is the presence of large areas of land and sea that interferes with the major air currents. Land heats up and cools down more quickly than the sea, so the continents are hotter than the sea in summer and cooler than the sea in winter. This effect brings the monsoon winds to India and other tropical areas. As the land becomes intensely hot in summer, the air rises, forming a low-pressure area. Cool, moist air sweeps in from the ocean, bringing torrential rain. In winter, the air cools rapidly over the land and moves toward the low-pressure areas over the warmer seas.

This same phenomenon causes daily sea breezes in coastal areas in hot, sunny weather. In the late afternoon, breezes blow shoreward as cooler air from the sea moves in to replace the rising hot air above the land; in the morning, breezes blow seaward as air moves away from the cooler land to the warmer sea.

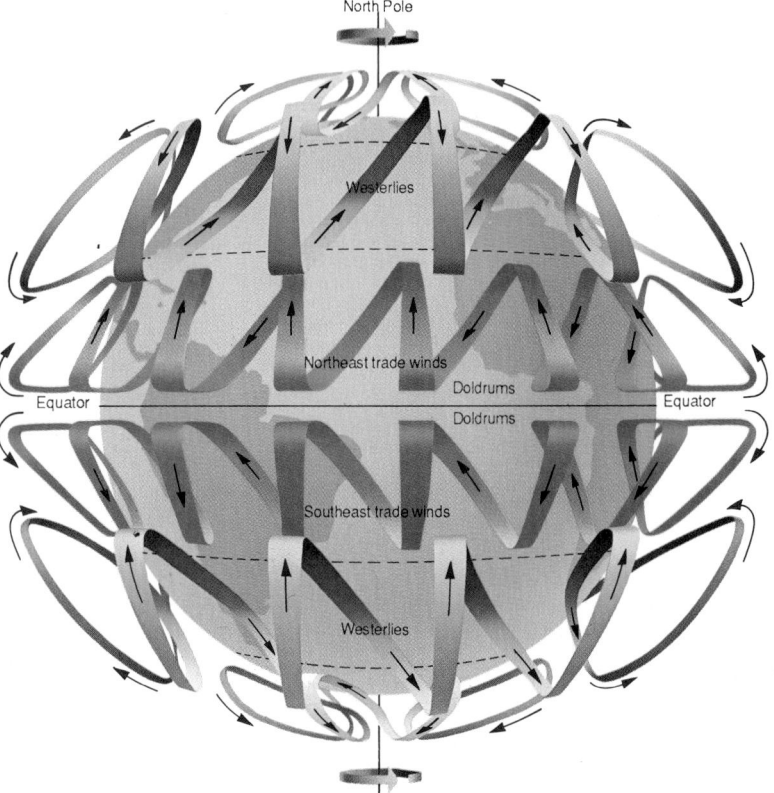

MAJOR WIND PATTERNS *Each hemisphere has three major wind systems—the trade winds, the westerlies, and the polar winds. Along the equator, wind* *less regions known as the doldrums occur, where sailing ships can find themselves becalmed for long periods.*

---

wind-chill factor (wĭnd′chĭl′) *n. Meteorology.* A measure of the cooling power of the air in relation to wind speed and air temperature.

wind cone (wĭnd) *n.* A wind indicator, a **windsock** *(see).*

wind·ed (wĭn′dĭd) *adj.* **1.** Having breath or respiratory power: *short-winded.* **2.** Out of breath.

wind·er (wīn′dər) *n.* **1.** A person, thing, or mechanism that winds, especially: **a.** A key or other device for winding up a spring-driven mechanism. **b.** An engine for raising and lowering cages in a mine shaft. **2.** A spool, barrel, or other object around which material is wound. **3.** Any of the steps of a winding staircase. In this sense, compare **flier.**

Win·der·mere, Lake (wĭn′dər-mîr′). Lake in Cumbria, northwest England. Situated in the Lake District, it is the largest lake in England, being 17 kilometers (10.5 miles) long and 1.6 kilometers (1 mile) wide, and is drained by the Leven River into Morecambe Bay.

wind·fall (wĭnd′fôl′) *n.* **1.** Something that has been blown down by the wind, such as a ripened fruit. **2.** A sudden and unexpected piece of good fortune or financial gain.

wind·flaw (wĭnd′flô′) *n.* A sudden gust or blast of wind.

wind·flow·er (wĭnd′flou′ər) *n.* The **wood anemone** *(see).* [Translation of Greek *anemōnē*, ANEMONE, from Greek *anemos*, wind.]

wind·gall (wĭnd′gôl′) *n.* A soft tumor on a horse's leg just above the fetlock.

wind gauge *n.* **1.** See **anemometer** (sense 1). **2.** A device attached to the sights of a gun, enabling allowance to be made for the effect of wind on the projectile.

wind gap (wĭnd) *n.* A shallow gap or ravine on the side of a deep mountain ridge.

wind harp (wĭnd) *n.* An **Aeolian harp** *(see).*

Wind·hoek (vĭnt′hook′). Capital of Namibia. Situated on a plateau in the center of the country, it was the capital of South-West Africa (1892) until taken by South African troops during World War I.

wind·hov·er (wĭnd′hŭv′ər, -hŏv′ər) *n. British Regional.* A **kestrel** *(see).* [WIND + HOVER, from its habit of hovering in one spot.]

wind·ing (wīn′dĭng) *n.* **1. a.** The act of one that winds. **b.** One complete turn of something wound. **2. a.** A thing in a wound condition; a spiral. **b.** A curve or bend, as in a road. **3.** *Electricity.* **a.** Wire wound into a coil. **b.** The manner in which such a coil is wound. **c.** A single loop of such a coil.
~*adj.* **1.** Twisting or turning; sinuous. **2.** Spiral: *a winding staircase.* **—wind·ing·ly** *adv.*

winding sheet (wīn′dĭng) *n.* A sheet for wrapping a dead body; a shroud.

wind instrument (wĭnd) *n.* Any musical instrument, as a clarinet, trumpet, or harmonica, sounded by wind, especially by the player's breath.

wind·jam·mer (wĭnd′jăm′ər) *n.* **1.** A large sailing ship. **2.** A crew member of a windjammer. [From WIND + JAM (verb).]

wind·lass (wĭnd′ləs) *n.* Any of numerous hauling or lifting machines consisting essentially of a drum or cylinder wound with rope and turned by a crank.
~*tr.v.* **windlassed, -lassing, -lasses.** To raise with a windlass. [Middle English *wyndlas,* variant of *windas,* from Norman French, from Old Norse *vindáss : vinda,* to wind + *áss†,* pole.]

win·dle·straw (wĭn′dəl-strô′) *n. British Regional.* A thin dried grass stalk. [Middle English *windlestraw* (unattested), Old English *windelstrēaw : windel,* basket, from *windan,* to WIND + *strēaw,* STRAW.]

wind·mill (wĭnd′mĭl′) *n.* **1.** A mill or other machine that runs on the energy generated by a wheel of adjustable blades, slats, or sails rotated by the wind. **2.** Anything similar to a windmill in appearance or operation, as a toy pinwheel. **3.** A person or thing imagined to be threatening or evil. Used chiefly in the phrase *tilting at windmills.* [Sense 3 is a reference to Cervantes' Don Quixote, who imagined windmills were evil giants.]

win·dow (wĭn′dō) *n.* **1.** An opening constructed in a wall or roof, as of a building or vehicle, that functions to admit light or air to an enclosure and is usually framed and spanned with glass mounted to permit opening and closing. **2. a.** A framework enclosing a pane of glass; a sash. **b.** A pane of glass, clear plastic, or the like; a windowpane. **3.** Any opening that resembles a window in function or appearance, such as the transparent space on an envelope that reveals the address printed on the enclosure. **4.** A code name for strips of foil dropped from aircraft as a radar countermeasure; chaff. **5.** The area or space immediately behind a window, especially at the front of a shop. **6.** A part of the electromagnetic spectrum in which radiation passes through a specified medium; for example, the radio window in the ionosphere lies between 50 gigahertz and 15 megahertz. **7.** A brief period during which a specified event can take place: *a launch window.*
~*tr.v.* **windowed, -dowing, -dows.** To provide with or as if with a window. [Middle English *window(e),* from Old Norse *vindauga : vindr,* wind, air + *auga,* eye.]

window box *n.* **1.** A usually long and narrow box for growing plants typically placed outdoors on a windowsill or ledge. **2.** Either of the vertical grooves on the inner sides of a window frame for the weights that counterbalance a sliding sash.

win·dow-dress·ing (wĭn′dō-drĕs′ĭng) *n.* **1. a.** A decorative display of retail merchandise in shop windows. **b.** Goods and trimmings used in such displays. **2.** A superficially attractive presentation, as of statistics, ideas, or policies, intended to highlight what is favorable and to conceal what is unpalatable. **—win·dow-dress·er** *n.*

windmill

ENERGY FROM THE AIR

A machine from the past with relevance for the future

The windmill first appeared in Persia in the 7th century and had reached Europe by the late 12th century. Thereafter its use spread rapidly. Improvements over the centuries included the fantail to turn the sails automatically into the wind, and sails that could be regulated to control the amount of power delivered.

The familiar multivaned windmill was developed in the United States in the last half of the 19th century. It consisted of a number of metal vanes set radially in a wheel. During the early 20th century such windmills were in use on nearly every farm in the Midwest and West until the advent of rural electrification in the 1930's. Small-scale wind-powered systems suitable for providing electricity or mechanical power in rural areas are still commercially available.

Recent studies indicate that large-scale wind-powered systems, which are pollution-free, could conceivably provide the United States with 5 to 10 percent of its electric power needs, saving 2.2 billion barrels of oil per year.

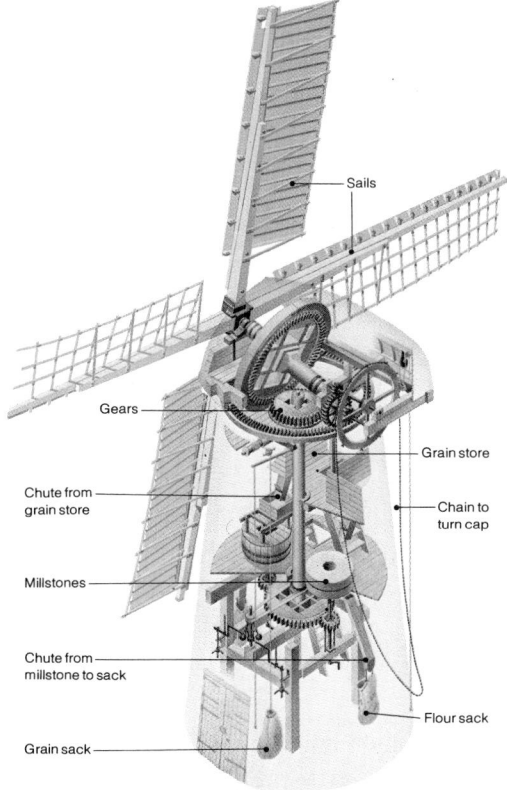

Sails

Gears

Grain store

Chute from grain store

Chain to turn cap

Millstones

Chute from millstone to sack

Flour sack

Grain sack

THE MECHANISM OF THE WINDMILL *The windmill at its most refined was a large and complex piece of machinery. The sails spanned up to 18 meters (60 feet) and weighed up to 5 tons. They made 10–15 revolutions a minute, and a gearing system turned the two millstones at 100 revolutions a minute.*

In the mill above, the miller had to turn the sails into the wind by pulling a looped chain that turned the cap on a cogged track, but in many mills a fantail did the task automatically. The miller could grind 270–320 kilograms (600–700 pounds) of grain an hour, but if the day was windless he would have to be prepared to work through the night.

window envelope *n.* An envelope with a transparent panel through which the address on the enclosure is visible.
win·dow·pane (wĭn′dō-pān′) *n.* A plate of glass in a window.
window seat *n.* Any place for sitting next to a window, as in the recess of a bay window or on a public transport vehicle.
window shade *n.* An opaque fabric, usually on rollers, mounted to cover or expose a window.
win·dow·shop (wĭn′dō-shŏp′) *intr.v.* **-shopped, -shopping, -shops.** To look at goods in store windows or showcases without making purchases. **—win·dow·shop·per** *n.*

win·dow·sill (wĭn′dō-sĭl′) *n.* The horizontal ledge at the base of a window opening.
wind·pipe (wĭnd′pīp′) *n. Anatomy.* The **trachea** (sense 1) *(see).*
wind·pol·li·nat·ed (wĭnd′pŏl′ə-nā′təd) *adj.* Pollinated by wind-borne pollen. Said of certain plants.
wind rose (wĭnd) *n.* Any of a class of meteorological diagrams depicting the distribution of wind direction over a period of time. [German *Windrose,* "a rose of winds," compass card.]
wind·row (wĭnd′rō′) *n.* **1.** A long row of cut hay or grain left to dry in a field before being bundled. **2.** A row, as of leaves or snow, heaped up by the wind. **~tr.v. windrowed, -rowing, -rows.** To shape or arrange into a windrow.
wind scale *n.* Any scale, as the Beaufort scale, that gives a numerical value to the force or speed of wind.
wind·screen (wĭnd′skrēn′) *n.* **1.** A screen that protects against the wind. **2.** *British.* An automobile windshield.
wind·shake (wĭnd′shāk′) *n.* A crack or separation between growth rings in timber, attributed to the straining of tree trunks in high winds.
wind·shield (wĭnd′shēld′) *n.* **1.** A framed pane of usually curved glass or other transparent shielding located in front of the occupants of a vehicle to protect them from the wind. **2.** Something placed to protect a person or object from the wind.
wind·sock (wĭnd′sŏk′) *n.* A large, tapered, open-ended sleeve, pivotally attached to a standard, that indicates the direction of the wind blowing through it. Also called "air sock," "drogue," "sock," "wind cone," "wind sleeve."
Wind·sor[1] (wĭn′zər). The family name of the British royal family since 1917.
Windsor[2]. Town in Berkshire, south-central England. Windsor Castle has been a royal residence since the time of William the Conqueror (11th century).
Windsor[3]. City in southern Ontario, Canada, on the Detroit River across from Detroit, Michigan. It is a port of entry and an important industrial center, producing automobiles, salt, and chemicals.
Windsor, Duke of. See **Edward VIII.**
Windsor, Wallis Warfield, Duchess of (1896–1986). U.S. socialite. In 1931, during her second marriage, she met the Prince of Wales, later King Edward VIII, and the two became companions. Choosing her love over his throne, Edward abdicated to George VI and became the Duke of Windsor (1936). When her divorce became final, the couple married (1937) and thereafter lived a highly publicized life until Edward's death in 1972.
Windsor chair *n.* A type of comfortable wooden chair typically having a high, curving, spoked back with arms and outward-slanting legs connected by a crossbar. [After *Windsor,* England.]
Windsor knot *n.* A wide, triangular tie knot.
Windsor tie *n.* A wide necktie tied in a loose bow.
wind sprint (wĭnd) *n.* A sprint run to develop breath.
wind·storm (wĭnd′stôrm′) *n.* A storm with high winds or violent gusts but little or no rain.
wind·suck·er (wĭnd′sŭk′ər) *n.* A horse given to noisily swallowing quantities of air. **—wind·suck·ing** *adj. & n.*
wind·surf·ing (wĭnd′sûrf′ĭng) *n.* The sport of sailing over water on a small, open vessel consisting of a large surfboard equipped with a sail. **—wind·surf** *v.* **—wind·surf·er** *n.*
wind·swept (wĭnd′swĕpt′) *adj.* **1.** Exposed to or moved by the force of the wind. **2.** Dishevelled by or as if by exposure to the wind: *a windswept appearance.*
wind tee (wĭnd) *n.* A large weather vane with a horizontal T-shaped wind indicator, commonly found at airfields.
wind tunnel (wĭnd) *n.* A chamber through which air is forced at controllable velocities in order to study the aerodynamic flow around and effects on airfoils, scale models, or other objects mounted within.
wind up (wĭnd) *tr.v.* To bring to an end; conclude; settle. **~intr.v. 1.** *Informal.* **a.** To come to a conclusion: *wound up by proposing a toast.* **b.** To come finally to a specified condition or situation: *wound up on the wrong side of the law.* **2.** *Baseball.* To make a pitching wind-up.
wind-up (wĭnd′ŭp′) *n.* **1. a.** The act of bringing something to a conclusion. **b.** The concluding part, as of an action, presentation, or speech. **2.** *Baseball.* The motions of a pitcher, such as swinging back the arm and raising the front foot, in preparation for pitching the ball. **~adj.** Having a spring wound up by hand: *a wind-up toy.*
wind·ward (wĭnd′wərd) *n.* **1.** The direction from which the wind blows. **2.** The side exposed to the wind. **—to the windward of.** Favorably situated with respect to. **~adj. 1.** Of or moving toward the quarter from which the wind blows. **2.** Of or on the side exposed to the wind or to prevailing winds. **~adv.** In a direction from which the wind blows; against the wind. Compare **leeward.**
Windward Islands. Archipelago of volcanic origin, southeast West Indies. The southern part of the Lesser Antilles, it extends southward from the Leeward Islands and includes Dominica, Grenada, St. Lucia, St. Vincent, and Martinique.
Windward Passage. Channel, *c.* 80 kilometers (50 miles) wide, between Cuba and Haiti, connecting the Atlantic Ocean and the Caribbean Sea. It provides a direct route from the eastern United States to the Panama Canal.

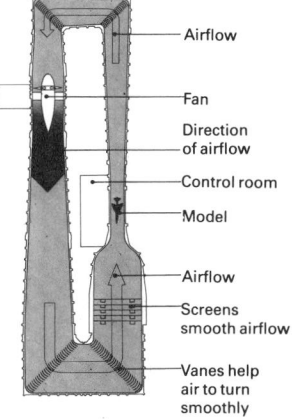

Airflow

Fan

Direction of airflow

Control room

Model

Airflow

Screens smooth airflow

Vanes help air to turn smoothly

wind tunnel *The artificially created airflow in a wind tunnel is used to study the aerodynamic performance of cars and aircraft. The study is usually carried out on small-scale models.*

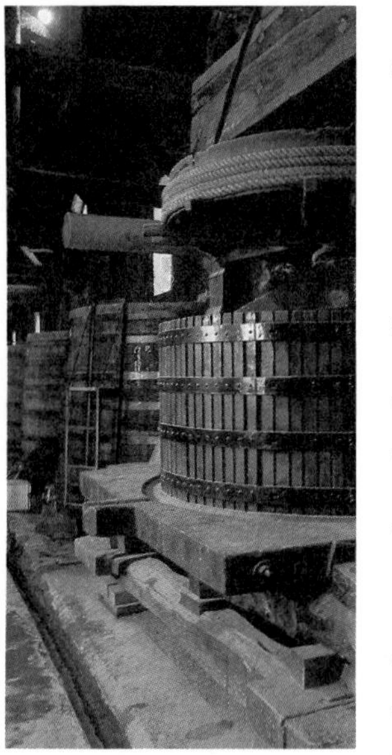

winepress *Juice was once extracted from grapes by treading them underfoot in large tubs, but today the grapes are more usually pressed by machine. Flowing through the slatted walls of the press, the juice is collected in vats and fermented into wine. This winepress is at the Château de la Chaise in France.*

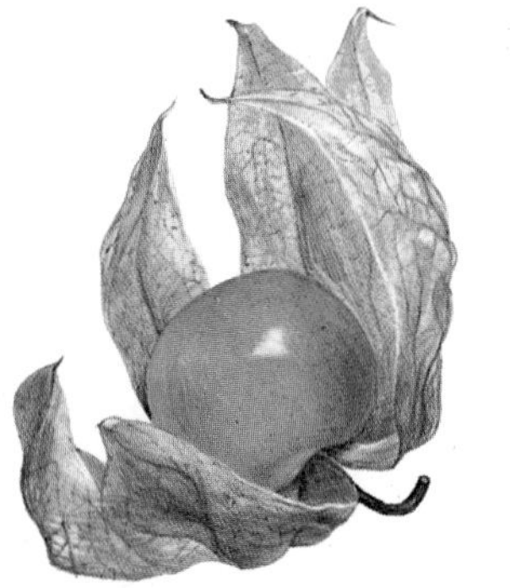

winter cherry *Sometimes called Chinese lantern plant, this creeping perennial has small white flowers in summer and orange-red berries in winter. In autumn the berries are enclosed in a red, lanternlike casing.*

wind·y (wĭn'dē) *adj.* **-ier, -iest. 1.** Characterized by the prevalence of strong winds: *a windy day.* **2.** Exposed to or swept by the wind. **3. a.** Characterized by lack of substance; empty; airy. **b.** Characterized by long-windedness, self-importance, or verbosity. **4.** Affected by or causing flatulence. **—wind·i·ly** *adv.* **—wind·i·ness** *n.*

wine (wīn) *n.* **1.** The fermented juice of any of various kinds of grapes making an alcoholic drink. **2.** The fermented juice of any of various other fruits or plants: *pear wine.* **3.** Something that intoxicates or exhilarates. **4.** The dark purplish color of red wine. **—new wine in old bottles.** New thought or principles that cannot be integrated with old traditional ways.
~*v.* **wined, wining, wines.** —*tr.* To provide or entertain with wines: *The guests were wined and dined.* —*intr.* To drink wine. [Middle English *win(e),* Old English *wīn,* from West Germanic *wīna-* (unattested), from Latin *vīnum.*]

wine·bib·ber (wīn'bĭb'ər) *n.* One who drinks excessive amounts of wine. [WINE + BIB, in archaic verbal sense, to drink.] **—wine·bib·bing** *adj. & n.*

wine cellar *n.* **1.** A place, especially a cellar, for storing wine. **2.** A stock of wines.

wine gallon *n.* A former unit of liquid measure used for wine, equivalent to the modern U.S. gallon (231 cubic inches or 3.79 liters).

wine·glass (wīn'glăs', -gläs') *n.* **1.** A glass from which wine is drunk; especially, a stemmed glass of a standard size having a capacity of approximately one sixth of a standard bottle of wine. **2.** The amount a wineglass will hold. In this sense, also called a "wineglassful."

wine·grow·er (wīn'grō'ər) *n.* One who owns a vineyard and produces wine. **—wine·grow·ing** *adj.* & *n.*

wine palm *n.* Any of various palm trees having sap or juice from which wine is prepared.

wine·press (wīn'prĕs') *n.* A vat in which the juice is pressed from grapes.

win·er·y (wī'nə-rē) *n., pl.* **-ies.** A winemaking establishment.

Wine·sap (wīn'săp') *n.* A variety of apple having fruit with dark-red skin.

wine·skin (wīn'skĭn') *n.* A bag for holding and dispensing wine, made from goatskin or other animal skin.

wine-tast·ing (wīn'tās'tĭng) *n.* The act or occasion of evaluating the quality of wine by tasting it. **—wine-tast·er** *n.*

wing (wĭng) *n.* **1.** Either of a pair of specialized organs of flight, as: **a.** The feather-covered modified forelimb of a bird. **b.** The membranous tissue supported by the elongated digits of the forelimb of a bat. **c.** A veined, membranous structure extending from the thorax of an insect. **d.** The enlarged pectoral fin of a flying fish. **2.** Any organ or structure homologous to or resembling a wing. **3.** *Botany.* **a.** A thin or membranous extension, as of the fruit of the sycamore or ash or along a twig or stem. **b.** Any of the lateral petals of the flower of a pea or related plant. **4.** Either of two winglike appendages believed to be part of the bodies of supernatural or fabulous creatures, such as angels, demons, or dragons. **5.** An airfoil whose principal function is providing lift; especially, either of two such airfoils symmetrically positioned on each side of the fuselage of an aircraft. **6.** Anything that resembles a wing in appearance, function, or position relative to a main body: *water wings.* **7.** A means of flight or of rapid movement: *Fear lent wings to his feet.* **8.** Something that is moved by or moves against the air, as a weather vane. **9.** *Chiefly British.* The fender of an automobile. **10.** An airfoil fitted to a racing car to help it hold the road. **11.** A folding section, as of a double door or of a movable partition. **12.** In the theater: **a.** A flat of scenery projecting onto the stage from the side. **b. wings.** The unseen backstage area on either side of the stage. **13.** A section of a building or structure projecting from the main or central part. **14.** Either of the two side projections on the back of a wing chair. **15.** A group affiliated with or subordinate to an older or larger organization. **16.** A section of a party or other group holding distinct, especially radical, political views: *the right wing; the left wing.* **17.** *Military.* Either the left or right flank of an army or a naval fleet lined up for battle. **18.** *Sports.* **a.** Either of the forward positions played near the sideline, as in soccer or hockey. **b.** One playing in such a position. **19.** An airforce unit larger than a group but smaller than a division or command. **20. wings.** Emblematic wings worn on the jacket by one who has qualified as an air pilot. **—clip someone's wings.** To restrict the movement, activity, or freedom of. **—in the wings.** Ready to come forward when required. **—on the wing. 1.** In flight; flying. **2.** Moving; traveling. **—spread (or stretch) one's wings.** To develop or exploit one's talents to the full. **—take wing. 1.** To fly off; soar away. **2.** To leave in a rush. **—under one's wing.** Under one's protection; in one's care.
~*v.* **winged, winging, wings.** —*intr.* To move on or as if on wings; fly. —*tr.* **1.** To furnish with wings. **2.** To feather (an arrow). **3. a.** To send (an arrow, for example) in flight. **b.** To cause or enable to move quickly; speed. **4.** To make (one's way) swiftly by or as if by flying. **5.** To wound superficially, as in the wing or arm. **6.** To furnish (a building, for example) with side or subordinate extensions. **—wing it.** *Informal.* To improvise or ad-lib, as in a theatrical performance. [Middle English *wenge(n),* from Old Norse *vængi,* accusative plural of *vængr,* bird's wing.]

wing and wing *adv. Nautical.* With sails extended on both sides.

Win·gate (wĭn'gāt'), **Orde Charles** (1903–44). British general. He worked with Jewish guerrillas in Palestine (1935–39) and during World War II defeated the Italians in Ethiopia (1941). In Burma he organized the specially trained Chindit forces.

wing·back (wĭng'băk') *n. Football.* **1.** A back positioned on offense behind or outside of an end. **2.** The position itself.

wing·bow (wĭng'bō') *n.* A mark of color on the bend of the wing in a domestic fowl.

wing-case (wĭng'kās') *n.* Either of the two hard, leathery, modified forewings that cover and protect the delicate hindwings of certain insects at rest, especially beetles.

wing chair *n.* An armchair with a high back from which project large, enclosing sidepieces or wings.

wing commander *n. Abbr.* **W/Cdr.** An officer of the British air force and certain other air forces, ranking between a group captain and a squadron leader.

wing·ding (wĭng'dĭng') *n.* A lavish or lively party or celebration. [20th century : origin obscure.]

winged (wĭngd, wĭng'ĭd) *adj.* **1.** Having wings or winglike appendages. **2.** Moving on or as if on wings; flying. **3.** Soaring; elevated; sublime. **4.** Swift; fleet.

wing·er (wĭng'ər) *n.* **1.** *Chiefly British.* A forward playing on the wing, as in soccer or hockey. **2.** One who belongs to the specified political wing of a party or other group. Used in combination: *left-wingers.*

wing-foot·ed (wĭng'fo͝ot'ĭd) *adj.* Swift; fleet.

wing·less (wĭng'lĭs) *adj.* Having no wings or having only rudimentary wings. Said especially of primitive insects of the subclass Apterygota, which includes the springtails and bristletails.

wing·let (wĭng'lĭt) *n.* A small or rudimentary wing.

wing loading *n.* The gross weight of an aircraft divided by the wing area. Used in stress analysis.

wing nut *n.* A nut with winglike projections for thumb and forefinger leverage in turning. Also called "butterfly nut."

wing·o·ver (wĭng'ō'vər) *n.* A flight maneuver or stunt in which an aircraft enters a climbing turn until almost stalled and is allowed to fall while the turn is continued until normal flight is attained in a direction opposite the original heading.

wing·span (wĭng'spăn') *n.* The linear distance from wing tip to wing tip of an aircraft, bird, or insect. Also called "wingspread."

wing tip *n.* **1.** A shoe part, often perforated, that covers the toe and extends backward along the sides of the shoe from a point at the center. **2.** A style of shoe having a wing tip. **3.** *Usually* **wingtip.** The extreme edge of a wing, as of a bird or aircraft.

wink¹ (wĭngk) *v.* **winked, winking, winks.** —*intr.* **1.** To close and open the eyelid of one eye deliberately, as to convey a message, signal, or suggestion. **2.** To close and open the eyelids of both eyes; blink. **3. a.** To shine fitfully; twinkle: *winking stars.* **b.** To flash intermittently, as the direction indicator on a car does. —*tr.* **1.** To close and open (an eye or the eyes) rapidly. **2.** To signal or express as by the winking of an eye or by flashing a light. **—wink at.** To pretend not to see: *winked at corruption in his ministry.*
~*n.* **1.** An act of winking. **2.** The extremely brief time required for a wink. **3.** A signal or hint conveyed by winking. **4.** A gleam; a twinkle. **5.** *Informal.* A brief moment of sleep. [Middle English *winken,* Old English *wincian,* to close one's eyes.]

wink² *n.* Any of the small, round disks used in the game of tiddlywinks. [Shortened from TIDDLYWINKS.]

wink·er (wĭngk'ər) *n.* **1.** One that winks. **2.** A horse's blinder.

win·kle (wĭng'kəl) *n.* A snail, the **periwinkle** *(see).*
~*tr.v.* **winkled, -kling, -kles.** *Chiefly British Informal.* To prize out; extract. Usually used with *out.* [Shortened from PERIWINKLE.]

Win·ne·ba·go (wĭn'ə-bā'gō) *n., pl.* **Winnebagos** or **-goes** or collectively **Winnebago. 1.** A tribe of North American Indians, inhabiting eastern Wisconsin. **2.** A member of the Winnebago. **3.** The Siouan language of the Winnebago.

Win·ne·ba·go, Lake (wĭn'ə-bā'gō). Lake, 557 square kilometers (215 square miles), in eastern Wisconsin. Fed and drained by the Fox River, it is part of an all-water route between the Great Lakes and the Mississippi River.

win·ner (wĭn'ər) *n.* **1.** One that wins, especially in a sports contest. **2.** *Informal.* One that is assured of success: *His latest film is a winner.* **3.** *Slang.* One of exceptionally poor quality or character: *That guy's a real winner.*

win·ning (wĭn'ĭng) *adj.* **1.** Successful; victorious. **2.** Charming; engaging: *a winning personality.*
~*n.* **1.** The act of one that wins; victory. **2. winnings.** Something that has been won; especially, money won by gambling. **3.** A section of a mine that has been recently prepared or opened for working. **—win·ning·ly** *adv.* **—win·ning·ness** *n.*

winning gallery *n.* In court tennis, an opening below the side penthouse. A ball played into this opening is counted as a win.

winning post *n.* The post at the end of a racecourse.

Win·ni·peg (wĭn'ə-pĕg'). Capital of Manitoba, south-central Canada. Situated at the confluence of the Red and Assiniboine rivers and south of Lake Winnipeg, it is the main wheat market and commercial center for the Prairie Provinces.

Winnipeg, Lake. Lake, 24,514 square kilometers (9,465 square miles) in area, in south-central Manitoba, Canada. It is the third-largest lake of Canada and has extensive fishing resources.

Win·ni·pe·sau·kee, Lake (wĭn'ə-pə-sô'kē). Lake, 184 square kilometers (71 square miles) in area, in east-central New Hampshire. The largest lake of New Hampshire, it is surrounded by a popular summer resort area.

win·now (wĭn'ō) *v.* **-nowed, -nowing, -nows.** —*tr.* **1.** To separate

the chaff from (grain) by means of a current of air. **2.** To blow (chaff) off or away. **3.** To scatter or disperse by blowing. **4.** To blow upon; cause to flutter or fly: *hair winnowed by the breeze.* **5.** To examine closely in order to separate the good from the bad; analyze; sift. **6.** To separate (a desirable or undesirable part); eliminate by sorting. Often used with *out.* —*intr.* **1.** To separate grain from chaff. **2.** To separate the good from the bad.
—*n.* **1.** A device for winnowing grain. **2.** An act of winnowing. [Middle English *windowen, wynwen,* Old English *windwian,* from *wind,* WIND.] —**win·now·er** *n.*

win·o (wī'nō) *n., pl.* **winos.** *Slang.* A person, especially a tramp or vagrant, who is habitually drunk on wine.

win·some (wĭn'səm) *adj.* Winning; charming; engaging. [Middle English *winsum,* Old English *wynsum* : *wyn,* joy + *-sum,* -SOME.] —**win·some·ly** *adv.* —**win·some·ness** *n.*

Win·ston-Sa·lem (wĭn'stən-sā'ləm). City in north-central North Carolina. It is the chief tobacco-manufacturing center of the United States. Salem was built by Moravians in 1766 and Winston was established in 1849 as the county seat. The two communities were united in 1913.

win·ter (wĭn'tər) *n.* **1.** The usually coldest season of the year, occurring between autumn and spring. In the Northern Hemisphere it extends from the winter solstice to the vernal (or spring) equinox and is popularly considered to comprise December, January, and February; in the Southern Hemisphere it falls between the summer solstice and the autumnal equinox, or, popularly, June, July, and August. **2.** A year as expressed through the recurrence of this season. **3.** Any period characterized by coldness, misery, barrenness, or death.
—*v.* **wintered, -tering, -ters.** —*intr.* To pass or spend the winter. —*tr.* To lodge, keep, or care for during the winter: *wintering the sheep in the stable.*
—*adj.* **1.** Pertaining to, characteristic of, suitable for, or occurring in winter: *a winter coat; winter weather.* **2. a.** Capable of being stored for use during the winter. Said of fruits or vegetables. **b.** Planted in the autumn and harvested in the spring or summer: *winter barley.* [Middle English, Old English *winter,* from Germanic *wentrus* (unattested), akin to WET.] —**win·ter·er** *n.* —**win·ter·less** *adj.* —**win·ter·ly** *adj.*

winter aconite *n.* A frequently cultivated European plant, *Eranthis hyemalis,* having a solitary yellow flower that blooms in winter or early spring.

win·ter·ber·ry (wĭn'tər-bĕr'ē) *n., pl.* **-ries.** Any of several North American shrubs of the genus *Ilex,* having showy red berries.

winter cherry *n.* A frequently cultivated Eurasian plant, *Physalis alkekengi,* having red berries enclosed in inflated papery, orange-red seed cases. Also called "Chinese lantern plant."

win·ter·feed (wĭn'tər-fēd') *tr.v.* **-fed** (-fĕd'), **-feeding, -feeds.** To feed (livestock) when grazing is not possible.

win·ter·green (wĭn'tər-grēn') *n.* **1. a.** A low-growing evergreen plant, *Gaultheria procumbens,* of eastern North America, having white or pinkish flowers, aromatic leaves, and spicy, edible red berries. Also called "checkerberry," "teaberry." **b.** A medicinal oil or flavoring obtained from this plant. **2. a.** Any of several similar or related plants. **b.** Any plant of the genus *Pyrola,* such as *P.minor,* having round pink flowers. [Translation of Dutch *wintergroen.*]

win·ter·ize (wĭn'tə-rīz') *tr.v.* **-ized, -izing, -izes.** To prepare or equip (a house or car, for example) for winter weather.

winter jasmine *n.* A shrub, *Jasminum nudiflorum,* native to China but widely cultivated for its yellow, winter-blooming flowers.

win·ter·kill (wĭn'tər-kĭl') *v.* **-killed, -killing, -kills.** —*tr.* To kill (plants, for example) by exposing to extremely cold winter weather. —*intr.* To die from exposure to cold winter weather. Used especially of plants. —**winterkill** *n.*

winter melon *n.* A variety of melon, *Cucumis melo inodorus,* having fruit with sweet, usually light-colored flesh. Also called "casaba." [Translation of Chinese *tung¹ kua¹.*]

Winter Olympic Games *pl.n.* An international sporting event in which representatives of different countries compete in winter sports, held in the same year as the **Olympic Games** *(see).* Also called "Winter Olympics."

winter rose *n.* A plant, the **Christmas rose** *(see).*

winter savory *n.* See **savory** (plant).

winter solstice *n. Astronomy.* A **solstice** *(see).*

winter sports *n.* Sports, such as skiing or bobsledding, that take place on snow and ice.

winter squash *n.* Any of several thick-rinded varieties of squash, such as the acorn squash, that can be stored for long periods.

win·ter·time (wĭn'tər-tīm') *n.* The winter season.

winter wheat *n.* Wheat planted in the autumn and harvested the following spring or early summer.

Win·throp (wĭn'thrəp). Family of colonial administrators in America, including **John** (1588-1649), a founder of the Massachusetts Bay Company who moved to the colony in 1630, served as its first governor (1629-33), and was re-elected several times. His son **John** (1606-76) was a major figure in the settlement of Connecticut, where he served as governor (1657 and 1659-76); his son **Fitz-John** (1638-1707) also served as Connecticut's governor (1698-1707).

win·try (wĭn'trē) *adj.* **-trier, -triest.** Also **win·ter·y** (wĭn'tə-rē) **-ier, -iest. 1.** Characteristic of winter; cold. **2.** Suggestive of winter; cheerless. [Old English *wintrig.*] —**win·tri·ly** *adv.* —**win·tri·ness** *n.*

win·y (wī'nē) *adj.* **-ier, -iest.** Having the qualities or taste of wine; intoxicating; heady.

---

wine

"READING" A WINE BOTTLE

The shape alone often reveals the place where the contents were made

Traditionally, different types of wine are associated with different-shaped bottles.

Bordeaux wines have tall, narrow bottles with squarish shoulders and are colored green for red wine (claret), green or clear for white.

Burgundy wines have wider bottles with sloping shoulders; they are dark green for red wine, lighter green for white.

German and Alsace wines have tall, slender bottles with no shoulders. Rhine (hock) bottles are reddish-brown, Moselle and Alsace bottles are green.

Port and sherry bottles are similar to Bordeaux bottles, but are squatter with squarer shoulders and longer necks; they are green, dark brown, or black.

Chianti may still sometimes be sold in green flasks in straw jackets, but Bordeaux-shaped bottles are more often used.

Champagnes and sparkling wines are in Burgundy-type bottles, but made of much thicker glass; they have tinfoil around the neck and a wired-on cork.

The standard wine bottle contains 750 milliliters of wine, but there are also larger versions with special names: magnum = 2 ordinary bottles; flagon = 3; double magnum or Jeroboam = 4; Rehoboam = 6; Champagne and Burgundy Impériale or Methuselah = 8 (Bordeaux 6); Salmanazar = 12; Balthazar = 16; Nebuchadnezzar = 20.

The label on the bottle should give the name of the country of origin, the region, château, or estate from which the wine comes, probably the vintage (the year in which it was made), and the name of the shipper or producer.

Within the large regions—such as Bordeaux,

Burgundy, or the Rhine—are areas or villages famous for their wine (such as Médoc or Sauternes, Chablis or Beaujolais, Nierstein or Hochheim), and within them again are the individual vineyards. In France, Germany, and Italy strict laws govern the use of these names.

The words *Appellation Contrôlée* on French bottles mean that the wine comes from the place named and was made according to local custom. *Vins Délimités de Qualité Supérieure* are not generally of such high standard but are of better quality than *vins ordinaires.*

Mise au château, Mise au domaine, or *Mise en bouteilles au château* means that the wine was bottled on the estate that produced it. *Cru* means growth, and some wines are classified by quality as *grand cru, premier cru,* and so on. Some labels name the grape—Cabernet Sauvignon, for instance, Riesling, or Gewürztraminer.

On German labels, *Kellerabzug* and *Originalabzug* mean estate-bottled. German wine is divided into *Tafelwein* (table wine), which can be purely German or a Common Market blend, *Qualitätswein* (quality wine), and *Qualitätswein mit Prädikat* (quality wine of distinction). With the last of these an indication will be given of the condition of the grapes: *Spätlese* (made from late-gathered grapes) is not as good as *Auslese* (made from selected, fully ripe grapes); even more expensive are *Beerenauslese* (made from individually selected overripe grapes) and *Trockenbeerenauslese* (made from grapes left on the vine until shrunken and highly enriched).

A characteristically shaped bottle of central Germany is the *Bocksbeutel,* or Franconian flagon, containing the white "stone wine" of Würzburg.

Bordeaux red   Burgundy   Burgundy pot   Chianti   Côte de Provence   Franconian flagon   Loire

Rhine   Moselle   Alsace   Bordeaux white   Champagne   Vintage port   Port

THE COMMONEST SHAPES *Above are 14 of the commonest shapes of wine bottles. On the top left are three of the traditional bottles of France, then Chianti of Italy in its old-style wicker basket—now fast disappearing. On the bottom far right are the squat, long-necked port bottles.*

winze (wĭnz) *n.* In mining, an inclined or vertical shaft or passage between levels. [Variant of earlier *winds,* probably from *wind,* windlass, from Middle Dutch or Middle Low German *winde* and from WIND (to wrap around, turn).]

wipe (wīp) *tr.v.* **wiped, wiping, wipes. 1.** To subject to light rubbing or friction, as with a cloth or paper, in order to clean or dry: *wipe the dishes; wipe the table.* **2. a.** To remove or get rid of by or as if by wiping. Usually used with *off* or *away*: *wiped away her tears; Wipe that smile off your face.* **b.** To remove; eradicate: *wipe out a memory.* **3.** To rub, move, or spread over something: *wiped his shoes on the mat.* **4.** In plumbing, to form (a joint) by spreading solder with a piece of cloth or leather. **—wipe out 1.** To destroy; annihilate: *wiped out a tribe.* **2.** *Informal.* To murder. **3.** In surfing, to lose balance and fall or jump off a surfboard.
~*n.* **1.** The act of wiping. **2.** Something used for wiping, as: **a.** A commercially produced treated cloth or tissue: *a box of baby wipes.* **b.** *Slang.* A handkerchief. **3.** *Informal.* **a.** A blow; a swipe. **b.** A jeer; a gibe. [Middle English *wipen,* Old English *wīpian.*]

wipe out *tr.v.* **1.** To destroy; annihilate: *wiped out a tribe.* **2.** To remove; eradicate: *wipe out a memory.* —*intr.v. Slang.* In surfing, to lose balance and fall or jump off a surfboard.

wipe-out (wīp′out′) *n.* **1.** The act or an instance of wiping out. **2.** A fall or jump off a surfboard. **3.** Total loss of radio reception as a result of interference by another signal.

wip·er (wī′pər) *n.* **1.** One that wipes. **2.** A device designed for wiping, such as a windshield wiper. **3.** In a machine, a cam that projects from a rotating horizontal shaft to activate another part. **4.** *Electricity.* A movable electrical contact, as in a rheostat.

wire (wīr) *n.* **1. a.** A usually pliable metallic strand or rod made in many lengths and diameters, sometimes clad and often electrically insulated, used chiefly for structural support or to conduct electricity. **b.** Such strands collectively, used as a fencing material, for example. **2.** A group of such strands bundled or twisted together as a functional unit; a cable. **3.** Something resembling a wire, as in slenderness or stiffness. **4.** The telegraph service: *sent it by wire.* **5.** A telegram. **6.** The screen on which sheets of paper are formed in a papermaking machine. **7.** A metal snare, as for catching rabbits. **8.** The finishing line of a racetrack. **—get (or get in) under the wire.** To arrive somewhere or finish something just in the nick of time. **—pull wires.** To use secret or underhand means to accomplish something; pull strings.
~*adj.* Made of or resembling a wire or wires: *a wire brush.*
~*v.* **wired, wiring, wires.** —*tr.* **1.** To bind, connect, or attach with a wire or wires. **2.** To equip with a system of electrical wires. **3. a.** To send by telegraph: *wire congratulations.* **b.** To send a telegram to. **4.** To snare with a wire. **5.** In croquet, to hit (a ball) behind a hoop and block an opponent's shot. —*intr.* To send a telegram; telegraph. [Middle English *wir(e),* Old English *wīr.*]

wire cloth *n.* A mesh woven of fine wire.

wire-draw (wīr′drô′) *tr.v.* **-drew** (-dro͞o′), **-drawn** (-drôn′), **-drawing, -draws. 1.** To draw (metal) into wire. **2.** To protract (a subject, for example) inordinately; spin out. **—wire·draw·er** *n.*

wire gauge *n.* **1.** A gauge for measuring the diameter of wire, usually in the form of a disk having variously sized slots in its periphery or a long graduated plate with similar slots along its edge. **2.** A standardized system of wire sizes.

wire gauze *n.* A material woven of very fine wires.

wire glass *n.* Sheet glass reinforced with wire-netting.

wire·grass (wīr′grăs′, -gräs′) *n.* Any of various grasses having tough, wiry roots or rootstocks, such as **Bermuda grass** *(see).*

wire-haired (wīr′hârd′) *adj.* Having a coat of stiff, wiry hair. Said of breeds of dogs: *a wire-haired terrier.*

wire·less (wīr′lĭs) *adj.* **1.** Without wires. **2.** *Chiefly British Archaic.* Radio.
~*n.* **1.** A radio telegraph or telephone system. **2.** A message transmitted by wireless telegraph or telephone. **3.** *Chiefly British Archaic.* Radio.
~*v.* **wirelessed, -lessing, -lesses.** —*tr.* To communicate with by wireless telegraphy or radiotelephone. —*intr.* To communicate in this way; radio.

wireless telegraphy *n.* Telegraphy by radio rather than by long-distance transmission lines. Also called "radiotelegraphy," "wireless telegraph."

wireless telephone *n.* **Radiotelephone** *(see).*

wire·man (wīr′mən) *n., pl.* **-men** (-mĭn). One who works with electric wiring; a lineman.

wire netting *n.* Netting made of woven wire, as for fences.

wire·pull·er (wīr′po͝ol′ər) *n.* One who pulls wires or strings, as of puppets. **2.** One who uses subterfuge, private influence, or underhand means in order to reach a goal. **—wire·pull·ing** *n.*

wire recorder *n.* A forerunner of the tape recorder that recorded sound on a spool of wire rather than on magnetic tape.

wire rope *n.* A rope composed of twisted strands of wire.

wire·tap (wīr′tăp′) *n.* **1.** A concealed listening or recording device connected to a communications circuit. **2.** The installation of such a device.
~*v.* **wiretapped, -tapping, -taps.** —*tr.* **1.** To connect a wiretap to. **2.** To monitor (a telephone line) by means of a wiretap. —*intr.* To install or monitor by a wiretap. **—wire·tap** *adj.* **—wire·tap·per** *n.*

wire wool *n.* A tangled mass of fine wire used to rub metal surfaces to remove dirt or rust.

wire·work (wīr′wûrk′) *n.* **1.** Wire fabric. **2.** Articles made of wire or wire fabric.

wire·worm (wīr′wûrm′) *n.* The wirelike larva of various click beetles that cause severe damage by boring into the roots of many plants.

wire-wove (wīr′wōv′) *adj.* **1.** Designating a high-grade writing paper with a smooth finish. **2.** Made of woven wire.

wir·ing (wīr′ĭng) *n.* **1.** The act of attaching, connecting, or installing wires. **2.** A system of electric wires, as in a building.

wir·ra (wĭr′ə) *interj. Irish.* Used to express sorrow or perplexity. [From Irish Gaelic *a Muire,* "Oh, Mary."]

Wir·ral, the (wîr′əl). Peninsula in Merseyside, northwestern England. Situated between the Mersey and Dee estuaries, it includes Wallasey, Birkenhead, Ellesmere Port, and Port Sunlight.

wir·y (wīr′ē) *adj.* **-ier, -iest. 1.** Made of or consisting of wire. **2.** Resembling wire, as in fineness and stiffness: *wiry hair.* **3.** Sinewy and lean; slender but tough. Said of people and animals. **—wir·i·ly** *adv.* **—wir·i·ness** *n.*

Wis·con·sin (wĭs-kŏn′sən). *Abbr.* **Wis.** State in the north-central United States. Extending from the Mississippi River to Lakes Superior and Michigan, it has more than 8,500 lakes and is mainly low-lying with extensive forests. It is the chief dairy state of the United States. The capital is Madison.

Wisconsin. River, *c.* 690 kilometers (430 miles) long, rising in the lake district of northeastern Wisconsin and flowing generally southwest across central Wisconsin to the Mississippi River. There are many hydroelectric power facilities on the river as well as the scenic Wisconsin Dells, a famous gorge.

wis·dom (wĭz′dəm) *n.* **1.** Enlightened understanding of what is true or right, usually acquired through long experience, as distinguished from a partial or specialized knowledge: *"The only wisdom we can hope to acquire/ Is the wisdom of humility"* (T.S. Eliot). **2.** Common sense; sagacity; good judgment. **3.** Accumulated learning; erudition. **4.** Wise sayings or teaching: *the wisdom of the ancients.* —See Synonyms at **knowledge.** [Middle English *wisedom,* Old English *wīsdōm* : *wīs,* WISE + *-dōm,* -dom.]

Wisdom of Jesus, the Son of Si·rach (sîr′ăk′) *n.* A book of the Apocrypha, **Ecclesiasticus** *(see).*

Wisdom of Solomon *n.* A book of the Apocrypha.

wisdom tooth *n.* Any of four molars, the last on each side of both jaws, usually erupting much later than the others. [From New Latin *dentes sapientiae* (plural), teeth of wisdom, from their usually being cut around the age of 20.]

wise[1] (wīz) *adj.* **wiser, wisest. 1.** Imbued with, based on, or suggestive of wisdom or discernment for what is true or right: *a wise decision.* **2.** Possessed of or showing common sense; prudent; sensible: *It would be wise not to mention this to anyone.* **3.** Shrewd; crafty: *a wise move.* **4.** Having knowledge or information; informed; aware: *came away none the wiser; soon got wise to his plan.* **5.** *Archaic.* Having magical or occult powers. **6.** *Slang.* Offensively self-assured; arrogant. **—get wise.** *Slang.* **1.** To learn the facts or become aware: *Get wise and stop fighting the system.* **2.** To become provocatively insolent: *a student who got wise with the teacher.* **—wise up.** *Slang.* To become aware or sophisticated. Often used with *to.* [Middle English *wis(e),* Old English *wīs.*] **—wise·ly** *adv.*

wise[2] *n.* **1.** Method or manner of doing; fashion; way; respect: *in no wise; in any wise.* [Middle English *wise,* Old English *wīse, wīs,* manner.]

-wise *suffix.* Indicates: **1.** Manner, direction, or position; for example, **clockwise. 2.** With reference to; for example, **taxwise.** [Middle English *-wise,* in a certain manner, Old English *-wīsan,* from *wīse,* WISE (manner).]

Usage: The suffix *-wise* has a long history of use in the sense "in the manner or direction of": *clockwise, likewise, otherwise, slantwise.* In recent times, *-wise* has been in vogue as a suffix meaning "with relation to" and attachable to any noun: *saleswise, inflationwise.* But indiscriminate use of these coinages can lead to confusion, as the exact nature of the relation the writer intends is not always clear from the context. Most new or temporary coinages of this sort are thus unacceptable in writing, and are considered by many to be inappropriate in speech.

wise·a·cre (wīz′ā′kər) *n. Informal.* An offensively self-assured person who affects to be wise. [Middle Dutch *wijsseggher,* soothsayer, alteration of Old High German *wīssago, wīzago,* seer.]

wise·crack (wīz′krăk′) *n. Informal.* A flippant, cleverly sardonic remark or retort; a joke or gibe. —See Synonyms at **joke.**
~*intr.v.* **wisecracked, -cracking, -cracks.** *Informal.* To make a wisecrack. **—wise·crack·er** *n.*

wise guy *n. Informal.* A self-assured person who affects an air of superior knowledge; a know-it-all.

wis·en·heim·er or **weis·en·heim·er** (wīz′ən-hī′mər) *n. Informal.* An offensively self-assured person. [From WISE + German *-enheimer* (as in German surnames such as *Oppenheimer.*)]

wi·sent (vē′zĕnt′) *n.* The European bison, *Bison bonasus.* See **bison.** [German *Wisent,* from Old High German *wisunt.*]

wish (wĭsh) *n.* **1.** A feeling of longing or desire for something. **2. a.** An expression, often unspoken, or confession of such a desire: *make a wish.* **b.** A known or expressed aspiration or request: *went against my wishes.* **3.** An object of desire; something wished for: *You've got your wish.* **4.** *Usually* **wishes.** An expressed desire for the welfare, happiness, or health of someone: *Send her my best wishes.*
~*v.* **wished, wishing, wishes.** —*tr.* **1.** To have as a wish, as: **a.** To want: *I wish to leave now.* **b.** To desire (something unattainable): *I wish I'd never been born.* **c.** To desire or request (someone) to do something: *I wish you'd come to the point.* **d.** To desire or long for (someone or something) to be in a specified state: *wished him a*

PRONUNCIATION KEY

ă, pat; ā, pay; âr, care;
ä, father, are; b, bib;
ch, church; d, deed; ĕ, pet;
ē, be; f, fife; g, gag; h, hat;
hw, which; ĭ, pit; ī, pie;
îr, pier; j, judge; k, kick;
l, lid, needle; m, mum;
n, no, sudden; ng, thing;
ŏ, pot; ō, toe; ô, paw, for;
oi, noise; ou, out; o͝o, book;
o͞o, boot; p, pop; r, roar;
s, sauce; sh, ship, dish;
t, tight; th, thin, path;
th, this, bathe; ŭ, cut; ûr, fur;
v, valve; w, with; y, yes;
z, zebra, size; zh, vision;
ə, about, item, edible,
gallop, circus, peaceful

IN FOREIGN WORDS:

à, *Fr.* ami; œ, *Fr.* feu, *Ger.* schön; ü, *Fr.* tu, *Ger.* über;
KH, *Ger.* ich, *Scot.* loch;
N, *Fr.* bon; y′, *Fr.* Compiègne

STRESS MARKS:

Primary stress: ′
in·cite′ (ĭn-sīt′)
Secondary stress: ′
in′sight′ (ĭn′sīt′)

thousand miles away; I wish this job were finished. **2.** To entertain or express a hope that a specified state or quality will befall or be enjoyed by (someone): *wish you all a Happy New Year; wished him no harm.* **3.** To confer or impose; foist. Used with *on*: *wouldn't wish him on my worst enemy.* —*intr.* **1.** To have or feel a desire. Usually used with *for*: *wish for the moon.* **2.** To express a wish. [Middle English *wisshen,* Old English *wȳscan.*] **—wish·er** *n.*

wish·bone (wĭsh′bōn′) *n.* The forked bone, or furcula, anterior to the breastbone of most birds, formed by the fusion of the clavicles. [So called from its use as a wish token. When it is snapped apart by two people, the person getting the longer piece will supposedly have his wish fulfilled.]

wish·ful (wĭsh′fəl) *adj.* Having or expressing a wish or longing. **—wish·ful·ly** *adv.* **—wish·ful·ness** *n.*

wish fulfillment *n.* **1.** The gratification of a desire. **2.** In psychoanalysis, the mind's enactment of a suppressed or frustrated desire, as in dreaming or fantasy.

wishful thinking *n.* Belief based on what one wishes to be true, rather than on what is actually true. **—wishful thinker** *n.*

wish-wash (wĭsh′wŏsh′, -wôsh′) *n. Informal.* **1.** A thin, watery drink. **2.** Insipid talk or writing. [Reduplication of WASH.]

wish·y-wash·y (wĭsh′ē-wŏsh′ē, -wô′shē) *adj.* **-ier, -iest.** *Informal.* **1.** Watery; thin; weak. **2.** Lacking in substance, quality, or force; feeble; insipid. [Reduplication of *washy,* from WASH.]

Wisla. See **Vistula.**

wisp (wĭsp) *n.* **1.** A small bunch or bundle, as of straw, hair, or grass. **2. a.** Someone or something thin, frail, slight, or brief: *a wisp of a smile; a wisp of a girl.* **b.** A thin or faint streak or fragment, as of smoke or clouds. **3.** A flock of birds, especially of snipe.

~*v.* **wisped, wisping, wisps.** —*tr.* To twist into a wisp. —*intr.* To move or drift in the manner of a wisp of smoke. [Middle English *wisp, wips*†.] **—wisp·y** *adj.*

wist. *Archaic.* Past tense and past participle of **wit** (to know).

wis·ter·i·a (wĭ-stîr′ē-ə) *n.* Any of several climbing woody vines of the genus *Wisteria,* having compound leaves and drooping clusters of showy purplish or white flowers. [New Latin *Wisteria,* after Caspar *Wistar* (1761–1818), U.S. anatomist.]

wist·ful (wĭst′fəl) *adj.* Full of a melancholy yearning; longing pensively. [Originally "attentive," from obsolete *wistly*† (influenced by *wishful*).] **—wist·ful·ly** *adv.* **—wist·ful·ness** *n.*

wit[1] (wĭt) *n.* **1.** The natural ability to perceive or know; understanding; intelligence; good sense: *had the wit to wrap up in the cold weather.* **2.** *Usually* **wits. a.** Ingenuity; resourcefulness: *using one's wits; live by one's wits.* **b.** Sound mental faculties; mind; sanity: *scared out of one's wits.* **3. a.** The ability to perceive and express in an ingeniously humorous manner the relationship or similarity between seemingly incongruous or disparate things. **b.** One noted for this ability; especially, one skilled in repartee. **c.** This quality of wit as manifested in speech or writing. —See Synonyms at **mind.** **—at one's wits' end.** At the limit of one's mental resources; utterly at a loss. **—have (or keep) one's wits about one.** To remain alert or calm, especially in a crisis. [Middle English, Old English.]

Synonyms: *humor, irony, repartee, sarcasm.*

wit[2] *v.* **wist** (wĭst), **witting,** present indicative **I wot** (wŏt), **thou wost** (wŏst), **he wot, we, you, they wite** (wĭt) or **witen** (wĭt′n). *Archaic.* —*tr.* To be or become aware of; know; learn. —*intr.* To know. **—to wit.** That is to say; namely. [Middle English *witen,* Old English *witan.*]

wit·an (wĭt′ăn) *pl.n.* In Anglo-Saxon England, the **witenagemot** *(see).* [Old English *witan,* plural of *wita,* councilor.]

witch (wĭch) *n.* **1.** A woman who practices black magic and sorcery or is believed to have dealings with the devil. **2.** An ugly or vicious old woman. **3.** *Informal.* A bewitching young woman or girl.

~*tr.v.* **witched, witching, witches.** **1.** To work or cast a spell upon; bewitch. **2.** To cause, bring, or effect by witchcraft. [Middle English *wicche,* Old English *wicce* (feminine), *wicca* (masculine).]

witch·craft (wĭch′krăft′, -kräft′) *n.* **1.** The practices of a witch; black magic; sorcery. **2.** A fascinating or irresistible influence, attraction, or charm. —See Synonyms at **magic.**

witch doctor *n.* A medicine man or shaman, especially among African peoples, reputedly having powers both to heal and to harm through sorcery and herbalism.

witch elm. Variant of **wych elm.**

witch·er·y (wĭch′ə-rē) *n., pl.* **-ies.** **1.** Sorcery; witchcraft. **2.** Power to charm or fascinate.

witch·es-broom (wĭch′ĭz-bro͞om′, -bro͝om′) *n.* An abnormal, brushlike growth of weak, closely clustered shoots or branches on a tree or woody plant, caused by fungi or viruses.

witches' Sabbath *n.* A midnight meeting of demons, witches, and sorcerers, supposedly presided over by Satan and marked by orgies and demonic rites. Also called "sabbat."

witch grass *n.* A North American grass, *Panicum capillare,* having branching, purplish panicles.

witch hazel, wych hazel *n.* **1.** Any of several shrubs of the genus *Hamamelis*; especially, *H. virginiana,* of eastern North America, having yellow flowers that bloom in late autumn or winter. **2.** An alcoholic solution containing an extract of the bark and leaves of this shrub, applied externally as a mild astringent. [Middle English *wyche,* WYCH (ELM) + HAZEL.]

witch hunt *n.* **1.** A rigorous search to detect witches, especially in the Middle Ages. **2.** A campaign launched on the pretext of investigating subversive or dishonest activities but aimed at exposing and harassing political opponents or holders of dissenting views. **—witch-hunt·er** *n.* **—witch-hunt·ing** *adj.* & *n.*

witch·ing (wĭch′ĭng) *adj.* **1.** Pertaining to or appropriate for witchcraft: *the witching hour.* **2.** Having power to charm or enchant; bewitching.

~*n.* Witchcraft. **—witch·ing·ly** *adv.*

witch moth *n.* Any of several large moths of the genus *Erebus,* of the southern United States and tropical America. [From its nocturnal habits.]

witch of Ag·nes·i (ăn-yā′zē) *n.* A plane mathematical curve with the equation $x^2y = 4a^2(2a-y)$. [After Maria Gaetana *Agnesi* (1718–99), Italian mathematician; probably referring to the resemblance of the curve to a witch's hat.]

wite[1] (wīt) *n. Chiefly Scottish.* Blame; fault. [Middle English *wite,* Old English *wīte,* fine, penalty.]

wite[2]. *Archaic.* Also **wit·en.** First, second, and third person plural present indicative of **wit** (to know).

wit·e·na·ge·mot (wĭt′n-ə-gə-mōt′) *n.* **1.** An Anglo-Saxon advisory council to the king, composed of about 100 nobles, prelates, and other officials, convened at intervals to discuss administrative and judicial affairs. **2.** The members of this council. In both senses, also called "witan." [Old English *witena gemōt* : *witena,* genitive plural of *wita,* councilor + *gemōt,* meeting, assembly; see **moot.**]

with (wĭth, wĭth) *prep. Abbr.* **w.** **1. a.** As a companion of; accompanying: *Who went with him?* **b.** In the partnership of: *painted the house with a friend.* **2.** In the company or house of: *spent the weekend with her sister.* **3.** Having as a possession, attribute, or characteristic: *a man with a mustache; the woman with the umbrella.* **4.** In a manner characterized by: *perform with skill; spoke with confidence.* **5.** In the charge or keeping of: *She left the letter with the doorman.* **6.** In the opinion or estimation of: *if it's all right with you.* **7. a.** In support of; on the side of: *voted with the opposition.* **b.** Of the same opinion or belief as: *He is with us on that.* **8.** In the same way as; like: *He believes, with Orwell, that some animals are more equal than others.* **9.** In the same group or mixture as; among: *Mix the flour with the eggs. Go and stand with the others.* **10.** In the membership or employment of: *He is with a publishing company.* **11. a.** By the means or agency of: *spattered with mud; threatened him with dismissal; eat with a fork.* **b.** Using as a material or ingredient: *filled his glass with beer; made it with fruit from the garden.* **12. a.** In spite of; notwithstanding: *With all his talent, he could not get a job.* **b.** Taking into account; in view of: *With all his talent, he ought to get a job. With our luck, it'll probably rain.* **13.** In the same direction as: *bend with the wind.* **14.** At the same time as: *rise with the sun.* **15.** In the matter of or in regard to: *satisfied with her progress.* **16.** In comparison or contrast to: *a dress identical with the one she has just bought.* **17.** In a harmonious relationship to: *The curtains don't really go with the carpet.* **18.** Having received: *With her permission, he left.* **19. a.** And; plus; added to: *beans with bacon.* **b.** Inclusive of; counting: *That makes ten of us, with the children.* **20.** In opposition or antagonism to; against: *wrestling with an opponent; quarreled with his neighbor.* **21.** To; onto: *Couple the first car with the second.* **22.** So as to be free of or separated from: *part with a friend.* **23.** In the course of: *We grow older with the hours.* **24.** In proportion to: *wines that improve with age.* **25.** *Informal.* Understanding; following the line of thought of: *Are you still with me?* **26.** As well as; in favorable comparison to: *She sings with the best of them.* **27. a.** Under the influence of; because of: *trembling with fear.* **b.** As a result of; thanks to: *With improved medical facilities, many of these patients now live longer.* **c.** Immediately following or attendant upon: *With the death of his brother, he inherited the title. He tore up the contract and, with that, stormed out.* **28.** In a situation in which there is or are: *He scored the winning goal with only seconds to go.* **29.** In the case of; as far as concerns: *With most people, voting is determined by economic factors.* **30.** Used to indicate the other party in any type of transaction or relationship: *chatting with his neighbor; works with handicapped children.* **31.** Used without a verb in expressions having the force of a wish or command: *On with the show!* **—in with.** In league or association with: *He is in with the wrong crowd.* **—with it.** *Informal.* **1.** Aware of modern trends; up-to-date. **2.** Alert and understanding: *I'm not with it this morning.* [Middle English *with,* with, against, by means of, Old English *wiþ,* against or in opposition to, together with.]

Usage: When *with* introduces a phrase following a singular subject, the verb is governed by that subject and remains singular: *The king, with his two sons, has arrived.* In casual speech, the plural meaning of the whole sometimes causes speakers to make the verb plural, but this is better avoided. See also **together, well.**

with·al (wĭth-ôl′, wĭth-) *adv.* **1.** Besides; in addition. **2.** Despite that; nevertheless. **3.** *Archaic.* Therewith.

~*prep. Archaic.* With. [Middle English *with al(le)* : WITH + ALL.]

with·draw (wĭth-drô′, wĭth-) *v.* **-drew** (-dro͞o′), **-drawn** (-drôn′), **-drawing, -draws.** —*tr.* **1.** To take back or away; remove: *withdrew fifty dollars from his account.* **2.** To recall; retract: *withdrew the charges.* —*intr.* **1.** To move or draw back; retreat; retire. **2. a.** To remove oneself from activity or a social environment. **b.** To remove the center of one's concern away from external activity; become detached. [Middle English *withdrawen* : *with,* away from, WITH + *drawen,* to pull, DRAW.]

with·draw·al (wĭth-drô′əl, wĭth-) *n.* Also **with·draw·ment** (-drô′mənt). **1.** The act or an instance of withdrawing, especially: **a.** A retreat, retirement, or disengagement. **b.** A detachment, as from emotional involvement. **c.** A removal of something that has been

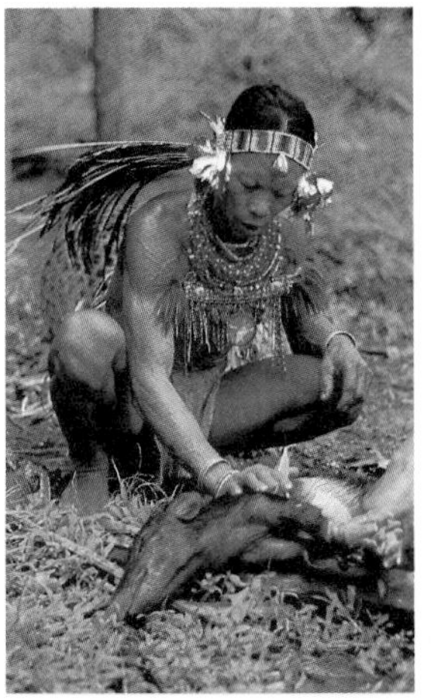

witch doctor *A Sumatran witch doctor, or medicine man, preparing a pig for sacrifice.*

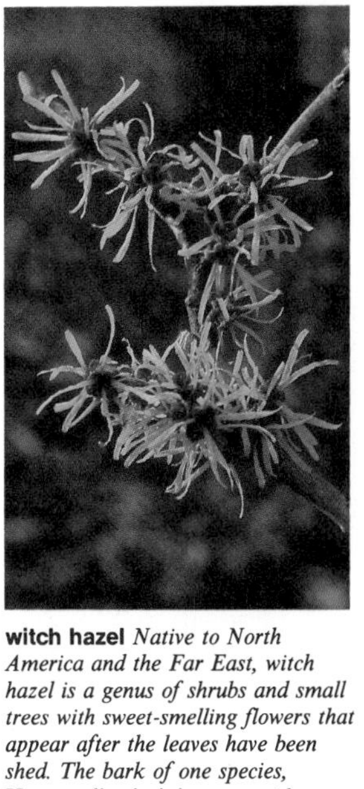

witch hazel *Native to North America and the Far East, witch hazel is a genus of shrubs and small trees with sweet-smelling flowers that appear after the leaves have been shed. The bark of one species,* Hamamelis virginiana, *provides an astringent liquid used as an antiseptic and skin cleanser. The species shown here is the Chinese witch hazel,* Hamamelis mollis.

deposited: *made a large withdrawal from her account.* **2.** Termination of the administration of a habit-forming substance, which usually precipitates specific mental and physical *withdrawal symptoms.* **3.** The act of **coitus interruptus** *(see).*

with·drawn (wĭth-drôn′, wĭth-). Past participle of **withdraw.** —*adj.* **1.** Remote; isolated. **2.** Socially retiring; introverted; shy. **3.** Detached; preoccupied.

withe (wĭth, wĭth, wīth) *n.* A tough, supple twig, especially a willow twig, used for binding things together; a withy. —*tr.v.* **withed, withing, withes.** To bind with withes. [Middle English *witthe, withe,* Old English *withthe.*]

with·er (wĭth′ər) *v.* **-ered, -ering, -ers.** —*intr.* **1.** To dry up or shrivel from or as if from loss of moisture: *The flowers withered in the sun.* **2.** To lose freshness, vitality, or strength; fade: *withered under his sarcasm; Hope withered away.* —*tr.* **1.** To cause to shrivel or fade. **2.** To cause to feel belittled; cut down; abash: *withered her with a glance.* [Middle English *widderen,* perhaps alteration of *wederen,* to weather, from *weder,* WEATHER.]

with·er·ite (wĭth′ə-rīt′) *n.* A white, yellow, or gray vitreous mineral, barium carbonate, $BaCO_3$. [After William *Withering* (1741–99), English physician.]

withe rod *n.* A shrub, *Viburnum cassinoides,* of eastern North America, having clusters of small white flowers and bluish-black fruit.

with·ers (wĭth′ərz) *pl.n.* The high point of the back of a horse, or of a similar or related animal, at the base of the neck and between the shoulder blades. [Perhaps from obsolete *wither-,* denoting opposition (the withers resist or "oppose" a load), from Middle English *wither-,* Old English *wither-,* from *wither,* against.]

with·er·shins (wĭth′ər-shĭnz′) *adv.* Also **wid·der·shins** (wĭd′-). *Chiefly Scottish.* In a direction opposite to the course of the sun; anticlockwise. [Middle Low German *weddersin(ne)s,* from Middle High German *widersinnes,* "countercourse" : *wider,* against + *sinnes,* genitive of *sin,* journey, direction.]

with·hold (wĭth-hōld′, wĭth-) *v.* **-held** (-hĕld′), **-holding, -holds.** —*tr.* **1.** To keep in check; restrain. **2.** To refrain from giving, granting, or permitting: *withhold permission.* —*intr.* To refrain; forbear. —See Synonyms at **keep.** [Middle English *withholden* : *with,* back, away from, WITH + *holden,* to HOLD.] —**with·hold′er** *n.*

with·hold·ing tax *n.* A portion of an employee's pay withheld by his employer, who then pays it to the government as partial payment of the employee's income tax.

with·in (wĭth-ĭn′, wĭth-) *adv.* **1.** In or into the inner part; inside. **2.** In or belonging to a community or group. **3.** Inside the body, mind, heart, or soul; inwardly. —*prep.* **1.** In the inner part or parts of; inside: *resentment within him.* **2.** Inside the limits or extent of in time, degree, or distance: *within ten miles of home; separated within a year of their marriage.* **3.** Inside the fixed limits of; not exceeding or transgressing: *within the laws of the land.* **4.** In the scope, sphere, or range of: *within the medical profession; within sight but not within reach.*

with·in·doors (wĭth-ĭn′dôrz′, -dōrz′, wĭth-) *adv.* Indoors.

with·it (wĭth′ĭt′, wĭth′-) *adj. Informal.* Up-to-date; hip.

with·out (wĭth-out′, wĭth-) *adv.* **1.** In or on the outside. **2.** Externally; outwardly. **3.** With something lacking or missing: *We can get along without.* —*prep.* **1.** Not having; lacking: *a family without a car.* **2. a.** With no or none of; in the absence of: *without help.* **b.** Not accompanied by: *no smoke without fire.* **3.** At, on, to, or toward the outside or exterior of: *without the walls.* **4.** With neglect or avoidance of: *went by without speaking to us.* —*conj. Regional.* Unless: "*You don't know about me without you have read a book by the name of* The Adventures of Tom Sawyer" (Mark Twain). [Middle English *withouten,* Old English *withūtan* : *with,* not together with, separated, WITH + *ūtan,* outside of, from *ūt,* OUT.]

with·out·doors (wĭth-out′dôrz′, -dōrz′, wĭth-) *adv.* Outside of a house or shelter; outdoors.

with·stand (wĭth-stănd′, wĭth-) *v.* **-stood, -standing, -stands.** —*tr.* **1.** To oppose with effort or force; resist. **2.** To resist or endure successfully; stand up to: *withstood years of hard wear.* —*intr.* To offer resistance. —See Synonyms at **oppose.** [Middle English *withstanden,* Old English *withstandan* : *with,* against, WITH + *standan,* to STAND.] —**with·stand′er** *n.*

with·y (wĭth′ē, wĭth′ē) *adj.* Resembling a withe in wiriness or toughness: *a withy young boxer.* —*n., pl.* **withies. 1.** A rope or band made of withes. **2.** A long, flexible twig, such as that of an osier. **3.** A tree or shrub having such twigs. [Middle English *wythy,* flexible twig, willow wand, Old English *withig.*]

wit·less (wĭt′lĭs) *adj.* Lacking intelligence or wit; stupid. —**wit·less·ly** *adv.* —**wit·less·ness** *n.*

wit·ling (wĭt′lĭng) *n.* **1.** One who thinks himself a wit. **2.** One who has little wit.

wit·ness (wĭt′nĭs) *n.* **1.** One who has seen or heard something and who can give evidence for its occurrence: *Were there any witnesses to the accident?* **2.** Anything that serves as evidence; a testimony. **3.** *Law.* **a.** One who is called upon to testify before a court. **b.** One who is called upon to be present at a transaction in order to attest to what took place. **c.** One who signs his name to a document for the purpose of attesting to its authenticity. **4.** An attestation to a fact, statement, or event. —*v.* **witnessed, -nessing, -nesses.** —*tr.* **1.** To be present at or have direct personal knowledge of (an event, for example). **2.** To

provide or serve as evidence of. **3.** To be the setting or site of: *This auditorium witnesses many ceremonies.* **4.** To attest to the legality or authenticity of (a document) by signing one's name. **5.** To consider as evidence or proof. Used parenthetically in the imperative: *The industry (witness its recent report) is clearly losing patience with the government.* —*intr.* To furnish or serve as evidence; testify. [Middle English *witnes(se),* Old English *witnes,* witness, knowledge, from *wit,* knowledge, WIT.] —**wit·ness·er** *n.*

witness box *n. Chiefly British.* Witness stand.

witness stand *n.* The place in a courtroom from which a witness presents testimony.

wit·ted (wĭt′ĭd) *adj.* Having wits or understanding as specified. Used in combination: *dim-witted; half-witted.*

Wit·ten·berg (wĭt′n-bûrg′, vĭt′n-bĕrk′). Town of Halle district, central East Germany. On the Elbe River, it is where Martin Luther nailed his 95 theses to the door of the Schlosskirche (1517), thus initiating the Protestant Reformation.

Witt·gen·stein (vĭt′gən-shtīn′, -stīn′), **Ludwig Johann Josef** (1889–1951). Austrian philosopher. He worked on theories of language and in his *Tractatus Logico-Philosophicus* (1921) helped develop logical positivism. His other important work, *Philosophical Investigations,* published (1953) after his death, examined linguistic ambiguities in philosophical statements.

wit·ti·cism (wĭt′ĭ-sĭz′əm) *n.* A witty remark or saying. —See Synonyms at **joke.** [From WITTY (influenced by CRITICISM).]

wit·ting (wĭt′ĭng). *Archaic.* Present participle of **wit** (to know). —*adj.* **1.** Aware or conscious. **2.** Done intentionally or with premeditation; deliberate. —**wit·ting·ly** *adv.*

wit·tol (wĭt′l) *n. Archaic.* A man who tolerates his wife's infidelity. [Middle English *wetewold* : *weten, witen,* to WIT (know) + *(coke)wold,* CUCKOLD.]

wit·ty (wĭt′ē) *adj.* **-tier, -tiest. 1.** Possessing, characterized by, or demonstrating wit in speech or writing; ingenious and humorous. **2.** *Archaic.* Intelligent. —**wit·ti·ly** *adv.* —**wit·ti·ness** *n.*

Wit·wa·ters·rand (wĭt-wô′tərz-rănd′, -ränd′, -wŏt′ərz-). Region of southern Transvaal, Republic of South Africa, also informally known as the Rand. Dominated by ridges forming the watershed of the Vaal and Olifants rivers, its gold reserves, exploited since 1886, account for almost one third of the world's output.

wive (wīv) *v.* **wived, wiving, wives.** —*tr.* **1.** To marry (a woman); take as a wife. **2.** To provide a wife for. —*intr.* To marry a woman. [Middle English *wiven,* Old English *wīfian,* from *wīf,* WIFE.]

wivern. Variant of **wyvern.**

wives. Plural of **wife.**

wiz (wĭz) *n. Informal.* A person considered exceptionally gifted or skilled; a wizard. [Short for WIZARD.]

wiz·ard (wĭz′ərd) *n.* **1.** A male witch; a sorcerer or magician. **2.** A person who is skillful or clever at a particular activity: *a wizard at cooking.* **3.** *Archaic.* A wise man or sage. —*adj.* **1.** Of or pertaining to wizards or wizardry. **2.** *Chiefly British Informal.* Excellent; wonderful. [Middle English *wysard* : *wys, wis,* WISE + -ARD.]

wiz·ard·ry (wĭz′ər-drē) *n.* The art, skill, or practice of a wizard; witchcraft; sorcery.

wiz·en (wĭz′ən) *v.* **-ened, -ening, -ens.** —*intr.* To wither or sear; dry up; shrivel. —*tr.* To cause to wither or dry up. —*adj.* Variant of **wizened.** [Middle English *wisenen,* Old English *wisnian.*]

wiz·ened (wĭz′ənd) *adj.* Also **wizen.** Shriveled or dried up, as through age; withered.

wk. 1. weak. **2.** week.

wkly. weekly.

WL, w.l. waterline.

wmk. watermark.

W.M.O World Meteorological Organization.

WNW west-northwest.

WO, W.O. 1. warrant officer. **2.** wireless operator.

woad (wōd) *n.* **1.** An Old World plant, *Isatis tinctoria,* formerly cultivated for its leaves that yield a blue dye. **2.** The dye obtained from this plant. [Middle English *wod(e),* Old English *wād†.*]

woad·wax·en (wōd′wăk′sən) *n.* A shrub, **dyer's greenweed** *(see).* [Variant (influenced by WOAD) of WOODWAXEN.]

wob·be·gong (wŏb′ĭ-gŏng′) *n.* Any of various Australian sharks of the family Orectolobidae, having brown and white markings. [From a native Australian language.]

wob·ble, wab·ble (wŏb′əl) *v.* **-bled, -bling, -bles.** —*intr.* **1.** To move or sway unsteadily from side to side. **2.** To tremble or quaver; shake: *Her voice wobbled with emotion.* **3.** To waver or vacillate in one's opinions, feelings, or the like. —*tr.* To cause to wobble. —*n.* The act or an instance of wobbling, as in a movement or sound. —See Synonyms at **shake.** [Perhaps from Low German *wabbeln.*] —**wob·bler** *n.*

wobble board *n.* In Australia, a flexible, rectangular sheet, as of masonite, used as a musical instrument, that produces a low booming sound when bent back and forward.

wob·bly (wŏb′lē) *adj.* **-blier, -bliest.** Tending to wobble; unsteady; shaky.

Wob·bly (wŏb′lē) *n., pl.* **-blies.** A member of the Industrial Workers of the World (I.W.W.). [20th century : origin obscure.]

w.o.c. without compensation.

Wode·house (wŏod′hous′), **Sir Pelham Grenville,** known as "P.G. Wodehouse" (1881–1975). British comic novelist. He introduced his most famous characters, the aristocratic Bertie Wooster and his manservant Jeeves, in *The Inimitable Jeeves* (1923).

Wo·den, Wo·dan (wōd'n) *n.* The chief god in Anglo-Saxon mythology, often identified with the Norse god Odin. [Old English *Wōden.*]

wodge. Variant of **wadge.**

woe (wō) *n.* **1.** Deep sorrow; grief. **2.** Misfortune; calamity. **3.** *Usually* **woes.** A difficulty; trouble: *Life is full of woes.* —See Synonyms at **regret.**

~*interj.* Used to express sorrow or dismay: *Woe is me!* [Middle English *wo(e),* Old English *wā* (interjection).]

woe·be·gone (wō'bĭ-gôn', -gŏn') *adj.* **1.** Mournful, sorrowful, or pathetic in appearance. **2.** Being in a sorry state: *a run-down, woebegone old shack.* [Middle English *wo begon* : *wo(e),* WOE + *begon,* beset, from *begon,* to beset, go about : *be-,* about + *gon,* to GO.]

woe·ful (wō'fəl) *adj.* **1.** Afflicted with woe; mournful. **2.** Pitiful, wretched, or deplorable: *a woeful attempt at a poem.* **—woe·ful·ly** *adv.* **—woe·ful·ness** *n.*

wok (wŏk) *n.* A large bowl-shaped metal pan used, especially in Chinese cooking, for frying, steaming, and the like. [Cantonese.]

woke. Past tense and *chiefly British & regional* past participle of **wake.**

wok·en. Alternate past participle of **wake.**

wold (wōld) *n.* A stretch of open, unforested, rolling countryside or moorland. [Middle English *wold,* a forest, hill, Old English *weald, wald,* from Germanic *walthus* (unattested).]

Wolds, the (wōldz). Range of chalk hills along the coasts of Lincolnshire and Yorkshire, England.

wolf (wo͝olf) *n., pl.* **wolves** (wo͝olvz). **1. a.** Either of two carnivorous mammals, *Canis lupus,* of northern regions, or *C. rufus* or *C. niger,* of southwestern North America, related to and resembling the dogs. **b.** The fur of such an animal. **2.** Any of various similar or related mammals. **3.** The destructive larva of any of various moths, beetles, or flies. **4. a.** One who is rapacious, predatory, and fierce. **b.** *Informal.* A man given to avid amatory pursuit of women. **5.** *Music.* **a.** A harshness in some notes of a bowed stringed instrument produced by defective vibration. **b.** Dissonance in some intervals of a keyboard instrument tuned to a system of unequal temperament. **—cry wolf.** To raise a false alarm. **—have (or hold) a wolf by the ears.** To be in a dangerous or precarious situation. **—keep the wolf from the door.** To ward off or avert hunger or poverty. **—throw to the wolves.** To abandon to certain destruction. **—wolf in sheep's clothing.** A person who conceals his malicious nature or intentions under a friendly exterior.

~*tr.v.* **wolfed, wolfing, wolfs.** To eat voraciously. Often used with *down.* [Middle English *wolf(e),* Old English *wulf.*] **—wolf·ish** *adj.* **—wolf·ish·ly** *adv.*

Wolf (vôlf), **Hugo** (1860–1903). Austrian composer. Chiefly a composer of songs, he set the poetry of Goethe and Italian and Spanish writers to music and wrote the opera *Der Corregidor* (1895).

wolf·ber·ry (wo͝olf'bĕr'ē) *n.* A shrub, *Symphoricarpos occidentalis,* of western North America, having white berries.

Wolf Cub *n. Chiefly British.* Formerly, a Cub Scout.

wolf dog *n.* **1.** A dog trained to hunt or ward off wolves. **2.** The offspring of a dog and a wolf.

Wolfe (wo͝olf), **James** (1727–59). British army officer. He led the successful assault on the French stronghold of Louisbourg in Nova Scotia. He was killed at the Battle of the Plains of Abraham (1759), in which Britain won the city of Quebec and New France.

Wolfe, Thomas Clayton (1900–38). U.S. novelist. His works include *Look Homeward, Angel* (1929) and the posthumously published *You Can't Go Home Again* (1940).

Wolff·i·an body (wo͝ol'fē-ən) *n.* The **mesonephros** *(see).* [After Kasper Friedrich *Wolff* (1733–94), German embryologist.]

wolf fish *n.* Any of several northern slender marine fishes of the genus *Anarhichas,* having sharp, powerful teeth and no pelvic fins.

wolf·hound (wo͝olf'hound') *n.* Any of various large dogs trained to hunt wolves or other large game. See **borzoi, Irish wolfhound.**

wolf pack *n.* Submarines or aircraft that attack as a group.

wolf·ram (wo͝ol'frəm) *n.* The element **tungsten** *(see).* [German *Wolfram* : perhaps Middle High German *wolf,* wolf, + *rām,* dirt, black, probably akin to Sanskrit *Rāma,* RAMA.]

wolf·ram·ite (wo͝ol'frə-mīt') *n.* Any of several red-brown to black minerals with the general formula $(Fe,Mn)WO_4$, a major source of tungsten. [German *Wolframit,* from WOLFRAM.]

wolfs·bane (wo͝olfs'bān') *n.* A plant, the **monkshood** *(see).*

wolf spider *n.* Any spider of the family Lycosidae, having long stout legs and hunting their prey. Also called "hunting spider."

wolf whistle *n.* A short, distinctive whistle rising to a high note and then diminishing again to a low note, used by a man to express sexual admiration for a woman. **—wolf-whistle** *v.*

wol·las·ton·ite (wo͝ol'ə-stə-nīt') *n.* A mineral, calcium silicate, $CaSiO_3$, found in metamorphic rocks and used in various ceramics, paints, plastics, and cements. [After William Hyde *Wollaston* (1766–1828), British physicist.]

Wol·las·ton prism (wo͝ol'ə-stən) *n.* A prism cut from quartz that separates the ordinary and extraordinary components of unpolarized light. [After W. H. *Wollaston;* see **wollastonite.**]

Woll·stone·craft (wo͝ol'stən-krăft'), **Mary** (1759–97). British radical and feminist. As a publisher's adviser, she met various radicals, including Tom Paine and her husband, William Godwin. Her works include *A Vindication of the Rights of Women* (1792) and a reply to Burke in *A View of the French Revolution* (1794). She died giving birth to her daughter, who became Mary Shelley.

Wo·lof (wō'lŏf') *n.* A West Atlantic language of Senegal. **—Wo·lof** *adj.*

Wolse·ley (wo͝olz'lē), **Garnet Joseph, 1st Viscount** (1833–1913). British field marshal. He won the Battle of Tall al Kabir (1882), led the expedition to relieve Gen. Gordon at Khartoum (1884–85), and became commander in chief of the army (1895–99).

Wol·sey (wo͝ol'zē), **Thomas** (*c.* 1475–1530). English cardinal. He rose to become the bishop of Lincoln and archbishop of York (1514) and a cardinal and Lord Chancellor of England (1515). Wolsey controlled foreign policy and worked for the increase of England's power. He was indecisive over Henry VIII's wish to divorce Catherine of Aragon, was prosecuted (1529), and arrested for high treason (1530).

wol·ver·ine (wo͝ol'və-rēn') *n.* A carnivorous mammal, *Gulo gulo* (or *G. luscus*), of northern regions, having dark fur and a bushy tail. Also called "glutton," *Canadian* "carcajou." [Earlier *wolvering,* irregularly from WOLF.]

wolves. Plural of **wolf.**

wom·an (wo͝om'ən) *n., pl.* **women** (wĭm'ĭn). **1. a.** An adult female human being. **b.** A woman of a specified status or occupation or concerned with a specified sphere of activity. Used in combination: *a noblewoman; a policewoman.* **2.** Women collectively; womankind: *Woman is wise.* **3.** Feminine quality or aspect; womanliness: *brought out the woman in him.* **4.** A female employed to do household duties. **5. a.** *Informal.* A wife or girlfriend. **b.** A mistress; paramour.

~*adj.* Female as opposed to male. [Middle English *wumman, wimman,* Old English *wīfmann* : *wīf,* WIFE + *man(n),* person, MAN.]

wom·an·hood (wo͝om'ən-ho͝od') *n.* **1.** The state of being a woman. **2.** Feminine nature or qualities. **3.** Womankind.

wom·an·ish (wo͝om'ə-nĭsh) *adj.* **1.** Characteristic of a woman; womanly. **2.** Considered more typical of or appropriate to the nature of a woman than of a man; effeminate; weak. **—wom·an·ish·ly** *adv.* **—wom·an·ish·ness** *n.*

wom·an·ize (wo͝om'ə-nīz') *v.* **-ized, -izing, -izes.** *—tr.* To give feminine characteristics to. *—intr.* To indulge in casual affairs with women habitually or excessively. Used of a man. **—wom·an·iz·er** *n.*

wom·an·kind (wo͝om'ən-kīnd') *n.* Female human beings collectively; women.

wom·an·ly (wo͝om'ən-lē) *adj.* **-lier, -liest.** Having the qualities, such as warmth and compassion, thought of as being typical of or appropriate to a woman. **—wom·an·li·ness** *n.*

wom·an·pow·er (wo͝om'ən-pou'ər) *n.* Power in terms of the women available to a particular group or required for a particular task.

woman suffrage *n.* The right of women to vote. **—wom·an-suf·fra·gist** *n.*

womb (wo͞om) *n.* **1.** The **uterus** *(see).* **2. a.** A place where something is generated or developed. **b.** Any protective and confining organ, receptacle, or place. **3.** *Obsolete.* The belly. [Middle English *womb(e),* Old English *wamb,* from Germanic *wambō* (unattested).]

wom·bat (wŏm'băt') *n.* An Australian marsupial, as *Phascolomis ursinus* or *Lasiorhinus latifrons,* somewhat resembling small bears. [Native Australian name.]

wom·en·folk (wĭm'ĭn-fōk') *pl.n.* **1.** Women collectively. **2.** A particular group of women, as those belonging to one family.

Women's Liberation Movement *n.* The social and political movement that originated in Europe and the United States in the 19th century seeking to bring into effect the principles of **feminism** *(see).* Among the early exponents of the movement were emancipated black slaves in the United States and suffragettes in Britain. Also called "Women's movement," informally "Women's Lib." **—wom·en's liberationist** *n.*

women's rights *pl.n.* **1.** Economic, political, legal, and social rights for women equal to those granted men. **2.** A movement in support of women's rights; feminism. Also called "woman's rights."

womera *n.* Variant of **woomera.**

won[1] (wŭn) *intr.v.* **wonned, wonning, wons.** *Archaic.* To dwell; abide. [Middle English *won(i)en,* Old English *wunian.*]

won[2] (wôn) *n., pl.* **won. 1.** The basic monetary unit of South Korea, equal to 100 jeon or jun or chon. **2.** The basic monetary unit of North Korea, equal to 100 jeon or jun or chon. See feature at **currency.** [Korean.]

won[3]**.** Past tense and past participle of **win.**

won·der (wŭn'dər) *n.* **1.** That which arouses awe, astonishment, or admiration; a marvel. Also used adjectivally: *a wonder cure; a wonder horse.* **2.** The feeling or emotion aroused by a wonder, characterized by admiration, awe, and sometimes bewilderment. **3.** A matter for surprise: *It's a wonder you weren't killed. No wonder it's not working—you haven't plugged it in.* **4. wonders.** *Informal.* Something miraculous or impressively successful in effect: *The ad did wonders for sales.* **—for a wonder.** Surprisingly. **—small wonder.** It is hardly surprising.

~*v.* **wondered, -dering, -ders.** *—intr.* **1. a.** To ponder with curiosity; speculate. **b.** To entertain doubts: *I often wonder about his honesty.* **2.** To have a feeling of awe or admiration; marvel. *—tr.* **1.** To feel curiosity about. **2.** *Chiefly British.* To feel surprise at: *I wonder that you're still awake.* **3.** Used to express a polite inquiry or request: *I wonder whether you would mind shutting the door.* [Middle English *wonder,* Old English *wundor.*] **—won·der·er** *n.*

won·der·ful (wŭn'dər-fəl) *adj.* **1.** Capable of exciting wonder; aston-

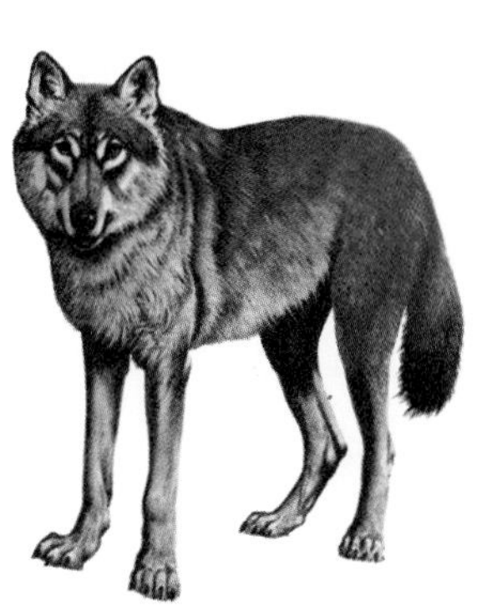

wolf *Wolves, which were once common in Eurasia and North America, are now found only in remote forests. They live in packs within specific territories and feed chiefly on mice and carrion as well as large hoofed mammals, such as deer.*

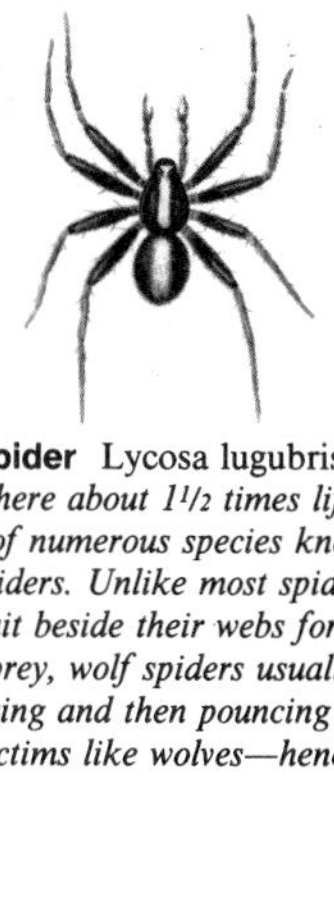

wolf spider Lycosa lugubris, *drawn here about 1 1/2 times life size, is one of numerous species known as wolf spiders. Unlike most spiders that wait beside their webs for their insect prey, wolf spiders usually hunt by chasing and then pouncing on their victims like wolves—hence their name.*

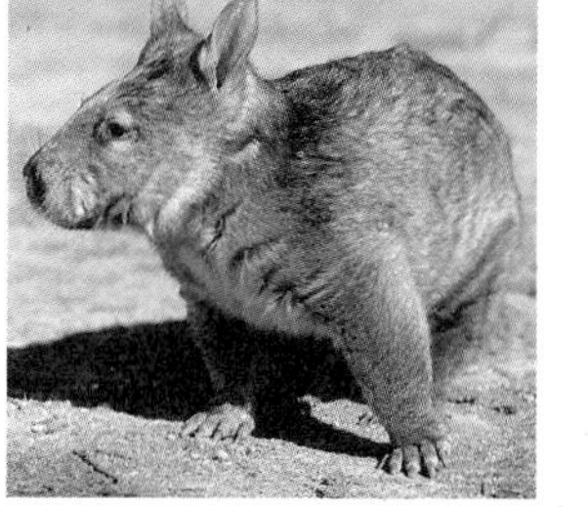

wombat *An Australian burrowing marsupial, the wombat has a rearward-facing pouch. A kangaroo's pouch, by contrast, opens forward. Wombats have rodentlike teeth and feed mainly on grass and roots.*

woodchuck *Also known as a ground hog, the woodchuck is a type of marmot native to the woodlands of North America. Woodchucks live in colonies underground and hibernate each winter.*

woodcock *Scolopax rusticola, the European woodcock (above), is a wading bird that is common in woods with wet or boggy ground in Europe and Asia. Its russet plumage provides excellent camouflage as it sits among the fallen leaves on the woodland floor.*

Wonders of the Ancient World

ACHIEVEMENTS OF ANTIQUITY

Seven marvels that astounded the ancient Greeks

In the 2nd century B.C., the Greek writer Antipater of Sidon was one of several who listed the greatest buildings and monuments of his day. Because seven was a magic number in Greek, Hebrew, and Chinese cultures, he selected seven of these wonders.

The Egyptian pyramids These are the only wonders still surviving and are now more than 4,000 years old.

The hanging gardens of Babylon Built by Nebuchadnezzar II in the 7th century B.C., they consisted of a series of terraces on which trees and flowers were grown. They stretched along the banks of the Euphrates, from which they were watered by irrigation channels.

The statue of Zeus at Olympia A colossal figure with an ivory body and gold cloak, created in the 5th century B.C. by the Athenian Phidias. It burned down in A.D. 475.

The temple of Artemis at Ephesus, Asia Minor Built of marble in the 6th century B.C., it was rebuilt in the 4th century B.C. and finally destroyed in the 3rd century A.D. There are fragments in the British Museum, London.

The Mausoleum at Halicarnassus, Asia Minor The tomb of Mausolus, a ruler of the city in the 4th century B.C. It was destroyed by an earthquake before the 15th century.

The Colossus of Rhodes A huge statue of the sun god, standing about 36 meters (120 feet) high at the mouth of Rhodes harbor. It was erected about 305 B.C. and destroyed by an earthquake in the 3rd century B.C.

The Pharos of Alexandria Thought to be the first lighthouse in the world, and to have stood 122 meters (400 feet) high, with a spiral ramp leading to the beacon. It was built in 270 B.C. on the island of Pharos at the entrance to the harbor of Alexandria, Egypt, and was destroyed in the 14th century.

THE GREAT PYRAMIDS *Standing on the west bank of the Nile near Cairo, they were built by slave labor between 3000 and 1800 B.C. as tombs for the Egyptian pharaohs. Inside, the mummified bodies were surrounded with treasure.*

---

ishing: *amazed at the scheme's wonderful simplicity.* **2.** Fine; excellent. —**won·der·ful·ly** *adv.* —**won·der·ful·ness** *n.*

won·der·land (wŭn′dər-lănd′) *n.* **1.** A marvelous imaginary realm. **2.** A marvelous place or scene that is real and not imaginary.

won·der·ment (wŭn′dər-mənt) *n.* **1.** Astonishment, awe, or surprise. **2.** Puzzlement or curiosity. **3.** Something that produces wonder; a marvel.

Wonders of the Ancient World *pl.n.* Seven monuments of the ancient world that appeared on various lists of late antiquity; most commonly, the Colossus of Rhodes, the Pharos at Alexandria, the Hanging Gardens (and Walls) of Babylon, the temple of Artemis at Ephesus, the pyramids of Giza, the tomb of Mausolus at Halicarnassus, and the statue of Zeus at Olympia. Also called "Seven Wonders of the World."

won·der·work·er (wŭn′dər-wûrk′ər) *n.* One who performs miracles or achieves exceptional success. —**won·der·work** *n.* —**won·der·work·ing** *adj.*

won·drous (wŭn′drəs) *adj.* Wonderful.

~*adv.* Archaic. To a wonderful or remarkable extent. —**won·drous·ly** *adv.*

won·ga-won·ga (wŏng′gə-wŏng′gə) *n.* **1.** A large pigeon, *Leucosarcia melanoleuca*, of Australia. **2.** Any of several Australian vines of the genus *Pandorea*; especially, *P. pandorea.* [From a native Australian language.]

wont (wônt, wŏnt, wŭnt) *adj.* Accustomed or used to. Usually used with an infinitive: *He was wont to drink port after dinner.*

~*n.* Usage or custom: *rose early, as was her wont.*

~*v.* **wont, wont** or **wonted, wonting, wonts.** —*tr.* To accustom. —*intr.* To be in the habit of. [Middle English *wont,* from the past participle of *wonen,* to be accustomed, dwell, to WON.]

won't (wōnt). Contraction of *will not.*

wont·ed (wôn′tĭd, wŏn′-, wŭn′-) *adj.* Accustomed; usual: *at the wonted hour.*

won ton (wŏn′tŏn′) *n., pl.* **won tons. 1.** In Chinese cookery, a noodle-dough dumpling filled with spiced minced pork, usually served in soup. **2.** Soup containing won tons. [Cantonese *wan tan.*]

woo (wōō) *v.* **wooed, wooing, woos.** —*tr.* **1.** To seek the affection of with intent to marry. **2. a.** To seek to achieve; try to gain; court: *wooed the favor of the public with tax cuts.* **b.** To make efforts to gain the favor or compliance of; tempt: *wooing the electorate.* **3.** To entreat, solicit, or importune. —*intr.* To court a woman. [Middle English *wowen,* Old English *wōgian†.*] —**woo·er** *n.*

wood¹ (wŏŏd) *n.* **1. a.** The tough, fibrous cellular substance constituting the xylem of trees and shrubs, lying beneath the bark and consisting largely of cellulose and lignin. **b.** Such a substance used for any of a wide variety of purposes, as for building material or fuel. **2.** *Often* **woods.** A dense growth of trees; a small forest. **3.** An object or part made of wood, especially: **a.** *Music.* A woodwind instrument. **b.** A golf club having a wooden head. **c.** The frame of a tennis racket, as opposed to its strings. —**out of the woods.** Free of difficulties or dangers. —**knock** (or **touch**) **wood. 1.** To place the hand against or strike a wooden object in an act of superstition to avert bad luck or misfortune, especially after having made a positive statement about someone or something. **2.** Used as an interjection in place of or as well as the act of knocking wood.

~*adj.* **1.** Made or consisting of wood; wooden. **2.** Associated with, used on, or containing wood: *a wood screw; a wood box.* **3.** Growing or living in woods or forests.

~*v.* **wooded, wooding, woods.** —*tr.* **1.** To supply or fuel with wood. **2.** To cover with trees; forest. —*intr.* To gather or be supplied with wood. [Middle English *wode,* Old English *wudu.*]

wood² *adj. Archaic.* Violently insane. [Middle English *wo(o)d,* Old English *wōd.*]

Wood (wŏŏd), **Grant** (1892–1942). U.S. artist. Influenced by the realistic works of 16th-century Flemish painters, he rejected the innovations of modernism and concentrated on capturing scenes from life in the American Midwest. His most recognized work, *American Gothic,* was completed in 1930.

wood alcohol *n.* **Methanol** *(see).*

wood anemone *n.* Either of two plants, *Anemone nemorosa,* of Europe, or *A. quinquefolia,* of eastern North America, having deeply divided leaves and a solitary white or pink flower. Also called "windflower."

wood ant *n.* A reddish European ant, *Formica rufa,* whose anthills are found in woodlands.

wood betony *n.* A plant, the **lousewort** *(see).*

wood·bin (wŏŏd′bĭn′) *n.* A bin for holding firewood.

wood·bine (wŏŏd′bīn′) *n.* Any of various climbing vines, especially: **1.** An Old World honeysuckle, *Lonicera periclymenum,* having yellowish flowers. **2.** See **Virginia creeper** (sense 1). [Middle English *wodebinde,* Old English *wudubinde* : *wudu,* WOOD + *bindan,* to BIND.]

wood·block (wŏŏd′blŏk′) *n.* **1.** A woodcut. **2.** *Music.* A partially hollowed out block of hard wood struck with a drumstick to produce percussive effects in an orchestra.

wood·bor·er (wŏŏd′bôr′ər, -bōr′ər) *n.* Any of various insects, insect larvae, or mollusks that bore into wood.

Wood Buffalo National Park. Vast unfenced region in northeastern Alberta and southern Mackenzie District, Canada, just west of Lake Athabaska. It has forestland, open plains, and numerous lakes and is a refuge for buffalo, bears, caribou, deer, moose, and waterfowl.

wood·carv·ing (wŏŏd′kär′vĭng) *n.* **1.** The art of carving in wood. **2.** An object carved from wood. —**wood·carv·er** *n.*

wood·chat (wŏŏd′chăt′) *n.* An Old World bird, *Lanius senator,* having black and white plumage with a reddish crown.

wood·chuck (wŏŏd′chŭk′) *n.* A common rodent, *Marmota monax,* of northern and eastern North America, having a short-legged, heavy-set body and grizzled brownish fur. Also called "ground hog." [Variant (by folk etymology) of Algonquian word; compare Cree *ocĕk,* fisher.]

wood coal *n.* **1.** Charcoal. **2.** Lignite.

wood·cock (wŏŏd′kŏk′) *n., pl.* **-cocks** or collectively **woodcock.** Either of two related game birds, *Scolopax rusticola,* of the Old World, or *Philohela minor,* of North America, having brownish plumage, short legs, and a long bill. [Middle English *wodecok,* Old English *wuducocc* : *wudu,* WOOD + *cocc,* COCK.]

wood·craft (wŏŏd′krăft′, -kräft′) *n.* **1.** The act, process, or art of working with wood. **2.** Skill and experience in matters pertaining to the woods, such as hunting, fishing, or camping.

wood·cut (wŏŏd′kŭt′) *n.* **1.** A piece of wood upon which a design for printing is engraved, especially along the grain. Also called "woodblock." **2.** A print made from such a piece of wood. Also called "woodblock," "woodprint."

wood·cut·ter (wo͝od'kŭt'ər) *n.* A person who cuts wood or trees. **—wood·cut·ting** *n.*

wood·ed (wo͝od'ĭd) *adj.* Having or covered with trees or woods.

wood·en (wo͝od'n) *adj.* **1.** Made or consisting of wood. **2.** Stiff; inflexible. **3.** Lifeless; expressionless. **—wood·en·ly** *adv.* **—wood·en·ness** *n.*

wood engraving *n.* **1.** A piece of wood upon which a design for printing is engraved, usually across the grain. **2.** The art or process of making wood engravings. **3.** A print made from such a piece of wood.

wood·en·head (wo͝od'n-hĕd') *n.* A stupid person; a blockhead. **—wood·en-head·ed** *adj.*

Wooden Horse *n.* The **Trojan horse** *(see).*

wooden Indian *n.* A wood effigy of an American Indian brave holding a cluster of cigars and used formerly as the emblem of a tobacconist.

Wood·hull (wo͝od'hŭl'), **Victoria Clafin** (1838–1927). U.S. publisher and feminist. Along with her sister, Tennessee Clafin (1846–1923), she founded a women's-rights magazine that advocated equal rights and free love (1870). An outspoken feminist, she was the first woman to be nominated for president (1872). In 1877 the sisters moved to England where they both married and worked for equality and various charitable institutions.

wood ibis *n.* Any of several large wading birds of the subfamily Mycteriinae, related to and resembling the storks; especially, *Mycteria americana* of the New World.

wood·land (wo͝od'lənd, -lănd') *n.* Land having a cover of trees and shrubs.
~*adj.* Of or indigenous to such a wooded area. **—wood·land·er** *n.*

wood·lark (wo͝od'lärk') *n.* An Old World songbird, *Lullula arborea,* resembling but smaller than the skylark.

wood lot *n.* An area restricted to the growing of forest trees.

wood louse *n.* Any of various small terrestrial crustaceans having a flattened segmented body and found in damp, shady places, especially under logs and stones. Also called "pill bug," "slater," "sow bug."

wood·man (wo͝od'mən) *n., pl.* **-men** (-mĭn). A woodsman.

wood·note (wo͝od'nōt') *n.* **1.** A song or call characteristic of a woodland bird. **2.** A piece of music or poetry resembling a bird's song in its spontaneity.

wood nymph *n.* A nymph of the forest; a dryad.

wood·peck·er (wo͝od'pĕk'ər) *n.* Any of various birds of the family Picidae, having strong claws and a stiff tail adapted for clinging to and climbing trees, and a chisellike bill for drilling through bark and wood.

wood pigeon *n.* A large Eurasian pigeon, *Columba palumbus,* having a white band on each wing. Also called "ringdove."

wood·pile (wo͝od'pīl') *n.* A pile of wood, especially when stacked for use as fuel.

wood·print (wo͝od'prĭnt') *n.* A **woodcut** *(see).*

wood pulp *n.* Any of various cellulose pulps ground from wood, chemically processed, and used to make paper.

wood pussy *n. Informal.* A skunk.

wood·ruff (wo͝od'rəf, -rŭf') *n.* Any of various plants of the genera *Galium* and *Asperula* in the bedstraw family; especially, *A. odorata,* native to Eurasia, having small white flowers and narrow, fragrant leaves used as flavoring and in sachets. [Middle English *woderofe,* Old English *wudurofe* : *wudu,* WOOD + *-rofe,* of uncertain origin; perhaps akin to Middle Low German *röve,* turnip.]

wood·rush (wo͝od'rŭsh) *n.* Any of various plants of the genus *Luzula,* resembling rushes but having long white hairs on the leaves and stems and generally found in drier habitats.

Woods, Lake of the. Lake, 3,846 square kilometers (1,485 square miles) in area, in southwestern Ontario, Canada, and north-central Minnesota. It has approximately 14,000 islands.

wood·screw (wo͝od'skro͞o') *n.* A tapered metal screw that is driven into wood, plaster, and the like with a screwdriver.

wood·shed (wo͝od'shĕd') *n.* A shed in which firewood is stored.

Woods Hole. Seaport in southeastern Massachusetts, at the southwestern extremity of Cape Cod. It is the site of an important marine biology laboratory and an oceanographic institution.

woods·man (wo͝odz'mən) *n., pl.* **-men** (-mĭn). One who works or lives in the woods or is versed in woodcraft; a forester.

wood sorrel *n.* Any of various plants of the genus *Oxalis,* having compound leaves with three leaflets; especially, *O. acetosella,* which has mauve-veined white flowers.

wood spirit *n.* **Methanol** *(see).*

Wood·stock[1] (wo͝od'stŏk'). Town of Oxfordshire, south-central England. Situated north of Oxford, it was the site of a royal palace where Elizabeth I was imprisoned by Mary I (1554). Nearby Blenheim Palace (1724) was designed by Sir John Vanbrugh.

Woodstock[2]**.** Town in southeastern New York. It was the site (1969) of a huge rock music festival.

wood sugar *n.* **Xylose** *(see).*

woods·y (wo͝od'zē) *adj.* **-ier, -iest.** Of, relating to, or suggestive of the woods.

wood tar *n.* A black, syruplike viscous fluid that is a by-product of the destructive distillation of wood and is used in pitch, wood preserving oils, preservatives, and medicines.

wood tick *n.* Any of various ticks of the genus *Dermacentor* that transmit the microorganism that causes Rocky Mountain spotted fever and tularemia in humans.

wood thrush *n.* A North American thrush, *Hylocichla mustelina,* having a melodious song.

wood·turn·ing (wo͝od'tûr'nĭng) *n.* The art or process of shaping wood into various forms on a lathe. **—wood·turn·er** *n.*

wood vinegar *n. Chemistry.* **Pyroligneous acid** *(see).*

wood warbler *n.* A woodland bird, *Phylloscopus sibilatrix,* having a yellow breast and distinct yellow eyestripe.

Wood·ward (wo͝od'wərd), **Robert Burns** (1917–79). U.S. chemist. The first scientist to synthesize various organic compounds, including quinine, cortisone, and chlorophyll, he was awarded the Nobel Prize in chemistry (1965).

wood·wax·en (wo͝od'wăk'sən) *n.* A shrub, the **dyer's greenweed** *(see).* [Middle English *wodewexen,* Old English *wudu weaxe* : *wudu,* WOOD + probably *weaxan,* to grow, WAX.]

wood·wind (wo͝od'wĭnd') *n.* **1.** Any of a group of musical wind instruments, formerly made of wood but now often of metal or plastic, that includes the bassoons, clarinets, flutes, oboes, and sometimes the saxophones. **2. woodwinds.** *Used with a singular or plural verb.* The section of an orchestra composed of woodwind instruments. **—wood·wind** *adj.* See feature, next page.

wood·work (wo͝od'wûrk') *n.* **1.** The art or skill of woodcarving or carpentry. **2.** Objects made of or work done in wood; especially, wooden interior fittings in a house, such as doors, staircases, or windowsills. **—wood·work·er** *n.* **—wood·work·ing** *n. & adj.*

wood·worm (wo͝od'wûrm') *n.* **1.** Any of various insect larvae that bore into wood, especially those of the furniture beetle and deathwatch beetle. **2.** The riddled effect produced in wood by such larvae.

wood·y (wo͝od'ē) *adj.* **-ier, -iest.** **1.** Forming or consisting of wood; ligneous: *woody tissue.* **2.** Characterized by the presence of wood or xylem: *woody plants.* **3.** Characteristic or suggestive of wood: *a woody smell.* **4.** Covered with trees; wooded.
~*n.* Also **wood·ie,** *pl.* **-ies.** A station wagon with exterior wood paneling. **—wood·i·ness** *n.*

woody nightshade *n.* See **bittersweet** (sense 1).

woof[1] (wo͝of, wo͞of) *n.* **1.** The threads that run crosswise in a woven fabric, at right angles to the warp threads; the weft. **2.** The texture of a woven fabric. [Alteration of Middle English *oof,* Old English *ōwef* : *ō-,* from *on,* ON + *wefan,* to weave.]

woof[2] (wo͝of) *n.* **1.** The deep, gruff bark of a dog. **2.** A sound similar to this.
~*intr.v.* **woofed, woof·ing, woofs.** To utter a woof. [Imitative.]

woof·er (wo͝of'ər) *n.* A loudspeaker designed to reproduce bass frequencies. Compare **tweeter.** [From WOOF (sound).]

wool (wo͝ol) *n.* **1.** The dense, soft, often curly hair forming the coat of sheep and certain other mammals. **2. a.** Yarn carded, spun, and processed from this for use in woven, knitted, and embroidered textiles. **b.** Loosely, any yarn used for knitting, even when mixed with synthetic fibers. **3.** Any filamentous or fibrous covering or substance suggestive of the texture or appearance of wool: *steel wool.* **—pull the wool over someone's eyes.** To deceive or trick someone.
~*adj.* Of, pertaining to, or consisting of wool or woolen material. [Middle English *wolle, wull,* Old English *wull.*]

wool-clip (wo͝ol'klĭp') *n.* The annual yield of wool.

wool·en (wo͝ol'ən) *adj.* Also **wool·len.** Of, pertaining to, or consisting of wool.
~*n.* Fabric or clothing made from wool, especially when knitted.

Woolf (wo͝olf), **Leonard Sidney** (1880–1969). British writer, the husband of Virginia Woolf. A member of the Fabians and cofounder with his wife of the Hogarth Press (1917), his works include *After the Deluge* (1931–39) and a five-volume autobiography (1960–69).

Woolf, (Adeline) Virginia, born Adeline Virginia Stephen (1882–1941). British novelist and member of the Bloomsbury group. Written in an experimental stream-of-consciousness style, her work includes *Mrs. Dalloway* (1925), *To the Lighthouse* (1927), *The Waves* (1931), and the posthumous *The Moment* (1948). She also wrote essays and critical works.

wool fat *n.* **Lanolin** *(see).*

wool·gath·er·ing (wo͝ol'găth'ər-ĭng) *n.* Absent-minded indulgence in fanciful daydreams. **—wool·gath·er·er** *n.*

wool·grow·er (wo͝ol'grō'ər) *n.* A person who breeds sheep or other animals for the production of wool. **—wool·grow·ing** *adj.*

wool in the grease *n.* See **grease** (sense 3b).

Wooll·cott (wo͝ol'kət, -kŏt'), **Alexander** (1887–1943). U.S. critic. The pre-eminent literary critic for several New York newspapers between 1914 and 1928, he was one of the original contributors to the *New Yorker* magazine and hosted a radio interview show from 1920 to 1942. His influential and widely read critical essays were also published in collections, such as *Shouts and Murmurs* (1922).

wool·ly, wool·y (wo͝ol'ē) *adj.* **-lier, -liest** or **-ier, -iest.** **1. a.** Pertaining to, consisting of, or covered with wool. **b.** Resembling wool. **2. a.** Lacking clarity or definition; hazy; fuzzy: *woolly thinking.* **b.** Lacking decisiveness resolution, or commitment. **3.** Having the characteristics of the rough, generally lawless atmosphere of frontier America: *wild and woolly.*
~*n., pl.* **woollies, woolies.** **1.** A garment made of wool; especially, a cardigan, sweater, or the like. **2.** *Western U.S. & Australian.* A sheep. **—wool·li·ly** *adv.* **—wool·li·ness** *n.*

woolly aphid *n.* Any aphid, such as those of the genera *Eriosoma*

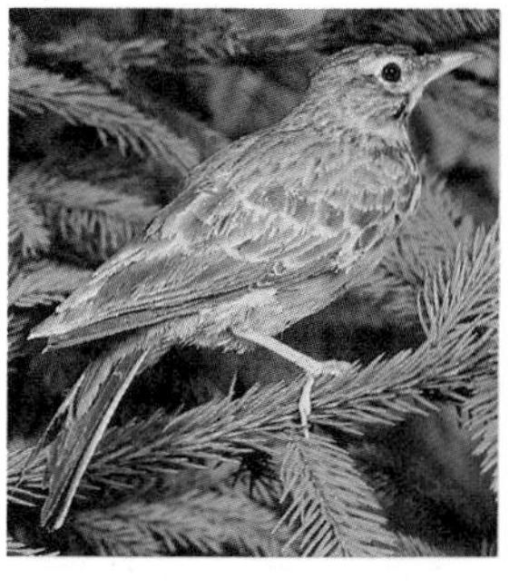

woodlark *The woodlark,* Lullula arborea, *lives on bush-sprinkled heaths and at the edges of forests throughout Europe. It often sings from treetops.*

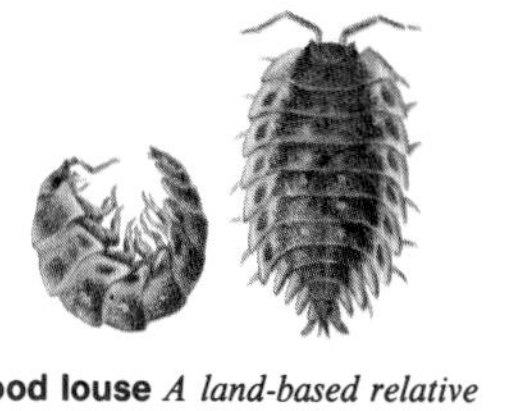

wood louse *A land-based relative of crabs and shrimp that lives in damp places. It avoids sunlight and dies within a few hours if its body becomes dry.*

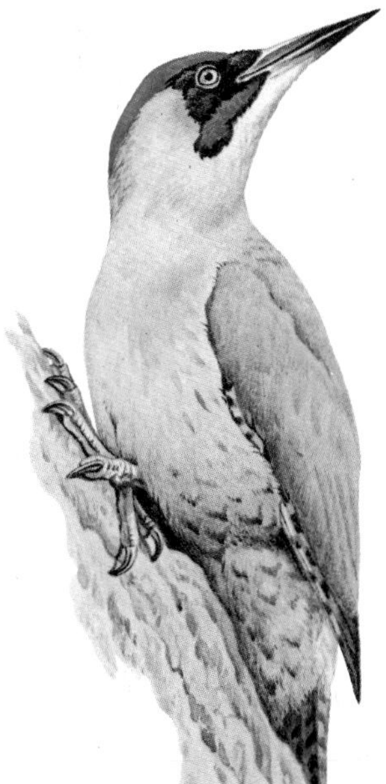

woodpecker *Most woodpeckers hammer the bark off trees with their beaks to feed on larvae and grubs concealed beneath it, but the European green woodpecker (above) often feeds from ants' nests on the ground.*

woodwind

SOUND OF THE WOODWINDS
The instrument's length governs its musical range

Woodwind instruments, once made of wood (except for the saxophone), are now also made of metal or plastic. They are played either through a mouth hole, as with the flute and recorder, or by means of a vibrating reed, as with the saxophone and clarinet. Oboes and bassoons have double reeds, which help to roughen the tone. Players vary the pitch by closing and opening holes in the instrument's body. The instrument's length dictates its range—a longer body produces lower notes.

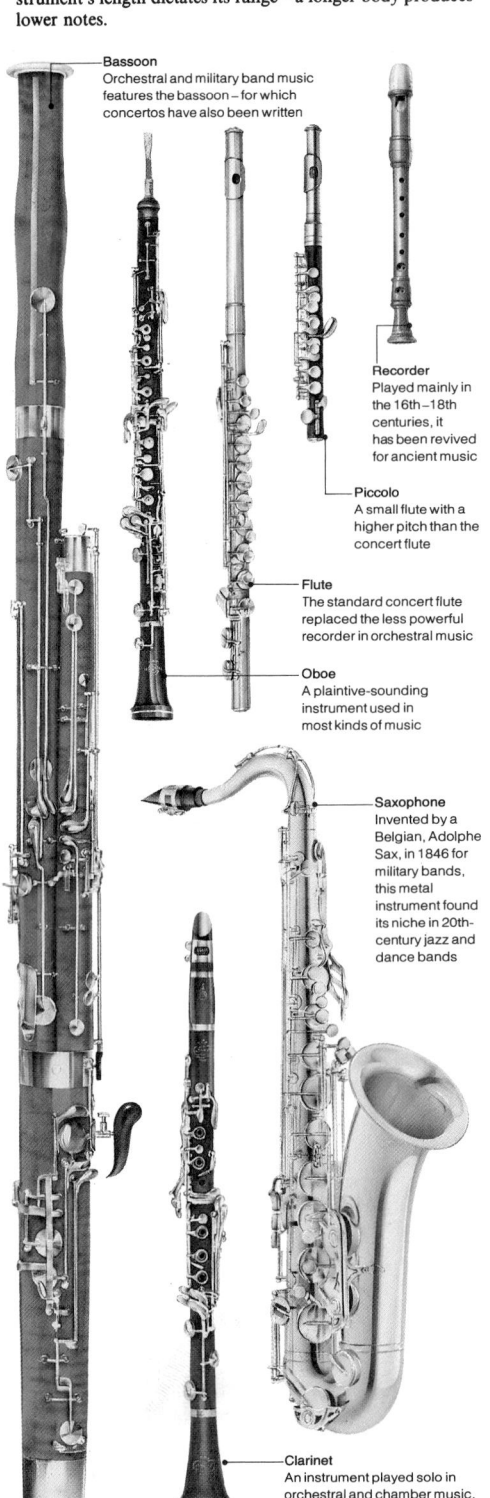

Bassoon
Orchestral and military band music features the bassoon – for which concertos have also been written

Recorder
Played mainly in the 16th–18th centuries, it has been revived for ancient music

Piccolo
A small flute with a higher pitch than the concert flute

Flute
The standard concert flute replaced the less powerful recorder in orchestral music

Oboe
A plaintive-sounding instrument used in most kinds of music

Saxophone
Invented by a Belgian, Adolphe Sax, in 1846 for military bands, this metal instrument found its niche in 20th-century jazz and dance bands

Clarinet
An instrument played solo in orchestral and chamber music, and in military and dance bands

woolly bear *Named because of its hairy appearance, this caterpillar is the juvenile form of a moth. Its adult form is better known as the garden tiger moth.*

and *Prociphalus,* that secretes white, waxy strands around its body.

woolly bear *n.* The hairy caterpillar of any of various tiger moths, especially that of *Isia isabella.*

woolly mammoth *n.* See **mammoth.**

Wool·man (wŏŏl′mən), **John** (1720–72). U.S. clergyman and abolitionist. A devout Quaker, he traveled around the colonies to spread the Quaker doctrine and convince people of the evils of slavery. He published several influential works, including *Some Considerations on the Keeping of Negroes* (1754).

wool·pack (wŏŏl′păk′) *n.* **1.** A large bag used for packing wool or fleeces for shipment. **2.** A cumulus cloud.

wool·sack (wŏŏl′săk′) *n.* **1.** A sack for wool. **2. a.** The official seat of the Lord Chancellor in the House of Lords. **b.** The Lord Chancellorship. Preceded by *the.*

wool·shed (wŏŏl′shĕd′) *n.* A building or complex of buildings in which sheep are sheared and wool is prepared for market.

wool·skin (wŏŏl′skĭn′) *n.* A sheepskin with the wool still on it.

wool·sort·er's disease (wŏŏl′sôr′tərz) *n.* A type of pneumonia resulting from infection of the lungs with anthrax bacilli.

wool·sta·pler (wŏŏl′stā′plər) *n.* A dealer in wool; especially, one who buys wool from the producer, grades it, and sells it to a manufacturer. **—wool·sta·pling** *adj. & n.*

Wool·worth (wŏŏl′wûrth′), **Frank Winfield** (1852–1919). U.S. merchant. At the age of 21 he persuaded his employer to include a five-cent-counter for slightly damaged or overstocked goods. By 1879 Woolworth had opened his own store in Lancaster, Pennsylvania, offering goods at prices up to 10 cents. The store was immediately successful and became the first in a chain of profitable five-and-tens stretching across the country.

wooly. Variant of **woolly.**

woom·e·ra, wom·e·ra (wŏŏm′ə-rə) *n. Australian.* A notched stick used by Australian Aborigines to hold a spear, giving increased leverage. [From an Australian native name (New South Wales).]

woo·zy (wŏŏ′zē, wŏŏz′ē) *adj.* **-i·er, -i·est. 1.** Dazed; stunned; confused. **2.** Dizzy or queasy, as from drink. [Perhaps alteration of OOZY.] **—woo·zi·ly** *adv.* **—woo·zi·ness** *n.*

Worces·ter[1] (wŏŏs′tər). County town of Hereford and Worcester, west-central England. On the Severn River, it has a 14th-century cathedral with a Norman crypt and was the site of Cromwell's defeat of Charles II and the Scots (1651). Its industries include Royal Worcester porcelain, sauce, gloves, and machinery.

Worcester[2] *n.* A fine china or porcelain made in Worcester from 1751. Also called "Worcester porcelain," "Worcester china."

Worces·ter·shire (wŏŏs′tər-shîr′, -shər). Former county of west-central England. In 1974 it was included in the new county of Hereford and Worcester. The county town was Worcester.

Worcestershire sauce *n.* A piquant sauce made from soy, vinegar, and spices, originally made in Worcester.

word (wûrd) *n.* **1. a.** A sound or a combination of sounds that symbolizes and communicates a meaning and may consist of a single morpheme or of a combination of morphemes. **b.** A written or printed representation of this. **2.** Something that is said; a short conversation or discussion: *Could I have a quick word with you?* **3. words.** The text of a vocal musical composition; the lyrics. **4.** An assurance or promise; a declared intention: *said he'd do it and was as good as his word; I give you my word.* **5. a.** A command or direction; an order: *executed at the general's word.* **b.** A verbal signal; a password or watchword. **6. a.** News or information: *the latest word.* **b.** Rumor: *Word has it he's married.* **7.** *Computer Science.* A sequence of 32, 36, 48, or 64 bits used to store or operate upon information in a computer system. **8. words.** Hostile or angry remarks made back and forth; a quarrel: *Words were exchanged between umpire and batter.* **9. Word. a.** See **Logos** (sense 2). **b.** The Scriptures or Gospel of the Christian Church: *the Word of God.* **—in a word.** In short. **—in so many words.** Precisely as stated; exactly. **—of few words.** Not given to talking; laconic. **—of one's word.** That can be depended on to keep a promise: *She's a woman of her word.* **—put in a (good) word for.** To recommend; speak favorably of. **—take one at one's word.** To be convinced of another's sincerity and act in accordance with his statement. **—upon my word.** Indeed; assuredly: *Upon my word, I've never seen anything like it.* **—word for word. 1.** Repeated in the same words; verbatim. **2.** Finding an equivalent translation for each word in turn. ~*tr.v.* **worded, wording, words.** To express in words. [Middle English *word,* Old English *word.*]

word·age (wûr′dĭj) *n.* **1.** The use of an excessive number of words; verbiage. **2.** The number of words used, as in a novel or an article. **3.** Wording.

word association *n.* **1.** An early psychoanalytical technique in which the patient says the first word to come into his mind in response to a key word. **2.** A party game in which players in turn say a word connected with the previous one.

word blindness *n.* Either of two disorders causing difficulties with reading and writing, **alexia** or **dyslexia** *(both of which see).* **—word-blind** *adj.*

word·book (wûrd′bŏŏk′) *n.* A vocabulary; a dictionary.

word·break (wûrd′brāk′) *n. Printing.* The point of division of a word when it is run on from one line to the next.

word class *n. Linguistics.* A part of speech, such as a noun, verb, or adjective.

word deafness *n.* A form of aphasia in which information in the form of speech is incomprehensible. **—word-deaf** *adj.*

word·ing (wûr′dĭng) *n.* **1.** The act or style of expressing in words;

phraseology; diction. **2.** The words themselves as they are deployed or arranged.

word·less (wûrd′lĭs) *adj.* Without words; unspoken; inarticulate; silent. —**word·less·ly** *adv.* —**word·less·ness** *n.*

word·mon·ger (wûrd′mŭng′gər, -mŏng′-) *n.* A writer or speaker who uses languge pretentiously or carelessly.

word order *n.* The syntactic arrangement of words in a sentence, clause, or phrase.

word-per·fect (wûrd′pûr′fĭkt) *adj.* **1.** Memorized perfectly: *a word-perfect recitation.* **2.** Remembering or repeating one's words perfectly.

word play *n.* **1.** Verbal wit. **2.** A play on words; a pun.

word processor *n.* An electronic device consisting of a keyboard similar to a typewriter, a microprocessor, and a cathode-ray screen that together enable copy, as for letters or documents, to be stored on magnetic disk, corrected, and printed. —**word processing** *n.*

word square *n.* **1.** A group of words arranged in a square that read the same vertically and horizontally. **2.** A puzzle whose solution is a word square.

Words·worth (wûrdz′wûrth′), **William** (1770–1850). British poet. Two important influences on his work were his early life in the Lake District and the optimism of postrevolutionary France. Conveying a mystical feeling of unity with nature, his works include *Poems in Two Volumes* (1807), containing "Ode to Immortality" and "The Daffodils," and his verse autobiography, *The Prelude* (written 1805, published 1850). He became poet laureate in 1843.

word·y (wûr′dē) *adj.* **-i·er, -i·est. 1.** Expressed in or using more words than are necessary. **2.** Pertaining to, consisting of, or having the nature of words; verbal. —See Synonyms at **talkative.** —**word·i·ly** *adv.* —**word·i·ness** *n.*

wore. 1. Past tense of **wear** (to be clothed in). **2.** Past tense of **wear** (to turn. Used of a ship).

work (wûrk) *n.* **1.** Physical or mental effort or activity directed toward the production or accomplishment of something; toil; labor. **2.** Employment; a job: *look for work.* **3.** The means by which one earns one's livelihood; a trade, craft, business, or profession. **4. a.** Something that is being or must be done, made, or performed, especially as a part of one's occupation; a duty or task: *begin the day's work.* **b.** The amount of this done or required. **5. a.** Something done, made, or performed through the agency, effort, or activity of a person or thing: *said the killings were the work of a vicious maniac; a work of genius.* **b.** A task or action occupying the specified amount of time: *It was the work of a few minutes.* **6. a.** Often **works.** The output of an artist or artisan considered or collected as a whole: *the works of Verdi.* **b.** A piece of needlework or embroidery. **7.** Any material or piece being processed in a machine during manufacture; a workpiece. **8. a.** A place of employment: *Don't phone me at work.* **b.** The part of a day during which one works: *met her after work; late for work.* **9.** The manner or style of working or the quality of treatment; workmanship: *good work.* **10.** Action producing an intended or expected effect: *waited for the poison to do its work.* **11.** A froth produced during the process of fermentation, as on vinegar, cider, or other liquid. **12.** *Physics. Abbr.* **w, W** The transfer of energy from one physical system to another; especially, the transfer of energy to a body by the application of force, usually calculated as the product of the force and the distance moved by the point of application in the direction of the force. —See **works.** —**have one's work cut out.** Have a lot to do. —**make short work of.** *Informal.* **1.** To deal with very quickly or easily. **2.** To overcome (an opponent). —**out of work.** Unemployed. —**set to work.** To begin doing something.
~*v.* **worked** or *archaic* **wrought** (rôt), **working, works.** —*intr.* **1.** To exert one's efforts for the purpose of doing, making, or achieving something; labor or toil. **2. a.** To be employed; have a job. **b.** To have an influence, result, or effect, as on a person, the mind, or the like: *The plea for help worked on their compassion.* **3. a.** To operate; function. **b.** To operate effectively: *Is the phone working? The plan didn't work.* **c.** To arrive at or be brought to a specified state, especially gradually or by repeated movement: *The stitches worked loose.* **4.** To proceed or progress slowly and laboriously. **5.** To move or contort from emotion or pain: *His mouth worked with fear.* **6.** To behave or respond in a specified way when handled or processed: *Not all metals work easily.* **7.** To ferment. **8.** *Nautical.* **a.** To be under strain in heavy seas so that seams loosen and fastenings become slack. **b.** To sail against the wind. **9.** To undergo small motions that result in friction and wear: *The gears work against each other.* **10.** To attempt to influence or persuade. Used with *on* or *upon.* —*tr.* **1.** To cause or effect; bring about: *I can't work miracles.* **2.** To cause to operate or function; handle or use: *work a power mower.* **3.** To make or force to work or to do work: *She works her employees hard.* **4.** To excite, rouse, or provoke: *He worked me into a rage.* **5.** *Informal.* To arrange, especially by somewhat devious means; contrive: *Try to work it so we both get our vacation at the same time.* **6.** *Informal.* To use or employ for one's own ends or purposes; exploit: *You have to learn how to work the system.* **7.** *Informal.* To practice trickery or deception on; cheat. **8.** To carry on one's occupation in; cover: *This postman works our street.* **9.** To cause to ferment. —**work off.** To get rid of by work or effort: *work off extra pounds; work off a debt.* —**work over.** *Slang.* To inflict severe physical damage upon; beat up. —**work up. 1.** To develop or proceed gradually toward a point: *The film works up to a thrilling climax.* **2.** To arouse the emotions of; excite; stir up: *worked up the crowd into a frenzy.* **3.** To produce by working: *work up an appetite.*

[Middle English *werke, worke,* Old English *we(o)rc,* act, deed, work.]

Synonyms: drudgery, labor, toil.

-work *suffix.* Indicates: **1.** Work done using the specified tools or materials; for example, **needlework. 2.** A product of work done in the specified medium; for example, **woodwork. 3.** Work performed in a specified way or of a specified type; for example, **nightwork, piecework.**

work·a·ble (wûrk′ə-bəl) *adj.* **1.** Capable of being worked, dealt with, or handled. **2.** Capable of working effectively or successfully; practicable or feasible. —See Synonyms at **possible.** —**work·a·bil·i·ty, work·a·ble·ness** *n.* —**work·a·bly** *adv.*

work·a·day (wûrk′ə-dā′) *adj.* **1.** Pertaining or appropriate to working days; everyday. **2.** Mundane; commonplace: *the workaday world.* [Middle English *werkeday,* a workday : *werke,* WORK + DAY.]

work·a·hol·ic (wûr′kə-hô′lĭk, -hŏl′ĭk) *n.* A person who suffers from a compulsive need to work excessively hard. [WORK + (ALC)O-HOLIC.] —**work·a·hol·ism** *n.*

work·bag (wûrk′băg′) *n.* A bag to hold material, such as needlework, on which one is working, or implements needed for work.

work·bench (wûrk′bĕnch′) *n.* A sturdy table or bench at which a machinist, mechanic, or carpenter works.

work·book (wûrk′bŏŏk′) *n.* **1.** A booklet containing problems and exercises, typically one that is published in conjunction with a textbook and has spaces in which answers are to be written. **2.** A manual containing operating instructions, as for an appliance or a machine. **3.** A book in which a record is kept of work proposed or accomplished.

work·box (wûrk′bŏks′) *n.* A box or basket for implements or materials used in sewing or other work. Also called "work basket."

work·day (wûrk′dā′) *n.* **1.** The part of a day set aside for work: *an eight-hour workday.* **2.** A day on which work is usually done, as opposed to a weekend or holiday. ~*adj.* Workaday.

work·er (wûr′kər) *n.* **1. a.** One that works. **b.** One who works in a specified way or at a specified occupation: *a fast worker; an office worker.* **2. a.** An employee, as opposed to an employer or manager. **b.** One who does manual or industrial labor. **3.** One who belongs to the working class. **4.** One of the sterile females of certain social insects, such as the ant or bee, that performs specialized work.

work·er-priest (wûr′kər-prēst′) *n. Roman Catholic Church.* A priest, especially in France, who spends time in secular employment for missionary purposes.

workers' compensation *n.* Payments required by law to be made to an employee who is injured in the course of work.

workers' cooperative *n.* An enterprise in which all workers share control over production, distribution, and exchange, often with equal profit-sharing, regardless of individual function.

work ethic *n.* A belief in the virtues of dutiful hard work and its moral superiority to leisure, play, or other activities that are considered unproductive.

work·folk (wûrk′fōk′) *pl.n.* Also **work·folks** (-fōks′). Laborers, especially farm laborers.

work force *n.* **1.** Those workers employed in a specific project; a staff. **2.** All workers potentially available to a nation, project, industry, or the like.

work function *n.* The energy required to remove an electron from a solid; especially, the work exerted against coulomb forces in removing an electron from just inside to just outside the surface of a metal.

work hardening *n.* The increase in strength that sometimes accompanies plastic deformation of a solid, especially a metal. —**work-hard·en** (wûrk′här′dn) *v.*

work·horse (wûrk′hôrs′) *n.* **1.** A horse that is used for labor rather than for racing or riding. **2.** *Informal.* A person who works tirelessly, especially at difficult or arduous tasks.

work·house (wûrk′hous′) *n.* **1.** A prison in which limited sentences are served by manual labor. **2.** A former public institution in Britain in which the poor were fed and housed in return for labor.

work in *tr.v.* **1.** To insert by adjustment, ingenious contrivance, or effort. **2.** To introduce unobtrusively: *worked in a request for money.*

work-in *n.* A method of industrial action where workers prevent the closure of a plant or office by occupying and running it themselves. Compare **sit-in.**

work·ing (wûr′kĭng) *adj.* **1.** Pertaining to, used for, or spent in working: *a working breakfast; a working uniform.* **2.** Adequate or appropriate for performing work or achieving effective results: *in working order; a working majority.* **3.** Capable of being used as the basis of further work: *a working hypothesis.*
~*n.* **1.** *Usually* **workings.** The way in which something works. **2.** The excavations in a mine or quarry or the part of them being worked.

working capital *n.* **1.** The assets of a business enterprise that can be applied to its operation. **2.** The current assets of an individual or business enterprise as opposed to the current liabilities.

working class *n.* Often **working classes.** The part of society whose income is from wages; the proletariat. —**working-class** *adj.*

working day *n.* A workday.

working drawing *n.* An engineering drawing, architect's plan, or the like, that is used by a machinist, builder, or other worker to make or build the subject of the drawing.

working fluid *n.* A **working substance** *(see)* that is a fluid.

THE WORLD (POLITICAL)

work·ing·man (wûr′kĭng-măn′) *n., pl.* **-men** (-mĕn′). A man who works for wages, especially at manual labor.

working papers *pl.n.* Legal documents necessary in certain countries to guarantee the right of an individual to employment.

working storage *n. Computer Science.* The part of a computer's data-storage disk that is reserved for data to be temporarily stored during the running of a program.

working substance *n.* **1.** A substance, especially a fluid, that undergoes changes of pressure, temperature, and volume in a heat engine. Also called "working fluid." **2.** The substance in a thermometer that expands and contracts.

work·less (wûrk′lĭs) *adj.* Unemployed.

work·load (wûrk′lōd′) *n.* The amount of work assigned to or done by a machine, worker, or unit of workers in a given time period.

work·man (wûrk′mən) *n., pl.* **-men** (-mĭn). **1.** A man who performs some form of manual or industrial labor. **2.** A person who works in a specified way: *A bad workman blames his tools.*

work·man·like (wûrk′mən-līk′) *adj.* Also **work·man·ly** (-lē). **1.** Characteristic of or befitting a skilled workman or craftsman: *workmanlike pottery.* **2.** Of satisfactory but not outstanding quality: *a workmanlike performance.*

work·man·ship (wûrk′mən-shĭp′) *n.* **1.** The art, skill, or technique of a workman. **2.** The quality of such art, skill, or technique: *silver of*

poor workmanship. **3.** Something produced or achieved by work or effort; handiwork.

workmen's compensation *n.* Workers' compensation.

work of art *n.* **1.** A piece of artistic work deemed valuable or superior. **2.** Anything likened to this in beauty or workmanship.

work out *tr.v.* **1.** To find a solution for; solve. **2.** To formulate or develop: *work out a plan.* **3.** To exhaust (a mine, soil, or the like). **4.** To fulfill (an obligation or debt, for example) by working instead of paying money. **5.** To accomplish by work or effort. —*intr.v.* **1.** To make its way or come out: *a nail working out of a board.* **2.** To have a specified result: *work out badly.* **3.** To prove successful, effective, or satisfactory: *Did your job work out?* **4.** To perform a series of exercises or drills: *works out at a gym.*

work·out (wûrk′out′) *n.* A period of exercise or practice, especially in athletics.

work·peo·ple (wûrk′pē′pəl) *pl.n. Chiefly British.* Those who work for wages.

work·piece (wûrk′pēs′) *n.* Any piece or part in the process of manufacture by machine or by hand.

work·room (wûrk′rōōm′, -rōōm′) *n.* A room where work is done, especially manual work.

works *pl.n. Used with a singular or plural verb.* **1.** A factory, plant, or similar building or complex of buildings where a usually speci-

fied type of industry is carried on. Often used in combination: *a gasworks; a steelworks.* **2.** The internal mechanism of an object: *the works of a watch.* **3.** Engineering structures, such as bridges or dams. **4.** A structure for fortification or defense. **—in the works.** *Informal.* Being processed or prepared. **—the works.** *Informal.* **1.** Everything; the whole of a set: *He had the works, from the avocado to the port and cigars.* **2.** Extreme punitive treatment.

work·shar·ing (wûrk′shâr′ĭng) *n.* The practice of **job-sharing** (see).

work·shop (wûrk′shŏp′) *n.* **1.** An area, room, or establishment in which manual or industrial work is done. **2. a.** A group of people who meet for a seminar in some specialized field: *a creative-writing workshop.* **b.** A meeting or seminar held by such a group.

work·shy (wûrk′shī′) *adj.* Habitually avoiding work.

work stoppage *n.* A protest measure by a group of workers that is marked by cessation of work and is usually less serious than a formal strike.

work·stud·y program (wûrk′stŭd′ē) *n.* A program designed to provide high school or college students with work experience.

work·ta·ble (wûrk′tā′bəl) *n.* A table designed for a specific task or activity, such as needlework or graphic arts.

work·week (wûrk′wēk′) *n.* The number of hours worked or required to be worked in a week.

work·wom·an (wûrk′wŏŏm′ən) *n., pl.* **-women** (-wĭm′ĭn). A woman who works.

world (wûrld) *n.* **1.** The earth. **2.** The universe. **3.** The earth and its inhabitants collectively. Also used adjectivally: *world champion; world peace.* **4.** The human race. **5. a.** Humankind considered as social creatures; human society: *turned her back on the world.* **b.** People as a whole; the public: *The story burst upon the world.* **6.** *Often* **World.** A specified part of the earth: *the Western World.* **7.** A particular period in history, including its people, culture, and social order: *the Victorian world.* **8.** Any realm, domain, or kingdom: *the insect world.* **9.** A field or sphere of human activity: *the world of advertising.* **10.** Everything that concerns or contributes to the life of an individual: *felt his whole world collapsing around him.* **11.** A specified way of life or state of being: *the world of the rich.* **12.** Secular life and its morality as distinguished from the religious or spiritual life: *a man of the world.* **13. a.** Human existence; mortal life: *came into the world.* **b.** A supposed state of existence beyond death: *the next world.* **14.** *Often* **worlds.** A large amount; much: *did him a world of good; worlds apart.* **15.** A planet or other celestial body: *the possibility of life on another world.* **—dead to the world.** Fast asleep or unconscious. **—for all the world.** *Informal.* To all intents and purposes; for all practical purposes: *He looked for all the world like a movie star.* **—on top of the world.** *Informal.* Elated,

THE WORLD (PHYSICAL)

exultant, or blissful. **—out of this world.** *Informal.* Excellent: *Dinner was out of this world.* **—world without end.** Forever and ever. [Middle English w(e)orld, Old English world, weorold, from Germanic, from weraz (unattested), man + aldh- (unattested), age.]
World Bank n. An international bank founded in 1945 to assist the economic development of the Third World by means of loans from richer nations. Also officially called "International Bank for Reconstruction and Development."
world-class (wûrld′klăs′) adj. Being one of or worthy of the best in the world.
World Council of Churches n. Abbr. **W.C.C.** An ecumenical grouping of Christian Churches, excluding the Roman Catholics, founded in 1948 to further the aims of Christian unity.
World Court n. **1.** The Permanent Court of International Justice, established by the League of Nations (1920). **2.** The **International Court of Justice** (see).
World Cup n. **1.** A soccer championship competition, held every four years, between 24 national teams selected in a qualifying competition. **2.** The trophy awarded to the winners of this competition.
World Health Organization n. Abbr. **W.H.O.** A United Nations agency, founded in 1948 and based in Geneva, that serves to coordinate and improve health activities worldwide.

world line n. Physics. The line representing the path of an object through the four-dimensional space-time continuum.
world·ling (wûrld′lĭng) n. A person absorbed in or devoted to this world; a worldly person.
world·ly (wûrld′lē) adj. **-lier, -liest. 1.** Of, pertaining to, or devoted to the temporal world; not spiritual or religious; secular. **2.** Sophisticated or cosmopolitan; worldly-wise. —See Usage note at **earthly.** **—world·li·ness** n.
world·ly-wise (wûrld′lē-wīz′) adj. Experienced in the ways of the world; sophisticated and shrewd, often to the point of cynicism.
world power n. A political entity whose actions consistently influence or change the course of international events.
World Series n. The series of professional baseball games played each fall between the championship teams of the American League and the National League.
world-shak·ing (wûrld′shā′kĭng) adj. Of great significance.
world soul n. A spiritual principle relating to the world as the human soul relates to a human being.
world view n. A particular way of viewing and interpreting the world; a philosophy of life.
World War I n. Abbr. **W.W.I** A war fought from 1914 to 1918, in which Great Britain, France, Russia, Belgium, Italy, Japan, the United States, and other allies defeated Germany, Austria-

Hungary, Turkey, and Bulgaria. Also called "First World War," "Great War."

World War II *n. Abbr.* **W.W.II** A war fought from 1939 to 1945, in which Great Britain, France, the Soviet Union, the United States, and other allies defeated Germany, Italy, and Japan. Also called "Second World War."

world-wea-ry (wûrld′wîr′ē) *adj.* **-rier, -riest.** Tired of the world and the pleasures afforded by it. —**world-wea-ri-ness** *n.*

world-wide (wûrld′wîd′) *adj.* Reaching or extending throughout the world; universal. —**world-wide** *adv.*

World Wildlife Fund *n. Abbr.* **WWF.** An organization founded in 1961 to raise money for the protection and conservation of wildlife throughout the world.

worm (wûrm) *n.* **1.** Any of various invertebrates, such as those of the phyla Annelida, Nematoda, or Platyhelminthes, having a long, flexible rounded or flattened body, often without obvious appendages. **2.** Any of various insect larvae having a soft, elongated body. **3.** Any of various unrelated animals resembling a worm in habit or appearance, as the shipworm or the slowworm. **4.** An object or device that is like a worm in appearance or action, such as a threaded screw, a spiral-shaped tube in a heat exchanger, or a condenser in a still. **5.** A shaft with a helical groove cut in it so that it can function as part of a worm gear. **6.** An insidiously tormenting

or devouring force: *"The worm of conscience still begnaw thy soul"* (Shakespeare). **7.** *Informal.* **a.** A pitiable creature; a poor wretch. **b.** A contemptible despicable person; one of no moral worth. **8. worms.** *Pathology.* Intestinal infestation with worms or wormlike parasites. In this sense, also called "helminthiasis."
—*v.* **wormed, worming, worms.** —*tr.* **1.** To make (one's way) with or as if with the sinuous crawling motion of a worm. **2.** To elicit by artful or devious means. Used with *out.* **3.** To cure of intestinal worms. **4.** *Nautical.* To wrap yarn or twine around (rope). —*intr.* **1.** To move in a sinuous manner suggestive of a worm. **2.** To make one's way by artful or devious means. Used with *into* or *out of.* [Middle English *worm,* Old English *wyrm,* worm, serpent.]

worm-eat-en (wûrm′ēt′n) *adj.* **1.** Bored through or gnawed by worms. **2.** Full of wormholes. **3.** Decayed; worn-out; decrepit.

worm fence *n.* A fence of crossed rails supporting one another and forming a zigzag pattern. Also called "snake fence," "Virginia fence," "Virginia rail fence."

worm gear *n.* **1.** A gear consisting of a threaded shaft and a wheel with teeth that mesh into it. **2.** A worm wheel.

worm-hole (wûrm′hōl′) *n.* A hole made by a burrowing worm. —**worm-holed** *adj.*

worm screw *n.* The threaded shaft of a worm gear. Also called "worm."

worm·seed (wûrm′sēd′) *n.* **1.** A tropical American plant, *Chenopodium ambrosioides,* yielding an oil used as an anthelmintic. **2.** Any of several other plants similarly used.

worm's-eye view (wûrmz′ī′) *n.* A view from below or from a lowly or grass-roots level.

worm wheel *n.* The toothed wheel of a worm gear. Also called "worm gear."

worm·wood (wûrm′wo͝od′) *n.* **1.** Any of several aromatic plants of the genus *Artemisia;* especially, *A. absinthium,* native to Europe, yielding a bitter extract used in making absinthe and in flavoring certain wines. Also called "absinthe." **2.** Something distressing or embittering. [Middle English *wormwode,* variant (influenced by WORM and WOOD) of *wermode,* Old English *wermōd,* from Germanic *wer-mōd-, wor-mōd-* (unattested). See also **vermouth.**]

worm·y (wûr′mē) *adj.* **-ier, -iest. 1.** Infested with or damaged by worms. **2.** Suggestive of a worm; especially, groveling or insinuating. **—worm·i·ness** *n.*

worn (wôrn, wōrn). Past participle of **wear.**
— *adj.* **1.** Affected by wear or use. **2.** Impaired or damaged by wear or use: *worn elbows on a coat.* **3. a.** Exhausted; spent. **b.** Showing exhaustion; drawn. **—See Synonyms at haggard.** [Middle English, past participle of *weren,* to WEAR.]

worn-out (wôrn′out′, wōrn′-) *adj.* **1.** Worn or used until no longer usable: *a worn-out suit.* **2.** Thoroughly exhausted; spent.

wor·ri·ment (wûr′ē-mənt) *n. Informal.* **1.** The act of worrying or state of being worried. **2.** A source of anxiety; a worry.

wor·ri·some (wûr′ē-səm) *adj.* **1.** Causing worry or anxiety. **2.** Tending to worry; anxious. **—wor·ri·some·ly** *adv.*

wor·ry (wûr′ē) *v.* **-ried, -rying, -ries. —** *intr.* **1.** To feel uneasy about some uncertain or threatening matter; be troubled or agitated. **2.** To pull, bite, or tear at something: *The dog worried at the bone.* **3.** To work or proceed doggedly in the face of difficulty or hardship; struggle: *worried away at a problem.* —*tr.* **1.** To cause to feel anxious, distressed, or troubled. **2.** To bother; annoy: *Don't worry me with your complaints.* **3. a.** To seize with the teeth and shake or tug at repeatedly: *a dog worrying a bone.* **b.** To attack roughly and repeatedly; harass. **c.** To touch, move, or handle idly; toy with: *worrying the sore tooth with his tongue.*
— *n., pl.* **worries. 1.** The act of worrying or the condition of being worried; mental uneasiness or anxiety. **2.** A source of nagging concern or uneasiness. **—See Synonyms at anxiety.** [Middle English *worien, wirien,* to seize by the throat, harass, Old English *wyrgan,* to strangle.] **—wor·ried·ly** *adv.* **—wor·ri·er** *n.*

worry beads *pl.n.* A bead bracelet kept in the hand and constantly toyed with to relieve boredom or tension, originally used by men in Greece and the Middle East.

wor·ry·wart (wûr′ē-wôrt′) *n. Informal.* One who tends to worry excessively and needlessly.

worse (wûrs). **1.** Comparative of **bad. 2.** Comparative of **ill.**
— *adj.* Also *obsolete* **wors·er** (wûr′sər). **1.** More inferior, as in quality, condition, or effect. **2.** More severe or unfavorable. **3.** Further from a standard; less desirable or satisfactory. **—the worse for wear.** Shoddy or rundown. **—worse luck.** *Informal.* Unfortunately.
— *adv.* In a worse way.
— *n.* Something that is worse. **—for the worse.** Into a worse state or condition. [Middle English *wors(e),* Old English *wyrsa.*]

wors·en (wûr′sən) *v.* **-ened, -ening, -ens.** —*intr.* To be or become worse. —*tr.* To make worse.

wor·ship (wûr′shĭp) *n.* **1.** The reverent love and allegiance accorded a deity, idol, or sacred object. **2.** A set of ceremonies, prayers, or other religious forms by which this love is expressed. **3.** Ardent devotion; adoration. **4.** *Often* **Worship.** *Chiefly British.* A title or form of address for magistrates, mayors, and certain other dignitaries. Used with *His, Her, Your,* or *Their.*
— *v.* **worshiped** or **worshipped, -shiping** or **-shipping, -ships.** —*tr.* **1.** To honor and love as a deity; venerate. **2.** To regard with great admiration or devotion; idolize. —*intr.* **1.** To participate in religious rites of worship. **2.** To perform any act of worship. —**See Synonyms at revere.** [Middle English *worschipe,* Old English *weorthscipe,* honor, dignity, reverence : *weorth,* WORTH + -SHIP.] **—wor·ship·er, wor·ship·per** *n.*

wor·ship·ful (wûr′shĭp-fəl) *adj.* **1.** Given to or expressive of worship; reverent or adoring. **2.** *Chiefly British.* Worthy of honor and respect; distinguished. Used especially as an honorific title. **—wor·ship·ful·ly** *adv.* **—wor·ship·ful·ness** *n.*

worst (wûrst). **1.** Superlative of **bad. 2.** Superlative of **ill.**
— *adj.* **1.** Most inferior, as in quality, condition, or effect. **2.** Most severe or unfavorable. **3.** Furthest from an ideal or standard; least desirable or satisfactory.
— *n.* Something that is worst: *at one's worst; do one's worst.* **—at worst. 1.** Under the worst foreseeable circumstances; if the worst should happen. **2.** From the least favorable point of view. **—get the worst of it.** To suffer a defeat or disadvantage. **—if (the) worst comes to (the) worst.** At the very worst.
— *adv.* In the worst manner or degree.
— *tr.v.* **worsted, worsting, worsts.** To gain the advantage over; defeat. [Middle English *worste, wurst,* Old English *wyrsta.*]

wor·sted (wo͝os′tĭd, wûr′stĭd) *n.* **1.** Firm-textured, compactly twisted woolen yarn made from long-staple fibers. **2.** Fabric made from such yarn. [Middle English *worsted,* first made in *Worthstede* (now Worstead), a village in Norfolk.] **—wor·sted** *adj.*

wort (wûrt, wôrt) *n.* **1.** A plant, especially one formerly used as a medicinal herb. Now used only in combination: *liverwort; milkwort.* **2.** An infusion of malt fermented to make beer. [Middle English *wort, wurt,* Old English *wyrt,* plant, herb.]

worth¹ (wûrth) *n.* **1.** The quality of something that renders it desirable, useful, or valuable: *the worth of higher education.* **2.** The material or market value of something: *have a worth of ten million dollars.* **3.** The number or quantity of something that may be purchased for a specified sum: *five dollars' worth of gas.* **4.** The quality within a person that commands respect; merit.
— *adj.* **1.** Equal in value to something specified: *He's not worth her little finger.* **2.** Deserving of; meriting: *a proposal worth consideration.* **3.** Having wealth or riches amounting to: *He's worth a quarter of a million.* **—for all one is worth.** To the utmost of one's powers or ability. **—for what it's worth.** Even though it may not be important. [Middle English *worth,* Old English *weorth.*]

worth² *intr.v.* **worthed, worthing, worths.** *Archaic.* To befall; betide: *"Howl ye, Woe worth the day!"* (Ezekiel 30:2). [Middle English *worthen,* Old English *weorthan.*]

worth·less (wûrth′lĭs) *adj.* **1.** Without worth, use, or value. **2.** Without moral worth; low and despicable. **—worth·less·ly** *adv.* **—worth·less·ness** *n.*

worth·while, worth-while (wûrth′hwīl′, -wīl′) *adj.* Sufficiently valuable or important to justify the expenditure of time or effort.

wor·thy (wûr′thē) *adj.* **-thier, -thiest. 1.** Having worth, merit, or value; useful or valuable. **2.** Honorable; admirable: *a worthy fellow.* **3.** Having sufficient worth; deserving: *worthy to be revered; worthy of acclaim.* **4.** Appropriate; suitable: *a large crowd, worthy of this great occasion.*
— *n., pl.* **worthies. 1.** A person esteemed for his worth, dignity, or importance. **2.** An eminent or distinguished person. Often used humorously: *local worthies.* **—wor·thi·ly** *adv.* **—wor·thi·ness** *n.*

-worthy *suffix.* Indicates: **1.** Of sufficient worth or importance for; for example, **newsworthy. 2.** Deserving of; for example, **blameworthy. 3.** Safe or suitable for travel by means of; for example, **roadworthy.**

wost. *Archaic.* Second person singular present tense of **wit** (to know).

wot. *Archaic.* First and third person singular present tense of **wit** (to know).

Wo·tan (vō′tän). A Teutonic god identified with Woden.

Wot·ton (wŏt′n, wo͝ot′n), **Sir Henry** (1568–1639). English diplomat and author. A member of Parliament (1614 and 1625), he was an ambassador for James II (1604–23) and spent several years in Venice, where he developed an appreciation of the fine arts. His poem "You Meaner Beauties of the Night" and a short book, *The Elements of Architecture* (1624), are among his few extant works.

Wouk (wōk), **Herman** (1915–). U.S. author. A World War II veteran, he combined meticulous research with his personal military experience to write highly popular war novels, including his Pulitzer Prize winner, *The Caine Mutiny* (1951).

would (wo͝od). Past tense of **will** (defective verb), often used as an auxiliary verb expressing various shades of attendant meaning indicating: **1.** A habitual action or custom in the past: *In her young days she would go skiing every winter.* **2.** *Chiefly British.* A stubborn action in the past: *Well, you would go and discuss politics with the barber.* **3.** A polite request or command: *Would you step this way, please.* **4.** Attempt or intention: *Those who would disregard the rules must bear the consequences.* **5.** Desire or preference: *Treat others as you would have them treat you.* **6.** *Archaic.* A heartfelt wish: *Would that he were in my arms again.* **7.** *Chiefly British.* Approximation or estimate: *That house would cost about $80,000.* **8. a.** Probability: *He would be a millionaire by now if he had taken my advice.* **b.** Condition; contingency of one condition upon another: *If you would only get home in time, we could have dinner together now and then.* **9.** Doubt, disdain, cynicism, or the like: *It would seem that I am under arrest again.* **10.** Moderation of the directness or bluntness of a request or statement: *My client would like to take issue with you there.*

    Usage: **Would have** is sometimes used in conditional clauses introduced by *if,* but standard English prefers *had,* both in formal speech and in writing: *If John had gone, he would have seen her* (not *If John would have gone*). Similarly, following the verb *wish, had* is the preferred form: *I wish that she had* (not *would have*) *gone.*

would-be (wo͝od′bē) *adj.* Desiring or pretending to be: *a would-be hero.*

would·n't (wo͝od′ənt). Contraction of *would not.*

wouldst, would·est. *Archaic.* Second person singular past tense of **will** (defective verb).

Woulfe bottle (wo͝olf) *n.* A glass laboratory bottle with two necks or sometimes more, used for bubbling a gas through a liquid. [After Peter *Woulfe* (died 1803), British chemist.]

wound¹ (wo͝ond) *n.* **1.** An injury to a person or animal in which the skin or other external organic surface is torn, pierced, cut, or otherwise broken, as a result of violence, accident, or surgery. **2.** An injury to the tissue of a plant. **3.** An injury to the feelings.
— *v.* **wounded, wounding, wounds.** —*tr.* To inflict a wound or wounds upon. —*intr.* To inflict a wound or wounds. **—See Synonyms at injure.** [Middle English *wound(e),* Old English *wund.*]

wound² (wound). **1.** Past tense and past participle of **wind** (to wrap). **2.** Alternate past tense and past participle of **wind** (to sound).

Wound·ed Knee (wo͝on′dĭd). Creek in southwestern South Dakota. It was the site of the last major battle of the Indian Wars (December 29, 1890), when some 200 Sioux men, women, and children were killed by the U.S. 7th Cavalry.

wound·wort (wōōnd′wûrt′, -wôrt′) n. **1.** Any of several plants of the genus *Stachys*, having downy leaves formerly used to treat wounds. **2.** Any of several similarly used plants.

wove. Past tense and rare past participle of **weave.**

woven. Past participle of **weave.**

wove paper n. Paper made on a closely woven wire roller or mold and having a very faint mesh pattern or none at all. Compare **laid paper.**

wow¹ (wou) interj. Informal. Used in expressing wonder, amazement, or the like.
—n. Informal. An outstanding success.
—tr.v. **wowed, wowing, wows.** Informal. To have a strong and usually pleasurable impact on.

wow² n. A slow variation in the pitch of sound reproduced by a record player or tape recorder, usually the result of irregular movement of a mechanical part. [Imitative.]

wow·ser (wou′zər) n. Australian Slang. An extremely puritanical person; a prude, killjoy, or teetotaler. [20th century : from English dialect *wow* (imitative), to wail, whine, complain.]

WPA Work Projects Administration.

W particle n. A large elementary participle hypothesized to be responsible for weak interaction.

w.p.m. words per minute.

W.r. Medicine. Wassermann reaction.

wrack¹ (răk) n. **1.** A remnant or vestige of something destroyed. **2. a.** Wreckage, especially of a ship cast ashore. **b.** Regional. Violent destruction of a building or vehicle. **3.** A tangled mass of seaweed or other marine vegetation, cast ashore or floating. **4.** Variant of **rack** (ruin).
—tr.v. **wracked, wracking, wracks.** To cause the ruin of; wreck. [Middle English *wrack*, Old English *wræc*, punishment, vengeance, and Middle Dutch *wrak*, wreckage, wrecked ship.]

wrack² Variant of **rack** (clouds).

wraith (rāth) n. **1.** An apparition of a living person, supposed to appear just before he dies. **2.** The ghost of a dead person. **3.** Anything pale and insubstantial. [16th century Scottish : origin obscure.]

Wran·gel or **Wran·gell Island** (răng′gəl). Island, 4,507 square kilometers (1,740 square miles), in the Arctic Ocean between the East Siberian Sea and the Chukchi Sea, off northeastern U.S.S.R. It is a breeding ground for polar bears, polar foxes, and seals.

Wrangell Mountains Range in southern Alaska, extending c. 160 kilometers (100 miles) southeast from the Copper River to the Canadian border. Mt. Blackburn (5,040 meters; 16,523 feet) is the highest peak.

wran·gle (răng′gəl) v. **-gled, -gling, -gles.** —intr. **1.** To dispute noisily or angrily; quarrel; bicker. **2.** To engage in debate or controversy. —tr. **1. a.** To win or obtain by argument. **b.** To force or persuade (someone) by argument. **2.** Western U.S. To herd (horses or other livestock). —See Synonyms at **argue.**
—n. **1.** An angry, noisy, or vehement argument or dispute. **2.** The act of wrangling. [Middle English *wranglen,* probably from Low German origin; akin to Low German *wrangeln.*]

wran·gler (răng′glər) n. **1.** One who wrangles. **2.** A cowboy, especially one who tends saddle horses. **3.** In Britain, a student who gains first-class honors in mathematics at Cambridge University.

wrap (răp) v. **wrapped** or **wrapt, wrapping, wraps.** —tr. **1.** To arrange or fold about in order to cover or protect something: *She wrapped her coat around her.* **2.** To cover, envelop, pack, or encase. **3.** To clasp, fold, or coil about something: *She wrapped her arms around his neck.* **4.** To envelop and obscure, often with the effect of concealing or disguising the nature of: *Fog wrapped the countryside.* **5.** To immerse in a specified condition. Usually used in the passive: *wrapped in grief; wrapped in thought.* —intr. **1.** To coil, wind, or twist about or around something: *The flag wrapped around the pole.* **2.** To put on warm clothing. Usually used with **up.**
—n. **1. a.** A garment to be wrapped or folded about a person, especially about the shoulders, such as a cloak or shawl. **b. wraps.** Warm outer clothing. **2.** A blanket. **3.** A wrapping or wrapper. **4.** Computer Science. A single turn of metallic magnetic tape in a tape-wound magnetic core. —**keep under wraps.** To keep secret or concealed. —**take the wraps off.** To disclose to the public; reveal. [Middle English *wrappen.*]

wrap·a·round (răp′ə-round′) adj. **1.** Having ends that curve back or that overlap the sides: *wraparound sunglasses.* **2.** Designating a garment, such as a skirt, that is open to the hem and wrapped around the body before being fastened.
—n. **1.** A wraparound garment. **2.** Printing. A flexible relief plate wrapped around a cylinder in letterpress printing.

wrap·per (răp′ər) n. **1.** One that wraps. **2.** The paper or other material in which something is wrapped: *a candy wrapper.* **3.** The paper encircling a magazine or newspaper sent by post. **4.** Chiefly British. A book jacket. **5.** The tobacco leaf covering a cigar. **6.** A loose dressing gown or negligee.

wrap·ping (răp′ĭng) n. Sometimes **wrappings.** The material in which something is wrapped.

wrapt. Alternate past tense of **wrap.**

wrap up tr.v. **1.** To settle finally or successfully; conclude; summarize: *wrap up a business deal.* **2.** To encompass in a few words; summarize.
—**wrapped up.** Immersed or absorbed: *wrapped up in his research.*

wrap-up (răp′ŭp′) n. A brief summary of the news.

wrasse (răs) n. Any of numerous chiefly tropical, often brightly colored marine fishes of the family Labridae. [Cornish and Welsh *gwrach†,* "old woman."]

wrath (răth, räth) n. **1.** Violent, resentful anger; rage; fury. **2.** Divine retribution. **3.** Archaic. A fit of violent anger. —See Synonyms at **anger.**
—adj. Archaic. Wrathful. [Middle English *wrath(th)e,* Old English *wrǣththu,* from *wrāth,* angry.]

Wrath, Cape. Promontory on the northwestern extremity of the Scottish mainland. The headland, 112 meters (368 feet) high, has a lighthouse.

wrath·ful (răth′fəl, räth′-) adj. **1.** Full of wrath; fiercely angry. **2.** Proceeding from or expressing wrath: *wrathful vengeance.* —**wrath·ful·ly** adv. —**wrath·ful·ness** n.

wreak (rēk) tr.v. **wreaked, wreaking, wreaks. 1.** To inflict (vengeance or punishment) upon a person. **2.** To express or gratify (anger, malevolence, or resentment); vent. **3.** To bring about; cause: *wreak havoc.* **4.** Archaic. To take vengeance for; avenge. [Middle English *wreken,* Old English *wrecan,* to drive, expel.] —**wreak·er** n.

wreath (rēth) n., pl. **wreaths** (rēthz). **1. a.** A ring or circlet of flowers or leaves worn on the head, placed as a memorial, or used as a decoration. **b.** A representation of this, as in woodwork. **2.** A curling shape; a ring: *wreaths of smoke.* [Middle English *wrethe,* Old English *writha,* from weak grade of *writhan,* to WRITE.]

wreathe (rēth) v. **wreathed, wreathing, wreathes.** —tr. **1.** To twist, coil, or entwine into a wreath or a wreathlike shape or contour. **2.** To crown, decorate, or encircle with or as if with a wreath. **3.** To coil or curl. **4.** To form a wreath around. —intr. **1.** To assume the form of a wreath. **2.** To curl, writhe, or spiral: *The smoke wreathed upward.* [From WREATH.]

wreck (rĕk) n. **1. a.** The action of wrecking or the condition of being wrecked; destruction. **b.** The accidental destruction of a ship; shipwreck. **2.** The stranded hulk of a ship that has been gravely damaged, as by being driven onto rocks. **3.** The remains of something that has been wrecked or ruined. **4.** Fragments of a ship or its cargo cast ashore by the sea after a shipwreck; wreckage. **5.** A person, animal, or thing in a shattered, dilapidated, or debilitated state: *He's a nervous wreck.*
—v. **wrecked, wrecking, wrecks.** —tr. **1.** To cause to undergo shipwreck. **2.** To bring to a state of ruin; disable or destroy; undermine. —intr. To suffer destruction, ruin, or shipwreck. —See Synonyms at **ruin.** [Middle English *wrek,* from Norman French *wrec,* from Scandinavian; akin to Old Norse *(v)rek,* wreckage.]

wreck·age (rĕk′ĭj) n. **1.** The act of wrecking or the condition of being wrecked. **2.** The debris of anything wrecked.

wreck·er (rĕk′ər) n. **1.** One that wrecks or destroys: *a wrecker of dreams.* **2.** A person who demolishes buildings or breaks up motor vehicles for a living. **3. a.** A person, piece of equipment, or vehicle employed in recovering or removing a wreck. **b.** One who salvages wrecked cargo or parts. **4. a.** Formerly, one who lured a vessel to destruction, as on a rocky coastline, in order to plunder. **b.** Archaic. A plunderer.

wreck·fish (rĕk′fĭsh′) n., pl. **-fishes** or collectively **wreckfish.** The stone bass (see). [From its often being found near wrecks.]

wrecking bar n. A small crowbar with a claw at one end and a slight curve at the other.

wren (rĕn) n. **1.** Any of various small, brownish birds of the family Troglodytidae. **2.** Any of various similar birds. [Middle English *wrenne,* Old English *wrenna,* from Germanic *wrend(il)a-* (unattested).]

Wren (rĕn) n. British Informal. A member of the Women's Royal Naval Service.

Wren (rĕn), **Sir Christopher** (1632–1723). English architect and mathematician. Educated at Oxford, he became professor of astronomy at both London (1657) and Oxford (1661) universities and helped form the Royal Society. He designed St. Paul's Cathedral, Greenwich Hospital, and the Pembroke College chapel at Cambridge. See feature, next page.

wrench (rĕnch) n. **1.** A sudden sharp, forcible twist or turn. **2.** An injury produced by twisting or straining. **3.** A sudden tug at one's emotions; a surge of sorrow, anguish, or similar emotion. **4. a.** A break in relations or a parting that causes emotional distress. **b.** The pain this causes. **5.** A deliberate distortion in the original form or meaning of something written or spoken. **6.** Any of various tools with fixed or adjustable jaws for gripping, especially for gripping a nut, bolt, or pipe, and a long handle for effective leverage in turning.
—v. **wrenched, wrenching, wrenches.** —tr. **1. a.** To twist or turn suddenly and forcibly. **b.** To twist and sprain: *wrenched her knee.* **2. a.** To force free by pulling at; yank; wrest. Usually used with *off* or *away.* **b.** To pull with a wrench. **3.** To pull at the feelings or emotions of; distress: *It wrenched her to say good-bye.* **4.** To distort or twist the original character or import of: *wrenched the text to prove her point.* —intr. To give a wrench, twist, or turn. [Middle English *wrenchen,* to twist, wrench, Old English *wrencan,* to twist.]

wrest (rĕst) tr.v. **wrested, wresting, wrests. 1.** To obtain by or as if by pulling with violent twisting movements: *wrest a book out of another's hands.* **2.** To usurp forcefully: *wrest power.* **3.** To obtain or extract by extortion, guile, or persistent effort: *wrest the meaning from an obscure poem.* **4. a.** To distort or twist the nature or meaning of: *wrested my words out of context.* **b.** To misapply.
—n. **1.** The action or an instance of wresting. **2.** A small key formerly used to turn the wrest pins of a harp or piano. [Middle

wren One of the smallest North American songbirds, Troglodytes troglodytes (above) lives under uprooted tree stumps or under stream banks, feeding mostly on insects. It is also known as the winter wren.

ST. PAUL'S: MONUMENT TO A GENIUS

Wren planned his dome to rival St. Peter's, Rome

The dome of St. Paul's Cathedral dignifies the heart of London, a glorious memorial to England's greatest architect, Sir Christopher Wren (1632–1723). Wren was one of the geniuses of the age of learning that swept Europe after the Renaissance. He was a brilliant Oxford student, described by Isaac Newton as one of the greatest geometricians of his age. Wren was first a scientist, working in physics, and became professor of astronomy at Oxford when only 29.

His career as an architect began in 1663 when his uncle, the Bishop of Ely, asked him to design the chapel for Pembroke College, Cambridge. He went to France to study architecture in 1665.

The Fire of London (1666) gave Wren the op-portunity to exercise his creative genius. He was one of the commissioners in charge of rebuilding, and although his ideas for sweeping avenues and spacious squares were not accepted, many of his 52 churches, built between 1670 and 1686 in distinctive classical styles, are still noted London landmarks.

St. Paul's, Wren's masterpiece, was begun in 1675, and his son Christopher laid the last stone in 1710. Wren himself was the first man to be buried there. Other Wren buildings include Trinity College Library, Cambridge (1676–84), Chelsea Hospital (1682–92), and the south and east wings of Hampton Court Palace (1689–94). Wren was knighted in 1673.

SHELDONIAN THEATRE *This D-shaped theater in Oxford, built between 1664 and 1669, was one of Wren's earliest buildings.*

THE FIRST DESIGN *The façade of Pembroke College chapel, Cambridge, Wren's first building (left). It led Wren to his life's work as an architect.*

PINNACLE OF GENIUS *Wren's great dome of St. Paul's has a bowl-shaped inner dome around which a brick cone supports an outer dome and the surmounting lantern. Only the windows at the base of the lantern are visible through the eye of the inner dome, casting light some 83 meters (274 feet) to the nave floor.*

English *wresten,* Old English *wrǣstan,* to twist; akin to WRIST.]
—**wrest·er** *n.*

wres·tle (rĕs′əl) *v.* **-tled, -tling, -tles.** —*intr.* **1.** To take part in a fight or competition consisting of grappling and attempting to throw or immobilize one's opponent, especially under certain contest rules. **2.** To contend; struggle; grapple. Used with *with* or *against: city planners wrestling with budget cuts.* **3.** To strive in an effort to gain mastery: *wrestle with temptation.* —*tr.* **1. a.** To take part in (a wrestling match). **b.** To wrestle with. **2.** To make (one's way, for example) by or as if by wrestling: *wrestled her way through the crowd.* **3.** *Western U.S.* To throw (a calf or other animal) for branding.
~*n.* **1.** An act of wrestling; especially, a wrestling match. **2.** A struggle. [Middle English *wrest(e)len,* Old English *wrǣstlian.*]
—**wres·tler** *n.*

wres·tling (rĕs′lĭng) *n.* Any of various gymnastic exercises or contests between two competitors and sometimes teams who attempt to throw or immobilize each other by grappling.

wrest pin *n.* Any of the pins to which the strings, especially of a keyboard stringed instrument, are attached and by which they are tuned.

wretch (rĕch) *n.* **1.** A miserable, unfortunate, or unhappy person. **2.** A base, mean, or despicable person: *"A stony adversary, an inhuman wretch"* (Shakespeare). [Middle English *wrecche,* Old English *wrecca,* wretch, exile.]

wretch·ed (rĕch′ĭd) *adj.* **1.** Living in degradation and misery; miserable: *wretched beggars huddling on the pavement.* **2.** Attended by misery and woes: *a wretched life.* **3.** Of a poor or mean character; dismal: *a wretched building.* **4.** Contemptible; despicable: *wretched treatment of prisoners.* **5.** Inferior in performance or quality: *a wretched translation.* **6.** Very unpleasant; deplorable. **7.** Used as an intensive: *a wretched nuisance.* —See Synonyms at **sad.** [Middle English *wrecched,* irregularly from *wrecche,* WRETCH.] —**wretch·ed·ly** *adv.* —**wretch·ed·ness** *n.*

wri·er. Alternate comparative of **wry.**

wri·est. Alternate superlative of **wry.**

wrig·gle (rĭg′əl) *v.* **-gled, -gling, -gles.** —*intr.* **1.** To turn or twist the body with sinuous writhing motions; squirm. **2.** To proceed with writhing motions. **3.** To worm one's way into or out of a situation; insinuate or extricate oneself by sly or subtle means: *He's always wriggling out of his responsibilities.* —*tr.* **1.** To move with a wriggling motion: *wriggle a toe.* **2.** To make (one's way, for example) by wriggling: *He wriggled his way into favor.*
~*n.* **1.** A wriggling movement. **2.** A sinuous path, line, marking, or the like. [Middle English *wrigglen,* from Middle Low German *wriggeln.*] —**wrig·gler** *n.* —**wrig·gly** *adj.*

wright (rīt) *n.* A person who constructs or repairs something. Now used only in combination: *playwright; shipwright.* [Middle English *wright,* Old English *wryhta, wyrhta.*]

Wright (rīt), **Frank Lloyd** (1869–1959). U.S. architect. He studied civil engineering and adapted its methods to architecture. Famous examples of his work include the Robie House (1909) in Chicago and the inside of the Guggenheim Museum (1946–56).

Wright, Orville (1871–1948) and **Wilbur** (1867–1912). U.S. pioneer aviators. The brothers ran a bicycle firm until they made the first successful powered flight in a heavier-than-air machine (1903).

Wright, Richard (1908–60). U.S. author. Recognized as a major writer after the publication of his novel *Native Son* (1940), he wrote several novels, primarily about life as a black American. While living as an expatriate in Europe, he wrote *The Outsider* (1953), considered by many to be the first existential novel by an American.

wring (rĭng) *v.* **wrung** (rŭng) *or rare* **winged, wringing, wrings.** —*tr.* **1.** To twist, squeeze, or compress, especially so as to extract liquid. Often used with *out.* **2.** To extract (liquid) by twisting or compressing. **3.** To wrench or twist forcibly or painfully: *wring someone's neck.* **4.** To clasp and twist or squeeze (one's hands), as in distress. **5.** To take hold of and shake energetically, as in congratulation: *The mayor wrung my hand.* **6.** To cause distress to; affect with painful emotion: *wring someone's heart.* **7.** To obtain or extract by applying force or pressure: *wring the truth out of a person.* —*intr.* To writhe or squirm, as in pain.
~*n.* The act or an instance of wringing; a squeeze or twist. [Middle English *wringen,* Old English *wringan.*]

wring·er (rĭng′ər) *n.* One that wrings; especially, a device in which laundry is pressed between rollers to extract water.

wring·ing (rĭng′ĭng) *adv.* Used as in intensive in the phrase *wringing wet.*

wrin·kle¹ (rĭng′kəl) *n.* **1.** A small furrow, ridge, or crease on a normally smooth surface, caused by crumpling, folding, or shrinking. **2.** A line or crease in the skin, as from age.
~*v.* **wrinkled, -kling, -kles.** —*tr.* **1.** To make a wrinkle or wrinkles in. **2.** To draw up so as to form wrinkles; pucker: *wrinkle one's nose in disdain.* —*intr.* To acquire or be affected with wrinkles. [Middle English, back-formation from *wrinkled,* wrinkled, probably Old English *gewrinclod,* serrated, winding, participle of *gewrinclian,* to wind.] —**wrin·kly** *adj.*

wrin·kle² *n. Informal.* An ingenious trick or method; a clever innovation. [Middle English *wrinkel,* crooked action, trick, specialized use of *wrinkle,* WRINKLE.]

wrist (rĭst) *n.* **1. a.** The junction between the hand and forearm. **b.** *Anatomy.* The system of bones forming this junction. Also called "carpus." **2.** The part of a sleeve or glove that encircles the wrist. [Middle English *wrist,* Old English *wrist.*]

Wright

BUILDINGS FOR A "NEW TOMORROW"

Pioneer of open-plan interiors in homes and offices

After studying civil engineering at the University of Wisconsin, Frank Lloyd Wright (1869-1959) worked for Louis H. Sullivan, the great Chicago architect. He became Sullivan's chief assistant and took an active part in some of the great achievements in Chicago's commercial architecture. In 1889 Wright began accepting commissions of his own and set up his Oak Park, Illinois, studio. During the next 20 years he built his revolutionary "Prairie houses," characterized by low-slung roof planes, ribbon windows, and terraces that extend the house into the landscape. The Prairie house demonstrated Wright's theory of "organic architecture," according to which buildings should blend naturally with their surroundings.

Wright was a structural innovator as well, experimenting with steel cantilevers and poured concrete. He was the first to introduce open planning by eliminating confining walls in buildings and create dynamic interiors with spiral ramps. The Johnson Wax Building in Racine, Wisconsin (1939), Taliesin West, his Arizona winter home and studio (1938), the Kaufmann House in Pennsylvania (1936), and the Guggenheim Museum in New York City (1960) are striking examples of Wright's creative genius.

In a professional career spanning 70 years, Wright built close to 500 structures and designed scores more. His work was daring and controversial, but always in the forefront of modern architecture. He once summed it up: "I am not interested in the architecture of yesterday, or today even, I am constructing a new tomorrow."

FALLING WATER *Built for the Pittsburgh department store owner Edgar Kaufmann, this house at Bear Run, Pennsylvania, is cantilevered out over a natural waterfall. The core of the house is a rocky ledge that forms the hearth of the fireplace.*

wrist·band (rĭst'bănd') *n.* A band, as on a long sleeve or on a wristwatch, that encircles the wrist.

wrist·drop (rĭst'drŏp') *n.* Paralysis of the muscles that raise back the hand, caused by compression of the nerve or by damage to the nerve, as in lead poisoning.

wrist·let (rĭst'lĭt) *n.* **1.** A band of material worn around the wrist for warmth or support. **2.** A bracelet.

wrist·lock (rĭst'lŏk') *n.* A wrestling hold in which an opponent's wrist is gripped and twisted to immobilize him.

wrist pin *n.* **1.** A pin attached to a wheel parallel to its axle, to function as a bearing for a crank. **2.** A pin that joins a piston to its connecting rod. In this sense, also called "gudgeon pin."

wrist·watch (rĭst'wŏch') *n.* A watch on a band worn about the wrist.

wris·ty (rĭs'tē) *adj.* Using or characterized by flexible movements of the wrist: *a wristy conducting style.*

writ¹ (rĭt) *n.* **1.** *Law.* A written order issued by a court, commanding the person to whom it is addressed to perform or cease performing some stated act. **2.** *Archaic.* Writings: *Holy Writ.* [Middle English *writ,* Old English *writ,* from Germanic *wrītan* (unattested), to scratch. See **write.**]

writ². *Archaic.* Past tense and past participle of **write.** —**writ large.** On a magnified scale; in a large or emphasized form: *He treated war just as a childhood game writ large.*

write (rīt) *v.* **wrote** (rōt) or *archaic* **writ** (rĭt), **written** (rĭt'n) or *archaic* **writ, writing, writes.** —*tr.* **1.** To form (letters, symbols, words, or sentences) on a surface such as paper, using a pen, pencil, or other tool. **2.** To spell: *How do you write your name?* **3.** To form (words) in cursive rather than printed script. **4.** To compose, especially as an author or musician: *write a memo; write a symphony; write one's memoirs.* **5.** To draw up in legal form; draft: *write a will.* **6.** To fill in with the required information: *write a check.* **7.** To cover with writing: *wrote five pages in an hour.* **8.** To set down; record: *write one's thoughts.* **9.** To relate or communicate by writing: *wrote that he was planning to extend his vacation.* **10.** To underwrite (an insurance policy). **11.** To have sufficient knowledge of (a language or writing system) to be able to compose in it in writing: *able to read German but not write it. She can speak Chinese but can't write it.* **12.** To depict clearly; mark: *"Utter dejection was written on every face"* (Winston Churchill). **13.** To ordain by fate or prophecy: *It is written that the Empire will fall.* **14.** *Computer Science.* To record (data) in a computer storage device. **15.** To send a letter to. —*intr.* **1.** To trace or form letters, words, or symbols on paper or another surface. **2.** To produce articles, books, or other matter to be read. **3.** To compose a letter or letters; communicate by letter: *wrote to say he'd be three days late.* —**write out.** **1.** To set down fully in writing. **2.** To remove (a character) from a long-running radio or television serial. [Middle English *writen,* Old English *wrītan,* from Germanic *wrītan* (unattested), to tear, scratch.]

write down *tr.v.* **1.** To put into writing. **2.** To reduce in rank, value, or price. **3.** To disparage in writing. **4.** To write in an affectedly simple or condescending style. Often used with *to.*

write-down (rīt'doun') *n. Accounting.* A reduction of the book value of an asset.

write in *intr.v.* To communicate or make a request by letter. —*tr.* **1.** To cast a vote for (one not listed on a ballot), as by inserting his name. **2.** To cast (a vote) in this way.

write-in (rīt'ĭn') *n.* **1.** A vote for one not listed on a ballot, usually cast by the insertion of his name in a space provided. **2.** A candidate voted for in this way. Also used adjectively: *a write-in campaign.*

write off *tr.v.* **1.** To reduce to zero the book value of (an asset that has become worthless). **2.** To cancel from accounts as a loss. **3.** To consider with resignation as a loss or failure.

write-off (rīt'ôf', -ŏf') *n.* **1. a.** A cancellation in account books. **b.** The amount canceled or lost. **2.** A reduction or depreciation of the entered value of an item.

writ·er (rī'tər) *n.* **1.** A person who has written (something specified): *the writer of the note.* **2.** A person who writes as an occupation; an author.

writer's cramp *n.* A cramp chiefly affecting the muscles of the thumb and two adjacent fingers after prolonged writing.

write up *tr.v.* **1.** To write a report or description of, as for publication. **2.** To bring (a journal, for example) up to date. **3.** To report (someone) for breaking the law or violating certain rules. **4.** To overstate the value of (assets).

write-up (rīt'ŭp') *n.* **1.** A published account, review, or notice, especially a favorable one. **2.** An illegal over-evaluation of a corporation's assets.

writhe (rīth) *v.* **writhed, writhed** or *archaic* **writhen** (rĭth'ən), **writhing, writhes.** —*intr.* **1.** To twist or squirm, as in pain, struggle, or embarrassment. **2.** To move with a twisting or contorted motion. —*tr.* To cause to twist or squirm; contort: *"He writhed himself quite off his stool in the excitement of his feelings"* (Charles Dickens). ~*n.* An act or instance of writhing; a contortion. [Middle English *writhen,* Old English *wrīthan.*] —**writh·er** *n.*

writ·ing (rī'tĭng) *n.* **1.** Written form: *Put it in writing.* **2. a.** Language symbols or characters written or imprinted on a surface. **b.** The art of using such symbols as a means of communication: *the invention of writing.* **3.** Any written work; especially, a literary composition. **4.** The activity, art, or occupation of a writer. **5.** Handwriting or handwritten matter: *couldn't read his writing.* —**the writing (or handwriting) on the wall.** An indication of approaching defeat or catastrophe. ~*adj.* Of, pertaining to, or used in writing: *writing paper.*

Writ·ings (rī'tĭngz) *pl.n.* Hagiographa (*see*). Preceded by *the.*

writ of election *n. Law.* A writ issued by a governor or other executive authority requiring that an election be held, especially a special election to fill a vacancy.

writ of error *n. Law.* A writ commissioning an appellate court to review the proceedings of another court and correct the judgment given if deemed necessary.

writ of execution *n. Law.* A writ ordering the enforcement of a judgment.

writ of prohibition *n. Law.* An order issued by a higher court,

Wyeth

THE PAINTER WHO REJECTED THE MODERN WORLD

Millions of Americans flock to Wyeth's exhibitions to view his vision of the past

The appeal of Andrew Wyeth—America's most popular living painter—is based on his rejection of the modern, commercialized world. His detailed and realistic canvases show artifacts and buildings that were made to last—such as rural houses in which generations of workers lived and died. His nostalgia for a lost America and his emphasis on the value of old-fashioned craftsmanship have drawn millions to his exhibitions. In the United States only Picasso's works have a greater mass appeal.

Born in 1917, he learned his craft from his father Newell Convers Wyeth, a painter and book illustrator. He was 20 when he held his first one-man show, in Philadelphia. As a mature artist, he has confined his work to rural areas in Maine and Pennsylvania. Working mainly in tempera (a mixture of powder color and egg yolk), he paints with a visionary quality that lifts his work above simple naturalism.

His major paintings include *Wind from the Sea* (1947), *Christina's World* (1948), *The Patriot* (1964), and *Witching Hour* (1977).

CHRISTINA'S WORLD *Christina Olson, a New England polio victim, reminded Wyeth of a "wounded seagull." He watched her hauling herself back home after gathering vegetables in a nearby field. The picture, he said, was more than just her portrait. "It really was her whole life."*

commanding a lower court to cease from proceeding in some matter not within its jurisdiction.

writ of summons *n. Law.* A writ directing a person to appear in court to answer a complaint.

writ·ten. Past participle of **write**.

wrnt. warrant.

Wroc·law (vrôt′släf′). Capital and port of Wroclaw province, southwestern Poland, on the Oder River. It was a Hanseatic city (1368–1474) before passing to the Hapsburgs (1526) and Prussia (1742).

wrong (rông, rŏng) *adj.* **1.** Not correct; erroneous. **2. a.** Contrary to conscience, morality, or law; wicked; immoral. **b.** Unfair or unjust. **3.** Not required, intended, or wanted: *We took a wrong turn.* **4.** Not fitting or suitable; inappropriate; improper: *the wrong moment.* **5.** Not in accordance with an established usage, method, or procedure. **6.** Not functioning properly; out of order; amiss. **7.** Unacceptable or undesirable according to social convention. ~*adv.* **1.** In a wrong manner or direction; mistakenly; erroneously. **2.** Immorally or unjustly: *behaved wrong.* —**do someone wrong.** To be unfaithful. —**go wrong. 1.** To take a wrong turn or make a wrong move: *Where did we go wrong?* **2.** To go astray morally. **3.** To happen or turn out badly; go amiss. ~*n.* **1. a.** That which is morally wrong: *to know right from wrong.* **b.** An unjust, injurious, or immoral act or circumstance. **2. a.** An invasion or violation of another's legal rights. **b.** *Law.* An infringement, especially one leading to a civil action; a tort. **3.** The condition of being mistaken or to blame: *in the wrong.* —See Synonyms at **injustice.** ~*tr.v.* **wronged, wronging, wrongs. 1.** To treat unjustly or injuriously. **2.** To discredit unjustly; malign. **3.** To treat dishonorably; especially, to seduce (a woman). [Middle English *wrang, wrong,* probably from Scandinavian; akin to Danish *vrang,* Old Norse *rangr* and *vrangr* (unattested), awry; akin to WRING.] —**wrong·er** *n.* —**wrong·ly** *adv.*

Usage: The adverbs *wrong* and *wrongly* are frequently interchangeable, especially in the sense of "erroneously." *Wrong* is more common in that sense except when the adverb occurs before the verb or the participle that it modifies: *She advised us wrong* (less often *wrongly. He spelled it wrong* (less often *wrongly.) Wrongly* is preferred in: *a wrongly conceived plan; a wrongly arranged compartment.*

wrong·do·er (rông′dōō′ər, rŏng′-) *n.* One who does wrong morally or legally. —**wrong·do·ing** *n.*

wrong font *n. Abbr.* **wf** *Printing.* The incorrect font. Used, as in proofreading, to indicate a typeface of the wrong kind.

wrong·foot (rông′fŏŏt′, rŏng′-) *tr.v.* **-footed, -footing, -foots. 1.** In tennis and various other sports, to mislead (one's opponent) into balancing on the wrong foot, and thereby pass him on the other side. **2.** To mislead or surprise (a person) into an embarrassing or foolish action: *He wrong-footed me with a surprise question.*

wrong·ful (rông′fəl, rŏng′-) *adj.* **1.** Wrong; injurious; marked by injustice or unfairness: *wrongful dismissal.* **2.** Contrary to law; unlawful; illegal. —**wrong·ful·ly** *adv.* —**wrong·ful·ness** *n.*

wrong-head·ed (rông'hĕd'ĭd, rŏng'-) adj. 1. Persistently erroneous in judgment. 2. Wrong in stubborn defiance of the evidence. —**wrong-head·ed·ly** adv. —**wrong-head·ed·ness** n.

wrote. Past tense of **write.**

wroth (rôth) adj. Archaic. Wrathful; angry. [Middle English wrath, wroth, Old English wrāth.]

wrought (rôt). Archaic. Past tense and past participle of **work.**
~adj. 1. Created or put together with care and deliberation. 2. Shaped by hammering with tools, rather than by casting. Said of metals or metalwork. 3. Made or embellished delicately or elaborately. —**wrought up.** Agitated; excited.

wrought iron n. An easily welded or forged iron containing approximately 0.2 percent carbon and total impurities less than approximately 0.5 percent. —**wrought-i·ron** adj.

wrung. Past tense and past participle of **wring.**

wry (rī) adj. **wrier** or **wryer, wriest** or **wryest.** 1. Temporarily twisted in an expression of distaste or displeasure: On tasting the wine, she made a wry face. 2. Drily humorous, often with a touch of irony. 3. Abnormally twisted or bent to one side; crooked. Said of the features or the neck. 4. At variance with what is right, proper, or suitable; perverse. [Middle English wrien, to bend, twist, turn aside, Old English wrīgian, to proceed, turn.] —**wry·ly** adv. —**wry·ness** n.

wry·bill (rī'bĭl') n. A plover native to New Zealand, Anarhynchus frontalis, having a right-handed twist to its beak.

wry·neck (rī'nĕk') n. 1. Either of two Old World birds, Jynx torquilla or J. ruficollis, that are capable of twisting the neck all the way around to look backward. 2. Pathology. **Torticollis** (see).

WSW west-southwest.

wt. weight.

Wu (woo) n. Any of various Chinese dialects spoken in the valley and delta regions of the Chang Jiang (Yangtze River.) [Mandarin, wú.]

Wu·han (woo'hän'). Capital and port of Hubei province, People's Republic of China. Situated at the confluence of the Chang Jiang and the Han Shui, it is formed from the cities of Hanyang, Wuchang, and Hankou Yangtze.

Wuhsien. See **Suzhou.**

wul·fen·ite (wool'fə-nīt') n. A yellow to orange-red or brown mineral, PbMoO₄, used as a molybdenum ore. [German Wulfenit, after Franz X. von Wulfen (1728–1805), Austrian mineralogist.]

Wun·der·kind (woon'dər-kĭnt') n., pl. **-kinds** or **-kinder** (-kĭn'dər). Sometimes wunderkind. 1. A person who attains great success or an advanced position in his profession, art, or the like at a relatively early age. 2. A child prodigy. [German, "wonder child."]

wurst (wûrst, woorst) n. A large sausage of seasoned and usually cooked meat, of a type produced in German-speaking countries. [German Wurst, from Old High German wurst.]

Würt·tem·berg (wûr'təm-bûrg'). Former kingdom of southwest West Germany. A duchy from 1495, it was a kingdom (1806–1918) and joined the German Reich in 1870. It was incorporated (1952) into the newly formed state of Baden-Württemberg.

wuth·er·ing (wŭth'ər-ĭng) adj. Northern British. 1. Affected by swirling wind; blustery. 2. Blowing strongly and noisily. Said of the wind. [Variant of dialect whithering, from whither, to bluster, from Scandinavian; akin to Old Norse hvitha, squall of wind, Old English hwitha, breeze.]

Wutsin. See **Changzhou.**

Wuxian. See **Suzhou.**

WV West Virginia (used with a Zip Code).

W. Va. West Virginia.

W.W.I World War I.

W.W.II World War II.

WWF World Wildlife Fund.

WY Wyoming (used with a Zip Code).

Wy·an·dot, Wy·an·dotte (wī'ən-dŏt') n., pl. **-dots** or collectively **Wyandot, -dottes** or collectively **Wyandotte.** 1. A North American Indian of a tribe in the Huron confederacy. 2. The Iroquoian language spoken by the Wyandot. [Wyandot wädát, tribal name.]

Wy·an·dotte (wī'ən-dŏt') n. 1. A domestic fowl of a breed developed in North America. 2. Variant of **Wyandot.**

Wy·att (wī'ət), **Sir Thomas** (c. 1503–42). English poet and courtier. In Henry VIII's favor, he was sent on various missions abroad but was twice imprisoned on a charge of being the lover of Anne Boleyn (1536) and for suspected treason (1541). He is credited with the introduction of the Petrarchan sonnet into English poetry.

wych elm, witch elm (wĭch) n. 1. An Old World elm, Ulmus glabra, often planted as a shade tree. 2. The wood of this tree. [Middle English wyche, Old English wice.]

wych hazel. Variant of **witch hazel.**

Wyc·liffe (wĭk'lĭf), **John** (c. 1329–84). English religious reformer. He spoke out against Church abuses and despite papal censure issued a condemnation of absolution, penances, and indulgences, denied transubstantiation, and issued the first translation of the Bible in English. He sent out itinerant preachers to spread his philosophy, but his followers, called Lollards, were imprisoned, although Wycliffe remained untouched. After his death, his works were again condemned by the Church.

wye (wī) n. 1. The letter y. 2. A Y-shaped object.

Wye (wī). River, c. 210 kilometers (130 miles) long, of eastern Wales and western England. Rising on Plynlimon Mt. in Wales, it flows generally southeast to the estuary of the Severn River. It is noted for its beautiful valley.

Wy·eth (wī'əth), **Andrew Newell** (1917–). U.S. painter. Working mainly in water color and egg tempera, he painted American landscapes and people in a restrained, naturalistic style. His many works include Christina's World (1948), That Gentleman (1960), Garret Room (1962), and Day of the Fair (1963).

Wyeth, James Browning, known as "Jamie" (1946–). U.S. artist. The son of Andrew Wyeth, he is known for his representational and richly detailed works, including a portrait of John F. Kennedy (1968) and numerous paintings of animals, such as Newfoundland (1971) and Angus (1974).

Wy·ler (wī'lər), **William** (1902–81). U.S. filmmaker. Generally considered one of the foremost Hollywood directors of the 1940's and 1950's, he received Academy Awards for his direction of Mrs. Miniver (1942), The Best Years of Our Lives (1946), and Ben-Hur (1959).

wynd (wīnd) n. Scottish. A narrow lane; an alley. [Middle English, probably from wynden, to go, Old English windan, to WIND.]

Wy·o·ming (wī-ō'mĭng). Abbr. Wyo. State of the western United States. With the Great Plains in the northeast and crossed by the Rocky Mts. in the west, it is rich in mineral reserves. Its capital is Cheyenne.

wy·vern, wi·vern (wī'vərn)n. A two-legged dragon with wings and a barbed and knotted tail. [17th century : Variant of earlier wyver, from Old French, from Latin vīpera, VIPER.]

wryneck A European bird, the wryneck is a member of the woodpecker family and lives on insects that it picks from tree bark with its long tongue. It twists its head into odd angles when startled and also during its courtship display.

x, X (ĕks) *n., pl.* **x's** (ĕk'sĭz) or **X's. 1.** The 24th letter of the modern English alphabet. **2.** Any of the speech sounds represented by this letter. **3.** Something shaped like the letter X. **4.** The mark X inscribed to represent the signature of an illiterate person. **5.** An unknown or unnamed factor, thing, or person. **6.** The 24th in a series; 23rd when *J* is omitted. **7.** The first in a series consisting of *x, y,* and *z.*

~*tr.v.* **x'd** (ĕkst), **x'ing** (ĕk'sĭng), **x's** (ĕk'sĭz) or **x-ed, x-ing, x's. 1.** To mark or sign with an x. **2.** To delete, cancel, or obliterate with a series of x's. Usually used with *out.*

x, X, x., X. *Note:* As an abbreviation or symbol, *x* may be a small or a capital letter, with or without a period. Established forms or those generally preferred precede the definition. When no form is given, all four forms are in general use in that sense. **1. X** A symbol for Christ or Christian. **2. x.** *Finance.* ex. **3. x** *Printing.* A symbol used, as in proofreading, to indicate a mechanical defect in type. **4. X** The symbol for a kiss. **5. X** A symbol placed on a map or diagram to mark the location or position of a point. **6. X** A symbol placed on a ballot paper, questionnaire, or the like, to indicate one's preference among alternatives. **7. x, X** The Roman numeral for ten. **8. x** A symbol used in marking school exercises, examination papers, or the like, to indicate an error. **9.** *Mathematics.* **x** The symbol for: **a.** An unknown number. **b.** An algebraic variable. **10. X** The symbol for reactance. **11.** *Biology.* Hybrid (cross).

X (ĕks) *n., pl.* **X's.** A rating assigned to motion pictures to which persons under a certain age, usually 17, may not be admitted. Also used adjectivally: *an X movie; an X rating.*

xan·thate (zăn'thāt') *n.* A salt or ester of a xanthic acid; especially, a simple xanthic acid salt, as of sodium or potassium, used as a flotation collector for copper, silver, and gold. [XANTH(O)- + -ATE.] —**xan·tha·tion** (zăn-thā'shən) *n.*

xan·thic acid (zăn'thĭk) *n.* Any of various unstable acids of the form ROC(S)SH, in which R is usually an alkyl radical. [Greek *xanthos†,* yellow (referring to the color of its salts).]

xan·thine (zăn'thēn', -thĭn) *n.* A yellowish-white purine base, $C_5H_4N_4O_2$, found in blood, urine, and some plants. [French *xanthine* : XANTH(O)- + -INE.]

Xan·thip·pe (zăn-tĭp'ē). The wife of Socrates; proverbial as a shrewish and scolding woman.

xantho-, xanth– *prefix.* Indicates the color yellow; for example, **xanthoma.** [New Latin, from Greek *xanthos†,* yellow.]

xan·tho·chroid (zăn'thə-kroid') *adj.* Having a light complexion and light hair.
~*n.* A xanthochroid individual. [New Latin *xanthochroi,* light-haired, fair-skinned people : XANTH(O)- + Greek *ōkhros,* pale, wan + -OID.]

xan·tho·ma (zăn-thō'mə) *n.* A skin disease characterized by nodular yellowish patches, especially on the eyelids. [New Latin : XANTH(O)- + -OMA.]

xan·tho·phyll (zăn'thə-fĭl') *n.* Any of a class of yellow carotenoid pigments, the commonest of which is lutein, found with chlorophyll in green plants and in egg yolk. [French *xanthophylle* : XANTHO- + -PHYLL.]

xan·thous (zăn'thəs) *adj.* **1.** Yellow. **2.** Having light-brown or yellowish skin. Compare **melanous.** [Greek *xanthos†,* yellow.]

Xan·thus (zăn'thəs). Ancient city of Lycia, western Asia Minor. On the Xanthus River in modern Turkey, it was captured by the Persians (*c.* 546 B.C.) and later the Romans (*c.* 42 B.C.).

Xavier, Saint Francis. See Saint Francis Xavier.

x-ax·is (ĕks'ăk'sĭs) *n., pl.* **x-axes** (-sēz). **1.** The horizontal axis of a two-dimensional Cartesian coordinate system. **2.** One of three axes in a three-dimensional Cartesian coordinate system.

X-chro·mo·some (ĕks'krō'mə-sōm') *n.* The larger of the two types of sex chromosome. It is associated with female characteristics in most animals, including humans, and occurs paired in the body cells of such female animals and paired with the **Y-chromosome** (see) in males.

Xe The symbol for the element xenon.

xe·bec, ze·bec, ze·beck (zē'bĕk') *n.* A small three-masted Mediterranean vessel with both square and triangular sails, once used commonly by Arab corsairs. [Earlier *chebec,* from French, from Italian *sciabecco,* from Arabic *shabbāk.*]

xe·ni·a (zē'nē-ə) *n. Botany.* An effect produced on a structure by the introduction of male genes; for example, a visible change in the endosperm of a seed caused by the pollen nucleus when it fuses with the endosperm nucleus. [New Latin, from Greek, the condition of a guest, from *xenos,* stranger, guest.]

xeno-, xen- *prefix.* Indicates strange, foreign, or different; for example, **xenolith, xenophobe.** [New Latin, from Greek *xenos,* stranger.]

xe·no·cryst (zĕn'ə-krĭst') *n.* A crystal foreign to the igneous rock in which it occurs. [XENO- + CRYST(AL).]

xe·nog·a·my (zĭ-nŏg'ə-mē) *n. Botany.* The transfer of pollen from one plant to another; cross-pollination. [XENO- + -GAMY.] —**xe·nog·a·mous** (zĭ-nŏg'ə-məs) *adj.*

xen·o·gen·e·sis (zĕn'ə-jĕn'ə-sĭs) *n. Biology.* **1.** The supposed production of offspring markedly different from and showing no relationship to either of its parents. **2. Alternation of generations** (see). [XENO- + -GENESIS.] —**xen·o·ge·net·ic** (zĕn'ə-jə-nĕt'ĭk), **xen·o·gen·ic** (zĕn'ə-jĕn'ĭk) *adj.*

xen·o·graft (zĕn'ə-grăft') *n.* A type of tissue graft, a **heterograft** (see). [XENO- + GRAFT.]

xen·o·lith (zĕn'ə-lĭth') *n.* A rock fragment foreign to the igneous mass in which it occurs. [XENO- + -LITH.]

xen·o·mor·phic (zĕn'ə-môr'fĭk) *adj.* Designating a mineral constituent of an igneous rock that lacks its characteristic crystal form as a result of deformation. [XENO- + -MORPHIC.]

xe·non (zē'nŏn') *n. Symbol* **Xe** A colorless, odorless, highly unreactive gaseous element found in minute quantities in the atmosphere, extracted commercially from liquefied air, and used in stroboscopic, bactericidal, and flash lamps and lasers. Atomic number 54, atomic weight 131.30, melting point –111.9°C, boiling point –108.1°C, density (gas) 5.887 grams per liter, specific gravity (liquid) 3.52 (–109°C). [Greek, neuter of *xenos,* stranger.]

xen·o·phobe (zĕn'ə-fōb') *n.* A person unduly fearful or contemptuous of strangers or foreigners or of foreign ideas and cultures, especially as reflected in his political or cultural views. [XENO- + -PHOBE.] —**xen·o·pho·bi·a** (zĕn'ə-fō'bē-ə) *n.* —**xen·o·pho·bic** (zĕn'ə-fō'bĭk) *adj.*

Xen·o·phon (zĕn'ə-fən) (*c.* 430–354 B.C.). Greek soldier, essayist, and historian. In his *Apology,* he gave an account of the death of Socrates, of whom he was a friend and pupil. He accompanied the expedition of Cyrus the Younger against King Artaxerxes Mnemon of Persia and on the death of Cyrus (401 B.C.) assumed command of 10,000 men. He led his troops from the center of the Persian Empire to the Black Sea and recorded their harrowing journey in the *Anabasis.*

xen·o·pus (zĕn'ə-pəs) *n.* A clawed toad of the African genus *Xenopus;* especially *X. laevis,* which has been used in pregnancy testing since it produces eggs when injected with the urine of a pregnant woman. In its native southern Africa the species *Xenopus laevis* is called the "platanna." [New Latin : XENO- + -*pus,* foot (see **-pod**).]

xer·ic (zĕr'ĭk, zîr'-) *adj.* Of, characterized by, or adapted to an extremely dry habitat. [Greek *xēros,* dry.]

xero-, xer- *prefix.* Indicates dryness; for example, **xerophyte, xerosis.** [New Latin, from Greek *xēros,* dry.]

xer·o·der·ma (zîr'ō-dûr'mə) *n.* Also **xer·o·der·mi·a** (-mē-ə). **1.** Abnormal dryness of the skin. **2.** A skin disease, **ichthyosis** (see). [New Latin : XERO- + -DERMA.] —**xer·o·der·mat·ic** (zîr'ō-dər-măt'ĭk), **xer·o·der·ma·tous** (zîr'ō-dûr'mə-təs) *adj.*

xe·rog·ra·phy (zĭ-rŏg'rə-fē) *n.* A dry photographic or photocopying process in which a negative image formed by a resinous powder on an electrically charged plate is electrically transferred to and thermally fixed as positive on a paper or other copying surface. [XERO- + -GRAPHY.] —**xer·o·graph·ic** (zîr'ə-grăf'ĭk) *adj.* —**xe·rog·raph·er** (zĭ-rŏg'rə-fər) *n.*

xe·roph·i·lous (zĭ-rŏf'ə-ləs) *adj.* Flourishing in or able to withstand a dry, hot environment. [XERO- + -PHILOUS.]

xer·oph·thal·mi·a (zîr′əf-thăl′mē-ə) *n.* Extreme dryness of the conjunctiva, thought to result from vitamin A deficiency. [Late Latin *xerophthalmia,* from Greek *xērophthalmia* : XER(O)- + OPHTHALMIA.] —**xer·oph·thal·mic** (zîr′əf-thăl′mĭk) *adj.*

xer·o·phyte (zîr′ə-fīt′) *n.* A plant, such as a cactus, that grows in and is adapted to an environment deficient in moisture. Compare **hydrophyte, mesophyte.** [XERO- + -PHYTE.] —**xer·o·phyt·ic** (zîr′ə-fĭt′ĭk) *adj.* —**xer·o·phyt·i·cal·ly** *adv.*

xer·o·sere (zîr′ə-sîr′) *n.* A sequence of ecological communities beginning in a dry area. [XERO- + SERE (series).]

xe·ro·sis (zĭ-rō′sĭs) *n.* Abnormal dryness, especially of the skin, conjunctiva, or mucous membranes. [New Latin : XER(O)- + -OSIS.] —**xe·rot·ic** (zĭ-rŏt′ĭk) *adj.*

Xer·ox (zîr′ŏks) *n.* **1.** A trademark for a photocopying process or machine using xerography. **2.** A copy made on a Xerox machine. ~*tr.v.* **Xeroxed, -oxing, -oxes.** To reproduce or print by means of a Xerox machine. —**Xer·ox** *adj.*

Xerx·es I (zûrk′sēz) (*c.* 519–465 B.C.). King of Persia (486–465 B.C.). Succeeding to the throne on the death of his father, Darius I, he organized a vast army that defeated the Greeks at Thermopylae and destroyed Athens (480 B.C.), but on the defeat of his navy at Salamis (480 B.C.) and of his army at Plataea (479 B.C.), he retreated to Persia, where he was later assassinated.

x-height (ĕks′hīt′) *n. Printing.* The height of a lower-case *x.*

Xho·sa (kō′sä) *n., pl.* **-sas** or collectively **Xhosa. 1.** A member of a southern African Bantu people living mainly in the Cape Province of the Republic of South Africa. **2.** The Bantu language spoken by the Xhosa, akin to Zulu.

xi (zī, sī; *Greek* ksē) *n., pl.* **xis. 1.** The 14th letter in the Greek alphabet, written Ξ, ξ. Transliterated in English as *X, x,* or *ks.* See feature at **alphabet. 2.** *Symbol* Ξ *Physics.* Any of four elementary particles in the baryon family.

Xia·men or **Hsia·men** (syä′mŭn′). Also **A·moy** (ə-moi′). Port of southeastern China. Situated in Fujian province on Xiamen Island, it stands opposite Taiwan. After its capture by the British during the Opium War (1841), it became a treaty port (1842). Formerly a chief port of the tea trade, it is today an important industrial city and tourist center.

Xi·an, Hsi-an, or **Sian** (shē′än′). Formerly **Chang·an** (chäng′än′). Capital of Shaanxi province, northwestern China. Situated in the valley of the Wei Ho, it was the capital of the Qin dynasty (255–206 B.C.) and at times of the Han and Tang dynasties. Jiang Jieshi, leader of the Kuomintang, was held hostage here (1936) until he agreed to join with the Communists against the Japanese.

Xi·ang Jiang, Hsi·ang Chiang, or **Si·ang Kiang** (shē′äng′ jyäng′). River of south-central China. It flows 1,150 kilometers (715 miles) through Hunan to the Dongting Hu (lake). Its valley is an extensive farming area.

Xi Jiang, Hsi Jiang, or **Si Kiang** (sē′ jyäng′). River of southern China. Rising in Yunnan province, southwestern China, it flows 1,900 kilometers (1,200 miles) eastward to enter the South China Sea through a delta. Navigable by large ships, it passes Guangzhou (Canton).

Xin·jiang Ui·gur Zi·zhi·qu (shĭn′jē-äng′ wē′gər zŭ′jŭ′chōō′). Also **Sin-kiang Ui·ghur Autonomous Region.** Region of western China. It is a high plateau enclosed by the Pamirs, Kunlun Shan, Altun Shan, and Tian Shan and includes the wastes of the Takla Makan desert with the Tarim basin and many salt lakes. Its many oases produce wheat, maize, and millet. There are considerable reserves of coal, tungsten, molybdenum, and oil. Most of the people are Turkic-speaking Muslims. The region came under Chinese control in the 16th century but was later contested by Russia. Urumqi is the capital.

xiphi-, xiph- *prefix.* Indicates sword; for example, **xiphisternum.** [New Latin, from Greek *xiphos,* sword, probably of Oriental origin.]

xiph·i·ster·num (zĭf′ə-stûr′nəm) *n., pl.* **-na** (-nə). The lowest or hindmost and smallest of the three divisions of the breastbone. Also called "xiphoid," "xiphoid process." [Greek *xiphos,* sword + STERNUM.]

xiph·oid (zĭf′oid′) *adj.* **1.** Having the shape of a sword. **2.** Of or pertaining to the xiphisternum. ~*n.* The xiphisternum. [Greek *xiphoeidēs,* "sword-shaped" : XIPHI- + -OID.]

xiph·o·su·ran (zĭf′ə-sŏŏr′ən) *n.* An arthropod of the order Xiphosura, which includes the horseshoe crab and many extinct forms. ~*adj.* Of or belonging to the order Xiphosura. [New Latin *Xiphosura,* "sword-tailed ones" : XIPHI- + *-ura,* plural of *-urus,* -UROUS.]

Xizang. See **Tibet.**

XL extra large.

X·mas (krĭs′məs, ĕks′məs) *n. Informal.* Christmas. [From the Greek letter X, transliterated as *Kh* (see **chi**) and representing Greek *Khristos,* CHRIST.]
Usage: This form occurs mainly in commercial writing, as on Christmas cards, and is not generally used in other contexts, unless there is a concern to save space (as in newspaper headlines).

XP. See **chi-rho.**

x-ra·di·a·tion, X-ra·di·a·tion (ĕks′rā′dē-ā′shən) *n.* **1.** Treatment with or exposure to x-rays. **2.** Radiation composed of x-rays.

x-ray, X-ray (ĕks′rā′) *n.* **1. a.** A relatively high-energy photon with wavelength in the approximate range from 0.05 angstroms to 100 angstroms. **b.** *Usually* **x-rays.** A stream of such photons, used for their penetrating power in radiography, radiology, radiotherapy, and research. **2.** A photograph taken with x-rays. In this sense, also called "x-ray photograph."
~*tr.v.* **x-rayed, x-raying, x-rays** or **X-rayed, X-raying, X-rays. 1.** To irradiate with x-rays. **2.** To photograph by means of x-rays. [Translation of German *X Strahlen* (plural), so called because their exact nature was not known.] —**x-ray** *adj.*

x-ray astronomy *n.* The study of the x-rays emitted by celestial bodies as detected by satellites and rockets above the earth's atmosphere.

x-ray crystallography *n.* The study of crystal structure by means of x-ray diffraction.

x-ray diffraction *n.* The diffraction of x-rays by the atoms or ions of a crystal according to a characteristic pattern that enables information to be obtained about the structure of the crystal.

x-ray microscope *n.* An instrument used to render a highly magnified image of the atomic structure of a crystalline system by means of the contrasts arising from the differences in absorption or emission of x-rays by the structure.

x-ray star *n.* A star that emits most of its radiation in the x-ray part of the electromagnetic spectrum.

x-ray therapy *n.* Radiotherapy with x-rays.

x-ray tube *n.* A vacuum tube containing electrodes that accelerate electrons and direct them to a metal anode, where their impacts produce x-rays.

xu (sōō) *n., pl.* **xu.** A monetary unit of Vietnam, equal to ¹/₁₀₀ of the dong. Also called "sau." See feature at **currency.** [Vietnamese, from French *sou.*]

xy·lan (zī′lən) *n.* A yellow, gummy pentosan found in plant cell walls and yielding xylose upon hydrolysis. [XYL(O)- + -AN.]

xy·lem (zī′ləm) *n. Botany.* The supporting and water-conducting tissue of vascular plants, consisting primarily of tracheids and vessels; woody tissue. Compare **phloem.** [German *Xylem,* from Greek *xulon,* wood.]

xy·lene (zī′lēn′) *n.* **1.** Any of three flammable isomeric hydrocarbons, $C_6H_4(CH_3)_2$, of the benzene series, obtained from wood and coal tar. Also called "xylol." **2.** A mixture of these isomers used as a solvent in making lacquers and rubber cement and as an aviation fuel. [XYL(O)- + -ENE.]

xy·li·dine (zī′lə-dēn′, -dĭn, zĭl′-) *n.* **1.** Any of six toxic isomers, $(CH_3)_2C_6H_3NH_2$, derived from xylene, used chiefly as dye intermediates. **2.** Any of various mixtures of these isomers. [XYL(O)- + -ID + -INE.]

xylo-, xyl- *prefix.* Indicates: **1.** Wood; for example, **xylograph; xylophone. 2.** Xylene; for example, **xylidine.** [Greek *xulont,* wood.]

xy·lo·graph (zī′lə-grăf′, -gräf′) *n.* **1.** An engraving on wood. **2.** An impression from a wood block. ~*tr.v.* **xylographed, -graphing, -graphs.** To print from a wood engraving. —**xy·log·ra·pher** (zī-lŏg′rə-fər) *n.*

xy·log·ra·phy (zī-lŏg′rə-fē) *n.* **1.** Wood engraving, especially of an early period. **2.** The art of printing texts or illustrations, sometimes with color, from wood blocks, as distinct from typography. [French *xylographie* : XYLO- + -GRAPHY.] —**xy·lo·graph·ic** (zī′lə-grăf′ĭk) *adj.* —**xy·lo·graph·i·cal·ly** *adv.*

xy·loid (zī′loid′) *adj.* Of or similar to wood. [XYL(O)- + -OID.]

xy·lol (zī′lôl′) *n.* A hydrocarbon, **xylene** (see). [XYL(O)- + -OL.]

xy·loph·a·gous (zī-lŏf′ə-gəs) *adj.* Feeding on wood. Said especially of certain insects. [Greek *xylophagos* : XYLO- + -PHAGOUS.]

xy·lo·phone (zī′lə-fōn′) *n.* A musical percussion instrument consisting of a mounted row of wooden bars graduated in length to sound a chromatic scale, played with two small mallets. [XYLO- + -PHONE.] —**xy·lo·phon·ic** (zī′lə-fŏn′ĭk) *adj.* —**xy·lo·phon·ist** (zī′lə-fō′nĭst) *n.*

xy·lose (zī′lōs′) *n.* A white crystalline aldose sugar, $C_5H_{10}O_5$, used in dyeing and tanning and in diabetic diets. Also called "wood sugar." [XYL(O)- + -OSE.]

xy·lot·o·my (zī-lŏt′ə-mē) *n.* The preparation of sections of wood for microscopic study. [XYLO- + -TOMY.]

xyst (zĭst) *n.* Also **xys·tus** (zĭs′təs). **1.** In ancient Greece, a covered portico used by athletes for exercise. **2.** In ancient Rome, a long tree-lined garden walk or terrace. [Latin *xystus,* from Greek *xustos,* "scraped smooth," from *xuein,* to scrape.]

xys·ter (zĭs′tər) *n.* A surgical instrument for scraping bones. [New Latin, from Greek *xuster,* scraper, from *xuein,* to scrape.]

PRONUNCIATION KEY

ă, pat; ā, pay; âr, care;
ä, father, are; b, bib;
ch, church; d, deed; ĕ, pet;
ē, be; f, fife; g, gag; h, hat;
hw, which; ĭ, pit; ī, pie;
îr, pier; j, judge; k, kick;
l, lid, needle; m, mum;
n, no, sudden; ng, thing;
ŏ, pot; ō, toe; ô, paw, for;
oi, noise; ou, out; ŏŏ, book;
ōō, boot; p, pop; r, roar;
s, sauce; sh, ship, dish;
t, tight; th, thin, path;
th, this, bathe; ŭ, cut; ûr, fur;
v, valve; w, with; y, yes;
z, zebra, size; zh, vision;
ə, about, item, edible,
gallop, circus, peaceful

IN FOREIGN WORDS:

à, *Fr.* ami; œ, *Fr.* feu, *Ger.*
schön; ü, *Fr.* tu, *Ger.* über;
KH, *Ger.* ich, *Scot.* loch;
N, *Fr.* bon; y′, *Fr.* Compiègne

STRESS MARKS:

Primary stress: ′
in·cite′ (ĭn-sīt′)
Secondary stress: ′
in′sight′ (ĭn′sīt′)

Y

yak *This domestic yak is much smaller than its wild cousin and is distributed widely through central Asia. It is well suited to high altitudes because of its relatively small appetite and its ability to withstand extreme cold.*

y, Y (wī) *n., pl.* **y's** or **Y's. 1.** The 25th letter of the modern English alphabet. **2.** Any of the speech sounds represented by this letter. **3.** Anything shaped like the letter Y. **4.** The 25th in a series; the 24th when *J* is omitted. **5.** The second in a series that consists of *x, y,* and *z.*

y, Y, y., Y. *Note:* As an abbreviation or symbol, *y* may be a small or a capital letter, with or without a period. Established forms or those generally preferred precede the definition. When no form is given, all four forms are in general use in that sense. **1. Y** hypercharge. **2. y** ordinate. **3. y.** year. **4. Y** yen (currency). **5. Y, Y.** A shortened form of the abbreviations Y.M.C.A., Y.W.C.A. **6. Y** The symbol for the element yttrium. **7.** *Mathematics.* The symbol for an algebraic variable.

y-, i- *prefix. Archaic.* Indicates the past participle; for example, **yclept.** [Middle English *i-, y-,* Old English *ge-,* from Germanic *ga-* (unattested).]

-y¹, -ey *suffix.* Indicates: **1.** The existence, possibility, or possession of something specified; for example, **curly, rainy. 2.** A relationship or resemblance to something specified; for example, **glassy, watery.** [Middle English *-ie, -y, -ey,* Old English *-ig, -æg,* from Common Germanic *-iga, -aga* (unattested).]

-y² *suffix.* Indicates: **1.** A condition, state of being, or quality; for example, **beggary, jealousy. 2.** An instance or result of engaging in a specified activity; for example, **entreaty, delivery.** [Middle English *-ie,* from Old French, from Latin *-ia,* -IA.]

-y³, -ey, -ie *suffix.* Indicates: **1.** Smallness or diminutiveness in a person or thing; for example, **kiddy, doggy. 2.** Familiarity or endearment; for example, **sweetie, daddy. 3.** A relationship or resemblance of a person or thing to a quality or thing specified; for example, **bookie, trendy.** [Middle English *-ie.*]

yab·ber (yăb'ər) *intr.v.* **-bered, -bering, -bers.** *Australian & New Zealand. Informal.* To jabber. [Alteration of JABBER.]

yacht (yät) *n.* Any of various sailing or powered vessels, generally with smart, graceful lines, used for pleasure cruises or racing.
~*intr.v.* **yachted, yachting, yachts.** To race, sail, or cruise in a yacht. [Earlier *yaught,* from obsolete Dutch *jaghte,* short for *jaght-(schip),* "chasing (ship)," from *jagen,* to chase, hunt, from Germanic *jagojan* (unattested).] **—yacht·ing** *n. & adj.*

yacht club *n.* A club that promotes and supports yachting, sailing, and boating.

yachts·man (yäts'mən) *n., pl.* **-men** (-mĭn). A person who owns or sails a yacht. **—yachts·man·ship** *n.*

yachts·wom·an (yäts'wŏom'ən) *n., pl.* **-women** (-wĭm'ĭn). A woman who owns or sails a yacht.

yack·e·ty-yak (yăk'ĭ-tē-yăk') *n. Slang.* See **yap** (sense 2). [Imitative.]

Yafa. See **Jaffa.**

YAG (yăg) *n.* A hard synthetic yttrium aluminum garnet used in laser technology and as a gemstone. [Y(TTRIUM) + A(LUMINUM) + G(ARNET).]

ya·gi (yä'gē, yäg'ē) *n. Electronics.* A directional radio and television antenna consisting of a horizontal conductor with several insulated dipoles parallel to and in the plane of the conductor. Also called "yagi antenna." [After H. *Yagi* (1888–1976), Japanese engineer.]

yah (yä) *adv. Informal.* Yes. [Variant of YEA.]

ya·hoo (yä'hōō, yä'-, yä-hōō') *n., pl.* **-hoos.** A crude or brutish person. [After the *Yahoos,* a race representing the brutish side of humanity in Jonathan Swift's *Gulliver's Travels.*]

Yahr·zeit (yär'tsīt, yôr'-) *n. Judaism.* Any of the anniversary days of the death of a close relative, observed by saying Kaddish, lighting a memorial candle, and sometimes fasting. [Yiddish, from Middle High German *jārzīt,* anniversary : *jār,* YEAR + *zīt,* time, TIDE.]

Yah·weh, Jah·weh (yä'-wä). Also **Yah·veh** (yä'vä) or **Jah·veh.** A name for God assumed by modern scholars to be a rendering of the pronunciation of the **Tetragrammaton** (*see*). Compare **Elohim.**

Yah·wist, Jah·wist (yä'wĭst) *n.* Also **Yah·vist** (yä'vĭst), **Jah·vist.** The author of the earliest sources of the Hexateuch, in which God is called Yahweh. Also called "Jehovist." Compare **Elohist. —Yah·wist, Yah·wis·tic** (yä-wĭs'tĭk) *adj.*

yak¹ (yăk) *n.* A long-haired bovine mammal, *Bos grunniens,* of the mountains of central Asia, where it is often domesticated. [Tibetan *gyag.*]

yak², yack *intr.v.* **yakked, yakking, yaks** or **yacked, yacking, yacks.** *Slang.* To talk or chatter persistently and meaninglessly. ~*n. Slang.* Continuous, meaningless chatter. [Imitative.]

Yak·i·ma¹ (yăk'ə-mə, yăk'ə-mô'). City in south-central Washington, on the Yakima River. It is the trade and shipping center of an irrigated agricultural valley noted for its fruit, hops, and mint.

Yakima² River, rising in the Cascade Range, central Washington, and flowing 327 kilometers (203 miles) southeast past Yakima to the Columbia River near Kennewick.

ya·ki·to·ri (yä'kĭ-tôr'ē) *n.* A dish consisting of bite-sized marinated chicken pieces that are grilled on small skewers. [Japanese : *yaki,* roasting + *tori,* bird.]

Ya·kut (yä-kōōt') *n.* **1.** A member of a people living in the Yakut Autonomous Soviet Socialist Republic. **2.** The Turkic language of this people, of the Altaic family of languages.

Yakut Autonomous Soviet Socialist Republic. Also **Ya·kutsk** (yä-kōōtsk'). Constituent republic of the U.S.S.R., in northeastern Siberia. Its capital is Yakutsk. Diamond mining is the republic's main industry.

Ya·kutsk (yä-kōōtsk'). Capital of Yakut A.S.S.R. In eastern Siberian U.S.S.R., it is a port on the Lena River. It is also a highway center and has tanneries, sawmills, and brickworks.

Yale (yāl), **Elihu** (1649–1721). Colonial-born English merchant and college benefactor. Born in Massachusetts and raised in England, he became a successful merchant and generous philanthropist. He made a series of contributions to the Collegiate School in Connecticut that was renamed in Yale's honor (1718) and developed into a prestigious university.

Yale lock *n.* A trademark for a door lock having a revolving barrel operated by a flat, serrated key. Compare **deadlock, mortise lock.**

y'all. Variant of **you-all.**

Yal·ta (yäl'tə). City of the U.S.S.R. On the Black Sea in the Crimea, it is a health and holiday resort. It was the site of the Yalta Conference (1945) attended by Churchill, Stalin, and Roosevelt.

Ya·lu (yä'lōō). River, rising in the Ch'ang-pai Mountains in Kirin province, northeastern China, and flowing 805 kilometers (c. 500 miles) southwest to the Bay of Korea at Tan-tung. It forms part of the China-North Korea border.

yam (yăm) *n.* **1.** Any of various chiefly tropical vines of the genus *Dioscorea,* many of which have edible tuberous roots. **2.** The starchy root of such a vine, used in the tropics as food. **3.** A sweet potato having reddish flesh. [Portuguese *inhame,* "edible," perhaps from Fulani *nyami,* to eat.]

Ya·mal Peninsula (yə-mäl'). A peninsula of the Soviet Union, in northwestern Siberia, extending north some 644 kilometers (400 miles) between the Kara Sea and the Gulf of Ob.

Ya·ma·mo·to (yä'mə-mô'tō), **Isoroku** (1884–1943). Japanese naval officer and statesman. Convinced that the U.S. fleet had to be destroyed before Japan could conquer the South Pacific, he planned and commanded the attack of Pearl Harbor (1941). He was killed later in the war when his plane was shot down over the Solomon Islands.

Ya·ma·sa·ki (yä'mə-sä'kē), **Minoru** (1912–). U.S. architect. Breaking from the trend toward austerity in post-World War II architecture, he designed buildings of sensuous appeal. Among his many projects are the Lambert Field-St. Louis Municipal Airport terminal (1951), the U.S. Science Pavillion for the Seattle World's Fair (1962), and the World Trade Center in New York City (1972).

ya·men (yä'mən) *n.* The office or residence of any public official in the Chinese Empire. [Mandarin Chinese *yá mén* : *yá,* office of a magistrate + *mén,* door.]

yam·mer (yăm'ər) *v.* **-mered, -mering, -mers.** *Informal.* —*intr.* **1.** To complain peevishly or whimperingly. **2.** To talk volubly and loudly. —*tr.* To utter or say in a complaining or clamorous tone. ~*n. Informal.* An act of yammering. [Alteration of earlier *yomer,*

Middle English *yomeren,* Old English *geōmrian,* to lament, from *gēomor,* sorrowful, from Common Germanic.] **—yam·mer·er** *n.*
Yamuna. See **Jumna.**
Yan'an, Yen-an, or **Yen·an** (yä'nän'). Industrial city of Shaanxi province, east-central China. It was the refuge of the Chinese Communists following the Long March and was their capital from World War II until they captured Beijing (Peking) in 1949.
yang (yäng) *n. Sometimes* **Yang.** In Chinese dualistic philosophy, the active, male cosmic element, force, or principle that is opposite but complementary to **yin** *(see).* [Mandarin Chinese *yáng,* the sun, masculine element.]
Yang (yäng), **Chen Ning** (1922–). U.S. physicist; born in China. Through numerous experiments he showed that parity, an intrinsic symmetry property of subatomic particles, is subject to violating factors and is not a constant force as was once thought. For this discovery, he and fellow researcher Tsung-Dao Lee (born 1926) received the 1957 Nobel Prize for physics.
Yangtze Kiang. See **Chang Jiang.**
yank (yăngk) *v.* **yanked, yanking, yanks.** *Informal.* *—tr.* To pull or extract suddenly; jerk: *yanked her out of the chair.* *—intr.* To pull on something suddenly; jerk.
~n. A sudden vigorous pull; a jerk. [19th century : origin obscure.]
Yank (yăngk) *n. Informal.* A Yankee. [Short for YANKEE.]
Yan·kee (yăng'kē) *n.* **1.** A native or inhabitant of New England. **2.** A native or inhabitant of a Northern state of the United States; especially, a Union soldier during the Civil War. **3.** A native or inhabitant of the United States; an American. Sometimes used derogatorily in all senses. [Perhaps from Dutch *Janke,* diminutive of *Jan,* John (used derisively of the Dutch in the 17th century, applied to inhabitants of New England in the 18th century.] **—Yan·kee** *adj.*
Yan·kee·dom (yăng'kē-dəm) *n.* **1.** The Northern states or New England. **2.** The United States. **3.** Yankees as a group.
Yankee Doo·dle (do͞od'l) *n.* A Yankee. [From the title of a song popular during the American Revolution.]
Yan·kee·ism (yăng'kē-ĭz'əm) *n.* **1.** The quality of being a Yankee, as in one's character or way of thinking. **2.** A Yankee custom or characteristic. **3.** A Yankee peculiarity, as of language or pronunciation.
Ya·oun·dé (yä-o͞on-dā'). Capital of Cameroon, in west-central Africa. Founded by German traders (1888), it was the capital of French Cameroon (1922–40 and 1946–60).
yap (yăp) *n.* **1.** A sharp, shrill bark, as of a small dog; a yelp. **2.** *Slang.* Noisy, stupid, or scolding talk; jabbering. Also called "yackety-yak." **3.** *Slang.* A crude, loud, stupid person. **4.** *Slang.* The mouth.
~v. **yapped, yapping, yaps.** *—intr.* **1.** To emit a yap or yaps; bark shrilly; yelp. **2.** *Slang.* To talk noisily, stupidly, annoyingly, or at excessive length; jabber. *—tr.* To utter or express by yapping: *The Queen of Hearts yapped her disapproval to Alice.* [Imitative.]
Yap (yăp, yäp). An island group, 65 square kilometers (*c.* 25 square miles) in area in the western Caroline Islands, western Pacific. It consists of 4 large and 10 small islands surrounded by a coral reef.
ya·pok, ya·pock (yə-pŏk') *n.* An aquatic marsupial mammal, *Chironectes minimus,* of tropical America, having dense fur, webbed hind feet, and a long tail. [After *Oyapock,* river in north Brazil.]
Ya·qui (yä'kē) *n., pl.* **-quis** or collectively **Yaqui. 1. a.** A tribe of North American Indians now living in Sonora, Mexico. **b.** A member of this tribe. **2.** The Uto-Aztecan language of the Yaqui.
Yar·bor·ough (yär'bər-ō, -bər-ə) *n. Sometimes* **yarborough.** A full hand of 13 cards in bridge or whist containing no card higher than a nine. [After Charles Anderson Worsley (1809–97), 2nd Earl of *Yarborough,* who is said to have unsuccessfully bet 1,000 to 1 that such a hand would not occur.]
yard¹ (yärd) *n.* **1.** *Abbr.* **yd** A unit of length in both the U.S. Customary System and the British Imperial System, equal to 0.9144 meter (3 feet). **2.** *Nautical.* A long, tapering spar slung usually at right angles to a mast to support and spread the head of a square sail, lugsail, or lateen. [Middle English *yerde, yarde,* Old English *gerd,* staff, twig, measuring rod, from West Germanic *gazdjō* (unattested).]
yard² *n.* **1.** A tract of ground adjacent to, surrounding, or surrounded by a building or group of buildings. **2.** A tract of ground, often enclosed, used for a specific type of work, business, or other activity. Often used in combination: *shipyard; graveyard.* **3.** An area provided with a system of tracks where railroad trains are made up and cars are switched, stored, and serviced. **4.** A winter pasture for deer or other grazing animals. **5.** An enclosed tract of ground in which animals, such as chickens or pigs, are kept. **6.** The garden of a house, especially if relatively small. **—the Yard.** *Informal.* In Britain, **Scotland Yard** *(see).*
~v. **yarded, yarding, yards.** *—tr.* To enclose, collect, or put in or as if in a yard. *—intr.* To gather in or as if in a yard. [Middle English *yarde, yard,* Old English *geard,* enclosure, residence, from Germanic *gardaz* (unattested).]
yard·age¹ (yär'dĭj) *n.* **1.** The amount or length of something measured in yards. **2.** Cloth sold by the yard.
yardage² *n.* **1.** The use of a railroad yard for loading and transporting cattle. **2.** The fee paid for such use.
yard·arm (yärd'ärm') *n.* Either end of the yard of a square sail.
yard bird *n. Slang.* **1. a.** A low-ranking enlisted man who is untrained. **b.** An enlisted man who is confined to base and is assigned menial tasks as punishment. **2.** A convict; prisoner.
yard goods *pl.n.* Cloth sold by the yard; **piece goods** (see).
yard grass *n.* Any of several weedy grasses of the genus *Eleusine.*
yard·man (yärd'mən) *n., pl.* **-men** (-mĭn). A man employed in a yard, especially a railroad yard.
yard·mas·ter (yärd'măs'tər, -mäs'tər) *n.* A railroad employee in charge of a yard.
yard of ale *n.* **1.** A slender drinking glass, about a yard long, and having a volume usually of two or three pints. **2.** The beer or ale held by such a glass, sometimes drained in one draft in competitions in British pubs.
yard sale *n.* A sale of used household belongings on the front or back lawn of a house.
yard·stick (yärd'stĭk') *n.* **1.** A graduated measuring stick one yard in length. **2.** Any test or standard used in measurement, comparison, or judgment; criterion.
yare (yâr) *adj. Archaic.* **1.** Responding easily; manageable; maneuverable. Said of a sea vessel. **2.** Bright; lively; quick. **3.** Ready; prepared.
~adv. Archaic. Soon; quickly; promptly. [Middle English *yare,* Old English *gearo, gearu,* finished, ready.] **—yare·ly** *adv.*
Yarmouth. See **Great Yarmouth.**
yar·mul·ke (yär'məl-kə, yä'məl-) *n., pl.* **-kes.** A small skullcap worn by male Jews on religious and celebratory occasions and by male Orthodox Jews at all times. [Yiddish, from Polish and Ukrainian *yarmulka,* perhaps from Turkish *yağmurluk,* raincoat, from *yağmur,* rain.]
yarn (yärn) *n.* **1.** A continuous strand of twisted threads of natural or synthetic material, such as wool, cotton, flax, or nylon, used in weaving or knitting. **2.** *Informal.* A long, involved story or a tale of real or fictitious adventures.
~intr.v. **yarned, yarning, yarns.** *Informal.* To tell a long, complicated story; spin a yarn. [Middle English *yarn,* Old English *gearn.*]
yarn-dyed (yärn'dīd') *adj.* Woven from yarn already dyed.
Ya·ro·slavl (yə-rō-släv'əl). Capital of Yaroslavl oblast, eastern European U.S.S.R., on the upper Volga River. It is a river port, a major rail junction, and an industrial and commercial center.
yar·row (yăr'ō) *n.* Any of several plants of the genus *Achillea;* especially, *A. millefolium,* native to Eurasia, having finely dissected foliage and flat clusters of usually white flowers. Also called "milfoil." [Middle English *yar(ro)we,* Old English *gearwe,* from West Germanic *garw-* (unattested).]
yash·mak, yash·mac (yäsh-mäk', yăsh'măk) *n.* A veil worn by Muslim women in public to cover their faces. [Arabic *yashmaq, yashmak.*]
yat·a·ghan, yat·a·gan (yăt'ə-găn', -gən) *n.* Also **at·a·ghan** (ăt'ə-găn'). A Turkish single-edged sword or scimitar having a slightly S-shaped blade with a pommel or knob on the end and lacking a handle guard. [Turkish *yatağan.*]
yau·pon (yô'pən) *n.* A holly, *Ilex vomitoria,* of the southeastern United States, having scarlet fruit and evergreen leaves, once used medicinally. [Catawba *yopun,* diminutive of *yop,* tree.]
yau·ti·a (you'tē-ə) *n.* **1.** Any of various tropical American plants of the genus *Xanthosoma;* especially *X. sagittifolium,* which is cultivated for its starchy tubers. **2.** One of these tubers. [American Spanish, from Taino.]
yaw (yô) *v.* **yawed, yawing, yaws.** *—intr.* **1.** To deviate temporarily from the intended course. Used of a ship. **2.** To turn about the vertical axis. Used of an aircraft or projectile. *—tr.* To cause to yaw.
~n. **1.** The action of yawing. **2.** The extent of this movement, measured in degrees. [16th century : origin obscure.]
yawl (yôl) *n.* **1.** A two-masted fore-and-aft-rigged sailing vessel similar to the ketch but having a smaller jigger mast stepped abaft the rudder. Also called "dandy." **2.** A ship's small boat, manned by oarsmen. Compare **ketch.** [Middle Low German *jolle†.*]
yawn (yôn) *v.* **yawned, yawning, yawns.** *—intr.* **1.** To open the mouth wide with a deep intake of air, usually involuntarily, from drowsiness, fatigue, or boredom. **2.** To open wide; gape: *The chasm yawned at our feet.* *—tr.* To utter wearily, as if in yawning.
~n. **1.** An act or instance of yawning. **2.** *Informal.* A dull or boring event or person. [Middle English *yonen, yenen,* Old English *geonian, ginian.*] **—yawn·er** *n.* **—yawn·ing·ly** *adv.*
yawp (yôp) *intr.v.* **yawped, yawping, yawps. 1.** To utter a sharp cry; bark; yelp. **2.** *Slang.* To talk loudly and stupidly.
~n. **1.** A bark; a yelp. **2.** *Slang.* Loud, stupid talk. [Middle English *yolpen,* perhaps variant of *yelpen,* YELP.]
yaws (yôz) *n. Used with a singular verb.* An infectious tropical skin disease, caused by a spirochete, *Treponema pertenue,* and characterized by multiple red pimples. Also called "frambesia". [17th century : of Cariban origin.]
y-ax·is (wī'ăk'sĭs) *n., pl.* **y-axes** (-sēz). **1.** The vertical axis of a two-dimensional Cartesian coordinate system. **2.** One of three axes in a three-dimensional Cartesian coordinate system.
Ya·zoo (yă-zo͞o', yăz'o͞o). River of Mississippi, rising in the northwest and flowing 303 kilometers (188 miles) generally southwest to the Mississippi River near Vicksburg.
Yb The symbol for the element ytterbium.
Y-chro·mo·some (wī'krō'mə-sōm') *n.* The smaller of the two types of sex chromosome, associated with male characteristics in most animals, including humans, and occurring paired with one **X-chromosome** *(see)* in the body cells of such male animals.
y·clept, y·cleped (ĭ-klĕpt'). *Archaic.* Past participle of **clepe.**
~adj. Archaic. Known as; named; called. [Middle English *ycleped,*

yashmak *These veils, which have been worn since very ancient times, are thought to have developed originally as a way of protecting the face from sun and sand. Muslim custom later decreed that they should be worn by women in public—as here, by an Egyptian woman—as a gesture of modesty.*

yawl *Yawls are two-masted sailing boats with a fore-and-aft rig. The smaller mast is usually set behind the rudder post.*

PRONUNCIATION KEY
ă, pat; ā, pay; âr, care;
ä, father, are; b, bib;
ch, church; d, deed; ĕ, pet;
ē, be; f, fife; g, gag; h, hat;
hw, which; ĭ, pit; ī, pie;
îr, pier; j, judge; k, kick;
l, lid, needle; m, mum;
n, no, sudden; ng, thing;
ŏ, pot; ō, toe; ô, paw, for;
oi, noise; ou, out; o͝o, book;
o͞o, boot; p, pop; r, roar;
s, sauce; sh, ship, dish;
t, tight; th, thin, path;
th, this, bathe; ŭ, cut; ûr, fur;
v, valve; w, with; y, yes;
z, zebra, size; zh, vision;
ə, about, item, edible, gallop, circus, peaceful

IN FOREIGN WORDS:
à, *Fr.* ami; œ, *Fr.* feu, *Ger.* schön; ü, *Fr.* tu, *Ger.* über; KH, *Ger.* ich, *Scot.* loch; N, *Fr.* bon; y', *Fr.* Compiègne

STRESS MARKS:
Primary stress: ′
in·cite′ (ĭn-sīt′)
Secondary stress: ′
in′sight′ (ĭn′sīt′)

Old English *gecleopod,* past participle of *clipian, cleopian,* to speak, call, CLEPE.]

yd yard (measurement).

ye[1] (*thē*) *adj. Archaic.* The. Still used in names to suggest antiquity or quaintness: *ye olde taverne.* [Incorrect transcription resulting from the resemblance between the runic letter called thorn (properly transcribed as *th*) and the letter *y* in certain Middle English manuscripts. See **thorn.**]

ye[2] (yē) *pron.* **1.** *Poetic & Archaic.* You (plural). **2.** *Regional.* You (singular). [Middle English, Old English *gē.*]

yea (yā) *adv.* **1.** Yes; aye. Now archaic except in recording or expressing a vote. **2.** *Archaic.* Indeed; truly.

~*n.* **1.** A statement or vote in favor of a motion. **2.** One who votes in favor of a motion: *The yeas have it.* [Middle English *ye, ya,* Old English *gēa,* yes.]

Yea·ger (yā′gər), **Charles Elwood,** known as "Chuck" (1923–). U.S. Air Force officer and test pilot. A highly decorated World War II fighter pilot, he made aviation history with his 1947 flight that broke the sound barrier and his 1953 flight that reached two and a half times the speed of sound.

yeah (yĕ′ə, yă′ə, yā′ə) *adv. Informal.* Yes. [Informal pronunciation of *yes.*]

yean (yēn) *v.* **yeaned, yeaning, yeans.** —*intr.* To bear young. Used of sheep and goats. —*tr.* To bear; give birth to. [Middle English *yenen,* Old English *geēanian* (unattested) : *ge-,* Y- + *ēanian,* to bear young, to lamb.]

yean·ling (yēn′lĭng) *n.* The young of a sheep or goat; a lamb or kid. [YEAN + -LING (little).] **—yean·ling** *adj.*

year (yîr) *n. Abbr.* **y., yr. 1.** The period of time as measured by the Gregorian calendar in which the earth completes a single revolution around the sun. It is divided into 12 months, 52 weeks, or 365 or 366 days, and begins on January 1 and ends on December 31. Also called "calendar year." **2.** See **sidereal year. 3.** See **tropical year. 4.** A period of about equal length in other calendars. **5.** Any period of approximately this duration: *We were married a year ago.* **6.** A period equal to the calendar year but beginning on a different date: *a fiscal year.* **7.** A set period of time, usually shorter than 12 months, devoted to some special activity: *the academic year.* **8.** A class of students at a school or college. **9. years.** Age; especially, old age: *feeling his years.* **10. years.** Time; especially, a long time: *It will take years to do it.* **—year in, year out.** Continuously or regularly over a long period of time. [Middle English *year, yere,* Old English *gēar.*]

year·book (yîr′bo͝ok′) *n.* **1.** A documentary, memorial, or historical book published every year, containing information about the previous year and sometimes for the current year. **2.** A yearly publication compiled by the graduating class of a high school or college, providing a record of the academic year, usually with photographs of students and faculty.

year-end, year·end (yîr′ĕnd′) *n.* The end of a fiscal year.

year·ling (yîr′lĭng) *n.* **1.** An animal that is one year old or has not completed its second year. **2.** A thoroughbred racehorse, regarded as a colt or filly one year old dating from January 1 of the year that it was foaled. **—year·ling** *adj.*

year·long (yîr′lông′, -lŏng′) *adj.* Lasting through one year.

year·ly (yîr′lē) *adj.* **1.** Occurring once a year or every year; annual. **2.** Of or lasting for a year.

~*adv.* Once a year; annually.

~*n., pl.* **yearlies.** A publication issued once a year.

yearn (yûrn) *intr.v.* **yearned, yearning, yearns. 1.** To have a strong or deep desire; be filled with longing. Usually used with *for* or *to: yearns for his native land.* **2.** To feel deep pity, sympathy, or tenderness: *"he yearns after/you protectively/hopelessly wanting nothing"* (William Carlos Williams). [Middle English *yernen,* Old English *gyrnan, giernan,* to strive, desire.] **—yearn·ing·ly** *adv.*

Synonyms: *hanker, hunger, long, pine, thirst.*

yearn·ing (yûr′nĭng) *n.* A deep longing.

year-round (yîr′round′) *adj.* Existing, active, or continuous throughout the year; during all seasons.

yea-say·er (yā′sā′ər) *n.* **1.** One who is confidently affirmative in attitude. **2.** One who uncritically agrees.

yeast (yēst) *n.* **1.** Any of various unicellular fungi of the genus *Saccharomyces* and related genera, reproducing by budding and capable of fermenting carbohydrates. **2.** Froth consisting of yeast cells together with the carbon dioxide they produce in the process of fermentation, present in or added to fruit juices and other substances in the production of alcoholic beverages. **3.** A commercial preparation, either in powdered or compressed form, containing yeast cells and inert material such as meal, and used especially as a leavening agent or as a dietary supplement to treat vitamin B deficiency. **4.** Foam; froth. **5.** An agent of ferment or activity.

~*intr.v.* **yeasted, yeasting, yeasts. 1.** To ferment. **2.** To froth or foam. [Middle English *yest,* Old English *gist, gyst.*]

yeast·y (yē′stē) *adj.* **-ier, -iest. 1.** Of, similar to, or containing yeast. **2.** Causing or characterized by a ferment. **3.** Restless; turbulent. **4.** Frothy; frivolous. **—yeast·i·ly** *adv.* **—yeast·i·ness** *n.*

Yeats (yāts), **William Butler** (1865–1939). Irish poet and playwright. He helped found the Irish National Theatre Company at the Abbey Theatre, Dublin; he wrote many short plays, mostly on mythological themes. His poetry is varied, ranging from early love lyrics to the complex symbolist poems of such later collections as *The Winding Stair* (1929) and *Last Poems* (1939), reflecting his deep interests in the occult, art, Celtic mythology, and Irish politics. He was awarded the Nobel Prize for literature (1923).

yecch, yech (yĕKH, yŭKH, yĕk, yŭk) *interj. Slang.* Used to express strong disgust or contempt.

~*n. Slang.* Something disgusting.

~*adj. Slang.* Disgusting; sickening. [Imitative.] **—yech·y** *adj.*

yegg (yĕg) *n. Slang.* A thief; especially, a burglar or safecracker. [20th century : origin unknown.]

yell (yĕl) *v.* **yelled, yelling, yells.** —*intr.* To cry out loudly, as in pain, fright, surprise, or enthusiasm. —*tr.* To utter loudly; shout.

~*n.* **1.** A loud cry; a shriek; a shout. **2.** A rhythmic cheer uttered or chanted in unison by a group: *a college yell.* [Middle English *yellen,* Old English *giellan,* to sound, shout, from Germanic *gel-, gal-* (unattested).] **—yell·er** *n.*

yel·low (yĕl′ō) *n.* **1.** Any of a group of colors of a hue resembling that of ripe lemons and varying in lightness and saturation; the hue of that portion of the spectrum lying between green and orange; one of the psychological primary hues, evoked in the normal observer by radiant energy of wavelength approximately 580 nanometers; also one of the subtractive primaries. **2.** A pigment or dye having this hue. **3.** Something that has this hue. **4.** The yolk of an egg. **5. yellows.** Any of various plant diseases usually caused by fungi of the genus *Fusarium* or viruses of the genus *Chlorogenus* and characterized by yellow or yellowish discoloration.

~*adj.* **1.** Of the color yellow. **2.** Designating a person or a people, such as the mongoloid race, having yellowish skin. **3.** *Slang.* Cowardly. **4.** Treating news material in a sensational, exaggerated way. Said of newspapers and journalism.

~*v.* **yellowed, -lowing, -lows.** —*tr.* To make or render yellow. —*intr.* To become yellow. [Middle English *yelwa, yelow,* Old English *geolu.*] **—yel·low·ly** *adv.* **—yel·low·ness** *n.* **—yel·low·y** *adj.*

yel·low·bark (yĕl′ō-bärk′) *n.* A kind of tree bark, **calisaya** *(see).*

yel·low-bel·lied (yĕl′ō-bĕl′ēd) *adj.* **1.** Having a belly yellow or yellowish in color, as certain birds and fish do. **2.** *Slang.* Cowardly.

yellow birch *n.* A North American tree, *Betula lutea,* having yellowish bark and hard, light-colored wood used for furniture and flooring.

yel·low·bird (yĕl′ō-bûrd′) *n.* Any of various yellow or predominantly yellow birds, such as the goldfinch or the yellow warbler.

yellow cake *n.* The final precipitate formed in the milling of uranium ore.

yellow card *n. Sports.* A card raised by a referee in soccer, indicating a player's violation.

yel·low-dog contract (yĕl′ō-dôg′, -dŏg′) *n.* An employer-employee contract no longer legal, by which the employee agrees not to join a union while employed.

yellow fever *n.* An acute infectious disease of subtropical and tropical New World areas, caused by a virus transmitted by a mosquito of the genus *Aëdes* and characterized by jaundice and dark-colored vomit resulting from hemorrhages. Also called "yellow jack."

yellow flag *n.* A common yellow-flowered iris, *Iris pseudacorus,* found by streams and on marshy land in Europe and northern Africa.

yel·low·ham·mer (yĕl′ō-hăm′ər) *n.* A Eurasian bird, *Emberiza citrinella,* having brown and yellow plumage. Also called "yellow bunting." [Earlier *yelambre* : perhaps YELLOW + *-ambre,* ultimately from Old English *amore, omer,* an unidentified bird.]

yel·low·ish (yĕl′ō-ĭsh) *adj.* Somewhat yellow; tinged with yellow. **—yel·low·ish·ness** *n.*

yellow jack *n.* **1. Yellow fever.** (see). **2.** *Nautical.* A yellow flag hoisted to request pratique or to warn of disease on board.

yellow jacket *n.* Any of several small wasps of the family Vespidae, having yellow and black markings and usually nesting on the ground.

yellow journalism *n.* Journalism that exploits, distorts, or exaggerates the news to create sensations and attract readers. [From the use of yellow ink in printing "Yellow Kid," a cartoon strip in the *New York World,* a newspaper noted for sensationalism.]

Yel·low·knife (yĕl′ō-nīf′). Capital of Northwest Territories, northern Canada. Situated on the Great Slave Lake, it was founded (1935) after the discovery of gold and is a mining and commercial center.

yel·low·legs (yĕl′ō-lĕgz′) *n., pl.* **yellowlegs.** Either of two North American wading birds: **1.** The greater yellowlegs, *Tringa melanoleuca,* having yellow legs and a long, narrow bill. **2.** The lesser yellowlegs, *T. flavipes,* a similar bird with a shorter bill.

yellow metal *n.* **1.** A form of brass containing about 60 percent copper and 40 percent zinc. **2.** Gold.

yellow ocher *n.* **1.** A yellow pigment, usually containing limonite. **2.** A moderate orange with yellow overtones.

yellow pages, Yellow Pages *pl.n.* A telephone directory or section of a directory, usually printed on yellow pages, that lists businesses, services, and products alphabetically according to the service they provide.

yellow peril, Yellow Peril *n.* The threatened expansion of the Oriental peoples, as magnified in the Western imagination.

yellow pimpernel *n.* See **pimpernel** (sense 2).

yellow pine *n.* **1.** Any of several North American evergreen trees having yellowish wood, such as *Pinus echinata,* of the southeasten United States, or the ponderosa pine. **2.** The wood of the yellow pine.

yellow poplar *n.* The **tulip tree** *(see).*

yellow rattle *n.* A semiparasitic annual plant, *Rhinanthus minor,*

PRONUNCIATION KEY

ă, pat; ā, pay; âr, care;
ä, father, are; b, bib;
ch, church; d, deed; ĕ, pet;
ē, be; f, fife; g, gag; h, hat;
hw, which; ĭ, pit; ī, pie;
îr, pier; j, judge; k, kick;
l, lid, needle; m, mum;
n, no, sudden; ng, thing;
ŏ, pot; ō, toe; ô, paw, for;
oi, noise; ou, out; o͝o, book;
o͞o, boot; p, pop; r, roar;
s, sauce; sh, ship, dish;
t, tight; th, thin, path;
th, this, bathe; ŭ, cut; ûr, fur;
v, valve; w, with; y, yes;
z, zebra, size; zh, vision;
ə, about, item, edible, gallop, circus, peaceful

IN FOREIGN WORDS:

à, *Fr.* ami; œ, *Fr.* feu, *Ger.* schön; ü, *Fr.* tu, *Ger.* über;
KH, *Ger.* ich, *Scot.* loch;
N, *Fr.* bon; y′, *Fr.* Compiègne

STRESS MARKS:

Primary stress: ′
in·cite′ (ĭn-sīt′)
Secondary stress: ′
in′sight′ (ĭn′sīt′)

having two-lipped yellow flowers and an inflated fruit inside which the ripened seeds rattle.

Yellow River. See **Huang He.**

Yellow Sea. Inlet of the western Pacific Ocean between Korea and northeast China. It receives its name from the yellow silt carried into it by the Huang He (Yellow River), Yalü Jiang, and Liao He.

yellow spot *n.* A part of the human retina, the **macula lutea** (*see*).

Yel·low·stone National Park (yĕl′ō-stōn′). The oldest and largest national park of the United States. Lying mainly in Wyoming, with small areas in Idaho and Montana, it is chiefly a volcanic plateau in the Rocky Mts. Established in 1872, it has more than 3,000 geysers and hot springs, the best-known being Old Faithful, which was so named in 1870 because it was thought to erupt once every 65 to 70 minutes. The eruptions are actually much more irregular, with intervals ranging from 33 to 148 minutes.

Yellowstone River. River rising in northwestern Wyoming and flowing 1,080 kilometers (671 miles) north through Yellowstone Lake and into Montana and then northeast to the Missouri River on the North Dakota border.

yellow streak *n.* A proneness to cowardice and disloyalty.

yel·low·tail (yĕl′ō-tāl′) *n.* Any of several fishes having a yellowish tail; especially, a marine game fish, *Seriola dorsalis,* of coastal waters of southern California and Mexico.

yel·low·throat (yĕl′ō-thrōt′) *n.* Any of several small New World birds of the genus *Geothlypis;* especially, the common yellowthroat, *G. trichas,* having a brownish back, a bright yellow throat, and, in the male, a black facial mask.

yellow warbler *n.* A New World warbler, *Dendroica petechia,* having predominantly yellow plumage.

yellow water lily *n.* A yellow-flowered aquatic plant, *Nuphar lutea,* having large floating leaves. Also called "brandy bottle."

yel·low·weed (yĕl′ō-wēd′) *n.* Any of various plants having yellow flowers, such as the dyer's rocket.

yel·low·wood (yĕl′ō-wŏŏd′) *n.* **1.** A tree, *Cladrastis lutea,* of the southeastern United States, having compound leaves, drooping clusters of white flowers, and yellow wood yielding a yellow dye. Also called "gopherwood." **2.** Any of various other trees having yellow wood. **3.** The wood of any of these trees.

yelp (yĕlp) *v.* **yelped, yelping, yelps.** —*intr.* To utter a sharp, short bark or cry, as in pain or surprise. Used especially of a dog. —*tr.* To utter by yelping. ~*n.* A sharp, short cry or bark. [Middle English *yelpen,* to cry aloud, Old English *gielpan,* to boast, exult (imitative).] —**yelp·er** *n.*

Yem·en (yĕm′ən). Mountainous country in the southwestern Arabian Peninsula of southwest Asia. A poor country, it is largely agricultural, cotton and coffee (from the fertile, well-watered coastal plain) and hides and skins being its chief exports. However, considerable foreign aid is being used for agricultural, fishing, and industrial development. The country was part of the Ottoman Empire (1517–1919). Republican army officers overthrew the imam (1962), but strife occurred until 1969. A military coup took place in 1974, but instability and fluctuating relations with its neighbors continue. A union with South Yemen has been proposed. Area, 195,000 square kilometers (75,270 square miles). Population, 6,500,000. Capital, San'a.

yen¹ (yĕn) *intr.v.* **yenned, yenning, yens.** *Informal.* To yearn; long. ~*n.* *Informal.* A yearning; a longing. [Cantonese *yan,* craving, corresponding to Mandarin Chinese *yǐn.*]

yen² *n., pl.* **yen. 1.** *Symbol* **Y** The basic monetary unit of Japan. See feature at **currency. 2.** A coin or note worth one yen. [Japanese *en,* from Mandarin Chinese *yuán,* "round (piece)," dollar.]

Yen-an or **Yenan.** See **Yan'an.**

yen·ta (yĕn′tə) *n. Slang.* A gossipy woman, especially one who pries into the affairs of others. [Yiddish *yente,* from the name *Yente.*]

yeo·man (yō′mən) *n., pl.* -men (-mĭn). **1.** An independent farmer; especially, a member of a former class of small freeholding farmers below the gentry in England. **2.** A **yeoman of the guard** (*see*). **3.** Formerly, an attendant, servant, or lesser official in a royal or noble household. **4. a.** A petty officer in the U.S. Navy concerned chiefly with clerical duties. **b.** A petty officer in the British Royal Navy concerned chiefly with signaling. **5.** *Archaic.* An assistant or other subordinate, as of a sheriff or craftsman. **6.** A member of the

British volunteer yeomanry. **7.** A diligent and dependable worker. [Middle English *yoman, yuman,* perhaps contraction of *yongman* : YOUNG + MAN.] —**yeo·man** *adj.*

yeo·man·ly (yō′mən-lē) *adj.* **1.** Pertaining to or ranking as a yeoman. **2.** Characteristic of or befitting a yeoman; sturdy, staunch, or workmanlike. —**yeo·man·ly** *adv.*

yeoman of the guard *n.* A member of a ceremonial guard attending the British sovereign and royal family, consisting of 100 yeomen with their officers.

yeo·man·ry (yō′mən-rē) *n.* **1.** The class or a body of yeomen. **2.** A British volunteer cavalry force organized in 1761 to serve as a home guard and later incorporated into the Territorial Army (1907).

yep (yĕp) *adv.* Also **yup** (yŭp). *Informal.* Yes. [From YES (after NOPE).]

yer·ba ma·té (yâr′bə mä-tā′, yûr′bə) *n.* A tealike South American beverage, **maté** (*see*). [Spanish *yerba,* herb, from Latin *herba,* plant, HERB.]

Yer·by (yûr′bē), **Frank Garvin** (1916–). U.S. novelist. His numerous best-selling historical novels, such as *The Foxes of Harrow* (1946) and *A Darkness at Ingraham's Crest* (1979), are characterized by complex plots, colorful language, and what have been criticized as sometimes contrived resolutions.

Ye·re·van (yĕ-rĕ-vän′). Capital of the Armenian S.S.R., southwest U.S.S.R., on the Razdan River. It passed several times between Persia and Turkey until ceded to Russia (1828). It is an industrial center.

Yerk·ish (yûr′kĭsh) *n.* An artificial language using geometric forms to represent words that was created for communication between chimpanzees and humans. [After the *Yerkes* Regional Primate Center in Georgia.]

yes (yĕs) *adv.* **1.** It is so; as you say or ask. Used in expressing affirmation, agreement, positive confirmation, or consent. **2.** Indeed; what is more. Used to introduce a more emphatic phrase: *I could do with a drink, yes, a very strong drink.* **3.** I hear you and am listening. Used in response to being addressed or summoned. ~*n., pl.* **yeses. 1.** An affirmative or consenting response. **2.** An affirmative vote or voter. [Middle English, Old English *gēse.*]

ye·shi·va, ye·shi·vah (yə-shē′və) *n., pl.* -**vas** or -**voth** (yə-shē-vōt′). **1.** An Orthodox Jewish school devoted to rabbinical and Talmudic studies. **2.** A Jewish day school providing religious and secular education. [Hebrew *yĕshībhāh,* from *yāshábh,* he sat down.]

Ye·şil Ir·mak (yĕ-shēl′ ĭr-mäk′). Ancient name **I·ris** (ī′rĭs). River of Turkey, rising in the north and flowing 420 kilometers (c. 260 miles) northwest, then northeast, past Tokat and Amasya into the Black Sea near Samsun.

yes man *n., pl.* **yes men.** *Informal.* A person who slavishly agrees with his superior; a sycophant.

yester– *prefix.* Indicates: **1.** The day before the present day; for example, *yestermorning.* **2.** A previous and indeterminate period of time; for example, **yesteryear.** [Middle English *yister-,* Old English *geostra(n).*]

yes·ter·day (yĕs′tər-dā′, -dē) *n.* **1.** The day before the present day. **2.** *Sometimes* **yesterdays.** Time in the immediate or recent past. ~*adv.* **1.** On the day before the present day. **2.** A short while ago. [Middle English *yesterdai,* Old English *geostran dæg* : YESTER- + DAY.]

yes·ter·eve·ning (yĕs′tər-ēv′nĭng) *n.* Also **yes·ter·eve** (-ēv′) or **yes·ter·e·ven** (-ē′vən). The evening of yesterday. —**yes·ter·eve·ning** *adv.*

yes·ter·morn·ing (yĕs′tər-môr′nĭng) *n.* Also **yes·ter·morn** (-môrn′). Yesterday morning. —**yes·ter·morn·ing** *adv.*

yes·ter·night (yĕs′tər-nīt′) *n.* Last night. —**yes·ter·night** *adv.*

yes·ter·year (yĕs′tər-yîr′) *n.* **1.** The year before the current one. **2.** Time past; yore. —**yes·ter·year** *adv.*

yes·treen (yĕs-trēn′) *n. Scottish.* Yesterday evening. [Middle English : YESTER- + E'EN (evening).] —**yes·treen** *adj.*

yet (yĕt) *adv.* **1.** At this time; for the present; now: *Don't sing yet.* **2.** Up to a particular time; thus far: *The end had not yet come.* **3.** In the time remaining; still: *There is yet a solution to be found.* **4.** Besides; in addition: *Play the tape yet another time.* **5.** Even; still: *a yet sadder tale.* **6.** Nevertheless; but despite this: *young yet wise.* **7.** At some future time; eventually: *They may yet score a goal.* —**as yet.** Up to the present time; up to now. ~*conj.* Nevertheless; and despite this: *He said he would be late, yet he arrived early.* [Middle English *yet, yit,* Old English *gīet(a)†.*]

Usage: Yet, as an adverb of time in the sense "up to the present," occurs with the perfect tenses: *Have they arrived yet?* However, it is often used, mainly in informal English, with the simple past tense: *Did you eat yet?*

ye·ti (yĕt′ē) *n.* The **abominable snowman** (*see*). [Alteration of Tibetan *miti* : *mi,* person + *ti,* a kind of animal.]

Yev·tu·shen·ko (yĕv′tə-shĕng′kō), **Yevgeny Alexandrovich** (1933–). Russian poet. His works contain criticisms of the U.S.S.R. and include *A Precocious Autobiography* (1963) and *Stolen Apples* (1972).

yew (yōō) *n.* **1.** Any of several evergreen trees or shrubs of the genus *Taxus,* of which the flat, dark-green needles and often the scarlet berries are poisonous. **2.** The wood of a yew; especially, the durable, fine-grained wood of an Old World species, *T. baccata,* used in cabinetmaking and for archery bows. [Middle English *ew,* Old English *ēow, īw.*]

Ygg·dra·sil, Yg·dra·sil (ĭg′drə-sĭl, üg′-) *n. Norse Mythology.* The

Yellowstone National Park *The first of the U.S. national parks (set up in 1872), Yellowstone covers almost 9,000 square kilometers (3,475 square miles), containing thousands of geysers, boiling pools, and hot springs. At Mammoth Hot Springs, shown here, the springs bubble over terraces built of limestone deposited by the mineral-rich water.*

yew Taxus baccata, *the common yew (above), is an evergreen conifer native to Eurasia and Mediterranean Africa. Sacred in European mythology, yews are often found in churchyards and may have been planted on pagan sites before Christians built churches there. Because of its strong, closely grained wood, the yew was used in the Middle Ages for making longbows.*

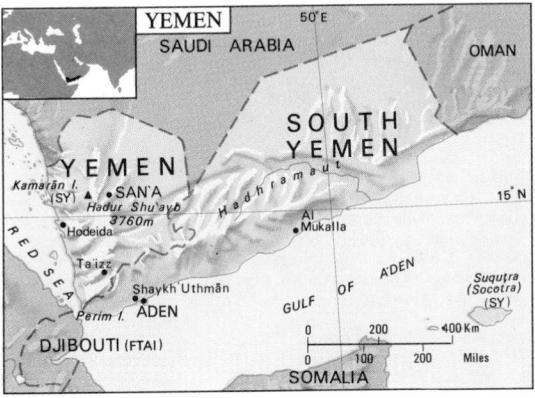

YEMEN
SAUDI ARABIA
OMAN
YEMEN
SOUTH YEMEN
Kamarān I. (SY)
SAN'A ▲ Hadur Shu'ayb 3760m
Hodeida
Ta'izz
Al Mukalla
Hadhramaut
ADEN
Shaykh 'Uthmān
ADEN
GULF OF ADEN
Suquţra (Socotra) (SY)
Perim I.
DJIBOUTI (FTAI)
SOMALIA
RED SEA
50′E
15′N
0 200 400 Km
0 100 200 Miles

great ash tree that holds together earth, heaven, and hell by its roots and branches. [Old Norse.]

YHWH, YHVH, JHWH, JHVH The Hebrew Tetragrammaton representing the name of God.

Yid·dish (yĭd′ĭsh) *n.* A High German language with additional vocabulary drawn from Hebrew and from Slavic that is written in Hebrew characters and spoken chiefly as a vernacular in eastern European Jewish communities and by emigrants from these communities throughout the world. Also called "Judeo-German." [Yiddish *Yidish,* from Middle High German *jüdisch,* Jewish, from *Jüde,* Jew, from Old High German *judo,* from Latin *Jūdaeus,* JEW.] —**Yid·dish** *adj.*

Yid·dish·ism (yĭd′ĭ-shĭz′əm) *n.* **1.** The advocacy or promotion of Yiddish language and literature. **2.** A word, expression, or usage characteristic of Yiddish.

yield (yēld) *v.* **yielded, yielding, yields.** —*tr.* **1.** To give forth by or as if by a natural process, especially by cultivation: *a field that yields much corn.* **2.** To provide or give in return; be productive of: *an investment that yields six percent.* **3.** To surrender (something) in deference or defeat; relinquish: *yielded the field to a rival.* **4.** To grant or concede: *yield right of way; yield the point in the argument.* —*intr.* **1.** To provide or give a return; be productive. **2.** To give up; surrender; submit. **3.** To give way to pressure, force, or persuasion. **4.** To give way to what is stronger or better; be overcome. Used with *to: "Wrong opinions and practices gradually yield to fact and argument"* (John Stuart Mill). —See Synonyms at **relinquish.** ~*n.* **1.** The amount yielded or produced; a product. **2.** The profit obtained from investment; a return. **3.** The energy released by an explosion, especially by a nuclear explosion, expressed in units of weight of TNT required to produce an equivalent release: *a 100-megaton yield.* **4.** The amount of a specific product produced by a chemical reaction, often expressed as a percentage of the stoichiometric quantity obtainable. [Middle English *yieldan,* Old English *gieldan,* to yield, pay, from Germanic *geldhan* (unattested), to pay.] —**yield·er** *n.*
  Synonyms: *bow, capitulate, defer, relent, submit.*

yield·ing (yēl′dĭng) *adj.* Inclined to yield; submissive. —**yield·ing·ly** *adv.* —**yield·ing·ness** *n.*

yield point *n.* The point, beyond the elastic limit of a material, at which a sudden increase in strain occurs with only a small increase in stress.

yin (yĭn) *n. Sometimes* **Yin.** The passive, female cosmic element, force, or principle that is opposite but complementary to **yang** *(see)* in Chinese dualistic philosophy. [Mandarin Chinese *yīn,* the moon, shade, femininity.]

yip (yĭp) *n.* A sharp, high-pitched bark; a yelp. ~*intr.v.* **yipped, yipping, yips.** To make such sounds; yelp. [Imitative.]

yipe (yīp) *interj. Also* **yipes** (yīps). Used to express surprise, fear or dismay.

yip·pee (yĭp′ē) *interj.* Used to express joy, elation, or excitement. [Perhaps related to HIP (a cheer).]

-yl *suffix. Chemistry.* Indicates a radical; for example, **carbonyl, ethyl.** [French *-yle,* from Greek *hulē,* wood, matter.]

y·lang-y·lang, i·lang-i·lang (ē′läng-ē′läng) *n.* **1.** A tropical Asian tree, *Cananga odorata* (or *Canangium odoratum*), having fragrant greenish-yellow flowers that yield an oil used in perfumery. **2.** An oil or perfume obtained from the flowers of this tree. [Tagalog *alang-ilang.*]

y·lem (ī′ləm) *n.* A form of matter hypothesized by proponents of the big bang theory to have existed before the formation of the chemical elements. [Middle English, from Old French, from Latin *hȳlē,* from Greek *hulē,* matter.]

Y.M.C.A. Young Men's Christian Association.

Y.M.H.A. Young Men's Hebrew Association.

-yne *suffix. Chemistry.* Indicates a triple bond in a compound; for example, **alkyne, ethyne.** [Alteration of -INE (indicating chemical substances).]

yock (yŏk, yŭk) *Slang.* —*intr. v.* **yocked, yock·ing, yocks.** To laugh or joke, especially in a rowdy manner. ~*n.* A joke; laugh: *"it contains a few yocks, but the humor . . . never emerges"* (*Variety*). [Imitative.]

yod[1], **yodh** (yŏd, yŏod) *n.* The tenth letter of the Hebrew alphabet. See feature at **alphabet.** [Hebrew *yōdh,* from *yādh,* hand.]

yod[2] *n.* The sound (y), especially when considered as a historical phonetic development. [Probably from YOD (Hebrew letter).]

yo·del (yŏd′l) *v.* **-deled, -deling, -dels** or *chiefly British* **-delled, -delling, -dels.** —*intr.* To sing so that the voice fluctuates between the normal chest voice and a falsetto. —*tr.* To sing (a melody without words) in this fashion. ~*n.* A song or cry that is yodeled. [German *jodeln* (imitative).] —**yo·del·er** *n.*

yo·ga (yŏ′gə) *n.* **1.** *Often* **Yoga.** A Hindu discipline aimed at training the consciousness for a state of perfect spiritual insight and union with the universal spirit. **2.** A system of exercises practiced as part of this discipline to promote control of the body and mind. Also called "hatha yoga." [Sanskrit, union, yoking.] —**yo·gic** (yŏ′gĭk) *adj.* —**yo·gism** *n.*

yogh (yŏкн) *n.* The Middle English letter ȝ, representing a velar or palatal fricative, usually voiced. [Middle English *yogh, yok,* perhaps from *yok,* YOKE (from its shape).]

yo·gi (yŏ′gē) *n., pl.* **-gis. 1.** One who practices yoga. **2.** One who teaches or is a master of yoga. [Hindi, from Sanskrit *yogin,* from *yoga,* YOGA.]

yog·urt, yog·hurt (yŏ′gərt, -gŏŏrt) *n.* A food of a custardlike consistency, prepared from milk curdled by bacteria, especially *Lactobacillus bulgaricus* and *Streptococcus thermophilus,* and often sweetened or flavored with fruit. [Turkish *yoğurt.*]

yo·him·bine (yŏ-hĭm′bēn′) *n.* A poisonous alkaloid, $C_{21}H_{26}N_2O_3$, derived from the bark of a tree, *Corynanthe yohimbe,* and formerly used as an aphrodisiac. [New Latin *yohimbe* (the tree), from Bantu.]

yoicks (yoiks) *interj.* Used as a hunting cry to urge the hounds after the fox.

yoke (yŏk) *n., pl.* **yokes** or **yoke** (for sense 2). **1.** A crossbar with two U-shaped pieces that encircle the necks of a pair of oxen, mules, or other draft animals working in a team. **2.** A pair of draft animals joined by such a device or trained to work together. **3.** A frame or crossbar designed to be carried across a person's shoulders with equally weighed loads, such as buckets of water, suspended from each end. **4.** A bar used with a double harness to connect the collar of each horse to the tongue of a wagon, coach, or other trailer. **5.** *Nautical.* A crossbar on a ship's rudder to which the steering cables are connected. **6.** A clamp or vise that holds a part in place or controls its movement or that holds two parts together. **7.** A piece of a garment that is closely fitted, either around the neck and shoulders or at the hips, and from which an unfitted or gathered part of the garment falls. **8.** Something that connects or joins together; a bond: *the yoke of marriage.* **9.** A structure made of two upright spears with a third laid across them, under which conquered enemies of ancient Rome were forced to march in subjection. **10.** Any form or symbol of subjugation or bondage: *under the yoke of a dictator.* —See Synonyms at **couple.** ~*v.* **yoked, yoking, yokes.** —*tr.* **1.** To fit or join with a yoke. **2. a.** To harness a draft animal to. **b.** To harness (a draft animal) to something. **3.** To connect, join, or bind together. **4.** To force into bondage or servitude; oppress. —*intr.* To become connected, joined, or bound together. [Middle English *yok,* Old English *geoc.*]

yoke·fel·low (yŏk′fĕl′ō) *n.* A companion or partner, as in work or marriage. Also called "yokemate."

yo·kel (yŏ′kəl) *n.* A country bumpkin or rustic; especially, one who is gullible or naive. [Perhaps from dialectal *yokel,* green woodpecker (probably imitative of its note).]

yoke·mate (yŏk′māt′) *n.* A yokefellow.

Yo·ko·ha·ma (yŏ′kə-hä′mə). Capital and port of Kanagawa prefecture, Honshu island, Japan. Situated on Tokyo Bay, it was badly damaged by an earthquake (1923) and bombing in World War II.

yo·ko·zu·na (yŏ′kō-zŏŏ-nä′) *n.* A champion sumo wrestler. [Japanese.]

yolk (yŏk) *n.* **1.** The nutritive material of an animal ovum, consisting primarily of protein and fat; especially, the yellow, usually spheroidal mass of the egg of a bird or reptile, surrounded by the albumen. **2.** A greasy substance found in unprocessed sheep's wool. [Middle English *yolke,* Old English *geoloca, geolca,* from *geolu,* YELLOW.] —**yolked** *adv.* —**yolk·y** *adj.*

yolk sac *n. Zoology.* A membranous sac attached to the embryo and providing early nourishment in the form of yolk in bony fishes, sharks, reptiles, birds, and primitive mammals, and functioning as the circulatory system of the human embryo prior to the initiation of internal circulation by the pumping of the heart.

Yom Kip·pur (yŏm′kĭp′ər, yŏm′ kĭ-pŏŏr′) *n.* The holiest Jewish holiday, celebrated on the tenth day of Tishri, on which fasting and prayer for the atonement of sins are prescribed. Also called "Day of Atonement." [Hebrew *yōm kippūr : yōm,* day + *kippūr,* atonement, from *kippēr,* they covered, they made atonement.]

yon (yŏn) *adj.* Yonder. ~*pron. Regional.* That one or those yonder. ~*adv.* Yonder. [Middle English *yon,* Old English *geon.*]

yond (yŏnd) *adj. Archaic.* Yonder. ~*adv. Archaic.* Yonder. [Middle English, from Old English *geon.*]

yon·der (yŏn′dər) *adj.* Being at an indicated distance, usually within sight. ~*adv.* In or at that indicated relatively distant place; over there. [Middle English *yonder,* from *yond,* YOND.]

yo·ni (yŏ′nē) *n.* In Hinduism, a representation of the vulva, symbolizing the feminine principle. [Sanskrit *yoni†,* abode, womb.]

Yon·kers (yŏng′kərz). City of southeastern New York, on the east bank of the Hudson River. It is an industrial city and a residential center for workers commuting to New York City. Sarah Lawrence College is here.

yoo-hoo (yŏŏ′hŏŏ′) *interj.* Used to attract someone's attention.

yore (yôr, yŏr) *n.* Time long past. Used in the phrase *days of yore.* [Middle English *yore,* Old English *gēara,* formerly, once, from *gēar,* YEAR.]

York[1] (yôrk). The royal house that held the English throne from 1461 to 1485.

York[2]. City of North Yorkshire, northeast England. Situated at the confluence of the Ouse and Foss rivers, it was a Roman military post (Eboracum) and is where Constantine I was proclaimed emperor (A.D. 306). An important market for the wool trade during the Middle Ages, York is a walled city with many medieval remains and is overlooked by the cathedral York Minster (13th–15th century).

York, Alvin Cullum, known as "Sergeant York" (1887–1964). U.S. Soldier. Drafted in World War I despite his conscientious objection to war, he is famous for his heroic single-handed attack on a German post during which he killed 25 of the enemy and captured 132. He was decorated with more than 50 medals and was portrayed by Gary Cooper in the 1940 film *Sergeant York*.

York, Richard Plantagenet, 3rd Duke of (1411–60). English nobleman. A descendant of the third son of Edward III, he was named by Henry VI as heir to the throne until Henry himself had a son. His claims led to the outbreak of the Wars of the Roses (1455) between the Yorkists and Lancastrians, and after Yorkist victories he was reinstated as heir. He was killed in battle at Wakefield.

York·ist (yôr′kĭst) *n.* A supporter of the House of York in its contention with the House of Lancaster during the Wars of the Roses (1455–85). —**York·ist** *adj.*

York·shire (yôrk′shîr′, -shər). Former county of northeast England, bordering the North Sea. In 1974 its area was redistributed between the counties of Humberside, North Yorkshire, West Yorkshire, and South Yorkshire. It was a center of the woolen industry during the Middle Ages and developed around its western coal field during the Industrial Revolution.

Yorkshire fog *n.* A tall, tufted European grass, *Holcus lanatus*, having downy stems and leaves. [From the foggy impression made by its leaves and from its prevalence in Yorkshire.]

Yorkshire Ouse. See **Ouse** (Sense 2).

Yorkshire pudding *n.* A light, baked pudding made from a batter of eggs, flour, and milk, and traditionally served with roast beef.

Yorkshire terrier *n.* A toy terrier of a breed developed in Yorkshire, having a long, bluish-gray and tan coat.

Yorkshire tyke *n. Informal.* A native or inhabitant of Yorkshire. Also called "**tyke**."

York·town (yôrk′toun′). A historic town of southeastern Virginia, on the York River near its mouth on Chesapeake Bay. The town was the site of the final campaign of the American Revolution (1781). The battlefield surrounds the town, which is included in the Colonial National Historical Park.

Yo·ru·ba (yō′rōō-bä) *n., pl.* **-bas** or collectively **Yoruba**. **1.** A member of a West African Negro people living chiefly in southwestern Nigeria. **2.** The Kwa language of this African people. —**Yo·ru·ban** (yō′rōō-bən) *adj.*

Yo·sem·i·te National Park (yō-sĕm′ə-tē). Park in eastern California. It is a mountainous region with many lakes, rivers, gorges, and falls, including Yosemite Falls, the highest in North America (739 meters; 2,425 feet).

you (yōō; *unstressed* yə) *pron.* The second person singular or plural pronoun in the nominative or objective case. **1.** Used to represent the one or ones addressed by the speaker: **a.** As subject: *You are always hounding me.* **b.** As the direct object of a verb: *I'll lift you.* **c.** As the indirect object of verb: *My friend will give you a thrashing.* **d.** As the object of a preposition: *He'll sing for you.* **2.** Used in apposition before a noun to indicate address: *You fool!* **3.** *Informal.* Used in place of the reflexive pronouns *yourself* or *yourselves*, as the indirect object of a verb: *You went and bought you a new tractor.* **4.** Used in various elliptical, absolute, or interjectional phrases in which it is neither subject nor object: *You and your so-called friends!* **5.** Used to represent unspecified persons or people in general: *You have to be ruthless in a ruthless world.* In more formal contexts, the pronoun *one* is often preferred. —**you know what** (or **who**). One that is unspecified but felt by the speaker to be known to the person addressed.
~*n.* The individuality or image of the person being addressed: *the real you; That shirt is really you.* —See Usage note at **me.** [Middle English *you, eow,* Old English *ēow,* dative and accusative of *gē,* ye.]

you-all (yōō-ôl′, yôl) *pl.* also **y'all** (yôl). *Regional.* You. Used in addressing two or more persons or referring to two or more persons, one of whom is addressed.

you'd (yōōd; *unstressed* yəd). Contraction of *you had* or *you would:* *I knew you'd understand.*

you'll (yōōl; *unstressed* yəl). Contraction of *you will* or *you shall:* *You'll be late.*

young (yŭng) *adj.* **young·er** (yŭng′gər), **young·est** (yŭng′gĭst). **1.** Being in the early or undeveloped period of life or growth; not old. **2. a.** Newly begun or formed; not advanced: *The evening is young.* **b.** Recently introduced; not long established: *a young firm.* **3. a.** Pertaining to or suggestive of youth or early life: *young for her age.* **b.** Vigorous or fresh; youthful. **c.** Lacking experience; immature; green: *Her sophistication made him feel very young.* **4.** Designating the junior of two people having the same name. Usually used in the comparative: *Pitt the younger.* **5.** *Geology.* Being of an early stage in a geological cycle. Said of bodies of water and land formations.
~*n., pl.* **young. 1.** *Used with a plural verb.* Young persons collectively; youth. **2.** Offspring; brood: *a lioness with her young.* —**with young.** Pregnant. Said of an animal. [Middle English *yong,* Old English *geong.*] —**young·ish** *adj.*

Synonyms: *adolescent, juvenile, teenager, youth.*

Young (yŭng), **Brigham** (1801–77). U.S. Mormon leader. One of the original Twelve Apostles of the Mormon Church, he became the leader of the religion after the assassination of its founder, Joseph Smith (1844). He led an exodus of the Mormons from their troubled settlement in Illinois to the site of the present-day Salt Lake City, Utah (1847), where they established a permanent home for the church.

Young, Denton True, known as "Cy" (1867–1955). U.S. baseball player. In his 22 years as a major-league pitcher, he won a record 511 games and pitched 76 no-hitters, including modern baseball's

first perfect game (1904). He was elected to the Hall of Fame in 1937.

Young, Edward (1683–1765). English poet. His most popular work, *The Complaint: or, Night Thoughts* (1742–45), a dramatic monologue, was inspired by the successive deaths of three family members, including his wife. He also wrote several unsuccessful dramas and a critical essay, *Conjectures on Original Composition* (1759).

Young, Thomas (1773–1829). English physicist and physician. He revived the wave theory of light and postulated the three-color theory of color vision. Also an Egyptologist, he helped decipher the hieroglyphics on the Rosetta Stone.

Young (yŭng), **Whitney Moore** (1921–71). U.S. civil-rights leader. As director of the National Urban League (1961–71), he played the primary role in the fight for equal opportunity for blacks in industry and government jobs. He also advised presidents John F. Kennedy and Lyndon B. Johnson on equal-rights issues.

young·ber·ry (yŭng′bĕr′ē) *n.* **1.** A trailing, prickly hybrid between a blackberry and a dewberry, cultivated in the western United States. **2.** The edible, dark-red berry of the youngberry. [After B. M. Young, 20th-century American fruit grower.]

young blood *n.* Young people with energy, enthusiasm, fresh ideas, and similar qualities.

Young·er (yŭng′gər), **Thomas Coleman,** known as "Cole" (1844–1916). U.S. outlaw. After fighting as a Confederate guerrilla in the Civil War, he joined the notorious gang led by Jesse James. He was sentenced to life in prison after an attempted bank heist in 1876 but was paroled in 1901.

young·ling (yŭng′lĭng) *n.* **1.** A young person. **2.** A young animal. **3.** A young plant. [Middle English *yongling,* Old English *geongling* : YOUNG + -LING (noun suffix).] —**young·ling** *adj.*

young man *n.* A male lover or boyfriend.

Young's modulus *n.* The ratio of the stress per unit area of cross section on a wire or rod under tension or compression to the longitudinal strain. Also called "Young's modulus of elasticity." [After Thomas YOUNG.]

Young Pretender. See Charles Edward **Stuart.**

young·ster (yŭng′stər) *n.* **1.** A young person or child. **2.** A young animal. **3.** A midshipman of the second-year class in the U.S. Naval Academy.

Youngs·town (yŭngz′toun′). City of northeastern Ohio. In an extensive coal and iron region, it is one of the largest iron and steel centers in the country.

Young Turk *n.* A progressive or rebellious member of a political party or other organized group. [Originally a member of a Turkish revolutionary party in the early 20th century.]

young woman *n.* A female lover or girlfriend.

youn·ker (yŭng′kər) *n.* A young man; a youngster. [Dutch *jonker,* from Middle Dutch *jonckher, jonchere,* young nobleman : *jonc,* young + *here,* master, lord.]

your (yŏŏr, yôr, yər; *unstressed* yər). The possessive form of the pronoun *you. Abbr.* **yr. 1.** Used to indicate possession, agency, or reception of an action by the one or ones addressed by the speaker: *your wallet; pursuing your tasks; suffered your first rebuff.* **2.** Used to designate something having special significance to you: *Today is your day.* **3.** *Informal.* Used with little or no sense of possession but suggesting mutual knowledge or experience: *He is not one of your scatterbrained philosophers.* **4.** Used to indicate possession, agency, or reception of an action by any unspecified person or persons: *The house is on your right.* In more formal contexts, the pronoun *one's* is often preferred in this sense. [Middle English *your,* Old English *ēower,* genitive of *gē,* ye. See **you.**]

you're (yŏŏr; *unstressed* yər). Contraction of *you are.*

yours (yŏŏrz, yôrz, yōrz; *unstressed* yərz). *Used with a singular or plural verb.* **1.** That or those belonging to you: *I can't find my scarf anywhere, so I'll borrow yours. My books are on the couch and yours are on the dining room table.* **2.** Used in the complimentary closing of letters, especially in such phrases as *yours sincerely, yours faithfully,* and *yours truly.* —**of yours.** Belonging or pertaining to you: *a friend of yours.* —**you and yours.** You and your family. [Middle English *youres,* genitive of YOUR.]

your·self (yŏŏr-sĕlf′, yôr′-, yōr′-, yər-) *pron.* **1.** That one identical with you. Used: **a.** Reflexively as the direct or indirect object of a verb or the object of a preposition: *Don't hurt yourself. Give yourself plenty of time. Are you talking to yourself?* **b.** For emphasis: *You yourself must insist upon his compliance.* **c.** In an absolute construction: *Yourself a victim of fraud, you can certainly understand how they feel.* **2.** Your normal or healthy condition or state: *You have not been yourself lately.* **3.** Oneself.

Usage: *Yourself* is not acceptable as a substitute for *you* in formal style, though it is commonly so used informally: *She wants to see Joan and yourself; Yourself and the others will be expected later; How's yourself?* It is particularly common in Irish English. It is with *yourself* and *yourselves* that standard English now distinguishes singular from plural in the second person: *You yourself know your duty; You yourselves know your duty.*

your·selves (yŏŏr-sĕlvz′, yôr-, yōr-, yər-) *pron.* **1.** Those that are identical with you. Used: **a.** Reflexively as the direct or indirect object of a verb or the object of a preposition: *Help yourselves. Have yourselves a good time. You should all watch out for yourselves.* **b.** For emphasis: *You should take care of the matter yourselves.* **c.** In an absolute construction. **2.** Your normal or healthy condition or state. —See Usage note at **yourself.**

yours truly *pron. Informal.* I; myself; me: *Yours truly had to pay.*

youse (yōōz) *pl. pron. Nonstandard.* You (plural).
youth (yōōth) *n., pl.* **youths** (yōōths, yōōthz). **1.** The condition or quality of being young. **2.** A quality, such as vigor, enthusiasm, rashness, inexperience, or freshness, typically associated with youth. **3.** An early period of development or existence. **4. a.** The time of life between childhood and maturity. **b.** *Used with a plural verb.* Young people collectively. **c.** A young person; especially, a young man. —See Synonyms at **young.** [Middle English *youthe,* Old English *geoguth.*]
youth·ful (yōōth′fəl) *adj.* **1.** Possessing youth; still young. **2.** Characteristic of youth; vigorous; fresh; active. **3.** Of or belonging to youth. **4.** In an early stage of development; new. **5.** *Geology.* Young. —**youth·ful·ly** *adv.* —**youth·ful·ness** *n.*
youth hostel *n.* A place offering simple accommodation and sometimes food to usually young travelers. Also called "hostel."
you've (yōōv; *unstressed* yəv). Contraction of *you have.*
yow (you) *interj.* Used to express alarm, pain, or surprise. [Possibly Middle English *yowe* (probably imitative).]
yowl (youl) *v.* **yowled, yowling, yowls.** —*intr.* To utter a loud, long cry; howl; wail. —*tr.* To say or utter with such a cry. —*n.* A loud, mournful cry; a wail. [Middle English *youlen* (imitative).]
yo-yo (yō′yō′) *n., pl.* **-yos. 1.** A toy in the shape of a spool, around which a string is wound. The string is attached to the finger, and the yo-yo is spun up and down by moving the hand. **2.** *Informal.* One that vacillates. **3.** *Slang.* A silly or stupid person. —*intr.v.* **-yoed, -yoing, -yos.** *Informal.* To shift repeatedly between positions or opinions; vacillate. [Originally a trademark.]
Y·pres (ē′prə). Town of West Flanders, southwestern Belgium. On the Yperlee River, it was a prosperous textile center during the Middle Ages and was the site of three battles during World War I.
Y·quem (ē-kĕm′) *n.* A variety of Sauterne wine. [After Château d'*Yquem,* an estate in southwestern France, where it is produced.]
yr. 1. year. **2.** younger. **3.** your.
yrs. 1. years. **2.** yours.
Yseult. Variant of **Iseult.**
Yssel. See **Ijssel.**
Ysselmeer. See **Ijsselmeer.**
yt·ter·bi·a (ĭ-tûr′bē-ə) *n.* Ytterbium oxide. [New Latin, from YTTERBIUM.]
yt·ter·bite (ĭ-tûr′bīt′) *n.* A mineral, **gadolinite** *(see).*
yt·ter·bi·um (ĭ-tûr′bē-əm) *n. Symbol* **Yb** A soft, bright, silvery rare-earth element occurring in two allotropic forms and used as an x-ray source for portable irradiation devices, in some laser materials, and in some special alloys. Atomic number 70, atomic weight 173.04, melting point 824°C, boiling point 1,427 °C, specific gravity 6.977 or 6.54 depending on allotropic form, valences 2, 3. [New Latin; discovered at *Ytterby,* Sweden.] —**yt·ter·bic** *adj.*
ytterbium oxide *n.* A colorless hygroscopic compound, Yb_2O_3, used in certain alloys. Also called "ytterbia."
yt·tri·a (ĭt′rē-ə) *n.* **Yttrium oxide** *(see).* [New Latin, after *Ytterby,* Sweden. See **ytterbium.**]
yt·tri·um (ĭt′rē-əm) *n. Symbol* **Y** A silvery, lustrous metallic element, not a rare earth but occurring in nearly all rare-earth minerals and resembling them chemically, used in various metallurgical applications, notably to increase the strength of magnesium and aluminum alloys. Atomic number 39, atomic weight 88.905, melting point 1,509°C, boiling point 3,338 °C, specific gravity 4.47, valence 3. [New Latin, from YTTR(IA).] —**yt·tric** (ĭt′rĭk) *adj.*
yttrium oxide *n.* A yellowish powder, Y_2O_3, used in optical glasses, ceramics, and color-television tubes. Also called "yttria."

yucca *There are about 40 species of yucca, ranging from small shrubs to trees that can reach 15 meters (50 feet). Native to southern North America and Central America, some species have leaves that are made into cloth, and the roots of others were once used as soap by American Indians.*

yu·an (yü-än′) *n., pl.* **yuan. 1. a.** The basic monetary unit of the People's Republic of China, equal to 10 chiao or jiao or 100 fen. **b.** The basic monetary unit of Taiwan, equal to 100 cents. See feature at **currency. 2.** A coin or note worth one yuan. [Mandarin Chinese *yuán,* round (piece), dollar.]
Yü·an (yü-än′). A Chinese dynasty that ruled from 1271 to 1368.
Yu·ca·tán Peninsula (yōō′kə-tän′). Peninsula of Central America. Separating the Gulf of Mexico from the Caribbean Sea, it is mainly a limestone plateau situated largely in southeastern Mexico. It includes Belize and northern Guatemala and was once the center of the Mayan civilization, of which there are many remains. Lumbering and fishing are its chief industries, and tourism is important.
Yuc·a·tec (yōō′kə-tĕk′) *n., pl.* **-tecs** or collectively **Yucatec. 1.** A member of an American Indian people inhabiting the Yucatán Peninsula. **2.** The Mayan language of this people.
yuc·ca (yŭk′ə) *n.* Any of various New World plants of the genus *Yucca,* often tall and stout-stemmed, and having a terminal cluster of white flowers. [Spanish *yuca,* of American Indian origin.]
Yucca House National Monument. Area of *c.* 4 hectares (10 acres) in southwestern Colorado, set aside to preserve the ruins of a prehistoric Indian village.
Yu·chi (yōō′chē) *n., pl.* **Yuchis** or collectively **Yuchi. 1.** A North American Indian language family consisting only of the language of the Yuchi tribe. **2.** A tribe of Yuchi-speaking North American Indians formerly inhabiting eastern Georgia. **3.** A member of this tribe. **4.** The language of this tribe.
yuck, yuk (yŭk, yōōKH) *interj. Informal.* Used to express disgust or distaste. [Imitative.]
yuck·y, yuk·ky (yŭk′ē) *adj.* **-ier, -iest.** *Slang.* Disgusting; revolting.
Yue, Yüeh (yōō-ä′) *n.* Cantonese *(see).*
Yu·ga (yōōg′ə) *n.* Also **Yug** (yōōg) *Hinduism.* One of the four ages constituting the cycle of history. [Sanskrit, yoke, pair, age.]
Yu·go·sla·vi·a Also **Ju·go·sla·vi·a** (yōō′gō-slä′vē-ə). Federal republic of southeastern Europe. Situated in the Balkan Peninsula and bordering the Adriatic Sea, it is chiefly mountainous except in the northeast, where fertile lowlands are drained by the Danube River. It was formed in 1918 as the Kingdom of the Serbs, Croats, and Slovenes and gained its present name in 1927. It was occupied by the Germans during World War II, after which Tito, a Communist, became president; he later broke with the U.S.S.R. (1948). Almost half the population is involved with agriculture: grains, potatoes, sugar beet, fruit, tobacco, and olives are grown. Mineral resources include copper, iron, gold, and coal, and industries include iron and steel, sugar refining, cement, textiles, and chemicals. Fishing and tourism are important on the Adriatic coast. Area, 255,804 square kilometers (96,766 square miles). Population, 22,400,000. Capital, Belgrade. —**Yu·go·slav, Yu·go·sla·vi·an** *n. & adj.*
Yu·ka·wa (yōō-kä′wə), Hideki (1907–81). Japanese nuclear physicist. In 1935 he predicted the existence of the meson, later observed by scientists. He also made important contributions to strong interaction and elementary-particle theory. He received the Nobel Prize for physics (1949).
Yu·kon¹ (yōō′kŏn). Territory of northwestern Canada, on the Beaufort Sea. It includes Mt. Logan, Canada's highest peak (6,050 meters; 19,850 feet) and is sparsely populated. It was the site of the Klondike gold rush in the 1890's. Its capital is Whitehorse.
Yukon². River of North America. Formed by the confluence of the Lewes and Pelly rivers in south-central Yukon, Canada, it flows 3,220 kilometers (2,000 miles), first northwest to Alaska, then southwest to the Bering Sea.
Yukon Time *n.* Time at the 135th meridian west of Greenwich, England, and in the ninth time zone based on it in North America. It is nine hours earlier than Greenwich time.
yu·lan (yōō′län; *Chinese* yü′län′) *n.* A tree, *Magnolia denudata,* native to China and often cultivated for its large, cup-shaped, fragrant white flowers. [Mandarin Chinese *yù lán,* "jade orchid" : *yù,* jade + *lán²,* orchid.]
Yule (yōōl) *n.* Christmas or the season or feast celebrating Christmas. [Middle English *yole, yule,* Old English *gēol(a)*†.]
yule log *n.* A large log traditionally burned in the fireplace at Christmas.
Yule·tide (yōōl′tīd′) *n.* The Christmas season.
Yu·ma (yōō′mə) *n., pl.* **-mas** or collectively **Yuma. 1.** A member of a Yuman-speaking North American Indian people of southwestern Arizona and the adjacent parts of California and Mexico. **2.** The language of this people. [Spanish *Yuma*†.]
Yu·man (yōō′mən) *n.* A language family comprising the languages of the Yuma and Mohave Indians and other North American Indian languages. —**Yu·man** *adj.*
yum·my (yŭm′ē) *adj.* **-mier, -miest.** *Informal.* Delightful; delicious. [From *yum,* imitative of the sound made by smacking lips.]
Yun·nan or **Yün·nan** (yōō′nän′). Province of southwest China. It is chiefly mountainous and is crossed by the Huang, Lancang (Mekong), and Nu (Salween) rivers. Its capital is Kunming.
yup. Variant of **yep.**
yup·pie (yŭp′ē) *n. Informal.* A young urban dweller with a professional career. [Abbreviation of *young urban professional* + -IE.]
yurt (yûrt) *n., pl.* **yurta** (yūr′tə). A circular, domed, portable tent used by the nomadic Mongols of Siberia. [Russian *yurta,* from Turkic; akin to Turkish *yurt,* home.]
Y.W.C.A. Young Women's Christian Association.
Y.W.H.A. Young Women's Hebrew Association.
ywis. Variant of **iwis.**

YUGOSLAVIA

HUNGARY

Maribor · Triglav 2863m · Jesenice · Karawanken · Ljubljana
Postojna · Koper · Pula · Cres · Krk · Rijeka · Sušak · Zagreb
SLOVENIA · Kupa · Drava · Pannonia · Subotica
VOJVODINA · Novi Sad · Dunav (Danube)
CROATIA · Brod · Sava · Zemun · BELGRADE
Gulf of Venice · Banja Luka · Tuzla · Smed. · Iron Gate
ROMANIA
BOSNIA · Zenica · Sarajevo · Morava · Kragujevac · 44°N
Split · HERCEGOVINA · DALMATIA · SERBIA
Solta · Brač · Hvar · Sjenica · Niš
MONTENEGRO · Mljet · Nikšić · Priština · Leskovac
ADRIATIC SEA · Dubrovnik · Titograd · Ibar
ITALY · Bar · 2702m Rudoke · Skopje · 42°N
Plan. · BULGARIA
ALBANIA · MACEDONIA
Bitole · Vardar · GREECE

0 100 200 300 Km
0 50 100 150 Miles
16°E 18°E 20°E 22°E 24°E

Z

z, Z (zē; *British* zĕd) *n., pl.* **z's** or **Z's.** **1.** The 26th letter of the modern English alphabet. **2.** Any of the speech sounds represented by this letter. **3.** Anything shaped like the letter *z*, such as a **z-bend** *(see).* **4.** The 26th in a series; 25th when *J* is omitted. **5.** The third in a series consisting of *x, y,* and *z.*

z, Z, z., Z. *Note:* As an abbreviation or symbol, *z* may be a small or a capital letter, with or without a period. Established forms or those generally preferred precede the definition. When no form is given, all four forms are in general use in that sense. **1. Z** atomic number. **2. Z** impedance. **3. z.** zero. **4. z.** zone. **5.** The symbol of an algebraic variable, especially the third variable in a tertiary equation.

za·ba·glio·ne (zä′bəl-yō′nē; *Italian* tzä-bä-lyō′nä) *n.* A dessert consisting of egg yolks, sugar, and wine, usually Marsala wine, beaten until thick and frothy and served either hot or cold. Also called "sabayon." [Italian *zaba(gl)ione.*]

Zach·a·ri·as (zăk′ə-rī′əs). Also **Zach·a·ri·ah** (-rī′ə). The husband of Elizabeth and father of John the Baptist. Luke 1:5.

Zad·kine (zăd′kēn′), **Ossip** (1890-1967). French sculptor. Born in Russia, he moved to Paris (1909) where he was heavily influenced by cubism in his representations of the human form. His most famous work is the memorial to the destruction of Rotterdam in World War II, *The Destroyed City* (1954).

zaf·fer, zaf·fre (zăf′ər) *n.* An impure oxide of cobalt, used to produce a blue color in enamel and in the making of smalt. [Italian *zaffera,* from Old French *safre,* from Arabic *ṣufr,* yellow copper.]

zaf·tig, zof·tig (zäf′tĭk, -tĭg) *adj. Slang.* **1.** Full-bosomed. **2.** Having a comfortably ample figure. [Yiddish, "plump."]

zag (zăg) *n.* A sharp turn in a different direction.
~*intr.v.* **zagged, zagging, zags.** To make a sharp turn or change of course. [Shortened from ZIGZAG.]

Za·greb (zä′grĕb′). Capital of Croatia, north-central Yugoslavia. On the Sava River, it was a Roman city and became a center for Yugoslav nationalism in the 19th century.

Zag·re·us (zăg′rē-əs). *Greek Mythology.* A god worshiped in Orphic cults and identified with Dionysus.

zai·bat·su (zī′bät-sōō′) *n., pl.* **zaibatsu.** Any of the powerful, family-controlled commercial combines of Japan. [Japanese, from Chinese *cái fá,* plutocrat : *cái,* wealth + *fá,* powerful person or family.]

za·ire (zīr, zä-îr′) *n.* The basic monetary unit of Zaire, equal to 100 makuta or 10,000 sengi. See feature at **currency.** [Portugese, from Kongo *nzadi,* large river.]

Za·ire¹ (zī′îr, zä-îr′). Also **Con·go** (kŏng′gō). River of central Africa. Formed by the confluence of the Lualaba and Luvua rivers near the Zaire–Zambian border, it flows 4,667 kilometers (2,900 miles) west and southwest to form the Zaire-Congo border and enter the Atlantic Ocean through a wide delta at Boma. It was explored by Capt. J. Tuckey (1816), David Livingstone (1871), and Henry Stanley (1874-77). It is navigable by shipping to Matadi and is the second-longest river of Africa.

Zaire². Formerly **Belgian Congo, Democratic Republic of the Congo.** Republic of central Africa. Situated almost entirely in the basin of the Zaire River, with a small coastline on the Atlantic ocean, it is largely equatorial rain forest, with the Ruwenzori Mts. in the southeast and savannah in the north and south. Discovered by the Portuguese (15th century), it was a source of slaves (17th to 19th century) and in 1908 was annexed by Belgium, from whom independence was gained in 1960. The secession of Katanga region (1960) led to civil war and U.N. intervention. In 1965 Mobutu Sese Seko seized power and later defeated attempts by Katanganese forces, backed by Cuba and Angola, to assume power (1977-78). Crops include tea, coffee, rubber, cocoa, palm oil, and cotton, and there are reserves of copper, zinc, cobalt, diamonds, oil, and natural gas. Area, 2,345,409 square kilometers (905,568 square miles). Population, 28,000,000. Capital, Kinshasa. —**Za·ir·e·an, Za·ir·ese** *n. & adj.*

za·kat (zə-kät′) *n.* A proportion of the income of a devout Muslim set aside to be devoted to the poor. [Arabic.]

Zam·be·zi (zăm-bē′zē). River of southern Africa. Rising in northwest Zambia, it flows 2,735 kilometers (1,700 miles) chiefly east-ward, forming the Zambia–Zimbabwe border, and enters the Indian Ocean through a wide delta near Chinde, Mozambique. Despite the many rapids along its length, it is navigable in stretches; it includes Victoria Falls and the Kariba and Cabora Bassa dams.

Zam·bi·a (zăm′bē-ə). Republic of south-central Africa. It consists chiefly of plateau, with mountains to the north and northeast and the basins of the Zambezi and Kafue rivers to the west. It produces maize, groundnuts, cotton, tobacco, and sugar, while cattle raising is important in the east. Copper, zinc, cobalt, and emeralds are mined, and there are unexploited iron deposits. Explored by Livingstone (1850's to 1870's), it became the British protectorate of Northern Rhodesia (1911), was incorporated into the Federation of Rhodesia and Nyasaland (1953-63), and achieved independence in 1964. Area, 752,614 square kilometers (290,586 square miles). Population, 5,700,000. Capital, Lusaka. —**Zam·bi·an** *n. & adj.*

za·mi·a (zā′mē-ə) *n.* Any of various chiefly tropical American cycads of the genus *Zamia,* having a thick, usually underground trunk and a crown of palmlike terminal leaves. [New Latin *Zamia,* from a misreading of *(nūces) azāniae,* pine (nuts), probably from Greek *azainein,* to dry, parch.]

za·min·dar, ze·min·dar (zə-mĕn-där′) *n.* **1.** An official in India during the Mogul empire assigned to collect the land taxes of his district. **2.** A native landholder in British colonial India, responsible for collecting and paying to the government the taxes on the land under his jurisdiction. [Persian *zamīndār : zamīn,* earth, land + *-dār,* holder, from Old Persian *dār-,* to hold.]

za·min·da·ri (zə-mĕn-där′ē) *n., pl.* **-is.** Also **ze·min·da·ry** (zə-mĕn-där′ē, zĕm′ən-där′ē) *pl.* **-ies.** **1.** The system of tax collection by zamindars. **2.** The area administered by a zamindar. [Hindi *zamīndāri,* from Persian, from *zamīndār,* ZAMINDAR.]

zanana. Variant of **zenana.**

Z.A.N.U., ZANU (zä′nōō). Zimbabwe African National Union.

Zan·uck (zăn′ək), **Darryl Francis** (1902-79). U.S. motion-picture producer. The producer of *The Jazz Singer* (1927), the first feature-length film with sound sequences, he became known for his socially

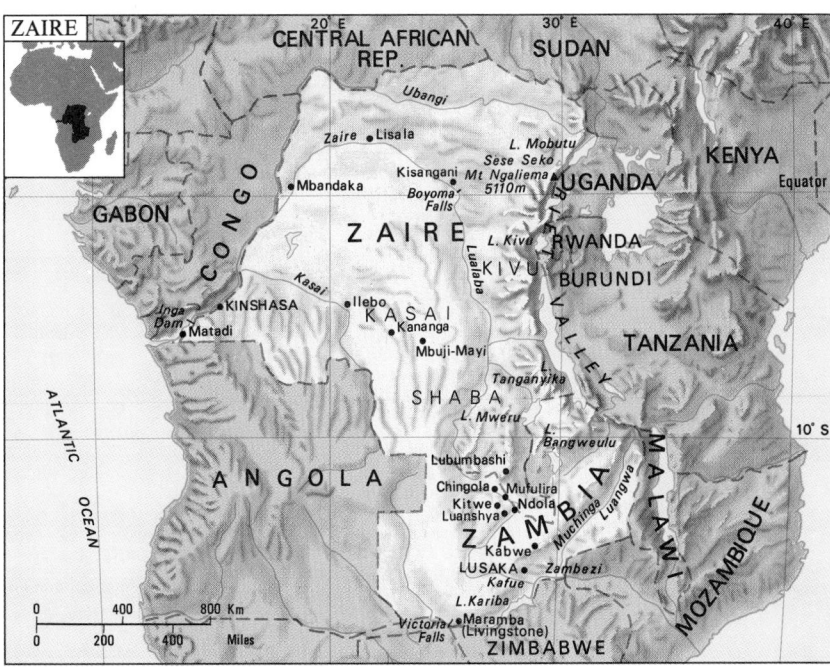

zebra *Of the three types of zebra in Africa, Burchell's zebra (above)—named after a 19th-century English naturalist—is the most common, ranging over most of the south and east of the continent.*

zebra finch *One of the Australian weaver finches, the zebra finch has been widely bred as a cage bird. In the wild it lives on open grassland.*

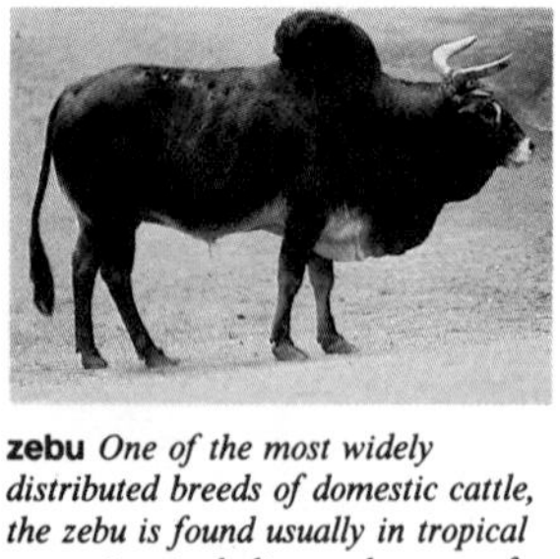

zebu *One of the most widely distributed breeds of domestic cattle, the zebu is found usually in tropical or semitropical climates because of its ability to cope with heat and its resistance to some tropical diseases. It is used as a beast of burden and reared for its milk and meat. The hump on the zebu's back is composed of muscle fibers that may once have strengthened its shoulder muscles but which now seem to serve no useful purpose. Males have larger humps than females.*

significant motion pictures. Associated with Twentieth Century-Fox for much of his career, he produced several classic films, including *Grapes of Wrath* (1940) and *Gentlemen's Agreement* (1947).

za·ny (zā′nē) *n., pl.* **-nies. 1.** A ludicrous, buffoonish character in old comedies who attempts feebly to mimic the tricks of the clown. **2.** A comical person given to extravagant or outlandish behavior. *~adj.* **zanier, -niest. 1.** Inventively and eccentrically humorous; bizarrely funny. **2.** Ludicrously comical; clownish; droll. [Italian *zani, zanni,* buffoon, from *Zanni,* dialectal variant of *Gianni,* pet form for *Giovanni,* John.]

Zan·zi·bar (zăn′zə-bär′). Coral island of Tanzania, eastern Africa, situated in the Indian Ocean. It was ruled by the Portuguese after 1503, before passing to the Arabs of Oman in 1698, and became a British protectorate in 1890. It achieved independence in 1963 and, with the exile of its sultan (1964), was united with Tanganyika to form Tanzania. Cocoa, rice, cloves, and copra are exported. **—Zan·zi·bar·i** *n. & adj.*

zap (zăp) *v.* **zapped, zapping, zaps.** *Slang.* *—tr.* **1.** To destroy or kill suddenly and violently, as with a burst of gunfire, flame, or electric current. **2.** To attack with heavy firepower; strafe or bombard. **3.** To hit suddenly and violently. *—intr.* To move very fast: *zapped along the road.*
~n. Slang. Vigor; vitality.
~interj. Slang. Used to indicate a sudden occurrence. [Imitative.]

Zapadnaya Dvina. See **Dvina, Western.**

Za·pa·ta (sä-pä′tä), **Emiliano** (*c.* 1877–1919). Mexican revolutionary. For the cause of agrarian reform he led an American Indian revolt (1910–15); he ruled the state of Morelos and occupied Mexico City three times.

za·pa·te·a·do (zä-pä-tā-ä′dō) *n., pl.* **-dos.** *Spanish.* **1.** The rhythmic stamping of the heels characteristic of Spanish flamenco dances. **2.** A Spanish flamenco dance in which the performer stamps rhythmically with his heels. [Spanish, from *zapatear,* to tap with the shoe, from *zapáto,* shoe.]

Zap·o·tec (zä′pə-tĕk′, sä′-) *n.* Any of a group of Central American languages spoken in southern Mexico. **—Zap·o·tec** *adj.*

zap·per (zăp′ər) *n.* **1.** A device used for directing radiation at a target, especially insects or weeds. **2.** *Slang.* A forcefully critical remark.

Z.A.P.U., ZAPU (zä′po͞o). Zimbabwe African People's Union.

Za·ra·go·za (sä′rä-gô′sä). *English* **Sar·a·gos·sa** (săr′ə-gŏs′ə). Capital of Zaragoza province, northeast Spain. On the Ebro River, it is in an agricultural region for which it is a market center. Its industries include textiles, food processing, and leather goods. Held by the Moors (8th to early 12th century), it was capital of Aragon (12th to 15th century) and resisted sieges by the French (1808–09) during the Peninsula War.

Zarathustra. See **Zoroaster.**

zar·a·tite (zăr′ə-tīt′) *n.* A green amorphous form of hydrated nickel carbonate, $NiCO_3 \cdot 2Ni(OH)_2 \cdot 4H_2O$. [Spanish *zaratita,* after G. *Zárate,* 19th-century Spanish mineralogist.]

za·re·ba, za·ri·ba, za·ree·ba (zə-rē′bə) *n.* **1.** An enclosure of bushes or stakes protecting a campsite or village in northeastern Africa. **2.** A campsite or village so protected. [Arabic *zarībah,* pen for cattle, from *zarb,* sheepfold.]

zarf (zärf) *n.* A chalicelike holder for a hot coffee cup, typically made of ornamented metal, used in the Middle East. [Arabic *ẓarf,* "container."]

zastruga. Variant of **sastruga.**

z-ax·is (zē′ăk′sĭs) *n., pl.* **z-axes** (-ăk′sēz′). **1.** One of the three axes in a three-dimensional Cartesian coordinate system. **2.** The vertical axis of an aircraft.

za·yin (zä′yĭn) *n.* The seventh letter of the Hebrew alphabet. See feature at **alphabet.** [Hebrew *zayin,* "weapon," from Aramaic.]

z-bend (zē′bĕnd′) *n.* A pair of successive sharp bends on a road.

zeal (zēl) *n.* Enthusiastic and diligent devotion in pursuit of a cause, ideal, or goal; fervent adherence or service; ardent commitment: *religious zeal.* —See Synonyms at **passion.** [Middle English *zele,* from Late Latin *zēlus,* from Greek *zēlos.*]

Zealand. See **Sjaelland.**

zeal·ot (zĕl′ət) *n.* **1.** One who is zealous; a fanatically committed person. See Synonyms at **fanatic. 2. Zealot.** A member of a Jewish sect that resisted Roman rule in Palestine during the 1st century A.D. [Late Latin *zēlōtes,* from Greek *zēlōtēs,* from *zēlos,* ardor, fervor, ZEAL.]

zeal·ot·ry (zĕl′ə-trē) *n.* Excessive zeal; fanaticism.

zeal·ous (zĕl′əs) *adj.* Filled with or motivated by zeal; ardent; enthusiastic; fervent. —See Synonyms at **eager. —zeal·ous·ly** *adv.* **—zeal·ous·ness** *n.*

ze·a·tin (zē′ə-tĭn) *n. Botany.* A naturally occurring cytokinin (a plant growth substance) found in corn kernels. [New Latin *Zea,* genus name for maize (see **zein**) + *-tin,* as in *kinetin.*]

zebec, zebeck. Variants of **xebec.**

Zeb·e·dee (zĕb′ə-dē). A fisherman whose sons James and John became disciples of Jesus. Matthew 4:21.

ze·bra (zē′brə) *n.* Any of several horselike African mammals of the genus *Equus,* having characteristic overall markings of conspicuous dark and whitish stripes. [Portuguese, from Old Spanish *zebra, zebro†,* wild ass.]

zebra finch *n.* A small Australian bird, *Poephila castanotis* (or *Taeniopygia castanotis* or *T. guttata),* having black and white striped markings and popular as a cage bird.

zebra fish *n.* A small freshwater tropical fish, *Brachydanio rerio,* of India, having horizontal dark-blue and silvery stripes and popular in home aquariums. Also called "zebra danio."

ze·bra·wood (zē′brə-wo͝od′) *n.* **1.** Any of several African or tropical American trees having striped wood, especially *Connarus guianensis.* **2.** The wood of such a tree, used in cabinetmaking.

ze·bu (zē′byo͞o) *n.* A domesticated bovine mammal, *Bos indicus,* of Asia and Africa, having a prominent hump on the back and a large dewlap. [French *zébu†.*]

Zeb·u·lon[1], Zeb·u·lun (zĕb′yə-lən). A son of Jacob and Leah. Genesis 30:20. [Hebrew *Zəbhūlōn,* from *zəbhūl,* dwelling, from *zābhal,* he dwelt.]

Zebulon[2], Zebulun *n.* A tribe of Israel descended from Zebulon.

zec·chi·no (zĕk-kē′nō) *n., pl.* **-ni** (-nē) or **-nos.** Also **zec·chin** (zĕk′ĭn), **zech·in.** A coin, a **sequin** *(see).* [Italian, SEQUIN.]

Zech. Zechariah (Old Testament).

Zech·a·ri·ah[1] (zĕk′ə-rī′ə). A Hebrew prophet of the 6th century B.C.

Zechariah[2] *n. Abbr.* **Zech.** A book of the Old Testament.

zed (zĕd) *n. Chiefly British.* The letter *z.* [Middle English *zed,* from Old French *zede,* from Late Latin *zēta,* ZETA.]

Zed·e·ki·ah (zĕd′ə-kī′ə). The last king of Judah (597–586 B.C.), who died in captivity at Babylon. II Kings 24:17. [Hebrew, *Ṣidqīyāh(ū),* "the Lord is righteousness."]

zed·o·ar·y (zĕd′ō-ĕr′ē) *n.* The dried rhizome of a tropical Asian plant, *Curcuma zedoaria,* used as a stimulant and condiment and in cosmetics. [Middle English *zeodoarye,* from Medieval Latin *zeodoaria,* from Arabic *zadwār,* from Persian *zedwārt†.*]

zee (zē) *n.* The letter *z.* [Variant (17th-century) of ZED.]

Zee·land (zē′lənd). Province of southwestern Netherlands. On the Scheldt estuary, it is bordered by Belgium in the south and includes the islands of Walcheren and North and South Beveland. It produces sugar beet, grains, flax, and fruit and has chemical and automobile industries. Its capital is Middelburg.

Zee·man (zē′mən), **Pieter** (1865–1943). Dutch physicist. Famous for his work on magneto-optics, he discovered the Zeeman effect. In 1902 he shared the Nobel Prize for physics with H.A. Lorentz.

Zeeman effect *n.* The splitting of single spectral lines of an emission spectrum into three or more polarized components when the radiation source is in a magnetic field. [After Pieter ZEEMAN.]

Zef·fi·rel·li (zĕf′ə-rĕl′ē), **Franco** (1923–). Italian stage and film director. Beginning his career as an actor and stage designer, he achieved recognition for directing a series of operas, including *La Cenerentola* (1953) at La Scala and *I Pagliacci* (1959) at Covent Garden. His films include *The Taming of the Shrew* (1966), *Romeo and Juliet* (1967), and *Jesus of Nazareth* (1977).

ze·in (zē′ĭn) *n.* A prolamine protein derived from corn and used in the manufacture of various plastics, coatings, and lacquers. [New Latin *Zea,* genus name for corn, from Greek *zea, zeia,* one-seeded wheat + -IN.]

Zeiss (zīs), **Carl** (1816–88). German industrialist and optician. After establishing his first workshop at Jena (1846), he joined Ernst Abbe (1840–1905) in 1866 to produce field glasses, microscopes, and later cameras using new optical techniques and materials, including heat-resistant glass.

Zeit·geist (tsīt′gīst′) *n.* The spirit of the time; the taste and outlook characteristic of a period or generation. [German, "time-spirit."]

zek (zĕk) *n.* An inmate of a Soviet labor camp. [Russian, from *zaklyuchenny,* prisoner.]

zemindar. Variant of **zamindar.**

zemindary. Variant of **zamindari.**

zemst·vo (zĕms′tvō) *n., pl.* **-vos.** An elective council responsible for the local administration of a provincial district in czarist Russia. [Russian, from *zemlya,* land.]

ze·na·na, za·na·na (zə-nä′nə) *n.* The part of a house in Asian countries such as India and Pakistan reserved for the women of the household. [Hindi *zenāna,* from Persian, from *zan,* woman.]

Zen (zĕn) *n.* A Chinese and Japanese school of Mahayana Buddhism that asserts that enlightenment can be attained through meditation, self-contemplation, and intuition rather than through the scriptures. Also called "Zen Buddhism." [Japanese *zen,* meditation, from Chinese *chan*; akin to Sanskrit *dhyāna,* he meditates.] **—Zen Buddhist** *n. & adj.*

Zend (zĕnd) *n.* **1.** The Zend-Avesta. **2.** Formerly, a language, **Avestan** *(see).*

Zend-A·ves·ta (zĕnd′ə-vĕs′tə) *n.* The entire body of sacred writings of the Zoroastrian religion. Also called "Zend." [Persian *zandavastā, zendastā,* from *Avesta-va-zend,* Avesta with an interpretation : Middle Persian *apastāk,* AVESTA + *va,* with + *zend†,* interpretation.] **—Zend-A·ves·ta·ic** (zĕnd′ə-vĕs′tā′ĭk) *adj.*

Ze·ner current (zē′nər) *n.* A current in certain p-n junctions produced, at the point of **Zener breakdown,** by electrons from the valence band that have been excited into the conduction band as a result of the application of a strong electric field. [After C.M. *Zener* (1905–), U.S. physicist.]

Zener diode *n.* A semiconductor diode used as a voltage regulator, in which at a specific reverse voltage there is a sharp increase in reverse current. [After C.M. *Zener;* see **Zener current.**]

Zeng·er (zĕng′ər, -gər), **John Peter** (1697–1746). U.S. printer and journalist, born in Germany. As editor of the *New York Weekly Journal* (1733–46), an antigovernment newspaper, he was arrested for seditious libel against the governor. He was acquitted in a trial that laid the foundations for freedom of the press and the right to criticize one's government and its officials (1735).

ze·nith (zē′nĭth) *n.* **1.** The point on the celestial sphere that is di-

Zen

JAPAN'S FORM OF BUDDHISM

Enlightenment through meditation and paradox

Zen is a branch of the Buddhist religion that has about nine million followers worldwide, most of whom live in Japan. In the 6th century B.C. Buddhism was brought from India to China where it was influenced by Taoism. In the 12th century it was transferred in its new form to Japan.

The aim of Zen is the same as that of mainstream Buddhism —to achieve nirvana, or enlightenment, and release from the cycle of death and rebirth that binds man to the world. This release is said to be reached by looking beyond the reality of the world and becoming aware of one's own immortal nature. The two main branches of Zen believe different aspects of Buddhism to be the fundamental truth. In Soto Zen meditation is the gradual path to self-awareness and liberation. In Rinzai Zen mental concepts produced by language are seen as the chief barrier to spiritual development. Paradoxes, called koans, are used to destroy the hold of language on the mind and bring a person to liberation through a sudden awakening. An example is: "Imagine the sound of one hand clapping."

Zen, with its rejection of the intellect, developed partly as a reaction against the idolization of scripture in mainstream Buddhism. Zen states that nirvana is possible for all people, not just reclusive monks, and aims to engender tranquillity, fearlessness, and spontaneity through a life of hard work and social concern.

Zen was the main religion of Japan in the 14th and 15th centuries and considerably influenced poetry, calligraphy, and painting. Disciplined spontaneity was developed by archery, flower arranging, and landscape gardening.

STONE GARDEN *A Zen stone garden is a place for meditation that goes beyond the normal concepts of conscious thought. The raked sand may represent the emptiness of mind that brings nirvana; the rocks may represent thoughts that obscure this enlightened state.*

STRICT REGIME *A monk sits in contemplation, part of the strict regime of the Koninji Temple, which is the cradle of Rinzai Zen in Japan.*

rectly above the observer. **2.** The highest point above the observer's horizon attained by a celestial body. **3.** The highest point of any path or course; a point of culmination; a peak; a summit. —See Synonyms at **summit.** [Middle English, from Old French *cenith,* from Old Spanish *zenit,* from Arabic *samt,* road, in *samt ar-ra's,* road (over) the head.] —**ze·nith·al** (zē′nĭth-əl) *adj.*

zenithal projection *n.* A form of map projection in which a part of the earth's surface is projected onto a plane tangential to it such that all points have their true compass bearings from the central point.

Ze·no·bi·a (zə-nō′bē-ə) (3rd century A.D.). Queen of Palmyra (part of Syria) from 267 A.D. Acceding to the throne after the death of her husband, Odenathus, she acted as regent for her son and extended her empire to include Syria, Egypt, and part of Asia Minor. In 272 she was defeated and captured by the Roman emperor Aurelian.

Ze·no of Cit·i·um (zē′no; sĭt′ē-əm) (*c.* 334-262 B.C.). Greek philosopher. He founded the Stoic school of philosophy, which taught that virtue is necessarily good and that most objects of desire, such as material possessions, family, and honors, are morally indifferent or at best only relatively good.

Zeno of E·le·a (ē′lē′ə) (*c.* 495-430 B.C.). Greek philosopher. Referred to by Aristotle as the inventor of dialectic, he formulated numerous paradoxes that seem to refute pluralism and the existence of motion and change. His arguments provided rigorous challenges for philosophers and mathematicians.

ze·o·lite (zē′ə-līt′) *n.* Any of a large group of hydrous calcium and aluminum silicate minerals or their corresponding synthetic compounds, used chiefly as molecular filters, water-softeners, and ion-exchange agents. [Swedish *zeolit,* "boiling stone" (because it swells and boils under the blowpipe) : Greek *zeein,* to boil + -LITE.]

Zeph. Zephaniah (Old Testament).

Zeph·a·ni·ah[1] (zĕf′ə-nī′ə). Hebrew prophet of the 7th century B.C.

Zephaniah[2] *n. Abbr.* **Zeph.** A book of the Old Testament containing the prophecies of Zephaniah.

zeph·yr (zĕf′ər) *n.* **1. a.** A gentle breeze. **b.** The west wind. **2.** Any of various light, soft fabrics, yarns, or garments. **3.** Any airy, insubstantial. or passing thing. —See Synonyms at **wind.** [Middle English *Zephirus,* from Latin *zephyrus,* from Greek *zephyros,* akin to *zophos†,* darkness, west.]

zephyr lily *n.* Any of several plants of the genus *Zephyranthes,* native to tropical America, having grasslike leaves and variously colored flowers.

Zeph·y·rus (zĕf′ər-əs). *Greek Mythology.* A god personifying the gentle west wind. [Latin, from Greek *Zephuros,* from *zephuros,* ZEPHYR.]

zep·pe·lin (zĕp′ə-lĭn; *German* tsĕp′ə-lēn′) *n. Sometimes* **Zeppelin.** A rigid airship having a long, cylindrical body supported by internal gas cells. [After its inventor, Ferdinand von ZEPPELIN.]

Zeppelin, Count Ferdinand von (1838–1917). German inventor. After retiring from the army (1891), he designed and built the first motorized, rigid-frame dirigible balloon.

Zer·matt (zĕr′mät). Resort of Valais canton, south Switzerland. Situated at the foot of the Matterhorn, it is a mountaineering and winter sports center.

ze·ro (zîr′ō, zē′rō) *n., pl.* **-ros** or **-roes.** *Abbr.* **z. 1.** The numeral, or numerical symbol, "0"; a naught. **2.** *Mathematics.* **a.** An element of a set that when added to any other element in the set produces a sum identical with the element to which it is added. **b.** A cardinal number indicating the absence of any or all units under consideration. **c.** An ordinal number indicating an initial point or origin. **d.** An argument at which the value of a function vanishes. **3. a.** The starting point on a scale of measurement. **b.** The position on a scale marking the point between positive and negative values. **4.** The temperature indicated by the numeral 0 on a thermometer. **5.** A sight setting that enables a firearm to shoot on target. **6.** One having no influence or importance; a nonentity; a nobody. **7.** The lowest point: *His prospects were set at zero.* **8.** Nothing; nil. ~*adj.* **1.** Of, pertaining to, or being zero. **2. a.** Having no measurable or otherwise determinable value: *zero economic growth.* **b.** Absent, inoperative, or irrelevant in specified circumstances: *zero energy.* **3. a.** Limited by cloud cover to little or no vertical visibility. **b.** Permitting little or no horizontal visibility. **4.** *Informal.* No; not any: *She showed zero interest in my problems.* ~*tr.v.* **zeroed, -roing, -roes.** To adjust (an instrument or device) to zero value. —**zero in. 1.** To aim or concentrate firepower on an exact target location. **2.** To adjust the aim or sight of by repeated firings. **3.** To converge intently; move near; close in: *The children zeroed in on the toy display.* [French *zéro,* from Italian *zero,* from Medieval Latin *zephirum,* from Arabic *şifr,* zero, CIPHER.]

zero gravity *n.* The state of weightlessness; the condition of not experiencing the effects of gravity.

zero hour *n.* The scheduled time for the start of an operation or action, especially a concerted military attack. Also called "H-hour."

ze·ro-point energy (zîr′ō-point′, zē′rō-) *n.* The irreducible minimum energy possessed by a substance at the temperature of absolute zero.

zero population growth *n. Abbr.* **ZPG** The limiting of population increase to the number of live births needed to maintain the existing population level.

ze·roth (zîr′ōth, zē′rōth) *n.* Anything, such as an element or term, that is considered to come before the first in a series. [ZERO + -TH (suffix of ordinals and fractions).] —**ze·roth** *adj. & adv.*

zest (zĕst) *n.* **1.** Added flavor or interest; piquancy; charm. **2.** Spir-

ited enjoyment; enthusiasm; gusto: "*At fifty-three he retains all the heady zest of adolescence*" (Kenneth Tynan). **3.** The outermost part of the rind of an orange or lemon, used as flavoring.
~*tr.v.* **zested, zesting, zests.** To give zest, charm, or spirit to. [French *zest†,* orange or lemon peel.] —**zest·ful** *adj.*

ze·ta (zā′tə, zē′-) *n.* The sixth letter in the Greek alphabet, written Z, ζ. Transliterated in English as Z, z. See feature at **alphabet.** [Late Latin *zēta,* from Greek, probably from Semitic, akin to Hebrew *zayit,* Aramaic *zētā.*]

ZETA (zē′tə) *n.* A torus-shaped ring in which a plasma is contained by magnetic fields in order that thermonuclear reactions may be examined. [*Z*ero-*e*nergy *t*hermonuclear *a*pparatus.]

zeug·ma (zōōg′mə) *n.* **1.** The use of a single word, especially a verb or adjective, to apply to two or more nouns, when its sense is appropriate to only one of them; for example, *He held his tongue and his oath; Pedal your bicycle rather than your car.* **2.** Loosely, a syllepsis. Compare **syllepsis.** [Latin, from Greek *zeugma,* a joining, uniting, yoking.]

Zeus (zōōs). The presiding god of the Greek pantheon, ruler of the heavens and father of other gods and mortal heroes. [Greek.]

Zeux·is (zōōk′sĭs) (*fl.* 5th century B.C.). Greek painter. One of the first Athenian artists to use shading in his work, he produced paintings of mythological figures and genre subjects that appeared highly realistic when compared with the traditional Greek works of simple outline.

Zhan·jiang (jän′jyäng′). Seaport in Guangdong province, south China, having a large harbor. In 1898 it was made a French foreign concession, and its architecture still retains some foreign influence.

Zhe·jiang (jŭ′jyäng′). China's smallest, most densely populated province, on the East China Sea coast. The north is part of the Chang Jiang valley, and the south, apart from the Fuchun Jiang valley, is mountainous. Zhejiang is a major rice, soy bean, wheat, cotton, and tea producing area. Its capital is the industrial port of Hangzhou.

Zheng·zhou, Cheng-chou, Cheng-chow (jŭng′jō′). Capital of Henan province, south-central China. An important industrial city and rail center on the Huang He, it produces heavy machinery and textiles.

Zhou or **Chou** (jō). A Chinese dynasty that ruled from c. 1027 to 221 B.C., enlarging the empire and promoting philosophy.

Zhou En-lai, Chou En-Lai (jō′ ĕn-lī′) (1898–1976). Chinese statesman. After studying in Japan and Europe, he became an increasingly important leader of the Chinese Communist Party. He organized a general strike in Shanghai (1927) and later an insurrection in Nanjing. He was the first prime minister (1949–76) and foreign minister (1949–58) of the People's Republic of China.

Zhu Du (jōō′ dŭ′) (1886–1976). Chinese Communist leader. After joining the Communist Party while studying in Germany (1922–26), he returned to his homeland where he took part in an unsuccessful rebellion that is regarded as the birth of the Chinese Red Army (1927). He joined Mao Ze-dong's efforts later that year and retained command of Chinese Communist military forces until 1954.

Zhu·jiang, Chu-chiang (jōō′jyäng′). River of southeast China. On its large, fertile delta lie the cities of Guangzhou (Canton) and Macao and the colony of Hong Kong.

Zhukiang. See **Chukiang.**

Zhu·kov (zhōō′kôv), **Georgi Konstantinovich** (1896–1974). Marshal of the U.S.S.R. Joining the Red Army in 1918, he rose to army chief of staff (1941). He directed the counteroffensive at Stalingrad (1943), relieved Leningrad (1943), and captured Berlin (1945). He served under Khrushchev as defense minister (1955–57) but was attacked for "political mistakes" (1957).

Zi·a ul-Haq (zē′ə ōōl-häk′), **Mohammed** (1924–). President of Pakistan. An army general, he led the military coup that overthrew President Bhutto (1977) and became martial-law administrator and then president (1978). Under his rule, general elections were postponed, Bhutto was executed, and strict Islamic laws were introduced.

zib·e·line, zib·el·line (zĭb′ə-lēn′, -lĭn) *n.* **1.** A thick, lustrous, soft fabric of wool and other animal hair, such as mohair, having a silky nap. **2.** *Rare.* The sable or its fur. [Old French, from Old Italian *zibellino,* from Slavic, akin to Russian *sobol†.*]

zib·et, zib·eth (zĭb′ĭt) *n.* A civet cat, *Viverra zibetha,* of southeastern Asia. [Italian *zibetto,* from Medieval Latin *zibethum,* from Arabic *zabād,* CIVET.]

Zieg·feld (zĕg′fĕld′, zĭg′-), **Florenz** (1867–1932). U.S. theater manager. Adapting the style of the Parisian Folies-Bergère, he became famous for his extravagant revues, known as the Ziegfeld Follies (1907–32). The discoverer of many entertainers, including Eddie Cantor and W.C. Fields, he produced musicals such as *Show Boat* (1927) and *Bitter Sweet* (1929).

Zieg·ler (zĕg′lər), **Karl** (1898–1973). German organic chemist. For his work on long-chain polymers and the use of catalysts to control polymerization in plastics production, he shared the Nobel Prize (1963).

Ziegler catalyst *n. Chemistry.* Any of a class of industrial catalysts that are mixed metal halides and organometallic compounds, used for promoting polymerization reactions to make stereospecific plastics with improved strength and other properties. The original such catalyst was a mixture of titanium chloride ($TiCl_4$) and aluminum trimethyl ($Al(CH_3)_3$), used to make high-density polythene from ethylene. [After Karl ZIEGLER.]

zig·gu·rat (zĭg′ŏŏ-răt′) *n.* Also **zik·ku·rat** (zĭk′-). A temple tower of the ancient Assyrians and Babylonians, having the form of a terraced pyramid of successively receding stories. [Assyrian *ziqquratu,* summit, mountain top, from *zaqaru-,* to be high.]

zig·zag (zĭg′zăg′) *n.* **1.** A line or course that proceeds by sharp turns in alternating directions. **2.** Any of a series of such sharp turns. **3.** Something exhibiting one or a series of sharp turns, such as a road or design.
~*adj.* Having or moving in a zigzag.
~*adv.* In a zigzag manner or pattern.
~*v.* **zigzagged, -zagging, -zags.** —*intr.* To move in or form a zigzag. —*tr.* To cause to move in or form a zigzag. [French, probably from German *Zickzack,* expressive formation.]

zig·zag·ger (zĭg′zăg′ər) *n.* **1.** A person or thing that zigzags. **2.** A sewing-machine attachment for sewing zigzag stitches.

zilch (zĭlch) *n. Slang.* **1.** Zero; nothing. **2.** An insignificant person; a nonentity. [20th century: origin obscure.]

zil·lion (zĭl′yən) *n. Informal.* An extremely large indefinite number. Used humorously.
~*adj. Informal.* Very many. [*z-* (perhaps representing the largest conceivable number) + (M)ILLION.]

Zil·pah (zĭl′pə). The servant of Leah who bore Jacob two sons, Gad and Asher. Genesis 30:9-13.

Zim·bab·we (zĭm-bä′bwĕ, -bwä). Formerly **Rho·de·sia** (rō-dē′zhə). Landlocked country of south-central Africa. It is made up of four main plateaus, including the Limpopo lowlands and forested Zambezi valley. Agriculture, mainly at subsistence level, accounts for only 16 percent of its gross domestic product, and manufacturing 25 percent. U.N. sanctions (imposed 1965) led to considerable diversification of manufacturing. The country has major reserves of timber and minerals, including coal. Its chief exports are gold, tobacco, iron and steel, chrome ore, asbestos, cotton, and nickel. Tourism is also important. Cecil Rhodes and his British South Africa Company obtained mineral rights in and claimed what are now Matabeleland and Mashonaland in the 1880's. After 1898 these formed the British colony of Southern Rhodesia, which became self-governing in 1923. The area was part of the Federation of Rhodesia and Nyasaland (1953–63), which broke up largely because of African opposition to the dominance of Southern Rhodesia's white minority. Led by Ian Smith, the minority government failed to arrive at an independence settlement with Britain, largely because it would not accept black majority rule, and made an illegal unilateral declaration of independence (1965). A republic was declared (1970), but Rhodesia was increasingly isolated in the world, and the government faced a protracted guerrilla war from the Zimbabwe African People's Union (ZAPU), led by Joshua Nkomo, and the Zimbabwe African National Union (ZANU), led by Robert Mugabe. Eventually, as an outcome of the Commonwealth Conference of 1979, a peace formula involving majority rule was agreed on, and under British supervision, elections were held (March 1980). Mugabe became independent Zimbabwe's first prime minister (April 1980). Area, 390,580 square kilometers (150,764 square miles). Population, 7,400,000. Capital, Harare (formerly Salisbury). —**Zim·bab·we·an, Zim·bab·wi·an** *adj.* & *n.*

Zim·mer (zĭm′ər) *n.* A trademark for a lightweight, sturdy, metal frame that has four rubber-tipped feet and a wide, curved crossbar that is easy to hold, used as a support when walking.

zinc (zĭngk) *n. Symbol* **Zn** A bluish-white, lustrous metallic element that is brittle at room temperatures but malleable when heated. It is used to form a wide variety of alloys including brass, bronze, German silver, various solders, and nickel silver, in galvanizing iron and other metals, for electric fuses, anodes, and meter cases, and in roofing, gutters, and various household objects. Atomic number 30,

Zeus *In Greek mythology, Zeus became king of the gods after he led them to victory over the Titans—the giants who were the offspring of Heaven and Earth. This detail from an Athenian cup made in about 550 B.C. shows the birth of his daughter Athena, who sprang fully armed from Zeus's brow when Hephaestus, the god of fire, split it open with an ax.*

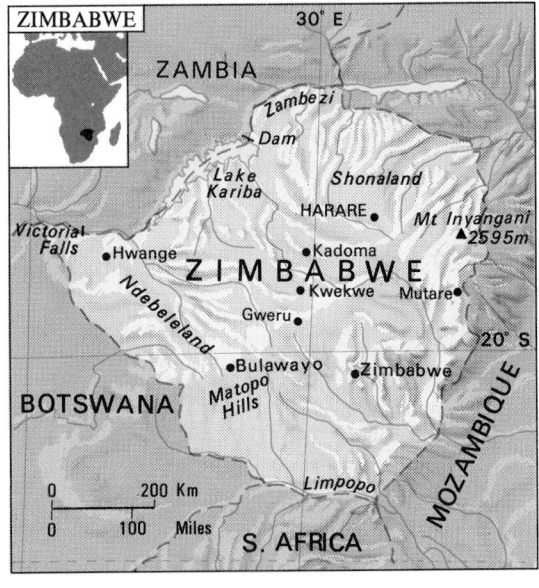

atomic weight 65.37, melting point 419.4°C, boiling point 907°C, specific gravity 7.133 (25°C), valence 2.

~*tr.v.* **zinced** or **zincked, zincing** or **zincking, zincs.** To coat or treat with zinc; galvanize. [German *Zink,* perhaps from *Zinke,* prong (so named because it becomes jagged in the furnace), from Old High German *zinko.*]

zinc·ate (zĭng′kāt′) *n.* Any of several chemical compounds derived from the reaction of zinc or zinc oxide with certain alkali solutions.

zinc blende *n.* A mineral, **sphalerite** (*see*).

zinc chloride *n.* A white soluble salt, $ZnCl_2$, used as a wood preservative, soldering flux, and medical astringent.

zinc·if·er·ous (zĭng-kĭf′ər-əs) *adj.* Designating a compound, ore, or mineral that contains zinc.

zinc·ite (zĭng′kīt′) *n.* A red to yellow-orange zinc ore, essentially ZnO.

zinc·o·graph (zĭng′kə-grăf′, -gräf′) *n.* **1.** A prepared zinc plate used in zincography. **2.** A print or picture obtained from such a plate. [ZINC + -GRAPH.]

zinc·og·ra·phy (zĭng-kŏg′rə-fē) *n.* The process of engraving zinc printing plates. [ZINC + -GRAPHY.] —**zinc·og·ra·pher** *n.* —**zinc·o·graph·ic** (zĭng′kə-grăf′ĭk), **zinc·o·graph·i·cal** *adj.*

zinc ointment *n. Medicine.* A salve consisting of about 20 percent zinc oxide with beeswax or paraffin and petrolatum, used in the treatment of skin diseases.

zinc oxide *n.* An amorphous white or yellowish powder, ZnO, used as a pigment, in compounding rubber, in the manufacture of plastics, and in pharmaceuticals and cosmetics. Also called "Chinese white," "zinc white."

zinc spinel *n.* A mineral, **gahnite** (*see*).

zinc sulfate *n.* A colorless crystalline compound, $ZnSO_4·7H_2O$, used medicinally as an emetic and astringent, as a fungicide, and in wood and skin preservatives. Also called "white vitriol."

zinc white *n.* A paint pigment, **zinc oxide** (*see*).

zin·fan·del (zĭn′făn-dĕl′) *n. Sometimes* **Zinfandel.** A dry red table wine from California. [Late 19th century : origin obscure.]

zing (zĭng) *n.* **1.** A brief high-pitched humming or buzzing sound, such as that made by a swiftly passing object. **2.** Zest; vigor.

~*intr.v.* **zinged, zinging, zings.** *Informal.* **1.** To make or move with such a sound. **2.** To move quickly or vigorously. [Imitative.]

zin·ga·ro (tsēn′gä-rō′) *n., pl.* **-ri** (-rē′). *Feminine* **zin·ga·ra** (tsēn′gä-rä′) *pl.* **-re** (-rē). A Gypsy. [Italian *zingaro,* probably from Greek *Athinganoi†* (plural), name of an oriental people.]

zin·jan·thro·pus (zĭn-jăn-thrō′pəs) *n.* Any extinct primate of the genus *Zinjanthropus.* See **australopithecine.** [New Latin : Arabic *Zinj,* East Africa + Greek *anthrōpos,* man.]

zink·en·ite, zinck·en·ite (zĭng′kə-nīt′) *n.* A steel-gray mineral, essentially $Pb_6Sb_{14}S_{27}$. [German *Zinkenit,* after J.K.L. *Zinken* (1790-1862), German mineralogist.]

zin·ni·a (zĭn′ē-ə) *n.* Any of various plants of the genus *Zinnia,* native to tropical America; especially, *Z. elegans,* widely cultivated for its showy, variously colored flowers. [New Latin *Zinnia,* after Johann Gottfried *Zinn* (1727-59), German botanist and physician.]

Zi·nov·iev (zĭ-nôf′yəf), **Gregory Evseyevich** (1883-1936). Soviet politician. Chairman of the Comintern after 1919, he was an influential government member until expelled from the party (1927). He was executed in a Stalinist purge. The publication in Britain of a forged letter allegedly from him contributed to the downfall of the Labour government (1924).

Zi·on (zī′ən) *n.* Also **Si·on.** **1. a.** The Jewish people; the Israelites. **b.** The Jewish homeland as a symbol of Judaism. **c.** Ancient Jerusalem. **2. a.** A place or religious community regarded as sacredly devoted to God; a city of God. **b.** Heaven. **3.** An idealized harmonious community; a utopia. **4.** In Rastafarian ideology, the promised land. Compare **Babylon.** [Middle English *Sion,* Old English, from Late Latin *Sīōn,* from Greek *Seiōn,* from Hebrew *Ṣīyōn.*]

Zion, Mount. **1.** The part of Jerusalem that was the City of David. **2.** The hill in Jerusalem on which Solomon's temple was built.

Zi·on·ism (zī′ə-nĭz′əm) *n.* A movement originally aimed at the reestablishment of a Jewish national homeland and state in Palestine and now concerned with the development of Israel. —**Zi·on·ist** *adj.* & *n.* —**Zi·on·is·tic** (zī′ə-nĭs′tĭk) *adj.*

Zion National Park. Scenic area, 59,550 hectares (147,035 acres), in southwestern Utah. It is noted for its many trails and its vividly colored cliffs, rock formations, and deep canyons. Zion Canyon, the park's main attraction, is a multicolored gorge 24 kilometers (15 miles) long and .8 kilometers (.5 miles) wide.

zip (zĭp) *n.* **1.** A brief, sharp, hissing sound, such as that made by a flying arrow. **2.** Energetic activity; zest; vim.

~*v.* **zipped, zipping, zips.** —*intr.* **1. a.** To move or act with a speed that makes or suggests a brief, sharp, hissing sound: *The cars zipped by endlessly.* **b.** To act or proceed swiftly and energetically. **2.** To become fastened by a zipper. Often used with *up.* —*tr.* To fasten with a zipper. Often used with *up.* [Imitative.]

Zip Code, zip code, ZIP Code *n.* Any of the multidigit code numbers assigned to postal delivery areas in the United States to expedite the sorting and delivery of mail. Also called "ZIP." [*Z*one *I*mprovement *P*lan.]

zip gun *n.* A crude homemade pistol.

zip·per (zĭp′ər) *n.* A fastening device consisting of parallel rows of metal or nylon teeth on adjacent edges of an opening that are interlocked by a sliding tab. [From ZIP.]

zip·py (zĭp′ē) *adj.* **-pier, -piest.** Full of energy; brisk; lively; snappy.

zir·con (zûr′kŏn′) *n.* A brown to colorless mineral, essentially

$ZrSiO_4$, which is heated, cut, and polished to form a brilliant blue-white gem. [German *Zirkon,* from French *jargon,* from Italian *giargone,* from Arabic *zarqūn,* from Persian *zargūn,* gold-coloured : *zar,* gold + *gūn-†.*]

zir·con·ate (zûr′kə-nāt′) *n.* Any of several chemical compounds formed by heating zirconium oxide with a metal carbonate or oxide in the presence of an acid. [ZIRCON + -ATE.]

zir·co·ni·um (zûr-kō′nē-əm) *n. Symbol* **Zr** A lustrous, grayish-white, strong, ductile metallic element obtained primarily from zircon and used chiefly in ceramic and refractory compounds, as an alloying agent, in nuclear reactors, and in medical prostheses. Atomic number 40, atomic weight 91.22, melting point 1,171°C, boiling point 4,377°C, specific gravity 6.53 (calculated), principal valence 4. [New Latin, from ZIRCON.]

zirconium oxide *n.* A hard, white, amorphous powder, ZrO_2, derived from zirconium and also found naturally, used chiefly in pigments, refractories, ceramics, and as an abrasive. Also called "zirconia."

zit (zĭt) *n. Slang.* A pimple. [20th century : origin obscure.]

zith·er (zĭth′ər, zĭth′-) *n.* Also **zith·ern** (-ərn). A musical instrument consisting of a flat sounding box with about 30 to 40 strings stretched over it and played horizontally with the fingertips or a plectrum. [German *Zither,* from Old High German *zithera, cithera,* from Latin *cithara,* from Greek *kithara,* CITHARA.] —**zith·er·ist** *n.*

zi·ti (zē′tē; *Italian* tsē′tē) *n.* A tubular pasta. [Italian, from plural of *zito,* boy.]

zi·zith (tsē-tsēt′, tsī′tsīs) *pl.n.* The tassels or fringes of thread on the four corners of ceremonial garments worn by Orthodox Jewish males. [Hebrew *ṣīṣīth,* tassel.]

zlo·ty (zlô′tē) *n., pl.* **-tys** or **zloty.** **1.** The basic monetary unit of Poland, equal to 100 groszy. See feature at **currency. 2.** A coin worth one zloty. [Polish *złoty,* "golden," from *złoto,* gold.]

Zn The symbol for the element zinc.

zo. Variant of **dzo.**

zo–. Variant of **zoo-.**

–zoa *suffix.* Indicates certain animal organisms or taxonomic groups; for example, **entozoa, Protozoa.** [New Latin, from Greek *zōia,* plural of *zōion,* animal.]

–zoan *suffix. Zoology.* Indicates animals within a taxonomic group; for example, **protozoan.** [From -ZOA.]

zo·di·ac (zō′dē-ăk′) *n.* **1. a.** *Astronomy.* A band of the celestial sphere, extending about eight degrees to either side of the ecliptic, that represents the path of the principal planets, the moon, and the sun. **b.** *Sometimes* **Zodiac.** In astrology, this band divided into 12 equal parts called signs, each 30 degrees wide, bearing the name of a constellation for which it was originally named but with which it no longer coincides owing to the precession of the equinoxes. **2.** A diagram or figure representing the signs of the zodiac. **3.** A complete circuit; a circle. [Middle English, from Old French *zodiaque,* from Latin *zōdiacus,* from Greek *zōidiakos (kuklos),* "(circle) of the zodiac," from *zōidion,* small represented figure, sign of the zodiac, diminutive of *zōion,* living being.] —**zo·di·a·cal** (zō-dī′ə-kəl) *adj.* See feature, next page.

zodiacal light *n.* A faint hazy cone of light, often visible in the west just after sunset or in the east just before sunrise, apparently caused by the reflection of sunlight from meteoric particles surrounding the sun.

zo·e·trope (zō′ə-trōp′) *n.* An optical toy consisting of a case containing a revolving cylinder bearing pictures that appear to move as they are viewed through a slit. [Originally a trademark; from Greek *zōē,* life + *tropos,* a turning, from *trepein,* to turn.]

Zof·fa·ny (zŏf′ə-nē), **Johann** (c. 1733-1810). German painter. Living chiefly in London after 1761, he secured royal patronage and painted many royal portraits as well as theatrical scenes.

zoftig. Variant of **zaftig.**

Zog I (zŏg) (1895-1961). King of Albania (1928-43). Educated in Istanbul, he served as prime minister (1922-24) and president (1925-28) but fled the country after its invasion by Italy (1939). He first settled in England and later moved to Egypt and France. He abdicated in 1943.

–zoic *suffix.* Indicates: **1.** A specified kind of animal existence; for example, **holozoic. 2.** A specified geological division; for example, **Mesozoic.** [Greek *zōikos,* of animals, from *zōion,* animal.]

zois·ite (zoi′sīt′) *n.* A gray or pink mineral, essentially $Ca_2Al_3(SiO_4)_3(OH)$. [German *Zoisit,* named after its discoverer, Baron S. *Zois* von Edelstein (1747-1819), Slovenian nobleman.]

Zo·la (zō′lə), **Émile Édouard Charles Antoine** (1840-1902). French novelist. Leader of the naturalist movement, he worked as a clerk and journalist before establishing his reputation with *Thérèse Raquin* (1867). Through the portrayal of a single extended family in *Les Rougon-Macquart,* a series of 20 novels including *L'Assommoir* (1877), *Nana* (1880), and *Germinal* (1885), he provided a detailed account of contemporary social problems. He was obliged to flee France after publishing *J'accuse* (1898), a defense of Alfred Dreyfus.

zoll·ver·ein (tsôl′fər-īn, zŏl′fə-rīn′) *n.* **1.** *Often* **Zollverein.** A union of German states during the 19th century that established a uniform tariff on imports from nonmembers and free trade among themselves. **2.** Any customs or tariff union. [German *Zollverein,* "custom union."]

zom·bie, zom·bi (zŏm′bē) *n.* **1.** A snake god of voodoo cults in West Africa, Haiti, and the southern United States. **2. a.** A supernatural power or spell that according to voodoo belief can enter

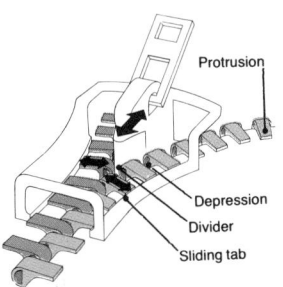

zipper *The zipper was invented by an American in 1893 as a quicker means of fastening boots, in place of buttons. It was unreliable until perfected by a Swede in 1912. The most common type of modern zipper fastener consists of two tapes with rows of teeth joined by a slide, or sliding tab. When the zipper is closed, the slide draws together the rows of teeth, so that the protrusions and depressions of opposite teeth mesh. When the zipper is opened, a divider on the slide pushes the teeth apart.*

Protrusion

Depression

Divider

Sliding tab

zodiac

HOW ASTROLOGERS SEEK TO PREDICT HUMAN DESTINY

A 5,000-year-old Babylonian system based on the planets and constellations

The zodiac with its 12 signs was devised about 3000 B.C. by Babylonian priests. The priests observed that the sun, moon, and planets seemed to move around the earth in a yearly course that passed through 12 constellations. They divided the course into 12 parts and called them after the constellations.

The Babylonians also saw that the sun seemed to

rise in a different part of the zodiac each month, and on that basis they compiled a calendar. They also believed that the movements of the sun, stars, and planets could be used to predict events on earth and the destiny of individuals. Although the constellations have been moving apart since the system was devised, astrologers today still use the Babylonians' basic ideas.

Astrologers cast horoscopes to analyze a person's character and future by linking the date, place, and time of birth with the exact position of the moon and planets at the time. Then they calculate how the characteristics they associate with the sun, moon, and planets may affect the person's future. Below is a summary of the zodiac signs' significance.

ARIES (Mar. 21 – Apr. 19)

Ruler: Mars. Positive traits: energetic, brave, direct. Negative traits: impatient, selfish, unsubtle. Suggested partner: Gemini or Sagittarius.

TAURUS (Apr. 20 – May 20)

Ruler: Venus. Positive traits: warm, determined. Negative traits: stubborn, possessive. Suggested partner: Taurus, Capricorn, or Pisces.

GEMINI (May 21 – June 20)

Ruler: Mercury. Positive traits: lively, versatile. Negative traits: superficial, inconsistent. Suggested partner: Gemini, Aries, or Libra.

CANCER (June 21 – July 22)

Ruler: Moon. Positive traits: kind, imaginative, sensitive. Negative traits: overemotional, possessive. Suggested partner: Taurus or Capricorn.

LEO (July 23 – Aug. 22)

Ruler: Sun. Positive traits: strong, generous, creative. Negative traits: intolerant, pompous, conceited. Suggested partner: Aries or Libra.

VIRGO (Aug. 23 – Sept. 22)

Ruler: Mercury. Positive traits: modest, practical. Negative traits: aloof, fussy, overcritical. Suggested partner: Virgo, Capricorn, or Taurus.

LIBRA (Sept. 23 – Oct. 22)

Ruler: Venus. Positive traits: idealistic, charming, romantic. Negative traits: indecisive, frivolous. Suggested partner: Leo or Aquarius.

SCORPIO (Oct. 23 – Nov. 21)

Rulers: Pluto and Mars. Positive traits: passionate, purposeful. Negative traits: jealous, secretive. Suggested partner: Capricorn or Cancer.

SAGITTARIUS (Nov. 22 – Dec. 21)

Ruler: Jupiter. Positive traits: optimistic, active. Negative traits: lack of tact, restlessness. Suggested partner: Libra or Aquarius.

CAPRICORN (Dec. 22 – Jan. 19)

Ruler: Saturn. Positive traits: careful, ambitious, determined. Negative traits: mean, pessimistic, rigid. Suggested partner: Taurus, Cancer, or Virgo.

AQUARIUS (Jan. 20 – Feb. 18)

Rulers: Uranus and Saturn. Positive traits: independent, original. Negative traits: perverse, obstinate. Suggested partner: Gemini or Libra.

PISCES (Feb. 19 – Mar. 20)

Rulers: Neptune and Jupiter. Positive traits: caring, intuitive, kind. Negative traits: vague, weak-willed. Suggested partner: Taurus or Cancer.

---

into and reanimate a dead body. **b.** A corpse revived in this way. **3.** One who appears lifeless, apathetic, or stupid. [Akin to Kongo *zumbi,* "fetish," *nzambi,* god.]

zo·nal (zō′nəl) *adj.* Also **zo·na·ry** (zō′nər-ē) **1.** Of or associated with a zone or zones. **2.** Divided into zones. **—zo·nal·ly** *adv.*

zonal soil *n.* A soil with a profile that depends largely on the type of vegetation it supports and the climate to which it is exposed.

zo·nate (zō′nāt′) *adj.* Also **zo·nat·ed** (zō′nā′tĭd). Having zones; belted, striped, or ringed.

zo·na·tion (zō-nā′shən) *n.* **1.** Arrangement or formation in zones; zonate structure. **2.** *Ecology.* The distribution of organisms in biogeographic zones.

zone (zōn) *n. Abbr.* **z. 1.** An area, region, or division distinguished from adjacent parts by some distinctive feature or character: *a danger zone; an erogenous zone.* **2. a.** *Geography.* Any of the five regions of the surface of the earth that are loosely divided according to prevailing climate and latitude, including the Torrid Zone, the North and South Temperate Zones, and the North and South Frigid Zones. **b.** A similar division on any planet. **3.** In geometry, a

portion of a sphere bounded by the intersections of two parallel planes with the sphere. **4.** *Ecology.* An area characterized by distinct physical conditions and populated by communities of certain kinds of organisms. **5.** *Geology.* A region or stratum distinguished by composition or content. **6. a.** A section or division of an area or territory established to distinguish it from other similar areas for a specific purpose: *a fare zone.* **b.** A municipal area in a city designated for a particular type of building, enterprise, or activity: *residential zone.* **7.** *Archaic.* A belt or girdle. **—See Synonyms at area.** ~*tr.v.* **zoned, zoning, zones. 1.** To divide into zones. **2.** To designate or mark off into zones. **3.** To surround or encircle with or as if with a belt or girdle. [Latin *zōna,* girdle, zone, from Greek *zōnē.*]

zone refining *n.* A method of redistributing the impurities in a semiconductor material by melting a small section or zone of a bar of the material and causing the molten zone to move along the length of the bar. Purification can be achieved by concentrating the impurities at the end of the bar, which is later removed. Also called "zone melting."

zone·time (zōn'tīm') *n.* Standard time used at sea according to the time zone in which a ship is located.

zonk (zŏngk, zôngk) *v.* **zonked, zonk·ing, zonks.** *Slang.* —*tr.* **1.** To stupefy; stun. **2.** To intoxicate with drugs or alcohol: *"zonk their patients with tranquilizers."* (Psychology Today). —*intr.* To be intoxicated with drugs or alcohol. [From the interjection *zonk,* of imitative origin.]

zonked (zŏngkt) *adj. Slang.* **1.** Intoxicated by alcohol or drugs. **2.** Dazed or stupefied. [From ZONK.]

zoo (zōō) *n., pl.* **zoos.** A public park or institution in which living animals are kept, bred, and exhibited to the public. Also called "zoological garden." [Short for ZOOLOGICAL GARDEN.]

zoo-, **zo-** *prefix.* Indicates animals or animal forms; for example, zoology, zoogeography, zooid. [Greek *zōio-,* from *zōion, zōon,* living being, animal.]

zo·o·chem·is·try (zō'ō-kěm'ĭs-trē) *n.* Animal biochemistry.

zo·o·chore (zō'ə-kôr', -kōr') *n.* A plant dispersed by animals. [ZOO- + -CHORE.]

zoogeog. zoogeography.

zoogeographic region *n.* An extensive region of the earth, such as central and southern Africa, characterized by the dominance of certain kinds of animal life.

zo·o·ge·og·ra·phy (zō'ə-jē-ŏg'rə-fē) *n. Abbr.* **zoogeog.** The biological study of the geographical distribution of animals. —**zo·o·ge·og·ra·pher** *n.* —**zo·o·ge·o·graph·ic** (zō'ə-jē'ə-grăf'ĭk), **zo·o·ge·o·graph·i·cal** *adj.* —**zo·o·ge·o·graph·i·cal·ly** *adv.*

zo·o·gloe·a, **zo·o·gle·a** (zō'ə-glē'ə) *n., pl.* **-gloeae, -gleae** (-glē'ē') or **-as.** Any of various bacteria of the genus *Zoogloea,* forming colonies in a jellylike secretion. [New Latin : ZOO- + Medieval Greek *glia,* gum, from Greek *gloios.*]

zo·og·ra·phy (zō-ŏg'rə-fē) *n.* The biological description of animals. [ZOO- + -GRAPHY.] —**zo·og·ra·pher** *n.* —**zo·o·graph·ic** (zō'ə-grăf'ĭk), **zo·o·graph·i·cal** *adj.*

zo·oid (zō'oid') *n.* **1.** *Biology.* An organic cell or organized body that has independent movement within a living organism; especially, a motile gamete such as a spermatozoon. **2.** *Zoology.* Any of the usually microscopic animals forming an aggregate or colony, as of hydrozoans. [ZO(O)- + -OID.] —**zo·oi·dal** (zō-oid'l) *adj.*

zool. zoological; zoology.

zo·ol·a·try (zō-ŏl'ə-trē) *n., pl.* **-tries.** The worship of animals. [New Latin *zoolatria* : ZOO- + -LATRY.] —**zo·ol·a·ter** *n.* —**zo·ol·a·trous** (zō-ŏl'ə-trəs) *adj.*

zo·o·log·i·cal (zō'ə-lŏj'ĭ-kəl) *adj.* Also **zo·o·log·ic** (zō'ə-lŏj'ĭk). *Abbr.* **zool. 1.** Of or pertaining to animals or animal life. **2.** Of or pertaining to the science of zoology. —**zo·o·log·i·cal·ly** *adv.*

zoological garden *n.* A zoo (see).

zo·ol·o·gist (zō-ŏl'ə-jĭst) *n.* One who specializes in the study of animals.

zo·ol·o·gy (zō-ŏl'ə-jē) *n., pl.* **-gies.** *Abbr.* **zool. 1.** The biological study of animals. **2.** The animal life of a particular area. **3.** The characteristics of an animal group or category: *the zoology of fish.* **4.** A book or scholarly work on animals. [New Latin *zoologia* : ZOO- + -LOGY.]

zoom (zōōm) *v.* **zoomed, zooming, zooms.** —*intr.* **1.** To make a continuous low-pitched buzzing or humming sound. **2.** To move while making such a sound. **3.** To climb suddenly and sharply in an airplane. **4.** To move or act very rapidly: *zoom up to town.* **5. a.** To move rapidly toward or away from a photographic subject. Used of a camera. Often used with *in* or *out.* **b.** To simulate such a movement, as by means of a zoom lens. Often used with *in* or *out.* —*tr.* To cause to zoom.

~*n.* The act or sound of zooming. [Imitative.]

zo·om·e·try (zō-ŏm'ə-trē) *n.* Measurement and comparison of the sizes of animals or animal parts, especially the measurement of bulk. [ZOO- + -METRY.] —**zo·o·met·ric** (zō'ə-mět'rĭk), **zo·o·met·ri·cal** *adj.* —**zo·o·met·ri·cal·ly** *adv.*

zoom lens *n.* A camera lens whose focal length can be rapidly changed, allowing rapid change in the size of an image.

zo·o·mor·phism (zō'ə-môr'fĭz'əm) *n.* Also **zo·o·mor·phy** (-môr'fē). **1.** The attribution of animal characteristics or qualities to a god or gods. **2.** The use of animal forms in symbolism, literature, or art. [ZOO- + -MORPH + -ISM.] —**zo·o·mor·phic** *adj.*

-zoon *suffix.* Indicates an individual animal or independently moving organic unit; for example, spermatozoon. [New Latin, from Greek *zōion, zōon,* living being, animal.]

zo·on·o·sis (zō-ŏn'ə-sĭs) *n., pl.* **-ses** (-sēz). A disease such as rabies or malaria that can be transmitted from animals to man. [New Latin : ZOO- + Greek *nosos,* illness.]

zo·oph·a·gous (zō-ŏf'ə-gəs) *adj.* Feeding on animal matter. [ZOO- + -PHAGOUS.]

zo·o·phile (zō'ə-fīl', -fĭl) *n.* A lover of animals; especially, one opposed to vivisection. [ZOO- + -PHILE.] —**zo·o·phil·ic** (zō'ə-fĭl'ĭk) *adj.* —**zo·oph·i·lism** (zō-ŏf'ə-lĭz'əm) *n.*

zo·oph·i·lous (zō-ŏf'ə-ləs) *adj.* **1.** *Botany.* Pollinated by animals. **2.** Of, pertaining to, or characterized by zoophilism.

zo·o·pho·bi·a (zō'ə-fō'bē-ə) *n.* An irrational fear of animals. [New Latin : ZOO- + -PHOBIA.] —**zo·oph·o·bous** (zō-ŏf'ə-bəs) *adj.*

zo·o·phyte (zō'ə-fīt') *n.* An invertebrate animal such as a sea anemone or sponge that remains attached to a surface and superficially resembles a plant. [Greek *zōophuton* : ZOO- + -PHYTE.] —**zo·o·phyt·ic** (zō'ə-fĭt'ĭk), **zo·o·phyt·i·cal** *adj.*

zo·o·plank·ton (zō'ə-plăngk'tən) *n.* Small crustaceans, fish larvae, and other, often microscopic, aquatic animals that make up the animal part of plankton.

zo·o·plas·ty (zō'ə-plăs'tē) *n.* Surgical transfer of tissue from an animal to man. [ZOO- + -PLASTY.] —**zo·o·plas·tic** (zō'ə-plăs'tĭk) *adj.*

zo·o·sperm (zō'ə-spûrm') *n. Biology.* A spermatozoon (see). [ZOO- + -SPERM.]

zo·o·spo·ran·gi·um (zō'ə-spə-răn'jē-əm) *n., pl.* **-gia** (-jē-ə). *Botany.* A sporangium in which zoospores develop.

zo·o·spore (zō'ə-spôr', -spōr') *n.* A motile, flagellated asexual spore, as of certain algae and fungi. [ZOO- + -SPORE.] —**zo·o·spor·ic** (zō'ə-spôr'ĭk, -spōr'ĭk), **zo·o·spor·ous** (zō'ə-spôr'əs, -spōr'əs) *adj.*

zo·os·ter·ol (zō-ŏs'tə-rôl') *n. Biochemistry.* Any of several animal sterols, such as cholesterol.

zo·o·tech·nics (zō'ə-těk'nĭks) *n. Used with a singular or plural verb.* Zootechny. [ZOO- + Greek *tekhnē,* art.]

zo·o·tech·ny (zō'ə-těk'nē) *n.* The domestication, breeding, and improvement of animals; the technology of animal husbandry. Also called "zootechnics." [ZOO- + Greek *tekhnē,* art.] —**zo·o·tech·ni·cal** (zō'ə-těk'nĭ-kəl) *adj.* —**zo·o·tech·ni·cian** (zō'ə-těk-nĭsh'ən) *n.*

zo·ot·o·my (zō-ŏt'ə-mē) *n.* **1.** Dissection of animals other than man. **2.** Comparative anatomy. [ZOO- + -TOMY.] —**zo·o·tom·ic** (zō'ə-tŏm'ĭk), **zo·o·tom·i·cal** *adj.* —**zo·o·tom·i·cal·ly** *adv.* —**zo·ot·o·mist** (zō-ŏt'ə-mĭst) *n.*

zoot suit (zōōt) *n. Slang.* A man's suit, popular especially in the early 1940's, characterized by full-legged, tight-cuffed trousers and a long jacket with wide lapels and wide, heavily padded shoulders. [*Zoot,* rhyming formation based on SUIT.]

zor·ille, **zor·il** (zôr'ĭl, zōr'-) *n.* Also **zo·ril·la** (zə-rĭl'ə). An African mammal, *Ictonyx striatus,* resembling the skunk in appearance and defensive action. [French, from Spanish *zorrillo, zorrilla,* "small fox," from *zorro,* fox, from Old Spanish *zorra†,* to drag.]

Zor·o·as·ter (zôr'ō-ăs'tər) (c. 628–551 B.C.). Also **Zar·a·thus·tra** (zăr'ə-thōōs'trə). Persian prophet. As a priest in northwest Persia, he founded the religion Zoroastrianism after he had a divine vision. He wrote the Gathas, a collection of hymns in honor of the god Ormazd. See feature, next page.

Zor·o·as·tri·an·ism (zôr'ō-ăs'trē-ə-nĭz'əm, zôr'-) *n.* The dualistic religious system founded in Persia by Zoroaster and set forth in the Zend-Avesta, teaching the worship of Ormazd, god of creation, light, and goodness, who is engaged in a continual struggle against Ahriman, spirit of evil and darkness. Also called "Mazdaism." —**Zo·ro·as·tri·an** *adj. & n.*

zos·ter (zŏs'tər) *n.* **1.** A belt or girdle worn by men in ancient Greece. **2.** A viral infection, shingles (see). [Latin, from Greek *zōstēr,* girdle.]

Zou·ave (zōō-äv', swäv) *n.* **1.** A member of a French infantry unit, formerly composed of Algerian recruits, characterized by colorful oriental uniforms and precision drilling. **2.** A member of any group modeled on the French Zouaves; especially, a member of such a unit of the Union Army in the Civil War. [French, from Berber *zwāwa,* an Algerian tribe.]

zounds (zoundz) *interj.* Also **swounds** (zwoundz, zoundz), **swouns** (zwounz, zounz). Used to express anger, surprise, or indignation. [Shortening and alteration of *by God's wounds.*]

zoy·si·a (zoi'zē-ə) *n.* Any of several creeping grasses of the genus *Zoysia,* native to Asia and Australia, and widely cultivated as a lawn grass. [New Latin *Zoysia;* after Karl von *Zois* (1756–1800), German botanist.]

ZPG zero population growth.

Zr The symbol for the element zirconium.

Z-pro·pyl·pi·per·i·dine (zē'prō'pĭl-pĭ-pěr'ə-dēn', -dĭn) *n.* A poisonous alkaloid, coniine (see).

zuc·chet·to (zōō-kět'ō; *Italian* tsōōk-kět'tō) *n., pl.* **-tos.** *Roman Catholic Church.* A skullcap worn by clergymen, varying in color according to the rank of the wearer. It is white, red, or purple for a pope, cardinal, or bishop respectively. [Italian, diminutive of *zucca,* gourd, head, from Late Latin *cucutia,* gourd, probably from Latin *cucurbita,* GOURD.]

zuc·chi·ni (zōō-kē'nē) *n., pl.* **zucchini. 1.** A variety of summer squash having an elongated shape and a smooth, thin, dark-green rind. **2.** The bushy plant that bears it. [Italian, plural of *zuchino,* diminutive of *zucca,* gourd. See zucchetto.]

Zuck·er·man (zŭk'ər-mən), **Solly, Baron** (1904–). South African-born British scientist. Trained as an anatomist, he served as chief scientific adviser to the British government (1964–71). His books include *Scientists and War* (1966) and *From Apes to Warlords* (1978).

Zug·spit·ze (zōōg'spĭt-sə). Mountain of southern West Germany. Situated in the Bavarian Alps near the Austrian border, it is the highest peak (2,963 meters; 9,721 feet) of West Germany.

zug·zwang (tsōōk'tsväng) *n.* In chess, a situation in which a player must take his turn, even though it is to his disadvantage.

~*tr.v.* **zugzwanged, -zwanging, -zwangs.** To force (one's opponent) into such a situation. [German : *Zug,* move (in chess) + *Zwang,* force, compulsion.]

Zui·der Zee (zī'dər zē'). Former inlet of the North Sea, northeastern Netherlands. A drainage project (begun 1920) separated the inlet from the sea by a dike (completed 1932), dividing it into the Ijsselmeer and the Waddenzee.

Zu·lu (zōō'lōō) *n., pl.* **-lus** or collectively **Zulu. 1.** A member of a large Bantu nation of southeastern Africa, formerly a powerful warrior nation, and now living chiefly in northeastern Natal. **2.** The Bantu language spoken by the Zulu people. —**Zu·lu** *adj.*

zucchini *A vigorously flowering squash plant, whose fruits are picked and eaten while young and small.*

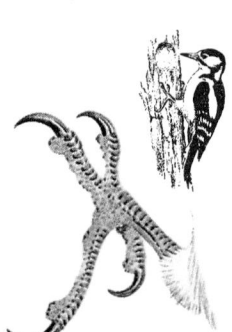

zygodactyl *Several types of climbing birds have zygodactyl feet—ones with four toes, two pointing forward and two backward—to help them balance against vertical surfaces, such as tree trunks. This is the foot of a great spotted woodpecker.*

Zoroaster

THE ONE GOD OF PERSIA

A religion that unified an empire

The ancient Persian mystic Zoroaster (*c.* 628–*c.* 551 B.C.), known by both this Greek form of his name and Zarathustra (the Persian form), originated a religion named after him. Virtually nothing is known of his life, except that his homeland was northwestern Persia, from where he fled to achieve acceptance in eastern Persia. There Zoroastrianism was adopted by the Achaemenid rulers. Darius the Great (522–486 B.C.) saw it as a means of unifying his empire.

The original tenets of Zoroastrianism are obscure—its sacred text, the Zend-Avesta, is a body of oral tradition probably not written until about A.D. 400—but it broke sharply with the Persians' previous belief in many gods. It taught that there is one God, Ormazd, assisted by a hierarchy of subordinate spirits. Ormazd created two opposing forces, Truth and Untruth, and rewarded or condemned men after death according to their actions on earth. In certain respects the religion seems to be a parallel to Judaism and a predecessor of Christianity. The priests were known as Magi, a term inherited from the previous Persian religion, from which comes the word "magic." Central to its rituals were the use of fire, the sacrifice of bulls, and the drinking of an intoxicant, "haoma."

Zoroastrianism was undermined when Alexander the Great conquered Persia in 330 B.C., but flourished again under Persia's Sassanid dynasty from A.D. 224 until 642, when the Muslims overran Persia. It is now practiced by 10,000 in Iran and 85,000 Parsees ("Persians") in India, descendants of those who fled Muslim rule.

ZOROASTRIAN GOD *Ormazd, the source of truth, was symbolized by the pure light of the sun. The earliest representations of the god were as a winged disk—from which various hovering, winged figures were developed.*

Zu·lu·land (zōō′lōō-lănd′). Southern African region, formerly in northeastern Natal province. The historic home of the Zulus, it rose to power during the early 19th century, resisting the Boer settlers until its final defeat by the British (1879). Part of Natal from 1897, it now corresponds approximately to the Bantu homeland of Kwa-Zulu.

zup·pa in·gle·se (tsōōp′pə ĭng-glā′sā) *n.* A dessert made of rum-flavored sponge cake and custard with cream and a fruit topping. [Italian, "English soup."]

Zu·rich (zŏŏr′ĭk). Capital of Zurich canton, northeastern Switzerland. On the Limmat River on the north shore of Lake Zurich, it is the cultural center of German-speaking Switzerland and is best known for its banking and financial facilities.

Zweig (zwīg, swīg, tsvīKH), **Stefan** (1881–1942). Austrian writer. Influenced by Freud, he was a prolific and popular writer of both fiction and nonfiction. His best-known work is the novel *Beware of Pity* (1939).

zwie·back (swē′băk′, -bäk′, swī′-, zwē′-, zwī′-) *n.* A type of bread, usually sweetened, baked first as a loaf and later cut into slices and toasted. [German : *zwie-*, twice + *baken*, to bake.]

Zwing·li (zwĭng′lē, swĭng′-, tsvĭng′-), **Ulrich** (1484–1531). Swiss Protestant reformer. Ordained as a Roman Catholic priest (1506), he became a preacher in Zurich (1518), where he spoke out against the selling of indulgences. He became leader of the Reformation in Switzerland but was killed in an attack on Zurich by the Catholic forest cantons. He predated Luther in many of his ideas and greatly influenced Calvin.

Zwing·li·an (zwĭng′lē-ən, swĭng′-, tsvĭng′-) *adj.* Of or pertaining to Zwingli or to his theological system, especially his doctrine that the physical body of Christ is not present in the Eucharist and that the ceremony is merely a symbolic commemoration of Christ's death. ~*n.* A follower of Ulrich Zwingli. —**Zwing·li·an·ism** *n.* —**Zwing·li·an·ist** *n.*

zwit·ter·i·on (zvĭt′ər-ī′ən, swĭt′-, tsvĭt′-) *n. Physics.* An ion carrying both a positive and a negative charge, thus forming an electrically neutral molecule. [German *Zwitterion*, "mongrel ion" : *Zwitter*, mongrel, hybrid, from Old High German *zwitar(a)n*, from *zwi-*, twice + ION.] —**zwit·ter·i·on·ic** (tsvĭt′ər-ī-ŏn′ĭk) *adj.*

Zwor·y·kin (zwôr′ə-kĭn), **Vladimir Kosma** (1889–1982). U.S. physicist. Born in Russia, he became a U.S. citizen in 1924. He invented the iconoscope (1938), the first practical television camera, and helped develop the electron microscope (1939).

zyg·a·poph·y·sis (zĭg′ə-pŏf′ə-sĭs, zī′gə-) *n., pl.* **-ses** (-sēz′). *Anatomy.* Either of two usually paired processes of a vertebra that articulate with corresponding parts of adjacent vertebrae. [ZYG(O)- + APOPHYSIS.] —**zyg·a·poph·y·se·al** (zĭg′ə-pŏf′ə-sē′əl, -pə-fĭz′ē-əl) *adj.*

zygo-, **zyg-** *prefix.* Indicates: **1.** Yoke or pair; for example, **zygodactyl**, **zygapophysis**. **2.** Union or fusion; for example, **zygospore**, **zygomorphic**. [New Latin, from Greek *zugon*, yoke.]

zy·go·dac·tyl (zī′gō-dăk′tĭl) *adj.* Also **zy·go·dac·tyl·ous** (-dăk-tĭl′əs). Having two toes projecting forward and two projecting backward. ~*n.* A zygodactyl bird.

zy·go·ma (zī-gō′mə) *n., pl.* **-mata** (-mə-tə) or **-mas. 1.** The zygomatic bone. **2.** The zygomatic arch. [New Latin, from Greek *zugōma*, bolt, bar, yoke, from *zugoun*, to yoke, connect.] —**zy·go·mat·ic** (zī′gə-măt′ĭk) *adj.*

zygomatic arch *n.* The bony arch in vertebrates that extends along the side or front of the skull beneath the orbit. Also called "zygoma."

zygomatic bone *n.* A small quadrangular bone in vertebrates on the side of the face below the eye, forming, in mammals, part of the orbit and part of the zygomatic arch. Also called "cheekbone," "jugal," "malar," "zygoma."

zy·go·mor·phic (zī′gō-môr′fĭk) *adj.* Also **zy·go·mor·phous** (-fəs). Bilaterally symmetrical so as to be capable of being symmetrically divided only along a single longitudinal plane. Said of flowers. Compare **actinomorphic.** [ZYGO- + -MORPHIC.] —**zy·go·mor·phism** *n.*

zy·go·sis (zī-gō′sĭs) *n., pl.* **-ses** (-sēz). The union of gametes to form a zygote; conjugation. [ZYG(O)- + -OSIS.]

zy·go·spore (zī′gō-spôr′, -spōr′) *n.* A thick-walled spore formed from the zygote in certain algae or fungi.

zy·gote (zī′gōt′) *n.* The cell formed by the union of two gametes. [Greek *zugōtos*, joined, yoked, from *zugoun*, to join, to yoke.] —**zy·got·ic** (zī-gŏt′ĭk) *adj.* —**zy·got·i·cal·ly** *adv.*

zy·go·tene (zī′gə-tēn′) *n.* The second stage of meiotic prophase during which the homologous chromosomes pair to form bivalents. [ZYGO(TE) + -TENE.]

zy·mase (zī′mās′, -māz′) *n.* The enzyme complex, first isolated from yeast, that converts hexose sugars to ethanol and carbon dioxide. [ZYM(O)- + -ASE.]

-zyme *suffix.* Indicates an enzyme; for example, **lysozyme.** [Greek *zumē*, leaven.]

zymo-, **zym-** *prefix.* Indicates fermentation; for example, **zymolysis**, **zymase**. [New Latin, from Greek *zumē*, leaven.]

zy·mo·gen (zī′mə-jən) *n.* The inactive protein precursor of an enzyme. [ZYMO- + -GEN.]

zy·mo·gen·ic (zī′mə-jĕn′ĭk) *adj.* Also **zy·mog·e·nous** (zī-mŏj′ə-nəs). **1.** Of or pertaining to a zymogen. **2.** Capable of causing fermentation. **3.** Enzyme-producing.

zy·mol·o·gy (zī-mŏl′ə-jē) *n.* The chemistry of fermentation. [New Latin *zymologia* : ZYMO- + -LOGY.] —**zy·mo·log·ic** (zī′mə-lŏj′ĭk), **zy·mo·log·i·cal** *adj.* —**zy·mol·o·gist** (zī-mŏl′ə-jĭst) *n.*

zy·mol·y·sis (zī-mŏl′ə-sĭs) *n.* Fermentation. Also called "zymosis." [ZYMO- + -LYSIS.] —**zy·mo·lyt·ic** (zī′mə-lĭt′ĭk) *adj.*

zy·mom·e·ter (zī-mŏm′ə-tər) *n.* An instrument used for determining the degree of fermentation. [ZYMO- + -METER.]

zy·mo·scope (zī′mə-skōp′) *n.* An instrument used to determine fermentation efficiency by measuring the amount of carbon dioxide produced. [ZYMO- + -SCOPE.]

zy·mo·sis (zī-mō′sĭs) *n.* **1.** Zymolysis. **2.** *Medicine.* The process of infection or an infectious disease. [New Latin, from Greek *zumōsis*, fermentation, from *zumoun*, to leaven, ferment, from *zumē*, leaven.] —**zy·mot·ic** (zī-mŏt′ĭk) *adj.* —**zy·mot·i·cal·ly** *adv.*

zy·mur·gy (zī′mûr-jē) *n.* The branch of chemistry concerned with fermentation processes in brewing. [ZYM(O)- + -URGY.]

zyz·zy·va (zĭz′ə-və) *n.* Any of various tropical American weevils of the genus *Zyzzyva*, often destructive to plants. [New Latin *Zyzzyva*, genus name.]

Acknowledgments

The artwork illustrating the entries listed below is reproduced by kind permission of the Publishers. Features are shown in capital letters.

ARNOLDO MONDADORI LTD:

Aardvark, Abyssinian cat, Agrimony, Anteater, Armadillo, Asparagus, Bedbug, Bryophyte, Drone, Emu, Ermine, Euphorbia, Fig, FISH, Fox, Hackney, HORSE, INSECT (Life Cycle of a Fly), Larva, Lemon, Manx cat, Mole-rat, Okapi, Olive, Pomegranate, Porcupine, Prickly pear, Remora, REPTILE, Shrew, Siamese cat, SNAKE, Square, Sugar cane, Tuatara, Vole, Walnut, Winter aconite, Winter cherry, Wolf.

Some of the illustrations in this dictionary are taken or adapted from the following books, first published by Reader's Digest.

ABC's of the Human Body; ABC's of Nature; Back to Basics; Book of British Birds; Book of the British Countryside; Book of the Car; Complete Guide to Needlework; Do It Yourself; Family Health Guide; Food from Your Garden; Heritage of Britain; Household Manual; Illustrated Guide to Britain; Inventions that Changed the World; The Last Two Million Years; Library of Modern Knowledge; Living World of Animals; Nature Lover's Library; North American Wildlife; The Past All Around Us; Success with House Plants; Things to Make and Do.

Artwork specially commissioned for this work was produced by the artists listed below.

Howard S. Friedman, Hayward and Martin Ltd, Walter Hortens, Mike Jackson, Pavel Kostal, Edward R. Lipinski, Malcolm McGregor, Eric Robson, Ray Skibinski, Judy Skorpel, Ted Williams.

Photographs appearing in this work came from the sources listed below.

Entries are identified by the headword.
Features are shown in capital letters.
Work commissioned by Reader's Digest is shown in italics.
Where necessary, photographs in features are also identified by position within the feature: *T*-**Top**, *B*-**Bottom**, *L*-**Left**, *R*-**Right**, *C*-**Center**, *I*-**Inset.**

Aardwolf: Simon Trevor/Bruce Coleman Ltd. **Abalone:** Jane Burton/Bruce Coleman Ltd. **Abu Simbel:** Gunter Heil/ZEFA. **Acanthus:** Michael Holford. **Accipiter:** Hans Reinhard/Bruce Coleman Ltd. **Acorn:** John Markham/Bruce Coleman Ltd. **Acorn Barnacle:** David & Katie Urry/Ardea London. **ADAM** Both from National Trust, London, England. **Adobe:** Gene Ahrens/Bruce Coleman Ltd. **Aeolipile:** Mary Evans Picture Library. **African Marigold:** Eric Crichton/Bruce Coleman Ltd. **African Violets:** Eric Crichton/Bruce Coleman Ltd. **Agama:** Mark N. Boulton/Bruce Coleman Ltd. **Agamemnon:** Konrad Helbig/ZEFA. **Agave:** B & C Calhoun/Bruce Coleman Ltd. **Ageratum:** Eric Crichton/Bruce Coleman Ltd. **Agouti:** Michael Freeman/Bruce Coleman Ltd. **Ajax:** Michael Holford. **Alabaster:** Michael Holford. **Alderfly:** Jane Burton/Bruce Coleman Ltd. **Alexanders:** Eric Crichton/Bruce Coleman Ltd. **Alexander the Great:** P.H. Teuffen/ZEFA. **Ali Baba:** Mary Evans Picture Library. **ALLEGORY** Reproduced by courtesy of the Trustees, The National Gallery, London. **Aloe:** M.P. Kahl/Bruce Coleman Ltd. **Altamira:** Michael Holford. **Alyssum:** Eric Crichton/Bruce Coleman Ltd. **Amaranth:** Eric Crichton/Bruce Coleman Ltd. **Amaryllis:** Francisco Futil/Bruce Coleman Ltd. **Amazons:** Michael Holford. **Ambulacrum:** Jane Burton/Bruce Coleman Ltd. **Amethyst:** Institute of Geological Sciences. **AMERICAN REVOLUTION** *TL* American Antiquarian Society, *TC* Charles Wilson Peale, Pennsylvania Academy of Fine Art, *TR* Metropolitan Museum of Art, Gift of William H. Huntington, 1823, *CL* Rembrandt Peale, United States Information Service, London, *BL* National Gallery of Art, Washington, D.C.; gift of Edgar William and Bernice Chrysler Garbisch, 1953, *BR* John Trumbull, Yale University Art Gallery. **Ammonite:** J. Fennell/Bruce Coleman Ltd. **Amoeba:** John Clegg/Ardea London. **Amphipod:** Inigo Everson/Bruce Coleman Ltd. **Amphitheater:** Nick Holt/ZEFA. **Andes:** Michael Freeman/Bruce Coleman Ltd. **Andrea del Sarto Painting:** Robert Harding Picture Library/Louvre. **Anemone:** B & C Calhoun/Bruce Coleman Ltd. **Angel Fall:** Adrian Warren/Ardea London. **Angelfish:** Jane Burton/Bruce Coleman Ltd. **Angle Shades:** John Fennell/Bruce Coleman Ltd. **Annual Ring** A.J. Deane/Bruce Coleman Ltd. **Anopheles:** Kim Taylor/Bruce Coleman Ltd. **Ansate Cross:** Michael Holford. **ANT** Graham Pizzey/Bruce Coleman Ltd. **Antarctica:** Edwin Mickleburgh/Ardea London. **Anthurium:** Eric Crichton/Bruce Coleman Ltd. **Antler:** Martin W. Grosnick/Ardea London. **Anubis:** Michael Holford. **Aphrodite:** Michael Holford. **Apis:** Michael Holford. **Apricot:** S. Roberts/Ardea London. **Aqueduct:** I.R. Beames/Ardea London. **Archaeopteryx:** Peter Green/Ardea London. **Archaic Smile:** Acropolis Museum, Athens/Robert Harding Picture Library. **Archerfish:** P. Morris/Ardea London. **Arctic Fox:** Brian Hawkes/Robert Harding Picture Library. **Ard:** Foto Leidmann/ZEFA. **Aril:** Eric Lindgren/Ardea London. **Arjuna:** Michael Holford. **Armadillo:** Francois Gohier/Ardea London. **Armillary Sphere:** Michael Holford. **Armorial Bearing:** Mary Evans Picture Library. **Arrowhead:** Bob Gibbons/Ardea London. **ART DECO** *TL* Angelo Hornak/Vision International, *TR* Angelo Hornak/Vision International, *CL* Richard Bryant, *BL* Angelo Hornak/Vision International, *BR* H.E. Kiessling/Bridgeman Art Library. **ARTHURIAN LEGEND** *TL* Bibliothèque Nationale, Paris Ms FR95 fol 159V, *TR* Bibliothèque Nationale, Paris Ms R577 fol 74V, *B* British Museum Add Ms 10294 fol 94. **ART NOUVEAU** *TL* Angelo Hornak/Vision International, *TC* Angelo Hornak/Vision International, *TR* Hunterian Art Gallery, University of Glasgow, Mackintosh Collection, *CL* ZEFA, *R* Bridgeman Art Library, *BL* and *BC* Bridgeman Art Library. **Ash:** Eric Crichton/Bruce Coleman Ltd. **Aspen:** Jeff Foott/Bruce Coleman Ltd. **Atahualpa:** Mary Evans Picture Library. **Athena:** National Museum Athens/Robert Harding Picture Library. **Aubrieta:** Eric Crichton/Bruce Coleman Ltd. **Audubon:** Michael Holford. **Augustus:** British Museum/Robert Harding Picture Library. **Aurochs:** Mary Evans Picture Library. **Avatar:** Michael Holford. **Avocado:** Eric Crichton/Bruce Coleman Ltd. **Avocet:** M.P. Kahl/Bruce Coleman Ltd. **Axolotl:** Jane Burton/Bruce Coleman Ltd. **Ayers Rock:** Eric Crichton/Bruce Coleman Ltd. **AZTEC** *T* Biblioteca Nazionale, Florence, *B* Ianthe Ruthven/Michael Holford. **Azalea:** Eric Crichton/Bruce Coleman Ltd.

Ba: Michael Holford. **Baboon:** Norman Myers/Bruce Coleman Ltd. **Babylon:** L. Schranner/ZEFA. **Bacchae:** Michael Holford. **BACH** From the Collection of William H. Scheide, Princeton, New Jersey. **BACTERIUM** all Tony Brain/Science Photo Library. **Bactrian Camel:** J. Bitsch/ZEFA. **Badlands:** R. Everts/ZEFA. **BADGER** J.P. Ferrero/Ardea London. **Bagworm:** Peter Ward/Bruce Coleman Ltd. **Bald Eagle:** Jeff Foott/Bruce Coleman Ltd. **Balloon:** M.P. Kahl/Bruce Coleman Ltd. **Balm:** John Mason/Ardea London. **Baltimore Oriole:** John Dunning/Ardea London. **Bamboo:** Sybil Sassoon/Robert Harding Picture Library. **Banana:** Richard Nicholas/ZEFA. **Bandicoot:** Bruce Coleman Ltd. **Baneberry:** A.P. Paterson/Ardea London. **Banjo Clock:** Michael Holford. **Baobab:** Jane Burton/Bruce Coleman Ltd. **Barbary Ape:** Bruce Coleman Ltd. **Barge:** Starfoto/ZEFA. **Bargeboard:** Andy Williams/Robert Harding Picture Library. **Bark:** N. Bahnsen/ZEFA. **Barn Owl:** John Markham/Bruce Coleman Ltd. **Barometer:** Michael Holford. **BAROQUE** *L* Bridgeman Art Library, *TR* Reproduced by courtesy of the Trustees, The National Gallery, London, *BR* James Austin/Robert Harding Picture Library. **Barracuda:** P. Morris/Ardea London. **Barrier Reef:** M.T.O'Keefe/Bruce Coleman Ltd. **Bartizan:** K. Praedel/ZEFA. **Basalt:** Trevor Wood/Robert Harding Picture Library. **Bascule:** Eric Crichton/Bruce Coleman Ltd. **Basilisk:** P. Morris/Ardea London. **Bas-Relief:** Caroline Weaver/Ardea London. **Basset Hound:** Hans Reinhard/Bruce Coleman Ltd. **Bat:** R.J. Tulloch/Bruce Coleman Ltd. **Beagle:** Hans Reinhard/Bruce Coleman Ltd. **Bearberry:** J. Wightman/Ardea London. **Beardsley Lithograph:** Mary Evans Picture Library. **Bearskin:** Jessica Anne Ehlers/Bruce Coleman Ltd. **BEAVER** Jack Swedberg/Ardea London. **Beefeaters:** Bruce Coleman Ltd. **Bellerophon:** Michael Holford. **Bellflower:** J.P. Ferrero/Ardea London. **Bell Jar:** Michael Holford. **Beluga:** Pat Morris/Ardea London. **Benin:** Michael Holford. **BERNINI** Dimitri Kessel, Life. © Time Inc/Colorific! **Bezant:** Michael Holford. **Bib:** Michael Holford. **Bilberry:** John Markham/Bruce Coleman Ltd. **Bird of Paradise:** Brian J. Coates/Bruce Coleman Ltd. **Bird of Paradise Flower:** M.P.L. Fogden/Bruce Coleman Ltd. **Bison:** Francisco Erize/Bruce Coleman Ltd. **Bittern:** Bruce Coleman Ltd. **Bittersweet:** Bob Gibbons/Ardea London. **Blackbird:** P.A. Hinchliffe/Bruce Coleman Ltd. **Black Currant:** Eric Crichton/Bruce Coleman Ltd. **BLACK HOLE** Dr. W.H. Fu/University of California/Science Photo Library. **Black Grouse:** Gunter Ziesler/Bruce Coleman Ltd. **Black Widow:** Jack Dermid/Bruce Coleman Ltd. **Bladder Campion:** Hans Reinhard/Bruce Coleman Ltd. **Bleeding Heart:** Bob & Clara Calhoun/Bruce Coleman Ltd. **Blesbok:** Ardea London. **Blister Beetle:** Jane Burton/Bruce Coleman Ltd. **BLOOD** *T* London Scientific Fotos, C Science Photo Library, *B* Dr. G.F. Leedale/Biophotos. **Bluebell:** Adrian Davies/Bruce Coleman Ltd. **Blueberry:** Pekka Helo/Bruce Coleman Ltd. **Blue Jay:** Bill Brooks/Bruce Coleman Ltd. **Bobcat:** Kenneth W. Fink/Ardea London. **Boll:** R. Bond/ZEFA. **Bonnet Monkey:** G.K. Brown/Ardea London. **Booby:** Brian Hawkes/Robert Harding Picture Library. **Bottle-Nosed Dolphin:** Norman Tomalin/Bruce Coleman Ltd. **Bowerbird:** Cyril Laubscher/Bruce Coleman Ltd. **Bow Street Runner:** Mary Evans Picture Library. **Boxer:** Hans Reinhard/Bruce Coleman Ltd. **Bracken:** Sinclair Stammers/Bruce Coleman Ltd. **Brazil Nuts:** Denis Moore/Robert Harding Picture Library. **Breadfruit:** A.F. Soper/Bruce Coleman Ltd. **Breaker:** Dr. D. James/ZEFA. **Bream:** Allan Power/Bruce Coleman Ltd. **Bridle:** Blume/ZEFA. **Broad Bean:** Eric Crichton/Bruce Coleman Ltd. **Broadbill:** Norman Tomalin/Bruce Coleman Ltd. **Broccoli:** Eric Crichton/Bruce Coleman Ltd. **Bromeliad:** John Mason/Ardea London. **BRONZE AGE** Hirmer Fotoarchiv. **Brooch:** Michael Holford. **Brown Bear:** Bruce Coleman Ltd. **BRUEGEL** Kunsthistorisches Museum, Vienna. **BRUNELLESCHI** both Scala. **Bryony:** J.A. Bailey/Ardea London. **Buck:** S.C. Porter/Bruce Coleman Ltd. **Buckeye:** Wardene Weisser/Ardea London. **BUDDHISM** *L* British Museum, *R* Bill O'Connor/Robert Harding Picture Library. **Budgerigar:** Bruce Coleman Ltd. **Buffalo:** Peter Davey/Bruce Coleman Ltd. **Bufflehead:** Joseph van Wormen/Bruce Coleman Ltd. **Bugloss:** Bob Gibbons/Ardea London. **Bulldog:** S. McKenna/ZEFA. **Bullfinch:** Bruce Coleman Ltd. **Bullfrog:** Hans & Judy Beste/Ardea London. **Burnoose:** Konrad Helbig/ZEFA. **Bush Baby:** P. Davey/Bruce Coleman Ltd. **Bustard:** L.R. Dawson/Bruce Coleman Ltd. **Bustle:** Victoria & Albert Museum/Robert Harding Picture Library. **BUTTERFLY** All photographs by Eric Lingren/Ardea London except *B* Ian Beames/Ardea London. **Butterfly Fish:** Allan Power/Bruce Coleman Ltd. **BYZANTIUM** *TR* Scala, *B* Stylitzes Codex, Biblioteca Nacional, Madrid.

Cabbage: Bruce Coleman Ltd. **Cabriole:** Michael Holford. **Cacao:** M.P.L. Fogden/Bruce Coleman Ltd. **Cacomistle:** Kenneth W. Fink/Ardea London. **Caddis Worm:** Dr. R. Sauer/ZEFA. **Caesar:** Michael Holford. **Calculator:** Michael Holford. **California Poppy:** Robert P. Carr/Bruce Coleman Ltd. **Camel:** G.K. Brown/Ardea London. **Camellia:** A.P. Paterson/Ardea London. **Camouflage:** G. Ziesler/ZEFA. **Campanile:** John Ross/Robert Harding Picture Library. **Canada Goose:** Jack Dermid/Bruce Coleman Ltd. **Canary:** John Markham/Bruce Coleman Ltd. **Cannabis:** G. Mabbs/ZEFA. **Canoe:** Brian J. Coates/Bruce Coleman Ltd. **Capital:** Mary Evans Picture Library. **Capybara:** Francisco Erize/Bruce Coleman Ltd. **Caracal:** R.I.M. Campbell/Bruce Coleman Ltd. **Caracara:** Francisco Erize/Bruce Coleman Ltd. **Caribou:** Martin W. Grosnick/Bruce Coleman Ltd. **Carnation:** Eric Crichton/Bruce Coleman Ltd. **Carnelian:** Institute of Geological Sciences. **Carrion Crow:** P.A. Hinchliffe/Bruce Coleman Ltd. **CARTIER-BRESSON** Henri Cartier-Bresson/John Hillelson Agency Ltd. **Cartouche:** ZEFA. **Caryatid:** Michael Holford. **Cashew:** T. Lancefield/ZEFA. **Cassowary:** Rod Williams/Bruce Coleman Ltd. **Catalpa:** Eric Crichton/Bruce Coleman Ltd. **Catfish:** Hans Reinhard/Bruce Coleman Ltd. **Cauliflower:** Bruce Coleman Ltd. **Cave Painting:** ZEFA. **Cedar of Lebanon:** Eric Crichton/Bruce Coleman Ltd. **CELL DIVISION** All: Eric V. Grave/Science Photo Library. **Centaur:** Mary Evans Picture Library. **Centipede:** C.S. Frith/Bruce Coleman Ltd. **Chalice:** Michael Holford. **Chambered Nautilus:** J.L. Mason/Ardea London. **Chameleon:** P. Davey/Bruce Coleman Ltd. **Chamois:** J.P. Ferrero/Ardea London. **Chariot:** Michael Holford. **CHARTRES** All: Sonia Halliday. **Château:** Ronald Sheridan/ZEFA. **Chaucer:** Mary Evans Picture Library. **Cheetah:** M.P. Kahl/Bruce Coleman Ltd. **Cherry:** Eric Crichton/Bruce Coleman Ltd. **Cheshire Cat:** Mary Evans Picture Library. **Chicory:** Hans Reinhard/Bruce Coleman Ltd. **Chili:** Sybil Sassoon/Robert Harding Picture Library. **Chimpanzee:** Peter Jackson/Bruce Coleman Ltd. **Chinchilla:** Jane Burton/Bruce Coleman Ltd. **Chinoiserie:** Michael Holford. **Chiton:** Michael Holford. **CHRISTIANITY** *L* Bridgeman Art Library, *R* Scala. **Christmas Rose:** Hans Reinhard/Bruce Coleman Ltd. **Chrysalis:** W. Kratz/ZEFA. **Chrysanthemum:** Eric Crichton/Bruce Coleman Ltd. **Churn:** Mary Evans Picture Library. **Cicada:** John R. Brownlie/Bruce Coleman Ltd. **Cichlid:** P. Morris/Ardea London. **Cinquefoil:** Charlie Ott/Bruce Coleman Ltd. **Cithara:** Michael Holford. **Civet:** Francisco Erize/Bruce Coleman Ltd. **CIVIL WAR** The Metropolitan Museum of Art, Gift of Mrs. Frank B. Porter, 1922. **Clavichord:** Mary Evans Picture Library. **Clematis:** Eric Crichton/Bruce Coleman Ltd. **Cloisonné:** Michael Holford. **Cloisters:** Michael Holford. **CLOUD** Cirrus, Stratocumulus, Cirrostratus & Cumulus R.K.

Pilsbury/Bruce Coleman Ltd. Nimbostratus, Cirrocumulus, Altocumulus, Altostratus & Cumulonimbus Alan Watts and Stratus Professor Scorer. **CLOWN** *L* BBC Hulton Picture Library, *R* Sylvie Mercier. **Cobra:** Dr. Frieder Sauer/Bruce Coleman Ltd. **Cobweb:** John Shaw/Bruce Coleman Ltd. **Cockatoo:** John R. Brownlie/Bruce Coleman Ltd. **Cockle:** Jane Burton/Bruce Coleman Ltd. **Cock-of-the-Rock:** L.C. Marigo/Bruce Coleman Ltd. **Coconut Palm:** Adrian Warren/Ardea London. **Coffee:** L.C. Marigo/Bruce Coleman Ltd. **Colobus Monkey:** R. Williams/Bruce Coleman Ltd. **Colorado Beetle:** Udo Hirsch/Bruce Coleman Ltd. **COLOSSEUM** Pubbli Aer Foto. **Colossus:** Michael Holford. **Columbine:** Wayne Lankinen/Bruce Coleman Ltd. **Compass:** B. Benjamin/ZEFA. **Composite Order:** Mary Evans Picture Library. **Compound Eye:** G. Dore/Bruce Coleman Ltd. **Conch:** Nicholas Devore III/Bruce Coleman Ltd. **Condor:** J. van Wormer/Bruce Coleman Ltd. **Confucius:** Mary Evans Picture Library. **CONSTABLE** Reproduced by Courtesy of the Trustees, The National Gallery, London. **Container:** Robert Harding Picture Library. **Contrail:** Walter Rawlings/Robert Harding Picture Library. **Coot:** Gordon Langsbury/Bruce Coleman Ltd. **Cope:** Michael Holford. **Coracle:** *Patrick Thurston.* **Coral:** Bill Wood/Robert Harding Picture Library. **Coral Snake:** Jack Dermid/Bruce Coleman Ltd. **Corinthian Order:** Michael Holford. **Cormorant:** M. Dohrn/Bruce Coleman Ltd. **Corydalis:** Hans Reinhard/Bruce Coleman Ltd. **Cotton:** Stephen J. Krasemann/Bruce Coleman Ltd. **Cottontail:** Leonard Lee Rue III/Bruce Coleman Ltd. **Cowberry:** N.A. Callow/Robert Harding Picture Library. **Cowry:** Adrian Davies/Bruce Coleman Ltd. **Cowslip:** E. Duscher/Bruce Coleman Ltd. **Coyote:** Tom Willock/Ardea London. **Crab:** Neville Fox-Davies/Bruce Coleman Ltd. **Crane:** Bruce Coleman Ltd. **Crater:** ZEFA. **Creeping Jennie:** Hans Reinhard/Bruce Coleman Ltd. **Crocodile:** Simon Trevor/Bruce Coleman Ltd. **Crocus:** R. Carr/Bruce Coleman Ltd. **Crookes Radiometer:** Michael Holford. **Crossbill:** W. Lankinen/Bruce Coleman Ltd. **Crosswort:** Eric Crichton/Bruce Coleman Ltd. **Crystal:** ZEFA. **Cubism:** Collection: State Museum Kroller-Muller, Otterlo, The Netherlands © A.D.A.G.P. 1984. **Cuckoo:** Hans Reinhard/Bruce Coleman Ltd. **Cuneiform:** Jennifer Fry/Bruce Coleman Ltd. **Cupid:** Michael Holford. **Curassow:** Hans Reinhard/Bruce Coleman Ltd. **Curlew:** Gordon Langsbury/Bruce Coleman Ltd. **Cuscus:** J.P. Ferrero/Ardea London. **Custard Apple:** J.L. Mason/Ardea London. **Cuttlefish:** P. Morris/Ardea London. **Cycad:** Jan Taylor/Bruce Coleman Ltd.

DADA *T* Courtesy Sidney Janis Gallery, N.Y. © A.D.A.G.P. 1984. *B* Lord's Gallery, London © S.P.A.D.E.M. 1984. **Dado:** Duchov Castle/Robert Harding Picture Library. **Dagger:** Michael Holford. **Daisy:** Geoff Dore/Bruce Coleman Ltd. **Damascene:** Michael Holford. **Damson:** Eric Crichton/Bruce Coleman Ltd. **Dandelion:** Eric Crichton/Bruce Coleman Ltd. **Darwin:** Ardea London. **Davy Lamp:** Michael Holford. **DEAD SEA SCROLLS** Israel Museum, Jerusalem. **Deathwatch Beetle:** J.L. Mason/Ardea London. **Decoy:** J.L. Mason/Ardea London. **Degas:** Courtauld Institute Galleries, London. (Courtauld Collection). **Delphi:** Michael Holford. **Delphinium:** Eric Crichton/Bruce Coleman Ltd. **Demeter:** Michael Holford. **Denarius:** Michael Holford. **Dendrites:** Jane Burton/Bruce Coleman Ltd. **Derringer:** Rainbird/Robert Harding Picture Library. **DESERT** *T* Leidmann/ZEFA, *C* and *B* Tony Morrison. **Diamond:** Institute of Geological Sciences. **Diamondback:** Jack Dermid/Bruce Coleman Ltd. **DICKENS** Michael Holford. **Diffraction:** Michael Holford. **Dike-Sea:** E. Winter/ZEFA. **Dike-Inland:** D.H. Teuffen/ZEFA. **Dill:** Starfoto/ZEFA. **Dingo:** Jen & Des Bartlett/Bruce Coleman Ltd. **Diogenes:** Mary Evans Picture Library. **Dionysus:** Michael Holford. **Dip:** M. Pitner/ZEFA. **Dolphin:** Alain Compost/Bruce Coleman Ltd. **DOME** *T* Michael Holford, *B* Mike Yamashita/Aspect Picture Library. **Donjon:** Michael Holford. **Donkey:** ZEFA. **Doric Order:** Mary Evans Picture Library. **Dormer:** Margaret Collier/Robert Harding Picture Library. **Dormouse:** Hans Reinhard/Bruce Coleman Ltd. **Douroucouli:** Bruce Coleman Ltd. **Dove:** Bruce Coleman Ltd. **Downing Street:** Bruce Coleman Ltd. **DRAGON** *L* Narodni Galerie V Praze, *R* Gulbenkian Museum of Oriental Art, University of Durham. **Dragon Tree:** Brian Hawkes/Robert Harding Picture Library. **Dromedary:** K. Goebel/ZEFA. **Druids:** Bruce Coleman Ltd. **Drum:** Michael Holford. **Druse:** H. Schumacher/ZEFA. **Drydock:** Robert Harding Picture Library. **Duiker:** Wardene Weisser/Ardea London. **Dunes:** Carol Hughes/Bruce Coleman Ltd. **DÜRER** Michael Holford. **Dutchman's-Breeches:** Lynn M. Stone/Bruce Coleman Ltd.

EARTHQUAKE Stan Wayman/Life April, 1964/Time Inc. ©/Colorific! **Easter Egg:** Michael Holford. **Easter Island:** Colin Caket/ZEFA. **Echidna:** John Markham/Bruce Coleman Ltd. **Eclosion:** Dr. F. Sauer/ZEFA. **Edelweiss:** Eric Crichton/Bruce Coleman Ltd. **Eggplant:** Eric Crichton/Bruce Coleman Ltd. **Egret:** Kenneth W. Fink/Ardea London. **EGYPT** all Michael Holford. **Eland:** Mark N. Boulton/Bruce Coleman Ltd. **Electrostatic Generator:** Michael Holford. **Elephant:** Lee Lyon/Bruce Coleman Ltd. **Elephant Seal:** Brian Hawkes/Robert Harding Picture Library. **Ely:** *Patrick Thurston.* **Embrasure:** Michael Holford. **Embroidery:** Michael Holford. **Enamel:** Michael Holford. **Endomorph:** Manfred Becker/ZEFA. **ENGLISH CIVIL WAR** Weidenfeld & Nicolson. **ENGRAVING** The Metropolitan Museum of Art, Fletcher Fund, 1919. **Epstein Sculpture:** Robert Harding Picture Library. **Equestrian:** Konrad Helbig/ZEFA. **Escapement:** Michael Holford. **ETRUSCAN** *T* Michael Holford, *B* Scala. **Evert Lloyd, Christine:** Tony Duffy/All Sport. **Ewer:** George Rainbird/American Museum in Britain, Bath/Robert Harding Picture Library. **Excavator:** Schlodien/ZEFA.

Fabergé Egg: Collection of Wartski's/Michael Holford. **Faience:** Michael Holford. **Falconry:** M. Freeman/Bruce Coleman Ltd. **Fallow Deer:** Leonard Lee Rue/Bruce Coleman Ltd. **Fan:** Victoria & Albert Museum/Robert Harding Picture Library. **Fanlight:** Robert Harding Picture Library. **Fantail:** Jane Burton/Bruce Coleman Ltd. **Fan Vaulting:** Michael Holford. **FAUVISM** Museum of Modern Art, New York. Gift of Mr. and Mrs. Charles Zadok © S.P.A.D.E.M. 1984. Oil on canvas, 26 inches x 39 inches. **Feather:** Frieder Sauer/Bruce Coleman Ltd. **Feather Palm:** Knight & Hunt Photo/ZEFA. **Felucca:** Ardea London. **Fencing:** Ung. Werbestudio/ZEFA. **FERN** Paul Wakefield/Bruce Coleman Ltd. **Fiddler Crab:** G.B. Frittie/Bruce Coleman Ltd. **Fig Bird:** Brian Coates/Bruce Coleman Ltd. **Figurine:** Michael Holford. **Filefish:** Jane Burton/Bruce Coleman Ltd. **Filigree:** Michael Holford. **Fingerboard:** Michael Holford. **Fjord:** Ziesmann/ZEFA. **Fireworks:** H. Armstrong/ZEFA. **Flight Deck:** Jack Novak/ZEFA. **Flint:** Adrian Davies/Bruce Coleman Ltd. **Flintlock:** Photo by Bill Monaghan © George Rainbird Ltd/Robert Harding Picture Library. **Floe:** Geoff Renner/Robert Harding Picture Library. **Fluting:** Michael Holford. **Font:** Mary Evans Picture Library. **Fore-and-Aft Rig:** Sassoon/Robert Harding Picture Library. **Forge:** *Neil Holmes.* **Fork:** Michael Holford. **Fosbury Flop:** UWS/ZEFA. **Four-Poster:** Christina Gascoigne/Robert Harding Picture Library. **Frame:** Ardea London. **Fresco:** Michael Holford. **Friarbird:** Ellis McNamara/Ardea London. **Frost:** Robert Harding Picture Library. **Fruit Bat:** Bruce Coleman Ltd. **Fruit Fly:** Anthony Healy/Bruce Coleman Ltd. **Fuchsia:** Udo Hirch/Bruce Coleman Ltd. **Fur Seal:** Clem Haagner/Ardea London. **FUTURISM** Mr. and Mrs. Estorick/Photo Herbert Michel.

Gable: F.A.H. Bloemendal/ZEFA. **GALAXY** *T* © 1961 California Institute of Technology & Carnegie Institution of Washington. *BL* Space Frontiers, *BR* Science Photo Library. **Galley:** Michael Holford. **Gannet:** Gordon Langsbury/Bruce Coleman Ltd. **Garnet:** Institute of Geological Sciences. **Gargoyle:** Michael Holford. **Gazelle:** Joe van Wormer/Bruce Coleman Ltd. **Gecko:** Eric Lindgren/Ardea London. **GEM** all photographs from the Institute of Geological Sciences. **Gemsbok:** Francisco Erize/Bruce Coleman Ltd. **Genet:** Clem Haagner/Ardea London. **Geode:** ZEFA. **Geothermal:** Paolo Koch/ZEFA. **Gerbil:** James Simon/Bruce Coleman Ltd. **Geyser:** James Simon/Bruce Coleman Ltd. **Gibbon:** Norman Tomalin/Bruce Coleman Ltd. **Gila Monster:** Norman Myers/Bruce Coleman Ltd. **Giraffe:** Leonard Lee Rue/Bruce Coleman Ltd. **Girandole:** Michael Holford. **Glacier:** M.N. Boulton/Bruce Coleman Ltd. **Gladiolus:** Ardea London. **Glassfish:** Jane Burton/Bruce Coleman Ltd. **Glastonbury:** *Malcolm Aird.* **Globe Thistle:** Peter Ward/Bruce Coleman Ltd. **Glowworm:** P.A. Hinchliffe/Bruce Coleman Ltd. **Gloxinia:** William McPherson/Bruce Coleman Ltd. **Glyph:** Ziesmann/ZEFA. **Gnu:** Kenneth W. Fink/Ardea London. **Goat:** Hans Reinhard/Bruce Coleman Ltd. **Goaway Bird:** Bruce Coleman Ltd. **Goldfish:** Hans Reinhard/Bruce Coleman Ltd. **Gondola:** Charles Henneghien/Bruce Coleman Ltd. **Gorilla:** Norman Tomalin/Bruce Coleman Ltd. **GOTHIC** all Michael Holford. **Gourd:** Eric Crichton/Bruce Coleman Ltd. **Grand Canyon:** Stella Martin. **Grapefruit:** Norman Tomalin/Bruce Coleman Ltd. **Grape Hyacinth:** Eric Crichton/Bruce Coleman Ltd. **Great Auk:** Mary Evans Picture Library. **Great Dane:** Hans Reinhard/Bruce Coleman Ltd. **Great Wall of China:** Norman Myers/Bruce Coleman Ltd. **Green Algae:** Jane Burton/Bruce Coleman Ltd. **Grimaldi, Joseph:** Mary Evans Picture Library. **Grizzly Bear:** Stouffer Productions/Bruce Coleman Ltd. **Ground Squirrel:** Ardea London. **Guinea Fowl:** M.P. Kahl/Bruce Coleman Ltd. **Guinea Pig:** J.P. Ferrero/Ardea London.

Hackle: R. Bond/ZEFA. **Haddock:** P. Morris/Ardea London. **Hadrian:** Michael Holford. **Hadrian's Wall:** Bergmann/ZEFA. **Halo:** Bruce Coleman Ltd. **Halter:** G. Mabbs/ZEFA. **Hammerhead Shark:** Ron & Valerie Taylor/Ardea London. **Hang Glider:** Eric Crichton/Bruce Coleman Ltd. **Harlequin:** Michael Holford. **Harebell:** Hans Reinhard/Bruce Coleman Ltd. **Harpy Eagle:** Kenneth W. Fink/Ardea London. **Harvester:** G. Heilman/ZEFA. **Hathor:** Mary Evans Picture Library. **Hauberk:** Stadtbibliothek Nuremberg/Robert Harding Picture Library. **Hawksbill:** J.L. Mason/Ardea London. **HEAVEN & HELL** *T* Michael Holford, *B* M. Thonig/ZEFA. **Hebe:** Eric Crichton/Bruce Coleman Ltd. **Hedgehog:** Hans Reinhard/Bruce Coleman Ltd. **Helicopter:** Jane Burton/Bruce Coleman Ltd. **Helmet:** Michael Holford. **Henge:** *Penny Tweedie.* **Herbaceous Border:** Ardea London. **Hercules:** Michael Holford. **Hibiscus:** Eric Crichton/Bruce Coleman Ltd. **Hieratic:** Michael Holford. **Hieroglyphic:** Charles Henneghien/Bruce Coleman Ltd. **High Relief:** Michael Holford. **Hilt:** Michael Holford. **Hind:** Brian Hawkes/Robert Harding Picture Library. **HINDUISM** all Michael Holford. **Hippodrome:** Ardea London. **Hippopotamus:** M.D. England/Ardea London. **HOCKNEY** 'A Bigger Splash' Acrylic on canvas, © David Hockney 1967, Courtesy Petersburg Press/Bridgeman Art Library. **Honesty:** John Flowerdew/ZEFA. **Honeycomb:** W. Kratz/ZEFA. **Honey Mushroom:** Adrian Davies/Bruce Coleman Ltd. **Honeysuckle:** John Fennell/Bruce Coleman Ltd. **Honiton Lace:** *Patrick Thurston.* **Hooded Seal:** Nir Lightfoot/Bruce Coleman Ltd. **Horn:** Mary Evans Picture Library. **Hornbill:** Sassoon/Robert Harding Picture Library. **Horned Owl:** P. Morris/Ardea London. **Horse Brass:** G. Mabbs/ZEFA. **Horseshoe Crab:** C.B. Frith/Bruce Coleman Ltd. **Horus:** Michael Holford. **HOVERCRAFT** Paul Kamper/ZEFA. **Howdah:** Michael Holford. **Hull:** Dr. K. Heydermann/Mulle/ZEFA. **Hummingbird:** Wardene Weisser/Ardea London. **Hydroplane:** W. Ostgathe/ZEFA. **Hypocaust:** Michael Holford. **Hyrax:** Kenneth W. Fink/Ardea London.

Ibex: Leonard Lee Rue/Bruce Coleman Ltd. **Iceberg:** Francisco Erize/Bruce Coleman Ltd. **I Ching:** Michael Holford. **Icicle:** Gordon Langsbury/Bruce Coleman Ltd. **Iguana:** Harold Schultz/Bruce Coleman Ltd. **Imbricate:** Michael Allen Bolton/ZEFA. **Impala:** M.F. Soper/Bruce Coleman Ltd. **IMPRESSIONISM** *TR* Musée Marmottan, *BL* Musée du Louvre/Cliché Musées Nationaux Paris, *BR* Louvre/Cliché Musées Nationaux Paris. **INCA:** Tony Morrison. **Incuse:** Michael Holford. **INDUSTRIAL REVOLUTION** *T* Science Museum, *B* Alan Hutchison Library. **INDUS VALLEY** *T* & *C* Robert Harding Picture Library, both *B* pictures Scala **Ingot:** Goebel/ZEFA. **Intarsia:** Michael Holford. **Intrusion:** Travel Photo International. **Ionic Order:** Mary Evans Picture Library. **Ironstone:** Neville Fox-Davies/Bruce Coleman Ltd. **ISLAM** *TL* A. Duncan/MEPhA, *TR* A. Duncan/MEPhA, *BL* British Museum, *BR* Metropolitan Museum of Art, Rogers Fund. **Ivory:** Michael Holford. **Ivy:** Ake Lindau/Ardea London.

Jackal: Ian Beames/Ardea London. **Jack-in-the-box:** *Eileen Tweedy*/Art Gallery & Museums, Brighton. **Jack Rabbit:** Stephen J. Krasemann/Bruce Coleman Ltd. **Jaguar:** Revers-Widaver/ZEFA. **Janus:** Michael Holford. **JELLYFISH** *L* Ron & Valerie Taylor/Ardea London, *R* Anthony & Elizabeth Bomford/Ardea London. **Jet:** *Michael Freeman.* **Joshua Tree:** P. Morris/Ardea London. **JUDAISM** *TR* Israel Museum, Jerusalem, *BL* Staats und Universitätsbibliothek, Hamburg (Ralph Kleinkempe from Aldus Books Ltd), *BR* Jewish Museum, London. **Juggernaut:** J. Pfaff/ZEFA. **Juggernaut:** Michael Holford. **Jumping Jack:** *Graham Henderson*/Museum of London. **Junco:** Kenneth W. Fink/Ardea London. **Junk:** Sassoon/Robert Harding Picture Library. **JUPITER** Both pictures NASA.

Kabuki: R. Halin/ZEFA. **Kale:** Eric Crichton/Bruce Coleman Ltd. **Kangaroo:** P. Morris/Ardea London. **Kapok:** Norman Myers/Bruce Coleman Ltd. **Katydid:** Donald D. Burgess/Ardea London. **Kayak:** R. Theissen/ZEFA. **Kilauea:** Hawaii-Corn/ZEFA. **Kiln:** Joy Langsbury/Bruce Coleman Ltd. **Kimono:** Michael Holford. **Kiwi:** Jeff Foott/Bruce Coleman Ltd. **Kiwi Fruit:** R. Smith/ZEFA. **Klee Painting:** Michael Holford © A.D.A.G.P., Cosmo Press 1984. **Koala:** Jen & Des Bartlett/Bruce Coleman Ltd. **Kohlrabi:** Eric Crichton/Bruce Coleman Ltd. **Kongoni:** Mark Boulton/Bruce Coleman Ltd. **Kookaburra:** Rainbird/Robert Harding Picture Library. **Krishna:** Michael Holford. **Kudu:** Clem Haagner/Ardea London.

Lace: *Patrick Thurston.* **Lacquer:** Michael Holford. **Ladybug:** W. Kratz/ZEFA. **LASER** © F. Goro/Life Magazine 1965/Colorific! **Lateen:** Sarah King/Robert Harding Picture Library. **Lattice:** Nedra Westwater/Robert Harding Picture Library. **Launcher:** Photri/ZEFA. **Lavender:** Eric Crichton/Bruce Coleman Ltd. **Leaf Insect:** Anton Thau/ZEFA. **LE CORBUSIER:** ZEFA. **Leeboard:** B. Fleumer/ZEFA. **Leech:** Jane Burton/Bruce Coleman Ltd. **Leg-of-Mutton:** Mary Evans Picture Library. **Lei:** Erwin Christian/ZEFA. **Lemur:** Kenneth W. Fink/Ardea London. **LENS** Eaglemoss Publications Ltd. **Leopard:** Peter Jackson/Bruce Coleman Ltd. **LEONARDO DA VINCI** *L* Reproduced by courtesy of the Trustees, The National Gallery, London, *R* Reproduced by Gracious Permission of Her Majesty the Queen. **Lichen:** J.L. Mason/Ardea London. **Life Guards:** Clive Sawyer/ZEFA. **Lighthouse:** Robert Harding Picture Library. **LIGHTNING** C. Voit/ZEFA. **Lilac:** Eric Crichton/Bruce Coleman Ltd. **Lintel:** Michael Holford. **Lion:** Michael Putland/Ardea London. **Litchi:** Eric Crichton/Bruce Coleman Ltd. **Little Auk:** L.R. Dawson/Bruce Coleman Ltd. **Llama:** Bruce Coleman Ltd. **Lock:** Ingrid Rangnow/ZEFA. **Locust:** John Markham/Bruce Coleman Ltd. **Lodestone:** Michael Holford. **Longhorn:** V. Wentzel/ZEFA. **Longship:** Puck-Kornetzki/ZEFA. **Loris:** Rod Williams/Bruce Coleman Ltd. **Lotus:** Joanna Van Gruist/Ardea London. **Lungwort:** Hans Reinhard/Bruce Coleman Ltd. **Lupine:** M. Thonig/ZEFA. **Lynx:** W. Layer/ZEFA.

Macaque: Sassoon/Robert Harding Picture Library. **Macaw:** Hans Reinhard/Bruce Coleman Ltd. **Mace:** *Patrick Thurston.* **Mace:** Starfoto/ZEFA. **MACHINE GUN** *TL&R* The Granger Collection, New York, *B* U.S. Signal Corps Photo III-SC-31994. **Magnolia:** Ardea London. **Majolica:** Michael Holford. **Malachite:** Adrian Davies/Bruce Coleman Ltd. **Mandala:** Michael Holford. **Mandrill:** Kenneth W. Fink/Ardea London. **Mangrove:** Bruce Coleman Ltd. **Mantis:**

Martin Dohrn/Bruce Coleman Ltd. **Marabou:** Carol Hughes/Bruce Coleman Ltd. **Marduk:** Michael Holford. **Mare:** ZEFA. **Marionette:** R. Bond/ZEFA. **Marmot:** Wardene Weisser/Ardea London. **MARS** both NASA. **Marten:** ZEFA. **MASK** *TR* Michael Holford, *BL* Bob Croxford/ZEFA and *BC* and *BR* both Michael Holford. **MATISSE:** Cliché Musées Nationaux Paris: Photo Bulloz © S.P.A.D.E.M. 1984. **Matterhorn:** Toni Hiebeler/ZEFA. **MAYA** *L* Michael Holford, *R* Ianthe Ruthven/Michael Holford. **Meadowlark:** Des Bartlett/Bruce Coleman Ltd. **Medicine Man:** Michael Holford. **Medusa:** Michael Holford. **Megalith:** Michael Holford. **Melon:** Ernst A. Weber/ZEFA. **MERCURY:** both NASA. **Mesopotamia:** Michael Holford. **MICHELANGELO:** Ted Spiegel/John Hillelson Agency. **MICROFILM:** University Microfilms International/Business Week. **Milkweed:** Bob & Clara Calhoun/Bruce Coleman Ltd. **MILKY WAY** *T* Space Frontiers Ltd., *B* Science Photo Library. **Minaret:** Ch. Fetzer/ZEFA. **Miniature:** Michael Holford. **Minotaur:** Michael Holford. **Minstrel:** British Museum/Robert Harding Picture Library. **Mistletoe:** Bob Gibbons/Ardea London. **Miter:** Michael Holford. **Moat:** Robert Harding Picture Library. **Moccasin:** Rod Williams/Bruce Coleman Ltd. **Mockingbird:** Joe Van Wormer/Bruce Coleman Ltd. **Mold:** Adrian Davies/Bruce Coleman Ltd. **MONEY** *TL* Michael Holford, *TR* Alan Hutchison Library. **Monkey Puzzle:** Ardea London. **Monolith:** Michael Holford. **Monorail:** B. Anderson/ZEFA. **Monstera:** William McPherson/Bruce Coleman Ltd. **Montezuma II:** Museo de America, Madrid/Robert Harding Picture Library. **MOON** *T* Space Frontiers, *BL* Space Frontiers, *BC* Science Photo Library, *BR* Space Frontiers. **Moonstone:** Institute of Geological Sciences. **MOORE** Walter Rawlings/Robert Harding Picture Library. **Moose:** Jeff Foott/Bruce Coleman Ltd. **Morel:** Hans Reinhard/Bruce Coleman Ltd. **Mosaic:** Michael Holford. **MOSQUE** *L* Paolo Koch/Shostal Associates, *R* Ray Manley/Shostal Associates, *BI* Jill Brown/Shostal Associates. **Mountaineer:** Chris Bonnington/Bruce Coleman Ltd. **Mount Rushmore National Memorial:** M.P.L. Fogden/Bruce Coleman Ltd. **Mule:** J.L.G. Grande/Bruce Coleman Ltd. **Mullion:** Robert Harding Picture Library. **Mummy:** Michael Holford. **Murillo Painting:** Michael Holford. **Muse:** Michael Holford. **Musk Ox:** Kenneth W. Fink/Ardea London.

Natterjack: J.P. Ferrero/Ardea London. **Neanderthal Man:** Rainbird/Robert Harding Picture Library. **NEBULA** © 1959 by California Institute of Technology and Carnegie Institution of Washington. **Nectarine:** Robert Harding Picture Library. **Nematode:** Dr. F. Sauer/ZEFA. **NEOCLASSICISM** *TL* © 1980 By the Metropolitan Museum of Art. *TR* Ole Woldbye/Thorvaldsens Museum, *BL Malcolm Aird, BR A. Howarth.* **Neptune:** Michael Holford. **Netsuke:** Michael Holford. **Newel:** *Malcolm Aird.* **Newt:** W. Kratz/ZEFA. **Niche:** Konrad Helbig/ZEFA. **Night Heron:** E. Hummel/ZEFA. **Nolan Painting:** Marlborough Fine Art, London/Bridgeman Art Library. **NUCLEAR WEAPON** U.S. Dept. of Environment/Science Photo Library (1 to 4), Aspect Picture Library (5). **Nutmeg:** Starfoto/ZEFA.

Oasis: Foto Leidmann/ZEFA. **Ocelot:** Norman Tomalin/Bruce Coleman Ltd. **Octagon:** Michael Holford. **Ogee:** Michael Holford. **Okra:** John Mason/Ardea London. **Olivine:** Institute of Geological Sciences. **Onion:** ZEFA. **Opal:** Institute of Geological Sciences. **OP ART** The Tate Gallery, London. **Opossum:** Leonard Lee Rue III/Bruce Coleman Ltd. **Opuntia:** Eric Crichton/Bruce Coleman Ltd. **Orangutan:** ZEFA. **Organ:** G.M. Wilkins/Robert Harding Picture Library. **Oriel:** Michael Holford. **Oryx:** B. Croxford/ZEFA. **Osiris:** Michael Holford. **Ostrich:** W. Layer/ZEFA. **OTTOMAN EMPIRE** Sonia Halliday. **Outcrop:** Dr. Hans Kramarz/ZEFA. **Ovenbird:** Gunter Ziesler/Bruce Coleman Ltd.

Paddle Wheel: Klaus Benser/ZEFA. **Paddy:** Starfoto/ZEFA. **Pagoda:** Christina Gascoigne/Robert Harding Picture Library. **Painted Lady:** L.R. Dawson/Bruce Coleman Ltd. **PALLADIAN** John Bethall. **Palomino:** J.P. Ferrero/Ardea London. **Panda:** WWF/Kojo Tanaka/Bruce Coleman Ltd. **Pangolin:** R. Borland/Bruce Coleman Ltd. **PANTHEON** John Flowerdew/ZEFA. **Papyrus:** Michael Holford. **Parabola:** J. Pfaff/ZEFA. **Parachute:** A. Hubrick/ZEFA. **Parasite:** P. Morris/Ardea London. **Pargeting:** G.M. Wilkins/Robert Harding Picture Library. **Parrot:** Geoff Kalt/ZEFA. **Parsnip:** Eric Crichton/Bruce Coleman Ltd. **PARTHENON** Michael Holford. **Passionflower:** Christian Zuber/Bruce Coleman Ltd. **Patchwork:** Michael Holford. **Peacock:** Wardene Weisser/Ardea London. **Pearl:** Orion Press/ZEFA. **Peat:** Hed Wiesner/ZEFA. **Peccary:** Hans D. Dessenbach/Ardea London. **Pegasus:** Michael Holford. **Pelican:** David Goulston/Bruce Coleman Ltd. **Penguin:** Jen & Des Bartlett/Bruce Coleman Ltd. **Pericles:** Michael Holford. **PERPENDICULAR** *T* John Bethall, *B* Angelo Hornak. **PERSIA** © Eric Lessing, Magnum. **Persimmon:** J.L. Mason/Ardea London. **PERSPECTIVE** Scala. **Petrified Forest:** ZEFA. **Pewter:** American Museum, Bath/Robert Harding Picture Library. **Pharaoh:** Robert Harding Picture Library. **Phonograph:** Michael Holford. **Photomicrograph:** Dr. David Corke/ZEFA. **Phrygian Cap:** Michael Holford. **PICASSO:** MAS © S.P.A.D.E.M. 1984. **Pigmentation:** Dr. David Corke/ZEFA. **Pilaster:** G. Archibold/Robert Harding Picture Library. **Pineapple:** William E. Townsend Jnr./Bruce Coleman Ltd. **Pinnacle:** P. Bond/ZEFA. **Pistol:** Robert Harding Picture Library. **Pitcher Plant:** Jack Dermid/Bruce Coleman Ltd. **PLAYING CARDS:** 1500 *Michael Holford*/Courtesy of Intercol. 1678 Yasha Beresiner, Intercol, London. Iran *Michael Holford*/Courtesy of Intercol. 1840 Tony Hutchins/Sunday Times. Modern *Michael Holford*/Waddingtons. India *Michael Holford*/Courtesy of Intercol. **Plum:** Eric Crichton/Bruce Coleman Ltd. **PLUTO** both by courtesy of the Royal Astronomical Society, London. **Polar Bear:** Thor Larsen/Bruce Coleman Ltd. **Polo:** E.M. Bordis/ZEFA. **Polyphemus Moth:** George Laycock/Bruce Coleman Ltd. **Pompeii:** J. Schorken/ZEFA. **POP ART** *L* The Tate Gallery, London © S.P.A.D.E.M. 1984, *R* Collection, The Museum of Modern Art, New York. Elizabeth Bliss Parkinson Fund © S.P.A.D.E.M. 1984. Oil silk--screened on canvas, 361/8 inches x 241/8 inches. **PORCELAIN** *TL* Robert Harding Picture Library. *TR* Bridgeman Art Library. *BL* Michael Holford/Victoria & Albert Museum, *BR* Michael Holford/Victoria & Albert Museum. **Portico:** Christina Gascoigne/Robert Harding Picture Library. **POSTIMPRESSIONISM:** *TL* Kunsthalle Bremen, *TR* Museum Folkwang Essen, *BL* The Metropolitan Museum of Art, Bequest of Mrs. H.O. Havemeyer, 1929. The H.O. Havemeyer Collection. **Potter's Wheel:** G.M. Wilkins/Robert Harding Picture Library. **POTTERY** *TR* Robert Harding Picture Library. *BL* John Bethell. *BR* Victoria & Albert Museum. **Powder Horn:** *Patrick Thurston.* **Prairie Dog:** M.P.L. Fogden/Bruce Coleman Ltd. **Pre-Columbian Pottery:** Robert Harding Picture Library. **Pre-Raphaelite Painting:** Photo John Webb/The Tate Gallery, London. **Primrose:** S.C. Porter/Bruce Coleman Ltd. **Proboscis:** E. Bleicher/ZEFA. **Prominence:** ZEFA. **Pronghorn:** Kenneth W. Fink/Ardea London. **Protective Coloring:** Kim Taylor/Bruce Coleman Ltd. **Pseudomorph:** ZEFA. **Pueblo:** Steenmanns/ZEFA. **Puffball:** Ake Lindau/Ardea London. **Puffer:** ZEFA. **PUGIN** John Bethell. **Puma:** W. Weisser/Ardea London. **Pupa:** Dr. Sauer/ZEFA. **Puppet:** Dr. G. Haasch/ZEFA. **Pyramid:** Kim Taylor/Bruce Coleman Ltd. **Pyrite:** Hed Wiesner/ZEFA. **Pyrotechnics:** Starfoto/ZEFA.

Quarry: R. Jensen/ZEFA. **Quern:** Mary Evans Picture Library. **Quetzalcoatl:** Michael Holford.

Ra: Michael Holford. **Rabbit:** Ian Beames/Ardea London. **Raccoon:** Hans Reinhard/ZEFA. **RADAR** Paul Brierley. **Radial Symmetry:** J.E. Rhodes/Robert Harding Picture Library. **Radio Telescope:** V. Stapelberg/ZEFA. **Ragged Robin:** Bob Gibbons/Ardea London. **Rainbow:** ZEFA. **Ram:** Leonard Lee Rue III/Bruce Coleman Ltd. **Ram God of Mendes:** Mary Evans Picture Library. **Rameses:** Michael Holford. **Rape:** Ian Sumner/Robert Harding Picture Library. **RAPHAEL** Scala. **Rattle:** Michael Holford. **Rattlesnake:** WWF/Urs Woy/Bruce Coleman Ltd. **Rayleigh Scattering:** K.D. Frohlich/ZEFA. **Red Currant:** John Mason/Ardea London. **Red Deer:** W. Ostgate/ZEFA. **Red Fox:** H. Reinhard/ZEFA. **Red Squirrel:** Leonard Lee Rue III/Bruce Coleman Ltd. **Reed:** Norman Tomalin/Bruce Coleman Ltd. **Regency:** Michael Holford. **Reindeer:** Herta Grondal/ZEFA. **Reliquary:** Michael Holford. **REMBRANDT** The Greater London Council as Trustees of the Iveagh Bequest, Kenwood. **RENAISSANCE** *L* Scala. *R* National Gallery of Art, Washington; Ailsa Mellon Bruce Fund. **Resin:** Bert Leidmann/ZEFA. **Retort:** Michael Holford. **Rhea:** Bruce Coleman Ltd. **Rhesus Monkey:** Ardea London. **Rhinoceros:** ZEFA. **Rickshaw:** Sybil Sassoon/Robert Harding Picture Library. **Roadrunner:** Charlie Ott/Bruce Coleman Ltd. **Robin:** W. Layer/ZEFA. **Rocking Horse:** Mary Evans Picture Library. **ROCOCO** *TL* Michael Holford. *TR* Wallace Collection. *BL* M. Thonig/ZEFA. **RODIN** Musée Rodin. **Roe Deer:** ZEFA.**ROMANESQUE** S.H. & D.H. Cavanaugh/Robert Harding Picture Library. **Romulus & Remus:** ZEFA. **Rood Screen:** Michael Holford. **Rotifer:** Dr. F. Sauer/ZEFA. **Rotunda:** Michael Holford. **Royal Palm:** Bruce Coleman Ltd. **Rubber Tree:** J. Bitsch/ZEFA. **Ruff:** Michael Holford. **RUISDAEL** From the Collections of J. Smith, London & A. van der Hoop, Amsterdam, donated to the City of Amsterdam in 1854, on loan since 1885, courtesy of the Rijksmuseum, Amsterdam. **Russet:** Eric Crichton/Bruce Coleman Ltd. **RUSSIAN REVOLUTION** e.t. archive. **Rye:** Prato/Bruce Coleman Ltd.

Sable Antelope: Simon Trevor/Bruce Coleman Ltd. **Sage Grouse:** Leonard Lee Rue III/Bruce Coleman Ltd. **Saiga:** Jane Burton/Bruce Coleman Ltd. **Salamander:** W. Layer/ZEFA. **Salmon:** Hans Reinhard/Bruce Coleman Ltd. **Sampler:** Michael Holford. **Samurai:** Michael Holford. **SAN ANDREAS FAULT** John Shelton. **Sand Dollars:** Alan Weaving/Ardea London. **Sand Dunes:** R. Bond/ZEFA. **Sandstone:** Gunter Heil/ZEFA. **Sand Yacht:** ZEFA. **SATELLITE** NASA/Science Photo Library. **SATURN** both NASA. **Satyr:** Michael Holford. **Scale:** Eric Lindgren/Ardea London. **Scallop:** John Gregg/Arlea London. **Scarab** *T* Jane Burton/Bruce Coleman Ltd., *B* Michael Holford. **Scat:** R. Beames/Ardea London. **Screamer:** Sullivan & Rogers/Bruce Coleman Ltd. **Scrimshaw:** François Gohier/Ardea London. **Sculpture:** ZEFA. **Sea Anemone:** Dr. Sauer/ZEFA. **Sea Cucumber:** Ron & Valerie Taylor/Ardea London. **Seaplane:** ZEFA. **Seashell:** John Ker/ZEFA. **Sea Snake:** Ron & Valerie Taylor/Ardea London. **Sea Urchin:** Adrian Davies/Bruce Coleman Ltd. **Secretary Bird:** ZEFA. **Seed:** N. Fox-Davies/Bruce Coleman Ltd. **Self-heal:** John Markham/Bruce Coleman Ltd. **Serow:** Kenneth W. Fink/Ardea London. **Seventeen-year Locust:** Leonard Lee Rue III/Bruce Coleman Ltd. **Sèvres Plate:** Michael Holford. **SEVEN DEADLY SINS** Prado, Madrid. **Shark:** Ron & Valerie Taylor/Ardea London. **Sheep:** ZEFA. **Sheepdog:** S. McKenna/ZEFA. **SHELLS** Mourning Cowrie: Heather Angel/Biofotos, Giant Clam: Heather Angel/Biofotos, Paper Nautilus: Ken Lucas/Seaphot, Queen Conch: Ken Lucas/Seaphot, others RD copyright. **Shield:** Michael Holford. **Ship Canal:** K. Kerth/ZEFA. **Shire Horse:** John S. Adams/ZEFA. **Shoebill:** Ian Beames/Ardea London. **Shofar:** F. Paul/ZEFA. **SIGN LANGUAGE** Reprinted from "Indian Sign Language" by William Tomkins, Dover Publications, 1969, reprinted with the permission of the publisher. **Silkworm:** Dr. P. Thiele/ZEFA. **Silverfish:** J.L. Mason/Ardea London. **Skimmer:** J.B. & S. Bottomley/Ardea London. **Skink:** Hans & Judy Beste/Ardea London. **Skunk Cabbage:** Gene Arens/Bruce Coleman Ltd. **Skylark:** Gunter Ziesler/Bruce Coleman Ltd. **Sloth:** Francisco Erize/Bruce Coleman Ltd. **Slowworm:** J.L. Mason/Ardea London. **Slug:** Ardea London. **Smelting:** ZEFA. **Snail:** Eric Lingren/Ardea London. **Snake:** Donald Burgess/Ardea London. **Snake Charmer:** M. Freeman/Bruce Coleman Ltd. **Snipe:** Roger Wilmshurst/Bruce Coleman Ltd. **Snow Leopard:** Kenneth W. Fink/Ardea London. **Snowplow:** ZEFA. **Snuffbox:** Royal Naval Museum, Portsmouth/Robert Harding Picture Library. **SOCIALIST REALISM** Scala/Art Resource. **SOLAR POWER** ZEFA. **SPACE SHUTTLE** © 1981 Douglas Kirkland/Colorific! **Sparrow Hawk:** W. Layer/ZEFA. **Spawn:** Jane Burton/Bruce Coleman Ltd. **Speedboat:** ZEFA. **SPIDER** John H. Gerard. **Spider Crab:** Neville Coleman/Bruce Coleman Ltd. **Spinnaker:** A. Roberts/ZEFA. **Spinning Wheel:** Michael Holford. **Spire:** Michael Holford. **Spirogyra:** Bruce Coleman Ltd. **Spleenwort:** Prato/Bruce Coleman Ltd. **Spoonbill:** M.P. Kahl/Bruce Coleman Ltd. **Springbok:** Goetz D. Plage/Bruce Coleman Ltd. **Spurge:** Roger Wilmshurst/Bruce Coleman Ltd. **Squirrel:** Kenneth W. Fink/Ardea London. **Squirrel Monkey:** Michael Freeman/Bruce Coleman Ltd. **Stack:** P.J. Sharpe/ZEFA. **Stadium:** Michael Holford. **STAINED GLASS** *L* Gottfried Frenzel/Institut für Glasgemäldeforschung und Restaurierung, Nuremberg, *R* Dr. Wolff Kolnerdom/Sonia Halliday. **Stalagmites and Stalactites:** W. Ernest/ZEFA. **Stallion:** J.P. Ferrero/Ardea London. **Starfish:** Sybil Sassoon/Robert Harding Picture Library. **Star-of-Bethlehem:** Hans Reinhard/Bruce Coleman Ltd. **Steam:** Walter Rawlings/Robert Harding Picture Library. **Steam Engine:** J.M. Jarvis/ZEFA. **Steamroller:** Derek Cattani/ZEFA. **Steinbok:** Peter Steyn/Ardea London. **Stele:** Michael Holford. **Stereoscope:** Michael Holford. **Stilt:** Graeme Chapman/Ardea London. **Stoa:** Michael Holford. **Stoat:** Hans Reinhard/Bruce Coleman Ltd. **Stock Dove:** Hans Reinhard/Bruce Coleman Ltd. **STONE AGE** Flint handax: Trustees of the British Museum (Natural History), Flint dagger, stone battle-ax and flint arrowhead: Devizes Museum, *Eileen Tweedy,* Nambicuara Indian and stone axhead: Jesco Von Puttkamer/Alan Hutchison Library. **Stonechat:** R.K. Murton/Bruce Coleman Ltd. **Stone Marten:** ZEFA. **Stork:** ZEFA. **Stupa:** J.L. Peyromaure/Alan Hutchison Library. **Suffolk:** J.P. Ferrero/Ardea London. **SUN** ZEFA. **Sun Bittern:** G. Ziesler/Bruce Coleman Ltd. **Sundial:** Nedra Westwater/Robert Harding Picture Library. **Supernova:** © 1959 by California Institute of Technology & Carnegie Institution of Washington. **Surgeon Fish:** Jane Burton/Bruce Coleman Ltd. **Suricate:** M.P. Kahl/Bruce Coleman Ltd. **SURREALISM** The Minneapolis Institute of Arts, Minneapolis, Minnesota © A.D.A.G.P. 1984. **Swan:** Hans D. Dossenbach/Ardea London. **Sweet Pea:** Eric Crichton/Bruce Coleman Ltd. **Sweet William:** Bruce Coleman Ltd. **Swordbill:** A.J. Mabbs/Bruce Coleman Ltd. **SYNAGOGUE** *Titanic Photography.*

Tahr: Bruce Coleman Ltd. **Talapoin:** Norman Tomalin/Bruce Coleman Ltd. **Tamandua:** Francisco Erize/Bruce Coleman Ltd. **Tanager:** Hans Reinhard: Bruce Coleman Ltd. **Tankard:** Robert Harding Picture Library. **Tanker:** Orion Press/ZEFA. **TAOISM:** Trustees of the British Museum. **Tapestry:** The Metropolitan Museum of Art, The Cloisters Collection, Gift of John D. Rockefeller, Jr., 1937/Robert Harding Picture Library. **Tapir:** ZEFA. **TAROT:** Victoria & Albert Museum, London. **Tarsier:** J. Mackinnon/Bruce Coleman Ltd. **Telegraph:** Michael Holford. **TELESCOPE:** *L* Firenze Museum della Scienza/Scala, *R* John Walsh/Aspect. **Temple:** Bob Croxford/ZEFA. **Tepee:** K.H. Kurz/ZEFA. **Termitarium:** Peter Ward/Bruce Coleman Ltd. **Termite:** Peter Ward/Bruce Coleman Ltd. **Tern:** Wayne Lankinen/Bruce Coleman Ltd. **Terpsichore:** Michael Holford. **Terra Cotta:** Michael Holford. **Terrapin:** Hans Reinhard/Bruce Coleman Ltd. **Thatch:** Colin Caket/ZEFA. **Thimble:** Michael Holford. **Thoth:** Michael Holford. **TIGER** *TL* Stan Wayman/Photo Researchers, *TR* John Pontier/Animals Animals, *B* Kenneth W. Fink/Bruce Coleman Ltd. **Tiki:** Michael Holford. **Tinamou:** Jen & Des Bartlett/Bruce Coleman Ltd. **TITIAN** Scala. **Toad:** ZEFA. **Toga:** Michael Holford. **Tomb:** ZEFA. **Topaz:** Institute of Geological Sciences. **Topiary:** Eric Crichton/Bruce Coleman Ltd. **Toucan:** Francisco Erize/Bruce Coleman Ltd. **Tragopan:** P. Morris/Ardea London. **TRAIN** all The Granger Collection, New York. **Trap-door Spider:** Jen & Des Bartlett/Bruce Coleman Ltd. **Tree Frog:** Pat Morris/Ardea London.**Triggerfish:** I.R. Beames/Ardea London. **Trillium:** Eric Crichton/Bruce Coleman Ltd. **Trilobite:** J. Fennell/Bruce Coleman Ltd. **Tripod:** Michael Holford. **Triptych:** ZEFA. **Trogon:** B & C Calhoun/Bruce Coleman Ltd. **Trompe L'Oeil:** Michael Holford. **Trotter:** ZEFA. **Trumpeter Swan:** Joe Van Wormer/Bruce Coleman Ltd. **Tsetse Fly:** Kim Taylor/Bruce Coleman Ltd. **TSUNAMI** Michael

Holford. **Turkey:** D.A.J. Mabbs/Bruce Coleman Ltd. **Turkey:** Kenneth W. Fink/Ardea London. **TURNER:** National Gallery of Art, Washington: Widener Collection. **Turnip:** Eric Crichton/Bruce Coleman Ltd. **Turtledove:** J.L.G. Grande/Bruce Coleman Ltd. **Tuscan Order:** Mary Evans Picture Library. **Tutu:** ZEFA. **Tympanum:** Michael Holford.

Undercroft: Michael Holford. **UNICORN:** Musée de Cluny/Cliché Musées Nationaux Paris. **UNITED NATIONS:** *L* Frank Spooner, *R* Klaus Benser/ZEFA. **Untouchable:** Alan Hutchison Library. **Uraeus:** ZEFA.

Vampire Bat: Rod Williams/Bruce Coleman Ltd. **VAN GOGH** From the Collection of Mr. & Mrs. Leigh B. Block, Chicago. **Vase:** Michael Holford. **VENUS** NASA. **Venus's Flower Basket:** Jane Burton/Bruce Coleman Ltd. **Venus's Flytrap:** ZEFA. **Verbena:** Eric Crichton/Bruce Coleman Ltd. **Vervet:** Peter Davey/Bruce Coleman Ltd. **Viaduct:** S. Sammer/ZEFA. **Viburnum:** Eric Crichton/Bruce Coleman Ltd. **Victoriana:** Photograph by kind permission of the Victorian Society, of Linley Sambourne House, open to the public, details from the Victorian Society, 01-994-1019. **VIKING** Ray Sutcliffe. **Vineyard:** ZEFA. **Virginia Creeper:** Eric Crichton/Bruce Coleman Ltd. **Viscacha:** G. Ziesler/Bruce Coleman Ltd. **VOLCANO:** Frank W. Lane. **Volute:** Neville Coleman/Bruce Coleman Ltd. **Vulture:** Peter Steyn/Ardea London.

Wailing Wall: H.J. Kreuger/ZEFA. **Wallaby:** F. Park/ZEFA. **Wall Creeper:** Hans Reinhard/Bruce Coleman Ltd. **Walrus:** Leonard Lee Rue III/Bruce Coleman Ltd. **Wapiti:** Kenneth W. Fink/Ardea London. **War Bonnet:** A. Roberts/ZEFA. **Wart Hog:** Mark Boulton/Bruce Coleman Ltd. **Wasp Pupae:** Dr. David Corke/ZEFA. **Water Beetle:** Jane Burton/Bruce Coleman Ltd. **Water Boatman:** John Clegg/Ardea London. **Waterbuck:** Alan Weaving/Ardea London. **Waterfall:** ZEFA. **Waxbill:** John Markham/Bruce Coleman Ltd. **Weather:** Dept. of Electrical Engineering & Electronics, Dundee University. **Weather Vane:** Robert Harding Picture Library. **Weaver Bird:** Pat Morris/Ardea London. **Wedgwood:** *John Cook (Whitecross Studios).* **Weevil:** Dr. Sauer/ZEFA. **White Clover:** Eric Crichton/Bruce Coleman Ltd. **White-Eye:** Alan Paterson/Ardea London. **Whydah:** Bruce Coleman Ltd. **Wild Boar:** Leonard Lee Rue III/Bruce Coleman Ltd. **Winepress:** C. Maher/ZEFA. **Witch Doctor:** Robert Harding Picture Library. **Witch Hazel:** Eric Crichton/Bruce Coleman Ltd. **Wombat:** J.P. Ferrero/Ardea London. **Woodchuck:** P. Morris/Ardea London. **Woodcock:** Hans Reinhard/Bruce Coleman Ltd. **WONDERS OF THE ANCIENT WORLD** Adam Woolfitt/Susan Griggs Agency. **Woodlark:** Hans Reinhard/Bruce Coleman Ltd. **Woolly Bear Caterpillar:** Bob Gibbons/Ardea London. **WREN** *TL* John Bethell, *TR* John Bethell, *B* Rainbird/Robert Harding Picture Library. **FRANK LLOYD WRIGHT** Richard Bryant. **WYETH:** Collection, The Museum of Modern Art, New York. Tempera on gesso panel, 32¼ inches x 47¼ inches. Purchase. **Wryneck:** R.M. Bloomfield/Ardea London.

Yak: Robert Harding Picture Library. **Yashmak:** ZEFA. **Yawl:** ZEFA. **Yellowstone National Park:** Hans Schmied/ZEFA. **Yucca:** Timothy O'Keefe/Bruce Coleman Ltd.

Zebra: Peter Steyne/Ardea London. **Zebra Finch:** John Markham/Bruce Coleman Ltd. **Zebu:** Bruce Coleman Ltd. **ZEN** *T* Carol Jopp/Robert Harding Picture Library, *B* © Elliott Erwitt—Magnum/John Hilleson Agency. **Zeus:** Michael Holford. **ZODIAC** Hunterian Collection, Library of University of Glasgow. **ZOROASTER** William McQuitty. **Zucchini:** Norman Owen Tomalin/Bruce Coleman Ltd.

The publishers also wish to thank the following for assistance in verifying scientific entries:
Jeremy Bartlett, Mary Bickley, David Ellesmere, Anne Haysom, Bruce Ingram, Michael Malone, Veronique Mott, Christopher Townshend, Linda Young.